The
MacArthur
Topical
Bible

The

MacArthur
Topical
Bible

John MacArthur

AUTHOR AND GENERAL EDITOR

NEW KING JAMES VERSION®

Thomas Nelson
Since 1798

NASHVILLE   DALLAS   MEXICO CITY   RIO DE JANEIRO

THE MACARTHUR TOPICAL BIBLE

© 2010 by John MacArthur.

Published in Nashville, Tennessee, by Thomas Nelson. Thomas Nelson is a registered trademark of Thomas Nelson, Inc.

Thomas Nelson, Inc., titles may be purchased in bulk for educational, business, fund-raising, or sales promotional use. For information, please e-mail SpecialMarkets@ThomasNelson.com.

ISBN-13: 9-781-4185-4376-1

Printed in the United States of America

10 11 12 13 14 – 5 4 3 2

Foreword
by
John MacArthur

When I wrote *The MacArthur Study Bible* in 1997, one of my goals was to create a tool that could help all Bible students understand what God was saying through His Word. As a result, all of the tools in *The MacArthur Study Bible*, including the notes on the verses, the introductions to each book, the maps, the charts, the special chapters on the Bible, the overview of theology, the topical index, and all the other assorted helps, were designed to further that goal.

One of my personal favorites is the topical index. It is taken from the *New Topical Textbook*, and it has been a vital tool throughout my years as both a student and teacher of God's Word. That's because it fulfills a significant role in the process of studying the Bible—a tool you need to effectively learn what God is teaching you in every passage you study. Let me explain.

As you study your Bible, you ought to be interpreting it. In Acts 8:30, Philip asked the Ethiopian eunuch, "Do you understand what you are reading?" In a similar way, you need to ask yourself, "What does the Bible mean by what it says?" You need to know what each passage means before you can apply it to your life. And the basic principle you should follow to do that is the analogy of faith, which means you should interpret the Bible with the Bible.

Four basic principles follow from that one overarching one: literal, historical, grammatical, and synthesis. The literal principle means that in general, the Bible speaks in literal terms, and you need to allow it to speak for itself. The historical principle means you interpret all passages in their historical context. The grammatical principle requires you to understand the basic grammatical structure of each sentence in the original language. And the final principle—the synthesis principle—is where this topical Bible becomes a vital asset to your study.

This principle is what the Reformers called the *analogia scriptura*. It means that the Bible does not contradict itself. If you find your interpretation of a particular passage contradicts a truth taught elsewhere in God's Word, then your interpretation cannot be right. You need to compare Scripture with Scripture to truly discover what the Bible means by what it says.

In truth the Bible is actually one book written by one Divine Author, although it was written over a period of 1,500 years by almost 40 human writers. During that time God progressively revealed Himself and His purposes through these men He inspired. As a result, His Word is perfectly cohesive and never contradictory. So Scripture is your best resource for completing your understanding of any passage you study. That's why I always use other Bible passages, both Old and New Testaments, as illustrations when I prepare my sermons each week.

It is for those reasons that you hold in your hands *The MacArthur Topical Bible*. The topical index in *The MacArthur Study Bible* is the main source for this topical Bible. But it has been edited, updated, and expanded to cover all the important and contemporary issues facing Christianity today.

Now that you have this tool in your hands, how should you use it? I would suggest you start by following the first three interpretation principles I outlined for you previously. Once you've interpreted the text, then you should make a list of the key subjects you've discovered that directly relate to the passage. Then take that list and look up each subject in this topical Bible to trace all that God has said about each of those subjects throughout Scripture. That's when you'll discover how each topic fits into the greater picture of God's intent.

To see what I mean, take a look at Romans 3:23-24, which says, "For all have sinned and fall short of the glory of God, being justified freely by His grace through the redemption that is in Christ Jesus." Now there are two verses full of some of the richest and most important truths in all of Scripture! Out of the many that stand out, let's take the word "justified" as an example.

If you look up the verb "justified" in this Topical Bible you'll find the root noun form, "justification." Under this major heading you'll see there are a number of main headings with their own subheadings, which will help you to further understand all that God has to say about that topic. Use what you discover to help you interpret what God is teaching in Romans 3:23-24. But you don't have to stop there. As you read each comparative passage, you can trace other subjects that relate to justification, which will give you an even greater understanding of what God is teaching in each text. If you are stumped by a particular passage, use the notes in *The MacArthur Study Bible*, commentaries, and other Bible study tools to help you in your search.

Basically, there is no limit to what you can discover by tracing topics throughout the Bible. It is my prayer that *The MacArthur Topical Bible* will become a resource you will turn to again and again as you mine the spiritual riches contained in God's precious Word. After all, it *is* God's Word to you, and you need to know all He has in it for you. May you receive it with great wonder and joy.

John MacArthur

Abbreviations
to the
Books of the Bible

1 Chr . . . . . . 1 Chronicles	Esth . . . . Esther	Mal . . . . Malachi
1 Cor . . . . . 1 Corinthians	Ex. . . . . Exodus	Mark . . . . Mark
1 John . . . . 1 John	Ezek . . . . Ezekiel	Matt. . . . . Matthew
1 Kin . . . . 1 Kings	Ezra . . . . Ezra	Mic. . . . . Micah
1 Pet . . . . 1 Peter	Gal . . . . Galatians	Nah . . . . Nahum
1 Sam . . . . 1 Samuel	Gen . . . . Genesis	Neh. . . . . Nehemiah
1 Thess. . 1 Thessalonians	Hab. . . . . Habakkuk	Num . . . . Numbers
1 Tim . . . . 1 Timothy	Hag . . . . Haggai	Obad . . . . Obadiah
2 Chr . . . . . . 2 Chronicles	Heb . . . . Hebrews	1 Pet . . . . 1 Peter
2 Cor . . . . . 2 Corinthians	Hos . . . . Hosea	2 Pet . . . . 2 Peter
2 John . . . . 2 John	Is. . . . . Isaiah	Phil . . . . Philippians
2 Kin . . . . 2 Kings	James . . . . James	Philem . . . . Philemon
2 Pet . . . . 2 Peter	Jer . . . . Jeremiah	Prov. . . . . Proverbs
2 Sam . . . . 2 Samuel	Job. . . . . Job	Ps . . . . Psalms
2 Thess. . 2 Thessalonians	Joel . . . . Joel	Rev . . . . Revelation
2 Tim . . . . 2 Timothy	John . . . . John	Rom . . . . Romans
3 John . . . . 3 John	1 John . . . . 1 John	Ruth . . . . Ruth
Acts. . . . . Acts	2 John . . . . 2 John	1 Sam . . . . 1 Samuel
Amos . . . . Amos	3 John . . . . 3 John	2 Sam . . . . 2 Samuel
1 Chr . . . . . . 1 Chronicles	Jon. . . . . Jonah	Song. . . Song of Solomon
2 Chr . . . . . . 2 Chronicles	Josh . . . . Joshua	1 Thess. . 1 Thessalonians
Col . . . . Colossians	Jude . . . . Jude	2 Thess. . 2 Thessalonians
1 Cor . . . . . 1 Corinthians	Judg . . . . Judges	1 Tim . . . . 1 Timothy
2 Cor . . . . . 2 Corinthians	1 Kin . . . . 1 Kings	2 Tim . . . . 2 Timothy
Dan . . . . Daniel	2 Kin . . . . 2 Kings	Titus. . . . . Titus
Deut . . . . . Deuteronomy	Lam . . . . . Lamentations	Zech. . . . . Zechariah
Eccl . . . . Ecclesiastes	Lev . . . . Leviticus	Zeph. . . . . Zephaniah
Eph . . . . Ephesians	Luke. . . . . Luke	

AARON

As spokesman and leader.

Ex 4:16 So he shall be your spokesman to the people. And he himself shall be as a mouth for you, and you shall be to him as God.

Ex 4:28–30 So Moses told Aaron all the words of the LORD who had sent him, and all the signs which He had commanded him. **29** Then Moses and Aaron went and gathered together all the elders of the children of Israel. **30** And Aaron spoke all the words which the LORD had spoken to Moses. Then he did the signs in the sight of the people.

Ex 5:1 Afterward Moses and Aaron went in and told Pharaoh, "Thus says the LORD God of Israel: 'Let My people go, that they may hold a feast to Me in the wilderness.' "

Ex 7:2 You shall speak all that I command you. And Aaron your brother shall tell Pharaoh to send the children of Israel out of his land.

Mic 6:4 For I brought you up from the land of Egypt, I redeemed you from the house of bondage; And I sent before you Moses, Aaron, and Miriam.

Genealogy of.

Ex 6:20–27 Now Amram took for himself Jochebed, his father's sister, as wife; and she bore him Aaron and Moses. And the years of the life of Amram *were* one hundred and thirty-seven. **21** The sons of Izhar *were* Korah, Nepheg, and Zichri. **22** And the sons of Uzziel *were* Mishael, Elzaphan, and Zithri. **23** Aaron took to himself Elisheba, daughter of Amminadab, sister of Nahshon, as wife; and she bore him Nadab, Abihu, Eleazar, and Ithamar. **24** And the sons of Korah *were* Assir, Elkanah, and Abiasaph. These are the families of the Korahites. **25** Eleazar, Aaron's son, took for himself one of the daughters of Putiel as wife; and she bore him Phinehas. These *are* the heads of the fathers' houses of the Levites according to their families. **26** These *are the same* Aaron and Moses to whom the LORD said, "Bring out the children of Israel from the land of Egypt according to their armies." **27** These *are* the ones who spoke to Pharaoh king of Egypt, to bring out the children of Israel from Egypt. These *are the same* Moses and Aaron.

With Moses before Pharaoh.

Ex 10:3 So Moses and Aaron came in to Pharaoh and said to him, "Thus says the LORD God of the Hebrews: 'How long will you refuse to humble yourself before Me? Let My people go, that they may serve Me.

Ex 10:16 Then Pharaoh called for Moses and Aaron in haste, and said, "I have sinned against the LORD your God and against you.

Ex 10:27–28 But the LORD hardened Pharaoh's heart, and he would not let them go. **28** Then Pharaoh said to him, "Get away from me! Take heed to yourself and see my face no more! For in the day you see my face you shall die!"

Death of.

Num 20:22–29 Now the children of Israel, the whole congregation, journeyed from Kadesh and came to Mount Hor. **23** And the LORD spoke to Moses and Aaron in Mount Hor by the border of the land of Edom, saying: **24** "Aaron shall be gathered to his people, for he shall not enter the land which I have given to the children of Israel, because you rebelled against My word at the water of Meribah. **25** Take Aaron and Eleazar his son, and bring them up to Mount Hor; **26** and strip Aaron of his garments and put them on Eleazar his son; for Aaron shall be gathered *to his people* and die there." **27** So Moses did just as the LORD commanded, and they went up to Mount Hor in the sight of all the congregation. **28** Moses stripped Aaron of his garments and put them on Eleazar his son; and Aaron died there on the top of the mountain. Then Moses and Eleazar came down from the mountain. **29** Now when all the congregation saw that Aaron was dead, all the house of Israel mourned for Aaron thirty days.

Num 33:38 Then Aaron the priest went up to Mount Hor at the command of the LORD, and died there in the fortieth year after the children of Israel had come out of the land of Egypt, on the first *day* of the fifth month.

As priest.

Ex 28:1–3 "Now take Aaron your brother, and his sons with him, from among the children of Israel, that he may minister to Me as priest, Aaron *and* Aaron's sons: Nadab, Abihu, Eleazar, and Ithamar. **2** And you shall make holy garments for Aaron your brother, for glory and for beauty. **3** So you shall speak to all *who are* gifted artisans, whom I have filled with the spirit of wisdom, that they may make Aaron's garments, to consecrate him, that he may minister to Me as priest.

Ex 28:30 And you shall put in the breastplate of judgment the Urim and the Thummim, and they shall be over Aaron's heart when he goes in before the LORD. So Aaron shall bear the judgment of the children of Israel over his heart before the LORD continually.

Heb 5:4 And no man takes this honor to himself, but he who is called by God, just as Aaron *was*.

Cf. Lev 8:1–36

And making of gold calf.

Ex 32:1–6 Now when the people saw that Moses delayed coming down from the mountain, the people gathered together to Aaron, and said to him, "Come, make us gods that shall go before us; for *as for* this Moses, the man who brought us up out of the land of Egypt, we do not know what has become of him." 2 And Aaron said to them, "Break off the golden earrings which *are* in the ears of your wives, your sons, and your daughters, and bring *them* to me." 3 So all the people broke off the golden earrings which *were* in their ears, and brought *them* to Aaron. 4 And he received *the gold* from their hand, and he fashioned it with an engraving tool, and made a molded calf. Then they said, "This *is* your god, O Israel, that brought you out of the land of Egypt!" 5 So when Aaron saw *it*, he built an altar before it. And Aaron made a proclamation and said, "Tomorrow *is* a feast to the LORD." 6 Then they rose early on the next day, offered burnt offerings, and brought peace offerings; and the people sat down to eat and drink, and rose up to play.

Ex 32:22–24 So Aaron said, "Do not let the anger of my lord become hot. You know the people, that they *are* set on evil. 23 For they said to me, 'Make us gods that shall go before us; *as for* this Moses, the man who brought us out of the land of Egypt, we do not know what has become of him.' 24 And I said to them, 'Whoever has any gold, let them break *it* off.' So they gave *it* to me, and I cast it into the fire, and this calf came out."

Deut 9:20–21 And the LORD was very angry with Aaron *and* would have destroyed him; so I prayed for Aaron also at the same time. 21 Then I took your sin, the calf which you had made, and burned it with fire and crushed it *and* ground *it* very small, until it was as fine as dust; and I threw its dust into the brook that descended from the mountain.

Ps 106:19–23 They made a calf in Horeb, And worshiped the molded image. 20 Thus they changed their glory Into the image of an ox that eats grass. 21 They forgot God their Savior, Who had done great things in Egypt, 22 Wondrous works in the land of Ham, Awesome things by the Red Sea. 23 Therefore He said that He would destroy them, Had not Moses His chosen one stood before Him in the breach, To turn away His wrath, lest He destroy *them*.

Sons of.

Lev 1:5 He shall kill the bull before the LORD; and the priests, Aaron's sons, shall bring the blood and sprinkle the blood all around on the altar that *is by* the door of the tabernacle of meeting.

Reaction to death of sons.

Lev 10:16–20 Then Moses made careful inquiry about the goat of the sin offering, and there it was—burned up. And he was angry with Eleazar and Ithamar, the sons of Aaron *who were* left, saying, 17 "Why have you not eaten the sin offering in a holy place, since it *is* most holy, and *God* has given it to you to bear the guilt of the congregation, to make atonement for them before the LORD? 18 See! Its blood was not brought inside the holy *place*; indeed you should have eaten it in a holy *place*, as I commanded." 19 And Aaron said to Moses, "Look, this day they have offered their sin offering and their burnt offering before the LORD, and such things have befallen me! *If* I had eaten the sin offering today, would it have been accepted in the sight of the

LORD?" 20 So when Moses heard *that*, he was content.

Relationship to tribe of Levi.

Num 3:6 "Bring the tribe of Levi near, and present them before Aaron the priest, that they may serve him.

Rebellion with Miriam. Num 12:1–12

Blossoming of his rod.

Num 17:8 Now it came to pass on the next day that Moses went into the tabernacle of witness, and behold, the rod of Aaron, of the house of Levi, had sprouted and put forth buds, had produced blossoms and yielded ripe almonds.

Denied entrance to Promised Land.

Num 20:12 Then the LORD spoke to Moses and Aaron, "Because you did not believe Me, to hallow Me in the eyes of the children of Israel, therefore you shall not bring this assembly into the land which I have given them."

Ps 106:32–33 They angered *Him* also at the waters of strife, So that it went ill with Moses on account of them; 33 Because they rebelled against His Spirit, So that he spoke rashly with his lips.

Admonition for house of, to praise God.

Ps 118:3 Let the house of Aaron now say, "His mercy *endures* forever."

Ps 135:19 Bless the LORD, O house of Israel! Bless the LORD, O house of Aaron!

Parents of John the Baptist descended from.

Luke 1:5 There was in the days of Herod, the king of Judea, a certain priest named Zacharias, of the division of Abijah. His wife *was* of the daughters of Aaron, and her name *was* Elizabeth.

ABANDON, ABANDONMENT

By God.

1 Kin 9:6–9 *But* if you or your sons at all turn from following Me, and do not keep My commandments *and* My statutes which I have set before you, but go and serve other gods and worship them, 7 then I will cut off Israel from the land which I have given them; and this house which I have consecrated for My name I will cast out of My sight. Israel will be a proverb and a byword among all peoples. 8 And *as for* this house, *which* is exalted, everyone who passes by it will be astonished and will hiss, and say, 'Why has the LORD done thus to this land and to this house?' 9 Then they will answer, 'Because they forsook the LORD their God, who brought their fathers out of the land of Egypt, and have embraced other gods, and worshiped them and served them; therefore the LORD has brought all this calamity on them.' "

Ps 73:27 For indeed, those who are far from You shall perish; You have destroyed all those who desert You for harlotry.

Matt 13:20–21 But he who received the seed on stony places, this is he who hears the word and immediately receives it with joy; 21 yet he has no root in himself, but endures only for a while. For when tribulation or persecution arises because of the word, immediately he stumbles.

2 Cor 11:3 But I fear, lest somehow, as the serpent de-

ceived Eve by his craftiness, so your minds may be corrupted from the simplicity that is in Christ.

Cf. Judg 10:13; 1 Kin 11:1–13; 2 Chr 15:2; 24:20; Ps 81:11–12; Hos 4:17; Matt 15:14; John 6:66; Acts 7:38–42; 14:16; 1 Tim 4:1

Results of.

Judg 16:20–21 And she said, "The Philistines *are* upon you, Samson!" So he awoke from his sleep, and said, "I will go out as before, at other times, and shake myself free!" But he did not know that the LORD had departed from him. **21** Then the Philistines took him and put out his eyes, and brought him down to Gaza. They bound him with bronze fetters, and he became a grinder in the prison.

1 Kin 22:20–23 And the LORD said, 'Who will persuade Ahab to go up, that he may fall at Ramoth Gilead?' So one spoke in this manner, and another spoke in that manner. **21** Then a spirit came forward and stood before the LORD, and said, 'I will persuade him.' **22** The LORD said to him, 'In what way?' So he said, 'I will go out and be a lying spirit in the mouth of all his prophets.' And the LORD said, 'You shall persuade *him,* and also prevail. Go out and do so.' **23** Therefore look! The LORD has put a lying spirit in the mouth of all these prophets of yours, and the LORD has declared disaster against you."

Ps 22:1 My God, My God, why have You forsaken Me? *Why are You so* far from helping Me, *And from* the words of My groaning?

2 Thess 2:11 And for this reason God will send them strong delusion, that they should believe the lie,

Cf. Matt 27:46; Mark 15:34; Rom 1:18–32

By family, friends.

Ps 27:10 When my father and my mother forsake me, Then the LORD will take care of me.

Ps 38:11 My loved ones and my friends stand aloof from my plague, And my relatives stand afar off.

Ps 142:4 Look on *my* right hand and see, For *there is* no one who acknowledges me; Refuge has failed me; No one cares for my soul.

2 Tim 1:15 This you know, that all those in Asia have turned away from me, among whom are Phygellus and Hermogenes.

2 Tim 4:9–12 Be diligent to come to me quickly; **10** for Demas has forsaken me, having loved this present world, and has departed for Thessalonica—Crescens for Galatia, Titus for Dalmatia. **11** Only Luke is with me. Get Mark and bring him with you, for he is useful to me for ministry. **12** And Tychicus I have sent to Ephesus.

2 Tim 4:16 At my first defense no one stood with me, but all forsook me. May it not be charged against them.

Of ministry.

2 Tim 4:9–10 Be diligent to come to me quickly; **10** for Demas has forsaken me, having loved this present world, and has departed for Thessalonica—Crescens for Galatia, Titus for Dalmatia.

Can involve apostasy.

2 Thess 2:3 Let no one deceive you by any means; for *that Day will not come* unless the falling away comes

first, and the man of sin is revealed, the son of perdition,

Heb 6:1–6 Therefore, leaving the discussion of the elementary *principles* of Christ, let us go on to perfection, not laying again the foundation of repentance from dead works and of faith toward God, **2** of the doctrine of baptisms, of laying on of hands, of resurrection of the dead, and of eternal judgment. **3** And this we will do if God permits. **4** For *it is* impossible for those who were once enlightened, and have tasted the heavenly gift, and have become partakers of the Holy Spirit, **5** and have tasted the good word of God and the powers of the age to come, **6** if they fall away, to renew them again to repentance, since they crucify again for themselves the Son of God, and put *Him* to an open shame.

Exhortation to, regarding world.

Luke 14:33 So likewise, whoever of you does not forsake all that he has cannot be My disciple.

Rev 18:4 And I heard another voice from heaven saying, "Come out of her, my people, lest you share in her sins, and lest you receive of her plagues.

Of proper role, results of.

Gen 3:17–19 Then to Adam He said, "Because you have heeded the voice of your wife, and have eaten from the tree of which I commanded you, saying, 'You shall not eat of it': "Cursed *is* the ground for your sake; In toil you shall eat *of* it All the days of your life. **18** Both thorns and thistles it shall bring forth for you, And you shall eat the herb of the field. **19** In the sweat of your face you shall eat bread Till you return to the ground, For out of it you were taken; For dust you *are,* And to dust you shall return."

ABIDE, ABIDING

In Christ.

John 8:31 Then Jesus said to those Jews who believed Him, "If you abide in My word, you are My disciples indeed.

John 15:1–10 "I am the true vine, and My Father is the vinedresser. **2** Every branch in Me that does not bear fruit He takes away; and every *branch* that bears fruit He prunes, that it may bear more fruit. **3** You are already clean because of the word which I have spoken to you. **4** Abide in Me, and I in you. As the branch cannot bear fruit of itself, unless it abides in the vine, neither can you, unless you abide in Me. **5** "I am the vine, you *are* the branches. He who abides in Me, and I in him, bears much fruit; for without Me you can do nothing. **6** If anyone does not abide in Me, he is cast out as a branch and is withered; and they gather them and throw *them* into the fire, and they are burned. **7** If you abide in Me, and My words abide in you, you will ask what you desire, and it shall be done for you. **8** By this My Father is glorified, that you bear much fruit; so you will be My disciples. **9** "As the Father loved Me, I also have loved you; abide in My love. **10** If you keep My commandments, you will abide in My love, just as I have kept My Father's commandments and abide in His love.

1 John 2:17 And the world is passing away, and the lust of it; but he who does the will of God abides forever.

1 John 2:27–29 But the anointing which you have received from Him abides in you, and you do not need that anyone teach you; but as the same anointing teaches you concerning all things, and is true, and is not a lie, and just as it has taught you, you will abide in Him. **28** And now, little children, abide in Him, that when He appears, we may have confidence and not be ashamed before Him at His coming. **29** If you know that He is righteous, you know that everyone who practices righteousness is born of Him.

1 John 3:24 Now he who keeps His commandments abides in Him, and He in him. And by this we know that He abides in us, by the Spirit whom He has given us.

2 John 1:9 Whoever transgresses and does not abide in the doctrine of Christ does not have God. He who abides in the doctrine of Christ has both the Father and the Son.

Of Holy Spirit.

John 14:16 And I will pray the Father, and He will give you another Helper, that He may abide with you forever—

Rom 8:9 But you are not in the flesh but in the Spirit, if indeed the Spirit of God dwells in you. Now if anyone does not have the Spirit of Christ, he is not His.

1 Cor 6:19–20 Or do you not know that your body is the temple of the Holy Spirit *who is* in you, whom you have from God, and you are not your own? **20** For you were bought at a price; therefore glorify God in your body and in your spirit, which are God's.

1 Cor 12:13 For by one Spirit we were all baptized into one body—whether Jews or Greeks, whether slaves or free—and have all been made to drink into one Spirit.

ABILITY

To save, solely with God.

John 6:37 All that the Father gives Me will come to Me, and the one who comes to Me I will by no means cast out.

John 6:44 No one can come to Me unless the Father who sent Me draws him; and I will raise him up at the last day.

John 6:65 And He said, "Therefore I have said to you that no one can come to Me unless it has been granted to him by My Father."

John 17:6 "I have manifested Your name to the men whom You have given Me out of the world. They were Yours, You gave them to Me, and they have kept Your word.

John 17:12 While I was with them in the world, I kept them in Your name. Those whom You gave Me I have kept; and none of them is lost except the son of perdition, that the Scripture might be fulfilled.

John 17:24 "Father, I desire that they also whom You gave Me may be with Me where I am, that they may behold My glory which You have given Me; for You loved Me before the foundation of the world.

Rom 8:29–30 For whom He foreknew, He also predestined *to be* conformed to the image of His Son, that He might be the firstborn among many brethren. **30** Moreover whom He predestined, these He also

called; whom He called, these He also justified; and whom He justified, these He also glorified.

Eph 1:3–6 Blessed *be* the God and Father of our Lord Jesus Christ, who has blessed us with every spiritual blessing in the heavenly *places* in Christ, **4** just as He chose us in Him before the foundation of the world, that we should be holy and without blame before Him in love, **5** having predestined us to adoption as sons by Jesus Christ to Himself, according to the good pleasure of His will, **6** to the praise of the glory of His grace, by which He made us accepted in the Beloved.

Col 2:13–14 And you, being dead in your trespasses and the uncircumcision of your flesh, He has made alive together with Him, having forgiven you all trespasses, **14** having wiped out the handwriting of requirements that was against us, which was contrary to us. And He has taken it out of the way, having nailed it to the cross.

1 Pet 1:2 elect according to the foreknowledge of God the Father, in sanctification of the Spirit, for obedience and sprinkling of the blood of Jesus Christ: Grace to you and peace be multiplied.

Cf. Rom 9:10–24

To minister, from God.

2 Cor 3:5 Not that we are sufficient of ourselves to think of anything as *being* from ourselves, but our sufficiency *is* from God,

And the grace of giving.

2 Cor 8:3–7 For I bear witness that according to *their* ability, yes, and beyond *their* ability, *they were* freely willing, **4** imploring us with much urgency that we would receive the gift and the fellowship of the ministering to the saints. **5** And not *only* as we had hoped, but they first gave themselves to the Lord, and *then* to us by the will of God. **6** So we urged Titus, that as he had begun, so he would also complete this grace in you as well. **7** But as you abound in everything—in faith, in speech, in knowledge, in all diligence, and in your love for us—*see* that you abound in this grace also.

ABOMINATION, ABOMINATIONS

Of Egyptian sacrifices.

Ex 8:26 And Moses said, "It is not right to do so, for we would be sacrificing the abomination of the Egyptians to the Lord our God. If we sacrifice the abomination of the Egyptians before their eyes, then will they not stone us?

Equated with homosexuality.

Lev 18:22 You shall not lie with a male as with a woman. It *is* an abomination.

Lev 20:13 If a man lies with a male as he lies with a woman, both of them have committed an abomination. They shall surely be put to death. Their blood *shall be* upon them.

Incompatible with God's nature.

Prov 3:32 For the perverse *person is* an abomination to the Lord, But His secret counsel *is* with the upright.

Prov 6:16–19 These six *things* the Lord hates, Yes, seven *are* an abomination to Him: **17** A proud look, A lying tongue, Hands that shed innocent blood, **18** A heart that devises wicked plans, Feet that are swift in running to evil, **19** A false witness *who* speaks lies, And one who sows discord among brethren.

Prov 11:20 Those who are of a perverse heart *are* an abomination to the LORD, But *the* blameless in their ways *are* His delight.

Of desolation (end times).

Dan 9:27 Then he shall confirm a covenant with many for one week; But in the middle of the week He shall bring an end to sacrifice and offering. And on the wing of abominations shall be one who makes desolate, Even until the consummation, which is determined, Is poured out on the desolate."

Matt 24:15 "Therefore when you see the 'abomination of desolation,' spoken of by Daniel the prophet, standing in the holy place" (whoever reads, let him understand),

Mark 13:14 "So when you see the 'abomination of desolation,' spoken of by Daniel the prophet, standing where it ought not" (let the reader understand), "then let those who are in Judea flee to the mountains.

2 Thess 2:3–4 Let no one deceive you by any means; for *that Day will not come* unless the falling away comes first, and the man of sin is revealed, the son of perdition, **4** who opposes and exalts himself above all that is called God or that is worshiped, so that he sits as God in the temple of God, showing himself that he is God.

Profaning the temple.

Dan 11:31 And forces shall be mustered by him, and they shall defile the sanctuary fortress; then they shall take away the daily *sacrifices*, and place *there* the abomination of desolation.

ABRAM, ABRAHAM

Called by God.

Gen 12:1–3 Now the LORD had said to Abram: "Get out of your country, From your family And from your father's house, To a land that I will show you. **2** I will make you a great nation; I will bless you And make your name great; And you shall be a blessing. **3** I will bless those who bless you, And I will curse him who curses you; And in you all the families of the earth shall be blessed."

Acts 7:2–4 And he said, "Brethren and fathers, listen: The God of glory appeared to our father Abraham when he was in Mesopotamia, before he dwelt in Haran, **3** and said to him, 'Get out of your country and from your relatives, and come to a land that I will show you.' **4** Then he came out of the land of the Chaldeans and dwelt in Haran. And from there, when his father was dead, He moved him to this land in which you now dwell.

God promised him Canaan.

Gen 12:1 Now the LORD had said to Abram: "Get out of your country, From your family And from your father's house, To a land that I will show you.

Gen 12:7 Then the LORD appeared to Abram and said, "To your descendants I will give this land." And there he built an altar to the LORD, who had appeared to him.

Received Melchizedek's blessing.

Gen 14:18–20 Then Melchizedek king of Salem brought out bread and wine; He *was* the priest of God Most High. **19** And he blessed him and said: "Blessed be Abram of God Most High, Possessor of heaven and earth; **20** And blessed be God Most High, Who has delivered your enemies into your hand." And he gave him a tithe of all.

God renewed covenant to,

Promised him a son. **Gen 15:1–21; 17:15–19**

Renamed him Abraham.

Gen 17:1–8 When Abram was ninety-nine years old, the LORD appeared to Abram and said to him, "I *am* Almighty God; walk before Me and be blameless. **2** And I will make My covenant between Me and you, and will multiply you exceedingly." **3** Then Abram fell on his face, and God talked with him, saying: **4** "As for Me, behold, My covenant is with you, and you shall be a father of many nations. **5** No longer shall your name be called Abram, but your name shall be Abraham; for I have made you a father of many nations. **6** I will make you exceedingly fruitful; and I will make nations of you, and kings shall come from you. **7** And I will establish My covenant between Me and you and your descendants after you in their generations, for an everlasting covenant, to be God to you and your descendants after you. **8** Also I give to you and your descendants after you the land in which you are a stranger, all the land of Canaan, as an everlasting possession; and I will be their God."

Justified by faith.

Gen 15:6 And he believed in the LORD, and He accounted it to him for righteousness.

Rom 4:1–12 What then shall we say that Abraham our father has found according to the flesh? **2** For if Abraham was justified by works, he has *something* to boast about, but not before God. **3** For what does the Scripture say? "Abraham believed God, and it was accounted to him for righteousness." **4** Now to him who works, the wages are not counted as grace but as debt. **5** But to him who does not work but believes on Him who justifies the ungodly, his faith is accounted for righteousness, **6** just as David also describes the blessedness of the man to whom God imputes righteousness apart from works: **7** "Blessed are those whose lawless deeds are forgiven, And whose sins are covered; **8** Blessed is the man to whom the LORD shall not impute sin." **9** Does this blessedness then *come* upon the circumcised *only*, or upon the uncircumcised also? For we say that faith was accounted to Abraham for righteousness. **10** How then was it accounted? While he was circumcised, or uncircumcised? Not while circumcised, but while uncircumcised. **11** And he received the sign of circumcision, a seal of the righteousness of the faith which *he had while still* uncircumcised, that he might be the father of all those who believe, though they are uncircumcised, that righteousness might be imputed to them also, **12** and the father of circumcision to those who not only *are* of the circumcision, but who also walk in the steps of the faith which our father Abraham *had while still* uncircumcised.

Cf. James 2:21–23

Interceded for Sodom. Gen 18:16–33

Son of promise, Isaac, born to.

Gen 21:1–8 And the LORD visited Sarah as He had said, and the LORD did for Sarah as He had spoken. **2** For Sarah conceived and bore Abraham a son in his old age, at the set time of which God had spoken to him. **3** And Abraham called the name of his son who was born to him—whom Sarah bore to him—Isaac. **4** Then Abraham circumcised his son Isaac when he was eight days old, as God had commanded him. **5** Now Abraham was one hundred years old when his son Isaac was born to him. **6** And Sarah said, "God has made me laugh, *and* all who hear will laugh with me." **7** She also said, "Who would have said to Abraham that Sarah would nurse children? For I have borne *him* a son in his old age." **8** So the child grew and was weaned. And Abraham made a great feast on the same day that Isaac was weaned.

Sent Hagar and Ishmael away.

Gen 21:9–21 And Sarah saw the son of Hagar the Egyptian, whom she had borne to Abraham, scoffing. **10** Therefore she said to Abraham, "Cast out this bondwoman and her son; for the son of this bondwoman shall not be heir with my son, *namely* with Isaac." **11** And the matter was very displeasing in Abraham's sight because of his son. **12** But God said to Abraham, "Do not let it be displeasing in your sight because of the lad or because of your bondwoman. Whatever Sarah has said to you, listen to her voice; for in Isaac your seed shall be called. **13** Yet I will also make a nation of the son of the bondwoman, because he *is* your seed." **14** So Abraham rose early in the morning, and took bread and a skin of water; and putting *it* on her shoulder, he gave *it* and the boy to Hagar, and sent her away. Then she departed and wandered in the Wilderness of Beersheba. **15** And the water in the skin was used up, and she placed the boy under one of the shrubs. **16** Then she went and sat down across from *him* at a distance of about a bowshot; for she said to herself, "Let me not see the death of the boy." So she sat opposite *him*, and lifted her voice and wept. **17** And God heard the voice of the lad. Then the angel of God called to Hagar out of heaven, and said to her, "What ails you, Hagar? Fear not, for God has heard the voice of the lad where he *is*. **18** Arise, lift up the lad and hold him with your hand, for I will make him a great nation." **19** Then God opened her eyes, and she saw a well of water. And she went and filled the skin with water, and gave the lad a drink. **20** So God was with the lad; and he grew and dwelt in the wilderness, and became an archer. **21** He dwelt in the Wilderness of Paran; and his mother took a wife for him from the land of Egypt.

Tested by God regarding Isaac. Gen 22:1–19

A hero of faith.

Heb 11:8–10 By faith Abraham obeyed when he was called to go out to the place which he would receive as an inheritance. And he went out, not knowing where he was going. **9** By faith he dwelt in the land of promise as *in* a foreign country, dwelling in tents with Isaac and Jacob, the heirs with him of the same promise; **10** for he waited for the city which has foundations, whose builder and maker *is* God.

Foresaw Christ's day and the gospel.

John 8:56 Your father Abraham rejoiced to see My day, and he saw *it* and was glad."

Gal 3:8 And the Scripture, foreseeing that God would justify the Gentiles by faith, preached the gospel to Abraham beforehand, *saying, "In you all the nations shall be blessed."*

Father of all believers.

Gal 3:7 Therefore know that *only* those who are of faith are sons of Abraham.

Gal 3:29 And if you *are* Christ's, then you are Abraham's seed, and heirs according to the promise.

Cf. Matt 8:11; Rom 4:11–25

Obtained wife for Isaac.

Gen 24:1–9 Now Abraham was old, well advanced in age; and the LORD had blessed Abraham in all things. **2** So Abraham said to the oldest servant of his house, who ruled over all that he had, "Please, put your hand under my thigh, **3** and I will make you swear by the LORD, the God of heaven and the God of the earth, that you will not take a wife for my son from the daughters of the Canaanites, among whom I dwell; **4** but you shall go to my country and to my family, and take a wife for my son Isaac." **5** And the servant said to him, "Perhaps the woman will not be willing to follow me to this land. Must I take your son back to the land from which you came?" **6** But Abraham said to him, "Beware that you do not take my son back there. **7** The LORD God of heaven, who took me from my father's house and from the land of my family, and who spoke to me and swore to me, saying, 'To your descendants I give this land,' He will send His angel before you, and you shall take a wife for my son from there. **8** And if the woman is not willing to follow you, then you will be released from this oath; only do not take my son back there." **9** So the servant put his hand under the thigh of Abraham his master, and swore to him concerning this matter.

ABUNDANCE

In Promised Land.

Deut 8:6–10 "Therefore you shall keep the commandments of the LORD your God, to walk in His ways and to fear Him. **7** For the LORD your God is bringing you into a good land, a land of brooks of water, of fountains and springs, that flow out of valleys and hills; **8** a land of wheat and barley, of vines and fig trees and pomegranates, a land of olive oil and honey; **9** a land in which you will eat bread without scarcity, in which you will lack nothing; a land whose stones *are* iron and out of whose hills you can dig copper. **10** When you have eaten and are full, then you shall bless the LORD your God for the good land which He has given you.

Included in blessings promised to Israel.

Deut 28:3–14 "Blessed *shall* you *be* in the city, and blessed *shall* you *be* in the country. **4** "Blessed *shall be* the fruit of your body, the produce of your ground and the increase of your herds, the increase of your cattle and the offspring of your flocks. **5** "Blessed *shall be* your basket and your kneading bowl. **6** "Blessed *shall* you *be* when you come in, and blessed *shall* you *be* when you go out. **7** "The LORD will cause your enemies who rise against you to be defeated before your face; they shall come out against you one way and flee before you seven ways. **8** "The LORD will command the blessing on you in your storehouses and in all to which you set your hand, and He will bless you in the land which the LORD your God is giving you. **9** "The LORD will establish you as a holy people to Himself, just as He has sworn to you, if you keep the commandments of the LORD your God and walk in His ways. **10** Then all peoples of the earth shall see that you are called by the name of the LORD, and they shall be afraid of you. **11** And the LORD will grant you plenty of goods, in the fruit of your body, in the increase of your livestock, and in the produce of your ground, in the land of which the LORD swore to your fathers to give you. **12** The LORD will open to you His good treasure, the heavens, to give the rain to your land in its season, and to bless all the work of your hand. You shall lend to many nations, but you shall not borrow. **13** And the LORD will make you the head and not the tail; you shall be above only, and not be beneath, if you heed the commandments of the LORD your God, which I command you today, and are careful to observe *them*. **14** So you shall not turn aside from any of the words which I command you this day, *to* the right or the left, to go after other gods to serve them.

Restored.

Joel 2:19–24 The LORD will answer and say to His people, "Behold, I will send you grain and new wine and oil, And you will be satisfied by them; I will no longer make you a reproach among the nations. **20** "But I will remove far from you the northern *army*, And will drive him away into a barren and desolate land, With his face toward the eastern sea And his back toward the western sea; His stench will come up, And his foul odor will rise, Because he has done monstrous things." **21** Fear not, O land; Be glad and rejoice, For the LORD has done marvelous things! **22** Do not be afraid, you beasts of the field; For the open pastures are springing up, And the tree bears its fruit; The fig tree and the vine yield their strength. **23** Be glad then, you children of Zion, And rejoice in the LORD your God; For He has given you the former rain faithfully, And He will cause the rain to come down for you— The former rain, And the latter rain in the first *month*. **24** The threshing floors shall be full of wheat, And the vats shall overflow with new wine and oil.

Mal 3:10–12 Bring all the tithes into the storehouse, That there may be food in My house, And try Me now in this," Says the LORD of hosts, "If I will not open for you the windows of heaven And pour out for you *such* blessing That *there will* not *be room* enough *to receive it*. **11** "And I will rebuke the devourer for your sakes, So that he will not destroy the fruit of your ground, Nor shall the vine fail to bear fruit for you in the field," Says the LORD of hosts; **12** And all nations will call you blessed, For you will be a delightful land," Says the LORD of hosts.

Equated with wealth.

Luke 21:4 for all these out of their abundance have put in offerings for God, but she out of her poverty put in all the livelihood that she had."

Related to surplus of spiritual virtue.

2 Cor 8:2 that in a great trial of affliction the abundance of their joy and their deep poverty abounded in the riches of their liberality.

2 Cor 9:8 And God *is* able to make all grace abound toward you, that you, always having all sufficiency in all *things*, may have an abundance for every good work.

ACCEPTABLE

God shows what is and is not, with first sacrifices.

Gen 4:4–7 Abel also brought of the firstborn of his flock and of their fat. And the LORD respected Abel and his offering, **5** but He did not respect Cain and his offering. And Cain was very angry, and his countenance fell. **6** So the LORD said to Cain, "Why are you angry? And why has your countenance fallen? **7** If you do well, will you not be accepted? And if you do not do well, sin lies at the door. And its desire *is* for you, but you should rule over it."

Cf. Eph 4:18; 1 John 3:12

For sacrifices to be, God demanded perfect animals.

Lev 22:21 And whoever offers a sacrifice of a peace offering to the LORD, to fulfill *his* vow, or a freewill offering from the cattle or the sheep, it must be perfect to be accepted; there shall be no defect in it.

Cf. Heb 9:13–14

Plea for life to be.

Ps 19:14 Let the words of my mouth and the meditation of my heart Be acceptable in Your sight, O LORD, my strength and my Redeemer.

Rom 12:1–2 I beseech you therefore, brethren, by the mercies of God, that you present your bodies a living sacrifice, holy, acceptable to God, *which is* your reasonable service. **2** And do not be conformed to this world, but be transformed by the renewing of your mind, that you may prove what *is* that good and acceptable and perfect will of God.

Eph 5:8–10 For you were once darkness, but now *you are* light in the Lord. Walk as children of light **9** (for the fruit of the Spirit *is* in all goodness, righteousness, and truth), **10** finding out what is acceptable to the Lord.

Applies to time of salvation.

Is 49:8 Thus says the LORD: "In an acceptable time I have heard You, And in the day of salvation I have helped You; I will preserve You and give You As a covenant to the people, To restore the earth, To cause them to inherit the desolate heritages;

Is 61:1–2 "The Spirit of the Lord GOD *is* upon Me, Because the LORD has anointed Me To preach good tidings to the poor; He has sent Me to heal the brokenhearted, To proclaim liberty to the captives, And the opening of the prison to *those who are* bound; **2** To proclaim the acceptable year of the LORD, And the day of vengeance of our God; To comfort all who mourn,

Luke 4:19 *To proclaim the acceptable year of the LORD."*

2 Cor 6:1–2 We then, *as* workers together *with Him* also plead with *you* not to receive the grace of God in vain. **2** For He says: *"In an acceptable time I have heard you, And in the day of salvation I have helped you."* Behold, now *is* the accepted time; behold, now *is* the day of salvation.

ACCEPTANCE

By Christ, of His deity and messiahship.

Luke 4:16–21 So He came to Nazareth, where He had been brought up. And as His custom was, He went into the synagogue on the Sabbath day, and stood up to read. **17** And He was handed the book of the prophet Isaiah. And when He had opened the book, He found the place where it was written: **18** *"The Spirit of the Lord is upon Me, Because He has anointed Me To preach the gospel to the poor; He has sent Me to heal the brokenhearted, To proclaim liberty to the captives And recovery of sight to the blind, To set at liberty those who are oppressed; **19** To proclaim the acceptable year of the Lord."* **20** Then He closed the book, and gave *it* back to the attendant and sat down. And the eyes of all who were in the synagogue were fixed on Him. **21** And He began to say to them, "Today this Scripture is fulfilled in your hearing."

John 4:25–26 The woman said to Him, "I know that Messiah is coming" (who is called Christ). "When He comes, He will tell us all things." **26** Jesus said to her, "I who speak to you am *He*."

John 5:17–18 But Jesus answered them, "My Father has been working until now, and I have been working." **18** Therefore the Jews sought all the more to kill Him, because He not only broke the Sabbath, but also said that God was His Father, making Himself equal with God.

John 8:58 Jesus said to them, "Most assuredly, I say to you, before Abraham was, I AM."

Before God, based on grace, not law.

Rom 3:19–26 Now we know that whatever the law says, it says to those who are under the law, that every mouth may be stopped, and all the world may become guilty before God. **20** Therefore by the deeds of the law no flesh will be justified in His sight, for by the law *is* the knowledge of sin. **21** But now the righteousness of God apart from the law is revealed, being witnessed by the Law and the Prophets, **22** even the righteousness of God, through faith in Jesus Christ, to all and on all who believe. For there is no difference; **23** for all have sinned and fall short of the glory of God, **24** being justified freely by His grace through the redemption that is in Christ Jesus, **25** whom God set forth *as* a propitiation by His blood, through faith, to demonstrate His righteousness, because in His forbearance God had passed over the sins that were previously committed, **26** to demonstrate at the present time His righteousness, that He might be just and the justifier of the one who has faith in Jesus.

Rom 7:6 But now we have been delivered from the law, having died to what we were held by, so that we should serve in the newness of the Spirit and not *in* the oldness of the letter.

Rom 8:1–4 *There is* therefore now no condemnation to those who are in Christ Jesus, who do not walk according to the flesh, but according to the Spirit. **2** For the law of the Spirit of life in Christ Jesus has made me free from the law of sin and death. **3** For what the law could not do in that it was weak through the flesh, God *did* by sending His own Son in the likeness of sinful flesh, on account of sin: He condemned sin in the flesh, **4** that the righteous requirement of the law might be fulfilled in us who do not walk according to the flesh but according to the Spirit.

Gal 3:10–13 For as many as are of the works of the law are under the curse; for it is written, *"Cursed is everyone who does not continue in all things which are written in the book of the law, to do them."* **11** But that no one is justified by the law in the sight of God *is* evident, for *"the just shall live by faith."* **12** Yet the law is not of faith, but *"the man who does them shall live by them."* **13** Christ has redeemed us from the curse of the law, having become a curse for us (for it is written, *"Cursed is everyone who hangs on a tree"*),

Between believers.

Rom 14:1–12 Receive one who is weak in the faith, *but* not to disputes over doubtful things. **2** For one believes he may eat all things, but he who is weak eats *only* vegetables. **3** Let not him who eats despise him who does not eat, and let not him who does not eat judge him who eats; for God has received him. **4** Who are you to judge another's servant? To his own master he stands or falls. Indeed, he will be made to stand, for God is able to make him stand. **5** One person esteems *one* day above another; another esteems every day *alike*. Let each be fully convinced in his own mind. **6** He who observes the day, observes *it* to the Lord; and he who does not observe the day, to the Lord he does not observe *it*. He who eats, eats to the Lord, for he gives God thanks; and he who does not eat, to the Lord he does not eat, and gives God thanks. **7** For none of us lives to himself, and no one dies to himself. **8** For if we live, we live to the Lord; and if we die, we die to the Lord. Therefore, whether we live or die, we are the Lord's. **9** For to this end Christ died and rose and lived again, that He might be Lord of both the dead and the living. **10** But why do you judge your brother? Or why do you show contempt for your brother? For we shall all stand before the judgment seat of Christ. **11** For it is written: *"As I live, says the Lord, Every knee shall bow to Me, And every tongue shall confess to God."* **12** So then each of us shall give account of himself to God.

1 Cor 8:1–13 Now concerning things offered to idols: We know that we all have knowledge. Knowledge puffs up, but love edifies. **2** And if anyone thinks that he knows anything, he knows nothing yet as he ought to know. **3** But if anyone loves God, this one is known by Him. **4** Therefore concerning the eating of things offered to idols, we know that an idol *is* nothing in the world, and that *there is* no other God but one. **5** For even if there are so-called gods, whether in heaven or on earth (as there are many gods and many lords), **6** yet for us *there is* one God, the Father, of whom *are* all things, and we for Him; and one Lord Jesus Christ, through whom *are* all things, and through whom we *live*. **7** However, *there is* not in everyone that knowledge; for some, with consciousness of the idol, until now eat *it* as a thing offered to an idol; and their conscience, being weak, is defiled. **8** But food does not commend us to God; for neither if we eat are we the better, nor if we do not eat are we the worse. **9** But beware lest somehow this liberty of yours become a stumbling block to those who are weak. **10** For if anyone sees you who have knowledge eating in an idol's temple, will not the conscience of him who is weak be emboldened to eat those things offered to idols? **11** And because of your knowledge shall the weak brother perish, for whom Christ died? **12** But when you thus sin against the brethren, and wound their weak conscience, you sin against Christ. **13** Therefore, if food makes my brother stumble, I will never again eat meat, lest I make my brother stumble.

Worthy of, key gospel truths.

1 Tim 1:15 This *is* a faithful saying and worthy of all acceptance, that Christ Jesus came into the world to save sinners, of whom I am chief.

1 Tim 4:9–10 This *is* a faithful saying and worthy of all acceptance. **10** For to this *end* we both labor and suffer reproach, because we trust in the living God, who is *the* Savior of all men, especially of those who believe.

2 Tim 2:11–13 This is a faithful saying: For if we died with *Him,* We shall also live with *Him.* **12** If we endure, We shall also reign with *Him.* If we deny *Him,* He also will deny us. **13** If we are faithless, He remains faithful; He cannot deny Himself.

Titus 3:8 This is a faithful saying, and these things I want you to affirm constantly, that those who have believed in God should be careful to maintain good works. These things are good and profitable to men.

ACCOMPLISH, ACCOMPLISHED
God's Word will.

Is 55:11 So shall My word be that goes forth from My mouth; It shall not return to Me void, But it shall accomplish what I please, And it shall prosper *in the thing* for which I sent it.

Mark 14:49 I was daily with you in the temple teaching, and you did not seize Me. But the Scriptures must be fulfilled."

Christ's mission will be.

Luke 9:51 Now it came to pass, when the time had come for Him to be received up, that He steadfastly set His face to go to Jerusalem,

Luke 12:50 But I have a baptism to be baptized with, and how distressed I am till it is accomplished!

Cf. John 12:27

Prayer will.

James 5:16 Confess *your* trespasses to one another, and pray for one another, that you may be healed. The effective, fervent prayer of a righteous man avails much.

ACCUSATION
Letter of, against Jews. Ezra 4:6–16
And Satan's role.

Zech 3:1–2 Then he showed me Joshua the high priest standing before the Angel of the LORD, and Satan standing at his right hand to oppose him. **2** And the LORD said to Satan, "The LORD rebuke you, Satan! The LORD who has chosen Jerusalem rebuke you! *Is* this not a brand plucked from the fire?"

Cf. Job 1–2; Rev 12:10

Against Jesus
By the scribes and Pharisees.

Mark 3:20–30 Then the multitude came together again, so that they could not so much as eat bread. **21** But when His own people heard *about this,* they went out to lay hold of Him, for they said, "He is out of His mind." **22** And the scribes who came down from Jerusalem said, "He has Beelzebub," and, "By the ruler of the demons He casts out demons." **23** So He called them to *Himself* and said to them in parables: "How can Satan cast out Satan? **24** If a kingdom is divided against itself, that kingdom cannot stand. **25** And if a house is divided against itself, that house cannot stand. **26** And if Satan has risen up against himself, and is divided, he cannot stand, but has an end. **27** No one can enter a strong man's house and plunder his goods, unless he first binds the strong man. And then he will plunder his house. **28** "Assuredly, I say to you, all sins will be forgiven the sons of men, and whatever blasphemies they may utter; **29** but he who blasphemes against the Holy Spirit never has forgiveness, but is subject to eternal condemnation"— **30** because they said, "He has an unclean spirit."

Cf. Matt 12:22–37

On the cross.

Matt 27:37 And they put up over His head the accusation written against Him: THIS IS JESUS THE KING OF THE JEWS.

Cf. Mark 15:26; Luke 23:38

Legally.

John 18:29 Pilate then went out to them and said, "What accusation do you bring against this Man?"

Against angelic beings.

2 Pet 2:11 whereas angels, who are greater in power and might, do not bring a reviling accusation against them before the Lord.

Jude 1:9 Yet Michael the archangel, in contending with the devil, when he disputed about the body of Moses, dared not bring against him a reviling accusation, but said, "The Lord rebuke you!"

ACKNOWLEDGMENT
Of faith in Christ.

Matt 10:32–33 "Therefore whoever confesses Me before men, him I will also confess before My Father who is in heaven. **33** But whoever denies Me before men, him I will also deny before My Father who is in heaven.

Luke 12:8–9 "Also I say to you, whoever confesses Me before men, him the Son of Man also will confess before the angels of God. **9** But he who denies Me before men will be denied before the angels of God.

John 9:35–38 Jesus heard that they had cast him out; and when He had found him, He said to him, "Do you believe in the Son of God?" **36** He answered and said, "Who is He, Lord, that I may believe in Him?" **37** And Jesus said to him, "You have both seen Him and it is He who is talking with you." **38** Then he said, "Lord, I believe!" And he worshiped Him.

Rom 10:9–13 that if you confess with your mouth the Lord Jesus and believe in your heart that God has raised Him from the dead, you will be saved. **10** For with the heart one believes unto righteousness, and with the mouth confession is made unto salvation. **11** For the Scripture says, *"Whoever believes on Him will not be put to shame."* **12** For there is no distinction between Jew and Greek, for the same Lord over all is rich to all who call upon Him. **13** For *"whoever calls on the name of the LORD shall be saved."*

Practical, of spiritual truth.

Philem 1:6 that the sharing of your faith may become effective by the acknowledgment of every good thing which is in you in Christ Jesus.

ACTIVITY, ACTIVITIES

God's creative.

Ps 74:13 You divided the sea by Your strength; You broke the heads of the sea serpents in the waters.

Cf. Gen 1:1—2:3

Wearisome ones of life.

Eccl 1:2–11 "Vanity of vanities," says the Preacher; "Vanity of vanities, all *is* vanity." **3** What profit has a man from all his labor In which he toils under the sun? **4** *One* generation passes away, and *another* generation comes; But the earth abides forever. **5** The sun also rises, and the sun goes down, And hastens to the place from which it arose. **6** The wind goes toward the south, And turns around to the north; The wind whirls about continually, And comes again on its circuit. **7** All the rivers run into the sea, Yet the sea *is* not full; To the place from which the rivers come, There they return again. **8** All things *are* full of labor; Man cannot express *it.* The eye is not satisfied with seeing, Nor the ear filled with hearing. **9** That which has been *is* what will be, That which *is* done is what will be done, And *there is* nothing new under the sun. **10** Is there anything of which it may be said, "See, this *is* new"? It has already been in ancient times before us. **11** *There is* no remembrance of former *things,* Nor will there be any remembrance of *things* that are to come By *those* who will come after.

All has a time.

Eccl 3:11 He has made everything beautiful in its time. Also He has put eternity in their hearts, except that no one can find out the work that God does from beginning to end.

On the Sabbath.

Matt 12:2–8 And when the Pharisees saw *it,* they said to Him, "Look, Your disciples are doing what is not lawful to do on the Sabbath!" **3** But He said to them, "Have you not read what David did when he was hungry, he and those who were with him: **4** how he entered the house of God and ate the showbread which was not lawful for him to eat, nor for those who were with him, but only for the priests? **5** Or have you not read in the law that on the Sabbath the priests in the temple profane the Sabbath, and are blameless? **6** Yet I say to you that in this place there is *One* greater than the temple. **7** But if you had known what *this* means, '*I desire mercy and not sac-*

rifice,' you would not have condemned the guiltless. **8** For the Son of Man is Lord even of the Sabbath."

Mark 2:27–28 And He said to them, "The Sabbath was made for man, and not man for the Sabbath. **28** Therefore the Son of Man is also Lord of the Sabbath."

Luke 6:9 Then Jesus said to them, "I will ask you one thing: Is it lawful on the Sabbath to do good or to do evil, to save life or to destroy?"

John 5:8–10 Jesus said to him, "Rise, take up your bed and walk." **9** And immediately the man was made well, took up his bed, and walked. And that day was the Sabbath. **10** The Jews therefore said to him who was cured, "It is the Sabbath; it is not lawful for you to carry your bed."

Sinful, lists of.

Rom 1:24–32 Therefore God also gave them up to uncleanness, in the lusts of their hearts, to dishonor their bodies among themselves, **25** who exchanged the truth of God for the lie, and worshiped and served the creature rather than the Creator, who is blessed forever. Amen. **26** For this reason God gave them up to vile passions. For even their women exchanged the natural use for what is against nature. **27** Likewise also the men, leaving the natural use of the woman, burned in their lust for one another, men with men committing what is shameful, and receiving in themselves the penalty of their error which was due. **28** And even as they did not like to retain God in *their* knowledge, God gave them over to a debased mind, to do those things which are not fitting; **29** being filled with all unrighteousness, sexual immorality, wickedness, covetousness, maliciousness; full of envy, murder, strife, deceit, evil-mindedness; *they are* whisperers, **30** backbiters, haters of God, violent, proud, boasters, inventors of evil things, disobedient to parents, **31** undiscerning, untrustworthy, unloving, unforgiving, unmerciful; **32** who, knowing the righteous judgment of God, that those who practice such things are deserving of death, not only do the same but also approve of those who practice them.

1 Cor 6:9–10 Do you not know that the unrighteous will not inherit the kingdom of God? Do not be deceived. Neither fornicators, nor idolaters, nor adulterers, nor homosexuals, nor sodomites, **10** nor thieves, nor covetous, nor drunkards, nor revilers, nor extortioners will inherit the kingdom of God.

Gal 5:19–21 Now the works of the flesh are evident, which are: adultery, fornication, uncleanness, lewdness, **20** idolatry, sorcery, hatred, contentions, jealousies, outbursts of wrath, selfish ambitions, dissensions, heresies, **21** envy, murders, drunkenness, revelries, and the like; of which I tell you beforehand, just as I also told *you* in time past, that those who practice such things will not inherit the kingdom of God.

Varied, concerning spiritual gifts.

1 Cor 12:6 And there are diversities of activities, but it is the same God who works all in all.

ADAM

Genealogy of. Gen 5:1–32; 6:1–8; 1 Chr 1:1–4; Jude 1:14

Used for "mankind."

Job 31:33 If I have covered my transgressions as Adam, By hiding my iniquity in my bosom,

Part of Christ's genealogy.

Luke 3:23–38 Now Jesus Himself began *His ministry at* about thirty years of age, being (as was supposed) *the* son of Joseph, *the son* of Heli, **24** *the son* of Matthat, *the son* of Levi, *the son* of Melchi, *the son* of Janna, *the* son of Joseph, **25** *the son* of Mattathiah, *the son* of Amos, *the son* of Nahum, *the son* of Esli, *the son* of Naggai, **26** *the son* of Maath, *the son* of Mattathiah, *the son* of Semei, *the son* of Joseph, *the son* of Judah, **27** *the son* of Joannas, *the son* of Rhesa, *the son* of Zerubbabel, *the son* of Shealtiel, *the son* of Neri, **28** *the son* of Melchi, *the son* of Addi, *the son* of Cosam, *the son* of Elmodam, *the son* of Er, **29** *the son* of Jose, *the son* of Eliezer, *the son* of Jorim, *the son* of Matthat, *the son* of Levi, **30** *the son* of Simeon, *the son* of Judah, *the* son of Joseph, *the son* of Jonan, *the son* of Eliakim, **31** *the son* of Melea, *the son* of Menan, *the son* of Mattathah, *the son* of Nathan, *the son* of David, **32** *the son of* Jesse, *the son* of Obed, *the son* of Boaz, *the son* of Salmon, *the son* of Nahshon, **33** *the son* of Amminadab, *the son* of Ram, *the son* of Hezron, *the son* of Perez, *the* son of Judah, **34** *the son* of Jacob, *the son* of Isaac, *the* son of Abraham, *the son* of Terah, *the son* of Nahor, **35** *the son* of Serug, *the son* of Reu, *the son* of Peleg, *the* son of Eber, *the son* of Shelah, **36** *the son* of Cainan, *the* son of Arphaxad, *the son* of Shem, *the son* of Noah, *the son* of Lamech, **37** *the son* of Methuselah, *the son* of Enoch, *the son* of Jared, *the son* of Mahalalel, *the son* of Cainan, **38** *the son* of Enosh, *the son* of Seth, *the* son of Adam, *the son* of God.

Consequences of his sin, for mankind.

Rom 5:12–19 Therefore, just as through one man sin entered the world, and death through sin, and thus death spread to all men, because all sinned— **13** (For until the law sin was in the world, but sin is not imputed when there is no law. **14** Nevertheless death reigned from Adam to Moses, even over those who had not sinned according to the likeness of the transgression of Adam, who is a type of Him who was to come. **15** But the free gift *is* not like the offense. For if by the one man's offense many died, much more the grace of God and the gift by the grace of the one Man, Jesus Christ, abounded to many. **16** And the gift *is* not like *that which came* through the one who sinned. For the judgment *which came* from one *offense resulted* in condemnation, but the free gift *which came* from many offenses *resulted* in justification. **17** For if by the one man's offense death reigned through the one, much more those who receive abundance of grace and of the gift of righteousness will reign in life through the One, Jesus Christ.) **18** Therefore, as through one man's offense *judgment* came to all men, resulting in condemnation, even so through one Man's righteous act *the free gift came* to all men, resulting in justification of life. **19** For as by one man's disobedience many were made sinners, so also by one Man's obedience many will be made righteous.

Cf. 1 Cor 15:21–22; Col 3:9; 1 Tim 2:13–14

Comparison to Christ.

1 Cor 15:45–49 And so it is written, *"The first man Adam became a living being."* The last Adam *became* a life-giving spirit. **46** However, the spiritual is not first, but the natural, and afterward the spiritual. **47** The first man *was* of the earth, *made* of dust; the second Man *is* the Lord from heaven. **48** As *was* the *man* of dust, so also *are* those *who are made* of dust; and as *is* the heavenly *Man,* so also *are* those *who are* heavenly. **49** And as we have borne the image of the *man* of dust, we shall also bear the image of the heavenly *Man.*

ADMINISTRATION

By Moses and early judges. Ex 18:13–26; Deut 16:18
Of law, to be just.

Deut 24:17–18 "You shall not pervert justice due the stranger or the fatherless, nor take a widow's garment as a pledge. **18** But you shall remember that you were a slave in Egypt, and the LORD your God redeemed you from there; therefore I command you to do this thing.

Spiritual gift of leadership.

1 Cor 12:28 And God has appointed these in the church: first apostles, second prophets, third teachers, after that miracles, then gifts of healings, helps, administrations, varieties of tongues.

And spiritual service, enterprise.

2 Cor 9:12 For the administration of this service not only supplies the needs of the saints, but also is abounding through many thanksgivings to God,

Cf. Eph 3:2

ADOPTION

Explained.

2 Cor 6:18 *"I will be a Father to you, And you shall be My sons and daughters, Says the LORD Almighty."*

Is according to promise.

Rom 9:8 That is, those who *are* the children of the flesh, these *are* not the children of God; but the children of the promise are counted as the seed.

Gal 3:29 And if you *are* Christ's, then you are Abraham's seed, and heirs according to the promise.

Is by faith.

Gal 3:7 Therefore know that *only* those who are of faith are sons of Abraham.

Gal 3:26 For you are all sons of God through faith in Christ Jesus.

Is of God's grace.

Ezek 16:3–6 and say, 'Thus says the Lord GOD to Jerusalem: "Your birth and your nativity *are* from the land of Canaan; your father *was* an Amorite and your mother a Hittite. **4** *As for* your nativity, on the day you were born your navel cord was not cut, nor were you washed in water to cleanse *you;* you were not rubbed with salt nor wrapped in swaddling cloths. **5** No eye pitied you, to do any of these things for you, to have compassion on you; but you were thrown out into the open field, when you yourself were loathed on the day you were born. **6** "And when I passed by you and saw you struggling in your own blood, I said to you in your blood, 'Live!' Yes, I said to you in your blood, 'Live!'

Rom 4:16–17 Therefore *it is* of faith that *it might be ac-*

cording to grace, so that the promise might be sure to all the seed, not only to those who are of the law, but also to those who are of the faith of Abraham, who is the father of us all **17** (as it is written, *"I have made you a father of many nations"*) in the presence of Him whom he believed—God, who gives life to the dead and calls those things which do not exist as though they did;

Eph 1:5–6 having predestined us to adoption as sons by Jesus Christ to Himself, according to the good pleasure of His will, **6** to the praise of the glory of His grace, by which He made us accepted in the Beloved.

Eph 1:11 In Him also we have obtained an inheritance, being predestined according to the purpose of Him who works all things according to the counsel of His will,

Is through Christ.

John 1:12 But as many as received Him, to them He gave the right to become children of God, to those who believe in His name:

Gal 4:4–5 But when the fullness of the time had come, God sent forth His Son, born of a woman, born under the law, **5** to redeem those who were under the law, that we might receive the adoption as sons.

Eph 1:5 having predestined us to adoption as sons by Jesus Christ to Himself, according to the good pleasure of His will,

Heb 2:10 For it was fitting for Him, for whom *are* all things and by whom *are* all things, in bringing many sons to glory, to make the captain of their salvation perfect through sufferings.

Heb 2:13 And again: *"I will put My trust in Him."* And again: *"Here am I and the children whom God has given Me."*

Saints predestined to.

Rom 8:29 For whom He foreknew, He also predestined *to be* conformed to the image of His Son, that He might be the firstborn among many brethren.

Eph 1:5 having predestined us to adoption as sons by Jesus Christ to Himself, according to the good pleasure of His will,

Eph 1:11 In Him also we have obtained an inheritance, being predestined according to the purpose of Him who works all things according to the counsel of His will,

Of Gentiles, predicted.

Hos 2:23 Then I will sow her for Myself in the earth, And I will have mercy on *her who had* not obtained mercy; Then I will say to *those who were* not My people, 'You *are* My people!' And they shall say, 'You *are* my God!' "

Rom 9:24–26 *even* us whom He called, not of the Jews only, but also of the Gentiles? **25** As He says also in Hosea: *"I will call them My people, who were not My people, And her beloved, who was not beloved."* **26** *"And it shall come to pass in the place where it was said to them, 'You are not My people,' There they shall be called sons of the living God."*

Eph 3:6 that the Gentiles should be fellow heirs, of the same body, and partakers of His promise in Christ through the gospel,

The adopted are gathered together in one by Christ.

John 11:52 and not for that nation only, but also that He would gather together in one the children of God who were scattered abroad.

New birth connected with.

John 1:12–13 But as many as received Him, to them He gave the right to become children of God, to those who believe in His name: **13** who were born, not of blood, nor of the will of the flesh, nor of the will of man, but of God.

The Holy Spirit is a witness of.

Rom 8:16 The Spirit Himself bears witness with our spirit that we are children of God,

Being led by the Spirit is an evidence of.

Rom 8:14 For as many as are led by the Spirit of God, these are sons of God.

Saints receive the Spirit of.

Rom 8:15 For you did not receive the spirit of bondage again to fear, but you received the Spirit of adoption by whom we cry out, "Abba, Father."

Gal 4:6 And because you are sons, God has sent forth the Spirit of His Son into your hearts, crying out, "Abba, Father!"

A privilege of saints.

John 1:12 But as many as received Him, to them He gave the right to become children of God, to those who believe in His name:

1 John 3:1 Behold what manner of love the Father has bestowed on us, that we should be called children of God! Therefore the world does not know us, because it did not know Him.

Saints become brethren of Christ by.

Heb 2:11–12 For both He who sanctifies and those who are being sanctified *are* all of one, for which reason He is not ashamed to call them brethren, **12** saying: *"I will declare Your name to My brethren; In the midst of the assembly I will sing praise to You."*

Saints wait for final consummation of.

Rom 8:19 For the earnest expectation of the creation eagerly waits for the revealing of the sons of God.

Rom 8:23 Not only *that,* but we also who have the firstfruits of the Spirit, even we ourselves groan within ourselves, eagerly waiting for the adoption, the redemption of our body.

1 John 3:2 Beloved, now we are children of God; and it has not yet been revealed what we shall be, but we know that when He is revealed, we shall be like Him, for we shall see Him as He is.

Subjects saints to the fatherly discipline of God.

Deut 8:5 You should know in your heart that as a man chastens his son, *so* the LORD your God chastens you.

Prov 3:11–12 My son, do not despise the chastening of the LORD, Nor detest His correction; **12** For whom the LORD loves He corrects, Just as a father the son *in whom* he delights.

Heb 12:5–11 And you have forgotten the exhortation which speaks to you as to sons: *"My son, do not despise the chastening of the LORD, Nor be discouraged when you are rebuked by Him; 6 For whom the LORD loves He chastens, And scourges every son whom*

He receives." 7 If you endure chastening, God deals with you as with sons; for what son is there whom a father does not chasten? 8 But if you are without chastening, of which all have become partakers, then you are illegitimate and not sons. 9 Furthermore, we have had human fathers who corrected *us,* and we paid *them* respect. Shall we not much more readily be in subjection to the Father of spirits and live? 10 For they indeed for a few days chastened *us* as seemed *best* to them, but He for *our* profit, that *we* may be partakers of His holiness. 11 Now no chastening seems to be joyful for the present, but painful; nevertheless, afterward it yields the peaceable fruit of righteousness to those who have been trained by it.

Should lead to holiness.

2 Cor 6:17–18 Therefore *"Come out from among them And be separate, says the Lord. Do not touch what is unclean, And I will receive you."* 18 *"I will be a Father to you, And you shall be My sons and daughters, Says the LORD Almighty."*

2 Cor 7:1 Therefore, having these promises, beloved, let us cleanse ourselves from all filthiness of the flesh and spirit, perfecting holiness in the fear of God.

Phil 2:15 that you may become blameless and harmless, children of God without fault in the midst of a crooked and perverse generation, among whom you shine as lights in the world,

1 John 3:2–3 Beloved, now we are children of God; and it has not yet been revealed what we shall be, but we know that when He is revealed, we shall be like Him, for we shall see Him as He is. 3 And everyone who has this hope in Him purifies himself, just as He is pure.

Should produce

Likeness to God.

Matt 5:44–45 But I say to you, love your enemies, bless those who curse you, do good to those who hate you, and pray for those who spitefully use you and persecute you, 45 that you may be sons of your Father in heaven; for He makes His sun rise on the evil and on the good, and sends rain on the just and on the unjust.

Matt 5:48 Therefore you shall be perfect, just as your Father in heaven is perfect.

Eph 5:1 Therefore be imitators of God as dear children.

Childlike confidence in God.

Matt 6:25–34 "Therefore I say to you, do not worry about your life, what you will eat or what you will drink; nor about your body, what you will put on. Is not life more than food and the body more than clothing? 26 Look at the birds of the air, for they neither sow nor reap nor gather into barns; yet your heavenly Father feeds them. Are you not of more value than they? 27 Which of you by worrying can add one cubit to his stature? 28 "So why do you worry about clothing? Consider the lilies of the field, how they grow: they neither toil nor spin; 29 and yet I say to you that even Solomon in all his glory was not arrayed like one of these. 30 Now if God so clothes the grass of the field, which today is, and tomorrow is thrown into the oven, *will He* not much more *clothe* you, O you of little faith? 31 "Therefore do not worry, saying, 'What shall we eat?' or 'What shall we drink?' or 'What shall we wear?' 32 For after all these things the Gentiles seek. For your heavenly Father knows that you need all these things. 33 But seek first the kingdom of God and His righteousness, and all these things shall be added to you. 34 Therefore do not worry about tomorrow, for tomorrow will worry about its own things. Sufficient for the day *is* its own trouble.

A desire for God's glory.

Matt 5:16 Let your light so shine before men, that they may see your good works and glorify your Father in heaven.

A spirit of prayer.

Matt 7:7–11 "Ask, and it will be given to you; seek, and you will find; knock, and it will be opened to you. 8 For everyone who asks receives, and he who seeks finds, and to him who knocks it will be opened. 9 Or what man is there among you who, if his son asks for bread, will give him a stone? 10 Or if he asks for a fish, will he give him a serpent? 11 If you then, being evil, know how to give good gifts to your children, how much more will your Father who is in heaven give good things to those who ask Him!

A love of peace.

Matt 5:9 Blessed *are* the peacemakers, For they shall be called sons of God.

A forgiving spirit.

Matt 6:14 "For if you forgive men their trespasses, your heavenly Father will also forgive you.

A merciful spirit.

Luke 6:35–36 But love your enemies, do good, and lend, hoping for nothing in return; and your reward will be great, and you will be sons of the Most High. For He is kind to the unthankful and evil. 36 Therefore be merciful, just as your Father also is merciful.

An avoidance of ostentation.

Matt 6:1–4 "Take heed that you do not do your charitable deeds before men, to be seen by them. Otherwise you have no reward from your Father in heaven. 2 Therefore, when you do a charitable deed, do not sound a trumpet before you as the hypocrites do in the synagogues and in the streets, that they may have glory from men. Assuredly, I say to you, they have their reward. 3 But when you do a charitable deed, do not let your left hand know what your right hand is doing, 4 that your charitable deed may be in secret; and your Father who sees in secret will Himself reward you openly.

Matt 6:6 But you, when you pray, go into your room, and when you have shut your door, pray to your Father who *is* in the secret *place;* and your Father who sees in secret will reward you openly.

Matt 6:18 so that you do not appear to men to be fasting, but to your Father who *is* in the secret *place;* and your Father who sees in secret will reward you openly.

Safety of those who receive.

Prov 14:26 In the fear of the LORD *there is* strong confidence, And His children will have a place of refuge.

Confers a new name. *See also* **Believers, Titles and Names of.**

Num 6:27 "So they shall put My name on the children of Israel, and I will bless them."

Is 62:2 The Gentiles shall see your righteousness, And all kings your glory. You shall be called by a new name, Which the mouth of the LORD will name.

Acts 15:17 *So that the rest of mankind may seek the LORD, Even all the Gentiles who are called by My name, Says the LORD who does all these things.'*

Entitles to an inheritance.

Rom 8:17 and if children, then heirs—heirs of God and joint heirs with Christ, if indeed we suffer with *Him,* that we may also be glorified together.

Gal 3:29 And if you *are* Christ's, then you are Abraham's seed, and heirs according to the promise.

Gal 4:7 Therefore you are no longer a slave but a son, and if a son, then an heir of God through Christ.

Eph 3:6 that the Gentiles should be fellow heirs, of the same body, and partakers of His promise in Christ through the gospel,

Is to be acknowledged in prayer.

Is 63:16 Doubtless You *are* our Father, Though Abraham was ignorant of us, And Israel does not acknowledge us. You, O LORD, *are* our Father; Our Redeemer from Everlasting *is* Your name.

Matt 6:9 In this manner, therefore, pray: Our Father in heaven, Hallowed be Your name.

Illustrated by

Joseph's sons.

Gen 48:5 And now your two sons, Ephraim and Manasseh, who were born to you in the land of Egypt before I came to you in Egypt, *are* mine; as Reuben and Simeon, they shall be mine.

Gen 48:14 Then Israel stretched out his right hand and laid *it* on Ephraim's head, who *was* the younger, and his left hand on Manasseh's head, guiding his hands knowingly, for Manasseh *was* the firstborn.

Gen 48:16 The Angel who has redeemed me from all evil, Bless the lads; Let my name be named upon them, And the name of my fathers Abraham and Isaac; And let them grow into a multitude in the midst of the earth."

Gen 48:22 Moreover I have given to you one portion above your brothers, which I took from the hand of the Amorite with my sword and my bow."

Moses.

Ex 2:10 And the child grew, and she brought him to Pharaoh's daughter, and he became her son. So she called his name Moses, saying, "Because I drew him out of the water."

Esther.

Esth 2:7 And *Mordecai* had brought up Hadassah, that *is,* Esther, his uncle's daughter, for she had neither father nor mother. The young woman *was* lovely and beautiful. When her father and mother died, Mordecai took her as his own daughter.

Typified by

Israel.

Ex 4:22 Then you shall say to Pharaoh, 'Thus says the LORD: "Israel *is* My son, My firstborn.

Hos 11:1 "When Israel *was* a child, I loved him, And out of Egypt I called My son.

Rom 9:4 who are Israelites, to whom *pertain* the adop-

tion, the glory, the covenants, the giving of the law, the service *of God,* and the promises;

Exemplified by

Solomon.

1 Chr 28:6 Now He said to me, 'It is your son Solomon *who* shall build My house and My courts; for I have chosen him *to be* My son, and I will be his Father.

ADULTERY

Joseph resists.

Gen 39:7–12 And it came to pass after these things that his master's wife cast longing eyes on Joseph, and she said, "Lie with me." 8 But he refused and said to his master's wife, "Look, my master does not know what *is* with me in the house, and he has committed all that he has to my hand. 9 *There is* no one greater in this house than I, nor has he kept back anything from me but you, because you *are* his wife. How then can I do this great wickedness, and sin against God?" 10 So it was, as she spoke to Joseph day by day, that he did not heed her, to lie with her *or* to be with her. 11 But it happened about this time, when Joseph went into the house to do his work, and none of the men of the house *was* inside, 12 that she caught him by his garment, saying, "Lie with me." But he left his garment in her hand, and fled and ran outside.

Forbidden.

Ex 20:14 "You shall not commit adultery.

Lev 20:10 'The man who commits adultery with *another* man's wife, *he* who commits adultery with his neighbor's wife, the adulterer and the adulteress, shall surely be put to death.

Deut 5:18 'You shall not commit adultery.

1 Cor 6:9–10 Do you not know that the unrighteous will not inherit the kingdom of God? Do not be deceived. Neither fornicators, nor idolaters, nor adulterers, nor homosexuals, nor sodomites, 10 nor thieves, nor covetous, nor drunkards, nor revilers, nor extortioners will inherit the kingdom of God.

Cf. Gen 20:9; Matt 5:27; James 2:11

Punishable by death.

Deut 22:22 "If a man is found lying with a woman married to a husband, then both of them shall die—the man that lay with the woman, and the woman; so you shall put away the evil from Israel.

Cf. Lev 20:10–21

David's sin of.

2 Sam 11:2–5 Then it happened one evening that David arose from his bed and walked on the roof of the king's house. And from the roof he saw a woman bathing, and the woman *was* very beautiful to behold. 3 So David sent and inquired about the woman. And *someone* said, "Is this not Bathsheba, the daughter of Eliam, the wife of Uriah the Hittite?" 4 Then David sent messengers, and took her; and she came to him, and he lay with her, for she was cleansed from her impurity; and she returned to her house. 5 And the woman conceived; so she sent and told David, and said, "I *am* with child."

Poetic warnings against.

Prov 5:1–14 My son, pay attention to my wisdom; Lend your ear to my understanding, 2 That you may preserve discretion, And your lips may keep knowledge. 3 For the lips of an immoral woman drip honey, And her mouth *is* smoother than oil; 4 But in the end she is bitter as wormwood, Sharp as a two-edged sword. 5 Her feet go down to death, Her steps lay hold of hell. 6 Lest you ponder *her* path of life— Her ways are unstable; You do not know *them.* 7 Therefore hear me now, *my* children, And do not depart from the words of my mouth. 8 Remove your way far from her, And do not go near the door of her house, 9 Lest you give your honor to others, And your years to the cruel *one;* 10 Lest aliens be filled with your wealth, And your labors *go* to the house of a foreigner; 11 And you mourn at last, When your flesh and your body are consumed, 12 And say: "How I have hated instruction, And my heart despised correction! 13 I have not obeyed the voice of my teachers, Nor inclined my ear to those who instructed me! 14 I was on the verge of total ruin, In the midst of the assembly and congregation."

Prov 6:20–35 My son, keep your father's command, And do not forsake the law of your mother. 21 Bind them continually upon your heart; Tie them around your neck. 22 When you roam, they will lead you; When you sleep, they will keep you; And *when* you awake, they will speak with you. 23 For the commandment *is* a lamp, And the law a light; Reproofs of instruction *are* the way of life, 24 To keep you from the evil woman, From the flattering tongue of a seductress. 25 Do not lust after her beauty in your heart, Nor let her allure you with her eyelids. 26 For by means of a harlot *A man is reduced* to a crust of bread; And an adulteress will prey upon his precious life. 27 Can a man take fire to his bosom, And his clothes not be burned? 28 Can one walk on hot coals, And his feet not be seared? 29 So *is* he who goes in to his neighbor's wife; Whoever touches her shall not be innocent. 30 *People* do not despise a thief If he steals to satisfy himself when he is starving. 31 Yet *when* he is found, he must restore sevenfold; He may have to give up all the substance of his house. 32 Whoever commits adultery with a woman lacks understanding; He *who* does so destroys his own soul. 33 Wounds and dishonor he will get, And his reproach will not be wiped away. 34 For jealousy *is* a husband's fury; Therefore he will not spare in the day of vengeance. 35 He will accept no recompense, Nor will he be appeased though you give many gifts.

Metaphor for idolatry.

Is 57:3 "But come here, You sons of the sorceress, You offspring of the adulterer and the harlot!

Spiritual, by Israel against God.

Jer 3:6 The LORD said also to me in the days of Josiah the king: "Have you seen what backsliding Israel has done? She has gone up on every high mountain and under every green tree, and there played the harlot.

Jer 5:7 "How shall I pardon you for this? Your children have forsaken Me And sworn by *those* that are *not* gods. When I had fed them to the full, Then they committed adultery And assembled themselves by troops in the harlots' houses.

Hos 2:5 For their mother has played the harlot; She who conceived them has behaved shamefully. For she said, 'I will go after my lovers, Who give *me* my bread and my water, My wool and my linen, My oil and my drink.'

Hos 4:12 My people ask counsel from their wooden *idols,* And their staff informs them. For the spirit of harlotry has caused *them* to stray, And they have played the harlot against their God.

Cf. Ezek 16:15–34; Mal 2:11; Matt 12:39

And divorce.

Matt 5:32 But I say to you that whoever divorces his wife for any reason except sexual immorality causes her to commit adultery; and whoever marries a woman who is divorced commits adultery.

Matt 19:8–9 He said to them, "Moses, because of the hardness of your hearts, permitted you to divorce your wives, but from the beginning it was not so. 9 And I say to you, whoever divorces his wife, except for sexual immorality, and marries another, commits adultery; and whoever marries her who is divorced commits adultery."

Mark 10:10–12 In the house His disciples also asked Him again about the same *matter.* 11 So He said to them, "Whoever divorces his wife and marries another commits adultery against her. 12 And if a woman divorces her husband and marries another, she commits adultery."

Luke 16:18 "Whoever divorces his wife and marries another commits adultery; and whoever marries her who is divorced from *her* husband commits adultery.

Synonym for uncontrolled lust.

2 Pet 2:14 having eyes full of adultery and that cannot cease from sin, enticing unstable souls. *They have* a heart trained in covetous practices, *and are* accursed children.

ADVENT, FIRST

Rejected by the Jews.

Is 8:15 And many among them shall stumble; They shall fall and be broken, Be snared and taken."

Anticipated.

Is 9:6–7 For unto us a Child is born, Unto us a Son is given; And the government will be upon His shoulder. And His name will be called Wonderful, Counselor, Mighty God, Everlasting Father, Prince of Peace. 7 Of the increase of *His* government and peace *There will be* no end, Upon the throne of David and over His kingdom, To order it and establish it with judgment and justice From that time forward, even forever. The zeal of the Lord of hosts will perform this.

Is 42:1–3 "Behold! My Servant whom I uphold, My Elect One *in whom* My soul delights! I have put My Spirit upon Him; He will bring forth justice to the Gentiles. 2 He will not cry out, nor raise *His voice,* Nor cause His voice to be heard in the street. 3 A bruised reed He will not break, And smoking flax He will not quench; He will bring forth justice for truth.

Is 49:5–12 "And now the LORD says, Who formed Me from the womb *to be* His Servant, To bring Jacob back to Him, So that Israel is gathered to Him (For I shall be glorious in the eyes of the LORD, And My God shall be My strength), 6 Indeed He says, 'It is too small a thing that You should be My Servant To raise up the tribes of Jacob, And to restore the preserved ones of Israel; I will also give You as a light to the Gentiles, That You should be My salvation to the ends of the earth.' " 7 Thus says the LORD, The Redeemer of Israel, their Holy One, To Him whom man despises, To Him whom the nation abhors, To the Servant of rulers: "Kings shall see and arise, Princes also shall worship, Because of the LORD who is faithful, The Holy One of Israel; And He has chosen You." 8 Thus says the LORD: "In an acceptable time I have heard You, And in the day of salvation I have helped You; I will preserve You and give You As a covenant to the people, To restore the earth, To cause them to inherit the desolate heritages; 9 That You may say to the prisoners, 'Go forth,' To those who are in darkness, 'Show yourselves.' "They shall feed along the roads, And their pastures shall be on all desolate heights. 10 They shall neither hunger nor thirst, Neither heat nor sun shall strike them; For He who has mercy on them will lead them, Even by the springs of water He will guide them. 11 I will make each of My mountains a road, And My highways shall be elevated. 12 Surely these shall come from afar; Look! Those from the north and the west, And these from the land of Sinim."

Mic 5:2 "But you, Bethlehem Ephrathah, *Though* you are little among the thousands of Judah, *Yet* out of you shall come forth to Me The One to be Ruler in Israel, Whose goings forth *are* from of old, From everlasting."

Zech 9:9 "Rejoice greatly, O daughter of Zion! Shout, O daughter of Jerusalem! Behold, your King is coming to you; He *is* just and having salvation, Lowly and riding on a donkey, A colt, the foal of a donkey.

Results of, mentioned.

Joel 2:28–29 "And it shall come to pass afterward That I will pour out My Spirit on all flesh; Your sons and your daughters shall prophesy, Your old men shall dream dreams, Your young men shall see visions. 29 And also on *My* menservants and on *My* maidservants I will pour out My Spirit in those days.

ADVENT, SECOND

Anticipated.

Ps 110:1 The LORD said to my Lord, "Sit at My right hand, Till I make Your enemies Your footstool."

Is 2:2–4 Now it shall come to pass in the latter days *That* the mountain of the LORD's house Shall be established on the top of the mountains, And shall be exalted above the hills; And all nations shall flow to it. 3 Many people shall come and say, "Come, and let us go up to the mountain of the LORD, To the house of the God of Jacob; He will teach us His ways, And we shall walk in His paths." For out of Zion shall go forth the law, And the word of the LORD from Jerusalem. 4 He shall judge between the nations, And rebuke many people; They shall beat their swords into plowshares, And their spears into pruning hooks; Nation shall not lift up sword against nation, Neither shall they learn war anymore.

Is 42:4 He will not fail nor be discouraged, Till He has established justice in the earth; And the coastlands shall wait for His law."

Dan 7:13–14 "I was watching in the night visions, And behold, *One* like the Son of Man, Coming with the clouds of heaven! He came to the Ancient of Days, And they brought Him near before Him. 14 Then to Him was given dominion and glory and a kingdom, That all peoples, nations, and languages should serve Him. His dominion *is* an everlasting dominion, Which shall not pass away, And His kingdom *the one* Which shall not be destroyed.

Joel 2:30–32 "And I will show wonders in the heavens and in the earth: Blood and fire and pillars of smoke. 31 The sun shall be turned into darkness, And the moon into blood, Before the coming of the great and awesome day of the LORD. 32 And it shall come to pass *That* whoever calls on the name of the LORD Shall be saved. For in Mount Zion and in Jerusalem there shall be deliverance, As the LORD has said, Among the remnant whom the LORD calls.

Zech 14:3–4 Then the LORD will go forth And fight against those nations, As He fights in the day of battle. 4 And in that day His feet will stand on the Mount of Olives, Which faces Jerusalem on the east. And the Mount of Olives shall be split in two, From east to west, *Making* a very large valley; Half of the mountain shall move toward the north And half of it toward the south.

Mal 3:1 "Behold, I send My messenger, And he will prepare the way before Me. And the Lord, whom you seek, Will suddenly come to His temple, Even the Messenger of the covenant, In whom you delight. Behold, He is coming," Says the LORD of hosts.

Heb 9:28 so Christ was offered once to bear the sins of many. To those who eagerly wait for Him He will appear a second time, apart from sin, for salvation.

Time prior to, mentioned.

Jer 30:7 Alas! For that day *is* great, So that none *is* like it; And it *is* the time of Jacob's trouble, But he shall be saved out of it.

Jer 51:8 Babylon has suddenly fallen and been destroyed. Wail for her! Take balm for her pain; Perhaps she may be healed.

Dan 9:27 Then he shall confirm a covenant with many for one week; But in the middle of the week He shall bring an end to sacrifice and offering. And on the wing of abominations shall be one who makes desolate, Even until the consummation, which is determined, Is poured out on the desolate."

Results of, mentioned.

Ezek 20:33–44 "*As* I live," says the Lord GOD, "surely with a mighty hand, with an outstretched arm, and with fury poured out, I will rule over you. 34 I will bring you out from the peoples and gather you out of the countries where you are scattered, with a mighty hand, with an outstretched arm, and with fury poured out. 35 And I will bring you into the wilderness of the peoples, and there I will plead My case with you face to face. 36 Just as I pleaded My case with your fathers in the wilderness of the land of Egypt, so I will plead My case with you," says the Lord GOD. 37 "I will make you pass under the rod, and I will bring you into the bond of the covenant; 38 I will purge the rebels from among you, and those who transgress against Me; I will bring them out of the country where they dwell, but they shall not enter the land of Israel. Then you will know that I *am* the LORD. 39 "As for you, O house of Israel," thus says the Lord GOD: "Go, serve every one of you his idols—and hereafter—if you will not obey Me; but profane My holy name no more with your gifts and your idols. **40** For on My holy mountain, on the mountain height of Israel," says the Lord GOD, "there all the house of Israel, all of them in the land, shall serve Me; there I will accept them, and there I will require your offerings and the firstfruits of your sacrifices, together with all your holy things. **41** I will accept you as a sweet aroma when I bring you out from the peoples and gather you out of the countries where you have been scattered; and I will be hallowed in you before the Gentiles. **42** Then you shall know that I *am* the LORD, when I bring you into the land of Israel, into the country *for* which I raised My hand in an oath to give to your fathers. **43** And there you shall remember your ways and all your doings with which you were defiled; and you shall loathe yourselves in your own sight because of all the evils that you have committed. **44** Then you shall know that I *am* the LORD, when I have dealt with you for My name's sake, not according to your wicked ways nor according to your corrupt doings, O house of Israel," says the Lord GOD.' "

Ezek 39:29 And I will not hide My face from them anymore; for I shall have poured out My Spirit on the house of Israel,' says the Lord GOD."

Cf. Ezek 43:1–12

ADVERSARY

Meaning of Satan's name.

Job 1:6 Now there was a day when the sons of God came to present themselves before the LORD, and Satan also came among them.

Zech 3:1 Then he showed me Joshua the high priest standing before the Angel of the LORD, and Satan standing at his right hand to oppose him.

Mark 1:13 And He was there in the wilderness forty days, tempted by Satan, and was with the wild beasts; and the angels ministered to Him.

1 Pet 5:8 Be sober, be vigilant; because your adversary the devil walks about like a roaring lion, seeking whom he may devour.

Cf. Mark 8:33; Luke 22:3; John 6:70; 13:2,27; 1 Thess 2:18; Rev 12:9

Job's reference to God.

Job 16:9 He tears *me* in His wrath, and hates me; He gnashes at me with His teeth; My adversary sharpens His gaze on me.

ADVICE

Of Jethro to Moses. Ex 18:13–27

Quality of Ahithophel's.

2 Sam 16:23 Now the advice of Ahithophel, which he gave in those days, *was* as if one had inquired at the oracle of God. So *was* all the advice of Ahithophel both with David and with Absalom.

Foolish, to Rehoboam.

1 Kin 12:8–15 But he rejected the advice which the elders had given him, and consulted the young men who had grown up with him, who stood before him. **9** And he said to them, "What advice do you give?

How should we answer this people who have spoken to me, saying, 'Lighten the yoke which your father put on us'?" **10** Then the young men who had grown up with him spoke to him, saying, "Thus you should speak to this people who have spoken to you, saying, 'Your father made our yoke heavy, but you make *it* lighter on us'—thus you shall say to them: 'My little *finger* shall be thicker than my father's waist! **11** And now, whereas my father put a heavy yoke on you, I will add to your yoke; my father chastised you with whips, but I will chastise you with scourges!' " **12** So Jeroboam and all the people came to Rehoboam the third day, as the king had directed, saying, "Come back to me the third day." **13** Then the king answered the people roughly, and rejected the advice which the elders had given him; **14** and he spoke to them according to the advice of the young men, saying, "My father made your yoke heavy, but I will add to your yoke; my father chastised you with whips, but I will chastise you with scourges!" **15** So the king did not listen to the people; for the turn *of events* was from the LORD, that He might fulfill His word, which the LORD had spoken by Ahijah the Shilonite to Jeroboam the son of Nebat.

2 Chr 10:8–15 But he rejected the advice which the elders had given him, and consulted the young men who had grown up with him, who stood before him. **9** And he said to them, "What advice do you give? How should we answer this people who have spoken to me, saying, 'Lighten the yoke which your father put on us'?" **10** Then the young men who had grown up with him spoke to him, saying, "Thus you should speak to the people who have spoken to you, saying, 'Your father made our yoke heavy, but you make *it* lighter on us'—thus you shall say to them: 'My little *finger* shall be thicker than my father's waist! **11** And now, whereas my father put a heavy yoke on you, I will add to your yoke; my father chastised you with whips, but I *will chastise you* with scourges!' " **12** So Jeroboam and all the people came to Rehoboam on the third day, as the king had directed, saying, "Come back to me the third day." **13** Then the king answered them roughly. King Rehoboam rejected the advice of the elders, **14** and he spoke to them according to the advice of the young men, saying, "My father made your yoke heavy, but I will add to it; my father chastised you with whips, but I *will chastise you* with scourges!" **15** So the king did not listen to the people; for the turn *of events* was from God, that the LORD might fulfill His word, which He had spoken by the hand of Ahijah the Shilonite to Jeroboam the son of Nebat.

Cf. Prov 13:10

AFFECTION

Of Joseph for his brothers.

Gen 45:14–15 Then he fell on his brother Benjamin's neck and wept, and Benjamin wept on his neck. **15** Moreover he kissed all his brothers and wept over them, and after that his brothers talked with him.

Gen 50:15–21 When Joseph's brothers saw that their father was dead, they said, "Perhaps Joseph will hate us, and may actually repay us for all the evil which we did to him." **16** So they sent *messengers* to Joseph, saying, "Before your father died he commanded, saying, **17** 'Thus you shall say to Joseph: "I beg you, please forgive the trespass of your brothers and their sin; for they did evil to you." ' Now, please, forgive the trespass of the servants of the God of your father." And Joseph wept when they spoke to him. **18** Then his brothers also went and fell down before his face, and they said, "Behold, we *are* your servants." **19** Joseph said to them, "Do not be afraid, for *am* I in the place of God? **20** But as for you, you meant evil against me; *but* God meant it for good, in order to bring it about as *it is* this day, to save many people alive. **21** Now therefore, do not be afraid; I will provide for you and your little ones." And he comforted them and spoke kindly to them.

Between Jonathan and David.

1 Sam 20:17 Now Jonathan again caused David to vow, because he loved him; for he loved him as he loved his own soul.

1 Sam 20:41–42 As soon as the lad had gone, David arose from *a place* toward the south, fell on his face to the ground, and bowed down three times. And they kissed one another; and they wept together, but David more so. **42** Then Jonathan said to David, "Go in peace, since we have both sworn in the name of the LORD, saying, 'May the LORD be between you and me, and between your descendants and my descendants, forever.' " So he arose and departed, and Jonathan went into the city.

For God's Word.

Ps 119:47–48 And I will delight myself in Your commandments, Which I love. **48** My hands also I will lift up to Your commandments, Which I love, And I will meditate on Your statutes.

Cf. Ps 119:97,113,127,140,159,163,167

Kiss as sign of.

Mark 14:44–45 Now His betrayer had given them a signal, saying, "Whomever I kiss, He is the One; seize Him and lead *Him* away safely." **45** As soon as he had come, immediately he went up to Him and said to Him, "Rabbi, Rabbi!" and kissed Him.

Cf. Acts 20:37; 1 Thess 5:26

In marriage, essential.

1 Cor 7:3 Let the husband render to his wife the affection due her, and likewise also the wife to her husband.

Eph 5:28–29 So husbands ought to love their own wives as their own bodies; he who loves his wife loves himself. **29** For no one ever hated his own flesh, but nourishes and cherishes it, just as the Lord *does* the church.

Of Paul for the churches.

Phil 1:8 For God is my witness, how greatly I long for you all with the affection of Jesus Christ.

Phil 2:1–2 Therefore if *there is* any consolation in Christ, if any comfort of love, if any fellowship of the Spirit, if any affection and mercy, **2** fulfill my joy by being like-minded, having the same love, *being* of one accord, of one mind.

1 Thess 2:7–8 But we were gentle among you, just as a nursing *mother* cherishes her own children. **8** So, affectionately longing for you, we were well pleased to impart to you not only the gospel of God, but also our own lives, because you had become dear to us.

Among believers.

2 Pet 1:7 to godliness brotherly kindness, and to brotherly kindness love.

1 John 4:7–10 Beloved, let us love one another, for love is of God; and everyone who loves is born of God and knows God. **8** He who does not love does not know God, for God is love. **9** In this the love of God was manifested toward us, that God has sent His only begotten Son into the world, that we might live through Him. **10** In this is love, not that we loved God, but that He loved us and sent His Son *to be* the propitiation for our sins.

AFFECTIONS, THE

Should be supremely set upon God.

Deut 6:3 Therefore hear, O Israel, and be careful to observe *it*, that it may be well with you, and that you may multiply greatly as the LORD God of your fathers has promised you—'a land flowing with milk and honey.'

Ps 42:1 As the deer pants for the water brooks, So pants my soul for You, O God.

Ps 73:25 Whom have I in heaven *but You*? And *there is* none upon earth *that* I desire besides You.

Ps 119:10 With my whole heart I have sought You; Oh, let me not wander from Your commandments!

Mark 12:30 *And you shall love the LORD your God with all your heart, with all your soul, with all your mind, and with all your strength.'* This *is* the first commandment.

Should be set

Upon the commandments of God.

Ps 19:8–10 The statutes of the LORD *are* right, rejoicing the heart; The commandment of the LORD *is* pure, enlightening the eyes; **9** The fear of the LORD *is* clean, enduring forever; The judgments of the LORD *are* true *and* righteous altogether. **10** More to be desired *are they* than gold, Yea, than much fine gold; Sweeter also than honey and the honeycomb.

Ps 119:20 My soul breaks with longing For Your judgments at all times.

Ps 119:97 Oh, how I love Your law! It *is* my meditation all the day.

Ps 119:103 How sweet are Your words to my taste, *Sweeter* than honey to my mouth!

Ps 119:167 My soul keeps Your testimonies, And I love them exceedingly.

Upon the house and worship of God.

1 Chr 29:3 Moreover, because I have set my affection on the house of my God, I have given to the house of my God, over and above all that I have prepared for the holy house, my own special treasure of gold and silver:

Ps 26:8 LORD, I have loved the habitation of Your house, And the place where Your glory dwells.

Ps 27:4 One *thing* I have desired of the LORD, That will I seek: That I may dwell in the house of the LORD All the days of my life, To behold the beauty of the LORD, And to inquire in His temple.

Ps 84:1–2 How lovely *is* Your tabernacle, O LORD of hosts! **2** My soul longs, yes, even faints For the courts of the LORD; My heart and my flesh cry out for the living God.

Upon the people of God.

Ps 16:3 As for the saints who *are* on the earth, "They are the excellent ones, in whom is all my delight."

Rom 12:10 *Be* kindly affectionate to one another with brotherly love, in honor giving preference to one another;

2 Cor 7:13–15 Therefore we have been comforted in your comfort. And we rejoiced exceedingly more for the joy of Titus, because his spirit has been refreshed by you all. **14** For if in anything I have boasted to him about you, I am not ashamed. But as we spoke all things to you in truth, even so our boasting to Titus was found true. **15** And his affections are greater for you as he remembers the obedience of you all, how with fear and trembling you received him.

1 Thess 2:8 So, affectionately longing for you, we were well pleased to impart to you not only the gospel of God, but also our own lives, because you had become dear to us.

Upon heavenly things.

Col 3:1–2 If then you were raised with Christ, seek those things which are above, where Christ is, sitting at the right hand of God. **2** Set your mind on things above, not on things on the earth.

Should be zealously engaged for God.

Ps 69:9 Because zeal for Your house has eaten me up, And the reproaches of those who reproach You have fallen on me.

Ps 119:139 My zeal has consumed me, Because my enemies have forgotten Your words.

Gal 4:18 But it is good to be zealous in a good thing always, and not only when I am present with you.

Christ claims the first place in.

Matt 10:37 He who loves father or mother more than Me is not worthy of Me. And he who loves son or daughter more than Me is not worthy of Me.

Luke 14:26 "If anyone comes to Me and does not hate his father and mother, wife and children, brothers and sisters, yes, and his own life also, he cannot be My disciple.

Energized by communion with Christ.

Luke 24:32 And they said to one another, "Did not our heart burn within us while He talked with us on the road, and while He opened the Scriptures to us?"

Blessedness of making God the object of.

Ps 91:14 "Because he has set his love upon Me, therefore I will deliver him; I will set him on high, because he has known My name.

Should not grow cold.

Ps 106:12–13 Then they believed His words; They sang His praise. **13** They soon forgot His works; They did not wait for His counsel,

Matt 24:12 And because lawlessness will abound, the love of many will grow cold.

Gal 4:15 What then was the blessing you *enjoyed*? For I bear you witness that, if possible, you would have plucked out your own eyes and given them to me.

Rev 2:4 Nevertheless I have *this* against you, that you have left your first love.

Of the wicked, not sincerely set on God.

Is 29:13 Therefore the Lord said: "Inasmuch as these people draw near with their mouths And honor Me with their lips, But have removed their hearts far from Me, And their fear toward Me is taught by the commandment of men,

Is 58:1–2 "Cry aloud, spare not; Lift up your voice like a trumpet; Tell My people their transgression, And the house of Jacob their sins. **2** Yet they seek Me daily, And delight to know My ways, As a nation that did righteousness, And did not forsake the ordinance of their God. They ask of Me the ordinances of justice; They take delight in approaching God.

Ezek 33:31–32 So they come to you as people do, they sit before you *as* My people, and they hear your words, but they do not do them; for with their mouth they show much love, *but* their hearts pursue their *own* gain. **32** Indeed you *are* to them as a very lovely song of one who has a pleasant voice and can play well on an instrument; for they hear your words, but they do not do them.

Matt 15:8–9 'These people draw near to Me with their mouth, And honor Me with their lips, But their heart is far from Me. **9** And in vain they worship Me, Teaching as doctrines the commandments of men.' "

Luke 8:13 But the ones on the rock *are those* who, when they hear, receive the word with joy; and these have no root, who believe for a while and in time of temptation fall away.

Carnal affections should be mortified.

Rom 8:13 For if you live according to the flesh you will die; but if by the Spirit you put to death the deeds of the body, you will live.

Rom 13:14 But put on the Lord Jesus Christ, and make no provision for the flesh, to *fulfill its* lusts.

1 Cor 9:27 But I discipline my body and bring *it* into subjection, lest, when I have preached to others, I myself should become disqualified.

Col 3:5 Therefore put to death your members which are on the earth: fornication, uncleanness, passion, evil desire, and covetousness, which is idolatry.

1 Thess 4:5 not in passion of lust, like the Gentiles who do not know God;

Carnal affections crucified in saints.

Rom 6:6 knowing this, that our old man was crucified with *Him*, that the body of sin might be done away with, that we should no longer be slaves of sin.

Gal 5:24 And those *who are* Christ's have crucified the flesh with its passions and desires.

False teachers seek to captivate.

Gal 1:10 For do I now persuade men, or God? Or do I seek to please men? For if I still pleased men, I would not be a bondservant of Christ.

Gal 4:17 They zealously court you, *but* for no good; yes, they want to exclude you, that you may be zealous for them.

2 Tim 3:6 For of this sort are those who creep into households and make captives of gullible women loaded down with sins, led away by various lusts,

2 Pet 2:3 By covetousness they will exploit you with deceptive words; for a long time their judgment has not been idle, and their destruction does not slumber.

2 Pet 2:18 For when they speak great swelling *words* of emptiness, they allure through the lusts of the flesh, through lewdness, the ones who have actually escaped from those who live in error.

Rev 2:14 But I have a few things against you, because you have there those who hold the doctrine of Balaam, who taught Balak to put a stumbling block before the children of Israel, to eat things sacrificed to idols, and to commit sexual immorality.

Rev 2:20 Nevertheless I have a few things against you, because you allow that woman Jezebel, who calls herself a prophetess, to teach and seduce My servants to commit sexual immorality and eat things sacrificed to idols.

Of the wicked, are unnatural and perverted.

Rom 1:31 undiscerning, untrustworthy, unloving, unforgiving, unmerciful;

2 Tim 3:3 unloving, unforgiving, slanderers, without self-control, brutal, despisers of good,

2 Pet 2:10 and especially those who walk according to the flesh in the lust of uncleanness and despise authority. *They are* presumptuous, self-willed. They are not afraid to speak evil of dignitaries,

AFFIRMATION

Of Jesus' deity.

Matt 17:5 While he was still speaking, behold, a bright cloud overshadowed them; and suddenly a voice came out of the cloud, saying, "This is My beloved Son, in whom I am well pleased. Hear Him!"

Mark 9:7 And a cloud came and overshadowed them; and a voice came out of the cloud, saying, "This is My beloved Son. Hear Him!"

Luke 9:35 And a voice came out of the cloud, saying, "This is My beloved Son. Hear Him!"

2 Pet 1:17 For He received from God the Father honor and glory when such a voice came to Him from the Excellent Glory: "This is My beloved Son, in whom I am well pleased."

Cf. Luke 18:38; 1 Cor 8:6; Eph 4:4–6; Col 1:3; 1 John 1:1–4

Of Scripture's power and effect.

Matt 5:17–19 "Do not think that I came to destroy the Law or the Prophets. I did not come to destroy but to fulfill. **18** For assuredly, I say to you, till heaven and earth pass away, one jot or one tittle will by no means pass from the law till all is fulfilled. **19** Whoever therefore breaks one of the least of these commandments, and teaches men so, shall be called least in the kingdom of heaven; but whoever does and teaches *them,* he shall be called great in the kingdom of heaven.

John 10:35 If He called them gods, to whom the word of God came (and the Scripture cannot be broken),

Amen, basic word of.

Matt 6:13 And do not lead us into temptation, But deliver us from the evil one. For Yours is the kingdom and the power and the glory forever. Amen.

Rom 1:25 who exchanged the truth of God for the lie, and worshiped and served the creature rather than the Creator, who is blessed forever. Amen.

2 Cor 1:20 For all the promises of God in Him *are* Yes, and in Him Amen, to the glory of God through us.

Phil 4:23 The grace of our Lord Jesus Christ be with you all. Amen.

Public, to ministry.

1 Tim 4:14 Do not neglect the gift that is in you, which was given to you by prophecy with the laying on of the hands of the eldership.

AFFLICTED, DUTY TOWARD THE

To pray for them.

Acts 12:5 Peter was therefore kept in prison, but constant prayer was offered to God for him by the church.

Phil 1:19 For I know that this will turn out for my deliverance through your prayer and the supply of the Spirit of Jesus Christ,

James 5:14–16 Is anyone among you sick? Let him call for the elders of the church, and let them pray over him, anointing him with oil in the name of the Lord. **15** And the prayer of faith will save the sick, and the Lord will raise him up. And if he has committed sins, he will be forgiven. **16** Confess *your* trespasses to one another, and pray for one another, that you may be healed. The effective, fervent prayer of a righteous man avails much.

To sympathize with them.

Rom 12:15 Rejoice with those who rejoice, and weep with those who weep.

Gal 6:2 Bear one another's burdens, and so fulfill the law of Christ.

To show kindness to them.

Job 6:14 "To him who is afflicted, kindness *should be shown* by his friend, Even though he forsakes the fear of the Almighty.

To bear them in mind.

Heb 13:3 Remember the prisoners as if chained with them—those who are mistreated—since you yourselves are in the body also.

To visit them.

James 1:27 Pure and undefiled religion before God and the Father is this: to visit orphans and widows in their trouble, *and* to keep oneself unspotted from the world.

To comfort them.

Job 16:5 *But* I would strengthen you with my mouth, And the comfort of my lips would relieve *your* grief.

2 Cor 1:4 who comforts us in all our tribulation, that we may be able to comfort those who are in any trouble, with the comfort with which we ourselves are comforted by God.

1 Thess 4:18 Therefore comfort one another with these words.

To relieve them.

Job 31:19–20 If I have seen anyone perish for lack of clothing, Or any poor *man* without covering; **20** If his heart has not blessed me, And *if* he was *not* warmed with the fleece of my sheep;

Is 58:10 *If* you extend your soul to the hungry And satisfy the afflicted soul, Then your light shall dawn in the darkness, And your darkness shall *be* as the noonday.

Phil 4:14 Nevertheless you have done well that you shared in my distress.

1 Tim 5:10 well reported for good works: if she has brought up children, if she has lodged strangers, if she has washed the saints' feet, if she has relieved the afflicted, if she has diligently followed every good work.

To protect them.

Ps 82:3 Defend the poor and fatherless; Do justice to the afflicted and needy.

Prov 22:22 Do not rob the poor because he *is* poor, Nor oppress the afflicted at the gate;

Prov 31:5 Lest they drink and forget the law, And pervert the justice of all the afflicted.

AFFLICTION, CONSOLATION UNDER

God is the Author and Giver of.

Ps 23:4 Yea, though I walk through the valley of the shadow of death, I will fear no evil; For You *are* with me; Your rod and Your staff, they comfort me.

2 Cor 7:6 Nevertheless God, who comforts the downcast, comforted us by the coming of Titus,

Col 1:11 strengthened with all might, according to His glorious power, for all patience and longsuffering with joy;

2 Thess 2:16–17 Now may our Lord Jesus Christ Himself, and our God and Father, who has loved us and given *us* everlasting consolation and good hope by grace, **17** comfort your hearts and establish you in every good word and work.

Christ is the Author and Giver of.

Is 61:2 To proclaim the acceptable year of the LORD, And the day of vengeance of our God; To comfort all who mourn,

2 Cor 1:5 For as the sufferings of Christ abound in us, so our consolation also abounds through Christ.

The Holy Spirit is the Author and Giver of.

John 14:16–17 And I will pray the Father, and He will give you another Helper, that He may abide with you forever— **17** the Spirit of truth, whom the world cannot receive, because it neither sees Him nor knows Him; but you know Him, for He dwells with you and will be in you.

John 15:26 "But when the Helper comes, whom I shall send to you from the Father, the Spirit of truth who proceeds from the Father, He will testify of Me.

John 16:7 Nevertheless I tell you the truth. It is to your advantage that I go away; for if I do not go away, the Helper will not come to you; but if I depart, I will send Him to you.

Acts 9:31 Then the churches throughout all Judea, Galilee, and Samaria had peace and were edified. And walking in the fear of the Lord and in the comfort of the Holy Spirit, they were multiplied.

Promised.

Is 51:3 For the LORD will comfort Zion, He will comfort all her waste places; He will make her wilderness like Eden, And her desert like the garden of the LORD; Joy and gladness will be found in it, Thanksgiving and the voice of melody.

Is 51:12 "I, *even* I, *am* He who comforts you. Who *are* you that you should be afraid Of a man *who* will die, And of the son of a man *who* will be made like grass?

Is 66:13 As one whom his mother comforts, So I will comfort you; And you shall be comforted in Jerusalem."

Ezek 14:22–23 Yet behold, there shall be left in it a remnant who will be brought out, *both* sons and daughters; surely they will come out to you, and you will see their ways and their doings. Then you will be comforted concerning the disaster that I have brought upon Jerusalem, all that I have brought upon it. **23** And they will comfort you, when you see their ways and their doings; and you shall know that I have done nothing without cause that I have done in it," says the Lord GOD.

Hos 2:14 "Therefore, behold, I will allure her, Will bring her into the wilderness, And speak comfort to her.

Zech 1:17 "Again proclaim, saying, 'Thus says the LORD of hosts: "My cities shall again spread out through prosperity; The LORD will again comfort Zion, And will again choose Jerusalem." ' "

Through the Holy Scriptures.

Ps 119:50 This *is* my comfort in my affliction, For Your word has given me life.

Ps 119:76 Let, I pray, Your merciful kindness be for my comfort, According to Your word to Your servant.

Rom 15:4 For whatever things were written before were written for our learning, that we through the patience and comfort of the Scriptures might have hope.

By ministers of the gospel.

Is 40:1–2 "Comfort, yes, comfort My people!" Says your God. **2** "Speak comfort to Jerusalem, and cry out to her, That her warfare is ended, That her iniquity is pardoned; For she has received from the LORD's hand Double for all her sins."

1 Cor 14:3 But he who prophesies speaks edification and exhortation and comfort to men.

2 Cor 1:4 who comforts us in all our tribulation, that we may be able to comfort those who are in any trouble, with the comfort with which we ourselves are comforted by God.

2 Cor 1:6 Now if we are afflicted, *it is* for your consolation and salvation, which is effective for enduring the same sufferings which we also suffer. Or if we are comforted, *it is* for your consolation and salvation.

Is abundant.

Ps 71:21 You shall increase my greatness, And comfort me on every side.

Is 66:11 That you may feed and be satisfied With the consolation of her bosom, That you may drink deeply and be delighted With the abundance of her glory."

Is strong.

Heb 6:18 that by two immutable things, in which it *is* impossible for God to lie, we might have strong consolation, who have fled for refuge to lay hold of the hope set before *us*.

Is everlasting.

2 Thess 2:16 Now may our Lord Jesus Christ Himself, and our God and Father, who has loved us and given *us* everlasting consolation and good hope by grace,

Is a cause of praise.

Is 12:1 And in that day you will say: "O LORD, I will praise You; Though You were angry with me, Your anger is turned away, and You comfort me.

Is 49:13 Sing, O heavens! Be joyful, O earth! And break out in singing, O mountains! For the LORD has comforted His people, And will have mercy on His afflicted.

Pray for.

Ps 119:82 My eyes fail *from searching* Your word, Saying, "When will You comfort me?"

Saints should administer to each other.

1 Thess 4:18 Therefore comfort one another with these words.

1 Thess 5:11 Therefore comfort each other and edify one another, just as you also are doing.

1 Thess 5:14 Now we exhort you, brethren, warn those who are unruly, comfort the fainthearted, uphold the weak, be patient with all.

Is sought in vain from the world.

Ps 69:20 Reproach has broken my heart, And I am full of heaviness; I looked *for someone* to take pity, but *there was* none; And for comforters, but I found none.

Eccl 4:1 Then I returned and considered all the oppression that is done under the sun: And look! The tears of the oppressed, But they have no comforter— On the side of their oppressors *there is* power, But they have no comforter.

Lam 1:2 She weeps bitterly in the night, Her tears *are* on her cheeks; Among all her lovers She has none to comfort *her.* All her friends have dealt treacherously with her; They have become her enemies.

To those who mourn for sin.

Ps 51:17 The sacrifices of God *are* a broken spirit, A broken and a contrite heart— These, O God, You will not despise.

Is 1:18 "Come now, and let us reason together," Says the LORD, "Though your sins are like scarlet, They shall be as white as snow; Though they are red like crimson, They shall be as wool.

Is 40:1-2 "Comfort, yes, comfort My people!" Says your God. 2 "Speak comfort to Jerusalem, and cry out to her, That her warfare is ended, That her iniquity is pardoned; For she has received from the LORD's hand Double for all her sins."

Is 61:1 "The Spirit of the Lord GOD *is* upon Me, Because the LORD has anointed Me To preach good tidings to the poor; He has sent Me to heal the brokenhearted, To proclaim liberty to the captives, And the opening of the prison to *those who are* bound;

Mic 7:18-19 Who *is* a God like You, Pardoning iniquity And passing over the transgression of the remnant of His heritage? He does not retain His anger forever, Because He delights *in* mercy. 19 He will again have compassion on us, And will subdue our iniquities. You will cast all our sins Into the depths of the sea.

Luke 4:18 *"The Spirit of the LORD is upon Me, Because*

He has anointed Me To preach the gospel to the poor; He has sent Me to heal the brokenhearted, To proclaim liberty to the captives And recovery of sight to the blind, To set at liberty those who are oppressed;

To the troubled in mind.

Ps 42:5 Why are you cast down, O my soul? And *why* are you disquieted within me? Hope in God, for I shall yet praise Him *For* the help of His countenance.

Ps 94:19 In the multitude of my anxieties within me, Your comforts delight my soul.

John 14:1 "Let not your heart be troubled; you believe in God, believe also in Me.

John 14:27 Peace I leave with you, My peace I give to you; not as the world gives do I give to you. Let not your heart be troubled, neither let it be afraid.

John 16:20 Most assuredly, I say to you that you will weep and lament, but the world will rejoice; and you will be sorrowful, but your sorrow will be turned into joy.

John 16:22 Therefore you now have sorrow; but I will see you again and your heart will rejoice, and your joy no one will take from you.

To those deserted by friends.

Ps 27:10 When my father and my mother forsake me, Then the LORD will take care of me.

Ps 41:9-12 Even my own familiar friend in whom I trusted, Who ate my bread, Has lifted up *his* heel against me. 10 But You, O LORD, be merciful to me, and raise me up, That I may repay them. 11 By this I know that You are well pleased with me, Because my enemy does not triumph over me. 12 As for me, You uphold me in my integrity, And set me before Your face forever.

John 15:18-19 "If the world hates you, you know that it hated Me before *it hated* you. 19 If you were of the world, the world would love its own. Yet because you are not of the world, but I chose you out of the world, therefore the world hates you.

To the persecuted.

Deut 33:27 The eternal God *is your* refuge, And underneath *are* the everlasting arms; He will thrust out the enemy from before you, And will say, 'Destroy!'

To the poor.

Ps 10:14 But You have seen, for You observe trouble and grief, To repay *it* by Your hand. The helpless commits himself to You; You are the helper of the fatherless.

Ps 34:9-10 Oh, fear the LORD, you His saints! *There is* no want to those who fear Him. 10 The young lions lack and suffer hunger; But those who seek the LORD shall not lack any good *thing.*

To the sick.

Ps 41:3 The LORD will strengthen him on his bed of illness; You will sustain him on his sickbed.

To the tempted.

Rom 16:20 And the God of peace will crush Satan under your feet shortly. The grace of our Lord Jesus Christ *be* with you. Amen.

1 Cor 10:13 No temptation has overtaken you except such as is common to man; but God *is* faithful, who will not allow you to be tempted beyond what you are able, but with the temptation will also make the way of escape, that you may be able to bear *it*.

2 Cor 12:9 And He said to me, "My grace is sufficient for you, for My strength is made perfect in weakness." Therefore most gladly I will rather boast in my infirmities, that the power of Christ may rest upon me.

James 1:12 Blessed *is* the man who endures temptation; for when he has been approved, he will receive the crown of life which the Lord has promised to those who love Him.

James 4:7 Therefore submit to God. Resist the devil and he will flee from you.

2 Pet 2:9 *then* the Lord knows how to deliver the godly out of temptations and to reserve the unjust under punishment for the day of judgment,

Rev 2:10 Do not fear any of those things which you are about to suffer. Indeed, the devil is about to throw *some* of you into prison, that you may be tested, and you will have tribulation ten days. Be faithful until death, and I will give you the crown of life.

In prospect of death.

Job 19:25–26 For I know *that* my Redeemer lives, And He shall stand at last on the earth; **26** And after my skin is destroyed, this *I know*, That in my flesh I shall see God,

Ps 23:4 Yea, though I walk through the valley of the shadow of death, I will fear no evil; For You *are* with me; Your rod and Your staff, they comfort me.

John 14:2 In My Father's house are many mansions; if *it were* not *so*, I would have told you. I go to prepare a place for you.

2 Cor 5:1 For we know that if our earthly house, *this* tent, is destroyed, we have a building from God, a house not made with hands, eternal in the heavens.

1 Thess 4:14 For if we believe that Jesus died and rose again, even so God will bring with Him those who sleep in Jesus.

Heb 4:9 There remains therefore a rest for the people of God.

Rev 7:14–17 And I said to him, "Sir, you know." So he said to me, "These are the ones who come out of the great tribulation, and washed their robes and made them white in the blood of the Lamb. **15** Therefore they are before the throne of God, and serve Him day and night in His temple. And He who sits on the throne will dwell among them. **16** They shall neither hunger anymore nor thirst anymore; the sun shall not strike them, nor any heat; **17** for the Lamb who is in the midst of the throne will shepherd them and lead them to living fountains of waters. And God will wipe away every tear from their eyes."

Rev 14:13 Then I heard a voice from heaven saying to me, "Write: 'Blessed *are* the dead who die in the Lord from now on.' " "Yes," says the Spirit, "that they may rest from their labors, and their works follow them."

Under the infirmities of age.

Ps 71:9 Do not cast me off in the time of old age; Do not forsake me when my strength fails.

Ps 71:18 Now also when *I am* old and grayheaded, O God, do not forsake me, Until I declare Your strength

to *this* generation, Your power to everyone *who* is to come.

AFFLICTION, PRAYER UNDER

Exhortation to.

James 5:13 Is anyone among you suffering? Let him pray. Is anyone cheerful? Let him sing psalms.

That God would consider our trouble.

2 Kin 19:16 Incline Your ear, O LORD, and hear; open Your eyes, O LORD, and see; and hear the words of Sennacherib, which he has sent to reproach the living God.

Neh 9:32 "Now therefore, our God, The great, the mighty, and awesome God, Who keeps covenant and mercy: Do not let all the trouble seem small before You That has come upon us, Our kings and our princes, Our priests and our prophets, Our fathers and on all Your people, From the days of the kings of Assyria until this day.

Ps 9:13 Have mercy on me, O LORD! Consider my trouble from those who hate me, You who lift me up from the gates of death,

Lam 5:1 Remember, O LORD, what has come upon us; Look, and behold our reproach!

For the presence and support of God.

Ps 10:1 Why do You stand afar off, O LORD? *Why* do You hide in times of trouble?

Ps 102:2 Do not hide Your face from me in the day of my trouble; Incline Your ear to me; In the day that I call, answer me speedily.

For divine comfort.

Ps 4:6 *There are* many who say, "Who will show us *any* good?" LORD, lift up the light of Your countenance upon us.

Ps 119:76 Let, I pray, Your merciful kindness be for my comfort, According to Your word to Your servant.

For mitigation of troubles.

Ps 39:12–13 "Hear my prayer, O LORD, And give ear to my cry; Do not be silent at my tears; For I *am* a stranger with You, A sojourner, as all my fathers *were*. **13** Remove Your gaze from me, that I may regain strength, Before I go away and am no more."

For deliverance.

Ps 25:17 The troubles of my heart have enlarged; Bring me out of my distresses!

Ps 25:22 Redeem Israel, O God, Out of all their troubles!

Ps 39:10 Remove Your plague from me; I am consumed by the blow of Your hand.

Is 64:9–12 Do not be furious, O LORD, Nor remember iniquity forever; Indeed, please look—we all *are* Your people! **10** Your holy cities are a wilderness, Zion is a wilderness, Jerusalem a desolation. **11** Our holy and beautiful temple, Where our fathers praised You, Is burned up with fire; And all our pleasant things are laid waste. **12** Will You restrain Yourself because of these *things*, O LORD? Will You hold Your peace, and afflict us very severely?

Jer 17:14 Heal me, O LORD, and I shall be healed; Save me, and I shall be saved, For You *are* my praise.

For pardon and deliverance from sin.

Ps 39:8 Deliver me from all my transgressions; Do not make me the reproach of the foolish.

Ps 51:1 Have mercy upon me, O God, According to Your lovingkindness; According to the multitude of Your tender mercies, Blot out my transgressions.

Ps 79:8 Oh, do not remember former iniquities against us! Let Your tender mercies come speedily to meet us, For we have been brought very low.

That we may be turned to God.

Ps 80:7 Restore us, O God of hosts; Cause Your face to shine, And we shall be saved!

Ps 85:4–6 Restore us, O God of our salvation, And cause Your anger toward us to cease. 5 Will You be angry with us forever? Will You prolong Your anger to all generations? 6 Will You not revive us again, That Your people may rejoice in You?

Jer 31:18 "I have surely heard Ephraim bemoaning himself: 'You have chastised me, and I was chastised, Like an untrained bull; Restore me, and I will return, For You are the LORD my God.

For divine teaching and direction.

Job 34:32 Teach me what I do not see; If I have done iniquity, I will do no more'?

Ps 27:11 Teach me Your way, O LORD, And lead me in a smooth path, because of my enemies.

Ps 143:10 Teach me to do Your will, For You are my God; Your Spirit is good. Lead me in the land of uprightness.

For increase of faith.

Mark 9:24 Immediately the father of the child cried out and said with tears, "Lord, I believe; help my unbelief!"

For mercy.

Ps 6:2 Have mercy on me, O LORD, for I am weak; O LORD, heal me, for my bones are troubled.

Hab 3:2 O LORD, I have heard Your speech and was afraid; O LORD, revive Your work in the midst of the years! In the midst of the years make it known; In wrath remember mercy.

For restoration to joy.

Ps 51:8 Make me hear joy and gladness, That the bones You have broken may rejoice.

Ps 51:12 Restore to me the joy of Your salvation, And uphold me by Your generous Spirit.

Ps 69:29 But I am poor and sorrowful; Let Your salvation, O God, set me up on high.

Ps 90:14–15 Oh, satisfy us early with Your mercy, That we may rejoice and be glad all our days! 15 Make us glad according to the days in which You have afflicted us, The years in which we have seen evil.

For protection and preservation from enemies.

2 Kin 19:19 Now therefore, O LORD our God, I pray, save us from his hand, that all the kingdoms of the earth may know that You are the LORD God, You alone."

2 Chr 20:12 O our God, will You not judge them? For we have no power against this great multitude that is coming against us; nor do we know what to do, but our eyes are upon You."

Ps 17:8–9 Keep me as the apple of Your eye; Hide me under the shadow of Your wings, 9 From the wicked who oppress me, From my deadly enemies who surround me.

That we may know the causes of our trouble.

Job 10:2 I will say to God, 'Do not condemn me; Show me why You contend with me.

Job 13:23–24 How many are my iniquities and sins? Make me know my transgression and my sin. 24 Why do You hide Your face, And regard me as Your enemy?

That we may be taught the uncertainty of life.

Ps 39:4 "LORD, make me to know my end, And what is the measure of my days, That I may know how frail I am.

That we may be quickened.

Ps 143:11 Revive me, O LORD, for Your name's sake! For Your righteousness' sake bring my soul out of trouble.

AFFLICTIONS

God appoints.

2 Kin 6:33 And while he was still talking with them, there was the messenger, coming down to him; and then the king said, "Surely this calamity is from the LORD; why should I wait for the LORD any longer?"

Job 5:6 For affliction does not come from the dust, Nor does trouble spring from the ground;

Job 5:17 "Behold, happy is the man whom God corrects; Therefore do not despise the chastening of the Almighty.

Ps 66:11 You brought us into the net; You laid affliction on our backs.

Amos 3:6 If a trumpet is blown in a city, will not the people be afraid? If there is calamity in a city, will not the LORD have done it?

Mic 6:9 The LORD's voice cries to the city— Wisdom shall see Your name: "Hear the rod! Who has appointed it?

God dispenses, as He will.

Job 11:10 "If He passes by, imprisons, and gathers to judgment, Then who can hinder Him?

Is 10:15 Shall the ax boast itself against him who chops with it? Or shall the saw exalt itself against him who saws with it? As if a rod could wield itself against those who lift it up, Or as if a staff could lift up, as if it were not wood!

Is 45:7 I form the light and create darkness, I make peace and create calamity; I, the LORD, do all these things.'

God regulates the measure of.

Ps 80:5 You have fed them with the bread of tears, And given them tears to drink in great measure.

Is 9:1 Nevertheless the gloom will not be upon her who is distressed, As when at first He lightly esteemed The land of Zebulun and the land of Naphtali, And afterward more heavily oppressed her, By the way of the sea, beyond the Jordan, In Galilee of the Gentiles.

Jer 46:28 Do not fear, O Jacob My servant," says the LORD, "For I am with you; For I will make a complete end of all the nations To which I have driven you,

But I will not make a complete end of you. I will rightly correct you, For I will not leave you wholly unpunished."

God determines the continuance of.

Gen 15:13–14 Then He said to Abram: "Know certainly that your descendants will be strangers in a land *that is* not theirs, and will serve them, and they will afflict them four hundred years. **14** And also the nation whom they serve I will judge; afterward they shall come out with great possessions.

Num 14:33 And your sons shall be shepherds in the wilderness forty years, and bear the brunt of your infidelity, until your carcasses are consumed in the wilderness.

Is 10:25 For yet a very little while and the indignation will cease, as will My anger in their destruction."

Jer 29:10 For thus says the LORD: After seventy years are completed at Babylon, I will visit you and perform My good word toward you, and cause you to return to this place.

God does not willingly send.

Lam 3:33 For He does not afflict willingly, Nor grieve the children of men.

Man is born to.

Job 5:6–7 For affliction does not come from the dust, Nor does trouble spring from the ground; **7** Yet man is born to trouble, As the sparks fly upward.

Job 14:1 "Man *who is* born of woman Is of few days and full of trouble.

Saints appointed to.

John 16:33 These things I have spoken to you, that in Me you may have peace. In the world you will have tribulation; but be of good cheer, I have overcome the world."

Acts 14:22 strengthening the souls of the disciples, exhorting *them* to continue in the faith, and *saying,* "We must through many tribulations enter the kingdom of God."

Phil 1:29 For to you it has been granted on behalf of Christ, not only to believe in Him, but also to suffer for His sake,

1 Thess 3:3 that no one should be shaken by these afflictions; for you yourselves know that we are appointed to this.

Consequent upon the Fall.

Gen 3:16–19 To the woman He said: "I will greatly multiply your sorrow and your conception; In pain you shall bring forth children; Your desire *shall be* for your husband, And he shall rule over you." **17** Then to Adam He said, "Because you have heeded the voice of your wife, and have eaten from the tree of which I commanded you, saying, 'You shall not eat of it': "Cursed *is* the ground for your sake; In toil you shall eat *of* it All the days of your life. **18** Both thorns and thistles it shall bring forth for you, And you shall eat the herb of the field. **19** In the sweat of your face you shall eat bread Till you return to the ground, For out of it you were taken; For dust you *are,* And to dust you shall return."

Sin produces.

Job 4:8 Even as I have seen, Those who plow iniquity And sow trouble reap the same.

Job 20:11 His bones are full of his youthful vigor, But it will lie down with him in the dust.

Prov 1:31 Therefore they shall eat the fruit of their own way, And be filled to the full with their own fancies.

1 Cor 11:29–30 For he who eats and drinks in an unworthy manner eats and drinks judgment to himself, not discerning the Lord's body. **30** For this reason many *are* weak and sick among you, and many sleep.

Sin visited with.

2 Sam 12:14 However, because by this deed you have given great occasion to the enemies of the LORD to blaspheme, the child also *who is* born to you shall surely die."

Ps 89:30–32 "If his sons forsake My law And do not walk in My judgments, **31** If they break My statutes And do not keep My commandments, **32** Then I will punish their transgression with the rod, And their iniquity with stripes.

Is 57:17 For the iniquity of his covetousness I was angry and struck him; I hid and was angry, And he went on backsliding in the way of his heart.

Acts 13:10–11 and said, "O full of all deceit and all fraud, *you* son of the devil, *you* enemy of all righteousness, will you not cease perverting the straight ways of the Lord? **11** And now, indeed, the hand of the Lord *is* upon you, and you shall be blind, not seeing the sun for a time." And immediately a dark mist fell on him, and he went around seeking someone to lead him by the hand.

Often severe.

Job 16:7–16 But now He has worn me out; You have made desolate all my company. **8** You have shriveled me up, And it is a witness *against me;* My leanness rises up against me *And* bears witness to my face. **9** He tears *me* in His wrath, and hates me; He gnashes at me with His teeth; My adversary sharpens His gaze on me. **10** They gape at me with their mouth, They strike me reproachfully on the cheek, They gather together against me. **11** God has delivered me to the ungodly, And turned me over to the hands of the wicked. **12** I was at ease, but He has shattered me; He also has taken *me* by my neck, and shaken me to pieces; He has set me up for His target, **13** His archers surround me. He pierces my heart and does not pity; He pours out my gall on the ground. **14** He breaks me with wound upon wound; He runs at me like a warrior. **15** "I have sewn sackcloth over my skin, And laid my head in the dust. **16** My face is flushed from weeping, And on my eyelids *is* the shadow of death;

Ps 42:7 Deep calls unto deep at the noise of Your waterfalls; All Your waves and billows have gone over me.

Ps 66:12 You have caused men to ride over our heads; We went through fire and through water; But You brought us out to rich *fulfillment.*

Jon 2:3 For You cast me into the deep, Into the heart of the seas, And the floods surrounded me; All Your billows and Your waves passed over me.

Rev 7:14 And I said to him, "Sir, you know." So he said to me, "These are the ones who come out of the great tribulation, and washed their robes and made them white in the blood of the Lamb.

Always less than we deserve.

Ezra 9:13 And after all that has come upon us for our evil deeds and for our great guilt, since You our God have punished us less than our iniquities *deserve*, and have given us *such* deliverance as this,

Ps 103:10 He has not dealt with us according to our sins, Nor punished us according to our iniquities.

Frequently terminate in good.

Gen 50:20 But as for you, you meant evil against me; *but* God meant it for good, in order to bring it about as *it is* this day, to save many people alive.

Ex 1:11–12 Therefore they set taskmasters over them to afflict them with their burdens. And they built for Pharaoh supply cities, Pithom and Raamses. 12 But the more they afflicted them, the more they multiplied and grew. And they were in dread of the children of Israel.

Deut 8:15–16 who led you through that great and terrible wilderness, *in which were* fiery serpents and scorpions and thirsty land where there was no water; who brought water for you out of the flinty rock; 16 who fed you in the wilderness with manna, which your fathers did not know, that He might humble you and that He might test you, to do you good in the end—

James 1:2–3 My brethren, count it all joy when you fall into various trials, 3 knowing that the testing of your faith produces patience.

1 Pet 3:14 But even if you should suffer for righteousness' sake, *you are* blessed. *"And do not be afraid of their threats, nor be troubled."*

1 Pet 4:13 but rejoice to the extent that you partake of Christ's sufferings, that when His glory is revealed, you may also be glad with exceeding joy.

Tempered with mercy.

Ps 78:38–39 But He, *being* full of compassion, forgave *their* iniquity, And did not destroy *them*. Yes, many a time He turned His anger away, And did not stir up all His wrath; 39 For He remembered that they *were but* flesh, A breath that passes away and does not come again.

Ps 106:43–46 Many times He delivered them; But they rebelled in their counsel, And were brought low for their iniquity. 44 Nevertheless He regarded their affliction, When He heard their cry; 45 And for their sake He remembered His covenant, And relented according to the multitude of His mercies. 46 He also made them to be pitied By all those who carried them away captive.

Is 30:18–21 Therefore the LORD will wait, that He may be gracious to you; And therefore He will be exalted, that He may have mercy on you. For the LORD *is* a God of justice; Blessed *are* all those who wait for Him. 19 For the people shall dwell in Zion at Jerusalem; You shall weep no more. He will be very gracious to you at the sound of your cry; When He hears it, He will answer you. 20 And *though* the Lord gives you The bread of adversity and the water of affliction, Yet your teachers will not be moved into a corner anymore, But your eyes shall see your teachers. 21 Your ears shall hear a word behind you, saying, "This *is* the way, walk in it,"

Whenever you turn to the right hand Or whenever you turn to the left.

Lam 3:32 Though He causes grief, Yet He will show compassion According to the multitude of His mercies.

Mic 7:7–9 Therefore I will look to the LORD; I will wait for the God of my salvation; My God will hear me. 8 Do not rejoice over me, my enemy; When I fall, I will arise; When I sit in darkness, The LORD *will be* a light to me. 9 I will bear the indignation of the LORD, Because I have sinned against Him, Until He pleads my case And executes justice for me. He will bring me forth to the light; I will see His righteousness.

Nah 1:12 Thus says the LORD: "Though *they are* safe, and likewise many, Yet in this manner they will be cut down When he passes through. Though I have afflicted you, I will afflict you no more;

Of saints, are comparatively light.

Acts 20:23–24 except that the Holy Spirit testifies in every city, saying that chains and tribulations await me. 24 But none of these things move me; nor do I count my life dear to myself, so that I may finish my race with joy, and the ministry which I received from the Lord Jesus, to testify to the gospel of the grace of God.

Rom 8:18 For I consider that the sufferings of this present time are not worthy *to be compared* with the glory which shall be revealed in us.

2 Cor 4:17 For our light affliction, which is but for a moment, is working for us a far more exceeding *and* eternal weight of glory,

Of saints, are but temporary.

Ps 30:5 For His anger *is but for* a moment, His favor *is for* life; Weeping may endure for a night, But joy *comes* in the morning.

Ps 103:9 He will not always strive *with us*, Nor will He keep *His anger* forever.

Is 54:7–8 "For a mere moment I have forsaken you, But with great mercies I will gather you. 8 With a little wrath I hid My face from you for a moment; But with everlasting kindness I will have mercy on you," Says the LORD, your Redeemer.

John 16:20 Most assuredly, I say to you that you will weep and lament, but the world will rejoice; and you will be sorrowful, but your sorrow will be turned into joy.

1 Pet 1:6 In this you greatly rejoice, though now for a little while, if need be, you have been grieved by various trials,

1 Pet 5:10 But may the God of all grace, who called us to His eternal glory by Christ Jesus, after you have suffered a while, perfect, establish, strengthen, and settle *you*.

Saints have joy under.

Job 5:17 "Behold, happy *is* the man whom God corrects; Therefore do not despise the chastening of the Almighty.

James 5:11 Indeed we count them blessed who endure. You have heard of the perseverance of Job and seen the end *intended by* the Lord—that the Lord is very compassionate and merciful.

Of saints, end in joy and blessedness.

Ps 126:5–6 Those who sow in tears Shall reap in joy. **6** He who continually goes forth weeping, Bearing seed for sowing, Shall doubtless come again with rejoicing, Bringing his sheaves *with him.*

1 Pet 4:13–14 but rejoice to the extent that you partake of Christ's sufferings, that when His glory is revealed, you may also be glad with exceeding joy. **14** If you are reproached for the name of Christ, blessed *are you,* for the Spirit of glory and of God rests upon you. On their part He is blasphemed, but on your part He is glorified.

Often arise from the profession of the gospel.

Matt 24:9 "Then they will deliver you up to tribulation and kill you, and you will be hated by all nations for My name's sake.

John 15:21 But all these things they will do to you for My name's sake, because they do not know Him who sent Me.

Phil 1:16 The former preach Christ from selfish ambition, not sincerely, supposing to add affliction to my chains;

2 Tim 3:11–12 persecutions, afflictions, which happened to me at Antioch, at Iconium, at Lystra—what persecutions I endured. And out of *them* all the Lord delivered me. **12** Yes, and all who desire to live godly in Christ Jesus will suffer persecution.

Exhibit the love and faithfulness of God.

Deut 8:5 You should know in your heart that as a man chastens his son, *so* the LORD your God chastens you.

Ps 119:75 I know, O LORD, that Your judgments *are* right, And *that* in faithfulness You have afflicted me.

Prov 3:12 For whom the LORD loves He corrects, Just as a father the son *in whom* he delights.

1 Cor 11:32 But when we are judged, we are chastened by the Lord, that we may not be condemned with the world.

Heb 12:6–7 *For whom the LORD loves He chastens, And scourges every son whom He receives."* **7** If you endure chastening, God deals with you as with sons; for what son is there whom a father does not chasten?

Rev 3:19 As many as I love, I rebuke and chasten. Therefore be zealous and repent.

AFFLICTIONS, BENEFITS OF
In promoting the glory of God.

John 9:1–3 Now as *Jesus* passed by, He saw a man who was blind from birth. **2** And His disciples asked Him, saying, "Rabbi, who sinned, this man or his parents, that he was born blind?" **3** Jesus answered, "Neither this man nor his parents sinned, but that the works of God should be revealed in him.

John 11:3–4 Therefore the sisters sent to Him, saying, "Lord, behold, he whom You love is sick." **4** When Jesus heard *that,* He said, "This sickness is not unto death, but for the glory of God, that the Son of God may be glorified through it."

John 21:18–19 Most assuredly, I say to you, when you were younger, you girded yourself and walked where you wished; but when you are old, you will stretch out your hands, and another will gird you

and carry *you* where you do not wish." **19** This He spoke, signifying by what death he would glorify God. And when He had spoken this, He said to him, "Follow Me."

In exhibiting the power and faithfulness of God.

Ps 34:19 Many *are* the afflictions of the righteous, But the LORD delivers him out of them all.

2 Cor 4:8–11 *We are* hard-pressed on every side, yet not crushed; *we are* perplexed, but not in despair; **9** persecuted, but not forsaken; struck down, but not destroyed— **10** always carrying about in the body the dying of the Lord Jesus, that the life of Jesus also may be manifested in our body. **11** For we who live are always delivered to death for Jesus' sake, that the life of Jesus also may be manifested in our mortal flesh.

2 Cor 12:9–10 And He said to me, "My grace is sufficient for you, for My strength is made perfect in weakness." Therefore most gladly I will rather boast in my infirmities, that the power of Christ may rest upon me. **10** Therefore I take pleasure in infirmities, in reproaches, in needs, in persecutions, in distresses, for Christ's sake. For when I am weak, then I am strong.

In teaching us the will of God.

Ps 119:71 *It is* good for me that I have been afflicted, That I may learn Your statutes.

Is 26:9 With my soul I have desired You in the night, Yes, by my spirit within me I will seek You early; For when Your judgments *are* in the earth, The inhabitants of the world will learn righteousness.

In turning us to God.

Deut 4:30–31 When you are in distress, and all these things come upon you in the latter days, when you turn to the LORD your God and obey His voice **31** (for the LORD your God *is* a merciful God), He will not forsake you nor destroy you, nor forget the covenant of your fathers which He swore to them.

Neh 1:8–9 Remember, I pray, the word that You commanded Your servant Moses, saying, 'If you are unfaithful, I will scatter you among the nations; **9** but *if* you return to Me, and keep My commandments and do them, though some of you were cast out to the farthest part of the heavens, *yet* I will gather them from there, and bring them to the place which I have chosen as a dwelling for My name.'

Ps 78:34 When He slew them, then they sought Him; And they returned and sought earnestly for God.

Is 10:20–21 And it shall come to pass in that day *That* the remnant of Israel, And such as have escaped of the house of Jacob, Will never again depend on him who defeated them, But will depend on the LORD, the Holy One of Israel, in truth. **21** The remnant will return, the remnant of Jacob, To the Mighty God.

Hos 2:6–7 "Therefore, behold, I will hedge up your way with thorns, And wall her in, So that she cannot find her paths. **7** She will chase her lovers, But not overtake them; Yes, she will seek them, but not find *them.* Then she will say, 'I will go and return to my first husband, For then *it was* better for me than now.'

In keeping us from again departing from God.

Job 34:31–32 "For has *anyone* said to God, 'I have borne *chastening;* I will offend no more; **32** Teach me *what* I do not see; If I have done iniquity, I will do no more'?

Is 10:20 And it shall come to pass in that day *That* the remnant of Israel, And such as have escaped of the house of Jacob, Will never again depend on him who defeated them, But will depend on the LORD, the Holy One of Israel, in truth.

Ezek 14:10–11 And they shall bear their iniquity; the punishment of the prophet shall be the same as the punishment of the one who inquired, **11** that the house of Israel may no longer stray from Me, nor be profaned anymore with all their transgressions, but that they may be My people and I may be their God," says the Lord GOD.' "

In leading us to seek God in prayer.

Judg 4:3 And the children of Israel cried out to the LORD; for Jabin had nine hundred chariots of iron, and for twenty years he had harshly oppressed the children of Israel.

Jer 31:18 "I have surely heard Ephraim bemoaning himself: 'You have chastised me, and I was chastised, Like an untrained bull; Restore me, and I will return, For You *are* the LORD my God.

Lam 2:17–19 The LORD has done what He purposed; He has fulfilled His word Which He commanded in days of old. He has thrown down and has not pitied, And He has caused an enemy to rejoice over you; He has exalted the horn of your adversaries. **18** Their heart cried out to the Lord, "O wall of the daughter of Zion, Let tears run down like a river day and night; Give yourself no relief; Give your eyes no rest. **19** "Arise, cry out in the night, At the beginning of the watches; Pour out your heart like water before the face of the Lord. Lift your hands toward Him For the life of your young children, Who faint from hunger at the head of every street."

Hos 5:14–15 For I *will* be like a lion to Ephraim, And like a young lion to the house of Judah. I, *even* I, will tear *them* and go away; I will take *them* away, and no one shall rescue. **15** I will return again to My place Till they acknowledge their offense. Then they will seek My face; In their affliction they will earnestly seek Me."

Jon 2:1 Then Jonah prayed to the LORD his God from the fish's belly.

In convincing us of sin.

Job 36:8–9 And if *they are* bound in fetters, Held in the cords of affliction, **9** Then He tells them their work and their transgressions— That they have acted defiantly.

Ps 119:67 Before I was afflicted I went astray, But now I keep Your word.

Luke 15:16–18 And he would gladly have filled his stomach with the pods that the swine ate, and no one gave him *anything.* **17** "But when he came to himself, he said, 'How many of my father's hired servants have bread enough and to spare, and I perish with hunger! **18** I will arise and go to my father, and will say to him, "Father, I have sinned against heaven and before you,

In leading us to confession of sin.

Num 21:7 Therefore the people came to Moses, and said, "We have sinned, for we have spoken against

the LORD and against you; pray to the LORD that He take away the serpents from us." So Moses prayed for the people.

Ps 32:5 I acknowledged my sin to You, And my iniquity I have not hidden. I said, "I will confess my transgressions to the LORD," And You forgave the iniquity of my sin. Selah

Ps 51:3 For I acknowledge my transgressions, And my sin *is* always before me.

In testing and exhibiting our sincerity.

Job 23:10 But He knows the way that I take; *When* He has tested me, I shall come forth as gold.

Ps 66:10 For You, O God, have tested us; You have refined us as silver is refined.

Prov 17:3 The refining pot *is* for silver and the furnace for gold, But the LORD tests the hearts.

In trying our faith and obedience.

Gen 22:1–2 Now it came to pass after these things that God tested Abraham, and said to him, "Abraham!" And he said, "Here I am." **2** Then He said, "Take now your son, your only *son* Isaac, whom you love, and go to the land of Moriah, and offer him there as a burnt offering on one of the mountains of which I shall tell you."

Deut 8:2 And you shall remember that the LORD your God led you all the way these forty years in the wilderness, to humble you *and* test you, to know what *was* in your heart, whether you would keep His commandments or not.

Deut 8:16 who fed you in the wilderness with manna, which your fathers did not know, that He might humble you and that He might test you, to do you good in the end—

Heb 11:17 By faith Abraham, when he was tested, offered up Isaac, and he who had received the promises offered up his only begotten *son,*

1 Pet 1:7 that the genuineness of your faith, *being* much more precious than gold that perishes, though it is tested by fire, may be found to praise, honor, and glory at the revelation of Jesus Christ,

Rev 2:10 Do not fear any of those things which you are about to suffer. Indeed, the devil is about to throw *some* of you into prison, that you may be tested, and you will have tribulation ten days. Be faithful until death, and I will give you the crown of life.

In humbling us.

Deut 8:3 So He humbled you, allowed you to hunger, and fed you with manna which you did not know nor did your fathers know, that He might make you know that man shall not live by bread alone; but man lives by every *word* that proceeds from the mouth of the LORD.

Deut 8:16 who fed you in the wilderness with manna, which your fathers did not know, that He might humble you and that He might test you, to do you good in the end—

2 Chr 7:13–14 When I shut up heaven and there is no rain, or command the locusts to devour the land, or send pestilence among My people, **14** if My people who are called by My name will humble themselves, and pray and seek My face, and turn from their wicked ways, then I will hear from heaven, and will forgive their sin and heal their land.

Lam 3:19–20 Remember my affliction and roaming, The wormwood and the gall. **20** My soul still remembers And sinks within me.

2 Cor 12:7 And lest I should be exalted above measure by the abundance of the revelations, a thorn in the flesh was given to me, a messenger of Satan to buffet me, lest I be exalted above measure.

In purifying us.

Eccl 7:2–3 Better to go to the house of mourning Than to go to the house of feasting, For that *is* the end of all men; And the living will take *it* to heart. **3** Sorrow *is* better than laughter, For by a sad countenance the heart is made better.

In exercising our patience.

Ps 40:1 I waited patiently for the LORD; And He inclined to me, And heard my cry.

Rom 5:3 And not only *that*, but we also glory in tribulations, knowing that tribulation produces perseverance;

James 1:3 knowing that the testing of your faith produces patience.

1 Pet 2:20 For what credit *is it* if, when you are beaten for your faults, you take it patiently? But when you do good and suffer, if you take it patiently, this *is* commendable before God.

In rendering us fruitful in good works.

John 15:2 Every branch in Me that does not bear fruit He takes away; and every *branch* that bears fruit He prunes, that it may bear more fruit.

Heb 12:10–11 For they indeed for a few days chastened *us* as seemed *best* to them, but He for *our* profit, that *we* may be partakers of His holiness. **11** Now no chastening seems to be joyful for the present, but painful; nevertheless, afterward it yields the peaceable fruit of righteousness to those who have been trained by it.

In furthering the gospel.

Acts 8:3–4 As for Saul, he made havoc of the church, entering every house, and dragging off men and women, committing *them* to prison. **4** Therefore those who were scattered went everywhere preaching the word.

Acts 11:19–21 Now those who were scattered after the persecution that arose over Stephen traveled as far as Phoenicia, Cyprus, and Antioch, preaching the word to no one but the Jews only. **20** But some of them were men from Cyprus and Cyrene, who, when they had come to Antioch, spoke to the Hellenists, preaching the Lord Jesus. **21** And the hand of the Lord was with them, and a great number believed and turned to the Lord.

Phil 1:12 But I want you to know, brethren, that the things *which happened* to me have actually turned out for the furtherance of the gospel,

2 Tim 2:9–10 for which I suffer trouble as an evildoer, *even* to the point of chains; but the word of God is not chained. **10** Therefore I endure all things for the sake of the elect, that they also may obtain the salvation which is in Christ Jesus with eternal glory.

2 Tim 4:16–17 At my first defense no one stood with me, but all forsook me. May it not be charged against them. **17** But the Lord stood with me and strengthened me, so that the message might be preached fully through me, and *that* all the Gentiles might hear. Also I was delivered out of the mouth of the lion.

Exemplified by

Joseph.

Gen 45:5 But now, do not therefore be grieved or angry with yourselves because you sold me here; for God sent me before you to preserve life.

Gen 45:7–8 And God sent me before you to preserve a posterity for you in the earth, and to save your lives by a great deliverance. **8** So now it *was* not you *who* sent me here, but God; and He has made me a father to Pharaoh, and lord of all his house, and a ruler throughout all the land of Egypt.

Israel.

Deut 8:3 So He humbled you, allowed you to hunger, and fed you with manna which you did not know nor did your fathers know, that He might make you know that man shall not live by bread alone; but man lives by every *word* that proceeds from the mouth of the LORD.

Deut 8:5 You should know in your heart that as a man chastens his son, *so* the LORD your God chastens you.

Hezekiah.

2 Chr 32:25–26 But Hezekiah did not repay according to the favor *shown* him, for his heart was lifted up; therefore wrath was looming over him and over Judah and Jerusalem. **26** Then Hezekiah humbled himself for the pride of his heart, he and the inhabitants of Jerusalem, so that the wrath of the LORD did not come upon them in the days of Hezekiah.

Manasseh.

2 Chr 33:12 Now when he was in affliction, he implored the LORD his God, and humbled himself greatly before the God of his fathers,

Jonah.

Jon 2:7 "When my soul fainted within me, I remembered the LORD; And my prayer went *up* to You, Into Your holy temple.

Prodigal son.

Luke 15:21 And the son said to him, 'Father, I have sinned against heaven and in your sight, and am no longer worthy to be called your son.'

AFRAID

Should not be.

Ex 14:13 And Moses said to the people, "Do not be afraid. Stand still, and see the salvation of the LORD, which He will accomplish for you today. For the Egyptians whom you see today, you shall see again no more forever.

Deut 20:1 "When you go out to battle against your enemies, and see horses and chariots *and* people more numerous than you, do not be afraid of them; for the LORD your God *is* with you, who brought you up from the land of Egypt.

2 Kin 19:6 And Isaiah said to them, "Thus you shall say to your master, 'Thus says the LORD: "Do not be afraid of the words which you have heard, with which the servants of the king of Assyria have blasphemed Me.

Prov 3:25–26 Do not be afraid of sudden terror, Nor of trouble from the wicked when it comes; **26** For the LORD will be your confidence, And will keep your foot from being caught.

Is 37:6 And Isaiah said to them, "Thus you shall say to your master, 'Thus says the LORD: "Do not be afraid of the words which you have heard, with which the servants of the king of Assyria have blasphemed Me.

Luke 1:30 Then the angel said to her, "Do not be afraid, Mary, for you have found favor with God.

Luke 2:10 Then the angel said to them, "Do not be afraid, for behold, I bring you good tidings of great joy which will be to all people.

1 Pet 3:5–6 For in this manner, in former times, the holy women who trusted in God also adorned themselves, being submissive to their own husbands, **6** as Sarah obeyed Abraham, calling him lord, whose daughters you are if you do good and are not afraid with any terror.

1 Pet 3:14 But even if you should suffer for righteousness' sake, *you are* blessed. *"And do not be afraid of their threats, nor be troubled."*

Moab was.

Num 22:3 And Moab was exceedingly afraid of the people because they *were* many, and Moab was sick with dread because of the children of Israel.

Israel was.

1 Sam 7:7 Now when the Philistines heard that the children of Israel had gathered together at Mizpah, the lords of the Philistines went up against Israel. And when the children of Israel heard *of it*, they were afraid of the Philistines.

1 Sam 17:11 When Saul and all Israel heard these words of the Philistine, they were dismayed and greatly afraid.

King Saul was,

Of David.

1 Sam 18:12 Now Saul was afraid of David, because the LORD was with him, but had departed from Saul.

Of man.

1 Sam 28:5 When Saul saw the army of the Philistines, he was afraid, and his heart trembled greatly.

Nehemiah was.

Neh 2:2 Therefore the king said to me, "Why *is* your face sad, since you *are* not sick? This *is* nothing but sorrow of heart." So I became dreadfully afraid,

God never is.

Is 31:4 For thus the LORD has spoken to me: "As a lion roars, And a young lion over his prey (When a multitude of shepherds is summoned against him, *He* will not be afraid of their voice Nor be disturbed by their noise), So the LORD of hosts will come down To fight for Mount Zion and for its hill.

When awakened, sinners are, of God.

Is 33:14 The sinners in Zion are afraid; Fearfulness has seized the hypocrites: "Who among us shall dwell with the devouring fire? Who among us shall dwell with everlasting burnings?"

Daniel was, in response to an angel.

Dan 8:15–17 Then it happened, when I, Daniel, had seen the vision and was seeking the meaning, that suddenly there stood before me one having the appearance of a man. **16** And I heard a man's voice between *the banks of* the Ulai, who called, and said, "Gabriel, make this *man* understand the vision." **17** So he came near where I stood, and when he came I was afraid and fell on my face; but he said to me, "Understand, son of man, that the vision *refers* to the time of the end."

Sailors were, in response to a storm.

Jon 1:4–5 But the LORD sent out a great wind on the sea, and there was a mighty tempest on the sea, so that the ship was about to be broken up. **5** Then the mariners were afraid; and every man cried out to his god, and threw the cargo that *was* in the ship into the sea, to lighten the load. But Jonah had gone down into the lowest parts of the ship, had lain down, and was fast asleep.

Disciples were,

In response to a storm.

Matt 8:23–27 Now when He got into a boat, His disciples followed Him. **24** And suddenly a great tempest arose on the sea, so that the boat was covered with the waves. But He was asleep. **25** Then His disciples came to *Him* and awoke Him, saying, "Lord, save us! We are perishing!" **26** But He said to them, "Why are you fearful, O you of little faith?" Then He arose and rebuked the winds and the sea, and there was a great calm. **27** So the men marveled, saying, "Who can this be, that even the winds and the sea obey Him?"

Mark 4:37–41 And a great windstorm arose, and the waves beat into the boat, so that it was already filling. **38** But He was in the stern, asleep on a pillow. And they awoke Him and said to Him, "Teacher, do You not care that we are perishing?" **39** Then He arose and rebuked the wind, and said to the sea, "Peace, be still!" And the wind ceased and there was a great calm. **40** But He said to them, "Why are you so fearful? How *is it* that you have no faith?" **41** And they feared exceedingly, and said to one another, "Who can this be, that even the wind and the sea obey Him!"

Luke 8:23–25 But as they sailed He fell asleep. And a windstorm came down on the lake, and they were filling *with water,* and were in jeopardy. **24** And they came to Him and awoke Him, saying, "Master, Master, we are perishing!" Then He arose and rebuked the wind and the raging of the water. And they ceased, and there was a calm. **25** But He said to them, "Where is your faith?" And they were afraid, and marveled, saying to one another, "Who can this be? For He commands even the winds and water, and they obey Him!"

In response to an angel.

Mark 16:8 So they went out quickly and fled from the tomb, for they trembled and were amazed. And they said nothing to anyone, for they were afraid.

Nicodemus was.

John 3:2 This man came to Jesus by night and said to Him, "Rabbi, we know that You are a teacher come from God; for no one can do these signs that You do unless God is with him."

Pilate was.

John 19:7–8 The Jews answered him, "We have a law, and according to our law He ought to die, because He made Himself the Son of God." **8** Therefore, when Pilate heard that saying, he was the more afraid,

Early church was.

Acts 5:5 Then Ananias, hearing these words, fell down and breathed his last. So great fear came upon all those who heard these things.

Felix was.

Acts 24:25 Now as he reasoned about righteousness, self-control, and the judgment to come, Felix was afraid and answered, "Go away for now; when I have a convenient time I will call for you."

Timothy tended to be.

2 Tim 1:7 For God has not given us a spirit of fear, but of power and of love and of a sound mind.

AGREEMENT

Same as vow.

Num 30:2 If a man makes a vow to the LORD, or swears an oath to bind himself by some agreement, he shall not break his word; he shall do according to all that proceeds out of his mouth.

Cf. Matt 5:33

Often equal to amen.

Deut 27:15 'Cursed *is* the one who makes a carved or molded image, an abomination to the LORD, the work of the hands of the craftsman, and sets *it* up in secret.' "And all the people shall answer and say, 'Amen!'

Binding covenant.

2 Sam 23:5 "Although my house *is* not so with God, Yet He has made with me an everlasting covenant, Ordered in all *things* and secure. For *this is* all my salvation and all *my* desire; Will He not make *it* increase?

2 Kin 11:17 Then Jehoiada made a covenant between the LORD, the king, and the people, that they should be the LORD's people, and *also* between the king and the people.

Neh 9:38 "And because of all this, We make a sure *covenant* and write *it;* Our leaders, our Levites, *and* our priests seal *it.*"

Rom 9:4 who are Israelites, to whom *pertain* the adoption, the glory, the covenants, the giving of the law, the service *of God,* and the promises;

Can be none, between truth and idols.

2 Cor 6:16 And what agreement has the temple of God with idols? For you are the temple of the living God. As God has said: *"I will dwell in them And walk among them. I will be their God, And they shall be My people."*

AGRICULTURE

The cultivation of the earth.

Gen 3:23 therefore the LORD God sent him out of the garden of Eden to till the ground from which he was taken.

The occupation of man before the Fall.

Gen 2:15 Then the LORD God took the man and put him in the garden of Eden to tend and keep it.

Rendered laborious by the curse on the earth.

Gen 3:17–19 Then to Adam He said, "Because you have heeded the voice of your wife, and have eaten from the tree of which I commanded you, saying, 'You shall not eat of it': "Cursed *is* the ground for your sake; In toil you shall eat *of* it All the days of your life. **18** Both thorns and thistles it shall bring forth for you, And you shall eat the herb of the field. **19** In the sweat of your face you shall eat bread Till you return to the ground, For out of it you were taken; For dust you *are,* And to dust you shall return."

Man doomed to labor in, after the Fall.

Gen 3:23 therefore the LORD God sent him out of the garden of Eden to till the ground from which he was taken.

Contributes to the support of all.

Eccl 5:9 Moreover the profit of the land is for all; *even* the king is served from the field.

The providence of God to be acknowledged in the produce of.

Jer 5:24 They do not say in their heart, "Let us now fear the LORD our God, Who gives rain, both the former and the latter, in its season. He reserves for us the appointed weeks of the harvest."

Hos 2:8 For she did not know That I gave her grain, new wine, and oil, And multiplied her silver and gold— *Which* they prepared for Baal.

Requires

Wisdom.

Is 28:26 For He instructs him in right judgment, His God teaches him.

Diligence.

Prov 27:23–27 Be diligent to know the state of your flocks, *And* attend to your herds; **24** For riches *are* not forever, Nor does a crown *endure* to all generations. **25** *When* the hay is removed, and the tender grass shows itself, And the herbs of the mountains are gathered in, **26** The lambs *will provide* your clothing, And the goats the price of a field; **27** *You shall have* enough goats' milk for your food, For the food of your household, And the nourishment of your maidservants.

Eccl 11:6 In the morning sow your seed, And in the evening do not withhold your hand; For you do not know which will prosper, Either this or that, Or whether both alike *will be* good.

Toil.

2 Tim 2:6 The hardworking farmer must be first to partake of the crops.

Patience in waiting.

James 5:7 Therefore be patient, brethren, until the coming of the Lord. See *how* the farmer waits for the precious fruit of the earth, waiting patiently for it until it receives the early and latter rain.

Diligence in, abundantly recompensed.

Prov 12:11 He who tills his land will be satisfied with

bread, But he who follows frivolity *is* devoid of understanding.

Prov 13:23 Much food *is in* the fallow *ground* of the poor, And for lack of justice there is waste.

Prov 28:19 He who tills his land will have plenty of bread, But he who follows frivolity will have poverty enough!

Heb 6:7 For the earth which drinks in the rain that often comes upon it, and bears herbs useful for those by whom it is cultivated, receives blessing from God;

Persons engaged in, called

Tillers of the ground.

Gen 4:2 Then she bore again, this time his brother Abel. Now Abel was a keeper of sheep, but Cain was a tiller of the ground.

Farmers.

2 Chr 26:10 Also he built towers in the desert. He dug many wells, for he had much livestock, both in the lowlands and in the plains; *he also had* farmers and vinedressers in the mountains and in Carmel, for he loved the soil.

Laborers.

Matt 9:37 Then He said to His disciples, "The harvest truly *is* plentiful, but the laborers *are* few.

Matt 20:1 "For the kingdom of heaven is like a landowner who went out early in the morning to hire laborers for his vineyard.

Peace favorable to.

Is 2:4 He shall judge between the nations, And rebuke many people; They shall beat their swords into plowshares, And their spears into pruning hooks; Nation shall not lift up sword against nation, Neither shall they learn war anymore.

Jer 31:24 And there shall dwell in Judah itself, and in all its cities together, farmers and those going out with flocks.

War destructive to.

Jer 50:16 Cut off the sower from Babylon, And him who handles the sickle at harvest time. For fear of the oppressing sword Everyone shall turn to his own people, And everyone shall flee to his own land.

Jer 51:23 With you also I will break in pieces the shepherd and his flock; With you I will break in pieces the farmer and his yoke of oxen; And with you I will break in pieces governors and rulers.

Patriarchs engaged in.

Gen 4:2 Then she bore again, this time his brother Abel. Now Abel was a keeper of sheep, but Cain was a tiller of the ground.

Gen 9:20 And Noah began *to be* a farmer, and he planted a vineyard.

The labor of, supposed to be lessened by Noah.

Gen 5:29 And he called his name Noah, saying, "This *one* will comfort us concerning our work and the toil of our hands, because of the ground which the LORD has cursed."

Gen 9:20 And Noah began *to be* a farmer, and he planted a vineyard.

Soil of Canaan suited to.

Gen 13:10 And Lot lifted his eyes and saw all the plain of Jordan, that it *was* well watered everywhere (before the LORD destroyed Sodom and Gomorrah) like the garden of the LORD, like the land of Egypt as you go toward Zoar.

Deut 8:7–9 For the LORD your God is bringing you into a good land, a land of brooks of water, of fountains and springs, that flow out of valleys and hills; **8** a land of wheat and barley, of vines and fig trees and pomegranates, a land of olive oil and honey; **9** a land in which you will eat bread without scarcity, in which you will lack nothing; a land whose stones *are* iron and out of whose hills you can dig copper.

Climate of Canaan favorable to.

Deut 11:10–11 For the land which you go to possess *is* not like the land of Egypt from which you have come, where you sowed your seed and watered *it* by foot, as a vegetable garden; **11** but the land which you cross over to possess *is* a land of hills and valleys, which drinks water from the rain of heaven,

Was promoted among the Jews by

Allotments to each family.

Num 36:7–9 So the inheritance of the children of Israel shall not change hands from tribe to tribe, for every one of the children of Israel shall keep the inheritance of the tribe of his fathers. **8** And every daughter who possesses an inheritance in any tribe of the children of Israel shall be the wife of one of the family of her father's tribe, so that the children of Israel each may possess the inheritance of his fathers. **9** Thus no inheritance shall change hands from *one* tribe to another, but every tribe of the children of Israel shall keep its own inheritance."

The rights of redemption.

Lev 25:23–28 'The land shall not be sold permanently, for the land *is* Mine; for you *are* strangers and sojourners with Me. **24** And in all the land of your possession you shall grant redemption of the land. **25** 'If one of your brethren becomes poor, and has sold *some* of his possession, and if his redeeming relative comes to redeem it, then he may redeem what his brother sold. **26** Or if the man has no one to redeem it, but he himself becomes able to redeem it, **27** then let him count the years since its sale, and restore the remainder to the man to whom he sold it, that he may return to his possession. **28** But if he is not able to have *it* restored to himself, then what was sold shall remain in the hand of him who bought it until the Year of Jubilee; and in the Jubilee it shall be released, and he shall return to his possession.

Separation from other nations.

Ex 33:16 For how then will it be known that Your people and I have found grace in Your sight, except You go with us? So we shall be separate, Your people and I, from all the people who *are* upon the face of the earth."

The prohibition against usury.

Ex 22:25 "If you lend money to *any of* My people *who are* poor among you, you shall not be like a moneylender to him; you shall not charge him interest.

The promises of God's blessings on.

Lev 26:4 then I will give you rain in its season, the land shall yield its produce, and the trees of the field shall yield their fruit.

Deut 7:13 And He will love you and bless you and multiply you; He will also bless the fruit of your womb and the fruit of your land, your grain and your new wine and your oil, the increase of your cattle and the offspring of your flock, in the land of which He swore to your fathers to give you.

Deut 11:14–15 then I will give *you* the rain for your land in its season, the early rain and the latter rain, that you may gather in your grain, your new wine, and your oil. **15** And I will send grass in your fields for your livestock, that you may eat and be filled.'

Enactments to protect,

Not to covet the fields of another.

Deut 5:21 'You shall not covet your neighbor's wife; and you shall not desire your neighbor's house, his field, his male servant, his female servant, his ox, his donkey, or anything that *is* your neighbor's.'

Not to move landmarks.

Deut 19:14 "You shall not remove your neighbor's landmark, which the men of old have set, in your inheritance which you will inherit in the land that the LORD your God is giving you to possess.

Prov 22:28 Do not remove the ancient landmark Which your fathers have set.

Not to cut down crops of another.

Deut 23:25 When you come into your neighbor's standing grain, you may pluck the heads with your hand, but you shall not use a sickle on your neighbor's standing grain.

Against the trespass of cattle.

Ex 22:5 "If a man causes a field or vineyard to be grazed, and lets loose his animal, and it feeds in another man's field, he shall make restitution from the best of his own field and the best of his own vineyard.

Against injuring the produce of.

Ex 22:5 "If a man causes a field or vineyard to be grazed, and lets loose his animal, and it feeds in another man's field, he shall make restitution from the best of his own field and the best of his own vineyard.

Often performed by hirelings.

1 Chr 27:26 Ezri the son of Chelub was over those who did the work of the field for tilling the ground.

2 Chr 26:10 Also he built towers in the desert. He dug many wells, for he had much livestock, both in the lowlands and in the plains; *he also had* farmers and vinedressers in the mountains and in Carmel, for he loved the soil.

Matt 20:8 "So when evening had come, the owner of the vineyard said to his steward, 'Call the laborers and give them *their* wages, beginning with the last to the first.'

Luke 17:7 And which of you, having a servant plowing or tending sheep, will say to him when he has come in from the field, 'Come at once and sit down to eat'?

Not to be engaged in during the Sabbatical year.

Ex 23:10–11 "Six years you shall sow your land and gather in its produce, **11** but the seventh *year* you shall let it rest and lie fallow, that the poor of your people may eat; and what they leave, the beasts of the field may eat. In like manner you shall do with your vineyard *and* your olive grove.

Produce of, given as rent for land.

Matt 21:33–34 "Hear another parable: There was a certain landowner who planted a vineyard and set a hedge around it, dug a winepress in it and built a tower. And he leased it to vinedressers and went into a far country. **34** Now when vintage-time drew near, he sent his servants to the vinedressers, that they might receive its fruit.

Produce of, often wasted because of sin.

Is 5:10 For ten acres of vineyard shall yield one bath, And a homer of seed shall yield one ephah."

Is 7:23 It shall happen in that day, *That* wherever there could be a thousand vines *Worth* a thousand *shekels* of silver, It will be for briers and thorns.

Jer 12:13 They have sown wheat but reaped thorns; They have put themselves to pain *but* do not profit. But be ashamed of your harvest Because of the fierce anger of the LORD."

Joel 1:10–11 The field is wasted, The land mourns; For the grain is ruined, The new wine is dried up, The oil fails. **11** Be ashamed, you farmers, Wail, you vinedressers, For the wheat and the barley; Because the harvest of the field has perished.

Grief occasioned by the failure of the fruits of.

Joel 1:11 Be ashamed, you farmers, Wail, you vinedressers, For the wheat and the barley; Because the harvest of the field has perished.

Amos 5:16–17 Therefore the LORD God of hosts, the Lord, says this: "*There shall be* wailing in all streets, And they shall say in all the highways, 'Alas! Alas!' They shall call the farmer to mourning, And skillful lamenters to wailing. **17** In all vineyards *there shall be* wailing, For I will pass through you," Says the LORD.

Produce of, exported.

1 Kin 5:11 And Solomon gave Hiram twenty thousand kors of wheat *as* food for his household, and twenty kors of pressed oil. Thus Solomon gave to Hiram year by year.

Ezek 27:17 Judah and the land of Israel *were* your traders. They traded for your merchandise wheat of Minnith, millet, honey, oil, and balm.

Operations in,

Hedging.

Is 5:2 He dug it up and cleared out its stones, And planted it with the choicest vine. He built a tower in its midst, And also made a winepress in it; So He expected *it* to bring forth *good* grapes, But it brought forth wild grapes.

Is 5:5 And now, please let Me tell you what I will do to My vineyard: I will take away its hedge, and it shall be burned; *And* break down its wall, and it shall be trampled down.

Hos 2:6 "Therefore, behold, I will hedge up your way with thorns, And wall her in, So that she cannot find her paths.

Plowing.

1 Kin 19:19 So he departed from there, and found Elisha the son of Shaphat, who *was* plowing *with* twelve yoke *of oxen* before him, and he was with the twelfth.

Then Elijah passed by him and threw his mantle on him.

Job 1:14 and a messenger came to Job and said, "The oxen were plowing and the donkeys feeding beside them,

Job 39:10 Can you bind the wild ox in the furrow with ropes? Or will he plow the valleys behind you?

Is 28:24 Does the plowman keep plowing all day to sow? Does he keep turning his soil and breaking the clods?

Digging.

Is 5:6 I will lay it waste; It shall not be pruned or dug, But there shall come up briers and thorns. I will also command the clouds That they rain no rain on it."

Luke 13:8 But he answered and said to him, 'Sir, let it alone this year also, until I dig around it and fertilize it.

Luke 16:3 "Then the steward said within himself, 'What shall I do? For my master is taking the stewardship away from me. I cannot dig; I am ashamed to beg.

Gathering out the stones.

Is 5:2 He dug it up and cleared out its stones, And planted it with the choicest vine. He built a tower in its midst, And also made a winepress in it; So He expected *it* to bring forth *good* grapes, But it brought forth wild grapes.

Sowing.

Eccl 11:4 He who observes the wind will not sow, And he who regards the clouds will not reap.

Is 32:20 Blessed *are* you who sow beside all waters, Who send out freely the feet of the ox and the donkey.

Matt 13:3 Then He spoke many things to them in parables, saying: "Behold, a sower went out to sow.

Planting.

Prov 31:16 She considers a field and buys it; From her profits she plants a vineyard.

Is 44:14 He cuts down cedars for himself, And takes the cypress and the oak; He secures *it* for himself among the trees of the forest. He plants a pine, and the rain nourishes *it*.

Jer 31:5 You shall yet plant vines on the mountains of Samaria; The planters shall plant and eat *them* as ordinary food.

Watering.

Deut 11:10 For the land which you go to possess *is* not like the land of Egypt from which you have come, where you sowed your seed and watered *it* by foot, as a vegetable garden;

1 Cor 3:6–8 I planted, Apollos watered, but God gave the increase. 7 So then neither he who plants is anything, nor he who waters, but God who gives the increase. 8 Now he who plants and he who waters are one, and each one will receive his own reward according to his own labor.

Weeding.

Matt 13:28 He said to them, 'An enemy has done this.' The servants said to him, 'Do you want us then to go and gather them up?'

Grafting.

Rom 11:17–19 And if some of the branches were broken off, and you, being a wild olive tree, were grafted in among them, and with them became a partaker of the root and fatness of the olive tree, **18** do not boast against the branches. But if you do boast, *remember that* you do not support the root, but the root supports you. **19** You will say then, "Branches were broken off that I might be grafted in."

Rom 11:24 For if you were cut out of the olive tree which is wild by nature, and were grafted contrary to nature into a cultivated olive tree, how much more will these, who *are* natural *branches*, be grafted into their own olive tree?

Pruning.

Lev 25:3 Six years you shall sow your field, and six years you shall prune your vineyard, and gather its fruit;

Is 5:6 I will lay it waste; It shall not be pruned or dug, But there shall come up briers and thorns. I will also command the clouds That they rain no rain on it."

John 15:2 Every branch in Me that does not bear fruit He takes away; and every *branch* that bears fruit He prunes, that it may bear more fruit.

Mowing.

Amos 7:1 Thus the Lord GOD showed me: Behold, He formed locust swarms at the beginning of the late crop; indeed *it was* the late crop after the king's mowings.

Reaping.

Ps 129:7 With which the reaper does not fill his hand, Nor he who binds sheaves, his arms.

Is 17:5 It shall be as when the harvester gathers the grain, And reaps the heads with his arm; It shall be as he who gathers heads of grain In the Valley of Rephaim.

Binding.

Gen 37:7 There we were, binding sheaves in the field. Then behold, my sheaf arose and also stood upright; and indeed your sheaves stood all around and bowed down to my sheaf."

Matt 13:30 Let both grow together until the harvest, and at the time of harvest I will say to the reapers, "First gather together the tares and bind them in bundles to burn them, but gather the wheat into my barn." ' "

Gleaning.

Lev 19:9 'When you reap the harvest of your land, you shall not wholly reap the corners of your field, nor shall you gather the gleanings of your harvest.

Ruth 2:3 Then she left, and went and gleaned in the field after the reapers. And she happened to come to the part of the field *belonging* to Boaz, who *was* of the family of Elimelech.

Stacking.

Ex 22:6 "If fire breaks out and catches in thorns, so that stacked grain, standing grain, or the field is consumed, he who kindled the fire shall surely make restitution.

Threshing.

Deut 25:4 "You shall not muzzle an ox while it treads out *the grain*.

Judg 6:11 Now the Angel of the LORD came and sat

under the terebinth tree which *was* in Ophrah, which *belonged* to Joash the Abiezrite, while his son Gideon threshed wheat in the winepress, in order to hide *it* from the Midianites.

Winnowing.

Ruth 3:2 Now Boaz, whose young women you were with, *is he* not our relative? In fact, he is winnowing barley tonight at the threshing floor.

Matt 3:12 His winnowing fan *is* in His hand, and He will thoroughly clean out His threshing floor, and gather His wheat into the barn; but He will burn up the chaff with unquenchable fire."

Storing in barns.

Matt 6:26 Look at the birds of the air, for they neither sow nor reap nor gather into barns; yet your heavenly Father feeds them. Are you not of more value than they?

Matt 13:30 Let both grow together until the harvest, and at the time of harvest I will say to the reapers, "First gather together the tares and bind them in bundles to burn them, but gather the wheat into my barn." ' "

Beasts used in,

The ox.

Deut 25:4 "You shall not muzzle an ox while it treads out *the grain.*

The donkey.

Deut 22:10 "You shall not plow with an ox and a donkey together.

The horse.

Is 28:28 Bread *flour* must be ground; Therefore he does not thresh it forever, Break *it with* his cartwheel, Or crush it *with* his horsemen.

Implements of,

The plowshare.

1 Sam 13:20 But all the Israelites would go down to the Philistines to sharpen each man's plowshare, his mattock, his ax, and his sickle;

The mattock.

1 Sam 13:20 But all the Israelites would go down to the Philistines to sharpen each man's plowshare, his mattock, his ax, and his sickle;

Is 7:25 And to any hill which could be dug with the hoe, You will not go there for fear of briers and thorns; But it will become a range for oxen And a place for sheep to roam.

The sickle.

Deut 16:9 "You shall count seven weeks for yourself; begin to count the seven weeks from *the time* you begin *to put* the sickle to the grain.

Deut 23:25 When you come into your neighbor's standing grain, you may pluck the heads with your hand, but you shall not use a sickle on your neighbor's standing grain.

The pruning hook.

Is 18:5 For before the harvest, when the bud is perfect And the sour grape is ripening in the flower, He will both cut off the sprigs with pruning hooks And take away *and* cut down the branches.

Joel 3:10 Beat your plowshares into swords And your pruning hooks into spears; Let the weak say, 'I *am* strong.' "

The fork.

1 Sam 13:21 and the charge for a sharpening was a pim for the plowshares, the mattocks, the forks, and the axes, and to set the points of the goads.

The ax.

1 Sam 13:20 But all the Israelites would go down to the Philistines to sharpen each man's plowshare, his mattock, his ax, and his sickle;

The sharp-toothed sledge.

Is 41:15 "Behold, I will make you into a new threshing sledge with sharp teeth; You shall thresh the mountains and beat *them* small, And make the hills like chaff.

The stick, etc.

Is 28:27 For the black cummin is not threshed with a threshing sledge, Nor is a cartwheel rolled over the cummin; But the black cummin is beaten out with a stick, And the cummin with a rod.

The cart.

1 Sam 6:7 Now therefore, make a new cart, take two milk cows which have never been yoked, and hitch the cows to the cart; and take their calves home, away from them.

Is 28:27–28 For the black cummin is not threshed with a threshing sledge, Nor is a cartwheel rolled over the cummin; But the black cummin is beaten out with a stick, And the cummin with a rod. **28** Bread *flour* must be ground; Therefore he does not thresh it forever, Break *it with* his cartwheel, Or crush it *with* his horsemen.

The shovel.

Is 30:24 Likewise the oxen and the young donkeys that work the ground Will eat cured fodder, Which has been winnowed with the shovel and fan.

The sieve.

Amos 9:9 "For surely I will command, And will sift the house of Israel among all nations, As *grain* is sifted in a sieve; Yet not the smallest grain shall fall to the ground.

The fan.

Is 30:24 Likewise the oxen and the young donkeys that work the ground Will eat cured fodder, Which has been winnowed with the shovel and fan.

Matt 3:12 His winnowing fan *is* in His hand, and He will thoroughly clean out His threshing floor, and gather His wheat into the barn; but He will burn up the chaff with unquenchable fire."

Illustrative of

Culture of the church.

1 Cor 3:9 For we are God's fellow workers; you are God's field, *you are* God's building.

Culture of the heart.

Jer 4:3 For thus says the LORD to the men of Judah and Jerusalem: "Break up your fallow ground, And do not sow among thorns.

Hos 10:12 Sow for yourselves righteousness; Reap in mercy; Break up your fallow ground, For *it is* time to seek the LORD, Till He comes and rains righteousness on you.

ALMS

To be given humbly.

Luke 11:41 But rather give alms of such things as you have; then indeed all things are clean to you.

Cf. Matt 6:1–4

Giving of, commanded.

Luke 12:33 Sell what you have and give alms; provide yourselves money bags which do not grow old, a treasure in the heavens that does not fail, where no thief approaches nor moth destroys.

Requested by underprivileged.

Acts 3:2 And a certain man lame from his mother's womb was carried, whom they laid daily at the gate of the temple which is called Beautiful, to ask alms from those who entered the temple;

Sometimes collected for poor.

Acts 24:17 "Now after many years I came to bring alms and offerings to my nation,

Cf. 2 Cor 8:16—9:5

ALMIGHTY

Term related to God's sovereign power.

Gen 17:1 When Abram was ninety-nine years old, the LORD appeared to Abram and said to him, "I *am* Almighty God; walk before Me and be blameless.

Gen 28:3 "May God Almighty bless you, And make you fruitful and multiply you, That you may be an assembly of peoples;

Ex 6:3 I appeared to Abraham, to Isaac, and to Jacob, as God Almighty, but *by* My name LORD I was not known to them.

Rev 4:8 *The* four living creatures, each having six wings, were full of eyes around and within. And they do not rest day or night, saying: "Holy, holy, holy, Lord God Almighty, Who was and is and is to come!"

Rev 15:3 They sing the song of Moses, the servant of God, and the song of the Lamb, saying: "Great and marvelous *are* Your works, Lord God Almighty! Just and true *are* Your ways, O King of the saints!

Synonym for God.

Job 6:4 For the arrows of the Almighty *are* within me; My spirit drinks in their poison; The terrors of God are arrayed against me.

Job 8:3 Does God subvert judgment? Or does the Almighty pervert justice?

Job 29:5 When the Almighty *was* yet with me, *When* my children *were* around me;

Ps 68:14 When the Almighty scattered kings in it, It was *white* as snow in Zalmon.

Ps 91:1 He who dwells in the secret place of the Most High Shall abide under the shadow of the Almighty.

Ezek 1:24 When they went, I heard the noise of their wings, like the noise of many waters, like the voice of the Almighty, a tumult like the noise of an army; and when they stood still, they let down their wings.

Joel 1:15 Alas for the day! For the day of the LORD *is* at hand; It shall come as destruction from the Almighty.

Rev 1:8 "I am the Alpha and the Omega, *the* Beginning and *the* End," says the Lord, "who is and who was and who is to come, the Almighty."

Rev 4:8 *The* four living creatures, each having six wings, were full of eyes around and within. And they do not rest day or night, saying: "Holy, holy, holy, Lord God Almighty, Who was and is and is to come!"

Rev 11:17 saying: "We give You thanks, O Lord God Almighty, The One who is and who was and who is to come, Because You have taken Your great power and reigned.

Rev 15:3 They sing the song of Moses, the servant of God, and the song of the Lamb, saying: "Great and marvelous *are* Your works, Lord God Almighty! Just and true *are* Your ways, O King of the saints!

Rev 16:7 And I heard another from the altar saying, "Even so, Lord God Almighty, true and righteous *are* Your judgments."

Rev 16:14 For they are spirits of demons, performing signs, *which* go out to the kings of the earth and of the whole world, to gather them to the battle of that great day of God Almighty.

Rev 19:15 Now out of His mouth goes a sharp sword, that with it He should strike the nations. And He Himself will rule them with a rod of iron. He Himself treads the winepress of the fierceness and wrath of Almighty God.

Rev 21:22 But I saw no temple in it, for the Lord God Almighty and the Lamb are its temple.

Associated with Battle of Armageddon.

Rev 16:14 For they are spirits of demons, performing signs, *which* go out to the kings of the earth and of the whole world, to gather them to the battle of that great day of God Almighty.

ALTARS

Designed for sacrifice.

Ex 20:24 An altar of earth you shall make for Me, and you shall sacrifice on it your burnt offerings and your peace offerings, your sheep and your oxen. In every place where I record My name I will come to you, and I will bless you.

To be made of earth, or unhewn stone.

Ex 20:24–25 An altar of earth you shall make for Me, and you shall sacrifice on it your burnt offerings and your peace offerings, your sheep and your oxen. In every place where I record My name I will come to you, and I will bless you. 25 And if you make Me an altar of stone, you shall not build it of hewn stone; for if you use your tool on it, you have profaned it.

Deut 27:5–6 And there you shall build an altar to the LORD your God, an altar of stones; you shall not use an iron *tool* on them. 6 You shall build with whole stones the altar of the LORD your God, and offer burnt offerings on it to the LORD your God.

Of brick, hateful to God.

Is 65:3 A people who provoke Me to anger continually to My face; Who sacrifice in gardens, And burn incense on altars of brick;

Natural rocks sometimes used as.

Judg 6:19–21 So Gideon went in and prepared a young goat, and unleavened bread from an ephah of flour. The meat he put in a basket, and he put the broth in a pot; and he brought *them* out to Him under the terebinth tree and presented *them*. 20 The Angel of God said to him, "Take the meat and the unleavened bread and lay *them* on this rock, and pour out the broth." And he did so. **21** Then the Angel of the LORD put out the end of the staff that *was* in His hand, and touched the meat and the unleavened bread; and fire rose out of the rock and consumed the meat and the unleavened bread. And the Angel of the LORD departed out of his sight.

Judg 13:19–20 So Manoah took the young goat with the grain offering, and offered it upon the rock to the LORD. And He did a wondrous thing while Manoah and his wife looked on— **20** it happened as the flame went up toward heaven from the altar—the Angel of the LORD ascended in the flame of the altar! When Manoah and his wife saw *this,* they fell on their faces to the ground.

Were not to have steps up to them.

Ex 20:26 Nor shall you go up by steps to My altar, that your nakedness may not be exposed on it.'

For idolatrous worship, often erected on roofs of houses.

2 Kin 23:12 The altars that *were* on the roof, the upper chamber of Ahaz, which the kings of Judah had made, and the altars which Manasseh had made in the two courts of the house of the LORD, the king broke down and pulverized there, and threw their dust into the Brook Kidron.

Jer 19:13 And the houses of Jerusalem and the houses of the kings of Judah shall be defiled like the place of Tophet, because of all the houses on whose roofs they have burned incense to all the host of heaven, and poured out drink offerings to other gods." ' "

Jer 32:29 And the Chaldeans who fight against this city shall come and set fire to this city and burn it, with the houses on whose roofs they have offered incense to Baal and poured out drink offerings to other gods, to provoke Me to anger;

Idolaters planted groves near.

Judg 6:30 Then the men of the city said to Joash, "Bring out your son, that he may die, because he has torn down the altar of Baal, and because he has cut down the wooden image that *was* beside it."

1 Kin 16:32–33 Then he set up an altar for Baal in the temple of Baal, which he had built in Samaria. **33** And Ahab made a wooden image. Ahab did more to provoke the LORD God of Israel to anger than all the kings of Israel who were before him.

2 Kin 21:3 For he rebuilt the high places which Hezekiah his father had destroyed; he raised up altars for Baal, and made a wooden image, as Ahab king of Israel had done; and he worshiped all the host of heaven and served them.

The Jews not to plant groves near.

Deut 16:21 "You shall not plant for yourself any tree, as a wooden image, near the altar which you build for yourself to the LORD your God.

For idolatrous worship, to be destroyed.

Ex 34:13 But you shall destroy their altars, break their *sacred* pillars, and cut down their wooden images

Deut 7:5 But thus you shall deal with them: you shall destroy their altars, and break down their *sacred* pillars, and cut down their wooden images, and burn their carved images with fire.

Probable origin of inscriptions on.

Deut 27:8 And you shall write very plainly on the stones all the words of this law."

Mentioned in Scripture, of

Noah.

Gen 8:20 Then Noah built an altar to the LORD, and took of every clean animal and of every clean bird, and offered burnt offerings on the altar.

Abraham.

Gen 12:7–8 Then the LORD appeared to Abram and said, "To your descendants I will give this land." And there he built an altar to the LORD, who had appeared to him. **8** And he moved from there to the mountain east of Bethel, and he pitched his tent *with* Bethel on the west and Ai on the east; there he built an altar to the LORD and called on the name of the LORD.

Gen 13:18 Then Abram moved *his* tent, and went and dwelt by the terebinth trees of Mamre, which *are* in Hebron, and built an altar there to the LORD.

Gen 22:9 Then they came to the place of which God had told him. And Abraham built an altar there and placed the wood in order; and he bound Isaac his son and laid him on the altar, upon the wood.

Isaac.

Gen 26:25 So he built an altar there and called on the name of the LORD, and he pitched his tent there; and there Isaac's servants dug a well.

Jacob.

Gen 33:20 Then he erected an altar there and called it El Elohe Israel.

Gen 35:1 Then God said to Jacob, "Arise, go up to Bethel and dwell there; and make an altar there to God, who appeared to you when you fled from the face of Esau your brother."

Gen 35:3 Then let us arise and go up to Bethel; and I will make an altar there to God, who answered me in the day of my distress and has been with me in the way which I have gone."

Gen 35:7 And he built an altar there and called the place El Bethel, because there God appeared to him when he fled from the face of his brother.

Moses.

Ex 17:15 And Moses built an altar and called its name, The-LORD-Is-My-Banner;

Ex 24:4 And Moses wrote all the words of the LORD. And he rose early in the morning, and built an altar at the foot of the mountain, and twelve pillars according to the twelve tribes of Israel.

Balaam.

Num 23:1 Then Balaam said to Balak, "Build seven altars for me here, and prepare for me here seven bulls and seven rams."

Num 23:14 So he brought him to the field of Zophim, to the top of Pisgah, and built seven altars, and offered a bull and a ram on *each* altar.

Num 23:29 Then Balaam said to Balak, "Build for me here seven altars, and prepare for me here seven bulls and seven rams."

Joshua.

Josh 8:30–31 Now Joshua built an altar to the LORD God

of Israel in Mount Ebal, **31** as Moses the servant of the LORD had commanded the children of Israel, as it is written in the Book of the Law of Moses: "an altar of whole stones over which no man has wielded an iron *tool*." And they offered on it burnt offerings to the LORD, and sacrificed peace offerings.

The temple of Solomon.

2 Chr 4:1 Moreover he made a bronze altar: twenty cubits was its length, twenty cubits its width, and ten cubits its height.

2 Chr 4:19 Thus Solomon had all the furnishings made for the house of God: the altar of gold and the tables on which *was* the showbread;

The second temple.

Ezra 3:2–3 Then Jeshua the son of Jozadak and his brethren the priests, and Zerubbabel the son of Shealtiel and his brethren, arose and built the altar of the God of Israel, to offer burnt offerings on it, as *it is* written in the Law of Moses the man of God. **3** Though fear *had come* upon them because of the people of those countries, they set the altar on its bases; and they offered burnt offerings on it to the LORD, *both* the morning and evening burnt offerings.

Reubenites, etc. east of Jordan.

Josh 22:10 And when they came to the region of the Jordan which *is* in the land of Canaan, the children of Reuben, the children of Gad, and half the tribe of Manasseh built an altar there by the Jordan—a great, impressive altar.

Gideon.

Judg 6:26–27 and build an altar to the LORD your God on top of this rock in the proper arrangement, and take the second bull and offer a burnt sacrifice with the wood of the image which you shall cut down." **27** So Gideon took ten men from among his servants and did as the LORD had said to him. But because he feared his father's household and the men of the city too much to do *it* by day, he did *it* by night.

The people of Israel.

Judg 21:4 So it was, on the next morning, that the people rose early and built an altar there, and offered burnt offerings and peace offerings.

Samuel.

1 Sam 7:17 But he always returned to Ramah, for his home *was* there. There he judged Israel, and there he built an altar to the LORD.

David.

2 Sam 24:21 Then Araunah said, "Why has my lord the king come to his servant?" And David said, "To buy the threshing floor from you, to build an altar to the LORD, that the plague may be withdrawn from the people."

2 Sam 24:25 And David built there an altar to the LORD, and offered burnt offerings and peace offerings. So the LORD heeded the prayers for the land, and the plague was withdrawn from Israel.

Jeroboam at Bethel.

1 Kin 12:33 So he made offerings on the altar which he had made at Bethel on the fifteenth day of the eighth month, in the month which he had devised in his own heart. And he ordained a feast for the children

of Israel, and offered sacrifices on the altar and burned incense.

Ahaz.

2 Kin 16:10–12 Now King Ahaz went to Damascus to meet Tiglath-Pileser king of Assyria, and saw an altar that *was* at Damascus; and King Ahaz sent to Urijah the priest the design of the altar and its pattern, according to all its workmanship. **11** Then Urijah the priest built an altar according to all that King Ahaz had sent from Damascus. So Urijah the priest made *it* before King Ahaz came back from Damascus. **12** And when the king came back from Damascus, the king saw the altar; and the king approached the altar and made offerings on it.

The Athenians.

Acts 17:23 for as I was passing through and considering the objects of your worship, I even found an altar with this inscription: TO THE UNKNOWN GOD. Therefore, the One whom you worship without knowing, Him I proclaim to you:

The burnt offering.

Ex 27:1–8 "You shall make an altar of acacia wood, five cubits long and five cubits wide—the altar shall be square—and its height *shall be* three cubits. **2** You shall make its horns on its four corners; its horns shall be of one piece with it. And you shall overlay it with bronze. **3** Also you shall make its pans to receive its ashes, and its shovels and its basins and its forks and its firepans; you shall make all its utensils of bronze. **4** You shall make a grate for it, a network of bronze; and on the network you shall make four bronze rings at its four corners. **5** You shall put it under the rim of the altar beneath, that the network may be midway up the altar. **6** And you shall make poles for the altar, poles of acacia wood, and overlay them with bronze. **7** The poles shall be put in the rings, and the poles shall be on the two sides of the altar to bear it. **8** You shall make it hollow with boards; as it was shown you on the mountain, so shall they make *it*.

Incense.

Ex 30:1–6 "You shall make an altar to burn incense on; you shall make it of acacia wood. **2** A cubit *shall be* its length and a cubit its width—it shall be square—and two cubits *shall be* its height. Its horns *shall be* of one piece with it. **3** And you shall overlay its top, its sides all around, and its horns with pure gold; and you shall make for it a molding of gold all around. **4** Two gold rings you shall make for it, under the molding on both its sides. You shall place *them* on its two sides, and they will be holders for the poles with which to bear it. **5** You shall make the poles of acacia wood, and overlay them with gold. **6** And you shall put it before the veil that *is* before the ark of the Testimony, before the mercy seat that *is* over the Testimony, where I will meet with you.

Protection afforded by.

1 Kin 1:50–51 Now Adonijah was afraid of Solomon; so he arose, and went and took hold of the horns of the altar. **51** And it was told Solomon, saying, "Indeed Adonijah is afraid of King Solomon; for look, he has taken hold of the horns of the altar, saying, 'Let King Solomon swear to me today that he will not put his servant to death with the sword.'"

Afforded no protection to murderers.

Ex 21:14 "But if a man acts with premeditation against his neighbor, to kill him by treachery, you shall take him from My altar, that he may die.

Cf. 1 Kin 2:18–34

ALTAR OF BURNT OFFERING, THE
Dimensions, etc. of.

Ex 27:1 "You shall make an altar of acacia wood, five cubits long and five cubits wide—the altar shall be square—and its height *shall be* three cubits.

Ex 38:1 He made the altar of burnt offering of acacia wood; five cubits *was* its length and five cubits its width—*it was* square—and its height *was* three cubits.

Horns on the corners of.

Ex 27:2 You shall make its horns on its four corners; its horns shall be of one piece with it. And you shall overlay it with bronze.

Ex 38:2 He made its horns on its four corners; the horns were *of one piece* with it. And he overlaid it with bronze.

Covered with bronze.

Ex 27:2 You shall make its horns on its four corners; its horns shall be of one piece with it. And you shall overlay it with bronze.

All its vessels of bronze.

Ex 27:3 Also you shall make its pans to receive its ashes, and its shovels and its basins and its forks and its firepans; you shall make all its utensils of bronze.

Ex 38:3 He made all the utensils for the altar: the pans, the shovels, the basins, the forks, and the firepans; all its utensils he made of bronze.

A network grate of bronze placed in.

Ex 27:4–5 You shall make a grate for it, a network of bronze; and on the network you shall make four bronze rings at its four corners. **5** You shall put it under the rim of the altar beneath, that the network may be midway up the altar.

Ex 38:4 And he made a grate of bronze network for the altar, under its rim, midway from the bottom.

Furnished with rings and poles.

Ex 27:6–7 And you shall make poles for the altar, poles of acacia wood, and overlay them with bronze. **7** The poles shall be put in the rings, and the poles shall be on the two sides of the altar to bear it.

Ex 38:5–7 He cast four rings for the four corners of the bronze grating, *as* holders for the poles. **6** And he made the poles of acacia wood, and overlaid them with bronze. **7** Then he put the poles into the rings on the sides of the altar, with which to bear it. He made the altar hollow with boards.

Made after a divine pattern.

Ex 27:8 You shall make it hollow with boards; as it was shown you on the mountain, so shall they make *it.*

Called

The bronze altar.

Ex 39:39 the bronze altar, its grate of bronze, its poles, and all its utensils; the laver with its base;

1 Kin 8:64 On the same day the king consecrated the middle of the court that *was* in front of the house of the LORD; for there he offered burnt offerings, grain offerings, and the fat of the peace offerings, because the bronze altar that *was* before the LORD *was* too small to receive the burnt offerings, the grain offerings, and the fat of the peace offerings.

The altar of God.

Ps 43:4 Then I will go to the altar of God, To God my exceeding joy; And on the harp I will praise You, O God, my God.

The altar of the Lord.

Mal 2:13 And this is the second thing you do: You cover the altar of the LORD with tears, With weeping and crying; So He does not regard the offering anymore, Nor receive *it* with goodwill from your hands.

Placed in the court before the door of the tabernacle.

Ex 40:6 Then you shall set the altar of the burnt offering before the door of the tabernacle of the tent of meeting.

Ex 40:29 And he put the altar of burnt offering *before* the door of the tabernacle of the tent of meeting, and offered upon it the burnt offering and the grain offering, as the LORD had commanded Moses.

Sanctified by God.

Ex 29:44 So I will consecrate the tabernacle of meeting and the altar. I will also consecrate both Aaron and his sons to minister to Me as priests.

Anointed and sanctified with holy oil.

Ex 40:10 You shall anoint the altar of the burnt offering and all its utensils, and consecrate the altar. The altar shall be most holy.

Lev 8:10–11 Also Moses took the anointing oil, and anointed the tabernacle and all that *was* in it, and consecrated them. **11** He sprinkled some of it on the altar seven times, anointed the altar and all its utensils, and the laver and its base, to consecrate them.

Cleansed and purified with blood.

Ex 29:36–37 And you shall offer a bull every day *as* a sin offering for atonement. You shall cleanse the altar when you make atonement for it, and you shall anoint it to sanctify it. **37** Seven days you shall make atonement for the altar and sanctify it. And the altar shall be most holy. Whatever touches the altar must be holy.

Was most holy.

Ex 40:10 You shall anoint the altar of the burnt offering and all its utensils, and consecrate the altar. The altar shall be most holy.

All sacrifices to be offered on.

Ex 29:38–42 "Now this *is* what you shall offer on the altar: two lambs of the first year, day by day continually. **39** One lamb you shall offer in the morning, and the other lamb you shall offer at twilight. **40** With the one lamb shall be one-tenth *of an ephah* of flour mixed with one-fourth of a hin of pressed oil, and one-fourth of a hin of wine *as* a drink offering. **41** And the other lamb you shall offer at twilight; and you shall offer with it the grain offering and the drink offering, as in the morning, for a sweet aroma, an offering made by fire to the LORD. **42** *This shall be* a continual burnt offering throughout your generations *at* the door of the tabernacle of meeting before the LORD, where I will meet you to speak with you.

Is 56:7 Even them I will bring to My holy mountain, And make them joyful in My house of prayer. Their burnt offerings and their sacrifices *Will be* accepted on My altar; For My house shall be called a house of prayer for all nations."

All gifts to be presented at.

Matt 5:23–24 Therefore if you bring your gift to the altar, and there remember that your brother has something against you, **24** leave your gift there before the altar, and go your way. First be reconciled to your brother, and then come and offer your gift.

Nothing polluted or defective to be offered on.

Lev 22:22 Those *that are* blind or broken or maimed, or have an ulcer or eczema or scabs, you shall not offer to the LORD, nor make an offering by fire of them on the altar to the LORD.

Mal 1:7–8 "You offer defiled food on My altar, But say, 'In what way have we defiled You?' By saying, 'The table of the LORD is contemptible.' **8** And when you offer the blind as a sacrifice, *Is it* not evil? And when you offer the lame and sick, *Is it* not evil? Offer it then to your governor! Would he be pleased with you? Would he accept you favorably?" Says the LORD of hosts.

Offering at the dedication of. Num 7:1–89

The fire upon,

Came from before the Lord.

Lev 9:24 and fire came out from before the LORD and consumed the burnt offering and the fat on the altar. When all the people saw *it,* they shouted and fell on their faces.

Was continually burning.

Lev 6:13 A fire shall always be burning on the altar; it shall never go out.

Consumed the sacrifices.

Lev 1:8–9 Then the priests, Aaron's sons, shall lay the parts, the head, and the fat in order on the wood that *is* on the fire upon the altar; **9** but he shall wash its entrails and its legs with water. And the priest shall burn all on the altar as a burnt sacrifice, an offering made by fire, a sweet aroma to the LORD.

Sacrifices bound to the horns of.

Ps 118:27 God *is* the LORD, And He has given us light; Bind the sacrifice with cords to the horns of the altar.

The blood of sacrifices put on the horns and poured at the foot of.

Ex 29:12 You shall take *some* of the blood of the bull and put *it* on the horns of the altar with your finger, and pour all the blood beside the base of the altar.

Lev 4:7 And the priest shall put some of the blood on the horns of the altar of sweet incense before the LORD, which is in the tabernacle of meeting; and he shall pour the remaining blood of the bull at the base of the altar of the burnt offering, which is at the door of the tabernacle of meeting.

Lev 4:18 And he shall put *some* of the blood on the horns of the altar which *is* before the LORD, which *is* in the tabernacle of meeting; and he shall pour the remaining blood at the base of the altar of burnt of-

fering, which is at the door of the tabernacle of meeting.

Lev 4:25 The priest shall take some of the blood of the sin offering with his finger, put *it* on the horns of the altar of burnt offering, and pour its blood at the base of the altar of burnt offering.

Lev 8:15 and Moses killed *it.* Then he took the blood, and put *some* on the horns of the altar all around with his finger, and purified the altar. And he poured the blood at the base of the altar, and consecrated it, to make atonement for it.

The priests,\

The only ones to serve.

Num 18:3 They shall attend to your needs and all the needs of the tabernacle; but they shall not come near the articles of the sanctuary and the altar, lest they die—they and you also.

Num 18:7 Therefore you and your sons with you shall attend to your priesthood for everything at the altar and behind the veil; and you shall serve. I give your priesthood *to you* as a gift for service, but the outsider who comes near shall be put to death."

Derived support from offerings on.

1 Cor 9:13 Do you not know that those who minister the holy things eat *of the things* of the temple, and those who serve at the altar partake of *the offerings of* the altar?

Ahaz removed and profaned.

2 Kin 16:10–16 Now King Ahaz went to Damascus to meet Tiglath-Pileser king of Assyria, and saw an altar that *was* at Damascus; and King Ahaz sent to Urijah the priest the design of the altar and its pattern, according to all its workmanship. **11** Then Urijah the priest built an altar according to all that King Ahaz had sent from Damascus. So Urijah the priest made *it* before King Ahaz came back from Damascus. **12** And when the king came back from Damascus, the king saw the altar; and the king approached the altar and made offerings on it. **13** So he burned his burnt offering and his grain offering; and he poured his drink offering and sprinkled the blood of his peace offerings on the altar. **14** He also brought the bronze altar which *was* before the LORD, from the front of the temple—from between the *new* altar and the house of the LORD—and put it on the north side of the *new* altar. **15** Then King Ahaz commanded Urijah the priest, saying, "On the great *new* altar burn the morning burnt offering, the evening grain offering, the king's burnt sacrifice, and his grain offering, with the burnt offering of all the people of the land, their grain offering, and their drink offerings; and sprinkle on it all the blood of the burnt offering and all the blood of the sacrifice. And the bronze altar shall be for me to inquire *by.*" **16** Thus did Urijah the priest, according to all that King Ahaz commanded.

The Jews condemned for swearing lightly by.

Matt 23:18–19 And, 'Whoever swears by the altar, it is nothing; but whoever swears by the gift that is on it, he is obliged *to perform it.*' **19** Fools and blind! For which is greater, the gift or the altar that sanctifies the gift?

Equivalent to the sacrifice of Christ.

Heb 13:10 We have an altar from which those who serve the tabernacle have no right to eat.

ALTAR OF INCENSE, THE
Dimensions, etc. of.

Ex 30:1–2 "You shall make an altar to burn incense on; you shall make it of acacia wood. 2 A cubit *shall be* its length and a cubit its width—it shall be square—and two cubits *shall be* its height. Its horns *shall be* of one piece with it.

Ex 37:25 He made the incense altar of acacia wood. Its length *was* a cubit and its width a cubit—*it was* square—and two cubits *was* its height. Its horns were *of one piece* with it.

Covered with gold.

Ex 30:3 And you shall overlay its top, its sides all around, and its horns with pure gold; and you shall make for it a molding of gold all around.

Ex 37:26 And he overlaid it with pure gold: its top, its sides all around, and its horns. He also made for it a molding of gold all around it.

Top of, surrounded with a crown of gold.

Ex 30:3 And you shall overlay its top, its sides all around, and its horns with pure gold; and you shall make for it a molding of gold all around.

Ex 37:26 And he overlaid it with pure gold: its top, its sides all around, and its horns. He also made for it a molding of gold all around it.

Had four rings of gold under the crown for the poles.

Ex 30:4 Two gold rings you shall make for it, under the molding on both its sides. You shall place *them* on its two sides, and they will be holders for the poles with which to bear it.

Ex 37:27 He made two rings of gold for it under its molding, by its two corners on both sides, as holders for the poles with which to bear it.

Poles of, covered with gold.

Ex 30:5 You shall make the poles of acacia wood, and overlay them with gold.

Called the gold altar.

Ex 39:38 the gold altar, the anointing oil, and the sweet incense; the screen for the tabernacle door;

Placed before the veil in the outer sanctuary.

Ex 30:6 And you shall put it before the veil that *is* before the ark of the Testimony, before the mercy seat that *is* over the Testimony, where I will meet with you.

Ex 40:5 You shall also set the altar of gold for the incense before the ark of the Testimony, and put up the screen for the door of the tabernacle.

Ex 40:26 He put the gold altar in the tabernacle of meeting in front of the veil;

Said to be before the Lord.

Lev 4:7 And the priest shall put some of the blood on the horns of the altar of sweet incense before the LORD, which is in the tabernacle of meeting; and he shall pour the remaining blood of the bull at the base of the altar of the burnt offering, which is at the door of the tabernacle of meeting.

1 Kin 9:25 Now three times a year Solomon offered burnt offerings and peace offerings on the altar which he had built for the LORD, and he burned incense with them *on the altar* that *was* before the LORD. So he finished the temple.

Anointed with holy oil.

Ex 30:26–27 With it you shall anoint the tabernacle of meeting and the ark of the Testimony; **27** the table and all its utensils, the lampstand and its utensils, and the altar of incense;

The priest burned incense on every morning and evening.

Ex 30:7–8 "Aaron shall burn on it sweet incense every morning; when he tends the lamps, he shall burn incense on it. **8** And when Aaron lights the lamps at twilight, he shall burn incense on it, a perpetual incense before the LORD throughout your generations.

No strange incense nor any sacrifice to be offered on.

Ex 30:9 You shall not offer strange incense on it, or a burnt offering, or a grain offering; nor shall you pour a drink offering on it.

Atonement made upon, by the high priest once every year.

Ex 30:10 And Aaron shall make atonement upon its horns once a year with the blood of the sin offering of atonement; once a year he shall make atonement upon it throughout your generations. It *is* most holy to the LORD."

Lev 16:18–19 And he shall go out to the altar that *is* before the LORD, and make atonement for it, and shall take some of the blood of the bull and some of the blood of the goat, and put it on the horns of the altar all around. **19** Then he shall sprinkle some of the blood on it with his finger seven times, cleanse it, and consecrate it from the uncleanness of the children of Israel.

The blood of all sin offerings put on the horns of.

Lev 4:7 And the priest shall put some of the blood on the horns of the altar of sweet incense before the LORD, which is in the tabernacle of meeting; and he shall pour the remaining blood of the bull at the base of the altar of the burnt offering, which is at the door of the tabernacle of meeting.

Lev 4:18 And he shall put *some* of the blood on the horns of the altar which *is* before the LORD, which is* in the tabernacle of meeting; and he shall pour the remaining blood at the base of the altar of burnt offering, which is at the door of the tabernacle of meeting.

Punishment for

Offering profane fire on.

Lev 10:1–2 Then Nadab and Abihu, the sons of Aaron, each took his censer and put fire in it, put incense on it, and offered profane fire before the LORD, which He had not commanded them. **2** So fire went out from the LORD and devoured them, and they died before the LORD.

Unauthorized offering on.

2 Chr 26:16–19 But when he was strong his heart was lifted up, to *his* destruction, for he transgressed against the LORD his God by entering the temple of the Lord to burn incense on the altar of incense. **17** So Azariah the priest went in after him, and with him were eighty priests of the Lord—valiant men. **18** And they withstood King Uzziah, and said to him, *"It is* not for you, Uzziah, to burn incense to the Lord, but for the priests, the sons of Aaron, who are consecrated to burn incense. Get out of the sanctuary, for you have trespassed! You *shall have* no honor from the Lord God." **19** Then Uzziah became furious; and he *had* a censer in his hand to burn incense. And while he was angry with the priests, leprosy broke out on his forehead, before the priests in the house of the Lord, beside the incense altar.

Covered by the priest before removal from the sanctuary.

Num 4:11 "Over the golden altar they shall spread a blue cloth, and cover it with a covering of badger skins; and they shall insert its poles.

AMALEK
Grandson of Esau and father of Amalekites.

Gen 36:12 Now Timna was the concubine of Eliphaz, Esau's son, and she bore Amalek to Eliphaz. These *were* the sons of Adah, Esau's wife.

Ex 17:8 Now Amalek came and fought with Israel in Rephidim.

Cf. 1 Sam 15:2,5; 2 Chr 4:43

Land of, later taken by Ephraim.

Judg 5:14 From Ephraim *were* those whose roots were in Amalek. After you, Benjamin, with your peoples, From Machir rulers came down, And from Zebulun those who bear the recruiter's staff.

Descendant of, claimed to kill King Saul.

2 Sam 1:5–10 So David said to the young man who told him, "How do you know that Saul and Jonathan his son are dead?" **6** Then the young man who told him said, "As I happened by chance *to be* on Mount Gilboa, there was Saul, leaning on his spear; and indeed the chariots and horsemen followed hard after him. **7** Now when he looked behind him, he saw me and called to me. And I answered, 'Here I am.' **8** And he said to me, 'Who *are* you?' So I answered him, 'I *am* an Amalekite.' **9** He said to me again, 'Please stand over me and kill me, for anguish has come upon me, but my life still *remains* in me.' **10** So I stood over him and killed him, because I was sure that he could not live after he had fallen. And I took the crown that *was* on his head and the bracelet that *was* on his arm, and have brought them here to my lord."

AMALEKITES, THE
Descent of.

Gen 36:12 Now Timna was the concubine of Eliphaz, Esau's son, and she bore Amalek to Eliphaz. These *were* the sons of Adah, Esau's wife.

Gen 36:16 Chief Korah, Chief Gatam, *and* Chief Amalek. These *were* the chiefs of Eliphaz in the land of Edom. They *were* the sons of Adah.

Character of,
Wicked.

1 Sam 15:18 Now the Lord sent you on a mission, and said, 'Go, and utterly destroy the sinners, the Ama-

lekites, and fight against them until they are consumed.'

Oppressive.

Judg 10:12 Also the Sidonians and Amalekites and Maonites oppressed you; and you cried out to Me, and I delivered you from their hand.

Warlike and cruel.

1 Sam 15:33 But Samuel said, "As your sword has made women childless, so shall your mother be childless among women." And Samuel hacked Agag in pieces before the Lord in Gilgal.

Governed by kings.

1 Sam 15:20 And Saul said to Samuel, "But I have obeyed the voice of the Lord, and gone on the mission on which the Lord sent me, and brought back Agag king of Amalek; I have utterly destroyed the Amalekites.

1 Sam 15:32 Then Samuel said, "Bring Agag king of the Amalekites here to me." So Agag came to him cautiously. And Agag said, "Surely the bitterness of death is past."

A powerful and influential nation.

Num 24:7 He shall pour water from his buckets, And his seed *shall be* in many waters. "His king shall be higher than Agag, And his kingdom shall be exalted.

Possessed cities.

1 Sam 15:5 And Saul came to a city of Amalek, and lay in wait in the valley.

Country of,
In the south of Canaan.

Num 13:29 The Amalekites dwell in the land of the South; the Hittites, the Jebusites, and the Amorites dwell in the mountains; and the Canaanites dwell by the sea and along the banks of the Jordan."

1 Sam 27:8 And David and his men went up and raided the Geshurites, the Girzites, and the Amalekites. For those nations were the inhabitants of the land from of old, as you go to Shur, even as far as the land of Egypt.

Extended from Havilah to Shur.

1 Sam 15:7 And Saul attacked the Amalekites, from Havilah all the way to Shur, which is east of Egypt.

Was the scene of ancient warfare.

Gen 14:7 Then they turned back and came to En Mishpat (that *is*, Kadesh), and attacked all the country of the Amalekites, and also the Amorites who dwelt in Hazezon Tamar.

Part of the Kenites dwelt among.

1 Sam 15:6 Then Saul said to the Kenites, "Go, depart, get down from among the Amalekites, lest I destroy you with them. For you showed kindness to all the children of Israel when they came up out of Egypt." So the Kenites departed from among the Amalekites.

Were the first to oppose Israel.

Ex 17:8 Now Amalek came and fought with Israel in Rephidim.

Defeated at Rephidim through the intercession of Moses.

Ex 17:9–13 And Moses said to Joshua, "Choose us some men and go out, fight with Amalek. Tomorrow I will stand on the top of the hill with the rod of God in my hand." **10** So Joshua did as Moses said to him, and fought with Amalek. And Moses, Aaron, and Hur went up to the top of the hill. **11** And so it was, when Moses held up his hand, that Israel prevailed; and when he let down his hand, Amalek prevailed. **12** But Moses' hands *became* heavy; so they took a stone and put *it* under him, and he sat on it. And Aaron and Hur supported his hands, one on one side, and the other on the other side; and his hands were steady until the going down of the sun. **13** So Joshua defeated Amalek and his people with the edge of the sword.

Doomed to utter destruction for opposing Israel.

Ex 17:14 Then the LORD said to Moses, "Write this *for a* memorial in the book and recount *it* in the hearing of Joshua, that I will utterly blot out the remembrance of Amalek from under heaven."

Ex 17:16 for he said, "Because the LORD has sworn: the LORD *will have* war with Amalek from generation to generation."

Num 24:20 Then he looked on Amalek, and he took up his oracle and said: "Amalek *was* first among the nations, But *shall be* last until he perishes."

Deut 25:19 Therefore it shall be, when the LORD your God has given you rest from your enemies all around, in the land which the LORD your God is giving you to possess *as* an inheritance, *that* you will blot out the remembrance of Amalek from under heaven. You shall not forget.

Presumption of Israel punished by.

Num 14:45 Then the Amalekites and the Canaanites who dwelt in that mountain came down and attacked them, and drove them back as far as Hormah.

United with Eglon against Israel.

Judg 3:13 Then he gathered to himself the people of Ammon and Amalek, went and defeated Israel, and took possession of the City of Palms.

Part of their possessions taken by Ephraim.

Judg 5:14 From Ephraim *were* those whose roots were in Amalek. After you, Benjamin, with your peoples, From Machir rulers came down, And from Zebulun those who bear the recruiter's staff.

Judg 12:15 Then Abdon the son of Hillel the Pirathonite died and was buried in Pirathon in the land of Ephraim, in the mountains of the Amalekites.

With Midian, oppressed Israel.

Judg 6:3–5 So it was, whenever Israel had sown, Midianites would come up; also Amalekites and the people of the East would come up against them. **4** Then they would encamp against them and destroy the produce of the earth as far as Gaza, and leave no sustenance for Israel, neither sheep nor ox nor donkey. **5** For they would come up with their livestock and their tents, coming in as numerous as locusts; both they and their camels were without number; and they would enter the land to destroy it.

Overcome by Gideon.

Judg 6:33–34 Then all the Midianites and Amalekites, the people of the East, gathered together; and they crossed over and encamped in the Valley of Jezreel. **34** But the Spirit of the LORD came upon Gideon; then

he blew the trumpet, and the Abiezrites gathered behind him.

Judg 7:21–22 And every man stood in his place all around the camp; and the whole army ran and cried out and fled. **22** When the three hundred blew the trumpets, the LORD set every man's sword against his companion throughout the whole camp; and the army fled to Beth Acacia, toward Zererah, as far as the border of Abel Meholah, by Tabbath.

Saul

Overcame, and delivered Israel.

1 Sam 14:48 And he gathered an army and attacked the Amalekites, and delivered Israel from the hands of those who plundered them.

Commissioned to destroy.

1 Sam 15:1–3 Samuel also said to Saul, "The LORD sent me to anoint you king over His people, over Israel. Now therefore, heed the voice of the words of the LORD. **2** Thus says the LORD of hosts: 'I will punish Amalek *for* what he did to Israel, how he ambushed him on the way when he came up from Egypt. **3** Now go and attack Amalek, and utterly destroy all that they have, and do not spare them. But kill both man and woman, infant and nursing child, ox and sheep, camel and donkey.' "

Massacred.

1 Sam 15:4–8 So Saul gathered the people together and numbered them in Telaim, two hundred thousand foot soldiers and ten thousand men of Judah. **5** And Saul came to a city of Amalek, and lay in wait in the valley. **6** Then Saul said to the Kenites, "Go, depart, get down from among the Amalekites, lest I destroy you with them. For you showed kindness to all the children of Israel when they came up out of Egypt." So the Kenites departed from among the Amalekites. **7** And Saul attacked the Amalekites, from Havilah all the way to Shur, which is east of Egypt. **8** He also took Agag king of the Amalekites alive, and utterly destroyed all the people with the edge of the sword.

Condemned for not utterly destroying.

1 Sam 15:9–26; 28:18

Agag, king of, slain by Samuel.

1 Sam 15:32–33 Then Samuel said, "Bring Agag king of the Amalekites here to me." So Agag came to him cautiously. And Agag said, "Surely the bitterness of death is past." **33** But Samuel said, "As your sword has made women childless, so shall your mother be childless among women." And Samuel hacked Agag in pieces before the LORD in Gilgal.

Invaded by David.

1 Sam 27:8–9 And David and his men went up and raided the Geshurites, the Girzites, and the Amalekites. For those nations were the inhabitants of the land from of old, as you go to Shur, even as far as the land of Egypt. **9** Whenever David attacked the land, he left neither man nor woman alive, but took away the sheep, the oxen, the donkeys, the camels, and the apparel, and returned and came to Achish.

Pillaged and burned Ziklag.

1 Sam 30:1–2 Now it happened, when David and his men came to Ziklag, on the third day, that the Amalekites had invaded the South and Ziklag, attacked

Ziklag and burned it with fire, **2** and had taken captive the women and those who *were* there, from small to great; they did not kill anyone, but carried *them* away and went their way.

Pursued and slain by David.

1 Sam 30:10–20 But David pursued, he and four hundred men; for two hundred stayed *behind*, who were so weary that they could not cross the Brook Besor. **11** Then they found an Egyptian in the field, and brought him to David; and they gave him bread and he ate, and they let him drink water. **12** And they gave him a piece of a cake of figs and two clusters of raisins. So when he had eaten, his strength came back to him; for he had eaten no bread nor drunk water for three days and three nights. **13** Then David said to him, "To whom do you *belong*, and where *are* you from?" And he said, "I *am* a young man from Egypt, servant of an Amalekite; and my master left me behind, because three days ago I fell sick. **14** We made an invasion of the southern *area* of the Cherethites, in the *territory* which *belongs* to Judah, and of the southern *area* of Caleb; and we burned Ziklag with fire." **15** And David said to him, "Can you take me down to this troop?" So he said, "Swear to me by God that you will neither kill me nor deliver me into the hands of my master, and I will take you down to this troop." **16** And when he had brought him down, there they were, spread out over all the land, eating and drinking and dancing, because of all the great spoil which they had taken from the land of the Philistines and from the land of Judah. **17** Then David attacked them from twilight until the evening of the next day. Not a man of them escaped, except four hundred young men who rode on camels and fled. **18** So David recovered all that the Amalekites had carried away, and David rescued his two wives. **19** And nothing of theirs was lacking, either small or great, sons or daughters, spoil or anything which they had taken from them; David recovered all. **20** Then David took all the flocks and herds they had driven before those *other* livestock, and said, "This *is* David's spoil."

Spoil taken from, consecrated.

2 Sam 8:11–12 King David also dedicated these to the LORD, along with the silver and gold that he had dedicated from all the nations which he had subdued— **12** from Syria, from Moab, from the people of Ammon, from the Philistines, from Amalek, and from the spoil of Hadadezer the son of Rehob, king of Zobah.

Confederated against Israel.

Ps 83:7 Gebal, Ammon, and Amalek; Philistia with the inhabitants of Tyre;

Remnant of, completely destroyed during the reign of Hezekiah.

1 Chr 4:41–43 These recorded by name came in the days of Hezekiah king of Judah; and they attacked their tents and the Meunites who were found there, and utterly destroyed them, as it is to this day. So they dwelt in their place, because *there was* pasture for their flocks there. **42** Now *some* of them, five hundred men of the sons of Simeon, went to Mount Seir, having as their captains Pelatiah, Neariah, Rephaiah, and Uzziel, the sons of Ishi. **43** And they defeated the rest of the Amalekites who had escaped. They have dwelt there to this day.

AMAZIAH

Son of Joash.

2 Kin 12:21 For Jozachar the son of Shimeath and Jehozabad the son of Shomer, his servants, struck him. So he died, and they buried him with his fathers in the City of David. Then Amaziah his son reigned in his place.

King of Judah. 2 Kin 14:1–22; 2 Chr 25:1–28

At war with Jehoash.

2 Kin 13:12 Now the rest of the acts of Joash, all that he did, and his might with which he fought against Amaziah king of Judah, *are* they not written in the book of the chronicles of the kings of Israel?

AMBITION

God condemns.

Gen 11:7 Come, let Us go down and there confuse their language, that they may not understand one another's speech."

Is 5:8 Woe to those who join house to house; They add field to field, Till *there is* no place Where they may dwell alone in the midst of the land!

Christ condemns.

Matt 18:1–4 At that time the disciples came to Jesus, saying, "Who then is greatest in the kingdom of heaven?" **2** Then Jesus called a little child to Him, set him in the midst of them, **3** and said, "Assuredly, I say to you, unless you are converted and become as little children, you will by no means enter the kingdom of heaven. **4** Therefore whoever humbles himself as this little child is the greatest in the kingdom of heaven.

Matt 20:25–26 But Jesus called them to *Himself* and said, "You know that the rulers of the Gentiles lord it over them, and those who are great exercise authority over them. **26** Yet it shall not be so among you; but whoever desires to become great among you, let him be your servant.

Matt 23:11–12 But he who is greatest among you shall be your servant. **12** And whoever exalts himself will be humbled, and he who humbles himself will be exalted.

Saints avoid.

Ps 131:1–2 LORD, my heart is not haughty, Nor my eyes lofty. Neither do I concern myself with great matters, Nor with things too profound for me. **2** Surely I have calmed and quieted my soul, Like a weaned child with his mother; Like a weaned child *is* my soul within me.

Vanity of.

Job 20:5–9 That the triumphing of the wicked is short, And the joy of the hypocrite is *but* for a moment? **6** Though his haughtiness mounts up to the heavens, And his head reaches to the clouds, **7** *Yet* he will perish forever like his own refuse; Those who have seen him will say, 'Where is he?' **8** He will fly away like a dream, and not be found; Yes, he will be chased away like a vision of the night. **9** The eye *that* saw him will *see him* no more, Nor will his place behold him anymore.

Job 24:24 They are exalted for a little while, Then they are gone. They are brought low; They are taken out of the way like all *others;* They dry out like the heads of grain.

Ps 49:11–20 Their inner thought *is that* their houses *will last* forever, Their dwelling places to all generations; They call *their* lands after their own names. **12** Nevertheless man, *though* in honor, does not remain; He is like the beasts *that* perish. **13** This is the way of those who *are* foolish, And of their posterity who approve their sayings. Selah **14** Like sheep they are laid in the grave; Death shall feed on them; The upright shall have dominion over them in the morning; And their beauty shall be consumed in the grave, far from their dwelling. **15** But God will redeem my soul from the power of the grave, For He shall receive me. Selah **16** Do not be afraid when one becomes rich, When the glory of his house is increased; **17** For when he dies he shall carry nothing away; His glory shall not descend after him. **18** Though while he lives he blesses himself (For *men* will praise you when you do well for yourself), **19** He shall go to the generation of his fathers; They shall never see light. **20** A man *who is* in honor, yet does not understand, Is like the beasts *that* perish.

Leads to strife and contention.

James 4:1–2 Where do wars and fights *come* from among you? Do *they* not *come* from your *desires for* pleasure that war in your members? **2** You lust and do not have. You murder and covet and cannot obtain. You fight and war. Yet you do not have because you do not ask.

Punishment of.

Prov 17:19 He who loves transgression loves strife, And he who exalts his gate seeks destruction.

Is 14:12–15 "How you are fallen from heaven, O Lucifer, son of the morning! *How* you are cut down to the ground, You who weakened the nations! **13** For you have said in your heart: 'I will ascend into heaven, I will exalt my throne above the stars of God; I will also sit on the mount of the congregation On the farthest sides of the north; **14** I will ascend above the heights of the clouds, I will be like the Most High.' **15** Yet you shall be brought down to Sheol, To the lowest depths of the Pit.

Ezek 31:10–11 "Therefore thus says the Lord GOD: 'Because you have increased in height, and it set its top among the thick boughs, and its heart was lifted up in its height, **11** therefore I will deliver it into the hand of the mighty one of the nations, and he shall surely deal with it; I have driven it out for its wickedness.

Obad 1:3–4 The pride of your heart has deceived you, *You* who dwell in the clefts of the rock, Whose habitation is high; *You* who say in your heart, 'Who will bring me down to the ground?' **4** Though you ascend *as* high as the eagle, And though you set your nest among the stars, From there I will bring you down," says the LORD.

Connected with
Pride.

Hab 2:5 "Indeed, because he transgresses by wine, *He is* a proud man, And he does not stay at home. Because he enlarges his desire as hell, And he *is* like death, and cannot be satisfied, He gathers to himself all nations And heaps up for himself all peoples.

Covetousness.

Hab 2:8–9 Because you have plundered many nations, All the remnant of the people shall plunder you, Because of men's blood And the violence of the land *and* the city, And of all who dwell in it. **9** "Woe to him who covets evil gain for his house, That he may set his nest on high, That he may be delivered from the power of disaster!

Cruelty.

Hab 2:12 "Woe to him who builds a town with bloodshed, Who establishes a city by iniquity!

Examples of,
Adam and Eve.

Gen 3:5–6 For God knows that in the day you eat of it your eyes will be opened, and you will be like God, knowing good and evil." **6** So when the woman saw that the tree *was* good for food, that it *was* pleasant to the eyes, and a tree desirable to make *one* wise, she took of its fruit and ate. She also gave to her husband with her, and he ate.

Builders of Babel.

Gen 11:4 And they said, "Come, let us build ourselves a city, and a tower whose top *is* in the heavens; let us make a name for ourselves, lest we be scattered abroad over the face of the whole earth."

Miriam and Aaron.

Num 12:2 So they said, "Has the LORD indeed spoken only through Moses? Has He not spoken through us also?" And the LORD heard *it.*

Korah, etc.

Num 16:3 They gathered together against Moses and Aaron, and said to them, "*You take* too much upon yourselves, for all the congregation *is* holy, every one of them, and the LORD *is* among them. Why then do you exalt yourselves above the assembly of the LORD?"

Absalom.

2 Sam 15:4 Moreover Absalom would say, "Oh, that I were made judge in the land, and everyone who has any suit or cause would come to me; then I would give him justice."

2 Sam 18:18 Now Absalom in his lifetime had taken and set up a pillar for himself, which *is* in the King's Valley. For he said, "I have no son to keep my name in remembrance." He called the pillar after his own name. And to this day it is called Absalom's Monument.

Adonijah.

1 Kin 1:5 Then Adonijah the son of Haggith exalted himself, saying, "I will be king"; and he prepared for himself chariots and horsemen, and fifty men to run before him.

Sennacherib.

2 Kin 19:23 By your messengers you have reproached the Lord, And said: "By the multitude of my chariots I have come up to the height of the mountains, To the limits of Lebanon; I will cut down its tall cedars *And* its choice cypress trees; I will enter the extremity of its borders, *To* its fruitful forest.

Shebna.

Is 22:16 'What have you here, and whom have you here, That you have hewn a sepulcher here, *As* he who hews himself a sepulcher on high, Who carves a tomb for himself in a rock?

Sons of Zebedee.

Matt 20:21 And He said to her, "What do you wish?" She said to Him, "Grant that these two sons of mine may sit, one on Your right hand and the other on the left, in Your kingdom."

Antichrist.

2 Thess 2:4 who opposes and exalts himself above all that is called God or that is worshiped, so that he sits as God in the temple of God, showing himself that he is God.

Diotrephes.

3 John 1:9 I wrote to the church, but Diotrephes, who loves to have the preeminence among them, does not receive us.

AMBITION, GODLY

To grow.

Phil 3:12–14 Not that I have already attained, or am already perfected; but I press on, that I may lay hold of that for which Christ Jesus has also laid hold of me. 13 Brethren, I do not count myself to have apprehended; but one thing *I do,* forgetting those things which are behind and reaching forward to those things which are ahead, 14 I press toward the goal for the prize of the upward call of God in Christ Jesus.

To extend the gospel.

Rom 15:17–20 Therefore I have reason to glory in Christ Jesus in the things *which pertain* to God. 18 For I will not dare to speak of any of those things which Christ has not accomplished through me, in word and deed, to make the Gentiles obedient— 19 in mighty signs and wonders, by the power of the Spirit of God, so that from Jerusalem and round about to Illyricum I have fully preached the gospel of Christ. 20 And so I have made it my aim to preach the gospel, not where Christ was named, lest I should build on another man's foundation,

To please God.

1 Cor 5:9 I wrote to you in my epistle not to keep company with sexually immoral people.

To lead a quiet life.

1 Thess 4:11 that you also aspire to lead a quiet life, to mind your own business, and to work with your own hands, as we commanded you,

AMMON

Descendants of Ben-Ammi.

Gen 19:38 And the younger, she also bore a son and called his name Ben-Ammi; he *is* the father of the people of Ammon to this day.

Amos 1:13 Thus says the LORD: "For three transgressions of the people of Ammon, and for four, I will not turn away its *punishment,* Because they ripped open

the women with child in Gilead, That they might enlarge their territory.

Wanted to dethrone Jehoshaphat.

2 Chr 20:1–2 It happened after this *that* the people of Moab with the people of Ammon, and *others* with them besides the Ammonites, came to battle against Jehoshaphat. 2 Then some came and told Jehoshaphat, saying, "A great multitude is coming against you from beyond the sea, from Syria; and they are in Hazazon Tamar" (which *is* En Gedi).

Received judgment.

Is 1:13–15 Bring no more futile sacrifices; Incense is an abomination to Me. The New Moons, the Sabbaths, and the calling of assemblies— I cannot endure iniquity and the sacred meeting. 14 Your New Moons and your appointed feasts My soul hates; They are a trouble to Me, I am weary of bearing *them.* 15 When you spread out your hands, I will hide My eyes from you; Even though you make many prayers, I will not hear. Your hands are full of blood.

Is 25:1–7 O LORD, You *are* my God. I will exalt You, I will praise Your name, For You have done wonderful *things; Your* counsels of old *are* faithfulness *and* truth. 2 For You have made a city a ruin, A fortified city a ruin, A palace of foreigners to be a city no more; It will never be rebuilt. 3 Therefore the strong people will glorify You; The city of the terrible nations will fear You. 4 For You have been a strength to the poor, A strength to the needy in his distress, A refuge from the storm, A shade from the heat; For the blast of the terrible ones *is* as a storm *against* the wall. 5 You will reduce the noise of aliens, As heat in a dry place; *As* heat in the shadow of a cloud, The song of the terrible ones will be diminished. 6 And in this mountain The LORD of hosts will make for all people A feast of choice pieces, A feast of wines on the lees, Of fat things full of marrow, Of well-refined wines on the lees. 7 And He will destroy on this mountain The surface of the covering cast over all people, And the veil that is spread over all nations.

Is 49:1–6 "Listen, O coastlands, to Me, And take heed, you peoples from afar! The LORD has called Me from the womb; From the matrix of My mother He has made mention of My name. 2 And He has made My mouth like a sharp sword; In the shadow of His hand He has hidden Me, And made Me a polished shaft; In His quiver He has hidden Me." 3 "And He said to me, 'You *are* My servant, O Israel, In whom I will be glorified.' 4 Then I said, 'I have labored in vain, I have spent my strength for nothing and in vain; Yet surely my just reward *is* with the LORD, And my work with my God.' " 5 "And now the LORD says, Who formed Me from the womb *to be* His Servant, To bring Jacob back to Him, So that Israel is gathered to Him (For I shall be glorious in the eyes of the LORD, And My God shall be My strength), 6 Indeed He says, 'It is too small a thing that You should be My Servant To raise up the tribes of Jacob, And to restore the preserved ones of Israel; I will also give You as a light to the Gentiles, That You should be My salvation to the ends of the earth.' "

Jeremiah's prophecy against.

Jer 49:1–6 Against the Ammonites. Thus says the LORD: "Has Israel no sons? Has he no heir? Why *then* does

Milcom inherit Gad, And his people dwell in its cities? **2** Therefore behold, the days are coming," says the LORD, "That I will cause to be heard an alarm of war In Rabbah of the Ammonites; It shall be a desolate mound, And her villages shall be burned with fire. Then Israel shall take possession of his inheritance," says the LORD. **3** "Wail, O Heshbon, for Ai is plundered! Cry, you daughters of Rabbah, Gird yourselves with sackcloth! Lament and run to and fro by the walls; For Milcom shall go into captivity With his priests and his princes together. **4** Why do you boast in the valleys, Your flowing valley, O backsliding daughter? Who trusted in her treasures, *saying,* 'Who will come against me?' **5** Behold, I will bring fear upon you," Says the Lord GOD of hosts, "From all those who are around you; You shall be driven out, everyone headlong, And no one will gather those who wander off. **6** But afterward I will bring back The captives of the people of Ammon," says the LORD.

Ezekiel's prophecy against.

Ezek 25:1–7 The word of the LORD came to me, saying, **2** "Son of man, set your face against the Ammonites, and prophesy against them. **3** Say to the Ammonites, 'Hear the word of the Lord GOD! Thus says the Lord GOD: "Because you said, 'Aha!' against My sanctuary when it was profaned, and against the land of Israel when it was desolate, and against the house of Judah when they went into captivity, **4** indeed, therefore, I will deliver you as a possession to the men of the East, and they shall set their encampments among you and make their dwellings among you; they shall eat your fruit, and they shall drink your milk. **5** And I will make Rabbah a stable for camels and Ammon a resting place for flocks. Then you shall know that I *am* the LORD." **6** 'For thus says the Lord GOD: "Because you clapped *your* hands, stamped your feet, and rejoiced in heart with all your disdain for the land of Israel, **7** indeed, therefore, I will stretch out My hand against you, and give you as plunder to the nations; I will cut you off from the peoples, and I will cause you to perish from the countries; I will destroy you, and you shall know that I *am* the LORD."

Zephaniah's prophecy against.

Zeph 2:8–11 "I have heard the reproach of Moab, And the insults of the people of Ammon, With which they have reproached My people, And made arrogant threats against their borders. **9** Therefore, as I live," Says the LORD of hosts, the God of Israel, "Surely Moab shall be like Sodom, And the people of Ammon like Gomorrah— Overrun with weeds and saltpits, And a perpetual desolation. The residue of My people shall plunder them, And the remnant of My people shall possess them." **10** This they shall have for their pride, Because they have reproached and made arrogant threats Against the people of the LORD of hosts. **11** The LORD *will be* awesome to them, For He will reduce to nothing all the gods of the earth; *People* shall worship Him, Each one from his place, Indeed all the shores of the nations.

AMMONITES, THE

Descent of.

Gen 19:38 And the younger, she also bore a son and called his name Ben-Ammi; he *is* the father of the people of Ammon to this day.

Called the

Descendants of Lot.

Deut 2:19 And *when* you come near the people of Ammon, do not harass them or meddle with them, for I will not give you *any* of the land of the people of Ammon *as* a possession, because I have given it to the descendants of Lot *as* a possession.' "

Descendants of Ammon.

Jer 25:21 Edom, Moab, and the people of Ammon;

Governed by hereditary kings.

2 Sam 10:1 It happened after this that the king of the people of Ammon died, and Hanun his son reigned in his place.

Country of,

Belonged to the Zamzummim.

Deut 2:20–21 (That was also regarded as a land of giants; giants formerly dwelt there. But the Ammonites call them Zamzummim, **21** a people as great and numerous and tall as the Anakim. But the LORD destroyed them before them, and they dispossessed them and dwelt in their place,

Bordered that of the Amorites.

Num 21:24 Then Israel defeated him with the edge of the sword, and took possession of his land from the Arnon to the Jabbok, as far as the people of Ammon; for the border of the people of Ammon *was* fortified.

Was fertile.

Jer 49:4 Why do you boast in the valleys, Your flowing valley, O backsliding daughter? Who trusted in her treasures, *saying,* 'Who will come against me?'

Well fortified.

Num 21:24 Then Israel defeated him with the edge of the sword, and took possession of his land from the Arnon to the Jabbok, as far as the people of Ammon; for the border of the people of Ammon *was* fortified.

Half of, given to the Gadites.

Josh 13:25 Their territory was Jazer, and all the cities of Gilead, and half the land of the Ammonites as far as Aroer, which *is* before Rabbah,

Character of,

Cruel and covetous.

Amos 1:13 Thus says the LORD: "For three transgressions of the people of Ammon, and for four, I will not turn away its *punishment,* Because they ripped open the women with child in Gilead, That they might enlarge their territory.

Proud and reproachful.

Zeph 2:10 This they shall have for their pride, Because they have reproached and made arrogant threats Against the people of the LORD of hosts.

Vindictive.

Ezek 25:3 Say to the Ammonites, 'Hear the word of the Lord GOD! Thus says the Lord GOD: "Because you said, 'Aha!' against My sanctuary when it was profaned, and against the land of Israel when it was desolate, and against the house of Judah when they went into captivity,

Ezek 25:6 'For thus says the Lord GOD: "Because you

clapped *your* hands, stamped your feet, and rejoiced in heart with all your disdain for the land of Israel,

Fond of ornaments.

2 Chr 20:25 When Jehoshaphat and his people came to take away their spoil, they found among them an abundance of valuables on the dead bodies, and precious jewelry, which they stripped off for themselves, more than they could carry away; and they were three days gathering the spoil because there was so much.

Idolatrous.

Judg 10:6 Then the children of Israel again did evil in the sight of the LORD, and served the Baals and the Ashtoreths, the gods of Syria, the gods of Sidon, the gods of Moab, the gods of the people of Ammon, and the gods of the Philistines; and they forsook the LORD and did not serve Him.

1 Kin 11:7 Then Solomon built a high place for Chemosh the abomination of Moab, on the hill that *is* east of Jerusalem, and for Molech the abomination of the people of Ammon.

1 Kin 11:33 because they have forsaken Me, and worshiped Ashtoreth the goddess of the Sidonians, Chemosh the god of the Moabites, and Milcom the god of the people of Ammon, and have not walked in My ways to do *what is* right in My eyes and *keep* My statutes and My judgments, as *did* his father David.

2 Kin 23:13 Then the king defiled the high places that *were* east of Jerusalem, which *were* on the south of the Mount of Corruption, which Solomon king of Israel had built for Ashtoreth the abomination of the Sidonians, for Chemosh the abomination of the Moabites, and for Milcom the abomination of the people of Ammon.

Superstitious.

Jer 27:3 and send them to the king of Edom, the king of Moab, the king of the Ammonites, the king of Tyre, and the king of Sidon, by the hand of the messengers who come to Jerusalem to Zedekiah king of Judah.

Jer 27:9 Therefore do not listen to your prophets, your diviners, your dreamers, your soothsayers, or your sorcerers, who speak to you, saying, "You shall not serve the king of Babylon."

Chief cities of.

2 Sam 12:26–27 Now Joab fought against Rabbah of the people of Ammon, and took the royal city. **27** And Joab sent messengers to David, and said, "I have fought against Rabbah, and I have taken the city's water *supply.*

Jer 49:3 "Wail, O Heshbon, for Ai is plundered! Cry, you daughters of Rabbah, Gird yourselves with sackcloth! Lament and run to and fro by the walls; For Milcom shall go into captivity With his priests and his princes together.

Jewish laws respecting,

Perpetual exclusion from the congregation.

Deut 23:3 "An Ammonite or Moabite shall not enter the assembly of the LORD; even to the tenth generation none of his *descendants* shall enter the assembly of the LORD forever,

Neh 13:1 On that day they read from the Book of Moses in the hearing of the people, and in it was found written that no Ammonite or Moabite should ever come into the assembly of God,

No covenant to be made with.

Deut 23:6 You shall not seek their peace nor their prosperity all your days forever.

Not to be distressed.

Deut 2:19 And *when* you come near the people of Ammon, do not harass them or meddle with them, for I will not give you *any* of the land of the people of Ammon *as* a possession, because I have given it to the descendants of Lot *as* a possession.' "

2 Chr 20:10 And now, here are the people of Ammon, Moab, and Mount Seir—whom You would not let Israel invade when they came out of the land of Egypt, but they turned from them and did not destroy them—

Assisted Eglon against Israel.

Judg 3:12–13 And the children of Israel again did evil in the sight of the LORD. So the LORD strengthened Eglon king of Moab against Israel, because they had done evil in the sight of the LORD. **13** Then he gathered to himself the people of Ammon and Amalek, went and defeated Israel, and took possession of the City of Palms.

With the Philistines oppressed Israel for eighteen years.

Judg 10:6–9 Then the children of Israel again did evil in the sight of the LORD, and served the Baals and the Ashtoreths, the gods of Syria, the gods of Sidon, the gods of Moab, the gods of the people of Ammon, and the gods of the Philistines; and they forsook the LORD and did not serve Him. **7** So the anger of the LORD was hot against Israel; and He sold them into the hands of the Philistines and into the hands of the people of Ammon. **8** From that year they harassed and oppressed the children of Israel for eighteen years—all the children of Israel who *were* on the other side of the Jordan in the land of the Amorites, in Gilead. **9** Moreover the people of Ammon crossed over the Jordan to fight against Judah also, against Benjamin, and against the house of Ephraim, so that Israel was severely distressed.

Jephthah raised up to deliver Israel from.
Judg 10:15–18; 11:4–33

Proposed a disgraceful treaty to Jabesh Gilead.

1 Sam 11:1–3 Then Nahash the Ammonite came up and encamped against Jabesh Gilead; and all the men of Jabesh said to Nahash, "Make a covenant with us, and we will serve you." **2** And Nahash the Ammonite answered them, "On this *condition* I will make *a covenant* with you, that I may put out all your right eyes, and bring reproach on all Israel." **3** Then the elders of Jabesh said to him, "Hold off for seven days, that we may send messengers to all the territory of Israel. And then, if *there is* no one to save us, we will come out to you."

Saul's victories over.

1 Sam 11:11 So it was, on the next day, that Saul put the people in three companies; and they came into the midst of the camp in the morning watch, and killed Ammonites until the heat of the day. And it happened that those who survived were scattered, so that no two of them were left together.

1 Sam 14:47 So Saul established his sovereignty over Israel, and fought against all his enemies on every side, against Moab, against the people of Ammon, against Edom, against the kings of Zobah, and against the Philistines. Wherever he turned, he harassed *them*.

Ill-treated David's ambassadors.

2 Sam 10:1–4 It happened after this that the king of the people of Ammon died, and Hanun his son reigned in his place. **2** Then David said, "I will show kindness to Hanun the son of Nahash, as his father showed kindness to me." So David sent by the hand of his servants to comfort him concerning his father. And David's servants came into the land of the people of Ammon. **3** And the princes of the people of Ammon said to Hanun their lord, "Do you think that David really honors your father because he has sent comforters to you? Has David not *rather* sent his servants to you to search the city, to spy it out, and to overthrow it?" **4** Therefore Hanun took David's servants, shaved off half of their beards, cut off their garments in the middle, at their buttocks, and sent them away.

Hired the Syrians against David.

2 Sam 10:6 When the people of Ammon saw that they had made themselves repulsive to David, the people of Ammon sent and hired the Syrians of Beth Rehob and the Syrians of Zoba, twenty thousand foot soldiers; and from the king of Maacah one thousand men, and from Ish-Tob twelve thousand men.

Victories of Joab over.

2 Sam 10:7–14 Now when David heard *of it*, he sent Joab and all the army of the mighty men. **8** Then the people of Ammon came out and put themselves in battle array at the entrance of the gate. And the Syrians of Zoba, Beth Rehob, Ish-Tob, and Maacah *were* by themselves in the field. **9** When Joab saw that the battle line was against him before and behind, he chose some of Israel's best and put *them* in battle array against the Syrians. **10** And the rest of the people he put under the command of Abishai his brother, that he might set *them* in battle array against the people of Ammon. **11** Then he said, "If the Syrians are too strong for me, then you shall help me; but if the people of Ammon are too strong for you, then I will come and help you. **12** Be of good courage, and let us be strong for our people and for the cities of our God. And may the LORD do *what is* good in His sight." **13** So Joab and the people who *were* with him drew near for the battle against the Syrians, and they fled before him. **14** When the people of Ammon saw that the Syrians were fleeing, they also fled before Abishai, and entered the city. So Joab returned from the people of Ammon and went to Jerusalem.

2 Sam 12:26–29 Now Joab fought against Rabbah of the people of Ammon, and took the royal city. **27** And Joab sent messengers to David, and said, "I have fought against Rabbah, and I have taken the city's water *supply*. **28** Now therefore, gather the rest of the people together and encamp against the city and take it, lest I take the city and it be called after my name." **29** So David gathered all the people together and went to Rabbah, fought against it, and took it.

The royal treasure of, taken.

2 Sam 12:30 Then he took their king's crown from his head. Its weight *was* a talent of gold, with precious stones. And it was *set* on David's head. Also he brought out the spoil of the city in great abundance.

Spoil of, consecrated to God.

2 Sam 8:11–12 King David also dedicated these to the LORD, along with the silver and gold that he had dedicated from all the nations which he had subdued— **12** from Syria, from Moab, from the people of Ammon, from the Philistines, from Amalek, and from the spoil of Hadadezer the son of Rehob, king of Zobah.

One of David's mighty men was of.

2 Sam 23:37 Zelek the Ammonite, Naharai the Beerothite (armorbearer of Joab the son of Zeruiah),

Solomon intermarried with, and introduced idols of, into Israel.

1 Kin 11:1–5 But King Solomon loved many foreign women, as well as the daughter of Pharaoh: women of the Moabites, Ammonites, Edomites, Sidonians, *and* Hittites— **2** from the nations of whom the LORD had said to the children of Israel, "You shall not intermarry with them, nor they with you. Surely they will turn away your hearts after their gods." Solomon clung to these in love. **3** And he had seven hundred wives, princesses, and three hundred concubines; and his wives turned away his heart. **4** For it was so, when Solomon was old, that his wives turned his heart after other gods; and his heart was not loyal to the LORD his God, as *was* the heart of his father David. **5** For Solomon went after Ashtoreth the goddess of the Sidonians, and after Milcom the abomination of the Ammonites.

Confederated against Jehoshaphat.

2 Chr 20:1 It happened after this *that* the people of Moab with the people of Ammon, and *others* with them besides the Ammonites, came to battle against Jehoshaphat.

Ps 83:7 Gebal, Ammon, and Amalek; Philistia with the inhabitants of Tyre;

Miraculous defeat of. 2 Chr 20:5–24

Submitted to Uzziah.

2 Chr 26:8 Also the Ammonites brought tribute to Uzziah. His fame spread as far as the entrance of Egypt, for he became exceedingly strong.

Defeated by Jotham.

2 Chr 27:5 He also fought with the king of the Ammonites and defeated them. And the people of Ammon gave him in that year one hundred talents of silver, ten thousand kors of wheat, and ten thousand of barley. The people of Ammon paid this to him in the second and third years also.

Seized upon the possessions of Gad.

Jer 49:1 Against the Ammonites. Thus says the LORD: "Has Israel no sons? Has he no heir? Why *then* does Milcom inherit Gad, And his people dwell in its cities?

Aided the Chaldeans against Judah.

2 Kin 24:2 And the LORD sent against him *raiding* bands of Chaldeans, bands of Syrians, bands of Moabites, and bands of the people of Ammon; He sent them against Judah to destroy it, according to the word of the LORD which He had spoken by His servants the prophets.

Vexed the Jews after captivity.

Neh 4:3 Now Tobiah the Ammonite *was* beside him, and he said, "Whatever they build, if even a fox goes up *on it,* he will break down their stone wall."

Neh 4:7–8 Now it happened, when Sanballat, Tobiah, the Arabs, the Ammonites, and the Ashdodites heard that the walls of Jerusalem were being restored and the gaps were beginning to be closed, that they became very angry, **8** and all of them conspired together to come *and* attack Jerusalem and create confusion.

The Jews reprobated for intermarrying with.

Ezra 9:1–3 When these things were done, the leaders came to me, saying, "The people of Israel and the priests and the Levites have not separated themselves from the peoples of the lands, with respect to the abominations of the Canaanites, the Hittites, the Perizzites, the Jebusites, the Ammonites, the Moabites, the Egyptians, and the Amorites. **2** For they have taken some of their daughters *as wives* for themselves and their sons, so that the holy seed is mixed with the peoples of *those* lands. Indeed, the hand of the leaders and rulers has been foremost in this trespass." **3** So when I heard this thing, I tore my garment and my robe, and plucked out some of the hair of my head and beard, and sat down astonished.

Neh 13:23–28 In those days I also saw Jews *who* had married women of Ashdod, Ammon, *and* Moab. **24** And half of their children spoke the language of Ashdod, and could not speak the language of Judah, but spoke according to the language of one or the other people. **25** So I contended with them and cursed them, struck some of them and pulled out their hair, and made them swear by God, *saying,* "You shall not give your daughters as wives to their sons, nor take their daughters for your sons or yourselves. **26** Did not Solomon king of Israel sin by these things? Yet among many nations there was no king like him, who was beloved of his God; and God made him king over all Israel. Nevertheless pagan women caused even him to sin. **27** Should we then hear of your doing all this great evil, transgressing against our God by marrying pagan women?" **28** And *one* of the sons of Joiada, the son of Eliashib the high priest, *was* a son-in-law of Sanballat the Horonite; therefore I drove him from me.

Predictions respecting,

Subjection to Babylon.

Jer 27:3 and send them to the king of Edom, the king of Moab, the king of the Ammonites, the king of Tyre, and the king of Sidon, by the hand of the messengers who come to Jerusalem to Zedekiah king of Judah.

Jer 27:6 And now I have given all these lands into the hand of Nebuchadnezzar the king of Babylon, My servant; and the beasts of the field I have also given him to serve him.

Cf. Jer 25:9–21

Destruction because of hatred for Israel.

Ezek 25:2–10 "Son of man, set your face against the Ammonites, and prophesy against them. **3** Say to the Ammonites, 'Hear the word of the Lord GOD! Thus says the Lord GOD: "Because you said, 'Aha!' against My sanctuary when it was profaned, and against the land of Israel when it was desolate, and against the house of Judah when they went into captivity, **4** indeed, therefore, I will deliver you as a possession to the men of the East, and they shall set their encampments among you and make their dwellings among you; they shall eat your fruit, and they shall drink your milk. **5** And I will make Rabbah a stable for camels and Ammon a resting place for flocks. Then you shall know that I *am* the LORD." **6** 'For thus says the Lord GOD: "Because you clapped *your* hands, stamped your feet, and rejoiced in heart with all your disdain for the land of Israel, **7** indeed, therefore, I will stretch out My hand against you, and give you as plunder to the nations; I will cut you off from the peoples, and I will cause you to perish from the countries; I will destroy you, and you shall know that I *am* the LORD." **8** 'Thus says the Lord GOD: "Because Moab and Seir say, 'Look! The house of Judah *is* like all the nations,' **9** therefore, behold, I will clear the territory of Moab of cities, of the cities on its frontier, the glory of the country, Beth Jeshimoth, Baal Meon, and Kirjathaim. **10** To the men of the East I will give it as a possession, together with the Ammonites, that the Ammonites may not be remembered among the nations.

Zeph 2:8–9 "I have heard the reproach of Moab, And the insults of the people of Ammon, With which they have reproached My people, And made arrogant threats against their borders. **9** Therefore, *as* I live," Says the LORD of hosts, the God of Israel, "Surely Moab shall be like Sodom, And the people of Ammon like Gomorrah— Overrun with weeds and saltpits, And a perpetual desolation. The residue of My people shall plunder them, And the remnant of My people shall possess them."

Punishment for oppressive cruelty.

Jer 49:1–5 Against the Ammonites. Thus says the LORD: "Has Israel no sons? Has he no heir? Why *then* does Milcom inherit Gad, And his people dwell in its cities? **2** Therefore behold, the days are coming," says the LORD, "That I will cause to be heard an alarm of war In Rabbah of the Ammonites; It shall be a desolate mound, And her villages shall be burned with fire. Then Israel shall take possession of his inheritance," says the LORD. **3** "Wail, O Heshbon, for Ai is plundered! Cry, you daughters of Rabbah, Gird yourselves with sackcloth! Lament and run to and fro by the walls; For Milcom shall go into captivity With his priests and his princes together. **4** Why do you boast in the valleys, Your flowing valley, O backsliding daughter? Who trusted in her treasures, *saying,* 'Who will come against me?' **5** Behold, I will bring fear upon you," Says the Lord GOD of hosts, "From all those who are around you; You shall be driven out, everyone headlong, And no one will gather those who wander off.

Amos 1:13–15 Thus says the LORD: "For three transgressions of the people of Ammon, and for four, I will not turn away its *punishment,* Because they ripped open the women with child in Gilead, That they might enlarge their territory. **14** But I will kindle a fire in the wall of Rabbah, And it shall devour its palaces, Amid shouting in the day of battle, And a tempest in the day of the whirlwind. **15** Their king

shall go into captivity, He and his princes together,"
Says the LORD.

Restoration.

Jer 49:6 But afterward I will bring back The captives of
the people of Ammon," says the LORD.

Subjection to the Jews.

Is 11:14 But they shall fly down upon the shoulder of
the Philistines toward the west; Together they shall
plunder the people of the East; They shall lay their
hand on Edom and Moab; And the people of
Ammon shall obey them.

AMORITES, THE

Descent of.

Gen 10:15–16 Canaan begot Sidon his firstborn, and
Heth; **16** the Jebusite, the Amorite, and the Girgashite;

1 Chr 1:13–14 Canaan begot Sidon, his firstborn, and
Heth; **14** the Jebusite, the Amorite, and the Girgashite;

One of the seven nations of Canaan.

Gen 15:21 the Amorites, the Canaanites, the Girgashites, and the Jebusites."

Ex 3:8 So I have come down to deliver them out of the
hand of the Egyptians, and to bring them up from
that land to a good and large land, to a land flowing
with milk and honey, to the place of the Canaanites
and the Hittites and the Amorites and the Perizzites
and the Hivites and the Jebusites.

Ex 3:17 and I have said I will bring you up out of the affliction of Egypt to the land of the Canaanites and the
Hittites and the Amorites and the Perizzites and the
Hivites and the Jebusites, to a land flowing with milk
and honey." '

Governed by many independent kings.

Josh 5:1 So it was, when all the kings of the Amorites
who *were* on the west side of the Jordan, and all the
kings of the Canaanites who *were* by the sea, heard
that the LORD had dried up the waters of the Jordan
from before the children of Israel until we had
crossed over, that their heart melted; and there was
no spirit in them any longer because of the children
of Israel.

Josh 9:10 and all that He did to the two kings of the
Amorites who *were* beyond the Jordan—to Sihon
king of Heshbon, and Og king of Bashan, who was at
Ashtaroth.

Kings of, great and powerful.

Ps 136:18 And slew famous kings, For His mercy *endures* forever—

Ps 136:20 And Og king of Bashan, For His mercy *endures* forever—

Originally inhabited a mountain district in the south.

Num 13:29 The Amalekites dwell in the land of the
South; the Hittites, the Jebusites, and the Amorites
dwell in the mountains; and the Canaanites dwell by
the sea and along the banks of the Jordan."

Deut 1:7 Turn and take your journey, and go to the
mountains of the Amorites, to all the neighboring
places in the plain, in the mountains and in the low-

land, in the South and on the seacoast, to the land of
the Canaanites and to Lebanon, as far as the great
river, the River Euphrates.

Deut 1:20 And I said to you, 'You have come to the
mountains of the Amorites, which the LORD our God
is giving us.

Judg 1:36 Now the boundary of the Amorites *was* from
the Ascent of Akrabbim, from Sela, and upward.

Acquired an extensive territory from Moab east of Jordan.

Num 21:26 For Heshbon *was* the city of Sihon king of
the Amorites, who had fought against the former
king of Moab, and had taken all his land from his
hand as far as the Arnon.

Num 21:30 "But we have shot at them; Heshbon has
perished as far as Dibon. Then we laid waste as far as
Nophah, Which *reaches* to Medeba."

Had many and strong cities.

Num 32:17 but we ourselves will be armed, ready *to go*
before the children of Israel until we have brought
them to their place; and our little ones will dwell in
the fortified cities because of the inhabitants of the
land.

Num 32:33 So Moses gave to the children of Gad, to the
children of Reuben, and to half the tribe of Manasseh
the son of Joseph, the kingdom of Sihon king of the
Amorites and the kingdom of Og king of Bashan, the
land with its cities within the borders, the cities of
the surrounding country.

Of gigantic strength and stature.

Amos 2:9 "Yet *it was* I *who* destroyed the Amorite before
them, Whose height *was* like the height of the cedars,
And he *was as* strong as the oaks; Yet I destroyed his
fruit above And his roots beneath.

Character of,

Profane and wicked.

Gen 15:16 But in the fourth generation they shall return
here, for the iniquity of the Amorites *is* not yet complete."

Idolatrous.

Josh 24:15 And if it seems evil to you to serve the LORD,
choose for yourselves this day whom you will serve,
whether the gods which your fathers served that
were on the other side of the River, or the gods of the
Amorites, in whose land you dwell. But as for me
and my house, we will serve the LORD."

Defeated by Chedorlaomer, etc.

Gen 14:7 Then they turned back and came to En Mishpat (that *is*, Kadesh), and attacked all the country of
the Amalekites, and also the Amorites who dwelt in
Hazezon Tamar.

Joined Abraham against the kings.

Gen 14:13 Then one who had escaped came and told
Abram the Hebrew, for he dwelt by the terebinth
trees of Mamre the Amorite, brother of Eshcol and
brother of Aner; and they *were* allies with Abram.

Gen 14:24 except only what the young men have eaten,
and the portion of the men who went with me: Aner,
Eshcol, and Mamre; let them take their portion."

Jacob took a portion from.

Gen 48:22 Moreover I have given to you one portion

above your brothers, which I took from the hand of the Amorite with my sword and my bow."

Forbearance of God toward.

Gen 15:16 But in the fourth generation they shall return here, for the iniquity of the Amorites *is* not yet complete."

Doomed to utter destruction.

Deut 20:17–18 but you shall utterly destroy them: the Hittite and the Amorite and the Canaanite and the Perizzite and the Hivite and the Jebusite, just as the LORD your God has commanded you, **18** lest they teach you to do according to all their abominations which they have done for their gods, and you sin against the LORD your God.

Refused a passage to Israel.

Num 21:21–23 Then Israel sent messengers to Sihon king of the Amorites, saying, **22** "Let me pass through your land. We will not turn aside into fields or vineyards; we will not drink water from wells. We will go by the King's Highway until we have passed through your territory." **23** But Sihon would not allow Israel to pass through his territory. So Sihon gathered all his people together and went out against Israel in the wilderness, and he came to Jahaz and fought against Israel.

Deut 2:30 "But Sihon king of Heshbon would not let us pass through, for the LORD your God hardened his spirit and made his heart obstinate, that He might deliver him into your hand, as *it is* this day.

Deprived of their eastern territory by Israel.

Num 21:24–35 Then Israel defeated him with the edge of the sword, and took possession of his land from the Arnon to the Jabbok, as far as the people of Ammon; for the border of the people of Ammon *was* fortified. **25** So Israel took all these cities, and Israel dwelt in all the cities of the Amorites, in Heshbon and in all its villages. **26** For Heshbon *was* the city of Sihon king of the Amorites, who had fought against the former king of Moab, and had taken all his land from his hand as far as the Arnon. **27** Therefore those who speak in proverbs say: "Come to Heshbon, let it be built; Let the city of Sihon be repaired. **28** "For fire went out from Heshbon, A flame from the city of Sihon; It consumed Ar of Moab, The lords of the heights of the Arnon. **29** Woe to you, Moab! You have perished, O people of Chemosh! He has given his sons as fugitives, And his daughters into captivity, To Sihon king of the Amorites. **30** "But we have shot at them; Heshbon has perished as far as Dibon. Then we laid waste as far as Nophah, Which *reaches* to Medeba." **31** Thus Israel dwelt in the land of the Amorites. **32** Then Moses sent to spy out Jazer; and they took its villages and drove out the Amorites who *were* there. **33** And they turned and went up by the way to Bashan. So Og king of Bashan went out against them, he and all his people, to battle at Edrei. **34** Then the LORD said to Moses, "Do not fear him, for I have delivered him into your hand, with all his people and his land; and you shall do to him as you did to Sihon king of the Amorites, who dwelt at Heshbon." **35** So they defeated him, his sons, and all his people, until there was no survivor left him; and they took possession of his land.

Land of, given to Reubenites, etc. Josh 13:15–31

Western kings of, confederated against Israel.

Josh 10:1–5 Now it came to pass when Adoni-Zedek king of Jerusalem heard how Joshua had taken Ai and had utterly destroyed it—as he had done to Jericho and its king, so he had done to Ai and its king— and how the inhabitants of Gibeon had made peace with Israel and were among them, **2** that they feared greatly, because Gibeon *was* a great city, like one of the royal cities, and because it *was* greater than Ai, and all its men *were* mighty. **3** Therefore Adoni-Zedek king of Jerusalem sent to Hoham king of Hebron, Piram king of Jarmuth, Japhia king of Lachish, and Debir king of Eglon, saying, **4** "Come up to me and help me, that we may attack Gibeon, for it has made peace with Joshua and with the children of Israel." **5** Therefore the five kings of the Amorites, the king of Jerusalem, the king of Hebron, the king of Jarmuth, the king of Lachish, *and* the king of Eglon, gathered together and went up, they and all their armies, and camped before Gibeon and made war against it.

Miraculous overthrow of.

Josh 10:11–14 And it happened, as they fled before Israel *and* were on the descent of Beth Horon, that the LORD cast down large hailstones from heaven on them as far as Azekah, and they died. *There were* more who died from the hailstones than the children of Israel killed with the sword. **12** Then Joshua spoke to the LORD in the day when the LORD delivered up the Amorites before the children of Israel, and he said in the sight of Israel: "Sun, stand still over Gibeon; And Moon, in the Valley of Aijalon." **13** So the sun stood still, And the moon stopped, Till the people had revenge Upon their enemies. *Is* this not written in the Book of Jasher? So the sun stood still in the midst of heaven, and did not hasten to go *down* for about a whole day. **14** And there has been no day like that, before it or after it, that the LORD heeded the voice of a man; for the LORD fought for Israel.

Kings of, degraded and slain.

Josh 10:24–27 So it was, when they brought out those kings to Joshua, that Joshua called for all the men of Israel, and said to the captains of the men of war who went with him, "Come near, put your feet on the necks of these kings." And they drew near and put their feet on their necks. **25** Then Joshua said to them, "Do not be afraid, nor be dismayed; be strong and of good courage, for thus the LORD will do to all your enemies against whom you fight." **26** And afterward Joshua struck them and killed them, and hanged them on five trees; and they were hanging on the trees until evening. **27** So it was at the time of the going down of the sun *that* Joshua commanded, and they took them down from the trees, cast them into the cave where they had been hidden, and laid large stones against the cave's mouth, *which remain* until this very day.

The Gibeonites a tribe of, deceived Israel into making a covenant.

Josh 9:3–16 But when the inhabitants of Gibeon heard what Joshua had done to Jericho and Ai, **4** they worked craftily, and went and pretended to be ambassadors. And they took old sacks on their donkeys, old wineskins torn and mended, **5** old and patched sandals on their feet, and old garments on themselves; and all the bread of their provision was dry *and* moldy. **6** And they went to Joshua, to the camp at Gilgal, and said to him and to the men of Israel, "We have come from a far country; now therefore, make a covenant with us." **7** Then the men of Israel said to the Hivites, "Perhaps you dwell among us; so how can we make a covenant with you?" **8** But they said to Joshua, "We *are* your servants." And Joshua said to them, "Who *are* you, and where do you come from?" **9** So they said to him: "From a very far country your servants have come, because of the name of the LORD your God; for we have heard of His fame, and all that He did in Egypt, **10** and all that He did to the two kings of the Amorites who *were* beyond the Jordan—to Sihon king of Heshbon, and Og king of Bashan, who was at Ashtaroth. **11** Therefore our elders and all the inhabitants of our country spoke to us, saying, 'Take provisions with you for the journey, and go to meet them, and say to them, "We *are* your servants; now therefore, make a covenant with us." ' **12** This bread of ours we took hot *for* our provision from our houses on the day we departed to come to you. But now look, it is dry and moldy. **13** And these wineskins which we filled *were* new, and see, they are torn; and these our garments and our sandals have become old because of the very long journey." **14** Then the men of Israel took some of their provisions; but they did not ask counsel of the LORD. **15** So Joshua made peace with them, and made a covenant with them to let them live; and the rulers of the congregation swore to them. **16** And it happened at the end of three days, after they had made a covenant with them, that they heard that they *were* their neighbors who dwelt near them.

2 Sam 21:2 So the king called the Gibeonites and spoke to them. Now the Gibeonites *were* not of the children of Israel, but of the remnant of the Amorites; the children of Israel had sworn protection to them, but Saul had sought to kill them in his zeal for the children of Israel and Judah.

The Israelites unable to expel, but extracted tribute from.

Judg 1:34–35 And the Amorites forced the children of Dan into the mountains, for they would not allow them to come down to the valley; **35** and the Amorites were determined to dwell in Mount Heres, in Aijalon, and in Shaalbim; yet when the strength of the house of Joseph became greater, they were put under tribute.

Had peace with Israel in the days of Samuel.

1 Sam 7:14 Then the cities which the Philistines had taken from Israel were restored to Israel, from Ekron to Gath; and Israel recovered its territory from the hands of the Philistines. Also there was peace between Israel and the Amorites.

Brought into bondage by Solomon.

1 Kin 9:20–21 All the people *who were* left of the Amorites, Hittites, Perizzites, Hivites, and Jebusites, who *were* not of the children of Israel— **21** that is, their descendants who were left in the land after them, whom the children of Israel had not been able to destroy completely—from these Solomon raised forced labor, as it is to this day.

Ahab followed the abominations of.

1 Kin 21:26 And he behaved very abominably in following idols, according to all *that* the Amorites had done, whom the LORD had cast out before the children of Israel.

Manasseh exceeded the abominations of.

2 Kin 21:11 "Because Manasseh king of Judah has done these abominations (he has acted more wickedly than all the Amorites who *were* before him, and has also made Judah sin with his idols),

The Jews after the captivity condemned for intermarrying with.

Ezra 9:1–2 When these things were done, the leaders came to me, saying, "The people of Israel and the priests and the Levites have not separated themselves from the peoples of the lands, with respect to the abominations of the Canaanites, the Hittites, the Perizzites, the Jebusites, the Ammonites, the Moabites, the Egyptians, and the Amorites. **2** For they have taken some of their daughters *as wives* for themselves and their sons, so that the holy seed is mixed with the peoples of *those* lands. Indeed, the hand of the leaders and rulers has been foremost in this trespass."

AMOS

Prophesied of Israel's salvation.

Amos 9:11–15 "On that day I will raise up The tabernacle of David, which has fallen down, And repair its damages; I will raise up its ruins, And rebuild it as in the days of old; **12** That they may possess the remnant of Edom, And all the Gentiles who are called by My name," Says the LORD who does this thing. **13** "Behold, the days are coming," says the LORD, "When the plowman shall overtake the reaper, And the treader of grapes him who sows seed; The mountains shall drip with sweet wine, And all the hills shall flow *with it*. **14** I will bring back the captives of My people Israel; They shall build the waste cities and inhabit *them*; They shall plant vineyards and drink wine from them; They shall also make gardens and eat fruit from them. **15** I will plant them in their land, And no longer shall they be pulled up From the land I have given them," Says the LORD your God.

Ministered to the northern kingdom.

Amos 1:1 The words of Amos, who was among the sheepbreeders of Tekoa, which he saw concerning Israel in the days of Uzziah king of Judah, and in the days of Jeroboam the son of Joash, king of Israel, two years before the earthquake.

From Tekoa.

Amos 1:1 The words of Amos, who was among the sheepbreeders of Tekoa, which he saw concerning Israel in the days of Uzziah king of Judah, and in the days of Jeroboam the son of Joash, king of Israel, two years before the earthquake.

Cf. Jer 6:1

Quoted by Stephen.

Acts 7:42–43 Then God turned and gave them up to worship the host of heaven, as it is written in the book of the Prophets: *'Did you offer Me slaughtered animals and sacrifices during forty years in the wilderness, O house of Israel?* **43** *You also took up the tabernacle of Moloch, And the star of your god Remphan, Images which you made to worship; And I will carry you away beyond Babylon.'*

Vision of

Locusts.

Amos 7:1–3 Thus the Lord GOD showed me: Behold, He formed locust swarms at the beginning of the late crop; indeed *it was* the late crop after the king's mowings. **2** And so it was, when they had finished eating the grass of the land, that I said: "O Lord GOD, forgive, I pray! Oh, that Jacob may stand, For he *is* small!" **3** *So* the LORD relented concerning this. "It shall not be," said the LORD.

Fire.

Amos 7:4–6 Thus the Lord GOD showed me: Behold, the Lord GOD called for conflict by fire, and it consumed the great deep and devoured the territory. **5** Then I said: "O Lord GOD, cease, I pray! Oh, that Jacob may stand, For he *is* small!" **6** *So* the LORD relented concerning this. "This also shall not be," said the Lord GOD.

The plumb line.

Amos 7:7–9 Thus He showed me: Behold, the Lord stood on a wall *made* with a plumb line, with a plumb line in His hand. **8** And the LORD said to me, "Amos, what do you see?" And I said, "A plumb line." Then the Lord said: "Behold, I am setting a plumb line In the midst of My people Israel; I will not pass by them anymore. **9** The high places of Isaac shall be desolate, And the sanctuaries of Israel shall be laid waste. I will rise with the sword against the house of Jeroboam."

The summer fruit.

Amos 8:1–14 Thus the Lord GOD showed me: Behold, a basket of summer fruit. **2** And He said, "Amos, what do you see?" So I said, "A basket of summer fruit." Then the LORD said to me: "The end has come upon My people Israel; I will not pass by them anymore. **3** And the songs of the temple Shall be wailing in that day," Says the Lord GOD— "Many dead bodies everywhere, They shall be thrown out in silence." **4** Hear this, you who swallow up the needy, And make the poor of the land fail, **5** Saying: "When will the New Moon be past, That we may sell grain? And the Sabbath, That we may trade wheat? Making the ephah small and the shekel large, Falsifying the scales by deceit, **6** That we may buy the poor for silver, And the needy for a pair of sandals— Even sell the bad wheat?" **7** The LORD has sworn by the pride of Jacob: "Surely I will never forget any of their works. **8** Shall the land not tremble for this, And everyone mourn who dwells in it? All of it shall swell like the River, Heave and subside Like the River of Egypt. **9** "And it shall come to pass in that day," says the Lord GOD, "That I will make the sun go down at noon, And I will darken the earth in broad daylight; **10** I will turn your feasts into mourning, And all your songs into lamentation; I will bring sackcloth on every waist, And baldness on every head; I will make it like mourning for an only *son,* And its end like a bitter day. **11** "Behold, the days are coming," says the Lord GOD, "That I will send a famine on the land, Not a famine of bread, Nor a thirst for water, But of hearing the words of the LORD. **12** They shall wander from sea to sea, And from north to east; They shall run to and fro, seeking the word of the LORD, But shall not find *it.* **13** "In that day the fair virgins And strong young men Shall faint from thirst. **14** Those who swear by the sin of Samaria, Who say, 'As your god lives, O Dan!' And, 'As the way of Beersheba lives!' They shall fall and never rise again."

The Lord.

Amos 9:1–10 I saw the Lord standing by the altar, and He said: "Strike the doorposts, that the thresholds may shake, And break them on the heads of them all. I will slay the last of them with the sword. He who flees from them shall not get away, And he who escapes from them shall not be delivered. **2** "Though they dig into hell, From there My hand shall take them; Though they climb up to heaven, From there I will bring them down; **3** And though they hide themselves on top of Carmel, From there I will search and take them; Though they hide from My sight at the bottom of the sea, From there I will command the serpent, and it shall bite them; **4** Though they go into captivity before their enemies, From there I will command the sword, And it shall slay them. I will set My eyes on them for harm and not for good." **5** The Lord GOD of hosts, He who touches the earth and it melts, And all who dwell there mourn; All of it shall swell like the River, And subside like the River of Egypt. **6** He who builds His layers in the sky, And has founded His strata in the earth; Who calls for the waters of the sea, And pours them out on the face of the earth— The LORD *is* His name. **7** "*Are* you not like the people of Ethiopia to Me, O children of Israel?" says the LORD. "Did I not bring up Israel from the land of Egypt, The Philistines from Caphtor, And the Syrians from Kir? **8** "Behold, the eyes of the Lord GOD *are* on the sinful kingdom, And I will destroy it from the face of the earth; Yet I will not utterly destroy the house of Jacob," Says the LORD. **9** "For surely I will command, And will sift the house of Israel among all nations, As *grain* is sifted in a sieve; Yet not the smallest grain shall fall to the ground. **10** All the sinners of My people shall die by the sword, Who say, 'The calamity shall not overtake nor confront us.'

AMUSEMENTS AND PLEASURES, WORLDLY
Belong to the works of the flesh.

Gal 5:19 Now the works of the flesh are evident, which are: adultery, fornication, uncleanness, lewdness,

Gal 5:21 envy, murders, drunkenness, revelries, and the like; of which I tell you beforehand, just as I also told *you* in time past, that those who practice such things will not inherit the kingdom of God.

Are transitory.

Job 21:12–13 They sing to the tambourine and harp, And rejoice to the sound of the flute. **13** They spend their days in wealth, And in a moment go down to the grave.

Heb 11:25 choosing rather to suffer affliction with the people of God than to enjoy the passing pleasures of sin,

Are all vanity.

Eccl 2:11 Then I looked on all the works that my hands had done And on the labor in which I had toiled; And indeed all *was* vanity and grasping for the wind. *There was* no profit under the sun.

Choke the word of God in the heart.

Luke 8:14 Now the ones *that* fell among thorns are those who, when they have heard, go out and are choked with cares, riches, and pleasures of life, and bring no fruit to maturity.

Formed a part of idolatrous worship.

Ex 32:4 And he received *the gold* from their hand, and he fashioned it with an engraving tool, and made a molded calf. Then they said, "This *is* your god, O Israel, that brought you out of the land of Egypt!"

Ex 32:6 Then they rose early on the next day, offered burnt offerings, and brought peace offerings; and the people sat down to eat and drink, and rose up to play.

Ex 32:19 So it was, as soon as he came near the camp, that he saw the calf *and* the dancing. So Moses' anger became hot, and he cast the tablets out of his hands and broke them at the foot of the mountain.

Judg 16:23–25 Now the lords of the Philistines gathered together to offer a great sacrifice to Dagon their god, and to rejoice. And they said: "Our god has delivered into our hands Samson our enemy!" 24 When the people saw him, they praised their god; for they said: "Our god has delivered into our hands our enemy, The destroyer of our land, And the one who multiplied our dead." 25 So it happened, when their hearts were merry, that they said, "Call for Samson, that he may perform for us." So they called for Samson from the prison, and he performed for them. And they stationed him between the pillars.

1 Cor 10:7 And do not become idolaters as *were* some of them. As it is written, *"The people sat down to eat and drink, and rose up to play."*

Lead to

Rejection of God.

Job 21:14–15 Yet they say to God, 'Depart from us, For we do not desire the knowledge of Your ways. 15 Who *is* the Almighty, that we should serve Him? And what profit do we have if we pray to Him?'

Poverty.

Prov 21:17 He who loves pleasure *will be* a poor man; He who loves wine and oil will not be rich.

Disregard of the judgments and works of God.

Is 5:12 The harp and the strings, The tambourine and flute, And wine are in their feasts; But they do not regard the work of the LORD, Nor consider the operation of His hands.

Amos 6:1–6 Woe to you *who are* at ease in Zion, And trust in Mount Samaria, Notable persons in the chief nation, To whom the house of Israel comes! 2 Go over to Calneh and see; And from there go to Hamath the great; Then go down to Gath of the Philistines. *Are you* better than these kingdoms? Or is their territory greater than your territory? 3 *Woe to* you who put far off the day of doom, Who cause the seat of violence to come near; 4 Who lie on beds of ivory, Stretch out on your couches, Eat lambs from the flock And calves from the midst of the stall; 5 Who sing

idly to the sound of stringed instruments, *And* invent for yourselves musical instruments like David; 6 Who drink wine from bowls, And anoint yourselves with the best ointments, But are not grieved for the affliction of Joseph.

Terminate in sorrow.

Prov 14:13 Even in laughter the heart may sorrow, And the end of mirth *may be* grief.

Are likely to lead to greater evil.

Matt 14:6–8 But when Herod's birthday was celebrated, the daughter of Herodias danced before them and pleased Herod. 7 Therefore he promised with an oath to give her whatever she might ask. 8 So she, having been prompted by her mother, said, "Give me John the Baptist's head here on a platter."

The wicked seek for happiness in.

Eccl 2:1 I said in my heart, "Come now, I will test you with mirth; therefore enjoy pleasure"; but surely, this also *was* vanity.

Eccl 2:8 I also gathered for myself silver and gold and the special treasures of kings and of the provinces. I acquired male and female singers, the delights of the sons of men, *and* musical instruments of all kinds.

Indulgence in,

A proof of folly.

Eccl 7:4 The heart of the wise *is* in the house of mourning, But the heart of fools *is* in the house of mirth.

A characteristic of the wicked.

Is 47:8 "Therefore hear this now, *you who are* given to pleasures, Who dwell securely, Who say in your heart, 'I *am*, and *there is* no one else besides me; I shall not sit *as* a widow, Nor shall I know the loss of children';

Eph 4:17 This I say, therefore, and testify in the Lord, that you should no longer walk as the rest of the Gentiles walk, in the futility of their mind,

Eph 4:19 who, being past feeling, have given themselves over to lewdness, to work all uncleanness with greediness.

2 Tim 3:4 traitors, headstrong, haughty, lovers of pleasure rather than lovers of God,

Titus 3:3 For we ourselves were also once foolish, disobedient, deceived, serving various lusts and pleasures, living in malice and envy, hateful and hating one another.

1 Pet 4:3 For we *have spent* enough of our past lifetime in doing the will of the Gentiles—when we walked in lewdness, lusts, drunkenness, revelries, drinking parties, and abominable idolatries.

A proof of spiritual death.

1 Tim 5:6 But she who lives in pleasure is dead while she lives.

An abuse of riches.

James 5:1 Come now, *you* rich, weep and howl for your miseries that are coming upon *you!*

James 5:5 You have lived on the earth in pleasure and luxury; you have fattened your hearts as in a day of slaughter.

Wisdom of abstaining from.

Eccl 7:2–3 Better to go to the house of mourning Than

to go to the house of feasting, For that *is* the end of all men; And the living will take *it* to heart. 3 Sorrow *is* better than laughter, For by a sad countenance the heart is made better.

Shunned by the saints.

1 Pet 4:3 For we *have spent* enough of our past lifetime in doing the will of the Gentiles—when we walked in lewdness, lusts, drunkenness, revelries, drinking parties, and abominable idolatries.

Abstinence from, seems strange to the wicked.

1 Pet 4:4 In regard to these, they think it strange that you do not run with *them* in the same flood of dissipation, speaking evil of *you*.

Denounced by God.

Is 5:11–12 Woe to those who rise early in the morning, *That* they may follow intoxicating drink; Who continue until night, *till* wine inflames them! 12 The harp and the strings, The tambourine and flute, And wine are in their feasts; But they do not regard the work of the LORD, Nor consider the operation of His hands.

Punishment of.

Eccl 11:9 Rejoice, O young man, in your youth, And let your heart cheer you in the days of your youth; Walk in the ways of your heart, And in the sight of your eyes; But know that for all these God will bring you into judgment.

2 Pet 2:13 *and* will receive the wages of unrighteousness, *as* those who count it pleasure to carouse in the daytime. *They are* spots and blemishes, carousing in their own deceptions while they feast with you,

Renunciation of, exemplified by Moses.

Heb 11:25 choosing rather to suffer affliction with the people of God than to enjoy the passing pleasures of sin,

ANAKIM, THE

Descent of.

Num 13:22 And they went up through the South and came to Hebron; Ahiman, Sheshai, and Talmai, the descendants of Anak, *were* there. (Now Hebron was built seven years before Zoan in Egypt.)

Josh 15:13 Now to Caleb the son of Jephunneh he gave a share among the children of Judah, according to the commandment of the LORD to Joshua, *namely*, Kirjath Arba, which *is* Hebron (*Arba was* the father of Anak).

Were called

The descendants of Anak.

Num 13:33 There we saw the giants (the descendants of Anak came from the giants); and we were like grasshoppers in our own sight, and so we were in their sight."

The sons of the Anakim.

Deut 1:28 Where can we go up? Our brethren have discouraged our hearts, saying, "The people *are* greater and taller than we; the cities *are* great and fortified up to heaven; moreover we have seen the sons of the Anakim there." '

The descendants of the Anakim.

Deut 9:2 a people great and tall, the descendants of the Anakim, whom you know, and *of whom* you heard *it*

said, 'Who can stand before the descendants of Anak?'

Divided into three tribes.

Josh 15:14 Caleb drove out the three sons of Anak from there: Sheshai, Ahiman, and Talmai, the children of Anak.

Inhabited the mountains of Judah.

Josh 11:21 And at that time Joshua came and cut off the Anakim from the mountains: from Hebron, from Debir, from Anab, from all the mountains of Judah, and from all the mountains of Israel; Joshua utterly destroyed them with their cities.

Hebron, chief city of.

Josh 14:15 And the name of Hebron formerly was Kirjath Arba (*Arba was* the greatest man among the Anakim). Then the land had rest from war.

Josh 21:11 And they gave them Kirjath Arba (*Arba was* the father of Anak), which *is* Hebron, in the mountains of Judah, with the common-land surrounding it.

Of gigantic strength and stature.

Deut 2:10–11 (The Emim had dwelt there in times past, a people as great and numerous and tall as the Anakim. 11 They were also regarded as giants, like the Anakim, but the Moabites call them Emim.

Deut 2:21 a people as great and numerous and tall as the Anakim. But the LORD destroyed them before them, and they dispossessed them and dwelt in their place,

Israel terrified by.

Num 13:33 There we saw the giants (the descendants of Anak came from the giants); and we were like grasshoppers in our own sight, and so we were in their sight."

Num 14:1 So all the congregation lifted up their voices and cried, and the people wept that night.

Hebron a possession of, given to Caleb for his faithfulness.

Josh 14:6–14 Then the children of Judah came to Joshua in Gilgal. And Caleb the son of Jephunneh the Kenizzite said to him: "You know the word which the LORD said to Moses the man of God concerning you and me in Kadesh Barnea. 7 I *was* forty years old when Moses the servant of the LORD sent me from Kadesh Barnea to spy out the land, and I brought back word to him as *it was* in my heart. 8 Nevertheless my brethren who went up with me made the heart of the people melt, but I wholly followed the LORD my God. 9 So Moses swore on that day, saying, 'Surely the land where your foot has trodden shall be your inheritance and your children's forever, because you have wholly followed the LORD my God.' 10 And now, behold, the LORD has kept me alive, as He said, these forty-five years, ever since the LORD spoke this word to Moses while Israel wandered in the wilderness; and now, here I am this day, eighty-five years old. 11 As yet I *am* as strong this day as on the day that Moses sent me; just as my strength *was* then, so now *is* my strength for war, both for going out and for coming in. 12 Now therefore, give me this mountain of which the LORD spoke in that day; for you heard in that day how the Anakim *were* there, and *that* the cities *were* great *and* fortified. It may be that the LORD *will be* with me, and I shall be able to drive them out as the LORD said." 13 And Joshua blessed him, and gave Hebron to Caleb the son of Jephunneh as an inheritance. 14 Hebron therefore became the inheritance of Caleb the son of Jephunneh the Kenizzite to this day, because he wholly followed the LORD God of Israel.

Driven from Hebron by Caleb.

Josh 15:13–14 Now to Caleb the son of Jephunneh he gave a share among the children of Judah, according to the commandment of the LORD to Joshua, *namely,* Kirjath Arba, which *is* Hebron (*Arba was* the father of Anak). 14 Caleb drove out the three sons of Anak from there: Sheshai, Ahiman, and Talmai, the children of Anak.

Driven from Kirjath Sepher or Debir by Othniel.

Josh 15:15–17 Then he went up from there to the inhabitants of Debir (formerly the name of Debir *was* Kirjath Sepher). 16 And Caleb said, "He who attacks Kirjath Sepher and takes it, to him I will give Achsah my daughter as wife." 17 So Othniel the son of Kenaz, the brother of Caleb, took it; and he gave him Achsah his daughter as wife.

Judg 1:12–13 Then Caleb said, "Whoever attacks Kirjath Sepher and takes it, to him I will give my daughter Achsah as wife." 13 And Othniel the son of Kenaz, Caleb's younger brother, took it; so he gave him his daughter Achsah as wife.

Almost annihilated.

Josh 11:21–22 And at that time Joshua came and cut off the Anakim from the mountains: from Hebron, from Debir, from Anab, from all the mountains of Judah, and from all the mountains of Israel; Joshua utterly destroyed them with their cities. 22 None of the Anakim were left in the land of the children of Israel; they remained only in Gaza, in Gath, and in Ashdod.

ANDREW

Brother of Peter.

Matt 4:18 And Jesus, walking by the Sea of Galilee, saw two brothers, Simon called Peter, and Andrew his brother, casting a net into the sea; for they were fishermen.

Mark 1:16 And as He walked by the Sea of Galilee, He saw Simon and Andrew his brother casting a net into the sea; for they were fishermen.

Mark 1:29 Now as soon as they had come out of the synagogue, they entered the house of Simon and Andrew, with James and John.

An apostle.

Matt 10:2 Now the names of the twelve apostles are these: first, Simon, who is called Peter, and Andrew his brother; James the *son* of Zebedee, and John his brother;

Mark 13:3 Now as He sat on the Mount of Olives opposite the temple, Peter, James, John, and Andrew asked Him privately,

From Bethsaida.

John 1:44 Now Philip was from Bethsaida, the city of Andrew and Peter.

ANGEL OF GOD, THE

Named

Angel of God.

Gen 21:17 And God heard the voice of the lad. Then the angel of God called to Hagar out of heaven, and said to her, "What ails you, Hagar? Fear not, for God has heard the voice of the lad where he *is.*

Angel of the Lord.

Gen 22:11 But the Angel of the LORD called to him from heaven and said, "Abraham, Abraham!" So he said, "Here I am."

Captain of the army of the Lord.

Josh 5:14 So He said, "No, but *as* Commander of the army of the LORD I have now come." And Joshua fell on his face to the earth and worshiped, and said to Him, "What does my Lord say to His servant?"

Appeared to

Hagar.

Gen 16:7–8 Now the Angel of the LORD found her by a spring of water in the wilderness, by the spring on the way to Shur. 8 And He said, "Hagar, Sarai's maid, where have you come from, and where are you going?" She said, "I am fleeing from the presence of my mistress Sarai."

Gen 21:17 And God heard the voice of the lad. Then the angel of God called to Hagar out of heaven, and said to her, "What ails you, Hagar? Fear not, for God has heard the voice of the lad where he *is.*

Abraham.

Gen 22:11 But the Angel of the LORD called to him from heaven and said, "Abraham, Abraham!" So he said, "Here I am."

Eliezer.

Gen 24:7 The LORD God of heaven, who took me from my father's house and from the land of my family, and who spoke to me and swore to me, saying, 'To your descendants I give this land,' He will send His angel before you, and you shall take a wife for my son from there.

Gen 24:40 But he said to me, 'The LORD, before whom I walk, will send His angel with you and prosper your way; and you shall take a wife for my son from my family and from my father's house.

Jacob.

Gen 31:11–13 Then the Angel of God spoke to me in a dream, saying, 'Jacob.' And I said, 'Here I am.' 12 And He said, 'Lift your eyes now and see, all the rams which leap on the flocks *are* streaked, speckled, and gray-spotted; for I have seen all that Laban is doing to you. 13 I *am* the God of Bethel, where you anointed the pillar *and* where you made a vow to Me. Now arise, get out of this land, and return to the land of your family.' "

Gen 32:24–30 Then Jacob was left alone; and a Man wrestled with him until the breaking of day. 25 Now when He saw that He did not prevail against him, He touched the socket of his hip; and the socket of Jacob's hip was out of joint as He wrestled with him. 26 And He said, "Let Me go, for the day breaks." But he said, "I will not let You go unless You bless me!" 27 So He said to him, "What *is* your name?" He said,

"Jacob." **28** And He said, "Your name shall no longer be called Jacob, but Israel; for you have struggled with God and with men, and have prevailed." **29** Then Jacob asked, saying, "Tell *me* Your name, I pray." And He said, "Why *is* it *that* you ask about My name?" And He blessed him there. **30** So Jacob called the name of the place Peniel: "For I have seen God face to face, and my life is preserved."

Moses.

Ex 3:2 And the Angel of the LORD appeared to him in a flame of fire from the midst of a bush. So he looked, and behold, the bush was burning with fire, but the bush *was* not consumed.

Nation of Israel.

Ex 13:21–22 And the LORD went before them by day in a pillar of cloud to lead the way, and by night in a pillar of fire to give them light, so as to go by day and night. **22** He did not take away the pillar of cloud by day or the pillar of fire by night *from* before the people.

Ex 14:19 And the Angel of God, who went before the camp of Israel, moved and went behind them; and the pillar of cloud went from before them and stood behind them.

Balaam.

Num 22:22–35 Then God's anger was aroused because he went, and the Angel of the LORD took His stand in the way as an adversary against him. And he was riding on his donkey, and his two servants *were* with him. **23** Now the donkey saw the Angel of the LORD standing in the way with His drawn sword in His hand, and the donkey turned aside out of the way and went into the field. So Balaam struck the donkey to turn her back onto the road. **24** Then the Angel of the LORD stood in a narrow path between the vineyards, *with* a wall on this side and a wall on that side. **25** And when the donkey saw the Angel of the LORD, she pushed herself against the wall and crushed Balaam's foot against the wall; so he struck her again. **26** Then the Angel of the LORD went further, and stood in a narrow place where there *was* no way to turn either to the right hand or to the left. **27** And when the donkey saw the Angel of the LORD, she lay down under Balaam; so Balaam's anger was aroused, and he struck the donkey with his staff. **28** Then the LORD opened the mouth of the donkey, and she said to Balaam, "What have I done to you, that you have struck me these three times?" **29** And Balaam said to the donkey, "Because you have abused me. I wish there were a sword in my hand, for now I would kill you!" **30** So the donkey said to Balaam, "*Am* I not your donkey on which you have ridden, ever since *I became* yours, to this day? Was I ever disposed to do this to you?" And he said, "No." **31** Then the LORD opened Balaam's eyes, and he saw the Angel of the LORD standing in the way with His drawn sword in His hand; and he bowed his head and fell flat on his face. **32** And the Angel of the LORD said to him, "Why have you struck your donkey these three times? Behold, I have come out to stand against you, because *your* way is perverse before Me. **33** The donkey saw Me and turned aside from Me these three times. If she had not turned aside from Me, surely I would also have killed you by now, and

let her live." **34** And Balaam said to the Angel of the LORD, "I have sinned, for I did not know You stood in the way against me. Now therefore, if it displeases You, I will turn back." **35** Then the Angel of the LORD said to Balaam, "Go with the men, but only the word that I speak to you, that you shall speak." So Balaam went with the princes of Balak.

Joshua.

Judg 2:1 Then the Angel of the LORD came up from Gilgal to Bochim, and said: "I led you up from Egypt and brought you to the land of which I swore to your fathers; and I said, 'I will never break My covenant with you.

David.

1 Chr 21:16–18 Then David lifted his eyes and saw the angel of the LORD standing between earth and heaven, having in his hand a drawn sword stretched out over Jerusalem. So David and the elders, clothed in sackcloth, fell on their faces. **17** And David said to God, "Was it not I who commanded the people to be numbered? I am the one who has sinned and done evil indeed; but these sheep, what have they done? Let Your hand, I pray, O LORD my God, be against me and my father's house, but not against Your people that they should be plagued." **18** Therefore, the angel of the LORD commanded Gad to say to David that David should go and erect an altar to the LORD on the threshing floor of Ornan the Jebusite.

ANGELS

Created by God and Christ.

Neh 9:6 You alone *are* the LORD; You have made heaven, The heaven of heavens, with all their host, The earth and everything on it, The seas and all that is in them, And You preserve them all. The host of heaven worships You.

Col 1:16 For by Him all things were created that are in heaven and that are on earth, visible and invisible, whether thrones or dominions or principalities or powers. All things were created through Him and for Him.

Worship God and Christ.

Neh 9:6 You alone *are* the LORD; You have made heaven, The heaven of heavens, with all their host, The earth and everything on it, The seas and all that is in them, And You preserve them all. The host of heaven worships You.

Phil 2:9–11 Therefore God also has highly exalted Him and given Him the name which is above every name, **10** that at the name of Jesus every knee should bow, of those in heaven, and of those on earth, and of those under the earth, **11** and *that* every tongue should confess that Jesus Christ *is* Lord, to the glory of God the Father.

Heb 1:6 But when He again brings the firstborn into the world, He says: *"Let all the angels of God worship Him."*

Are ministering spirits.

1 Kin 19:5 Then as he lay and slept under a broom tree, suddenly an angel touched him, and said to him, "Arise *and* eat."

Ps 104:4 Who makes His angels spirits, His ministers a flame of fire.

Luke 16:22 So it was that the beggar died, and was carried by the angels to Abraham's bosom. The rich man also died and was buried.

Acts 12:7–11 Now behold, an angel of the Lord stood by *him,* and a light shone in the prison; and he struck Peter on the side and raised him up, saying, "Arise quickly!" And his chains fell off *his* hands. **8** Then the angel said to him, "Gird yourself and tie on your sandals"; and so he did. And he said to him, "Put on your garment and follow me." **9** So he went out and followed him, and did not know that what was done by the angel was real, but thought he was seeing a vision. **10** When they were past the first and the second guard posts, they came to the iron gate that leads to the city, which opened to them of its own accord; and they went out and went down one street, and immediately the angel departed from him. **11** And when Peter had come to himself, he said, "Now I know for certain that the Lord has sent His angel, and has delivered me from the hand of Herod and *from* all the expectation of the Jewish people."

Acts 27:23 For there stood by me this night an angel of the God to whom I belong and whom I serve,

Heb 1:7 And of the angels He says: *"Who makes His angels spirits And His ministers a flame of fire."*

Heb 1:14 Are they not all ministering spirits sent forth to minister for those who will inherit salvation?

Communicate the will of God and Christ.

Dan 8:16–17 And I heard a man's voice between *the banks of* the Ulai, who called, and said, "Gabriel, make this *man* understand the vision." **17** So he came near where I stood, and when he came I was afraid and fell on my face; but he said to me, "Understand, son of man, that the vision *refers* to the time of the end."

Dan 9:21–23 yes, while I *was* speaking in prayer, the man Gabriel, whom I had seen in the vision at the beginning, being caused to fly swiftly, reached me about the time of the evening offering. **22** And he informed *me,* and talked with me, and said, "O Daniel, I have now come forth to give you skill to understand. **23** At the beginning of your supplications the command went out, and I have come to tell *you,* for you *are* greatly beloved; therefore consider the matter, and understand the vision:

Dan 10:11 And he said to me, "O Daniel, man greatly beloved, understand the words that I speak to you, and stand upright, for I have now been sent to you." While he was speaking this word to me, I stood trembling.

Dan 12:6–7 And *one* said to the man clothed in linen, who *was* above the waters of the river, "How long shall the fulfillment of these wonders *be?*" **7** Then I heard the man clothed in linen, who *was* above the waters of the river, when he held up his right hand and his left hand to heaven, and swore by Him who lives forever, that *it shall be* for a time, times, and half *a time;* and when the power of the holy people has been completely shattered, all these *things* shall be finished.

Matt 2:13 Now when they had departed, behold, an angel of the Lord appeared to Joseph in a dream, saying, "Arise, take the young Child and His mother, flee to Egypt, and stay there until I bring you word; for Herod will seek the young Child to destroy Him."

Matt 2:20 saying, "Arise, take the young Child and His mother, and go to the land of Israel, for those who sought the young Child's life are dead."

Luke 1:19 And the angel answered and said to him, "I am Gabriel, who stands in the presence of God, and was sent to speak to you and bring you these glad tidings.

Luke 1:28 And having come in, the angel said to her, "Rejoice, highly favored *one,* the Lord *is* with you; blessed *are* you among women!"

Acts 5:20 "Go, stand in the temple and speak to the people all the words of this life."

Acts 8:26 Now an angel of the Lord spoke to Philip, saying, "Arise and go toward the south along the road which goes down from Jerusalem to Gaza." This is desert.

Acts 10:5 Now send men to Joppa, and send for Simon whose surname is Peter.

Acts 27:23 For there stood by me this night an angel of the God to whom I belong and whom I serve,

Rev 1:1 The Revelation of Jesus Christ, which God gave Him to show His servants—things which must shortly take place. And He sent and signified *it* by His angel to His servant John,

Obey the will of God.

Ps 103:20 Bless the LORD, you His angels, Who excel in strength, who do His word, Heeding the voice of His word.

Matt 6:10 Your kingdom come. Your will be done On earth as *it is* in heaven.

Execute the purposes of God.

Num 22:22 Then God's anger was aroused because he went, and the Angel of the LORD took His stand in the way as an adversary against him. And he was riding on his donkey, and his two servants *were* with him.

Ps 103:21 Bless the LORD, all *you* His hosts, *You* ministers of His, who do His pleasure.

Matt 13:39–42 The enemy who sowed them is the devil, the harvest is the end of the age, and the reapers are the angels. **40** Therefore as the tares are gathered and burned in the fire, so it will be at the end of this age. **41** The Son of Man will send out His angels, and they will gather out of His kingdom all things that offend, and those who practice lawlessness, **42** and will cast them into the furnace of fire. There will be wailing and gnashing of teeth.

Matt 28:2 And behold, there was a great earthquake; for an angel of the Lord descended from heaven, and came and rolled back the stone from the door, and sat on it.

John 5:4 For an angel went down at a certain time into the pool and stirred up the water; then whoever stepped in first, after the stirring of the water, was made well of whatever disease he had.

Rev 5:2 Then I saw a strong angel proclaiming with a loud voice, "Who is worthy to open the scroll and to loose its seals?"

Execute the judgments of God.

2 Sam 24:16 And when the angel stretched out His hand over Jerusalem to destroy it, the LORD relented from the destruction, and said to the angel who was destroying the people, "It is enough; now restrain your hand." And the angel of the LORD was by the threshing floor of Araunah the Jebusite.

2 Kin 19:35 And it came to pass on a certain night that the angel of the LORD went out, and killed in the camp of the Assyrians one hundred and eighty-five thousand; and when *people* arose early in the morning, there were the corpses—all dead.

Ps 35:5–6 Let them be like chaff before the wind, And let the angel of the LORD chase *them*. 6 Let their way be dark and slippery, And let the angel of the LORD pursue them.

Acts 12:23 Then immediately an angel of the Lord struck him, because he did not give glory to God. And he was eaten by worms and died.

Rev 16:1 Then I heard a loud voice from the temple saying to the seven angels, "Go and pour out the bowls of the wrath of God on the earth."

Celebrate the praises of God.

Job 38:7 When the morning stars sang together, And all the sons of God shouted for joy?

Ps 148:2 Praise Him, all His angels; Praise Him, all His hosts!

Is 6:3 And one cried to another and said: "Holy, holy, holy *is* the LORD of hosts; The whole earth *is* full of His glory!"

Luke 2:13–14 And suddenly there was with the angel a multitude of the heavenly host praising God and saying: 14 "Glory to God in the highest, And on earth peace, goodwill toward men!"

Rev 5:11–12 Then I looked, and I heard the voice of many angels around the throne, the living creatures, and the elders; and the number of them was ten thousand times ten thousand, and thousands of thousands, 12 saying with a loud voice: "Worthy is the Lamb who was slain To receive power and riches and wisdom, And strength and honor and glory and blessing!"

Rev 7:11–12 All the angels stood around the throne and the elders and the four living creatures, and fell on their faces before the throne and worshiped God, 12 saying: "Amen! Blessing and glory and wisdom, Thanksgiving and honor and power and might, *Be* to our God forever and ever. Amen."

The law given by the ministration of.

Acts 7:53 who have received the law by the direction of angels and have not kept *it*."

Heb 2:2 For if the word spoken through angels proved steadfast, and every transgression and disobedience received a just reward,

Announced

The conception of Christ.

Matt 1:20–21 But while he thought about these things, behold, an angel of the Lord appeared to him in a dream, saying, "Joseph, son of David, do not be afraid to take to you Mary your wife, for that which is conceived in her is of the Holy Spirit. 21 And she will bring forth a Son, and you shall call His name JESUS, for He will save His people from their sins."

Luke 1:31 And behold, you will conceive in your womb and bring forth a Son, and shall call His name JESUS.

The birth of Christ.

Luke 2:10–12 Then the angel said to them, "Do not be afraid, for behold, I bring you good tidings of great joy which will be to all people. 11 For there is born to you this day in the city of David a Savior, who is Christ the Lord. 12 And this *will be* the sign to you: You will find a Babe wrapped in swaddling cloths, lying in a manger."

The resurrection of Christ.

Matt 28:5–7 But the angel answered and said to the women, "Do not be afraid, for I know that you seek Jesus who was crucified. 6 He is not here; for He is risen, as He said. Come, see the place where the Lord lay. 7 And go quickly and tell His disciples that He is risen from the dead, and indeed He is going before you into Galilee; there you will see Him. Behold, I have told you."

Luke 24:23 When they did not find His body, they came saying that they had also seen a vision of angels who said He was alive.

The ascension and second coming of Christ.

Acts 1:11 who also said, "Men of Galilee, why do you stand gazing up into heaven? This *same* Jesus, who was taken up from you into heaven, will so come in like manner as you saw Him go into heaven."

The conception of John the Baptist.

Luke 1:13 But the angel said to him, "Do not be afraid, Zacharias, for your prayer is heard; and your wife Elizabeth will bear you a son, and you shall call his name John.

Luke 1:36 Now indeed, Elizabeth your relative has also conceived a son in her old age; and this is now the sixth month for her who was called barren.

Minister to Christ.

Matt 4:11 Then the devil left Him, and behold, angels came and ministered to Him.

Luke 22:43 Then an angel appeared to Him from heaven, strengthening Him.

John 1:51 And He said to him, "Most assuredly, I say to you, hereafter you shall see heaven open, and the angels of God ascending and descending upon the Son of Man."

Are subject to Christ.

Eph 1:21 far above all principality and power and might and dominion, and every name that is named, not only in this age but also in that which is to come.

Col 1:16 For by Him all things were created that are in heaven and that are on earth, visible and invisible, whether thrones or dominions or principalities or powers. All things were created through Him and for Him.

Col 2:10 and you are complete in Him, who is the head of all principality and power.

1 Pet 3:22 who has gone into heaven and is at the right hand of God, angels and authorities and powers having been made subject to Him.

Shall execute the purposes of Christ.

Matt 13:41 The Son of Man will send out His angels, and they will gather out of His kingdom all things that offend, and those who practice lawlessness,

Matt 24:31 And He will send His angels with a great

sound of a trumpet, and they will gather together His elect from the four winds, from one end of heaven to the other.

Shall attend Christ at his second coming.

Matt 16:27 For the Son of Man will come in the glory of His Father with His angels, and then He will reward each according to his works.

Matt 25:31 "When the Son of Man comes in His glory, and all the holy angels with Him, then He will sit on the throne of His glory.

Mark 8:38 For whoever is ashamed of Me and My words in this adulterous and sinful generation, of him the Son of Man also will be ashamed when He comes in the glory of His Father with the holy angels."

2 Thess 1:7 and to *give* you who are troubled rest with us when the Lord Jesus is revealed from heaven with His mighty angels,

Know and delight in the gospel of Christ.

Eph 3:9–10 and to make all see what *is* the fellowship of the mystery, which from the beginning of the ages has been hidden in God who created all things through Jesus Christ; **10** to the intent that now the manifold wisdom of God might be made known by the church to the principalities and powers in the heavenly *places*,

1 Tim 3:16 And without controversy great is the mystery of godliness: God was manifested in the flesh, Justified in the Spirit, Seen by angels, Preached among the Gentiles, Believed on in the world, Received up in glory.

1 Pet 1:12 To them it was revealed that, not to themselves, but to us they were ministering the things which now have been reported to you through those who have preached the gospel to you by the Holy Spirit sent from heaven—things which angels desire to look into.

Ministration of, obtained by prayer.

Matt 26:53 Or do you think that I cannot now pray to My Father, and He will provide Me with more than twelve legions of angels?

Acts 12:5–7 Peter was therefore kept in prison, but constant prayer was offered to God for him by the church. **6** And when Herod was about to bring him out, that night Peter was sleeping, bound with two chains between two soldiers; and the guards before the door were keeping the prison. **7** Now behold, an angel of the Lord stood by *him*, and a light shone in the prison; and he struck Peter on the side and raised him up, saying, "Arise quickly!" And his chains fell off *his* hands.

Rejoice over every repentant sinner.

Luke 15:7 I say to you that likewise there will be more joy in heaven over one sinner who repents than over ninety-nine just persons who need no repentance.

Luke 15:10 Likewise, I say to you, there is joy in the presence of the angels of God over one sinner who repents."

Have charge over the children of God.

Ps 34:7 The angel of the Lord encamps all around those who fear Him, And delivers them.

Ps 91:11–12 For He shall give His angels charge over you, To keep you in all your ways. **12** In *their* hands they shall bear you up, Lest you dash your foot against a stone.

Dan 6:22 My God sent His angel and shut the lions' mouths, so that they have not hurt me, because I was found innocent before Him; and also, O king, I have done no wrong before you."

Matt 18:10 "Take heed that you do not despise one of these little ones, for I say to you that in heaven their angels always see the face of My Father who is in heaven.

Are of different orders.

Is 6:2 Above it stood seraphim; each one had six wings: with two he covered his face, with two he covered his feet, and with two he flew.

Rom 8:38 For I am persuaded that neither death nor life, nor angels nor principalities nor powers, nor things present nor things to come,

1 Cor 15:24 Then *comes* the end, when He delivers the kingdom to God the Father, when He puts an end to all rule and all authority and power.

Col 1:16 For by Him all things were created that are in heaven and that are on earth, visible and invisible, whether thrones or dominions or principalities or powers. All things were created through Him and for Him.

1 Thess 4:16 For the Lord Himself will descend from heaven with a shout, with the voice of an archangel, and with the trumpet of God. And the dead in Christ will rise first.

1 Pet 3:22 who has gone into heaven and is at the right hand of God, angels and authorities and powers having been made subject to Him.

Jude 1:9 Yet Michael the archangel, in contending with the devil, when he disputed about the body of Moses, dared not bring against him a reviling accusation, but said, "The Lord rebuke you!"

Rev 12:7 And war broke out in heaven: Michael and his angels fought with the dragon; and the dragon and his angels fought,

Are not to be worshiped.

Col 2:18 Let no one cheat you of your reward, taking delight in *false* humility and worship of angels, intruding into those things which he has not seen, vainly puffed up by his fleshly mind,

Rev 19:10 And I fell at his feet to worship him. But he said to me, "See *that you do* not *do that!* I am your fellow servant, and of your brethren who have the testimony of Jesus. Worship God! For the testimony of Jesus is the spirit of prophecy."

Rev 22:9 Then he said to me, "See *that you do* not *do that.* For I am your fellow servant, and of your brethren the prophets, and of those who keep the words of this book. Worship God."

Are examples of meekness.

2 Pet 2:11 whereas angels, who are greater in power and might, do not bring a reviling accusation against them before the Lord.

Jude 1:9 Yet Michael the archangel, in contending with the devil, when he disputed about the body of Moses, dared not bring against him a reviling accusation, but said, "The Lord rebuke you!"

Are wise.

2 Sam 14:20 To bring about this change of affairs your servant Joab has done this thing; but my lord *is* wise, according to the wisdom of the angel of God, to know everything that *is* in the earth."

Are mighty.

Ps 103:20 Bless the LORD, you His angels, Who excel in strength, who do His word, Heeding the voice of His word.

Are holy.

Matt 25:31 "When the Son of Man comes in His glory, and all the holy angels with Him, then He will sit on the throne of His glory.

Are innumerable.

Job 25:3 Is there any number to His armies? Upon whom does His light not rise?

Heb 12:22 But you have come to Mount Zion and to the city of the living God, the heavenly Jerusalem, to an innumerable company of angels,

Some are elect.

1 Tim 5:21 I charge *you* before God and the Lord Jesus Christ and the elect angels that you observe these things without prejudice, doing nothing with partiality.

ANGER

Forbidden, if unjust or uncontrolled.

Eccl 7:9 Do not hasten in your spirit to be angry, For anger rests in the bosom of fools.

Matt 5:22 But I say to you that whoever is angry with his brother without a cause shall be in danger of the judgment. And whoever says to his brother, 'Raca!' shall be in danger of the council. But whoever says, 'You fool!' shall be in danger of hell fire.

Rom 12:19 Beloved, do not avenge yourselves, but *rather* give place to wrath; for it is written, *"Vengeance is Mine, I will repay,"* says the Lord.

A work of the flesh.

Gal 5:20 idolatry, sorcery, hatred, contentions, jealousies, outbursts of wrath, selfish ambitions, dissensions, heresies,

A characteristic of fools.

Prov 12:16 A fool's wrath is known at once, But a prudent *man* covers shame.

Prov 14:29 He who *is* slow to wrath has great understanding, But he who *is* impulsive exalts folly.

Prov 27:3 A stone *is* heavy and sand *is* weighty, But a fool's wrath *is* heavier than both of them.

Eccl 7:9 Do not hasten in your spirit to be angry, For anger rests in the bosom of fools.

Connected with

Pride.

Prov 21:24 A proud *and* haughty *man*—"Scoffer" *is* his name; He acts with arrogant pride.

Cruelty.

Gen 49:7 Cursed *be* their anger, for *it is* fierce; And their wrath, for it is cruel! I will divide them in Jacob And scatter them in Israel.

Prov 27:3–4 A stone *is* heavy and sand *is* weighty, But a fool's wrath *is* heavier than both of them. 4 Wrath *is*

cruel and anger a torrent, But who *is* able to stand before jealousy?

Clamor and evil speaking.

Eph 4:31 Let all bitterness, wrath, anger, clamor, and evil speaking be put away from you, with all malice.

Malice and blasphemy.

Col 3:8 But now you yourselves are to put off all these: anger, wrath, malice, blasphemy, filthy language out of your mouth.

Strife and contention.

Prov 21:19 Better to dwell in the wilderness, Than with a contentious and angry woman.

Prov 29:22 An angry man stirs up strife, And a furious man abounds in transgression.

Prov 30:33 For *as* the churning of milk produces butter, And wringing the nose produces blood, So the forcing of wrath produces strife.

Brings its own punishment.

Job 5:2 For wrath kills a foolish man, And envy slays a simple one.

Prov 19:19 *A man of* great wrath will suffer punishment; For if you rescue *him*, you will have to do it again.

Prov 25:28 Whoever *has* no rule over his own spirit *Is* like a city broken down, without walls.

Grievous words stir up.

Judg 12:4 Now Jephthah gathered together all the men of Gilead and fought against Ephraim. And the men of Gilead defeated Ephraim, because they said, "You Gileadites *are* fugitives of Ephraim among the Ephraimites *and* among the Manassites."

2 Sam 19:43 And the men of Israel answered the men of Judah, and said, "We have ten shares in the king; therefore we also have more *right* to David than you. Why then do you despise us—were we not the first to advise bringing back our king?" Yet the words of the men of Judah were fiercer than the words of the men of Israel.

Prov 15:1 A soft answer turns away wrath, But a harsh word stirs up anger.

Should not betray us into sin.

Ps 37:8 Cease from anger, and forsake wrath; Do not fret—*it* only *causes* harm.

Eph 4:26 *"Be angry, and do not sin"*: do not let the sun go down on your wrath,

In prayer be free from.

1 Tim 2:8 I desire therefore that the men pray everywhere, lifting up holy hands, without wrath and doubting;

May be averted by wisdom.

Prov 29:8 Scoffers set a city aflame, But wise *men* turn away wrath.

Meekness pacifies.

Prov 15:1 A soft answer turns away wrath, But a harsh word stirs up anger.

Eccl 10:4 If the spirit of the ruler rises against you, Do not leave your post; For conciliation pacifies great offenses.

Children should not be provoked to.

Eph 6:4 And you, fathers, do not provoke your children

to wrath, but bring them up in the training and admonition of the Lord.

Col 3:21 Fathers, do not provoke your children, lest they become discouraged.

Be slow to.

Prov 15:18 A wrathful man stirs up strife, But *he who is* slow to anger allays contention.

Prov 16:32 *He who is* slow to anger *is* better than the mighty, And he who rules his spirit than he who takes a city.

Prov 19:11 The discretion of a man makes him slow to anger, And his glory *is* to overlook a transgression.

Titus 1:7 For a bishop must be blameless, as a steward of God, not self-willed, not quick-tempered, not given to wine, not violent, not greedy for money,

James 1:19 So then, my beloved brethren, let every man be swift to hear, slow to speak, slow to wrath;

Avoid those given to.

Gen 49:6 Let not my soul enter their council; Let not my honor be united to their assembly; For in their anger they slew a man, And in their self-will they hamstrung an ox.

Prov 22:24 Make no friendship with an angry man, And with a furious man do not go,

Justifiable—Illustrated by

Our Lord.

Mark 3:5 And when He had looked around at them with anger, being grieved by the hardness of their hearts, He said to the man, "Stretch out your hand." And he stretched *it* out, and his hand was restored as whole as the other.

Jacob.

Gen 31:36 Then Jacob was angry and rebuked Laban, and Jacob answered and said to Laban: "What *is* my trespass? What *is* my sin, that you have so hotly pursued me?

Moses.

Ex 11:8 And all these your servants shall come down to me and bow down to me, saying, 'Get out, and all the people who follow you!' After that I will go out." Then he went out from Pharaoh in great anger.

Ex 32:19 So it was, as soon as he came near the camp, that he saw the calf *and* the dancing. So Moses' anger became hot, and he cast the tablets out of his hands and broke them at the foot of the mountain.

Lev 10:16 Then Moses made careful inquiry about the goat of the sin offering, and there it was—burned up. And he was angry with Eleazar and Ithamar, the sons of Aaron *who were* left, saying,

Num 16:15 Then Moses was very angry, and said to the LORD, "Do not respect their offering. I have not taken one donkey from them, nor have I hurt one of them."

Nehemiah.

Neh 5:6 And I became very angry when I heard their outcry and these words.

Neh 13:17 Then I contended with the nobles of Judah, and said to them, "What evil thing *is* this that you do, by which you profane the Sabbath day?

Neh 13:25 So I contended with them and cursed them, struck some of them and pulled out their hair, and

made them swear by God, *saying,* "You shall not give your daughters as wives to their sons, nor take their daughters for your sons or yourselves.

Sinful—Illustrated by

Cain.

Gen 4:5–6 but He did not respect Cain and his offering. And Cain was very angry, and his countenance fell. **6** So the LORD said to Cain, "Why are you angry? And why has your countenance fallen?

Esau.

Gen 27:45 until your brother's anger turns away from you, and he forgets what you have done to him; then I will send and bring you from there. Why should I be bereaved also of you both in one day?"

Simeon and Levi.

Gen 49:5–7 "Simeon and Levi *are* brothers; Instruments of cruelty *are in* their dwelling place. **6** Let not my soul enter their council; Let not my honor be united to their assembly; For in their anger they slew a man, And in their self-will they hamstrung an ox. **7** Cursed *be* their anger, for *it is* fierce; And their wrath, for it is cruel! I will divide them in Jacob And scatter them in Israel.

Moses.

Num 20:10–11 And Moses and Aaron gathered the assembly together before the rock; and he said to them, "Hear now, you rebels! Must we bring water for you out of this rock?" **11** Then Moses lifted his hand and struck the rock twice with his rod; and water came out abundantly, and the congregation and their animals drank.

Balaam.

Num 22:27 And when the donkey saw the Angel of the LORD, she lay down under Balaam; so Balaam's anger was aroused, and he struck the donkey with his staff.

Saul.

1 Sam 20:30 Then Saul's anger was aroused against Jonathan, and he said to him, "You son of a perverse, rebellious *woman!* Do I not know that you have chosen the son of Jesse to your own shame and to the shame of your mother's nakedness?

Ahab.

1 Kin 21:4 So Ahab went into his house sullen and displeased because of the word which Naboth the Jezreelite had spoken to him; for he had said, "I will not give you the inheritance of my fathers." And he lay down on his bed, and turned away his face, and would eat no food.

Naaman.

2 Kin 5:11 But Naaman became furious, and went away and said, "Indeed, I said to myself, 'He will surely come out *to me,* and stand and call on the name of the LORD his God, and wave his hand over the place, and heal the leprosy.'

Asa.

2 Chr 16:10 Then Asa was angry with the seer, and put him in prison, for *he was* enraged at him because of this. And Asa oppressed *some* of the people at that time.

Uzziah.

2 Chr 26:19 Then Uzziah became furious; and he *had* a

censer in his hand to burn incense. And while he was angry with the priests, leprosy broke out on his forehead, before the priests in the house of the LORD, beside the incense altar.

Haman.

Esth 3:5 When Haman saw that Mordecai did not bow or pay him homage, Haman was filled with wrath.

Nebuchadnezzar.

Dan 3:13 Then Nebuchadnezzar, in rage and fury, gave the command to bring Shadrach, Meshach, and Abed-Nego. So they brought these men before the king.

Jonah.

Jon 4:4 Then the LORD said, "*Is it* right for you to be angry?"

Herod.

Matt 2:16 Then Herod, when he saw that he was deceived by the wise men, was exceedingly angry; and he sent forth and put to death all the male children who were in Bethlehem and in all its districts, from two years old and under, according to the time which he had determined from the wise men.

Jews.

Luke 4:28 So all those in the synagogue, when they heard these things, were filled with wrath,

High priest, etc.

Acts 5:17 Then the high priest rose up, and all those who *were* with him (which is the sect of the Sadducees), and they were filled with indignation,

Acts 7:54 When they heard these things they were cut to the heart, and they gnashed at him with *their* teeth.

ANNAS

Former high priest in Jesus' time.

John 18:13 And they led Him away to Annas first, for he was the father-in-law of Caiaphas who was high priest that year.

Controlled high priest's office.

Luke 3:2 while Annas and Caiaphas were high priests, the word of God came to John the son of Zacharias in the wilderness.

Acts 4:6 as well as Annas the high priest, Caiaphas, John, and Alexander, and as many as were of the family of the high priest, were gathered together at Jerusalem.

ANOINTING, FOR EVERYDAY PURPOSES

With oil.

Ps 92:10 But my horn You have exalted like a wild ox; I have been anointed with fresh oil.

John 11:2 It was *that* Mary who anointed the Lord with fragrant oil and wiped His feet with her hair, whose brother Lazarus was sick.

Was used for

Decorating the person.

Ruth 3:3 Therefore wash yourself and anoint yourself, put on your *best* garment and go down to the threshing floor; *but* do not make yourself known to the man until he has finished eating and drinking.

Refreshing the body.

2 Chr 28:15 Then the men who were designated by

name rose up and took the captives, and from the spoil they clothed all who were naked among them, dressed them and gave them sandals, gave them food and drink, and anointed them; and they let all the feeble ones ride on donkeys. So they brought them to their brethren at Jericho, the city of palm trees. Then they returned to Samaria.

Purifying the body.

Esth 2:12 Each young woman's turn came to go in to King Ahasuerus after she had completed twelve months' preparation, according to the regulations for the women, for thus were the days of their preparation apportioned: six months with oil of myrrh, and six months with perfumes and preparations for beautifying women.

Is 57:9 You went to the king with ointment, And increased your perfumes; You sent your messengers far off, And *even* descended to Sheol.

Curing the sick.

Mark 6:13 And they cast out many demons, and anointed with oil many who were sick, and healed *them.*

Healing wounds.

Is 1:6 From the sole of the foot even to the head, *There is* no soundness in it, *But* wounds and bruises and putrefying sores; They have not been closed or bound up, Or soothed with ointment.

Luke 10:34 So he went to *him* and bandaged his wounds, pouring on oil and wine; and he set him on his own animal, brought him to an inn, and took care of him.

Preparing weapons for war.

Is 21:5 Prepare the table, Set a watchman in the tower, Eat and drink. Arise, you princes, Anoint the shield!

Preparing the dead for burial.

Matt 26:12 For in pouring this fragrant oil on My body, she did *it* for My burial.

Mark 16:1 Now when the Sabbath was past, Mary Magdalene, Mary *the mother* of James, and Salome bought spices, that they might come and anoint Him.

Luke 23:56 Then they returned and prepared spices and fragrant oils. And they rested on the Sabbath according to the commandment.

The Jews were very fond of.

Prov 27:9 Ointment and perfume delight the heart, And the sweetness of a man's friend *gives delight* by hearty counsel.

Amos 6:6 Who drink wine from bowls, And anoint yourselves with the best ointments, But are not grieved for the affliction of Joseph.

Was applied to

The head.

Ps 23:5 You prepare a table before me in the presence of my enemies; You anoint my head with oil; My cup runs over.

Eccl 9:8 Let your garments always be white, And let your head lack no oil.

The face.

Ps 104:15 And wine *that* makes glad the heart of man, Oil to make *his* face shine, And bread *which* strengthens man's heart.

The feet.

Luke 7:38–39 and stood at His feet behind *Him* weeping; and she began to wash His feet with her tears, and wiped *them* with the hair of her head; and she kissed His feet and anointed *them* with the fragrant oil. **39** Now when the Pharisee who had invited Him saw *this,* he spoke to himself, saying, "This Man, if He were a prophet, would know who and what manner of woman *this is* who is touching Him, for she is a sinner."

John 12:3 Then Mary took a pound of very costly oil of spikenard, anointed the feet of Jesus, and wiped His feet with her hair. And the house was filled with the fragrance of the oil.

The eyes.

Rev 3:18 I counsel you to buy from Me gold refined in the fire, that you may be rich; and white garments, that you may be clothed, *that* the shame of your nakedness may not be revealed; and anoint your eyes with eye salve, that you may see.

Ointment for,

Richly perfumed.

Song 4:10 How fair is your love, My sister, *my* spouse! How much better than wine is your love, And the scent of your perfumes Than all spices!

John 12:3 Then Mary took a pound of very costly oil of spikenard, anointed the feet of Jesus, and wiped His feet with her hair. And the house was filled with the fragrance of the oil.

Most expensive.

2 Kin 20:13 And Hezekiah was attentive to them, and showed them all the house of his treasures—the silver and gold, the spices and precious ointment, and all his armory—all that was found among his treasures. There was nothing in his house or in all his dominion that Hezekiah did not show them.

Amos 6:6 Who drink wine from bowls, And anoint yourselves with the best ointments, But are not grieved for the affliction of Joseph.

John 12:3 Then Mary took a pound of very costly oil of spikenard, anointed the feet of Jesus, and wiped His feet with her hair. And the house was filled with the fragrance of the oil.

John 12:5 "Why was this fragrant oil not sold for three hundred denarii and given to the poor?"

Prepared by the perfumer.

Eccl 10:1 Dead flies putrefy the perfumer's ointment, And cause it to give off a foul odor; *So does* a little folly to one respected for wisdom *and* honor.

An article of commerce.

Ezek 27:17 Judah and the land of Israel *were* your traders. They traded for your merchandise wheat of Minnith, millet, honey, oil, and balm.

Rev 18:13 and cinnamon and incense, fragrant oil and frankincense, wine and oil, fine flour and wheat, cattle and sheep, horses and chariots, and bodies and souls of men.

Neglected in times of affliction.

2 Sam 12:20 So David arose from the ground, washed and anointed himself, and changed his clothes; and he went into the house of the LORD and worshiped.

Then he went to his own house; and when he requested, they set food before him, and he ate.

2 Sam 14:2 And Joab sent to Tekoa and brought from there a wise woman, and said to her, "Please pretend to be a mourner, and put on mourning apparel; do not anoint yourself with oil, but act like a woman who has been mourning a long time for the dead.

Dan 10:3 I ate no pleasant food, no meat or wine came into my mouth, nor did I anoint myself at all, till three whole weeks were fulfilled.

Neglect of, to guests, a mark of disrespect.

Luke 7:46 You did not anoint My head with oil, but this woman has anointed My feet with fragrant oil.

A token of joy.

Eccl 9:7–8 Go, eat your bread with joy, And drink your wine with a merry heart; For God has already accepted your works. **8** Let your garments always be white, And let your head lack no oil.

Deprivation of, threatened as a punishment.

Deut 28:40 You shall have olive trees throughout all your territory, but you shall not anoint *yourself* with the oil; for your olives shall drop off.

Mic 6:15 "You shall sow, but not reap; You shall tread the olives, but not anoint yourselves with oil; And *make* sweet wine, but not drink wine.

Why recommended by Christ in times of fasting.

Matt 6:17–18 But you, when you fast, anoint your head and wash your face, **18** so that you do not appear to men to be fasting, but to your Father who *is* in the secret *place;* and your Father who sees in secret will reward you openly.

ANOINTING, SACRED

Antiquity of.

Gen 28:18 Then Jacob rose early in the morning, and took the stone that he had put at his head, set it up as a pillar, and poured oil on top of it.

Gen 35:14 So Jacob set up a pillar in the place where He talked with him, a pillar of stone; and he poured a drink offering on it, and he poured oil on it.

Consecrates to God's service.

Ex 30:29 You shall consecrate them, that they may be most holy; whatever touches them must be holy.

Persons who received,

Prophets.

1 Kin 19:16 Also you shall anoint Jehu the son of Nimshi *as* king over Israel. And Elisha the son of Shaphat of Abel Meholah you shall anoint *as* prophet in your place.

Priests.

Ex 40:13–15 You shall put the holy garments on Aaron, and anoint him and consecrate him, that he may minister to Me as priest. **14** And you shall bring his sons and clothe them with tunics. **15** You shall anoint them, as you anointed their father, that they may minister to Me as priests; for their anointing shall surely be an everlasting priesthood throughout their generations."

Kings.

Judg 9:8 "The trees once went forth to anoint a king

over them. And they said to the olive tree, 'Reign over us!'

1 Sam 9:16 "Tomorrow about this time I will send you a man from the land of Benjamin, and you shall anoint him commander over My people Israel, that he may save My people from the hand of the Philistines; for I have looked upon My people, because their cry has come to Me."

1 Kin 1:34 There let Zadok the priest and Nathan the prophet anoint him king over Israel; and blow the horn, and say, '*Long* live King Solomon!'

Things which received,

Tabernacle, etc.

Ex 30:26–27 With it you shall anoint the tabernacle of meeting and the ark of the Testimony; **27** the table and all its utensils, the lampstand and its utensils, and the altar of incense;

Ex 40:9 "And you shall take the anointing oil, and anoint the tabernacle and all that *is* in it; and you shall hallow it and all its utensils, and it shall be holy.

Bronze altar.

Ex 29:36 And you shall offer a bull every day *as* a sin offering for atonement. You shall cleanse the altar when you make atonement for it, and you shall anoint it to sanctify it.

Ex 40:10 You shall anoint the altar of the burnt offering and all its utensils, and consecrate the altar. The altar shall be most holy.

Bronze laver.

Ex 40:11 And you shall anoint the laver and its base, and consecrate it.

Those who partook of,

Protected by God.

1 Chr 16:22 *Saying,* "Do not touch My anointed ones, And do My prophets no harm."

Ps 105:15 *Saying,* "Do not touch My anointed ones, And do My prophets no harm."

Not to be injured or insulted.

1 Sam 24:6 And he said to his men, "The LORD forbid that I should do this thing to my master, the LORD's anointed, to stretch out my hand against him, seeing he *is* the anointed of the LORD."

1 Sam 26:9 But David said to Abishai, "Do not destroy him; for who can stretch out his hand against the LORD's anointed, and be guiltless?"

2 Sam 1:14–15 So David said to him, "How was it you were not afraid to put forth your hand to destroy the LORD's anointed?" **15** Then David called one of the young men and said, "Go near, *and* execute him!" And he struck him so that he died.

2 Sam 19:21 But Abishai the son of Zeruiah answered and said, "Shall not Shimei be put to death for this, because he cursed the LORD's anointed?"

Oil or ointment for,

Divinely prescribed.

Ex 30:23–25 "Also take for yourself quality spices—five hundred *shekels* of liquid myrrh, half as much sweet-smelling cinnamon (two hundred and fifty *shekels*), two hundred and fifty *shekels* of sweet-smelling cane, **24** five hundred *shekels* of cassia, according to the shekel of the sanctuary, and a hin of olive oil. **25** And

you shall make from these a holy anointing oil, an ointment compounded according to the art of the perfumer. It shall be a holy anointing oil.

Compounded by the priests.

1 Chr 9:30 And *some* of the sons of the priests made the ointment of the spices.

A holy anointing oil for ever.

Ex 30:25 And you shall make from these a holy anointing oil, an ointment compounded according to the art of the perfumer. It shall be a holy anointing oil.

Ex 30:31 "And you shall speak to the children of Israel, saying: 'This shall be a holy anointing oil to Me throughout your generations.

Not to be imitated.

Ex 30:32 It shall not be poured on man's flesh; nor shall you make *any other* like it, according to its composition. It *is* holy, *and* it shall be holy to you.

To be put on no outsider.

Ex 30:33 Whoever compounds *any* like it, or whoever puts *any* of it on an outsider, shall be cut off from his people.' "

Jews condemned for imitating.

Ezek 23:41 You sat on a stately couch, with a table prepared before it, on which you had set My incense and My oil.

Typified.

Ex 40:13–15 You shall put the holy garments on Aaron, and anoint him and consecrate him, that he may minister to Me as priest. **14** And you shall bring his sons and clothe them with tunics. **15** You shall anoint them, as you anointed their father, that they may minister to Me as priests; for their anointing shall surely be an everlasting priesthood throughout their generations."

Lev 8:12 And he poured some of the anointing oil on Aaron's head and anointed him, to consecrate him.

1 Sam 16:13 Then Samuel took the horn of oil and anointed him in the midst of his brothers; and the Spirit of the LORD came upon David from that day forward. So Samuel arose and went to Ramah.

1 Kin 19:16 Also you shall anoint Jehu the son of Nimshi *as* king over Israel. And Elisha the son of Shaphat of Abel Meholah you shall anoint *as* prophet in your place.

ANTICHRIST

Denies the Father and the Son.

1 John 2:22 Who is a liar but he who denies that Jesus is the Christ? He is antichrist who denies the Father and the Son.

Denies the incarnation of Christ.

1 John 4:3 and every spirit that does not confess that Jesus Christ has come in the flesh is not of God. And this is the *spirit* of the Antichrist, which you have heard was coming, and is now already in the world.

2 John 1:7 For many deceivers have gone out into the world who do not confess Jesus Christ *as* coming in the flesh. This is a deceiver and an antichrist.

Prevalent in apostolic times.

1 John 2:18 Little children, it is the last hour; and as you have heard that the Antichrist is coming, even now many antichrists have come, by which we know that it is the last hour.

Deceit, a characteristic of.

2 John 1:7 For many deceivers have gone out into the world who do not confess Jesus Christ *as* coming in the flesh. This is a deceiver and an antichrist.

Eschatological opponent of Christ

Called man of sin.

2 Thess 2:3 Let no one deceive you by any means; for *that Day will not come* unless the falling away comes first, and the man of sin is revealed, the son of perdition,

Called son of perdition.

2 Thess 2:3 Let no one deceive you by any means; for *that Day will not come* unless the falling away comes first, and the man of sin is revealed, the son of perdition,

Called lawless one.

2 Thess 2:8 And then the lawless one will be revealed, whom the Lord will consume with the breath of His mouth and destroy with the brightness of His coming.

Called beast.

Rev 11:7 When they finish their testimony, the beast that ascends out of the bottomless pit will make war against them, overcome them, and kill them.

Will work miracles.

2 Thess 2:9 The coming of the *lawless one* is according to the working of Satan, with all power, signs, and lying wonders,

Will deceive many.

2 John 1:7 For many deceivers have gone out into the world who do not confess Jesus Christ *as* coming in the flesh. This is a deceiver and an antichrist.

Rev 19:20 Then the beast was captured, and with him the false prophet who worked signs in his presence, by which he deceived those who received the mark of the beast and those who worshiped his image. These two were cast alive into the lake of fire burning with brimstone.

Will persecute Christians.

Rev 13:7 It was granted to him to make war with the saints and to overcome them. And authority was given him over every tribe, tongue, and nation.

Will be energized by Satan.

2 Thess 2:9 The coming of the *lawless one* is according to the working of Satan, with all power, signs, and lying wonders,

Will seek to be worshiped.

2 Thess 2:4 who opposes and exalts himself above all that is called God or that is worshiped, so that he sits as God in the temple of God, showing himself that he is God.

Is now restrained.

2 Thess 2:6 And now you know what is restraining, that he may be revealed in his own time.

Will be destroyed at Christ's second coming.

2 Thess 2:8 And then the lawless one will be revealed, whom the Lord will consume with the breath of His mouth and destroy with the brightness of His coming.

Rev 19:20 Then the beast was captured, and with him the false prophet who worked signs in his presence, by which he deceived those who received the mark of the beast and those who worshiped his image. These two were cast alive into the lake of fire burning with brimstone.

Will be consigned to the lake of fire for eternity.

Rev 20:10 The devil, who deceived them, was cast into the lake of fire and brimstone where the beast and the false prophet *are*. And they will be tormented day and night forever and ever.

APOSTATES

Described.

Deut 13:13 'Corrupt men have gone out from among you and enticed the inhabitants of their city, saying, "Let us go and serve other gods" '—which you have not known—

Heb 3:12 Beware, brethren, lest there be in any of you an evil heart of unbelief in departing from the living God;

Persecution tends to make.

Matt 24:9–10 "Then they will deliver you up to tribulation and kill you, and you will be hated by all nations for My name's sake. **10** And then many will be offended, will betray one another, and will hate one another.

Luke 8:13 But the ones on the rock *are those* who, when they hear, receive the word with joy; and these have no root, who believe for a while and in time of temptation fall away.

A worldly spirit tends to make.

2 Tim 4:10 for Demas has forsaken me, having loved this present world, and has departed for Thessalonica—Crescens for Galatia, Titus for Dalmatia.

Never belonged to Christ.

1 John 2:19 They went out from us, but they were not of us; for if they had been of us, they would have continued with us; but *they went out* that they might be made manifest, that none of them were of us.

Saints do not become.

Ps 44:18–19 Our heart has not turned back, Nor have our steps departed from Your way; **19** But You have severely broken us in the place of jackals, And covered us with the shadow of death.

Heb 6:9 But, beloved, we are confident of better things concerning you, yes, things that accompany salvation, though we speak in this manner.

Heb 10:39 But we are not of those who draw back to perdition, but of those who believe to the saving of the soul.

It is impossible to restore.

Heb 6:4–6 For *it is* impossible for those who were once enlightened, and have tasted the heavenly gift, and have become partakers of the Holy Spirit, **5** and have tasted the good word of God and the powers of the age to come, **6** if they fall away, to renew them again to repentance, since they crucify again for themselves the Son of God, and put *Him* to an open shame.

Guilt and punishment of.

Zeph 1:4–6 "I will stretch out My hand against Judah,

And against all the inhabitants of Jerusalem. I will cut off every trace of Baal from this place, The names of the idolatrous priests with the *pagan* priests— 5 Those who worship the host of heaven on the housetops; Those who worship and swear *oaths* by the Lord, But who *also* swear by Milcom; 6 Those who have turned back from *following* the Lord, And have not sought the Lord, nor inquired of Him."

Heb 10:25–31 not forsaking the assembling of ourselves together, as *is* the manner of some, but exhorting *one another*, and so much the more as you see the Day approaching. 26 For if we sin willfully after we have received the knowledge of the truth, there no longer remains a sacrifice for sins, 27 but a certain fearful expectation of judgment, and fiery indignation which will devour the adversaries. 28 Anyone who has rejected Moses' law dies without mercy on the testimony of two or three witnesses. 29 Of how much worse punishment, do you suppose, will he be thought worthy who has trampled the Son of God underfoot, counted the blood of the covenant by which he was sanctified a common thing, and insulted the Spirit of grace? 30 For we know Him who said, *"Vengeance is Mine, I will repay,"* says the Lord. And again, *"The Lord will judge His people."* 31 It is a fearful thing to fall into the hands of the living God.

Heb 10:39 But we are not of those who draw back to perdition, but of those who believe to the saving of the soul.

2 Pet 2:17 These are wells without water, clouds carried by a tempest, for whom is reserved the blackness of darkness forever.

2 Pet 2:20–22 For if, after they have escaped the pollutions of the world through the knowledge of the Lord and Savior Jesus Christ, they are again entangled in them and overcome, the latter end is worse for them than the beginning. 21 For it would have been better for them not to have known the way of righteousness, than having known *it,* to turn from the holy commandment delivered to them. 22 But it has happened to them according to the true proverb: *"A dog returns to his own vomit,"* and, "a sow, having washed, to her wallowing in the mire."

Cautions against becoming.

Heb 3:12 Beware, brethren, lest there be in any of you an evil heart of unbelief in departing from the living God;

2 Pet 3:17 You therefore, beloved, since you know *this* beforehand, beware lest you also fall from your own steadfastness, being led away with the error of the wicked;

Shall abound in the latter days.

Matt 24:12 And because lawlessness will abound, the love of many will grow cold.

2 Thess 2:3 Let no one deceive you by any means; for *that Day will not come* unless the falling away comes first, and the man of sin is revealed, the son of perdition,

1 Tim 4:1–3 Now the Spirit expressly says that in latter times some will depart from the faith, giving heed to deceiving spirits and doctrines of demons, 2 speaking lies in hypocrisy, having their own conscience

seared with a hot iron, 3 forbidding to marry, *and commanding* to abstain from foods which God created to be received with thanksgiving by those who believe and know the truth.

Examples of,

Amaziah.

2 Chr 25:14 Now it was so, after Amaziah came from the slaughter of the Edomites, that he brought the gods of the people of Seir, set them up *to be* his gods, and bowed down before them and burned incense to them.

2 Chr 25:27 After the time that Amaziah turned away from following the Lord, they made a conspiracy against him in Jerusalem, and he fled to Lachish; but they sent after him to Lachish and killed him there.

Professed disciples.

John 6:66 From that *time* many of His disciples went back and walked with Him no more.

Hymenaeus and Alexander.

1 Tim 1:19–20 having faith and a good conscience, which some having rejected, concerning the faith have suffered shipwreck, 20 of whom are Hymenaeus and Alexander, whom I delivered to Satan that they may learn not to blaspheme.

APOSTLES, THE

Christ pre-eminently called "the Apostle."

Heb 3:1 Therefore, holy brethren, partakers of the heavenly calling, consider the Apostle and High Priest of our confession, Christ Jesus,

Appointed by Christ.

Mark 3:14 Then He appointed twelve, that they might be with Him and that He might send them out to preach,

John 15:16 You did not choose Me, but I chose you and appointed you that you should go and bear fruit, and *that* your fruit should remain, that whatever you ask the Father in My name He may give you.

Received their title from Christ.

Luke 6:13 And when it was day, He called His disciples to *Himself;* and from them He chose twelve whom He also named apostles:

Called by

God.

1 Cor 1:1 Paul, called *to be* an apostle of Jesus Christ through the will of God, and Sosthenes *our* brother,

1 Cor 12:28 And God has appointed these in the church: first apostles, second prophets, third teachers, after that miracles, then gifts of healings, helps, administrations, varieties of tongues.

Gal 1:1 Paul, an apostle (not from men nor through man, but through Jesus Christ and God the Father who raised Him from the dead),

Gal 1:15–16 But when it pleased God, who separated me from my mother's womb and called *me* through His grace, 16 to reveal His Son in me, that I might preach Him among the Gentiles, I did not immediately confer with flesh and blood,

Christ.

Matt 10:1 And when He had called His twelve disciples to *Him,* He gave them power *over* unclean spirits, to cast them out, and to heal all kinds of sickness and all kinds of disease.

Mark 3:13 And He went up on the mountain and called to *Him* those He Himself wanted. And they came to Him.

Acts 20:24 But none of these things move me; nor do I count my life dear to myself, so that I may finish my race with joy, and the ministry which I received from the Lord Jesus, to testify to the gospel of the grace of God.

Rom 1:5 Through Him we have received grace and apostleship for obedience to the faith among all nations for His name,

Some were unlearned men.

Acts 4:13 Now when they saw the boldness of Peter and John, and perceived that they were uneducated and untrained men, they marveled. And they realized that they had been with Jesus.

Selected from obscure stations.

Matt 4:18 And Jesus, walking by the Sea of Galilee, saw two brothers, Simon called Peter, and Andrew his brother, casting a net into the sea; for they were fishermen.

Sent first to the house of Israel.

Matt 10:5–6 These twelve Jesus sent out and commanded them, saying: "Do not go into the way of the Gentiles, and do not enter a city of the Samaritans. 6 But go rather to the lost sheep of the house of Israel.

Luke 24:47 and that repentance and remission of sins should be preached in His name to all nations, beginning at Jerusalem.

Acts 13:46 Then Paul and Barnabas grew bold and said, "It was necessary that the word of God should be spoken to you first; but since you reject it, and judge yourselves unworthy of everlasting life, behold, we turn to the Gentiles.

Sent to preach the gospel to all nations.

Matt 28:19–20 Go therefore and make disciples of all the nations, baptizing them in the name of the Father and of the Son and of the Holy Spirit, 20 teaching them to observe all things that I have commanded you; and lo, I am with you always, *even* to the end of the age." Amen.

Mark 16:15 And He said to them, "Go into all the world and preach the gospel to every creature.

2 Tim 1:11 to which I was appointed a preacher, an apostle, and a teacher of the Gentiles.

Christ always present with.

Matt 28:20 teaching them to observe all things that I have commanded you; and lo, I am with you always, *even* to the end of the age." Amen.

Warned against a timid profession of Christ.

Matt 10:27–33 "Whatever I tell you in the dark, speak in the light; and what you hear in the ear, preach on the housetops. 28 And do not fear those who kill the body but cannot kill the soul. But rather fear Him who is able to destroy both soul and body in hell. 29 Are not two sparrows sold for a copper coin? And not one of them falls to the ground apart from your Father's will. 30 But the very hairs of your head are all numbered. 31 Do not fear therefore; you are of more value than many sparrows. 32 "Therefore who-

ever confesses Me before men, him I will also confess before My Father who is in heaven. 33 But whoever denies Me before men, him I will also deny before My Father who is in heaven.

The Holy Spirit given to.

John 20:22 And when He had said this, He breathed on *them,* and said to them, "Receive the Holy Spirit.

Acts 2:1–4 When the Day of Pentecost had fully come, they were all with one accord in one place. 2 And suddenly there came a sound from heaven, as of a rushing mighty wind, and it filled the whole house where they were sitting. 3 Then there appeared to them divided tongues, as of fire, and *one* sat upon each of them. 4 And they were all filled with the Holy Spirit and began to speak with other tongues, as the Spirit gave them utterance.

Acts 9:17 And Ananias went his way and entered the house; and laying his hands on him he said, "Brother Saul, the Lord Jesus, who appeared to you on the road as you came, has sent me that you may receive your sight and be filled with the Holy Spirit."

Guided by the Spirit into all truth.

John 14:26 But the Helper, the Holy Spirit, whom the Father will send in My name, He will teach you all things, and bring to your remembrance all things that I said to you.

John 15:26 "But when the Helper comes, whom I shall send to you from the Father, the Spirit of truth who proceeds from the Father, He will testify of Me.

John 16:13 However, when He, the Spirit of truth, has come, He will guide you into all truth; for He will not speak on His own *authority,* but whatever He hears He will speak; and He will tell you things to come.

Instructed by the Spirit to answer adversaries.

Matt 10:19–20 But when they deliver you up, do not worry about how or what you should speak. For it will be given to you in that hour what you should speak; 20 for it is not you who speak, but the Spirit of your Father who speaks in you.

Luke 12:11–12 "Now when they bring you to the synagogues and magistrates and authorities, do not worry about how or what you should answer, or what you should say. 12 For the Holy Spirit will teach you in that very hour what you ought to say."

Specially devoted to the office of the ministry.

Acts 6:4 but we will give ourselves continually to prayer and to the ministry of the word."

Acts 20:27 For I have not shunned to declare to you the whole counsel of God.

Humility urged upon.

Matt 20:26–27 Yet it shall not be so among you; but whoever desires to become great among you, let him be your servant. 27 And whoever desires to be first among you, let him be your slave—

Mark 9:33–37 Then He came to Capernaum. And when He was in the house He asked them, "What was it you disputed among yourselves on the road?" 34 But they kept silent, for on the road they had disputed among themselves who *would be the* greatest. 35 And He sat down, called the twelve, and said to them, "If anyone desires to be first, he shall be last of all and servant of all." 36 Then He took a little child and set him in the midst of them. And when He had taken him in His arms, He said to them, **37** "Whoever receives one of these little children in My name receives Me; and whoever receives Me, receives not Me but Him who sent Me."

Luke 22:24–30 Now there was also a dispute among them, as to which of them should be considered the greatest. **25** And He said to them, "The kings of the Gentiles exercise lordship over them, and those who exercise authority over them are called 'benefactors.' **26** But not so *among* you; on the contrary, he who is greatest among you, let him be as the younger, and he who governs as he who serves. **27** For who *is* greater, he who sits at the table, or he who serves? *Is* it not he who sits at the table? Yet I am among you as the One who serves. **28** "But you are those who have continued with Me in My trials. **29** And I bestow upon you a kingdom, just as My Father bestowed *one* upon Me, **30** that you may eat and drink at My table in My kingdom, and sit on thrones judging the twelve tribes of Israel."

Self-denial urged upon.

Matt 10:37–39 He who loves father or mother more than Me is not worthy of Me. And he who loves son or daughter more than Me is not worthy of Me. **38** And he who does not take his cross and follow after Me is not worthy of Me. **39** He who finds his life will lose it, and he who loses his life for My sake will find it.

Mutual love urged upon.

John 15:17 These things I command you, that you love one another.

Equal authority given to each of.

Matt 16:19 And I will give you the keys of the kingdom of heaven, and whatever you bind on earth will be bound in heaven, and whatever you loose on earth will be loosed in heaven."

Matt 18:18 "Assuredly, I say to you, whatever you bind on earth will be bound in heaven, and whatever you loose on earth will be loosed in heaven.

2 Cor 11:5 For I consider that I am not at all inferior to the most eminent apostles.

Were not of the world.

John 15:19 If you were of the world, the world would love its own. Yet because you are not of the world, but I chose you out of the world, therefore the world hates you.

John 17:16 They are not of the world, just as I am not of the world.

Were hated by the world.

Matt 10:22 And you will be hated by all for My name's sake. But he who endures to the end will be saved.

Matt 24:9 "Then they will deliver you up to tribulation and kill you, and you will be hated by all nations for My name's sake.

John 15:18 "If the world hates you, you know that it hated Me before *it hated* you.

Persecutions and sufferings of.

Matt 10:16 "Behold, I send you out as sheep in the midst of wolves. Therefore be wise as serpents and harmless as doves.

Matt 10:18 You will be brought before governors and kings for My sake, as a testimony to them and to the Gentiles.

Luke 21:16 You will be betrayed even by parents and brothers, relatives and friends; and they will put *some* of you to death.

John 15:20 Remember the word that I said to you, 'A servant is not greater than his master.' If they persecuted Me, they will also persecute you. If they kept My word, they will keep yours also.

John 16:2 They will put you out of the synagogues; yes, the time is coming that whoever kills you will think that he offers God service.

Saw Christ in the flesh.

Luke 1:2 just as those who from the beginning were eyewitnesses and ministers of the word delivered them to us,

Acts 1:22 beginning from the baptism of John to that day when He was taken up from us, one of these must become a witness with us of His resurrection."

1 Cor 9:1 Am I not an apostle? Am I not free? Have I not seen Jesus Christ our Lord? Are you not my work in the Lord?

1 John 1:1 That which was from the beginning, which we have heard, which we have seen with our eyes, which we have looked upon, and our hands have handled, concerning the Word of life—

Witnesses of the resurrection and ascension of Christ.

Luke 24:33–41 So they rose up that very hour and returned to Jerusalem, and found the eleven and those *who were* with them gathered together, **34** saying, "The Lord is risen indeed, and has appeared to Simon!" **35** And they told about the things *that had happened* on the road, and how He was known to them in the breaking of bread. **36** Now as they said these things, Jesus Himself stood in the midst of them, and said to them, "Peace to you." **37** But they were terrified and frightened, and supposed they had seen a spirit. **38** And He said to them, "Why are you troubled? And why do doubts arise in your hearts? **39** Behold My hands and My feet, that it is I Myself. Handle Me and see, for a spirit does not have flesh and bones as you see I have." **40** When He had said this, He showed them His hands and His feet. **41** But while they still did not believe for joy, and marveled, He said to them, "Have you any food here?"

Luke 24:51 Now it came to pass, while He blessed them, that He was parted from them and carried up into heaven.

Acts 1:2–9 until the day in which He was taken up, after He through the Holy Spirit had given commandments to the apostles whom He had chosen, **3** to whom He also presented Himself alive after His suffering by many infallible proofs, being seen by them during forty days and speaking of the things pertaining to the kingdom of God. **4** And being assembled together with *them*, He commanded them not to depart from Jerusalem, but to wait for the Promise of the Father, "which," He said, "you have heard from Me; **5** for John truly baptized with water, but you shall be baptized with the Holy Spirit not many days from now." **6** Therefore, when they had come together, they asked Him, saying, "Lord, will You at this time restore the kingdom to Israel?" **7** And He said to them, "It is not for you to know times or seasons which the Father has put in His own authority. **8** But you shall receive power when the Holy Spirit has come upon you; and you shall be witnesses to Me in Jerusalem, and in all Judea and Samaria, and to the end of the earth." **9** Now when He had spoken these things, while they watched, He was taken up, and a cloud received Him out of their sight.

Acts 10:40–41 Him God raised up on the third day, and showed Him openly, **41** not to all the people, but to witnesses chosen before by God, *even* to us who ate and drank with Him after He arose from the dead.

1 Cor 15:8 Then last of all He was seen by me also, as by one born out of due time.

Empowered to work miracles.

Matt 10:1 And when He had called His twelve disciples to *Him,* He gave them power *over* unclean spirits, to cast them out, and to heal all kinds of sickness and all kinds of disease.

Matt 10:8 Heal the sick, cleanse the lepers, raise the dead, cast out demons. Freely you have received, freely give.

Mark 16:20 And they went out and preached everywhere, the Lord working with *them* and confirming the word through the accompanying signs. Amen.

Luke 9:1 Then He called His twelve disciples together and gave them power and authority over all demons, and to cure diseases.

Acts 2:43 Then fear came upon every soul, and many wonders and signs were done through the apostles.

ARK OF THE COVENANT, THE

Called the

Ark of God.

1 Sam 3:3 and before the lamp of God went out in the tabernacle of the LORD where the ark of God *was,* and while Samuel was lying down,

Ark of God's strength.

2 Chr 6:41 "Now therefore, Arise, O LORD God, to Your resting place, You and the ark of Your strength. Let Your priests, O LORD God, be clothed with salvation, And let Your saints rejoice in goodness.

Ps 132:8 Arise, O LORD, to Your resting place, You and the ark of Your strength.

Ark of the covenant of the Lord.

Num 10:33 So they departed from the mountain of the LORD on a journey of three days; and the ark of the covenant of the LORD went before them for the three days' journey, to search out a resting place for them.

Ark of the Testimony.

Ex 30:6 And you shall put it before the veil that *is* before the ark of the Testimony, before the mercy seat that *is* over the Testimony, where I will meet with you.

Num 7:89 Now when Moses went into the tabernacle of meeting to speak with Him, he heard the voice of One speaking to him from above the mercy seat that *was* on the ark of the Testimony, from between the two cherubim; thus He spoke to him.

Dimensions of.

Ex 25:10 "And they shall make an ark of acacia wood;

two and a half cubits *shall be* its length, a cubit and a half its width, and a cubit and a half its height.

Ex 37:1 Then Bezalel made the ark of acacia wood; two and a half cubits *was* its length, a cubit and a half its width, and a cubit and a half its height.

Entirely covered with gold.

Ex 25:11 And you shall overlay it with pure gold, inside and out you shall overlay it, and shall make on it a molding of gold all around.

Ex 37:2 He overlaid it with pure gold inside and outside, and made a molding of gold all around it.

Surrounded with a molding of gold.

Ex 25:11 And you shall overlay it with pure gold, inside and out you shall overlay it, and shall make on it a molding of gold all around.

Furnished with rings and poles.

Ex 25:12–15 You shall cast four rings of gold for it, and put *them* in its four corners; two rings *shall be* on one side, and two rings on the other side. **13** And you shall make poles *of* acacia wood, and overlay them with gold. **14** You shall put the poles into the rings on the sides of the ark, that the ark may be carried by them. **15** The poles shall be in the rings of the ark; they shall not be taken from it.

Ex 37:3–5 And he cast for it four rings of gold *to be set* in its four corners: two rings on one side, and two rings on the other side of it. **4** He made poles of acacia wood, and overlaid them with gold. **5** And he put the poles into the rings at the sides of the ark, to bear the ark.

Tables of Testimony placed in.

Ex 25:16 And you shall put into the ark the Testimony which I will give you.

Ex 25:21 You shall put the mercy seat on top of the ark, and in the ark you shall put the Testimony that I will give you.

1 Kin 8:9 Nothing *was* in the ark except the two tablets of stone which Moses put there at Horeb, when the LORD made *a covenant* with the children of Israel, when they came out of the land of Egypt.

1 Kin 8:21 And there I have made a place for the ark, in which *is* the covenant of the LORD which He made with our fathers, when He brought them out of the land of Egypt."

2 Chr 5:10 Nothing was in the ark except the two tablets which Moses put *there* at Horeb, when the LORD made *a covenant* with the children of Israel, when they had come out of Egypt.

Heb 9:4 which had the golden censer and the ark of the covenant overlaid on all sides with gold, in which *were* the golden pot that had the manna, Aaron's rod that budded, and the tablets of the covenant;

Mercy seat laid upon.

Ex 25:21 You shall put the mercy seat on top of the ark, and in the ark you shall put the Testimony that I will give you.

Ex 26:34 You shall put the mercy seat upon the ark of the Testimony in the Most Holy.

Placed in the Holy of Holies.

Ex 26:33 And you shall hang the veil from the clasps. Then you shall bring the ark of the Testimony in there, behind the veil. The veil shall be a divider for you between the holy *place* and the Most Holy.

Ex 40:21 And he brought the ark into the tabernacle, hung up the veil of the covering, and partitioned off the ark of the Testimony, as the LORD had commanded Moses.

Heb 9:3–4 and behind the second veil, the part of the tabernacle which is called the Holiest of All, **4** which had the golden censer and the ark of the covenant overlaid on all sides with gold, in which *were* the golden pot that had the manna, Aaron's rod that budded, and the tablets of the covenant;

The pot of manna and Aaron's rod laid up before.

Ex 16:33–34 And Moses said to Aaron, "Take a pot and put an omer of manna in it, and lay it up before the LORD, to be kept for your generations." **34** As the LORD commanded Moses, so Aaron laid it up before the Testimony, to be kept.

Num 17:10 And the LORD said to Moses, "Bring Aaron's rod back before the Testimony, to be kept as a sign against the rebels, that you may put their complaints away from Me, lest they die."

Heb 9:4 which had the golden censer and the ark of the covenant overlaid on all sides with gold, in which *were* the golden pot that had the manna, Aaron's rod that budded, and the tablets of the covenant;

A copy of the Law laid beside.

Deut 31:26 "Take this Book of the Law, and put it beside the ark of the covenant of the LORD your God, that it may be there as a witness against you;

Anointed with sacred oil.

Ex 30:26 With it you shall anoint the tabernacle of meeting and the ark of the Testimony;

Covered with the veil by the priests before removal.

Num 4:5–6 When the camp prepares to journey, Aaron and his sons shall come, and they shall take down the covering veil and cover the ark of the Testimony with it. **6** Then they shall put on it a covering of badger skins, and spread over *that* a cloth entirely of blue; and they shall insert its poles.

A symbol of the presence and glory of God.

Num 14:43–44 For the Amalekites and the Canaanites *are* there before you, and you shall fall by the sword; because you have turned away from the LORD, the LORD will not be with you." **44** But they presumed to go up to the mountaintop. Nevertheless, neither the ark of the covenant of the LORD nor Moses departed from the camp.

1 Sam 14:18–19 And Saul said to Ahijah, "Bring the ark of God here" (for at that time the ark of God was with the children of Israel). **19** Now it happened, while Saul talked to the priest, that the noise which *was* in the camp of the Philistines continued to increase; so Saul said to the priest, "Withdraw your hand."

Ps 132:8 Arise, O LORD, to Your resting place, You and the ark of Your strength.

Esteemed the glory of Israel.

1 Sam 4:21–22 Then she named the child Ichabod, saying, "The glory has departed from Israel!" because the ark of God had been captured and because of her father-in-law and her husband. **22** And she said, "The glory has departed from Israel, for the ark of God has been captured."

Was holy.

2 Chr 35:3 Then he said to the Levites who taught all Israel, who were holy to the LORD: "Put the holy ark in the house which Solomon the son of David, king of Israel, built. *It shall* no longer *be* a burden on *your* shoulders. Now serve the LORD your God and His people Israel.

Sanctified its resting place.

2 Chr 8:11 Now Solomon brought the daughter of Pharaoh up from the City of David to the house he had built for her, for he said, "My wife shall not dwell in the house of David king of Israel, because *the places* to which the ark of the LORD has come are holy."

The Israelites enquired of the Lord before.

Josh 7:6–9 Then Joshua tore his clothes, and fell to the earth on his face before the ark of the LORD until evening, he and the elders of Israel; and they put dust on their heads. **7** And Joshua said, "Alas, Lord GOD, why have You brought this people over the Jordan at all—to deliver us into the hand of the Amorites, to destroy us? Oh, that we had been content, and dwelt on the other side of the Jordan! **8** O Lord, what shall I say when Israel turns its back before its enemies? **9** For the Canaanites and all the inhabitants of the land will hear *it*, and surround us, and cut off our name from the earth. Then what will You do for Your great name?"

Judg 20:27 So the children of Israel inquired of the LORD (the ark of the covenant of God *was* there in those days,

1 Chr 13:3 and let us bring the ark of our God back to us, for we have not inquired at it since the days of Saul."

Was carried

By priests of Levites alone.

Deut 10:8 At that time the LORD separated the tribe of Levi to bear the ark of the covenant of the LORD, to stand before the LORD to minister to Him and to bless in His name, to this day.

Josh 3:14 So it was, when the people set out from their camp to cross over the Jordan, with the priests bearing the ark of the covenant before the people,

2 Sam 15:24 There was Zadok also, and all the Levites with him, bearing the ark of the covenant of God. And they set down the ark of God, and Abiathar went up until all the people had finished crossing over from the city.

1 Chr 15:2 Then David said, "No one may carry the ark of God but the Levites, for the LORD has chosen them to carry the ark of God and to minister before Him forever."

Before the Israelites in their journeys.

Num 10:33 So they departed from the mountain of the LORD on a journey of three days; and the ark of the covenant of the LORD went before them for the three days' journey, to search out a resting place for them.

Josh 3:6 Then Joshua spoke to the priests, saying, "Take up the ark of the covenant and cross over before the people." So they took up the ark of the covenant and went before the people.

Sometimes to the camp in war.

1 Sam 4:4–5 So the people sent to Shiloh, that they might bring from there the ark of the covenant of the LORD of hosts, who dwells *between* the cherubim. And the two sons of Eli, Hophni and Phinehas, *were* there with the ark of the covenant of God. 5 And when the ark of the covenant of the LORD came into the camp, all Israel shouted so loudly that the earth shook.

Profanation of, punished.

Num 4:5 When the camp prepares to journey, Aaron and his sons shall come, and they shall take down the covering veil and cover the ark of the Testimony with it.

Num 4:15 And when Aaron and his sons have finished covering the sanctuary and all the furnishings of the sanctuary, when the camp is set to go, then the sons of Kohath shall come to carry *them;* but they shall not touch any holy thing, lest they die. "These *are* the things in the tabernacle of meeting which the sons of Kohath are to carry.

1 Sam 6:19 Then He struck the men of Beth Shemesh, because they had looked into the ark of the LORD. He struck fifty thousand and seventy men of the people, and the people lamented because the LORD had struck the people with a great slaughter.

1 Chr 15:13 For because you *did* not *do it* the first *time,* the LORD our God broke out against us, because we did not consult Him about the proper order."

Protecting of, rewarded.

1 Chr 13:14 The ark of God remained with the family of Obed-Edom in his house three months. And the LORD blessed the house of Obed-Edom and all that he had.

Captured by the Philistines.

1 Sam 4:11 Also the ark of God was captured; and the two sons of Eli, Hophni and Phinehas, died.

Miracles connected with,

Jordan divided.

Josh 4:7 Then you shall answer them that the waters of the Jordan were cut off before the ark of the covenant of the LORD; when it crossed over the Jordan, the waters of the Jordan were cut off. And these stones shall be for a memorial to the children of Israel forever."

Fall of the walls of Jericho. **Josh 6:6–20**

Fall of Dagon.

1 Sam 5:1–4 Then the Philistines took the ark of God and brought it from Ebenezer to Ashdod. 2 When the Philistines took the ark of God, they brought it into the house of Dagon and set it by Dagon. 3 And when the people of Ashdod arose early in the morning, there was Dagon, fallen on its face to the earth before the ark of the LORD. So they took Dagon and set it in its place again. 4 And when they arose early the next morning, there was Dagon, fallen on its face to the ground before the ark of the LORD. The head of Dagon and both the palms of its hands *were* bro-

ken off on the threshold; only Dagon's torso was left of it.

Philistines plagued.

1 Sam 5:6–12 But the hand of the LORD was heavy on the people of Ashdod, and He ravaged them and struck them with tumors, *both* Ashdod and its territory. 7 And when the men of Ashdod saw how *it was,* they said, "The ark of the God of Israel must not remain with us, for His hand is harsh toward us and Dagon our god." 8 Therefore they sent and gathered to themselves all the lords of the Philistines, and said, "What shall we do with the ark of the God of Israel?" And they answered, "Let the ark of the God of Israel be carried away to Gath." So they carried the ark of the God of Israel away. 9 So it was, after they had carried it away, that the hand of the LORD was against the city with a very great destruction; and He struck the men of the city, both small and great, and tumors broke out on them. 10 Therefore they sent the ark of God to Ekron. So it was, as the ark of God came to Ekron, that the Ekronites cried out, saying, "They have brought the ark of the God of Israel to us, to kill us and our people!" 11 So they sent and gathered together all the lords of the Philistines, and said, "Send away the ark of the God of Israel, and let it go back to its own place, so that it does not kill us and our people." For there was a deadly destruction throughout all the city; the hand of God was very heavy there. 12 And the men who did not die were stricken with the tumors, and the cry of the city went up to heaven.

Manner of its restoration. **1 Sam 6:1–18**

At Kirjath Jearim twenty years.

1 Sam 7:1–2 Then the men of Kirjath Jearim came and took the ark of the LORD, and brought it into the house of Abinadab on the hill, and consecrated Eleazar his son to keep the ark of the LORD. 2 So it was that the ark remained in Kirjath Jearim a long time; it was there twenty years. And all the house of Israel lamented after the LORD.

Removed from Kirjath Jearim to the house of Obed-Edom. 2 Sam 6:1–11

David made a tent for.

2 Sam 6:17 So they brought the ark of the LORD, and set it in its place in the midst of the tabernacle that David had erected for it. Then David offered burnt offerings and peace offerings before the LORD.

1 Chr 15:1 *David* built houses for himself in the City of David; and he prepared a place for the ark of God, and pitched a tent for it.

Brought into the city of David.

2 Sam 6:12–15 Now it was told King David, saying, "The LORD has blessed the house of Obed-Edom and all that *belongs* to him, because of the ark of God." So David went and brought up the ark of God from the house of Obed-Edom to the City of David with gladness. 13 And so it was, when those bearing the ark of the LORD had gone six paces, that he sacrificed oxen and fatted sheep. 14 Then David danced before the LORD with all *his* might; and David *was* wearing a linen ephod. 15 So David and all the house of Israel brought up the ark of the LORD with shouting and with the sound of the trumpet.

1 Chr 15:25–28 So David, the elders of Israel, and the captains over thousands went to bring up the ark of the covenant of the LORD from the house of Obed-Edom with joy. **26** And so it was, when God helped the Levites who bore the ark of the covenant of the LORD, that they offered seven bulls and seven rams. **27** David was clothed with a robe of fine linen, as were all the Levites who bore the ark, the singers, and Chenaniah the music master *with* the singers. David also wore a linen ephod. **28** Thus all Israel brought up the ark of the covenant of the LORD with shouting and with the sound of the horn, with trumpets and with cymbals, making music with stringed instruments and harps.

Brought by Solomon into the temple with great solemnity.

1 Kin 8:1–6 Now Solomon assembled the elders of Israel and all the heads of the tribes, the chief fathers of the children of Israel, to King Solomon in Jerusalem, that they might bring up the ark of the covenant of the LORD from the City of David, which *is* Zion. **2** Therefore all the men of Israel assembled with King Solomon at the feast in the month of Ethanim, which *is* the seventh month. **3** So all the elders of Israel came, and the priests took up the ark. **4** Then they brought up the ark of the LORD, the tabernacle of meeting, and all the holy furnishings that *were* in the tabernacle. The priests and the Levites brought them up. **5** Also King Solomon, and all the congregation of Israel who were assembled with him, *were* with him before the ark, sacrificing sheep and oxen that could not be counted or numbered for multitude. **6** Then the priests brought in the ark of the covenant of the LORD to its place, into the inner sanctuary of the temple, to the Most Holy *Place*, under the wings of the cherubim.

2 Chr 5:2–9 Now Solomon assembled the elders of Israel and all the heads of the tribes, the chief fathers of the children of Israel, in Jerusalem, that they might bring the ark of the covenant of the LORD up from the City of David, which *is* Zion. **3** Therefore all the men of Israel assembled with the king at the feast, which *was* in the seventh month. **4** So all the elders of Israel came, and the Levites took up the ark. **5** Then they brought up the ark, the tabernacle of meeting, and all the holy furnishings that *were* in the tabernacle. The priests and the Levites brought them up. **6** Also King Solomon, and all the congregation of Israel who were assembled with him, were sacrificing sheep and oxen that could not be counted or numbered for multitude. **7** Then the priests brought in the ark of the covenant of the LORD to its place, into the inner sanctuary of the temple, to the Most Holy *Place*, under the wings of the cherubim. **8** For the cherubim spread *their* wings over the place of the ark, and the cherubim overshadowed the ark and its poles. **9** The poles extended so that the ends of the poles of the ark could be seen from *the holy place*, in front of the inner sanctuary; but they could not be seen from outside. And they are there to this day.

ARMAGEDDON, BATTLE OF, THE
Old Testament allusions to.

Joel 3:2 I will also gather all nations, And bring them down to the Valley of Jehoshaphat; And I will enter into judgment with them there On account of My people, My heritage Israel, Whom they have scattered among the nations; They have also divided up My land.

Mic 4:11–13 Now also many nations have gathered against you, Who say, "Let her be defiled, And let our eye look upon Zion." **12** But they do not know the thoughts of the LORD, Nor do they understand His counsel; For He will gather them like sheaves to the threshing floor. **13** "Arise and thresh, O daughter of Zion; For I will make your horn iron, And I will make your hooves bronze; You shall beat in pieces many peoples; I will consecrate their gain to the LORD, And their substance to the Lord of the whole earth."

Zech 12:3 And it shall happen in that day that I will make Jerusalem a very heavy stone for all peoples; all who would heave it away will surely be cut in pieces, though all nations of the earth are gathered against it.

Zech 14:2 For I will gather all the nations to battle against Jerusalem; The city shall be taken, The houses rifled, And the women ravished. Half of the city shall go into captivity, But the remnant of the people shall not be cut off from the city.

New Testament allusions to.

Rev 14:18–20 And another angel came out from the altar, who had power over fire, and he cried with a loud cry to him who had the sharp sickle, saying, "Thrust in your sharp sickle and gather the clusters of the vine of the earth, for her grapes are fully ripe." **19** So the angel thrust his sickle into the earth and gathered the vine of the earth, and threw *it* into the great winepress of the wrath of God. **20** And the winepress was trampled outside the city, and blood came out of the winepress, up to the horses' bridles, for one thousand six hundred furlongs.

Rev 16:14 For they are spirits of demons, performing signs, *which* go out to the kings of the earth and of the whole world, to gather them to the battle of that great day of God Almighty.

Rev 17:14 These will make war with the Lamb, and the Lamb will overcome them, for He is Lord of lords and King of kings; and those *who are* with Him *are* called, chosen, and faithful."

Rev 19:17–21 Then I saw an angel standing in the sun; and he cried with a loud voice, saying to all the birds that fly in the midst of heaven, "Come and gather together for the supper of the great God, **18** that you may eat the flesh of kings, the flesh of captains, the flesh of mighty men, the flesh of horses and of those who sit on them, and the flesh of all *people*, free and slave, both small and great." **19** And I saw the beast, the kings of the earth, and their armies, gathered together to make war against Him who sat on the horse and against His army. **20** Then the beast was captured, and with him the false prophet who worked signs in his presence, by which he deceived those who received the mark of the beast and those who worshiped his image. These two were cast alive into the lake of fire burning with brimstone. **21** And the rest were killed with the sword which proceeded from the mouth of Him who sat on the horse. And all the birds were filled with their flesh.

Place of, identified.

Rev 16:16 And they gathered them together to the place called in Hebrew, Armageddon.

ARMIES

Antiquity of.

Gen 14:1–8 And it came to pass in the days of Amraphel king of Shinar, Arioch king of Ellasar, Chedorlaomer king of Elam, and Tidal king of nations, 2 *that* they made war with Bera king of Sodom, Birsha king of Gomorrah, Shinab king of Admah, Shemeber king of Zeboiim, and the king of Bela (that is, Zoar). 3 All these joined together in the Valley of Siddim (that is, the Salt Sea). 4 Twelve years they served Chedorlaomer, and in the thirteenth year they rebelled. 5 In the fourteenth year Chedorlaomer and the kings that *were* with him came and attacked the Rephaim in Ashteroth Karnaim, the Zuzim in Ham, the Emim in Shaveh Kiriathaim, 6 and the Horites in their mountain of Seir, as far as El Paran, which *is* by the wilderness. 7 Then they turned back and came to En Mishpat (that *is*, Kadesh), and attacked all the country of the Amalekites, and also the Amorites who dwelt in Hazezon Tamar. 8 And the king of Sodom, the king of Gomorrah, the king of Admah, the king of Zeboiim, and the king of Bela (that *is*, Zoar) went out and joined together in battle in the Valley of Siddim

Ancient, often numerous.

Josh 11:4 So they went out, they and all their armies with them, *as* many people *as* the sand that *is* on the seashore in multitude, with very many horses and chariots.

1 Sam 13:5 Then the Philistines gathered together to fight with Israel, thirty thousand chariots and six thousand horsemen, and people as the sand which *is* on the seashore in multitude. And they came up and encamped in Michmash, to the east of Beth Aven.

Of different nations often confederated.

Josh 9:2 that they gathered together to fight with Joshua and Israel with one accord.

Josh 10:5 Therefore the five kings of the Amorites, the king of Jerusalem, the king of Hebron, the king of Jarmuth, the king of Lachish, *and* the king of Eglon, gathered together and went up, they and all their armies, and camped before Gibeon and made war against it.

Judg 3:13 Then he gathered to himself the people of Ammon and Amalek, went and defeated Israel, and took possession of the City of Palms.

1 Kin 20:1 Now Ben-Hadad the king of Syria gathered all his forces together; thirty-two kings *were* with him, with horses and chariots. And he went up and besieged Samaria, and made war against it.

Troops often hired for.

1 Chr 19:7 So they hired for themselves thirty-two thousand chariots, with the king of Maacah and his people, who came and encamped before Medeba. Also the people of Ammon gathered together from their cities, and came to battle.

2 Chr 25:6 He also hired one hundred thousand mighty men of valor from Israel for one hundred talents of silver.

Were composed of

Bowmen and slingers.

1 Chr 12:2 armed with bows, using both the right hand and the left in *hurling* stones and *shooting* arrows with the bow. *They were* of Benjamin, Saul's brethren.

Jer 4:29 The whole city shall flee from the noise of the horsemen and bowmen. They shall go into thickets and climb up on the rocks. Every city *shall be* forsaken, And not a man shall dwell in it.

Spearmen or heavily armed troops.

Ps 68:30 Rebuke the beasts of the reeds, The herd of bulls with the calves of the peoples, *Till everyone* submits himself with pieces of silver. Scatter the peoples *who* delight in war.

Acts 23:23 And he called for two centurions, saying, "Prepare two hundred soldiers, seventy horsemen, and two hundred spearmen to go to Caesarea at the third hour of the night;

Cavalry.

Ex 14:9 So the Egyptians pursued them, all the horses *and* chariots of Pharaoh, his horsemen and his army, and overtook them camping by the sea beside Pi Hahiroth, before Baal Zephon.

1 Kin 20:20 And each one killed his man; so the Syrians fled, and Israel pursued them; and Ben-Hadad the king of Syria escaped on a horse with the cavalry.

War chariots.

Josh 17:16 But the children of Joseph said, "The mountain country is not enough for us; and all the Canaanites who dwell in the land of the valley have chariots of iron, *both those* who *are* of Beth Shean and its towns and *those* who *are* of the Valley of Jezreel."

Judg 4:3 And the children of Israel cried out to the Lord; for Jabin had nine hundred chariots of iron, and for twenty years he had harshly oppressed the children of Israel.

Often consisted of the whole effective strength of nations.

Num 21:23 But Sihon would not allow Israel to pass through his territory. So Sihon gathered all his people together and went out against Israel in the wilderness, and he came to Jahaz and fought against Israel.

1 Sam 29:1 Then the Philistines gathered together all their armies at Aphek, and the Israelites encamped by a fountain which *is* in Jezreel.

Furnished with standards.

Song 6:4 O my love, you *are as* beautiful as Tirzah, Lovely as Jerusalem, Awesome as *an army* with banners!

Jer 4:21 How long will I see the standard, *And* hear the sound of the trumpet?

Accompanied by beasts of burden and wagons for baggage.

Judg 7:12 Now the Midianites and Amalekites, all the people of the East, were lying in the valley as numerous as locusts; and their camels *were* without number, as the sand by the seashore in multitude.

2 Kin 7:7 Therefore they arose and fled at twilight, and left the camp intact—their tents, their horses, and their donkeys—and they fled for their lives.

Ezek 23:24 And they shall come against you With chariots, wagons, and war-horses, With a horde of people. They shall array against you Buckler, shield, and helmet all around. 'I will delegate judgment to them, And they shall judge you according to their judgments

Were led by experienced captains.

2 Kin 18:17 Then the king of Assyria sent *the* Tartan, *the* Rabsaris, *and the* Rabshakeh from Lachish, with a great army against Jerusalem, to King Hezekiah. And they went up and came to Jerusalem. When they had come up, they went and stood by the aqueduct from the upper pool, which *was* on the highway to the Fuller's Field.

2 Kin 18:24 How then will you repel one captain of the least of my master's servants, and put your trust in Egypt for chariots and horsemen?

Called the

Wings of a nation.

Is 8:8 He will pass through Judah, He will overflow and pass over, He will reach up to the neck; And the stretching out of his wings Will fill the breadth of Your land, O Immanuel.

Jer 48:40 For thus says the LORD: "Behold, one shall fly like an eagle, And spread his wings over Moab.

Forces of kings.

2 Chr 32:9 After this Sennacherib king of Assyria sent his servants to Jerusalem (but he and all the forces with him *laid siege* against Lachish), to Hezekiah king of Judah, and to all Judah who *were* in Jerusalem, saying,

Bands.

2 Kin 24:2 And the LORD sent against him *raiding* bands of Chaldeans, bands of Syrians, bands of Moabites, and bands of the people of Ammon; He sent them against Judah to destroy it, according to the word of the LORD which He had spoken by His servants the prophets.

Troops.

1 Chr 7:4 And with them, by their generations, according to their fathers' houses, *were* thirty-six thousand troops ready for war; for they had many wives and sons.

Began their campaigns in the spring.

2 Sam 11:1 It happened in the spring of the year, at the time when kings go out *to battle*, that David sent Joab and his servants with him, and all Israel; and they destroyed the people of Ammon and besieged Rabbah. But David remained at Jerusalem.

Often went on foreign service.

Jer 5:15 Behold, I will bring a nation against you from afar, O house of Israel," says the LORD. "It *is* a mighty nation, It *is* an ancient nation, A nation whose language you do not know, Nor can you understand what they say.

Jer 50:3 For out of the north a nation comes up against her, Which shall make her land desolate, And no one shall dwell therein. They shall move, they shall depart, Both man and beast.

Marched

With order and precision.

Is 5:27 No one will be weary or stumble among them,

No one will slumber or sleep; Nor will the belt on their loins be loosed, Nor the strap of their sandals be broken;

Joel 2:7–8 They run like mighty men, They climb the wall like men of war; Every one marches in formation, And they do not break ranks. **8** They do not push one another; Every one marches in his own column. Though they lunge between the weapons, They are not cut down.

With rapidity.

Jer 48:40 For thus says the LORD: "Behold, one shall fly like an eagle, And spread his wings over Moab.

Hab 1:8 Their horses also are swifter than leopards, And more fierce than evening wolves. Their chargers charge ahead; Their cavalry comes from afar; They fly as the eagle *that* hastens to eat.

With noise and tumult.

Is 17:12–13 Woe to the multitude of many people *Who* make a noise like the roar of the seas, And to the rushing of nations *That* make a rushing like the rushing of mighty waters! **13** The nations will rush like the rushing of many waters; But *God* will rebuke them and they will flee far away, And be chased like the chaff of the mountains before the wind, Like a rolling thing before the whirlwind.

Joel 2:5 With a noise like chariots Over mountaintops they leap, Like the noise of a flaming fire that devours the stubble, Like a strong people set in battle array.

Employed in

Fighting battles.

1 Sam 17:2–3 And Saul and the men of Israel were gathered together, and they encamped in the Valley of Elah, and drew up in battle array against the Philistines. **3** The Philistines stood on a mountain on one side, and Israel stood on a mountain on the other side, with a valley between them.

1 Chr 19:17 When it was told David, he gathered all Israel, crossed over the Jordan and came upon them, and set up in battle array against them. So when David had set up in *battle* array against the Syrians, they fought with him.

Besieging cities.

Deut 20:12 Now if *the city* will not make peace with you, but war against you, then you shall besiege it.

Is 29:3 I will encamp against you all around, I will lay siege against you with a mound, And I will raise siegeworks against you.

Assaulting cities.

Josh 7:3–4 And they returned to Joshua and said to him, "Do not let all the people go up, but let about two or three thousand men go up and attack Ai. Do not weary all the people there, for *the people of Ai are* few." **4** So about three thousand men went up there from the people, but they fled before the men of Ai.

Judg 9:45 So Abimelech fought against the city all that day; he took the city and killed the people who *were* in it; and he demolished the city and sowed it with salt.

Often surprised their enemies.

Josh 8:2 And you shall do to Ai and its king as you did to Jericho and its king. Only its spoil and its cattle you shall take as booty for yourselves. Lay an ambush for the city behind it."

2 Chr 13:15 Then the men of Judah gave a shout; and as the men of Judah shouted, it happened that God struck Jeroboam and all Israel before Abijah and Judah.

Jer 51:12 Set up the standard on the walls of Babylon; Make the guard strong, Set up the watchmen, Prepare the ambushes. For the LORD has both devised and done What He spoke against the inhabitants of Babylon.

Commenced battles with a shout.

1 Sam 17:20 So David rose early in the morning, left the sheep with a keeper, and took *the things* and went as Jesse had commanded him. And he came to the camp as the army was going out to the fight and shouting for the battle.

2 Chr 13:15 Then the men of Judah gave a shout; and as the men of Judah shouted, it happened that God struck Jeroboam and all Israel before Abijah and Judah.

Jer 51:14 The LORD of hosts has sworn by Himself: "Surely I will fill you with men, as with locusts, And they shall lift up a shout against you."

Toil and fatigue often endured by.

Ezek 29:18 "Son of man, Nebuchadnezzar king of Babylon caused his army to labor strenuously against Tyre; every head *was* made bald, and every shoulder rubbed raw; yet neither he nor his army received wages from Tyre, for the labor which they expended on it.

Divided the spoil.

Ex 15:9 The enemy said, 'I will pursue, I will overtake, I will divide the spoil; My desire shall be satisfied on them. I will draw my sword, My hand shall destroy them.'

Josh 22:8 and spoke to them, saying, "Return with much riches to your tents, with very much livestock, with silver, with gold, with bronze, with iron, and with very much clothing. Divide the spoil of your enemies with your brethren."

Judg 5:30 'Are they not finding and dividing the spoil: To every man a girl *or* two; For Sisera, plunder of dyed garments, Plunder of garments embroidered and dyed, Two pieces of dyed embroidery for the neck of the looter?'

Zech 14:1 Behold, the day of the LORD is coming, And your spoil will be divided in your midst.

Sent out foraging parties.

2 Kin 5:2 And the Syrians had gone out on raids, and had brought back captive a young girl from the land of Israel. She waited on Naaman's wife.

2 Kin 13:20 Then Elisha died, and they buried him. And the *raiding* bands from Moab invaded the land in the spring of the year.

Exercised savage cruelties on the vanquished.

Jer 50:42 They shall hold the bow and the lance; They *are* cruel and shall not show mercy. Their voice shall roar like the sea; They shall ride on horses, Set in array, like a man for the battle, Against you, O daughter of Babylon.

Lam 5:11–13 They ravished the women in Zion, The

maidens in the cities of Judah. **12** Princes were hung up by their hands, And elders were not respected. **13** Young men ground at the millstones; Boys staggered under *loads of* wood.

Amos 1:13 Thus says the LORD: "For three transgressions of the people of Ammon, and for four, I will not turn away its *punishment,* Because they ripped open the women with child in Gilead, That they might enlarge their territory.

The instrument of God's vengeance.

Is 13:5 They come from a far country, From the end of heaven— The LORD and His weapons of indignation, To destroy the whole land.

In latter ages received pay.

Luke 3:14 Likewise the soldiers asked him, saying, "And what shall we do?" So he said to them, "Do not intimidate anyone or accuse falsely, and be content with your wages."

1 Cor 9:7 Who ever goes to war at his own expense? Who plants a vineyard and does not eat of its fruit? Or who tends a flock and does not drink of the milk of the flock?

Encamped

In the open fields.

2 Sam 11:11 And Uriah said to David, "The ark and Israel and Judah are dwelling in tents, and my lord Joab and the servants of my lord are encamped in the open fields. Shall I then go to my house to eat and drink, and to lie with my wife? *As* you live, and *as* your soul lives, I will not do this thing."

1 Chr 11:15 Now three of the thirty chief men went down to the rock to David, into the cave of Adullam; and the army of the Philistines encamped in the Valley of Rephaim.

Before cities.

Josh 10:5 Therefore the five kings of the Amorites, the king of Jerusalem, the king of Hebron, the king of Jarmuth, the king of Lachish, *and* the king of Eglon, gathered together and went up, they and all their armies, and camped before Gibeon and made war against it.

1 Sam 11:1 Then Nahash the Ammonite came up and encamped against Jabesh Gilead; and all the men of Jabesh said to Nahash, "Make a covenant with us, and we will serve you."

Fear occasioned by.

Num 22:3 And Moab was exceedingly afraid of the people because they *were* many, and Moab was sick with dread because of the children of Israel.

Jer 6:25 Do not go out into the field, Nor walk by the way. Because of the sword of the enemy, Fear *is* on every side.

Devastation occasioned by.

Is 37:18 Truly, LORD, the kings of Assyria have laid waste all the nations and their lands,

Jer 5:17 And they shall eat up your harvest and your bread, *Which* your sons and daughters should eat. They shall eat up your flocks and your herds; They shall eat up your vines and your fig trees; They shall destroy your fortified cities, In which you trust, with the sword.

Often destroyed by

Their enemies.

Ex 17:13 So Joshua defeated Amalek and his people with the edge of the sword.

Josh 10:10 So the LORD routed them before Israel, killed them with a great slaughter at Gibeon, chased them along the road that goes to Beth Horon, and struck them down as far as Azekah and Makkedah.

Josh 10:20 Then it happened, while Joshua and the children of Israel made an end of slaying them with a very great slaughter, till they had finished, that those who escaped entered fortified cities.

Judg 11:33 And he defeated them from Aroer as far as Minnith—twenty cities—and to Abel Keramim, with a very great slaughter. Thus the people of Ammon were subdued before the children of Israel.

2 Sam 18:7 The people of Israel were overthrown there before the servants of David, and a great slaughter of twenty thousand took place there that day.

1 Kin 20:21 Then the king of Israel went out and attacked the horses and chariots, and killed the Syrians with a great slaughter.

Themselves through divine intervention.

Judg 7:22 When the three hundred blew the trumpets, the LORD set every man's sword against his companion throughout the whole camp; and the army fled to Beth Acacia, toward Zererah, as far as the border of Abel Meholah, by Tabbath.

1 Sam 14:15–16 And there was trembling in the camp, in the field, and among all the people. The garrison and the raiders also trembled; and the earth quaked, so that it was a very great trembling. **16** Now the watchmen of Saul in Gibeah of Benjamin looked, and *there* was the multitude, melting away; and they went here and there.

2 Chr 20:23 For the people of Ammon and Moab stood up against the inhabitants of Mount Seir to utterly kill and destroy *them*. And when they had made an end of the inhabitants of Seir, they helped to destroy one another.

Supernatural means.

Josh 10:11 And it happened, as they fled before Israel *and* were on the descent of Beth Horon, that the LORD cast down large hailstones from heaven on them as far as Azekah, and they died. *There were* more who died from the hailstones than the children of Israel killed with the sword.

2 Kin 19:35 And it came to pass on a certain night that the angel of the LORD went out, and killed in the camp of the Assyrians one hundred and eighty-five thousand; and when *people* arose early in the morning, there were the corpses—all dead.

Brought their idols with them.

1 Chr 14:12 And when they left their gods there, David gave a commandment, and they were burned with fire.

Compared to

Whirlwinds.

Jer 25:32 Thus says the LORD of hosts: "Behold, disaster shall go forth From nation to nation, And a great whirlwind shall be raised up From the farthest parts of the earth.

Waters of a river.

Is 8:7 Now therefore, behold, the Lord brings up over them The waters of the River, strong and mighty— The king of Assyria and all his glory; He will go up over all his channels And go over all his banks.

Grasshoppers.

Judg 6:3–5 So it was, whenever Israel had sown, Midianites would come up; also Amalekites and the people of the East would come up against them. **4** Then they would encamp against them and destroy the produce of the earth as far as Gaza, and leave no sustenance for Israel, neither sheep nor ox nor donkey. **5** For they would come up with their livestock and their tents, coming in as numerous as locusts; both they and their camels were without number; and they would enter the land to destroy it.

Judg 7:12 Now the Midianites and Amalekites, all the people of the East, were lying in the valley as numerous as locusts; and their camels *were* without number, as the sand by the seashore in multitude.

Locusts.

Is 33:4 And Your plunder shall be gathered *Like* the gathering of the caterpillar; As the running to and fro of locusts, He shall run upon them.

Jer 51:14 The LORD of hosts has sworn by Himself: "Surely I will fill you with men, as with locusts, And they shall lift up a shout against you."

Jer 51:27 Set up a banner in the land, Blow the trumpet among the nations! Prepare the nations against her, Call the kingdoms together against her: Ararat, Minni, and Ashkenaz. Appoint a general against her; Cause the horses to come up like the bristling locusts.

Flies.

Is 7:18–19 And it shall come to pass in that day *That* the LORD will whistle for the fly That *is* in the farthest part of the rivers of Egypt, And for the bee that *is* in the land of Assyria. **19** They will come, and all of them will rest In the desolate valleys and in the clefts of the rocks, And on all thorns and in all pastures.

Clouds.

Ezek 38:9–16 You will ascend, coming like a storm, covering the land like a cloud, you and all your troops and many peoples with you." **10** 'Thus says the Lord GOD: "On that day it shall come to pass *that* thoughts will arise in your mind, and you will make an evil plan: **11** You will say, 'I will go up against a land of unwalled villages; I will go to a peaceful people, who dwell safely, all of them dwelling without walls, and having neither bars nor gates'— **12** to take plunder and to take booty, to stretch out your hand against the waste places *that are again* inhabited, and against a people gathered from the nations, who have acquired livestock and goods, who dwell in the midst of the land. **13** Sheba, Dedan, the merchants of Tarshish, and all their young lions will say to you, 'Have you come to take plunder? Have you gathered your army to take booty, to carry away silver and gold, to take away livestock and goods, to take great plunder?' " ' **14** "Therefore, son of man, prophesy and say to Gog, 'Thus says the Lord GOD: "On that day when My people Israel dwell safely, will you not know *it*? **15** Then you will come from your place out of the far north, you and many peoples with you, all of them riding on horses, a great company and a mighty army. **16** You will come up against My people Israel like a cloud, to cover the land. It will be in the latter days that I will bring you against My land, so that the nations may know Me, when I am hallowed in you, O Gog, before their eyes."

Overflowing torrents.

Is 28:2 Behold, the Lord has a mighty and strong one, Like a tempest of hail and a destroying storm, Like a flood of mighty waters overflowing, Who will bring *them* down to the earth with *His* hand.

Dan 11:10 However his sons shall stir up strife, and assemble a multitude of great forces; and *one* shall certainly come and overwhelm and pass through; then he shall return to his fortress and stir up strife.

Dan 11:26 Yes, those who eat of the portion of his delicacies shall destroy him; his army shall be swept away, and many shall fall down slain.

ARMOR
Sometimes part of spoils of warfare.

2 Sam 2:21 And Abner said to him, "Turn aside to your right hand or to your left, and lay hold on one of the young men and take his armor for yourself." But Asahel would not turn aside from following him.

Symbolic of righteousness.

Rom 13:12 The night is far spent, the day is at hand. Therefore let us cast off the works of darkness, and let us put on the armor of light.

2 Cor 6:7 by the word of truth, by the power of God, by the armor of righteousness on the right hand and on the left,

Spiritual, described.

Eph 6:10–17 Finally, my brethren, be strong in the Lord and in the power of His might. **11** Put on the whole armor of God, that you may be able to stand against the wiles of the devil. **12** For we do not wrestle against flesh and blood, but against principalities, against powers, against the rulers of the darkness of this age, against spiritual *hosts* of wickedness in the heavenly *places*. **13** Therefore take up the whole armor of God, that you may be able to withstand in the evil day, and having done all, to stand. **14** Stand therefore, having girded your waist with truth, having put on the breastplate of righteousness, **15** and having shod your feet with the preparation of the gospel of peace; **16** above all, taking the shield of faith with which you will be able to quench all the fiery darts of the wicked one. **17** And take the helmet of salvation, and the sword of the Spirit, which is the word of God;

ARROGANCE
Should not be displayed before God.

1 Sam 2:3 "Talk no more so very proudly; Let no arrogance come from your mouth, For the LORD *is* the God of knowledge; And by Him actions are weighed.

Prov 8:13 The fear of the LORD *is* to hate evil; Pride and arrogance and the evil way And the perverse mouth I hate.

Of the wicked.

Ps 94:3–7 LORD, how long will the wicked, How long will the wicked triumph? **4** They utter speech, *and* speak insolent things; All the workers of iniquity boast in themselves. **5** They break in pieces Your people, O LORD, And afflict Your heritage. **6** They slay the widow and the stranger, And murder the fatherless. **7** Yet they say, "The LORD does not see, Nor does the God of Jacob understand."

And Israel.

Is 9:8–10 The Lord sent a word against Jacob, And it has fallen on Israel. **9** All the people will know— Ephraim and the inhabitant of Samaria— Who say in pride and arrogance of heart: **10** "The bricks have fallen down, But we will rebuild with hewn stones; The sycamores are cut down, But we will replace *them* with cedars."

God punishes.

Is 13:11 "I will punish the world for *its* evil, And the wicked for their iniquity; I will halt the arrogance of the proud, And will lay low the haughtiness of the terrible.

Satan's described.

Is 14:12–14 "How you are fallen from heaven, O Lucifer, son of the morning! *How* you are cut down to the ground, You who weakened the nations! **13** For you have said in your heart: 'I will ascend into heaven, I will exalt my throne above the stars of God; I will also sit on the mount of the congregation On the farthest sides of the north; **14** I will ascend above the heights of the clouds, I will be like the Most High.'

Reason for Tyre's overthrow.

Is 23:8–9 Who has taken this counsel against Tyre, the crowning *city,* Whose merchants *are* princes, Whose traders *are* the honorable of the earth? **9** The LORD of hosts has purposed it, To bring to dishonor the pride of all glory, To bring into contempt all the honorable of the earth.

A problem in the Corinthian church.

1 Cor 4:6 Now these things, brethren, I have figuratively transferred to myself and Apollos for your sakes, that you may learn in us not to think beyond what is written, that none of you may be puffed up on behalf of one against the other.

1 Cor 4:18–19 Now some are puffed up, as though I were not coming to you. **19** But I will come to you shortly, if the Lord wills, and I will know, not the word of those who are puffed up, but the power.

1 Cor 5:2 And you are puffed up, and have not rather mourned, that he who has done this deed might be taken away from among you.

1 Cor 8:1 Now concerning things offered to idols: We know that we all have knowledge. Knowledge puffs up, but love edifies.

1 Cor 13:4 Love suffers long *and* is kind; love does not envy; love does not parade itself, is not puffed up;

2 Cor 12:20 For I fear lest, when I come, I shall not find you such as I wish, and *that* I shall be found by you such as you do not wish; lest *there be* contentions, jealousies, outbursts of wrath, selfish ambitions, backbitings, whisperings, conceits, tumults;

Characteristic of false teachers.

2 Pet 2:10 and especially those who walk according to the flesh in the lust of uncleanness and despise authority. *They are* presumptuous, self-willed. They are not afraid to speak evil of dignitaries,

ARROWS

Deadly and destructive weapons.

Prov 26:18 Like a madman who throws firebrands, arrows, and death,

Called shafts.

Is 49:2 And He has made My mouth like a sharp sword; In the shadow of His hand He has hidden Me, And made Me a polished shaft; In His quiver He has hidden Me."

Sharp.

Ps 120:4 Sharp arrows of the warrior, With coals of the broom tree!

Is 5:28 Whose arrows *are* sharp, And all their bows bent; Their horses' hooves will seem like flint, And their wheels like a whirlwind.

Bright and polished.

Is 49:2 And He has made My mouth like a sharp sword; In the shadow of His hand He has hidden Me, And made Me a polished shaft; In His quiver He has hidden Me."

Jer 51:11 Make the arrows bright! Gather the shields! The LORD has raised up the spirit of the kings of the Medes. For His plan *is* against Babylon to destroy it, Because it *is* the vengeance of the LORD, The vengeance for His temple.

Sometimes poisoned.

Job 6:4 For the arrows of the Almighty *are* within me; My spirit drinks in their poison; The terrors of God are arrayed against me.

Carried in a quiver.

Gen 27:3 Now therefore, please take your weapons, your quiver and your bow, and go out to the field and hunt game for me.

Is 49:2 And He has made My mouth like a sharp sword; In the shadow of His hand He has hidden Me, And made Me a polished shaft; In His quiver He has hidden Me."

Jer 5:16 Their quiver *is* like an open tomb; They *are* all mighty men.

Lam 3:13 He has caused the arrows of His quiver To pierce my loins.

Discharged

From a bow.

Ps 11:2 For look! The wicked bend *their* bow, They make ready their arrow on the string, That they may shoot secretly at the upright in heart.

Is 7:24 With arrows and bows men will come there, Because all the land will become briers and thorns.

From engines.

2 Chr 26:15 And he made devices in Jerusalem, invented by skillful men, to be on the towers and the corners, to shoot arrows and large stones. So his fame spread far and wide, for he was marvelously helped till he became strong.

At a mark for amusement.

1 Sam 20:20–22 Then I will shoot three arrows to the side, as though I shot at a target; **21** and there I will send a lad, *saying,* 'Go, find the arrows.' If I expressly say to the lad, 'Look, the arrows *are* on this side of you; get them and come'—then, as the LORD lives, *there is* safety for you and no harm. **22** But if I say thus to the young man, 'Look, the arrows *are* beyond you'—go your way, for the LORD has sent you away.

At the beasts of the earth.

Gen 27:3 Now therefore, please take your weapons, your quiver and your bow, and go out to the field and hunt game for me.

Against enemies.

2 Kin 19:32 "Therefore thus says the LORD concerning the king of Assyria: 'He shall not come into this city, Nor shoot an arrow there, Nor come before it with shield, Nor build a siege mound against it.

Jer 50:14 "Put yourselves in array against Babylon all around, All you who bend the bow; Shoot at her, spare no arrows, For she has sinned against the LORD.

With great force.

Num 24:8 "God brings him out of Egypt; He has strength like a wild ox; He shall consume the nations, his enemies; He shall break their bones And pierce *them* with his arrows.

2 Kin 9:24 Now Jehu drew his bow with full strength and shot Jehoram between his arms; and the arrow came out at his heart, and he sank down in his chariot.

Fleetness of, alluded to.

Zech 9:14 Then the LORD will be seen over them, And His arrow will go forth like lightning. The Lord GOD will blow the trumpet, And go with whirlwinds from the south.

The ancients used for divination.

Ezek 21:21 For the king of Babylon stands at the parting of the road, at the fork of the two roads, to use divination: he shakes the arrows, he consults the images, he looks at the liver.

Illustrative of

Christ.

Is 49:2 And He has made My mouth like a sharp sword; In the shadow of His hand He has hidden Me, And made Me a polished shaft; In His quiver He has hidden Me."

The word of Christ.

Ps 45:5 Your arrows *are* sharp in the heart of the King's enemies; The peoples fall under You.

God's judgment.

Deut 32:23 'I will heap disasters on them; I will spend My arrows on them.

Ps 7:13 He also prepares for Himself instruments of death; He makes His arrows into fiery shafts.

Ps 21:12 Therefore You will make them turn their back; You will make ready *Your arrows* on Your string toward their faces.

Ps 64:7 But God shall shoot at them *with* an arrow; Suddenly they shall be wounded.

Ezek 5:16 When I send against them the terrible arrows of famine which shall be for destruction, which I will send to destroy you, I will increase the famine upon you and cut off your supply of bread.

Severe afflictions.

Job 6:4 For the arrows of the Almighty *are* within me; My spirit drinks in their poison; The terrors of God are arrayed against me.

Ps 38:2 For Your arrows pierce me deeply, And Your hand presses me down.

Bitter words.

Ps 64:3 Who sharpen their tongue like a sword, And bend *their bows to shoot* their arrows—bitter words,

Slanderous tongues.

Jer 9:8 Their tongue *is* an arrow shot out; It speaks deceit; *One* speaks peaceably to his neighbor with his mouth, But in his heart he lies in wait.

False witnesses.

Prov 25:18 A man who bears false witness against his neighbor *Is like* a club, a sword, and a sharp arrow.

Devices of the wicked.

Ps 11:2 For look! The wicked bend *their* bow, They make ready their arrow on the string, That they may shoot secretly at the upright in heart.

Young children.

Ps 127:5 Happy *is* the man who has his quiver full of them; They shall not be ashamed, But shall speak with their enemies in the gate.

Lightnings.

Ps 77:17–18 The clouds poured out water; The skies sent out a sound; Your arrows also flashed about. **18** The voice of Your thunder *was* in the whirlwind; The lightnings lit up the world; The earth trembled and shook.

Hab 3:11 The sun and moon stood still in their habitation; At the light of Your arrows they went, At the shining of Your glittering spear.

Destruction of power.

Ps 76:3 There He broke the arrows of the bow, The shield and sword of battle. Selah

(Falling from the hand) of paralyzing power.

Ezek 39:3 Then I will knock the bow out of your left hand, and cause the arrows to fall out of your right hand.

ARTAXERXES

Corresponded with opponents of Jews.
Ezra 4:7–23

Helped Ezra with temple project.

Ezra 6:14 So the elders of the Jews built, and they prospered through the prophesying of Haggai the prophet and Zechariah the son of Iddo. And they built and finished *it*, according to the commandment of the God of Israel, and according to the command of Cyrus, Darius, and Artaxerxes king of Persia.

Cf. Ezra 7:11–26

Persian king.

Ezra 7:1 Now after these things, in the reign of Artaxerxes king of Persia, Ezra the son of Seraiah, the son of Azariah, the son of Hilkiah,

Granted Nehemiah letters of passage to Judah.

Neh 2:1–8 And it came to pass in the month of Nisan, in the twentieth year of King Artaxerxes, *when* wine *was* before him, that I took the wine and gave it to the king. Now I had never been sad in his presence before. **2** Therefore the king said to me, "Why *is* your face sad, since you *are* not sick? This *is* nothing but sorrow of heart." So I became dreadfully afraid, **3** and said to the king, "May the king live forever! Why should my face not be sad, when the city, the place of my fathers' tombs, *lies* waste, and its gates are burned with fire?" **4** Then the king said to me, "What do you request?" So I prayed to the God of heaven. **5** And I said to the king, "If it pleases the king, and if your servant has found favor in your sight, I ask that you send me to Judah, to the city of my fathers' tombs, that I may rebuild it." **6** Then the king said to me (the queen also sitting beside him), "How long will your journey be? And when will you return?" So it pleased the king to send me; and I set him a time. **7** Furthermore I said to the king, "If it pleases the king, let letters be given to me for the governors *of the region* beyond the River, that they must permit me to pass through till I come to Judah, **8** and a letter to Asaph the keeper of the king's forest, that he must give me timber to make beams for the gates of the citadel which *pertains* to the temple, for the city wall, and for the house that I will occupy." And the king granted *them* to me according to the good hand of my God upon me.

Provided ongoing assistance to Nehemiah.

Neh 5:14 Moreover, from the time that I was appointed to be their governor in the land of Judah, from the twentieth year until the thirty-second year of King Artaxerxes, twelve years, neither I nor my brothers ate the governor's provisions.

ASHER, THE TRIBE OF
Descended from Jacob's eighth son.

Gen 30:12–13 And Leah's maid Zilpah bore Jacob a second son. **13** Then Leah said, "I am happy, for the daughters will call me blessed." So she called his name Asher.

Predictions concerning.

Gen 49:20 "Bread from Asher *shall be* rich, And he shall yield royal dainties.

Deut 33:24–25 And of Asher he said: "Asher *is* most blessed of sons; Let him be favored by his brothers, And let him dip his foot in oil. **25** Your sandals *shall be* iron and bronze; As your days, *so shall* your strength *be.*

Strength of, on leaving Egypt.

Num 1:40–41 From the children of Asher, their genealogies by their families, by their fathers' house, according to the number of names, from twenty years old and above, all who *were able to* go to war: **41** those who were numbered of the tribe of Asher *were* forty-one thousand five hundred.

Persons selected from,

To number the people.

Num 1:13 from Asher, Pagiel the son of Ocran;

To spy out the land.

Num 13:13 from the tribe of Asher, Sethur the son of Michael;

To divide the land.

Num 34:27 a leader from the tribe of the children of Asher, Ahihud the son of Shelomi;

The center of the fourth division of Israel in its journeys.

Num 10:25–26 Then the standard of the camp of the children of Dan (the rear guard of all the camps) set out according to their armies; over their army *was* Ahiezer the son of Ammishaddai. 26 Over the army of the tribe of the children of Asher *was* Pagiel the son of Ocran.

Encamped next to, and under the standard of Dan, north of the tabernacle.

Num 2:25 "The standard of the forces with Dan *shall be* on the north side according to their armies, and the leader of the children of Dan *shall be* Ahiezer the son of Ammishaddai."

Num 2:27 "Those who camp next to him *shall be* the tribe of Asher, and the leader of the children of Asher *shall be* Pagiel the son of Ocran."

Offering of, at the dedication.

Num 7:72–77 On the eleventh day Pagiel the son of Ocran, leader of the children of Asher, *presented an offering.* 73 His offering *was* one silver platter, the weight of which *was* one hundred and thirty *shekels*, and one silver bowl of seventy shekels, according to the shekel of the sanctuary, both of them full of fine flour mixed with oil as a grain offering; 74 one gold pan of ten *shekels*, full of incense; 75 one young bull, one ram, and one male lamb in its first year, as a burnt offering; 76 one kid of the goats as a sin offering; 77 and as the sacrifice of peace offerings: two oxen, five rams, five male goats, and five male lambs in their first year. This *was* the offering of Pagiel the son of Ocran.

Families of.

Num 26:44–47 The sons of Asher according to their families *were:* of Jimna, the family of the Jimnites; of Jesui, the family of the Jesuites; of Beriah, the family of the Beriites. 45 Of the sons of Beriah: of Heber, the family of the Heberites; of Malchiel, the family of the Malchielites. 46 And the name of the daughter of Asher *was* Serah. 47 These *are* the families of the sons of Asher according to those who were numbered of them: fifty-three thousand four hundred.

Strength of, on entering Canaan.

Num 26:47 These *are* the families of the sons of Asher according to those who were numbered of them: fifty-three thousand four hundred.

On Ebal, said amen to the curses of the law.

Deut 27:13 and these shall stand on Mount Ebal to curse: Reuben, Gad, Asher, Zebulun, Dan, and Naphtali.

Bounds of their inheritance.

Josh 19:24–31 The fifth lot came out for the tribe of the children of Asher according to their families. 25 And their territory included Helkath, Hali, Beten, Achshaph, 26 Alammelech, Amad, and Mishal; it reached to Mount Carmel westward, along *the Brook* Shihor Libnath. 27 It turned toward the sunrise to Beth Dagon; and it reached to Zebulun and to the Valley of Jiphthah El, then northward beyond Beth Emek and Neiel, bypassing Cabul *which was* on the left, 28 including Ebron, Rehob, Hammon, and Kanah, as far as Greater Sidon. 29 And the border turned to Ramah and to the fortified city of Tyre; then the border turned to Hosah, and ended at the sea by the region of Achzib. 30 Also Ummah, Aphek, and Rehob *were* included: twenty-two cities with their villages. 31 This *was* the inheritance of the tribe of the children of Asher according to their families, these cities with their villages.

Bordered on the sea.

Josh 19:29 And the border turned to Ramah and to the fortified city of Tyre; then the border turned to Hosah, and ended at the sea by the region of Achzib.

Judg 5:17 Gilead stayed beyond the Jordan, And why did Dan remain on ships? Asher continued at the seashore, And stayed by his inlets.

Did not fully drive out Canaanites.

Judg 1:31–32 Nor did Asher drive out the inhabitants of Acco or the inhabitants of Sidon, or of Ahlab, Achzib, Helbah, Aphik, or Rehob. 32 So the Asherites dwelt among the Canaanites, the inhabitants of the land; for they did not drive them out.

Reproved for not aiding against Sisera.

Judg 5:17 Gilead stayed beyond the Jordan, And why did Dan remain on ships? Asher continued at the seashore, And stayed by his inlets.

Assisted Gideon against the Midianites.

Judg 6:35 And he sent messengers throughout all Manasseh, who also gathered behind him. He also sent messengers to Asher, Zebulun, and Naphtali; and they came up to meet them.

Judg 7:23 And the men of Israel gathered together from Naphtali, Asher, and all Manasseh, and pursued the Midianites.

Some of, at the coronation of David.

1 Chr 12:36 of Asher, those who could go out to war, able to keep battle formation, forty thousand;

Officers placed over, by Solomon.

1 Kin 4:16 Baanah the son of Hushai, in Asher and Aloth;

Aided in Hezekiah's reformation.

2 Chr 30:11 Nevertheless some from Asher, Manasseh, and Zebulun humbled themselves and came to Jerusalem.

Remarkable persons of.

1 Chr 7:30–40 The sons of Asher *were* Imnah, Ishvah, Ishvi, Beriah, and their sister Serah. 31 The sons of Beriah *were* Heber and Malchiel, who was the father of Birzaith. 32 And Heber begot Japhlet, Shomer, Hotham, and their sister Shua. 33 The sons of Japhlet *were* Pasach, Bimhal, and Ashvath. These *were* the children of Japhlet. 34 The sons of Shemer *were* Ahi, Rohgah, Jehubbah, and Aram. 35 And the sons of his brother Helem *were* Zophah, Imna, Shelesh, and Amal. 36 The sons of Zophah *were* Suah, Harnepher, Shual, Beri, Imrah, 37 Bezer, Hod, Shamma, Shilshah, Jithran, and Beera. 38 The sons of Jether *were* Jephunneh, Pispah, and Ara. 39 The sons of Ulla *were* Arah, Haniel, and Rizia. **40** All these *were* the children of Asher, heads of *their* fathers' houses, choice men, mighty men of valor, chief leaders. And they were recorded by genealogies among the army fit for battle; their number *was* twenty-six thousand.

Luke 2:36 Now there was one, Anna, a prophetess, the daughter of Phanuel, of the tribe of Asher. She was of a great age, and had lived with a husband seven years from her virginity;

ASHES

Expression of humility and mourning.

Gen 18:27 Then Abraham answered and said, "Indeed now, I who *am but* dust and ashes have taken it upon myself to speak to the Lord:

2 Sam 13:19 Then Tamar put ashes on her head, and tore her robe of many colors that *was* on her, and laid her hand on her head and went away crying bitterly.

Esth 4:1 When Mordecai learned all that had happened, he tore his clothes and put on sackcloth and ashes, and went out into the midst of the city. He cried out with a loud and bitter cry.

Job 42:6 Therefore I abhor *myself*, And repent in dust and ashes."

Jer 6:26 O daughter of my people, Dress in sackcloth And roll about in ashes! Make mourning *as for* an only son, most bitter lamentation; For the plunderer will suddenly come upon us.

Dan 9:3 Then I set my face toward the Lord God to make request by prayer and supplications, with fasting, sackcloth, and ashes.

Jon 3:6 Then word came to the king of Nineveh; and he arose from his throne and laid aside his robe, covered *himself* with sackcloth and sat in ashes.

Matt 11:21 "Woe to you, Chorazin! Woe to you, Bethsaida! For if the mighty works which were done in you had been done in Tyre and Sidon, they would have repented long ago in sackcloth and ashes.

Cf. Job 2:8; Mal 4:3

From sacrifices, needed proper disposal.

Lev 4:12 the whole bull he shall carry outside the camp to a clean place, where the ashes are poured out, and burn it on wood with fire; where the ashes are poured out it shall be burned.

Lev 6:10–11 And the priest shall put on his linen garment, and his linen trousers he shall put on his body, and take up the ashes of the burnt offering which the fire has consumed on the altar, and he shall put them beside the altar. **11** Then he shall take off his garments, put on other garments, and carry the ashes outside the camp to a clean place.

1 Kin 13:3 And he gave a sign the same day, saying, "This *is* the sign which the LORD has spoken: Surely the altar shall split apart, and the ashes on it shall be poured out."

Cf. 2 Kin 23:4; Heb 9:13

ASIA MINOR (MODERN TURKEY)

Origin of many pilgrims who witnessed Pentecost.

Acts 2:9–10 Parthians and Medes and Elamites, those dwelling in Mesopotamia, Judea and Cappadocia, Pontus and Asia, **10** Phrygia and Pamphylia, Egypt and the parts of Libya adjoining Cyrene, visitors from Rome, both Jews and proselytes,

Some of Stephen's debating foes from there.

Acts 6:9 Then there arose some from what is called the Synagogue of the Freedmen (Cyrenians, Alexandrians, and those from Cilicia and Asia), disputing with Stephen.

Holy Spirit prevented Paul, for a time, from going there.

Acts 16:6 Now when they had gone through Phrygia and the region of Galatia, they were forbidden by the Holy Spirit to preach the word in Asia.

Area of, north of Ephesus, referred to.

Acts 19:1 And it happened, while Apollos was at Corinth, that Paul, having passed through the upper regions, came to Ephesus. And finding some disciples

Gospel spread throughout.

Acts 19:10 And this continued for two years, so that all who dwelt in Asia heard the word of the Lord Jesus, both Jews and Greeks.

Roman officials from, mentioned.

Acts 19:31 Then some of the officials of Asia, who were his friends, sent to him pleading that he would not venture into the theater.

Representatives from churches there, traveled with Paul.

Acts 20:4 And Sopater of Berea accompanied him to Asia—also Aristarchus and Secundus of the Thessalonians, and Gaius of Derbe, and Timothy, and Tychicus and Trophimus of Asia.

Paul's probable farewell statement from.

Acts 20:25 "And indeed, now I know that you all, among whom I have gone preaching the kingdom of God, will see my face no more.

Jewish pilgrims from there opposed Paul.

Acts 21:27–29 Now when the seven days were almost ended, the Jews from Asia, seeing him in the temple, stirred up the whole crowd and laid hands on him, **28** crying out, "Men of Israel, help! This is the man who teaches all *men* everywhere against the people, the law, and this place; and furthermore he also brought Greeks into the temple and has defiled this holy place." **29** (For they had previously seen Trophimus the Ephesian with him in the city, whom they supposed that Paul had brought into the temple.)

Acts 24:18 in the midst of which some Jews from Asia found me purified in the temple, neither with a mob nor with tumult.

In province within, many defected from the faith.

2 Tim 1:15 This you know, that all those in Asia have turned away from me, among whom are Phygellus and Hermogenes.

Home of seven churches in John's vision.

Rev 1:4 John, to the seven churches which are in Asia: Grace to you and peace from Him who is and who was and who is to come, and from the seven Spirits who are before His throne,

ASSEMBLY (CONGREGATION)
Reference to
Israel.

Lev 16:17 There shall be no man in the tabernacle of meeting when he goes in to make atonement in the Holy *Place,* until he comes out, that he may make atonement for himself, for his household, and for all the assembly of Israel.

Num 20:12 Then the LORD spoke to Moses and Aaron, "Because you did not believe Me, to hallow Me in the eyes of the children of Israel, therefore you shall not bring this assembly into the land which I have given them."

Deut 23:1 "He who is emasculated by crushing or mutilation shall not enter the assembly of the LORD.

1 Kin 8:14–22 Then the king turned around and blessed the whole assembly of Israel, while all the assembly of Israel was standing. **15** And he said: "Blessed *be* the LORD God of Israel, who spoke with His mouth to my father David, and with His hand has fulfilled *it,* saying, **16** 'Since the day that I brought My people Israel out of Egypt, I have chosen no city from any tribe of Israel *in which* to build a house, that My name might be there; but I chose David to be over My people Israel.' **17** Now it was in the heart of my father David to build a temple for the name of the LORD God of Israel. **18** But the LORD said to my father David, 'Whereas it was in your heart to build a temple for My name, you did well that it was in your heart. **19** Nevertheless you shall not build the temple, but your son who will come from your body, he shall build the temple for My name.' **20** So the LORD has fulfilled His word which He spoke; and I have filled the position of my father David, and sit on the throne of Israel, as the LORD promised; and I have built a temple for the name of the LORD God of Israel. **21** And there I have made a place for the ark, in which *is* the covenant of the LORD which He made with our fathers, when He brought them out of the land of Egypt." **22** Then Solomon stood before the altar of the LORD in the presence of all the assembly of Israel, and spread out his hands toward heaven;

Cf. 1 Kin 8:54–66; 1 Chr 28:1—29:20; 2 Chr 7:1–11; Ezra 3:1–12; 10:1–15; Ps 149:1–4

World leaders.

Ps 82:1 God stands in the congregation of the mighty; He judges among the gods.

Believers.

Ps 89:7 God is greatly to be feared in the assembly of the saints, And to be held in reverence by all *those* around Him.

Angels.

Heb 12:23 to the general assembly and church of the firstborn *who are* registered in heaven, to God the Judge of all, to the spirits of just men made perfect,

In the midst of, a time for praise.
Ps 22:22 I will declare Your name to My brethren; In the midst of the assembly I will praise You.

As a public that witnesses sin.
Prov 5:14 I was on the verge of total ruin, In the midst of the assembly and congregation."

Of opposing army.
Lam 1:15 "The Lord has trampled underfoot all my mighty *men* in my midst; He has called an assembly against me To crush my young men; The Lord trampled *as* in a winepress The virgin daughter of Judah.

For sacred purposes.
Num 10:3 When they blow both of them, all the congregation shall gather before you at the door of the tabernacle of meeting.

2 Chr 7:9 And on the eighth day they held a sacred assembly, for they observed the dedication of the altar seven days, and the feast seven days.

Neh 8:18 Also day by day, from the first day until the last day, he read from the Book of the Law of God. And they kept the feast seven days; and on the eighth day *there was* a sacred assembly, according to the *prescribed* manner.

Joel 1:14 Consecrate a fast, Call a sacred assembly; Gather the elders *And* all the inhabitants of the land *Into* the house of the LORD your God, And cry out to the LORD.

Cf. Zeph 3:18

Involved in spiritual discipline.
Matt 18:15–19 "Moreover if your brother sins against you, go and tell him his fault between you and him alone. If he hears you, you have gained your brother. **16** But if he will not hear, take with you one or two more, that *'by the mouth of two or three witnesses every word may be established.'* **17** And if he refuses to hear them, tell *it* to the church. But if he refuses even to hear the church, let him be to you like a heathen and a tax collector. **18** "Assuredly, I say to you, whatever you bind on earth will be bound in heaven, and whatever you loose on earth will be loosed in heaven. **19** "Again I say to you that if two of you agree on earth concerning anything that they ask, it will be done for them by My Father in heaven.

Related to church.
Acts 5:11 So great fear came upon all the church and upon all who heard these things.

James 2:2–3 For if there should come into your assembly a man with gold rings, in fine apparel, and there should also come in a poor man in filthy clothes, **3** and you pay attention to the one wearing the fine clothes and say to him, "You sit here in a good place," and say to the poor man, "You stand there," or, "Sit here at my footstool,"

ASSURANCE
Produced by faith.
Eph 3:12 in whom we have boldness and access with confidence through faith in Him.

2 Tim 1:12 For this reason I also suffer these things; nevertheless I am not ashamed, for I know whom I have believed and am persuaded that He is able to keep what I have committed to Him until that Day.

Heb 10:22 let us draw near with a true heart in full assurance of faith, having our hearts sprinkled from an evil conscience and our bodies washed with pure water.

Made full by hope.
Heb 6:11 And we desire that each one of you show the

same diligence to the full assurance of hope until the end,

Heb 6:19 This *hope* we have as an anchor of the soul, both sure and steadfast, and which enters the Presence *behind* the veil,

Confirmed by love.

1 John 3:14 We know that we have passed from death to life, because we love the brethren. He who does not love *his* brother abides in death.

1 John 3:19 And by this we know that we are of the truth, and shall assure our hearts before Him.

1 John 4:18 There is no fear in love; but perfect love casts out fear, because fear involves torment. But he who fears has not been made perfect in love.

Is abundant in the understanding of the gospel.

Col 2:2 that their hearts may be encouraged, being knit together in love, and *attaining* to all riches of the full assurance of understanding, to the knowledge of the mystery of God, both of the Father and of Christ,

1 Thess 1:5 For our gospel did not come to you in word only, but also in power, and in the Holy Spirit and in much assurance, as you know what kind of men we were among you for your sake.

Saints privileged to have, of

Their election.

Ps 4:3 But know that the LORD has set apart for Himself him who is godly; The LORD will hear when I call to Him.

1 Thess 1:4 knowing, beloved brethren, your election by God.

Their redemption.

Job 19:25 For I know *that* my Redeemer lives, And He shall stand at last on the earth;

Their adoption.

Rom 8:16 The Spirit Himself bears witness with our spirit that we are children of God,

1 John 3:2 Beloved, now we are children of God; and it has not yet been revealed what we shall be, but we know that when He is revealed, we shall be like Him, for we shall see Him as He is.

Their salvation.

Is 12:2 Behold, God *is* my salvation, I will trust and not be afraid; 'For YAH, the LORD, *is* my strength and song; He also has become my salvation.' "

Eternal life.

1 John 5:13 These things I have written to you who believe in the name of the Son of God, that you may know that you have eternal life, and that you may *continue to* believe in the name of the Son of God.

The unalienable love of God.

Rom 8:38–39 For I am persuaded that neither death nor life, nor angels nor principalities nor powers, nor things present nor things to come, **39** nor height nor depth, nor any other created thing, shall be able to separate us from the love of God which is in Christ Jesus our Lord.

Union with God and Christ.

1 Cor 6:15 Do you not know that your bodies are members of Christ? Shall I then take the members of Christ and make *them* members of a harlot? Certainly not!

2 Cor 13:5 Examine yourselves *as to* whether you are in the faith. Test yourselves. Do you not know yourselves, that Jesus Christ is in you?—unless indeed you are disqualified.

Eph 5:30 For we are members of His body, of His flesh and of His bones.

1 John 2:5 But whoever keeps His word, truly the love of God is perfected in him. By this we know that we are in Him.

1 John 4:13 By this we know that we abide in Him, and He in us, because He has given us of His Spirit.

Peace with God by Christ.

Rom 5:1 Therefore, having been justified by faith, we have peace with God through our Lord Jesus Christ,

Preservation.

Ps 3:6 I will not be afraid of ten thousands of people Who have set *themselves* against me all around.

Ps 3:8 Salvation *belongs* to the LORD. Your blessing *is* upon Your people. Selah

Ps 27:3–5 Though an army may encamp against me, My heart shall not fear; Though war may rise against me, In this I *will be* confident. **4** One *thing* I have desired of the LORD, That will I seek: That I may dwell in the house of the LORD All the days of my life, To behold the beauty of the LORD, And to inquire in His temple. **5** For in the time of trouble He shall hide me in His pavilion; In the secret place of His tabernacle He shall hide me; He shall set me high upon a rock.

Ps 46:1–3 God *is* our refuge and strength, A very present help in trouble. **2** Therefore we will not fear, Even though the earth be removed, And though the mountains be carried into the midst of the sea; **3** *Though* its waters roar *and* be troubled, *Though* the mountains shake with its swelling. Selah

Answers to prayer.

1 John 3:22 And whatever we ask we receive from Him, because we keep His commandments and do those things that are pleasing in His sight.

1 John 5:14–15 Now this is the confidence that we have in Him, that if we ask anything according to His will, He hears us. **15** And if we know that He hears us, whatever we ask, we know that we have the petitions that we have asked of Him.

Continuance in grace.

Phil 1:6 being confident of this very thing, that He who has begun a good work in you will complete *it* until the day of Jesus Christ;

Comfort in affliction.

Ps 73:26 My flesh and my heart fail; *But* God *is* the strength of my heart and my portion forever.

Luke 4:18–19 *"The Spirit of the LORD is upon Me, Because He has anointed Me To preach the gospel to the poor; He has sent Me to heal the brokenhearted, To proclaim liberty to the captives And recovery of sight to the blind, To set at liberty those who are oppressed;* **19** *To proclaim the acceptable year of the* LORD.*"*

2 Cor 4:8–10 *We are* hard-pressed on every side, yet not crushed; *we are* perplexed, but not in despair; **9** persecuted, but not forsaken; struck down, but not destroyed— **10** always carrying about in the body the dying of the Lord Jesus, that the life of Jesus also may be manifested in our body.

2 Cor 4:16–18 Therefore we do not lose heart. Even though our outward man is perishing, yet the inward *man* is being renewed day by day. **17** For our light affliction, which is but for a moment, is working for us a far more exceeding *and* eternal weight of glory, **18** while we do not look at the things which are seen, but at the things which are not seen. For the things which are seen *are* temporary, but the things which are not seen *are* eternal.

Support in death.

Ps 23:4 Yea, though I walk through the valley of the shadow of death, I will fear no evil; For You *are* with me; Your rod and Your staff, they comfort me.

A glorious resurrection.

Job 19:26 And after my skin is destroyed, this *I know,* That in my flesh I shall see God,

Phil 3:21 who will transform our lowly body that it may be conformed to His glorious body, according to the working by which He is able even to subdue all things to Himself.

1 John 3:2 Beloved, now we are children of God; and it has not yet been revealed what we shall be, but we know that when He is revealed, we shall be like Him, for we shall see Him as He is.

A kingdom.

Heb 12:28 Therefore, since we are receiving a kingdom which cannot be shaken, let us have grace, by which we may serve God acceptably with reverence and godly fear.

Rev 5:10 And have made us kings and priests to our God; And we shall reign on the earth."

A crown.

2 Tim 4:7–8 I have fought the good fight, I have finished the race, I have kept the faith. **8** Finally, there is laid up for me the crown of righteousness, which the Lord, the righteous Judge, will give to me on that Day, and not to me only but also to all who have loved His appearing.

James 1:12 Blessed *is* the man who endures temptation; for when he has been approved, he will receive the crown of life which the Lord has promised to those who love Him.

Give diligence to attain to.

2 Pet 1:10–11 Therefore, brethren, be even more diligent to make your call and election sure, for if you do these things you will never stumble; **11** for so an entrance will be supplied to you abundantly into the everlasting kingdom of our Lord and Savior Jesus Christ.

Strive to maintain.

Heb 3:14 For we have become partakers of Christ if we hold the beginning of our confidence steadfast to the end,

Heb 3:18 And to whom did He swear that they would not enter His rest, but to those who did not obey?

Confident hope in God restores.

Ps 42:11 Why are you cast down, O my soul? And why are you disquieted within me? Hope in God; For I shall yet praise Him, The help of my countenance and my God.

Exemplified by

David.

Ps 23:4 Yea, though I walk through the valley of the shadow of death, I will fear no evil; For You *are* with me; Your rod and Your staff, they comfort me.

Ps 73:24–26 You will guide me with Your counsel, And afterward receive me *to* glory. **25** Whom have I in heaven *but* You? And *there is* none upon earth *that* I desire besides You. **26** My flesh and my heart fail; *But* God *is* the strength of my heart and my portion forever.

Paul.

2 Tim 1:12 For this reason I also suffer these things; nevertheless I am not ashamed, for I know whom I have believed and am persuaded that He is able to keep what I have committed to Him until that Day.

2 Tim 4:18 And the Lord will deliver me from every evil work and preserve *me* for His heavenly kingdom. To Him *be* glory forever and ever. Amen!

ASSYRIA

Antiquity and origin of.

Gen 10:8–11 Cush begot Nimrod; he began to be a mighty one on the earth. **9** He was a mighty hunter before the LORD; therefore it is said, "Like Nimrod the mighty hunter before the LORD." **10** And the beginning of his kingdom was Babel, Erech, Accad, and Calneh, in the land of Shinar. **11** From that land he went to Assyria and built Nineveh, Rehoboth Ir, Calah,

Situated beyond the Euphrates.

Is 7:20 In the same day the Lord will shave with a hired razor, With those from beyond the River, with the king of Assyria, The head and the hair of the legs, And will also remove the beard.

Watered by the river Tigris.

Gen 2:14 The name of the third river *is* Hiddekel; it *is* the one which goes toward the east of Assyria. The fourth river *is* the Euphrates.

Called

The land of Nimrod.

Mic 5:6 They shall waste with the sword the land of Assyria, And the land of Nimrod at its entrances; Thus He shall deliver *us* from the Assyrian, When he comes into our land And when he treads within our borders.

Shinar.

Gen 11:2 And it came to pass, as they journeyed from the east, that they found a plain in the land of Shinar, and they dwelt there.

Gen 14:1 And it came to pass in the days of Amraphel king of Shinar, Arioch king of Ellasar, Chedorlaomer king of Elam, and Tidal king of nations,

Nineveh, chief city of.

Gen 10:11 From that land he went to Assyria and built Nineveh, Rehoboth Ir, Calah,

2 Kin 19:36 So Sennacherib king of Assyria departed and went away, returned *home,* and remained at Nineveh.

Governed by kings.

2 Kin 15:19 Pul king of Assyria came against the land; and Menahem gave Pul a thousand talents of silver, that his hand might be with him to strengthen the kingdom under his control.

2 Kin 15:29 In the days of Pekah king of Israel, Tiglath-Pileser king of Assyria came and took Ijon, Abel Beth Maachah, Janoah, Kedesh, Hazor, Gilead, and Galilee, all the land of Naphtali; and he carried them captive to Assyria.

Celebrated for

Fertility.

2 Kin 18:32 until I come and take you away to a land like your own land, a land of grain and new wine, a land of bread and vineyards, a land of olive groves and honey, that you may live and not die. But do not listen to Hezekiah, lest he persuade you, saying, "The LORD will deliver us."

Is 36:17 until I come and take you away to a land like your own land, a land of grain and new wine, a land of bread and vineyards.

Extent of conquests.

2 Kin 18:33–35 Has any of the gods of the nations at all delivered its land from the hand of the king of Assyria? **34** Where *are* the gods of Hamath and Arpad? Where *are* the gods of Sepharvaim and Hena and Ivah? Indeed, have they delivered Samaria from my hand? **35** Who among all the gods of the lands have delivered their countries from my hand, that the LORD should deliver Jerusalem from my hand?' "

2 Kin 19:11–13 Look! You have heard what the kings of Assyria have done to all lands by utterly destroying them; and shall you be delivered? **12** Have the gods of the nations delivered those whom my fathers have destroyed, Gozan and Haran and Rezeph, and the people of Eden who *were* in Telassar? **13** Where *is* the king of Hamath, the king of Arpad, and the king of the city of Sepharvaim, Hena, and Ivah?' "

Is 10:9–14 *Is* not Calno like Carchemish? *Is* not Hamath like Arpad? *Is* not Samaria like Damascus? **10** As my hand has found the kingdoms of the idols, Whose carved images excelled those of Jerusalem and Samaria, **11** As I have done to Samaria and her idols, Shall I not do also to Jerusalem and her idols?' " **12** Therefore it shall come to pass, when the Lord has performed all His work on Mount Zion and on Jerusalem, *that He will say,* "I will punish the fruit of the arrogant heart of the king of Assyria, and the glory of his haughty looks." **13** For he says: "By the strength of my hand I have done *it,* And by my wisdom, for I am prudent; Also I have removed the boundaries of the people, And have robbed their treasuries; So I have put down the inhabitants like a valiant *man.* **14** My hand has found like a nest the riches of the people, And as one gathers eggs *that are* left, I have gathered all the earth; And there was no one who moved *his* wing, Nor opened *his* mouth with even a peep."

Extensive commerce.

Ezek 27:23–24 Haran, Canneh, Eden, the merchants of Sheba, Assyria, *and* Chilmad *were* your merchants. **24** These *were* your merchants in choice items—in purple clothes, in embroidered garments, in chests of multicolored apparel, in sturdy woven cords, which were in your marketplace.

Idolatry, the religion of.

2 Kin 19:37 Now it came to pass, as he was worshiping in the temple of Nisroch his god, that his sons Adrammelech and Sharezer struck him down with the sword; and they escaped into the land of Ararat. Then Esarhaddon his son reigned in his place.

As a power, was

Most formidable.

Is 28:2 Behold, the Lord has a mighty and strong one, Like a tempest of hail and a destroying storm, Like a flood of mighty waters overflowing, Who will bring *them* down to the earth with *His* hand.

Intolerant and oppressive.

Nah 3:19 Your injury *has* no healing, Your wound is severe. All who hear news of you Will clap *their* hands over you, For upon whom has not your wickedness passed continually?

Cruel and destructive.

Is 10:7 Yet he does not mean so, Nor does his heart think so; But *it is* in his heart to destroy, And cut off not a few nations.

Unfaithful, etc.

2 Chr 28:20–21 Also Tiglath-Pileser king of Assyria came to him and distressed him, and did not assist him. **21** For Ahaz took part *of the treasures* from the house of the LORD, from the house of the king, and from the leaders, and he gave *it* to the king of Assyria; but he did not help him.

Proud and haughty.

2 Kin 19:22–24 'Whom have you reproached and blasphemed? Against whom have you raised *your* voice, And lifted up your eyes on high? Against the Holy *One* of Israel. **23** By your messengers you have reproached the Lord, And said: "By the multitude of my chariots I have come up to the height of the mountains, To the limits of Lebanon; I will cut down its tall cedars *And* its choice cypress trees; I will enter the extremity of its borders, *To* its fruitful forest. **24** I have dug and drunk strange water, And with the soles of my feet I have dried up All the brooks of defense."

Is 10:8 For he says, 'Are not my princes altogether kings?

An instrument of God's vengeance.

Is 7:18–19 And it shall come to pass in that day *That* the LORD will whistle for the fly That *is* in the farthest part of the rivers of Egypt, And for the bee that *is* in the land of Assyria. **19** They will come, and all of them will rest In the desolate valleys and in the clefts of the rocks, And on all thorns and in all pastures.

Is 10:5–6 "Woe to Assyria, the rod of My anger And the staff in whose hand is My indignation. **6** I will send him against an ungodly nation, And against the people of My wrath I will give him charge, To seize the spoil, to take the prey, And to tread them down like the mire of the streets.

Chief men of, described.

Ezek 23:6 *Who were* clothed in purple, Captains and rulers, All of them desirable young men, Horsemen riding on horses.

Ezek 23:12 "She lusted for the neighboring Assyrians, Captains and rulers, Clothed most gorgeously, Horsemen riding on horses, All of them desirable young men.

Ezek 23:23 The Babylonians, All the Chaldeans, Pekod, Shoa, Koa, All the Assyrians with them, All of them desirable young men, Governors and rulers, Captains and men of renown, All of them riding on horses.

Armies of, described.

Is 5:26–29 He will lift up a banner to the nations from afar, And will whistle to them from the end of the earth; Surely they shall come with speed, swiftly. **27** No one will be weary or stumble among them, No one will slumber or sleep; Nor will the belt on their loins be loosed, Nor the strap of their sandals be broken; **28** Whose arrows *are* sharp, And all their bows bent; Their horses' hooves will seem like flint, And their wheels like a whirlwind. **29** Their roaring *will be* like a lion, They will roar like young lions; Yes, they will roar And lay hold of the prey; They will carry *it* away safely, And no one will deliver.

Pul, king of, bought off by Menahem.

2 Kin 15:19–20 Pul king of Assyria came against the land; and Menahem gave Pul a thousand talents of silver, that his hand might be with him to strengthen the kingdom under his control. **20** And Menahem exacted the money from Israel, from all the very wealthy, from each man fifty shekels of silver, to give to the king of Assyria. So the king of Assyria turned back, and did not stay there in the land.

Tiglath-Pileser, king of,

Ravaged Israel.

2 Kin 15:29 In the days of Pekah king of Israel, Tiglath-Pileser king of Assyria came and took Ijon, Abel Beth Maachah, Janoah, Kedesh, Hazor, Gilead, and Galilee, all the land of Naphtali; and he carried them captive to Assyria.

Asked to aid Ahaz against Syria.

2 Kin 16:7–8 So Ahaz sent messengers to Tiglath-Pileser king of Assyria, saying, "I *am* your servant and your son. Come up and save me from the hand of the king of Syria and from the hand of the king of Israel, who rise up against me." **8** And Ahaz took the silver and gold that was found in the house of the LORD, and in the treasuries of the king's house, and sent *it as* a present to the king of Assyria.

Took money from Ahaz, but strengthened him not.

2 Chr 28:20–21 Also Tiglath-Pileser king of Assyria came to him and distressed him, and did not assist him. **21** For Ahaz took part *of the treasures* from the house of the LORD, from the house of the king, and from the leaders, and he gave *it* to the king of Assyria; but he did not help him.

Conquered Syria.

2 Kin 16:9 So the king of Assyria heeded him; for the king of Assyria went up against Damascus and took it, carried *its people* captive to Kir, and killed Rezin.

Shalmaneser, king of,

Reduced Israel to tribute.

2 Kin 17:3 Shalmaneser king of Assyria came up against him; and Hoshea became his vassal, and paid him tribute money.

Was conspired against by Hoshea.

2 Kin 17:4 And the king of Assyria uncovered a conspiracy by Hoshea; for he had sent messengers to So, king of Egypt, and brought no tribute to the king of Assyria, as *he had done* year by year. Therefore the king of Assyria shut him up, and bound him in prison.

Imprisoned Hoshea.

2 Kin 17:4 And the king of Assyria uncovered a conspiracy by Hoshea; for he had sent messengers to So, king of Egypt, and brought no tribute to the king of Assyria, as *he had done* year by year. Therefore the king of Assyria shut him up, and bound him in prison.

Carried Israel captive.

2 Kin 17:5–6 Now the king of Assyria went throughout all the land, and went up to Samaria and besieged it for three years. **6** In the ninth year of Hoshea, the king of Assyria took Samaria and carried Israel away to Assyria, and placed them in Halah and by the Habor, the River of Gozan, and in the cities of the Medes.

Re-peopled Samaria from Assyria.

2 Kin 17:24 Then the king of Assyria brought *people* from Babylon, Cuthah, Ava, Hamath, and from Sepharvaim, and placed *them* in the cities of Samaria instead of the children of Israel; and they took possession of Samaria and dwelt in its cities.

Sennacherib, king of,

Invaded Judah.

2 Kin 18:13 And in the fourteenth year of King Hezekiah, Sennacherib king of Assyria came up against all the fortified cities of Judah and took them.

Bought off by Hezekiah.

2 Kin 18:14–16 Then Hezekiah king of Judah sent to the king of Assyria at Lachish, saying, "I have done wrong; turn away from me; whatever you impose on me I will pay." And the king of Assyria assessed Hezekiah king of Judah three hundred talents of silver and thirty talents of gold. **15** So Hezekiah gave *him* all the silver that was found in the house of the LORD and in the treasuries of the king's house. **16** At that time Hezekiah stripped *the gold from* the doors of the temple of the LORD, and *from* the pillars which Hezekiah king of Judah had overlaid, and gave it to the king of Assyria.

Insulted and threatened Judah.

2 Kin 19:10–13 "Thus you shall speak to Hezekiah king of Judah, saying: 'Do not let your God in whom you trust deceive you, saying, "Jerusalem shall not be given into the hand of the king of Assyria." **11** Look! You have heard what the kings of Assyria have done to all lands by utterly destroying them; and shall you be delivered? **12** Have the gods of the nations delivered those whom my fathers have destroyed, Gozan and Haran and Rezeph, and the people of Eden who *were* in Telassar? **13** Where *is* the king of Hamath, the king of Arpad, and the king of the city of Sepharvaim, Hena, and Ivah?' "

Cf. 2 Kin 18:17–32

Blasphemed the Lord.

2 Kin 18:33–35 Has any of the gods of the nations at all delivered its land from the hand of the king of Assyria? **34** Where *are* the gods of Hamath and Arpad? Where *are* the gods of Sepharvaim and Hena and Ivah? Indeed, have they delivered Samaria from my hand? **35** Who among all the gods of the lands have delivered their countries from my hand, that the LORD should deliver Jerusalem from my hand?' "

Prayed against by Hezekiah.

2 Kin 19:14–19 And Hezekiah received the letter from the hand of the messengers, and read it; and Hezekiah went up to the house of the LORD, and spread it before the LORD. **15** Then Hezekiah prayed before the LORD, and said: "O LORD God of Israel, *the One* who dwells *between* the cherubim, You are God, You alone, of all the kingdoms of the earth. You have made heaven and earth. **16** Incline Your ear, O LORD, and hear; open Your eyes, O LORD, and see; and hear the words of Sennacherib, which he has sent to reproach the living God. **17** Truly, LORD, the kings of Assyria have laid waste the nations and their lands, **18** and have cast their gods into the fire; for they *were* not gods, but the work of men's hands—wood and stone. Therefore they destroyed them. **19** Now therefore, O LORD our God, I pray, save us from his hand, that all the kingdoms of the earth may know that You *are* the LORD God, You alone."

Reproved for pride and blasphemy.

Is 37:21–29 Then Isaiah the son of Amoz sent to Hezekiah, saying, "Thus says the LORD God of Israel, 'Because you have prayed to Me against Sennacherib king of Assyria, **22** this *is* the word which the LORD has spoken concerning him: "The virgin, the daughter of Zion, Has despised you, laughed you to scorn; The daughter of Jerusalem Has shaken *her* head behind your back! **23** "Whom have you reproached and blasphemed? Against whom have you raised *your* voice, And lifted up your eyes on high? Against the Holy One of Israel. **24** By your servants you have reproached the Lord, And said, 'By the multitude of my chariots I have come up to the height of the mountains, To the limits of Lebanon; I will cut down its tall cedars *And* its choice cypress trees; I will enter its farthest height, To its fruitful forest. **25** I have dug and drunk water, And with the soles of my feet I have dried up All the brooks of defense.' **26** "Did you not hear long ago *How* I made it, From ancient times that I formed it? Now I have brought it to pass, That you should be For crushing fortified cities *into* heaps of ruins. **27** Therefore their inhabitants *had* little power; They were dismayed and confounded; They were *as* the grass of the field And the green herb, *As* the grass on the housetops And grain blighted before it is grown. **28** "But I know your dwelling place, Your going out and your coming in, And your rage against Me. **29** Because your rage against Me and your tumult Have come up to My ears, Therefore I will put My hook in your nose And My bridle in your lips, And I will turn you back By the way which you came." '

Cf. 2 Kin 19:12–34

His army destroyed by God.

2 Kin 19:35 And it came to pass on a certain night that the angel of the LORD went out, and killed in the camp of the Assyrians one hundred and eighty-five

thousand; and when *people* arose early in the morning, there were the corpses—all dead.

Assassinated by his sons.

2 Kin 19:37 Now it came to pass, as he was worshiping in the temple of Nisroch his god, that his sons Adrammelech and Sharezer struck him down with the sword; and they escaped into the land of Ararat. Then Esarhaddon his son reigned in his place.

Condemned for oppressing God's people.

Is 52:4 For thus says the Lord GOD: "My people went down at first Into Egypt to dwell there; Then the Assyrian oppressed them without cause.

Manasseh taken captive to.

2 Chr 33:11 Therefore the LORD brought upon them the captains of the army of the king of Assyria, who took Manasseh with hooks, bound him with bronze *fetters,* and carried him off to Babylon.

The re-peopling of Samaria from, completed by Osnapper.

Ezra 4:10 and the rest of the nations whom the great and noble Osnapper took captive and settled in the cities of Samaria and the remainder beyond the River—and so forth.

Idolatry of, brought into Samaria.

2 Kin 17:29 However every nation continued to make gods of its own, and put *them* in the shrines on the high places which the Samaritans had made, *every* nation in the cities where they dwelt.

Judah condemned for trusting.

Jer 2:18 And now why take the road to Egypt, To drink the waters of Sihor? Or why take the road to Assyria, To drink the waters of the River?

Jer 2:36 Why do you gad about so much to change your way? Also you shall be ashamed of Egypt as you were ashamed of Assyria.

Israel condemned for trusting.

Hos 5:13 "When Ephraim saw his sickness, And Judah *saw* his wound, Then Ephraim went to Assyria And sent to King Jareb; Yet he cannot cure you, Nor heal you of your wound.

Hos 7:11 "Ephraim also is like a silly dove, without sense— They call to Egypt, They go to Assyria.

Hos 8:9 For they have gone up to Assyria, *Like* a wild donkey alone by itself; Ephraim has hired lovers.

The Jews condemned for following the idolatries of.

Ezek 16:28 You also played the harlot with the Assyrians, because you were insatiable; indeed you played the harlot with them and still were not satisfied.

Cf. Ezek 23:5,7–49

The greatness, extent, duration, and fall, illustrated.

Ezek 31:3–17 Indeed Assyria *was* a cedar in Lebanon, With fine branches that shaded the forest, And of high stature; And its top was among the thick boughs. **4** The waters made it grow; Underground waters gave it height, With their rivers running around the place where it was planted, And sent out rivulets to all the trees of the field. **5** Therefore its height was exalted above all the trees of the field; Its boughs were multiplied, And its branches became long because of the abundance of water, As it sent them out. **6** All the birds of the heavens made their nests in its boughs; Under its branches all the beasts of the field brought forth their young; And in its shadow all great nations made their home. **7** 'Thus it was beautiful in greatness and in the length of its branches, Because its roots reached to abundant waters. **8** The cedars in the garden of God could not hide it; The fir trees were not like its boughs, And the chestnut trees were not like its branches; No tree in the garden of God was like it in beauty. **9** I made it beautiful with a multitude of branches, So that all the trees of Eden envied it, That *were* in the garden of God.' **10** "Therefore thus says the Lord GOD: 'Because you have increased in height, and it set its top among the thick boughs, and its heart was lifted up in its height, **11** therefore I will deliver it into the hand of the mighty one of the nations, and he shall surely deal with it; I have driven it out for its wickedness. **12** And aliens, the most terrible of the nations, have cut it down and left it; its branches have fallen on the mountains and in all the valleys; its boughs lie broken by all the rivers of the land; and all the peoples of the earth have gone from under its shadow and left it. **13** 'On its ruin will remain all the birds of the heavens, And all the beasts of the field will come to its branches— **14** 'So that no trees by the waters may ever again exalt themselves for their height, nor set their tops among the thick boughs, that no tree which drinks water may ever be high enough to reach up to them. 'For they have all been delivered to death, To the depths of the earth, Among the children of men who go down to the Pit.' **15** "Thus says the Lord GOD: 'In the day when it went down to hell, I caused mourning. I covered the deep because of it. I restrained its rivers, and the great waters were held back. I caused Lebanon to mourn for it, and all the trees of the field wilted because of it. **16** I made the nations shake at the sound of its fall, when I cast it down to hell together with those who descend into the Pit; and all the trees of Eden, the choice and best of Lebanon, all that drink water, were comforted in the depths of the earth. **17** They also went down to hell with it, with those *slain* by the sword; and *those who were* its *strong* arm dwelt in its shadows among the nations.

Predictions respecting

Conquest of the Kenites by.

Num 24:22 Nevertheless Kain shall be burned. How long until Asshur carries you away captive?"

Conquest of Syria by.

Is 8:4 for before the child shall have knowledge to cry 'My father' and 'My mother,' the riches of Damascus and the spoil of Samaria will be taken away before the king of Assyria."

Conquest and captivity of Israel by.

Is 8:4 for before the child shall have knowledge to cry 'My father' and 'My mother,' the riches of Damascus and the spoil of Samaria will be taken away before the king of Assyria."

Hos 9:3 They shall not dwell in the LORD's land, But Ephraim shall return to Egypt, And shall eat unclean *things* in Assyria.

Hos 10:6 *The idol* also shall be carried to Assyria As a

present for King Jareb. Ephraim shall receive shame, And Israel shall be ashamed of his own counsel.

Hos 11:5 "He shall not return to the land of Egypt; But the Assyrian shall be his king, Because they refused to repent.

Invasion of Judah by.

Is 5:26 He will lift up a banner to the nations from afar, And will whistle to them from the end of the earth; Surely they shall come with speed, swiftly.

Is 7:17–20 The LORD will bring the king of Assyria upon you and your people and your father's house—days that have not come since the day that Ephraim departed from Judah." **18** And it shall come to pass in that day *That* the LORD will whistle for the fly That *is* in the farthest part of the rivers of Egypt, And for the bee that *is* in the land of Assyria. **19** They will come, and all of them will rest In the desolate valleys and in the clefts of the rocks, And on all thorns and in all pastures. **20** In the same day the Lord will shave with a hired razor, With those from beyond the River, with the king of Assyria, The head and the hair of the legs, And will also remove the beard.

Is 8:8 He will pass through Judah, He will overflow and pass over, He will reach up to the neck; And the stretching out of his wings Will fill the breadth of Your land, O Immanuel.

Is 10:5–6 "Woe to Assyria, the rod of My anger And the staff in whose hand is My indignation. **6** I will send him against an ungodly nation, And against the people of My wrath I will give him charge, To seize the spoil, to take the prey, And to tread them down like the mire of the streets.

Is 10:12 Therefore it shall come to pass, when the Lord has performed all His work on Mount Zion and on Jerusalem, *that He will say*, "I will punish the fruit of the arrogant heart of the king of Assyria, and the glory of his haughty looks."

Restoration of Israel from.

Is 27:12–13 And it shall come to pass in that day *That* the LORD will thresh, From the channel of the River to the Brook of Egypt; And you will be gathered one by one, O you children of Israel. **13** So it shall be in that day: The great trumpet will be blown; They will come, who are about to perish in the land of Assyria, And they who are outcasts in the land of Egypt, And shall worship the LORD in the holy mount at Jerusalem.

Hos 11:11 They shall come trembling like a bird from Egypt, Like a dove from the land of Assyria. And I will let them dwell in their houses," Says the LORD.

Zech 10:10 I will also bring them back from the land of Egypt, And gather them from Assyria. I will bring them into the land of Gilead and Lebanon, Until no *more room* is found for them.

Destruction of.

Is 10:12–19 Therefore it shall come to pass, when the Lord has performed all His work on Mount Zion and on Jerusalem, *that He will say*, "I will punish the fruit of the arrogant heart of the king of Assyria, and the glory of his haughty looks." **13** For he says: "By the strength of my hand I have done *it*, And by my wisdom, for I am prudent; Also I have removed the boundaries of the people, And have robbed their treasuries; So I have put down the inhabitants like a valiant *man.* **14** My hand has found like a nest the riches of the people, And as one gathers eggs *that are* left, I have gathered all the earth; And there was no one who moved *his* wing, Nor opened *his* mouth with even a peep." **15** Shall the ax boast itself against him who chops with it? *Or* shall the saw exalt itself against him who saws with it? As if a rod could wield *itself* against those who lift it up, *Or* as if a staff could lift up, *as if it were* not wood! **16** Therefore the Lord, the Lord of hosts, Will send leanness among his fat ones; And under his glory He will kindle a burning Like the burning of a fire. **17** So the Light of Israel will be for a fire, And his Holy One for a flame; It will burn and devour His thorns and his briers in one day. **18** And it will consume the glory of his forest and of his fruitful field, Both soul and body; And they will be as when a sick man wastes away. **19** Then the rest of the trees of his forest Will be so few in number That a child may write them.

Is 14:24–25 The LORD of hosts has sworn, saying, "Surely, as I have thought, so it shall come to pass, And as I have purposed, *so* it shall stand: **25** That I will break the Assyrian in My land, And on My mountains tread him underfoot. Then his yoke shall be removed from them, And his burden removed from their shoulders.

Is 30:31–33 For through the voice of the LORD Assyria will be beaten down, As He strikes with the rod. **32** And *in* every place where the staff of punishment passes, Which the LORD lays on him, *It* will be with tambourines and harps; And in battles of brandishing He will fight with it. **33** For Tophet *was* established of old, Yes, for the king it is prepared. He has made *it* deep and large; Its pyre *is* fire with much wood; The breath of the LORD, like a stream of brimstone, Kindles it.

Is 31:8–9 "Then Assyria shall fall by a sword not of man, And a sword not of mankind shall devour him. But he shall flee from the sword, And his young men shall become forced labor. **9** He shall cross over to his stronghold for fear, And his princes shall be afraid of the banner," Says the LORD, Whose fire *is* in Zion And whose furnace *is* in Jerusalem.

Zech 10:11 He shall pass through the sea with affliction, And strike the waves of the sea: All the depths of the River shall dry up. Then the pride of Assyria shall be brought down, And the scepter of Egypt shall depart.

Participation in the blessings of the gospel.

Is 19:23–25 In that day there will be a highway from Egypt to Assyria, and the Assyrian will come into Egypt and the Egyptian into Assyria, and the Egyptians will serve with the Assyrians. **24** In that day Israel will be one of three with Egypt and Assyria—a blessing in the midst of the land, **25** whom the LORD of hosts shall bless, saying, "Blessed *is* Egypt My people, and Assyria the work of My hands, and Israel My inheritance."

Mic 7:12 *In* that day they shall come to you From Assyria and the fortified cities, From the fortress to the River, From sea to sea, And mountain *to* mountain.

ATONEMENT, THE

Explained.

Rom 5:8–11 But God demonstrates His own love toward us, in that while we were still sinners, Christ died for us. **9** Much more then, having now been justified by His blood, we shall be saved from wrath through Him. **10** For if when we were enemies we were reconciled to God through the death of His Son, much more, having been reconciled, we shall be saved by His life. **11** And not only *that,* but we also rejoice in God through our Lord Jesus Christ, through whom we have now received the reconciliation.

2 Cor 5:18–19 Now all things *are* of God, who has reconciled us to Himself through Jesus Christ, and has given us the ministry of reconciliation, **19** that is, that God was in Christ reconciling the world to Himself, not imputing their trespasses to them, and has committed to us the word of reconciliation.

Gal 1:4 who gave Himself for our sins, that He might deliver us from this present evil age, according to the will of our God and Father,

1 John 2:2 And He Himself is the propitiation for our sins, and not for ours only but also for the whole world.

1 John 4:10 In this is love, not that we loved God, but that He loved us and sent His Son *to be* the propitiation for our sins.

Foreordained.

Rom 3:25 whom God set forth *as* a propitiation by His blood, through faith, to demonstrate His righteousness, because in His forbearance God had passed over the sins that were previously committed,

1 Pet 1:11 searching what, or what manner of time, the Spirit of Christ who was in them was indicating when He testified beforehand the sufferings of Christ and the glories that would follow.

1 Pet 1:20 He indeed was foreordained before the foundation of the world, but was manifest in these last times for you

Rev 13:8 All who dwell on the earth will worship him, whose names have not been written in the Book of Life of the Lamb slain from the foundation of the world.

Foretold.

Is 53:4–6 Surely He has borne our griefs And carried our sorrows; Yet we esteemed Him stricken, Smitten by God, and afflicted. **5** But He *was* wounded for our transgressions, *He was* bruised for our iniquities; The chastisement for our peace *was* upon Him, And by His stripes we are healed. **6** All we like sheep have gone astray; We have turned, every one, to his own way; And the LORD has laid on Him the iniquity of us all.

Is 53:8–12 He was taken from prison and from judgment, And who will declare His generation? For He was cut off from the land of the living; For the transgressions of My people He was stricken. **9** And they made His grave with the wicked— But with the rich at His death, Because He had done no violence, Nor *was any* deceit in His mouth. **10** Yet it pleased the LORD to bruise Him; He has put *Him* to grief. When You make His soul an offering for sin, He shall see *His* seed, He shall prolong *His* days, And the pleasure of the LORD shall prosper in His hand. **11** He shall see the labor of His soul, *and* be satisfied. By His knowledge My righteous Servant shall justify many, For He shall bear their iniquities. **12** Therefore I will divide Him a portion with the great, And He shall divide the spoil with the strong, Because He poured out His soul unto death, And He was numbered with the transgressors, And He bore the sin of many, And made intercession for the transgressors.

Dan 9:24–27 "Seventy weeks are determined For your people and for your holy city, To finish the transgression, To make an end of sins, To make reconciliation for iniquity, To bring in everlasting righteousness, To seal up vision and prophecy, And to anoint the Most Holy. 25 "Know therefore and understand, *That* from the going forth of the command To restore and build Jerusalem Until Messiah the Prince, *There shall be* seven weeks and sixty-two weeks; The street shall be built again, and the wall, Even in troublesome times. 26 "And after the sixty-two weeks Messiah shall be cut off, but not for Himself; And the people of the prince who is to come Shall destroy the city and the sanctuary. The end of it *shall be* with a flood, And till the end of the war desolations are determined. 27 Then he shall confirm a covenant with many for one week; But in the middle of the week He shall bring an end to sacrifice and offering. And on the wing of abominations shall be one who makes desolate, Even until the consummation, which is determined, Is poured out on the desolate."

Zech 13:1 "In that day a fountain shall be opened for the house of David and for the inhabitants of Jerusalem, for sin and for uncleanness.

Zech 13:7 "Awake, O sword, against My Shepherd, Against the Man who is My Companion," Says the LORD of hosts. "Strike the Shepherd, And the sheep will be scattered; Then I will turn My hand against the little ones.

John 11:50–51 nor do you consider that it is expedient for us that one man should die for the people, and not that the whole nation should perish." 51 Now this he did not say on his own *authority*; but being high priest that year he prophesied that Jesus would die for the nation,

Effected by Christ alone.

John 1:29 The next day John saw Jesus coming toward him, and said, "Behold! The Lamb of God who takes away the sin of the world!

John 1:36 And looking at Jesus as He walked, he said, "Behold the Lamb of God!"

Acts 4:10 let it be known to you all, and to all the people of Israel, that by the name of Jesus Christ of Nazareth, whom you crucified, whom God raised from the dead, by Him this man stands here before you whole.

Acts 4:12 Nor is there salvation in any other, for there is no other name under heaven given among men by which we must be saved."

1 Thess 1:10 and to wait for His Son from heaven, whom He raised from the dead, *even* Jesus who delivers us from the wrath to come.

1 Tim 2:5–6 For *there is* one God and one Mediator between God and men, *the* Man Christ Jesus, 6 who gave Himself a ransom for all, to be testified in due time,

Heb 2:9 But we see Jesus, who was made a little lower than the angels, for the suffering of death crowned with glory and honor, that He, by the grace of God, might taste death for everyone.

1 Pet 2:24 who Himself bore our sins in His own body on the tree, that we, having died to sins, might live for righteousness—by whose stripes you were healed.

Was voluntary.

Ps 40:6–8 Sacrifice and offering You did not desire; My ears You have opened. Burnt offering and sin offering You did not require. 7 Then I said, "Behold, I come; In the scroll of the book *it is* written of me. 8 I delight to do Your will, O my God, And Your law *is* within my heart."

John 10:11 "I am the good shepherd. The good shepherd gives His life for the sheep.

John 10:15 As the Father knows Me, even so I know the Father; and I lay down My life for the sheep.

John 10:17–18 "Therefore My Father loves Me, because I lay down My life that I may take it again. 18 No one takes it from Me, but I lay it down of Myself. I have power to lay it down, and I have power to take it again. This command I have received from My Father."

Heb 10:5–9 Therefore, when He came into the world, He said: *"Sacrifice and offering You did not desire, But a body You have prepared for Me. 6 In burnt offerings and sacrifices for sin You had no pleasure. 7 Then I said, 'Behold, I have come— In the volume of the book it is written of Me— To do Your will, O God.' "* 8 Previously saying, *"Sacrifice and offering, burnt offerings, and offerings for sin You did not desire, nor had pleasure in them"* (which are offered according to the law), 9 then He said, *"Behold, I have come to do Your will, O God."* He takes away the first that He may establish the second.

Exhibits the

Grace and mercy of God.

Rom 8:32 He who did not spare His own Son, but delivered Him up for us all, how shall He not with Him also freely give us all things?

Eph 2:4–5 But God, who is rich in mercy, because of His great love with which He loved us, 5 even when we were dead in trespasses, made us alive together with Christ (by grace you have been saved),

Eph 2:7 that in the ages to come He might show the exceeding riches of His grace in *His* kindness toward us in Christ Jesus.

1 Tim 2:4 who desires all men to be saved and to come to the knowledge of the truth.

Heb 2:9 But we see Jesus, who was made a little lower than the angels, for the suffering of death crowned with glory and honor, that He, by the grace of God, might taste death for everyone.

Love of God.

Rom 5:8 But God demonstrates His own love toward us, in that while we were still sinners, Christ died for us.

1 John 4:9–10 In this the love of God was manifested toward us, that God has sent His only begotten Son into the world, that we might live through Him. 10 In this is love, not that we loved God, but that He loved us and sent His Son *to be* the propitiation for our sins.

Love of Christ.

John 15:13 Greater love has no one than this, than to lay down one's life for his friends.

Gal 2:20 I have been crucified with Christ; it is no longer I who live, but Christ lives in me; and the *life* which I now live in the flesh I live by faith in the Son of God, who loved me and gave Himself for me.

Eph 5:2 And walk in love, as Christ also has loved us and given Himself for us, an offering and a sacrifice to God for a sweet-smelling aroma.

Eph 5:25 Husbands, love your wives, just as Christ also loved the church and gave Himself for her,

Rev 1:5 and from Jesus Christ, the faithful witness, the firstborn from the dead, and the ruler over the kings of the earth. To Him who loved us and washed us from our sins in His own blood,

Reconciles the justice and mercy of God.

Is 45:21 Tell and bring forth *your case;* Yes, let them take counsel together. Who has declared this from ancient time? *Who* has told it from that time? *Have* not I, the LORD? And *there is* no other God besides Me, A just God and a Savior; *There is* none besides Me.

Rom 3:25–26 whom God set forth *as* a propitiation by His blood, through faith, to demonstrate His righteousness, because in His forbearance God had passed over the sins that were previously committed, **26** to demonstrate at the present time His righteousness, that He might be just and the justifier of the one who has faith in Jesus.

Necessity for.

Is 59:16 He saw that *there was* no man, And wondered that *there was* no intercessor; Therefore His own arm brought salvation for Him; And His own righteousness, it sustained Him.

Luke 19:10 for the Son of Man has come to seek and to save that which was lost."

Heb 9:22 And according to the law almost all things are purified with blood, and without shedding of blood there is no remission.

Made but once.

Heb 7:27 who does not need daily, as those high priests, to offer up sacrifices, first for His own sins and then for the people's, for this He did once for all when He offered up Himself.

Heb 9:24–28 For Christ has not entered the holy places made with hands, *which are* copies of the true, but into heaven itself, now to appear in the presence of God for us; **25** not that He should offer Himself often, as the high priest enters the Most Holy Place every year with blood of another— **26** He then would have had to suffer often since the foundation of the world; but now, once at the end of the ages, He has appeared to put away sin by the sacrifice of Himself. **27** And as it is appointed for men to die once, but after this the judgment, **28** so Christ was offered once to bear the sins of many. To those who eagerly wait for Him He will appear a second time, apart from sin, for salvation.

Heb 10:10 By that will we have been sanctified through the offering of the body of Jesus Christ once *for all.*

Heb 10:12 But this Man, after He had offered one sacri-fice for sins forever, sat down at the right hand of God,

Heb 10:14 For by one offering He has perfected forever those who are being sanctified.

1 Pet 3:18 For Christ also suffered once for sins, the just for the unjust, that He might bring us to God, being put to death in the flesh but made alive by the Spirit,

Acceptable to God.

Eph 5:2 And walk in love, as Christ also has loved us and given Himself for us, an offering and a sacrifice to God for a sweet-smelling aroma.

Reconciliation to God effected by.

Rom 5:10 For if when we were enemies we were reconciled to God through the death of His Son, much more, having been reconciled, we shall be saved by His life.

2 Cor 5:18–20 Now all things *are* of God, who has reconciled us to Himself through Jesus Christ, and has given us the ministry of reconciliation, **19** that is, that God was in Christ reconciling the world to Himself, not imputing their trespasses to them, and has committed to us the word of reconciliation. **20** Now then, we are ambassadors for Christ, as though God were pleading through us: we implore *you* on Christ's behalf, be reconciled to God.

Eph 2:13–16 But now in Christ Jesus you who once were far off have been brought near by the blood of Christ. **14** For He Himself is our peace, who has made both one, and has broken down the middle wall of separation, **15** having abolished in His flesh the enmity, *that is,* the law of commandments *contained* in ordinances, so as to create in Himself one new man *from* the two, *thus* making peace, **16** and that He might reconcile them both to God in one body through the cross, thereby putting to death the enmity.

Col 1:20–22 and by Him to reconcile all things to Himself, by Him, whether things on earth or things in heaven, having made peace through the blood of His cross. **21** And you, who once were alienated and enemies in your mind by wicked works, yet now He has reconciled **22** in the body of His flesh through death, to present you holy, and blameless, and above reproach in His sight—

Heb 2:17 Therefore, in all things He had to be made like *His* brethren, that He might be a merciful and faithful High Priest in things *pertaining* to God, to make propitiation for the sins of the people.

1 Pet 3:18 For Christ also suffered once for sins, the just for the unjust, that He might bring us to God, being put to death in the flesh but made alive by the Spirit,

Access to God by.

Heb 10:19–20 Therefore, brethren, having boldness to enter the Holiest by the blood of Jesus, **20** by a new and living way which He consecrated for us, through the veil, that is, His flesh,

Remission of sins by.

John 1:29 The next day John saw Jesus coming toward him, and said, "Behold! The Lamb of God who takes away the sin of the world!

Rom 3:25 whom God set forth *as* a propitiation by His blood, through faith, to demonstrate His righteousness, because in His forbearance God had passed over the sins that were previously committed,

Eph 1:7 In Him we have redemption through His blood, the forgiveness of sins, according to the riches of His grace

1 John 1:7 But if we walk in the light as He is in the light, we have fellowship with one another, and the blood of Jesus Christ His Son cleanses us from all sin.

Rev 1:5 and from Jesus Christ, the faithful witness, the firstborn from the dead, and the ruler over the kings of the earth. To Him who loved us and washed us from our sins in His own blood,

Justification by.

Rom 5:9 Much more then, having now been justified by His blood, we shall be saved from wrath through Him.

2 Cor 5:21 For He made Him who knew no sin *to be* sin for us, that we might become the righteousness of God in Him.

Sanctification by.

2 Cor 5:15 and He died for all, that those who live should live no longer for themselves, but for Him who died for them and rose again.

Eph 5:26–27 that He might sanctify and cleanse her with the washing of water by the word, **27** that He might present her to Himself a glorious church, not having spot or wrinkle or any such thing, but that she should be holy and without blemish.

Titus 2:14 who gave Himself for us, that He might redeem us from every lawless deed and purify for Himself *His* own special people, zealous for good works.

Heb 10:10 By that will we have been sanctified through the offering of the body of Jesus Christ once *for all*.

Heb 13:12 Therefore Jesus also, that He might sanctify the people with His own blood, suffered outside the gate.

Redemption by.

Matt 20:28 just as the Son of Man did not come to be served, but to serve, and to give His life a ransom for many."

Acts 20:28 Therefore take heed to yourselves and to all the flock, among which the Holy Spirit has made you overseers, to shepherd the church of God which He purchased with His own blood.

1 Tim 2:6 who gave Himself a ransom for all, to be testified in due time,

Heb 9:12 Not with the blood of goats and calves, but with His own blood He entered the Most Holy Place once for all, having obtained eternal redemption.

Rev 5:9 And they sang a new song, saying: "You are worthy to take the scroll, And to open its seals; For You were slain, And have redeemed us to God by Your blood Out of every tribe and tongue and people and nation,

Has delivered saints from the

Power of sin.

Rom 8:3 For what the law could not do in that it was weak through the flesh, God *did* by sending His own Son in the likeness of sinful flesh, on account of sin: He condemned sin in the flesh,

1 Pet 1:18–19 knowing that you were not redeemed with corruptible things, *like* silver or gold, from your aimless conduct *received* by tradition from your fathers, **19** but with the precious blood of Christ, as of a lamb without blemish and without spot.

Power of the world.

Gal 1:4 who gave Himself for our sins, that He might deliver us from this present evil age, according to the will of our God and Father,

Gal 6:14 But God forbid that I should boast except in the cross of our Lord Jesus Christ, by whom the world has been crucified to me, and I to the world.

Power of the devil.

Col 2:15 Having disarmed principalities and powers, He made a public spectacle of them, triumphing over them in it.

Heb 2:14–15 Inasmuch then as the children have partaken of flesh and blood, He Himself likewise shared in the same, that through death He might destroy him who had the power of death, that is, the devil, **15** and release those who through fear of death were all their lifetime subject to bondage.

Saints glorify God for.

1 Cor 6:20 For you were bought at a price; therefore glorify God in your body and in your spirit, which are God's.

Gal 2:20 I have been crucified with Christ; it is no longer I who live, but Christ lives in me; and the *life* which I now live in the flesh I live by faith in the Son of God, who loved me and gave Himself for me.

Phil 1:20–21 according to my earnest expectation and hope that in nothing I shall be ashamed, but with all boldness, as always, so now also Christ will be magnified in my body, whether by life or by death. **21** For to me, to live *is* Christ, and to die *is* gain.

Saints rejoice in God for.

Rom 5:11 And not only *that*, but we also rejoice in God through our Lord Jesus Christ, through whom we have now received the reconciliation.

Saints praise God for.

Rev 5:9–13 And they sang a new song, saying: "You are worthy to take the scroll, And to open its seals; For You were slain, And have redeemed us to God by Your blood Out of every tribe and tongue and people and nation, **10** And have made us kings and priests to our God; And we shall reign on the earth." **11** Then I looked, and I heard the voice of many angels around the throne, the living creatures, and the elders; and the number of them was ten thousand times ten thousand, and thousands of thousands, **12** saying with a loud voice: "Worthy is the Lamb who was slain To receive power and riches and wisdom, And strength and honor and glory and blessing!" **13** And every creature which is in heaven and on the earth and under the earth and such as are in the sea, and all that are in them, I heard saying: "Blessing and honor and glory and power *Be* to Him who sits on the throne, And to the Lamb, forever and ever!"

Faith in, indispensable.

Rom 3:25 whom God set forth *as* a propitiation by His

blood, through faith, to demonstrate His righteousness, because in His forbearance God had passed over the sins that were previously committed,

Gal 3:13–14 Christ has redeemed us from the curse of the law, having become a curse for us (for it is written, *"Cursed is everyone who hangs on a tree"*), **14** that the blessing of Abraham might come upon the Gentiles in Christ Jesus, that we might receive the promise of the Spirit through faith.

Commemorated in the Lord's Supper.

Matt 26:26–28 And as they were eating, Jesus took bread, blessed and broke *it*, and gave *it* to the disciples and said, "Take, eat; this is My body." **27** Then He took the cup, and gave thanks, and gave *it* to them, saying, "Drink from it, all of you. **28** For this is My blood of the new covenant, which is shed for many for the remission of sins.

1 Cor 11:23–26 For I received from the Lord that which I also delivered to you: that the Lord Jesus on the *same* night in which He was betrayed took bread; **24** and when He had given thanks, He broke *it* and said, "Take, eat; this is My body which is broken for you; do this in remembrance of Me." **25** In the same manner *He* also *took* the cup after supper, saying, "This cup is the new covenant in My blood. This do, as often as you drink *it*, in remembrance of Me." **26** For as often as you eat this bread and drink this cup, you proclaim the Lord's death till He comes.

Ministers should fully set forth.

Acts 5:29–31 But Peter and the *other* apostles answered and said: "We ought to obey God rather than men. **30** The God of our fathers raised up Jesus whom you murdered by hanging on a tree. **31** Him God has exalted to His right hand *to be* Prince and Savior, to give repentance to Israel and forgiveness of sins.

Acts 5:42 And daily in the temple, and in every house, they did not cease teaching and preaching Jesus *as* the Christ.

1 Cor 15:3 For I delivered to you first of all that which I also received: that Christ died for our sins according to the Scriptures,

2 Cor 5:18–21 Now all things *are* of God, who has reconciled us to Himself through Jesus Christ, and has given us the ministry of reconciliation, **19** that is, that God was in Christ reconciling the world to Himself, not imputing their trespasses to them, and has committed to us the word of reconciliation. **20** Now then, we are ambassadors for Christ, as though God were pleading through us: we implore *you* on Christ's behalf, be reconciled to God. **21** For He made Him who knew no sin *to be* sin for us, that we might become the righteousness of God in Him.

Typified.

Gen 4:4 Abel also brought of the firstborn of his flock and of their fat. And the Lord respected Abel and his offering,

Heb 11:4 By faith Abel offered to God a more excellent sacrifice than Cain, through which he obtained witness that he was righteous, God testifying of his gifts; and through it he being dead still speaks.

Gen 22:2 Then He said, "Take now your son, your only *son* Isaac, whom you love, and go to the land of Mo-

riah, and offer him there as a burnt offering on one of the mountains of which I shall tell you."

Heb 11:17 By faith Abraham, when he was tested, offered up Isaac, and he who had received the promises offered up his only begotten *son,*

Heb 11:19 concluding that God *was* able to raise *him* up, even from the dead, from which he also received him in a figurative sense.

Ex 12:5 Your lamb shall be without blemish, a male of the first year. You may take *it* from the sheep or from the goats.

Ex 12:11 And thus you shall eat it: *with* a belt on your waist, your sandals on your feet, and your staff in your hand. So you shall eat it in haste. It *is* the Lord's Passover.

Ex 12:14 'So this day shall be to you a memorial; and you shall keep it as a feast to the Lord throughout your generations. You shall keep it as a feast by an everlasting ordinance.

1 Cor 5:7 Therefore purge out the old leaven, that you may be a new lump, since you truly are unleavened. For indeed Christ, our Passover, was sacrificed for us.

Ex 24:8 And Moses took the blood, sprinkled *it* on the people, and said, "This is the blood of the covenant which the Lord has made with you according to all these words."

Heb 9:20 saying, *"This is the blood of the covenant which God has commanded you."*

Lev 16:30 For on that day *the priest* shall make atonement for you, to cleanse you, *that* you may be clean from all your sins before the Lord.

Lev 16:34 This shall be an everlasting statute for you, to make atonement for the children of Israel, for all their sins, once a year." And he did as the Lord commanded Moses.

Heb 9:7 But into the second part the high priest *went* alone once a year, not without blood, which he offered for himself and *for* the people's sins *committed* in ignorance;

Heb 9:12 Not with the blood of goats and calves, but with His own blood He entered the Most Holy Place once for all, having obtained eternal redemption.

Heb 9:28 so Christ was offered once to bear the sins of many. To those who eagerly wait for Him He will appear a second time, apart from sin, for salvation.

Lev 17:11 For the life of the flesh *is* in the blood, and I have given it to you upon the altar to make atonement for your souls; for it *is* the blood *that* makes atonement for the soul.'

Heb 9:22 And according to the law almost all things are purified with blood, and without shedding of blood there is no remission.

ATONEMENT, THE DAY OF
Tenth day of seventh month.

Lev 23:26–27 And the Lord spoke to Moses, saying: **27** "Also the tenth *day* of this seventh month *shall be* the Day of Atonement. It shall be a holy convocation for you; you shall afflict your souls, and offer an offering made by fire to the Lord.

A day of humiliation.

Lev 16:29 *"This* shall be a statute forever for you: In the seventh month, on the tenth *day* of the month, you shall afflict your souls, and do no work at all, *whether* a native of your own country or a stranger who dwells among you.

Lev 16:31 It *is* a sabbath of solemn rest for you, and you shall afflict your souls. *It is* a statute forever.

Lev 23:27 "Also the tenth *day* of this seventh month *shall be* the Day of Atonement. It shall be a holy convocation for you; you shall afflict your souls, and offer an offering made by fire to the LORD.

Observed as a sabbath.

Lev 23:28 And you shall do no work on that same day, for it *is* the Day of Atonement, to make atonement for you before the LORD your God.

Lev 23:32 It *shall be* to you a sabbath of *solemn* rest, and you shall afflict your souls; on the ninth *day* of the month at evening, from evening to evening, you shall celebrate your sabbath."

Offerings to be made on.

Lev 16:3 "Thus Aaron shall come into the Holy *Place:* with *the blood of* a young bull as a sin offering, and *of* a ram as a burnt offering.

Lev 16:5–15 And he shall take from the congregation of the children of Israel two kids of the goats as a sin offering, and one ram as a burnt offering. 6 "Aaron shall offer the bull as a sin offering, which *is* for himself, and make atonement for himself and for his house. 7 He shall take the two goats and present them before the LORD *at* the door of the tabernacle of meeting. 8 Then Aaron shall cast lots for the two goats: one lot for the LORD and the other lot for the scapegoat. 9 And Aaron shall bring the goat on which the LORD's lot fell, and offer it *as* a sin offering. 10 But the goat on which the lot fell to be the scapegoat shall be presented alive before the LORD, to make atonement upon it, *and* to let it go as the scapegoat into the wilderness. 11 "And Aaron shall bring the bull of the sin offering, which is for himself, and make atonement for himself and for his house, and shall kill the bull as the sin offering which *is* for himself. 12 Then he shall take a censer full of burning coals of fire from the altar before the LORD, with his hands full of sweet incense beaten fine, and bring *it* inside the veil. 13 And he shall put the incense on the fire before the LORD, that the cloud of incense may cover the mercy seat that *is* on the Testimony, lest he die. 14 He shall take some of the blood of the bull and sprinkle *it* with his finger on the mercy seat on the east *side;* and before the mercy seat he shall sprinkle some of the blood with his finger seven times. 15 "Then he shall kill the goat of the sin offering, which *is* for the people, bring its blood inside the veil, do with that blood as he did with the blood of the bull, and sprinkle it on the mercy seat and before the mercy seat.

The high priest entered into the holy place on.

Lev 16:2–3 and the LORD said to Moses: "Tell Aaron your brother not to come into *just* any time into the Holy *Place* inside the veil, before the mercy seat which *is* on the ark, lest he die; for I will appear in the cloud above the mercy seat. 3 "Thus Aaron shall

come into the Holy *Place:* with *the blood of* a young bull as a sin offering, and *of* a ram as a burnt offering.

Heb 9:7 But into the second part the high priest *went* alone once a year, not without blood, which he offered for himself and *for* the people's sins *committed* in ignorance;

Atonement made on.

For the holy place.

Ex 30:10 And Aaron shall make atonement upon its horns once a year with the blood of the sin offering of atonement; once a year he shall make atonement upon it throughout your generations. It *is* most holy to the LORD."

Lev 16:15–16 "Then he shall kill the goat of the sin offering, which *is* for the people, bring its blood inside the veil, do with that blood as he did with the blood of the bull, and sprinkle it on the mercy seat and before the mercy seat. 16 So he shall make atonement for the Holy *Place,* because of the uncleanness of the children of Israel, and because of their transgressions, for all their sins; and so he shall do for the tabernacle of meeting which remains among them in the midst of their uncleanness.

For the high priest.

Lev 16:11 "And Aaron shall bring the bull of the sin offering, which is for himself, and make atonement for himself and for his house, and shall kill the bull as the sin offering which *is* for himself.

Heb 9:7 But into the second part the high priest *went* alone once a year, not without blood, which he offered for himself and *for* the people's sins *committed* in ignorance;

For the whole congregation.

Lev 16:17 There shall be no man in the tabernacle of meeting when he goes in to make atonement in the Holy *Place,* until he comes out, that he may make atonement for himself, for his household, and for all the assembly of Israel.

Lev 16:24 And he shall wash his body with water in a holy place, put on his garments, come out and offer his burnt offering and the burnt offering of the people, and make atonement for himself and for the people.

Heb 9:7 But into the second part the high priest *went* alone once a year, not without blood, which he offered for himself and *for* the people's sins *committed* in ignorance;

The sins of the people borne off by the scapegoat on.

Lev 16:21 Aaron shall lay both his hands on the head of the live goat, confess over it all the iniquities of the children of Israel, and all their transgressions, concerning all their sins, putting them on the head of the goat, and shall send *it* away into the wilderness by the hand of a suitable man.

Punishment for not observing.

Lev 23:29–30 For any person who is not afflicted *in soul* on that same day shall be cut off from his people. 30 And any person who does any work on that same day, that person I will destroy from among his people.

Year of Jubilee commenced on.

Lev 25:9 Then you shall cause the trumpet of the Jubilee to sound on the tenth *day* of the seventh month; on the Day of Atonement you shall make the trumpet to sound throughout all your land.

Typical.

Heb 9:8 the Holy Spirit indicating this, that the way into the Holiest of All was not yet made manifest while the first tabernacle was still standing.

Heb 9:24 For Christ has not entered the holy places made with hands, *which are* copies of the true, but into heaven itself, now to appear in the presence of God for us;

ATONEMENT, UNDER THE LAW

Made by sacrifice.

Lev 1:4–5 Then he shall put his hand on the head of the burnt offering, and it will be accepted on his behalf to make atonement for him. 5 He shall kill the bull before the LORD; and the priests, Aaron's sons, shall bring the blood and sprinkle the blood all around on the altar that *is by* the door of the tabernacle of meeting.

By priests alone.

1 Chr 6:49 But Aaron and his sons offered sacrifices on the altar of burnt offering and on the altar of incense, for all the work of the Most Holy *Place,* and to make atonement for Israel, according to all that Moses the servant of God had commanded.

2 Chr 29:24 And the priests killed them; and they presented their blood on the altar as a sin offering to make an atonement for all Israel, for the king commanded *that* the burnt offering and the sin offering *be made* for all Israel.

Necessary for

Propitiating God.

Ex 32:30 Now it came to pass on the next day that Moses said to the people, "You have committed a great sin. So now I will go up to the LORD; perhaps I can make atonement for your sin."

Lev 23:27–28 "Also the tenth *day* of this seventh month *shall be* the Day of Atonement. It shall be a holy convocation for you; you shall afflict your souls, and offer an offering made by fire to the LORD. 28 And you shall do no work on that same day, for it *is* the Day of Atonement, to make atonement for you before the LORD your God.

2 Sam 21:3 Therefore David said to the Gibeonites, "What shall I do for you? And with what shall I make atonement, that you may bless the inheritance of the LORD?"

Ransoming.

Ex 30:15–16 The rich shall not give more and the poor shall not give less than half a shekel, when *you* give an offering to the LORD, to make atonement for yourselves. 16 And you shall take the atonement money of the children of Israel, and shall appoint it for the service of the tabernacle of meeting, that it may be a memorial for the children of Israel before the LORD, to make atonement for yourselves."

Job 33:24 Then He is gracious to him, and says, 'Deliver him from going down to the Pit; I have found a ransom';

Purifying.

Ex 29:36 And you shall offer a bull every day *as* a sin offering for atonement. You shall cleanse the altar when you make atonement for it, and you shall anoint it to sanctify it.

Offered for

The congregation.

Num 15:25 So the priest shall make atonement for the whole congregation of the children of Israel, and it shall be forgiven them, for it was unintentional; they shall bring their offering, an offering made by fire to the LORD, and their sin offering before the LORD, for their unintended sin.

2 Chr 29:24 And the priests killed them; and they presented their blood on the altar as a sin offering to make an atonement for all Israel, for the king commanded *that* the burnt offering and the sin offering *be made* for all Israel.

The priests.

Ex 29:31–33 "And you shall take the ram of the consecration and boil its flesh in the holy place. 32 Then Aaron and his sons shall eat the flesh of the ram, and the bread that *is* in the basket, *by* the door of the tabernacle of meeting. 33 They shall eat those things with which the atonement was made, to consecrate *and* to sanctify them; but an outsider shall not eat *them,* because they *are* holy.

Lev 8:34 As he has done this day, *so* the LORD has commanded to do, to make atonement for you.

Persons sinning ignorantly. **Lev 4:20–35**

Persons sinning willfully.

Lev 6:7 So the priest shall make atonement for him before the LORD, and he shall be forgiven for any one of these things that he may have done in which he trespasses."

Persons swearing rashly.

Lev 5:4 'Or if a person swears, speaking thoughtlessly with *his* lips to do evil or to do good, whatever *it is* that a man may pronounce by an oath, and he is unaware of it—when he realizes *it,* then he shall be guilty in any of these *matters.*

Lev 5:6 and he shall bring his trespass offering to the LORD for his sin which he has committed, a female from the flock, a lamb or a kid of the goats as a sin offering. So the priest shall make atonement for him concerning his sin.

Persons withholding evidence.

Lev 5:1 'If a person sins in hearing the utterance of an oath, and *is* a witness, whether he has seen or known *of the matter*—if he does not tell *it,* he bears guilt.

Lev 5:6 and he shall bring his trespass offering to the LORD for his sin which he has committed, a female from the flock, a lamb or a kid of the goats as a sin offering. So the priest shall make atonement for him concerning his sin.

Unclean persons.

Lev 5:2–3 'Or if a person touches any unclean thing, whether *it is* the carcass of an unclean beast, or the carcass of unclean livestock, or the carcass of unclean creeping things, and he is unaware of it, he also shall be unclean and guilty. 3 Or if he touches human uncleanness—whatever uncleanness with which a man may be defiled, and he is unaware of it—when he realizes *it*, then he shall be guilty.

Lev 5:6 and he shall bring his trespass offering to the LORD for his sin which he has committed, a female from the flock, a lamb or a kid of the goats as a sin offering. So the priest shall make atonement for him concerning his sin.

Women after childbirth.

Lev 12:8 'And if she is not able to bring a lamb, then she may bring two turtledoves or two young pigeons— one as a burnt offering and the other as a sin offering. So the priest shall make atonement for her, and she will be clean.' "

The altar.

Ex 29:36–37 And you shall offer a bull every day *as* a sin offering for atonement. You shall cleanse the altar when you make atonement for it, and you shall anoint it to sanctify it. **37** Seven days you shall make atonement for the altar and sanctify it. And the altar shall be most holy. Whatever touches the altar must be holy.

Lev 16:18–19 And he shall go out to the altar that *is* before the LORD, and make atonement for it, and shall take some of the blood of the bull and some of the blood of the goat, and put it on the horns of the altar all around. **19** Then he shall sprinkle some of the blood on it with his finger seven times, cleanse it, and consecrate it from the uncleanness of the children of Israel.

The holy place.

Lev 16:16–17 So he shall make atonement for the Holy *Place*, because of the uncleanness of the children of Israel, and because of their transgressions, for all their sins; and so he shall do for the tabernacle of meeting which remains among them in the midst of their uncleanness. **17** There shall be no man in the tabernacle of meeting when he goes in to make atonement in the Holy *Place*, until he comes out, that he may make atonement for himself, for his household, and for all the assembly of Israel.

The healed leper.

Lev 14:18 The rest of the oil that *is* in the priest's hand he shall put on the head of him who is to be cleansed. So the priest shall make atonement for him before the LORD.

The leprous house healed.

Lev 14:53 Then he shall let the living bird loose outside the city in the open field, and make atonement for the house, and it shall be clean.

Extraordinary cases of.

Ex 32:30–34 Now it came to pass on the next day that Moses said to the people, "You have committed a great sin. So now I will go up to the LORD; perhaps I can make atonement for your sin." **31** Then Moses returned to the LORD and said, "Oh, these people have committed a great sin, and have made for themselves a god of gold! **32** Yet now, if You will forgive their sin—but if not, I pray, blot me out of Your book which You have written." **33** And the LORD said to Moses, "Whoever has sinned against Me, I will blot him out of My book. **34** Now therefore, go, lead the people to *the place* of which I have spoken to you. Behold, My Angel shall go before you. Nevertheless, in

the day when I visit for punishment, I will visit punishment upon them for their sin."

Num 16:47 Then Aaron took *it* as Moses commanded, and ran into the midst of the assembly; and already the plague had begun among the people. So he put in the incense and made atonement for the people.

Num 25:10–13 Then the LORD spoke to Moses, saying: **11** "Phinehas the son of Eleazar, the son of Aaron the priest, has turned back My wrath from the children of Israel, because he was zealous with My zeal among them, so that I did not consume the children of Israel in My zeal. **12** Therefore say, 'Behold, I give to him My covenant of peace; **13** and it shall be to him and his descendants after him a covenant of an everlasting priesthood, because he was zealous for his God, and made atonement for the children of Israel.' "

Typical of Christ's atonement.

Rom 5:6–11 For when we were still without strength, in due time Christ died for the ungodly. **7** For scarcely for a righteous man will one die; yet perhaps for a good man someone would even dare to die. **8** But God demonstrates His own love toward us, in that while we were still sinners, Christ died for us. **9** Much more then, having now been justified by His blood, we shall be saved from wrath through Him. **10** For if when we were enemies we were reconciled to God through the death of His Son, much more, having been reconciled, we shall be saved by His life. **11** And not only *that*, but we also rejoice in God through our Lord Jesus Christ, through whom we have now received the reconciliation.

ATTITUDE

Cain's, of indifference.

Gen 4:9 Then the LORD said to Cain, "Where *is* Abel your brother?" He said, "I do not know. *Am* I my brother's keeper?"

Rebekah's, of a true servant.

Gen 24:15–20 And it happened, before he had finished speaking, that behold, Rebekah, who was born to Bethuel, son of Milcah, the wife of Nahor, Abraham's brother, came out with her pitcher on her shoulder. **16** Now the young woman *was* very beautiful to behold, a virgin; no man had known her. And she went down to the well, filled her pitcher, and came up. **17** And the servant ran to meet her and said, "Please let me drink a little water from your pitcher." **18** So she said, "Drink, my lord." Then she quickly let her pitcher down to her hand, and gave him a drink. **19** And when she had finished giving him a drink, she said, "I will draw *water* for your camels also, until they have finished drinking." **20** Then she quickly emptied her pitcher into the trough, ran back to the well to draw *water*, and drew for all his camels.

Israel's,

Of complaint.

Ex 16:2–3 Then the whole congregation of the children of Israel complained against Moses and Aaron in the wilderness. **3** And the children of Israel said to them, "Oh, that we had died by the hand of the LORD in the land of Egypt, when we sat by the pots of meat *and* when we ate bread to the full! For you have brought us out into this wilderness to kill this whole assembly with hunger."

Cf. Deut 9:1–24

Of unbelief.

Num 13:31–33 But the men who had gone up with him said, "We are not able to go up against the people, for they *are* stronger than we." **32** And they gave the children of Israel a bad report of the land which they had spied out, saying, "The land through which we have gone as spies *is* a land that devours its inhabitants, and all the people whom we saw in it *are* men of *great* stature. **33** There we saw the giants (the descendants of Anak came from the giants); and we were like grasshoppers in our own sight, and so we were in their sight."

Num 14:1–4 So all the congregation lifted up their voices and cried, and the people wept that night. **2** And all the children of Israel complained against Moses and Aaron, and the whole congregation said to them, "If only we had died in the land of Egypt! Or if only we had died in this wilderness! **3** Why has the LORD brought us to this land to fall by the sword, that our wives and children should become victims? Would it not be better for us to return to Egypt?" **4** So they said to one another, "Let us select a leader and return to Egypt."

Tested by God.

Deut 8:2–5 And you shall remember that the LORD your God led you all the way these forty years in the wilderness, to humble you *and* test you, to know what *was* in your heart, whether you would keep His commandments or not. **3** So He humbled you, allowed you to hunger, and fed you with manna which you did not know nor did your fathers know, that He might make you know that man shall not live by bread alone; but man lives by every *word* that proceeds from the mouth of the LORD. **4** Your garments did not wear out on you, nor did your foot swell these forty years. **5** You should know in your heart that as a man chastens his son, *so* the LORD your God chastens you.

Cf. 1 Chr 29:17

Of self-centeredness.

Deut 12:8 "You shall not at all do as we are doing here today—every man doing whatever *is* right in his own eyes—

Judg 17:6 In those days *there was* no king in Israel; everyone did *what was* right in his own eyes.

Judg 21:25 In those days *there was* no king in Israel; everyone did *what was* right in his own eyes.

Of the heart is most important.

1 Sam 15:22 So Samuel said: "Has the LORD *as great* delight in burnt offerings and sacrifices, As in obeying the voice of the LORD? Behold, to obey is better than sacrifice, *And* to heed than the fat of rams.

2 Chr 30:18–20 For a multitude of the people, many from Ephraim, Manasseh, Issachar, and Zebulun, had not cleansed themselves, yet they ate the Passover contrary to what was written. But Hezekiah prayed for them, saying, "May the good LORD provide atonement for everyone **19** *who* prepares his heart to seek God, the LORD God of his fathers, though *he is* not *cleansed* according to the purification

of the sanctuary." **20** And the LORD listened to Hezekiah and healed the people.

Ps 19:14 Let the words of my mouth and the meditation of my heart Be acceptable in Your sight, O LORD, my strength and my Redeemer.

Ps 40:6–8 Sacrifice and offering You did not desire; My ears You have opened. Burnt offering and sin offering You did not require. **7** Then I said, "Behold, I come; In the scroll of the book *it is* written of me. **8** I delight to do Your will, O my God, And Your law *is* within my heart."

Ps 51:15–17 O Lord, open my lips, And my mouth shall show forth Your praise. **16** For You do not desire sacrifice, or else I would give *it;* You do not delight in burnt offering. **17** The sacrifices of God *are* a broken spirit, A broken and a contrite heart— These, O God, You will not despise.

Ps 69:30–31 I will praise the name of God with a song, And will magnify Him with thanksgiving. **31** *This* also shall please the LORD better than an ox *or* bull, Which has horns and hooves.

Is 1:10–15 Hear the word of the LORD, You rulers of Sodom; Give ear to the law of our God, You people of Gomorrah: **11** "To what purpose *is* the multitude of your sacrifices to Me?" Says the LORD. "I have had enough of burnt offerings of rams And the fat of fed cattle. I do not delight in the blood of bulls, Or of lambs or goats. **12** "When you come to appear before Me, Who has required this from your hand, To trample My courts? **13** Bring no more futile sacrifices; Incense is an abomination to Me. The New Moons, the Sabbaths, and the calling of assemblies— I cannot endure iniquity and the sacred meeting. **14** Your New Moons and your appointed feasts My soul hates; They are a trouble to Me, I am weary of bearing *them.* **15** When you spread out your hands, I will hide My eyes from you; Even though you make many prayers, I will not hear. Your hands are full of blood.

Hos 6:6 For I desire mercy and not sacrifice, And the knowledge of God more than burnt offerings.

Amos 5:21–24 "I hate, I despise your feast days, And I do not savor your sacred assemblies. **22** Though you offer Me burnt offerings and your grain offerings, I will not accept *them,* Nor will I regard your fattened peace offerings. **23** Take away from Me the noise of your songs, For I will not hear the melody of your stringed instruments. **24** But let justice run down like water, And righteousness like a mighty stream.

Mic 6:6–8 With what shall I come before the LORD, *And* bow myself before the High God? Shall I come before Him with burnt offerings, With calves a year old? **7** Will the LORD be pleased with thousands of rams, Ten thousand rivers of oil? Shall I give my firstborn *for* my transgression, The fruit of my body *for* the sin of my soul? **8** He has shown you, O man, what *is* good; And what does the LORD require of you But to do justly, To love mercy, And to walk humbly with your God?

Matt 23:23 "Woe to you, scribes and Pharisees, hypocrites! For you pay tithe of mint and anise and cummin, and have neglected the weightier *matters* of the law: justice and mercy and faith. These you ought to have done, without leaving the others undone.

Cf. Ps 50:7–15; Jer 7:21–26

Of God, toward specific sins.

Prov 6:16–19 These six *things* the LORD hates, Yes, seven *are* an abomination to Him: **17** A proud look, A lying tongue, Hands that shed innocent blood, **18** A heart that devises wicked plans, Feet that are swift in running to evil, **19** A false witness *who* speaks lies, And one who sows discord among brethren.

Cf. Prov 3:32

Of Jonah, toward Nineveh's repentance.

Jon 4:1–11 But it displeased Jonah exceedingly, and he became angry. **2** So he prayed to the LORD, and said, "Ah, LORD, was not this what I said when I was still in my country? Therefore I fled previously to Tarshish; for I know that You *are* a gracious and merciful God, slow to anger and abundant in lovingkindness, One who relents from doing harm. **3** Therefore now, O LORD, please take my life from me, for *it is* better for me to die than to live!" **4** Then the LORD said, "*Is it* right for you to be angry?" **5** So Jonah went out of the city and sat on the east side of the city. There he made himself a shelter and sat under it in the shade, till he might see what would become of the city. **6** And the LORD God prepared a plant and made it come up over Jonah, that it might be shade for his head to deliver him from his misery. So Jonah was very grateful for the plant. **7** But as morning dawned the next day God prepared a worm, and it *so* damaged the plant that it withered. **8** And it happened, when the sun arose, that God prepared a vehement east wind; and the sun beat on Jonah's head, so that he grew faint. Then he wished death for himself, and said, "*It is* better for me to die than to live." **9** Then God said to Jonah, "*Is it* right for you to be angry about the plant?" And he said, "*It is* right for me to be angry, even to death!" **10** But the LORD said, "You have had pity on the plant for which you have not labored, nor made it grow, which came up in a night and perished in a night. **11** And should I not pity Nineveh, that great city, in which are more than one hundred and twenty thousand persons who cannot discern between their right hand and their left—and much livestock?"

Of God and Jesus, compassion toward sinners.

Ex 33:19 Then He said, "I will make all My goodness pass before you, and I will proclaim the name of the LORD before you. I will be gracious to whom I will be gracious, and I will have compassion on whom I will have compassion."

Ps 86:15 But You, O Lord, *are* a God full of compassion, and gracious, Longsuffering and abundant in mercy and truth.

Jer 9:1 Oh, that my head were waters, And my eyes a fountain of tears, That I might weep day and night For the slain of the daughter of my people!

Jer 13:17 But if you will not hear it, My soul will weep in secret for *your* pride; My eyes will weep bitterly And run down with tears, Because the LORD's flock has been taken captive.

Jer 14:17 "Therefore you shall say this word to them: 'Let my eyes flow with tears night and day, And let them not cease; For the virgin daughter of my people Has been broken with a mighty stroke, with a very severe blow.

Matt 9:36 But when He saw the multitudes, He was moved with compassion for them, because they were weary and scattered, like sheep having no shepherd.

Luke 13:34 "O Jerusalem, Jerusalem, the one who kills the prophets and stones those who are sent to her! How often I wanted to gather your children together, as a hen *gathers* her brood under *her* wings, but you were not willing!

Luke 19:41 Now as He drew near, He saw the city and wept over it,

Of Jesus toward sin.

Matt 21:12–13 Then Jesus went into the temple of God and drove out all those who bought and sold in the temple, and overturned the tables of the money changers and the seats of those who sold doves. **13** And He said to them, "It is written, '*My house shall be called a house of prayer,*' but you have made it a '*den of thieves.*' "

Mark 11:15–18 So they came to Jerusalem. Then Jesus went into the temple and began to drive out those who bought and sold in the temple, and overturned the tables of the money changers and the seats of those who sold doves. **16** And He would not allow anyone to carry wares through the temple. **17** Then He taught, saying to them, "Is it not written, '*My house shall be called a house of prayer for all nations*'? But you have made it a '*den of thieves.*'" **18** And the scribes and chief priests heard it and sought how they might destroy Him; for they feared Him, because all the people were astonished at His teaching.

Luke 19:45–48 Then He went into the temple and began to drive out those who bought and sold in it, **46** saying to them, "It is written, '*My house is a house of prayer,*' but you have made it a '*den of thieves.*'" **47** And He was teaching daily in the temple. But the chief priests, the scribes, and the leaders of the people sought to destroy Him, **48** and were unable to do anything; for all the people were very attentive to hear Him.

Of sinners toward truth.

Ps 95:8 "Do not harden your hearts, as in the rebellion, As *in* the day of trial in the wilderness,

Mark 3:5 And when He had looked around at them with anger, being grieved by the hardness of their hearts, He said to the man, "Stretch out your hand." And he stretched *it* out, and his hand was restored as whole as the other.

Mark 16:14 Later He appeared to the eleven as they sat at the table; and He rebuked their unbelief and hardness of heart, because they did not believe those who had seen Him after He had risen.

Rom 9:18 Therefore He has mercy on whom He wills, and whom He wills He hardens.

Heb 3:8 *Do not harden your hearts as in the rebellion, In the day of trial in the wilderness,*

Heb 3:15 while it is said: "*Today, if you will hear His voice, Do not harden your hearts as in the rebellion.*"

Of proper worship.

John 4:21–24 Jesus said to her, "Woman, believe Me, the hour is coming when you will neither on this mountain, nor in Jerusalem, worship the Father. **22** You worship what you do not know; we know what we worship, for salvation is of the Jews. **23** But the hour is coming, and now is, when the true worshipers will worship the Father in spirit and truth; for the Father is seeking such to worship Him. **24** God *is* Spirit, and those who worship Him must worship in spirit and truth."

Of proper giving.

Mark 12:41–44 Now Jesus sat opposite the treasury and saw how the people put money into the treasury. And many *who were* rich put in much. **42** Then one poor widow came and threw in two mites, which make a quadrans. **43** So He called His disciples to *Himself* and said to them, "Assuredly, I say to you that this poor widow has put in more than all those who have given to the treasury; **44** for they all put in out of their abundance, but she out of her poverty put in all that she had, her whole livelihood."

2 Cor 8:12 For if there is first a willing mind, *it is* accepted according to what one has, *and* not according to what he does not have.

2 Cor 9:7 *So let* each one *give* as he purposes in his heart, not grudgingly or of necessity; for God loves a cheerful giver.

Christ's, of humility.

Phil 2:6–11 who, being in the form of God, did not consider it robbery to be equal with God, **7** but made Himself of no reputation, taking the form of a bondservant, *and* coming in the likeness of men. **8** And being found in appearance as a man, He humbled Himself and became obedient to *the point of* death, even the death of the cross. **9** Therefore God also has highly exalted Him and given Him the name which is above every name, **10** that at the name of Jesus every knee should bow, of those in heaven, and of those on earth, and of those under the earth, **11** and *that* every tongue should confess that Jesus Christ *is* Lord, to the glory of God the Father.

Proper one, of mind.

Phil 4:6–9 Be anxious for nothing, but in everything by prayer and supplication, with thanksgiving, let your requests be made known to God; **7** and the peace of God, which surpasses all understanding, will guard your hearts and minds through Christ Jesus. **8** Finally, brethren, whatever things are true, whatever things *are* noble, whatever things *are* just, whatever things *are* pure, whatever things *are* lovely, whatever things *are* of good report, if *there is* any virtue and if *there is* anything praiseworthy—meditate on these things. **9** The things which you learned and received and heard and saw in me, these do, and the God of peace will be with you.

Col 3:12 Therefore, as *the* elect of God, holy and beloved, put on tender mercies, kindness, humility, meekness, longsuffering;

Cf. 1 Pet 3:8

Caution against one of apostasy.

Heb 12:15–17 looking carefully lest anyone fall short of the grace of God; lest any root of bitterness springing up cause trouble, and by this many become defiled; **16** lest there *be* any fornicator or profane person like Esau, who for one morsel of food sold his birthright. **17** For you know that afterward, when he wanted to

inherit the blessing, he was rejected, for he found no place for repentance, though he sought it diligently with tears.

Of impartiality.

James 2:1–13 My brethren, do not hold the faith of our Lord Jesus Christ, *the Lord* of glory, with partiality. **2** For if there should come into your assembly a man with gold rings, in fine apparel, and there should also come in a poor man in filthy clothes, **3** and you pay attention to the one wearing the fine clothes and say to him, "You sit here in a good place," and say to the poor man, "You stand there," or, "Sit here at my footstool," **4** have you not shown partiality among yourselves, and become judges with evil thoughts? **5** Listen, my beloved brethren: Has God not chosen the poor of this world *to be* rich in faith and heirs of the kingdom which He promised to those who love Him? **6** But you have dishonored the poor man. Do not the rich oppress you and drag you into the courts? **7** Do they not blaspheme that noble name by which you are called? **8** If you really fulfill *the* royal law according to the Scripture, *"You shall love your neighbor as yourself,"* you do well; **9** but if you show partiality, you commit sin, and are convicted by the law as transgressors. **10** For whoever shall keep the whole law, and yet stumble in one *point*, he is guilty of all. **11** For He who said, *"Do not commit adultery,"* also said, *"Do not murder."* Now if you do not commit adultery, but you do murder, you have become a transgressor of the law. **12** So speak and so do as those who will be judged by the law of liberty. **13** For judgment is without mercy to the one who has shown no mercy. Mercy triumphs over judgment.

Cf. James 3:13–18

Proper, toward

Government.

Rom 13:1–7 Let every soul be subject to the governing authorities. For there is no authority except from God, and the authorities that exist are appointed by God. **2** Therefore whoever resists the authority resists the ordinance of God, and those who resist will bring judgment on themselves. **3** For rulers are not a terror to good works, but to evil. Do you want to be unafraid of the authority? Do what is good, and you will have praise from the same. **4** For he is God's minister to you for good. But if you do evil, be afraid; for he does not bear the sword in vain; for he is God's minister, an avenger to *execute* wrath on him who practices evil. **5** Therefore *you* must be subject, not only because of wrath but also for conscience' sake. **6** For because of this you also pay taxes, for they are God's ministers attending continually to this very thing. **7** Render therefore to all their due: taxes to whom taxes *are due*, customs to whom customs, fear to whom fear, honor to whom honor.

1 Pet 2:13–17 Therefore submit yourselves to every ordinance of man for the Lord's sake, whether to the king as supreme, **14** or to governors, as to those who are sent by him for the punishment of evildoers and *for the* praise of those who do good. **15** For this is the will of God, that by doing good you may put to silence the ignorance of foolish men— **16** as free, yet not using liberty as a cloak for vice, but as bondservants of God. **17** Honor all *people.* Love the brotherhood. Fear God. Honor the king.

Hostile employer.

1 Pet 2:18 Servants, *be* submissive to *your* masters with all fear, not only to the good and gentle, but also to the harsh.

Unjust suffering.

1 Pet 3:13–17 And who *is* he who will harm you if you become followers of what is good? **14** But even if you should suffer for righteousness' sake, *you are* blessed. *"And do not be afraid of their threats, nor be troubled."* **15** But sanctify the Lord God in your hearts, and always *be* ready to *give* a defense to everyone who asks you a reason for the hope that is in you, with meekness and fear; **16** having a good conscience, that when they defame you as evildoers, those who revile your good conduct in Christ may be ashamed. **17** For *it is* better, if it is the will of God, to suffer for doing good than for doing evil.

Submission.

1 Cor 16:15 I urge you, brethren—you know the household of Stephanas, that it is the firstfruits of Achaia, and *that* they have devoted themselves to the ministry of the saints—

1 Thess 5:12–14 And we urge you, brethren, to recognize those who labor among you, and are over you in the Lord and admonish you, **13** and to esteem them very highly in love for their work's sake. Be at peace among yourselves. **14** Now we exhort you, brethren, warn those who are unruly, comfort the fainthearted, uphold the weak, be patient with all.

Titus 3:1–2 Remind them to be subject to rulers and authorities, to obey, to be ready for every good work, **2** to speak evil of no one, to be peaceable, gentle, showing all humility to all men.

Heb 13:7 Remember those who rule over you, who have spoken the word of God to you, whose faith follow, considering the outcome of *their* conduct.

Heb 13:17 Obey those who rule over you, and be submissive, for they watch out for your souls, as those who must give account. Let them do so with joy and not with grief, for that would be unprofitable for you.

1 Pet 5:5–7 Likewise you younger people, submit yourselves to *your* elders. Yes, all of *you* be submissive to one another, and be clothed with humility, for *"God resists the proud, But gives grace to the humble."* **6** Therefore humble yourselves under the mighty hand of God, that He may exalt you in due time, **7** casting all your care upon Him, for He cares for you.

AUTHORITY

Of Scripture.

Ps 12:6 The words of the LORD *are* pure words, *Like* silver tried in a furnace of earth, Purified seven times.

Ps 119:140 Your word *is* very pure; Therefore Your servant loves it.

Prov 30:5 Every word of God *is* pure; He *is* a shield to those who put their trust in Him.

John 10:35 If He called them gods, to whom the word of God came (and the Scripture cannot be broken),

2 Tim 3:16–17 All Scripture *is* given by inspiration of God, and *is* profitable for doctrine, for reproof, for correction, for instruction in righteousness, **17** that the man of God may be complete, thoroughly equipped for every good work.

2 Pet 1:20–21 knowing this first, that no prophecy of Scripture is of any private interpretation, **21** for prophecy never came by the will of man, but holy men of God spoke *as they were* moved by the Holy Spirit.

Cf. Is 55:11; 2 Pet 1:3–4

Of Joseph in Egypt.

Gen 39:2–6 The LORD was with Joseph, and he was a successful man; and he was in the house of his master the Egyptian. **3** And his master saw that the LORD *was* with him and that the LORD made all he did to prosper in his hand. **4** So Joseph found favor in his sight, and served him. Then he made him overseer of his house, and all *that* he had he put under his authority. **5** So it was, from the time *that* he had made him overseer of his house and all that he had, that the LORD blessed the Egyptian's house for Joseph's sake; and the blessing of the LORD was on all that he had in the house and in the field. **6** Thus he left all that he had in Joseph's hand, and he did not know what he had except for the bread which he ate. Now Joseph was handsome in form and appearance.

Gen 39:20–21 Then Joseph's master took him and put him into the prison, a place where the king's prisoners *were* confined. And he was there in the prison. **21** But the LORD was with Joseph and showed him mercy, and He gave him favor in the sight of the keeper of the prison.

Gen 41:55–56 So when all the land of Egypt was famished, the people cried to Pharaoh for bread. Then Pharaoh said to all the Egyptians, "Go to Joseph; whatever he says to you, do." **56** The famine was over all the face of the earth, and Joseph opened all the storehouses and sold to the Egyptians. And the famine became severe in the land of Egypt.

Of the priests.

Deut 21:5 Then the priests, the sons of Levi, shall come near, for the LORD your God has chosen them to minister to Him and to bless in the name of the LORD; by their word every controversy and every assault shall be *settled.*

Of God, over the nations and governments.

Gen 10:32 These *were* the families of the sons of Noah, according to their generations, in their nations; and from these the nations were divided on the earth after the flood.

Gen 11:9 Therefore its name is called Babel, because there the LORD confused the language of all the earth; and from there the LORD scattered them abroad over the face of all the earth.

Gen 14:18 Then Melchizedek king of Salem brought out bread and wine; he *was* the priest of God Most High.

Num 24:16 The utterance of him who hears the words of God, And has the knowledge of the Most High, *Who* sees the vision of the Almighty, *Who* falls down, with eyes wide open:

Deut 32:8–9 When the Most High divided their inheritance to the nations, When He separated the sons of Adam, He set the boundaries of the peoples According to the number of the children of Israel. **9** For the

LORD's portion *is* His people; Jacob *is* the place of His inheritance.

Ps 2:1–12 Why do the nations rage, And the people plot a vain thing? **2** The kings of the earth set themselves, And the rulers take counsel together, Against the LORD and against His Anointed, *saying,* **3** "Let us break Their bonds in pieces And cast away Their cords from us." **4** He who sits in the heavens shall laugh; The LORD shall hold them in derision. **5** Then He shall speak to them in His wrath, And distress them in His deep displeasure: **6** "Yet I have set My King On My holy hill of Zion." **7** "I will declare the decree: The LORD has said to Me, 'You *are* My Son, Today I have begotten You. **8** Ask of Me, and I will give *You* The nations *for* Your inheritance, And the ends of the earth *for* Your possession. **9** You shall break them with a rod of iron; You shall dash them to pieces like a potter's vessel.' " **10** Now therefore, be wise, O kings; Be instructed, you judges of the earth. **11** Serve the LORD with fear, And rejoice with trembling. **12** Kiss the Son, lest He be angry, And you perish *in* the way, When His wrath is kindled but a little. Blessed *are* all those who put their trust in Him.

Ps 82:8 Arise, O God, judge the earth; For You shall inherit all nations.

Rom 13:1 Let every soul be subject to the governing authorities. For there is no authority except from God, and the authorities that exist are appointed by God.

Of Christ,

Challenged by the Jewish leaders.

Matt 21:23–27 Now when He came into the temple, the chief priests and the elders of the people confronted Him as He was teaching, and said, "By what authority are You doing these things? And who gave You this authority?" **24** But Jesus answered and said to them, "I also will ask you one thing, which if you tell Me, I likewise will tell you by what authority I do these things: **25** The baptism of John—where was it from? From heaven or from men?" And they reasoned among themselves, saying, "If we say, 'From heaven,' He will say to us, 'Why then did you not believe him?' **26** But if we say, 'From men,' we fear the multitude, for all count John as a prophet." **27** So they answered Jesus and said, "We do not know." And He said to them, "Neither will I tell you by what authority I do these things.

Matt 22:15–22 Then the Pharisees went and plotted how they might entangle Him in *His* talk. **16** And they sent to Him their disciples with the Herodians, saying, "Teacher, we know that You are true, and teach the way of God in truth; nor do You care about anyone, for You do not regard the person of men. **17** Tell us, therefore, what do You think? Is it lawful to pay taxes to Caesar, or not?" **18** But Jesus perceived their wickedness, and said, "Why do you test Me, *you* hypocrites? **19** Show Me the tax money." So they brought Him a denarius. **20** And He said to them, "Whose image and inscription *is* this?" **21** They said to Him, "Caesar's." And He said to them, "Render therefore to Caesar the things that are Caesar's, and to God the things that are God's." **22** When they had heard *these words,* they marveled, and left Him and went their way.

Cf. Mark 11:27–33; 12:13–17; Luke 20:1–8; 20:20–26

Challenged by the Sadducees.

Matt 22:23–33 The same day the Sadducees, who say there is no resurrection, came to Him and asked Him, **24** saying: "Teacher, Moses said that if a man dies, having no children, his brother shall marry his wife and raise up offspring for his brother. **25** Now there were with us seven brothers. The first died after he had married, and having no offspring, left his wife to his brother. **26** Likewise the second also, and the third, even to the seventh. **27** Last of all the woman died also. **28** Therefore, in the resurrection, whose wife of the seven will she be? For they all had her." **29** Jesus answered and said to them, "You are mistaken, not knowing the Scriptures nor the power of God. **30** For in the resurrection they neither marry nor are given in marriage, but are like angels of God in heaven. **31** But concerning the resurrection of the dead, have you not read what was spoken to you by God, saying, **32** *'I am the God of Abraham, the God of Isaac, and the God of Jacob'*? God is not the God of the dead, but of the living." **33** And when the multitudes heard *this,* they were astonished at His teaching.

Cf. Mark 12:18–27; Luke 20:27–40

Challenged by a Pharisee scribe.

Matt 22:34–40 But when the Pharisees heard that He had silenced the Sadducees, they gathered together. **35** Then one of them, a lawyer, asked *Him a question,* testing Him, and saying, **36** "Teacher, which *is* the great commandment in the law?" **37** Jesus said to him, " *'You shall love the LORD your God with all your heart, with all your soul, and with all your mind.'* **38** This is *the* first and great commandment. **39** And *the* second *is* like it: *'You shall love your neighbor as yourself.'* **40** On these two commandments hang all the Law and the Prophets."

Cf. Mark 12:28–34

Affirmed.

Matt 8:8–9 The centurion answered and said, "Lord, I am not worthy that You should come under my roof. But only speak a word, and my servant will be healed. **9** For I also am a man under authority, having soldiers under me. And I say to this *one,* 'Go,' and he goes; and to another, 'Come,' and he comes; and to my servant, 'Do this,' and he does *it*."

Luke 7:7–8 Therefore I did not even think myself worthy to come to You. But say the word, and my servant will be healed. **8** For I also am a man placed under authority, having soldiers under me. And I say to one, 'Go,' and he goes; and to another, 'Come,' and he comes; and to my servant, 'Do this,' and he does *it*."

Extent of.

Matt 28:18 And Jesus came and spoke to them, saying, "All authority has been given to Me in heaven and on earth.

John 3:35 The Father loves the Son, and has given all things into His hand.

John 5:27 and has given Him authority to execute judgment also, because He is the Son of Man.

John 17:2 as You have given Him authority over all flesh, that He should give eternal life to as many as You have given Him.

Phil 2:9–11 Therefore God also has highly exalted Him

and given Him the name which is above every name, **10** that at the name of Jesus every knee should bow, of those in heaven, and of those on earth, and of those under the earth, **11** and *that* every tongue should confess that Jesus Christ *is* Lord, to the glory of God the Father.

Heb 1:1–4 God, who at various times and in various ways spoke in time past to the fathers by the prophets, **2** has in these last days spoken to us by *His* Son, whom He has appointed heir of all things, through whom also He made the worlds; **3** who being the brightness of *His* glory and the express image of His person, and upholding all things by the word of His power, when He had by Himself purged our sins, sat down at the right hand of the Majesty on high, **4** having become so much better than the angels, as He has by inheritance obtained a more excellent name than they.

Cf. Matt 11:27

People's response to.

Matt 7:28–29 And so it was, when Jesus had ended these sayings, that the people were astonished at His teaching, **29** for He taught them as one having authority, and not as the scribes.

Matt 13:54 When He had come to His own country, He taught them in their synagogue, so that they were astonished and said, "Where did this *Man* get this wisdom and *these* mighty works?

Mark 1:22 And they were astonished at His teaching, for He taught them as one having authority, and not as the scribes.

Mark 1:27 Then they were all amazed, so that they questioned among themselves, saying, "What is this? What new doctrine *is* this? For with authority He commands even the unclean spirits, and they obey Him."

Luke 4:3 And the devil said to Him, "If You are the Son of God, command this stone to become bread."

Over the Sabbath.

Matt 12:8 For the Son of Man is Lord even of the Sabbath."

Mark 2:27–28 And He said to them, "The Sabbath was made for man, and not man for the Sabbath. **28** Therefore the Son of Man is also Lord of the Sabbath."

Luke 6:5 And He said to them, "The Son of Man is also Lord of the Sabbath."

Given to believers in the church.

Matt 16:18–19 And I also say to you that you are Peter, and on this rock I will build My church, and the gates of Hades shall not prevail against it. **19** And I will give you the keys of the kingdom of heaven, and whatever you bind on earth will be bound in heaven, and whatever you loose on earth will be loosed in heaven."

John 20:23 If you forgive the sins of any, they are forgiven them; if you retain the *sins* of any, they are retained."

Cf. Matt 18:15–17

As exercised by unbelievers.

Matt 20:25 But Jesus called them to *Himself* and said, "You know that the rulers of the Gentiles lord it over them, and those who are great exercise authority over them.

Mark 10:42 But Jesus called them to *Himself* and said to them, "You know that those who are considered rulers over the Gentiles lord it over them, and their great ones exercise authority over them.

Of men, over women in the church.

1 Cor 11:8–9 For man is not from woman, but woman from man. **9** Nor was man created for the woman, but woman for the man.

1 Tim 2:11–15 Let a woman learn in silence with all submission. **12** And I do not permit a woman to teach or to have authority over a man, but to be in silence. **13** For Adam was formed first, then Eve. **14** And Adam was not deceived, but the woman being deceived, fell into transgression. **15** Nevertheless she will be saved in childbearing if they continue in faith, love, and holiness, with self-control.

Cf. Is 3:12; Eph 5:22–33

Of Paul, as an apostle.

2 Cor 10:1–18 Now I, Paul, myself am pleading with you by the meekness and gentleness of Christ—who in presence *am* lowly among you, but being absent am bold toward you. **2** But I beg *you* that when I am present I may not be bold with that confidence by which I intend to be bold against some, who think of us as if we walked according to the flesh. **3** For though we walk in the flesh, we do not war according to the flesh. **4** For the weapons of our warfare *are* not carnal but mighty in God for pulling down strongholds, **5** casting down arguments and every high thing that exalts itself against the knowledge of God, bringing every thought into captivity to the obedience of Christ, **6** and being ready to punish all disobedience when your obedience is fulfilled. **7** Do you look at things according to the outward appearance? If anyone is convinced in himself that he is Christ's, let him again consider this in himself, that just as he *is* Christ's, even so we *are* Christ's. **8** For even if I should boast somewhat more about our authority, which the Lord gave us for edification and not for your destruction, I shall not be ashamed— **9** lest I seem to terrify you by letters. **10** "For *his* letters," they say, "*are* weighty and powerful, but *his* bodily presence *is* weak, and *his* speech contemptible." **11** Let such a person consider this, that what we are in word by letters when we are absent, such *we will* also *be* in deed when we are present. **12** For we dare not class ourselves or compare ourselves with those who commend themselves. But they, measuring themselves by themselves, and comparing themselves among themselves, are not wise. **13** We, however, will not boast beyond measure, but within the limits of the sphere which God appointed us—a sphere which especially includes you. **14** For we are not overextending ourselves (as though *our authority* did not extend to you), for it was to you that we came with the gospel of Christ; **15** not boasting of things beyond measure, *that is,* in other men's labors, but having hope, *that* as your faith is increased, we shall be greatly enlarged by you in our sphere, **16** to preach the gospel in the *regions* beyond you, *and* not to boast in another man's sphere of accomplishment. **17** But *"he who glories, let him glory in the* LORD." **18** For not he who commends himself is approved, but whom the Lord commends.

B

BAAL
Prophets of, contended with Elijah.

1 Kin 18:9–42 So he said, "How have I sinned, that you are delivering your servant into the hand of Ahab, to kill me? **10** *As* the LORD your God lives, there is no nation or kingdom where my master has not sent someone to hunt for you; and when they said, '*He is not here*,' he took an oath from the kingdom or nation that they could not find you. **11** And now you say, 'Go, tell your master, "Elijah *is here*" '! **12** And it shall come to pass, *as soon as* I am gone from you, that the Spirit of the LORD will carry you to a place I do not know; so when I go and tell Ahab, and he cannot find you, he will kill me. But I your servant have feared the LORD from my youth. **13** Was it not reported to my lord what I did when Jezebel killed the prophets of the LORD, how I hid one hundred men of the LORD's prophets, fifty to a cave, and fed them with bread and water? **14** And now you say, 'Go, tell your master, "Elijah *is here*." ' He will kill me!" **15** Then Elijah said, "*As* the LORD of hosts lives, before whom I stand, I will surely present myself to him today." **16** So Obadiah went to meet Ahab, and told him; and Ahab went to meet Elijah. **17** Then it happened, when Ahab saw Elijah, that Ahab said to him, "*Is that* you, O troubler of Israel?" **18** And he answered, "I have not troubled Israel, but you and your father's house *have*, in that you have forsaken the commandments of the LORD and have followed the Baals. **19** Now therefore, send *and* gather all Israel to me on Mount Carmel, the four hundred and fifty prophets of Baal, and the four hundred prophets of Asherah, who eat at Jezebel's table." **20** So Ahab sent for all the children of Israel, and gathered the prophets together on Mount Carmel. **21** And Elijah came to all the people, and said, "How long will you falter between two opinions? If the LORD *is* God, follow Him; but if Baal, follow him." But the people answered him not a word. **22** Then Elijah said to the people, "I alone am left a prophet of the LORD; but Baal's prophets *are* four hundred and fifty men. **23** Therefore let them give us two bulls; and let them choose one bull for themselves, cut it in pieces, and lay *it* on the wood, but put no fire *under it*; and I will prepare the other bull, and lay *it* on the wood, but put no fire *under it*. **24** Then you call on the name of your gods, and I will call on the name of the LORD; and the God who answers by fire, He is God." So all the people answered and said, "It is well spoken." **25** Now Elijah said to the prophets of Baal, "Choose one bull for yourselves and prepare *it* first, for you *are* many; and call on the name of your god, but put no fire *under it*." **26** So they took the bull which was given them, and they prepared *it*, and called on the name of Baal from morning even till noon, saying, "O Baal, hear us!"

But *there was* no voice; no one answered. Then they leaped about the altar which they had made. **27** And so it was, at noon, that Elijah mocked them and said, "Cry aloud, for he *is* a god; either he is meditating, or he is busy, or he is on a journey, *or* perhaps he is sleeping and must be awakened." **28** So they cried aloud, and cut themselves, as was their custom, with knives and lances, until the blood gushed out on them. **29** And when midday was past, they prophesied until the *time* of the offering of the *evening* sacrifice. But *there was* no voice; no one answered, no one paid attention. **30** Then Elijah said to all the people, "Come near to me." So all the people came near to him. And he repaired the altar of the LORD *that was* broken down. **31** And Elijah took twelve stones, according to the number of the tribes of the sons of Jacob, to whom the word of the LORD had come, saying, "Israel shall be your name." **32** Then with the stones he built an altar in the name of the LORD; and he made a trench around the altar large enough to hold two seahs of seed. **33** And he put the wood in order, cut the bull in pieces, and laid *it* on the wood, and said, "Fill four waterpots with water, and pour *it* on the burnt sacrifice and on the wood." **34** Then he said, "Do *it* a second time," and they did *it* a second time; and he said, "Do *it* a third time," and they did *it* a third time. **35** So the water ran all around the altar; and he also filled the trench with water. **36** And it came to pass, at *the time of* the offering of the *evening* sacrifice, that Elijah the prophet came near and said, "LORD God of Abraham, Isaac, and Israel, let it be known this day that You *are* God in Israel and I *am* Your servant, and *that* I have done all these things at Your word. **37** Hear me, O LORD, hear me, that this people may know that You *are* the LORD God, and *that* You have turned their hearts back *to You* again." **38** Then the fire of the LORD fell and consumed the burnt sacrifice, and the wood and the stones and the dust, and it licked up the water that *was* in the trench. **39** Now when all the people saw *it*, they fell on their faces; and they said, "The LORD, He *is* God! The LORD, He *is* God!" **40** And Elijah said to them, "Seize the prophets of Baal! Do not let one of them escape!" So they seized them; and Elijah brought them down to the Brook Kishon and executed them there. **41** Then Elijah said to Ahab, "Go up, eat and drink; for *there is* the sound of abundance of rain." **42** So Ahab went up to eat and drink. And Elijah went up to the top of Carmel; then he bowed down on the ground, and put his face between his knees,

Gideon destroyed altar of.

Judg 6:25–32 Now it came to pass the same night that the LORD said to him, "Take your father's young bull, the second bull of seven years old, and tear down the altar of Baal that your father has, and cut down the wooden image that *is* beside it; 26 and build an altar to the LORD your God on top of this rock in the proper arrangement, and take the second bull and offer a burnt sacrifice with the wood of the image which you shall cut down." 27 So Gideon took ten men from among his servants and did as the LORD had said to him. But because he feared his father's household and the men of the city too much to do *it* by day, he did *it* by night. 28 And when the men of the city arose early in the morning, there was the altar of Baal, torn down; and the wooden image that *was* beside it was cut down, and the second bull was being offered on the altar *which had been* built. 29 So they said to one another, "Who has done this thing?" And when they had inquired and asked, they said, "Gideon the son of Joash has done this thing." 30 Then the men of the city said to Joash, "Bring out your son, that he may die, because he has torn down the altar of Baal, and because he has cut down the wooden image that *was* beside it." 31 But Joash said to all who stood against him, "Would you plead for Baal? Would you save him? Let the one who would plead for him be put to death by morning! If he *is* a god, let him plead for himself, because his altar has been torn down!" 32 Therefore on that day he called him Jerubbaal, saying, "Let Baal plead against him, because he has torn down his altar."

Samuel preached against.

1 Sam 7:3–4 Then Samuel spoke to all the house of Israel, saying, "If you return to the LORD with all your hearts, *then* put away the foreign gods and the Ashtoreths from among you, and prepare your hearts for the LORD, and serve Him only; and He will deliver you from the hand of the Philistines." 4 So the children of Israel put away the Baals and the Ashtoreths, and served the LORD only.

Jehu killed worshipers of.

2 Kin 10:18–28 Then Jehu gathered all the people together, and said to them, "Ahab served Baal a little, Jehu will serve him much. 19 Now therefore, call to me all the prophets of Baal, all his servants, and all his priests. Let no one be missing, for I have a great sacrifice for Baal. Whoever is missing shall not live." But Jehu acted deceptively, with the intent of destroying the worshipers of Baal. 20 And Jehu said, "Proclaim a solemn assembly for Baal." So they proclaimed *it*. 21 Then Jehu sent throughout all Israel; and all the worshipers of Baal came, so that there was not a man left who did not come. So they came into the temple of Baal, and the temple of Baal was full from one end to the other. 22 And he said to the one in charge of the wardrobe, "Bring out vestments for all the worshipers of Baal." So he brought out vestments for them. 23 Then Jehu and Jehonadab the son of Rechab went into the temple of Baal, and said to the worshipers of Baal, "Search and see that no servants of the LORD are here with you, but only the worshipers of Baal." 24 So they went in to offer sacrifices and burnt offerings. Now Jehu had appointed for himself eighty men on the outside, and had said, "*If* any of the men whom I have brought into your hands escapes, *whoever lets him escape, it shall be* his life for the life of the other." 25 Now it happened, as soon as he had made an end of offering the burnt offering, that Jehu said to the guard and to the cap-

tains, "Go in *and* kill them; let no one come out!" And they killed them with the edge of the sword; then the guards and the officers threw *them* out, and went into the inner room of the temple of Baal. 26 And they brought the *sacred* pillars out of the temple of Baal and burned them. 27 Then they broke down the *sacred* pillar of Baal, and tore down the temple of Baal and made it a refuse dump to this day. 28 Thus Jehu destroyed Baal from Israel.

Jehoiada destroyed temple of.

2 Kin 11:17–18 Then Jehoiada made a covenant between the LORD, the king, and the people, that they should be the LORD's people, and *also* between the king and the people. 18 And all the people of the land went to the temple of Baal, and tore it down. They thoroughly broke in pieces its altars and images, and killed Mattan the priest of Baal before the altars. And the priest appointed officers over the house of the LORD.

Of Peor; Israel punished for worshiping.

Num 25:1–9 Now Israel remained in Acacia Grove, and the people began to commit harlotry with the women of Moab. 2 They invited the people to the sacrifices of their gods, and the people ate and bowed down to their gods. 3 So Israel was joined to Baal of Peor, and the anger of the LORD was aroused against Israel. 4 Then the LORD said to Moses, "Take all the leaders of the people and hang the offenders before the LORD, out in the sun, that the fierce anger of the LORD may turn away from Israel." 5 So Moses said to the judges of Israel, "Every one of you kill his men who were joined to Baal of Peor." 6 And indeed, one of the children of Israel came and presented to his brethren a Midianite woman in the sight of Moses and in the sight of all the congregation of the children of Israel, who *were* weeping at the door of the tabernacle of meeting. 7 Now when Phinehas the son of Eleazar, the son of Aaron the priest, saw *it*, he rose from among the congregation and took a javelin in his hand; 8 and he went after the man of Israel into the tent and thrust both of them through, the man of Israel, and the woman through her body. So the plague was stopped among the children of Israel. 9 And those who died in the plague were twenty-four thousand.

Deut 4:3–4 Your eyes have seen what the LORD did at Baal Peor; for the LORD your God has destroyed from among you all the men who followed Baal of Peor. 4 But you who held fast to the LORD your God *are* alive today, every one of you.

Ps 106:28–30 They joined themselves also to Baal of Peor, And ate sacrifices made to the dead. 29 Thus they provoked *Him* to anger with their deeds, And the plague broke out among them. 30 Then Phinehas stood up and intervened, And the plague was stopped.

Cf. Hos 9:10

Perazim; David defeated Philistines there.

2 Sam 5:20–21 So David went to Baal Perazim, and David defeated them there; and he said, "The LORD has broken through my enemies before me, like a breakthrough of water." Therefore he called the name of that place Baal Perazim. 21 And they left their images there, and David and his men carried them away.

Worship of,

Introduced in Israel.

1 Kin 16:23–34 In the thirty-first year of Asa king of Judah, Omri became king over Israel, *and reigned* twelve years. Six years he reigned in Tirzah. **24** And he bought the hill of Samaria from Shemer for two talents of silver; then he built on the hill, and called the name of the city which he built, Samaria, after the name of Shemer, owner of the hill. **25** Omri did evil in the eyes of the LORD, and did worse than all who *were* before him. **26** For he walked in all the ways of Jeroboam the son of Nebat, and in his sin by which he had made Israel sin, provoking the LORD God of Israel to anger with their idols. **27** Now the rest of the acts of Omri which he did, and the might that he showed, *are* they not written in the book of the chronicles of the kings of Israel? **28** So Omri rested with his fathers and was buried in Samaria. Then Ahab his son reigned in his place. **29** In the thirty-eighth year of Asa king of Judah, Ahab the son of Omri became king over Israel; and Ahab the son of Omri reigned over Israel in Samaria twenty-two years. **30** Now Ahab the son of Omri did evil in the sight of the LORD, more than all who *were* before him. **31** And it came to pass, as though it had been a trivial thing for him to walk in the sins of Jeroboam the son of Nebat, that he took as wife Jezebel the daughter of Ethbaal, king of the Sidonians; and he went and served Baal and worshiped him. **32** Then he set up an altar for Baal in the temple of Baal, which he had built in Samaria. **33** And Ahab made a wooden image. Ahab did more to provoke the LORD God of Israel to anger than all the kings of Israel who were before him. **34** In his days Hiel of Bethel built Jericho. He laid its foundation with Abiram his firstborn, and with his youngest *son* Segub he set up its gates, according to the word of the LORD, which He had spoken through Joshua the son of Nun.

Cf. Hos 2:8

By Ahaziah.

1 Kin 22:51–53 Ahaziah the son of Ahab became king over Israel in Samaria in the seventeenth year of Jehoshaphat king of Judah, and reigned two years over Israel. **52** He did evil in the sight of the LORD, and walked in the way of his father and in the way of his mother and in the way of Jeroboam the son of Nebat, who had made Israel sin; **53** for he served Baal and worshiped him, and provoked the LORD God of Israel to anger, according to all that his father had done.

Opposed by God.

Zeph 1:4–6 "I will stretch out My hand against Judah, And against all the inhabitants of Jerusalem. I will cut off every trace of Baal from this place, The names of the idolatrous priests with the *pagan* priests— **5** Those who worship the host of heaven on the housetops; Those who worship and swear *oaths* by the LORD, But who *also* swear by Milcom; **6** Those who have turned back from *following* the LORD, And have not sought the LORD, nor inquired of Him."

Hezekiah destroyed idols of.

2 Kin 18:4 He removed the high places and broke the *sacred* pillars, cut down the wooden image and broke in pieces the bronze serpent that Moses had made;

for until those days the children of Israel burned incense to it, and called it Nehushtan.

Manasseh rebuilds high places to.

2 Kin 21:3–7 For he rebuilt the high places which Hezekiah his father had destroyed; he raised up altars for Baal, and made a wooden image, as Ahab king of Israel had done; and he worshiped all the host of heaven and served them. **4** He also built altars in the house of the LORD, of which the LORD had said, "In Jerusalem I will put My name." **5** And he built altars for all the host of heaven in the two courts of the house of the LORD. **6** Also he made his son pass through the fire, practiced soothsaying, used witchcraft, and consulted spiritists and mediums. He did much evil in the sight of the LORD, to provoke *Him* to anger. **7** He even set a carved image of Asherah that he had made, in the house of which the LORD had said to David and to Solomon his son, "In this house and in Jerusalem, which I have chosen out of all the tribes of Israel, I will put My name forever;

Josiah destroyed altars of.

2 Chr 34:3–7 For in the eighth year of his reign, while he was still young, he began to seek the God of his father David; and in the twelfth year he began to purge Judah and Jerusalem of the high places, the wooden images, the carved images, and the molded images. **4** They broke down the altars of the Baals in his presence, and the incense altars which *were* above them he cut down; and the wooden images, the carved images, and the molded images he broke in pieces, and made dust of them and scattered *it* on the graves of those who had sacrificed to them. **5** He also burned the bones of the priests on their altars, and cleansed Judah and Jerusalem. **6** And *so he did* in the cities of Manasseh, Ephraim, and Simeon, as far as Naphtali and all around, with axes. **7** When he had broken down the altars and the wooden images, had beaten the carved images into powder, and cut down all the incense altars throughout all the land of Israel, he returned to Jerusalem.

BABYLON

Origin of.

Gen 10:8 Cush begot Nimrod; he began to be a mighty one on the earth.

Gen 10:10 And the beginning of his kingdom was Babel, Erech, Accad, and Calneh, in the land of Shinar.

Origin of the name.

Gen 11:8–9 So the LORD scattered them abroad from there over the face of all the earth, and they ceased building the city. **9** Therefore its name is called Babel, because there the LORD confused the language of all the earth; and from there the LORD scattered them abroad over the face of all the earth.

Was called

Land of the Chaldeans.

Jer 25:12 'Then it will come to pass, when seventy years are completed, *that* I will punish the king of Babylon and that nation, the land of the Chaldeans, for their iniquity,' says the LORD; 'and I will make it a perpetual desolation.

Ezek 12:13 I will also spread My net over him, and he

shall be caught in My snare. I will bring him to Babylon, *to* the land of the Chaldeans; yet he shall not see it, though he shall die there.

Land of Shinar.

Dan 1:2 And the Lord gave Jehoiakim king of Judah into his hand, with some of the articles of the house of God, which he carried into the land of Shinar to the house of his god; and he brought the articles into the treasure house of his god.

Zech 5:11 And he said to me, "To build a house for it in the land of Shinar; when it is ready, *the basket* will be set there on its base."

Land of Merathaim.

Jer 50:1 The word that the LORD spoke against Babylon *and* against the land of the Chaldeans by Jeremiah the prophet.

Jer 50:21 "Go up against the land of Merathaim, against it, And against the inhabitants of Pekod. Waste and utterly destroy them," says the LORD, "And do according to all that I have commanded you.

Wilderness of the sea.

Is 21:1 The burden against the Wilderness of the Sea. As whirlwinds in the South pass through, *So* it comes from the desert, from a terrible land.

Is 21:9 And look, here comes a chariot of men *with a* pair of horsemen!" Then he answered and said, "Babylon is fallen, is fallen! And all the carved images of her gods He has broken to the ground."

Sheshach.

Jer 25:26 all the kings of the north, far and near, one with another; and all the kingdoms of the world which *are* on the face of the earth. Also the king of Sheshach shall drink after them.

Lady of kingdoms.

Is 47:5 "Sit in silence, and go into darkness, O daughter of the Chaldeans; For you shall no longer be called The Lady of Kingdoms.

Situated beyond the Euphrates.

Gen 11:31 And Terah took his son Abram and his grandson Lot, the son of Haran, and his daughter-in-law Sarai, his son Abram's wife, and they went out with them from Ur of the Chaldeans to go to the land of Canaan; and they came to Haran and dwelt there.

Josh 24:2–3 And Joshua said to all the people, "Thus says the LORD God of Israel: 'Your fathers, *including* Terah, the father of Abraham and the father of Nahor, dwelt on the other side of the River in old times; and they served other gods. 3 Then I took your father Abraham from the other side of the River, led him throughout all the land of Canaan, and multiplied his descendants and gave him Isaac.

Formerly a part of Mesopotamia.

Acts 7:2 And he said, "Brethren and fathers, listen: The God of glory appeared to our father Abraham when he was in Mesopotamia, before he dwelt in Haran,

Watered by the rivers Euphrates and Tigris.

Ps 137:1 By the rivers of Babylon, There we sat down, yea, we wept When we remembered Zion.

Jer 51:13 O you who dwell by many waters, Abundant in treasures, Your end has come, The measure of your covetousness.

Composed of many nations.

Dan 3:4 Then a herald cried aloud: "To you it is commanded, O peoples, nations, and languages,

Dan 3:29 Therefore I make a decree that any people, nation, or language which speaks anything amiss against the God of Shadrach, Meshach, and Abed-Nego shall be cut in pieces, and their houses shall be made an ash heap; because there is no other God who can deliver like this."

Governed by kings.

2 Kin 20:12 At that time Berodach-Baladan the son of Baladan, king of Babylon, sent letters and a present to Hezekiah, for he heard that Hezekiah had been sick.

Dan 5:1 Belshazzar the king made a great feast for a thousand of his lords, and drank wine in the presence of the thousand.

With Media and Persia divided by Darius into 120 provinces.

Dan 6:1 It pleased Darius to set over the kingdom one hundred and twenty satraps, to be over the whole kingdom;

Administrators placed over.

Dan 2:48 Then the king promoted Daniel and gave him many great gifts; and he made him ruler over the whole province of Babylon, and chief administrator over all the wise *men* of Babylon.

Dan 6:1 It pleased Darius to set over the kingdom one hundred and twenty satraps, to be over the whole kingdom;

Babylon the chief province of.

Dan 3:1 Nebuchadnezzar the king made an image of gold, whose height *was* sixty cubits *and* its width six cubits. He set it up in the plain of Dura, in the province of Babylon.

Babylon the capital of,

Its antiquity.

Gen 11:4 And they said, "Come, let us build ourselves a city, and a tower whose top *is* in the heavens; let us make a name for ourselves, lest we be scattered abroad over the face of the whole earth."

Gen 11:9 Therefore its name is called Babel, because there the LORD confused the language of all the earth; and from there the LORD scattered them abroad over the face of all the earth.

Enlarged by Nebuchadnezzar.

Dan 4:30 The king spoke, saying, "Is not this great Babylon, that I have built for a royal dwelling by my mighty power and for the honor of my majesty?"

Surrounded with a great wall and fortified.

Jer 51:53 Though Babylon were to mount up to heaven, And though she were to fortify the height of her strength, Yet from Me plunderers would come to her," says the LORD.

Jer 51:58 Thus says the LORD of hosts: "The broad walls of Babylon shall be utterly broken, And her high gates shall be burned with fire; The people will labor in vain, And the nations, because of the fire; And they shall be weary."

Called the golden city.

Is 14:4 that you will take up this proverb against the

king of Babylon, and say: "How the oppressor has ceased, The golden city ceased!

Called the glory of kingdoms.

Is 13:19 And Babylon, the glory of kingdoms, The beauty of the Chaldeans' pride, Will be as when God overthrew Sodom and Gomorrah.

Called beauty of Chaldees, etc.

Is 13:19 And Babylon, the glory of kingdoms, The beauty of the Chaldeans' pride, Will be as when God overthrew Sodom and Gomorrah.

Called the city of merchants.

Ezek 17:4 He cropped off its topmost young twig And carried it to a land of trade; He set it in a city of merchants.

Called Babylon the great.

Dan 4:30 The king spoke, saying, "Is not this great Babylon, that I have built for a royal dwelling by my mighty power and for the honor of my majesty?"

Remarkable for

Antiquity.

Jer 5:15 Behold, I will bring a nation against you from afar, O house of Israel," says the LORD. "It *is* a mighty nation, It *is* an ancient nation, A nation whose language you do not know, Nor can you understand what they say.

Naval power.

Is 43:14 Thus says the LORD, your Redeemer, The Holy One of Israel: "For your sake I will send to Babylon, And bring them all down as fugitives— The Chaldeans, who rejoice in their ships.

Military power.

Jer 5:16 Their quiver *is* like an open tomb; They *are* all mighty men.

Jer 50:23 How the hammer of the whole earth has been cut apart and broken! How Babylon has become a desolation among the nations! I have laid a snare for you;

National greatness.

Is 13:19 And Babylon, the glory of kingdoms, The beauty of the Chaldeans' pride, Will be as when God overthrew Sodom and Gomorrah.

Jer 51:41 "Oh, how Sheshach is taken! Oh, how the praise of the whole earth is seized! How Babylon has become desolate among the nations!

Wealth.

Jer 50:37 A sword *is* against their horses, Against their chariots, And against all the mixed peoples who *are* in her midst; And they will become like women. A sword *is* against her treasures, and they will be robbed.

Jer 51:13 O you who dwell by many waters, Abundant in treasures, Your end has come, The measure of your covetousness.

Commerce.

Ezek 17:4 He cropped off its topmost young twig And carried it to a land of trade; He set it in a city of merchants.

Wisdom.

Is 47:10 "For you have trusted in your wickedness; You have said, 'No one sees me'; Your wisdom and your

knowledge have warped you; And you have said in your heart, 'I *am*, and *there is* no one else besides me.'

Jer 50:35 "A sword *is* against the Chaldeans," says the LORD, "Against the inhabitants of Babylon, And against her princes and her wise men.

Inhabitants of,

Idolatrous.

Jer 50:38 A drought *is* against her waters, and they will be dried up. For it *is* the land of carved images, And they are insane with *their* idols.

Dan 3:18 But if not, let it be known to you, O king, that we do not serve your gods, nor will we worship the gold image which you have set up."

Given to magic.

Is 47:9 But these two *things* shall come to you In a moment, in one day: The loss of children, and widowhood. They shall come upon you in their fullness Because of the multitude of your sorceries, For the great abundance of your enchantments.

Is 47:12–13 "Stand now with your enchantments And the multitude of your sorceries, In which you have labored from your youth— Perhaps you will be able to profit, Perhaps you will prevail. **13** You are wearied in the multitude of your counsels; Let now the astrologers, the stargazers, *And* the monthly prognosticators Stand up and save you From what shall come upon you.

Dan 2:1–2 Now in the second year of Nebuchadnezzar's reign, Nebuchadnezzar had dreams; and his spirit was *so* troubled that his sleep left him. **2** Then the king gave the command to call the magicians, the astrologers, the sorcerers, and the Chaldeans to tell the king his dreams. So they came and stood before the king.

Profane and sacrilegious.

Dan 5:1–3 Belshazzar the king made a great feast for a thousand of his lords, and drank wine in the presence of the thousand. **2** While he tasted the wine, Belshazzar gave the command to bring the gold and silver vessels which his father Nebuchadnezzar had taken from the temple which *had been* in Jerusalem, that the king and his lords, his wives, and his concubines might drink from them. **3** Then they brought the gold vessels that had been taken from the temple of the house of God which *had been* in Jerusalem; and the king and his lords, his wives, and his concubines drank from them.

Wicked.

Is 47:10 "For you have trusted in your wickedness; You have said, 'No one sees me'; Your wisdom and your knowledge have warped you; And you have said in your heart, 'I *am*, and *there is* no one else besides me.'

As a power was

Arrogant.

Is 14:13–14 For you have said in your heart: 'I will ascend into heaven, I will exalt my throne above the stars of God; I will also sit on the mount of the congregation On the farthest sides of the north; **14** I will ascend above the heights of the clouds, I will be like the Most High.'

Jer 50:29 "Call together the archers against Babylon. All you who bend the bow, encamp against it all around;

Let none of them escape. Repay her according to her work; According to all she has done, do to her; For she has been proud against the LORD, Against the Holy One of Israel.

Jer 50:31–32 "Behold, I *am* against you, O most haughty one!" says the Lord GOD of hosts; "For your day has come, The time *that* I will punish you. **32** The most proud shall stumble and fall, And no one will raise him up; I will kindle a fire in his cities, And it will devour all around him."

Secure and self-confident.

Is 47:7–8 And you said, 'I shall be a lady forever,' *So* that you did not take these *things* to heart, Nor remember the latter end of them. **8** "Therefore hear this now, *you who are* given to pleasures, Who dwell securely, Who say in your heart, 'I *am*, and *there is* no one else besides me; I shall not sit *as* a widow, Nor shall I know the loss of children';

Grand and stately.

Is 47:1 "Come down and sit in the dust, O virgin daughter of Babylon; Sit on the ground without a throne, O daughter of the Chaldeans! For you shall no more be called Tender and delicate.

Is 47:5 "Sit in silence, and go into darkness, O daughter of the Chaldeans; For you shall no longer be called The Lady of Kingdoms.

Covetous.

Jer 51:13 O you who dwell by many waters, Abundant in treasures, Your end has come, The measure of your covetousness.

Oppressive.

Is 14:4 that you will take up this proverb against the king of Babylon, and say: "How the oppressor has ceased, The golden city ceased!

Cruel and destructive.

Is 14:17 Who made the world as a wilderness And destroyed its cities, *Who* did not open the house of his prisoners?'

Is 47:6 I was angry with My people; I have profaned My inheritance, And given them into your hand. You showed them no mercy; On the elderly you laid your yoke very heavily.

Jer 51:25 "Behold, I *am* against you, O destroying mountain, Who destroys all the earth," says the LORD. "And I will stretch out My hand against you, Roll you down from the rocks, And make you a burnt mountain.

Hab 1:6–7 For indeed I am raising up the Chaldeans, A bitter and hasty nation Which marches through the breadth of the earth, To possess dwelling places *that are* not theirs. **7** They are terrible and dreadful; Their judgment and their dignity proceed from themselves.

An instrument of God's vengeance on other nations.

Is 47:6 I was angry with My people; I have profaned My inheritance, And given them into your hand. You showed them no mercy; On the elderly you laid your yoke very heavily.

Jer 51:7 Babylon *was* a golden cup in the LORD's hand, That made all the earth drunk. The nations drank her wine; Therefore the nations are deranged.

Languages spoken in.

Dan 1:4 young men in whom *there was* no blemish, but good-looking, gifted in all wisdom, possessing knowledge and quick to understand, who *had* ability to serve in the king's palace, and whom they might teach the language and literature of the Chaldeans.

Dan 2:4 Then the Chaldeans spoke to the king in Aramaic, "O king, live forever! Tell your servants the dream, and we will give the interpretation."

Armies of, described.

Hab 1:7–9 They are terrible and dreadful; Their judgment and their dignity proceed from themselves. **8** Their horses also are swifter than leopards, And more fierce than evening wolves. Their chargers charge ahead; Their cavalry comes from afar; They fly as the eagle *that* hastens to eat. **9** "They all come for violence; Their faces are set *like* the east wind. They gather captives like sand.

Represented by

A great eagle.

Ezek 17:3 and say, 'Thus says the Lord GOD: "A great eagle with large wings and long pinions, Full of feathers of various colors, Came to Lebanon And took from the cedar the highest branch.

A head of gold.

Dan 2:32 This image's head *was* of fine gold, its chest and arms of silver, its belly and thighs of bronze,

Dan 2:37–38 You, O king, *are* a king of kings. For the God of heaven has given you a kingdom, power, strength, and glory; **38** and wherever the children of men dwell, or the beasts of the field and the birds of the heaven, He has given *them* into your hand, and has made you ruler over them all—you *are* this head of gold.

A lion with eagle's wings.

Dan 7:4 The first *was* like a lion, and had eagle's wings. I watched till its wings were plucked off; and it was lifted up from the earth and made to stand on two feet like a man, and a man's heart was given to it.

Ambassadors of, sent to Hezekiah.

2 Kin 20:12 At that time Berodach-Baladan the son of Baladan, king of Babylon, sent letters and a present to Hezekiah, for he heard that Hezekiah had been sick.

Nebuchadnezzar king of,

Made Jehoiakim tributary.

2 Kin 24:1 In his days Nebuchadnezzar king of Babylon came up, and Jehoiakim became his vassal *for* three years. Then he turned and rebelled against him.

Besieged Jerusalem.

2 Kin 24:10–11 At that time the servants of Nebuchadnezzar king of Babylon came up against Jerusalem, and the city was besieged. **11** And Nebuchadnezzar king of Babylon came against the city, as his servants were besieging it.

Took Jehoiachin, etc. captive to Babylon.

2 Kin 24:12 Then Jehoiachin king of Judah, his mother, his servants, his princes, and his officers went out to the king of Babylon; and the king of Babylon, in the eighth year of his reign, took him prisoner.

2 Kin 24:14–16 Also he carried into captivity all Jerusalem: all the captains and all the mighty men of valor, ten thousand captives, and all the craftsmen and smiths. None remained except the poorest people of the land. **15** And he carried Jehoiachin captive to Babylon. The king's mother, the king's wives, his officers, and the mighty of the land he carried into captivity from Jerusalem to Babylon. **16** All the valiant men, seven thousand, and craftsmen and smiths, one thousand, all *who were* strong *and* fit for war, these the king of Babylon brought captive to Babylon.

2 Chr 36:10 At the turn of the year King Nebuchadnezzar summoned *him* and took him to Babylon, with the costly articles from the house of the LORD, and made Zedekiah, *Jehoiakim's* brother, king over Judah and Jerusalem.

Made Zedekiah king.

2 Kin 24:17 Then the king of Babylon made Mattaniah, *Jehoiachin's* uncle, king in his place, and changed his name to Zedekiah.

Rebelled against by Zedekiah.

2 Kin 24:20 For because of the anger of the LORD *this* happened in Jerusalem and Judah, that He finally cast them out from His presence. Then Zedekiah rebelled against the king of Babylon.

Besieged and took Jerusalem.

2 Kin 25:1–4 Now it came to pass in the ninth year of his reign, in the tenth month, on the tenth *day* of the month, *that* Nebuchadnezzar king of Babylon and all his army came against Jerusalem and encamped against it; and they built a siege wall against it all around. **2** So the city was besieged until the eleventh year of King Zedekiah. **3** By the ninth *day* of the *fourth* month the famine had become so severe in the city that there was no food for the people of the land. **4** Then the city wall was broken through, and all the men of war *fled* at night by way of the gate between two walls, which was by the king's garden, even though the Chaldeans *were* still encamped all around against the city. And *the king* went by way of the plain.

2 Kin 25:9–10 He burned the house of the LORD and the king's house; all the houses of Jerusalem, that is, all the houses of the great, he burned with fire. **10** And all the army of the Chaldeans who *were with* the captain of the guard broke down the walls of Jerusalem all around.

Took Zedekiah, etc. captive to Babylon.

2 Kin 25:7 Then they killed the sons of Zedekiah before his eyes, put out the eyes of Zedekiah, bound him with bronze fetters, and took him to Babylon.

2 Kin 25:11 Then Nebuzaradan the captain of the guard carried away captive the rest of the people *who* remained in the city and the defectors who had deserted to the king of Babylon, with the rest of the multitude.

2 Kin 25:18–21 And the captain of the guard took Seraiah the chief priest, Zephaniah the second priest, and the three doorkeepers. **19** He also took out of the city an officer who had charge of the men of war, five men of the king's close associates who were found in the city, the chief recruiting officer of the army, who mustered the people of the land, and sixty men of the people of the land *who were* found in the city. **20** So

Nebuzaradan, captain of the guard, took these and brought them to the king of Babylon at Riblah. **21** Then the king of Babylon struck them and put them to death at Riblah in the land of Hamath. Thus Judah was carried away captive from its own land.

2 Chr 36:20 And those who escaped from the sword he carried away to Babylon, where they became servants to him and his sons until the rule of the kingdom of Persia,

Spoiled and burned the temple.

2 Kin 24:13 And he carried out from there all the treasures of the house of the LORD and the treasures of the king's house, and he cut in pieces all the articles of gold which Solomon king of Israel had made in the temple of the LORD, as the LORD had said.

2 Kin 25:9 He burned the house of the LORD and the king's house; all the houses of Jerusalem, that is, all the houses of the great, he burned with fire.

2 Kin 25:13–17 The bronze pillars that *were* in the house of the LORD, and the carts and the bronze Sea that *were* in the house of the LORD, the Chaldeans broke in pieces, and carried their bronze to Babylon. **14** They also took away the pots, the shovels, the trimmers, the spoons, and all the bronze utensils with which the priests ministered. **15** The firepans and the basins, the things of solid gold and solid silver, the captain of the guard took away. **16** The two pillars, one Sea, and the carts, which Solomon had made for the house of the LORD, the bronze of all these articles was beyond measure. **17** The height of one pillar *was* eighteen cubits, and the capital on it *was* of bronze. The height of the capital was three cubits, and the network and pomegranates all around the capital were all of bronze. The second pillar was the same, with a network.

2 Chr 36:18–19 And all the articles from the house of God, great and small, the treasures of the house of the LORD, and the treasures of the king and of his leaders, all *these* he took to Babylon. **19** Then they burned the house of God, broke down the wall of Jerusalem, burned all its palaces with fire, and destroyed all its precious possessions.

Revolt of the Jews from, and their punishment illustrated. Ezek 17:1–24

The Jews exhorted to be subject to, and settle in.

Jer 27:17 Do not listen to them; serve the king of Babylon, and live! Why should this city be laid waste?

Jer 29:1–7 Now these *are* the words of the letter that Jeremiah the prophet sent from Jerusalem to the remainder of the elders who were carried away captive—to the priests, the prophets, and all the people whom Nebuchadnezzar had carried away captive from Jerusalem to Babylon. **2** (This happened after Jeconiah the king, the queen mother, the eunuchs, the princes of Judah and Jerusalem, the craftsmen, and the smiths had departed from Jerusalem.) **3** *The letter was sent* by the hand of Elasah the son of Shaphan, and Gemariah the son of Hilkiah, whom Zedekiah king of Judah sent to Babylon, to Nebuchadnezzar king of Babylon, saying, **4** Thus says the LORD of hosts, the God of Israel, to all who were carried away captive, whom I have caused to be carried away from Jerusalem to Babylon: **5** Build houses and dwell *in them;* plant gardens and eat their fruit.

6 Take wives and beget sons and daughters; and take wives for your sons and give your daughters to husbands, so that they may bear sons and daughters—that you may be increased there, and not diminished. 7 And seek the peace of the city where I have caused you to be carried away captive, and pray to the LORD for it; for in its peace you will have peace.

Treatment of the Jews in.

2 Kin 25:27–30 Now it came to pass in the thirty-seventh year of the captivity of Jehoiachin king of Judah, in the twelfth month, on the twenty-seventh *day* of the month, *that* Evil-Merodach king of Babylon, in the year that he began to reign, released Jehoiachin king of Judah from prison. 28 He spoke kindly to him, and gave him a more prominent seat than those of the kings who *were* with him in Babylon. 29 So Jehoiachin changed from his prison garments, and he ate bread regularly before the king all the days of his life. 30 And as for his provisions, *there was* a regular ration given him by the king, a portion for each day, all the days of his life.

Dan 1:3–7 Then the king instructed Ashpenaz, the master of his eunuchs, to bring some of the children of Israel and some of the king's descendants and some of the nobles, 4 young men in whom *there was* no blemish, but good-looking, gifted in all wisdom, possessing knowledge and quick to understand, who *had* ability to serve in the king's palace, and whom they might teach the language and literature of the Chaldeans. 5 And the king appointed for them a daily provision of the king's delicacies and of the wine which he drank, and three years of training for them, so that at the end of *that time* they might serve before the king. 6 Now from among those of the sons of Judah were Daniel, Hananiah, Mishael, and Azariah. 7 To them the chief of the eunuchs gave names: he gave Daniel *the name* Belteshazzar; to Hananiah, Shadrach; to Mishael, Meshach; and to Azariah, Abed-Nego.

Grief of the Jews in.

Ps 137:1–6 By the rivers of Babylon, There we sat down, yea, we wept When we remembered Zion. 2 We hung our harps Upon the willows in the midst of it. 3 For there those who carried us away captive asked of us a song, And those who plundered us *requested* mirth, *Saying,* "Sing us *one* of the songs of Zion!" 4 How shall we sing the LORD's song In a foreign land? 5 If I forget you, O Jerusalem, Let my right hand forget *its skill!* 6 If I do not remember you, Let my tongue cling to the roof of my mouth— If I do not exalt Jerusalem Above my chief joy.

Destroyed by the Medes.

Dan 5:30–31 That very night Belshazzar, king of the Chaldeans, was slain. 31 And Darius the Mede received the kingdom, *being* about sixty-two years old.

Restoration of the Jews from.

2 Chr 36:23 Thus says Cyrus king of Persia: All the kingdoms of the earth the LORD God of heaven has given me. And He has commanded me to build Him a house at Jerusalem which is in Judah. Who *is* among you of all His people? May the LORD his God *be* with him, and let him go up!

Cf. Ezra 1:1–11; 2:1–67

Predictions respecting,

Conquests by.

Jer 21:3–10 Then Jeremiah said to them, "Thus you shall say to Zedekiah, 4 'Thus says the LORD God of Israel: "Behold, I will turn back the weapons of war that *are* in your hands, with which you fight against the king of Babylon and the Chaldeans who besiege you outside the walls; and I will assemble them in the midst of this city. 5 I Myself will fight against you with an outstretched hand and with a strong arm, even in anger and fury and great wrath. 6 I will strike the inhabitants of this city, both man and beast; they shall die of a great pestilence. 7 And afterward," says the LORD, "I will deliver Zedekiah king of Judah, his servants and the people, and such as are left in this city from the pestilence and the sword and the famine, into the hand of Nebuchadnezzar king of Babylon, into the hand of their enemies, and into the hand of those who seek their life; and he shall strike them with the edge of the sword. He shall not spare them, or have pity or mercy." ' 8 "Now you shall say to this people, 'Thus says the LORD: "Behold, I set before you the way of life and the way of death. 9 He who remains in this city shall die by the sword, by famine, and by pestilence; but he who goes out and defects to the Chaldeans who besiege you, he shall live, and his life shall be as a prize to him. 10 For I have set My face against this city for adversity and not for good," says the LORD. "It shall be given into the hand of the king of Babylon, and he shall burn it with fire." '

Jer 27:2–6 "Thus says the LORD to me: 'Make for yourselves bonds and yokes, and put them on your neck, 3 and send them to the king of Edom, the king of Moab, the king of the Ammonites, the king of Tyre, and the king of Sidon, by the hand of the messengers who come to Jerusalem to Zedekiah king of Judah. 4 And command them to say to their masters, "Thus says the LORD of hosts, the God of Israel—thus you shall say to your masters: 5 'I have made the earth, the man and the beast that *are* on the ground, by My great power and by My outstretched arm, and have given it to whom it seemed proper to Me. 6 And now I have given all these lands into the hand of Nebuchadnezzar the king of Babylon, My servant; and the beasts of the field I have also given him to serve him.

Jer 49:28–33 Against Kedar and against the kingdoms of Hazor, which Nebuchadnezzar king of Babylon shall strike. Thus says the LORD: "Arise, go up to Kedar, And devastate the men of the East! 29 Their tents and their flocks they shall take away. They shall take for themselves their curtains, All their vessels and their camels; And they shall cry out to them, 'Fear *is* on every side!' 30 "Flee, get far away! Dwell in the depths, O inhabitants of Hazor!" says the LORD. "For Nebuchadnezzar king of Babylon has taken counsel against you, And has conceived a plan against you. 31 "Arise, go up to the wealthy nation that dwells securely," says the LORD, "Which has neither gates nor bars, Dwelling alone. 32 Their camels shall be for booty, And the multitude of their cattle for plunder. I will scatter to all winds those in the farthest corners, And I will bring their calamity from all its sides," says the LORD. 33 "Hazor shall be a dwelling for jackals, a desolation forever; No one shall reside there, Nor son of man dwell in it."

Cf. Ezek 21:19–32; 29:18–20

Captivity of the Jews by.

Jer 20:4–6 For thus says the LORD: 'Behold, I will make you a terror to yourself and to all your friends; and they shall fall by the sword of their enemies, and your eyes shall see *it*. I will give all Judah into the hand of the king of Babylon, and he shall carry them captive to Babylon and slay them with the sword. **5** Moreover I will deliver all the wealth of this city, all its produce, and all its precious things; all the treasures of the kings of Judah I will give into the hand of their enemies, who will plunder them, seize them, and carry them to Babylon. **6** And you, Pashhur, and all who dwell in your house, shall go into captivity. You shall go to Babylon, and there you shall die, and be buried there, you and all your friends, to whom you have prophesied lies.' "

Jer 22:20–26 "Go up to Lebanon, and cry out, And lift up your voice in Bashan; Cry from Abarim, For all your lovers are destroyed. **21** I spoke to you in your prosperity, *But* you said, 'I will not hear.' This *has been* your manner from your youth, That you did not obey My voice. **22** The wind shall eat up all your rulers, And your lovers shall go into captivity; Surely then you will be ashamed and humiliated For all your wickedness. **23** O inhabitant of Lebanon, Making your nest in the cedars, How gracious will you be when pangs come upon you, Like the pain of a woman in labor? **24** "*As* I live," says the LORD, "though Coniah the son of Jehoiakim, king of Judah, were the signet on My right hand, yet I would pluck you off; **25** and I will give you into the hand of those who seek your life, and into the hand *of those* whose face you fear—the hand of Nebuchadnezzar king of Babylon and the hand of the Chaldeans. **26** So I will cast you out, and your mother who bore you, into another country where you were not born; and there you shall die.

Jer 25:9–11 behold, I will send and take all the families of the north,' says the LORD, 'and Nebuchadnezzar the king of Babylon, My servant, and will bring them against this land, against its inhabitants, and against these nations all around, and will utterly destroy them, and make them an astonishment, a hissing, and perpetual desolations. **10** Moreover I will take from them the voice of mirth and the voice of gladness, the voice of the bridegroom and the voice of the bride, the sound of the millstones and the light of the lamp. **11** And this whole land shall be a desolation *and* an astonishment, and these nations shall serve the king of Babylon seventy years.

Mic 4:10 Be in pain, and labor to bring forth, O daughter of Zion, Like a woman in birth pangs. For now you shall go forth from the city, You shall dwell in the field, And to Babylon you shall go. There you shall be delivered; There the LORD will redeem you From the hand of your enemies.

Restoration of the Jews from.

Is 14:1–4 For the LORD will have mercy on Jacob, and will still choose Israel, and settle them in their own land. The strangers will be joined with them, and they will cling to the house of Jacob. **2** Then people

will take them and bring them to their place, and the house of Israel will possess them for servants and maids in the land of the LORD; they will take them captive whose captives they were, and rule over their oppressors. **3** It shall come to pass in the day the LORD gives you rest from your sorrow, and from your fear and the hard bondage in which you were made to serve, **4** that you will take up this proverb against the king of Babylon, and say: "How the oppressor has ceased, The golden city ceased!

Is 44:28 Who says of Cyrus, '*He is* My shepherd, And he shall perform all My pleasure, Saying to Jerusalem, "You shall be built," And to the temple, "Your foundation shall be laid." '

Is 48:20 Go forth from Babylon! Flee from the Chaldeans! With a voice of singing, Declare, proclaim this, Utter it to the end of the earth; Say, "The LORD has redeemed His servant Jacob!"

Jer 29:10 For thus says the LORD: After seventy years are completed at Babylon, I will visit you and perform My good word toward you, and cause you to return to this place.

Jer 50:4 "In those days and in that time," says the LORD, "The children of Israel shall come, They and the children of Judah together; With continual weeping they shall come, And seek the LORD their God.

Jer 50:8 "Move from the midst of Babylon, Go out of the land of the Chaldeans; And be like the rams before the flocks.

Jer 50:19 But I will bring back Israel to his home, And he shall feed on Carmel and Bashan; His soul shall be satisfied on Mount Ephraim and Gilead.

Destruction of (**Is 13:1–22; 14:4–22; 21:1–10; 47:1–15; Jer 25:12; 50:1–46; 51:1–64**).

Perpetual desolation of.

Is 13:19–22 And Babylon, the glory of kingdoms, The beauty of the Chaldeans' pride, Will be as when God overthrew Sodom and Gomorrah. **20** It will never be inhabited, Nor will it be settled from generation to generation; Nor will the Arabian pitch tents there, Nor will the shepherds make their sheepfolds there. **21** But wild beasts of the desert will lie there, And their houses will be full of owls; Ostriches will dwell there, And wild goats will caper there. **22** The hyenas will howl in their citadels, And jackals in their pleasant palaces. Her time *is* near to come, And her days will not be prolonged."

Is 14:22–23 "For I will rise up against them," says the LORD of hosts, "And cut off from Babylon the name and remnant, And offspring and posterity," says the LORD. **23** "I will also make it a possession for the porcupine, And marshes of muddy water; I will sweep it with the broom of destruction," says the LORD of hosts.

Jer 50:13 Because of the wrath of the LORD She shall not be inhabited, But she shall be wholly desolate. Everyone who goes by Babylon shall be horrified And hiss at all her plagues.

Jer 50:39 "Therefore the wild desert beasts shall dwell *there* with the jackals, And the ostriches shall dwell in it. It shall be inhabited no more forever, Nor shall it be dwelt in from generation to generation.

Jer 51:37 Babylon shall become a heap, A dwelling place

for jackals, An astonishment and a hissing, Without an inhabitant.

Preaching of the gospel in.

Ps 87:4 "I will make mention of Rahab and Babylon to those who know Me; Behold, O Philistia and Tyre, with Ethiopia: 'This *one* was born there.' "

BALAAM

Was asked to curse Israel.

Num 22:5–6 Then he sent messengers to Balaam the son of Beor at Pethor, which *is* near the River in the land of the sons of his people, to call him, saying: "Look, a people has come from Egypt. See, they cover the face of the earth, and are settling next to me! 6 Therefore please come at once, curse this people for me, for they *are* too mighty for me. Perhaps I shall be able to defeat them and drive them out of the land, for I know that he whom you bless *is* blessed, and he whom you curse is cursed."

Josh 24:9–10 Then Balak the son of Zippor, king of Moab, arose to make war against Israel, and sent and called Balaam the son of Beor to curse you. 10 But I would not listen to Balaam; therefore he continued to bless you. So I delivered you out of his hand.

Neh 13:2 because they had not met the children of Israel with bread and water, but hired Balaam against them to curse them. However, our God turned the curse into a blessing.

Ps 106:28–31 They joined themselves also to Baal of Peor, And ate sacrifices made to the dead. 29 Thus they provoked *Him* to anger with their deeds, And the plague broke out among them. 30 Then Phinehas stood up and intervened, And the plague was stopped. 31 And that was accounted to him for righteousness To all generations forevermore.

Mic 6:5 O My people, remember now What Balak king of Moab counseled, And what Balaam the son of Beor answered him, From Acacia Grove to Gilgal, That you may know the righteousness of the LORD."

Claimed to know God.

Num 22:18 Then Balaam answered and said to the servants of Balak, "Though Balak were to give me his house full of silver and gold, I could not go beyond the word of the LORD my God, to do less or more.

With his donkey and the angel.

Num 22:22–40 Then God's anger was aroused because he went, and the Angel of the LORD took His stand in the way as an adversary against him. And he was riding on his donkey, and his two servants *were* with him. 23 Now the donkey saw the Angel of the LORD standing in the way with His drawn sword in His hand, and the donkey turned aside out of the way and went into the field. So Balaam struck the donkey to turn her back onto the road. 24 Then the Angel of the LORD stood in a narrow path between the vineyards, *with* a wall on this side and a wall on that side. 25 And when the donkey saw the Angel of the LORD, she pushed herself against the wall and crushed Balaam's foot against the wall; so he struck her again. 26 Then the Angel of the LORD went further, and stood in a narrow place where there *was* no way to turn either to the right hand or to the left. 27 And when the donkey saw the Angel of the LORD, she lay down under Balaam; so Balaam's anger was aroused, and he struck the donkey with his staff. 28 Then the LORD opened the mouth of the donkey, and she said to Balaam, "What have I done to you, that you have struck me these three times?" 29 And Balaam said to the donkey, "Because you have abused me. I wish there were a sword in my hand, for now I would kill you!" 30 So the donkey said to Balaam, "*Am* I not your donkey on which you have ridden, ever since I *became* yours, to this day? Was I ever disposed to do this to you?" And he said, "No." 31 Then the LORD opened Balaam's eyes, and he saw the Angel of the LORD standing in the way with His drawn sword in His hand; and he bowed his head and fell flat on his face. 32 And the Angel of the LORD said to him, "Why have you struck your donkey these three times? Behold, I have come out to stand against you, because *your* way is perverse before Me. 33 The donkey saw Me and turned aside from Me these three times. If she had not turned aside from Me, surely I would also have killed you by now, and let her live." 34 And Balaam said to the Angel of the LORD, "I have sinned, for I did not know You stood in the way against me. Now therefore, if it displeases You, I will turn back." 35 Then the Angel of the LORD said to Balaam, "Go with the men, but only the word that I speak to you, that you shall speak." So Balaam went with the princes of Balak. 36 Now when Balak heard that Balaam was coming, he went out to meet him at the city of Moab, which *is* on the border at the Arnon, the boundary of the territory. 37 Then Balak said to Balaam, "Did I not earnestly send to you, calling for you? Why did you not come to me? Am I not able to honor you?" 38 And Balaam said to Balak, "Look, I have come to you! Now, have I any power at all to say anything? The word that God puts in my mouth, that I must speak." 39 So Balaam went with Balak, and they came to Kirjath Huzoth. 40 Then Balak offered oxen and sheep, and he sent *some* to Balaam and to the princes who *were* with him.

Called a false prophet.

Deut 23:3–6 "An Ammonite or Moabite shall not enter the assembly of the LORD; even to the tenth generation none of his *descendants* shall enter the assembly of the LORD forever, 4 because they did not meet you with bread and water on the road when you came out of Egypt, and because they hired against you Balaam the son of Beor from Pethor of Mesopotamia, to curse you. 5 Nevertheless the LORD your God would not listen to Balaam, but the LORD your God turned the curse into a blessing for you, because the LORD your God loves you. 6 You shall not seek their peace nor their prosperity all your days forever.

Josh 13:22 The children of Israel also killed with the sword Balaam the son of Beor, the soothsayer, among those who were killed by them.

Josh 24:9–10 Then Balak the son of Zippor, king of Moab, arose to make war against Israel, and sent and called Balaam the son of Beor to curse you. 10 But I would not listen to Balaam; therefore he continued to bless you. So I delivered you out of his hand.

Cf. Neh 13:1–3; Mic 6:5; 2 Pet 2:15–16; Jude 11; Rev 2:14

Was killed by Israel.

Josh 13:22 The children of Israel also killed with the

sword Balaam the son of Beor, the soothsayer, among those who were killed by them.

BAPTISM

As administered by John.

Matt 3:5–12 Then Jerusalem, all Judea, and all the region around the Jordan went out to him **6** and were baptized by him in the Jordan, confessing their sins. **7** But when he saw many of the Pharisees and Sadducees coming to his baptism, he said to them, "Brood of vipers! Who warned you to flee from the wrath to come? **8** Therefore bear fruits worthy of repentance, **9** and do not think to say to yourselves, 'We have Abraham as *our* father.' For I say to you that God is able to raise up children to Abraham from these stones. **10** And even now the ax is laid to the root of the trees. Therefore every tree which does not bear good fruit is cut down and thrown into the fire. **11** I indeed baptize you with water unto repentance, but He who is coming after me is mightier than I, whose sandals I am not worthy to carry. He will baptize you with the Holy Spirit and fire. **12** His winnowing fan *is* in His hand, and He will thoroughly clean out His threshing floor, and gather His wheat into the barn; but He will burn up the chaff with unquenchable fire."

John 3:23 Now John also was baptizing in Aenon near Salim, because there was much water there. And they came and were baptized.

Acts 13:24 after John had first preached, before His coming, the baptism of repentance to all the people of Israel.

Acts 19:4 Then Paul said, "John indeed baptized with a baptism of repentance, saying to the people that they should believe on Him who would come after him, that is, on Christ Jesus."

Sanctioned by Christ's submission to it.

Matt 3:13–15 Then Jesus came from Galilee to John at the Jordan to be baptized by him. **14** And John *tried to* prevent Him, saying, "I need to be baptized by You, and are You coming to me?" **15** But Jesus answered and said to him, "Permit *it to be so* now, for thus it is fitting for us to fulfill all righteousness." Then he allowed Him.

Luke 3:21 When all the people were baptized, it came to pass that Jesus also was baptized; and while He prayed, the heaven was opened.

Adopted by Christ.

John 3:22 After these things Jesus and His disciples came into the land of Judea, and there He remained with them and baptized.

John 4:1–2 Therefore, when the Lord knew that the Pharisees had heard that Jesus made and baptized more disciples than John **2** (though Jesus Himself did not baptize, but His disciples),

Appointed an ordinance of the Christian church.

Matt 28:19–20 Go therefore and make disciples of all the nations, baptizing them in the name of the Father and of the Son and of the Holy Spirit, **20** teaching them to observe all things that I have commanded you; and lo, I am with you always, *even* to the end of the age." Amen.

Mark 16:15–16 And He said to them, "Go into all the world and preach the gospel to every creature. **16** He who believes and is baptized will be saved; but he who does not believe will be condemned.

To be administered in the name of the Father, Son, and Holy Spirit.

Matt 28:19 Go therefore and make disciples of all the nations, baptizing them in the name of the Father and of the Son and of the Holy Spirit,

Water, the outward and visible sign in.

Acts 8:36 Now as they went down the road, they came to some water. And the eunuch said, "See, *here is* water. What hinders me from being baptized?"

Acts 10:47 "Can anyone forbid water, that these should not be baptized who have received the Holy Spirit just as we *have?*"

Remission of sins, signified by.

Acts 2:38 Then Peter said to them, "Repent, and let every one of you be baptized in the name of Jesus Christ for the remission of sins; and you shall receive the gift of the Holy Spirit.

Acts 22:16 And now why are you waiting? Arise and be baptized, and wash away your sins, calling on the name of the Lord.'

Rom 6:3–4 Or do you not know that as many of us as were baptized into Christ Jesus were baptized into His death? **4** Therefore we were buried with Him through baptism into death, that just as Christ was raised from the dead by the glory of the Father, even so we also should walk in newness of life.

Unity of the church effected by.

1 Cor 12:13 For by one Spirit we were all baptized into one body—whether Jews or Greeks, whether slaves or free—and have all been made to drink into one Spirit.

Gal 3:27–28 For as many of you as were baptized into Christ have put on Christ. **28** There is neither Jew nor Greek, there is neither slave nor free, there is neither male nor female; for you are all one in Christ Jesus.

Confession of sin necessary to.

Matt 3:6 and were baptized by him in the Jordan, confessing their sins.

Repentance necessary to.

Acts 2:38 Then Peter said to them, "Repent, and let every one of you be baptized in the name of Jesus Christ for the remission of sins; and you shall receive the gift of the Holy Spirit.

Faith necessary to.

Acts 8:37 Then Philip said, "If you believe with all your heart, you may." And he answered and said, "I believe that Jesus Christ is the Son of God."

Acts 18:8 Then Crispus, the ruler of the synagogue, believed on the Lord with all his household. And many of the Corinthians, hearing, believed and were baptized.

There is but one.

Eph 4:5 one Lord, one faith, one baptism;

Administered to

Individuals.

Acts 8:38 So he commanded the chariot to stand still. And both Philip and the eunuch went down into the water, and he baptized him.

Acts 9:18 Immediately there fell from his eyes *something* like scales, and he received his sight at once; and he arose and was baptized.

Households.

Acts 16:15 And when she and her household were baptized, she begged *us*, saying, "If you have judged me to be faithful to the Lord, come to my house and stay." So she persuaded us.

Acts 16:33 And he took them the same hour of the night and washed *their* stripes. And immediately he and all his family were baptized.

1 Cor 1:16 Yes, I also baptized the household of Stephanas. Besides, I do not know whether I baptized any other.

Only to professing believers.

Acts 2:38 Then Peter said to them, "Repent, and let every one of you be baptized in the name of Jesus Christ for the remission of sins; and you shall receive the gift of the Holy Spirit.

Matt 3:6 and were baptized by him in the Jordan, confessing their sins.

Mark 16:16 He who believes and is baptized will be saved; but he who does not believe will be condemned.

Acts 8:12 But when they believed Philip as he preached the things concerning the kingdom of God and the name of Jesus Christ, both men and women were baptized.

Acts 8:36–37 Now as they went down the road, they came to some water. And the eunuch said, "See, *here is* water. What hinders me from being baptized?" **37** Then Philip said, "If you believe with all your heart, you may." And he answered and said, "I believe that Jesus Christ is the Son of God."

Acts 10:47–48 "Can anyone forbid water, that these should not be baptized who have received the Holy Spirit just as we *have*?" **48** And he commanded them to be baptized in the name of the Lord. Then they asked him to stay a few days.

Administered by immersing the whole body of the person in water.

Matt 3:16 When He had been baptized, Jesus came up immediately from the water; and behold, the heavens were opened to Him, and He saw the Spirit of God descending like a dove and alighting upon Him.

Acts 8:38–39 So he commanded the chariot to stand still. And both Philip and the eunuch went down into the water, and he baptized him. **39** Now when they came up out of the water, the Spirit of the Lord caught Philip away, so that the eunuch saw him no more; and he went on his way rejoicing.

Emblematic of the influences of the Holy Spirit.

Matt 3:11 I indeed baptize you with water unto repentance, but He who is coming after me is mightier than I, whose sandals I am not worthy to carry. He will baptize you with the Holy Spirit and fire.

Titus 3:5 not by works of righteousness which we have done, but according to His mercy He saved us, through the washing of regeneration and renewing of the Holy Spirit,

Typified.

1 Cor 10:2 all were baptized into Moses in the cloud and in the sea,

1 Pet 3:20–21 who formerly were disobedient, when once the Divine longsuffering waited in the days of Noah, while *the* ark was being prepared, in which a few, that is, eight souls, were saved through water. **21** There is also an antitype which now saves us—baptism (not the removal of the filth of the flesh, but the answer of a good conscience toward God), through the resurrection of Jesus Christ,

BARNABAS

Parted ways with Paul.

Acts 15:38–40 But Paul insisted that they should not take with them the one who had departed from them in Pamphylia, and had not gone with them to the work. **39** Then the contention became so sharp that they parted from one another. And so Barnabas took Mark and sailed to Cyprus; **40** but Paul chose Silas and departed, being commended by the brethren to the grace of God.

Donated proceeds to apostles.

Acts 4:36–37 And Joses, who was also named Barnabas by the apostles (which is translated Son of Encouragement), a Levite of the country of Cyprus, **37** having land, sold *it*, and brought the money and laid *it* at the apostles' feet.

Introduced Paul to other apostles.

Acts 9:27 But Barnabas took him and brought *him* to the apostles. And he declared to them how he had seen the Lord on the road, and that He had spoken to him, and how he had preached boldly at Damascus in the name of Jesus.

Cousin to John Mark.

Col 4:10 Aristarchus my fellow prisoner greets you, with Mark the cousin of Barnabas (about whom you received instructions: if he comes to you, welcome him),

Cf. Acts 12:25

Accompanied by Mark to Cyprus.

Acts 15:39 Then the contention became so sharp that they parted from one another. And so Barnabas took Mark and sailed to Cyprus;

Cf. Acts 13:5

Ministered with Paul at Antioch.

Acts 11:19–30 Now those who were scattered after the persecution that arose over Stephen traveled as far as Phoenicia, Cyprus, and Antioch, preaching the word to no one but the Jews only. **20** But some of them were men from Cyprus and Cyrene, who, when they had come to Antioch, spoke to the Hellenists, preaching the Lord Jesus. **21** And the hand of the Lord was with them, and a great number believed and turned to the Lord. **22** Then news of these things came to the ears of the church in Jerusalem, and they sent out Barnabas to go as far as Antioch. **23** When he came and had seen the grace of God, he was glad, and encouraged them all that with purpose of heart they should continue with the Lord. **24** For he was a good man, full of the Holy Spirit and of faith. And a great many people were added to the Lord. **25** Then Barnabas departed for Tarsus to seek Saul. **26** And when he had found him, he brought him to Antioch. So it was that for a whole year they assembled with the church and taught a great many people. And the disciples were first called Christians in Antioch. **27** And in these days prophets came from Jerusalem to Antioch. **28** Then one of them, named Agabus, stood up and showed by the Spirit that there was going to be a great famine throughout all the world, which also happened in the days of Claudius Caesar. **29** Then the disciples, each according to his ability, determined to send relief to the brethren dwelling in Judea. **30** This they also did, and sent it to the elders by the hands of Barnabas and Saul.

Sent out from Antioch with Paul.

Acts 13:1–5 Now in the church that was at Antioch there were certain prophets and teachers: Barnabas, Simeon who was called Niger, Lucius of Cyrene, Manaen who had been brought up with Herod the tetrarch, and Saul. **2** As they ministered to the Lord and fasted, the Holy Spirit said, "Now separate to Me Barnabas and Saul for the work to which I have called them." **3** Then, having fasted and prayed, and laid hands on them, they sent *them* away. **4** So, being sent out by the Holy Spirit, they went down to Seleucia, and from there they sailed to Cyprus. **5** And when they arrived in Salamis, they preached the word of God in the synagogues of the Jews. They also had John as *their* assistant.

With Paul at Lystra.

Acts 14:8–18 And in Lystra a certain man without strength in his feet was sitting, a cripple from his mother's womb, who had never walked. **9** *This* man heard Paul speaking. Paul, observing him intently and seeing that he had faith to be healed, **10** said with a loud voice, "Stand up straight on your feet!" And he leaped and walked. **11** Now when the people saw what Paul had done, they raised their voices, saying in the Lycaonian *language,* "The gods have come down to us in the likeness of men!" **12** And Barnabas they called Zeus, and Paul, Hermes, because he was the chief speaker. **13** Then the priest of Zeus, whose temple was in front of their city, brought oxen and garlands to the gates, intending to sacrifice with the multitudes. **14** But when the apostles Barnabas and Paul heard this, they tore their clothes and ran in among the multitude, crying out **15** and saying, "Men, why are you doing these things? We also are men with the same nature as you, and preach to you that you should turn from these useless things to the living God, who made the heaven, the earth, the sea, and all things that are in them, **16** who in bygone generations allowed all nations to walk in their own ways. **17** Nevertheless He did not leave Himself without witness, in that He did good, gave us rain from heaven and fruitful seasons, filling our hearts with food and gladness." **18** And with these sayings they could scarcely restrain the multitudes from sacrificing to them.

With Paul at Corinth.

1 Cor 9:6 Or *is it* only Barnabas and I *who* have no right to refrain from working?

At the Jerusalem Council.

Acts 15:12 Then all the multitude kept silent and lis-tened to Barnabas and Paul declaring how many miracles and wonders God had worked through them among the Gentiles.

Cf. Gal 2:1

Commended, with Paul, in ministry to Gentiles.

Gal 2:9 and when James, Cephas, and John, who seemed to be pillars, perceived the grace that had been given to me, they gave me and Barnabas the right hand of fellowship, that we *should go* to the Gentiles and they to the circumcised.

Influenced by Peter's hypocrisy at Antioch.

Gal 2:13 And the rest of the Jews also played the hypo-crite with him, so that even Barnabas was carried away with their hypocrisy.

BATHSHEBA

David's adultery with.

2 Sam 11:1–5 It happened in the spring of the year, at the time when kings go out *to battle,* that David sent Joab and his servants with him, and all Israel; and they de-stroyed the people of Ammon and besieged Rabbah. But David remained at Jerusalem. **2** Then it happened one evening that David arose from his bed and walked on the roof of the king's house. And from the roof he saw a woman bathing, and the woman *was* very beautiful to behold. **3** So David sent and inquired about the woman. And *someone* said, "Is this not Bath-sheba, the daughter of Eliam, the wife of Uriah the Hittite?" **4** Then David sent messengers, and took her; and she came to him, and he lay with her, for she was cleansed from her impurity; and she returned to her house. **5** And the woman conceived; so she sent and told David, and said, "I *am* with child."

Mother of Solomon.

1 Kin 1:11 So Nathan spoke to Bathsheba the mother of Solomon, saying, "Have you not heard that Adonijah the son of Haggith has become king, and David our lord does not know *it?*

Cf. Song 3:11

Hears Adonijah's request for a wife.

1 Kin 2:13–25 Now Adonijah the son of Haggith came to Bathsheba the mother of Solomon. So she said, "Do you come peaceably?" And he said, "Peaceably." **14** Moreover he said, "I have something *to say* to you." And she said, "Say it." **15** Then he said, "You know that the kingdom was mine, and all Israel had set their expectations on me, that I should reign. How-ever, the kingdom has been turned over, and has be-come my brother's; for it was his from the LORD. **16** Now I ask one petition of you; do not deny me." And she said to him, "Say it." **17** Then he said, "Please speak to King Solomon, for he will not refuse you, that he may give me Abishag the Shunammite as wife." **18** So Bathsheba said, "Very well, I will speak for you to the king." **19** Bathsheba therefore went to King Solomon, to speak to him for Adonijah. And the king rose up to meet her and bowed down to her, and sat down on his throne and had a throne set for the king's mother; so she sat at his right hand. **20** Then she said, "I desire one small petition of you; do not re-fuse me." And the king said to her, "Ask it, my moth-er, for I will not refuse you." **21** So she said, "Let Abi-shag the Shunammite be given to Adonijah your brother as wife." **22** And King Solomon answered and said to his mother, "Now why do you ask Abishag the Shunammite for Adonijah? Ask for him the kingdom also—for he *is* my older brother—for him, and for Abiathar the priest, and for Joab the son of Zeruiah." **23** Then King Solomon swore by the LORD, saying, "May God do so to me, and more also, if Adonijah has not spoken this word against his own life! **24** Now therefore, *as* the LORD lives, who has confirmed me and set me on the throne of David my father, and who has established a house for me, as He promised, Adonijah shall be put to death today!" **25** So King Solomon sent by the hand of Benaiah the son of Jehoiada; and he struck him down, and he died.

In Matthew's genealogy of Christ.

Matt 1:6 and Jesse begot David the king. David the king begot Solomon by her *who had been the wife* of Uriah.

BEAR, THE

Described as

Voracious.

Dan 7:5 "And suddenly another beast, a second, like a bear. It was raised up on one side, and *had* three ribs in its mouth between its teeth. And they said thus to it: 'Arise, devour much flesh!'

Cunning.

Lam 3:10 He *has been* to me a bear lying in wait, *Like* a lion in ambush.

Attacking people.

2 Kin 2:24 So he turned around and looked at them, and pronounced a curse on them in the name of the LORD. And two female bears came out of the woods and mauled forty-two of the youths.

Amos 5:19 It *will be* as though a man fled from a lion, And a bear met him! Or *as though* he went into the house, Leaned his hand on the wall, And a serpent bit him!

Particularly fierce when deprived of its young.

2 Sam 17:8 For," said Hushai, "you know your father and his men, that they *are* mighty men, and they *are* enraged in their minds, like a bear robbed of her cubs in the field; and your father *is* a man of war, and will not camp with the people.

Prov 17:12 Let a man meet a bear robbed of her cubs, Rather than a fool in his folly.

Killed by David.

1 Sam 17:36–37 Your servant has killed both lion and bear; and this uncircumcised Philistine will be like one of them, seeing he has defied the armies of the living God." **37** Moreover David said, "The LORD, who delivered me from the paw of the lion and from the paw of the bear, He will deliver me from the hand of this Philistine." And Saul said to David, "Go, and the LORD be with you!"

Illustrative of

God in his judgments.

Lam 3:10 He *has been* to me a bear lying in wait, *Like* a lion in ambush.

Hos 13:8 I will meet them like a bear deprived *of her cubs;* I will tear open their rib cage, And there I will devour them like a lion. The wild beast shall tear them.

Wicked rulers.

Prov 28:15 *Like* a roaring lion and a charging bear *Is* a wicked ruler over poor people.

The kingdom of Medo-Persia.

Dan 7:5 "And suddenly another beast, a second, like a bear. It was raised up on one side, and *had* three ribs in its mouth between its teeth. And they said thus to it: 'Arise, devour much flesh!'

The kingdom of Antichrist.

Rev 13:2 Now the beast which I saw was like a leopard, his feet were like *the feet of* a bear, and his mouth like the mouth of a lion. The dragon gave him his power, his throne, and great authority.

BEARD, THE

The Jews never appeared without.

2 Sam 10:5 When they told David, he sent to meet them, because the men were greatly ashamed. And the king said, "Wait at Jericho until your beards have grown, and *then* return."

Worn even by the priests.

Ps 133:2 *It is* like the precious oil upon the head, Running down on the beard, The beard of Aaron, Running down on the edge of his garments.

Laying hold of, a token of respect.

2 Sam 20:9 Then Joab said to Amasa, "*Are* you in health, my brother?" And Joab took Amasa by the beard with his right hand to kiss him.

Shaving of, a great offense.

2 Sam 10:4 Therefore Hanun took David's servants, shaved off half of their beards, cut off their garments in the middle, at their buttocks, and sent them away.

2 Sam 10:6–7 When the people of Ammon saw that they had made themselves repulsive to David, the people of Ammon sent and hired the Syrians of Beth Rehob and the Syrians of Zoba, twenty thousand foot soldiers; and from the king of Maacah one thousand men, and from Ish-Tob twelve thousand men. **7** Now when David heard *of it,* he sent Joab and all the army of the mighty men.

Plucking of, a sign of scorn.

Is 50:6 I gave My back to those who struck *Me,* And My cheeks to those who plucked out the beard; I did not hide My face from shame and spitting.

Dribbling on, a sign of derangement.

1 Sam 21:13 So he changed his behavior before them, pretended madness in their hands, scratched on the doors of the gate, and let his saliva fall down on his beard.

In affliction,

Was neglected and untrimmed.

2 Sam 19:24 Now Mephibosheth the son of Saul came down to meet the king. And he had not cared for his feet, nor trimmed his mustache, nor washed his clothes, from the day the king departed until the day he returned in peace.

Was clipped or shaved.

Jer 41:5 that certain men came from Shechem, from Shiloh, and from Samaria, eighty men with their beards shaved and their clothes torn, having cut themselves, with offerings and incense in their hand, to bring *them* to the house of the LORD.

Jer 48:37 "For every head *shall be* bald, and every beard clipped; On all the hands *shall be* cuts, and on the loins sackcloth—

Sometimes plucked out.

Ezra 9:3 So when I heard this thing, I tore my garment and my robe, and plucked out some of the hair of my head and beard, and sat down astonished.

Corners of, not to be marred for the dead.

Lev 19:27 You shall not shave around the sides of your head, nor shall you disfigure the edges of your beard.

Lev 21:5 'They shall not make any bald *place* on their heads, nor shall they shave the edges of their beards nor make any cuttings in their flesh.

Subject to leprosy.

Lev 13:29–30 "If a man or woman has a sore on the head or the beard, **30** then the priest shall examine the sore; and indeed if it appears deeper than the skin, *and there is* in it thin yellow hair, then the priest shall pronounce him unclean. It *is* a scaly leprosy of the head or beard.

Of the healed leper to be shaved.

Lev 14:9 But on the seventh day he shall shave all the hair off his head and his beard and his eyebrows—all his hair he shall shave off. He shall wash his clothes and wash his body in water, and he shall be clean.

Shaving, illustrative of severe judgments.

Is 7:20 In the same day the Lord will shave with a hired razor, With those from beyond the River, with the king of Assyria, The head and the hair of the legs, And will also remove the beard.

Is 15:2 He has gone up to the temple and Dibon, To the high places to weep. Moab will wail over Nebo and over Medeba; On all their heads *will be* baldness, *And* every beard cut off.

Ezek 5:1 "And you, son of man, take a sharp sword, take it as a barber's razor, and pass *it* over your head and your beard; then take scales to weigh and divide the hair.

BEASTS

Created by God.

Gen 1:24–25 Then God said, "Let the earth bring forth the living creature according to its kind: cattle and creeping thing and beast of the earth, *each* according to its kind"; and it was so. **25** And God made the beast of the earth according to its kind, cattle according to its kind, and everything that creeps on the earth according to its kind. And God saw that *it was* good.

Gen 2:19 Out of the ground the LORD God formed every beast of the field and every bird of the air, and brought *them* to Adam to see what he would call them. And whatever Adam called each living creature, that *was* its name.

Creation of, exhibits God's power.

Jer 27:5 'I have made the earth, the man and the beast that *are* on the ground, by My great power and by My outstretched arm, and have given it to whom it seemed proper to Me.

Made for the praise and glory of God.

Ps 148:10 Beasts and all cattle; Creeping things and flying fowl;

Differ in flesh from birds and fishes.

1 Cor 15:39 All flesh *is* not the same flesh, but *there is* one *kind of* flesh of men, another flesh of animals, another of fish, *and* another of birds.

Herbs of the field given to, for food.

Gen 1:30 Also, to every beast of the earth, to every bird of the air, and to everything that creeps on the earth, in which *there is* life, *I have given* every green herb for food"; and it was so.

Power over, given to man.

Gen 1:26 Then God said, "Let Us make man in Our image, according to Our likeness; let them have dominion over the fish of the sea, over the birds of the air, and over the cattle, over all the earth and over every creeping thing that creeps on the earth."

Gen 1:28 Then God blessed them, and God said to them, "Be fruitful and multiply; fill the earth and subdue it; have dominion over the fish of the sea, over the birds of the air, and over every living thing that moves on the earth."

Ps 8:7 All sheep and oxen— Even the beasts of the field,

Instinctively fear man.

Gen 9:2 And the fear of you and the dread of you shall be on every beast of the earth, on every bird of the air, on all that move *on* the earth, and on all the fish of the sea. They are given into your hand.

Received their names from Adam.

Gen 2:19–20 Out of the ground the LORD God formed every beast of the field and every bird of the air, and brought *them* to Adam to see what he would call them. And whatever Adam called each living creature, that *was* its name. **20** So Adam gave names to all cattle, to the birds of the air, and to every beast of the field. But for Adam there was not found a helper comparable to him.

Given to man for food after the Flood.

Gen 9:3 Every moving thing that lives shall be food for you. I have given you all things, even as the green herbs.

Not to be eaten with blood.

Gen 9:4 But you shall not eat flesh with its life, *that is,* its blood.

Deut 12:16 Only you shall not eat the blood; you shall pour it on the earth like water.

Deut 12:23 Only be sure that you do not eat the blood, for the blood *is* the life; you may not eat the life with the meat.

That died naturally or were torn, not to be eaten.

Ex 22:31 "And you shall be holy men to Me: you shall not eat meat torn *by beasts* in the field; you shall throw it to the dogs.

Lev 17:15 "And every person who eats what died *naturally* or what was torn *by beasts, whether he is* a native of your own country or a stranger, he shall both wash his clothes and bathe in water, and be unclean until evening. Then he shall be clean.

Lev 22:8 Whatever dies *naturally* or is torn *by beasts* he shall not eat, to defile himself with it: I *am* the LORD.

Supply clothing to man.

Gen 3:21 Also for Adam and his wife the LORD God made tunics of skin, and clothed them.

Job 31:20 If his heart has not blessed me, And *if he was not* warmed with the fleece of my sheep;

The property of God.

Ps 50:10 For every beast of the forest *is* Mine, And the cattle on a thousand hills.

Subjects of God's care.

Ps 36:6 Your righteousness *is* like the great mountains; Your judgments *are* a great deep; O LORD, You preserve man and beast.

Ps 104:10–11 He sends the springs into the valleys; They flow among the hills. **11** They give drink to every beast of the field; The wild donkeys quench their thirst.

Described as

Devoid of speech.

2 Pet 2:16 but he was rebuked for his iniquity: a dumb donkey speaking with a man's voice restrained the madness of the prophet.

Devoid of understanding.

Ps 32:9 Do not be like the horse *or* like the mule, *Which* have no understanding, Which must be harnessed with bit and bridle, Else they will not come near you.

Ps 73:22 I *was* so foolish and ignorant; I was *like* a beast before You.

Devoid of immortality.

Ps 49:12–15 Nevertheless man, *though* in honor, does not remain; He is like the beasts *that* perish. **13** This is the way of those who *are* foolish, And of their posterity who approve their sayings. Selah **14** Like sheep they are laid in the grave; Death shall feed on them; The upright shall have dominion over them in the morning; And their beauty shall be consumed in the grave, far from their dwelling. **15** But God will redeem my soul from the power of the grave, For He shall receive me. Selah

Possessed of instinct.

Is 1:3 The ox knows its owner And the donkey its master's crib; *But* Israel does not know, My people do not consider."

Being four-footed.

Acts 10:12 In it were all kinds of four-footed animals of the earth, wild beasts, creeping things, and birds of the air.

By nature wild, etc.

Ps 50:11 I know all the birds of the mountains, And the wild beasts of the field *are* Mine.

Mark 1:13 And He was there in the wilderness forty days, tempted by Satan, and was with the wild beasts; and the angels ministered to Him.

Capable of being tamed.

James 3:7 For every kind of beast and bird, of reptile and creature of the sea, is tamed and has been tamed by mankind.

‑‑ ‑f, noisome and destructive.

ill give peace in the land, and you shall lie d none will make *you* afraid; I will rid the land of evil beasts, and the sword will not go through your land.

Ezek 5:17 So I will send against you famine and wild beasts, and they will bereave you. Pestilence and blood shall pass through you, and I will bring the sword against you. I, the LORD, have spoken.' "

Many kinds of, domestic.

Gen 36:6 Then Esau took his wives, his sons, his daughters, and all the persons of his household, his cattle and all his animals, and all his goods which he had gained in the land of Canaan, and went to a country away from the presence of his brother Jacob.

Gen 45:17 And Pharaoh said to Joseph, "Say to your brothers, 'Do this: Load your animals and depart; go to the land of Canaan.

Lessons of wisdom to be learned from.

Job 12:7 "But now ask the beasts, and they will teach you; And the birds of the air, and they will tell you;

Found in

Deserts.

Is 13:21 But wild beasts of the desert will lie there, And their houses will be full of owls; Ostriches will dwell there, And wild goats will caper there.

Fields.

Deut 7:22 And the LORD your God will drive out those nations before you little by little; you will be unable to destroy them at once, lest the beasts of the field become *too* numerous for you.

Joel 2:22 Do not be afraid, you beasts of the field; For the open pastures are springing up, And the tree bears its fruit; The fig tree and the vine yield their strength.

Mountains.

Song 4:8 Come with me from Lebanon, *my* spouse, With me from Lebanon. Look from the top of Amana, From the top of Senir and Hermon, From the lions' dens, From the mountains of the leopards.

Forests.

Is 56:9 All you beasts of the field, come to devour, All you beasts in the forest.

Mic 5:8 And the remnant of Jacob Shall be among the Gentiles, In the midst of many peoples, Like a lion among the beasts of the forest, Like a young lion among flocks of sheep, Who, if he passes through, Both treads down and tears in pieces, And none can deliver.

Habitations of,

Dens and caves.

Job 37:8 The beasts go into dens, And remain in their lairs.

Job 38:40 When they crouch in *their* dens, Or lurk in their lairs to lie in wait?

Under spreading trees.

Dan 4:12 Its leaves *were* lovely, Its fruit abundant, And in it *was* food for all. The beasts of the field found shade under it, The birds of the heavens dwelt in its branches, And all flesh was fed from it.

Deserted cities.

Is 13:21–22 But wild beasts of the desert will lie there, And their houses will be full of owls; Ostriches will dwell there, And wild goats will caper there. **22** The hyenas will howl in their citadels, And jackals in their pleasant palaces. Her time *is* near to come, And her days will not be prolonged."

Zeph 2:15 This is the rejoicing city That dwelt securely, That said in her heart, "I *am* it, and *there is* none besides me." How has she become a desolation, A place for beasts to lie down! Everyone who passes by her Shall hiss and shake his fist.

Frequently suffered on account of the sins of men.

Joel 1:18 How the animals groan! The herds of cattle are restless, Because they have no pasture; Even the flocks of sheep suffer punishment.

Joel 1:20 The beasts of the field also cry out to You, For the water brooks are dried up, And fire has devoured the open pastures.

Hag 1:11 For I called for a drought on the land and the mountains, on the grain and the new wine and the oil, on whatever the ground brings forth, on men and livestock, and on all the labor of *your* hands."

Often destroyed for the sins of men.

Gen 6:7 So the LORD said, "I will destroy man whom I have created from the face of the earth, both man and beast, creeping thing and birds of the air, for I am sorry that I have made them."

Gen 7:23 So He destroyed all living things which were on the face of the ground: both man and cattle, creeping thing and bird of the air. They were destroyed from the earth. Only Noah and those who *were* with him in the ark remained *alive*.

Ex 11:5 and all the firstborn in the land of Egypt shall die, from the firstborn of Pharaoh who sits on his throne, even to the firstborn of the female servant who *is* behind the handmill, and all the firstborn of the animals.

Hos 4:3 Therefore the land will mourn; And everyone who dwells there will waste away With the beasts of the field And the birds of the air; Even the fish of the sea will be taken away.

Early distinguished into clean and unclean.

Gen 7:2 You shall take with you seven each of every clean animal, a male and his female; two each of animals that *are* unclean, a male and his female;

Clean,
Named.

Ex 21:28 "If an ox gores a man or a woman to death, then the ox shall surely be stoned, and its flesh shall not be eaten; but the owner of the ox *shall be* acquitted.

Deut 14:4–6 "These *are* the animals which you may eat: the ox, the sheep, the goat, **5** the deer, the gazelle, the roe deer, the wild goat, the mountain goat, the antelope, and the mountain sheep. **6** And you may eat every animal with cloven hooves, having the hoof split into two parts, *and that* chews the cud, among the animals.

2 Sam 2:18 Now the three sons of Zeruiah were there: Joab and Abishai and Asahel. And Asahel *was as* fleet of foot as a wild gazelle.

Job 39:1 "Do you know the time when the wild mountain goats bear young? *Or* can you mark when the deer gives birth?

How distinguished.

Lev 11:3 Among the animals, whatever divides the hoof, having cloven hooves *and* chewing the cud—that you may eat.

Deut 14:6 And you may eat every animal with cloven hooves, having the hoof split into two parts, *and that* chews the cud, among the animals.

Used for food.

Lev 11:2 "Speak to the children of Israel, saying, 'These *are* the animals which you may eat among all the animals that *are* on the earth:

Deut 12:15 "However, you may slaughter and eat meat within all your gates, whatever your heart desires, according to the blessing of the LORD your God which He has given you; the unclean and the clean may eat of it, of the gazelle and the deer alike.

Used for sacrifice.

Gen 8:20 Then Noah built an altar to the LORD, and took of every clean animal and of every clean bird, and offered burnt offerings on the altar.

Firstborn, not redeemed.

Num 18:17 But the firstborn of a cow, the firstborn of a sheep, or the firstborn of a goat you shall not redeem; they *are* holy. You shall sprinkle their blood on the altar, and burn their fat *as* an offering made by fire for a sweet aroma to the LORD.

Unclean,
Named.

Ex 22:31 "And you shall be holy men to Me: you shall not eat meat torn *by beasts* in the field; you shall throw it to the dogs.

Lev 11:4–7 Nevertheless these you shall not eat among those that chew the cud or those that have cloven hooves: the camel, because it chews the cud but does not have cloven hooves, is unclean to you; **5** the rock hyrax, because it chews the cud but does not have cloven hooves, *is* unclean to you; **6** the hare, because it chews the cud but does not have cloven hooves, *is* unclean to you; **7** and the swine, though it divides the hoof, having cloven hooves, yet does not chew the cud, *is* unclean to you.

Lev 11:29–30 'These also *shall be* unclean to you among the creeping things that creep on the earth: the mole, the mouse, and the large lizard after its kind; **30** the gecko, the monitor lizard, the sand reptile, the sand lizard, and the chameleon.

Deut 14:7 Nevertheless, of those that chew the cud or have cloven hooves, you shall not eat, *such as* these: the camel, the hare, and the rock hyrax; for they chew the cud but do not have cloven hooves; they *are* unclean for you.

Is 66:17 "Those who sanctify themselves and purify themselves, *To* go to the gardens After an *idol* in the midst, Eating swine's flesh and the abomination and the mouse, Shall be consumed together," says the LORD.

How distinguished.

Lev 11:26 *The carcass* of any animal which divides the foot, but is not cloven-hoofed or does not chew the cud, *is* unclean to you. Everyone who touches it shall be unclean.

Not eaten.

Lev 11:4–8 Nevertheless these you shall not eat among those that chew the cud or those that have cloven hooves: the camel, because it chews the cud but does not have cloven hooves, is unclean to you; **5** the rock hyrax, because it chews the cud but does not have cloven hooves, *is* unclean to you; **6** the hare, because it chews the cud but does not have cloven hooves, *is* unclean to you; **7** and the swine, though it divides the hoof, having cloven hooves, yet does not chew the cud, *is* unclean to you. **8** Their flesh you shall not eat, and their carcasses you shall not touch. They *are* unclean to you.

Deut 14:7–8 Nevertheless, of those that chew the cud or have cloven hooves, you shall not eat, *such as* these: the camel, the hare, and the rock hyrax; for they chew the cud but do not have cloven hooves; they *are* unclean for you. **8** Also the swine is unclean for you, because it has cloven hooves, yet *does* not *chew* the cud; you shall not eat their flesh or touch their dead carcasses.

Not offered in sacrifice.

Lev 27:11 If *it is* an unclean animal which they do not offer as a sacrifice to the LORD, then he shall present the animal before the priest;

Firstborn, redeemed.

Num 18:15 "Everything that first opens the womb of all flesh, which they bring to the LORD, whether man or beast, shall be yours; nevertheless the firstborn of man you shall surely redeem, and the firstborn of unclean animals you shall redeem.

Caused uncleanness when dead.

Lev 5:2 'Or if a person touches any unclean thing, whether *it is* the carcass of an unclean beast, or the carcass of unclean livestock, or the carcass of unclean creeping things, and he is unaware of it, he also shall be unclean and guilty.

Domestic,

To enjoy the Sabbath.

Ex 20:10 but the seventh day *is* the Sabbath of the LORD your God. *In it* you shall do no work: you, nor your son, nor your daughter, nor your male servant, nor your female servant, nor your cattle, nor your stranger who *is* within your gates.

Deut 5:14 but the seventh day *is* the Sabbath of the LORD your God. *In it* you shall do no work: you, nor your son, nor your daughter, nor your male servant, nor your female servant, nor your ox, nor your donkey, nor any of your cattle, nor your stranger who *is* within your gates, that your male servant and your female servant may rest as well as you.

To be taken care of.

Lev 25:7 for your livestock and the beasts that *are* in your land—all its produce shall be for food.

Deut 25:4 "You shall not muzzle an ox while it treads out *the* grain.

Not to be cruelly used.

Prov 12:10 A righteous *man* regards the life of his animal, But the tender mercies of the wicked *are* cruel.

No likeness of, to be worshiped.

Deut 4:17 the likeness of any animal that *is* on the earth or the likeness of any winged bird that flies in the air,

Representations of, worshiped by the heathen.

Rom 1:23 and changed the glory of the incorruptible God into an image made like corruptible man—and birds and four-footed animals and creeping things.

Spoken of by Solomon.

1 Kin 4:33 Also he spoke of trees, from the cedar tree of Lebanon even to the hyssop that springs out of the wall; he spoke also of animals, of birds, of creeping things, and of fish.

Often used as instruments of punishment.

Lev 26:22 I will also send wild beasts among you, which shall rob you of your children, destroy your livestock, and make you few in number; and your highways shall be desolate.

Deut 32:24 *They shall be* wasted with hunger, Devoured by pestilence and bitter destruction; I will also send against them the teeth of beasts, With the poison of serpents of the dust.

Jer 15:3 "And I will appoint over them four forms *of destruction*," says the LORD: "the sword to slay, the dogs to drag, the birds of the heavens and the beasts of the earth to devour and destroy.

Ezek 5:17 So I will send against you famine and wild beasts, and they will bereave you. Pestilence and blood shall pass through you, and I will bring the sword against you. I, the LORD, have spoken.' "

Man by nature no better than.

Eccl 3:18–19 I said in my heart, "Concerning the condition of the sons of men, God tests them, that they may see that they themselves are *like* animals." **19** For what happens to the sons of men also happens to animals; one thing befalls them: as one dies, so dies the other. Surely, they all have one breath; man has no advantage over animals, for all *is* vanity.

Illustrative of

The wicked.

Ps 49:20 A man *who is* in honor, yet does not understand, Is like the beasts *that* perish.

Titus 1:12 One of them, a prophet of their own, said, "Cretans *are* always liars, evil beasts, lazy gluttons."

False teachers.

2 Pet 2:12 But these, like natural brute beasts made to be caught and destroyed, speak evil of the things they do not understand, and will utterly perish in their own corruption,

Jude 1:10 But these speak evil of whatever they do not know; and whatever they know naturally, like brute beasts, in these things they corrupt themselves.

Persecutors.

1 Cor 15:32 If, in the manner of men, I have fought with beasts at Ephesus, what advantage *is it* to me? If *the* dead do not rise, *"Let us eat and drink, for tomorrow we die!"*

2 Tim 4:17 But the Lord stood with me and strengthened me, so that the message might be preached fully through me, and *that* all the Gentiles might hear. Also I was delivered out of the mouth of the lion.

Kingdoms.

Dan 7:11 "I watched then because of the sound of the pompous words which the horn was speaking; I watched till the beast was slain, and its body destroyed and given to the burning flame.

Dan 7:17 'Those great beasts, which are four, *are* four kings *which* arise out of the earth.

Dan 8:4 I saw the ram pushing westward, northward, and southward, so that no animal could withstand him; nor *was there any* that could deliver from his hand, but he did according to his will and became great.

People of different nations.

Dan 4:12 Its leaves *were* lovely, Its fruit abundant, And in it *was* food for all. The beasts of the field found shade under it, The birds of the heavens dwelt in its branches, And all flesh was fed from it.

Dan 4:21–22 whose leaves *were* lovely and its fruit abundant, in which *was* food for all, under which the beasts of the field dwelt, and in whose branches the birds of the heaven had their home— **22** it *is* you, O king, who have grown and become strong; for your greatness has grown and reaches to the heavens, and your dominion to the end of the earth.

Antichrist.

Rev 13:2 Now the beast which I saw was like a leopard, his feet were like *the feet of* a bear, and his mouth like the mouth of a lion. The dragon gave him his power, his throne, and great authority.

Rev 20:4 And I saw thrones, and they sat on them, and judgment was committed to them. Then *I saw* the souls of those who had been beheaded for their witness to Jesus and for the word of God, who had not worshiped the beast or his image, and had not received *his* mark on their foreheads or on their hands. And they lived and reigned with Christ for a thousand years.

BEDS

Antiquity of.

Gen 47:31 Then he said, "Swear to me." And he swore to him. So Israel bowed himself on the head of the bed.

Ex 8:3 So the river shall bring forth frogs abundantly, which shall go up and come into your house, into your bedroom, on your bed, into the houses of your servants, on your people, into your ovens, and into your kneading bowls.

Couches or divans used as.

Job 7:13 When I say, 'My bed will comfort me, My couch will ease my complaint,'

Ps 6:6 I am weary with my groaning; All night I make my bed swim; I drench my couch with my tears.

A small pallet or mattress used as.

1 Sam 19:15 Then Saul sent the messengers *back* to see David, saying, "Bring him up to me in the bed, that I may kill him."

Considered necessary.

2 Kin 4:10 Please, let us make a small upper room on the wall; and let us put a bed for him there, and a table and a chair and a lampstand; so it will be, whenever he comes to us, he can turn in there."

Made of

Iron.

Deut 3:11 "For only Og king of Bashan remained of the

remnant of the giants. Indeed his bedstead *was* an iron bedstead. (*Is* it not in Rabbah of the people of Ammon?) Nine cubits *is* its length and four cubits its width, according to the standard cubit.

Ivory.

Amos 6:4 Who lie on beds of ivory, Stretch out on your couches, Eat lambs from the flock And calves from the midst of the stall;

Gold and silver.

Esth 1:6 *There were* white and blue linen *curtains* fastened with cords of fine linen and purple on silver rods and marble pillars; *and the* couches *were* of gold and silver on a *mosaic* pavement of alabaster, turquoise, and white and black marble.

Covered with tapestry and linen.

Prov 7:16 I have spread my bed with tapestry, Colored coverings of Egyptian linen.

Often perfumed.

Prov 7:17 I have perfumed my bed With myrrh, aloes, and cinnamon.

Ezek 23:41 You sat on a stately couch, with a table prepared before it, on which you had set My incense and My oil.

Of the poor, covered with upper garment.

Ex 22:26–27 If you ever take your neighbor's garment as a pledge, you shall return it to him before the sun goes down. **27** For that *is* his only covering, it *is* his garment for his skin. What will he sleep in? And it will be that when he cries to Me, I will hear, for I *am* gracious.

Deut 24:12–13 And if the man *is* poor, you shall not keep his pledge overnight. **13** You shall in any case return the pledge to him again when the sun goes down, that he may sleep in his own garment and bless you; and it shall be righteousness to you before the LORD your God.

Used for

Sleeping on.

Job 33:15 In a dream, in a vision of the night, When deep sleep falls upon men, While slumbering on their beds,

Luke 11:7 and he will answer from within and say, 'Do not trouble me; the door is now shut, and my children are with me in bed; I cannot rise and give to you'?

Reclining on by day.

2 Sam 4:5 Then the sons of Rimmon the Beerothite, Rechab and Baanah, set out and came at about the heat of the day to the house of Ishbosheth, who was lying on his bed at noon.

2 Sam 11:2 Then it happened one evening that David arose from his bed and walked on the roof of the king's house. And from the roof he saw a woman bathing, and the woman *was* very beautiful to behold.

Reclining on at meals.

1 Sam 28:23–25 But he refused and said, "I will not eat." So his servants, together with the woman, urged him; and he heeded their voice. Then he arose from the ground and sat on the bed. **24** Now the woman had a fatted calf in the house, and she hastened to kill it. And she took flour and kneaded *it*, and baked unleavened bread from it. **25** So she brought *it* before Saul and his servants, and they ate. Then they rose and went away that night.

Amos 6:4–6 Who lie on beds of ivory, Stretch out on your couches, Eat lambs from the flock And calves from the midst of the stall; **5** Who sing idly to the sound of stringed instruments, *And* invent for yourselves musical instruments like David; **6** Who drink wine from bowls, And anoint yourselves with the best ointments, But are not grieved for the affliction of Joseph.

Luke 7:36–38 Then one of the Pharisees asked Him to eat with him. And He went to the Pharisee's house, and sat down to eat. **37** And behold, a woman in the city who was a sinner, when she knew that *Jesus* sat at the table in the Pharisee's house, brought an alabaster flask of fragrant oil, **38** and stood at His feet behind *Him* weeping; and she began to wash His feet with her tears, and wiped *them* with the hair of her head; and she kissed His feet and anointed *them* with the fragrant oil.

John 13:23 Now there was leaning on Jesus' bosom one of His disciples, whom Jesus loved.

Not used in affliction.

2 Sam 12:16 David therefore pleaded with God for the child, and David fasted and went in and lay all night on the ground.

2 Sam 13:31 So the king arose and tore his garments and lay on the ground, and all his servants stood by with their clothes torn.

Persons sometimes took to, in grief.

1 Kin 21:4 So Ahab went into his house sullen and displeased because of the word which Naboth the Jezreelite had spoken to him; for he had said, "I will not give you the inheritance of my fathers." And he lay down on his bed, and turned away his face, and would eat no food.

Hos 7:14 They did not cry out to Me with their heart When they wailed upon their beds. "They assemble together for grain and new wine, They rebel against Me;

Saints meditate and praise God while on.

Ps 4:4 Be angry, and do not sin. Meditate within your heart on your bed, and be still. Selah

Ps 149:5 Let the saints be joyful in glory; Let them sing aloud on their beds.

The wicked devise mischief while on.

Ps 36:4 He devises wickedness on his bed; He sets himself in a way *that is* not good; He does not abhor evil.

Mic 2:1 Woe to those who devise iniquity, And work out evil on their beds! At morning light they practice it, Because it is in the power of their hand.

The lazy too fond of.

Prov 26:14 *As* a door turns on its hinges, So *does* the lazy *man* on his bed.

Of the poor, often sold for debt.

Prov 22:27 If you have nothing *with which* to pay, Why should he take away your bed from under you?

Subject to ceremonial defilement.

Lev 15:4 Every bed is unclean on which he who has the

discharge lies, and everything on which he sits shall be unclean.

Purification of.

Mark 7:4 *When they come* from the marketplace, they do not eat unless they wash. And there are many other things which they have received and hold, *like* the washing of cups, pitchers, copper vessels, and couches.

Illustrative of

The grave.

Is 57:2 He shall enter into peace; They shall rest in their beds, *Each one* walking *in* his uprightness.

(Made in darkness) extreme misery.

Job 17:13 If I wait *for* the grave *as* my house, If I make my bed in the darkness,

(Made in sickness) divine support and comfort.

Ps 41:3 The LORD will strengthen him on his bed of illness; You will sustain him on his sickbed.

(Too short) plans which afford no rest or peace.

Is 28:20 For the bed is too short to stretch out *on*, And the covering so narrow that one cannot wrap himself *in it.*

BEERSHEBA

Wilderness where Hagar and Ishmael wandered.

Gen 21:14 So Abraham rose early in the morning, and took bread and a skin of water; and putting *it* on her shoulder, he gave *it* and the boy to Hagar, and sent her away. Then she departed and wandered in the Wilderness of Beersheba.

Place of oath between Abraham and Abimelech.

Gen 21:31–32 Therefore he called that place Beersheba, because the two of them swore an oath there. **32** Thus they made a covenant at Beersheba. So Abimelech rose with Phichol, the commander of his army, and they returned to the land of the Philistines.

Cf. Gen 26:33; 2 Sam 24:7; 1 Kin 19:3

Southern border of Canaan.

Judg 20:1 So all the children of Israel came out, from Dan to Beersheba, as well as from the land of Gilead, and the congregation gathered together as one man before the LORD at Mizpah.

1 Sam 3:20 And all Israel from Dan to Beersheba knew that Samuel *had been* established as a prophet of the LORD.

2 Sam 3:10 to transfer the kingdom from the house of Saul, and set up the throne of David over Israel and over Judah, from Dan to Beersheba."

2 Sam 17:11 Therefore I advise that all Israel be fully gathered to you, from Dan to Beersheba, like the sand that *is* by the sea for multitude, and that you go to battle in person.

2 Sam 24:2 So the king said to Joab the commander of the army who *was* with him, "Now go throughout all the tribes of Israel, from Dan to Beersheba, and count the people, that I may know the number of the people."

1 Kin 4:25 And Judah and Israel dwelt safely, each man under his vine and his fig tree, from Dan as far as Beersheba, all the days of Solomon.

2 Chr 30:5 So they resolved to make a proclamation throughout all Israel, from Beersheba to Dan, that they should come to keep the Passover to the LORD God of Israel at Jerusalem, since they had not done *it* for a long *time* in the *prescribed* manner.

Cf. 2 Kin 23:8; Amos 5:5; 8:14

Samuel's sons judged there.

1 Sam 8:2 The name of his firstborn was Joel, and the name of his second, Abijah; *they were* judges in Beersheba.

Isaac heard from God at, made covenant there.

Gen 26:23–25 Then he went up from there to Beersheba. **24** And the LORD appeared to him the same night and said, "I *am* the God of your father Abraham; do not fear, for I *am* with you. I will bless you and multiply your descendants for My servant Abraham's sake." **25** So he built an altar there and called on the name of the LORD, and he pitched his tent there; and there Isaac's servants dug a well.

BELIEVERS, AFFLICTED

God is with.

Ps 46:5 God *is* in the midst of her, she shall not be moved; God shall help her, just at the break of dawn.

Ps 46:7 The LORD of hosts *is* with us; The God of Jacob *is* our refuge. Selah

God is a refuge and strength to.

Ps 27:5–6 For in the time of trouble He shall hide me in His pavilion; In the secret place of His tabernacle He shall hide me; He shall set me high upon a rock. **6** And now my head shall be lifted up above my enemies all around me; Therefore I will offer sacrifices of joy in His tabernacle; I will sing, yes, I will sing praises to the LORD.

Ps 46:1–2 God *is* our refuge and strength, A very present help in trouble. **2** Therefore we will not fear, Even though the earth be removed, And though the mountains be carried into the midst of the sea;

Is 25:4 For You have been a strength to the poor, A strength to the needy in his distress, A refuge from the storm, A shade from the heat; For the blast of the terrible ones *is* as a storm *against* the wall.

Jer 16:19 O LORD, my strength and my fortress, My refuge in the day of affliction, The Gentiles shall come to You From the ends of the earth and say, "Surely our fathers have inherited lies, Worthlessness and unprofitable *things.*"

Nah 1:7 The LORD *is* good, A stronghold in the day of trouble; And He knows those who trust in Him.

God comforts.

Is 49:13 Sing, O heavens! Be joyful, O earth! And break out in singing, O mountains! For the LORD has comforted His people, And will have mercy on His afflicted.

Is 61:2 To proclaim the acceptable year of the LORD, And the day of vengeance of our God; To comfort all who mourn,

Jer 31:13 "Then shall the virgin rejoice in the dance, And the young men and the old, together; For I will turn their mourning to joy, Will comfort them, And make them rejoice rather than sorrow.

Matt 5:4 Blessed *are* those who mourn, For they shall be comforted.

2 Cor 1:4–5 who comforts us in all our tribulation, that we may be able to comfort those who are in any trouble, with the comfort with which we ourselves are comforted by God. **5** For as the sufferings of Christ abound in us, so our consolation also abounds through Christ.

2 Cor 7:6 Nevertheless God, who comforts the downcast, comforted us by the coming of Titus,

God preserves and delivers.

Ps 34:4 I sought the LORD, and He heard me, And delivered me from all my fears.

Ps 34:19–20 Many *are* the afflictions of the righteous, But the LORD delivers him out of them all. **20** He guards all his bones; Not one of them is broken.

Prov 12:13 The wicked is ensnared by the transgression of *his* lips, But the righteous will come through trouble.

Jer 39:17–18 But I will deliver you in that day," says the LORD, "and you shall not be given into the hand of the men of whom you *are* afraid. **18** For I will surely deliver you, and you shall not fall by the sword; but your life shall be as a prize to you, because you have put your trust in Me," says the LORD.' "

Christ supports.

2 Tim 4:17 But the Lord stood with me and strengthened me, so that the message might be preached fully through me, and *that* all the Gentiles might hear. Also I was delivered out of the mouth of the lion.

Heb 2:18 For in that He Himself has suffered, being tempted, He is able to aid those who are tempted.

Christ comforts.

Matt 11:28–30 Come to Me, all *you* who labor and are heavy laden, and I will give you rest. **29** Take My yoke upon you and learn from Me, for I am gentle and lowly in heart, and you will find rest for your souls. **30** For My yoke *is* easy and My burden is light."

Luke 7:13 When the Lord saw her, He had compassion on her and said to her, "Do not weep."

John 14:1 "Let not your heart be troubled; you believe in God, believe also in Me.

John 16:33 These things I have spoken to you, that in Me you may have peace. In the world you will have tribulation; but be of good cheer, I have overcome the world."

Christ preserves.

Is 63:9 In all their affliction He was afflicted, And the Angel of His Presence saved them; In His love and in His pity He redeemed them; And He bore them and carried them All the days of old.

Christ delivers.

Rev 3:10 Because you have kept My command to persevere, I also will keep you from the hour of trial which shall come upon the whole world, to test those who dwell on the earth.

Should praise God.

Ps 13:5–6 But I have trusted in Your mercy; My heart shall rejoice in Your salvation. **6** I will sing to the LORD, Because He has dealt bountifully with me.

Ps 56:8–10 You number my wanderings; Put my tears into Your bottle; *Are they* not in Your book? **9** When I cry out *to You*, Then my enemies will turn back; This I know, because God *is* for me. **10** In God (I will praise *His* word), In the LORD (I will praise *His* word),

Ps 57:6–7 They have prepared a net for my steps; My soul is bowed down; They have dug a pit before me; Into the midst of it they *themselves* have fallen. Selah **7** My heart is steadfast, O God, my heart is steadfast; I will sing and give praise.

Ps 71:20–23 *You*, who have shown me great and severe troubles, Shall revive me again, And bring me up again from the depths of the earth. **21** You shall increase my greatness, And comfort me on every side. **22** Also with the lute I will praise You— *And* Your faithfulness, O my God! To You I will sing with the harp, O Holy One of Israel. **23** My lips shall greatly rejoice when I sing to You, And my soul, which You have redeemed.

Should imitate Christ.

Heb 12:1–3 Therefore we also, since we are surrounded by so great a cloud of witnesses, let us lay aside every weight, and the sin which so easily ensnares *us*, and let us run with endurance the race that is set before us, **2** looking unto Jesus, the author and finisher of *our* faith, who for the joy that was set before Him endured the cross, despising the shame, and has sat down at the right hand of the throne of God. **3** For consider Him who endured such hostility from sinners against Himself, lest you become weary and discouraged in your souls.

1 Pet 2:21–23 For to this you were called, because Christ also suffered for us, leaving us an example, that you should follow His steps: **22** *"Who committed no sin, Nor was deceit found in His mouth"*; **23** who, when He was reviled, did not revile in return; when He suffered, He did not threaten, but committed *Himself* to Him who judges righteously;

Should imitate the prophets.

James 5:10 My brethren, take the prophets, who spoke in the name of the Lord, as an example of suffering and patience.

Should be patient.

Rom 12:12 rejoicing in hope, patient in tribulation, continuing steadfastly in prayer;

2 Thess 1:4 so that we ourselves boast of you among the churches of God for your patience and faith in all your persecutions and tribulations that you endure,

James 1:4 But let patience have *its* perfect work, that you may be perfect and complete, lacking nothing.

1 Pet 2:20 For what credit *is it* if, when you are beaten for your faults, you take it patiently? But when you do good and suffer, if you take it patiently, this *is* commendable before God.

Should be resigned.

Job 1:21 And he said: "Naked I came from my mother's womb, And naked shall I return there. The LORD gave, and the LORD has taken away; Blessed be the name of the LORD."

Job 2:10 But he said to her, "You speak as one of the foolish women speaks. Shall we indeed accept good

from God, and shall we not accept adversity?" In all this Job did not sin with his lips.

Should not despise chastening.

Job 5:17 "Behold, happy *is* the man whom God corrects; Therefore do not despise the chastening of the Almighty.

Ps 39:9 I was mute, I did not open my mouth, Because it was You who did *it*.

Prov 3:11 My son, do not despise the chastening of the LORD, Nor detest His correction;

Heb 12:5 And you have forgotten the exhortation which speaks to you as to sons: *"My son, do not despise the chastening of the LORD, Nor be discouraged when you are rebuked by Him;*

Should acknowledge the justice of their chastisements.

Neh 9:33 However You *are* just in all that has befallen us; For You have dealt faithfully, But we have done wickedly.

Is 64:5–7 You meet him who rejoices and does righteousness, *Who* remembers You in Your ways. You are indeed angry, for we have sinned— In these ways we continue; And we need to be saved. **6** But we are all like an unclean *thing*, And all our righteousnesses *are* like filthy rags; We all fade as a leaf, And our iniquities, like the wind, Have taken us away. **7** And *there is* no one who calls on Your name, Who stirs himself up to take hold of You; For You have hidden Your face from us, And have consumed us because of our iniquities.

Lam 3:39 Why should a living man complain, A man for the punishment of his sins?

Mic 7:9 I will bear the indignation of the LORD, Because I have sinned against Him, Until He pleads my case And executes justice for me. He will bring me forth to the light; I will see His righteousness.

Should trust in the goodness of God.

Job 13:15 Though He slay me, yet will I trust Him. Even so, I will defend my own ways before Him.

Ps 71:20 *You*, who have shown me great and severe troubles, Shall revive me again, And bring me up again from the depths of the earth.

2 Cor 1:9 Yes, we had the sentence of death in ourselves, that we should not trust in ourselves but in God who raises the dead,

1 Pet 2:23 who, when He was reviled, did not revile in return; when He suffered, He did not threaten, but committed *Himself* to Him who judges righteously;

Should turn and devote themselves to God.

Ps 116:7–9 Return to your rest, O my soul, For the LORD has dealt bountifully with you. **8** For You have delivered my soul from death, My eyes from tears, *And* my feet from falling. **9** I will walk before the LORD In the land of the living.

Should keep the pious resolutions made during afflictions.

Ps 66:13–15 I will go into Your house with burnt offerings; I will pay You my vows, **14** Which my lips have uttered And my mouth has spoken when I was in trouble. **15** I will offer You burnt sacrifices of fat animals, With the sweet aroma of rams; I will offer bulls with goats. Selah

Should be frequent in prayer. See "Affliction, Prayer Under."

Ps 50:15–17 Call upon Me in the day of trouble; I will deliver you, and you shall glorify Me." **16** But to the wicked God says: "What *right* have you to declare My statutes, Or take My covenant in your mouth, **17** Seeing you hate instruction And cast My words behind you?

Should take encouragement from former mercies.

Ps 27:9 Do not hide Your face from me; Do not turn Your servant away in anger; You have been my help; Do not leave me nor forsake me, O God of my salvation.

2 Cor 1:10 who delivered us from so great a death, and does deliver us; in whom we trust that He will still deliver *us,*

Examples of,

Joseph.

Gen 39:20–23 Then Joseph's master took him and put him into the prison, a place where the king's prisoners *were* confined. And he was there in the prison. **21** But the LORD was with Joseph and showed him mercy, and He gave him favor in the sight of the keeper of the prison. **22** And the keeper of the prison committed to Joseph's hand all the prisoners who *were* in the prison; whatever they did there, it was his doing. **23** The keeper of the prison did not look into anything *that was* under *Joseph's* authority, because the LORD was with him; and whatever he did, the LORD made *it* prosper.

Ps 105:17–19 He sent a man before them— Joseph—*who* was sold as a slave. **18** They hurt his feet with fetters, He was laid in irons. **19** Until the time that his word came to pass, The word of the LORD tested him.

Moses.

Heb 11:25 choosing rather to suffer affliction with the people of God than to enjoy the passing pleasures of sin,

Job.

Job 1:20–22 Then Job arose, tore his robe, and shaved his head; and he fell to the ground and worshiped. **21** And he said: "Naked I came from my mother's womb, And naked shall I return there. The LORD gave, and the LORD has taken away; Blessed be the name of the LORD." **22** In all this Job did not sin nor charge God with wrong.

David.

2 Sam 12:15–23 Then Nathan departed to his house. And the LORD struck the child that Uriah's wife bore to David, and it became ill. **16** David therefore pleaded with God for the child, and David fasted and went in and lay all night on the ground. **17** So the elders of his house arose *and went* to him, to raise him up from the ground. But he would not, nor did he eat food with them. **18** Then on the seventh day it came to pass that the child died. And the servants of David were afraid to tell him that the child was dead. For they said, "Indeed, while the child was alive, we spoke to him, and he would not heed our voice. How can we tell him that the child is dead? He may do some harm!" **19** When David saw that his servants were whispering, David perceived that the child was dead. Therefore David said to his servants, "Is the child dead?" And they said, "He is dead." **20** So David arose from the ground, washed and anointed himself, and changed his clothes; and he went into the house of the LORD and worshiped. Then he went to his own house; and when he requested, they set food before him, and he ate. **21** Then his servants said to him, "What *is* this that you have done? You fasted and wept for the child *while he was* alive, but when the child died, you arose and ate food." **22** And he said, "While the child was alive, I fasted and wept; for I said, 'Who can tell *whether* the LORD will be gracious to me, that the child may live?' **23** But now he is dead; why should I fast? Can I bring him back again? I shall go to him, but he shall not return to me."

Paul.

Acts 20:22–24 And see, now I go bound in the spirit to Jerusalem, not knowing the things that will happen to me there, **23** except that the Holy Spirit testifies in every city, saying that chains and tribulations await me. **24** But none of these things move me; nor do I count my life dear to myself, so that I may finish my race with joy, and the ministry which I received from the Lord Jesus, to testify to the gospel of the grace of God.

Acts 21:13 Then Paul answered, "What do you mean by weeping and breaking my heart? For I am ready not only to be bound, but also to die at Jerusalem for the name of the Lord Jesus."

The Apostles.

1 Cor 4:13 being defamed, we entreat. We have been made as the filth of the world, the offscouring of all things until now.

2 Cor 6:4–10 But in all *things* we commend ourselves as ministers of God: in much patience, in tribulations, in needs, in distresses, **5** in stripes, in imprisonments, in tumults, in labors, in sleeplessness, in fastings; **6** by purity, by knowledge, by longsuffering, by kindness, by the Holy Spirit, by sincere love, **7** by the word of truth, by the power of God, by the armor of righteousness on the right hand and on the left, **8** by honor and dishonor, by evil report and good report; as deceivers, and *yet* true; **9** as unknown, and *yet* well known; as dying, and behold we live; as chastened, and *yet* not killed; **10** as sorrowful, yet always rejoicing; as poor, yet making many rich; as having nothing, and *yet* possessing all things.

BELIEVERS, CHARACTER OF

Attentive to Christ's voice.

John 10:3–4 To him the doorkeeper opens, and the sheep hear his voice; and he calls his own sheep by name and leads them out. **4** And when he brings out his own sheep, he goes before them; and the sheep follow him, for they know his voice.

Blameless and harmless.

Phil 2:15 that you may become blameless and harmless, children of God without fault in the midst of a crooked and perverse generation, among whom you shine as lights in the world,

Bold.

Prov 28:1 The wicked flee when no one pursues, But the righteous are bold as a lion.

Rom 13:3 For rulers are not a terror to good works, but to evil. Do you want to be unafraid of the authority? Do what is good, and you will have praise from the same.

Contrite.

Is 57:15 For thus says the High and Lofty One Who inhabits eternity, whose name *is* Holy: "I dwell in the high and holy *place*, With him *who* has a contrite and humble spirit, To revive the spirit of the humble, And to revive the heart of the contrite ones.

Is 66:2 For all those *things* My hand has made, And all those *things* exist," Says the LORD. "But on this *one* will I look: On *him who is* poor and of a contrite spirit, And who trembles at My word.

Devout.

Acts 8:2 And devout men carried Stephen *to his burial,* and made great lamentation over him.

Acts 22:12 "Then a certain Ananias, a devout man according to the law, having a good testimony with all the Jews who dwelt *there,*

Faithful.

Rev 17:14 These will make war with the Lamb, and the Lamb will overcome them, for He is Lord of lords and King of kings; and those *who are* with Him *are* called, chosen, and faithful."

Follow Christ.

John 10:4 And when he brings out his own sheep, he goes before them; and the sheep follow him, for they know his voice.

John 10:27 My sheep hear My voice, and I know them, and they follow Me.

Godly.

Ps 4:3 But know that the LORD has set apart for Himself him who is godly; The LORD will hear when I call to Him.

Matt 3:16 When He had been baptized, Jesus came up immediately from the water; and behold, the heavens were opened to Him, and He saw the Spirit of God descending like a dove and alighting upon Him.

Acts 10:2 a devout *man* and one who feared God with all his household, who gave alms generously to the people, and prayed to God always.

2 Pet 2:9 *then* the Lord knows how to deliver the godly out of temptations and to reserve the unjust under punishment for the day of judgment,

Guileless.

John 1:47 Jesus saw Nathanael coming toward Him, and said of him, "Behold, an Israelite indeed, in whom is no deceit!"

Holy.

Deut 7:6 "For you *are* a holy people to the LORD your God; the LORD your God has chosen you to be a people for Himself, a special treasure above all the peoples on the face of the earth.

Deut 14:2 For you *are* a holy people to the LORD your God, and the LORD has chosen you to be a people for Himself, a special treasure above all the peoples who *are* on the face of the earth.

Col 3:12 Therefore, as *the* elect of God, holy and beloved, put on tender mercies, kindness, humility, meekness, longsuffering;

Humble.

Ps 34:2 My soul shall make its boast in the LORD; The humble shall hear *of it* and be glad.

1 Pet 5:5 Likewise you younger people, submit yourselves to *your* elders. Yes, all of *you* be submissive to one another, and be clothed with humility, for *"God resists the proud, But gives grace to the humble."*

Hunger after righteousness.

Matt 5:6 Blessed *are* those who hunger and thirst for righteousness, For they shall be filled.

Just.

Gen 6:9 This is the genealogy of Noah. Noah was a just man, perfect in his generations. Noah walked with God.

Hab 2:4 "Behold the proud, His soul is not upright in him; But the just shall live by his faith.

Luke 2:25 And behold, there was a man in Jerusalem whose name was Simeon, and this man was just and devout, waiting for the Consolation of Israel, and the Holy Spirit was upon him.

Led by the Spirit.

Rom 8:14 For as many as are led by the Spirit of God, these are sons of God.

Generous.

Is 32:8 But a generous man devises generous things, And by generosity he shall stand.

2 Cor 9:13 while, through the proof of this ministry, they glorify God for the obedience of your confession to the gospel of Christ, and for *your* liberal sharing with them and all *men,*

Loving.

Col 1:4 since we heard of your faith in Christ Jesus and of your love for all the saints;

1 Thess 4:9 But concerning brotherly love you have no need that I should write to you, for you yourselves are taught by God to love one another;

Lowly.

Prov 16:19 Better *to be* of a humble spirit with the lowly, Than to divide the spoil with the proud.

Meek.

Is 29:19 The humble also shall increase *their* joy in the LORD, And the poor among men shall rejoice In the Holy One of Israel.

Matt 5:5 Blessed *are* the meek, For they shall inherit the earth.

Merciful.

Ps 37:26 *He is* ever merciful, and lends; And his descendants *are* blessed.

Matt 5:7 Blessed *are* the merciful, For they shall obtain mercy.

New creatures.

2 Cor 5:17 Therefore, if anyone *is* in Christ, *he is* a new creation; old things have passed away; behold, all things have become new.

Eph 2:10 For we are His workmanship, created in Christ Jesus for good works, which God prepared beforehand that we should walk in them.

Obedient.

Rom 16:19 For your obedience has become known to

all. Therefore I am glad on your behalf; but I want you to be wise in what is good, and simple concerning evil.

1 Pet 1:14 as obedient children, not conforming yourselves to the former lusts, *as* in your ignorance;

Poor in spirit.

Ps 51:17 The sacrifices of God *are* a broken spirit, A broken and a contrite heart— These, O God, You will not despise.

Matt 5:3 "Blessed *are* the poor in spirit, For theirs is the kingdom of heaven.

Prudent.

Prov 16:21 The wise in heart will be called prudent, And sweetness of the lips increases learning.

Pure in heart.

Matt 5:8 Blessed *are* the pure in heart, For they shall see God.

1 John 3:3 And everyone who has this hope in Him purifies himself, just as He is pure.

Righteous.

Is 60:21 Also your people *shall* all *be* righteous; They shall inherit the land forever, The branch of My planting, The work of My hands, That I may be glorified.

Luke 1:6 And they were both righteous before God, walking in all the commandments and ordinances of the Lord blameless.

Sincere.

2 Cor 1:12 For our boasting is this: the testimony of our conscience that we conducted ourselves in the world in simplicity and godly sincerity, not with fleshly wisdom but by the grace of God, and more abundantly toward you.

2 Cor 2:17 For we are not, as so many, peddling the word of God; but as of sincerity, but as from God, we speak in the sight of God in Christ.

Steadfast.

Acts 2:42 And they continued steadfastly in the apostles' doctrine and fellowship, in the breaking of bread, and in prayers.

Col 2:5 For though I am absent in the flesh, yet I am with you in spirit, rejoicing to see your *good* order and the steadfastness of your faith in Christ.

Taught of God.

Is 54:13 All your children *shall be* taught by the LORD, And great *shall be* the peace of your children.

1 John 2:27 But the anointing which you have received from Him abides in you, and you do not need that anyone teach you; but as the same anointing teaches you concerning all things, and is true, and is not a lie, and just as it has taught you, you will abide in Him.

True.

2 Cor 6:8 by honor and dishonor, by evil report and good report; as deceivers, and *yet* true;

Undefiled.

Ps 119:1 Blessed *are* the undefiled in the way, Who walk in the law of the LORD!

Upright.

1 Kin 3:6 And Solomon said: "You have shown great mercy to Your servant David my father, because he walked before You in truth, in righteousness, and in uprightness of heart with You; You have continued this great kindness for him, and You have given him a son to sit on his throne, as *it is* this day.

Ps 15:2 He who walks uprightly, And works righteousness, And speaks the truth in his heart;

Watchful.

Luke 12:37 Blessed *are* those servants whom the master, when he comes, will find watching. Assuredly, I say to you that he will gird himself and have them sit down *to eat*, and will come and serve them.

Zealous of good works.

Titus 2:14 who gave Himself for us, that He might redeem us from every lawless deed and purify for Himself *His* own special people, zealous for good works.

Titus 3:8 This is a faithful saying, and these things I want you to affirm constantly, that those who have believed in God should be careful to maintain good works. These things are good and profitable to men.

BELIEVERS, COMPARED TO

The sun.

Judg 5:31 "Thus let all Your enemies perish, O LORD! But *let* those who love Him *be* like the sun When it comes out in full strength." So the land had rest for forty years.

Matt 13:43 Then the righteous will shine forth as the sun in the kingdom of their Father. He who has ears to hear, let him hear!

Stars.

Dan 12:3 Those who are wise shall shine Like the brightness of the firmament, And those who turn many to righteousness Like the stars forever and ever.

Lights.

Matt 5:14 "You are the light of the world. A city that is set on a hill cannot be hidden.

Phil 2:15 that you may become blameless and harmless, children of God without fault in the midst of a crooked and perverse generation, among whom you shine as lights in the world,

Mount Zion.

Ps 125:1–2 Those who trust in the LORD *Are* like Mount Zion, *Which* cannot be moved, *but* abides forever. 2 As the mountains surround Jerusalem, So the LORD surrounds His people From this time forth and forever.

Lebanon.

Hos 14:5–7 I will be like the dew to Israel; He shall grow like the lily, And lengthen his roots like Lebanon. 6 His branches shall spread; His beauty shall be like an olive tree, And his fragrance like Lebanon. 7 Those who dwell under his shadow shall return; They shall be revived *like* grain, And grow like a vine. Their scent *shall be* like the wine of Lebanon.

Treasure.

Ex 19:5 Now therefore, if you will indeed obey My voice and keep My covenant, then you shall be a special treasure to Me above all people; for all the earth *is* Mine.

Ps 135:4 For the Lord has chosen Jacob for Himself, Israel for His special treasure.

Jewels.

Mal 3:17 "They shall be Mine," says the Lord of hosts, "On the day that I make them My jewels. And I will spare them As a man spares his own son who serves him."

Gold.

Job 23:10 But He knows the way that I take; *When* He has tested me, I shall come forth as gold.

Lam 4:2 The precious sons of Zion, Valuable as fine gold, How they are regarded as clay pots, The work of the hands of the potter!

Vessels of gold and silver.

2 Tim 2:20 But in a great house there are not only vessels of gold and silver, but also of wood and clay, some for honor and some for dishonor.

Jewels of a crown.

Zech 9:16 The Lord their God will save them in that day, As the flock of His people. For they *shall be like* the jewels of a crown, Lifted like a banner over His land—

Living stones.

1 Pet 2:5 you also, as living stones, are being built up a spiritual house, a holy priesthood, to offer up spiritual sacrifices acceptable to God through Jesus Christ.

Babes.

Matt 11:25 At that time Jesus answered and said, "I thank You, Father, Lord of heaven and earth, that You have hidden these things from *the* wise and prudent and have revealed them to babes.

1 Pet 2:2 as newborn babes, desire the pure milk of the word, that you may grow thereby,

Little children.

Matt 18:3 and said, "Assuredly, I say to you, unless you are converted and become as little children, you will by no means enter the kingdom of heaven.

1 Cor 14:20 Brethren, do not be children in understanding; however, in malice be babes, but in understanding be mature.

Obedient children.

1 Pet 1:14 as obedient children, not conforming yourselves to the former lusts, *as* in your ignorance;

Members of a body.

1 Cor 12:20 But now indeed *there are* many members, yet one body.

1 Cor 12:27 Now you are the body of Christ, and members individually.

Soldiers.

2 Tim 2:3–4 You therefore must endure hardship as a good soldier of Jesus Christ. 4 No one engaged in warfare entangles himself with the affairs of *this* life, that he may please him who enlisted him as a soldier.

Runners in a race.

1 Cor 9:24 Do you not know that those who run in a race all run, but one receives the prize? Run in such a way that you may obtain *it.*

Heb 12:1 Therefore we also, since we are surrounded by so great a cloud of witnesses, let us lay aside every weight, and the sin which so easily ensnares *us,* and let us run with endurance the race that is set before us,

Athletes.

2 Tim 2:5 And also if anyone competes in athletics, he is not crowned unless he competes according to the rules.

Good servants.

Matt 25:21 His lord said to him, 'Well *done,* good and faithful servant; you were faithful over a few things, I will make you ruler over many things. Enter into the joy of your lord.'

Sojourners and pilgrims.

1 Pet 2:11 Beloved, I beg *you* as sojourners and pilgrims, abstain from fleshly lusts which war against the soul,

Sheep.

Ps 78:52 But He made His own people go forth like sheep, And guided them in the wilderness like a flock;

Matt 25:33 And He will set the sheep on His right hand, but the goats on the left.

John 10:4 And when he brings out his own sheep, he goes before them; and the sheep follow him, for they know his voice.

Lambs.

Is 40:11 He will feed His flock like a shepherd; He will gather the lambs with His arm, And carry *them* in His bosom, *And* gently lead those who are with young.

John 21:15 So when they had eaten breakfast, Jesus said to Simon Peter, "Simon, *son* of Jonah, do you love Me more than these?" He said to Him, "Yes, Lord; You know that I love You." He said to him, "Feed My lambs."

Calves of the stall.

Mal 4:2 But to you who fear My name The Sun of Righteousness shall arise With healing in His wings; And you shall go out And grow fat like stall-fed calves.

Lions.

Prov 28:1 The wicked flee when no one pursues, But the righteous are bold as a lion.

Mic 5:8 And the remnant of Jacob Shall be among the Gentiles, In the midst of many peoples, Like a lion among the beasts of the forest, Like a young lion among flocks of sheep, Who, if he passes through, Both treads down and tears in pieces, And none can deliver.

Eagles.

Ps 103:5 Who satisfies your mouth with good *things,* So *that* your youth is renewed like the eagle's.

Is 40:31 But those who wait on the Lord Shall renew *their* strength; They shall mount up with wings like eagles, They shall run and not be weary, They shall walk and not faint.

Doves.

Ps 68:13 Though you lie down among the sheepfolds, *You will be* like the wings of a dove covered with silver, And her feathers with yellow gold."

Is 60:8 "Who *are* these *who* fly like a cloud, And like doves to their roosts?

Thirsting deer.

Ps 42:1 As the deer pants for the water brooks, So pants my soul for You, O God.

Good fish.

Matt 13:48 which, when it was full, they drew to shore; and they sat down and gathered the good into vessels, but threw the bad away.

Dew and showers.

Mic 5:7 Then the remnant of Jacob Shall be in the midst of many peoples, Like dew from the LORD, Like showers on the grass, That tarry for no man Nor wait for the sons of men.

Watered gardens.

Is 58:11 The LORD will guide you continually, And satisfy your soul in drought, And strengthen your bones; You shall be like a watered garden, And like a spring of water, whose waters do not fail.

Unfailing springs.

Is 58:11 The LORD will guide you continually, And satisfy your soul in drought, And strengthen your bones; You shall be like a watered garden, And like a spring of water, whose waters do not fail.

Vines.

Hos 14:7 Those who dwell under his shadow shall return; They shall be revived *like* grain, And grow like a vine. Their scent *shall be* like the wine of Lebanon.

Branches of a vine.

John 15:2 Every branch in Me that does not bear fruit He takes away; and every *branch* that bears fruit He prunes, that it may bear more fruit.

John 15:4–5 Abide in Me, and I in you. As the branch cannot bear fruit of itself, unless it abides in the vine, neither can you, unless you abide in Me. 5 "I am the vine, you *are* the branches. He who abides in Me, and I in him, bears much fruit; for without Me you can do nothing.

Pomegranates.

Song 4:13 Your plants *are* an orchard of pomegranates With pleasant fruits, Fragrant henna with spikenard,

Good figs.

Jer 24:2–7 One basket *had* very good figs, like the figs *that are* first ripe; and the other basket *had* very bad figs which could not be eaten, they were so bad. 3 Then the LORD said to me, "What do you see, Jeremiah?" And I said, "Figs, the good figs, very good; and the bad, very bad, which cannot be eaten, they are so bad." 4 Again the word of the LORD came to me, saying, 5 "Thus says the LORD, the God of Israel: 'Like these good figs, so will I acknowledge those who are carried away captive from Judah, whom I have sent out of this place for *their own* good, into the land of the Chaldeans. 6 For I will set My eyes on them for good, and I will bring them back to this land; I will build them and not pull *them* down, and I will plant them and not pluck *them* up. 7 Then I will give them a heart to know Me, that I *am* the LORD; and they shall be My people, and I will be their God, for they shall return to Me with their whole heart.

Lilies.

Hos 14:5 I will be like the dew to Israel; He shall grow like the lily, And lengthen his roots like Lebanon.

Willows by the watercourses.

Is 44:4 They will spring up among the grass Like willows by the watercourses.'

Trees planted by rivers.

Ps 1:3 He shall be like a tree Planted by the rivers of water, That brings forth its fruit in its season, Whose leaf also shall not wither; And whatever he does shall prosper.

Cedars in Lebanon.

Ps 92:12 The righteous shall flourish like a palm tree, He shall grow like a cedar in Lebanon.

Palm trees.

Ps 92:12 The righteous shall flourish like a palm tree, He shall grow like a cedar in Lebanon.

Green olive trees.

Ps 52:8 But I *am* like a green olive tree in the house of God; I trust in the mercy of God forever and ever.

Hos 14:6 His branches shall spread; His beauty shall be like an olive tree, And his fragrance like Lebanon.

Fruitful trees.

Ps 1:3 He shall be like a tree Planted by the rivers of water, That brings forth its fruit in its season, Whose leaf also shall not wither; And whatever he does shall prosper.

Jer 17:8 For he shall be like a tree planted by the waters, Which spreads out its roots by the river, And will not fear when heat comes; But its leaf will be green, And will not be anxious in the year of drought, Nor will cease from yielding fruit.

Grain.

Hos 14:7 Those who dwell under his shadow shall return; They shall be revived *like* grain, And grow like a vine. Their scent *shall be* like the wine of Lebanon.

Wheat.

Matt 3:12 His winnowing fan *is* in His hand, and He will thoroughly clean out His threshing floor, and gather His wheat into the barn; but He will burn up the chaff with unquenchable fire."

Matt 13:29–30 But he said, 'No, lest while you gather up the tares you also uproot the wheat with them. 30 Let both grow together until the harvest, and at the time of harvest I will say to the reapers, "First gather together the tares and bind them in bundles to burn them, but gather the wheat into my barn." ' "

Salt.

Matt 5:13 "You are the salt of the earth; but if the salt loses its flavor, how shall it be seasoned? It is then good for nothing but to be thrown out and trampled underfoot by men.

BELIEVERS, DEATH OF

Also called being asleep in Christ.

1 Cor 15:18 Then also those who have fallen asleep in Christ have perished.

1 Thess 4:14 For if we believe that Jesus died and rose again, even so God will bring with Him those who sleep in Jesus.

Is blessed.

Rev 14:13 Then I heard a voice from heaven saying to me, "Write: 'Blessed *are* the dead who die in the Lord from now on.' " "Yes," says the Spirit, "that they may rest from their labors, and their works follow them."

Is gain.

Phil 1:21 For to me, to live *is* Christ, and to die *is* gain.

Is full of

Faith.

Heb 11:13 These all died in faith, not having received the promises, but having seen them afar off were assured of them, embraced *them* and confessed that they were strangers and pilgrims on the earth.

Peace.

Is 57:2 He shall enter into peace; They shall rest in their beds, *Each one* walking *in* his uprightness.

Hope.

Prov 14:32 The wicked is banished in his wickedness, But the righteous has a refuge in his death.

Sometimes desired.

Job 14:14 If a man dies, shall he live *again?* All the days of my hard service I will wait, Till my change comes.

Luke 2:29 "Lord, now You are letting Your servant depart in peace, According to Your word;

Met with resignation.

Gen 50:24 And Joseph said to his brethren, "I am dying; but God will surely visit you, and bring you out of this land to the land of which He swore to Abraham, to Isaac, and to Jacob."

Josh 23:14 "Behold, this day I *am* going the way of all the earth. And you know in all your hearts and in all your souls that not one thing has failed of all the good things which the LORD your God spoke concerning you. All have come to pass for you; not one word of them has failed.

1 Kin 2:2 "I go the way of all the earth; be strong, therefore, and prove yourself a man.

Met without fear.

1 Cor 15:55 "O Death, where is your sting? O Hades, where is your victory?"

Precious in God's sight.

Ps 116:15 Precious in the sight of the LORD *Is* the death of His saints.

God is present in the.

Ps 23:4 Yea, though I walk through the valley of the shadow of death, I will fear no evil; For You *are* with me; Your rod and Your staff, they comfort me.

Ps 48:14 For this *is* God, Our God forever and ever; He will be our guide *Even* to death.

Removes from coming evil.

2 Kin 22:20 Surely, therefore, I will gather you to your fathers, and you shall be gathered to your grave in peace; and your eyes shall not see all the calamity which I will bring on this place." ' " So they brought back word to the king.

Is 57:1 The righteous perishes, And no man takes *it* to heart; Merciful men *are* taken away, While no one considers That the righteous is taken away from evil.

Leads to

Rest.

Job 3:17 There the wicked cease *from* troubling, And there the weary are at rest.

2 Thess 1:7 and to *give* you who are troubled rest with us when the Lord Jesus is revealed from heaven with His mighty angels,

Comfort.

Luke 16:25 But Abraham said, 'Son, remember that in your lifetime you received your good things, and likewise Lazarus evil things; but now he is comforted and you are tormented.

Christ's presence.

2 Cor 5:8 We are confident, yes, well pleased rather to be absent from the body and to be present with the Lord.

Phil 1:23 For I am hard-pressed between the two, having a desire to depart and be with Christ, *which is* far better.

A crown of life.

2 Tim 4:8 Finally, there is laid up for me the crown of righteousness, which the Lord, the righteous Judge, will give to me on that Day, and not to me only but also to all who have loved His appearing.

Rev 2:10 Do not fear any of those things which you are about to suffer. Indeed, the devil is about to throw *some* of you into prison, that you may be tested, and you will have tribulation ten days. Be faithful until death, and I will give you the crown of life.

A joyful resurrection.

Is 26:19 Your dead shall live; *Together with* my dead body they shall arise. Awake and sing, you who dwell in dust; For your dew *is like* the dew of herbs, And the earth shall cast out the dead.

Dan 12:2 And many of those who sleep in the dust of the earth shall awake, Some to everlasting life, Some to shame *and* everlasting contempt.

Disregarded by the wicked.

Is 57:1 The righteous perishes, And no man takes *it* to heart; Merciful men *are* taken away, While no one considers That the righteous is taken away from evil.

Survivors consoled for.

1 Thess 4:13–18 But I do not want you to be ignorant, brethren, concerning those who have fallen asleep, lest you sorrow as others who have no hope. **14** For if we believe that Jesus died and rose again, even so God will bring with Him those who sleep in Jesus. **15** For this we say to you by the word of the Lord, that we who are alive *and* remain until the coming of the Lord will by no means precede those who are asleep. **16** For the Lord Himself will descend from heaven with a shout, with the voice of an archangel, and with the trumpet of God. And the dead in Christ will rise first. **17** Then we who are alive *and* remain shall be caught up together with them in the clouds to meet the Lord in the air. And thus we shall always be with the Lord. **18** Therefore comfort one another with these words.

The wicked wish theirs to resemble.

Num 23:10 "Who can count the dust of Jacob, Or number one-fourth of Israel? Let me die the death of the righteous, And let my end be like his!"

Illustrated.

Luke 16:22 So it was that the beggar died, and was carried by the angels to Abraham's bosom. The rich man also died and was buried.

Exemplified by

Abraham.

Gen 25:8 Then Abraham breathed his last and died in a good old age, an old man and full *of years,* and was gathered to his people.

Isaac.

Gen 35:29 So Isaac breathed his last and died, and was gathered to his people, *being* old and full of days. And his sons Esau and Jacob buried him.

Jacob.

Gen 49:33 And when Jacob had finished commanding his sons, he drew his feet up into the bed and breathed his last, and was gathered to his people.

Aaron.

Num 20:28 Moses stripped Aaron of his garments and put them on Eleazar his son; and Aaron died there on the top of the mountain. Then Moses and Eleazar came down from the mountain.

Moses.

Deut 34:5 So Moses the servant of the LORD died there in the land of Moab, according to the word of the LORD.

Joshua.

Josh 24:29 Now it came to pass after these things that Joshua the son of Nun, the servant of the LORD, died, *being* one hundred and ten years old.

Elisha.

2 Kin 13:14 Elisha had become sick with the illness of which he would die. Then Joash the king of Israel came down to him, and wept over his face, and said, "O my father, my father, the chariots of Israel and their horsemen!"

2 Kin 13:20 Then Elisha died, and they buried him. And the *raiding* bands from Moab invaded the land in the spring of the year.

One thief on the cross.

Luke 23:43 And Jesus said to him, "Assuredly, I say to you, today you will be with Me in Paradise."

Dorcas.

Acts 9:37 But it happened in those days that she became sick and died. When they had washed her, they laid *her* in an upper room.

BELIEVERS, PRIVILEGES OF

Abiding in Christ.

John 15:4–5 Abide in Me, and I in you. As the branch cannot bear fruit of itself, unless it abides in the vine, neither can you, unless you abide in Me. **5** "I am the vine, you *are* the branches. He who abides in Me, and I in him, bears much fruit; for without Me you can do nothing.

Partaking of the divine nature.

2 Pet 1:4 by which have been given to us exceedingly great and precious promises, that through these you may be partakers of the divine nature, having escaped the corruption *that is* in the world through lust.

Access to God by Christ.

Eph 3:12 in whom we have boldness and access with confidence through faith in Him.

Being part of the church.

Eph 2:19 Now, therefore, you are no longer strangers and foreigners, but fellow citizens with the saints and members of the household of God,

Heb 12:23 to the general assembly and church of the firstborn *who are* registered in heaven, to God the Judge of all, to the spirits of just men made perfect,

Having

Union in God and Christ.

John 17:21 that they all may be one, as You, Father, *are* in Me, and I in You; that they also may be one in Us, that the world may believe that You sent Me.

Christ for their shepherd.

Is 40:11 He will feed His flock like a shepherd; He will gather the lambs with His arm, And carry *them* in His bosom, *And* gently lead those who are with young.

John 10:14 I am the good shepherd; and I know My *sheep,* and am known by My own.

John 10:16 And other sheep I have which are not of this fold; them also I must bring, and they will hear My voice; and there will be one flock *and* one shepherd.

Christ for their intercessor.

Rom 8:34 Who *is* he who condemns? *It is* Christ who died, and furthermore is also risen, who is even at the right hand of God, who also makes intercession for us.

Heb 7:25 Therefore He is also able to save to the uttermost those who come to God through Him, since He always lives to make intercession for them.

1 John 2:1 My little children, these things I write to you, so that you may not sin. And if anyone sins, we have an Advocate with the Father, Jesus Christ the righteous.

The promises of God.

2 Cor 7:1 Therefore, having these promises, beloved, let us cleanse ourselves from all filthiness of the flesh and spirit, perfecting holiness in the fear of God.

2 Pet 1:4 by which have been given to us exceedingly great and precious promises, that through these you may be partakers of the divine nature, having escaped the corruption *that is* in the world through lust.

All things.

1 Cor 3:21–22 Therefore let no one boast in men. For all things are yours: **22** whether Paul or Apollos or Cephas, or the world or life or death, or things present or things to come—all are yours.

All things working together for their good.

Rom 8:28 And we know that all things work together for good to those who love God, to those who are the called according to *His* purpose.

2 Cor 4:15–17 For all things *are* for your sakes, that grace, having spread through the many, may cause thanksgiving to abound to the glory of God. **16** Therefore we do not lose heart. Even though our outward man is perishing, yet the inward *man* is being renewed day by day. **17** For our light affliction, which is but for a moment, is working for us a far more exceeding *and* eternal weight of glory,

Their names written in the Book of Life.

Rev 13:8 All who dwell on the earth will worship him,

whose names have not been written in the Book of Life of the Lamb slain from the foundation of the world.

Rev 20:15 And anyone not found written in the Book of Life was cast into the lake of fire.

Having God for their

King.

Ps 5:2 Give heed to the voice of my cry, My King and my God, For to You I will pray.

Ps 44:4 You are my King, O God; Command victories for Jacob.

Is 44:6 "Thus says the LORD, the King of Israel, And his Redeemer, the LORD of hosts: 'I *am* the First and I *am* the Last; Besides Me *there is* no God.

Glory.

Ps 3:3 But You, O LORD, *are* a shield for me, My glory and the One who lifts up my head.

Is 60:19 "The sun shall no longer be your light by day, Nor for brightness shall the moon give light to you; But the LORD will be to you an everlasting light, And your God your glory.

Salvation.

Ps 18:2 The LORD is my rock and my fortress and my deliverer; My God, my strength, in whom I will trust; My shield and the horn of my salvation, my stronghold.

Ps 27:1 The LORD *is* my light and my salvation; Whom shall I fear? The LORD *is* the strength of my life; Of whom shall I be afraid?

Is 12:2 Behold, God *is* my salvation, I will trust and not be afraid; 'For YAH, the LORD, *is* my strength and song; He also has become my salvation.' "

Father.

Deut 32:6 Do you thus deal with the LORD, O foolish and unwise people? *Is* He not your Father, *who* bought you? Has He not made you and established you?

Is 63:16 Doubtless You *are* our Father, Though Abraham was ignorant of us, And Israel does not acknowledge us. You, O LORD, *are* our Father; Our Redeemer from Everlasting *is* Your name.

Is 64:8 But now, O LORD, You *are* our Father; We *are* the clay, and You our potter; And all we *are* the work of Your hand.

Redeemer.

Ps 19:14 Let the words of my mouth and the meditation of my heart Be acceptable in Your sight, O LORD, my strength and my Redeemer.

Is 43:14 Thus says the LORD, your Redeemer, The Holy One of Israel: "For your sake I will send to Babylon, And bring them all down as fugitives— The Chaldeans, who rejoice in their ships.

Friend.

2 Chr 20:7 *Are* You not our God, *who* drove out the inhabitants of this land before Your people Israel, and gave it to the descendants of Abraham Your friend forever?

James 2:23 And the Scripture was fulfilled which says, *"Abraham believed God, and it was accounted to him for righteousness."* And he was called the friend of God.

Helper.

Ps 33:20 Our soul waits for the LORD; He *is* our help and our shield.

Heb 13:6 So we may boldly say: *"The LORD is my helper; I will not fear. What can man do to me?"*

Keeper.

Ps 121:4–5 Behold, He who keeps Israel Shall neither slumber nor sleep. 5 The LORD *is* your keeper; The LORD *is* your shade at your right hand.

Deliverer.

2 Sam 22:2 And he said: "The LORD *is* my rock and my fortress and my deliverer;

Ps 18:2 The LORD is my rock and my fortress and my deliverer; My God, my strength, in whom I will trust; My shield and the horn of my salvation, my stronghold.

Strength.

Ps 18:2 The LORD is my rock and my fortress and my deliverer; My God, my strength, in whom I will trust; My shield and the horn of my salvation, my stronghold.

Ps 27:1 The LORD *is* my light and my salvation; Whom shall I fear? The LORD *is* the strength of my life; Of whom shall I be afraid?

Ps 46:1 God *is* our refuge and strength, A very present help in trouble.

Refuge.

Ps 46:1 God *is* our refuge and strength, A very present help in trouble.

Ps 46:11 The LORD of hosts *is* with us; The God of Jacob *is* our refuge. Selah

Is 25:4 For You have been a strength to the poor, A strength to the needy in his distress, A refuge from the storm, A shade from the heat; For the blast of the terrible ones *is* as a storm *against* the wall.

Shield.

Gen 15:1 After these things the word of the LORD came to Abram in a vision, saying, "Do not be afraid, Abram. I *am* your shield, your exceedingly great reward."

Ps 84:11 For the LORD God *is* a sun and shield; The LORD will give grace and glory; No good *thing* will He withhold From those who walk uprightly.

Tower.

2 Sam 22:3 The God of my strength, in whom I will trust; My shield and the horn of my salvation, My stronghold and my refuge; My Savior, You save me from violence.

Ps 61:3 For You have been a shelter for me, A strong tower from the enemy.

Light.

Ps 27:1 The LORD *is* my light and my salvation; Whom shall I fear? The LORD *is* the strength of my life; Of whom shall I be afraid?

Is 60:19 "The sun shall no longer be your light by day, Nor for brightness shall the moon give light to you; But the LORD will be to you an everlasting light, And your God your glory.

Mic 7:8 Do not rejoice over me, my enemy; When I fall, I will arise; When I sit in darkness, The LORD *will be* a light to me.

Guide.

Ps 48:14 For this *is* God, Our God forever and ever; He will be our guide *Even* to death.

Is 58:11 The LORD will guide you continually, And satisfy your soul in drought, And strengthen your bones; You shall be like a watered garden, And like a spring of water, whose waters do not fail.

Lawgiver.

Neh 9:13–14 "You came down also on Mount Sinai, And spoke with them from heaven, And gave them just ordinances and true laws, Good statutes and commandments. 14 You made known to them Your holy Sabbath, And commanded them precepts, statutes and laws, By the hand of Moses Your servant.

Is 33:22 (For the LORD *is* our Judge, The LORD *is* our Lawgiver, The LORD *is* our King; He will save us);

Habitation.

Ps 90:1 LORD, You have been our dwelling place in all generations.

Ps 91:9 Because you have made the LORD, *who is* my refuge, *Even* the Most High, your dwelling place,

Portion.

Ps 73:26 My flesh and my heart fail; *But* God *is* the strength of my heart and my portion forever.

Lam 3:24 "The LORD *is* my portion," says my soul, "Therefore I hope in Him!"

Committing themselves to God.

Ps 31:5 Into Your hand I commit my spirit; You have redeemed me, O LORD God of truth.

Acts 7:59 And they stoned Stephen as he was calling on God and saying, "Lord Jesus, receive my spirit."

2 Tim 1:12 For this reason I also suffer these things; nevertheless I am not ashamed, for I know whom I have believed and am persuaded that He is able to keep what I have committed to Him until that Day.

Calling upon God in trouble.

Ps 50:15 Call upon Me in the day of trouble; I will deliver you, and you shall glorify Me."

Suffering for Christ.

Acts 5:41 So they departed from the presence of the council, rejoicing that they were counted worthy to suffer shame for His name.

Phil 1:29 For to you it has been granted on behalf of Christ, not only to believe in Him, but also to suffer for His sake,

Profiting by chastisement.

Ps 119:67 Before I was afflicted I went astray, But now I keep Your word.

Heb 12:10–11 For they indeed for a few days chastened *us* as seemed *best* to them, but He for *our* profit, that *we* may be partakers of His holiness. 11 Now no chastening seems to be joyful for the present, but painful; nevertheless, afterward it yields the peaceable fruit of righteousness to those who have been trained by it.

Secure during public calamities.

Job 5:20 In famine He shall redeem you from death, And in war from the power of the sword.

Job 5:23 For you shall have a covenant with the stones of the field, And the beasts of the field shall be at peace with you.

Ps 27:1–5 The LORD *is* my light and my salvation; Whom shall I fear? The LORD *is* the strength of my life; Of whom shall I be afraid? 2 When the wicked came against me To eat up my flesh, My enemies and foes, They stumbled and fell. 3 Though an army may encamp against me, My heart shall not fear; Though war may rise against me, In this I *will be* confident. 4 One *thing* I have desired of the LORD, That will I seek: That I may dwell in the house of the LORD All the days of my life, To behold the beauty of the LORD, And to inquire in His temple. 5 For in the time of trouble He shall hide me in His pavilion; In the secret place of His tabernacle He shall hide me; He shall set me high upon a rock.

Ps 91:5–10 You shall not be afraid of the terror by night, Nor of the arrow *that* flies by day, 6 Nor of the pestilence *that* walks in darkness, Nor of the destruction *that* lays waste at noonday. 7 A thousand may fall at your side, And ten thousand at your right hand; *But* it shall not come near you. 8 Only with your eyes shall you look, And see the reward of the wicked. 9 Because you have made the LORD, *who is* my refuge, *Even* the Most High, your dwelling place, 10 No evil shall befall you, Nor shall any plague come near your dwelling;

Interceding for others.

Gen 18:23–33 And Abraham came near and said, "Would You also destroy the righteous with the wicked? 24 Suppose there were fifty righteous within the city; would You also destroy the place and not spare *it* for the fifty righteous that were in it? 25 Far be it from You to do such a thing as this, to slay the righteous with the wicked, so that the righteous should be as the wicked; far be it from You! Shall not the Judge of all the earth do right?" 26 So the LORD said, "If I find in Sodom fifty righteous within the city, then I will spare all the place for their sakes." 27 Then Abraham answered and said, "Indeed now, I who *am but* dust and ashes have taken it upon myself to speak to the Lord: 28 Suppose there were five less than the fifty righteous; would You destroy all of the city for *lack of* five?" So He said, "If I find there forty-five, I will not destroy *it*." 29 And he spoke to Him yet again and said, "Suppose there should be forty found there?" So He said, "I will not do *it* for the sake of forty." 30 Then he said, "Let not the Lord be angry, and I will speak: Suppose thirty should be found there?" So He said, "I will not do *it* if I find thirty there." 31 And he said, "Indeed now, I have taken it upon myself to speak to the Lord: Suppose twenty should be found there?" So He said, "I will not destroy *it* for the sake of twenty." 32 Then he said, "Let not the Lord be angry, and I will speak but once more: Suppose ten should be found there?" And He said, "I will not destroy *it* for the sake of ten." 33 So the LORD went His way as soon as He had finished speaking with Abraham; and Abraham returned to his place.

James 5:16 Confess *your* trespasses to one another, and pray for one another, that you may be healed. The effective, fervent prayer of a righteous man avails much.

BELIEVERS, TEMPORAL HAPPINESS OF

Is in God.

Ps 73:25–26 Whom have I in heaven *but You?* And *there is* none upon earth *that* I desire besides You. **26** My flesh and my heart fail; *But* God *is* the strength of my heart and my portion forever.

Only found in the ways of wisdom.

Prov 3:17–18 Her ways *are* ways of pleasantness, And all her paths *are* peace. **18** She *is* a tree of life to those who take hold of her, And happy *are* all who retain her.

Described by Christ in the beatitudes.

Matt 5:3–12 "Blessed *are* the poor in spirit, For theirs is the kingdom of heaven. **4** Blessed *are* those who mourn, For they shall be comforted. **5** Blessed *are* the meek, For they shall inherit the earth. **6** Blessed *are* those who hunger and thirst for righteousness, For they shall be filled. **7** Blessed *are* the merciful, For they shall obtain mercy. **8** Blessed *are* the pure in heart, For they shall see God. **9** Blessed *are* the peacemakers, For they shall be called sons of God. **10** Blessed are those who are persecuted for righteousness' sake, For theirs is the kingdom of heaven. **11** "Blessed are you when they revile and persecute you, and say all kinds of evil against you falsely for My sake. **12** Rejoice and be exceedingly glad, for great *is* your reward in heaven, for so they persecuted the prophets who were before you.

Is derived from

Fear of God.

Ps 128:1–2 Blessed *is* every one who fears the LORD, Who walks in His ways. **2** When you eat the labor of your hands, You *shall be* happy, and *it shall be* well with you.

Prov 28:14 Happy *is* the man who is always reverent, But he who hardens his heart will fall into calamity.

Trust in God.

Prov 16:20 He who heeds the word wisely will find good, And whoever trusts in the LORD, happy *is* he.

Phil 4:6–7 Be anxious for nothing, but in everything by prayer and supplication, with thanksgiving, let your requests be made known to God; **7** and the peace of God, which surpasses all understanding, will guard your hearts and minds through Christ Jesus.

The words of Christ.

John 17:13 But now I come to You, and these things I speak in the world, that they may have My joy fulfilled in themselves.

Obedience to God.

Ps 40:8 I delight to do Your will, O my God, And Your law *is* within my heart."

John 13:17 If you know these things, blessed are you if you do them.

Salvation.

Deut 33:29 Happy *are* you, O Israel! Who *is* like you, a people saved by the LORD, The shield of your help And the sword of your majesty! Your enemies shall submit to you, And you shall tread down their high places."

Is 12:2–3 Behold, God *is* my salvation, I will trust and not be afraid; 'For YAH, the LORD, *is* my strength and

song; He also has become my salvation.' " **3** Therefore with joy you will draw water From the wells of salvation.

Hope in the Lord.

Ps 146:5 Happy *is* he who *has* the God of Jacob for his help, Whose hope *is* in the LORD his God,

Hope of glory.

Rom 5:2 through whom also we have access by faith into this grace in which we stand, and rejoice in hope of the glory of God.

God being their Lord.

Ps 144:15 Happy *are* the people who are in such a state; Happy *are* the people whose God *is* the LORD!

God being their help.

Ps 146:5 Happy *is* he who *has* the God of Jacob for his help, Whose hope *is* in the LORD his God,

Praising God.

Ps 135:3 Praise the LORD, for the LORD *is* good; Sing praises to His name, for *it is* pleasant.

Their mutual love.

Ps 133:1 Behold, how good and how pleasant *it is* For brethren to dwell together in unity!

Divine chastening.

Job 5:17 "Behold, happy *is* the man whom God corrects; Therefore do not despise the chastening of the Almighty.

James 5:11 Indeed we count them blessed who endure. You have heard of the perseverance of Job and seen the end *intended by* the Lord—that the Lord is very compassionate and merciful.

Suffering for Christ.

2 Cor 12:10 Therefore I take pleasure in infirmities, in reproaches, in needs, in persecutions, in distresses, for Christ's sake. For when I am weak, then I am strong.

1 Pet 3:14 But even if you should suffer for righteousness' sake, *you are* blessed. *"And do not be afraid of their threats, nor be troubled."*

1 Pet 4:13–14 but rejoice to the extent that you partake of Christ's sufferings, that when His glory is revealed, you may also be glad with exceeding joy. **14** If you are reproached for the name of Christ, blessed *are* you, for the Spirit of glory and of God rests upon you. On their part He is blasphemed, but on your part He is glorified.

Having mercy on the poor.

Prov 14:21 He who despises his neighbor sins; But he who has mercy on the poor, happy *is* he.

Finding wisdom.

Prov 3:13 Happy *is* the man *who* finds wisdom, And the man *who* gains understanding;

Is abundant and satisfying.

Ps 36:8 They are abundantly satisfied with the fullness of Your house, And You give them drink from the river of Your pleasures.

Ps 63:5 My soul shall be satisfied as with marrow and fatness, And my mouth shall praise You with joyful lips.

BELIEVERS, TITLES AND NAMES OF

Believers.

Acts 5:14 And believers were increasingly added to the Lord, multitudes of both men and women,

1 Tim 4:12 Let no one despise your youth, but be an example to the believers in word, in conduct, in love, in spirit, in faith, in purity.

Beloved of God.

Rom 1:7 To all who are in Rome, beloved of God, called *to be* saints: Grace to you and peace from God our Father and the Lord Jesus Christ.

Beloved brethren.

1 Cor 15:58 Therefore, my beloved brethren, be steadfast, immovable, always abounding in the work of the Lord, knowing that your labor is not in vain in the Lord.

James 2:5 Listen, my beloved brethren: Has God not chosen the poor of this world *to be* rich in faith and heirs of the kingdom which He promised to those who love Him?

Blessed of the Lord.

Gen 24:31 And he said, "Come in, O blessed of the Lord! Why do you stand outside? For I have prepared the house, and a place for the camels."

Gen 26:29 that you will do us no harm, since we have not touched you, and since we have done nothing to you but good and have sent you away in peace. You *are* now the blessed of the Lord.' "

Blessed of the Father.

Matt 25:34 Then the King will say to those on His right hand, 'Come, you blessed of My Father, inherit the kingdom prepared for you from the foundation of the world:

Brethren, brothers.

Matt 23:8 But you, do not be called 'Rabbi'; for One is your Teacher, the Christ, and you are all brethren.

Luke 8:21 But He answered and said to them, "My mother and My brothers are these who hear the word of God and do it."

John 20:17 Jesus said to her, "Do not cling to Me, for I have not yet ascended to My Father; but go to My brethren and say to them, 'I am ascending to My Father and your Father, and *to* My God and your God.' "

Acts 12:17 But motioning to them with his hand to keep silent, he declared to them how the Lord had brought him out of the prison. And he said, "Go, tell these things to James and to the brethren." And he departed and went to another place.

Called of Jesus Christ.

Rom 1:6 among whom you also are the called of Jesus Christ;

Children of the Lord.

Deut 14:1 "You *are* the children of the Lord your God; you shall not cut yourselves nor shave the front of your head for the dead.

Children of God.

John 1:12 But as many as received Him, to them He gave the right to become children of God, to those who believe in His name:

John 11:52 and not for that nation only, but also that He would gather together in one the children of God who were scattered abroad.

Phil 2:15 that you may become blameless and harmless, children of God without fault in the midst of a crooked and perverse generation, among whom you shine as lights in the world,

1 John 3:1–2 Behold what manner of love the Father has bestowed on us, that we should be called children of God! Therefore the world does not know us, because it did not know Him. **2** Beloved, now we are children of God; and it has not yet been revealed what we shall be, but we know that when He is revealed, we shall be like Him, for we shall see Him as He is.

1 John 3:10 In this the children of God and the children of the devil are manifest: Whoever does not practice righteousness is not of God, nor *is* he who does not love his brother.

Sons of the living God.

Rom 9:26 *"And it shall come to pass in the place where it was said to them, 'You are not My people,' There they shall be called sons of the living God."*

Sons of the Father.

Matt 5:45 that you may be sons of your Father in heaven; for He makes His sun rise on the evil and on the good, and sends rain on the just and on the unjust.

Sons of the Most High.

Luke 6:35 But love your enemies, do good, and lend, hoping for nothing in return; and your reward will be great, and you will be sons of the Most High. For He is kind to the unthankful and evil.

Sons of Abraham.

Gal 3:7 Therefore know that *only* those who are of faith are sons of Abraham.

Children of Jacob.

Ps 105:6 O seed of Abraham His servant, You children of Jacob, His chosen ones!

Children of promise.

Rom 9:8 That is, those who *are* the children of the flesh, these *are* not the children of God; but the children of the promise are counted as the seed.

Gal 4:28 Now we, brethren, as Isaac *was*, are children of promise.

Children of the free woman.

Gal 4:31 So then, brethren, we are not children of the bondwoman but of the free.

Sons of the kingdom.

Matt 13:38 The field is the world, the good seeds are the sons of the kingdom, but the tares are the sons of the wicked *one*.

Children of Zion.

Ps 149:2 Let Israel rejoice in their Maker; Let the children of Zion be joyful in their King.

Joel 2:23 Be glad then, you children of Zion, And rejoice in the Lord your God; For He has given you the former rain faithfully, And He will cause the rain to come down for you— The former rain, And the latter rain in the first *month*.

Friends of the bridegroom.

Matt 9:15 And Jesus said to them, "Can the friends of

the bridegroom mourn as long as the bridegroom is with them? But the days will come when the bridegroom will be taken away from them, and then they will fast.

Children of light.

Eph 5:8 For you were once darkness, but now *you are* light in the Lord. Walk as children of light

Sons of light and day.

Luke 16:8 So the master commended the unjust steward because he had dealt shrewdly. For the sons of this world are more shrewd in their generation than the sons of light.

1 Thess 5:5 You are all sons of light and sons of the day. We are not of the night nor of darkness.

Sons of the resurrection.

Luke 20:36 nor can they die anymore, for they are equal to the angels and are sons of God, being sons of the resurrection.

Chosen generation.

1 Pet 2:9 But you *are* a chosen generation, a royal priesthood, a holy nation, His own special people, that you may proclaim the praises of Him who called you out of darkness into His marvelous light;

Chosen ones.

1 Chr 16:13 O seed of Israel His servant, You children of Jacob, His chosen ones!

Chosen vessels.

Acts 9:15 But the Lord said to him, "Go, for he is a chosen vessel of Mine to bear My name before Gentiles, kings, and the children of Israel.

Christians.

Acts 11:26 And when he had found him, he brought him to Antioch. So it was that for a whole year they assembled with the church and taught a great many people. And the disciples were first called Christians in Antioch.

Acts 26:28 Then Agrippa said to Paul, "You almost persuade me to become a Christian."

Dear children.

Eph 5:1 Therefore be imitators of God as dear children.

Disciples of Christ.

John 8:31 Then Jesus said to those Jews who believed Him, "If you abide in My word, you are My disciples indeed.

John 15:8 By this My Father is glorified, that you bear much fruit; so you will be My disciples.

Elect of God.

Col 3:12 Therefore, as *the* elect of God, holy and beloved, put on tender mercies, kindness, humility, meekness, longsuffering;

Titus 1:1 Paul, a bondservant of God and an apostle of Jesus Christ, according to the faith of God's elect and the acknowledgment of the truth which accords with godliness,

Epistles of Christ.

2 Cor 3:3 clearly *you are* an epistle of Christ, ministered by us, written not with ink but by the Spirit of the living God, not on tablets of stone but on tablets of flesh, *that is,* of the heart.

Excellent ones.

Ps 16:3 As for the saints who *are* on the earth, "They are the excellent ones, in whom is all my delight."

Faithful brethren in Christ.

Col 1:2 To the saints and faithful brethren in Christ *who are* in Colosse: Grace to you and peace from God our Father and the Lord Jesus Christ.

Faithful, The.

Ps 12:1 Help, LORD, for the godly man ceases! For the faithful disappear from among the sons of men.

Faithful of the land.

Ps 101:6 My eyes *shall be* on the faithful of the land, That they may dwell with me; He who walks in a perfect way, He shall serve me.

Fellow citizens with the saints.

Eph 2:19 Now, therefore, you are no longer strangers and foreigners, but fellow citizens with the saints and members of the household of God,

Fellow heirs.

Eph 3:6 that the Gentiles should be fellow heirs, of the same body, and partakers of His promise in Christ through the gospel,

Fellow servants.

Rev 6:11 Then a white robe was given to each of them; and it was said to them that they should rest a little while longer, until both *the number of* their fellow servants and their brethren, who would be killed as they *were,* was completed.

Friends of God.

2 Chr 20:7 *Are* You not our God, *who* drove out the inhabitants of this land before Your people Israel, and gave it to the descendants of Abraham Your friend forever?

James 2:23 And the Scripture was fulfilled which says, *"Abraham believed God, and it was accounted to him for righteousness."* And he was called the friend of God.

Friends of Christ.

John 15:15 No longer do I call you servants, for a servant does not know what his master is doing; but I have called you friends, for all things that I heard from My Father I have made known to you.

Godly, The.

Ps 4:3 But know that the LORD has set apart for Himself him who is godly; The LORD will hear when I call to Him.

2 Pet 2:9 *then* the Lord knows how to deliver the godly out of temptations and to reserve the unjust under punishment for the day of judgment,

Heirs of God.

Rom 8:17 and if children, then heirs—heirs of God and joint heirs with Christ, if indeed we suffer with *Him,* that we may also be glorified together.

Gal 4:7 Therefore you are no longer a slave but a son, and if a son, then an heir of God through Christ.

Heirs of the grace of life.

1 Pet 3:7 Husbands, likewise, dwell with *them* with understanding, giving honor to the wife, as to the weaker vessel, and as *being* heirs together of the grace of life, that your prayers may not be hindered.

Heirs of the kingdom.

James 2:5 Listen, my beloved brethren: Has God not chosen the poor of this world *to be* rich in faith and heirs of the kingdom which He promised to those who love Him?

Heirs of promise.

Heb 6:17 Thus God, determining to show more abundantly to the heirs of promise the immutability of His counsel, confirmed *it* by an oath,

Gal 3:29 And if you *are* Christ's, then you are Abraham's seed, and heirs according to the promise.

Heirs of salvation.

Heb 1:14 Are they not all ministering spirits sent forth to minister for those who will inherit salvation?

Holy brethren.

1 Thess 5:27 I charge you by the Lord that this epistle be read to all the holy brethren.

Heb 3:1 Therefore, holy brethren, partakers of the heavenly calling, consider the Apostle and High Priest of our confession, Christ Jesus,

Holy nation.

Ex 19:6 And you shall be to Me a kingdom of priests and a holy nation.' These *are* the words which you shall speak to the children of Israel."

1 Pet 2:9 But you *are* a chosen generation, a royal priesthood, a holy nation, His own special people, that you may proclaim the praises of Him who called you out of darkness into His marvelous light;

Holy people.

Deut 26:19 and that He will set you high above all nations which He has made, in praise, in name, and in honor, and that you may be a holy people to the LORD your God, just as He has spoken."

Is 62:12 And they shall call them The Holy People, The Redeemed of the LORD; And you shall be called Sought Out, A City Not Forsaken.

Holy priesthood.

1 Pet 2:5 you also, as living stones, are being built up a spiritual house, a holy priesthood, to offer up spiritual sacrifices acceptable to God through Jesus Christ.

Joint heirs with Christ.

Rom 8:17 and if children, then heirs—heirs of God and joint heirs with Christ, if indeed we suffer with *Him,* that we may also be glorified together.

Just, The.

Hab 2:4 "Behold the proud, His soul is not upright in him; But the just shall live by his faith.

Kings and priests to God.

Rev 1:6 and has made us kings and priests to His God and Father, to Him *be* glory and dominion forever and ever. Amen.

Kingdom of priests.

Ex 19:6 And you shall be to Me a kingdom of priests and a holy nation.' These *are* the words which you shall speak to the children of Israel."

Lambs.

Is 40:11 He will feed His flock like a shepherd; He will gather the lambs with His arm, And carry *them* in His bosom, *And* gently lead those who are with young.

John 21:15

So when they had eaten breakfast, Jesus said to Simon Peter, "Simon, *son* of Jonah, do you love Me more than these?" He said to Him, "Yes, Lord; You know that I love You." He said to him, "Feed My lambs."

Lights of the world.

Matt 5:14 "You are the light of the world. A city that is set on a hill cannot be hidden.

Little children.

John 13:33 Little children, I shall be with you a little while longer. You will seek Me; and as I said to the Jews, 'Where I am going, you cannot come,' so now I say to you.

1 John 2:1 My little children, these things I write to you, so that you may not sin. And if anyone sins, we have an Advocate with the Father, Jesus Christ the righteous.

Living stones.

1 Pet 2:5 you also, as living stones, are being built up a spiritual house, a holy priesthood, to offer up spiritual sacrifices acceptable to God through Jesus Christ.

Members of Christ.

1 Cor 6:15 Do you not know that your bodies are members of Christ? Shall I then take the members of Christ and make *them* members of a harlot? Certainly not!

Eph 5:30 For we are members of His body, of His flesh and of His bones.

Men of God.

Deut 33:1 Now this *is* the blessing with which Moses the man of God blessed the children of Israel before his death.

1 Tim 6:11 But you, O man of God, flee these things and pursue righteousness, godliness, faith, love, patience, gentleness.

2 Tim 3:17 that the man of God may be complete, thoroughly equipped for every good work.

Obedient children.

1 Pet 1:14 as obedient children, not conforming yourselves to the former lusts, *as* in your ignorance;

Special people.

Deut 14:2 For you *are* a holy people to the LORD your God, and the LORD has chosen you to be a people for Himself, a special treasure above all the peoples who *are* on the face of the earth.

Titus 2:14 who gave Himself for us, that He might redeem us from every lawless deed and purify for Himself *His* own special people, zealous for good works.

1 Pet 2:9 But you *are* a chosen generation, a royal priesthood, a holy nation, His own special people, that you may proclaim the praises of Him who called you out of darkness into His marvelous light;

Special treasure.

Ex 19:5 Now therefore, if you will indeed obey My voice and keep My covenant, then you shall be a special treasure to Me above all people; for all the earth *is* Mine.

Ps 135:4 For the LORD has chosen Jacob for Himself, Israel for His special treasure.

People of God.

Heb 4:9 There remains therefore a rest for the people of God.

1 Pet 2:10 who once *were* not a people but *are* now the people of God, who had not obtained mercy but now have obtained mercy.

People near to God.

Ps 148:14 And He has exalted the horn of His people, The praise of all His saints— Of the children of Israel, A people near to Him. Praise the Lord!

People saved by the Lord.

Deut 33:29 Happy *are* you, O Israel! Who *is* like you, a people saved by the Lord, The shield of your help And the sword of your majesty! Your enemies shall submit to you, And you shall tread down their high places."

Pillars in the temple of God.

Rev 3:12 He who overcomes, I will make him a pillar in the temple of My God, and he shall go out no more. I will write on him the name of My God and the name of the city of My God, the New Jerusalem, which comes down out of heaven from My God. And *I will write on him* My new name.

Is 35:10 And the ransomed of the Lord shall return, And come to Zion with singing, With everlasting joy on their heads. They shall obtain joy and gladness, And sorrow and sighing shall flee away.

Redeemed of the Lord.

Is 51:11 So the ransomed of the Lord shall return, And come to Zion with singing, With everlasting joy on their heads. They shall obtain joy and gladness; Sorrow and sighing shall flee away.

Royal priesthood.

1 Pet 2:9 But you *are* a chosen generation, a royal priesthood, a holy nation, His own special people, that you may proclaim the praises of Him who called you out of darkness into His marvelous light;

Salt of the earth.

Matt 5:13 "You are the salt of the earth; but if the salt loses its flavor, how shall it be seasoned? It is then good for nothing but to be thrown out and trampled underfoot by men.

Servants (slaves) of Christ.

1 Cor 7:22 For he who is called in the Lord *while* a slave is the Lord's freedman. Likewise he who is called *while* free is Christ's slave.

Eph 6:6 not with eyeservice, as men-pleasers, but as bondservants of Christ, doing the will of God from the heart,

Slaves of righteousness.

Rom 6:18 And having been set free from sin, you became slaves of righteousness.

Sheep of Christ.

John 10:1–16 "Most assuredly, I say to you, he who does not enter the sheepfold by the door, but climbs up some other way, the same is a thief and a robber. 2 But he who enters by the door is the shepherd of the sheep. 3 To him the doorkeeper opens, and the sheep hear his voice; and he calls his own sheep by name and leads them out. 4 And when he brings out his own sheep, he goes before them; and the sheep follow him, for they know his voice. 5 Yet they will by no means follow a stranger, but will flee from him, for they do not know the voice of strangers." 6 Jesus used this illustration, but they did not understand the things which He spoke to them. 7 Then Jesus said to them again, "Most assuredly, I say to you, I am the door of the sheep. 8 All who *ever* came before Me are thieves and robbers, but the sheep did not hear them. 9 I am the door. If anyone enters by Me, he will be saved, and will go in and out and find pasture. 10 The thief does not come except to steal, and to kill, and to destroy. I have come that they may have life, and that they may have *it* more abundantly. 11 "I am the good shepherd. The good shepherd gives His life for the sheep. 12 But a hireling, *he who is* not the shepherd, one who does not own the sheep, sees the wolf coming and leaves the sheep and flees; and the wolf catches the sheep and scatters them. 13 The hireling flees because he is a hireling and does not care about the sheep. 14 I am the good shepherd; and I know My *sheep*, and am known by My own. 15 As the Father knows Me, even so I know the Father; and I lay down My life for the sheep. 16 And other sheep I have which are not of this fold; them also I must bring, and they will hear My voice; and there will be one flock *and* one shepherd.

John 21:16 He said to him again a second time, "Simon, *son* of Jonah, do you love Me?" He said to Him, "Yes, Lord; You know that I love You." He said to him, "Tend My sheep."

Sojourners with God.

Lev 25:23 'The land shall not be sold permanently, for the land *is* Mine; for you *are* strangers and sojourners with Me.

Ps 39:12 "Hear my prayer, O Lord, And give ear to my cry; Do not be silent at my tears; For I *am* a stranger with You, A sojourner, as all my fathers *were*.

The Lord's freemen.

1 Cor 7:22 For he who is called in the Lord *while* a slave is the Lord's freedman. Likewise he who is called *while* free is Christ's slave.

Trees of righteousness.

Is 61:3 To console those who mourn in Zion, To give them beauty for ashes, The oil of joy for mourning, The garment of praise for the spirit of heaviness; That they may be called trees of righteousness, The planting of the Lord, that He may be glorified."

Vessels to honor.

2 Tim 2:21 Therefore if anyone cleanses himself from the latter, he will be a vessel for honor, sanctified and useful for the Master, prepared for every good work.

Vessels of mercy.

Rom 9:23 and that He might make known the riches of His glory on the vessels of mercy, which He had prepared beforehand for glory,

Witnesses for God.

Is 44:8 Do not fear, nor be afraid; Have I not told you from that time, and declared *it*? You *are* My witnesses. Is there a God besides Me? Indeed *there is* no other Rock; I know not *one*.' "

BELIEVERS, WARFARE OF

Is not after the flesh.

2 Cor 10:3 For though we walk in the flesh, we do not war according to the flesh.

Is called good.

1 Tim 1:18–19 This charge I commit to you, son Timothy, according to the prophecies previously made concerning you, that by them you may wage the good warfare, **19** having faith and a good conscience, which some having rejected, concerning the faith have suffered shipwreck,

Is called the good fight of faith.

1 Tim 6:12 Fight the good fight of faith, lay hold on eternal life, to which you were also called and have confessed the good confession in the presence of many witnesses.

Is against

The devil.

Gen 3:15 And I will put enmity Between you and the woman, And between your seed and her Seed; He shall bruise your head, And you shall bruise His heel."

2 Cor 2:11 lest Satan should take advantage of us; for we are not ignorant of his devices.

Eph 6:12 For we do not wrestle against flesh and blood, but against principalities, against powers, against the rulers of the darkness of this age, against spiritual *hosts* of wickedness in the heavenly *places*.

James 4:7 Therefore submit to God. Resist the devil and he will flee from you.

1 Pet 5:8 Be sober, be vigilant; because your adversary the devil walks about like a roaring lion, seeking whom he may devour.

Rev 12:17 And the dragon was enraged with the woman, and he went to make war with the rest of her offspring, who keep the commandments of God and have the testimony of Jesus Christ.

The flesh.

Rom 7:23 But I see another law in my members, warring against the law of my mind, and bringing me into captivity to the law of sin which is in my members.

1 Cor 9:25–27 And everyone who competes *for the prize* is temperate in all things. Now they *do it* to obtain a perishable crown, but we *for* an imperishable *crown*. **26** Therefore I run thus: not with uncertainty. Thus I fight: not as *one who* beats the air. **27** But I discipline my body and bring *it* into subjection, lest, when I have preached to others, I myself should become disqualified.

Gal 5:17 For the flesh lusts against the Spirit, and the Spirit against the flesh; and these are contrary to one another, so that you do not do the things that you wish.

1 Pet 2:11 Beloved, I beg *you* as sojourners and pilgrims, abstain from fleshly lusts which war against the soul,

Enemies.

Ps 38:19 But my enemies *are* vigorous, *and* they are strong; And those who hate me wrongfully have multiplied.

Ps 56:2 My enemies would hound *me* all day, For *there are* many who fight against me, O Most High.

Ps 59:3 For look, they lie in wait for my life; The mighty gather against me, Not *for* my transgression nor *for* my sin, O LORD.

The world.

John 16:33 These things I have spoken to you, that in Me you may have peace. In the world you will have tribulation; but be of good cheer, I have overcome the world."

1 John 5:4–5 For whatever is born of God overcomes the world. And this is the victory that has overcome the world—our faith. **5** Who is he who overcomes the world, but he who believes that Jesus is the Son of God?

Death.

1 Cor 15:26 The last enemy *that* will be destroyed *is* death.

Heb 2:14–15 Inasmuch then as the children have partaken of flesh and blood, He Himself likewise shared in the same, that through death He might destroy him who had the power of death, that is, the devil, **15** and release those who through fear of death were all their lifetime subject to bondage.

Often arises from the opposition of friends or relatives.

Mic 7:6 For son dishonors father, Daughter rises against her mother, Daughter-in-law against her mother-in-law; A man's enemies *are* the men of his own household.

Matt 10:35–36 For I have come to *'set a man against his father, a daughter against her mother, and a daughter-in-law against her mother-in-law'*; **36** and *'a man's enemies will be those of his own household.'*

To be carried on

Under Christ, as our captain.

Heb 2:10 For it was fitting for Him, for whom *are* all things and by whom *are* all things, in bringing many sons to glory, to make the captain of their salvation perfect through sufferings.

Under the Lord's banner.

Ps 60:4 You have given a banner to those who fear You, That it may be displayed because of the truth. Selah

With faith and a good conscience.

1 Tim 1:18–19 This charge I commit to you, son Timothy, according to the prophecies previously made concerning you, that by them you may wage the good warfare, **19** having faith and a good conscience, which some having rejected, concerning the faith have suffered shipwreck,

With steadfastness in the faith.

1 Cor 16:13 Watch, stand fast in the faith, be brave, be strong.

Heb 10:23 Let us hold fast the confession of *our* hope without wavering, for He who promised *is* faithful.

1 Pet 5:9 Resist him, steadfast in the faith, knowing that the same sufferings are experienced by your brotherhood in the world.

With earnestness.

Jude 1:3 Beloved, while I was very diligent to write to you concerning our common salvation, I found it necessary to write to you exhorting you to contend earnestly for the faith which was once for all delivered to the saints.

With watchfulness.

1 Cor 16:13 Watch, stand fast in the faith, be brave, be strong.

1 Pet 5:8 Be sober, be vigilant; because your adversary the devil walks about like a roaring lion, seeking whom he may devour.

With sobriety.

1 Thess 5:6 Therefore let us not sleep, as others *do,* but let us watch and be sober.

1 Pet 5:8 Be sober, be vigilant; because your adversary the devil walks about like a roaring lion, seeking whom he may devour.

With endurance.

2 Tim 2:3 You therefore must endure hardship as a good soldier of Jesus Christ.

2 Tim 2:10 Therefore I endure all things for the sake of the elect, that they also may obtain the salvation which is in Christ Jesus with eternal glory.

With self-denial.

1 Cor 9:25–27 And everyone who competes *for the prize* is temperate in all things. Now they *do it* to obtain a perishable crown, but we *for* an imperishable *crown.* **26** Therefore I run thus: not with uncertainty. Thus I fight: not as *one who* beats the air. **27** But I discipline my body and bring *it* into subjection, lest, when I have preached to others, I myself should become disqualified.

With confidence in God.

Ps 27:1–3 The LORD *is* my light and my salvation; Whom shall I fear? The LORD *is* the strength of my life; Of whom shall I be afraid? **2** When the wicked came against me To eat up my flesh, My enemies and foes, They stumbled and fell. **3** Though an army may encamp against me, My heart shall not fear; Though war may rise against me, In this I *will be* confident.

With prayer.

Ps 35:1–3 Plead *my cause,* O LORD, with those who strive with me; Fight against those who fight against me. **2** Take hold of shield and buckler, And stand up for my help. **3** Also draw out the spear, And stop those who pursue me. Say to my soul, "I *am* your salvation."

Eph 6:18 praying always with all prayer and supplication in the Spirit, being watchful to this end with all perseverance and supplication for all the saints—

Without earthly entanglements.

2 Tim 2:4 No one engaged in warfare entangles himself with the affairs of *this* life, that he may please him who enlisted him as a soldier.

Mere professors do not maintain.

Jer 9:3 "And *like* their bow they have bent their tongues *for* lies. They are not valiant for the truth on the earth. For they proceed from evil to evil, And they do not know Me," says the LORD.

Are all engaged in.

Phil 1:30 having the same conflict which you saw in me and now hear *is* in me.

Must stand firm in.

Eph 6:13–14 Therefore take up the whole armor of God,

that you may be able to withstand in the evil day, and having done all, to stand. **14** Stand therefore, having girded your waist with truth, having put on the breastplate of righteousness,

Exhorted to diligence.

1 Tim 6:12 Fight the good fight of faith, lay hold on eternal life, to which you were also called and have confessed the good confession in the presence of many witnesses.

Jude 1:3 Beloved, while I was very diligent to write to you concerning our common salvation, I found it necessary to write to you exhorting you to contend earnestly for the faith which was once for all delivered to the saints.

Encouraged in.

Is 41:11–12 "Behold, all those who were incensed against you Shall be ashamed and disgraced; They shall be as nothing, And those who strive with you shall perish. **12** You shall seek them and not find them— Those who contended with you. Those who war against you Shall be as nothing, As a nonexistent thing.

Is 51:12 "I, *even* I, *am* He who comforts you. Who *are* you that you should be afraid Of a man *who* will die, And of the son of a man *who* will be made like grass?

Mic 7:8 Do not rejoice over me, my enemy; When I fall, I will arise; When I sit in darkness, The LORD *will be* a light to me.

1 John 4:4 You are of God, little children, and have overcome them, because He who is in you is greater than he who is in the world.

Helped by God in.

Ps 20:2 May He send you help from the sanctuary, And strengthen you out of Zion;

Ps 27:14 Wait on the LORD; Be of good courage, And He shall strengthen your heart; Wait, I say, on the LORD!

Ps 118:13 You pushed me violently, that I might fall, But the LORD helped me.

Ps 140:7 O GOD the Lord, the strength of my salvation, You have covered my head in the day of battle.

Is 41:10 Fear not, for I *am* with you; Be not dismayed, for I *am* your God. I will strengthen you, Yes, I will help you, I will uphold you with My righteous right hand.'

Is 41:13–14 For I, the LORD your God, will hold your right hand, Saying to you, 'Fear not, I will help you.' **14** "Fear not, you worm Jacob, You men of Israel! I will help you," says the LORD And your Redeemer, the Holy One of Israel.

2 Cor 7:5–6 For indeed, when we came to Macedonia, our bodies had no rest, but we were troubled on every side. Outside *were* conflicts, inside *were* fears. **6** Nevertheless God, who comforts the downcast, comforted us by the coming of Titus,

Strengthened by Christ in.

2 Cor 12:9 And He said to me, "My grace is sufficient for you, for My strength is made perfect in weakness." Therefore most gladly I will rather boast in my infirmities, that the power of Christ may rest upon me.

2 Tim 4:17 But the Lord stood with me and strengthened me, so that the message might be preached fully through me, and *that* all the Gentiles might hear. Also I was delivered out of the mouth of the lion.

Delivered by Christ in.

2 Tim 4:18 And the Lord will deliver me from every evil work and preserve *me* for His heavenly kingdom. To Him *be* glory forever and ever. Amen!

Thank God for victory in.

Rom 7:25 I thank God—through Jesus Christ our Lord! So then, with the mind I myself serve the law of God, but with the flesh the law of sin.

1 Cor 15:57 But thanks *be* to God, who gives us the victory through our Lord Jesus Christ.

2 Cor 2:14 Now thanks *be* to God who always leads us in triumph in Christ, and through us diffuses the fragrance of His knowledge in every place.

Armor for,

Girdle of truth.

Eph 6:14 Stand therefore, having girded your waist with truth, having put on the breastplate of righteousness,

Breastplate of righteousness.

Eph 6:14 Stand therefore, having girded your waist with truth, having put on the breastplate of righteousness,

Preparation of the gospel.

Eph 6:15 and having shod your feet with the preparation of the gospel of peace;

Shield of faith.

Eph 6:16 above all, taking the shield of faith with which you will be able to quench all the fiery darts of the wicked one.

Helmet of salvation.

Eph 6:17 And take the helmet of salvation, and the sword of the Spirit, which is the word of God;

1 Thess 5:8 But let us who are of the day be sober, putting on the breastplate of faith and love, and *as* a helmet the hope of salvation.

Sword of the Spirit.

Eph 6:17 And take the helmet of salvation, and the sword of the Spirit, which is the word of God;

Not carnal.

2 Cor 10:4 For the weapons of our warfare *are* not carnal but mighty in God for pulling down strongholds,

Mighty through God.

2 Cor 10:4–5 For the weapons of our warfare *are* not carnal but mighty in God for pulling down strongholds, **5** casting down arguments and every high thing that exalts itself against the knowledge of God, bringing every thought into captivity to the obedience of Christ,

The whole, is required.

Eph 6:13 Therefore take up the whole armor of God, that you may be able to withstand in the evil day, and having done all, to stand.

Victory in, is

Through Christ.

Rom 7:25 I thank God—through Jesus Christ our Lord! So then, with the mind I myself serve the law of God, but with the flesh the law of sin.

1 Cor 15:27 For *"He has put all things under His feet."* But when He says "all things are put under *Him*," *it is* evident that He who put all things under Him is excepted.

2 Cor 12:9 And He said to me, "My grace is sufficient for you, for My strength is made perfect in weakness." Therefore most gladly I will rather boast in my infirmities, that the power of Christ may rest upon me.

Rev 12:11 And they overcame him by the blood of the Lamb and by the word of their testimony, and they did not love their lives to the death.

By faith.

Heb 11:33–37 who through faith subdued kingdoms, worked righteousness, obtained promises, stopped the mouths of lions, **34** quenched the violence of fire, escaped the edge of the sword, out of weakness were made strong, became valiant in battle, turned to flight the armies of the aliens. **35** Women received their dead raised to life again. Others were tortured, not accepting deliverance, that they might obtain a better resurrection. **36** Still others had trial of mockings and scourgings, yes, and of chains and imprisonment. **37** They were stoned, they were sawn in two, were tempted, were slain with the sword. They wandered about in sheepskins and goatskins, being destitute, afflicted, tormented—

1 John 5:4–5 For whatever is born of God overcomes the world. And this is the victory that has overcome the world—our faith. **5** Who is he who overcomes the world, but he who believes that Jesus is the Son of God?

Over the devil.

Rom 16:20 And the God of peace will crush Satan under your feet shortly. The grace of our Lord Jesus Christ *be* with you. Amen.

1 John 2:14 I have written to you, fathers, Because you have known Him *who is* from the beginning. I have written to you, young men, Because you are strong, and the word of God abides in you, And you have overcome the wicked one.

Over the flesh.

Rom 7:24–25 O wretched man that I am! Who will deliver me from this body of death? **25** I thank God—through Jesus Christ our Lord! So then, with the mind I myself serve the law of God, but with the flesh the law of sin.

Gal 5:24 And those *who are* Christ's have crucified the flesh with its passions and desires.

Over the world.

1 John 5:4–5 For whatever is born of God overcomes the world. And this is the victory that has overcome the world—our faith. **5** Who is he who overcomes the world, but he who believes that Jesus is the Son of God?

Over all that exalts itself.

2 Cor 10:5 casting down arguments and every high thing that exalts itself against the knowledge of God, bringing every thought into captivity to the obedience of Christ,

Over death and the grave.

Is 25:8 He will swallow up death forever, And the Lord GOD will wipe away tears from all faces; The rebuke

of His people He will take away from all the earth;
For the LORD has spoken.

Is 26:19 Your dead shall live; *Together with* my dead body they shall arise. Awake and sing, you who dwell in dust; For your dew *is like* the dew of herbs, And the earth shall cast out the dead.

Hos 13:14 "I will ransom them from the power of the grave; I will redeem them from death. O Death, I will be your plagues! O Grave, I will be your destruction! Pity is hidden from My eyes."

1 Cor 15:54–55 So when this corruptible has put on incorruption, and this mortal has put on immortality, then shall be brought to pass the saying that is written: *"Death is swallowed up in victory."* **55** *"O Death, where is your sting? O Hades, where is your victory?"*

All-encompassing.

Rom 8:37 Yet in all these things we are more than conquerors through Him who loved us.

2 Cor 10:5 casting down arguments and every high thing that exalts itself against the knowledge of God, bringing every thought into captivity to the obedience of Christ,

They who overcome in, shall

Eat of the hidden manna.

Rev 2:17 "He who has an ear, let him hear what the Spirit says to the churches. To him who overcomes I will give some of the hidden manna to eat. And I will give him a white stone, and on the stone a new name written which no one knows except him who receives *it.*" '

Eat of the tree of life.

Rev 2:7 "He who has an ear, let him hear what the Spirit says to the churches. To him who overcomes I will give to eat from the tree of life, which is in the midst of the Paradise of God." '

Be clothed in white raiment.

Rev 3:5 He who overcomes shall be clothed in white garments, and I will not blot out his name from the Book of Life; but I will confess his name before My Father and before His angels.

Be pillars in the temple of God.

Rev 3:12 He who overcomes, I will make him a pillar in the temple of My God, and he shall go out no more. I will write on him the name of My God and the name of the city of My God, the New Jerusalem, which comes down out of heaven from My God. And *I will write on him* My new name.

Sit with Christ on his throne.

Rev 3:21 To him who overcomes I will grant to sit with Me on My throne, as I also overcame and sat down with My Father on His throne.

Have a white stone and, in it, a new name written.

Rev 2:17 "He who has an ear, let him hear what the Spirit says to the churches. To him who overcomes I will give some of the hidden manna to eat. And I will give him a white stone, and on the stone a new name written which no one knows except him who receives *it.*" '

Have power over the nations.

Rev 2:26 And he who overcomes, and keeps My works until the end, to him I will give power over the nations—

Have the name of God written upon them by Christ.

Rev 3:12 He who overcomes, I will make him a pillar in the temple of My God, and he shall go out no more. I will write on him the name of My God and the name of the city of My God, the New Jerusalem, which comes down out of heaven from My God. And *I will write on him* My new name.

Have God as their God.

Rev 21:7 He who overcomes shall inherit all things, and I will be his God and he shall be My son.

Have the morning star.

Rev 2:28 and I will give him the morning star.

Inherit all things.

Rev 21:7 He who overcomes shall inherit all things, and I will be his God and he shall be My son.

Be confessed by Christ before God the Father.

Rev 3:5 He who overcomes shall be clothed in white garments, and I will not blot out his name from the Book of Life; but I will confess his name before My Father and before His angels.

Be sons of God.

Rev 21:7 He who overcomes shall inherit all things, and I will be his God and he shall be My son.

Not be hurt by the second death.

Rev 2:11 "He who has an ear, let him hear what the Spirit says to the churches. He who overcomes shall not be hurt by the second death." '

Not have their names blotted out of the Book of Life.

Rev 3:5 He who overcomes shall be clothed in white garments, and I will not blot out his name from the Book of Life; but I will confess his name before My Father and before His angels.

Illustrated.

Is 9:5 For every warrior's sandal from the noisy battle, And garments rolled in blood, Will be used for burning *and* fuel of fire.

Zech 10:5 They shall be like mighty men, Who tread down *their enemies* In the mire of the streets in the battle. They shall fight because the LORD is with them, And the riders on horses shall be put to shame.

BELOVED

Described David's feelings toward Saul and Jonathan.

2 Sam 1:23 "Saul and Jonathan *were* beloved and pleasant in their lives, And in their death they were not divided; They were swifter than eagles, They were stronger than lions.

Probable reference to David.

Ps 60:5 That Your beloved may be delivered, Save *with* Your right hand, and hear me.

Term of endearment in marriage.

Song 2:16 My beloved *is* mine, and I *am* his. He feeds *his* flock among the lilies.

Song 7:10 I *am* my beloved's, And his desire *is* toward me.

Described God's love

For Israel.

Jer 11:15 "What has My beloved to do in My house,

Having done lewd deeds with many? And the holy flesh has passed from you. When you do evil, then you rejoice.

Jer 12:7 "I have forsaken My house, I have left My heritage; I have given the dearly beloved of My soul into the hand of her enemies.

For Jesus Christ.

Matt 3:17 And suddenly a voice *came* from heaven, saying, "This is My beloved Son, in whom I am well pleased."

Mark 9:7 And a cloud came and overshadowed them; and a voice came out of the cloud, saying, "This is My beloved Son. Hear Him!"

Luke 9:35 And a voice came out of the cloud, saying, "This is My beloved Son. Hear Him!"

Cf. Mark 12:6; Luke 3:22; 20:13; 2 Pet 1:17

Synonym for believers.

Rom 1:7 To all who are in Rome, beloved of God, called *to be* saints: Grace to you and peace from God our Father and the Lord Jesus Christ.

Col 3:12 Therefore, as *the* elect of God, holy and beloved, put on tender mercies, kindness, humility, meekness, longsuffering;

Heb 6:9 But, beloved, we are confident of better things concerning you, yes, things that accompany salvation, though we speak in this manner.

James 1:16 Do not be deceived, my beloved brethren.

James 1:19 So then, my beloved brethren, let every man be swift to hear, slow to speak, slow to wrath;

James 2:5 Listen, my beloved brethren: Has God not chosen the poor of this world *to be* rich in faith and heirs of the kingdom which He promised to those who love Him?

Cf. Acts 15:25; 2 Pet 3:1,14; 1 John 4:1; 3 John 1–2,5,11; Jude 3

Described Paul's love for his converts.

1 Cor 4:14 I do not write these things to shame you, but as my beloved children I warn *you.*

Phil 4:1 Therefore, my beloved and longed-for brethren, my joy and crown, so stand fast in the Lord, beloved.

2 Thess 2:13 But we are bound to give thanks to God always for you, brethren beloved by the Lord, because God from the beginning chose you for salvation through sanctification by the Spirit and belief in the truth,

Cf. 2 Tim 1:2; Philem 1–2,16

Synonym for Christ.

Eph 1:6 to the praise of the glory of His grace, by which He made us accepted in the Beloved.

Described Jerusalem.

Rev 20:9 They went up on the breadth of the earth and surrounded the camp of the saints and the beloved city. And fire came down from God out of heaven and devoured them.

Cf. Ps 78:68; 87:2

BELTS (GIRDLES, SASHES)
Worn around the waist.

1 Kin 2:5 "Moreover you know also what Joab the son

of Zeruiah did to me, *and* what he did to the two commanders of the armies of Israel, to Abner the son of Ner and Amasa the son of Jether, whom he killed. And he shed the blood of war in peacetime, and put the blood of war on his belt that *was* around his waist, and on his sandals that *were* on his feet.

Jer 13:1 Thus the LORD said to me: "Go and get yourself a linen sash, and put it around your waist, but do not put it in water."

Jer 13:11 For as the sash clings to the waist of a man, so I have caused the whole house of Israel and the whole house of Judah to cling to Me,' says the LORD, 'that they may become My people, for renown, for praise, and for glory; but they would not hear.'

Worn by priests about the chest.

Rev 1:13 and in the midst of the seven lampstands *One* like the Son of Man, clothed with a garment down to the feet and girded about the chest with a golden band.

Made of
Fine linen.

Ezek 16:10 I clothed you in embroidered cloth and gave you sandals of badger skin; I clothed you with fine linen and covered you with silk.

Woven linen with blue, purple, etc.

Ex 39:29 and a sash of fine woven linen with blue, purple, and scarlet *thread,* made by a weaver, as the LORD had commanded Moses.

Gold.

Rev 1:13 and in the midst of the seven lampstands *One* like the Son of Man, clothed with a garment down to the feet and girded about the chest with a golden band.

Rev 15:6 And out of the temple came the seven angels having the seven plagues, clothed in pure bright linen, and having their chests girded with golden bands.

Leather.

2 Kin 1:8 So they answered him, "A hairy man wearing a leather belt around his waist." And he said, "It *is* Elijah the Tishbite."

Matt 3:4 Now John himself was clothed in camel's hair, with a leather belt around his waist; and his food was locusts and wild honey.

Sackcloth.

Is 3:24 And so it shall be: Instead of a sweet smell there will be a stench; Instead of a sash, a rope; Instead of well-set hair, baldness; Instead of a rich robe, a girding of sackcloth; And branding instead of beauty.

Lam 2:10 The elders of the daughter of Zion Sit on the ground *and* keep silence; They throw dust on their heads And gird themselves with sackcloth. The virgins of Jerusalem Bow their heads to the ground.

Made for sale by industrious women.

Prov 31:24 She makes linen garments and sells *them,* And supplies sashes for the merchants.

Used for
Strengthening the loins.

Prov 31:17 She girds herself with strength, And strengthens her arms.

Is 22:21 I will clothe him with your robe And strengthen him with your belt; I will commit your responsibility into his hand. He shall be a father to the inhabitants of Jerusalem And to the house of Judah.

Girding up the garments when walking.

1 Kin 18:46 Then the hand of the LORD came upon Elijah; and he girded up his loins and ran ahead of Ahab to the entrance of Jezreel.

2 Kin 4:29 Then he said to Gehazi, "Get yourself ready, and take my staff in your hand, and be on your way. If you meet anyone, do not greet him; and if anyone greets you, do not answer him; but lay my staff on the face of the child."

Girding up the garments when working.

Luke 12:37 Blessed *are* those servants whom the master, when he comes, will find watching. Assuredly, I say to you that he will gird himself and have them sit down *to eat,* and will come and serve them.

Luke 17:8 But will he not rather say to him, 'Prepare something for my supper, and gird yourself and serve me till I have eaten and drunk, and afterward you will eat and drink'?

John 13:4 rose from supper and laid aside His garments, took a towel and girded Himself.

Carrying the sword.

2 Sam 20:8 When they *were* at the large stone which *is* in Gibeon, Amasa came before them. Now Joab was dressed in battle armor; on it was a belt *with* a sword fastened in its sheath at his hips; and as he was going forward, it fell out.

Neh 4:18 Every one of the builders had his sword girded at his side as he built. And the one who sounded the trumpet *was* beside me.

Carrying the inkhorn.

Ezek 9:2 And suddenly six men came from the direction of the upper gate, which faces north, each with his battle-ax in his hand. One man among them *was* clothed with linen and had a writer's inkhorn at his side. They went in and stood beside the bronze altar.

Holding money.

Matt 10:9 Provide neither gold nor silver nor copper in your money belts,

Mark 6:8 He commanded them to take nothing for the journey except a staff—no bag, no bread, no copper in *their* money belts—

Taken off when at rest.

Is 5:27 No one will be weary or stumble among them, No one will slumber or sleep; Nor will the belt on their loins be loosed, Nor the strap of their sandals be broken;

Given as

A token of friendship.

1 Sam 18:4 And Jonathan took off the robe that *was* on him and gave it to David, with his armor, even to his sword and his bow and his belt.

A reward of military service.

2 Sam 18:11 So Joab said to the man who told him, "You just saw *him!* And why did you not strike him there to the ground? I would have given you ten *shekels* of silver and a belt."

Illustrative of

Strength.

Ps 18:39 For You have armed me with strength for the battle; You have subdued under me those who rose up against me.

Is 22:21 I will clothe him with your robe And strengthen him with your belt; I will commit your responsibility into his hand. He shall be a father to the inhabitants of Jerusalem And to the house of Judah.

Gladness.

Ps 30:11 You have turned for me my mourning into dancing; You have put off my sackcloth and clothed me with gladness,

Righteousness and faithfulness of Christ.

Is 11:5 Righteousness shall be the belt of His loins, And faithfulness the belt of His waist.

Truth.

Eph 6:14 Stand therefore, having girded your waist with truth, having put on the breastplate of righteousness,

BENEDICTION

Solomon's.

1 Kin 8:54–61 And so it was, when Solomon had finished praying all this prayer and supplication to the LORD, that he arose from before the altar of the LORD, from kneeling on his knees with his hands spread up to heaven. **55** Then he stood and blessed all the assembly of Israel with a loud voice, saying: **56** "Blessed *be* the LORD, who has given rest to His people Israel, according to all that He promised. There has not failed one word of all His good promise, which He promised through His servant Moses. **57** May the LORD our God be with us, as He was with our fathers. May He not leave us nor forsake us, **58** that He may incline our hearts to Himself, to walk in all His ways, and to keep His commandments and His statutes and His judgments, which He commanded our fathers. **59** And may these words of mine, with which I have made supplication before the LORD, be near the LORD our God day and night, that He may maintain the cause of His servant and the cause of His people Israel, as each day may require, **60** that all the peoples of the earth may know that the LORD *is* God; *there is* no other. **61** Let your heart therefore be loyal to the LORD our God, to walk in His statutes and keep His commandments, as at this day."

For God's kingdom rule.

Ps 100:1–5 Make a joyful shout to the LORD, all you lands! **2** Serve the LORD with gladness; Come before His presence with singing. **3** Know that the LORD, He *is* God; *It is* He *who* has made us, and not we ourselves; *We are* His people and the sheep of His pasture. **4** Enter into His gates with thanksgiving, *And* into His courts with praise. Be thankful to Him, *and* bless His name. **5** For the LORD *is* good; His mercy *is* everlasting, And His truth *endures* to all generations.

To God the Creator.

Ps 104:31–35 May the glory of the LORD endure forever; May the LORD rejoice in His works. **32** He looks on the earth, and it trembles; He touches the hills, and they smoke. **33** I will sing to the LORD as long as I live; I will sing praise to my God while I have my being. **34** May my meditation be sweet to Him; I will be glad in the LORD. **35** May sinners be consumed from the earth, And the wicked be no more. Bless the LORD, O my soul! Praise the LORD!

Zacharias's.

Luke 1:68–79 "Blessed *is* the Lord God of Israel, For He has visited and redeemed His people, **69** And has raised up a horn of salvation for us In the house of His servant David, **70** As He spoke by the mouth of His holy prophets, Who *have been* since the world began, **71** That we should be saved from our enemies And from the hand of all who hate us, **72** To perform the mercy *promised* to our fathers And to remember His holy covenant, **73** The oath which He swore to our father Abraham: **74** To grant us that we, Being delivered from the hand of our enemies, Might serve Him without fear, **75** In holiness and righteousness before Him all the days of our life. **76** "And you, child, will be called the prophet of the Highest; For you will go before the face of the Lord to prepare His ways, **77** To give knowledge of salvation to His people By the remission of their sins, **78** Through the tender mercy of our God, With which the Dayspring from on high has visited us; **79** To give light to those who sit in darkness and the shadow of death, To guide our feet into the way of peace."

Paul's,

To the Romans.

Rom 16:25–27 Now to Him who is able to establish you according to my gospel and the preaching of Jesus Christ, according to the revelation of the mystery kept secret since the world began **26** but now made manifest, and by the prophetic Scriptures made known to all nations, according to the commandment of the everlasting God, for obedience to the faith— **27** to God, alone wise, *be* glory through Jesus Christ forever. Amen.

To the Corinthians.

2 Cor 13:11–14 Finally, brethren, farewell. Become complete. Be of good comfort, be of one mind, live in peace; and the God of love and peace will be with you. **12** Greet one another with a holy kiss. **13** All the saints greet you. **14** The grace of the Lord Jesus Christ, and the love of God, and the communion of the Holy Spirit *be* with you all. Amen.

Cf. 2 Cor 1:3

To the Galatians.

Gal 6:18 Brethren, the grace of our Lord Jesus Christ *be* with your spirit. Amen.

To the Ephesians.

Eph 3:20–21 Now to Him who is able to do exceedingly abundantly above all that we ask or think, according to the power that works in us, **21** to Him *be* glory in the church by Christ Jesus to all generations, forever and ever. Amen.

Eph 6:21–24 But that you also may know my affairs *and* how I am doing, Tychicus, a beloved brother and faithful minister in the Lord, will make all things known to you; **22** whom I have sent to you for this very purpose, that you may know our affairs, and *that* he may comfort your hearts. **23** Peace to the brethren, and love with faith, from God the Father and the Lord Jesus Christ. **24** Grace *be* with all those who love our Lord Jesus Christ in sincerity. Amen.

To the Thessalonians.

1 Thess 5:23–24 Now may the God of peace Himself sanctify you completely; and may your whole spirit, soul, and body be preserved blameless at the coming of our Lord Jesus Christ. **24** He who calls you *is* faithful, who also will do *it.*

2 Thess 3:16–18 Now may the Lord of peace Himself give you peace always in every way. The Lord *be* with you all. **17** The salutation of Paul with my own hand, which is a sign in every epistle; so I write. **18** The grace of our Lord Jesus Christ *be* with you all. Amen.

To Timothy.

1 Tim 6:21 by professing it some have strayed concerning the faith. Grace *be* with you. Amen.

2 Tim 4:22 The Lord Jesus Christ be with your spirit. Grace be with you. Amen.

To Titus.

Titus 3:15 All who *are* with me greet you. Greet those who love us in the faith. Grace *be* with you all. Amen.

By author of Hebrews.

Heb 13:20–21 Now may the God of peace who brought up our Lord Jesus from the dead, that great Shepherd of the sheep, through the blood of the everlasting covenant, **21** make you complete in every good work to do His will, working in you what is well pleasing in His sight, through Jesus Christ, to whom *be* glory forever and ever. Amen.

By Jude, to believers.

Jude 1:24–25 Now to Him who is able to keep you from stumbling, And to present *you* faultless Before the presence of His glory with exceeding joy, **25** To God our Savior, Who alone is wise, *Be* glory and majesty, Dominion and power, Both now and forever. Amen.

BEN-HADAD
Ruler of Syrian kingdom (Ben-Hadad I); treaty with Asa.

1 Kin 15:18–20 Then Asa took all the silver and gold *that was* left in the treasuries of the house of the LORD and the treasuries of the king's house, and delivered them into the hand of his servants. And King Asa sent them to Ben-Hadad the son of Tabrimmon, the son of Hezion, king of Syria, who dwelt in Damascus, saying, **19** "Let there *be* a treaty between you and me, as there was between my father and your father. See, I have sent you a present of silver and gold. Come and break your treaty with Baasha king of Israel, so that he will withdraw from me." **20** So Ben-Hadad heeded King Asa, and sent the captains of his armies against the cities of Israel. He attacked Ijon, Dan, Abel Beth Maachah, and all Chinneroth, with all the land of Naphtali.

2 Chr 16:2–6 Then Asa brought silver and gold from the treasuries of the house of the LORD and of the king's house, and sent to Ben-Hadad king of Syria, who dwelt in Damascus, saying, **3** "Let there *be* a treaty between you and me, as there was between my father and your father. See, I have sent you silver and gold;

come, break your treaty with Baasha king of Israel, so that he will withdraw from me." 4 So Ben-Hadad heeded King Asa, and sent the captains of his armies against the cities of Israel. They attacked Ijon, Dan, Abel Maim, and all the storage cities of Naphtali. 5 Now it happened, when Baasha heard *it*, that he stopped building Ramah and ceased his work. 6 Then King Asa took all Judah, and they carried away the stones and timber of Ramah, which Baasha had used for building; and with them he built Geba and Mizpah.

Opposed Ahab (Ben-Hadad II).

1 Kin 20:1–12 Now Ben-Hadad the king of Syria gathered all his forces together; thirty-two kings *were* with him, with horses and chariots. And he went up and besieged Samaria, and made war against it. 2 Then he sent messengers into the city to Ahab king of Israel, and said to him, "Thus says Ben-Hadad: 3 'Your silver and your gold *are* mine; your loveliest wives and children are mine.' " 4 And the king of Israel answered and said, "My lord, O king, just as you say, I and all that I have *are* yours." 5 Then the messengers came back and said, "Thus speaks Ben-Hadad, saying, 'Indeed I have sent to you, saying, "You shall deliver to me your silver and your gold, your wives and your children"; 6 but I will send my servants to you tomorrow about this time, and they shall search your house and the houses of your servants. And it shall be, *that* whatever is pleasant in your eyes, they will put *it* in their hands and take it.' " 7 So the king of Israel called all the elders of the land, and said, "Notice, please, and see how this *man* seeks trouble, for he sent to me for my wives, my children, my silver, and my gold; and I did not deny him." 8 And all the elders and all the people said to him, "Do not listen or consent." 9 Therefore he said to the messengers of Ben-Hadad, "Tell my lord the king, 'All that you sent for to your servant the first time I will do, but this thing I cannot do.' " And the messengers departed and brought back word to him. 10 Then Ben-Hadad sent to him and said, "The gods do so to me, and more also, if enough dust is left of Samaria for a handful for each of the people who follow me." 11 So the king of Israel answered and said, "Tell *him*, 'Let not the one who puts on *his* armor boast like the one who takes *it off.*' " 12 And it happened when *Ben-Hadad* heard this message, as he and the kings *were* drinking at the command post, that he said to his servants, "Get ready." And they got ready to attack the city.

1 Kin 20:26–30 So it was, in the spring of the year, that Ben-Hadad mustered the Syrians and went up to Aphek to fight against Israel. 27 And the children of Israel were mustered and given provisions, and they went against them. Now the children of Israel encamped before them like two little flocks of goats, while the Syrians filled the countryside. 28 Then a man of God came and spoke to the king of Israel, and said, "Thus says the LORD: 'Because the Syrians have said, "The LORD *is* God of the hills, but He *is* not God of the valleys," therefore I will deliver all this great multitude into your hand, and you shall know that I *am* the LORD.' " 29 And they encamped opposite each other for seven days. So it was that on the seventh day the battle was joined; and the children of Israel

killed one hundred thousand foot soldiers *of* the Syrians in one day. 30 But the rest fled to Aphek, into the city; then a wall fell on twenty-seven thousand of the men *who were* left. And Ben-Hadad fled and went into the city, into an inner chamber.

Cf. 2 Kin 6:24

Treaty with Ahab.

1 Kin 20:31–34 Then his servants said to him, "Look now, we have heard that the kings of the house of Israel *are* merciful kings. Please, let us put sackcloth around our waists and ropes around our heads, and go out to the king of Israel; perhaps he will spare your life." 32 So they wore sackcloth around their waists and *put* ropes around their heads, and came to the king of Israel and said, "Your servant Ben-Hadad says, 'Please let me live.' " And he said, "*Is* he still alive? He *is* my brother." 33 Now the men were watching closely to see whether *any sign of mercy would come* from him; and they quickly grasped *at this word* and said, "Your brother Ben-Hadad." So he said, "Go, bring him." Then Ben-Hadad came out to him; and he had him come up into the chariot. 34 So *Ben-Hadad* said to him, "The cities which my father took from your father I will restore; and you may set up marketplaces for yourself in Damascus, as my father did in Samaria." Then *Ahab said*, "I will send you away with this treaty." So he made a treaty with him and sent him away.

Final battle with Ahab.

1 Kin 22:31–38 Now the king of Syria had commanded the thirty-two captains of his chariots, saying, "Fight with no one small or great, but only with the king of Israel." 32 So it was, when the captains of the chariots saw Jehoshaphat, that they said, "Surely it *is* the king of Israel!" Therefore they turned aside to fight against him, and Jehoshaphat cried out. 33 And it happened, when the captains of the chariots saw that it *was* not the king of Israel, that they turned back from pursuing him. 34 Now a *certain* man drew a bow at random, and struck the king of Israel between the joints of his armor. So he said to the driver of his chariot, "Turn around and take me out of the battle, for I am wounded." 35 The battle increased that day; and the king was propped up in his chariot, facing the Syrians, and died at evening. The blood ran out from the wound onto the floor of the chariot. 36 Then, as the sun was going down, a shout went throughout the army, saying, "Every man to his city, and every man to his own country!" 37 So the king died, and was brought to Samaria. And they buried the king in Samaria. 38 Then *someone* washed the chariot at a pool in Samaria, and the dogs licked up his blood while the harlots bathed, according to the word of the LORD which He had spoken.

Ruled at time of Naaman and Elisha.

2 Kin 5:1 Now Naaman, commander of the army of the king of Syria, was a great and honorable man in the eyes of his master, because by him the LORD had given victory to Syria. He was also a mighty man of valor, *but* a leper.

2 Kin 6:8–12 Now the king of Syria was making war against Israel; and he consulted with his servants, saying, "My camp *will be* in such and such a place." 9 And the man of God sent to the king of Israel, saying, "Beware that you do not pass this place, for the Syrians are coming down there." **10** Then the king of Israel sent *someone* to the place of which the man of God had told him. Thus he warned him, and he was watchful there, not just once or twice. **11** Therefore the heart of the king of Syria was greatly troubled by this thing; and he called his servants and said to them, "Will you not show me which of us *is* for the king of Israel?" **12** And one of his servants said, "None, my lord, O king; but Elisha, the prophet who *is* in Israel, tells the king of Israel the words that you speak in your bedroom."

Cf. 2 Kin 13:3

Death of.

2 Kin 8:7–15 Then Elisha went to Damascus, and Ben-Hadad king of Syria was sick; and it was told him, saying, "The man of God has come here." **8** And the king said to Hazael, "Take a present in your hand, and go to meet the man of God, and inquire of the LORD by him, saying, 'Shall I recover from this disease?' " **9** So Hazael went to meet him and took a present with him, of every good thing of Damascus, forty camel-loads; and he came and stood before him, and said, "Your son Ben-Hadad king of Syria has sent me to you, saying, 'Shall I recover from this disease?' " **10** And Elisha said to him, "Go, say to him, 'You shall certainly recover.' However the LORD has shown me that he will really die." **11** Then he set his countenance in a stare until he was ashamed; and the man of God wept. **12** And Hazael said, "Why is my lord weeping?" He answered, "Because I know the evil that you will do to the children of Israel: Their strongholds you will set on fire, and their young men you will kill with the sword; and you will dash their children, and rip open their women with child." **13** So Hazael said, "But what *is* your servant—a dog, that he should do this gross thing?" And Elisha answered, "The LORD has shown me that you *will become* king over Syria." **14** Then he departed from Elisha, and came to his master, who said to him, "What did Elisha say to you?" And he answered, "He told me you would surely recover." **15** But it happened on the next day that he took a thick cloth and dipped *it* in water, and spread *it* over his face so that he died; and Hazael reigned in his place.

Reference to idols of Syria.

Jer 49:27 "I will kindle a fire in the wall of Damascus, And it shall consume the palaces of Ben-Hadad."

Cf. Amos 1:4

BENJAMIN, THE TRIBE OF

Descended from Jacob's twelfth son.

Gen 35:18 And so it was, as her soul was departing (for she died), that she called his name Ben-Oni; but his father called him Benjamin.

Predictions respecting.

Gen 49:27 "Benjamin is a ravenous wolf; In the morning he shall devour the prey, And at night he shall divide the spoil."

Deut 33:12 Of Benjamin he said: "The beloved of the LORD shall dwell in safety by Him, *Who* shelters him all the day long; And he shall dwell between His shoulders."

Persons selected from,

To number the people.

Num 1:11 from Benjamin, Abidan the son of Gideoni;

To spy out the land.

Num 13:9 from the tribe of Benjamin, Palti the son of Raphu;

To divide the land.

Num 34:21 from the tribe of Benjamin, Elidad the son of Chislon;

Strength of, on leaving Egypt.

Num 1:36–37 From the children of Benjamin, their genealogies by their families, by their fathers' house, according to the number of names, from twenty years old and above, all who *were able to* go to war: **37** those who were numbered of the tribe of Benjamin *were* thirty-five thousand four hundred.

Formed the rear of the third division of Israel in their journeys.

Num 10:22 And the standard of the camp of the children of Ephraim set out according to their armies; over their army *was* Elishama the son of Ammihud.

Num 10:24 And over the army of the tribe of the children of Benjamin *was* Abidan the son of Gideoni.

Encamped on west side of the tabernacle under the standard of Ephraim.

Num 2:18 "On the west side *shall be* the standard of the forces with Ephraim according to their armies, and the leader of the children of Ephraim *shall be* Elishama the son of Ammihud."

Num 2:22 "Then *comes* the tribe of Benjamin, and the leader of the children of Benjamin *shall be* Abidan the son of Gideoni."

Offering of, at dedication.

Num 7:60–65 On the ninth day Abidan the son of Gideoni, leader of the children of Benjamin, *presented an offering*. **61** His offering *was* one silver platter, the weight of which *was* one hundred and thirty *shekels*, and one silver bowl of seventy shekels, according to the shekel of the sanctuary, both of them full of fine flour mixed with oil as a grain offering; **62** one gold pan of ten *shekels*, full of incense; **63** one young bull, one ram, and one male lamb in its first year, as a burnt offering; **64** one kid of the goats as a sin offering; **65** and as the sacrifice of peace offerings: two oxen, five rams, five male goats, and five male lambs in their first year. This *was* the offering of Abidan the son of Gideoni.

Families of.

Num 26:38–40 The sons of Benjamin according to their families were: of Bela, the family of the Belaites; of Ashbel, the family of the Ashbelites; of Ahiram, the family of the Ahiramites; **39** of Shupham, the family of the Shuphamites; of Hupham, the family of the Huphamites. **40** And the sons of Bela were Ard and Naaman: *of Ard,* the family of the Ardites; of Naaman, the family of the Naamites.

Strength of, entering Canaan.

Num 26:41 These *are* the sons of Benjamin according to their families; and those who were numbered of them *were* forty-five thousand six hundred.

On Gerizim, said amen to the blessings.

Deut 27:12 "These shall stand on Mount Gerizim to bless the people, when you have crossed over the Jordan: Simeon, Levi, Judah, Issachar, Joseph, and Benjamin;

Cities and bounds of their inheritance.
Josh 18:11–28

Celebrated as bowmen and slingers.

1 Chr 12:2 armed with bows, using both the right hand and the left in *hurling* stones and *shooting* arrows with the bow. *They were* of Benjamin, Saul's brethren.

Assisted against Sisera.

Judg 5:14 From Ephraim *were* those whose roots were in Amalek. After you, Benjamin, with your peoples, From Machir rulers came down, And from Zebulun those who bear the recruiter's staff.

Oppressed by the Ammonites.

Judg 10:9 Moreover the people of Ammon crossed over the Jordan to fight against Judah also, against Benjamin, and against the house of Ephraim, so that Israel was severely distressed.

Almost annihilated for protecting the men of Gibeah. Judg 20:12–48

Remnant of, provided with wives to preserve the tribe. Judg 21:1–23

Furnished the first king to Israel.

1 Sam 9:1–2 There was a man of Benjamin whose name *was* Kish the son of Abiel, the son of Zeror, the son of Bechorath, the son of Aphiah, a Benjamite, a mighty man of power. **2** And he had a choice and handsome son whose name *was* Saul. *There was* not a more handsome person than he among the children of Israel. From his shoulders upward *he was* taller than any of the people.

1 Sam 9:15–17 Now the LORD had told Samuel in his ear the day before Saul came, saying, **16** "Tomorrow about this time I will send you a man from the land of Benjamin, and you shall anoint him commander over My people Israel, that he may save My people from the hand of the Philistines; for I have looked upon My people, because their cry has come to Me." **17** So when Samuel saw Saul, the LORD said to him, "There he is, the man of whom I spoke to you. This one shall reign over My people."

1 Sam 10:20–21 And when Samuel had caused all the tribes of Israel to come near, the tribe of Benjamin was chosen. **21** When he had caused the tribe of Benjamin to come near by their families, the family of Matri was chosen. And Saul the son of Kish was chosen. But when they sought him, he could not be found.

Adhered for a time to the house of Saul against David.

2 Sam 2:8–10 But Abner the son of Ner, commander of Saul's army, took Ishbosheth the son of Saul and brought him over to Mahanaim; **9** and he made him king over Gilead, over the Ashurites, over Jezreel, over Ephraim, over Benjamin, and over all Israel. **10** Ishbosheth, Saul's son, *was* forty years old when he began to reign over Israel, and he reigned two years. Only the house of Judah followed David.

2 Sam 2:15 So they arose and went over by number, twelve from Benjamin, *followers* of Ishbosheth the son of Saul, and twelve from the servants of David.

2 Sam 2:25 Now the children of Benjamin gathered together behind Abner and became a unit, and took their stand on top of a hill.

2 Sam 2:31 But the servants of David had struck down, of Benjamin and Abner's men, three hundred and sixty men who died.

Some of, assisted David.

1 Chr 12:1–7 Now these *were* the men who came to David at Ziklag while he was still a fugitive from Saul the son of Kish; and they *were* among the mighty men, helpers in the war, **2** armed with bows, using both the right hand and the left in *hurling* stones and *shooting* arrows with the bow. *They were* of Benjamin, Saul's brethren. **3** The chief *was* Ahiezer, then Joash, the sons of Shemaah the Gibeathite; Jeziel and Pelet the sons of Azmaveth; Berachah, and Jehu the Anathothite; **4** Ishmaiah the Gibeonite, a mighty man among the thirty, and over the thirty; Jeremiah, Jahaziel, Johanan, and Jozabad the Gederathite; **5** Eluzai, Jerimoth, Bealiah, Shemariah, and Shephatiah the Haruphite; **6** Elkanah, Jisshiah, Azarel, Joezer, and Jashobeam, the Korahites; **7** and Joelah and Zebadiah the sons of Jeroham of Gedor.

1 Chr 12:16 Then some of the sons of Benjamin and Judah came to David at the stronghold.

Revolted from the house of Saul.

2 Sam 3:19 And Abner also spoke in the hearing of Benjamin. Then Abner also went to speak in the hearing of David in Hebron all that seemed good to Israel and the whole house of Benjamin.

Some of, at David's coronation.

1 Chr 12:29 of the sons of Benjamin, relatives of Saul, three thousand (until then the greatest part of them had remained loyal to the house of Saul);

A thousand of, with Shimei came to meet David on his return to Jerusalem.

2 Sam 19:16–17 And Shimei the son of Gera, a Benjamite, who *was* from Bahurim, hurried and came down with the men of Judah to meet King David. **17** *There were* a thousand men of Benjamin with him, and Ziba the servant of the house of Saul, and his fifteen sons and his twenty servants with him; and they went over the Jordan before the king.

Very numerous in David's time.

1 Chr 7:6–12 *The sons* of Benjamin *were* Bela, Becher, and Jediael—three *in all*. **7** The sons of Bela were Ezbon, Uzzi, Uzziel, Jerimoth, and Iri—five *in all*. They *were* heads of *their* fathers' houses, and they were listed by their genealogies, twenty-two thousand and thirty-four mighty men of valor. **8** The sons of Becher *were* Zemirah, Joash, Eliezer, Elioenai, Omri, Jerimoth, Abijah, Anathoth, and Alemeth. All these *are* the sons of Becher. **9** And they were recorded by genealogy according to their generations, heads of their fathers' houses, twenty thousand two hundred mighty men of valor. **10** The son of Jediael *was* Bilhan, and the sons of Bilhan *were* Jeush, Benjamin, Ehud, Chenaanah, Zethan, Tharshish, and Ahishahar. **11** All these sons of Jediael *were* heads of their fathers' houses; *there were* seventeen thousand two hundred mighty men of valor fit to go out for war *and* battle. **12** Shuppim and Huppim *were* the sons of Ir, *and* Hushim *was* the son of Aher.

Captains appointed over.

1 Kin 4:18 Shimei the son of Elah, in Benjamin;

1 Chr 27:12 The ninth *captain* for the ninth month *was* Abiezer the Anathothite, of the Benjamites; in his division *were* twenty-four thousand.

Remained faithful to Judah.

1 Kin 12:21 And when Rehoboam came to Jerusalem, he assembled all the house of Judah with the tribe of Benjamin, one hundred and eighty thousand chosen *men* who were warriors, to fight against the house of Israel, that he might restore the kingdom to Rehoboam the son of Solomon.

Furnished an army to Jehoshaphat.

2 Chr 17:17 Of Benjamin: Eliada a mighty man of valor, and with him two hundred thousand men armed with bow and shield;

Numbers of, returned from the captivity and dwelt at Jerusalem.

Ezra 1:5 Then the heads of the fathers' *houses* of Judah and Benjamin, and the priests and the Levites, with all whose spirits God had moved, arose to go up and build the house of the LORD which *is* in Jerusalem.

Neh 11:4 Also in Jerusalem dwelt *some* of the children of Judah and of the children of Benjamin. The children of Judah: Athaiah the son of Uzziah, the son of Zechariah, the son of Amariah, the son of Shephatiah, the son of Mahalalel, of the children of Perez;

Celebrated persons of,

Ehud.

Judg 3:15 But when the children of Israel cried out to the LORD, the LORD raised up a deliverer for them: Ehud the son of Gera, the Benjamite, a left-handed man. By him the children of Israel sent tribute to Eglon king of Moab.

Kish.

1 Sam 9:1 There was a man of Benjamin whose name *was* Kish the son of Abiel, the son of Zeror, the son of Bechorath, the son of Aphiah, a Benjamite, a mighty man of power.

Saul.

1 Sam 9:1 There was a man of Benjamin whose name *was* Kish the son of Abiel, the son of Zeror, the son of Bechorath, the son of Aphiah, a Benjamite, a mighty man of power.

1 Sam 10:1 Then Samuel took a flask of oil and poured *it* on his head, and kissed him and said: "*Is it* not because the LORD has anointed you commander over His inheritance?

Abner.

1 Sam 14:51 Kish *was* the father of Saul, and Ner the father of Abner *was* the son of Abiel.

1 Sam 17:55 When Saul saw David going out against the Philistine, he said to Abner, the commander of the army, "Abner, whose son *is* this youth?" And Abner said, "As your soul lives, O king, I do not know."

Elhanan.

2 Sam 21:19 Again there was war at Gob with the Philistines, where Elhanan the son of Jaare-Oregim the

Bethlehemite killed *the brother of* Goliath the Gittite, the shaft of whose spear *was* like a weaver's beam.

Paul.

Phil 3:5 circumcised the eighth day, of the stock of Israel, *of* the tribe of Benjamin, a Hebrew of the Hebrews; concerning the law, a Pharisee;

BETHEL

Place named by Abraham.

Gen 12:8 And he moved from there to the mountain east of Bethel, and he pitched his tent *with* Bethel on the west and Ai on the east; there he built an altar to the LORD and called on the name of the LORD.

Place renamed as, by Jacob.

Gen 28:19 And he called the name of that place Bethel; but the name of that city had been Luz previously.

Cf. Gen 31:13; Amos 4:4; 5:5

Jacob's return to.

Gen 35:1–15 Then God said to Jacob, "Arise, go up to Bethel and dwell there; and make an altar there to God, who appeared to you when you fled from the face of Esau your brother." 2 And Jacob said to his household and to all who *were* with him, "Put away the foreign gods that *are* among you, purify yourselves, and change your garments. 3 Then let us arise and go up to Bethel; and I will make an altar there to God, who answered me in the day of my distress and has been with me in the way which I have gone." 4 So they gave Jacob all the foreign gods which *were* in their hands, and the earrings which *were* in their ears; and Jacob hid them under the terebinth tree which *was* by Shechem. 5 And they journeyed, and the terror of God was upon the cities that *were* all around them, and they did not pursue the sons of Jacob. 6 So Jacob came to Luz (that *is*, Bethel), which *is* in the land of Canaan, he and all the people who *were* with him. 7 And he built an altar there and called the place El Bethel, because there God appeared to him when he fled from the face of his brother. 8 Now Deborah, Rebekah's nurse, died, and she was buried below Bethel under the terebinth tree. So the name of it was called Allon Bachuth. 9 Then God appeared to Jacob again, when he came from Padan Aram, and blessed him. 10 And God said to him, "Your name *is* Jacob; your name shall not be called Jacob anymore, but Israel shall be your name." So He called his name Israel. 11 Also God said to him: "I *am* God Almighty. Be fruitful and multiply; a nation and a company of nations shall proceed from you, and kings shall come from your body. 12 The land which I gave Abraham and Isaac I give to you; and to your descendants after you I give this land." 13 Then God went up from him in the place where He talked with him. 14 So Jacob set up a pillar in the place where He talked with him, a pillar of stone; and he poured a drink offering on it, and he poured oil on it. 15 And Jacob called the name of the place where God spoke with him, Bethel.

Jeroboam placed idol there.

1 Kin 12:28–29 Therefore the king asked advice, made two calves of gold, and said to the people, "It is too much for you to go up to Jerusalem. Here are your gods, O Israel, which brought you up from the land of Egypt!" **29** And he set up one in Bethel, and the other he put in Dan.

Cf. 2 Kin 2:2; Amos 3:14

Ashes of idolatrous articles sent there.

2 Kin 23:4 And the king commanded Hilkiah the high priest, the priests of the second order, and the doorkeepers, to bring out of the temple of the LORD all the articles that were made for Baal, for Asherah, and for all the host of heaven; and he burned them outside Jerusalem in the fields of Kidron, and carried their ashes to Bethel.

Cf. 2 Kin 23:15

Abijah recaptured.

2 Chr 13:19 And Abijah pursued Jeroboam and took cities from him: Bethel with its villages, Jeshanah with its villages, and Ephrain with its villages.

BETHLEHEM

In Judah

Home of Ruth's father-in-law.

Ruth 1:1 Now it came to pass, in the days when the judges ruled, that there was a famine in the land. And a certain man of Bethlehem, Judah, went to dwell in the country of Moab, he and his wife and his two sons.

Ruth and Naomi return there.

Ruth 1:15–22 And she said, "Look, your sister-in-law has gone back to her people and to her gods; return after your sister-in-law." **16** But Ruth said: "Entreat me not to leave you, *Or to* turn back from following after you; For wherever you go, I will go; And wherever you lodge, I will lodge; Your people *shall be* my people, And your God, my God. **17** Where you die, I will die, And there will I be buried. The LORD do so to me, and more also, If *anything but* death parts you and me." **18** When she saw that she was determined to go with her, she stopped speaking to her. **19** Now the two of them went until they came to Bethlehem. And it happened, when they had come to Bethlehem, that all the city was excited because of them; and the women said, "*Is* this Naomi?" **20** But she said to them, "Do not call me Naomi; call me Mara, for the Almighty has dealt very bitterly with me. **21** I went out full, and the LORD has brought me home again empty. Why do you call me Naomi, since the LORD has testified against me, and the Almighty has afflicted me?" **22** So Naomi returned, and Ruth the Moabitess her daughter-in-law with her, who returned from the country of Moab. Now they came to Bethlehem at the beginning of barley harvest.

Cf. Ruth 4:11

Later called "city of David."

Luke 2:4 Joseph also went up from Galilee, out of the city of Nazareth, into Judea, to the city of David, which is called Bethlehem, because he was of the house and lineage of David,

Luke 2:11 For there is born to you this day in the city of David a Savior, who is Christ the Lord.

Cf. 1 Sam 16:1

Christ born there.

Mic 5:2 "But you, Bethlehem Ephrathah, *Though* you are little among the thousands of Judah, *Yet* out of

you shall come forth to Me The One to be Ruler in Israel, Whose goings forth *are* from of old, From everlasting."

Luke 2:4–7 Joseph also went up from Galilee, out of the city of Nazareth, into Judea, to the city of David, which is called Bethlehem, because he was of the house and lineage of David, **5** to be registered with Mary, his betrothed wife, who was with child. **6** So it was, that while they were there, the days were completed for her to be delivered. **7** And she brought forth her firstborn Son, and wrapped Him in swaddling cloths, and laid Him in a manger, because there was no room for them in the inn.

Wise men visit Christ there.

Matt 2:1–12 Now after Jesus was born in Bethlehem of Judea in the days of Herod the king, behold, wise men from the East came to Jerusalem, **2** saying, "Where is He who has been born King of the Jews? For we have seen His star in the East and have come to worship Him." **3** When Herod the king heard *this,* he was troubled, and all Jerusalem with him. **4** And when he had gathered all the chief priests and scribes of the people together, he inquired of them where the Christ was to be born. **5** So they said to him, "In Bethlehem of Judea, for thus it is written by the prophet: **6** '*But you, Bethlehem, in the land of Judah, Are not the least among the rulers of Judah; For out of you shall come a Ruler Who will shepherd My people Israel.*'" **7** Then Herod, when he had secretly called the wise men, determined from them what time the star appeared. **8** And he sent them to Bethlehem and said, "Go and search carefully for the young Child, and when you have found *Him,* bring back word to me, that I may come and worship Him also." **9** When they heard the king, they departed; and behold, the star which they had seen in the East went before them, till it came and stood over where the young Child was. **10** When they saw the star, they rejoiced with exceedingly great joy. **11** And when they had come into the house, they saw the young Child with Mary His mother, and fell down and worshiped Him. And when they had opened their treasures, they presented gifts to Him: gold, frankincense, and myrrh. **12** Then, being divinely warned in a dream that they should not return to Herod, they departed for their own country another way.

Herod slaughtered the infants there.

Matt 2:16 Then Herod, when he saw that he was deceived by the wise men, was exceedingly angry; and he sent forth and put to death all the male children who were in Bethlehem and in all its districts, from two years old and under, according to the time which he had determined from the wise men.

In Zebulun.

Josh 19:15 Included were Kattath, Nahallal, Shimron, Idalah, and Bethlehem: twelve cities with their villages.

BETHANY

Jesus' arrival there.

John 12:1 Then, six days before the Passover, Jesus came to Bethany, where Lazarus was who had been dead, whom He had raised from the dead.

Mary, sister of Martha and Lazarus, anointed Jesus there.

Matt 26:6–13 And when Jesus was in Bethany at the house of Simon the leper, 7 a woman came to Him having an alabaster flask of very costly fragrant oil, and she poured *it* on His head as He sat *at the table.* 8 But when His disciples saw *it,* they were indignant, saying, "Why this waste? 9 For this fragrant oil might have been sold for much and given to *the* poor." 10 But when Jesus was aware of *it,* He said to them, "Why do you trouble the woman? For she has done a good work for Me. 11 For you have the poor with you always, but Me you do not have always. 12 For in pouring this fragrant oil on My body, she did *it* for My burial. 13 Assuredly, I say to you, wherever this gospel is preached in the whole world, what this woman has done will also be told as a memorial to her."

Cf. Mark 14:3–9; John 12:2–8

Located near Jerusalem and Mount of Olives.

Mark 11:1 Now when they drew near Jerusalem, to Bethphage and Bethany, at the Mount of Olives, He sent two of His disciples;

Luke 19:29 And it came to pass, when He drew near to Bethphage and Bethany, at the mountain called Olivet, *that* He sent two of His disciples,

Home of Mary and Martha.

Luke 10:38–42 Now it happened as they went that He entered a certain village; and a certain woman named Martha welcomed Him into her house. 39 And she had a sister called Mary, who also sat at Jesus' feet and heard His word. 40 But Martha was distracted with much serving, and she approached Him and said, "Lord, do You not care that my sister has left me to serve alone? Therefore tell her to help me." 41 And Jesus answered and said to her, "Martha, Martha, you are worried and troubled about many things. 42 But one thing is needed, and Mary has chosen that good part, which will not be taken away from her."

John 11:1 Now a certain *man* was sick, Lazarus of Bethany, the town of Mary and her sister Martha.

Site of the ascension.

Luke 24:50–51 And He led them out as far as Bethany, and He lifted up His hands and blessed them. 51 Now it came to pass, while He blessed them, that He was parted from them and carried up into heaven.

BETHSAIDA

Rebuked by Jesus.

Matt 11:21 "Woe to you, Chorazin! Woe to you, Bethsaida! For if the mighty works which were done in you had been done in Tyre and Sidon, they would have repented long ago in sackcloth and ashes.

Blind man healed there.

Mark 8:22–26 Then He came to Bethsaida; and they brought a blind man to Him, and begged Him to touch him. 23 So He took the blind man by the hand and led him out of the town. And when He had spit on his eyes and put His hands on him, He asked him if he saw anything. 24 And he looked up and said, "I see men like trees, walking." 25 Then He put *His* hands on his eyes again and made him look up. And he was restored and saw everyone clearly. 26 Then He sent him away to his house, saying, "Neither go into the town, nor tell anyone in the town."

Located on Sea of Galilee.

Mark 6:45 Immediately He made His disciples get into the boat and go before Him to the other side, to Bethsaida, while He sent the multitude away.

Near there, Jesus and disciples sought to retreat from crowds.

Luke 9:10–11 And the apostles, when they had returned, told Him all that they had done. Then He took them and went aside privately into a deserted place belonging to the city called Bethsaida. 11 But when the multitudes knew *it,* they followed Him; and He received them and spoke to them about the kingdom of God, and healed those who had need of healing.

Original home of Peter and Andrew.

John 1:44 Now Philip was from Bethsaida, the city of Andrew and Peter.

BIRDS

Created by God.

Gen 1:20–21 Then God said, "Let the waters abound with an abundance of living creatures, and let birds fly above the earth across the face of the firmament of the heavens." 21 So God created great sea creatures and every living thing that moves, with which the waters abounded, according to their kind, and every winged bird according to its kind. And God saw that *it was* good.

Gen 2:19 Out of the ground the LORD God formed every beast of the field and every bird of the air, and brought *them* to Adam to see what he would call them. And whatever Adam called each living creature, that *was* its name.

Herbs of the field given as food to.

Gen 1:30 Also, to every beast of the earth, to every bird of the air, and to everything that creeps on the earth, in which *there is* life, *I have given* every green herb for food"; and it was so.

Differ in flesh from beasts and fishes.

1 Cor 15:39 All flesh *is* not the same flesh, but *there is* one *kind of* flesh of men, another flesh of animals, another of fish, *and* another of birds.

Power over given to man.

Gen 1:26 Then God said, "Let Us make man in Our image, according to Our likeness; let them have dominion over the fish of the sea, over the birds of the air, and over the cattle, over all the earth and over every creeping thing that creeps on the earth."

Ps 8:8 The birds of the air, And the fish of the sea That pass through the paths of the seas.

Names given to, by Adam.

Gen 2:19–20 Out of the ground the LORD God formed every beast of the field and every bird of the air, and brought *them* to Adam to see what he would call them. And whatever Adam called each living creature, that *was* its name. 20 So Adam gave names to all cattle, to the birds of the air, and to every beast of the field. But for Adam there was not found a helper comparable to him.

Instinctively fear man.

Gen 9:2 And the fear of you and the dread of you shall be on every beast of the earth, on every bird of the air, on all that move *on* the earth, and on all the fish of the sea. They are given into your hand.

Instinct of, inferior to man's reason.

Job 35:11 Who teaches us more than the beasts of the earth, And makes us wiser than the birds of heaven?'

Lessons of wisdom to be learned from.

Job 12:7 "But now ask the beasts, and they will teach you; And the birds of the air, and they will tell you;

Can all be tamed.

James 3:7 For every kind of beast and bird, of reptile and creature of the sea, is tamed and has been tamed by mankind.

Given as food to man.

Gen 9:2–3 And the fear of you and the dread of you shall be on every beast of the earth, on every bird of the air, on all that move *on* the earth, and on all the fish of the sea. They are given into your hand. **3** Every moving thing that lives shall be food for you. I have given you all things, even as the green herbs.

The blood of, not to be eaten.

Lev 7:26 Moreover you shall not eat any blood in any of your dwellings, *whether* of bird or beast.

The property of God.

Ps 50:11 I know all the birds of the mountains, And the wild beasts of the field *are* Mine.

God provides for.

Ps 104:1–12 Bless the LORD, O my soul! O LORD my God, You are very great: You are clothed with honor and majesty, **2** Who cover *Yourself* with light as *with* a garment, Who stretch out the heavens like a curtain. **3** He lays the beams of His upper chambers in the waters, Who makes the clouds His chariot, Who walks on the wings of the wind, **4** Who makes His angels spirits, His ministers a flame of fire. **5** *You who* laid the foundations of the earth, So *that* it should not be moved forever, **6** You covered it with the deep as *with* a garment; The waters stood above the mountains. **7** At Your rebuke they fled; At the voice of Your thunder they hastened away. **8** They went up over the mountains; They went down into the valleys, To the place which You founded for them. **9** You have set a boundary that they may not pass over, That they may not return to cover the earth. **10** He sends the springs into the valleys; They flow among the hills. **11** They give drink to every beast of the field; The wild donkeys quench their thirst. **12** By them the birds of the heavens have their home; They sing among the branches.

Matt 6:26 Look at the birds of the air, for they neither sow nor reap nor gather into barns; yet your heavenly Father feeds them. Are you not of more value than they?

Luke 12:23–24 Life is more than food, and the body *is more* than clothing. **24** Consider the ravens, for they neither sow nor reap, which have neither storehouse nor barn; and God feeds them. Of how much more value are you than the birds?

Called

Birds of the air.

Gen 7:3 also seven each of birds of the air, male and female, to keep the species alive on the face of all the earth.

Matt 8:20 And Jesus said to him, "Foxes have holes and birds of the air *have* nests, but the Son of Man has nowhere to lay *His* head."

Birds of heaven.

Job 35:11 Who teaches us more than the beasts of the earth, And makes us wiser than the birds of heaven?'

Feathered fowl.

Ezek 39:17 "And as for you, son of man, thus says the Lord GOD, 'Speak to every sort of bird and to every beast of the field: "Assemble yourselves and come; Gather together from all sides to My sacrificial meal Which I am sacrificing for you, A great sacrificial meal on the mountains of Israel, That you may eat flesh and drink blood.

Winged bird.

Deut 4:17 the likeness of any animal that *is* on the earth or the likeness of any winged bird that flies in the air,

Food of.

Gen 15:11 And when the vultures came down on the carcasses, Abram drove them away.

Gen 40:19 Within three days Pharaoh will lift off your head from you and hang you on a tree; and the birds will eat your flesh from you."

Deut 28:26 Your carcasses shall be food for all the birds of the air and the beasts of the earth, and no one shall frighten *them* away.

Matt 13:4 And as he sowed, some *seed* fell by the wayside; and the birds came and devoured them.

Furnished with claws.

Dan 4:33 That very hour the word was fulfilled concerning Nebuchadnezzar; he was driven from men and ate grass like oxen; his body was wet with the dew of heaven till his hair had grown like eagles' *feathers* and his nails like birds' *claws.*

Make, and dwell in nests.

Matt 8:20 And Jesus said to him, "Foxes have holes and birds of the air *have* nests, but the Son of Man has nowhere to lay *His* head."

Are hostile to strange kinds.

Jer 12:9 My heritage *is* to Me *like* a speckled vulture; The vultures all around *are* against her. Come, assemble all the beasts of the field, Bring them to devour!

Each have their peculiar note or song.

Ps 104:12 By them the birds of the heavens have their home; They sing among the branches.

Eccl 12:4 When the doors are shut in the streets, And the sound of grinding is low; When one rises up at the sound of a bird, And all the daughters of music are brought low.

Song 2:12 The flowers appear on the earth; The time of singing has come, And the voice of the turtledove Is heard in our land.

Fly above the earth.

Gen 1:20 Then God said, "Let the waters abound with an abundance of living creatures, and let birds fly above the earth across the face of the firmament of the heavens."

Rapid flight of, alluded to.

Is 31:5 Like birds flying about, So will the Lord of hosts defend Jerusalem. Defending, He will also deliver *it*; Passing over, He will preserve *it*."

Hos 9:11 *As for* Ephraim, their glory shall fly away like a bird— No birth, no pregnancy, and no conception!

Hos 11:11 They shall come trembling like a bird from Egypt, Like a dove from the land of Assyria. And I will let them dwell in their houses," Says the Lord.

Many kinds of, migratory.

Jer 8:7 "Even the stork in the heavens Knows her appointed times; And the turtledove, the swift, and the swallow Observe the time of their coming. But My people do not know the judgment of the Lord.

Often remove from places suffering calamities.

Jer 4:25 I beheld, and indeed *there was* no man, And all the birds of the heavens had fled.

Jer 9:10 I will take up a weeping and wailing for the mountains, And for the dwelling places of the wilderness a lamentation, Because they are burned up, So that no one can pass through; Nor can *men* hear the voice of the cattle. Both the birds of the heavens and the beasts have fled; They are gone.

Rest on trees.

Dan 4:12 Its leaves *were* lovely, Its fruit abundant, And in it *was* food for all. The beasts of the field found shade under it, The birds of the heavens dwelt in its branches, And all flesh was fed from it.

Matt 13:32 which indeed is the least of all the seeds; but when it is grown it is greater than the herbs and becomes a tree, so that the birds of the air come and nest in its branches."

Inhabit

Mountains.

Ps 50:11 I know all the birds of the mountains, And the wild beasts of the field *are* Mine.

Deserts.

Ps 102:6 I am like a pelican of the wilderness; I am like an owl of the desert.

Deserted cities.

Is 34:11 But the pelican and the porcupine shall possess it, Also the owl and the raven shall dwell in it. And He shall stretch out over it The line of confusion and the stones of emptiness.

Is 34:14–15 The wild beasts of the desert shall also meet with the jackals, And the wild goat shall bleat to its companion; Also the night creature shall rest there, And find for herself a place of rest. **15** There the arrow snake shall make her nest and lay *eggs* And hatch, and gather *them* under her shadow; There also shall the hawks be gathered, Every one with her mate.

Make their nests

In trees.

Ps 104:17 Where the birds make their nests; The stork has her home in the fir trees.

Ezek 31:6 All the birds of the heavens made their nests in its boughs; Under its branches all the beasts of the field brought forth their young; And in its shadow all great nations made their home.

On the ground.

Deut 22:6 "If a bird's nest happens to be before you along the way, in any tree or on the ground, with young ones or eggs, with the mother sitting on the young or on the eggs, you shall not take the mother with the young;

In clefts of rocks.

Num 24:21 Then he looked on the Kenites, and he took up his oracle and said: "Firm is your dwelling place, And your nest is set in the rock;

Jer 48:28 You who dwell in Moab, Leave the cities and dwell in the rock, And be like the dove *which* makes her nest In the sides of the cave's mouth.

In deserted cities.

Is 34:15 There the arrow snake shall make her nest and lay *eggs* And hatch, and gather *them* under her shadow; There also shall the hawks be gathered, Every one with her mate.

Under the roofs of houses.

Ps 84:3 Even the sparrow has found a home, And the swallow a nest for herself, Where she may lay her young— *Even* Your altars, O Lord of hosts, My King and my God.

Early distinguished into clean and unclean.

Gen 8:20 Then Noah built an altar to the Lord, and took of every clean animal and of every clean bird, and offered burnt offerings on the altar.

Clean,

Names of.

Ex 16:12–13 "I have heard the complaints of the children of Israel. Speak to them, saying, 'At twilight you shall eat meat, and in the morning you shall be filled with bread. And you shall know that I *am* the Lord your God.' " **13** So it was that quails came up at evening and covered the camp, and in the morning the dew lay all around the camp.

Lev 1:14 'And if the burnt sacrifice of his offering to the Lord *is* of birds, then he shall bring his offering of turtledoves or young pigeons.

Lev 12:6 'When the days of her purification are fulfilled, whether for a son or a daughter, she shall bring to the priest a lamb of the first year as a burnt offering, and a young pigeon or a turtledove as a sin offering, to the door of the tabernacle of meeting.

Lev 14:4 then the priest shall command to take for him who is to be cleansed two living *and* clean birds, cedar wood, scarlet, and hyssop.

Lev 14:22 and two turtledoves or two young pigeons, such as he is able to afford: one shall be a sin offering and the other a burnt offering.

Num 11:31–32 Now a wind went out from the Lord, and it brought quail from the sea and left *them* fluttering near the camp, about a day's journey on this side and about a day's journey on the other side, all around the camp, and about two cubits above the surface of the ground. **32** And the people stayed up all that day, all night, and all the next day, and gathered the quail (he who gathered least gathered ten homers); and they spread *them* out for themselves all around the camp.

Song 2:12 The flowers appear on the earth; The time of singing has come, And the voice of the turtledove Is heard in our land.

To be eaten.

Deut 14:11 "All clean birds you may eat.

Deut 14:20 "You may eat all clean birds.

Offered in sacrifice.

Gen 8:20 Then Noah built an altar to the LORD, and took of every clean animal and of every clean bird, and offered burnt offerings on the altar.

Lev 1:14 'And if the burnt sacrifice of his offering to the LORD *is* of birds, then he shall bring his offering of turtledoves or young pigeons.

Unclean,

Names of.

Lev 11:13–18 'And these you shall regard as an abomination among the birds; they shall not be eaten, they *are* an abomination: the eagle, the vulture, the buzzard, **14** the kite, and the falcon after its kind; **15** every raven after its kind, **16** the ostrich, the short-eared owl, the sea gull, and the hawk after its kind; **17** the little owl, the fisher owl, and the screech owl; **18** the white owl, the jackdaw, and the carrion vulture;

Deut 14:13 the red kite, the falcon, and the kite after their kinds;

Not to be eaten.

Lev 11:13 'And these you shall regard as an abomination among the birds; they shall not be eaten, they *are* an abomination: the eagle, the vulture, the buzzard,

Lev 11:17 the little owl, the fisher owl, and the screech owl;

Deut 14:12 But these you shall not eat: the eagle, the vulture, the buzzard,

Not to be eaten with their young.

Deut 22:6–7 "If a bird's nest happens to be before you along the way, in any tree or on the ground, with young ones or eggs, with the mother sitting on the young or on the eggs, you shall not take the mother with the young; **7** you shall surely let the mother go, and take the young for yourself, that it may be well with you and *that* you may prolong *your* days.

Taken in snares or nets.

Prov 1:17 Surely, in vain the net is spread In the sight of any bird;

Often suffered for man's sin.

Gen 6:7 So the LORD said, "I will destroy man whom I have created from the face of the earth, both man and beast, creeping thing and birds of the air, for I am sorry that I have made them."

Jer 12:4 How long will the land mourn, And the herbs of every field wither? The beasts and birds are consumed, For the wickedness of those who dwell there, Because they said, "He will not see our final end."

Ezek 38:20 so that the fish of the sea, the birds of the heavens, the beasts of the field, all creeping things that creep on the earth, and all men who *are* on the face of the earth shall shake at My presence. The mountains shall be thrown down, the steep places shall fall, and every wall shall fall to the ground.'

Hos 4:3 Therefore the land will mourn; And everyone who dwells there will waste away With the beasts of the field And the birds of the air; Even the fish of the sea will be taken away.

Solomon wrote the history of.

1 Kin 4:33 Also he spoke of trees, from the cedar tree of Lebanon even to the hyssop that springs out of the wall; he spoke also of animals, of birds, of creeping things, and of fish.

Confinement of, in cages alluded to.

Jer 5:27 As a cage is full of birds, So their houses *are* full of deceit. Therefore they have become great and grown rich.

No likeness of, to be made for worship.

Deut 4:17 the likeness of any animal that *is* on the earth or the likeness of any winged bird that flies in the air,

Often worshiped by idolaters.

Rom 1:23 and changed the glory of the incorruptible God into an image made like corruptible man—and birds and four-footed animals and creeping things.

Illustrative of

Cruel and rapacious kings.

Is 46:11 Calling a bird of prey from the east, The man who executes My counsel, from a far country. Indeed I have spoken *it*; I will also bring it to pass. I have purposed *it*; I will also do it.

Hostile nations.

Jer 12:9 My heritage *is* to Me *like* a speckled vulture; The vultures all around *are* against her. Come, assemble all the beasts of the field, Bring them to devour!

People of different countries.

Ezek 31:6 All the birds of the heavens made their nests in its boughs; Under its branches all the beasts of the field brought forth their young; And in its shadow all great nations made their home.

Matt 13:32 which indeed is the least of all the seeds; but when it is grown it is greater than the herbs and becomes a tree, so that the birds of the air come and nest in its branches."

An unsettled person, etc.

Prov 27:8 Like a bird that wanders from its nest *Is* a man who wanders from his place.

Is 16:2 For it shall be as a wandering bird thrown out of the nest; *So* shall be the daughters of Moab at the fords of the Arnon.

The devil and his spirits.

Matt 13:4 And as he sowed, some *seed* fell by the wayside; and the birds came and devoured them.

Matt 13:19 When anyone hears the word of the kingdom, and does not understand *it*, then the wicked *one* comes and snatches away what was sown in his heart. This is he who received seed by the wayside.

(Snaring) death.

Eccl 9:12 For man also does not know his time: Like fish taken in a cruel net, Like birds caught in a snare, So the sons of men *are* snared in an evil time, When it falls suddenly upon them.

(Snaring) the designs of the wicked.

Ps 124:7 Our soul has escaped as a bird from the snare of the fowlers; The snare is broken, and we have escaped.

Prov 1:10–17 My son, if sinners entice you, Do not consent. **11** If they say, "Come with us, Let us lie in wait to *shed* blood; Let us lurk secretly for the innocent without cause; **12** Let us swallow them alive like Sheol, And whole, like those who go down to the Pit; **13** We shall find all *kinds* of precious possessions, We shall fill our houses with spoil; **14** Cast in your lot among us, Let us all have one purse"— **15** My son, do not walk in the way with them, Keep your foot from their path; **16** For their feet run to evil, And they make haste to shed blood. **17** Surely, in vain the net is spread In the sight of any bird;

Prov 7:23 Till an arrow struck his liver. As a bird hastens to the snare, He did not know it *would cost* his life.

BLASPHEMY

Christ assailed with.

Matt 10:25 It is enough for a disciple that he be like his teacher, and a servant like his master. If they have called the master of the house Beelzebub, how much more *will they call* those of his household!

Luke 22:64–65 And having blindfolded Him, they struck Him on the face and asked Him, saying, "Prophesy! Who is the one who struck You?" **65** And many other things they blasphemously spoke against Him.

1 Pet 4:14 If you are reproached for the name of Christ, blessed *are you*, for the Spirit of glory and of God rests upon you. On their part He is blasphemed, but on your part He is glorified.

Charged upon Christ.

Matt 9:2–3 Then behold, they brought to Him a paralytic lying on a bed. When Jesus saw their faith, He said to the paralytic, "Son, be of good cheer; your sins are forgiven you." **3** And at once some of the scribes said within themselves, "This Man blasphemes!"

Matt 26:64–65 Jesus said to him, "*It is as* you said. Nevertheless, I say to you, hereafter you will see the Son of Man sitting at the right hand of the Power, and coming on the clouds of heaven." **65** Then the high priest tore his clothes, saying, "He has spoken blasphemy! What further need do we have of witnesses? Look, now you have heard His blasphemy!

John 10:33 The Jews answered Him, saying, "For a good work we do not stone You, but for blasphemy, and because You, being a Man, make Yourself God."

John 10:36 do you say of Him whom the Father sanctified and sent into the world, 'You are blaspheming,' because I said, 'I am the Son of God'?

Charged upon saints.

Acts 6:11 Then they secretly induced men to say, "We have heard him speak blasphemous words against Moses and God."

Acts 6:13 They also set up false witnesses who said, "This man does not cease to speak blasphemous words against this holy place and the law;

Proceeds from the heart.

Matt 15:19 For out of the heart proceed evil thoughts, murders, adulteries, fornications, thefts, false witness, blasphemies.

Forbidden.

Ex 20:7 "You shall not take the name of the Lord your God in vain, for the Lord will not hold *him* guiltless who takes His name in vain.

Col 3:8 But now you yourselves are to put off all these: anger, wrath, malice, blasphemy, filthy language out of your mouth.

The wicked practice it.

Ps 74:18 Remember this, *that* the enemy has reproached, O Lord, And *that* a foolish people has blasphemed Your name.

Is 52:5 Now therefore, what have I here," says the Lord, "That My people are taken away for nothing? Those who rule over them Make them wail," says the Lord, "And My name *is* blasphemed continually every day.

2 Tim 3:2 For men will be lovers of themselves, lovers of money, boasters, proud, blasphemers, disobedient to parents, unthankful, unholy,

Idolatry counted as.

Is 65:7 Your iniquities and the iniquities of your fathers together," Says the Lord, "Who have burned incense on the mountains And blasphemed Me on the hills; Therefore I will measure their former work into their bosom."

Ezek 20:27–28 "Therefore, son of man, speak to the house of Israel, and say to them, 'Thus says the Lord God: "In this too your fathers have blasphemed Me, by being unfaithful to Me. **28** When I brought them into the land *concerning* which I had raised My hand in an oath to give them, and they saw all the high hills and all the thick trees, there they offered their sacrifices and provoked Me with their offerings. There they also sent up their sweet aroma and poured out their drink offerings.

Hypocrisy counted as.

Rev 2:9 "I know your works, tribulation, and poverty (but you are rich); and *I know* the blasphemy of those who say they are Jews and are not, but *are* a synagogue of Satan.

Saints grieved to hear.

Ps 44:15–16 My dishonor *is* continually before me, And the shame of my face has covered me, **16** Because of the voice of him who reproaches and reviles, Because of the enemy and the avenger.

Ps 74:10 O God, how long will the adversary reproach? Will the enemy blaspheme Your name forever?

Ps 74:18 Remember this, *that* the enemy has reproached, O Lord, And *that* a foolish people has blasphemed Your name.

Ps 74:22 Arise, O God, plead Your own cause; Remember how the foolish man reproaches You daily.

Saints give no occasion for.

2 Sam 12:14 However, because by this deed you have given great occasion to the enemies of the Lord to blaspheme, the child also *who is* born to you shall surely die."

1 Tim 6:1 Let as many bondservants as are under the yoke count their own masters worthy of all honor, so that the name of God and *His* doctrine may not be blasphemed.

Against the Holy Spirit, unpardonable.

Matt 12:31–32 "Therefore I say to you, every sin and blasphemy will be forgiven men, but the blasphemy *against* the Spirit will not be forgiven men. 32 Anyone who speaks a word against the Son of Man, it will be forgiven him; but whoever speaks against the Holy Spirit, it will not be forgiven him, either in this age or in the *age* to come.

Connected with folly and pride.

2 Kin 19:22 'Whom have you reproached and blasphemed? Against whom have you raised *your* voice, And lifted up your eyes on high? Against the Holy One of Israel.

Ps 74:18 Remember this, *that* the enemy has reproached, O LORD, And *that* a foolish people has blasphemed Your name.

Characteristic of false teachers.

2 Pet 2:10–11 and especially those who walk according to the flesh in the lust of uncleanness and despise authority. *They are* presumptuous, self-willed. They are not afraid to speak evil of dignitaries, 11 whereas angels, who are greater in power and might, do not bring a reviling accusation against them before the Lord.

Punishment of.

Lev 24:16 And whoever blasphemes the name of the LORD shall surely be put to death. All the congregation shall certainly stone him, the stranger as well as him who is born in the land. When he blasphemes the name *of the* LORD, he shall be put to death.

Is 65:7 Your iniquities and the iniquities of your fathers together," Says the LORD, "Who have burned incense on the mountains And blasphemed Me on the hills; Therefore I will measure their former work into their bosom."

Ezek 20:27–33 "Therefore, son of man, speak to the house of Israel, and say to them, 'Thus says the Lord GOD: "In this too your fathers have blasphemed Me, by being unfaithful to Me. 28 When I brought them into the land *concerning* which I had raised My hand in an oath to give them, and they saw all the high hills and all the thick trees, there they offered their sacrifices and provoked Me with their offerings. There they also sent up their sweet aroma and poured out their drink offerings. 29 Then I said to them, 'What *is* this high place to which you go?' So its name is called Bamah to this day." ' 30 Therefore say to the house of Israel, 'Thus says the Lord GOD: "Are you defiling yourselves in the manner of your fathers, and committing harlotry according to their abominations? 31 For when you offer your gifts and make your sons pass through the fire, you defile yourselves with all your idols, even to this day. So shall I be inquired of by you, O house of Israel? *As* I live," says the Lord GOD, "I will not be inquired of by you. 32 What you have in your mind shall never be, when you say, 'We will be like the Gentiles, like the families in other countries, serving wood and stone.' 33 "*As* I live," says the Lord GOD, "surely with a mighty hand, with an outstretched arm, and with fury poured out, I will rule over you.

Ezek 35:11–12 therefore, *as* I live," says the Lord GOD, "I will do according to your anger and according to the envy which you showed in your hatred against them; and I will make Myself known among them when I judge you. 12 Then you shall know that I *am* the LORD. I have heard all your blasphemies which you

have spoken against the mountains of Israel, saying, 'They are desolate; they are given to us to consume.'

Illustrated by

The Danite.

Lev 24:11 And the Israelite woman's son blasphemed the name *of the* LORD and cursed; and so they brought him to Moses. (His mother's name *was* Shelomith the daughter of Dibri, of the tribe of Dan.)

Sennacherib.

2 Kin 19:4 It may be that the LORD your God will hear all the words of *the* Rabshakeh, whom his master the king of Assyria has sent to reproach the living God, and will rebuke the words which the LORD your God has heard. Therefore lift up *your* prayer for the remnant that is left.' "

2 Kin 19:10 "Thus you shall speak to Hezekiah king of Judah, saying: 'Do not let your God in whom you trust deceive you, saying, "Jerusalem shall not be given into the hand of the king of Assyria."

2 Kin 19:22 'Whom have you reproached and blasphemed? Against whom have you raised *your* voice, And lifted up your eyes on high? Against the Holy One of Israel.

The Jews.

Luke 22:65 And many other things they blasphemously spoke against Him.

Hymenaeus.

1 Tim 1:20 of whom are Hymenaeus and Alexander, whom I delivered to Satan that they may learn not to blaspheme.

The reprobate.

Rev 16:10–11 Then the fifth angel poured out his bowl on the throne of the beast, and his kingdom became full of darkness; and they gnawed their tongues because of the pain. 11 They blasphemed the God of heaven because of their pains and their sores, and did not repent of their deeds.

Rev 17:3 So he carried me away in the Spirit into the wilderness. And I saw a woman sitting on a scarlet beast *which was* full of names of blasphemy, having seven heads and ten horns.

BLESSED, THE

Whom God chooses and calls.

Ps 65:4 Blessed *is the man* You choose, And cause to approach *You, That* he may dwell in Your courts. We shall be satisfied with the goodness of Your house, Of Your holy temple.

Is 51:2 Look to Abraham your father, And to Sarah *who* bore you; For I called him alone, And blessed him and increased him."

Eph 1:3–4 Blessed *be* the God and Father of our Lord Jesus Christ, who has blessed us with every spiritual blessing in the heavenly *places* in Christ, 4 just as He chose us in Him before the foundation of the world, that we should be holy and without blame before Him in love,

Rev 19:9 Then he said to me, "Write: 'Blessed *are* those who are called to the marriage supper of the Lamb!' " And he said to me, "These are the true sayings of God."

Who know Christ and the gospel.

Ps 89:15 Blessed *are* the people who know the joyful sound! They walk, O LORD, in the light of Your countenance.

Matt 11:6 And blessed is he who is not offended because of Me."

Matt 16:16–17 Simon Peter answered and said, "You are the Christ, the Son of the living God." **17** Jesus answered and said to him, "Blessed are you, Simon Bar-Jonah, for flesh and blood has not revealed *this* to you, but My Father who is in heaven.

Who believe.

Luke 1:45 Blessed *is* she who believed, for there will be a fulfillment of those things which were told her from the Lord."

Gal 3:9 So then those who *are* of faith are blessed with believing Abraham.

Whose sins are forgiven.

Ps 32:1–2 Blessed *is he whose* transgression *is* forgiven, *Whose* sin *is* covered. **2** Blessed *is* the man to whom the LORD does not impute iniquity, And in whose spirit *there is* no deceit.

Rom 4:7 *"Blessed are those whose lawless deeds are forgiven, And whose sins are covered;*

To whom God imputes righteousness without works.

Rom 4:6–9 just as David also describes the blessedness of the man to whom God imputes righteousness apart from works: **7** *"Blessed are those whose lawless deeds are forgiven, And whose sins are covered;* **8** *Blessed is the man to whom the LORD shall not impute sin."* **9** *Does* this blessedness then *come* upon the circumcised *only,* or upon the uncircumcised also? For we say that faith was accounted to Abraham for righteousness.

Whom God chastens.

Job 5:17 "Behold, happy *is* the man whom God corrects; Therefore do not despise the chastening of the Almighty.

Ps 94:12 Blessed *is* the man whom You instruct, O LORD, And teach out of Your law,

Who suffer for Christ.

Luke 6:22 Blessed are you when men hate you, And when they exclude you, And revile *you,* and cast out your name as evil, For the Son of Man's sake.

Who trust in God.

Is 30:18 Therefore the LORD will wait, that He may be gracious to you; And therefore He will be exalted, that He may have mercy on you. For the LORD *is* a God of justice; Blessed *are* all those who wait for Him.

Ps 2:12 Kiss the Son, lest He be angry, And you perish *in* the way, When His wrath is kindled but a little. Blessed *are* all those who put their trust in Him.

Ps 34:8 Oh, taste and see that the LORD *is* good; Blessed *is* the man *who* trusts in Him!

Ps 40:4 Blessed *is* that man who makes the LORD his trust, And does not respect the proud, nor such as turn aside to lies.

Ps 84:5 Blessed *is* the man whose strength *is* in You, Whose heart *is* set on pilgrimage.

Ps 84:12 O LORD of hosts, Blessed *is* the man who trusts in You!

Ps 144:15 Happy *are* the people who are in such a state; Happy *are* the people whose God *is* the LORD!

Jer 17:7 "Blessed *is* the man who trusts in the LORD, And whose hope is the LORD.

Who fear God and keep His word.

Ps 112:1 Praise the LORD! Blessed *is* the man *who* fears the LORD, Who delights greatly in His commandments.

Ps 119:2 Blessed *are* those who keep His testimonies, Who seek Him with the whole heart!

Ps 128:1 Blessed *is* every one who fears the LORD, Who walks in His ways.

Ps 128:4 Behold, thus shall the man be blessed Who fears the LORD.

Matt 13:16 But blessed *are* your eyes for they see, and your ears for they hear;

Luke 11:28 But He said, "More than that, blessed *are* those who hear the word of God and keep it!"

James 1:24 for he observes himself, goes away, and immediately forgets what kind of man he was.

Rev 1:3 Blessed *is* he who reads and those who hear the words of this prophecy, and keep those things which are written in it; for the time *is* near.

Rev 22:7 "Behold, I am coming quickly! Blessed *is* he who keeps the words of the prophecy of this book."

Who delight in the commandments of God.

Ps 112:1 Praise the LORD! Blessed *is* the man *who* fears the LORD, Who delights greatly in His commandments.

Matt 5:6 Blessed *are* those who hunger and thirst for righteousness, For they shall be filled.

Rev 22:14 Blessed *are* those who do His commandments, that they may have the right to the tree of life, and may enter through the gates into the city.

Who avoid wicked companionship.

Ps 1:1 Blessed *is* the man Who walks not in the counsel of the ungodly, Nor stands in the path of sinners, Nor sits in the seat of the scornful;

Prov 24:25 But those who rebuke *the wicked* will have delight, And a good blessing will come upon them.

Who endure and guard against temptation.

James 1:12 Blessed *is* the man who endures temptation; for when he has been approved, he will receive the crown of life which the Lord has promised to those who love Him.

Rev 16:15 "Behold, I am coming as a thief. Blessed *is* he who watches, and keeps his garments, lest he walk naked and they see his shame."

Who watch for the Lord.

Luke 12:37 Blessed *are* those servants whom the master, when he comes, will find watching. Assuredly, I say to you that he will gird himself and have them sit down *to eat,* and will come and serve them.

Who die in the Lord.

Rev 14:13 Then I heard a voice from heaven saying to me, "Write: 'Blessed *are* the dead who die in the Lord from now on.' " "Yes," says the Spirit, "that they may rest from their labors, and their works follow them."

Rev 20:6 Blessed and holy *is* he who has part in the first resurrection. Over such the second death has no power, but they shall be priests of God and of Christ, and shall reign with Him a thousand years.

Who favor saints.

Gen 12:3 I will bless those who bless you, And I will curse him who curses you; And in you all the families of the earth shall be blessed."

The just and pure.

Ps 5:12 For You, O LORD, will bless the righteous; With favor You will surround him as *with* a shield.

Ps 10:6 He has said in his heart, "I shall not be moved; I shall never be in adversity."

Ps 106:3 Blessed *are* those who keep justice, And he who does righteousness at all times!

Ps 119:1 Blessed *are* the undefiled in the way, Who walk in the law of the LORD!

Matt 5:8 Blessed *are* the pure in heart, For they shall see God.

The children of the righteous.

Ps 112:2 His descendants will be mighty on earth; The generation of the upright will be blessed.

Prov 20:7 The righteous *man* walks in his integrity; His children *are* blessed after him.

Those with godly attitudes.

Prov 28:20 A faithful man will abound with blessings, But he who hastens to be rich will not go unpunished.

Matt 5:3–5 "Blessed *are* the poor in spirit, For theirs is the kingdom of heaven. **4** Blessed *are* those who mourn, For they shall be comforted. **5** Blessed *are* the meek, For they shall inherit the earth.

Matt 5:7 Blessed *are* the merciful, For they shall obtain mercy.

Matt 5:9 Blessed *are* the peacemakers, For they shall be called sons of God.

Luke 6:21 Blessed *are you* who hunger now, For you shall be filled. Blessed *are you* who weep now, For you shall laugh."

The generous.

Deut 15:10 You shall surely give to him, and your heart should not be grieved when you give to him, because for this thing the LORD your God will bless you in all your works and in all to which you put your hand.

Ps 41:1 Blessed *is* he who considers the poor; The LORD will deliver him in time of trouble.

Prov 22:9 He who has a generous eye will be blessed, For he gives of his bread to the poor.

Luke 14:13–14 But when you give a feast, invite *the* poor, *the* maimed, *the* lame, *the* blind. **14** And you will be blessed, because they cannot repay you; for you shall be repaid at the resurrection of the just."

Saints at the judgment day.

Matt 25:34 Then the King will say to those on His right hand, 'Come, you blessed of My Father, inherit the kingdom prepared for you from the foundation of the world:

Luke 14:15 Now when one of those who sat at the table with Him heard these things, he said to Him,

"Blessed *is* he who shall eat bread in the kingdom of God!"

Rev 19:9 Then he said to me, "Write: 'Blessed *are* those who are called to the marriage supper of the Lamb!' " And he said to me, "These are the true sayings of God."

BLINDNESS, SPIRITUAL

Explained.

1 Cor 2:14 But the natural man does not receive the things of the Spirit of God, for they are foolishness to him; nor can he know *them,* because they are spiritually discerned.

The effect of sin.

Is 29:10 For the LORD has poured out on you The spirit of deep sleep, And has closed your eyes, namely, the prophets; And He has covered your heads, *namely,* the seers.

Matt 6:23 But if your eye is bad, your whole body will be full of darkness. If therefore the light that is in you is darkness, how great *is* that darkness!

John 3:19–20 And this is the condemnation, that the light has come into the world, and men loved darkness rather than light, because their deeds were evil. **20** For everyone practicing evil hates the light and does not come to the light, lest his deeds should be exposed.

The effect of unbelief.

Rom 11:8 Just as it is written: *"God has given them a spirit of stupor, Eyes that they should not see And ears that they should not hear, To this very day."*

2 Cor 4:3–4 But even if our gospel is veiled, it is veiled to those who are perishing, **4** whose minds the god of this age has blinded, who do not believe, lest the light of the gospel of the glory of Christ, who is the image of God, should shine on them.

A proof of lack of love.

1 John 2:9 He who says he is in the light, and hates his brother, is in darkness until now.

1 John 2:11 But he who hates his brother is in darkness and walks in darkness, and does not know where he is going, because the darkness has blinded his eyes.

A work of the devil.

2 Cor 4:4 whose minds the god of this age has blinded, who do not believe, lest the light of the gospel of the glory of Christ, who is the image of God, should shine on them.

Leads to all evil.

Eph 4:17–19 This I say, therefore, and testify in the Lord, that you should no longer walk as the rest of the Gentiles walk, in the futility of their mind, **18** having their understanding darkened, being alienated from the life of God, because of the ignorance that is in them, because of the blindness of their heart; **19** who, being past feeling, have given themselves over to lewdness, to work all uncleanness with greediness.

Is inconsistent with communion with God.

1 John 1:6–7 If we say that we have fellowship with Him, and walk in darkness, we lie and do not practice the truth. **7** But if we walk in the light as He is in the light, we have fellowship with one another, and the blood of Jesus Christ His Son cleanses us from all sin.

Of ministers, fatal to themselves and to the people.

Matt 15:14 Let them alone. They are blind leaders of the blind. And if the blind leads the blind, both will fall into a ditch."

The wicked are in.

Ps 82:5 They do not know, nor do they understand; They walk about in darkness; All the foundations of the earth are unstable.

Is 26:11 LORD, *when* Your hand is lifted up, they will not see. But they will see and be ashamed For *their* envy of people; Yes, the fire of Your enemies shall devour them.

Jer 5:21 'Hear this now, O foolish people, Without understanding, Who have eyes and see not, And who have ears and hear not:

Rom 1:19–21 because what may be known of God is manifest in them, for God has shown *it* to them. **20** For since the creation of the world His invisible *attributes* are clearly seen, being understood by the things that are made, *even* His eternal power and Godhead, so that they are without excuse, **21** because, although they knew God, they did not glorify *Him* as God, nor were thankful, but became futile in their thoughts, and their foolish hearts were darkened.

The self-righteous are in.

Matt 23:19 Fools and blind! For which is greater, the gift or the altar that sanctifies the gift?

Matt 23:26 Blind Pharisee, first cleanse the inside of the cup and dish, that the outside of them may be clean also.

Rev 3:17 Because you say, 'I am rich, have become wealthy, and have need of nothing'—and do not know that you are wretched, miserable, poor, blind, and naked—

Judicially inflicted.

Ps 69:23 Let their eyes be darkened, so that they do not see; And make their loins shake continually.

Is 29:10 For the LORD has poured out on you The spirit of deep sleep, And has closed your eyes, namely, the prophets; And He has covered your heads, *namely,* the seers.

Is 44:18 They do not know nor understand; For He has shut their eyes, so that they cannot see, *And* their hearts, so that they cannot understand.

Matt 13:13–14 Therefore I speak to them in parables, because seeing they do not see, and hearing they do not hear, nor do they understand. **14** And in them the prophecy of Isaiah is fulfilled, which says: 'Hearing *you will hear and shall not understand, And seeing you will see and not perceive;*

John 12:40 *"He has blinded their eyes and hardened their hearts, Lest they should see with their eyes, Lest they should understand with their hearts and turn, So that I should heal them."*

Pray for the removal of.

Ps 13:3 Consider *and* hear me, O LORD my God; Enlighten my eyes, Lest I sleep the *sleep of* death;

Ps 119:18 Open my eyes, that I may see Wondrous things from Your law.

Christ appointed to remove.

Is 42:7 To open blind eyes, To bring out prisoners from the prison, Those who sit in darkness from the prison house.

Luke 4:18 *"The Spirit of the LORD is upon Me, Because He has anointed Me To preach the gospel to the poor; He has sent Me to heal the brokenhearted, To proclaim liberty to the captives And recovery of sight to the blind, To set at liberty those who are oppressed;*

John 8:12 Then Jesus spoke to them again, saying, "I am the light of the world. He who follows Me shall not walk in darkness, but have the light of life."

John 9:39 And Jesus said, "For judgment I have come into this world, that those who do not see may see, and that those who see may be made blind."

2 Cor 4:6 For it is the God who commanded light to shine out of darkness, who has shone in our hearts to *give* the light of the knowledge of the glory of God in the face of Jesus Christ.

Christ's ministers are lights to remove.

Matt 5:14 "You are the light of the world. A city that is set on a hill cannot be hidden.

Acts 26:18 to open their eyes, *in order* to turn *them* from darkness to light, and *from* the power of Satan to God, that they may receive forgiveness of sins and an inheritance among those who are sanctified by faith in Me.'

Saints are delivered from.

John 8:12 Then Jesus spoke to them again, saying, "I am the light of the world. He who follows Me shall not walk in darkness, but have the light of life."

Eph 5:8 For you were once darkness, but now *you are* light in the Lord. Walk as children of light

Col 1:13 He has delivered us from the power of darkness and conveyed *us* into the kingdom of the Son of His love,

1 Thess 5:4–5 But you, brethren, are not in darkness, so that this Day should overtake you as a thief. **5** You are all sons of light and sons of the day. We are not of the night nor of darkness.

1 Pet 2:9 But you *are* a chosen generation, a royal priesthood, a holy nation, His own special people, that you may proclaim the praises of Him who called you out of darkness into His marvelous light;

Removal of, illustrated.

John 9:7 And He said to him, "Go, wash in the pool of Siloam" (which is translated, Sent). So he went and washed, and came back seeing.

John 9:11 He answered and said, "A Man called Jesus made clay and anointed my eyes and said to me, 'Go to the pool of Siloam and wash.' So I went and washed, and I received sight."

John 9:25 He answered and said, "Whether He is a sinner *or not* I do not know. One thing I know: that though I was blind, now I see."

Acts 9:18 Immediately there fell from his eyes *something* like scales, and he received his sight at once; and he arose and was baptized.

Rev 3:18 I counsel you to buy from Me gold refined in

the fire, that you may be rich; and white garments, that you may be clothed, *that* the shame of your nakedness may not be revealed; and anoint your eyes with eye salve, that you may see.

Examples of,

Israel.

Rom 11:25 For I do not desire, brethren, that you should be ignorant of this mystery, lest you should be wise in your own opinion, that blindness in part has happened to Israel until the fullness of the Gentiles has come in.

2 Cor 3:15 But even to this day, when Moses is read, a veil lies on their heart.

Scribes and Pharisees.

Matt 23:16 "Woe to you, blind guides, who say, 'Whoever swears by the temple, it is nothing; but whoever swears by the gold of the temple, he is obliged *to perform it.*'

Matt 23:24 Blind guides, who strain out a gnat and swallow a camel!

Churches of Laodicea.

Rev 3:17 Because you say, 'I am rich, have become wealthy, and have need of nothing'—and do not know that you are wretched, miserable, poor, blind, and naked—

BLOOD

The life of animals.

Gen 9:4 But you shall not eat flesh with its life, *that is,* its blood.

Lev 17:11 For the life of the flesh *is* in the blood, and I have given it to you upon the altar to make atonement for your souls; for it *is* the blood *that* makes atonement for the soul.'

Lev 17:14 for *it is* the life of all flesh. Its blood sustains its life. Therefore I said to the children of Israel, 'You shall not eat the blood of any flesh, for the life of all flesh is its blood. Whoever eats it shall be cut off.'

Of all men the same.

Acts 17:26 And He has made from one blood every nation of men to dwell on all the face of the earth, and has determined their preappointed times and the boundaries of their dwellings,

Eating of, forbidden to

Man after the Flood.

Gen 9:4 But you shall not eat flesh with its life, *that is,* its blood.

The Israelites under the law.

Lev 3:17 'This shall be a perpetual statute throughout your generations in all your dwellings: you shall eat neither fat nor blood.' "

Lev 17:10 'And whatever man of the house of Israel, or of the strangers who dwell among you, who eats any blood, I will set My face against that person who eats blood, and will cut him off from among his people.

Lev 17:12 Therefore I said to the children of Israel, 'No one among you shall eat blood, nor shall any stranger who dwells among you eat blood.'

The early Christians.

Acts 15:20 but that we write to them to abstain from

things polluted by idols, *from* sexual immorality, *from* things strangled, and *from* blood.

Acts 15:29 that you abstain from things offered to idols, from blood, from things strangled, and from sexual immorality. If you keep yourselves from these, you will do well. Farewell.

The Jews often guilty of eating.

Ezek 33:25 "Therefore say to them, 'Thus says the Lord GOD: "You eat *meat* with blood, you lift up your eyes toward your idols, and shed blood. Should you then possess the land?

Of animals slain for good to be poured on the earth and covered.

Lev 17:13 "Whatever man of the children of Israel, or of the strangers who dwell among you, who hunts and catches any animal or bird that may be eaten, he shall pour out its blood and cover it with dust;

Deut 12:16 Only you shall not eat the blood; you shall pour it on the earth like water.

Deut 12:24 You shall not eat it; you shall pour it on the earth like water.

Animals of prey delight in.

Num 23:24 Look, a people rises like a lioness, And lifts itself up like a lion; It shall not lie down until it devours the prey, And drinks the blood of the slain."

Job 39:30 Its young ones suck up blood; And where the slain *are,* there it *is.*"

Ps 68:23 That your foot may crush *them* in blood, And the tongues of your dogs *may have* their portion from *your* enemies."

Shedding of human,

Forbidden.

Gen 9:5 Surely for your lifeblood I will demand *a reckoning;* from the hand of every beast I will require it, and from the hand of man. From the hand of every man's brother I will require the life of man.

Hateful to God.

Prov 6:16–17 These six *things* the LORD hates, Yes, seven *are* an abomination to Him: 17 A proud look, A lying tongue, Hands that shed innocent blood,

Defiling to the land.

Ps 106:38 And shed innocent blood, The blood of their sons and daughters, Whom they sacrificed to the idols of Canaan; And the land was polluted with blood.

Defiling to the person.

Is 59:3 For your hands are defiled with blood, And your fingers with iniquity; Your lips have spoken lies, Your tongue has muttered perversity.

Jews often guilty of.

Jer 22:17 "Yet your eyes and your heart *are* for nothing but your covetousness, For shedding innocent blood, And practicing oppression and violence."

Ezek 22:4 You have become guilty by the blood which you have shed, and have defiled yourself with the idols which you have made. You have caused your days to draw near, and have come to *the end of* your years; therefore I have made you a reproach to the nations, and a mockery to all countries.

Always punished.

Gen 9:6 "Whoever sheds man's blood, By man his

blood shall be shed; For in the image of God He made man.

Mode of clearing those accused of.

Deut 21:1–9 "If *anyone* is found slain, lying in the field in the land which the LORD your God is giving you to possess, *and* it is not known who killed him, **2** then your elders and your judges shall go out and measure *the distance* from the slain man to the surrounding cities. **3** And it shall be *that* the elders of the city nearest to the slain man will take a heifer which has not been worked *and* which has not pulled with a yoke. **4** The elders of that city shall bring the heifer down to a valley with flowing water, which is neither plowed nor sown, and they shall break the heifer's neck there in the valley. **5** Then the priests, the sons of Levi, shall come near, for the LORD your God has chosen them to minister to Him and to bless in the name of the LORD; by their word every controversy and every assault shall be *settled*. **6** And all the elders of that city nearest to the slain *man* shall wash their hands over the heifer whose neck was broken in the valley. **7** Then they shall answer and say, 'Our hands have not shed this blood, nor have our eyes seen *it*. **8** Provide atonement, O LORD, for Your people Israel, whom You have redeemed, and do not lay innocent blood to the charge of Your people Israel.' And atonement shall be provided on their behalf for the blood. **9** So you shall put away the *guilt of* innocent blood from among you when you do *what is* right in the sight of the LORD.

The price of, not to be consecrated.

Matt 27:6 But the chief priests took the silver pieces and said, "It is not lawful to put them into the treasury, because they are the price of blood."

Of legal sacrifices,

For atonement.

Ex 30:10 And Aaron shall make atonement upon its horns once a year with the blood of the sin offering of atonement; once a year he shall make atonement upon it throughout your generations. It *is* most holy to the LORD."

Lev 17:11 For the life of the flesh *is* in the blood, and I have given it to you upon the altar to make atonement for your souls; for it *is* the blood *that* makes atonement for the soul.'

For purification.

Heb 9:13 For if the blood of bulls and goats and the ashes of a heifer, sprinkling the unclean, sanctifies for the purifying of the flesh,

Heb 9:19–22 For when Moses had spoken every precept to all the people according to the law, he took the blood of calves and goats, with water, scarlet wool, and hyssop, and sprinkled both the book itself and all the people, **20** saying, *"This is the blood of the covenant which God has commanded you."* **21** Then likewise he sprinkled with blood both the tabernacle and all the vessels of the ministry. **22** And according to the law almost all things are purified with blood, and without shedding of blood there is no remission.

How disposed of.

Ex 29:12 You shall take *some* of the blood of the bull and put *it* on the horns of the altar with your finger, and pour all the blood beside the base of the altar.

Lev 4:7 And the priest shall put some of the blood on the horns of the altar of sweet incense before the LORD, which is in the tabernacle of meeting; and he shall pour the remaining blood of the bull at the base of the altar of the burnt offering, which is at the door of the tabernacle of meeting.

Not offered with leaven.

Ex 23:18 "You shall not offer the blood of My sacrifice with leavened bread; nor shall the fat of My sacrifice remain until morning.

Ex 34:25 "You shall not offer the blood of My sacrifice with leaven, nor shall the sacrifice of the Feast of the Passover be left until morning.

Ineffectual to remove sin.

Heb 10:4 For *it is* not possible that the blood of bulls and goats could take away sins.

Idolaters made drink offerings of.

Ps 16:4 Their sorrows shall be multiplied who hasten *after* another *god;* Their drink offerings of blood I will not offer, Nor take up their names on my lips.

Water turned into, as a sign.

Ex 4:9 And it shall be, if they do not believe even these two signs, or listen to your voice, that you shall take water from the river and pour *it* on the dry *land.* And the water which you take from the river will become blood on the dry *land.*"

Waters of Egypt turned into, as a judgment.

Ex 7:17–21 Thus says the LORD: "By this you shall know that I *am* the LORD. Behold, I will strike the waters which *are* in the river with the rod that *is* in my hand, and they shall be turned to blood. **18** And the fish that *are* in the river shall die, the river shall stink, and the Egyptians will loathe to drink the water of the river." ' " **19** Then the LORD spoke to Moses, "Say to Aaron, 'Take your rod and stretch out your hand over the waters of Egypt, over their streams, over their rivers, over their ponds, and over all their pools of water, that they may become blood. And there shall be blood throughout all the land of Egypt, both in *buckets of* wood and *pitchers of* stone.' " **20** And Moses and Aaron did so, just as the LORD commanded. So he lifted up the rod and struck the waters that *were* in the river, in the sight of Pharaoh and in the sight of his servants. And all the waters that *were* in the river were turned to blood. **21** The fish that *were* in the river died, the river stank, and the Egyptians could not drink the water of the river. So there was blood throughout all the land of Egypt.

Illustrative of

(Washing the feet in) victories.

Ps 58:10 The righteous shall rejoice when he sees the vengeance; He shall wash his feet in the blood of the wicked,

Ps 68:23 That your foot may crush *them* in blood, And the tongues of your dogs *may have* their portion from *your* enemies."

(Building with) oppression and cruelty.

Hab 2:12 "Woe to him who builds a town with bloodshed, Who establishes a city by iniquity!

(Preparing for) ripening for destruction.

Ezek 35:6 therefore, *as* I live," says the Lord GOD, "I will prepare you for blood, and blood shall pursue you;

since you have not hated blood, therefore blood shall pursue you.

(On one's own head) guilt.

Lev 20:9 'For everyone who curses his father or his mother shall surely be put to death. He has cursed his father or his mother. His blood *shall be* upon him.

2 Sam 1:16 So David said to him, "Your blood *is* on your own head, for your own mouth has testified against you, saying, 'I have killed the LORD's anointed.' "

Ezek 18:13 If he has exacted usury Or taken increase— Shall he then live? He shall not live! If he has done any of these abominations, He shall surely die; His blood shall be upon him.

(Given to drink) severe judgments.

Ezek 16:38 And I will judge you as women who break wedlock or shed blood are judged; I will bring blood upon you in fury and jealousy.

Rev 16:6 For they have shed the blood of saints and prophets, And You have given them blood to drink. For it is their just due."

BOAZ

Ruth's kinsman-redeemer. Ruth 4:1–12
Got acquainted with Ruth.

Ruth 2:8–16 Then Boaz said to Ruth, "You will listen, my daughter, will you not? Do not go to glean in another field, nor go from here, but stay close by my young women. **9** *Let* your eyes *be* on the field which they reap, and go after them. Have I not commanded the young men not to touch you? And when you are thirsty, go to the vessels and drink from what the young men have drawn." **10** So she fell on her face, bowed down to the ground, and said to him, "Why have I found favor in your eyes, that you should take notice of me, since I *am* a foreigner?" **11** And Boaz answered and said to her, "It has been fully reported to me, all that you have done for your mother-in-law since the death of your husband, and *how* you have left your father and your mother and the land of your birth, and have come to a people whom you did not know before. **12** The LORD repay your work, and a full reward be given you by the LORD God of Israel, under whose wings you have come for refuge." **13** Then she said, "Let me find favor in your sight, my lord; for you have comforted me, and have spoken kindly to your maidservant, though I am not like one of your maidservants." **14** Now Boaz said to her at mealtime, "Come here, and eat of the bread, and dip your piece of bread in the vinegar." So she sat beside the reapers, and he passed parched *grain* to her; and she ate and was satisfied, and kept some back. **15** And when she rose up to glean, Boaz commanded his young men, saying, "Let her glean even among the sheaves, and do not reproach her. **16** Also let *grain* from the bundles fall purposely for her; leave *it* that she may glean, and do not rebuke her."

Romance with Ruth. Ruth 3:1–18
Had son in the line of David.

Ruth 4:13–17 So Boaz took Ruth and she became his wife; and when he went in to her, the LORD gave her conception, and she bore a son. **14** Then the women said to Naomi, "Blessed *be* the LORD, who has not left you this day without a close relative; and may his name be famous in Israel! **15** And may he be to you a restorer of life and a nourisher of your old age; for your daughter-in-law, who loves you, who is better to you than seven sons, has borne him." **16** Then Naomi took the child and laid him on her bosom, and became a nurse to him. **17** Also the neighbor women gave him a name, saying, "There is a son born to Naomi." And they called his name Obed. He *is* the father of Jesse, the father of David.

Matt 1:5–6 Salmon begot Boaz by Rahab, Boaz begot Obed by Ruth, Obed begot Jesse, **6** and Jesse begot David the king. David the king begot Solomon by her *who had been the wife* of Uriah.

Same name symbolically attached to temple pillar.

1 Kin 7:21 Then he set up the pillars by the vestibule of the temple; he set up the pillar on the right and called its name Jachin, and he set up the pillar on the left and called its name Boaz.

2 Chr 3:17 Then he set up the pillars before the temple, one on the right hand and the other on the left; he called the name of the one on the right hand Jachin, and the name of the one on the left Boaz.

BOLDNESS, HOLY

Christ set an example of.

John 7:26 But look! He speaks boldly, and they say nothing to Him. Do the rulers know indeed that this is truly the Christ?

Is through faith in Christ.

Eph 3:12 in whom we have boldness and access with confidence through faith in Him.

Heb 10:19 Therefore, brethren, having boldness to enter the Holiest by the blood of Jesus,

A characteristic of saints.

Prov 28:1 The wicked flee when no one pursues, But the righteous are bold as a lion.

Produced by

Trust in God.

Is 50:7 "For the Lord GOD will help Me; Therefore I will not be disgraced; Therefore I have set My face like a flint, And I know that I will not be ashamed.

The fear of God.

Acts 4:19 But Peter and John answered and said to them, "Whether it is right in the sight of God to listen to you more than to God, you judge.

Acts 5:29 But Peter and the *other* apostles answered and said: "We ought to obey God rather than men.

Faithfulness to God.

1 Tim 3:13 For those who have served well as deacons obtain for themselves a good standing and great boldness in the faith which is in Christ Jesus.

Express your trust in God with.

Heb 13:6 So we may boldly say: *"The LORD is my helper; I will not fear. What can man do to me?"*

Have, in prayer.

Eph 3:12 in whom we have boldness and access with confidence through faith in Him.

Heb 4:16 Let us therefore come boldly to the throne of grace, that we may obtain mercy and find grace to help in time of need.

Saints shall have, in judgment.

1 John 4:17 Love has been perfected among us in this: that we may have boldness in the day of judgment; because as He is, so are we in this world.

Exhortations to.

Josh 1:7 Only be strong and very courageous, that you may observe to do according to all the law which Moses My servant commanded you; do not turn from it to the right hand or to the left, that you may prosper wherever you go.

2 Chr 19:11 And take notice: Amariah the chief priest *is* over you in all matters of the LORD; and Zebadiah the son of Ishmael, the ruler of the house of Judah, for all the king's matters; also the Levites *will be* officials before you. Behave courageously, and the LORD will be with the good.

Jer 1:8 Do not be afraid of their faces, For I *am* with you to deliver you," says the LORD.

Ezek 3:9 Like adamant stone, harder than flint, I have made your forehead; do not be afraid of them, nor be dismayed at their looks, though they *are* a rebellious house."

Pray for.

Acts 4:29 Now, Lord, look on their threats, and grant to Your servants that with all boldness they may speak Your word,

Eph 6:19–20 and for me, that utterance may be given to me, that I may open my mouth boldly to make known the mystery of the gospel, **20** for which I am an ambassador in chains; that in it I may speak boldly, as I ought to speak.

Ministers should exhibit, in

Faithfulness to their people.

2 Cor 7:4 Great *is* my boldness of speech toward you, great *is* my boasting on your behalf. I am filled with comfort. I am exceedingly joyful in all our tribulation.

2 Cor 10:1 Now I, Paul, myself am pleading with you by the meekness and gentleness of Christ—who in presence *am* lowly among you, but being absent am bold toward you.

Preaching.

Acts 4:31 And when they had prayed, the place where they were assembled together was shaken; and they were all filled with the Holy Spirit, and they spoke the word of God with boldness.

Phil 1:14 and most of the brethren in the Lord, having become confident by my chains, are much more bold to speak the word without fear.

Reproving sin.

Is 58:1 "Cry aloud, spare not; Lift up your voice like a trumpet; Tell My people their transgression, And the house of Jacob their sins.

Mic 3:8 But truly I am full of power by the Spirit of the LORD, And of justice and might, To declare to Jacob his transgression And to Israel his sin.

The face of opposition.

Acts 13:46 Then Paul and Barnabas grew bold and said, "It was necessary that the word of God should be spoken to you first; but since you reject it, and judge yourselves unworthy of everlasting life, behold, we turn to the Gentiles.

1 Thess 2:2 But even after we had suffered before and were spitefully treated at Philippi, as you know, we were bold in our God to speak to you the gospel of God in much conflict.

Exemplified by

Abraham.

Gen 18:22–32 Then the men turned away from there and went toward Sodom, but Abraham still stood before the LORD. **23** And Abraham came near and said, "Would You also destroy the righteous with the wicked? **24** Suppose there were fifty righteous within the city; would You also destroy the place and not spare *it* for the fifty righteous that were in it? **25** Far be it from You to do such a thing as this, to slay the righteous with the wicked, so that the righteous should be as the wicked; far be it from You! Shall not the Judge of all the earth do right?" **26** So the LORD said, "If I find in Sodom fifty righteous within the city, then I will spare all the place for their sakes." **27** Then Abraham answered and said, "Indeed now, I who *am but* dust and ashes have taken it upon myself to speak to the Lord: **28** Suppose there were five less than the fifty righteous; would You destroy all of the city for *lack of* five?" So He said, "If I find there forty-five, I will not destroy *it.*" **29** And he spoke to Him yet again and said, "Suppose there should be forty found there?" So He said, "I will not do *it* for the sake of forty." **30** Then he said, "Let not the Lord be angry, and I will speak: Suppose thirty should be found there?" So He said, "I will not do *it* if I find thirty there." **31** And he said, "Indeed now, I have taken it upon myself to speak to the Lord: Suppose twenty should be found there?" So He said, "I will not destroy *it* for the sake of twenty." **32** Then he said, "Let not the Lord be angry, and I will speak but once more: Suppose ten should be found there?" And He said, "I will not destroy *it* for the sake of ten."

Jacob.

Gen 32:24–29 Then Jacob was left alone; and a Man wrestled with him until the breaking of day. **25** Now when He saw that He did not prevail against him, He touched the socket of his hip; and the socket of Jacob's hip was out of joint as He wrestled with him. **26** And He said, "Let Me go, for the day breaks." But he said, "I will not let You go unless You bless me!" **27** So He said to him, "What *is* your name?" He said, "Jacob." **28** And He said, "Your name shall no longer be called Jacob, but Israel; for you have struggled with God and with men, and have prevailed." **29** Then Jacob asked, saying, "Tell *me* Your name, I pray." And He said, "Why *is it that* you ask about My name?" And He blessed him there.

Moses.

Ex 32:31–32 Then Moses returned to the LORD and said, "Oh, these people have committed a great sin, and have made for themselves a god of gold! **32** Yet now, if You will forgive their sin—but if not, I pray, blot me out of Your book which You have written."

Ex 33:18 And he said, "Please, show me Your glory."

Aaron.

Num 16:47–48 Then Aaron took *it* as Moses commanded, and ran into the midst of the assembly; and already the plague had begun among the people. So he put in the incense and made atonement for the people. **48** And he stood between the dead and the living; so the plague was stopped.

David.

1 Sam 17:45 Then David said to the Philistine, "You come to me with a sword, with a spear, and with a javelin. But I come to you in the name of the Lord of hosts, the God of the armies of Israel, whom you have defied.

Elijah.

1 Kin 18:15 Then Elijah said, "*As* the Lord of hosts lives, before whom I stand, I will surely present myself to him today."

1 Kin 18:18 And he answered, "I have not troubled Israel, but you and your father's house *have*, in that you have forsaken the commandments of the Lord and have followed the Baals.

Nehemiah.

Neh 6:11 And I said, "Should such a man as I flee? And who *is there* such as I who would go into the temple to save his life? I will not go in!"

Shadrach.

Dan 3:17–18 If that *is the case*, our God whom we serve is able to deliver us from the burning fiery furnace, and He will deliver *us* from your hand, O king. **18** But if not, let it be known to you, O king, that we do not serve your gods, nor will we worship the gold image which you have set up."

Daniel.

Dan 6:10 Now when Daniel knew that the writing was signed, he went home. And in his upper room, with his windows open toward Jerusalem, he knelt down on his knees three times that day, and prayed and gave thanks before his God, as was his custom since early days.

Joseph of Arimathea.

Mark 15:43 Joseph of Arimathea, a prominent council member, who was himself waiting for the kingdom of God, coming and taking courage, went in to Pilate and asked for the body of Jesus.

Peter and John.

Acts 4:8–13 Then Peter, filled with the Holy Spirit, said to them, "Rulers of the people and elders of Israel: **9** If we this day are judged for a good deed *done* to a helpless man, by what means he has been made well, **10** let it be known to you all, and to all the people of Israel, that by the name of Jesus Christ of Nazareth, whom you crucified, whom God raised from the dead, by Him this man stands here before you whole. **11** This is the *'stone which was rejected by you builders, which has become the chief cornerstone.'* **12** Nor is there salvation in any other, for there is no other name under heaven given among men by which we must be saved." **13** Now when they saw the boldness of Peter and John, and perceived that they were uneducated and untrained men, they marveled. And they realized that they had been with Jesus.

Stephen.

Acts 7:51 "*You* stiff-necked and uncircumcised in heart and ears! You always resist the Holy Spirit; as your fathers *did*, so *do* you.

Paul.

Acts 9:27 But Barnabas took him and brought *him* to the apostles. And he declared to them how he had seen the Lord on the road, and that He had spoken to him, and how he had preached boldly at Damascus in the name of Jesus.

Acts 9:29 And he spoke boldly in the name of the Lord Jesus and disputed against the Hellenists, but they attempted to kill him.

Acts 19:8 And he went into the synagogue and spoke boldly for three months, reasoning and persuading concerning the things of the kingdom of God.

Barnabas.

Acts 14:3 Therefore they stayed there a long time, speaking boldly in the Lord, who was bearing witness to the word of His grace, granting signs and wonders to be done by their hands.

Apollos.

Acts 18:26 So he began to speak boldly in the synagogue. When Aquila and Priscilla heard him, they took him aside and explained to him the way of God more accurately.

BONDAGE, SPIRITUAL

Is to the devil.

2 Tim 2:26 and *that* they may come to their senses *and escape* the snare of the devil, having been taken captive by him to *do* his will.

Is to the fear of death.

Heb 2:14–15 Inasmuch then as the children have partaken of flesh and blood, He Himself likewise shared in the same, that through death He might destroy him who had the power of death, that is, the devil, **15** and release those who through fear of death were all their lifetime subject to bondage.

Is to sin.

John 8:34 Jesus answered them, "Most assuredly, I say to you, whoever commits sin is a slave of sin.

Acts 8:23 For I see that you are poisoned by bitterness and bound by iniquity."

Rom 6:16 Do you not know that to whom you present yourselves slaves to obey, you are that one's slaves whom you obey, whether of sin *leading* to death, or of obedience *leading* to righteousness?

Rom 7:23 But I see another law in my members, warring against the law of my mind, and bringing me into captivity to the law of sin which is in my members.

Gal 4:3 Even so we, when we were children, were in bondage under the elements of the world.

2 Pet 2:19 While they promise them liberty, they themselves are slaves of corruption; for by whom a person is overcome, by him also he is brought into bondage.

Deliverance from, promised.

Is 42:6–7 "I, the Lord, have called You in righteousness, And will hold Your hand; I will keep You and give You as a covenant to the people, As a light to the Gentiles, **7** To open blind eyes, To bring out prisoners from the prison, Those who sit in darkness from the prison house.

Christ delivers from.

Luke 4:18 "*The Spirit of the Lord is upon Me, Because He has anointed Me To preach the gospel to the* *poor; He has sent Me to heal the brokenhearted, To proclaim liberty to the captives And recovery of sight to the blind, To set at liberty those who are oppressed;*

Luke 4:21 And He began to say to them, "Today this Scripture is fulfilled in your hearing."

John 8:36 Therefore if the Son makes you free, you shall be free indeed.

Rom 7:24–25 O wretched man that I am! Who will deliver me from this body of death? 25 I thank God— through Jesus Christ our Lord! So then, with the mind I myself serve the law of God, but with the flesh the law of sin.

Eph 4:8 Therefore He says: *"When He ascended on high, He led captivity captive, And gave gifts to men."*

The gospel, the instrument of deliverance from.

John 8:32 And you shall know the truth, and the truth shall make you free."

Rom 8:2 For the law of the Spirit of life in Christ Jesus has made me free from the law of sin and death.

Saints are delivered from.

Deut 4:20 But the LORD has taken you and brought you out of the iron furnace, out of Egypt, to be His people, an inheritance, as you are this day.

Rom 6:18 And having been set free from sin, you became slaves of righteousness.

Rom 6:22 But now having been set free from sin, and having become slaves of God, you have your fruit to holiness, and the end, everlasting life.

Typified Israel in Egypt.

Ex 1:13–14 So the Egyptians made the children of Israel serve with rigor. 14 And they made their lives bitter with hard bondage—in mortar, in brick, and in all manner of service in the field. All their service in which they made them serve *was* with rigor.

BOOKS

Earliest mention of.

Job 19:23–24 "Oh, that my words were written! Oh, that they were inscribed in a book! 24 That they were engraved on a rock With an iron pen and lead, forever!

Made of

Papyrus or paper reed.

Is 19:7 The papyrus reeds by the River, by the mouth of the River, And everything sown by the River, Will wither, be driven away, and be no more.

Parchment.

2 Tim 4:13 Bring the cloak that I left with Carpus at Troas when you come—and the books, especially the parchments.

Made in a roll.

Is 34:4 All the host of heaven shall be dissolved, And the heavens shall be rolled up like a scroll; All their host shall fall down As the leaf falls from the vine, And as *fruit* falling from a fig tree.

Jer 36:2 "Take a scroll of a book and write on it all the words that I have spoken to you against Israel, against Judah, and against all the nations, from the day I spoke to you, from the days of Josiah even to this day.

Ezek 2:9 Now when I looked, there was a hand stretched out to me; and behold, a scroll of a book *was* in it.

Written with pen and ink.

Jer 36:18 So Baruch answered them, "He proclaimed with his mouth all these words to me, and I wrote *them* with ink in the book."

3 John 1:13 I had many things to write, but I do not wish to write to you with pen and ink;

Often written on both sides.

Ezek 2:10 Then He spread it before me; and *there was* writing on the inside and on the outside, and written on it *were* lamentations and mourning and woe.

Of prophecy, sometimes sealed.

Is 29:11 The whole vision has become to you like the words of a book that is sealed, which *men* deliver to one who is literate, saying, "Read this, please." And he says, "I cannot, for it *is* sealed."

Dan 12:4 "But you, Daniel, shut up the words, and seal the book until the time of the end; many shall run to and fro, and knowledge shall increase."

Rev 5:1 And I saw in the right *hand* of Him who sat on the throne a scroll written inside and on the back, sealed with seven seals.

Often dedicated to persons of distinction.

Luke 1:3 it seemed good to me also, having had perfect understanding of all things from the very first, to write to you an orderly account, most excellent Theophilus,

Acts 1:1 The former account I made, O Theophilus, of all that Jesus began both to do and teach,

Were numerous and expensive.

Acts 19:19 Also, many of those who had practiced magic brought their books together and burned *them* in the sight of all. And they counted up the value of them, and *it* totaled fifty thousand *pieces* of silver.

Divine communications recorded in.

Ex 17:14 Then the LORD said to Moses, "Write this *for* a memorial in the book and recount *it* in the hearing of Joshua, that I will utterly blot out the remembrance of Amalek from under heaven.

Is 30:8 Now go, write it before them on a tablet, And note it on a scroll, That it may be for time to come, Forever and ever:

Jer 36:2 "Take a scroll of a book and write on it all the words that I have spoken to you against Israel, against Judah, and against all the nations, from the day I spoke to you, from the days of Josiah even to this day.

Rev 1:19 Write the things which you have seen, and the things which are, and the things which will take place after this.

Important events recorded in.

Ezra 4:15 that search may be made in the book of the records of your fathers. And you will find in the book of the records and know that this city *is* a rebellious city, harmful to kings and provinces, and that they have incited sedition within the city in former times, for which cause this city was destroyed.

Ezra 6:1–2 Then King Darius issued a decree, and a search was made in the archives, where the treasures were stored in Babylon. **2** And at Achmetha, in the palace that *is* in the province of Media, a scroll was found, and in it a record *was* written thus:

Esth 2:23 And when an inquiry was made into the matter, it was confirmed, and both were hanged on a gallows; and it was written in the book of the chronicles in the presence of the king.

Erasures in, alluded to.

Ex 32:33 And the LORD said to Moses, "Whoever has sinned against Me, I will blot him out of My book.

Num 5:23 Then the priest shall write these curses in a book, and he shall scrape *them* off into the bitter water.

Not extant, but mentioned in Scripture

Wars of the Lord.

Num 21:14 Therefore it is said in the Book of the Wars of the LORD: "Waheb in Suphah, The brooks of the Arnon,

Jasher.

Josh 10:13 So the sun stood still, And the moon stopped, Till the people had revenge Upon their enemies. *Is* this not written in the Book of Jasher? So the sun stood still in the midst of heaven, and did not hasten to go *down* for about a whole day.

2 Sam 1:18 and he told *them* to teach the children of Judah *the Song of* the Bow; indeed *it is* written in the Book of Jasher:

Samuel concerning the kingdom.

1 Sam 10:25 Then Samuel explained to the people the behavior of royalty, and wrote *it* in a book and laid *it* up before the LORD. And Samuel sent all the people away, every man to his house.

Chronicles of David.

1 Chr 27:24 Joab the son of Zeruiah began a census, but he did not finish, for wrath came upon Israel because of this census; nor was the number recorded in the account of the chronicles of King David.

Acts of Solomon.

1 Kin 11:41 Now the rest of the acts of Solomon, all that he did, and his wisdom, *are* they not written in the book of the acts of Solomon?

Natural history by Solomon.

1 Kin 4:32–33 He spoke three thousand proverbs, and his songs were one thousand and five. **33** Also he spoke of trees, from the cedar tree of Lebanon even to the hyssop that springs out of the wall; he spoke also of animals, of birds, of creeping things, and of fish.

History of the kings.

1 Chr 9:1 So all Israel was recorded by genealogies, and indeed, they *were* inscribed in the book of the kings of Israel. But Judah was carried away captive to Babylon because of their unfaithfulness.

Samuel the seer.

1 Chr 29:29 Now the acts of King David, first and last, indeed they *are* written in the book of Samuel the seer, in the book of Nathan the prophet, and in the book of Gad the seer,

Nathan.

1 Chr 29:29 Now the acts of King David, first and last,

indeed they *are* written in the book of Samuel the seer, in the book of Nathan the prophet, and in the book of Gad the seer,

2 Chr 9:29 Now the rest of the acts of Solomon, first and last, *are* they not written in the book of Nathan the prophet, in the prophecy of Ahijah the Shilonite, and in the visions of Iddo the seer concerning Jeroboam the son of Nebat?

Shemaiah.

2 Chr 12:15 The acts of Rehoboam, first and last, *are* they not written in the book of Shemaiah the prophet, and of Iddo the seer concerning genealogies? And *there were* wars between Rehoboam and Jeroboam all their days.

Gad the seer.

1 Chr 29:29 Now the acts of King David, first and last, indeed they *are* written in the book of Samuel the seer, in the book of Nathan the prophet, and in the book of Gad the seer,

Ahijah the Shilonite.

2 Chr 9:29 Now the rest of the acts of Solomon, first and last, *are* they not written in the book of Nathan the prophet, in the prophecy of Ahijah the Shilonite, and in the visions of Iddo the seer concerning Jeroboam the son of Nebat?

Visions of Iddo.

2 Chr 9:29 Now the rest of the acts of Solomon, first and last, *are* they not written in the book of Nathan the prophet, in the prophecy of Ahijah the Shilonite, and in the visions of Iddo the seer concerning Jeroboam the son of Nebat?

2 Chr 12:15 The acts of Rehoboam, first and last, *are* they not written in the book of Shemaiah the prophet, and of Iddo the seer concerning genealogies? And *there were* wars between Rehoboam and Jeroboam all their days.

Jehu the son of Hanani.

2 Chr 20:34 Now the rest of the acts of Jehoshaphat, first and last, indeed they *are* written in the book of Jehu the son of Hanani, which *is* mentioned in the book of the kings of Israel.

Sayings of the seers.

2 Chr 33:19 Also his prayer and *how God* received his entreaty, and all his sin and trespass, and the sites where he built high places and set up wooden images and carved images, before he was humbled, indeed they *are* written among the sayings of Hozai.

Illustrative of

Memorials of God's providence.

Ps 56:8 You number my wanderings; Put my tears into Your bottle; *Are they* not in Your book?

Ps 139:16 Your eyes saw my substance, being yet unformed. And in Your book they all were written, The days fashioned for me, When *as yet there were* none of them.

Memorials of conversation and conduct of men.

Dan 7:10 A fiery stream issued And came forth from before Him. A thousand thousands ministered to Him; Ten thousand times ten thousand stood before Him. The court was seated, And the books were opened.

Mal 3:16 Then those who feared the LORD spoke to one another, And the LORD listened and heard *them;* So a book of remembrance was written before Him For those who fear the LORD And who meditate on His name.

Rev 20:12 And I saw the dead, small and great, standing before God, and books were opened. And another book was opened, which is *the Book* of Life. And the dead were judged according to their works, by the things which were written in the books.

The record of the church of Christ.

Heb 12:23 to the general assembly and church of the firstborn *who are* registered in heaven, to God the Judge of all, to the spirits of just men made perfect,

Rev 20:12 And I saw the dead, small and great, standing before God, and books were opened. And another book was opened, which is *the Book* of Life. And the dead were judged according to their works, by the things which were written in the books.

Rev 20:15 And anyone not found written in the Book of Life was cast into the lake of fire.

Rev 22:19 and if anyone takes away from the words of the book of this prophecy, God shall take away his part from the Book of Life, from the holy city, and *from* the things which are written in this book.

BORROWING. *See* INTEREST

BOTTLES (SKINS, JUGS)
First mention of, in Scripture.

Gen 21:14 So Abraham rose early in the morning, and took bread and a skin of water; and putting *it* on her shoulder, he gave *it* and the boy to Hagar, and sent her away. Then she departed and wandered in the Wilderness of Beersheba.

Used for holding

Water.

Gen 21:14–15 So Abraham rose early in the morning, and took bread and a skin of water; and putting *it* on her shoulder, he gave *it* and the boy to Hagar, and sent her away. Then she departed and wandered in the Wilderness of Beersheba. **15** And the water in the skin was used up, and she placed the boy under one of the shrubs.

Gen 21:19 Then God opened her eyes, and she saw a well of water. And she went and filled the skin with water, and gave the lad a drink.

Milk.

Judg 4:19 Then he said to her, "Please give me a little water to drink, for I am thirsty." So she opened a jug of milk, gave him a drink, and covered him.

Wine.

1 Sam 1:24 Now when she had weaned him, she took him up with her, with three bulls, one ephah of flour, and a skin of wine, and brought him to the house of the LORD in Shiloh. And the child *was* young.

1 Sam 16:20 And Jesse took a donkey *loaded with* bread, a skin of wine, and a young goat, and sent *them* by his son David to Saul.

Some, made of earthenware.

Jer 19:1 Thus says the LORD: "Go and get a potter's

earthen flask, and *take* some of the elders of the people and some of the elders of the priests.

Made of skins,

Marred by age and use.

Josh 9:13–14 And these wineskins which we filled *were* new, and see, they are torn; and these our garments and our sandals have become old because of the very long journey." **14** Then the men of Israel took some of their provisions; but they did not ask counsel of the LORD.

When old, unfit for holding new wine.

Matt 9:17 Nor do they put new wine into old wineskins, or else the wineskins break, the wine is spilled, and the wineskins are ruined. But they put new wine into new wineskins, and both are preserved."

Mark 2:22 And no one puts new wine into old wineskins; or else the new wine bursts the wineskins, the wine is spilled, and the wineskins are ruined. But new wine must be put into new wineskins."

Sometimes probably of large dimensions.

1 Sam 25:18 Then Abigail made haste and took two hundred *loaves* of bread, two skins of wine, five sheep already dressed, five seahs of roasted *grain,* one hundred clusters of raisins, and two hundred cakes of figs, and loaded *them* on donkeys.

2 Sam 16:1 When David was a little past the top *of the mountain,* there was Ziba the servant of Mephibosheth, who met him with a couple of saddled donkeys, and on them two hundred *loaves* of bread, one hundred clusters of raisins, one hundred summer fruits, and a skin of wine.

Illustrative of

The clouds.

Job 38:37 Who can number the clouds by wisdom? Or who can pour out the bottles of heaven,

God's remembrance.

Ps 56:8 You number my wanderings; Put my tears into Your bottle; *Are they* not in Your book?

Sinners ripe for judgment.

Jer 13:12–14 "Therefore you shall speak to them this word: 'Thus says the LORD God of Israel: "Every bottle shall be filled with wine." ' "And they will say to you, 'Do we not certainly know that every bottle will be filled with wine?' **13** "Then you shall say to them, 'Thus says the LORD: "Behold, I will fill all the inhabitants of this land—even the kings who sit on David's throne, the priests, the prophets, and all the inhabitants of Jerusalem—with drunkenness! **14** And I will dash them one against another, even the fathers and the sons together," says the LORD. "I will not pity nor spare nor have mercy, but will destroy them." ' "

(Dried up) the afflicted.

Ps 119:83 For I have become like a wineskin in smoke, Yet I do not forget Your statutes.

(Ready to burst) the impatient.

Job 32:19 Indeed my belly *is* like wine *that* has no vent; It is ready to burst like new wineskins.

(Broken) severe judgments.

Is 30:14 And He shall break it like the breaking of the potter's vessel, Which is broken in pieces; He shall not spare. So there shall not be found among its fragments A shard to take fire from the hearth, Or to take water from the cistern."

Jer 19:10 "Then you shall break the flask in the sight of the men who go with you,

Jer 48:12 "Therefore behold, the days are coming," says the LORD, "That I shall send him wine-workers Who will tip him over And empty his vessels And break the bottles.

BOW, THE

An instrument of war.

Gen 48:22 Moreover I have given to you one portion above your brothers, which I took from the hand of the Amorite with my sword and my bow."

Is 7:24 With arrows and bows men will come there, Because all the land will become briers and thorns.

Zech 9:10 I will cut off the chariot from Ephraim And the horse from Jerusalem; The battle bow shall be cut off. He shall speak peace to the nations; His dominion *shall be* 'from sea to sea, And from the River to the ends of the earth.'

Sometimes used in hunting.

Gen 27:3 Now therefore, please take your weapons, your quiver and your bow, and go out to the field and hunt game for me.

For shooting arrows.

1 Chr 12:2 armed with bows, using both the right hand and the left in *hurling* stones and *shooting* arrows with the bow. *They were* of Benjamin, Saul's brethren.

Those who used, called

Bowmen.

Jer 4:29 The whole city shall flee from the noise of the horsemen and bowmen. They shall go into thickets and climb up on the rocks. Every city *shall be* forsaken, And not a man shall dwell in it.

Archers.

1 Sam 31:3 The battle became fierce against Saul. The archers hit him, and he was severely wounded by the archers.

Jer 51:3 Against *her* let the archer bend his bow, And lift himself up against *her* in his armor. Do not spare her young men; Utterly destroy all her army.

Usually of bronze.

2 Sam 22:35 He teaches my hands to make war, So that my arms can bend a bow of bronze.

Job 20:24 He will flee from the iron weapon; A bronze bow will pierce him through.

Held in the left hand.

Ezek 39:3 Then I will knock the bow out of your left hand, and cause the arrows to fall out of your right hand.

Drawn with full force.

2 Kin 9:24 Now Jehu drew his bow with full strength and shot Jehoram between his arms; and the arrow came out at his heart, and he sank down in his chariot.

The Jews taught to use.

2 Sam 1:18 and he told *them* to teach the children of Judah *the Song of* the Bow; indeed *it is* written in the Book of Jasher:

Used expertly by

Lydians.

Jer 46:9 Come up, O horses, and rage, O chariots! And let the mighty men come forth: The Ethiopians and the Libyans who handle the shield, And the Lydians who handle *and* bend the bow.

Elamites.

Jer 49:35 "Thus says the LORD of hosts: 'Behold, I will break the bow of Elam, The foremost of their might.

Philistines.

1 Sam 31:2–3 Then the Philistines followed hard after Saul and his sons. And the Philistines killed Jonathan, Abinadab, and Malchishua, Saul's sons. 3 The battle became fierce against Saul. The archers hit him, and he was severely wounded by the archers.

Sons of Reuben, Gad, and Manasseh.

1 Chr 5:18 The sons of Reuben, the Gadites, and half the tribe of Manasseh *had* forty-four thousand seven hundred and sixty valiant men, men able to bear shield and sword, to shoot with the bow, and skillful in war, who went to war.

Benjamites.

1 Chr 12:2 armed with bows, using both the right hand and the left in *hurling* stones and *shooting* arrows with the bow. *They were* of Benjamin, Saul's brethren.

2 Chr 14:8 And Asa had an army of three hundred thousand from Judah who carried shields and spears, and from Benjamin two hundred and eighty thousand men who carried shields and drew bows; all these *were* mighty men of valor.

Given as a token of friendship.

1 Sam 18:4 And Jonathan took off the robe that *was* on him and gave it to David, with his armor, even to his sword and his bow and his belt.

Often furnished by the state.

2 Chr 26:14 Then Uzziah prepared for them, for the entire army, shields, spears, helmets, body armor, bows, and slings *to cast* stones.

Of the vanquished, broken and burned.

Ps 37:15 Their sword shall enter their own heart, And their bows shall be broken.

Ezek 39:9 "Then those who dwell in the cities of Israel will go out and set on fire and burn the weapons, both the shields and bucklers, the bows and arrows, the javelins and spears; and they will make fires with them for seven years.

Illustrative

Of strength and power.

Job 29:20 My glory *is* fresh within me, And my bow is renewed in my hand.'

Of the tongue of the wicked.

Ps 11:2 For look! The wicked bend *their* bow, They make ready their arrow on the string, That they may shoot secretly at the upright in heart.

Jer 9:3 "And *like* their bow they have bent their tongues *for* lies. They are not valiant for the truth on the earth. For they proceed from evil to evil, And they do not know Me," says the LORD.

(When deceitful) of the hypocrite.

Ps 78:57 But turned back and acted unfaithfully like

their fathers; They were turned aside like a deceitful bow.

Hos 7:16 They return, *but* not to the Most High; They are like a treacherous bow. Their princes shall fall by the sword For the cursings of their tongue. This *shall be* their derision in the land of Egypt.

(When broken) of the overthrow of power.

1 Sam 2:4 "The bows of the mighty men *are* broken, And those who stumbled are girded with strength.

Jer 49:35 "Thus says the LORD of hosts: 'Behold, I will break the bow of Elam, The foremost of their might.

Hos 1:5 It shall come to pass in that day That I will break the bow of Israel in the Valley of Jezreel."

Hos 2:18 In that day I will make a covenant for them With the beasts of the field, With the birds of the air, And *with* the creeping things of the ground. Bow and sword of battle I will shatter from the earth, To make them lie down safely.

BRANCHES
Pictured spiritual deadness or deficiency.

Jer 5:10 "Go up on her walls and destroy, But do not make a complete end. Take away her branches, For they *are* not the LORD's.

Jer 11:16–17 The LORD called your name, Green Olive Tree, Lovely *and* of Good Fruit. With the noise of a great tumult He has kindled fire on it, And its branches are broken. 17 "For the LORD of hosts, who planted you, has pronounced doom against you for the evil of the house of Israel and of the house of Judah, which they have done against themselves to provoke Me to anger in offering incense to Baal."

John 15:2 Every branch in Me that does not bear fruit He takes away; and every *branch* that bears fruit He prunes, that it may bear more fruit.

John 15:6 If anyone does not abide in Me, he is cast out as a branch and is withered; and they gather them and throw *them* into the fire, and they are burned.

Name for Messiah.

Ezek 18:22–24 None of the transgressions which he has committed shall be remembered against him; because of the righteousness which he has done, he shall live. 23 Do I have any pleasure at all that the wicked should die?" says the Lord GOD, "*and* not that he should turn from his ways and live? 24 "But when a righteous man turns away from his righteousness and commits iniquity, and does according to all the abominations that the wicked *man* does, shall he live? All the righteousness which he has done shall not be remembered; because of the unfaithfulness of which he is guilty and the sin which he has committed, because of them he shall die.

Cf. Is 4:2; Jer 23:5; 33:15; Zech 3:8; 6:12

Represent high spiritual leadership.

Zech 4:12–14 And I further answered and said to him, "What *are these* two olive branches that *drip* into the receptacles of the two gold pipes from which the golden *oil* drains?" 13 Then he answered me and said, "Do you not know what these *are*?" And I said, "No, my lord." 14 So he said, "These *are* the two anointed ones, who stand beside the Lord of the whole earth."

Were spread in worship before Christ.

Matt 21:8 And a very great multitude spread their clothes on the road; others cut down branches from the trees and spread *them* on the road.

Mark 11:8 And many spread their clothes on the road, and others cut down leafy branches from the trees and spread *them* on the road.

John 12:13 took branches of palm trees and went out to meet Him, and cried out: "Hosanna! *'Blessed is He who comes in the name of the LORD!'* The King of Israel!"

Cf. Rev 7:9

Represent believers who must abide in Christ.

John 15:1–17 "I am the true vine, and My Father is the vinedresser. 2 Every branch in Me that does not bear fruit He takes away; and every *branch* that bears fruit He prunes, that it may bear more fruit. 3 You are already clean because of the word which I have spoken to you. 4 Abide in Me, and I in you. As the branch cannot bear fruit of itself, unless it abides in the vine, neither can you, unless you abide in Me. 5 "I am the vine, you *are* the branches. He who abides in Me, and I in him, bears much fruit; for without Me you can do nothing. 6 If anyone does not abide in Me, he is cast out as a branch and is withered; and they gather them and throw *them* into the fire, and they are burned. 7 If you abide in Me, and My words abide in you, you will ask what you desire, and it shall be done for you. 8 By this My Father is glorified, that you bear much fruit; so you will be My disciples. 9 "As the Father loved Me, I also have loved you; abide in My love. 10 If you keep My commandments, you will abide in My love, just as I have kept My Father's commandments and abide in His love. 11 "These things I have spoken to you, that My joy may remain in you, and *that* your joy may be full. 12 This is My commandment, that you love one another as I have loved you. 13 Greater love has no one than this, than to lay down one's life for his friends. 14 You are My friends if you do whatever I command you. 15 No longer do I call you servants, for a servant does not know what his master is doing; but I have called you friends, for all things that I heard from My Father I have made known to you. 16 You did not choose Me, but I chose you and appointed you that you should go and bear fruit, and *that* your fruit should remain, that whatever you ask the Father in My name He may give you. 17 These things I command you, that you love one another.

Picture those who are and are not part of God's covenant.

Rom 11:16–24 For if the firstfruit *is* holy, the lump *is* also *holy;* and if the root *is* holy, so *are* the branches. 17 And if some of the branches were broken off, and you, being a wild olive tree, were grafted in among them, and with them became a partaker of the root and fatness of the olive tree, 18 do not boast against the branches. But if you do boast, *remember that* you do not support the root, but the root supports you. 19 You will say then, "Branches were broken off that I might be grafted in." 20 Well *said.* Because of unbelief they were broken off, and you stand by faith. Do not be haughty, but fear. 21 For if God did not spare the natural branches, He may not spare you either.

22 Therefore consider the goodness and severity of God: on those who fell, severity; but toward you, goodness, if you continue in *His* goodness. Otherwise you also will be cut off. **23** And they also, if they do not continue in unbelief, will be grafted in, for God is able to graft them in again. **24** For if you were cut out of the olive tree which is wild by nature, and were grafted contrary to nature into a cultivated olive tree, how much more will these, who *are* natural *branches,* be grafted into their own olive tree?

BREAD

Given by God.

Ruth 1:6 Then she arose with her daughters-in-law that she might return from the country of Moab, for she had heard in the country of Moab that the LORD had visited His people by giving them bread.

Matt 6:11 Give us this day our daily bread.

Yielded by the earth.

Job 28:5 *As* for the earth, from it comes bread, But underneath it is turned up as by fire;

Is 55:10 "For as the rain comes down, and the snow from heaven, And do not return there, But water the earth, And make it bring forth and bud, That it may give seed to the sower And bread to the eater,

Made of

Wheat.

Ex 29:2 and unleavened bread, unleavened cakes mixed with oil, and unleavened wafers anointed with oil (you shall make them of wheat flour).

Ps 81:16 He would have fed them also with the finest of wheat; And with honey from the rock I would have satisfied you."

Barley.

Judg 7:13 And when Gideon had come, there was a man telling a dream to his companion. He said, "I have had a dream: *To my* surprise, a loaf of barley bread tumbled into the camp of Midian; it came to a tent and struck it so that it fell and overturned, and the tent collapsed."

John 6:9 "There is a lad here who has five barley loaves and two small fish, but what are they among so many?"

Beans, millet, etc.

Ezek 4:9 "Also take for yourself wheat, barley, beans, lentils, millet, and spelt; put them into one vessel, and make bread of them for yourself. *During* the number of days that you lie on your side, three hundred and ninety days, you shall eat it.

Manna (in the wilderness).

Num 11:8 The people went about and gathered *it,* ground *it* on millstones or beat *it* in the mortar, cooked *it* in pans, and made cakes of it; and its taste was like the taste of pastry prepared with oil.

Was kneaded.

Gen 18:6 So Abraham hurried into the tent to Sarah and said, "Quickly, make ready three measures of fine meal; knead *it* and make cakes."

Jer 7:18 The children gather wood, the fathers kindle the fire, and the women knead dough, to make cakes for the queen of heaven; and *they* pour out drink of-

ferings to other gods, that they may provoke Me to anger.

Hos 7:4 "They *are* all adulterers. Like an oven heated by a baker— He ceases stirring *the fire* after kneading the dough, Until it is leavened.

Bowls used for kneading.

Ex 12:34 So the people took their dough before it was leavened, having their kneading bowls bound up in their clothes on their shoulders.

Usually leavened.

Lev 23:17 You shall bring from your dwellings two wave *loaves* of two-tenths *of an ephah.* They shall be of fine flour; they shall be baked with leaven. *They are* the firstfruits to the LORD.

Matt 13:33 Another parable He spoke to them: "The kingdom of heaven is like leaven, which a woman took and hid in three measures of meal till it was all leavened."

Sometimes unleavened.

Ex 12:18 In the first *month,* on the fourteenth day of the month at evening, you shall eat unleavened bread, until the twenty-first day of the month at evening.

1 Cor 5:8 Therefore let us keep the feast, not with old leaven, nor with the leaven of malice and wickedness, but with the unleavened *bread* of sincerity and truth.

Was formed into

Loaves.

1 Sam 10:3–4 Then you shall go on forward from there and come to the terebinth tree of Tabor. There three men going up to God at Bethel will meet you, one carrying three young goats, another carrying three loaves of bread, and another carrying a skin of wine. **4** And they will greet you and give you two *loaves* of bread, which you shall receive from their hands.

Matt 14:17 And they said to Him, "We have here only five loaves and two fish."

Cakes.

1 Kin 17:13 And Elijah said to her, "Do not fear; go *and* do as you have said, but make me a small cake from it first, and bring *it* to me; and afterward make *some* for yourself and your son.

Wafers.

Ex 16:31 And the house of Israel called its name Manna. And it *was* like white coriander seed, and the taste of it *was* like wafers *made* with honey.

Ex 29:23 one loaf of bread, one cake *made with* oil, and one wafer from the basket of the unleavened bread that *is* before the LORD;

Was baked

On hearths.

Gen 18:6 So Abraham hurried into the tent to Sarah and said, "Quickly, make ready three measures of fine meal; knead *it* and make cakes."

On coals of fire.

Is 44:19 And no one considers in his heart, Nor *is there* knowledge nor understanding to say, "I have burned half of it in the fire, Yes, I have also baked bread on its coals; I have roasted meat and eaten *it*; And shall I make the rest of it an abomination? Shall I fall down before a block of wood?"

John 21:9 Then, as soon as they had come to land, they saw a fire of coals there, and fish laid on it, and bread.

In ovens.

Lev 26:26 When I have cut off your supply of bread, ten women shall bake your bread in one oven, and they shall bring back your bread by weight, and you shall eat and not be satisfied.

Hos 7:4–7 "They *are* all adulterers. Like an oven heated by a baker— He ceases stirring *the fire* after kneading the dough, Until it is leavened. **5** In the day of our king Princes have made *him* sick, inflamed with wine; He stretched out his hand with scoffers. **6** They prepare their heart like an oven, While they lie in wait; Their baker sleeps all night; In the morning it burns like a flaming fire. **7** They are all hot, like an oven, And have devoured their judges; All their kings have fallen. None among them calls upon Me.

Making of, a trade.

Gen 40:2 And Pharaoh was angry with his two officers, the chief butler and the chief baker.

Jer 37:21 Then Zedekiah the king commanded that they should commit Jeremiah to the court of the prison, and that they should give him daily a piece of bread from the bakers' street, until all the bread in the city was gone. Thus Jeremiah remained in the court of the prison.

Ordinary, called common bread.

1 Sam 21:4 And the priest answered David and said, *"There is* no common bread on hand; but there is holy bread, if the young men have at least kept themselves from women."

Sacred, called holy bread.

1 Sam 21:4 And the priest answered David and said, *"There is* no common bread on hand; but there is holy bread, if the young men have at least kept themselves from women."

1 Sam 21:6 So the priest gave him holy *bread;* for there was no bread there but the showbread which had been taken from before the LORD, in order to put hot bread *in its place* on the day when it was taken away.

Nutritious and strengthening.

Ps 104:15 And wine *that* makes glad the heart of man, Oil to make *his* face shine, And bread *which* strengthens man's heart.

Often represents the whole sustenance of man.

Gen 3:19 In the sweat of your face you shall eat bread Till you return to the ground, For out of it you were taken; For dust you *are,* And to dust you shall return."

Gen 39:6 Thus he left all that he had in Joseph's hand, and he did not know what he had except for the bread which he ate. Now Joseph was handsome in form and appearance.

Matt 6:11 Give us this day our daily bread.

The principal food used by the ancients.

Gen 18:5 And I will bring a morsel of bread, that you may refresh your hearts. After that you may pass by, inasmuch as you have come to your servant." They said, "Do as you have said."

Gen 21:14 So Abraham rose early in the morning, and took bread and a skin of water; and putting *it* on her shoulder, he gave *it* and the boy to Hagar, and sent her away. Then she departed and wandered in the Wilderness of Beersheba.

Gen 27:17 Then she gave the savory food and the bread, which she had prepared, into the hand of her son Jacob.

Judg 19:5 Then it came to pass on the fourth day that they arose early in the morning, and he stood to depart; but the young woman's father said to his son-in-law, "Refresh your heart with a morsel of bread, and afterward go your way."

Broken for use.

Lam 4:4 The tongue of the infant clings To the roof of its mouth for thirst; The young children ask for bread, *But* no one breaks *it* for them.

Matt 14:19 Then He commanded the multitudes to sit down on the grass. And He took the five loaves and the two fish, and looking up to heaven, He blessed and broke and gave the loaves to the disciples; and the disciples gave to the multitudes.

Kept in baskets.

Gen 40:16 When the chief baker saw that the interpretation was good, he said to Joseph, "I also *was* in my dream, and there *were* three white baskets on my head.

Ex 29:32 Then Aaron and his sons shall eat the flesh of the ram, and the bread that *is* in the basket, *by* the door of the tabernacle of meeting.

Publicly sold.

Matt 14:15 When it was evening, His disciples came to Him, saying, "This is a deserted place, and the hour is already late. Send the multitudes away, that they may go into the villages and buy themselves food."

Matt 15:33 Then His disciples said to Him, "Where could we get enough bread in the wilderness to fill such a great multitude?"

In times of scarcity, sold by weight.

Lev 26:26 When I have cut off your supply of bread, ten women shall bake your bread in one oven, and they shall bring back your bread by weight, and you shall eat and not be satisfied.

Ezek 4:16 Moreover He said to me, "Son of man, surely I will cut off the supply of bread in Jerusalem; they shall eat bread by weight and with anxiety, and shall drink water by measure and with dread,

Scarceness of, sent as a punishment.

Ps 105:16 Moreover He called for a famine in the land; He destroyed all the provision of bread.

Is 3:1 For behold, the Lord, the LORD of hosts, Takes away from Jerusalem and from Judah The stock and the store, The whole supply of bread and the whole supply of water;

Ezek 5:16 When I send against them the terrible arrows of famine which shall be for destruction, which I will send to destroy you, I will increase the famine upon you and cut off your supply of bread.

Plenty of, promised to the obedient.

Lev 26:5 Your threshing shall last till the time of vintage, and the vintage shall last till the time of sowing; you shall eat your bread to the full, and dwell in your land safely.

Often given as a present.

1 Sam 25:18 Then Abigail made haste and took two hundred *loaves* of bread, two skins of wine, five sheep already dressed, five seahs of roasted *grain*, one hundred clusters of raisins, and two hundred cakes of figs, and loaded *them* on donkeys.

1 Chr 12:40 Moreover those who were near to them, from as far away as Issachar and Zebulun and Naphtali, were bringing food on donkeys and camels, on mules and oxen—provisions of flour and cakes of figs and cakes of raisins, wine and oil and oxen and sheep abundantly, for *there was* joy in Israel.

Served after funerals.

Ezek 24:17–22 Sigh in silence, make no mourning for the dead; bind your turban on your head, and put your sandals on your feet; do not cover *your* lips, and do not eat man's bread *of sorrow*." **18** So I spoke to the people in the morning, and at evening my wife died; and the next morning I did as I was commanded. **19** And the people said to me, "Will you not tell us what these *things signify* to us, that you behave so?" **20** Then I answered them, "The word of the LORD came to me, saying, **21** 'Speak to the house of Israel, "Thus says the Lord GOD: 'Behold, I will profane My sanctuary, your arrogant boast, the desire of your eyes, the delight of your soul; and your sons and daughters whom you left behind shall fall by the sword. **22** And you shall do as I have done; you shall not cover *your* lips nor eat man's bread *of sorrow*.

With water, the food of prisons.

1 Kin 22:27 and say, 'Thus says the king: "Put this *fellow* in prison, and feed him with bread of affliction and water of affliction, until I come in peace." ' "

First fruit of, offered to God.

Num 15:19–20 then it will be, when you eat of the bread of the land, that you shall offer up a heave offering to the LORD. **20** You shall offer up a cake of the first of your ground meal *as* a heave offering; as a heave offering of the threshing floor, so shall you offer it up.

Offered with sacrifices.

Ex 29:2 and unleavened bread, unleavened cakes mixed with oil, and unleavened wafers anointed with oil (you shall make them of wheat flour).

Ex 29:23 one loaf of bread, one cake *made with* oil, and one wafer from the basket of the unleavened bread that *is* before the LORD;

Num 28:2 "Command the children of Israel, and say to them, 'My offering, My food for My offerings made by fire as a sweet aroma to Me, you shall be careful to offer to Me at their appointed time.'

Placed on table of showbread.

Ex 25:30 And you shall set the showbread on the table before Me always.

Multitudes miraculously fed by Christ with.

Matt 14:19–21 Then He commanded the multitudes to sit down on the grass. And He took the five loaves and the two fish, and looking up to heaven, He blessed and broke and gave the loaves to the disciples; and the disciples gave to the multitudes. **20** So they all ate and were filled, and they took up twelve baskets full of the fragments that remained. **21** Now

those who had eaten were about five thousand men, besides women and children.

Matt 15:34–37 Jesus said to them, "How many loaves do you have?" And they said, "Seven, and a few little fish." **35** So He commanded the multitude to sit down on the ground. **36** And He took the seven loaves and the fish and gave thanks, broke *them* and gave *them* to His disciples; and the disciples *gave* to the multitude. **37** So they all ate and were filled, and they took up seven large baskets full of the fragments that were left.

Illustrative of

Christ.

John 6:33–35 For the bread of God is He who comes down from heaven and gives life to the world." **34** Then they said to Him, "Lord, give us this bread always." **35** And Jesus said to them, "I am the bread of life. He who comes to Me shall never hunger, and he who believes in Me shall never thirst.

(When broken) the death of Christ.

Matt 26:26 And as they were eating, Jesus took bread, blessed and broke *it*, and gave *it* to the disciples and said, "Take, eat; this is My body."

1 Cor 11:23–24 For I received from the Lord that which I also delivered to you: that the Lord Jesus on the *same* night in which He was betrayed took bread; **24** and when He had given thanks, He broke *it* and said, "Take, eat; this is My body which is broken for you; do this in remembrance of Me."

(Partaking of) communion of saints.

Acts 2:46 So continuing daily with one accord in the temple, and breaking bread from house to house, they ate their food with gladness and simplicity of heart,

1 Cor 10:17 For we, *though* many, are one bread *and* one body; for we all partake of that one bread.

(Lack of) extreme poverty.

Prov 12:9 Better *is the one* who is slighted but has a servant, Than he who honors himself but lacks bread.

Is 3:7 In that day he will protest, saying, "I cannot cure *your* ills, For in my house *is* neither food nor clothing; Do not make me a ruler of the people."

(Seeking of) extreme poverty.

1 Sam 2:36 And it shall come to pass that everyone who is left in your house will come *and* bow down to him for a piece of silver and a morsel of bread, and say, "Please, put me in one of the priestly positions, that I may eat a piece of bread." ' "

Ps 37:25 I have been young, and *now* am old; Yet I have not seen the righteous forsaken, Nor his descendants begging bread.

Lam 1:11 All her people sigh, They seek bread; They have given their valuables for food to restore life. "See, O LORD, and consider, For I am scorned."

(Fullness of) abundance.

Deut 8:9 a land in which you will eat bread without scarcity, in which you will lack nothing; a land whose stones *are* iron and out of whose hills you can dig copper.

Ezek 16:49 Look, this was the iniquity of your sister Sodom: She and her daughter had pride, fullness of food, and abundance of idleness; neither did she strengthen the hand of the poor and needy.

(Of adversity) heavy affliction.

Is 30:20 And *though* the Lord gives you The bread of adversity and the water of affliction, Yet your teachers will not be moved into a corner anymore, But your eyes shall see your teachers.

(Of tears) sorrow.

Ps 80:5 You have fed them with the bread of tears, And given them tears to drink in great measure.

(Of deceit) unlawful gain.

Prov 20:17 Bread gained by deceit *is* sweet to a man, But afterward his mouth will be filled with gravel.

(Of idleness) sloth.

Prov 31:27 She watches over the ways of her household, And does not eat the bread of idleness.

BREASTPLATE

A part of defensive armor.

1 Kin 22:34 Now a *certain* man drew a bow at random, and struck the king of Israel between the joints of his armor. So he said to the driver of his chariot, "Turn around and take me out of the battle, for I am wounded."

A part of the high priest's dress.

Ex 28:4 And these *are* the garments which they shall make: a breastplate, an ephod, a robe, a skillfully woven tunic, a turban, and a sash. So they shall make holy garments for Aaron your brother and his sons, that he may minister to Me as priest.

For the high priest,

Materials of.

Ex 28:15 "You shall make the breastplate of judgment. Artistically woven according to the workmanship of the ephod you shall make it: of gold, blue, purple, and scarlet *thread,* and fine woven linen, you shall make it.

Ex 39:8 And he made the breastplate, artistically woven like the workmanship of the ephod, of gold, blue, purple, and scarlet *thread,* and of fine woven linen.

Form and dimensions of.

Ex 28:16 It shall be doubled into a square: a span *shall be* its length, and a span *shall be* its width.

Ex 39:9 They made the breastplate square by doubling it; a span *was* its length and a span its width when doubled.

Made from the offering of the people.

Ex 35:9 onyx stones, and stones to be set in the ephod and in the breastplate.

Had names of the tribes engraved on precious stones.

Ex 28:17–21 And you shall put settings of stones in it, four rows of stones: *The first* row *shall be* a sardius, a topaz, and an emerald; *this shall be* the first row; **18** the second row *shall be* a turquoise, a sapphire, and a diamond; **19** the third row, a jacinth, an agate, and an amethyst; **20** and the fourth row, a beryl, an onyx, and a jasper. They shall be set in gold settings. **21** And the stones shall have the names of the sons of Israel, twelve according to their names, *like* the engravings of a signet, each one with its own name; they shall be according to the twelve tribes.

Ex 39:10 And they set in it four rows of stones: a row with a sardius, a topaz, and an emerald was the first row;

Ex 39:14 *There were* twelve stones according to the names of the sons of Israel: according to their names, *engraved like* a signet, each one with its own name according to the twelve tribes.

Inseparably united to the ephod.

Ex 28:22–28 "You shall make chains for the breastplate at the end, like braided cords of pure gold. **23** And you shall make two rings of gold for the breastplate, and put the two rings on the two ends of the breastplate. **24** Then you shall put the two braided *chains* of gold in the two rings which are on the ends of the breastplate; **25** and the *other* two ends of the two braided *chains* you shall fasten to the two settings, and put them on the shoulder straps of the ephod in the front. **26** "You shall make two rings of gold, and put them on the two ends of the breastplate, on the edge of it, which is on the inner side of the ephod. **27** And two *other* rings of gold you shall make, and put them on the two shoulder straps, underneath the ephod toward its front, right at the seam above the intricately woven band of the ephod. **28** They shall bind the breastplate by means of its rings to the rings of the ephod, using a blue cord, so that it is above the intricately woven band of the ephod, and so that the breastplate does not come loose from the ephod.

Ex 39:15–21 And they made chains for the breastplate at the ends, like braided cords of pure gold. **16** They also made two settings of gold and two gold rings, and put the two rings on the two ends of the breastplate. **17** And they put the two braided *chains* of gold in the two rings on the ends of the breastplate. **18** The two ends of the two braided *chains* they fastened in the two settings, and put them on the shoulder straps of the ephod in the front. **19** And they made two rings of gold and put *them* on the two ends of the breastplate, on the edge of it, which *was* on the inward side of the ephod. **20** They made two *other* gold rings and put them on the two shoulder straps, underneath the ephod toward its front, right at the seam above the intricately woven band of the ephod. **21** And they bound the breastplate by means of its rings to the rings of the ephod with a blue cord, so that it would be above the intricately woven band of the ephod, and that the breastplate would not come loose from the ephod, as the LORD had commanded Moses.

The Urim and Thummim placed in.

Ex 28:30 And you shall put in the breastplate of judgment the Urim and the Thummim, and they shall be over Aaron's heart when he goes in before the LORD. So Aaron shall bear the judgment of the children of Israel over his heart before the LORD continually.

Lev 8:8 Then he put the breastplate on him, and he put the Urim and the Thummim in the breastplate.

Worn as a memorial.

Ex 28:29 "So Aaron shall bear the names of the sons of Israel on the breastplate of judgment over his heart, when he goes into the holy *place,* as a memorial before the LORD continually.

Is 49:16 See, I have inscribed you on the palms *of My hands;* Your walls *are* continually before Me.

Illustrative of the

Righteous judgment of Christ.

Is 59:17 For He put on righteousness as a breastplate, And a helmet of salvation on His head; He put on the garments of vengeance for clothing, And was clad with zeal as a cloak.

Defense of righteousness.

Eph 6:14 Stand therefore, having girded your waist with truth, having put on the breastplate of righteousness,

Defense of faith and love.

1 Thess 5:8 But let us who are of the day be sober, putting on the breastplate of faith and love, and *as* a helmet the hope of salvation.

BRONZE, OR COPPER

Dug out of the mountains.

Deut 8:9 a land in which you will eat bread without scarcity, in which you will lack nothing; a land whose stones *are* iron and out of whose hills you can dig copper.

Purified by smelting.

Job 28:2 Iron is taken from the earth, And copper *is* smelted *from* ore.

Characterized by

Strength.

Job 40:18 His bones *are like* beams of bronze, His ribs like bars of iron.

Hardness.

Lev 26:19 I will break the pride of your power; I will make your heavens like iron and your earth like bronze.

Yellow color.

Ezra 8:27 twenty gold basins *worth* a thousand drachmas, and two vessels of fine polished bronze, precious as gold.

Fusibility.

Ezek 22:18 "Son of man, the house of Israel has become dross to Me; they *are* all bronze, tin, iron, and lead, in the midst of a furnace; they have become dross from silver.

Ezek 22:20 *As men* gather silver, bronze, iron, lead, and tin into the midst of a furnace, to blow fire on it, to melt *it;* so I will gather *you* in My anger and in My fury, and I will leave *you there* and melt you.

Takes a high polish.

2 Chr 4:16 also the pots, the shovels, the forks—and all their articles Huram his master *craftsman* made of burnished bronze for King Solomon for the house of the LORD.

Ezek 1:7 Their legs *were* straight, and the soles of their feet *were* like the soles of calves' feet. They sparkled like the color of burnished bronze.

Inferior in value to gold and silver.

Is 60:17 "Instead of bronze I will bring gold, Instead of iron I will bring silver, Instead of wood, bronze, And instead of stones, iron. I will also make your officers peace, And your magistrates righteousness.

Dan 2:32 This image's head *was* of fine gold, its chest and arms of silver, its belly and thighs of bronze,

Dan 2:39 But after you shall arise another kingdom inferior to yours; then another, a third kingdom of bronze, which shall rule over all the earth.

Antiquity of working in.

Gen 4:22 And as for Zillah, she also bore Tubal-Cain, an instructor of every craftsman in bronze and iron. And the sister of Tubal-Cain *was* Naamah.

Extensive commerce in.

Ezek 27:13 Javan, Tubal, and Meshech *were* your traders. They bartered human lives and vessels of bronze for your merchandise.

Rev 18:12 merchandise of gold and silver, precious stones and pearls, fine linen and purple, silk and scarlet, every kind of citron wood, every kind of object of ivory, every kind of object of most precious wood, bronze, iron, and marble;

Working in, a trade.

Gen 4:22 And as for Zillah, she also bore Tubal-Cain, an instructor of every craftsman in bronze and iron. And the sister of Tubal-Cain *was* Naamah.

1 Kin 7:14 He *was* the son of a widow from the tribe of Naphtali, and his father *was* a man of Tyre, a bronze worker; he was filled with wisdom and understanding and skill in working with all kinds of bronze work. So he came to King Solomon and did all his work.

2 Chr 24:12 The king and Jehoiada gave it to those who did the work of the service of the house of the LORD; and they hired masons and carpenters to repair the house of the LORD, and also those who worked in iron and bronze to restore the house of the LORD.

2 Tim 4:14 Alexander the coppersmith did me much harm. May the Lord repay him according to his works.

Canaan abounded in.

Deut 8:9 a land in which you will eat bread without scarcity, in which you will lack nothing; a land whose stones *are* iron and out of whose hills you can dig copper.

Deut 33:25 Your sandals *shall be* iron and bronze; As your days, *so shall* your strength *be.*

Taken in war,

Often in great quantities.

Josh 22:8 and spoke to them, saying, "Return with much riches to your tents, with very much livestock, with silver, with gold, with bronze, with iron, and with very much clothing. Divide the spoil of your enemies with your brethren."

2 Sam 8:8 Also from Betah and from Berothai, cities of Hadadezer, King David took a large amount of bronze.

2 Kin 25:13–16 The bronze pillars that *were* in the house of the LORD, and the carts and the bronze Sea that *were* in the house of the LORD, the Chaldeans broke in pieces, and carried their bronze to Babylon. **14** They also took away the pots, the shovels, the trimmers, the spoons, and all the bronze utensils with which the priests ministered. **15** The firepans and the basins, the things of solid gold and solid silver, the captain of the guard took away. **16** The two pillars, one Sea, and the carts, which Solomon had made for the house of the LORD, the bronze of all these articles was beyond measure.

Cleansed by fire.

Num 31:21–23 Then Eleazar the priest said to the men of war who had gone to the battle, "This *is* the ordinance of the law which the LORD commanded Moses: **22** "Only the gold, the silver, the bronze, the iron, the tin, and the lead, **23** everything that can endure fire, you shall put through the fire, and it shall be clean; and it shall be purified with the water of purification. But all that cannot endure fire you shall put through water.

Generally consecrated to God.

Josh 6:19 But all the silver and gold, and vessels of bronze and iron, *are* consecrated to the LORD; they shall come into the treasury of the LORD."

Josh 6:24 But they burned the city and all that *was* in it with fire. Only the silver and gold, and the vessels of bronze and iron, they put into the treasury of the house of the LORD.

2 Sam 8:10–11 then Toi sent Joram his son to King David, to greet him and bless him, because he had fought against Hadadezer and defeated him (for Hadadezer had been at war with Toi); and *Joram* brought with him articles of silver, articles of gold, and articles of bronze. **11** King David also dedicated these to the LORD, along with the silver and gold that he had dedicated from all the nations which he had subdued—

Offerings of, for the tabernacle.

Ex 38:29 The offering of bronze *was* seventy talents and two thousand four hundred shekels.

Collected by David for the temple.

1 Chr 22:3 And David prepared iron in abundance for the nails of the doors of the gates and for the joints, and bronze in abundance beyond measure,

1 Chr 22:14 Indeed I have taken much trouble to prepare for the house of the LORD one hundred thousand talents of gold and one million talents of silver, and bronze and iron beyond measure, for it is so abundant. I have prepared timber and stone also, and you may add to them.

1 Chr 22:16 Of gold and silver and bronze and iron *there is* no limit. Arise and begin working, and the LORD be with you."

1 Chr 29:2 Now for the house of my God I have prepared with all my might: gold for *things to be made of* gold, silver for *things of* silver, bronze for *things of* bronze, iron for *things of* iron, wood for *things of* wood, onyx stones, *stones* to be set, glistening stones of various colors, all kinds of precious stones, and marble slabs in abundance.

Offerings of, for the temple.

1 Chr 29:6–7 Then the leaders of the fathers' *houses,* leaders of the tribes of Israel, the captains of thousands and of hundreds, with the officers over the king's work, offered willingly. **7** They gave for the work of the house of God five thousand talents and ten thousand darics of gold, ten thousand talents of silver, eighteen thousand talents of bronze, and one hundred thousand talents of iron.

Coined for money.

Matt 10:9 Provide neither gold nor silver nor copper in your money belts,

Mark 12:41–42 Now Jesus sat opposite the treasury and saw how the people put money into the treasury. And many *who were* rich put in much. **42** Then one poor widow came and threw in two mites, which make a quadrans.

Made into

Mirrors.

Ex 38:8 He made the laver of bronze and its base of bronze, from the bronze mirrors of the serving women who assembled at the door of the tabernacle of meeting.

Gates.

Ps 107:16 For He has broken the gates of bronze, And cut the bars of iron in two.

Is 45:2 'I will go before you And make the crooked places straight; I will break in pieces the gates of bronze And cut the bars of iron.

Bars for gates.

1 Kin 4:13 Ben-Geber, in Ramoth Gilead; to him *belonged* the towns of Jair the son of Manasseh, in Gilead; to him *also belonged* the region of Argob in Bashan—sixty large cities with walls and bronze gate-bars;

Fetters.

Judg 16:21 Then the Philistines took him and put out his eyes, and brought him down to Gaza. They bound him with bronze fetters, and he became a grinder in the prison.

2 Kin 25:7 Then they killed the sons of Zedekiah before his eyes, put out the eyes of Zedekiah, bound him with bronze fetters, and took him to Babylon.

Shields.

1 Kin 14:27 Then King Rehoboam made bronze shields in their place, and committed *them* to the hands of the captains of the guard, who guarded the doorway of the king's house.

2 Chr 12:10 Then King Rehoboam made bronze shields in their place, and committed *them* to the hands of the captains of the guard, who guarded the doorway of the king's house.

Helmets.

1 Sam 17:5 *He had* a bronze helmet on his head, and he *was* armed with a coat of mail, and the weight of the coat *was* five thousand shekels of bronze.

Armor for the legs.

1 Sam 17:6 And *he had* bronze armor on his legs and a bronze javelin between his shoulders.

Household vessels.

Mark 7:4 *When they come* from the marketplace, they do not eat unless they wash. And there are many other things which they have received and hold, *like* the washing of cups, pitchers, copper vessels, and couches.

Sacred vessels.

Ex 27:3 Also you shall make its pans to receive its ashes, and its shovels and its basins and its forks and its firepans; you shall make all its utensils of bronze.

1 Kin 7:45 the pots, the shovels, and the bowls. All these articles which Huram made for King Solomon for the house of the LORD were of burnished bronze.

Altars.

Ex 27:2 You shall make its horns on its four corners; its horns shall be of one piece with it. And you shall overlay it with bronze.

Ex 39:39 the bronze altar, its grate of bronze, its poles, and all its utensils; the laver with its base;

Sockets for pillars.

Ex 38:10–11 There were twenty pillars for them, with twenty bronze sockets. The hooks of the pillars and their bands were silver. 11 On the north side the hangings were one hundred cubits long, with twenty pillars and their twenty bronze sockets. The hooks of the pillars and their bands were silver.

Ex 38:17 The sockets for the pillars were bronze, the hooks of the pillars and their bands were silver, and the overlay of their capitals was silver; and all the pillars of the court had bands of silver.

Lavers.

Ex 30:18 "You shall also make a laver of bronze, with its base also of bronze, for washing. You shall put it between the tabernacle of meeting and the altar. And you shall put water in it,

1 Kin 7:38 Then he made ten lavers of bronze; each laver contained forty baths, and each laver was four cubits. On each of the ten carts was a laver.

Pillars.

1 Kin 7:15–16 And he cast two pillars of bronze, each one eighteen cubits high, and a line of twelve cubits measured the circumference of each. 16 Then he made two capitals of cast bronze, to set on the tops of the pillars. The height of one capital was five cubits, and the height of the other capital was five cubits.

Idols.

Dan 5:4 They drank wine, and praised the gods of gold and silver, bronze and iron, wood and stone.

Rev 9:20 But the rest of mankind, who were not killed by these plagues, did not repent of the works of their hands, that they should not worship demons, and idols of gold, silver, brass, stone, and wood, which can neither see nor hear nor walk.

Instruments of music.

1 Chr 15:19 the singers, Heman, Asaph, and Ethan, were to sound the cymbals of bronze;

Moses made the serpent of.

Num 21:9 So Moses made a bronze serpent, and put it on a pole; and so it was, if a serpent had bitten anyone, when he looked at the bronze serpent, he lived.

2 Kin 18:4 He removed the high places and broke the sacred pillars, cut down the wooden image and broke in pieces the bronze serpent that Moses had made; for until those days the children of Israel burned incense to it, and called it Nehushtan.

Illustrative of

Obstinate sinners.

Is 48:4 Because I knew that you were obstinate, And your neck was an iron sinew, And your brow bronze,

Jer 6:28 They are all stubborn rebels, walking as slanderers. They are bronze and iron, They are all corrupters;

The judgment of God.

Zech 6:1 Then I turned and raised my eyes and looked, and behold, four chariots were coming from between two mountains, and the mountains were mountains of bronze.

The strength and firmness of Christ.

Dan 10:6 His body was like beryl, his face like the appearance of lightning, his eyes like torches of fire, his arms and feet like burnished bronze in color, and the sound of his words like the voice of a multitude.

Rev 1:15 His feet were like fine brass, as if refined in a furnace, and His voice as the sound of many waters;

Strength given to saints.

Jer 15:20 And I will make you to this people a fortified bronze wall; And they will fight against you, But they shall not prevail against you; For I am with you to save you And deliver you," says the LORD.

Mic 4:13 "Arise and thresh, O daughter of Zion; For I will make your horn iron, And I will make your hooves bronze; You shall beat in pieces many peoples; I will consecrate their gain to the LORD, And their substance to the Lord of the whole earth."

Macedonian empire.

Dan 2:39 But after you shall arise another kingdom inferior to yours; then another, a third kingdom of bronze, which shall rule over all the earth.

Extreme drought.

Deut 28:23 And your heavens which are over your head shall be bronze, and the earth which is under you shall be iron.

The earth made barren.

Lev 26:19 I will break the pride of your power; I will make your heavens like iron and your earth like bronze.

BROOKS

Canaan abounded with.

Deut 8:7 For the LORD your God is bringing you into a good land, a land of brooks of water, of fountains and springs, that flow out of valleys and hills;

Borders of, favorable to

Grass.

1 Kin 18:5 And Ahab had said to Obadiah, "Go into the land to all the springs of water and to all the brooks; perhaps we may find grass to keep the horses and mules alive, so that we will not have to kill any livestock."

Willows.

Lev 23:40 And you shall take for yourselves on the first day the fruit of beautiful trees, branches of palm trees, the boughs of leafy trees, and willows of the brook; and you shall rejoice before the LORD your God for seven days.

Job 40:22 The lotus trees cover him with their shade; The willows by the brook surround him.

Reeds.

Is 19:7 The papyrus reeds by the River, by the mouth of the River, And everything sown by the River, Will wither, be driven away, and be no more.

Abounded with fish.

Is 19:8 The fishermen also will mourn; All those will lament who cast hooks into the River, And they will languish who spread nets on the waters.

Afforded protection to a country.

Is 19:6 The rivers will turn foul; The brooks of defense will be emptied and dried up; The reeds and rushes will wither.

Those mentioned in Scripture

Arnon.

Num 21:14–15 Therefore it is said in the Book of the Wars of the LORD: "Waheb in Suphah, The brooks of the Arnon, 15 And the slope of the brooks That reaches to the dwelling of Ar, And lies on the border of Moab."

Besor.

1 Sam 30:9 So David went, he and the six hundred men who *were* with him, and came to the Brook Besor, where those stayed who were left behind.

Gaash.

2 Sam 23:30 Benaiah a Pirathonite, Hiddai from the brooks of Gaash,

1 Chr 11:32 Hurai of the brooks of Gaash, Abiel the Arbathite,

Cherith.

1 Kin 17:3 "Get away from here and turn eastward, and hide by the Brook Cherith, which flows into the Jordan.

1 Kin 17:5 So he went and did according to the word of the LORD, for he went and stayed by the Brook Cherith, which flows into the Jordan.

Eshcol.

Num 13:23–24 Then they came to the Valley of Eshcol, and there cut down a branch with one cluster of grapes; they carried it between two of them on a pole. They also *brought* some of the pomegranates and figs. 24 The place was called the Valley of Eshcol, because of the cluster which the men of Israel cut down there.

Kidron.

2 Sam 15:23 And all the country wept with a loud voice, and all the people crossed over. The king himself also crossed over the Brook Kidron, and all the people crossed over toward the way of the wilderness.

1 Kin 15:13 Also he removed Maachah his grandmother from *being* queen mother, because she had made an obscene image of Asherah. And Asa cut down her obscene image and burned *it* by the Brook Kidron.

John 18:1 When Jesus had spoken these words, He went out with His disciples over the Brook Kidron, where there was a garden, which He and His disciples entered.

Kishon.

1 Kin 18:40 And Elijah said to them, "Seize the prophets of Baal! Do not let one of them escape!" So they seized them; and Elijah brought them down to the Brook Kishon and executed them there.

Ps 83:9 Deal with them as *with* Midian, As *with* Sisera, As *with* Jabin at the Brook Kishon,

Zered.

Deut 2:13 " 'Now rise and cross over the Valley of the Zered.' So we crossed over the Valley of the Zered.

Of the willows.

Is 15:7 Therefore the abundance they have gained, And what they have laid up, They will carry away to the Brook of the Willows.

Illustrative of

Wisdom.

Prov 18:4 The words of a man's mouth *are* deep waters; The wellspring of wisdom *is* a flowing brook.

Temporal abundance.

Job 20:17 He will not see the streams, The rivers flowing with honey and cream.

(Deceptive) false friends.

Job 6:15 My brothers have dealt deceitfully like a brook, Like the streams of the brooks that pass away,

(Drinking from, by the wayside) help in distress.

Ps 110:7 He shall drink of the brook by the wayside; Therefore He shall lift up the head.

BURIAL

First mention of.

Gen 4:9–10 Then the LORD said to Cain, "Where *is* Abel your brother?" He said, "I do not know. *Am* I my brother's keeper?" 10 And He said, "What have you done? The voice of your brother's blood cries out to Me from the ground.

Design of.

Gen 23:3–4 Then Abraham stood up from before his dead, and spoke to the sons of Heth, saying, 4 "I *am* a foreigner and a visitor among you. Give me property for a burial place among you, that I may bury my dead out of my sight."

Attended by

Family of the dead.

Gen 50:5–6 'My father made me swear, saying, "Behold, I am dying; in my grave which I dug for myself in the land of Canaan, there you shall bury me." Now therefore, please let me go up and bury my father, and I will come back.' " 6 And Pharaoh said, "Go up and bury your father, as he made you swear."

Gen 50:8 as well as all the house of Joseph, his brothers, and his father's house. Only their little ones, their flocks, and their herds they left in the land of Goshen.

Matt 8:21 Then another of His disciples said to Him, "Lord, let me first go and bury my father."

Numbers of friends, etc.

Gen 50:7 So Joseph went up to bury his father; and with him went up all the servants of Pharaoh, the elders of his house, and all the elders of the land of Egypt,

Gen 50:9 And there went up with him both chariots and horsemen, and it was a very great gathering.

2 Sam 3:31 Then David said to Joab and to all the people who were with him, "Tear your clothes, gird yourselves with sackcloth, and mourn for Abner." And King David followed the coffin.

Luke 7:12 And when He came near the gate of the city, behold, a dead man was being carried out, the only son of his mother; and she was a widow. And a large crowd from the city was with her.

Female friends.

Mark 15:47 And Mary Magdalene and Mary *the mother* of Joses observed where He was laid.

Luke 7:13 When the Lord saw her, He had compassion on her and said to her, "Do not weep."

Hired mourners.

Jer 9:17–18 Thus says the LORD of hosts: "Consider and call for the mourning women, That they may come; And send for skillful wailing women, That they may come. **18** Let them make haste And take up a wailing for us, That our eyes may run with tears, And our eyelids gush with water.

Great lamentation at.

Gen 50:10–11 Then they came to the threshing floor of Atad, which *is* beyond the Jordan, and they mourned there with a great and very solemn lamentation. He observed seven days of mourning for his father. **11** And when the inhabitants of the land, the Canaanites, saw the mourning at the threshing floor of Atad, they said, "This *is* a deep mourning of the Egyptians." Therefore its name was called Abel Mizraim, which *is* beyond the Jordan.

2 Sam 3:31–32 Then David said to Joab and to all the people who were with him, "Tear your clothes, gird yourselves with sackcloth, and mourn for Abner." And King David followed the coffin. **32** So they buried Abner in Hebron; and the king lifted up his voice and wept at the grave of Abner, and all the people wept.

Orations sometimes made at.

2 Sam 3:33–34 And the king sang *a lament* over Abner and said: "Should Abner die as a fool dies? **34** Your hands were not bound Nor your feet put into fetters; As a man falls before wicked men, *so* you fell." Then all the people wept over him again.

The body was

Washed before.

Acts 9:37 But it happened in those days that she became sick and died. When they had washed her, they laid *her* in an upper room.

Anointed for.

Matt 26:12 For in pouring this fragrant oil on My body, she did *it* for My burial.

Wound in linen for.

John 11:44 And he who had died came out bound hand and foot with graveclothes, and his face was wrapped with a cloth. Jesus said to them, "Loose him, and let him go."

John 19:40 Then they took the body of Jesus, and bound it in strips of linen with the spices, as the custom of the Jews is to bury.

Preserved with spices for.

John 19:39–40 And Nicodemus, who at first came to Jesus by night, also came, bringing a mixture of myrrh and aloes, about a hundred pounds. **40** Then they took the body of Jesus, and bound it in strips of linen with the spices, as the custom of the Jews is to bury.

Sometimes burned before.

1 Sam 31:12 all the valiant men arose and traveled all night, and took the body of Saul and the bodies of his sons from the wall of Beth Shan; and they came to Jabesh and burned them there.

Carried in a coffin to.

2 Sam 3:31 Then David said to Joab and to all the people who were with him, "Tear your clothes, gird yourselves with sackcloth, and mourn for Abner." And King David followed the coffin.

Luke 7:14 Then He came and touched the open coffin, and those who carried *him* stood still. And He said, "Young man, I say to you, arise."

Perfumes burned at.

2 Chr 16:14 They buried him in his own tomb, which he had made for himself in the City of David; and they laid him in the bed which was filled with spices and various ingredients prepared in a mixture of ointments. They made a very great burning for him.

Jer 34:5 You shall die in peace; as in the ceremonies of your fathers, the former kings who were before you, so they shall burn incense for you and lament for you, *saying*, "Alas, lord!" For I have pronounced the word, says the LORD.' "

Antiquity of coffins for.

Gen 50:26 So Joseph died, *being* one hundred and ten years old; and they embalmed him, and he was put in a coffin in Egypt.

Often took place immediately after death.

John 11:17 So when Jesus came, He found that he had already been in the tomb four days.

John 11:39 Jesus said, "Take away the stone." Martha, the sister of him who was dead, said to Him, "Lord, by this time there is a stench, for he has been *dead* four days."

Acts 5:6 And the young men arose and wrapped him up, carried *him* out, and buried *him.*

Acts 5:10 Then immediately she fell down at his feet and breathed her last. And the young men came in and found her dead, and carrying *her* out, buried *her* by her husband.

Of persons hanged, always on the day of execution.

Deut 21:23 his body shall not remain overnight on the tree, but you shall surely bury him that day, so that you do not defile the land which the LORD your God is giving you *as* an inheritance; for he who is hanged *is* accursed of God.

John 19:31 Therefore, because it was the Preparation *Day,* that the bodies should not remain on the cross on the Sabbath (for that Sabbath was a high day), the Jews asked Pilate that their legs might be broken, and *that* they might be taken away.

Of enemies, sometimes performed by the conquerors.

1 Kin 11:15 For it happened, when David was in Edom, and Joab the commander of the army had gone up to bury the slain, after he had killed every male in Edom

Ezek 39:11–14 "It will come to pass in that day *that* I will give Gog a burial place there in Israel, the valley of those who pass by east of the sea; and it will obstruct travelers, because there they will bury Gog and all his multitude. Therefore they will call *it* the Valley of Hamon Gog. **12** For seven months the house of Israel will be burying them, in order to cleanse the land. **13** Indeed all the people of the land will be burying, and they will gain renown for it on the day that I am glorified," says the Lord GOD. **14** "They will set apart men regularly employed, with the help of a search party, to pass through the land and bury those bodies remaining on the ground, in order to cleanse it. At the end of seven months they will make a search.

Of the friendless, a kind act.

2 Sam 2:5 So David sent messengers to the men of Jabesh Gilead, and said to them, "You *are* blessed of the LORD, for you have shown this kindness to your lord, to Saul, and have buried him.

Places used for,

Natural caves.

Gen 23:19 And after this, Abraham buried Sarah his wife in the cave of the field of Machpelah, before Mamre (that *is,* Hebron) in the land of Canaan.

John 11:38 Then Jesus, again groaning in Himself, came to the tomb. It was a cave, and a stone lay against it.

Caves hewn out of rocks.

Is 22:16 'What have you here, and whom have you here, That you have hewn a sepulcher here, *As* he who hews himself a sepulcher on high, Who carves a tomb for himself in a rock?

Matt 27:60 and laid it in his new tomb which he had hewn out of the rock; and he rolled a large stone against the door of the tomb, and departed.

Gardens.

2 Kin 21:18 So Manasseh rested with his fathers, and was buried in the garden of his own house, in the garden of Uzza. Then his son Amon reigned in his place.

2 Kin 21:26 And he was buried in his tomb in the garden of Uzza. Then Josiah his son reigned in his place.

John 19:41 Now in the place where He was crucified there was a garden, and in the garden a new tomb in which no one had yet been laid.

Under trees.

Gen 35:8 Now Deborah, Rebekah's nurse, died, and she was buried below Bethel under the terebinth tree. So the name of it was called Allon Bachuth.

1 Sam 31:13 Then they took their bones and buried *them* under the tamarisk tree at Jabesh, and fasted seven days.

Tops of the hills.

Josh 24:33 And Eleazar the son of Aaron died. They buried him in a hill *belonging to* Phinehas his son, which was given to him in the mountains of Ephraim.

2 Kin 23:16 As Josiah turned, he saw the tombs that *were* there on the mountain. And he sent and took the bones out of the tombs and burned *them* on the altar, and defiled it according to the word of the LORD which the man of God proclaimed, who proclaimed these words.

Houses of the deceased.

1 Sam 25:1 Then Samuel died; and the Israelites gathered together and lamented for him, and buried him at his home in Ramah. And David arose and went down to the Wilderness of Paran.

1 Kin 2:34 So Benaiah the son of Jehoiada went up and

struck and killed him; and he was buried in his own house in the wilderness.

The city of David for the kings of Judah.

1 Kin 2:10 So David rested with his fathers, and was buried in the City of David.

2 Chr 21:20 He was thirty-two years old when he became king. He reigned in Jerusalem eight years and, to no one's sorrow, departed. However they buried him in the City of David, but not in the tombs of the kings.

2 Chr 24:16 And they buried him in the City of David among the kings, because he had done good in Israel, both toward God and His house.

Antiquity of purchasing places for.

Gen 23:7–16 Then Abraham stood up and bowed himself to the people of the land, the sons of Heth. **8** And he spoke with them, saying, "If it is your wish that I bury my dead out of my sight, hear me, and meet with Ephron the son of Zohar for me, **9** that he may give me the cave of Machpelah which he has, which *is* at the end of his field. Let him give it to me at the full price, as property for a burial place among you." **10** Now Ephron dwelt among the sons of Heth; and Ephron the Hittite answered Abraham in the presence of the sons of Heth, all who entered at the gate of his city, saying, **11** "No, my lord, hear me: I give you the field and the cave that *is* in it; I give it to you in the presence of the sons of my people. I give it to you. Bury your dead!" **12** Then Abraham bowed himself down before the people of the land; **13** and he spoke to Ephron in the hearing of the people of the land, saying, "If you *will give it,* please hear me. I will give you money for the field; take *it* from me and I will bury my dead there." **14** And Ephron answered Abraham, saying to him, **15** "My lord, listen to me; the land *is worth* four hundred shekels of silver. What *is* that between you and me? So bury your dead." **16** And Abraham listened to Ephron; and Abraham weighed out the silver for Ephron which he had named in the hearing of the sons of Heth, four hundred shekels of silver, currency of the merchants.

Places of,

Frequently prepared and pointed out during life.

Gen 50:5 'My father made me swear, saying, "Behold, I am dying; in my grave which I dug for myself in the land of Canaan, there you shall bury me." Now therefore, please let me go up and bury my father, and I will come back.' "

2 Chr 16:14 They buried him in his own tomb, which he had made for himself in the City of David; and they laid him in the bed which was filled with spices and various ingredients prepared in a mixture of ointments. They made a very great burning for him.

Matt 27:60 and laid it in his new tomb which he had hewn out of the rock; and he rolled a large stone against the door of the tomb, and departed.

Members of a family interred in the same.

Gen 25:10 the field which Abraham purchased from the sons of Heth. There Abraham was buried, and Sarah his wife.

Gen 49:31 There they buried Abraham and Sarah his wife, there they buried Isaac and Rebekah his wife, and there I buried Leah.

2 Sam 2:32 Then they took up Asahel and buried him in his father's tomb, which *was* in Bethlehem. And Joab and his men went all night, and they came to Hebron at daybreak.

Held in high veneration.

Neh 2:3 and said to the king, "May the king live forever! Why should my face not be sad, when the city, the place of my fathers' tombs, *lies* waste, and its gates are burned with fire?"

Neh 2:5 And I said to the king, "If it pleases the king, and if your servant has found favor in your sight, I ask that you send me to Judah, to the city of my fathers' tombs, that I may rebuild it."

Provided for the common people.

Jer 26:23 And they brought Urijah from Egypt and brought him to Jehoiakim the king, who killed him with the sword and cast his dead body into the graves of the common people.

Provided for aliens and strangers.

Matt 27:7 And they consulted together and bought with them the potter's field, to bury strangers in.

Visited by sorrowing friends.

John 11:31 Then the Jews who were with her in the house, and comforting her, when they saw that Mary rose up quickly and went out, followed her, saying, "She is going to the tomb to weep there."

Pillars erected on.

Gen 35:20 And Jacob set a pillar on her grave, which *is* the pillar of Rachel's grave to this day.

Tombs erected over.

Matt 23:27–29 "Woe to you, scribes and Pharisees, hypocrites! For you are like whitewashed tombs which indeed appear beautiful outwardly, but inside are full of dead *men's* bones and all uncleanness. 28 Even so you also outwardly appear righteous to men, but inside you are full of hypocrisy and lawlessness. 29 "Woe to you, scribes and Pharisees, hypocrites! Because you build the tombs of the prophets and adorn the monuments of the righteous,

Sometimes had inscriptions.

2 Kin 23:17 Then he said, "What gravestone *is* this that I see?" So the men of the city told him, "*It is* the tomb of the man of God who came from Judah and proclaimed these things which you have done against the altar of Bethel."

Sometimes not apparent.

Luke 11:44 Woe to you, scribes and Pharisees, hypocrites! For you are like graves which are not seen, and the men who walk over *them* are not aware *of them.*"

Were ceremonially unclean.

Num 19:16 Whoever in the open field touches one who is slain by a sword or who has died, or a bone of a man, or a grave, shall be unclean seven days.

Num 19:18 A clean person shall take hyssop and dip *it* in the water, sprinkle *it* on the tent, on all the vessels, on the persons who were there, or on the one who touched a bone, the slain, the dead, or a grave.

Often desecrated by idolatry.

Is 65:3–4 A people who provoke Me to anger continually to My face; Who sacrifice in gardens, And burn incense on altars of brick; 4 Who sit among the graves, And spend the night in the tombs; Who eat swine's flesh, And the broth of abominable things is *in* their vessels;

The Jews anxious to be interred in their family places of.

Gen 47:29–31 When the time drew near that Israel must die, he called his son Joseph and said to him, "Now if I have found favor in your sight, please put your hand under my thigh, and deal kindly and truly with me. Please do not bury me in Egypt, 30 but let me lie with my fathers; you shall carry me out of Egypt and bury me in their burial place." And he said, "I will do as you have said." 31 Then he said, "Swear to me." And he swore to him. So Israel bowed himself on the head of the bed.

Gen 49:29–30 Then he charged them and said to them: "I am to be gathered to my people; bury me with my fathers in the cave that *is* in the field of Ephron the Hittite, 30 in the cave that *is* in the field of Machpelah, which *is* before Mamre in the land of Canaan, which Abraham bought with the field of Ephron the Hittite as a possession for a burial place.

Gen 50:25 Then Joseph took an oath from the children of Israel, saying, "God will surely visit you, and you shall carry up my bones from here."

2 Sam 19:37 Please let your servant turn back again, that I may die in my own city, near the grave of my father and mother. But here is your servant Chimham; let him cross over with my lord the king, and do for him what seems good to you."

Followed by a feast.

2 Sam 3:35 And when all the people came to persuade David to eat food while it was still day, David took an oath, saying, "God do so to me, and more also, if I taste bread or anything else till the sun goes down!"

Jer 16:7–8 Nor shall *men* break *bread* in mourning for them, to comfort them for the dead; nor shall *men* give them the cup of consolation to drink for their father or their mother. 8 Also you shall not go into the house of feasting to sit with them, to eat and drink."

Hos 9:4 They shall not offer wine *offerings* to the LORD, Nor shall their sacrifices be pleasing to Him. *It shall be* like bread of mourners to them; All who eat it shall be defiled. For their bread *shall be* for their *own* life; It shall not come into the house of the LORD.

Privation of, considered a calamity.

Eccl 6:3 If a man begets a hundred *children* and lives many years, so that the days of his years are many, but his soul is not satisfied with goodness, or indeed he has no burial, I say *that* a stillborn child *is* better than he—

Privation of, threatened as a punishment.

2 Kin 9:10 The dogs shall eat Jezebel on the plot *of ground* at Jezreel, and *there shall be* none to bury *her.'*" And he opened the door and fled.

Jer 8:2 They shall spread them before the sun and the moon and all the host of heaven, which they have loved and which they have served and after which they have walked, which they have sought and which they have worshiped. They shall not be gathered nor buried; they shall be like refuse on the face of the earth.

Jer 16:4 "They shall die gruesome deaths; they shall not be lamented nor shall they be buried, *but* they shall be like refuse on the face of the earth. They shall be consumed by the sword and by famine, and their corpses shall be meat for the birds of heaven and for the beasts of the earth."

An ignominious, compared to the burial of a donkey.

Jer 22:19 He shall be buried with the burial of a donkey, Dragged and cast out beyond the gates of Jerusalem.

BUSYBODIES

The idle are.

2 Thess 3:11 For we hear that there are some who walk among you in a disorderly manner, not working at all, but are busybodies.

1 Tim 5:13 And besides they learn *to be* idle, wandering about from house to house, and not only idle but also gossips and busybodies, saying things which they ought not.

Are mischievous talebearers.

1 Tim 5:13 And besides they learn *to be* idle, wandering about from house to house, and not only idle but also gossips and busybodies, saying things which they ought not.

Bring mischief upon themselves.

2 Kin 14:10 You have indeed defeated Edom, and your heart has lifted you up. Glory *in that*, and stay at home; for why should you meddle with trouble so that you fall—you and Judah with you?"

Prov 26:17 He who passes by *and* meddles in a quarrel not his own *Is like* one who takes a dog by the ears.

Christians must not be.

1 Pet 4:15 But let none of you suffer as a murderer, a thief, an evildoer, or as a busybody in other people's matters.

Caesar

Augustus, name commonly applied to.

Luke 2:1 And it came to pass in those days *that* a decree went out from Caesar Augustus that all the world should be registered.

Acts 25:21 But when Paul appealed to be reserved for the decision of Augustus, I commanded him to be kept till I could send him to Caesar."

Taxes owed to.

Matt 22:17 Tell us, therefore, what do You think? Is it lawful to pay taxes to Caesar, or not?"

Luke 20:22–25 Is it lawful for us to pay taxes to Caesar or not?" **23** But He perceived their craftiness, and said to them, "Why do you test Me? **24** Show Me a denarius. Whose image and inscription does it have?" They answered and said, "Caesar's." **25** And He said to them, "Render therefore to Caesar the things that are Caesar's, and to God the things that are God's."

Limited authority of.

Matt 22:21 They said to Him, "Caesar's." And He said to them, "Render therefore to Caesar the things that are Caesar's, and to God the things that are God's."

Rom 13:1–7 Let every soul be subject to the governing authorities. For there is no authority except from God, and the authorities that exist are appointed by God. **2** Therefore whoever resists the authority resists the ordinance of God, and those who resist will bring judgment on themselves. **3** For rulers are not a terror to good works, but to evil. Do you want to be unafraid of the authority? Do what is good, and you will have praise from the same. **4** For he is God's minister to you for good. But if you do evil, be afraid; for he does not bear the sword in vain; for he is God's minister, an avenger to *execute* wrath on him who practices evil. **5** Therefore *you* must be subject, not only because of wrath but also for conscience' sake. **6** For because of this you also pay taxes, for they are God's ministers attending continually to this very thing. **7** Render therefore to all their due: taxes to whom taxes *are due*, customs to whom customs, fear to whom fear, honor to whom honor.

1 Pet 2:13–17 Therefore submit yourselves to every ordinance of man for the Lord's sake, whether to the king as supreme, **14** or to governors, as to those who are sent by him for the punishment of evildoers and *for the* praise of those who do good. **15** For this is the will of God, that by doing good you may put to silence the ignorance of foolish men— **16** as free, yet not using liberty as a cloak for vice, but as bondservants of God. **17** Honor all *people.* Love the brotherhood. Fear God. Honor the king.

Claudius.

Acts 11:28 Then one of them, named Agabus, stood up and showed by the Spirit that there was going to be a great famine throughout all the world, which also happened in the days of Claudius Caesar.

The Jews' phony allegiance to.

John 19:15 But they cried out, "Away with *Him,* away with *Him!* Crucify Him!" Pilate said to them, "Shall I crucify your King?" The chief priests answered, "We have no king but Caesar!"

Paul's appeal to.

Acts 25:11–12 For if I am an offender, or have committed anything deserving of death, I do not object to dying; but if there is nothing in these things of which these men accuse me, no one can deliver me to them. I appeal to Caesar." **12** Then Festus, when he had conferred with the council, answered, "You have appealed to Caesar? To Caesar you shall go!"

Acts 27:24 saying, 'Do not be afraid, Paul; you must be brought before Caesar; and indeed God has granted you all those who sail with you.'

Acts 28:19 But when the Jews spoke against *it,* I was compelled to appeal to Caesar, not that I had anything of which to accuse my nation.

Calf, The

The young of the herd.

Jer 31:12 Therefore they shall come and sing in the height of Zion, Streaming to the goodness of the Lord— For wheat and new wine and oil, For the young of the flock and the herd; Their souls shall be like a well-watered garden, And they shall sorrow no more at all.

Playfulness of, alluded to.

Ps 29:6 He makes them also skip like a calf, Lebanon and Sirion like a young wild ox.

Fattened in stalls, etc.

1 Sam 28:24 Now the woman had a fatted calf in the house, and she hastened to kill it. And she took flour and kneaded *it,* and baked unleavened bread from it.

Is 27:10 Yet the fortified city *will be* desolate, The habitation forsaken and left like a wilderness; There the calf will feed, and there it will lie down And consume its branches.

Amos 6:4 Who lie on beds of ivory, Stretch out on your couches, Eat lambs from the flock And calves from the midst of the stall;

Offered in sacrifice.

Lev 9:2–3 And he said to Aaron, "Take for yourself a young bull as a sin offering and a ram as a burnt offering, without blemish, and offer *them* before the

LORD. **3** And to the children of Israel you shall speak, saying, 'Take a kid of the goats as a sin offering, and a calf and a lamb, *both* of the first year, without blemish, as a burnt offering,

Mic 6:6 With what shall I come before the LORD, *And* bow myself before the High God? Shall I come before Him with burnt offerings, With calves a year old?

Heb 9:12 Not with the blood of goats and calves, but with His own blood He entered the Most Holy Place once for all, having obtained eternal redemption.

Heb 9:19 For when Moses had spoken every precept to all the people according to the law, he took the blood of calves and goats, with water, scarlet wool, and hyssop, and sprinkled both the book itself and all the people,

If firstborn, not redeemed.

Num 18:17 But the firstborn of a cow, the firstborn of a sheep, or the firstborn of a goat you shall not redeem; they *are* holy. You shall sprinkle their blood on the altar, and burn their fat *as* an offering made by fire for a sweet aroma to the LORD.

Eaten in the patriarchal age.

Gen 18:7–8 And Abraham ran to the herd, took a tender and good calf, gave *it* to a young man, and he hastened to prepare it. **8** So he took butter and milk and the calf which he had prepared, and set *it* before them; and he stood by them under the tree as they ate.

When fattened, considered a delicacy.

1 Sam 28:24–25 Now the woman had a fatted calf in the house, and she hastened to kill it. And she took flour and kneaded *it*, and baked unleavened bread from it. **25** So she brought *it* before Saul and his servants, and they ate. Then they rose and went away that night.

Amos 6:4 Who lie on beds of ivory, Stretch out on your couches, Eat lambs from the flock And calves from the midst of the stall;

Luke 15:23 And bring the fatted calf here and kill *it*, and let us eat and be merry;

Luke 15:27 And he said to him, 'Your brother has come, and because he has received him safe and sound, your father has killed the fatted calf.'

Illustrative of believers nourished by grace.

Mal 4:2 But to you who fear My name The Sun of Righteousness shall arise With healing in His wings; And you shall go out And grow fat like stall-fed calves.

CALF, THE GOLDEN
Made when Moses was delayed on the mountain.

Ex 32:1 Now when the people saw that Moses delayed coming down from the mountain, the people gathered together to Aaron, and said to him, "Come, make us gods that shall go before us; for *as for* this Moses, the man who brought us up out of the land of Egypt, we do not know what has become of him."

Was made
Of the ornaments of the women, etc.

Ex 32:2–3 And Aaron said to them, "Break off the golden earrings which *are* in the ears of your wives, your sons, and your daughters, and bring *them* to me."

3 So all the people broke off the golden earrings which *were* in their ears, and brought *them* to Aaron.

To represent God.

Ex 32:4–5 And he received *the gold* from their hand, and he fashioned it with an engraving tool, and made a molded calf. Then they said, "This *is* your god, O Israel, that brought you out of the land of Egypt!" **5** So when Aaron saw *it*, he built an altar before it. And Aaron made a proclamation and said, "Tomorrow *is* a feast to the LORD."

After an Egyptian model.

Acts 7:39 whom our fathers would not obey, but rejected. And in their hearts they turned back to Egypt,

Acts 7:41 And they made a calf in those days, offered sacrifices to the idol, and rejoiced in the works of their own hands.

Molded in the fire.

Ex 32:4 And he received *the gold* from their hand, and he fashioned it with an engraving tool, and made a molded calf. Then they said, "This *is* your god, O Israel, that brought you out of the land of Egypt!"

Ps 106:19 They made a calf in Horeb, And worshiped the molded image.

An altar built before.

Ex 32:5 So when Aaron saw *it*, he built an altar before it. And Aaron made a proclamation and said, "Tomorrow *is* a feast to the LORD."

Sacrifices offered to.

Ex 32:6 Then they rose early on the next day, offered burnt offerings, and brought peace offerings; and the people sat down to eat and drink, and rose up to play.

Acts 7:41 And they made a calf in those days, offered sacrifices to the idol, and rejoiced in the works of their own hands.

Worshiped with profane revelry.

Ex 32:6 Then they rose early on the next day, offered burnt offerings, and brought peace offerings; and the people sat down to eat and drink, and rose up to play.

Ex 32:18–19 But he said: "*It is* not the noise of the shout of victory, Nor the noise of the cry of defeat, *But* the sound of singing I hear." **19** So it was, as soon as he came near the camp, that he saw the calf *and* the dancing. So Moses' anger became hot, and he cast the tablets out of his hands and broke them at the foot of the mountain.

Ex 32:25 Now when Moses saw that the people *were* unrestrained (for Aaron had not restrained them, to *their* shame among their enemies),

1 Cor 10:7 And do not become idolaters *as were* some of them. As it is written, *"The people sat down to eat and drink, and rose up to play."*

Making of,
A very great sin.

Ex 32:21 And Moses said to Aaron, "What did this people do to you that you have brought *so* great a sin upon them?"

Ex 32:30–31 Now it came to pass on the next day that Moses said to the people, "You have committed a great sin. So now I will go up to the LORD; perhaps I can make atonement for your sin." **31** Then Moses returned to the LORD and said, "Oh, these people have committed a great sin, and have made for themselves a god of gold!

A forgetting of God.

Ps 106:20–21 Thus they changed their glory Into the image of an ox that eats grass. **21** They forgot God their Savior, Who had done great things in Egypt,

A turning aside from the divine command.

Ex 32:8 They have turned aside quickly out of the way which I commanded them. They have made themselves a molded calf, and worshiped it and sacrificed to it, and said, 'This *is* your god, O Israel, that brought you out of the land of Egypt!' "

Deut 9:12 "Then the LORD said to me, 'Arise, go down quickly from here, for your people whom you brought out of Egypt have acted corruptly; they have quickly turned aside from the way which I commanded them; they have made themselves a molded image.'

Deut 9:16 And I looked, and behold, you had sinned against the LORD your God—had made for yourselves a molded calf! You had turned aside quickly from the way which the LORD had commanded you.

Excited wrath against Aaron.

Deut 9:20 And the LORD was very angry with Aaron *and* would have destroyed him; so I prayed for Aaron also at the same time.

Excited wrath against Israel.

Ex 32:10 Now therefore, let Me alone, that My wrath may burn hot against them and I may consume them. And I will make of you a great nation."

Deut 9:14 Let Me alone, that I may destroy them and blot out their name from under heaven; and I will make of you a nation mightier and greater than they.'

Deut 9:19 For I was afraid of the anger and hot displeasure with which the LORD was angry with you, to destroy you. But the LORD listened to me at that time also.

Caused Moses to break the tablets.

Ex 32:19 So it was, as soon as he came near the camp, that he saw the calf *and* the dancing. So Moses' anger became hot, and he cast the tablets out of his hands and broke them at the foot of the mountain.

Deut 9:17 Then I took the two tablets and threw them out of my two hands and broke them before your eyes.

Israel punished for.

Ex 32:26–29 then Moses stood in the entrance of the camp, and said, "Whoever *is* on the LORD's side—*come* to me!" And all the sons of Levi gathered themselves together to him. **27** And he said to them, "Thus says the LORD God of Israel: 'Let every man put his sword on his side, and go in and out from entrance to entrance throughout the camp, and let every man kill his brother, every man his companion, and every man his neighbor.' " **28** So the sons of Levi did according to the word of Moses. And about three thousand men of the people fell that day. **29** Then Moses said, "Consecrate yourselves today to the LORD, that He may bestow on you a blessing this day, for every man has opposed his son and his brother."

Ex 32:35 So the LORD plagued the people because of what they did with the calf which Aaron made.

Moses interceded for those who worshiped.

Ex 32:11–14 Then Moses pleaded with the LORD his God, and said: "LORD, why does Your wrath burn hot against Your people whom You have brought out of the land of Egypt with great power and with a mighty hand? **12** Why should the Egyptians speak, and say, 'He brought them out to harm them, to kill them in the mountains, and to consume them from the face of the earth'? Turn from Your fierce wrath, and relent from this harm to Your people. **13** Remember Abraham, Isaac, and Israel, Your servants, to whom You swore by Your own self, and said to them, 'I will multiply your descendants as the stars of heaven; and all this land that I have spoken of I give to your descendants, and they shall inherit *it* forever.' " **14** So the LORD relented from the harm which He said He would do to His people.

Ex 32:30–34 Now it came to pass on the next day that Moses said to the people, "You have committed a great sin. So now I will go up to the LORD; perhaps I can make atonement for your sin." **31** Then Moses returned to the LORD and said, "Oh, these people have committed a great sin, and have made for themselves a god of gold! **32** Yet now, if You will forgive their sin—but if not, I pray, blot me out of Your book which You have written." **33** And the LORD said to Moses, "Whoever has sinned against Me, I will blot him out of My book. **34** Now therefore, go, lead the people to *the place* of which I have spoken to you. Behold, My Angel shall go before you. Nevertheless, in the day when I visit for punishment, I will visit punishment upon them for their sin."

Deut 9:18–20 And I fell down before the LORD, as at the first, forty days and forty nights; I neither ate bread nor drank water, because of all your sin which you committed in doing wickedly in the sight of the LORD, to provoke Him to anger. **19** For I was afraid of the anger and hot displeasure with which the LORD was angry with you, to destroy you. But the LORD listened to me at that time also. **20** And the LORD was very angry with Aaron *and* would have destroyed him; so I prayed for Aaron also at the same time.

Destroyed by Moses.

Ex 32:20 Then he took the calf which they had made, burned *it* in the fire, and ground *it* to powder; and he scattered *it* on the water and made the children of Israel drink *it*.

Deut 9:21 Then I took your sin, the calf which you had made, and burned it with fire and crushed it *and* ground *it* very small, until it was as fine as dust; and I threw its dust into the brook that descended from the mountain.

Used as a warning to others.

1 Cor 10:5–7 But with most of them God was not well pleased, for *their bodies* were scattered in the wilderness. **6** Now these things became our examples, to the intent that we should not lust after evil things as they also lusted. **7** And do not become idolaters as *were* some of them. As it is written, *"The people sat down to eat and drink, and rose up to play."*

CALL OF GOD, THE

By Christ.

Is 55:5 Surely you shall call a nation you do not know, And nations *who* do not know you shall run to you, Because of the LORD your God, And the Holy One of Israel; For He has glorified you."

Rom 1:6 among whom you also are the called of Jesus Christ;

By His Spirit.

Rev 22:17 And the Spirit and the bride say, "Come!" And let him who hears say, "Come!" And let him who thirsts come. Whoever desires, let him take the water of life freely.

By His works.

Ps 19:2–3 Day unto day utters speech, And night unto night reveals knowledge. **3** *There is* no speech nor language *Where* their voice is not heard.

Rom 1:20 For since the creation of the world His invisible *attributes* are clearly seen, being understood by the things that are made, *even* His eternal power and Godhead, so that they are without excuse,

By His ministers.

Jer 35:15 I have also sent to you all My servants the prophets, rising up early and sending *them*, saying, 'Turn now everyone from his evil way, amend your doings, and do not go after other gods to serve them; then you will dwell in the land which I have given you and your fathers.' But you have not inclined your ear, nor obeyed Me.

2 Cor 5:20 Now then, we are ambassadors for Christ, as though God were pleading through us: we implore *you* on Christ's behalf, be reconciled to God.

By His gospel.

2 Thess 2:14 to which He called you by our gospel, for the obtaining of the glory of our Lord Jesus Christ.

Is from darkness.

1 Pet 2:9 But you *are* a chosen generation, a royal priesthood, a holy nation, His own special people, that you may proclaim the praises of Him who called you out of darkness into His marvelous light;

Addressed to all.

Is 45:22 "Look to Me, and be saved, All you ends of the earth! For I *am* God, and *there is* no other.

Matt 20:16 So the last will be first, and the first last. For many are called, but few chosen."

Most reject.

Prov 1:24 Because I have called and you refused, I have stretched out my hand and no one regarded,

Matt 20:16 So the last will be first, and the first last. For many are called, but few chosen."

Effectual to believers.

Acts 2:47 praising God and having favor with all the people. And the Lord added to the church daily those who were being saved.

Acts 13:48 Now when the Gentiles heard this, they were glad and glorified the word of the Lord. And as many as had been appointed to eternal life believed.

1 Cor 1:24 but to those who are called, both Jews and Greeks, Christ the power of God and the wisdom of God.

To man is

Of grace.

Gal 1:15 But when it pleased God, who separated me from my mother's womb and called *me* through His grace,

2 Tim 1:9 who has saved us and called *us* with a holy calling, not according to our works, but according to His own purpose and grace which was given to us in Christ Jesus before time began,

According to the purpose of God.

Rom 8:28 And we know that all things work together for good to those who love God, to those who are the called according to *His* purpose.

Rom 9:11 (for *the children* not yet being born, nor having done any good or evil, that the purpose of God according to election might stand, not of works but of Him who calls),

Rom 9:23–24 and that He might make known the riches of His glory on the vessels of mercy, which He had prepared beforehand for glory, **24** *even* us whom He called, not of the Jews only, but also of the Gentiles?

Heavenly.

Phil 3:14 I press toward the goal for the prize of the upward call of God in Christ Jesus.

Heb 3:1 Therefore, holy brethren, partakers of the heavenly calling, consider the Apostle and High Priest of our confession, Christ Jesus,

To fellowship with Christ.

1 Cor 1:9 God *is* faithful, by whom you were called into the fellowship of His Son, Jesus Christ our Lord.

To holiness.

1 Thess 4:7 For God did not call us to uncleanness, but in holiness.

To liberty.

Gal 5:13 For you, brethren, have been called to liberty; only do not *use* liberty as an opportunity for the flesh, but through love serve one another.

To peace.

1 Cor 7:15 But if the unbeliever departs, let him depart; a brother or a sister is not under bondage in such *cases*. But God has called us to peace.

Col 3:15 And let the peace of God rule in your hearts, to which also you were called in one body; and be thankful.

To glory and virtue.

2 Pet 1:3 as His divine power has given to us all things that *pertain* to life and godliness, through the knowledge of Him who called us by glory and virtue,

To the eternal glory of Christ.

2 Thess 2:14 to which He called you by our gospel, for the obtaining of the glory of our Lord Jesus Christ.

1 Pet 5:10 But may the God of all grace, who called us to His eternal glory by Christ Jesus, after you have suffered a while, perfect, establish, strengthen, and settle *you*.

To eternal life.

1 Tim 6:12 Fight the good fight of faith, lay hold on eternal life, to which you were also called and have confessed the good confession in the presence of many witnesses.

Partakers of, are justified.

Rom 8:30 Moreover whom He predestined, these He also called; whom He called, these He also justified; and whom He justified, these He also glorified.

Walk worthy of.

Eph 4:1 I, therefore, the prisoner of the Lord, beseech you to walk worthy of the calling with which you were called,

Blessedness of receiving.

Rev 19:9 Then he said to me, "Write: 'Blessed *are* those who are called to the marriage supper of the Lamb!' " And he said to me, "These are the true sayings of God."

Praise God for.

1 Pet 2:9 But you *are* a chosen generation, a royal priesthood, a holy nation, His own special people, that you may proclaim the praises of Him who called you out of darkness into His marvelous light;

Rejection of, leads to

Judicial blindness.

Is 6:9 And He said, "Go, and tell this people: 'Keep on hearing, but do not understand; Keep on seeing, but do not perceive.'

Acts 28:24–27 And some were persuaded by the things which were spoken, and some disbelieved. **25** So when they did not agree among themselves, they departed after Paul had said one word: "The Holy Spirit spoke rightly through Isaiah the prophet to our fathers, **26** saying, *'Go to this people and say: "Hearing you will hear, and shall not understand; And seeing you will see, and not perceive; **27** For the hearts of this people have grown dull. Their ears are hard of hearing, And their eyes they have closed, Lest they should see with their eyes and hear with their ears, Lest they should understand with their hearts and turn, So that I should heal them." '*

Rom 11:8–10 Just as it is written: *"God has given them a spirit of stupor, Eyes that they should not see And ears that they should not hear, To this very day."* **9** And David says: *"Let their table become a snare and a trap, A stumbling block and a recompense to them. **10** Let their eyes be darkened, so that they do not see, And bow down their back always."*

Delusion.

Is 66:4 So will I choose their delusions, And bring their fears on them; Because, when I called, no one answered, When I spoke they did not hear; But they did evil before My eyes, And chose *that* in which I do not delight."

2 Thess 2:10–11 and with all unrighteous deception among those who perish, because they did not receive the love of the truth, that they might be saved. **11** And for this reason God will send them strong delusion, that they should believe the lie,

Temporal judgments.

Is 28:12 To whom He said, "This *is* the rest *with which* You may cause the weary to rest," And, "This *is* the refreshing"; Yet they would not hear.

Jer 6:16 Thus says the LORD: "Stand in the ways and see, And ask for the old paths, where the good way *is*, And walk in it; Then you will find rest for your souls. But they said, 'We will not walk *in it.'*

Jer 6:19 Hear, O earth! Behold, I will certainly bring calamity on this people— The fruit of their thoughts, Because they have not heeded My words Nor My law, but rejected it.

Jer 35:17 "Therefore thus says the LORD God of hosts, the God of Israel: 'Behold, I will bring on Judah and on all the inhabitants of Jerusalem all the doom that I have pronounced against them; because I have spoken to them but they have not heard, and I have called to them but they have not answered.' "

Zech 7:12–14 Yes, they made their hearts like flint, refusing to hear the law and the words which the LORD of hosts had sent by His Spirit through the former prophets. Thus great wrath came from the LORD of hosts. **13** Therefore it happened, *that* just as He proclaimed and they would not hear, so they called out and I would not listen," says the LORD of hosts. **14** "But I scattered them with a whirlwind among all the nations which they had not known. Thus the land became desolate after them, so that no one passed through or returned; for they made the pleasant land desolate."

Rejection by God.

Prov 1:14–32 Cast in your lot among us, Let us all have one purse"— **15** My son, do not walk in the way with them, Keep your foot from their path; **16** For their feet run to evil, And they make haste to shed blood. **17** Surely, in vain the net is spread In the sight of any bird; **18** But they lie in wait for their *own* blood, They lurk secretly for their *own* lives. **19** So *are* the ways of everyone who is greedy for gain; It takes away the life of its owners. **20** Wisdom calls aloud outside; She raises her voice in the open squares. **21** She cries out in the chief concourses, At the openings of the gates in the city She speaks her words: **22** "How long, you simple ones, will you love simplicity? For scorners delight in their scorning, And fools hate knowledge. **23** Turn at my rebuke; Surely I will pour out my spirit on you; I will make my words known to you. **24** Because I have called and you refused, I have stretched out my hand and no one regarded, **25** Because you disdained all my counsel, And would have none of my rebuke, **26** I also will laugh at your calamity; I will mock when your terror comes, **27** When your terror comes like a storm, And your destruction comes like a whirlwind, When distress and anguish come upon you. **28** "Then they will call on me, but I will not answer; They will seek me diligently, but they will not find me. **29** Because they hated knowledge And did not choose the fear of the LORD, **30** They would have none of my counsel *And* despised my every rebuke. **31** Therefore they shall eat the fruit of their own way, And be filled to the full with their own fancies. **32** For the turning away of the simple will slay them, And the complacency of fools will destroy them;

Jer 6:19 Hear, O earth! Behold, I will certainly bring calamity on this people— The fruit of their thoughts, Because they have not heeded My words Nor My law, but rejected it.

Jer 6:30 *People* will call them rejected silver, Because the LORD has rejected them."

Condemnation.

John 12:48 He who rejects Me, and does not receive My words, has that which judges him—the word that I have spoken will judge him in the last day.

Heb 2:1–3 Therefore we must give the more earnest heed to the things we have heard, lest we drift away. **2** For if the word spoken through angels proved steadfast, and every transgression and disobedience received a just reward, **3** how shall we escape if we neglect so great a salvation, which at the first began to be spoken by the Lord, and was confirmed to us by those who heard *Him,*

Heb 12:25 See that you do not refuse Him who speaks. For if they did not escape who refused Him who spoke on earth, much more *shall we not escape* if we turn away from Him who *speaks* from heaven,

Destruction.

Prov 29:1 He who is often rebuked, *and* hardens *his* neck, Will suddenly be destroyed, and that without remedy.

Matt 22:3–7 and sent out his servants to call those who were invited to the wedding; and they were not willing to come. **4** Again, he sent out other servants, saying, 'Tell those who are invited, "See, I have prepared my dinner; my oxen and fatted cattle *are* killed, and all things *are* ready. Come to the wedding." ' **5** But they made light of it and went their ways, one to his own farm, another to his business. **6** And the rest seized his servants, treated *them* spitefully, and killed *them.* **7** But when the king heard *about it,* he was furious. And he sent out his armies, destroyed those murderers, and burned up their city.

Withdrawal of the means of grace.

Jer 26:4–6 And you shall say to them, 'Thus says the LORD: "If you will not listen to Me, to walk in My law which I have set before you, **5** to heed the words of My servants the prophets whom I sent to you, both rising up early and sending *them* (but you have not heeded), **6** then I will make this house like Shiloh, and will make this city a curse to all the nations of the earth." ' "

Acts 13:46 Then Paul and Barnabas grew bold and said, "It was necessary that the word of God should be spoken to you first; but since you reject it, and judge yourselves unworthy of everlasting life, behold, we turn to the Gentiles.

Acts 18:6 But when they opposed him and blasphemed, he shook *his* garments and said to them, "Your blood *be* upon your *own* heads; I *am* clean. From now on I will go to the Gentiles."

Rev 2:5 Remember therefore from where you have fallen; repent and do the first works, or else I will come to you quickly and remove your lampstand from its place—unless you repent.

CAMEL, THE

Unclean.

Lev 11:4 Nevertheless these you shall not eat among those that chew the cud or those that have cloven hooves: the camel, because it chews the cud but does not have cloven hooves, is unclean to you;

Deut 14:7 Nevertheless, of those that chew the cud or have cloven hooves, you shall not eat, *such as* these: the camel, the hare, and the rock hyrax; for they chew the cud but do not have cloven hooves; they *are* unclean for you.

Characterized by

The humps on its back.

Is 30:6 The burden against the beasts of the South. Through a land of trouble and anguish, From which *came* the lioness and lion, The viper and fiery flying serpent, They will carry their riches on the backs of young donkeys, And their treasures on the humps of camels, To a people *who* shall not profit;

Its docility.

Gen 24:11 And he made his camels kneel down outside the city by a well of water at evening time, the time when women go out to draw *water.*

Abounded in the east.

1 Chr 5:21 Then they took away their livestock—fifty thousand of their camels, two hundred and fifty thousand of their sheep, and two thousand of their donkeys—also one hundred thousand of their men;

Is 60:6 The multitude of camels shall cover your *land,* The dromedaries of Midian and Ephah; All those from Sheba shall come; They shall bring gold and incense, And they shall proclaim the praises of the LORD.

A part of patriarchal wealth.

Gen 12:16 He treated Abram well for her sake. He had sheep, oxen, male donkeys, male and female servants, female donkeys, and camels.

Gen 30:43 Thus the man became exceedingly prosperous, and had large flocks, female and male servants, and camels and donkeys.

Job 1:3 Also, his possessions were seven thousand sheep, three thousand camels, five hundred yoke of oxen, five hundred female donkeys, and a very large household, so that this man was the greatest of all the people of the East.

Kept in numbers by kings.

1 Chr 27:30 Obil the Ishmaelite *was* over the camels, Jehdeiah the Meronothite *was* over the donkeys,

Used for

Riding.

Gen 24:61 Then Rebekah and her maids arose, and they rode on the camels and followed the man. So the servant took Rebekah and departed.

Drawing chariots.

Is 21:7 And he saw a chariot *with* a pair of horsemen, A chariot of donkeys, *and* a chariot of camels, And he listened earnestly with great care.

Carrying burdens.

Gen 37:25 And they sat down to eat a meal. Then they lifted their eyes and looked, and there was a company of Ishmaelites, coming from Gilead with their camels, bearing spices, balm, and myrrh, on their way to carry *them* down to Egypt.

1 Kin 10:2 She came to Jerusalem with a very great retinue, with camels that bore spices, very much gold, and precious stones; and when she came to Solomon, she spoke with him about all that was in her heart.

2 Kin 8:9 So Hazael went to meet him and took a present with him, of every good thing of Damascus, forty camel-loads; and he came and stood before him, and said, "Your son Ben-Hadad king of Syria has sent me to you, saying, 'Shall I recover from this disease?' "

War.

Judg 7:12 Now the Midianites and Amalekites, all the people of the East, were lying in the valley as numerous as locusts; and their camels *were* without number, as the sand by the seashore in multitude.

1 Sam 30:17 Then David attacked them from twilight until the evening of the next day. Not a man of them escaped, except four hundred young men who rode on camels and fled.

Of the rich, adorned with chains.

Judg 8:21 So Zebah and Zalmunna said, "Rise yourself, and kill us; for as a man *is, so is* his strength." So Gideon arose and killed Zebah and Zalmunna, and took the crescent ornaments that *were* on their camels' necks.

Judg 8:26 Now the weight of the gold earrings that he requested was one thousand seven hundred *shekels* of gold, besides the crescent ornaments, pendants, and purple robes which *were* on the kings of Midian, and besides the chains that *were* around their camels' necks.

Subject to plagues.

Ex 9:3 behold, the hand of the LORD will be on your cattle in the field, on the horses, on the donkeys, on the camels, on the oxen, and on the sheep—a very severe pestilence.

Zech 14:15 Such also shall be the plague On the horse *and* the mule, On the camel and the donkey, And on all the cattle that will be in those camps. So *shall* this plague *be.*

Treated with great care.

Gen 24:31–32 And he said, "Come in, O blessed of the LORD! Why do you stand outside? For I have prepared the house, and a place for the camels." **32** Then the man came to the house. And he unloaded the camels, and provided straw and feed for the camels, and water to wash his feet and the feet of the men who *were* with him.

Esteemed a valuable booty.

1 Chr 5:20–21 And they were helped against them, and the Hagrites were delivered into their hand, and all who *were* with them, for they cried out to God in the battle. He heeded their prayer, because they put their trust in Him. **21** Then they took away their livestock—fifty thousand of their camels, two hundred and fifty thousand of their sheep, and two thousand of their donkeys—also one hundred thousand of their men;

2 Chr 14:15 They also attacked the livestock enclosures, and carried off sheep and camels in abundance, and returned to Jerusalem.

Job 1:17 While he *was* still speaking, another also came and said, "The Chaldeans formed three bands, raided the camels and took them away, yes, and killed the servants with the edge of the sword; and I alone have escaped to tell you!"

Jer 49:29 Their tents and their flocks they shall take away. They shall take for themselves their curtains, All their vessels and their camels; And they shall cry out to them, 'Fear *is* on every side!'

Jer 49:32 Their camels shall be for booty, And the multitude of their cattle for plunder. I will scatter to all winds those in the farthest corners, And I will bring their calamity from all its sides," says the LORD.

Coarse cloth made from its hair.

Matt 3:4 Now John himself was clothed in camel's hair, with a leather belt around his waist; and his food was locusts and wild honey.

Referred to in illustrations by Christ.

Matt 19:24 And again I say to you, it is easier for a camel to go through the eye of a needle than for a rich man to enter the kingdom of God."

Matt 23:24 Blind guides, who strain out a gnat and swallow a camel!

CANAANITES, THE

Lineage and composition.

Gen 9:25–26 Then he said: "Cursed *be* Canaan; A servant of servants He shall be to his brethren." **26** And he said: "Blessed *be* the LORD, The God of Shem, And may Canaan be his servant.

Gen 10:6 The sons of Ham *were* Cush, Mizraim, Put, and Canaan.

Gen 10:15–18 Canaan begot Sidon his firstborn, and Heth; **16** the Jebusite, the Amorite, and the Girgashite; **17** the Hivite, the Arkite, and the Sinite; **18** the Arvadite, the Zemarite, and the Hamathite. Afterward the families of the Canaanites were dispersed.

Included seven distinct nations.

Deut 7:1 "When the LORD your God brings you into the land which you go to possess, and has cast out many nations before you, the Hittites and the Girgashites and the Amorites and the Canaanites and the Perizzites and the Hivites and the Jebusites, seven nations greater and mightier than you,

Borders of their country.

Gen 10:19 And the border of the Canaanites was from Sidon as you go toward Gerar, as far as Gaza; then as you go toward Sodom, Gomorrah, Admah, and Zeboiim, as far as Lasha.

Country of, fertile.

Ex 3:17 and I have said I will bring you up out of the affliction of Egypt to the land of the Canaanites and the Hittites and the Amorites and the Perizzites and the Hivites and the Jebusites, to a land flowing with milk and honey.' '

Num 13:27 Then they told him, and said: "We went to the land where you sent us. It truly flows with milk and honey, and this *is* its fruit.

Described as

Powerful and numerous.

Num 13:28 Nevertheless the people who dwell in the land *are* strong; the cities *are* fortified *and* very large; moreover we saw the descendants of Anak there.

Deut 7:1 "When the LORD your God brings you into the land which you go to possess, and has cast out many nations before you, the Hittites and the Girgashites and the Amorites and the Canaanites and the Perizzites and the Hivites and the Jebusites, seven nations greater and mightier than you,

Deut 7:17 "If you should say in your heart, 'These nations are greater than I; how can I dispossess them?'—

Idolatrous.

Deut 29:17 and you saw their abominations and their idols which *were* among them—wood and stone and silver and gold);

Superstitious.

Deut 18:9–11 "When you come into the land which the LORD your God is giving you, you shall not learn to follow the abominations of those nations. **10** There shall not be found among you *anyone* who makes his son or his daughter pass through the fire, *or one* who practices witchcraft, *or* a soothsayer, or one who interprets omens, or a sorcerer, **11** or one who conjures spells, or a medium, or a spiritist, or one who calls up the dead.

Profane and wicked.

Lev 18:27 (for all these abominations the men of the land have done, who *were* before you, and thus the land is defiled),

Had many strong cities.

Num 13:28 Nevertheless the people who dwell in the land *are* strong; the cities *are* fortified *and* very large; moreover we saw the descendants of Anak there.

Deut 1:28 Where can we go up? Our brethren have discouraged our hearts, saying, "The people *are* greater and taller than we; the cities *are* great and fortified up to heaven; moreover we have seen the sons of the Anakim there." '

Expelled for wickedness.

Deut 9:4 "Do not think in your heart, after the LORD your God has cast them out before you, saying, 'Because of my righteousness the LORD has brought me in to possess this land'; but *it is* because of the wickedness of these nations *that* the LORD is driving them out from before you.

Deut 18:12 For all who do these things *are* an abomination to the LORD, and because of these abominations the LORD your God drives them out from before you.

And Abraham

Was called to dwell among.

Gen 12:1–5 Now the LORD had said to Abram: "Get out of your country, From your family And from your father's house, To a land that I will show you. **2** I will make you a great nation; I will bless you And make your name great; And you shall be a blessing. **3** I will bless those who bless you, And I will curse him who curses you; And in you all the families of the earth shall be blessed." **4** So Abram departed as the LORD had spoken to him, and Lot went with him. And Abram *was* seventy-five years old when he departed from Haran. **5** Then Abram took Sarai his wife and Lot his brother's son, and all their possessions that they had gathered, and the people whom they had acquired in Haran, and they departed to go to the land of Canaan. So they came to the land of Canaan.

Gen 12:6 Abram passed through the land to the place of Shechem, as far as the terebinth tree of Moreh. And the Canaanites *were* then in the land.

Gen 13:7 And there was strife between the herdsmen of Abram's livestock and the herdsmen of Lot's livestock. The Canaanites and the Perizzites then dwelt in the land.

Was promised Canaan for inheritance.

Gen 13:14–17 And the LORD said to Abram, after Lot had separated from him: "Lift your eyes now and look from the place where you are—northward, southward, eastward, and westward; **15** for all the land which you see I give to you and your descendants forever. **16** And I will make your descendants as the dust of the earth; so that if a man could number the dust of the earth, *then* your descendants also could be numbered. **17** Arise, walk in the land through its length and its width, for I give it to you."

Gen 15:18 On the same day the LORD made a covenant with Abram, saying: "To your descendants I have given this land, from the river of Egypt to the great river, the River Euphrates—

Gen 17:8 Also I give to you and your descendants after you the land in which you are a stranger, all the land of Canaan, as an everlasting possession; and I will be their God."

Kind to the patriarchs.

Gen 14:13 Then one who had escaped came and told Abram the Hebrew, for he dwelt by the terebinth trees of Mamre the Amorite, brother of Eshcol and brother of Aner; and they *were* allies with Abram.

Gen 23:6 "Hear us, my lord: You *are* a mighty prince among us; bury your dead in the choicest of our burial places. None of us will withhold from you his burial place, that you may bury your dead."

Israel commanded

Not to make a covenant with.

Deut 7:2 and when the LORD your God delivers them over to you, you shall conquer them *and* utterly destroy them. You shall make no covenant with them nor show mercy to them.

Judg 2:2 And you shall make no covenant with the inhabitants of this land; you shall tear down their altars.' But you have not obeyed My voice. Why have you done this?

Not to intermarry with.

Deut 7:3 Nor shall you make marriages with them. You shall not give your daughter to their son, nor take their daughter for your son.

Josh 23:12 Or else, if indeed you do go back, and cling to the remnant of these nations—these that remain among you—and make marriages with them, and go in to them and they to you,

Not to follow idols of.

Ex 23:24 You shall not bow down to their gods, nor serve them, nor do according to their works; but you shall utterly overthrow them and completely break down their *sacred* pillars.

Deut 7:25 You shall burn the carved images of their gods with fire; you shall not covet the silver or gold *that is* on them, nor take *it* for yourselves, lest you be snared by it; for it *is* an abomination to the LORD your God.

Not to follow customs of.

Lev 18:26–27 You shall therefore keep My statutes and My judgments, and shall not commit *any* of these abominations, *either* any of your own nation or any stranger who dwells among you **27** (for all these abominations the men of the land have done, who *were* before you, and thus the land is defiled),

To destroy, without mercy.

Deut 7:2 and when the LORD your God delivers them over to you, you shall conquer them *and* utterly destroy them. You shall make no covenant with them nor show mercy to them.

Deut 7:24 And He will deliver their kings into your hand, and you will destroy their name from under heaven; no one shall be able to stand against you until you have destroyed them.

To destroy all vestiges of their idolatry.

Ex 23:24 You shall not bow down to their gods, nor serve them, nor do according to their works; but you shall utterly overthrow them and completely break down their *sacred* pillars.

Deut 7:5 But thus you shall deal with them: you shall destroy their altars, and break down their *sacred* pillars, and cut down their wooden images, and burn their carved images with fire.

Deut 7:25 You shall burn the carved images of their gods with fire; you shall not covet the silver or gold *that is* on them, nor take *it* for yourselves, lest you be snared by it; for it *is* an abomination to the LORD your God.

Not to fear.

Deut 7:17–18 "If you should say in your heart, 'These nations are greater than I; how can I dispossess them?'— **18** you shall not be afraid of them, *but* you shall remember well what the LORD your God did to Pharaoh and to all Egypt:

Deut 31:7 Then Moses called Joshua and said to him in the sight of all Israel, "Be strong and of good courage, for you must go with this people to the land which the LORD has sworn to their fathers to give them, and you shall cause them to inherit it.

Terrified at the approach of Israel.

Ex 15:15–16 Then the chiefs of Edom will be dismayed; The mighty men of Moab, Trembling will take hold of them; All the inhabitants of Canaan will melt away. **16** Fear and dread will fall on them; By the greatness of Your arm They will be *as* still as a stone, Till Your people pass over, O LORD, Till the people pass over Whom You have purchased.

Josh 2:9–11 and said to the men: "I know that the LORD has given you the land, that the terror of you has fallen on us, and that all the inhabitants of the land are fainthearted because of you. **10** For we have heard how the LORD dried up the water of the Red Sea for you when you came out of Egypt, and what you did to the two kings of the Amorites who *were* on the other side of the Jordan, Sihon and Og, whom you utterly destroyed. **11** And as soon as we heard *these things*, our hearts melted; neither did there remain any more courage in anyone because of you, for the LORD your God, He *is* God in heaven above and on earth beneath.

Josh 5:1 So it was, when all the kings of the Amorites who *were* on the west side of the Jordan, and all the kings of the Canaanites who *were* by the sea, heard that the LORD had dried up the waters of the Jordan from before the children of Israel until we had crossed over, that their heart melted; and there was no spirit in them any longer because of the children of Israel.

Partially subdued by Israel. Josh 10:1—11:23; Judg 1:1–36

Part of their country left

To try Israel.

Judg 2:3 Therefore I also said, 'I will not drive them out before you; but they shall be *thorns* in your side, and their gods shall be a snare to you.' "

Judg 2:21–22 I also will no longer drive out before them any of the nations which Joshua left when he died, **22** so that through them I may test Israel, whether they will keep the ways of the LORD, to walk in them as their fathers kept *them*, or not."

Judg 3:1–4 Now these *are* the nations which the LORD left, that He might test Israel by them, *that is*, all who had not known any of the wars in Canaan **2** (*this was* only so that the generations of the children of Israel might be taught to know war, at least those who had not formerly known it), **3** *namely*, five lords of the Philistines, all the Canaanites, the Sidonians, and the Hivites who dwelt in Mount Lebanon, from Mount Baal Hermon to the entrance of Hamath. **4** And they were *left, that He might* test Israel by them, to know whether they would obey the commandments of the LORD, which He had commanded their fathers by the hand of Moses.

To chastise Israel.

Num 33:55 But if you do not drive out the inhabitants of the land from before you, then it shall be that those whom you let remain *shall be* irritants in your eyes and thorns in your sides, and they shall harass you in the land where you dwell.

Judg 4:2 So the LORD sold them into the hand of Jabin king of Canaan, who reigned in Hazor. The commander of his army *was* Sisera, who dwelt in Harosheth Hagoyim.

Israel ensnared by.

Judg 2:3 Therefore I also said, 'I will not drive them out before you; but they shall be *thorns* in your side, and their gods shall be a snare to you.' "

Judg 2:19 And it came to pass, when the judge was dead, that they reverted and behaved more corruptly than their fathers, by following other gods, to serve them and bow down to them. They did not cease from their own doings nor from their stubborn way.

Ps 106:36–38 They served their idols, Which became a snare to them. **37** They even sacrificed their sons And their daughters to demons, **38** And shed innocent blood, The blood of their sons and daughters, Whom they sacrificed to the idols of Canaan; And the land was polluted with blood.

Some descendants of, in our Lord's time.

Matt 15:22 And behold, a woman of Canaan came from that region and cried out to Him, saying, "Have mercy on me, O Lord, Son of David! My daughter is severely demon-possessed."

Mark 7:26 The woman was a Greek, a Syro-Phoenician by birth, and she kept asking Him to cast the demon out of her daughter.

CAPITAL PUNISHMENT

Invoked on every beast.

Gen 9:5 Surely for your lifeblood I will demand *a reckoning;* from the hand of every beast I will require it, and from the hand of man. From the hand of every man's brother I will require the life of man.

Ex 21:28 "If an ox gores a man or a woman to death, then the ox shall surely be stoned, and its flesh shall not be eaten; but the owner of the ox *shall be* acquitted.

Invoked on man.

Gen 9:5 Surely for your lifeblood I will demand *a reckoning;* from the hand of every beast I will require it, and from the hand of man. From the hand of every man's brother I will require the life of man.

Lev 24:17 'Whoever kills any man shall surely be put to death.

Matt 26:52 But Jesus said to him, "Put your sword in its place, for all who take the sword will perish by the sword.

John 19:11 Jesus answered, "You could have no power at all against Me unless it had been given you from above. Therefore the one who delivered Me to you has the greater sin."

Acts 25:11 For if I am an offender, or have committed anything deserving of death, I do not object to dying; but if there is nothing in these things of which these men accuse me, no one can deliver me to them. I appeal to Caesar."

Rom 13:4 For he is God's minister to you for good. But if you do evil, be afraid; for he does not bear the sword in vain; for he is God's minister, an avenger to *execute* wrath on him who practices evil.

Invoked on rebellious sons.

Deut 21:18–21 "If a man has a stubborn and rebellious son who will not obey the voice of his father or the voice of his mother, and *who,* when they have chastened him, will not heed them, **19** then his father and his mother shall take hold of him and bring him out to the elders of his city, to the gate of his city. **20** And they shall say to the elders of his city, 'This son of ours is stubborn and rebellious; he will not obey our voice; he is a glutton and a drunkard.' **21** Then all the men of his city shall stone him to death with stones; so you shall put away the evil from among you, and all Israel shall hear and fear.

Performed on the evidence of two or three witnesses.

Deut 17:6–7 Whoever is deserving of death shall be put to death on the testimony of two or three witnesses; he shall not be put to death on the testimony of one witness. **7** The hands of the witnesses shall be the first against him to put him to death, and afterward the hands of all the people. So you shall put away the evil from among you.

Figure of speech regarding.

Judg 8:2 So he said to them, "What have I done now in comparison with you? *Is not the gleaning of the grapes* of Ephraim better than the vintage of Abiezer?

Reserved right of the Romans.

John 18:31 Then Pilate said to them, "You take Him and judge Him according to your law." Therefore the Jews said to him, "It is not lawful for us to put anyone to death,"

CAPTIVITY

Babylonian,

Predictions concerning.

Lev 26:31–35 I will lay your cities waste and bring your sanctuaries to desolation, and I will not smell the fragrance of your sweet aromas. **32** I will bring the land to desolation, and your enemies who dwell in it shall be astonished at it. **33** I will scatter you among the nations and draw out a sword after you; your land shall be desolate and your cities waste. **34** Then the land shall enjoy its sabbaths as long as it lies desolate and you *are* in your enemies' land; then the land shall rest and enjoy its sabbaths. **35** As long as *it* lies desolate it shall rest— for the time it did not rest on your sabbaths when you dwelt in it.

Lev 26:38 You shall perish among the nations, and the land of your enemies shall eat you up.

2 Kin 20:16–17 Then Isaiah said to Hezekiah, "Hear the word of the LORD: **17** 'Behold, the days are coming when all that *is* in your house, and what your fathers have accumulated until this day, shall be carried to Babylon; nothing shall be left,' says the LORD.

Is 39:5–6 Then Isaiah said to Hezekiah, "Hear the word of the LORD of hosts: **6** 'Behold, the days are coming when all that *is* in your house, and what your fathers have accumulated until this day, shall be carried to Babylon; nothing shall be left,' says the LORD.

Length of.

Jer 25:11 And this whole land shall be a desolation *and* an astonishment, and these nations shall serve the king of Babylon seventy years.

Dan 9:2 in the first year of his reign I, Daniel, understood by the books the number of the years *specified* by the word of the LORD through Jeremiah the prophet, that He would accomplish seventy years in the desolations of Jerusalem.

Beginning of "times of the Gentiles."

Luke 21:24 And they will fall by the edge of the sword, and be led away captive into all nations. And Jerusalem will be trampled by Gentiles until the times of the Gentiles are fulfilled.

God as sanctuary during.

Ezek 11:16 Therefore say, 'Thus says the Lord GOD: "Although I have cast them far off among the Gentiles, and although I have scattered them among the countries, yet I shall be a little sanctuary for them in the countries where they have gone." '

God removes priestly leadership.

Ezek 21:26 thus says the Lord GOD: "Remove the turban, and take off the crown; Nothing *shall remain* the same. Exalt the humble, and humble the exalted.

Description of.

2 Kin 24:12–16 Then Jehoiachin king of Judah, his mother, his servants, his princes, and his officers went out to the king of Babylon; and the king of Babylon, in the eighth year of his reign, took him prisoner. **13** And he carried out from there all the treasures of the house of the LORD and the treasures of the king's house, and he cut in pieces all the articles of gold which Solomon king of Israel had made in the temple of the LORD, as the LORD had said. **14** Also he carried into captivity all Jerusalem: all the captains and all the mighty men of valor, ten thousand captives, and all the craftsmen and smiths. None remained except the poorest people of the land. **15** And he carried Jehoiachin captive to Babylon. The king's mother, the king's wives, his officers, and the mighty of the land he carried into captivity from Jerusalem to Babylon. **16** All the valiant men, seven thousand, and craftsmen and smiths, one thousand, all *who were* strong *and* fit for war, these the king of Babylon brought captive to Babylon.

Ps 137:1–9 By the rivers of Babylon, There we sat down, yea, we wept When we remembered Zion. **2** We hung our harps Upon the willows in the midst of it. **3** For there those who carried us away captive asked of us a song, And those who plundered us *requested* mirth, Saying, "Sing us *one* of the songs of Zion!" **4** How shall we sing the LORD's song In a foreign land? **5** If I forget you, O Jerusalem, Let my right hand forget *its skill!* **6** If I do not remember you, Let my tongue cling to the roof of my mouth— If I do not exalt Jerusalem Above my chief joy. **7** Remember, O LORD, against the sons of Edom The day of Jerusalem, Who said, "Raze *it,* raze *it,* To its very foundation!" **8** O daughter of Babylon, who are to be destroyed, Happy the one who repays you as you have served us! **9** Happy the one who takes and dashes Your little ones against the rock!

Reasons for.

1 Chr 9:1 So all Israel was recorded by genealogies, and indeed, they *were* inscribed in the book of the kings of Israel. But Judah was carried away captive to Babylon because of their unfaithfulness.

Is 27:8 In measure, by sending it away, You contended with it. He removes *it* by His rough wind In the day of the east wind.

Return from.

Ps 126:1–5 When the LORD brought back the captivity of Zion, We were like those who dream. **2** Then our mouth was filled with laughter, And our tongue with singing. Then they said among the nations, "The LORD has done great things for them." **3** The LORD has done great things for us, *And* we are glad. **4** Bring back our captivity, O LORD, As the streams in the South. **5** Those who sow in tears Shall reap in joy.

Ps 129:1–4 "Many a time they have afflicted me from my youth," Let Israel now say— **2** "Many a time they have afflicted me from my youth; Yet they have not prevailed against me. **3** The plowers plowed on my back; They made their furrows long." **4** The LORD *is* righteous; He has cut in pieces the cords of the wicked.

End of.

Ezek 1:1–5 Now it came to pass in the thirtieth year, in the fourth *month,* on the fifth *day* of the month, as I *was* among the captives by the River Chebar, *that* the heavens were opened, and I saw visions of God. **2** On the fifth *day* of the month, which *was* in the fifth year of King Jehoiachin's captivity, **3** the word of the LORD came expressly to Ezekiel the priest, the son of Buzi, in the land of the Chaldeans by the River Chebar; and the hand of the LORD was upon him there. **4** Then I looked, and behold, a whirlwind was coming out of the north, a great cloud with raging fire engulfing itself; and brightness *was* all around it and radiating out of its midst like the color of amber, out of the midst of the fire. **5** Also from within it *came* the likeness of four living creatures. And this *was* their appearance: they had the likeness of a man.

Ezek 3:8 Behold, I have made your face strong against their faces, and your forehead strong against their foreheads.

Idols taken into.

Is 46:1–2 Bel bows down, Nebo stoops; Their idols were on the beasts and on the cattle. Your carriages *were* heavily loaded, A burden to the weary *beast.* **2** They stoop, they bow down together; They could not deliver the burden, But have themselves gone into captivity.

Promise of deliverance from.

Is 40:2 "Speak comfort to Jerusalem, and cry out to her, That her warfare is ended, That her iniquity is pardoned; For she has received from the LORD's hand Double for all her sins."

Is 43:12 I have declared and saved, I have proclaimed, And *there was* no foreign *god* among you; Therefore you *are* My witnesses," Says the LORD, "that I *am* God.

Is 46:11 Calling a bird of prey from the east, The man who executes My counsel, from a far country. Indeed I have spoken *it;* I will also bring it to pass. I have purposed *it;* I will also do it.

Is 49:10–11 They shall neither hunger nor thirst, Neither heat nor sun shall strike them; For He who has mercy on them will lead them, Even by the springs of water He will guide them. **11** I will make each of My mountains a road, And My highways shall be elevated.

Is 49:24–26 Shall the prey be taken from the mighty, Or the captives of the righteous be delivered? **25** But thus says the LORD: "Even the captives of the mighty shall be taken away, And the prey of the terrible be delivered; For I will contend with him who contends with you, And I will save your children. **26** I will feed those who oppress you with their own flesh, And they shall be drunk with their own blood as with sweet wine. All flesh shall know That I, the LORD, *am* your Savior, And your Redeemer, the Mighty One of Jacob."

God's care during.

Is 40:27–31 Why do you say, O Jacob, And speak, O Israel: "My way is hidden from the LORD, And my just claim is passed over by my God"? **28** Have you not known? Have you not heard? The everlasting God, the LORD, The Creator of the ends of the earth, Neither faints nor is weary. His understanding is unsearchable. **29** He gives power to the weak, And to *those who have* no might He increases strength.

30 Even the youths shall faint and be weary, And the young men shall utterly fall, **31** But those who wait on the LORD Shall renew *their* strength; They shall mount up with wings like eagles, They shall run and not be weary, They shall walk and not faint.

Assyrian,

Prediction concerning.

Ezek 7:8 Now upon you I will soon pour out My fury, And spend My anger upon you; I will judge you according to your ways, And I will repay you for all your abominations.

Ezek 7:17 Every hand will be feeble, And every knee will be *as* weak *as* water.

Reasons for. **2 Kin 17:5–23**

Prayer for restoration from.

Ps 80:1–3 Give ear, O Shepherd of Israel, You who lead Joseph like a flock; You who dwell *between* the cherubim, shine forth! **2** Before Ephraim, Benjamin, and Manasseh, Stir up Your strength, And come *and* save us! **3** Restore us, O God; Cause Your face to shine, And we shall be saved!

Ps 80:16–19 *It is* burned with fire, *it is* cut down; They perish at the rebuke of Your countenance. **17** Let Your hand be upon the man of Your right hand, Upon the son of man *whom* You made strong for Yourself. **18** Then we will not turn back from You; Revive us, and we will call upon Your name. **19** Restore us, O LORD God of hosts; Cause Your face to shine, And we shall be saved!

Living in tents during.

Hos 12:9 "But I *am* the LORD your God, Ever since the land of Egypt; I will again make you dwell in tents, As in the days of the appointed feast.

Prophecies of deliverance from. Deut 30:1–10

CARES, EXCESSIVE

About earthly things, forbidden.

Matt 6:25 "Therefore I say to you, do not worry about your life, what you will eat or what you will drink; nor about your body, what you will put on. Is not life more than food and the body more than clothing?

Luke 12:22 Then He said to His disciples, "Therefore I say to you, do not worry about your life, what you will eat; nor about the body, what you will put on.

Luke 12:29 "And do not seek what you should eat or what you should drink, nor have an anxious mind.

John 6:27 Do not labor for the food which perishes, but for the food which endures to everlasting life, which the Son of Man will give you, because God the Father has set His seal on Him."

Should be cast on God.

Ps 37:5 Commit your way to the LORD, Trust also in Him, And He shall bring *it* to pass.

Ps 55:22 Cast your burden on the LORD, And He shall sustain you; He shall never permit the righteous to be moved.

Prov 16:3 Commit your works to the LORD, And your thoughts will be established.

1 Pet 5:7 casting all your care upon Him, for He cares for you.

An obstruction to the gospel.

Matt 13:22 Now he who received seed among the thorns is he who hears the word, and the cares of this world and the deceitfulness of riches choke the word, and he becomes unfruitful.

Luke 8:14 Now the ones *that* fell among thorns are those who, when they have heard, go out and are choked with cares, riches, and pleasures of life, and bring no fruit to maturity.

Luke 14:18–20 But they all with one *accord* began to make excuses. The first said to him, 'I have bought a piece of ground, and I must go and see it. I ask you to have me excused.' **19** And another said, 'I have bought five yoke of oxen, and I am going to test them. I ask you to have me excused.' **20** Still another said, 'I have married a wife, and therefore I cannot come.'

Believers should be without.

Jer 17:7–8 "Blessed *is* the man who trusts in the LORD, And whose hope is the LORD. **8** For he shall be like a tree planted by the waters, Which spreads out its roots by the river, And will not fear when heat comes; But its leaf will be green, And will not be anxious in the year of drought, Nor will cease from yielding fruit.

Dan 3:16–17 Shadrach, Meshach, and Abed-Nego answered and said to the king, "O Nebuchadnezzar, we have no need to answer you in this matter. **17** If that *is the case*, our God whom we serve is able to deliver us from the burning fiery furnace, and He will deliver *us* from your hand, O king.

Matt 6:26 Look at the birds of the air, for they neither sow nor reap nor gather into barns; yet your heavenly Father feeds them. Are you not of more value than they?

Matt 6:28 "So why do you worry about clothing? Consider the lilies of the field, how they grow: they neither toil nor spin;

Matt 6:30 Now if God so clothes the grass of the field, which today is, and tomorrow is thrown into the oven, *will He* not much more *clothe* you, O you of little faith?

Luke 22:35 And He said to them, "When I sent you without money bag, knapsack, and sandals, did you lack anything?" So they said, "Nothing."

1 Cor 7:32 But I want you to be without care. He who is unmarried cares for the things of the Lord—how he may please the Lord.

Phil 4:6 Be anxious for nothing, but in everything by prayer and supplication, with thanksgiving, let your requests be made known to God;

Heb 13:5 *Let your* conduct *be* without covetousness; *be* content with such things as you have. For He Himself has said, *"I will never leave you nor forsake you."*

Unbecoming in Christians.

2 Tim 2:4 No one engaged in warfare entangles himself with the affairs of *this* life, that he may please him who enlisted him as a soldier.

Uselessness of.

Matt 6:27 Which of you by worrying can add one cubit to his stature?

Luke 12:25–26 And which of you by worrying can add

one cubit to his stature? **26** If you then are not able to do *the* least, why are you anxious for the rest?

Vanity of.

Ps 39:6 Surely every man walks about like a shadow; Surely they busy themselves in vain; He heaps up *riches,* And does not know who will gather them.

Eccl 4:8 There is one alone, without companion: He has neither son nor brother. Yet *there is* no end to all his labors, Nor is his eye satisfied with riches. *But he never asks,* "For whom do I toil and deprive myself of good?" This also *is* vanity and a grave misfortune.

Warning against.

Luke 21:34 "But take heed to yourselves, lest your hearts be weighed down with carousing, drunkenness, and cares of this life, and that Day come on you unexpectedly.

Sent as a punishment to the wicked.

Ezek 4:16 Moreover He said to me, "Son of man, surely I will cut off the supply of bread in Jerusalem; they shall eat bread by weight and with anxiety, and shall drink water by measure and with dread,

Ezek 12:19 And say to the people of the land, 'Thus says the Lord GOD to the inhabitants of Jerusalem *and* to the land of Israel: "They shall eat their bread with anxiety, and drink their water with dread, so that her land may be emptied of all who are in it, because of the violence of all those who dwell in it.

Illustrated by Martha.

Luke 10:41 And Jesus answered and said to her, "Martha, Martha, you are worried and troubled about many things.

CAVES

Natural.

Heb 11:38 of whom the world was not worthy. They wandered in deserts and mountains, *in* dens and caves of the earth.

Man-made.

Judg 6:2 and the hand of Midian prevailed against Israel. Because of the Midianites, the children of Israel made for themselves the dens, the caves, and the strongholds which *are* in the mountains.

Found in the

Open fields.

Gen 23:20 So the field and the cave that *is* in it were deeded to Abraham by the sons of Heth as property for a burial place.

Rocks.

Is 2:19 They shall go into the holes of the rocks, And into the caves of the earth, From the terror of the LORD And the glory of His majesty, When He arises to shake the earth mightily.

Were used as

Dwelling-places.

Gen 19:30 Then Lot went up out of Zoar and dwelt in the mountains, and his two daughters were with him; for he was afraid to dwell in Zoar. And he and his two daughters dwelt in a cave.

Places of concealment.

1 Sam 13:6 When the men of Israel saw that they were

in danger (for the people were distressed), then the people hid in caves, in thickets, in rocks, in holes, and in pits.

1 Sam 14:11 So both of them showed themselves to the garrison of the Philistines. And the Philistines said, "Look, the Hebrews are coming out of the holes where they have hidden."

1 Kin 18:4 For so it was, while Jezebel massacred the prophets of the LORD, that Obadiah had taken one hundred prophets and hidden them, fifty to a cave, and had fed them with bread and water.)

Heb 11:38 of whom the world was not worthy. They wandered in deserts and mountains, *in* dens and caves of the earth.

Resting places.

1 Sam 24:3 So he came to the sheepfolds by the road, where there *was* a cave; and Saul went in to attend to his needs. (David and his men were staying in the recesses of the cave.)

1 Kin 19:9 And there he went into a cave, and spent the night in that place; and behold, the word of the LORD *came* to him, and He said to him, "What are you doing here, Elijah?"

Burial places.

Gen 23:19 And after this, Abraham buried Sarah his wife in the cave of the field of Machpelah, before Mamre (that *is,* Hebron) in the land of Canaan.

John 11:38 Then Jesus, again groaning in Himself, came to the tomb. It was a cave, and a stone lay against it.

Hiding places of wild beasts.

Nah 2:12 The lion tore in pieces enough for his cubs, Killed for his lionesses, Filled his caves with prey, And his dens with flesh.

Often spacious.

1 Sam 22:1–2 David therefore departed from there and escaped to the cave of Adullam. So when his brothers and all his father's house heard *it,* they went down there to him. **2** And everyone *who was* in distress, everyone who *was* in debt, and everyone *who was* discontented gathered to him. So he became captain over them. And there were about four hundred men with him.

1 Sam 24:3 So he came to the sheepfolds by the road, where there *was* a cave; and Saul went in to attend to his needs. (David and his men were staying in the recesses of the cave.)

Afford no protection from the judgments of God.

Is 2:19 They shall go into the holes of the rocks, And into the caves of the earth, From the terror of the LORD And the glory of His majesty, When He arises to shake the earth mightily.

Ezek 33:27 "Say thus to them, 'Thus says the Lord GOD: "*As* I live, surely those who *are* in the ruins shall fall by the sword, and the one who *is* in the open field I will give to the beasts to be devoured, and those who *are* in the strongholds and caves shall die of the pestilence.

Rev 6:15 And the kings of the earth, the great men, the rich men, the commanders, the mighty men, every slave and every free man, hid themselves in the caves and in the rocks of the mountains,

Those mentioned in Scripture

Adullam.

1 Sam 22:1 David therefore departed from there and escaped to the cave of Adullam. So when his brothers and all his father's house heard *it*, they went down there to him.

En Gedi.

1 Sam 23:29 Then David went up from there and dwelt in strongholds at En Gedi.

1 Sam 24:1 Now it happened, when Saul had returned from following the Philistines, that it was told him, saying, "Take note! David *is* in the Wilderness of En Gedi."

1 Sam 24:3 So he came to the sheepfolds by the road, where there *was* a cave; and Saul went in to attend to his needs. (David and his men were staying in the recesses of the cave.)

Machpelah.

Gen 23:9 that he may give me the cave of Machpelah which he has, which *is* at the end of his field. Let him give it to me at the full price, as property for a burial place among you."

Makkedah.

Josh 10:16–27 But these five kings had fled and hidden themselves in a cave at Makkedah. **17** And it was told Joshua, saying, "The five kings have been found hidden in the cave at Makkedah." **18** So Joshua said, "Roll large stones against the mouth of the cave, and set men by it to guard them. **19** And do not stay *there* yourselves, *but* pursue your enemies, and attack their rear *guard*. Do not allow them to enter their cities, for the LORD your God has delivered them into your hand." **20** Then it happened, while Joshua and the children of Israel made an end of slaying them with a very great slaughter, till they had finished, that those who escaped entered fortified cities. **21** And all the people returned to the camp, to Joshua at Makkedah, in peace. No one moved his tongue against any of the children of Israel. **22** Then Joshua said, "Open the mouth of the cave, and bring out those five kings to me from the cave." **23** And they did so, and brought out those five kings to him from the cave: the king of Jerusalem, the king of Hebron, the king of Jarmuth, the king of Lachish, *and* the king of Eglon. **24** So it was, when they brought out those kings to Joshua, that Joshua called for all the men of Israel, and said to the captains of the men of war who went with him, "Come near, put your feet on the necks of these kings." And they drew near and put their feet on their necks. **25** Then Joshua said to them, "Do not be afraid, nor be dismayed; be strong and of good courage, for thus the LORD will do to all your enemies against whom you fight." **26** And afterward Joshua struck them and killed them, and hanged them on five trees; and they were hanging on the trees until evening. **27** So it was at the time of the going down of the sun *that* Joshua commanded, and they took them down from the trees, cast them into the cave where they had been hidden, and laid large stones against the cave's mouth, *which remain* until this very day.

CEDAR, THE

Planted by God.

Ps 104:16 The trees of the LORD are full *of sap*, The cedars of Lebanon which He planted,

Is 41:19 I will plant in the wilderness the cedar and the acacia tree, The myrtle and the oil tree; I will set in the desert the cypress tree *and* the pine And the box tree together,

Lebanon celebrated for.

Judg 9:15 And the bramble said to the trees, 'If in truth you anoint me as king over you, *Then* come *and* take shelter in my shade; But if not, let fire come out of the bramble And devour the cedars of Lebanon!'

Ps 92:12 The righteous shall flourish like a palm tree, He shall grow like a cedar in Lebanon.

Banks of rivers favorable to the growth of.

Num 24:6 Like valleys that stretch out, Like gardens by the riverside, Like aloes planted by the LORD, Like cedars beside the waters.

Imported largely by Solomon.

1 Kin 10:27 The king made silver *as common* in Jerusalem as stones, and he made cedar trees as abundant as the sycamores which *are* in the lowland.

Described as

High.

Is 37:24 By your servants you have reproached the Lord, And said, 'By the multitude of my chariots I have come up to the height of the mountains, To the limits of Lebanon; I will cut down its tall cedars *And* its choice cypress trees; I will enter its farthest height, To its fruitful forest.

Ezek 17:22 Thus says the Lord GOD: "I will take also *one* of the highest branches of the high cedar and set *it* out. I will crop off from the topmost of its young twigs a tender one, and will plant *it* on a high and prominent mountain.

Amos 2:9 "Yet *it was* I *who* destroyed the Amorite before them, Whose height *was* like the height of the cedars, And he *was as* strong as the oaks; Yet I destroyed his fruit above And his roots beneath.

Spreading.

Ps 80:10–11 The hills were covered with its shadow, And the mighty cedars with its boughs. **11** She sent out her boughs to the Sea, And her branches to the River.

Fragrant.

Song 4:11 Your lips, O *my* spouse, Drip as the honeycomb; Honey and milk *are* under your tongue; And the fragrance of your garments *Is* like the fragrance of Lebanon.

Graceful and beautiful.

Ps 80:10 The hills were covered with its shadow, And the mighty cedars with its boughs.

Ezek 17:23 On the mountain height of Israel I will plant it; and it will bring forth boughs, and bear fruit, and be a majestic cedar. Under it will dwell birds of every sort; in the shadow of its branches they will dwell.

Strong and durable.

Is 9:10 "The bricks have fallen down, But we will rebuild with hewn stones; The sycamores are cut down, But we will replace *them* with cedars."

Considered the first of trees.

1 Kin 4:33 Also he spoke of trees, from the cedar tree of Lebanon even to the hyssop that springs out of the wall; he spoke also of animals, of birds, of creeping things, and of fish.

Extensive commerce in.

1 Kin 5:10–11 Then Hiram gave Solomon cedar and cypress logs *according to* all his desire. 11 And Solomon gave Hiram twenty thousand kors of wheat *as* food for his household, and twenty kors of pressed oil. Thus Solomon gave to Hiram year by year.

Ezra 3:7 They also gave money to the masons and the carpenters, and food, drink, and oil to the people of Sidon and Tyre to bring cedar logs from Lebanon to the sea, to Joppa, according to the permission which they had from Cyrus king of Persia.

Used in

Building temples.

1 Kin 5:5–6 And behold, I propose to build a house for the name of the LORD my God, as the LORD spoke to my father David, saying, "Your son, whom I will set on your throne in your place, he shall build the house for My name." 6 Now therefore, command that they cut down cedars for me from Lebanon; and my servants will be with your servants, and I will pay you wages for your servants according to whatever you say. For you know *there is* none among us who has skill to cut timber like the Sidonians.

1 Kin 6:9–10 So he built the temple and finished it, and he paneled the temple with beams and boards of cedar. 10 And he built side chambers against the entire temple, each five cubits high; they were attached to the temple with cedar beams.

Building palaces.

2 Sam 5:11 Then Hiram king of Tyre sent messengers to David, and cedar trees, and carpenters and masons. And they built David a house.

1 Kin 7:2–3 He also built the House of the Forest of Lebanon; its length *was* one hundred cubits, its width fifty cubits, and its height thirty cubits, with four rows of cedar pillars, and cedar beams on the pillars. 3 And *it was* paneled with cedar above the beams that *were* on forty-five pillars, fifteen *to* a row.

Making masts of ships.

Ezek 27:5 They made all *your* planks of fir trees from Senir; They took a cedar from Lebanon to make you a mast.

Making chariots.

Song 3:9 Of the wood of Lebanon Solomon the King Made himself a palanquin:

Purifying the leper.

Lev 14:4–7 then the priest shall command to take for him who is to be cleansed two living *and* clean birds, cedar wood, scarlet, and hyssop. 5 And the priest shall command that one of the birds be killed in an earthen vessel over running water. 6 As for the living bird, he shall take it, the cedar wood and the scarlet and the hyssop, and dip them and the living bird in the blood of the bird *that was* killed over the running water. 7 And he shall sprinkle it seven times on him

who is to be cleansed from the leprosy, and shall pronounce him clean, and shall let the living bird loose in the open field.

Lev 14:49–52 And he shall take, to cleanse the house, two birds, cedar wood, scarlet, and hyssop. 50 Then he shall kill one of the birds in an earthen vessel over running water; 51 and he shall take the cedar wood, the hyssop, the scarlet, and the living bird, and dip them in the blood of the slain bird and in the running water, and sprinkle the house seven times. 52 And he shall cleanse the house with the blood of the bird and the running water and the living bird, with the cedar wood, the hyssop, and the scarlet.

Preparing the water of separation.

Num 19:6 And the priest shall take cedar wood and hyssop and scarlet, and cast *them* into the midst of the fire burning the heifer.

Making idols.

Is 44:14 He cuts down cedars for himself, And takes the cypress and the oak; He secures *it* for himself among the trees of the forest. He plants a pine, and the rain nourishes *it*.

And the eagle

Perched on the high branches of.

Ezek 17:3 and say, 'Thus says the Lord GOD: "A great eagle with large wings and long pinions, Full of feathers of various colors, Came to Lebanon And took from the cedar the highest branch.

Instrumental in propagating the tree.

Ezek 17:4–5 He cropped off its topmost young twig And carried it to a land of trade; He set it in a city of merchants. 5 Then he took some of the seed of the land And planted it in a fertile field; He placed *it* by abundant waters *And* set it like a willow tree.

Destruction of.

Ps 29:5 The voice of the LORD breaks the cedars, Yes, the LORD splinters the cedars of Lebanon.

Jer 22:7 I will prepare destroyers against you, Everyone with his weapons; They shall cut down your choice cedars And cast *them* into the fire.

Illustrative of

Majesty, strength, and glory of Christ.

Ezek 17:22–23 Thus says the Lord GOD: "I will take also *one* of the highest branches of the high cedar and set it out. I will crop off from the topmost of its young twigs a tender one, and will plant *it* on a high and prominent mountain. 23 On the mountain height of Israel I will plant it; and it will bring forth boughs, and bear fruit, and be a majestic cedar. Under it will dwell birds of every sort; in the shadow of its branches they will dwell.

Beauty and glory of Israel.

Num 24:6 Like valleys that stretch out, Like gardens by the riverside, Like aloes planted by the LORD, Like cedars beside the waters.

Saints in their rapid growth.

Ps 92:12 The righteous shall flourish like a palm tree, He shall grow like a cedar in Lebanon.

Powerful nations.

Ezek 31:3 Indeed Assyria *was* a cedar in Lebanon, With

fine branches that shaded the forest, And of high stature; And its top was among the thick boughs.

Amos 2:9 "Yet *it was* I *who* destroyed the Amorite before them, Whose height *was* like the height of the cedars, And he *was as* strong as the oaks; Yet I destroyed his fruit above And his roots beneath.

Arrogant rulers.

Is 2:13 Upon all the cedars of Lebanon *that are* high and lifted up, And upon all the oaks of Bashan;

Is 10:33–34 Behold, the Lord, The LORD of hosts, Will lop off the bough with terror; Those of high stature *will be* hewn down, And the haughty will be humbled. **34** He will cut down the thickets of the forest with iron, And Lebanon will fall by the Mighty One.

CELEBRATIONS

Often great.

Gen 21:8 So the child grew and was weaned. And Abraham made a great feast on the same day that Isaac was weaned.

Dan 5:1 Belshazzar the king made a great feast for a thousand of his lords, and drank wine in the presence of the thousand.

Luke 5:29 Then Levi gave Him a great feast in his own house. And there were a great number of tax collectors and others who sat down with them.

Given on occasions of

Marriages.

Matt 22:2 "The kingdom of heaven is like a certain king who arranged a marriage for his son,

Birthdays.

Mark 6:21 Then an opportune day came when Herod on his birthday gave a feast for his nobles, the high officers, and the chief *men* of Galilee.

Weaning children.

Gen 21:8 So the child grew and was weaned. And Abraham made a great feast on the same day that Isaac was weaned.

Departing from friends.

1 Kin 19:21 So *Elisha* turned back from him, and took a yoke of oxen and slaughtered them and boiled their flesh, using the oxen's equipment, and gave it to the people, and they ate. Then he arose and followed Elijah, and became his servant.

Return of friends.

2 Sam 12:4 And a traveler came to the rich man, who refused to take from his own flock and from his own herd to prepare one for the wayfaring man who had come to him; but he took the poor man's lamb and prepared it for the man who had come to him."

Luke 15:23 And bring the fatted calf here and kill *it*, and let us eat and be merry;

Ratifying covenants.

Gen 26:30 So he made them a feast, and they ate and drank.

Gen 31:54 Then Jacob offered a sacrifice on the mountain, and called his brethren to eat bread. And they ate bread and stayed all night on the mountain.

Sheep-shearing.

1 Sam 25:2 Now *there was* a man in Maon whose business *was* in Carmel, and the man *was* very rich. He had three thousand sheep and a thousand goats. And he was shearing his sheep in Carmel.

1 Sam 25:36 Now Abigail went to Nabal, and there he was, holding a feast in his house, like the feast of a king. And Nabal's heart *was* merry within him, for he *was* very drunk; therefore she told him nothing, little or much, until morning light.

2 Sam 13:23 And it came to pass, after two full years, that Absalom had sheepshearers in Baal Hazor, which *is* near Ephraim; so Absalom invited all the king's sons.

Harvest.

Ruth 3:2–7 Now Boaz, whose young women you were with, *is he* not our relative? In fact, he is winnowing barley tonight at the threshing floor. **3** Therefore wash yourself and anoint yourself, put on your *best* garment and go down to the threshing floor; *but do* not make yourself known to the man until he has finished eating and drinking. **4** Then it shall be, when he lies down, that you shall notice the place where he lies; and you shall go in, uncover his feet, and lie down; and he will tell you what you should do." **5** And she said to her, "All that you say to me I will do." **6** So she went down to the threshing floor and did according to all that her mother-in-law instructed her. **7** And after Boaz had eaten and drunk, and his heart was cheerful, he went to lie down at the end of the heap of grain; and she came softly, uncovered his feet, and lay down.

Is 9:3 You have multiplied the nation *And* increased its joy; They rejoice before You According to the joy of harvest, As *men* rejoice when they divide the spoil.

Grape harvest.

Judg 9:27 So they went out into the fields, and gathered *grapes* from their vineyards and trod *them*, and made merry. And they went into the house of their god, and ate and drank, and cursed Abimelech.

Coronation of kings.

1 Kin 1:9 And Adonijah sacrificed sheep and oxen and fattened cattle by the stone of Zoheleth, which *is* by En Rogel; he also invited all his brothers, the king's sons, and all the men of Judah, the king's servants.

1 Kin 1:18–19 So now, look! Adonijah has become king; and now, my lord the king, you do not know about *it*. **19** He has sacrificed oxen and fattened cattle and sheep in abundance, and has invited all the sons of the king, Abiathar the priest, and Joab the commander of the army; but Solomon your servant he has not invited.

1 Chr 12:39–40 And they were there with David three days, eating and drinking, for their brethren had prepared for them. **40** Moreover those who were near to them, from as far away as Issachar and Zebulun and Naphtali, were bringing food on donkeys and camels, on mules and oxen—provisions of flour and cakes of figs and cakes of raisins, wine and oil and oxen and sheep abundantly, for *there was* joy in Israel.

Hos 7:5 In the day of our king Princes have made *him* sick, inflamed with wine; He stretched out his hand with scoffers.

Offering voluntary sacrifice.

Gen 31:54 Then Jacob offered a sacrifice on the mountain, and called his brethren to eat bread. And they ate bread and stayed all night on the mountain.

Deut 12:6–7 There you shall take your burnt offerings, your sacrifices, your tithes, the heave offerings of your hand, your vowed offerings, your freewill offerings, and the firstborn of your herds and flocks. 7 And there you shall eat before the LORD your God, and you shall rejoice in all to which you have put your hand, you and your households, in which the LORD your God has blessed you.

1 Sam 1:4–5 And whenever the time came for Elkanah to make an offering, he would give portions to Peninnah his wife and to all her sons and daughters. 5 But to Hannah he would give a double portion, for he loved Hannah, although the LORD had closed her womb.

1 Sam 1:9 So Hannah arose after they had finished eating and drinking in Shiloh. Now Eli the priest was sitting on the seat by the doorpost of the tabernacle of the LORD.

Festivals.

1 Sam 20:5 And David said to Jonathan, "Indeed tomorrow *is* the New Moon, and I should not fail to sit with the king to eat. But let me go, that I may hide in the field until the third *day* at evening.

1 Sam 20:24–26 Then David hid in the field. And when the New Moon had come, the king sat down to eat the feast. 25 Now the king sat on his seat, as at other times, on a seat by the wall. And Jonathan arose, and Abner sat by Saul's side, but David's place was empty. 26 Nevertheless Saul did not say anything that day, for he thought, "Something has happened to him; he *is* unclean, surely he *is* unclean."

National deliverance.

Esth 8:17 And in every province and city, wherever the king's command and decree came, the Jews had joy and gladness, a feast and a holiday. Then many of the people of the land became Jews, because fear of the Jews fell upon them.

Esth 9:17–19 *This was* on the thirteenth day of the month of Adar. And on the fourteenth of *the month* they rested and made it a day of feasting and gladness. 18 But the Jews who *were* at Shushan assembled together on the thirteenth *day*, as well as on the fourteenth; and on the fifteenth of *the month* they rested, and made it a day of feasting and gladness. 19 Therefore the Jews of the villages who dwelt in the unwalled towns celebrated the fourteenth day of the month of Adar *with* gladness and feasting, as a holiday, and for sending presents to one another.

Preparations made for.

Gen 18:6–7 So Abraham hurried into the tent to Sarah and said, "Quickly, make ready three measures of fine meal; knead *it* and make cakes." 7 And Abraham ran to the herd, took a tender and good calf, gave *it* to a young man, and he hastened to prepare it.

Prov 9:2 She has slaughtered her meat, She has mixed her wine, She has also furnished her table.

Matt 22:4 Again, he sent out other servants, saying, 'Tell those who are invited, "See, I have prepared my dinner; my oxen and fatted cattle *are* killed, and all things *are* ready. Come to the wedding." '

Luke 15:23 And bring the fatted calf here and kill *it*, and let us eat and be merry;

Kinds of, mentioned in Scripture

Dinner or supper.

Gen 43:16 When Joseph saw Benjamin with them, he said to the steward of his house, "Take *these* men to my home, and slaughter an animal and make ready; for *these* men will dine with me at noon."

Matt 22:4 Again, he sent out other servants, saying, 'Tell those who are invited, "See, I have prepared my dinner; my oxen and fatted cattle *are* killed, and all things *are* ready. Come to the wedding." '

Luke 14:12 Then He also said to him who invited Him, "When you give a dinner or a supper, do not ask your friends, your brothers, your relatives, nor rich neighbors, lest they also invite you back, and you be repaid.

John 12:2 There they made Him a supper; and Martha served, but Lazarus was one of those who sat at the table with Him.

Banquet of wine.

Esth 5:6 At the banquet of wine the king said to Esther, "What *is* your petition? It shall be granted you. What *is* your request, up to half the kingdom? It shall be done!"

Under the direction of a master of the feast.

John 2:8–9 And He said to them, "Draw *some* out now, and take *it* to the master of the feast." And they took *it*. 9 When the master of the feast had tasted the water that was made wine, and did not know where it came from (but the servants who had drawn the water knew), the master of the feast called the bridegroom.

Hired servants and family members helped with.

Gen 18:7-8 And Abraham ran to the herd, took a tender and good calf, gave it to a young man, and he hastened to prepare it. 8 So he took butter and milk and the calf which he had prepared, and set *it* before them; and he stood by them under the tree as they ate.

Matt 22:13 Then the king said to the servants, 'Bind him hand and foot, take him away, and cast *him* into outer darkness; there will be weeping and gnashing of teeth.'

Luke 10:40 But Martha was distracted with much serving, and she approached Him and said, "Lord, do You not care that my sister has left me to serve alone? Therefore tell her to help me."

John 2:5 His mother said to the servants, "Whatever He says to you, do *it*."

John 12:2 There they made Him a supper; and Martha served, but Lazarus was one of those who sat at the table with Him.

Invitations to,

Often addressed to many.

Luke 14:16 Then He said to him, "A certain man gave a great supper and invited many,

Often only to relatives and friends.

1 Kin 1:9 And Adonijah sacrificed sheep and oxen and fattened cattle by the stone of Zoheleth, which *is* by

En Rogel; he also invited all his brothers, the king's sons, and all the men of Judah, the king's servants.

Luke 14:12 Then He also said to him who invited Him, "When you give a dinner or a supper, do not ask your friends, your brothers, your relatives, nor rich neighbors, lest they also invite you back, and you be repaid.

Often by the master in person.

2 Sam 13:24 Then Absalom came to the king and said, "Kindly note, your servant has sheepshearers; please, let the king and his servants go with your servant."

Esth 5:4 So Esther answered, "If it pleases the king, let the king and Haman come today to the banquet that I have prepared for him."

Zeph 1:7 Be silent in the presence of the Lord GOD; For the day of the LORD *is* at hand, For the LORD has prepared a sacrifice; He has invited His guests.

Luke 7:36 Then one of the Pharisees asked Him to eat with him. And He went to the Pharisee's house, and sat down to eat.

Repeated through servants when all things were ready.

Prov 9:1–5 Wisdom has built her house, She has hewn out her seven pillars; **2** She has slaughtered her meat, She has mixed her wine, She has also furnished her table. **3** She has sent out her maidens, She cries out from the highest places of the city, **4** "Whoever *is* simple, let him turn in here!" *As for* him who lacks understanding, she says to him, **5** "Come, eat of my bread And drink of the wine I have mixed.

Luke 14:17 and sent his servant at supper time to say to those who were invited, 'Come, for all things are now ready.'

Should be sent to the poor, etc.

Deut 14:29 And the Levite, because he has no portion nor inheritance with you, and the stranger and the fatherless and the widow who *are* within your gates, may come and eat and be satisfied, that the LORD your God may bless you in all the work of your hand which you do.

Luke 14:13 But when you give a feast, invite *the* poor, *the* maimed, *the* lame, *the* blind.

Often held in

The house.

Luke 5:29 Then Levi gave Him a great feast in his own house. And there were a great number of tax collectors and others who sat down with them.

Luke 7:36–37 Then one of the Pharisees asked Him to eat with him. And He went to the Pharisee's house, and sat down to eat. **37** And behold, a woman in the city who was a sinner, when she knew that *Jesus* sat at the table in the Pharisee's house, brought an alabaster flask of fragrant oil,

The outdoors, beside fountains.

1 Kin 1:9 And Adonijah sacrificed sheep and oxen and fattened cattle by the stone of Zoheleth, which *is* by En Rogel; he also invited all his brothers, the king's sons, and all the men of Judah, the king's servants.

The court of the house.

Esth 1:5–6 And when these days were completed, the king made a feast lasting seven days for all the people who were present in Shushan the citadel, from great to small, in the court of the garden of the king's palace. **6** *There were* white and blue linen *curtains* fastened with cords of fine linen and purple on silver rods and marble pillars; *and the* couches *were* of gold and silver on a *mosaic* pavement of alabaster, turquoise, and white and black marble.

The upper room or guest chamber.

Mark 14:14–15 Wherever he goes in, say to the master of the house, 'The Teacher says, "Where is the guest room in which I may eat the Passover with My disciples?" ' **15** Then he will show you a large upper room, furnished *and* prepared; there make ready for us."

Guests at,

Greeted by the master.

Luke 7:45 You gave Me no kiss, but this woman has not ceased to kiss My feet since the time I came in.

Usually anointed.

Ps 23:5 You prepare a table before me in the presence of my enemies; You anoint my head with oil; My cup runs over.

Luke 7:46 You did not anoint My head with oil, but this woman has anointed My feet with fragrant oil.

Had their feet washed when they came a distance.

Gen 18:4 Please let a little water be brought, and wash your feet, and rest yourselves under the tree.

Gen 43:24 So the man brought the men into Joseph's house and gave *them* water, and they washed their feet; and he gave their donkeys feed.

Luke 7:38 and stood at His feet behind *Him* weeping; and she began to wash His feet with her tears, and wiped *them* with the hair of her head; and she kissed His feet and anointed *them* with the fragrant oil.

Luke 7:44 Then He turned to the woman and said to Simon, "Do you see this woman? I entered your house; you gave Me no water for My feet, but she has washed My feet with her tears and wiped *them* with the hair of her head.

Arranged according to rank.

Gen 43:33 And they sat before him, the firstborn according to his birthright and the youngest according to his youth; and the men looked in astonishment at one another.

1 Sam 9:22 Now Samuel took Saul and his servant and brought them into the hall, and had them sit in the place of honor among those who were invited; there *were* about thirty persons.

Luke 14:10 But when you are invited, go and sit down in the lowest place, so that when he who invited you comes he may say to you, 'Friend, go up higher.' Then you will have glory in the presence of those who sit at the table with you.

Often had separate dishes.

Gen 43:34 Then he took servings to them from before him, but Benjamin's serving was five times as much as any of theirs. So they drank and were merry with him.

1 Sam 1:4 And whenever the time came for Elkanah to make an offering, he would give portions to Peninnah his wife and to all her sons and daughters.

Often ate from the same dish.

Matt 26:23 He answered and said, "He who dipped *his* hand with Me in the dish will betray Me.

Insistence on having best seats at, condemned.

Matt 23:6 They love the best places at feasts, the best seats in the synagogues,

Luke 14:7–8 So He told a parable to those who were invited, when He noted how they chose the best places, saying to them: 8 "When you are invited by anyone to a wedding feast, do not sit down in the best place, lest one more honorable than you be invited by him;

A choice portion reserved in, for principal guests.

Gen 43:34 Then he took servings to them from before him, but Benjamin's serving was five times as much as any of theirs. So they drank and were merry with him.

1 Sam 1:5 But to Hannah he would give a double portion, for he loved Hannah, although the Lord had closed her womb.

1 Sam 9:23–24 And Samuel said to the cook, "Bring the portion which I gave you, of which I said to you, 'Set it apart.' " 24 So the cook took up the thigh with its upper part and set *it* before Saul. And *Samuel* said, "Here it is, what was kept back. *It* was set apart for you. Eat; for until this time it has been kept for you, since I said I invited the people." So Saul ate with Samuel that day.

Custom of presenting the bread at, to one of the guests, alluded to.

John 13:26 Jesus answered, "It is he to whom I shall give a piece of bread when I have dipped *it*." And having dipped the bread, He gave *it* to Judas Iscariot, *the son* of Simon.

Portions of, often sent to the absent.

2 Sam 11:8 And David said to Uriah, "Go down to your house and wash your feet." So Uriah departed from the king's house, and a gift *of food* from the king followed him.

Neh 8:10 Then he said to them, "Go your way, eat the fat, drink the sweet, and send portions to those for whom nothing is prepared; for *this* day *is* holy to our Lord. Do not sorrow, for the joy of the Lord is your strength."

Esth 9:19 Therefore the Jews of the villages who dwelt in the unwalled towns celebrated the fourteenth day of the month of Adar *with* gladness and feasting, as a holiday, and for sending presents to one another.

Offense given by refusing to go to.

Luke 14:18 But they all with one *accord* began to make excuses. The first said to him, 'I have bought a piece of ground, and I must go and see it. I ask you to have me excused.'

Luke 14:24 For I say to you that none of those men who were invited shall taste my supper.' "

Anxiety to have many guests at, alluded to.

Luke 14:22–23 And the servant said, 'Master, it is done as you commanded, and still there is room.' 23 Then the master said to the servant, 'Go out into the highways and hedges, and compel *them* to come in, that my house may be filled.

Men and women did not usually meet at.

Esth 1:8–9 In accordance with the law, the drinking was not compulsory; for so the king had ordered all the officers of his household, that they should do according to each man's pleasure. 9 Queen Vashti also made a feast for the women *in* the royal palace which *belonged* to King Ahasuerus.

Mark 6:21 Then an opportune day came when Herod on his birthday gave a feast for his nobles, the high officers, and the chief *men* of Galilee.

None admitted to, after the master had risen and shut the door.

Luke 13:24–25 "Strive to enter through the narrow gate, for many, I say to you, will seek to enter and will not be able. 25 When once the Master of the house has risen up and shut the door, and you begin to stand outside and knock at the door, saying, 'Lord, Lord, open for us,' and He will answer and say to you, 'I do not know you, where you are from,'

Began with thanksgiving.

1 Sam 9:13 As soon as you come into the city, you will surely find him before he goes up to the high place to eat. For the people will not eat until he comes, because he must bless the sacrifice; afterward those who are invited will eat. Now therefore, go up, for about this time you will find him."

Mark 8:6 So He commanded the multitude to sit down on the ground. And He took the seven loaves and gave thanks, broke *them* and gave *them* to His disciples to set before *them;* and they set *them* before the multitude.

Concluded with a hymn.

Mark 14:26 And when they had sung a hymn, they went out to the Mount of Olives.

None asked to eat or drink more than he liked at.

Esth 1:8 In accordance with the law, the drinking was not compulsory; for so the king had ordered all the officers of his household, that they should do according to each man's pleasure.

Music and dancing often introduced at.

Amos 6:5 Who sing idly to the sound of stringed instruments, *And* invent for yourselves musical instruments like David;

Mark 6:22 And when Herodias' daughter herself came in and danced, and pleased Herod and those who sat with him, the king said to the girl, "Ask me whatever you want, and I will give *it* to you."

Luke 15:25 "Now his older son was in the field. And as he came and drew near to the house, he heard music and dancing.

Often had scenes of great intemperance.

1 Sam 25:36 Now Abigail went to Nabal, and there he was, holding a feast in his house, like the feast of a king. And Nabal's heart *was* merry within him, for he *was* very drunk; therefore she told him nothing, little or much, until morning light.

Dan 5:3–4 Then they brought the gold vessels that had been taken from the temple of the house of God which *had been* in Jerusalem; and the king and his lords, his wives, and his concubines drank from them. 4 They drank wine, and praised the gods of gold and silver, bronze and iron, wood and stone.

Hos 7:5 In the day of our king Princes have made *him* sick, inflamed with wine; He stretched out his hand with scoffers.

Given by the guests in return.

Job 1:4 And his sons would go and feast *in their* houses, each on his *appointed* day, and would send and invite their three sisters to eat and drink with them.

Luke 14:12 Then He also said to him who invited Him, "When you give a dinner or a supper, do not ask your friends, your brothers, your relatives, nor rich neighbors, lest they also invite you back, and you be repaid.

CELIBACY

Must be optional.

Matt 19:10–12 His disciples said to Him, "If such is the case of the man with *his* wife, it is better not to marry." **11** But He said to them, "All cannot accept this saying, but only *those* to whom it has been given: **12** For there are eunuchs who were born thus from *their* mother's womb, and there are eunuchs who were made eunuchs by men, and there are eunuchs who have made themselves eunuchs for the kingdom of heaven's sake. He who is able to accept *it*, let him accept *it*."

1 Tim 4:3 forbidding to marry, *and commanding* to abstain from foods which God created to be received with thanksgiving by those who believe and know the truth.

Cf. Gen 2:18

Reasons for.

1 Cor 7:7–9 For I wish that all men were even as I myself. But each one has his own gift from God, one in this manner and another in that. **8** But I say to the unmarried and to the widows: It is good for them if they remain even as I am; **9** but if they cannot exercise self-control, let them marry. For it is better to marry than to burn *with passion.*

CENSERS

For burning incense.

Lev 10:1 Then Nadab and Abihu, the sons of Aaron, each took his censer and put fire in it, put incense on it, and offered profane fire before the LORD, which He had not commanded them.

2 Chr 26:19 Then Uzziah became furious; and he *had* a censer in his hand to burn incense. And while he was angry with the priests, leprosy broke out on his forehead, before the priests in the house of the LORD, beside the incense altar.

Made of

Bronze.

Num 16:39 So Eleazar the priest took the bronze censers, which those who were burned up had presented, and they were hammered out as a covering on the altar,

Gold.

1 Kin 7:50 the basins, the trimmers, the bowls, the ladles, and the censers of pure gold; and the hinges of gold, *both* for the doors of the inner room (the Most Holy *Place*) *and* for the doors of the main hall of the temple.

One of gold in the most holy place.

Heb 9:4 which had the golden censer and the ark of the covenant overlaid on all sides with gold, in which *were* the golden pot that had the manna, Aaron's rod that budded, and the tablets of the covenant;

Often used in idolatrous worship.

Ezek 8:11 And there stood before them seventy men of the elders of the house of Israel, and in their midst stood Jaazaniah the son of Shaphan. Each man had a censer in his hand, and a thick cloud of incense went up.

Made into plates to cover the altar.

Num 16:39 So Eleazar the priest took the bronze censers, which those who were burned up had presented, and they were hammered out as a covering on the altar,

Typical of Christ's intercession.

Rev 8:3 Then another angel, having a golden censer, came and stood at the altar. He was given much incense, that he should offer *it* with the prayers of all the saints upon the golden altar which was before the throne.

Rev 8:5 Then the angel took the censer, filled it with fire from the altar, and threw *it* to the earth. And there were noises, thunderings, lightnings, and an earthquake.

CENSUS

Taken of the sons of Israel.

Ex 30:12 "When you take the census of the children of Israel for their number, then every man shall give a ransom for himself to the LORD, when you number them, that there may be no plague among them when *you* number them.

Ex 38:25–28 And the silver from those who were numbered of the congregation *was* one hundred talents and one thousand seven hundred and seventy-five shekels, according to the shekel of the sanctuary: **26** a bekah for each man (*that is,* half a shekel, according to the shekel of the sanctuary), for everyone included in the numbering from twenty years old and above, for six hundred thousand and three thousand, five hundred and fifty *men.* **27** And from the hundred talents of silver were cast the sockets of the sanctuary and the bases of the veil: one hundred sockets from the hundred talents, one talent for each socket. **28** Then from the one thousand seven hundred and seventy-five *shekels* he made hooks for the pillars, overlaid their capitals, and made bands for them.

To make roster of fighting men in Israel.

Num 1:2–3 "Take a census of all the congregation of the children of Israel, by their families, by their fathers' houses, according to the number of names, every male individually, **3** from twenty years old and above—all who *are able to* go to war in Israel. You and Aaron shall number them by their armies.

Num 26:1–2 And it came to pass, after the plague, that the LORD spoke to Moses and Eleazar the son of Aaron the priest, saying: **2** "Take a census of all the congregation of the children of Israel from twenty years old and above, by their fathers' houses, all who are able to go to war in Israel."

Of Levite males.

Num 3:15 "Number the children of Levi by their fathers' houses, by their families; you shall number every male from a month old and above."

Num 4:3 from thirty years old and above, even to fifty years old, all who enter the service to do the work in the tabernacle of meeting.

David's sinful.

2 Sam 24:1 Again the anger of the LORD was aroused against Israel, and He moved David against them to say, "Go, number Israel and Judah."

1 Chr 21:1 Now Satan stood up against Israel, and moved David to number Israel.

1 Chr 27:3–4 *he was* of the children of Perez, and the chief of all the captains of the army for the first month. 4 Over the division of the second month *was* Dodai an Ahohite, and of his division Mikloth also *was* the leader; in his division *were* twenty-four thousand.

Universal, at birth of Christ.

Luke 2:1–3 And it came to pass in those days *that* a decree went out from Caesar Augustus that all the world should be registered. 2 This census first took place while Quirinius was governing Syria. 3 So all went to be registered, everyone to his own city.

Acts 5:37 After this man, Judas of Galilee rose up in the days of the census, and drew away many people after him. He also perished, and all who obeyed him were dispersed.

CHARIOTS

Carriages for traveling, etc.

Gen 46:29 So Joseph made ready his chariot and went up to Goshen to meet his father Israel; and he presented himself to him, and fell on his neck and wept on his neck a good while.

Carriages used in war.

1 Kin 20:25 and you shall muster an army like the army that you have lost, horse for horse and chariot for chariot. Then we will fight against them in the plain; surely we will be stronger than they." And he listened to their voice and did so.

Wheels of, described.

1 Kin 7:33 The workmanship of the wheels *was* like the workmanship of a chariot wheel; their axle pins, their rims, their spokes, and their hubs *were* all of cast *bronze.*

Bound with harnesses.

Mic 1:13 O inhabitant of Lachish, Harness the chariot to the swift steeds (She *was* the beginning of sin to the daughter of Zion), For the transgressions of Israel were found in you.

Drawn by

Horses.

2 Kin 10:2 Now as soon as this letter comes to you, since your master's sons *are* with you, and you have chariots and horses, a fortified city also, and weapons,

Song 1:9 I have compared you, my love, To my filly among Pharaoh's chariots.

Donkeys and camels.

Is 21:7 And he saw a chariot *with* a pair of horsemen, A chariot of donkeys, *and* a chariot of camels, And he listened earnestly with great care.

Value of, in Solomon's time.

1 Kin 10:29 Now a chariot that was imported from Egypt cost six hundred *shekels* of silver, and a horse one hundred and fifty; and thus, through their agents, they exported *them* to all the kings of the Hittites and the kings of Syria.

Drivers generally employed for.

1 Kin 22:34 Now a *certain* man drew a bow at random, and struck the king of Israel between the joints of his armor. So he said to the driver of his chariot, "Turn around and take me out of the battle, for I am wounded."

2 Chr 18:33 Now a certain man drew a bow at random, and struck the king of Israel between the joints of his armor. So he said to the driver of his chariot, "Turn around and take me out of the battle, for I am wounded."

Sometimes driven by the owners.

2 Kin 9:16 So Jehu rode in a chariot and went to Jezreel, for Joram was laid up there; and Ahaziah king of Judah had come down to see Joram.

Sometimes driven furiously.

2 Kin 9:20 So the watchman reported, saying, "He went up to them and is not coming back; and the driving *is* like the driving of Jehu the son of Nimshi, for he drives furiously!"

Is 5:28 Whose arrows *are* sharp, And all their bows bent; Their horses' hooves will seem like flint, And their wheels like a whirlwind.

Jer 4:13 "Behold, he shall come up like clouds, And his chariots like a whirlwind. His horses are swifter than eagles. Woe to us, for we are plundered!"

Bounding motion of, referred to.

Nah 3:2 The noise of a whip And the noise of rattling wheels, Of galloping horses, Of clattering chariots!

Noise of, referred to.

2 Kin 7:6 For the LORD had caused the army of the Syrians to hear the noise of chariots and the noise of horses—the noise of a great army; so they said to one another, "Look, the king of Israel has hired against us the kings of the Hittites and the kings of the Egyptians to attack us!"

Joel 2:5 With a noise like chariots Over mountaintops they leap, Like the noise of a flaming fire that devours the stubble, Like a strong people set in battle array.

Nah 3:2 The noise of a whip And the noise of rattling wheels, Of galloping horses, Of clattering chariots!

Rev 9:9 And they had breastplates like breastplates of iron, and the sound of their wings *was* like the sound of chariots with many horses running into battle.

Introduced into Israel by David.

2 Sam 8:4 David took from him one thousand *chariots,* seven hundred horsemen, and twenty thousand foot soldiers. Also David hamstrung all the chariot horses, except that he spared *enough* of them for one hundred chariots.

Multiplied by Solomon.

1 Kin 10:26 And Solomon gathered chariots and horsemen; he had one thousand four hundred chariots and twelve thousand horsemen, whom he stationed in the chariot cities and with the king at Jerusalem.

Imported from Egypt.

1 Kin 10:28–29 Also Solomon had horses imported from Egypt and Keveh; the king's merchants bought them in Keveh at the *current* price. **29** Now a chariot that was imported from Egypt cost six hundred *shekels* of silver, and a horse one hundred and fifty; and thus, through their agents, they exported *them* to all the kings of the Hittites and the kings of Syria.

Strategic aspects

Armed with iron.

Josh 17:16 But the children of Joseph said, "The mountain country is not enough for us; and all the Canaanites who dwell in the land of the valley have chariots of iron, *both those* who *are* of Beth Shean and its towns and *those* who *are* of the Valley of Jezreel."

Judg 1:19 So the LORD was with Judah. And they drove out the mountaineers, but they could not drive out the inhabitants of the lowland, because they had chariots of iron.

Lighted by night with torches.

Nah 2:3 The shields of his mighty men *are* made red, The valiant men *are* in scarlet. The chariots *come* with flaming torches In the day of his preparation, And the spears are brandished.

Commanded by captains.

Ex 14:7 Also, he took six hundred choice chariots, and all the chariots of Egypt with captains over every one of them.

1 Kin 16:9 Now his servant Zimri, commander of half *his* chariots, conspired against him as he was in Tirzah drinking himself drunk in the house of Arza, steward of *his* house in Tirzah.

Advantageously maneuvered in a flat country.

Judg 1:19 So the LORD was with Judah. And they drove out the mountaineers, but they could not drive out the inhabitants of the lowland, because they had chariots of iron.

1 Kin 20:23–25 Then the servants of the king of Syria said to him, "Their gods *are* gods of the hills. Therefore they were stronger than we; but if we fight against them in the plain, surely we will be stronger than they. **24** So do this thing: Dismiss the kings, each from his position, and put captains in their places; **25** and you shall muster an army like the army that you have lost, horse for horse and chariot for chariot. Then we will fight against them in the plain; surely we will be stronger than they." And he listened to their voice and did so.

Formed part of the line of battle.

1 Kin 20:25 and you shall muster an army like the army that you have lost, horse for horse and chariot for chariot. Then we will fight against them in the plain; surely we will be stronger than they." And he listened to their voice and did so.

Used in pursuing enemies.

Ex 14:9 So the Egyptians pursued them, all the horses *and* chariots of Pharaoh, his horsemen and his army, and overtook them camping by the sea beside Pi Hahiroth, before Baal Zephon.

2 Sam 1:6 Then the young man who told him said, "As I happened by chance *to be* on Mount Gilboa, there was Saul, leaning on his spear; and indeed the chariots and horsemen followed hard after him.

Kept in chariot cities.

1 Kin 9:19 all the storage cities that Solomon had, cities for his chariots and cities for his cavalry, and whatever Solomon desired to build in Jerusalem, in Lebanon, and in all the land of his dominion.

1 Kin 10:26 And Solomon gathered chariots and horsemen; he had one thousand four hundred chariots and twelve thousand horsemen, whom he stationed in the chariot cities and with the king at Jerusalem.

Kings rode in, to battle.

1 Kin 22:35 The battle increased that day; and the king was propped up in his chariot, facing the Syrians, and died at evening. The blood ran out from the wound onto the floor of the chariot.

Used in war by the

Egyptians.

Ex 14:7 Also, he took six hundred choice chariots, and all the chariots of Egypt with captains over every one of them.

2 Kin 18:24 How then will you repel one captain of the least of my master's servants, and put your trust in Egypt for chariots and horsemen?

Canaanites.

Josh 17:16 But the children of Joseph said, "The mountain country is not enough for us; and all the Canaanites who dwell in the land of the valley have chariots of iron, *both those* who *are* of Beth Shean and its towns and *those* who *are* of the Valley of Jezreel."

Judg 4:3 And the children of Israel cried out to the LORD; for Jabin had nine hundred chariots of iron, and for twenty years he had harshly oppressed the children of Israel.

Philistines.

1 Sam 13:5 Then the Philistines gathered together to fight with Israel, thirty thousand chariots and six thousand horsemen, and people as the sand which *is* on the seashore in multitude. And they came up and encamped in Michmash, to the east of Beth Aven.

Syrians.

2 Sam 10:18 Then the Syrians fled before Israel; and David killed seven hundred charioteers and forty thousand horsemen of the Syrians, and struck Shobach the commander of their army, who died there.

1 Kin 20:1 Now Ben-Hadad the king of Syria gathered all his forces together; thirty-two kings *were* with him, with horses and chariots. And he went up and besieged Samaria, and made war against it.

Assyrians.

2 Kin 19:23 By your messengers you have reproached the Lord, And said: "By the multitude of my chariots I have come up to the height of the mountains, To the limits of Lebanon; I will cut down its tall cedars *And* its choice cypress trees; I will enter the extremity of its borders, *To* its fruitful forest.

Ethiopians.

2 Chr 14:9 Then Zerah the Ethiopian came out against them with an army of a million men and three hundred chariots, and he came to Mareshah.

2 Chr 16:8 Were the Ethiopians and the Lubim not a huge army with very many chariots and horsemen? Yet, because you relied on the Lord, He delivered them into your hand.

Babylonians.

Ezek 23:24 And they shall come against you With chariots, wagons, and war-horses, With a horde of people. They shall array against you Buckler, shield, and helmet all around. 'I will delegate judgment to them, And they shall judge you according to their judgments.

Ezek 26:7 "For thus says the Lord God: 'Behold, I will bring against Tyre from the north Nebuchadnezzar king of Babylon, king of kings, with horses, with chariots, and with horsemen, and an army with many people.

Jews.

2 Kin 8:21 So Joram went to Zair, and all his chariots with him. Then he rose by night and attacked the Edomites who had surrounded him and the captains of the chariots; and the troops fled to their tents.

2 Kin 10:2 Now as soon as this letter comes to you, since your master's sons *are* with you, and you have chariots and horses, a fortified city also, and weapons,

Used by

Kings, regularly.

1 Kin 12:18 Then King Rehoboam sent Adoram, who *was* in charge of the revenue; but all Israel stoned him with stones, and he died. Therefore King Rehoboam mounted his chariot in haste to flee to Jerusalem.

1 Kin 18:44 Then it came to pass the seventh *time*, that he said, "There is a cloud, as small as a man's hand, rising out of the sea!" So he said, "Go up, say to Ahab, 'Prepare *your chariot*, and go down before the rain stops you.'"

Persons of distinction.

Gen 41:43 And he had him ride in the second chariot which he had; and they cried out before him, "Bow the knee!" So he set him over all the land of Egypt.

2 Kin 5:9 Then Naaman went with his horses and chariot, and he stood at the door of Elisha's house.

2 Kin 5:21 So Gehazi pursued Naaman. When Naaman saw *him* running after him, he got down from the chariot to meet him, and said, "*Is* all well?"

Jer 17:25 then shall enter the gates of this city kings and princes sitting on the throne of David, riding in chariots and on horses, they and their princes, accompanied by the men of Judah and the inhabitants of Jerusalem; and this city shall remain forever.

Acts 8:27–28 So he arose and went. And behold, a man of Ethiopia, a eunuch of great authority under Candace the queen of the Ethiopians, who had charge of all her treasury, and had come to Jerusalem to worship, **28** was returning. And sitting in his chariot, he was reading Isaiah the prophet.

Often attended by running footmen.

1 Sam 8:11 And he said, "This will be the behavior of the king who will reign over you: He will take your sons and appoint *them* for his own chariots and *to be* his horsemen, and *some* will run before his chariots.

2 Sam 15:1 After this it happened that Absalom provided himself with chariots and horses, and fifty men to run before him.

1 Kin 1:5 Then Adonijah the son of Haggith exalted himself, saying, "I will be king"; and he prepared for himself chariots and horsemen, and fifty men to run before him.

Consecrated to the sun.

2 Kin 23:11 Then he removed the horses that the kings of Judah had dedicated to the sun, at the entrance to the house of the Lord, by the chamber of Nathan-Melech, the officer who *was* in the court; and he burned the chariots of the sun with fire.

The Jews condemned for

Multiplying.

Is 2:7 Their land is also full of silver and gold, And there is no end to their treasures; Their land is also full of horses, And there is no end to their chariots.

Trusting in.

Is 22:18 He will surely turn violently and toss you like a ball Into a large country; There you shall die, and there your glorious chariots *Shall be* the shame of your master's house.

Is 31:1 Woe to those who go down to Egypt for help, *And* rely on horses, Who trust in chariots because *they are* many, And in horsemen because they are very strong, But who do not look to the Holy One of Israel, Nor seek the Lord!

Taken in war, often destroyed.

Josh 11:6 But the Lord said to Joshua, "Do not be afraid because of them, for tomorrow about this time I will deliver all of them slain before Israel. You shall hamstring their horses and burn their chariots with fire."

Josh 11:9 So Joshua did to them as the Lord had told him: he hamstrung their horses and burned their chariots with fire.

Jer 51:21 With you I will break in pieces the horse and its rider; With you I will break in pieces the chariot and its rider;

Mic 5:10 "And it shall be in that day," says the Lord, "That I will cut off your horses from your midst And destroy your chariots.

Nah 2:13 "Behold, I *am* against you," says the Lord of hosts, "I will burn your chariots in smoke, and the sword shall devour your young lions; I will cut off your prey from the earth, and the voice of your messengers shall be heard no more."

Illustrative of

The clouds.

Ps 104:3 He lays the beams of His upper chambers in the waters, Who makes the clouds His chariot, Who walks on the wings of the wind,

The judgments of God.

Is 66:15 For behold, the Lord will come with fire And with His chariots, like a whirlwind, To render His anger with fury, And His rebuke with flames of fire.

Angels.

2 Kin 6:16–17 So he answered, "Do not fear, for those who *are* with us *are* more than those who *are* with them." **17** And Elisha prayed, and said, "Lord, I pray, open his eyes that he may see." Then the Lord opened the eyes of the young man, and he saw. And behold, the mountain *was* full of horses and chariots of fire all around Elisha.

Ps 68:17 The chariots of God *are* twenty thousand, *Even* thousands of thousands; The Lord is among them *as in* Sinai, in the Holy *Place.*

Prophets.

2 Kin 2:12 And Elisha saw *it*, and he cried out, "My father, my father, the chariot of Israel and its horsemen!" So he saw him no more. And he took hold of his own clothes and tore them into two pieces.

2 Kin 13:14 Elisha had become sick with the illness of which he would die. Then Joash the king of Israel came down to him, and wept over his face, and said, "O my father, my father, the chariots of Israel and their horsemen!"

Elijah taken to heaven in one of fire.

2 Kin 2:11 Then it happened, as they continued on and talked, that suddenly a chariot of fire *appeared* with horses of fire, and separated the two of them; and Elijah went up by a whirlwind into heaven.

CHARITY *SEE* LOVE TO MAN

CHASTITY

Commanded.

Ex 20:14 "You shall not commit adultery.

Prov 31:3 Do not give your strength to women, Nor your ways to that which destroys kings.

Acts 15:20 but that we write to them to abstain from things polluted by idols, *from* sexual immorality, *from* things strangled, and *from* blood.

Rom 13:13 Let us walk properly, as in the day, not in revelry and drunkenness, not in lewdness and lust, not in strife and envy.

Col 3:5 Therefore put to death your members which are on the earth: fornication, uncleanness, passion, evil desire, and covetousness, which is idolatry.

1 Thess 4:3 For this is the will of God, your sanctification: that you should abstain from sexual immorality;

Required in vision.

Job 31:1 "I have made a covenant with my eyes; Why then should I look upon a young woman?

Matt 5:28 But I say to you that whoever looks at a woman to lust for her has already committed adultery with her in his heart.

Required in heart.

Prov 6:25 Do not lust after her beauty in your heart, Nor let her allure you with her eyelids.

Required in speech.

Eph 5:3 But fornication and all uncleanness or covetousness, let it not even be named among you, as is fitting for saints;

Keep the body in.

1 Cor 6:13 Foods for the stomach and the stomach for foods, but God will destroy both it and them. Now the body *is* not for sexual immorality but for the Lord, and the Lord for the body.

1 Cor 6:15–18 Do you not know that your bodies are members of Christ? Shall I then take the members of

Christ and make *them* members of a harlot? Certainly not! 16 Or do you not know that he who is joined to a harlot is one body *with her?* For *"the two,"* He says, *"shall become one flesh."* 17 But he who is joined to the Lord is one spirit *with Him.* 18 Flee sexual immorality. Every sin that a man does is outside the body, but he who commits sexual immorality sins against his own body.

Preserved by wisdom.

Prov 2:10–11 When wisdom enters your heart, And knowledge is pleasant to your soul, 11 Discretion will preserve you; Understanding will keep you,

Prov 2:16 To deliver you from the immoral woman, From the seductress *who* flatters with her words,

Prov 7:1–5 My son, keep my words, And treasure my commands within you. 2 Keep my commands and live, And my law as the apple of your eye. 3 Bind them on your fingers; Write them on the tablet of your heart. 4 Say to wisdom, "You *are* my sister," And call understanding *your* nearest kin, 5 That they may keep you from the immoral woman, From the seductress *who* flatters with her words.

Saints are kept in.

Eccl 7:26 And I find more bitter than death The woman whose heart *is* snares and nets, Whose hands *are* fetters. He who pleases God shall escape from her, But the sinner shall be trapped by her.

Advantages of.

1 Pet 3:1–2 Wives, likewise, *be* submissive to your own husbands, that even if some do not obey the word, they, without a word, may be won by the conduct of their wives, 2 when they observe your chaste conduct *accompanied* by fear.

Shun those devoid of.

1 Cor 5:11 But now I have written to you not to keep company with anyone named a brother, who is sexually immoral or covetous, or an idolater, or a reviler, or a drunkard, or an extortioner—not even to eat with such a person.

1 Pet 4:3 For we *have spent* enough of our past lifetime in doing the will of the Gentiles—when we walked in lewdness, lusts, drunkenness, revelries, drinking parties, and abominable idolatries.

The wicked are devoid of.

Rom 1:29 being filled with all unrighteousness, sexual immorality, wickedness, covetousness, maliciousness; full of envy, murder, strife, deceit, evil-mindedness; *they are* whisperers,

Eph 4:19 who, being past feeling, have given themselves over to lewdness, to work all uncleanness with greediness.

2 Pet 2:14 having eyes full of adultery and that cannot cease from sin, enticing unstable souls. *They have* a heart trained in covetous practices, *and are* accursed children.

Jude 1:8 Likewise also these dreamers defile the flesh, reject authority, and speak evil of dignitaries.

Dangerous to deviate from.

2 Sam 11:2–4 Then it happened one evening that David arose from his bed and walked on the roof of the king's house. And from the roof he saw a woman bathing, and the woman *was* very beautiful to behold. **3** So David sent and inquired about the woman. And *someone* said, "*Is* this not Bathsheba, the daughter of Eliam, the wife of Uriah the Hittite?" **4** Then David sent messengers, and took her; and she came to him, and he lay with her, for she was cleansed from her impurity; and she returned to her house.

Consequences of associating with those devoid of.

Prov 7:25–27 Do not let your heart turn aside to her ways, Do not stray into her paths; **26** For she has cast down many wounded, And all who were slain by her were strong *men*. **27** Her house *is* the way to hell, Descending to the chambers of death.

Prov 22:14 The mouth of an immoral woman *is* a deep pit; He who is abhorred by the LORD will fall there.

Lack of, excludes from heaven.

Gal 5:19–21 Now the works of the flesh are evident, which are: adultery, fornication, uncleanness, lewdness, **20** idolatry, sorcery, hatred, contentions, jealousies, outbursts of wrath, selfish ambitions, dissensions, heresies, **21** envy, murders, drunkenness, revelries, and the like; of which I tell you beforehand, just as I also told *you* in time past, that those who practice such things will not inherit the kingdom of God.

Drunkenness destructive to.

Prov 23:31–33 Do not look on the wine when it is red, When it sparkles in the cup, *When* it swirls around smoothly; **32** At the last it bites like a serpent, And stings like a viper. **33** Your eyes will see strange things, And your heart will utter perverse things.

Breach of, punished.

1 Cor 3:16–17 Do you not know that you are the temple of God and *that* the Spirit of God dwells in you? **17** If anyone defiles the temple of God, God will destroy him. For the temple of God is holy, which *temple* you are.

Eph 5:5–6 For this you know, that no fornicator, unclean person, nor covetous man, who is an idolater, has any inheritance in the kingdom of Christ and God. **6** Let no one deceive you with empty words, for because of these things the wrath of God comes upon the sons of disobedience.

Heb 13:4 Marriage *is* honorable among all, and the bed undefiled; but fornicators and adulterers God will judge.

Rev 22:15 But outside *are* dogs and sorcerers and sexually immoral and murderers and idolaters, and whoever loves and practices a lie.

Motives for.

1 Cor 6:19 Or do you not know that your body is the temple of the Holy Spirit *who is* in you, whom you have from God, and you are not your own?

1 Thess 4:7 For God did not call us to uncleanness, but in holiness.

Exemplified by

Abimelech.

Gen 20:4–5 But Abimelech had not come near her; and he said, "Lord, will You slay a righteous nation also? **5** Did he not say to me, 'She *is* my sister'? And she, even she herself said, 'He *is* my brother.' In the integrity of my heart and innocence of my hands I have done this."

Gen 26:10–11 And Abimelech said, "What *is* this you have done to us? One of the people might soon have lain with your wife, and you would have brought guilt on us." **11** So Abimelech charged all *his* people, saying, "He who touches this man or his wife shall surely be put to death."

Joseph.

Gen 39:7–10 And it came to pass after these things that his master's wife cast longing eyes on Joseph, and she said, "Lie with me." **8** But he refused and said to his master's wife, "Look, my master does not know what *is* with me in the house, and he has committed all that he has to my hand. **9** *There is* no one greater in this house than I, nor has he kept back anything from me but you, because you *are* his wife. How then can I do this great wickedness, and sin against God?" **10** So it was, as she spoke to Joseph day by day, that he did not heed her, to lie with her *or* to be with her.

Ruth.

Ruth 3:10–11 Then he said, "Blessed *are* you of the LORD, my daughter! For you have shown more kindness at the end than at the beginning, in that you did not go after young men, whether poor or rich. **11** And now, my daughter, do not fear. I will do for you all that you request, for all the people of my town know that you *are* a virtuous woman.

Boaz.

Ruth 3:13 Stay this night, and in the morning it shall be *that* if he will perform the duty of a close relative for you—good; let him do it. But if he does not want to perform the duty for you, then I will perform the duty for you, *as* the LORD lives! Lie down until morning."

CHERUBIM
Form and appearance of.

Ezek 1:5–11 Also from within it *came* the likeness of four living creatures. And this *was* their appearance: they had the likeness of a man. **6** Each one had four faces, and each one had four wings. **7** Their legs *were* straight, and the soles of their feet *were* like the soles of calves' feet. They sparkled like the color of burnished bronze. **8** The hands of a man *were* under their wings on their four sides; and each of the four had faces and wings. **9** Their wings touched one another. *The creatures* did not turn when they went, but each one went straight forward. **10** As for the likeness of their faces, *each* had the face of a man; each of the four had the face of a lion on the right side, each of the four had the face of an ox on the left side, and each of the four had the face of an eagle. **11** Thus *were* their faces. Their wings stretched upward; two *wings* of each one touched one another, and two covered their bodies.

Ezek 1:13–14 As for the likeness of the living creatures, their appearance *was* like burning coals of fire, like the appearance of torches going back and forth among the living creatures. The fire was bright, and out of the fire went lightning. **14** And the living creatures ran back and forth, in appearance like a flash of lightning.

Animated by the Spirit of God.

Ezek 1:12 And each one went straight forward; they went wherever the spirit wanted to go, and they did not turn when they went.

Ezek 1:20 Wherever the spirit wanted to go, they went, *because* there the spirit went; and the wheels were lifted together with them, for the spirit of the living creatures *was* in the wheels.

Engaged in accomplishing the purposes of God.

Ezek 1:15 Now as I looked at the living creatures, behold, a wheel *was* on the earth beside each living creature with its four faces.

Ezek 1:21 When those went, *these* went; when those stood, *these* stood; and when those were lifted up from the earth, the wheels were lifted up together with them, for the spirit of the living creatures *was* in the wheels.

Ezek 10:9–11 And when I looked, there were four wheels by the cherubim, one wheel by one cherub and another wheel by each other cherub; the wheels appeared *to have* the color of a beryl stone. **10** *As for* their appearance, all four looked alike—as it were, a wheel in the middle of a wheel. **11** When they went, they went toward *any* of their four directions; they did not turn aside when they went, but followed in the direction the head was facing. They did not turn aside when they went.

Ezek 10:16–17 When the cherubim went, the wheels went beside them; and when the cherubim lifted their wings to mount up from the earth, the same wheels also did not turn from beside them. **17** When *the cherubim* stood still, *the wheels* stood still, and when *one* was lifted up, *the other* lifted itself up, for the spirit of the living creature *was* in them.

The glory of God exhibited upon.

Ezek 1:22 The likeness of the firmament above the heads of the living creatures *was* like the color of an awesome crystal, stretched out over their heads.

Ezek 1:26–28 And above the firmament over their heads *was* the likeness of a throne, in appearance like a sapphire stone; on the likeness of the throne *was* a likeness with the appearance of a man high above it. **27** Also from the appearance of His waist and upward I saw, as it were, the color of amber with the appearance of fire all around within it; and from the appearance of His waist and downward I saw, as it were, the appearance of fire with brightness all around. **28** Like the appearance of a rainbow in a cloud on a rainy day, so *was* the appearance of the brightness all around it. This *was* the appearance of the likeness of the glory of the LORD. So when I saw *it*, I fell on my face, and I heard a voice of One speaking.

Ezek 10:4 Then the glory of the LORD went up from the cherub, *and paused* over the threshold of the temple; and the house was filled with the cloud, and the court was full of the brightness of the LORD's glory.

Ezek 10:18 Then the glory of the LORD departed from the threshold of the temple and stood over the cherubim.

Ezek 10:20 This *is* the living creature I saw under the God of Israel by the River Chebar, and I knew they *were* cherubim.

Sound of their wings was as the voice of God.

Ezek 1:24 When they went, I heard the noise of their wings, like the noise of many waters, like the voice of the Almighty, a tumult like the noise of an army; and when they stood still, they let down their wings.

Ezek 10:5 And the sound of the wings of the cherubim was heard *even* in the outer court, like the voice of Almighty God when He speaks.

Placed at the entrance of Eden.

Gen 3:24 So He drove out the man; and He placed cherubim at the east of the garden of Eden, and a flaming sword which turned every way, to guard the way to the tree of life.

Of gold

Formed out of, and at each end of the mercy seat.

Ex 25:18–20 And you shall make two cherubim of gold; of hammered work you shall make them at the two ends of the mercy seat. **19** Make one cherub at one end, and the other cherub at the other end; you shall make the cherubim at the two ends of it *of one piece* with the mercy seat. **20** And the cherubim shall stretch out *their* wings above, covering the mercy seat with their wings, and they shall face one another; the faces of the cherubim *shall be* toward the mercy seat.

Placed over the ark of the covenant.

1 Sam 4:4 So the people sent to Shiloh, that they might bring from there the ark of the covenant of the LORD of hosts, who dwells *between* the cherubim. And the two sons of Eli, Hophni and Phinehas, *were* there with the ark of the covenant of God.

1 Kin 8:6–7 Then the priests brought in the ark of the covenant of the LORD to its place, into the inner sanctuary of the temple, to the Most Holy *Place*, under the wings of the cherubim. **7** For the cherubim spread *their* two wings over the place of the ark, and the cherubim overshadowed the ark and its poles.

2 Chr 5:7–8 Then the priests brought in the ark of the covenant of the LORD to its place, into the inner sanctuary of the temple, to the Most Holy *Place*, under the wings of the cherubim. **8** For the cherubim spread *their* wings over the place of the ark, and the cherubim overshadowed the ark and its poles.

God's presence manifested between.

2 Sam 6:2 And David arose and went with all the people who *were* with him from Baale Judah to bring up from there the ark of God, whose name is called by the Name, the LORD of Hosts, who dwells *between* the cherubim.

2 Kin 19:15 Then Hezekiah prayed before the LORD, and said: "O LORD God of Israel, *the One* who dwells *between* the cherubim, You are God, You alone, of all the kingdoms of the earth. You have made heaven and earth.

Ps 80:1 Give ear, O Shepherd of Israel, You who lead Joseph like a flock; You who dwell *between* the cherubim, shine forth!

Ps 99:1 The LORD reigns; Let the peoples tremble! He dwells *between* the cherubim; Let the earth be moved!

The oracles or answers of God delivered from between.

Ex 25:22 And there I will meet with you, and I will

speak with you from above the mercy seat, from between the two cherubim which *are* on the ark of the Testimony, about everything which I will give you in commandment to the children of Israel.

Num 7:89 Now when Moses went into the tabernacle of meeting to speak with Him, he heard the voice of One speaking to him from above the mercy seat that *was* on the ark of the Testimony, from between the two cherubim; thus He spoke to him.

Called the cherubim of glory.

Heb 9:5 and above it were the cherubim of glory overshadowing the mercy seat. Of these things we cannot now speak in detail.

Representations of, made on the

Curtains of the tabernacle.

Ex 26:1 "Moreover you shall make the tabernacle *with* ten curtains *of* fine woven linen and blue, purple, and scarlet *thread*; with artistic designs of cherubim you shall weave them.

Ex 26:31 "You shall make a veil woven of blue, purple, and scarlet *thread,* and fine woven linen. It shall be woven with an artistic design of cherubim.

Veil of the tabernacle.

Ex 26:31 "You shall make a veil woven of blue, purple, and scarlet *thread,* and fine woven linen. It shall be woven with an artistic design of cherubim.

Veil of the temple.

2 Chr 3:14 And he made the veil of blue, purple, crimson, and fine linen, and wove cherubim into it.

Doors of the temple.

1 Kin 6:32 The two doors *were of* olive wood; and he carved on them figures of cherubim, palm trees, and open flowers, and overlaid *them* with gold; and he spread gold on the cherubim and on the palm trees.

1 Kin 6:35 Then he carved cherubim, palm trees, and open flowers *on them,* and overlaid *them* with gold applied evenly on the carved work.

Walls of the temple.

2 Chr 3:7 He also overlaid the house—the beams and doorposts, its walls and doors—with gold; and he carved cherubim on the walls.

Riding on, illustrative of majesty and power of God.

2 Sam 22:11 He rode upon a cherub, and flew; And He was seen upon the wings of the wind.

Ps 18:10 And He rode upon a cherub, and flew; He flew upon the wings of the wind.

CHILDREN

Christ was an example to.

Luke 2:51 Then He went down with them and came to Nazareth, and was subject to them, but His mother kept all these things in her heart.

Are a gift from God.

Gen 33:5 And he lifted his eyes and saw the women and children, and said, "Who *are* these with you?" So he said, "The children whom God has graciously given your servant."

Ps 127:3 Behold, children *are* a heritage from the LORD, The fruit of the womb *is* a reward.

Are capable of glorifying God.

Ps 8:2 Out of the mouth of babes and nursing infants You have ordained strength, Because of Your enemies, That You may silence the enemy and the avenger.

Ps 148:12–13 Both young men and maidens; Old men and children. **13** Let them praise the name of the LORD, For His name alone is exalted; His glory *is* above the earth and heaven.

Matt 21:15–16 But when the chief priests and scribes saw the wonderful things that He did, and the children crying out in the temple and saying, "Hosanna to the Son of David!" they were indignant **16** and said to Him, "Do You hear what these are saying?" And Jesus said to them, "Yes. Have you never read, *'Out of the mouth of babes and nursing infants You have perfected praise'?* "

Should be

Brought to Christ.

Mark 10:13–16 Then they brought little children to Him, that He might touch them; but the disciples rebuked those who brought *them.* **14** But when Jesus saw *it,* He was greatly displeased and said to them, "Let the little children come to Me, and do not forbid them; for of such is the kingdom of God. **15** Assuredly, I say to you, whoever does not receive the kingdom of God as a little child will by no means enter it." **16** And He took them up in His arms, laid *His* hands on them, and blessed them.

Brought early to the house of God.

1 Sam 1:24 Now when she had weaned him, she took him up with her, with three bulls, one ephah of flour, and a skin of wine, and brought him to the house of the LORD in Shiloh. And the child *was* young.

Instructed in the ways of God.

Deut 31:12–13 Gather the people together, men and women and little ones, and the stranger who *is* within your gates, that they may hear and that they may learn to fear the LORD your God and carefully observe all the words of this law, **13** and *that* their children, who have not known *it,* may hear and learn to fear the LORD your God as long as you live in the land which you cross the Jordan to possess."

Prov 22:6 Train up a child in the way he should go, And when he is old he will not depart from it.

Judiciously trained.

Prov 22:15 Foolishness *is* bound up in the heart of a child; The rod of correction will drive it far from him.

Prov 29:17 Correct your son, and he will give you rest; Yes, he will give delight to your soul.

Eph 6:4 And you, fathers, do not provoke your children to wrath, but bring them up in the training and admonition of the Lord.

Should

Fear and obey God.

Deut 30:2 and you return to the LORD your God and obey His voice, according to all that I command you today, you and your children, with all your heart and with all your soul,

Prov 24:21 My son, fear the LORD and the king; Do not associate with those given to change;

Eccl 12:1 Remember now your Creator in the days of your youth, Before the difficult days come, And the years draw near when you say, "I have no pleasure in them":

Honor and obey parents.

Ex 20:12 "Honor your father and your mother, that your days may be long upon the land which the LORD your God is giving you.

Lev 19:3 'Every one of you shall revere his mother and his father, and keep My Sabbaths: I *am* the LORD your God.

Prov 1:8–9 My son, hear the instruction of your father, And do not forsake the law of your mother; **9** For they *will be* a graceful ornament on your head, And chains about your neck.

Prov 6:20 My son, keep your father's command, And do not forsake the law of your mother.

Eph 6:1 Children, obey your parents in the Lord, for this is right.

Heb 12:9 Furthermore, we have had human fathers who corrected *us,* and we paid *them* respect. Shall we not much more readily be in subjection to the Father of spirits and live?

Take care of parents.

1 Tim 5:4 But if any widow has children or grandchildren, let them first learn to show piety at home and to repay their parents; for this is good and acceptable before God.

Honor the aged.

Lev 19:32 'You shall rise before the gray headed and honor the presence of an old man, and fear your God: I *am* the LORD.

1 Pet 5:5 Likewise you younger people, submit yourselves to *your* elders. Yes, all of *you* be submissive to one another, and be clothed with humility, for *"God resists the proud, But gives grace to the humble."*

Not imitate bad parents.

Ezek 20:18 "But I said to their children in the wilderness, 'Do not walk in the statutes of your fathers, nor observe their judgments, nor defile yourselves with their idols.

Are a heritage from the Lord.

Ps 113:9 He grants the barren woman a home, Like a joyful mother of children. Praise the LORD!

Ps 127:3 Behold, children *are* a heritage from the LORD, The fruit of the womb *is* a reward.

Often prayed for.

1 Sam 1:10–11 And she *was* in bitterness of soul, and prayed to the LORD and wept in anguish. **11** Then she made a vow and said, "O LORD of hosts, if You will indeed look on the affliction of Your maidservant and remember me, and not forget Your maidservant, but will give Your maidservant a male child, then I will give him to the LORD all the days of his life, and no razor shall come upon his head."

Luke 1:13 But the angel said to him, "Do not be afraid, Zacharias, for your prayer is heard; and your wife Elizabeth will bear you a son, and you shall call his name John.

Often given in answer to prayer.

Gen 25:21 Now Isaac pleaded with the LORD for his

wife, because she *was* barren; and the LORD granted his plea, and Rebekah his wife conceived.

1 Sam 1:27 For this child I prayed, and the LORD has granted me my petition which I asked of Him.

Luke 1:13 But the angel said to him, "Do not be afraid, Zacharias, for your prayer is heard; and your wife Elizabeth will bear you a son, and you shall call his name John.

Mostly nursed by the mothers.

1 Sam 1:22 But Hannah did not go up, for she said to her husband, "*Not* until the child is weaned; then I will take him, that he may appear before the LORD and remain there forever."

1 Kin 3:21 And when I rose in the morning to nurse my son, there he was, dead. But when I had examined him in the morning, indeed, he was not my son whom I had borne."

Ps 22:9 But You *are* He who took Me out of the womb; You made Me trust *while* on My mother's breasts.

Song 8:1 Oh, that you were like my brother, Who nursed at my mother's breasts! *If* I should find you outside, I would kiss you; I would not be despised.

Weaning of, a time of joy and feasting.

Gen 21:8 So the child grew and was weaned. And Abraham made a great feast on the same day that Isaac was weaned.

1 Sam 1:24 Now when she had weaned him, she took him up with her, with three bulls, one ephah of flour, and a skin of wine, and brought him to the house of the LORD in Shiloh. And the child *was* young.

Circumcised on the eighth day.

Phil 3:5 circumcised the eighth day, of the stock of Israel, *of* the tribe of Benjamin, a Hebrew of the Hebrews; concerning the law, a Pharisee;

Named at circumcision.

Luke 1:59 So it was, on the eighth day, that they came to circumcise the child; and they would have called him by the name of his father, Zacharias.

Luke 2:21 And when eight days were completed for the circumcision of the Child, His name was called JESUS, the name given by the angel before He was conceived in the womb.

Were named

After relatives.

Luke 1:59 So it was, on the eighth day, that they came to circumcise the child; and they would have called him by the name of his father, Zacharias.

Luke 1:61 But they said to her, "There is no one among your relatives who is called by this name."

From remarkable events.

Gen 18:13 And the LORD said to Abraham, "Why did Sarah laugh, saying, 'Shall I surely bear *a child,* since I am old?'

Gen 21:3 And Abraham called the name of his son who was born to him—whom Sarah bore to him—Isaac.

Gen 21:6 And Sarah said, "God has made me laugh, *and* all who hear will laugh with me."

Ex 2:10 And the child grew, and she brought him to Pharaoh's daughter, and he became her son. So she called his name Moses, saying, "Because I drew him out of the water."

Ex 18:3–4 with her two sons, of whom the name of one *was* Gershom (for he said, "I have been a stranger in a foreign land") **4** and the name of the other *was* Eliezer (for *he said*, "The God of my father *was* my help, and delivered me from the sword of Pharaoh");

From circumstances connected with their birth.

Gen 25:25–26 And the first came out red. *He was* like a hairy garment all over; so they called his name Esau. **26** Afterward his brother came out, and his hand took hold of Esau's heel; so his name was called Jacob. Isaac *was* sixty years old when she bore them.

Gen 35:18 And so it was, as her soul was departing (for she died), that she called his name Ben-Oni; but his father called him Benjamin.

1 Chr 4:9 Now Jabez was more honorable than his brothers, and his mother called his name Jabez, saying, "Because I bore *him* in pain."

Often by God.

Is 8:3 Then I went to the prophetess, and she conceived and bore a son. Then the LORD said to me, "Call his name Maher-Shalal-Hash-Baz;

Hos 1:4 Then the LORD said to him: "Call his name Jezreel, For in a little *while* I will avenge the bloodshed of Jezreel on the house of Jehu, And bring an end to the kingdom of the house of Israel.

Hos 1:6 And she conceived again and bore a daughter. Then *God* said to him: "Call her name Lo-Ruhamah, For I will no longer have mercy on the house of Israel, But I will utterly take them away.

Hos 1:9 Then *God* said: "Call his name Lo-Ammi, For you *are* not My people, And I will not be your *God*.

Often numerous.

2 Kin 10:1 Now Ahab had seventy sons in Samaria. And Jehu wrote and sent letters to Samaria, to the rulers of Jezreel, to the elders, and to those who reared Ahab's *sons*, saying:

1 Chr 4:27 Shimei had sixteen sons and six daughters; but his brothers did not have many children, nor did any of their families multiply as much as the children of Judah.

Numerous, considered a special blessing.

Ps 115:14 May the LORD give you increase more and more, You and your children.

Ps 127:4–5 Like arrows in the hand of a warrior, So *are* the children of one's youth. **5** Happy *is* the man who has his quiver full of them; They shall not be ashamed, But shall speak with their enemies in the gate.

Sometimes born when parents were old.

Gen 15:3 Then Abram said, "Look, You have given me no offspring; indeed one born in my house is my heir!"

Gen 15:6 And he believed in the LORD, and He accounted it to him for righteousness.

Gen 17:17 Then Abraham fell on his face and laughed, and said in his heart, "Shall *a child* be born to a man who is one hundred years old? And shall Sarah, who is ninety years old, bear *a child?*"

Luke 1:18 And Zacharias said to the angel, "How shall

I know this? For I am an old man, and my wife is well advanced in years."

Male,

If firstborn, belonged to God and were redeemed.

Ex 13:12–13 that you shall set apart to the LORD all that open the womb, that is, every firstborn that comes from an animal which you have; the males *shall be* the LORD's. **13** But every firstborn of a donkey you shall redeem with a lamb; and if you will not redeem *it*, then you shall break its neck. And all the firstborn of man among your sons you shall redeem.

Ex 13:15 And it came to pass, when Pharaoh was stubborn about letting us go, that the LORD killed all the firstborn in the land of Egypt, both the firstborn of man and the firstborn of beast. Therefore I sacrifice to the LORD all males that open the womb, but all the firstborn of my sons I redeem.'

Under the care of tutors, till they came of age.

2 Kin 10:1 Now Ahab had seventy sons in Samaria. And Jehu wrote and sent letters to Samaria, to the rulers of Jezreel, to the elders, and to those who reared Ahab's *sons*, saying:

Gal 4:1–2 Now I say *that* the heir, as long as he is a child, does not differ at all from a slave, though he is master of all, **2** but is under guardians and stewards until the time appointed by the father.

Inherited the possessions of their father.

Deut 21:16–17 then it shall be, on the day he bequeaths his possessions to his sons, *that* he must not bestow firstborn status on the son of the loved wife in preference to the son of the unloved, the *true* firstborn. **17** But he shall acknowledge the son of the unloved wife *as* the firstborn by giving him a double portion of all that he has, for he *is* the beginning of his strength; the right of the firstborn *is* his.

Luke 12:13–14 Then one from the crowd said to Him, "Teacher, tell my brother to divide the inheritance with me." **14** But He said to him, "Man, who made Me a judge or an arbitrator over you?"

Received the blessing of their father before his death.

Gen 27:1–4 Now it came to pass, when Isaac was old and his eyes were so dim that he could not see, that he called Esau his older son and said to him, "My son." And he answered him, "Here I am." **2** Then he said, "Behold now, I am old. I do not know the day of my death. **3** Now therefore, please take your weapons, your quiver and your bow, and go out to the field and hunt game for me. **4** And make me savory food, such as I love, and bring *it* to me that I may eat, that my soul may bless you before I die."

Gen 48:15 And he blessed Joseph, and said: "God, before whom my fathers Abraham and Isaac walked, The God who has fed me all my life long to this day,

Cf. Gen 49:1–33

Female inherited property in default of sons.

Num 27:1–8 Then came the daughters of Zelophehad the son of Hepher, the son of Gilead, the son of Machir, the son of Manasseh, from the families of Manasseh the son of Joseph; and these *were* the names of his daughters: Mahlah, Noah, Hoglah, Milcah, and Tirzah. **2** And they stood before Moses, before Eleazar the priest, and before the leaders and all the congregation, *by* the doorway of the tabernacle of meeting, saying: 3 "Our father died in the wilderness; but he was not in the company of those who gathered together against the LORD, in company with Korah, but he died in his own sin; and he had no sons. 4 Why should the name of our father be removed from among his family because he had no son? Give us a possession among our father's brothers." 5 So Moses brought their case before the LORD. 6 And the LORD spoke to Moses, saying: 7 "The daughters of Zelophehad speak *what is* right; you shall surely give them a possession of inheritance among their father's brothers, and cause the inheritance of their father to pass to them. 8 And you shall speak to the children of Israel, saying: 'If a man dies and has no son, then you shall cause his inheritance to pass to his daughter.

Josh 17:1–6 There was also a lot for the tribe of Manasseh, for he *was* the firstborn of Joseph: *namely* for Machir the firstborn of Manasseh, the father of Gilead, because he was a man of war; therefore he was given Gilead and Bashan. 2 And there was *a lot* for the rest of the children of Manasseh according to their families: for the children of Abiezer, the children of Helek, the children of Asriel, the children of Shechem, the children of Hepher, and the children of Shemida; these *were* the male children of Manasseh the son of Joseph according to their families. 3 But Zelophehad the son of Hepher, the son of Gilead, the son of Machir, the son of Manasseh, had no sons, but only daughters. And these *are* the names of his daughters: Mahlah, Noah, Hoglah, Milcah, and Tirzah. 4 And they came near before Eleazar the priest, before Joshua the son of Nun, and before the rulers, saying, "The LORD commanded Moses to give us an inheritance among our brothers." Therefore, according to the commandment of the LORD, he gave them an inheritance among their father's brothers. 5 Ten shares fell to Manasseh, besides the land of Gilead and Bashan, which *were* on the other side of the Jordan, 6 because the daughters of Manasseh received an inheritance among his sons; and the rest of Manasseh's sons had the land of Gilead.

Mother's care for.

Ex 2:2–10 So the woman conceived and bore a son. And when she saw that he *was* a beautiful *child,* she hid him three months. 3 But when she could no longer hide him, she took an ark of bulrushes for him, daubed it with asphalt and pitch, put the child in it, and laid *it* in the reeds by the river's bank. 4 And his sister stood afar off, to know what would be done to him. 5 Then the daughter of Pharaoh came down to bathe at the river. And her maidens walked along the riverside; and when she saw the ark among the reeds, she sent her maid to get it. 6 And when she opened *it,* she saw the child, and behold, the baby wept. So she had compassion on him, and said, "This is one of the Hebrews' children." 7 Then his sister said to Pharaoh's daughter, "Shall I go and call a nurse for you from the Hebrew women, that she may nurse the child for you?" 8 And Pharaoh's daughter said to her, "Go." So the maiden went and called the child's mother. 9 Then Pharaoh's daughter said to her, "Take this child away and nurse him for me, and I will give *you* your wages." So the woman took the

child and nursed him. 10 And the child grew, and she brought him to Pharaoh's daughter, and he became her son. So she called his name Moses, saying, "Because I drew him out of the water."

1 Sam 2:19 Moreover his mother used to make him a little robe, and bring *it* to him year by year when she came up with her husband to offer the yearly sacrifice.

1 Kin 3:27 So the king answered and said, "Give the first woman the living child, and by no means kill him; she *is* his mother."

Is 49:15 "Can a woman forget her nursing child, And not have compassion on the son of her womb? Surely they may forget, Yet I will not forget you.

1 Thess 2:7–8 But we were gentle among you, just as a nursing *mother* cherishes her own children. 8 So, affectionately longing for you, we were well pleased to impart to you not only the gospel of God, but also our own lives, because you had become dear to us.

Of God's people, holy.

Ezra 9:2 For they have taken some of their daughters *as wives* for themselves and their sons, so that the holy seed is mixed with the peoples of *those* lands. Indeed, the hand of the leaders and rulers has been foremost in this trespass."

1 Cor 7:14 For the unbelieving husband is sanctified by the wife, and the unbelieving wife is sanctified by the husband; otherwise your children would be unclean, but now they are holy.

Of God's people, interested in the promises.

Deut 29:29 "The secret *things belong* to the LORD our God, but those *things which are* revealed *belong* to us and to our children forever, that *we* may do all the words of this law.

Acts 2:39 For the promise is to you and to your children, and to all who are afar off, as many as the Lord our God will call."

Prosperity of, dependent on parents' obedience.

Deut 4:40 You shall therefore keep His statutes and His commandments which I command you today, that it may go well with you and with your children after you, and that you may prolong *your* days in the land which the LORD your God is giving you for all time."

Deut 12:25 You shall not eat it, that it may go well with you and your children after you, when you do *what is* right in the sight of the LORD.

Deut 12:28 Observe and obey all these words which I command you, that it may go well with you and your children after you forever, when you do *what is* good and right in the sight of the LORD your God.

Ps 128:1–3 Blessed *is* every one who fears the LORD, Who walks in His ways. 2 When you eat the labor of your hands, You *shall be* happy, and *it shall be* well with you. 3 Your wife *shall be* like a fruitful vine In the very heart of your house, Your children like olive plants All around your table.

Frequently bore the curse of parents.

Ex 20:5 you shall not bow down to them nor serve them. For I, the LORD your God, *am* a jealous God, visiting the iniquity of the fathers upon the children to the third and fourth *generations* of those who hate Me,

214

Ps 109:9–10 Let his children be fatherless, And his wife a widow. **10** Let his children continually be vagabonds, and beg; Let them seek *their bread* also from their desolate places.

Schooling of.

Luke 2:46 Now so it was *that* after three days they found Him in the temple, sitting in the midst of the teachers, both listening to them and asking them questions.

Acts 22:3 "I am indeed a Jew, born in Tarsus of Cilicia, but brought up in this city at the feet of Gamaliel, taught according to the strictness of our fathers' law, and was zealous toward God as you all are today.

Power of parents over, during the patriarchal age.

Gen 9:24–25 So Noah awoke from his wine, and knew what his younger son had done to him. **25** Then he said: "Cursed *be* Canaan; A servant of servants He shall be to his brethren."

Gen 21:14 So Abraham rose early in the morning, and took bread and a skin of water; and putting *it* on her shoulder, he gave *it* and the boy to Hagar, and sent her away. Then she departed and wandered in the Wilderness of Beersheba.

Gen 38:24 And it came to pass, about three months after, that Judah was told, saying, "Tamar your daughter-in-law has played the harlot; furthermore she *is* with child by harlotry." So Judah said, "Bring her out and let her be burned!"

Rebellion punished by the civil power.

Ex 21:15–17 "And he who strikes his father or his mother shall surely be put to death. **16** "He who kidnaps a man and sells him, or if he is found in his hand, shall surely be put to death. **17** "And he who curses his father or his mother shall surely be put to death.

Deut 21:18–21 "If a man has a stubborn and rebellious son who will not obey the voice of his father or the voice of his mother, and *who,* when they have chastened him, will not heed them, **19** then his father and his mother shall take hold of him and bring him out to the elders of his city, to the gate of his city. **20** And they shall say to the elders of his city, 'This son of ours is stubborn and rebellious; he will not obey our voice; he is a glutton and a drunkard.' **21** Then all the men of his city shall stone him to death with stones; so you shall put away the evil from among you, and all Israel shall hear and fear.

Sometimes tried to avoid supporting parents.

Matt 15:5 But you say, 'Whoever says to his father or mother, "Whatever profit you might have received from me *is* a gift *to God*"—

Mark 7:11–12 But you say, 'If a man says to his father or mother, "Whatever profit you might have received from me *is* Corban"—' (that is, a gift *to God*), **12** then you no longer let him do anything for his father or his mother,

Sometimes offered to idols.

2 Kin 17:31 and the Avites made Nibhaz and Tartak; and the Sepharvites burned their children in fire to Adrammelech and Anammelech, the gods of Sepharvaim.

2 Chr 28:3 He burned incense in the Valley of the Son of Hinnom, and burned his children in the fire, according to the abominations of the nations whom the LORD had cast out before the children of Israel.

2 Chr 33:6 Also he caused his sons to pass through the fire in the Valley of the Son of Hinnom; he practiced soothsaying, used witchcraft and sorcery, and consulted mediums and spiritists. He did much evil in the sight of the LORD, to provoke Him to anger.

Illegitimate,

Had no inheritance.

Gen 21:10 Therefore she said to Abraham, "Cast out this bondwoman and her son; for the son of this bondwoman shall not be heir with my son, *namely* with Isaac."

Gen 21:14 So Abraham rose early in the morning, and took bread and a skin of water; and putting *it* on her shoulder, he gave *it* and the boy to Hagar, and sent her away. Then she departed and wandered in the Wilderness of Beersheba.

Gal 4:30 Nevertheless what does the Scripture say? *"Cast out the bondwoman and her son, for the son of the bondwoman shall not be heir with the son of the freewoman."*

Not cared for by the father.

Heb 12:8 But if you are without chastening, of which all have become partakers, then you are illegitimate and not sons.

Excluded from the congregation.

Deut 23:2 "One of illegitimate birth shall not enter the assembly of the LORD; even to the tenth generation none of his *descendants* shall enter the assembly of the LORD.

Sometimes sent away with gifts.

Gen 25:6 But Abraham gave gifts to the sons of the concubines which Abraham had; and while he was still living he sent them eastward, away from Isaac his son, to the country of the east.

Despised by their brethren.

Judg 11:2 Gilead's wife bore sons; and when his wife's sons grew up, they drove Jephthah out, and said to him, "You shall have no inheritance in our father's house, for you *are* the son of another woman."

Grief caused by loss of.

Gen 37:35 And all his sons and all his daughters arose to comfort him; but he refused to be comforted, and he said, "For I shall go down into the grave to my son in mourning." Thus his father wept for him.

Gen 44:27–29 Then your servant my father said to us, 'You know that my wife bore me two sons; **28** and the one went out from me, and I said, "Surely he is torn to pieces"; and I have not seen him since. **29** But if you take this one also from me, and calamity befalls him, you shall bring down my gray hair with sorrow to the grave.'

2 Sam 13:37 But Absalom fled and went to Talmai the son of Ammihud, king of Geshur. And *David* mourned for his son every day.

Jer 6:26 O daughter of my people, Dress in sackcloth And roll about in ashes! Make mourning *as for an* only son, most bitter lamentation; For the plunderer will suddenly come upon us.

Jer 31:15 Thus says the LORD: "A voice was heard in Ramah, Lamentation *and* bitter weeping, Rachel weeping for her children, Refusing to be comforted for her children, Because they *are* no more."

Resignation manifested by loss of.

Lev 10:19–20 And Aaron said to Moses, "Look, this day they have offered their sin offering and their burnt offering before the LORD, and such things have befallen me! *If* I had eaten the sin offering today, would it have been accepted in the sight of the LORD?" **20** So when Moses heard *that,* he was content.

2 Sam 12:18–23 Then on the seventh day it came to pass that the child died. And the servants of David were afraid to tell him that the child was dead. For they said, "Indeed, while the child was alive, we spoke to him, and he would not heed our voice. How can we tell him that the child is dead? He may do some harm!" **19** When David saw that his servants were whispering, David perceived that the child was dead. Therefore David said to his servants, "Is the child dead?" And they said, "He is dead." **20** So David arose from the ground, washed and anointed himself, and changed his clothes; and he went into the house of the LORD and worshiped. Then he went to his own house; and when he requested, they set food before him, and he ate. **21** Then his servants said to him, "What *is* this that you have done? You fasted and wept for the child *while he was* alive, but when the child died, you arose and ate food." **22** And he said, "While the child was alive, I fasted and wept; for I said, 'Who can tell *whether* the LORD will be gracious to me, that the child may live?' **23** But now he is dead; why should I fast? Can I bring him back again? I shall go to him, but he shall not return to me."

Job 1:19–21 and suddenly a great wind came from across the wilderness and struck the four corners of the house, and it fell on the young people, and they are dead; and I alone have escaped to tell you!" **20** Then Job arose, tore his robe, and shaved his head; and he fell to the ground and worshiped. **21** And he said: "Naked I came from my mother's womb, And naked shall I return there. The LORD gave, and the LORD has taken away; Blessed be the name of the LORD."

CHILDREN, GOOD

The Lord is with.

1 Sam 3:19 So Samuel grew, and the LORD was with him and let none of his words fall to the ground.

Obey the truth.

Prov 28:7 Whoever keeps the law *is* a discerning son, But a companion of gluttons shames his father.

Acts 2:39 For the promise is to you and to your children, and to all who are afar off, as many as the Lord our God will call."

Matt 18:4 Therefore whoever humbles himself as this little child is the greatest in the kingdom of heaven.

2 Tim 3:15 and that from childhood you have known the Holy Scriptures, which are able to make you wise for salvation through faith which is in Christ Jesus.

Shall be blessed.

Prov 3:1–4 My son, do not forget my law, But let your heart keep my commands; **2** For length of days and

long life And peace they will add to you. **3** Let not mercy and truth forsake you; Bind them around your neck, Write them on the tablet of your heart, **4** *And* so find favor and high esteem In the sight of God and man.

Eph 6:2–3 *"Honor your father and mother,"* which is the first commandment with promise: **3** *"that it may be well with you and you may live long on the earth."*

Honor parents.

Gen 28:7 and that Jacob had obeyed his father and his mother and had gone to Padan Aram.

Gen 45:9 "Hurry and go up to my father, and say to him, 'Thus says your son Joseph: "God has made me lord of all Egypt; come down to me, do not tarry.

Gen 45:11 There I will provide for you, lest you and your household, and all that you have, come to poverty; for *there are* still five years of famine." '

Gen 46:29 So Joseph made ready his chariot and went up to Goshen to meet his father Israel; and he presented himself to him, and fell on his neck and wept on his neck a good while.

Gen 47:12 Then Joseph provided his father, his brothers, and all his father's household with bread, according to the number in *their* families.

Gen 47:30 but let me lie with my fathers; you shall carry me out of Egypt and bury me in their burial place." And he said, "I will do as you have said."

Prov 10:1 The proverbs of Solomon: A wise son makes a glad father, But a foolish son *is* the grief of his mother.

Prov 13:1 A wise son *heeds* his father's instruction, But a scoffer does not listen to rebuke.

Prov 29:17 Correct your son, and he will give you rest; Yes, he will give delight to your soul.

Col 3:20 Children, obey your parents in all things, for this is well pleasing to the Lord.

Heb 12:9 Furthermore, we have had human fathers who corrected *us,* and we paid *them* respect. Shall we not much more readily be in subjection to the Father of spirits and live?

Spirit of, a requisite for the kingdom of heaven.

Matt 18:3 and said, "Assuredly, I say to you, unless you are converted and become as little children, you will by no means enter the kingdom of heaven.

Exemplified by

Isaac.

Gen 22:6–10 So Abraham took the wood of the burnt offering and laid *it* on Isaac his son; and he took the fire in his hand, and a knife, and the two of them went together. **7** But Isaac spoke to Abraham his father and said, "My father!" And he said, "Here I am, my son." Then he said, "Look, the fire and the wood, but where *is* the lamb for a burnt offering?" **8** And Abraham said, "My son, God will provide for Himself the lamb for a burnt offering." So the two of them went together. **9** Then they came to the place of which God had told him. And Abraham built an altar there and placed the wood in order; and he bound Isaac his son and laid him on the altar, upon the wood. **10** And Abraham stretched out his hand and took the knife to slay his son.

Joseph.

Gen 45:9 "Hurry and go up to my father, and say to him, 'Thus says your son Joseph: "God has made me lord of all Egypt; come down to me, do not tarry.

Gen 46:29 So Joseph made ready his chariot and went up to Goshen to meet his father Israel; and he presented himself to him, and fell on his neck and wept on his neck a good while.

Samson.

Judg 13:24 So the woman bore a son and called his name Samson; and the child grew, and the LORD blessed him.

Samuel.

1 Sam 3:19 So Samuel grew, and the LORD was with him and let none of his words fall to the ground.

Obadiah.

1 Kin 18:12 And it shall come to pass, *as soon as* I am gone from you, that the Spirit of the LORD will carry you to a place I do not know; so when I go and tell Ahab, and he cannot find you, he will kill me. But I your servant have feared the LORD from my youth.

Josiah.

2 Chr 34:3 For in the eighth year of his reign, while he was still young, he began to seek the God of his father David; and in the twelfth year he began to purge Judah and Jerusalem of the high places, the wooden images, the carved images, and the molded images.

Esther.

Esth 2:20 *Now* Esther had not revealed her family and her people, just as Mordecai had charged her, for Esther obeyed the command of Mordecai as when she was brought up by him.

David.

1 Sam 17:20 So David rose early in the morning, left the sheep with a keeper, and took *the things* and went as Jesse had commanded him. And he came to the camp as the army was going out to the fight and shouting for the battle.

Ps 71:5 For You are my hope, O Lord GOD; *You are* my trust from my youth.

Daniel.

Dan 1:6 Now from among those of the sons of Judah were Daniel, Hananiah, Mishael, and Azariah.

John the Baptist.

Luke 1:80 So the child grew and became strong in spirit, and was in the deserts till the day of his manifestation to Israel.

Timothy.

2 Tim 3:15 and that from childhood you have known the Holy Scriptures, which are able to make you wise for salvation through faith which is in Christ Jesus.

CHILDREN, EVIL

No respect for parents.

1 Sam 2:25 If one man sins against another, God will judge him. But if a man sins against the LORD, who will intercede for him?" Nevertheless they did not heed the voice of their father, because the LORD desired to kill them.

Prov 15:5 A fool despises his father's instruction, But he who receives correction is prudent.

Prov 15:20 A wise son makes a father glad, But a foolish man despises his mother.

Prov 17:25 A foolish son *is* a grief to his father, And bitterness to her who bore him.

Prov 19:13 A foolish son *is* the ruin of his father, And the contentions of a wife *are* a continual dripping.

Prov 19:26 He who mistreats *his* father *and* chases away *his* mother Is a son who causes shame and brings reproach.

Prov 28:24 Whoever robs his father or his mother, And says, "*It is* no transgression," The same *is* companion to a destroyer.

Prov 30:11 *There is* a generation *that* curses its father, And does not bless its mother.

Is 3:5 The people will be oppressed, Every one by another and every one by his neighbor; The child will be insolent toward the elder, And the base toward the honorable."

Ezek 22:7 In you they have made light of father and mother; in your midst they have oppressed the stranger; in you they have mistreated the fatherless and the widow.

Punishment of.

Ex 21:15 "And he who strikes his father or his mother shall surely be put to death.

Deut 21:20–21 And they shall say to the elders of his city, 'This son of ours is stubborn and rebellious; he will not obey our voice; he is a glutton and a drunkard.' 21 Then all the men of his city shall stone him to death with stones; so you shall put away the evil from among you, and all Israel shall hear and fear.

Deut 27:16 'Cursed *is* the one who treats his father or his mother with contempt.' "And all the people shall say, 'Amen!'

2 Kin 2:23–24 Then he went up from there to Bethel; and as he was going up the road, some youths came from the city and mocked him, and said to him, "Go up, you baldhead! Go up, you baldhead!" 24 So he turned around and looked at them, and pronounced a curse on them in the name of the LORD. And two female bears came out of the woods and mauled forty-two of the youths.

Prov 30:17 The eye *that* mocks *his* father, And scorns obedience to *his* mother, The ravens of the valley will pick it out, And the young eagles will eat it.

Mark 7:10 For Moses said, *'Honor your father and your mother'*; and, *'He who curses father or mother, let him be put to death.'*

Exemplified by

Esau.

Gen 26:34–35 When Esau was forty years old, he took as wives Judith the daughter of Beeri the Hittite, and Basemath the daughter of Elon the Hittite. 35 And they were a grief of mind to Isaac and Rebekah.

Sons of Eli.

1 Sam 2:12 Now the sons of Eli *were* corrupt; they did not know the LORD.

1 Sam 2:17 Therefore the sin of the young men was very

great before the LORD, for men abhorred the offering of the LORD.

Sons of Samuel.

1 Sam 8:3 But his sons did not walk in his ways; they turned aside after dishonest gain, took bribes, and perverted justice.

Absalom.

2 Sam 15:10 Then Absalom sent spies throughout all the tribes of Israel, saying, "As soon as you hear the sound of the trumpet, then you shall say, 'Absalom reigns in Hebron!' "

Adonijah.

1 Kin 1:5–6 Then Adonijah the son of Haggith exalted himself, saying, "I will be king"; and he prepared for himself chariots and horsemen, and fifty men to run before him. **6** (And his father had not rebuked him at any time by saying, "Why have you done so?" He *was* also very good-looking. *His mother* had borne him after Absalom.)

Children at Bethel.

2 Kin 2:23 Then he went up from there to Bethel; and as he was going up the road, some youths came from the city and mocked him, and said to him, "Go up, you baldhead! Go up, you baldhead!"

Adrammelech and Sharezer.

2 Kin 19:37 Now it came to pass, as he was worshiping in the temple of Nisroch his god, that his sons Adrammelech and Sharezer struck him down with the sword; and they escaped into the land of Ararat. Then Esarhaddon his son reigned in his place.

CHOICES, HUMAN

Abram and Lot.

Gen 13:8–12 So Abram said to Lot, "Please let there be no strife between you and me, and between my herdsmen and your herdsmen; for we *are* brethren. **9** *Is* not the whole land before you? Please separate from me. If *you take* the left, then I will go to the right; or, if *you go* to the right, then I will go to the left." **10** And Lot lifted his eyes and saw all the plain of Jordan, that it *was* well watered everywhere (before the LORD destroyed Sodom and Gomorrah) like the garden of the LORD, like the land of Egypt as you go toward Zoar. **11** Then Lot chose for himself all the plain of Jordan, and Lot journeyed east. And they separated from each other. **12** Abram dwelt in the land of Canaan, and Lot dwelt in the cities of the plain and pitched *his* tent even as far as Sodom.

Moses appoints wise men.

Deut 1:13 Choose wise, understanding, and knowledgeable men from among your tribes, and I will make them heads over you.'

Of life.

Deut 30:15–19 "See, I have set before you today life and good, death and evil, **16** in that I command you today to love the LORD your God, to walk in His ways, and to keep His commandments, His statutes, and His judgments, that you may live and multiply; and the LORD your God will bless you in the land which you go to possess. **17** But if your heart turns away so that you do not hear, and are drawn away, and worship other gods and serve them, **18** I an-

nounce to you today that you shall surely perish; you shall not prolong *your* days in the land which you cross over the Jordan to go in and possess. **19** I call heaven and earth as witnesses today against you *that* I have set before you life and death, blessing and cursing; therefore choose life, that both you and your descendants may live;

To follow God.

Josh 24:15 And if it seems evil to you to serve the LORD, choose for yourselves this day whom you will serve, whether the gods which your fathers served that *were* on the other side of the River, or the gods of the Amorites, in whose land you dwell. But as for me and my house, we will serve the LORD."

1 Kin 18:21 And Elijah came to all the people, and said, "How long will you falter between two opinions? If the LORD *is* God, follow Him; but if Baal, follow him." But the people answered him not a word.

Hos 14:9 Who *is* wise? Let him understand these things. *Who is* prudent? Let him know them. For the ways of the LORD *are* right; The righteous walk in them, But transgressors stumble in them.

Repentance and obedience.

Is 1:19–20 If you are willing and obedient, You shall eat the good of the land; **20** But if you refuse and rebel, You shall be devoured by the sword"; For the mouth of the LORD has spoken.

Responsible.

Prov 1:3–4 To receive the instruction of wisdom, Justice, judgment, and equity; **4** To give prudence to the simple, To the young man knowledge and discretion—

Paul's, to preach the gospel.

1 Cor 9:16–19 For if I preach the gospel, I have nothing to boast of, for necessity is laid upon me; yes, woe is me if I do not preach the gospel! **17** For if I do this willingly, I have a reward; but if against my will, I have been entrusted with a stewardship. **18** What is my reward then? That when I preach the gospel, I may present the gospel of Christ without charge, that I may not abuse my authority in the gospel. **19** For though I am free from all *men*, I have made myself a servant to all, that I might win the more;

CHRISTIAN LIBERTY

Foretold.

Is 42:7 To open blind eyes, To bring out prisoners from the prison, Those who sit in darkness from the prison house.

Is 61:1 "The Spirit of the Lord GOD *is* upon Me, Because the LORD has anointed Me To preach good tidings to the poor; He has sent Me to heal the brokenhearted, To proclaim liberty to the captives, And the opening of the prison to *those who are* bound;

Conferred

By God.

Col 1:13 He has delivered us from the power of darkness and conveyed *us* into the kingdom of the Son of His love,

By Christ.

1 Cor 7:22 For he who is called in the Lord *while* a slave is the Lord's freedman. Likewise he who is called *while* free is Christ's slave.

Gal 4:3–5 Even so we, when we were children, were in bondage under the elements of the world. 4 But when the fullness of the time had come, God sent forth His Son, born of a woman, born under the law, 5 to redeem those who were under the law, that we might receive the adoption as sons.

Gal 5:1 Stand fast therefore in the liberty by which Christ has made us free, and do not be entangled again with a yoke of bondage.

By the Holy Spirit.

Rom 8:15 For you did not receive the spirit of bondage again to fear, but you received the Spirit of adoption by whom we cry out, "Abba, Father."

2 Cor 3:17 Now the Lord is the Spirit; and where the Spirit of the Lord *is*, there *is* liberty.

Proclaimed by Christ.

Luke 4:18 *"The Spirit of the LORD is upon Me, Because He has anointed Me To preach the gospel to the poor; He has sent Me to heal the brokenhearted, To proclaim liberty to the captives And recovery of sight to the blind, To set at liberty those who are oppressed;*

John 8:32 And you shall know the truth, and the truth shall make you free."

Is freedom from

The law.

Rom 7:6 But now we have been delivered from the law, having died to what we were held by, so that we should serve in the newness of the Spirit and not *in* the oldness of the letter.

Rom 8:2 For the law of the Spirit of life in Christ Jesus has made me free from the law of sin and death.

Gal 3:13 Christ has redeemed us from the curse of the law, having become a curse for us (for it is written, *"Cursed is everyone who hangs on a tree"*),

The fear of death.

Heb 2:15 and release those who through fear of death were all their lifetime subject to bondage.

Sin.

Rom 6:7 For he who has died has been freed from sin.

Rom 6:18 And having been set free from sin, you became slaves of righteousness.

Corruption.

Rom 8:21 because the creation itself also will be delivered from the bondage of corruption into the glorious liberty of the children of God.

Bondage of man.

1 Cor 9:19 For though I am free from all *men,* I have made myself a servant to all, that I might win the more;

Jewish ordinances.

Gal 4:3 Even so we, when we were children, were in bondage under the elements of the world.

Col 2:20 Therefore, if you died with Christ from the basic principles of the world, why, as *though* living in the world, do you subject yourselves to regulations—

Called the glorious liberty of the children of God.

Rom 8:21 because the creation itself also will be delivered from the bondage of corruption into the glorious liberty of the children of God.

Saints should

Praise God for.

Ps 116:16–17 O LORD, truly I *am* Your servant; I *am* Your servant, the son of Your maidservant; You have loosed my bonds. 17 I will offer to You the sacrifice of thanksgiving, And will call upon the name of the LORD.

Assert.

Ps 119:45 And I will walk at liberty, For I seek Your precepts.

1 Cor 10:29 "Conscience," I say, not your own, but that of the other. For why is my liberty judged by another *man's* conscience?

Stand fast in.

Gal 2:5 to whom we did not yield submission even for an hour, that the truth of the gospel might continue with you.

Gal 5:1 Stand fast therefore in the liberty by which Christ has made us free, and do not be entangled again with a yoke of bondage.

Not abuse.

1 Cor 8:9 But beware lest somehow this liberty of yours become a stumbling block to those who are weak.

1 Cor 10:29 "Conscience," I say, not your own, but that of the other. For why is my liberty judged by another *man's* conscience?

1 Cor 10:32 Give no offense, either to the Jews or to the Greeks or to the church of God,

Gal 5:13 For you, brethren, have been called to liberty; only do not *use* liberty as an opportunity for the flesh, but through love serve one another.

1 Pet 2:16 as free, yet not using liberty as a cloak for vice, but as bondservants of God.

Portrait of new life.

James 1:25 But he who looks into the perfect law of liberty and continues *in it,* and is not a forgetful hearer but a doer of the work, this one will be blessed in what he does.

James 2:12 So speak and so do as those who will be judged by the law of liberty.

False teachers

Promise, to others.

2 Pet 2:19 While they promise them liberty, they themselves are slaves of corruption; for by whom a person is overcome, by him also he is brought into bondage.

Abuse.

Jude 1:4 For certain men have crept in unnoticed, who long ago were marked out for this condemnation, ungodly men, who turn the grace of our God into lewdness and deny the only Lord God and our Lord Jesus Christ.

Try to destroy.

Gal 2:4 And *this occurred* because of false brethren secretly brought in (who came in by stealth to spy out our liberty which we have in Christ Jesus, that they might bring us into bondage),

The wicked, devoid of.

John 8:34 Jesus answered them, "Most assuredly, I say to you, whoever commits sin is a slave of sin.

Rom 6:20 For when you were slaves of sin, you were free in regard to righteousness.

Typified.

Lev 25:10–17 And you shall consecrate the fiftieth year, and proclaim liberty throughout *all* the land to all its inhabitants. It shall be a Jubilee for you; and each of you shall return to his possession, and each of you shall return to his family. **11** That fiftieth year shall be a Jubilee to you; in it you shall neither sow nor reap what grows of its own accord, nor gather *the grapes* of your untended vine. **12** For it *is* the Jubilee; it shall be holy to you; you shall eat its produce from the field. **13** 'In this Year of Jubilee, each of you shall return to his possession. **14** And if you sell anything to your neighbor or buy from your neighbor's hand, you shall not oppress one another. **15** According to the number of years after the Jubilee you shall buy from your neighbor, and according to the number of years of crops he shall sell to you. **16** According to the multitude of years you shall increase its price, and according to the fewer number of years you shall diminish its price; for he sells to you *according* to the number *of the years* of the crops. **17** Therefore you shall not oppress one another, but you shall fear your God; for I *am* the LORD your God.

Gal 4:22–26 For it is written that Abraham had two sons: the one by a bondwoman, the other by a freewoman. **23** But he *who was* of the bondwoman was born according to the flesh, and he of the freewoman through promise, **24** which things are symbolic. For these are the two covenants: the one from Mount Sinai which gives birth to bondage, which is Hagar— **25** for this Hagar is Mount Sinai in Arabia, and corresponds to Jerusalem which now is, and is in bondage with her children— **26** but the Jerusalem above is free, which is the mother of us all.

Gal 4:31 So then, brethren, we are not children of the bondwoman but of the free.

CHRISTIAN SERVICE

In seeking the edification of others.

Rom 14:19 Therefore let us pursue the things *which make* for peace and the things by which one may edify another.

Rom 15:2 Let each of us please *his* neighbor for *his* good, leading to edification.

1 Thess 5:11 Therefore comfort each other and edify one another, just as you also are doing.

In admonishing and reproving others.

Lev 19:17 'You shall not hate your brother in your heart. You shall surely rebuke your neighbor, and not bear sin because of him.

Eph 5:11 And have no fellowship with the unfruitful works of darkness, but rather expose *them*.

1 Thess 5:14 Now we exhort you, brethren, warn those who are unruly, comfort the fainthearted, uphold the weak, be patient with all.

2 Thess 3:15 Yet do not count *him* as an enemy, but admonish *him* as a brother.

In teaching and exhorting.

Ps 34:11 Come, you children, listen to me; I will teach you the fear of the LORD.

Ps 51:13 *Then* I will teach transgressors Your ways, And sinners shall be converted to You.

Col 3:16 Let the word of Christ dwell in you richly in all wisdom, teaching and admonishing one another in psalms and hymns and spiritual songs, singing with grace in your hearts to the Lord.

Heb 3:13 but exhort one another daily, while it is called *"Today,"* lest any of you be hardened through the deceitfulness of sin.

Heb 10:25 not forsaking the assembling of ourselves together, as *is* the manner of some, but exhorting *one another,* and so much the more as you see the Day approaching.

In interceding for others.

Col 4:3 meanwhile praying also for us, that God would open to us a door for the word, to speak the mystery of Christ, for which I am also in chains,

Heb 13:18 Pray for us; for we are confident that we have a good conscience, in all things desiring to live honorably.

James 5:16 Confess *your* trespasses to one another, and pray for one another, that you may be healed. The effective, fervent prayer of a righteous man avails much.

In aiding ministers in their labors.

Rom 16:3 Greet Priscilla and Aquila, my fellow workers in Christ Jesus,

Rom 16:9 Greet Urbanus, our fellow worker in Christ, and Stachys, my beloved.

2 Cor 11:9 And when I was present with you, and in need, I was a burden to no one, for what I lacked the brethren who came from Macedonia supplied. And in everything I kept myself from being burdensome to you, and so I will keep *myself*.

Phil 4:14–16 Nevertheless you have done well that you shared in my distress. **15** Now you Philippians know also that in the beginning of the gospel, when I departed from Macedonia, no church shared with me concerning giving and receiving but you only. **16** For even in Thessalonica you sent *aid* once and again for my necessities.

3 John 1:6 who have borne witness of your love before the church. *If* you send them forward on their journey in a manner worthy of God, you will do well,

In encouraging the weak.

Is 35:3–4 Strengthen the weak hands, And make firm the feeble knees. **4** Say to those *who are* fearful-hearted, "Be strong, do not fear! Behold, your God will come *with* vengeance, *With* the recompense of God; He will come and save you."

Rom 14:1 Receive one who is weak in the faith, *but* not to disputes over doubtful things.

Rom 15:1 We then who are strong ought to bear with the scruples of the weak, and not to please ourselves.

1 Thess 5:14 Now we exhort you, brethren, warn those who are unruly, comfort the fainthearted, uphold the weak, be patient with all.

In visiting and relieving the poor, the sick, etc.

Lev 25:35 'If one of your brethren becomes poor, and falls into poverty among you, then you shall help him, like a stranger or a sojourner, that he may live with you.

Ps 112:9 He has dispersed abroad, He has given to the

poor; His righteousness endures forever; His horn will be exalted with honor.

Matt 25:36 I *was* naked and you clothed Me; I was sick and you visited Me; I was in prison and you came to Me.'

Acts 20:35 I have shown you in every way, by laboring like this, that you must support the weak. And remember the words of the Lord Jesus, that He said, 'It is more blessed to give than to receive.' "

2 Cor 9:9 As it is written: *"He has dispersed abroad, He has given to the poor; His righteousness endures forever."*

James 1:27 Pure and undefiled religion before God and the Father is this: to visit orphans and widows in their trouble, *and* to keep oneself unspotted from the world.

Should be done willingly and generously.

Ex 35:29 The children of Israel brought a freewill offering to the LORD, all the men and women whose hearts were willing to bring *material* for all kinds of work which the LORD, by the hand of Moses, had commanded to be done.

Ex 36:5–7 and they spoke to Moses, saying, "The people bring much more than enough for the service of the work which the LORD commanded *us* to do." **6** So Moses gave a commandment, and they caused it to be proclaimed throughout the camp, saying, "Let neither man nor woman do any more work for the offering of the sanctuary." And the people were restrained from bringing, **7** for the material they had was sufficient for all the work to be done—indeed too much.

1 Chr 29:9 Then the people rejoiced, for they had offered willingly, because with a loyal heart they had offered willingly to the LORD; and King David also rejoiced greatly.

1 Chr 29:14 But who *am* I, and who *are* my people, That we should be able to offer so willingly as this? For all things *come* from You, And of Your own we have given You.

2 Cor 8:3 For I bear witness that according to *their* ability, yes, and beyond *their* ability, *they were* freely willing,

Encouragement to.

Prov 11:25 The generous soul will be made rich, And he who waters will also be watered himself.

Prov 11:30 The fruit of the righteous *is a* tree of life, And he who wins souls *is* wise.

1 Cor 1:27 But God has chosen the foolish things of the world to put to shame the wise, and God has chosen the weak things of the world to put to shame the things which are mighty;

James 5:19–20 Brethren, if anyone among you wanders from the truth, and someone turns him back, **20** let him know that he who turns a sinner from the error of his way will save a soul from death and cover a multitude of sins.

Illustrated.

Matt 25:14 "For *the kingdom of heaven is* like a man traveling to a far country, *who* called his own servants and delivered his goods to them.

Luke 19:13 So he called ten of his servants, delivered to them ten minas, and said to them, 'Do business till I come.'

CHRISTLIKENESS

Complete.

Rom 8:18 For I consider that the sufferings of this present time are not worthy *to be compared* with the glory which shall be revealed in us.

The goal of salvation.

Rom 8:29 For whom He foreknew, He also predestined *to be* conformed to the image of His Son, that He might be the firstborn among many brethren.

Gal 4:19 My little children, for whom I labor in birth again until Christ is formed in you,

Pursuit of sanctification.

Phil 3:12–14 Not that I have already attained, or am already perfected; but I press on, that I may lay hold of that for which Christ Jesus has also laid hold of me. **13** Brethren, I do not count myself to have apprehended; but one thing I *do*, forgetting those things which are behind and reaching forward to those things which are ahead, **14** I press toward the goal for the prize of the upward call of God in Christ Jesus.

Leaders set the example of.

1 Cor 4:16 Therefore I urge you, imitate me.

Phil 3:17 Brethren, join in following my example, and note those who so walk, as you have us for a pattern.

1 Tim 4:12 Let no one despise your youth, but be an example to the believers in word, in conduct, in love, in spirit, in faith, in purity.

Heb 13:7 Remember those who rule over you, who have spoken the word of God to you, whose faith follow, considering the outcome of *their* conduct.

Progressive transformation into.

2 Cor 3:18 But we all, with unveiled face, beholding as in a mirror the glory of the Lord, are being transformed into the same image from glory to glory, just as by the Spirit of the Lord.

Eph 3:16–20 that He would grant you, according to the riches of His glory, to be strengthened with might through His Spirit in the inner man, **17** that Christ may dwell in your hearts through faith; that you, being rooted and grounded in love, **18** may be able to comprehend with all the saints what *is* the width and length and depth and height— **19** to know the love of Christ which passes knowledge; that you may be filled with all the fullness of God. **20** Now to Him who is able to do exceedingly abundantly above all that we ask or think, according to the power that works in us,

Col 3:9–10 Do not lie to one another, since you have put off the old man with his deeds, **10** and have put on the new *man* who is renewed in knowledge according to the image of Him who created him,

1 Tim 4:15 Meditate on these things; give yourself entirely to them, that your progress may be evident to all.

CHURCH, THE

Belongs to God.

Matt 16:18 And I also say to you that you are Peter, and on this rock I will build My church, and the gates of Hades shall not prevail against it.

Eph 3:21 to Him *be* glory in the church by Christ Jesus to all generations, forever and ever. Amen.

1 Tim 3:15 but if I am delayed, *I write* so that you may know how you ought to conduct yourself in the house of God, which is the church of the living God, the pillar and ground of the truth.

Displays the wisdom of God.

Eph 3:10 to the intent that now the manifold wisdom of God might be made known by the church to the principalities and powers in the heavenly *places,*

Elect.

1 Pet 5:13 She who is in Babylon, elect together with *you,* greets you; and *so does* Mark my son.

Glorious.

Eph 5:27 that He might present her to Himself a glorious church, not having spot or wrinkle or any such thing, but that she should be holy and without blemish.

Clothed in righteousness.

Rev 19:8 And to her it was granted to be arrayed in fine linen, clean and bright, for the fine linen is the righteous acts of the saints.

Believers continually added to, by the Lord.

Acts 2:27 *For You will not leave my soul in Hades, Nor will You allow Your Holy One to see corruption.*

Acts 5:14 And believers were increasingly added to the Lord, multitudes of both men and women,

Acts 11:24 For he was a good man, full of the Holy Spirit and of faith. And a great many people were added to the Lord.

Unity of.

Rom 12:5 so we, *being* many, are one body in Christ, and individually members of one another.

1 Cor 10:17 For we, *though* many, are one bread *and* one body; for we all partake of that one bread.

1 Cor 12:12 For as the body is one and has many members, but all the members of that one body, being many, are one body, so also *is* Christ.

Gal 3:28 There is neither Jew nor Greek, there is neither slave nor free, there is neither male nor female; for you are all one in Christ Jesus.

Saints baptized into, by one Spirit.

1 Cor 12:13 For by one Spirit we were all baptized into one body—whether Jews or Greeks, whether slaves or free—and have all been made to drink into one Spirit.

Ministers commanded to feed.

Acts 20:28 Therefore take heed to yourselves and to all the flock, among which the Holy Spirit has made you overseers, to shepherd the church of God which He purchased with His own blood.

Is edified by the Word.

1 Cor 14:4 He who speaks in a tongue edifies himself, but he who prophesies edifies the church.

1 Cor 14:13 Therefore let him who speaks in a tongue pray that he may interpret.

Eph 4:15–16 but, speaking the truth in love, may grow up in all things into Him who is the head—Christ—

16 from whom the whole body, joined and knit together by what every joint supplies, according to the effective working by which every part does its share, causes growth of the body for the edifying of itself in love.

The wicked persecute.

Acts 8:1–3 Now Saul was consenting to his death. At that time a great persecution arose against the church which was at Jerusalem; and they were all scattered throughout the regions of Judea and Samaria, except the apostles. **2** And devout men carried Stephen *to his burial*, and made great lamentation over him. **3** As for Saul, he made havoc of the church, entering every house, and dragging off men and women, committing *them* to prison.

1 Thess 2:14–15 For you, brethren, became imitators of the churches of God which are in Judea in Christ Jesus. For you also suffered the same things from your own countrymen, just as they *did* from the Judeans, **15** who killed both the Lord Jesus and their own prophets, and have persecuted us; and they do not please God and are contrary to all men,

Not to be despised.

1 Cor 11:22 What! Do you not have houses to eat and drink in? Or do you despise the church of God and shame those who have nothing? What shall I say to you? Shall I praise you in this? I do not praise *you.*

CHURCH DISCIPLINE

Ministers authorized to establish.

Matt 16:19 And I will give you the keys of the kingdom of heaven, and whatever you bind on earth will be bound in heaven, and whatever you loose on earth will be loosed in heaven."

Matt 18:18 "Assuredly, I say to you, whatever you bind on earth will be bound in heaven, and whatever you loose on earth will be loosed in heaven.

Consists in

Maintaining sound doctrine.

1 Tim 1:3 As I urged you when I went into Macedonia—remain in Ephesus that you may charge some that they teach no other doctrine,

Titus 1:13 This testimony is true. Therefore rebuke them sharply, that they may be sound in the faith,

Ordering its affairs.

1 Cor 11:34 But if anyone is hungry, let him eat at home, lest you come together for judgment. And the rest I will set in order when I come.

Titus 1:5 For this reason I left you in Crete, that you should set in order the things that are lacking, and appoint elders in every city as I commanded you—

Rebuking offenders.

1 Tim 5:20 Those who are sinning rebuke in the presence of all, that the rest also may fear.

2 Tim 4:2 Preach the word! Be ready in season *and* out of season. Convince, rebuke, exhort, with all longsuffering and teaching.

Removing obstinate offenders.

1 Cor 5:3–5 For I indeed, as absent in body but present in spirit, have already judged (as though I were present) him who has so done this deed. **4** In the name of our Lord Jesus Christ, when you are gathered together, along with my spirit, with the power of our Lord Jesus Christ, 5 deliver such a one to Satan for the destruction of the flesh, that his spirit may be saved in the day of the Lord Jesus.

1 Cor 5:13 But those who are outside God judges. Therefore *"put away from yourselves the evil person."*

1 Tim 1:20 of whom are Hymenaeus and Alexander, whom I delivered to Satan that they may learn not to blaspheme.

Should be submitted to.

Heb 13:17 Obey those who rule over you, and be submissive, for they watch out for your souls, as those who must give account. Let them do so with joy and not with grief, for that would be unprofitable for you.

Is for edification.

2 Cor 10:8 For even if I should boast somewhat more about our authority, which the Lord gave us for edification and not for your destruction, I shall not be ashamed—

2 Cor 13:10 Therefore I write these things being absent, lest being present I should use sharpness, according to the authority which the Lord has given me for edification and not for destruction.

Decency and order, the objects of.

1 Cor 14:40 Let all things be done decently and in order.

Exercise, in a spirit of charity.

2 Cor 2:6–8 This punishment which *was inflicted* by the majority *is* sufficient for such a man, 7 so that, on the contrary, you *ought* rather to forgive and comfort *him,* lest perhaps such a one be swallowed up with too much sorrow. 8 Therefore I urge you to reaffirm *your* love to him.

Prohibits women preaching.

1 Cor 14:34 Let your women keep silent in the churches, for they are not permitted to speak; but *they are* to be submissive, as the law also says.

1 Tim 2:12 And I do not permit a woman to teach or to have authority over a man, but to be in silence.

CHURCH, EXCELLENCY AND GLORY OF THE

Derived from Christ.

Luke 2:34 Then Simeon blessed them, and said to Mary His mother, "Behold, this *Child* is destined for the fall and rising of many in Israel, and for a sign which will be spoken against

Consist in its

Being the temple of God.

1 Cor 3:16–17 Do you not know that you are the temple of God and *that* the Spirit of God dwells in you? 17 If anyone defiles the temple of God, God will destroy him. For the temple of God is holy, which *temple* you are.

Eph 2:21–22 in whom the whole building, being fitted together, grows into a holy temple in the Lord, 22 in whom you also are being built together for a dwelling place of God in the Spirit.

Being the body of Christ.

Eph 1:22–23 And He put all *things* under His feet, and gave Him *to be* head over all *things* to the church,

23 which is His body, the fullness of Him who fills all in all.

Being the bride of Christ.

Rev 19:7–8 Let us be glad and rejoice and give Him glory, for the marriage of the Lamb has come, and His wife has made herself ready." 8 And to her it was granted to be arrayed in fine linen, clean and bright, for the fine linen is the righteous acts of the saints.

Rev 21:2 Then I, John, saw the holy city, New Jerusalem, coming down out of heaven from God, prepared as a bride adorned for her husband.

Members being righteous.

Rev 19:8 And to her it was granted to be arrayed in fine linen, clean and bright, for the fine linen is the righteous acts of the saints.

Sanctification.

Eph 5:26–27 that He might sanctify and cleanse her with the washing of water by the word, 27 that He might present her to Himself a glorious church, not having spot or wrinkle or any such thing, but that she should be holy and without blemish.

CHURCH, TITLES AND NAMES OF THE

Assembly of the saints.

Ps 89:7 God is greatly to be feared in the assembly of the saints, And to be held in reverence by all *those* around Him.

Assembly of the upright.

Ps 111:1 Praise the LORD! I will praise the LORD with *my* whole heart, In the assembly of the upright and *in* the congregation.

Body of Christ.

Eph 1:22–23 And He put all *things* under His feet, and gave Him *to be* head over all *things* to the church, 23 which is His body, the fullness of Him who fills all in all.

Col 1:24 I now rejoice in my sufferings for you, and fill up in my flesh what is lacking in the afflictions of Christ, for the sake of His body, which is the church,

Bride of Christ.

Rev 21:9 Then one of the seven angels who had the seven bowls filled with the seven last plagues came to me and talked with me, saying, "Come, I will show you the bride, the Lamb's wife."

Church of God.

Acts 20:28 Therefore take heed to yourselves and to all the flock, among which the Holy Spirit has made you overseers, to shepherd the church of God which He purchased with His own blood.

Church of the Living God.

1 Tim 3:15 but if I am delayed, *I write* so that you may know how you ought to conduct yourself in the house of God, which is the church of the living God, the pillar and ground of the truth.

Church of the firstborn.

Heb 12:23 to the general assembly and church of the firstborn *who are* registered in heaven, to God the Judge of all, to the spirits of just men made perfect,

City of the Living God.

Heb 12:22 But you have come to Mount Zion and to the

city of the living God, the heavenly Jerusalem, to an innumerable company of angels,

Congregation of saints.

Ps 149:1 Praise the LORD! Sing to the LORD a new song, *And* His praise in the assembly of saints.

Dwelling place of God.

Eph 2:22 in whom you also are being built together for a dwelling place of God in the Spirit.

Family in heaven and earth.

Eph 3:15 from whom the whole family in heaven and earth is named,

Flock of God.

1 Pet 5:2–3 Shepherd the flock of God which is among you, serving as overseers, not by compulsion but willingly, not for dishonest gain but eagerly; **3** nor as being lords over those entrusted to you, but being examples to the flock;

Fold of Christ.

John 10:16 And other sheep I have which are not of this fold; them also I must bring, and they will hear My voice; and there will be one flock *and* one shepherd.

General assembly of the firstborn.

Heb 12:23 to the general assembly and church of the firstborn *who are* registered in heaven, to God the Judge of all, to the spirits of just men made perfect,

Golden lampstand.

Rev 1:20 The mystery of the seven stars which you saw in My right hand, and the seven golden lampstands: The seven stars are the angels of the seven churches, and the seven lampstands which you saw are the seven churches.

God's building.

1 Cor 3:9 For we are God's fellow workers; you are God's field, *you are* God's building.

God's field.

1 Cor 3:9 For we are God's fellow workers; you are God's field, *you are* God's building.

Heavenly Jerusalem.

Gal 4:26 but the Jerusalem above is free, which is the mother of us all.

Heb 12:22 But you have come to Mount Zion and to the city of the living God, the heavenly Jerusalem, to an innumerable company of angels,

Holy city.

Rev 21:2 Then I, John, saw the holy city, New Jerusalem, coming down out of heaven from God, prepared as a bride adorned for her husband.

Holy hill.

Ps 15:1 LORD, who may abide in Your tabernacle? Who may dwell in Your holy hill?

House of God.

1 Tim 3:15 but if I am delayed, *I write* so that you may know how you ought to conduct yourself in the house of God, which is the church of the living God, the pillar and ground of the truth.

Heb 10:21 and *having* a High Priest over the house of God,

House of Christ.

Heb 3:6 but Christ as a Son over His own house, whose

house we are if we hold fast the confidence and the rejoicing of the hope firm to the end.

Household of God.

Eph 2:19 Now, therefore, you are no longer strangers and foreigners, but fellow citizens with the saints and members of the household of God,

Inheritance.

Ps 28:9 Save Your people, And bless Your inheritance; Shepherd them also, And bear them up forever.

Israel of God.

Gal 6:16 And as many as walk according to this rule, peace and mercy *be* upon them, and upon the Israel of God.

Lamb's wife.

Rev 19:7 Let us be glad and rejoice and give Him glory, for the marriage of the Lamb has come, and His wife has made herself ready."

Rev 21:9 Then one of the seven angels who had the seven bowls filled with the seven last plagues came to me and talked with me, saying, "Come, I will show you the bride, the Lamb's wife."

Mount Zion.

Heb 12:22 But you have come to Mount Zion and to the city of the living God, the heavenly Jerusalem, to an innumerable company of angels,

Mountain of the Lord's house.

Is 2:2 Now it shall come to pass in the latter days *That* the mountain of the LORD's house Shall be established on the top of the mountains, And shall be exalted above the hills; And all nations shall flow to it.

New Jerusalem.

Rev 21:2 Then I, John, saw the holy city, New Jerusalem, coming down out of heaven from God, prepared as a bride adorned for her husband.

Pillar and ground of the truth.

1 Tim 3:15 but if I am delayed, *I write* so that you may know how you ought to conduct yourself in the house of God, which is the church of the living God, the pillar and ground of the truth.

Spiritual house.

1 Pet 2:5 you also, as living stones, are being built up a spiritual house, a holy priesthood, to offer up spiritual sacrifices acceptable to God through Jesus Christ.

Temple of God.

1 Cor 3:16–17 Do you not know that you are the temple of God and *that* the Spirit of God dwells in you? **17** If anyone defiles the temple of God, God will destroy him. For the temple of God is holy, which *temple* you are.

Temple of the living God.

2 Cor 6:16 And what agreement has the temple of God with idols? For you are the temple of the living God. As God has said: *"I will dwell in them And walk among them. I will be their God, And they shall be My people."*

Vineyard.

Matt 21:41 They said to Him, "He will destroy those wicked men miserably, and lease *his* vineyard to other vinedressers who will render to him the fruits in their seasons."

CIRCUMCISION

Instituted by God.

Gen 17:9–10 And God said to Abraham: "As for you, you shall keep My covenant, you and your descendants after you throughout their generations. **10** This is My covenant which you shall keep, between Me and you and your descendants after you: Every male child among you shall be circumcised;

Described.

Gen 17:11 and you shall be circumcised in the flesh of your foreskins, and it shall be a sign of the covenant between Me and you.

Ex 4:25 Then Zipporah took a sharp stone and cut off the foreskin of her son and cast it at Moses' feet, and said, "Surely you are a husband of blood to me!"

Related to the law.

Lev 12:3 And on the eighth day the flesh of his foreskin shall be circumcised.

John 7:22 Moses therefore gave you circumcision (not that it is from Moses, but from the fathers), and you circumcise a man on the Sabbath.

Gal 5:3 And I testify again to every man who becomes circumcised that he is a debtor to keep the whole law.

Called the

Covenant of circumcision.

Acts 7:8 Then He gave him the covenant of circumcision; and so Abraham begot Isaac and circumcised him on the eighth day; and Isaac begot Jacob, and Jacob begot the twelve patriarchs.

Circumcision in the flesh.

Eph 2:11 Therefore remember that you, once Gentiles in the flesh—who are called Uncircumcision by what is called the Circumcision made in the flesh by hands—

A painful and bloody rite.

Ex 4:26 So He let him go. Then she said, "You are a husband of blood!"—because of the circumcision.

Josh 5:8 So it was, when they had finished circumcising all the people, that they stayed in their places in the camp till they were healed.

Promises to Abraham previous to.

Rom 4:9 Does this blessedness then come upon the circumcised only, or upon the uncircumcised also? For we say that faith was accounted to Abraham for righteousness.

Rom 4:13 For the promise that he would be the heir of the world was not to Abraham or to his seed through the law, but through the righteousness of faith.

A seal of the covenant.

Gen 17:11 and you shall be circumcised in the flesh of your foreskins, and it shall be a sign of the covenant between Me and you.

Rom 4:11 And he received the sign of circumcision, a seal of the righteousness of the faith which he had while still uncircumcised, that he might be the father of all those who believe, though they are uncircumcised, that righteousness might be imputed to them also,

Spiritual significance of.

Rom 2:28–29 For he is not a Jew who is one outwardly, nor is circumcision that which is outward in the flesh;

29 but he is a Jew who is one inwardly; and circumcision is that of the heart, in the Spirit, not in the letter; whose praise is not from men but from God.

Phil 3:3 For we are the circumcision, who worship God in the Spirit, rejoice in Christ Jesus, and have no confidence in the flesh,

Col 2:11 In Him you were also circumcised with the circumcision made without hands, by putting off the body of the sins of the flesh, by the circumcision of Christ,

Necessary to enjoying the privileges of the Jewish state.

Ex 12:48 And when a stranger dwells with you and wants to keep the Passover to the LORD, let all his males be circumcised, and then let him come near and keep it; and he shall be as a native of the land. For no uncircumcised person shall eat it.

Ezek 44:7 When you brought in foreigners, uncircumcised in heart and uncircumcised in flesh, to be in My sanctuary to defile it—My house—and when you offered My food, the fat and the blood, then they broke My covenant because of all your abominations.

Was performed

On males home-born and bought.

Gen 17:12–13 He who is eight days old among you shall be circumcised, every male child in your generations, he who is born in your house or bought with money from any foreigner who is not your descendant. **13** He who is born in your house and he who is bought with your money must be circumcised, and My covenant shall be in your flesh for an everlasting covenant.

On the eighth day.

Gen 17:12 He who is eight days old among you shall be circumcised, every male child in your generations, he who is born in your house or bought with money from any foreigner who is not your descendant.

Lev 12:3 And on the eighth day the flesh of his foreskin shall be circumcised.

Even on the sabbath day.

John 7:22–23 Moses therefore gave you circumcision (not that it is from Moses, but from the fathers), and you circumcise a man on the Sabbath. **23** If a man receives circumcision on the Sabbath, so that the law of Moses should not be broken, are you angry with Me because I made a man completely well on the Sabbath?

With knives of flint.

Ex 4:25 Then Zipporah took a sharp stone and cut off the foreskin of her son and cast it at Moses' feet, and said, "Surely you are a husband of blood to me!"

Josh 5:3 So Joshua made flint knives for himself, and circumcised the sons of Israel at the hill of the foreskins.

By the heads of families.

Gen 17:23 So Abraham took Ishmael his son, all who were born in his house and all who were bought with his money, every male among the men of Abraham's house, and circumcised the flesh of their foreskins that very same day, as God had said to him.

Ex 4:25 Then Zipporah took a sharp stone and cut off

the foreskin of her son and cast *it* at *Moses'* feet, and said, "Surely you *are* a husband of blood to me!"

By persons in authority.

Josh 5:3 So Joshua made flint knives for himself, and circumcised the sons of Israel at the hill of the foreskins.

In the presence of the family, etc.

Luke 1:58–61 When her neighbors and relatives heard how the Lord had shown great mercy to her, they rejoiced with her. **59** So it was, on the eighth day, that they came to circumcise the child; and they would have called him by the name of his father, Zacharias. **60** His mother answered and said, "No; he shall be called John." **61** But they said to her, "There is no one among your relatives who is called by this name."

First on Abraham and his family.

Gen 17:24–27 Abraham *was* ninety-nine years old when he was circumcised in the flesh of his foreskin. **25** And Ishmael his son *was* thirteen years old when he was circumcised in the flesh of his foreskin. **26** That very same day Abraham was circumcised, and his son Ishmael; **27** and all the men of his house, born in the house or bought with money from a foreigner, were circumcised with him.

Not in the wilderness.

Josh 5:5 For all the people who came out had been circumcised, but all the people born in the wilderness, on the way as they came out of Egypt, had not been circumcised.

By Joshua at Gilgal.

Josh 5:2 At that time the LORD said to Joshua, "Make flint knives for yourself, and circumcise the sons of Israel again the second time."

Josh 5:7 Then Joshua circumcised their sons *whom* He raised up in their place; for they were uncircumcised, because they had not been circumcised on the way.

Accompanied with naming the child.

Gen 21:3–4 And Abraham called the name of his son who was born to him—whom Sarah bore to him—Isaac. **4** Then Abraham circumcised his son Isaac when he was eight days old, as God had commanded him.

Luke 1:59 So it was, on the eighth day, that they came to circumcise the child; and they would have called him by the name of his father, Zacharias.

Luke 2:21 And when eight days were completed for the circumcision of the Child, His name was called JESUS, the name given by the angel before He was conceived in the womb.

Punishment for neglecting.

Gen 17:14 And the uncircumcised male child, who is not circumcised in the flesh of his foreskin, that person shall be cut off from his people; he has broken My covenant."

Ex 4:24 And it came to pass on the way, at the encampment, that the LORD met him and sought to kill him.

Ex 4:26 So He let him go. Then she said, "*You are* a husband of blood!"—because of the circumcision.

Without faith, vain.

Rom 3:30 since *there is* one God who will justify the cir-

cumcised by faith and the uncircumcised through faith.

Gal 5:6 For in Christ Jesus neither circumcision nor uncircumcision avails anything, but faith working through love.

Without obedience, vain.

Rom 2:25 For circumcision is indeed profitable if you keep the law; but if you are a breaker of the law, your circumcision has become uncircumcision.

1 Cor 7:19 Circumcision is nothing and uncircumcision is nothing, but keeping the commandments of God *is what matters.*

The Jews

Identified by.

Acts 10:45 And those of the circumcision who believed were astonished, as many as came with Peter, because the gift of the Holy Spirit had been poured out on the Gentiles also.

Gal 2:9 and when James, Cephas, and John, who seemed to be pillars, perceived the grace that had been given to me, they gave me and Barnabas the right hand of fellowship, that we *should go* to the Gentiles and they to the circumcised.

Held it unlawful to intermarry with the uncircumcised.

Gen 34:14 And they said to them, "We cannot do this thing, to give our sister to one who is uncircumcised, for that *would be* a reproach to us.

Judg 14:3 Then his father and mother said to him, "*Is there* no woman among the daughters of your brethren, or among all my people, that you must go and get a wife from the uncircumcised Philistines?" And Samson said to his father, "Get her for me, for she pleases me well."

Had no interaction with the uncircumcised.

Acts 10:28 Then he said to them, "You know how unlawful it is for a Jewish man to keep company with or go to one of another nation. But God has shown me that I should not call any man common or unclean.

Acts 11:3 saying, "You went in to uncircumcised men and ate with them!"

Gal 2:12 for before certain men came from James, he would eat with the Gentiles; but when they came, he withdrew and separated himself, fearing those who were of the circumcision.

Despised the uncircumcised.

1 Sam 14:6 Then Jonathan said to the young man who bore his armor, "Come, let us go over to the garrison of these uncircumcised; it may be that the LORD will work for us. For nothing restrains the LORD from saving by many or by few."

1 Sam 17:26 Then David spoke to the men who stood by him, saying, "What shall be done for the man who kills this Philistine and takes away the reproach from Israel? For who *is* this uncircumcised Philistine, that he should defy the armies of the living God?"

Matt 15:26–27 But He answered and said, "It is not good to take the children's bread and throw *it* to the little dogs." **27** And she said, "Yes, Lord, yet even the little dogs eat the crumbs which fall from their masters' table."

Eph 2:11 Therefore remember that you, once Gentiles in the flesh—who are called Uncircumcision by what is called the Circumcision made in the flesh by hands—

Eph 2:15 having abolished in His flesh the enmity, *that is,* the law of commandments *contained* in ordinances, so as to create in Himself one new man *from* the two, *thus* making peace,

Sometimes performed on slain enemies.

1 Sam 18:25–27 Then Saul said, "Thus you shall say to David: 'The king does not desire any dowry but one hundred foreskins of the Philistines, to take vengeance on the king's enemies.' " But Saul thought to make David fall by the hand of the Philistines. **26** So when his servants told David these words, it pleased David well to become the king's son-in-law. Now the days had not expired; **27** therefore David arose and went, he and his men, and killed two hundred men of the Philistines. And David brought their foreskins, and they gave them in full count to the king, that he might become the king's son-in-law. Then Saul gave him Michal his daughter as a wife.

2 Sam 3:14 So David sent messengers to Ishbosheth, Saul's son, saying, "Give *me* my wife Michal, whom I betrothed to myself for a hundred foreskins of the Philistines."

Abolished by the gospel.

Eph 2:11 Therefore remember that you, once Gentiles in the flesh—who are called Uncircumcision by what is called the Circumcision made in the flesh by hands—

Eph 2:15 having abolished in His flesh the enmity, *that is,* the law of commandments *contained* in ordinances, so as to create in Himself one new man *from* the two, *thus* making peace,

Col 3:11 where there is neither Greek nor Jew, circumcised nor uncircumcised, barbarian, Scythian, slave *nor* free, but Christ *is* all and in all.

Performed on Timothy for sake of the Jews.

Acts 16:3 Paul wanted to have him go on with him. And he took *him* and circumcised him because of the Jews who were in that region, for they all knew that his father was Greek.

Necessity of, denied by Paul.

Gal 2:3–5 Yet not even Titus who *was* with me, being a Greek, was compelled to be circumcised. **4** And *this occurred because* of false brethren secretly brought in (who came in by stealth to spy out our liberty which we have in Christ Jesus, that they might bring us into bondage), **5** to whom we did not yield submission even for an hour, that the truth of the gospel might continue with you.

Necessity of, asserted by false teachers.

Acts 15:24 Since we have heard that some who went out from us have troubled you with words, unsettling your souls, saying, "You *must* be circumcised and keep the law"—to whom we gave no *such* commandment—

Gal 6:12 As many as desire to make a good showing in the flesh, these *would* compel you to be circumcised, only that they may not suffer persecution for the cross of Christ.

Phil 3:2 Beware of dogs, beware of evil workers, beware of the mutilation!

Titus 1:10 For there are many insubordinate, both idle talkers and deceivers, especially those of the circumcision,

Trusting in, a denial of Christ.

Gal 3:3–4 Are you so foolish? Having begun in the Spirit, are you now being made perfect by the flesh? **4** Have you suffered so many things in vain—if indeed *it was* in vain?

Gal 5:3–4 And I testify again to every man who becomes circumcised that he is a debtor to keep the whole law. **4** You have become estranged from Christ, you who *attempt to* be justified by law; you have fallen from grace.

Paul denounced for opposing.

Acts 21:21 but they have been informed about you that you teach all the Jews who are among the Gentiles to forsake Moses, saying that they ought not to circumcise *their* children nor to walk according to the customs.

Illustrative of

Readiness to hear and obey.

Jer 6:10 To whom shall I speak and give warning, That they may hear? Indeed their ear *is* uncircumcised, And they cannot give heed. Behold, the word of the LORD is a reproach to them; They have no delight in it.

Purity of heart.

Deut 10:16 Therefore circumcise the foreskin of your heart, and be stiff-necked no longer.

Deut 30:6 And the LORD your God will circumcise your heart and the heart of your descendants, to love the LORD your God with all your heart and with all your soul, that you may live.

Purity of speech.

Ex 6:12 And Moses spoke before the LORD, saying, "The children of Israel have not heeded me. How then shall Pharaoh heed me, for I *am* of uncircumcised lips?"

CITIES

First mention of.

Gen 4:17 And Cain knew his wife, and she conceived and bore Enoch. And he built a city, and called the name of the city after the name of his son—Enoch.

Designed for dwellings.

Ps 107:7 And He led them forth by the right way, That they might go to a city for a dwelling place.

Ps 107:36 There He makes the hungry dwell, That they may establish a city for a dwelling place,

Construction features

Stone and wood.

Ps 102:14 For Your servants take pleasure in her stones, And show favor to her dust.

Ezek 26:12 They will plunder your riches and pillage your merchandise; they will break down your walls and destroy your pleasant houses; they will lay your stones, your timber, and your soil in the midst of the water.

Brick and mortar.

Gen 11:3 Then they said to one another, "Come, let us

make bricks and bake *them* thoroughly." They had brick for stone, and they had asphalt for mortar.

Ex 1:11 Therefore they set taskmasters over them to afflict them with their burdens. And they built for Pharaoh supply cities, Pithom and Raamses.

Ex 1:14 And they made their lives bitter with hard bondage—in mortar, in brick, and in all manner of service in the field. All their service in which they made them serve *was* with rigor.

Solid foundations.

Ezra 6:3 In the first year of King Cyrus, King Cyrus issued a decree *concerning* the house of God at Jerusalem: "Let the house be rebuilt, the place where they offered sacrifices; and let the foundations of it be firmly laid, its height sixty cubits *and* its width sixty cubits,

Rev 21:14 Now the wall of the city had twelve foundations, and on them were the names of the twelve apostles of the Lamb.

Compact.

Ps 122:3 Jerusalem is built As a city that is compact together,

Often of a square form.

Rev 21:16 The city is laid out as a square; its length is as great as its breadth. And he measured the city with the reed: twelve thousand furlongs. Its length, breadth, and height are equal.

Arranged in streets and lanes.

Num 22:39 So Balaam went with Balak, and they came to Kirjath Huzoth.

Zech 8:5 The streets of the city Shall be full of boys and girls Playing in its streets.'

Luke 14:21 So that servant came and reported these things to his master. Then the master of the house, being angry, said to his servant, 'Go out quickly into the streets and lanes of the city, and bring in here *the* poor and *the* maimed and *the* lame and *the* blind.'

Entered through gates.

Gen 34:24 And all who went out of the gate of his city heeded Hamor and Shechem his son; every male was circumcised, all who went out of the gate of his city.

Neh 13:19 So it was, at the gates of Jerusalem, as it began to be dark before the Sabbath, that I commanded the gates to be shut, and charged that they must not be opened till after the Sabbath. Then I posted *some* of my servants at the gates, *so that* no burdens would be brought in on the Sabbath day.

Neh 13:22 And I commanded the Levites that they should cleanse themselves, and that they should go and guard the gates, to sanctify the Sabbath day. Remember me, O my God, *concerning* this also, and spare me according to the greatness of Your mercy!

Surrounded with walls.

Deut 1:28 Where can we go up? Our brethren have discouraged our hearts, saying, "The people *are* greater and taller than we; the cities *are* great and fortified up to heaven; moreover we have seen the sons of the Anakim there." '

Deut 3:5 All these cities *were* fortified with high walls, gates, and bars, besides a great many rural towns.

Often fortified.

2 Chr 11:5–10 So Rehoboam dwelt in Jerusalem, and built cities for defense in Judah. **6** And he built Bethlehem, Etam, Tekoa, **7** Beth Zur, Sochoh, Adullam, **8** Gath, Mareshah, Ziph, **9** Adoraim, Lachish, Azekah, **10** Zorah, Aijalon, and Hebron, which are in Judah and Benjamin, fortified cities.

2 Chr 11:23 He dealt wisely, and dispersed some of his sons throughout all the territories of Judah and Benjamin, to every fortified city; and he gave them provisions in abundance. He also sought many wives *for them.*

Ps 48:12–13 Walk about Zion, And go all around her. Count her towers; **13** Mark well her bulwarks; Consider her palaces; That you may tell *it* to the generation following.

Jer 4:5 Declare in Judah and proclaim in Jerusalem, and say: "Blow the trumpet in the land; Cry, 'Gather together,' And say, 'Assemble yourselves, And let us go into the fortified cities.'

Dan 11:15 So the king of the North shall come and build a siege mound, and take a fortified city; and the forces of the South shall not withstand *him.* Even his choice troops *shall have* no strength to resist.

Sometimes had suburbs.

Num 35:2 "Command the children of Israel that they give the Levites cities to dwell in from the inheritance of their possession, and you shall *also* give the Levites common-land around the cities.

Josh 21:3 So the children of Israel gave to the Levites from their inheritance, at the commandment of the LORD, these cities and their common-lands:

Artificial mode of supplying water to.

2 Kin 18:17 Then the king of Assyria sent *the* Tartan, *the* Rabsaris, *and the* Rabshakeh from Lachish, with a great army against Jerusalem, to King Hezekiah. And they went up and came to Jerusalem. When they had come up, they went and stood by the aqueduct from the upper pool, which *was* on the highway to the Fuller's Field.

2 Kin 20:20 Now the rest of the acts of Hezekiah—all his might, and how he made a pool and a tunnel and brought water into the city—*are* they not written in the book of the chronicles of the kings of Judah?

Furnished with supplies.

2 Chr 11:11–12 And he fortified the strongholds, and put captains in them, and stores of food, oil, and wine. **12** Also in every city *he put* shields and spears, and made them very strong, having Judah and Benjamin on his side.

Garrisoned in war.

2 Chr 17:2 And he placed troops in all the fortified cities of Judah, and set garrisons in the land of Judah and in the cities of Ephraim which Asa his father had taken.

2 Chr 17:19 These served the king, besides those the king put in the fortified cities throughout all Judah.

Often had citadels.

Judg 9:51 But there was a strong tower in the city, and all the men and women—all the people of the city—fled there and shut themselves in; then they went up to the top of the tower.

Location features

Beside rivers.

Ps 137:1 By the rivers of Babylon, There we sat down, yea, we wept When we remembered Zion.

On hills.

Matt 5:14 "You are the light of the world. A city that is set on a hill cannot be hidden.

Luke 4:29 and rose up and thrust Him out of the city; and they led Him to the brow of the hill on which their city was built, that they might throw Him down over the cliff.

Rev 17:9 "Here *is* the mind which has wisdom: The seven heads are seven mountains on which the woman sits.

In plains.

Gen 11:2 And it came to pass, as they journeyed from the east, that they found a plain in the land of Shinar, and they dwelt there.

Gen 11:4 And they said, "Come, let us build ourselves a city, and a tower whose top *is* in the heavens; let us make a name for ourselves, lest we be scattered abroad over the face of the whole earth."

Gen 13:12 Abram dwelt in the land of Canaan, and Lot dwelt in the cities of the plain and pitched *his* tent even as far as Sodom.

In desert places.

2 Chr 8:4 He also built Tadmor in the wilderness, and all the storage cities which he built in Hamath.

Ps 107:35–36 He turns a wilderness into pools of water, And dry land into watersprings. 36 There He makes the hungry dwell, That they may establish a city for a dwelling place,

In pleasant situations.

2 Kin 2:19 Then the men of the city said to Elisha, "Please notice, the situation of this city *is* pleasant, as my lord sees; but the water *is* bad, and the ground barren."

Ps 48:2 Beautiful in elevation, The joy of the whole earth, *Is* Mount Zion *on* the sides of the north, The city of the great King.

Were named after

The family of the founder.

Gen 4:17 And Cain knew his wife, and she conceived and bore Enoch. And he built a city, and called the name of the city after the name of his son—Enoch.

Judg 18:29 And they called the name of the city Dan, after the name of Dan their father, who was born to Israel. However, the name of the city formerly *was* Laish.

The proprietor of the land.

1 Kin 16:24 And he bought the hill of Samaria from Shemer for two talents of silver; then he built on the hill, and called the name of the city which he built, Samaria, after the name of Shemer, owner of the hill.

The country in which built.

Dan 4:29–30 At the end of the twelve months he was walking about the royal palace of Babylon. 30 The king spoke, saying, "Is not this great Babylon, that I have built for a royal dwelling by my mighty power and for the honor of my majesty?"

Numerous.

Josh 15:21 The cities at the limits of the tribe of the children of Judah, toward the border of Edom in the South, were Kabzeel, Eder, Jagur,

1 Chr 2:22 Segub begot Jair, who had twenty-three cities in the land of Gilead.

Jer 2:28 But where *are* your gods that you have made for yourselves? Let them arise, If they can save you in the time of your trouble; For *according to* the number of your cities Are your gods, O Judah.

Densely populated.

Jon 4:11 And should I not pity Nineveh, that great city, in which are more than one hundred and twenty thousand persons who cannot discern between their right hand and their left—and much livestock?"

Often impressive.

Gen 10:12 and Resen between Nineveh and Calah (that *is* the principal city).

Deut 6:10 "So it shall be, when the LORD your God brings you into the land of which He swore to your fathers, to Abraham, Isaac, and Jacob, to give you large and beautiful cities which you did not build,

Dan 4:30 The king spoke, saying, "Is not this great Babylon, that I have built for a royal dwelling by my mighty power and for the honor of my majesty?"

Jon 3:3 So Jonah arose and went to Nineveh, according to the word of the LORD. Now Nineveh was an exceedingly great city, a three-day journey *in extent.*

Of great antiquity.

Gen 10:11–12 From that land he went to Assyria and built Nineveh, Rehoboth Ir, Calah, 12 and Resen between Nineveh and Calah (that *is* the principal city).

Sometimes insignificant.

Gen 19:20 See now, this city *is* near *enough* to flee to, and it *is* a little one; please let me escape there (*is* it not a little one?) and my soul shall live."

Eccl 9:14 *There was* a little city with few men in it; and a great king came against it, besieged it, and built great snares around it.

Different kinds of,

Royal.

Num 21:26 For Heshbon *was* the city of Sihon king of the Amorites, who had fought against the former king of Moab, and had taken all his land from his hand as far as the Arnon.

Josh 10:2 that they feared greatly, because Gibeon *was* a great city, like one of the royal cities, and because it *was* greater than Ai, and all its men *were* mighty.

2 Sam 12:26 Now Joab fought against Rabbah of the people of Ammon, and took the royal city.

Fenced.

Josh 10:20 Then it happened, while Joshua and the children of Israel made an end of slaying them with a very great slaughter, till they had finished, that those who escaped entered fortified cities.

Is 36:1 Now it came to pass in the fourteenth year of King Hezekiah *that* Sennacherib king of Assyria came up against all the fortified cities of Judah and took them.

Supply.

Ex 1:11 Therefore they set taskmasters over them to afflict them with their burdens. And they built for Pharaoh supply cities, Pithom and Raamses.

Commercial.

Is 23:11 He stretched out His hand over the sea, He shook the kingdoms; The LORD has given a commandment against Canaan To destroy its strongholds.

Ezek 27:3 and say to Tyre, 'You who are situated at the entrance of the sea, merchant of the peoples on many coastlands, thus says the Lord GOD: "O Tyre, you have said, 'I *am* perfect in beauty.'

Chariot.

2 Chr 1:14 And Solomon gathered chariots and horsemen; he had one thousand four hundred chariots and twelve thousand horsemen, whom he stationed in the chariot cities and with the king in Jerusalem.

2 Chr 9:25 Solomon had four thousand stalls for horses and chariots, and twelve thousand horsemen whom he stationed in the chariot cities and with the king at Jerusalem.

Store.

2 Chr 8:4 He also built Tadmor in the wilderness, and all the storage cities which he built in Hamath.

2 Chr 8:6 also Baalath and all the storage cities that Solomon had, and all the chariot cities and the cities of the cavalry, and all that Solomon desired to build in Jerusalem, in Lebanon, and in all the land of his dominion.

Levitical.

Lev 25:32–33 Nevertheless the cities of the Levites, *and* the houses in the cities of their possession, the Levites may redeem at any time. **33** And if a man purchases a house from the Levites, then the house that was sold in the city of his possession shall be released in the Jubilee; for the houses in the cities of the Levites *are* their possession among the children of Israel.

Num 35:7–8 So all the cities you will give to the Levites *shall be* forty-eight; these *you shall give* with their common-land. **8** And the cities which you will give *shall be* from the possession of the children of Israel; from the larger *tribe* you shall give many, from the smaller you shall give few. Each shall give some of its cities to the Levites, in proportion to the inheritance that each receives."

Refuge.

Num 35:6 "Now among the cities which you will give to the Levites *you shall appoint* six cities of refuge, to which a manslayer may flee. And to these you shall add forty-two cities.

Prosperity of.

Gen 49:13 "Zebulun shall dwell by the haven of the sea; He *shall become* a haven for ships, And his border shall adjoin Sidon.

Deut 33:18–19 And of Zebulun he said: "Rejoice, Zebulun, in your going out, And Issachar in your tents! **19** They shall call the peoples *to* the mountain; There they shall offer sacrifices of righteousness; For they shall partake *of* the abundance of the seas And *of* treasures hidden in the sand."

Ezek 28:5 By your great wisdom in trade you have increased your riches, And your heart is lifted up because of your riches),"

Infested by dogs.

1 Kin 14:11 The dogs shall eat whoever belongs to Jeroboam and dies in the city, and the birds of the air shall eat whoever dies in the field; for the LORD has spoken!" '

Ps 59:6 At evening they return, They growl like a dog, And go all around the city.

Ps 59:14 And at evening they return, They growl like a dog, And go all around the city.

Under governors.

2 Chr 33:14 After this he built a wall outside the City of David on the west side of Gihon, in the valley, as far as the entrance of the Fish Gate; and *it* enclosed Ophel, and he raised it to a very great height. Then he put military captains in all the fortified cities of Judah.

2 Cor 11:32 In Damascus the governor, under Aretas the king, was guarding the city of the Damascenes with a garrison, desiring to arrest me;

Provided with judges.

Deut 16:18 "You shall appoint judges and officers in all your gates, which the LORD your God gives you, according to your tribes, and they shall judge the people with just judgment.

2 Chr 19:5 Then he set judges in the land throughout all the fortified cities of Judah, city by city,

Protected at night by watchmen.

Ps 127:1 Unless the LORD builds the house, They labor in vain who build it; Unless the LORD guards the city, The watchman stays awake in vain.

Song 5:7 The watchmen who went about the city found me. They struck me, they wounded me; The keepers of the walls Took my veil away from me.

Is 21:11 The burden against Dumah. He calls to me out of Seir, "Watchman, what of the night? Watchman, what of the night?"

Afforded refuge in times of danger.

Jer 8:14–16 "Why do we sit still? Assemble yourselves, And let us enter the fortified cities, And let us be silent there. For the LORD our God has put us to silence And given us water of gall to drink, Because we have sinned against the LORD. **15** "We looked for peace, but no good *came;* And for a time of health, and there was trouble! **16** The snorting of His horses was heard from Dan. The whole land trembled at the sound of the neighing of His strong ones; For they have come and devoured the land and all that is in it, The city and those who dwell in it."

Often deserted on the approach of an enemy.

1 Sam 31:7 And when the men of Israel who *were* on the other side of the valley, and *those* who *were* on the other side of the Jordan, saw that the men of Israel had fled and that Saul and his sons were dead, they forsook the cities and fled; and the Philistines came and dwelt in them.

Jer 4:20 Destruction upon destruction is cried, For the whole land is plundered. Suddenly my tents are plundered, *And* my curtains in a moment.

Frequently

Stormed.

Josh 8:3–7 So Joshua arose, and all the people of war, to go up against Ai; and Joshua chose thirty thousand mighty men of valor and sent them away by night. **4** And he commanded them, saying: "Behold, you shall lie in ambush against the city, behind the city. Do not go very far from the city, but all of you be ready. **5** Then I and all the people who *are* with me will approach the city; and it will come about, when they come out against us as at the first, that we shall flee before them. **6** For they will come out after us till we have drawn them from the city, for they will say, *'They are* fleeing before us as at the first.' Therefore we will flee before them. **7** Then you shall rise from the ambush and seize the city, for the LORD your God will deliver it into your hand.

Judg 9:44 Then Abimelech and the company that *was* with him rushed forward and stood at the entrance of the gate of the city; and the *other* two companies rushed upon all who *were* in the fields and killed them.

Besieged.

Deut 28:52 "They shall besiege you at all your gates until your high and fortified walls, in which you trust, come down throughout all your land; and they shall besiege you at all your gates throughout all your land which the LORD your God has given you.

2 Kin 19:24–25 I have dug and drunk strange water, And with the soles of my feet I have dried up All the brooks of defense." **25** 'Did you not hear long ago *How* I made it, From ancient times that I formed it? Now I have brought it to pass, That you should be For crushing fortified cities *into* heaps of ruins.

Pillaged.

Is 13:16 Their children also will be dashed to pieces before their eyes; Their houses will be plundered And their wives ravished.

Jer 20:5 Moreover I will deliver all the wealth of this city, all its produce, and all its precious things; all the treasures of the kings of Judah I will give into the hand of their enemies, who will plunder them, seize them, and carry them to Babylon.

Wasted by pestilence.

1 Sam 5:11 So they sent and gathered together all the lords of the Philistines, and said, "Send away the ark of the God of Israel, and let it go back to its own place, so that it does not kill us and our people." For there was a deadly destruction throughout all the city; the hand of God was very heavy there.

Wasted by famine.

Jer 52:6 By the fourth month, on the ninth day of the month, the famine had become so severe in the city that there was no food for the people of the land.

Amos 4:6 "Also I gave you cleanness of teeth in all your cities. And lack of bread in all your places; Yet you have not returned to Me," Says the LORD.

Depopulated.

Is 17:9 In that day his strong cities will be as a forsaken bough And an uppermost branch, Which they left because of the children of Israel; And there will be desolation.

Ezek 26:19 "For thus says the Lord GOD: 'When I make you a desolate city, like cities that are not inhabited, when I bring the deep upon you, and great waters cover you,

Burned.

Judg 20:38 Now the appointed signal between the men of Israel and the men in ambush was that they would make a great cloud of smoke rise up from the city,

Judg 20:40 But when the cloud began to rise from the city in a column of smoke, the Benjamites looked behind them, and there was the whole city going up *in smoke* to heaven.

Is 1:7 Your country *is* desolate, Your cities *are* burned with fire; Strangers devour your land in your presence; And *it is* desolate, as overthrown by strangers.

Destroyed.

Judg 9:45 So Abimelech fought against the city all that day; he took the city and killed the people who *were* in it; and he demolished the city and sowed it with salt.

Is 25:2 For You have made a city a ruin, A fortified city a ruin, A palace of foreigners to be a city no more; It will never be rebuilt.

Difficulty of taking, alluded to.

Prov 18:19 A brother offended *is harder to win* than a strong city, And contentions *are* like the bars of a castle.

Jer 1:18–19 For behold, I have made you this day A fortified city and an iron pillar, And bronze walls against the whole land— Against the kings of Judah, Against its princes, Against its priests, And against the people of the land. **19** They will fight against you, But they shall not prevail against you. For I *am* with you," says the LORD, "to deliver you."

Illustrative of

Believers.

Matt 5:14 "You are the light of the world. A city that is set on a hill cannot be hidden.

Church triumphant.

Rev 21:2 Then I, John, saw the holy city, New Jerusalem, coming down out of heaven from God, prepared as a bride adorned for her husband.

Rev 22:19 and if anyone takes away from the words of the book of this prophecy, God shall take away his part from the Book of Life, from the holy city, and *from* the things which are written in this book.

Heavenly inheritance.

Heb 11:16 But now they desire a better, that is, a heavenly *country.* Therefore God is not ashamed to be called their God, for He has prepared a city for them.

The apostasy.

Rev 16:10 Then the fifth angel poured out his bowl on the throne of the beast, and his kingdom became full of darkness; and they gnawed their tongues because of the pain.

Rev 17:18 And the woman whom you saw is that great city which reigns over the kings of the earth."

Riches.

Prov 10:15 The rich man's wealth *is* his strong city; The destruction of the poor *is* their poverty.

CITIES OF REFUGE

Purpose of.

Ex 21:13 However, if he did not lie in wait, but God delivered *him* into his hand, then I will appoint for you a place where he may flee.

Num 35:11 then you shall appoint cities to be cities of refuge for you, that the manslayer who kills any person accidentally may flee there.

Josh 20:3 that the slayer who kills a person accidentally *or* unintentionally may flee there; and they shall be your refuge from the avenger of blood.

Names of.

Deut 4:41–43 Then Moses set apart three cities on this side of the Jordan, toward the rising of the sun, **42** that the manslayer might flee there, who kills his neighbor unintentionally, without having hated him in time past, and that by fleeing to one of these cities he might live: **43** Bezer in the wilderness on the plateau for the Reubenites, Ramoth in Gilead for the Gadites, and Golan in Bashan for the Manassites.

Josh 20:7–8 So they appointed Kedesh in Galilee, in the mountains of Naphtali, Shechem in the mountains of Ephraim, and Kirjath Arba (which *is* Hebron) in the mountains of Judah. **8** And on the other side of the Jordan, by Jericho eastward, they assigned Bezer in the wilderness on the plain, from the tribe of Reuben, Ramoth in Gilead, from the tribe of Gad, and Golan in Bashan, from the tribe of Manasseh.

Required to be

Easy of access.

Deut 19:3 You shall prepare roads for yourself, and divide into three parts the territory of your land which the LORD your God is giving you to inherit, that any manslayer may flee there.

Is 62:10 Go through, Go through the gates! Prepare the way for the people; Build up, Build up the highway! Take out the stones, Lift up a banner for the peoples!

Open to all who unintentionally killed someone.

Josh 20:4 And when he flees to one of those cities, and stands at the entrance of the gate of the city, and declares his case in the hearing of the elders of that city, they shall take him into the city as one of them, and give him a place, that he may dwell among them.

Strangers might take advantage of.

Num 35:15 These six cities shall be for refuge for the children of Israel, for the stranger, and for the sojourner among them, that anyone who kills a person accidentally may flee there.

Those admitted to,

Were put on trial.

Num 35:12 They shall be cities of refuge for you from the avenger, that the manslayer may not die until he stands before the congregation in judgment.

Num 35:24 then the congregation shall judge between the manslayer and the avenger of blood according to these judgments.

Not protected outside of.

Num 35:26–27 But if the manslayer at any time goes outside the limits of the city of refuge where he fled, **27** and the avenger of blood finds him outside the limits of his city of refuge, and the avenger of blood kills the manslayer, he shall not be guilty of blood,

Obliged to remain in, until the high priest's death.

Num 35:25 So the congregation shall deliver the manslayer from the hand of the avenger of blood, and the congregation shall return him to the city of refuge where he had fled, and he shall remain there until the death of the high priest who was anointed with the holy oil.

Num 35:28 because he should have remained in his city of refuge until the death of the high priest. But after the death of the high priest the manslayer may return to the land of his possession.

Afforded no asylum to murderers.

Ex 21:14 "But if a man acts with premeditation against his neighbor, to kill him by treachery, you shall take him from My altar, that he may die.

Num 35:16–21 'But if he strikes him with an iron implement, so that he dies, he *is* a murderer; the murderer shall surely be put to death. **17** And if he strikes him with a stone in the hand, by which one could die, and he does die, he *is* a murderer; the murderer shall surely be put to death. **18** Or *if* he strikes him with a wooden hand weapon, by which one could die, and he does die, he *is* a murderer; the murderer shall surely be put to death. **19** The avenger of blood himself shall put the murderer to death; when he meets him, he shall put him to death. **20** If he pushes him out of hatred or, while lying in wait, hurls something at him so that he dies, **21** or in enmity he strikes him with his hand so that he dies, the one who struck *him* shall surely be put to death. He *is* a murderer. The avenger of blood shall put the murderer to death when he meets him.

Illustrative of

The hope of the gospel.

Heb 6:18 that by two immutable things, in which it *is* impossible for God to lie, we might have strong consolation, who have fled for refuge to lay hold of the hope set before *us.*

(The way to) Christ.

John 14:6 Jesus said to him, "I am the way, the truth, and the life. No one comes to the Father except through Me.

CITIZENSHIP

Qualities of good.

Prov 24:21 My son, fear the LORD and the king; Do not associate with those given to change;

1 Pet 1:17 And if you call on the Father, who without partiality judges according to each one's work, conduct yourselves throughout the time of your stay *here* in fear;

1 Pet 2:13–17 Therefore submit yourselves to every ordinance of man for the Lord's sake, whether to the king as supreme, **14** or to governors, as to those who are sent by him for the punishment of evildoers and *for the* praise of those who do good. **15** For this is the will of God, that by doing good you may put to silence the ignorance of foolish men— **16** as free, yet not using liberty as a cloak for vice, but as bondservants of God. **17** Honor all *people.* Love the brotherhood. Fear God. Honor the king.

Paul's Roman.

Acts 16:37 But Paul said to them, "They have beaten us openly, uncondemned Romans, *and* have thrown *us* into prison. And now do they put us out secretly? No indeed! Let them come themselves and get us out."

Acts 22:25–29 And as they bound him with thongs, Paul said to the centurion who stood by, "Is it lawful for you to scourge a man who is a Roman, and uncondemned?" **26** When the centurion heard *that,* he went and told the commander, saying, "Take care what you do, for this man is a Roman." **27** Then the commander came and said to him, "Tell me, are you a Roman?" He said, "Yes." **28** The commander answered, "With a large sum I obtained this citizenship." And Paul said, "But I was born *a citizen.*" **29** Then immediately those who were about to examine him withdrew from him; and the commander was also afraid after he found out that he was a Roman, and because he had bound him.

The believer's heavenly.

Phil 3:20 For our citizenship is in heaven, from which we also eagerly wait for the Savior, the Lord Jesus Christ,

Rev 3:12 He who overcomes, I will make him a pillar in the temple of My God, and he shall go out no more. I will write on him the name of My God and the name of the city of My God, the New Jerusalem, which comes down out of heaven from My God. And *I will write on him* My new name.

CLEAN, CLEANSE

Spiritually.

Lev 11:44–45 For I *am* the LORD your God. You shall therefore consecrate yourselves, and you shall be holy; for I *am* holy. Neither shall you defile yourselves with any creeping thing that creeps on the earth. **45** For I *am* the LORD who brings you up out of the land of Egypt, to be your God. You shall therefore be holy, for I *am* holy.

Ceremonial.

Lev 14:2 "This shall be the law of the leper for the day of his cleansing: He shall be brought to the priest.

Lev 16:30 For on that day *the priest* shall make atonement for you, to cleanse you, *that* you may be clean from all your sins before the LORD.

Regarding the law of leprosy.

Lev 13:59 "This *is* the law of the leprous plague in a garment of wool or linen, either in the warp or woof, or in anything made of leather, to pronounce it clean or to pronounce it unclean."

Lev 14:57 to teach when *it is* unclean and when *it is* clean. This *is* the law of leprosy."

Portrayal of what is.

Is 1:18 "Come now, and let us reason together," Says the LORD, "Though your sins are like scarlet, They shall be as white as snow; Though they are red like crimson, They shall be as wool.

All foods declared.

Acts 10:12–15 In it were all kinds of four-footed animals of the earth, wild beasts, creeping things, and birds of the air. **13** And a voice came to him, "Rise, Peter; kill and eat." **14** But Peter said, "Not so, Lord! For I have never eaten anything common or unclean." **15** And a voice *spoke* to him again the second time, "What God has cleansed you must not call common."

From disease.

Luke 17:11–19 Now it happened as He went to Jerusalem that He passed through the midst of Samaria and Galilee. **12** Then as He entered a certain village, there met Him ten men who were lepers, who stood afar off. **13** And they lifted up *their* voices and said, "Jesus, Master, have mercy on us!" **14** So when He saw *them,* He said to them, "Go, show yourselves to the priests." And so it was that as they went, they were cleansed. **15** And one of them, when he saw that he was healed, returned, and with a loud voice glorified God, **16** and fell down on *his* face at His feet, giving Him thanks. And he was a Samaritan. **17** So Jesus answered and said, "Were there not ten cleansed? But where *are* the nine? **18** Were there not any found who returned to give glory to God except this foreigner?" **19** And He said to him, "Arise, go your way. Your faith has made you well."

Morally pure.

Phil 4:8 Finally, brethren, whatever things are true, whatever things *are* noble, whatever things *are* just, whatever things *are* pure, whatever things *are* lovely, whatever things *are* of good report, if *there is* any virtue and if *there is* anything praiseworthy—meditate on these things.

CLOUDS

Formed from the sea.

1 Kin 18:44 Then it came to pass the seventh *time,* that he said, "There is a cloud, as small as a man's hand, rising out of the sea!" So he said, "Go up, say to Ahab, 'Prepare *your chariot,* and go down before the rain stops you.' "

Amos 9:6 He who builds His layers in the sky, And has founded His strata in the earth; Who calls for the waters of the sea, And pours them out on the face of the earth— The LORD *is* His name.

Power and wisdom of God exhibited.

Gen 9:14 It shall be, when I bring a cloud over the earth, that the rainbow shall be seen in the cloud;

Job 26:8–9 He binds up the water in His thick clouds, Yet the clouds are not broken under it. **9** He covers the face of *His* throne, *And* spreads His cloud over it.

Job 36:27–28 For He draws up drops of water, Which distill as rain from the mist, **28** Which the clouds drop down *And* pour abundantly on man.

Job 37:10–11 By the breath of God ice is given, And the broad waters are frozen. **11** Also with moisture He saturates the thick clouds; He scatters His bright clouds.

Job 37:15–16 Do you know when God dispatches them, And causes the light of His cloud to shine? **16** Do you know how the clouds are balanced, Those wondrous works of Him who is perfect in knowledge?

Ps 135:6–7 Whatever the LORD pleases He does, In heaven and in earth, In the seas and in all deep places. **7** He causes the vapors to ascend from the ends of the earth; He makes lightning for the rain; He brings the wind out of His treasuries.

Ps 147:5 Great *is* our Lord, and mighty in power; His understanding *is* infinite.

Ps 147:8 Who covers the heavens with clouds, Who prepares rain for the earth, Who makes grass to grow on the mountains.

Prov 3:20 By His knowledge the depths were broken up, And clouds drop down the dew.

Prov 8:28 When He established the clouds above, When He strengthened the fountains of the deep,

Jer 10:13 When He utters His voice, *There is* a multitude of waters in the heavens: "And He causes the vapors to ascend from the ends of the earth. He makes lightning for the rain, He brings the wind out of His treasuries."

Jer 51:16 When He utters *His* voice— *There is* a multitude of waters in the heavens: "He causes the vapors to ascend from the ends of the earth; He makes lightnings for the rain; He brings the wind out of His treasuries."

Made for the glory of God.

Ps 148:4 Praise Him, you heavens of heavens, And you waters above the heavens!

Called the

Clouds of heaven.

Dan 7:13 "I was watching in the night visions, And behold, *One* like the Son of Man, Coming with the clouds of heaven! He came to the Ancient of Days, And they brought Him near before Him.

Matt 24:30 Then the sign of the Son of Man will appear in heaven, and then all the tribes of the earth will mourn, and they will see the Son of Man coming on the clouds of heaven with power and great glory.

Windows of heaven.

Gen 7:11 In the six hundredth year of Noah's life, in the second month, the seventeenth day of the month, on that day all the fountains of the great deep were broken up, and the windows of heaven were opened.

Is 24:18 And it shall be *That* he who flees from the noise of the fear Shall fall into the pit, And he who comes up from the midst of the pit Shall be caught in the snare; For the windows from on high are open, And the foundations of the earth are shaken.

Bottles of heaven.

Job 38:37 Who can number the clouds by wisdom? Or who can pour out the bottles of heaven,

Chambers of God.

Ps 104:3 He lays the beams of His upper chambers in the waters, Who makes the clouds His chariot, Who walks on the wings of the wind,

Ps 104:13 He waters the hills from His upper chambers; The earth is satisfied with the fruit of Your works.

Waters above the firmament.

Gen 1:7 Thus God made the firmament, and divided the waters which *were* under the firmament from the waters which *were* above the firmament; and it was so.

Dust of God's feet.

Nah 1:3 The LORD *is* slow to anger and great in power, And will not at all acquit *the wicked.* The LORD has His way In the whirlwind and in the storm, And the clouds *are* the dust of His feet.

Different kinds of, mentioned

White.

Rev 14:14 Then I looked, and behold, a white cloud, and on the cloud sat *One* like the Son of Man, having on His head a golden crown, and in His hand a sharp sickle.

Bright.

Job 37:11 Also with moisture He saturates the thick clouds; He scatters His bright clouds.

Zech 10:1 Ask the LORD for rain In the time of the latter rain. The LORD will make flashing clouds; He will give them showers of rain, Grass in the field for everyone.

Thick.

Job 22:14 Thick clouds cover Him, so that He cannot see, And He walks above the circle of heaven.'

Job 37:11 Also with moisture He saturates the thick clouds; He scatters His bright clouds.

Black.

1 Kin 18:45 Now it happened in the meantime that the sky became black with clouds and wind, and there was a heavy rain. So Ahab rode away and went to Jezreel.

Swift.

Is 19:1 The burden against Egypt. Behold, the LORD rides on a swift cloud, And will come into Egypt; The idols of Egypt will totter at His presence, And the heart of Egypt will melt in its midst.

Great.

Ezek 1:4 Then I looked, and behold, a whirlwind was coming out of the north, a great cloud with raging fire engulfing itself; and brightness *was* all around it and radiating out of its midst like the color of amber, out of the midst of the fire.

Small.

1 Kin 18:44 Then it came to pass the seventh *time,* that he said, "There is a cloud, as small as a man's hand, rising out of the sea!" So he said, "Go up, say to Ahab, 'Prepare *your chariot,* and go down before the rain stops you.' "

Activities of,

Often cover the heavens.

Ps 147:8 Who covers the heavens with clouds, Who prepares rain for the earth, Who makes grass to grow on the mountains.

Often obscure the sun, etc.

Job 36:32 He covers *His* hands with lightning, And commands it to strike.

Ezek 32:7 When I put out your light, I will cover the heavens, and make its stars dark; I will cover the sun with a cloud, And the moon shall not give her light.

Often dispersed by the wind.

Hos 13:3 Therefore they shall be like the morning cloud And like the early dew that passes away, Like chaff blown off from a threshing floor And like smoke from a chimney.

To give rain.

Judg 5:4 "LORD, when You went out from Seir, When You marched from the field of Edom, The earth trembled and the heavens poured, The clouds also poured water;

1 Kin 18:44–45 Then it came to pass the seventh *time*, that he said, "There is a cloud, as small as a man's hand, rising out of the sea!" So he said, "Go up, say to Ahab, 'Prepare *your chariot*, and go down before the rain stops you.'" **45** Now it happened in the meantime that the sky became black with clouds and wind, and there was a heavy rain. So Ahab rode away and went to Jezreel.

Ps 104:13–14 He waters the hills from His upper chambers; The earth is satisfied with the fruit of Your works. **14** He causes the grass to grow for the cattle, And vegetation for the service of man, That he may bring forth food from the earth,

Luke 12:54 Then He also said to the multitudes, "Whenever *you see* a cloud rising out of the west, immediately you say, 'A shower is coming'; and so it is.

To supply dew.

Prov 3:20 By His knowledge the depths were broken up, And clouds drop down the dew.

Is 18:4 For so the LORD said to me, "I will take My rest, And I will look from My dwelling place Like clear heat in sunshine, Like a cloud of dew in the heat of harvest."

To moderate heat.

Is 25:5 You will reduce the noise of aliens, As heat in a dry place; *As* heat in the shadow of a cloud, The song of the terrible ones will be diminished.

Produce thunder and lightning.

Ps 77:17–18 The clouds poured out water; The skies sent out a sound; Your arrows also flashed about. **18** The voice of Your thunder *was* in the whirlwind; The lightnings lit up the world; The earth trembled and shook.

The rainbow appears in.

Gen 9:13–14 I set My rainbow in the cloud, and it shall be for the sign of the covenant between Me and the earth. **14** It shall be, when I bring a cloud over the earth, that the rainbow shall be seen in the cloud;

Sometimes the instrument of God's judgments.

Gen 7:11–12 In the six hundredth year of Noah's life, in the second month, the seventeenth day of the month, on that day all the fountains of the great deep were broken up, and the windows of heaven were opened. **12** And the rain was on the earth forty days and forty nights.

Job 37:13 He causes it to come, Whether for correction, Or for His land, Or for mercy.

Ps 77:17 The clouds poured out water; The skies sent out a sound; Your arrows also flashed about.

Man's knowledge of.

Job 36:29 Indeed, can *anyone* understand the spreading of clouds, The thunder from His canopy?

Job 37:15–16 Do you know when God dispatches them, And causes the light of His cloud to shine? **16** Do you know how the clouds are balanced, Those wondrous works of Him who is perfect in knowledge?

Job 38:34 "Can you lift up your voice to the clouds, That an abundance of water may cover you?

Job 38:37 Who can number the clouds by wisdom? Or who can pour out the bottles of heaven,

Illustrative of

Hostile armies.

Jer 4:13 "Behold, he shall come up like clouds, And his chariots like a whirlwind. His horses are swifter than eagles. Woe to us, for we are plundered!"

Ezek 38:9 You will ascend, coming like a storm, covering the land like a cloud, you and all your troops and many peoples with you."

Ezek 38:16 You will come up against My people Israel like a cloud, to cover the land. It will be in the latter days that I will bring you against My land, so that the nations may know Me, when I am hallowed in you, O Gog, before their eyes."

The sins of men.

Is 44:22 I have blotted out, like a thick cloud, your transgressions, And like a cloud, your sins. Return to Me, for I have redeemed you."

The judgments of God.

Lam 2:1 How the Lord has covered the daughter of Zion With a cloud in His anger! He cast down from heaven to the earth The beauty of Israel, And did not remember His footstool In the day of His anger.

Ezek 30:3 For the day *is* near, Even the day of the LORD *is* near; It will be a day of clouds, the time of the Gentiles.

Ezek 34:12 As a shepherd seeks out his flock on the day he is among his scattered sheep, so will I seek out My sheep and deliver them from all the places where they were scattered on a cloudy and dark day.

Joel 2:2 A day of darkness and gloominess, A day of clouds and thick darkness, Like the morning *clouds* spread over the mountains. A people *come*, great and strong, The like of whom has never been; Nor will there ever be any *such* after them, Even for many successive generations.

The unsearchableness of God.

2 Sam 22:12 He made darkness canopies around Him, Dark waters *and* thick clouds of the skies.

Ps 97:2 Clouds and darkness surround Him; Righteousness and justice *are* the foundation of His throne.

Ezek 1:4 Then I looked, and behold, a whirlwind was coming out of the north, a great cloud with raging fire engulfing itself; and brightness *was* all around it and radiating out of its midst like the color of amber, out of the midst of the fire.

The power and greatness of God.

Ps 104:3 He lays the beams of His upper chambers in the waters, Who makes the clouds His chariot, Who walks on the wings of the wind,

Is 19:1 The burden against Egypt. Behold, the LORD rides on a swift cloud, And will come into Egypt; The idols of Egypt will totter at His presence, And the heart of Egypt will melt in its midst.

The goodness and prosperity of hypocrites.

Hos 6:4 "O Ephraim, what shall I do to you? O Judah, what shall I do to you? For your faithfulness is like a morning cloud, And like the early dew it goes away.

Hos 13:3 Therefore they shall be like the morning cloud And like the early dew that passes away, Like chaff blown off from a threshing floor And like smoke from a chimney.

False teachers.

2 Pet 2:17 These are wells without water, clouds carried by a tempest, for whom is reserved the blackness of darkness forever.

Jude 1:12 These are spots in your love feasts, while they feast with you without fear, serving *only* themselves. *They are* clouds without water, carried about by the winds; late autumn trees without fruit, twice dead, pulled up by the roots;

The fraudulent.

Prov 25:14 Whoever falsely boasts of giving *Is like* clouds and wind without rain.

Wise and good rulers.

2 Sam 23:3–4 The God of Israel said, The Rock of Israel spoke to me: 'He who rules over men *must be* just, Ruling in the fear of God. **4** And *he shall be* like the light of the morning *when* the sun rises, A morning without clouds, *Like* the tender grass *springing* out of the earth, By clear shining after rain.'

Prov 16:15 In the light of the king's face *is* life, And his favor *is* like a cloud of the latter rain.

CLOUD OF GLORY

First manifestation of.

Ex 13:20–21 So they took their journey from Succoth and camped in Etham at the edge of the wilderness. **21** And the LORD went before them by day in a pillar of cloud to lead the way, and by night in a pillar of fire to give them light, so as to go by day and night.

Names for,

The cloud.

Ex 34:5 Now the LORD descended in the cloud and stood with him there, and proclaimed the name of the LORD.

Pillar of cloud and fire.

Ex 13:22 He did not take away the pillar of cloud by day or the pillar of fire by night *from* before the people.

Cloudy pillar.

Ex 33:9–10 And it came to pass, when Moses entered the tabernacle, that the pillar of cloud descended and stood *at* the door of the tabernacle, and *the* LORD talked with Moses. **10** All the people saw the pillar of cloud standing *at* the tabernacle door, and all the people rose and worshiped, each man *in* his tent door.

Cloud of the Lord.

Num 10:34 And the cloud of the LORD *was* above them by day when they went out from the camp.

The presence of God.

Ex 33:14–15 And He said, "My Presence will go *with you,* and I will give you rest." **15** Then he said to Him, "If Your Presence does not go *with us,* do not bring us up from here.

God's glory manifested in.

Ex 16:10 Now it came to pass, as Aaron spoke to the whole congregation of the children of Israel, that they looked toward the wilderness, and behold, the glory of the LORD appeared in the cloud.

Ex 24:16 Now the glory of the LORD rested on Mount Sinai, and the cloud covered it six days. And on the seventh day He called to Moses out of the midst of the cloud.

Ex 34:5 Now the LORD descended in the cloud and stood with him there, and proclaimed the name of the LORD.

Ex 40:35 And Moses was not able to enter the tabernacle of meeting, because the cloud rested above it, and the glory of the LORD filled the tabernacle.

Num 11:25 Then the LORD came down in the cloud, and spoke to him, and took of the Spirit that *was* upon him, and placed *the same* upon the seventy elders; and it happened, when the Spirit rested upon them, that they prophesied, although they never did *so* again.

Ps 99:7 He spoke to them in the cloudy pillar; They kept His testimonies and the ordinance He gave them.

Was designed to

Guide Israel.

Ex 13:21–22 And the LORD went before them by day in a pillar of cloud to lead the way, and by night in a pillar of fire to give them light, so as to go by day and night. **22** He did not take away the pillar of cloud by day or the pillar of fire by night *from* before the people.

Ex 40:36–38 Whenever the cloud was taken up from above the tabernacle, the children of Israel would go onward in all their journeys. **37** But if the cloud was not taken up, then they did not journey till the day that it was taken up. **38** For the cloud of the LORD *was* above the tabernacle by day, and fire was over it by night, in the sight of all the house of Israel, throughout all their journeys.

Num 9:17–23 Whenever the cloud was taken up from above the tabernacle, after that the children of Israel would journey; and in the place where the cloud settled, there the children of Israel would pitch their tents. **18** At the command of the LORD the children of Israel would journey, and at the command of the LORD they would camp; as long as the cloud stayed above the tabernacle they remained encamped. **19** Even when the cloud continued long, many days above the tabernacle, the children of Israel kept the charge of the LORD and did not journey. **20** So it was, when the cloud was above the tabernacle a few days: according to the command of the LORD they would remain encamped, and according to the command of the LORD they would journey. **21** So it was, when the cloud remained only from evening until morning: when the cloud was taken up in the morning, then they would journey; whether by day or by night, whenever the cloud was taken up, they would journey. **22** *Whether it was* two days, a month, or a year that the cloud remained above the tabernacle, the children of Israel would remain encamped and not journey; but when it was taken up, they would journey. **23** At the command of the LORD they remained encamped, and at the command of the LORD they journeyed; they kept the charge of the LORD, at the command of the LORD by the hand of Moses.

Neh 9:19 Yet in Your manifold mercies You did not forsake them in the wilderness. The pillar of the cloud did not depart from them by day, To lead them on the road; Nor the pillar of fire by night, To show them light, And the way they should go.

Ps 105:39 He spread a cloud for a covering, And fire to give light in the night.

Defend Israel.

Ex 14:19 And the Angel of God, who went before the camp of Israel, moved and went behind them; and the pillar of cloud went from before them and stood behind them.

Ps 105:39 He spread a cloud for a covering, And fire to give light in the night.

Cover the tabernacle.

Ex 40:34 Then the cloud covered the tabernacle of meeting, and the glory of the LORD filled the tabernacle.

Num 9:15 Now on the day that the tabernacle was raised up, the cloud covered the tabernacle, the tent of the Testimony; from evening until morning it was above the tabernacle like the appearance of fire.

Was dark to the enemies of Israel.

Ex 14:20 So it came between the camp of the Egyptians and the camp of Israel. Thus it was a cloud and darkness *to the one*, and it gave light by night *to the other*, so that the one did not come near the other all that night.

Was the Shekinah over the mercy seat.

Lev 16:2 and the LORD said to Moses: "Tell Aaron your brother not to come at *just* any time into the Holy *Place* inside the veil, before the mercy seat which *is* on the ark, lest he die; for I will appear in the cloud above the mercy seat.

Manifested in the temple of Solomon.

1 Kin 8:10–11 And it came to pass, when the priests came out of the holy *place,* that the cloud filled the house of the LORD, **11** so that the priests could not continue ministering because of the cloud; for the glory of the LORD filled the house of the LORD.

2 Chr 5:13 indeed it came to pass, when the trumpeters and singers *were* as one, to make one sound to be heard in praising and thanking the LORD, and when they lifted up their voice with the trumpets and cymbals and instruments of music, and praised the LORD, *saying:* "For He *is* good, For His mercy *endures* forever," that the house, the house of the LORD, was filled with a cloud,

Ezek 10:4 Then the glory of the LORD went up from the cherub, *and paused* over the threshold of the temple; and the house was filled with the cloud, and the court was full of the brightness of the LORD's glory.

Special appearances of,

At the murmuring for bread.

Ex 16:10 Now it came to pass, as Aaron spoke to the whole congregation of the children of Israel, that they looked toward the wilderness, and behold, the glory of the LORD appeared in the cloud.

At the giving of the law.

Ex 19:9 And the LORD said to Moses, "Behold, I come to you in the thick cloud, that the people may hear when I speak with you, and believe you forever." So Moses told the words of the people to the LORD.

Ex 19:16 Then it came to pass on the third day, in the morning, that there were thunderings and lightnings, and a thick cloud on the mountain; and the sound of the trumpet was very loud, so that all the people who *were* in the camp trembled.

Ex 24:16–18 Now the glory of the LORD rested on Mount Sinai, and the cloud covered it six days. And on the seventh day He called to Moses out of the midst of the cloud. **17** The sight of the glory of the LORD *was* like a consuming fire on the top of the mountain in the eyes of the children of Israel. **18** So Moses went into the midst of the cloud and went up into the mountain. And Moses was on the mountain forty days and forty nights.

At the sedition of Aaron and Miriam.

Num 12:5 Then the LORD came down in the pillar of cloud and stood *in* the door of the tabernacle, and called Aaron and Miriam. And they both went forward.

At the murmuring of Israel on the report of the spies.

Num 14:10 And all the congregation said to stone them with stones. Now the glory of the LORD appeared in the tabernacle of meeting before all the children of Israel.

At the rebellion of Korah, etc.

Num 16:19 And Korah gathered all the congregation against them at the door of the tabernacle of meeting. Then the glory of the LORD appeared to all the congregation.

At the murmuring of Israel on account of Korah's death.

Num 16:42 Now it happened, when the congregation had gathered against Moses and Aaron, that they turned toward the tabernacle of meeting; and suddenly the cloud covered it, and the glory of the LORD appeared.

At Christ's transfiguration.

Matt 17:5 While he was still speaking, behold, a bright cloud overshadowed them; and suddenly a voice came out of the cloud, saying, "This is My beloved Son, in whom I am well pleased. Hear Him!"

At Christ's ascension.

Acts 1:9 Now when He had spoken these things, while they watched, He was taken up, and a cloud received Him out of their sight.

Our Lord shall make his second appearance in.

Luke 21:27 Then they will see the Son of Man coming in a cloud with power and great glory.

Acts 1:11 who also said, "Men of Galilee, why do you stand gazing up into heaven? This *same* Jesus, who was taken up from you into heaven, will so come in like manner as you saw Him go into heaven."

Illustrative of

The glory of Christ.

Rev 10:1 I saw still another mighty angel coming down from heaven, clothed with a cloud. And a rainbow *was* on his head, his face *was* like the sun, and his feet like pillars of fire.

The protection of God's people.

Is 4:5 then the LORD will create above every dwelling place of Mount Zion, and above her assemblies, a cloud and smoke by day and the shining of a flaming fire by night. For over all the glory there *will be a* covering.

COMFORT

Through Noah.

Gen 5:29 And he called his name Noah, saying, "This

one will comfort us concerning our work and the toil of our hands, because of the ground which the Lord has cursed."

Failure of Job's friends to.

Job 16:2–5 "I have heard many such things; Miserable comforters *are* you all! **3** Shall words of wind have an end? Or what provokes you that you answer? **4** I also could speak as you *do*, If your soul were in my soul's place. I could heap up words against you, And shake my head at you; **5** *But* I would strengthen you with my mouth, And the comfort of my lips would relieve *your* grief.

Divine.

Ps 37:24 Though he fall, he shall not be utterly cast down; For the Lord upholds *him with* His hand.

Ps 145:14 The Lord upholds all who fall, And raises up all *who are* bowed down.

Mic 7:8 Do not rejoice over me, my enemy; When I fall, I will arise; When I sit in darkness, The Lord *will be* a light to me.

Found in God's Word.

Ps 119:50 This *is* my comfort in my affliction, For Your word has given me life.

For the captives.

Is 40:1–2 "Comfort, yes, comfort My people!" Says your God. **2** "Speak comfort to Jerusalem, and cry out to her, That her warfare is ended, That her iniquity is pardoned; For she has received from the Lord's hand Double for all her sins."

Zech 1:17 "Again proclaim, saying, 'Thus says the Lord of hosts: "My cities shall again spread out through prosperity; The Lord will again comfort Zion, And will again choose Jerusalem." ' "

For the weak and oppressed.

Is 42:3 A bruised reed He will not break, And smoking flax He will not quench; He will bring forth justice for truth.

For those who mourn over sin.

Matt 5:4 Blessed *are* those who mourn, For they shall be comforted.

Provided by Christ.

Is 61:1–2 "The Spirit of the Lord God *is* upon Me, Because the Lord has anointed Me To preach good tidings to the poor; He has sent Me to heal the brokenhearted, To proclaim liberty to the captives, And the opening of the prison to *those who are* bound; **2** To proclaim the acceptable year of the Lord, And the day of vengeance of our God; To comfort all who mourn,

Phil 2:1 Therefore if *there is* any consolation in Christ, if any comfort of love, if any fellowship of the Spirit, if any affection and mercy,

Provided by the Spirit.

John 16:7 Nevertheless I tell you the truth. It is to your advantage that I go away; for if I do not go away, the Helper will not come to you; but if I depart, I will send Him to you.

As encouragement.

Rom 15:4 For whatever things were written before were written for our learning, that we through the patience and comfort of the Scriptures might have hope.

2 Cor 1:3–6 Blessed *be* the God and Father of our Lord Jesus Christ, the Father of mercies and God of all comfort, **4** who comforts us in all our tribulation, that we may be able to comfort those who are in any trouble, with the comfort with which we ourselves are comforted by God. **5** For as the sufferings of Christ abound in us, so our consolation also abounds through Christ. **6** Now if we are afflicted, *it is* for your consolation and salvation, which is effective for enduring the same sufferings which we also suffer. Or if we are comforted, *it is* for your consolation and salvation.

Heb 10:24–25 And let us consider one another in order to stir up love and good works, **25** not forsaking the assembling of ourselves together, as *is* the manner of some, but exhorting *one another,* and so much the more as you see the Day approaching.

1 Thess 4:18 Therefore comfort one another with these words.

COMMERCE

Described.

1 Kin 5:8 Then Hiram sent to Solomon, saying: I have considered *the message* which you sent me, *and* I will do all you desire concerning the cedar and cypress logs.

1 Kin 5:11 And Solomon gave Hiram twenty thousand kors of wheat *as* food for his household, and twenty kors of pressed oil. Thus Solomon gave to Hiram year by year.

1 Kin 10:28–29 Also Solomon had horses imported from Egypt and Keveh; the king's merchants bought them in Keveh at the *current* price. **29** Now a chariot that was imported from Egypt cost six hundred *shekels* of silver, and a horse one hundred and fifty; and thus, through their agents, they exported *them* to all the kings of the Hittites and the kings of Syria.

Ezek 27:19 Dan and Javan paid for your wares, traversing back and forth. Wrought iron, cassia, and cane were among your merchandise.

Defined as

Trade.

Gen 34:10 So you shall dwell with us, and the land shall be before you. Dwell and trade in it, and acquire possessions for yourselves in it."

Gen 42:34 And bring your youngest brother to me; so I shall know that you *are* not spies, but *that* you *are* honest *men.* I will grant your brother to you, and you may trade in the land.' "

Ezek 17:4 He cropped off its topmost young twig And carried it to a land of trade; He set it in a city of merchants.

Matt 25:16 Then he who had received the five talents went and traded with them, and made another five talents.

Buying and selling.

James 4:13 Come now, you who say, "Today or tomorrow we will go to such and such a city, spend a year there, buy and sell, and make a profit";

Articles of, called

Merchandise.

Ezek 26:12 They will plunder your riches and pillage

your merchandise; they will break down your walls and destroy your pleasant houses; they will lay your stones, your timber, and your soil in the midst of the water.

Wares.

Jer 10:17 Gather up your wares from the land, O inhabitant of the fortress!

Ezek 27:16 Syria *was* your merchant because of the abundance of goods you made. They gave you for your wares emeralds, purple, embroidery, fine linen, corals, and rubies.

Cargo.

Jon 1:5 Then the mariners were afraid; and every man cried out to his god, and threw the cargo that *was* in the ship into the sea, to lighten the load. But Jonah had gone down into the lowest parts of the ship, had lain down, and was fast asleep.

Persons engaged in, called

Merchants.

Gen 37:28 Then Midianite traders passed by; so *the brothers* pulled Joseph up and lifted him out of the pit, and sold him to the Ishmaelites for twenty *shekels* of silver. And they took Joseph to Egypt.

2 Chr 9:14 besides *what* the traveling merchants and traders brought. And all the kings of Arabia and governors of the country brought gold and silver to Solomon.

Prov 31:24 She makes linen garments and sells *them*, And supplies sashes for the merchants.

Is 23:8 Who has taken this counsel against Tyre, the crowning *city*, Whose merchants *are* princes, Whose traders *are* the honorable of the earth?

Sellers and buyers.

Is 24:2 And it shall be: As with the people, so with the priest; As with the servant, so with his master; As with the maid, so with her mistress; As with the buyer, so with the seller; As with the lender, so with the borrower; As with the creditor, so with the debtor.

Carried on in marketplaces.

Ezek 27:12 "Tarshish *was* your merchant because of your many luxury goods. They gave you silver, iron, tin, and lead for your goods.

Matt 11:16 "But to what shall I liken this generation? It is like children sitting in the marketplaces and calling to their companions,

Inland, by caravans.

Job 6:19 The caravans of Tema look, The travelers of Sheba hope for them.

Is 21:13 The burden against Arabia. In the forest in Arabia you will lodge, O you traveling companies of Dedanites.

Maritime, by ships.

2 Chr 8:18 And Hiram sent him ships by the hand of his servants, and servants who knew the sea. They went with the servants of Solomon to Ophir, and acquired four hundred and fifty talents of gold from there, and brought it to King Solomon.

2 Chr 9:21 For the king's ships went to Tarshish with the servants of Hiram. Once every three years the merchant ships came, bringing gold, silver, ivory, apes, and monkeys.

Increased the wealth of nations and individuals.

2 Chr 9:20–22 All King Solomon's drinking vessels *were* gold, and all the vessels of the House of the Forest of Lebanon *were* pure gold. Not *one was* silver, for this was accounted as nothing in the days of Solomon. **21** For the king's ships went to Tarshish with the servants of Hiram. Once every three years the merchant ships came, bringing gold, silver, ivory, apes, and monkeys. **22** So King Solomon surpassed all the kings of the earth in riches and wisdom.

Prov 31:14–18 She is like the merchant ships, She brings her food from afar. **15** She also rises while it is yet night, And provides food for her household, And a portion for her maidservants. **16** She considers a field and buys it; From her profits she plants a vineyard. **17** She girds herself with strength, And strengthens her arms. **18** She perceives that her merchandise *is* good, And her lamp does not go out by night.

Ezek 28:4–5 With your wisdom and your understanding You have gained riches for yourself, And gathered gold and silver into your treasuries; **5** By your great wisdom in trade you have increased your riches, And your heart is lifted up because of your riches),"

Carried on by the

Ishmaelites.

Gen 37:25 And they sat down to eat a meal. Then they lifted their eyes and looked, and there was a company of Ishmaelites, coming from Gilead with their camels, bearing spices, balm, and myrrh, on their way to carry *them* down to Egypt.

Egyptians. Gen 42:2–34

Ethiopians.

Is 45:14 Thus says the LORD: "The labor of Egypt and merchandise of Cush And of the Sabeans, men of stature, Shall come over to you, and they shall be yours; They shall walk behind you, They shall come over in chains; And they shall bow down to you. They will make supplication to you, *saying*, 'Surely God *is* in you, And *there is* no other; *There is* no other God.' "

Ninevites.

Nah 3:16 You have multiplied your merchants more than the stars of heaven. The locust plunders and flies away.

Syrians.

Ezek 27:16 Syria *was* your merchant because of the abundance of goods you made. They gave you for your wares emeralds, purple, embroidery, fine linen, corals, and rubies.

Ezek 27:18 Damascus *was* your merchant because of the abundance of goods you made, because of your many luxury items, with the wine of Helbon and with white wool.

People of Tarshish.

Ezek 27:25 "The ships of Tarshish were carriers of your merchandise. You were filled and very glorious in the midst of the seas.

People of Tyre.

Ezek 28:5 By your great wisdom in trade you have increased your riches, And your heart is lifted up because of your riches),"

Ezek 28:13 You were in Eden, the garden of God; Every precious stone *was* your covering: The sardius, topaz, and diamond, Beryl, onyx, and jasper, Sapphire, turquoise, and emerald with gold. The workmanship of your timbrels and pipes Was prepared for you on the day you were created.

Ezek 28:16 "By the abundance of your trading You became filled with violence within, And you sinned; Therefore I cast you as a profane thing Out of the mountain of God; And I destroyed you, O covering cherub, From the midst of the fiery stones.

Of the Jews,
Under strict laws.

Lev 19:36–37 You shall have honest scales, honest weights, an honest ephah, and an honest hin: I *am* the LORD your God, who brought you out of the land of Egypt. **37** 'Therefore you shall observe all My statutes and all My judgments, and perform them: I *am* the LORD.' "

Lev 25:14 And if you sell anything to your neighbor or buy from your neighbor's hand, you shall not oppress one another.

Lev 25:17 Therefore you shall not oppress one another, but you shall fear your God; for I *am* the LORD your God.

Commenced after their settlement in Canaan.

Gen 49:13 "Zebulun shall dwell by the haven of the sea; He *shall become* a haven for ships, And his border shall adjoin Sidon.

Judg 5:17 Gilead stayed beyond the Jordan, And why did Dan remain on ships? Asher continued at the seashore, And stayed by his inlets.

Greatly extended by Solomon.

1 Kin 9:26–27 King Solomon also built a fleet of ships at Ezion Geber, which *is* near Elath on the shore of the Red Sea, in the land of Edom. **27** Then Hiram sent his servants with the fleet, seamen who knew the sea, to work with the servants of Solomon.

2 Chr 9:21 For the king's ships went to Tarshish with the servants of Hiram. Once every three years the merchant ships came, bringing gold, silver, ivory, apes, and monkeys.

Checked in Jehoshaphat's time.

1 Kin 22:48–49 Jehoshaphat made merchant ships to go to Ophir for gold; but they never sailed, for the ships were wrecked at Ezion Geber. **49** Then Ahaziah the son of Ahab said to Jehoshaphat, "Let my servants go with your servants in the ships." But Jehoshaphat would not.

Sins connected with.

Prov 20:14 "*It is* good for nothing," cries the buyer; But when he has gone his way, then he boasts.

Ezek 22:13 "Behold, therefore, I beat My fists at the dishonest profit which you have made, and at the bloodshed which has been in your midst.

Ezek 28:2 "Son of man, say to the prince of Tyre, 'Thus says the Lord GOD: "Because your heart *is* lifted up, And you say, 'I *am* a god, I sit *in* the seat of gods, In the midst of the seas,' Yet you *are* a man, and not a god, Though you set your heart as the heart of a god

Ezek 28:16–18 "By the abundance of your trading You became filled with violence within, And you sinned;

Therefore I cast you as a profane thing Out of the mountain of God; And I destroyed you, O covering cherub, From the midst of the fiery stones. **17** "Your heart was lifted up because of your beauty; You corrupted your wisdom for the sake of your splendor; I cast you to the ground, I laid you before kings, That they might gaze at you. **18** "You defiled your sanctuaries By the multitude of your iniquities, By the iniquity of your trading; Therefore I brought fire from your midst; It devoured you, And I turned you to ashes upon the earth In the sight of all who saw you.

Hos 12:7 "A cunning Canaanite! Deceitful scales *are* in his hand; He loves to oppress.

Denunciations for abuses of.

Is 23:11 He stretched out His hand over the sea, He shook the kingdoms; The LORD has given a commandment against Canaan To destroy its strongholds.

Ezek 7:12–13 The time has come, The day draws near. 'Let not the buyer rejoice, Nor the seller mourn, For wrath *is* on their whole multitude. **13** For the seller shall not return to what has been sold, Though he may still be alive; For the vision concerns the whole multitude, And it shall not turn back; No one will strengthen himself Who lives in iniquity.

Ezek 27:32–36 In their wailing for you They will take up a lamentation, And lament for you: 'What *city is* like Tyre, Destroyed in the midst of the sea? **33** 'When your wares went out by sea, You satisfied many people; You enriched the kings of the earth With your many luxury goods and your merchandise. **34** But you are broken by the seas in the depths of the waters; Your merchandise and the entire company will fall in your midst. **35** All the inhabitants of the isles will be astonished at you; Their kings will be greatly afraid, And *their* countenance will be troubled. **36** The merchants among the peoples will hiss at you; You will become a horror, and *be* no more forever.' " ' "

Ezek 28:16–18 "By the abundance of your trading You became filled with violence within, And you sinned; Therefore I cast you as a profane thing Out of the mountain of God; And I destroyed you, O covering cherub, From the midst of the fiery stones. **17** "Your heart was lifted up because of your beauty; You corrupted your wisdom for the sake of your splendor; I cast you to the ground, I laid you before kings, That they might gaze at you. **18** "You defiled your sanctuaries By the multitude of your iniquities, By the iniquity of your trading; Therefore I brought fire from your midst; It devoured you, And I turned you to ashes upon the earth In the sight of all who saw you.

Articles of,
Purple cloth.

Ezek 27:16 Syria *was* your merchant because of the abundance of goods you made. They gave you for your wares emeralds, purple, embroidery, fine linen, corals, and rubies.

Ezek 27:24 These *were* your merchants in choice items— in purple clothes, in embroidered garments, in chests of multicolored apparel, in sturdy woven cords, which were in your marketplace.

Bronze.

Ezek 27:13 Javan, Tubal, and Meshech *were* your

traders. They bartered human lives and vessels of bronze for your merchandise.

Wheat.

1 Kin 5:11 And Solomon gave Hiram twenty thousand kors of wheat *as* food for his household, and twenty kors of pressed oil. Thus Solomon gave to Hiram year by year.

Ezek 27:17 Judah and the land of Israel *were* your traders. They traded for your merchandise wheat of Minnith, millet, honey, oil, and balm.

Livestock.

Ezek 27:21 Arabia and all the princes of Kedar *were* your regular merchants. They traded with you in lambs, rams, and goats.

Chests of rich apparel.

Ezek 27:24 These *were* your merchants in choice items—in purple clothes, in embroidered garments, in chests of multicolored apparel, in sturdy woven cords, which were in your marketplace.

Chariots, etc.

1 Kin 10:29 Now a chariot that was imported from Egypt cost six hundred *shekels* of silver, and a horse one hundred and fifty; and thus, through their agents, they exported *them* to all the kings of the Hittites and the kings of Syria.

Ezek 27:20 Dedan *was* your merchant in saddlecloths for riding.

Embroidery.

Ezek 27:16 Syria *was* your merchant because of the abundance of goods you made. They gave you for your wares emeralds, purple, embroidery, fine linen, corals, and rubies.

Ezek 27:24 These *were* your merchants in choice items—in purple clothes, in embroidered garments, in chests of multicolored apparel, in sturdy woven cords, which were in your marketplace.

Gold.

2 Chr 8:18 And Hiram sent him ships by the hand of his servants, and servants who knew the sea. They went with the servants of Solomon to Ophir, and acquired four hundred and fifty talents of gold from there, and brought it to King Solomon.

Honey.

Ezek 27:17 Judah and the land of Israel *were* your traders. They traded for your merchandise wheat of Minnith, millet, honey, oil, and balm.

Horses.

1 Kin 10:28–29 Also Solomon had horses imported from Egypt and Keveh; the king's merchants bought them in Keveh at the *current* price. **29** Now a chariot that was imported from Egypt cost six hundred *shekels* of silver, and a horse one hundred and fifty; and thus, through their agents, they exported *them* to all the kings of the Hittites and the kings of Syria.

Ezek 27:14 Those from the house of Togarmah traded for your wares with horses, steeds, and mules.

Ivory.

2 Chr 9:21 For the king's ships went to Tarshish with the servants of Hiram. Once every three years the merchant ships came, bringing gold, silver, ivory, apes, and monkeys.

Ezek 27:15 The men of Dedan *were* your traders; many isles *were* the market of your hand. They brought you ivory tusks and ebony as payment.

Iron and steel.

Ezek 27:12 "Tarshish *was* your merchant because of your many luxury goods. They gave you silver, iron, tin, and lead for your goods.

Ezek 27:19 Dan and Javan paid for your wares, traversing back and forth. Wrought iron, cassia, and cane were among your merchandise.

Land.

Gen 23:13–16 and he spoke to Ephron in the hearing of the people of the land, saying, "If you *will give it,* please hear me. I will give you money for the field; take *it* from me and I will bury my dead there." **14** And Ephron answered Abraham, saying to him, **15** "My lord, listen to me; the land *is worth* four hundred shekels of silver. What *is* that between you and me? So bury your dead." **16** And Abraham listened to Ephron; and Abraham weighed out the silver for Ephron which he had named in the hearing of the sons of Heth, four hundred shekels of silver, currency of the merchants.

Ruth 4:3 Then he said to the close relative, "Naomi, who has come back from the country of Moab, sold the piece of land which *belonged* to our brother Elimelech.

Lead.

Ezek 27:12 "Tarshish *was* your merchant because of your many luxury goods. They gave you silver, iron, tin, and lead for your goods.

Oil.

1 Kin 5:11 And Solomon gave Hiram twenty thousand kors of wheat *as* food for his household, and twenty kors of pressed oil. Thus Solomon gave to Hiram year by year.

Ezek 27:17 Judah and the land of Israel *were* your traders. They traded for your merchandise wheat of Minnith, millet, honey, oil, and balm.

Perfumes.

Song 3:6 Who *is* this coming out of the wilderness Like pillars of smoke, Perfumed with myrrh and frankincense, With all the merchant's fragrant powders?

Precious stones.

Ezek 27:16 Syria *was* your merchant because of the abundance of goods you made. They gave you for your wares emeralds, purple, embroidery, fine linen, corals, and rubies.

Ezek 27:22 The merchants of Sheba and Raamah *were* your merchants. They traded for your wares the choicest spices, all kinds of precious stones, and gold.

Ezek 28:13 You were in Eden, the garden of God; Every precious stone *was* your covering: The sardius, topaz, and diamond, Beryl, onyx, and jasper, Sapphire, turquoise, and emerald with gold. The workmanship of your timbrels and pipes Was prepared for you on the day you were created.

Ezek 28:16 "By the abundance of your trading You became filled with violence within, And you sinned; Therefore I cast you as a profane thing Out of the mountain of God; And I destroyed you, O covering cherub, From the midst of the fiery stones.

Slaves.

Gen 37:28 Then Midianite traders passed by; so *the brothers* pulled Joseph up and lifted him out of the pit, and sold him to the Ishmaelites for twenty *shekels* of silver. And they took Joseph to Egypt.

Gen 37:36 Now the Midianites had sold him in Egypt to Potiphar, an officer of Pharaoh *and* captain of the guard.

Deut 24:7 "If a man is found kidnapping any of his brethren of the children of Israel, and mistreats him or sells him, then that kidnapper shall die; and you shall put away the evil from among you.

Silver.

2 Chr 9:21 For the king's ships went to Tarshish with the servants of Hiram. Once every three years the merchant ships came, bringing gold, silver, ivory, apes, and monkeys.

Timber.

1 Kin 5:6 Now therefore, command that they cut down cedars for me from Lebanon; and my servants will be with your servants, and I will pay you wages for your servants according to whatever you say. For you know *there is* none among us who has skill to cut timber like the Sidonians.

1 Kin 5:8 Then Hiram sent to Solomon, saying: I have considered *the message* which you sent me, *and* I will do all you desire concerning the cedar and cypress logs.

Tin.

Ezek 27:12 "Tarshish *was* your merchant because of your many luxury goods. They gave you silver, iron, tin, and lead for your goods.

White wool.

Ezek 27:18 Damascus *was* your merchant because of the abundance of goods you made, because of your many luxury items, with the wine of Helbon and with white wool.

Wine.

2 Chr 2:15 Now therefore, the wheat, the barley, the oil, and the wine which my lord has spoken of, let him send to his servants.

Ezek 27:18 Damascus *was* your merchant because of the abundance of goods you made, because of your many luxury items, with the wine of Helbon and with white wool.

COMMITMENT

God's call of.

Ex 34:14–15 (for you shall worship no other god, for the LORD, whose name *is* Jealous, *is* a jealous God), **15** lest you make a covenant with the inhabitants of the land, and they play the harlot with their gods and make sacrifice to their gods, and *one of them* invites you and you eat of his sacrifice,

David's prayer of.

1 Chr 29:16–20 "O LORD our God, all this abundance that we have prepared to build You a house for Your holy name is from Your hand, and *is* all Your own. **17** I know also, my God, that You test the heart and have pleasure in uprightness. As for me, in the uprightness of my heart I have willingly offered all these *things*; and now with joy I have seen Your people, who are present here to offer willingly to You. **18** O LORD God of Abraham, Isaac, and Israel, our fathers, keep this forever in the intent of the thoughts of the heart of Your people, and fix their heart toward You. **19** And give my son Solomon a loyal heart to keep Your commandments and Your testimonies and Your statutes, to do all *these things*, and to build the temple for which I have made provision." **20** Then David said to all the assembly, "Now bless the LORD your God." So all the assembly blessed the LORD God of their fathers, and bowed their heads and prostrated themselves before the LORD and the king.

To God's Word.

Neh 8:8 So they read distinctly from the book, in the Law of God; and they gave the sense, and helped *them* to understand the reading.

John 15:7–10 If you abide in Me, and My words abide in you, you will ask what you desire, and it shall be done for you. **8** By this My Father is glorified, that you bear much fruit; so you will be My disciples. **9** "As the Father loved Me, I also have loved you; abide in My love. **10** If you keep My commandments, you will abide in My love, just as I have kept My Father's commandments and abide in His love.

Renewal of.

Neh 9:36–38 "Here we *are*, servants today! And the land that You gave to our fathers, To eat its fruit and its bounty, Here we *are*, servants in it! **37** And it yields much increase to the kings You have set over us, Because of our sins; Also they have dominion over our bodies and our cattle At their pleasure; And we *are* in great distress. **38** "And because of all this, We make a sure *covenant* and write *it;* Our leaders, our Levites, *and* our priests seal *it.*"

Hab 3:16–19 When I heard, my body trembled; My lips quivered at *the* voice; Rottenness entered my bones; And I trembled in myself, That I might rest in the day of trouble. When he comes up to the people, He will invade them with his troops. **17** Though the fig tree may not blossom, Nor fruit be on the vines; Though the labor of the olive may fail, And the fields yield no food; Though the flock may be cut off from the fold, And there be no herd in the stalls— **18** Yet I will rejoice in the LORD, I will joy in the God of my salvation. **19** The LORD God is my strength; He will make my feet like deer's *feet*, And He will make me walk on my high hills. To the Chief Musician. With my stringed instruments.

To trust in the Lord.

Ps 40:3–4 He has put a new song in my mouth— Praise to our God; Many will see *it* and fear, And will trust in the LORD. **4** Blessed *is* that man who makes the LORD his trust, And does not respect the proud, nor such as turn aside to lies.

Ps 63:8 My soul follows close behind You; Your right hand upholds me.

To praise.

Ps 145:1–2 I will extol You, my God, O King; And I will bless Your name forever and ever. **2** Every day I will bless You, And I will praise Your name forever and ever.

Ps 146:1–2 Praise the Lord! Praise the Lord, O my soul! **2** While I live I will praise the Lord; I will sing praises to my God while I have my being.

To truth.

Eph 6:14 Stand therefore, having girded your waist with truth, having put on the breastplate of righteousness,

Demanded by Christ of His followers.

Matt 10:37–38 He who loves father or mother more than Me is not worthy of Me. And he who loves son or daughter more than Me is not worthy of Me. **38** And he who does not take his cross and follow after Me is not worthy of Me.

Matt 16:24–26 Then Jesus said to His disciples, "If anyone desires to come after Me, let him deny himself, and take up his cross, and follow Me. **25** For whoever desires to save his life will lose it, but whoever loses his life for My sake will find it. **26** For what profit is it to a man if he gains the whole world, and loses his own soul? Or what will a man give in exchange for his soul?

Luke 14:33 So likewise, whoever of you does not forsake all that he has cannot be My disciple.

John 21:15–17 So when they had eaten breakfast, Jesus said to Simon Peter, "Simon, *son* of Jonah, do you love Me more than these?" He said to Him, "Yes, Lord; You know that I love You." He said to him, "Feed My lambs." **16** He said to him again a second time, "Simon, *son* of Jonah, do you love Me?" He said to Him, "Yes, Lord; You know that I love You." He said to him, "Tend My sheep." **17** He said to him the third time, "Simon, *son* of Jonah, do you love Me?" Peter was grieved because He said to him the third time, "Do you love Me?" And he said to Him, "Lord, You know all things; You know that I love You." Jesus said to him, "Feed My sheep.

Call to carry one's cross, a picture of total.

Matt 10:38 And he who does not take his cross and follow after Me is not worthy of Me.

Luke 14:27 And whoever does not bear his cross and come after Me cannot be My disciple.

Encouragement toward greater.

Heb 10:24 And let us consider one another in order to stir up love and good works,

James 5:8 You also be patient. Establish your hearts, for the coming of the Lord is at hand.

Undivided.

James 3:17 But the wisdom that is from above is first pure, then peaceable, gentle, willing to yield, full of mercy and good fruits, without partiality and without hypocrisy.

Superficial.

Matt 13:20 But he who received the seed on stony places, this is he who hears the word and immediately receives it with joy;

COMMUNICATION—A BIBLICAL APPROACH

The power of words.

Prov 11:9 The hypocrite with *his* mouth destroys his neighbor, But through knowledge the righteous will be delivered.

Prov 12:18 There is one who speaks like the piercings of a sword, But the tongue of the wise *promotes* health.

Prov 15:4 A wholesome tongue *is* a tree of life, But perverseness in it breaks the spirit.

Prov 18:21 Death and life *are* in the power of the tongue, And those who love it will eat its fruit.

Matt 12:37 For by your words you will be justified, and by your words you will be condemned."

James 3:1–8 My brethren, let not many of you become teachers, knowing that we shall receive a stricter judgment. **2** For we all stumble in many things. If anyone does not stumble in word, he *is* a perfect man, able also to bridle the whole body. **3** Indeed, we put bits in horses' mouths that they may obey us, and we turn their whole body. **4** Look also at ships: although they are so large and are driven by fierce winds, they are turned by a very small rudder wherever the pilot desires. **5** Even so the tongue is a little member and boasts great things. See how great a forest a little fire kindles! **6** And the tongue *is* a fire, a world of iniquity. The tongue is so set among our members that it defiles the whole body, and sets on fire the course of nature; and it is set on fire by hell. **7** For every kind of beast and bird, of reptile and creature of the sea, is tamed and has been tamed by mankind. **8** But no man can tame the tongue. *It is* an unruly evil, full of deadly poison.

The value of words.

Prov 20:15 There is gold and a multitude of rubies, But the lips of knowledge *are* a precious jewel.

Prov 25:11–14 A word fitly spoken *is like* apples of gold In settings of silver. **12** *Like* an earring of gold and an ornament of fine gold *Is* a wise rebuker to an obedient ear. **13** Like the cold of snow in time of harvest *Is* a faithful messenger to those who send him, For he refreshes the soul of his masters. **14** Whoever falsely boasts of giving *Is like* clouds and wind without rain.

The source of words.

Prov 6:12 A worthless person, a wicked man, Walks with a perverse mouth;

Prov 15:28 The heart of the righteous studies how to answer, But the mouth of the wicked pours forth evil.

Prov 16:23–24 The heart of the wise teaches his mouth, And adds learning to his lips. **24** Pleasant words *are like* a honeycomb, Sweetness to the soul and health to the bones.

Matt 12:34 Brood of vipers! How can you, being evil, speak good things? For out of the abundance of the heart the mouth speaks.

Communication guidelines

Positives and negatives.

Prov 10:11–14 The mouth of the righteous *is* a well of life, But violence covers the mouth of the wicked. **12** Hatred stirs up strife, But love covers all sins. **13** Wisdom is found on the lips of him who has understanding, But a rod *is* for the back of him who is devoid of understanding. **14** Wise *people* store up knowledge, But the mouth of the foolish *is* near destruction.

Prov 10:18–21 Whoever hides hatred *has* lying lips, And whoever spreads slander *is* a fool. **19** In the multitude of words sin is not lacking, But he who restrains his lips *is* wise. **20** The tongue of the righteous *is* choice silver; The heart of the wicked *is worth* little. **21** The lips of the righteous feed many, But fools die for lack of wisdom.

Prov 25:11–14 A word fitly spoken *is like* apples of gold In settings of silver. **12** *Like* an earring of gold and an ornament of fine gold *Is* a wise rebuker to an obedient ear. **13** Like the cold of snow in time of harvest *Is* a faithful messenger to those who send him, For he refreshes the soul of his masters. **14** Whoever falsely boasts of giving *Is like* clouds and wind without rain.

Prov 26:17–28 He who passes by *and* meddles in a quarrel not his own *Is like* one who takes a dog by the ears. **18** Like a madman who throws firebrands, arrows, and death, **19** *Is* the man *who* deceives his neighbor, And says, "I was only joking!" **20** Where *there is* no wood, the fire goes out; And where *there is* no talebearer, strife ceases. **21** *As* charcoal *is* to burning coals, and wood to fire, So *is* a contentious man to kindle strife. **22** The words of a talebearer *are* like tasty trifles, And they go down into the inmost body. **23** Fervent lips with a wicked heart *Are like* earthenware covered with silver dross. **24** He who hates, disguises *it* with his lips, And lays up deceit within himself; **25** When he speaks kindly, do not believe him, For *there are* seven abominations in his heart; **26** *Though his* hatred is covered by deceit, His wickedness will be revealed before the assembly. **27** Whoever digs a pit will fall into it, And he who rolls a stone will have it roll back on him. **28** A lying tongue hates *those who are* crushed by it, And a flattering mouth works ruin.

Be listening.

Prov 18:13 He who answers a matter before he hears *it,* It *is* folly and shame to him.

Prov 19:20 Listen to counsel and receive instruction, That you may be wise in your latter days.

James 1:19 So then, my beloved brethren, let every man be swift to hear, slow to speak, slow to wrath;

Do not talk too much.

Prov 10:19 In the multitude of words sin is not lacking, But he who restrains his lips *is* wise.

Prov 13:2–3 A man shall eat well by the fruit of *his* mouth, But the soul of the unfaithful feeds on violence. **3** He who guards his mouth preserves his life, *But* he who opens wide his lips shall have destruction.

Prov 17:27–28 He who has knowledge spares his words, *And* a man of understanding is of a calm spirit. **28** Even a fool is counted wise when he holds his peace; *When* he shuts his lips, *he is considered* perceptive.

Eccl 10:12–14 The words of a wise man's mouth *are* gracious, But the lips of a fool shall swallow him up; **13** The words of his mouth begin with foolishness, And the end of his talk *is* raving madness. **14** A fool also multiplies words. No man knows what is to be; Who can tell him what will be after him?

Col 4:6 *Let* your speech always *be* with grace, seasoned with salt, that you may know how you ought to answer each one.

Do not nag.

Prov 21:19 Better to dwell in the wilderness, Than with a contentious and angry woman.

Prov 26:21 *As* charcoal *is* to burning coals, and wood to fire, So *is* a contentious man to kindle strife.

Do not meddle.

Prov 26:27 Whoever digs a pit will fall into it, And he who rolls a stone will have it roll back on him.

Do not gossip.

Prov 11:13 A talebearer reveals secrets, But he who is of a faithful spirit conceals a matter.

Prov 20:19 He who goes about *as* a talebearer reveals secrets; Therefore do not associate with one who flatters with his lips.

Prov 26:20 Where *there is* no wood, the fire goes out; And where *there is* no talebearer, strife ceases.

Do not brag.

Prov 14:23 In all labor there is profit, But idle chatter *leads* only to poverty.

Prov 27:2 Let another man praise you, and not your own mouth; A stranger, and not your own lips.

Be slow to speak.

Prov 15:28 The heart of the righteous studies how to answer, But the mouth of the wicked pours forth evil.

Prov 29:20 Do you see a man hasty in his words? *There is* more hope for a fool than for him.

James 1:19 So then, my beloved brethren, let every man be swift to hear, slow to speak, slow to wrath;

Be wise in timing.

Prov 15:23 A man has joy by the answer of his mouth, And a word *spoken* in due season, how good *it is!*

Eph 4:29 Let no corrupt word proceed out of your mouth, but what is good for necessary edification, that it may impart grace to the hearers.

Admit wrongs.

Prov 29:23 A man's pride will bring him low, But the humble in spirit will retain honor.

James 5:16 Confess *your* trespasses to one another, and pray for one another, that you may be healed. The effective, fervent prayer of a righteous man avails much.

Do not lie.

Ps 34:13 Keep your tongue from evil, And your lips from speaking deceit.

Prov 12:19 The truthful lip shall be established forever, But a lying tongue *is* but for a moment.

Prov 12:22 Lying lips *are* an abomination to the LORD, But those who deal truthfully *are* His delight.

Prov 26:18–19 Like a madman who throws firebrands, arrows, and death, **19** *Is* the man *who* deceives his neighbor, And says, "I was only joking!"

Eph 4:15 but, speaking the truth in love, may grow up in all things into Him who is the head—Christ—

Eph 4:25 Therefore, putting away lying, "Let each one of you speak truth with his neighbor," for we are members of one another.

Do not respond in anger.

Prov 15:1 A soft answer turns away wrath, But a harsh word stirs up anger.

Eph 4:26 *"Be angry, and do not sin"*: do not let the sun go down on your wrath,

Avoid quarrels.

Prov 17:14 The beginning of strife *is like* releasing water; Therefore stop contention before a quarrel starts.

Prov 20:3 *It is* honorable for a man to stop striving, Since any fool can start a quarrel.

Set a guard over my lips.

Ps 141:3 Set a guard, O LORD, over my mouth; Keep watch over the door of my lips.

Deliver me from lying lips.

Ps 120:3 What shall be given to you, Or what shall be done to you, You false tongue?

May my lips offer up a sacrifice of praise.

Heb 13:15 Therefore by Him let us continually offer the sacrifice of praise to God, that is, the fruit of *our* lips, giving thanks to His name.

Let me speak encouragingly.

Eph 4:29 Let no corrupt word proceed out of your mouth, but what is good for necessary edification, that it may impart grace to the hearers.

Bridle my tongue.

James 1:26 If anyone among you thinks he is religious, and does not bridle his tongue but deceives his own heart, this one's religion *is* useless.

COMMUNION WITH GOD

Is communion with the Father.

1 John 1:3 that which we have seen and heard we declare to you, that you also may have fellowship with us; and truly our fellowship *is* with the Father and with His Son Jesus Christ.

Is communion with the Son.

1 Cor 1:9 God *is* faithful, by whom you were called into the fellowship of His Son, Jesus Christ our Lord.

1 John 1:3 that which we have seen and heard we declare to you, that you also may have fellowship with us; and truly our fellowship *is* with the Father and with His Son Jesus Christ.

Rev 3:20 Behold, I stand at the door and knock. If anyone hears My voice and opens the door, I will come in to him and dine with him, and he with Me.

Is communion with the Holy Spirit.

1 Cor 12:13 For by one Spirit we were all baptized into one body—whether Jews or Greeks, whether slaves or free—and have all been made to drink into one Spirit.

2 Cor 13:14 The grace of the Lord Jesus Christ, and the love of God, and the communion of the Holy Spirit *be* with you all. Amen.

Phil 2:1 Therefore if *there is* any consolation in Christ, if any comfort of love, if any fellowship of the Spirit, if any affection and mercy,

Holiness essential to.

2 Cor 6:14–16 Do not be unequally yoked together with unbelievers. For what fellowship has righteousness with lawlessness? And what communion has light with darkness? 15 And what accord has Christ with Belial? Or what part has a believer with an unbeliever? 16 And what agreement has the temple of God with idols? For you are the temple of the living God. As God has said: *"I will dwell in them And walk among them. I will be their God, And they shall be My people."*

Promised to the obedient.

John 14:23 Jesus answered and said to him, "If anyone loves Me, he will keep My word; and My Father will love him, and We will come to him and make Our home with him.

True for believers.

Ps 16:8 I have set the LORD always before me; Because *He is* at my right hand I shall not be moved.

Ps 42:1 As the deer pants for the water brooks, So pants my soul for You, O God.

Ps 63:5–6 My soul shall be satisfied as with marrow and fatness, And my mouth shall praise You with joyful lips. 6 When I remember You on my bed, I meditate on You in the *night* watches.

John 14:16–18 And I will pray the Father, and He will give you another Helper, that He may abide with you forever— 17 the Spirit of truth, whom the world cannot receive, because it neither sees Him nor knows Him; but you know Him, for He dwells with you and will be in you. 18 I will not leave you orphans; I will come to you.

1 Cor 10:16 The cup of blessing which we bless, is it not the communion of the blood of Christ? The bread which we break, is it not the communion of the body of Christ?

Phil 1:23 For I am hard-pressed between the two, having a desire to depart and be with Christ, *which is* far better.

Heb 4:16 Let us therefore come boldly to the throne of grace, that we may obtain mercy and find grace to help in time of need.

Exemplified by

Enoch.

Gen 5:24 And Enoch walked with God; and he *was* not, for God took him.

Noah.

Gen 6:9 This is the genealogy of Noah. Noah was a just man, perfect in his generations. Noah walked with God.

Abraham.

Gen 18:33 So the LORD went His way as soon as He had finished speaking with Abraham; and Abraham returned to his place.

Jacob.

Gen 32:24–29 Then Jacob was left alone; and a Man wrestled with him until the breaking of day. 25 Now when He saw that He did not prevail against him, He touched the socket of his hip; and the socket of Jacob's hip was out of joint as He wrestled with him. 26 And He said, "Let Me go, for the day breaks." But he said, "I will not let You go unless You bless me!" 27 So He said to him, "What *is* your name?" He said, "Jacob." 28 And He said, "Your name shall no longer be called Jacob, but Israel; for you have struggled with God and with men, and have prevailed."

29 Then Jacob asked, saying, "Tell *me* Your name, I pray." And He said, "Why *is* it *that* you ask about My name?" And He blessed him there.

Moses.

Ex 33:11–23 So the LORD spoke to Moses face to face, as a man speaks to his friend. And he would return to the camp, but his servant Joshua the son of Nun, a young man, did not depart from the tabernacle. **12** Then Moses said to the LORD, "See, You say to me, 'Bring up this people.' But You have not let me know whom You will send with me. Yet You have said, 'I know you by name, and you have also found grace in My sight.' **13** Now therefore, I pray, if I have found grace in Your sight, show me now Your way, that I may know You and that I may find grace in Your sight. And consider that this nation *is* Your people." **14** And He said, "My Presence will go *with you,* and I will give you rest." **15** Then he said to Him, "If Your Presence does not go *with us,* do not bring us up from here. **16** For how then will it be known that Your people and I have found grace in Your sight, except You go with us? So we shall be separate, Your people and I, from all the people who *are* upon the face of the earth." **17** So the LORD said to Moses, "I will also do this thing that you have spoken; for you have found grace in My sight, and I know you by name." **18** And he said, "Please, show me Your glory." **19** Then He said, "I will make all My goodness pass before you, and I will proclaim the name of the LORD before you. I will be gracious to whom I will be gracious, and I will have compassion on whom I will have compassion." **20** But He said, "You cannot see My face; for no man shall see Me, and live." **21** And the LORD said, "Here is a place by Me, and you shall stand on the rock. **22** So it shall be, while My glory passes by, that I will put you in the cleft of the rock, and will cover you with My hand while I pass by. **23** Then I will take away My hand, and you shall see My back; but My face shall not be seen."

COMPASSION AND SYMPATHY

Christ set an example of.

Luke 19:41–42 Now as He drew near, He saw the city and wept over it, **42** saying, "If you had known, even you, especially in this your day, the things *that make* for your peace! But now they are hidden from your eyes.

Heb 5:2 He can have compassion on those who are ignorant and going astray, since he himself is also subject to weakness.

Exhortation to.

Rom 12:15 Rejoice with those who rejoice, and weep with those who weep.

1 Pet 3:8 Finally, all *of you be* of one mind, having compassion for one another; love as brothers, *be* tenderhearted, *be* courteous;

Exercise, toward

The afflicted.

Job 6:14 "To him who is afflicted, kindness *should be shown* by his friend, Even though he forsakes the fear of the Almighty.

Heb 13:3 Remember the prisoners as if chained with them—those who are mistreated—since you yourselves are in the body also.

The chastened.

Is 22:4 Therefore I said, "Look away from me, I will weep bitterly; Do not labor to comfort me Because of the plundering of the daughter of my people."

Jer 9:1 Oh, that my head were waters, And my eyes a fountain of tears, That I might weep day and night For the slain of the daughter of my people!

Enemies.

Ps 35:13 But as for me, when they were sick, My clothing *was* sackcloth; I humbled myself with fasting; And my prayer would return to my own heart.

The poor.

Prov 19:17 He who has pity on the poor lends to the LORD, And He will pay back what he has given.

The weak.

2 Cor 11:29 Who is weak, and I am not weak? Who is made to stumble, and I do not burn *with indignation?*

Gal 6:2 Bear one another's burdens, and so fulfill the law of Christ.

Believers.

1 Cor 12:25–26 that there should be no schism in the body, but *that* the members should have the same care for one another. **26** And if one member suffers, all the members suffer with *it;* or if one member is honored, all the members rejoice with *it.*

Inseparable from love to God.

John 4:20 Our fathers worshiped on this mountain, and you *Jews* say that in Jerusalem is the place where one ought to worship."

1 John 3:17 But whoever has this world's goods, and sees his brother in need, and shuts up his heart from him, how does the love of God abide in him?

Promise to those who show.

Prov 19:17 He who has pity on the poor lends to the LORD, And He will pay back what he has given.

Matt 10:42 And whoever gives one of these little ones only a cup of cold *water* in the name of a disciple, assuredly, I say to you, he shall by no means lose his reward."

Illustrated.

Ex 2:6 And when she opened *it,* she saw the child, and behold, the baby wept. So she had compassion on him, and said, "This is one of the Hebrews' children."

2 Sam 17:27–29 Now it happened, when David had come to Mahanaim, that Shobi the son of Nahash from Rabbah of the people of Ammon, Machir the son of Ammiel from Lo Debar, and Barzillai the Gileadite from Rogelim, **28** brought beds and basins, earthen vessels and wheat, barley and flour, parched *grain* and beans, lentils and parched *seeds,* **29** honey and curds, sheep and cheese of the herd, for David and the people who *were* with him to eat. For they said, "The people are hungry and weary and thirsty in the wilderness."

1 Kin 17:18–19 So she said to Elijah, "What have I to do with you, O man of God? Have you come to me to bring my sin to remembrance, and to kill my son?" **19** And he said to her, "Give me your son." So he took him out of her arms and carried him to the upper room where he was staying, and laid him on his own bed.

Neh 1:4 So it was, when I heard these words, that I sat down and wept, and mourned *for many* days; I was fasting and praying before the God of heaven.

Job 2:11 Now when Job's three friends heard of all this adversity that had come upon him, each one came from his own place—Eliphaz the Temanite, Bildad the Shuhite, and Zophar the Naamathite. For they had made an appointment together to come and mourn with him, and to comfort him.

Job 30:25 Have I not wept for him who was in trouble? Has *not* my soul grieved for the poor?

Ps 35:13–14 But as for me, when they were sick, My clothing *was* sackcloth; I humbled myself with fasting; And my prayer would return to my own heart. **14** I paced about as though *he were* my friend *or* brother; I bowed down heavily, as one who mourns *for his* mother.

Luke 10:33 But a certain Samaritan, as he journeyed, came where he was. And when he saw him, he had compassion.

Luke 15:20 "And he arose and came to his father. But when he was still a great way off, his father saw him and had compassion, and ran and fell on his neck and kissed him.

John 11:19 And many of the Jews had joined the women around Martha and Mary, to comfort them concerning their brother.

1 Cor 9:22 to the weak I became as weak, that I might win the weak. I have become all things to all *men,* that I might by all means save some.

COMPLAINING

Forbidden.

1 Cor 10:10 nor complain, as some of them also complained, and were destroyed by the destroyer.

Phil 2:14 Do all things without complaining and disputing,

Against

The sovereignty of God.

Prov 19:3 The foolishness of a man twists his way, And his heart frets against the LORD.

Rom 9:19–20 You will say to me then, "Why does He still find fault? For who has resisted His will?" **20** But indeed, O man, who are you to reply against God? Will the thing formed say to him who formed *it,* "Why have you made me like this?"

The service of God.

Mal 3:14 You have said, 'It is useless to serve God; What profit *is it* that we have kept His ordinance, And that we have walked as mourners Before the LORD of hosts?

Christ.

Luke 5:30 And their scribes and the Pharisees complained against His disciples, saying, "Why do You eat and drink with tax collectors and sinners?"

Luke 15:2 And the Pharisees and scribes complained, saying, "This Man receives sinners and eats with them."

Luke 19:7 But when they saw *it,* they all complained, saying, "He has gone to be a guest with a man who is a sinner."

John 6:41–43 The Jews then complained about Him, because He said, "I am the bread which came down from heaven." **42** And they said, "Is not this Jesus, the son of Joseph, whose father and mother we know? How is it then that He says, 'I have come down from heaven'?" **43** Jesus therefore answered and said to them, "Do not murmur among yourselves.

John 6:52 The Jews therefore quarreled among themselves, saying, "How can this Man give us *His* flesh to eat?"

Ministers of God.

Ex 17:3 And the people thirsted there for water, and the people complained against Moses, and said, "Why *is* it you have brought us up out of Egypt, to kill us and our children and our livestock with thirst?"

Num 16:41 On the next day all the congregation of the children of Israel complained against Moses and Aaron, saying, "You have killed the people of the LORD."

Disciples of Christ.

Matt 7:2 For with what judgment you judge, you will be judged; and with the measure you use, it will be measured back to you.

Luke 5:30 And their scribes and the Pharisees complained against His disciples, saying, "Why do You eat and drink with tax collectors and sinners?"

Luke 6:2 And some of the Pharisees said to them, "Why are you doing what is not lawful to do on the Sabbath?"

Unreasonableness of.

Lam 3:39 Why should a living man complain, A man for the punishment of his sins?

Tempts God.

Ex 17:2 Therefore the people contended with Moses, and said, "Give us water, that we may drink." So Moses said to them, "Why do you contend with me? Why do you tempt the LORD?"

Provokes God.

Num 14:2 And all the children of Israel complained against Moses and Aaron, and the whole congregation said to them, "If only we had died in the land of Egypt! Or if only we had died in this wilderness!

Num 14:11 Then the LORD said to Moses: "How long will these people reject Me? And how long will they not believe Me, with all the signs which I have performed among them?

Deut 9:8 Also in Horeb you provoked the LORD to wrath, so that the LORD was angry *enough* with you to have destroyed you.

Deut 9:22 "Also at Taberah and Massah and Kibroth Hattaavah you provoked the LORD to wrath.

Believers should cease from.

Is 29:23–24 But when he sees his children, The work of My hands, in his midst, They will hallow My name, And hallow the Holy One of Jacob, And fear the God of Israel. **24** These also who erred in spirit will come to understanding, And those who complained will learn doctrine."

Guilt of encouraging others in.

Num 13:31–33 But the men who had gone up with him said, "We are not able to go up against the people, for they *are* stronger than we." **32** And they gave the children of Israel a bad report of the land which they had spied out, saying, "The land through which we have gone as spies *is* a land that devours its inhabitants, and all the people whom we saw in it *are* men of *great* stature. **33** There we saw the giants (the descendants of Anak came from the giants); and we were like grasshoppers in our own sight, and so we were in their sight."

Num 14:36–37 Now the men whom Moses sent to spy out the land, who returned and made all the congregation complain against him by bringing a bad report of the land, **37** those very men who brought the evil report about the land, died by the plague before the Lord.

Punishment of.

Num 11:1 Now *when* the people complained, it displeased the Lord; for the Lord heard *it,* and His anger was aroused. So the fire of the Lord burned among them, and consumed *some* in the outskirts of the camp.

Num 14:27–29 "How long *shall I bear with* this evil congregation who complain against Me? I have heard the complaints which the children of Israel make against Me. **28** Say to them, 'As I live,' says the Lord, 'just as you have spoken in My hearing, so I will do to you: **29** The carcasses of you who have complained against Me shall fall in this wilderness, all of you who were numbered, according to your entire number, from twenty years old and above.

Num 16:45–46 "Get away from among this congregation, that I may consume them in a moment." And they fell on their faces. **46** So Moses said to Aaron, "Take a censer and put fire in it from the altar, put incense *on it,* and take it quickly to the congregation and make atonement for them; for wrath has gone out from the Lord. The plague has begun."

Ps 106:25–26 But complained in their tents, *And* did not heed the voice of the Lord. **26** Therefore He raised His hand *in an oath* against them, To overthrow them in the wilderness,

Illustrated.

Matt 20:11 And when they had received *it,* they complained against the landowner,

Luke 15:29–30 So he answered and said to *his* father, 'Lo, these many years I have been serving you; I never transgressed your commandment at any time; and yet you never gave me a young goat, that I might make merry with my friends. **30** But as soon as this son of yours came, who has devoured your livelihood with harlots, you killed the fatted calf for him.'

Jude 1:16 These are grumblers, complainers, walking according to their own lusts; and they mouth great swelling *words,* flattering people to gain advantage.

Examples of,

Cain.

Gen 4:13–14 And Cain said to the Lord, "My punishment *is* greater than I can bear! **14** Surely You have driven me out this day from the face of the ground; I

shall be hidden from Your face; I shall be a fugitive and a vagabond on the earth, and it will happen *that* anyone who finds me will kill me."

Moses.

Ex 5:22–23 So Moses returned to the Lord and said, "Lord, why have You brought trouble on this people? Why *is* it You have sent me? **23** For since I came to Pharaoh to speak in Your name, he has done evil to this people; neither have You delivered Your people at all."

The Israelites.

Ex 14:11 Then they said to Moses, "Because *there were* no graves in Egypt, have you taken us away to die in the wilderness? Why have you so dealt with us, to bring us up out of Egypt?

Ex 15:24 And the people complained against Moses, saying, "What shall we drink?"

Ex 16:2 Then the whole congregation of the children of Israel complained against Moses and Aaron in the wilderness.

Ex 17:2–3 Therefore the people contended with Moses, and said, "Give us water, that we may drink." So Moses said to them, "Why do you contend with me? Why do you tempt the Lord?" **3** And the people thirsted there for water, and the people complained against Moses, and said, "Why *is* it you have brought us up out of Egypt, to kill us and our children and our livestock with thirst?"

Num 11:1–4 Now *when* the people complained, it displeased the Lord; for the Lord heard *it,* and His anger was aroused. So the fire of the Lord burned among them, and consumed *some* in the outskirts of the camp. **2** Then the people cried out to Moses, and when Moses prayed to the Lord, the fire was quenched. **3** So he called the name of the place Taberah, because the fire of the Lord had burned among them. **4** Now the mixed multitude who were among them yielded to intense craving; so the children of Israel also wept again and said: "Who will give us meat to eat?

Num 21:5 And the people spoke against God and against Moses: "Why have you brought us up out of Egypt to die in the wilderness? For *there is* no food and no water, and our soul loathes this worthless bread."

Aaron, etc.

Num 12:1–2 Then Miriam and Aaron spoke against Moses because of the Ethiopian woman whom he had married; for he had married an Ethiopian woman. **2** So they said, "Has the Lord indeed spoken only through Moses? Has He not spoken through us also?" And the Lord heard *it.*

Num 12:8 I speak with him face to face, Even plainly, and not in dark sayings; And he sees the form of the Lord. Why then were you not afraid To speak against My servant Moses?"

Korah, etc.

Num 16:3 They gathered together against Moses and Aaron, and said to them, "*You take* too much upon yourselves, for all the congregation *is* holy, every one of them, and the Lord *is* among them. Why then do you exalt yourselves above the assembly of the Lord?"

Elijah.

1 Kin 19:4 But he himself went a day's journey into the wilderness, and came and sat down under a broom tree. And he prayed that he might die, and said, "It is enough! Now, LORD, take my life, for I *am* no better than my fathers!"

Job.

Job 3:1–26 After this Job opened his mouth and cursed the day of his *birth.* **2** And Job spoke, and said: **3** "May the day perish on which I was born, And the night *in which* it was said, 'A male child is conceived.' **4** May that day be darkness; May God above not seek it, Nor the light shine upon it. **5** May darkness and the shadow of death claim it; May a cloud settle on it; May the blackness of the day terrify it. **6** *As for* that night, may darkness seize it; May it not rejoice among the days of the year, May it not come into the number of the months. **7** Oh, may that night be barren! May no joyful shout come into it! **8** May those curse it who curse the day, Those who are ready to arouse Leviathan. **9** May the stars of its morning be dark; May it look for light, but *have* none, And not see the dawning of the day; **10** Because it did not shut up the doors of my *mother's* womb, Nor hide sorrow from my eyes. **11** "Why did I not die at birth? *Why* did I *not* perish when I came from the womb? **12** Why did the knees receive me? Or why the breasts, that I should nurse? **13** For now I would have lain still and been quiet, I would have been asleep; Then I would have been at rest **14** With kings and counselors of the earth, Who built ruins for themselves, **15** Or with princes who had gold, Who filled their houses *with* silver; **16** Or *why* was I not hidden like a stillborn child, Like infants who never saw light? **17** There the wicked cease *from* troubling, And there the weary are at rest. **18** *There* the prisoners rest together; They do not hear the voice of the oppressor. **19** The small and great are there, And the servant *is* free from his master. **20** "Why is light given to him who is in misery, And life to the bitter of soul, **21** Who long for death, but it does not *come,* And search for it more than hidden treasures; **22** Who rejoice exceedingly, *And* are glad when they can find the grave? **23** *Why is light given* to a man whose way is hidden, And whom God has hedged in? **24** For my sighing comes before I eat, And my groanings pour out like water. **25** For the thing I greatly feared has come upon me, And what I dreaded has happened to me. **26** I am not at ease, nor am I quiet; I have no rest, for trouble comes."

Jeremiah.

Jer 20:14–18 Cursed *be* the day in which I was born! Let the day not be blessed in which my mother bore me! **15** Let the man *be* cursed Who brought news to my father, saying, "A male child has been born to you!" Making him very glad. **16** And let that man be like the cities Which the LORD overthrew, and did not relent; Let him hear the cry in the morning And the shouting at noon, **17** Because he did not kill me from the womb, That my mother might have been my grave, And her womb always enlarged *with me.* **18** Why did I come forth from the womb to see labor and sorrow, That my days should be consumed with shame?

Jonah.

Jon 4:8–9 And it happened, when the sun arose, that

God prepared a vehement east wind; and the sun beat on Jonah's head, so that he grew faint. Then he wished death for himself, and said, "It is better for me to die than to live." **9** Then God said to Jonah, "Is it right for you to be angry about the plant?" And he said, "It is right for me to be angry, even to death!"

The disciples.

Mark 14:4–5 But there were some who were indignant among themselves, and said, "Why was this fragrant oil wasted? **5** For it might have been sold for more than three hundred denarii and given to the poor." And they criticized her sharply.

John 6:61 When Jesus knew in Himself that His disciples complained about this, He said to them, "Does this offend you?

The Pharisees.

Luke 15:2 And the Pharisees and scribes complained, saying, "This Man receives sinners and eats with them."

Luke 19:7 But when they saw *it,* they all complained, saying, "He has gone to be a guest with a man who is a sinner."

The Jews.

John 6:41–43 The Jews then complained about Him, because He said, "I am the bread which came down from heaven." **42** And they said, "Is not this Jesus, the son of Joseph, whose father and mother we know? How is it then that He says, 'I have come down from heaven'?" **43** Jesus therefore answered and said to them, "Do not murmur among yourselves.

The Greek believers.

Acts 6:1 Now in those days, when *the number of* the disciples was multiplying, there arose a complaint against the Hebrews by the Hellenists, because their widows were neglected in the daily distribution.

CONDEMNATION

Inseparable consequence of sin.

Prov 12:2 A good *man* obtains favor from the LORD, But a man of wicked intentions He will condemn.

Matt 25:41 "Then He will also say to those on the left hand, 'Depart from Me, you cursed, into the everlasting fire prepared for the devil and his angels:

Rom 5:12 Therefore, just as through one man sin entered the world, and death through sin, and thus death spread to all men, because all sinned—

Rom 5:16 And the gift *is* not like *that which came* through the one who sinned. For the judgment *which came* from one *offense resulted* in condemnation, but the free gift *which came* from many offenses *resulted* in justification.

Rom 5:18 Therefore, as through one man's offense *judgment* came to all men, resulting in condemnation, even so through one Man's righteous act *the free gift came* to all men, resulting in justification of life.

Rom 6:23 For the wages of sin *is* death, but the gift of God *is* eternal life in Christ Jesus our Lord.

Increased by

Impenitence.

Matt 11:20–24 Then He began to rebuke the cities in

which most of His mighty works had been done, because they did not repent: **21** "Woe to you, Chorazin! Woe to you, Bethsaida! For if the mighty works which were done in you had been done in Tyre and Sidon, they would have repented long ago in sackcloth and ashes. **22** But I say to you, it will be more tolerable for Tyre and Sidon in the day of judgment than for you. **23** And you, Capernaum, who are exalted to heaven, will be brought down to Hades; for if the mighty works which were done in you had been done in Sodom, it would have remained until this day. **24** But I say to you that it shall be more tolerable for the land of Sodom in the day of judgment than for you."

Unbelief.

John 3:18–19 "He who believes in Him is not condemned; but he who does not believe is condemned already, because he has not believed in the name of the only begotten Son of God. **19** And this is the condemnation, that the light has come into the world, and men loved darkness rather than light, because their deeds were evil.

Pride.

1 Tim 3:6 not a novice, lest being puffed up with pride he fall into the *same* condemnation as the devil.

Oppression.

James 5:1–5 Come now, *you* rich, weep and howl for your miseries that are coming upon *you!* **2** Your riches are corrupted, and your garments are moth-eaten. **3** Your gold and silver are corroded, and their corrosion will be a witness against you and will eat your flesh like fire. You have heaped up treasure in the last days. **4** Indeed the wages of the laborers who mowed your fields, which you kept back by fraud, cry out; and the cries of the reapers have reached the ears of the Lord of Sabaoth. **5** You have lived on the earth in pleasure and luxury; you have fattened your hearts as in a day of slaughter.

Hypocrisy.

Matt 23:14 Woe to you, scribes and Pharisees, hypocrites! For you devour widows' houses, and for a pretense make long prayers. Therefore you will receive greater condemnation.

Conscience testifies to the justice of.

Job 9:20 Though I were righteous, my own mouth would condemn me; Though I *were* blameless, it would prove me perverse.

Rom 2:1 Therefore you are inexcusable, O man, whoever you are who judge, for in whatever you judge another you condemn yourself; for you who judge practice the same things.

Titus 3:11 knowing that such a person is warped and sinning, being self-condemned.

Sinners deserve it.

Matt 12:37 For by your words you will be justified, and by your words you will be condemned."

2 Cor 11:15 Therefore it *is* no great thing if his ministers also transform themselves into ministers of righteousness, whose end will be according to their works.

Saints are delivered from, by Christ.

John 3:18 "He who believes in Him is not condemned;

but he who does not believe is condemned already, because he has not believed in the name of the only begotten Son of God.

John 5:24 "Most assuredly, I say to you, he who hears My word and believes in Him who sent Me has everlasting life, and shall not come into judgment, but has passed from death into life.

Rom 8:1 *There is* therefore now no condemnation to those who are in Christ Jesus, who do not walk according to the flesh, but according to the Spirit.

Rom 8:33–34 Who shall bring a charge against God's elect? *It is* God who justifies. **34** Who *is* he who condemns? *It is* Christ who died, and furthermore is also risen, who is even at the right hand of God, who also makes intercession for us.

Of the wicked, an example.

2 Pet 2:7 and delivered righteous Lot, *who was* oppressed by the filthy conduct of the wicked

Jude 1:7 as Sodom and Gomorrah, and the cities around them in a similar manner to these, having given themselves over to sexual immorality and gone after strange flesh, are set forth as an example, suffering the vengeance of eternal fire.

Chastisements are designed to rescue us from.

Ps 94:12–13 Blessed *is* the man whom You instruct, O Lord, And teach out of Your law, **13** That You may give him rest from the days of adversity, Until the pit is dug for the wicked.

1 Cor 11:32 But when we are judged, we are chastened by the Lord, that we may not be condemned with the world.

Apostates and unbelievers destined for.

John 3:18 "He who believes in Him is not condemned; but he who does not believe is condemned already, because he has not believed in the name of the only begotten Son of God.

John 3:36 He who believes in the Son has everlasting life; and he who does not believe the Son shall not see life, but the wrath of God abides on him."

Jude 1:4 For certain men have crept in unnoticed, who long ago were marked out for this condemnation, ungodly men, who turn the grace of our God into lewdness and deny the only Lord God and our Lord Jesus Christ.

The law is the ministration of.

Rom 3:19 Now we know that whatever the law says, it says to those who are under the law, that every mouth may be stopped, and all the world may become guilty before God.

2 Cor 3:9 For if the ministry of condemnation *had* glory, the ministry of righteousness exceeds much more in glory.

CONDUCT, CHRISTIAN

Believing God.

Mark 11:22 So Jesus answered and said to them, "Have faith in God.

John 14:11–12 Believe Me that I *am* in the Father and the Father in Me, or else believe Me for the sake of the works themselves. **12** "Most assuredly, I say to you, he who believes in Me, the works that I do he will do also; and greater *works* than these he will do, because I go to My Father.

Obeying God.

Deut 6:5 You shall love the LORD your God with all your heart, with all your soul, and with all your strength.

Eccl 12:13 Let us hear the conclusion of the whole matter: Fear God and keep His commandments, For this is man's all.

Mic 6:8 He has shown you, O man, what *is* good; And what does the LORD require of you But to do justly, To love mercy, And to walk humbly with your God?

Matt 22:37 Jesus said to him, " *'You shall love the LORD your God with all your heart, with all your soul, and with all your mind.'*

Luke 1:6 And they were both righteous before God, walking in all the commandments and ordinances of the Lord blameless.

Eph 5:1 Therefore be imitators of God as dear children.

1 Pet 1:15–16 but as He who called you *is* holy, you also be holy in all *your* conduct, **16** because it is written, *"Be holy, for I am holy."*

1 Pet 2:17 Honor all *people*. Love the brotherhood. Fear God. Honor the king.

1 John 5:3 For this is the love of God, that we keep His commandments. And His commandments are not burdensome.

Rejoicing in God.

Ps 33:1 Rejoice in the LORD, O you righteous! *For* praise from the upright is beautiful.

Hab 3:18 Yet I will rejoice in the LORD, I will joy in the God of my salvation.

Believing in Christ.

John 6:29 Jesus answered and said to them, "This is the work of God, that you believe in Him whom He sent."

1 John 3:23 And this is His commandment: that we should believe on the name of His Son Jesus Christ and love one another, as He gave us commandment.

Loving Christ.

John 21:15 So when they had eaten breakfast, Jesus said to Simon Peter, "Simon, *son* of Jonah, do you love Me more than these?" He said to Him, "Yes, Lord; You know that I love You." He said to him, "Feed My lambs."

1 Pet 1:7–8 that the genuineness of your faith, *being* much more precious than gold that perishes, though it is tested by fire, may be found to praise, honor, and glory at the revelation of Jesus Christ, **8** whom having not seen you love. Though now you do not see *Him,* yet believing, you rejoice with joy inexpressible and full of glory,

Obeying Christ.

John 13:15 For I have given you an example, that you should do as I have done to you.

John 14:21 He who has My commandments and keeps them, it is he who loves Me. And he who loves Me will be loved by My Father, and I will love him and manifest Myself to him."

John 15:14 You are My friends if you do whatever I command you.

Rom 6:18 And having been set free from sin, you became slaves of righteousness.

Rom 14:8 For if we live, we live to the Lord; and if we die, we die to the Lord. Therefore, whether we live or die, we are the Lord's.

2 Cor 5:15 and He died for all, that those who live should live no longer for themselves, but for Him who died for them and rose again.

1 Pet 2:21–24 For to this you were called, because Christ also suffered for us, leaving us an example, that you should follow His steps: **22** *"Who committed no sin, Nor was deceit found in His mouth"*; **23** who, when He was reviled, did not revile in return; when He suffered, He did not threaten, but committed *Himself* to Him who judges righteously; **24** who Himself bore our sins in His own body on the tree, that we, having died to sins, might live for righteousness—by whose stripes you were healed.

Walking

Honestly.

1 Thess 4:12 that you may walk properly toward those who are outside, and *that* you may lack nothing.

Worthy of God.

1 Thess 2:12 that you would walk worthy of God who calls you into His own kingdom and glory.

Worthy of the Lord.

Col 1:10 that you may walk worthy of the Lord, fully pleasing *Him,* being fruitful in every good work and increasing in the knowledge of God;

In the Spirit.

Gal 5:25 If we live in the Spirit, let us also walk in the Spirit.

After the Spirit.

Rom 8:1 *There is* therefore now no condemnation to those who are in Christ Jesus, who do not walk according to the flesh, but according to the Spirit.

In newness of life.

Rom 6:4 Therefore we were buried with Him through baptism into death, that just as Christ was raised from the dead by the glory of the Father, even so we also should walk in newness of life.

Worthy of vocation.

Eph 4:1 I, therefore, the prisoner of the Lord, beseech you to walk worthy of the calling with which you were called,

As children of light.

Eph 5:8 For you were once darkness, but now *you are* light in the Lord. Walk as children of light

Rejoicing in Christ.

Phil 3:1 Finally, my brethren, rejoice in the Lord. For me to write the same things to you *is* not tedious, but for you *it is* safe.

Phil 4:4 Rejoice in the Lord always. Again I will say, rejoice!

Loving one another.

John 15:12 This is My commandment, that you love one another as I have loved you.

Rom 12:10 *Be* kindly affectionate to one another with brotherly love, in honor giving preference to one another;

1 Cor 13:1–13 Though I speak with the tongues of men and of angels, but have not love, I have become sounding brass or a clanging cymbal. **2** And though I have *the gift of* prophecy, and understand all mysteries and all knowledge, and though I have all faith, so that I could remove mountains, but have not love, I am nothing. **3** And though I bestow all my goods to feed *the poor,* and though I give my body to be burned, but have not love, it profits me nothing. **4** Love suffers long *and* is kind; love does not envy; love does not parade itself, is not puffed up; **5** does not behave rudely, does not seek its own, is not provoked, thinks no evil; **6** does not rejoice in iniquity, but rejoices in the truth; **7** bears all things, believes all things, hopes all things, endures all things. **8** Love never fails. But whether *there are* prophecies, they will fail; whether *there are* tongues, they will cease; whether *there is* knowledge, it will vanish away. **9** For we know in part and we prophesy in part. **10** But when that which is perfect has come, then that which is in part will be done away. **11** When I was a child, I spoke as a child, I understood as a child, I thought as a child; but when I became a man, I put away childish things. **12** For now we see in a mirror, dimly, but then face to face. Now I know in part, but then I shall know just as I also am known. **13** And now abide faith, hope, love, these three; but the greatest of these *is* love.

Eph 5:2 And walk in love, as Christ also has loved us and given Himself for us, an offering and a sacrifice to God for a sweet-smelling aroma.

Heb 13:1 Let brotherly love continue.

Striving for the faith.

Phil 1:27 Only let your conduct be worthy of the gospel of Christ, so that whether I come and see you or am absent, I may hear of your affairs, that you stand fast in one spirit, with one mind striving together for the faith of the gospel,

Jude 1:3 Beloved, while I was very diligent to write to you concerning our common salvation, I found it necessary to write to you exhorting you to contend earnestly for the faith which was once for all delivered to the saints.

Putting away all sin.

1 Cor 5:7 Therefore purge out the old leaven, that you may be a new lump, since you truly are unleavened. For indeed Christ, our Passover, was sacrificed for us.

1 Cor 9:27 But I discipline my body and bring *it* into subjection, lest, when I have preached to others, I myself should become disqualified.

Eph 4:26 *"Be angry, and do not sin":* do not let the sun go down on your wrath,

Col 3:5 Therefore put to death your members which are on the earth: fornication, uncleanness, passion, evil desire, and covetousness, which is idolatry.

1 Thess 5:22 Abstain from every form of evil.

Heb 12:1 Therefore we also, since we are surrounded by so great a cloud of witnesses, let us lay aside every weight, and the sin which so easily ensnares *us,* and let us run with endurance the race that is set before us,

Jude 1:23 but others save with fear, pulling *them* out of the fire, hating even the garment defiled by the flesh.

Following after holiness and goodness.

Matt 5:16 Let your light so shine before men, that they may see your good works and glorify your Father in heaven.

Matt 5:48 Therefore you shall be perfect, just as your Father in heaven is perfect.

2 Cor 7:1 Therefore, having these promises, beloved, let us cleanse ourselves from all filthiness of the flesh and spirit, perfecting holiness in the fear of God.

Phil 4:8 Finally, brethren, whatever things are true, whatever things *are* noble, whatever things *are* just, whatever things *are* pure, whatever things *are* lovely, whatever things *are* of good report, if *there is* any virtue and if *there is* anything praiseworthy—meditate on these things.

1 Thess 5:15 See that no one renders evil for evil to anyone, but always pursue what is good both for yourselves and for all.

1 Tim 4:12 Let no one despise your youth, but be an example to the believers in word, in conduct, in love, in spirit, in faith, in purity.

1 Tim 6:11 But you, O man of God, flee these things and pursue righteousness, godliness, faith, love, patience, gentleness.

2 Tim 3:17 that the man of God may be complete, thoroughly equipped for every good work.

Titus 2:7 in all things showing yourself *to be* a pattern of good works; in doctrine *showing* integrity, reverence, incorruptibility,

Titus 2:10 not pilfering, but showing all good fidelity, that they may adorn the doctrine of God our Savior in all things.

James 1:19 So then, my beloved brethren, let every man be swift to hear, slow to speak, slow to wrath;

1 Pet 2:12 having your conduct honorable among the Gentiles, that when they speak against you as evildoers, they may, by *your* good works which they observe, glorify God in the day of visitation.

Overcoming the world.

Ps 1:1 Blessed *is* the man Who walks not in the counsel of the ungodly, Nor stands in the path of sinners, Nor sits in the seat of the scornful;

2 Thess 3:6 But we command you, brethren, in the name of our Lord Jesus Christ, that you withdraw from every brother who walks disorderly and not according to the tradition which he received from us.

Titus 2:12 teaching us that, denying ungodliness and worldly lusts, we should live soberly, righteously, and godly in the present age,

1 John 5:4–5 For whatever is born of God overcomes the world. And this is the victory that has overcome the world—our faith. **5** Who is he who overcomes the world, but he who believes that Jesus is the Son of God?

Abounding in the work of the Lord.

1 Cor 15:58 Therefore, my beloved brethren, be steadfast, immovable, always abounding in the work of the Lord, knowing that your labor is not in vain in the Lord.

2 Cor 8:7 But as you abound in everything—in faith, in

speech, in knowledge, in all diligence, and in your love for us—*see* that you abound in this grace also.

1 Thess 4:1 Finally then, brethren, we urge and exhort in the Lord Jesus that you should abound more and more, just as you received from us how you ought to walk and to please God;

Forgiving wrongs.

Matt 5:39–41 But I tell you not to resist an evil person. But whoever slaps you on your right cheek, turn the other to him also. **40** If anyone wants to sue you and take away your tunic, let him have *your* cloak also. **41** And whoever compels you to go one mile, go with him two.

Matt 6:14 "For if you forgive men their trespasses, your heavenly Father will also forgive you.

Rom 12:20 Therefore *"If your enemy is hungry, feed him; If he is thirsty, give him a drink; For in so doing you will heap coals of fire on his head."*

1 Cor 6:7 Now therefore, it is already an utter failure for you that you go to law against one another. Why do you not rather accept wrong? Why do you not rather *let yourselves* be cheated?

Living peaceably with all.

Rom 12:18 If it is possible, as much as depends on you, live peaceably with all men.

Heb 12:14 Pursue peace with all *people,* and holiness, without which no one will see the Lord:

Visiting the afflicted.

Matt 25:36 I *was* naked and you clothed Me; I was sick and you visited Me; I was in prison and you came to Me.'

James 1:27 Pure and undefiled religion before God and the Father is this: to visit orphans and widows in their trouble, *and* to keep oneself unspotted from the world.

Extending fair treatment.

Matt 7:12 Therefore, whatever you want men to do to you, do also to them, for this is the Law and the Prophets.

Luke 6:31 And just as you want men to do to you, you also to do to them likewise.

Sympathizing with others.

Gal 6:2 Bear one another's burdens, and so fulfill the law of Christ.

1 Thess 5:14 Now we exhort you, brethren, warn those who are unruly, comfort the fainthearted, uphold the weak, be patient with all.

Honoring others.

Ps 15:4 In whose eyes a vile person is despised, But he honors those who fear the LORD; He *who* swears to his own hurt and does not change;

Rom 12:10 *Be* kindly affectionate to one another with brotherly love, in honor giving preference to one another;

Fulfilling domestic duties.

Eph 6:1–8 Children, obey your parents in the Lord, for this is right. **2** *"Honor your father and mother,"* which is the first commandment with promise: **3** *"that it may be well with you and you may live long on the earth."* **4** And you, fathers, do not provoke your children to wrath, but bring them up in the

training and admonition of the Lord. **5** Bondservants, be obedient to those who are your masters according to the flesh, with fear and trembling, in sincerity of heart, as to Christ; **6** not with eyeservice, as men-pleasers, but as bondservants of Christ, doing the will of God from the heart, **7** with goodwill doing service, as to the Lord, and not to men, **8** knowing that whatever good anyone does, he will receive the same from the Lord, whether *he is* a slave or free.

1 Pet 3:1–7 Wives, likewise, *be* submissive to your own husbands, that even if some do not obey the word, they, without a word, may be won by the conduct of their wives, **2** when they observe your chaste conduct *accompanied* by fear. **3** Do not let your adornment be *merely* outward—arranging the hair, wearing gold, or putting on *fine* apparel— **4** rather *let it be* the hidden person of the heart, with the incorruptible *beauty* of a gentle and quiet spirit, which is very precious in the sight of God. **5** For in this manner, in former times, the holy women who trusted in God also adorned themselves, being submissive to their own husbands, **6** as Sarah obeyed Abraham, calling him lord, whose daughters you are if you do good and are not afraid with any terror. **7** Husbands, likewise, dwell with *them* with understanding, giving honor to the wife, as to the weaker vessel, and as *being* heirs together of the grace of life, that your prayers may not be hindered.

Submitting to authorities.

Rom 13:1–7 Let every soul be subject to the governing authorities. For there is no authority except from God, and the authorities that exist are appointed by God. **2** Therefore whoever resists the authority resists the ordinance of God, and those who resist will bring judgment on themselves. **3** For rulers are not a terror to good works, but to evil. Do you want to be unafraid of the authority? Do what is good, and you will have praise from the same. **4** For he is God's minister to you for good. But if you do evil, be afraid; for he does not bear the sword in vain; for he is God's minister, an avenger to *execute* wrath on him who practices evil. **5** Therefore *you* must be subject, not only because of wrath but also for conscience' sake. **6** For because of this you also pay taxes, for they are God's ministers attending continually to this very thing. **7** Render therefore to all their due: taxes to whom taxes *are due,* customs to whom customs, fear to whom fear, honor to whom honor.

Being generous to others.

Acts 20:35 I have shown you in every way, by laboring like this, that you must support the weak. And remember the words of the Lord Jesus, that He said, 'It is more blessed to give than to receive.' "

Rom 12:13 distributing to the needs of the saints, given to hospitality.

Being contented.

Phil 4:11 Not that I speak in regard to need, for I have learned in whatever state I am, to be content:

Heb 13:5 *Let your* conduct *be* without covetousness; *be* content with such things as you have. For He Himself has said, *"I will never leave you nor forsake you."*

Blessedness of persevering.

Ps 1:1–3 Blessed *is* the man Who walks not in the counsel of the ungodly, Nor stands in the path of sinners, Nor sits in the seat of the scornful; **2** But his delight *is* in the law of the LORD, And in His law he meditates day and night. **3** He shall be like a tree Planted by the rivers of water, That brings forth its fruit in its season, Whose leaf also shall not wither; And whatever he does shall prosper.

Ps 19:9–11 The fear of the LORD *is* clean, enduring forever; The judgments of the LORD *are* true *and* righteous altogether. **10** More to be desired *are they* than gold, Yea, than much fine gold; Sweeter also than honey and the honeycomb. **11** Moreover by them Your servant is warned, *And* in keeping them *there is* great reward.

Ps 50:23 Whoever offers praise glorifies Me; And to him who orders *his* conduct *aright* I will show the salvation of God."

Matt 5:3–12 "Blessed *are* the poor in spirit, For theirs is the kingdom of heaven. **4** Blessed *are* those who mourn, For they shall be comforted. **5** Blessed *are* the meek, For they shall inherit the earth. **6** Blessed *are* those who hunger and thirst for righteousness, For they shall be filled. **7** Blessed *are* the merciful, For they shall obtain mercy. **8** Blessed *are* the pure in heart, For they shall see God. **9** Blessed *are* the peacemakers, For they shall be called sons of God. **10** Blessed are those who are persecuted for righteousness' sake, For theirs is the kingdom of heaven. **11** "Blessed are you when they revile and persecute you, and say all kinds of evil against you falsely for My sake. **12** Rejoice and be exceedingly glad, for great *is* your reward in heaven, for so they persecuted the prophets who were before you.

John 15:10 If you keep My commandments, you will abide in My love, just as I have kept My Father's commandments and abide in His love.

CONFESSING CHRIST

Influences of the Holy Spirit necessary to.

1 Cor 12:3 Therefore I make known to you that no one speaking by the Spirit of God calls Jesus accursed, and no one can say that Jesus is Lord except by the Holy Spirit.

1 John 4:2 By this you know the Spirit of God: Every spirit that confesses that Jesus Christ has come in the flesh is of God,

Evidence of salvation.

Rom 10:9–10 that if you confess with your mouth the Lord Jesus and believe in your heart that God has raised Him from the dead, you will be saved. **10** For with the heart one believes unto righteousness, and with the mouth confession is made unto salvation.

1 John 2:23 Whoever denies the Son does not have the Father either; he who acknowledges the Son has the Father also.

1 John 4:15 Whoever confesses that Jesus is the Son of God, God abides in him, and he in God.

Ensures His confessing us.

Matt 10:32–33 "Therefore whoever confesses Me before men, him I will also confess before My Father who is in heaven. **33** But whoever denies Me before men, him I will also deny before My Father who is in heaven.

Hindrances to.

Mark 8:35 For whoever desires to save his life will lose it, but whoever loses his life for My sake and the gospel's will save it.

John 7:13 However, no one spoke openly of Him for fear of the Jews.

John 12:42–43 Nevertheless even among the rulers many believed in Him, but because of the Pharisees they did not confess *Him*, lest they should be put out of the synagogue; **43** for they loved the praise of men more than the praise of God.

2 Tim 2:12 If we endure, We shall also reign with *Him*. If we deny *Him*, He also will deny us.

Exemplified by

Nathanael.

John 1:49 Nathanael answered and said to Him, "Rabbi, You are the Son of God! You are the King of Israel!"

Peter.

John 6:68–69 But Simon Peter answered Him, "Lord, to whom shall we go? You have the words of eternal life. **69** Also we have come to believe and know that You are the Christ, the Son of the living God."

Cf. Acts 2:22–36

The man born blind.

John 9:25 He answered and said, "Whether He is a sinner *or not* I do not know. One thing I know: that though I was blind, now I see."

John 9:33 If this Man were not from God, He could do nothing."

Martha.

John 11:27 She said to Him, "Yes, Lord, I believe that You are the Christ, the Son of God, who is to come into the world."

Peter and John.

Acts 4:7–12 And when they had set them in the midst, they asked, "By what power or by what name have you done this?" **8** Then Peter, filled with the Holy Spirit, said to them, "Rulers of the people and elders of Israel: **9** If we this day are judged for a good deed *done* to a helpless man, by what means he has been made well, **10** let it be known to you all, and to all the people of Israel, that by the name of Jesus Christ of Nazareth, whom you crucified, whom God raised from the dead, by Him this man stands here before you whole. **11** This is the *'stone which was rejected by you builders, which has become the chief cornerstone.'* **12** Nor is there salvation in any other, for there is no other name under heaven given among men by which we must be saved."

The apostles.

Acts 5:29–32 But Peter and the *other* apostles answered and said: "We ought to obey God rather than men. **30** The God of our fathers raised up Jesus whom you murdered by hanging on a tree. **31** Him God has exalted to His right hand *to be* Prince and Savior, to give repentance to Israel and forgiveness of sins. **32** And we are His witnesses to these things, and *so* also *is* the Holy Spirit whom God has given to those who obey Him."

Acts 5:42 And daily in the temple, and in every house,

they did not cease teaching and preaching Jesus *as* the Christ.

Stephen.

Acts 7:52 Which of the prophets did your fathers not persecute? And they killed those who foretold the coming of the Just One, of whom you now have become the betrayers and murderers,

Acts 7:59 And they stoned Stephen as he was calling on God and saying, "Lord Jesus, receive my spirit."

Paul.

Acts 9:29 And he spoke boldly in the name of the Lord Jesus and disputed against the Hellenists, but they attempted to kill him.

Timothy.

1 Tim 6:12 Fight the good fight of faith, lay hold on eternal life, to which you were also called and have confessed the good confession in the presence of many witnesses.

John.

Rev 1:9 I, John, both your brother and companion in the tribulation and kingdom and patience of Jesus Christ, was on the island that is called Patmos for the word of God and for the testimony of Jesus Christ.

The Church in Pergamos.

Rev 2:13 "I know your works, and where you dwell, where Satan's throne *is.* And you hold fast to My name, and did not deny My faith even in the days in which Antipas *was* My faithful martyr, who was killed among you, where Satan dwells.

Martyrs.

Rev 20:4 And I saw thrones, and they sat on them, and judgment was committed to them. Then *I saw* the souls of those who had been beheaded for their witness to Jesus and for the word of God, who had not worshiped the beast or his image, and had not received *his* mark on their foreheads or on their hands. And they lived and reigned with Christ for a thousand years.

CONFESSION OF SIN

God regards.

Lev 26:40–42 'But if they confess their iniquity and the iniquity of their fathers, with their unfaithfulness in which they were unfaithful to Me, and that they also have walked contrary to Me, **41** and *that* I also have walked contrary to them and have brought them into the land of their enemies; if their uncircumcised hearts are humbled, and they accept their guilt— **42** then I will remember My covenant with Jacob, and My covenant with Isaac and My covenant with Abraham I will remember; I will remember the land.

Job 33:27–28 Then he looks at men and says, 'I have sinned, and perverted *what was* right, And it did not profit me.' **28** He will redeem his soul from going down to the Pit, And his life shall see the light.

Prov 28:13 He who covers his sins will not prosper, But whoever confesses and forsakes *them* will have mercy.

Dan 9:20–23 Now while I *was* speaking, praying, and confessing my sin and the sin of my people Israel, and presenting my supplication before the LORD my God for the holy mountain of my God, **21** yes, while I *was* speaking in prayer, the man Gabriel, whom I

had seen in the vision at the beginning, being caused to fly swiftly, reached me about the time of the evening offering. **22** And he informed *me,* and talked with me, and said, "O Daniel, I have now come forth to give you skill to understand. **23** At the beginning of your supplications the command went out, and I have come to tell *you,* for you *are* greatly beloved; therefore consider the matter, and understand the vision:

Exhortation to.

Lev 5:5 'And it shall be, when he is guilty in any of these *matters,* that he shall confess that he has sinned in that *thing;*

Josh 7:19 Now Joshua said to Achan, "My son, I beg you, give glory to the LORD God of Israel, and make confession to Him, and tell me now what you have done; do not hide *it* from me."

Jer 3:13 Only acknowledge your iniquity, That you have transgressed against the LORD your God, And have scattered your charms To alien deities under every green tree, And you have not obeyed My voice,' says the LORD.

Hos 5:15 I will return again to My place Till they acknowledge their offense. Then they will seek My face; In their affliction they will earnestly seek Me."

James 5:16 Confess *your* trespasses to one another, and pray for one another, that you may be healed. The effective, fervent prayer of a righteous man avails much.

Should be accompanied with

Willingness to suffer.

Lev 26:41 and *that* I also have walked contrary to them and have brought them into the land of their enemies; if their uncircumcised hearts are humbled, and they accept their guilt—

Ezra 9:13 And after all that has come upon us for our evil deeds and for our great guilt, since You our God have punished us less than our iniquities *deserve,* and have given us *such* deliverance as this,

Neh 9:33 However You *are* just in all that has befallen us; For You have dealt faithfully, But we have done wickedly.

Prayer for forgiveness.

2 Sam 24:10 And David's heart condemned him after he had numbered the people. So David said to the LORD, "I have sinned greatly in what I have done; but now, I pray, O LORD, take away the iniquity of Your servant, for I have done very foolishly."

Ps 25:11 For Your name's sake, O LORD, Pardon my iniquity, for it *is* great.

Ps 51:1 Have mercy upon me, O God, According to Your lovingkindness; According to the multitude of Your tender mercies, Blot out my transgressions.

Jer 14:7–9 O LORD, though our iniquities testify against us, Do it for Your name's sake; For our backslidings are many, We have sinned against You. **8** O the Hope of Israel, his Savior in time of trouble, Why should You be like a stranger in the land, And like a traveler *who* turns aside to tarry for a night? **9** Why should You be like a man astonished, Like a mighty one *who* cannot save? Yet You, O LORD, *are* in our midst, And we are called by Your name; Do not leave us!

Jer 14:20 We acknowledge, O Lord, our wickedness *And* the iniquity of our fathers, For we have sinned against You.

Self-abasement.

Is 64:5–6 You meet him who rejoices and does righteousness, *Who* remembers You in Your ways. You are indeed angry, for we have sinned— In these ways we continue; And we need to be saved. **6** But we are all like an unclean *thing*, And all our righteousnesses *are* like filthy rags; We all fade as a leaf, And our iniquities, like the wind, Have taken us away.

Jer 3:25 We lie down in our shame, And our reproach covers us. For we have sinned against the Lord our God, We and our fathers, From our youth even to this day, And have not obeyed the voice of the Lord our God."

Godly sorrow.

Ps 38:18 For I will declare my iniquity; I will be in anguish over my sin.

Lam 1:20 "See, O Lord, that I *am* in distress; My soul is troubled; My heart is overturned within me, For I have been very rebellious. Outside the sword bereaves, At home *it is* like death.

Forsaking sin.

Prov 28:13 He who covers his sins will not prosper, But whoever confesses and forsakes *them* will have mercy.

Willingness to make restitution.

Num 5:6–7 "Speak to the children of Israel: 'When a man or woman commits any sin that men commit in unfaithfulness against the Lord, and that person is guilty, **7** then he shall confess the sin which he has committed. He shall make restitution for his trespass in full, plus one-fifth of it, and give *it* to the one he has wronged.

Should be full and unreserved.

Ps 32:5 I acknowledged my sin to You, And my iniquity I have not hidden. I said, "I will confess my transgressions to the Lord," And You forgave the iniquity of my sin. Selah

Ps 51:3 For I acknowledge my transgressions, And my sin *is* always before me.

Ps 106:6 We have sinned with our fathers, We have committed iniquity, We have done wickedly.

Followed by pardon.

Ps 32:5 I acknowledged my sin to You, And my iniquity I have not hidden. I said, "I will confess my transgressions to the Lord," And You forgave the iniquity of my sin. Selah

1 John 1:9 If we confess our sins, He is faithful and just to forgive us *our* sins and to cleanse us from all unrighteousness.

Illustrated by

Aaron.

Num 12:11 So Aaron said to Moses, "Oh, my lord! Please do not lay *this* sin on us, in which we have done foolishly and in which we have sinned.

The Israelites.

Num 21:6–7 So the Lord sent fiery serpents among the people, and they bit the people; and many of the people of Israel died. **7** Therefore the people came to Mo-

ses, and said, "We have sinned, for we have spoken against the Lord and against you; pray to the Lord that He take away the serpents from us." So Moses prayed for the people.

1 Sam 7:6 So they gathered together at Mizpah, drew water, and poured *it* out before the Lord. And they fasted that day, and said there, "We have sinned against the Lord." And Samuel judged the children of Israel at Mizpah.

1 Sam 12:19 And all the people said to Samuel, "Pray for your servants to the Lord your God, that we may not die; for we have added to all our sins the evil of asking a king for ourselves."

Saul.

1 Sam 15:24 Then Saul said to Samuel, "I have sinned, for I have transgressed the commandment of the Lord and your words, because I feared the people and obeyed their voice.

David.

2 Sam 24:10 And David's heart condemned him after he had numbered the people. So David said to the Lord, "I have sinned greatly in what I have done; but now, I pray, O Lord, take away the iniquity of Your servant, for I have done very foolishly."

Ezra.

Ezek 9:6 Utterly slay old *and* young men, maidens and little children and women; but do not come near anyone on whom *is* the mark; and begin at My sanctuary." So they began with the elders who *were* before the temple.

Nehemiah.

Neh 1:6–7 please let Your ear be attentive and Your eyes open, that You may hear the prayer of Your servant which I pray before You now, day and night, for the children of Israel Your servants, and confess the sins of the children of Israel which we have sinned against You. Both my father's house and I have sinned. **7** We have acted very corruptly against You, and have not kept the commandments, the statutes, nor the ordinances which You commanded Your servant Moses.

The Levites.

Neh 9:4 Then Jeshua, Bani, Kadmiel, Shebaniah, Bunni, Sherebiah, Bani, *and* Chenani stood on the stairs of the Levites and cried out with a loud voice to the Lord their God.

Neh 9:33–34 However You *are* just in all that has befallen us; For You have dealt faithfully, But we have done wickedly. **34** Neither our kings nor our princes, Our priests nor our fathers, Have kept Your law, Nor heeded Your commandments and Your testimonies, With which You testified against them.

Job.

Job 7:20 Have I sinned? What have I done to You, O watcher of men? Why have You set me as Your target, So that I am a burden to myself?

Daniel.

Dan 9:4 And I prayed to the Lord my God, and made confession, and said, "O Lord, great and awesome God, who keeps His covenant and mercy with those who love Him, and with those who keep His commandments,

Peter.

Luke 5:8 When Simon Peter saw *it*, he fell down at Jesus' knees, saying, "Depart from me, for I am a sinful man, O Lord!"

The prodigal son.

Luke 15:21 And the son said to him, 'Father, I have sinned against heaven and in your sight, and am no longer worthy to be called your son.'

The tax collector.

Luke 18:13 And the tax collector, standing afar off, would not so much as raise *his* eyes to heaven, but beat his breast, saying, 'God, be merciful to me a sinner!'

The thief.

Luke 23:41 And we indeed justly, for we receive the due reward of our deeds; but this Man has done nothing wrong."

CONFIDENCE

In God's wisdom.

Prov 3:26 For the LORD will be your confidence, And will keep your foot from being caught.

In God's sovereign control.

Acts 4:24–30 So when they heard that, they raised their voice to God with one accord and said: "Lord, You *are* God, who made heaven and earth and the sea, and all that is in them, **25** who by the mouth of Your servant David have said: *'Why did the nations rage, And the people plot vain things?* **26** *The kings of the earth took their stand, And the rulers were gathered together Against the LORD and against His Christ.'* **27** "For truly against Your holy Servant Jesus, whom You anointed, both Herod and Pontius Pilate, with the Gentiles and the people of Israel, were gathered together **28** to do whatever Your hand and Your purpose determined before to be done. **29** Now, Lord, look on their threats, and grant to Your servants that with all boldness they may speak Your word, **30** by stretching out Your hand to heal, and that signs and wonders may be done through the name of Your holy Servant Jesus."

In God's support.

Is 50:8–9 *He is* near who justifies Me; Who will contend with Me? Let us stand together. Who *is* My adversary? Let him come near Me. **9** Surely the Lord GOD will help Me; Who *is* he *who* will condemn Me? Indeed they will all grow old like a garment; The moth will eat them up.

In prayer.

Zech 10:1 Ask the LORD for rain In the time of the latter rain. The LORD will make flashing clouds; He will give them showers of rain, Grass in the field for everyone.

1 John 5:14 Now this is the confidence that we have in Him, that if we ask anything according to His will, He hears us.

In one's access to God.

Eph 3:12 in whom we have boldness and access with confidence through faith in Him.

Heb 10:19 Therefore, brethren, having boldness to enter the Holiest by the blood of Jesus,

To reckon as true.

Rom 6:11 Likewise you also, reckon yourselves to be dead indeed to sin, but alive to God in Christ Jesus our Lord.

Boldness.

2 Cor 3:12 Therefore, since we have such hope, we use great boldness of speech—

2 Cor 7:4 Great *is* my boldness of speech toward you, great *is* my boasting on your behalf. I am filled with comfort. I am exceedingly joyful in all our tribulation.

Not in one's humanness.

Phil 3:3 For we are the circumcision, who worship God in the Spirit, rejoice in Christ Jesus, and have no confidence in the flesh,

In the return of Christ.

1 John 2:28 And now, little children, abide in Him, that when He appears, we may have confidence and not be ashamed before Him at His coming.

CONFUSION

As a metaphor, wine of.

Ps 60:3 You have shown Your people hard things; You have made us drink the wine of confusion.

As a curse.

Deut 28:28 The LORD will strike you with madness and blindness and confusion of heart.

Zech 12:4 In that day," says the LORD, "I will strike every horse with confusion, and its rider with madness; I will open My eyes on the house of Judah, and will strike every horse of the peoples with blindness.

Of the disciples regarding Jesus' departure.

John 13:36 Simon Peter said to Him, "Lord, where are You going?" Jesus answered him, "Where I am going you cannot follow Me now, but you shall follow Me afterward."

John 14:5 Thomas said to Him, "Lord, we do not know where You are going, and how can we know the way?"

God is not the author of.

1 Cor 14:33 For God is not *the author* of confusion but of peace, as in all the churches of the saints.

Result of human wisdom.

James 3:14–16 But if you have bitter envy and self-seeking in your hearts, do not boast and lie against the truth. **15** This wisdom does not descend from above, but *is* earthly, sensual, demonic. **16** For where envy and self-seeking *exist*, confusion and every evil thing *are* there.

CONSCIENCE

Witnesses in man.

Prov 20:27 The spirit of a man *is* the lamp of the LORD, Searching all the inner depths of his heart.

Rom 2:15 who show the work of the law written in their hearts, their conscience also bearing witness, and between themselves *their* thoughts accusing or else excusing *them*)

Accuses of sin.

Gen 42:21 Then they said to one another, "We *are* truly guilty concerning our brother, for we saw the anguish of his soul when he pleaded with us, and we would not hear; therefore this distress has come upon us."

2 Sam 24:10 And David's heart condemned him after he had numbered the people. So David said to the LORD, "I have sinned greatly in what I have done; but now, I pray, O LORD, take away the iniquity of Your servant, for I have done very foolishly."

Matt 27:3 Then Judas, His betrayer, seeing that He had been condemned, was remorseful and brought back the thirty pieces of silver to the chief priests and elders,

Acts 2:37 Now when they heard *this*, they were cut to the heart, and said to Peter and the rest of the apostles, "Men *and* brethren, what shall we do?"

Should affirm believers.

Job 27:6 My righteousness I hold fast, and will not let it go; My heart shall not reproach *me* as long as I live.

Acts 23:1 Then Paul, looking earnestly at the council, said, "Men *and* brethren, I have lived in all good conscience before God until this day."

Acts 24:16 This *being* so, I myself always strive to have a conscience without offense toward God and men.

Acts 26:9 "Indeed, I myself thought I must do many things contrary to the name of Jesus of Nazareth.

Rom 9:1 I tell the truth in Christ, I am not lying, my conscience also bearing me witness in the Holy Spirit,

Rom 14:22 Do you have faith? Have *it* to yourself before God. Happy *is* he who does not condemn himself in what he approves.

Heb 13:18 Pray for us; for we are confident that we have a good conscience, in all things desiring to live honorably.

1 Pet 3:16 having a good conscience, that when they defame you as evildoers, those who revile your good conduct in Christ may be ashamed.

1 Pet 3:21 There is also an antitype which now saves us—baptism (not the removal of the filth of the flesh, but the answer of a good conscience toward God), through the resurrection of Jesus Christ,

Only Christ's blood can purify.

Heb 9:14 how much more shall the blood of Christ, who through the eternal Spirit offered Himself without spot to God, cleanse your conscience from dead works to serve the living God?

Heb 10:2–10 For then would they not have ceased to be offered? For the worshipers, once purified, would have had no more consciousness of sins. **3** But in those *sacrifices there is* a reminder of sins every year. **4** For *it is* not possible that the blood of bulls and goats could take away sins. **5** Therefore, when He came into the world, He said: *"Sacrifice and offering You did not desire, But a body You have prepared for Me.* **6** *In burnt offerings and sacrifices for sin You had no pleasure.* **7** *Then I said, 'Behold, I have come— In the volume of the book it is written of Me— To do Your will, O God.'* **8** Previously saying, *"Sacrifice and offering, burnt offerings, and offerings for sin You did not desire, nor had pleasure in them"* (which are offered according to the law), **9** then He said, *"Behold, I have come to do Your will, O God."*

He takes away the first that He may establish the second. **10** By that will we have been sanctified through the offering of the body of Jesus Christ once *for all.*

Heb 10:22 let us draw near with a true heart in full assurance of faith, having our hearts sprinkled from an evil conscience and our bodies washed with pure water.

Walk obediently for sake of.

Rom 13:5 Therefore *you* must be subject, not only because of wrath but also for conscience' sake.

2 Cor 1:12 For our boasting is this: the testimony of our conscience that we conducted ourselves in the world in simplicity and godly sincerity, not with fleshly wisdom but by the grace of God, and more abundantly toward you.

1 Tim 1:19 having faith and a good conscience, which some having rejected, concerning the faith have suffered shipwreck,

1 Tim 3:9 holding the mystery of the faith with a pure conscience.

1 Pet 2:19 For this *is* commendable, if because of conscience toward God one endures grief, suffering wrongfully.

1 John 3:21 Beloved, if our heart does not condemn us, we have confidence toward God.

Of others, not to be offended.

Rom 14:21 *It is* good neither to eat meat nor drink wine nor *do anything* by which your brother stumbles or is offended or is made weak.

1 Cor 10:28–32 But if anyone says to you, "This was offered to idols," do not eat it for the sake of the one who told you, and for conscience' sake; for *"the earth is the LORD's, and all its fullness."* **29** "Conscience," I say, not your own, but that of the other. For why is my liberty judged by another *man's* conscience? **30** But if I partake with thanks, why am I evil spoken of for *the food* over which I give thanks? **31** Therefore, whether you eat or drink, or whatever you do, do all to the glory of God. **32** Give no offense, either to the Jews or to the Greeks or to the church of God,

Ministers should commend themselves to that of their people.

2 Cor 4:2 But we have renounced the hidden things of shame, not walking in craftiness nor handling the word of God deceitfully, but by manifestation of the truth commending ourselves to every man's conscience in the sight of God.

2 Cor 5:11 Knowing, therefore, the terror of the Lord, we persuade men; but we are well known to God, and I also trust are well known in your consciences.

Of wicked unbelievers.

1 Tim 4:2 speaking lies in hypocrisy, having their own conscience seared with a hot iron,

Titus 1:15 To the pure all things are pure, but to those who are defiled and unbelieving nothing is pure; but even their mind and conscience are defiled.

CONTEMPT

Sin of.

Job 31:13–14 "If I have despised the cause of my male or female servant When they complained against me, **14** What then shall I do when God rises up? When He punishes, how shall I answer Him?

Prov 11:12 He who is devoid of wisdom despises his neighbor, But a man of understanding holds his peace.

Prov 14:21 He who despises his neighbor sins; But he who has mercy on the poor, happy *is* he.

A characteristic of the wicked.

Prov 18:3 When the wicked comes, contempt comes also; And with dishonor *comes* reproach.

Is 5:24 Therefore, as the fire devours the stubble, And the flame consumes the chaff, *So* their root will be as rottenness, And their blossom will ascend like dust; Because they have rejected the law of the LORD of hosts, And despised the word of the Holy One of Israel.

2 Tim 3:3 unloving, unforgiving, slanderers, without self-control, brutal, despisers of good,

Forbidden toward

Parents.

Prov 23:22 Listen to your father who begot you, And do not despise your mother when she is old.

Christ's little ones.

Matt 18:10 "Take heed that you do not despise one of these little ones, for I say to you that in heaven their angels always see the face of My Father who is in heaven.

Weak brethren.

Rom 14:3 Let not him who eats despise him who does not eat, and let not him who does not eat judge him who eats; for God has received him.

Young ministers.

1 Cor 16:11 Therefore let no one despise him. But send him on his journey in peace, that he may come to me; for I am waiting for him with the brethren.

1 Tim 4:12 Let no one despise your youth, but be an example to the believers in word, in conduct, in love, in spirit, in faith, in purity.

Believing masters.

1 Tim 6:2 And those who have believing masters, let them not despise *them* because they are brethren, but rather serve *them* because those who are benefited are believers and beloved. Teach and exhort these things.

The poor.

James 2:1–3 My brethren, do not hold the faith of our Lord Jesus Christ, *the Lord* of glory, with partiality. **2** For if there should come into your assembly a man with gold rings, in fine apparel, and there should also come in a poor man in filthy clothes, **3** and you pay attention to the one wearing the fine clothes and say to him, "You sit here in a good place," and say to the poor man, "You stand there," or, "Sit here at my footstool,"

Self-righteous pride leads to.

Ps 123:4 Our soul is exceedingly filled With the scorn of those who are at ease, With the contempt of the proud.

Is 65:5 Who say, 'Keep to yourself, Do not come near me, For I am holier than you!' These *are* smoke in My nostrils, A fire that burns all the day.

Luke 18:9 Also He spoke this parable to some who trusted in themselves that they were righteous, and despised others:

Luke 18:11 The Pharisee stood and prayed thus with himself, 'God, I thank You that I am not like other men—extortioners, unjust, adulterers, or even as this tax collector.

Of ministers, is a despising of God.

Luke 10:16 He who hears you hears Me, he who rejects you rejects Me, and he who rejects Me rejects Him who sent Me."

1 Thess 4:8 Therefore he who rejects *this* does not reject man, but God, who has also given us His Holy Spirit.

Causes believers to cry to God.

Neh 4:4 Hear, O our God, for we are despised; turn their reproach on their own heads, and give them as plunder to a land of captivity!

Ps 123:3 Have mercy on us, O LORD, have mercy on us! For we are exceedingly filled with contempt.

The wicked exhibit toward

Christ.

Ps 22:6 But I *am* a worm, and no man; A reproach of men, and despised by the people.

Is 53:3 He is despised and rejected by men, A Man of sorrows and acquainted with grief. And we hid, as it were, *our* faces from Him; He was despised, and we did not esteem Him.

Matt 27:29 When they had twisted a crown of thorns, they put *it* on His head, and a reed in His right hand. And they bowed the knee before Him and mocked Him, saying, "Hail, King of the Jews!"

Believers.

Ps 119:141 I *am* small and despised, *Yet* I do not forget Your precepts.

Authorities.

2 Pet 2:10 and especially those who walk according to the flesh in the lust of uncleanness and despise authority. *They are* presumptuous, self-willed. They are not afraid to speak evil of dignitaries,

Jude 1:8 Likewise also these dreamers defile the flesh, reject authority, and speak evil of dignitaries.

Parents.

Prov 15:5 A fool despises his father's instruction, But he who receives correction is prudent.

Prov 15:20 A wise son makes a father glad, But a foolish man despises his mother.

The afflicted.

Job 19:18 Even young children despise me; I arise, and they speak against me.

The poor.

Ps 14:6 You shame the counsel of the poor, But the LORD is his refuge.

Eccl 9:16 Then I said: "Wisdom *is* better than strength. Nevertheless the poor man's wisdom *is* despised, And his words are not heard.

Illustrated by

Hagar.

Gen 16:4 So he went in to Hagar, and she conceived. And when she saw that she had conceived, her mistress became despised in her eyes.

Children of Belial.

1 Sam 10:27 But some rebels said, "How can this man save us?" So they despised him, and brought him no presents. But he held his peace.

Nabal.

1 Sam 25:10–11 Then Nabal answered David's servants, and said, "Who *is* David, and who *is* the son of Jesse? There are many servants nowadays who break away each one from his master. **11** Shall I then take my bread and my water and my meat that I have killed for my shearers, and give *it* to men when I do not know where they *are* from?"

Michal.

2 Sam 6:16 Now as the ark of the Lord came into the City of David, Michal, Saul's daughter, looked through a window and saw King David leaping and whirling before the Lord; and she despised him in her heart.

Sanballat, etc.

Neh 2:19 But when Sanballat the Horonite, Tobiah the Ammonite official, and Geshem the Arab heard *of it,* they laughed at us and despised us, and said, "What *is* this thing that you are doing? Will you rebel against the king?"

Neh 4:2–3 And he spoke before his brethren and the army of Samaria, and said, "What are these feeble Jews doing? Will they fortify themselves? Will they offer sacrifices? Will they complete it in a day? Will they revive the stones from the heaps of rubbish— *stones* that are burned?" **3** Now Tobiah the Ammonite *was* beside him, and he said, "Whatever they build, if even a fox goes up *on it,* he will break down their stone wall."

False teachers.

2 Cor 10:10 "For *his* letters," they say, "*are* weighty and powerful, but *his* bodily presence *is* weak, and *his* speech contemptible."

CONTENTMENT

Believers should exhibit.

Ps 37:16 A little that a righteous man has *Is* better than the riches of many wicked.

Luke 3:14 Likewise the soldiers asked him, saying, "And what shall we do?" So he said to them, "Do not intimidate anyone or accuse falsely, and be content with your wages."

1 Cor 7:20 Let each one remain in the same calling in which he was called.

1 Tim 6:6 Now godliness with contentment is great gain.

1 Tim 6:8 And having food and clothing, with these we shall be content.

Heb 13:5 *Let your* conduct *be* without covetousness; *be* content with such things as you have. For He Himself has said, *"I will never leave you nor forsake you."*

The wicked lack.

Eccl 5:10 He who loves silver will not be satisfied with silver; Nor he who loves abundance, with increase. This also *is* vanity.

Is 5:8 Woe to those who join house to house; They add field to field, Till *there is* no place Where they may dwell alone in the midst of the land!

Exemplified by

Barzillai.

2 Sam 19:33–37 And the king said to Barzillai, "Come across with me, and I will provide for you while you are with me in Jerusalem." **34** But Barzillai said to the king, "How long have I to live, that I should go up with the king to Jerusalem? **35** I *am* today eighty years old. Can I discern between the good and bad? Can your servant taste what I eat or what I drink? Can I hear any longer the voice of singing men and singing women? Why then should your servant be a further burden to my lord the king? **36** Your servant will go a little way across the Jordan with the king. And why should the king repay me *with* such a reward? **37** Please let your servant turn back again, that I may die in my own city, near the grave of my father and mother. But here is your servant Chimham; let him cross over with my lord the king, and do for him what seems good to you."

A Shunammite.

2 Kin 4:13 And he said to him, "Say now to her, 'Look, you have been concerned for us with all this care. What *can I* do for you? Do you want me to speak on your behalf to the king or to the commander of the army?' " She answered, "I dwell among my own people."

David.

Ps 16:6 The lines have fallen to me in pleasant *places;* Yes, I have a good inheritance.

Agur.

Prov 30:8–9 Remove falsehood and lies far from me; Give me neither poverty nor riches— Feed me with the food allotted to me; **9** Lest I be full and deny *You,* And say, "Who *is* the Lord?" Or lest I be poor and steal, And profane the name of my God.

Paul.

Phil 4:11–12 Not that I speak in regard to need, for I have learned in whatever state I am, to be content: **12** I know how to be abased, and I know how to abound. Everywhere and in all things I have learned both to be full and to be hungry, both to abound and to suffer need.

CONTRACTS

Formal ones were written on scroll(s).

Rev 5:1 And I saw in the right *hand* of Him who sat on the throne a scroll written inside and on the back, sealed with seven seals.

Cf. Jer 32:10–15

Jacob's with Laban.

Gen 29:18–30 Now Jacob loved Rachel; so he said, "I will serve you seven years for Rachel your younger daughter." **19** And Laban said, "*It is* better that I give her to you than that I should give her to another man. Stay with me." **20** So Jacob served seven years for Rachel, and they seemed *only* a few days to him because of the love he had for her. **21** Then Jacob said to Laban, "Give *me* my wife, for my days are fulfilled, that I may go in to her." **22** And Laban gathered together all the men of the place and made a feast. **23** Now it came to pass in the evening, that he took Leah his daughter and brought her to Jacob; and he went in to her. **24** And Laban gave his maid Zilpah to his daughter Leah *as* a maid. **25** So it came to pass in the morning, that behold, it *was* Leah. And he said to Laban, "What is this you have done to me? Was it not for Rachel that I served you? Why then have you deceived me?" **26** And Laban said, "It must not be done so in our country, to give the younger before the firstborn. **27** Fulfill her week, and we will give you this one also for the service which you will serve with me still another seven years." **28** Then Jacob did so and fulfilled her week. So he gave him his daughter Rachel as wife also. **29** And Laban gave his maid Bilhah to his daughter Rachel as a maid. **30** Then *Jacob* also went in to Rachel, and he also loved Rachel more than Leah. And he served with Laban still another seven years.

Gen 30:25–43 And it came to pass, when Rachel had borne Joseph, that Jacob said to Laban, "Send me away, that I may go to my own place and to my country. **26** Give *me* my wives and my children for whom I have served you, and let me go; for you know my service which I have done for you." **27** And Laban said to him, "Please *stay*, if I have found favor in your eyes, *for* I have learned by experience that the LORD has blessed me for your sake." **28** Then he said, "Name me your wages, and I will give *it.*" **29** So *Jacob* said to him, "You know how I have served you and how your livestock has been with me. **30** For what you had before I *came was* little, and it has increased to a great amount; the LORD has blessed you since my coming. And now, when shall I also provide for my own house?" **31** So he said, "What shall I give you?" And Jacob said, "You shall not give me anything. If you will do this thing for me, I will again feed and keep your flocks: **32** Let me pass through all your flock today, removing from there all the speckled and spotted sheep, and all the brown ones among the lambs, and the spotted and speckled among the goats; and *these* shall be my wages. **33** So my righteousness will answer for me in time to come, when the subject of my wages comes before you: every one that *is* not speckled and spotted among the goats, and brown among the lambs, will be considered stolen, if *it is* with me." **34** And Laban said, "Oh, that it were according to your word!" **35** So he removed that day the male goats that were speckled and spotted, all the female goats that were speckled and spotted, every one that had *some* white in it, and all the brown ones among the lambs, and gave *them* into the hand of his sons. **36** Then he put three days' journey between himself and Jacob, and Jacob fed the rest of Laban's flocks. **37** Now Jacob took for himself rods of green poplar and of the almond and chestnut trees, peeled white strips in them, and exposed the white which *was* in the rods. **38** And the rods which he had peeled, he set before the flocks in the gutters, in the watering troughs where the flocks came to drink, so that they should conceive when they came to drink. **39** So the flocks conceived before the rods, and the flocks brought forth streaked, speckled, and spotted. **40** Then Jacob separated the lambs, and made the flocks face toward the streaked and all the brown in the flock of Laban; but he put his own flocks by themselves and did not put them with Laban's flock. **41** And it came to pass, whenever the stronger livestock conceived, that Jacob placed the rods before the eyes of the livestock in the gutters, that they might conceive among the rods. **42** But when the flocks were feeble, he did not put *them* in; so the feebler were Laban's and the stronger Jacob's. **43** Thus the man became exceedingly prosperous, and had large flocks, female and male servants, and camels and donkeys.

Gen 31:1–9 Now *Jacob* heard the words of Laban's sons, saying, "Jacob has taken away all that was our father's, and from what was our father's he has acquired all this wealth." **2** And Jacob saw the countenance of Laban, and indeed it *was not favorable* toward him as before. **3** Then the LORD said to Jacob, "Return to the land of your fathers and to your family, and I will be with you." **4** So Jacob sent and called Rachel and Leah to the field, to his flock, **5** and said to them, "I see your father's countenance, that it *is* not *favorable* toward me as before; but the God of my father has been with me. **6** And you know that with all my might I have served your father. **7** Yet your father has deceived me and changed my wages ten times, but God did not allow him to hurt me. **8** If he said thus: 'The speckled shall be your wages,' then all the flocks bore speckled. And if he said thus: 'The streaked shall be your wages,' then all the flocks bore streaked. **9** So God has taken away the livestock of your father and given *them* to me.

As the marriage agreement.

Gen 2:24 Therefore a man shall leave his father and mother and be joined to his wife, and they shall become one flesh.

Mal 2:14 Yet you say, "For what reason?" Because the LORD has been witness Between you and the wife of your youth, With whom you have dealt treacherously; Yet she is your companion And your wife by covenant.

Cf. Gen 31:50; Prov 2:17

CONVERSION

Divine origin of.

1 Kin 18:37 Hear me, O LORD, hear me, that this people may know that You *are* the LORD God, and *that* You have turned their hearts back *to You* again."

Prov 1:23 Turn at my rebuke; Surely I will pour out my spirit on you; I will make my words known to you.

John 6:44 No one can come to Me unless the Father who sent Me draws him; and I will raise him up at the last day.

Acts 3:26 To you first, God, having raised up His Servant Jesus, sent Him to bless you, in turning away every one *of you* from your iniquities."

Acts 11:21 And the hand of the Lord was with them, and a great number believed and turned to the Lord.

Acts 11:23 When he came and had seen the grace of God, he was glad, and encouraged them all that with purpose of heart they should continue with the Lord.

Acts 21:19 When he had greeted them, he told in detail those things which God had done among the Gentiles through his ministry.

Rom 15:18 For I will not dare to speak of any of those things which Christ has not accomplished through me, in word and deed, to make the Gentiles obedient—

Is the result of faith and repentance.

Acts 3:19 Repent therefore and be converted, that your sins may be blotted out, so that times of refreshing may come from the presence of the Lord,

Acts 11:21 And the hand of the Lord was with them, and a great number believed and turned to the Lord.

Acts 26:20 but declared first to those in Damascus and in Jerusalem, and throughout all the region of Judea, and *then* to the Gentiles, that they should repent, turn to God, and do works befitting repentance.

Through the instrumentality of

The Scriptures.

Ps 19:7 The law of the LORD *is* perfect, converting the soul; The testimony of the LORD *is* sure, making wise the simple;

Ministers.

Acts 26:18 to open their eyes, *in order* to turn *them* from darkness to light, and *from* the power of Satan to God, that they may receive forgiveness of sins and an inheritance among those who are sanctified by faith in Me.'

1 Thess 1:9 For they themselves declare concerning us what manner of entry we had to you, and how you turned to God from idols to serve the living and true God,

Self-examination.

Ps 119:59 I thought about my ways, And turned my feet to Your testimonies.

Lam 3:40 Let us search out and examine our ways, And turn back to the LORD;

Affliction.

Ps 78:34 When He slew them, then they sought Him; And they returned and sought earnestly for God.

Of sinners, a cause for joy

To God.

Ezek 18:23 Do I have any pleasure at all that the wicked should die?" says the Lord GOD, "*and* not that he should turn from his ways and live?

Luke 15:32 It was right that we should make merry and be glad, for your brother was dead and is alive again, and was lost and is found.' "

To believers.

Acts 15:3 So, being sent on their way by the church, they passed through Phoenicia and Samaria, describing the conversion of the Gentiles; and they caused great joy to all the brethren.

Gal 1:23–24 But they were hearing only, "He who formerly persecuted us now preaches the faith which he once *tried to* destroy." 24 And they glorified God in me.

Exhortations to.

Job 36:10 He also opens their ear to instruction, And commands that they turn from iniquity.

Prov 1:23 Turn at my rebuke; Surely I will pour out my spirit on you; I will make my words known to you.

Is 31:6 Return *to Him* against whom the children of Israel have deeply revolted.

Is 55:7 Let the wicked forsake his way, And the unrigh-

teous man his thoughts; Let him return to the LORD, And He will have mercy on him; And to our God, For He will abundantly pardon.

Jer 3:7 And I said, after she had done all these *things*, 'Return to Me.' But she did not return. And her treacherous sister Judah saw it.

Ezek 33:11 Say to them: '*As* I live,' says the Lord GOD, 'I have no pleasure in the death of the wicked, but that the wicked turn from his way and live. Turn, turn from your evil ways! For why should you die, O house of Israel?'

Matt 18:3 and said, "Assuredly, I say to you, unless you are converted and become as little children, you will by no means enter the kingdom of heaven.

Promises connected with.

Neh 1:9 but *if* you return to Me, and keep My commandments and do them, though some of you were cast out to the farthest part of the heavens, *yet* I will gather them from there, and bring them to the place which I have chosen as a dwelling for My name.'

Is 1:27 Zion shall be redeemed with justice, And her penitents with righteousness.

Jer 3:14 "Return, O backsliding children," says the LORD; "for I am married to you. I will take you, one from a city and two from a family, and I will bring you to Zion.

Ezek 18:27 Again, when a wicked *man* turns away from the wickedness which he committed, and does what is lawful and right, he preserves himself alive.

Pray for.

Ps 80:7 Restore us, O God of hosts; Cause Your face to shine, And we shall be saved!

Ps 85:4 Restore us, O God of our salvation, And cause Your anger toward us to cease.

Jer 31:18 "I have surely heard Ephraim bemoaning himself: 'You have chastised me, and I was chastised, Like an untrained bull; Restore me, and I will return, For You *are* the LORD my God.

Lam 5:21 Turn us back to You, O LORD, and we will be restored; Renew our days as of old,

Is accompanied by confession of sin, and prayer.

1 Kin 8:35 "When the heavens are shut up and there is no rain because they have sinned against You, when they pray toward this place and confess Your name, and turn from their sin because You afflict them,

Danger of neglecting.

Ps 7:12 If he does not turn back, He will sharpen His sword; He bends His bow and makes it ready.

Jer 44:5 But they did not listen or incline their ear to turn from their wickedness, to burn no incense to other gods.

Jer 44:11 "Therefore thus says the LORD of hosts, the God of Israel: 'Behold, I will set My face against you for catastrophe and for cutting off all Judah.

Ezek 3:19 Yet, if you warn the wicked, and he does not turn from his wickedness, nor from his wicked way, he shall die in his iniquity; but you have delivered your soul.

Encouragement for leading sinners to.

Ps 51:13 *Then* I will teach transgressors Your ways, And sinners shall be converted to You.

Dan 12:3 Those who are wise shall shine Like the brightness of the firmament, And those who turn many to righteousness Like the stars forever and ever.

James 5:19–20 Brethren, if anyone among you wanders from the truth, and someone turns him back, **20** let him know that he who turns a sinner from the error of his way will save a soul from death and cover a multitude of sins.

Of Gentiles, predicted.

Is 2:2 Now it shall come to pass in the latter days *That* the mountain of the LORD's house Shall be established on the top of the mountains, And shall be exalted above the hills; And all nations shall flow to it.

Is 11:10 "And in that day there shall be a Root of Jesse, Who shall stand as a banner to the people; For the Gentiles shall seek Him, And His resting place shall be glorious."

Is 60:5 Then you shall see and become radiant, And your heart shall swell with joy; Because the abundance of the sea shall be turned to you, The wealth of the Gentiles shall come to you.

Is 66:12 For thus says the LORD: "Behold, I will extend peace to her like a river, And the glory of the Gentiles like a flowing stream. Then you shall feed; On *her* sides shall you be carried, And be dandled on *her* knees.

Of Israel, predicted.

Ezek 36:25–27 Then I will sprinkle clean water on you, and you shall be clean; I will cleanse you from all your filthiness and from all your idols. **26** I will give you a new heart and put a new spirit within you; I will take the heart of stone out of your flesh and give you a heart of flesh. **27** I will put My Spirit within you and cause you to walk in My statutes, and you will keep My judgments and do *them*.

CORRUPTION

Woe to those who lead someone into.

Prov 28:10 Whoever causes the upright to go astray in an evil way, He himself will fall into his own pit; But the blameless will inherit good.

Matt 5:19 Whoever therefore breaks one of the least of these commandments, and teaches men so, shall be called least in the kingdom of heaven; but whoever does and teaches *them*, he shall be called great in the kingdom of heaven.

Matt 23:15 "Woe to you, scribes and Pharisees, hypocrites! For you travel land and sea to win one proselyte, and when he is won, you make him twice as much a son of hell as yourselves.

Of spiritual leaders.

Hab 1:4 Therefore the law is powerless, And justice never goes forth. For the wicked surround the righteous; Therefore perverse judgment proceeds.

2 Pet 2:19 While they promise them liberty, they themselves are slaves of corruption; for by whom a person is overcome, by him also is he brought into bondage.

People enticed by fruits of.

Zeph 3:6–7 "I have cut off nations, Their fortresses are devastated; I have made their streets desolate, With none passing by. Their cities are destroyed; *There is*

no one, no inhabitant. **7** I said, 'Surely you will fear Me, You will receive instruction'— So that her dwelling would not be cut off, *Despite* everything for which I punished her. But they rose early and corrupted all their deeds.

The result of sin.

Rom 6:23 For the wages of sin *is* death, but the gift of God *is* eternal life in Christ Jesus our Lord.

Gal 6:8 For he who sows to his flesh will of the flesh reap corruption, but he who sows to the Spirit will of the Spirit reap everlasting life.

Opposite of sanctification.

1 Tim 4:5 for it is sanctified by the word of God and prayer.

Titus 1:15 To the pure all things are pure, but to those who are defiled and unbelieving nothing is pure; but even their mind and conscience are defiled.

The believer escapes.

2 Pet 1:4 by which have been given to us exceedingly great and precious promises, that through these you may be partakers of the divine nature, having escaped the corruption *that is* in the world through lust.

COURAGE

Infused with, from God.

Judg 7:15 And so it was, when Gideon heard the telling of the dream and its interpretation, that he worshiped. He returned to the camp of Israel, and said, "Arise, for the LORD has delivered the camp of Midian into your hand."

Essential for leadership.

2 Chr 19:11 And take notice: Amariah the chief priest *is* over you in all matters of the LORD; and Zebadiah the son of Ishmael, the ruler of the house of Judah, for all the king's matters; also the Levites *will be* officials before you. Behave courageously, and the LORD will be with the good."

Necessary for obeying God.

Josh 1:7 Only be strong and very courageous, that you may observe to do according to all the law which Moses My servant commanded you; do not turn from it to the right hand or to the left, that you may prosper wherever you go.

Ps 31:24 Be of good courage, And He shall strengthen your heart, All you who hope in the LORD.

Synonym for being of good cheer.

Matt 9:2 Then behold, they brought to Him a paralytic lying on a bed. When Jesus saw their faith, He said to the paralytic, "Son, be of good cheer; your sins are forgiven you."

Mark 6:50 for they all saw Him and were troubled. But immediately He talked with them and said to them, "Be of good cheer! It is I; do not be afraid."

Cf. Luke 8:48; John 16:33

In spite of severe trouble or persecution.

2 Cor 1:8–10 For we do not want you to be ignorant, brethren, of our trouble which came to us in Asia: that we were burdened beyond measure, above strength, so that we despaired even of life. **9** Yes, we had the sentence of death in ourselves, that we should not trust in ourselves but in God who raises the dead, **10** who delivered us from so great a death, and does deliver us; in whom we trust that He will still deliver *us*,

James 5:8 You also be patient. Establish your hearts, for the coming of the Lord is at hand.

Exemplified by Jeremiah.

Jer 26:12–14 Then Jeremiah spoke to all the princes and all the people, saying: "The LORD sent me to prophesy against this house and against this city with all the words that you have heard. **13** Now therefore, amend your ways and your doings, and obey the voice of the LORD your God; then the LORD will relent concerning the doom that He has pronounced against you. **14** As for me, here I am, in your hand; do with me as seems good and proper to you.

COURTS OF JUSTICE

Secular, have authority from God.

Rom 13:1–5 Let every soul be subject to the governing authorities. For there is no authority except from God, and the authorities that exist are appointed by God. **2** Therefore whoever resists the authority resists the ordinance of God, and those who resist will bring judgment on themselves. **3** For rulers are not a terror to good works, but to evil. Do you want to be unafraid of the authority? Do what is good, and you will have praise from the same. **4** For he is God's minister to you for good. But if you do evil, be afraid; for he does not bear the sword in vain; for he is God's minister, an avenger to *execute* wrath on him who practices evil. **5** Therefore *you* must be subject, not only because of wrath but also for conscience' sake.

Superior court

Held first by Moses alone in the wilderness.

Ex 18:13–20 And so it was, on the next day, that Moses sat to judge the people; and the people stood before Moses from morning until evening. **14** So when Moses' father-in-law saw all that he did for the people, he said, "What *is* this thing that you are doing for the people? Why do you alone sit, and all the people stand before you from morning until evening?" **15** And Moses said to his father-in-law, "Because the people come to me to inquire of God. **16** When they have a difficulty, they come to me, and I judge between one and another; and I make known the statutes of God and His laws." **17** So Moses' father-in-law said to him, "The thing that you do *is* not good. **18** Both you and these people who *are* with you will surely wear yourselves out. For this thing *is* too much for you; you are not able to perform it by yourself. **19** Listen now to my voice; I will give you counsel, and God will be with you: Stand before God for the people, so that you may bring the difficulties to God. **20** And you shall teach them the statutes and the laws, and show them the way in which they must walk and the work they must do.

Consisted subsequently of priests, Levites, and judges.

Deut 17:9 And you shall come to the priests, the Levites, and to the judge *there* in those days, and inquire *of them;* they shall pronounce upon you the sentence of judgment.

Deut 17:12 Now the man who acts presumptuously

and will not heed the priest who stands to minister there before the LORD your God, or the judge, that man shall die. So you shall put away the evil from Israel.

Judg 4:4–5 Now Deborah, a prophetess, the wife of Lapidoth, was judging Israel at that time. **5** And she would sit under the palm tree of Deborah between Ramah and Bethel in the mountains of Ephraim. And the children of Israel came up to her for judgment.

Mal 2:7 "For the lips of a priest should keep knowledge, And *people* should seek the law from his mouth; For he is the messenger of the LORD of hosts.

Decided on all appeals and difficult cases.

Ex 18:26 So they judged the people at all times; the hard cases they brought to Moses, but they judged every small case themselves.

Deut 1:17 You shall not show partiality in judgment; you shall hear the small as well as the great; you shall not be afraid in any man's presence, for the judgment is God's. The case that is too hard for you, bring to me, and I will hear it.'

Deut 17:8–9 "If a matter arises which is too hard for you to judge, between degrees of guilt for bloodshed, between one judgment or another, or between one punishment or another, matters of controversy within your gates, then you shall arise and go up to the place which the LORD your God chooses. **9** And you shall come to the priests, the Levites, and to the judge *there* in those days, and inquire *of them;* they shall pronounce upon you the sentence of judgment.

Decisions of, conclusive.

Deut 17:10–11 You shall do according to the sentence which they pronounce upon you in that place which the LORD chooses. And you shall be careful to do according to all that they order you. **11** According to the sentence of the law in which they instruct you, according to the judgment which they tell you, you shall do; you shall not turn aside *to* the right hand or *to* the left from the sentence which they pronounce upon you.

Inferior court

In all cities.

Deut 16:18 "You shall appoint judges and officers in all your gates, which the LORD your God gives you, according to your tribes, and they shall judge the people with just judgment.

2 Chr 19:5–7 Then he set judges in the land throughout all the fortified cities of Judah, city by city, **6** and said to the judges, "Take heed to what you are doing, for you do not judge for man but for the LORD, who *is* with you in the judgment. **7** Now therefore, let the fear of the LORD be upon you; take care and do *it*, for *there is* no iniquity with the LORD our God, no partiality, nor taking of bribes."

Held at the gates.

Gen 34:20 And Hamor and Shechem his son came to the gate of their city, and spoke with the men of their city, saying:

Deut 16:18 "You shall appoint judges and officers in all your gates, which the LORD your God gives you, according to your tribes, and they shall judge the people with just judgment.

Deut 21:19 then his father and his mother shall take hold of him and bring him out to the elders of his city, to the gate of his city.

Judges of, appointed by the governor.

Ex 18:21 Moreover you shall select from all the people able men, such as fear God, men of truth, hating covetousness; and place *such* over them *to be* rulers of thousands, rulers of hundreds, rulers of fifties, and rulers of tens.

Ex 18:25 And Moses chose able men out of all Israel, and made them heads over the people: rulers of thousands, rulers of hundreds, rulers of fifties, and rulers of tens.

Deut 1:9–15 "And I spoke to you at that time, saying: 'I alone am not able to bear you. **10** The LORD your God has multiplied you, and here you *are* today, as the stars of heaven in multitude. **11** May the LORD God of your fathers make you a thousand times more numerous than you are, and bless you as He has promised you! **12** How can I alone bear your problems and your burdens and your complaints? **13** Choose wise, understanding, and knowledgeable men from among your tribes, and I will make them heads over you.' **14** And you answered me and said, 'The thing which you have told *us* to do *is* good.' **15** So I took the heads of your tribes, wise and knowledgeable men, and made them heads over you, leaders of thousands, leaders of hundreds, leaders of fifties, leaders of tens, and officers for your tribes.

2 Sam 15:3 Then Absalom would say to him, "Look, your case *is* good and right; but *there is* no deputy of the king to hear you."

All minor cases decided by.

Ex 18:26 So they judged the people at all times; the hard cases they brought to Moses, but they judged every small case themselves.

2 Sam 15:4 Moreover Absalom would say, "Oh, that I were made judge in the land, and everyone who has any suit or cause would come to me; then I would give him justice."

All transfers of property made before.

Gen 23:17–20 So the field of Ephron which *was* in Machpelah, which *was* before Mamre, the field and the cave which *was* in it, and all the trees that *were* in the field, which *were* within all the surrounding borders, were deeded **18** to Abraham as a possession in the presence of the sons of Heth, before all who went in at the gate of his city. **19** And after this, Abraham buried Sarah his wife in the cave of the field of Machpelah, before Mamre (that *is*, Hebron) in the land of Canaan. **20** So the field and the cave that *is* in it were deeded to Abraham by the sons of Heth as property for a burial place.

Ruth 4:1–2 Now Boaz went up to the gate and sat down there; and behold, the close relative of whom Boaz had spoken came by. So Boaz said, "Come aside, friend, sit down here." So he came aside and sat down. **2** And he took ten men of the elders of the city, and said, "Sit down here." So they sat down.

Re-established by Jehoshaphat.

2 Chr 19:5–10 Then he set judges in the land throughout all the fortified cities of Judah, city by city, **6** and said to the judges, "Take heed to what you are doing, for you do not judge for man but for the LORD, who *is* with you in the judgment. **7** Now therefore, let the fear of the LORD be upon you; take care and do *it*, for *there is* no iniquity with the LORD our God, no partiality, nor taking of bribes." **8** Moreover in Jerusalem, for the judgment of the LORD and for controversies, Jehoshaphat appointed some of the Levites and priests, and some of the chief fathers of Israel, when they returned to Jerusalem. **9** And he commanded them, saying, "Thus you shall act in the fear of the LORD, faithfully and with a loyal heart: **10** Whatever case comes to you from your brethren who dwell in their cities, whether of bloodshed or offenses against law or commandment, against statutes or ordinances, you shall warn them, lest they trespass against the LORD and wrath come upon you and your brethren. Do this, and you will not be guilty.

Re-established by Ezra.

Ezra 7:25 And you, Ezra, according to your God-given wisdom, set magistrates and judges who may judge all the people who *are in the region* beyond the River, all such as know the laws of your God; and teach those who do not know *them.*

Of the Romans in Judea

Presided over by the governor or deputy.

Matt 27:2 And when they had bound Him, they led Him away and delivered Him to Pontius Pilate the governor.

Matt 27:11 Now Jesus stood before the governor. And the governor asked Him, saying, "Are You the King of the Jews?" Jesus said to him, "*It is as you say.*"

Acts 18:12 When Gallio was proconsul of Achaia, the Jews with one accord rose up against Paul and brought him to the judgment seat,

Place of, called the hall of judgment.

John 18:28 Then they led Jesus from Caiaphas to the Praetorium, and it was early morning. But they themselves did not go into the Praetorium, lest they should be defiled, but that they might eat the Passover.

John 18:33 Then Pilate entered the Praetorium again, called Jesus, and said to Him, "Are You the King of the Jews?"

John 19:9 and went again into the Praetorium, and said to Jesus, "Where are You from?" But Jesus gave him no answer.

Regarding religion.

Acts 18:14–15 And when Paul was about to open *his* mouth, Gallio said to the Jews, "If it were a matter of wrongdoing or wicked crimes, O Jews, there would be reason why I should bear with you. **15** But if it is a question of words and names and your own law, look *to it* yourselves; for I do not want to be a judge of such *matters.*"

Acts 24:8 commanding his accusers to come to you. By examining him yourself you may ascertain all these things of which we accuse him."

Could alone award death.

John 18:31 Then Pilate said to them, "You take Him and judge Him according to your law." Therefore the Jews said to him, "It is not lawful for us to put anyone to death,"

Had privileges.

Acts 22:25–29 And as they bound him with thongs, Paul said to the centurion who stood by, "Is it lawful for you to scourge a man who is a Roman, and uncondemned?" **26** When the centurion heard *that*, he went and told the commander, saying, "Take care what you do, for this man is a Roman." **27** Then the commander came and said to him, "Tell me, are you a Roman?" He said, "Yes." **28** The commander answered, "With a large sum I obtained this citizenship." And Paul said, "But I was born *a citizen.*" **29** Then immediately those who were about to examine him withdrew from him; and the commander was also afraid after he found out that he was a Roman, and because he had bound him.

Appeals from, made to the emperor.

Acts 25:11 For if I am an offender, or have committed anything deserving of death, I do not object to dying; but if there is nothing in these things of which these men accuse me, no one can deliver me to them. I appeal to Caesar."

Acts 26:32 Then Agrippa said to Festus, "This man might have been set free if he had not appealed to Caesar."

Acts 28:19 But when the Jews spoke against *it,* I was compelled to appeal to Caesar, not that I had anything of which to accuse my nation.

Generally held in the morning.

Jer 21:12 O house of David! Thus says the LORD: "Execute judgment in the morning; And deliver *him who is* plundered Out of the hand of the oppressor, Lest My fury go forth like fire And burn so that no one can quench *it,* Because of the evil of your doings.

Matt 27:1 When morning came, all the chief priests and elders of the people plotted against Jesus to put Him to death.

Luke 22:66 As soon as it was day, the elders of the people, both chief priests and scribes, came together and led Him into their council, saying,

Acts 5:21 And when they heard *that,* they entered the temple early in the morning and taught. But the high priest and those with him came and called the council together, with all the elders of the children of Israel, and sent to the prison to have them brought.

Sometimes held in synagogues.

Matt 10:17 But beware of men, for they will deliver you up to councils and scourge you in their synagogues.

Acts 22:19 So I said, 'Lord, they know that in every synagogue I imprisoned and beat those who believe on You.

Acts 26:11 And I punished them often in every synagogue and compelled *them* to blaspheme; and being exceedingly enraged against them, I persecuted *them* even to foreign cities.

James 2:2 For if there should come into your assembly a man with gold rings, in fine apparel, and there should also come in a poor man in filthy clothes,

Provided with

Judges.

Deut 16:18 "You shall appoint judges and officers in all your gates, which the LORD your God gives you, according to your tribes, and they shall judge the people with just judgment.

Matt 5:25 Agree with your adversary quickly, while you are on the way with him, lest your adversary deliver you to the judge, the judge hand you over to the officer, and you be thrown into prison.

Executioners.

Matt 18:34 And his master was angry, and delivered him to the torturers until he should pay all that was due to him.

Judges of,

Called elders.

Deut 25:7 But if the man does not want to take his brother's wife, then let his brother's wife go up to the gate to the elders, and say, 'My husband's brother refuses to raise up a name to his brother in Israel; he will not perform the duty of my husband's brother.'

1 Sam 16:4 So Samuel did what the LORD said, and went to Bethlehem. And the elders of the town trembled at his coming, and said, "Do you come peaceably?"

Called magistrates.

Luke 12:58 When you go with your adversary to the magistrate, make every effort along the way to settle with him, lest he drag you to the judge, the judge deliver you to the officer, and the officer throw you into prison.

To judge righteously.

Lev 19:15 'You shall do no injustice in judgment. You shall not be partial to the poor, nor honor the person of the mighty. In righteousness you shall judge your neighbor.

Deut 1:6 "The LORD our God spoke to us in Horeb, saying: 'You have dwelt long enough at this mountain.

2 Chr 19:6–7 and said to the judges, "Take heed to what you are doing, for you do not judge for man but for the LORD, who *is* with you in the judgment. **7** Now therefore, let the fear of the LORD be upon you; take care and do *it,* for *there is* no iniquity with the LORD our God, no partiality, nor taking of bribes."

2 Chr 19:9 And he commanded them, saying, "Thus you shall act in the fear of the LORD, faithfully and with a loyal heart:

To judge impartially.

Ex 23:3 You shall not show partiality to a poor man in his dispute.

Ex 23:6 "You shall not pervert the judgment of your poor in his dispute.

Ex 23:8 And you shall take no bribe, for a bribe blinds the discerning and perverts the words of the righteous.

Lev 19:15 'You shall do no injustice in judgment. You shall not be partial to the poor, nor honor the person of the mighty. In righteousness you shall judge your neighbor.

Deut 1:17 You shall not show partiality in judgment; you shall hear the small as well as the great; you shall not be afraid in any man's presence, for the judgment *is* God's. The case that is too hard for you, bring to me, and I will hear it.'

Deut 16:19 You shall not pervert justice; you shall not show partiality, nor take a bribe, for a bribe blinds the eyes of the wise and twists the words of the righteous.

Prov 22:22 Do not rob the poor because he *is* poor, Nor oppress the afflicted at the gate;

To decide according to the law.

Deut 19:18 And the judges shall make careful inquiry, and indeed, *if* the witness *is* a false witness, who has testified falsely against his brother,

Ezek 44:24 In controversy they shall stand as judges, *and* judge it according to My judgments. They shall keep My laws and My statutes in all My appointed meetings, and they shall hallow My Sabbaths.

To promote peace.

Zech 8:16 These *are* the things you shall do: Speak each man the truth to his neighbor; Give judgment in your gates for truth, justice, and peace;

Sat on the judgment seat while hearing cases.

Ex 18:13 And so it was, on the next day, that Moses sat to judge the people; and the people stood before Moses from morning until evening.

Is 28:6 For a spirit of justice to him who sits in judgment, And for strength to those who turn back the battle at the gate.

Matt 27:19 While he was sitting on the judgment seat, his wife sent to him, saying, "Have nothing to do with that just Man, for I have suffered many things today in a dream because of Him."

Conferred together before giving judgment.

Acts 5:34–40 Then one in the council stood up, a Pharisee named Gamaliel, a teacher of the law held in respect by all the people, and commanded them to put the apostles outside for a little while. 35 And he said to them: "Men of Israel, take heed to yourselves what you intend to do regarding these men. 36 For some time ago Theudas rose up, claiming to be somebody. A number of men, about four hundred, joined him. He was slain, and all who obeyed him were scattered and came to nothing. 37 After this man, Judas of Galilee rose up in the days of the census, and drew away many people after him. He also perished, and all who obeyed him were dispersed. 38 And now I say to you, keep away from these men and let them alone; for if this plan or this work is of men, it will come to nothing; 39 but if it is of God, you cannot overthrow it—lest you even be found to fight against God." 40 And they agreed with him, and when they had called for the apostles and beaten *them*, they commanded that they should not speak in the name of Jesus, and let them go.

Acts 25:12 Then Festus, when he had conferred with the council, answered, "You have appealed to Caesar? To Caesar you shall go!"

Acts 26:30–31 When he had said these things, the king stood up, as well as the governor and Bernice and those who sat with them; 31 and when they had gone aside, they talked among themselves, saying, "This man is doing nothing deserving of death or chains."

Pronounced the judgment of the court.

Matt 26:65–66 Then the high priest tore his clothes, saying, "He has spoken blasphemy! What further need do we have of witnesses? Look, now you have heard His blasphemy! 66 What do you think?" They answered and said, "He is deserving of death."

Luke 23:24 So Pilate gave sentence that it should be as they requested.

Acts 5:40 And they agreed with him, and when they had called for the apostles and beaten *them*, they commanded that they should not speak in the name of Jesus, and let them go.

Both the accusers and accused required to appear before.

Deut 25:1 "If there is a dispute between men, and they come to court, that *the judges* may judge them, and they justify the righteous and condemn the wicked,

Acts 25:16 To them I answered, 'It is not the custom of the Romans to deliver any man to destruction before the accused meets the accusers face to face, and has opportunity to answer for himself concerning the charge against him.'

The accused

Stood before the judge.

Num 35:12 They shall be cities of refuge for you from the avenger, that the manslayer may not die until he stands before the congregation in judgment.

Matt 27:11 Now Jesus stood before the governor. And the governor asked Him, saying, "Are You the King of the Jews?" Jesus said to him, "*It is as* you say."

Permitted to plead their own cause.

1 Kin 3:17–22 And one woman said, "O my lord, this woman and I dwell in the same house; and I gave birth while she *was* in the house. 18 Then it happened, the third day after I had given birth, that this woman also gave birth. And we *were* together; no one *was* with us in the house, except the two of us in the house. 19 And this woman's son died in the night, because she lay on him. 20 So she arose in the middle of the night and took my son from my side, while your maidservant slept, and laid him in her bosom, and laid her dead child in my bosom. 21 And when I rose in the morning to nurse my son, there he was, dead. But when I had examined him in the morning, indeed, he was not my son whom I had borne." 22 Then the other woman said, "No! But the living one *is* my son, and the dead one *is* your son." And the first woman said, "No! But the dead one *is* your son, and the living one *is* my son." Thus they spoke before the king.

Acts 24:10 Then Paul, after the governor had nodded to him to speak, answered: "Inasmuch as I know that you have been for many years a judge of this nation, I do the more cheerfully answer for myself,

Acts 26:1 Then Agrippa said to Paul, "You are permitted to speak for yourself." So Paul stretched out his hand and answered for himself:

Might have advocates.

Prov 31:8–9 Open your mouth for the speechless, In the cause of all *who are* appointed to die. 9 Open your mouth, judge righteously, And plead the cause of the poor and needy.

Is 1:17 Learn to do good; Seek justice, Rebuke the oppressor; Defend the fatherless, Plead for the widow.

Acts 24:1 Now after five days Ananias the high priest came down with the elders and a certain orator *named* Tertullus. These gave evidence to the governor against Paul.

Exhorted to confess.

Josh 7:19 Now Joshua said to Achan, "My son, I beg you, give glory to the LORD God of Israel, and make confession to Him, and tell me now what you have done; do not hide *it* from me."

Examined under oath.

Lev 5:1 'If a person sins in hearing the utterance of an oath, and *is* a witness, whether he has seen or known *of the matter*—if he does not tell *it*, he bears guilt.

Matt 26:63 But Jesus kept silent. And the high priest answered and said to Him, "I put You under oath by the living God: Tell us if You are the Christ, the Son of God!"

Sometimes treated with insult or torture.

Matt 26:67 Then they spat in His face and beat Him; and others struck *Him* with the palms of their hands,

John 18:22–23 And when He had said these things, one of the officers who stood by struck Jesus with the palm of his hand, saying, "Do You answer the high priest like that?" 23 Jesus answered him, "If I have spoken evil, bear witness of the evil; but if well, why do you strike Me?"

Acts 16:19–21 But when her masters saw that their hope of profit was gone, they seized Paul and Silas and dragged *them* into the marketplace to the authorities. 20 And they brought them to the magistrates, and said, "These men, being Jews, exceedingly trouble our city; 21 and they teach customs which are not lawful for us, being Romans, to receive or observe."

Acts 22:24 the commander ordered him to be brought into the barracks, and said that he should be examined under scourging, so that he might know why they shouted so against him.

Acts 23:2–3 And the high priest Ananias commanded those who stood by him to strike him on the mouth. 3 Then Paul said to him, "God will strike you, *you* whitewashed wall! For you sit to judge me according to the law, and do you command me to be struck contrary to the law?"

The evidence of two or more witnesses required.

Deut 17:6 Whoever is deserving of death shall be put to death on the testimony of two or three witnesses; he shall not be put to death on the testimony of one witness.

Deut 19:15 "One witness shall not rise against a man concerning any iniquity or any sin that he commits; by the mouth of two or three witnesses the matter shall be established.

John 8:17 It is also written in your law that the testimony of two men is true.

2 Cor 13:1 This *will be* the third *time* I am coming to you. *"By the mouth of two or three witnesses every word shall be established."*

Witnesses sometimes laid their hands on the criminal's head before punishment.

Lev 24:14 "Take outside the camp him who has cursed; then let all who heard *him* lay their hands on his head, and let all the congregation stone him.

Fate of witnesses in.

Deut 19:19 then you shall do to him as he thought to have done to his brother; so you shall put away the evil from among you.

Corruption and bribery often practiced in.

Is 10:1 "Woe to those who decree unrighteous decrees, Who write misfortune, *Which* they have prescribed

Amos 5:12 For I know your manifold transgressions And your mighty sins: Afflicting the just *and* taking bribes; Diverting the poor *from justice* at the gate.

Amos 8:6 That we may buy the poor for silver, And the needy for a pair of sandals— Even sell the bad wheat?"

The judgment of,

Not given till accused was heard.

John 7:51 "Does our law judge a man before it hears him and knows what he is doing?"

Immediately executed.

Deut 25:2 then it shall be, if the wicked man deserves to be beaten, that the judge will cause him to lie down and be beaten in his presence, according to his guilt, with a certain number of blows.

Josh 7:25 And Joshua said, "Why have you troubled us? The LORD will trouble you this day." So all Israel stoned him with stones; and they burned them with fire after they had stoned them with stones.

Mark 15:15–20 So Pilate, wanting to gratify the crowd, released Barabbas to them; and he delivered Jesus, after he had scourged *Him,* to be crucified. 16 Then the soldiers led Him away into the hall called Praetorium, and they called together the whole garrison. 17 And they clothed Him with purple; and they twisted a crown of thorns, put it on His *head,* 18 and began to salute Him, "Hail, King of the Jews!" 19 Then they struck Him on the head with a reed and spat on Him; and bowing the knee, they worshiped Him. 20 And when they had mocked Him, they took the purple off Him, put His own clothes on Him, and led Him out to crucify Him.

Witnesses first to execute.

Deut 17:7 The hands of the witnesses shall be the first against him to put him to death, and afterward the hands of all the people. So you shall put away the evil from among you.

Acts 7:58 and they cast *him* out of the city and stoned *him.* And the witnesses laid down their clothes at the feet of a young man named Saul.

Allusions to.

Job 5:4 His sons are far from safety, They are crushed in the gate, And *there is* no deliverer.

Matt 5:22 But I say to you that whoever is angry with his brother without a cause shall be in danger of the judgment. And whoever says to his brother, 'Raca!' shall be in danger of the council. But whoever says, 'You fool!' shall be in danger of hell fire.

Illustrative of the last judgment.

Matt 19:28 So Jesus said to them, "Assuredly I say to you, that in the regeneration, when the Son of Man sits on the throne of His glory, you who have followed Me will also sit on twelve thrones, judging the twelve tribes of Israel.

Rom 14:10 But why do you judge your brother? Or why do you show contempt for your brother? For we shall all stand before the judgment seat of Christ.

1 Cor 6:2 Do you not know that the saints will judge the world? And if the world will be judged by you, are you unworthy to judge the smallest matters?

COVENANTS

Agreements between two parties.

Gen 26:28 But they said, "We have certainly seen that the LORD is with you. So we said, 'Let there now be an oath between us, between you and us; and let us make a covenant with you,

Dan 11:6 And at the end of *some* years they shall join forces, for the daughter of the king of the South shall go to the king of the North to make an agreement; but she shall not retain the power of her authority, and neither he nor his authority shall stand; but she shall be given up, with those who brought her, and with him who begot her, and with him who strengthened her in *those* times.

Designed for

Establishing friendship.

1 Sam 18:3 Then Jonathan and David made a covenant, because he loved him as his own soul.

Mutual protection in war and peace.

Gen 26:28–29 But they said, "We have certainly seen that the LORD is with you. So we said, 'Let there now be an oath between us, between you and us; and let us make a covenant with you, 29 that you will do us no harm, since we have not touched you, and since we have done nothing to you but good and have sent you away in peace. You *are* now the blessed of the LORD.' "

Gen 31:50–52 If you afflict my daughters, or if you take *other* wives besides my daughters, *although* no man *is* with us—see, God *is* witness between you and me!" 51 Then Laban said to Jacob, "Here is this heap and here is *this* pillar, which I have placed between you and me. 52 This heap *is* a witness, and *this* pillar *is* a witness, that I will not pass beyond this heap to you, and you will not pass beyond this heap and this pillar to me, for harm.

Josh 9:15–16 So Joshua made peace with them, and made a covenant with them to let them live; and the rulers of the congregation swore to them. 16 And it happened at the end of three days, after they had made a covenant with them, that they heard that they *were* their neighbors who dwelt near them.

1 Kin 5:12 So the LORD gave Solomon wisdom, as He had promised him; and there was peace between Hiram and Solomon, and the two of them made a treaty together.

1 Kin 15:18–19 Then Asa took all the silver and gold *that was* left in the treasuries of the house of the LORD and the treasuries of the king's house, and delivered them into the hand of his servants. And King Asa sent them to Ben-Hadad the son of Tabrimmon, the son of Hezion, king of Syria, who dwelt in Damascus, saying, 19 "*Let there be* a treaty between you and me, as there was between my father and your father. See, I have sent you a present of silver and gold. Come and break your treaty with Baasha king of Israel, so that he will withdraw from me."

2 Kin 17:41 So these nations feared the LORD, yet served their carved images; also their children and their children's children have continued doing as their fathers did, even to this day.

Economic reasons.

Gen 23:14–16 And Ephron answered Abraham, saying to him, 15 "My lord, listen to me; the land *is worth* four hundred shekels of silver. What *is* that between you and me? So bury your dead." 16 And Abraham listened to Ephron; and Abraham weighed out the silver for Ephron which he had named in the hearing of the sons of Heth, four hundred shekels of silver, currency of the merchants.

1 Kin 5:6–11 Now therefore, command that they cut down cedars for me from Lebanon; and my servants will be with your servants, and I will pay you wages for your servants according to whatever you say. For you know *there is* none among us who has skill to cut timber like the Sidonians. 7 So it was, when Hiram heard the words of Solomon, that he rejoiced greatly and said, Blessed *be* the LORD this day, for He has given David a wise son over this great people! 8 Then Hiram sent to Solomon, saying: I have considered *the message* which you sent me, *and* I will do all you desire concerning the cedar and cypress logs. 9 My servants shall bring *them* down from Lebanon to the sea; I will float them in rafts by sea to the place you indicate to me, and will have them broken apart there; then you can take *them* away. And you shall fulfill my desire by giving food for my household. 10 Then Hiram gave Solomon cedar and cypress logs *according to* all his desire. 11 And Solomon gave Hiram twenty thousand kors of wheat *as* food for his household, and twenty kors of pressed oil. Thus Solomon gave to Hiram year by year.

Conditions of,

Clearly specified.

1 Sam 11:1–2 Then Nahash the Ammonite came up and encamped against Jabesh Gilead; and all the men of Jabesh said to Nahash, "Make a covenant with us, and we will serve you." 2 And Nahash the Ammonite answered them, "On this *condition* I will make *a covenant* with you, that I may put out all your right eyes, and bring reproach on all Israel."

Confirmed by oath.

Gen 21:23 Now therefore, swear to me by God that you will not deal falsely with me, with my offspring, or with my posterity; but that according to the kindness that I have done to you, you will do to me and to the land in which you have dwelt."

Gen 21:31 Therefore he called that place Beersheba, because the two of them swore an oath there.

Gen 26:31 Then they arose early in the morning and swore an oath with one another; and Isaac sent them away, and they departed from him in peace.

Witnessed.

Gen 23:17–18 So the field of Ephron which *was* in Machpelah, which *was* before Mamre, the field and the cave which *was* in it, and all the trees that *were* in the field, which *were* within all the surrounding borders, were deeded 18 to Abraham as a possession in the presence of the sons of Heth, before all who went in at the gate of his city.

Ruth 4:9–11 And Boaz said to the elders and all the people, "You *are* witnesses this day that I have bought all that was Elimelech's, and all that *was* Chilion's and Mahlon's, from the hand of Naomi. 10 Moreover,

Ruth the Moabitess, the widow of Mahlon, I have acquired as my wife, to perpetuate the name of the dead through his inheritance, that the name of the dead may not be cut off from among his brethren and from his position at the gate. You *are* witnesses this day." **11** And all the people who *were* at the gate, and the elders, said, "*We are* witnesses. The LORD make the woman who is coming to your house like Rachel and Leah, the two who built the house of Israel; and may you prosper in Ephrathah and be famous in Bethlehem.

Ratification of,

Written and sealed.

Neh 9:38 "And because of all this, We make a sure *covenant* and write *it;* Our leaders, our Levites, *and* our priests seal *it.*"

Neh 10:1 Now those who placed *their* seal on *the document were:* Nehemiah the governor, the son of Hacaliah, and Zedekiah,

God often called to witness.

Gen 31:50 If you afflict my daughters, or if you take *other* wives besides my daughters, *although* no man *is* with us—see, God *is* witness between you and me!"

Gen 31:53 The God of Abraham, the God of Nahor, and the God of their father judge between us." And Jacob swore by the Fear of his father Isaac.

When confirmed, unalterable.

Gal 3:15 Brethren, I speak in the manner of men: Though *it is* only a man's covenant, yet *if it is* confirmed, no one annuls or adds to it.

Made by passing between the pieces of the divided sacrifices.

Gen 15:9–17 So He said to him, "Bring Me a three-year-old heifer, a three-year-old female goat, a three-year-old ram, a turtledove, and a young pigeon." **10** Then he brought all these to Him and cut them in two, down the middle, and placed each piece opposite the other; but he did not cut the birds in two. **11** And when the vultures came down on the carcasses, Abram drove them away. **12** Now when the sun was going down, a deep sleep fell upon Abram; and behold, horror *and* great darkness fell upon him. **13** Then He said to Abram: "Know certainly that your descendants will be strangers in a land *that is* not theirs, and will serve them, and they will afflict them four hundred years. **14** And also the nation whom they serve I will judge; afterward they shall come out with great possessions. **15** Now as for you, you shall go to your fathers in peace; you shall be buried at a good old age. **16** But in the fourth generation they shall return here, for the iniquity of the Amorites *is* not yet complete." **17** And it came to pass, when the sun went down and it was dark, that behold, there appeared a smoking oven and a burning torch that passed between those pieces.

Jer 34:18–19 And I will give the men who have transgressed My covenant, who have not performed the words of the covenant which they made before Me, when they cut the calf in two and passed between the parts of it— **19** the princes of Judah, the princes of Jerusalem, the eunuchs, the priests, and all the people of the land who passed between the parts of the calf—

Tokens of,

Salt.

Num 18:19 "All the heave offerings of the holy things, which the children of Israel offer to the LORD, I have given to you and your sons and daughters with you as an ordinance forever; *it is* a covenant of salt forever before the LORD with you and your descendants with you."

2 Chr 13:5 Should you not know that the LORD God of Israel gave the dominion over Israel to David forever, to him and his sons, by a covenant of salt?

Joining of hands.

Prov 11:21 *Though they join* forces, the wicked will not go unpunished; But the posterity of the righteous will be delivered.

Ezek 17:18 Since he despised the oath by breaking the covenant, and in fact gave his hand and still did all these *things,* he shall not escape.' "

Feasts.

Gen 26:30 So he made them a feast, and they ate and drank.

Gen 31:54 Then Jacob offered a sacrifice on the mountain, and called his brethren to eat bread. And they ate bread and stayed all night on the mountain.

Gifts.

Gen 21:27–30 So Abraham took sheep and oxen and gave them to Abimelech, and the two of them made a covenant. **28** And Abraham set seven ewe lambs of the flock by themselves. **29** Then Abimelech asked Abraham, "What *is the meaning of* these seven ewe lambs which you have set by themselves?" **30** And he said, "You will take *these* seven ewe lambs from my hand, that they may be my witness that I have dug this well."

1 Sam 18:3–4 Then Jonathan and David made a covenant, because he loved him as his own soul. **4** And Jonathan took off the robe that *was* on him and gave it to David, with his armor, even to his sword and his bow and his belt.

Pillars.

Gen 31:45–46 So Jacob took a stone and set it up *as* a pillar. **46** Then Jacob said to his brethren, "Gather stones." And they took stones and made a heap, and they ate there on the heap.

Places named for.

Gen 21:31 Therefore he called that place Beersheba, because the two of them swore an oath there.

Gen 31:47–49 Laban called it Jegar Sahadutha, but Jacob called it Galeed. **48** And Laban said, "This heap *is* a witness between you and me this day." Therefore its name was called Galeed, **49** also Mizpah, because he said, "May the LORD watch between you and me when we are absent one from another.

The Jews

Not to make, with idolatrous nations.

Ex 23:32 You shall make no covenant with them, nor with their gods.

Deut 7:2 and when the LORD your God delivers them over to you, you shall conquer them *and* utterly destroy them. You shall make no covenant with them nor show mercy to them.

Is 30:2–5 Who walk to go down to Egypt, And have not asked My advice, To strengthen themselves in the strength of Pharaoh, And to trust in the shadow of Egypt! **3** Therefore the strength of Pharaoh Shall be your shame, And trust in the shadow of Egypt Shall be *your* humiliation. **4** For his princes were at Zoan, And his ambassadors came to Hanes. **5** They were all ashamed of a people *who* could not benefit them, Or be help or benefit, But a shame and also a reproach."

Hos 12:1 "Ephraim feeds on the wind, And pursues the east wind; He daily increases lies and desolation. Also they make a covenant with the Assyrians, And oil is carried to Egypt.

Regarded as sacred.

Josh 9:16–19 And it happened at the end of three days, after they had made a covenant with them, that they heard that they *were* their neighbors who dwelt near them. **17** Then the children of Israel journeyed and came to their cities on the third day. Now their cities *were* Gibeon, Chephirah, Beeroth, and Kirjath Jearim. **18** But the children of Israel did not attack them, because the rulers of the congregation had sworn to them by the LORD God of Israel. And all the congregation complained against the rulers. **19** Then all the rulers said to all the congregation, "We have sworn to them by the LORD God of Israel; now therefore, we may not touch them.

Ps 15:4 In whose eyes a vile person is despised, But he honors those who fear the LORD; He *who* swears to his own hurt and does not change;

Illustrative of

The marriage contract.

Mal 2:14 Yet you say, "For what reason?" Because the LORD has been witness Between you and the wife of your youth, With whom you have dealt treacherously; Yet she is your companion And your wife by covenant.

God's promises to man.

Gen 9:9–11 "And as for Me, behold, I establish My covenant with you and with your descendants after you, **10** and with every living creature that *is* with you: the birds, the cattle, and every beast of the earth with you, of all that go out of the ark, every beast of the earth. **11** Thus I establish My covenant with you: Never again shall all flesh be cut off by the waters of the flood; never again shall there be a flood to destroy the earth."

Eph 2:12 that at that time you were without Christ, being aliens from the commonwealth of Israel and strangers from the covenants of promise, having no hope and without God in the world.

The Jews' united determination to serve God.

2 Kin 11:17 Then Jehoiada made a covenant between the LORD, the king, and the people, that they should be the LORD's people, and *also* between the king and the people.

2 Chr 15:12 Then they entered into a covenant to seek the LORD God of their fathers with all their heart and with all their soul;

Neh 10:29 these joined with their brethren, their nobles, and entered into a curse and an oath to walk in God's Law, which was given by Moses the servant of God,

and to observe and do all the commandments of the LORD our Lord, and His ordinances and His statutes:

Good resolutions.

Job 31:1 "I have made a covenant with my eyes; Why then should I look upon a young woman?

(With death and hell) carnal security.

Is 28:15 Because you have said, "We have made a covenant with death, And with Sheol we are in agreement. When the overflowing scourge passes through, It will not come to us, For we have made lies our refuge, And under falsehood we have hidden ourselves."

Is 28:18 Your covenant with death will be annulled, And your agreement with Sheol will not stand; When the overflowing scourge passes through, Then you will be trampled down by it.

(With stones and beasts, of the earth) peace and prosperity.

Job 5:23 For you shall have a covenant with the stones of the field, And the beasts of the field shall be at peace with you.

Hos 2:18 In that day I will make a covenant for them With the beasts of the field, With the birds of the air, And *with* the creeping things of the ground. Bow and sword of battle I will shatter from the earth, To make them lie down safely.

COVETOUSNESS

Heart is origin of.

Ezek 33:31 So they come to you as people do, they sit before you *as* My people, and they hear your words, but they do not do them; for with their mouth they show much love, *but* their hearts pursue their *own* gain.

Mark 7:22–23 thefts, covetousness, wickedness, deceit, lewdness, an evil eye, blasphemy, pride, foolishness. **23** All these evil things come from within and defile a man."

2 Pet 2:14 having eyes full of adultery and that cannot cease from sin, enticing unstable souls. *They have* a heart trained in covetous practices, *and are* accursed children.

Is idolatry.

Eph 5:5 For this you know, that no fornicator, unclean person, nor covetous man, who is an idolater, has any inheritance in the kingdom of Christ and God.

Col 3:5 Therefore put to death your members which are on the earth: fornication, uncleanness, passion, evil desire, and covetousness, which is idolatry.

Is never satisfied.

Eccl 5:10 He who loves silver will not be satisfied with silver; Nor he who loves abundance, with increase. This also *is* vanity.

Hab 2:5 "Indeed, because he transgresses by wine, *He is* a proud man, And he does not stay at home. Because he enlarges his desire as hell, And he *is* like death, and cannot be satisfied, He gathers to himself all nations And heaps up for himself all peoples.

Is vanity.

Ps 39:6 Surely every man walks about like a shadow; Surely they busy themselves in vain; He heaps up *riches*, And does not know who will gather them.

Eccl 4:8 There is one alone, without companion: He has neither son nor brother. Yet *there is* no end to all his labors, Nor is his eye satisfied with riches. *But he never asks,* "For whom do I toil and deprive myself of good?" This also *is* vanity and a grave misfortune.

Is inconsistent for believers.

Eph 5:3 But fornication and all uncleanness or covetousness, let it not even be named among you, as is fitting for saints;

1 Tim 3:3 not given to wine, not violent, not greedy for money, but gentle, not quarrelsome, not covetous;

Heb 13:5 *Let your* conduct *be* without covetousness; *be* content with such things as you have. For He Himself has said, *"I will never leave you nor forsake you."*

Leads to

Injustice and oppression.

Prov 28:20 A faithful man will abound with blessings, But he who hastens to be rich will not go unpunished.

Mic 2:2 They covet fields and take *them* by violence, Also houses, and seize *them*. So they oppress a man and his house, A man and his inheritance.

Foolish and hurtful lusts.

1 Tim 6:9 But those who desire to be rich fall into temptation and a snare, and *into* many foolish and harmful lusts which drown men in destruction and perdition.

Departure from the faith.

1 Tim 6:10 For the love of money is a root of all *kinds of* evil, for which some have strayed from the faith in their greediness, and pierced themselves through with many sorrows.

Lying.

2 Kin 5:22–25 And he said, "All *is* well. My master has sent me, saying, 'Indeed, just now two young men of the sons of the prophets have come to me from the mountains of Ephraim. Please give them a talent of silver and two changes of garments.' " **23** So Naaman said, "Please, take two talents." And he urged him, and bound two talents of silver in two bags, with two changes of garments, and handed *them* to two of his servants; and they carried *them* on ahead of him. **24** When he came to the citadel, he took *them* from their hand, and stored *them* away in the house; then he let the men go, and they departed. **25** Now he went in and stood before his master. Elisha said to him, "Where *did you go*, Gehazi?" And he said, "Your servant did not go anywhere."

Murder.

Prov 1:18–19 But they lie in wait for their *own* blood, They lurk secretly for their *own* lives. **19** So *are* the ways of everyone who is greedy for gain; It takes away the life of its owners.

Ezek 22:12 In you they take bribes to shed blood; you take usury and increase; you have made profit from your neighbors by extortion, and have forgotten Me," says the Lord GOD.

Theft.

Josh 7:21 When I saw among the spoils a beautiful Babylonian garment, two hundred shekels of silver, and a wedge of gold weighing fifty shekels, I coveted

them and took them. And there they are, hidden in the earth in the midst of my tent, with the silver under it."

Poverty.

Prov 28:22 A man with an evil eye hastens after riches, And does not consider that poverty will come upon him.

Domestic troubles.

Prov 15:27 He who is greedy for gain troubles his own house, But he who hates bribes will live.

Forbidden.

Ex 20:17 "You shall not covet your neighbor's house; you shall not covet your neighbor's wife, nor his male servant, nor his female servant, nor his ox, nor his donkey, nor anything that *is* your neighbor's."

A characteristic of the wicked.

Ps 10:3 For the wicked boasts of his heart's desire; He blesses the greedy *and* renounces the LORD.

Prov 21:26 He covets greedily all day long, But the righteous gives and does not spare.

Rom 1:29 being filled with all unrighteousness, sexual immorality, wickedness, covetousness, maliciousness; full of envy, murder, strife, deceit, evil-mindedness; *they are* whisperers,

1 Cor 6:10 nor thieves, nor covetous, nor drunkards, nor revilers, nor extortioners will inherit the kingdom of God.

Eph 5:5 For this you know, that no fornicator, unclean person, nor covetous man, who is an idolater, has any inheritance in the kingdom of Christ and God.

To be opposed by believers.

Ex 18:21 Moreover you shall select from all the people able men, such as fear God, men of truth, hating covetousness; and place *such* over them *to be* rulers of thousands, rulers of hundreds, rulers of fifties, and rulers of tens.

Acts 20:33 I have coveted no one's silver or gold or apparel.

Col 3:5 Therefore put to death your members which are on the earth: fornication, uncleanness, passion, evil desire, and covetousness, which is idolatry.

Prophets denounced.

Is 5:8 Woe to those who join house to house; They add field to field, Till *there is* no place Where they may dwell alone in the midst of the land!

Hab 2:9 "Woe to him who covets evil gain for his house, That he may set his nest on high, That he may be delivered from the power of disaster!

Punishment of.

Job 20:15 He swallows down riches And vomits them up again; God casts them out of his belly.

Is 57:17 For the iniquity of his covetousness I was angry and struck him; I hid and was angry, And he went on backsliding in the way of his heart.

Jer 22:17–19 "Yet your eyes and your heart *are* for nothing but your covetousness, For shedding innocent blood, And practicing oppression and violence." **18** Therefore thus says the LORD concerning Jehoiakim the son of Josiah, king of Judah: "They shall not lament for him, *Saying,* 'Alas, my brother!' or 'Alas, my sister!' They shall not lament for him, *Saying,*

'Alas, master!' or 'Alas, his glory!' **19** He shall be buried with the burial of a donkey, Dragged and cast out beyond the gates of Jerusalem.

Mic 2:2–3 They covet fields and take *them* by violence, Also houses, and seize *them*. So they oppress a man and his house, A man and his inheritance. **3** Therefore thus says the LORD: "Behold, against this family I am devising disaster, From which you cannot remove your necks; Nor shall you walk haughtily, For this *is* an evil time.

Avoid.

Ps 119:36 Incline my heart to Your testimonies, And not to covetousness.

Luke 12:15 And He said to them, "Take heed and beware of covetousness, for one's life does not consist in the abundance of the things he possesses."

1 Cor 5:11 But now I have written to you not to keep company with anyone named a brother, who is sexually immoral, or covetous, or an idolater, or a reviler, or a drunkard, or an extortioner—not even to eat with such a person.

Reward of those who hate.

Prov 28:16 A ruler who lacks understanding *is* a great oppressor, *But* he who hates covetousness will prolong *his* days.

Shall abound in the last days.

2 Tim 3:2 For men will be lovers of themselves, lovers of money, boasters, proud, blasphemers, disobedient to parents, unthankful, unholy,

2 Pet 2:1–3 But there were also false prophets among the people, even as there will be false teachers among you, who will secretly bring in destructive heresies, even denying the Lord who bought them, *and* bring on themselves swift destruction. **2** And many will follow their destructive ways, because of whom the way of truth will be blasphemed. **3** By covetousness they will exploit you with deceptive words; for a long time their judgment has not been idle, and their destruction does not slumber.

Illustrated by

Laban.

Gen 31:41 Thus I have been in your house twenty years; I served you fourteen years for your two daughters, and six years for your flock, and you have changed my wages ten times.

Achan.

Josh 7:21 When I saw among the spoils a beautiful Babylonian garment, two hundred shekels of silver, and a wedge of gold weighing fifty shekels, I coveted them and took them. And there they are, hidden in the earth in the midst of my tent, with the silver under it."

Eli's sons.

1 Sam 2:12–14 Now the sons of Eli *were* corrupt; they did not know the LORD. **13** And the priests' custom with the people *was that* when any man offered a sacrifice, the priest's servant would come with a three-pronged fleshhook in his hand while the meat was boiling. **14** Then he would thrust *it* into the pan, or kettle, or caldron, or pot; and the priest would take for himself all that the fleshhook brought up. So they did in Shiloh to all the Israelites who came there.

Samuel's sons.

1 Sam 8:3 But his sons did not walk in his ways; they turned aside after dishonest gain, took bribes, and perverted justice.

Saul.

1 Sam 15:9 But Saul and the people spared Agag and the best of the sheep, the oxen, the fatlings, the lambs, and all *that was* good, and were unwilling to utterly destroy them. But everything despised and worthless, that they utterly destroyed.

1 Sam 15:19 Why then did you not obey the voice of the LORD? Why did you swoop down on the spoil, and do evil in the sight of the LORD?"

Ahab.

1 Kin 21:2–4 So Ahab spoke to Naboth, saying, "Give me your vineyard, that I may have it for a vegetable garden, because it *is* near, next to my house; and for it I will give you a vineyard better than it. *Or,* if it seems good to you, I will give you its worth in money." **3** But Naboth said to Ahab, "The LORD forbid that I should give the inheritance of my fathers to you!" **4** So Ahab went into his house sullen and displeased because of the word which Naboth the Jezreelite had spoken to him; for he had said, "I will not give you the inheritance of my fathers." And he lay down on his bed, and turned away his face, and would eat no food.

Gehazi.

2 Kin 5:20–24 But Gehazi, the servant of Elisha the man of God, said, "Look, my master has spared Naaman this Syrian, while not receiving from his hands what he brought; but *as* the LORD lives, I will run after him and take something from him." **21** So Gehazi pursued Naaman. When Naaman saw *him* running after him, he got down from the chariot to meet him, and said, "*Is* all well?" **22** And he said, "All *is* well. My master has sent me, saying, 'Indeed, just now two young men of the sons of the prophets have come to me from the mountains of Ephraim. Please give them a talent of silver and two changes of garments.' " **23** So Naaman said, "Please, take two talents." And he urged him, and bound two talents of silver in two bags, with two changes of garments, and handed *them* to two of his servants; and they carried *them* on ahead of him. **24** When he came to the citadel, he took *them* from their hand, and stored *them* away in the house; then he let the men go, and they departed.

Nobles of the Jews.

Neh 5:7 After serious thought, I rebuked the nobles and rulers, and said to them, "Each of you is exacting usury from his brother." So I called a great assembly against them.

Is 1:23 Your princes *are* rebellious, And companions of thieves; Everyone loves bribes, And follows after rewards. They do not defend the fatherless, Nor does the cause of the widow come before them.

The Jewish people.

Is 56:11 Yes, *they are* greedy dogs *Which* never have enough. And they *are* shepherds Who cannot understand; They all look to their own way, Every one for his *own* gain, From his *own* territory.

Jer 6:13 "Because from the least of them even to the

greatest of them, Everyone *is* given to covetousness; And from the prophet even to the priest, Everyone deals falsely.

Babylon.

Jer 51:13 O you who dwell by many waters, Abundant in treasures, Your end has come, The measure of your covetousness.

The rich young man.

Matt 19:22 But when the young man heard that saying, he went away sorrowful, for he had great possessions.

Mark 10:17–22 Now as He was going out on the road, one came running, knelt before Him, and asked Him, "Good Teacher, what shall I do that I may inherit eternal life?" **18** So Jesus said to him, "Why do you call Me good? No one *is* good but One, *that is,* God. **19** You know the commandments: *'Do not commit adultery,' 'Do not murder,' 'Do not steal,' 'Do not bear false witness,' 'Do not defraud,' 'Honor your father and your mother.'"* **20** And he answered and said to Him, "Teacher, all these things I have kept from my youth." **21** Then Jesus, looking at him, loved him, and said to him, "One thing you lack: Go your way, sell whatever you have and give to the poor, and you will have treasure in heaven; and come, take up the cross, and follow Me." **22** But he was sad at this word, and went away sorrowful, for he had great possessions.

Judas.

Matt 26:14–15 Then one of the twelve, called Judas Iscariot, went to the chief priests **15** and said, "What are you willing to give me if I deliver Him to you?" And they counted out to him thirty pieces of silver.

John 12:6 This he said, not that he cared for the poor, but because he was a thief, and had the money box; and he used to take what was put in it.

Pharisees.

Luke 16:14 Now the Pharisees, who were lovers of money, also heard all these things, and they derided Him.

Ananias and Sapphira.

Acts 5:1–10 But a certain man named Ananias, with Sapphira his wife, sold a possession. **2** And he kept back *part* of the proceeds, his wife also being aware *of it,* and brought a certain part and laid *it* at the apostles' feet. **3** But Peter said, "Ananias, why has Satan filled your heart to lie to the Holy Spirit and keep back *part* of the price of the land for yourself? **4** While it remained, was it not your own? And after it was sold, was it not in your own control? Why have you conceived this thing in your heart? You have not lied to men but to God." **5** Then Ananias, hearing these words, fell down and breathed his last. So great fear came upon all those who heard these things. **6** And the young men arose and wrapped him up, carried *him* out, and buried *him.* **7** Now it was about three hours later when his wife came in, not knowing what had happened. **8** And Peter answered her, "Tell me whether you sold the land for so much?" She said, "Yes, for so much." **9** Then Peter said to her, "How is it that you have agreed together to test the Spirit of the Lord? Look, the feet of those who have buried your husband *are* at the door, and

they will carry you out." **10** Then immediately she fell down at his feet and breathed her last. And the young men came in and found her dead, and carrying *her* out, buried *her* by her husband.

Felix.

Acts 24:26 Meanwhile he also hoped that money would be given him by Paul, that he might release him. Therefore he sent for him more often and conversed with him.

Balaam.

2 Pet 2:15 They have forsaken the right way and gone astray, following the way of Balaam the *son* of Beor, who loved the wages of unrighteousness;

Jude 1:11 Woe to them! For they have gone in the way of Cain, have run greedily in the error of Balaam for profit, and perished in the rebellion of Korah.

CRAFTS AND TRADES

Perfumer.

Ex 30:25 And you shall make from these a holy anointing oil, an ointment compounded according to the art of the perfumer. It shall be a holy anointing oil.

Ex 30:35 You shall make of these an incense, a compound according to the art of the perfumer, salted, pure, *and* holy.

Armorer.

1 Sam 8:12 He will appoint captains over his thousands and captains over his fifties, *will set some* to plow his ground and reap his harvest, and *some* to make his weapons of war and equipment for his chariots.

Baker.

Gen 40:1 It came to pass after these things *that* the butler and the baker of the king of Egypt offended their lord, the king of Egypt.

1 Sam 8:13 He will take your daughters *to be* perfumers, cooks, and bakers.

Brickmaker.

Gen 11:3 Then they said to one another, "Come, let us make bricks and bake *them* thoroughly." They had brick for stone, and they had asphalt for mortar.

Ex 5:7–8 "You shall no longer give the people straw to make brick as before. Let them go and gather straw for themselves. **8** And you shall lay on them the quota of bricks which they made before. You shall not reduce it. For they are idle; therefore they cry out, saying, 'Let us go *and* sacrifice to our God.'

Ex 5:18 Therefore go now *and* work; for no straw shall be given you, yet you shall deliver the quota of bricks."

Coppersmith.

2 Tim 4:14 Alexander the coppersmith did me much harm. May the Lord repay him according to his works.

Blacksmith.

Gen 4:22 And as for Zillah, she also bore Tubal-Cain, an instructor of every craftsman in bronze and iron. And the sister of Tubal-Cain *was* Naamah.

1 Sam 13:19 Now there was no blacksmith to be found throughout all the land of Israel, for the Philistines said, "Lest the Hebrews make swords or spears."

Carver.

Ex 31:5 in cutting jewels for setting, in carving wood, and to work in all *manner of* workmanship.

1 Kin 6:18 The inside of the temple was cedar, carved with ornamental buds and open flowers. All *was* cedar; there was no stone *to be* seen.

Carpenter.

2 Sam 5:11 Then Hiram king of Tyre sent messengers to David, and cedar trees, and carpenters and masons. And they built David a house.

Mark 6:3 Is this not the carpenter, the Son of Mary, and brother of James, Joses, Judas, and Simon? And are not His sisters here with us?" So they were offended at Him.

Caulker.

Ezek 27:9 Elders of Gebal and its wise men Were in you to caulk your seams; All the ships of the sea And their oarsmen were in you To market your merchandise.

Ezek 27:27 "Your riches, wares, and merchandise, Your mariners and pilots, Your caulkers and merchandisers, All your men of war who *are* in you, And the entire company which *is* in your midst, Will fall into the midst of the seas on the day of your ruin.

Dyer.

Ex 25:5 ram skins dyed red, badger skins, and acacia wood;

Embroiderer.

Ex 35:35 He has filled them with skill to do all manner of work of the engraver and the designer and the tapestry maker, in blue, purple, and scarlet *thread*, and fine linen, and of the weaver—those who do every work and those who design artistic works.

Ex 38:23 And with him *was* Aholiab the son of Ahisamach, of the tribe of Dan, an engraver and designer, a weaver of blue, purple, and scarlet *thread*, and of fine linen.

Embalmer.

Gen 50:2–3 And Joseph commanded his servants the physicians to embalm his father. So the physicians embalmed Israel. **3** Forty days were required for him, for such are the days required for those who are embalmed; and the Egyptians mourned for him seventy days.

Gen 50:26 So Joseph died, *being* one hundred and ten years old; and they embalmed him, and he was put in a coffin in Egypt.

Engraver.

Ex 28:11 With the work of an engraver in stone, *like* the engravings of a signet, you shall engrave the two stones with the names of the sons of Israel. You shall set them in settings of gold.

Is 49:16 See, I have inscribed you on the palms *of My hands;* Your walls *are* continually before Me.

2 Cor 3:7 But if the ministry of death, written *and* engraved on stones, was glorious, so that the children of Israel could not look steadily at the face of Moses because of the glory of his countenance, which *glory* was passing away,

Launderer.

Mark 9:3 His clothes became shining, exceedingly white, like snow, such as no launderer on earth can whiten them.

Gardener.

Jer 29:5 Build houses and dwell *in them;* plant gardens and eat their fruit.

John 20:15 Jesus said to her, "Woman, why are you weeping? Whom are you seeking?" She, supposing Him to be the gardener, said to Him, "Sir, if You have carried Him away, tell me where You have laid Him, and I will take Him away."

Goldsmith.

Is 40:19 The workman molds an image, The goldsmith overspreads it with gold, And the silversmith casts silver chains.

Farmer, herdsman.

Gen 4:2 Then she bore again, this time his brother Abel. Now Abel was a keeper of sheep, but Cain was a tiller of the ground.

Gen 9:20 And Noah began *to be* a farmer, and he planted a vineyard.

Mariner, etc.

Ezek 27:8–9 "Inhabitants of Sidon and Arvad were your oarsmen; Your wise men, O Tyre, were in you; They became your pilots. **9** Elders of Gebal and its wise men Were in you to caulk your seams; All the ships of the sea And their oarsmen were in you To market your merchandise.

Mason.

2 Sam 5:11 Then Hiram king of Tyre sent messengers to David, and cedar trees, and carpenters and masons. And they built David a house.

2 Chr 24:12 The king and Jehoiada gave it to those who did the work of the service of the house of the LORD; and they hired masons and carpenters to repair the house of the LORD, and also those who worked in iron and bronze to restore the house of the LORD.

Musician.

1 Sam 18:6 Now it had happened as they were coming *home,* when David was returning from the slaughter of the Philistine, that the women had come out of all the cities of Israel, singing and dancing, to meet King Saul, with tambourines, with joy, and with musical instruments.

1 Chr 15:16 Then David spoke to the leaders of the Levites to appoint their brethren *to be* the singers accompanied by instruments of music, stringed instruments, harps, and cymbals, by raising the voice with resounding joy.

Potter.

Is 64:8 But now, O LORD, You *are* our Father; We *are* the clay, and You our potter; And all we *are* the work of Your hand.

Jer 18:3 Then I went down to the potter's house, and there he was, making something at the wheel.

Lam 4:2 The precious sons of Zion, Valuable as fine gold, How they are regarded as clay pots, The work of the hands of the potter!

Zech 11:13 And the LORD said to me, "Throw it to the potter"—that princely price they set on me. So I took the thirty *pieces* of silver and threw them into the house of the LORD for the potter.

Recruiter.

Judg 5:14 From Ephraim *were* those whose roots were in Amalek. After you, Benjamin, with your peoples, From Machir rulers came down, And from Zebulun those who bear the recruiter's staff.

Refiner and smelter of metals.

1 Chr 28:18 and refined gold by weight for the altar of incense, and for the construction of the chariot, that is, the gold cherubim that spread *their wings* and overshadowed the ark of the covenant of the LORD.

Job 28:2 Iron is taken from the earth, And copper *is* smelted *from* ore.

Mal 3:2–3 "But who can endure the day of His coming? And who can stand when He appears? For He *is* like a refiner's fire And like launderers' soap. 3 He will sit as a refiner and a purifier of silver; He will purify the sons of Levi, And purge them as gold and silver, That they may offer to the LORD An offering in righteousness.

Rope maker.

Judg 16:11 So he said to her, "If they bind me securely with new ropes that have never been used, then I shall become weak, and be like any *other* man."

Silversmith.

Judg 17:4 Thus he returned the silver to his mother. Then his mother took two hundred *shekels* of silver and gave them to the silversmith, and he made it into a carved image and a molded image; and they were in the house of Micah.

Acts 19:24 For a certain man named Demetrius, a silversmith, who made silver shrines of Diana, brought no small profit to the craftsmen.

Stonecutter.

Ex 20:25 And if you make Me an altar of stone, you shall not build it of hewn stone; for if you use your tool on it, you have profaned it.

1 Chr 22:15 Moreover *there are* workmen with you in abundance: woodsmen and stonecutters, and all types of skillful men for every kind of work.

Ship builder.

1 Kin 9:26 King Solomon also built a fleet of ships at Ezion Geber, which *is* near Elath on the shore of the Red Sea, in the land of Edom.

Spinner.

Ex 35:25 All the women *who were* gifted artisans spun yarn with their hands, and brought what they had spun, of blue, purple, *and* scarlet, and fine linen.

Prov 31:19 She stretches out her hands to the distaff, And her hand holds the spindle.

Tailor.

Ex 28:3 So you shall speak to all *who are* gifted artisans, whom I have filled with the spirit of wisdom, that they may make Aaron's garments, to consecrate him, that he may minister to Me as priest.

Tanner.

Acts 9:43 So it was that he stayed many days in Joppa with Simon, a tanner.

Acts 10:6 He is lodging with Simon, a tanner, whose house is by the sea. He will tell you what you must do."

Tentmaker.

Gen 4:20 And Adah bore Jabal. He was the father of those who dwell in tents and have livestock.

Acts 18:3 So, because he was of the same trade, he stayed with them and worked; for by occupation they were tentmakers.

Weaver.

Ex 35:35 He has filled them with skill to do all manner of work of the engraver and the designer and the tapestry maker, in blue, purple, and scarlet *thread,* and fine linen, and of the weaver—those who do every work and those who design artistic works.

John 19:23 Then the soldiers, when they had crucified Jesus, took His garments and made four parts, to each soldier a part, and also the tunic. Now the tunic was without seam, woven from the top in one piece.

Wine-maker.

Neh 13:15 In those days I saw *people* in Judah treading wine presses on the Sabbath, and bringing in sheaves, and loading donkeys with wine, grapes, figs, and all *kinds of* burdens, which they brought into Jerusalem on the Sabbath day. And I warned *them* about the day on which they were selling provisions.

Is 63:3 "I have trodden the winepress alone, And from the peoples no one *was* with Me. For I have trodden them in My anger, And trampled them in My fury; Their blood is sprinkled upon My garments, And I have stained all My robes.

CREATION

Definition of.

Rom 4:17 (as it is written, *"I have made you a father of many nations"*) in the presence of Him whom he believed—God, who gives life to the dead and calls those things which do not exist as though they did;

Heb 11:3 By faith we understand that the worlds were framed by the word of God, so that the things which are seen were not made of things which are visible.

Effected

By God.

Gen 1:1 In the beginning God created the heavens and the earth.

Gen 2:4–5 This *is* the history of the heavens and the earth when they were created, in the day that the LORD God made the earth and the heavens, 5 before any plant of the field was in the earth and before any herb of the field had grown. For the LORD God had not caused it to rain on the earth, and *there was* no man to till the ground;

Ps 19:4 Their line has gone out through all the earth, And their words to the end of the world. In them He has set a tabernacle for the sun,

Ps 33:9 For He spoke, and it was *done;* He commanded, and it stood fast.

Ps 135:6 Whatever the LORD pleases He does, In heaven and in earth, In the seas and in all deep places.

Prov 16:4 The LORD has made all for Himself, Yes, even the wicked for the day of doom.

Prov 26:10 The great *God* who formed everything Gives the fool *his* hire and the transgressor *his* wages.

Is 42:5 Thus says God the LORD, Who created the heavens and stretched them out, Who spread forth the earth and that which comes from it, Who gives breath to the people on it, And spirit to those who walk on it:

Heb 11:3 By faith we understand that the worlds were framed by the word of God, so that the things which are seen were not made of things which are visible.

2 Pet 3:5 For this they willfully forget: that by the word of God the heavens were of old, and the earth standing out of water and in the water,

Rev 4:11 "You are worthy, O Lord, To receive glory and honor and power; For You created all things, And by Your will they exist and were created."

By Christ.

John 1:3 All things were made through Him, and without Him nothing was made that was made.

John 1:10 He was in the world, and the world was made through Him, and the world did not know Him.

Col 1:16 For by Him all things were created that are in heaven and that are on earth, visible and invisible, whether thrones or dominions or principalities or powers. All things were created through Him and for Him.

By the Holy Spirit.

Job 26:13 By His Spirit He adorned the heavens; His hand pierced the fleeing serpent.

Ps 104:30 You send forth Your Spirit, they are created; And You renew the face of the earth.

In the beginning.

Gen 1:1 In the beginning God created the heavens and the earth.

Matt 24:21 For then there will be great tribulation, such as has not been since the beginning of the world until this time, no, nor ever shall be.

In six normal days.

Ex 20:11 For *in* six days the LORD made the heavens and the earth, the sea, and all that *is* in them, and rested the seventh day. Therefore the LORD blessed the Sabbath day and hallowed it.

Ex 31:17 It *is* a sign between Me and the children of Israel forever; for *in* six days the LORD made the heavens and the earth, and on the seventh day He rested and was refreshed.' "

Order of,

First day, making light and dividing it from darkness.

Gen 1:3–5 Then God said, "Let there be light"; and there was light. **4** And God saw the light, that *it was* good; and God divided the light from the darkness. **5** God called the light Day, and the darkness He called Night. So the evening and the morning were the first day.

2 Cor 4:6 For it is the God who commanded light to shine out of darkness, who has shone in our hearts to *give* the light of the knowledge of the glory of God in the face of Jesus Christ.

Second day, making the firmament or atmosphere, and separating the waters.

Gen 1:6–8 Then God said, "Let there be a firmament in the midst of the waters, and let it divide the waters from the waters." **7** Thus God made the firmament, and divided the waters which *were* under the firmament from the waters which *were* above the firmament; and it was so. **8** And God called the firmament Heaven. So the evening and the morning were the second day.

Third day, separating the land from the water, and making it fruitful.

Gen 1:9–13 Then God said, "Let the waters under the heavens be gathered together into one place, and let the dry *land* appear"; and it was so. **10** And God called the dry *land* Earth, and the gathering together of the waters He called Seas. And God saw that *it was* good. **11** Then God said, "Let the earth bring forth grass, the herb *that* yields seed, *and* the fruit tree *that* yields fruit according to its kind, whose seed *is* in itself, on the earth"; and it was so. **12** And the earth brought forth grass, the herb *that* yields seed according to its kind, and the tree *that* yields fruit, whose seed *is* in itself according to its kind. And God saw that *it was* good. **13** So the evening and the morning were the third day.

Fourth day, placing the sun, moon, and stars to give light, etc.

Gen 1:14–19 Then God said, "Let there be lights in the firmament of the heavens to divide the day from the night; and let them be for signs and seasons, and for days and years; **15** and let them be for lights in the firmament of the heavens to give light on the earth"; and it was so. **16** Then God made two great lights: the greater light to rule the day, and the lesser light to rule the night. *He made* the stars also. **17** God set them in the firmament of the heavens to give light on the earth, **18** and to rule over the day and over the night, and to divide the light from the darkness. And God saw that *it was* good. **19** So the evening and the morning were the fourth day.

Fifth day, making birds, insects, and fishes.

Gen 1:20–23 Then God said, "Let the waters abound with an abundance of living creatures, and let birds fly above the earth across the face of the firmament of the heavens." **21** So God created great sea creatures and every living thing that moves, with which the waters abounded, according to their kind, and every winged bird according to its kind. And God saw that *it was* good. **22** And God blessed them, saying, "Be fruitful and multiply, and fill the waters in the seas, and let birds multiply on the earth." **23** So the evening and the morning were the fifth day.

Sixth day, making beasts of the earth, and man.

Gen 1:24 Then God said, "Let the earth bring forth the living creature according to its kind: cattle and creeping thing and beast of the earth, *each* according to its kind"; and it was so.

Gen 1:28 Then God blessed them, and God said to them, "Be fruitful and multiply; fill the earth and subdue it; have dominion over the fish of the sea, over the birds of the air, and over every living thing that moves on the earth."

Gen 1:31 Then God saw everything that He had made, and indeed *it was* very good. So the evening and the morning were the sixth day.

Seventh day, God rested.

Gen 2:2–3 And on the seventh day God ended His work which He had done, and He rested on the seventh day from all His work which He had done. 3 Then God blessed the seventh day and sanctified it, because in it He rested from all His work which God had created and made.

Exhibits

The existence of God.

Rom 1:20 For since the creation of the world His invisible *attributes* are clearly seen, being understood by the things that are made, *even* His eternal power and Godhead, so that they are without excuse,

The power of God.

Is 40:26 Lift up your eyes on high, And see who has created these *things*, Who brings out their host by number; He calls them all by name, By the greatness of His might And the strength of *His* power; Not one is missing.

Is 40:28 Have you not known? Have you not heard? The everlasting God, the LORD, The Creator of the ends of the earth, Neither faints nor is weary. His understanding is unsearchable.

Rom 1:20 For since the creation of the world His invisible *attributes* are clearly seen, being understood by the things that are made, *even* His eternal power and Godhead, so that they are without excuse,

The glory and handiwork of God.

Ps 19:1 The heavens declare the glory of God; And the firmament shows His handiwork.

The wisdom of God.

Ps 104:24 O LORD, how manifold are Your works! In wisdom You have made them all. The earth is full of Your possessions—

Ps 136:5 To Him who by wisdom made the heavens, For His mercy *endures* forever;

The goodness of God.

Ps 33:5 He loves righteousness and justice; The earth is full of the goodness of the LORD.

God as the sole object of worship.

Is 45:16 They shall be ashamed And also disgraced, all of them; They shall go in confusion together, *Who are* makers of idols.

Is 45:18 For thus says the LORD, Who created the heavens, Who is God, Who formed the earth and made it, Who has established it, Who did not create it in vain, Who formed it to be inhabited: "I *am* the LORD, and *there is* no other.

Acts 17:24 God, who made the world and everything in it, since He is Lord of heaven and earth, does not dwell in temples made with hands.

Acts 17:27 so that they should seek the Lord, in the hope that they might grope for Him and find Him, though He is not far from each one of us;

God to be praised for.

Neh 9:6 You alone *are* the LORD; You have made heaven, The heaven of heavens, with all their host, The earth and everything on it, The seas and all that is in them, And You preserve them all. The host of heaven worships You.

Ps 146:5–6 Happy *is* he who *has* the God of Jacob for his help, Whose hope *is* in the LORD his God, 6 Who made heaven and earth, The sea, and all that *is in* them; Who keeps truth forever,

Ps 145:10 All Your works shall praise You, O LORD, And Your saints shall bless You.

Ps 148:5 Let them praise the name of the LORD, For He commanded and they were created.

Leads to confidence in God.

Ps 124:8 Our help *is* in the name of the LORD, Who made heaven and earth.

Ps 146:5–6 Happy *is* he who *has* the God of Jacob for his help, Whose hope *is* in the LORD his God, 6 Who made heaven and earth, The sea, and all that *is* in them; Who keeps truth forever,

Insignificance of man seen from.

Ps 8:3–4 When I consider Your heavens, the work of Your fingers, The moon and the stars, which You have ordained, 4 What is man that You are mindful of him, And the son of man that You visit him?

Is 40:12 Who has measured the waters in the hollow of His hand, Measured heaven with a span And calculated the dust of the earth in a measure? Weighed the mountains in scales And the hills in a balance?

Is 40:17 All nations before Him *are* as nothing, And they are counted by Him less than nothing and worthless.

Groans because of sin.

Rom 8:22 For we know that the whole creation groans and labors with birth pangs together until now.

Illustrative of

The new birth.

2 Cor 5:17 Therefore, if anyone *is* in Christ, *he is* a new creation; old things have passed away; behold, all things have become new.

Eph 2:10 For we are His workmanship, created in Christ Jesus for good works, which God prepared beforehand that we should walk in them.

Daily renewal of saints.

Ps 51:10 Create in me a clean heart, O God, And renew a steadfast spirit within me.

Eph 4:24 and that you put on the new man which was created according to God, in true righteousness and holiness.

Renewal of the earth.

Is 65:17 "For behold, I create new heavens and a new earth; And the former shall not be remembered or come to mind.

2 Pet 3:11 Therefore, since all these things will be dissolved, what manner *of persons* ought you to be in holy conduct and godliness,

2 Pet 3:13 Nevertheless we, according to His promise, look for new heavens and a new earth in which righteousness dwells.

CREDITORS

Defined.

Philem 1:18 But if he has wronged you or owes anything, put that on my account.

Might demand

Pledges.

Ex 22:26–27 If you ever take your neighbor's garment as

a pledge, you shall return it to him before the sun goes down. 27 For that *is* his only covering, it *is* his garment for his skin. What will he sleep in? And it will be that when he cries to Me, I will hear, for I *am* gracious.

Deut 24:10–13 "When you lend your brother anything, you shall not go into his house to get his pledge. 11 You shall stand outside, and the man to whom you lend shall bring the pledge out to you. 12 And if the man *is* poor, you shall not keep his pledge overnight. 13 You shall in any case return the pledge to him again when the sun goes down, that he may sleep in his own garment and bless you; and it shall be righteousness to you before the LORD your God.

Prov 6:1 My son, if you become surety for your friend, *If* you have shaken hands in pledge for a stranger,

Prov 22:26–27 Do not be one of those who shakes hands in a pledge, One of those who is surety for debts; 27 If you have nothing *with which* to pay, Why should he take away your bed from under you?

Ezek 18:7 If he has not oppressed anyone, *But* has restored to the debtor his pledge; Has robbed no one by violence, *But* has given his bread to the hungry And covered the naked with clothing;

Ezek 18:12 If he has oppressed the poor and needy, Robbed by violence, Not restored the pledge, Lifted his eyes to the idols, *Or* committed abomination;

Mortgages on property.

Neh 5:3 There were also *some* who said, "We have mortgaged our lands and vineyards and houses, that we might buy grain because of the famine."

Bills or promissory notes.

Luke 16:6–7 And he said, 'A hundred measures of oil.' So he said to him, 'Take your bill, and sit down quickly and write fifty.' 7 Then he said to another, 'And how much do you owe?' So he said, 'A hundred measures of wheat.' And he said to him, 'Take your bill, and write eighty.'

Interest from strangers.

Deut 23:20 To a foreigner you may charge interest, but to your brother you shall not charge interest, that the LORD your God may bless you in all to which you set your hand in the land which you are entering to possess.

Prohibited from

Taking millstones in pledge.

Deut 24:6 "No man shall take the lower or the upper millstone in pledge, for he takes *one's* living in pledge.

Violently selecting pledges.

Deut 24:10 "When you lend your brother anything, you shall not go into his house to get his pledge.

Exacting usury from God's people.

Ex 22:25 "If you lend money to *any of* My people *who are* poor among you, you shall not be like a money-lender to him; you shall not charge him interest.

Lev 25:36–37 Take no usury or interest from him; but fear your God, that your brother may live with you. 37 You shall not lend him your money for usury, nor lend him your food at a profit.

Exacting debts from God's people during sabbatical year.

Deut 15:2–3 And this *is* the form of the release: Every creditor who has lent *anything* to his neighbor shall release *it*; he shall not require *it* of his neighbor or his brother, because it is called the LORD's release. 3 Of a foreigner you may require *it*; but you shall give up your claim to what is owed by your brother,

Sometimes entirely remitted debts.

Neh 5:10–12 I also, *with* my brethren and my servants, am lending them money and grain. Please, let us stop this usury! 11 Restore now to them, even this day, their lands, their vineyards, their olive groves, and their houses, also a hundredth of the money and the grain, the new wine and the oil, that you have charged them." 12 So they said, "We will restore *it*, and will require nothing from them; we will do as you say." Then I called the priests, and required an oath from them that they would do according to this promise.

Matt 18:27 Then the master of that servant was moved with compassion, released him, and forgave him the debt.

Luke 7:42 And when they had nothing with which to repay, he freely forgave them both. Tell Me, therefore, which of them will love him more?"

Often exacted debts

Cruelly.

Neh 5:7–9 After serious thought, I rebuked the nobles and rulers, and said to them, "Each of you is exacting usury from his brother." So I called a great assembly against them. 8 And I said to them, "According to our ability we have redeemed our Jewish brethren who were sold to the nations. Now indeed, will you even sell your brethren? Or should they be sold to us?" Then they were silenced and found nothing *to* say. 9 Then I said, "What you are doing *is* not good. Should you not walk in the fear of our God because of the reproach of the nations, our enemies?

Job 24:3–9 They drive away the donkey of the fatherless; They take the widow's ox as a pledge. 4 They push the needy off the road; All the poor of the land are forced to hide. 5 Indeed, *like* wild donkeys in the desert, They go out to their work, searching for food. The wilderness *yields* food for them *and* for *their* children. 6 They gather their fodder in the field And glean in the vineyard of the wicked. 7 They spend the night naked, without clothing, And have no covering in the cold. 8 They are wet with the showers of the mountains, And huddle around the rock for want of shelter. 9 "*Some* snatch the fatherless from the breast, And take a pledge from the poor.

Matt 18:28–30 "But that servant went out and found one of his fellow servants who owed him a hundred denarii; and he laid hands on him and took *him* by the throat, saying, 'Pay me what you owe!' 29 So his fellow servant fell down at his feet and begged him, saying, 'Have patience with me, and I will pay you all.' 30 And he would not, but went and threw him into prison till he should pay the debt.

By selling the debtor or taking him for a servant.

Ex 21:2 If you buy a Hebrew servant, he shall serve six

years; and in the seventh he shall go out free and pay nothing.

Matt 18:25 But as he was not able to pay, his master commanded that he be sold, with his wife and children and all that he had, and that payment be made.

By selling the debtor's property.

Matt 18:25 But as he was not able to pay, his master commanded that he be sold, with his wife and children and all that he had, and that payment be made.

By selling the debtor's family.

2 Kin 4:1 A certain woman of the wives of the sons of the prophets cried out to Elisha, saying, "Your servant my husband is dead, and you know that your servant feared the LORD. And the creditor is coming to take my two sons to be his slaves."

Job 24:9 *"Some* snatch the fatherless from the breast, And take a pledge from the poor.

Matt 18:25 But as he was not able to pay, his master commanded that he be sold, with his wife and children and all that he had, and that payment be made.

By imprisonment.

Matt 5:25–26 Agree with your adversary quickly, while you are on the way with him, lest your adversary deliver you to the judge, the judge hand you over to the officer, and you be thrown into prison. **26** Assuredly, I say to you, you will by no means get out of there till you have paid the last penny.

Matt 18:34 And his master was angry, and delivered him to the torturers until he should pay all that was due to him.

From the sureties.

Prov 11:15 He who is surety for a stranger will suffer, But one who hates being surety is secure.

Prov 22:26–27 Do not be one of those who shakes hands in a pledge, One of those who is surety for debts; **27** If you have nothing *with which* to pay, Why should he take away your bed from under you?

Were sometimes defrauded.

Luke 16:5–7 "So he called every one of his master's debtors to *him,* and said to the first, 'How much do you owe my master?' **6** And he said, 'A hundred measures of oil.' So he said to him, 'Take your bill, and sit down quickly and write fifty.' **7** Then he said to another, 'And how much do you owe?' So he said, 'A hundred measures of wheat.' And he said to him, 'Take your bill, and write eighty.'

Illustrative of

God's claim upon men.

Matt 5:25–26 Agree with your adversary quickly, while you are on the way with him, lest your adversary deliver you to the judge, the judge hand you over to the officer, and you be thrown into prison. **26** Assuredly, I say to you, you will by no means get out of there till you have paid the last penny.

Matt 18:23 Therefore the kingdom of heaven is like a certain king who wanted to settle accounts with his servants.

Matt 18:25 But as he was not able to pay, his master commanded that he be sold, with his wife and children and all that he had, and that payment be made.

Luke 7:41 "There was a certain creditor who had two debtors. One owed five hundred denarii, and the other fifty.

Luke 7:47 Therefore I say to you, her sins, *which are* many, are forgiven, for she loved much. But to whom little is forgiven, *the same* loves little."

The demands of the law.

Gal 5:3 And I testify again to every man who becomes circumcised that he is a debtor to keep the whole law.

CROSS, THE

Message of, redemption.

1 Cor 1:18 For the message of the cross is foolishness to those who are perishing, but to us who are being saved it is the power of God.

Referred to as a tree.

Acts 13:29 Now when they had fulfilled all that was written concerning Him, they took *Him* down from the tree and laid *Him* in a tomb.

Breeds opposition.

Gal 5:11 And I, brethren, if I still preach circumcision, why do I still suffer persecution? Then the offense of the cross has ceased.

Boasting in.

Gal 6:14 But God forbid that I should boast except in the cross of our Lord Jesus Christ, by whom the world has been crucified to me, and I to the world.

The instrument of Christ's death. *See* "Jesus Christ, Crucifixion of."

Phil 2:8 And being found in appearance as a man, He humbled Himself and became obedient to *the point of* death, even the death of the cross.

Believer's death nailed to.

Col 2:14 having wiped out the handwriting of requirements that was against us, which was contrary to us. And He has taken it out of the way, having nailed it to the cross.

CURSE

On creation.

Gen 3:14–19 So the LORD God said to the serpent: "Because you have done this, You *are* cursed more than all cattle, And more than every beast of the field; On your belly you shall go, And you shall eat dust All the days of your life. **15** And I will put enmity Between you and the woman, And between your seed and her Seed; He shall bruise your head, And you shall bruise His heel." **16** To the woman He said: "I will greatly multiply your sorrow and your conception; In pain you shall bring forth children; Your desire *shall be* for your husband, And he shall rule over you." **17** Then to Adam He said, "Because you have heeded the voice of your wife, and have eaten from the tree of which I commanded you, saying, 'You shall not eat of it': "Cursed *is* the ground for your sake; In toil you shall eat *of* it All the days of your life. **18** Both thorns and thistles it shall bring forth for you, And you shall eat the herb of the field. **19** In the sweat of your face you shall eat bread Till you return to the ground, For out of it you were taken; For dust you *are,* And to dust you shall return."

Rom 8:20–22 For the creation was subjected to futility, not willingly, but because of Him who subjected *it* in hope; **21** because the creation itself also will be delivered from the bondage of corruption into the glorious liberty of the children of God. **22** For we know that the whole creation groans and labors with birth pangs together until now.

Rev 22:3 And there shall be no more curse, but the throne of God and of the Lamb shall be in it, and His servants shall serve Him.

Of the law.

Deut 27:26 'Cursed *is* the one who does not confirm *all* the words of this law.' "And all the people shall say, 'Amen!' "

Gal 3:10 For as many as are of the works of the law are under the curse; for it is written, *"Cursed is everyone who does not continue in all things which are written in the book of the law, to do them."*

Gal 3:13 Christ has redeemed us from the curse of the law, having become a curse for us (for it is written, *"Cursed is everyone who hangs on a tree"*),

In human speech.

Judg 17:2 And he said to his mother, "The eleven hundred *shekels* of silver that were taken from you, and on which you put a curse, even saying it in my ears—here *is* the silver with me; I took it." And his mother said, *"May you be* blessed by the LORD, my son!"

2 Sam 16:9–11 Then Abishai the son of Zeruiah said to the king, "Why should this dead dog curse my lord the king? Please, let me go over and take off his head!" **10** But the king said, "What have I to do with you, you sons of Zeruiah? So let him curse, because the LORD has said to him, 'Curse David.' Who then shall say, 'Why have you done so?' " **11** And David said to Abishai and all his servants, "See how my son who came from my own body seeks my life. How much more now *may this* Benjamite? Let him alone, and let him curse; for so the LORD has ordered him.

Job 2:9 Then his wife said to him, "Do you still hold fast to your integrity? Curse God and die!"

Matt 26:74 Then he began to curse and swear, *saying,* "I do not know the Man!" Immediately a rooster crowed.

James 3:9 With it we bless our God and Father, and with it we curse men, who have been made in the similitude of God.

DAMASCUS

Center of fine merchandise.

2 Kin 8:9 So Hazael went to meet him and took a present with him, of every good thing of Damascus, forty camel-loads; and he came and stood before him, and said, "Your son Ben-Hadad king of Syria has sent me to you, saying, 'Shall I recover from this disease?' "

Capital of Syria.

2 Chr 28:5 Therefore the LORD his God delivered him into the hand of the king of Syria. They defeated him, and carried away a great multitude of them as captives, and brought *them* to Damascus. Then he was also delivered into the hand of the king of Israel, who defeated him with a great slaughter.

Object of God's judgments.

Is 17:1 The burden against Damascus. "Behold, Damascus will cease from *being* a city, And it will be a ruinous heap.

Zech 9:1 The burden of the word of the LORD Against the land of Hadrach, And Damascus its resting place (For the eyes of men And all the tribes of Israel Are on the LORD);

Paul's escape from.

2 Cor 11:32–33 In Damascus the governor, under Aretas the king, was guarding the city of the Damascenes with a garrison, desiring to arrest me; 33 but I was let down in a basket through a window in the wall, and escaped from his hands.

DAN, THE TRIBE OF

Descended from Jacob's fifth son.

Gen 30:6 Then Rachel said, "God has judged my case; and He has also heard my voice and given me a son." Therefore she called his name Dan.

Predictions respecting.

Gen 49:16–17 "Dan shall judge his people As one of the tribes of Israel. 17 Dan shall be a serpent by the way, A viper by the path, That bites the horse's heels So that its rider shall fall backward.

Deut 33:22 And of Dan he said: "Dan *is* a lion's whelp; He shall leap from Bashan."

Persons selected from,

To number the people.

Num 1:12 from Dan, Ahiezer the son of Ammishaddai;

To spy out the land.

Num 13:12 from the tribe of Dan, Ammiel the son of Gemalli;

To divide the land.

Num 34:22 a leader from the tribe of the children of Dan, Bukki the son of Jogli;

Strength of, on leaving Egypt.

Num 1:38–39 From the children of Dan, their genealogies by their families, by their fathers' house, according to the number of names, from twenty years old and above, all who *were able to* go to war: 39 those who were numbered of the tribe of Dan *were* sixty-two thousand seven hundred.

Led the fourth and last division of Israel.

Num 2:31 "All who were numbered of the forces with Dan, one hundred and fifty-seven thousand six hundred—they shall break camp last, with their standards."

Num 10:25 Then the standard of the camp of the children of Dan (the rear guard of all the camps) set out according to their armies; over their army *was* Ahiezer the son of Ammishaddai.

Encamped north of the tabernacle.

Num 2:25 "The standard of the forces with Dan *shall be* on the north side according to their armies, and the leader of the children of Dan *shall be* Ahiezer the son of Ammishaddai."

Offering of, at dedication.

Num 7:66–71 On the tenth day Ahiezer the son of Ammishaddai, leader of the children of Dan, *presented an offering.* 67 His offering *was* one silver platter, the weight of which *was* one hundred and thirty *shekels*, and one silver bowl of seventy shekels, according to the shekel of the sanctuary, both of them full of fine flour mixed with oil as a grain offering; 68 one gold pan of ten *shekels*, full of incense; 69 one young bull, one ram, and one male lamb in its first year, as a burnt offering; 70 one kid of the goats as a sin offering; 71 and as the sacrifice of peace offerings: two oxen, five rams, five male goats, and five male lambs in their first year. This *was* the offering of Ahiezer the son of Ammishaddai.

Families of.

Num 26:42 These *are* the sons of Dan according to their families: of Shuham, the family of the Shuhamites. These *are* the families of Dan according to their families.

Strength of, entering Canaan.

Num 26:43 All the families of the Shuhamites, according to those who were numbered of them, *were* sixty-four thousand four hundred.

On Ebal, said amen to the curses.

Deut 27:13 and these shall stand on Mount Ebal to curse: Reuben, Gad, Asher, Zebulun, Dan, and Naphtali.

Borders of its inheritance.

Josh 19:40–46 The seventh lot came out for the tribe of the children of Dan according to their families. **41** And the territory of their inheritance was Zorah, Eshtaol, Ir Shemesh, **42** Shaalabbin, Aijalon, Jethlah, **43** Elon, Timnah, Ekron, **44** Eltekeh, Gibbethon, Baalath, **45** Jehud, Bene Berak, Gath Rimmon, **46** Me Jarkon, and Rakkon, with the region near Joppa.

A commercial people.

Judg 5:17 Gilead stayed beyond the Jordan, And why did Dan remain on ships? Asher continued at the seashore, And stayed by his inlets.

Ezek 27:19 Dan and Javan paid for your wares, traversing back and forth. Wrought iron, cassia, and cane were among your merchandise.

Restricted to the hills by the Amorites.

Judg 1:34 And the Amorites forced the children of Dan into the mountains, for they would not allow them to come down to the valley;

A part of,

Sent to seek new settlements.

Judg 18:1–2 In those days *there was* no king in Israel. And in those days the tribe of the Danites was seeking an inheritance for itself to dwell in; for until that day *their* inheritance among the tribes of Israel had not fallen to them. **2** So the children of Dan sent five men of their family from their territory, men of valor from Zorah and Eshtaol, to spy out the land and search it. They said to them, "Go, search the land." So they went to the mountains of Ephraim, to the house of Micah, and lodged there.

Took Leshem (Laish) and called it Dan.

Josh 19:47 And the border of the children of Dan went beyond these, because the children of Dan went up to fight against Leshem and took it; and they struck it with the edge of the sword, took possession of it, and dwelt in it. They called Leshem, Dan, after the name of Dan their father.

Judg 18:8–13 Then *the* spies came back to their brethren at Zorah and Eshtaol, and their brethren said to them, "What *is* your *report?*" **9** So they said, "Arise, let us go up against them. For we have seen the land, and indeed it *is* very good. *Would* you *do* nothing? Do not hesitate to go, *and* enter to possess the land. **10** When you go, you will come to a secure people and a large land. For God has given it into your hands, a place where *there is* no lack of anything that *is* on the earth." **11** And six hundred men of the family of the Danites went from there, from Zorah and Eshtaol, armed with weapons of war. **12** Then they went up and encamped in Kirjath Jearim in Judah. (Therefore they call that place Mahaneh Dan to this day. There *it is*, west of Kirjath Jearim.) **13** And they passed from there to the mountains of Ephraim, and came to the house of Micah.

Judg 18:27–29 So they took *the things* Micah had made, and the priest who had belonged to him, and went to Laish, to a people quiet and secure; and they struck them with the edge of the sword and burned the city with fire. **28** *There was* no deliverer, because it *was* far from Sidon, and they had no ties with anyone. It was in the valley that belongs to Beth Rehob. So they rebuilt the city and dwelt there. **29** And they called the name of the city Dan, after the name of Dan their father, who was born to Israel. However, the name of the city formerly *was* Laish.

Plundered Micah of his idols and his ephod.

Judg 18:17–21 Then the five men who had gone to spy out the land went up. Entering there, they took the carved image, the ephod, the household idols, and the molded image. The priest stood at the entrance of the gate with the six hundred men *who were* armed with weapons of war. **18** When these went into Micah's house and took the carved image, the ephod, the household idols, and the molded image, the priest said to them, "What are you doing?" **19** And they said to him, "Be quiet, put your hand over your mouth, and come with us; be a father and a priest to us. *Is it* better for you to be a priest to the household of one man, or that you be a priest to a tribe and a family in Israel?" **20** So the priest's heart was glad; and he took the ephod, the household idols, and the carved image, and took his place among the people. **21** Then they turned and departed, and put the little ones, the livestock, and the goods in front of them.

Judg 18:27 So they took *the things* Micah had made, and the priest who had belonged to him, and went to Laish, to a people quiet and secure; and they struck them with the edge of the sword and burned the city with fire.

Set up Micah's idols in Dan.

Judg 18:30–31 Then the children of Dan set up for themselves the carved image; and Jonathan the son of Gershom, the son of Manasseh, and his sons were priests to the tribe of Dan until the day of the captivity of the land. **31** So they set up for themselves Micah's carved image which he made, all the time that the house of God was in Shiloh.

Reproved for not aiding against Sisera.

Judg 5:17 Gilead stayed beyond the Jordan, And why did Dan remain on ships? Asher continued at the seashore, And stayed by his inlets.

Samson was of.

Judg 13:2 Now there was a certain man from Zorah, of the family of the Danites, whose name *was* Manoah; and his wife *was* barren and had no children.

Judg 13:24–25 So the woman bore a son and called his name Samson; and the child grew, and the LORD blessed him. **25** And the Spirit of the LORD began to move upon him at Mahaneh Dan between Zorah and Eshtaol.

Number of, who first supported David.

1 Chr 12:35 of the Danites who could keep battle formation, twenty-eight thousand six hundred;

Ruler appointed over, by David.

1 Chr 27:22 *over* Dan, Azarel the son of Jeroham. These *were* the leaders of the tribes of Israel.

DARKNESS

Created by God.

Job 38:8–9 "Or *who* shut in the sea with doors, When it burst forth *and* issued from the womb; **9** When I made the clouds its garment, And thick darkness its swaddling band;

Ps 104:20 You make darkness, and it is night, In which all the beasts of the forest creep about.

Is 45:7 I form the light and create darkness, I make peace and create calamity; I, the Lord, do all these *things*.'

Originally covered the earth.

Gen 1:2 The earth was without form, and void; and darkness *was* on the face of the deep. And the Spirit of God was hovering over the face of the waters.

Separated from the light.

Gen 1:4 And God saw the light, that *it was* good; and God divided the light from the darkness.

Called night.

Gen 1:5 God called the light Day, and the darkness He called Night. So the evening and the morning were the first day.

Occurred after sunset.

Gen 15:17 And it came to pass, when the sun went down and it was dark, that behold, there appeared a smoking oven and a burning torch that passed between those pieces.

John 6:17 got into the boat, and went over the sea toward Capernaum. And it was already dark, and Jesus had not come to them.

Inexplicable nature of.

Job 38:19–20 "Where *is* the way *to* the dwelling of light? And darkness, where *is* its place, **20** That you may take it to its territory, That you may know the paths *to* its home?

Degrees of, mentioned

Great.

Gen 15:12 Now when the sun was going down, a deep sleep fell upon Abram; and behold, horror *and* great darkness fell upon him.

That may be felt.

Ex 10:21 Then the Lord said to Moses, "Stretch out your hand toward heaven, that there may be darkness over the land of Egypt, darkness *which* may even be felt."

Thick.

Deut 5:22 "These words the Lord spoke to all your assembly, in the mountain from the midst of the fire, the cloud, and the thick darkness, with a loud voice; and He added no more. And He wrote them on two tablets of stone and gave them to me.

Joel 2:2 A day of darkness and gloominess, A day of clouds and thick darkness, Like the morning *clouds* spread over the mountains. A people *come*, great and strong, The like of whom has never been; Nor will there ever be any *such* after them, Even for many successive generations.

Dense.

Jer 13:16 Give glory to the Lord your God Before He causes darkness, And before your feet stumble On the dark mountains, And while you are looking for light, He turns it into the shadow of death *And* makes *it* dense darkness.

Outer or extreme.

Matt 8:12 But the sons of the kingdom will be cast out into outer darkness. There will be weeping and gnashing of teeth."

Effects of,

Keeps us from seeing objects.

Ex 10:23 They did not see one another; nor did anyone rise from his place for three days. But all the children of Israel had light in their dwellings.

Causes us to go astray.

John 12:35 Then Jesus said to them, "A little while longer the light is with you. Walk while you have the light, lest darkness overtake you; he who walks in darkness does not know where he is going.

1 John 2:11 But he who hates his brother is in darkness and walks in darkness, and does not know where he is going, because the darkness has blinded his eyes.

Causes us to stumble.

Is 59:10 We grope for the wall like the blind, And we grope as if *we had* no eyes; We stumble at noonday as at twilight; *We are* as dead *men* in desolate places.

Sometimes synonym for night.

Ps 91:6 *Nor* of the pestilence *that* walks in darkness, *Nor* of the destruction *that* lays waste at noonday.

Cannot hide us from God.

Ps 139:11–12 If I say, "Surely the darkness shall fall on me," Even the night shall be light about me; **12** Indeed, the darkness shall not hide from You, But the night shines as the day; The darkness and the light *are* both alike *to* You.

And the wicked

The children of.

1 Thess 5:5 You are all sons of light and sons of the day. We are not of the night nor of darkness.

Live in.

Ps 107:10 Those who sat in darkness and in the shadow of death, Bound in affliction and irons—

Walk in.

Ps 82:5 They do not know, nor do they understand; They walk about in darkness; All the foundations of the earth are unstable.

Perpetuate their designs in.

Job 24:16 In the dark they break into houses Which they marked for themselves in the daytime; They do not know the light.

Are full of.

Matt 6:23 But if your eye is bad, your whole body will be full of darkness. If therefore the light that is in you is darkness, how great *is* that darkness!

Miraculous presence of,

On Mount Sinai.

Ex 19:16 Then it came to pass on the third day, in the morning, that there were thunderings and lightnings, and a thick cloud on the mountain; and the sound of the trumpet was very loud, so that all the people who *were* in the camp trembled.

Heb 12:18 For you have not come to the mountain that may be touched and that burned with fire, and to blackness and darkness and tempest,

Over the land of Egypt.

Ex 10:21–22 Then the Lord said to Moses, "Stretch out your hand toward heaven, that there may be darkness over the land of Egypt, darkness *which* may even be felt." **22** So Moses stretched out his hand toward heaven, and there was thick darkness in all the land of Egypt three days.

At the death of Christ.

Matt 27:45 Now from the sixth hour until the ninth hour there was darkness over all the land.

Before the destruction of Jerusalem.

Matt 24:29 "Immediately after the tribulation of those days the sun will be darkened, and the moon will not give its light; the stars will fall from heaven, and the powers of the heavens will be shaken.

Illustrative of

Greatness and unsearchableness of God.

Ex 20:21 So the people stood afar off, but Moses drew near the thick darkness where God *was*.

2 Sam 22:10 He bowed the heavens also, and came down With darkness under His feet.

2 Sam 22:12 He made darkness canopies around Him, Dark waters *and* thick clouds of the skies.

1 Kin 8:12 Then Solomon spoke: "The LORD said He would dwell in the dark cloud.

Ps 97:2 Clouds and darkness surround Him; Righteousness and justice *are* the foundation of His throne.

Mysterious and deep subjects.

Job 28:3 *Man* puts an end to darkness, And searches every recess For ore in the darkness and the shadow of death.

Secrecy.

Is 45:19 I have not spoken in secret, In a dark place of the earth; I did not say to the seed of Jacob, 'Seek Me in vain'; I, the LORD, speak righteousness, I declare things that are right.

Matt 10:27 "Whatever I tell you in the dark, speak in the light; and what you hear in the ear, preach on the housetops.

Ignorance and error.

Job 37:19 "Teach us what we should say to Him, *For* we can prepare nothing because of the darkness.

Is 60:2 For behold, the darkness shall cover the earth, And deep darkness the people; But the LORD will arise over you, And His glory will be seen upon you.

John 1:5 And the light shines in the darkness, and the darkness did not comprehend it.

John 3:19 And this is the condemnation, that the light has come into the world, and men loved darkness rather than light, because their deeds were evil.

John 12:35 Then Jesus said to them, "A little while longer the light is with you. Walk while you have the light, lest darkness overtake you; he who walks in darkness does not know where he is going.

Acts 26:18 to open their eyes, *in order* to turn *them* from darkness to light, and *from* the power of Satan to God, that they may receive forgiveness of sins and an inheritance among those who are sanctified by faith in Me.'

Anything hateful.

Job 3:4–9 May that day be darkness; May God above not seek it, Nor the light shine upon it. 5 May darkness and the shadow of death claim it; May a cloud settle on it; May the blackness of the day terrify it.

6 *As for* that night, may darkness seize it; May it not rejoice among the days of the year, May it not come into the number of the months. 7 Oh, may that night be barren! May no joyful shout come into it! 8 May those curse it who curse the day, Those who are ready to arouse Leviathan. 9 May the stars of its morning be dark; May it look for light, but *have* none, And not see the dawning of the day;

A course of sin.

Prov 2:13 From those who leave the paths of uprightness To walk in the ways of darkness;

Eph 5:11 And have no fellowship with the unfruitful works of darkness, but rather expose *them*.

Heavy afflictions.

Job 23:17 Because I was not cut off from the presence of darkness, And He did *not* hide deep darkness from my face.

Ps 112:4 Unto the upright there arises light in the darkness; *He is* gracious, and full of compassion, and righteous.

Eccl 5:17 All his days he also eats in darkness, And *he has* much sorrow and sickness and anger.

Is 5:30 In that day they will roar against them Like the roaring of the sea. And if *one* looks to the land, Behold, darkness *and* sorrow; And the light is darkened by the clouds.

Is 8:22 Then they will look to the earth, and see trouble and darkness, gloom of anguish; and *they will be* driven into darkness.

Is 59:9 Therefore justice is far from us, Nor does righteousness overtake us; We look for light, but there is darkness! For brightness, *but* we walk in blackness!

The power of Satan.

Eph 6:12 For we do not wrestle against flesh and blood, but against principalities, against powers, against the rulers of the darkness of this age, against spiritual *hosts* of wickedness in the heavenly *places*.

Col 1:13 He has delivered us from the power of darkness and conveyed *us* into the kingdom of the Son of His love,

The grave.

1 Sam 2:9 He will guard the feet of His saints, But the wicked shall be silent in darkness. "For by strength no man shall prevail.

Job 10:21–22 Before I go *to the place from which* I shall not return, To the land of darkness and the shadow of death, 22 A land as dark as darkness *itself*, As the shadow of death, without any order, *Where* even the light *is* like darkness.' "

The punishment of devils and wicked men.

Matt 22:13 Then the king said to the servants, 'Bind him hand and foot, take him away, and cast *him* into outer darkness; there will be weeping and gnashing of teeth.'

2 Pet 2:4 For if God did not spare the angels who sinned, but cast *them* down to hell and delivered *them* into chains of darkness, to be reserved for judgment;

2 Pet 2:17 These are wells without water, clouds carried by a tempest, for whom is reserved the blackness of darkness forever.

Jude 1:6 And the angels who did not keep their proper domain, but left their own abode, He has reserved in everlasting chains under darkness for the judgment of the great day;

Jude 1:13 raging waves of the sea, foaming up their own shame; wandering stars for whom is reserved the blackness of darkness forever.

DAVID

Genealogy of.

1 Chr 2:3–15 The sons of Judah *were* Er, Onan, and Shelah. *These* three were born to him by the daughter of Shua, the Canaanitess. Er, the firstborn of Judah, was wicked in the sight of the LORD; so He killed him. **4** And Tamar, his daughter-in-law, bore him Perez and Zerah. All the sons of Judah *were* five. **5** The sons of Perez *were* Hezron and Hamul. **6** The sons of Zerah *were* Zimri, Ethan, Heman, Calcol, and Dara—five of them in all. **7** The son of Carmi *was* Achar, the troubler of Israel, who transgressed in the accursed thing. **8** The son of Ethan *was* Azariah. **9** Also the sons of Hezron who were born to him *were* Jerahmeel, Ram, and Chelubai. **10** Ram begot Amminadab, and Amminadab begot Nahshon, leader of the children of Judah; **11** Nahshon begot Salma, and Salma begot Boaz; **12** Boaz begot Obed, and Obed begot Jesse; **13** Jesse begot Eliab his firstborn, Abinadab the second, Shimea the third, **14** Nethanel the fourth, Raddai the fifth, **15** Ozem the sixth, *and* David the seventh.

Youngest son of Jesse.

1 Sam 16:10–13 Thus Jesse made seven of his sons pass before Samuel. And Samuel said to Jesse, "The LORD has not chosen these." **11** And Samuel said to Jesse, "Are all the young men here?" Then he said, "There remains yet the youngest, and there he is, keeping the sheep." And Samuel said to Jesse, "Send and bring him. For we will not sit down till he comes here." **12** So he sent and brought him in. Now he *was* ruddy, with bright eyes, and good-looking. And the LORD said, "Arise, anoint him; for this *is* the one!" **13** Then Samuel took the horn of oil and anointed him in the midst of his brothers; and the Spirit of the LORD came upon David from that day forward. So Samuel arose and went to Ramah.

Chosen by God.

1 Sam 16:1 Now the LORD said to Samuel, "How long will you mourn for Saul, seeing I have rejected him from reigning over Israel? Fill your horn with oil, and go; I am sending you to Jesse the Bethlehemite. For I have provided Myself a king among his sons."

1 Sam 16:13 Then Samuel took the horn of oil and anointed him in the midst of his brothers; and the Spirit of the LORD came upon David from that day forward. So Samuel arose and went to Ramah.

Killed Goliath.

1 Sam 17:40–49 Then he took his staff in his hand; and he chose for himself five smooth stones from the brook, and put them in a shepherd's bag, in a pouch which he had, and his sling was in his hand. And he drew near to the Philistine. **41** So the Philistine came, and began drawing near to David, and the man who bore the shield *went* before him. **42** And when the Philistine looked about and saw David, he disdained

him; for he was *only* a youth, ruddy and good-looking. **43** So the Philistine said to David, "*Am* I a dog, that you come to me with sticks?" And the Philistine cursed David by his gods. **44** And the Philistine said to David, "Come to me, and I will give your flesh to the birds of the air and the beasts of the field!" **45** Then David said to the Philistine, "You come to me with a sword, with a spear, and with a javelin. But I come to you in the name of the LORD of hosts, the God of the armies of Israel, whom you have defied. **46** This day the LORD will deliver you into my hand, and I will strike you and take your head from you. And this day I will give the carcasses of the camp of the Philistines to the birds of the air and the wild beasts of the earth, that all the earth may know that there is a God in Israel. **47** Then all this assembly shall know that the LORD does not save with sword and spear; for the battle *is* the LORD's, and He will give you into our hands." **48** So it was, when the Philistine arose and came and drew near to meet David, that David hurried and ran toward the army to meet the Philistine. **49** Then David put his hand in his bag and took out a stone; and he slung *it* and struck the Philistine in his forehead, so that the stone sank into his forehead, and he fell on his face to the earth.

Bond with Jonathan.

1 Sam 18:1–4 Now when he had finished speaking to Saul, the soul of Jonathan was knit to the soul of David, and Jonathan loved him as his own soul. **2** Saul took him that day, and would not let him go home to his father's house anymore. **3** Then Jonathan and David made a covenant, because he loved him as his own soul. **4** And Jonathan took off the robe that *was* on him and gave it to David, with his armor, even to his sword and his bow and his belt.

Cf. 1 Sam 20:1–42; 23:16–18

Flight from Saul.

1 Sam 19:1–18 Now Saul spoke to Jonathan his son and to all his servants, that they should kill David; but Jonathan, Saul's son, delighted greatly in David. **2** So Jonathan told David, saying, "My father Saul seeks to kill you. Therefore please be on your guard until morning, and stay in a secret *place* and hide. **3** And I will go out and stand beside my father in the field where you *are*, and I will speak with my father about you. Then what I observe, I will tell you." **4** Thus Jonathan spoke well of David to Saul his father, and said to him, "Let not the king sin against his servant, against David, because he has not sinned against you, and because his works *have been* very good toward you. **5** For he took his life in his hands and killed the Philistine, and the LORD brought about a great deliverance for all Israel. You saw *it* and rejoiced. Why then will you sin against innocent blood, to kill David without a cause?" **6** So Saul heeded the voice of Jonathan, and Saul swore, "*As* the LORD lives, he shall not be killed." **7** Then Jonathan called David, and Jonathan told him all these things. So Jonathan brought David to Saul, and he was in his presence as in times past. **8** And there was war again; and David went out and fought with the Philistines, and struck them with a mighty blow, and they fled from him. **9** Now the distressing spirit from the LORD came upon Saul as he sat in his house with his spear in his hand. And David was playing *music* with *his* hand. **10** Then Saul sought to pin David to the wall with the spear, but he slipped away from Saul's presence; and he drove the spear into the wall. So David fled and escaped that night. **11** Saul also sent messengers to David's house to watch him and to kill him in the morning. And Michal, David's wife, told him, saying, "If you do not save your life tonight, tomorrow you will be killed." **12** So Michal let David down through a window. And he went and fled and escaped. **13** And Michal took an image and laid *it* in the bed, put a cover of goats' *hair* for his head, and covered *it* with clothes. **14** So when Saul sent messengers to take David, she said, "He *is* sick." **15** Then Saul sent the messengers *back* to see David, saying, "Bring him up to me in the bed, that I may kill him." **16** And when the messengers had come in, there was the image in the bed, with a cover of goats' *hair* for his head. **17** Then Saul said to Michal, "Why have you deceived me like this, and sent my enemy away, so that he has escaped?" And Michal answered Saul, "He said to me, 'Let me go! Why should I kill you?' " **18** So David fled and escaped, and went to Samuel at Ramah, and told him all that Saul had done to him. And he and Samuel went and stayed in Naioth.

Twice spared Saul's life.

1 Sam 24:1–7 Now it happened, when Saul had returned from following the Philistines, that it was told him, saying, "Take note! David *is* in the Wilderness of En Gedi." **2** Then Saul took three thousand chosen men from all Israel, and went to seek David and his men on the Rocks of the Wild Goats. **3** So he came to the sheepfolds by the road, where there *was* a cave; and Saul went in to attend to his needs. (David and his men were staying in the recesses of the cave.) **4** Then the men of David said to him, "This is the day of which the LORD said to you, 'Behold, I will deliver your enemy into your hand, that you may do to him as it seems good to you.' " And David arose and secretly cut off a corner of Saul's robe. **5** Now it happened afterward that David's heart troubled him because he had cut Saul's *robe*. **6** And he said to his men, "The LORD forbid that I should do this thing to my master, the LORD's anointed, to stretch out my hand against him, seeing he *is* the anointed of the LORD." **7** So David restrained his servants with *these* words, and did not allow them to rise against Saul. And Saul got up from the cave and went on *his* way.

1 Sam 26:5–12 So David arose and came to the place where Saul had encamped. And David saw the place where Saul lay, and Abner the son of Ner, the commander of his army. Now Saul lay within the camp, with the people encamped all around him. **6** Then David answered, and said to Ahimelech the Hittite and to Abishai the son of Zeruiah, brother of Joab, saying, "Who will go down with me to Saul in the camp?" And Abishai said, "I will go down with you." **7** So David and Abishai came to the people by night; and there Saul lay sleeping within the camp, with his spear stuck in the ground by his head. And Abner and the people lay all around him. **8** Then Abishai said to David, "God has delivered your enemy into your hand this day. Now therefore, please, let me strike him at once with the spear, right to the earth; and I will not *have to strike* him a second time!" **9** But David said to Abishai, "Do not destroy him; for who can stretch out his hand against the LORD's anointed, and be guiltless?" **10** David said furthermore, "*As* the LORD lives, the LORD shall strike him, or his day shall come to die, or he shall go out to battle and perish. **11** The LORD forbid that I should stretch out my hand against the LORD's anointed. But please, take now the spear and the jug of water that *are* by his head, and let us go." **12** So David took the spear and the jug of water *by* Saul's head, and they got away; and no man saw or knew *it* or awoke. For they *were* all asleep, because a deep sleep from the LORD had fallen on them.

Mourned for Saul.

2 Sam 1:17–27 Then David lamented with this lamentation over Saul and over Jonathan his son, **18** and he told *them* to teach the children of Judah *the Song of* the Bow; indeed *it is* written in the Book of Jasher: **19** "The beauty of Israel is slain on your high places! How the mighty have fallen! **20** Tell *it* not in Gath, Proclaim *it* not in the streets of Ashkelon— Lest the daughters of the Philistines rejoice, Lest the daughters of the uncircumcised triumph. **21** "O mountains of Gilboa, *Let there be* no dew nor rain upon you, Nor fields of offerings. For the shield of the mighty is cast away there! The shield of Saul, not anointed with oil. **22** From the blood of the slain, From the fat of the mighty, The bow of Jonathan did not turn back, And the sword of Saul did not return empty. **23** "Saul and Jonathan *were* beloved and pleasant in their lives, And in their death they were not divided; They were swifter than eagles, They were stronger than lions. **24** "O daughters of Israel, weep over Saul, Who clothed you in scarlet, with luxury; Who put ornaments of gold on your apparel. **25** "How the mighty have fallen in the midst of the battle! Jonathan *was* slain in your high places. **26** I am distressed for you, my brother Jonathan; You have been very pleasant to me; Your love to me was wonderful, Surpassing the love of women. **27** "How the mighty have fallen, And the weapons of war perished!"

Anointed king of Judah at Hebron.

2 Sam 2:1–4 It happened after this that David inquired of the LORD, saying, "Shall I go up to any of the cities of Judah?" And the LORD said to him, "Go up." David said, "Where shall I go up?" And He said, "To Hebron." **2** So David went up there, and his two wives also, Ahinoam the Jezreelitess, and Abigail the widow of Nabal the Carmelite. **3** And David brought up the men who *were* with him, every man with his household. So they dwelt in the cities of Hebron. **4** Then the men of Judah came, and there they anointed David king over the house of Judah. And they told David, saying, "The men of Jabesh Gilead *were the ones* who buried Saul."

2 Sam 2:11 And the time that David was king in Hebron over the house of Judah was seven years and six months.

Recognized as king of all Israel; captured Zion.

2 Sam 5:1–10 Then all the tribes of Israel came to David at Hebron and spoke, saying, "Indeed we *are* your bone and your flesh. **2** Also, in time past, when Saul was king over us, you were the one who led Israel out and brought them in; and the LORD said to you, 'You shall shepherd My people Israel, and be ruler over Israel.' " **3** Therefore all the elders of Israel came to the king at Hebron, and King David made a covenant with them at Hebron before the LORD. And they anointed David king over Israel. **4** David *was* thirty years old when he began to reign, *and* he reigned forty years. **5** In Hebron he reigned over Judah seven years and six months, and in Jerusalem he reigned thirty-three years over all Israel and Judah. **6** And the king and his men went to Jerusalem against the Jebusites, the inhabitants of the land, who spoke to David, saying, "You shall not come in here; but the blind and the lame will repel you," thinking, "David cannot come in here." **7** Nevertheless David took the stronghold of Zion (that *is*, the City of David). **8** Now David said on that day, "Whoever climbs up by way of the water shaft and defeats the Jebusites (the lame and the blind, *who are* hated by David's soul), *he shall be chief and captain*." Therefore they say, "The blind and the lame shall not come into the house." **9** Then David dwelt in the stronghold, and called it the City of David. And David built all around from the Millo and inward. **10** So David went on and became great, and the LORD God of hosts *was* with him.

Cf. 1 Chr 11:1–9

Led ark to Jerusalem.

2 Sam 6:1–16 Again David gathered all *the* choice *men* of Israel, thirty thousand. **2** And David arose and went with all the people who *were* with him from Baale Judah to bring up from there the ark of God, whose name is called by the Name, the LORD of Hosts, who dwells *between* the cherubim. **3** So they set the ark of God on a new cart, and brought it out of the house of Abinadab, which *was* on the hill; and Uzzah and Ahio, the sons of Abinadab, drove the new cart. **4** And they brought it out of the house of Abinadab, which *was* on the hill, accompanying the ark of God; and Ahio went before the ark. **5** Then David and all the house of Israel played *music* before the LORD on all kinds of *instruments* of fir wood, on harps, on stringed instruments, on tambourines, on sistrums, and on cymbals. **6** And when they came to Nachon's threshing floor, Uzzah put out *his hand* to the ark of God and took hold of it, for the oxen stumbled. **7** Then the anger of the LORD was aroused against Uzzah, and God struck him there for *his* error; and he died there by the ark of God. **8** And David became angry because of the LORD's outbreak against Uzzah; and he called the name of the place Perez Uzzah to this day. **9** David was afraid of the LORD that day; and he said, "How can the ark of the LORD come to me?" **10** So David would not move the ark of the LORD with him into the City of David; but David took it aside into the house of Obed-Edom the Gittite. **11** The ark of the LORD remained in the house of Obed-Edom the Gittite three months. And the LORD blessed Obed-Edom and all his household. **12** Now it was told King David, saying, "The LORD has blessed the house of Obed-Edom and all that *belongs* to him, because of the ark of God." So David went and brought up the ark of God from the house of Obed-Edom to the City of David with gladness. **13** And so it was, when those bearing the ark of the LORD had gone six paces, that he sacrificed oxen and fatted sheep. **14** Then David danced before the LORD with all *his* might; and David *was* wearing a linen ephod.

15 So David and all the house of Israel brought up the ark of the LORD with shouting and with the sound of the trumpet. **16** Now as the ark of the LORD came into the City of David, Michal, Saul's daughter, looked through a window and saw King David leaping and whirling before the LORD; and she despised him in her heart.

Cf. 1 Chr 13:1–14; 15:25–28

Received covenant from God.

2 Sam 7:1–17 Now it came to pass when the king was dwelling in his house, and the LORD had given him rest from all his enemies all around, **2** that the king said to Nathan the prophet, "See now, I dwell in a house of cedar, but the ark of God dwells inside tent curtains." **3** Then Nathan said to the king, "Go, do all that *is* in your heart, for the LORD *is* with you." **4** But it happened that night that the word of the LORD came to Nathan, saying, **5** "Go and tell My servant David, 'Thus says the LORD: "Would you build a house for Me to dwell in? **6** For I have not dwelt in a house since the time that I brought the children of Israel up from Egypt, even to this day, but have moved about in a tent and in a tabernacle. **7** Wherever I have moved about with all the children of Israel, have I ever spoken a word to anyone from the tribes of Israel, whom I commanded to shepherd My people Israel, saying, 'Why have you not built Me a house of cedar?' " ' **8** Now therefore, thus shall you say to My servant David, 'Thus says the LORD of hosts: "I took you from the sheepfold, from following the sheep, to be ruler over My people, over Israel. **9** And I have been with you wherever you have gone, and have cut off all your enemies from before you, and have made you a great name, like the name of the great men who *are* on the earth. **10** Moreover I will appoint a place for My people Israel, and will plant them, that they may dwell in a place of their own and move no more; nor shall the sons of wickedness oppress them anymore, as previously, **11** since the time that I commanded judges *to be* over My people Israel, and have caused you to rest from all your enemies. Also the LORD tells you that He will make you a house. **12** "When your days are fulfilled and you rest with your fathers, I will set up your seed after you, who will come from your body, and I will establish his kingdom. **13** He shall build a house for My name, and I will establish the throne of his kingdom forever. **14** I will be his Father, and he shall be My son. If he commits iniquity, I will chasten him with the rod of men and with the blows of the sons of men. **15** But My mercy shall not depart from him, as I took *it* from Saul, whom I removed from before you. **16** And your house and your kingdom shall be established forever before you. Your throne shall be established forever." ' " **17** According to all these words and according to all this vision, so Nathan spoke to David.

Cf. 1 Chr 17:3–15

Committed adultery with Bathsheba.

2 Sam 11:1–27 It happened in the spring of the year, at the time when kings go out *to battle,* that David sent Joab and his servants with him, and all Israel; and they destroyed the people of Ammon and besieged Rabbah. But David remained at Jerusalem. **2** Then it happened one evening that David arose from his bed and walked on the roof of the king's house. And from the roof he saw a woman bathing, and the woman *was* very beautiful to behold. 3 So David sent and inquired about the woman. And *someone* said, "*Is* this not Bathsheba, the daughter of Eliam, the wife of Uriah the Hittite?" 4 Then David sent messengers, and took her; and she came to him, and he lay with her, for she was cleansed from her impurity; and she returned to her house. 5 And the woman conceived; so she sent and told David, and said, "I *am* with child." 6 Then David sent to Joab, *saying,* "Send me Uriah the Hittite." And Joab sent Uriah to David. 7 When Uriah had come to him, David asked how Joab was doing, and how the people were doing, and how the war prospered. 8 And David said to Uriah, "Go down to your house and wash your feet." So Uriah departed from the king's house, and a gift *of food* from the king followed him. 9 But Uriah slept at the door of the king's house with all the servants of his lord, and did not go down to his house. 10 So when they told David, saying, "Uriah did not go down to his house," David said to Uriah, "Did you not come from a journey? Why did you not go down to your house?" 11 And Uriah said to David, "The ark and Israel and Judah are dwelling in tents, and my lord Joab and the servants of my lord are encamped in the open fields. Shall I then go to my house to eat and drink, and to lie with my wife? *As* you live, and *as* your soul lives, I will not do this thing." 12 Then David said to Uriah, "Wait here today also, and tomorrow I will let you depart." So Uriah remained in Jerusalem that day and the next. 13 Now when David called him, he ate and drank before him; and he made him drunk. And at evening he went out to lie on his bed with the servants of his lord, but he did not go down to his house. 14 In the morning it happened that David wrote a letter to Joab and sent *it* by the hand of Uriah. 15 And he wrote in the letter, saying, "Set Uriah in the forefront of the hottest battle, and retreat from him, that he may be struck down and die." 16 So it was, while Joab besieged the city, that he assigned Uriah to a place where he knew there *were* valiant men. 17 Then the men of the city came out and fought with Joab. And *some* of the people of the servants of David fell; and Uriah the Hittite died also. 18 Then Joab sent and told David all the things concerning the war, 19 and charged the messenger, saying, "When you have finished telling the matters of the war to the king, 20 if it happens that the king's wrath rises, and he says to you: 'Why did you approach so near to the city when you fought? Did you not know that they would shoot from the wall? 21 Who struck Abimelech the son of Jerubbesheth? Was it not a woman who cast a piece of a millstone on him from the wall, so that he died in Thebez? Why did you go near the wall?'—then you shall say, 'Your servant Uriah the Hittite is dead also.' 22 So the messenger went, and came and told David all that Joab had sent by him. 23 And the messenger said to David, "Surely the men prevailed against us and came out to us in the field; then we drove them back as far as the entrance of the gate. 24 The archers shot from the wall at your servants; and *some* of the king's servants are dead, and your servant Uriah the Hittite is dead also." 25 Then David said to the messenger, "Thus you shall say to Joab: 'Do not let this thing displease you, for the sword devours one as well as another. Strengthen your attack against the city, and overthrow it.' So encourage him." 26 When the wife of Uriah heard that Uriah her husband was dead, she mourned for her husband. 27 And when her mourning was over, David sent and brought her to his house, and she became his wife and bore him a son. But the thing that David had done displeased the LORD.

Rebuked by Nathan.

2 Sam 12:1–14 Then the LORD sent Nathan to David. And he came to him, and said to him: "There were two men in one city, one rich and the other poor. 2 The rich *man* had exceedingly many flocks and herds. 3 But the poor *man* had nothing, except one little ewe lamb which he had bought and nourished; and it grew up together with him and with his children. It ate of his own food and drank from his own cup and lay in his bosom; and it was like a daughter to him. 4 And a traveler came to the rich man, who refused to take from his own flock and from his own herd to prepare one for the wayfaring man who had come to him; but he took the poor man's lamb and prepared it for the man who had come to him." 5 So David's anger was greatly aroused against the man, and he said to Nathan, "*As* the LORD lives, the man who has done this shall surely die! 6 And he shall restore fourfold for the lamb, because he did this thing and because he had no pity." 7 Then Nathan said to David, "You *are* the man! Thus says the LORD God of Israel: 'I anointed you king over Israel, and I delivered you from the hand of Saul. 8 I gave you your master's house and your master's wives into your keeping, and gave you the house of Israel and Judah. And if *that had been* too little, I also would have given you much more! 9 Why have you despised the commandment of the LORD, to do evil in His sight? You have killed Uriah the Hittite with the sword; you have taken his wife *to be* your wife, and have killed him with the sword of the people of Ammon. 10 Now therefore, the sword shall never depart from your house, because you have despised Me, and have taken the wife of Uriah the Hittite to be your wife.' 11 Thus says the LORD: 'Behold, I will raise up adversity against you from your own house; and I will take your wives before your eyes and give *them* to your neighbor, and he shall lie with your wives in the sight of this sun. 12 For you did *it* secretly, but I will do this thing before all Israel, before the sun.' " 13 So David said to Nathan, "I have sinned against the LORD." And Nathan said to David, "The LORD also has put away your sin; you shall not die. 14 However, because by this deed you have given great occasion to the enemies of the LORD to blaspheme, the child also *who is* born to you shall surely die."

Absalom rebelled against.

2 Sam 15:1–12 After this it happened that Absalom provided himself with chariots and horses, and fifty men to run before him. 2 Now Absalom would rise early and stand beside the way to the gate. *So* it was, whenever anyone who had a lawsuit came to the king for a decision, that Absalom would call to him and say, "What city *are* you from?" And he would say, "Your servant *is* from such and such a tribe of Israel." **3** Then Absalom would say to him, "Look, your case *is* good and right; but *there is* no deputy of the king to hear you." **4** Moreover Absalom would say, "Oh, that I were made judge in the land, and everyone who has any suit or cause would come to me; then I would give him justice." **5** And *so* it was, whenever anyone came near to bow down to him, that he would put out his hand and take him and kiss him. **6** In this manner Absalom acted toward all Israel who came to the king for judgment. So Absalom stole the hearts of the men of Israel. **7** Now it came to pass after forty years that Absalom said to the king, "Please, let me go to Hebron and pay the vow which I made to the LORD. **8** For your servant took a vow while I dwelt at Geshur in Syria, saying, 'If the LORD indeed brings me back to Jerusalem, then I will serve the LORD.' " **9** And the king said to him, "Go in peace." So he arose and went to Hebron. **10** Then Absalom sent spies throughout all the tribes of Israel, saying, "As soon as you hear the sound of the trumpet, then you shall say, 'Absalom reigns in Hebron!' " **11** And with Absalom went two hundred men invited from Jerusalem, and they went along innocently and did not know anything. **12** Then Absalom sent for Ahithophel the Gilonite, David's counselor, from his city—from Giloh—while he offered sacrifices. And the conspiracy grew strong, for the people with Absalom continually increased in number.

Returned to Jerusalem.

2 Sam 19:15–18 Then the king returned and came to the Jordan. And Judah came to Gilgal, to go to meet the king, to escort the king across the Jordan. **16** And Shimei the son of Gera, a Benjamite, who *was* from Bahurim, hurried and came down with the men of Judah to meet King David. **17** *There were* a thousand men of Benjamin with him, and Ziba the servant of the house of Saul, and his fifteen sons and his twenty servants with him; and they went over the Jordan before the king. **18** Then a ferryboat went across to carry over the king's household, and to do what he thought good. Now Shimei the son of Gera fell down before the king when he had crossed the Jordan.

His last words.

2 Sam 23:1–7 Now these *are* the last words of David. *Thus* says David the son of Jesse; *Thus* says the man raised up on high, The anointed of the God of Jacob, And the sweet psalmist of Israel: **2** "The Spirit of the LORD spoke by me, And His word *was* on my tongue. **3** The God of Israel said, The Rock of Israel spoke to me: 'He who rules over men *must be* just, Ruling in the fear of God. **4** And *he shall be* like the light of the morning *when* the sun rises, A morning without clouds, *Like* the tender grass *springing* out of the earth, By clear shining after rain.' **5** "Although my house *is* not so with God, Yet He has made with me an everlasting covenant, Ordered in all *things* and secure. For *this is* all my salvation and all *my* desire; Will He not make *it* increase? **6** But *the sons* of rebellion *shall* all *be* as thorns thrust away, Because they cannot be taken with hands. **7** But the man *who* touches them Must be armed with iron and the shaft of a spear, And they shall be utterly burned with fire in *their* place."

Dying charge to Solomon.

1 Kin 2:1–11 Now the days of David drew near that he should die, and he charged Solomon his son, saying, **2** "I go the way of all the earth; be strong, therefore, and prove yourself a man. **3** And keep the charge of the LORD your God: to walk in His ways, to keep His statutes, His commandments, His judgments, and His testimonies, as it is written in the Law of Moses, that you may prosper in all that you do and wherever you turn; **4** that the LORD may fulfill His word which He spoke concerning me, saying, 'If your sons take heed to their way, to walk before Me in truth with all their heart and with all their soul,' He said, 'you shall not lack a man on the throne of Israel.' **5** "Moreover you know also what Joab the son of Zeruiah did to me, *and* what he did to the two commanders of the armies of Israel, to Abner the son of Ner and Amasa the son of Jether, whom he killed. And he shed the blood of war in peacetime, and put the blood of war on his belt that *was* around his waist, and on his sandals that *were* on his feet. **6** Therefore do according to your wisdom, and do not let his gray hair go down to the grave in peace. **7** "But show kindness to the sons of Barzillai the Gileadite, and let them be among those who eat at your table, for so they came to me when I fled from Absalom your brother. **8** "And see, *you have* with you Shimei the son of Gera, a Benjamite from Bahurim, who cursed me with a malicious curse in the day when I went to Mahanaim. But he came down to meet me at the Jordan, and I swore to him by the LORD, saying, 'I will not put you to death with the sword.' **9** Now therefore, do not hold him guiltless, for you *are* a wise man and know what you ought to do to him; but bring his gray hair down to the grave with blood." **10** So David rested with his fathers, and was buried in the City of David. **11** The period that David reigned over Israel *was* forty years; seven years he reigned in Hebron, and in Jerusalem he reigned thirty-three years.

Eternal kingdom of.

Mark 11:10 Blessed *is* the kingdom of our father David That comes in the name of the Lord! Hosanna in the highest!"

Luke 1:32 He will be great, and will be called the Son of the Highest; and the Lord God will give Him the throne of His father David.

Acts 15:16 'After this I will return And will rebuild the *tabernacle of David, which has fallen down; I will re-build its ruins, And I will set it up;*

Hero of faith.

Heb 11:32–33 And what more shall I say? For the time would fail me to tell of Gideon and Barak and Samson and Jephthah, also *of* David and Samuel and the prophets: **33** who through faith subdued kingdoms, worked righteousness, obtained promises, stopped the mouths of lions,

DAY

The light first called.

Gen 1:5 God called the light Day, and the darkness He called Night. So the evening and the morning were the first day.

Natural, from evening to evening.

Gen 1:5 God called the light Day, and the darkness He called Night. So the evening and the morning were the first day.

Lev 23:32 It *shall be* to you a sabbath of *solemn* rest, and you shall afflict your souls; on the ninth *day* of the month at evening, from evening to evening, you shall celebrate your sabbath."

Measured by the sun's continuance above the horizon.

Gen 31:39–40 That which was torn *by beasts* I did not bring to you; I bore the loss of it. You required it from my hand, *whether* stolen by day or stolen by night. **40** *There* I was! In the day the drought consumed me, and the frost by night, and my sleep departed from my eyes.

Neh 4:21–22 So we labored in the work, and half of *the men* held the spears from daybreak until the stars appeared. **22** At the same time I also said to the people, "Let each man and his servant stay at night in Jerusalem, that they may be our guard by night and a working party by day."

Prophetical, a year.

Ezek 4:6 And when you have completed them, lie again on your right side; then you shall bear the iniquity of the house of Judah forty days. I have laid on you a day for each year.

Dan 12:12 Blessed *is* he who waits, and comes to the one thousand three hundred and thirty-five days.

Commonly divided into

Break of.

Gen 32:24 Then Jacob was left alone; and a Man wrestled with him until the breaking of day.

Gen 32:26 And He said, "Let Me go, for the day breaks." But he said, "I will not let You go unless You bless me!"

Song 2:17 Until the day breaks And the shadows flee away, Turn, my beloved, And be like a gazelle Or a young stag Upon the mountains of Bether.

Morning.

Ex 29:39 One lamb you shall offer in the morning, and the other lamb you shall offer at twilight.

2 Sam 23:4 And *he shall be* like the light of the morning *when* the sun rises, A morning without clouds, *Like* the tender grass *springing* out of the earth, By clear shining after rain.'

Noon.

Gen 43:16 When Joseph saw Benjamin with them, he said to the steward of his house, "Take *these* men to my home, and slaughter an animal and make ready; for *these* men will dine with me at noon."

Ps 55:17 Evening and morning and at noon I will pray, and cry aloud, And He shall hear my voice.

Decline of.

Judg 19:8–9 Then he arose early in the morning on the fifth day to depart, but the young woman's father said, "Please refresh your heart." So they delayed until afternoon; and both of them ate. **9** And when the man stood to depart—he and his concubine and his servant—his father-in-law, the young woman's father, said to him, "Look, the day is now drawing toward evening; please spend the night. See, the day is coming to an end; lodge here, that your heart may be merry. Tomorrow go your way early, so that you may get home."

Luke 9:12 When the day began to wear away, the twelve came and said to Him, "Send the multitude away, that they may go into the surrounding towns and country, and lodge and get provisions; for we are in a deserted place here."

Luke 24:29 But they constrained Him, saying, "Abide with us, for it is toward evening, and the day is far spent." And He went in to stay with them.

Evening.

Gen 8:11 Then the dove came to him in the evening, and behold, a freshly plucked olive leaf *was* in her mouth; and Noah knew that the waters had receded from the earth.

Ps 104:23 Man goes out to his work And to his labor until the evening.

Jer 6:4 "Prepare war against her; Arise, and let us go up at noon. Woe to us, for the day goes away, For the shadows of the evening are lengthening."

Sometimes divided into four parts.

Neh 9:3 And they stood up in their place and read from the Book of the Law of the Lord their God *for one-fourth* of the day; and *for another* fourth they confessed and worshiped the Lord their God.

Later subdivided into twelve hours.

Matt 20:3 And he went out about the third hour and saw others standing idle in the marketplace,

Matt 20:5–6 Again he went out about the sixth and the ninth hour, and did likewise. **6** And about the eleventh hour he went out and found others standing idle, and said to them, 'Why have you been standing here idle all day?'

John 11:9 Jesus answered, "Are there not twelve hours in the day? If anyone walks in the day, he does not stumble, because he sees the light of this world.

Time of, ascertained by the sundial.

2 Kin 20:11 So Isaiah the prophet cried out to the Lord, and He brought the shadow ten degrees backward, by which it had gone down on the sundial of Ahaz.

Succession of, secured by covenant.

Gen 8:22 "While the earth remains, Seedtime and harvest, Cold and heat, Winter and summer, And day and night Shall not cease."

Made for the glory of God.

Ps 19:2 Day unto day utters speech, And night unto night reveals knowledge.

Ps 74:16 The day *is* Yours, the night also *is* Yours; You have prepared the light and the sun.

Under the control of God.

Amos 5:8 He made the Pleiades and Orion; He turns the shadow of death into morning And makes the day dark as night; He calls for the waters of the sea And pours them out on the face of the earth; The Lord *is* His name.

Amos 8:9 "And it shall come to pass in that day," says the Lord God, "That I will make the sun go down at noon, And I will darken the earth in broad daylight;

A time of judgment called a day of

Anger.

Lam 2:21 "Young and old lie On the ground in the streets; My virgins and my young men Have fallen by the sword; You have slain *them* in the day of Your anger, You have slaughtered *and* not pitied.

Wrath.

Job 20:28 The increase of his house will depart, *And his goods* will flow away in the day of His wrath.

Zeph 1:15 That day *is* a day of wrath, A day of trouble and distress, A day of devastation and desolation, A day of darkness and gloominess, A day of clouds and thick darkness,

Zeph 1:18 Neither their silver nor their gold Shall be able to deliver them In the day of the LORD's wrath; But the whole land shall be devoured By the fire of His jealousy, For He will make speedy riddance Of all those who dwell in the land.

Rom 2:5 But in accordance with your hardness and your impenitent heart you are treasuring up for yourself wrath in the day of wrath and revelation of the righteous judgment of God,

Your watchman.

Mic 7:4 The best of them *is* like a brier; The most upright *is sharper* than a thorn hedge; The day of your watchman and your punishment comes; Now shall be their perplexity.

Doom.

Job 21:30 For the wicked are reserved for the day of doom; They shall be brought out on the day of wrath.

Jer 17:17 Do not be a terror to me; You *are* my hope in the day of doom.

Amos 6:3 *Woe to* you who put far off the day of doom, Who cause the seat of violence to come near;

Darkness.

Joel 2:2 A day of darkness and gloominess, A day of clouds and thick darkness, Like the morning *clouds* spread over the mountains. A people *come,* great and strong, The like of whom has never been; Nor will there ever be any *such* after them, Even for many successive generations.

Zeph 1:15 That day *is* a day of wrath, A day of trouble and distress, A day of devastation and desolation, A day of darkness and gloominess, A day of clouds and thick darkness,

Trouble.

Ps 102:2 Do not hide Your face from me in the day of my trouble; Incline Your ear to me; In the day that I call, answer me speedily.

Calamity.

Deut 32:35 Vengeance is Mine, and recompense; Their foot shall slip in *due* time; For the day of their calamity *is* at hand, And the things to come hasten upon them.'

Jer 18:17 I will scatter them as with an east wind before the enemy; I will show them the back and not the face In the day of their calamity."

Adversity.

Prov 24:10 *If* you faint in the day of adversity, Your strength *is* small.

Vengeance.

Prov 6:34 For jealousy *is* a husband's fury; Therefore he will not spare in the day of vengeance.

Is 61:2 To proclaim the acceptable year of the LORD, And the day of vengeance of our God; To comfort all who mourn,

Slaughter.

Is 30:25 There will be on every high mountain And on every high hill Rivers *and* streams of waters, In the day of the great slaughter, When the towers fall.

Jer 12:3 But You, O LORD, know me; You have seen me, And You have tested my heart toward You. Pull them out like sheep for the slaughter, And prepare them for the day of slaughter.

Evil.

Eph 6:13 Therefore take up the whole armor of God, that you may be able to withstand in the evil day, and having done all, to stand.

The Lord.

Is 2:12 For the day of the LORD of hosts *Shall come* upon everything proud and lofty, Upon everything lifted up— And it shall be brought low—

Is 13:6 Wail, for the day of the LORD *is* at hand! It will come as destruction from the Almighty.

Zeph 1:14 The great day of the LORD *is* near; *It is* near and hastens quickly. The noise of the day of the LORD is bitter; There the mighty men shall cry out.

A time of mercy called a day of

Salvation.

2 Cor 6:2 For He says: *"In an acceptable time I have heard you, And in the day of salvation I have helped you."* Behold, now *is* the accepted time; behold, now *is* the day of salvation.

Redemption.

Eph 4:30 And do not grieve the Holy Spirit of God, by whom you were sealed for the day of redemption.

Visitation.

Jer 27:22 'They shall be carried to Babylon, and there they shall be until the day that I visit them,' says the LORD. 'Then I will bring them up and restore them to this place.' "

1 Pet 2:12 having your conduct honorable among the Gentiles, that when they speak against you as evildoers, they may, by *your* good works which they observe, glorify God in the day of visitation.

God's power.

Ps 110:3 Your people *shall be* volunteers In the day of Your power; In the beauties of holiness, from the womb of the morning, You have the dew of Your youth.

A time of festivity called a

Holiday.

Esth 8:17 And in every province and city, wherever the king's command and decree came, the Jews had joy and gladness, a feast and a holiday. Then many of the people of the land became Jews, because fear of the Jews fell upon them.

Esth 9:19 Therefore the Jews of the villages who dwelt in the unwalled towns celebrated the fourteenth day of the month of Adar *with* gladness and feasting, as a holiday, and for sending presents to one another.

Day of good news.

2 Kin 7:9 Then they said to one another, "We are not doing right. This day *is* a day of good news, and we remain silent. If we wait until morning light, some punishment will come upon us. Now therefore, come, let us go and tell the king's household."

Day the Lord has made.

Ps 118:24 This *is* the day the LORD has made; We will rejoice and be glad in it.

Appointed day.

Hos 9:5 What will you do in the appointed day, And in the day of the feast of the LORD?

Day of gladness.

Num 10:10 Also in the day of your gladness, in your appointed feasts, and at the beginning of your months, you shall blow the trumpets over your burnt offerings and over the sacrifices of your peace offerings; and they shall be a memorial for you before your God: I *am* the LORD your God."

The time for labor.

Ps 104:23 Man goes out to his work And to his labor until the evening.

Wild beasts hide during the.

Ps 104:22 *When* the sun rises, they gather together And lie down in their dens.

Illustrative of

Time of judgment.

1 Cor 3:13 each one's work will become clear; for the Day will declare it, because it will be revealed by fire; and the fire will test each one's work, of what sort it is.

1 Cor 4:3 But with me it is a very small thing that I should be judged by you or by a human court. In fact, I do not even judge myself.

Spiritual light.

1 Thess 5:5 You are all sons of light and sons of the day. We are not of the night nor of darkness.

1 Thess 5:8 But let us who are of the day be sober, putting on the breastplate of faith and love, and *as* a helmet the hope of salvation.

2 Pet 1:19 And so we have the prophetic word confirmed, which you do well to heed as a light that shines in a dark place, until the day dawns and the morning star rises in your hearts;

The path of the just.

Prov 4:18 But the path of the just *is* like the shining sun, That shines ever brighter unto the perfect day.

DEAD, THE

Those who have departed this life.

Gen 23:2 So Sarah died in Kirjath Arba (that *is,* Hebron) in the land of Canaan, and Abraham came to mourn for Sarah and to weep for her.

Gen 25:8 Then Abraham breathed his last and died in a good old age, an old man and full *of years,* and was gathered to his people.

Job 1:19 and suddenly a great wind came from across the wilderness and struck the four corners of the house, and it fell on the young people, and they are dead; and I alone have escaped to tell you!"

Other terms used for,

Corpses.

1 Kin 13:24 When he was gone, a lion met him on the road and killed him. And his corpse was thrown on the road, and the donkey stood by it. The lion also stood by the corpse.

2 Kin 19:35 And it came to pass on a certain night that the angel of the LORD went out, and killed in the camp of the Assyrians one hundred and eighty-five thousand; and when *people* arose early in the morning, there were the corpses—all dead.

Nah 3:3 Horsemen charge with bright sword and glittering spear. *There is* a multitude of slain, A great number of bodies, Countless corpses— They stumble over the corpses—

Carcasses.

Num 14:29 The carcasses of you who have complained against Me shall fall in this wilderness, all of you who were numbered, according to your entire number, from twenty years old and above.

Num 14:32–33 But *as for* you, your carcasses shall fall in this wilderness. 33 And your sons shall be shepherds in the wilderness forty years, and bear the brunt of your infidelity, until your carcasses are consumed in the wilderness.

Those who are no more.

Matt 2:18 *"A voice was heard in Ramah, Lamentation, weeping, and great mourning, Rachel weeping for her children, Refusing to be comforted, Because they are no more."*

Deceased, died.

Is 26:14 *They are* dead, they will not live; *They are* deceased, they will not rise. Therefore You have punished and destroyed them, And made all their memory to perish.

Matt 22:25 Now there were with us seven brothers. The first died after he had married, and having no offspring, left his wife to his brother.

Characterized by

Being without a spirit.

James 2:26 For as the body without the spirit is dead, so faith without works is dead also.

Being incapable of motion.

Matt 28:4 And the guards shook for fear of him, and became like dead *men.*

Rev 1:17 And when I saw Him, I fell at His feet as dead. But He laid His right hand on me, saying to me, "Do not be afraid; I am the First and the Last.

Ignorance of all human affairs.

Eccl 9:5 For the living know that they will die; But the dead know nothing, And they have no more reward, For the memory of them is forgotten.

Absence of all human passions.

Eccl 9:6 Also their love, their hatred, and their envy have now perished; Nevermore will they have a share In anything done under the sun.

Inability to glorify God.

Ps 115:17 The dead do not praise the LORD, Nor any who go down into silence.

Do not return to this life.

Job 7:9–10 *As* the cloud disappears and vanishes away, So he who goes down to the grave does not come up. **10** He shall never return to his house, Nor shall his place know him anymore.

Job 14:10 But man dies and is laid away; Indeed he breathes his last And where *is* he?

Job 14:14 If a man dies, shall he live *again?* All the days of my hard service I will wait, Till my change comes.

Eyes of, closed by nearest relatives.

Gen 46:4 I will go down with you to Egypt, and I will also surely bring you up *again;* and Joseph will put his hand on your eyes."

Bodies carefully prepared.

John 19:40 Then they took the body of Jesus, and bound it in strips of linen with the spices, as the custom of the Jews is to bury.

Acts 9:37 But it happened in those days that she became sick and died. When they had washed her, they laid *her* in an upper room.

Mourning for, often

Very great.

Jer 16:6 Both the great and the small shall die in this land. They shall not be buried; neither shall men lament for them, cut themselves, nor make themselves bald for them.

Jer 31:15 Thus says the Lᴏʀᴅ: "A voice was heard in Ramah, Lamentation *and* bitter weeping, Rachel weeping for her children, Refusing to be comforted for her children, Because they *are* no more."

Matt 2:18 *"A voice was heard in Ramah, Lamentation, weeping, and great mourning, Rachel weeping for her children, Refusing to be comforted, Because they are no more."*

John 11:33 Therefore, when Jesus saw her weeping, and the Jews who came with her weeping, He groaned in the spirit and was troubled.

Loud and clamorous.

Mark 5:38 Then He came to the house of the ruler of the synagogue, and saw a tumult and those who wept and wailed loudly.

By hired mourners.

Jer 9:17–18 Thus says the Lᴏʀᴅ of hosts: "Consider and call for the mourning women, That they may come; And send for skillful wailing women, That they may come. **18** Let them make haste And take up a wailing for us, That our eyes may run with tears, And our eyelids gush with water.

Amos 5:16 Therefore the Lᴏʀᴅ God of hosts, the Lord, says this: *"There shall be* wailing in all streets, And they shall say in all the highways, 'Alas! Alas!' They shall call the farmer to mourning, And skillful lamenters to wailing.

With plaintive music.

Jer 48:36 Therefore My heart shall wail like flutes for Moab, And like flutes My heart shall wail For the men of Kir Heres. Therefore the riches they have acquired have perished.

Matt 9:23 When Jesus came into the ruler's house, and saw the flute players and the noisy crowd wailing,

Testified by change of apparel.

2 Sam 14:2 And Joab sent to Tekoa and brought from there a wise woman, and said to her, "Please pretend to be a mourner, and put on mourning apparel; do not anoint yourself with oil, but act like a woman who has been mourning a long time for the dead.

Testified by breaking of bread.

Jer 16:7 Nor shall *men* break *bread* in mourning for them, to comfort them for the dead; nor shall *men* give them the cup of consolation to drink for their father or their mother.

Testified by covering the head.

2 Sam 19:4 But the king covered his face, and the king cried out with a loud voice, "O my son Absalom! O Absalom, my son, my son!"

Testified by tearing the garments.

Gen 37:34 Then Jacob tore his clothes, put sackcloth on his waist, and mourned for his son many days.

2 Sam 3:31 Then David said to Joab and to all the people who were with him, "Tear your clothes, gird yourselves with sackcloth, and mourn for Abner." And King David followed the coffin.

Lasted many days.

Gen 37:34 Then Jacob tore his clothes, put sackcloth on his waist, and mourned for his son many days.

Gen 50:3 Forty days were required for him, for such are the days required for those who are embalmed; and the Egyptians mourned for him seventy days.

Gen 50:10 Then they came to the threshing floor of Atad, which *is* beyond the Jordan, and they mourned there with a great and very solemn lamentation. He observed seven days of mourning for his father.

Regard often shown to the memory of.

Ruth 1:8 And Naomi said to her two daughters-in-law, "Go, return each to her mother's house. The Lᴏʀᴅ deal kindly with you, as you have dealt with the dead and with me.

Too soon forgotten.

Ps 31:12 I am forgotten like a dead man, out of mind; I am like a broken vessel.

Eccl 9:5 For the living know that they will die; But the dead know nothing, And they have no more reward, For the memory of them is forgotten.

Pagan expressions of grief for, forbidden.

Lev 19:28 You shall not make any cuttings in your flesh for the dead, nor tattoo any marks on you: I *am* the Lᴏʀᴅ.

Deut 14:1–2 "You *are* the children of the Lᴏʀᴅ your God; you shall not cut yourselves nor shave the front of your head for the dead. **2** For you *are* a holy people to the Lᴏʀᴅ your God, and the Lᴏʀᴅ has chosen you to be a people for Himself, a special treasure above all the peoples who *are* on the face of the earth.

All offerings to, forbidden.

Deut 26:14 I have not eaten any of it when in mourning, nor have I removed *any* of it for an unclean *use,* nor given *any* of it for the dead. I have obeyed the voice of the Lᴏʀᴅ my God, and have done according to all that You have commanded me.

Touching of, caused uncleanness.

Num 19:11 'He who touches the dead body of anyone shall be unclean seven days.

Num 19:13 Whoever touches the body of anyone who has died, and does not purify himself, defiles the tabernacle of the LORD. That person shall be cut off from Israel. He shall be unclean, because the water of purification was not sprinkled on him; his uncleanness *is* still on him.

Num 19:16 Whoever in the open field touches one who is slain by a sword or who has died, or a bone of a man, or a grave, shall be unclean seven days.

Num 9:6–7 Now there were *certain* men who were defiled by a human corpse, so that they could not keep the Passover on that day; and they came before Moses and Aaron that day. 7 And those men said to him, "We *became* defiled by a human corpse. Why are we kept from presenting the offering of the LORD at its appointed time among the children of Israel?"

In a house, rendered it unclean.

Num 19:14–15 'This *is* the law when a man dies in a tent: All who come into the tent and all who *are* in the tent shall be unclean seven days; 15 and every open vessel, which has no cover fastened on it, *is* unclean.

Even bones of, caused uncleanness.

Num 19:16 Whoever in the open field touches one who is slain by a sword or who has died, or a bone of a man, or a grave, shall be unclean seven days.

2 Chr 34:5 He also burned the bones of the priests on their altars, and cleansed Judah and Jerusalem.

A priest not to mourn for, except when close relative.

Lev 21:1–3 And the LORD said to Moses, "Speak to the priests, the sons of Aaron, and say to them: 'None shall defile himself for the dead among his people, 2 except for his relatives who are nearest to him: his mother, his father, his son, his daughter, and his brother; 3 also his virgin sister who is near to him, who has had no husband, for her he may defile himself.

Ezek 44:25 "They shall not defile *themselves* by coming near a dead person. Only for father or mother, for son or daughter, for brother or unmarried sister may they defile themselves.

High priest in no case to mourn for.

Lev 21:10–11 'He who is the high priest among his brethren, on whose head the anointing oil was poured and who is consecrated to wear the garments, shall not uncover his head nor tear his clothes; 11 nor shall he go near any dead body, nor defile himself for his father or his mother;

Nazirites not to touch or mourn for.

Num 6:6–7 All the days that he separates himself to the LORD he shall not go near a dead body. 7 He shall not make himself unclean even for his father or his mother, for his brother or his sister, when they die, because his separation to God *is* on his head.

Those defiled by, removed from the camp.

Num 5:2 "Command the children of Israel that they put out of the camp every leper, everyone who has a discharge, and whoever becomes defiled by a corpse.

Uncleanness contracted from, removed by the water separation.

Num 19:12 He shall purify himself with the water on the third day and on the seventh day; *then* he will be clean. But if he does not purify himself on the third day and on the seventh day, he will not be clean.

Num 19:18 A clean person shall take hyssop and dip *it* in the water, sprinkle *it* on the tent, on all the vessels, on the persons who were there, or on the one who touched a bone, the slain, the dead, or a grave.

Many idolaters

Offered sacrifices for.

Ps 106:28 They joined themselves also to Baal of Peor, And ate sacrifices made to the dead.

Invoked and consulted.

1 Sam 28:7–8 Then Saul said to his servants, "Find me a woman who is a medium, that I may go to her and inquire of her." And his servants said to him, "In fact, *there is* a woman who is a medium at En Dor." 8 So Saul disguised himself and put on other clothes, and he went, and two men with him; and they came to the woman by night. And he said, "Please conduct a séance for me, and bring up for me the one I shall name to you."

Consecrated part of their crops to.

Deut 26:14 I have not eaten any of it when in mourning, nor have I removed *any* of it for an unclean *use*, nor given *any* of it for the dead. I have obeyed the voice of the LORD my God, and have done according to all that You have commanded me.

The Jews looked for a resurrection from.

Is 26:19 Your dead shall live; *Together with* my dead body they shall arise. Awake and sing, you who dwell in dust; For your dew *is like* the dew of herbs, And the earth shall cast out the dead.

Acts 24:15 I have hope in God, which they themselves also accept, that there will be a resurrection of *the* dead, both of *the* just and *the* unjust.

Instances of, restored to life in Old Testament.

1 Kin 17:22 Then the LORD heard the voice of Elijah; and the soul of the child came back to him, and he revived.

2 Kin 4:34–36 And he went up and lay on the child, and put his mouth on his mouth, his eyes on his eyes, and his hands on his hands; and he stretched himself out on the child, and the flesh of the child became warm. 35 He returned and walked back and forth in the house, and again went up and stretched himself out on him; then the child sneezed seven times, and the child opened his eyes. 36 And he called Gehazi and said, "Call this Shunammite woman." So he called her. And when she came in to him, he said, "Pick up your son."

2 Kin 13:21 So it was, as they were burying a man, that suddenly they spied a band *of raiders;* and they put the man in the tomb of Elisha; and when the man was let down and touched the bones of Elisha, he revived and stood on his feet.

Instances of, restored by Christ.

Matt 9:25 But when the crowd was put outside, He went in and took her by the hand, and the girl arose.

Luke 7:15 So he who was dead sat up and began to speak. And He presented him to his mother.

John 11:44 And he who had died came out bound hand and foot with graveclothes, and his face was wrapped with a cloth. Jesus said to them, "Loose him, and let him go."

Acts 9:40 But Peter put them all out, and knelt down and prayed. And turning to the body he said, "Tabitha, arise." And she opened her eyes, and when she saw Peter she sat up.

Acts 20:12 And they brought the young man in alive, and they were not a little comforted.

Illustrative of

Man's state by nature.

2 Cor 5:4 For we who are in *this* tent groan, being burdened, not because we want to be unclothed, but further clothed, that mortality may be swallowed up by life.

Eph 2:1 And you *He made alive,* who were dead in trespasses and sins,

Eph 2:5 even when we were dead in trespasses, made us alive together with Christ (by grace you have been saved),

A state of deep affliction, etc.

Gen 20:3 But God came to Abimelech in a dream by night, and said to him, "Indeed you *are* a dead man because of the woman whom you have taken, for she *is* a man's wife."

Ps 88:5–6 Adrift among the dead, Like the slain who lie in the grave, Whom You remember no more, And who are cut off from Your hand. **6** You have laid me in the lowest pit, In darkness, in the depths.

Ps 143:3 For the enemy has persecuted my soul; He has crushed my life to the ground; He has made me dwell in darkness, Like those who have long been dead.

Is 59:10 We grope for the wall like the blind, And we grope as if *we had* no eyes; We stumble at noonday as at twilight; *We are* as dead *men* in desolate places.

Freedom from the power of sin.

Rom 6:2 Certainly not! How shall we who died to sin live any longer in it?

Rom 6:8 Now if we died with Christ, we believe that we shall also live with Him,

Rom 6:11 Likewise you also, reckon yourselves to be dead indeed to sin, but alive to God in Christ Jesus our Lord.

Col 3:3 For you died, and your life is hidden with Christ in God.

Freedom from the law.

Rom 7:4 Therefore, my brethren, you also have become dead to the law through the body of Christ, that you may be married to another—to Him who was raised from the dead, that we should bear fruit to God.

Faith without works.

1 Tim 5:6 But she who lives in pleasure is dead while she lives.

James 2:17 Thus also faith by itself, if it does not have works, is dead.

James 2:26 For as the body without the spirit is dead, so faith without works is dead also.

Those who consult the occult.

Is 8:19 And when they say to you, "Seek those who are mediums and wizards, who whisper and mutter," should not a people seek their God? *Should they seek* the dead on behalf of the living?

Beyond child-bearing age.

Rom 4:19 And not being weak in faith, he did not consider his own body, already dead (since he was about a hundred years old), and the deadness of Sarah's womb.

DEATH, ETERNAL

The necessary consequence of sin.

Rom 6:16 Do you not know that to whom you present yourselves slaves to obey, you are that one's slaves whom you obey, whether of sin *leading* to death, or of obedience *leading* to righteousness?

Rom 6:21 What fruit did you have then in the things of which you are now ashamed? For the end of those things *is* death.

Rom 6:23 For the wages of sin *is* death, but the gift of God *is* eternal life in Christ Jesus our Lord.

Rom 8:13 For if you live according to the flesh you will die; but if by the Spirit you put to death the deeds of the body, you will live.

James 1:15 Then, when desire has conceived, it gives birth to sin; and sin, when it is full-grown, brings forth death.

The portion of the wicked.

Matt 25:41 "Then He will also say to those on the left hand, 'Depart from Me, you cursed, into the everlasting fire prepared for the devil and his angels:

Matt 25:46 And these will go away into everlasting punishment, but the righteous into eternal life."

Rom 1:32 who, knowing the righteous judgment of God, that those who practice such things are deserving of death, not only do the same but also approve of those who practice them.

The way to, described.

Ps 9:17 The wicked shall be turned into hell, *And* all the nations that forget God.

Prov 14:12 There is a way *that seems* right to a man, But its end *is* the way of death.

Matt 7:13 "Enter by the narrow gate; for wide *is* the gate and broad *is* the way that leads to destruction, and there are many who go in by it.

God alone can inflict.

Matt 10:28 And do not fear those who kill the body but cannot kill the soul. But rather fear Him who is able to destroy both soul and body in hell.

James 4:12 There is one Lawgiver, who is able to save and to destroy. Who are you to judge another?

Is described as

Banishment from God.

2 Thess 1:9 These shall be punished with everlasting destruction from the presence of the Lord and from the glory of His power,

A lake of fire.

Rev 19:20 Then the beast was captured, and with him the false prophet who worked signs in his presence, by which he deceived those who received the mark of the beast and those who worshiped his image. These two were cast alive into the lake of fire burning with brimstone.

Rev 21:8 But the cowardly, unbelieving, abominable, murderers, sexually immoral, sorcerers, idolaters, and all liars shall have their part in the lake which burns with fire and brimstone, which is the second death."

The worm that dies not.

Mark 9:44 where *'Their worm does not die And the fire is not quenched.'*

Outer darkness.

Matt 25:30 And cast the unprofitable servant into the outer darkness. There will be weeping and gnashing of teeth.'

The blackness of darkness forever.

2 Pet 2:17 These are wells without water, clouds carried by a tempest, for whom is reserved the blackness of darkness forever.

Indignation, wrath, etc.

Rom 2:8–9 but to those who are self-seeking and do not obey the truth, but obey unrighteousness—indignation and wrath, **9** tribulation and anguish, on every soul of man who does evil, of the Jew first and also of the Greek;

Other names for,

Destruction.

Rom 9:22 *What* if God, wanting to show *His* wrath and to make His power known, endured with much longsuffering the vessels of wrath prepared for destruction,

2 Thess 1:9 These shall be punished with everlasting destruction from the presence of the Lord and from the glory of His power,

Perishing.

2 Pet 2:12 But these, like natural brute beasts made to be caught and destroyed, speak evil of the things they do not understand, and will utterly perish in their own corruption,

The wrath to come.

1 Thess 1:10 and to wait for His Son from heaven, whom He raised from the dead, *even* Jesus who delivers us from the wrath to come.

The second death.

Rev 2:11 "He who has an ear, let him hear what the Spirit says to the churches. He who overcomes shall not be hurt by the second death." '

The resurrection of condemnation.

John 5:29 and come forth—those who have done good, to the resurrection of life, and those who have done evil, to the resurrection of condemnation.

A resurrection to shame and contempt.

Dan 12:2 And many of those who sleep in the dust of the earth shall awake, Some to everlasting life, Some to shame *and* everlasting contempt.

Condemnation of hell.

Matt 23:33 Serpents, brood of vipers! How can you escape the condemnation of hell?

Everlasting punishment.

Matt 25:46 And these will go away into everlasting punishment, but the righteous into eternal life."

Shall be inflicted by Christ.

Matt 25:31 "When the Son of Man comes in His glory, and all the holy angels with Him, then He will sit on the throne of His glory.

Matt 25:41 "Then He will also say to those on the left hand, 'Depart from Me, you cursed, into the everlasting fire prepared for the devil and his angels:

2 Thess 1:7–8 and to *give* you who are troubled rest with us when the Lord Jesus is revealed from heaven with His mighty angels, **8** in flaming fire taking vengeance on those who do not know God, and on those who do not obey the gospel of our Lord Jesus Christ.

Christ, the only way of escape from.

John 3:16 For God so loved the world that He gave His only begotten Son, that whoever believes in Him should not perish but have everlasting life.

John 8:51 Most assuredly, I say to you, if anyone keeps My word he shall never see death."

Acts 4:12 Nor is there salvation in any other, for there is no other name under heaven given among men by which we must be saved."

Believers shall escape.

Rev 2:11 "He who has an ear, let him hear what the Spirit says to the churches. He who overcomes shall not be hurt by the second death." '

Rev 20:6 Blessed and holy *is* he who has part in the first resurrection. Over such the second death has no power, but they shall be priests of God and of Christ, and shall reign with Him a thousand years.

Should strive to save others from.

James 5:20 let him know that he who turns a sinner from the error of his way will save a soul from death and cover a multitude of sins.

Illustrated.

Luke 16:23–26 And being in torments in Hades, he lifted up his eyes and saw Abraham afar off, and Lazarus in his bosom. **24** "Then he cried and said, 'Father Abraham, have mercy on me, and send Lazarus that he may dip the tip of his finger in water and cool my tongue; for I am tormented in this flame.' **25** But Abraham said, 'Son, remember that in your lifetime you received your good things, and likewise Lazarus evil things; but now he is comforted and you are tormented. **26** And besides all this, between us and you there is a great gulf fixed, so that those who want to pass from here to you cannot, nor can those from there pass to us.'

DEATH, NATURAL

By Adam.

Gen 3:19 In the sweat of your face you shall eat bread Till you return to the ground, For out of it you were taken; For dust you *are*, And to dust you shall return."

1 Cor 15:21–22 For since by man *came* death, by Man also *came* the resurrection of the dead. **22** For as in Adam all die, even so in Christ all shall be made alive.

Consequence of sin.

Gen 2:17 but of the tree of the knowledge of good and evil you shall not eat, for in the day that you eat of it you shall surely die."

Rom 5:12 Therefore, just as through one man sin entered the world, and death through sin, and thus death spread to all men, because all sinned—

Comes to all.

Eccl 8:8 No one has power over the spirit to retain the spirit, And no one has power in the day of death. *There is* no release from that war, And wickedness will not deliver those who are given to it.

Heb 9:27 And as it is appointed for men to die once, but after this the judgment,

Ordered by God.

Deut 32:39 'Now see that I, *even* I, *am* He, And *there is* no God besides Me; I kill and I make alive; I wound and I heal; Nor *is there any* who can deliver from My hand.

Job 14:5 Since his days *are* determined, The number of his months *is* with You; You have appointed his limits, so that he cannot pass.

Puts an end to earthly projects.

Eccl 9:10 Whatever your hand finds to do, do *it* with your might; for *there is* no work or device or knowledge or wisdom in the grave where you are going.

Strips of earthly possessions.

Job 1:21 And he said: "Naked I came from my mother's womb, And naked shall I return there. The Lord gave, and the Lord has taken away; Blessed be the name of the Lord."

1 Tim 6:7 For we brought nothing into *this* world, *and it is* certain we can carry nothing out.

Levels all ranks.

Job 3:17–19 There the wicked cease *from* troubling, And there the weary are at rest. **18** *There* the prisoners rest together; They do not hear the voice of the oppressor. **19** The small and great are there, And the servant *is* free from his master.

Conquered by Christ.

Rom 6:9 knowing that Christ, having been raised from the dead, dies no more. Death no longer has dominion over Him.

2 Tim 1:10 but has now been revealed by the appearing of our Savior Jesus Christ, *who* has abolished death and brought life and immortality to light through the gospel,

Heb 2:15 and release those who through fear of death were all their lifetime subject to bondage.

Rev 1:18 I *am* He who lives, and was dead, and behold, I am alive forevermore. Amen. And I have the keys of Hades and of Death.

Shall finally be destroyed by Christ.

Hos 13:14 "I will ransom them from the power of the grave; I will redeem them from death. O Death, I will be your plagues! O Grave, I will be your destruction! Pity is hidden from My eyes."

1 Cor 15:26 The last enemy *that* will be destroyed *is* death.

Regard as at hand.

Job 14:1–2 "Man *who is* born of woman Is of few days

and full of trouble. **2** He comes forth like a flower and fades away; He flees like a shadow and does not continue.

Ps 39:4–5 "Lord, make me to know my end, And what *is* the measure of my days, *That* I may know how frail I *am*. **5** Indeed, You have made my days *as* handbreadths, And my age *is* as nothing before You; Certainly every man at his best state *is* but vapor. Selah

Ps 90:9 For all our days have passed away in Your wrath; We finish our years like a sigh.

1 Pet 1:24 because *"All flesh is as grass, And all the glory of man as the flower of the grass. The grass withers, And its flower falls away,*

Prepare for.

2 Kin 20:1 In those days Hezekiah was sick and near death. And Isaiah the prophet, the son of Amoz, went to him and said to him, "Thus says the Lord: 'Set your house in order, for you shall die, and not live.' "

Ps 39:4 "Lord, make me to know my end, And what *is* the measure of my days, *That* I may know how frail I *am*.

Ps 39:13 Remove Your gaze from me, that I may regain strength, Before I go away and am no more."

Ps 90:12 So teach *us* to number our days, That we may gain a heart of wisdom.

Consideration of, a motive to diligence.

Eccl 9:10 Whatever your hand finds to do, do *it* with your might; for *there is* no work or device or knowledge or wisdom in the grave where you are going.

John 9:4 I must work the works of Him who sent Me while it is day; *the* night is coming when no one can work.

When averted for a season, is a motive to increased devotedness.

Ps 56:12–13 Vows *made* to You *are binding* upon me, O God; I will render praises to You, **13** For You have delivered my soul from death. *Have You* not *kept* my feet from falling, That I may walk before God In the light of the living?

Ps 118:17 I shall not die, but live, And declare the works of the Lord.

Is 38:18 For Sheol cannot thank You, Death cannot praise You; Those who go down to the pit cannot hope for Your truth.

Is 38:20 "The Lord *was ready* to save me; Therefore we will sing my songs with stringed instruments All the days of our life, in the house of the Lord."

Enoch and Elijah were exempted from.

Gen 5:24 And Enoch walked with God; and he *was* not, for God took him.

2 Kin 2:11 Then it happened, as they continued on and talked, that suddenly a chariot of fire *appeared* with horses of fire, and separated the two of them; and Elijah went up by a whirlwind into heaven.

Heb 11:5 By faith Enoch was taken away so that he did not see death, *"and was not found, because God had taken him"*; for before he was taken he had this testimony, that he pleased God.

All shall be raised from.

Acts 24:15 I have hope in God, which they themselves

also accept, that there will be a resurrection of *the* dead, both of *the* just and *the* unjust.

None subject to in heaven.

Luke 20:36 nor can they die anymore, for they are equal to the angels and are sons of God, being sons of the resurrection.

Rev 21:4 And God will wipe away every tear from their eyes; there shall be no more death, nor sorrow, nor crying. There shall be no more pain, for the former things have passed away."

Illustrates the change produced in conversion.

Rom 6:2 Certainly not! How shall we who died to sin live any longer in it?

Col 2:20 Therefore, if you died with Christ from the basic principles of the world, why, as *though* living in the world, do you subject yourselves to regulations—

Is described as

Rest and sleep.

Deut 31:16 And the LORD said to Moses: "Behold, you will rest with your fathers; and this people will rise and play the harlot with the gods of the foreigners of the land, where they go *to be* among them, and they will forsake Me and break My covenant which I have made with them.

John 11:11 These things He said, and after that He said to them, "Our friend Lazarus sleeps, but I go that I may wake him up."

Our earthly house, this tent, being destroyed.

2 Cor 5:1 For we know that if our earthly house, *this* tent, is destroyed, we have a building from God, a house not made with hands, eternal in the heavens.

Putting off this tent.

2 Pet 1:14 knowing that shortly I *must* put off my tent, just as our Lord Jesus Christ showed me.

God requiring the soul.

Luke 12:20 But God said to him, 'Fool! This night your soul will be required of you; then whose will those things be which you have provided?'

Going the way of no return.

Job 16:22 For when a few years are finished, I shall go the way of no return.

Gathering to one's people.

Gen 49:33 And when Jacob had finished commanding his sons, he drew his feet up into the bed and breathed his last, and was gathered to his people.

Going down into silence.

Ps 115:17 The dead do not praise the LORD, Nor any who go down into silence.

Breathing one's last.

Acts 5:10 Then immediately she fell down at his feet and breathed her last. And the young men came in and found her dead, and carrying *her* out, buried *her* by her husband.

Returning to dust.

Gen 3:19 In the sweat of your face you shall eat bread Till you return to the ground, For out of it you were taken; For dust you *are*, And to dust you shall return."

Ps 104:29 You hide Your face, they are troubled; You

take away their breath, they die and return to their dust.

Fading away and fleeing.

Job 14:2 He comes forth like a flower and fades away; He flees like a shadow and does not continue.

Departing.

Phil 1:23 For I am hard-pressed between the two, having a desire to depart and be with Christ, *which is* far better.

DEATH, SPIRITUAL

Alienation from God is.

Eph 4:18 having their understanding darkened, being alienated from the life of God, because of the ignorance that is in them, because of the blindness of their heart;

Carnal-mindedness is.

Rom 8:6 For to be carnally minded *is* death, but to be spiritually minded *is* life and peace.

Walking in trespasses and sins is.

Eph 2:1 And you He made alive, who were dead in trespasses and sins,

Col 2:13 And you, being dead in your trespasses and the uncircumcision of your flesh, He has made alive together with Him, having forgiven you all trespasses,

Spiritual ignorance is.

Is 9:2 The people who walked in darkness Have seen a great light; Those who dwelt in the land of the shadow of death, Upon them a light has shined.

Matt 4:16 *The people who sat in darkness have seen a great light, And upon those who sat in the region and shadow of death Light has dawned."*

Luke 1:79 To give light to those who sit in darkness and the shadow of death, To guide our feet into the way of peace."

Unbelief is.

John 3:36 He who believes in the Son has everlasting life; and he who does not believe the Son shall not see life, but the wrath of God abides on him."

1 John 5:12 He who has the Son has life; he who does not have the Son of God does not have life.

Living in pleasure is.

1 Tim 5:6 But she who lives in pleasure is dead while she lives.

Hypocrisy is.

Rev 3:1–2 "And to the angel of the church in Sardis write, 'These things says He who has the seven Spirits of God and the seven stars: "I know your works, that you have a name that you are alive, but you are dead. 2 Be watchful, and strengthen the things which remain, that are ready to die, for I have not found your works perfect before God.

Is a consequence of the Fall.

Rom 5:15 But the free gift *is* not like the offense. For if by the one man's offense many died, much more the grace of God and the gift by the grace of the one Man, Jesus Christ, abounded to many.

Is the state of all men by nature.

Rom 6:13 And do not present your members *as* instruments of unrighteousness to sin, but present yourselves to God as being alive from the dead, and your members *as* instruments of righteousness to God.

Rom 8:6 For to be carnally minded *is* death, but to be spiritually minded *is* life and peace.

The fruits of, are dead works.

Heb 6:1 Therefore, leaving the discussion of the elementary *principles* of Christ, let us go on to perfection, not laying again the foundation of repentance from dead works and of faith toward God,

Heb 9:14 how much more shall the blood of Christ, who through the eternal Spirit offered Himself without spot to God, cleanse your conscience from dead works to serve the living God?

A call to arise from.

Eph 5:14 Therefore He says: "Awake, you who sleep, Arise from the dead, And Christ will give you light."

Deliverance from, is through Christ.

John 5:24–25 "Most assuredly, I say to you, he who hears My word and believes in Him who sent Me has everlasting life, and shall not come into judgment, but has passed from death into life. 25 Most assuredly, I say to you, the hour is coming, and now is, when the dead will hear the voice of the Son of God; and those who hear will live.

Eph 2:5 even when we were dead in trespasses, made us alive together with Christ (by grace you have been saved),

1 John 5:12 He who has the Son has life; he who does not have the Son of God does not have life.

Believers are raised from.

Rom 6:13 And do not present your members *as* instruments of unrighteousness to sin, but present yourselves to God as being alive from the dead, and your members *as* instruments of righteousness to God.

Love of the brethren, a proof of passing from.

1 John 3:14 We know that we have passed from death to life, because we love the brethren. He who does not love *his* brother abides in death.

Deliverance from, illustrated.

Ezek 37:2–3 Then He caused me to pass by them all around, and behold, *there were* very many in the open valley; and indeed *they were* very dry. 3 And He said to me, "Son of man, can these bones live?" So I answered, "O Lord GOD, You know."

Luke 15:24 for this my son was dead and is alive again; he was lost and is found.' And they began to be merry.

DEBT

People were freed from, during the Year of Jubilee.

Lev 25:23–38 'The land shall not be sold permanently, for the land *is* Mine; for you *are* strangers and sojourners with Me. 24 And in all the land of your possession you shall grant redemption of the land. 25 'If one of your brethren becomes poor, and has sold

some of his possession, and if his redeeming relative comes to redeem it, then he may redeem what his brother sold. 26 Or if the man has no one to redeem it, but he himself becomes able to redeem it, 27 then let him count the years since its sale, and restore the remainder to the man to whom he sold it, that he may return to his possession. 28 But if he is not able to have *it* restored to himself, then what was sold shall remain in the hand of him who bought it until the Year of Jubilee; and in the Jubilee it shall be released, and he shall return to his possession. 29 'If a man sells a house in a walled city, then he may redeem it within a whole year after it is sold; *within* a full year he may redeem it. 30 But if it is not redeemed within the space of a full year, then the house in the walled city shall belong permanently to him who bought it, throughout his generations. It shall not be released in the Jubilee. 31 However the houses of villages which have no wall around them shall be counted as the fields of the country. They may be redeemed, and they shall be released in the Jubilee. 32 Nevertheless the cities of the Levites, *and* the houses in the cities of their possession, the Levites may redeem at any time. 33 And if a man purchases a house from the Levites, then the house that was sold in the city of his possession shall be released in the Jubilee; for the houses in the cities of the Levites *are* their possession among the children of Israel. 34 But the field of the common-land of their cities may not be sold, for it *is* their perpetual possession. 35 'If one of your brethren becomes poor, and falls into poverty among you, then you shall help him, like a stranger or a sojourner, that he may live with you. 36 Take no usury or interest from him; but fear your God, that your brother may live with you. 37 You shall not lend him your money for usury, nor lend him your food at a profit. 38 I *am* the LORD your God, who brought you out of the land of Egypt, to give you the land of Canaan *and* to be your God.

Could be worked off.

Ex 21:2–4 If you buy a Hebrew servant, he shall serve six years; and in the seventh he shall go out free and pay nothing. 3 If he comes in by himself, he shall go out by himself; if he *comes in* married, then his wife shall go out with him. 4 If his master has given him a wife, and she has borne him sons or daughters, the wife and her children shall be her master's, and he shall go out by himself.

Deut 15:12–18 "If your brother, a Hebrew man, or a Hebrew woman, is sold to you and serves you six years, then in the seventh year you shall let him go free from you. 13 And when you send him away free from you, you shall not let him go away empty-handed; 14 you shall supply him liberally from your flock, from your threshing floor, and from your winepress. *From what* the LORD has blessed you with, you shall give to him. 15 You shall remember that you were a slave in the land of Egypt, and the LORD your God redeemed you; therefore I command you this thing today. 16 And if it happens that he says to you, 'I will not go away from you,' because he loves you and your house, since he prospers with you, 17 then you shall take an awl and thrust *it* through his ear to the door, and he shall be your servant forever. Also to your female servant you shall do likewise. 18 It shall not seem hard to you when you send him away free from you; for he has been worth a double hired servant in serving you six years. Then the LORD your God will bless you in all that you do.

Danger of becoming surety for another's.

Prov 6:1–5 My son, if you become surety for your friend, *If* you have shaken hands in pledge for a stranger, 2 You are snared by the words of your mouth; You are taken by the words of your mouth. 3 So do this, my son, and deliver yourself; For you have come into the hand of your friend: Go and humble yourself; Plead with your friend. 4 Give no sleep to your eyes, Nor slumber to your eyelids. 5 Deliver yourself like a gazelle from the hand *of the hunter,* And like a bird from the hand of the fowler.

Prov 22:26–27 Do not be one of those who shakes hands in a pledge, One of those who is surety for debts; 27 If you have nothing *with which* to pay, Why should he take away your bed from under you?

Parable about forgiveness of.

Matt 18:21–35 Then Peter came to Him and said, "Lord, how often shall my brother sin against me, and I forgive him? Up to seven times?" 22 Jesus said to him, "I do not say to you, up to seven times, but up to seventy times seven. 23 Therefore the kingdom of heaven is like a certain king who wanted to settle accounts with his servants. 24 And when he had begun to settle accounts, one was brought to him who owed him ten thousand talents. 25 But as he was not able to pay, his master commanded that he be sold, with his wife and children and all that he had, and that payment be made. 26 The servant therefore fell down before him, saying, 'Master, have patience with me, and I will pay you all.' 27 Then the master of that servant was moved with compassion, released him, and forgave him the debt. 28 "But that servant went out and found one of his fellow servants who owed him a hundred denarii; and he laid hands on him and took *him* by the throat, saying, 'Pay me what you owe!' 29 So his fellow servant fell down at his feet and begged him, saying, 'Have patience with me, and I will pay you all.' 30 And he would not, but went and threw him into prison till he should pay the debt. 31 So when his fellow servants saw what had been done, they were very grieved, and came and told their master all that had been done. 32 Then his master, after he had called him, said to him, 'You wicked servant! I forgave you all that debt because you begged me. 33 Should you not also have had compassion on your fellow servant, just as I had pity on you?' 34 And his master was angry, and delivered him to the torturers until he should pay all that was due to him. 35 "So My heavenly Father also will do to you if each of you, from his heart, does not forgive his brother his trespasses."

Cf. Col 2:13–14

DECEIT

Is falsehood.

Ps 119:118 You reject all those who stray from Your statutes, For their deceit *is* falsehood.

The tongue, the instrument of.

Rom 3:13 *"Their throat is an open tomb; With their tongues they have practiced deceit"; "The poison of asps is under their lips";*

Characteristic of the heart.

Jer 17:9 "The heart *is* deceitful above all *things,* And desperately wicked; Who can know it?

Mark 7:21–22 For from within, out of the heart of men, proceed evil thoughts, adulteries, fornications, murders, 22 thefts, covetousness, wickedness, deceit, lewdness, an evil eye, blasphemy, pride, foolishness.

God abhors.

Ps 5:6 You shall destroy those who speak falsehood; The LORD abhors the bloodthirsty and deceitful man.

Forbidden.

Prov 24:28 Do not be a witness against your neighbor without cause, For would you deceive with your lips?

1 Pet 3:10 For *"He who would love life And see good days, Let him refrain his tongue from evil, And his lips from speaking deceit.*

Christ was perfectly free from.

Is 53:9 And they made His grave with the wicked— But with the rich at His death, Because He had done no violence, Nor *was any* deceit in His mouth.

1 Pet 2:22 *"Who committed no sin, Nor was deceit found in His Mouth";*

Believers

Free from.

Ps 24:4 He who has clean hands and a pure heart, Who has not lifted up his soul to an idol, Nor sworn deceitfully.

Zeph 3:13 The remnant of Israel shall do no unrighteousness And speak no lies, Nor shall a deceitful tongue be found in their mouth; For they shall feed *their* flocks and lie down, And no one shall make *them* afraid."

Rev 14:5 And in their mouth was found no deceit, for they are without fault before the throne of God.

Purposed against.

Job 27:4 My lips will not speak wickedness, Nor my tongue utter deceit.

Avoid.

Job 31:5 "If I have walked with falsehood, Or if my foot has hastened to deceit,

Shun those addicted to.

Ps 101:7 He who works deceit shall not dwell within my house; He who tells lies shall not continue in my presence.

Pray for deliverance from those who use.

Ps 43:1 Vindicate me, O God, And plead my cause against an ungodly nation; Oh, deliver me from the deceitful and unjust man!

Ps 120:2 Deliver my soul, O LORD, from lying lips *And* from a deceitful tongue.

Should beware of those who teach.

Eph 5:6 Let no one deceive you with empty words, for because of these things the wrath of God comes upon the sons of disobedience.

Col 2:4 Now this I say lest anyone should deceive you with persuasive words.

Col 2:8 Beware lest anyone cheat you through philosophy and empty deceit, according to the tradition of men, according to the basic principles of the world, and not according to Christ.

1 John 3:7 Little children, let no one deceive you. He who practices righteousness is righteous, just as He is righteous.

Should lay aside, in seeking truth.

2 Cor 4:2 But we have renounced the hidden things of shame, not walking in craftiness nor handling the word of God deceitfully, but by manifestation of the truth commending ourselves to every man's conscience in the sight of God.

1 Thess 2:3 For our exhortation *did* not *come* from error or uncleanness, nor *was it* in deceit.

1 Pet 2:1 Therefore, laying aside all malice, all deceit, hypocrisy, envy, and all evil speaking,

The wicked

Are full of.

Rom 1:29 being filled with all unrighteousness, sexual immorality, wickedness, covetousness, maliciousness; full of envy, murder, strife, deceit, evil-mindedness; *they are* whisperers,

Devise.

Ps 35:20 For they do not speak peace, But they devise deceitful matters Against *the* quiet ones in the land.

Ps 38:12 Those also who seek my life lay snares *for me;* Those who seek my hurt speak of destruction, And plan deception all the day long.

Prov 12:5 The thoughts of the righteous *are* right, *But* the counsels of the wicked *are* deceitful.

Utter.

Ps 10:7 His mouth is full of cursing and deceit and oppression; Under his tongue *is* trouble and iniquity.

Ps 36:3 The words of his mouth *are* wickedness and deceit; He has ceased to be wise *and* to do good.

Work.

Prov 11:18 The wicked *man* does deceptive work, But he who sows righteousness *will have* a sure reward.

Increase in.

2 Tim 3:13 But evil men and impostors will grow worse and worse, deceiving and being deceived.

Use, to each other.

Jer 9:5 Everyone will deceive his neighbor, And will not speak the truth; They have taught their tongue to speak lies; They weary themselves to commit iniquity.

Use, to themselves.

Jer 37:9 Thus says the LORD: 'Do not deceive yourselves, saying, "The Chaldeans will surely depart from us," for they will not depart.

Obad 1:3 The pride of your heart has deceived you, *You* who dwell in the clefts of the rock, Whose habitation is high; *You* who say in your heart, 'Who will bring me down to the ground?'

Obad 1:7 All the men in your confederacy Shall force you to the border; The men at peace with you Shall deceive you *and* prevail against you. *Those who eat* your bread shall lay a trap for you. No one is aware of it.

Delight in.

Prov 20:17 Bread gained by deceit *is* sweet to a man, But afterward his mouth will be filled with gravel.

False teachers

Are workers of.

2 Cor 11:13 For such *are* false apostles, deceitful workers, transforming themselves into apostles of Christ.

Preach.

Jer 14:14 And the LORD said to me, "The prophets prophesy lies in My name. I have not sent them, commanded them, nor spoken to them; they prophesy to you a false vision, divination, a worthless thing, and the deceit of their heart.

Jer 23:26 How long will *this* be in the heart of the prophets who prophesy lies? Indeed *they are* prophets of the deceit of their own heart,

Impose on others by.

Rom 16:18 For those who are such do not serve our Lord Jesus Christ, but their own belly, and by smooth words and flattering speech deceive the hearts of the simple.

Eph 4:14 that we should no longer be children, tossed to and fro and carried about with every wind of doctrine, by the trickery of men, in the cunning craftiness of deceitful plotting,

Entertain themselves with.

2 Pet 2:13 *and* will receive the wages of unrighteousness, *as* those who count it pleasure to carouse in the daytime. *They are* spots and blemishes, carousing in their own deceptions while they feast with you,

Hypocrites devise.

Job 15:35 They conceive trouble and bring forth futility; Their womb prepares deceit."

Hos 11:12 "Ephraim has encircled Me with lies, And the house of Israel with deceit; But Judah still walks with God, Even with the Holy One *who is* faithful.

False witnesses use.

Prov 12:17 He *who* speaks truth declares righteousness, But a false witness, deceit.

Prov 14:5 A faithful witness does not lie, But a false witness will utter lies.

A characteristic of Antichrist.

2 John 1:7 For many deceivers have gone out into the world who do not confess Jesus Christ *as* coming in the flesh. This is a deceiver and an antichrist.

A characteristic of end times.

2 Thess 2:10 and with all unrighteous deception among those who perish, because they did not receive the love of the truth, that they might be saved.

Evil of,

Keeps from knowledge of God.

Jer 9:6 Your dwelling place *is* in the midst of deceit; Through deceit they refuse to know Me," says the LORD.

Keeps from turning to God.

Jer 8:5 Why has this people slidden back, Jerusalem, in a perpetual backsliding? They hold fast to deceit, They refuse to return.

Leads to pride and oppression.

Jer 5:27–28 As a cage is full of birds, So their houses *are* full of deceit. Therefore they have become great and grown rich. **28** They have grown fat, they are sleek; Yes, they surpass the deeds of the wicked; They do not plead the cause, The cause of the fatherless; Yet they prosper, And the right of the needy they do not defend.

Leads to lying.

Prov 14:25 A true witness delivers souls, But a deceitful *witness* speaks lies.

Often accompanied by fraud and injustice.

Ps 10:7 His mouth is full of cursing and deceit and oppression; Under his tongue *is* trouble and iniquity.

Ps 43:1 Vindicate me, O God, And plead my cause against an ungodly nation; Oh, deliver me from the deceitful and unjust man!

Hatred often concealed by.

Prov 26:24–28 He who hates, disguises *it* with his lips, And lays up deceit within himself; **25** When he speaks kindly, do not believe him, For *there are* seven abominations in his heart; **26** *Though his* hatred is covered by deceit, His wickedness will be revealed before the assembly. **27** Whoever digs a pit will fall into it, And he who rolls a stone will have it roll back on him. **28** A lying tongue hates *those who are* crushed by it, And a flattering mouth works ruin.

The folly of fools is.

Prov 14:8 The wisdom of the prudent *is* to understand his way, But the folly of fools *is* deceit.

The kisses of an enemy are.

Prov 27:6 Faithful *are* the wounds of a friend, But the kisses of an enemy *are* deceitful.

Blessedness of being free from.

Ps 24:4–5 He who has clean hands and a pure heart, Who has not lifted up his soul to an idol, Nor sworn deceitfully. **5** He shall receive blessing from the LORD, And righteousness from the God of his salvation.

Ps 32:2 Blessed *is* the man to whom the LORD does not impute iniquity, And in whose spirit *there is* no deceit.

Punishment of.

Ps 55:23 But You, O God, shall bring them down to the pit of destruction; Bloodthirsty and deceitful men shall not live out half their days; But I will trust in You.

Jer 9:7–9 Therefore thus says the LORD of hosts: "Behold, I will refine them and try them; For how shall I deal with the daughter of My people? **8** Their tongue *is* an arrow shot out; It speaks deceit; *One* speaks peaceably to his neighbor with his mouth, But in his heart he lies in wait. **9** Shall I not punish them for these *things?*" says the LORD. "Shall I not avenge Myself on such a nation as this?"

Illustrated by

The devil.

Gen 3:1 Now the serpent was more cunning than any beast of the field which the LORD God had made. And he said to the woman, "Has God indeed said, 'You shall not eat of every tree of the garden'?"

Gen 3:4–5 Then the serpent said to the woman, "You will not surely die. **5** For God knows that in the day you eat of it your eyes will be opened, and you will be like God, knowing good and evil."

John 8:44 You are of *your* father the devil, and the desires of your father you want to do. He was a murderer from the beginning, and does not stand in the truth, because there is no truth in him. When he speaks a lie, he speaks from his own *resources*, for he is a liar and the father of it.

Rebekah and Jacob.

Gen 27:9 Go now to the flock and bring me from there two choice kids of the goats, and I will make savory food from them for your father, such as he loves.

Gen 27:19 Jacob said to his father, "I *am* Esau your firstborn; I have done just as you told me; please arise, sit and eat of my game, that your soul may bless me."

Laban.

Gen 31:7 Yet your father has deceived me and changed my wages ten times, but God did not allow him to hurt me.

Joseph's brothers.

Gen 37:31–32 So they took Joseph's tunic, killed a kid of the goats, and dipped the tunic in the blood. **32** Then they sent the tunic of *many* colors, and they brought *it* to their father and said, "We have found this. Do you know whether it *is* your son's tunic or not?"

Pharaoh.

Ex 8:29 Then Moses said, "Indeed I am going out from you, and I will entreat the LORD, that the swarms *of flies* may depart tomorrow from Pharaoh, from his servants, and from his people. But let Pharaoh not deal deceitfully anymore in not letting the people go to sacrifice to the LORD."

David.

1 Sam 21:13 So he changed his behavior before them, pretended madness in their hands, scratched on the doors of the gate, and let his saliva fall down on his beard.

Job's friends.

Job 6:15 My brothers have dealt deceitfully like a brook, Like the streams of the brooks that pass away,

Doeg.

Ps 52:1–2 Why do you boast in evil, O mighty man? The goodness of God *endures* continually. **2** Your tongue devises destruction, Like a sharp razor, working deceitfully.

Herod.

Matt 2:8 And he sent them to Bethlehem and said, "Go and search carefully for the young Child, and when you have found *Him*, bring back word to me, that I may come and worship Him also."

The Pharisees.

Matt 22:16 And they sent to Him their disciples with the Herodians, saying, "Teacher, we know that You are true, and teach the way of God in truth; nor do You care about anyone, for You do not regard the person of men.

The chief priests.

Mark 14:1 After two days it was the Passover and *the Feast* of Unleavened Bread. And the chief priests and the scribes sought how they might take Him by trickery and put *Him* to death.

DECISIVENESS

Necessary to the service of God.

Luke 9:62 But Jesus said to him, "No one, having put his hand to the plow, and looking back, is fit for the kingdom of God."

Exhortations to.

Josh 24:14–15 "Now therefore, fear the LORD, serve Him in sincerity and in truth, and put away the gods which your fathers served on the other side of the River and in Egypt. Serve the LORD! **15** And if it seems evil to you to serve the LORD, choose for yourselves this day whom you will serve, whether the gods which your fathers served that *were* on the other side of the River, or the gods of the Amorites, in whose land you dwell. But as for me and my house, we will serve the LORD."

Exhibited in

Seeking God with the heart.

2 Chr 15:12 Then they entered into a covenant to seek the LORD God of their fathers with all their heart and with all their soul;

Keeping the commandments of God.

Neh 10:29 these joined with their brethren, their nobles, and entered into a curse and an oath to walk in God's Law, which was given by Moses the servant of God, and to observe and do all the commandments of the LORD our Lord, and His ordinances and His statutes:

Being on the Lord's side.

Ex 32:26 then Moses stood in the entrance of the camp, and said, "Whoever *is* on the LORD's side—*come* to me!" And all the sons of Levi gathered themselves together to him.

Following God fully.

Num 14:24 But My servant Caleb, because he has a different spirit in him and has followed Me fully, I will bring into the land where he went, and his descendants shall inherit it.

Num 32:12 except Caleb the son of Jephunneh, the Kenizzite, and Joshua the son of Nun, for they have wholly followed the LORD.'

Deut 6:5 You shall love the LORD your God with all your heart, with all your soul, and with all your strength.

Josh 14:8 Nevertheless my brethren who went up with me made the heart of the people melt, but I wholly followed the LORD my God.

Is 56:6 "Also the sons of the foreigner Who join themselves to the LORD, to serve Him, And to love the name of the LORD, to be His servants— Everyone who keeps from defiling the Sabbath, And holds fast My covenant—

Blessedness of.

Josh 1:7 Only be strong and very courageous, that you may observe to do according to all the law which Moses My servant commanded you; do not turn from it to the right hand or to the left, that you may prosper wherever you go.

Opposed to

A divided service.

Matt 6:24 "No one can serve two masters; for either he will hate the one and love the other, or else he will be loyal to the one and despise the other. You cannot serve God and mammon.

Double-mindedness.

James 1:8 *he is* a double-minded man, unstable in all his ways.

Wavering between two opinions.

1 Kin 18:21 And Elijah came to all the people, and said, "How long will you falter between two opinions? If the LORD *is* God, follow Him; but if Baal, follow him." But the people answered him not a word.

Turning to the right or left.

Deut 5:32 "Therefore you shall be careful to do as the LORD your God has commanded you; you shall not turn aside to the right hand or to the left.

Not setting the heart aright.

Ps 78:8 And may not be like their fathers, A stubborn and rebellious generation, A generation *that* did not set its heart aright, And whose spirit was not faithful to God.

Ps 78:37 For their heart was not steadfast with Him, Nor were they faithful in His covenant.

Exemplified by

Moses.

Ex 32:26 then Moses stood in the entrance of the camp, and said, "Whoever *is* on the LORD's side—*come* to me!" And all the sons of Levi gathered themselves together to him.

Caleb.

Num 13:30 Then Caleb quieted the people before Moses, and said, "Let us go up at once and take possession, for we are well able to overcome it."

Joshua.

Josh 24:15 And if it seems evil to you to serve the LORD, choose for yourselves this day whom you will serve, whether the gods which your fathers served that *were* on the other side of the River, or the gods of the Amorites, in whose land you dwell. But as for me and my house, we will serve the LORD."

Ruth.

Ruth 1:16 But Ruth said: "Entreat me not to leave you, *Or to* turn back from following after you; For wherever you go, I will go; And wherever you lodge, I will lodge; Your people *shall be* my people, And your God, my God.

Asa.

2 Chr 15:8 And when Asa heard these words and the prophecy of Oded the prophet, he took courage, and removed the abominable idols from all the land of Judah and Benjamin and from the cities which he had taken in the mountains of Ephraim; and he restored the altar of the LORD that *was* before the vestibule of the LORD.

David.

Ps 17:3 You have tested my heart; You have visited *me* in the night; You have tried me and have found nothing; I have purposed that my mouth shall not transgress.

Peter.

John 6:68 But Simon Peter answered Him, "Lord, to whom shall we go? You have the words of eternal life.

Paul.

Acts 21:13 Then Paul answered, "What do you mean by weeping and breaking my heart? For I am ready not only to be bound, but also to die at Jerusalem for the name of the Lord Jesus."

Abraham.

Heb 11:8 By faith Abraham obeyed when he was called to go out to the place which he would receive as an inheritance. And he went out, not knowing where he was going.

DEDICATION

Consecration of a place of worship.

2 Chr 2:4 Behold, I am building a temple for the name of the LORD my God, to dedicate it to Him, to burn before Him sweet incense, for the continual show-bread, for the burnt offerings morning and evening, on the Sabbaths, on the New Moons, and on the set feasts of the LORD our God. This *is an ordinance* forever to Israel.

Solemn confirmation of a covenant.

Heb 9:18 Therefore not even the first *covenant* was dedicated without blood.

Devoting anything to sacred uses.

1 Chr 28:12 and the plans for all that he had by the Spirit, of the courts of the house of the LORD, of all the chambers all around, of the treasuries of the house of God, and of the treasuries for the dedicated things;

Subjects of,

Tabernacle.

Num 7:1–6 Now it came to pass, when Moses had finished setting up the tabernacle, that he anointed it and consecrated it and all its furnishings, and the altar and all its utensils; so he anointed them and consecrated them. 2 Then the leaders of Israel, the heads of their fathers' houses, who *were* the leaders of the tribes and over those who were numbered, made an offering. 3 And they brought their offering before the LORD, six covered carts and twelve oxen, a cart for *every* two of the leaders, and for each one an ox; and they presented them before the tabernacle. 4 Then the LORD spoke to Moses, saying, 5 "Accept *these* from them, that they may be used in doing the work of the tabernacle of meeting; and you shall give them to the Levites, *to* every man according to his service." 6 So Moses took the carts and the oxen, and gave them to the Levites.

Temple of Solomon.

2 Chr 7:5 King Solomon offered a sacrifice of twenty-two thousand bulls and one hundred and twenty thousand sheep. So the king and all the people dedicated the house of God.

Cf. 1 Kin 8:1–63

Second temple.

Ezra 6:16–17 Then the children of Israel, the priests and the Levites and the rest of the descendants of the captivity, celebrated the dedication of this house of God with joy. 17 And they offered sacrifices at the dedication of this house of God, one hundred bulls, two hundred rams, four hundred lambs, and as a sin offering for all Israel twelve male goats, according to the number of the tribes of Israel.

Persons.

Ex 22:29 "You shall not delay *to offer* the first of your ripe produce and your juices. The firstborn of your sons you shall give to Me.

1 Sam 1:11 Then she made a vow and said, "O LORD of hosts, if You will indeed look on the affliction of Your maidservant and remember me, and not forget Your maidservant, but will give Your maidservant a male child, then I will give him to the LORD all the days of his life, and no razor shall come upon his head."

Property.

Lev 27:28 'Nevertheless no devoted *offering* that a man may devote to the LORD of all that he has, *both* man and beast, or the field of his possession, shall be sold or redeemed; every devoted *offering is* most holy to the LORD.

Matt 15:5 But you say, 'Whoever says to his father or mother, "Whatever profit you might have received from me *is a gift to God*"—

Spoils of war.

2 Sam 8:11 King David also dedicated these to the LORD, along with the silver and gold that he had dedicated from all the nations which he had subdued—

1 Chr 18:11 King David also dedicated these to the LORD, along with the silver and gold that he had brought from all *these* nations—from Edom, from Moab, from the people of Ammon, from the Philistines, and from Amalek.

Tribute from foreigners.

2 Sam 8:10–11 then Toi sent Joram his son to King David, to greet him and bless him, because he had fought against Hadadezer and defeated him (for Hadadezer had been at war with Toi); and *Joram* brought with him articles of silver, articles of gold, and articles of bronze. 11 King David also dedicated these to the LORD, along with the silver and gold that he had dedicated from all the nations which he had subdued—

Walls of cities.

Neh 12:27 Now at the dedication of the wall of Jerusalem they sought out the Levites in all their places, to bring them to Jerusalem to celebrate the dedication with gladness, both with thanksgivings and singing, *with* cymbals and stringed instruments and harps.

Houses when built.

Deut 20:5 "Then the officers shall speak to the people, saying: 'What man *is there* who has built a new house and has not dedicated it? Let him go and return to his house, lest he die in the battle and another man dedicate it.

Ps 30:1 I will extol You, O LORD, for You have lifted me up, And have not let my foes rejoice over me.

By idolaters in setting up idols.

Dan 3:2–3 And King Nebuchadnezzar sent *word* to gather together the satraps, the administrators, the governors, the counselors, the treasurers, the judges, the magistrates, and all the officials of the provinces, to come to the dedication of the image which King Nebuchadnezzar had set up. 3 So the satraps, the administrators, the governors, the counselors, the treasurers, the judges, the magistrates, and all the officials of the provinces gathered together for the dedication of the image that King Nebuchadnezzar had set up; and they stood before the image that Nebuchadnezzar had set up.

Things dedicated to God

Esteemed holy.

Lev 27:28 'Nevertheless no devoted *offering* that a man may devote to the LORD of all that he has, *both* man and beast, or the field of his possession, shall be sold or redeemed; every devoted *offering is* most holy to the LORD.

2 Kin 12:18 And Jehoash king of Judah took all the sacred things that his fathers, Jehoshaphat and Jehoram and Ahaziah, kings of Judah, had dedicated, and his own sacred things, and all the gold found in the treasuries of the house of the LORD and in the king's house, and sent *them* to Hazael king of Syria. Then he went away from Jerusalem.

Placed with the treasures of the Lord's house.

1 Kin 7:51 So all the work that King Solomon had done for the house of the LORD was finished; and Solomon brought in the things which his father David had dedicated: the silver and the gold and the furnishings. He put them in the treasuries of the house of the LORD.

2 Chr 5:1 So all the work that Solomon had done for the house of the LORD was finished; and Solomon brought in the things which his father David had dedicated: the silver and the gold and all the furnishings. And he put *them* in the treasuries of the house of God.

Special rooms prepared for.

2 Chr 31:11–12 Now Hezekiah commanded *them* to prepare rooms in the house of the LORD, and they prepared them. **12** Then they faithfully brought in the offerings, the tithes, and the dedicated things; Cononiah the Levite had charge of them, and Shimei his brother *was* the next.

Levites placed over.

1 Chr 26:20 Of the Levites, Ahijah *was* over the treasuries of the house of God and over the treasuries of the dedicated things.

1 Chr 26:26 This Shelomith and his brethren *were* over all the treasuries of the dedicated things which King David and the heads of fathers' *houses,* the captains over thousands and hundreds, and the captains of the army, had dedicated.

2 Chr 31:12 Then they faithfully brought in the offerings, the tithes, and the dedicated things; Cononiah the Levite had charge of them, and Shimei his brother *was* the next.

Applied to the repair and maintenance of the temple.

2 Kin 12:4–5 And Jehoash said to the priests, "All the money of the dedicated gifts that are brought into the house of the LORD—each man's census money, each man's assessment money—*and* all the money that a man purposes in his heart to bring into the house of the LORD, **5** let the priests take *it* themselves, each from his constituency; and let them repair the damages of the temple, wherever any dilapidation is found."

1 Chr 26:27 Some of the spoils won in battles they dedicated to maintain the house of the LORD.

For support of priests.

Num 18:14 "Every devoted thing in Israel shall be yours.

Ezek 44:29 They shall eat the grain offering, the sin offering, and the trespass offering; every dedicated thing in Israel shall be theirs.

Given to propitiate enemies.

2 Kin 12:17–18 Hazael king of Syria went up and fought against Gath, and took it; then Hazael set his face to go up to Jerusalem. **18** And Jehoash king of Judah took all the sacred things that his fathers, Jehoshaphat and Jehoram and Ahaziah, kings of Judah, had dedicated, and his own sacred things, and all the gold found in the treasuries of the house of the LORD and in the king's house, and sent *them* to Hazael king of Syria. Then he went away from Jerusalem.

Of property, often perverted.

Mark 7:9–13 He said to them, "*All too* well you reject the commandment of God, that you may keep your tradition. **10** For Moses said, '*Honor your father and your mother'*; and, '*He who curses father or mother, let him be put to death.'* **11** But you say, 'If a man says to his father or mother, "Whatever profit you might have received from me *is* Corban"—' (that is, a gift *to* God), **12** then you no longer let him do anything for his father or his mother, **13** making the word of God of no effect through your tradition which you have handed down. And many such things you do."

Illustrated devotedness to God.

Ps 119:38 Establish Your word to Your servant, Who *is* devoted to fearing You.

DEER, THE

Clean and used as food.

Deut 12:15 "However, you may slaughter and eat meat within all your gates, whatever your heart desires, according to the blessing of the LORD your God which He has given you; the unclean and the clean may eat of it, of the gazelle and the deer alike.

Deut 14:5 the deer, the gazelle, the roe deer, the wild goat, the mountain goat, the antelope, and the mountain sheep.

Often hunted.

Lam 1:6 And from the daughter of Zion All her splendor has departed. Her princes have become like deer *That* find no pasture, That flee without strength Before the pursuer.

Male of, called the roebuck.

1 Kin 4:23 ten fatted oxen, twenty oxen from the pastures, and one hundred sheep, besides deer, gazelles, roebucks, and fatted fowl.

Female of,

Called the doe.

Song 2:7 I charge you, O daughters of Jerusalem, By the gazelles or by the does of the field, Do not stir up nor awaken love Until it pleases.

Loving and graceful.

Prov 5:19 *As a* loving deer and a graceful doe, Let her breasts satisfy you at all times; And always be enraptured with her love.

Brings forth at appointed time.

Job 39:1–2 "Do you know the time when the wild

mountain goats bear young? *Or* can you mark when the deer gives birth? **2** Can you number the months *that* they fulfill? Or do you know the time when they bear young?

Brings forth with difficulty.

Job 39:3 They bow down, They bring forth their young, They deliver their offspring.

Brings forth at the voice of God.

Ps 29:9 The voice of the LORD makes the deer give birth, And strips the forests bare; And in His temple everyone says, "Glory!"

Forsakes her young in famine.

Jer 14:5 Yes, the deer also gave birth in the field, But left because there was no grass.

Wild.

2 Sam 2:18 Now the three sons of Zeruiah were there: Joab and Abishai and Asahel. And Asahel *was as* fleet of foot as a wild gazelle.

Inhabits the mountains.

1 Chr 12:8 *Some* Gadites joined David at the stronghold in the wilderness, mighty men of valor, men trained for battle, who could handle shield and spear, whose faces *were like* the faces of lions, and *were* as swift as gazelles on the mountains:

Often hunted by men.

Prov 6:5 Deliver yourself like a gazelle from the hand *of the hunter,* And like a bird from the hand of the fowler.

Young of, abundantly provided for.

Job 39:4 Their young ones are healthy, They grow strong with grain; They depart and do not return to them.

Illustrative of

Converted sinners.

Is 35:6 Then the lame shall leap like a deer, And the tongue of the dumb sing. For waters shall burst forth in the wilderness, And streams in the desert.

(Sure-footedness of) experienced believers.

Ps 18:33 He makes my feet like the *feet of* deer, And sets me on my high places.

Hab 3:19 The LORD God is my strength; He will make my feet like deer's *feet,* And He will make me walk on my high hills. To the Chief Musician. With my stringed instruments.

(Panting for water) believers longing for God.

Ps 42:1–2 As the deer pants for the water brooks, So pants my soul for You, O God. **2** My soul thirsts for God, for the living God. When shall I come and appear before God?

(Without pasture) the persecuted.

Lam 1:6 And from the daughter of Zion All her splendor has departed. Her princes have become like deer *That* find no pasture, That flee without strength Before the pursuer.

DEFILEMENT

Forbidden to the Jews.

Lev 11:44–45 For I *am* the LORD your God. You shall therefore consecrate yourselves, and you shall be holy; for I *am* holy. Neither shall you defile yourselves with any creeping thing that creeps on the earth. **45** For I *am* the LORD who brings you up out of the land of Egypt, to be your God. You shall therefore be holy, for I *am* holy.

Things liable to,

The person.

Lev 5:3 Or if he touches human uncleanness—whatever uncleanness with which a man may be defiled, and he is unaware of it—when he realizes *it,* then he shall be guilty.

Garments.

Lev 13:59 "This *is* the law of the leprous plague in a garment of wool or linen, either in the warp or woof, or in anything made of leather, to pronounce it clean or to pronounce it unclean."

Furniture, etc.

Lev 15:9–10 Any saddle on which he who has the discharge rides shall be unclean. **10** Whoever touches anything that was under him shall be unclean until evening. He who carries *any of* those things shall wash his clothes and bathe in water, and be unclean until evening.

Num 19:14–15 'This *is* the law when a man dies in a tent: All who come into the tent and all who *are* in the tent shall be unclean seven days; **15** and every open vessel, which has no cover fastened on it, *is* unclean.

Houses.

Lev 14:44 then the priest shall come and look; and indeed *if* the plague has spread in the house, it *is* an active leprosy in the house. It *is* unclean.

The land.

Lev 18:25 For the land is defiled; therefore I visit the punishment of its iniquity upon it, and the land vomits out its inhabitants.

Deut 21:23 his body shall not remain overnight on the tree, but you shall surely bury him that day, so that you do not defile the land which the LORD your God is giving you *as* an inheritance; for he who is hanged *is* accursed of God.

The sanctuary.

Lev 20:3 I will set My face against that man, and will cut him off from his people, because he has given *some* of his descendants to Molech, to defile My sanctuary and profane My holy name.

Zeph 3:4 Her prophets are insolent, treacherous people; Her priests have polluted the sanctuary, They have done violence to the law.

Caused by

Eating unclean things.

Lev 11:8 Their flesh you shall not eat, and their carcasses you shall not touch. They *are* unclean to you.

Acts 10:11 and saw heaven opened and an object like a great sheet bound at the four corners, descending to him and let down to the earth.

Acts 10:14 But Peter said, "Not so, Lord! For I have never eaten anything common or unclean."

Eating things that died.

Lev 17:15 "And every person who eats what died *naturally* or what was torn *by beasts, whether he is* a native of your own country or a stranger, he shall both wash his clothes and bathe in water, and be unclean until evening. Then he shall be clean.

Touching a dead body or a bone.

Num 9:6–7 Now there were *certain* men who were defiled by a human corpse, so that they could not keep the Passover on that day; and they came before Moses and Aaron that day. 7 And those men said to him, "We *became* defiled by a human corpse. Why are we kept from presenting the offering of the LORD at its appointed time among the children of Israel?"

Num 19:11 'He who touches the dead body of anyone shall be unclean seven days.

Num 19:16 Whoever in the open field touches one who is slain by a sword or who has died, or a bone of a man, or a grave, shall be unclean seven days.

Touching a grave.

Num 19:16 Whoever in the open field touches one who is slain by a sword or who has died, or a bone of a man, or a grave, shall be unclean seven days.

Touching a dead beast.

Lev 5:2 'Or if a person touches any unclean thing, whether *it is* the carcass of an unclean beast, or the carcass of unclean livestock, or the carcass of unclean creeping things, and he is unaware of it, he also shall be unclean and guilty.

Lev 11:24–28 'By these you shall become unclean; whoever touches the carcass of any of them shall be unclean until evening; 25 whoever carries part of the carcass of any of them shall wash his clothes and be unclean until evening: 26 *The carcass* of any animal which divides the foot, but is not cloven-hoofed or does not chew the cud, *is* unclean to you. Everyone who touches it shall be unclean. 27 And whatever goes on its paws, among all kinds of animals that go on *all* fours, those *are* unclean to you. Whoever touches any such carcass shall be unclean until evening. 28 Whoever carries *any such* carcass shall wash his clothes and be unclean until evening. It *is* unclean to you.

Being alone with a dead body.

Num 19:14 'This *is* the law when a man dies in a tent: All who come into the tent and all who *are* in the tent shall be unclean seven days;

Mourning for the dead.

Lev 21:1–3 And the LORD said to Moses, "Speak to the priests, the sons of Aaron, and say to them: 'None shall defile himself for the dead among his people, 2 except for his relatives who are nearest to him: his mother, his father, his son, his daughter, and his brother; 3 also his virgin sister who is near to him, who has had no husband, for her he may defile himself.

Having leprosy.

Lev 13:3 The priest shall examine the sore on the skin of the body; and if the hair on the sore has turned white, and the sore appears *to be* deeper than the skin of his body, it *is* a leprous sore. Then the priest shall examine him, and pronounce him unclean.

Lev 13:11 it *is* an old leprosy on the skin of his body. The priest shall pronounce him unclean, and shall not isolate him, for he *is* unclean.

Num 5:2–3 "Command the children of Israel that they put out of the camp every leper, everyone who has a discharge, and whoever becomes defiled by a corpse. 3 You shall put out both male and female; you shall put them outside the camp, that they may not defile their camps in the midst of which I dwell."

Having a discharge, etc.

Lev 15:2 "Speak to the children of Israel, and say to them: 'When any man has a discharge from his body, his discharge *is* unclean.

Num 5:2 "Command the children of Israel that they put out of the camp every leper, everyone who has a discharge, and whoever becomes defiled by a corpse.

Touching anything defiled by a discharge, etc.

Lev 15:5–11 And whoever touches his bed shall wash his clothes and bathe in water, and be unclean until evening. 6 He who sits on anything on which he who has the discharge sat shall wash his clothes and bathe in water, and be unclean until evening. 7 And he who touches the body of him who has the discharge shall wash his clothes and bathe in water, and be unclean until evening. 8 If he who has the discharge spits on him who is clean, then he shall wash his clothes and bathe in water, and be unclean until evening. 9 Any saddle on which he who has the discharge rides shall be unclean. 10 Whoever touches anything that was under him shall be unclean until evening. He who carries *any of* those things shall wash his clothes and bathe in water, and be unclean until evening. 11 And whomever the one who has the discharge touches, and has not rinsed his hands in water, he shall wash his clothes and bathe in water, and be unclean until evening.

Going into a leprous house.

Lev 14:46 Moreover he who goes into the house at all while it is shut up shall be unclean until evening.

Sacrificing the red heifer.

Num 19:7 Then the priest shall wash his clothes, he shall bathe in water, and afterward he shall come into the camp; the priest shall be unclean until evening.

Burning the red heifer.

Num 19:8 And the one who burns it shall wash his clothes in water, bathe in water, and shall be unclean until evening.

Gathering the ashes of the red heifer.

Num 19:10 And the one who gathers the ashes of the heifer shall wash his clothes, and be unclean until evening. It shall be a statute forever to the children of Israel and to the stranger who dwells among them.

Touching an unclean person.

Num 19:22 Whatever the unclean *person* touches shall be unclean; and the person who touches *it* shall be unclean until evening.' "

Childbearing.

Lev 12:2 "Speak to the children of Israel, saying: 'If a woman has conceived, and borne a male child, then she shall be unclean seven days; as in the days of her customary impurity she shall be unclean.

Causes of, improperly enlarged by tradition.

Matt 15:20 These are *the things* which defile a man, but to eat with unwashed hands does not defile a man."

Mark 7:2 Now when they saw some of His disciples eat bread with defiled, that is, with unwashed hands, they found fault.

Moral, caused by

Following the sins of the nations.

Lev 18:24 'Do not defile yourselves with any of these things; for by all these the nations are defiled, which I am casting out before you.

Seeking after mediums, etc.

Lev 19:31 'Give no regard to mediums and familiar spirits; do not seek after them, to be defiled by them: I *am* the LORD your God.

Giving children to Molech.

Lev 20:3 I will set My face against that man, and will cut him off from his people, because he has given *some* of his descendants to Molech, to defile My sanctuary and profane My holy name.

Making and serving idols.

Ezek 20:17–18 Nevertheless My eye spared them from destruction. I did not make an end of them in the wilderness. 18 "But I said to their children in the wilderness, 'Do not walk in the statutes of your fathers, nor observe their judgments, nor defile yourselves with their idols.

Ezek 22:3–4 Then say, 'Thus says the Lord GOD: "The city sheds blood in her own midst, that her time may come; and she makes idols within herself to defile herself. 4 You have become guilty by the blood which you have shed, and have defiled yourself with the idols which you have made. You have caused your days to draw near, and have come to *the end of* your years; therefore I have made you a reproach to the nations, and a mockery to all countries.

Ezek 23:7 Thus she committed her harlotry with them, All of them choice men of Assyria; And with all for whom she lusted, With all their idols, she defiled herself.

Blood shedding.

Is 59:3 For your hands are defiled with blood, And your fingers with iniquity; Your lips have spoken lies, Your tongue has muttered perversity.

Moral, punished.

Lev 18:24–25 'Do not defile yourselves with any of these things; for by all these the nations are defiled, which I am casting out before you. 25 For the land is defiled; therefore I visit the punishment of its iniquity upon it, and the land vomits out its inhabitants.

Lev 18:28–29 lest the land vomit you out also when you defile it, as it vomited out the nations that *were* before you. 29 For whoever commits any of these abominations, the persons who commit *them* shall be cut off from among their people.

Those under, removed from the camp.

Num 5:3–4 You shall put out both male and female; you shall put them outside the camp, that they may not defile their camps in the midst of which I dwell." 4 And the children of Israel did so, and put them outside the camp; as the LORD spoke to Moses, so the children of Israel did.

Deut 23:14 For the LORD your God walks in the midst of your camp, to deliver you and give your enemies over to you; therefore your camp shall be holy, that He may see no unclean thing among you, and turn away from you.

Priests

To decide in all cases of.

Lev 10:10 that you may distinguish between holy and unholy, and between unclean and clean,

Lev 13:3 The priest shall examine the sore on the skin of the body; and if the hair on the sore has turned white, and the sore appears *to be* deeper than the skin of his body, it *is* a leprous sore. Then the priest shall examine him, and pronounce him unclean.

Specially required to avoid.

Lev 21:1–6 And the LORD said to Moses, "Speak to the priests, the sons of Aaron, and say to them: 'None shall defile himself for the dead among his people, 2 except for his relatives who are nearest to him: his mother, his father, his son, his daughter, and his brother; 3 also his virgin sister who is near to him, who has had no husband, for her he may defile himself. 4 *Otherwise* he shall not defile himself, *being* a chief man among his people, to profane himself. 5 'They shall not make any bald *place* on their heads, nor shall they shave the edges of their beards nor make any cuttings in their flesh. 6 They shall be holy to their God and not profane the name of their God, for they offer the offerings of the LORD made by fire, *and* the bread of their God; therefore they shall be holy.

Lev 21:11–12 nor shall he go near any dead body, nor defile himself for his father or his mother; 12 nor shall he go out of the sanctuary, nor profane the sanctuary of his God; for the consecration of the anointing oil of his God *is* upon him: I *am* the LORD.

Not to eat holy things while under.

Lev 22:2 "Speak to Aaron and his sons, that they separate themselves from the holy things of the children of Israel, and that they do not profane My holy name by what they dedicate to Me: I *am* the LORD.

Lev 22:4–6 'Whatever man of the descendants of Aaron, who *is* a leper or has a discharge, shall not eat the holy offerings until he is clean. And whoever touches anything made unclean *by* a corpse, or a man who has had an emission of semen, 5 or whoever touches any creeping thing by which he would be made unclean, or any person by whom he would become unclean, whatever his uncleanness may be— 6 the person who has touched any such thing shall be unclean until evening, and shall not eat the holy *offerings* unless he washes his body with water.

Punished for eating of the holy things while under.

Lev 22:3 Say to them: 'Whoever of all your descendants throughout your generations, who goes near the holy things which the children of Israel dedicate to the LORD, while he has uncleanness upon him, that person shall be cut off from My presence: I *am* the LORD.

Cleansed by legal offerings.

Num 19:18–19 A clean person shall take hyssop and dip *it* in the water, sprinkle *it* on the tent, on all the vessels, on the persons who were there, or on the one who touched a bone, the slain, the dead, or a grave. 19 The clean *person* shall sprinkle the unclean on the third day and on the seventh day; and on the seventh day he shall purify himself, wash his clothes, and bathe in water; and at evening he shall be clean.

Heb 9:13 For if the blood of bulls and goats and the ashes of a heifer, sprinkling the unclean, sanctifies for the purifying of the flesh,

Neglecting purification from, punished by cutting off.

Num 19:13 Whoever touches the body of anyone who has died, and does not purify himself, defiles the tabernacle of the LORD. That person shall be cut off from Israel. He shall be unclean, because the water of purification was not sprinkled on him; his uncleanness *is* still on him.

Num 19:20 'But the man who is unclean and does not purify himself, that person shall be cut off from among the assembly, because he has defiled the sanctuary of the LORD. The water of purification has not been sprinkled on him; he *is* unclean.

Ceremonial, abolished under the gospel.

Acts 10:15 And a voice *spoke* to him again the second time, "What God has cleansed you must not call common."

Rom 14:14 I know and am convinced by the Lord Jesus that *there is* nothing unclean of itself; but to him who considers anything to be unclean, to him *it is* unclean.

Col 2:20–22 Therefore, if you died with Christ from the basic principles of the world, why, as *though* living in the world, do you subject yourselves to regulations— **21** "Do not touch, do not taste, do not handle," **22** which all concern things which perish with the using—according to the commandments and doctrines of men?

Illustrative of

Sin.

Matt 15:11 Not what goes into the mouth defiles a man; but what comes out of the mouth, this defiles a man."

Matt 15:18 But those things which proceed out of the mouth come from the heart, and they defile a man.

Jude 1:8 Likewise also these dreamers defile the flesh, reject authority, and speak evil of dignitaries.

Unholy doctrines.

1 Cor 3:16–17 Do you not know that you are the temple of God and *that* the Spirit of God dwells in you? **17** If anyone defiles the temple of God, God will destroy him. For the temple of God is holy, which *temple* you are.

DELIGHTING IN GOD

Commanded.

Ps 37:4 Delight yourself also in the LORD, And He shall give you the desires of your heart.

Reconciliation leads to.

Job 22:21 "Now acquaint yourself with Him, and be at peace; Thereby good will come to you.

Job 22:26 For then you will have your delight in the Almighty, And lift up your face to God.

Observing the Sabbath leads to.

Is 58:13–14 "If you turn away your foot from the Sabbath, *From* doing your pleasure on My holy day, And call the Sabbath a delight, The holy *day* of the LORD honorable, And shall honor Him, not doing your own ways, Nor finding your own pleasure, Nor speaking *your own* words, **14** Then you shall delight yourself in the LORD; And I will cause you to ride on the high hills of the earth, And feed you with the heritage of Jacob your father. The mouth of the LORD has spoken."

Believers' experience in

Communion with God.

Song 2:3 Like an apple tree among the trees of the woods, So *is* my beloved among the sons. I sat down in his shade with great delight, And his fruit *was* sweet to my taste.

The law of God.

Ps 1:2 But his delight *is* in the law of the LORD, And in His law he meditates day and night.

Ps 119:24 Your testimonies also *are* my delight *And* my counselors.

Ps 119:35 Make me walk in the path of Your commandments, For I delight in it.

The goodness of God.

Neh 9:25 And they took strong cities and a rich land, And possessed houses full of all goods, Cisterns *already* dug, vineyards, olive groves, And fruit trees in abundance. So they ate and were filled and grew fat, And delighted themselves in Your great goodness.

Blessedness.

Ps 112:1 Praise the LORD! Blessed *is* the man *who* fears the LORD, *Who* delights greatly in His commandments.

The comforts of God.

Ps 94:19 In the multitude of my anxieties within me, Your comforts delight my soul.

Hypocrites

Pretend to.

Is 58:2 Yet they seek Me daily, And delight to know My ways, As a nation that did righteousness, And did not forsake the ordinance of their God. They ask of Me the ordinances of justice; They take delight in approaching God.

In heart despise.

Job 27:10 Will he delight himself in the Almighty? Will he always call on God?

Jer 6:10 To whom shall I speak and give warning, That they may hear? Indeed their ear *is* uncircumcised, And they cannot give heed. Behold, the word of the LORD is a reproach to them; They have no delight in it.

Promise to.

Ps 37:4 Delight yourself also in the LORD, And He shall give you the desires of your heart.

DEMONS

Evil force of fallen angels.

Deut 32:17 They sacrificed to demons, not to God, *To gods* they did not know, To new *gods*, new arrivals That your fathers did not fear.

Followed Satan in rebellion against God.

Rev 12:4 His tail drew a third of the stars of heaven and threw them to the earth. And the dragon stood before the woman who was ready to give birth, to devour her Child as soon as it was born.

Rebellion of.

1 Pet 3:19–20 by whom also He went and preached to the spirits in prison, **20** who formerly were disobedient, when once the Divine longsuffering waited in the days of Noah, while *the* ark was being prepared, in which a few, that is, eight souls, were saved through water.

2 Pet 2:4 For if God did not spare the angels who sinned, but cast *them* down to hell and delivered *them* into chains of darkness, to be reserved for judgment;

Took wives from human race.

Gen 6:1–4 Now it came to pass, when men began to multiply on the face of the earth, and daughters were born to them, **2** that the sons of God saw the daughters of men, that they *were* beautiful; and they took wives for themselves of all whom they chose. **3** And the LORD said, "My Spirit shall not strive with man forever, for he *is* indeed flesh; yet his days shall be one hundred and twenty years." **4** There were giants on the earth in those days, and also afterward, when the sons of God came in to the daughters of men and they bore *children* to them. Those *were* the mighty men who *were* of old, men of renown.

Cf. 2 Pet 2:4; Jude 6

Abode of, in hell.

1 Pet 3:19 by whom also He went and preached to the spirits in prison,

2 Pet 2:4 For if God did not spare the angels who sinned, but cast *them* down to hell and delivered *them* into chains of darkness, to be reserved for judgment;

Held for judgment by God.

2 Pet 2:4 For if God did not spare the angels who sinned, but cast *them* down to hell and delivered *them* into chains of darkness, to be reserved for judgment;

Jude 1:6 And the angels who did not keep their proper domain, but left their own abode, He has reserved in everlasting chains under darkness for the judgment of the great day;

Called

Familiar spirits.

Lev 20:6 'And the person who turns to mediums and familiar spirits, to prostitute himself with them, I will set My face against that person and cut him off from his people.

Unclean spirits.

Acts 5:16 Also a multitude gathered from the surrounding cities to Jerusalem, bringing sick people and those who were tormented by unclean spirits, and they were all healed.

Principalities.

Rom 8:38 For I am persuaded that neither death nor life, nor angels nor principalities nor powers, nor things present nor things to come,

Cf. Eph 6:12; Col 2:15

Spirits in prison.

1 Pet 3:19 by whom also He went and preached to the spirits in prison,

DENIAL OF CHRIST

In doctrine.

Mark 8:38 For whoever is ashamed of Me and My words in this adulterous and sinful generation, of him the Son of Man also will be ashamed when He comes in the glory of His Father with the holy angels."

2 Tim 1:8 Therefore do not be ashamed of the testimony of our Lord, nor of me His prisoner, but share with me in the sufferings for the gospel according to the power of God,

In practice.

Phil 3:10 that I may know Him and the power of His resurrection, and the fellowship of His sufferings, being conformed to His death,

Phil 3:18 For many walk, of whom I have told you often, and now tell you even weeping, *that they are* the enemies of the cross of Christ:

Titus 1:16 They profess to know God, but in works they deny Him, being abominable, disobedient, and disqualified for every good work.

A characteristic of false teachers.

2 Pet 2:1 But there were also false prophets among the people, even as there will be false teachers among you, who will secretly bring in destructive heresies, even denying the Lord who bought them, *and* bring on themselves swift destruction.

Jude 1:4 For certain men have crept in unnoticed, who long ago were marked out for this condemnation, ungodly men, who turn the grace of our God into lewdness and deny the only Lord God and our Lord Jesus Christ.

Is the spirit of Antichrist.

1 John 2:22–23 Who is a liar but he who denies that Jesus is the Christ? He is antichrist who denies the Father and the Son. **23** Whoever denies the Son does not have the Father either; he who acknowledges the Son has the Father also.

1 John 4:3 and every spirit that does not confess that Jesus Christ has come in the flesh is not of God. And this is the *spirit* of the Antichrist, which you have heard was coming, and is now already in the world.

Christ will deny those guilty of.

Matt 10:33 But whoever denies Me before men, him I will also deny before My Father who is in heaven.

2 Tim 2:12 If we endure, We shall also reign with *Him.* If we deny *Him,* He also will deny us.

Leads to destruction.

2 Pet 2:1 But there were also false prophets among the people, even as there will be false teachers among you, who will secretly bring in destructive heresies, even denying the Lord who bought them, *and* bring on themselves swift destruction.

Jude 1:4 For certain men have crept in unnoticed, who long ago were marked out for this condemnation, ungodly men, who turn the grace of our God into lewdness and deny the only Lord God and our Lord Jesus Christ.

Jude 1:15 to execute judgment on all, to convict all who are ungodly among them of all their ungodly deeds which they have committed in an ungodly way, and of all the harsh things which ungodly sinners have spoken against Him."

Illustrated by

Peter.

Matt 26:69–75 Now Peter sat outside in the courtyard. And a servant girl came to him, saying, "You also were with Jesus of Galilee." **70** But he denied it before *them* all, saying, "I do not know what you are saying." **71** And when he had gone out to the gateway, another *girl* saw him and said to those *who were* there, "This *fellow* also was with Jesus of Nazareth." **72** But again he denied with an oath, "I do not know the Man!" **73** And a little later those who stood by came up and said to Peter, "Surely you also are *one* of them, for your speech betrays you." **74** Then he began to curse and swear, *saying*, "I do not know the Man!" Immediately a rooster crowed. **75** And Peter remembered the word of Jesus who had said to him, "Before the rooster crows, you will deny Me three times." So he went out and wept bitterly.

The Jews.

John 18:40 Then they all cried again, saying, "Not this Man, but Barabbas!" Now Barabbas was a robber.

Acts 3:13–14 The God of Abraham, Isaac, and Jacob, the God of our fathers, glorified His Servant Jesus, whom you delivered up and denied in the presence of Pilate, when he was determined to let *Him* go. **14** But you denied the Holy One and the Just, and asked for a murderer to be granted to you,

DESERTS

Vast, barren plains.

Ex 5:3 So they said, "The God of the Hebrews has met with us. Please, let us go three days' journey into the desert and sacrifice to the LORD our God, lest He fall upon us with pestilence or with the sword."

Uninhabited places.

Matt 14:15 When it was evening, His disciples came to Him, saying, "This is a deserted place, and the hour is already late. Send the multitudes away, that they may go into the villages and buy themselves food."

Mark 6:31 And He said to them, "Come aside by yourselves to a deserted place and rest a while." For there were many coming and going, and they did not even have time to eat.

Described as

Uninhabited and lonely.

Jer 2:6 Neither did they say, 'Where *is* the LORD, Who brought us up out of the land of Egypt, Who led us through the wilderness, Through a land of deserts and pits, Through a land of drought and the shadow of death, Through a land that no one crossed And where no one dwelt?'

Uncultivated.

Num 20:5 And why have you made us come up out of Egypt, to bring us to this evil place? It *is* not a place of grain or figs or vines or pomegranates; nor *is* there any water to drink."

Jer 2:2 "Go and cry in the hearing of Jerusalem, saying, 'Thus says the LORD: "I remember you, The kindness of your youth, The love of your betrothal, When you went after Me in the wilderness, In a land not sown.

Desolate.

Ezek 6:14 So I will stretch out My hand against them and make the land desolate, yes, more desolate than the wilderness toward Diblah, in all their dwelling places. Then they shall know that I *am* the LORD.' " ' "

Dry and without water.

Ex 17:1 Then all the congregation of the children of Israel set out on their journey from the Wilderness of Sin, according to the commandment of the LORD, and camped in Rephidim; but *there was* no water for the people to drink.

Deut 8:15 who led you through that great and terrible wilderness, *in which were* fiery serpents and scorpions and thirsty land where there was no water; who brought water for you out of the flinty rock;

Trackless.

Is 43:19 Behold, I will do a new thing, Now it shall spring forth; Shall you not know it? I will even make a road in the wilderness *And* rivers in the desert.

Great and terrible.

Deut 1:19 "So we departed from Horeb, and went through all that great and terrible wilderness which you saw on the way to the mountains of the Amorites, as the LORD our God had commanded us. Then we came to Kadesh Barnea.

Wasteland and howling wilderness.

Deut 32:10 "He found him in a desert land And in the wasteland, a howling wilderness; He encircled him, He instructed him, He kept him as the apple of His eye.

Full of wild beasts.

Is 13:21 But wild beasts of the desert will lie there, And their houses will be full of owls; Ostriches will dwell there, And wild goats will caper there.

Mark 1:13 And He was there in the wilderness forty days, tempted by Satan, and was with the wild beasts; and the angels ministered to Him.

Contained serpents and scorpions.

Deut 8:15 who led you through that great and terrible wilderness, *in which were* fiery serpents and scorpions and thirsty land where there was no water; who brought water for you out of the flinty rock;

Infested with robbers.

Jer 3:2 "Lift up your eyes to the desolate heights and see: Where have you not lain *with men*? By the road you have sat for them Like an Arabian in the wilderness; And you have polluted the land With your harlotries and your wickedness.

Lam 4:19 Our pursuers were swifter Than the eagles of the heavens. They pursued us on the mountains And lay in wait for us in the wilderness.

Danger of travelling in.

Ex 14:3 For Pharaoh will say of the children of Israel, 'They *are* bewildered by the land; the wilderness has closed them in.'

2 Cor 11:26 *in* journeys often, *in* perils of waters, *in* perils of robbers, *in* perils of *my own* countrymen, *in* perils of the Gentiles, *in* perils in the city, *in* perils in the wilderness, *in* perils in the sea, *in* perils among false brethren;

Guides required in.

Num 10:31 So *Moses* said, "Please do not leave, inasmuch as you know how we are to camp in the wilderness, and you can be our eyes.

Deut 32:10 "He found him in a desert land And in the wasteland, a howling wilderness; He encircled him, He instructed him, He kept him as the apple of His eye.

Phenomena of, alluded to

Mirage or deceptive appearance of water.

Jer 15:18 Why is my pain perpetual And my wound incurable, *Which* refuses to be healed? Will You surely be to me like an unreliable stream, *As* waters *that* fail?

Dry wind (spirit).

2 Kin 19:7 Surely I will send a spirit upon him, and he shall hear a rumor and return to his own land; and I will cause him to fall by the sword in his own land." ' "

Jer 4:11 At that time it will be said To this people and to Jerusalem, "A dry wind of the desolate heights *blows* in the wilderness Toward the daughter of My people— Not to fan or to cleanse—

Whirlwinds and clouds.

Is 21:1 The burden against the Wilderness of the Sea. As whirlwinds in the South pass through, *So* it comes from the desert, from a terrible land.

Jer 4:12–13 A wind too strong for these will come for Me; Now I will also speak judgment against them." **13** "Behold, he shall come up like clouds, And his chariots like a whirlwind. His horses are swifter than eagles. Woe to us, for we are plundered!"

Clouds of power and dust.

Deut 28:24 The LORD will change the rain of your land to powder and dust; from the heaven it shall come down on you until you are destroyed.

Those mentioned in Scripture

Arabian or great desert.

Ex 23:31 And I will set your bounds from the Red Sea to the sea, Philistia, and from the desert to the River. For I will deliver the inhabitants of the land into your hand, and you shall drive them out before you.

Beth Aven.

Josh 18:12 Their border on the north side began at the Jordan, and the border went up to the side of Jericho on the north, and went up through the mountains westward; it ended at the Wilderness of Beth Aven.

Beersheba.

Gen 21:14 So Abraham rose early in the morning, and took bread and a skin of water; and putting *it* on her shoulder, he gave *it* and the boy to Hagar, and sent her away. Then she departed and wandered in the Wilderness of Beersheba.

1 Kin 19:3–4 And when he saw *that*, he arose and ran for his life, and went to Beersheba, which *belongs* to Judah, and left his servant there. **4** But he himself went a day's journey into the wilderness, and came and sat down under a broom tree. And he prayed that he might die, and said, "It is enough! Now, LORD, take my life, for I *am* no better than my fathers!"

Damascus.

1 Kin 19:15 Then the LORD said to him: "Go, return on your way to the Wilderness of Damascus; and when you arrive, anoint Hazael *as* king over Syria.

Edom.

2 Kin 3:8 Then he said, "Which way shall we go up?" And he answered, "By way of the Wilderness of Edom."

En Gedi.

1 Sam 24:1 Now it happened, when Saul had returned from following the Philistines, that it was told him, saying, "Take note! David *is* in the Wilderness of En Gedi."

Gibeon.

2 Sam 2:24 Joab and Abishai also pursued Abner. And the sun was going down when they came to the hill of Ammah, which *is* before Giah by the road to the Wilderness of Gibeon.

Judea.

Matt 3:1 In those days John the Baptist came preaching in the wilderness of Judea,

Jeruel.

2 Chr 20:16 Tomorrow go down against them. They will surely come up by the Ascent of Ziz, and you will find them at the end of the brook before the Wilderness of Jeruel.

Kedemoth.

Deut 2:26 "And I sent messengers from the Wilderness of Kedemoth to Sihon king of Heshbon, with words of peace, saying,

Kadesh.

Ps 29:8 The voice of the LORD shakes the wilderness; The LORD shakes the Wilderness of Kadesh.

Maon.

1 Sam 23:24–25 So they arose and went to Ziph before Saul. But David and his men *were* in the Wilderness of Maon, in the plain on the south of Jeshimon. **25** When Saul and his men went to seek *him*, they told David. Therefore he went down to the rock, and stayed in the Wilderness of Maon. And when Saul heard *that*, he pursued David in the Wilderness of Maon.

Paran.

Gen 21:21 He dwelt in the Wilderness of Paran; and his mother took a wife for him from the land of Egypt.

Num 10:12 And the children of Israel set out from the Wilderness of Sinai on their journeys; then the cloud settled down in the Wilderness of Paran.

Shur.

Gen 16:7 Now the Angel of the LORD found her by a spring of water in the wilderness, by the spring on the way to Shur.

Sin.

Ex 16:1 And they journeyed from Elim, and all the congregation of the children of Israel came to the Wilderness of Sin, which is between Elim and Sinai, on the fifteenth day of the second month after they departed from the land of Egypt.

Sinai.

Ex 19:1–2 In the third month after the children of Israel had gone out of the land of Egypt, on the same day,

DESPAIR

they came *to* the Wilderness of Sinai. 2 For they had departed from Rephidim, had come *to* the Wilderness of Sinai, and camped in the wilderness. So Israel camped there before the mountain.

Num 33:16 They moved from the Wilderness of Sinai and camped at Kibroth Hattaavah.

Ziph.

1 Sam 23:14–15 And David stayed in strongholds in the wilderness, and remained in the mountains in the Wilderness of Ziph. Saul sought him every day, but God did not deliver him into his hand. 15 So David saw that Saul had come out to seek his life. And David *was* in the Wilderness of Ziph in a forest.

Zin.

Num 20:1 Then the children of Israel, the whole congregation, came into the Wilderness of Zin in the first month, and the people stayed in Kadesh; and Miriam died there and was buried there.

Num 27:14 For in the Wilderness of Zin, during the strife of the congregation, you rebelled against My command to hallow Me at the waters before their eyes." (These *are* the waters of Meribah, at Kadesh in the Wilderness of Zin.)

Of the Red Sea.

Ex 13:18 So God led the people around *by* way of the wilderness of the Red Sea. And the children of Israel went up in orderly ranks out of the land of Egypt.

Near Gaza.

Acts 8:26 Now an angel of the Lord spoke to Philip, saying, "Arise and go toward the south along the road which goes down from Jerusalem to Gaza." This is desert.

Shrubs often found in.

Jer 17:6 For he shall be like a shrub in the desert, And shall not see when good comes, But shall inhabit the parched places in the wilderness, In a salt land *which is* not inhabited.

Parts of, afforded pasture.

Gen 36:24 These *were* the sons of Zibeon: both Ajah and Anah. This *was the* Anah who found the water in the wilderness as he pastured the donkeys of his father Zibeon.

Ex 3:1 Now Moses was tending the flock of Jethro his father-in-law, the priest of Midian. And he led the flock to the back of the desert, and came to Horeb, the mountain of God.

Inhabited by wandering tribes.

Gen 21:20–21 So God was with the lad; and he grew and dwelt in the wilderness, and became an archer. 21 He dwelt in the Wilderness of Paran; and his mother took a wife for him from the land of Egypt.

Ps 72:9 Those who dwell in the wilderness will bow before Him, And His enemies will lick the dust.

Jer 25:24 all the kings of Arabia and all the kings of the mixed multitude who dwell in the desert;

The persecuted fled to.

1 Sam 23:14 And David stayed in strongholds in the wilderness, and remained in the mountains in the Wilderness of Ziph. Saul sought him every day, but God did not deliver him into his hand.

Heb 11:38 of whom the world was not worthy. They

wandered in deserts and mountains, *in* dens and caves of the earth.

The disaffected fled to.

1 Sam 22:2 And everyone *who was* in distress, everyone who *was* in debt, and everyone *who was* discontented gathered to him. So he became captain over them. And there were about four hundred men with him.

Acts 21:38 Are you not the Egyptian who some time ago stirred up a rebellion and led the four thousand assassins out into the wilderness?"

Illustrative of

Barrenness.

Ps 106:9 He rebuked the Red Sea also, and it dried up; So He led them through the depths, As through the wilderness.

Ps 107:33 He turns rivers into a wilderness, And the watersprings into dry ground;

Ps 107:35 He turns a wilderness into pools of water, And dry land into watersprings.

Those deprived of blessings.

Hos 2:3 Lest I strip her naked And expose her, as in the day she was born, And make her like a wilderness, And set her like a dry land, And slay her with thirst.

The Gentiles.

Is 35:1 The wilderness and the wasteland shall be glad for them, And the desert shall rejoice and blossom as the rose;

Is 35:6 Then the lame shall leap like a deer, And the tongue of the dumb sing. For waters shall burst forth in the wilderness, And streams in the desert.

Is 41:19 I will plant in the wilderness the cedar and the acacia tree, The myrtle and the oil tree; I will set in the desert the cypress tree *and* the pine And the box tree together,

What affords no support.

Jer 2:31 "O generation, see the word of the LORD! Have I been a wilderness to Israel, Or a land of darkness? Why do My people say, 'We are lords; We will come no more to You'?

Desolation by armies.

Jer 12:10–13 "Many rulers have destroyed My vineyard, They have trodden My portion underfoot; They have made My pleasant portion a desolate wilderness. 11 They have made it desolate; Desolate, it mourns to Me; The whole land is made desolate, Because no one takes *it* to heart. 12 The plunderers have come On all the desolate heights in the wilderness, For the sword of the LORD shall devour From *one* end of the land to the *other* end of the land; No flesh shall have peace. 13 They have sown wheat but reaped thorns; They have put themselves to pain *but* do not profit. But be ashamed of your harvest Because of the fierce anger of the LORD."

Jer 50:12 Your mother shall be deeply ashamed; She who bore you shall be ashamed. Behold, the least of the nations *shall be* a wilderness, A dry land and a desert.

DESPAIR

Produced in the wicked by divine judgments.

Deut 28:34 So you shall be driven mad because of the sight which your eyes see.

DESPAIR

314

Deut 28:67 In the morning you shall say, 'Oh, that it were evening!' And at evening you shall say, 'Oh, that it were morning!' because of the fear which terrifies your heart, and because of the sight which your eyes see.

Rev 9:6 In those days men will seek death and will not find it; they will desire to die, and death will flee from them.

Rev 16:10 Then the fifth angel poured out his bowl on the throne of the beast, and his kingdom became full of darkness; and they gnawed their tongues because of the pain.

Sinful.

Job 3:1–3 After this Job opened his mouth and cursed the day of his *birth.* **2** And Job spoke, and said: **3** "May the day perish on which I was born, And the night *in which* it was said, 'A male child is conceived.'

Jer 20:14–15 Cursed *be* the day in which I was born! Let the day not be blessed in which my mother bore me! **15** Let the man *be* cursed Who brought news to my father, saying, "A male child has been born to you!" Making him very glad.

Leads to

Questioning God.

Ps 10:1 Why do You stand afar off, O LORD? *Why* do You hide in times of trouble?

Continuing in sin.

Jer 2:25 Withhold your foot from being unshod, and your throat from thirst. But you said, 'There is no hope. No! For I have loved aliens, and after them I will go.'

Jer 18:12 And they said, "That is hopeless! So we will walk according to our own plans, and we will every one obey the dictates of his evil heart."

Blasphemy.

Is 8:21 They will pass through it hard-pressed and hungry; and it shall happen, when they are hungry, that they will be enraged and curse their king and their God, and look upward.

Rev 16:10–11 Then the fifth angel poured out his bowl on the throne of the beast, and his kingdom became full of darkness; and they gnawed their tongues because of the pain. **11** They blasphemed the God of heaven because of their pains and their sores, and did not repent of their deeds.

Shall seize upon the wicked at the appearing of Christ.

Rev 6:16 and said to the mountains and rocks, "Fall on us and hide us from the face of Him who sits on the throne and from the wrath of the Lamb!

Believers sometimes tempted to.

Job 7:6 "My days are swifter than a weaver's shuttle, And are spent without hope.

Lam 3:18 And I said, "My strength and my hope Have perished from the LORD."

Believers enabled to overcome.

2 Cor 4:8–9 *We are* hard-pressed on every side, yet not crushed; *we are* perplexed, but not in despair; **9** persecuted, but not forsaken; struck down, but not destroyed—

Trust in God, a preservative against.

Ps 42:5 Why are you cast down, O my soul? And *why* are you disquieted within me? Hope in God, for I shall yet praise Him *For* the help of His countenance.

Ps 42:11 Why are you cast down, O my soul? And why are you disquieted within me? Hope in God; For I shall yet praise Him, The help of my countenance and my God.

Exemplified by

Cain.

Gen 4:13–14 And Cain said to the LORD, "My punishment *is* greater than I can bear! **14** Surely You have driven me out this day from the face of the ground; I shall be hidden from Your face; I shall be a fugitive and a vagabond on the earth, and it will happen *that* anyone who finds me will kill me."

Job.

Job 3:1–11 After this Job opened his mouth and cursed the day of his *birth.* **2** And Job spoke, and said: **3** "May the day perish on which I was born, And the night *in which* it was said, 'A male child is conceived.' **4** May that day be darkness; May God above not seek it, Nor the light shine upon it. **5** May darkness and the shadow of death claim it; May a cloud settle on it; May the blackness of the day terrify it. **6** *As for* that night, may darkness seize it; May it not rejoice among the days of the year, May it not come into the number of the months. **7** Oh, may that night be barren! May no joyful shout come into it! **8** May those curse it who curse the day, Those who are ready to arouse Leviathan. **9** May the stars of its morning be dark; May it look for light, but *have* none, And not see the dawning of the day; **10** Because it did not shut up the doors of my *mother's* womb, Nor hide sorrow from my eyes. **11** "Why did I not die at birth? *Why* did I *not* perish when I came from the womb?

Job 3:24–26 For my sighing comes before I eat, And my groanings pour out like water. **25** For the thing I greatly feared has come upon me, And what I dreaded has happened to me. **26** I am not at ease, nor am I quiet; I have no rest, for trouble comes."

Ahithophel.

2 Sam 17:23 Now when Ahithophel saw that his advice was not followed, he saddled a donkey, and arose and went home to his house, to his city. Then he put his household in order, and hanged himself, and died; and he was buried in his father's tomb.

Elijah.

1 Kin 19:3–4 And when he saw *that,* he arose and ran for his life, and went to Beersheba, which *belongs* to Judah, and left his servant there. **4** But he himself went a day's journey into the wilderness, and came and sat down under a broom tree. And he prayed that he might die, and said, "It is enough! Now, LORD, take my life, for I *am* no better than my fathers!"

Judas Iscariot.

Matt 27:5 Then he threw down the pieces of silver in the temple and departed, and went and hanged himself.

DEVIL, THE

Sinned against God.

2 Pet 2:4 For if God did not spare the angels who sinned, but cast *them* down to hell and delivered *them* into chains of darkness, to be reserved for judgment;

1 John 3:8 He who sins is of the devil, for the devil has sinned from the beginning. For this purpose the Son of God was manifested, that He might destroy the works of the devil.

Cast out of heaven and down to hell.

Luke 10:18 And He said to them, "I saw Satan fall like lightning from heaven.

2 Pet 2:4 For if God did not spare the angels who sinned, but cast *them* down to hell and delivered *them* into chains of darkness, to be reserved for judgment;

Jude 1:6 And the angels who did not keep their proper domain, but left their own abode, He has reserved in everlasting chains under darkness for the judgment of the great day;

The author of the Fall.

Gen 3:1 Now the serpent was more cunning than any beast of the field which the LORD God had made. And he said to the woman, "Has God indeed said, 'You shall not eat of every tree of the garden'?"

Gen 3:6 So when the woman saw that the tree *was* good for food, that it *was* pleasant to the eyes, and a tree desirable to make *one* wise, she took of its fruit and ate. She also gave to her husband with her, and he ate.

Gen 3:14 So the LORD God said to the serpent: "Because you have done this, You *are* cursed more than all cattle, And more than every beast of the field; On your belly you shall go, And you shall eat dust All the days of your life.

Gen 3:24 So He drove out the man; and He placed cherubim at the east of the garden of Eden, and a flaming sword which turned every way, to guard the way to the tree of life.

Tempted Christ.

Matt 4:3–10 Now when the tempter came to Him, he said, "If You are the Son of God, command that these stones become bread." **4** But He answered and said, "It is written, *'Man shall not live by bread alone, but by every word that proceeds from the mouth of God.'"* **5** Then the devil took Him up into the holy city, set Him on the pinnacle of the temple, **6** and said to Him, "If You are the Son of God, throw Yourself down. For it is written: *'He shall give His angels charge over you,'* and, *'In their hands they shall bear you up, Lest you dash your foot against a stone.'"* **7** Jesus said to him, "It is written again, *'You shall not tempt the LORD your God.'"* **8** Again, the devil took Him up on an exceedingly high mountain, and showed Him all the kingdoms of the world and their glory. **9** And he said to Him, "All these things I will give You if You will fall down and worship me." **10** Then Jesus said to him, "Away with you, Satan! For it is written, *'You shall worship the LORD your God, and Him only you shall serve.'"*

Perverts the Scripture.

Ps 91:11–12 For He shall give His angels charge over you, To keep you in all your ways. **12** In *their* hands they shall bear you up, Lest you dash your foot against a stone.

Matt 4:6 and said to Him, "If You are the Son of God,

throw Yourself down. For it is written: *'He shall give His angels charge over you,'* and, *'In their hands they shall bear you up, Lest you dash your foot against a stone.'"*

Opposes God's work.

Zech 3:1 Then he showed me Joshua the high priest standing before the Angel of the LORD, and Satan standing at his right hand to oppose him.

Matt 13:19 When anyone hears the word of the kingdom, and does not understand *it*, then the wicked *one* comes and snatches away what was sown in his heart. This is he who received seed by the wayside.

2 Cor 4:4 whose minds the god of this age has blinded, who do not believe, lest the light of the gospel of the glory of Christ, who is the image of God, should shine on them.

1 Thess 2:18 Therefore we wanted to come to you— even I, Paul, time and again—but Satan hindered us.

Works lying wonders.

2 Thess 2:9 The coming of the *lawless one* is according to the working of Satan, with all power, signs, and lying wonders,

Rev 16:14 For they are spirits of demons, performing signs, *which* go out to the kings of the earth and of the whole world, to gather them to the battle of that great day of God Almighty.

Assumes the form of an angel of light.

2 Cor 11:14 And no wonder! For Satan himself transforms himself into an angel of light.

The wicked

Are the children of.

Matt 13:38 The field is the world, the good seeds are the sons of the kingdom, but the tares are the sons of the wicked *one*.

Acts 13:10 and said, "O full of all deceit and all fraud, *you* son of the devil, *you* enemy of all righteousness, will you not cease perverting the straight ways of the Lord?

1 John 3:10 In this the children of God and the children of the devil are manifest: Whoever does not practice righteousness is not of God, nor *is* he who does not love his brother.

Turn aside after.

1 Tim 5:15 For some have already turned aside after Satan.

Do the lusts of.

John 8:44 You are of *your* father the devil, and the desires of your father you want to do. He was a murderer from the beginning, and does not stand in the truth, because there is no truth in him. When he speaks a lie, he speaks from his own *resources,* for he is a liar and the father of it.

Possessed by.

Luke 22:3 Then Satan entered Judas, surnamed Iscariot, who was numbered among the twelve.

Acts 5:3 But Peter said, "Ananias, why has Satan filled your heart to lie to the Holy Spirit and keep back *part* of the price of the land for yourself?

Eph 2:2 in which you once walked according to the course of this world, according to the prince of the power of the air, the spirit who now works in the sons of disobedience,

Blinded by.

2 Cor 4:4 whose minds the god of this age has blinded, who do not believe, lest the light of the gospel of the glory of Christ, who is the image of God, should shine on them.

Deceived by.

1 Kin 22:21–22 Then a spirit came forward and stood before the LORD, and said, 'I will persuade him.' **22** The LORD said to him, 'In what way?' So he said, 'I will go out and be a lying spirit in the mouth of all his prophets.' And the LORD said, 'You shall persuade *him*, and also prevail. Go out and do so.'

Rev 20:7–8 Now when the thousand years have expired, Satan will be released from his prison **8** and will go out to deceive the nations which are in the four corners of the earth, Gog and Magog, to gather them together to battle, whose number *is* as the sand of the sea.

Ensnared by.

1 Tim 3:7 Moreover he must have a good testimony among those who are outside, lest he fall into reproach and the snare of the devil.

2 Tim 2:26 and *that* they may come to their senses *and* escape the snare of the devil, having been taken captive by him to *do* his will.

Troubled by.

1 Sam 16:14 But the Spirit of the LORD departed from Saul, and a distressing spirit from the LORD troubled him.

Punished, together with.

Matt 25:41 "Then He will also say to those on the left hand, 'Depart from Me, you cursed, into the everlasting fire prepared for the devil and his angels:

Believers

Afflicted by, only as God permits.

Job 1:12 And the LORD said to Satan, "Behold, all that he has *is* in your power; only do not lay a hand on his *person*." So Satan went out from the presence of the LORD.

Job 2:4–7 So Satan answered the LORD and said, "Skin for skin! Yes, all that a man has he will give for his life. **5** But stretch out Your hand now, and touch his bone and his flesh, and he will surely curse You to Your face!" **6** And the LORD said to Satan, "Behold, he is in your hand, but spare his life." **7** So Satan went out from the presence of the LORD, and struck Job with painful boils from the sole of his foot to the crown of his head.

Tempted by.

1 Chr 21:1 Now Satan stood up against Israel, and moved David to number Israel.

1 Thess 3:5 For this reason, when I could no longer endure it, I sent to know your faith, lest by some means the tempter had tempted you, and our labor might be in vain.

Sifted by.

Luke 22:31 And the Lord said, "Simon, Simon! Indeed, Satan has asked for you, that he may sift *you* as wheat.

Should resist.

James 4:7 Therefore submit to God. Resist the devil and he will flee from you.

1 Pet 5:9 Resist him, steadfast in the faith, knowing that the same sufferings are experienced by your brotherhood in the world.

Should be armed against.

Eph 6:11–16 Put on the whole armor of God, that you may be able to stand against the wiles of the devil. **12** For we do not wrestle against flesh and blood, but against principalities, against powers, against the rulers of the darkness of this age, against spiritual *hosts* of wickedness in the heavenly *places*. **13** Therefore take up the whole armor of God, that you may be able to withstand in the evil day, and having done all, to stand. **14** Stand therefore, having girded your waist with truth, having put on the breastplate of righteousness, **15** and having shod your feet with the preparation of the gospel of peace; **16** above all, taking the shield of faith with which you will be able to quench all the fiery darts of the wicked one.

Should be watchful against.

2 Cor 2:11 lest Satan should take advantage of us; for we are not ignorant of his devices.

Overcome.

Rom 16:20 And the God of peace will crush Satan under your feet shortly. The grace of our Lord Jesus Christ *be* with you. Amen.

1 John 2:13 I write to you, fathers, Because you have known Him *who is* from the beginning. I write to you, young men, Because you have overcome the wicked one. I write to you, little children, Because you have known the Father.

Rev 12:10–11 Then I heard a loud voice saying in heaven, "Now salvation, and strength, and the kingdom of our God, and the power of His Christ have come, for the accuser of our brethren, who accused them before our God day and night, has been cast down. **11** And they overcame him by the blood of the Lamb and by the word of their testimony, and they did not love their lives to the death.

Triumph over, by Christ

Predicted.

Gen 3:15 And I will put enmity Between you and the woman, And between your seed and her Seed; He shall bruise your head, And you shall bruise His heel."

In resisting his temptations.

Matt 4:11 Then the devil left Him, and behold, angels came and ministered to Him.

In casting out the spirits of.

Luke 11:20 But if I cast out demons with the finger of God, surely the kingdom of God has come upon you.

Luke 13:32 And He said to them, "Go, tell that fox, 'Behold, I cast out demons and perform cures today and tomorrow, and the third *day* I shall be perfected.'

In empowering his disciples to cast out.

Matt 10:1 And when He had called His twelve disciples to *Him*, He gave them power *over* unclean spirits, to cast them out, and to heal all kinds of sickness and all kinds of disease.

Mark 16:17 And these signs will follow those who believe: In My name they will cast out demons; they will speak with new tongues;

In destroying the works of.

1 John 3:8 He who sins is of the devil, for the devil has sinned from the beginning. For this purpose the Son of God was manifested, that He might destroy the works of the devil.

Completed by His death.

Col 2:15 Having disarmed principalities and powers, He made a public spectacle of them, triumphing over them in it.

Heb 2:14 Inasmuch then as the children have partaken of flesh and blood, He Himself likewise shared in the same, that through death He might destroy him who had the power of death, that is, the devil,

Illustrated.

Luke 11:21–22 When a strong man, fully armed, guards his own palace, his goods are in peace. **22** But when a stronger than he comes upon him and overcomes him, he takes from him all his armor in which he trusted, and divides his spoils.

Character of,

Presumptuous.

Job 1:6 Now there was a day when the sons of God came to present themselves before the LORD, and Satan also came among them.

Matt 4:5–6 Then the devil took Him up into the holy city, set Him on the pinnacle of the temple, **6** and said to Him, "If You are the Son of God, throw Yourself down. For it is written: *'He shall give His angels charge over you,'* and, *'In their hands they shall bear you up, Lest you dash your foot against a stone.'*"

Proud.

1 Tim 3:6 not a novice, lest being puffed up with pride he fall into the *same* condemnation as the devil.

Powerful.

Eph 2:2 in which you once walked according to the course of this world, according to the prince of the power of the air, the spirit who now works in the sons of disobedience,

Eph 6:12 For we do not wrestle against flesh and blood, but against principalities, against powers, against the rulers of the darkness of this age, against spiritual *hosts* of wickedness in the heavenly *places.*

Wicked.

1 John 2:13 I write to you, fathers, Because you have known Him *who is* from the beginning. I write to you, young men, Because you have overcome the wicked one. I write to you, little children, Because you have known the Father.

Cynical.

Job 1:9 So Satan answered the LORD and said, "Does Job fear God for nothing?

Job 2:4 So Satan answered the LORD and said, "Skin for skin! Yes, all that a man has he will give for his life.

Crafty.

Gen 3:1 Now the serpent was more cunning than any beast of the field which the LORD God had made. And he said to the woman, "Has God indeed said, 'You shall not eat of every tree of the garden'?"

2 Cor 11:3 But I fear, lest somehow, as the serpent deceived Eve by his craftiness, so your minds may be corrupted from the simplicity that is in Christ.

Deceitful.

2 Cor 11:14 And no wonder! For Satan himself transforms himself into an angel of light.

Eph 6:11 Put on the whole armor of God, that you may be able to stand against the wiles of the devil.

Fierce and cruel.

Luke 8:29 For He had commanded the unclean spirit to come out of the man. For it had often seized him, and he was kept under guard, bound with chains and shackles; and he broke the bonds and was driven by the demon into the wilderness.

Luke 9:39 And behold, a spirit seizes him, and he suddenly cries out; it convulses him so that he foams *at the mouth;* and it departs from him with great difficulty, bruising him.

Luke 9:42 And as he was still coming, the demon threw him down and convulsed *him.* Then Jesus rebuked the unclean spirit, healed the child, and gave him back to his father.

1 Pet 5:8 Be sober, be vigilant; because your adversary the devil walks about like a roaring lion, seeking whom he may devour.

Cowardly.

James 4:7 Therefore submit to God. Resist the devil and he will flee from you.

The Antichrist is of.

2 Thess 2:9 The coming of the *lawless one* is according to the working of Satan, with all power, signs, and lying wonders,

1 John 4:3 and every spirit that does not confess that Jesus Christ has come in the flesh is not of God. And this is the *spirit* of the Antichrist, which you have heard was coming, and is now already in the world.

Shall be condemned at the judgment.

Jude 1:6 And the angels who did not keep their proper domain, but left their own abode, He has reserved in everlasting chains under darkness for the judgment of the great day;

Rev 20:10 The devil, who deceived them, was cast into the lake of fire and brimstone where the beast and the false prophet *are.* And they will be tormented day and night forever and ever.

Everlasting fire is prepared for.

Matt 25:41 "Then He will also say to those on the left hand, 'Depart from Me, you cursed, into the everlasting fire prepared for the devil and his angels:

Compared to

A fowler.

Ps 91:3 Surely He shall deliver you from the snare of the fowler *And* from the perilous pestilence.

Birds.

Matt 13:4 And as he sowed, some *seed* fell by the wayside; and the birds came and devoured them.

A sower of tares.

Matt 13:25 but while men slept, his enemy came and sowed tares among the wheat and went his way.

Matt 13:28 He said to them, 'An enemy has done this.'

The servants said to him, 'Do you want us then to go and gather them up?'

A wolf.

John 10:12 But a hireling, *he who is* not the shepherd, one who does not own the sheep, sees the wolf coming and leaves the sheep and flees; and the wolf catches the sheep and scatters them.

A roaring lion.

1 Pet 5:8 Be sober, be vigilant; because your adversary the devil walks about like a roaring lion, seeking whom he may devour.

A serpent.

Gen 3:1 Now the serpent was more cunning than any beast of the field which the LORD God had made. And he said to the woman, "Has God indeed said, 'You shall not eat of every tree of the garden'?"

Rev 12:9 So the great dragon was cast out, that serpent of old, called the Devil and Satan, who deceives the whole world; he was cast to the earth, and his angels were cast out with him.

Rev 20:2 He laid hold of the dragon, that serpent of old, who is *the* Devil and Satan, and bound him for a thousand years;

DEVIL, TITLES AND NAMES OF THE

Abaddon.

Rev 9:11 And they had as king over them the angel of the bottomless pit, whose name in Hebrew *is* Abaddon, but in Greek he has the name Apollyon.

Accuser of our brethren.

Rev 12:10 Then I heard a loud voice saying in heaven, "Now salvation, and strength, and the kingdom of our God, and the power of His Christ have come, for the accuser of our brethren, who accused them before our God day and night, has been cast down.

Adversary.

1 Pet 5:8 Be sober, be vigilant; because your adversary the devil walks about like a roaring lion, seeking whom he may devour.

Angel of the bottomless pit.

Rev 9:11 And they had as king over them the angel of the bottomless pit, whose name in Hebrew *is* Abaddon, but in Greek he has the name Apollyon.

Apollyon.

Rev 9:11 And they had as king over them the angel of the bottomless pit, whose name in Hebrew *is* Abaddon, but in Greek he has the name Apollyon.

Beelzebub.

Matt 12:24 Now when the Pharisees heard *it* they said, "This *fellow* does not cast out demons except by Beelzebub, the ruler of the demons."

Belial.

2 Cor 6:15 And what accord has Christ with Belial? Or what part has a believer with an unbeliever?

Distressing spirit.

1 Sam 16:14 But the Spirit of the LORD departed from Saul, and a distressing spirit from the LORD troubled him.

Dragon.

Rev 20:2 He laid hold of the dragon, that serpent of old, who is *the* Devil and Satan, and bound him for a thousand years;

Enemy.

Matt 13:39 The enemy who sowed them is the devil, the harvest is the end of the age, and the reapers are the angels.

Father of lies.

John 8:44 You are of *your* father the devil, and the desires of your father you want to do. He was a murderer from the beginning, and does not stand in the truth, because there is no truth in him. When he speaks a lie, he speaks from his own *resources*, for he is a liar and the father of it.

Fleeing serpent.

Is 27:1 In that day the LORD with His severe sword, great and strong, Will punish Leviathan the fleeing serpent, Leviathan that twisted serpent; And He will slay the reptile that *is* in the sea.

Great red dragon.

Rev 12:3 And another sign appeared in heaven: behold, a great, fiery red dragon having seven heads and ten horns, and seven diadems on his heads.

Leviathan.

Is 27:1 In that day the LORD with His severe sword, great and strong, Will punish Leviathan the fleeing serpent, Leviathan that twisted serpent; And He will slay the reptile that *is* in the sea.

Liar.

John 8:44 You are of *your* father the devil, and the desires of your father you want to do. He was a murderer from the beginning, and does not stand in the truth, because there is no truth in him. When he speaks a lie, he speaks from his own *resources*, for he is a liar and the father of it.

Lying spirit.

1 Kin 22:22 The LORD said to him, 'In what way?' So he said, 'I will go out and be a lying spirit in the mouth of all his prophets.' And the LORD said, 'You shall persuade *him*, and also prevail. Go out and do so.'

Murderer.

John 8:44 You are of *your* father the devil, and the desires of your father you want to do. He was a murderer from the beginning, and does not stand in the truth, because there is no truth in him. When he speaks a lie, he speaks from his own *resources*, for he is a liar and the father of it.

Prince of the power of the air.

Eph 2:2 in which you once walked according to the course of this world, according to the prince of the power of the air, the spirit who now works in the sons of disobedience,

Reptile.

Is 27:1 In that day the LORD with His severe sword, great and strong, Will punish Leviathan the fleeing serpent, Leviathan that twisted serpent; And He will slay the reptile that *is* in the sea.

Ruler of the darkness of this world.

Eph 6:12 For we do not wrestle against flesh and blood, but against principalities, against powers, against the rulers of the darkness of this age, against spiritual *hosts* of wickedness in the heavenly *places*.

Ruler of the demons.

Matt 12:24 Now when the Pharisees heard *it* they said, "This *fellow* does not cast out demons except by Beelzebub, the ruler of the demons."

Ruler of this world.

John 14:30 I will no longer talk much with you, for the ruler of this world is coming, and he has nothing in Me.

Satan.

1 Chr 21:1 Now Satan stood up against Israel, and moved David to number Israel.

Job 1:6 Now there was a day when the sons of God came to present themselves before the LORD, and Satan also came among them.

Serpent.

Gen 3:4 Then the serpent said to the woman, "You will not surely die.

Gen 3:13–14 And the LORD God said to the woman, "What *is* this you have done?" The woman said, "The serpent deceived me, and I ate." **14** So the LORD God said to the serpent: "Because you have done this, You *are* cursed more than all cattle, And more than every beast of the field; On your belly you shall go, And you shall eat dust All the days of your life.

2 Cor 11:3 But I fear, lest somehow, as the serpent deceived Eve by his craftiness, so your minds may be corrupted from the simplicity that is in Christ.

Serpent of old.

Rev 12:9 So the great dragon was cast out, that serpent of old, called the Devil and Satan, who deceives the whole world; he was cast to the earth, and his angels were cast out with him.

Rev 20:2 He laid hold of the dragon, that serpent of old, who is *the* Devil and Satan, and bound him for a thousand years;

Spirit who works in the sons of disobedience.

Eph 2:2 in which you once walked according to the course of this world, according to the prince of the power of the air, the spirit who now works in the sons of disobedience,

Tempter.

Matt 4:3 Now when the tempter came to Him, he said, "If You are the Son of God, command that these stones become bread."

1 Thess 3:5 For this reason, when I could no longer endure it, I sent to know your faith, lest by some means the tempter had tempted you, and our labor might be in vain.

The god of this age.

2 Cor 4:4 whose minds the god of this age has blinded, who do not believe, lest the light of the gospel of the glory of Christ, who is the image of God, should shine on them.

Twisted serpent.

Is 27:1 In that day the LORD with His severe sword, great and strong, Will punish Leviathan the fleeing serpent, Leviathan that twisted serpent; And He will slay the reptile that *is* in the sea.

Wicked one.

Matt 13:19 When anyone hears the word of the kingdom, and does not understand *it*, then the wicked *one* comes and snatches away what was sown in his heart. This is he who received seed by the wayside.

Matt 13:38 The field is the world, the good seeds are the sons of the kingdom, but the tares are the sons of the wicked *one*.

DEVOTION TO GOD

A characteristic of believers.

Job 23:12 I have not departed from the commandment of His lips; I have treasured the words of His mouth More than my necessary *food*.

Christ, an example of.

John 4:34 Jesus said to them, "My food is to do the will of Him who sent Me, and to finish His work.

John 17:4 I have glorified You on the earth. I have finished the work which You have given Me to do.

Grounded upon

The mercies of God.

Rom 12:1 I beseech you therefore, brethren, by the mercies of God, that you present your bodies a living sacrifice, holy, acceptable to God, *which is* your reasonable service.

The goodness of God.

1 Sam 12:24 Only fear the LORD, and serve Him in truth with all your heart; for consider what great things He has done for you.

The call of God.

1 Thess 2:12 that you would walk worthy of God who calls you into His own kingdom and glory.

The death of Christ.

2 Cor 5:15 and He died for all, that those who live should live no longer for themselves, but for Him who died for them and rose again.

Our creation.

Ps 86:9 All nations whom You have made Shall come and worship before You, O Lord, And shall glorify Your name.

Our preservation.

Is 46:4 Even to *your* old age, I *am* He, And *even* to gray hairs I will carry *you!* I have made, and I will bear; Even I will carry, and will deliver *you*.

Our redemption.

1 Cor 6:19–20 Or do you not know that your body is the temple of the Holy Spirit *who is* in you, whom you have from God, and you are not your own? **20** For you were bought at a price; therefore glorify God in your body and in your spirit, which are God's.

Should be

With our spirit.

1 Cor 6:20 For you were bought at a price; therefore glorify God in your body and in your spirit, which are God's.

1 Pet 4:6 For this reason the gospel was preached also to those who are dead, that they might be judged according to men in the flesh, but live according to God in the spirit.

With our bodies.

Rom 12:1 I beseech you therefore, brethren, by the mercies of God, that you present your bodies a living sacrifice, holy, acceptable to God, *which is* your reasonable service.

1 Cor 6:20 For you were bought at a price; therefore glorify God in your body and in your spirit, which are God's.

With our members.

Rom 6:12–13 Therefore do not let sin reign in your mortal body, that you should obey it in its lusts. **13** And do not present your members *as* instruments of unrighteousness to sin, but present yourselves to God as being alive from the dead, and your members *as* instruments of righteousness to God.

1 Pet 4:2 that he no longer should live the rest of *his* time in the flesh for the lusts of men, but for the will of God.

With our substance.

Ex 22:29 "You shall not delay *to offer* the first of your ripe produce and your juices. The firstborn of your sons you shall give to Me.

Prov 3:9 Honor the LORD with your possessions, And with the firstfruits of all your increase;

Unreserved.

Matt 6:24 "No one can serve two masters; for either he will hate the one and love the other, or else he will be loyal to the one and despise the other. You cannot serve God and mammon.

Luke 14:33 So likewise, whoever of you does not forsake all that he has cannot be My disciple.

Abounding.

1 Thess 4:1 Finally then, brethren, we urge and exhort in the Lord Jesus that you should abound more and more, just as you received from us how you ought to walk and to please God;

Persevering.

Luke 1:74–75 To grant us that we, Being delivered from the hand of our enemies, Might serve Him without fear, **75** In holiness and righteousness before Him all the days of our life.

Luke 9:62 But Jesus said to him, "No one, having put his hand to the plow, and looking back, is fit for the kingdom of God."

In life and death.

Rom 14:8 For if we live, we live to the Lord; and if we die, we die to the Lord. Therefore, whether we live or die, we are the Lord's.

Phil 1:20 according to my earnest expectation and hope that in nothing I shall be ashamed, but with all boldness, as always, so now also Christ will be magnified in my body, whether by life or by death.

Should be exhibited in

Loving God.

Deut 6:5 You shall love the LORD your God with all your heart, with all your soul, and with all your strength.

Luke 10:27 So he answered and said, "'You shall love the LORD your God with all your heart, with all your soul, with all your strength, and with all your mind,' and 'your neighbor as yourself.'"

Serving God.

1 Sam 12:24 Only fear the LORD, and serve Him in truth with all your heart; for consider what great things He has done for you.

Rom 12:11 not lagging in diligence, fervent in spirit, serving the Lord;

Walking worthy of God.

1 Thess 2:12 that you would walk worthy of God who calls you into His own kingdom and glory.

Doing all to God's glory.

1 Cor 10:31 Therefore, whether you eat or drink, or whatever you do, do all to the glory of God.

Self-denial and bearing the cross.

Mark 8:34 When He had called the people to *Himself*, with His disciples also, He said to them, "Whoever desires to come after Me, let him deny himself, and take up his cross, and follow Me.

Living for Christ.

2 Cor 5:15 and He died for all, that those who live should live no longer for themselves, but for Him who died for them and rose again.

Giving up all for Christ.

Matt 19:21 Jesus said to him, "If you want to be perfect, go, sell what you have and give to the poor, and you will have treasure in heaven; and come, follow Me."

Matt 19:28–29 So Jesus said to them, "Assuredly I say to you, that in the regeneration, when the Son of Man sits on the throne of His glory, you who have followed Me will also sit on twelve thrones, judging the twelve tribes of Israel. **29** And everyone who has left houses or brothers or sisters or father or mother or wife or children or lands, for My name's sake, shall receive a hundredfold, and inherit eternal life.

Lack of, condemned.

Rev 3:16 So then, because you are lukewarm, and neither cold nor hot, I will vomit you out of My mouth.

Exemplified by

Joshua.

Josh 24:15 And if it seems evil to you to serve the LORD, choose for yourselves this day whom you will serve, whether the gods which your fathers served that *were* on the other side of the River, or the gods of the Amorites, in whose land you dwell. But as for me and my house, we will serve the LORD."

Peter, Andrew, James, John.

Matt 4:20–22 They immediately left *their* nets and followed Him. **21** Going on from there, He saw two other brothers, James *the son* of Zebedee, and John his brother, in the boat with Zebedee their father, mending their nets. He called them, **22** and immediately they left the boat and their father, and followed Him.

Joanna, etc.

Luke 8:3 and Joanna the wife of Chuza, Herod's steward, and Susanna, and many others who provided for Him from their substance.

Paul.

Phil 1:21 For to me, to live *is* Christ, and to die *is* gain.

Timothy.

Phil 2:19–22 But I trust in the Lord Jesus to send Timothy to you shortly, that I also may be encouraged when I know your state. **20** For I have no one like-minded, who will sincerely care for your state. **21** For all seek their own, not the things which are of Christ Jesus. **22** But you know his proven character, that as a son with *his* father he served with me in the gospel.

Epaphroditus.

Phil 2:30 because for the work of Christ he came close to death, not regarding his life, to supply what was lacking in your service toward me.

DILIGENCE

Christ, an example of.

Seeking Him.

Mark 1:35 Now in the morning, having risen a long while before daylight, He went out and departed to a solitary place; and there He prayed.

Luke 2:49 And He said to them, "Why did you seek Me? Did you not know that I must be about My Father's business?"

Required by God in

Seeking Him.

1 Chr 22:19 Now set your heart and your soul to seek the Lord your God. Therefore arise and build the sanctuary of the Lord God, to bring the ark of the covenant of the Lord and the holy articles of God into the house that is to be built for the name of the Lord."

Heb 11:6 But without faith *it is* impossible to please Him, for he who comes to God must believe that He is, and *that* He is a rewarder of those who diligently seek Him.

Obeying Him.

Deut 6:17 You shall diligently keep the commandments of the Lord your God, His testimonies, and His statutes which He has commanded you.

Deut 11:13 'And it shall be that if you earnestly obey My commandments which I command you today, to love the Lord your God and serve Him with all your heart and with all your soul,

Is 55:2 Why do you spend money for *what is* not bread, And your wages for *what* does not satisfy? Listen carefully to Me, and eat *what is* good, And let your soul delight itself in abundance.

Pursuing sanctification.

Deut 4:9 Only take heed to yourself, and diligently keep yourself, lest you forget the things your eyes have seen, and lest they depart from your heart all the days of your life. And teach them to your children and your grandchildren,

Ps 77:6 I call to remembrance my song in the night; I meditate within my heart, And my spirit makes diligent search.

Prov 4:23 Keep your heart with all diligence, For out of it *spring* the issues of life.

Phil 3:13–14 Brethren, I do not count myself to have apprehended; but one thing *I do,* forgetting those things which are behind and reaching forward to those things which are ahead, **14** I press toward the goal for the prize of the upward call of God in Christ Jesus.

2 Pet 1:5 But also for this very reason, giving all diligence, add to your faith virtue, to virtue knowledge,

2 Pet 1:10 Therefore, brethren, be even more diligent to make your call and election sure, for if you do these things you will never stumble;

2 Pet 3:14 Therefore, beloved, looking forward to these things, be diligent to be found by Him in peace, without spot and blameless;

Labors of love.

1 Tim 5:10 well reported for good works: if she has brought up children, if she has lodged strangers, if she has washed the saints' feet, if she has relieved the afflicted, if she has diligently followed every good work.

Heb 6:10–12 For God *is* not unjust to forget your work and labor of love which you have shown toward His name, *in that* you have ministered to the saints, and do minister. **11** And we desire that each one of you show the same diligence to the full assurance of hope until the end, **12** that you do not become sluggish, but imitate those who through faith and patience inherit the promises.

Guarding against defilement.

Heb 12:15 looking carefully lest anyone fall short of the grace of God; lest any root of bitterness springing up cause trouble, and by this many become defiled;

Lawful business.

Prov 27:23 Be diligent to know the state of your flocks, *And* attend to your herds;

Eccl 9:10 Whatever your hand finds to do, do *it* with your might; for *there is* no work or device or knowledge or wisdom in the grave where you are going.

Teaching doctrine.

Deut 11:19 You shall teach them to your children, speaking of them when you sit in your house, when you walk by the way, when you lie down, and when you rise up.

2 Tim 4:2 Preach the word! Be ready in season *and* out of season. Convince, rebuke, exhort, with all longsuffering and teaching.

Jude 1:3 Beloved, while I was very diligent to write to you concerning our common salvation, I found it necessary to write to you exhorting you to contend earnestly for the faith which was once for all delivered to the saints.

Discharging official duties.

Deut 19:18 And the judges shall make careful inquiry, and indeed, *if* the witness *is* a false witness, who has testified falsely against his brother,

Believers should abound in.

2 Cor 8:7 But as you abound in everything—in faith, in speech, in knowledge, in all diligence, and in your love for us—*see* that you abound in this grace also.

In the service of God,

Should be persevered in.

Gal 6:9 And let us not grow weary while doing good, for in due season we shall reap if we do not lose heart.

Is not in vain.

1 Cor 15:58 Therefore, my beloved brethren, be steadfast, immovable, always abounding in the work of the Lord, knowing that your labor is not in vain in the Lord.

Preserves from evil.

Ex 15:26 and said, "If you diligently heed the voice of the Lord your God and do what is right in His sight, give ear to His commandments and keep all His statutes, I will put none of the diseases on you which I have brought on the Egyptians. For I *am* the LORD who heals you."

Leads to assured hope.

Heb 6:11 And we desire that each one of you show the same diligence to the full assurance of hope until the end,

God rewards.

Deut 11:14 then I will give *you* the rain for your land in its season, the early rain and the latter rain, that you may gather in your grain, your new wine, and your oil.

Heb 11:6 But without faith *it is* impossible to please *Him,* for he who comes to God must believe that He is, and *that* He is a rewarder of those who diligently seek Him.

In temporal matters, leads to

Favor.

Prov 11:27 He who earnestly seeks good finds favor, But trouble will come to him who seeks *evil.*

Prosperity.

Prov 10:4 He who has a slack hand becomes poor, But the hand of the diligent makes rich.

Prov 13:4 The soul of a lazy *man* desires, and *has* nothing; But the soul of the diligent shall be made rich.

Honor.

Prov 12:24 The hand of the diligent will rule, But the lazy *man* will be put to forced labor.

Prov 22:29 Do you see a man *who* excels in his work? He will stand before kings; He will not stand before unknown *men.*

Illustrated.

Prov 6:6–8 Go to the ant, you sluggard! Consider her ways and be wise, **7** Which, having no captain, Overseer or ruler, **8** Provides her supplies in the summer, *And* gathers her food in the harvest.

Exemplified by

Jacob.

Gen 31:40 *There* I was! In the day the drought consumed me, and the frost by night, and my sleep departed from my eyes.

Ruth.

Ruth 2:17 So she gleaned in the field until evening, and beat out what she had gleaned, and it was about an ephah of barley.

Hezekiah.

2 Chr 31:21 And in every work that he began in the service of the house of God, in the law and in the commandment, to seek his God, he did *it* with all his heart. So he prospered.

Nehemiah, etc.

Neh 4:6 So we built the wall, and the entire wall was joined together up to half its *height,* for the people had a mind to work.

The Psalmist.

Ps 119:60 I made haste, and did not delay To keep Your commandments.

The apostles.

Acts 5:42 And daily in the temple, and in every house,

they did not cease teaching and preaching Jesus *as* the Christ.

Apollos.

Acts 18:25 This man had been instructed in the way of the Lord; and being fervent in spirit, he spoke and taught accurately the things of the Lord, though he knew only the baptism of John.

Titus.

2 Cor 8:22 And we have sent with them our brother whom we have often proved diligent in many things, but now much more diligent, because of the great confidence which *we have* in you.

Paul.

1 Thess 2:9 For you remember, brethren, our labor and toil; for laboring night and day, that we might not be a burden to any of you, we preached to you the gospel of God.

Onesiphorus.

2 Tim 1:17 but when he arrived in Rome, he sought me out very zealously and found *me.*

DILIGENCE IN WORK

Commanded.

Eph 4:28 Let him who stole steal no longer, but rather let him labor, working with *his* hands what is good, that he may have something to give him who has need.

1 Thess 4:11 that you also aspire to lead a quiet life, to mind your own business, and to work with your own hands, as we commanded you,

Required of man before and after the Fall.

Gen 2:15 Then the LORD God took the man and put him in the garden of Eden to tend and keep it.

Gen 3:23 therefore the LORD God sent him out of the garden of Eden to till the ground from which he was taken.

To be suspended on the Sabbath.

Ex 20:10 but the seventh day *is* the Sabbath of the LORD your God. *In it* you shall do no work: you, nor your son, nor your daughter, nor your male servant, nor your female servant, nor your cattle, nor your stranger who *is* within your gates.

Characteristic of godly women.

Prov 31:13–31 She seeks wool and flax, And willingly works with her hands. **14** She is like the merchant ships, She brings her food from afar. **15** She also rises while it is yet night, And provides food for her household, And a portion for her maidservants. **16** She considers a field and buys it; From her profits she plants a vineyard. **17** She girds herself with strength, And strengthens her arms. **18** She perceives that her merchandise *is* good, And her lamp does not go out by night. **19** She stretches out her hands to the distaff, And her hand holds the spindle. **20** She extends her hand to the poor, Yes, she reaches out her hands to the needy. **21** She is not afraid of snow for her household, For all her household *is* clothed with scarlet. **22** She makes tapestry for herself; Her clothing *is* fine linen and purple. **23** Her husband is known in the gates, When he sits among the elders of the land. **24** She makes linen garments and sells *them,* And supplies sashes for the merchants. **25** Strength and honor *are* her clothing; She shall rejoice in time to come. **26** She opens her mouth with wisdom, And on her tongue *is* the law of kindness. **27** She watches over the ways of her household, And does not eat the bread of idleness. **28** Her children rise up and call her blessed; Her husband *also,* and he praises her: **29** "Many daughters have done well, But you excel them all." **30** Charm *is* deceitful and beauty *is* passing, But a woman *who* fears the LORD, she shall be praised. **31** Give her of the fruit of her hands, And let her own works praise her in the gates.

Early rising necessary to.

Prov 31:15 She also rises while it is yet night, And provides food for her household, And a portion for her maidservants.

Requisite to supply

Our own needs.

Acts 20:34 Yes, you yourselves know that these hands have provided for my necessities, and for those who were with me.

1 Thess 2:9 For you remember, brethren, our labor and toil; for laboring night and day, that we might not be a burden to any of you, we preached to you the gospel of God.

Needs of others.

Acts 20:35 I have shown you in every way, by laboring like this, that you must support the weak. And remember the words of the Lord Jesus, that He said, 'It is more blessed to give than to receive.' "

Eph 4:28 Let him who stole steal no longer, but rather let him labor, working with *his* hands what is good, that he may have something to give him who has need.

The lazy devoid of.

Prov 24:30–31 I went by the field of the lazy *man,* And by the vineyard of the man devoid of understanding; **31** And there it was, all overgrown with thorns; Its surface was covered with nettles; Its stone wall was broken down.

Leads to

Increase of substance.

Prov 13:11 Wealth *gained by* dishonesty will be diminished, But he who gathers by labor will increase.

Affection of relatives.

Prov 31:28 Her children rise up and call her blessed; Her husband *also,* and he praises her:

General commendation.

Prov 31:31 Give her of the fruit of her hands, And let her own works praise her in the gates.

Illustrated.

Prov 6:6–8 Go to the ant, you sluggard! Consider her ways and be wise, **7** Which, having no captain, Overseer or ruler, **8** Provides her supplies in the summer, *And* gathers her food in the harvest.

Exemplified by

Rachel.

Gen 29:9 Now while he was still speaking with them, Rachel came with her father's sheep, for she was a shepherdess.

Jacob.

Gen 31:6 And you know that with all my might I have served your father.

Jethro's daughters.

Ex 2:10 And the child grew, and she brought him to Pharaoh's daughter, and he became her son. So she called his name Moses, saying, "Because I drew him out of the water."

Ruth.

Ruth 2:2–3 So Ruth the Moabitess said to Naomi, "Please let me go to the field, and glean heads of grain after *him* in whose sight I may find favor." And she said to her, "Go, my daughter." **3** Then she left, and went and gleaned in the field after the reapers. And she happened to come to the part of the field *belonging* to Boaz, who *was* of the family of Elimelech.

Jeroboam.

1 Kin 11:28 The man Jeroboam *was* a mighty man of valor; and Solomon, seeing that the young man was industrious, made him the officer over all the labor force of the house of Joseph.

David.

1 Sam 16:11 And Samuel said to Jesse, "Are all the young men here?" Then he said, "There remains yet the youngest, and there he is, keeping the sheep." And Samuel said to Jesse, "Send and bring him. For we will not sit down till he comes here."

The Jewish elders.

Ezra 6:14–15 So the elders of the Jews built, and they prospered through the prophesying of Haggai the prophet and Zechariah the son of Iddo. And they built and finished *it,* according to the commandment of the God of Israel, and according to the command of Cyrus, Darius, and Artaxerxes king of Persia. **15** Now the temple was finished on the third day of the month of Adar, which was in the sixth year of the reign of King Darius.

Dorcas.

Acts 9:39 Then Peter arose and went with them. When he had come, they brought *him* to the upper room. And all the widows stood by him weeping, showing the tunics and garments which Dorcas had made while she was with them.

Paul.

Acts 18:3 So, because he was of the same trade, he stayed with them and worked; for by occupation they were tentmakers.

1 Cor 4:12 And we labor, working with our own hands. Being reviled, we bless; being persecuted, we endure;

DISCERNMENT

Moral insight and application of knowledge.

Phil 1:9 And this I pray, that your love may abound still more and more in knowledge and all discernment,

To differentiate between good and evil.

Heb 5:14 But solid food belongs to those who are of full age, *that is,* those who by reason of use have their senses exercised to discern both good and evil.

A plea to know.

Prov 2:3 Yes, if you cry out for discernment, *And* lift up your voice for understanding,

Regarding false doctrine.

1 Thess 5:21–22 Test all things; hold fast what is good. **22** Abstain from every form of evil.

Rev 2:2 "I know your works, your labor, your patience, and that you cannot bear those who are evil. And you have tested those who say they are apostles and are not, and have found them liars;

Believers have, regarding spiritual truth.

1 Cor 2:14 But the natural man does not receive the things of the Spirit of God, for they are foolishness to him; nor can he know *them*, because they are spiritually discerned.

Gift of.

1 Cor 12:10 to another the working of miracles, to another prophecy, to another discerning of spirits, to another *different* kinds of tongues, to another the interpretation of tongues.

DISEASES

Often sent as punishment.

Deut 28:21 The LORD will make the plague cling to you until He has consumed you from the land which you are going to possess.

John 5:14 Afterward Jesus found him in the temple, and said to him, "See, you have been made well. Sin no more, lest a worse thing come upon you."

Often brought from other countries.

Deut 7:15 And the LORD will take away from you all sickness, and will afflict you with none of the terrible diseases of Egypt which you have known, but will lay *them* on all those who hate you.

Often through Satan.

1 Sam 16:14–16 But the Spirit of the LORD departed from Saul, and a distressing spirit from the LORD troubled him. 15 And Saul's servants said to him, "Surely, a distressing spirit from God is troubling you. 16 Let our master now command your servants, *who are* before you, to seek out a man *who is* a skillful player on the harp. And it shall be that he will play it with his hand when the distressing spirit from God is upon you, and you shall be well."

Job 2:7 So Satan went out from the presence of the LORD, and struck Job with painful boils from the sole of his foot to the crown of his head.

Regarded as visitations.

Job 2:7–10 So Satan went out from the presence of the LORD, and struck Job with painful boils from the sole of his foot to the crown of his head. 8 And he took for himself a potsherd with which to scrape himself while he sat in the midst of the ashes. 9 Then his wife said to him, "Do you still hold fast to your integrity? Curse God and die!" 10 But he said to her, "You speak as one of the foolish women speaks. Shall we indeed accept good from God, and shall we not accept adversity?" In all this Job did not sin with his lips.

Ps 38:2 For Your arrows pierce me deeply, And Your hand presses me down.

Ps 38:7 For my loins are full of inflammation, And *there is* no soundness in my flesh.

Intemperance a cause of.

Hos 7:5 In the day of our king Princes have made *him* sick, inflamed with wine; He stretched out his hand with scoffers.

Sins of youth a cause of.

Job 20:11 His bones are full of his youthful vigor, But it will lie down with him in the dust.

Overexcitement a cause of.

Dan 8:27 And I, Daniel, fainted and was sick for days; afterward I arose and went about the king's business. I was astonished by the vision, but no one understood it.

Were many and varied.

Matt 4:24 Then His fame went throughout all Syria; and they brought to Him all sick people who were afflicted with various diseases and torments, and those who were demon-possessed, epileptics, and paralytics; and He healed them.

Those mentioned in Scripture

Atrophy.

Job 16:8 You have shriveled me up, And it is a witness *against me*; My leanness rises up against me *And* bears witness to my face.

Job 19:20 My bone clings to my skin and to my flesh, And I have escaped by the skin of my teeth.

Blindness.

Job 29:15 I *was* eyes to the blind, And I *was* feet to the lame.

Matt 9:27 When Jesus departed from there, two blind men followed Him, crying out and saying, "Son of David, have mercy on us!"

Boils and sores.

Ex 9:10 Then they took ashes from the furnace and stood before Pharaoh, and Moses scattered *them* toward heaven. And *they* caused boils that break out in sores on man and beast.

2 Kin 20:7 Then Isaiah said, "Take a lump of figs." So they took and laid *it* on the boil, and he recovered.

Is 1:6 From the sole of the foot even to the head, *There is* no soundness in it, *But* wounds and bruises and putrefying sores; They have not been closed or bound up, Or soothed with ointment.

Luke 16:20 But there was a certain beggar named Lazarus, full of sores, who was laid at his gate,

Consumption and fever.

Lev 26:16 I also will do this to you: I will even appoint terror over you, wasting disease and fever which shall consume the eyes and cause sorrow of heart. And you shall sow your seed in vain, for your enemies shall eat it.

Deut 28:22 The LORD will strike you with consumption, with fever, with inflammation, with severe burning fever, with the sword, with scorching, and with mildew; they shall pursue you until you perish.

Matt 8:14 Now when Jesus had come into Peter's house, He saw his wife's mother lying sick with a fever.

Demon possession.

Matt 15:22 And behold, a woman of Canaan came from that region and cried out to Him, saying, "Have mercy on me, O Lord, Son of David! My daughter is severely demon-possessed."

Mark 5:15 Then they came to Jesus, and saw the one *who had been* demon-possessed and had the legion, sitting and clothed and in his right mind. And they were afraid.

Deafness.

Ps 38:13 But I, like a deaf *man*, do not hear; And *I am* like a mute *who* does not open his mouth.

Mark 7:32 Then they brought to Him one who was deaf and had an impediment in his speech, and they begged Him to put His hand on him.

Debility.

Ps 102:23 He weakened my strength in the way; He shortened my days.

Ezek 7:17 Every hand will be feeble, And every knee will be *as* weak *as* water.

Depression.

1 Sam 16:14 But the Spirit of the LORD departed from Saul, and a distressing spirit from the LORD troubled him.

Dropsy.

Luke 14:2 And behold, there was a certain man before Him who had dropsy.

Dysentery.

2 Chr 21:12–19 And a letter came to him from Elijah the prophet, saying, Thus says the LORD God of your father David: Because you have not walked in the ways of Jehoshaphat your father, or in the ways of Asa king of Judah, **13** but have walked in the way of the kings of Israel, and have made Judah and the inhabitants of Jerusalem to play the harlot like the harlotry of the house of Ahab, and also have killed your brothers, those of your father's household, *who were* better than yourself, **14** behold, the LORD will strike your people with a serious affliction—your children, your wives, and all your possessions; **15** and you *will become* very sick with a disease of your intestines, until your intestines come out by reason of the sickness, day by day. **16** Moreover the LORD stirred up against Jehoram the spirit of the Philistines and the Arabians who *were* near the Ethiopians. **17** And they came up into Judah and invaded it, and carried away all the possessions that were found in the king's house, and also his sons and his wives, so that there was not a son left to him except Jehoahaz, the youngest of his sons. **18** After all this the LORD struck him in his intestines with an incurable disease. **19** Then it happened in the course of time, after the end of two years, that his intestines came out because of his sickness; so he died in severe pain. And his people made no burning for him, like the burning for his fathers.

Acts 28:8 And it happened that the father of Publius lay sick of a fever and dysentery. Paul went in to him and prayed, and he laid his hands on him and healed him.

Epilepsy.

Matt 4:24 Then His fame went throughout all Syria; and they brought to Him all sick people who were afflicted with various diseases and torments, and those who were demon-possessed, epileptics, and paralytics; and He healed them.

Matt 17:15 "Lord, have mercy on my son, for he is an epileptic and suffers severely; for he often falls into the fire and often into the water.

Hemorrhage.

Matt 9:20 And suddenly, a woman who had a flow of blood for twelve years came from behind and touched the hem of His garment.

Itch.

Deut 28:27 The LORD will strike you with the boils of Egypt, with tumors, with the scab, and with the itch, from which you cannot be healed.

Inflammation.

Deut 28:22 The LORD will strike you with consumption, with fever, with inflammation, with severe burning fever, with the sword, with scorching, and with mildew; they shall pursue you until you perish.

Lameness.

2 Sam 4:4 Jonathan, Saul's son, had a son *who was* lame in *his* feet. He was five years old when the news about Saul and Jonathan came from Jezreel; and his nurse took him up and fled. And it happened, as she made haste to flee, that he fell and became lame. His name *was* Mephibosheth.

2 Chr 16:12 And in the thirty-ninth year of his reign, Asa became diseased in his feet, and his malady was severe; yet in his disease he did not seek the LORD, but the physicians.

Leprosy.

Lev 13:2 "When a man has on the skin of his body a swelling, a scab, or a bright spot, and it becomes on the skin of his body *like* a leprous sore, then he shall be brought to Aaron the priest or to one of his sons the priests.

2 Kin 5:1 Now Naaman, commander of the army of the king of Syria, was a great and honorable man in the eyes of his master, because by him the LORD had given victory to Syria. He was also a mighty man of valor, *but* a leper.

Loss of appetite.

Job 33:20 So that his life abhors bread, And his soul succulent food.

Ps 107:18 Their soul abhorred all manner of food, And they drew near to the gates of death.

Plague.

Num 11:33 But while the meat *was* still between their teeth, before it was chewed, the wrath of the LORD was aroused against the people, and the LORD struck the people with a very great plague.

2 Sam 24:15 So the LORD sent a plague upon Israel from the morning till the appointed time. From Dan to Beersheba seventy thousand men of the people died.

2 Sam 24:21 Then Araunah said, "Why has my lord the king come to his servant?" And David said, "To buy the threshing floor from you, to build an altar to the LORD, that the plague may be withdrawn from the people."

2 Sam 24:25 And David built there an altar to the LORD, and offered burnt offerings and peace offerings. So the LORD heeded the prayers for the land, and the plague was withdrawn from Israel.

Paralysis.

Matt 8:6 saying, "Lord, my servant is lying at home paralyzed, dreadfully tormented."

Matt 9:2 Then behold, they brought to Him a paralytic

lying on a bed. When Jesus saw their faith, He said to the paralytic, "Son, be of good cheer; your sins are forgiven you."

Scab.

Deut 28:27 The LORD will strike you with the boils of Egypt, with tumors, with the scab, and with the itch, from which you cannot be healed.

Speech impairment.

Prov 31:8 Open your mouth for the speechless, In the cause of all *who are* appointed to die.

Matt 9:32 As they went out, behold, they brought to Him a man, mute and demon-possessed.

Mark 7:32 Then they brought to Him one who was deaf and had an impediment in his speech, and they begged Him to put His hand on him.

Sunstroke.

2 Kin 4:18–20 And the child grew. Now it happened one day that he went out to his father, to the reapers. **19** And he said to his father, "My head, my head!" So he said to a servant, "Carry him to his mother." **20** When he had taken him and brought him to his mother, he sat on her knees till noon, and *then* died.

Is 49:10 They shall neither hunger nor thirst, Neither heat nor sun shall strike them; For He who has mercy on them will lead them, Even by the springs of water He will guide them.

Tumors.

Deut 28:27 The LORD will strike you with the boils of Egypt, with tumors, with the scab, and with the itch, from which you cannot be healed.

1 Sam 5:6 But the hand of the LORD was heavy on the people of Ashdod, and He ravaged them and struck them with tumors, *both* Ashdod and its territory.

1 Sam 5:12 And the men who did not die were stricken with the tumors, and the cry of the city went up to heaven.

Worms.

Acts 12:23 Then immediately an angel of the Lord struck him, because he did not give glory to God. And he was eaten by worms and died.

Children subject to.

2 Sam 12:15 Then Nathan departed to his house. And the LORD struck the child that Uriah's wife bore to David, and it became ill.

1 Kin 17:17 Now it happened after these things *that* the son of the woman who owned the house became sick. And his sickness was so serious that there was no breath left in him.

Frequently were

Loathsome.

Ps 38:7 For my loins are full of inflammation, And *there is* no soundness in my flesh.

Ps 41:8 "An evil disease," *they say*, "clings to him. And *now* that he lies down, he will rise up no more."

Painful.

2 Chr 21:15 and you *will become* very sick with a disease of your intestines, until your intestines come out by reason of the sickness, day by day.

Job 33:19 "*Man* is also chastened with pain on his bed, And with strong *pain* in many of his bones,

Prolonged.

Deut 28:59 then the LORD will bring upon you and your descendants extraordinary plagues—great and prolonged plagues—and serious and prolonged sicknesses.

John 5:5 Now a certain man was there who had an infirmity thirty-eight years.

Luke 13:16 So ought not this woman, being a daughter of Abraham, whom Satan has bound—think of it—for eighteen years, be loosed from this bond on the Sabbath?"

Complicated.

Deut 28:60–61 Moreover He will bring back on you all the diseases of Egypt, of which you were afraid, and they shall cling to you. **61** Also every sickness and every plague, which *is* not written in this Book of the Law, will the LORD bring upon you until you are destroyed.

Acts 28:8 And it happened that the father of Publius lay sick of a fever and dysentery. Paul went in to him and prayed, and he laid his hands on him and healed him.

Incurable.

2 Chr 21:18 After all this the LORD struck him in his intestines with an incurable disease.

Jer 14:19 Have You utterly rejected Judah? Has Your soul loathed Zion? Why have You stricken us so that *there is* no healing for us? We looked for peace, but *there was* no good; And for the time of healing, and there was trouble.

Physicians undertook the cure of.

Jer 8:22 *Is there* no balm in Gilead, *Is there* no physician there? Why then is there no recovery For the health of the daughter of my people?

Matt 9:12 When Jesus heard *that*, He said to them, "Those who are well have no need of a physician, but those who are sick.

Luke 4:23 He said to them, "You will surely say this proverb to Me, 'Physician, heal yourself! Whatever we have heard done in Capernaum, do also here in Your country.' "

Medicine used for curing.

Prov 17:22 A merry heart does good, *like* medicine, But a broken spirit dries the bones.

Is 1:6 From the sole of the foot even to the head, *There is* no soundness in it, *But* wounds and bruises and putrefying sores; They have not been closed or bound up, Or soothed with ointment.

Art of curing, defective.

Job 13:4 But you forgers of lies, You *are* all worthless physicians.

Mark 5:26 and had suffered many things from many physicians. She had spent all that she had and was no better, but rather grew worse.

God often entreated to cure.

2 Sam 12:16 David therefore pleaded with God for the child, and David fasted and went in and lay all night on the ground.

2 Kin 20:1–3 In those days Hezekiah was sick and near death. And Isaiah the prophet, the son of Amoz, went to him and said to him, "Thus says the LORD:

'Set your house in order, for you shall die, and not live.' " 2 Then he turned his face toward the wall, and prayed to the LORD, saying, 3 "Remember now, O LORD, I pray, how I have walked before You in truth and with a loyal heart, and have done *what was good* in Your sight." And Hezekiah wept bitterly.

Ps 6:2 Have mercy on me, O LORD, for I *am* weak; O LORD, heal me, for my bones are troubled.

James 5:14 Is anyone among you sick? Let him call for the elders of the church, and let them pray over him, anointing him with oil in the name of the Lord.

Not looking to God in, condemned.

2 Chr 16:12 And in the thirty-ninth year of his reign, Asa became diseased in his feet, and his malady was severe; yet in his disease he did not seek the LORD, but the physicians.

Those afflicted with, were

Anointed.

Mark 6:13 And they cast out many demons, and anointed with oil many who were sick, and healed *them.*

Often laid in the streets to receive advice from passers by.

Mark 6:56 Wherever He entered, into villages, cities, or the country, they laid the sick in the marketplaces, and begged Him that they might just touch the hem of His garment. And as many as touched Him were made well.

Acts 5:15 so that they brought the sick out into the streets and laid *them* on beds and couches, that at least the shadow of Peter passing by might fall on some of them.

Often divinely supported.

Ps 41:3 The LORD will strengthen him on his bed of illness; You will sustain him on his sickbed.

Often divinely cured.

2 Kin 20:5 "Return and tell Hezekiah the leader of My people, 'Thus says the LORD, the God of David your father: "I have heard your prayer, I have seen your tears; surely I will heal you. On the third day you shall go up to the house of the LORD.

Illustrative of sin.

Is 1:5 Why should you be stricken again? You will revolt more and more. The whole head is sick, And the whole heart faints.

DISOBEDIENCE TO GOD

Provokes His anger.

Ps 78:10 They did not keep the covenant of God; They refused to walk in His law,

Ps 78:40 How often they provoked Him in the wilderness, *And* grieved Him in the desert!

Is 3:8 For Jerusalem stumbled, And Judah is fallen, Because their tongue and their doings *Are* against the LORD, To provoke the eyes of His glory.

Forfeits His promised blessings.

Josh 5:6 For the children of Israel walked forty years in the wilderness, till all the people *who were* men of war, who came out of Egypt, were consumed, because they did not obey the voice of the LORD—to whom the LORD swore that He would not show them the land which the LORD had sworn to their fathers

that He would give us, "a land flowing with milk and honey."

1 Sam 2:30 Therefore the LORD God of Israel says: 'I said indeed *that* your house and the house of your father would walk before Me forever.' But now the LORD says: 'Far be it from Me; for those who honor Me I will honor, and those who despise Me shall be lightly esteemed.

1 Sam 13:14 But now your kingdom shall not continue. The LORD has sought for Himself a man after His own heart, and the LORD has commanded him *to be* commander over His people, because you have not kept what the LORD commanded you."

Jer 18:10 if it does evil in My sight so that it does not obey My voice, then I will relent concerning the good with which I said I would benefit it.

Brings a curse.

Deut 11:28 and the curse, if you do not obey the commandments of the LORD your God, but turn aside from the way which I command you today, to go after other gods which you have not known.

Deut 28:15 "But it shall come to pass, if you do not obey the voice of the LORD your God, to observe carefully all His commandments and His statutes which I command you today, that all these curses will come upon you and overtake you:

A characteristic of the wicked.

Jer 2:21 Yet I had planted you a noble vine, a seed of highest quality. How then have you turned before Me Into the degenerate plant of an alien vine?

Eph 2:2 in which you once walked according to the course of this world, according to the prince of the power of the air, the spirit who now works in the sons of disobedience,

Titus 1:16 They profess to know God, but in works they deny Him, being abominable, disobedient, and disqualified for every good work.

Titus 3:3 For we ourselves were also once foolish, disobedient, deceived, serving various lusts and pleasures, living in malice and envy, hateful and hating one another.

Heinousness of, illustrated.

Jer 35:14 "The words of Jonadab the son of Rechab, which he commanded his sons, not to drink wine, are performed; for to this day they drink none, and obey their father's commandment. But although I have spoken to you, rising early and speaking, you did not obey Me.

Men prone to excuse.

Gen 3:12–13 Then the man said, "The woman whom You gave *to be* with me, she gave me of the tree, and I ate." 13 And the LORD God said to the woman, "What *is* this you have done?" The woman said, "The serpent deceived me, and I ate."

Shall be punished.

Is 42:24–25 Who gave Jacob for plunder, and Israel to the robbers? Was it not the LORD, He against whom we have sinned? For they would not walk in His ways, Nor were they obedient to His law. 25 Therefore He has poured on him the fury of His anger And the strength of battle; It has set him on fire all around, Yet he did not know; And it burned him, Yet he did not take *it* to heart.

Heb 2:2 For if the word spoken through angels proved steadfast, and every transgression and disobedience received a just reward,

Men acknowledge the punishment of, to be just.

Neh 9:32–33 "Now therefore, our God, The great, the mighty, and awesome God, Who keeps covenant and mercy: Do not let all the trouble seem small before You That has come upon us, Our kings and our princes, Our priests and our prophets, Our fathers and on all Your people, From the days of the kings of Assyria until this day. 33 However You *are* just in all that has befallen us; For You have dealt faithfully, But we have done wickedly.

Dan 9:10–11 We have not obeyed the voice of the LORD our God, to walk in His laws, which He set before us by His servants the prophets. 11 Yes, all Israel has transgressed Your law, and has departed so as not to obey Your voice; therefore the curse and the oath written in the Law of Moses the servant of God have been poured out on us, because we have sinned against Him.

Dan 9:14 Therefore the LORD has kept the disaster in mind, and brought it upon us; for the LORD our God *is* righteous in all the works which He does, though we have not obeyed His voice.

Warnings against.

1 Sam 12:15 However, if you do not obey the voice of the LORD, but rebel against the commandment of the LORD, then the hand of the LORD will be against you, as *it was* against your fathers.

Jer 12:17 But if they do not obey, I will utterly pluck up and destroy that nation," says the LORD.

Bitter results of, illustrated.

Jer 9:13 And the LORD said, "Because they have forsaken My law which I set before them, and have not obeyed My voice, nor walked according to it,

Jer 9:15 therefore thus says the LORD of hosts, the God of Israel: "Behold, I will feed them, this people, with wormwood, and give them water of gall to drink.

Exemplified by

Adam and Eve.

Gen 3:6 So when the woman saw that the tree *was* good for food, that it *was* pleasant to the eyes, and a tree desirable to make *one* wise, she took of its fruit and ate. She also gave to her husband with her, and he ate.

Gen 3:11 And He said, "Who told you that you *were* naked? Have you eaten from the tree of which I commanded you that you should not eat?"

Pharaoh.

Ex 5:2 And Pharaoh said, "Who *is* the LORD, that I should obey His voice to let Israel go? I do not know the LORD, nor will I let Israel go."

Nadab and Abihu.

Lev 10:1 Then Nadab and Abihu, the sons of Aaron, each took his censer and put fire in it, put incense on it, and offered profane fire before the LORD, which He had not commanded them.

Moses and Aaron.

Num 20:8 "Take the rod; you and your brother Aaron gather the congregation together. Speak to the rock before their eyes, and it will yield its water; thus you shall bring water for them out of the rock, and give drink to the congregation and their animals."

Num 20:11 Then Moses lifted his hand and struck the rock twice with his rod; and water came out abundantly, and the congregation and their animals drank.

Num 20:24 "Aaron shall be gathered to his people, for he shall not enter the land which I have given to the children of Israel, because you rebelled against My word at the water of Meribah.

Saul.

1 Sam 28:18 Because you did not obey the voice of the LORD nor execute His fierce wrath upon Amalek, therefore the LORD has done this thing to you this day.

The prophet.

1 Kin 13:20–23 Now it happened, as they sat at the table, that the word of the LORD came to the prophet who had brought him back; 21 and he cried out to the man of God who had come from Judah, saying, "Thus says the LORD: 'Because you have disobeyed the word of the LORD, and have not kept the commandment which the LORD your God commanded you, 22 but you came back, ate bread, and drank water in the place of which *the* LORD said to you, "Eat no bread and drink no water," your corpse shall not come to the tomb of your fathers.' " 23 So it was, after he had eaten bread and after he had drunk, that he saddled the donkey for him, the prophet whom he had brought back.

Israel.

2 Kin 18:9–12 Now it came to pass in the fourth year of King Hezekiah, which *was* the seventh year of Hoshea the son of Elah, king of Israel, *that* Shalmaneser king of Assyria came up against Samaria and besieged it. 10 And at the end of three years they took it. In the sixth year of Hezekiah, that *is*, the ninth year of Hoshea king of Israel, Samaria was taken. 11 Then the king of Assyria carried Israel away captive to Assyria, and put them in Halah and by the Habor, the River of Gozan, and in the cities of the Medes, 12 because they did not obey the voice of the LORD their God, but transgressed His covenant *and* all that Moses the servant of the LORD had commanded; and they would neither hear nor do *them*.

Jonah.

Jon 1:2–3 "Arise, go to Nineveh, that great city, and cry out against it; for their wickedness has come up before Me." 3 But Jonah arose to flee to Tarshish from the presence of the LORD. He went down to Joppa, and found a ship going to Tarshish; so he paid the fare, and went down into it, to go with them to Tarshish from the presence of the LORD.

DIVINATION

An abominable practice.

Deut 18:12 For all who do these things *are* an abomination to the LORD, and because of these abominations the LORD your God drives them out from before you.

1 Sam 15:23 For rebellion *is as* the sin of witchcraft, And stubbornness *is as* iniquity and idolatry. Because you have rejected the word of the LORD, He also has rejected you from *being* king."

Practiced by

Diviners.

Deut 18:14 For these nations which you will dispossess listened to soothsayers and diviners; but as for you, the LORD your God has not appointed such for you.

Interpreters of omens.

Deut 18:10 There shall not be found among you *anyone* who makes his son or his daughter pass through the fire, *or one* who practices witchcraft, *or* a soothsayer, or one who interprets omens, or a sorcerer,

Conjurers.

Deut 18:11 or one who conjures spells, or a medium, or a spiritist, or one who calls up the dead.

Mediums and spiritists.

Deut 18:11 or one who conjures spells, or a medium, or a spiritist, or one who calls up the dead.

1 Sam 28:3 Now Samuel had died, and all Israel had lamented for him and buried him in Ramah, in his own city. And Saul had put the mediums and the spiritists out of the land.

Magicians.

Gen 41:8 Now it came to pass in the morning that his spirit was troubled, and he sent and called for all the magicians of Egypt and all its wise men. And Pharaoh told them his dreams, but *there was* no one who could interpret them for Pharaoh.

Dan 4:7 Then the magicians, the astrologers, the Chaldeans, and the soothsayers came in, and I told them the dream; but they did not make known to me its interpretation.

Astrologers.

Is 47:13 You are wearied in the multitude of your counsels; Let now the astrologers, the stargazers, *And* the monthly prognosticators Stand up and save you From what shall come upon you.

Dan 4:7 Then the magicians, the astrologers, the Chaldeans, and the soothsayers came in, and I told them the dream; but they did not make known to me its interpretation.

Sorcerers and sorceresses.

Ex 22:18 "You shall not permit a sorceress to live.

Deut 18:10 There shall not be found among you *anyone* who makes his son or his daughter pass through the fire, *or one* who practices witchcraft, *or* a soothsayer, or one who interprets omens, or a sorcerer,

Jer 27:9 Therefore do not listen to your prophets, your diviners, your dreamers, your soothsayers, or your sorcerers, who speak to you, saying, "You shall not serve the king of Babylon."

Acts 13:6 Now when they had gone through the island to Paphos, they found a certain sorcerer, a false prophet, a Jew whose name *was* Bar-Jesus,

Acts 13:8 But Elymas the sorcerer (for so his name is translated) withstood them, seeking to turn the proconsul away from the faith.

Necromancers.

Deut 18:11 or one who conjures spells, or a medium, or a spiritist, or one who calls up the dead.

Soothsayers.

Is 2:6 For You have forsaken Your people, the house of Jacob, Because they are filled with eastern ways; They *are* soothsayers like the Philistines, And they are pleased with the children of foreigners.

Jer 27:9 Therefore do not listen to your prophets, your diviners, your dreamers, your soothsayers, or your sorcerers, who speak to you, saying, "You shall not serve the king of Babylon."

Dan 2:27 Daniel answered in the presence of the king, and said, "The secret which the king has demanded, the wise *men*, the astrologers, the magicians, and the soothsayers cannot declare to the king.

False prophets.

Jer 14:14 And the LORD said to me, "The prophets prophesy lies in My name. I have not sent them, commanded them, nor spoken to them; they prophesy to you a false vision, divination, a worthless thing, and the deceit of their heart.

Ezek 13:3 Thus says the Lord GOD: "Woe to the foolish prophets, who follow their own spirit and have seen nothing!

Ezek 13:6 They have envisioned futility and false divination, saying, 'Thus says the LORD!' But the LORD has not sent them; yet they hope that the word may be confirmed.

Effected through

Enchantments.

Ex 7:11 But Pharaoh also called the wise men and the sorcerers; so the magicians of Egypt, they also did in like manner with their enchantments.

Sorcery.

Num 24:1 Now when Balaam saw that it pleased the LORD to bless Israel, he did not go as at other times, to seek to use sorcery, but he set his face toward the wilderness.

Is 47:12 "Stand now with your enchantments And the multitude of your sorceries, In which you have labored from your youth— Perhaps you will be able to profit, Perhaps you will prevail.

Acts 8:11 And they heeded him because he had astonished them with his sorceries for a long time.

Soothsaying.

2 Kin 21:6 Also he made his son pass through the fire, practiced soothsaying, used witchcraft, and consulted spiritists and mediums. He did much evil in the sight of the LORD, to provoke *Him* to anger.

Raising the dead.

1 Sam 28:11–12 Then the woman said, "Whom shall I bring up for you?" And he said, "Bring up Samuel for me." **12** When the woman saw Samuel, she cried out with a loud voice. And the woman spoke to Saul, saying, "Why have you deceived me? For you *are* Saul!"

Inspecting animal organs.

Ezek 21:21 For the king of Babylon stands at the parting of the road, at the fork of the two roads, to use divination: he shakes the arrows, he consults the images, he looks at the liver.

The flight of arrows.

Ezek 21:21–22 For the king of Babylon stands at the

parting of the road, at the fork of the two roads, to use divination: he shakes the arrows, he consults the images, he looks at the liver. 22 In his right hand is the divination for Jerusalem: to set up battering rams, to call for a slaughter, to lift the voice with shouting, to set battering rams against the gates, to heap up a *siege* mound, and to build a wall.

Cups.

Gen 44:2 Also put my cup, the silver cup, in the mouth of the sack of the youngest, and his grain money." So he did according to the word that Joseph had spoken.

Gen 44:5 Is not this *the one* from which my lord drinks, and with which he indeed practices divination? You have done evil in so doing.' "

Rods.

Hos 4:12 My people ask counsel from their wooden *idols*, And their staff informs them. For the spirit of harlotry has caused *them* to stray, And they have played the harlot against their God.

Dreams.

Jer 29:8 For thus says the LORD of hosts, the God of Israel: Do not let your prophets and your diviners who are in your midst deceive you, nor listen to your dreams which you cause to be dreamed.

Zech 10:2 For the idols speak delusion; The diviners envision lies, And tell false dreams; They comfort in vain. Therefore *the people* wend their way like sheep; They are in trouble because *there is* no shepherd.

Connected with idolatry.

2 Chr 33:5–6 And he built altars for all the host of heaven in the two courts of the house of the LORD. 6 Also he caused his sons to pass through the fire in the Valley of the Son of Hinnom; he practiced soothsaying, used witchcraft and sorcery, and consulted mediums and spiritists. He did much evil in the sight of the LORD, to provoke Him to anger.

Books of, numerous and expensive.

Acts 19:19 Also, many of those who had practiced magic brought their books together and burned *them* in the sight of all. And they counted up the value of them, and *it* totaled fifty thousand *pieces* of silver.

A lucrative employment.

Num 22:7 So the elders of Moab and the elders of Midian departed with the diviner's fee in their hand, and they came to Balaam and spoke to him the words of Balak.

Acts 16:16 Now it happened, as we went to prayer, that a certain slave girl possessed with a spirit of divination met us, who brought her masters much profit by fortune-telling.

Those who practiced,

Regarded as wise men.

Dan 2:12 For this reason the king was angry and very furious, and gave the command to destroy all the wise *men* of Babylon.

Dan 2:27 Daniel answered in the presence of the king, and said, "The secret which the king has demanded, the wise *men*, the astrologers, the magicians, and the soothsayers cannot declare to the king.

Regarded with awe.

Acts 8:9 But there was a certain man called Simon, who previously practiced sorcery in the city and astonished the people of Samaria, claiming that he was someone great,

Acts 8:11 And they heeded him because he had astonished them with his sorceries for a long time.

Consulted in difficulties.

Dan 2:2 Then the king gave the command to call the magicians, the astrologers, the sorcerers, and the Chaldeans to tell the king his dreams. So they came and stood before the king.

Dan 2:4–7 Therefore I issued a decree to bring in all the wise *men* of Babylon before me, that they might make known to me the interpretation of the dream. 7 Then the magicians, the astrologers, the Chaldeans, and the soothsayers came in, and I told them the dream; but they did not make known to me its interpretation.

Used mysterious words and gestures.

Is 8:19 And when they say to you, "Seek those who are mediums and wizards, who whisper and mutter," should not a people seek their God? *Should they seek* the dead on behalf of the living?

A system of fraud.

Ezek 13:6–7 They have envisioned futility and false divination, saying, 'Thus says the LORD!' But the LORD has not sent them; yet they hope that the word may be confirmed. 7 Have you not seen a futile vision, and have you not spoken false divination? You say, 'The LORD says,' but I have not spoken."

Jer 29:8 For thus says the LORD of hosts, the God of Israel: Do not let your prophets and your diviners who are in your midst deceive you, nor listen to your dreams which you cause to be dreamed.

Frustrated by God.

Is 44:25 Who frustrates the signs of the babblers, And drives diviners mad; Who turns wise men backward, And makes their knowledge foolishness;

Could not injure the Lord's people.

Num 23:23 "For *there is* no sorcery against Jacob, Nor any divination against Israel. It now must be said of Jacob And of Israel, 'Oh, what God has done!'

The law

Forbade to the Israelites the practice of.

Lev 19:26 'You shall not eat *anything* with the blood, nor shall you practice divination or soothsaying.

Deut 18:10–11 There shall not be found among you *anyone* who makes his son or his daughter pass through the fire, *or one* who practices witchcraft, *or a* soothsayer, or one who interprets omens, or a sorcerer, 11 or one who conjures spells, or a medium, or a spiritist, or one who calls up the dead.

Forbade seeking after.

Lev 19:31 'Give no regard to mediums and familiar spirits; do not seek after them, to be defiled by them: I *am* the LORD your God.

Deut 18:14 For these nations which you will dispossess listened to soothsayers and diviners; but as for you, the LORD your God has not appointed such for you.

Punished with death those who practiced.

Ex 22:18 "You shall not permit a sorceress to live.

Lev 20:27 'A man or a woman who is a medium, or who

has familiar spirits, shall surely be put to death; they shall stone them with stones. Their blood *shall be* upon them.' "

Punished those who turned to.

Lev 20:6 'And the person who turns to mediums and familiar spirits, to prostitute himself with them, I will set My face against that person and cut him off from his people.

The Jews sometimes succumbed to.

2 Kin 17:17 And they caused their sons and daughters to pass through the fire, practiced witchcraft and soothsaying, and sold themselves to do evil in the sight of the LORD, to provoke Him to anger.

Is 2:6 For You have forsaken Your people, the house of Jacob, Because they are filled with eastern ways; They *are* soothsayers like the Philistines, And they are pleased with the children of foreigners.

DIVISIONS

Forbidden in the church.

1 Cor 1:10–13 Now I plead with you, brethren, by the name of our Lord Jesus Christ, that you all speak the same thing, and *that* there be no divisions among you, but *that* you be perfectly joined together in the same mind and in the same judgment. **11** For it has been declared to me concerning you, my brethren, by those of Chloe's *household*, that there are contentions among you. **12** Now I say this, that each of you says, "I am of Paul," or "I am of Apollos," or "I am of Cephas," or "I am of Christ." **13** Is Christ divided? Was Paul crucified for you? Or were you baptized in the name of Paul?

1 Cor 11:18 For first of all, when you come together as a church, I hear that there are divisions among you, and in part I believe it.

1 Cor 12:24–25 but our presentable *parts* have no need. But God composed the body, having given greater honor to that *part* which lacks it, **25** that there should be no schism in the body, but *that* the members should have the same care for one another.

Are contrary to the

Unity of Christ.

1 Cor 1:13 Is Christ divided? Was Paul crucified for you? Or were you baptized in the name of Paul?

1 Cor 12:13 For by one Spirit we were all baptized into one body—whether Jews or Greeks, whether slaves or free—and have all been made to drink into one Spirit.

Desire of Christ.

John 17:21–23 that they all may be one, as You, Father, *are* in Me, and I in You; that they also may be one in Us, that the world may believe that You sent Me. **22** And the glory which You gave Me I have given them, that they may be one just as We are one: **23** I in them, and You in Me; that they may be made perfect in one, and that the world may know that You have sent Me, and have loved them as You have loved Me.

Purpose of Christ.

John 10:16 And other sheep I have which are not of this fold; them also I must bring, and they will hear My voice; and there will be one flock *and* one shepherd.

Spirit of the church.

1 Cor 11:16 But if anyone seems to be contentious, we have no such custom, nor *do* the churches of God.

Are proof of a carnal spirit.

1 Cor 3:3 for you are still carnal. For where *there are* envy, strife, and divisions among you, are you not carnal and behaving like *mere* men?

Believers should avoid those who cause.

Rom 16:17 Now I urge you, brethren, note those who cause divisions and offenses, contrary to the doctrine which you learned, and avoid them.

Evil of, illustrated.

Matt 12:25 But Jesus knew their thoughts, and said to them: "Every kingdom divided against itself is brought to desolation, and every city or house divided against itself will not stand.

DIVORCE

Law of marriage is against.

Gen 2:24 Therefore a man shall leave his father and mother and be joined to his wife, and they shall become one flesh.

Matt 19:6 So then, they are no longer two but one flesh. Therefore what God has joined together, let not man separate."

Permitted

By the Mosaic law.

Deut 24:1 "When a man takes a wife and marries her, and it happens that she finds no favor in his eyes because he has found some uncleanness in her, and he writes her a certificate of divorce, puts *it* in her hand, and sends her out of his house,

On account of hardness of heart.

Matt 19:8 He said to them, "Moses, because of the hardness of your hearts, permitted you to divorce your wives, but from the beginning it was not so.

Often sought by the Jews.

Mic 2:9 The women of My people you cast out From their pleasant houses; From their children You have taken away My glory forever.

Mal 2:14 Yet you say, "For what reason?" Because the LORD has been witness Between you and the wife of your youth, With whom you have dealt treacherously; Yet she is your companion And your wife by covenant.

Sought on slight grounds.

Matt 5:31 "Furthermore it has been said, 'Whoever divorces his wife, let him give her a certificate of divorce.'

Matt 19:3 The Pharisees also came to Him, testing Him, and saying to Him, "Is it lawful for a man to divorce his wife for *just* any reason?"

Not allowed to those who falsely accused their wives.

Deut 22:18–19 Then the elders of that city shall take that man and punish him; **19** and they shall fine him one hundred *shekels* of silver and give *them* to the father of the young woman, because he has brought a bad name on a virgin of Israel. And she shall be his wife; he cannot divorce her all his days.

Women

Could obtain.

Prov 2:17 Who forsakes the companion of her youth, And forgets the covenant of her God.

Mark 10:12 And if a woman divorces her husband and marries another, she commits adultery."

Could marry after obtaining.

Deut 24:2 when she has departed from his house, and goes and becomes another man's *wife*,

Responsible for vows following.

Num 30:9 "Also any vow of a widow or a divorced woman, by which she has bound herself, shall stand against her.

Married after, could not return to first husband.

Deut 24:3–4 *if* the latter husband detests her and writes her a certificate of divorce, puts *it* in her hand, and sends her out of his house, or if the latter husband dies who took her as his wife, 4 *then* her former husband who divorced her must not take her back to be his wife after she has been defiled; for that *is* an abomination before the LORD, and you shall not bring sin on the land which the LORD your God is giving you *as* an inheritance.

Jer 3:1 "They say, 'If a man divorces his wife, And she goes from him And becomes another man's, May he return to her again?' Would not that land be greatly polluted? But you have played the harlot with many lovers; Yet return to Me," says the LORD.

Afflicted by.

Is 54:4 "Do not fear, for you will not be ashamed; Neither be disgraced, for you will not be put to shame; For you will forget the shame of your youth, And will not remember the reproach of your widowhood anymore.

Is 54:6 For the LORD has called you Like a woman forsaken and grieved in spirit, Like a youthful wife when you were refused," Says your God.

Priests not to marry women after.

Lev 21:14 A widow or a divorced woman or a defiled woman *or* a harlot—these he shall not marry; but he shall take a virgin of his own people as wife.

Of servants, regulated by law.

Ex 21:7 "And if a man sells his daughter to be a female slave, she shall not go out as the male slaves do.

Ex 21:11 And if he does not do these three for her, then she shall go out free, without *paying* money.

Of captives, regulated by law.

Deut 21:13–14 She shall put off the clothes of her captivity, remain in your house, and mourn her father and her mother a full month; after that you may go in to her and be her husband, and she shall be your wife. 14 And it shall be, if you have no delight in her, then you shall set her free, but you certainly shall not sell her for money; you shall not treat her brutally, because you have humbled her.

Forced on those who had idolatrous wives.

Neh 13:23 In those days I also saw Jews *who* had married women of Ashdod, Ammon, *and* Moab.

Neh 13:30 Thus I cleansed them of everything pagan. I also assigned duties to the priests and the Levites, each to his service,

Cf. Ezra 10:2–17

Jews condemned for love of.

Mal 2:14–16 Yet you say, "For what reason?" Because the LORD has been witness Between you and the wife of your youth, With whom you have dealt treacherously; Yet she is your companion And your wife by covenant. 15 But did He not make *them* one, Having a remnant of the Spirit? And why one? He seeks godly offspring. Therefore take heed to your spirit, And let none deal treacherously with the wife of his youth. 16 "For the LORD God of Israel says That He hates divorce, For it covers one's garment with violence," Says the LORD of hosts. "Therefore take heed to your spirit, That you do not deal treacherously."

Forbidden by Christ except for adultery.

Matt 5:32 But I say to you that whoever divorces his wife for any reason except sexual immorality causes her to commit adultery; and whoever marries a woman who is divorced commits adultery.

Matt 19:9 And I say to you, whoever divorces his wife, except for sexual immorality, and marries another, commits adultery; and whoever marries her who is divorced commits adultery."

Prohibition of, offended the Jews.

Matt 19:10 His disciples said to Him, "If such is the case of the man with *his* wife, it is better not to marry."

Illustrative of God's casting off the Jews.

Is 50:1 Thus says the LORD: "Where *is* the certificate of your mother's divorce, Whom I have put away? Or which of My creditors *is it* to whom I have sold you? For your iniquities you have sold yourselves, And for your transgressions your mother has been put away.

Jer 3:8 Then I saw that for all the causes for which backsliding Israel had committed adultery, I had put her away and given her a certificate of divorce; yet her treacherous sister Judah did not fear, but went and played the harlot also.

DOCTRINES, FALSE

Destructive to faith.

2 Tim 2:18 who have strayed concerning the truth, saying that the resurrection is already past; and they overthrow the faith of some.

Hateful to God.

Rev 2:14–15 But I have a few things against you, because you have there those who hold the doctrine of Balaam, who taught Balak to put a stumbling block before the children of Israel, to eat things sacrificed to idols, and to commit sexual immorality. 15 Thus you also have those who hold the doctrine of the Nicolaitans, which thing I hate.

Unprofitable and useless.

Titus 3:9 But avoid foolish disputes, genealogies, contentions, and strivings about the law; for they are unprofitable and useless.

Heb 13:9 Do not be carried about with various and strange doctrines. For *it is* good that the heart be established by grace, not with foods which have not profited those who have been occupied with them.

Should be avoided by

Ministers.

1 Tim 1:4 nor give heed to fables and endless genealogies, which cause disputes rather than godly edification which is in faith.

1 Tim 6:20 O Timothy! Guard what was committed to your trust, avoiding the profane *and* idle babblings and contradictions of what is falsely called knowledge—

Believers.

Eph 4:14 that we should no longer be children, tossed to and fro and carried about with every wind of doctrine, by the trickery of men, in the cunning craftiness of deceitful plotting,

Col 2:8 Beware lest anyone cheat you through philosophy and empty deceit, according to the tradition of men, according to the basic principles of the world, and not according to Christ.

All men.

Jer 23:16 Thus says the LORD of hosts: "Do not listen to the words of the prophets who prophesy to you. They make you worthless; They speak a vision of their own heart, Not from the mouth of the LORD.

Jer 29:8 For thus says the LORD of hosts, the God of Israel: Do not let your prophets and your diviners who are in your midst deceive you, nor listen to your dreams which you cause to be dreamed.

The wicked love to believe.

2 Thess 2:11 And for this reason God will send them strong delusion, that they should believe the lie,

2 Tim 4:3–4 For the time will come when they will not endure sound doctrine, but according to their own desires, *because* they have itching ears, they will heap up for themselves teachers; 4 and they will turn *their* ears away from the truth, and be turned aside to fables.

Teachers of,

Not to be received.

2 John 1:10 If anyone comes to you and does not bring this doctrine, do not receive him into your house nor greet him;

Should be avoided.

Rom 16:17–18 Now I urge you, brethren, note those who cause divisions and offenses, contrary to the doctrine which you learned, and avoid them. **18** For those who are such do not serve our Lord Jesus Christ, but their own belly, and by smooth words and flattering speech deceive the hearts of the simple.

Bring reproach on the truth.

2 Pet 2:2 And many will follow their destructive ways, because of whom the way of truth will be blasphemed.

Speak perverse things.

Acts 20:30 Also from among yourselves men will rise up, speaking perverse things, to draw away the disciples after themselves.

Attract many.

2 Pet 2:2 And many will follow their destructive ways, because of whom the way of truth will be blasphemed.

Deceive many.

Matt 24:5 For many will come in My name, saying, 'I am the Christ,' and will deceive many.

Shall abound in the latter days.

1 Tim 4:1 Now the Spirit expressly says that in latter times some will depart from the faith, giving heed to deceiving spirits and doctrines of demons,

Pervert the gospel of Christ.

Gal 1:6–7 I marvel that you are turning away so soon from Him who called you in the grace of Christ, to a different gospel, **7** which is not another; but there are some who trouble you and want to pervert the gospel of Christ.

Shall be exposed.

2 Tim 3:9 but they will progress no further, for their folly will be manifest to all, as theirs also was.

Teachers of, are described as

Cruel.

Acts 20:29 For I know this, that after my departure savage wolves will come in among you, not sparing the flock.

Deceitful.

2 Cor 11:13 For such *are* false apostles, deceitful workers, transforming themselves into apostles of Christ.

Covetous.

Titus 1:11 whose mouths must be stopped, who subvert whole households, teaching things which they ought not, for the sake of dishonest gain.

2 Pet 2:3 By covetousness they will exploit you with deceptive words; for a long time their judgment has not been idle, and their destruction does not slumber.

Ungodly.

Judg 1:4 Then Judah went up, and the LORD delivered the Canaanites and the Perizzites into their hand; and they killed ten thousand men at Bezek.

Proud and ignorant.

1 Tim 6:3–4 If anyone teaches otherwise and does not consent to wholesome words, *even* the words of our Lord Jesus Christ, and to the doctrine which accords with godliness, **4** he is proud, knowing nothing, but is obsessed with disputes and arguments over words, from which come envy, strife, reviling, evil suspicions,

Corrupt and reprobate.

2 Tim 3:8 Now as Jannes and Jambres resisted Moses, so do these also resist the truth: men of corrupt minds, disapproved concerning the faith;

Should be tested by Scripture.

Is 8:20 To the law and to the testimony! If they do not speak according to this word, *it is* because *there is* no light in them.

1 John 4:1 Beloved, do not believe every spirit, but test the spirits, whether they are of God; because many false prophets have gone out into the world.

Curse on those who teach.

Gal 1:8–9 But even if we, or an angel from heaven, preach any other gospel to you than what we have preached to you, let him be accursed. **9** As we have said before, so now I say again, if anyone preaches any other gospel to you than what you have received, let him be accursed.

Punishment on those who teach.

Mic 3:6–7 "Therefore you shall have night without vision, And you shall have darkness without divination; The sun shall go down on the prophets, And the day shall be dark for them. **7** So the seers shall be ashamed, And the diviners abashed; Indeed they shall all cover their lips; For *there is* no answer from God."

2 Pet 2:1 But there were also false prophets among the people, even as there will be false teachers among you, who will secretly bring in destructive heresies, even denying the Lord who bought them, *and* bring on themselves swift destruction.

2 Pet 2:3 By covetousness they will exploit you with deceptive words; for a long time their judgment has not been idle, and their destruction does not slumber.

DOG, THE

Despised by the Jews.

2 Sam 3:8 Then Abner became very angry at the words of Ishbosheth, and said, "*Am* I a dog's head that belongs to Judah? Today I show loyalty to the house of Saul your father, to his brothers, and to his friends, and have not delivered you into the hand of David; and you charge me today with a fault concerning this woman?

Described as

An object of abuse.

Prov 26:17 He who passes by *and* meddles in a quarrel not his own *Is like* one who takes a dog by the ears.

Unclean.

Luke 16:21 desiring to be fed with the crumbs which fell from the rich man's table. Moreover the dogs came and licked his sores.

2 Pet 2:22 But it has happened to them according to the true proverb: *"A dog returns to his own vomit,"* and, "a sow, having washed, to her wallowing in the mire."

Carnivorous.

1 Kin 14:11 The dogs shall eat whoever belongs to Jeroboam and dies in the city, and the birds of the air shall eat whoever dies in the field; for the LORD has spoken!" '

2 Kin 9:35–36 So they went to bury her, but they found no more of her than the skull and the feet and the palms of *her* hands. **36** Therefore they came back and told him. And he said, "This *is* the word of the LORD, which He spoke by His servant Elijah the Tishbite, saying, 'On the plot *of ground* at Jezreel dogs shall eat the flesh of Jezebel;

Fond of blood.

1 Kin 21:19 You shall speak to him, saying, 'Thus says the LORD: "Have you murdered and also taken possession?" ' And you shall speak to him, saying, 'Thus says the LORD: "In the place where dogs licked the blood of Naboth, dogs shall lick your blood, even yours." ' "

1 Kin 22:38 Then *someone* washed the chariot at a pool in Samaria, and the dogs licked up his blood while the harlots bathed, according to the word of the LORD which He had spoken.

Dangerous and destructive.

Ps 22:16 For dogs have surrounded Me; The congregation of the wicked has enclosed Me. They pierced My hands and My feet;

Infested cities by night.

Ps 59:14–15 And at evening they return, They growl like a dog, And go all around the city. **15** They wander up and down for food, And howl if they are not satisfied.

Nothing holy to be given to.

Matt 7:6 "Do not give what is holy to the dogs; nor cast your pearls before swine, lest they trample them under their feet, and turn and tear you in pieces.

Matt 15:26 But He answered and said, "It is not good to take the children's bread and throw *it* to the little dogs."

Things torn by beasts given to.

Ex 22:31 "And you shall be holy men to Me: you shall not eat meat torn *by beasts* in the field; you shall throw it to the dogs.

Sacrificing of, an abomination.

Is 66:3 "He who kills a bull *is as if* he slays a man; He who sacrifices a lamb, *as if* he breaks a dog's neck; He who offers a grain offering, *as if he offers* swine's blood; He who burns incense, *as if* he blesses an idol. Just as they have chosen their own ways, And their soul delights in their abominations,

Price of, not to be consecrated.

Deut 23:18 You shall not bring the wages of a harlot or the price of a dog to the house of the LORD your God for any vowed offering, for both of these *are* an abomination to the LORD your God.

When domesticated,

Employed in watching flocks.

Job 30:1 "But now they mock at me, *men* younger than I, Whose fathers I disdained to put with the dogs of my flock.

Fed with the crumbs, etc.

Matt 15:27 And she said, "Yes, Lord, yet even the little dogs eat the crumbs which fall from their masters' table."

Manner of, in drinking, alluded to.

Judg 7:5 So he brought the people down to the water. And the LORD said to Gideon, "Everyone who laps from the water with his tongue, as a dog laps, you shall set apart by himself; likewise everyone who gets down on his knees to drink."

Illustrative of

Gentiles.

Matt 15:22 And behold, a woman of Canaan came from that region and cried out to Him, saying, "Have mercy on me, O Lord, Son of David! My daughter is severely demon-possessed."

Matt 15:26 But He answered and said, "It is not good to take the children's bread and throw *it* to the little dogs."

Covetous ministers.

Is 56:11 Yes, *they are* greedy dogs *Which* never have enough. And they *are* shepherds Who cannot understand; They all look to their own way, Every one for his own gain, From his *own* territory.

Fools.

Prov 26:11 As a dog returns to his own vomit, *So* a fool repeats his folly.

Apostates.

2 Pet 2:22 But it has happened to them according to the true proverb: *"A dog returns to his own vomit,"* and, "a sow, having washed, to her wallowing in the mire."

Persecutors.

Ps 22:16 For dogs have surrounded Me; The congregation of the wicked has enclosed Me. They pierced My hands and My feet;

Ps 22:20 Deliver Me from the sword, My precious *life* from the power of the dog.

Obstinate sinners.

Matt 7:6 "Do not give what is holy to the dogs; nor cast your pearls before swine, lest they trample them under their feet, and turn and tear you in pieces.

Rev 22:15 But outside *are* dogs and sorcerers and sexually immoral and murderers and idolaters, and whoever loves and practices a lie.

False teachers.

Phil 3:2 Beware of dogs, beware of evil workers, beware of the mutilation!

(Dumb) unfaithful ministers.

Is 56:10 His watchmen *are* blind, They are all ignorant; They *are* all dumb dogs, They cannot bark; Sleeping, lying down, loving to slumber.

(Dead) the worthless person.

1 Sam 24:14 After whom has the king of Israel come out? Whom do you pursue? A dead dog? A flea?

2 Sam 9:8 Then he bowed himself, and said, "What *is* your servant, that you should look upon such a dead dog as I?"

DONKEY, THE DOMESTIC

Unclean.

Ex 13:13 But every firstborn of a donkey you shall redeem with a lamb; and if you will not redeem *it*, then you shall break its neck. And all the firstborn of man among your sons you shall redeem.

Lev 11:2–3 "Speak to the children of Israel, saying, 'These *are* the animals which you may eat among all the animals that *are* on the earth: 3 Among the animals, whatever divides the hoof, having cloven hooves *and* chewing the cud—that you may eat.

Lev 11:26 *The carcass* of any animal which divides the foot, but is not cloven-hoofed or does not chew the cud, *is* unclean to you. Everyone who touches it shall be unclean.

Described as

Not devoid of instinct.

Is 1:3 The ox knows its owner And the donkey its master's crib; *But* Israel does not know, My people do not consider."

Strong.

Gen 49:14 "Issachar is a strong donkey, Lying down between two burdens;

Fond of ease.

Gen 49:14–15 "Issachar is a strong donkey, Lying down between two burdens; 15 He saw that rest *was* good, And that the land *was* pleasant; He bowed his shoulder to bear *a burden*, And became a band of slaves.

Often fed on vine leaves.

Gen 49:11 Binding his donkey to the vine, And his donkey's colt to the choice vine, He washed his garments in wine, And his clothes in the blood of grapes.

Formed a part of patriarchal wealth.

Gen 12:16 He treated Abram well for her sake. He had sheep, oxen, male donkeys, male and female servants, female donkeys, and camels.

Gen 30:43 Thus the man became exceedingly prosperous, and had large flocks, female and male servants, and camels and donkeys.

Job 1:3 Also, his possessions were seven thousand sheep, three thousand camels, five hundred yoke of oxen, five hundred female donkeys, and a very large household, so that this man was the greatest of all the people of the East.

Job 42:12 Now the LORD blessed the latter *days* of Job more than his beginning; for he had fourteen thousand sheep, six thousand camels, one thousand yoke of oxen, and one thousand female donkeys.

Was used

In agriculture.

Is 30:6 The burden against the beasts of the South. Through a land of trouble and anguish, From which *came* the lioness and lion, The viper and fiery flying serpent, They will carry their riches on the backs of young donkeys, And their treasures on the humps of camels, To a people *who* shall not profit;

Is 30:24 Likewise the oxen and the young donkeys that work the ground Will eat cured fodder, Which has been winnowed with the shovel and fan.

For bearing burdens.

Gen 42:26 So they loaded their donkeys with the grain and departed from there.

1 Sam 25:18 Then Abigail made haste and took two hundred *loaves* of bread, two skins of wine, five sheep already dressed, five seahs of roasted *grain*, one hundred clusters of raisins, and two hundred cakes of figs, and loaded *them* on donkeys.

For riding.

Gen 22:3 So Abraham rose early in the morning and saddled his donkey, and took two of his young men with him, and Isaac his son; and he split the wood for the burnt offering, and arose and went to the place of which God had told him.

Num 22:21 So Balaam rose in the morning, saddled his donkey, and went with the princes of Moab.

In harness.

Is 21:7 And he saw a chariot *with* a pair of horsemen, A chariot of donkeys, *and* a chariot of camels, And he listened earnestly with great care.

In war.

2 Kin 7:7 Therefore they arose and fled at twilight, and left the camp intact—their tents, their horses, and their donkeys—and they fled for their lives.

2 Kin 7:10 So they went and called to the gatekeepers of the city, and told them, saying, "We went to the Syrian camp, and surprisingly no one *was* there, not a human sound—only horses and donkeys tied, and the tents intact."

Governed by a bridle.

Prov 26:3 A whip for the horse, A bridle for the donkey, And a rod for the fool's back.

Urged on with a staff.

Num 22:23 Now the donkey saw the Angel of the LORD standing in the way with His drawn sword in His hand, and the donkey turned aside out of the way and went into the field. So Balaam struck the donkey to turn her back onto the road.

Num 22:27 And when the donkey saw the Angel of the LORD, she lay down under Balaam; so Balaam's anger was aroused, and he struck the donkey with his staff.

Women often rode on.

Josh 15:18 Now it was so, when she came *to him,* that she persuaded him to ask her father for a field. So she dismounted from *her* donkey, and Caleb said to her, "What do you wish?"

1 Sam 25:20 So it was, *as* she rode on the donkey, that she went down under cover of the hill; and there were David and his men, coming down toward her, and she met them.

Persons of rank rode on.

Judg 10:3–4 After him arose Jair, a Gileadite; and he judged Israel twenty-two years. **4** Now he had thirty sons who rode on thirty donkeys; they also had thirty towns, which are called "Havoth Jair" to this day, which *are* in the land of Gilead.

2 Sam 16:2 And the king said to Ziba, "What do you mean to do with these?" So Ziba said, "The donkeys *are* for the king's household to ride on, the bread and summer fruit for the young men to eat, and the wine for those who are faint in the wilderness to drink."

Judges of Israel rode on white ones.

Judg 5:10 "Speak, you who ride on white donkeys, Who sit in judges' attire, And who walk along the road.

Young, most valued for labor.

Is 30:6 The burden against the beasts of the South. Through a land of trouble and anguish, From which *came* the lioness and lion, The viper and fiery flying serpent, They will carry their riches on the backs of young donkeys, And their treasures on the humps of camels, To a people *who* shall not profit;

Is 30:24 Likewise the oxen and the young donkeys that work the ground Will eat cured fodder, Which has been winnowed with the shovel and fan.

Trustworthy persons appointed to take care of.

Gen 36:24 These *were* the sons of Zibeon: both Ajah and Anah. This *was the* Anah who found the water in the wilderness as he pastured the donkeys of his father Zibeon.

1 Sam 9:3 Now the donkeys of Kish, Saul's father, were lost. And Kish said to his son Saul, "Please take one of the servants with you, and arise, go and look for the donkeys."

1 Chr 27:30 Obil the Ishmaelite *was* over the camels, Jehdeiah the Meronothite *was* over the donkeys,

Often taken unlawfully by corrupt rulers.

Num 16:15 Then Moses was very angry, and said to the LORD, "Do not respect their offering. I have not taken one donkey from them, nor have I hurt one of them."

1 Sam 8:16 And he will take your male servants, your female servants, your finest young men, and your donkeys, and put *them* to his work.

1 Sam 12:3 Here I am. Witness against me before the LORD and before His anointed: Whose ox have I taken, or whose donkey have I taken, or whom have I cheated? Whom have I oppressed, or from whose hand have I received *any* bribe with which to blind my eyes? I will restore *it* to you."

Later counted as an ignoble creature.

Jer 22:19 He shall be buried with the burial of a donkey, Dragged and cast out beyond the gates of Jerusalem.

Eaten during famine in Samaria.

2 Kin 6:25 And there was a great famine in Samaria; and indeed they besieged it until a donkey's head was *sold* for eighty *shekels* of silver, and one-fourth of a kab of dove droppings for five *shekels* of silver.

Laws respecting,

Not to be coveted.

Ex 20:17 "You shall not covet your neighbor's house; you shall not covet your neighbor's wife, nor his male servant, nor his female servant, nor his ox, nor his donkey, nor anything that *is* your neighbor's."

If fallen under a burden, to be assisted.

Ex 23:5 If you see the donkey of one who hates you lying under its burden, and you would refrain from helping it, you shall surely help him with it.

If astray, to be brought back to its owners or taken care of until its owners appeared.

Ex 23:4 "If you meet your enemy's ox or his donkey going astray, you shall surely bring it back to him again.

Deut 22:1–3 "You shall not see your brother's ox or his sheep going astray, and hide yourself from them; you shall certainly bring them back to your brother. **2** And if your brother *is* not near you, or if you do not know him, then you shall bring it to your own house, and it shall remain with you until your brother seeks it; then you shall restore it to him. **3** You shall do the same with his donkey, and so shall you do with his garment; with any lost thing of your brother's, which he has lost and you have found, you shall do likewise; you must not hide yourself.

Not to be yoked with an ox.

Deut 22:10 "You shall not plow with an ox and a donkey together.

To enjoy the rest of the Sabbath.

Deut 5:14 but the seventh day *is* the Sabbath of the LORD your God. *In it* you shall do no work: you, nor your son, nor your daughter, nor your male servant, nor your female servant, nor your ox, nor your donkey, nor any of your cattle, nor your stranger who *is* within your gates, that your male servant and your female servant may rest as well as you.

Firstborn of, if not redeemed, to have its neck broken.

Ex 13:13 But every firstborn of a donkey you shall redeem with a lamb; and if you will not redeem *it,* then you shall break its neck. And all the firstborn of man among your sons you shall redeem.

Ex 34:20 But the firstborn of a donkey you shall redeem with a lamb. And if you will not redeem *him,* then you shall break his neck. All the firstborn of your sons you shall redeem. "And none shall appear before Me empty-handed.

Christ entered Jerusalem on.

Zech 9:9 "Rejoice greatly, O daughter of Zion! Shout, O daughter of Jerusalem! Behold, your King is coming to you; He *is* just and having salvation, Lowly and riding on a donkey, A colt, the foal of a donkey.

John 12:14 Then Jesus, when He had found a young donkey, sat on it; as it is written:

Miracles connected with

Mouth of Balaam's opened to speak.

Num 22:28 Then the LORD opened the mouth of the donkey, and she said to Balaam, "What have I done to you, that you have struck me these three times?"

2 Pet 2:16 but he was rebuked for his iniquity: a dumb donkey speaking with a man's voice restrained the madness of the prophet.

A thousand men slain by Samson with a jawbone of.

Judg 15:15 He found a fresh jawbone of a donkey, reached out his hand and took it, and killed a thousand men with it.

Not torn by a lion.

1 Kin 13:28 Then he went and found his corpse thrown on the road, and the donkey and the lion standing by the corpse. The lion had not eaten the corpse nor torn the donkey.

DONKEY, THE WILD

Inhabits wild and solitary places.

Job 39:5–6 "Who set the wild donkey free? Who loosed the bonds of the onager, 6 Whose home I have made the wilderness, And the barren land his dwelling?

Is 32:14 Because the palaces will be forsaken, The bustling city will be deserted. The forts and towers will become lairs forever, A joy of wild donkeys, a pasture of flocks—

Dan 5:21 Then he was driven from the sons of men, his heart was made like the beasts, and his dwelling *was* with the wild donkeys. They fed him with grass like oxen, and his body was wet with the dew of heaven, till he knew that the Most High God rules in the kingdom of men, and appoints over it whomever He chooses.

Ranges the mountains for food.

Job 39:8 The range of the mountains *is* his pasture, And he searches after every green thing.

Brays when hungry.

Job 6:5 Does the wild donkey bray when it has grass, Or does the ox low over its fodder?

Suffers in time of scarcity.

Jer 14:6 And the wild donkeys stood in the desolate heights; They sniffed at the wind like jackals; Their eyes failed because *there was* no grass."

Described as

Fond of liberty.

Job 39:5 "Who set the wild donkey free? Who loosed the bonds of the onager,

Intractable.

Job 11:12 For an empty-headed man will be wise, When a wild donkey's colt is born a man.

Unsocial.

Hos 8:9 For they have gone up to Assyria, *Like* a wild donkey alone by itself; Ephraim has hired lovers.

Despises his pursuers.

Job 39:7 He scorns the tumult of the city; He does not heed the shouts of the driver.

Supported by God.

Ps 104:10–11 He sends the springs into the valleys; They flow among the hills. 11 They give drink to every beast of the field; The wild donkeys quench their thirst.

Illustrative of

Intractableness of natural man.

Job 11:12 For an empty-headed man will be wise, When a wild donkey's colt is born a man.

The wicked in their pursuit of sin.

Job 24:5 Indeed, *like* wild donkeys in the desert, They go out to their work, searching for food. The wilderness *yields* food for them *and* for *their* children.

Israel in their love of idols.

Jer 2:23–24 "How can you say, 'I am not polluted, I have not gone after the Baals'? See your way in the valley; Know what you have done: *You are* a swift dromedary breaking loose in her ways, 24 A wild donkey used to the wilderness, *That* sniffs at the wind in her desire; In her time of mating, who can turn her away? All those who seek her will not weary themselves; In her month they will find her.

The Assyrian power.

Hos 8:9 For they have gone up to Assyria, *Like* a wild donkey alone by itself; Ephraim has hired lovers.

The Ishmaelites (Hebrew).

Gen 16:12 He shall be a wild man; His hand *shall be* against every man, And every man's hand against him. And he shall dwell in the presence of all his brethren."

DOVE, THE

Clean and used as food.

Deut 14:11 "All clean birds you may eat.

Offered in sacrifice.

Gen 15:9 So He said to him, "Bring Me a three-year-old heifer, a three-year-old female goat, a three-year-old ram, a turtledove, and a young pigeon."

Lev 1:14 'And if the burnt sacrifice of his offering to the LORD *is* of birds, then he shall bring his offering of turtledoves or young pigeons.

Impiously sold in the court of the temple.

Matt 21:12 Then Jesus went into the temple of God and drove out all those who bought and sold in the temple, and overturned the tables of the money changers and the seats of those who sold doves.

John 2:16 And He said to those who sold doves, "Take these things away! Do not make My Father's house a house of merchandise!"

Characterized by

Simplicity.

Matt 10:16 "Behold, I send you out as sheep in the midst of wolves. Therefore be wise as serpents and harmless as doves.

Lovely faces.

Song 2:14 "O my dove, in the clefts of the rock, In the secret *places* of the cliff, Let me see your face, Let me hear your voice; For your voice *is* sweet, And your face *is* lovely."

Softness of eyes.

Song 1:15 Behold, you *are* fair, my love! Behold, you *are* fair! You *have* dove's eyes.

Sweetness of voice.

Song 2:14 "O my dove, in the clefts of the rock, In the secret *places* of the cliff, Let me see your face, Let me hear your voice; For your voice *is* sweet, And your face *is* lovely."

Richness of plumage.

Ps 68:13 Though you lie down among the sheepfolds, *You will be* like the wings of a dove covered with silver, And her feathers with yellow gold."

Mournful sound of, alluded to.

Nah 2:7 It is decreed: She shall be led away captive, She shall be brought up; And her maidservants shall lead *her* as with the voice of doves, Beating their breasts.

Dwells in rocks.

Song 2:14 "O my dove, in the clefts of the rock, In the secret *places* of the cliff, Let me see your face, Let me hear your voice; For your voice *is* sweet, And your face *is* lovely."

Jer 48:28 You who dwell in Moab, Leave the cities and dwell in the rock, And be like the dove *which* makes her nest In the sides of the cave's mouth.

Frequents streams and rivers.

Song 5:12 His eyes *are* like doves By the rivers of waters, Washed with milk, *And* fitly set.

Sent from the ark by Noah.

Gen 8:8 He also sent out from himself a dove, to see if the waters had receded from the face of the ground.

Gen 8:10 And he waited yet another seven days, and again he sent the dove out from the ark.

Gen 8:12 So he waited yet another seven days and sent out the dove, which did not return again to him anymore.

Why considered the emblem of peace.

Gen 8:11 Then the dove came to him in the evening, and behold, a freshly plucked olive leaf *was* in her mouth; and Noah knew that the waters had receded from the earth.

The harbinger of spring.

Song 2:12 The flowers appear on the earth; The time of singing has come, And the voice of the turtledove Is heard in our land.

Illustrative of

The Holy Spirit.

Matt 3:16 When He had been baptized, Jesus came up immediately from the water; and behold, the heavens were opened to Him, and He saw the Spirit of God descending like a dove and alighting upon Him.

John 1:32 And John bore witness, saying, "I saw the Spirit descending from heaven like a dove, and He remained upon Him.

Mourners.

Is 38:14 Like a crane *or* a swallow, so I chattered; I mourned like a dove; My eyes fail *from looking* upward. O LORD, I am oppressed; Undertake for me!

Is 59:11 We all growl like bears, And moan sadly like doves; We look for justice, but *there is* none; For salvation, *but* it is far from us.

(In its flight) the return of Israel from captivity.

Hos 11:11 They shall come trembling like a bird from Egypt, Like a dove from the land of Assyria. And I will let them dwell in their houses," Says the LORD.

DREAMS

Visions in sleep.

Job 33:15 In a dream, in a vision of the night, When deep sleep falls upon men, While slumbering on their beds,

Dan 2:28 But there is a God in heaven who reveals secrets, and He has made known to King Nebuchadnezzar what will be in the latter days. Your dream, and the visions of your head upon your bed, were these:

Often imaginary.

Job 20:8 He will fly away like a dream, and not be found; Yes, he will be chased away like a vision of the night.

Is 29:8 It shall even be as when a hungry man dreams, And look—he eats; But he awakes, and his soul is still empty; Or as when a thirsty man dreams, And look—he drinks; But he awakes, and indeed *he is* faint, And his soul still craves: So the multitude of all the nations shall be, Who fight against Mount Zion."

Excess of business frequently leads to.

Eccl 5:3 For a dream comes through much activity, And a fool's voice *is known* by *his* many words.

God's will often revealed in.

Num 12:6 Then He said, "Hear now My words: If there is a prophet among you, *I*, the LORD, make Myself known to him in a vision; I speak to him in a dream.

1 Sam 28:6 And when Saul inquired of the LORD, the LORD did not answer him, either by dreams or by Urim or by the prophets.

Job 33:15–16 In a dream, in a vision of the night, When deep sleep falls upon men, While slumbering on their beds, **16** Then He opens the ears of men, And seals their instruction.

False prophets

Pretend to have.

Jer 23:25–28 "I have heard what the prophets have said who prophesy lies in My name, saying, 'I have dreamed, I have dreamed!' **26** How long will *this* be in the heart of the prophets who prophesy lies? Indeed *they are* prophets of the deceit of their own heart, **27** who try to make My people forget My name by their dreams which everyone tells his neighbor, as their fathers forgot My name for Baal. **28** "The prophet who has a dream, let him tell a dream; And he who has My word, let him speak My word faithfully. What *is* the chaff to the wheat?" says the LORD.

Jer 29:8 For thus says the LORD of hosts, the God of Israel: Do not let your prophets and your diviners who are in your midst deceive you, nor listen to your dreams which you cause to be dreamed.

Theirs not to be regarded.

Deut 13:1–3 "If there arises among you a prophet or a

dreamer of dreams, and he gives you a sign or a wonder, **2** and the sign or the wonder comes to pass, of which he spoke to you, saying, 'Let us go after other gods'—which you have not known—'and let us serve them,' **3** you shall not listen to the words of that prophet or that dreamer of dreams, for the LORD your God is testing you to know whether you love the LORD your God with all your heart and with all your soul.

Jer 27:9 Therefore do not listen to your prophets, your diviners, your dreamers, your soothsayers, or your sorcerers, who speak to you, saying, "You shall not serve the king of Babylon."

Condemned for false ones.

Jer 23:32 Behold, I *am* against those who prophesy false dreams," says the LORD, "and tell them, and cause My people to err by their lies and by their recklessness. Yet I did not send them or command them; therefore they shall not profit this people at all," says the LORD.

Vanity of trusting to natural.

Eccl 5:7 For in the multitude of dreams and many words *there is* also vanity. But fear God.

The ancients

Put great faith in.

Judg 7:15 And so it was, when Gideon heard the telling of the dream and its interpretation, that he worshiped. He returned to the camp of Israel, and said, "Arise, for the LORD has delivered the camp of Midian into your hand."

Often perplexed by.

Gen 40:5–6 Then the butler and the baker of the king of Egypt, who were confined in the prison, had a dream, both of them, each man's dream in one night and each man's dream with its own interpretation. **6** And Joseph came in to them in the morning and looked at them, and saw that they *were* sad.

Gen 41:8 Now it came to pass in the morning that his spirit was troubled, and he sent and called for all the magicians of Egypt and all its wise men. And Pharaoh told them his dreams, but *there was* no one who could interpret them for Pharaoh.

Job 7:14 Then You scare me with dreams And terrify me with visions,

Dan 2:1 Now in the second year of Nebuchadnezzar's reign, Nebuchadnezzar had dreams; and his spirit was *so* troubled that his sleep left him.

Dan 4:5 I saw a dream which made me afraid, and the thoughts on my bed and the visions of my head troubled me.

Anxious to have them explained.

Gen 40:8 And they said to him, "We each have had a dream, and *there is* no interpreter of it." So Joseph said to them, "Do not interpretations belong to God? Tell *them* to me, please."

Dan 2:3 And the king said to them, "I have had a dream, and my spirit is anxious to know the dream."

Consulted magicians on.

Gen 41:8 Now it came to pass in the morning that his spirit was troubled, and he sent and called for all the magicians of Egypt and all its wise men. And Pharaoh told them his dreams, but *there was* no one who could interpret them for Pharaoh.

Dan 2:2–4 Then the king gave the command to call the magicians, the astrologers, the sorcerers, and the Chaldeans to tell the king his dreams. So they came and stood before the king. **3** And the king said to them, "I have had a dream, and my spirit is anxious to know the dream." **4** Then the Chaldeans spoke to the king in Aramaic, "O king, live forever! Tell your servants the dream, and we will give the interpretation."

God the only interpreter of.

Gen 40:8 And they said to him, "We each have had a dream, and *there is* no interpreter of it." So Joseph said to them, "Do not interpretations belong to God? Tell *them* to me, please."

Gen 41:16 So Joseph answered Pharaoh, saying, "*It is* not in me; God will give Pharaoh an answer of peace."

Dan 2:27–30 Daniel answered in the presence of the king, and said, "The secret which the king has demanded, the wise *men*, the astrologers, the magicians, and the soothsayers cannot declare to the king. **28** But there is a God in heaven who reveals secrets, and He has made known to King Nebuchadnezzar what will be in the latter days. Your dream, and the visions of your head upon your bed, were these: **29** As for you, O king, thoughts came *to* your *mind while* on your bed, *about* what would come to pass after this; and He who reveals secrets has made known to you what will be. **30** But as for me, this secret has not been revealed to me because I have more wisdom than anyone living, but for *our* sakes who make known the interpretation to the king, and that you may know the thoughts of your heart.

Dan 7:16 I came near to one of those who stood by, and asked him the truth of all this. So he told me and made known to me the interpretation of these things:

Mentioned in Scripture of

Abimelech.

Gen 20:3–7 But God came to Abimelech in a dream by night, and said to him, "Indeed you *are* a dead man because of the woman whom you have taken, for she *is* a man's wife." **4** But Abimelech had not come near her; and he said, "Lord, will You slay a righteous nation also? **5** Did he not say to me, 'She *is* my sister'? And she, even she herself said, 'He *is* my brother.' In the integrity of my heart and innocence of my hands I have done this." **6** And God said to him in a dream, "Yes, I know that you did this in the integrity of your heart. For I also withheld you from sinning against Me; therefore I did not let you touch her. **7** Now therefore, restore the man's wife; for he *is* a prophet, and he will pray for you and you shall live. But if you do not restore *her*, know that you shall surely die, you and all who *are* yours."

Jacob.

Gen 28:12 Then he dreamed, and behold, a ladder *was* set up on the earth, and its top reached to heaven; and there the angels of God were ascending and descending on it.

Gen 31:10 "And it happened, at the time when the flocks conceived, that I lifted my eyes and saw in a dream, and behold, the rams which leaped upon the flocks *were* streaked, speckled, and gray-spotted.

Laban.

Gen 31:24 But God had come to Laban the Syrian in a

dream by night, and said to him, "Be careful that you speak to Jacob neither good nor bad."

Joseph.

Gen 37:5–9 Now Joseph had a dream, and he told *it* to his brothers; and they hated him even more. **6** So he said to them, "Please hear this dream which I have dreamed: **7** There we were, binding sheaves in the field. Then behold, my sheaf arose and also stood upright; and indeed your sheaves stood all around and bowed down to my sheaf." **8** And his brothers said to him, "Shall you indeed reign over us? Or shall you indeed have dominion over us?" So they hated him even more for his dreams and for his words. **9** Then he dreamed still another dream and told it to his brothers, and said, "Look, I have dreamed another dream. And this time, the sun, the moon, and the eleven stars bowed down to me."

Pharaoh's butler and baker.

Gen 40:5–19 Then the butler and the baker of the king of Egypt, who *were* confined in the prison, had a dream, both of them, each man's dream in one night *and* each man's dream with its *own* interpretation. **6** And Joseph came in to them in the morning and looked at them, and saw that they *were* sad. **7** So he asked Pharaoh's officers who *were* with him in the custody of his lord's house, saying, "Why do you look *so* sad today?" **8** And they said to him, "We each have had a dream, and *there is* no interpreter of it." So Joseph said to them, "Do not interpretations belong to God? Tell *them* to me, please." **9** Then the chief butler told his dream to Joseph, and said to him, "Behold, in my dream a vine *was* before me, **10** and in the vine *were* three branches; it *was* as though it budded, its blossoms shot forth, and its clusters brought forth ripe grapes. **11** Then Pharaoh's cup *was* in my hand; and I took the grapes and pressed them into Pharaoh's cup, and placed the cup in Pharaoh's hand." **12** And Joseph said to him, "This *is* the interpretation of it: The three branches *are* three days. **13** Now within three days Pharaoh will lift up your head and restore you to your place, and you will put Pharaoh's cup in his hand according to the former manner, when you were his butler. **14** But remember me when it is well with you, and please show kindness to me; make mention of me to Pharaoh, and get me out of this house. **15** For indeed I was stolen away from the land of the Hebrews; and also I have done nothing here that they should put me into the dungeon." **16** When the chief baker saw that the interpretation was good, he said to Joseph, "I also *was* in my dream, and there *were* three white baskets on my head. **17** In the uppermost basket *were* all kinds of baked goods for Pharaoh, and the birds ate them out of the basket on my head." **18** So Joseph answered and said, "This *is* the interpretation of it: The three baskets *are* three days. **19** Within three days Pharaoh will lift off your head from you and hang you on a tree; and the birds will eat your flesh from you."

Pharaoh.

Gen 41:1–7 Then it came to pass, at the end of two full years, that Pharaoh had a dream; and behold, he stood by the river. **2** Suddenly there came up out of the river seven cows, fine looking and fat; and they fed in the meadow. **3** Then behold, seven other cows came up after them out of the river, ugly and gaunt, and stood by the *other* cows on the bank of the river. **4** And the ugly and gaunt cows ate up the seven fine looking and fat cows. So Pharaoh awoke. **5** He slept and dreamed a second time; and suddenly seven heads of grain came up on one stalk, plump and good. **6** Then behold, seven thin heads, blighted by the east wind, sprang up after them. **7** And the seven thin heads devoured the seven plump and full heads. So Pharaoh awoke, and indeed, *it was* a dream.

Midianite.

Judg 7:13–15 And when Gideon had come, there was a man telling a dream to his companion. He said, "I have had a dream: *To my* surprise, a loaf of barley bread tumbled into the camp of Midian; it came to a tent and struck it so that it fell and overturned, and the tent collapsed." **14** Then his companion answered and said, "This *is* nothing else but the sword of Gideon the son of Joash, a man of Israel! Into his hand God has delivered Midian and the whole camp." **15** And so it was, when Gideon heard the telling of the dream and its interpretation, that he worshiped. He returned to the camp of Israel, and said, "Arise, for the LORD has delivered the camp of Midian into your hand."

Solomon.

1 Kin 3:5–15 At Gibeon the LORD appeared to Solomon in a dream by night; and God said, "Ask! What shall I give you?" **6** And Solomon said: "You have shown great mercy to Your servant David my father, because he walked before You in truth, in righteousness, and in uprightness of heart with You; You have continued this great kindness for him, and You have given him a son to sit on his throne, as *it is* this day. **7** Now, O LORD my God, You have made Your servant king instead of my father David, but I *am* a little child; I do not know *how* to go out or come in. **8** And Your servant *is* in the midst of Your people whom You have chosen, a great people, too numerous to be numbered or counted. **9** Therefore give to Your servant an understanding heart to judge Your people, that I may discern between good and evil. For who is able to judge this great people of Yours?" **10** The speech pleased the LORD, that Solomon had asked this thing. **11** Then God said to him: "Because you have asked this thing, and have not asked long life for yourself, nor have asked riches for yourself, nor have asked the life of your enemies, but have asked for yourself understanding to discern justice, **12** behold, I have done according to your words; see, I have given you a wise and understanding heart, so that there has not been anyone like you before you, nor shall any like you arise after you. **13** And I have also given you what you have not asked: both riches and honor, so that there shall not be anyone like you among the kings all your days. **14** So if you walk in My ways, to keep My statutes and My commandments, as your father David walked, then I will lengthen your days." **15** Then Solomon awoke; and indeed it had been a dream. And he came to Jerusalem and stood before the ark of the covenant of the LORD, offered up burnt offerings, offered peace offerings, and made a feast for all his servants.

Nebuchadnezzar.

Dan 2:1 Now in the second year of Nebuchadnezzar's reign, Nebuchadnezzar had dreams; and his spirit was *so* troubled that his sleep left him.

Dan 2:31 "You, O king, were watching; and behold, a great image! This great image, whose splendor *was* excellent, stood before you; and its form *was* awesome.

Dan 4:5 I saw a dream which made me afraid, and the thoughts on my bed and the visions of my head troubled me.

Dan 4:8 But at last Daniel came before me (his name *is* Belteshazzar, according to the name of my god; in him *is* the Spirit of the Holy God), and I told the dream before him, *saying:*

Daniel.

Dan 7:1 In the first year of Belshazzar king of Babylon, Daniel had a dream and visions of his head *while* on his bed. Then he wrote down the dream, telling the main facts.

Joseph, earthly father of Jesus.

Matt 1:20–21 But while he thought about these things, behold, an angel of the Lord appeared to him in a dream, saying, "Joseph, son of David, do not be afraid to take to you Mary your wife, for that which is conceived in her is of the Holy Spirit. **21** And she will bring forth a Son, and you shall call His name JESUS, for He will save His people from their sins."

Matt 2:13 Now when they had departed, behold, an angel of the Lord appeared to Joseph in a dream, saying, "Arise, take the young Child and His mother, flee to Egypt, and stay there until I bring you word; for Herod will seek the young Child to destroy Him."

Matt 2:19–20 Now when Herod was dead, behold, an angel of the Lord appeared in a dream to Joseph in Egypt, **20** saying, "Arise, take the young Child and His mother, and go to the land of Israel, for those who sought the young Child's life are dead."

Wise men.

Matt 2:11–12 And when they had come into the house, they saw the young Child with Mary His mother, and fell down and worshiped Him. And when they had opened their treasures, they presented gifts to Him: gold, frankincense, and myrrh. **12** Then, being divinely warned in a dream that they should not return to Herod, they departed for their own country another way.

Pilate's wife.

Matt 27:19 While he was sitting on the judgment seat, his wife sent to him, saying, "Have nothing to do with that just Man, for I have suffered many things today in a dream because of Him."

Illustrative of

Prosperity of sinners.

Job 20:5–8 That the triumphing of the wicked is short, And the joy of the hypocrite is *but* for a moment? **6** Though his haughtiness mounts up to the heavens, And his head reaches to the clouds, **7** *Yet* he will perish forever like his own refuse; Those who have seen him will say, 'Where is he?' **8** He will fly away like a dream, and not be found; Yes, he will be chased away like a vision of the night.

Ps 73:19–20 Oh, how they are *brought* to desolation, as in a moment! They are utterly consumed with terrors. **20** As a dream when *one* awakes, So, Lord, when You awake, You shall despise their image.

Impure thoughts.

Jude 1:8 Likewise also these dreamers defile the flesh, reject authority, and speak evil of dignitaries.

Enemies of God's people.

Is 29:7–8 The multitude of all the nations who fight against Ariel, Even all who fight against her and her fortress, And distress her, Shall be as a dream of a night vision. **8** It shall even be as when a hungry man dreams, And look—he eats; But he awakes, and his soul is still empty; Or as when a thirsty man dreams, And look—he drinks; But he awakes, and indeed *he is* faint, And his soul still craves: So the multitude of all the nations shall be, Who fight against Mount Zion."

DROUGHT

Judgment on Ahab's idolatry.

1 Kin 17:1 And Elijah the Tishbite, of the inhabitants of Gilead, said to Ahab, "*As* the LORD God of Israel lives, before whom I stand, there shall not be dew nor rain these years, except at my word."

James 5:17 Elijah was a man with a nature like ours, and he prayed earnestly that it would not rain; and it did not rain on the land for three years and six months.

God's punishment

On those who fail to worship.

Zech 14:17 And it shall be *that* whichever of the families of the earth do not come up to Jerusalem to worship the King, the LORD of hosts, on them there will be no rain.

During the Tribulation.

Rev 11:6 These have power to shut heaven, so that no rain falls in the days of their prophecy; and they have power over waters to turn them to blood, and to strike the earth with all plagues, as often as they desire.

Effect of.

Ps 107:33–34 He turns rivers into a wilderness, And the watersprings into dry ground; **34** A fruitful land into barrenness, For the wickedness of those who dwell in it.

Jer 14:1–6 The word of the LORD that came to Jeremiah concerning the droughts. **2** "Judah mourns, And her gates languish; They mourn for the land, And the cry of Jerusalem has gone up. **3** Their nobles have sent their lads for water; They went to the cisterns *and* found no water. They returned with their vessels empty; They were ashamed and confounded And covered their heads. **4** Because the ground is parched, For there was no rain in the land, The plowmen were ashamed; They covered their heads. **5** Yes, the deer also gave birth in the field, But left because there was no grass. **6** And the wild donkeys stood in the desolate heights; They sniffed at the wind like jackals; Their eyes failed because *there was* no grass."

Elijah prayed for God to end.

James 5:18 And he prayed again, and the heaven gave rain, and the earth produced its fruit.

DRUGS. *See* OCCULT, THE

DRUNKENNESS

Forbidden.

Luke 21:34 "But take heed to yourselves, lest your hearts be weighed down with carousing, drunkenness, and cares of this life, and that Day come on you unexpectedly.

Eph 5:18 And do not be drunk with wine, in which is dissipation; but be filled with the Spirit,

Is a work of the flesh.

Gal 5:21 envy, murders, drunkenness, revelries, and the like; of which I tell you beforehand, just as I also told you in time past, that those who practice such things will not inherit the kingdom of God.

Is debasing.

Is 28:8 For all tables are full of vomit *and* filth; No place *is* clean.

Is inflaming.

Is 5:11 Woe to those who rise early in the morning, *That* they may follow intoxicating drink; Who continue until night, *till* wine inflames them!

Enslaves the heart.

Hos 4:11 "Harlotry, wine, and new wine enslave the heart.

Leads to

Poverty.

Prov 21:17 He who loves pleasure *will be* a poor man; He who loves wine and oil will not be rich.

Prov 23:21 For the drunkard and the glutton will come to poverty, And drowsiness will clothe *a man* with rags.

Strife.

Prov 23:29–30 Who has woe? Who has sorrow? Who has contentions? Who has complaints? Who has wounds without cause? Who has redness of eyes? 30 Those who linger long at the wine, Those who go in search of mixed wine.

Woe and sorrow.

Prov 23:29–30 Who has woe? Who has sorrow? Who has contentions? Who has complaints? Who has wounds without cause? Who has redness of eyes? 30 Those who linger long at the wine, Those who go in search of mixed wine.

Error.

Is 28:7 But they also have erred through wine, And through intoxicating drink are out of the way; The priest and the prophet have erred through intoxicating drink, They are swallowed up by wine, They are out of the way through intoxicating drink; They err in vision, they stumble *in* judgment.

Contempt of God's works.

Is 5:12 The harp and the strings, The tambourine and flute, And wine are in their feasts; But they do not regard the work of the LORD, Nor consider the operation of His hands.

Scorning.

Hos 7:5 In the day of our king Princes have made *him* sick, inflamed with wine; He stretched out his hand with scoffers.

Revelry and lust.

Rom 13:13 Let us walk properly, as in the day, not in revelry and drunkenness, not in lewdness and lust, not in strife and envy.

The wicked addicted to.

Is 56:12 "Come," *one says,* "I will bring wine, And we will fill ourselves with intoxicating drink; Tomorrow will be as today, *And* much more abundant."

Dan 5:1–4 Belshazzar the king made a great feast for a thousand of his lords, and drank wine in the presence of the thousand. 2 While he tasted the wine, Belshazzar gave the command to bring the gold and silver vessels which his father Nebuchadnezzar had taken from the temple which *had been* in Jerusalem, that the king and his lords, his wives, and his concubines might drink from them. 3 Then they brought the gold vessels that had been taken from the temple of the house of God which *had been* in Jerusalem; and the king and his lords, his wives, and his concubines drank from them. 4 They drank wine, and praised the gods of gold and silver, bronze and iron, wood and stone.

Folly of yielding to.

Prov 20:1 Wine *is* a mocker, Strong drink *is* a brawler, And whoever is led astray by it is not wise.

Avoid those given to.

Prov 23:20 Do not mix with winebibbers, *Or* with gluttonous eaters of meat;

1 Cor 5:11 But now I have written to you not to keep company with anyone named a brother, who is sexually immoral, or covetous, or an idolater, or a reviler, or a drunkard, or an extortioner—not even to eat with such a person.

Denunciations against,

Those given to.

Is 5:11–12 Woe to those who rise early in the morning, *That* they may follow intoxicating drink; Who continue until night, *till* wine inflames them! 12 The harp and the strings, The tambourine and flute, And wine are in their feasts; But they do not regard the work of the LORD, Nor consider the operation of His hands.

Is 28:1–3 Woe to the crown of pride, to the drunkards of Ephraim, Whose glorious beauty *is* a fading flower Which *is* at the head of the verdant valleys, To those who are overcome with wine! 2 Behold, the Lord has a mighty and strong one, Like a tempest of hail and a destroying storm, Like a flood of mighty waters overflowing, Who will bring *them* down to the earth with *His* hand. 3 The crown of pride, the drunkards of Ephraim, Will be trampled underfoot;

Those who encourage.

Hab 2:15 "Woe to him who gives drink to his neighbor, Pressing *him to* your bottle, Even to make *him* drunk, That you may look on his nakedness!

Excludes from heaven.

1 Cor 6:10 nor thieves, nor covetous, nor drunkards, nor revilers, nor extortioners will inherit the kingdom of God.

Gal 5:21 envy, murders, drunkenness, revelries, and the like; of which I tell you beforehand, just as I also told *you* in time past, that those who practice such things will not inherit the kingdom of God.

Punishment of.

Deut 21:20 And they shall say to the elders of his city, 'This son of ours is stubborn and rebellious; he will not obey our voice; he is a glutton and a drunkard.'

Joel 1:5–6 Awake, you drunkards, and weep; And wail, all you drinkers of wine, Because of the new wine, For it has been cut off from your mouth. **6** For a nation has come up against My land, Strong, and without number; His teeth *are* the teeth of a lion, And he has the fangs of a fierce lion.

Amos 6:6–7 Who drink wine from bowls, And anoint yourselves with the best ointments, But are not grieved for the affliction of Joseph. **7** Therefore they shall now go captive as the first of the captives, And those who recline at banquets shall be removed.

Matt 24:49–51 and begins to beat *his* fellow servants, and to eat and drink with the drunkards, **50** the master of that servant will come on a day when he is not looking for *him* and at an hour that he is not aware of, **51** and will cut him in two and appoint *him* his portion with the hypocrites. There shall be weeping and gnashing of teeth.

Exemplified by

Noah.

Gen 9:21 Then he drank of the wine and was drunk, and became uncovered in his tent.

Nabal.

1 Sam 25:36 Now Abigail went to Nabal, and there he was, holding a feast in his house, like the feast of a king. And Nabal's heart *was* merry within him, for he *was* very drunk; therefore she told him nothing, little or much, until morning light.

Uriah.

2 Sam 11:13 Now when David called him, he ate and drank before him; and he made him drunk. And at evening he went out to lie on his bed with the servants of his lord, but he did not go down to his house.

Elah.

1 Kin 16:8–10 In the twenty-sixth year of Asa king of Judah, Elah the son of Baasha became king over Israel, *and reigned* two years in Tirzah. **9** Now his servant Zimri, commander of half *his* chariots, conspired against him as he was in Tirzah drinking himself drunk in the house of Arza, steward of *his* house in Tirzah. **10** And Zimri went in and struck him and killed him in the twenty-seventh year of Asa king of Judah, and reigned in his place.

Ben Hadad.

1 Kin 20:16 So they went out at noon. Meanwhile Ben-Hadad and the thirty-two kings helping him were getting drunk at the command post.

Belshazzar.

Dan 5:4 They drank wine, and praised the gods of gold and silver, bronze and iron, wood and stone.

The Corinthians.

1 Cor 11:21 For in eating, each one takes his own supper ahead of *others;* and one is hungry and another is drunk.

EAGLE, THE

A bird of prey.

Job 9:26 They pass by like swift ships, Like an eagle swooping on its prey.

Matt 24:28 For wherever the carcass is, there the eagles will be gathered together.

Unclean.

Lev 11:13 'And these you shall regard as an abomination among the birds; they shall not be eaten, they *are* an abomination: the eagle, the vulture, the buzzard,

Cf. Deut 14:12

Different kinds.

Lev 11:13 'And these you shall regard as an abomination among the birds; they shall not be eaten, they *are* an abomination: the eagle, the vulture, the buzzard,

Lev 11:18 the white owl, the jackdaw, and the carrion vulture;

Ezek 17:3 and say, 'Thus says the Lord GOD: "A great eagle with large wings and long pinions, Full of feathers of various colors, Came to Lebanon And took from the cedar the highest branch.

Lived in the heavens.

Lam 4:19 Our pursuers were swifter Than the eagles of the heavens. They pursued us on the mountains And lay in wait for us in the wilderness.

Described as

Farsighted.

Job 39:29 From there it spies out the prey; Its eyes observe from afar.

Swift.

2 Sam 1:23 "Saul and Jonathan *were* beloved and pleasant in their lives, And in their death they were not divided; They were swifter than eagles, They were stronger than lions.

Soaring to heaven.

Prov 23:5 Will you set your eyes on that which is not? For *riches* certainly make themselves wings; They fly away like an eagle *toward* heaven.

Strength of its feathers alluded to.

Dan 4:33 That very hour the word was fulfilled concerning Nebuchadnezzar; he was driven from men and ate grass like oxen; his body was wet with the dew of heaven till his hair had grown like eagles' *feathers* and his nails like birds' *claws.*

Greatness of its wings alluded to.

Ezek 17:3 and say, 'Thus says the Lord GOD: "A great eagle with large wings and long pinions, Full of

feathers of various colors, Came to Lebanon And took from the cedar the highest branch.

Ezek 17:7 "But there was another great eagle with large wings and many feathers; And behold, this vine bent its roots toward him, And stretched its branches toward him, From the garden terrace where it had been planted, That he might water it.

Uniqueness of its flight alluded to.

Prov 30:19 The way of an eagle in the air, The way of a serpent on a rock, The way of a ship in the midst of the sea, And the way of a man with a virgin.

Delights in the lofty cedars.

Ezek 17:3–4 and say, 'Thus says the Lord GOD: "A great eagle with large wings and long pinions, Full of feathers of various colors, Came to Lebanon And took from the cedar the highest branch. 4 He cropped off its topmost young twig And carried it to a land of trade; He set it in a city of merchants.

Dwells in the high rocks.

Job 39:27–28 Does the eagle mount up at your command, And make its nest on high? 28 On the rock it dwells and resides, On the crag of the rock and the stronghold.

Its young eat blood.

Job 39:29–30 From there it spies out the prey; Its eyes observe from afar. 30 Its young ones suck up blood; And where the slain *are,* there it *is.*"

Illustrative of

Wisdom and zeal of God's ministers.

Ezek 1:10 As for the likeness of their faces, *each* had the face of a man; each of the four had the face of a lion on the right side, each of the four had the face of an ox on the left side, and each of the four had the face of an eagle.

Rev 4:7 The first living creature *was* like a lion, the second living creature like a calf, the third living creature had a face like a man, and the fourth living creature *was* like a flying eagle.

Great and powerful kings.

Ezek 17:3 and say, 'Thus says the Lord GOD: "A great eagle with large wings and long pinions, Full of feathers of various colors, Came to Lebanon And took from the cedar the highest branch.

Hos 8:1 "Set the trumpet to your mouth! *He shall come* like an eagle against the house of the LORD, Because they have transgressed My covenant And rebelled against My law.

(Renewed strength and beauty of) the renewal of believers.

Ps 103:5 Who satisfies your mouth with good *things,* So *that* your youth is renewed like the eagle's.

Is 40:31 But those who wait on the LORD Shall renew *their* strength; They shall mount up with wings like eagles, They shall run and not be weary, They shall walk and not faint.

(Mode of teaching her young to fly) God's care of His people.

Ex 19:4 'You have seen what I did to the Egyptians, and *how* I bore you on eagles' wings and brought you to Myself.

Deut 32:11 As an eagle stirs up its nest, Hovers over its young, Spreading out its wings, taking them up, Carrying them on its wings,

(Wings of) protection afforded to the church.

Rev 12:14 But the woman was given two wings of a great eagle, that she might fly into the wilderness to her place, where she is nourished for a time and times and half a time, from the presence of the serpent.

(Swiftness of) the melting away of riches.

Prov 23:5 Will you set your eyes on that which is not? For *riches* certainly make themselves wings; They fly away like an eagle *toward* heaven.

(Swiftness of) the swiftness of hostile armies.

Deut 28:49 The LORD will bring a nation against you from afar, from the end of the earth, *as swift* as the eagle flies, a nation whose language you will not understand,

Jer 4:13 "Behold, he shall come up like clouds, And his chariots like a whirlwind. His horses are swifter than eagles. Woe to us, for we are plundered!"

Jer 48:40 For thus says the LORD: "Behold, one shall fly like an eagle, And spread his wings over Moab.

Lam 4:19 Our pursuers were swifter Than the eagles of the heavens. They pursued us on the mountains And lay in wait for us in the wilderness.

(Height and security of its dwelling) the false security of the wicked.

Jer 49:16 Your fierceness has deceived you, The pride of your heart, O you who dwell in the clefts of the rock, Who hold the height of the hill! Though you make your nest as high as the eagle, I will bring you down from there," says the LORD.

Obad 1:4 Though you ascend *as* high as the eagle, And though you set your nest among the stars, From there I will bring you down," says the LORD.

(Increased baldness of, in the moulting season) calamities.

Mic 1:16 Make yourself bald and cut off your hair, Because of your precious children; Enlarge your baldness like an eagle, For they shall go from you into captivity.

(Swooping on its prey) the swiftness of man's days.

Job 9:26 They pass by like swift ships, Like an eagle swooping on its prey.

Sign of the times.

Matt 24:28 For wherever the carcass is, there the eagles will be gathered together.

EAR, THE

The organ of hearing.

Job 13:1 "Behold, my eye has seen all *this*, My ear ha heard and understood it.

Job 29:11 When the ear heard, then it blessed me, An when the eye saw, then it approved me;

Capable of testing and distinguishing words.

Job 12:11 Does not the ear test words And the mouth taste its food?

God

Made.

Prov 20:12 The hearing ear and the seeing eye, The LORD has made them both.

Planted.

Ps 94:9 He who planted the ear, shall He not hear? He who formed the eye, shall He not see?

Opens.

Job 33:16 Then He opens the ears of men, And seals their instruction.

Job 36:10 He also opens their ear to instruction, And commands that they turn from iniquity.

Judicially closed.

Is 6:10 "Make the heart of this people dull, And their ears heavy, And shut their eyes; Lest they see with their eyes, And hear with their ears, And understand with their heart, And return and be healed."

Matt 13:15 *For the hearts of this people have grown dull. Their ears are hard of hearing, And their eyes they have closed, Lest they should see with their eyes and hear with their ears, Lest they should understand with their hearts and turn, So that I should heal them.'*

Christ opens.

Is 35:5 Then the eyes of the blind shall be opened, And the ears of the deaf shall be unstopped.

Is 43:8 Bring out the blind people who have eyes, And the deaf who have ears.

Instruction received through.

Is 30:21 Your ears shall hear a word behind you, saying, "This *is* the way, walk in it," Whenever you turn to the right hand Or whenever you turn to the left.

That hears and receives the Word of God, blessed.

Ex 15:26 and said, "If you diligently heed the voice of the LORD your God and do what is right in His sight, give ear to His commandments and keep all His statutes, I will put none of the diseases on you which I have brought on the Egyptians. For I *am* the LORD who heals you."

Matt 13:16 But blessed *are* your eyes for they see, and your ears for they hear;

Of believers should

Seek knowledge.

Prov 18:15 The heart of the prudent acquires knowledge, And the ear of the wise seeks knowledge.

Be bowed down to instructions.

Prov 5:1 My son, pay attention to my wisdom; Lend your ear to my understanding,

Be inclined to wisdom.

Prov 2:2 So that you incline your ear to wisdom, *And* apply your heart to understanding;

Be given to the law of God.

Is 1:10 Hear the word of the LORD, You rulers of Sodom; Give ear to the law of our God, You people of Gomorrah:

Receive the word of God.

Jer 9:20 Yet hear the word of the LORD, O women, And let your ear receive the word of His mouth; Teach your daughters wailing, And everyone her neighbor a lamentation.

Hear and obey rebukes.

Prov 15:31 The ear that hears the rebukes of life Will abide among the wise.

Prov 25:12 *Like* an earring of gold and an ornament of fine gold *Is* a wise rebuker to an obedient ear.

Sometimes dissatisfied.

Eccl 1:8 All things *are* full of labor; Man cannot express *it*. The eye is not satisfied with seeing, Nor the ear filled with hearing.

Of the wicked,

Uncircumcised.

Jer 6:10 To whom shall I speak and give warning, That they may hear? Indeed their ear *is* uncircumcised, And they cannot give heed. Behold, the word of the LORD is a reproach to them; They have no delight in it.

Acts 7:51 "You stiff-necked and uncircumcised in heart and ears! You always resist the Holy Spirit; as your fathers *did,* so *do* you.

Itching.

2 Tim 4:3 For the time will come when they will not endure sound doctrine, but according to their own desires, *because* they have itching ears, they will heap up for themselves teachers;

Not inclined to hear God.

Jer 7:24 Yet they did not obey or incline their ear, but followed the counsels *and* the dictates of their evil hearts, and went backward and not forward.

Jer 35:15 I have also sent to you all My servants the prophets, rising up early and sending *them,* saying, 'Turn now everyone from his evil way, amend your doings, and do not go after other gods to serve them; then you will dwell in the land which I have given you and your fathers.' But you have not inclined your ear, nor obeyed Me.

Turned away from God's law.

Prov 28:9 One who turns away his ear from hearing the law, Even his prayer *is* an abomination.

Stopped against God's word.

Ps 58:4 Their poison *is* like the poison of a serpent; *They are* like the deaf cobra *that* stops its ear,

Zech 7:11 But they refused to heed, shrugged their shoulders, and stopped their ears so that they could not hear.

Not to be stopped at cry of the poor.

Prov 21:13 Whoever shuts his ears to the cry of the poor Will also cry himself and not be heard.

Blood put on the right ear of

Priests at consecration.

Ex 29:20 Then you shall kill the ram, and take some of its blood and put *it* on the tip of the right ear of Aaron and on the tip of the right ear of his sons, on the thumb of their right hand and on the big toe of their right foot, and sprinkle the blood all around on the altar.

Lev 8:23 and Moses killed *it.* Also he took *some* of its blood and put it on the tip of Aaron's right ear, on the thumb of his right hand, and on the big toe of his right foot.

The healed leper in cleansing him.

Lev 14:14 The priest shall take *some* of the blood of the trespass offering, and the priest shall put *it* on the tip of the right ear of him who is to be cleansed, on the thumb of his right hand, and on the big toe of his right foot.

Often adorned with rings.

Ezek 16:12 And I put a jewel in your nose, earrings in your ears, and a beautiful crown on your head.

Hos 2:13 I will punish her For the days of the Baals to which she burned incense. She decked herself with her earrings and jewelry, And went after her lovers; But Me she forgot," says the LORD.

Of servants who refused to leave their masters, drilled to the door.

Ex 21:6 then his master shall bring him to the judges. He shall also bring him to the door, or to the doorpost, and his master shall pierce his ear with an awl; and he shall serve him forever.

Deut 15:17 then you shall take an awl and thrust *it* through his ear to the door, and he shall be your servant forever. Also to your female servant you shall do likewise.

EARLY RISING

Christ set an example of.

Mark 1:35 Now in the morning, having risen a long while before daylight, He went out and departed to a solitary place; and there He prayed.

Luke 21:38 Then early in the morning all the people came to Him in the temple to hear Him.

John 8:2 Now early in the morning He came again into the temple, and all the people came to Him; and He sat down and taught them.

Requisite for

Devotion.

Ps 5:3 My voice You shall hear in the morning, O LORD; In the morning I will direct *it* to You, And I will look up.

Ps 59:16 But I will sing of Your power; Yes, I will sing aloud of Your mercy in the morning; For You have been my defense And refuge in the day of my trouble.

Ps 63:1 O God, You *are* my God; Early will I seek You; My soul thirsts for You; My flesh longs for You In a dry and thirsty land Where there is no water.

Ps 88:13 But to You I have cried out, O LORD, And in the morning my prayer comes before You.

Is 26:9 With my soul I have desired You in the night, Yes, by my spirit within me I will seek You early; For when Your judgments *are* in the earth, The inhabitants of the world will learn righteousness.

Executing God's commands.

Gen 22:3 So Abraham rose early in the morning and saddled his donkey, and took two of his young men with him, and Isaac his son; and he split the wood for the burnt offering, and arose and went to the place of which God had told him.

Discharge of daily duties.

Prov 31:15 She also rises while it is yet night, And provides food for her household, And a portion for her maidservants.

Neglect of, leads to poverty.

Prov 6:9–11 How long will you slumber, O sluggard? When will you rise from your sleep? **10** A little sleep, a little slumber, A little folding of the hands to sleep— **11** So shall your poverty come on you like a prowler, And your need like an armed man.

Practiced by the wicked for

Deceit.

Prov 27:14 He who blesses his friend with a loud voice, rising early in the morning, It will be counted a curse to him.

Executing plans of evil.

Mic 2:1 Woe to those who devise iniquity, And work out evil on their beds! At morning light they practice it, Because it is in the power of their hand.

Illustrates spiritual diligence.

Rom 13:11–12 And *do* this, knowing the time, that now *it is* high time to awake out of sleep; for now our salvation *is* nearer than when we *first* believed. **12** The night is far spent, the day is at hand. Therefore let us cast off the works of darkness, and let us put on the armor of light.

Exemplified by

Abraham.

Gen 19:27 And Abraham went early in the morning to the place where he had stood before the LORD.

Isaac, etc.

Gen 26:31 Then they arose early in the morning and swore an oath with one another; and Isaac sent them away, and they departed from him in peace.

Jacob.

Gen 28:18 Then Jacob rose early in the morning, and took the stone that he had put at his head, set it up as a pillar, and poured oil on top of it.

Joshua, etc.

Josh 3:1 Then Joshua rose early in the morning; and they set out from Acacia Grove and came to the Jordan, he and all the children of Israel, and lodged there before they crossed over.

Gideon.

Judg 6:38 And it was so. When he rose early the next morning and squeezed the fleece together, he wrung the dew out of the fleece, a bowlful of water.

Samuel.

1 Sam 15:12 So when Samuel rose early in the morning to meet Saul, it was told Samuel, saying, "Saul went to Carmel, and indeed, he set up a monument for

himself; and he has gone on around, passed by, and gone down to Gilgal."

David.

1 Sam 17:20 So David rose early in the morning, left the sheep with a keeper, and took *the things* and went as Jesse had commanded him. And he came to the camp as the army was going out to the fight and shouting for the battle.

Mary, etc.

Mark 16:2 Very early in the morning, on the first *day* of the week, they came to the tomb when the sun had risen.

The apostles.

Acts 5:21 And when they heard *that,* they entered the temple early in the morning and taught. But the high priest and those with him came and called the council together, with all the elders of the children of Israel, and sent to the prison to have them brought.

EARTH, THE

The world in general.

Gen 1:2 The earth was without form, and void; and darkness *was* on the face of the deep. And the Spirit of God was hovering over the face of the waters.

The dry land as divided from waters.

Gen 1:10 And God called the dry *land* Earth, and the gathering together of the waters He called Seas. And God saw that *it was* good.

God

Created.

Gen 1:1 In the beginning God created the heavens and the earth.

Neh 9:6 You alone *are* the LORD; You have made heaven, The heaven of heavens, with all their host, The earth and everything on it, The seas and all that is in them, And You preserve them all. The host of heaven worships You.

Laid the foundation of.

Job 38:4 "Where were you when I laid the foundations of the earth? Tell *Me,* if you have understanding.

Ps 102:25 Of old You laid the foundation of the earth, And the heavens *are* the work of Your hands.

Formed.

Ps 90:2 Before the mountains were brought forth, Or ever You had formed the earth and the world, Even from everlasting to everlasting, You *are* God.

Spread abroad.

Is 42:5 Thus says God the LORD, Who created the heavens and stretched them out, Who spread forth the earth and that which comes from it, Who gives breath to the people on it, And spirit to those who walk on it:

Is 44:24 Thus says the LORD, your Redeemer, And He who formed you from the womb: "I *am* the LORD, who makes all *things,* Who stretches out the heavens all alone, Who spreads abroad the earth by Myself;

Suspended in space.

Job 26:7 He stretches out the north over empty space; *He* hangs the earth on nothing.

Supports.

Ps 75:3 The earth and all its inhabitants are dissolved; I set up its pillars firmly. Selah

Establishes.

Ps 78:69 And He built His sanctuary like the heights, Like the earth which He has established forever.

Ps 119:90 Your faithfulness *endures* to all generations; You established the earth, and it abides.

Illumines.

Gen 1:14–16 Then God said, "Let there be lights in the firmament of the heavens to divide the day from the night; and let them be for signs and seasons, and for days and years; **15** and let them be for lights in the firmament of the heavens to give light on the earth"; and it was so. **16** Then God made two great lights: the greater light to rule the day, and the lesser light to rule the night. *He made* the stars also.

Jer 33:25 "Thus says the LORD: 'If My covenant *is* not with day and night, *and if* I have not appointed the ordinances of heaven and earth,

Waters.

Ps 65:9 You visit the earth and water it, You greatly enrich it; The river of God is full of water; You provide their grain, For so You have prepared it.

Ps 147:8 Who covers the heavens with clouds, Who prepares rain for the earth, Who makes grass to grow on the mountains.

Makes fruitful.

Gen 1:11 Then God said, "Let the earth bring forth grass, the herb *that* yields seed, *and* the fruit tree *that* yields fruit according to its kind, whose seed *is* in itself, on the earth"; and it was so.

Gen 27:28 Therefore may God give you Of the dew of heaven, Of the fatness of the earth, And plenty of grain and wine.

Inspects.

Zech 4:10 For who has despised the day of small things? For these seven rejoice to see The plumb line in the hand of Zerubbabel. They are the eyes of the LORD, Which scan to and fro throughout the whole earth."

Governs supremely.

Job 34:13 Who gave Him charge over the earth? Or who appointed *Him over* the whole world?

Ps 135:6 Whatever the LORD pleases He does, In heaven and in earth, In the seas and in all deep places.

Reigns in.

Ex 8:22 And in that day I will set apart the land of Goshen, in which My people dwell, that no swarms *of flies* shall be there, in order that you may know that I *am* the LORD in the midst of the land.

Ps 97:1 The LORD reigns; Let the earth rejoice; Let the multitude of isles be glad!

Shall be exalted in.

Ps 46:10 Be still, and know that I *am* God; I will be exalted among the nations, I will be exalted in the earth!

Owns.

Ex 9:29 So Moses said to him, "As soon as I have gone out of the city, I will spread out my hands to the LORD; the thunder will cease, and there will be no more hail, that you may know that the earth *is* the LORD's.

1 Cor 10:26 for *"the earth is the LORD's, and all its fullness."*

Created, to be inhabited.

Is 45:18 For thus says the LORD, Who created the heavens, Who is God, Who formed the earth and made it, Who has established it, Who did not create it in vain, Who formed it to be inhabited: "I *am* the LORD, and *there is* no other.

First division of.

Gen 10:25 To Eber were born two sons: the name of one *was* Peleg, for in his days the earth was divided; and his brother's name *was* Joktan.

Size of, worthy of respect.

Job 11:9 Their measure *is* longer than the earth And broader than the sea.

Job 38:18 Have you comprehended the breadth of the earth? Tell *Me*, if you know all this.

Prov 25:3 *As* the heavens for height and the earth for depth, So the heart of kings *is* unsearchable.

Diversified by hills and mountains.

Hab 3:6 He stood and measured the earth; He looked and startled the nations. And the everlasting mountains were scattered, The perpetual hills bowed. His ways *are* everlasting.

Full of minerals.

Deut 8:9 a land in which you will eat bread without scarcity, in which you will lack nothing; a land whose stones *are* iron and out of whose hills you can dig copper.

Job 28:1–5 "Surely there is a mine for silver, And a place *where* gold is refined. **2** Iron is taken from the earth, And copper *is* smelted *from* ore. **3** *Man* puts an end to darkness, And searches every recess For ore in the darkness and the shadow of death. **4** He breaks open a shaft away from people; *In places* forgotten by feet They hang far away from men; They swing to and fro. **5** *As* for the earth, from it comes bread, But underneath it is turned up as by fire;

Job 28:15–19 It cannot be purchased for gold, Nor can silver be weighed *for* its price. **16** It cannot be valued in the gold of Ophir, In precious onyx or sapphire. **17** Neither gold nor crystal can equal it, Nor can it be exchanged for jewelry of fine gold. **18** No mention shall be made of coral or quartz, For the price of wisdom *is* above rubies. **19** The topaz of Ethiopia cannot equal it, Nor can it be valued in pure gold.

Described as

God's footstool.

Is 66:1 Thus says the LORD: "Heaven *is* My throne, And earth *is* My footstool. Where *is* the house that you will build Me? And where *is* the place of My rest?

Matt 5:35 nor by the earth, for it is His footstool; nor by Jerusalem, for it is the city of the great King.

Full of God's goodness.

Ps 33:5 He loves righteousness and justice; The earth is full of the goodness of the LORD.

Full of God's riches.

Ps 104:24 O LORD, how manifold are Your works! In

wisdom You have made them all. The earth is full of Your possessions—

Full of God's mercy.

Ps 119:64 The earth, O LORD, is full of Your mercy; Teach me Your statutes.

Full of God's glory.

Num 14:21 but truly, as I live, all the earth shall be filled with the glory of the LORD—

Is 6:3 And one cried to another and said: "Holy, holy, holy *is* the LORD of hosts; The whole earth *is* full of His glory!"

Shining with God's glory.

Ezek 43:2 And behold, the glory of the God of Israel came from the way of the east. His voice *was* like the sound of many waters; and the earth shone with His glory.

Trembling before God.

Ps 68:8 The earth shook; The heavens also dropped *rain* at the presence of God; Sinai itself *was moved* at the presence of God, the God of Israel.

Jer 10:10 But the LORD *is* the true God; He *is* the living God and the everlasting King. At His wrath the earth will tremble, And the nations will not be able to endure His indignation.

Melting at God's voice.

Ps 46:6 The nations raged, the kingdoms were moved; He uttered His voice, the earth melted.

Burning at God's presence.

Nah 1:5 The mountains quake before Him, The hills melt, And the earth heaves at His presence, Yes, the world and all who dwell in it.

Man

Formed out of.

Gen 2:7 And the LORD God formed man *of* the dust of the ground, and breathed into his nostrils the breath of life; and man became a living being.

Ps 103:14 For He knows our frame; He remembers that we *are* dust.

1 Cor 15:47–48 The first man *was* of the earth, *made* of dust; the second Man *is* the Lord from heaven. **48** As *was* the *man* of dust, so also *are* those *who are made* of dust; and as *is* the heavenly *Man,* so also *are* those *who are* heavenly.

Given dominion over.

Gen 1:26 Then God said, "Let Us make man in Our image, according to Our likeness; let them have dominion over the fish of the sea, over the birds of the air, and over the cattle, over all the earth and over every creeping thing that creeps on the earth."

Ps 115:16 The heaven, *even* the heavens, *are* the LORD's; But the earth He has given to the children of men.

By nature minds the things of.

Phil 3:19 whose end *is* destruction, whose god *is their* belly, and *whose* glory *is* in their shame—who set their mind on earthly things.

Brought a curse on.

Gen 3:17 Then to Adam He said, "Because you have heeded the voice of your wife, and have eaten from the tree of which I commanded you, saying, 'You

shall not eat of it': "Cursed *is* the ground for your sake; In toil you shall eat *of* it All the days of your life.

Shall return to.

Gen 3:19 In the sweat of your face you shall eat bread Till you return to the ground, For out of it you were taken; For dust you *are,* And to dust you shall return."

Ps 146:4 His spirit departs, he returns to his earth; In that very day his plans perish.

Subject to God's judgments.

Ps 46:8 Come, behold the works of the LORD, Who has made desolations in the earth.

Is 11:4 But with righteousness He shall judge the poor, And decide with equity for the meek of the earth; He shall strike the earth with the rod of His mouth, And with the breath of His lips He shall slay the wicked.

Corrupted by sin.

Gen 6:11–12 The earth also was corrupt before God, and the earth was filled with violence. **12** So God looked upon the earth, and indeed it was corrupt; for all flesh had corrupted their way on the earth.

Is 24:5 The earth is also defiled under its inhabitants, Because they have transgressed the laws, Changed the ordinance, Broken the everlasting covenant.

Made barren by sin.

Deut 28:23 And your heavens which *are* over your head shall be bronze, and the earth which is under you *shall be* iron.

Ps 107:34 A fruitful land into barrenness, For the wickedness of those who dwell in it.

Made to mourn and languish because of sin.

Is 24:4 The earth mourns *and* fades away, The world languishes *and* fades away; The haughty people of the earth languish.

Jer 4:28 For this shall the earth mourn, And the heavens above be black, Because I have spoken. I have purposed and will not relent, Nor will I turn back from it.

Jer 12:4 How long will the land mourn, And the herbs of every field wither? The beasts and birds are consumed, For the wickedness of those who dwell there, Because they said, "He will not see our final end."

Hos 4:3 Therefore the land will mourn; And everyone who dwells there will waste away With the beasts of the field And the birds of the air; Even the fish of the sea will be taken away.

Satan roams over.

Job 1:7 And the LORD said to Satan, "From where do you come?" So Satan answered the LORD and said, "From going to and fro on the earth, and from walking back and forth on it."

1 Pet 5:8 Be sober, be vigilant; because your adversary the devil walks about like a roaring lion, seeking whom he may devour.

Shall be filled with the knowledge of God.

Is 11:9 They shall not hurt nor destroy in all My holy mountain, For the earth shall be full of the knowledge of the LORD As the waters cover the sea.

Hab 2:14 For the earth will be filled With the knowledge of the glory of the LORD, As the waters cover the sea.

Once flooded.

Gen 7:17–24 Now the flood was on the earth forty days. The waters increased and lifted up the ark, and it rose high above the earth. **18** The waters prevailed and greatly increased on the earth, and the ark moved about on the surface of the waters. **19** And the waters prevailed exceedingly on the earth, and all the high hills under the whole heaven were covered. **20** The waters prevailed fifteen cubits upward, and the mountains were covered. **21** And all flesh died that moved on the earth: birds and cattle and beasts and every creeping thing that creeps on the earth, and every man. **22** All in whose nostrils *was* the breath of the spirit of life, all that *was* on the dry *land*, died. **23** So He destroyed all living things which were on the face of the ground: both man and cattle, creeping thing and bird of the air. They were destroyed from the earth. Only Noah and those who *were* with him in the ark remained *alive*. **24** And the waters prevailed on the earth one hundred and fifty days.

Never again to be totally flooded.

Gen 9:11 Thus I establish My covenant with you: Never again shall all flesh be cut off by the waters of the flood; never again shall there be a flood to destroy the earth."

2 Pet 3:6–7 by which the world *that* then existed perished, being flooded with water. **7** But the heavens and the earth *which* are now preserved by the same word, are reserved for fire until the day of judgment and perdition of ungodly men.

To be dissolved by fire.

2 Pet 3:7 But the heavens and the earth *which* are now preserved by the same word, are reserved for fire until the day of judgment and perdition of ungodly men.

2 Pet 3:10 But the day of the Lord will come as a thief in the night, in which the heavens will pass away with a great noise, and the elements will melt with fervent heat; both the earth and the works that are in it will be burned up.

2 Pet 3:12 looking for and hastening the coming of the day of God, because of which the heavens will be dissolved, being on fire, and the elements will melt with fervent heat?

To be renewed.

Is 65:17 "For behold, I create new heavens and a new earth; And the former shall not be remembered or come to mind.

2 Pet 3:13 Nevertheless we, according to His promise, look for new heavens and a new earth in which righteousness dwells.

Rev 21:1 Now I saw a new heaven and a new earth, for the first heaven and the first earth had passed away. Also there was no more sea.

Saints shall inherit.

Ps 25:13 He himself shall dwell in prosperity, And his descendants shall inherit the earth.

Matt 5:5 Blessed *are* the meek, For they shall inherit the earth.

EARTHQUAKES

Islands and mountainous districts liable to.

Ps 114:4 The mountains skipped like rams, The little hills like lambs.

Ps 114:6 O mountains, *that* you skipped like rams? O little hills, like lambs?

Rev 6:14 Then the sky receded as a scroll when it is rolled up, and every mountain and island was moved out of its place.

Rev 16:18 And there were noises and thunderings and lightnings; and there was a great earthquake, such a mighty and great earthquake as had not occurred since men were on the earth.

Rev 16:20 Then every island fled away, and the mountains were not found.

Frequently accompanied by

Volcanic eruptions.

Ps 104:32 He looks on the earth, and it trembles; He touches the hills, and they smoke.

Nah 1:5 The mountains quake before Him, The hills melt, And the earth heaves at His presence, Yes, the world and all who dwell in it.

Convulsion and receding of the sea.

2 Sam 22:8 "Then the earth shook and trembled; The foundations of heaven quaked and were shaken, Because He was angry.

2 Sam 22:16 Then the channels of the sea were seen, The foundations of the world were uncovered, At the rebuke of the LORD, At the blast of the breath of His nostrils.

Ps 18:7 Then the earth shook and trembled; The foundations of the hills also quaked and were shaken, Because He was angry.

Ps 18:15 Then the channels of the sea were seen, The foundations of the world were uncovered At Your rebuke, O LORD, At the blast of the breath of Your nostrils.

Ps 46:3 *Though* its waters roar *and* be troubled, *Though* the mountains shake with its swelling. Selah

Opening of the earth.

Num 16:31–32 Now it came to pass, as he finished speaking all these words, that the ground split apart under them, **32** and the earth opened its mouth and swallowed them up, with their households and all the men with Korah, with all *their* goods.

Overturning of mountains.

Ps 46:2 Therefore we will not fear, Even though the earth be removed, And though the mountains be carried into the midst of the sea;

Zech 14:4 And in that day His feet will stand on the Mount of Olives, Which faces Jerusalem on the east. And the Mount of Olives shall be split in two, From east to west, *Making* a very large valley; Half of the mountain shall move toward the north And half of it toward the south.

Splitting of rocks.

Matt 27:51 Then, behold, the veil of the temple was torn in two from top to bottom; and the earth quaked, and the rocks were split,

Men always terrified by.

Num 16:34 Then all Israel who *were* around them fled at their cry, for they said, "Lest the earth swallow us up *also!*"

Zech 14:5 Then you shall flee *through* My mountain valley, For the mountain valley shall reach to Azal. Yes, you shall flee As you fled from the earthquake In the days of Uzziah king of Judah. Thus the LORD my God will come, *And* all the saints with You.

Matt 27:54 So when the centurion and those with him, who were guarding Jesus, saw the earthquake and the things that had happened, they feared greatly, saying, "Truly this was the Son of God!"

Rev 11:13 In the same hour there was a great earthquake, and a tenth of the city fell. In the earthquake seven thousand people were killed, and the rest were afraid and gave glory to the God of heaven.

Mentioned in Scripture

At Mount Sinai.

Ex 19:18 Now Mount Sinai *was* completely in smoke, because the LORD descended upon it in fire. Its smoke ascended like the smoke of a furnace, and the whole mountain quaked greatly.

In the wilderness.

Num 16:31–32 Now it came to pass, as he finished speaking all these words, that the ground split apart under them, **32** and the earth opened its mouth and swallowed them up, with their households and all the men with Korah, with all *their* goods.

In strongholds of the Philistines.

1 Sam 14:15 And there was trembling in the camp, in the field, and among all the people. The garrison and the raiders also trembled; and the earth quaked, so that it was a very great trembling.

When Elijah fled from Jezebel.

1 Kin 19:11 Then He said, "Go out, and stand on the mountain before the LORD." And behold, the LORD passed by, and a great and strong wind tore into the mountains and broke the rocks in pieces before the LORD, *but* the LORD *was* not in the wind; and after the wind an earthquake, *but* the LORD *was* not in the earthquake;

In Uzziah's reign.

Amos 1:1 The words of Amos, who was among the sheepbreeders of Tekoa, which he saw concerning Israel in the days of Uzziah king of Judah, and in the days of Jeroboam the son of Joash, king of Israel, two years before the earthquake.

Zech 14:5 Then you shall flee *through* My mountain valley, For the mountain valley shall reach to Azal. Yes, you shall flee As you fled from the earthquake In the days of Uzziah king of Judah. Thus the LORD my God will come, *And* all the saints with You.

At our Lord's death.

Matt 27:51 Then, behold, the veil of the temple was torn in two from top to bottom; and the earth quaked, and the rocks were split,

At our Lord's resurrection.

Matt 28:2 And behold, there was a great earthquake; for an angel of the Lord descended from heaven, and came and rolled back the stone from the door, and sat on it.

At Philippi.

Acts 16:26 Suddenly there was a great earthquake, so that the foundations of the prison were shaken; and immediately all the doors were opened and everyone's chains were loosed.

Before the destruction of Jerusalem, predicted.

Matt 24:7 For nation will rise against nation, and kingdom against kingdom. And there will be famines, pestilences, and earthquakes in various places.

Luke 21:11 And there will be great earthquakes in various places, and famines and pestilences; and there will be fearful sights and great signs from heaven.

At Christ's second coming, predicted.

Zech 14:4 And in that day His feet will stand on the Mount of Olives, Which faces Jerusalem on the east. And the Mount of Olives shall be split in two, From east to west, *Making* a very large valley; Half of the mountain shall move toward the north And half of it toward the south.

Illustrative of

God's power.

Job 9:6 He shakes the earth out of its place, And its pillars tremble;

Heb 12:26 whose voice then shook the earth; but now He has promised, saying, *"Yet once more I shake not only the earth, but also heaven."*

God's presence.

Ps 68:7–8 O God, when You went out before Your people, When You marched through the wilderness, Selah **8** The earth shook; The heavens also dropped *rain* at the presence of God; Sinai itself *was moved* at the presence of God, the God of Israel.

Ps 114:7 Tremble, O earth, at the presence of the Lord, At the presence of the God of Jacob,

God's anger.

Ps 18:7 Then the earth shook and trembled; The foundations of the hills also quaked and were shaken, Because He was angry.

Ps 60:2 You have made the earth tremble; You have broken it; Heal its breaches, for it is shaking.

Is 13:13 Therefore I will shake the heavens, And the earth will move out of her place, In the wrath of the LORD of hosts And in the day of His fierce anger.

The judgments of God.

Is 24:19–20 The earth is violently broken, The earth is split open, The earth is shaken exceedingly. **20** The earth shall reel to and fro like a drunkard, And shall totter like a hut; Its transgression shall be heavy upon it, And it will fall, and not rise again.

Is 29:6 You will be punished by the LORD of hosts With thunder and earthquake and great noise, *With* storm and tempest And the flame of devouring fire.

Jer 4:24 I beheld the mountains, and indeed they trembled, And all the hills moved back and forth.

Rev 8:5 Then the angel took the censer, filled it with fire from the altar, and threw *it* to the earth. And there were noises, thunderings, lightnings, and an earthquake.

The overthrow of kingdoms.

Hag 2:6 "For thus says the LORD of hosts: 'Once more (it *is* a little while) I will shake heaven and earth, the sea and dry land;

Hag 2:21–22 "Speak to Zerubbabel, governor of Judah, saying: 'I will shake heaven and earth. **22** I will overthrow the throne of kingdoms; I will destroy the strength of the Gentile kingdoms. I will overthrow the chariots And those who ride in them; The horses and their riders shall come down, Every one by the sword of his brother.

Rev 6:12–13 I looked when He opened the sixth seal, and behold, there was a great earthquake; and the sun became black as sackcloth of hair, and the moon became like blood. **13** And the stars of heaven fell to the earth, as a fig tree drops its late figs when it is shaken by a mighty wind.

Rev 16:18–19 And there were noises and thunderings and lightnings; and there was a great earthquake, such a mighty and great earthquake as had not occurred since men were on the earth. **19** Now the great city was divided into three parts, and the cities of the nations fell. And great Babylon was remembered before God, to give her the cup of the wine of the fierceness of His wrath.

EDIFICATION

Described.

Eph 4:12–16 for the equipping of the saints for the work of ministry, for the edifying of the body of Christ, **13** till we all come to the unity of the faith and of the knowledge of the Son of God, to a perfect man, to the measure of the stature of the fullness of Christ; **14** that we should no longer be children, tossed to and fro and carried about with every wind of doctrine, by the trickery of men, in the cunning craftiness of deceitful plotting, **15** but, speaking the truth in love, may grow up in all things into Him who is the head—Christ— **16** from whom the whole body, joined and knit together by what every joint supplies, according to the effective working by which every part does its share, causes growth of the body for the edifying of itself in love.

Is the object of

The ministerial office.

Eph 4:11–12 And He Himself gave some *to be* apostles, some prophets, some evangelists, and some pastors and teachers, **12** for the equipping of the saints for the work of ministry, for the edifying of the body of Christ,

Ministerial gifts.

1 Cor 14:3–5 But he who prophesies speaks edification and exhortation and comfort to men. **4** He who speaks in a tongue edifies himself, but he who prophesies edifies the church. **5** I wish you all spoke with tongues, but even more that you prophesied; for he who prophesies *is* greater than he who speaks with tongues, unless indeed he interprets, that the church may receive edification.

1 Cor 14:12 Even so you, since you are zealous for spiritual *gifts, let it be* for the edification of the church *that* you seek to excel.

Ministerial authority.

2 Cor 10:8 For even if I should boast somewhat more about our authority, which the Lord gave us for edification and not for your destruction, I shall not be ashamed—

2 Cor 13:10 Therefore I write these things being absent, lest being present I should use sharpness, according to the authority which the Lord has given me for edification and not for destruction.

The church's union in Christ.

Eph 4:16 from whom the whole body, joined and knit together by what every joint supplies, according to the effective working by which every part does its share, causes growth of the body for the edifying of itself in love.

The gospel, the instrument of.

Acts 20:32 "So now, brethren, I commend you to God and to the word of His grace, which is able to build you up and give you an inheritance among all those who are sanctified.

Love leads to.

1 Cor 8:1 Now concerning things offered to idols: We know that we all have knowledge. Knowledge puffs up, but love edifies.

Exhortation to.

Jude 1:20–21 But you, beloved, building yourselves up on your most holy faith, praying in the Holy Spirit, **21** keep yourselves in the love of God, looking for the mercy of our Lord Jesus Christ unto eternal life.

Mutual, commanded.

Rom 14:19 Therefore let us pursue the things *which make* for peace and the things by which one may edify another.

1 Thess 5:11 Therefore comfort each other and edify one another, just as you also are doing.

All to be done to.

2 Cor 12:19 Again, do you think that we excuse ourselves to you? We speak before God in Christ. But *we do* all things, beloved, for your edification.

Eph 4:29 Let no corrupt word proceed out of your mouth, but what is good for necessary edification, that it may impart grace to the hearers.

Use self-denial to promote, in others.

1 Cor 10:23 All things are lawful for me, but not all things are helpful; all things are lawful for me, but not all things edify.

1 Cor 10:33 just as I also please all *men* in all *things,* not seeking my own profit, but the *profit* of many, that they may be saved.

The peace of the church favors.

Acts 9:31 Then the churches throughout all Judea, Galilee, and Samaria had peace and were edified. And walking in the fear of the Lord and in the comfort of the Holy Spirit, they were multiplied.

Foolish questions opposed to.

1 Tim 1:4 nor give heed to fables and endless genealogies, which cause disputes rather than godly edification which is in faith.

EDOMITES, THE

Descended from Esau.

Gen 36:9 And this *is* the genealogy of Esau the father of the Edomites in Mount Seir.

Dwelt in Mount Seir.

Gen 32:3 Then Jacob sent messengers before him to Esau his brother in the land of Seir, the country of Edom.

Deut 2:4–5 And command the people, saying, "You *are about to* pass through the territory of your brethren, the descendants of Esau, who live in Seir; and they will be afraid of you. Therefore watch yourselves carefully. 5 Do not meddle with them, for I will not give you *any* of their land, no, not so much as one footstep, because I have given Mount Seir to Esau *as* a possession.

Other names for,

Descendants of Esau.

Deut 2:4 And command the people, saying, "You *are about to* pass through the territory of your brethren, the descendants of Esau, who live in Seir; and they will be afraid of you. Therefore watch yourselves carefully.

Brethren of Israel.

Num 20:14 Now Moses sent messengers from Kadesh to the king of Edom. "Thus says your brother Israel: 'You know all the hardship that has befallen us,

Governed by chiefs.

Gen 36:15–30 These *were* the chiefs of the sons of Esau. The sons of Eliphaz, the firstborn *son* of Esau, were Chief Teman, Chief Omar, Chief Zepho, Chief Kenaz, 16 Chief Korah, Chief Gatam, *and* Chief Amalek. These *were* the chiefs of Eliphaz in the land of Edom. They *were* the sons of Adah. 17 These *were* the sons of Reuel, Esau's son: Chief Nahath, Chief Zerah, Chief Shammah, and Chief Mizzah. These *were* the chiefs of Reuel in the land of Edom. These *were* the sons of Basemath, Esau's wife. 18 And these *were* the sons of Aholibamah, Esau's wife: Chief Jeush, Chief Jaalam, and Chief Korah. These *were* the chiefs *who descended* from Aholibamah, Esau's wife, the daughter of Anah. 19 These *were* the sons of Esau, who is Edom, and these *were* their chiefs. 20 These *were* the sons of Seir the Horite who inhabited the land: Lotan, Shobal, Zibeon, Anah, 21 Dishon, Ezer, and Dishan. These *were* the chiefs of the Horites, the sons of Seir, in the land of Edom. 22 And the sons of Lotan were Hori and Hemam. Lotan's sister *was* Timna. 23 These *were* the sons of Shobal: Alvan, Manahath, Ebal, Shepho, and Onam. 24 These *were* the sons of Zibeon: both Ajah and Anah. This *was the* Anah who found the water in the wilderness as he pastured the donkeys of his father Zibeon. 25 These *were* the children of Anah: Dishon and Aholibamah the daughter of Anah. 26 These *were* the sons of Dishon: Hemdan, Eshban, Ithran, and Cheran. 27 These *were* the sons of Ezer: Bilhan, Zaavan, and Akan. 28 These *were* the sons of Dishan: Uz and Aran. 29 These *were* the chiefs of the Horites: Chief Lotan, Chief Shobal, Chief Zibeon, Chief Anah, 30 Chief Dishon, Chief Ezer, and Chief Dishan. These *were* the chiefs of the Horites, according to their chiefs in the land of Seir.

Gen 36:40–43 And these *were* the names of the chiefs of Esau, according to their families and their places, by their names: Chief Timnah, Chief Alvah, Chief Jetheth, 41 Chief Aholibamah, Chief Elah, Chief Pinon, 42 Chief Kenaz, Chief Teman, Chief Mibzar, 43 Chief Magdiel, and Chief Iram. These *were* the chiefs of Edom, according to their dwelling places in the land of their possession. Esau *was* the father of the Edomites.

Ex 15:15 Then the chiefs of Edom will be dismayed; The mighty men of Moab, Trembling will take hold of them; All the inhabitants of Canaan will melt away.

Afterwards had kings.

Num 20:14 Now Moses sent messengers from Kadesh to the king of Edom. "Thus says your brother Israel: 'You know all the hardship that has befallen us,

Under a deputy while subject to Judah.

1 Kin 22:47 *There was* then no king in Edom, only a deputy of the king.

Character of,

Wise.

Jer 49:7 Against Edom. Thus says the LORD of hosts: "*Is* wisdom no more in Teman? Has counsel perished from the prudent? Has their wisdom vanished?

Proud and self-confident.

Jer 49:16 Your fierceness has deceived you, The pride of your heart, O you who dwell in the clefts of the rock, Who hold the height of the hill! Though you make your nest as high as the eagle, I will bring you down from there," says the LORD.

Obad 1:3 The pride of your heart has deceived you, *You* who dwell in the clefts of the rock, Whose habitation is high; *You* who say in your heart, 'Who will bring me down to the ground?'

Lion-like.

Jer 49:19 "Behold, he shall come up like a lion from the floodplain of the Jordan Against the dwelling place of the strong; But I will suddenly make him run away from her. And who *is* a chosen *man that* I may appoint over her? For who *is* like Me? Who will arraign Me? And who *is* that shepherd Who will withstand Me?"

Vindictive.

Ezek 25:12 'Thus says the Lord GOD: "Because of what Edom did against the house of Judah by taking vengeance, and has greatly offended by avenging itself on them,"

Idolatrous.

2 Chr 25:14 Now it was so, after Amaziah came from the slaughter of the Edomites, that he brought the gods of the people of Seir, set them up *to be* his gods, and bowed down before them and burned incense to them.

2 Chr 25:20 But Amaziah would not heed, for it *came* from God, that He might give them into the hand *of their enemies*, because they sought the gods of Edom.

Superstitious.

Jer 27:9 Therefore do not listen to your prophets, your diviners, your dreamers, your soothsayers, or your sorcerers, who speak to you, saying, "You shall not serve the king of Babylon."

Carried on extensive commerce.

Ezek 27:20 Dedan *was* your merchant in saddlecloths for riding.

Country of,

Specially given to them.

Deut 2:5 Do not meddle with them, for I will not give you *any* of their land, no, not so much as one footstep, because I have given Mount Seir to Esau *as a* possession.

Fertile and rich.

Gen 27:39 Then Isaac his father answered and said to him: "Behold, your dwelling shall be of the fatness of the earth, And of the dew of heaven from above.

Mountainous and rocky.

Jer 49:16 Your fierceness has deceived you, The pride of your heart, O you who dwell in the clefts of the rock, Who hold the height of the hill! Though you make your nest as high as the eagle, I will bring you down from there," says the LORD.

Mal 1:3 But Esau I have hated, And laid waste his mountains and his heritage For the jackals of the wilderness."

Traversed by roads.

Num 20:17 Please let us pass through your country. We will not pass through fields or vineyards, nor will we drink water from wells; we will go along the King's Highway; we will not turn aside to the right hand or to the left until we have passed through your territory.' "

Well fortified.

Ps 60:9 Who will bring me *to* the strong city? Who will lead me to Edom?

Called Mount Seir.

Ezek 35:2 "Son of man, set your face against Mount Seir and prophesy against it,

Called Mount of Esau.

Obad 1:21 Then saviors shall come to Mount Zion To judge the mountains of Esau, And the kingdom shall be the LORD's.

Called Dumah.

Is 21:11 The burden against Dumah. He calls to me out of Seir, "Watchman, what of the night? Watchman, what of the night?"

Called Idumea.

Mark 3:8 and Jerusalem and Idumea and beyond the Jordan; and those from Tyre and Sidon, a great multitude, when they heard how many things He was doing, came to Him.

Called Edom.

Is 34:6 The sword of the LORD is filled with blood, It is made overflowing with fatness, With the blood of lambs and goats, With the fat of the kidneys of rams. For the LORD has a sacrifice in Bozrah, And a great slaughter in the land of Edom.

Is 63:1 Who *is* this who comes from Edom, With dyed garments from Bozrah, This *One who is* glorious in His apparel, Traveling in the greatness of His strength?— "I who speak in righteousness, mighty to save."

Cities of,

Dinhabah or Dedan.

Gen 36:32 Bela the son of Beor reigned in Edom, and the name of his city *was* Dinhabah.

Jer 49:8 Flee, turn back, dwell in the depths, O inhabitants of Dedan! For I will bring the calamity of Esau upon him, The time *that* I will punish him.

Avith.

Gen 36:35 And when Husham died, Hadad the son of Bedad, who attacked Midian in the field of Moab, reigned in his place. And the name of his city *was* Avith.

Pau.

Gen 36:39 And when Baal-Hanan the son of Achbor died, Hadar reigned in his place; and the name of his city *was* Pau. His wife's name *was* Mehetabel, the daughter of Matred, the daughter of Mezahab.

Bozrah.

Jer 49:22 Behold, He shall come up and fly like the eagle, And spread His wings over Bozrah; The heart of the mighty men of Edom in that day shall be Like the heart of a woman in birth pangs.

Amos 1:12 But I will send a fire upon Teman, Which shall devour the palaces of Bozrah."

Teman.

Jer 49:7 Against Edom. Thus says the LORD of hosts: "*Is* wisdom no more in Teman? Has counsel perished from the prudent? Has their wisdom vanished?

Ezek 25:13 therefore thus says the Lord GOD: "I will also stretch out My hand against Edom, cut off man and beast from it, and make it desolate from Teman; Dedan shall fall by the sword.

Ezion Geber, a seaport.

1 Kin 9:26 King Solomon also built a fleet of ships at Ezion Geber, which *is* near Elath on the shore of the Red Sea, in the land of Edom.

Implacable enemies of Israel.

Ezek 35:5 "Because you have had an ancient hatred, and have shed *the blood of* the children of Israel by the power of the sword at the time of their calamity, *when* their iniquity *came to an* end,

Israel forbidden to hate.

Deut 23:7 "You shall not abhor an Edomite, for he *is* your brother. You shall not abhor an Egyptian, because you were an alien in his land.

Israel forbidden to destroy.

Deut 2:4–6 And command the people, saying, "You *are about to* pass through the territory of your brethren, the descendants of Esau, who live in Seir; and they will be afraid of you. Therefore watch yourselves carefully. 5 Do not meddle with them, for I will not give you *any* of their land, no, not so much as one footstep, because I have given Mount Seir to Esau *as* a possession. 6 You shall buy food from them with money, that you may eat; and you shall also buy water from them with money, that you may drink.

2 Chr 20:10 And now, here are the people of Ammon, Moab, and Mount Seir—whom You would not let Israel invade when they came out of the land of Egypt, but they turned from them and did not destroy them—

Might be received into the congregation in third generation.

> **Deut 23:8** The children of the third generation born to them may enter the assembly of the LORD.

Refused Israel a passage.

> **Num 20:21** Thus Edom refused to give Israel passage through his territory; so Israel turned away from him.

> **Judg 11:17** Then Israel sent messengers to the king of Edom, saying, "Please let me pass through your land." But the king of Edom would not heed. And in like manner they sent to the king of Moab, but he would not *consent*. So Israel remained in Kadesh.

Saul made war against.

> **1 Sam 14:47** So Saul established his sovereignty over Israel, and fought against all his enemies on every side, against Moab, against the people of Ammon, against Edom, against the kings of Zobah, and against the Philistines. Wherever he turned, he harassed *them*.

David subdued.

> **2 Sam 8:14** He also put garrisons in Edom; throughout all Edom he put garrisons, and all the Edomites became David's servants. And the LORD preserved David wherever he went.

> **1 Chr 18:11** King David also dedicated these to the LORD, along with the silver and gold that he had brought from all *these* nations—from Edom, from Moab, from the people of Ammon, from the Philistines, and from Amalek.

> **1 Chr 18:13** He also put garrisons in Edom, and all the Edomites became David's servants. And the LORD preserved David wherever he went.

Slaughter of, by Joab and Abishai.

> **1 Kin 11:16** (because for six months Joab remained there with all Israel, until he had cut down every male in Edom),

> **1 Chr 18:12** Moreover Abishai the son of Zeruiah killed eighteen thousand Edomites in the Valley of Salt.

Took refuge in Egypt.

> **1 Kin 11:17–19** that Hadad fled to go to Egypt, he and certain Edomites of his father's servants with him. Hadad *was* still a little child. 18 Then they arose from Midian and came to Paran; and they took men with them from Paran and came to Egypt, to Pharaoh king of Egypt, who gave him a house, apportioned food for him, and gave him land. 19 And Hadad found great favor in the sight of Pharaoh, so that he gave him as wife the sister of his own wife, that is, the sister of Queen Tahpenes.

Returned after David's death.

> **1 Kin 11:21–22** So when Hadad heard in Egypt that David rested with his fathers, and that Joab the commander of the army was dead, Hadad said to Pharaoh, "Let me depart, that I may go to my own country." 22 Then Pharaoh said to him, "But what have you lacked with me, that suddenly you seek to go to your own country?" So he answered, "Nothing, but do let me go anyway."

Were stirred up against Solomon.

> **1 Kin 11:14** Now the LORD raised up an adversary against Solomon, Hadad the Edomite; he *was* a descendant of the king in Edom.

Confederated with enemies of Israel against Jehoshaphat.

> **2 Chr 20:10** And now, here are the people of Ammon, Moab, and Mount Seir—whom You would not let Israel invade when they came out of the land of Egypt, but they turned from them and did not destroy them—

> **Ps 83:4–6** They have said, "Come, and let us cut them off from *being* a nation, That the name of Israel may be remembered no more." 5 For they have consulted together with one consent; They form a confederacy against You: 6 The tents of Edom and the Ishmaelites; Moab and the Hagrites;

Miraculous overthrow of.

> **2 Chr 20:22** Now when they began to sing and to praise, the LORD set ambushes against the people of Ammon, Moab, and Mount Seir, who had come against Judah; and they were defeated.

Revolted against Joram, king of Judah.

> **2 Kin 8:20–22** In his days Edom revolted against Judah's authority, and made a king over themselves. 21 So Joram went to Zair, and all his chariots with him. Then he rose by night and attacked the Edomites who had surrounded him and the captains of the chariots; and the troops fled to their tents. 22 Thus Edom has been in revolt against Judah's authority to this day. And Libnah revolted at that time.

> **2 Chr 21:8–10** In his days Edom revolted against Judah's authority, and made a king over themselves. 9 So Jehoram went out with his officers, and all his chariots with him. And he rose by night and attacked the Edomites who had surrounded him and the captains of the chariots. 10 Thus Edom has been in revolt against Judah's authority to this day. At that time Libnah revolted against his rule, because he had forsaken the LORD God of his fathers.

Reconquered by Amaziah.

> **2 Kin 14:7** He killed ten thousand Edomites in the Valley of Salt, and took Sela by war, and called its name Joktheel to this day.

> **2 Kin 14:10** You have indeed defeated Edom, and your heart has lifted you up. Glory *in that*, and stay at home; for why should you meddle with trouble so that you fall—you and Judah with you?"

> **2 Chr 25:11–12** Then Amaziah strengthened himself, and leading his people, he went to the Valley of Salt and killed ten thousand of the people of Seir. 12 Also the children of Judah took captive ten thousand alive, brought them to the top of the rock, and cast them down from the top of the rock, so that they all were dashed in pieces.

The Jews ensnared by the idols of, and punished.

> **2 Chr 25:14–15** Now it was so, after Amaziah came from the slaughter of the Edomites, that he brought the gods of the people of Seir, set them up *to be* his gods, and bowed down before them and burned incense to them. 15 Therefore the anger of the LORD was aroused against Amaziah, and He sent him a prophet who said to him, "Why have you sought the gods of the people, which could not rescue their own people from your hand?"

> **2 Chr 25:20** But Amaziah would not heed, for it *came* from God, that He might give them into the hand *of their enemies*, because they sought the gods of Edom.

Rebelled against Ahaz.

2 Chr 28:17 For again the Edomites had come, attacked Judah, and carried away captives.

Aided Babylon against Judah.

Ps 137:7 Remember, O LORD, against the sons of Edom The day of Jerusalem, Who said, "Raze it, raze it, To its very foundation!"

Obad 1:11 In the day that you stood on the other side— In the day that strangers carried captive his forces, When foreigners entered his gates And cast lots for Jerusalem— Even you *were* as one of them.

Predictions respecting,

Subjection to Israel.

Gen 25:23 And the LORD said to her: "Two nations *are* in your womb, Two peoples shall be separated from your body; *One* people shall be stronger than the other, And the older shall serve the younger."

Gen 27:29 Let peoples serve you, And nations bow down to you. Be master over your brethren, And let your mother's sons bow down to you. Cursed *be* everyone who curses you, And blessed *be* those who bless you!"

Gen 27:37 Then Isaac answered and said to Esau, "Indeed I have made him your master, and all his brethren I have given to him as servants; with grain and wine I have sustained him. What shall I do now for you, my son?"

Is 11:14 But they shall fly down upon the shoulder of the Philistines toward the west; Together they shall plunder the people of the East; They shall lay their hand on Edom and Moab; And the people of Ammon shall obey them.

Amos 9:12 That they may possess the remnant of Edom, And all the Gentiles who are called by My name," Says the LORD who does this thing.

Revolt from Israel.

Gen 27:40 By your sword you shall live, And you shall serve your brother; And it shall come to pass, when you become restless, That you shall break his yoke from your neck."

Israel's occupation of their country.

Num 24:18 "And Edom shall be a possession; Seir also, his enemies, shall be a possession, While Israel does valiantly.

Obad 1:17–19 "But on Mount Zion there shall be deliverance, And there shall be holiness; The house of Jacob shall possess their possessions. **18** The house of Jacob shall be a fire, And the house of Joseph a flame; But the house of Esau *shall be* stubble; They shall kindle them and devour them, And no survivor shall *remain* of the house of Esau," For the LORD has spoken. **19** The South shall possess the mountains of Esau, And the Lowland shall possess Philistia. They shall possess the fields of Ephraim And the fields of Samaria. Benjamin *shall possess* Gilead.

To share in the punishment of the nations.

Jer 9:26 Egypt, Judah, Edom, the people of Ammon, Moab, and all *who are* in the farthest corners, who dwell in the wilderness. For all *these* nations *are* uncircumcised, and all the house of Israel *are* uncircumcised in the heart."

Ezek 32:29 "There is Edom, Her kings and all her princes, Who despite their might Are laid beside *those* slain by the sword; They shall lie with the uncircumcised, And with those who go down to the Pit.

Cf. Jer 25:15–27

Punishment for persecuting Israel.

Is 34:5–8 "For My sword shall be bathed in heaven; Indeed it shall come down on Edom, And on the people of My curse, for judgment. **6** The sword of the LORD is filled with blood, It is made overflowing with fatness, With the blood of lambs and goats, With the fat of the kidneys of rams. For the LORD has a sacrifice in Bozrah, And a great slaughter in the land of Edom. **7** The wild oxen shall come down with them, And the young bulls with the mighty bulls; Their land shall be soaked with blood, And their dust saturated with fatness." **8** For *it is* the day of the LORD's vengeance, The year of recompense for the cause of Zion.

Is 63:1–4 Who *is* this who comes from Edom, With dyed garments from Bozrah, This *One who is* glorious in His apparel, Traveling in the greatness of His strength?— "I who speak in righteousness, mighty to save." **2** Why *is* Your apparel red, And Your garments like one who treads in the winepress? **3** "I have trodden the winepress alone, And from the peoples no one *was* with Me. For I have trodden them in My anger, And trampled them in My fury; Their blood is sprinkled upon My garments, And I have stained all My robes. **4** For the day of vengeance *is* in My heart, And the year of My redeemed has come.

Lam 4:21 Rejoice and be glad, O daughter of Edom, *You* who dwell in the land of Uz! The cup shall also pass over to you And you shall become drunk and make yourself naked.

Ezek 25:13–14 therefore thus says the Lord GOD: "I will also stretch out My hand against Edom, cut off man and beast from it, and make it desolate from Teman; Dedan shall fall by the sword. **14** I will lay My vengeance on Edom by the hand of My people Israel, that they may do in Edom according to My anger and according to My fury; and they shall know My vengeance," says the Lord GOD.

Amos 1:11–12 Thus says the LORD: "For three transgressions of Edom, and for four, I will not turn away its *punishment*, Because he pursued his brother with the sword, And cast off all pity; His anger tore perpetually, And he kept his wrath forever. **12** But I will send a fire upon Teman, Which shall devour the palaces of Bozrah."

Obad 1:10 "For violence against your brother Jacob, Shame shall cover you, And you shall be cut off forever.

Obad 1:15 "For the day of the LORD upon all the nations *is* near; As you have done, it shall be done to you; Your reprisal shall return upon your own head.

Exterminating slaughter of.

Obad 1:18 The house of Jacob shall be a fire, And the house of Joseph a flame; But the house of Esau *shall be* stubble; They shall kindle them and devour them, And no survivor shall *remain* of the house of Esau," For the LORD has spoken.

Utter desolation of their country.

Is 34:9–17 Its streams shall be turned into pitch, And its dust into brimstone; Its land shall become burning pitch. **10** It shall not be quenched night or day; Its smoke shall ascend forever. From generation to generation it shall lie waste; No one shall pass through it forever and ever. **11** But the pelican and the porcupine shall possess it, Also the owl and the raven shall dwell in it. And He shall stretch out over it The line of confusion and the stones of emptiness. **12** They shall call its nobles to the kingdom, But none *shall be* there, and all its princes shall be nothing. **13** And thorns shall come up in its palaces, Nettles and brambles in its fortresses; It shall be a habitation of jackals, A courtyard for ostriches. **14** The wild beasts of the desert shall also meet with the jackals, And the wild goat shall bleat to its companion; Also the night creature shall rest there, And find for herself a place of rest. **15** There the arrow snake shall make her nest and lay *eggs* And hatch, and gather *them* under her shadow; There also shall the hawks be gathered, Every one with her mate. **16** "Search from the book of the LORD, and read: Not one of these shall fail; Not one shall lack her mate. For My mouth has commanded it, and His Spirit has gathered them. **17** He has cast the lot for them, And His hand has divided it among them with a measuring line. They shall possess it forever; From generation to generation they shall dwell in it."

Cf. Ezek 35:7–15

The king of Babylon an instrument of their punishment.

Jer 27:3–6 and send them to the king of Edom, the king of Moab, the king of the Ammonites, the king of Tyre, and the king of Sidon, by the hand of the messengers who come to Jerusalem to Zedekiah king of Judah. **4** And command them to say to their masters, "Thus says the LORD of hosts, the God of Israel—thus you shall say to your masters: **5** 'I have made the earth, the man and the beast that *are* on the ground, by My great power and by My outstretched arm, and have given it to whom it seemed proper to Me. **6** And now I have given all these lands into the hand of Nebuchadnezzar the king of Babylon, My servant; and the beasts of the field I have also given him to serve him.

Israel an instrument of their punishment.

Ezek 25:14 I will lay My vengeance on Edom by the hand of My people Israel, that they may do in Edom according to My anger and according to My fury; and they shall know My vengeance," says the Lord GOD.

Obad 1:18 The house of Jacob shall be a fire, And the house of Joseph a flame; But the house of Esau *shall be* stubble; They shall kindle them and devour them, And no survivor shall *remain* of the house of Esau," For the LORD has spoken.

Their ruin to be an astonishment.

Jer 49:17 "Edom also shall be an astonishment; Everyone who goes by it will be astonished And will hiss at all its plagues.

Jer 49:21 The earth shakes at the noise of their fall; At the cry its noise is heard at the Red Sea.

Remarkable persons of,

Doeg.

1 Sam 22:18 And the king said to Doeg, "You turn and kill the priests!" So Doeg the Edomite turned and struck the priests, and killed on that day eighty-five men who wore a linen ephod.

Hadad.

1 Kin 11:14 Now the LORD raised up an adversary against Solomon, Hadad the Edomite; he *was* a descendant of the king in Edom.

1 Kin 11:19 And Hadad found great favor in the sight of Pharaoh, so that he gave him as wife the sister of his own wife, that is, the sister of Queen Tahpenes.

Eliphaz.

Job 2:11 Now when Job's three friends heard of all this adversity that had come upon him, each one came from his own place—Eliphaz the Temanite, Bildad the Shuhite, and Zophar the Naamathite. For they had made an appointment together to come and mourn with him, and to comfort him.

EGYPT

Peopled by Mizraim's posterity.

Gen 10:6 The sons of Ham *were* Cush, Mizraim, Put, and Canaan.

Gen 10:13–14 Mizraim begot Ludim, Anamim, Lehabim, Naphtuhim, **14** Pathrusim, and Casluhim (from whom came the Philistines and Caphtorim).

Boundaries of.

Ezek 29:10 Indeed, therefore, I *am* against you and against your rivers, and I will make the land of Egypt utterly waste and desolate, from Migdol *to* Syene, as far as the border of Ethiopia.

Dry climate of.

Deut 11:10–11 For the land which you go to possess *is* not like the land of Egypt from which you have come, where you sowed your seed and watered *it* by foot, as a vegetable garden; **11** but the land which you cross over to possess *is* a land of hills and valleys, which drinks water from the rain of heaven,

Watered by the Nile.

Gen 41:1–3 Then it came to pass, at the end of two full years, that Pharaoh had a dream; and behold, he stood by the river. **2** Suddenly there came up out of the river seven cows, fine looking and fat; and they fed in the meadow. **3** Then behold, seven other cows came up after them out of the river, ugly and gaunt, and stood by the *other* cows on the bank of the river.

Ex 1:22 So Pharaoh commanded all his people, saying, "Every son who is born you shall cast into the river, and every daughter you shall save alive."

Flooding of, alluded to.

Amos 8:8 Shall the land not tremble for this, And everyone mourn who dwells in it? All of it shall swell like the River, Heave and subside Like the River of Egypt.

Subject to plague, etc.

Gen 41:30 but after them seven years of famine will arise, and all the plenty will be forgotten in the land of Egypt; and the famine will deplete the land.

Deut 7:15 And the LORD will take away from you all sickness, and will afflict you with none of the terrible diseases of Egypt which you have known, but will lay *them* on all those who hate you.

Deut 28:27 The LORD will strike you with the boils of Egypt, with tumors, with the scab, and with the itch, from which you cannot be healed.

Deut 28:60 Moreover He will bring back on you all the diseases of Egypt, of which you were afraid, and they shall cling to you.

Other names for,

The land of Ham.

Ps 105:23 Israel also came into Egypt, And Jacob dwelt in the land of Ham.

Ps 106:22 Wondrous works in the land of Ham, Awesome things by the Red Sea.

The South.

Jer 13:19 The cities of the South shall be shut up, And no one shall open *them;* Judah shall be carried away captive, all of it; It shall be wholly carried away captive.

Cf. Dan 11:14,25

Sihor.

Is 23:3 And on great waters the grain of Shihor, The harvest of the River, *is* her revenue; And she is a marketplace for the nations.

Rahab.

Ps 87:4 "I will make mention of Rahab and Babylon to those who know Me; Behold, O Philistia and Tyre, with Ethiopia: 'This *one* was born there.' "

Ps 89:10 You have broken Rahab in pieces, as one who is slain; You have scattered Your enemies with Your mighty arm.

House of bondage.

Ex 13:3 And Moses said to the people: "Remember this day in which you went out of Egypt, out of the house of bondage; for by strength of hand the LORD brought you out of this *place.* No leavened bread shall be eaten.

Ex 13:14 So it shall be, when your son asks you in time to come, saying, 'What *is* this?' that you shall say to him, 'By strength of hand the LORD brought us out of Egypt, out of the house of bondage.

Deut 7:8 but because the LORD loves you, and because He would keep the oath which He swore to your fathers, the LORD has brought you out with a mighty hand, and redeemed you from the house of bondage, from the hand of Pharaoh king of Egypt.

Celebrated for

Fertility.

Gen 13:10 And Lot lifted his eyes and saw all the plain of Jordan, that it *was* well watered everywhere (before the LORD destroyed Sodom and Gomorrah) like the garden of the LORD, like the land of Egypt as you go toward Zoar.

Gen 45:18 Bring your father and your households and come to me; I will give you the best of the land of Egypt, and you will eat the fat of the land.

Wealth.

Heb 11:26 esteeming the reproach of Christ greater riches than the treasures in Egypt; for he looked to the reward.

Literature.

1 Kin 4:30 Thus Solomon's wisdom excelled the wisdom of all the men of the East and all the wisdom of Egypt.

Acts 7:22 And Moses was learned in all the wisdom of the Egyptians, and was mighty in words and deeds.

Fine horses.

1 Kin 10:28–29 Also Solomon had horses imported from Egypt and Keveh; the king's merchants bought them in Keveh at the *current* price. **29** Now a chariot that was imported from Egypt cost six hundred *shekels* of silver, and a horse one hundred and fifty; and thus, through their agents, they exported *them* to all the kings of the Hittites and the kings of Syria.

Fine linen, etc.

Prov 7:16 I have spread my bed with tapestry, Colored coverings of Egyptian linen.

Is 19:9 Moreover those who work in fine flax And those who weave fine fabric will be ashamed;

Commerce.

Gen 41:57 So all countries came to Joseph in Egypt to buy *grain,* because the famine was severe in all lands.

Ezek 27:7 Fine embroidered linen from Egypt was what you spread for your sail; Blue and purple from the coasts of Elishah was what covered you.

Religion of, idolatrous.

Ex 12:12 'For I will pass through the land of Egypt on that night, and will strike all the firstborn in the land of Egypt, both man and beast; and against all the gods of Egypt I will execute judgment: I *am* the LORD.

Num 33:4 For the Egyptians were burying all *their* firstborn, whom the LORD had killed among them. Also on their gods the LORD had executed judgments.

Is 19:1 The burden against Egypt. Behold, the LORD rides on a swift cloud, And will come into Egypt; The idols of Egypt will totter at His presence, And the heart of Egypt will melt in its midst.

Idolatry of, followed by Israel.

Ex 32:4 And he received *the gold* from their hand, and he fashioned it with an engraving tool, and made a molded calf. Then they said, "This *is* your god, O Israel, that brought you out of the land of Egypt!"

Ezek 20:8 But they rebelled against Me and would not obey Me. They did not all cast away the abominations which were before their eyes, nor did they forsake the idols of Egypt. Then I said, 'I will pour out My fury on them and fulfill My anger against them in the midst of the land of Egypt.'

Ezek 20:19 I *am* the LORD your God: Walk in My statutes, keep My judgments, and do them;

Magic practiced in.

Ex 7:11–12 But Pharaoh also called the wise men and the sorcerers; so the magicians of Egypt, they also did in like manner with their enchantments. **12** For every man threw down his rod, and they became serpents. But Aaron's rod swallowed up their rods.

Ex 7:22 Then the magicians of Egypt did so with their enchantments; and Pharaoh's heart grew hard, and he did not heed them, as the LORD had said.

Ex 8:7 And the magicians did so with their enchantments, and brought up frogs on the land of Egypt.

Ruled by kings called the Pharaohs.

Gen 12:14–15 So it was, when Abram came into Egypt,

that the Egyptians saw the woman, that she *was* very beautiful. **15** The princes of Pharaoh also saw her and commended her to Pharaoh. And the woman was taken to Pharaoh's house.

Gen 40:1–2 It came to pass after these things *that* the butler and the baker of the king of Egypt offended their lord, the king of Egypt. **2** And Pharaoh was angry with his two officers, the chief butler and the chief baker.

Ex 1:8 Now there arose a new king over Egypt, who did not know Joseph.

Ex 1:22 So Pharaoh commanded all his people, saying, "Every son who is born you shall cast into the river, and every daughter you shall save alive."

Under a governor.

Gen 41:41–44 And Pharaoh said to Joseph, "See, I have set you over all the land of Egypt." **42** Then Pharaoh took his signet ring off his hand and put it on Joseph's hand; and he clothed him in garments of fine linen and put a gold chain around his neck. **43** And he had him ride in the second chariot which he had; and they cried out before him, "Bow the knee!" So he set him over all the land of Egypt. **44** Pharaoh also said to Joseph, "I *am* Pharaoh, and without your consent no man may lift his hand or foot in all the land of Egypt."

Had princes and counselors.

Gen 12:15 The princes of Pharaoh also saw her and commended her to Pharaoh. And the woman was taken to Pharaoh's house.

Is 19:11 Surely the princes of Zoan *are* fools; Pharaoh's wise counselors give foolish counsel. How do you say to Pharaoh, "I *am* the son of the wise, The son of ancient kings?"

National characteristics of,

Proud and arrogant.

Ezek 29:3 Speak, and say, 'Thus says the Lord GOD: "Behold, I *am* against you, O Pharaoh king of Egypt, O great monster who lies in the midst of his rivers, Who has said, 'My River *is* my own; I have made *it* for myself.'

Ezek 30:6 'Thus says the LORD: "Those who uphold Egypt shall fall, And the pride of her power shall come down. From Migdol *to* Syene Those within her shall fall by the sword," Says the Lord GOD.

Pompous.

Ezek 32:12 By the swords of the mighty warriors, all of them the most terrible of the nations, I will cause your multitude to fall. 'They shall plunder the pomp of Egypt, And all its multitude shall be destroyed.

Strong.

Is 30:2–3 Who walk to go down to Egypt, And have not asked My advice, To strengthen themselves in the strength of Pharaoh, And to trust in the shadow of Egypt! **3** Therefore the strength of Pharaoh Shall be your shame, And trust in the shadow of Egypt Shall be *your* humiliation.

Ambitious of conquests.

Jer 46:8 Egypt rises up like a flood, And *its* waters move like the rivers; And he says, 'I will go up *and* cover the earth, I will destroy the city and its inhabitants.'

Treacherous.

Is 29:6–7 You will be punished by the LORD of hosts With thunder and earthquake and great noise, *With* storm and tempest And the flame of devouring fire. **7** The multitude of all the nations who fight against Ariel, Even all who fight against her and her fortress, And distress her, Shall be as a dream of a night vision.

Is 36:6 Look! You are trusting in the staff of this broken reed, Egypt, on which if a man leans, it will go into his hand and pierce it. So *is* Pharaoh king of Egypt to all who trust in him.

Inhabitants of,

Superstitious.

Is 19:3 The spirit of Egypt will fail in its midst; I will destroy their counsel, And they will consult the idols and the charmers, The mediums and the sorcerers.

Hospitable.

Gen 47:5–6 Then Pharaoh spoke to Joseph, saying, "Your father and your brothers have come to you. **6** The land of Egypt *is* before you. Have your father and brothers dwell in the best of the land; let them dwell in the land of Goshen. And if you know *any* competent men among them, then make them chief herdsmen over my livestock."

1 Kin 11:18 Then they arose from Midian and came to Paran; and they took men with them from Paran and came to Egypt, to Pharaoh king of Egypt, who gave him a house, apportioned food for him, and gave him land.

Often intermarried with strangers.

Gen 21:21 He dwelt in the Wilderness of Paran; and his mother took a wife for him from the land of Egypt.

1 Kin 3:1 Now Solomon made a treaty with Pharaoh king of Egypt, and married Pharaoh's daughter; then he brought her to the City of David until he had finished building his own house, and the house of the LORD, and the wall all around Jerusalem.

1 Kin 11:19 And Hadad found great favor in the sight of Pharaoh, so that he gave him as wife the sister of his own wife, that is, the sister of Queen Tahpenes.

1 Chr 2:34–35 Now Sheshan had no sons, only daughters. And Sheshan had an Egyptian servant whose name *was* Jarha. **35** Sheshan gave his daughter to Jarha his servant as wife, and she bore him Attai.

Abhorred shepherds.

Gen 46:34 that you shall say, 'Your servants' occupation has been with livestock from our youth even till now, both we *and* also our fathers,' that you may dwell in the land of Goshen; for every shepherd *is* an abomination to the Egyptians."

Abhorred the sacrifice of oxen, etc.

Ex 8:26 And Moses said, "It is not right to do so, for we would be sacrificing the abomination of the Egyptians to the LORD our God. If we sacrifice the abomination of the Egyptians before their eyes, then will they not stone us?

Not to be abhorred by Israel.

Deut 23:7 "You shall not abhor an Edomite, for he *is* your brother. You shall not abhor an Egyptian, because you were an alien in his land.

Might be received into the congregation in the third generation.

Deut 23:8 The children of the third generation born to them may enter the assembly of the LORD.

Mode of entertaining in.

Gen 43:32–34 So they set him a place by himself, and them by themselves, and the Egyptians who ate with him by themselves; because the Egyptians could not eat food with the Hebrews, for that *is* an abomination to the Egyptians. **33** And they sat before him, the firstborn according to his birthright and the youngest according to his youth; and the men looked in astonishment at one another. **34** Then he took servings to them from before him, but Benjamin's serving was five times as much as any of theirs. So they drank and were merry with him.

Diet used in.

Num 11:5 We remember the fish which we ate freely in Egypt, the cucumbers, the melons, the leeks, the onions, and the garlic;

Mode of embalming in.

Gen 50:3 Forty days were required for him, for such are the days required for those who are embalmed; and the Egyptians mourned for him seventy days.

Often a refuge to strangers.

Gen 12:10 Now there was a famine in the land, and Abram went down to Egypt to dwell there, for the famine *was* severe in the land.

Gen 47:4 And they said to Pharaoh, "We have come to dwell in the land, because your servants have no pasture for their flocks, for the famine *is* severe in the land of Canaan. Now therefore, please let your servants dwell in the land of Goshen."

1 Kin 11:17 that Hadad fled to go to Egypt, he and certain Edomites of his father's servants with him. Hadad *was* still a little child.

1 Kin 11:40 Solomon therefore sought to kill Jeroboam. But Jeroboam arose and fled to Egypt, to Shishak king of Egypt, and was in Egypt until the death of Solomon.

2 Kin 25:26 And all the people, small and great, and the captains of the armies, arose and went to Egypt; for they were afraid of the Chaldeans.

Matt 2:12–13 Then, being divinely warned in a dream that they should not return to Herod, they departed for their own country another way. **13** Now when they had departed, behold, an angel of the Lord appeared to Joseph in a dream, saying, "Arise, take the young Child and His mother, flee to Egypt, and stay there until I bring you word; for Herod will seek the young Child to destroy Him."

The armies of,

Described.

Ex 14:7–9 Also, he took six hundred choice chariots, and all the chariots of Egypt with captains over every one of them. **8** And the LORD hardened the heart of Pharaoh king of Egypt, and he pursued the children of Israel; and the children of Israel went out with boldness. **9** So the Egyptians pursued them, all the horses *and* chariots of Pharaoh, his horsemen and his army, and overtook them camping by the sea beside Pi Hahiroth, before Baal Zephon.

Destroyed in the Red Sea.

Ex 14:23–28 And the Egyptians pursued and went after them into the midst of the sea, all Pharaoh's horses, his chariots, and his horsemen. **24** Now it came to pass, in the morning watch, that the LORD looked down upon the army of the Egyptians through the pillar of fire and cloud, and He troubled the army of the Egyptians. **25** And He took off their chariot wheels, so that they drove them with difficulty; and the Egyptians said, "Let us flee from the face of Israel, for the LORD fights for them against the Egyptians." **26** Then the LORD said to Moses, "Stretch out your hand over the sea, that the waters may come back upon the Egyptians, on their chariots, and on their horsemen." **27** And Moses stretched out his hand over the sea; and when the morning appeared, the sea returned to its full depth, while the Egyptians were fleeing into it. So the LORD overthrew the Egyptians in the midst of the sea. **28** Then the waters returned and covered the chariots, the horsemen, *and* all the army of Pharaoh that came into the sea after them. Not so much as one of them remained.

Captured and burned Gezer.

1 Kin 9:16 (Pharaoh king of Egypt had gone up and taken Gezer and burned it with fire, had killed the Canaanites who dwelt in the city, and had given it *as* a dowry to his daughter, Solomon's wife.)

Besieged and plundered Jerusalem in Rehoboam's time.

1 Kin 14:25–26 It happened in the fifth year of King Rehoboam *that* Shishak king of Egypt came up against Jerusalem. **26** And he took away the treasures of the house of the LORD and the treasures of the king's house; he took away everything. He also took away all the gold shields which Solomon had made.

Invaded Assyria and killed Josiah who assisted it.

2 Kin 23:29 In his days Pharaoh Necho king of Egypt went to the aid of the king of Assyria, to the River Euphrates; and King Josiah went against him. And *Pharaoh Necho* killed him at Megiddo when he confronted him.

Deposed Jehoahaz and made Judah pay tribute.

2 Kin 23:31–35 Jehoahaz *was* twenty-three years old when he became king, and he reigned three months in Jerusalem. His mother's name *was* Hamutal the daughter of Jeremiah of Libnah. **32** And he did evil in the sight of the LORD, according to all that his fathers had done. **33** Now Pharaoh Necho put him in prison at Riblah in the land of Hamath, that he might not reign in Jerusalem; and he imposed on the land a tribute of one hundred talents of silver and a talent of gold. **34** Then Pharaoh Necho made Eliakim the son of Josiah king in place of his father Josiah, and changed his name to Jehoiakim. And *Pharaoh* took Jehoahaz and went to Egypt, and he died there. **35** So Jehoiakim gave the silver and gold to Pharaoh; but he taxed the land to give money according to the command of Pharaoh; he exacted the silver and gold from the people of the land, from every one according to his assessment, to give *it* to Pharaoh Necho.

Assistance of, sought by Judah against the Chaldees.

Jer 37:5 Then Pharaoh's army came up from Egypt; and

when the Chaldeans who were besieging Jerusalem heard news of them, they departed from Jerusalem.

Jer 37:7 "Thus says the LORD, the God of Israel, 'Thus you shall say to the king of Judah, who sent you to Me to inquire of Me: "Behold, Pharaoh's army which has come up to help you will return to Egypt, to their own land.

Ezek 17:15 But he rebelled against him by sending his ambassadors to Egypt, that they might give him horses and many people. Will he prosper? Will he who does such *things* escape? Can he break a covenant and still be delivered?

History of Israel in,

Their sojourn in it, foretold.

Gen 15:13 Then He said to Abram: "Know certainly that your descendants will be strangers in a land *that is* not theirs, and will serve them, and they will afflict them four hundred years.

Joseph sold into.

Gen 37:28 Then Midianite traders passed by; so *the brothers* pulled Joseph up and lifted him out of the pit, and sold him to the Ishmaelites for twenty *shekels* of silver. And they took Joseph to Egypt.

Gen 39:1 Now Joseph had been taken down to Egypt. And Potiphar, an officer of Pharaoh, captain of the guard, an Egyptian, bought him from the Ishmaelites who had taken him down there.

Potiphar blessed for Joseph's sake.

Gen 39:2–6 The LORD was with Joseph, and he was a successful man; and he was in the house of his master the Egyptian. 3 And his master saw that the LORD *was* with him and that the LORD made all he did to prosper in his hand. 4 So Joseph found favor in his sight, and served him. Then he made him overseer of his house, and all *that* he had he put under his authority. 5 So it was, from the time *that* he had made him overseer of his house and all that he had, that the LORD blessed the Egyptian's house for Joseph's sake; and the blessing of the LORD was on all that he had in the house and in the field. 6 Thus he left all that he had in Joseph's hand, and he did not know what he had except for the bread which he ate. Now Joseph was handsome in form and appearance.

Joseph unjustly cast into prison.

Gen 39:7–20 And it came to pass after these things that his master's wife cast longing eyes on Joseph, and she said, "Lie with me." 8 But he refused and said to his master's wife, "Look, my master does not know what *is* with me in the house, and he has committed all that he has to my hand. 9 *There is* no one greater in this house than I, nor has he kept back anything from me but you, because you *are* his wife. How then can I do this great wickedness, and sin against God?" 10 So it was, as she spoke to Joseph day by day, that he did not heed her, to lie with her *or* to be with her. 11 But it happened about this time, when Joseph went into the house to do his work, and none of the men of the house *was* inside, 12 that she caught him by his garment, saying, "Lie with me." But he left his garment in her hand, and fled and ran outside. 13 And so it was, when she saw that he had left his garment in her hand and fled outside, 14 that she called to the men of her house and spoke to them,

saying, "See, he has brought in to us a Hebrew to mock us. He came in to me to lie with me, and I cried out with a loud voice. 15 And it happened, when he heard that I lifted my voice and cried out, that he left his garment with me, and fled and went outside." 16 So she kept his garment with her until his master came home. 17 Then she spoke to him with words like these, saying, "The Hebrew servant whom you brought to us came in to me to mock me; 18 so it happened, as I lifted my voice and cried out, that he left his garment with me and fled outside." 19 So it was, when his master heard the words which his wife spoke to him, saying, "Your servant did to me after this manner," that his anger was aroused. 20 Then Joseph's master took him and put him into the prison, a place where the king's prisoners *were* confined. And he was there in the prison.

Joseph interprets the chief baker's and the chief butler's dreams.

Gen 40:5–19 Then the butler and the baker of the king of Egypt, who *were* confined in the prison, had a dream, both of them, each man's dream in one night *and* each man's dream with its *own* interpretation. 6 And Joseph came in to them in the morning and looked at them, and saw that they *were* sad. 7 So he asked Pharaoh's officers who *were* with him in the custody of his lord's house, saying, "Why do you look *so* sad today?" 8 And they said to him, "We each have had a dream, and *there is* no interpreter of it." So Joseph said to them, "Do not interpretations belong to God? Tell *them* to me, please." 9 Then the chief butler told his dream to Joseph, and said to him, "Behold, in my dream a vine *was* before me, 10 and in the vine *were* three branches; it *was* as though it budded, its blossoms shot forth, and its clusters brought forth ripe grapes. 11 Then Pharaoh's cup *was* in my hand; and I took the grapes and pressed them into Pharaoh's cup, and placed the cup in Pharaoh's hand." 12 And Joseph said to him, "This *is* the interpretation of it: The three branches *are* three days. 13 Now within three days Pharaoh will lift up your head and restore you to your place, and you will put Pharaoh's cup in his hand according to the former manner, when you were his butler. 14 But remember me when it is well with you, and please show kindness to me; make mention of me to Pharaoh, and get me out of this house. 15 For indeed I was stolen away from the land of the Hebrews; and also I have done nothing here that they should put me into the dungeon." 16 When the chief baker saw that the interpretation was good, he said to Joseph, "I also *was* in my dream, and there *were* three white baskets on my head. 17 In the uppermost basket *were* all kinds of baked goods for Pharaoh, and the birds ate them out of the basket on my head." 18 So Joseph answered and said, "This *is* the interpretation of it: The three baskets *are* three days. 19 Within three days Pharaoh will lift off your head from you and hang you on a tree; and the birds will eat your flesh from you."

Joseph interprets Pharaoh's dreams.

Gen 41:14–32 Then Pharaoh sent and called Joseph, and they brought him quickly out of the dungeon; and he shaved, changed his clothing, and came to Pharaoh. 15 And Pharaoh said to Joseph, "I have had a dream, and *there is* no one who can interpret it. But I have heard it said of you *that* you can understand a dream, to interpret it." **16** So Joseph answered Pharaoh, saying, "*It is* not in me; God will give Pharaoh an answer of peace." **17** Then Pharaoh said to Joseph: "Behold, in my dream I stood on the bank of the river. **18** Suddenly seven cows came up out of the river, fine looking and fat; and they fed in the meadow. **19** Then behold, seven other cows came up after them, poor and very ugly and gaunt, such ugliness as I have never seen in all the land of Egypt. **20** And the gaunt and ugly cows ate up the first seven, the fat cows. **21** When they had eaten them up, no one would have known that they had eaten them, for they *were* just as ugly as at the beginning. So I awoke. **22** Also I saw in my dream, and suddenly seven heads came up on one stalk, full and good. **23** Then behold, seven heads, withered, thin, *and* blighted by the east wind, sprang up after them. **24** And the thin heads devoured the seven good heads. So I told *this* to the magicians, but *there was* no one who could explain *it* to me." **25** Then Joseph said to Pharaoh, "The dreams of Pharaoh *are* one; God has shown Pharaoh what He *is* about to do: **26** The seven good cows *are* seven years, and the seven good heads *are* seven years; the dreams *are* one. **27** And the seven thin and ugly cows which came up after them *are* seven years, and the seven empty heads blighted by the east wind are seven years of famine. **28** This *is* the thing which I have spoken to Pharaoh. God has shown Pharaoh what He *is* about to do. **29** Indeed seven years of great plenty will come throughout all the land of Egypt; **30** but after them seven years of famine will arise, and all the plenty will be forgotten in the land of Egypt; and the famine will deplete the land. **31** So the plenty will not be known in the land because of the famine following, for it *will be* very severe. **32** And the dream was repeated to Pharaoh twice because the thing *is* established by God, and God will shortly bring it to pass.

Joseph counsels Pharaoh.

Gen 41:33–36 "Now therefore, let Pharaoh select a discerning and wise man, and set him over the land of Egypt. **34** Let Pharaoh do *this*, and let him appoint officers over the land, to collect one-fifth *of the produce* of the land of Egypt in the seven plentiful years. **35** And let them gather all the food of those good years that are coming, and store up grain under the authority of Pharaoh, and let them keep food in the cities. **36** Then that food shall be as a reserve for the land for the seven years of famine which shall be in the land of Egypt, that the land may not perish during the famine."

Joseph made governor.

Gen 41:41–44 And Pharaoh said to Joseph, "See, I have set you over all the land of Egypt." **42** Then Pharaoh took his signet ring off his hand and put it on Joseph's hand; and he clothed him in garments of fine linen and put a gold chain around his neck. **43** And he had him ride in the second chariot which he had; and they cried out before him, "Bow the knee!" So he set him over all the land of Egypt. **44** Pharaoh also said to Joseph, "I *am* Pharaoh, and without your consent no man may lift his hand or foot in all the land of Egypt."

Joseph's successful provision against the years of famine.

Gen 41:46–56 Joseph was thirty years old when he

stood before Pharaoh king of Egypt. And Joseph went out from the presence of Pharaoh, and went throughout all the land of Egypt. **47** Now in the seven plentiful years the ground brought forth abundantly. **48** So he gathered up all the food of the seven years which were in the land of Egypt, and laid up the food in the cities; he laid up in every city the food of the fields which surrounded them. **49** Joseph gathered very much grain, as the sand of the sea, until he stopped counting, for *it was* immeasurable. **50** And to Joseph were born two sons before the years of famine came, whom Asenath, the daughter of Poti-Pherah priest of On, bore to him. **51** Joseph called the name of the firstborn Manasseh: "For God has made me forget all my toil and all my father's house." **52** And the name of the second he called Ephraim: "For God has caused me to be fruitful in the land of my affliction." **53** Then the seven years of plenty which were in the land of Egypt ended, **54** and the seven years of famine began to come, as Joseph had said. The famine was in all lands, but in all the land of Egypt there was bread. **55** So when all the land of Egypt was famished, the people cried to Pharaoh for bread. Then Pharaoh said to all the Egyptians, "Go to Joseph; whatever he says to you, do." **56** The famine was over all the face of the earth, and Joseph opened all the storehouses and sold to the Egyptians. And the famine became severe in the land of Egypt.

Joseph's ten brothers arrive.

Gen 42:1–6 When Jacob saw that there was grain in Egypt, Jacob said to his sons, "Why do you look at one another?" **2** And he said, "Indeed I have heard that there is grain in Egypt; go down to that place and buy for us there, that we may live and not die." **3** So Joseph's ten brothers went down to buy grain in Egypt. **4** But Jacob did not send Joseph's brother Benjamin with his brothers, for he said, "Lest some calamity befall him." **5** And the sons of Israel went to buy *grain* among those who journeyed, for the famine was in the land of Canaan. **6** Now Joseph *was* governor over the land; and it was he who sold to all the people of the land. And Joseph's brothers came and bowed down before him with *their* faces to the earth.

Joseph recognizes his brothers.

Gen 42:7–8 Joseph saw his brothers and recognized them, but he acted as a stranger to them and spoke roughly to them. Then he said to them, "Where do you come from?" And they said, "From the land of Canaan to buy food." **8** So Joseph recognized his brothers, but they did not recognize him.

Benjamin brought to.

Gen 43:15 So the men took that present and Benjamin, and they took double money in their hand, and arose and went down to Egypt; and they stood before Joseph.

Joseph makes himself known to his brothers.

Gen 45:1–8 Then Joseph could not restrain himself before all those who stood by him, and he cried out, "Make everyone go out from me!" So no one stood with him while Joseph made himself known to his brothers. **2** And he wept aloud, and the Egyptians and the house of Pharaoh heard *it*. **3** Then Joseph said to his brothers, "I *am* Joseph; does my father still live?" But his brothers could not answer him, for they were dismayed in his presence. **4** And Joseph said to his brothers, "Please come near to me." So they came near. Then he said: "I *am* Joseph your brother, whom you sold into Egypt. **5** But now, do not therefore be grieved or angry with yourselves because you sold me here; for God sent me before you to preserve life. **6** For these two years the famine *has been* in the land, and *there are* still five years in which *there will be* neither plowing nor harvesting. **7** And God sent me before you to preserve a posterity for you in the earth, and to save your lives by a great deliverance. **8** So now *it was* not you *who* sent me here, but God; and He has made me a father to Pharaoh, and lord of all his house, and a ruler throughout all the land of Egypt.

Joseph sends for his father.

Gen 45:9–11 "Hurry and go up to my father, and say to him, 'Thus says your son Joseph: "God has made me lord of all Egypt; come down to me, do not tarry. **10** You shall dwell in the land of Goshen, and you shall be near to me, you and your children, your children's children, your flocks and your herds, and all that you have. **11** There I will provide for you, lest you and your household, and all that you have, come to poverty; for *there are* still five years of famine." '

Pharaoh invites Jacob into the land.

Gen 45:16–20 Now the report of it was heard in Pharaoh's house, saying, "Joseph's brothers have come." So it pleased Pharaoh and his servants well. **17** And Pharaoh said to Joseph, "Say to your brothers, 'Do this: Load your animals and depart; go to the land of Canaan. **18** Bring your father and your households and come to me; I will give you the best of the land of Egypt, and you will eat the fat of the land. **19** Now you are commanded—do this: Take carts out of the land of Egypt for your little ones and your wives; bring your father and come. **20** Also do not be concerned about your goods, for the best of all the land of Egypt *is* yours.' "

Jacob's journey.

Gen 46:5–7 Then Jacob arose from Beersheba; and the sons of Israel carried their father Jacob, their little ones, and their wives, in the carts which Pharaoh had sent to carry him. **6** So they took their livestock and their goods, which they had acquired in the land of Canaan, and went to Egypt, Jacob and all his descendants with him. **7** His sons and his sons' sons, his daughters and his sons' daughters, and all his descendants he brought with him to Egypt.

Jacob and others presented to Pharaoh.

Gen 47:1–10 Then Joseph went and told Pharaoh, and said, "My father and my brothers, their flocks and their herds and all that they possess, have come from the land of Canaan; and indeed they *are* in the land of Goshen." **2** And he took five men from among his brothers and presented them to Pharaoh. **3** Then Pharaoh said to his brothers, "What *is* your occupation?" And they said to Pharaoh, "Your servants *are* shepherds, both we *and* also our fathers." **4** And they said to Pharaoh, "We have come to dwell in the land, because your servants have no pasture for their flocks, for the famine *is* severe in the land of Canaan. Now therefore, please let your servants dwell in the land of Goshen." **5** Then Pharaoh spoke to Joseph,

saying, "Your father and your brothers have come to you. **6** The land of Egypt *is* before you. Have your father and brothers dwell in the best of the land; let them dwell in the land of Goshen. And if you know *any* competent men among them, then make them chief herdsmen over my livestock." **7** Then Joseph brought in his father Jacob and set him before Pharaoh; and Jacob blessed Pharaoh. **8** Pharaoh said to Jacob, "How old *are* you?" **9** And Jacob said to Pharaoh, "The days of the years of my pilgrimage *are* one hundred and thirty years; few and evil have been the days of the years of my life, and they have not attained to the days of the years of the life of my fathers in the days of their pilgrimage." **10** So Jacob blessed Pharaoh, and went out from before Pharaoh.

Jacob placed in the land of Goshen.

Gen 46:34 that you shall say, 'Your servants' occupation has been with livestock from our youth even till now, both we *and* also our fathers,' that you may dwell in the land of Goshen; for every shepherd *is* an abomination to the Egyptians."

Gen 47:11 And Joseph situated his father and his brothers, and gave them a possession in the land of Egypt, in the best of the land, in the land of Rameses, as Pharaoh had commanded.

Gen 47:27 So Israel dwelt in the land of Egypt, in the country of Goshen; and they had possessions there and grew and multiplied exceedingly.

Joseph enriches the king of.

Gen 47:13–26 Now *there was* no bread in all the land; for the famine *was* very severe, so that the land of Egypt and the land of Canaan languished because of the famine. **14** And Joseph gathered up all the money that was found in the land of Egypt and in the land of Canaan, for the grain which they bought; and Joseph brought the money into Pharaoh's house. **15** So when the money failed in the land of Egypt and in the land of Canaan, all the Egyptians came to Joseph and said, "Give us bread, for why should we die in your presence? For the money has failed." **16** Then Joseph said, "Give your livestock, and I will give you *bread* for your livestock, if the money is gone." **17** So they brought their livestock to Joseph, and Joseph gave them bread *in exchange* for the horses, the flocks, the cattle of the herds, and for the donkeys. Thus he fed them with bread *in exchange* for all their livestock that year. **18** When that year had ended, they came to him the next year and said to him, "We will not hide from my lord that our money is gone; my lord also has our herds of livestock. There is nothing left in the sight of my lord but our bodies and our lands. **19** Why should we die before your eyes, both we and our land? Buy us and our land for bread, and we and our land will be servants of Pharaoh; give *us* seed, that we may live and not die, that the land may not be desolate." **20** Then Joseph bought all the land of Egypt for Pharaoh; for every man of the Egyptians sold his field, because the famine was severe upon them. So the land became Pharaoh's. **21** And as for the people, he moved them into the cities, from *one* end of the borders of Egypt to the *other* end. **22** Only the land of the priests he did not buy; for the priests had rations *allotted to them* by Pharaoh, and they ate their rations which Pharaoh gave them; therefore they did not sell their lands. **23** Then Joseph said to the people, "Indeed I have bought you and your land this day for Pharaoh. Look, *here is* seed for you, and you shall sow the land. **24** And it shall come to pass in the harvest that you shall give one-fifth to Pharaoh. Four-fifths shall be your own, as seed for the field and for your food, for those of your households and as food for your little ones." **25** So they said, "You have saved our lives; let us find favor in the sight of my lord, and we will be Pharaoh's servants." **26** And Joseph made it a law over the land of Egypt to this day, *that* Pharaoh should have one-fifth, except for the land of the priests only, *which* did not become Pharaoh's.

Jacob's death and burial.

Gen 49:33 And when Jacob had finished commanding his sons, he drew his feet up into the bed and breathed his last, and was gathered to his people.

Gen 50:1–13 Then Joseph fell on his father's face and wept over him, and kissed him. **2** And Joseph commanded his servants the physicians to embalm his father. So the physicians embalmed Israel. **3** Forty days were required for him, for such are the days required for those who are embalmed; and the Egyptians mourned for him seventy days. **4** Now when the days of his mourning were past, Joseph spoke to the household of Pharaoh, saying, "If now I have found favor in your eyes, please speak in the hearing of Pharaoh, saying, **5** 'My father made me swear, saying, "Behold, I am dying; in my grave which I dug for myself in the land of Canaan, there you shall bury me." Now therefore, please let me go up and bury my father, and I will come back.' " **6** And Pharaoh said, "Go up and bury your father, as he made you swear." **7** So Joseph went up to bury his father; and with him went up all the servants of Pharaoh, the elders of his house, and all the elders of the land of Egypt, **8** as well as all the house of Joseph, his brothers, and his father's house. Only their little ones, their flocks, and their herds they left in the land of Goshen. **9** And there went up with him both chariots and horsemen, and it was a very great gathering. **10** Then they came to the threshing floor of Atad, which *is* beyond the Jordan, and they mourned there with a great and very solemn lamentation. He observed seven days of mourning for his father. **11** And when the inhabitants of the land, the Canaanites, saw the mourning at the threshing floor of Atad, they said, "This *is* a deep mourning of the Egyptians." Therefore its name was called Abel Mizraim, which *is* beyond the Jordan. **12** So his sons did for him just as he had commanded them. **13** For his sons carried him to the land of Canaan, and buried him in the cave of the field of Machpelah, before Mamre, which Abraham bought with the field from Ephron the Hittite as property for a burial place.

Israelites increase and are oppressed.

Ex 1:1–14 Now these *are* the names of the children of Israel who came to Egypt; each man and his household came with Jacob: **2** Reuben, Simeon, Levi, and Judah; **3** Issachar, Zebulun, and Benjamin; **4** Dan, Naphtali, Gad, and Asher. **5** All those who were descendants of Jacob were seventy persons (for Joseph was in Egypt *already*). **6** And Joseph died, all his brothers, and all that generation. **7** But the children of Israel were fruitful and increased abundantly, multiplied and grew exceedingly mighty; and the land was filled with them. **8** Now there arose a new king over Egypt, who did not know Joseph. **9** And he said to his people, "Look, the people of the children of Israel *are* more and mightier than we; **10** come, let us deal shrewdly with them, lest they multiply, and it happen, in the event of war, that they also join our enemies and fight against us, and *so* go up out of the land." **11** Therefore they set taskmasters over them to afflict them with their burdens. And they built for Pharaoh supply cities, Pithom and Raamses. **12** But the more they afflicted them, the more they multiplied and grew. And they were in dread of the children of Israel. **13** So the Egyptians made the children of Israel serve with rigor. **14** And they made their lives bitter with hard bondage—in mortar, in brick, and in all manner of service in the field. All their service in which they made them serve *was* with rigor.

Male children destroyed.

Ex 1:15–22 Then the king of Egypt spoke to the Hebrew midwives, of whom the name of one *was* Shiphrah and the name of the other Puah; **16** and he said, "When you do the duties of a midwife for the Hebrew women, and see *them* on the birthstools, if it *is* a son, then you shall kill him; but if it *is* a daughter, then she shall live." **17** But the midwives feared God, and did not do as the king of Egypt commanded them, but saved the male children alive. **18** So the king of Egypt called for the midwives and said to them, "Why have you done this thing, and saved the male children alive?" **19** And the midwives said to Pharaoh, "Because the Hebrew women *are* not like the Egyptian women; for they *are* lively and give birth before the midwives come to them." **20** Therefore God dealt well with the midwives, and the people multiplied and grew very mighty. **21** And so it was, because the midwives feared God, that He provided households for them. **22** So Pharaoh commanded all his people, saying, "Every son who is born you shall cast into the river, and every daughter you shall save alive."

Moses born and hidden for three months.

Ex 2:2 So the woman conceived and bore a son. And when she saw that he *was* a beautiful *child,* she hid him three months.

Moses set afloat on the Nile.

Ex 2:3–4 But when she could no longer hide him, she took an ark of bulrushes for him, daubed it with asphalt and pitch, put the child in it, and laid *it* in the reeds by the river's bank. **4** And his sister stood afar off, to know what would be done to him.

Moses adopted and brought up by Pharaoh's daughter.

Ex 2:5–10 Then the daughter of Pharaoh came down to bathe at the river. And her maidens walked along the riverside; and when she saw the ark among the reeds, she sent her maid to get it. **6** And when she opened *it,* she saw the child, and behold, the baby wept. So she had compassion on him, and said, "This is one of the Hebrews' children." **7** Then his sister said to Pharaoh's daughter, "Shall I go and call a nurse for you from the Hebrew women, that she may nurse the child for you?" **8** And Pharaoh's daughter said to her, "Go." So the maiden went and called the child's mother. **9** Then Pharaoh's daughter said to her, "Take this child away and nurse him for me, and I will give *you* your wages." So the woman took the child and nursed him. **10** And the child grew, and she brought him to Pharaoh's daughter, and he became her son. So she called his name Moses, saying, "Because I drew him out of the water."

Moses slays an Egyptian.

Ex 2:11–12 Now it came to pass in those days, when Moses was grown, that he went out to his brethren and looked at their burdens. And he saw an Egyptian beating a Hebrew, one of his brethren. **12** So he looked this way and that way, and when he saw no one, he killed the Egyptian and hid him in the sand.

Moses flees to Midian.

Ex 2:15 When Pharaoh heard of this matter, he sought to kill Moses. But Moses fled from the face of Pharaoh and dwelt in the land of Midian; and he sat down by a well.

Moses sent to Pharaoh.

Ex 3:2–10 And the Angel of the LORD appeared to him in a flame of fire from the midst of a bush. So he looked, and behold, the bush was burning with fire, but the bush *was* not consumed. **3** Then Moses said, "I will now turn aside and see this great sight, why the bush does not burn." **4** So when the LORD saw that he turned aside to look, God called to him from the midst of the bush and said, "Moses, Moses!" And he said, "Here I am." **5** Then He said, "Do not draw near this place. Take your sandals off your feet, for the place where you stand *is* holy ground." **6** Moreover He said, "I *am* the God of your father—the God of Abraham, the God of Isaac, and the God of Jacob." And Moses hid his face, for he was afraid to look upon God. **7** And the LORD said: "I have surely seen the oppression of My people who *are* in Egypt, and have heard their cry because of their taskmasters, for I know their sorrows. **8** So I have come down to deliver them out of the hand of the Egyptians, and to bring them up from that land to a good and large land, to a land flowing with milk and honey, to the place of the Canaanites and the Hittites and the Amorites and the Perizzites and the Hivites and the Jebusites. **9** Now therefore, behold, the cry of the children of Israel has come to Me, and I have also seen the oppression with which the Egyptians oppress them. **10** Come now, therefore, and I will send you to Pharaoh that you may bring My people, the children of Israel, out of Egypt."

Pharaoh increases their affliction. **Ex 5:1–23**

Moses proves his divine mission by miracles.

Ex 4:29–31 Then Moses and Aaron went and gathered together all the elders of the children of Israel. **30** And Aaron spoke all the words which the LORD had spoken to Moses. Then he did the signs in the sight of the people. **31** So the people believed; and when they heard that the LORD had visited the children of Israel and that He had looked on their affliction, then they bowed their heads and worshiped.

Ex 7:10 So Moses and Aaron went in to Pharaoh, and they did so, just as the LORD commanded. And Aaron cast down his rod before Pharaoh and before his servants, and it became a serpent.

Egypt is plagued for Pharaoh's obstinacy. **Ex 7:14—10:29**

The Passover instituted. **Ex 12:1–28**

Destruction of the firstborn.

Ex 12:29–30 And it came to pass at midnight that the LORD struck all the firstborn in the land of Egypt, from the firstborn of Pharaoh who sat on his throne to the firstborn of the captive who *was* in the dungeon, and all the firstborn of livestock. **30** So Pharaoh rose in the night, he, all his servants, and all the Egyptians; and there was a great cry in Egypt, for *there was* not a house where *there was* not one dead.

Israel plunders the Egyptians.

Ex 12:35–36 Now the children of Israel had done according to the word of Moses, and they had asked from the Egyptians articles of silver, articles of gold, and clothing. **36** And the LORD had given the people favor in the sight of the Egyptians, so that they granted them *what they requested.* Thus they plundered the Egyptians.

Israel driven out of.

Ex 12:31–33 Then he called for Moses and Aaron by night, and said, "Rise, go out from among my people, both you and the children of Israel. And go, serve the LORD as you have said. **32** Also take your flocks and your herds, as you have said, and be gone; and bless me also." **33** And the Egyptians urged the people, that they might send them out of the land in haste. For they said, "We *shall* all *be* dead."

Date of the Exodus from.

Ex 12:41 And it came to pass at the end of the four hundred and thirty years—on that very same day—it came to pass that all the armies of the LORD went out from the land of Egypt.

Heb 11:27 By faith he forsook Egypt, not fearing the wrath of the king; for he endured as seeing Him who is invisible.

Pharaoh pursues Israel and is miraculously destroyed. **Ex 14:5–25**

Prophecies respecting,

Dismay of its inhabitants.

Is 19:1 The burden against Egypt. Behold, the LORD rides on a swift cloud, And will come into Egypt; The idols of Egypt will totter at His presence, And the heart of Egypt will melt in its midst.

Is 19:16–17 In that day Egypt will be like women, and will be afraid and fear because of the waving of the hand of the LORD of hosts, which He waves over it. **17** And the land of Judah will be a terror to Egypt; everyone who makes mention of it will be afraid in himself, because of the counsel of the LORD of hosts which He has determined against it.

Infatuation of its princes.

Is 19:3 The spirit of Egypt will fail in its midst; I will destroy their counsel, And they will consult the idols and the charmers, The mediums and the sorcerers.

Is 19:11–14 Surely the princes of Zoan *are* fools; Pharaoh's wise counselors give foolish counsel. How do you say to Pharaoh, "I *am* the son of the wise, The son of ancient kings?" **12** Where *are* they? Where are your wise men? Let them tell you now, And let them know what the LORD of hosts has purposed against

Egypt. **13** The princes of Zoan have become fools; The princes of Noph are deceived; They have also deluded Egypt, *Those who are* the mainstay of its tribes. **14** The LORD has mingled a perverse spirit in her midst; And they have caused Egypt to err in all her work, As a drunken man staggers in his vomit.

Failure of internal resources.

Is 19:5–10 The waters will fail from the sea, And the river will be wasted and dried up. **6** The rivers will turn foul; The brooks of defense will be emptied and dried up; The reeds and rushes will wither. **7** The papyrus reeds by the River, by the mouth of the River, And everything sown by the River, Will wither, be driven away, and be no more. **8** The fishermen also will mourn; All those will lament who cast hooks into the River, And they will languish who spread nets on the waters. **9** Moreover those who work in fine flax And those who weave fine fabric will be ashamed; **10** And its foundations will be broken. All who make wages *will be* troubled of soul.

Civil war and domestic strife.

Is 19:2 "I will set Egyptians against Egyptians; Everyone will fight against his brother, And everyone against his neighbor, City against city, kingdom against kingdom.

Armies destroyed by Babylon.

Jer 46:2–12 Against Egypt. Concerning the army of Pharaoh Necho, king of Egypt, which was by the River Euphrates in Carchemish, and which Nebuchadnezzar king of Babylon defeated in the fourth year of Jehoiakim the son of Josiah, king of Judah: **3** "Order the buckler and shield, And draw near to battle! **4** Harness the horses, And mount up, you horsemen! Stand forth with *your* helmets, Polish the spears, Put on the armor! **5** Why have I seen them dismayed *and* turned back? Their mighty ones are beaten down; They have speedily fled, And did not look back, *For* fear *was* all around," says the LORD. **6** "Do not let the swift flee away, Nor the mighty man escape; They will stumble and fall Toward the north, by the River Euphrates. **7** "Who *is* this coming up like a flood, Whose waters move like the rivers? **8** Egypt rises up like a flood, And *its* waters move like the rivers; And he says, 'I will go up *and* cover the earth, I will destroy the city and its inhabitants.' **9** Come up, O horses, and rage, O chariots! And let the mighty men come forth: The Ethiopians and the Libyans who handle the shield, And the Lydians who handle *and* bend the bow. **10** For this *is* the day of the Lord GOD of hosts, A day of vengeance, That He may avenge Himself on His adversaries. The sword shall devour; It shall be satiated and made drunk with their blood; For the Lord GOD of hosts has a sacrifice In the north country by the River Euphrates. **11** "Go up to Gilead and take balm, O virgin, the daughter of Egypt; In vain you will use many medicines; You shall not be cured. **12** The nations have heard of your shame, And your cry has filled the land; For the mighty man has stumbled against the mighty; They both have fallen together."

Invasion by Babylon.

Jer 46:13 The word that the LORD spoke to Jeremiah the prophet, how Nebuchadnezzar king of Babylon would come *and* strike the land of Egypt.

Jer 46:24 The daughter of Egypt shall be ashamed; She shall be delivered into the hand Of the people of the north."

Ezek 32:11 "For thus says the Lord GOD: 'The sword of the king of Babylon shall come upon you.

Destruction of its power.

Ezek 30:24–25 I will strengthen the arms of the king of Babylon and put My sword in his hand; but I will break Pharaoh's arms, and he will groan before him with the groanings of a mortally wounded *man.* **25** Thus I will strengthen the arms of the king of Babylon, but the arms of Pharaoh shall fall down; they shall know that I *am* the LORD, when I put My sword into the hand of the king of Babylon and he stretches it out against the land of Egypt.

Destruction of its cities.

Ezek 30:14–18 I will make Pathros desolate, Set fire to Zoan, And execute judgments in No. **15** I will pour My fury on Sin, the strength of Egypt; I will cut off the multitude of No, **16** And set a fire in Egypt; Sin shall have great pain, No shall be split open, And Noph *shall be in* distress daily. **17** The young men of Aven and Pi Beseth shall fall by the sword, And these *cities* shall go into captivity. **18** At Tehaphnehes the day shall also be darkened, When I break the yokes of Egypt there. And her arrogant strength shall cease in her; As for her, a cloud shall cover her, And her daughters shall go into captivity.

Destruction of its idols.

Jer 43:12–13 I will kindle a fire in the houses of the gods of Egypt, and he shall burn them and carry them away captive. And he shall array himself with the land of Egypt, as a shepherd puts on his garment, and he shall go out from there in peace. **13** He shall also break the sacred pillars of Beth Shemesh that *are* in the land of Egypt; and the houses of the gods of the Egyptians he shall burn with fire." ' "

Jer 46:25 The LORD of hosts, the God of Israel, says: "Behold, I will bring punishment on Amon of No, and Pharaoh and Egypt, with their gods and their kings—Pharaoh and those who trust in him.

Ezek 30:13 'Thus says the Lord GOD: "I will also destroy the idols, And cause the images to cease from Noph; There shall no longer be princes from the land of Egypt; I will put fear in the land of Egypt.

Spoil of, a reward to Babylon for services against Tyre.

Ezek 29:18–20 "Son of man, Nebuchadnezzar king of Babylon caused his army to labor strenuously against Tyre; every head *was* made bald, and every shoulder rubbed raw; yet neither he nor his army received wages from Tyre, for the labor which they expended on it. **19** Therefore thus says the Lord GOD: 'Surely I will give the land of Egypt to Nebuchadnezzar king of Babylon; he shall take away her wealth, carry off her spoil, and remove her pillage; and that will be the wages for his army. **20** I have given him the land of Egypt *for* his labor, because they worked for Me,' says the Lord GOD.

Captivity of its people.

Is 20:4 so shall the king of Assyria lead away the Egyptians as prisoners and the Ethiopians as captives, young and old, naked and barefoot, with their buttocks uncovered, to the shame of Egypt.

Jer 46:19 O you daughter dwelling in Egypt, Prepare yourself to go into captivity! For Noph shall be waste and desolate, without inhabitant.

Jer 46:24 The daughter of Egypt shall be ashamed; She shall be delivered into the hand Of the people of the north."

Jer 46:26 And I will deliver them into the hand of those who seek their lives, into the hand of Nebuchadnezzar king of Babylon and the hand of his servants. Afterward it shall be inhabited as in the days of old," says the LORD.

Ezek 30:4 The sword shall come upon Egypt, And great anguish shall be in Ethiopia, When the slain fall in Egypt, And they take away her wealth, And her foundations are broken down.

Utter desolation of, for forty years.

Ezek 29:8–12 'Therefore thus says the Lord GOD: "Surely I will bring a sword upon you and cut off from you man and beast. 9 And the land of Egypt shall become desolate and waste; then they will know that I *am* the LORD, because he said, 'The River *is* mine, and I have made *it.*' 10 Indeed, therefore, I *am* against you and against your rivers, and I will make the land of Egypt utterly waste and desolate, from Migdol *to* Syene, as far as the border of Ethiopia. 11 Neither foot of man shall pass through it nor foot of beast pass through it, and it shall be uninhabited forty years. 12 I will make the land of Egypt desolate in the midst of the countries *that are* desolate; and among the cities *that are* laid waste, her cities shall be desolate forty years; and I will scatter the Egyptians among the nations and disperse them throughout the countries."

Ezek 30:12 I will make the rivers dry, And sell the land into the hand of the wicked; I will make the land waste, and all that is in it, By the hand of aliens. I, the LORD, have spoken."

Ezek 32:15 'When I make the land of Egypt desolate, And the country is destitute of all that once filled it, When I strike all who dwell in it, Then they shall know that I *am* the LORD.

Allies to share its misfortunes.

Ezek 30:4 The sword shall come upon Egypt, And great anguish shall be in Ethiopia, When the slain fall in Egypt, And they take away her wealth, And her foundations are broken down.

Ezek 30:6 'Thus says the LORD: "Those who uphold Egypt shall fall, And the pride of her power shall come down. From Migdol *to* Syene Those within her shall fall by the sword," Says the Lord GOD.

The Jews who practiced its idolatry to share its punishments. **Jer 44:7–28**

Terror caused by its fall.

Ezek 32:9–10 'I will also trouble the hearts of many peoples, when I bring your destruction among the nations, into the countries which you have not known. 10 Yes, I will make many peoples astonished at you, and their kings shall be horribly afraid of you when I brandish My sword before them; and they shall tremble *every* moment, every man for his own life, in the day of your fall.'

Status forever reduced to low level.

Ezek 29:15 It shall be the lowliest of kingdoms; it shall

never again exalt itself above the nations, for I will diminish them so that they will not rule over the nations anymore.

Christ to be called out of.

Hos 11:1 "When Israel *was* a child, I loved him, And out of Egypt I called My son.

Matt 2:15 and was there until the death of Herod, that it might be fulfilled which was spoken by the Lord through the prophet, saying, *"Out of Egypt I called My Son."*

Conversion of.

Is 19:18–20 In that day five cities in the land of Egypt will speak the language of Canaan and swear by the LORD of hosts; one will be called the City of Destruction. 19 In that day there will be an altar to the LORD in the midst of the land of Egypt, and a pillar to the LORD at its border. 20 And it will be for a sign and for a witness to the LORD of hosts in the land of Egypt; for they will cry to the LORD because of the oppressors, and He will send them a Savior and a Mighty One, and He will deliver them.

To be numbered and blessed along with Israel.

Is 19:23–25 In that day there will be a highway from Egypt to Assyria, and the Assyrian will come into Egypt and the Egyptian into Assyria, and the Egyptians will serve with the Assyrians. 24 In that day Israel will be one of three with Egypt and Assyria—a blessing in the midst of the land, 25 whom the LORD of hosts shall bless, saying, "Blessed *is* Egypt My people, and Assyria the work of My hands, and Israel My inheritance."

Prophetic illustration of its destruction.

Jer 43:9–10 "Take large stones in your hand, and hide them in the sight of the men of Judah, in the clay in the brick courtyard which *is* at the entrance to Pharaoh's house in Tahpanhes; 10 and say to them, 'Thus says the LORD of hosts, the God of Israel: "Behold, I will send and bring Nebuchadnezzar the king of Babylon, My servant, and will set his throne above these stones that I have hidden. And he will spread his royal pavilion over them.

Ezek 30:21–22 "Son of man, I have broken the arm of Pharaoh king of Egypt; and see, it has not been bandaged for healing, nor a splint put on to bind it, to make it strong enough to hold a sword. 22 Therefore thus says the Lord GOD: 'Surely I *am* against Pharaoh king of Egypt, and will break his arms, both the strong one and the one that was broken; and I will make the sword fall out of his hand.

Ezek 32:4–6 Then I will leave you on the land; I will cast you out on the open fields, And cause to settle on you all the birds of the heavens. And with you I will fill the beasts of the whole earth. 5 I will lay your flesh on the mountains, And fill the valleys with your carcass. 6 'I will also water the land with the flow of your blood, *Even* to the mountains; And the riverbeds will be full of you.

ELDERS. *SEE ALSO* MINISTERS
Pastors and overseers of the church.

Acts 11:30 This they also did, and sent it to the elders by the hands of Barnabas and Saul.

Acts 21:18 On the following *day* Paul went in with us to James, and all the elders were present.

Cf. Acts 15:2

Work of.

1 Thess 5:12 And we urge you, brethren, to recognize those who labor among you, and are over you in the Lord and admonish you,

Group of, led Jerusalem church.

Acts 21:18 On the following *day* Paul went in with us to James, and all the elders were present.

Paul's concern for.

Acts 20:17–38 From Miletus he sent to Ephesus and called for the elders of the church. **18** And when they had come to him, he said to them: "You know, from the first day that I came to Asia, in what manner I always lived among you, **19** serving the Lord with all humility, with many tears and trials which happened to me by the plotting of the Jews; **20** how I kept back nothing that was helpful, but proclaimed it to you, and taught you publicly and from house to house, **21** testifying to Jews, and also to Greeks, repentance toward God and faith toward our Lord Jesus Christ. **22** And see, now I go bound in the spirit to Jerusalem, not knowing the things that will happen to me there, **23** except that the Holy Spirit testifies in every city, saying that chains and tribulations await me. **24** But none of these things move me; nor do I count my life dear to myself, so that I may finish my race with joy, and the ministry which I received from the Lord Jesus, to testify to the gospel of the grace of God. **25** "And indeed, now I know that you all, among whom I have gone preaching the kingdom of God, will see my face no more. **26** Therefore I testify to you this day that I *am* innocent of the blood of all *men.* **27** For I have not shunned to declare to you the whole counsel of God. **28** Therefore take heed to yourselves and to all the flock, among which the Holy Spirit has made you overseers, to shepherd the church of God which He purchased with His own blood. **29** For I know this, that after my departure savage wolves will come in among you, not sparing the flock. **30** Also from among yourselves men will rise up, speaking perverse things, to draw away the disciples after themselves. **31** Therefore watch, and remember that for three years I did not cease to warn everyone night and day with tears. **32** "So now, brethren, I commend you to God and to the word of His grace, which is able to build you up and give you an inheritance among all those who are sanctified. **33** I have coveted no one's silver or gold or apparel. **34** Yes, you yourselves know that these hands have provided for my necessities, and for those who were with me. **35** I have shown you in every way, by laboring like this, that you must support the weak. And remember the words of the Lord Jesus, that He said, 'It is more blessed to give than to receive.' " **36** And when he had said these things, he knelt down and prayed with them all. **37** Then they all wept freely, and fell on Paul's neck and kissed him, **38** sorrowing most of all for the words which he spoke, that they would see his face no more. And they accompanied him to the ship.

Qualifications of.

1 Tim 3:1–7 This *is* a faithful saying: If a man desires the position of a bishop, he desires a good work. **2** A bishop then must be blameless, the husband of one wife, temperate, sober-minded, of good behavior, hospitable, able to teach; **3** not given to wine, not violent, not greedy for money, but gentle, not quarrelsome, not covetous; **4** one who rules his own house well, having *his* children in submission with all reverence **5** (for if a man does not know how to rule his own house, how will he take care of the church of God?); **6** not a novice, lest being puffed up with pride he fall into the *same* condemnation as the devil. **7** Moreover he must have a good testimony among those who are outside, lest he fall into reproach and the snare of the devil.

Titus 1:5–9 For this reason I left you in Crete, that you should set in order the things that are lacking, and appoint elders in every city as I commanded you— **6** if a man is blameless, the husband of one wife, having faithful children not accused of dissipation or insubordination. **7** For a bishop must be blameless, as a steward of God, not self-willed, not quick-tempered, not given to wine, not violent, not greedy for money, **8** but hospitable, a lover of what is good, sober-minded, just, holy, self-controlled, **9** holding fast the faithful word as he has been taught, that he may be able, by sound doctrine, both to exhort and convict those who contradict.

Responsibilities of,

Lead and teach.

1 Tim 5:17 Let the elders who rule well be counted worthy of double honor, especially those who labor in the word and doctrine.

Help the spiritually weak.

1 Thess 5:12–14 And we urge you, brethren, to recognize those who labor among you, and are over you in the Lord and admonish you, **13** and to esteem them very highly in love for their work's sake. Be at peace among yourselves. **14** Now we exhort you, brethren, warn those who are unruly, comfort the fainthearted, uphold the weak, be patient with all.

Care for the church.

1 Tim 3:5 (for if a man does not know how to rule his own house, how will he take care of the church of God?);

1 Pet 5:1–2 The elders who are among you I exhort, I who am a fellow elder and a witness of the sufferings of Christ, and also a partaker of the glory that will be revealed: **2** Shepherd the flock of God which is among you, serving as overseers, not by compulsion but willingly, not for dishonest gain but eagerly;

Protect the church.

Acts 20:28–30 Therefore take heed to yourselves and to all the flock, among which the Holy Spirit has made you overseers, to shepherd the church of God which He purchased with His own blood. **29** For I know this, that after my departure savage wolves will come in among you, not sparing the flock. **30** Also from among yourselves men will rise up, speaking perverse things, to draw away the disciples after themselves.

Set an example for the flock.

1 Pet 5:3 nor as being lords over those entrusted to you, but being examples to the flock;

Ordain other elders.

1 Tim 4:14 Do not neglect the gift that is in you, which was given to you by prophecy with the laying on of the hands of the eldership.

Responsibility of congregation toward.

Heb 13:17 Obey those who rule over you, and be submissive, for they watch out for your souls, as those who must give account. Let them do so with joy and not with grief, for that would be unprofitable for you.

Worthy of

Double honor.

1 Tim 5:17 Let the elders who rule well be counted worthy of double honor, especially those who labor in the word and doctrine.

Esteem.

1 Thess 5:12–13 And we urge you, brethren, to recognize those who labor among you, and are over you in the Lord and admonish you, **13** and to esteem them very highly in love for their work's sake. Be at peace among yourselves.

Will be rewarded the crown of glory by the Chief Shepherd.

1 Pet 5:4 and when the Chief Shepherd appears, you will receive the crown of glory that does not fade away.

Rules for accusation of.

1 Tim 5:19 Do not receive an accusation against an elder except from two or three witnesses.

Rebuke of.

1 Tim 5:20 Those who are sinning rebuke in the presence of all, that the rest also may fear.

Also called

Bishops.

Phil 1:1 Paul and Timothy, bondservants of Jesus Christ, To all the saints in Christ Jesus who are in Philippi, with the bishops and deacons:

1 Tim 3:1 This *is* a faithful saying: If a man desires the position of a bishop, he desires a good work.

Titus 1:7 For a bishop must be blameless, as a steward of God, not self-willed, not quick-tempered, not given to wine, not violent, not greedy for money,

Overseers.

Acts 20:28 Therefore take heed to yourselves and to all the flock, among which the Holy Spirit has made you overseers, to shepherd the church of God which He purchased with His own blood.

1 Pet 5:2 Shepherd the flock of God which is among you, serving as overseers, not by compulsion but willingly, not for dishonest gain but eagerly;

Pastors (Shepherds).

Eph 4:11 And He Himself gave some *to be* apostles, some prophets, some evangelists, and some pastors and teachers,

1 Pet 5:2 Shepherd the flock of God which is among you, serving as overseers, not by compulsion but willingly, not for dishonest gain but eagerly;

ELECTION

Of Christ, as Messiah.

Is 42:1 "Behold! My Servant whom I uphold, My Elect One *in whom* My soul delights! I have put My Spirit upon Him; He will bring forth justice to the Gentiles.

1 Pet 2:6 Therefore it is also contained in the Scripture, *"Behold, I lay in Zion A chief cornerstone, elect, precious, And he who believes on Him will by no means be put to shame."*

Of good angels.

1 Tim 5:21 I charge *you* before God and the Lord Jesus Christ and the elect angels that you observe these things without prejudice, doing nothing with partiality.

Of Israel.

Deut 7:6 "For you *are* a holy people to the LORD your God; the LORD your God has chosen you to be a people for Himself, a special treasure above all the peoples on the face of the earth.

Is 45:5 I *am* the LORD, and *there is* no other; There is no God besides Me. I will gird you, though you have not known Me,

Of ministers.

Luke 6:13 And when it was day, He called His disciples to *Himself*; and from them He chose twelve whom He also named apostles:

Acts 9:15 But the Lord said to him, "Go, for he is a chosen vessel of Mine to bear My name before Gentiles, kings, and the children of Israel.

Of churches.

1 Pet 5:13 She who is in Babylon, elect together with *you*, greets you; and *so does* Mark my son.

Of believers is

By God.

1 Thess 1:4 knowing, beloved brethren, your election by God.

Titus 1:1 Paul, a bondservant of God and an apostle of Jesus Christ, according to the faith of God's elect and the acknowledgment of the truth which accords with godliness,

By Christ.

John 13:18 "I do not speak concerning all of you. I know whom I have chosen; but that the Scripture may be fulfilled, *'He who eats bread with Me has lifted up his heel against Me.'*

John 15:16 You did not choose Me, but I chose you and appointed you that you should go and bear fruit, and *that* your fruit should remain, that whatever you ask the Father in My name He may give you.

In Christ.

Eph 1:4 just as He chose us in Him before the foundation of the world, that we should be holy and without blame before Him in love,

Personal.

Matt 20:16 So the last will be first, and the first last. For many are called, but few chosen."

John 6:44 No one can come to Me unless the Father who sent Me draws him; and I will raise him up at the last day.

Acts 22:14 Then he said, 'The God of our fathers has chosen you that you should know His will, and see the Just One, and hear the voice of His mouth.

2 John 1:13 The children of your elect sister greet you. Amen.

According to the purpose of God.

Rom 9:11 (for *the children* not yet being born, nor having done any good or evil, that the purpose of God according to election might stand, not of works but of Him who calls),

Eph 1:11 In Him also we have obtained an inheritance, being predestined according to the purpose of Him who works all things according to the counsel of His will,

According to the foreknowledge of God.

Rom 8:29 For whom He foreknew, He also predestined *to be* conformed to the image of His Son, that He might be the firstborn among many brethren.

1 Pet 1:2 elect according to the foreknowledge of God the Father, in sanctification of the Spirit, for obedience and sprinkling of the blood of Jesus Christ: Grace to you and peace be multiplied.

Eternal.

Eph 1:4 just as He chose us in Him before the foundation of the world, that we should be holy and without blame before Him in love,

Sovereign.

Rom 9:15–16 For He says to Moses, *"I will have mercy on whomever I will have mercy, and I will have compassion on whomever I will have compassion."* **16** So then *it is* not of him who wills, nor of him who runs, but of God who shows mercy.

1 Cor 1:27 But God has chosen the foolish things of the world to put to shame the wise, and God has chosen the weak things of the world to put to shame the things which are mighty;

Eph 1:11 In Him also we have obtained an inheritance, being predestined according to the purpose of Him who works all things according to the counsel of His will,

Without regard to any human merit.

Rom 9:11 (for *the children* not yet being born, nor having done any good or evil, that the purpose of God according to election might stand, not of works but of Him who calls),

Of grace.

Rom 11:5 Even so then, at this present time there is a remnant according to the election of grace.

Recorded in heaven.

Luke 10:20 Nevertheless do not rejoice in this, that the spirits are subject to you, but rather rejoice because your names are written in heaven."

For the glory of God.

Eph 1:6 to the praise of the glory of His grace, by which He made us accepted in the Beloved.

Through sanctification of the Spirit and faith.

2 Thess 2:13 But we are bound to give thanks to God always for you, brethren beloved by the Lord, because God from the beginning chose you for salvation through sanctification by the Spirit and belief in the truth,

1 Pet 1:2 elect according to the foreknowledge of God the Father, in sanctification of the Spirit, for obedi-

ence and sprinkling of the blood of Jesus Christ: Grace to you and peace be multiplied.

To adoption.

Eph 1:5 having predestined us to adoption as sons by Jesus Christ to Himself, according to the good pleasure of His will,

To salvation.

2 Thess 2:13 But we are bound to give thanks to God always for you, brethren beloved by the Lord, because God from the beginning chose you for salvation through sanctification by the Spirit and belief in the truth,

To conformity with Christ.

Rom 8:29 For whom He foreknew, He also predestined *to be* conformed to the image of His Son, that He might be the firstborn among many brethren.

To good works.

Eph 2:10 For we are His workmanship, created in Christ Jesus for good works, which God prepared beforehand that we should walk in them.

To spiritual warfare.

2 Tim 2:4 No one engaged in warfare entangles himself with the affairs of *this* life, that he may please him who enlisted him as a soldier.

To eternal glory.

Rom 9:23 and that He might make known the riches of His glory on the vessels of mercy, which He had prepared beforehand for glory,

Ensures to believers

Effectual calling.

Rom 8:30 Moreover whom He predestined, these He also called; whom He called, these He also justified; and whom He justified, these He also glorified.

Divine teaching.

John 17:6 "I have manifested Your name to the men whom You have given Me out of the world. They were Yours, You gave them to Me, and they have kept Your word.

Belief in Christ.

Acts 13:48 Now when the Gentiles heard this, they were glad and glorified the word of the Lord. And as many as had been appointed to eternal life believed.

Acceptance with God.

Rom 11:7 What then? Israel has not obtained what it seeks; but the elect have obtained it, and the rest were blinded.

Protection.

Mark 13:20 And unless the Lord had shortened those days, no flesh would be saved; but for the elect's sake, whom He chose, He shortened the days.

Vindication of their wrongs.

Luke 18:7 And shall God not avenge His own elect who cry out day and night to Him, though He bears long with them?

Working of all things for good.

Rom 8:28 And we know that all things work together for good to those who love God, to those who are the called according to *His* purpose.

Blessedness.

Ps 33:12 Blessed *is* the nation whose God *is* the LORD, The people He has chosen as His own inheritance.

Ps 65:4 Blessed *is the man* You choose, And cause to approach *You, That* he may dwell in Your courts. We shall be satisfied with the goodness of Your house, Of Your holy temple.

The inheritance.

Is 65:9 I will bring forth descendants from Jacob, And from Judah an heir of My mountains; My elect shall inherit it, And My servants shall dwell there.

1 Pet 1:4–5 to an inheritance incorruptible and undefiled and that does not fade away, reserved in heaven for you, **5** who are kept by the power of God through faith for salvation ready to be revealed in the last time.

Should lead to cultivation of graces.

Col 3:12 Therefore, as *the* elect of God, holy and beloved, put on tender mercies, kindness, humility, meekness, longsuffering;

Should be evidenced by diligence.

2 Pet 1:10 Therefore, brethren, be even more diligent to make your call and election sure, for if you do these things you will never stumble;

Saints may have assurance of.

1 Thess 1:4 knowing, beloved brethren, your election by God.

Exemplified in

Isaac.

Gen 21:12 But God said to Abraham, "Do not let it be displeasing in your sight because of the lad or because of your bondwoman. Whatever Sarah has said to you, listen to her voice; for in Isaac your seed shall be called.

Abraham.

Neh 9:7 "You *are* the LORD God, Who chose Abram, And brought him out of Ur of the Chaldeans, And gave him the name Abraham;

Zerubbabel.

Hag 2:23 'In that day,' says the LORD of hosts, 'I will take you, Zerubbabel My servant, the son of Shealtiel,' says the LORD, 'and will make you like a signet *ring;* for I have chosen you,' says the LORD of hosts."

The apostles.

John 13:18 "I do not speak concerning all of you. I know whom I have chosen; but that the Scripture may be fulfilled, *'He who eats bread with Me has lifted up his heel against Me.'*

John 15:19 If you were of the world, the world would love its own. Yet because you are not of the world, but I chose you out of the world, therefore the world hates you.

Jacob.

Rom 9:12–13 it was said to her, *"The older shall serve the younger."* **13** As it is written, *"Jacob I have loved, but Esau I have hated."*

Rufus.

Rom 16:13 Greet Rufus, chosen in the Lord, and his mother and mine.

Paul.

Gal 1:15 But when it pleased God, who separated me from my mother's womb and called *me* through His grace,

ELIJAH

Gave challenges to Ahab.

1 Kin 17:1 And Elijah the Tishbite, of the inhabitants of Gilead, said to Ahab, "As the LORD God of Israel lives, before whom I stand, there shall not be dew nor rain these years, except at my word."

1 Kin 18:1–6 And it came to pass *after* many days that the word of the LORD came to Elijah, in the third year, saying, "Go, present yourself to Ahab, and I will send rain on the earth." **2** So Elijah went to present himself to Ahab; and *there was* a severe famine in Samaria. **3** And Ahab had called Obadiah, who *was* in charge of *his* house. (Now Obadiah feared the LORD greatly.) **4** For so it was, while Jezebel massacred the prophets of the LORD, that Obadiah had taken one hundred prophets and hidden them, fifty to a cave, and had fed them with bread and water.) **5** And Ahab had said to Obadiah, "Go into the land to all the springs of water and to all the brooks; perhaps we may find grass to keep the horses and mules alive, so that we will not have to kill any livestock." **6** So they divided the land between them to explore it; Ahab went one way by himself, and Obadiah went another way by himself.

1 Kin 21:17–29 Then the word of the LORD came to Elijah the Tishbite, saying, **18** "Arise, go down to meet Ahab king of Israel, who *lives* in Samaria. There *he is,* in the vineyard of Naboth, where he has gone down to take possession of it. **19** You shall speak to him, saying, 'Thus says the LORD: "Have you murdered and also taken possession?" ' And you shall speak to him, saying, 'Thus says the LORD: "In the place where dogs licked the blood of Naboth, dogs shall lick your blood, even yours." ' " **20** So Ahab said to Elijah, "Have you found me, O my enemy?" And he answered, "I have found *you,* because you have sold yourself to do evil in the sight of the LORD: **21** 'Behold, I will bring calamity on you. I will take away your posterity, and will cut off from Ahab every male in Israel, both bond and free. **22** I will make your house like the house of Jeroboam the son of Nebat, and like the house of Baasha the son of Ahijah, because of the provocation with which you have provoked *Me* to anger, and made Israel sin.' **23** And concerning Jezebel the LORD also spoke, saying, 'The dogs shall eat Jezebel by the wall of Jezreel.' **24** The dogs shall eat whoever belongs to Ahab and dies in the city, and the birds of the air shall eat whoever dies in the field." **25** But there was no one like Ahab who sold himself to do wickedness in the sight of the LORD, because Jezebel his wife stirred him up. **26** And he behaved very abominably in following idols, according to all *that* the Amorites had done, whom the LORD had cast out before the children of Israel. **27** So it was, when Ahab heard those words, that he tore his clothes and put sackcloth on his body, and fasted and lay in sackcloth, and went about mourning. **28** And the word of the LORD came to Elijah the Tishbite, saying, **29** "See how Ahab has humbled himself before Me? Because he has humbled himself before Me, I will not bring the calamity in his days. In the days of his son I will bring the calamity on his house."

Supplied by God with food.

1 Kin 17:3–6 "Get away from here and turn eastward, and hide by the Brook Cherith, which flows into the Jordan. **4** And it will be *that* you shall drink from the brook, and I have commanded the ravens to feed you there." **5** So he went and did according to the word of the LORD, for he went and stayed by the Brook Cherith, which flows into the Jordan. **6** The ravens brought him bread and meat in the morning, and bread and meat in the evening; and he drank from the brook.

1 Kin 19:4–8 But he himself went a day's journey into the wilderness, and came and sat down under a broom tree. And he prayed that he might die, and said, "It is enough! Now, LORD, take my life, for I *am* no better than my fathers!" **5** Then as he lay and slept under a broom tree, suddenly an angel touched him, and said to him, "Arise *and* eat." **6** Then he looked, and there by his head *was* a cake baked on coals, and a jar of water. So he ate and drank, and lay down again. **7** And the angel of the LORD came back the second time, and touched him, and said, "Arise *and* eat, because the journey *is* too great for you." **8** So he arose, and ate and drank; and he went in the strength of that food forty days and forty nights as far as Horeb, the mountain of God.

Raised widow's son from the dead.

1 Kin 17:17–24 Now it happened after these things *that* the son of the woman who owned the house became sick. And his sickness was so serious that there was no breath left in him. **18** So she said to Elijah, "What have I to do with you, O man of God? Have you come to me to bring my sin to remembrance, and to kill my son?" **19** And he said to her, "Give me your son." So he took him out of her arms and carried him to the upper room where he was staying, and laid him on his own bed. **20** Then he cried out to the LORD and said, "O LORD my God, have You also brought tragedy on the widow with whom I lodge, by killing her son?" **21** And he stretched himself out on the child three times, and cried out to the LORD and said, "O LORD my God, I pray, let this child's soul come back to him." **22** Then the LORD heard the voice of Elijah; and the soul of the child came back to him, and he revived. **23** And Elijah took the child and brought him down from the upper room into the house, and gave him to his mother. And Elijah said, "See, your son lives!" **24** Then the woman said to Elijah, "Now by this I know that you *are* a man of God, *and* that the word of the LORD in your mouth *is* the truth."

Defeated prophets of Baal. 1 Kin 18:17–46

His divine mission.

1 Kin 19:9–21 And there he went into a cave, and spent the night in that place; and behold, the word of the LORD *came* to him, and He said to him, "What are you doing here, Elijah?" **10** So he said, "I have been very zealous for the LORD God of hosts; for the children of Israel have forsaken Your covenant, torn down Your altars, and killed Your prophets with the sword. I alone am left; and they seek to take my life." **11** Then He said, "Go out, and stand on the mountain before

the LORD." And behold, the LORD passed by, and a great and strong wind tore into the mountains and broke the rocks in pieces before the LORD, *but* the LORD *was* not in the wind; and after the wind an earthquake, *but* the LORD *was* not in the earthquake; **12** and after the earthquake a fire, *but* the LORD *was* not in the fire; and after the fire a still small voice. **13** So it was, when Elijah heard *it*, that he wrapped his face in his mantle and went out and stood in the entrance of the cave. Suddenly a voice *came* to him, and said, "What are you doing here, Elijah?" **14** And he said, "I have been very zealous for the LORD God of hosts; because the children of Israel have forsaken Your covenant, torn down Your altars, and killed Your prophets with the sword. I alone am left; and they seek to take my life." **15** Then the LORD said to him: "Go, return on your way to the Wilderness of Damascus; and when you arrive, anoint Hazael *as* king over Syria. **16** Also you shall anoint Jehu the son of Nimshi *as* king over Israel. And Elisha the son of Shaphat of Abel Meholah you shall anoint *as* prophet in your place. **17** It shall be *that* whoever escapes the sword of Hazael, Jehu will kill; and whoever escapes the sword of Jehu, Elisha will kill. **18** Yet I have reserved seven thousand in Israel, all whose knees have not bowed to Baal, and every mouth that has not kissed him." **19** So he departed from there, and found Elisha the son of Shaphat, who *was* plowing *with* twelve yoke *of oxen* before him, and he was with the twelfth. Then Elijah passed by him and threw his mantle on him. **20** And he left the oxen and ran after Elijah, and said, "Please let me kiss my father and my mother, and *then* I will follow you." And he said to him, "Go back again, for what have I done to you?" **21** So *Elisha* turned back from him, and took a yoke of oxen and slaughtered them and boiled their flesh, using the oxen's equipment, and gave it to the people, and they ate. Then he arose and followed Elijah, and became his servant.

Taken up to heaven in a chariot of fire. 2 Kin 2:1–15

Was a type of John the Baptist.

Matt 11:14 And if you are willing to receive *it*, he is Elijah who is to come.

Luke 1:17 He will also go before Him in the spirit and power of Elijah, '*to turn the hearts of the fathers to the children,*' and the disobedient to the wisdom of the just, to make ready a people prepared for the Lord."

Cf. Mal 4:5–6; Mark 9:12–13

Appeared at the Transfiguration.

Matt 17:4 Then Peter answered and said to Jesus, "Lord, it is good for us to be here; if You wish, let us make here three tabernacles: one for You, one for Moses, and one for Elijah."

Mark 9:4–5 And Elijah appeared to them with Moses, and they were talking with Jesus. **5** Then Peter answered and said to Jesus, "Rabbi, it is good for us to be here; and let us make three tabernacles: one for You, one for Moses, and one for Elijah"—

Luke 9:30 And behold, two men talked with Him, who were Moses and Elijah,

Luke 9:33 Then it happened, as they were parting from Him, *that* Peter said to Jesus, "Master, it is good for us to be here; and let us make three tabernacles: one for You, one for Moses, and one for Elijah"—not knowing what he said.

ELISHA

Successor to Elijah.

1 Kin 19:16 Also you shall anoint Jehu the son of Nimshi *as* king over Israel. And Elisha the son of Shaphat of Abel Meholah you shall anoint *as* prophet in your place.

1 Kin 19:19–21 So he departed from there, and found Elisha the son of Shaphat, who *was* plowing *with* twelve yoke *of oxen* before him, and he was with the twelfth. Then Elijah passed by him and threw his mantle on him. **20** And he left the oxen and ran after Elijah, and said, "Please let me kiss my father and my mother, and *then* I will follow you." And he said to him, "Go back again, for what have I done to you?" **21** So *Elisha* turned back from him, and took a yoke of oxen and slaughtered them and boiled their flesh, using the oxen's equipment, and gave it to the people, and they ate. Then he arose and followed Elijah, and became his servant.

Saw Elijah taken up and was then designated a prophet. 2 Kin 2:1–22

Divided the Jordan River.

2 Kin 2:14 Then he took the mantle of Elijah that had fallen from him, and struck the water, and said, "Where *is* the LORD God of Elijah?" And when he also had struck the water, it was divided this way and that; and Elisha crossed over.

And the miracle of the increase of widow's oil.

2 Kin 4:1–7 A certain woman of the wives of the sons of the prophets cried out to Elisha, saying, "Your servant my husband is dead, and you know that your servant feared the LORD. And the creditor is coming to take my two sons to be his slaves." **2** So Elisha said to her, "What shall I do for you? Tell me, what do you have in the house?" And she said, "Your maidservant has nothing in the house but a jar of oil." **3** Then he said, "Go, borrow vessels from everywhere, from all your neighbors—empty vessels; do not gather just a few. **4** And when you have come in, you shall shut the door behind you and your sons; then pour it into all those vessels, and set aside the full ones." **5** So she went from him and shut the door behind her and her sons, who brought *the vessels* to her; and she poured *it* out. **6** Now it came to pass, when the vessels were full, that she said to her son, "Bring me another vessel." And he said to her, "*There is* not another vessel." So the oil ceased. **7** Then she came and told the man of God. And he said, "Go, sell the oil and pay your debt; and you *and* your sons live on the rest."

Raised the Shunammite's son from the dead.

2 Kin 4:18–37 And the child grew. Now it happened one day that he went out to his father, to the reapers. **19** And he said to his father, "My head, my head!" So he said to a servant, "Carry him to his mother." **20** When he had taken him and brought him to his mother, he sat on her knees till noon, and *then* died. **21** And she went up and laid him on the bed of the man of God, shut *the door* upon him, and went out. **22** Then she called to her husband, and said, "Please send me one of the young men and one of the don-

keys, that I may run to the man of God and come back." **23** So he said, "Why are you going to him today? *It is* neither the New Moon nor the Sabbath." And she said, "*It is* well." **24** Then she saddled a donkey, and said to her servant, "Drive, and go forward; do not slacken the pace for me unless I tell you." **25** And so she departed, and went to the man of God at Mount Carmel. So it was, when the man of God saw her afar off, that he said to his servant Gehazi, "Look, the Shunammite woman! **26** Please run now to meet her, and say to her, 'Is it well with you? *Is it* well with your husband? *Is it* well with the child?' " And she answered, "*It is* well." **27** Now when she came to the man of God at the hill, she caught him by the feet, but Gehazi came near to push her away. But the man of God said, "Let her alone; for her soul *is* in deep distress, and the LORD has hidden *it* from me, and has not told me." **28** So she said, "Did I ask a son of my lord? Did I not say, 'Do not deceive *me*'?" **29** Then he said to Gehazi, "Get yourself ready, and take my staff in your hand, and be on your way. If you meet anyone, do not greet him; and if anyone greets you, do not answer him; but lay my staff on the face of the child." **30** And the mother of the child said, "*As* the LORD lives, and *as* your soul lives, I will not leave you." So he arose and followed her. **31** Now Gehazi went on ahead of them, and laid the staff on the face of the child; but *there was* neither voice nor hearing. Therefore he went back to meet him, and told him, saying, "The child has not awakened." **32** When Elisha came into the house, there was the child, lying dead on his bed. **33** He went in therefore, shut the door behind the two of them, and prayed to the LORD. **34** And he went up and lay on the child, and put his mouth on his mouth, his eyes on his eyes, and his hands on his hands; and he stretched himself out on the child, and the flesh of the child became warm. **35** He returned and walked back and forth in the house, and again went up and stretched himself out on him; then the child sneezed seven times, and the child opened his eyes. **36** And he called Gehazi and said, "Call this Shunammite woman." So he called her. And when she came in to him, he said, "Pick up your son." **37** So she went in, fell at his feet, and bowed to the ground; then she picked up her son and went out.

Healed Naaman the leper. 2 Kin 5:1–19

Struck the Syrian army blind.

2 Kin 6:18–23 So when *the Syrians* came down to him, Elisha prayed to the LORD, and said, "Strike this people, I pray, with blindness." And He struck them with blindness according to the word of Elisha. **19** Now Elisha said to them, "This *is* not the way, nor *is* this the city. Follow me, and I will bring you to the man whom you seek." But he led them to Samaria. **20** So it was, when they had come to Samaria, that Elisha said, "LORD, open the eyes of these *men*, that they may see." And the LORD opened their eyes, and they saw; and there *they were*, inside Samaria! **21** Now when the king of Israel saw them, he said to Elisha, "My father, shall I kill *them*? Shall I kill *them*?" **22** But he answered, "You shall not kill *them*. Would you kill those whom you have taken captive with your sword and your bow? Set food and water before them, that they may eat and drink and go to their master." **23** Then he prepared a great feast for them; and after they ate and drank, he sent them away and they went to their master. So the bands of Syrian *raiders* came no more into the land of Israel.

Prophesied Ben-Hadad's death.

2 Kin 8:7–15 Then Elisha went to Damascus, and Ben-Hadad king of Syria was sick; and it was told him, saying, "The man of God has come here." **8** And the king said to Hazael, "Take a present in your hand, and go to meet the man of God, and inquire of the LORD by him, saying, 'Shall I recover from this disease?' " **9** So Hazael went to meet him and took a present with him, of every good thing of Damascus, forty camel-loads; and he came and stood before him, and said, "Your son Ben-Hadad king of Syria has sent me to you, saying, 'Shall I recover from this disease?' " **10** And Elisha said to him, "Go, say to him, 'You shall certainly recover.' However the LORD has shown me that he will really die." **11** Then he set his countenance in a stare until he was ashamed; and the man of God wept. **12** And Hazael said, "Why is my lord weeping?" He answered, "Because I know the evil that you will do to the children of Israel: Their strongholds you will set on fire, and their young men you will kill with the sword; and you will dash their children, and rip open their women with child." **13** So Hazael said, "But what *is* your servant—a dog, that he should do this gross thing?" And Elisha answered, "The LORD has shown me that you *will become* king over Syria." **14** Then he departed from Elisha, and came to his master, who said to him, "What did Elisha say to you?" And he answered, "He told me you would surely recover." **15** But it happened on the next day that he took a thick cloth and dipped *it* in water, and spread *it* over his face so that he died; and Hazael reigned in his place.

Prophesied Joash's victories.

2 Kin 13:14–19 Elisha had become sick with the illness of which he would die. Then Joash the king of Israel came down to him, and wept over his face, and said, "O my father, my father, the chariots of Israel and their horsemen!" **15** And Elisha said to him, "Take a bow and some arrows." So he took himself a bow and some arrows. **16** Then he said to the king of Israel, "Put your hand on the bow." So he put his hand *on it*, and Elisha put his hands on the king's hands. **17** And he said, "Open the east window"; and he opened *it*. Then Elisha said, "Shoot"; and he shot. And he said, "The arrow of the LORD's deliverance and the arrow of deliverance from Syria; for you must strike the Syrians at Aphek till you have destroyed *them*." **18** Then he said, "Take the arrows"; so he took *them*. And he said to the king of Israel, "Strike the ground"; so he struck three times, and stopped. **19** And the man of God was angry with him, and said, "You should have struck five or six times; then you would have struck Syria till you had destroyed *it*! But now you will strike Syria *only* three times."

EMBALMING

Unknown to early patriarchs.

Gen 23:4 "I *am* a foreigner and a visitor among you. Give me property for a burial place among you, that I may bury my dead out of my sight."

Learned by the Jews in Egypt.

Gen 50:2 And Joseph commanded his servants the physicians to embalm his father. So the physicians embalmed Israel.

Gen 50:26 So Joseph died, *being* one hundred and ten years old; and they embalmed him, and he was put in a coffin in Egypt.

Time required for.

Gen 50:3 Forty days were required for him, for such are the days required for those who are embalmed; and the Egyptians mourned for him seventy days.

How performed by the Jews.

2 Chr 16:14 They buried him in his own tomb, which he had made for himself in the City of David; and they laid him in the bed which was filled with spices and various ingredients prepared in a mixture of ointments. They made a very great burning for him.

Luke 23:56 Then they returned and prepared spices and fragrant oils. And they rested on the Sabbath according to the commandment.

John 19:40 Then they took the body of Jesus, and bound it in strips of linen with the spices, as the custom of the Jews is to bury.

Not always practiced by the Jews.

John 11:39 Jesus said, "Take away the stone." Martha, the sister of him who was dead, said to Him, "Lord, by this time there is a stench, for he has been *dead* four days."

An attempt to defeat God's purpose.

Gen 3:19 In the sweat of your face you shall eat bread Till you return to the ground, For out of it you were taken; For dust you *are*, And to dust you shall return."

ENCOURAGEMENT

Of Scripture to believers.

Rom 15:4 For whatever things were written before were written for our learning, that we through the patience and comfort of the Scriptures might have hope.

By Christ.

Phil 2:1 Therefore if *there is* any consolation in Christ, if any comfort of love, if any fellowship of the Spirit, if any affection and mercy,

By Paul.

1 Thess 3:2 and sent Timothy, our brother and minister of God, and our fellow laborer in the gospel of Christ, to establish you and encourage you concerning your faith,

Of Jonathan for David.

1 Sam 23:16 Then Jonathan, Saul's son, arose and went to David in the woods and strengthened his hand in God.

Of the strong for the weak.

1 Thess 5:14 Now we exhort you, brethren, warn those who are unruly, comfort the fainthearted, uphold the weak, be patient with all.

ENDURANCE

To remain under trials, without succumbing.

Rom 5:3 And not only *that*, but we also glory in tribulations, knowing that tribulation produces perseverance;

2 Thess 1:4 so that we ourselves boast of you among the churches of God for your patience and faith in all your persecutions and tribulations that you endure,

James 1:3–4 knowing that the testing of your faith produces patience. 4 But let patience have *its* perfect work, that you may be perfect and complete, lacking nothing.

James 1:12 Blessed *is* the man who endures temptation; for when he has been approved, he will receive the crown of life which the Lord has promised to those who love Him.

In the Christian life.

Heb 12:1 Therefore we also, since we are surrounded by so great a cloud of witnesses, let us lay aside every weight, and the sin which so easily ensnares *us*, and let us run with endurance the race that is set before us,

The proof of salvation.

Matt 24:13 But he who endures to the end shall be saved.

2 Tim 2:12 If we endure, We shall also reign with *Him*. If we deny *Him*, He also will deny us.

Cf. Matt 10:22

A characteristic of love.

1 Cor 13:7 bears all things, believes all things, hopes all things, endures all things.

Exemplified by

Abraham.

Heb 6:15 And so, after he had patiently endured, he obtained the promise.

Job.

James 5:11 Indeed we count them blessed who endure. You have heard of the perseverance of Job and seen the end *intended by* the Lord—that the Lord is very compassionate and merciful.

ENEMIES

Christ prayed for his.

Luke 23:34 Then Jesus said, "Father, forgive them, for they do not know what they do." And they divided His garments and cast lots.

The lives of, to be spared.

1 Sam 24:10 Look, this day your eyes have seen that the LORD delivered you today into my hand in the cave, and *someone* urged *me* to kill you. But *my eye* spared you, and I said, 'I will not stretch out my hand against my lord, for he *is* the LORD's anointed.'

2 Sam 16:10–11 But the king said, "What have I to do with you, you sons of Zeruiah? So let him curse, because the LORD has said to him, 'Curse David.' Who then shall say, 'Why have you done so?' " 11 And David said to Abishai and all his servants, "See how my son who came from my own body seeks my life. How much more now *may this* Benjamite? Let him alone, and let him curse; for so the LORD has ordered him.

The goods of, to be taken care of.

Ex 23:4–5 "If you meet your enemy's ox or his donkey going astray, you shall surely bring it back to him again. 5 If you see the donkey of one who hates you lying under its burden, and you would refrain from helping it, you shall surely help him with it.

Should be

Loved.

Matt 5:44 But I say to you, love your enemies, bless those who curse you, do good to those who hate you, and pray for those who spitefully use you and persecute you,

Prayed for.

Acts 7:60 Then he knelt down and cried out with a loud voice, "Lord, do not charge them with this sin." And when he had said this, he fell asleep.

Assisted.

Prov 25:21 If your enemy is hungry, give him bread to eat; And if he is thirsty, give him water to drink;

Rom 12:20 Therefore *"If your enemy is hungry, feed him; If he is thirsty, give him a drink; For in so doing you will heap coals of fire on his head."*

Overcome by kindness.

1 Sam 26:21 Then Saul said, "I have sinned. Return, my son David. For I will harm you no more, because my life was precious in your eyes this day. Indeed I have played the fool and erred exceedingly."

Do not rejoice at the misfortunes of.

Job 31:29 "If I have rejoiced at the destruction of him who hated me, Or lifted myself up when evil found him

Prov 24:17 Do not rejoice when your enemy falls, And do not let your heart be glad when he stumbles;

Do not desire the death of.

1 Kin 3:11 Then God said to him: "Because you have asked this thing, and have not asked long life for yourself, nor have asked riches for yourself, nor have asked the life of your enemies, but have asked for yourself understanding to discern justice,

Do not curse.

Job 31:30 (Indeed I have not allowed my mouth to sin By asking for a curse on his soul);

Be affectionately concerned for.

Ps 35:13 But as for me, when they were sick, My clothing *was* sackcloth; I humbled myself with fasting; And my prayer would return to my own heart.

The friendship of, deceitful.

2 Sam 20:9–10 Then Joab said to Amasa, "*Are* you in health, my brother?" And Joab took Amasa by the beard with his right hand to kiss him. 10 But Amasa did not notice the sword that *was* in Joab's hand. And he struck him with it in the stomach, and his entrails poured out on the ground; and he did not *strike* him again. Thus he died. Then Joab and Abishai his brother pursued Sheba the son of Bichri.

Prov 26:26 *Though his* hatred is covered by deceit, His wickedness will be revealed before the assembly.

Prov 27:6 Faithful *are* the wounds of a friend, But the kisses of an enemy *are* deceitful.

Matt 26:48–49 Now His betrayer had given them a sign, saying, "Whomever I kiss, He is the One; seize Him." 49 Immediately he went up to Jesus and said, "Greetings, Rabbi!" and kissed Him.

God defends against.

Ps 59:9 I will wait for You, O You his Strength; For God *is* my defense.

Ps 61:3 For You have been a shelter for me, A strong tower from the enemy.

God delivers from.

1 Sam 12:11 And the LORD sent Jerubbaal, Bedan, Jephthah, and Samuel, and delivered you out of the hand of your enemies on every side; and you dwelt in safety.

Ezra 8:31 Then we departed from the river of Ahava on the twelfth *day* of the first month, to go to Jerusalem. And the hand of our God was upon us, and He delivered us from the hand of the enemy and from ambush along the road.

Ps 18:48 He delivers me from my enemies. You also lift me up above those who rise against me; You have delivered me from the violent man.

Made to be at peace with believers.

Prov 16:7 When a man's ways please the LORD, He makes even his enemies to be at peace with him.

Pray for deliverance from.

1 Sam 12:10 Then they cried out to the LORD, and said, 'We have sinned, because we have forsaken the LORD and served the Baals and Ashtoreths; but now deliver us from the hand of our enemies, and we will serve You.'

Ps 17:9 From the wicked who oppress me, *From* my deadly enemies who surround me.

Ps 59:1 Deliver me from my enemies, O my God; Defend me from those who rise up against me.

Ps 64:1 Hear my voice, O God, in my meditation; Preserve my life from fear of the enemy.

Of believers, God will destroy.

Ps 60:12 Through God we will do valiantly, For *it is* He *who* shall tread down our enemies.

Praise God for deliverance from.

Ps 136:24 And rescued us from our enemies, For His mercy *endures* forever;

ENVY

Forbidden.

Prov 3:31 Do not envy the oppressor, And choose none of his ways;

Rom 13:13 Let us walk properly, as in the day, not in revelry and drunkenness, not in lewdness and lust, not in strife and envy.

Produced by foolish argumentation.

1 Tim 6:4 he is proud, knowing nothing, but is obsessed with disputes and arguments over words, from which come envy, strife, reviling, evil suspicions,

Excited by good deeds of others.

Eccl 4:4 Again, I saw that for all toil and every skillful work a man is envied by his neighbor. This also *is* vanity and grasping for the wind.

A work of the flesh.

Gal 5:21 envy, murders, drunkenness, revelries, and the like; of which I tell you beforehand, just as I also told *you* in time past, that those who practice such things will not inherit the kingdom of God.

James 4:5 Or do you think that the Scripture says in vain, "The Spirit who dwells in us yearns jealously"?

Harmful to the health.

Job 5:2 For wrath kills a foolish man, And envy slays a simple one.

Prov 14:30 A sound heart *is* life to the body, But envy *is* rottenness to the bones.

None can stand before.

Prov 27:4 Wrath *is* cruel and anger a torrent, But who *is* able to stand before jealousy?

A proof of carnal-mindedness.

1 Cor 3:1 And I, brethren, could not speak to you as to spiritual *people* but as to carnal, as to babes in Christ.

1 Cor 3:3 for you are still carnal. For where *there are* envy, strife, and divisions among you, are you not carnal and behaving like *mere* men?

Inconsistent with the gospel.

James 3:14 But if you have bitter envy and self-seeking in your hearts, do not boast and lie against the truth.

Hinders growth in grace.

1 Pet 2:1–2 Therefore, laying aside all malice, all deceit, hypocrisy, envy, and all evil speaking, **2** as newborn babes, desire the pure milk of the word, that you may grow thereby,

The wicked

Are full of.

Rom 1:29 being filled with all unrighteousness, sexual immorality, wickedness, covetousness, maliciousness; full of envy, murder, strife, deceit, evil-mindedness; *they are* whisperers,

Live in.

Titus 3:3 For we ourselves were also once foolish, disobedient, deceived, serving various lusts and pleasures, living in malice and envy, hateful and hating one another.

Leads to every evil work.

James 3:16 For where envy and self-seeking *exist*, confusion and every evil thing *are* there.

Prosperity of the wicked should not excite.

Ps 37:1 Do not fret because of evildoers, Nor be envious of the workers of iniquity.

Ps 37:35 I have seen the wicked in great power, And spreading himself like a native green tree.

Ps 73:3 For I *was* envious of the boastful, When I saw the prosperity of the wicked.

Ps 73:17–20 Until I went into the sanctuary of God; *Then* I understood their end. **18** Surely You set them in slippery places; You cast them down to destruction. **19** Oh, how they are *brought* to desolation, as in a moment! They are utterly consumed with terrors. **20** As a dream when *one* awakes, So, Lord, when You awake, You shall despise their image.

Punishment of.

Is 26:11 LORD, *when* Your hand is lifted up, they will not see. But they will see and be ashamed For *their* envy of people; Yes, the fire of Your enemies shall devour them.

Examples of,

Cain.

Gen 4:5 but He did not respect Cain and his offering. And Cain was very angry, and his countenance fell.

The Philistines.

Gen 26:14 for he had possessions of flocks and possessions of herds and a great number of servants. So the Philistines envied him.

Laban's sons.

Gen 31:1 Now *Jacob* heard the words of Laban's sons, saying, "Jacob has taken away all that was our father's, and from what was our father's he has acquired all this wealth."

Joseph's brothers.

Gen 37:11 And his brothers envied him, but his father kept the matter *in mind.*

Joshua.

Num 11:28–29 So Joshua the son of Nun, Moses' assistant, *one* of his choice men, answered and said, "Moses my lord, forbid them!" **29** Then Moses said to him, "Are you zealous for my sake? Oh, that all the Lord's people were prophets *and* that the Lord would put His Spirit upon them!"

Aaron, etc.

Num 12:2 So they said, "Has the Lord indeed spoken only through Moses? Has He not spoken through us also?" And the Lord heard *it.*

Korah, etc.

Num 16:3 They gathered together against Moses and Aaron, and said to them, "*You take* too much upon yourselves, for all the congregation *is* holy, every one of them, and the Lord *is* among them. Why then do you exalt yourselves above the assembly of the Lord?"

Ps 106:16 When they envied Moses in the camp, *And* Aaron the saint of the Lord,

Saul.

1 Sam 18:8 Then Saul was very angry, and the saying displeased him; and he said, "They have ascribed to David ten thousands, and to me they have ascribed *only* thousands. Now *what* more can he have but the kingdom?"

Sanballat, etc.

Neh 2:10 When Sanballat the Horonite and Tobiah the Ammonite official heard *of it,* they were deeply disturbed that a man had come to seek the well-being of the children of Israel.

Haman.

Esth 5:13 Yet all this avails me nothing, so long as I see Mordecai the Jew sitting at the king's gate."

The Edomites.

Ezek 35:11 therefore, *as* I live," says the Lord God, "I will do according to your anger and according to the envy which you showed in your hatred against them; and I will make Myself known among them when I judge you.

The princes of Babylon.

Dan 6:3–4 Then this Daniel distinguished himself above the governors and satraps, because an excellent spirit *was* in him; and the king gave thought to setting him over the whole realm. **4** So the governors and satraps sought to find *some* charge against Daniel concerning the kingdom; but they could find no charge or fault, because he *was* faithful; nor was there any error or fault found in him.

The chief priests.

Mark 15:10 For he knew that the chief priests had handed Him over because of envy.

The Jews.

Acts 13:45 But when the Jews saw the multitudes, they were filled with envy; and contradicting and blaspheming, they opposed the things spoken by Paul.

Acts 17:5 But the Jews who were not persuaded, becoming envious, took some of the evil men from the marketplace, and gathering a mob, set all the city in an uproar and attacked the house of Jason, and sought to bring them out to the people.

EPHOD, THE

The emblem of the priestly office.

Hos 3:4 For the children of Israel shall abide many days without king or prince, without sacrifice or sacred pillar, without ephod or teraphim.

Worn by

The high priest.

1 Sam 2:28 Did I not choose him out of all the tribes of Israel *to be* My priest, to offer upon My altar, to burn incense, and to wear an ephod before Me? And did I not give to the house of your father all the offerings of the children of Israel made by fire?

1 Sam 14:3 Ahijah the son of Ahitub, Ichabod's brother, the son of Phinehas, the son of Eli, the Lord's priest in Shiloh, was wearing an ephod. But the people did not know that Jonathan had gone.

Ordinary priests.

1 Sam 22:18 And the king said to Doeg, "You turn and kill the priests!" So Doeg the Edomite turned and struck the priests, and killed on that day eighty-five men who wore a linen ephod.

Generally made of linen.

1 Sam 2:18 But Samuel ministered before the Lord, *even as* a child, wearing a linen ephod.

2 Sam 6:14 Then David danced before the Lord with all *his* might; and David *was* wearing a linen ephod.

For the high priest,

Commanded to be made.

Ex 28:4 And these *are* the garments which they shall make: a breastplate, an ephod, a robe, a skillfully woven tunic, a turban, and a sash. So they shall make holy garments for Aaron your brother and his sons, that he may minister to Me as priest.

Made of offerings of the people.

Ex 25:4 blue, purple, and scarlet *thread,* fine linen, and goats' *hair;*

Ex 25:7 onyx stones, and stones to be set in the ephod and in the breastplate.

Made of gold, blue, purple, scarlet, etc.

Ex 28:6 and they shall make the ephod of gold, blue, purple, *and* scarlet *thread,* and fine woven linen, artistically worked.

Ex 39:2–3 He made the ephod of gold, blue, purple, and scarlet *thread,* and of fine woven linen. **3** nd they beat the gold into thin sheets and cut *it into* threads, to work *it in with* the blue, purple, and scarlet *thread* and the fine linen, *into* artistic designs.

Shoulders of, joined by onyx stones engraved with names of the twelve tribes of Israel.

Ex 28:7 It shall have two shoulder straps joined at its two edges, and *so* it shall be joined together.

Ex 28:9–12 "Then you shall take two onyx stones and engrave on them the names of the sons of Israel: **10** six of their names on one stone and six names on the other stone, in order of their birth. **11** With the work of an engraver in stone, *like* the engravings of a signet, you shall engrave the two stones with the names of the sons of Israel. You shall set them in settings of gold. **12** And you shall put the two stones on the shoulders of the ephod *as* memorial stones for the sons of Israel. So Aaron shall bear their names before the LORD on his two shoulders as a memorial.

Ex 39:4 They made shoulder straps for it to couple *it* together; it was coupled together at its two edges.

Ex 39:6–7 And they set onyx stones, enclosed in settings of gold; they were engraved, as signets are engraved, with the names of the sons of Israel. **7** He put them on the shoulders of the ephod *as* memorial stones for the sons of Israel, as the LORD had commanded Moses.

Had a girdle of intricate workmanship.

Ex 28:8 And the intricately woven band of the ephod, which *is* on it, shall be of the same workmanship, *made of* gold, blue, purple, and scarlet *thread,* and fine woven linen.

Breastplate of judgment inseparably united to.

Ex 28:25–28 and the *other* two ends of the two braided *chains* you shall fasten to the two settings, and put them on the shoulder straps of the ephod in the front. **26** "You shall make two rings of gold, and put them on the two ends of the breastplate, on the edge of it, which is on the inner side of the ephod. **27** And two *other* rings of gold you shall make, and put them on the two shoulder straps, underneath the ephod toward its front, right at the seam above the intricately woven band of the ephod. **28** They shall bind the breastplate by means of its rings to the rings of the ephod, using a blue cord, so that it is above the intricately woven band of the ephod, and so that the breastplate does not come loose from the ephod.

Ex 39:20–21 They made two *other* gold rings and put them on the two shoulder straps, underneath the ephod toward its front, right at the seam above the intricately woven band of the ephod. **21** And they bound the breastplate by means of its rings to the rings of the ephod with a blue cord, so that it would be above the intricately woven band of the ephod, and that the breastplate would not come loose from the ephod, as the LORD had commanded Moses.

Worn over the robe.

Ex 28:31 "You shall make the robe of the ephod all of blue.

Lev 8:7 And he put the tunic on him, girded him with the sash, clothed him with the robe, and put the ephod on him; and he girded him with the intricately woven band of the ephod, and with it tied *the ephod* on him.

Fastened on with its own sash.

Lev 8:7 And he put the tunic on him, girded him with the sash, clothed him with the robe, and put the ephod on him; and he girded him with the intricate-

ly woven band of the ephod, and with it tied *the ephod* on him.

Worn or held by him when consulted.

1 Sam 23:6 Now it happened, when Abiathar the son of Ahimelech fled to David at Keilah, *that* he went down *with* an ephod in his hand.

1 Sam 23:9–12 When David knew that Saul plotted evil against him, he said to Abiathar the priest, "Bring the ephod here." **10** Then David said, "O LORD God of Israel, Your servant has certainly heard that Saul seeks to come to Keilah to destroy the city for my sake. **11** Will the men of Keilah deliver me into his hand? Will Saul come down, as Your servant has heard? O LORD God of Israel, I pray, tell Your servant." And the LORD said, "He will come down." **12** Then David said, "Will the men of Keilah deliver me and my men into the hand of Saul?" And the LORD said, "They will deliver *you.*"

1 Sam 30:7–8 Then David said to Abiathar the priest, Ahimelech's son, "Please bring the ephod here to me." And Abiathar brought the ephod to David. **8** So David inquired of the LORD, saying, "Shall I pursue this troop? Shall I overtake them?" And He answered him, "Pursue, for you shall surely overtake *them* and without fail recover *all.*"

Used by idolatrous priests.

Judg 8:27 Then Gideon made it into an ephod and set it up in his city, Ophrah. And all Israel played the harlot with it there. It became a snare to Gideon and to his house.

Judg 17:5 The man Micah had a shrine, and made an ephod and household idols; and he consecrated one of his sons, who became his priest.

Judg 18:14 Then the five men who had gone to spy out the country of Laish answered and said to their brethren, "Do you know that there are in these houses an ephod, household idols, a carved image, and a molded image? Now therefore, consider what you should do."

Israel deprived of, for sin.

Hos 3:4 For the children of Israel shall abide many days without king or prince, without sacrifice or sacred pillar, without ephod or teraphim.

EPHRAIM, THE TRIBE OF

Descended from Joseph's second son adopted by Jacob.

Gen 41:52 And the name of the second he called Ephraim: "For God has caused me to be fruitful in the land of my affliction."

Gen 48:5 And now your two sons, Ephraim and Manasseh, who were born to you in the land of Egypt before I came to you in Egypt, *are* mine; as Reuben and Simeon, they shall be mine.

Predictions respecting.

Gen 48:20 So he blessed them that day, saying, "By you Israel will bless, saying, 'May God make you as Ephraim and as Manasseh!' " And thus he set Ephraim before Manasseh.

Deut 33:13–17 And of Joseph he said: "Blessed of the LORD *is* his land, With the precious things of heaven, with the dew, And the deep lying beneath, **14** With the precious fruits of the sun, With the precious produce of the months, 15 With the best things of the ancient mountains, With the precious things of the everlasting hills, 16 With the precious things of the earth and its fullness, And the favor of Him who dwelt in the bush. Let *the blessing* come 'on the head of Joseph, And on the crown of the head of him *who was* separate from his brothers.' 17 His glory *is like* a firstborn bull, And his horns *like* the horns of the wild ox; Together with them He shall push the peoples To the ends of the earth; They *are* the ten thousands of Ephraim, And they *are* the thousands of Manasseh."

Persons selected from,

To number the people.

Num 1:10 from the sons of Joseph: from Ephraim, Elishama the son of Ammihud; from Manasseh, Gamaliel the son of Pedahzur;

To spy out the land.

Num 13:8 from the tribe of Ephraim, Hoshea the son of Nun;

To divide the land.

Num 34:24 and a leader from the tribe of the children of Ephraim, Kemuel the son of Shiphtan;

Strength of, on leaving Egypt.

Num 1:32–33 From the sons of Joseph, the children of Ephraim, their genealogies by their families, by their fathers' house, according to the number of names, from twenty years old and above, all who *were able to* go to war: 33 those who were numbered of the tribe of Ephraim *were* forty thousand five hundred.

Led the third division of Israel.

Num 10:22 And the standard of the camp of the children of Ephraim set out according to their armies; over their army *was* Elishama the son of Ammihud.

Encamped west of the tabernacle.

Num 2:18 "On the west side *shall be* the standard of the forces with Ephraim according to their armies, and the leader of the children of Ephraim *shall be* Elishama the son of Ammihud."

Offering of, at the dedication.

Num 7:48–53 On the seventh day Elishama the son of Ammihud, leader of the children of Ephraim, *presented an offering.* 49 His offering *was* one silver platter, the weight of which *was* one hundred and thirty *shekels,* and one silver bowl of seventy shekels, according to the shekel of the sanctuary, both of them full of fine flour mixed with oil as a grain offering; 50 one gold pan of ten *shekels,* full of incense; 51 one young bull, one ram, and one male lamb in its first year, as a burnt offering; 52 one kid of the goats as a sin offering; 53 and as the sacrifice of peace offerings: two oxen, five rams, five male goats, and five male lambs in their first year. This *was* the offering of Elishama the son of Ammihud.

Families of.

Num 26:35–36 These *are* the sons of Ephraim according to their families: of Shuthelah, the family of the Shuthalhites; of Becher, the family of the Bachrites; of Tahan, the family of the Tahanites. 36 And these *are* the sons of Shuthelah: of Eran, the family of the Eranites.

Strength of, on entering Canaan.

Num 26:37 These *are* the families of the sons of Ephra-

im according to those who were numbered of them: thirty-two thousand five hundred. These *are* the sons of Joseph according to their families.

On Gerizim, said amen to blessings.

Deut 27:12 "These shall stand on Mount Gerizim to bless the people, when you have crossed over the Jordan: Simeon, Levi, Judah, Issachar, Joseph, and Benjamin;

Borders of its inheritance.

Josh 16:5–9 The border of the children of Ephraim, according to their families, was *thus:* The border of their inheritance on the east side was Ataroth Addar as far as Upper Beth Horon. 6 And the border went out toward the sea on the north side of Michmethath; then the border went around eastward to Taanath Shiloh, and passed by it on the east of Janohah. 7 Then it went down from Janohah to Ataroth and Naarah, reached to Jericho, and came out at the Jordan. 8 The border went out from Tappuah westward to the Brook Kanah, and it ended at the sea. This *was* the inheritance of the tribe of the children of Ephraim according to their families. 9 The separate cities for the children of Ephraim *were* among the inheritance of the children of Manasseh, all the cities with their villages.

Could not drive out the Canaanites but made them subservient.

Josh 16:10 And they did not drive out the Canaanites who dwelt in Gezer; but the Canaanites dwell among the Ephraimites to this day and have become forced laborers.

Judg 1:29 Nor did Ephraim drive out the Canaanites who dwelt in Gezer; so the Canaanites dwelt in Gezer among them.

Assisted

Manasseh in taking Bethel.

Judg 1:22–25 And the house of Joseph also went up against Bethel, and the LORD *was* with them. 23 So the house of Joseph sent men to spy out Bethel. (The name of the city *was* formerly Luz.) 24 And when the spies saw a man coming out of the city, they said to him, "Please show us the entrance to the city, and we will show you mercy." 25 So he showed them the entrance to the city, and they struck the city with the edge of the sword; but they let the man and all his family go.

Deborah and Barak against Sisera.

Judg 5:14 From Ephraim *were* those whose roots were in Amalek. After you, Benjamin, with your peoples, From Machir rulers came down, And from Zebulun those who bear the recruiter's staff.

Gideon against Midian.

Judg 7:24–25 Then Gideon sent messengers throughout all the mountains of Ephraim, saying, "Come down against the Midianites, and seize from them the watering places as far as Beth Barah and the Jordan." Then all the men of Ephraim gathered together and seized the watering places as far as Beth Barah and the Jordan. 25 And they captured two princes of the Midianites, Oreb and Zeeb. They killed Oreb at the rock of Oreb, and Zeeb they killed at the winepress of Zeeb. They pursued Midian and brought the heads of Oreb and Zeeb to Gideon on the other side of the Jordan.

Reprimanded Gideon for not calling them sooner against Midian.

Judg 8:1–3 Now the men of Ephraim said to him, "Why have you done this to us by not calling us when you went to fight with the Midianites?" And they reprimanded him sharply. **2** So he said to them, "What have I done now in comparison with you? Is not the gleaning of the grapes of Ephraim better than the vintage of Abiezer? **3** God has delivered into your hands the princes of Midian, Oreb and Zeeb. And what was I able to do in comparison with you?" Then their anger toward him subsided when he said that.

Quarreled with Jephthah for not seeking their aid against Ammon.

Judg 12:1–4 Then the men of Ephraim gathered together, crossed over toward Zaphon, and said to Jephthah, "Why did you cross over to fight against the people of Ammon, and did not call us to go with you? We will burn your house down on you with fire!" **2** And Jephthah said to them, "My people and I were in a great struggle with the people of Ammon; and when I called you, you did not deliver me out of their hands. **3** So when I saw that you would not deliver me, I took my life in my hands and crossed over against the people of Ammon; and the LORD delivered them into my hand. Why then have you come up to me this day to fight against me?" **4** Now Jephthah gathered together all the men of Gilead and fought against Ephraim. And the men of Gilead defeated Ephraim, because they said, "You Gileadites are fugitives of Ephraim among the Ephraimites and among the Manassites."

Were defeated and many slain.

Judg 12:5–6 The Gileadites seized the fords of the Jordan before the Ephraimites arrived. And when any Ephraimite who escaped said, "Let me cross over," the men of Gilead would say to him, "Are you an Ephraimite?" If he said, "No," **6** then they would say to him, "Then say, 'Shibboleth'!" And he would say, "Sibboleth," for he could not pronounce it right. Then they would take him and kill him at the fords of the Jordan. There fell at that time forty-two thousand Ephraimites.

Some of, at coronation of David.

1 Chr 12:30 of the sons of Ephraim twenty thousand eight hundred, mighty men of valor, famous men throughout their father's house;

Officers appointed over, by David.

1 Chr 27:10 The seventh captain for the seventh month was Helez the Pelonite, of the children of Ephraim; in his division were twenty-four thousand.

1 Chr 27:20 over the children of Ephraim, Hoshea the son of Azaziah; over the half-tribe of Manasseh, Joel the son of Pedaiah;

The leading tribe of the kingdom of Israel.

Jer 31:9 They shall come with weeping, And with supplications I will lead them. I will cause them to walk by the rivers of waters, In a straight way in which they shall not stumble; For I am a Father to Israel, And Ephraim is My firstborn.

Jer 31:20 Is Ephraim My dear son? Is he a pleasant child? For though I spoke against him, I earnestly remember him still; Therefore My heart yearns for him; I will surely have mercy on him, says the LORD.

Many of, joined Judah under Asa.

2 Chr 15:9 Then he gathered all Judah and Benjamin, and those who dwelt with them from Ephraim, Manasseh, and Simeon, for they came over to him in great numbers from Israel when they saw that the LORD his God was with him.

Many of, joined in Hezekiah's Passover and reformation.

2 Chr 30:18 For a multitude of the people, many from Ephraim, Manasseh, Issachar, and Zebulun, had not cleansed themselves, yet they ate the Passover contrary to what was written. But Hezekiah prayed for them, saying, "May the good LORD provide atonement for everyone

2 Chr 31:1 Now when all this was finished, all Israel who were present went out to the cities of Judah and broke the sacred pillars in pieces, cut down the wooden images, and threw down the high places and the altars—from all Judah, Benjamin, Ephraim, and Manasseh—until they had utterly destroyed them all. Then all the children of Israel returned to their own cities, every man to his possession.

The tabernacle continued a long time in Shiloh, a city of.

Josh 18:1 Now the whole congregation of the children of Israel assembled together at Shiloh, and set up the tabernacle of meeting there. And the land was subdued before them.

Josh 19:51 These were the inheritances which Eleazar the priest, Joshua the son of Nun, and the heads of the fathers of the tribes of the children of Israel divided as an inheritance by lot in Shiloh before the LORD, at the door of the tabernacle of meeting. So they made an end of dividing the country.

One of Jeroboam's calves set up in Bethel, a city of.

1 Kin 12:29 And he set up one in Bethel, and the other he put in Dan.

Remarkable persons of,

Joshua.

Num 13:8 from the tribe of Ephraim, Hoshea the son of Nun;

Josh 1:1 After the death of Moses the servant of the LORD, it came to pass that the LORD spoke to Joshua the son of Nun, Moses' assistant, saying:

Abdon.

Judg 12:13–15 After him, Abdon the son of Hillel the Pirathonite judged Israel. **14** He had forty sons and thirty grandsons, who rode on seventy young donkeys. He judged Israel eight years. **15** Then Abdon the son of Hillel the Pirathonite died and was buried in Pirathon in the land of Ephraim, in the mountains of the Amalekites.

Zichri.

2 Chr 28:7 Zichri, a mighty man of Ephraim, killed Maaseiah the king's son, Azrikam the officer over the house, and Elkanah who was second to the king.

EQUALITY

Of Christ with God the Father.

1 Cor 8:6 yet for us *there is* one God, the Father, of whom *are* all things, and we for Him; and one Lord Jesus Christ, through whom *are* all things, and through whom we *live.*

Phil 2:6 who, being in the form of God, did not consider it robbery to be equal with God,

Cf. John 5:19–47

In the kingdom of God.

Matt 20:1–16 "For the kingdom of heaven is like a landowner who went out early in the morning to hire laborers for his vineyard. **2** Now when he had agreed with the laborers for a denarius a day, he sent them into his vineyard. **3** And he went out about the third hour and saw others standing idle in the marketplace, **4** and said to them, 'You also go into the vineyard, and whatever is right I will give you.' So they went. **5** Again he went out about the sixth and the ninth hour, and did likewise. **6** And about the eleventh hour he went out and found others standing idle, and said to them, 'Why have you been standing here idle all day?' **7** They said to him, 'Because no one hired us.' He said to them, 'You also go into the vineyard, and whatever is right you will receive.' **8** "So when evening had come, the owner of the vineyard said to his steward, 'Call the laborers and give them *their* wages, beginning with the last to the first.' **9** And when those came who *were hired* about the eleventh hour, they each received a denarius. **10** But when the first came, they supposed that they would receive more; and they likewise received each a denarius. **11** And when they had received *it,* they complained against the landowner, **12** saying, 'These last *men* have worked *only* one hour, and you made them equal to us who have borne the burden and the heat of the day.' **13** But he answered one of them and said, 'Friend, I am doing you no wrong. Did you not agree with me for a denarius? **14** Take *what is* yours and go your way. I wish to give to this last man *the same* as to you. **15** Is it not lawful for me to do what I wish with my own things? Or is your eye evil because I am good?' **16** So the last will be first, and the first last. For many are called, but few chosen."

Mark 10:31 But many *who are* first will be last, and the last first."

Gal 3:28 There is neither Jew nor Greek, there is neither slave nor free, there is neither male nor female; for you are all one in Christ Jesus.

Cf. 2 Cor 8:13–15; Eph 4:4–6

ETERNAL LIFE

Christ is.

1 John 1:2 the life was manifested, and we have seen, and bear witness, and declare to you that eternal life which was with the Father and was manifested to us—

1 John 5:20 And we know that the Son of God has come and has given us an understanding, that we may know Him who is true; and we are in Him who is true, in His Son Jesus Christ. This is the true God and eternal life.

Defined.

John 17:3 And this is eternal life, that they may know You, the only true God, and Jesus Christ whom You have sent.

Given

By God.

Ps 133:3 *It is* like the dew of Hermon, Descending upon the mountains of Zion; For there the LORD commanded the blessing— Life forevermore.

John 17:2 as You have given Him authority over all flesh, that He should give eternal life to as many as You have given Him.

Rom 6:23 For the wages of sin *is* death, but the gift of God *is* eternal life in Christ Jesus our Lord.

By Christ.

John 6:27 Do not labor for the food which perishes, but for the food which endures to everlasting life, which the Son of Man will give you, because God the Father has set His seal on Him."

John 6:68 But Simon Peter answered Him, "Lord, to whom shall we go? You have the words of eternal life.

John 10:28 And I give them eternal life, and they shall never perish; neither shall anyone snatch them out of My hand.

Rom 5:21 so that as sin reigned in death, even so grace might reign through righteousness to eternal life through Jesus Christ our Lord.

Rom 6:23 For the wages of sin *is* death, but the gift of God *is* eternal life in Christ Jesus our Lord.

2 Tim 1:10 but has now been revealed by the appearing of our Savior Jesus Christ, *who* has abolished death and brought life and immortality to light through the gospel,

1 John 5:11 And this is the testimony: that God has given us eternal life, and this life is in His Son.

To those who believe.

John 3:15–16 that whoever believes in Him should not perish but have eternal life. **16** For God so loved the world that He gave His only begotten Son, that whoever believes in Him should not perish but have everlasting life.

John 5:24 "Most assuredly, I say to you, he who hears My word and believes in Him who sent Me has everlasting life, and shall not come into judgment, but has passed from death into life.

John 6:40 And this is the will of Him who sent Me, that everyone who sees the Son and believes in Him may have everlasting life; and I will raise him up at the last day."

John 6:47 Most assuredly, I say to you, he who believes in Me has everlasting life.

John 12:25 He who loves his life will lose it, and he who hates his life in this world will keep it for eternal life.

In answer to prayer.

Ps 21:4 He asked life from You, *and* You gave *it* to him— Length of days forever and ever.

Through the Scriptures.

John 5:39 You search the Scriptures, for in them you think you have eternal life; and these are they which testify of Me.

Results from

Drinking the water of life.

John 4:14 but whoever drinks of the water that I shall give him will never thirst. But the water that I shall give him will become in him a fountain of water springing up into everlasting life."

Eating the bread of life.

John 6:50–58 This is the bread which comes down from heaven, that one may eat of it and not die. **51** I am the living bread which came down from heaven. If anyone eats of this bread, he will live forever; and the bread that I shall give is My flesh, which I shall give for the life of the world." **52** The Jews therefore quarreled among themselves, saying, "How can this Man give us *His* flesh to eat?" **53** Then Jesus said to them, "Most assuredly, I say to you, unless you eat the flesh of the Son of Man and drink His blood, you have no life in you. **54** Whoever eats My flesh and drinks My blood has eternal life, and I will raise him up at the last day. **55** For My flesh is food indeed, and My blood is drink indeed. **56** He who eats My flesh and drinks My blood abides in Me, and I in him. **57** As the living Father sent Me, and I live because of the Father, so he who feeds on Me will live because of Me. **58** This is the bread which came down from heaven—not as your fathers ate the manna, and are dead. He who eats this bread will live forever."

Eating of the tree of life.

Rev 2:7 "He who has an ear, let him hear what the Spirit says to the churches. To him who overcomes I will give to eat from the tree of life, which is in the midst of the Paradise of God." '

They who are ordained to, believe the gospel.

Acts 13:48 Now when the Gentiles heard this, they were glad and glorified the word of the Lord. And as many as had been appointed to eternal life believed.

Believers

Have promises of.

1 Tim 4:8 For bodily exercise profits a little, but godliness is profitable for all things, having promise of the life that now is and of that which is to come.

2 Tim 1:1 Paul, an apostle of Jesus Christ by the will of God, according to the promise of life which is in Christ Jesus,

Titus 1:2 in hope of eternal life which God, who cannot lie, promised before time began,

Titus 3:7 that having been justified by His grace we should become heirs according to the hope of eternal life.

1 John 2:25 And this is the promise that He has promised us—eternal life.

Jude 1:21 keep yourselves in the love of God, looking for the mercy of our Lord Jesus Christ unto eternal life.

May have assurance of.

John 10:28–29 And I give them eternal life, and they shall never perish; neither shall anyone snatch them out of My hand. **29** My Father, who has given *them* to Me, is greater than all; and no one is able to snatch *them* out of My Father's hand.

2 Cor 5:1 For we know that if our earthly house, *this* tent, is destroyed, we have a building from God, a house not made with hands, eternal in the heavens.

1 John 5:13 These things I have written to you who believe in the name of the Son of God, that you may know that you have eternal life, and that you may *continue to* believe in the name of the Son of God.

Shall inherit.

Matt 19:29 And everyone who has left houses or brothers or sisters or father or mother or wife or children or lands, for My name's sake, shall receive a hundredfold, and inherit eternal life.

Gal 6:8 For he who sows to his flesh will of the flesh reap corruption, but he who sows to the Spirit will of the Spirit reap everlasting life.

Should lay hold of.

1 Tim 6:12 Fight the good fight of faith, lay hold on eternal life, to which you were also called and have confessed the good confession in the presence of many witnesses.

1 Tim 6:19 storing up for themselves a good foundation for the time to come, that they may lay hold on eternal life.

Shall rise to.

Dan 12:2 And many of those who sleep in the dust of the earth shall awake, Some to everlasting life, Some to shame *and* everlasting contempt.

Matt 25:46 And these will go away into everlasting punishment, but the righteous into eternal life."

John 5:29 and come forth—those who have done good, to the resurrection of life, and those who have done evil, to the resurrection of condemnation.

Shall reign in.

Dan 7:18 But the saints of the Most High shall receive the kingdom, and possess the kingdom forever, even forever and ever.'

Rom 5:17 For if by the one man's offense death reigned through the one, much more those who receive abundance of grace and of the gift of righteousness will reign in life through the One, Jesus Christ.)

Cannot be inherited by works.

Mark 10:17 Now as He was going out on the road, one came running, knelt before Him, and asked Him, "Good Teacher, what shall I do that I may inherit eternal life?"

Rom 2:7 eternal life to those who by patient continuance in doing good seek for glory, honor, and immortality;

Rom 3:10–19 As it is written: *"There is none righteous, no, not one;* **11** *There is none who understands; There is none who seeks after God.* **12** *They have all turned aside; They have together become unprofitable; There is none who does good, no, not one."* **13** *"Their throat is an open tomb; With their tongues they have practiced deceit"; "The poison of asps is under their lips";* **14** *"Whose mouth is full of cursing and bitterness."* **15** *"Their feet are swift to shed blood;* **16** *Destruction and misery are in their ways;* **17** *And the way of peace they have not known."* **18** *"There is no fear of God before their eyes."* **19** Now we know that whatever the law says, it says to those who are under the law, that every mouth may be stopped, and all the world may become guilty before God.

Rom 3:28 Therefore we conclude that a man is justified by faith apart from the deeds of the law.

The wicked

Do not have.

1 John 3:15 Whoever hates his brother is a murderer, and you know that no murderer has eternal life abiding in him.

Judge themselves unworthy of.

Acts 13:46 Then Paul and Barnabas grew bold and said, "It was necessary that the word of God should be spoken to you first; but since you reject it, and judge yourselves unworthy of everlasting life, behold, we turn to the Gentiles.

Exhortation to seek.

John 6:27 Do not labor for the food which perishes, but for the food which endures to everlasting life, which the Son of Man will give you, because God the Father has set His seal on Him."

EUPHRATES, THE

A branch of the river of Eden.

Gen 2:14 The name of the third river *is* Hiddekel; it *is* the one which goes toward the east of Assyria. The fourth river *is* the Euphrates.

Other names for,

The River.

Ex 23:31 And I will set your bounds from the Red Sea to the sea, Philistia, and from the desert to the River. For I will deliver the inhabitants of the land into your hand, and you shall drive them out before you.

Josh 24:2 And Joshua said to all the people, "Thus says the LORD God of Israel: 'Your fathers, *including* Terah, the father of Abraham and the father of Nahor, dwelt on the other side of the River in old times; and they served other gods.

Neh 2:7 Furthermore I said to the king, "If it pleases the king, let letters be given to me for the governors *of the region* beyond the River, that they must permit me to pass through till I come to Judah,

Ps 72:8 He shall have dominion also from sea to sea, And from the River to the ends of the earth.

The great river.

Gen 15:18 On the same day the LORD made a covenant with Abram, saying: "To your descendants I have given this land, from the river of Egypt to the great river, the River Euphrates—

Deut 1:7 Turn and take your journey, and go to the mountains of the Amorites, to all the neighboring *places* in the plain, in the mountains and in the lowland, in the South and on the seacoast, to the land of the Canaanites and to Lebanon, as far as the great river, the River Euphrates.

Waters of, considered wholesome.

Jer 2:18 And now why take the road to Egypt, To drink the waters of Sihor? Or why take the road to Assyria, To drink the waters of the River?

Often overflowed its banks.

Is 8:7–8 Now therefore, behold, the Lord brings up over them The waters of the River, strong and mighty— The king of Assyria and all his glory; He will go up over all his channels And go over all his banks. **8** He will pass through Judah, He will overflow and pass over, He will reach up to the neck;

And the stretching out of his wings Will fill the breadth of Your land, O Immanuel.

Assyria bounded by.

2 Kin 23:29 In his days Pharaoh Necho king of Egypt went to the aid of the king of Assyria, to the River Euphrates; and King Josiah went against him. And *Pharaoh Necho* killed him at Megiddo when he confronted him.

Is 7:20 In the same day the Lord will shave with a hired razor, With those from beyond the River, with the king of Assyria, The head and the hair of the legs, And will also remove the beard.

Babylon situated on.

Jer 51:12–13 Set up the standard on the walls of Babylon; Make the guard strong, Set up the watchmen, Prepare the ambushes. For the LORD has both devised and done What He spoke against the inhabitants of Babylon. **13** O you who dwell by many waters, Abundant in treasures, Your end has come, The measure of your covetousness.

Jer 51:36 Therefore thus says the LORD: "Behold, I will plead your case and take vengeance for you. I will dry up her sea and make her springs dry.

Extreme eastern boundary of the promised land.

Gen 15:18 On the same day the LORD made a covenant with Abram, saying: "To your descendants I have given this land, from the river of Egypt to the great river, the River Euphrates—

Deut 1:7 Turn and take your journey, and go to the mountains of the Amorites, to all the neighboring *places* in the plain, in the mountains and in the lowland, in the South and on the seacoast, to the land of the Canaanites and to Lebanon, as far as the great river, the River Euphrates.

Deut 11:24 Every place on which the sole of your foot treads shall be yours: from the wilderness and Lebanon, from the river, the River Euphrates, even to the Western Sea, shall be your territory.

Egyptian army destroyed at.

Jer 46:2 Against Egypt. Concerning the army of Pharaoh Necho, king of Egypt, which was by the River Euphrates in Carchemish, and which Nebuchadnezzar king of Babylon defeated in the fourth year of Jehoiakim the son of Josiah, king of Judah:

Jer 46:6 "Do not let the swift flee away, Nor the mighty man escape; They will stumble and fall Toward the north, by the River Euphrates.

Jer 46:10 For this *is* the day of the Lord GOD of hosts, A day of vengeance, That He may avenge Himself on His adversaries. The sword shall devour; It shall be satiated and made drunk with their blood; For the Lord GOD of hosts has a sacrifice In the north country by the River Euphrates.

Frequented by the captive Jews.

Ps 137:1 By the rivers of Babylon, There we sat down, yea, we wept When we remembered Zion.

Captivity of Judah represented by the marring of Jeremiah's sash in.

Jer 13:3–9 And the word of the LORD came to me the second time, saying, **4** "Take the sash that you acquired, which *is* around your waist, and arise, go to the Euphrates, and hide it there in a hole in the rock." **5** So

I went and hid it by the Euphrates, as the LORD commanded me. **6** Now it came to pass after many days that the LORD said to me, "Arise, go to the Euphrates, and take from there the sash which I commanded you to hide there." **7** Then I went to the Euphrates and dug, and I took the sash from the place where I had hidden it; and there was the sash, ruined. It was profitable for nothing. **8** Then the word of the LORD came to me, saying, **9** "Thus says the LORD: 'In this manner I will ruin the pride of Judah and the great pride of Jerusalem.

Prophecies respecting Babylon thrown into, as a sign.

Jer 51:63 Now it shall be, when you have finished reading this book, *that* you shall tie a stone to it and throw it out into the Euphrates.

Shall be the scene of future judgments.

Rev 16:12 Then the sixth angel poured out his bowl on the great river Euphrates, and its water was dried up, so that the way of the kings from the east might be prepared.

EVANGELISM, THE RESPONSIBILITY FOR

After the example of Christ.

Acts 10:38 how God anointed Jesus of Nazareth with the Holy Spirit and with power, who went about doing good and healing all who were oppressed by the devil, for God was with Him.

Belongs to all believers

Women and children as well as men.

Ps 8:2 Out of the mouth of babes and nursing infants You have ordained strength, Because of Your enemies, That You may silence the enemy and the avenger.

Prov 31:26 She opens her mouth with wisdom, And on her tongue *is* the law of kindness.

Matt 21:15–16 But when the chief priests and scribes saw the wonderful things that He did, and the children crying out in the temple and saying, "Hosanna to the Son of David!" they were indignant **16** and said to Him, "Do You hear what these are saying?" And Jesus said to them, "Yes. Have you never read, *'Out of the mouth of babes and nursing infants You have perfected praise'?* "

Phil 4:3 And I urge you also, true companion, help these women who labored with me in the gospel, with Clement also, and the rest of my fellow workers, whose names *are* in the Book of Life.

1 Tim 5:9–10 Do not let a widow under sixty years old be taken into the number, *and not unless* she has been the wife of one man, **10** well reported for good works: if she has brought up children, if she has lodged strangers, if she has washed the saints' feet, if she has relieved the afflicted, if she has diligently followed every good work.

Titus 2:3–5 the older women likewise, that they be reverent in behavior, not slanderers, not given to much wine, teachers of good things— **4** that they admonish the young women to love their husbands, to love their children, **5** to be discreet, chaste, homemakers, good, obedient to their own husbands, that the word of God may not be blasphemed.

1 Pet 3:1 Wives, likewise, *be* submissive to your own husbands, that even if some do not obey the word, they, without a word, may be won by the conduct of their wives,

On principle.

Ex 19:6 And you shall be to Me a kingdom of priests and a holy nation.' These *are* the words which you shall speak to the children of Israel."

Ps 66:16 Come *and* hear, all you who fear God, And I will declare what He has done for my soul.

Ps 116:16–19 O LORD, truly I *am* Your servant; I *am* Your servant, the son of Your maidservant; You have loosed my bonds. **17** I will offer to You the sacrifice of thanksgiving, And will call upon the name of the LORD. **18** I will pay my vows to the LORD Now in the presence of all His people, **19** In the courts of the LORD's house, In the midst of you, O Jerusalem. Praise the LORD!

2 Cor 5:14–15 For the love of Christ compels us, because we judge thus: that if One died for all, then all died; **15** and He died for all, that those who live should live no longer for themselves, but for Him who died for them and rose again.

1 Pet 2:9 But you *are* a chosen generation, a royal priesthood, a holy nation, His own special people, that you may proclaim the praises of Him who called you out of darkness into His marvelous light;

1 Pet 4:10–11 As each one has received a gift, minister it to one another, as good stewards of the manifold grace of God. **11** If anyone speaks, *let him speak* as the oracles of God. If anyone ministers, *let him do it* as with the ability which God supplies, that in all things God may be glorified through Jesus Christ, to whom belong the glory and the dominion forever and ever. Amen.

At all ages.

Deut 32:7 "Remember the days of old, Consider the years of many generations. Ask your father, and he will show you; Your elders, and they will tell you:

Ps 71:17–18 O God, You have taught me from my youth; And to this *day* I declare Your wondrous works. **18** Now also when I *am* old and grayheaded, O God, do not forsake me, Until I declare Your strength to *this* generation, Your power to everyone *who* is to come.

Ps 148:12–13 Both young men and maidens; Old men and children. **13** Let them praise the name of the LORD, For His name alone is exalted; His glory *is* above the earth and heaven.

In the family.

Deut 6:7 You shall teach them diligently to your children, and shall talk of them when you sit in your house, when you walk by the way, when you lie down, and when you rise up.

Ps 78:5–8 For He established a testimony in Jacob, And appointed a law in Israel, Which He commanded our fathers, That they should make them known to their children; **6** That the generation to come might know *them*, The children *who* would be born, *That* they may arise and declare *them* to their children, **7** That they may set their hope in God, And not forget the works of God, But keep His commandments; **8** And may not be like their fathers, A stubborn and rebellious generation, A generation *that* did not set its heart aright, And whose spirit was not faithful to God.

Is 38:19 The living, the living man, he shall praise You, As I *do* this day; The father shall make known Your truth to the children.

1 Cor 7:16 For how do you know, O wife, whether you will save *your* husband? Or how do you know, O husband, whether you will save *your* wife?

In their contact with the world.

Matt 5:16 Let your light so shine before men, that they may see your good works and glorify your Father in heaven.

Phil 2:15–16 that you may become blameless and harmless, children of God without fault in the midst of a crooked and perverse generation, among whom you shine as lights in the world, **16** holding fast the word of life, so that I may rejoice in the day of Christ that I have not run in vain or labored in vain.

1 Pet 2:12 having your conduct honorable among the Gentiles, that when they speak against you as evildoers, they may, by *your* good works which they observe, glorify God in the day of visitation.

Involves putting Christ first.

Luke 5:11 So when they had brought their boats to land, they forsook all and followed Him.

Luke 14:26–27 "If anyone comes to Me and does not hate his father and mother, wife and children, brothers and sisters, yes, and his own life also, he cannot be My disciple. **27** And whoever does not bear his cross and come after Me cannot be My disciple.

Luke 18:22 So when Jesus heard these things, He said to him, "You still lack one thing. Sell all that you have and distribute to the poor, and you will have treasure in heaven; and come, follow Me."

1 Cor 2:2 For I determined not to know anything among you except Jesus Christ and Him crucified.

Heb 10:34 for you had compassion on me in my chains, and joyfully accepted the plundering of your goods, knowing that you have a better and an enduring possession for yourselves in heaven.

Cf. Josh 24:15; 1 Chr 29:2,3,14,16; Ps 27:4; Eccl 11:1; Matt 6:19–20; Mark 12:44; Luke 12:33; Acts 2:45; 4:32–34

By life example.

Ps 37:30 The mouth of the righteous speaks wisdom, And his tongue talks of justice.

Prov 10:31 The mouth of the righteous brings forth wisdom, But the perverse tongue will be cut out.

Prov 15:7 The lips of the wise disperse knowledge, But the heart of the fool *does* not *do* so.

Matt 5:16 Let your light so shine before men, that they may see your good works and glorify your Father in heaven.

Eph 4:29 Let no corrupt word proceed out of your mouth, but what is good for necessary edification, that it may impart grace to the hearers.

Phil 2:15 that you may become blameless and harmless, children of God without fault in the midst of a crooked and perverse generation, among whom you shine as lights in the world,

Col 4:6 *Let* your speech always *be* with grace, seasoned with salt, that you may know how you ought to answer each one.

1 Thess 1:7 so that you became examples to all in Macedonia and Achaia who believe.

1 Pet 2:12 having your conduct honorable among the Gentiles, that when they speak against you as evildoers, they may, by *your* good works which they observe, glorify God in the day of visitation.

In talking about God's works and the gospel.

Ps 34:8 Oh, taste and see that the Lord *is* good; Blessed *is* the man *who* trusts in Him!

Ps 71:24 My tongue also shall talk of Your righteousness all the day long; For they are confounded, For they are brought to shame Who seek my hurt.

Ps 77:12 I will also meditate on all Your work, And talk of Your deeds.

Ps 119:27 Make me understand the way of Your precepts; So shall I meditate on Your wonderful works.

Ps 119:46 I will speak of Your testimonies also before kings, And will not be ashamed.

Ps 145:11–12 They shall speak of the glory of Your kingdom, And talk of Your power, **12** To make known to the sons of men His mighty acts, And the glorious majesty of His kingdom.

Is 43:1–2 But now, thus says the Lord, who created you, O Jacob, And He who formed you, O Israel: "Fear not, for I have redeemed you; I have called *you* by your name; You *are* Mine. **2** When you pass through the waters, I *will be* with you; And through the rivers, they shall not overflow you. When you walk through the fire, you shall not be burned, Nor shall the flame scorch you.

Matt 10:32 "Therefore whoever confesses Me before men, him I will also confess before My Father who is in heaven.

John 1:46 And Nathanael said to him, "Can anything good come out of Nazareth?" Philip said to him, "Come and see."

John 4:29 "Come, see a Man who told me all things that I ever did. Could this be the Christ?"

In giving a reason for their faith.

Ex 12:26–27 And it shall be, when your children say to you, 'What do you mean by this service?' **27** that you shall say, 'It *is* the Passover sacrifice of the Lord, who passed over the houses of the children of Israel in Egypt when He struck the Egyptians and delivered our households.' " So the people bowed their heads and worshiped.

Deut 6:20–21 "When your son asks you in time to come, saying, 'What *is the meaning of* the testimonies, the statutes, and the judgments which the Lord our God has commanded you?' **21** then you shall say to your son: 'We were slaves of Pharaoh in Egypt, and the Lord brought us out of Egypt with a mighty hand;

1 Pet 3:15 But sanctify the Lord God in your hearts, and always *be* ready to *give* a defense to everyone who asks you a reason for the hope that is in you, with meekness and fear;

Exemplified by

Shadrach, etc.

Dan 3:16–18 Shadrach, Meshach, and Abed-Nego answered and said to the king, "O Nebuchadnezzar, we have no need to answer you in this matter. **17** If that *is the case,* our God whom we serve is able to deliver us from the burning fiery furnace, and He will deliver *us* from your hand, O king. **18** But if not, let it be known to you, O king, that we do not serve your gods, nor will we worship the gold image which you have set up."

A restored demoniac.

Mark 5:20 And he departed and began to proclaim in Decapolis all that Jesus had done for him; and all marveled.

The shepherds.

Luke 2:17 Now when they had seen *Him,* they made widely known the saying which was told them concerning this Child.

Anna.

Luke 2:38 And coming in that instant she gave thanks to the Lord, and spoke of Him to all those who looked for redemption in Jerusalem.

A leper.

Luke 17:15 And one of them, when he saw that he was healed, returned, and with a loud voice glorified God,

The disciples.

Luke 19:37–38 Then, as He was now drawing near the descent of the Mount of Olives, the whole multitude of the disciples began to rejoice and praise God with a loud voice for all the mighty works they had seen, **38** saying: " *'Blessed is the King who comes in the name of the LORD!'* Peace in heaven and glory in the highest!"

A centurion.

Luke 23:47 So when the centurion saw what had happened, he glorified God, saying, "Certainly this was a righteous Man!"

Andrew.

John 1:41–42 He first found his own brother Simon, and said to him, "We have found the Messiah" (which is translated, the Christ). **42** And he brought him to Jesus. Now when Jesus looked at him, He said, "You are Simon the son of Jonah. You shall be called Cephas" (which is translated, A Stone).

Philip.

John 1:46 And Nathanael said to him, "Can anything good come out of Nazareth?" Philip said to him, "Come and see."

A woman of Samaria.

John 4:29 "Come, see a Man who told me all things that I ever did. Could this be the Christ?"

Barnabas.

Acts 4:36–37 And Joses, who was also named Barnabas by the apostles (which is translated Son of Encouragement), a Levite of the country of Cyprus, **37** having land, sold *it,* and brought the money and laid *it* at the apostles' feet.

The persecuted believers.

Acts 8:4 Therefore those who were scattered went everywhere preaching the word.

Acts 11:19–20 Now those who were scattered after the persecution that arose over Stephen traveled as far as Phoenicia, Cyprus, and Antioch, preaching the word to no one but the Jews only. **20** But some of them were men from Cyprus and Cyrene, who, when they

had come to Antioch, spoke to the Hellenists, preaching the Lord Jesus.

Apollos.

Acts 18:25 This man had been instructed in the way of the Lord; and being fervent in spirit, he spoke and taught accurately the things of the Lord, though he knew only the baptism of John.

Aquila and Priscilla.

Acts 18:26 So he began to speak boldly in the synagogue. When Aquila and Priscilla heard him, they took him aside and explained to him the way of God more accurately.

Onesiphorus.

2 Tim 1:16 The Lord grant mercy to the household of Onesiphorus, for he often refreshed me, and was not ashamed of my chain;

Philemon.

Philem 1:1–6 Paul, a prisoner of Christ Jesus, and Timothy *our* brother, To Philemon our beloved *friend* and fellow laborer, **2** to the beloved Apphia, Archippus our fellow soldier, and to the church in your house: **3** Grace to you and peace from God our Father and the Lord Jesus Christ. **4** I thank my God, making mention of you always in my prayers, **5** hearing of your love and faith which you have toward the Lord Jesus and toward all the saints, **6** that the sharing of your faith may become effective by the acknowledgment of every good thing which is in you in Christ Jesus.

EVENING, THE

The day originally began with.

Gen 1:5 God called the light Day, and the darkness He called Night. So the evening and the morning were the first day.

Divided into two, commencing at 3 o'clock, and sunset.

Ex 12:6 Now you shall keep it until the fourteenth day of the same month. Then the whole assembly of the congregation of Israel shall kill it at twilight.

Num 9:3 On the fourteenth day of this month, at twilight, you shall keep it at its appointed time. According to all its rites and ceremonies you shall keep it."

Mentioned in Scripture.

Gen 19:1 Now the two angels came to Sodom in the evening, and Lot was sitting in the gate of Sodom. When Lot saw *them,* he rose to meet them, and he bowed himself with his face toward the ground.

Deut 28:67 In the morning you shall say, 'Oh, that it were evening!' And at evening you shall say, 'Oh, that it were morning!' because of the fear which terrifies your heart, and because of the sight which your eyes see.

Josh 8:29 And the king of Ai he hanged on a tree until evening. And as soon as the sun was down, Joshua commanded that they should take his corpse down from the tree, cast it at the entrance of the gate of the city, and raise over it a great heap of stones *that remains* to this day.

Acts 4:3 And they laid hands on them, and put *them* in custody until the next day, for it was already evening.

Also called the cool of the day.

Gen 3:8 And they heard the sound of the LORD God walking in the garden in the cool of the day, and Adam and his wife hid themselves from the presence of the LORD God among the trees of the garden.

Stretches out its shadows.

Jer 6:4 "Prepare war against her; Arise, and let us go up at noon. Woe to us, for the day goes away, For the shadows of the evening are lengthening.

The outgoings of, praise God.

Ps 65:8 They also who dwell in the farthest parts are afraid of Your signs; You make the outgoings of the morning and evening rejoice.

Man ceases from labor in.

Ruth 2:17 So she gleaned in the field until evening, and beat out what she had gleaned, and it was about an ephah of barley.

Ps 104:23 Man goes out to his work And to his labor until the evening.

Wild beasts come forth in.

Ps 59:6 At evening they return, They growl like a dog, And go all around the city.

Ps 59:14 And at evening they return, They growl like a dog, And go all around the city.

Jer 5:6 Therefore a lion from the forest shall slay them, A wolf of the deserts shall destroy them; A leopard will watch over their cities. Everyone who goes out from there shall be torn in pieces, Because their transgressions are many; Their backslidings have increased.

A season for

Meditation.

Gen 24:63 And Isaac went out to meditate in the field in the evening; and he lifted his eyes and looked, and there, the camels *were* coming.

Prayer.

Ps 55:17 Evening and morning and at noon I will pray, and cry aloud, And He shall hear my voice.

Matt 14:15 When it was evening, His disciples came to Him, saying, "This is a deserted place, and the hour is already late. Send the multitudes away, that they may go into the villages and buy themselves food."

Matt 14:23 And when He had sent the multitudes away, He went up on the mountain by Himself to pray. Now when evening came, He was alone there.

Exercise.

2 Sam 11:2 Then it happened one evening that David arose from his bed and walked on the roof of the king's house. And from the roof he saw a woman bathing, and the woman *was* very beautiful to behold.

Taking food.

Mark 14:17–18 In the evening He came with the twelve. **18** Now as they sat and ate, Jesus said, "Assuredly, I say to you, one of you who eats with Me will betray Me."

Luke 24:29–30 But they constrained Him, saying, "Abide with us, for it is toward evening, and the day is far spent." And He went in to stay with them. **30** Now it came to pass, as He sat at the table with

them, that He took bread, blessed and broke *it*, and gave it to them.

Humiliation often continued until.

Josh 7:6 Then Joshua tore his clothes, and fell to the earth on his face before the ark of the LORD until evening, he and the elders of Israel; and they put dust on their heads.

Judg 20:23 Then the children of Israel went up and wept before the LORD until evening, and asked counsel of the LORD, saying, "Shall I again draw near for battle against the children of my brother Benjamin?" And the LORD said, "Go up against him."

Judg 20:26 Then all the children of Israel, that is, all the people, went up and came to the house of God and wept. They sat there before the LORD and fasted that day until evening; and they offered burnt offerings and peace offerings before the LORD.

Judg 21:2 Then the people came to the house of God, and remained there before God till evening. They lifted up their voices and wept bitterly,

Ezra 9:4–5 Then everyone who trembled at the words of the God of Israel assembled to me, because of the transgression of those who had been carried away captive, and I sat astonished until the evening sacrifice. **5** At the evening sacrifice I arose from my fasting; and having torn my garment and my robe, I fell on my knees and spread out my hands to the LORD my God.

Custom of sitting at the gates in.

Gen 19:1 Now the two angels came to Sodom in the evening, and Lot was sitting in the gate of Sodom. When Lot saw *them*, he rose to meet them, and he bowed himself with his face toward the ground.

All defiled persons unclean until.

Lev 11:24–28 'By these you shall become unclean; whoever touches the carcass of any of them shall be unclean until evening; **25** whoever carries part of the carcass of any of them shall wash his clothes and be unclean until evening: **26** *The carcass* of any animal which divides the foot, but is not cloven-hoofed or does not chew the cud, *is* unclean to you. Everyone who touches it shall be unclean. **27** And whatever goes on its paws, among all kinds of animals that go on *all* fours, those *are* unclean to you. Whoever touches any such carcass shall be unclean until evening. **28** Whoever carries *any such* carcass shall wash his clothes and be unclean until evening. It *is* unclean to you.

Lev 15:5–7 And whoever touches his bed shall wash his clothes and bathe in water, and be unclean until evening. **6** He who sits on anything on which he who has the discharge sat shall wash his clothes and bathe in water, and be unclean until evening. **7** And he who touches the body of him who has the discharge shall wash his clothes and bathe in water, and be unclean until evening.

Lev 17:15 "And every person who eats what died *naturally* or what was torn *by beasts, whether he is* a native of your own country or a stranger, he shall both wash his clothes and bathe in water, and be unclean until evening. Then he shall be clean.

Num 19:19 The clean *person* shall sprinkle the unclean on the third day and on the seventh day; and on the seventh day he shall purify himself, wash his clothes, and bathe in water; and at evening he shall be clean.

Part of the daily sacrifice offered in.

Ex 29:41 And the other lamb you shall offer at twilight; and you shall offer with it the grain offering and the drink offering, as in the morning, for a sweet aroma, an offering made by fire to the LORD.

Ps 141:2 Let my prayer be set before You *as* incense, The lifting up of my hands *as* the evening sacrifice.

Dan 9:21 yes, while I *was* speaking in prayer, the man Gabriel, whom I had seen in the vision at the beginning, being caused to fly swiftly, reached me about the time of the evening offering.

Paschal lamb killed in.

Ex 12:6 Now you shall keep it until the fourteenth day of the same month. Then the whole assembly of the congregation of Israel shall kill it at twilight.

Ex 12:18 In the first *month*, on the fourteenth day of the month at evening, you shall eat unleavened bread, until the twenty-first day of the month at evening.

The golden lamps lighted in.

Ex 27:20–21 "And you shall command the children of Israel that they bring you pure oil of pressed olives for the light, to cause the lamp to burn continually. **21** In the tabernacle of meeting, outside the veil which *is* before the Testimony, Aaron and his sons shall tend it from evening until morning before the LORD. *It shall be* a statute forever to their generations on behalf of the children of Israel.

Ex 30:8 And when Aaron lights the lamps at twilight, he shall burn incense on it, a perpetual incense before the LORD throughout your generations.

The sky red in, a token of fair weather.

Matt 16:2 He answered and said to them, "When it is evening you say, *'It will be* fair weather, for the sky is red';

EVIL

God is too pure to behold.

Hab 1:13 *You are* of purer eyes than to behold evil, And cannot look on wickedness. Why do You look on those who deal treacherously, *And* hold Your tongue when the wicked devours A *person* more righteous than he?

Men are by nature.

Matt 7:11 If you then, being evil, know how to give good gifts to your children, how much more will your Father who is in heaven give good things to those who ask Him!

Intent of man's heart.

Gen 6:5 Then the LORD saw that the wickedness of man *was* great in the earth, and *that* every intent of the thoughts of his heart *was* only evil continually.

Believer is to depart from.

Ps 34:14 Depart from evil and do good; Seek peace and pursue it.

Ps 37:27 Depart from evil, and do good; And dwell forevermore.

Believer hates.

Ps 97:10 You who love the LORD, hate evil! He preserves the souls of His saints; He delivers them out of the hand of the wicked.

Amos 5:14–15 Seek good and not evil, That you may live; So the LORD God of hosts will be with you, As you have spoken. **15** Hate evil, love good; Establish justice in the gate. It may be that the LORD God of hosts Will be gracious to the remnant of Joseph.

Rom 12:9 *Let* love *be* without hypocrisy. Abhor what is evil. Cling to what is good.

Believer is to abstain from.

1 Thess 5:22 Abstain from every form of evil.

Evidence of Jerusalem's ritualism.

Is 1:16 "Wash yourselves, make yourselves clean; Put away the evil of your doings from before My eyes. Cease to do evil,

Is to be overcome with good.

Rom 12:21 Do not be overcome by evil, but overcome evil with good.

Is the reverse of goodness.

Is 5:20 Woe to those who call evil good, and good evil; Who put darkness for light, and light for darkness; Who put bitter for sweet, and sweet for bitter!

Is not to be repaid in kind.

Rom 12:17 Repay no one evil for evil. Have regard for good things in the sight of all men.

1 Pet 3:9 not returning evil for evil or reviling for reviling, but on the contrary blessing, knowing that you were called to this, that you may inherit a blessing.

Is not to be imitated.

3 John 1:11 Beloved, do not imitate what is evil, but what is good. He who does good is of God, but he who does evil has not seen God.

Brings God's judgment.

Is 13:11 "I will punish the world for *its* evil, And the wicked for their iniquity; I will halt the arrogance of the proud, And will lay low the haughtiness of the terrible.

Characteristic of

The current world system.

Gal 1:4 who gave Himself for our sins, that He might deliver us from this present evil age, according to the will of our God and Father,

The immoral society.

Eph 5:16 redeeming the time, because the days are evil.

The Pharisees.

Matt 12:32 Anyone who speaks a word against the Son of Man, it will be forgiven him; but whoever speaks against the Holy Spirit, it will not be forgiven him, either in this age or in the *age* to come.

EXHORTATION

Gift of.

Rom 12:8 he who exhorts, in exhortation; he who gives, with liberality; he who leads, with diligence; he who shows mercy, with cheerfulness.

To completely identify with Christ.

Heb 3:13–14 but exhort one another daily, while it is called *"Today,"* lest any of you be hardened through the deceitfulness of sin. **14** For we have become partakers of Christ if we hold the beginning of our confidence steadfast to the end,

To obey God's Word.

Titus 1:9 holding fast the faithful word as he has been taught, that he may be able, by sound doctrine, both to exhort and convict those who contradict.

To apply God's Word.

1 Tim 4:13 Till I come, give attention to reading, to exhortation, to doctrine.

Titus 2:15 Speak these things, exhort, and rebuke with all authority. Let no one despise you.

To strengthen believers.

1 Tim 5:1 Do not rebuke an older man, but exhort *him* as a father, younger men as brothers,

Cf. Gal 6:1–2

In view of the coming of Christ.

Heb 10:24–25 And let us consider one another in order to stir up love and good works, **25** not forsaking the assembling of ourselves together, as *is* the manner of some, but exhorting *one another,* and so much the more as you see the Day approaching.

Paul's fatherly example of.

1 Thess 2:11 as you know how we exhorted, and comforted, and charged every one of you, as a father *does* his own children,

EYE, THE

The light of the body.

Matt 6:22 "The lamp of the body is the eye. If therefore your eye is good, your whole body will be full of light.

Luke 11:34 The lamp of the body is the eye. Therefore, when your eye is good, your whole body also is full of light. But when *your eye* is bad, your body also *is* full of darkness.

God

Made.

Prov 20:12 The hearing ear and the seeing eye, The LORD has made them both.

Formed.

Ps 94:9 He who planted the ear, shall He not hear? He who formed the eye, shall He not see?

Opens.

2 Kin 6:17 And Elisha prayed, and said, "LORD, I pray, open his eyes that he may see." Then the LORD opened the eyes of the young man, and he saw. And behold, the mountain *was* full of horses and chariots of fire all around Elisha.

Ps 146:8 The LORD opens *the eyes of* the blind; The LORD raises those who are bowed down; The LORD loves the righteous.

Enlightens.

Ezra 9:8 And now for a little while grace has been *shown* from the LORD our God, to leave us a remnant to escape, and to give us a peg in His holy place, that our God may enlighten our eyes and give us a measure of revival in our bondage.

Ps 13:3 Consider *and* hear me, O LORD my God; Enlighten my eyes, Lest I sleep the *sleep of* death;

Frequently bright.

1 Sam 16:12 So he sent and brought him in. Now he *was* ruddy, with bright eyes, and good-looking. And the LORD said, "Arise, anoint him; for this *is* the one!"

Sometimes delicate.

Gen 29:17 Leah's eyes *were* delicate, but Rachel was beautiful of form and appearance.

Sometimes defective.

Lev 21:20 or is a hunchback or a dwarf, or *a man* who has a defect in his eye, or eczema or scab, or is a eunuch.

Parts of, mentioned in Scripture

The lid.

Job 16:16 My face is flushed from weeping, And on my eyelids *is* the shadow of death;

The brow.

Lev 14:9 But on the seventh day he shall shave all the hair off his head and his beard and his eyebrows—all his hair he shall shave off. He shall wash his clothes and wash his body in water, and he shall be clean.

Actions of, mentioned in Scripture

Seeing.

Job 7:8 The eye of him who sees me will see me no *more; While* your *eyes* are upon me, I shall no longer *be.*

Job 28:10 He cuts out channels in the rocks, And his eye sees every precious thing.

Winking.

Prov 10:10 He who winks with the eye causes trouble, But a prating fool will fall.

Weeping.

Job 16:20 My friends scorn me; My eyes pour out *tears* to God.

Ps 88:9 My eye wastes away because of affliction. LORD, I have called daily upon You; I have stretched out my hands to You.

Lam 1:16 "For these *things* I weep; My eye, my eye overflows with water; Because the comforter, who should restore my life, Is far from me. My children are desolate Because the enemy prevailed."

Guiding.

Num 10:31 So *Moses* said, "Please do not leave, inasmuch as you know how we are to camp in the wilderness, and you can be our eyes.

Ps 32:8 I will instruct you and teach you in the way you should go; I will guide you with My eye.

The light of, rejoices the heart.

Prov 15:30 The light of the eyes rejoices the heart, *And* a good report makes the bones healthy.

Not satisfied with seeing.

Prov 27:20 Hell and Destruction are never full; So the eyes of man are never satisfied.

Eccl 1:8 All things *are* full of labor; Man cannot express *it.* The eye is not satisfied with seeing, Nor the ear filled with hearing.

Not satisfied with riches.

Eccl 4:8 There is one alone, without companion: He has neither son nor brother. Yet *there is* no end to all his labors, Nor is his eye satisfied with riches. *But he*

never asks, "For whom do I toil and deprive myself of good?" This also *is* vanity and a grave misfortune.

Nothing wicked to be set before.

Ps 101:3 I will set nothing wicked before my eyes; I hate the work of those who fall away; It shall not cling to me.

A guard to be set on.

Job 31:1 "I have made a covenant with my eyes; Why then should I look upon a young woman?

Prov 23:31 Do not look on the wine when it is red, When it sparkles in the cup, *When* it swirls around smoothly;

Made red by wine.

Gen 49:12 His eyes *are* darker than wine, And his teeth whiter than milk.

Prov 23:29 Who has woe? Who has sorrow? Who has contentions? Who has complaints? Who has wounds without cause? Who has redness of eyes?

Grows dim by sorrow.

Job 17:7 My eye has also grown dim because of sorrow, And all my members *are* like shadows.

Grows dim by age.

Gen 27:1 Now it came to pass, when Isaac was old and his eyes were so dim that he could not see, that he called Esau his older son and said to him, "My son." And he answered him, "Here I am."

1 Sam 3:2 And it came to pass at that time, while Eli *was* lying down in his place, and when his eyes had begun to grow so dim that he could not see,

Wasted by grief.

Ps 6:7 My eye wastes away because of grief; It grows old because of all my enemies.

Ps 31:9 Have mercy on me, O LORD, for I am in trouble; My eye wastes away with grief, *Yes,* my soul and my body!

Consumed by sickness.

Lev 26:16 I also will do this to you: I will even appoint terror over you, wasting disease and fever which shall consume the eyes and cause sorrow of heart. And you shall sow your seed in vain, for your enemies shall eat it.

The Jews

Wore their phylacteries between.

Ex 13:16 It shall be as a sign on your hand and as frontlets between your eyes, for by strength of hand the LORD brought us out of Egypt."

Matt 23:5 But all their works they do to be seen by men. They make their phylacteries broad and enlarge the borders of their garments.

Raised up, in prayer.

Ps 121:1 I will lift up my eyes to the hills— From whence comes my help?

Ps 123:1 Unto You I lift up my eyes, O You who dwell in the heavens.

Cast on the ground, in humiliation.

Luke 18:13 And the tax collector, standing afar off, would not so much as raise *his* eyes to heaven, but

beat his breast, saying, 'God, be merciful to me a sinner!'

The Jewish women often painted.

2 Kin 9:30 Now when Jehu had come to Jezreel, Jezebel heard *of it;* and she put paint on her eyes and adorned her head, and looked through a window.

Jer 4:30 "And *when* you *are* plundered, What will you do? Though you clothe yourself with crimson, Though you adorn *yourself* with ornaments of gold, Though you enlarge your eyes with paint, In vain you will make yourself fair; *Your* lovers will despise you; They will seek your life.

Ezek 23:40 "Furthermore you sent for men to come from afar, to whom a messenger *was* sent; and there they came. And you washed yourself for them, painted your eyes, and adorned yourself with ornaments.

Often put out as a punishment.

Judg 16:21 Then the Philistines took him and put out his eyes, and brought him down to Gaza. They bound him with bronze fetters, and he became a grinder in the prison.

1 Sam 11:2 And Nahash the Ammonite answered them, "On this *condition* I will make *a covenant* with you, that I may put out all your right eyes, and bring reproach on all Israel."

2 Kin 25:7 Then they killed the sons of Zedekiah before his eyes, put out the eyes of Zedekiah, bound him with bronze fetters, and took him to Babylon.

Punishment for injuring.

Ex 21:24 eye for eye, tooth for tooth, hand for hand, foot for foot,

Ex 21:26 "If a man strikes the eye of his male or female servant, and destroys it, he shall let him go free for the sake of his eye.

Lev 24:20 fracture for fracture, eye for eye, tooth for tooth; as he has caused disfigurement of a man, so shall it be done to him.

Matt 5:38 "You have heard that it was said, *'An eye for an eye and a tooth for a tooth.'*

Illustrative of

The mind.

Matt 6:22–23 "The lamp of the body is the eye. If therefore your eye is good, your whole body will be full of light. **23** But if your eye is bad, your whole body will be full of darkness. If therefore the light that is in you is darkness, how great *is* that darkness!

(Open) spiritual illumination.

Ps 119:18 Open my eyes, that I may see Wondrous things from Your law.

Ps 119:37 Turn away my eyes from looking at worthless things, *And* revive me in Your way.

(Anointing with eye salve) healing by the Spirit.

Rev 3:18 I counsel you to buy from Me gold refined in the fire, that you may be rich; and white garments, that you may be clothed, *that* the shame of your nakedness may not be revealed; and anoint your eyes with eye salve, that you may see.

F

FAITH

Definition of.

Heb 11:1 Now faith is the substance of things hoped for, the evidence of things not seen.

Commanded.

Mark 11:22 So Jesus answered and said to them, "Have faith in God.

1 John 3:23 And this is His commandment: that we should believe on the name of His Son Jesus Christ and love one another, as He gave us commandment.

The objects of, are

God.

John 14:1 "Let not your heart be troubled; you believe in God, believe also in Me.

Christ.

John 6:29 Jesus answered and said to them, "This is the work of God, that you believe in Him whom He sent."

Acts 20:21 testifying to Jews, and also to Greeks, repentance toward God and faith toward our Lord Jesus Christ.

Writings of Moses.

John 5:46 For if you believed Moses, you would believe Me; for he wrote about Me.

Acts 24:14 But this I confess to you, that according to the Way which they call a sect, so I worship the God of my fathers, believing all things which are written in the Law and in the Prophets.

Writings of the prophets.

2 Chr 20:20 So they rose early in the morning and went out into the Wilderness of Tekoa; and as they went out, Jehoshaphat stood and said, "Hear me, O Judah and you inhabitants of Jerusalem: Believe in the LORD your God, and you shall be established; believe His prophets, and you shall prosper."

Acts 26:27 King Agrippa, do you believe the prophets? I know that you do believe."

The gospel.

Mark 1:15 and saying, "The time is fulfilled, and the kingdom of God is at hand. Repent, and believe in the gospel."

Promises of God.

Rom 4:21 and being fully convinced that what He had promised He was also able to perform.

Heb 11:13 These all died in faith, not having received the promises, but having seen them afar off were assured of them, embraced *them* and confessed that they were strangers and pilgrims on the earth.

In Christ, is

The gift of God.

Rom 12:3 For I say, through the grace given to me, to everyone who is among you, not to think *of himself* more highly than he ought to think, but to think soberly, as God has dealt to each one a measure of faith.

Eph 2:8 For by grace you have been saved through faith, and that not of yourselves; *it is* the gift of God,

Eph 6:23 Peace to the brethren, and love with faith, from God the Father and the Lord Jesus Christ.

Phil 1:29 For to you it has been granted on behalf of Christ, not only to believe in Him, but also to suffer for His sake,

Righteousness from God.

Phil 3:9 and be found in Him, not having my own righteousness, which *is* from the law, but that which *is* through faith in Christ, the righteousness which is from God by faith;

The work of God.

Acts 11:21 And the hand of the Lord was with them, and a great number believed and turned to the Lord.

1 Cor 2:5 that your faith should not be in the wisdom of men but in the power of God.

Precious.

2 Pet 1:1 Simon Peter, a bondservant and apostle of Jesus Christ, To those who have obtained like precious faith with us by the righteousness of our God and Savior Jesus Christ:

Most holy.

Jude 1:20 But you, beloved, building yourselves up on your most holy faith, praying in the Holy Spirit,

Fruitful.

1 Thess 1:3 remembering without ceasing your work of faith, labor of love, and patience of hope in our Lord Jesus Christ in the sight of our God and Father,

Accompanied by repentance.

Mark 1:15 and saying, "The time is fulfilled, and the kingdom of God is at hand. Repent, and believe in the gospel."

Luke 24:47 and that repentance and remission of sins should be preached in His name to all nations, beginning at Jerusalem.

Followed by conversion.

Acts 11:21 And the hand of the Lord was with them, and a great number believed and turned to the Lord.

Christ is the author and finisher of.

Heb 12:2 looking unto Jesus, the author and finisher of *our* faith, who for the joy that was set before Him endured the cross, despising the shame, and has sat down at the right hand of the throne of God.

s a gift of the Holy Spirit.

1 Cor 12:9 to another faith by the same Spirit, to another gifts of healings by the same Spirit,

The Scriptures designed to produce.

John 20:31 but these are written that you may believe that Jesus is the Christ, the Son of God, and that believing you may have life in His name.

2 Tim 3:15 and that from childhood you have known the Holy Scriptures, which are able to make you wise for salvation through faith which is in Christ Jesus.

Preaching designed to produce.

John 17:20 "I do not pray for these alone, but also for those who will believe in Me through their word;

Acts 8:12 But when they believed Philip as he preached the things concerning the kingdom of God and the name of Jesus Christ, both men and women were baptized.

Rom 10:14–15 How then shall they call on Him in whom they have not believed? And how shall they believe in Him of whom they have not heard? And how shall they hear without a preacher? **15** And how shall they preach unless they are sent? As it is written: *"How beautiful are the feet of those who preach the gospel of peace, Who bring glad tidings of good things!"*

Rom 10:17 So then faith *comes* by hearing, and hearing by the word of God.

1 Cor 3:5 Who then is Paul, and who *is* Apollos, but ministers through whom you believed, as the Lord gave to each one?

Through it is

Remission of sins.

Acts 10:43 To Him all the prophets witness that, through His name, whoever believes in Him will receive remission of sins."

Rom 3:25 whom God set forth *as* a propitiation by His blood, through faith, to demonstrate His righteousness, because in His forbearance God had passed over the sins that were previously committed,

Justification.

Hab 2:4 "Behold the proud, His soul is not upright in him; But the just shall live by his faith.

Acts 13:39 and by Him everyone who believes is justified from all things from which you could not be justified by the law of Moses.

Rom 1:17 For in it the righteousness of God is revealed from faith to faith; as it is written, *"The just shall live by faith."*

Rom 3:21–22 But now the righteousness of God apart from the law is revealed, being witnessed by the Law and the Prophets, **22** even the righteousness of God, through faith in Jesus Christ, to all and on all who believe. For there is no difference; **23** for all have sinned and fall short of the glory of God, **24** being justified freely by His grace through the redemption that is in Christ Jesus,

Rom 3:28 Therefore we conclude that a man is justified by faith apart from the deeds of the law.

Rom 3:30 since *there is* one God who will justify the circumcised by faith and the uncircumcised through faith.

Rom 5:1 Therefore, having been justified by faith, we have peace with God through our Lord Jesus Christ,

Gal 2:16 knowing that a man is not justified by the works of the law but by faith in Jesus Christ, even we have believed in Christ Jesus, that we might be justified by faith in Christ and not by the works of the law; for by the works of the law no flesh shall be justified.

Cf. Rom 9:30; Gal 3:11,24; Heb 10:38–39

Salvation.

Mark 16:16 He who believes and is baptized will be saved; but he who does not believe will be condemned.

Acts 16:31 So they said, "Believe on the Lord Jesus Christ, and you will be saved, you and your household."

Sanctification.

Acts 15:9 and made no distinction between us and them, purifying their hearts by faith.

Acts 26:18 to open their eyes, *in order* to turn *them* from darkness to light, and *from* the power of Satan to God, that they may receive forgiveness of sins and an inheritance among those who are sanctified by faith in Me.'

Spiritual light.

John 12:36 While you have the light, believe in the light, that you may become sons of light." These things Jesus spoke, and departed, and was hidden from them.

John 12:46 I have come *as* a light into the world, that whoever believes in Me should not abide in darkness.

Spiritual life.

John 20:31 but these are written that you may believe that Jesus is the Christ, the Son of God, and that believing you may have life in His name.

Gal 2:20 I have been crucified with Christ; it is no longer I who live, but Christ lives in me; and the *life* which I now live in the flesh I live by faith in the Son of God, who loved me and gave Himself for me.

Eternal life.

John 3:15–16 that whoever believes in Him should not perish but have eternal life. **16** For God so loved the world that He gave His only begotten Son, that whoever believes in Him should not perish but have everlasting life.

John 6:40 And this is the will of Him who sent Me, that everyone who sees the Son and believes in Him may have everlasting life; and I will raise him up at the last day."

John 6:47 Most assuredly, I say to you, he who believes in Me has everlasting life.

Rest in heaven.

Heb 4:3 For we who have believed do enter that rest, as He has said: *"So I swore in My wrath, 'They shall not enter My rest,' "* although the works were finished from the foundation of the world.

Edification.

1 Tim 1:4 nor give heed to fables and endless genealogies, which cause disputes rather than godly edification which is in faith.

Jude 1:20 But you, beloved, building yourselves up on your most holy faith, praying in the Holy Spirit,

Preservation.

1 Pet 1:5 who are kept by the power of God through

faith for salvation ready to be revealed in the last time.

Adoption.

John 1:12 But as many as received Him, to them He gave the right to become children of God, to those who believe in His name:

Gal 3:26 For you are all sons of God through faith in Christ Jesus.

Access to God.

Rom 5:2 through whom also we have access by faith into this grace in which we stand, and rejoice in hope of the glory of God.

Eph 3:12 in whom we have boldness and access with confidence through faith in Him.

Inheritance of the promises.

Gal 3:22 But the Scripture has confined all under sin, that the promise by faith in Jesus Christ might be given to those who believe.

Heb 6:12 that you do not become sluggish, but imitate those who through faith and patience inherit the promises.

The gift of the Holy Spirit.

Acts 11:15–17 And as I began to speak, the Holy Spirit fell upon them, as upon us at the beginning. **16** Then I remembered the word of the Lord, how He said, 'John indeed baptized with water, but you shall be baptized with the Holy Spirit.' **17** If therefore God gave them the same gift as *He gave* us when we believed on the Lord Jesus Christ, who was I that I could withstand God?"

Gal 3:14 that the blessing of Abraham might come upon the Gentiles in Christ Jesus, that we might receive the promise of the Spirit through faith.

Eph 1:13 In Him you also *trusted,* after you heard the word of truth, the gospel of your salvation; in whom also, having believed, you were sealed with the Holy Spirit of promise,

Impossible to please God without.

Heb 11:6 But without faith *it is* impossible to please *Him,* for he who comes to God must believe that He is, and *that* He is a rewarder of those who diligently seek Him.

Justification is by, to be of grace.

Rom 4:16 Therefore *it is* of faith that *it might be* according to grace, so that the promise might be sure to all the seed, not only to those who are of the law, but also to those who are of the faith of Abraham, who is the father of us all

Essential to the profitable reception of the gospel.

Heb 4:2 For indeed the gospel was preached to us as well as to them; but the word which they heard did not profit them, not being mixed with faith in those who heard *it.*

Produces obedience.

Rom 1:5 Through Him we have received grace and apostleship for obedience to the faith among all nations for His name,

Necessary in spiritual warfare.

1 Tim 1:18–19 This charge I commit to you, son Timothy, according to the prophecies previously made concerning you, that by them you may wage the good warfare, **19** having faith and a good conscience, which some having rejected, concerning the faith have suffered shipwreck,

1 Tim 6:12 Fight the good fight of faith, lay hold on eternal life, to which you were also called and have confessed the good confession in the presence of many witnesses.

The Word is effectual in those who have.

1 Thess 2:13 For this reason we also thank God without ceasing, because when you received the word of God which you heard from us, you welcomed *it* not *as* the word of men, but as it is in truth, the word of God, which also effectively works in you who believe.

Excludes self-justification.

Rom 10:3–4 For they being ignorant of God's righteousness, and seeking to establish their own righteousness, have not submitted to the righteousness of God. **4** For Christ *is* the end of the law for righteousness to everyone who believes.

Excludes boasting.

Rom 3:27 Where *is* boasting then? It is excluded. By what law? Of works? No, but by the law of faith.

Works by love.

Gal 5:6 For in Christ Jesus neither circumcision nor uncircumcision avails anything, but faith working through love.

1 Tim 1:5 Now the purpose of the commandment is love from a pure heart, *from* a good conscience, and *from* sincere faith,

Philem 1:5 hearing of your love and faith which you have toward the Lord Jesus and toward all the saints,

Benefits of,

Hope.

Rom 5:2 through whom also we have access by faith into this grace in which we stand, and rejoice in hope of the glory of God.

Joy.

Acts 16:34 Now when he had brought them into his house, he set food before them; and he rejoiced, having believed in God with all his household.

1 Pet 1:8 whom having not seen you love. Though now you do not see *Him,* yet believing, you rejoice with joy inexpressible and full of glory,

Peace.

Rom 15:13 Now may the God of hope fill you with all joy and peace in believing, that you may abound in hope by the power of the Holy Spirit.

Confidence.

Is 28:16 Therefore thus says the Lord GOD: "Behold, I lay in Zion a stone for a foundation, A tried stone, a precious cornerstone, a sure foundation; Whoever believes will not act hastily.

1 Pet 2:6 Therefore it is also contained in the Scripture, *"Behold, I lay in Zion A chief cornerstone, elect, precious, And he who believes on Him will by no means be put to shame."*

Boldness in preaching.

Ps 116:10 I believed, therefore I spoke, "I am greatly afflicted."

2 Cor 4:13 And since we have the same spirit of faith,

according to what is written, *"I believed and therefore I spoke,"* we also believe and therefore speak,

Christ is precious to those having.

Eph 3:17 that Christ may dwell in your hearts through faith; that you, being rooted and grounded in love,

1 Pet 2:7 Therefore, to you who believe, *He is* precious; but to those who are disobedient, *"The stone which the builders rejected Has become the chief cornerstone,"*

Necessary in prayer.

Matt 21:22 And whatever things you ask in prayer, believing, you will receive."

James 1:6 But let him ask in faith, with no doubting, for he who doubts is like a wave of the sea driven and tossed by the wind.

Unbelievers do not have.

John 10:26–27 But you do not believe, because you are not of My sheep, as I said to you. **27** My sheep hear My voice, and I know them, and they follow Me.

An evidence of the new birth.

1 John 5:1 Whoever believes that Jesus is the Christ is born of God, and everyone who loves Him who begot also loves him who is begotten of Him.

Believers

Will live by.

Gal 2:20 I have been crucified with Christ; it is no longer I who live, but Christ lives in me; and the *life* which I now live in the flesh I live by faith in the Son of God, who loved me and gave Himself for me.

Will stand by.

Rom 11:20 Well *said.* Because of unbelief they were broken off, and you stand by faith. Do not be haughty, but fear.

2 Cor 1:24 Not that we have dominion over your faith, but are fellow workers for your joy; for by faith you stand.

Will walk by.

Rom 4:12 and the father of circumcision to those who not only *are* of the circumcision, but who also walk in the steps of the faith which our father Abraham *had while still* uncircumcised.

2 Cor 5:7 For we walk by faith, not by sight.

Obtain a good testimony by.

Heb 11:2 For by it the elders obtained a *good* testimony.

Overcome the world by.

1 John 5:4–5 For whatever is born of God overcomes the world. And this is the victory that has overcome the world—our faith. **5** Who is he who overcomes the world, but he who believes that Jesus is the Son of God?

Defeat the devil by.

Eph 6:16 above all, taking the shield of faith with which you will be able to quench all the fiery darts of the wicked one.

1 Pet 5:9 Resist him, steadfast in the faith, knowing that the same sufferings are experienced by your brotherhood in the world.

Delivered from power of sin by.

1 Pet 1:9 receiving the end of your faith—the salvation of *your* souls.

Are supported by.

Ps 27:13 *I would have lost heart,* unless I had believed That I would see the goodness of the LORD In the land of the living.

1 Tim 4:10 For to this *end* we both labor and suffer reproach, because we trust in the living God, who is *the* Savior of all men, especially of those who believe.

Will die in.

Heb 11:13 These all died in faith, not having received the promises, but having seen them afar off were assured of them, embraced *them* and confessed that they were strangers and pilgrims on the earth.

Should be sincere in.

1 Tim 1:5 Now the purpose of the commandment is love from a pure heart, *from* a good conscience, and *from* sincere faith,

2 Tim 1:5 when I call to remembrance the genuine faith that is in you, which dwelt first in your grandmother Lois and your mother Eunice, and I am persuaded is in you also.

Should abound in.

2 Cor 8:7 But as you abound in everything—in faith, in speech, in knowledge, in all diligence, and in your love for us—*see* that you abound in this grace also.

Should continue in.

Acts 14:22 strengthening the souls of the disciples, exhorting *them* to continue in the faith, and *saying,* "We must through many tribulations enter the kingdom of God."

Col 1:23 if indeed you continue in the faith, grounded and steadfast, and are not moved away from the hope of the gospel which you heard, which was preached to every creature under heaven, of which I, Paul, became a minister.

Should be strong in.

Rom 4:20–24 He did not waver at the promise of God through unbelief, but was strengthened in faith, giving glory to God, **21** and being fully convinced that what He had promised He was also able to perform. **22** And therefore *"it was accounted to him for righteousness."* **23** Now it was not written for his sake alone that it was imputed to him, **24** but also for us. It shall be imputed to us who believe in Him who raised up Jesus our Lord from the dead,

Should stand fast in.

1 Cor 16:13 Watch, stand fast in the faith, be brave, be strong.

Should be grounded and settled in.

Col 1:23 if indeed you continue in the faith, grounded and steadfast, and are not moved away from the hope of the gospel which you heard, which was preached to every creature under heaven, of which I, Paul, became a minister.

Should hold, with a good conscience.

1 Tim 1:19 having faith and a good conscience, which some having rejected, concerning the faith have suffered shipwreck,

Should pray for the increase of.

Luke 17:5 And the apostles said to the Lord, "Increase our faith."

Should have full assurance of.

2 Tim 1:12 For this reason I also suffer these things; nevertheless I am not ashamed, for I know whom I have believed and am persuaded that He is able to keep what I have committed to Him until that Day.

Heb 10:22 let us draw near with a true heart in full assurance of faith, having our hearts sprinkled from an evil conscience and our bodies washed with pure water.

Should examine whether they are in.

2 Cor 13:5 Examine yourselves *as to* whether you are in the faith. Test yourselves. Do you not know yourselves, that Jesus Christ is in you?—unless indeed you are disqualified.

True, evidenced by its works.

James 2:17 Thus also faith by itself, if it does not have works, is dead.

James 2:20–26 But do you want to know, O foolish man, that faith without works is dead? **21** Was not Abraham our father justified by works when he offered Isaac his son on the altar? **22** Do you see that faith was working together with his works, and by works faith was made perfect? **23** And the Scripture was fulfilled which says, *"Abraham believed God, and it was accounted to him for righteousness."* And he was called the friend of God. **24** You see then that a man is justified by works, and not by faith only. **25** Likewise, was not Rahab the harlot also justified by works when she received the messengers and sent *them* out another way? **26** For as the body without the spirit is dead, so faith without works is dead also.

All difficulties overcome by.

Matt 17:20 So Jesus said to them, "Because of your unbelief; for assuredly, I say to you, if you have faith as a mustard seed, you will say to this mountain, 'Move from here to there,' and it will move; and nothing will be impossible for you.

Matt 21:21 So Jesus answered and said to them, "Assuredly, I say to you, if you have faith and do not doubt, you will not only do what was done to the fig tree, but also if you say to this mountain, 'Be removed and be cast into the sea,' it will be done.

Mark 9:23 Jesus said to him, "If you can believe, all things *are* possible to him who believes."

All things should be done in.

Rom 14:22 Do you have faith? Have *it* to yourself before God. Happy *is* he who does not condemn himself in what he approves.

Whatever is not of, is sin.

Rom 14:23 But he who doubts is condemned if he eats, because *he does* not *eat* from faith; for whatever *is* not from faith is sin.

Often tried by affliction.

1 Pet 1:6–7 In this you greatly rejoice, though now for a little while, if need be, you have been grieved by various trials, **7** that the genuineness of your faith, *being* much more precious than gold that perishes, though it is tested by fire, may be found to praise, honor, and glory at the revelation of Jesus Christ,

Trial of, works patience.

James 1:3 knowing that the testing of your faith produces patience.

The wicked sometimes profess.

Acts 8:13 Then Simon himself also believed; and when he was baptized he continued with Philip, and was amazed, seeing the miracles and signs which were done.

Acts 8:21 You have neither part nor portion in this matter, for your heart is not right in the sight of God.

The wicked destitute of.

John 10:25 Jesus answered them, "I told you, and you do not believe. The works that I do in My Father's name, they bear witness of Me.

John 12:37 But although He had done so many signs before them, they did not believe in Him,

Acts 19:9 But when some were hardened and did not believe, but spoke evil of the Way before the multitude, he departed from them and withdrew the disciples, reasoning daily in the school of Tyrannus.

2 Thess 3:2 and that we may be delivered from unreasonable and wicked men; for not all have faith.

Protection of, illustrated as

A shield.

Eph 6:16 above all, taking the shield of faith with which you will be able to quench all the fiery darts of the wicked one.

A breastplate.

1 Thess 5:8 But let us who are of the day be sober, putting on the breastplate of faith and love, and *as* a helmet the hope of salvation.

Exemplified by

Caleb.

Num 13:30 Then Caleb quieted the people before Moses, and said, "Let us go up at once and take possession, for we are well able to overcome it."

Job.

Job 19:25 For I know *that* my Redeemer lives, And He shall stand at last on the earth;

Shadrach, etc.

Dan 3:17 If that *is the case,* our God whom we serve is able to deliver us from the burning fiery furnace, and He will deliver *us* from your hand, O king.

Daniel.

Dan 6:10 Now when Daniel knew that the writing was signed, he went home. And in his upper room, with his windows open toward Jerusalem, he knelt down on his knees three times that day, and prayed and gave thanks before his God, as was his custom since early days.

Dan 6:23 Now the king was exceedingly glad for him, and commanded that they should take Daniel up out of the den. So Daniel was taken up out of the den, and no injury whatever was found on him, because he believed in his God.

Peter.

Matt 16:16 Simon Peter answered and said, "You are the Christ, the Son of the living God."

A woman who was a sinner.

Luke 7:50 Then He said to the woman, "Your faith has saved you. Go in peace."

Nathanael.

John 1:49 Nathanael answered and said to Him,

"Rabbi, You are the Son of God! You are the King of Israel!"

The Samaritans.

John 4:39 And many of the Samaritans of that city believed in Him because of the word of the woman who testified, "He told me all that I *ever* did."

Martha.

John 11:27 She said to Him, "Yes, Lord, I believe that You are the Christ, the Son of God, who is to come into the world."

The disciples.

John 16:30 Now we are sure that You know all things, and have no need that anyone should question You. By this we believe that You came forth from God."

Thomas.

John 20:28 And Thomas answered and said to Him, "My Lord and my God!"

Stephen.

Acts 6:5 And the saying pleased the whole multitude. And they chose Stephen, a man full of faith and the Holy Spirit, and Philip, Prochorus, Nicanor, Timon, Parmenas, and Nicolas, a proselyte from Antioch,

Priests.

Acts 6:7 Then the word of God spread, and the number of the disciples multiplied greatly in Jerusalem, and a great many of the priests were obedient to the faith.

The Ethiopian.

Acts 8:37 Then Philip said, "If you believe with all your heart, you may." And he answered and said, "I believe that Jesus Christ is the Son of God."

Barnabas.

Acts 11:24 For he was a good man, full of the Holy Spirit and of faith. And a great many people were added to the Lord.

Sergius Paulus.

Acts 13:12 Then the proconsul believed, when he saw what had been done, being astonished at the teaching of the Lord.

The Philippian jailer.

Acts 16:31 So they said, "Believe on the Lord Jesus Christ, and you will be saved, you and your household."

Acts 16:34 Now when he had brought them into his house, he set food before them; and he rejoiced, having believed in God with all his household.

The Roman believers.

Rom 1:8 First, I thank my God through Jesus Christ for you all, that your faith is spoken of throughout the whole world.

The Colossian believers.

Col 1:4 since we heard of your faith in Christ Jesus and of your love for all the saints;

The Thessalonian believers.

1 Thess 1:3 remembering without ceasing your work of faith, labor of love, and patience of hope in our Lord Jesus Christ in the sight of our God and Father,

Lois.

2 Tim 1:5 when I call to remembrance the genuine faith that is in you, which dwelt first in your grandmother

Lois and your mother Eunice, and I am persuaded is in you also.

Paul.

2 Tim 4:7 I have fought the good fight, I have finished the race, I have kept the faith.

Abel.

Heb 11:4 By faith Abel offered to God a more excellent sacrifice than Cain, through which he obtained witness that he was righteous, God testifying of his gifts; and through it he being dead still speaks.

Enoch.

Heb 11:5 By faith Enoch was taken away so that he did not see death, *"and was not found, because God had taken him";* for before he was taken he had this testimony, that he pleased God.

Noah.

Heb 11:7 By faith Noah, being divinely warned of things not yet seen, moved with godly fear, prepared an ark for the saving of his household, by which he condemned the world and became heir of the righteousness which is according to faith.

Abraham.

Heb 11:8 By faith Abraham obeyed when he was called to go out to the place which he would receive as an inheritance. And he went out, not knowing where he was going.

Heb 11:17 By faith Abraham, when he was tested, offered up Isaac, and he who had received the promises offered up his only begotten *son,*

Isaac.

Heb 11:20 By faith Isaac blessed Jacob and Esau concerning things to come.

Jacob.

Heb 11:21 By faith Jacob, when he was dying, blessed each of the sons of Joseph, and worshiped, *leaning* on the top of his staff.

Joseph.

Heb 11:22 By faith Joseph, when he was dying, made mention of the departure of the children of Israel, and gave instructions concerning his bones.

Moses.

Heb 11:24 By faith Moses, when he became of age, refused to be called the son of Pharaoh's daughter,

Heb 11:27 By faith he forsook Egypt, not fearing the wrath of the king; for he endured as seeing Him who is invisible.

Rahab.

Heb 11:31 By faith the harlot Rahab did not perish with those who did not believe, when she had received the spies with peace.

Gideon, etc.

Heb 11:32–33 And what more shall I say? For the time would fail me to tell of Gideon and Barak and Samson and Jephthah, also *of* David and Samuel and the prophets: 33 who through faith subdued kingdoms, worked righteousness, obtained promises, stopped the mouths of lions,

Heb 11:39 And all these, having obtained a good testimony through faith, did not receive the promise,

FAITHFULNESS

A characteristic of believers.

Eph 1:1 Paul, an apostle of Jesus Christ by the will of God, To the saints who are in Ephesus, and faithful in Christ Jesus:

Col 1:2 To the saints and faithful brethren in Christ *who are* in Colosse: Grace to you and peace from God our Father and the Lord Jesus Christ.

1 Tim 6:2 And those who have believing masters, let them not despise *them* because they are brethren, but rather serve *them* because those who are benefited are believers and beloved. Teach and exhort these things.

Rev 17:14 These will make war with the Lamb, and the Lamb will overcome them, for He is Lord of lords and King of kings; and those *who are* with Him *are* called, chosen, and faithful."

A fruit of the Spirit.

Gal 5:22 But the fruit of the Spirit is love, joy, peace, longsuffering, kindness, goodness, faithfulness,

Exhibited in

The service of God.

Matt 24:45 "Who then is a faithful and wise servant, whom his master made ruler over his household, to give them food in due season?

Declaring the Word of God.

Jer 23:28 "The prophet who has a dream, let him tell a dream; And he who has My word, let him speak My word faithfully. What *is* the chaff to the wheat?" says the LORD.

2 Cor 2:17 For we are not, as so many, peddling the word of God; but as of sincerity, but as from God, we speak in the sight of God in Christ.

2 Cor 4:2 But we have renounced the hidden things of shame, not walking in craftiness nor handling the word of God deceitfully, but by manifestation of the truth commending ourselves to every man's conscience in the sight of God.

The care of dedicated things.

2 Chr 31:12 Then they faithfully brought in the offerings, the tithes, and the dedicated things; Cononiah the Levite had charge of them, and Shimei his brother *was* the next.

Helping the brethren.

3 John 1:5 Beloved, you do faithfully whatever you do for the brethren and for strangers,

Bearing witness.

Prov 14:5 A faithful witness does not lie, But a false witness will utter lies.

Reproving others.

Ps 141:5 Let the righteous strike me; *It shall be* a kindness. And let him rebuke me; *It shall be* as excellent oil; Let my head not refuse it. For still my prayer *is* against the deeds of the wicked.

Prov 27:6 Faithful *are* the wounds of a friend, But the kisses of an enemy *are* deceitful.

Situations of trust.

2 Kin 12:15 Moreover they did not require an account from the men into whose hand they delivered the money to be paid to workmen, for they dealt faithfully.

Neh 13:13 And I appointed as treasurers over the storehouse Shelemiah the priest and Zadok the scribe, and of the Levites, Pedaiah; and next to them *was* Hanan the son of Zaccur, the son of Mattaniah; for they were considered faithful, and their task *was* to distribute to their brethren.

Acts 6:1–3 Now in those days, when *the number of* the disciples was multiplying, there arose a complaint against the Hebrews by the Hellenists, because their widows were neglected in the daily distribution. **2** Then the twelve summoned the multitude of the disciples and said, "It is not desirable that we should leave the word of God and serve tables. **3** Therefore, brethren, seek out from among you seven men of *good* reputation, full of the Holy Spirit and wisdom, whom we may appoint over this business;

Doing work.

2 Chr 34:12 And the men did the work faithfully. Their overseers *were* Jahath and Obadiah the Levites, of the sons of Merari, and Zechariah and Meshullam, of the sons of the Kohathites, to supervise. *Others of* the Levites, all of whom were skillful with instruments of music,

Keeping secrets.

Prov 11:13 A talebearer reveals secrets, But he who is of a faithful spirit conceals a matter.

Conveying messages.

Prov 13:17 A wicked messenger falls into trouble, But a faithful ambassador *brings* health.

Prov 25:13 Like the cold of snow in time of harvest *Is* a faithful messenger to those who send him, For he refreshes the soul of his masters.

All things.

1 Tim 3:11 Likewise, *their* wives *must be* reverent, not slanderers, temperate, faithful in all things.

The smallest matters.

Luke 16:10–12 He who *is* faithful in *what is* least is faithful also in much; and he who is unjust in *what is* least is unjust also in much. **11** Therefore if you have not been faithful in the unrighteous mammon, who will commit to your trust the true *riches?* **12** And if you have not been faithful in what is another man's, who will give you what is your own?

God preserves those who exhibit.

Ps 31:23 Oh, love the LORD, all you His saints! *For* the LORD preserves the faithful, And fully repays the proud person.

Should be to death.

Rev 2:10 Do not fear any of those things which you are about to suffer. Indeed, the devil is about to throw *some* of you into prison, that you may be tested, and you will have tribulation ten days. Be faithful until death, and I will give you the crown of life.

Especially required in

Ministers.

1 Cor 4:2 Moreover it is required in stewards that one be found faithful.

2 Tim 2:2 And the things that you have heard from me among many witnesses, commit these to faithful men who will be able to teach others also.

The wives of ministers.

1 Tim 3:11 Likewise, *their* wives *must be* reverent, not slanderers, temperate, faithful in all things.

The children of ministers.

Titus 1:6 if a man is blameless, the husband of one wife, having faithful children not accused of dissipation or insubordination.

Difficulty of finding.

Prov 20:6 Most men will proclaim each his own goodness, But who can find a faithful man?

The wicked devoid of.

Ps 5:9 For *there is* no faithfulness in their mouth; Their inward part *is* destruction; Their throat *is* an open tomb; They flatter with their tongue.

Associate with those who exhibit.

Ps 101:6 My eyes *shall be* on the faithful of the land, That they may dwell with me; He who walks in a perfect way, He shall serve me.

Blessedness of.

1 Sam 26:23 May the LORD repay every man *for* his righteousness and his faithfulness; for the LORD delivered you into *my* hand today, but I would not stretch out my hand against the LORD's anointed.

Prov 28:20 A faithful man will abound with blessings, But he who hastens to be rich will not go unpunished.

Blessedness of, illustrated.

Matt 24:45–46 "Who then is a faithful and wise servant, whom his master made ruler over his household, to give them food in due season? **46** Blessed *is* that servant whom his master, when he comes, will find so doing.

Matt 25:21 His lord said to him, 'Well *done,* good and faithful servant; you were faithful over a few things, I will make you ruler over many things. Enter into the joy of your lord.'

Matt 25:23 His lord said to him, 'Well *done,* good and faithful servant; you have been faithful over a few things, I will make you ruler over many things. Enter into the joy of your lord.'

Exemplified by

Joseph.

Gen 39:22–23 And the keeper of the prison committed to Joseph's hand all the prisoners who *were* in the prison; whatever they did there, it was his doing. **23** The keeper of the prison did not look into anything *that was* under *Joseph's* authority, because the LORD was with him; and whatever he did, the LORD made *it* prosper.

Moses.

Num 12:7 Not so with My servant Moses; He *is* faithful in all My house.

Heb 3:2 who was faithful to Him who appointed Him, as Moses also *was faithful* in all His house.

Heb 3:5 And Moses indeed *was* faithful in all His house as a servant, for a testimony of those things which would be spoken *afterward,*

David.

1 Sam 22:14 So Ahimelech answered the king and said, "And who among all your servants *is as* faithful as David, who is the king's son-in-law, who goes at your bidding, and is honorable in your house?

Hananiah.

Neh 7:2 that I gave the charge of Jerusalem to my brother Hanani, and Hananiah the leader of the citadel, for he *was* a faithful man and feared God more than many.

Abraham.

Neh 9:8 You found his heart faithful before You, And made a covenant with him To give the land of the Canaanites, The Hittites, the Amorites, The Perizzites, the Jebusites, And the Girgashites— To give *it* to his descendants. You have performed Your words, For You *are* righteous.

Gal 3:9 So then those who *are* of faith are blessed with believing Abraham.

Daniel.

Dan 6:4 So the governors and satraps sought to find *some* charge against Daniel concerning the kingdom; but they could find no charge or fault, because he *was* faithful; nor was there any error or fault found in him.

Paul.

Acts 20:20 how I kept back nothing that was helpful, but proclaimed it to you, and taught you publicly and from house to house,

Acts 20:27 For I have not shunned to declare to you the whole counsel of God.

Timothy.

1 Cor 4:17 For this reason I have sent Timothy to you, who is my beloved and faithful son in the Lord, who will remind you of my ways in Christ, as I teach everywhere in every church.

Tychicus.

Eph 6:21 But that you also may know my affairs *and* how I am doing, Tychicus, a beloved brother and faithful minister in the Lord, will make all things known to you;

Epaphras.

Col 1:7 as you also learned from Epaphras, our dear fellow servant, who is a faithful minister of Christ on your behalf,

Onesimus.

Col 4:9 with Onesimus, a faithful and beloved brother, who is *one* of you. They will make known to you all things which *are happening* here.

Silvanus.

1 Pet 5:12 By Silvanus, our faithful brother as I consider him, I have written to you briefly, exhorting and testifying that this is the true grace of God in which you stand.

Antipas.

Rev 2:13 "I know your works, and where you dwell, where Satan's throne *is.* And you hold fast to My name, and did not deny My faith even in the days in which Antipas *was* My faithful martyr, who was killed among you, where Satan dwells.

FALL OF MAN, THE

By the disobedience of Adam.

Gen 3:6 So when the woman saw that the tree *was* good

for food, that it *was* pleasant to the eyes, and a tree desirable to make *one* wise, she took of its fruit and ate. She also gave to her husband with her, and he ate.

Gen 3:11–12 And He said, "Who told you that you *were* naked? Have you eaten from the tree of which I commanded you that you should not eat?" **12** Then the man said, "The woman whom You gave *to be* with me, she gave me of the tree, and I ate."

Rom 5:12 Therefore, just as through one man sin entered the world, and death through sin, and thus death spread to all men, because all sinned—

Rom 5:15 But the free gift *is* not like the offense. For if by the one man's offense many died, much more the grace of God and the gift by the grace of the one Man, Jesus Christ, abounded to many.

Rom 5:19 For as by one man's disobedience many were made sinners, so also by one Man's obedience many will be made righteous.

Through temptation of the devil.

Gen 3:1–5 Now the serpent was more cunning than any beast of the field which the LORD God had made. And he said to the woman, "Has God indeed said, 'You shall not eat of every tree of the garden'?" **2** And the woman said to the serpent, "We may eat the fruit of the trees of the garden; **3** but of the fruit of the tree which *is* in the midst of the garden, God has said, 'You shall not eat it, nor shall you touch it, lest you die.' " **4** Then the serpent said to the woman, "You will not surely die. **5** For God knows that in the day you eat of it your eyes will be opened, and you will be like God, knowing good and evil."

2 Cor 11:3 But I fear, lest somehow, as the serpent deceived Eve by his craftiness, so your minds may be corrupted from the simplicity that is in Christ.

1 Tim 2:14 And Adam was not deceived, but the woman being deceived, fell into transgression.

Man, in consequence of,

Made in the image of Adam.

Gen 5:3 And Adam lived one hundred and thirty years, and begot *a son* in his own likeness, after his image, and named him Seth.

1 Cor 15:48–49 As *was* the *man* of dust, so also *are* those *who are made* of dust; and as *is* the heavenly *Man*, so also *are* those *who are* heavenly. **49** And as we have borne the image of the *man* of dust, we shall also bear the image of the heavenly *Man*.

Born in sin.

Job 15:14 "What *is* man, that he could be pure? And *he who is* born of a woman, that he could be righteous?

Job 25:4 How then can man be righteous before God? Or how can he be pure *who is* born of a woman?

Ps 51:5 Behold, I was brought forth in iniquity, And in sin my mother conceived me.

Is 48:8 Surely you did not hear, Surely you did not know; Surely from long ago your ear was not opened. For I knew that you would deal very treacherously, And were called a transgressor from the womb.

John 3:6 That which is born of the flesh is flesh, and that which is born of the Spirit is spirit.

A child of wrath.

Eph 2:3 among whom also we all once conducted ourselves in the lusts of our flesh, fulfilling the desires of the flesh and of the mind, and were by nature children of wrath, just as the others.

Evil in heart.

Gen 6:5 Then the LORD saw that the wickedness of man *was* great in the earth, and *that* every intent of the thoughts of his heart *was* only evil continually.

Gen 8:21 And the LORD smelled a soothing aroma. Then the LORD said in His heart, "I will never again curse the ground for man's sake, although the imagination of man's heart *is* evil from his youth; nor will I again destroy every living thing as I have done.

Jer 16:12 And you have done worse than your fathers, for behold, each one follows the dictates of his own evil heart, so that no one listens to Me.

Matt 15:19 For out of the heart proceed evil thoughts, murders, adulteries, fornications, thefts, false witness, blasphemies.

Blinded in heart.

Eph 4:18 having their understanding darkened, being alienated from the life of God, because of the ignorance that is in them, because of the blindness of their heart;

Corrupt and perverse in his ways.

Gen 6:12 So God looked upon the earth, and indeed it was corrupt; for all flesh had corrupted their way on the earth.

Ps 10:5 His ways are always prospering; Your judgments *are* far above, out of his sight; *As for* all his enemies, he sneers at them.

Rom 3:12–16 *They have all turned aside; They have together become unprofitable; There is none who does good, no, not one." 13 "Their throat is an open tomb; With their tongues they have practiced deceit"; "The poison of asps is under their lips"; 14 "Whose mouth is full of cursing and bitterness." 15 "Their feet are swift to shed blood; 16 Destruction and misery are in their ways;*

Depraved in mind.

Rom 8:5–7 For those who live according to the flesh set their minds on the things of the flesh, but those *who live* according to the Spirit, the things of the Spirit. **6** For to be carnally minded *is* death, but to be spiritually minded *is* life and peace. **7** Because the carnal mind *is* enmity against God; for it is not subject to the law of God, nor indeed can be.

Eph 4:17 This I say, therefore, and testify in the Lord, that you should no longer walk as the rest of the Gentiles walk, in the futility of their mind,

Col 1:21 And you, who once were alienated and enemies in your mind by wicked works, yet now He has reconciled

Titus 1:15 To the pure all things are pure, but to those who are defiled and unbelieving nothing is pure; but even their mind and conscience are defiled.

Heb 10:22 let us draw near with a true heart in full assurance of faith, having our hearts sprinkled from an evil conscience and our bodies washed with pure water.

Without understanding.

Ps 14:2–3 The LORD looks down from heaven upon the children of men, To see if there are any who understand, who seek God. 3 They have all turned aside, They have together become corrupt; *There is* none who does good, No, not one.

Rom 1:31 undiscerning, untrustworthy, unloving, unforgiving, unmerciful;

Rom 3:11 *There is none who understands; There is none who seeks after God.*

Does not receive the things of God.

1 Cor 2:14 But the natural man does not receive the things of the Spirit of God, for they are foolishness to him; nor can he know *them*, because they are spiritually discerned.

Comes short of God's glory.

Rom 3:23 for all have sinned and fall short of the glory of God,

Intractable.

Job 11:12 For an empty-headed man will be wise, When a wild donkey's colt is born a man.

Estranged from God.

Gen 3:8 And they heard the sound of the LORD God walking in the garden in the cool of the day, and Adam and his wife hid themselves from the presence of the LORD God among the trees of the garden.

Ps 58:3 The wicked are estranged from the womb; They go astray as soon as they are born, speaking lies.

Eph 4:18 having their understanding darkened, being alienated from the life of God, because of the ignorance that is in them, because of the blindness of their heart;

Col 1:21 And you, who once were alienated and enemies in your mind by wicked works, yet now He has reconciled

In bondage to sin.

Rom 6:19 I speak in human *terms* because of the weakness of your flesh. For just as you presented your members *as* slaves of uncleanness, and of lawlessness *leading* to *more* lawlessness, so now present your members *as* slaves *of* righteousness for holiness.

Rom 7:5 For when we were in the flesh, the sinful passions which were aroused by the law were at work in our members to bear fruit to death.

Rom 7:23 But I see another law in my members, warring against the law of my mind, and bringing me into captivity to the law of sin which is in my members.

Gal 5:17 For the flesh lusts against the Spirit, and the Spirit against the flesh; and these are contrary to one another, so that you do not do the things that you wish.

Titus 3:3 For we ourselves were also once foolish, disobedient, deceived, serving various lusts and pleasures, living in malice and envy, hateful and hating one another.

In bondage to the devil.

2 Tim 2:26 and *that* they may come to their senses *and* escape the snare of the devil, having been taken captive by him to *do* his will.

Heb 2:14–15 Inasmuch then as the children have partaken of flesh and blood, He Himself likewise shared in the same, that through death He might destroy him who had the power of death, that is, the devil, 15 and release those who through fear of death were all their lifetime subject to bondage.

Constant in evil.

Ps 10:5 His ways are always prospering; Your judgments *are* far above, out of his sight; *As for* all his enemies, he sneers at them.

2 Pet 2:14 having eyes full of adultery and that cannot cease from sin, enticing unstable souls. *They have* a heart trained in covetous practices, *and are* accursed children.

Conscious of guilt.

Gen 3:7–8 Then the eyes of both of them were opened, and they knew that they *were* naked; and they sewed fig leaves together and made themselves coverings. 8 And they heard the sound of the LORD God walking in the garden in the cool of the day, and Adam and his wife hid themselves from the presence of the LORD God among the trees of the garden.

Gen 3:10 So he said, "I heard Your voice in the garden, and I was afraid because I was naked; and I hid myself."

Unrighteous.

Eccl 7:20 For *there is* not a just man on earth who does good And does not sin.

Rom 3:10 As it is written: *"There is none righteous, no, not one;*

Completely corrupt.

Job 15:16 How much less man, *who is* abominable and filthy, Who drinks iniquity like water!

Ps 14:3 They have all turned aside, They have together become corrupt; *There is* none who does good, No, not one.

Turned to his own way.

Is 53:6 All we like sheep have gone astray; We have turned, every one, to his own way; And the LORD has laid on Him the iniquity of us all.

Loves darkness.

John 3:19 And this is the condemnation, that the light has come into the world, and men loved darkness rather than light, because their deeds were evil.

Corrupt, etc., in speech.

Rom 3:13–14 *"Their throat is an open tomb; With their tongues they have practiced deceit"; "The poison of asps is under their lips"; 14 "Whose mouth is full of cursing and bitterness."*

Devoid of the fear of God.

Rom 3:18 *"There is no fear of God before their eyes."*

Totally depraved.

Gen 6:5 Then the LORD saw that the wickedness of man *was* great in the earth, and that every intent of the thoughts of his heart *was* only evil continually.

Rom 7:18 For I know that in me (that is, in my flesh) nothing good dwells; for to will is present with me, but *how* to perform what is good I do not find.

Eph 2:1 And you He *made alive*, who were dead in trespasses and sins,

Col 2:13 And you, being dead in your trespasses and the uncircumcision of your flesh, He has made alive together with Him, having forgiven you all trespasses,

All men partake of the effects of.

1 Kin 8:46 "When they sin against You (for *there is* no one who does not sin), and You become angry with them and deliver them to the enemy, and they take them captive to the land of the enemy, far or near;

Gal 3:22 But the Scripture has confined all under sin, that the promise by faith in Jesus Christ might be given to those who believe.

1 John 1:8 If we say that we have no sin, we deceive ourselves, and the truth is not in us.

1 John 5:19 We know that we are of God, and the whole world lies *under the sway of* the wicked one.

Man's punishment as a result of,

Banishment from paradise.

Gen 3:24 So He drove out the man; and He placed cherubim at the east of the garden of Eden, and a flaming sword which turned every way, to guard the way to the tree of life.

Assigned to difficult labor and troubles.

Gen 3:16 To the woman He said: "I will greatly multiply your sorrow and your conception; In pain you shall bring forth children; Your desire *shall be* for your husband, And he shall rule over you."

Gen 3:19 In the sweat of your face you shall eat bread Till you return to the ground, For out of it you were taken; For dust you *are,* And to dust you shall return."

Job 5:6–7 For affliction does not come from the dust, Nor does trouble spring from the ground; 7 Yet man is born to trouble, As the sparks fly upward.

Temporal death.

Gen 3:19 In the sweat of your face you shall eat bread Till you return to the ground, For out of it you were taken; For dust you *are,* And to dust you shall return."

Rom 5:12 Therefore, just as through one man sin entered the world, and death through sin, and thus death spread to all men, because all sinned—

1 Cor 15:22 For as in Adam all die, even so in Christ all shall be made alive.

Eternal death.

Job 21:30 For the wicked are reserved for the day of doom; They shall be brought out on the day of wrath.

Rom 5:18 Therefore, as through one man's offense *judgment* came to all men, resulting in condemnation, even so through one Man's righteous act *the free gift came* to all men, resulting in justification of life.

Rom 5:21 so that as sin reigned in death, even so grace might reign through righteousness to eternal life through Jesus Christ our Lord.

Rom 6:23 For the wages of sin *is* death, but the gift of God *is* eternal life in Christ Jesus our Lord.

Cannot be remedied by man.

Prov 20:9 Who can say, "I have made my heart clean, I am pure from my sin"?

Jer 2:22 For though you wash yourself with lye, and use much soap, *Yet* your iniquity is marked before Me," says the Lord GOD.

Jer 13:23 Can the Ethiopian change his skin or the leopard its spots? *Then* may you also do good who are accustomed to do evil.

Remedy for, provided by God.

Gen 3:15 And I will put enmity Between you and the woman, And between your seed and her Seed; He shall bruise your head, And you shall bruise His heel."

John 3:16 For God so loved the world that He gave His only begotten Son, that whoever believes in Him should not perish but have everlasting life.

FAMILIES

Of believers are blessed.

Ps 128:3–6 Your wife *shall be* like a fruitful vine In the very heart of your house, Your children like olive plants All around your table. 4 Behold, thus shall the man be blessed Who fears the LORD. 5 The LORD bless you out of Zion, And may you see the good of Jerusalem All the days of your life. 6 Yes, may you see your children's children. Peace *be* upon Israel!

Responsibilities of,

Be taught the Scriptures.

Deut 4:9–10 Only take heed to yourself, and diligently keep yourself, lest you forget the things your eyes have seen, and lest they depart from your heart all the days of your life. And teach them to your children and your grandchildren, 10 *especially concerning* the day you stood before the LORD your God in Horeb, when the LORD said to me, 'Gather the people to Me, and I will let them hear My words, that they may learn to fear Me all the days they live on the earth, and *that* they may teach their children.'

Worship God together.

1 Cor 16:19 The churches of Asia greet you. Aquila and Priscilla greet you heartily in the Lord, with the church that is in their house.

Be duly regulated.

Prov 31:27 She watches over the ways of her household, And does not eat the bread of idleness.

1 Tim 3:4–5 one who rules his own house well, having *his* children in submission with all reverence 5 (for if a man does not know how to rule his own house, how will he take care of the church of God?);

1 Tim 3:12 Let deacons be the husbands of one wife, ruling *their* children and their own houses well.

Live in unity.

Gen 45:24 So he sent his brothers away, and they departed; and he said to them, "See that you do not become troubled along the way."

Ps 133:1 Behold, how good and how pleasant *it is* For brethren to dwell together in unity!

Members forgive one another.

Gen 50:17–21 'Thus you shall say to Joseph: "I beg you, please forgive the trespass of your brothers and their sin; for they did evil to you." ' Now, please, forgive the trespass of the servants of the God of your father." And Joseph wept when they spoke to him. 18 Then his brothers also went and fell down before his face, and they said, "Behold, we *are* your servants." 19 Joseph said to them, "Do not be afraid, for *am* I in the place of God? 20 But as for you, you meant evil against me; *but* God meant it for good, in order to bring it about as *it is* this day, to save many people alive. 21 Now therefore, do not be afraid; I will provide for you and your little ones." And he comforted them and spoke kindly to them.

Matt 18:21–22 Then Peter came to Him and said, "Lord,

how often shall my brother sin against me, and I forgive him? Up to seven times?" **22** Jesus said to him, "I do not say to you, up to seven times, but up to seventy times seven.

Rejoice together before God.

Deut 14:26 And you shall spend that money for whatever your heart desires: for oxen or sheep, for wine or similar drink, for whatever your heart desires; you shall eat there before the LORD your God, and you shall rejoice, you and your household.

Deceivers and liars should be removed from.

Ps 101:7 He who works deceit shall not dwell within my house; He who tells lies shall not continue in my presence.

Warning against departing from God.

Deut 29:18 so that there may not be among you man or woman or family or tribe, whose heart turns away today from the LORD our God, to go *and* serve the gods of these nations, and that there may not be among you a root bearing bitterness or wormwood;

Punishment of unbelieving ones.

Jer 10:25 Pour out Your fury on the Gentiles, who do not know You, And on the families who do not call on Your name; For they have eaten up Jacob, Devoured him and consumed him, And made his dwelling place desolate.

Good—exemplified by

Abraham.

Gen 18:19 For I have known him, in order that he may command his children and his household after him, that they keep the way of the LORD, to do righteousness and justice, that the LORD may bring to Abraham what He has spoken to him."

Jacob.

Gen 35:2 And Jacob said to his household and to all who *were* with him, "Put away the foreign gods that *are* among you, purify yourselves, and change your garments.

Joshua.

Josh 24:15 And if it seems evil to you to serve the LORD, choose for yourselves this day whom you will serve, whether the gods which your fathers served that *were* on the other side of the River, or the gods of the Amorites, in whose land you dwell. But as for me and my house, we will serve the LORD."

David.

2 Sam 6:20 Then David returned to bless his household. And Michal the daughter of Saul came out to meet David, and said, "How glorious was the king of Israel today, uncovering himself today in the eyes of the maids of his servants, as one of the base fellows shamelessly uncovers himself!"

Job.

Job 1:5 So it was, when the days of feasting had run their course, that Job would send and sanctify them, and he would rise early in the morning and offer burnt offerings *according to* the number of them all. For Job said, "It may be that my sons have sinned and cursed God in their hearts." Thus Job did regularly.

Lazarus of Bethany.

John 11:1–5 Now a certain *man* was sick, Lazarus of Bethany, the town of Mary and her sister Martha. **2** It was *that* Mary who anointed the Lord with fragrant oil and wiped His feet with her hair, whose brother Lazarus was sick. **3** Therefore the sisters sent to Him, saying, "Lord, behold, he whom You love is sick." **4** When Jesus heard *that*, He said, "This sickness is not unto death, but for the glory of God, that the Son of God may be glorified through it." **5** Now Jesus loved Martha and her sister and Lazarus.

Cornelius.

Acts 10:2 a devout *man* and one who feared God with all his household, who gave alms generously to the people, and prayed to God always.

Acts 10:33 So I sent to you immediately, and you have done well to come. Now therefore, we are all present before God, to hear all the things commanded you by God."

Lydia.

Acts 16:15 And when she and her household were baptized, she begged *us*, saying, "If you have judged me to be faithful to the Lord, come to my house and stay." So she persuaded us.

The jailer of Philippi.

Acts 16:31–34 So they said, "Believe on the Lord Jesus Christ, and you will be saved, you and your household." **32** Then they spoke the word of the Lord to him and to all who were in his house. **33** And he took them the same hour of the night and washed *their* stripes. And immediately he and all his family were baptized. **34** Now when he had brought them into his house, he set food before them; and he rejoiced, having believed in God with all his household.

Crispus.

Acts 18:8 Then Crispus, the ruler of the synagogue, believed on the Lord with all his household. And many of the Corinthians, hearing, believed and were baptized.

Lois.

2 Tim 1:5 when I call to remembrance the genuine faith that is in you, which dwelt first in your grandmother Lois and your mother Eunice, and I am persuaded is in you also.

FAMINE

Sent by God.

Ps 10:16 The LORD *is* King forever and ever; The nations have perished out of His land.

Often because of sin.

Lev 26:21 Then, if you walk contrary to Me, and are not willing to obey Me, I will bring on you seven times more plagues, according to your sins.

Lev 26:26 When I have cut off your supply of bread, ten women shall bake your bread in one oven, and they shall bring back your bread by weight, and you shall eat and not be satisfied.

Lam 4:4–6 The tongue of the infant clings To the roof of its mouth for thirst; The young children ask for bread, *But* no one breaks *it* for them. **5** Those who ate delicacies Are desolate in the streets; Those who were brought up in scarlet Embrace ash heaps. **6** The punishment of the iniquity of the daughter of my people Is greater than the punishment of the sin of

Sodom, Which was overthrown in a moment, With no hand to help her!

One of God's four severe judgments on Jerusalem.

Ezek 14:21 For thus says the Lord GOD: "How much more it shall be when I send My four severe judgments on Jerusalem—the sword and famine and wild beasts and pestilence—to cut off man and beast from it?

Caused by

God's blessing withheld.

Hos 2:8–9 For she did not know That I gave her grain, new wine, and oil, And multiplied her silver and gold— *Which* they prepared for Baal. **9** "Therefore I will return and take away My grain in its time And My new wine in its season, And will take back My wool and My linen, *Given* to cover her nakedness.

Hag 1:6 "You have sown much, and bring in little; You eat, but do not have enough; You drink, but you are not filled with drink; You clothe yourselves, but no one is warm; And he who earns wages, Earns wages *to put* into a bag with holes."

Lack of seasonable rain.

1 Kin 17:1 And Elijah the Tishbite, of the inhabitants of Gilead, said to Ahab, "*As* the LORD God of Israel lives, before whom I stand, there shall not be dew nor rain these years, except at my word."

Jer 14:1–4 The word of the LORD that came to Jeremiah concerning the droughts. **2** "Judah mourns, And her gates languish; They mourn for the land, And the cry of Jerusalem has gone up. **3** Their nobles have sent their lads for water; They went to the cisterns *and* found no water. They returned with their vessels empty; They were ashamed and confounded And covered their heads. **4** Because the ground is parched, For there was no rain in the land, The plowmen were ashamed; They covered their heads.

Amos 4:7 "I also withheld rain from you, When *there were* still three months to the harvest. I made it rain on one city, I withheld rain from another city. One part was rained upon, And where it did not rain the part withered.

Rotting of the seed in the ground.

Joel 1:17 The seed shrivels under the clods, Storehouses are in shambles; Barns are broken down, For the grain has withered.

Swarms of locusts.

Deut 28:38 "You shall carry much seed out to the field but gather little in, for the locust shall consume it.

Deut 28:42 Locusts shall consume all your trees and the produce of your land.

Joel 1:4 What the chewing locust left, the swarming locust has eaten; What the swarming locust left, the crawling locust has eaten; And what the crawling locust left, the consuming locust has eaten.

Blight and mildew.

Amos 4:9 "I blasted you with blight and mildew. When your gardens increased, Your vineyards, Your fig trees, And your olive trees, The locust devoured *them*; Yet you have not returned to Me," Says the LORD.

Hag 2:17 I struck you with blight and mildew and hail

in all the labors of your hands; yet you did not *turn* to Me,' says the LORD.

Devastation by enemies.

Deut 28:33 A nation whom you have not known shall eat the fruit of your land and the produce of your labor, and you shall be only oppressed and crushed continually.

Deut 28:51 And they shall eat the increase of your livestock and the produce of your land, until you are destroyed; they shall not leave you grain or new wine or oil, *or* the increase of your cattle or the offspring of your flocks, until they have destroyed you.

Often long in duration.

Gen 41:27 And the seven thin and ugly cows which came up after them *are* seven years, and the seven empty heads blighted by the east wind are seven years of famine.

2 Kin 8:1–2 Then Elisha spoke to the woman whose son he had restored to life, saying, "Arise and go, you and your household, and stay wherever you can; for the LORD has called for a famine, and furthermore, it will come upon the land for seven years." **2** So the woman arose and did according to the saying of the man of God, and she went with her household and dwelt in the land of the Philistines seven years.

Often severe.

Gen 12:10 Now there was a famine in the land, and Abram went down to Egypt to dwell there, for the famine *was* severe in the land.

1 Kin 18:2 So Elijah went to present himself to Ahab; and *there was* a severe famine in Samaria.

Jer 52:6 By the fourth month, on the ninth day of the month, the famine had become so severe in the city that there was no food for the people of the land.

Expressed by

Taking away the supply of bread, etc.

Is 3:1 For behold, the Lord, the LORD of hosts, Takes away from Jerusalem and from Judah The stock and the store, The whole supply of bread and the whole supply of water;

Cleanness of teeth.

Amos 4:6 "Also I gave you cleanness of teeth in all your cities, And lack of bread in all your places; Yet you have not returned to Me," Says the LORD.

The arrows of destruction.

Ezek 5:16 When I send against them the terrible arrows of famine which shall be for destruction, which I will send to destroy you, I will increase the famine upon you and cut off your supply of bread.

Often accompanied by war.

Jer 14:15 Therefore thus says the LORD concerning the prophets who prophesy in My name, whom I did not send, and who say, 'Sword and famine shall not be in this land'—'By sword and famine those prophets shall be consumed!

Jer 29:18 And I will pursue them with the sword, with famine, and with pestilence; and I will deliver them to trouble among all the kingdoms of the earth—to be a curse, an astonishment, a hissing, and a reproach among all the nations where I have driven them,

Often followed by pestilence.

Jer 42:17 So shall it be with all the men who set their faces to go to Egypt to dwell there. They shall die by the sword, by famine, and by pestilence. And none of them shall remain or escape from the disaster that I will bring upon them.'

Ezek 7:15 The sword *is* outside, And the pestilence and famine within. Whoever *is* in the field Will die by the sword; And whoever *is* in the city, Famine and pestilence will devour him.

Matt 24:7 For nation will rise against nation, and kingdom against kingdom. And there will be famines, pestilences, and earthquakes in various places.

Things eaten during,

Wild herbs.

2 Kin 4:39–40 So one went out into the field to gather herbs, and found a wild vine, and gathered from it a lapful of wild gourds, and came and sliced *them* into the pot of stew, though they did not know *what they were.* **40** Then they served it to the men to eat. Now it happened, as they were eating the stew, that they cried out and said, "Man of God, *there is* death in the pot!" And they could not eat *it.*

Donkey's flesh.

2 Kin 6:25 And there was a great famine in Samaria; and indeed they besieged it until a donkey's head was *sold* for eighty *shekels* of silver, and one-fourth of a kab of dove droppings for five *shekels* of silver.

Dung.

2 Kin 6:25 And there was a great famine in Samaria; and indeed they besieged it until a donkey's head was *sold* for eighty *shekels* of silver, and one-fourth of a kab of dove droppings for five *shekels* of silver.

Lam 4:5 Those who ate delicacies Are desolate in the streets; Those who were brought up in scarlet Embrace ash heaps.

Human flesh.

Lev 26:29 You shall eat the flesh of your sons, and you shall eat the flesh of your daughters.

2 Kin 6:28–29 Then the king said to her, "What is troubling you?" And she answered, "This woman said to me, 'Give your son, that we may eat him today, and we will eat my son tomorrow.' **29** So we boiled my son, and ate him. And I said to her on the next day, 'Give your son, that we may eat him'; but she has hidden her son."

Provisions sold by weight during.

Ezek 4:16 Moreover He said to me, "Son of man, surely I will cut off the supply of bread in Jerusalem; they shall eat bread by weight and with anxiety, and shall drink water by measure and with dread,

Wild animals suffered from.

Jer 14:5–6 Yes, the deer also gave birth in the field, But left because there was no grass. **6** And the wild donkeys stood in the desolate heights; They sniffed at the wind like jackals; Their eyes failed because *there was* no grass."

Results from,

Burning and fever.

Deut 32:24 *They shall be* wasted with hunger, Devoured by pestilence and bitter destruction; I will also send

against them the teeth of beasts, With the poison of serpents of the dust.

Damaged skin.

Lam 4:8 *Now* their appearance is blacker than soot; They go unrecognized in the streets; Their skin clings to their bones, It has become as dry as wood.

Lam 5:10 Our skin is hot as an oven, Because of the fever of famine.

Grief and mourning.

Joel 1:11–13 Be ashamed, you farmers, Wail, you vinedressers, For the wheat and the barley; Because the harvest of the field has perished. **12** The vine has dried up, And the fig tree has withered; The pomegranate tree, The palm tree also, And the apple tree— All the trees of the field are withered; Surely joy has withered away from the sons of men. **13** Gird yourselves and lament, you priests; Wail, you who minister before the altar; Come, lie all night in sackcloth, You who minister to my God; For the grain offering and the drink offering Are withheld from the house of your God.

Faintness.

Gen 47:13 Now *there was* no bread in all the land; for the famine *was* very severe, so that the land of Egypt and the land of Canaan languished because of the famine.

Wasting of the body.

Lam 4:8 *Now* their appearance is blacker than soot; They go unrecognized in the streets; Their skin clings to their bones, It has become as dry as wood.

Ezek 4:17 that they may lack bread and water, and be dismayed with one another, and waste away because of their iniquity.

Death.

2 Kin 7:4 If we say, 'We will enter the city,' the famine *is* in the city, and we shall die there. And if we sit here, we die also. Now therefore, come, let us surrender to the army of the Syrians. If they keep us alive, we shall live; and if they kill us, we shall only die."

Jer 11:22 therefore thus says the LORD of hosts: 'Behold, I will punish them. The young men shall die by the sword, their sons and their daughters shall die by famine;

God provided for His people during.

1 Kin 17:4 And it will be *that* you shall drink from the brook, and I have commanded the ravens to feed you there."

1 Kin 17:9 "Arise, go to Zarephath, which *belongs* to Sidon, and dwell there. See, I have commanded a widow there to provide for you."

Job 5:20 In famine He shall redeem you from death, And in war from the power of the sword.

Ps 33:19 To deliver their soul from death, And to keep them alive in famine.

Ps 37:19 They shall not be ashamed in the evil time, And in the days of famine they shall be satisfied.

Instances of, in Scripture

In the days of Abraham.

Gen 12:10 Now there was a famine in the land, and Abram went down to Egypt to dwell there, for the famine *was* severe in the land.

In the days of Isaac.

Gen 26:1 There was a famine in the land, besides the first famine that was in the days of Abraham. And Isaac went to Abimelech king of the Philistines, in Gerar.

In the days of Joseph.

Gen 41:53–56 Then the seven years of plenty which were in the land of Egypt ended, **54** and the seven years of famine began to come, as Joseph had said. The famine was in all lands, but in all the land of Egypt there was bread. **55** So when all the land of Egypt was famished, the people cried to Pharaoh for bread. Then Pharaoh said to all the Egyptians, "Go to Joseph; whatever he says to you, do." **56** The famine was over all the face of the earth, and Joseph opened all the storehouses and sold to the Egyptians. And the famine became severe in the land of Egypt.

In the days of the judges.

Ruth 1:1 Now it came to pass, in the days when the judges ruled, that there was a famine in the land. And a certain man of Bethlehem, Judah, went to dwell in the country of Moab, he and his wife and his two sons.

In the reign of David.

2 Sam 21:1 Now there was a famine in the days of David for three years, year after year; and David inquired of the LORD. And the LORD answered, "*It is* because of Saul and *his* bloodthirsty house, because he killed the Gibeonites."

In the reign of Ahab.

1 Kin 17:1 And Elijah the Tishbite, of the inhabitants of Gilead, said to Ahab, "*As* the LORD God of Israel lives, before whom I stand, there shall not be dew nor rain these years, except at my word."

1 Kin 18:5 And Ahab had said to Obadiah, "Go into the land to all the springs of water and to all the brooks; perhaps we may find grass to keep the horses and mules alive, so that we will not have to kill any livestock."

In the time of Elisha.

2 Kin 4:38 And Elisha returned to Gilgal, and *there was* a famine in the land. Now the sons of the prophets *were* sitting before him; and he said to his servant, "Put on the large pot, and boil stew for the sons of the prophets."

During the siege of Samaria.

2 Kin 6:25 And there was a great famine in Samaria; and indeed they besieged it until a donkey's head was *sold* for eighty *shekels* of silver, and one-fourth of a kab of dove droppings for five *shekels* of silver.

Of seven years foretold by Elisha.

2 Kin 8:1 Then Elisha spoke to the woman whose son he had restored to life, saying, "Arise and go, you and your household, and stay wherever you can; for the LORD has called for a famine, and furthermore, it will come upon the land for seven years."

In the time of Jeremiah.

Jer 14:1 The word of the LORD that came to Jeremiah concerning the droughts.

During the siege of Jerusalem.

2 Kin 25:3 By the ninth *day* of the *fourth* month the famine had become so severe in the city that there was no food for the people of the land.

After the captivity.

Neh 5:3 There were also *some* who said, "We have mortgaged our lands and vineyards and houses, that we might buy grain because of the famine."

In the reign of Claudius Caesar.

Acts 11:28 Then one of them, named Agabus, stood up and showed by the Spirit that there was going to be a great famine throughout all the world, which also happened in the days of Claudius Caesar.

Before the destruction of Jerusalem.

Matt 24:7 For nation will rise against nation, and kingdom against kingdom. And there will be famines, pestilences, and earthquakes in various places.

In the end times.

Rev 6:5–6 When He opened the third seal, I heard the third living creature say, "Come and see." So I looked, and behold, a black horse, and he who sat on it had a pair of scales in his hand. **6** And I heard a voice in the midst of the four living creatures saying, "A quart of wheat for a denarius, and three quarts of barley for a denarius; and do not harm the oil and the wine."

Rev 18:8 Therefore her plagues will come in one day—death and mourning and famine. And she will be utterly burned with fire, for strong *is* the Lord God who judges her.

The Jews in their restored state not to be afflicted by.

Ezek 36:29–30 I will deliver you from all your uncleannesses. I will call for the grain and multiply it, and bring no famine upon you. **30** And I will multiply the fruit of your trees and the increase of your fields, so that you need never again bear the reproach of famine among the nations.

Illustrative of a dearth of hearing the Word of God.

Amos 8:11–12 "Behold, the days are coming," says the Lord GOD, "That I will send a famine on the land, Not a famine of bread, Nor a thirst for water, But of hearing the words of the LORD. **12** They shall wander from sea to sea, And from north to east; They shall run to and fro, seeking the word of the LORD, But shall not find *it.*

FASTING

Spirit of, explained.

Is 58:6–7 "*Is* this not the fast that I have chosen: To loose the bonds of wickedness, To undo the heavy burdens, To let the oppressed go free, And that you break every yoke? **7** *Is it* not to share your bread with the hungry, And that you bring to your house the poor who are cast out; When you see the naked, that you cover him, And not hide yourself from your own flesh?

Not to be made a subject of display.

Matt 6:16–18 "Moreover, when you fast, do not be like the hypocrites, with a sad countenance. For they disfigure their faces that they may appear to men to be fasting. Assuredly, I say to you, they have their reward. **17** But you, when you fast, anoint your head and wash your face, **18** so that you do not appear to men to be fasting, but to your Father who *is* in the secret *place;* and your Father who sees in secret will reward you openly.

Should be to God.

Zech 7:5 "Say to all the people of the land, and to the priests: 'When you fasted and mourned in the fifth and seventh *months* during those seventy years, did you really fast for Me—for Me?

Matt 6:18 so that you do not appear to men to be fasting, but to your Father who *is* in the secret *place;* and your Father who sees in secret will reward you openly.

For the chastening of the soul.

Ps 69:10 When I wept *and chastened* my soul with fasting, That became my reproach.

For the humbling of the soul.

Ps 35:13 But as for me, when they were sick, My clothing *was* sackcloth; I humbled myself with fasting; And my prayer would return to my own heart.

Occasions it was observed

Judgments of God.

Joel 1:14 Consecrate a fast, Call a sacred assembly; Gather the elders *And* all the inhabitants of the land *Into* the house of the LORD your God, And cry out to the LORD.

Joel 2:12 "Now, therefore," says the LORD, "Turn to Me with all your heart, With fasting, with weeping, and with mourning."

Public calamities.

2 Sam 1:12 And they mourned and wept and fasted until evening for Saul and for Jonathan his son, for the people of the LORD and for the house of Israel, because they had fallen by the sword.

Afflictions of the church.

Luke 5:33–35 Then they said to Him, "Why do the disciples of John fast often and make prayers, and likewise those of the Pharisees, but Yours eat and drink?" 34 And He said to them, "Can you make the friends of the bridegroom fast while the bridegroom is with them? 35 But the days will come when the bridegroom will be taken away from them; then they will fast in those days."

Afflictions of others.

Ps 35:13 But as for me, when they were sick, My clothing *was* sackcloth; I humbled myself with fasting; And my prayer would return to my own heart.

Dan 6:18 Now the king went to his palace and spent the night fasting; and no musicians were brought before him. Also his sleep went from him.

Private afflictions.

2 Sam 12:16 David therefore pleaded with God for the child, and David fasted and went in and lay all night on the ground.

Approaching danger.

Esth 4:16 "Go, gather all the Jews who are present in Shushan, and fast for me; neither eat nor drink for three days, night or day. My maids and I will fast likewise. And so I will go to the king, which *is* against the law; and if I perish, I perish!"

Ordination of ministers.

Acts 13:3 Then, having fasted and prayed, and laid hands on them, they sent *them* away.

Acts 14:23 So when they had appointed elders in every church, and prayed with fasting, they commended them to the Lord in whom they had believed.

Accompanied by

Prayer.

Ezra 8:23 So we fasted and entreated our God for this, and He answered our prayer.

Dan 9:3 Then I set my face toward the Lord God to make request by prayer and supplications, with fasting, sackcloth, and ashes.

Confession of sin.

1 Sam 7:6 So they gathered together at Mizpah, drew water, and poured *it* out before the LORD. And they fasted that day, and said there, "We have sinned against the LORD." And Samuel judged the children of Israel at Mizpah.

Neh 9:1–2 Now on the twenty-fourth day of this month the children of Israel were assembled with fasting, in sackcloth, and with dust on their heads. 2 Then those of Israelite lineage separated themselves from all foreigners; and they stood and confessed their sins and the iniquities of their fathers.

Mourning.

Joel 2:12 "Now, therefore," says the LORD, "Turn to Me with all your heart, With fasting, with weeping, and with mourning."

Humiliation.

Deut 9:18 And I fell down before the LORD, as at the first, forty days and forty nights; I neither ate bread nor drank water, because of all your sin which you committed in doing wickedly in the sight of the LORD, to provoke Him to anger.

Neh 9:1 Now on the twenty-fourth day of this month the children of Israel were assembled with fasting, in sackcloth, and with dust on their heads.

Promises connected with.

Is 58:8–12 Then your light shall break forth like the morning, Your healing shall spring forth speedily, And your righteousness shall go before you; The glory of the LORD shall be your rear guard. 9 Then you shall call, and the LORD will answer; You shall cry, and He will say, 'Here I *am*.' "If you take away the yoke from your midst, The pointing of the finger, and speaking wickedness, 10 *If* you extend your soul to the hungry And satisfy the afflicted soul, Then your light shall dawn in the darkness, And your darkness shall *be* as the noonday. 11 The LORD will guide you continually, And satisfy your soul in drought, And strengthen your bones; You shall be like a watered garden, And like a spring of water, whose waters do not fail. 12 Those from among you Shall build the old waste places; You shall raise up the foundations of many generations; And you shall be called the Repairer of the Breach, The Restorer of Streets to Dwell In.

Matt 6:18 so that you do not appear to men to be fasting, but to your Father who *is* in the secret *place;* and your Father who sees in secret will reward you openly.

By hypocrites

Described.

Is 58:4–5 Indeed you fast for strife and debate, And to strike with the fist of wickedness. You will not fast as *you do* this day, To make your voice heard on high. 5 Is it a fast that I have chosen, A day for a man to afflict his soul? *Is it* to bow down his head like a bulrush, And to spread out sackcloth and ashes? Would you call this a fast, And an acceptable day to the LORD?

They were ostentatious in.

Matt 6:16 "Moreover, when you fast, do not be like the hypocrites, with a sad countenance. For they disfigure their faces that they may appear to men to be fasting. Assuredly, I say to you, they have their reward.

They boasted of, before God.

Luke 18:12 I fast twice a week; I give tithes of all that I possess.'

Was rejected.

Is 58:3 'Why have we fasted,' *they say,* 'and You have not seen? *Why* have we afflicted our souls, and You take no notice?' "In fact, in the day of your fast you find pleasure, And exploit all your laborers.

Jer 14:12 When they fast, I will not hear their cry; and when they offer burnt offering and grain offering, I will not accept them. But I will consume them by the sword, by the famine, and by the pestilence."

Extraordinary—exemplified by

Our Lord.

Matt 4:2 And when He had fasted forty days and forty nights, afterward He was hungry.

Moses.

Ex 34:28 So he was there with the LORD forty days and forty nights; he neither ate bread nor drank water. And He wrote on the tablets the words of the covenant, the Ten Commandments.

Deut 9:9 When I went up into the mountain to receive the tablets of stone, the tablets of the covenant which the LORD made with you, then I stayed on the mountain forty days and forty nights. I neither ate bread nor drank water.

Deut 9:18 And I fell down before the LORD, as at the first, forty days and forty nights; I neither ate bread nor drank water, because of all your sin which you committed in doing wickedly in the sight of the LORD, to provoke Him to anger.

Elijah.

1 Kin 19:8 So he arose, and ate and drank; and he went in the strength of that food forty days and forty nights as far as Horeb, the mountain of God.

National—exemplified by

Israel.

Judg 20:26 Then all the children of Israel, that is, all the people, went up and came to the house of God and wept. They sat there before the LORD and fasted that day until evening; and they offered burnt offerings and peace offerings before the LORD.

Ezra 8:21 Then I proclaimed a fast there at the river of Ahava, that we might humble ourselves before our God, to seek from Him the right way for us and our little ones and all our possessions.

Esth 4:3 And in every province where the king's command and decree arrived, *there was* great mourning among the Jews, with fasting, weeping, and wailing; and many lay in sackcloth and ashes.

Esth 4:16 "Go, gather all the Jews who are present in Shushan, and fast for me; neither eat nor drink for three days, night or day. My maids and I will fast likewise. And so I will go to the king, which *is* against the law; and if I perish, I perish!"

Jer 36:9 Now it came to pass in the fifth year of Jehoiakim the son of Josiah, king of Judah, in the ninth month, *that* they proclaimed a fast before the LORD to all the people in Jerusalem, and to all the people who came from the cities of Judah to Jerusalem.

The men of Jabesh-gilead.

1 Sam 31:13 Then they took their bones and buried *them* under the tamarisk tree at Jabesh, and fasted seven days.

Ninevites.

Jon 3:5–8 So the people of Nineveh believed God, proclaimed a fast, and put on sackcloth, from the greatest to the least of them. **6** Then word came to the king of Nineveh; and he arose from his throne and laid aside his robe, covered *himself* with sackcloth and sat in ashes. **7** And he caused *it* to be proclaimed and published throughout Nineveh by the decree of the king and his nobles, saying, Let neither man nor beast, herd nor flock, taste anything; do not let them eat, or drink water. **8** But let man and beast be covered with sackcloth, and cry mightily to God; yes, let every one turn from his evil way and from the violence that is in his hands.

Of believers—exemplified by

David.

2 Sam 12:16 David therefore pleaded with God for the child, and David fasted and went in and lay all night on the ground.

Ps 109:24 My knees are weak through fasting, And my flesh is feeble from lack of fatness.

Nehemiah.

Neh 1:4 So it was, when I heard these words, that I sat down and wept, and mourned *for many* days; I was fasting and praying before the God of heaven.

Esther.

Esth 4:16 "Go, gather all the Jews who are present in Shushan, and fast for me; neither eat nor drink for three days, night or day. My maids and I will fast likewise. And so I will go to the king, which *is* against the law; and if I perish, I perish!"

Daniel.

Dan 9:3 Then I set my face toward the Lord God to make request by prayer and supplications, with fasting, sackcloth, and ashes.

The disciples of John.

Matt 9:14 Then the disciples of John came to Him, saying, "Why do we and the Pharisees fast often, but Your disciples do not fast?"

Anna.

Luke 2:37 and this woman *was* a widow of about eighty-four years, who did not depart from the temple, but served God with fastings and prayers night and day.

Cornelius.

Acts 10:30 So Cornelius said, "Four days ago I was fasting until this hour; and at the ninth hour I prayed in my house, and behold, a man stood before me in bright clothing,

The early Christians.

Acts 13:2 As they ministered to the Lord and fasted, the Holy Spirit said, "Now separate to Me Barnabas and Saul for the work to which I have called them."

The apostles.

2 Cor 6:5 in stripes, in imprisonments, in tumults, in labors, in sleeplessness, in fastings;

Paul.

2 Cor 11:27 in weariness and toil, in sleeplessness often, in hunger and thirst, in fastings often, in cold and nakedness—

Of the wicked—illustrated by

The elders of Jezreel.

1 Kin 21:12 They proclaimed a fast, and seated Naboth with high honor among the people.

Ahab.

1 Kin 21:27 So it was, when Ahab heard those words, that he tore his clothes and put sackcloth on his body, and fasted and lay in sackcloth, and went about mourning.

The Pharisees.

Mark 2:18 The disciples of John and of the Pharisees were fasting. Then they came and said to Him, "Why do the disciples of John and of the Pharisees fast, but Your disciples do not fast?"

Luke 18:12 I fast twice a week; I give tithes of all that I possess.'

FATHERLESS

Find mercy in God.

Hos 14:3 Assyria shall not save us, We will not ride on horses, Nor will we say anymore to the work of our hands, *'You are* our gods.' For in You the fatherless finds mercy."

God will

Be a father of.

Ps 68:5 A father of the fatherless, a defender of widows, *Is* God in His holy habitation.

Be a helper of.

Ps 10:14 But You have seen, for You observe trouble and grief, To repay *it* by Your hand. The helpless commits himself to You; You are the helper of the fatherless.

Hear the cry of.

Ex 22:23 If you afflict them in any way, *and* they cry at all to Me, I will surely hear their cry;

Administer justice for.

Deut 10:18 He administers justice for the fatherless and the widow, and loves the stranger, giving him food and clothing.

Ps 10:18 To do justice to the fatherless and the oppressed, That the man of the earth may oppress no more.

Punish those who oppress.

Ex 22:24 and My wrath will become hot, and I will kill you with the sword; your wives shall be widows, and your children fatherless.

Is 10:1–3 "Woe to those who decree unrighteous de-

crees, Who write misfortune, *Which* they have prescribed 2 To rob the needy of justice, And to take what is right from the poor of My people, That widows may be their prey, And *that* they may rob the fatherless. 3 What will you do in the day of punishment, And in the desolation *which* will come from afar? To whom will you flee for help? And where will you leave your glory?

Mal 3:5 And I will come near you for judgment; I will be a swift witness Against sorcerers, Against adulterers, Against perjurers, Against those who exploit wage earners and widows and orphans, And against those who turn away an alien— Because they do not fear Me," Says the LORD of hosts.

Punish those who do not defend.

Jer 5:28–29 They have grown fat, they are sleek; Yes, they surpass the deeds of the wicked; They do not plead the cause, The cause of the fatherless; Yet they prosper, And the right of the needy they do not defend. 29 Shall I not punish *them* for these *things?'* says the LORD. 'Shall I not avenge Myself on such a nation as this?'

Should be visited.

James 1:27 Pure and undefiled religion before God and the Father is this: to visit orphans and widows in their trouble, *and* to keep oneself unspotted from the world.

Should share in our blessings.

Deut 14:29 And the Levite, because he has no portion nor inheritance with you, and the stranger and the fatherless and the widow who *are* within your gates, may come and eat and be satisfied, that the LORD your God may bless you in all the work of your hand which you do.

Should be defended.

Ps 82:3 Defend the poor and fatherless; Do justice to the afflicted and needy.

Is 1:17 Learn to do good; Seek justice, Rebuke the oppressor; Defend the fatherless, Plead for the widow.

Should not be treated unjustly.

Deut 24:17 "You shall not pervert justice due the stranger or the fatherless, nor take a widow's garment as a pledge.

Should not be defrauded.

Prov 23:10 Do not remove the ancient landmark, Nor enter the fields of the fatherless;

Should not be afflicted.

Ex 22:22 "You shall not afflict any widow or fatherless child.

Should not be oppressed.

Zech 7:10 Do not oppress the widow or the fatherless, The alien or the poor. Let none of you plan evil in his heart Against his brother.'

Should not suffer violence.

Jer 22:3 Thus says the LORD: "Execute judgment and righteousness, and deliver the plundered out of the hand of the oppressor. Do no wrong and do no violence to the stranger, the fatherless, or the widow, nor shed innocent blood in this place.

Blessedness of taking care of.

Deut 14:29 And the Levite, because he has no portion

nor inheritance with you, and the stranger and the fatherless and the widow who *are* within your gates, may come and eat and be satisfied, that the LORD your God may bless you in all the work of your hand which you do.

Job 29:12–13 Because I delivered the poor who cried out, The fatherless and *the one who* had no helper. **13** The blessing of a perishing *man* came upon me, And I caused the widow's heart to sing for joy.

Jer 7:6–7 *if* you do not oppress the stranger, the fatherless, and the widow, and do not shed innocent blood in this place, or walk after other gods to your hurt, **7** then I will cause you to dwell in this place, in the land that I gave to your fathers forever and ever.

The wicked

Rob.

Is 10:2 To rob the needy of justice, And to take what is right from the poor of My people, That widows may be their prey, And *that* they may rob the fatherless.

Overwhelm.

Job 6:27 Yes, you overwhelm the fatherless, And you undermine your friend.

Mistreat.

Ezek 22:7 In you they have made light of father and mother; in your midst they have oppressed the stranger; in you they have mistreated the fatherless and the widow.

Oppress.

Job 24:3 They drive away the donkey of the fatherless; They take the widow's ox as a pledge.

Murder.

Ps 94:6 They slay the widow and the stranger, And murder the fatherless.

Do not defend.

Is 1:23 Your princes *are* rebellious, And companions of thieves; Everyone loves bribes, And follows after rewards. They do not defend the fatherless, Nor does the cause of the widow come before them.

Jer 5:28 They have grown fat, they are sleek; Yes, they surpass the deeds of the wicked; They do not plead the cause, The cause of the fatherless; Yet they prosper, And the right of the needy they do not defend.

A curse on those who oppress.

Deut 27:19 'Cursed *is* the one who perverts the justice due the stranger, the fatherless, and widow.' "And all the people shall say, 'Amen!'

Promises with respect to.

Jer 49:11 Leave your fatherless children, I will preserve *them* alive; And let your widows trust in Me."

Illustrative of Zion in affliction.

Lam 5:3 We have become orphans and waifs, Our mothers *are* like widows.

Examples of,

Lot.

Gen 11:27–28 This *is* the genealogy of Terah: Terah begot Abram, Nahor, and Haran. Haran begot Lot. **28** And Haran died before his father Terah in his native land, in Ur of the Chaldeans.

The daughters of Zelophehad.

Num 27:1–5 Then came the daughters of Zelophehad the son of Hepher, the son of Gilead, the son of Machir, the son of Manasseh, from the families of Manasseh the son of Joseph; and these *were* the names of his daughters: Mahlah, Noah, Hoglah, Milcah, and Tirzah. **2** And they stood before Moses, before Eleazar the priest, and before the leaders and all the congregation, *by* the doorway of the tabernacle of meeting, saying: **3** "Our father died in the wilderness; but he was not in the company of those who gathered together against the LORD, in company with Korah, but he died in his own sin; and he had no sons. **4** Why should the name of our father be removed from among his family because he had no son? Give us a possession among our father's brothers." **5** So Moses brought their case before the LORD.

Jotham.

Judg 9:16–21 "Now therefore, if you have acted in truth and sincerity in making Abimelech king, and if you have dealt well with Jerubbaal and his house, and have done to him as he deserves— **17** for my father fought for you, risked his life, and delivered you out of the hand of Midian; **18** but you have risen up against my father's house this day, and killed his seventy sons on one stone, and made Abimelech, the son of his female servant, king over the men of Shechem, because he is your brother— **19** if then you have acted in truth and sincerity with Jerubbaal and with his house this day, *then* rejoice in Abimelech, and let him also rejoice in you. **20** But if not, let fire come from Abimelech and devour the men of Shechem and Beth Millo; and let fire come from the men of Shechem and from Beth Millo and devour Abimelech!" **21** And Jotham ran away and fled; and he went to Beer and dwelt there, for fear of Abimelech his brother.

Mephibosheth.

2 Sam 9:3 Then the king said, "*Is* there not still someone of the house of Saul, to whom I may show the kindness of God?" And Ziba said to the king, "There is still a son of Jonathan *who is* lame in *his* feet."

Joash.

2 Kin 11:1–12 When Athaliah the mother of Ahaziah saw that her son was dead, she arose and destroyed all the royal heirs. **2** But Jehosheba, the daughter of King Joram, sister of Ahaziah, took Joash the son of Ahaziah, and stole him away from among the king's sons *who were* being murdered; and they hid him and his nurse in the bedroom, from Athaliah, so that he was not killed. **3** So he was hidden with her in the house of the LORD for six years, while Athaliah reigned over the land. **4** In the seventh year Jehoiada sent and brought the captains of hundreds—of the bodyguards and the escorts—and brought them into the house of the LORD to him. And he made a covenant with them and took an oath from them in the house of the LORD, and showed them the king's son. **5** Then he commanded them, saying, "This *is* what you shall do: One-third of you who come on duty on the Sabbath shall be keeping watch over the king's house, **6** one-third *shall be* at the gate of Sur, and one-third at the gate behind the escorts. You shall keep the watch of the house, lest it be broken down. **7** The two contingents of you who go off duty on the Sabbath shall keep the watch of the house of the LORD for the king. **8** But you shall surround the king on all sides, every man with his weapons in his hand; and whoever comes within range, let him be put to death. You are to be with the king as he goes out and as he comes in." **9** So the captains of the hundreds did according to all that Jehoiada the priest commanded. Each of them took his men who were to be on duty on the Sabbath, with those who were going off duty on the Sabbath, and came to Jehoiada the priest. **10** And the priest gave the captains of hundreds the spears and shields which *had belonged* to King David, that were in the temple of the LORD. **11** Then the escorts stood, every man with his weapons in his hand, all around the king, from the right side of the temple to the left side of the temple, by the altar and the house. **12** And he brought out the king's son, put the crown on him, and *gave him* the Testimony; they made him king and anointed him, and they clapped their hands and said, "Long live the king!"

Esther.

Esth 2:7 And *Mordecai* had brought up Hadassah, that *is,* Esther, his uncle's daughter, for she had neither father nor mother. The young woman *was* lovely and beautiful. When her father and mother died, Mordecai took her as his own daughter.

FATHERS
Instruct their sons.
Prov 1:8 My son, hear the instruction of your father, And do not forsake the law of your mother;

Prov 13:1 A wise son *heeds* his father's instruction, But a scoffer does not listen to rebuke.

Fools despise instruction of.
Prov 15:5 A fool despises his father's instruction, But he who receives correction is prudent.

Destruction on those who mock instruction of.
Prov 30:17 The eye *that* mocks *his* father, And scorns obedience to *his* mother, The ravens of the valley will pick it out, And the young eagles will eat it.

Are the glory of children.
Prov 17:6 Children's children *are* the crown of old men, And the glory of children *is* their father.

Are glad for wise children.
Prov 10:1 The proverbs of Solomon: A wise son makes a glad father, But a foolish son *is* the grief of his mother.

Are not to provoke their children.
Eph 6:4 And you, fathers, do not provoke your children to wrath, but bring them up in the training and admonition of the Lord.

Col 3:21 Fathers, do not provoke your children, lest they become discouraged.

Are respected if they correct their children.
Heb 12:9 Furthermore, we have had human fathers who corrected *us,* and we paid *them* respect. Shall we not much more readily be in subjection to the Father of spirits and live?

FEAR, GODLY
God is the object and author of.
Is 8:13 The LORD of hosts, Him you shall hallow; *Let* Him *be* your fear, And *let* Him *be* your dread.

Jer 32:39–40 then I will give them one heart and one way, that they may fear Me forever, for the good of them and their children after them. **40** And I will make an everlasting covenant with them, that I will not turn away from doing them good; but I will put My fear in their hearts so that they will not depart from Me.

Understood through Scripture.
Prov 2:3–5 Yes, if you cry out for discernment, *And* lift up your voice for understanding, **4** If you seek her as silver, And search for her as *for* hidden treasures; **5** Then you will understand the fear of the LORD, And find the knowledge of God.

Described as
The beginning of knowledge.

Prov 1:7 The fear of the LORD *is* the beginning of knowledge, *But* fools despise wisdom and instruction.

Prov 9:10 "The fear of the LORD *is* the beginning of wisdom, And the knowledge of the Holy One *is* understanding.

Prov 15:33 The fear of the LORD *is* the instruction of wisdom, And before honor *is* humility.

Hatred of evil.

Prov 8:13 The fear of the LORD *is* to hate evil; Pride and arrogance and the evil way And the perverse mouth I hate.

Wisdom.

Job 28:28 And to man He said, 'Behold, the fear of the Lord, that *is* wisdom, And to depart from evil *is* understanding.' "

Ps 111:10 The fear of the LORD *is* the beginning of wisdom; A good understanding have all those who do *His commandments.* His praise endures forever.

A treasure to saints.

Prov 15:16 Better *is* a little with the fear of the LORD, Than great treasure with trouble.

Is 33:6 Wisdom and knowledge will be the stability of your times, *And* the strength of salvation; The fear of the LORD *is* His treasure.

A fountain of life.

Prov 14:27 The fear of the LORD *is* a fountain of life, To turn *one* away from the snares of death.

Sanctifying.

Ps 19:9 The fear of the LORD *is* clean, enduring forever; The judgments of the LORD *are* true *and* righteous altogether.

Filial and reverential.

Heb 12:9 Furthermore, we have had human fathers who corrected *us,* and we paid *them* respect. Shall we not much more readily be in subjection to the Father of spirits and live?

Heb 12:28 Therefore, since we are receiving a kingdom which cannot be shaken, let us have grace, by which we may serve God acceptably with reverence and godly fear.

Commanded.
Deut 13:4 You shall walk after the LORD your God and fear Him, and keep His commandments and obey His voice; you shall serve Him and hold fast to Him.

Ps 2:11 Serve the Lord with fear, And rejoice with trembling.

Ps 22:23 You who fear the Lord, praise Him! All you descendants of Jacob, glorify Him, And fear Him, all you offspring of Israel!

Eccl 12:13 Let us hear the conclusion of the whole matter: Fear God and keep His commandments, For this is man's all.

1 Pet 2:17 Honor all *people*. Love the brotherhood. Fear God. Honor the king.

Motives to,

The holiness of God.

Rev 15:4 Who shall not fear You, O Lord, and glorify Your name? For *You* alone *are* holy. For all nations shall come and worship before You, For Your judgments have been manifested."

The greatness of God.

Deut 10:12 "And now, Israel, what does the Lord your God require of you, but to fear the Lord your God, to walk in all His ways and to love Him, to serve the Lord your God with all your heart and with all your soul,

Deut 10:17 For the Lord your God *is* God of gods and Lord of lords, the great God, mighty and awesome, who shows no partiality nor takes a bribe.

The goodness of God.

1 Sam 12:24 Only fear the Lord, and serve Him in truth with all your heart; for consider what great things He has done for you.

The forgiveness of God.

Ps 130:4 But *there is* forgiveness with You, That You may be feared.

Wondrous works of God.

Josh 4:23–24 for the Lord your God dried up the waters of the Jordan before you until you had crossed over, as the Lord your God did to the Red Sea, which He dried up before us until we had crossed over, **24** that all the peoples of the earth may know the hand of the Lord, that it *is* mighty, that you may fear the Lord your God forever."

Judgments of God.

Rev 14:7 saying with a loud voice, "Fear God and give glory to Him, for the hour of His judgment has come; and worship Him who made heaven and earth, the sea and springs of water."

A characteristic of believers.

Mal 3:16 Then those who feared the Lord spoke to one another, And the Lord listened and heard *them;* So a book of remembrance was written before Him For those who fear the Lord And who meditate on His name.

Necessary to

The worship of God.

Ps 5:7 But as for me, I will come into Your house in the multitude of Your mercy; In fear of You I will worship toward Your holy temple.

Ps 89:7 God is greatly to be feared in the assembly of the saints, And to be held in reverence by all *those* around Him.

The service of God.

Ps 2:11 Serve the Lord with fear, And rejoice with trembling.

Heb 12:28 Therefore, since we are receiving a kingdom which cannot be shaken, let us have grace, by which we may serve God acceptably with reverence and godly fear.

Avoiding of sin.

Ex 20:20 And Moses said to the people, "Do not fear; for God has come to test you, and that His fear may be before you, so that you may not sin."

Righteous government.

2 Sam 23:3 The God of Israel said, The Rock of Israel spoke to me: 'He who rules over men *must be* just, Ruling in the fear of God.

Impartial administration of justice.

2 Chr 19:6–9 and said to the judges, "Take heed to what you are doing, for you do not judge for man but for the Lord, who *is* with you in the judgment. **7** Now therefore, let the fear of the Lord be upon you; take care and do *it*, for *there is* no iniquity with the Lord our God, no partiality, nor taking of bribes." **8** Moreover in Jerusalem, for the judgment of the Lord and for controversies, Jehoshaphat appointed some of the Levites and priests, and some of the chief fathers of Israel, when they returned to Jerusalem. **9** And he commanded them, saying, "Thus you shall act in the fear of the Lord, faithfully and with a loyal heart:

Perfecting holiness.

2 Cor 7:1 Therefore, having these promises, beloved, let us cleanse ourselves from all filthiness of the flesh and spirit, perfecting holiness in the fear of God.

Those who have it

Give pleasure to God.

Ps 147:11 The Lord takes pleasure in those who fear Him, In those who hope in His mercy.

Are pitied by God.

Ps 103:13 As a father pities *his* children, *So* the Lord pities those who fear Him.

Are accepted by God.

Acts 10:35 But in every nation whoever fears Him and works righteousness is accepted by Him.

Receive mercy from God.

Ps 103:11 For as the heavens are high above the earth, *So* great is His mercy toward those who fear Him;

Ps 103:17 But the mercy of the Lord *is* from everlasting to everlasting On those who fear Him, And His righteousness to children's children,

Luke 1:50 And His mercy *is* on those who fear Him From generation to generation.

Are blessed.

Ps 112:1 Praise the Lord! Blessed *is* the man *who* fears the Lord, *Who* delights greatly in His commandments.

Ps 115:13 He will bless those who fear the Lord, *Both* small and great.

Confide in God.

Ps 115:11 You who fear the Lord, trust in the Lord; He *is* their help and their shield.

Prov 14:26 In the fear of the Lord *there is* strong confidence, And His children will have a place of refuge.

Depart from evil.

Prov 16:6 In mercy and truth Atonement is provided for iniquity; And by the fear of the Lord *one* departs from evil.

Converse together of holy things.

Mal 3:16 Then those who feared the Lord spoke to one another, And the Lord listened and heard *them;* So a book of remembrance was written before Him For those who fear the Lord And who meditate on His name.

Should not fear man.

Is 8:12–13 "Do not say, 'A conspiracy,' Concerning all that this people call a conspiracy, Nor be afraid of their threats, nor be troubled. **13** The Lord of hosts, Him you shall hallow; *Let* Him *be* your fear, And *let* Him *be* your dread.

Matt 10:28 And do not fear those who kill the body but cannot kill the soul. But rather fear Him who is able to destroy both soul and body in hell.

Desires of, fulfilled by God.

Ps 145:19 He will fulfill the desire of those who fear Him; He also will hear their cry and save them.

Days of, prolonged.

Prov 10:27 The fear of the Lord prolongs days, But the years of the wicked will be shortened.

Should be

Prayed for.

Ps 86:11 Teach me Your way, O Lord; I will walk in Your truth; Unite my heart to fear Your name.

Exhibited in our service.

Col 3:22 Bondservants, obey in all things your masters according to the flesh, not with eyeservice, as menpleasers, but in sincerity of heart, fearing God.

Exhibited in giving a reason for our hope.

1 Pet 3:15 But sanctify the Lord God in your hearts, and always *be* ready to *give* a defense to everyone who asks you a reason for the hope that is in you, with meekness and fear;

Constantly maintained.

Deut 14:23 And you shall eat before the Lord your God, in the place where He chooses to make His name abide, the tithe of your grain and your new wine and your oil, of the firstborn of your herds and your flocks, that you may learn to fear the Lord your God always.

Josh 4:24 that all the peoples of the earth may know the hand of the Lord, that it *is* mighty, that you may fear the Lord your God forever."

Prov 23:17 Do not let your heart envy sinners, But *be* zealous for the fear of the Lord all the day;

Taught to others.

Ps 34:11 Come, you children, listen to me; I will teach you the fear of the Lord.

Advantages of.

Prov 15:16 Better *is* a little with the fear of the Lord, Than great treasure with trouble.

Prov 19:23 The fear of the Lord *leads* to life, And *he who has it* will abide in satisfaction; He will not be visited with evil.

Eccl 8:12–13 Though a sinner does evil a hundred *times,* and his *days* are prolonged, yet I surely know that it will be well with those who fear God, who fear before Him. **13** But it will not be well with the wicked; nor will he prolong *his* days, *which are* as a shadow, because he does not fear before God.

The wicked destitute of.

Ps 36:1 An oracle within my heart concerning the transgression of the wicked: *There is* no fear of God before his eyes.

Prov 1:29 Because they hated knowledge And did not choose the fear of the Lord,

Jer 2:19 Your own wickedness will correct you, And your backslidings will rebuke you. Know therefore and see that *it is* an evil and bitter *thing* That you have forsaken the Lord your God, And the fear of Me *is* not in you," Says the Lord God of hosts.

Rom 3:18 *"There is no fear of God before their eyes."*

Exemplified by

Abraham.

Gen 22:12 And He said, "Do not lay your hand on the lad, or do anything to him; for now I know that you fear God, since you have not withheld your son, your only *son,* from Me."

Joseph.

Gen 39:9 *There is* no one greater in this house than I, nor has he kept back anything from me but you, because you *are* his wife. How then can I do this great wickedness, and sin against God?"

Gen 42:18 Then Joseph said to them the third day, "Do this and live, *for* I fear God:

Obadiah.

1 Kin 18:12 And it shall come to pass, *as soon as* I am gone from you, that the Spirit of the Lord will carry you to a place I do not know; so when I go and tell Ahab, and he cannot find you, he will kill me. But I your servant have feared the Lord from my youth.

Nehemiah.

Neh 5:15 But the former governors who *were* before me laid burdens on the people, and took from them bread and wine, besides forty shekels of silver. Yes, even their servants bore rule over the people, but I did not do so, because of the fear of God.

Job.

Job 1:1 There was a man in the land of Uz, whose name *was* Job; and that man was blameless and upright, and one who feared God and shunned evil.

Job 1:8 Then the Lord said to Satan, "Have you considered My servant Job, that *there is* none like him on the earth, a blameless and upright man, one who fears God and shuns evil?"

Christians.

Acts 9:31 Then the churches throughout all Judea, Galilee, and Samaria had peace and were edified. And walking in the fear of the Lord and in the comfort of the Holy Spirit, they were multiplied.

Cornelius.

Acts 10:2 a devout *man* and one who feared God with all his household, who gave alms generously to the people, and prayed to God always.

Noah.

Heb 11:7 By faith Noah, being divinely warned of things not yet seen, moved with godly fear, prepared an ark for the saving of his household, by which he condemned the world and became heir of the righteousness which is according to faith.

FEAR, UNHOLY

A characteristic of the wicked.

Rev 21:8 But the cowardly, unbelieving, abominable, murderers, sexually immoral, sorcerers, idolaters, and all liars shall have their part in the lake which burns with fire and brimstone, which is the second death."

Descriptions of,

A fear of idols.

2 Kin 17:38 And the covenant that I have made with you, you shall not forget, nor shall you fear other gods.

A fear of man.

1 Sam 15:24 Then Saul said to Samuel, "I have sinned, for I have transgressed the commandment of the LORD and your words, because I feared the people and obeyed their voice.

John 9:22 His parents said these *things* because they feared the Jews, for the Jews had agreed already that if anyone confessed *that* He *was* Christ, he would be put out of the synagogue.

A fear of judgments.

Is 2:19 They shall go into the holes of the rocks, And into the caves of the earth, From the terror of the LORD And the glory of His majesty, When He arises to shake the earth mightily.

Luke 21:26 men's hearts failing them from fear and the expectation of those things which are coming on the earth, for the powers of the heavens will be shaken.

Rev 6:16–17 and said to the mountains and rocks, "Fall on us and hide us from the face of Him who sits on the throne and from the wrath of the Lamb! **17** For the great day of His wrath has come, and who is able to stand?"

A fear of future punishment.

Heb 10:27 but a certain fearful expectation of judgment, and fiery indignation which will devour the adversaries.

Overwhelming.

Ex 15:16 Fear and dread will fall on them; By the greatness of Your arm They will be *as* still as a stone, Till Your people pass over, O LORD, Till the people pass over Whom You have purchased.

Job 15:21 Dreadful sounds *are* in his ears; In prosperity the destroyer comes upon him.

Job 15:24 Trouble and anguish make him afraid; They overpower him, like a king ready for battle.

Consuming.

Ps 73:19 Oh, how they are *brought* to desolation, as in a moment! They are utterly consumed with terrors.

A guilty conscience leads to.

Gen 3:8 And they heard the sound of the LORD God walking in the garden in the cool of the day, and Adam and his wife hid themselves from the presence of the LORD God among the trees of the garden.

Gen 3:10 So he said, "I heard Your voice in the garden, and I was afraid because I was naked; and I hid myself."

Ps 53:5 There they are in great fear *Where* no fear was, For God has scattered the bones of him who encamps against you; You have put *them* to shame, Because God has despised them.

Prov 28:1 The wicked flee when no one pursues, But the righteous are bold as a lion.

Seizes the wicked.

Job 15:24 Trouble and anguish make him afraid; They overpower him, like a king ready for battle.

Job 18:11 Terrors frighten him on every side, And drive him to his feet.

Surprises the hypocrite.

Is 33:14 The sinners in Zion are afraid; Fearfulness has seized the hypocrites: "Who among us shall dwell with the devouring fire? Who among us shall dwell with everlasting burnings?"

Is 33:18 Your heart will meditate on terror: "Where *is* the scribe? Where *is* he who weighs? Where *is* he who counts the towers?"

The wicked judicially filled with.

Lev 26:16–17 I also will do this to you: I will even appoint terror over you, wasting disease and fever which shall consume the eyes and cause sorrow of heart. And you shall sow your seed in vain, for your enemies shall eat it. **17** I will set My face against you, and you shall be defeated by your enemies. Those who hate you shall reign over you, and you shall flee when no one pursues you.

Deut 28:65–67 And among those nations you shall find no rest, nor shall the sole of your foot have a resting place; but there the LORD will give you a trembling heart, failing eyes, and anguish of soul. **66** Your life shall hang in doubt before you; you shall fear day and night, and have no assurance of life. **67** In the morning you shall say, 'Oh, that it were evening!' And at evening you shall say, 'Oh, that it were morning!' because of the fear which terrifies your heart, and because of the sight which your eyes see.

Jer 49:5 Behold, I will bring fear upon you," Says the Lord GOD of hosts, "From all those who are around you; You shall be driven out, everyone headlong, And no one will gather those who wander off.

Certain for unbelievers.

Prov 1:27 When your terror comes like a storm, And your destruction comes like a whirlwind, When distress and anguish come upon you.

Prov 10:24 The fear of the wicked will come upon him, And the desire of the righteous will be granted.

God mocks.

Prov 1:26 I also will laugh at your calamity; I will mock when your terror comes,

Believers sometimes tempted to.

Ps 55:5 Fearfulness and trembling have come upon me, And horror has overwhelmed me.

Believers delivered from.

Prov 1:33 But whoever listens to me will dwell safely, And will be secure, without fear of evil."

Is 14:3 It shall come to pass in the day the LORD gives

you rest from your sorrow, and from your fear and the hard bondage in which you were made to serve,

1 John 4:18 There is no fear in love; but perfect love casts out fear, because fear involves torment. But he who fears has not been made perfect in love.

Trust in God, a preservative from.

Ps 27:1 The LORD *is* my light and my salvation; Whom shall I fear? The LORD *is* the strength of my life; Of whom shall I be afraid?

Exhortations against.

Is 8:12 "Do not say, 'A conspiracy,' Concerning all that this people call a conspiracy, Nor be afraid of their threats, nor be troubled.

John 14:27 Peace I leave with you, My peace I give to you; not as the world gives do I give to you. Let not your heart be troubled, neither let it be afraid.

2 Tim 1:7–8 For God has not given us a spirit of fear, but of power and of love and of a sound mind. 8 Therefore do not be ashamed of the testimony of our Lord, nor of me His prisoner, but share with me in the sufferings for the gospel according to the power of God,

Illustrated by

Adam.

Gen 3:10 So he said, "I heard Your voice in the garden, and I was afraid because I was naked; and I hid myself."

Cain.

Gen 4:14 Surely You have driven me out this day from the face of the ground; I shall be hidden from Your face; I shall be a fugitive and a vagabond on the earth, and it will happen *that* anyone who finds me will kill me."

The Midianites.

Judg 7:21–22 And every man stood in his place all around the camp; and the whole army ran and cried out and fled. 22 When the three hundred blew the trumpets, the LORD set every man's sword against his companion throughout the whole camp; and the army fled to Beth Acacia, toward Zererah, as far as the border of Abel Meholah, by Tabbath.

The Philistines.

1 Sam 14:15 And there was trembling in the camp, in the field, and among all the people. The garrison and the raiders also trembled; and the earth quaked, so that it was a very great trembling.

Saul.

1 Sam 28:5 When Saul saw the army of the Philistines, he was afraid, and his heart trembled greatly.

1 Sam 28:20 Immediately Saul fell full length on the ground, and was dreadfully afraid because of the words of Samuel. And there was no strength in him, for he had eaten no food all day or all night.

Adonijah's guests.

1 Kin 1:49 So all the guests who were with Adonijah were afraid, and arose, and each one went his way.

Haman.

Esth 7:6 And Esther said, "The adversary and enemy *is* this wicked Haman!" So Haman was terrified before the king and queen.

Ahaz.

Is 7:2 And it was told to the house of David, saying, "Syria's forces are deployed in Ephraim." So his heart and the heart of his people were moved as the trees of the woods are moved with the wind.

Belshazzar.

Dan 5:6 Then the king's countenance changed, and his thoughts troubled him, so that the joints of his hips were loosened and his knees knocked against each other.

Pilate.

John 19:8 Therefore, when Pilate heard that saying, he was the more afraid,

Felix.

Acts 24:25 Now as he reasoned about righteousness, self-control, and the judgment to come, Felix was afraid and answered, "Go away for now; when I have a convenient time I will call for you."

FEAST OF DEDICATION, THE

To commemorate the cleansing of the temple after its defilement by Antiochus.

Dan 11:31 And forces shall be mustered by him, and they shall defile the sanctuary fortress; then they shall take away the daily *sacrifices,* and place *there* the abomination of desolation.

Held in the winter month, Chislev.

John 10:22 Now it was the Feast of Dedication in Jerusalem, and it was winter.

FEAST OF THE NEW MOON, THE

Held first day of the month.

Num 10:10 Also in the day of your gladness, in your appointed feasts, and at the beginning of your months, you shall blow the trumpets over your burnt offerings and over the sacrifices of your peace offerings; and they shall be a memorial for you before your God: I *am* the LORD your God."

Celebrated with blowing of trumpets.

Num 10:10 Also in the day of your gladness, in your appointed feasts, and at the beginning of your months, you shall blow the trumpets over your burnt offerings and over the sacrifices of your peace offerings; and they shall be a memorial for you before your God: I *am* the LORD your God."

Ps 81:3–4 Blow the trumpet at the time of the New Moon, At the full moon, on our solemn feast day. 4 For this *is* a statute for Israel, A law of the God of Jacob.

Sacrifices at.

Num 28:11–15 'At the beginnings of your months you shall present a burnt offering to the LORD: two young bulls, one ram, and seven lambs in their first year, without blemish; 12 three-tenths *of an ephah* of fine flour as a grain offering, mixed with oil, for each bull; two-tenths *of an ephah* of fine flour as a grain offering, mixed with oil, for the one ram; 13 and one-tenth *of an ephah* of fine flour, mixed with oil, as a grain offering for each lamb, as a burnt offering of sweet aroma, an offering made by fire to the LORD. 14 Their drink offering shall be half a hin of wine for a bull, one-third of a hin for a ram, and one-fourth of a hin for a lamb; this *is* the burnt offering for each month throughout the months of the year. **15** Also one kid of the goats as a sin offering to the LORD shall be offered, besides the regular burnt offering and its drink offering.

A season for

Inquiring of God's messengers.

2 Kin 4:23 So he said, "Why are you going to him today? *It is* neither the New Moon nor the Sabbath." And she said, "*It is* well."

Worship in God's house.

Is 66:23 And it shall come to pass *That* from one New Moon to another, And from one Sabbath to another, All flesh shall come to worship before Me," says the LORD.

Ezek 46:1 'Thus says the Lord GOD: "The gateway of the inner court that faces toward the east shall be shut the six working days; but on the Sabbath it shall be opened, and on the day of the New Moon it shall be opened.

Celebrations.

1 Sam 20:5 And David said to Jonathan, "Indeed tomorrow *is* the New Moon, and I should not fail to sit with the king to eat. But let me go, that I may hide in the field until the third *day* at evening.

1 Sam 20:18 Then Jonathan said to David, "Tomorrow *is* the New Moon; and you will be missed, because your seat will be empty.

Observed with great solemnity.

1 Chr 23:31 and at every presentation of a burnt offering to the LORD on the Sabbaths and on the New Moons and on the set feasts, by number according to the ordinance governing them, regularly before the LORD;

2 Chr 2:4 Behold, I am building a temple for the name of the LORD my God, to dedicate *it* to Him, to burn before Him sweet incense, for the continual showbread, for the burnt offerings morning and evening, on the Sabbaths, on the New Moons, and on the set feasts of the LORD our God. This *is an ordinance* forever for Israel.

2 Chr 8:13 according to the daily rate, offering according to the commandment of Moses, for the Sabbaths, the New Moons, and the three appointed yearly feasts—the Feast of Unleavened Bread, the Feast of Weeks, and the Feast of Tabernacles.

2 Chr 31:3 The king also *appointed* a portion of his possessions for the burnt offerings: for the morning and evening burnt offerings, the burnt offerings for the Sabbaths and the New Moons and the set feasts, as *it is* written in the Law of the LORD.

Restored after captivity.

Ezra 3:5 Afterwards *they offered* the regular burnt offering, and *those* for New Moons and for all the appointed feasts of the LORD that were consecrated, and *those* of everyone who willingly offered a freewill offering to the LORD.

Neh 10:33 for the showbread, for the regular grain offering, for the regular burnt offering of the Sabbaths, the New Moons, and the set feasts; for the holy things, for the sin offerings to make atonement for Israel, and all the work of the house of our God.

Mere outward observance of, hateful to God.

Is 1:13–14 Bring no more futile sacrifices; Incense is an abomination to Me. The New Moons, the Sabbaths, and the calling of assemblies— I cannot endure iniquity and the sacred meeting. **14** Your New Moons and your appointed feasts My soul hates; They are a trouble to Me, I am weary of bearing *them.*

Disliked by the ungodly.

Amos 8:5 Saying: "When will the New Moon be past, That we may sell grain? And the Sabbath, That we may trade wheat? Making the ephah small and the shekel large, Falsifying the scales by deceit,

The Jews deprived of, for sin.

Hos 2:11 I will also cause all her mirth to cease, Her feast days, Her New Moons, Her Sabbaths— All her appointed feasts.

Observance of, by Christians, unnecessary.

Gal 4:9–10 But now after you have known God, or rather are known by God, how *is it that* you turn again to the weak and beggarly elements, to which you desire again to be in bondage? **10** You observe days and months and seasons and years.

Col 2:16 So let no one judge you in food or in drink, or regarding a festival or a new moon or sabbaths,

FEAST OF THE PASSOVER, THE

Ordained by God.

Ex 12:1–2 Now the LORD spoke to Moses and Aaron in the land of Egypt, saying, **2** "This month *shall be* your beginning of months; it *shall be* the first month of the year to you.

Commenced the fourteenth day of the first month at twilight.

Ex 12:2 "This month *shall be* your beginning of months; it *shall be* the first month of the year to you.

Ex 12:6 Now you shall keep it until the fourteenth day of the same month. Then the whole assembly of the congregation of Israel shall kill it at twilight.

Ex 12:18 In the first *month,* on the fourteenth day of the month at evening, you shall eat unleavened bread, until the twenty-first day of the month at evening.

Lev 23:5 On the fourteenth *day* of the first month at twilight *is* the LORD's Passover.

Num 9:3 On the fourteenth day of this month, at twilight, you shall keep it at its appointed time. According to all its rites and ceremonies you shall keep it."

Lasted seven days.

Ex 12:15 Seven days you shall eat unleavened bread. On the first day you shall remove leaven from your houses. For whoever eats leavened bread from the first day until the seventh day, that person shall be cut off from Israel.

Lev 23:6 And on the fifteenth day of the same month *is* the Feast of Unleavened Bread to the LORD; seven days you must eat unleavened bread.

Various names for,

Passover.

Num 9:5 And they kept the Passover on the fourteenth day of the first month, at twilight, in the Wilderness of Sinai; according to all that the LORD commanded Moses, so the children of Israel did.

John 2:23 Now when He was in Jerusalem at the Passover, during the feast, many believed in His name when they saw the signs which He did.

Jew's Passover.

John 2:13 Now the Passover of the Jews was at hand, and Jesus went up to Jerusalem.

John 11:55 And the Passover of the Jews was near, and many went from the country up to Jerusalem before the Passover, to purify themselves.

Lord's Passover.

Ex 12:11 And thus you shall eat it: *with* a belt on your waist, your sandals on your feet, and your staff in your hand. So you shall eat it in haste. It *is* the LORD's Passover.

Ex 12:27 that you shall say, 'It *is* the Passover sacrifice of the LORD, who passed over the houses of the children of Israel in Egypt when He struck the Egyptians and delivered our households.' " So the people bowed their heads and worshiped.

Feast of Unleavened Bread.

Mark 14:1 After two days it was the Passover and *the Feast* of Unleavened Bread. And the chief priests and the scribes sought how they might take Him by trickery and put *Him* to death.

Luke 22:1 Now the Feast of Unleavened Bread drew near, which is called Passover.

Days of Unleavened Bread.

Acts 12:3 And because he saw that it pleased the Jews, he proceeded further to seize Peter also. Now it was *during* the Days of Unleavened Bread.

Acts 20:6 But we sailed away from Philippi after the Days of Unleavened Bread, and in five days joined them at Troas, where we stayed seven days.

All males to appear at.

Ex 23:17 "Three times in the year all your males shall appear before the Lord GOD.

Deut 16:16 "Three times a year all your males shall appear before the LORD your God in the place which He chooses: at the Feast of Unleavened Bread, at the Feast of Weeks, and at the Feast of Tabernacles; and they shall not appear before the LORD empty-handed.

Paschal lamb eaten first day of.

Ex 12:6 Now you shall keep it until the fourteenth day of the same month. Then the whole assembly of the congregation of Israel shall kill it at twilight.

Ex 12:8 Then they shall eat the flesh on that night; roasted in fire, with unleavened bread *and* with bitter *herbs* they shall eat it.

Unleavened bread eaten at.

Ex 12:15 Seven days you shall eat unleavened bread. On the first day you shall remove leaven from your houses. For whoever eats leavened bread from the first day until the seventh day, that person shall be cut off from Israel.

Deut 16:3 You shall eat no leavened bread with it; seven days you shall eat unleavened bread with it, *that is,* the bread of affliction (for you came out of the land of Egypt in haste), that you may remember the day in which you came out of the land of Egypt all the days of your life.

Leaven

Not to be in Jewish houses during.

Ex 12:19 For seven days no leaven shall be found in your houses, since whoever eats what is leavened, that same person shall be cut off from the congregation of Israel, whether *he is* a stranger or a native of the land.

Not to be in any of their quarters.

Ex 13:7 Unleavened bread shall be eaten seven days. And no leavened bread shall be seen among you, nor shall leaven be seen among you in all your quarters.

Deut 16:4 And no leaven shall be seen among you in all your territory for seven days, nor shall *any* of the meat which you sacrifice the first day at twilight remain overnight until morning.

Nothing with, to be eaten.

Ex 12:20 You shall eat nothing leavened; in all your dwellings you shall eat unleavened bread.' "

Punishment for eating.

Ex 12:15 Seven days you shall eat unleavened bread. On the first day you shall remove leaven from your houses. For whoever eats leavened bread from the first day until the seventh day, that person shall be cut off from Israel.

Ex 12:19 For seven days no leaven shall be found in your houses, since whoever eats what is leavened, that same person shall be cut off from the congregation of Israel, whether *he is* a stranger or a native of the land.

First and last days of, holy convocations.

Ex 12:16 On the first day *there shall be* a holy convocation, and on the seventh day there shall be a holy convocation for you. No manner of work shall be done on them; but *that* which everyone must eat—that only may be prepared by you.

Num 28:18 On the first day *you shall have* a holy convocation. You shall do no customary work.

Num 28:25 And on the seventh day you shall have a holy convocation. You shall do no customary work.

Sacrifices during.

Lev 23:8 But you shall offer an offering made by fire to the LORD for seven days. The seventh day *shall be* a holy convocation; you shall do no customary work *on it.*' "

Lev 23:10–14 "Speak to the children of Israel, and say to them: 'When you come into the land which I give to you, and reap its harvest, then you shall bring a sheaf of the firstfruits of your harvest to the priest. 11 He shall wave the sheaf before the LORD, to be accepted on your behalf; on the day after the Sabbath the priest shall wave it. 12 And you shall offer on that day, when you wave the sheaf, a male lamb of the first year, without blemish, as a burnt offering to the LORD. 13 Its grain offering *shall be* two-tenths *of an ephah* of fine flour mixed with oil, an offering made by fire to the LORD, for a sweet aroma; and its drink offering *shall be* of wine, one-fourth of a hin. 14 You shall eat neither bread nor parched grain nor fresh grain until the same day that you have brought an offering to your God; *it shall be* a statute forever throughout your generations in all your dwellings.

Num 28:19–24 And you shall present an offering made

by fire as a burnt offering to the LORD: two young bulls, one ram, and seven lambs in their first year. Be sure they are without blemish. **20** Their grain offering shall be of fine flour mixed with oil: three-tenths *of an ephah* you shall offer for a bull, and two-tenths for a ram; **21** you shall offer one-tenth *of an ephah* for each of the seven lambs; **22** also one goat *as* a sin offering, to make atonement for you. **23** You shall offer these besides the burnt offering of the morning, which *is* for a regular burnt offering. **24** In this manner you shall offer the food of the offering made by fire daily for seven days, as a sweet aroma to the LORD; it shall be offered besides the regular burnt offering and its drink offering.

Its commemorations,

Passing over the firstborn.

Ex 12:12–13 'For I will pass through the land of Egypt on that night, and will strike all the firstborn in the land of Egypt, both man and beast; and against all the gods of Egypt I will execute judgment: I *am* the LORD. **13** Now the blood shall be a sign for you on the houses where you *are*. And when I see the blood, I will pass over you; and the plague shall not be on you to destroy *you* when I strike the land of Egypt.

Deliverance of Israel from bondage of Egypt.

Ex 12:17 So you shall observe *the Feast of* Unleavened Bread, for on this same day I will have brought your armies out of the land of Egypt. Therefore you shall observe this day throughout your generations as an everlasting ordinance.

Ex 12:42 It *is* a night of solemn observance to the LORD for bringing them out of the land of Egypt. This *is* that night of the LORD, a solemn observance for all the children of Israel throughout their generations.

Ex 13:9 It shall be as a sign to you on your hand and as a memorial between your eyes, that the LORD's law may be in your mouth; for with a strong hand the LORD has brought you out of Egypt.

Deut 16:3 You shall eat no leavened bread with it; seven days you shall eat unleavened bread with it, *that is,* the bread of affliction (for you came out of the land of Egypt in haste), that you may remember the day in which you came out of the land of Egypt all the days of your life.

To be perpetually observed during the Mosaic age.

Ex 12:14 'So this day shall be to you a memorial; and you shall keep it as a feast to the LORD throughout your generations. You shall keep it as a feast by an everlasting ordinance.

Ex 13:10 You shall therefore keep this ordinance in its season from year to year.

Children to be taught the nature and design of.

Ex 12:26–27 And it shall be, when your children say to you, 'What do you mean by this service?' **27** that you shall say, 'It *is* the Passover sacrifice of the LORD, who passed over the houses of the children of Israel in Egypt when He struck the Egyptians and delivered our households.' " So the people bowed their heads and worshiped.

Ex 13:8 And you shall tell your son in that day, saying, 'This *is done* because of what the LORD did for me when I came up from Egypt.'

Purification necessary for the proper observance of.

2 Chr 30:15–19 Then they slaughtered the Passover *lambs* on the fourteenth *day* of the second month. The priests and the Levites were ashamed, and sanctified themselves, and brought the burnt offerings to the house of the LORD. **16** They stood in their place according to their custom, according to the Law of Moses the man of God; the priests sprinkled the blood *received* from the hand of the Levites. **17** For *there were* many in the assembly who had not sanctified themselves; therefore the Levites had charge of the slaughter of the Passover *lambs* for everyone *who was* not clean, to sanctify *them* to the LORD. **18** For a multitude of the people, many from Ephraim, Manasseh, Issachar, and Zebulun, had not cleansed themselves, yet they ate the Passover contrary to what was written. But Hezekiah prayed for them, saying, "May the good LORD provide atonement for everyone **19** *who* prepares his heart to seek God, the LORD God of his fathers, though *he is* not *cleansed* according to the purification of the sanctuary."

John 11:55 And the Passover of the Jews was near, and many went from the country up to Jerusalem before the Passover, to purify themselves.

Those who were unclean could celebrate later.

Num 9:6–11 Now there were *certain* men who were defiled by a human corpse, so that they could not keep the Passover on that day; and they came before Moses and Aaron that day. **7** And those men said to him, "We *became* defiled by a human corpse. Why are we kept from presenting the offering of the LORD at its appointed time among the children of Israel?" **8** And Moses said to them, "Stand still, that I may hear what the LORD will command concerning you." **9** Then the LORD spoke to Moses, saying, **10** "Speak to the children of Israel, saying: 'If anyone of you or your posterity is unclean because of a corpse, or *is* far away on a journey, he may still keep the LORD's Passover. **11** On the fourteenth day of the second month, at twilight, they may keep it. They shall eat it with unleavened bread and bitter herbs.

2 Chr 30:2–3 For the king and his leaders and all the assembly in Jerusalem had agreed to keep the Passover in the second month. **3** For they could not keep it at the regular time, because a sufficient number of priests had not consecrated themselves, nor had the people gathered together at Jerusalem.

2 Chr 30:15 Then they slaughtered the Passover *lambs* on the fourteenth *day* of the second month. The priests and the Levites were ashamed, and sanctified themselves, and brought the burnt offerings to the house of the LORD.

No uncircumcised person to keep.

Ex 12:43 And the LORD said to Moses and Aaron, "This *is* the ordinance of the Passover: No foreigner shall eat it.

Ex 12:45 A sojourner and a hired servant shall not eat it.

Strangers and servants, when circumcised, might keep.

Ex 12:44 But every man's servant who is bought for money, when you have circumcised him, then he may eat it.

Ex 12:48 And when a stranger dwells with you *and wants* to keep the Passover to the LORD, let all his males be circumcised, and then let him come near and keep it; and he shall be as a native of the land. For no uncircumcised person shall eat it.

Neglect of, punished with death.

Num 9:13 But the man who *is* clean and is not on a journey, and ceases to keep the Passover, that same person shall be cut off from among his people, because he did not bring the offering of the LORD at its appointed time; that man shall bear his sin.

Improper keeping of, punished.

2 Chr 30:18 For a multitude of the people, many from Ephraim, Manasseh, Issachar, and Zebulun, had not cleansed themselves, yet they ate the Passover contrary to what was written. But Hezekiah prayed for them, saying, "May the good LORD provide atonement for everyone

2 Chr 30:20 And the LORD listened to Hezekiah and healed the people.

Remarkable celebrations of,

On leaving Egypt.

Ex 12:28 Then the children of Israel went away and did *so;* just as the LORD had commanded Moses and Aaron, so they did.

Ex 12:50 Thus all the children of Israel did; as the LORD commanded Moses and Aaron, so they did.

In the wilderness of Sinai.

Num 9:3–5 On the fourteenth day of this month, at twilight, you shall keep it at its appointed time. According to all its rites and ceremonies you shall keep it." **4** So Moses told the children of Israel that they should keep the Passover. **5** And they kept the Passover on the fourteenth day of the first month, at twilight, in the Wilderness of Sinai; according to all that the LORD commanded Moses, so the children of Israel did.

On entering the land of promise.

Josh 5:10–11 Now the children of Israel camped in Gilgal, and kept the Passover on the fourteenth day of the month at twilight on the plains of Jericho. **11** And they ate of the produce of the land on the day after the Passover, unleavened bread and parched grain, on the very same day.

In Hezekiah's reign.

2 Chr 30:1 And Hezekiah sent to all Israel and Judah, and also wrote letters to Ephraim and Manasseh, that they should come to the house of the LORD at Jerusalem, to keep the Passover to the LORD God of Israel.

In Josiah's reign.

2 Kin 23:22–23 Such a Passover surely had never been held since the days of the judges who judged Israel, nor in all the days of the kings of Israel and the kings of Judah. **23** But in the eighteenth year of King Josiah this Passover was held before the LORD in Jerusalem.

2 Chr 35:1 Now Josiah kept a Passover to the LORD in Jerusalem, and they slaughtered the Passover *lambs* on the fourteenth *day* of the first month.

2 Chr 35:18 There had been no Passover kept in Israel like that since the days of Samuel the prophet; and none of the kings of Israel had kept such a Passover as Josiah kept, with the priests and the Levites, all Ju-

dah and Israel who were present, and the inhabitants of Jerusalem.

After the captivity.

Ezra 6:19–20 And the descendants of the captivity kept the Passover on the fourteenth *day* of the first month. **20** For the priests and the Levites had purified themselves; all of them *were ritually* clean. And they slaughtered the Passover *lambs* for all the descendants of the captivity, for their brethren the priests, and for themselves.

Before the death of Christ.

Luke 22:15 Then He said to them, "With *fervent* desire I have desired to eat this Passover with you before I suffer;

Moses kept through faith.

Heb 11:28 By faith he kept the Passover and the sprinkling of blood, lest he who destroyed the firstborn should touch them.

Christ always observed.

Matt 26:17–20 Now on the first *day of the Feast* of Unleavened Bread the disciples came to Jesus, saying to Him, "Where do You want us to prepare for You to eat the Passover?" **18** And He said, "Go into the city to a certain man, and say to him, 'The Teacher says, "My time is at hand; I will keep the Passover at your house with My disciples." ' " **19** So the disciples did as Jesus had directed them; and they prepared the Passover. **20** When evening had come, He sat down with the twelve.

Luke 22:15 Then He said to them, "With *fervent* desire I have desired to eat this Passover with you before I suffer;

John 2:13 Now the Passover of the Jews was at hand, and Jesus went up to Jerusalem.

John 2:23 Now when He was in Jerusalem at the Passover, during the feast, many believed in His name when they saw the signs which He did.

The people of Jerusalem lent their rooms to strangers for.

Luke 22:11–12 Then you shall say to the master of the house, 'The Teacher says to you, "Where is the guest room where I may eat the Passover with My disciples?" ' **12** Then he will show you a large, furnished upper room; there make ready."

The Lord's Supper instituted at.

Matt 26:26–28 And as they were eating, Jesus took bread, blessed and broke *it,* and gave *it* to the disciples and said, "Take, eat; this is My body." **27** Then He took the cup, and gave thanks, and gave *it* to them, saying, "Drink from it, all of you. **28** For this is My blood of the new covenant, which is shed for many for the remission of sins.

Custom of releasing a prisoner at.

Matt 27:15 Now at the feast the governor was accustomed to releasing to the multitude one prisoner whom they wished.

Luke 23:16–17 I will therefore chastise Him and release *Him*" **17** (for it was necessary for him to release one to them at the feast).

The Sabbath in, a high day.

John 19:31 Therefore, because it was the Preparation

Day, that the bodies should not remain on the cross on the Sabbath (for that Sabbath was a high day), the Jews asked Pilate that their legs might be broken, and *that* they might be taken away.

The day before the Sabbath in, called the Preparation Day.

John 19:14 Now it was the Preparation Day of the Passover, and about the sixth hour. And he said to the Jews, "Behold your King!"

John 19:31 Therefore, because it was the Preparation *Day*, that the bodies should not remain on the cross on the Sabbath (for that Sabbath was a high day), the Jews asked Pilate that their legs might be broken, and *that* they might be taken away.

Illustrative of redemption through Christ.

1 Cor 5:7–8 Therefore purge out the old leaven, that you may be a new lump, since you truly are unleavened. For indeed Christ, our Passover, was sacrificed for us. **8** Therefore let us keep the feast, not with old leaven, nor with the leaven of malice and wickedness, but with the unleavened *bread* of sincerity and truth.

FEAST OF PENTECOST, THE

Held fiftieth day after offering first sheaf of new grain harvest.

Lev 23:15–16 'And you shall count for yourselves from the day after the Sabbath, from the day that you brought the sheaf of the wave offering: seven Sabbaths shall be completed. **16** Count fifty days to the day after the seventh Sabbath; then you shall offer a new grain offering to the LORD.

Deut 16:9 "You shall count seven weeks for yourself; begin to count the seven weeks from *the time* you begin to *put* the sickle to the grain.

Other names for,

Feast of harvest.

Ex 23:16 and the Feast of Harvest, the firstfruits of your labors which you have sown in the field; and the Feast of Ingathering at the end of the year, when you have gathered in *the fruit of* your labors from the field.

Feast of weeks.

Ex 34:22 "And you shall observe the Feast of Weeks, of the firstfruits of wheat harvest, and the Feast of Ingathering at the year's end.

Deut 16:10 Then you shall keep the Feast of Weeks to the LORD your God with the tribute of a freewill offering from your hand, which you shall give as the LORD your God blesses you.

Day of the firstfruits.

Num 28:26 'Also on the day of the firstfruits, when you bring a new grain offering to the LORD at your *Feast of* Weeks, you shall have a holy convocation. You shall do no customary work.

Day of Pentecost.

Acts 2:1 When the Day of Pentecost had fully come, they were all with one accord in one place.

To be perpetually observed.

Lev 23:21 And you shall proclaim on the same day *that* it is a holy convocation to you. You shall do no customary work *on it. It shall be* a statute forever in all your dwellings throughout your generations.

All males to attend.

Ex 23:16–17 and the Feast of Harvest, the firstfruits of your labors which you have sown in the field; and the Feast of Ingathering at the end of the year, when you have gathered in *the fruit of* your labors from the field. **17** "Three times in the year all your males shall appear before the Lord GOD.

Deut 16:16 "Three times a year all your males shall appear before the LORD your God in the place which He chooses: at the Feast of Unleavened Bread, at the Feast of Weeks, and at the Feast of Tabernacles; and they shall not appear before the LORD empty-handed.

A holy convocation.

Lev 23:21 And you shall proclaim on the same day *that* it is a holy convocation to you. You shall do no customary work *on it. It shall be* a statute forever in all your dwellings throughout your generations.

Num 28:26 'Also on the day of the firstfruits, when you bring a new grain offering to the LORD at your *Feast of* Weeks, you shall have a holy convocation. You shall do no customary work.

A time of holy rejoicing.

Deut 16:11–12 You shall rejoice before the LORD your God, you and your son and your daughter, your male servant and your female servant, the Levite who *is* within your gates, the stranger and the fatherless and the widow who *are* among you, at the place where the LORD your God chooses to make His name abide. **12** And you shall remember that you were a slave in Egypt, and you shall be careful to observe these statutes.

The firstfruits of bread presented at.

Lev 23:17 You shall bring from your dwellings two wave *loaves* of two-tenths *of an ephah*. They shall be of fine flour; they shall be baked with leaven. *They are* the firstfruits to the LORD.

Deut 16:10 Then you shall keep the Feast of Weeks to the LORD your God with the tribute of a freewill offering from your hand, which you shall give as the LORD your God blesses you.

Sacrifices at.

Lev 23:18–19 And you shall offer with the bread seven lambs of the first year, without blemish, one young bull, and two rams. They shall be *as* a burnt offering to the LORD, with their grain offering and their drink offerings, an offering made by fire for a sweet aroma to the LORD. **19** Then you shall sacrifice one kid of the goats as a sin offering, and two male lambs of the first year as a sacrifice of a peace offering.

Num 28:27–31 You shall present a burnt offering as a sweet aroma to the LORD: two young bulls, one ram, and seven lambs in their first year, **28** with their grain offering of fine flour mixed with oil: three-tenths *of an ephah* for each bull, two-tenths for the one ram, **29** and one-tenth for each of the seven lambs; **30** *also* one kid of the goats, to make atonement for you. **31** Be sure they are without blemish. You shall present *them* with their drink offerings, besides the regular burnt offering with its grain offering.

The law given from Mount Sinai on.

Ex 12:6 Now you shall keep it until the fourteenth day

of the same month. Then the whole assembly of the congregation of Israel shall kill it at twilight.

Ex 12:12 'For I will pass through the land of Egypt on that night, and will strike all the firstborn in the land of Egypt, both man and beast; and against all the gods of Egypt I will execute judgment: I *am* the LORD.

Ex 19:1 In the third month after the children of Israel had gone out of the land of Egypt, on the same day, they came *to* the Wilderness of Sinai.

Ex 19:11 And let them be ready for the third day. For on the third day the LORD will come down upon Mount Sinai in the sight of all the people.

The Holy Spirit given to apostles at.

Acts 2:1–3 When the Day of Pentecost had fully come, they were all with one accord in one place. **2** And suddenly there came a sound from heaven, as of a rushing mighty wind, and it filled the whole house where they were sitting. **3** Then there appeared to them divided tongues, as of fire, and *one* sat upon each of them.

Observed by the early church.

Acts 20:16 For Paul had decided to sail past Ephesus, so that he would not have to spend time in Asia; for he was hurrying to be at Jerusalem, if possible, on the Day of Pentecost.

1 Cor 16:8 But I will tarry in Ephesus until Pentecost.

FEAST OF PURIM (LOTS), THE

Instituted by Mordecai.

Esth 9:20 And Mordecai wrote these things and sent letters to all the Jews, near and far, who *were* in all the provinces of King Ahasuerus,

To commemorate the defeat of Haman's wicked design.

Esth 3:7–15 In the first month, which is the month of Nisan, in the twelfth year of King Ahasuerus, they cast Pur (that *is*, the lot), before Haman to determine the day and the month, until *it fell on the* twelfth *month*, which *is* the month of Adar. **8** Then Haman said to King Ahasuerus, "There is a certain people scattered and dispersed among the people in all the provinces of your kingdom; their laws *are* different from all *other* people's, and they do not keep the king's laws. Therefore it *is* not fitting for the king to let them remain. **9** If it pleases the king, let *a decree* be written that they be destroyed, and I will pay ten thousand talents of silver into the hands of those who do the work, to bring *it* into the king's treasuries." **10** So the king took his signet ring from his hand and gave it to Haman, the son of Hammedatha the Agagite, the enemy of the Jews. **11** And the king said to Haman, "The money and the people *are* given to you, to do with them as seems good to you." **12** Then the king's scribes were called on the thirteenth day of the first month, and *a decree* was written according to all that Haman commanded—to the king's satraps, to the governors who *were* over each province, to the officials of all people, to every province according to its script, and to every people in their language. In the name of King Ahasuerus it was written, and sealed with the king's signet ring. **13** And the letters were sent by couriers into all the king's provinces, to destroy, to kill, and to annihilate all the Jews, both

young and old, little children and women, in one day, on the thirteenth *day* of the twelfth *month*, which *is* the month of Adar, and to plunder their possessions. **14** A copy of the document was to be issued as law in every province, being published for all people, that they should be ready for that day. **15** The couriers went out, hastened by the king's command; and the decree was proclaimed in Shushan the citadel. So the king and Haman sat down to drink, but the city of Shushan was perplexed.

Esth 9:24–26 because Haman, the son of Hammedatha the Agagite, the enemy of all the Jews, had plotted against the Jews to annihilate them, and had cast Pur (that *is*, the lot), to consume them and destroy them; **25** but when *Esther* came before the king, he commanded by letter that this wicked plot which *Haman* had devised against the Jews should return on his own head, and that he and his sons should be hanged on the gallows. **26** So they called these days Purim, after the name Pur. Therefore, because of all the words of this letter, what they had seen concerning this matter, and what had happened to them,

Began fourteenth day of the twelfth month.

Esth 9:17 *This was* on the thirteenth day of the month of Adar. And on the fourteenth of *the month* they rested and made it a day of feasting and gladness.

Lasted two days.

Esth 9:21 to establish among them that they should celebrate yearly the fourteenth and fifteenth days of the month of Adar,

Mode of celebrating.

Esth 9:17–19 *This was* on the thirteenth day of the month of Adar. And on the fourteenth of *the month* they rested and made it a day of feasting and gladness. **18** But the Jews who *were* at Shushan assembled together on the thirteenth *day*, as well as on the fourteenth; and on the fifteenth of *the month* they rested, and made it a day of feasting and gladness. **19** Therefore the Jews of the villages who dwelt in the unwalled towns celebrated the fourteenth day of the month of Adar *with* gladness and feasting, as a holiday, and for sending presents to one another.

Esth 9:22 as the days on which the Jews had rest from their enemies, as the month which was turned from sorrow to joy for them, and from mourning to a holiday; that they should make them days of feasting and joy, of sending presents to one another and gifts to the poor.

The Jews bound themselves to keep.

Esth 9:27–28 the Jews established and imposed it upon themselves and their descendants and all who would join them, that without fail they should celebrate these two days every year, according to the written *instructions* and according to the *prescribed* time, **28** *that* these days *should be* remembered and kept throughout every generation, every family, every province, and every city, that these days of Purim should not fail *to be observed* among the Jews, and *that* the memory of them should not perish among their descendants.

Confirmed by royal authority.

Esth 9:29–32 Then Queen Esther, the daughter of Abihail, with Mordecai the Jew, wrote with full authority to confirm this second letter about Purim. **30** And *Mordecai* sent letters to all the Jews, to the one hundred and twenty-seven provinces of the kingdom of Ahasuerus, *with* words of peace and truth, **31** to confirm these days of Purim at their *appointed* time, as Mordecai the Jew and Queen Esther had prescribed for them, and as they had decreed for themselves and their descendants concerning matters of their fasting and lamenting. **32** So the decree of Esther confirmed these matters of Purim, and it was written in the book.

FEAST OF TABERNACLES, THE

Held after grain and grape harvest.

Deut 16:13 "You shall observe the Feast of Tabernacles seven days, when you have gathered from your threshing floor and from your winepress.

Began fifteenth day of the seventh month.

Lev 23:34 "Speak to the children of Israel, saying: 'The fifteenth day of this seventh month *shall be* the Feast of Tabernacles *for* seven days to the LORD.

Lev 23:39 'Also on the fifteenth day of the seventh month, when you have gathered in the fruit of the land, you shall keep the feast of the LORD *for* seven days; on the first day *there shall be* a sabbath-*rest*, and on the eighth day a sabbath-*rest*.

Lasted seven days.

Lev 23:34 "Speak to the children of Israel, saying: 'The fifteenth day of this seventh month *shall be* the Feast of Tabernacles *for* seven days to the LORD.

Lev 23:41 You shall keep it as a feast to the LORD for seven days in the year. *It shall be* a statute forever in your generations. You shall celebrate it in the seventh month.

Deut 16:13 "You shall observe the Feast of Tabernacles seven days, when you have gathered from your threshing floor and from your winepress.

Deut 16:15 Seven days you shall keep a sacred feast to the LORD your God in the place which the LORD chooses, because the LORD your God will bless you in all your produce and in all the work of your hands, so that you surely rejoice.

Called the Feast of Ingathering.

Ex 23:16–17 and the Feast of Harvest, the firstfruits of your labors which you have sown in the field; and the Feast of Ingathering at the end of the year, when you have gathered in *the fruit of* your labors from the field. **17** "Three times in the year all your males shall appear before the Lord GOD.

All males obliged to appear at.

Ex 23:16–17 and the Feast of Harvest, the firstfruits of your labors which you have sown in the field; and the Feast of Ingathering at the end of the year, when you have gathered in *the fruit of* your labors from the field. **17** "Three times in the year all your males shall appear before the Lord GOD.

First and last days of, holy convocations.

Lev 23:35 On the first day *there shall be* a holy convocation. You shall do no customary work *on it.*

Lev 23:39 'Also on the fifteenth day of the seventh month, when you have gathered in the fruit of the land, you shall keep the feast of the LORD *for* seven

days; on the first day *there shall be* a sabbath-*rest*, and on the eighth day a sabbath-*rest*.

Num 29:12 'On the fifteenth day of the seventh month you shall have a holy convocation. You shall do no customary work, and you shall keep a feast to the LORD seven days.

Num 29:35 'On the eighth day you shall have a sacred assembly. You shall do no customary work.

Sacrifices during.

Lev 23:36–37 *For* seven days you shall offer an offering made by fire to the LORD. On the eighth day you shall have a holy convocation, and you shall offer an offering made by fire to the LORD. It *is* a sacred assembly, *and* you shall do no customary work *on it.* **37** 'These *are* the feasts of the LORD which you shall proclaim *to be* holy convocations, to offer an offering made by fire to the LORD, a burnt offering and a grain offering, a sacrifice and drink offerings, everything on its day—

Cf. Num 29:13–39

To be observed

With rejoicing.

Deut 16:14–15 And you shall rejoice in your feast, you and your son and your daughter, your male servant and your female servant and the Levite, the stranger and the fatherless and the widow, who *are* within your gates. **15** Seven days you shall keep a sacred feast to the LORD your God in the place which the LORD chooses, because the LORD your God will bless you in all your produce and in all the work of your hands, so that you surely rejoice.

Perpetually.

Lev 23:41 You shall keep it as a feast to the LORD for seven days in the year. *It shall be* a statute forever in your generations. You shall celebrate it in the seventh month.

The people dwelt in booths during.

Lev 23:42 You shall dwell in booths for seven days. All who are native Israelites shall dwell in booths,

Neh 8:15–16 and that they should announce and proclaim in all their cities and in Jerusalem, saying, "Go out to the mountain, and bring olive branches, branches of oil trees, myrtle branches, palm branches, and branches of leafy trees, to make booths, *as it is* written." **16** Then the people went out and brought *them* and made themselves booths, each one on the roof of his house, or in their courtyards or the courts of the house of God, and in the open square of the Water Gate and in the open square of the Gate of Ephraim.

The law publicly read every seventh year at.

Deut 31:10–12 And Moses commanded them, saying: "At the end of *every* seven years, at the appointed time in the year of release, at the Feast of Tabernacles, **11** when all Israel comes to appear before the LORD your God in the place which He chooses, you shall read this law before all Israel in their hearing. **12** Gather the people together, men and women and little ones, and the stranger who *is* within your gates, that they may hear and that they may learn to fear the LORD your God and carefully observe all the words of this law,

Neh 8:18 Also day by day, from the first day until the last day, he read from the Book of the Law of God. And they kept the feast seven days; and on the eighth day *there was* a sacred assembly, according to the *prescribed* manner.

Customs observed at,

Bearing branches of palms.

Lev 23:40 And you shall take for yourselves on the first day the fruit of beautiful trees, branches of palm trees, the boughs of leafy trees, and willows of the brook; and you shall rejoice before the LORD your God for seven days.

Rev 7:9 After these things I looked, and behold, a great multitude which no one could number, of all nations, tribes, peoples, and tongues, standing before the throne and before the Lamb, clothed with white robes, with palm branches in their hands,

Drawing water from the pool of Siloam.

John 7:2 Now the Jews' Feast of Tabernacles was at hand.

John 7:37–39 On the last day, that great *day* of the feast, Jesus stood and cried out, saying, "If anyone thirsts, let him come to Me and drink. **38** He who believes in Me, as the Scripture has said, out of his heart will flow rivers of living water." **39** But this He spoke concerning the Spirit, whom those believing in Him would receive; for the Holy Spirit was not yet *given*, because Jesus was not yet glorified.

Singing hosannas.

Ps 118:24–29 This *is* the day the LORD has made; We will rejoice and be glad in it. **25** Save now, I pray, O LORD; O LORD, I pray, send now prosperity. **26** Blessed *is* he who comes in the name of the LORD! We have blessed you from the house of the LORD. **27** God *is* the LORD, And He has given us light; Bind the sacrifice with cords to the horns of the altar. **28** You *are* my God, and I will praise You; *You are* my God, I will exalt You. **29** Oh, give thanks to the LORD, for *He is* good! For His mercy *endures* forever.

Matt 21:8–9 And a very great multitude spread their clothes on the road; others cut down branches from the trees and spread *them* on the road. **9** Then the multitudes who went before and those who followed cried out, saying: "Hosanna to the Son of David! *'Blessed is He who comes in the name of the LORD!'* Hosanna in the highest!"

To commemorate the sojourn of Israel in the desert.

Lev 23:43 that your generations may know that I made the children of Israel dwell in booths when I brought them out of the land of Egypt: I *am* the LORD your God.' "

Remarkable celebrations of,

At the dedication of Solomon's temple.

1 Kin 8:2 Therefore all the men of Israel assembled with King Solomon at the feast in the month of Ethanim, which *is* the seventh month.

1 Kin 8:65 At that time Solomon held a feast, and all Israel with him, a great assembly from the entrance of Hamath to the Brook of Egypt, before the LORD our God, seven days and seven *more* days—fourteen days.

After the captivity.

Ezra 3:4 They also kept the Feast of Tabernacles, as *it is* written, and *offered* the daily burnt offerings in the number required by ordinance for each day.

Neh 8:17 So the whole assembly of those who had returned from the captivity made booths and sat under the booths; for since the days of Joshua the son of Nun until that day the children of Israel had not done so. And there was very great gladness.

FEAST OF TRUMPETS, THE

Held the first day of the seventh month.

Lev 23:24 "Speak to the children of Israel, saying: 'In the seventh month, on the first *day* of the month, you shall have a sabbath-*rest*, a memorial of blowing of trumpets, a holy convocation.

Num 29:1 'And in the seventh month, on the first *day* of the month, you shall have a holy convocation. You shall do no customary work. For you it is a day of blowing the trumpets.

A memorial of blowing of trumpets.

Lev 23:24 "Speak to the children of Israel, saying: 'In the seventh month, on the first *day* of the month, you shall have a sabbath-*rest*, a memorial of blowing of trumpets, a holy convocation.

A holy convocation and rest.

Lev 23:24–25 "Speak to the children of Israel, saying: 'In the seventh month, on the first *day* of the month, you shall have a sabbath-*rest*, a memorial of blowing of trumpets, a holy convocation. **25** You shall do no customary work *on it*; and you shall offer an offering made by fire to the LORD.' "

Sacrifices at.

Num 29:2–6 You shall offer a burnt offering as a sweet aroma to the LORD: one young bull, one ram, *and* seven lambs in their first year, without blemish. **3** Their grain offering *shall be* fine flour mixed with oil: three-tenths *of an ephah* for the bull, two-tenths for the ram, **4** and one-tenth for each of the seven lambs; **5** also one kid of the goats *as* a sin offering, to make atonement for you; **6** besides the burnt offering with its grain offering for the New Moon, the regular burnt offering with its grain offering, and their drink offerings, according to their ordinance, as a sweet aroma, an offering made by fire to the LORD.

FEASTS, THE THREE ANNUAL

Instituted by God.

Ex 23:14 "Three times you shall keep a feast to Me in the year:

Enumerated.

Ex 23:15–16 You shall keep the Feast of Unleavened Bread (you shall eat unleavened bread seven days, as I commanded you, at the time appointed in the month of Abib, for in it you came out of Egypt; none shall appear before Me empty); **16** and the Feast of Harvest, the firstfruits of your labors which you have sown in the field; and the Feast of Ingathering at the end of the year, when you have gathered in *the fruit* of your labors from the field.

Various names for,

Appointed feasts.

Is 1:14 Your New Moons and your appointed feasts My soul hates; They are a trouble to Me, I am weary of bearing *them.*

Feasts of the Lord.

Lev 23:4 'These *are* the feasts of the LORD, holy convocations which you shall proclaim at their appointed times.

Solemn feasts.

2 Chr 8:13 according to the daily rate, offering according to the commandment of Moses, for the Sabbaths, the New Moons, and the three appointed yearly feasts—the Feast of Unleavened Bread, the Feast of Weeks, and the Feast of Tabernacles.

Lam 1:4 The roads to Zion mourn Because no one comes to the set feasts. All her gates are desolate; Her priests sigh, Her virgins are afflicted, And she *is* in bitterness.

Solemn meetings.

Is 1:13 Bring no more futile sacrifices; Incense is an abomination to Me. The New Moons, the Sabbaths, and the calling of assemblies— I cannot endure iniquity and the sacred meeting.

All males to attend.

Ex 23:17 "Three times in the year all your males shall appear before the Lord GOD.

Ex 34:23 "Three times in the year all your men shall appear before the Lord, the LORD God of Israel.

Children began attending, when twelve years old.

Luke 2:42 And when He was twelve years old, they went up to Jerusalem according to the custom of the feast.

Females often attended.

1 Sam 1:3–5 This man went up from his city yearly to worship and sacrifice to the LORD of hosts in Shiloh. Also the two sons of Eli, Hophni and Phinehas, the priests of the LORD, *were* there. 4 And whenever the time came for Elkanah to make an offering, he would give portions to Peninnah his wife and to all her sons and daughters. 5 But to Hannah he would give a double portion, for he loved Hannah, although the LORD had closed her womb.

1 Sam 1:9 So Hannah arose after they had finished eating and drinking in Shiloh. Now Eli the priest was sitting on the seat by the doorpost of the tabernacle of the LORD.

Luke 2:41 His parents went to Jerusalem every year at the Feast of the Passover.

The Jews attended gladly and in large companies.

Ps 42:4 When I remember these *things,* I pour out my soul within me. For I used to go with the multitude; I went with them to the house of God, With the voice of joy and praise, With a multitude that kept a pilgrim feast.

Ps 84:6–7 *As they* pass through the Valley of Baca, They make it a spring; The rain also covers it with pools. 7 They go from strength to strength; *Each one* appears before God in Zion.

Ps 122:1–2 I was glad when they said to me, "Let us go into the house of the LORD." 2 Our feet have been standing Within your gates, O Jerusalem!

Luke 2:44 but supposing Him to have been in the company, they went a day's journey, and sought Him among *their* relatives and acquaintances.

The land divinely protected during.

Ex 34:24 For I will cast out the nations before you and enlarge your borders; neither will any man covet your land when you go up to appear before the LORD your God three times in the year.

Offerings to be made at.

Ex 34:20 But the firstborn of a donkey you shall redeem with a lamb. And if you will not redeem *him,* then you shall break his neck. All the firstborn of your sons you shall redeem. "And none shall appear before Me empty-handed.

Deut 16:16–17 "Three times a year all your males shall appear before the LORD your God in the place which He chooses: at the Feast of Unleavened Bread, at the Feast of Weeks, and at the Feast of Tabernacles; and they shall not appear before the LORD empty-handed. 17 Every man *shall give* as he is able, according to the blessing of the LORD your God which He has given you.

Were seasons of

Joy and gladness.

Ps 42:4 When I remember these *things,* I pour out my soul within me. For I used to go with the multitude; I went with them to the house of God, With the voice of joy and praise, With a multitude that kept a pilgrim feast.

Is 30:20 And *though* the Lord gives you The bread of adversity and the water of affliction, Yet your teachers will not be moved into a corner anymore, But your eyes shall see your teachers.

Sacrificing.

1 Sam 1:3 This man went up from his city yearly to worship and sacrifice to the LORD of hosts in Shiloh. Also the two sons of Eli, Hophni and Phinehas, the priests of the LORD, *were* there.

1 Kin 9:25 Now three times a year Solomon offered burnt offerings and peace offerings on the altar which he had built for the LORD, and he burned incense with them *on the altar that was* before the LORD. So he finished the temple.

2 Chr 8:13 according to the daily rate, offering according to the commandment of Moses, for the Sabbaths, the New Moons, and the three appointed yearly feasts—the Feast of Unleavened Bread, the Feast of Weeks, and the Feast of Tabernacles.

Special meals.

1 Sam 1:4 And whenever the time came for Elkanah to make an offering, he would give portions to Peninnah his wife and to all her sons and daughters.

1 Sam 1:9 So Hannah arose after they had finished eating and drinking in Shiloh. Now Eli the priest was sitting on the seat by the doorpost of the tabernacle of the LORD.

The ten tribes seduced by Jeroboam from attending.

1 Kin 12:27 If these people go up to offer sacrifices in the house of the LORD at Jerusalem, then the heart of this people will turn back to their lord, Rehoboam king of Judah, and they will kill me and go back to Rehoboam king of Judah."

The Jews dispersed in distant lands often attended.

Acts 2:5–11 And there were dwelling in Jerusalem Jews, devout men, from every nation under heaven. **6** And when this sound occurred, the multitude came together, and were confused, because everyone heard them speak in his own language. **7** Then they were all amazed and marveled, saying to one another, "Look, are not all these who speak Galileans? **8** And how *is it that* we hear, each in our own language in which we were born? **9** Parthians and Medes and Elamites, those dwelling in Mesopotamia, Judea and Cappadocia, Pontus and Asia, **10** Phrygia and Pamphylia, Egypt and the parts of Libya adjoining Cyrene, visitors from Rome, both Jews and proselytes, **11** Cretans and Arabs—we hear them speaking in our own tongues the wonderful works of God."

Acts 8:27 So he arose and went. And behold, a man of Ethiopia, a eunuch of great authority under Candace the queen of the Ethiopians, who had charge of all her treasury, and had come to Jerusalem to worship,

Christ attended.

John 5:1 After this there was a feast of the Jews, and Jesus went up to Jerusalem.

John 7:10 But when His brothers had gone up, then He also went up to the feast, not openly, but as it were in secret.

Jews' sins caused God to reject.

Is 1:13–14 Bring no more futile sacrifices; Incense is an abomination to Me. The New Moons, the Sabbaths, and the calling of assemblies— I cannot endure iniquity and the sacred meeting. **14** Your New Moons and your appointed feasts My soul hates; They are a trouble to Me, I am weary of bearing *them*.

Amos 5:21 "I hate, I despise your feast days, And I do not savor your sacred assemblies.

Illustrative of general assembly of the church.

Heb 12:23 to the general assembly and church of the firstborn *who are* registered in heaven, to God the Judge of all, to the spirits of just men made perfect,

FEET, THE

Necessary members of the body.

1 Cor 12:15 If the foot should say, "Because I am not a hand, I am not of the body," is it therefore not of the body?

1 Cor 12:21 And the eye cannot say to the hand, "I have no need of you"; nor again the head to the feet, "I have no need of you."

Parts of, mentioned in Scripture

Heel.

Ps 41:9 Even my own familiar friend in whom I trusted, Who ate my bread, Has lifted up *his* heel against me.

Ps 49:5 Why should I fear in the days of evil, *When* the iniquity at my heels surrounds me?

Hos 12:3 He took his brother by the heel in the womb, And in his strength he struggled with God.

Sole.

Deut 11:24 Every place on which the sole of your foot

treads shall be yours: from the wilderness and Lebanon, from the river, the River Euphrates, even to the Western Sea, shall be your territory.

1 Kin 5:3 You know how my father David could not build a house for the name of the LORD his God because of the wars which were fought against him on every side, until the LORD put *his foes* under the soles of his feet.

Toes.

Ex 29:20 Then you shall kill the ram, and take some of its blood and put *it* on the tip of the right ear of Aaron and on the tip of the right ear of his sons, on the thumb of their right hand and on the big toe of their right foot, and sprinkle the blood all around on the altar.

2 Sam 21:20 Yet again there was war at Gath, where there was a man of *great* stature, who had six fingers on each hand and six toes on each foot, twenty-four in number; and he also was born to the giant.

Dan 2:41 Whereas you saw the feet and toes, partly of potter's clay and partly of iron, the kingdom shall be divided; yet the strength of the iron shall be in it, just as you saw the iron mixed with ceramic clay.

Often swift.

2 Sam 2:18 Now the three sons of Zeruiah were there: Joab and Abishai and Asahel. And Asahel *was as* fleet of foot as a wild gazelle.

2 Sam 22:34 He makes my feet like the *feet* of deer, And sets me on my high places.

Were liable to

Disease.

1 Kin 15:23 The rest of all the acts of Asa, all his might, all that he did, and the cities which he built, *are* they not written in the book of the chronicles of the kings of Judah? But in the time of his old age he was diseased in his feet.

Swelling from walking.

Deut 8:4 Your garments did not wear out on you, nor did your foot swell these forty years.

Injury from stones, etc.

Ps 91:12 In *their* hands they shall bear you up, Lest you dash your foot against a stone.

Early use of shoes.

Ex 12:11 And thus you shall eat it: *with* a belt on your waist, your sandals on your feet, and your staff in your hand. So you shall eat it in haste. It *is* the LORD's Passover.

Of women, often adorned with jingling ornaments.

Is 3:16 Moreover the LORD says: "Because the daughters of Zion are haughty, And walk with outstretched necks And wanton eyes, Walking and mincing *as* they go, Making a jingling with their feet,

Is 3:18 In that day the Lord will take away the finery: The jingling anklets, the scarves, and the crescents;

Of the Jews,

Neglected in affliction.

2 Sam 19:24 Now Mephibosheth the son of Saul came down to meet the king. And he had not cared for his feet, nor trimmed his mustache, nor washed his clothes, from the day the king departed until the day he returned in peace.

Ezek 24:17 Sigh in silence, make no mourning for the dead; bind your turban on your head, and put your sandals on your feet; do not cover *your* lips, and do not eat man's bread *of sorrow.*"

Bare in affliction.

2 Sam 15:30 So David went up by the Ascent of the *Mount of* Olives, and wept as he went up; and he had his head covered and went barefoot. And all the people who *were* with him covered their heads and went up, weeping as they went up.

Washed frequently.

2 Sam 11:8 And David said to Uriah, "Go down to your house and wash your feet." So Uriah departed from the king's house, and a gift *of food* from the king followed him.

Song 5:3 I have taken off my robe; How can I put it on *again?* I have washed my feet; How can I defile them?

Stamped on the ground in extreme joy or grief.

Ezek 6:11 'Thus says the Lord GOD: "Pound your fists and stamp your feet, and say, 'Alas, for all the evil abominations of the house of Israel! For they shall fall by the sword, by famine, and by pestilence.

Ezek 25:6 'For thus says the Lord GOD: "Because you clapped *your* hands, stamped your feet, and rejoiced in heart with all your disdain for the land of Israel,

Washing for others, a menial office.

1 Sam 25:41 Then she arose, bowed her face to the earth, and said, "Here is your maidservant, a servant to wash the feet of the servants of my lord."

John 13:5–14 After that, He poured water into a basin and began to wash the disciples' feet, and to wipe *them* with the towel with which He was girded. **6** Then He came to Simon Peter. And *Peter* said to Him, "Lord, are You washing my feet?" **7** Jesus answered and said to him, "What I am doing you do not understand now, but you will know after this." **8** Peter said to Him, "You shall never wash my feet!" Jesus answered him, "If I do not wash you, you have no part with Me." **9** Simon Peter said to Him, "Lord, not my feet only, but also *my* hands and *my* head!" **10** Jesus said to him, "He who is bathed needs only to wash *his* feet, but is completely clean; and you are clean, but not all of you." **11** For He knew who would betray Him; therefore He said, "You are not all clean." **12** So when He had washed their feet, taken His garments, and sat down again, He said to them, "Do you know what I have done to you? **13** You call Me Teacher and Lord, and you say well, for *so* I am. **14** If I then, *your* Lord and Teacher, have washed your feet, you also ought to wash one another's feet.

Of strangers and travelers, washed.

Gen 18:4 Please let a little water be brought, and wash your feet, and rest yourselves under the tree.

Gen 19:2 And he said, "Here now, my lords, please turn in to your servant's house and spend the night, and wash your feet; then you may rise early and go on your way." And they said, "No, but we will spend the night in the open square."

Gen 24:32 Then the man came to the house. And he unloaded the camels, and provided straw and feed for the camels, and water to wash his feet and the feet of the men who *were* with him.

1 Tim 5:10 well reported for good works: if she has brought up children, if she has lodged strangers, if she has washed the saints' feet, if she has relieved the afflicted, if she has diligently followed every good work.

Neglect of washing, disrespectful to guest.

Luke 7:44 Then He turned to the woman and said to Simon, "Do you see this woman? I entered your house, you gave Me no water for My feet, but she has washed My feet with her tears and wiped *them* with the hair of her head.

Respect for and subjection to persons, expressed by

Falling at.

1 Sam 25:24 So she fell at his feet and said: "On me, my lord, *on* me *let* this iniquity *be!* And please let your maidservant speak in your ears, and hear the words of your maidservant.

2 Kin 4:37 So she went in, fell at his feet, and bowed to the ground; then she picked up her son and went out.

Esth 8:3 Now Esther spoke again to the king, fell down at his feet, and implored him with tears to counteract the evil of Haman the Agagite, and the scheme which he had devised against the Jews.

Mark 5:22 And behold, one of the rulers of the synagogue came, Jairus by name. And when he saw Him, he fell at His feet

Acts 10:25 As Peter was coming in, Cornelius met him and fell down at his feet and worshiped *him.*

Kissing.

Luke 7:38 and stood at His feet behind *Him* weeping; and she began to wash His feet with her tears, and wiped *them* with the hair of her head; and she kissed His feet and anointed *them* with the fragrant oil.

Luke 7:45 You gave Me no kiss, but this woman has not ceased to kiss My feet since the time I came in.

Licking the dust of.

Is 49:23 Kings shall be your foster fathers, And their queens your nursing mothers; They shall bow down to you with *their* faces to the earth, And lick up the dust of your feet. Then you will know that I *am* the LORD, For they shall not be ashamed who wait for Me."

Condemnation expressed by shaking the dust from.

Matt 10:14 And whoever will not receive you nor hear your words, when you depart from that house or city, shake off the dust from your feet.

Mark 6:11 And whoever will not receive you nor hear you, when you depart from there, shake off the dust under your feet as a testimony against them. Assuredly, I say to you, it will be more tolerable for Sodom and Gomorrah in the day of judgment than for that city!"

Subjugation of enemies expressed by placing on their necks.

Josh 10:24 So it was, when they brought out those kings to Joshua, that Joshua called for all the men of Israel, and said to the captains of the men of war who went with him, "Come near, put your feet on the necks of these kings." And they drew near and put their feet on their necks.

Ps 110:1 The LORD said to my Lord, "Sit at My right hand, Till I make Your enemies Your footstool."

Origin of uncovering in consecrated places.

Ex 3:5 Then He said, "Do not draw near this place. Take your sandals off your feet, for the place where you stand *is* holy ground."

Josh 5:15 Then the Commander of the LORD's army said to Joshua, "Take your sandal off your foot, for the place where you stand *is* holy." And Joshua did so.

Of enemies, often maimed and cut off.

Judg 1:6–7 Then Adoni-Bezek fled, and they pursued him and caught him and cut off his thumbs and big toes. **7** And Adoni-Bezek said, "Seventy kings with their thumbs and big toes cut off used to gather *scraps* under my table; as I have done, so God has repaid me." Then they brought him to Jerusalem, and there he died.

2 Sam 4:12 So David commanded his young men, and they executed them, cut off their hands and feet, and hanged *them* by the pool in Hebron. But they took the head of Ishbosheth and buried *it* in the tomb of Abner in Hebron.

Of criminals

Bound with fetters.

Ps 105:18 They hurt his feet with fetters, He was laid in irons.

Placed in stocks.

Job 13:27 You put my feet in the stocks, And watch closely all my paths. You set a limit for the soles of my feet.

Acts 16:24 Having received such a charge, he put them into the inner prison and fastened their feet in the stocks.

Path of

To be pondered.

Prov 4:26 Ponder the path of your feet, And let all your ways be established.

To be kept from evil.

Prov 1:15 My son, do not walk in the way with them, Keep your foot from their path;

Heb 12:13 and make straight paths for your feet, so that what is lame may not be *dislocated*, but rather be healed.

To be turned to God's testimonies.

Ps 119:59 I thought about my ways, And turned my feet to Your testimonies.

To be directed by God's word.

Ps 119:105 Your word *is* a lamp to my feet And a light to my path.

To be guided by wisdom and discretion.

Prov 3:21–23 My son, let them not depart from your eyes—Keep sound wisdom and discretion; **22** So they will be life to your soul And grace to your neck. **23** Then you will walk safely in your way, And your foot will not stumble.

Prov 3:26 For the LORD will be your confidence, And will keep your foot from being caught.

Of the wicked

Swift to mischief.

Prov 6:18 A heart that devises wicked plans, Feet that are swift in running to evil,

Swift to shed blood.

Prov 1:16 For their feet run to evil, And they make haste to shed blood.

Rom 3:15 *"Their feet are swift to shed blood;*

Ensnared.

Job 18:8 For he is cast into a net by his own feet, And he walks into a snare.

Ps 9:15 The nations have sunk down in the pit *which* they made; In the net which they hid, their own foot is caught.

Of believers

At liberty.

Ps 18:36 You enlarged my path under me, So my feet did not slip.

Ps 31:8 And have not shut me up into the hand of the enemy; You have set my feet in a wide place.

Kept by God.

1 Sam 2:9 He will guard the feet of His saints, But the wicked shall be silent in darkness. "For by strength no man shall prevail.

Ps 66:9 Who keeps our soul among the living, And does not allow our feet to be moved.

Ps 116:8 For You have delivered my soul from death, My eyes from tears, *And* my feet from falling.

Ps 121:3 He will not allow your foot to be moved; He who keeps you will not slumber.

Guided by Christ.

Is 48:17 Thus says the LORD, your Redeemer, The Holy One of Israel: "I *am* the LORD your God, Who teaches you to profit, Who leads you by the way you should go.

Luke 1:79 To give light to those who sit in darkness and the shadow of death, To guide our feet into the way of peace."

Illustrative of

(Set on a rock) stability.

Ps 40:2 He also brought me up out of a horrible pit, Out of the miry clay, And set my feet upon a rock, And established my steps.

(Set in a wide place) liberty.

Ps 31:8 And have not shut me up into the hand of the enemy; You have set my feet in a wide place.

(Slipping) yielding to temptation.

Job 12:5 A lamp is despised in the thought of one who is at ease; It is made ready for those whose feet slip.

Ps 17:5 Uphold my steps in Your paths, That my footsteps may not slip.

Ps 38:16 For I said, *"Hear me,* lest they rejoice over me, Lest, when my foot slips, they exalt *themselves* against me."

Ps 94:18 If I say, "My foot slips," Your mercy, O LORD, will hold me up.

(Trampling under) complete destruction.

Is 18:7 In that time a present will be brought to the LORD of hosts From a people tall and smooth *of skin,* And from a people terrible from their beginning onward, A nation powerful and treading down, Whose land the rivers divide— To the place of the name of the LORD of hosts, To Mount Zion.

Lam 1:15 "The Lord has trampled underfoot all my mighty *men* in my midst; He has called an assembly against me To crush my young men; The Lord trampled *as* in a winepress The virgin daughter of Judah.

(Bathed or dipped in oil) abundance.

Deut 33:24 And of Asher he said: "Asher *is* most blessed of sons; Let him be favored by his brothers, And let him dip his foot in oil.

Job 29:6 When my steps were bathed with cream, And the rock poured out rivers of oil for me!

(Crushing the enemy in blood) victory.

Ps 68:23 That your foot may crush *them* in blood, And the tongues of your dogs *may have* their portion from *your* enemies."

FELLOWSHIP OF BELIEVERS, THE

God's will.

Mal 3:16 Then those who feared the LORD spoke to one another, And the LORD listened and heard *them;* So a book of remembrance was written before Him For those who fear the LORD And who meditate on His name.

Matt 18:20 For where two or three are gathered together in My name, I am there in the midst of them."

John 17:20–21 "I do not pray for these alone, but also for those who will believe in Me through their word; **21** that they all may be one, as You, Father, *are* in Me, and I in You; that they also may be one in Us, that the world may believe that You sent Me.

Occurs

With God.

1 John 1:3 that which we have seen and heard we declare to you, that you also may have fellowship with us; and truly our fellowship *is* with the Father and with His Son Jesus Christ.

With believers in heaven.

Heb 12:22–24 But you have come to Mount Zion and to the city of the living God, the heavenly Jerusalem, to an innumerable company of angels, **23** to the general assembly and church of the firstborn *who are* registered in heaven, to God the Judge of all, to the spirits of just men made perfect, **24** to Jesus the Mediator of the new covenant, and to the blood of sprinkling that speaks better things than *that of* Abel.

With each other.

Gal 2:9 and when James, Cephas, and John, who seemed to be pillars, perceived the grace that had been given to me, they gave me and Barnabas the right hand of fellowship, that we *should go* to the Gentiles and they to the circumcised.

1 John 1:3 that which we have seen and heard we declare to you, that you also may have fellowship with us; and truly our fellowship *is* with the Father and with His Son Jesus Christ.

1 John 1:7 But if we walk in the light as He is in the light, we have fellowship with one another, and the blood of Jesus Christ His Son cleanses us from all sin.

In public and social worship.

Ps 34:3 Oh, magnify the LORD with me, And let us exalt His name together.

Ps 55:14 We took sweet counsel together, *And* walked to the house of God in the throng.

Acts 1:14 These all continued with one accord in prayer and supplication, with the women and Mary the mother of Jesus, and with His brothers.

Heb 10:25 not forsaking the assembling of ourselves together, as *is* the manner of some, but exhorting *one another,* and so much the more as you see the Day approaching.

In the Lord's Supper.

1 Cor 10:17 For we, *though* many, are one bread *and* one body; for we all partake of that one bread.

In holy conversation.

Mal 3:16 Then those who feared the LORD spoke to one another, And the LORD listened and heard *them;* So a book of remembrance was written before Him For those who fear the LORD And who meditate on His name.

In prayer for each other.

2 Cor 1:11 you also helping together in prayer for us, that thanks may be given by many persons on our behalf for the gift *granted* to us through many.

Eph 6:18 praying always with all prayer and supplication in the Spirit, being watchful to this end with all perseverance and supplication for all the saints—

In exhortation.

Col 3:16 Let the word of Christ dwell in you richly in all wisdom, teaching and admonishing one another in psalms and hymns and spiritual songs, singing with grace in your hearts to the Lord.

Heb 10:25 not forsaking the assembling of ourselves together, as *is* the manner of some, but exhorting *one another,* and so much the more as you see the Day approaching.

In mutual comfort and edification.

1 Thess 4:18 Therefore comfort one another with these words.

1 Thess 5:11 Therefore comfort each other and edify one another, just as you also are doing.

In mutual sympathy and kindness.

Rom 12:15 Rejoice with those who rejoice, and weep with those who weep.

Eph 4:32 And be kind to one another, tenderhearted, forgiving one another, even as God in Christ forgave you.

In mutual love and concern.

1 Cor 12:26–27 And if one member suffers, all the members suffer with *it;* or if one member is honored, all the members rejoice with *it.* **27** Now you are the body of Christ, and members individually.

In mutual submission.

Eph 5:21 submitting to one another in the fear of God.

In mutual sharing of life.

Philem 1:6 that the sharing of your faith may become effective by the acknowledgment of every good thing which is in you in Christ Jesus.

The delight of.

Ps 16:3 As for the saints who *are* on the earth, "They are the excellent ones, in whom is all my delight."

Ps 42:4 When I remember these *things*, I pour out my soul within me. For I used to go with the multitude; I went with them to the house of God, With the voice of joy and praise, With a multitude that kept a pilgrim feast.

Ps 133:1–3 Behold, how good and how pleasant *it is* For brethren to dwell together in unity! **2** *It is* like the precious oil upon the head, Running down on the beard, The beard of Aaron, Running down on the edge of his garments. **3** *It is* like the dew of Hermon, Descending upon the mountains of Zion; For there the LORD commanded the blessing— Life forevermore.

Rom 15:32 that I may come to you with joy by the will of God, and may be refreshed together with you.

Exhortation to.

Eph 4:1–3 I, therefore, the prisoner of the Lord, beseech you to walk worthy of the calling with which you were called, **2** with all lowliness and gentleness, with longsuffering, bearing with one another in love, **3** endeavoring to keep the unity of the Spirit in the bond of peace.

Opposed to communion with the wicked.

2 Cor 6:14–17 Do not be unequally yoked together with unbelievers. For what fellowship has righteousness with lawlessness? And what communion has light with darkness? **15** And what accord has Christ with Belial? Or what part has a believer with an unbeliever? **16** And what agreement has the temple of God with idols? For you are the temple of the living God. As God has said: *"I will dwell in them And walk among them. I will be their God, And they shall be My people."* **17** Therefore *"Come out from among them And be separate, says the Lord. Do not touch what is unclean, And I will receive you."*

Eph 5:11 And have no fellowship with the unfruitful works of darkness, but rather expose *them*.

Exemplified by

Jonathan.

1 Sam 23:16 Then Jonathan, Saul's son, arose and went to David in the woods and strengthened his hand in God.

David.

Ps 119:63 I *am* a companion of all who fear You, And of those who keep Your precepts.

Daniel.

Dan 2:17–18 Then Daniel went to his house, and made the decision known to Hananiah, Mishael, and Azariah, his companions, **18** that they might seek mercies from the God of heaven concerning this secret, so that Daniel and his companions might not perish with the rest of the wise *men* of Babylon.

The apostles.

Acts 1:14 These all continued with one accord in prayer and supplication, with the women and Mary the mother of Jesus, and with His brothers.

The local church.

Acts 2:42 And they continued steadfastly in the apostles' doctrine and fellowship, in the breaking of bread, and in prayers.

Acts 5:12 And through the hands of the apostles many signs and wonders were done among the people. And they were all with one accord in Solomon's Porch.

Paul.

Acts 20:36–38 And when he had said these things, he knelt down and prayed with them all. **37** Then they all wept freely, and fell on Paul's neck and kissed him, **38** sorrowing most of all for the words which he spoke, that they would see his face no more. And they accompanied him to the ship.

FIG TREE, THE

Produces a rich, sweet fruit.

Judg 9:11 But the fig tree said to them, 'Should I cease my sweetness and my good fruit, And go to sway over trees?'

Not found in desert places.

Num 20:5 And why have you made us come up out of Egypt, to bring us to this evil place? It *is* not a place of grain or figs or vines or pomegranates; nor *is* there any water to drink."

Abounded in

Egypt.

Ps 105:33 He struck their vines also, and their fig trees, And splintered the trees of their territory.

Canaan.

Num 13:23 Then they came to the Valley of Eshcol, and there cut down a branch with one cluster of grapes; they carried it between two of them on a pole. *They* also *brought* some of the pomegranates and figs.

Deut 8:8 a land of wheat and barley, of vines and fig trees and pomegranates, a land of olive oil and honey;

Often grew wild.

Amos 7:14 Then Amos answered, and said to Amaziah: "I *was* no prophet, Nor *was* I a son of a prophet, But I *was* a sheepbreeder And a tender of sycamore fruit.

Sometimes planted in vineyards.

Luke 13:6 He also spoke this parable: "A certain *man* had a fig tree planted in his vineyard, and he came seeking fruit on it and found none.

Grown by the Jews.

Amos 4:9 "I blasted you with blight and mildew. When your gardens increased, Your vineyards, Your fig trees, And your olive trees, The locust devoured *them*; Yet you have not returned to Me," Says the LORD.

Required cultivation.

Luke 13:8 But he answered and said to him, 'Sir, let it alone this year also, until I dig around it and fertilize *it*.

Fruit of, formed after winter.

Song 2:11 For lo, the winter is past, The rain is over *and* gone.

Song 2:13 The fig tree puts forth her green figs, And the vines *with* the tender grapes Give a good smell. Rise up, my love, my fair one, And come away!

New leaves of, a sign of the approach of summer.

Matt 24:32 "Now learn this parable from the fig tree:

When its branch has already become tender and puts forth leaves, you know that summer *is* near.

Reasonableness of expecting fruit upon, when full of leaves.

Mark 11:13 And seeing from afar a fig tree having leaves, He went to see if perhaps He would find something on it. When He came to it, He found nothing but leaves, for it was not the season for figs.

Fruit of,

Eaten fresh from the tree.

Matt 21:18–19 Now in the morning, as He returned to the city, He was hungry. **19** And seeing a fig tree by the road, He came to it and found nothing on it but leaves, and said to it, "Let no fruit grow on you ever again." Immediately the fig tree withered away.

Eaten dried in cakes.

1 Sam 30:12 And they gave him a piece of a cake of figs and two clusters of raisins. So when he had eaten, his strength came back to him; for he had eaten no bread nor drunk water for three days and three nights.

Gathered and kept in baskets.

Jer 24:1 The LORD showed me, and there were two baskets of figs set before the temple of the LORD, after Nebuchadnezzar king of Babylon had carried away captive Jeconiah the son of Jehoiakim, king of Judah, and the princes of Judah with the craftsmen and smiths, from Jerusalem, and had brought them to Babylon.

First ripened ones, valued.

Jer 24:2 One basket *had* very good figs, like the figs *that are* first ripe; and the other basket *had* very bad figs which could not be eaten, they were so bad.

Hos 9:10 "I found Israel Like grapes in the wilderness; I saw your fathers As the firstfruits on the fig tree in its first season. *But* they went to Baal Peor, And separated themselves *to that* shame; They became an abomination like the thing they loved.

Used in the miraculous healing of Hezekiah.

2 Kin 20:7 Then Isaiah said, "Take a lump of figs." So they took and laid *it* on the boil, and he recovered.

Is 38:21 Now Isaiah had said, "Let them take a lump of figs, and apply *it* as a poultice on the boil, and he shall recover."

Sold in the markets.

Neh 13:15 In those days I saw *people* in Judah treading wine presses on the Sabbath, and bringing in sheaves, and loading donkeys with wine, grapes, figs, and all *kinds of* burdens, which they brought into Jerusalem on the Sabbath day. And I warned *them* about the day on which they were selling provisions.

Sent as presents.

1 Sam 25:18 Then Abigail made haste and took two hundred *loaves* of bread, two skins of wine, five sheep already dressed, five seahs of roasted *grain,* one hundred clusters of raisins, and two hundred cakes of figs, and loaded *them* on donkeys.

1 Chr 12:40 Moreover those who were near to them, from as far away as Issachar and Zebulun and Naphtali, were bringing food on donkeys and camels, on mules and oxen—provisions of flour and cakes of figs and cakes of raisins, wine and oil and oxen and sheep abundantly, for *there was* joy in Israel.

Leaves of, used by Adam for covering.

Gen 3:7 Then the eyes of both of them were opened, and they knew that they *were* naked; and they sewed fig leaves together and made themselves coverings.

Afforded a thick shade.

John 1:48 Nathanael said to Him, "How do You know me?" Jesus answered and said to him, "Before Philip called you, when you were under the fig tree, I saw you."

John 1:50 Jesus answered and said to him, "Because I said to you, 'I saw you under the fig tree,' do you believe? You will see greater things than these."

Sometimes unfruitful.

Luke 13:7 Then he said to the keeper of his vineyard, 'Look, for three years I have come seeking fruit on this fig tree and find none. Cut it down; why does it use up the ground?'

Failure of, a great calamity.

Hab 3:17 Though the fig tree may not blossom, Nor fruit be on the vines; Though the labor of the olive may fail, And the fields yield no food; Though the flock may be cut off from the fold, And there be no herd in the stalls—

The Jews punished

By breaking down the trees.

Hos 2:12 "And I will destroy her vines and her fig trees, Of which she has said, 'These *are* my wages that my lovers have given me.' So I will make them a forest, And the beasts of the field shall eat them.

By failure of fruit on the trees.

Jer 8:13 "I will surely consume them," says the LORD. "No grapes *shall be* on the vine, Nor figs on the fig tree, And the leaf shall fade; And *the things* I have given them shall pass away from them." ' "

Hag 2:19 Is the seed still in the barn? As yet the vine, the fig tree, the pomegranate, and the olive tree have not yielded *fruit. But* from this day I will bless *you.*' "

By enemies devouring fruit of.

Jer 5:17 And they shall eat up your harvest and your bread, *Which* your sons and daughters should eat. They shall eat up your flocks and your herds; They shall eat up your vines and your fig trees; They shall destroy your fortified cities, In which you trust, with the sword.

By locusts eating of the trees.

Joel 1:4 What the chewing locust left, the swarming locust has eaten; What the swarming locust left, the crawling locust has eaten; And what the crawling locust left, the consuming locust has eaten.

Joel 1:7 He has laid waste My vine, And ruined My fig tree; He has stripped it bare and thrown *it* away; Its branches are made white.

Joel 1:12 The vine has dried up, And the fig tree has withered; The pomegranate tree, The palm tree also, And the apple tree— All the trees of the field are withered; Surely joy has withered away from the sons of men.

Amos 4:9 "I blasted you with blight and mildew. When your gardens increased, Your vineyards, Your fig trees, And your olive trees, The locust devoured *them*; Yet you have not returned to Me," Says the LORD.

Illustrative of

(Barren) mere professors of religion.

Matt 21:19 And seeing a fig tree by the road, He came to it and found nothing on it but leaves, and said to it, "Let no fruit grow on you ever again." Immediately the fig tree withered away.

Luke 13:6–7 He also spoke this parable: "A certain *man* had a fig tree planted in his vineyard, and he came seeking fruit on it and found none. 7 Then he said to the keeper of his vineyard, 'Look, for three years I have come seeking fruit on this fig tree and find none. Cut it down; why does it use up the ground?'

(Sitting under one's own) prosperity and peace.

1 Kin 4:25 And Judah and Israel dwelt safely, each man under his vine and his fig tree, from Dan as far as Beersheba, all the days of Solomon.

Mic 4:4 But everyone shall sit under his vine and under his fig tree, And no one shall make *them* afraid; For the mouth of the LORD of hosts has spoken.

Fruit of, illustrative of

Good works.

Matt 7:16 You will know them by their fruits. Do men gather grapes from thornbushes or figs from thistles?

(Good) believers.

Jer 24:2–3 One basket *had* very good figs, like the figs *that are* first ripe; and the other basket *had* very bad figs which could not be eaten, they were so bad. 3 Then the LORD said to me, "What do you see, Jeremiah?" And I said, "Figs, the good figs, very good; and the bad, very bad, which cannot be eaten, they are so bad."

(Bad, rotten) wicked men.

Jer 24:2–8 One basket *had* very good figs, like the figs *that are* first ripe; and the other basket *had* very bad figs which could not be eaten, they were so bad. 3 Then the LORD said to me, "What do you see, Jeremiah?" And I said, "Figs, the good figs, very good; and the bad, very bad, which cannot be eaten, they are so bad." 4 Again the word of the LORD came to me, saying, 5 "Thus says the LORD, the God of Israel: 'Like these good figs, so will I acknowledge those who are carried away captive from Judah, whom I have sent out of this place for *their own* good, into the land of the Chaldeans. 6 For I will set My eyes on them for good, and I will bring them back to this land; I will build them and not pull *them* down, and I will plant them and not pluck *them* up. 7 Then I will give them a heart to know Me, that I *am* the LORD; and they shall be My people, and I will be their God, for they shall return to Me with their whole heart. 8 'And as the bad figs which cannot be eaten, they are so bad'—surely thus says the LORD—'so will I give up Zedekiah the king of Judah, his princes, the residue of Jerusalem who remain in this land, and those who dwell in the land of Egypt.

Jer 29:17 thus says the LORD of hosts: Behold, I will send on them the sword, the famine, and the pestilence, and will make them like rotten figs that cannot be eaten, they are so bad.

(First ripe) the fathers of Israel.

Hos 9:10 "I found Israel Like grapes in the wilderness; I saw your fathers As the firstfruits on the fig tree in its first season. *But* they went to Baal Peor, And separated themselves *to that* shame; They became an abomination like the thing they loved.

(Untimely and dropping) the wicked ripe for judgment.

Is 34:4 All the host of heaven shall be dissolved, And the heavens shall be rolled up like a scroll; All their host shall fall down As the leaf falls from the vine, And as *fruit* falling from a fig tree.

Nah 3:12 All your strongholds *are* fig trees with ripened figs: If they are shaken, They fall into the mouth of the eater.

Rev 6:13 And the stars of heaven fell to the earth, as a fig tree drops its late figs when it is shaken by a mighty wind.

FIRE

Can be increased in intensity.

Dan 3:19 Then Nebuchadnezzar was full of fury, and the expression on his face changed toward Shadrach, Meshach, and Abed-Nego. He spoke and commanded that they heat the furnace seven times more than it was usually heated.

Dan 3:22 Therefore, because the king's command was urgent, and the furnace exceedingly hot, the flame of the fire killed those men who took up Shadrach, Meshach, and Abed-Nego.

Though small, kindles a great matter.

James 3:5 Even so the tongue is a little member and boasts great things. See how great a forest a little fire kindles!

Things connected with,

Burning coals and wood.

Prov 26:21 *As* charcoal *is* to burning coals, and wood to fire, So *is* a contentious man to kindle strife.

Burning brush and boiling water.

Is 64:2 As fire burns brushwood, As fire causes water to boil— To make Your name known to Your adversaries, *That* the nations may tremble at Your presence!

Flame.

Job 18:5 "The light of the wicked indeed goes out, And the flame of his fire does not shine.

Song 8:6 Set me as a seal upon your heart, As a seal upon your arm; For love *is as* strong as death, Jealousy *as* cruel as the grave; Its flames *are* flames of fire, A most vehement flame.

Is 66:15 For behold, the LORD will come with fire And with His chariots, like a whirlwind, To render His anger with fury, And His rebuke with flames of fire.

Sparks.

Is 1:31 The strong shall be as tinder, And the work of it as a spark; Both will burn together, And no one shall quench *them.*

Ashes.

1 Kin 13:3 And he gave a sign the same day, saying, "This *is* the sign which the LORD has spoken: Surely the altar shall split apart, and the ashes on it shall be poured out."

2 Pet 2:6 and turning the cities of Sodom and Gomorrah into ashes, condemned *them* to destruction, making *them* an example to those who afterward would live ungodly;

Smoke.

Is 34:10 It shall not be quenched night or day; Its smoke shall ascend forever. From generation to generation it shall lie waste; No one shall pass through it forever and ever.

Joel 2:30 "And I will show wonders in the heavens and in the earth: Blood and fire and pillars of smoke.

Kept alive by fuel.

Prov 26:20 Where *there is* no wood, the fire goes out; And where *there is* no talebearer, strife ceases.

Is 9:5 For every warrior's sandal from the noisy battle, And garments rolled in blood, Will be used for burning *and* fuel of fire.

Characterized as

Bright.

Ezek 1:13 As for the likeness of the living creatures, their appearance *was* like burning coals of fire, like the appearance of torches going back and forth among the living creatures. The fire was bright, and out of the fire went lightning.

Spreading.

James 3:5 Even so the tongue is a little member and boasts great things. See how great a forest a little fire kindles!

Illuminating.

Ps 78:14 In the daytime also He led them with the cloud, And all the night with a light of fire.

Ps 105:39 He spread a cloud for a covering, And fire to give light in the night.

Heating.

Mark 14:54 But Peter followed Him at a distance, right into the courtyard of the high priest. And he sat with the servants and warmed himself at the fire.

Melting.

Ps 68:2 As smoke is driven away, So drive *them* away; As wax melts before the fire, *So* let the wicked perish at the presence of God.

Purifying.

Num 31:23 everything that can endure fire, you shall put through the fire, and it shall be clean; and it shall be purified with the water of purification. But all that cannot endure fire you shall put through water.

1 Pet 1:7 that the genuineness of your faith, *being* much more precious than gold that perishes, though it is tested by fire, may be found to praise, honor, and glory at the revelation of Jesus Christ,

Rev 3:18 I counsel you to buy from Me gold refined in the fire, that you may be rich; and white garments, that you may be clothed, *that* the shame of your nakedness may not be revealed; and anoint your eyes with eye salve, that you may see.

Drying.

Job 15:30 He will not depart from darkness; The flame will dry out his branches, And by the breath of His mouth he will go away.

Joel 1:20 The beasts of the field also cry out to You, For the water brooks are dried up, And fire has devoured the open pastures.

Consuming.

Judg 15:4–5 Then Samson went and caught three hundred foxes; and he took torches, turned *the foxes* tail to tail, and put a torch between each pair of tails. 5 When he had set the torches on fire, he let *the foxes* go into the standing grain of the Philistines, and burned up both the shocks and the standing grain, as well as the vineyards *and* olive groves.

Ps 46:9 He makes wars cease to the end of the earth; He breaks the bow and cuts the spear in two; He burns the chariot in the fire.

Is 10:16–17 Therefore the Lord, the Lord of hosts, Will send leanness among his fat ones; And under his glory He will kindle a burning Like the burning of a fire. 17 So the Light of Israel will be for a fire, And his Holy One for a flame; It will burn and devour His thorns and his briers in one day.

Insatiable.

Prov 30:16 The grave, The barren womb, The earth *that* is not satisfied with water— And the fire never says, "Enough!"

Sacred,

Came from before the Lord.

Lev 9:24 and fire came out from before the LORD and consumed the burnt offering and the fat on the altar. When all the people saw *it*, they shouted and fell on their faces.

Always burning on the altar.

Lev 6:13 A fire shall always be burning on the altar; it shall never go out.

All burnt offerings consumed by.

Lev 6:9 "Command Aaron and his sons, saying, 'This *is* the law of the burnt offering: The burnt offering *shall be* on the hearth upon the altar all night until morning, and the fire of the altar shall be kept burning on it.

Lev 6:12 And the fire on the altar shall be kept burning on it; it shall not be put out. And the priest shall burn wood on it every morning, and lay the burnt offering in order on it; and he shall burn on it the fat of the peace offerings.

Incense burned with.

Lev 16:12 Then he shall take a censer full of burning coals of fire from the altar before the LORD, with his hands full of sweet incense beaten fine, and bring *it* inside the veil.

Num 16:46 So Moses said to Aaron, "Take a censer and put fire in it from the altar, put incense *on it*, and take it quickly to the congregation and make atonement for them; for wrath has gone out from the LORD. The plague has begun."

Guilt of burning incense without.

Lev 10:1 Then Nadab and Abihu, the sons of Aaron, each took his censer and put fire in it, put incense on it, and offered profane fire before the LORD, which He had not commanded them.

Restored to the temple.

2 Chr 7:1–3 When Solomon had finished praying, fire came down from heaven and consumed the burnt offering and the sacrifices; and the glory of the LORD filled the temple. 2 And the priests could not enter the house of the LORD, because the glory of the LORD had filled the LORD's house. 3 When all the children of Israel saw how the fire came down, and the glory of the LORD on the temple, they bowed their faces to the ground on the pavement, and worshiped and praised the LORD, saying: "For He is good, For His mercy endures forever."

Frequently employed as an instrument of divine vengeance.

Ps 97:3 A fire goes before Him, And burns up His enemies round about.

Is 47:14 Behold, they shall be as stubble, The fire shall burn them; They shall not deliver themselves From the power of the flame; It shall not be a coal to be warmed by, Nor a fire to sit before!

Is 66:16 For by fire and by His sword The LORD will judge all flesh; And the slain of the LORD shall be many.

Miraculous,

In the burning bush.

Ex 3:2 And the Angel of the LORD appeared to him in a flame of fire from the midst of a bush. So he looked, and behold, the bush was burning with fire, but the bush was not consumed.

Plagued the Egyptians.

Ex 9:23–24 And Moses stretched out his rod toward heaven; and the LORD sent thunder and hail, and fire darted to the ground. And the LORD rained hail on the land of Egypt. 24 So there was hail, and fire mingled with the hail, so very heavy that there was none like it in all the land of Egypt since it became a nation.

Led the people of Israel in the desert.

Ex 13:22 He did not take away the pillar of cloud by day or the pillar of fire by night from before the people.

Ex 40:38 For the cloud of the LORD was above the tabernacle by day, and fire was over it by night, in the sight of all the house of Israel, throughout all their journeys.

On Mount Sinai at giving of law.

Deut 4:11 "Then you came near and stood at the foot of the mountain, and the mountain burned with fire to the midst of heaven, with darkness, cloud, and thick darkness.

Deut 4:36 Out of heaven He let you hear His voice, that He might instruct you; on earth He showed you His great fire, and you heard His words out of the midst of the fire.

Destroyed Nadab and Abihu.

Lev 10:1–2 Then Nadab and Abihu, the sons of Aaron, each took his censer and put fire in it, put incense on it, and offered profane fire before the LORD, which He had not commanded them. 2 So fire went out from the LORD and devoured them, and they died before the LORD.

Destroyed the people at Taberah.

Num 11:1 Now when the people complained, it displeased the LORD; for the LORD heard it, and His anger was aroused. So the fire of the LORD burned among them, and consumed some in the outskirts of the camp.

Consumed the company of Korah.

Num 16:35 And a fire came out from the LORD and consumed the two hundred and fifty men who were offering incense.

Consumed the sacrifice of Gideon.

Judg 6:21 Then the Angel of the LORD put out the end of the staff that was in His hand, and touched the meat and the unleavened bread; and fire rose out of the rock and consumed the meat and the unleavened bread. And the Angel of the LORD departed out of his sight.

Angel ascended in.

Judg 13:20 it happened as the flame went up toward heaven from the altar—the Angel of the LORD ascended in the flame of the altar! When Manoah and his wife saw this, they fell on their faces to the ground.

Consumed the sacrifice of Elijah.

1 Kin 18:38 Then the fire of the LORD fell and consumed the burnt sacrifice, and the wood and the stones and the dust, and it licked up the water that was in the trench.

Destroyed the enemies of Elijah.

2 Kin 1:10 So Elijah answered and said to the captain of fifty, "If I am a man of God, then let fire come down from heaven and consume you and your fifty men." And fire came down from heaven and consumed him and his fifty.

2 Kin 1:12 So Elijah answered and said to them, "If I am a man of God, let fire come down from heaven and consume you and your fifty men." And the fire of God came down from heaven and consumed him and his fifty.

Elijah taken up in a chariot of.

2 Kin 2:11 Then it happened, as they continued on and talked, that suddenly a chariot of fire appeared with horses of fire, and separated the two of them; and Elijah went up by a whirlwind into heaven.

God appeared in.

Ex 3:2 And the Angel of the LORD appeared to him in a flame of fire from the midst of a bush. So he looked, and behold, the bush was burning with fire, but the bush was not consumed.

Ex 19:18 Now Mount Sinai was completely in smoke, because the LORD descended upon it in fire. Its smoke ascended like the smoke of a furnace, and the whole mountain quaked greatly.

Christ shall appear in.

Dan 7:10 A fiery stream issued And came forth from before Him. A thousand thousands ministered to Him; Ten thousand times ten thousand stood before Him. The court was seated, And the books were opened.

2 Thess 1:8 in flaming fire taking vengeance on those who do not know God, and on those who do not obey the gospel of our Lord Jesus Christ.

Punishment of the wicked shall be in.

Matt 13:42 and will cast them into the furnace of fire. There will be wailing and gnashing of teeth.

Matt 25:41 "Then He will also say to those on the left hand, 'Depart from Me, you cursed, into the everlasting fire prepared for the devil and his angels:

In houses,

Lighted in the winter.

Jer 36:22 Now the king was sitting in the winter house in the ninth month, with *a fire* burning on the hearth before him.

Lighted on spring mornings.

John 18:18 Now the servants and officers who had made a fire of coals stood there, for it was cold, and they warmed themselves. And Peter stood with them and warmed himself.

Not to be lighted on the Sabbath.

Ex 35:3 You shall kindle no fire throughout your dwellings on the Sabbath day."

Made from charcoal.

John 18:18 Now the servants and officers who had made a fire of coals stood there, for it was cold, and they warmed themselves. And Peter stood with them and warmed himself.

Made from wood.

Acts 28:3 But when Paul had gathered a bundle of sticks and laid *them* on the fire, a viper came out because of the heat, and fastened on his hand.

Injury from, to be made good by the person who kindled it.

Ex 22:6 "If fire breaks out and catches in thorns, so that stacked grain, standing grain, or the field is consumed, he who kindled the fire shall surely make restitution.

Illustrative of

God's protection.

Num 9:16 So it was always: the cloud covered it *by day*, and the appearance of fire by night.

Zech 2:5 For I,' says the LORD, 'will be a wall of fire all around her, and I will be the glory in her midst.' "

God's vengeance.

Deut 4:24 For the LORD your God *is* a consuming fire, a jealous God.

Heb 12:29 For our God *is* a consuming fire.

Christ as judge.

Is 10:17 So the Light of Israel will be for a fire, And his Holy One for a flame; It will burn and devour His thorns and his briers in one day.

Mal 3:2 "But who can endure the day of His coming? And who can stand when He appears? For He *is* like a refiner's fire And like launderers' soap.

The Holy Spirit.

Is 4:4 When the Lord has washed away the filth of the daughters of Zion, and purged the blood of Jerusalem from her midst, by the spirit of judgment and by the spirit of burning,

Acts 2:3 Then there appeared to them divided tongues, as of fire, and *one* sat upon each of them.

God's people destroying their enemies.

Is 10:17 So the Light of Israel will be for a fire, And his Holy One for a flame; It will burn and devour His thorns and his briers in one day.

Obad 1:18 The house of Jacob shall be a fire, And the house of Joseph a flame; But the house of Esau *shall be* stubble; They shall kindle them and devour them,

And no survivor shall *remain* of the house of Esau," For the LORD has spoken.

The word of God.

Jer 5:14 Therefore thus says the LORD God of hosts: "Because you speak this word, Behold, I will make My words in your mouth fire, And this people wood, And it shall devour them.

Jer 23:29 *"Is* not My word like a fire?" says the LORD, "And like a hammer *that* breaks the rock in pieces?

Zeal of believers.

Ps 39:3 My heart was hot within me; While I was musing, the fire burned. *Then* I spoke with my tongue:

Ps 119:139 My zeal has consumed me, Because my enemies have forgotten Your words.

Zeal of angels.

Ps 104:4 Who makes His angels spirits, His ministers a flame of fire.

Heb 1:7 And of the angels He says: *"Who makes His angels spirits And His ministers a flame of fire."*

Lust.

Prov 6:27–28 Can a man take fire to his bosom, And his clothes not be burned? **28** Can one walk on hot coals, And his feet not be seared?

Wickedness.

Is 9:18 For wickedness burns as the fire; It shall devour the briers and thorns, And kindle in the thickets of the forest; They shall mount up *like* rising smoke.

The tongue.

Prov 16:27 An ungodly man digs up evil, And *it is* on his lips like a burning fire.

James 3:6 And the tongue *is* a fire, a world of iniquity. The tongue is so set among our members that it defiles the whole body, and sets on fire the course of nature; and it is set on fire by hell.

The self-righteous.

Is 65:5 Who say, 'Keep to yourself, Do not come near me, For I am holier than you!' These *are* smoke in My nostrils, A fire that burns all the day.

The hope of hypocrites.

Is 50:11 Look, all you who kindle a fire, Who encircle *yourselves* with sparks: Walk in the light of your fire and in the sparks you have kindled— This you shall have from My hand: You shall lie down in torment.

Persecution.

Luke 12:49–53 "I came to send fire on the earth, and how I wish it were already kindled! **50** But I have a baptism to be baptized with, and how distressed I am till it is accomplished! **51** Do *you* suppose that I came to give peace on earth? I tell you, not at all, but rather division. **52** For from now on five in one house will be divided: three against two, and two against three. **53** Father will be divided against son and son against father, mother against daughter and daughter against mother, mother-in-law against her daughter-in-law and daughter-in-law against her mother-in-law."

Affliction.

Is 43:2 When you pass through the waters, I *will be* with you; And through the rivers, they shall not overflow you. When you walk through the fire, you shall not be burned, Nor shall the flame scorch you.

Judgments.

Jer 48:45 "Those who fled stood under the shadow of Heshbon Because of exhaustion. But a fire shall come out of Heshbon, A flame from the midst of Sihon, And shall devour the brow of Moab, The crown of the head of the sons of tumult.

Lam 1:13 "From above He has sent fire into my bones, And it overpowered them; He has spread a net for my feet And turned me back; He has made me desolate *And* faint all the day.

Ezek 39:6 "And I will send fire on Magog and on those who live in security in the coastlands. Then they shall know that I *am* the LORD.

FIRSTBORN, THE

Of man and beast, dedicated to God.

Ex 13:2 "Consecrate to Me all the firstborn, whatever opens the womb among the children of Israel, *both* of man and beast; it is Mine."

Ex 13:12 that you shall set apart to the LORD all that open the womb, that is, every firstborn that comes from an animal which you have; the males *shall be* the LORD's.

Ex 22:29 "You shall not delay *to offer* the first of your ripe produce and your juices. The firstborn of your sons you shall give to Me.

Dedicated to commemorate the first Passover.

Ex 13:15 And it came to pass, when Pharaoh was stubborn about letting us go, that the LORD killed all the firstborn in the land of Egypt, both the firstborn of man and the firstborn of beast. Therefore I sacrifice to the LORD all males that open the womb, but all the firstborn of my sons I redeem.'

Num 3:13 because all the firstborn *are* Mine. On the day that I struck all the firstborn in the land of Egypt, I sanctified to Myself all the firstborn in Israel, both man and beast. They shall be Mine: I *am* the LORD."

Num 8:17 For all the firstborn among the children of Israel *are* Mine, *both* man and beast; on the day that I struck all the firstborn in the land of Egypt I sanctified them to Myself.

Of clean beasts

Not to labor.

Deut 15:19 "All the firstborn males that come from your herd and your flock you shall sanctify to the LORD your God; you shall do no work with the firstborn of your herd, nor shear the firstborn of your flock.

Not shorn.

Deut 15:19 "All the firstborn males that come from your herd and your flock you shall sanctify to the LORD your God; you shall do no work with the firstborn of your herd, nor shear the firstborn of your flock.

Not taken from the mother for seven days.

Ex 22:30 Likewise you shall do with your oxen *and* your sheep. It shall be with its mother seven days; on the eighth day you shall give it to Me.

Lev 22:27 "When a bull or a sheep or a goat is born, it shall be seven days with its mother; and from the eighth day and thereafter it shall be accepted as an offering made by fire to the LORD.

Offered in sacrifice.

Num 18:17 But the firstborn of a cow, the firstborn of a sheep, or the firstborn of a goat you shall not redeem; they *are* holy. You shall sprinkle their blood on the altar, and burn their fat *as* an offering made by fire for a sweet aroma to the LORD.

Could not be a free-will offering.

Lev 27:26 'But the firstborn of the animals, which should be the LORD's firstborn, no man shall dedicate; whether *it is* an ox or sheep, it *is* the LORD's.

Antiquity of offering.

Gen 4:4 Abel also brought of the firstborn of his flock and of their fat. And the LORD respected Abel and his offering,

Flesh of, the priest's portion.

Num 18:18 And their flesh shall be yours, just as the wave breast and the right thigh are yours.

Of unclean beasts

To be redeemed.

Num 18:15 "Everything that first opens the womb of all flesh, which they bring to the LORD, whether man or beast, shall be yours; nevertheless the firstborn of man you shall surely redeem, and the firstborn of unclean animals you shall redeem.

Law of redemption for.

Num 18:16 And those redeemed of the devoted things you shall redeem when one month old, according to your valuation, for five shekels of silver, according to the shekel of the sanctuary, which *is* twenty gerahs.

Of the donkey, to be redeemed with lamb, or its neck broken.

Ex 13:13 But every firstborn of a donkey you shall redeem with a lamb; and if you will not redeem *it*, then you shall break its neck. And all the firstborn of man among your sons you shall redeem.

Ex 34:20 But the firstborn of a donkey you shall redeem with a lamb. And if you will not redeem *him*, then you shall break his neck. All the firstborn of your sons you shall redeem. "And none shall appear before Me empty-handed.

Of Israel,

Tribe of Levi taken for.

Num 3:12 "Now behold, I Myself have taken the Levites from among the children of Israel instead of every firstborn who opens the womb among the children of Israel. Therefore the Levites shall be Mine,

Num 3:40–43 Then the LORD said to Moses: "Number all the firstborn males of the children of Israel from a month old and above, and take the number of their names. **41** And you shall take the Levites for Me—I *am* the LORD—instead of all the firstborn among the children of Israel, and the livestock of the Levites instead of all the firstborn among the livestock of the children of Israel." **42** So Moses numbered all the firstborn among the children of Israel, as the LORD commanded him. **43** And all the firstborn males, according to the number of names from a month old and above, of those who were numbered of them, were twenty-two thousand two hundred and seventy-three.

Num 8:18 I have taken the Levites instead of all the firstborn of the children of Israel.

To be redeemed.

Ex 34:20 But the firstborn of a donkey you shall redeem

with a lamb. And if you will not redeem *him*, then you shall break his neck. All the firstborn of your sons you shall redeem. "And none shall appear before Me empty-handed.

Num 18:15 "Everything that first opens the womb of all flesh, which they bring to the LORD, whether man or beast, shall be yours; nevertheless the firstborn of man you shall surely redeem, and the firstborn of unclean animals you shall redeem.

Price of redemption for.

Num 3:46–47 And for the redemption of the two hundred and seventy-three of the firstborn of the children of Israel, who are more than the number of the Levites, **47** you shall take five shekels for each one individually; you shall take *them* in the currency of the shekel of the sanctuary, the shekel of twenty gerahs.

Price of, given to the priests.

Num 3:48–51 And you shall give the money, with which the excess number of them is redeemed, to Aaron and his sons." **49** So Moses took the redemption money from those who were over and above those who were redeemed by the Levites. **50** From the firstborn of the children of Israel he took the money, one thousand three hundred and sixty-five *shekels*, according to the shekel of the sanctuary. **51** And Moses gave their redemption money to Aaron and his sons, according to the word of the LORD, as the LORD commanded Moses.

Laws respecting, restored after the captivity.

Neh 10:36 to bring the firstborn of our sons and our cattle, as *it is* written in the Law, and the firstborn of our herds and our flocks, to the house of our God, to the priests who minister in the house of our God;

Laws respecting, observed at Christ's birth.

Luke 2:22–23 Now when the days of her purification according to the law of Moses were completed, they brought Him to Jerusalem to present *Him* to the Lord **23** (as it is written in the law of the Lord, *"Every male who opens the womb shall be called holy to the LORD"*),

The beginning of strength and excellency of power.

Gen 49:3 "Reuben, you are my firstborn, My might and the beginning of my strength, The excellency of dignity and the excellency of power.

Deut 21:17 But he shall acknowledge the son of the unloved wife *as* the firstborn by giving him a double portion of all that he has, for he *is* the beginning of his strength; the right of the firstborn *is* his.

Precious and valuable.

Mic 6:7 Will the LORD be pleased with thousands of rams, Ten thousand rivers of oil? Shall I give my firstborn *for* my transgression, The fruit of my body *for* the sin of my soul?

Zech 12:10 "And I will pour on the house of David and on the inhabitants of Jerusalem the Spirit of grace and supplication; then they will look on Me whom they pierced. Yes, they will mourn for Him as one mourns for *his* only *son,* and grieve for Him as one grieves for a firstborn.

Objects of special love.

Gen 25:28 And Isaac loved Esau because he ate *of his* game, but Rebekah loved Jacob.

Jer 31:9 They shall come with weeping, And with supplications I will lead them. I will cause them to walk by the rivers of waters, In a straight way in which they shall not stumble; For I am a Father to Israel, And Ephraim *is* My firstborn.

Jer 31:20 *Is* Ephraim My dear son? *Is he* a pleasant child? For though I spoke against him, I earnestly remember him still; Therefore My heart yearns for him; I will surely have mercy on him, says the LORD.

Privileges of,

Precedence in the family.

Gen 48:13–14 And Joseph took them both, Ephraim with his right hand toward Israel's left hand, and Manasseh with his left hand toward Israel's right hand, and brought *them* near him. **14** Then Israel stretched out his right hand and laid *it* on Ephraim's head, who *was* the younger, and his left hand on Manasseh's head, guiding his hands knowingly, for Manasseh *was* the firstborn.

Authority over the younger children.

Gen 27:29 Let peoples serve you, And nations bow down to you. Be master over your brethren, And let your mother's sons bow down to you. Cursed *be* everyone who curses you, And blessed *be* those who bless you!"

1 Sam 20:29 And he said, 'Please let me go, for our family has a sacrifice in the city, and my brother has commanded me *to be there.* And now, if I have found favor in your eyes, please let me get away and see my brothers.' Therefore he has not come to the king's table."

Special blessing by the father.

Gen 27:4 And make me savory food, such as I love, and bring *it* to me that I may eat, that my soul may bless you before I die."

Gen 27:35 But he said, "Your brother came with deceit and has taken away your blessing."

The father's title and power.

2 Chr 21:3 Their father gave them great gifts of silver and gold and precious things, with fortified cities in Judah; but he gave the kingdom to Jehoram, because he *was* the firstborn.

A double portion of inheritance.

Deut 21:17 But he shall acknowledge the son of the unloved wife *as* the firstborn by giving him a double portion of all that he has, for he *is* the beginning of his strength; the right of the firstborn *is* his.

In case of death, the next brother to raise up offspring to.

Deut 25:5–6 "If brothers dwell together, and one of them dies and has no son, the widow of the dead man shall not be *married* to a stranger outside *the family;* her husband's brother shall go in to her, take her as his wife, and perform the duty of a husband's brother to her. **6** And it shall be *that* the firstborn son which she bears will succeed to the name of his dead brother, that his name may not be blotted out of Israel.

Matt 22:24–28 saying: "Teacher, Moses said that if a man dies, having no children, his brother shall marry his wife and raise up offspring for his brother. **25** Now there were with us seven brothers. The first died after he had married, and having no offspring, left his wife to his brother. **26** Likewise the second also, and the third, even to the seventh. **27** Last of all the woman died also. **28** Therefore, in the resurrection, whose wife of the seven will she be? For they all had her."

Not to be reallocated by parents through caprice.

Deut 21:15–16 "If a man has two wives, one loved and the other unloved, and they have borne him children, *both* the loved and the unloved, and *if* the firstborn son is of her who is unloved, **16** then it shall be, on the day he bequeaths his possessions to his sons, *that* he must not bestow firstborn status on the son of the loved wife in preference to the son of the unloved, the *true* firstborn.

Could be forfeited by misconduct.

Gen 49:3–4 "Reuben, you are my firstborn, My might and the beginning of my strength, The excellency of dignity and the excellency of power. **4** Unstable as water, you shall not excel, Because you went up to your father's bed; Then you defiled *it*— He went up to my couch.

Gen 49:8 "Judah, you *are he* whom your brothers shall praise; Your hand *shall be* on the neck of your enemies; Your father's children shall bow down before you.

1 Chr 5:1 Now the sons of Reuben the firstborn of Israel—he *was* indeed the firstborn, but because he defiled his father's bed, his birthright was given to the sons of Joseph, the son of Israel, so that the genealogy is not listed according to the birthright;

Could be sold.

Gen 25:31 But Jacob said, "Sell me your birthright as of this day."

Gen 25:33 Then Jacob said, "Swear to me as of this day." So he swore to him, and sold his birthright to Jacob.

Heb 12:16–17 lest there *be* any fornicator or profane person like Esau, who for one morsel of food sold his birthright. **17** For you know that afterward, when he wanted to inherit the blessing, he was rejected, for he found no place for repentance, though he sought it diligently with tears.

Instances of, superseded

Cain.

Gen 4:4–5 Abel also brought of the firstborn of his flock and of their fat. And the LORD respected Abel and his offering, **5** but He did not respect Cain and his offering. And Cain was very angry, and his countenance fell.

Japheth.

Gen 10:21 And *children* were born also to Shem, the father of all the children of Eber, the brother of Japheth the elder.

Ishmael.

Gen 17:19–21 Then God said: "No, Sarah your wife shall bear you a son, and you shall call his name Isaac; I will establish My covenant with him for an everlasting covenant, *and* with his descendants after him. **20** And as for Ishmael, I have heard you. Behold, I have blessed him, and will make him fruitful, and will multiply him exceedingly. He shall beget twelve princes, and I will make him a great nation.

21 But My covenant I will establish with Isaac, whom Sarah shall bear to you at this set time next year."

Esau.

Gen 25:23 And the LORD said to her: "Two nations *are* in your womb, Two peoples shall be separated from your body; *One* people shall be stronger than the other, And the older shall serve the younger."

Rom 9:12–13 it was said to her, *"The older shall serve the younger."* **13** As it is written, *"Jacob I have loved, but Esau I have hated."*

Manasseh.

Gen 48:15–20 And he blessed Joseph, and said: "God, before whom my fathers Abraham and Isaac walked, The God who has fed me all my life long to this day, **16** The Angel who has redeemed me from all evil, Bless the lads; Let my name be named upon them, And the name of my fathers Abraham and Isaac; And let them grow into a multitude in the midst of the earth." **17** Now when Joseph saw that his father laid his right hand on the head of Ephraim, it displeased him; so he took hold of his father's hand to remove it from Ephraim's head to Manasseh's head. **18** And Joseph said to his father, "Not so, my father, for this *one is* the firstborn; put your right hand on his head." **19** But his father refused and said, "I know, my son, I know. He also shall become a people, and he also shall be great; but truly his younger brother shall be greater than he, and his descendants shall become a multitude of nations." **20** So he blessed them that day, saying, "By you Israel will bless, saying, 'May God make you as Ephraim and as Manasseh!' " And thus he set Ephraim before Manasseh.

Reuben, etc.

1 Chr 5:1–2 Now the sons of Reuben the firstborn of Israel—he *was* indeed the firstborn, but because he defiled his father's bed, his birthright was given to the sons of Joseph, the son of Israel, so that the genealogy is not listed according to the birthright; **2** yet Judah prevailed over his brothers, and from him *came* a ruler, although the birthright was Joseph's—

Aaron.

Ex 7:1–2 So the LORD said to Moses: "See, I have made you *as* God to Pharaoh, and Aaron your brother shall be your prophet. **2** You shall speak all that I command you. And Aaron your brother shall tell Pharaoh to send the children of Israel out of his land.

Num 12:2 So they said, "Has the LORD indeed spoken only through Moses? Has He not spoken through us also?" And the LORD heard *it.*

Num 12:8 I speak with him face to face, Even plainly, and not in dark sayings; And he sees the form of the LORD. Why then were you not afraid To speak against My servant Moses?"

David's brothers.

1 Sam 16:6–12 So it was, when they came, that he looked at Eliab and said, "Surely the LORD's anointed *is* before Him!" **7** But the LORD said to Samuel, "Do not look at his appearance or at his physical stature, because I have refused him. For *the LORD does* not *see* as man sees; for man looks at the outward appearance, but the LORD looks at the heart." **8** So Jesse called Abinadab, and made him pass before Samuel. And he said, "Neither has the LORD chosen this one."

9 Then Jesse made Shammah pass by. And he said, "Neither has the LORD chosen this one." **10** Thus Jesse made seven of his sons pass before Samuel. And Samuel said to Jesse, "The LORD has not chosen these." **11** And Samuel said to Jesse, "Are all the young men here?" Then he said, "There remains yet the youngest, and there he is, keeping the sheep." And Samuel said to Jesse, "Send and bring him. For we will not sit down till he comes here." **12** So he sent and brought him in. Now he *was* ruddy, with bright eyes, and good-looking. And the LORD said, "Arise, anoint him; for this *is* the one!"

Adonijah.

1 Kin 2:15 Then he said, "You know that the kingdom was mine, and all Israel had set their expectations on me, that I should reign. However, the kingdom has been turned over, and has become my brother's; for it was his from the LORD.

1 Kin 2:22 And King Solomon answered and said to his mother, "Now why do you ask Abishag the Shunammite for Adonijah? Ask for him the kingdom also— for he *is* my older brother—for him, and for Abiathar the priest, and for Joab the son of Zeruiah."

Illustrative of

The dignity, etc., of Christ.

Ps 89:27 Also I will make him *My* firstborn, The highest of the kings of the earth.

Rom 8:29 For whom He foreknew, He also predestined *to be* conformed to the image of His Son, that He might be the firstborn among many brethren.

Col 1:18 And He is the head of the body, the church, who is the beginning, the firstborn from the dead, that in all things He may have the preeminence.

The dignity, etc., of the church.

Heb 12:23 to the general assembly and church of the firstborn *who are* registered in heaven, to God the Judge of all, to the spirits of just men made perfect,

FIRSTFRUITS, THE

To be brought to God's house.

Ex 34:26 "The first of the firstfruits of your land you shall bring to the house of the LORD your God. You shall not boil a young goat in its mother's milk."

Different kinds of,

Barley harvest.

Lev 23:10–14 "Speak to the children of Israel, and say to them: 'When you come into the land which I give to you, and reap its harvest, then you shall bring a sheaf of the firstfruits of your harvest to the priest. **11** He shall wave the sheaf before the LORD, to be accepted on your behalf; on the day after the Sabbath the priest shall wave it. **12** And you shall offer on that day, when you wave the sheaf, a male lamb of the first year, without blemish, as a burnt offering to the LORD. **13** Its grain offering *shall be* two-tenths *of an ephah* of fine flour mixed with oil, an offering made by fire to the LORD, for a sweet aroma; and its drink offering *shall be* of wine, one-fourth of a hin. **14** You shall eat neither bread nor parched grain nor fresh grain until the same day that you have brought an offering to your God; *it shall be* a statute forever throughout your generations in all your dwellings.

Wheat harvest.

Ex 23:16 and the Feast of Harvest, the firstfruits of your labors which you have sown in the field; and the Feast of Ingathering at the end of the year, when you have gathered in *the fruit of* your labors from the field.

Lev 23:16–17 Count fifty days to the day after the seventh Sabbath; then you shall offer a new grain offering to the LORD. **17** You shall bring from your dwellings two wave *loaves* of two-tenths *of an ephah.* They shall be of fine flour; they shall be baked with leaven. *They are* the firstfruits to the LORD.

Wine and oil.

Deut 18:4 The firstfruits of your grain and your new wine and your oil, and the first of the fleece of your sheep, you shall give him.

Wool.

Deut 18:4 The firstfruits of your grain and your new wine and your oil, and the first of the fleece of your sheep, you shall give him.

Honey.

2 Chr 31:5 As soon as the commandment was circulated, the children of Israel brought in abundance the firstfruits of grain and wine, oil and honey, and of all the produce of the field; and they brought in abundantly the tithe of everything.

Fruit of new trees in fourth year.

Lev 19:23–24 'When you come into the land, and have planted all kinds of trees for food, then you shall count their fruit as uncircumcised. Three years it shall be as uncircumcised to you. *It* shall not be eaten. **24** But in the fourth year all its fruit shall be holy, a praise to the LORD.

All agricultural produce.

Deut 26:2 that you shall take some of the first of all the produce of the ground, which you shall bring from your land that the LORD your God is giving you, and put *it* in a basket and go to the place where the LORD your God chooses to make His name abide.

To be the very best of their kind.

Num 18:12 "All the best of the oil, all the best of the new wine and the grain, their firstfruits which they offer to the LORD, I have given them to you.

Holy to the Lord.

Ezek 48:14 And they shall not sell or exchange any of it; they may not alienate this best *part* of the land, for *it* is holy to the LORD.

God honored by the offering of.

Prov 3:9 Honor the LORD with your possessions, And with the firstfruits of all your increase;

Offering of, consecrated the whole.

Rom 11:16 For if the firstfruit *is* holy, the lump *is* also *holy;* and if the root *is* holy, so *are* the branches.

To be offered

Without delay.

Ex 22:29 "You shall not delay *to offer* the first of your ripe produce and your juices. The firstborn of your sons you shall give to Me.

In a basket.

Deut 26:2 that you shall take some of the first of all the

produce of the ground, which you shall bring from your land that the LORD your God is giving you, and put *it* in a basket and go to the place where the LORD your God chooses to make His name abide.

With thanksgiving.

Deut 26:3–10 And you shall go to the one who is priest in those days, and say to him, 'I declare today to the LORD your God that I have come to the country which the LORD swore to our fathers to give us.' **4** "Then the priest shall take the basket out of your hand and set it down before the altar of the LORD your God. **5** And you shall answer and say before the LORD your God: 'My father *was* a Syrian, about to perish, and he went down to Egypt and dwelt there, few in number; and there he became a nation, great, mighty, and populous. **6** But the Egyptians mistreated us, afflicted us, and laid hard bondage on us. **7** Then we cried out to the LORD God of our fathers, and the LORD heard our voice and looked on our affliction and our labor and our oppression. **8** So the LORD brought us out of Egypt with a mighty hand and with an outstretched arm, with great terror and with signs and wonders. **9** He has brought us to this place and has given us this land, "a land flowing with milk and honey"; **10** and now, behold, I have brought the firstfruits of the land which you, O LORD, have given me.' "Then you shall set it before the LORD your God, and worship before the LORD your God.

Allotted to the priests.

Lev 23:20 The priest shall wave them with the bread of the firstfruits *as* a wave offering before the LORD, with the two lambs. They shall be holy to the LORD for the priest.

Num 18:12–13 "All the best of the oil, all the best of the new wine and the grain, their firstfruits which they offer to the LORD, I have given them to you. **13** Whatever first ripe fruit is in their land, which they bring to the LORD, shall be yours. Everyone who is clean in your house may eat it.

Deut 18:3–5 "And this shall be the priest's due from the people, from those who offer a sacrifice, whether *it is* bull or sheep: they shall give to the priest the shoulder, the cheeks, and the stomach. **4** The firstfruits of your grain and your new wine and your oil, and the first of the fleece of your sheep, you shall give him. **5** For the LORD your God has chosen him out of all your tribes to stand to minister in the name of the LORD, him and his sons forever.

Law of, restored after the captivity.

Neh 10:35 And *we made ordinances* to bring the firstfruits of our ground and the firstfruits of all fruit of all trees, year by year, to the house of the LORD;

Neh 10:37 to bring the firstfruits of our dough, our offerings, the fruit from all kinds of trees, *the* new wine and oil, to the priests, to the storerooms of the house of our God; and to bring the tithes of our land to the Levites, for the Levites should receive the tithes in all our farming communities.

Neh 13:31 and *to bringing* the wood offering and the firstfruits at appointed times. Remember me, O my God, for good!

Illustrative of

People of Israel.

Jer 2:3 Israel *was* holiness to the LORD, The firstfruits of His increase. All that devour him will offend; Disaster will come upon them," says the LORD.' "

First converts in any place.

Rom 16:5 Likewise *greet* the church that is in their house. Greet my beloved Epaenetus, who is the firstfruits of Achaia to Christ.

Church of Christ.

James 1:18 Of His own will He brought us forth by the word of truth, that we might be a kind of firstfruits of His creatures.

Rev 14:4 These are the ones who were not defiled with women, for they are virgins. These are the ones who follow the Lamb wherever He goes. These were redeemed from *among* men, *being* firstfruits to God and to the Lamb.

Resurrection of Christ.

1 Cor 15:20 But now Christ is risen from the dead, *and* has become the firstfruits of those who have fallen asleep.

1 Cor 15:23 But each one in his own order: Christ the firstfruits, afterward those *who are* Christ's at His coming.

FISH

Created by God.

Gen 1:20–21 Then God said, "Let the waters abound with an abundance of living creatures, and let birds fly above the earth across the face of the firmament of the heavens." **21** So God created great sea creatures and every living thing that moves, with which the waters abounded, according to their kind, and every winged bird according to its kind. And God saw that *it was* good.

Ex 20:11 For *in* six days the LORD made the heavens and the earth, the sea, and all that *is* in them, and rested the seventh day. Therefore the LORD blessed the Sabbath day and hallowed it.

Made for God's glory.

Job 12:8–9 Or speak to the earth, and it will teach you; And the fish of the sea will explain to you. **9** Who among all these does not know That the hand of the LORD has done this,

Ps 69:34 Let heaven and earth praise Him, The seas and everything that moves in them.

Inhabit

Seas.

Num 11:22 Shall flocks and herds be slaughtered for them, to provide enough for them? Or shall all the fish of the sea be gathered together for them, to provide enough for them?"

Ezek 47:10 It shall be *that* fishermen will stand by it from En Gedi to En Eglaim; they will be *places* for spreading their nets. Their fish will be of the same kinds as the fish of the Great Sea, exceedingly many.

Rivers.

Ex 7:18 And the fish that *are* in the river shall die, the river shall stink, and the Egyptians will loathe to drink the water of the river." ' "

Ezek 29:5 I will leave you in the wilderness, You and all the fish of your rivers; You shall fall on the open field; You shall not be picked up or gathered. I have given you as food To the beasts of the field And to the birds of the heavens.

Number and variety of.

Ps 104:25 This great and wide sea, In which *are* innumerable teeming things, Living things both small and great.

Different in flesh from beasts, etc.

1 Cor 15:39 All flesh *is* not the same flesh, but *there is* one *kind of* flesh of men, another flesh of animals, another of fish, *and* another of birds.

Cannot live without water.

Is 50:2 Why, when I came, *was there* no man? *Why*, when I called, *was there* none to answer? Is My hand shortened at all that it cannot redeem? Or have I no power to deliver? Indeed with My rebuke I dry up the sea, I make the rivers a wilderness; Their fish stink because *there is* no water, And die of thirst.

Man given dominion over.

Gen 1:26 Then God said, "Let Us make man in Our image, according to Our likeness; let them have dominion over the fish of the sea, over the birds of the air, and over the cattle, over all the earth and over every creeping thing that creeps on the earth."

Gen 1:28 Then God blessed them, and God said to them, "Be fruitful and multiply; fill the earth and subdue it; have dominion over the fish of the sea, over the birds of the air, and over every living thing that moves on the earth."

Ps 8:8 The birds of the air, And the fish of the sea That pass through the paths of the seas.

Man permitted to eat.

Gen 9:2–3 And the fear of you and the dread of you shall be on every beast of the earth, on every bird of the air, on all that move *on* the earth, and on all the fish of the sea. They are given into your hand. **3** Every moving thing that lives shall be food for you. I have given you all things, even as the green herbs.

Used as food

By the Egyptians.

Num 11:5 We remember the fish which we ate freely in Egypt, the cucumbers, the melons, the leeks, the onions, and the garlic;

By the Jews.

Matt 7:10 Or if he asks for a fish, will he give him a serpent?

Method of cooking alluded to.

Luke 24:42 So they gave Him a piece of a broiled fish and some honeycomb.

John 21:9 Then, as soon as they had come to land, they saw a fire of coals there, and fish laid on it, and bread.

The people of Tyre traded in.

Neh 13:16 Men of Tyre dwelt there also, who brought in fish and all kinds of goods, and sold *them* on the Sabbath to the children of Judah, and in Jerusalem.

Gate at Jerusalem associated with.

2 Chr 33:14 After this he built a wall outside the City of David on the west side of Gihon, in the valley, as far as the entrance of the Fish Gate; and *it* enclosed Ophel, and he raised it to a very great height. Then he put military captains in all the fortified cities of Judah.

Zeph 1:10 "And there shall be on that day," says the Lord, "The sound of a mournful cry from the Fish Gate, A wailing from the Second Quarter, And a loud crashing from the hills.

Distinction between clean and unclean.

Lev 11:9–12 These you may eat of all that *are* in the water: whatever in the water has fins and scales, whether in the seas or in the rivers—that you may eat. **10** But all in the seas or in the rivers that do not have fins and scales, all that move in the water or any living thing which *is* in the water, they *are* an abomination to you. **11** They shall be an abomination to you; you shall not eat their flesh, but you shall regard their carcasses as an abomination. **12** Whatever in the water does not have fins or scales—that *shall be* an abomination to you.

Deut 14:9–10 "These you may eat of all that *are* in the waters: you may eat all that have fins and scales. **10** And whatever does not have fins and scales you shall not eat; it *is* unclean for you.

Some were very large.

Gen 1:21 So God created great sea creatures and every living thing that moves, with which the waters abounded, according to their kind, and every winged bird according to its kind. And God saw that *it was* good.

Matt 12:40 For as Jonah was three days and three nights in the belly of the great fish, so will the Son of Man be three days and three nights in the heart of the earth.

Solomon wrote the history of.

1 Kin 4:33 Also he spoke of trees, from the cedar tree of Lebanon even to the hyssop that springs out of the wall; he spoke also of animals, of birds, of creeping things, and of fish.

No likeness of, to be made for worship.

Ex 20:4 "You shall not make for yourself a carved image—any likeness *of anything* that *is* in heaven above, or that *is* in the earth beneath, or that *is* in the water under the earth;

Deut 4:18 the likeness of anything that creeps on the ground or the likeness of any fish that *is* in the water beneath the earth.

Catching of, a trade.

Matt 4:18 And Jesus, walking by the Sea of Galilee, saw two brothers, Simon called Peter, and Andrew his brother, casting a net into the sea; for they were fishermen.

Luke 5:2 and saw two boats standing by the lake; but the fishermen had gone from them and were washing *their* nets.

Taken with

Nets.

Luke 5:4–6 When He had stopped speaking, He said to Simon, "Launch out into the deep and let down your nets for a catch." **5** But Simon answered and said to Him, "Master, we have toiled all night and caught nothing; nevertheless at Your word I will let down the net." **6** And when they had done this, they caught a great number of fish, and their net was breaking.

John 21:6–8 And He said to them, "Cast the net on the right side of the boat, and you will find *some*." So they cast, and now they were not able to draw it in because of the multitude of fish. **7** Therefore that disciple whom Jesus loved said to Peter, "It is the Lord!" Now when Simon Peter heard that it was the Lord, he put on *his* outer garment (for he had removed it), and plunged into the sea. **8** But the other disciples came in the little boat (for they were not far from land, but about two hundred cubits), dragging the net with fish.

Hooks.

Amos 4:2 The Lord GOD has sworn by His holiness: "Behold, the days shall come upon you When He will take you away with fishhooks, And your posterity with fishhooks.

Matt 17:27 Nevertheless, lest we offend them, go to the sea, cast in a hook, and take the fish that comes up first. And when you have opened its mouth, you will find a piece of money; take that and give it to them for Me and you."

Spears.

Job 41:7 Can you fill his skin with harpoons, Or his head with fishing spears?

Often suffered for man's sin.

Ex 7:21 The fish that *were* in the river died, the river stank, and the Egyptians could not drink the water of the river. So there was blood throughout all the land of Egypt.

Ezek 38:20 so that the fish of the sea, the birds of the heavens, the beasts of the field, all creeping things that creep on the earth, and all men who *are* on the face of the earth shall shake at My presence. The mountains shall be thrown down, the steep places shall fall, and every wall shall fall to the ground.'

Miracles connected with

Feeding the multitudes.

Matt 14:17–21 And they said to Him, "We have here only five loaves and two fish." **18** He said, "Bring them here to Me." **19** Then He commanded the multitudes to sit down on the grass. And He took the five loaves and the two fish, and looking up to heaven, He blessed and broke and gave the loaves to the disciples; and the disciples gave to the multitudes. **20** So they all ate and were filled, and they took up twelve baskets full of the fragments that remained. **21** Now those who had eaten were about five thousand men, besides women and children.

Matt 15:34 Jesus said to them, "How many loaves do you have?" And they said, "Seven, and a few little fish."

Immense catches of.

Luke 5:6 And when they had done this, they caught a great number of fish, and their net was breaking.

Luke 5:9 For he and all who were with him were astonished at the catch of fish which they had taken;

John 21:6 And He said to them, "Cast the net on the right side of the boat, and you will find *some*." So they cast, and now they were not able to draw it in because of the multitude of fish.

John 21:11 Simon Peter went up and dragged the net to land, full of large fish, one hundred and fifty-three;

and although there were so many, the net was not broken.

Procuring tribute money from.

Matt 17:27 Nevertheless, lest we offend them, go to the sea, cast in a hook, and take the fish that comes up first. And when you have opened its mouth, you will find a piece of money; take that and give it to them for Me and you."

Illustrative of

The whole population of Egypt.

Ezek 29:4–5 But I will put hooks in your jaws, And cause the fish of your rivers to stick to your scales; I will bring you up out of the midst of your rivers, And all the fish in your rivers will stick to your scales. **5** I will leave you in the wilderness, You and all the fish of your rivers; You shall fall on the open field; You shall not be picked up or gathered. I have given you as food To the beasts of the field And to the birds of the heavens.

Men ignorant of future events.

Eccl 9:12 For man also does not know his time: Like fish taken in a cruel net, Like birds caught in a snare, So the sons of men *are* snared in an evil time, When it falls suddenly upon them.

Those ensnared by the wicked.

Hab 1:14 *Why* do You make men like fish of the sea, Like creeping things *that have* no ruler over them?

(Good) believers.

Matt 13:48–49 which, when it was full, they drew to shore; and they sat down and gathered the good into vessels, but threw the bad away. **49** So it will be at the end of the age. The angels will come forth, separate the wicked from among the just,

(Bad) mere professing believers.

Matt 13:48–49 which, when it was full, they drew to shore; and they sat down and gathered the good into vessels, but threw the bad away. **49** So it will be at the end of the age. The angels will come forth, separate the wicked from among the just,

FLATTERY

Believers should not use.

Job 32:21–22 Let me not, I pray, show partiality to anyone; Nor let me flatter any man. **22** For I do not know how to flatter, *Else* my Maker would soon take me away.

Ministers should not use.

1 Thess 2:5 For neither at any time did we use flattering words, as you know, nor a cloak for covetousness—God *is* witness.

Unbelievers use, toward

Others.

Ps 5:9 For *there is* no faithfulness in their mouth; Their inward part *is* destruction; Their throat *is* an open tomb; They flatter with their tongue.

Ps 12:2 They speak idly everyone with his neighbor; *With* flattering lips *and* a double heart they speak.

Themselves.

Ps 36:2 For he flatters himself in his own eyes, When he finds out his iniquity *and* when he hates.

God.

Ps 78:36 Nevertheless they flattered Him with their mouth, And they lied to Him with their tongue;

Those in authority.

Dan 11:34 Now when they fall, they shall be aided with a little help; but many shall join with them by intrigue.

False prophets and teachers use.

Ezek 12:24 For no more shall there be any false vision or flattering divination within the house of Israel.

Rom 16:18 For those who are such do not serve our Lord Jesus Christ, but their own belly, and by smooth words and flattering speech deceive the hearts of the simple.

Wisdom, a preservative against.

Prov 4:5 Get wisdom! Get understanding! Do not forget, nor turn away from the words of my mouth.

Worldly advantage obtained by.

Dan 11:21–22 And in his place shall arise a vile person, to whom they will not give the honor of royalty; but he shall come in peaceably, and seize the kingdom by intrigue. **22** With the force of a flood they shall be swept away from before him and be broken, and also the prince of the covenant.

Seldom gains respect.

Prov 28:23 He who rebukes a man will find more favor afterward Than he who flatters with the tongue.

Avoid those given to.

Prov 20:19 He who goes about *as* a talebearer reveals secrets; Therefore do not associate with one who flatters with his lips.

Danger of.

Prov 7:21–23 With her enticing speech she caused him to yield, With her flattering lips she seduced him. **22** Immediately he went after her, as an ox goes to the slaughter, Or as a fool to the correction of the stocks, **23** Till an arrow struck his liver. As a bird hastens to the snare, He did not know it *would cost* his life.

Punishment of.

Job 17:5 He who speaks flattery to *his* friends, Even the eyes of his children will fail.

Ps 12:3 May the LORD cut off all flattering lips, *And* the tongue that speaks proud things,

Examples of,

The woman of Tekoah.

2 Sam 14:17 Your maidservant said, 'The word of my lord the king will now be comforting; for as the angel of God, so *is* my lord the king in discerning good and evil. And may the LORD your God be with you.' "

2 Sam 14:20 To bring about this change of affairs your servant Joab has done this thing; but my lord *is* wise, according to the wisdom of the angel of God, to know everything that *is* in the earth."

Absalom.

2 Sam 15:2–6 Now Absalom would rise early and stand beside the way to the gate. *So* it was, whenever anyone who had a lawsuit came to the king for a decision, that Absalom would call to him and say, "What city *are* you from?" And he would say, "Your servant *is* from such and such a tribe of Israel." **3** Then Absa-

lom would say to him, "Look, your case *is* good and right; but *there is* no deputy of the king to hear you." **4** Moreover Absalom would say, "Oh, that I were made judge in the land, and everyone who has any suit or cause would come to me; then I would give him justice." **5** And *so* it was, whenever anyone came near to bow down to him, that he would put out his hand and take him and kiss him. **6** In this manner Absalom acted toward all Israel who came to the king for judgment. So Absalom stole the hearts of the men of Israel.

The false prophets.

1 Kin 22:13 Then the messenger who had gone to call Micaiah spoke to him, saying, "Now listen, the words of the prophets with one accord encourage the king. Please, let your word be like the word of one of them, and speak encouragement."

Darius's courtiers.

Dan 6:7 All the governors of the kingdom, the administrators and satraps, the counselors and advisors, have consulted together to establish a royal statute and to make a firm decree, that whoever petitions any god or man for thirty days, except you, O king, shall be cast into the den of lions.

The Pharisees, etc.

Luke 20:20–21 So they watched *Him,* and sent spies who pretended to be righteous, that they might seize on His words, in order to deliver Him to the power and the authority of the governor. **21** Then they asked Him, saying, "Teacher, we know that You say and teach rightly, and You do not show personal favoritism, but teach the way of God in truth:

The people of Tyre, etc.

Acts 12:22 And the people kept shouting, "The voice of a god and not of a man!"

FLESH (MAN'S UNREDEEMED HUMANNESS), THE

Is weak in ability to practice righteousness.

Matt 26:41 Watch and pray, lest you enter into temptation. The spirit indeed *is* willing, but the flesh *is* weak."

Mark 14:38 Watch and pray, lest you enter into temptation. The spirit indeed *is* willing, but the flesh *is* weak."

Serves the law of sin.

Rom 7:25 I thank God—through Jesus Christ our Lord! So then, with the mind I myself serve the law of God, but with the flesh the law of sin.

Nothing good dwells in.

Rom 7:18 For I know that in me (that is, in my flesh) nothing good dwells; for to will is present with me, but *how* to perform what is good I do not find.

Weakness of, manifested in inability to discern spiritual truth.

Rom 6:19 I speak in human *terms* because of the weakness of your flesh. For just as you presented your members *as* slaves of uncleanness, and of lawlessness *leading* to *more* lawlessness, so now present your members *as* slaves *of* righteousness for holiness.

God condemned sin in, through sinless flesh of Christ.

Rom 8:3 For what the law could not do in that it was weak through the flesh, God *did* by sending His own Son in the likeness of sinful flesh, on account of sin: He condemned sin in the flesh,

Believers do not live according to.

Rom 8:4–6 that the righteous requirement of the law might be fulfilled in us who do not walk according to the flesh but according to the Spirit. **5** For those who live according to the flesh set their minds on the things of the flesh, but those *who live* according to the Spirit, the things of the Spirit. **6** For to be carnally minded *is* death, but to be spiritually minded *is* life and peace.

Rom 8:12–13 Therefore, brethren, we are debtors—not to the flesh, to live according to the flesh. **13** For if you live according to the flesh you will die; but if by the Spirit you put to death the deeds of the body, you will live.

Gal 5:13 For you, brethren, have been called to liberty; only do not *use* liberty as an opportunity for the flesh, but through love serve one another.

Gal 5:16–17 I say then: Walk in the Spirit, and you shall not fulfill the lust of the flesh. **17** For the flesh lusts against the Spirit, and the Spirit against the flesh; and these are contrary to one another, so that you do not do the things that you wish.

Believers are not to make any provision for.

Rom 13:14 But put on the Lord Jesus Christ, and make no provision for the flesh, to *fulfill its* lusts.

Believers have no confidence in.

Phil 3:3 For we are the circumcision, who worship God in the Spirit, rejoice in Christ Jesus, and have no confidence in the flesh,

Believers have crucified, through Christ.

Gal 5:24 And those *who are* Christ's have crucified the flesh with its passions and desires.

Believers are to cleanse themselves from the filthiness of the, associated with false religion.

2 Cor 7:1 Therefore, having these promises, beloved, let us cleanse ourselves from all filthiness of the flesh and spirit, perfecting holiness in the fear of God.

Sanctification cannot occur through.

Gal 3:3 Are you so foolish? Having begun in the Spirit, are you now being made perfect by the flesh?

Those who sow to, reap corruption.

Gal 6:8 For he who sows to his flesh will of the flesh reap corruption, but he who sows to the Spirit will of the Spirit reap everlasting life.

Unbelievers live according to.

Rom 8:5–6 For those who live according to the flesh set their minds on the things of the flesh, but those *who live* according to the Spirit, the things of the Spirit. **6** For to be carnally minded *is* death, but to be spiritually minded *is* life and peace.

False teachers live according to.

2 Pet 2:10 and especially those who walk according to the flesh in the lust of uncleanness and despise authority. *They are* presumptuous, self-willed. They are not afraid to speak evil of dignitaries,

The works of.

Gal 5:19–21 Now the works of the flesh are evident, which are: adultery, fornication, uncleanness, lewdness, **20** idolatry, sorcery, hatred, contentions, jealousies, outbursts of wrath, selfish ambitions, dissensions, heresies, **21** envy, murders, drunkenness, revelries, and the like; of which I tell you beforehand, just as I also told *you* in time past, that those who practice such things will not inherit the kingdom of God.

Satan uses the lust of, to incite sin.

1 John 2:16 For all that *is* in the world—the lust of the flesh, the lust of the eyes, and the pride of life—is not of the Father but is of the world.

"In the flesh" describes unregenerate people.

Rom 7:5 For when we were in the flesh, the sinful passions which were aroused by the law were at work in our members to bear fruit to death.

Rom 8:8 So then, those who are in the flesh cannot please God.

Also called

Body of death.

Rom 7:24 O wretched man that I am! Who will deliver me from this body of death?

Body of sin.

Rom 6:6 knowing this, that our old man was crucified with *Him,* that the body of sin might be done away with, that we should no longer be slaves of sin.

Mortal body.

Rom 6:12 Therefore do not let sin reign in your mortal body, that you should obey it in its lusts.

Carnal.

Rom 7:14 For we know that the law is spiritual, but I am carnal, sold under sin.

1 Cor 3:1 And I, brethren, could not speak to you as to spiritual *people* but as to carnal, as to babes in Christ.

FLOOD, THE

Sent as a punishment for the extreme wickedness of man.

Gen 6:5–7 Then the LORD saw that the wickedness of man *was* great in the earth, and *that* every intent of the thoughts of his heart *was* only evil continually. **6** And the LORD was sorry that He had made man on the earth, and He was grieved in His heart. **7** So the LORD said, "I will destroy man whom I have created from the face of the earth, both man and beast, creeping thing and birds of the air, for I am sorry that I have made them."

Gen 6:11–13 The earth also was corrupt before God, and the earth was filled with violence. **12** So God looked upon the earth, and indeed it was corrupt; for all flesh had corrupted their way on the earth. **13** And God said to Noah, "The end of all flesh has come before Me, for the earth is filled with violence through them; and behold, I will destroy them with the earth.

Gen 6:17 And behold, I Myself am bringing floodwaters on the earth, to destroy from under heaven all flesh in which *is* the breath of life; everything that *is* on the earth shall die.

Also called the waters of Noah.

Is 54:9 "For this *is* like the waters of Noah to Me; For as I have sworn That the waters of Noah would no longer cover the earth, So have I sworn That I would not be angry with you, nor rebuke you.

Noah forewarned of.

Gen 6:13 And God said to Noah, "The end of all flesh has come before Me, for the earth is filled with violence through them; and behold, I will destroy them with the earth.

Heb 11:7 By faith Noah, being divinely warned of things not yet seen, moved with godly fear, prepared an ark for the saving of his household, by which he condemned the world and became heir of the righteousness which is according to faith.

Longsuffering of God exhibited in deferring.

Gen 6:3 And the LORD said, "My Spirit shall not strive with man forever, for he *is* indeed flesh; yet his days shall be one hundred and twenty years."

1 Pet 3:20 who formerly were disobedient, when once the Divine longsuffering waited in the days of Noah, while *the* ark was being prepared, in which a few, that is, eight souls, were saved through water.

The wicked warned of.

1 Pet 3:19–20 by whom also He went and preached to the spirits in prison, **20** who formerly were disobedient, when once the Divine longsuffering waited in the days of Noah, while *the* ark was being prepared, in which a few, that is, eight souls, were saved through water.

2 Pet 2:5 and did not spare the ancient world, but saved Noah, *one of* eight *people,* a preacher of righteousness, bringing in the flood on the world of the ungodly;

Noah, etc., saved from.

Gen 6:18–22 But I will establish My covenant with you; and you shall go into the ark—you, your sons, your wife, and your sons' wives with you. **19** And of every living thing of all flesh you shall bring two of every *sort* into the ark, to keep *them* alive with you; they shall be male and female. **20** Of the birds after their kind, of animals after their kind, and of every creeping thing of the earth after its kind, two of every *kind* will come to you to keep *them* alive. **21** And you shall take for yourself of all food that is eaten, and you shall gather *it* to yourself; and it shall be food for you and for them." **22** Thus Noah did; according to all that God commanded him, so he did.

Gen 7:13–14 On the very same day Noah and Noah's sons, Shem, Ham, and Japheth, and Noah's wife and the three wives of his sons with them, entered the ark— **14** they and every beast after its kind, all cattle after their kind, every creeping thing that creeps on the earth after its kind, and every bird after its kind, every bird of every sort.

Gen 9:28 And Noah lived after the flood three hundred and fifty years.

Date of its commencement.

Gen 7:11 In the six hundredth year of Noah's life, in the second month, the seventeenth day of the month, on that day all the fountains of the great deep were broken up, and the windows of heaven were opened.

Came suddenly and unexpectedly.

Matt 24:38–39 For as in the days before the flood, they were eating and drinking, marrying and giving in marriage, until the day that Noah entered the ark, **39** and did not know until the flood came and took them all away, so also will the coming of the Son of Man be.

Produced by

Forty days' incessant rain.

Gen 7:4 For after seven more days I will cause it to rain on the earth forty days and forty nights, and I will destroy from the face of the earth all living things that I have made."

Gen 7:12 And the rain was on the earth forty days and forty nights.

Gen 7:17 Now the flood was on the earth forty days. The waters increased and lifted up the ark, and it rose high above the earth.

Opening up of the fountains of the great deep.

Gen 7:11 In the six hundredth year of Noah's life, in the second month, the seventeenth day of the month, on that day all the fountains of the great deep were broken up, and the windows of heaven were opened.

Increased gradually.

Gen 7:17–18 Now the flood was on the earth forty days. The waters increased and lifted up the ark, and it rose high above the earth. **18** The waters prevailed and greatly increased on the earth, and the ark moved about on the surface of the waters.

Extreme height of.

Gen 7:19–20 And the waters prevailed exceedingly on the earth, and all the high hills under the whole heaven were covered. **20** The waters prevailed fifteen cubits upward, and the mountains were covered.

Time of its increase and prevailing.

Gen 7:24 And the waters prevailed on the earth one hundred and fifty days.

Causes of its abatement.

Gen 8:1–2 Then God remembered Noah, and every living thing, and all the animals that *were* with him in the ark. And God made a wind to pass over the earth, and the waters subsided. **2** The fountains of the deep and the windows of heaven were also stopped, and the rain from heaven was restrained.

Decrease of, gradual.

Gen 8:3 And the waters receded continually from the earth. At the end of the hundred and fifty days the waters decreased.

Gen 8:5 And the waters decreased continually until the tenth month. In the tenth *month,* on the first *day* of the month, the tops of the mountains were seen.

Date of its complete removal.

Gen 8:13 And it came to pass in the six hundred and first year, in the first *month,* the first *day* of the month, that the waters were dried up from the earth; and Noah removed the covering of the ark and looked, and indeed the surface of the ground was dry.

Destroyed inhabitants of the whole earth.

Gen 7:23 So He destroyed all living things which were on the face of the ground: both man and cattle, creeping thing and bird of the air. They were destroyed from the earth. Only Noah and those who *were* with him in the ark remained *alive.*

Entire face of the earth changed by.

2 Pet 3:5–6 For this they willfully forget: that by the word of God the heavens were of old, and the earth standing out of water and in the water, **6** by which the world *that* then existed perished, being flooded with water.

Traditional notice of.

Job 22:15–17 Will you keep to the old way Which wicked men have trod, **16** Who were cut down before their time, Whose foundations were swept away by a flood? **17** They said to God, 'Depart from us! What can the Almighty do to them?'

That it shall never again occur

Promised.

Gen 8:21–22 And the LORD smelled a soothing aroma. Then the LORD said in His heart, "I will never again curse the ground for man's sake, although the imagination of man's heart *is* evil from his youth; nor will I again destroy every living thing as I have done. **22** "While the earth remains, Seedtime and harvest, Cold and heat, Winter and summer, And day and night Shall not cease."

Confirmed by covenant.

Gen 9:9–11 "And as for Me, behold, I establish My covenant with you and with your descendants after you, **10** and with every living creature that *is* with you: the birds, the cattle, and every beast of the earth with you, of all that go out of the ark, every beast of the earth. **11** Thus I establish My covenant with you: Never again shall all flesh be cut off by the waters of the flood; never again shall there be a flood to destroy the earth."

The rainbow a sign.

Gen 9:12–17 And God said: "This *is* the sign of the covenant which I make between Me and you, and every living creature that *is* with you, for perpetual generations: **13** I set My rainbow in the cloud, and it shall be for the sign of the covenant between Me and the earth. **14** It shall be, when I bring a cloud over the earth, that the rainbow shall be seen in the cloud; **15** and I will remember My covenant which *is* between Me and you and every living creature of all flesh; the waters shall never again become a flood to destroy all flesh. **16** The rainbow shall be in the cloud, and I will look on it to remember the everlasting covenant between God and every living creature of all flesh that *is* on the earth." **17** And God said to Noah, "This *is* the sign of the covenant which I have established between Me and all flesh that *is* on the earth."

A pledge of God's faithfulness.

Is 54:9–10 "For this *is* like the waters of Noah to Me; For as I have sworn That the waters of Noah would no longer cover the earth, So have I sworn That I would not be angry with you, nor rebuke you. **10** For the mountains shall depart And the hills be removed, But My kindness shall not depart from you, Nor shall My covenant of peace be removed," Says the LORD, who has mercy on you.

Illustrative of

The destruction of sinners.

Ps 32:6 For this cause everyone who is godly shall pray to You In a time when You may be found; Surely in a flood of great waters They shall not come near him.

Is 28:2 Behold, the Lord has a mighty and strong one, Like a tempest of hail and a destroying storm, Like a flood of mighty waters overflowing, Who will bring *them* down to the earth with *His* hand.

Is 28:18 Your covenant with death will be annulled, And your agreement with Sheol will not stand; When the overflowing scourge passes through, Then you will be trampled down by it.

Baptism.

1 Pet 3:20–21 who formerly were disobedient, when once the Divine longsuffering waited in the days of Noah, while *the* ark was being prepared, in which a few, that is, eight souls, were saved through water. **21** There is also an antitype which now saves us— baptism (not the removal of the filth of the flesh, but the answer of a good conscience toward God), through the resurrection of Jesus Christ,

(Unexpectedness of) suddenness of Christ's second coming.

Matt 24:36–39 "But of that day and hour no one knows, not even the angels of heaven, but My Father only. **37** But as the days of Noah *were,* so also will the coming of the Son of Man be. **38** For as in the days before the flood, they were eating and drinking, marrying and giving in marriage, until the day that Noah entered the ark, **39** and did not know until the flood came and took them all away, so also will the coming of the Son of Man be.

Luke 17:26–27 And as it was in the days of Noah, so it will be also in the days of the Son of Man: **27** They ate, they drank, they married wives, they were given in marriage, until the day that Noah entered the ark, and the flood came and destroyed them all.

Luke 17:30 Even so will it be in the day when the Son of Man is revealed.

FLOWERS

Wild in fields.

Ps 103:15 *As for* man, his days *are* like grass; As a flower of the field, so he flourishes.

Cultivated in gardens.

Song 6:2–3 My beloved has gone to his garden, To the beds of spices, To feed *his flock* in the gardens, And to gather lilies. **3** I *am* my beloved's, And my beloved *is* mine. He feeds *his flock* among the lilies.

Described as

Beautiful.

Matt 6:29 and yet I say to you that even Solomon in all his glory was not arrayed like one of these.

Scented.

Song 5:13 His cheeks *are* like a bed of spices, Banks of scented herbs. His lips *are* lilies, Dripping liquid myrrh.

Short-lived.

Ps 103:16 For the wind passes over it, and it is gone, And its place remembers it no more.

Is 40:8 The grass withers, the flower fades, But the word of our God stands forever."

Appearing in spring.

Song 2:12 The flowers appear on the earth; The time of singing has come, And the voice of the turtledove Is heard in our land.

Those mentioned in Scripture,

The lily.

Hos 14:5 I will be like the dew to Israel; He shall grow like the lily, And lengthen his roots like Lebanon.

Matt 6:28 "So why do you worry about clothing? Consider the lilies of the field, how they grow: they neither toil nor spin;

The lily of the valley.

Song 2:1 I *am* the rose of Sharon, *And* the lily of the valleys.

The rose of Sharon.

Song 2:1 I *am* the rose of Sharon, *And* the lily of the valleys.

Is 35:1 The wilderness and the wasteland shall be glad for them, And the desert shall rejoice and blossom as the rose;

Of the grass.

1 Pet 1:24 because *"All flesh is as grass, And all the glory of man as the flower of the grass. The grass withers, And its flower falls away,*

Garlands of, used in worship of idols.

Acts 14:13 Then the priest of Zeus, whose temple was in front of their city, brought oxen and garlands to the gates, intending to sacrifice with the multitudes.

Representations of, on the

Gold lampstand.

Ex 25:31 "You shall also make a lampstand of pure gold; the lampstand shall be of hammered work. Its shaft, its branches, its bowls, its *ornamental* knobs, and flowers shall be *of one piece.*

Ex 25:33 Three bowls *shall be* made like almond *blossoms* on one branch, *with* an *ornamental* knob and a flower, and three bowls made like almond *blossoms* on the other branch, *with* an *ornamental* knob and a flower— and so for the six branches that come out of the lampstand.

2 Chr 4:21 with the flowers and the lamps and the wick-trimmers of gold, of purest gold;

Sea of brass.

1 Kin 7:26 It *was* a handbreadth thick; and its brim was shaped like the brim of a cup, *like* a lily blossom. It contained two thousand baths.

2 Chr 4:5 It *was* a handbreadth thick; and its brim was shaped like the brim of a cup, *like* a lily blossom. It contained three thousand baths.

Woodwork of the temple.

1 Kin 6:18 The inside of the temple was cedar, carved with ornamental buds and open flowers. All *was* cedar; there was no stone *to be* seen.

1 Kin 6:29 Then he carved all the walls of the temple all around, both the inner and outer *sanctuaries,* with carved figures of cherubim, palm trees, and open flowers.

1 Kin 6:33 So for the door of the sanctuary he also made doorposts *of* olive wood, one-fourth *of the wall.*

1 Kin 6:35 Then he carved cherubim, palm trees, and open flowers *on them,* and overlaid *them* with gold applied evenly on the carved work.

Illustrative of

Shortness of man's life.

Job 14:2 He comes forth like a flower and fades away; He flees like a shadow and does not continue.

Ps 103:15 *As for* man, his days *are* like grass; As a flower of the field, so he flourishes.

Kingdom of Israel.

Is 28:1 Woe to the crown of pride, to the drunkards of Ephraim, Whose glorious beauty *is* a fading flower Which *is* at the head of the verdant valleys, To those who are overcome with wine!

Glory of man.

1 Pet 1:24 because *"All flesh is as grass, And all the glory of man as the flower of the grass. The grass withers, And its flower falls away,*

Rich men.

James 1:10–11 but the rich in his humiliation, because as a flower of the field he will pass away. **11** For no sooner has the sun risen with a burning heat than it withers the grass; its flower falls, and its beautiful appearance perishes. So the rich man also will fade away in his pursuits.

FOOLS

All men are, without the knowledge of God.

Titus 3:3 For we ourselves were also once foolish, disobedient, deceived, serving various lusts and pleasures, living in malice and envy, hateful and hating one another.

Deny God.

Ps 14:1 The fool has said in his heart, *"There is* no God." They are corrupt, They have done abominable works, There is none who does good.

Ps 53:1 The fool has said in his heart, *"There is* no God." They are corrupt, and have done abominable iniquity; *There is* none who does good.

Blaspheme God.

Ps 74:18 Remember this, *that* the enemy has reproached, O LORD, And *that* a foolish people has blasphemed Your name.

Ps 74:22 Arise, O God, plead Your own cause; Remember how the foolish man reproaches You daily.

Mock sin.

Prov 14:9 Fools mock at sin, But among the upright *there is* favor.

Hate knowledge and instruction.

Prov 1:7 The fear of the LORD *is* the beginning of knowledge, *But* fools despise wisdom and instruction.

Prov 1:22 "How long, you simple ones, will you love simplicity? For scorners delight in their scorning, And fools hate knowledge.

Prov 15:5 A fool despises his father's instruction, But he who receives correction is prudent.

Prov 16:22 Understanding *is* a wellspring of life to him who has it. But the correction of fools *is* folly.

Prov 18:2 A fool has no delight in understanding, But in expressing his own heart.

Die for lack of wisdom.

Prov 10:21 The lips of the righteous feed many, But fools die for lack of wisdom.

Feed on foolishness.

Prov 15:14 The heart of him who has understanding seeks knowledge, But the mouth of fools feeds on foolishness.

Display their folly.

Prov 13:16 Every prudent *man* acts with knowledge, But a fool lays open *his* folly.

Eccl 10:3 Even when a fool walks along the way, He lacks wisdom, And he shows everyone *that* he *is* a fool.

Produce folly.

Prov 14:24 The crown of the wise is their riches, *But* the foolishness of fools *is* folly.

Believers are not to walk like.

Eph 5:15 See then that you walk circumspectly, not as fools but as wise,

Make sport of mischief.

Prov 10:23 To do evil *is* like sport to a fool, But a man of understanding has wisdom.

Walk in darkness.

Eccl 2:14 The wise man's eyes *are* in his head, But the fool walks in darkness. Yet I myself perceived That the same event happens to them all.

Hate to depart from evil.

Prov 13:19 A desire accomplished is sweet to the soul, But *it is* an abomination to fools to depart from evil.

Worship of, evil to God.

Eccl 5:1 Walk prudently when you go to the house of God; and draw near to hear rather than to give the sacrifice of fools, for they do not know that they do evil.

Described as

Corrupt and abominable.

Ps 14:1 The fool has said in his heart, *"There is* no God." They are corrupt, They have done abominable works, There is none who does good.

Self-sufficient.

Prov 12:15 The way of a fool *is* right in his own eyes, But he who heeds counsel *is* wise.

Rom 1:22 Professing to be wise, they became fools,

Self-confident.

Prov 14:16 A wise *man* fears and departs from evil, But a fool rages and is self-confident.

Self-deceivers.

Prov 14:8 The wisdom of the prudent *is* to understand his way, But the folly of fools *is* deceit.

Mere professors of religion.

Matt 25:2–12 Now five of them were wise, and five *were* foolish. **3** Those who *were* foolish took their lamps and took no oil with them, **4** but the wise took oil in their vessels with their lamps. **5** But while the bridegroom was delayed, they all slumbered and slept. **6** "And at midnight a cry was *heard:* 'Behold, the bridegroom is coming; go out to meet him!' **7** Then all those virgins arose and trimmed their lamps. **8** And the foolish said to the wise, 'Give us *some* of your oil, for our lamps are going out.' **9** But the wise answered, saying, *'No,* lest there should not be enough for us and you; but go rather to those who sell, and buy for yourselves.' **10** And while they went to buy, the bridegroom came, and those who were ready went in with him to the wedding; and the door was shut. **11** "Afterward the other virgins came also, saying, 'Lord, Lord, open to us!' **12** But he answered and said, 'Assuredly, I say to you, I do not know you.'

Full of words.

Eccl 10:14 A fool also multiplies words. No man knows what is to be; Who can tell him what will be after him?

Given to quarreling.

Prov 20:3 *It is* honorable for a man to stop striving, Since any fool can start a quarrel.

Slanderers.

Prov 10:18 Whoever hides hatred *has* lying lips, And whoever spreads slander *is* a fool.

Liars.

Prov 10:18 Whoever hides hatred *has* lying lips, And whoever spreads slander *is* a fool.

Slothful.

Eccl 4:5 The fool folds his hands And consumes his own flesh.

Angry.

Eccl 7:9 Do not hasten in your spirit to be angry, For anger rests in the bosom of fools.

Contentious.

Prov 18:6 A fool's lips enter into contention, And his mouth calls for blows.

Proud.

Prov 14:3 In the mouth of a fool *is* a rod of pride, But the lips of the wise will preserve them.

A grief to parents.

Prov 17:25 A foolish son *is* a grief to his father, And bitterness to her who bore him.

Prov 19:13 A foolish son *is* the ruin of his father, And the contentions of a wife *are* a continual dripping.

Come to shame.

Prov 3:35 The wise shall inherit glory, But shame shall be the legacy of fools.

Destroy themselves by their speech.

Prov 10:8 The wise in heart will receive commands, But a prating fool will fall.

Prov 10:14 Wise *people* store up knowledge, But the mouth of the foolish *is* near destruction.

Eccl 10:12 The words of a wise man's mouth *are* gracious, But the lips of a fool shall swallow him up;

The company of, ruinous.

Prov 13:20 He who walks with wise *men* will be wise, But the companion of fools will be destroyed.

Lips of, a snare to the soul.

Prov 18:7 A fool's mouth *is* his destruction, And his lips *are* the snare of his soul.

Cling to their folly.

Prov 26:11 As a dog returns to his own vomit, So a fool repeats his folly.

Prov 27:22 Though you grind a fool in a mortar with a pestle along with crushed grain, *Yet* his foolishness will not depart from him.

Worship idols.

Jer 10:8 But they are altogether dull-hearted and foolish; A wooden idol *is* a worthless doctrine.

Rom 1:22–23 Professing to be wise, they became fools, 23 and changed the glory of the incorruptible God into an image made like corruptible man—and birds and four-footed animals and creeping things.

Trust in their own hearts.

Prov 28:26 He who trusts in his own heart is a fool, But whoever walks wisely will be delivered.

Depend upon their wealth.

Luke 12:20 But God said to him, 'Fool! This night your soul will be required of you; then whose will those things be which you have provided?'

Hear the gospel but do not obey it.

Matt 7:26 "But everyone who hears these sayings of Mine, and does not do them, will be like a foolish man who built his house on the sand:

The mouth of, pours out folly.

Prov 12:23 A prudent man conceals knowledge, But the heart of fools proclaims foolishness.

Prov 14:33 Wisdom rests in the heart of him who has understanding, But *what is* in the heart of fools is made known.

Prov 15:2 The tongue of the wise uses knowledge rightly, But the mouth of fools pours forth foolishness.

Honor is unbecoming for.

Prov 26:1 As snow in summer and rain in harvest, So honor is not fitting for a fool.

Prov 26:8 Like one who binds a stone in a sling *Is* he who gives honor to a fool.

God has no pleasure in.

Eccl 5:4 When you make a vow to God, do not delay to pay it; For *He has* no pleasure in fools. Pay what you have vowed—

Shall not stand in the presence of God.

Ps 5:5 The boastful shall not stand in Your sight; You hate all workers of iniquity.

Believers should avoid them.

Prov 9:6 Forsake foolishness and live, And go in the way of understanding.

Prov 14:7 Go from the presence of a foolish man, When you do not perceive *in him* the lips of knowledge.

Exhorted to seek wisdom.

Prov 8:5 O you simple ones, understand prudence, And you fools, be of an understanding heart.

Punishment of.

Ps 107:17 Fools, because of their transgression, And because of their iniquities, were afflicted.

Prov 19:29 Judgments are prepared for scoffers, And beatings for the backs of fools.

Prov 26:10 The great *God* who formed everything Gives the fool *his* hire and the transgressor *his* wages.

Examples of,
Rehoboam.

1 Kin 12:8 But he rejected the advice which the elders had given him, and consulted the young men who had grown up with him, who stood before him.

Israel.

Jer 4:22 "For My people *are* foolish, They have not known Me. They *are* silly children, And they have no understanding. They *are* wise to do evil, But to do good they have no knowledge."

The Pharisees.

Matt 23:17 Fools and blind! For which is greater, the gold or the temple that sanctifies the gold?

Matt 23:19 Fools and blind! For which is greater, the gift or the altar that sanctifies the gift?

FORESTS

Tracts of land covered with trees.

Is 44:14 He cuts down cedars for himself, And takes the cypress and the oak; He secures *it* for himself among the trees of the forest. He plants a pine, and the rain nourishes *it*.

Underbrush often in.

Is 9:18 For wickedness burns as the fire; It shall devour the briers and thorns, And kindle in the thickets of the forest; They shall mount up *like* rising smoke.

Inhabited by wild animals.

Ps 50:10 For every beast of the forest *is* Mine, *And* the cattle on a thousand hills.

Ps 104:20 You make darkness, and it is night, In which all the beasts of the forest creep about.

Is 56:9 All you beasts of the field, come to devour, All you beasts in the forest.

Jer 5:6 Therefore a lion from the forest shall slay them, A wolf of the deserts shall destroy them; A leopard will watch over their cities. Everyone who goes out from there shall be torn in pieces, Because their transgressions are many; Their backslidings have increased.

Mic 5:8 And the remnant of Jacob Shall be among the Gentiles, In the midst of many peoples, Like a lion among the beasts of the forest, Like a young lion among flocks of sheep, Who, if he passes through, Both treads down and tears in pieces, And none can deliver.

Abounded with wild honey.

1 Sam 14:25–26 Now all *the people* of the land came to a forest; and there was honey on the ground. 26 And when the people had come into the woods, there was the honey, dripping; but no one put his hand to his mouth, for the people feared the oath.

Often afforded pasture.

Mic 7:14 Shepherd Your people with Your staff, The flock of Your heritage, Who dwell solitarily *in* a woodland, In the midst of Carmel; Let them feed *in* Bashan and Gilead, As in days of old.

Those mentioned in Scripture,
Bashan.

Is 2:13 Upon all the cedars of Lebanon *that are* high and lifted up, And upon all the oaks of Bashan;

Ezek 27:6 *Of* oaks from Bashan they made your oars; The company of Ashurites have inlaid your planks *With* ivory from the coasts of Cyprus.

Zech 11:2 Wail, O cypress, for the cedar has fallen, Because the mighty *trees* are ruined. Wail, O oaks of Ba-shan, For the thick forest has come down.

Hereth.

1 Sam 22:5 Now the prophet Gad said to David, "Do not stay in the stronghold; depart, and go to the land of Judah." So David departed and went into the forest of Hereth.

Ephraim.

2 Sam 18:6 So the people went out into the field of battle against Israel. And the battle was in the woods of Ephraim.

2 Sam 18:8 For the battle there was scattered over the face of the whole countryside, and the woods devoured more people that day than the sword devoured.

Lebanon.

1 Kin 7:2 He also built the House of the Forest of Lebanon; its length *was* one hundred cubits, its width fifty cubits, and its height thirty cubits, with four rows of cedar pillars, and cedar beams on the pillars.

1 Kin 10:17 He also *made* three hundred shields *of* hammered gold; three minas of gold went into each shield. The king put them in the House of the Forest of Lebanon.

2 Kin 19:23 By your messengers you have reproached the Lord, And said: "By the multitude of my chariots I have come up to the height of the mountains, To the limits of Lebanon; I will cut down its tall cedars *And* its choice cypress trees; I will enter the extremity of its borders, *To* its fruitful forest.

Is 37:24 By your servants you have reproached the Lord, And said, 'By the multitude of my chariots I have come up to the height of the mountains, To the limits of Lebanon; I will cut down its tall cedars *And* its choice cypress trees; I will enter its farthest height, To its fruitful forest.

Arabian.

Is 21:13 The burden against Arabia. In the forest in Arabia you will lodge, O you traveling companies of Dedanites.

The South.

Ezek 20:46–47 "Son of man, set your face toward the south; preach against the south and prophesy against the forest land, the South, **47** and say to the forest of the South, 'Hear the word of the LORD! Thus says the Lord GOD: "Behold, I will kindle a fire in you, and it shall devour every green tree and every dry tree in you; the blazing flame shall not be quenched, and all faces from the south to the north shall be scorched by it.

The king's.

Neh 2:8 and a letter to Asaph the keeper of the king's forest, that he must give me timber to make beams for the gates of the citadel which *pertains* to the temple, for the city wall, and for the house that I will occupy." And the king granted *them* to me according to the good hand of my God upon me.

Supplied timber for building.

1 Kin 5:6–8 Now therefore, command that they cut down cedars for me from Lebanon; and my servants will be with your servants, and I will pay you wages for your servants according to whatever you say. For

you know *there is* none among us who has skill to cut timber like the Sidonians. **7** So it was, when Hiram heard the words of Solomon, that he rejoiced greatly and said, Blessed *be* the LORD this day, for He has given David a wise son over this great people! **8** Then Hiram sent to Solomon, saying: I have considered *the message* which you sent me, *and* I will do all you desire concerning the cedar and cypress logs.

Were places of refuge.

1 Sam 22:5 Now the prophet Gad said to David, "Do not stay in the stronghold; depart, and go to the land of Judah." So David departed and went into the forest of Hereth.

1 Sam 23:16 Then Jonathan, Saul's son, arose and went to David in the woods and strengthened his hand in God.

Jotham built towers, etc., in.

2 Chr 27:4 Moreover he built cities in the mountains of Judah, and in the forests he built fortresses and towers.

The power of God extends over.

Ps 29:9 The voice of the LORD makes the deer give birth, And strips the forests bare; And in His temple everyone says, "Glory!"

Called on to rejoice at God's mercy.

Is 44:23 Sing, O heavens, for the LORD has done *it!* Shout, you lower parts of the earth; Break forth into singing, you mountains, O forest, and every tree in it! For the LORD has redeemed Jacob, And glorified Himself in Israel.

Often destroyed by enemies.

2 Kin 19:23 By your messengers you have reproached the Lord, And said: "By the multitude of my chariots I have come up to the height of the mountains, To the limits of Lebanon; I will cut down its tall cedars *And* its choice cypress trees; I will enter the extremity of its borders, *To* its fruitful forest.

Is 37:24 By your servants you have reproached the Lord, And said, 'By the multitude of my chariots I have come up to the height of the mountains, To the limits of Lebanon; I will cut down its tall cedars *And* its choice cypress trees; I will enter its farthest height, To its fruitful forest.

Jer 46:23 "They shall cut down her forest," says the LORD, "Though it cannot be searched, Because they *are* innumerable, And more numerous than grasshoppers.

Illustrative of

The unfruitful world.

Is 32:19 Though hail comes down on the forest, And the city is brought low in humiliation.

(A fruitful field turned into) the Jews rejected by God.

Is 29:17 *Is* it not yet a very little while Till Lebanon shall be turned into a fruitful field, And the fruitful field be esteemed as a forest?

Is 32:15 Until the Spirit is poured upon us from on high, And the wilderness becomes a fruitful field, And the fruitful field is counted as a forest.

(Destroyed by fire) destruction of the wicked.

Is 9:18 For wickedness burns as the fire; It shall devour the briers and thorns, And kindle in the thickets of the forest; They shall mount up *like* rising smoke.

Is 10:17–18 So the Light of Israel will be for a fire, And his Holy One for a flame; It will burn and devour His thorns and his briers in one day. **18** And it will consume the glory of his forest and of his fruitful field, Both soul and body; And they will be as when a sick man wastes away.

Jer 21:14 But I will punish you according to the fruit of your doings," says the LORD; "I will kindle a fire in its forest, And it shall devour all things around it." ' "

FORGETTING GOD

A characteristic of the wicked.

Prov 2:17 Who forsakes the companion of her youth, And forgets the covenant of her God.

Is 65:11 "But you *are* those who forsake the LORD, Who forget My holy mountain, Who prepare a table for Gad, And who furnish a drink offering for Meni.

Backsliders are guilty of.

Jer 3:21–22 A voice was heard on the desolate heights, Weeping *and* supplications of the children of Israel. For they have perverted their way; They have forgotten the LORD their God. **22** "Return, you backsliding children, *And* I will heal your backslidings." "Indeed we do come to You, For You are the LORD our God.

Means not remembering His

Covenant.

Deut 4:23 Take heed to yourselves, lest you forget the covenant of the LORD your God which He made with you, and make for yourselves a carved image in the form of anything which the LORD your God has forbidden you.

2 Kin 17:38 And the covenant that I have made with you, you shall not forget, nor shall you fear other gods.

Works.

Ps 78:7 That they may set their hope in God, And not forget the works of God, But keep His commandments;

Ps 78:11 And forgot His works And His wonders that He had shown them.

Ps 106:13 They soon forgot His works; They did not wait for His counsel,

Benefits.

Ps 103:2 Bless the LORD, O my soul, And forget not all His benefits:

Ps 106:7 Our fathers in Egypt did not understand Your wonders; They did not remember the multitude of Your mercies, But rebelled by the sea—the Red Sea.

Word.

Heb 12:5 And you have forgotten the exhortation which speaks to you as to sons: *"My son, do not despise the chastening of the LORD, Nor be discouraged when you are rebuked by Him;*

James 1:25 But he who looks into the perfect law of liberty and continues *in it,* and is not a forgetful hearer but a doer of the work, this one will be blessed in what he does.

Law.

Ps 119:153 Consider my affliction and deliver me, For I do not forget Your law.

Ps 119:176 I have gone astray like a lost sheep; Seek

Your servant, For I do not forget Your commandments.

Hos 4:6 My people are destroyed for lack of knowledge. Because you have rejected knowledge, I also will reject you from being priest for Me; Because you have forgotten the law of your God, I also will forget your children.

Past deliverance.

Judg 8:34 Thus the children of Israel did not remember the LORD their God, who had delivered them from the hands of all their enemies on every side;

Ps 78:42 They did not remember His power: The day when He redeemed them from the enemy,

Power to deliver.

Is 51:13–15 And you forget the LORD your Maker, Who stretched out the heavens And laid the foundations of the earth; You have feared continually every day Because of the fury of the oppressor, When *he has* prepared to destroy. And where *is* the fury of the oppressor? **14** The captive exile hastens, that he may be loosed, That he should not die in the pit, And that his bread should not fail. **15** But I *am* the LORD your God, Who divided the sea whose waves roared—The LORD of hosts *is* His name.

Encouraged by false teachers.

Jer 23:27 who try to make My people forget My name by their dreams which everyone tells his neighbor, as their fathers forgot My name for Baal.

Prosperity often leads to.

Deut 8:12–14 lest—*when* you have eaten and are full, and have built beautiful houses and dwell *in them;* **13** and *when* your herds and your flocks multiply, and your silver and your gold are multiplied, and all that you have is multiplied; **14** when your heart is lifted up, and you forget the LORD your God who brought you out of the land of Egypt, from the house of bondage;

Hos 13:6 When they had pasture, they were filled; They were filled and their heart was exalted; Therefore they forgot Me.

Trials should not lead to.

Ps 44:17–20 All this has come upon us; But we have not forgotten You, Nor have we dealt falsely with Your covenant. **18** Our heart has not turned back, Nor have our steps departed from Your way; **19** But You have severely broken us in the place of jackals, And covered us with the shadow of death. **20** If we had forgotten the name of our God, Or stretched out our hands to a foreign god,

Should resolve against.

Ps 119:16 I will delight myself in Your statutes; I will not forget Your word.

Ps 119:93 I will never forget Your precepts, For by them You have given me life.

Cautions against.

Deut 6:12 *then* beware, lest you forget the LORD who brought you out of the land of Egypt, from the house of bondage.

Deut 8:11 "Beware that you do not forget the LORD your God by not keeping His commandments, His judgments, and His statutes which I command you today,

Exhortation to those guilty of.

Ps 50:22 "Now consider this, you who forget God, Lest I tear *you* in pieces, And *there be* none to deliver:

Punishment for.

Job 8:12–13 While it *is* yet green *and* not cut down, It withers before any *other* plant. **13** So *are* the paths of all who forget God; And the hope of the hypocrite shall perish,

Ps 9:17 The wicked shall be turned into hell, *And* all the nations that forget God.

Is 17:10–11 Because you have forgotten the God of your salvation, And have not been mindful of the Rock of your stronghold, Therefore you will plant pleasant plants And set out foreign seedlings; **11** In the day you will make your plant to grow, And in the morning you will make your seed to flourish; *But* the harvest *will be* a heap of ruins In the day of grief and desperate sorrow.

Ezek 23:35 "Therefore thus says the Lord GOD: 'Because you have forgotten Me and cast Me behind your back, Therefore you shall bear the *penalty Of* your lewdness and your harlotry.' "

Hos 8:14 "For Israel has forgotten his Maker, And has built temples; Judah also has multiplied fortified cities; But I will send fire upon his cities, And it shall devour his palaces."

FORGIVENESS OF INJURIES

Christ set an example of.

Luke 23:34 Then Jesus said, "Father, forgive them, for they do not know what they do." And they divided His garments and cast lots.

Commanded.

Mark 11:25 "And whenever you stand praying, if you have anything against anyone, forgive him, that your Father in heaven may also forgive you your trespasses.

Rom 12:19 Beloved, do not avenge yourselves, but *rather* give place to wrath; for it is written, *"Vengeance is Mine, I will repay,"* says the Lord.

1 Pet 4:8 And above all things have fervent love for one another, for *"love will cover a multitude of sins."*

To be unlimited.

Matt 18:22 Jesus said to him, "I do not say to you, up to seven times, but up to seventy times seven.

Luke 17:4 And if he sins against you seven times in a day, and seven times in a day returns to you, saying, 'I repent,' you shall forgive him."

A characteristic of believers.

Ps 7:4 If I have repaid evil to him who was at peace with me, Or have plundered my enemy without cause,

Prov 19:11 The discretion of a man makes him slow to anger, And his glory *is* to overlook a transgression.

Motives to,

The mercy of God.

Luke 6:36 Therefore be merciful, just as your Father also is merciful.

Our need of it.

Mark 11:25 "And whenever you stand praying, if you have anything against anyone, forgive him, that your Father in heaven may also forgive you your trespasses.

God's forgiveness of us.

Eph 4:32 And be kind to one another, tenderhearted, forgiving one another, even as God in Christ forgave you.

Christ's forgiveness of us.

Col 3:13 bearing with one another, and forgiving one another, if anyone has a complaint against another; even as Christ forgave you, so you also *must do.*

Should be accompanied by

Forbearance.

Col 3:13 bearing with one another, and forgiving one another, if anyone has a complaint against another; even as Christ forgave you, so you also *must do.*

Kindness.

Gen 45:5–11 But now, do not therefore be grieved or angry with yourselves because you sold me here; for God sent me before you to preserve life. **6** For these two years the famine *has been* in the land, and *there are* still five years in which *there will be* neither plowing nor harvesting. **7** And God sent me before you to preserve a posterity for you in the earth, and to save your lives by a great deliverance. **8** So now *it was* not you *who* sent me here, but God; and He has made me a father to Pharaoh, and lord of all his house, and a ruler throughout all the land of Egypt. **9** "Hurry and go up to my father, and say to him, 'Thus says your son Joseph: "God has made me lord of all Egypt; come down to me, do not tarry. **10** You shall dwell in the land of Goshen, and you shall be near to me, you and your children, your children's children, your flocks and your herds, and all that you have. **11** There I will provide for you, lest you and your household, and all that you have, come to poverty; for *there are* still five years of famine." '

Rom 12:20 Therefore *"If your enemy is hungry, feed him; If he is thirsty, give him a drink; For in so doing you will heap coals of fire on his head."*

Blessing and prayer.

Matt 5:44 But I say to you, love your enemies, bless those who curse you, do good to those who hate you, and pray for those who spitefully use you and persecute you,

Promises for.

Matt 6:14 "For if you forgive men their trespasses, your heavenly Father will also forgive you.

Luke 6:37 "Judge not, and you shall not be judged. Condemn not, and you shall not be condemned. Forgive, and you will be forgiven.

Must be extended to be received.

Matt 6:15 But if you do not forgive men their trespasses, neither will your Father forgive your trespasses.

James 2:13 For judgment is without mercy to the one who has shown no mercy. Mercy triumphs over judgment.

Illustrated.

Matt 18:23–35 Therefore the kingdom of heaven is like a certain king who wanted to settle accounts with his servants. **24** And when he had begun to settle accounts, one was brought to him who owed him ten thousand talents. **25** But as he was not able to pay, his master commanded that he be sold, with his wife and children and all that he had, and that payment be made. **26** The servant therefore fell down before him, saying, 'Master, have patience with me, and I will pay you all.' **27** Then the master of that servant was moved with compassion, released him, and forgave him the debt. **28** "But that servant went out and found one of his fellow servants who owed him a hundred denarii; and he laid hands on him and took *him* by the throat, saying, 'Pay me what you owe!' **29** So his fellow servant fell down at his feet and begged him, saying, 'Have patience with me, and I will pay you all.' **30** And he would not, but went and threw him into prison till he should pay the debt. **31** So when his fellow servants saw what had been done, they were very grieved, and came and told their master all that had been done. **32** Then his master, after he had called him, said to him, 'You wicked servant! I forgave you all that debt because you begged me. **33** Should you not also have had compassion on your fellow servant, just as I had pity on you?' **34** And his master was angry, and delivered him to the torturers until he should pay all that was due to him. **35** "So My heavenly Father also will do to you if each of you, from his heart, does not forgive his brother his trespasses."

2 Cor 2:5–11 But if anyone has caused grief, he has not grieved me, but all of you to some extent—not to be too severe. **6** This punishment which *was inflicted* by the majority *is* sufficient for such a man, **7** so that, on the contrary, you *ought* rather to forgive and comfort *him,* lest perhaps such a one be swallowed up with too much sorrow. **8** Therefore I urge you to reaffirm *your* love to him. **9** For to this end I also wrote, that I might put you to the test, whether you are obedient in all things. **10** Now whom you forgive anything, I also *forgive.* For if indeed I have forgiven anything, I have forgiven that one for your sakes in the presence of Christ, **11** lest Satan should take advantage of us; for we are not ignorant of his devices.

Exemplified by

Joseph.

Gen 50:20–21 But as for you, you meant evil against me; *but* God meant it for good, in order to bring it about as *it is* this day, to save many people alive. **21** Now therefore, do not be afraid; I will provide for you and your little ones." And he comforted them and spoke kindly to them.

David.

1 Sam 24:7 So David restrained his servants with *these* words, and did not allow them to rise against Saul. And Saul got up from the cave and went on *his* way.

2 Sam 18:5 Now the king had commanded Joab, Abishai, and Ittai, saying, "*Deal* gently for my sake with the young man Absalom." And all the people heard when the king gave all the captains orders concerning Absalom.

2 Sam 19:23 Therefore the king said to Shimei, "You shall not die." And the king swore to him.

Solomon.

1 Kin 1:53 So King Solomon sent them to bring him down from the altar. And he came and fell down be-

fore King Solomon; and Solomon said to him, "Go to your house."

Stephen.

Acts 7:60 Then he knelt down and cried out with a loud voice, "Lord, do not charge them with this sin." And when he had said this, he fell asleep.

Paul.

2 Tim 4:16 At my first defense no one stood with me, but all forsook me. May it not be charged against them.

FORSAKING GOD

Idolaters guilty of.

1 Sam 8:8 According to all the works which they have done since the day that I brought them up out of Egypt, even to this day—with which they have forsaken Me and served other gods—so they are doing to you also.

1 Kin 11:33 because they have forsaken Me, and worshiped Ashtoreth the goddess of the Sidonians, Chemosh the god of the Moabites, and Milcom the god of the people of Ammon, and have not walked in My ways to do *what is* right in My eyes and *keep* My statutes and My judgments, as *did* his father David.

The wicked guilty of.

Deut 28:20 "The LORD will send on you cursing, confusion, and rebuke in all that you set your hand to do, until you are destroyed and until you perish quickly, because of the wickedness of your doings in which you have forsaken Me.

Backsliders guilty of.

Jer 15:6 You have forsaken Me," says the LORD, "You have gone backward. Therefore I will stretch out My hand against you and destroy you; I am weary of relenting!

Means departing from

His house.

2 Chr 29:6 For our fathers have trespassed and done evil in the eyes of the LORD our God; they have forsaken Him, have turned their faces away from the dwelling place of the LORD, and turned *their* backs *on* Him.

His covenant.

Deut 29:25 Then *people* would say: 'Because they have forsaken the covenant of the LORD God of their fathers, which He made with them when He brought them out of the land of Egypt;

1 Kin 19:10 So he said, "I have been very zealous for the LORD God of hosts; for the children of Israel have forsaken Your covenant, torn down Your altars, and killed Your prophets with the sword. I alone am left; and they seek to take my life."

Jer 22:9 Then they will answer, 'Because they have forsaken the covenant of the LORD their God, and worshiped other gods and served them.' "

Dan 11:30 For ships from Cyprus shall come against him; therefore he shall be grieved, and return in rage against the holy covenant, and do *damage.* "So he shall return and show regard for those who forsake the holy covenant.

His commandments.

Ezra 9:10 And now, O our God, what shall we say after this? For we have forsaken Your commandments,

The right way.

2 Pet 2:15 They have forsaken the right way and gone astray, following the way of Balaam the *son* of Beor, who loved the wages of unrighteousness;

Trusting in man is.

Jer 17:5 Thus says the LORD: "Cursed *is* the man who trusts in man And makes flesh his strength, Whose heart departs from the LORD.

Leads men to follow their own devices.

Jer 2:13 "For My people have committed two evils: They have forsaken Me, the fountain of living waters, *And* hewn themselves cisterns—broken cisterns that can hold no water.

Prosperity tempts to.

Deut 31:20 When I have brought them to the land flowing with milk and honey, of which I swore to their fathers, and they have eaten and filled themselves and grown fat, then they will turn to other gods and serve them; and they will provoke Me and break My covenant.

Deut 32:15 "But Jeshurun grew fat and kicked; You grew fat, you grew thick, You are obese! Then he forsook God *who* made him, And scornfully esteemed the Rock of his salvation.

Wickedness of.

Jer 2:13 "For My people have committed two evils: They have forsaken Me, the fountain of living waters, *And* hewn themselves cisterns—broken cisterns that can hold no water.

Jer 5:7 "How shall I pardon you for this? Your children have forsaken Me And sworn by *those* that are *not* gods. When I had fed them to the full, Then they committed adultery And assembled themselves by troops in the harlots' houses.

Unreasonableness and ingratitude of.

Jer 2:5–6 Thus says the LORD: "What injustice have your fathers found in Me, That they have gone far from Me, Have followed idols, And have become idolaters? 6 Neither did they say, 'Where *is* the LORD, Who brought us up out of the land of Egypt, Who led us through the wilderness, Through a land of deserts and pits, Through a land of drought and the shadow of death, Through a land that no one crossed And where no one dwelt?'

Brings confusion.

Jer 17:13 O LORD, the hope of Israel, All who forsake You shall be ashamed. "Those who depart from Me Shall be written in the earth, Because they have forsaken the LORD, The fountain of living waters."

Followed by remorse.

Ezek 6:9 Then those of you who escape will remember Me among the nations where they are carried captive, because I was crushed by their adulterous heart which has departed from Me, and by their eyes which play the harlot after their idols; they will loathe themselves for the evils which they committed in all their abominations.

Brings down His wrath.

Ezra 8:22 For I was ashamed to request of the king an escort of soldiers and horsemen to help us against the enemy on the road, because we had spoken to the king, saying, "The hand of our God *is* upon all those for good who seek Him, but His power and His wrath *are* against all those who forsake Him."

Provokes God to forsake men.

Judg 10:13 Yet you have forsaken Me and served other gods. Therefore I will deliver you no more.

2 Chr 15:2 And he went out to meet Asa, and said to him: "Hear me, Asa, and all Judah and Benjamin. The LORD *is* with you while you are with Him. If you seek Him, He will be found by you; but if you forsake Him, He will forsake you.

2 Chr 24:20 Then the Spirit of God came upon Zechariah the son of Jehoiada the priest, who stood above the people, and said to them, "Thus says God: 'Why do you transgress the commandments of the LORD, so that you cannot prosper? Because you have forsaken the LORD, He also has forsaken you.' "

2 Chr 24:24 For the army of the Syrians came with a small company of men; but the LORD delivered a very great army into their hand, because they had forsaken the LORD God of their fathers. So they executed judgment against Joash.

People's resolve against.

Josh 24:16 So the people answered and said: "Far be it from us that we should forsake the LORD to serve other gods;

Cf. Neh 10:29–39

Curse pronounced upon.

Jer 17:5 Thus says the LORD: "Cursed *is* the man who trusts in man And makes flesh his strength, Whose heart departs from the LORD.

Sin of, to be confessed.

Ezra 9:10 And now, O our God, what shall we say after this? For we have forsaken Your commandments,

Warnings against.

Josh 24:20 If you forsake the LORD and serve foreign gods, then He will turn and do you harm and consume you, after He has done you good."

1 Chr 28:9 "As for you, my son Solomon, know the God of your father, and serve Him with a loyal heart and with a willing mind; for the LORD searches all hearts and understands all the intent of the thoughts. If you seek Him, He will be found by you; but if you forsake Him, He will cast you off forever.

Punishment for.

Deut 28:20 "The LORD will send on you cursing, confusion, and rebuke in all that you set your hand to do, until you are destroyed and until you perish quickly, because of the wickedness of your doings in which you have forsaken Me.

2 Kin 22:16–17 "Thus says the LORD: 'Behold, I will bring calamity on this place and on its inhabitants—all the words of the book which the king of Judah has read— 17 because they have forsaken Me and burned incense to other gods, that they might provoke Me to anger with all the works of their hands. Therefore My wrath shall be aroused against this place and shall not be quenched.' " '

Is 1:28 The destruction of transgressors and of sinners *shall be* together, And those who forsake the LORD shall be consumed.

Jer 1:16 I will utter My judgments Against them concerning all their wickedness, Because they have forsaken Me, Burned incense to other gods, And worshiped the works of their own hands.

Jer 5:19 And it will be when you say, 'Why does the Lᴏʀᴅ our God do all these *things* to us?' then you shall answer them, 'Just as you have forsaken Me and served foreign gods in your land, so you shall serve aliens in a land *that is* not yours.'

Illustrated by

The children of Israel.

1 Sam 12:10 Then they cried out to the Lᴏʀᴅ, and said, 'We have sinned, because we have forsaken the Lᴏʀᴅ and served the Baals and Ashtoreths; but now deliver us from the hand of our enemies, and we will serve You.'

Saul.

1 Sam 15:11 "I greatly regret that I have set up Saul *as* king, for he has turned back from following Me, and has not performed My commandments." And it grieved Samuel, and he cried out to the Lᴏʀᴅ all night.

Ahab.

1 Kin 18:18 And he answered, "I have not troubled Israel, but you and your father's house *have,* in that you have forsaken the commandments of the Lᴏʀᴅ and have followed the Baals.

Amon.

2 Kin 21:22 He forsook the Lᴏʀᴅ God of his fathers, and did not walk in the way of the Lᴏʀᴅ.

The kingdom of Judah.

2 Chr 12:1 Now it came to pass, when Rehoboam had established the kingdom and had strengthened himself, that he forsook the law of the Lᴏʀᴅ, and all Israel along with him.

2 Chr 12:5 Then Shemaiah the prophet came to Rehoboam and the leaders of Judah, who were gathered together in Jerusalem because of Shishak, and said to them, "Thus says the Lᴏʀᴅ: 'You have forsaken Me, and therefore I also have left you in the hand of Shishak.' "

2 Chr 21:10 Thus Edom has been in revolt against Judah's authority to this day. At that time Libnah revolted against his rule, because he had forsaken the Lᴏʀᴅ God of his fathers.

Is 1:4 Alas, sinful nation, A people laden with iniquity, A brood of evildoers, Children who are corrupters! They have forsaken the Lᴏʀᴅ, They have provoked to anger The Holy One of Israel, They have turned away backward.

Jer 15:6 You have forsaken Me," says the Lᴏʀᴅ, "You have gone backward. Therefore I will stretch out My hand against you and destroy you; I am weary of relenting!

The kingdom of Israel.

2 Chr 13:11 And they burn to the Lᴏʀᴅ every morning and every evening burnt sacrifices and sweet incense; *they* also *set* the showbread *in order on* the pure *gold* table, and the lampstand of gold with its lamps to burn every evening; for we keep the command of the Lᴏʀᴅ our God, but you have forsaken Him.

Cf. 2 Kin 17:7–18

Many disciples.

John 6:66 From that *time* many of His disciples went back and walked with Him no more.

Phygellus, etc.

2 Tim 1:15 This you know, that all those in Asia have turned away from me, among whom are Phygellus and Hermogenes.

Balaam.

2 Pet 2:15 They have forsaken the right way and gone astray, following the way of Balaam the *son* of Beor, who loved the wages of unrighteousness;

FORTRESSES

Places strong by nature.

Num 24:21 Then he looked on the Kenites, and he took up his oracle and said: "Firm is your dwelling place, And your nest is set in the rock;

Places fortified by design.

Jer 51:53 Though Babylon were to mount up to heaven, And though she were to fortify the height of her strength, *Yet* from Me plunderers would come to her," says the Lᴏʀᴅ.

A place of security.

Is 33:16 He will dwell on high; His place of defense *will be* the fortress of rocks; Bread will be given him, His water *will be* sure.

Dan 11:10 However his sons shall stir up strife, and assemble a multitude of great forces; and *one* shall certainly come and overwhelm and pass through; then he shall return to his fortress and stir up strife.

Places used as

Cities.

Judg 9:31 And he sent messengers to Abimelech secretly, saying, "Take note! Gaal the son of Ebed and his brothers have come to Shechem; and here they are, fortifying the city against you.

Neh 4:2 And he spoke before his brethren and the army of Samaria, and said, "What are these feeble Jews doing? Will they fortify themselves? Will they offer sacrifices? Will they complete it in a day? Will they revive the stones from the heaps of rubbish—*stones* that are burned?"

Strongholds.

Judg 6:2 and the hand of Midian prevailed against Israel. Because of the Midianites, the children of Israel made for themselves the dens, the caves, and the strongholds which *are* in the mountains.

2 Sam 5:9 Then David dwelt in the stronghold, and called it the City of David. And David built all around from the Millo and inward.

2 Chr 11:11 And he fortified the strongholds, and put captains in them, and stores of food, oil, and wine.

Is 25:12 The fortress of the high fort of your walls He will bring down, lay low, *And* bring to the ground, down to the dust.

Strong towers.

2 Chr 26:9 And Uzziah built towers in Jerusalem at the Corner Gate, at the Valley Gate, and at the corner buttress of the wall; then he fortified them.

Afforded protection against enemies.

Judg 6:2 and the hand of Midian prevailed against Israel. Because of the Midianites, the children of Israel made for themselves the dens, the caves, and the strongholds which *are* in the mountains.

Nah 2:1 He who scatters has come up before your face. Man the fort! Watch the road! Strengthen *your* flanks! Fortify *your* power mightily.

Frequent occurrences involving,

Entered by the enemy.

Dan 11:7 But from a branch of her roots *one* shall arise in his place, who shall come with an army, enter the fortress of the king of the North, and deal with them and prevail.

Plundered.

Hos 10:14 Therefore tumult shall arise among your people, And all your fortresses shall be plundered As Shalman plundered Beth Arbel in the day of battle— A mother dashed in pieces upon *her* children.

Leveled.

Is 25:12 The fortress of the high fort of your walls He will bring down, lay low, *And* bring to the ground, down to the dust.

Deserted, etc.

Is 34:13 And thorns shall come up in its palaces, Nettles and brambles in its fortresses; It shall be a habitation of jackals, A courtyard for ostriches.

Threatened destruction.

Is 17:3 The fortress also will cease from Ephraim, The kingdom from Damascus, And the remnant of Syria; They will be as the glory of the children of Israel," Says the LORD of hosts.

Illustrative of

God's protection.

Ps 18:2 The LORD is my rock and my fortress and my deliverer; My God, my strength, in whom I will trust; My shield and the horn of my salvation, my stronghold.

Jer 16:19 O LORD, my strength and my fortress, My refuge in the day of affliction, The Gentiles shall come to You From the ends of the earth and say, "Surely our fathers have inherited lies, Worthlessness and unprofitable *things*."

Christ, the defense of saints.

Is 33:16 He will dwell on high; His place of defense *will be* the fortress of rocks; Bread will be given him, His water *will be* sure.

Protection afforded to ministers.

Jer 6:27 "I have set you *as* an assayer *and* a fortress among My people, That you may know and test their way.

FOUNDATION

The lowest part of a building, and on which it rests.

Luke 14:29 lest, after he has laid the foundation, and is not able to finish, all who see *it* begin to mock him,

Acts 16:26 Suddenly there was a great earthquake, so that the foundations of the prison were shaken; and immediately all the doors were opened and everyone's chains were loosed.

Figuratively applied to

The heavens.

2 Sam 22:8 "Then the earth shook and trembled; The foundations of heaven quaked and were shaken, Because He was angry.

The earth (world).

Job 38:4 "Where were you when I laid the foundations of the earth? Tell *Me*, if you have understanding.

Ps 18:15 Then the channels of the sea were seen, The foundations of the world were uncovered At Your rebuke, O LORD, At the blast of the breath of Your nostrils.

Ps 104:5 *You who* laid the foundations of the earth, So *that* it should not be moved forever,

Matt 13:35 that it might be fulfilled which was spoken by the prophet, saying: *"I will open My mouth in parables; I will utter things kept secret from the foundation of the world."*

The mountains.

Deut 32:22 For a fire is kindled in My anger, And shall burn to the lowest hell; It shall consume the earth with her increase, And set on fire the foundations of the mountains.

The ocean.

Ps 104:8 They went up over the mountains; They went down into the valleys, To the place which You founded for them.

Kingdoms.

Ex 9:18 Behold, tomorrow about this time I will cause very heavy hail to rain down, such as has not been in Egypt since its founding until now.

Laid for

Cities.

Josh 6:26 Then Joshua charged *them* at that time, saying, "Cursed *be* the man before the LORD who rises up and builds this city Jericho; he shall lay its foundation with his firstborn, and with his youngest he shall set up its gates."

1 Kin 16:34 In his days Hiel of Bethel built Jericho. He laid its foundation with Abiram his firstborn, and with his youngest *son* Segub he set up its gates, according to the word of the LORD, which He had spoken through Joshua the son of Nun.

Walls.

Ezra 4:12 Let it be known to the king that the Jews who came up from you have come to us at Jerusalem, and are building the rebellious and evil city, and are finishing *its* walls and repairing the foundations.

Rev 21:14 Now the wall of the city had twelve foundations, and on them were the names of the twelve apostles of the Lamb.

Houses.

Luke 6:48 He is like a man building a house, who dug deep and laid the foundation on the rock. And when the flood arose, the stream beat vehemently against that house, and could not shake it, for it was founded on the rock.

Temples.

1 Kin 6:37 In the fourth year the foundation of the house of the Lord was laid, in the month of Ziv.

Ezra 3:10 When the builders laid the foundation of the temple of the Lord, the priests stood in their apparel with trumpets, and the Levites, the sons of Asaph, with cymbals, to praise the Lord, according to the ordinance of David king of Israel.

Towers.

Luke 14:28–29 For which of you, intending to build a tower, does not sit down first and count the cost, whether he has *enough* to finish *it*— **29** lest, after he has laid the foundation, and is not able to finish, all who see *it* begin to mock him,

Described as

Of stone.

1 Kin 5:17 And the king commanded them to quarry large stones, costly stones, *and* hewn stones, to lay the foundation of the temple.

Deep laid.

Luke 6:48 He is like a man building a house, who dug deep and laid the foundation on the rock. And when the flood arose, the stream beat vehemently against that house, and could not shake it, for it was founded on the rock.

Strongly laid.

Ezra 6:3 In the first year of King Cyrus, King Cyrus issued a decree *concerning* the house of God at Jerusalem: "Let the house be rebuilt, the place where they offered sacrifices; and let the foundations of it be firmly laid, its height sixty cubits *and* its width sixty cubits,

Joined together by corner stones.

Ezra 4:12 Let it be known to the king that the Jews who came up from you have come to us at Jerusalem, and are building the rebellious and evil city, and are finishing *its* walls and repairing the foundations.

Eph 2:20 having been built on the foundation of the apostles and prophets, Jesus Christ Himself being the chief corner*stone,*

1 Pet 2:6 Therefore it is also contained in the Scripture, *"Behold, I lay in Zion A chief cornerstone, elect, precious, And he who believes on Him will by no means be put to shame."*

Security afforded by.

Matt 7:25 and the rain descended, the floods came, and the winds blew and beat on that house; and it did not fall, for it was founded on the rock.

Cf. Luke 6:48

Illustrative of

Christ.

Is 28:16 Therefore thus says the Lord God: "Behold, I lay in Zion a stone for a foundation, A tried stone, a precious cornerstone, a sure foundation; Whoever believes will not act hastily.

1 Cor 3:11 For no other foundation can anyone lay than that which is laid, which is Jesus Christ.

Doctrines of the apostles, etc.

Eph 2:20 having been built on the foundation of the apostles and prophets, Jesus Christ Himself being the chief corner*stone,*

First principles of the gospel.

Heb 6:1–2 Therefore, leaving the discussion of the elementary *principles* of Christ, let us go on to perfection, not laying again the foundation of repentance from dead works and of faith toward God, **2** of the doctrine of baptisms, of laying on of hands, of resurrection of the dead, and of eternal judgment.

Decrees and purposes of God.

2 Tim 2:19 Nevertheless the solid foundation of God stands, having this seal: "The Lord knows those who are His," and, "Let everyone who names the name of Christ depart from iniquity."

Magistrates ("gods").

Ps 82:1–5 God stands in the congregation of the mighty; He judges among the gods. **2** How long will you judge unjustly, And show partiality to the wicked? Selah **3** Defend the poor and fatherless; Do justice to the afflicted and needy. **4** Deliver the poor and needy; Free them from the hand of the wicked. **5** They do not know, nor do they understand; They walk about in darkness; All the foundations of the earth are unstable.

The righteous.

Prov 10:25 When the whirlwind passes by, the wicked *is* no *more,* But the righteous *has* an everlasting foundation.

Hope of believers.

Ps 87:1 His foundation *is* in the holy mountains.

Security of believers' inheritance.

Heb 11:10 for he waited for the city which has foundations, whose builder and maker *is* God.

Fountains and Springs

Created by God.

Ps 74:15 You broke open the fountain and the flood; You dried up mighty rivers.

Ps 104:10 He sends the springs into the valleys; They flow among the hills.

God to be praised for.

Rev 14:7 saying with a loud voice, "Fear God and give glory to Him, for the hour of His judgment has come; and worship Him who made heaven and earth, the sea and springs of water."

Come from the great deep.

Gen 7:11 In the six hundredth year of Noah's life, in the second month, the seventeenth day of the month, on that day all the fountains of the great deep were broken up, and the windows of heaven were opened.

Job 38:16 "Have you entered the springs of the sea? Or have you walked in search of the depths?

Found in hills and valleys.

Deut 8:7 For the Lord your God is bringing you into a good land, a land of brooks of water, of fountains and springs, that flow out of valleys and hills;

Ps 104:10 He sends the springs into the valleys; They flow among the hills.

Each have only one kind of water.

James 3:11 Does a spring send forth fresh *water* and bitter from the same opening?

Provide

Drink to the beasts.

Ps 104:11 They give drink to every beast of the field; The wild donkeys quench their thirst.

Refreshment to the birds.

Ps 104:12 By them the birds of the heavens have their home; They sing among the branches.

Fruitfulness to the earth.

1 Kin 18:5 And Ahab had said to Obadiah, "Go into the land to all the springs of water and to all the brooks; perhaps we may find grass to keep the horses and mules alive, so that we will not have to kill any livestock."

Joel 3:18 And it will come to pass in that day *That* the mountains shall drip with new wine, The hills shall flow with milk, And all the brooks of Judah shall be flooded with water; A fountain shall flow from the house of the LORD And water the Valley of Acacias.

Frequented by travelers.

Gen 16:7 Now the Angel of the LORD found her by a spring of water in the wilderness, by the spring on the way to Shur.

Abound in Canaan.

Deut 8:7 For the LORD your God is bringing you into a good land, a land of brooks of water, of fountains and springs, that flow out of valleys and hills;

1 Kin 18:5 And Ahab had said to Obadiah, "Go into the land to all the springs of water and to all the brooks; perhaps we may find grass to keep the horses and mules alive, so that we will not have to kill any livestock."

Sometimes dried up.

Is 58:11 The LORD will guide you continually, And satisfy your soul in drought, And strengthen your bones; You shall be like a watered garden, And like a spring of water, whose waters do not fail.

Drying up of, a severe punishment.

Ps 107:33–34 He turns rivers into a wilderness, And the watersprings into dry ground; 34 A fruitful land into barrenness, For the wickedness of those who dwell in it.

Hos 13:15 Though he is fruitful among *his* brethren, An east wind shall come; The wind of the LORD shall come up from the wilderness. Then his spring shall become dry, And his fountain shall be dried up. He shall plunder the treasury of every desirable prize.

Constantly flowing, especially esteemed.

Is 58:11 The LORD will guide you continually, And satisfy your soul in drought, And strengthen your bones; You shall be like a watered garden, And like a spring of water, whose waters do not fail.

Could not be ceremonially defiled.

Lev 11:36 Nevertheless a spring or a cistern, *in which there is* plenty of water, shall be clean, but whatever touches any such carcass becomes unclean.

Sometimes stopped or turned off to distress enemies.

2 Chr 32:3–4 he consulted with his leaders and commanders to stop the water from the springs which *were* outside the city; and they helped him. 4 Thus many people gathered together who stopped all the springs and the brook that ran through the land, saying, "Why should the kings of Assyria come and find much water?"

Those mentioned in Scripture,

On the way to Shur.

Gen 16:7 Now the Angel of the LORD found her by a spring of water in the wilderness, by the spring on the way to Shur.

Of the waters of Nephtoah.

Josh 15:9 Then the border went around from the top of the hill to the fountain of the water of Nephtoah, and extended to the cities of Mount Ephron. And the border went around to Baalah (which *is* Kirjath Jearim).

Of Jezreel.

1 Sam 29:1 Then the Philistines gathered together all their armies at Aphek, and the Israelites encamped by a fountain which *is* in Jezreel.

Of Pisgah.

Deut 4:49 and all the plain on the east side of the Jordan as far as the Sea of the Arabah, below the slopes of Pisgah.

Upper and lower springs.

Josh 15:19 She answered, "Give me a blessing; since you have given me land in the South, give me also springs of water." So he gave her the upper springs and the lower springs.

Judg 1:15 So she said to him, "Give me a blessing; since you have given me land in the South, give me also springs of water." And Caleb gave her the upper springs and the lower springs.

Illustrative of

God.

Ps 36:9 For with You *is* the fountain of life; In Your light we see light.

Jer 2:13 "For My people have committed two evils: They have forsaken Me, the fountain of living waters, *And* hewn themselves cisterns—broken cisterns that can hold no water.

Jer 17:13 O LORD, the hope of Israel, All who forsake You shall be ashamed. "Those who depart from Me Shall be written in the earth, Because they have forsaken the LORD, The fountain of living waters."

Christ.

Zech 13:1 "In that day a fountain shall be opened for the house of David and for the inhabitants of Jerusalem, for sin and for uncleanness.

The Holy Spirit.

John 7:38–39 He who believes in Me, as the Scripture has said, out of his heart will flow rivers of living water." 39 But this He spoke concerning the Spirit, whom those believing in Him would receive; for the Holy Spirit was not yet *given*, because Jesus was not yet glorified.

Constant supplies of grace.

Ps 87:7 Both the singers and the players on instruments say, "All my springs *are* in you."

Eternal life.

John 4:14 but whoever drinks of the water that I shall give him will never thirst. But the water that I shall give him will become in him a fountain of water springing up into everlasting life."

Rev 21:6 And He said to me, "It is done! I am the Alpha and the Omega, the Beginning and the End. I will give of the fountain of the water of life freely to him who thirsts.

The means of grace.

Is 41:18 I will open rivers in desolate heights, And fountains in the midst of the valleys; I will make the wilderness a pool of water, And the dry land springs of water.

Joel 3:18 And it will come to pass in that day *That* the mountains shall drip with new wine, The hills shall flow with milk, And all the brooks of Judah shall be flooded with water; A fountain shall flow from the house of the LORD And water the Valley of Acacias.

A good wife.

Prov 5:18 Let your fountain be blessed, And rejoice with the wife of your youth.

A numerous posterity.

Deut 33:28 Then Israel shall dwell in safety, The fountain of Jacob alone, In a land of grain and new wine; His heavens shall also drop dew.

Spiritual wisdom.

Prov 16:22 Understanding *is* a wellspring of life to him who has it. But the correction of fools *is* folly.

Prov 18:4 The words of a man's mouth *are* deep waters; The wellspring of wisdom *is* a flowing brook.

The law of the wise.

Prov 13:14 The law of the wise *is* a fountain of life, To turn *one* away from the snares of death.

Godly fear.

Prov 14:27 The fear of the LORD *is* a fountain of life, To turn *one* away from the snares of death.

(Not failing) the church.

Is 58:11 The LORD will guide you continually, And satisfy your soul in drought, And strengthen your bones; You shall be like a watered garden, And like a spring of water, whose waters do not fail.

(Always flowing) unceasing wickedness of the Jews.

Jer 6:7 As a fountain wells up with water, So she wells up with her wickedness. Violence and plundering are heard in her. Before Me continually *are* grief and wounds.

The natural heart.

Matt 15:18–19 But those things which proceed out of the mouth come from the heart, and they defile a man. **19** For out of the heart proceed evil thoughts, murders, adulteries, fornications, thefts, false witness, blasphemies.

James 3:11 Does a spring send forth fresh *water* and bitter from the same opening?

(Troubled) believers led astray.

Prov 25:26 A righteous *man* who falters before the wicked *Is like* a murky spring and a polluted well.

FOX, THE

Found in deserts.

Ezek 13:4 O Israel, your prophets are like foxes in the deserts.

Abounded in Palestine.

Judg 15:4 Then Samson went and caught three hundred foxes; and he took torches, turned *the foxes* tail to tail, and put a torch between each pair of tails.

Lam 5:18 Because of Mount Zion which is desolate, With foxes walking about on it.

Described as

Active.

Neh 4:3 Now Tobiah the Ammonite *was* beside him, and he said, "Whatever they build, if even a fox goes up *on it*, he will break down their stone wall."

Crafty.

Luke 13:32 And He said to them, "Go, tell that fox, 'Behold, I cast out demons and perform cures today and tomorrow, and the third *day* I shall be perfected.'

Carnivorous.

Ps 63:10 They shall fall by the sword; They shall be a portion for jackals.

Destructive to vines.

Song 2:15 Catch us the foxes, The little foxes that spoil the vines, For our vines *have* tender grapes.

Dwells in holes.

Matt 8:20 And Jesus said to him, "Foxes have holes and birds of the air *have* nests, but the Son of Man has nowhere to lay *His* head."

Cf. Luke 9:58

Illustrative of

False prophets.

Ezek 13:4 O Israel, your prophets are like foxes in the deserts.

Cunning and deceitful persons.

Luke 13:32 And He said to them, "Go, tell that fox, 'Behold, I cast out demons and perform cures today and tomorrow, and the third *day* I shall be perfected.'

Used by Samson for annoying the Philistines.

Judg 15:4–6 Then Samson went and caught three hundred foxes; and he took torches, turned *the foxes* tail to tail, and put a torch between each pair of tails. **5** When he had set the torches on fire, he let *the foxes* go into the standing grain of the Philistines, and burned up both the shocks and the standing grain, as well as the vineyards *and* olive groves. **6** Then the Philistines said, "Who has done this?" And they answered, "Samson, the son-in-law of the Timnite, because he has taken his wife and given her to his companion." So the Philistines came up and burned her and her father with fire.

FREEDOM. SEE ALSO LIBERTY, CHRISTIAN

Christ's promise of.

John 8:31–36 Then Jesus said to those Jews who believed Him, "If you abide in My word, you are My disciples indeed. **32** And you shall know the truth, and the truth shall make you free." **33** They answered Him, "We are Abraham's descendants, and have never been in bondage to anyone. How *can* You say, 'You will be made free'?" **34** Jesus answered them, "Most assuredly, I say to you, whoever commits sin is a slave of sin. **35** And a slave does not abide in the house forever, *but* a son abides forever. **36** Therefore if the Son makes you free, you shall be free indeed.

From the penalty of the law.

Rom 7:4–6 Therefore, my brethren, you also have become dead to the law through the body of Christ, that you may be married to another—to Him who was raised from the dead, that we should bear fruit to God. **5** For when we were in the flesh, the sinful passions which were aroused by the law were at work in our members to bear fruit to death. **6** But now we have been delivered from the law, having died to what we were held by, so that we should serve in the newness of the Spirit and not *in* the oldness of the letter.

Gal 3:13–14 Christ has redeemed us from the curse of the law, having become a curse for us (for it is written, *"Cursed is everyone who hangs on a tree"*), **14** that the blessing of Abraham might come upon the Gentiles in Christ Jesus, that we might receive the promise of the Spirit through faith.

James 1:25 But he who looks into the perfect law of liberty and continues *in it*, and is not a forgetful hearer but a doer of the work, this one will be blessed in what he does.

Summarized by Paul.

Gal 5:6 For in Christ Jesus neither circumcision nor uncircumcision avails anything, but faith working through love.

Gal 5:13–14 For you, brethren, have been called to liberty; only do not *use* liberty as an opportunity for the flesh, but through love serve one another. **14** For all the law is fulfilled in one word, *even* in this: *"You shall love your neighbor as yourself."*

FRUITS

The produce of seeds, etc.

Deut 22:9 "You shall not sow your vineyard with different kinds of seed, lest the yield of the seed which you have sown and the fruit of your vineyard be defiled.

Ps 107:37 And sow fields and plant vineyards, That they may yield a fruitful harvest.

The produce of trees.

Gen 1:29 And God said, "See, I have given you every herb *that* yields seed which *is* on the face of all the earth, and every tree whose fruit yields seed; to you it shall be for food.

Eccl 2:5 I made myself gardens and orchards, and I planted all *kinds* of fruit trees in them.

Various names for,

Fruit of the ground.

Gen 4:3 And in the process of time it came to pass that Cain brought an offering of the fruit of the ground to the LORD.

Jer 7:20 Therefore thus says the Lord GOD: "Behold, My anger and My fury will be poured out on this place—on man and on beast, on the trees of the field and on the fruit of the ground. And it will burn and not be quenched."

Fruit of the earth.

Is 4:2 In that day the Branch of the LORD shall be beautiful and glorious; And the fruit of the earth *shall be* excellent and appealing For those of Israel who have escaped.

Increase of the land.

Ps 85:12 Yes, the LORD will give *what is* good; And our land will yield its increase.

Provided by God.

Mal 3:11 "And I will rebuke the devourer for your sakes, So that he will not destroy the fruit of your ground, Nor shall the vine fail to bear fruit for you in the field," Says the LORD of hosts;

Acts 14:17 Nevertheless He did not leave Himself without witness, in that He did good, gave us rain from heaven and fruitful seasons, filling our hearts with food and gladness."

Require

A fruitful land.

Ps 107:33–34 He turns rivers into a wilderness, And the watersprings into dry ground; **34** A fruitful land into barrenness, For the wickedness of those who dwell in it.

Rain from heaven.

Ps 104:13 He waters the hills from His upper chambers; The earth is satisfied with the fruit of Your works.

James 5:18 And he prayed again, and the heaven gave rain, and the earth produced its fruit.

Influence of the sun and moon.

Deut 33:14 With the precious fruits of the sun, With the precious produce of the months,

Produced in their due seasons.

Matt 21:41 They said to Him, "He will destroy those wicked men miserably, and lease *his* vineyard to other vinedressers who will render to him the fruits in their seasons."

First of, devoted to God.

Deut 26:2 that you shall take some of the first of all the produce of the ground, which you shall bring from your land that the LORD your God is giving you, and put *it* in a basket and go to the place where the LORD your God chooses to make His name abide.

Divided into

Early season.

Is 28:4 And the glorious beauty is a fading flower Which *is* at the head of the verdant valley, Like the first fruit before the summer, Which an observer sees; He eats it up while it is still in his hand.

Summer fruits.

2 Sam 16:1 When David was a little past the top *of the mountain,* there was Ziba the servant of Mephibosheth, who met him with a couple of saddled donkeys, and on them two hundred *loaves* of bread, one hundred clusters of raisins, one hundred summer fruits, and a skin of wine.

New and old.

Song 7:13 The mandrakes give off a fragrance, And at our gates *are* pleasant *fruits,* All manner, new and old, Which I have laid up for you, my beloved.

Good.

Jer 11:16 The LORD called your name, Green Olive Tree, Lovely *and* of Good Fruit. With the noise of a great tumult He has kindled fire on it, And its branches are broken.

Pleasant.

Song 4:16 Awake, O north *wind,* And come, O south! Blow upon my garden, *That* its spices may flow out. Let my beloved come to his garden And eat its pleasant fruits.

Precious.

Deut 33:14 With the precious fruits of the sun, With the precious produce of the months,

Bad.

Matt 7:17 Even so, every good tree bears good fruit, but a bad tree bears bad fruit.

To be waited for with patience.

James 5:7 Therefore be patient, brethren, until the coming of the Lord. See *how* the farmer waits for the precious fruit of the earth, waiting patiently for it until it receives the early and latter rain.

Often sent as presents.

Gen 43:11 And their father Israel said to them, "If *it must be* so, then do this: Take some of the best fruits of the land in your vessels and carry down a present for the man—a little balm and a little honey, spices and myrrh, pistachio nuts and almonds.

Often destroyed

In God's anger.

Jer 7:20 Therefore thus says the Lord GOD: "Behold, My anger and My fury will be poured out on this place—on man and on beast, on the trees of the field and on the fruit of the ground. And it will burn and not be quenched."

By blight.

Joel 1:12 The vine has dried up, And the fig tree has withered; The pomegranate tree, The palm tree also, And the apple tree— All the trees of the field are withered; Surely joy has withered away from the sons of men.

By locusts, etc.

Deut 28:38–39 "You shall carry much seed out to the field but gather little in, for the locust shall consume it. **39** You shall plant vineyards and tend *them,* but you shall neither drink *of* the wine nor gather the grapes; for the worms shall eat them.

Joel 1:4 What the chewing locust left, the swarming locust has eaten; What the swarming locust left, the crawling locust has eaten; And what the crawling locust left, the consuming locust has eaten.

By enemies.

Ezek 25:4 indeed, therefore, I will deliver you as a possession to the men of the East, and they shall set their encampments among you and make their dwellings among you; they shall eat your fruit, and they shall drink your milk.

By drought.

Hag 1:10 Therefore the heavens above you withhold the dew, and the earth withholds its fruit.

Illustrative of

The effects of repentance.

Matt 3:8 Therefore bear fruits worthy of repentance,

Works of the Spirit.

Gal 5:22–23 But the fruit of the Spirit is love, joy, peace, longsuffering, kindness, goodness, faithfulness, **23** gentleness, self-control. Against such there is no law.

Eph 5:9 (for the fruit of the Spirit *is* in all goodness, righteousness, and truth),

Good works.

Matt 7:17–18 Even so, every good tree bears good fruit, but a bad tree bears bad fruit. **18** A good tree cannot bear bad fruit, nor *can* a bad tree bear good fruit.

Phil 4:17 Not that I seek the gift, but I seek the fruit that abounds to your account.

Wise conversation.

Prov 12:14 A man will be satisfied with good by the fruit of *his* mouth, And the recompense of a man's hands will be rendered to him.

Prov 18:20 A man's stomach shall be satisfied from the fruit of his mouth; *From* the produce of his lips he shall be filled.

Praise.

Heb 13:15 Therefore by Him let us continually offer the sacrifice of praise to God, that is, the fruit of *our* lips, giving thanks to His name.

The example, etc., of the godly.

Prov 11:30 The fruit of the righteous *is* a tree of life, And he who wins souls *is* wise.

The effects of industry.

Prov 31:16 She considers a field and buys it; From her profits she plants a vineyard.

Prov 31:31 Give her of the fruit of her hands, And let her own works praise her in the gates.

The reward of believers.

Is 3:10 "Say to the righteous that *it shall be* well *with them,* For they shall eat the fruit of their doings.

The reward of the wicked.

Jer 17:9–10 "The heart *is* deceitful above all *things,* And desperately wicked; Who can know it? **10** I, the LORD, search the heart, *I* test the mind, Even to give every man according to his ways, According to the fruit of his doings.

New converts.

Ps 72:16 There will be an abundance of grain in the earth, On the top of the mountains; Its fruit shall wave like Lebanon; And *those* of the city shall flourish like grass of the earth.

John 4:36 And he who reaps receives wages, and gathers fruit for eternal life, that both he who sows and he who reaps may rejoice together.

(Bad) the conduct and conversation of evil men.

Matt 12:33 "Either make the tree good and its fruit good, or else make the tree bad and its fruit bad; for a tree is known by *its* fruit.

G

GAD, THE TRIBE OF

Descended from Jacob's seventh son.

Gen 30:11 Then Leah said, "A troop comes!" So she called his name Gad.

Predictions respecting.

Gen 49:19 "Gad, a troop shall tramp upon him, But he shall triumph at last.

Deut 33:20–21 And of Gad he said: "Blessed *is* he who enlarges Gad; He dwells as a lion, And tears the arm and the crown of his head. 21 He provided the first *part* for himself, Because a lawgiver's portion was reserved there. He came *with* the heads of the people; He administered the justice of the LORD, And His judgments with Israel."

Persons selected from,

To number the people.

Num 1:14 from Gad, Eliasaph the son of Deuel;

To spy out the land.

Num 13:15 from the tribe of Gad, Geuel the son of Machi.

Strength of, on leaving Egypt.

Num 1:24–25 From the children of Gad, their genealogies by their families, by their fathers' house, according to the number of names, from twenty years old and above, all who *were able to* go to war: 25 those who were numbered of the tribe of Gad *were* forty-five thousand six hundred and fifty.

The rear of second division of Israel in their journeys.

Num 10:18–20 And the standard of the camp of Reuben set out according to their armies; over their army *was* Elizur the son of Shedeur. 19 Over the army of the tribe of the children of Simeon *was* Shelumiel the son of Zurishaddai. 20 And over the army of the tribe of the children of Gad *was* Eliasaph the son of Deuel.

Encamped south of the tabernacle under the standard of Reuben.

Num 2:10 "On the south side *shall be* the standard of the forces with Reuben according to their armies, and the leader of the children of Reuben *shall be* Elizur the son of Shedeur."

Num 2:14 "Then *comes* the tribe of Gad, and the leader of the children of Gad *shall be* Eliasaph the son of Reuel."

Offering of, at the dedication.

Num 7:42–47 On the sixth day Eliasaph the son of Deuel, leader of the children of Gad, *presented an offering.* 43 His offering *was* one silver platter, the weight of which *was* one hundred and thirty *shekels,* and one silver bowl of seventy shekels, according to the shekel of the sanctuary, both of them full of fine flour mixed with oil as a grain offering; 44 one gold pan of ten *shekels,* full of incense; 45 one young bull, one ram, and one male lamb in its first year, as a burnt offering; 46 one kid of the goats as a sin offering; 47 and as the sacrifice of peace offerings: two oxen, five rams, five male goats, and five male lambs in their first year. This *was* the offering of Eliasaph the son of Deuel.

Families of.

Num 26:15–17 The sons of Gad according to their families *were:* of Zephon, the family of the Zephonites; *of* Haggi, the family of the Haggites; *of* Shuni, the family of the Shunites; 16 *of* Ozni, the family of the Oznites; *of* Eri, the family of the Erites; 17 *of* Arod, the family of the Arodites; *of* Areli, the family of the Arelites.

Strength of, on entering Canaan.

Num 26:18 These *are* the families of the sons of Gad according to those who were numbered of them: forty thousand five hundred.

On Ebal, said amen to the curse.

Deut 27:13 and these shall stand on Mount Ebal to curse: Reuben, Gad, Asher, Zebulun, Dan, and Naphtali.

Sought and obtained its inheritance east of the Jordan. Num 32:1–33

Borders of its inheritance.

Josh 13:24–28 Moses also had given *an inheritance* to the tribe of Gad, to the children of Gad according to their families. 25 Their territory was Jazer, and all the cities of Gilead, and half the land of the Ammonites as far as Aroer, which *is* before Rabbah, 26 and from Heshbon to Ramath Mizpah and Betonim, and from Mahanaim to the border of Debir, 27 and in the valley Beth Haram, Beth Nimrah, Succoth, and Zaphon, the rest of the kingdom of Sihon king of Heshbon, with the Jordan as *its* border, as far as the edge of the Sea of Chinnereth, on the other side of the Jordan eastward. 28 This *is* the inheritance of the children of Gad according to their families, the cities and their villages.

Cities built by.

Num 32:34–36 And the children of Gad built Dibon and Ataroth and Aroer, 35 Atroth and Shophan and Jazer and Jogbehah, 36 Beth Nimrah and Beth Haran, fortified cities, and folds for sheep.

Assisted in conquest of Canaan.

Josh 4:12–13 And the men of Reuben, the men of Gad, and half the tribe of Manasseh crossed over armed before the children of Israel, as Moses had spoken to them. 13 About forty thousand prepared for war crossed over before the LORD for battle, to the plains of Jericho.

Josh 22:9 So the children of Reuben, the children of

Gad, and half the tribe of Manasseh returned, and departed from the children of Israel at Shiloh, which *is* in the land of Canaan, to go to the country of Gilead, to the land of their possession, which they had obtained according to the word of the LORD by the hand of Moses.

Assisted in building the altar of witness.

Josh 22:10–29

Many from other tribes sought refuge with, from the Philistines.

1 Sam 13:7 And *some of* the Hebrews crossed over the Jordan to the land of Gad and Gilead. As for Saul, he *was* still in Gilgal, and all the people followed him trembling.

Eleven of, swam the Jordan, and joined David in the stronghold.

1 Chr 12:8–15 *Some* Gadites joined David at the stronghold in the wilderness, mighty men of valor, men trained for battle, who could handle shield and spear, whose faces *were like* the faces of lions, and *were* as swift as gazelles on the mountains: 9 Ezer the first, Obadiah the second, Eliab the third, 10 Mishmannah the fourth, Jeremiah the fifth, 11 Attai the sixth, Eliel the seventh, 12 Johanan the eighth, Elzabad the ninth, 13 Jeremiah the tenth, and Machbanai the eleventh. 14 These *were* from the sons of Gad, captains of the army; the least was over a hundred, and the greatest was over a thousand. 15 These *are* the ones who crossed the Jordan in the first month, when it had overflowed all its banks; and they put to flight all *those* in the valleys, to the east and to the west.

Some of, at coronation of David.

1 Chr 12:37–38 of the Reubenites and the Gadites and the half-tribe of Manasseh, from the other side of the Jordan, one hundred and twenty thousand armed for battle with every *kind* of weapon of war. 38 All these men of war, who could keep ranks, came to Hebron with a loyal heart, to make David king over all Israel; and all the rest of Israel *were* of one mind to make David king.

David appointed rulers over.

1 Chr 26:32 And his brethren *were* two thousand seven hundred able men, heads of fathers' *houses*, whom King David made officials over the Reubenites, the Gadites, and the half-tribe of Manasseh, for every matter pertaining to God and the affairs of the king.

Plundered the Hagrites.

1 Chr 5:18–22 The sons of Reuben, the Gadites, and half the tribe of Manasseh *had* forty-four thousand seven hundred and sixty valiant men, men able to bear shield and sword, to shoot with the bow, and skillful in war, who went to war. 19 They made war with the Hagrites, Jetur, Naphish, and Nodab. 20 And they were helped against them, and the Hagrites were delivered into their hand, and all who *were* with them, for they cried out to God in the battle. He heeded their prayer, because they put their trust in Him. 21 Then they took away their livestock—fifty thousand of their camels, two hundred and fifty thousand of their sheep, and two thousand of their donkeys—also one hundred thousand of their men; 22 for many fell dead, because the war *was* God's. And they dwelt in their place until the captivity.

Subdued by Hazael, king of Syria.

2 Kin 10:33 from the Jordan eastward: all the land of Gilead—Gad, Reuben, and Manasseh—from Aroer, which *is* by the River Arnon, including Gilead and Bashan.

Taken captive to Assyria.

2 Kin 15:29 In the days of Pekah king of Israel, Tiglath-Pileser king of Assyria came and took Ijon, Abel Beth Maachah, Janoah, Kedesh, Hazor, Gilead, and Galilee, all the land of Naphtali; and he carried them captive to Assyria.

1 Chr 5:22 for many fell dead, because the war *was* God's. And they dwelt in their place until the captivity.

1 Chr 5:26 So the God of Israel stirred up the spirit of Pul king of Assyria, that is, Tiglath-Pileser king of Assyria. He carried the Reubenites, the Gadites, and the half-tribe of Manasseh into captivity. He took them to Halah, Habor, Hara, and the river of Gozan to this day.

Land of, seized by the Moabites and Ammonites.

Jer 48:18–24 "O daughter inhabiting Dibon, Come down from *your* glory, And sit in thirst; For the plunderer of Moab has come against you, He has destroyed your strongholds. 19 O inhabitant of Aroer, Stand by the way and watch; Ask him who flees And her who escapes; Say, 'What has happened?' 20 Moab is shamed, for he is broken down. Wail and cry! Tell it in Arnon, that Moab is plundered. 21 "And judgment has come on the plain country: On Holon and Jahzah and Mephaath, 22 On Dibon and Nebo and Beth Diblathaim, 23 On Kirjathaim and Beth Gamul and Beth Meon, 24 On Kerioth and Bozrah, On all the cities of the land of Moab, Far or near.

Jer 49:1 Against the Ammonites. Thus says the LORD: "Has Israel no sons? Has he no heir? Why *then* does Milcom inherit Gad, And his people dwell in its cities?

GALILEE

Separated from Judea by Samaria.

John 4:3–4 He left Judea and departed again to Galilee. 4 But He needed to go through Samaria.

Upper part of, called Galilee of the Gentiles.

Is 9:1 Nevertheless the gloom *will* not *be* upon her who *is* distressed, As when at first He lightly esteemed The land of Zebulun and the land of Naphtali, And afterward more heavily oppressed *her*, By the way of the sea, beyond the Jordan, In Galilee of the Gentiles.

Matt 4:15 *"The land of Zebulun and the land of Naphtali, By the way of the sea, beyond the Jordan, Galilee of the Gentiles:*

Lake of Gennesaret, called the Sea of.

Matt 15:29 Jesus departed from there, skirted the Sea of Galilee, and went up on the mountain and sat down there.

Luke 5:1 So it was, as the multitude pressed about Him to hear the word of God, that He stood by the Lake of Gennesaret,

Kedesh the city of refuge for.

Josh 21:32 and from the tribe of Naphtali, Kedesh in Galilee with its common-land (a city of refuge for the slayer), Hammoth Dor with its common-land, and Kartan with its common-land: three cities.

Inhabitants of,

Called Galileans.

Acts 2:7 Then they were all amazed and marveled, saying to one another, "Look, are not all these who speak Galileans?

Had distinctive dialect.

Matt 26:73 And a little later those who stood by came up and said to Peter, "Surely you also are *one* of them, for your speech betrays you."

Mark 14:70 But he denied it again. And a little later those who stood by said to Peter again, "Surely you are *one* of them; for you are a Galilean, and your speech shows *it*."

Despised by the Jews.

John 7:41 Others said, "This is the Christ." But some said, "Will the Christ come out of Galilee?

John 7:52 They answered and said to him, "Are you also from Galilee? Search and look, for no prophet has arisen out of Galilee."

Opposed the Roman taxation.

Acts 5:37 After this man, Judas of Galilee rose up in the days of the census, and drew away many people after him. He also perished, and all who obeyed him were dispersed.

Cruelly treated by Pilate.

Luke 13:1 There were present at that season some who told Him about the Galileans whose blood Pilate had mingled with their sacrifices.

Twenty cities of, given to Hiram.

1 Kin 9:11 (Hiram the king of Tyre had supplied Solomon with cedar and cypress and gold, as much as he desired), *that* King Solomon then gave Hiram twenty cities in the land of Galilee.

Conquered by the Syrians.

1 Kin 15:20 So Ben-Hadad heeded King Asa, and sent the captains of his armies against the cities of Israel. He attacked Ijon, Dan, Abel Beth Maachah, and all Chinneroth, with all the land of Naphtali.

Conquered by the Assyrians.

2 Kin 15:29 In the days of Pekah king of Israel, Tiglath-Pileser king of Assyria came and took Ijon, Abel Beth Maachah, Janoah, Kedesh, Hazor, Gilead, and Galilee, all the land of Naphtali; and he carried them captive to Assyria.

Jurisdiction of, granted to Herod by the Romans.

Luke 3:1 Now in the fifteenth year of the reign of Tiberius Caesar, Pontius Pilate being governor of Judea, Herod being tetrarch of Galilee, his brother Philip tetrarch of Iturea and the region of Trachonitis, and Lysanias tetrarch of Abilene,

Luke 23:6-7 When Pilate heard of Galilee, he asked if the Man were a Galilean. 7 And as soon as he knew that He belonged to Herod's jurisdiction, he sent Him to Herod, who was also in Jerusalem at that time.

Supplied Tyre, etc. with provisions.

Acts 12:20 Now Herod had been very angry with the people of Tyre and Sidon; but they came to him with one accord, and having made Blastus the king's personal aide their friend, they asked for peace, because their country was supplied with food by the king's *country.*

Christ

Brought up in.

Matt 2:22 But when he heard that Archelaus was reigning over Judea instead of his father Herod, he was afraid to go there. And being warned by God in a dream, he turned aside into the region of Galilee.

Luke 2:39 So when they had performed all things according to the law of the Lord, they returned to Galilee, to their *own* city, Nazareth.

Luke 2:51 Then He went down with them and came to Nazareth, and was subject to them, but His mother kept all these things in her heart.

Despised as being from.

Matt 26:69 Now Peter sat outside in the courtyard. And a servant girl came to him, saying, "You also were with Jesus of Galilee."

John 7:52 They answered and said to him, "Are you also from Galilee? Search and look, for no prophet has arisen out of Galilee."

Chose His apostles from.

Matt 4:18 And Jesus, walking by the Sea of Galilee, saw two brothers, Simon called Peter, and Andrew his brother, casting a net into the sea; for they were fishermen.

Matt 4:21 Going on from there, He saw two other brothers, James *the son* of Zebedee, and John his brother, in the boat with Zebedee their father, mending their nets. He called them,

John 1:43-44 The following day Jesus wanted to go to Galilee, and He found Philip and said to him, "Follow Me." 44 Now Philip was from Bethsaida, the city of Andrew and Peter.

Acts 1:11 who also said, "Men of Galilee, why do you stand gazing up into heaven? This *same* Jesus, who was taken up from you into heaven, will so come in like manner as you saw Him go into heaven."

Preaching in, predicted.

Is 9:1-2 Nevertheless the gloom *will* not *be* upon her who *is* distressed, As when at first He lightly esteemed The land of Zebulun and the land of Naphtali, And afterward more heavily oppressed *her*, By the way of the sea, beyond the Jordan, In Galilee of the Gentiles. 2 The people who walked in darkness Have seen a great light; Those who dwelt in the land of the shadow of death, Upon them a light has shined.

Matt 4:14-15 that it might be fulfilled which was spoken by Isaiah the prophet, saying: 15 *"The land of Zebulun and the land of Naphtali, By the way of the sea, beyond the Jordan, Galilee of the Gentiles:*

Preached throughout.

Mark 1:39 And He was preaching in their synagogues throughout all Galilee, and casting out demons.

Luke 4:44 And He was preaching in the synagogues of Galilee.

Worked many miracles in.

Matt 4:23-24 And Jesus went about all Galilee, teaching in their synagogues, preaching the gospel of the kingdom, and healing all kinds of sickness and all kinds of disease among the people. **24** Then His fame went throughout all Syria; and they brought to Him all sick people who were afflicted with various diseases and torments, and those who were demon-possessed, epileptics, and paralytics; and He healed them.

Matt 15:29–31 Jesus departed from there, skirted the Sea of Galilee, and went up on the mountain and sat down there. **30** Then great multitudes came to Him, having with them *the* lame, blind, mute, maimed, and many others; and they laid them down at Jesus' feet, and He healed them. **31** So the multitude marveled when they saw *the* mute speaking, *the* maimed made whole, *the* lame walking, and *the* blind seeing; and they glorified the God of Israel.

Widely accepted in.

Matt 4:25 Great multitudes followed Him—from Galilee, and *from* Decapolis, Jerusalem, Judea, and beyond the Jordan.

John 4:45 So when He came to Galilee, the Galileans received Him, having seen all the things He did in Jerusalem at the feast; for they also had gone to the feast.

Ministered to by women of.

Matt 27:55 And many women who followed Jesus from Galilee, ministering to Him, were there looking on from afar,

Mark 15:41 who also followed Him and ministered to Him when He was in Galilee, and many other women who came up with Him to Jerusalem.

Luke 8:3 and Joanna the wife of Chuza, Herod's steward, and Susanna, and many others who provided for Him from their substance.

Sought refuge in.

John 4:1 Therefore, when the Lord knew that the Pharisees had heard that Jesus made and baptized more disciples than John

John 4:3 He left Judea and departed again to Galilee.

Appeared in, to His disciples after His resurrection.

Matt 26:32 But after I have been raised, I will go before you to Galilee."

Matt 28:7 And go quickly and tell His disciples that He is risen from the dead, and indeed He is going before you into Galilee; there you will see Him. Behold, I have told you."

Modern towns of,

Accho or Ptolemais.

Judg 1:31 Nor did Asher drive out the inhabitants of Acco or the inhabitants of Sidon, or of Ahlab, Achzib, Helbah, Aphik, or Rehob.

Tiberias.

John 6:23 however, other boats came from Tiberias, near the place where they ate bread after the Lord had given thanks—

Nazareth.

Matt 2:22–23 But when he heard that Archelaus was reigning over Judea instead of his father Herod, he was afraid to go there. And being warned by God in a dream, he turned aside into the region of Galilee. **23** And he came and dwelt in a city called Nazareth, that it might be fulfilled which was spoken by the prophets, "He shall be called a Nazarene."

Luke 1:26 Now in the sixth month the angel Gabriel was sent by God to a city of Galilee named Nazareth,

Cana.

John 2:1 On the third day there was a wedding in Cana of Galilee, and the mother of Jesus was there.

John 21:2 Simon Peter, Thomas called the Twin, Nathanael of Cana in Galilee, the *sons* of Zebedee, and two others of His disciples were together.

Capernaum.

Matt 4:13 And leaving Nazareth, He came and dwelt in Capernaum, which is by the sea, in the regions of Zebulun and Naphtali,

Chorazin.

Matt 11:21 "Woe to you, Chorazin! Woe to you, Bethsaida! For if the mighty works which were done in you had been done in Tyre and Sidon, they would have repented long ago in sackcloth and ashes.

Bethsaida.

Mark 6:45 Immediately He made His disciples get into the boat and go before Him to the other side, to Bethsaida, while He sent the multitude away.

John 1:44 Now Philip was from Bethsaida, the city of Andrew and Peter.

Nain.

Luke 7:11 Now it happened, the day after, *that* He went into a city called Nain; and many of His disciples went with Him, and a large crowd.

Caesarea.

Acts 9:30 When the brethren found out, they brought him down to Caesarea and sent him out to Tarsus.

Acts 10:24 And the following day they entered Caesarea. Now Cornelius was waiting for them, and had called together his relatives and close friends.

Caesarea Philippi.

Matt 16:13 When Jesus came into the region of Caesarea Philippi, He asked His disciples, saying, "Who do men say that I, the Son of Man, am?"

Mark 8:27 Now Jesus and His disciples went out to the towns of Caesarea Philippi; and on the road He asked His disciples, saying to them, "Who do men say that I am?"

Christian churches established in.

Acts 9:31 Then the churches throughout all Judea, Galilee, and Samaria had peace and were edified. And walking in the fear of the Lord and in the comfort of the Holy Spirit, they were multiplied.

GARDEN OF EDEN, THE
Planted by the Lord.

Gen 2:8 The LORD God planted a garden eastward in Eden, and there He put the man whom He had formed.

Other names for,

The garden of the Lord.

Gen 13:10 And Lot lifted his eyes and saw all the plain of Jordan, that it *was* well watered everywhere (before the LORD destroyed Sodom and Gomorrah) like the garden of the LORD, like the land of Egypt as you go toward Zoar.

The garden of God.

Ezek 28:13 You were in Eden, the garden of God; Every precious stone *was* your covering: The sardius, topaz, and diamond, Beryl, onyx, and jasper, Sapphire, turquoise, and emerald with gold. The workmanship of your timbrels and pipes Was prepared for you on the day you were created.

Had every tree good for food.

Gen 2:9 And out of the ground the LORD God made every tree grow that is pleasant to the sight and good for food. The tree of life *was* also in the midst of the garden, and the tree of the knowledge of good and evil.

Watered by a river.

Gen 2:10–14 Now a river went out of Eden to water the garden, and from there it parted and became four riverheads. **11** The name of the first *is* Pishon; it *is* the one which skirts the whole land of Havilah, where *there is* gold. **12** And the gold of that land *is* good. Bdellium and the onyx stone *are* there. **13** The name of the second river *is* Gihon; it *is* the one which goes around the whole land of Cush. **14** The name of the third river *is* Hiddekel; it *is* the one which goes toward the east of Assyria. The fourth river *is* the Euphrates.

Man placed in, to tend and keep.

Gen 2:8 The LORD God planted a garden eastward in Eden, and there He put the man whom He had formed.

Gen 2:15 Then the LORD God took the man and put him in the garden of Eden to tend and keep it.

Man driven from, after the Fall.

Gen 3:23–24 therefore the LORD God sent him out of the garden of Eden to till the ground from which he was taken. **24** So He drove out the man; and He placed cherubim at the east of the garden of Eden, and a flaming sword which turned every way, to guard the way to the tree of life.

Fertility of Canaan like.

Gen 13:10 And Lot lifted his eyes and saw all the plain of Jordan, that it *was* well watered everywhere (before the LORD destroyed Sodom and Gomorrah) like the garden of the LORD, like the land of Egypt as you go toward Zoar.

Joel 2:3 A fire devours before them, And behind them a flame burns; The land *is* like the Garden of Eden before them, And behind them a desolate wilderness; Surely nothing shall escape them.

The future state of the Jews shall be like.

Is 51:3 For the LORD will comfort Zion, He will comfort all her waste places; He will make her wilderness like Eden, And her desert like the garden of the LORD; Joy and gladness will be found in it, Thanksgiving and the voice of melody.

Ezek 36:35 So they will say, 'This land that was desolate has become like the garden of Eden; and the wasted, desolate, and ruined cities *are now* fortified *and* inhabited.'

GARDENS

Often made by the banks of rivers.

Num 24:6 Like valleys that stretch out, Like gardens by the riverside, Like aloes planted by the LORD, Like cedars beside the waters.

Kinds of, mentioned in Scripture

Vegetable.

Deut 11:10 For the land which you go to possess *is* not like the land of Egypt from which you have come, where you sowed your seed and watered *it* by foot, as a vegetable garden;

1 Kin 21:2 So Ahab spoke to Naboth, saying, "Give me your vineyard, that I may have it for a vegetable garden, because it *is* near, next to my house; and for it I will give you a vineyard better than it. *Or,* if it seems good to you, I will give you its worth in money."

Cucumber.

Is 1:8 So the daughter of Zion is left as a booth in a vineyard, As a hut in a garden of cucumbers, As a besieged city.

Fruit tree.

Eccl 2:5–6 I made myself gardens and orchards, and I planted all *kinds* of fruit trees in them. **6** I made myself water pools from which to water the growing trees of the grove.

Spices, etc.

Song 4:16 Awake, O north *wind,* And come, O south! Blow upon my garden, *That* its spices may flow out. Let my beloved come to his garden And eat its pleasant fruits.

Song 6:2 My beloved has gone to his garden, To the beds of spices, To feed *his flock* in the gardens, And to gather lilies.

Often enclosed.

Song 4:12 A garden enclosed *Is* my sister, *my* spouse, A spring shut up, A fountain sealed.

Often refreshed by fountains.

Song 4:15 A fountain of gardens, A well of living waters, And streams from Lebanon.

Taken care of by gardeners.

John 20:15 Jesus said to her, "Woman, why are you weeping? Whom are you seeking?" She, supposing Him to be the gardener, said to Him, "Sir, if You have carried Him away, tell me where You have laid Him, and I will take Him away."

Lodges erected in.

Is 1:8 So the daughter of Zion is left as a booth in a vineyard, As a hut in a garden of cucumbers, As a besieged city.

Often used for

Celebrations.

Song 5:1 I have come to my garden, my sister, *my* spouse; I have gathered my myrrh with my spice; I have eaten my honeycomb with my honey; I have drunk my wine with my milk. Eat, O friends! Drink, yes, drink deeply, O beloved ones!

Spiritual retreat.

John 18:1 When Jesus had spoken these words, He went out with His disciples over the Brook Kidron, where there was a garden, which He and His disciples entered.

Burial places.

2 Kin 21:18 So Manasseh rested with his fathers, and

was buried in the garden of his own house, in the garden of Uzza. Then his son Amon reigned in his place.

2 Kin 21:26 And he was buried in his tomb in the garden of Uzza. Then Josiah his son reigned in his place.

John 19:41 Now in the place where He was crucified there was a garden, and in the garden a new tomb in which no one had yet been laid.

Idolatrous worship.

Is 1:29 For they shall be ashamed of the terebinth trees Which you have desired; And you shall be embarrassed because of the gardens Which you have chosen.

Is 65:3 A people who provoke Me to anger continually to My face; Who sacrifice in gardens, And burn incense on altars of brick;

Blasting of, a punishment.

Amos 4:9 "I blasted you with blight and mildew. When your gardens increased, Your vineyards, Your fig trees, And your olive trees, The locust devoured *them*; Yet you have not returned to Me," Says the LORD.

Jews ordered to plant, in Babylon.

Jer 29:5 Build houses and dwell *in them*; plant gardens and eat their fruit.

Jer 29:28 For he has sent to us *in* Babylon, saying, 'This *captivity is* long; build houses and dwell *in them*, and plant gardens and eat their fruit.' "

Illustrative of

(Well watered) spiritual prosperity of God's people.

Is 58:11 The LORD will guide you continually, And satisfy your soul in drought, And strengthen your bones; You shall be like a watered garden, And like a spring of water, whose waters do not fail.

Jer 31:12 Therefore they shall come and sing in the height of Zion, Streaming to the goodness of the LORD— For wheat and new wine and oil, For the young of the flock and the herd; Their souls shall be like a well-watered garden, And they shall sorrow no more at all.

(When dried up) the wicked.

Is 1:30 For you shall be as a terebinth whose leaf fades, And as a garden that has no water.

GARMENT, OUTER

Law respecting fringes of.

Num 15:38 "Speak to the children of Israel: Tell them to make tassels on the corners of their garments throughout their generations, and to put a blue thread in the tassels of the corners.

Deut 22:12 "You shall make tassels on the four corners of the clothing with which you cover *yourself.*

Used by the poor as a covering by night.

Ex 22:26–27 If you ever take your neighbor's garment as a pledge, you shall return it to him before the sun goes down. **27** For that *is* his only covering, it *is* his garment for his skin. What will he sleep in? And it will be that when he cries to Me, I will hear, for I *am* gracious.

Deut 24:13 You shall in any case return the pledge to him again when the sun goes down, that he may

sleep in his own garment and bless you; and it shall be righteousness to you before the LORD your God.

Burdens bound up in.

Ex 12:34 So the people took their dough before it was leavened, having their kneading bowls bound up in their clothes on their shoulders.

The skirts of, used to hold things in.

2 Kin 4:39 So one went out into the field to gather herbs, and found a wild vine, and gathered from it a lapful of wild gourds, and came and sliced *them* into the pot of stew, though they did not know *what they were.*

Neh 5:13 Then I shook out the fold of my garment and said, "So may God shake out each man from his house, and from his property, who does not perform this promise. Even thus may he be shaken out and emptied." And all the assembly said, "Amen!" and praised the LORD. Then the people did according to this promise.

Hag 2:12 "If one carries holy meat in the fold of his garment, and with the edge he touches bread or stew, wine or oil, or any food, will it become holy?" ' " Then the priests answered and said, "No."

Luke 6:38 Give, and it will be given to you: good measure, pressed down, shaken together, and running over will be put into your bosom. For with the same measure that you use, it will be measured back to you."

Probably used by women as a veil.

Ruth 3:15 Also he said, "Bring the shawl that *is* on you and hold it." And when she held it, he measured six *ephahs* of barley, and laid *it* on her. Then she went into the city.

Required to be girded up

For running.

1 Kin 18:46 Then the hand of the LORD came upon Elijah; and he girded up his loins and ran ahead of Ahab to the entrance of Jezreel.

For labor.

Luke 17:8 But will he not rather say to him, 'Prepare something for my supper, and gird yourself and serve me till I have eaten and drunk, and afterward you will eat and drink'?

Often laid aside.

Matt 24:18 And let him who is in the field not go back to get his clothes.

Mark 10:50 And throwing aside his garment, he rose and came to Jesus.

The Jews said to be naked without.

2 Sam 6:20 Then David returned to bless his household. And Michal the daughter of Saul came out to meet David, and said, "How glorious was the king of Israel today, uncovering himself today in the eyes of the maids of his servants, as one of the base fellows shamelessly uncovers himself!"

Mark 14:51–52 Now a certain young man followed Him, having a linen cloth thrown around *his* naked *body.* And the young men laid hold of him, **52** and he left the linen cloth and fled from them naked.

John 21:7 Therefore that disciple whom Jesus loved said to Peter, "It is the Lord!" Now when Simon Peter heard that it was the Lord, he put on *his* outer garment (for he had removed it), and plunged into the sea.

Was the clothing

Torn in token of anger.

Matt 26:65 Then the high priest tore his clothes, saying, "He has spoken blasphemy! What further need do we have of witnesses? Look, now you have heard His blasphemy!

Torn in token of grief.

Joel 2:13 So rend your heart, and not your garments; Return to the LORD your God, For He *is* gracious and merciful, Slow to anger, and of great kindness; And He relents from doing harm.

Of Samuel, torn by Saul.

1 Sam 15:27 And as Samuel turned around to go away, *Saul* seized the edge of his robe, and it tore.

Of Saul, which David cut.

1 Sam 24:4–5 Then the men of David said to him, "This is the day of which the LORD said to you, 'Behold, I will deliver your enemy into your hand, that you may do to him as it seems good to you.' " And David arose and secretly cut off a corner of Saul's robe. **5** Now it happened afterward that David's heart troubled him because he had cut Saul's *robe.*

Of Jeroboam, torn by Ahijah.

1 Kin 11:30 Then Ahijah took hold of the new garment that *was* on him, and tore it *into* twelve pieces.

Laid aside by Christ.

John 13:4 rose from supper and laid aside His garments, took a towel and girded Himself.

Spread before Christ by the Jews.

Matt 21:8 And a very great multitude spread their clothes on the road; others cut down branches from the trees and spread *them* on the road.

The Jews condemned for making broad the borders of.

Matt 23:5 But all their works they do to be seen by men. They make their phylacteries broad and enlarge the borders of their garments.

GARMENTS

Origin of.

Gen 3:7 Then the eyes of both of them were opened, and they knew that they *were* naked; and they sewed fig leaves together and made themselves coverings.

Gen 3:21 Also for Adam and his wife the LORD God made tunics of skin, and clothed them.

Names for,

Clothes.

Prov 6:27 Can a man take fire to his bosom, And his clothes not be burned?

Ezek 16:39 I will also give you into their hand, and they shall throw down your shrines and break down your high places. They shall also strip you of your clothes, take your beautiful jewelry, and leave you naked and bare.

Clothing.

Gen 28:20 Then Jacob made a vow, saying, "If God will be with me, and keep me in this way that I am going, and give me bread to eat and clothing to put on,

Job 22:6 For you have taken pledges from your brother for no reason, And stripped the naked of their clothing.

Job 31:19 If I have seen anyone perish for lack of clothing, Or any poor *man* without covering;

Materials used for,

Wool.

Prov 27:26 The lambs *will provide* your clothing, And the goats the price of a field;

Ezek 34:3 You eat the fat and clothe yourselves with the wool; you slaughter the fatlings, *but* you do not feed the flock.

Linen.

Gen 41:42 Then Pharaoh took his signet ring off his hand and put it on Joseph's hand; and he clothed him in garments of fine linen and put a gold chain around his neck.

Lev 6:10 And the priest shall put on his linen garment, and his linen trousers he shall put on his body, and take up the ashes of the burnt offering which the fire has consumed on the altar, and he shall put them beside the altar.

Esth 8:15 So Mordecai went out from the presence of the king in royal apparel of blue and white, with a great crown of gold and a garment of fine linen and purple; and the city of Shushan rejoiced and was glad.

Prov 31:22 She makes tapestry for herself; Her clothing *is* fine linen and purple.

Camel's hair.

Matt 3:4 Now John himself was clothed in camel's hair, with a leather belt around his waist; and his food was locusts and wild honey.

Skins.

Heb 11:37 They were stoned, they were sawn in two, were tempted, were slain with the sword. They wandered about in sheepskins and goatskins, being destitute, afflicted, tormented—

Sackcloth.

2 Sam 3:31 Then David said to Joab and to all the people who were with him, "Tear your clothes, gird yourselves with sackcloth, and mourn for Abner." And King David followed the coffin.

2 Kin 19:1 And so it was, when King Hezekiah heard *it,* that he tore his clothes, covered himself with sackcloth, and went into the house of the LORD.

Not to be made of mixed materials.

Deut 22:11 "You shall not wear a garment of different sorts, *such as* wool and linen mixed together.

Of the sexes, not to be interchanged.

Deut 22:5 "A woman shall not wear anything that pertains to a man, nor shall a man put on a woman's garment, for all who do so *are* an abomination to the LORD your God.

Colors of, mentioned

White.

Eccl 9:8 Let your garments always be white, And let your head lack no oil.

Purple.

Ezek 23:6 *Who were* clothed in purple, Captains and

rulers, All of them desirable young men, Horsemen riding on horses.

Dan 5:7 The king cried aloud to bring in the astrologers, the Chaldeans, and the soothsayers. The king spoke, saying to the wise *men* of Babylon, "Whoever reads this writing, and tells me its interpretation, shall be clothed with purple and *have* a chain of gold around his neck; and he shall be the third ruler in the kingdom."

Luke 16:19 "There was a certain rich man who was clothed in purple and fine linen and fared sumptuously every day.

Scarlet.

2 Sam 1:24 "O daughters of Israel, weep over Saul, Who clothed you in scarlet, with luxury; Who put ornaments of gold on your apparel.

Varied colors.

Gen 37:3 Now Israel loved Joseph more than all his children, because he *was* the son of his old age. Also he made him a tunic of *many* colors.

2 Sam 13:18 Now she had on a robe of many colors, for the king's virgin daughters wore such apparel. And his servant put her out and bolted the door behind her.

Were often fringed and bordered.

Num 15:38 "Speak to the children of Israel: Tell them to make tassels on the corners of their garments throughout their generations, and to put a blue thread in the tassels of the corners.

Deut 22:12 "You shall make tassels on the four corners of the clothing with which you cover *yourself.*

Scribes and Pharisees condemned for making broad the borders of.

Matt 23:5 But all their works they do to be seen by men. They make their phylacteries broad and enlarge the borders of their garments.

Worn long and flowing.

Luke 20:46 "Beware of the scribes, who desire to go around in long robes, love greetings in the marketplaces, the best seats in the synagogues, and the best places at feasts,

Rev 1:13 and in the midst of the seven lampstands *One* like the Son of Man, clothed with a garment down to the feet and girded about the chest with a golden band.

Girded up during work.

Luke 17:8 But will he not rather say to him, 'Prepare something for my supper, and gird yourself and serve me till I have eaten and drunk, and afterward you will eat and drink'?

John 13:4 rose from supper and laid aside His garments, took a towel and girded Himself.

Those mentioned in Scripture,

Robe.

Rev 19:16 And He has on *His* robe and on His thigh a name written: KING OF KINGS AND LORD OF LORDS.

Clothes or outer garment.

Deut 24:13 You shall in any case return the pledge to him again when the sun goes down, that he may

sleep in his own garment and bless you; and it shall be righteousness to you before the LORD your God.

Matt 21:8 And a very great multitude spread their clothes on the road; others cut down branches from the trees and spread *them* on the road.

John 21:7 Therefore that disciple whom Jesus loved said to Peter, "It is the Lord!" Now when Simon Peter heard that it was the Lord, he put on *his* outer garment (for he had removed it), and plunged into the sea.

Tunic or cloak.

Luke 6:29 To him who strikes you on the *one* cheek, offer the other also. And from him who takes away your cloak, do not withhold *your* tunic either.

John 19:23 Then the soldiers, when they had crucified Jesus, took His garments and made four parts, to each soldier a part, and also the tunic. Now the tunic was without seam, woven from the top in one piece.

2 Tim 4:13 Bring the cloak that I left with Carpus at Troas when you come—and the books, especially the parchments.

Belt.

1 Sam 18:4 And Jonathan took off the robe that *was* on him and gave it to David, with his armor, even to his sword and his bow and his belt.

Acts 21:11 When he had come to us, he took Paul's belt, bound his *own* hands and feet, and said, "Thus says the Holy Spirit, 'So shall the Jews at Jerusalem bind the man who owns this belt, and deliver *him* into the hands of the Gentiles.' "

Turban or hat.

Lev 8:13 Then Moses brought Aaron's sons and put tunics on them, girded them with sashes, and put hats on them, as the LORD had commanded Moses.

Dan 3:21 Then these men were bound in their coats, their trousers, their turbans, and their *other* garments, and were cast into the midst of the burning fiery furnace.

Sandal.

Ex 3:5 Then He said, "Do not draw near this place. Take your sandals off your feet, for the place where you stand *is* holy ground."

Mark 6:9 but to wear sandals, and not to put on two tunics.

Veil.

Gen 24:65 for she had said to the servant, "Who *is* this man walking in the field to meet us?" The servant said, "It *is* my master." So she took a veil and covered herself.

Liable to plague and leprosy. Lev 13:47–59

Cleansed by water from ceremonial uncleanness.

Lev 11:32 Anything on which *any* of them falls, when they are dead shall be unclean, whether *it is* any item of wood or clothing or skin or sack, whatever item *it is*, in which *any* work is done, it must be put in water. And it shall be unclean until evening; then it shall be clean.

Num 31:20 Purify every garment, everything made of leather, everything woven of goats' *hair*, and everything made of wood."

Of the rich,

Of the finest materials.

Matt 11:8 But what did you go out to see? A man clothed in soft garments? Indeed, those who wear soft *clothing* are in kings' houses.

James 2:2 For if there should come into your assembly a man with gold rings, in fine apparel, and there should also come in a poor man in filthy clothes,

Gorgeous.

Luke 7:25 But what did you go out to see? A man clothed in soft garments? Indeed those who are gorgeously appareled and live in luxury are in kings' courts.

Acts 12:21 So on a set day Herod, arrayed in royal apparel, sat on his throne and gave an oration to them.

Embroidered and multi-colored.

Ps 45:14 She shall be brought to the King in robes of many colors; The virgins, her companions who follow her, shall be brought to You.

Ezek 16:18 You took your embroidered garments and covered them, and you set My oil and My incense before them.

Perfumed.

Ps 45:8 All Your garments are scented with myrrh and aloes *and* cassia, Out of the ivory palaces, by which they have made You glad.

Song 4:11 Your lips, O *my* spouse, Drip as the honeycomb; Honey and milk *are* under your tongue; And the fragrance of your garments *Is* like the fragrance of Lebanon.

Multiplied and piled up.

Job 27:17 He may pile *it* up, but the just will wear *it*, And the innocent will divide the silver.

Is 3:22 the festal apparel, and the mantles; The outer garments, the purses,

Often moth-eaten.

Job 13:28 "*Man* decays like a rotten thing, Like a garment that is moth-eaten.

James 5:2 Your riches are corrupted, and your garments are moth-eaten.

Of the poor,

Provided specially by God.

Deut 10:18 He administers justice for the fatherless and the widow, and loves the stranger, giving him food and clothing.

Filthy.

James 2:2 For if there should come into your assembly a man with gold rings, in fine apparel, and there should also come in a poor man in filthy clothes,

Used as a covering by night.

Deut 24:13 You shall in any case return the pledge to him again when the sun goes down, that he may sleep in his own garment and bless you; and it shall be righteousness to you before the LORD your God.

Not to be retained in pledge.

Deut 24:12–13 And if the man *is* poor, you shall not keep his pledge overnight. **13** You shall in any case return the pledge to him again when the sun goes down, that he may sleep in his own garment and

bless you; and it shall be righteousness to you before the LORD your God.

Grew old and wore out.

Josh 9:5 old and patched sandals on their feet, and old garments on themselves; and all the bread of their provision was dry *and* moldy.

Ps 102:26 They will perish, but You will endure; Yes, they will all grow old like a garment; Like a cloak You will change them, And they will be changed.

Of Israel, preserved for forty years.

Deut 8:4 Your garments did not wear out on you, nor did your foot swell these forty years.

Of those slain with a sword, not used.

Is 14:19 But you are cast out of your grave Like an abominable branch, *Like* the garment of those who are slain, Thrust through with a sword, Who go down to the stones of the pit, Like a corpse trodden underfoot.

Given as a token of covenants.

1 Sam 18:4 And Jonathan took off the robe that *was* on him and gave it to David, with his armor, even to his sword and his bow and his belt.

Given as presents.

Gen 45:22 He gave to all of them, to each man, changes of garments; but to Benjamin he gave three hundred *pieces* of silver and five changes of garments.

2 Kin 5:22 And he said, "All *is* well. My master has sent me, saying, 'Indeed, just now two young men of the sons of the prophets have come to me from the mountains of Ephraim. Please give them a talent of silver and two changes of garments.' "

Often torn in affliction.

2 Sam 15:32 Now it happened when David had come to the top *of the mountain*, where he worshiped God—there was Hushai the Archite coming to meet him with his robe torn and dust on his head.

Ezra 9:3 So when I heard this thing, I tore my garment and my robe, and plucked out some of the hair of my head and beard, and sat down astonished.

Ezra 9:5 At the evening sacrifice I arose from my fasting; and having torn my garment and my robe, I fell on my knees and spread out my hands to the LORD my God.

Illustrative of

(White) righteousness.

Matt 28:3 His countenance was like lightning, and his clothing as white as snow.

Rev 3:18 I counsel you to buy from Me gold refined in the fire, that you may be rich; and white garments, that you may be clothed, *that* the shame of your nakedness may not be revealed; and anoint your eyes with eye salve, that you may see.

(Rolled in blood) victory.

Is 9:5 For every warrior's sandal from the noisy battle, And garments rolled in blood, Will be used for burning *and* fuel of fire.

(Washed in wine) abundance.

Gen 49:11 Binding his donkey to the vine, And his donkey's colt to the choice vine, He washed his garments in wine, And his clothes in the blood of grapes.

GATES

Design of.

Is 62:10 Go through, Go through the gates! Prepare the way for the people; Build up, Build up the highway! Take out the stones, Lift up a banner for the peoples!

Made of

Bronze.

Ps 107:16 For He has broken the gates of bronze, And cut the bars of iron in two.

Is 45:2 'I will go before you And make the crooked places straight; I will break in pieces the gates of bronze And cut the bars of iron.

Iron.

Acts 12:10 When they were past the first and the second guard posts, they came to the iron gate that leads to the city, which opened to them of its own accord; and they went out and went down one street, and immediately the angel departed from him.

Often double-doored.

Is 45:1 "Thus says the LORD to His anointed, To Cyrus, whose right hand I have held— To subdue nations before him And loose the armor of kings, To open before him the double doors, So that the gates will not be shut:

Fastened with bars of iron.

Ps 107:16 For He has broken the gates of bronze, And cut the bars of iron in two.

Is 45:2 'I will go before you And make the crooked places straight; I will break in pieces the gates of bronze And cut the bars of iron.

Made for

Cities.

1 Kin 17:10 So he arose and went to Zarephath. And when he came to the gate of the city, indeed a widow *was* there gathering sticks. And he called to her and said, "Please bring me a little water in a cup, that I may drink."

Houses.

Luke 16:20 But there was a certain beggar named Lazarus, full of sores, who was laid at his gate,

Acts 12:14 When she recognized Peter's voice, because of *her* gladness she did not open the gate, but ran in and announced that Peter stood before the gate.

Temples.

Acts 3:2 And a certain man lame from his mother's womb was carried, whom they laid daily at the gate of the temple which is called Beautiful, to ask alms from those who entered the temple;

Palaces.

Esth 5:13 Yet all this avails me nothing, so long as I see Mordecai the Jew sitting at the king's gate."

Prisons.

Acts 12:10 When they were past the first and the second guard posts, they came to the iron gate that leads to the city, which opened to them of its own accord; and they went out and went down one street, and immediately the angel departed from him.

Camps.

Ex 32:26 then Moses stood in the entrance of the camp, and said, "Whoever *is* on the LORD's side—*come to*

me!" And all the sons of Levi gathered themselves together to him.

Rivers.

Nah 2:6 The gates of the rivers are opened, And the palace is dissolved.

Of cities,

Chief places of concourse.

Prov 1:21 She cries out in the chief concourses, At the openings of the gates in the city She speaks her words:

Courts of justice held at.

Deut 16:18 "You shall appoint judges and officers in all your gates, which the LORD your God gives you, according to your tribes, and they shall judge the people with just judgment.

2 Sam 15:2 Now Absalom would rise early and stand beside the way to the gate. *So* it was, whenever anyone who had a lawsuit came to the king for a decision, that Absalom would call to him and say, "What city *are* you from?" And he would say, "Your servant *is* from such and such a tribe of Israel."

Prov 22:22–23 Do not rob the poor because he *is* poor, Nor oppress the afflicted at the gate; 23 For the LORD will plead their cause, And plunder the soul of those who plunder them.

Land sold at.

Gen 23:10 Now Ephron dwelt among the sons of Heth; and Ephron the Hittite answered Abraham in the presence of the sons of Heth, all who entered at the gate of his city, saying,

Gen 23:16 And Abraham listened to Ephron; and Abraham weighed out the silver for Ephron which he had named in the hearing of the sons of Heth, four hundred shekels of silver, currency of the merchants.

Land redeemed at.

2 Kin 7:1 Then Elisha said, "Hear the word of the LORD. Thus says the LORD: 'Tomorrow about this time a seah of fine flour *shall be sold* for a shekel, and two seahs of barley for a shekel, at the gate of Samaria.' "

2 Kin 7:18 So it happened just as the man of God had spoken to the king, saying, "Two seahs of barley for a shekel, and a seah of fine flour for a shekel, shall be *sold* tomorrow about this time in the gate of Samaria."

Markets held at.

2 Kin 7:1 Then Elisha said, "Hear the word of the LORD. Thus says the LORD: 'Tomorrow about this time a seah of fine flour *shall be sold* for a shekel, and two seahs of barley for a shekel, at the gate of Samaria.' "

2 Kin 7:18 So it happened just as the man of God had spoken to the king, saying, "Two seahs of barley for a shekel, and a seah of fine flour for a shekel, shall be *sold* tomorrow about this time in the gate of Samaria."

Proclamations made at.

Prov 1:21 She cries out in the chief concourses, At the openings of the gates in the city She speaks her words:

Jer 17:19 Thus the LORD said to me: "Go and stand in the gate of the children of the people, by which the kings of Judah come in and by which they go out, and in all the gates of Jerusalem;

Councils of state held at.

2 Chr 18:9 The king of Israel and Jehoshaphat king of

Judah, clothed in *their* robes, sat each on his throne; and they sat at a threshing floor at the entrance of the gate of Samaria; and all the prophets prophesied before them.

Jer 39:3 Then all the princes of the king of Babylon came in and sat in the Middle Gate: Nergal-Sharezer, Samgar-Nebo, Sarsechim, Rabsaris, Nergal-Sarezer, Rabmag, with the rest of the princes of the king of Babylon.

Conferences held at.

Gen 34:20 And Hamor and Shechem his son came to the gate of their city, and spoke with the men of their city, saying:

2 Sam 3:27 Now when Abner had returned to Hebron, Joab took him aside in the gate to speak with him privately, and there stabbed him in the stomach, so that he died for the blood of Asahel his brother.

Public commendation given at.

Prov 31:23 Her husband is known in the gates, When he sits among the elders of the land.

Prov 31:31 Give her of the fruit of her hands, And let her own works praise her in the gates.

Public censure passed at.

Job 5:4 His sons are far from safety, They are crushed in the gate, And *there is* no deliverer.

Is 29:21 Who make a man an offender by a word, And lay a snare for him who reproves in the gate, And turn aside the just by empty words.

Shut at nightfall.

Josh 2:5 And it happened as the gate was being shut, when it was dark, that the men went out. Where the men went I do not know; pursue them quickly, for you may overtake them."

Neh 13:19 So it was, at the gates of Jerusalem, as it began to be dark before the Sabbath, that I commanded the gates to be shut, and charged that they must not be opened till after the Sabbath. Then I posted *some* of my servants at the gates, *so that* no burdens would be brought in on the Sabbath day.

Chief points of attack in war.

Judg 5:8 They chose new gods; Then *there was* war in the gates; Not a shield or spear was seen among forty thousand in Israel.

Is 22:7 It shall come to pass *that* your choicest valleys Shall be full of chariots, And the horsemen shall set themselves in array at the gate.

Ezek 21:15 I have set the point of the sword against all their gates, That the heart may melt and many may stumble. Ah! *It is* made bright; *It is* grasped for slaughter:

Battering rams used against.

Ezek 21:22 In his right hand is the divination for Jerusalem: to set up battering rams, to call for a slaughter, to lift the voice with shouting, to set battering rams against the gates, to heap up a *siege* mound, and to build a wall.

Experienced officers placed over.

2 Kin 7:17 Now the king had appointed the officer on whose hand he leaned to have charge of the gate. But the people trampled him in the gate, and he died,

just as the man of God had said, who spoke when the king came down to him.

Troops reviewed at, going to war.

2 Sam 18:4 Then the king said to them, "Whatever seems best to you I will do." So the king stood beside the gate, and all the people went out by hundreds and by thousands.

Often razed and burned.

Neh 1:3 And they said to me, "The survivors who are left from the captivity in the province *are* there in great distress and reproach. The wall of Jerusalem *is* also broken down, and its gates *are* burned with fire."

Lam 2:9 Her gates have sunk into the ground; He has destroyed and broken her bars. Her king and her princes *are* among the nations; The Law *is* no *more*, And her prophets find no vision from the LORD.

Idolatrous rites performed at.

Acts 14:13 Then the priest of Zeus, whose temple was in front of their city, brought oxen and garlands to the gates, intending to sacrifice with the multitudes.

Criminals punished at.

Deut 17:5 then you shall bring out to your gates that man or woman who has committed that wicked thing, and shall stone to death that man or woman with stones.

Jer 20:2 Then Pashhur struck Jeremiah the prophet, and put him in the stocks that *were* in the high gate of Benjamin, which *was* by the house of the LORD.

Custom of sitting at, in the evening, alluded to.

Gen 19:1 Now the two angels came to Sodom in the evening, and Lot was sitting in the gate of Sodom. When Lot saw *them,* he rose to meet them, and he bowed himself with his face toward the ground.

Of the temple,

Called roads to Zion.

Lam 1:4 The roads to Zion mourn Because no one comes to the set feasts. All her gates are desolate; Her priests sigh, Her virgins are afflicted, And she *is* in bitterness.

Called gates of righteousness.

Ps 118:19 Open to me the gates of righteousness; I will go through them, *And* I will praise the LORD.

Called gate of the Lord.

Ps 118:20 This is the gate of the LORD, Through which the righteous shall enter.

Overlaid with gold.

2 Kin 18:16 At that time Hezekiah stripped *the gold from* the doors of the temple of the LORD, and *from* the pillars which Hezekiah king of Judah had overlaid, and gave it to the king of Assyria.

One called Beautiful.

Acts 3:2 And a certain man lame from his mother's womb was carried, whom they laid daily at the gate of the temple which is called Beautiful, to ask alms from those who entered the temple;

Levites the porters of.

2 Chr 8:14 And, according to the order of David his father, he appointed the divisions of the priests for their service, the Levites for their duties (to praise and serve before the priests) as the duty of each day required, and the gatekeepers by their divisions at each gate; for so David the man of God had commanded.

2 Chr 23:4 This *is* what you shall do: One-third of you entering on the Sabbath, of the priests and the Levites, *shall be* keeping watch over the doors;

Charge of, given by lot.

1 Chr 26:13–19 And they cast lots for each gate, the small as well as the great, according to their father's house. **14** The lot for the East *Gate* fell to Shelemiah. Then they cast lots *for* his son Zechariah, a wise counselor, and his lot came out for the North Gate; **15** to Obed-Edom the South Gate, and to his sons the storehouse. **16** To Shuppim and Hosah *the lot came out* for the West Gate, with the Shallecheth Gate on the ascending highway—watchman opposite watchman. **17** On the east were *six* Levites, on the north four each day, on the south four each day, and for the storehouse two by two. **18** As for the Parbar on the west, *there were* four on the highway *and* two at the Parbar. **19** These were the divisions of the gatekeepers among the sons of Korah and among the sons of Merari.

The treasury placed at.

2 Chr 24:8 Then at the king's command they made a chest, and set it outside at the gate of the house of the LORD.

Mark 12:41 Now Jesus sat opposite the treasury and saw how the people put money into the treasury. And many *who were* rich put in much.

The pious Israelites delighted to enter.

Ps 100:4 Enter into His gates with thanksgiving, *And* into His courts with praise. Be thankful to Him, *and* bless His name.

Ps 118:19–20 Open to me the gates of righteousness; I will go through them, *And* I will praise the LORD. **20** This is the gate of the LORD, Through which the righteous shall enter.

Frequented by beggars.

Acts 3:2 And a certain man lame from his mother's womb was carried, whom they laid daily at the gate of the temple which is called Beautiful, to ask alms from those who entered the temple;

Of Jerusalem,

High gate of Benjamin.

Jer 20:2 Then Pashhur struck Jeremiah the prophet, and put him in the stocks that *were* in the high gate of Benjamin, which *was* by the house of the LORD.

Jer 37:13 And when he was in the Gate of Benjamin, a captain of the guard *was* there whose name *was* Irijah the son of Shelemiah, the son of Hananiah; and he seized Jeremiah the prophet, saying, "You are defecting to the Chaldeans!"

Fish Gate.

2 Chr 33:14 After this he built a wall outside the City of David on the west side of Gihon, in the valley, as far as the entrance of the Fish Gate; and *it* enclosed Ophel, and he raised it to a very great height. Then he put military captains in all the fortified cities of Judah.

Neh 3:3 Also the sons of Hassenaah built the Fish Gate; they laid its beams and hung its doors with its bolts and bars.

Sheep Gate.

Neh 3:1 Then Eliashib the high priest rose up with his brethren the priests and built the Sheep Gate; they consecrated it and hung its doors. They built as far as the Tower of the Hundred, *and* consecrated it, then as far as the Tower of Hananel.

John 5:2 Now there is in Jerusalem by the Sheep *Gate* a pool, which is called in Hebrew, Bethesda, having five porches.

Miphkad Gate.

Neh 3:31 After him Malchijah, one of the goldsmiths, made repairs as far as the house of the Nethinim and of the merchants, in front of the Miphkad Gate, and as far as the upper room at the corner.

Gate of Ephraim.

Neh 12:39 and above the Gate of Ephraim, above the Old Gate, above the Fish Gate, the Tower of Hananel, the Tower of the Hundred, as far as the Sheep Gate; and they stopped by the Gate of the Prison.

Valley Gate.

2 Chr 26:9 And Uzziah built towers in Jerusalem at the Corner Gate, at the Valley Gate, and at the corner buttress of the wall; then he fortified them.

Neh 2:13 And I went out by night through the Valley Gate to the Serpent Well and the Refuse Gate, and viewed the walls of Jerusalem which were broken down and its gates which were burned with fire.

Water Gate.

Neh 3:26 Moreover the Nethinim who dwelt in Ophel *made repairs* as far as *the place* in front of the Water Gate toward the east, and on the projecting tower.

Neh 8:3 Then he read from it in the open square that *was* in front of the Water Gate from morning until midday, before the men and women and those who could understand; and the ears of all the people *were* attentive to the Book of the Law.

Horse Gate.

2 Chr 23:15 So they seized her; and she went by way of the entrance of the Horse Gate *into* the king's house, and they killed her there.

Neh 3:28 Beyond the Horse Gate the priests made repairs, each in front of his *own* house.

Old Gate.

Neh 3:6 Moreover Jehoiada the son of Paseah and Meshullam the son of Besodeiah repaired the Old Gate; they laid its beams and hung its doors, with its bolts and bars.

Neh 12:39 and above the Gate of Ephraim, above the Old Gate, above the Fish Gate, the Tower of Hananel, the Tower of the Hundred, as far as the Sheep Gate; and they stopped by the Gate of the Prison.

Corner Gate.

2 Chr 26:9 And Uzziah built towers in Jerusalem at the Corner Gate, at the Valley Gate, and at the corner buttress of the wall; then he fortified them.

Refuse Gate.

Neh 3:14 Malchijah the son of Rechab, leader of the district of Beth Haccerem, repaired the Refuse Gate; he built it and hung its doors with its bolts and bars.

Neh 12:31 So I brought the leaders of Judah up on the wall, and appointed two large thanksgiving choirs.

One went to the right hand on the wall toward the Refuse Gate.

Fountain Gate.

Neh 3:15 Shallun the son of Col-Hozeh, leader of the district of Mizpah, repaired the Fountain Gate; he built it, covered it, hung its doors with its bolts and bars, and repaired the wall of the Pool of Shelah by the King's Garden, as far as the stairs that go down from the City of David.

Carcass of sin offering burned outside the.

Lev 4:12 the whole bull he shall carry outside the camp to a clean place, where the ashes are poured out, and burn it on wood with fire; where the ashes are poured out it shall be burned.

Heb 13:11–13 For the bodies of those animals, whose blood is brought into the sanctuary by the high priest for sin, are burned outside the camp. **12** Therefore Jesus also, that He might sanctify the people with His own blood, suffered outside the gate. **13** Therefore let us go forth to Him, outside the camp, bearing His reproach.

Criminals generally punished outside the.

Lev 24:23 Then Moses spoke to the children of Israel; and they took outside the camp him who had cursed, and stoned him with stones. So the children of Israel did as the LORD commanded Moses.

John 19:17 And He, bearing His cross, went out to a place called *the Place* of a Skull, which is called in Hebrew, Golgotha,

Heb 13:12 Therefore Jesus also, that He might sanctify the people with His own blood, suffered outside the gate.

Illustrative of

Christ.

John 10:9 I am the door. If anyone enters by Me, he will be saved, and will go in and out and find pasture.

(Of heaven) access to God.

Gen 28:12–17 Then he dreamed, and behold, a ladder *was* set up on the earth, and its top reached to heaven; and there the angels of God were ascending and descending on it. **13** And behold, the LORD stood above it and said: "I *am* the LORD God of Abraham your father and the God of Isaac; the land on which you lie I will give to you and your descendants. **14** Also your descendants shall be as the dust of the earth; you shall spread abroad to the west and the east, to the north and the south; and in you and in your seed all the families of the earth shall be blessed. **15** Behold, I *am* with you and will keep you wherever you go, and will bring you back to this land; for I will not leave you until I have done what I have spoken to you." **16** Then Jacob awoke from his sleep and said, "Surely the LORD is in this place, and I did not know *it*." **17** And he was afraid and said, "How awesome *is* this place! This *is* none other than the house of God, and this *is* the gate of heaven!"

(Of Hades) Satan's power.

Matt 16:18 And I also say to you that you are Peter, and on this rock I will build My church, and the gates of Hades shall not prevail against it.

(Of Sheol) death.

Is 38:10 I said, "In the prime of my life I shall go to the gates of Sheol; I am deprived of the remainder of my years."

(Narrow) the entrance to life.

Matt 7:14 Because narrow *is* the gate and difficult *is* the way which leads to life, and there are few who find it.

(Wide) the entrance to destruction.

Matt 7:13 "Enter by the narrow gate; for wide *is* the gate and bróad *is* the way that leads to destruction, and there are many who go in by it.

GENEALOGIES

The Jews reckoned by.

1 Chr 9:1 So all Israel was recorded by genealogies, and indeed, they *were* inscribed in the book of the kings of Israel. But Judah was carried away captive to Babylon because of their unfaithfulness.

2 Chr 31:19 Also for the sons of Aaron the priests, *who were* in the fields of the common-lands of their cities, in every single city, *there were* men who were designated by name to distribute portions to all the males among the priests and to all who were listed by genealogies among the Levites.

Public registers kept of.

2 Chr 12:15 The acts of Rehoboam, first and last, *are* they not written in the book of Shemaiah the prophet, and of Iddo the seer concerning genealogies? And *there were* wars between Rehoboam and Jeroboam all their days.

Neh 7:5 Then my God put it into my heart to gather the nobles, the rulers, and the people, that they might be registered by genealogy. And I found a register of the genealogy of those who had come up in the first *return*, and found written in it:

Of Christ,

Presented twice. **Matt 1:1–17; Luke 3:23–38**

Prove His descent from Judah.

Heb 7:14 For *it is* evident that our Lord arose from Judah, of which tribe Moses spoke nothing concerning priesthood.

Priests who could not prove their own, excluded from the priesthood.

Ezra 2:62 These sought their listing *among* those who were registered by genealogy, but they were not found; therefore they *were excluded* from the priesthood as defiled.

Neh 7:64 These sought their listing *among* those who were registered by genealogy, but it was not found; therefore they were excluded from the priesthood as defiled.

Subject of, to be avoided.

1 Tim 1:4 nor give heed to fables and endless genealogies, which cause disputes rather than godly edification which is in faith.

Titus 3:9 But avoid foolish disputes, genealogies, contentions, and strivings about the law; for they are unprofitable and useless.

Believers in the book of life, illustrates.

Luke 10:20 Nevertheless do not rejoice in this, that the spirits are subject to you, but rather rejoice because your names are written in heaven."

Heb 12:23 to the general assembly and church of the

firstborn *who are* registered in heaven, to God the Judge of all, to the spirits of just men made perfect,

Rev 3:5 He who overcomes shall be clothed in white garments, and I will not blot out his name from the Book of Life; but I will confess his name before My Father and before His angels.

GENEROSITY

Pleasing to God.

2 Cor 9:7 *So let* each one *give* as he purposes in his heart, not grudgingly or of necessity; for God loves a cheerful giver.

Heb 6:10 For God *is* not unjust to forget your work and labor of love which you have shown toward His name, *in that* you have ministered to the saints, and do minister.

Heb 13:16 But do not forget to do good and to share, for with such sacrifices God is well pleased.

Christ's example of.

2 Cor 8:9 For you know the grace of our Lord Jesus Christ, that though He was rich, yet for your sakes He became poor, that you through His poverty might become rich.

Should be exercised

With love.

1 Cor 13:3 And though I bestow all my goods to feed *the poor*, and though I give my body to be burned, but have not love, it profits me nothing.

In the service of God.

Ex 35:21–29 Then everyone came whose heart was stirred, and everyone whose spirit was willing, *and* they brought the LORD's offering for the work of the tabernacle of meeting, for all its service, and for the holy garments. **22** They came, both men and women, as many as had a willing heart, *and* brought earrings and nose rings, rings and necklaces, all jewelry of gold, that is, every man who *made* an offering of gold to the LORD. **23** And every man, with whom was found blue, purple, and scarlet *thread*, fine linen, goats' *hair*, red skins of rams, and badger skins, brought *them*. **24** Everyone who offered an offering of silver or bronze brought the LORD's offering. And everyone with whom was found acacia wood for any work of the service, brought *it*. **25** All the women *who were* gifted artisans spun yarn with their hands, and brought what they had spun, of blue, purple, *and* scarlet, and fine linen. **26** And all the women whose hearts stirred with wisdom spun yarn of goats' *hair*. **27** The rulers brought onyx stones, and the stones to be set in the ephod and in the breastplate, **28** and spices and oil for the light, for the anointing oil, and for the sweet incense. **29** The children of Israel brought a freewill offering to the LORD, all the men and women whose hearts were willing to bring *material* for all kinds of work which the LORD, by the hand of Moses, had commanded to be done.

Toward believers.

Rom 12:13 distributing to the needs of the saints, given to hospitality.

Gal 6:10 Therefore, as we have opportunity, let us do good to all, especially to those who are of the household of faith.

Toward servants.

Deut 15:12–14 "If your brother, a Hebrew man, or a Hebrew woman, is sold to you and serves you six years, then in the seventh year you shall let him go free from you. **13** And when you send him away free from you, you shall not let him go away empty-handed; **14** you shall supply him liberally from your flock, from your threshing floor, and from your winepress. *From what* the LORD has blessed you with, you shall give to him.

Toward the poor.

Lev 25:35 'If one of your brethren becomes poor, and falls into poverty among you, then you shall help him, like a stranger or a sojourner, that he may live with you.

Deut 15:11 For the poor will never cease from the land; therefore I command you, saying, 'You shall open your hand wide to your brother, to your poor and your needy, in your land.'

Ps 112:9 He has dispersed abroad, He has given to the poor; His righteousness endures forever; His horn will be exalted with honor.

Is 58:7 *Is it* not to share your bread with the hungry, And that you bring to your house the poor who are cast out; When you see the naked, that you cover him, And not hide yourself from your own flesh?

Matt 5:42 Give to him who asks you, and from him who wants to borrow from you do not turn away.

Luke 12:33 Sell what you have and give alms; provide yourselves money bags which do not grow old, a treasure in the heavens that does not fail, where no thief approaches nor moth destroys.

Toward enemies.

Prov 25:21 If your enemy is hungry, give him bread to eat; And if he is thirsty, give him water to drink;

Toward all men.

Is 32:8 But a generous man devises generous things, And by generosity he shall stand.

Gal 6:10 Therefore, as we have opportunity, let us do good to all, especially to those who are of the household of faith.

In supporting missions.

Phil 4:14–16 Nevertheless you have done well that you shared in my distress. **15** Now you Philippians know also that in the beginning of the gospel, when I departed from Macedonia, no church shared with me concerning giving and receiving but you only. **16** For even in Thessalonica you sent *aid* once and again for my necessities.

In rendering personal services.

Phil 2:30 because for the work of Christ he came close to death, not regarding his life, to supply what was lacking in your service toward me.

Without ostentation.

Matt 6:1–3 "Take heed that you do not do your charitable deeds before men, to be seen by them. Otherwise you have no reward from your Father in heaven. **2** Therefore, when you do a charitable deed, do not sound a trumpet before you as the hypocrites do in the synagogues and in the streets, that they may have glory from men. Assuredly, I say to you, they have their reward. **3** But when you do a charitable deed, do not let your left hand know what your right hand is doing,

According to ability.

Deut 16:10 Then you shall keep the Feast of Weeks to the LORD your God with the tribute of a freewill offering from your hand, which you shall give as the LORD your God blesses you.

Deut 16:17 Every man *shall give* as he is able, according to the blessing of the LORD your God which He has given you.

Rom 12:8 he who exhorts, in exhortation; he who gives, with liberality; he who leads, with diligence; he who shows mercy, with cheerfulness.

1 Cor 16:2 On the first *day* of the week let each one of you lay something aside, storing up as he may prosper, that there be no collections when I come.

Willingly.

Ex 25:2 "Speak to the children of Israel, that they bring Me an offering. From everyone who gives it willingly with his heart you shall take My offering.

2 Cor 8:12 For if there is first a willing mind, *it is* accepted according to what one has, *and* not according to what he does not have.

Abundantly.

2 Cor 8:7 But as you abound in everything—in faith, in speech, in knowledge, in all diligence, and in your love for us—*see* that you abound in this grace also.

2 Cor 9:11–13 while *you are* enriched in everything for all liberality, which causes thanksgiving through us to God. **12** For the administration of this service not only supplies the needs of the saints, but also is abounding through many thanksgivings to God, **13** while, through the proof of this ministry, they glorify God for the obedience of your confession to the gospel of Christ, and for *your* liberal sharing with them and all *men,*

It should encourage others toward.

2 Cor 9:2 for I know your willingness, about which I boast of you to the Macedonians, that Achaia was ready a year ago; and your zeal has stirred up the majority.

Labor to make possible.

Acts 20:35 I have shown you in every way, by laboring like this, that you must support the weak. And remember the words of the Lord Jesus, that He said, 'It is more blessed to give than to receive.' "

Eph 4:28 Let him who stole steal no longer, but rather let him labor, working with *his* hands what is good, that he may have something to give him who has need.

Lack of

Brings many a curse.

Prov 28:27 He who gives to the poor will not lack, But he who hides his eyes will have many curses.

A proof of not loving God.

1 John 3:17 But whoever has this world's goods, and sees his brother in need, and shuts up his heart from him, how does the love of God abide in him?

A proof of not having faith.

James 2:14–16 What *does it* profit, my brethren, if someone says he has faith but does not have works? Can faith save him? **15** If a brother or sister is naked and destitute of daily food, **16** and one of you says to them, "Depart in peace, be warmed and filled," but you do not give them the things which are needed for the body, what *does it* profit?

Blessings connected with.

Ps 41:1 Blessed *is* he who considers the poor; The LORD will deliver him in time of trouble.

Prov 22:9 He who has a generous eye will be blessed, For he gives of his bread to the poor.

Acts 20:35 I have shown you in every way, by laboring like this, that you must support the weak. And remember the words of the Lord Jesus, that He said, 'It is more blessed to give than to receive.' "

Promises to.

Ps 112:9 He has dispersed abroad, He has given to the poor; His righteousness endures forever; His horn will be exalted with honor.

Prov 11:25 The generous soul will be made rich, And he who waters will also be watered himself.

Prov 28:27 He who gives to the poor will not lack, But he who hides his eyes will have many curses.

Eccl 11:1–2 Cast your bread upon the waters, For you will find it after many days. **2** Give a serving to seven, and also to eight, For you do not know what evil will be on the earth.

Is 58:10 *If* you extend your soul to the hungry And satisfy the afflicted soul, Then your light shall dawn in the darkness, And your darkness shall *be* as the noonday.

Exhortations to.

Luke 3:11 He answered and said to them, "He who has two tunics, let him give to him who has none; and he who has food, let him do likewise."

Luke 11:41 But rather give alms of such things as you have; then indeed all things are clean to you.

Acts 20:35 I have shown you in every way, by laboring like this, that you must support the weak. And remember the words of the Lord Jesus, that He said, 'It is more blessed to give than to receive.' "

1 Cor 16:1 Now concerning the collection for the saints, as I have given orders to the churches of Galatia, so you must do also:

1 Tim 6:17–18 Command those who are rich in this present age not to be haughty, nor to trust in uncertain riches but in the living God, who gives us richly all things to enjoy. **18** *Let them* do good, that they be rich in good works, ready to give, willing to share,

Exemplified by

The leaders of Israel.

Num 7:2 Then the leaders of Israel, the heads of their fathers' houses, who *were* the leaders of the tribes and over those who were numbered, made an offering.

Boaz.

Ruth 2:16 Also let *grain* from the bundles fall purposely for her; leave *it* that she may glean, and do not rebuke her."

David.

2 Sam 9:7 So David said to him, "Do not fear, for I will surely show you kindness for Jonathan your father's sake, and will restore to you all the land of Saul your grandfather; and you shall eat bread at my table continually."

2 Sam 9:10 You therefore, and your sons and your servants, shall work the land for him, and you shall bring in *the harvest,* that your master's son may have food to eat. But Mephibosheth your master's son shall eat bread at my table always." Now Ziba had fifteen sons and twenty servants.

Barzillai, etc.

2 Sam 17:27–29 Now it happened, when David had come to Mahanaim, that Shobi the son of Nahash from Rabbah of the people of Ammon, Machir the son of Ammiel from Lo Debar, and Barzillai the Gileadite from Rogelim, **28** brought beds and basins, earthen vessels and wheat, barley and flour, parched *grain* and beans, lentils and parched *seeds,* **29** honey and curds, sheep and cheese of the herd, for David and the people who *were* with him to eat. For they said, "The people are hungry and weary and thirsty in the wilderness."

Araunah.

2 Sam 24:22 Now Araunah said to David, "Let my lord the king take and offer up whatever *seems* good to him. Look, *here are* oxen for burnt sacrifice, and threshing implements and the yokes of the oxen for wood.

A Shunammite.

2 Kin 4:8 Now it happened one day that Elisha went to Shunem, where there *was* a notable woman, and she persuaded him to eat some food. So it was, as often as he passed by, he would turn in there to eat some food.

2 Kin 4:10 Please, let us make a small upper room on the wall; and let us put a bed for him there, and a table and a chair and a lampstand; so it will be, whenever he comes to us, he can turn in there."

Judah.

2 Chr 24:10–11 Then all the leaders and all the people rejoiced, brought their contributions, and put *them* into the chest until all had given. **11** So it was, at that time, when the chest was brought to the king's official by the hand of the Levites, and when they saw that *there was* much money, that the king's scribe and the high priest's officer came and emptied the chest, and took it and returned it to its place. Thus they did day by day, and gathered money in abundance.

A governor.

Neh 7:70 And some of the heads of the fathers' houses gave to the work. The governor gave to the treasury one thousand gold drachmas, fifty basins, and five hundred and thirty priestly garments.

The Jews.

Neh 7:71–72 Some of the heads of the fathers' *houses* gave to the treasury of the work twenty thousand gold drachmas, and two thousand two hundred silver minas. **72** And that which the rest of the people gave *was* twenty thousand gold drachmas, two thousand silver minas, and sixty-seven priestly garments.

Job.

Job 29:15–16 I *was* eyes to the blind, And I *was* feet to the lame. **16** I *was* a father to the poor, And I searched out the case *that* I did not know.

Nebuzaradan.

Jer 40:4–5 And now look, I free you this day from the chains that *were* on your hand. If it seems good to you to come with me to Babylon, come, and I will look after you. But if it seems wrong for you to come with me to Babylon, remain here. See, all the land *is* before you; wherever it seems good and convenient for you to go, go there." **5** Now while Jeremiah had not yet gone back, *Nebuzaradan said,* "Go back to Gedaliah the son of Ahikam, the son of Shaphan, whom the king of Babylon has made governor over the cities of Judah, and dwell with him among the people. Or go wherever it seems convenient for you to go." So the captain of the guard gave him rations and a gift and let him go.

Joanna, etc.

Luke 8:3 and Joanna the wife of Chuza, Herod's steward, and Susanna, and many others who provided for Him from their substance.

Zacchaeus.

Luke 19:8 Then Zacchaeus stood and said to the Lord, "Look, Lord, I give half of my goods to the poor; and if I have taken anything from anyone by false accusation, I restore fourfold."

The early church.

Acts 2:45 and sold their possessions and goods, and divided them among all, as anyone had need.

Barnabas.

Acts 4:36–37 And Joses, who was also named Barnabas by the apostles (which is translated Son of Encouragement), a Levite of the country of Cyprus, **37** having land, sold *it,* and brought the money and laid *it* at the apostles' feet.

Dorcas.

Acts 9:36 At Joppa there was a certain disciple named Tabitha, which is translated Dorcas. This woman was full of good works and charitable deeds which she did.

Cornelius.

Acts 10:1–2 There was a certain man in Caesarea called Cornelius, a centurion of what was called the Italian Regiment, **2** a devout *man* and one who feared God with all his household, who gave alms generously to the people, and prayed to God always.

The church of Antioch.

Acts 11:29–30 Then the disciples, each according to his ability, determined to send relief to the brethren dwelling in Judea. **30** This they also did, and sent it to the elders by the hands of Barnabas and Saul.

Lydia.

Acts 16:15 And when she and her household were baptized, she begged *us,* saying, "If you have judged me to be faithful to the Lord, come to my house and stay." So she persuaded us.

Paul.

Acts 20:34 Yes, you yourselves know that these hands have provided for my necessities, and for those who were with me.

Stephanas, etc.

1 Cor 16:17 I am glad about the coming of Stephanas, Fortunatus, and Achaicus, for what was lacking on your part they supplied.

Extraordinary, exemplified by

The Israelites.

Ex 36:5 and they spoke to Moses, saying, "The people bring much more than enough for the service of the work which the LORD commanded *us* to do."

A poor widow.

Mark 12:42–44 Then one poor widow came and threw in two mites, which make a quadrans. **43** So He called His disciples to *Himself* and said to them, "Assuredly, I say to you that this poor widow has put in more than all those who have given to the treasury; **44** for they all put in out of their abundance, but she out of her poverty put in all that she had, her whole livelihood."

The churches of Macedonia.

2 Cor 8:1–5 Moreover, brethren, we make known to you the grace of God bestowed on the churches of Macedonia: **2** that in a great trial of affliction the abundance of their joy and their deep poverty abounded in the riches of their liberality. **3** For I bear witness that according to *their* ability, yes, and beyond *their* ability, *they were* freely willing, **4** imploring us with much urgency that we would receive the gift and the fellowship of the ministering to the saints. **5** And not *only* as we had hoped, but they first gave themselves to the Lord, and *then* to us by the will of God.

GENTILES, THE

Include all nations except the Jews.

Rom 2:9 tribulation and anguish, on every soul of man who does evil, of the Jew first and also of the Greek;

Rom 3:9 What then? Are we better *than they?* Not at all. For we have previously charged both Jews and Greeks that they are all under sin.

Rom 9:24 *even* us whom He called, not of the Jews only, but also of the Gentiles?

Other names for,

Nations.

Ps 2:1 Why do the nations rage, And the people plot a vain thing?

Ps 9:20 Put them in fear, O LORD, *That* the nations may know themselves *to be but* men. Selah

Ps 22:28 For the kingdom *is* the LORD's, And He rules over the nations.

Is 9:1 Nevertheless the gloom *will* not *be* upon her who *is* distressed, As when at first He lightly esteemed The land of Zebulun and the land of Naphtali, And afterward more heavily oppressed *her, By* the way of the sea, beyond the Jordan, In Galilee of the Gentiles.

Gal 3:8 And the Scripture, foreseeing that God would justify the Gentiles by faith, preached the gospel to Abraham beforehand, *saying, "In you all the nations shall be blessed."*

Uncircumcised.

1 Sam 14:6 Then Jonathan said to the young man who bore his armor, "Come, let us go over to the garrison of these uncircumcised; it may be that the LORD will work for us. For nothing restrains the LORD from saving by many or by few."

Is 52:1 Awake, awake! Put on your strength, O Zion; Put on your beautiful garments, O Jerusalem, the holy city! For the uncircumcised and the unclean Shall no longer come to you.

Rom 2:26 Therefore, if an uncircumcised man keeps the righteous requirements of the law, will not his uncircumcision be counted as circumcision?

Greeks.

Rom 1:16 For I am not ashamed of the gospel of Christ, for it is the power of God to salvation for everyone who believes, for the Jew first and also for the Greek.

Rom 10:12 For there is no distinction between Jew and Greek, for the same Lord over all is rich to all who call upon Him.

Strangers and foreigners.

Is 14:1 For the LORD will have mercy on Jacob, and will still choose Israel, and settle them in their own land. The strangers will be joined with them, and they will cling to the house of Jacob.

Is 60:10 "The sons of foreigners shall build up your walls, And their kings shall minister to you; For in My wrath I struck you, But in My favor I have had mercy on you.

Ruled by God.

2 Chr 20:6 and said: "O LORD God of our fathers, *are* You not God in heaven, and do You *not* rule over all the kingdoms of the nations, and in Your hand *is there not* power and might, so that no one is able to withstand You?

Ps 47:8 God reigns over the nations; God sits on His holy throne.

Rom 3:29–30 Or *is He* the God of the Jews only? *Is He* not also the God of the Gentiles? Yes, of the Gentiles also, **30** since *there is* one God who will justify the circumcised by faith and the uncircumcised through faith.

Chastised by God.

Ps 9:5 You have rebuked the nations, You have destroyed the wicked; You have blotted out their name forever and ever.

Ps 94:10 He who instructs the nations, shall He not correct, He who teaches man knowledge?

Counsel of, brought to nothing.

Ps 33:10 The LORD brings the counsel of the nations to nothing; He makes the plans of the peoples of no effect.

Characterized as

Ignorant of God.

Rom 1:21 because, although they knew God, they did not glorify *Him* as God, nor were thankful, but became futile in their thoughts, and their foolish hearts were darkened.

1 Thess 4:5 not in passion of lust, like the Gentiles who do not know God;

Refusing to know God.

Rom 1:28 And even as they did not like to retain God in *their* knowledge, God gave them over to a debased mind, to do those things which are not fitting;

Without the law.

Rom 2:14 for when Gentiles, who do not have the law, by nature do the things in the law, these, although not having the law, are a law to themselves,

Idolatrous.

Rom 1:23 and changed the glory of the incorruptible

God into an image made like corruptible man—and birds and four-footed animals and creeping things.

Rom 1:25 who exchanged the truth of God for the lie, and worshiped and served the creature rather than the Creator, who is blessed forever. Amen.

1 Cor 12:2 You know that you were Gentiles, carried away to these dumb idols, however you were led.

Superstitious.

Deut 18:14 For these nations which you will dispossess listened to soothsayers and diviners; but as for you, the LORD your God has not appointed such for you.

Depraved and wicked.

Rom 1:28–32 And even as they did not like to retain God in *their* knowledge, God gave them over to a debased mind, to do those things which are not fitting; **29** being filled with all unrighteousness, sexual immorality, wickedness, covetousness, maliciousness; full of envy, murder, strife, deceit, evil-mindedness; *they are* whisperers, **30** backbiters, haters of God, violent, proud, boasters, inventors of evil things, disobedient to parents, **31** undiscerning, untrustworthy, unloving, unforgiving, unmerciful; **32** who, knowing the righteous judgment of God, that those who practice such things are deserving of death, not only do the same but also approve of those who practice them.

Eph 4:19 who, being past feeling, have given themselves over to lewdness, to work all uncleanness with greediness.

Blasphemous.

Neh 5:9 Then I said, "What you are doing *is* not good. Should you not walk in the fear of our God because of the reproach of the nations, our enemies?

Loyal to false gods.

Jer 2:11 Has a nation changed *its* gods, Which *are* not gods? But My people have changed their Glory For *what* does not profit.

Hated and despised the Jews.

Esth 9:1 Now in the twelfth month, that *is*, the month of Adar, on the thirteenth day, *the time* came for the king's command and his decree to be executed. On the day that the enemies of the Jews had hoped to overpower them, the opposite occurred, in that the Jews themselves overpowered those who hated them.

Esth 9:5 Thus the Jews defeated all their enemies with the stroke of the sword, with slaughter and destruction, and did what they pleased with those who hated them.

Ps 44:13–14 You make us a reproach to our neighbors, A scorn and a derision to those all around us. **14** You make us a byword among the nations, A shaking of the head among the peoples.

Ps 123:3 Have mercy on us, O LORD, have mercy on us! For we are exceedingly filled with contempt.

Often ravaged and defiled the holy land and sanctuary.

Ps 79:1 O God, the nations have come into Your inheritance; Your holy temple they have defiled; They have laid Jerusalem in heaps.

Lam 1:10 The adversary has spread his hand Over all her pleasant things; For she has seen the nations enter her sanctuary, Those whom You commanded Not to enter Your assembly.

Israel

Was not to follow the ways of.

Lev 18:3 According to the doings of the land of Egypt, where you dwelt, you shall not do; and according to the doings of the land of Canaan, where I am bringing you, you shall not do; nor shall you walk in their ordinances.

Jer 10:2 Thus says the LORD: "Do not learn the way of the Gentiles; Do not be dismayed at the signs of heaven, For the Gentiles are dismayed at them.

Was not to intermarry with.

Deut 7:3 Nor shall you make marriages with them. You shall not give your daughter to their son, nor take their daughter for your son.

Permitted to have, as servants.

Lev 25:44 And as for your male and female slaves whom you may have—from the nations that are around you, from them you may buy male and female slaves.

Viewed them as dogs.

Matt 15:26 But He answered and said, "It is not good to take the children's bread and throw *it* to the little dogs."

Never associated with.

Acts 10:28 Then he said to them, "You know how unlawful it is for a Jewish man to keep company with or go to one of another nation. But God has shown me that I should not call any man common or unclean.

Acts 11:2–3 And when Peter came up to Jerusalem, those of the circumcision contended with him, **3** saying, "You went in to uncircumcised men and ate with them!"

Often corrupted by.

2 Kin 17:7–8 For so it was that the children of Israel had sinned against the LORD their God, who had brought them up out of the land of Egypt, from under the hand of Pharaoh king of Egypt; and they had feared other gods, **8** and had walked in the statutes of the nations whom the LORD had cast out from before the children of Israel, and of the kings of Israel, which they had made.

Dispersed among.

John 7:35 Then the Jews said among themselves, "Where does He intend to go that we shall not find Him? Does He intend to go to the Dispersion among the Greeks and teach the Greeks?

Excluded from Israel's privileges.

Eph 2:11–12 Therefore remember that you, once Gentiles in the flesh—who are called Uncircumcision by what is called the Circumcision made in the flesh by hands— **12** that at that time you were without Christ, being aliens from the commonwealth of Israel and strangers from the covenants of promise, having no hope and without God in the world.

Not allowed to enter the temple.

Acts 21:28–29 crying out, "Men of Israel, help! This is the man who teaches all *men* everywhere against the people, the law, and this place; and furthermore he also brought Greeks into the temple and has defiled this holy place." **29** (For they had previously seen Trophimus the Ephesian with him in the city, whom they supposed that Paul had brought into the temple.)

Outer court of temple for.

Eph 2:14 For He Himself is our peace, who has made both one, and has broken down the middle wall of separation,

Rev 11:2 But leave out the court which is outside the temple, and do not measure it, for it has been given to the Gentiles. And they will tread the holy city underfoot *for* forty-two months.

Given to Christ as His inheritance.

Ps 2:8 Ask of Me, and I will give *You* The nations *for* Your inheritance, And the ends of the earth *for* Your possession.

Christ given as a light to.

Is 42:6 "I, the LORD, have called You in righteousness, And will hold Your hand; I will keep You and give You as a covenant to the people, As a light to the Gentiles,

Luke 2:32 A light to *bring* revelation to the Gentiles, And the glory of Your people Israel."

Conversion of, predicted.

Is 2:2 Now it shall come to pass in the latter days *That* the mountain of the LORD's house Shall be established on the top of the mountains, And shall be exalted above the hills; And all nations shall flow to it.

Is 11:10 "And in that day there shall be a Root of Jesse, Who shall stand as a banner to the people; For the Gentiles shall seek Him, And His resting place shall be glorious."

Rom 11:11–13 I say then, have they stumbled that they should fall? Certainly not! But through their fall, to provoke them to jealousy, salvation *has come* to the Gentiles. 12 Now if their fall *is* riches for the world, and their failure riches for the Gentiles, how much more their fullness! 13 For I speak to you Gentiles; inasmuch as I am an apostle to the Gentiles, I magnify my ministry,

Mercy of God extended to.

Rom 15:9–12 and that the Gentiles might glorify God for *His* mercy, as it is written: *"For this reason I will confess to You among the Gentiles, And sing to Your name."* 10 And again he says: *"Rejoice, O Gentiles, with His people!"* 11 And again: *"Praise the LORD, all you Gentiles! Laud Him, all you peoples!"* 12 And again, Isaiah says: *"There shall be a root of Jesse; And He who shall rise to reign over the Gentiles, In Him the Gentiles shall hope."*

United with the Jews to crucify Christ.

Acts 4:27 "For truly against Your holy Servant Jesus, whom You anointed, both Herod and Pontius Pilate, with the Gentiles and the people of Israel, were gathered together

The gospel not to be preached to, until preached to the Jews.

Matt 10:5 These twelve Jesus sent out and commanded them, saying: "Do not go into the way of the Gentiles, and do not enter a city of the Samaritans.

Luke 24:47 and that repentance and remission of sins should be preached in His name to all nations, beginning at Jerusalem.

Acts 13:46 Then Paul and Barnabas grew bold and said, "It was necessary that the word of God should be spoken to you first; but since you reject it, and judge yourselves unworthy of everlasting life, behold, we turn to the Gentiles.

First special introduction of the gospel to.

Acts 10:34–45 Then Peter opened *his* mouth and said: "In truth I perceive that God shows no partiality. 35 But in every nation whoever fears Him and works righteousness is accepted by Him. 36 The word which *God* sent to the children of Israel, preaching peace through Jesus Christ—He is Lord of all— 37 that word you know, which was proclaimed throughout all Judea, and began from Galilee after the baptism which John preached: 38 how God anointed Jesus of Nazareth with the Holy Spirit and with power, who went about doing good and healing all who were oppressed by the devil, for God was with Him. 39 And we are witnesses of all things which He did both in the land of the Jews and in Jerusalem, whom they killed by hanging on a tree. 40 Him God raised up on the third day, and showed Him openly, 41 not to all the people, but to witnesses chosen before by God, *even* to us who ate and drank with Him after He arose from the dead. 42 And He commanded us to preach to the people, and to testify that it is He who was ordained by God *to be* Judge of the living and the dead. 43 To Him all the prophets witness that, through His name, whoever believes in Him will receive remission of sins." 44 While Peter was still speaking these words, the Holy Spirit fell upon all those who heard the word. 45 And those of the circumcision who believed were astonished, as many as came with Peter, because the gift of the Holy Spirit had been poured out on the Gentiles also.

Acts 15:14 Simon has declared how God at the first visited the Gentiles to take out of them a people for His name.

First general introduction of the gospel to.

Acts 13:48–49 Now when the Gentiles heard this, they were glad and glorified the word of the Lord. And as many as had been appointed to eternal life believed. 49 And the word of the Lord was being spread throughout all the region.

Acts 13:52 And the disciples were filled with joy and with the Holy Spirit.

Acts 15:12 Then all the multitude kept silent and listened to Barnabas and Paul declaring how many miracles and wonders God had worked through them among the Gentiles.

Paul was the apostle of.

Acts 9:15 But the Lord said to him, "Go, for he is a chosen vessel of Mine to bear My name before Gentiles, kings, and the children of Israel.

Gal 1:16 to reveal His Son in me, that I might preach Him among the Gentiles, I did not immediately confer with flesh and blood,

Gal 2:7–8 But on the contrary, when they saw that the gospel for the uncircumcised had been committed to me, as *the gospel* for the circumcised *was* to Peter 8 (for He who worked effectively in Peter for the apostleship to the circumcised also worked effectively in me toward the Gentiles),

Jerusalem trampled down by, etc.

Luke 21:24 And they will fall by the edge of the sword, and be led away captive into all nations. And Jerusalem will be trampled by Gentiles until the times of the Gentiles are fulfilled.

Fullness of, follows Israel's unbelief.

Rom 11:25 For I do not desire, brethren, that you should be ignorant of this mystery, lest you should be wise in your own opinion, that blindness in part has happened to Israel until the fullness of the Gentiles has come in.

GIBEONITES, THE

Descended from the Hivites and Amorites.

Josh 9:3 But when the inhabitants of Gibeon heard what Joshua had done to Jericho and Ai,

Josh 9:7 Then the men of Israel said to the Hivites, "Perhaps you dwell among us; so how can we make a covenant with you?"

2 Sam 21:2 So the king called the Gibeonites and spoke to them. Now the Gibeonites *were* not of the children of Israel, but of the remnant of the Amorites; the children of Israel had sworn protection to them, but Saul had sought to kill them in his zeal for the children of Israel and Judah.

A mighty and warlike people.

Josh 10:2 that they feared greatly, because Gibeon *was* a great city, like one of the royal cities, and because it *was* greater than Ai, and all its men *were* mighty.

Cities of.

Josh 9:17 Then the children of Israel journeyed and came to their cities on the third day. Now their cities *were* Gibeon, Chephirah, Beeroth, and Kirjath Jearim.

The Jews

Deceived by.

Josh 9:4–13 they worked craftily, and went and pretended to be ambassadors. And they took old sacks on their donkeys, old wineskins torn and mended, 5 old and patched sandals on their feet, and old garments on themselves; and all the bread of their provision was dry *and* moldy. 6 And they went to Joshua, to the camp at Gilgal, and said to him and to the men of Israel, "We have come from a far country; now therefore, make a covenant with us." 7 Then the men of Israel said to the Hivites, "Perhaps you dwell among us; so how can we make a covenant with you?" 8 But they said to Joshua, "We *are* your servants." And Joshua said to them, "Who *are* you, and where do you come from?" 9 So they said to him: "From a very far country your servants have come, because of the name of the LORD your God; for we have heard of His fame, and all that He did in Egypt, 10 and all that He did to the two kings of the Amorites who *were* beyond the Jordan—to Sihon king of Heshbon, and Og king of Bashan, who was at Ashtaroth. 11 Therefore our elders and all the inhabitants of our country spoke to us, saying, 'Take provisions with you for the journey, and go to meet them, and say to them, "We *are* your servants; now therefore, make a covenant with us." ' 12 This bread of ours we took hot *for* our provision from our houses on the day we departed to come to you. But now look, it is dry and moldy. 13 And these wineskins which we

filled *were* new, and see, they are torn; and these our garments and our sandals have become old because of the very long journey."

Made an agreement with.

Josh 9:15 So Joshua made peace with them, and made a covenant with them to let them live; and the rulers of the congregation swore to them.

Spared them on account of their oath.

Josh 9:18–19 But the children of Israel did not attack them, because the rulers of the congregation had sworn to them by the LORD God of Israel. And all the congregation complained against the rulers. 19 Then all the rulers said to all the congregation, "We have sworn to them by the LORD God of Israel; now therefore, we may not touch them.

Appointed them woodcutters, etc.

Josh 9:20–27 This we will do to them: We will let them live, lest wrath be upon us because of the oath which we swore to them." 21 And the rulers said to them, "Let them live, but let them be woodcutters and water carriers for all the congregation, as the rulers had promised them." 22 Then Joshua called for them, and he spoke to them, saying, "Why have you deceived us, saying, 'We *are* very far from you,' when you dwell near us? 23 Now therefore, you *are* cursed, and none of you shall be freed from being slaves—woodcutters and water carriers for the house of my God." 24 So they answered Joshua and said, "Because your servants were clearly told that the LORD your God commanded His servant Moses to give you all the land, and to destroy all the inhabitants of the land from before you; therefore we were very much afraid for our lives because of you, and have done this thing. 25 And now, here we are, in your hands; do with us as it seems good and right to do to us." 26 So he did to them, and delivered them out of the hand of the children of Israel, so that they did not kill them. 27 And that day Joshua made them woodcutters and water carriers for the congregation and for the altar of the LORD, in the place which He would choose, even to this day.

Attacked by the kings of Canaan.

Josh 10:1–5 Now it came to pass when Adoni-Zedek king of Jerusalem heard how Joshua had taken Ai and had utterly destroyed it—as he had done to Jericho and its king, so he had done to Ai and its king—and how the inhabitants of Gibeon had made peace with Israel and were among them, 2 that they feared greatly, because Gibeon *was* a great city, like one of the royal cities, and because it *was* greater than Ai, and all its men *were* mighty. 3 Therefore Adoni-Zedek king of Jerusalem sent to Hoham king of Hebron, Piram king of Jarmuth, Japhia king of Lachish, and Debir king of Eglon, saying, 4 "Come up to me and help me, that we may attack Gibeon, for it has made peace with Joshua and with the children of Israel." 5 Therefore the five kings of the Amorites, the king of Jerusalem, the king of Hebron, the king of Jarmuth, the king of Lachish, *and* the king of Eglon, gathered together and went up, they and all their armies, and camped before Gibeon and made war against it.

Delivered by Israel.

Josh 10:6–10 And the men of Gibeon sent to Joshua at the camp at Gilgal, saying, "Do not forsake your servants; come up to us quickly, save us and help us, for all the kings of the Amorites who dwell in the mountains have gathered together against us." 7 So Joshua ascended from Gilgal, he and all the people of war with him, and all the mighty men of valor. 8 And the LORD said to Joshua, "Do not fear them, for I have delivered them into your hand; not a man of them shall stand before you." 9 Joshua therefore came upon them suddenly, having marched all night from Gilgal. 10 So the LORD routed them before Israel, killed them with a great slaughter at Gibeon, chased them along the road that goes to Beth Horon, and struck them down as far as Azekah and Makkedah.

Saul sought to destroy.

2 Sam 21:2 So the king called the Gibeonites and spoke to them. Now the Gibeonites *were* not of the children of Israel, but of the remnant of the Amorites; the children of Israel had sworn protection to them, but Saul had sought to kill them in his zeal for the children of Israel and Judah.

Israel plagued for Saul's cruelty to.

2 Sam 21:1 Now there was a famine in the days of David for three years, year after year; and David inquired of the LORD. And the LORD answered, "*It is* because of Saul and *his* bloodthirsty house, because he killed the Gibeonites."

Effected the destruction of the remnant of Saul's house.

2 Sam 21:4–9 And the Gibeonites said to him, "We will have no silver or gold from Saul or from his house, nor shall you kill any man in Israel for us." So he said, "Whatever you say, I will do for you." 5 Then they answered the king, "As for the man who consumed us and plotted against us, *that* we should be destroyed from remaining in any of the territories of Israel, 6 let seven men of his descendants be delivered to us, and we will hang them before the LORD in Gibeah of Saul, *whom* the LORD chose." And the king said, "I will give *them*." 7 But the king spared Mephibosheth the son of Jonathan, the son of Saul, because of the LORD's oath that *was* between them, between David and Jonathan the son of Saul. 8 So the king took Armoni and Mephibosheth, the two sons of Rizpah the daughter of Aiah, whom she bore to Saul, and the five sons of Michal the daughter of Saul, whom she brought up for Adriel the son of Barzillai the Meholathite; 9 and he delivered them into the hands of the Gibeonites, and they hanged them on the hill before the LORD. So they fell, *all* seven together, and were put to death in the days of harvest, in the first *days*, in the beginning of barley harvest.

The office of the Nethinim probably originated in.

1 Chr 9:2 And the first inhabitants who *dwelt* in their possessions in their cities *were* Israelites, priests, Levites, and the Nethinim.

Part of, returned from the captivity.

Neh 7:25 the sons of Gibeon, ninety-five;

GIFTS (FROM GOD)

All blessings are.

James 1:17 Every good gift and every perfect gift is from above, and comes down from the Father of lights, with whom there is no variation or shadow of turning.

2 Pet 1:3 as His divine power has given to us all things that *pertain* to life and godliness, through the knowledge of Him who called us by glory and virtue,

Are dispensed according to His will.

Eccl 2:26 For *God* gives wisdom and knowledge and joy to a man who *is* good in His sight; but to the sinner He gives the work of gathering and collecting, that he may give to *him who is* good before God. This also *is* vanity and grasping for the wind.

Dan 2:21 And He changes the times and the seasons; He removes kings and raises up kings; He gives wisdom to the wise And knowledge to those who have understanding.

Rom 12:6 Having then gifts differing according to the grace that is given to us, *let us use them:* if prophecy, *let us prophesy* in proportion to our faith;

1 Cor 7:7 For I wish that all men were even as I myself. But each one has his own gift from God, one in this manner and another in that.

Are free and abundant.

Num 14:8 If the LORD delights in us, then He will bring us into this land and give it to us, 'a land which flows with milk and honey.'

Rom 8:32 He who did not spare His own Son, but delivered Him up for us all, how shall He not with Him also freely give us all things?

Spiritual ones

Christ the chief of.

Ps 68:18 You have ascended on high, You have led captivity captive; You have received gifts among men, Even *from* the rebellious, That the LORD God might dwell *there.*

Is 42:6 "I, the LORD, have called You in righteousness, And will hold Your hand; I will keep You and give You as a covenant to the people, As a light to the Gentiles,

Is 55:4 Indeed I have given him *as* a witness to the people, A leader and commander for the people.

John 3:16 For God so loved the world that He gave His only begotten Son, that whoever believes in Him should not perish but have everlasting life.

John 4:10 Jesus answered and said to her, "If you knew the gift of God, and who it is who says to you, 'Give Me a drink,' you would have asked Him, and He would have given you living water."

John 6:32–33 Then Jesus said to them, "Most assuredly, I say to you, Moses did not give you the bread from heaven, but My Father gives you the true bread from heaven. 33 For the bread of God is He who comes down from heaven and gives life to the world."

Eph 4:7–8 But to each one of us grace was given according to the measure of Christ's gift. 8 Therefore He says: "*When He ascended on high, He led captivity captive, And gave gifts to men.*"

John 6:27 Do not labor for the food which perishes, but for the food which endures to everlasting life, which the Son of Man will give you, because God the Father has set His seal on Him."

Are through the Holy Spirit.

Luke 11:13 If you then, being evil, know how to give good gifts to your children, how much more will *your* heavenly Father give the Holy Spirit to those who ask Him!"

Acts 8:20 But Peter said to him, "Your money perish with you, because you thought that the gift of God could be purchased with money!

Grace.

Ps 84:11 For the LORD God *is* a sun and shield; The LORD will give grace and glory; No good *thing* will He withhold From those who walk uprightly.

James 4:6 But He gives more grace. Therefore He says: "God resists the proud, But gives grace to the humble."

Wisdom.

Prov 2:6 For the LORD gives wisdom; From His mouth *come* knowledge and understanding;

James 1:5 If any of you lacks wisdom, let him ask of God, who gives to all liberally and without reproach, and it will be given to him.

Repentance.

Acts 11:18 When they heard these things they became silent; and they glorified God, saying, "Then God has also granted to the Gentiles repentance to life."

Faith.

Eph 2:8 For by grace you have been saved through faith, and that not of yourselves; *it is* the gift of God,

Phil 1:29 For to you it has been granted on behalf of Christ, not only to believe in Him, but also to suffer for His sake,

Righteousness.

Rom 5:16–17 And the gift *is* not like *that which came* through the one who sinned. For the judgment *which came* from one *offense resulted* in condemnation, but the free gift *which came* from many offenses *resulted* in justification. **17** For if by the one man's offense death reigned through the one, much more those who receive abundance of grace and of the gift of righteousness will reign in life through the One, Jesus Christ.)

Strength and power.

Ps 68:35 O God, *You are* more awesome than Your holy places. The God of Israel *is* He who gives strength and power to *His* people. Blessed *be* God!

A new heart.

Ezek 11:19 Then I will give them one heart, and I will put a new spirit within them, and take the stony heart out of their flesh, and give them a heart of flesh,

Peace.

Ps 29:11 The LORD will give strength to His people; The LORD will bless His people with peace.

Rest.

Matt 11:28 Come to Me, all *you* who labor and are heavy laden, and I will give you rest.

2 Thess 1:7 and to *give* you who are troubled rest with us when the Lord Jesus is revealed from heaven with His mighty angels,

Glory.

Ps 84:11 For the LORD God *is* a sun and shield; The LORD will give grace and glory; No good *thing* will He withhold From those who walk uprightly.

John 17:22 And the glory which You gave Me I have given them, that they may be one just as We are one:

Eternal life.

Rom 6:23 For the wages of sin *is* death, but the gift of God *is* eternal life in Christ Jesus our Lord.

Are not revoked.

Rom 11:29 For the gifts and the calling of God *are* irrevocable.

To be used for mutual profit.

1 Pet 4:10 As each one has received a gift, minister it to one another, as good stewards of the manifold grace of God.

Believers should pray for.

Matt 7:7 "Ask, and it will be given to you; seek, and you will find; knock, and it will be opened to you.

Matt 7:11 If you then, being evil, know how to give good gifts to your children, how much more will your Father who is in heaven give good things to those who ask Him!

John 16:23–24 "And in that day you will ask Me nothing. Most assuredly, I say to you, whatever you ask the Father in My name He will give you. **24** Until now you have asked nothing in My name. Ask, and you will receive, that your joy may be full.

Believers should acknowledge.

Ps 4:7 You have put gladness in my heart, More than in the season that their grain and wine increased.

Ps 21:2 You have given him his heart's desire, And have not withheld the request of his lips. Selah

Temporal ones

Life.

Is 42:5 Thus says God the LORD, Who created the heavens and stretched them out, Who spread forth the earth and that which comes from it, Who gives breath to the people on it, And spirit to those who walk on it:

Food and clothing.

Matt 6:25–33 "Therefore I say to you, do not worry about your life, what you will eat or what you will drink; nor about your body, what you will put on. Is not life more than food and the body more than clothing? **26** Look at the birds of the air, for they neither sow nor reap nor gather into barns; yet your heavenly Father feeds them. Are you not of more value than they? **27** Which of you by worrying can add one cubit to his stature? **28** "So why do you worry about clothing? Consider the lilies of the field, how they grow: they neither toil nor spin; **29** and yet I say to you that even Solomon in all his glory was not arrayed like one of these. **30** Now if God so clothes the grass of the field, which today is, and tomorrow is thrown into the oven, *will He* not much more *clothe* you, O you of little faith? **31** "Therefore do not worry, saying, 'What shall we eat?' or 'What shall we drink?' or 'What shall we wear?' **32** For after all these things the Gentiles seek. For your heavenly Father knows that you need all these things. **33** But seek first the kingdom of God and His righteousness, and all these things shall be added to you.

Rain and fruitful seasons.

Gen 27:28 Therefore may God give you Of the dew of heaven, Of the fatness of the earth, And plenty of grain and wine.

Lev 26:4–5 then I will give you rain in its season, the land shall yield its produce, and the trees of the field shall yield their fruit. **5** Your threshing shall last till the time of vintage, and the vintage shall last till the time of sowing; you shall eat your bread to the full, and dwell in your land safely.

Is 30:23 Then He will give the rain for your seed With which you sow the ground, And bread of the increase of the earth; It will be fat and plentiful. In that day your cattle will feed In large pastures.

Wisdom.

2 Chr 1:12 wisdom and knowledge *are* granted to you; and I will give you riches and wealth and honor, such as none of the kings have had who *were* before you, nor shall any after you have the like."

Peace.

Lev 26:6 I will give peace in the land, and you shall lie down, and none will make *you* afraid; I will rid the land of evil beasts, and the sword will not go through your land.

1 Chr 22:9 Behold, a son shall be born to you, who shall be a man of rest; and I will give him rest from all his enemies all around. His name shall be Solomon, for I will give peace and quietness to Israel in his days.

All good things.

Ps 34:10 The young lions lack and suffer hunger; But those who seek the LORD shall not lack any good thing.

1 Tim 6:17 Command those who are rich in this present age not to be haughty, nor to trust in uncertain riches but in the living God, who gives us richly all things to enjoy.

To be used and enjoyed.

Eccl 3:13 and also that every man should eat and drink and enjoy the good of all his labor—it *is* the gift of God.

Eccl 5:19–20 As for every man to whom God has given riches and wealth, and given him power to eat of it, to receive his heritage and rejoice in his labor—this *is* the gift of God. **20** For he will not dwell unduly on the days of his life, because God keeps *him* busy with the joy of his heart.

1 Tim 4:4–5 For every creature of God *is* good, and nothing is to be refused if it is received with thanksgiving; **5** for it is sanctified by the word of God and prayer.

Should cause us to remember God.

Deut 8:18 "And you shall remember the LORD your God, for *it is* He who gives you power to get wealth, that He may establish His covenant which He swore to your fathers, as *it is* this day.

All creatures partake of.

Ps 136:25 Who gives food to all flesh, For His mercy endures forever.

Ps 145:15–16 The eyes of all look expectantly to You, And You give them their food in due season. **16** You open Your hand And satisfy the desire of every living thing.

Believers should pray for.

Zech 10:1 Ask the LORD for rain In the time of the latter rain. The LORD will make flashing clouds; He will give them showers of rain, Grass in the field for everyone.

Matt 6:11 Give us this day our daily bread.

Illustrated.

Matt 25:15–30 And to one he gave five talents, to another two, and to another one, to each according to his own ability; and immediately he went on a journey. **16** Then he who had received the five talents went and traded with them, and made another five talents. **17** And likewise he who *had received* two gained two more also. **18** But he who had received one went and dug in the ground, and hid his lord's money. **19** After a long time the lord of those servants came and settled accounts with them. **20** "So he who had received five talents came and brought five other talents, saying, 'Lord, you delivered to me five talents; look, I have gained five more talents besides them.' **21** His lord said to him, 'Well *done*, good and faithful servant; you were faithful over a few things, I will make you ruler over many things. Enter into the joy of your lord.' **22** He also who had received two talents came and said, 'Lord, you delivered to me two talents; look, I have gained two more talents besides them.' **23** His lord said to him, 'Well *done*, good and faithful servant; you have been faithful over a few things, I will make you ruler over many things. Enter into the joy of your lord.' **24** "Then he who had received the one talent came and said, 'Lord, I knew you to be a hard man, reaping where you have not sown, and gathering where you have not scattered seed. **25** And I was afraid, and went and hid your talent in the ground. Look, *there* you have *what is* yours.' **26** "But his lord answered and said to him, 'You wicked and lazy servant, you knew that I reap where I have not sown, and gather where I have not scattered seed. **27** So you ought to have deposited my money with the bankers, and at my coming I would have received back my own with interest. **28** So take the talent from him, and give *it* to him who has ten talents. **29** 'For to everyone who has, more will be given, and he will have abundance; but from him who does not have, even what he has will be taken away. **30** And cast the unprofitable servant into the outer darkness. There will be weeping and gnashing of teeth.'

GLORIFICATION

Described.

Phil 3:20–21 For our citizenship is in heaven, from which we also eagerly wait for the Savior, the Lord Jesus Christ, **21** who will transform our lowly body that it may be conformed to His glorious body, according to the working by which He is able even to subdue all things to Himself.

1 John 3:2 Beloved, now we are children of God; and it has not yet been revealed what we shall be, but we know that when He is revealed, we shall be like Him, for we shall see Him as He is.

Future certainty for believers.

Rom 8:30 Moreover whom He predestined, these He also called; whom He called, these He also justified; and whom He justified, these He also glorified.

Final feature of redemption.

Rom 13:11 And *do* this, knowing the time, that now *it is* high time to awake out of sleep; for now our salvation *is* nearer than when we *first* believed.

GLORIFYING GOD

Commanded.

1 Chr 16:28 Give to the LORD, O families of the peoples, Give to the LORD glory and strength.

Ps 22:23 You who fear the LORD, praise Him! All you descendants of Jacob, glorify Him, And fear Him, all you offspring of Israel!

Is 42:12 Let them give glory to the LORD, And declare His praise in the coastlands.

Due to Him.

1 Chr 16:29 Give to the LORD the glory *due* His name; Bring an offering, and come before Him. Oh, worship the LORD in the beauty of holiness!

Should be done because of His

Holiness.

Ps 99:9 Exalt the LORD our God, And worship at His holy hill; For the LORD our God *is* holy.

Rev 15:4 Who shall not fear You, O Lord, and glorify Your name? For *You* alone *are* holy. For all nations shall come and worship before You, For Your judgments have been manifested."

Mercy and truth.

Ps 115:1 Not unto us, O LORD, not unto us, But to Your name give glory, Because of Your mercy, Because of Your truth.

Rom 15:9 and that the Gentiles might glorify God for *His* mercy, as it is written: *"For this reason I will confess to You among the Gentiles, And sing to Your name."*

Faithfulness and truth.

Is 25:1 O LORD, You *are* my God. I will exalt You, I will praise Your name, For You have done wonderful *things; Your* counsels of old *are* faithfulness *and* truth.

Wonderful works.

Matt 15:31 So the multitude marveled when they saw *the* mute speaking, *the* maimed made whole, *the* lame walking, and *the* blind seeing; and they glorified the God of Israel.

Acts 4:21 So when they had further threatened them, they let them go, finding no way of punishing them, because of the people, since they all glorified God for what had been done.

Judgments.

Is 25:3 Therefore the strong people will glorify You; The city of the terrible nations will fear You.

Ezek 28:22 and say, 'Thus says the Lord GOD: "Behold, I *am* against you, O Sidon; I will be glorified in your midst; And they shall know that I *am* the LORD, When I execute judgments in her and am hallowed in her.

Rev 14:7 saying with a loud voice, "Fear God and give glory to Him, for the hour of His judgment has come;

and worship Him who made heaven and earth, the sea and springs of water."

Deliverance.

Ps 50:15 Call upon Me in the day of trouble; I will deliver you, and you shall glorify Me."

Grace to others.

Acts 11:18 When they heard these things they became silent; and they glorified God, saying, "Then God has also granted to the Gentiles repentance to life."

2 Cor 9:13 while, through the proof of this ministry, they glorify God for the obedience of your confession to the gospel of Christ, and for *your* liberal sharing with them and all *men,*

Gal 1:24 And they glorified God in me.

Obligation of believers to.

1 Cor 6:20 For you were bought at a price; therefore glorify God in your body and in your spirit, which are God's.

Is acceptable through Christ.

Phil 1:11 being filled with the fruits of righteousness which *are* by Jesus Christ, to the glory and praise of God.

1 Pet 4:11 If anyone speaks, *let him speak* as the oracles of God. If anyone ministers, *let him do it* as with the ability which God supplies, that in all things God may be glorified through Jesus Christ, to whom belong the glory and the dominion forever and ever. Amen.

Christ, an example of.

John 17:4 I have glorified You on the earth. I have finished the work which You have given Me to do.

Accomplished by

Relying on His promises.

Rom 4:20 He did not waver at the promise of God through unbelief, but was strengthened in faith, giving glory to God,

Praising Him.

Ps 50:23 Whoever offers praise glorifies Me; And to him who orders *his* conduct *aright* I will show the salvation of God."

Dying for Him.

John 21:19 This He spoke, signifying by what death he would glorify God. And when He had spoken this, He said to him, "Follow Me."

Confessing Christ.

Phil 2:11 and *that* every tongue should confess that Jesus Christ *is* Lord, to the glory of God the Father.

Suffering for Christ.

1 Pet 4:14 If you are reproached for the name of Christ, blessed *are you,* for the Spirit of glory and of God rests upon you. On their part He is blasphemed, but on your part He is glorified.

1 Pet 4:16 Yet if *anyone suffers* as a Christian, let him not be ashamed, but let him glorify God in this matter.

Glorifying Christ.

Acts 19:17 This became known both to all Jews and Greeks dwelling in Ephesus; and fear fell on them all, and the name of the Lord Jesus was magnified.

2 Thess 1:12 that the name of our Lord Jesus Christ may

be glorified in you, and you in Him, according to the grace of our God and the Lord Jesus Christ.

Bringing forth fruits of righteousness.

John 15:8 By this My Father is glorified, that you bear much fruit; so you will be My disciples.

Phil 1:11 being filled with the fruits of righteousness which *are* by Jesus Christ, to the glory and praise of God.

Patience in affliction.

Is 24:15 Therefore glorify the Lord in the dawning light, The name of the Lord God of Israel in the coastlands of the sea.

Faithfulness.

1 Pet 4:11 If anyone speaks, *let him speak* as the oracles of God. If anyone ministers, *let him do it* as with the ability which God supplies, that in all things God may be glorified through Jesus Christ, to whom belong the glory and the dominion forever and ever. Amen.

Required in body and spirit.

1 Cor 6:20 For you were bought at a price; therefore glorify God in your body and in your spirit, which are God's.

Shall be universal.

Ps 86:9 All nations whom You have made Shall come and worship before You, O Lord, And shall glorify Your name.

Rev 5:13 And every creature which is in heaven and on the earth and under the earth and such as are in the sea, and all that are in them, I heard saying: "Blessing and honor and glory and power *Be* to Him who sits on the throne, And to the Lamb, forever and ever!"

Believers should

Resolve to.

Ps 69:30 I will praise the name of God with a song, And will magnify Him with thanksgiving.

Ps 118:28 You *are* my God, and I will praise You; *You are* my God, I will exalt You.

Unite in.

Ps 34:3 Oh, magnify the Lord with me, And let us exalt His name together.

Rom 15:6 that you may with one mind *and* one mouth glorify the God and Father of our Lord Jesus Christ.

Persevere in.

Ps 86:12 I will praise You, O Lord my God, with all my heart, And I will glorify Your name forevermore.

Do all to.

1 Cor 10:31 Therefore, whether you eat or drink, or whatever you do, do all to the glory of God.

All the blessings of God are designed to lead to.

Is 60:21 Also your people *shall* all *be* righteous; They shall inherit the land forever, The branch of My planting, The work of My hands, That I may be glorified.

Is 61:3 To console those who mourn in Zion, To give them beauty for ashes, The oil of joy for mourning, The garment of praise for the spirit of heaviness; That they may be called trees of righteousness, The planting of the Lord, that He may be glorified."

The holy example of believers may lead others to.

Matt 5:16 Let your light so shine before men, that they may see your good works and glorify your Father in heaven.

1 Pet 2:12 having your conduct honorable among the Gentiles, that when they speak against you as evildoers, they may, by *your* good works which they observe, glorify God in the day of visitation.

All, by nature, fail in.

Rom 3:23 for all have sinned and fall short of the glory of God,

The wicked averse to.

Dan 5:23 And you have lifted yourself up against the Lord of heaven. They have brought the vessels of His house before you, and you and your lords, your wives and your concubines, have drunk wine from them. And you have praised the gods of silver and gold, bronze and iron, wood and stone, which do not see or hear or know; and the God who *holds* your breath in His hand and owns all your ways, you have not glorified.

Rom 1:21 because, although they knew God, they did not glorify *Him* as God, nor were thankful, but became futile in their thoughts, and their foolish hearts were darkened.

Punishment for not.

Dan 5:23 And you have lifted yourself up against the Lord of heaven. They have brought the vessels of His house before you, and you and your lords, your wives and your concubines, have drunk wine from them. And you have praised the gods of silver and gold, bronze and iron, wood and stone, which do not see or hear or know; and the God who *holds* your breath in His hand and owns all your ways, you have not glorified.

Dan 5:30 That very night Belshazzar, king of the Chaldeans, was slain.

Mal 2:2 If you will not hear, And if you will not take *it* to heart, To give glory to My name," Says the Lord of hosts, "I will send a curse upon you, And I will curse your blessings. Yes, I have cursed them already, Because you do not take *it* to heart.

Acts 12:23 Then immediately an angel of the Lord struck him, because he did not give glory to God. And he was eaten by worms and died.

Rom 1:21 because, although they knew God, they did not glorify *Him* as God, nor were thankful, but became futile in their thoughts, and their foolish hearts were darkened.

Heavenly host engaged in.

Rev 4:11 "You are worthy, O Lord, To receive glory and honor and power; For You created all things, And by Your will they exist and were created."

Exemplified by

David.

Ps 57:5 Be exalted, O God, above the heavens; *Let* Your glory *be* above all the earth.

The multitude.

Matt 9:8 Now when the multitudes saw *it*, they marveled and glorified God, who had given such power to men.

Matt 15:31 So the multitude marveled when they saw *the* mute speaking, *the* maimed made whole, *the* lame walking, and *the* blind seeing; and they glorified the God of Israel.

Mary.

Luke 1:46 And Mary said: "My soul magnifies the Lord,

The angels.

Luke 2:14 "Glory to God in the highest, And on earth peace, goodwill toward men!"

The shepherds.

Luke 2:20 Then the shepherds returned, glorifying and praising God for all the things that they had heard and seen, as it was told them.

The paralytic.

Luke 5:25 Immediately he rose up before them, took up what he had been lying on, and departed to his own house, glorifying God.

The woman with an infirmity.

Luke 13:13 And He laid *His* hands on her, and immediately she was made straight, and glorified God.

The leper.

Luke 17:15 And one of them, when he saw that he was healed, returned, and with a loud voice glorified God,

The blind man.

Luke 18:43 And immediately he received his sight, and followed Him, glorifying God. And all the people, when they saw *it,* gave praise to God.

The centurion.

Luke 23:47 So when the centurion saw what had happened, he glorified God, saying, "Certainly this was a righteous Man!"

The church at Jerusalem.

Acts 11:18 When they heard these things they became silent; and they glorified God, saying, "Then God has also granted to the Gentiles repentance to life."

The Gentiles at Antioch.

Acts 13:48 Now when the Gentiles heard this, they were glad and glorified the word of the Lord. And as many as had been appointed to eternal life believed.

Abraham.

Rom 4:20 He did not waver at the promise of God through unbelief, but was strengthened in faith, giving glory to God,

Paul.

Rom 11:36 For of Him and through Him and to Him *are* all things, to whom *be* glory forever. Amen.

GLORY

God is, to His people.

Ps 3:3 But You, O LORD, *are* a shield for me, My glory and the One who lifts up my head.

Zech 2:5 For I,' says the LORD, 'will be a wall of fire all around her, and I will be the glory in her midst.' "

Christ is, to His people.

Is 60:1 Arise, shine; For your light has come! And the glory of the LORD is risen upon you.

Luke 2:32 A light to *bring* revelation to the Gentiles, And the glory of Your people Israel."

The gospel ordained to be, to believers.

1 Cor 2:7 But we speak the wisdom of God in a mystery, the hidden *wisdom* which God ordained before the ages for our glory,

Of the gospel, exceeds that of the law.

2 Cor 3:9–10 For if the ministry of condemnation *had* glory, the ministry of righteousness exceeds much more in glory. **10** For even what was made glorious had no glory in this respect, because of the glory that excels.

Is response of believers to Christ and the gospel.

1 Pet 1:8 whom having not seen you love. Though now you do not see *Him,* yet believing, you rejoice with joy inexpressible and full of glory,

Spiritual,

Is given by God.

Ps 84:11 For the LORD God *is* a sun and shield; The LORD will give grace and glory; No good *thing* will He withhold From those who walk uprightly.

Is given by Christ.

John 17:22 And the glory which You gave Me I have given them, that they may be one just as We are one:

Is the work of the Holy Spirit.

2 Cor 3:18 But we all, with unveiled face, beholding as in a mirror the glory of the Lord, are being transformed into the same image from glory to glory, just as by the Spirit of the Lord.

Eternal,

Accompanies salvation by Christ.

2 Tim 2:10 Therefore I endure all things for the sake of the elect, that they also may obtain the salvation which is in Christ Jesus with eternal glory.

Heb 2:10 For it was fitting for Him, for whom *are* all things and by whom *are* all things, in bringing many sons to glory, to make the captain of their salvation perfect through sufferings.

Inherited by believers.

1 Sam 2:8 He raises the poor from the dust *And* lifts the beggar from the ash heap, To set *them* among princes And make them inherit the throne of glory. "For the pillars of the earth *are* the LORD's, And He has set the world upon them.

Ps 73:24 You will guide me with Your counsel, And afterward receive me *to* glory.

Prov 3:35 The wise shall inherit glory, But shame shall be the legacy of fools.

Col 3:4 When Christ *who is* our life appears, then you also will appear with Him in glory.

1 Pet 5:10 But may the God of all grace, who called us to His eternal glory by Christ Jesus, after you have suffered a while, perfect, establish, strengthen, and settle *you.*

Believers called to.

Rom 9:23 and that He might make known the riches of His glory on the vessels of mercy, which He had prepared beforehand for glory,

2 Thess 2:14 to which He called you by our gospel, for the obtaining of the glory of our Lord Jesus Christ.

1 Pet 5:10 But may the God of all grace, who called us to His eternal glory by Christ Jesus, after you have suffered a while, perfect, establish, strengthen, and settle *you.*

Enhanced by present afflictions.

2 Cor 4:17 For our light affliction, which is but for a moment, is working for us a far more exceeding *and* eternal weight of glory,

Present afflictions not worthy to be compared with.

Rom 8:18 For I consider that the sufferings of this present time are not worthy *to be compared* with the glory which shall be revealed in us.

Of Israel, shall be rich and abundant.

Is 60:11–13 Therefore your gates shall be open continually; They shall not be shut day or night, That *men* may bring to you the wealth of the Gentiles, And their kings in procession. **12** For the nation and kingdom which will not serve you shall perish, And *those* nations shall be utterly ruined. **13** "The glory of Lebanon shall come to you, The cypress, the pine, and the box tree together, To beautify the place of My sanctuary; And I will make the place of My feet glorious.

The bodies of believers shall be raised in.

1 Cor 15:43 It is sown in dishonor, it is raised in glory. It is sown in weakness, it is raised in power.

Phil 3:21 who will transform our lowly body that it may be conformed to His glorious body, according to the working by which He is able even to subdue all things to Himself.

Believers shall be the, of their ministers.

1 Thess 2:19–20 For what *is* our hope, or joy, or crown of rejoicing? *Is it* not even you in the presence of our Lord Jesus Christ at His coming? **20** For you are our glory and joy.

Temporal,

Is given by God.

Dan 2:37 You, O king, *are* a king of kings. For the God of heaven has given you a kingdom, power, strength, and glory;

Passes away.

1 Pet 1:24 because *"All flesh is as grass, And all the glory of man as the flower of the grass. The grass withers, And its flower falls away,*

The devil tries to seduce by.

Matt 4:8 Again, the devil took Him up on an exceedingly high mountain, and showed Him all the kingdoms of the world and their glory.

Should not be sought from man.

Matt 6:2 Therefore, when you do a charitable deed, do not sound a trumpet before you as the hypocrites do in the synagogues and in the streets, that they may have glory from men. Assuredly, I say to you, they have their reward.

1 Thess 2:6 Nor did we seek glory from men, either from you or from others, when we might have made demands as apostles of Christ.

Of the wicked,

Is in their shame.

Hos 4:7 "The more they increased, The more they sinned against Me; I will change their glory into shame.

Phil 3:19 whose end *is* destruction, whose god *is their* belly, and *whose* glory *is* in their shame—who set their mind on earthly things.

Ends in destruction.

Is 5:14 Therefore Sheol has enlarged itself And opened its mouth beyond measure; Their glory and their multitude and their pomp, And he who is jubilant, shall descend into it.

GLUTTONY

Christ falsely accused of.

Matt 11:19 The Son of Man came eating and drinking, and they say, 'Look, a glutton and a winebibber, a friend of tax collectors and sinners!' But wisdom is justified by her children."

The wicked addicted to.

Phil 3:19 whose end *is* destruction, whose god *is their* belly, and *whose* glory *is* in their shame—who set their mind on earthly things.

Jude 1:12 These are spots in your love feasts, while they feast with you without fear, serving *only* themselves. *They are* clouds without water, carried about by the winds; late autumn trees without fruit, twice dead, pulled up by the roots;

Leads to

Carnal security.

Is 22:13 But instead, joy and gladness, Slaying oxen and killing sheep, Eating meat and drinking wine: "Let us eat and drink, for tomorrow we die!"

1 Cor 15:32 If, in the manner of men, I have fought with beasts at Ephesus, what advantage *is it* to me? If *the* dead do not rise, *"Let us eat and drink, for tomorrow we die!"*

Luke 12:19 And I will say to my soul, "Soul, you have many goods laid up for many years; take your ease; eat, drink, *and* be merry." '

Poverty.

Prov 23:21 For the drunkard and the glutton will come to poverty, And drowsiness will clothe *a man* with rags.

Of princes, ruinous to their people.

Eccl 10:16–17 Woe to you, O land, when your king *is* a child, And your princes feast in the morning! **17** Blessed *are* you, O land, when your king *is* the son of nobles, And your princes feast at the proper time— For strength and not for drunkenness!

A part of the past for believers.

1 Pet 4:3 For we *have spent* enough of our past lifetime in doing the will of the Gentiles—when we walked in lewdness, lusts, drunkenness, revelries, drinking parties, and abominable idolatries.

Caution against.

Prov 23:2–3 And put a knife to your throat If you *are* a man given to appetite. **3** Do not desire his delicacies, For they *are* deceptive food.

Luke 21:34 "But take heed to yourselves, lest your hearts be weighed down with carousing, drunkenness, and cares of this life, and that Day come on you unexpectedly.

Rom 13:13–14 Let us walk properly, as in the day, not in revelry and drunkenness, not in lewdness and lust, not in strife and envy. **14** But put on the Lord Jesus Christ, and make no provision for the flesh, to *fulfill its* lusts.

Pray against temptations to.

Ps 141:4 Do not incline my heart to any evil thing, To practice wicked works With men who work iniquity; And do not let me eat of their delicacies.

Punishment of.

Num 11:33–34 But while the meat *was* still between their teeth, before it was chewed, the wrath of the LORD was aroused against the people, and the LORD struck the people with a very great plague. 34 So he called the name of that place Kibroth Hattaavah, because there they buried the people who had yielded to craving.

Deut 21:21 Then all the men of his city shall stone him to death with stones; so you shall put away the evil from among you, and all Israel shall hear and fear.

Ps 78:31 The wrath of God came against them, And slew the stoutest of them, And struck down the choice *men* of Israel.

Amos 6:4 Who lie on beds of ivory, Stretch out on your couches, Eat lambs from the flock And calves from the midst of the stall;

Amos 6:7 Therefore they shall now go captive as the first of the captives, And those who recline at banquets shall be removed.

Danger of, illustrated.

Luke 12:45–46 But if that servant says in his heart, 'My master is delaying his coming,' and begins to beat the male and female servants, and to eat and drink and be drunk, 46 the master of that servant will come on a day when he is not looking for *him*, and at an hour when he is not aware, and will cut him in two and appoint *him* his portion with the unbelievers.

Examples of,

Esau.

Gen 25:30–34 And Esau said to Jacob, "Please feed me with that same red *stew*, for I *am* weary." Therefore his name was called Edom. 31 But Jacob said, "Sell me your birthright as of this day." 32 And Esau said, "Look, I *am* about to die; so what *is* this birthright to me?" 33 Then Jacob said, "Swear to me as of this day." So he swore to him, and sold his birthright to Jacob. 34 And Jacob gave Esau bread and stew of lentils; then he ate and drank, arose, and went his way. Thus Esau despised *his* birthright.

Heb 12:16–17 lest there *be* any fornicator or profane person like Esau, who for one morsel of food sold his birthright. 17 For you know that afterward, when he wanted to inherit the blessing, he was rejected, for he found no place for repentance, though he sought it diligently with tears.

Israel.

Num 11:4 Now the mixed multitude who were among them yielded to intense craving; so the children of Israel also wept again and said: "Who will give us meat to eat?

Ps 78:18 And they tested God in their heart By asking for the food of their fancy.

The sons of Eli.

1 Sam 2:12–17 Now the sons of Eli *were* corrupt; they did not know the LORD. 13 And the priests' custom with the people *was that* when any man offered a sacrifice, the priest's servant would come with a three-pronged fleshhook in his hand while the meat was boiling. 14 Then he would thrust *it* into the pan, or kettle, or caldron, or pot; and the priest would take for himself all that the fleshhook brought up. So they did in Shiloh to all the Israelites who came there. 15 Also, before they burned the fat, the priest's servant would come and say to the man who sacrificed, "Give meat for roasting to the priest, for he will not take boiled meat from you, but raw." 16 And *if* the man said to him, "They should really burn the fat first; *then* you may take *as much* as your heart desires," he would then answer him, "*No*, but you must give *it* now; and if not, I will take *it* by force." 17 Therefore the sin of the young men was very great before the LORD, for men abhorred the offering of the LORD.

Belshazzar.

Dan 5:1 Belshazzar the king made a great feast for a thousand of his lords, and drank wine in the presence of the thousand.

GOAT, THE

Clean and fit for food.

Deut 14:4–5 These *are* the animals which you may eat: the ox, the sheep, the goat, 5 the deer, the gazelle, the roe deer, the wild goat, the mountain goat, the antelope, and the mountain sheep.

Offered in sacrifice.

Gen 15:9 So He said to him, "Bring Me a three-year-old heifer, a three-year-old female goat, a three-year-old ram, a turtledove, and a young pigeon."

Lev 16:5 And he shall take from the congregation of the children of Israel two kids of the goats as a sin offering, and one ram as a burnt offering.

Lev 16:7 He shall take the two goats and present them before the LORD *at* the door of the tabernacle of meeting.

The male, best for sacrifice.

Lev 22:19 *you shall offer* of your own free will a male without blemish from the cattle, from the sheep, or from the goats.

Ps 50:9 I will not take a bull from your house, *Nor* goats out of your folds.

Firstborn of, not redeemed.

Num 18:17 But the firstborn of a cow, the firstborn of a sheep, or the firstborn of a goat you shall not redeem; they *are* holy. You shall sprinkle their blood on the altar, and burn their fat *as* an offering made by fire for a sweet aroma to the LORD.

Jews had large flocks of.

Gen 32:14 two hundred female goats and twenty male goats, two hundred ewes and twenty rams,

1 Sam 25:2 Now *there was* a man in Maon whose business *was* in Carmel, and the man *was* very rich. He had three thousand sheep and a thousand goats. And he was shearing his sheep in Carmel.

Most profitable to the owner.

Prov 27:26 The lambs *will provide* your clothing, And the goats the price of a field;

Milk of, used as food.

Prov 27:27 *You shall have* enough goats' milk for your

food, For the food of your household, And the nourishment of your maidservants.

The young of,

Called kids.

Gen 37:31 So they took Joseph's tunic, killed a kid of the goats, and dipped the tunic in the blood.

Kept in small flocks.

1 Kin 20:27 And the children of Israel were mustered and given provisions, and they went against them. Now the children of Israel encamped before them like two little flocks of goats, while the Syrians filled the countryside.

Fed near the shepherds' tents.

Song 1:8 If you do not know, O fairest among women, Follow in the footsteps of the flock, And feed your little goats Beside the shepherds' tents.

Not to be boiled in mother's milk.

Ex 23:19 The first of the firstfruits of your land you shall bring into the house of the LORD your God. You shall not boil a young goat in its mother's milk.

Offered in sacrifice.

Lev 4:23 or if his sin which he has committed comes to his knowledge, he shall bring as his offering a kid of the goats, a male without blemish.

Lev 5:6 and he shall bring his trespass offering to the LORD for his sin which he has committed, a female from the flock, a lamb or a kid of the goats as a sin offering. So the priest shall make atonement for him concerning his sin.

Offered at the Passover.

Ex 12:5 Your lamb shall be without blemish, a male of the first year. You may take *it* from the sheep or from the goats.

2 Chr 35:7 Then Josiah gave the *lay* people lambs and young goats from the flock, all for Passover *offerings* for all who were present, to the number of thirty thousand, as well as three thousand cattle; these *were* from the king's possessions.

Considered a delicacy.

Gen 27:9 Go now to the flock and bring me from there two choice kids of the goats, and I will make savory food from them for your father, such as he loves.

Judg 6:19 So Gideon went in and prepared a young goat, and unleavened bread from an ephah of flour. The meat he put in a basket, and he put the broth in a pot; and he brought *them* out to Him under the terebinth tree and presented *them.*

Given as a present.

Gen 38:17 And he said, "I will send a young goat from the flock." So she said, "Will you give *me* a pledge till you send *it?* "

Judg 15:1 After a while, in the time of wheat harvest, it happened that Samson visited his wife with a young goat. And he said, "Let me go in to my wife, into *her* room." But her father would not permit him to go in.

The hair of,

Offered for the tabernacle.

Ex 25:4 blue, purple, and scarlet *thread,* fine linen, and goats' *hair;*

Ex 35:23 And every man, with whom was found blue,

purple, and scarlet *thread,* fine linen, goats' *hair,* red skins of rams, and badger skins, brought *them.*

Made into curtains, for covering the tabernacle.

Ex 35:26 And all the women whose hearts stirred with wisdom spun yarn of goats' *hair.*

Ex 36:14–18 He made curtains of goats' *hair* for the tent over the tabernacle; he made eleven curtains. **15** The length of each curtain *was* thirty cubits, and the width of each curtain four cubits; the eleven curtains *were* the same size. **16** He coupled five curtains by themselves and six curtains by themselves. **17** And he made fifty loops on the edge of the curtain that is outermost in one set, and fifty loops he made on the edge of the curtain of the second set. **18** He also made fifty bronze clasps to couple the tent together, that it might be one.

Made into pillows.

1 Sam 19:13 And Michal took an image and laid *it* in the bed, put a cover of goats' *hair* for his head, and covered *it* with clothes.

Skin of, often used as clothing.

Heb 11:37 They were stoned, they were sawn in two, were tempted, were slain with the sword. They wandered about in sheepskins and goatskins, being destitute, afflicted, tormented—

Bashan celebrated for.

Deut 32:14 Curds from the cattle, and milk of the flock, With fat of lambs; And rams of the breed of Bashan, and goats, With the choicest wheat; And you drank wine, the blood of the grapes.

The Arabians traded in.

Ezek 27:21 Arabia and all the princes of Kedar *were* your regular merchants. They traded with you in lambs, rams, and goats.

Flocks of, always led by a male.

Jer 50:8 "Move from the midst of Babylon, Go out of the land of the Chaldeans; And be like the rams before the flocks.

When wild, dwelt in the hills and rocks.

1 Sam 24:2 Then Saul took three thousand chosen men from all Israel, and went to seek David and his men on the Rocks of the Wild Goats.

Job 39:1 "Do you know the time when the wild mountain goats bear young? *Or* can you mark when the deer gives birth?

Ps 104:18 The high hills *are* for the wild goats; The cliffs are a refuge for the rock badgers.

Illustrative of

The Macedonian empire.

Dan 8:5 And as I was considering, suddenly a male goat came from the west, across the surface of the whole earth, without touching the ground; and the goat *had* a notable horn between his eyes.

Dan 8:21 And the male goat *is* the kingdom of Greece. The large horn that *is* between its eyes *is* the first king.

The wicked.

Zech 10:3 "My anger is kindled against the shepherds, And I will punish the goatherds. For the LORD of hosts will visit His flock, The house of Judah, And will make them as His royal horse in the battle.

Matt 25:32–33 All the nations will be gathered before Him, and He will separate them one from another, as a shepherd divides *his* sheep from the goats. **33** And He will set the sheep on His right hand, but the goats on the left.

GOD

Is a spirit.

John 4:24 God *is* Spirit, and those who worship Him must worship in spirit and truth."

2 Cor 3:17 Now the Lord is the Spirit; and where the Spirit of the Lord *is*, there *is* liberty.

Is declared to be

Light.

Is 60:19 "The sun shall no longer be your light by day, Nor for brightness shall the moon give light to you; But the LORD will be to you an everlasting light, And your God your glory.

James 1:17 Every good gift and every perfect gift is from above, and comes down from the Father of lights, with whom there is no variation or shadow of turning.

1 John 1:5 This is the message which we have heard from Him and declare to you, that God is light and in Him is no darkness at all.

Love.

1 John 4:8 He who does not love does not know God, for God is love.

1 John 4:16 And we have known and believed the love that God has for us. God is love, and he who abides in love abides in God, and God in him.

Invisible.

Job 23:8–9 "Look, I go forward, but He is not *there*, And backward, but I cannot perceive Him; **9** When He works on the left hand, I cannot behold *Him*; When He turns to the right hand, I cannot see *Him*.

John 1:18 No one has seen God at any time. The only begotten Son, who is in the bosom of the Father, He has declared *Him*.

John 5:37 And the Father Himself, who sent Me, has testified of Me. You have neither heard His voice at any time, nor seen His form.

Col 1:15 He is the image of the invisible God, the firstborn over all creation.

1 Tim 1:17 Now to the King eternal, immortal, invisible, to God who alone is wise, *be* honor and glory forever and ever. Amen.

Unsearchable.

Job 11:7 "Can you search out the deep things of God? Can you find out the limits of the Almighty?

Job 37:23 *As for* the Almighty, we cannot find Him; *He is* excellent in power, *In* judgment and abundant justice; He does not oppress.

Ps 145:3 Great *is* the LORD, and greatly to be praised; And His greatness *is* unsearchable.

Is 40:28 Have you not known? Have you not heard? The everlasting God, the LORD, The Creator of the ends of the earth, Neither faints nor is weary. His understanding is unsearchable.

Rom 11:33 Oh, the depth of the riches both of the wisdom and knowledge of God! How unsearchable *are* His judgments and His ways past finding out!

Incorruptible.

Rom 1:23 and changed the glory of the incorruptible God into an image made like corruptible man—and birds and four-footed animals and creeping things.

Eternal.

Deut 33:27 The eternal God *is your* refuge, And underneath *are* the everlasting arms; He will thrust out the enemy from before you, And will say, 'Destroy!'

Ps 90:2 Before the mountains were brought forth, Or ever You had formed the earth and the world, Even from everlasting to everlasting, You *are* God.

Rev 4:8–10 *The* four living creatures, each having six wings, were full of eyes around and within. And they do not rest day or night, saying: "Holy, holy, holy, Lord God Almighty, Who was and is and is to come!" **9** Whenever the living creatures give glory and honor and thanks to Him who sits on the throne, who lives forever and ever, **10** the twenty-four elders fall down before Him who sits on the throne and worship Him who lives forever and ever, and cast their crowns before the throne, saying:

Immortal.

1 Tim 1:17 Now to the King eternal, immortal, invisible, to God who alone is wise, *be* honor and glory forever and ever. Amen.

1 Tim 6:16 who alone has immortality, dwelling in unapproachable light, whom no man has seen or can see, to whom *be* honor and everlasting power. Amen.

Omnipotent.

Gen 17:1 When Abram was ninety-nine years old, the LORD appeared to Abram and said to him, "I *am* Almighty God; walk before Me and be blameless.

Ex 6:3 I appeared to Abraham, to Isaac, and to Jacob, as God Almighty, but *by* My name LORD I was not known to them.

Omniscient.

Ps 139:1–6 O LORD, You have searched me and known *me.* **2** You know my sitting down and my rising up; You understand my thought afar off. **3** You comprehend my path and my lying down, And are acquainted with all my ways. **4** For *there is* not a word on my tongue, *But* behold, O LORD, You know it altogether. **5** You have hedged me behind and before, And laid Your hand upon me. **6** *Such* knowledge *is* too wonderful for me; It is high, I cannot *attain* it.

Prov 5:21 For the ways of man *are* before the eyes of the LORD, And He ponders all his paths.

Omnipresent.

Ps 139:7 Where can I go from Your Spirit? Or where can I flee from Your presence?

Jer 23:23 "*Am* I a God near at hand," says the LORD, "And not a God afar off?

Immutable.

Ps 102:26–27 They will perish, but You will endure; Yes, they will all grow old like a garment; Like a cloak You will change them, And they will be changed. **27** But You *are* the same, And Your years will have no end.

James 1:17 Every good gift and every perfect gift is from above, and comes down from the Father of lights, with whom there is no variation or shadow of turning.

Alone is wise.

Rom 16:27 to God, alone wise, *be* glory through Jesus Christ forever. Amen.

1 Tim 1:17 Now to the King eternal, immortal, invisible, to God who alone is wise, *be* honor and glory forever and ever. Amen.

Glorious.

Ex 15:11 "Who *is* like You, O LORD, among the gods? Who *is* like You, glorious in holiness, Fearful in praises, doing wonders?

Ps 145:5 I will meditate on the glorious splendor of Your majesty, And on Your wondrous works.

Most High.

Ps 83:18 That they may know that You, whose name alone *is* the LORD, *Are* the Most High over all the earth.

Acts 7:48 "However, the Most High does not dwell in temples made with hands, as the prophet says:

Perfect.

Matt 5:48 Therefore you shall be perfect, just as your Father in heaven is perfect.

Holy.

Ps 99:9 Exalt the LORD our God, And worship at His holy hill; For the LORD our God *is* holy.

Is 5:16 But the LORD of hosts shall be exalted in judgment, And God who is holy shall be hallowed in righteousness.

Just.

Deut 32:4 He *is* the Rock, His work *is* perfect; For all His ways *are* justice, A God of truth and without injustice; Righteous and upright *is* He.

Is 45:21 Tell and bring forth *your case;* Yes, let them take counsel together. Who has declared this from ancient time? *Who* has told it from that time? *Have* not I, the LORD? And *there is* no other God besides Me, A just God and a Savior; *There is* none besides Me.

True.

Jer 10:10 But the LORD *is* the true God; He *is* the living God and the everlasting King. At His wrath the earth will tremble, And the nations will not be able to endure His indignation.

John 17:3 And this is eternal life, that they may know You, the only true God, and Jesus Christ whom You have sent.

Upright.

Ps 25:8 Good and upright *is* the LORD; Therefore He teaches sinners in the way.

Ps 92:15 To declare that the LORD is upright; *He is* my rock, and *there is* no unrighteousness in Him.

Righteous.

Ezra 9:15 O LORD God of Israel, You *are* righteous, for we are left as a remnant, as *it is* this day. Here we *are* before You, in our guilt, though no one can stand before You because of this!"

Ps 145:17 The LORD *is* righteous in all His ways, Gracious in all His works.

Good.

Ps 25:8 Good and upright *is* the LORD; Therefore He teaches sinners in the way.

Ps 119:68 You *are* good, and do good; Teach me Your statutes.

Great.

2 Chr 2:5 And the temple which I build *will be* great, for our God is greater than all gods.

Ps 86:10 For You *are* great, and do wondrous things; You alone *are* God.

Gracious.

Ex 34:6 And the LORD passed before him and proclaimed, "The LORD, the LORD God, merciful and gracious, longsuffering, and abounding in goodness and truth,

Ps 116:5 Gracious *is* the LORD, and righteous; Yes, our God *is* merciful.

Faithful.

1 Cor 10:13 No temptation has overtaken you except such as is common to man; but God *is* faithful, who will not allow you to be tempted beyond what you are able, but with the temptation will also make the way of escape, that you may be able to bear *it.*

1 Pet 4:19 Therefore let those who suffer according to the will of God commit their souls *to Him* in doing good, as to a faithful Creator.

Merciful.

Ex 34:6–7 And the LORD passed before him and proclaimed, "The LORD, the LORD God, merciful and gracious, longsuffering, and abounding in goodness and truth, 7 keeping mercy for thousands, forgiving iniquity and transgression and sin, by no means clearing *the guilty,* visiting the iniquity of the fathers upon the children and the children's children to the third and the fourth generation."

Ps 86:5 For You, Lord, *are* good, and ready to forgive, And abundant in mercy to all those who call upon You.

Longsuffering.

Num 14:18 'The LORD is longsuffering and abundant in mercy, forgiving iniquity and transgression; but He by no means clears *the guilty,* visiting the iniquity of the fathers on the children to the third and fourth generation.'

Mic 7:1 Woe is me! For I am like those who gather summer fruits, Like those who glean vintage grapes; *There is no* cluster to eat Of the first-ripe fruit *which* my soul desires.

Jealous.

Josh 24:19 But Joshua said to the people, "You cannot serve the LORD, for He *is* a holy God. He *is* a jealous God; He will not forgive your transgressions nor your sins.

Nah 1:2 God *is* jealous, and the LORD avenges; The LORD avenges and *is* furious. The LORD will take vengeance on His adversaries, And He reserves *wrath* for His enemies;

Compassionate.

2 Kin 13:23 But the LORD was gracious to them, had compassion on them, and regarded them, because of His covenant with Abraham, Isaac, and Jacob, and would not yet destroy them or cast them from His presence.

A consuming fire.

Heb 12:29 For our God *is* a consuming fire.

None equal to Him.

Ex 9:14 for at this time I will send all My plagues to your very heart, and on your servants and on your people, that you may know that *there is* none like Me in all the earth.

Deut 4:35 To you it was shown, that you might know that the LORD Himself *is* God; *there is* none other besides Him.

Deut 33:26 *"There is* no one like the God of Jeshurun, *Who* rides the heavens to help you, And in His excellency on the clouds.

2 Sam 7:22 Therefore You are great, O Lord GOD. For *there is* none like You, nor *is there any* God besides You, according to all that we have heard with our ears.

Is 43:10 "You *are* My witnesses," says the LORD, "And My servant whom I have chosen, That you may know and believe Me, And understand that I *am* He. Before Me there was no God formed, Nor shall there be after Me.

Is 44:6 "Thus says the LORD, the King of Israel, And his Redeemer, the LORD of hosts: 'I *am* the First and I *am* the Last; Besides Me *there is* no God.

Is 46:5 "To whom will you liken Me, and make *Me* equal And compare Me, that we should be alike?

Is 46:9 Remember the former things of old, For I *am* God, and *there is* no other; *I am* God, and *there is* none like Me,

Jer 10:6 Inasmuch as *there is* none like You, O LORD (You *are* great, and Your name *is* great in might),

Matt 19:17 So He said to him, "Why do you call Me good? No one *is* good but One, *that is,* God. But if you want to enter into life, keep the commandments."

Fills heaven and earth.

1 Kin 8:27 "But will God indeed dwell on the earth? Behold, heaven and the heaven of heavens cannot contain You. How much less this temple which I have built!

Jer 23:24 Can anyone hide himself in secret places, So I shall not see him?" says the LORD; "Do I not fill heaven and earth?" says the LORD.

Should be worshiped in spirit and in truth.

John 4:24 God *is* Spirit, and those who worship Him must worship in spirit and truth."

GOD, ACCESS TO

Is initiated by Him.

Ps 65:4 Blessed *is the man* You choose, And cause to approach *You, That* he may dwell in Your courts. We shall be satisfied with the goodness of Your house, Of Your holy temple.

Is by Christ.

John 10:7 Then Jesus said to them again, "Most assuredly, I say to you, I am the door of the sheep.

John 10:9 I am the door. If anyone enters by Me, he will be saved, and will go in and out and find pasture.

John 14:6 Jesus said to him, "I am the way, the truth, and the life. No one comes to the Father except through Me.

Rom 5:2 through whom also we have access by faith into this grace in which we stand, and rejoice in hope of the glory of God.

Eph 2:13 But now in Christ Jesus you who once were far off have been brought near by the blood of Christ.

Eph 3:12 in whom we have boldness and access with confidence through faith in Him.

Col 1:21–22 And you, who once were alienated and enemies in your mind by wicked works, yet now He has reconciled **22** in the body of His flesh through death, to present you holy, and blameless, and above reproach in His sight—

Heb 7:25 Therefore He is also able to save to the uttermost those who come to God through Him, since He always lives to make intercession for them.

Heb 10:19 Therefore, brethren, having boldness to enter the Holiest by the blood of Jesus,

1 Pet 3:18 For Christ also suffered once for sins, the just for the unjust, that He might bring us to God, being put to death in the flesh but made alive by the Spirit,

Is by the Holy Spirit.

Eph 2:18 For through Him we both have access by one Spirit to the Father.

Obtained through faith.

Acts 14:27 Now when they had come and gathered the church together, they reported all that God had done with them, and that He had opened the door of faith to the Gentiles.

Rom 5:2 through whom also we have access by faith into this grace in which we stand, and rejoice in hope of the glory of God.

Eph 3:12 in whom we have boldness and access with confidence through faith in Him.

Heb 11:6 But without faith *it is* impossible to please *Him,* for he who comes to God must believe that He is, and *that* He is a rewarder of those who diligently seek Him.

In prayer. *See* Prayer.

Deut 4:7 "For what great nation *is there* that has God *so* near to it, as the LORD our God *is* to us, for whatever *reason* we may call upon Him?

Ps 145:18 The LORD *is* near to all who call upon Him, To all who call upon Him in truth.

Matt 6:6 But you, when you pray, go into your room, and when you have shut your door, pray to your Father who *is* in the secret *place;* and your Father who sees in secret will reward you openly.

1 Pet 1:17 And if you call on the Father, who without partiality judges according to each one's work, conduct yourselves throughout the time of your stay *here* in fear;

To obtain mercy and grace.

Heb 4:16 Let us therefore come boldly to the throne of grace, that we may obtain mercy and find grace to help in time of need.

A privilege of believers.

Deut 4:7 "For what great nation *is there* that has God *so* near to it, as the LORD our God *is* to us, for whatever *reason* we may call upon Him?

Ps 15:1 LORD, who may abide in Your tabernacle? Who may dwell in Your holy hill?

Ps 23:6 Surely goodness and mercy shall follow me All the days of my life; And I will dwell in the house of the LORD Forever.

Ps 24:3–4 Who may ascend into the hill of the LORD? Or who may stand in His holy place? **4** He who has clean hands and a pure heart, Who has not lifted up his soul to an idol, Nor sworn deceitfully.

Believers have, with confidence.

Eph 3:12 in whom we have boldness and access with confidence through faith in Him.

Heb 4:16 Let us therefore come boldly to the throne of grace, that we may obtain mercy and find grace to help in time of need.

Heb 10:19–20 Therefore, brethren, having boldness to enter the Holiest by the blood of Jesus, **20** by a new and living way which He consecrated for us, through the veil, that is, His flesh,

Promised to repenting sinners. *See* Repentance.

Hos 14:2 Take words with you, And return to the LORD. Say to Him, "Take away all iniquity; Receive *us* graciously, For we will offer the sacrifices of our lips.

Joel 2:12 "Now, therefore," says the LORD, "Turn to Me with all your heart, With fasting, with weeping, and with mourning."

The wicked commanded to seek.

Is 55:6 Seek the LORD while He may be found, Call upon Him while He is near.

James 4:8 Draw near to God and He will draw near to you. Cleanse *your* hands, *you* sinners; and purify *your* hearts, *you* double-minded.

Promises connected with.

Is 55:3 Incline your ear, and come to Me. Hear, and your soul shall live; And I will make an everlasting covenant with you— The sure mercies of David.

Matt 6:6 But you, when you pray, go into your room, and when you have shut your door, pray to your Father who *is* in the secret *place;* and your Father who sees in secret will reward you openly.

James 4:8 Draw near to God and He will draw near to you. Cleanse *your* hands, *you* sinners; and purify *your* hearts, *you* double-minded.

Blessedness connected with.

Ps 16:11 You will show me the path of life; In Your presence *is* fullness of joy; At Your right hand *are* pleasures forevermore.

Ps 65:4 Blessed *is the man* You choose, And cause to approach *You, That* he may dwell in Your courts. We shall be satisfied with the goodness of Your house, Of Your holy temple.

Typified.

Lev 16:12–15 Then he shall take a censer full of burning coals of fire from the altar before the LORD, with his hands full of sweet incense beaten fine, and bring *it* inside the veil. **13** And he shall put the incense on the fire before the LORD, that the cloud of incense may cover the mercy seat that *is* on the Testimony, lest he die. **14** He shall take some of the blood of the bull and sprinkle *it* with his finger on the mercy seat on the east *side;* and before the mercy seat he shall sprin-

kle some of the blood with his finger seven times. **15** "Then he shall kill the goat of the sin offering, which *is* for the people, bring its blood inside the veil, do with that blood as he did with the blood of the bull, and sprinkle it on the mercy seat and before the mercy seat.

Heb 10:19–22 Therefore, brethren, having boldness to enter the Holiest by the blood of Jesus, **20** by a new and living way which He consecrated for us, through the veil, that is, His flesh, **21** and *having* a High Priest over the house of God, **22** let us draw near with a true heart in full assurance of faith, having our hearts sprinkled from an evil conscience and our bodies washed with pure water.

Signified.

Matt 27:51 Then, behold, the veil of the temple was torn in two from top to bottom; and the earth quaked, and the rocks were split,

Mark 15:38 Then the veil of the temple was torn in two from top to bottom.

Luke 23:45 Then the sun was darkened, and the veil of the temple was torn in two.

John 1:51 And He said to him, "Most assuredly, I say to you, hereafter you shall see heaven open, and the angels of God ascending and descending upon the Son of Man."

Not fully realized under Old Covenant.

Heb 9:6–15 Now when these things had been thus prepared, the priests always went into the first part of the tabernacle, performing *the services.* **7** But into the second part the high priest *went* alone once a year, not without blood, which he offered for himself and *for* the people's sins *committed* in ignorance; **8** the Holy Spirit indicating this, that the way into the Holiest of All was not yet made manifest while the first tabernacle was still standing. **9** It *was* symbolic for the present time in which both gifts and sacrifices are offered which cannot make him who performed the service perfect in regard to the conscience— **10** *concerned* only with foods and drinks, various washings, and fleshly ordinances imposed until the time of reformation. **11** But Christ came *as* High Priest of the good things to come, with the greater and more perfect tabernacle not made with hands, that is, not of this creation. **12** Not with the blood of goats and calves, but with His own blood He entered the Most Holy Place once for all, having obtained eternal redemption. **13** For if the blood of bulls and goats and the ashes of a heifer, sprinkling the unclean, sanctifies for the purifying of the flesh, **14** how much more shall the blood of Christ, who through the eternal Spirit offered Himself without spot to God, cleanse your conscience from dead works to serve the living God? **15** And for this reason He is the Mediator of the new covenant, by means of death, for the redemption of the transgressions under the first covenant, that those who are called may receive the promise of the eternal inheritance.

Moses had.

Ex 24:2 And Moses alone shall come near the LORD, but they shall not come near; nor shall the people go up with him."

Ex 34:4–7 So he cut two tablets of stone like the first

ones. Then Moses rose early in the morning and went up Mount Sinai, as the LORD had commanded him; and he took in his hand the two tablets of stone. 5 Now the LORD descended in the cloud and stood with him there, and proclaimed the name of the LORD. 6 And the LORD passed before him and proclaimed, "The LORD, the LORD God, merciful and gracious, longsuffering, and abounding in goodness and truth, 7 keeping mercy for thousands, forgiving iniquity and transgression and sin, by no means clearing *the guilty,* visiting the iniquity of the fathers upon the children and the children's children to the third and the fourth generation."

GOD, THE COUNSELS AND PURPOSES OF

Excellence of.

Is 25:1 O LORD, You *are* my God. I will exalt You, I will praise Your name, For You have done wonderful *things; Your* counsels of old *are* faithfulness *and* truth.

Is 28:29 This also comes from the LORD of hosts, *Who* is wonderful in counsel *and* excellent in guidance.

Jer 32:19 *You are* great in counsel and mighty in work, for your eyes *are* open to all the ways of the sons of men, to give everyone according to his ways and according to the fruit of his doings.

Immutability of.

Ps 33:11 The counsel of the LORD stands forever, The plans of His heart to all generations.

Prov 19:21 There are many plans in a man's heart, Nevertheless the LORD's counsel—that will stand.

Is 14:24 The LORD of hosts has sworn, saying, "Surely, as I have thought, so it shall come to pass, And as I have purposed, *so* it shall stand:

Is 14:27 For the LORD of hosts has purposed, And who will annul *it?* His hand *is* stretched out, And who will turn it back?"

Is 46:11 Calling a bird of prey from the east, The man who executes My counsel, from a far country. Indeed I have spoken *it;* I will also bring it to pass. I have purposed *it;* I will also do it.

Jer 4:28 For this shall the earth mourn, And the heavens above be black, Because I have spoken. I have purposed and will not relent, Nor will I turn back from it.

Rom 9:11 (for *the children* not yet being born, nor having done any good or evil, that the purpose of God according to election might stand, not of works but of Him who calls)

Heb 6:17 Thus God, determining to show more abundantly to the heirs of promise the immutability of His counsel, confirmed *it* by an oath,

Sovereignty and eternality of.

Is 40:13–14 Who has directed the Spirit of the LORD, Or *as* His counselor has taught Him? **14** With whom did He take counsel, and *who* instructed Him, And taught Him in the path of justice? Who taught Him knowledge, And showed Him the way of understanding?

Dan 4:35 All the inhabitants of the earth *are* reputed as nothing; He does according to His will in the army of heaven And *among* the inhabitants of the earth. No one can restrain His hand Or say to Him, "What have You done?"

Eph 3:11 according to the eternal purpose which He accomplished in Christ Jesus our Lord,

Sufferings and death of Christ were according to.

Acts 2:23 Him, being delivered by the determined purpose and foreknowledge of God, you have taken by lawless hands, have crucified, and put to death;

Acts 4:28 to do whatever Your hand and Your purpose determined before to be done.

Believers saved and united according to.

Rom 8:28 And we know that all things work together for good to those who love God, to those who are the called according to *His* purpose.

Eph 1:9–11 having made known to us the mystery of His will, according to His good pleasure which He purposed in Himself, **10** that in the dispensation of the fullness of the times He might gather together in one all things in Christ, both which are in heaven and which are on earth—in Him. **11** In Him also we have obtained an inheritance, being predestined according to the purpose of Him who works all things according to the counsel of His will,

2 Tim 1:9 who has saved us and called *us* with a holy calling, not according to our works, but according to His own purpose and grace which was given to us in Christ Jesus before time began,

Should obey.

Jer 49:20 Therefore hear the counsel of the LORD that He has taken against Edom, And His purposes that He has proposed against the inhabitants of Teman: Surely the least of the flock shall draw them out; Surely He shall make their dwelling places desolate with them.

Jer 50:45 Therefore hear the counsel of the LORD that He has taken against Babylon, And His purposes that He has proposed against the land of the Chaldeans: Surely the least of the flock shall draw them out; Surely He will make their dwelling place desolate with them.

Mystery of.

Deut 29:29 "The secret *things belong* to the LORD our God, but those *things which are* revealed *belong* to us and to our children forever, that *we* may do all the words of this law.

Matt 24:36 "But of that day and hour no one knows, not even the angels of heaven, but My Father only.

Acts 1:7 And He said to them, "It is not for you to know times or seasons which the Father has put in His own authority.

The wicked

Do not understand.

Mic 4:12 But they do not know the thoughts of the LORD, Nor do they understand His counsel; For He will gather them like sheaves to the threshing floor.

Despise.

Is 5:19 That say, "Let Him make speed *and* hasten His work, That we may see *it;* And let the counsel of the Holy One of Israel draw near and come, That we may know *it.*"

Reject.

Luke 7:30 But the Pharisees and lawyers rejected the will of God for themselves, not having been baptized by him.

GOD, THE ETERNALITY OF

His nature is without beginning or end.

Ps 90:2 Before the mountains were brought forth, Or ever You had formed the earth and the world, Even from everlasting to everlasting, You *are* God.

Ps 106:48 Blessed *be* the LORD God of Israel From everlasting to everlasting! And let all the people say, "Amen!" Praise the LORD!

Rev 4:9–10 Whenever the living creatures give glory and honor and thanks to Him who sits on the throne, who lives forever and ever, **10** the twenty-four elders fall down before Him who sits on the throne and worship Him who lives forever and ever, and cast their crowns before the throne, saying:

Rev 16:5 And I heard the angel of the waters saying: "You are righteous, O Lord, The One who is and who was and who is to be, Because You have judged these things.

Shown in His creative work.

Ps 102:25–27 Of old You laid the foundation of the earth, And the heavens *are* the work of Your hands. **26** They will perish, but You will endure; Yes, they will all grow old like a garment; Like a cloak You will change them, And they will be changed. **27** But You *are* the same, And Your years will have no end.

As Father.

Is 9:6 For unto us a Child is born, Unto us a Son is given; And the government will be upon His shoulder. And His name will be called Wonderful, Counselor, Mighty God, Everlasting Father, Prince of Peace.

As King.

1 Tim 1:17 Now to the King eternal, immortal, invisible, to God who alone is wise, *be* honor and glory forever and ever. Amen.

Revealed in His power. *See* God, Power of.

Rom 1:20 For since the creation of the world His invisible *attributes* are clearly seen, being understood by the things that are made, *even* His eternal power and Godhead, so that they are without excuse,

GOD, THE FAITHFULNESS OF

Is part of His character.

Is 49:7 Thus says the LORD, The Redeemer of Israel, their Holy One, To Him whom man despises, To Him whom the nation abhors, To the Servant of rulers: "Kings shall see and arise, Princes also shall worship, Because of the LORD who is faithful, The Holy One of Israel; And He has chosen You."

1 Cor 1:9 God *is* faithful, by whom you were called into the fellowship of His Son, Jesus Christ our Lord.

1 Thess 5:24 He who calls you *is* faithful, who also will do *it*.

Is declared to be

Great.

Lam 3:23 *They are* new every morning; Great *is* Your faithfulness.

Established.

Ps 89:2 For I have said, "Mercy shall be built up forever; Your faithfulness You shall establish in the very heavens."

Incomparable.

Ps 89:8 O LORD God of hosts, Who *is* mighty like You, O LORD? Your faithfulness also surrounds You.

Unfailing.

Ps 89:33 Nevertheless My lovingkindness I will not utterly take from him, Nor allow My faithfulness to fail.

2 Tim 2:13 If we are faithless, He remains faithful; He cannot deny Himself.

Infinite.

Ps 36:5 Your mercy, O LORD, *is* in the heavens; Your faithfulness *reaches* to the clouds.

Everlasting.

Ps 119:90 Your faithfulness *endures* to all generations; You established the earth, and it abides.

Ps 146:6 Who made heaven and earth, The sea, and all that *is* in them; Who keeps truth forever,

Should be pleaded in prayer.

Ps 143:1 Hear my prayer, O LORD, Give ear to my supplications! In Your faithfulness answer me, *And* in Your righteousness.

Should be proclaimed.

Ps 40:10 I have not hidden Your righteousness within my heart; I have declared Your faithfulness and Your salvation; I have not concealed Your lovingkindness and Your truth From the great assembly.

Ps 89:1 I will sing of the mercies of the LORD forever; With my mouth will I make known Your faithfulness to all generations.

Manifested

In His counsels.

Is 25:1 O LORD, You *are* my God. I will exalt You, I will praise Your name, For You have done wonderful *things*; Your counsels of old *are* faithfulness *and* truth.

In afflicting believers.

Ps 119:75 I know, O LORD, that Your judgments *are* right, And *that* in faithfulness You have afflicted me.

In fulfilling His promises.

1 Kin 8:20 So the LORD has fulfilled His word which He spoke; and I have filled the position of my father David, and sit on the throne of Israel, as the LORD promised; and I have built a temple for the name of the LORD God of Israel.

Ps 132:11 The LORD has sworn *in* truth to David; He will not turn from it: "I will set upon your throne the fruit of your body.

Mic 7:20 You will give truth to Jacob *And* mercy to Abraham, Which You have sworn to our fathers From days of old.

Heb 10:23 Let us hold fast the confession of *our* hope without wavering, for He who promised *is* faithful.

In keeping His covenant.

Deut 7:9 "Therefore know that the LORD your God, He is God, the faithful God who keeps covenant and mercy for a thousand generations with those who love Him and keep His commandments;

Ps 111:5 He has given food to those who fear Him; He will ever be mindful of His covenant.

In executing His judgments.

Jer 23:20 The anger of the LORD will not turn back Until He has executed and performed the thoughts of His heart. In the latter days you will understand it perfectly.

Jer 51:29 And the land will tremble and sorrow; For every purpose of the LORD shall be performed against Babylon, To make the land of Babylon a desolation without inhabitant.

In helping believers endure temptations.

1 Cor 10:13 No temptation has overtaken you except such as is common to man; but God is faithful, who will not allow you to be tempted beyond what you are able, but with the temptation will also make the way of escape, that you may be able to bear *it*.

In forgiving sins.

1 John 1:9 If we confess our sins, He is faithful and just to forgive us *our* sins and to cleanse us from all unrighteousness.

To believers.

Ps 89:24 "But My faithfulness and My mercy *shall be* with him, And in My name his horn shall be exalted.

2 Thess 3:3 But the Lord is faithful, who will establish you and guard *you* from the evil one.

Believers encouraged to depend on.

1 Pet 4:19 Therefore let those who suffer according to the will of God commit their souls *to Him* in doing good, as to a faithful Creator.

Will be praised.

Ps 89:5 And the heavens will praise Your wonders, O LORD; Your faithfulness also in the assembly of the saints.

Ps 92:2 To declare Your lovingkindness in the morning, And Your faithfulness every night,

GOD, THE FAVOR OF

Christ the special object of.

Luke 2:52 And Jesus increased in wisdom and stature, and in favor with God and men.

Is the source of

Mercy.

Is 60:10 "The sons of foreigners shall build up your walls, And their kings shall minister to you; For in My wrath I struck you, But in My favor I have had mercy on you.

Spiritual life.

Ps 30:5 For His anger is *but for* a moment, His favor *is for* life; Weeping may endure for a night, But joy *comes* in the morning.

Spiritual wisdom leads to.

Prov 8:35 For whoever finds me finds life, And obtains favor from the LORD;

Mercy and truth lead to.

Prov 3:3–4 Let not mercy and truth forsake you; Bind them around your neck, Write them on the tablet of your heart, 4 *And* so find favor and high esteem In the sight of God and man.

Believers

Obtain.

Prov 12:2 A good *man* obtains favor from the LORD, But a man of wicked intentions He will condemn.

Surrounded by.

Ps 5:12 For You, O LORD, will bless the righteous; With favor You will surround him as *with* a shield.

Strengthened by.

Ps 30:7 LORD, by Your favor You have made my mountain stand strong; You hid Your face, *and* I was troubled.

Victorious through.

Ps 44:3 For they did not gain possession of the land by their own sword, Nor did their own arm save them; But it was Your right hand, Your arm, and the light of Your countenance, Because You favored them.

Preserved through.

Job 10:12 You have granted me life and favor, And Your care has preserved my spirit.

Exalted in.

Ps 89:17 For You *are* the glory of their strength, And in Your favor our horn is exalted.

Sometimes tempted to doubt.

Ps 77:7 Will the Lord cast off forever? And will He be favorable no more?

Should pray for.

Ex 33:12 Then Moses said to the LORD, "See, You say to me, 'Bring up this people.' But You have not let me know whom You will send with me. Yet You have said, 'I know you by name, and you have also found grace in My sight.'

Num 11:15 If You treat me like this, please kill me here and now—if I have found favor in Your sight—and do not let me see my wretchedness!"

Job 33:26 He shall pray to God, and He will delight in him, He shall see His face with joy, For He restores to man His righteousness.

Ps 106:4 Remember me, O LORD, with the favor *You have toward* Your people. Oh, visit me with Your salvation,

Ps 119:58 I entreated Your favor with *my* whole heart; Be merciful to me according to Your word.

Should acknowledge.

Ps 85:1 LORD, You have been favorable to Your land; You have brought back the captivity of Jacob.

Domestic blessings traced to.

Prov 18:22 *He who* finds a wife finds a good *thing,* And obtains favor from the LORD.

Defeat of enemies evidence of.

Ps 41:11 By this I know that You are well pleased with me, Because my enemy does not triumph over me.

The wicked

Uninfluenced by.

Is 26:10 Let grace be shown to the wicked, *Yet* he will not learn righteousness; In the land of uprightness he will deal unjustly, And will not behold the majesty of the LORD.

Do not obtain.

Is 27:11 When its boughs are withered, they will be broken off; The women come *and* set them on fire. For it *is* a people of no understanding; Therefore He who made them will not have mercy on them, And He who formed them will show them no favor.

Jer 16:13 Therefore I will cast you out of this land into a land that you do not know, neither you nor your fathers; and there you shall serve other gods day and night, where I will not show you favor.'

Examples of those who received,

Naphtali.

Deut 33:23 And of Naphtali he said: "O Naphtali, satisfied with favor, And full of the blessing of the LORD, Possess the west and the south."

Samuel.

1 Sam 2:26 And the child Samuel grew in stature, and in favor both with the LORD and men.

Job.

Job 10:12 You have granted me life and favor, And Your care has preserved my spirit.

Mary.

Luke 1:28 And having come in, the angel said to her, "Rejoice, highly favored *one*, the Lord *is* with you; blessed *are* you among women!"

Luke 1:30 Then the angel said to her, "Do not be afraid, Mary, for you have found favor with God.

David.

Acts 7:46 who found favor before God and asked to find a dwelling for the God of Jacob.

GOD, THE GLORY OF

The supreme purpose of redemption.

Eph 1:12 that we who first trusted in Christ should be to the praise of His glory.

Every tongue should confess Christ as Lord, to.

Phil 2:11 and *that* every tongue should confess that Jesus Christ *is* Lord, to the glory of God the Father.

Exhibited in Christ.

John 1:14 And the Word became flesh and dwelt among us, and we beheld His glory, the glory as of the only begotten of the Father, full of grace and truth.

2 Cor 4:6 For it is the God who commanded light to shine out of darkness, who has shone in our hearts to *give* the light of the knowledge of the glory of God in the face of Jesus Christ.

Heb 1:3 who being the brightness of *His* glory and the express image of His person, and upholding all things by the word of His power, when He had by Himself purged our sins, sat down at the right hand of the Majesty on high,

Exhibited in

His name.

Deut 28:58 "If you do not carefully observe all the words of this law that are written in this book, that you may fear this glorious and awesome name, THE LORD YOUR GOD,

Neh 9:5 And the Levites, Jeshua, Kadmiel, Bani, Hashabniah, Sherebiah, Hodijah, Shebaniah, *and* Pethahiah, said: "Stand up *and* bless the LORD your God Forever and ever! "Blessed be Your glorious name, Which is exalted above all blessing and praise!

His majesty.

Job 37:22 He comes from the north *as* golden *splendor*; With God *is* awesome majesty.

Ps 93:1 The LORD reigns, He is clothed with majesty; The LORD is clothed, He has girded Himself with strength. Surely the world is established, so that it cannot be moved.

Ps 104:1 Bless the LORD, O my soul! O LORD my God, You are very great: You are clothed with honor and majesty,

Ps 145:5 I will meditate on the glorious splendor of Your majesty, And on Your wondrous works.

Ps 145:12 To make known to the sons of men His mighty acts, And the glorious majesty of His kingdom.

Is 2:10 Enter into the rock, and hide in the dust, From the terror of the LORD And the glory of His majesty.

His power.

Ex 15:1 Then Moses and the children of Israel sang this song to the LORD, and spoke, saying: "I will sing to the LORD, For He has triumphed gloriously! The horse and its rider He has thrown into the sea!

Ex 15:6 "Your right hand, O LORD, has become glorious in power; Your right hand, O LORD, has dashed the enemy in pieces.

Rom 6:4 Therefore we were buried with Him through baptism into death, that just as Christ was raised from the dead by the glory of the Father, even so we also should walk in newness of life.

His works.

Ps 19:1 The heavens declare the glory of God; And the firmament shows His handiwork.

Ps 111:3 His work *is* honorable and glorious, And His righteousness endures forever.

His holiness.

Ex 15:11 "Who *is* like You, O LORD, among the gods? Who *is* like You, glorious in holiness, Fearful in praises, doing wonders?

Described as

Great.

Ps 138:5 Yes, they shall sing of the ways of the LORD, For great *is* the glory of the LORD.

Eternal.

Ps 104:31 May the glory of the LORD endure forever; May the LORD rejoice in His works.

Rich.

Eph 3:16 that He would grant you, according to the riches of His glory, to be strengthened with might through His Spirit in the inner man,

Highly exalted.

Ps 8:1 O LORD, our Lord, How excellent *is* Your name in all the earth, Who have set Your glory above the heavens!

Ps 113:4 The LORD *is* high above all nations, His glory above the heavens.

Exhibited to

Moses.

Ex 33:18–23 And he said, "Please, show me Your glory." **19** Then He said, "I will make all My goodness pass before you, and I will proclaim the name of the LORD before you. I will be gracious to whom I will be gracious, and I will have compassion on whom I will have compassion." **20** But He said, "You cannot see My face; for no man shall see Me, and live." **21** And the LORD said, "Here is a place by Me, and you shall stand on the rock. **22** So it shall be, while My glory passes by, that I will put you in the cleft of the rock, and will cover you with My hand while I pass by. **23** Then I will take away My hand, and you shall see My back; but My face shall not be seen."

Ex 34:5–7 Now the LORD descended in the cloud and stood with him there, and proclaimed the name of the LORD. **6** And the LORD passed before him and proclaimed, "The LORD, the LORD God, merciful and gracious, longsuffering, and abounding in goodness and truth, **7** keeping mercy for thousands, forgiving iniquity and transgression and sin, by no means clearing *the guilty*, visiting the iniquity of the fathers upon the children and the children's children to the third and the fourth generation."

Acts 7:2 And he said, "Brethren and fathers, listen: The God of glory appeared to our father Abraham when he was in Mesopotamia, before he dwelt in Haran,

Stephen.

Acts 7:55 But he, being full of the Holy Spirit, gazed into heaven and saw the glory of God, and Jesus standing at the right hand of God,

His people.

Lev 9:23 And Moses and Aaron went into the tabernacle of meeting, and came out and blessed the people. Then the glory of the LORD appeared to all the people,

Deut 5:24 And you said: 'Surely the LORD our God has shown us His glory and His greatness, and we have heard His voice from the midst of the fire. We have seen this day that God speaks with man; yet he *still* lives.

Ps 102:16 For the LORD shall build up Zion; He shall appear in His glory.

Enlightens the church.

Rev 21:11 having the glory of God. Her light *was* like a most precious stone, like a jasper stone, clear as crystal.

Rev 21:23 The city had no need of the sun or of the moon to shine in it, for the glory of God illuminated it. The Lamb *is* its light.

He shares it with no one.

Is 48:11 For My own sake, for My own sake, I will do *it*; For how should *My name* be profaned? And I will not give My glory to another.

Departure of, from the temple.

Ezek 9:3 Now the glory of the God of Israel had gone up from the cherub, where it had been, to the threshold of the temple. And He called to the man clothed with linen, who *had* the writer's inkhorn at his side;

Ezek 10:18–19 Then the glory of the LORD departed from the threshold of the temple and stood over the cherubim. **19** And the cherubim lifted their wings and mounted up from the earth in my sight. When they went out, the wheels *were* beside them; and they stood at the door of the east gate of the LORD's house, and the glory of the God of Israel *was* above them.

Ezek 11:23 And the glory of the LORD went up from the

midst of the city and stood on the mountain, which *is* on the east side of the city.

Believers desire to behold.

Ps 63:2 So I have looked for You in the sanctuary, To see Your power and Your glory.

Ps 90:16 Let Your work appear to Your servants, And Your glory to their children.

Guarded by Him.

Is 42:8 I *am* the LORD, that *is* My name; And My glory I will not give to another, Nor My praise to carved images.

Believers should

Reverence.

Is 59:19 So shall they fear The name of the LORD from the west, And His glory from the rising of the sun; When the enemy comes in like a flood, The Spirit of the LORD will lift up a standard against him.

Plead in prayer.

Ps 79:9 Help us, O God of our salvation, For the glory of Your name; And deliver us, and provide atonement for our sins, For Your name's sake!

Declare.

1 Chr 16:24 Declare His glory among the nations, His wonders among all peoples.

Ps 96:3 Declare His glory among the nations, His wonders among all peoples.

Ps 145:5 I will meditate on the glorious splendor of Your majesty, And on Your wondrous works.

Ps 145:11 They shall speak of the glory of Your kingdom, And talk of Your power,

Magnify.

Ps 57:5 Be exalted, O God, above the heavens; *Let* Your glory *be* above all the earth.

The earth is full of.

Is 6:3 And one cried to another and said: "Holy, holy, holy *is* the LORD of hosts; The whole earth *is* full of His glory!"

Hab 2:14 For the earth will be filled With the knowledge of the glory of the LORD, As the waters cover the sea.

Man made in the image and.

1 Cor 11:7 For a man indeed ought not to cover *his* head, since he is the image and glory of God; but woman is the glory of man.

Man falls short of.

Rom 3:23 for all have sinned and fall short of the glory of God,

Also called the glory of the Lord.

1 Kin 8:11 so that the priests could not continue ministering because of the cloud; for the glory of the LORD filled the house of the LORD.

GOD, THE GOODNESS OF

Is part of His character.

Ps 25:8 Good and upright *is* the LORD; Therefore He teaches sinners in the way.

Nah 1:7 The LORD *is* good, A stronghold in the day of trouble; And He knows those who trust in Him.

Matt 19:17 So He said to him, "Why do you call Me

good? No one *is* good but One, *that is,* God. But if you want to enter into life, keep the commandments."

Declared to be

Great.

Neh 9:35 For they have not served You in their kingdom, Or in the many good *things* that You gave them, Or in the large and rich land which You set before them; Nor did they turn from their wicked works.

Zech 9:17 For how great is its goodness And how great its beauty! Grain shall make the young men thrive, And new wine the young women.

Rich.

Ps 104:24 O LORD, how manifold are Your works! In wisdom You have made them all. The earth is full of Your possessions—

Rom 2:4 Or do you despise the riches of His goodness, forbearance, and longsuffering, not knowing that the goodness of God leads you to repentance?

Abundant.

Ex 34:6 And the LORD passed before him and proclaimed, "The LORD, the LORD God, merciful and gracious, longsuffering, and abounding in goodness and truth,

Ps 33:5 He loves righteousness and justice; The earth is full of the goodness of the LORD.

Satisfying.

Ps 65:4 Blessed *is the man* You choose, And cause to approach *You, That* he may dwell in Your courts. We shall be satisfied with the goodness of Your house, Of Your holy temple.

Jer 31:12 Therefore they shall come and sing in the height of Zion, Streaming to the goodness of the LORD— For wheat and new wine and oil, For the young of the flock and the herd; Their souls shall be like a well-watered garden, And they shall sorrow no more at all.

Jer 31:14 I will satiate the soul of the priests with abundance, And My people shall be satisfied with My goodness, says the LORD."

Enduring.

Ps 23:6 Surely goodness and mercy shall follow me All the days of my life; And I will dwell in the house of the LORD Forever.

Ps 52:1 Why do you boast in evil, O mighty man? The goodness of God *endures* continually.

Universal.

Ps 145:9 The LORD *is* good to all, And His tender mercies *are* over all His works.

Matt 5:45 that you may be sons of your Father in heaven; for He makes His sun rise on the evil and on the good, and sends rain on the just and on the unjust.

Ways it is manifested,

To His people.

Ps 31:19 Oh, how great *is* Your goodness, Which You have laid up for those who fear You, *Which* You have prepared for those who trust in You In the presence of the sons of men!

Lam 3:25 The LORD *is* good to those who wait for Him, To the soul *who* seeks Him.

In doing good.

Ps 119:68 You *are* good, and do good; Teach me Your statutes.

Ps 145:9 The LORD *is* good to all, And His tender mercies *are* over all His works.

In supplying temporal wants.

Acts 14:17 Nevertheless He did not leave Himself without witness, in that He did good, gave us rain from heaven and fruitful seasons, filling our hearts with food and gladness."

In providing for the poor.

Ps 68:10 Your congregation dwelt in it; You, O God, provided from Your goodness for the poor.

In forgiving sins.

2 Chr 30:18 For a multitude of the people, many from Ephraim, Manasseh, Issachar, and Zebulun, had not cleansed themselves, yet they ate the Passover contrary to what was written. But Hezekiah prayed for them, saying, "May the good LORD provide atonement for everyone

Ps 86:5 For You, Lord, *are* good, and ready to forgive, And abundant in mercy to all those who call upon You.

Leads to repentance.

Rom 2:4 Or do you despise the riches of His goodness, forbearance, and longsuffering, not knowing that the goodness of God leads you to repentance?

Recognize, in His dealings.

Ezra 8:18 Then, by the good hand of our God upon us, they brought us a man of understanding, of the sons of Mahli the son of Levi, the son of Israel, namely Sherebiah, with his sons and brothers, eighteen men;

Neh 2:18 And I told them of the hand of my God which had been good upon me, and also of the king's words that he had spoken to me. So they said, "Let us rise up and build." Then they set their hands to *this* good *work.*

Pray for the manifestation of.

2 Thess 1:11 Therefore we also pray always for you that our God would count you worthy of *this* calling, and fulfill all the good pleasure of *His* goodness and the work of faith with power,

Do not despise.

Rom 2:4 Or do you despise the riches of His goodness, forbearance, and longsuffering, not knowing that the goodness of God leads you to repentance?

Reverence.

Jer 33:9 Then it shall be to Me a name of joy, a praise, and an honor before all nations of the earth, who shall hear all the good that I do to them; they shall fear and tremble for all the goodness and all the prosperity that I provide for it.'

Hos 3:5 Afterward the children of Israel shall return and seek the LORD their God and David their king. They shall fear the LORD and His goodness in the latter days.

Magnify.

Ps 107:8 Oh, that *men* would give thanks to the LORD for His goodness, And *for* His wonderful works to the children of men!

Jer 33:11 the voice of joy and the voice of gladness, the voice of the bridegroom and the voice of the bride, the voice of those who will say: "Praise the LORD of hosts, For the LORD *is* good, For His mercy *endures*

forever"— *and* of those *who will* bring the sacrifice of praise into the house of the Lord. For I will cause the captives of the land to return as at the first,' says the Lord.

Urge others to confide in.

Ps 34:8 Oh, taste and see that the Lord *is* good; Blessed *is* the man *who* trusts in Him!

The wicked disregard.

Neh 9:35 For they have not served You in their kingdom, Or in the many good *things* that You gave them, Or in the large and rich land which You set before them; Nor did they turn from their wicked works.

GOD, THE HOLINESS OF

Is incomparable.

Ex 15:11 "Who *is* like You, O Lord, among the gods? Who *is* like You, glorious in holiness, Fearful in praises, doing wonders?

1 Sam 2:2 "No one is holy like the Lord, For *there is* none besides You, Nor *is there* any rock like our God.

Exhibited in His

Character.

Ps 22:3 But You *are* holy, Enthroned in the praises of Israel.

John 17:11 Now I am no longer in the world, but these are in the world, and I come to You. Holy Father, keep through Your name those whom You have given Me, that they may be one as We *are.*

Name.

Is 57:15 For thus says the High and Lofty One Who inhabits eternity, whose name *is* Holy: "I dwell in the high and holy *place,* With him *who* has a contrite and humble spirit, To revive the spirit of the humble, And to revive the heart of the contrite ones.

Luke 1:49 For He who is mighty has done great things for me, And holy *is* His name.

Words.

Ps 60:6 God has spoken in His holiness: "I will rejoice; I will divide Shechem And measure out the Valley of Succoth.

Jer 23:9 My heart within me is broken Because of the prophets; All my bones shake. I am like a drunken man, And like a man whom wine has overcome, Because of the Lord, And because of His holy words.

Works.

Ps 145:17 The Lord *is* righteous in all His ways, Gracious in all His works.

Kingdom.

Ps 47:8 God reigns over the nations; God sits on His holy throne.

Matt 13:41 The Son of Man will send out His angels, and they will gather out of His kingdom all things that offend, and those who practice lawlessness,

1 Cor 6:9–10 Do you not know that the unrighteous will not inherit the kingdom of God? Do not be deceived. Neither fornicators, nor idolaters, nor adulterers, nor homosexuals, nor sodomites, **10** nor thieves, nor covetous, nor drunkards, nor revilers, nor extortioners will inherit the kingdom of God.

Rev 21:27 But there shall by no means enter it anything that defiles, or causes an abomination or a lie, but only those who are written in the Lamb's Book of Life.

Is pledged for the fulfilment of

His promises.

Ps 89:35 Once I have sworn by My holiness; I will not lie to David:

His judgments.

Amos 4:2 The Lord God has sworn by His holiness: "Behold, the days shall come upon you When He will take you away with fishhooks, And your posterity with fishhooks.

Believers are commanded to imitate.

Lev 11:44 For I *am* the Lord your God. You shall therefore consecrate yourselves, and you shall be holy; for I *am* holy. Neither shall you defile yourselves with any creeping thing that creeps on the earth.

Josh 24:19 But Joshua said to the people, "You cannot serve the Lord, for He *is* a holy God. He *is* a jealous God; He will not forgive your transgressions nor your sins.

Ps 93:5 Your testimonies are very sure; Holiness adorns Your house, O Lord, forever.

1 Pet 1:15–16 but as He who called you *is* holy, you also be holy in all *your* conduct, **16** because it is written, *"Be holy, for I am holy."*

Believers should thank Him for.

Ps 30:4 Sing praise to the Lord, you saints of His, And give thanks at the remembrance of His holy name.

Should produce reverential fear.

Rev 15:4 Who shall not fear You, O Lord, and glorify Your name? For *You* alone *are* holy. For all nations shall come and worship before You, For Your judgments have been manifested."

Heavenly hosts adore.

Is 6:3 And one cried to another and said: "Holy, holy, holy *is* the Lord of hosts; The whole earth *is* full of His glory!"

Rev 4:8 *The* four living creatures, each having six wings, were full of eyes around and within. And they do not rest day or night, saying: "Holy, holy, holy, Lord God Almighty, Who was and is and is to come!"

Should be magnified.

1 Chr 16:10 Glory in His holy name; Let the hearts of those rejoice who seek the Lord!

Ps 48:1 Great *is* the Lord, and greatly to be praised In the city of our God, *In* His holy mountain.

Ps 99:3 Let them praise Your great and awesome name— He *is* holy.

Ps 99:5 Exalt the Lord our God, And worship at His footstool— He *is* holy.

Rev 15:4 Who shall not fear You, O Lord, and glorify Your name? For *You* alone *are* holy. For all nations shall come and worship before You, For Your judgments have been manifested."

GOD, THE JUSTICE OF

Is a part of His character.

Deut 32:4 *He is* the Rock, His work *is* perfect; For all His ways *are* justice, A God of truth and without injustice; Righteous and upright *is* He.

Is 45:21 Tell and bring forth *your case*; Yes, let them take counsel together. Who has declared this from ancient time? *Who* has told it from that time? *Have* not I, the LORD? And *there is* no other God besides Me, A just God and a Savior; *There is* none besides Me.

Declared to be

Abundant.

Job 37:23 As *for* the Almighty, we cannot find Him; *He is* excellent in power, *In* judgment and abundant justice; He does not oppress.

Incomparable.

Job 4:17 'Can a mortal be more righteous than God? Can a man be more pure than his Maker?

Incorruptible.

Deut 10:17 For the LORD your God *is* God of gods and Lord of lords, the great God, mighty and awesome, who shows no partiality nor takes a bribe.

2 Chr 19:7 Now therefore, let the fear of the LORD be upon you; take care and do *it*, for *there is* no iniquity with the LORD our God, no partiality, nor taking of bribes."

Impartial.

Jer 32:19 *You are* great in counsel and mighty in work, for your eyes *are* open to all the ways of the sons of men, to give everyone according to his ways and according to the fruit of his doings.

Rom 2:11 For there is no partiality with God.

Col 3:25 But he who does wrong will be repaid for what he has done, and there is no partiality.

1 Pet 1:17 And if you call on the Father, who without partiality judges according to each one's work, conduct yourselves throughout the time of your stay *here* in fear;

Unfailing.

Zeph 3:5 The LORD *is* righteous in her midst, He will do no unrighteousness. Every morning He brings His justice to light; He never fails, But the unjust knows no shame.

Undeviating.

Job 8:3 Does God subvert judgment? Or does the Almighty pervert justice?

Job 34:12 Surely God will never do wickedly, Nor will the Almighty pervert justice.

The foundation of His throne.

Ps 89:14 Righteousness and justice *are* the foundation of Your throne; Mercy and truth go before Your face.

Not to be sinned against.

Jer 50:7 All who found them have devoured them; And their adversaries said, 'We have not offended, Because they have sinned against the LORD, the habitation of justice, The LORD, the hope of their fathers.'

Denied by the ungodly.

Ezek 33:17 "Yet the children of your people say, 'The way of the LORD is not fair.' But it is their way which is not fair!

Ezek 33:20 Yet you say, 'The way of the LORD is not fair.' O house of Israel, I will judge every one of you according to his own ways."

Exhibited in

Forgiving sins.

1 John 1:9 If we confess our sins, He is faithful and just to forgive us *our* sins and to cleanse us from all unrighteousness.

Redemption.

Rom 3:26 to demonstrate at the present time His righteousness, that He might be just and the justifier of the one who has faith in Jesus.

His government.

Ps 9:4 For You have maintained my right and my cause; You sat on the throne judging in righteousness.

Jer 9:24 But let him who glories glory in this, That he understands and knows Me, That I *am* the LORD, exercising lovingkindness, judgment, and righteousness in the earth. For in these I delight," says the LORD.

His judgments.

Gen 18:25 Far be it from You to do such a thing as this, to slay the righteous with the wicked, so that the righteous should be as the wicked; far be it from You! Shall not the Judge of all the earth do right?"

Rev 19:2 For true and righteous *are* His judgments, because He has judged the great harlot who corrupted the earth with her fornication; and He has avenged on her the blood of His servants *shed* by her."

All His ways.

Ezek 18:25 "Yet you say, 'The way of the Lord is not fair.' Hear now, O house of Israel, is it not My way which is fair, and your ways which are not fair?

Ezek 18:29 Yet the house of Israel says, 'The way of the Lord is not fair.' O house of Israel, is it not My ways which are fair, and your ways which are not fair?

The final judgment.

Acts 17:31 because He has appointed a day on which He will judge the world in righteousness by the Man whom He has ordained. He has given assurance of this to all by raising Him from the dead."

Acknowledgment of.

Ps 51:4 Against You, You only, have I sinned, And done *this* evil in Your sight— That You may be found just when You speak, *And* blameless when You judge.

Ps 98:9 For He is coming to judge the earth. With righteousness He shall judge the world, And the peoples with equity.

Rom 3:4 Certainly not! Indeed, let God be true but every man a liar. As it is written: *"That You may be justified in Your words, And may overcome when You are judged."*

Should be praised.

Ps 99:3–4 Let them praise Your great and awesome name— He *is* holy. 4 The King's strength also loves justice; You have established equity; You have executed justice and righteousness in Jacob.

GOD, THE LONGSUFFERING OF

Is part of His character.

Ex 34:6 And the LORD passed before him and proclaimed, "The LORD, the LORD God, merciful and gracious, longsuffering, and abounding in goodness and truth,

Num 14:18 'The LORD is longsuffering and abundant in mercy, forgiving iniquity and transgression; but He by no means clears *the guilty,* visiting the iniquity of the fathers on the children to the third and fourth *generation.*'

Ps 86:15 But You, O Lord, *are* a God full of compassion, and gracious, Longsuffering and abundant in mercy and truth.

Should lead to repentance and salvation.

Joel 2:13 So rend your heart, and not your garments; Return to the LORD your God, For He *is* gracious and merciful, Slow to anger, and of great kindness; And He relents from doing harm.

Rom 2:4 Or do you despise the riches of His goodness, forbearance, and longsuffering, not knowing that the goodness of God leads you to repentance?

2 Pet 3:9 The Lord is not slack concerning *His* promise, as some count slackness, but is longsuffering toward us, not willing that any should perish but that all should come to repentance.

2 Pet 3:15 and consider *that* the longsuffering of our Lord *is* salvation—as also our beloved brother Paul, according to the wisdom given to him, has written to you,

Exercised toward

His people.

Is 30:18 Therefore the LORD will wait, that He may be gracious to you; And therefore He will be exalted, that He may have mercy on you. For the LORD *is* a God of justice; Blessed *are* all those who wait for Him.

Ezek 20:17 Nevertheless My eye spared them from destruction. I did not make an end of them in the wilderness.

Rom 3:25 whom God set forth *as* a propitiation by His blood, through faith, to demonstrate His righteousness, because in His forbearance God had passed over the sins that were previously committed,

The wicked.

Rom 9:22 *What* if God, wanting to show *His* wrath and to make His power known, endured with much longsuffering the vessels of wrath prepared for destruction,

1 Pet 3:20 who formerly were disobedient, when once the Divine longsuffering waited in the days of Noah, while *the* ark was being prepared, in which a few, that is, eight souls, were saved through water.

Plead in prayer.

Jer 15:15 O LORD, You know; Remember me and visit me, And take vengeance for me on my persecutors. In Your enduring patience, do not take me away. Know that for Your sake I have suffered rebuke.

Limits set to.

Gen 6:3 And the LORD said, "My Spirit shall not strive with man forever, for he *is* indeed flesh; yet his days shall be one hundred and twenty years."

Jer 44:22 So the LORD could no longer bear *it,* because of the evil of your doings *and* because of the abominations which you committed. Therefore your land is a desolation, an astonishment, a curse, and without an inhabitant, as *it is* this day.

The wicked

Abuse.

Eccl 8:11 Because the sentence against an evil work is not executed speedily, therefore the heart of the sons of men is fully set in them to do evil.

Matt 24:48–49 But if that evil servant says in his heart, 'My master is delaying his coming,' 49 and begins to beat *his* fellow servants, and to eat and drink with the drunkards,

Despise.

Rom 2:4 Or do you despise the riches of His goodness, forbearance, and longsuffering, not knowing that the goodness of God leads you to repentance?

Punished for despising.

Neh 9:30 Yet for many years You had patience with them, And testified against them by Your Spirit in Your prophets. Yet they would not listen; Therefore You gave them into the hand of the peoples of the lands.

Matt 24:48–51 But if that evil servant says in his heart, 'My master is delaying his coming,' 49 and begins to beat *his* fellow servants, and to eat and drink with the drunkards, 50 the master of that servant will come on a day when he is not looking for *him* and at an hour that he is not aware of, 51 and will cut him in two and appoint *him* his portion with the hypocrites. There shall be weeping and gnashing of teeth.

Rom 2:5 But in accordance with your hardness and your impenitent heart you are treasuring up for yourself wrath in the day of wrath and revelation of the righteous judgment of God,

Illustrated.

Luke 13:6–9 He also spoke this parable: "A certain *man* had a fig tree planted in his vineyard, and he came seeking fruit on it and found none. 7 Then he said to the keeper of his vineyard, 'Look, for three years I have come seeking fruit on this fig tree and find none. Cut it down; why does it use up the ground?' 8 But he answered and said to him, 'Sir, let it alone this year also, until I dig around it and fertilize *it.* 9 And if it bears fruit, *well.* But if not, after that you can cut it down.' "

Exemplified toward

Manasseh.

2 Chr 33:10–13 And the LORD spoke to Manasseh and his people, but they would not listen. 11 Therefore the LORD brought upon them the captains of the army of the king of Assyria, who took Manasseh with hooks, bound him with bronze *fetters,* and carried him off to Babylon. 12 Now when he was in affliction, he implored the LORD his God, and humbled himself greatly before the God of his fathers, 13 and prayed to Him; and He received his entreaty, heard his supplication, and brought him back to Jerusalem into his kingdom. Then Manasseh knew that the LORD *was* God.

Israel.

Ps 78:38 But He, *being* full of compassion, forgave *their* iniquity, And did not destroy *them.* Yes, many a time He turned His anger away, And did not stir up all His wrath;

Is 48:9 "For My name's sake I will defer My anger, And *for* My praise I will restrain it from you, So that I do not cut you off.

Jerusalem.

Matt 23:37 "O Jerusalem, Jerusalem, the one who kills

the prophets and stones those who are sent to her! How often I wanted to gather your children together, as a hen gathers her chicks under *her* wings, but you were not willing!

Paul.

1 Tim 1:16 However, for this reason I obtained mercy, that in me first Jesus Christ might show all longsuffering, as a pattern to those who are going to believe on Him for everlasting life.

GOD, THE LOVE OF

Part of His character.

2 Cor 13:11 Finally, brethren, farewell. Become complete. Be of good comfort, be of one mind, live in peace; and the God of love and peace will be with you.

1 John 4:8 He who does not love does not know God, for God is love.

Christ, the special object of.

John 15:9–10 "As the Father loved Me, I also have loved you; abide in My love. **10** If you keep My commandments, you will abide in My love, just as I have kept My Father's commandments and abide in His love.

John 17:26 And I have declared to them Your name, and will declare *it*, that the love with which You loved Me may be in them, and I in them."

Described as

Sovereign.

Deut 7:7–8 The LORD did not set His love on you nor choose you because you were more in number than any other people, for you were the least of all peoples; **8** but because the LORD loves you, and because He would keep the oath which He swore to your fathers, the LORD has brought you out with a mighty hand, and redeemed you from the house of bondage, from the hand of Pharaoh king of Egypt.

Deut 10:15 The LORD delighted only in your fathers, to love them; and He chose their descendants after them, you above all peoples, as *it is* this day.

Job 7:17 "What *is* man, that You should exalt him, *That* You should set Your heart on him,

Great.

Eph 2:4 But God, who is rich in mercy, because of His great love with which He loved us,

Abiding.

Zeph 3:17 The LORD your God in your midst, The Mighty One, will save; He will rejoice over you with gladness, He will quiet *you* with His love, He will rejoice over you with singing."

Unfailing and certain.

Is 49:15–16 "Can a woman forget her nursing child, And not have compassion on the son of her womb? Surely they may forget, Yet I will not forget you. **16** See, I have inscribed you on the palms *of My hands;* Your walls *are* continually before Me.

Rom 8:39 nor height nor depth, nor any other created thing, shall be able to separate us from the love of God which is in Christ Jesus our Lord.

Constraining.

Hos 11:4 I drew them with gentle cords, With bands of

love, And I was to them as those who take the yoke from their neck. I stooped *and* fed them.

Everlasting.

Jer 31:3 The LORD has appeared of old to me, *saying:* "Yes, I have loved you with an everlasting love; Therefore with lovingkindness I have drawn you.

Manifested toward

Perishing sinners.

John 3:16 For God so loved the world that He gave His only begotten Son, that whoever believes in Him should not perish but have everlasting life.

Titus 3:4 But when the kindness and the love of God our Savior toward man appeared,

His saints.

John 16:27 for the Father Himself loves you, because you have loved Me, and have believed that I came forth from God.

John 17:23 I in them, and You in Me; that they may be made perfect in one, and that the world may know that You have sent Me, and have loved them as You have loved Me.

2 Thess 2:16 Now may our Lord Jesus Christ Himself, and our God and Father, who has loved us and given *us* everlasting consolation and good hope by grace,

1 John 4:16 And we have known and believed the love that God has for us. God is love, and he who abides in love abides in God, and God in him.

The destitute.

Deut 10:18 He administers justice for the fatherless and the widow, and loves the stranger, giving him food and clothing.

The cheerful giver.

2 Cor 9:7 *So let* each one *give* as he purposes in his heart, not grudgingly or of necessity; for God loves a cheerful giver.

Exhibited in

The giving of Christ.

John 3:16 For God so loved the world that He gave His only begotten Son, that whoever believes in Him should not perish but have everlasting life.

Rom 5:8 But God demonstrates His own love toward us, in that while we were still sinners, Christ died for us.

1 John 4:9–10 In this the love of God was manifested toward us, that God has sent His only begotten Son into the world, that we might live through Him. **10** In this is love, not that we loved God, but that He loved us and sent His Son *to be* the propitiation for our sins.

Election.

Hos 11:4 I drew them with gentle cords, With bands of love, And I was to them as those who take the yoke from their neck. I stooped *and* fed them.

Mal 1:2–3 "I have loved you," says the LORD. "Yet you say, 'In what way have You loved us?' *Was* not Esau Jacob's brother?" Says the LORD. "Yet Jacob I have loved; **3** But Esau I have hated, And laid waste his mountains and his heritage For the jackals of the wilderness."

Rom 9:11–13 (for *the children* not yet being born, nor having done any good or evil, that the purpose of God according to election might stand, not of works but of Him who calls), **12** it was said to her, *"The older shall serve the younger."* **13** As it is written, *"Jacob I have loved, but Esau I have hated."*

Eph 2:4–5 But God, who is rich in mercy, because of His great love with which He loved us, **5** even when we were dead in trespasses, made us alive together with Christ (by grace you have been saved),

Titus 3:4–7 But when the kindness and the love of God our Savior toward man appeared, **5** not by works of righteousness which we have done, but according to His mercy He saved us, through the washing of regeneration and renewing of the Holy Spirit, **6** whom He poured out on us abundantly through Jesus Christ our Savior, **7** that having been justified by His grace we should become heirs according to the hope of eternal life.

1 John 4:19 We love Him because He first loved us.

Adoption.

1 John 3:1 Behold what manner of love the Father has bestowed on us, that we should be called children of God! Therefore the world does not know us, because it did not know Him.

Redemption of Israel.

Is 43:3–4 For I *am* the LORD your God, The Holy One of Israel, your Savior; I gave Egypt for your ransom, Ethiopia and Seba in your place. **4** Since you were precious in My sight, You have been honored, And I have loved you; Therefore I will give men for you, And people for your life.

Is 63:9 In all their affliction He was afflicted, And the Angel of His Presence saved them; In His love and in His pity He redeemed them; And He bore them and carried them All the days of old.

Forgiving sin.

Is 38:17 Indeed *it was* for *my own* peace *That* I had great bitterness; But You have lovingly *delivered* my soul from the pit of corruption, For You have cast all my sins behind Your back.

Temporal blessings.

Deut 7:13 And He will love you and bless you and multiply you; He will also bless the fruit of your womb and the fruit of your land, your grain and your new wine and your oil, the increase of your cattle and the offspring of your flock, in the land of which He swore to your fathers to give you.

Chastisements.

Heb 12:6 *For whom the LORD loves He chastens, And scourges every son whom He receives."*

Defeating evil counsels.

Deut 23:5 Nevertheless the LORD your God would not listen to Balaam, but the LORD your God turned the curse into a blessing for you, because the LORD your God loves you.

Poured out by the Holy Spirit.

Rom 5:5 Now hope does not disappoint, because the love of God has been poured out in our hearts by the Holy Spirit who was given to us.

Perfected in believers

By obedience.

1 John 2:5 But whoever keeps His word, truly the love

of God is perfected in him. By this we know that we are in Him.

1 John 4:16 And we have known and believed the love that God has for us. God is love, and he who abides in love abides in God, and God in him.

Jude 1:21 keep yourselves in the love of God, looking for the mercy of our Lord Jesus Christ unto eternal life.

By brotherly love.

1 John 4:12 No one has seen God at any time. If we love one another, God abides in us, and His love has been perfected in us.

GOD, THE LOVINGKINDNESS OF

Is through Christ.

Eph 2:7 that in the ages to come He might show the exceeding riches of His grace in *His* kindness toward us in Christ Jesus.

Titus 3:4–6 But when the kindness and the love of God our Savior toward man appeared, **5** not by works of righteousness which we have done, but according to His mercy He saved us, through the washing of regeneration and renewing of the Holy Spirit, **6** whom He poured out on us abundantly through Jesus Christ our Savior,

Described as

Abundant.

Neh 9:17 They refused to obey, And they were not mindful of Your wonders That You did among them. But they hardened their necks, And in their rebellion They appointed a leader To return to their bondage. But You *are* God, Ready to pardon, Gracious and merciful, Slow to anger, Abundant in kindness, And did not forsake them.

Is 63:7 I will mention the lovingkindnesses of the LORD And the praises of the LORD, According to all that the LORD has bestowed on us, And the great goodness toward the house of Israel, Which He has bestowed on them according to His mercies, According to the multitude of His lovingkindnesses.

Precious.

Ps 36:7 How precious *is* Your lovingkindness, O God! Therefore the children of men put their trust under the shadow of Your wings.

Good.

Ps 69:16 Hear me, O LORD, for Your lovingkindness *is* good; Turn to me according to the multitude of Your tender mercies.

Marvellous.

Ps 17:7 Show Your marvelous lovingkindness by Your right hand, O You who save those who trust *in You* From those who rise up *against them.*

Ps 31:21 Blessed *be* the LORD, For He has shown me His marvelous kindness in a strong city!

Everlasting.

Is 54:8 With a little wrath I hid My face from you for a moment; But with everlasting kindness I will have mercy on you," Says the LORD, your Redeemer.

Merciful.

Ps 117:2 For His merciful kindness is great toward us,

And the truth of the LORD *endures* forever. Praise the LORD!

Better than life.

Ps 63:3 Because Your lovingkindness *is* better than life, My lips shall praise You.

Believers

Have a knowledge of.

Ps 107:43 Whoever *is* wise will observe these *things*, And they will understand the lovingkindness of the LORD.

Are betrothed in.

Hos 2:19 "I will betroth you to Me forever; Yes, I will betroth you to Me In righteousness and justice, In lovingkindness and mercy;

Are drawn by.

Jer 31:3 The LORD has appeared of old to me, *saying:* "Yes, I have loved you with an everlasting love; Therefore with lovingkindness I have drawn you.

Are preserved by.

Ps 40:11 Do not withhold Your tender mercies from me, O LORD; Let Your lovingkindness and Your truth continually preserve me.

Are revived by.

Ps 119:88 Revive me according to Your lovingkindness, So that I may keep the testimony of Your mouth.

Are comforted by.

Ps 119:76 Let, I pray, Your merciful kindness be for my comfort, According to Your word to Your servant.

Look for mercy through.

Ps 51:1 Have mercy upon me, O God, According to Your lovingkindness; According to the multitude of Your tender mercies, Blot out my transgressions.

Receive mercy through.

Is 54:8 With a little wrath I hid My face from you for a moment; But with everlasting kindness I will have mercy on you," Says the LORD, your Redeemer.

Are heard according to.

Ps 119:149 Hear my voice according to Your lovingkindness; O LORD, revive me according to Your justice.

Are ever mindful of.

Ps 26:3 For Your lovingkindness *is* before my eyes, And I have walked in Your truth.

Ps 48:9 We have thought, O God, on Your lovingkindness, In the midst of Your temple.

Should expect, in affliction.

Ps 42:7–8 Deep calls unto deep at the noise of Your waterfalls; All Your waves and billows have gone over me. 8 The LORD will command His lovingkindness in the daytime, And in the night His song *shall be* with me— A prayer to the God of my life.

Are crowned with.

Ps 103:4 Who redeems your life from destruction, Who crowns you with lovingkindness and tender mercies,

Always have.

Ps 89:33 Nevertheless My lovingkindness I will not utterly take from him, Nor allow My faithfulness to fail.

Is 54:10 For the mountains shall depart And the hills be removed, But My kindness shall not depart from you, Nor shall My covenant of peace be removed," Says the LORD, who has mercy on you.

Pray for the

Former manifestations of.

Ps 25:6 Remember, O LORD, Your tender mercies and Your lovingkindnesses, For they *are* from of old.

Ps 89:49 Lord, where *are* Your former lovingkindnesses, *Which* You swore to David in Your truth?

Exhibition of.

Ps 17:7 Show Your marvelous lovingkindness by Your right hand, O You who save those who trust *in You* From those who rise up *against them.*

Ps 143:8 Cause me to hear Your lovingkindness in the morning, For in You do I trust; Cause me to know the way in which I should walk, For I lift up my soul to You.

Continuance of.

Ps 36:10 Oh, continue Your lovingkindness to those who know You, And Your righteousness to the upright in heart.

Extension of.

Gen 24:12 Then he said, "O LORD God of my master Abraham, please give me success this day, and show kindness to my master Abraham.

2 Sam 2:6 And now may the LORD show kindness and truth to you. I also will repay you this kindness, because you have done this thing.

Praise God for.

Ps 92:2 To declare Your lovingkindness in the morning, And Your faithfulness every night,

Ps 138:2 I will worship toward Your holy temple, And praise Your name For Your lovingkindness and Your truth; For You have magnified Your word above all Your name.

Proclaim.

Ps 40:10 I have not hidden Your righteousness within my heart; I have declared Your faithfulness and Your salvation; I have not concealed Your lovingkindness and Your truth From the great assembly.

GOD, THE MERCY OF

Part of His character.

Ex 34:6–7 And the LORD passed before him and proclaimed, "The LORD, the LORD God, merciful and gracious, longsuffering, and abounding in goodness and truth, 7 keeping mercy for thousands, forgiving iniquity and transgression and sin, by no means clearing *the guilty*, visiting the iniquity of the fathers upon the children and the children's children to the third and the fourth generation."

Neh 9:17 They refused to obey, And they were not mindful of Your wonders That You did among them. But they hardened their necks, And in their rebellion They appointed a leader To return to their bondage. But You *are* God, Ready to pardon, Gracious and merciful, Slow to anger, Abundant in kindness, And did not forsake them.

Ps 62:12 Also to You, O Lord, *belongs* mercy; For You render to each one according to his work.

Jon 4:2 So he prayed to the LORD, and said, "Ah, LORD,

was not this what I said when I was still in my country? Therefore I fled previously to Tarshish; for I know that You *are* a gracious and merciful God, slow to anger and abundant in lovingkindness, One who relents from doing harm.

Jon 4:10–11 But the LORD said, "You have had pity on the plant for which you have not labored, nor made it grow, which came up in a night and perished in a night. **11** And should I not pity Nineveh, that great city, in which are more than one hundred and twenty thousand persons who cannot discern between their right hand and their left—and much livestock?"

Mic 7:18 Who *is* a God like You, Pardoning iniquity And passing over the transgression of the remnant of His heritage? He does not retain His anger forever, Because He delights *in* mercy.

2 Cor 1:3 Blessed *be* the God and Father of our Lord Jesus Christ, the Father of mercies and God of all comfort,

Described as

Great.

Num 14:18 'The LORD is longsuffering and abundant in mercy, forgiving iniquity and transgression; but He by no means clears *the guilty,* visiting the iniquity of the fathers on the children to the third and fourth *generation.'*

Is 54:7 "For a mere moment I have forsaken you, But with great mercies I will gather you.

Rich.

Eph 2:4 But God, who is rich in mercy, because of His great love with which He loved us,

Abundant.

Neh 9:27 Therefore You delivered them into the hand of their enemies, Who oppressed them; And in the time of their trouble, When they cried to You, You heard from heaven; And according to Your abundant mercies You gave them deliverers who saved them From the hand of their enemies.

Ps 86:5 For You, Lord, *are* good, and ready to forgive, And abundant in mercy to all those who call upon You.

Ps 86:15 But You, O Lord, *are* a God full of compassion, and gracious, Longsuffering and abundant in mercy and truth.

Ps 103:8 The LORD *is* merciful and gracious, Slow to anger, and abounding in mercy.

Lam 3:32 Though He causes grief, Yet He will show compassion According to the multitude of His mercies.

1 Pet 1:3 Blessed *be* the God and Father of our Lord Jesus Christ, who according to His abundant mercy has begotten us again to a living hope through the resurrection of Jesus Christ from the dead,

Sure.

Is 55:3 Incline your ear, and come to Me. Hear, and your soul shall live; And I will make an everlasting covenant with you— The sure mercies of David.

Mic 7:20 You will give truth to Jacob *And* mercy to Abraham, Which You have sworn to our fathers From days of old.

Everlasting.

1 Chr 16:34 Oh, give thanks to the LORD, for *He is* good! For His mercy *endures* forever.

Ps 89:28 My mercy I will keep for him forever, And My covenant shall stand firm with him.

Ps 106:1 Praise the LORD! Oh, give thanks to the LORD, for *He is* good! For His mercy *endures* forever.

Ps 107:1 Oh, give thanks to the LORD, for *He is* good! For His mercy *endures* forever.

Cf. Ps 136:1–26

Tender.

Ps 25:6 Remember, O LORD, Your tender mercies and Your lovingkindnesses, For they *are* from of old.

Ps 103:4 Who redeems your life from destruction, Who crowns you with lovingkindness and tender mercies,

Luke 1:78 Through the tender mercy of our God, With which the Dayspring from on high has visited us;

New every morning.

Lam 3:22–23 *Through* the LORD's mercies we are not consumed, Because His compassions fail not. **23** *They are* new every morning; Great *is* Your faithfulness.

High as heaven.

Ps 36:5 Your mercy, O LORD, *is* in the heavens; Your faithfulness *reaches* to the clouds.

Ps 103:11 For as the heavens are high above the earth, *So* great is His mercy toward those who fear Him;

Everywhere.

Ps 119:64 The earth, O LORD, is full of Your mercy; Teach me Your statutes.

Ps 145:9 The LORD *is* good to all, And His tender mercies *are* over all His works.

Manifested

In the sending of Christ.

Luke 1:78 Through the tender mercy of our God, With which the Dayspring from on high has visited us;

In longsuffering.

Lam 3:22 *Through* the LORD's mercies we are not consumed, Because His compassions fail not.

Dan 9:9 To the Lord our God *belong* mercy and forgiveness, though we have rebelled against Him.

To His people.

Deut 32:43 "Rejoice, O Gentiles, *with* His people; For He will avenge the blood of His servants, And render vengeance to His adversaries; He will provide atonement for His land *and* His people."

1 Kin 8:23 and he said: "LORD God of Israel, *there is* no God in heaven above or on earth below like You, who keep *Your* covenant and mercy with Your servants who walk before You with all their hearts.

Ps 103:17 But the mercy of the LORD *is* from everlasting to everlasting On those who fear Him, And His righteousness to children's children,

Luke 1:50 And His mercy *is* on those who fear Him From generation to generation.

Titus 3:5 not by works of righteousness which we have done, but according to His mercy He saved us, through the washing of regeneration and renewing of the Holy Spirit,

To returning backsliders.

Jer 3:12 Go and proclaim these words toward the north, and say: 'Return, backsliding Israel,' says the LORD; 'I will not cause My anger to fall on you. For I *am* merciful,' says the LORD; 'I will not remain angry forever.

Hos 14:4 "I will heal their backsliding, I will love them freely, For My anger has turned away from him.

Joel 2:13 So rend your heart, and not your garments; Return to the LORD your God, For He *is* gracious and merciful, Slow to anger, and of great kindness; And He relents from doing harm.

To repentant sinners.

Ps 32:5 I acknowledged my sin to You, And my iniquity I have not hidden. I said, "I will confess my transgressions to the LORD," And You forgave the iniquity of my sin. Selah

Prov 28:13 He who covers his sins will not prosper, But whoever confesses and forsakes *them* will have mercy.

Is 55:7 Let the wicked forsake his way, And the unrighteous man his thoughts; Let him return to the LORD, And He will have mercy on him; And to our God, For He will abundantly pardon.

Luke 15:18–20 I will arise and go to my father, and will say to him, "Father, I have sinned against heaven and before you, **19** and I am no longer worthy to be called your son. Make me like one of your hired servants." ' **20** "And he arose and came to his father. But when he was still a great way off, his father saw him and had compassion, and ran and fell on his neck and kissed him.

To the afflicted.

Is 49:13 Sing, O heavens! Be joyful, O earth! And break out in singing, O mountains! For the LORD has comforted His people, And will have mercy on His afflicted.

Is 54:7 "For a mere moment I have forsaken you, But with great mercies I will gather you.

Hos 14:3 Assyria shall not save us, We will not ride on horses, Nor will we say anymore to the work of our hands, 'You *are* our gods.' For in You the fatherless finds mercy."

To whom He will.

Hos 2:23 Then I will sow her for Myself in the earth, And I will have mercy on *her who had* not obtained mercy; Then I will say to *those who were* not My people, 'You *are* My people!' And they shall say, 'You *are* my God!' "

Rom 9:15 For He says to Moses, *"I will have mercy on whomever I will have mercy, and I will have compassion on whomever I will have compassion."*

Rom 9:18 Therefore He has mercy on whom He wills, and whom He wills He hardens.

With everlasting kindness.

Is 54:8 With a little wrath I hid My face from you for a moment; But with everlasting kindness I will have mercy on you," Says the LORD, your Redeemer.

A ground of hope and trust.

Ps 52:8 But I *am* like a green olive tree in the house of God; I trust in the mercy of God forever and ever.

Ps 130:7 O Israel, hope in the LORD; For with the LORD

there is mercy, And with Him *is* abundant redemption.

Ps 147:11 The LORD takes pleasure in those who fear Him, In those who hope in His mercy.

Should be

Sought for ourselves and others.

Ps 6:2 Have mercy on me, O LORD, for I *am* weak; O LORD, heal me, for my bones are troubled.

Gal 6:16 And as many as walk according to this rule, peace and mercy *be* upon them, and upon the Israel of God.

1 Tim 1:2 To Timothy, a true son in the faith: Grace, mercy, *and* peace from God our Father and Jesus Christ our Lord.

2 Tim 1:18 The Lord grant to him that he may find mercy from the Lord in that Day—and you know very well how many ways he ministered *to me* at Ephesus.

Pleaded in prayer.

Ps 6:4 Return, O LORD, deliver me! Oh, save me for Your mercies' sake!

Ps 25:6 Remember, O LORD, Your tender mercies and Your lovingkindnesses, For they *are* from of old.

Ps 51:1 Have mercy upon me, O God, According to Your lovingkindness; According to the multitude of Your tender mercies, Blot out my transgressions.

Rejoiced in.

Ps 31:7 I will be glad and rejoice in Your mercy, For You have considered my trouble; You have known my soul in adversities,

Magnified.

1 Chr 16:34 Oh, give thanks to the LORD, for *He is* good! For His mercy *endures* forever.

Ps 115:1 Not unto us, O LORD, not unto us, But to Your name give glory, Because of Your mercy, Because of Your truth.

Ps 118:1–4 Oh, give thanks to the LORD, for *He is* good! For His mercy *endures* forever. **2** Let Israel now say, "His mercy *endures* forever." **3** Let the house of Aaron now say, "His mercy *endures* forever." **4** Let those who fear the LORD now say, "His mercy *endures* forever."

Ps 118:29 Oh, give thanks to the LORD, for *He is* good! For His mercy *endures* forever.

Jer 33:11 the voice of joy and the voice of gladness, the voice of the bridegroom and the voice of the bride, the voice of those who will say: "Praise the LORD of hosts, For the LORD *is* good, For His mercy *endures* forever"— *and* of those *who will* bring the sacrifice of praise into the house of the LORD. For I will cause the captives of the land to return as at the first,' says the LORD.

Demonstrated toward

Lot.

Gen 19:16 And while he lingered, the men took hold of his hand, his wife's hand, and the hands of his two daughters, the LORD being merciful to him, and they brought him out and set him outside the city.

Gen 19:19 Indeed now, your servant has found favor in your sight, and you have increased your mercy which you have shown me by saving my life; but I cannot escape to the mountains, lest some evil overtake me and I die.

Epaphroditus.

Phil 2:27 For indeed he was sick almost unto death; but God had mercy on him, and not only on him but on me also, lest I should have sorrow upon sorrow.

Paul.

1 Tim 1:13 although I was formerly a blasphemer, a persecutor, and an insolent man; but I obtained mercy because I did *it* ignorantly in unbelief.

GOD, THE POWER OF

One of His attributes.

Ps 62:11 God has spoken once, Twice I have heard this: That power *belongs* to God.

Expressed by the

Voice of God.

Ps 29:3 The voice of the LORD *is* over the waters; The God of glory thunders; The LORD *is* over many waters.

Ps 29:5 The voice of the LORD breaks the cedars, Yes, the LORD splinters the cedars of Lebanon.

Ps 68:33 To Him who rides on the heaven of heavens, *which were* of old! Indeed, He sends out His voice, a mighty voice.

Finger of God.

Ex 8:19 Then the magicians said to Pharaoh, "This *is* the finger of God." But Pharaoh's heart grew hard, and he did not heed them, just as the LORD had said.

Ps 8:3 When I consider Your heavens, the work of Your fingers, The moon and the stars, which You have ordained,

Hand of God.

Ex 9:3 behold, the hand of the LORD will be on your cattle in the field, on the horses, on the donkeys, on the camels, on the oxen, and on the sheep—a very severe pestilence.

Ex 9:15 Now if I had stretched out My hand and struck you and your people with pestilence, then you would have been cut off from the earth.

Is 48:13 Indeed My hand has laid the foundation of the earth, And My right hand has stretched out the heavens; *When* I call to them, They stand up together.

Arm of God.

Job 40:9 Have you an arm like God? Or can you thunder with a voice like His?

Is 52:10 The LORD has made bare His holy arm In the eyes of all the nations; And all the ends of the earth shall see The salvation of our God.

Thunder of His power.

Job 26:14 Indeed these *are* the mere edges of His ways, And how small a whisper we hear of Him! But the thunder of His power who can understand?"

Described as

Great.

Ps 79:11 Let the groaning of the prisoner come before You; According to the greatness of Your power Preserve those who are appointed to die;

Nah 1:3 The LORD *is* slow to anger and great in power, And will not at all acquit *the wicked.* The LORD has His way In the whirlwind and in the storm, And the clouds *are* the dust of His feet.

Strong.

Ps 89:13 You have a mighty arm; Strong is Your hand, *and* high is Your right hand.

Ps 136:12 With a strong hand, and with an outstretched arm, For His mercy *endures* forever;

Glorious.

Ex 15:6 "Your right hand, O LORD, has become glorious in power; Your right hand, O LORD, has dashed the enemy in pieces.

Is 63:12 Who led *them* by the right hand of Moses, With His glorious arm, Dividing the water before them To make for Himself an everlasting name,

Mighty.

Job 9:4 *God is* wise in heart and mighty in strength. Who has hardened *himself* against Him and prospered?

Ps 89:13 You have a mighty arm; Strong is Your hand, *and* high is Your right hand.

Everlasting.

Is 26:4 Trust in the LORD forever, For in YAH, the LORD, *is* everlasting strength.

Rom 1:20 For since the creation of the world His invisible *attributes* are clearly seen, being understood by the things that are made, *even* His eternal power and Godhead, so that they are without excuse,

Sovereign.

Rom 9:21 Does not the potter have power over the clay, from the same lump to make one vessel for honor and another for dishonor?

Effectual.

Is 43:13 Indeed before the day *was,* I *am* He; And *there is* no one who can deliver out of My hand; I work, and who will reverse it?"

Eph 3:7 of which I became a minister according to the gift of the grace of God given to me by the effective working of His power.

Irresistible.

Deut 32:39 'Now see that I, *even* I, *am* He, And *there is* no God besides Me; I kill and I make alive; I wound and I heal; Nor *is there any* who can deliver from My hand.

Dan 4:35 All the inhabitants of the earth *are* reputed as nothing; He does according to His will in the army of heaven And *among* the inhabitants of the earth. No one can restrain His hand Or say to Him, "What have You done?"

Incomparable.

Ex 15:11–12 "Who *is* like You, O LORD, among the gods? Who *is* like You, glorious in holiness, Fearful in praises, doing wonders? **12** You stretched out Your right hand; The earth swallowed them.

Deut 3:24 'O Lord GOD, You have begun to show Your servant Your greatness and Your mighty hand, for what god *is there* in heaven or on earth who can do *anything* like Your works and Your mighty *deeds?*

Job 40:9 Have you an arm like God? Or can you thunder with a voice like His?

Ps 89:8 O LORD God of hosts, Who *is* mighty like You, O LORD? Your faithfulness also surrounds You.

Unsearchable.

Job 5:9 Who does great things, and unsearchable, Marvelous things without number.

Job 9:10 He does great things past finding out, Yes, wonders without number.

Incomprehensible.

Job 26:14 Indeed these *are* the mere edges of His ways, And how small a whisper we hear of Him! But the thunder of His power who can understand?"

Eccl 3:11 He has made everything beautiful in its time. Also He has put eternity in their hearts, except that no one can find out the work that God does from beginning to end.

Can accomplish anything.

Gen 18:14 Is anything too hard for the LORD? At the appointed time I will return to you, according to the time of life, and Sarah shall have a son."

Jer 32:27 "Behold, I *am* the LORD, the God of all flesh. Is there anything too hard for Me?

Matt 19:26 But Jesus looked at *them* and said to them, "With men this is impossible, but with God all things are possible."

Can save by many or by few.

1 Sam 14:6 Then Jonathan said to the young man who bore his armor, "Come, let us go over to the garrison of these uncircumcised; it may be that the LORD will work for us. For nothing restrains the LORD from saving by many or by few."

Is the source of all other strength.

1 Chr 29:12 Both riches and honor *come* from You, And You reign over all. In Your hand *is* power and might; In Your hand *it is* to make great And to give strength to all.

Ps 68:35 O God, *You are* more awesome than Your holy places. The God of Israel *is* He who gives strength and power to *His* people. Blessed *be* God!

Exhibited in

Creation.

Ps 102:25 Of old You laid the foundation of the earth, And the heavens *are* the work of Your hands.

Jer 10:12 He has made the earth by His power, He has established the world by His wisdom, And has stretched out the heavens at His discretion.

Establishing and governing all things.

Ps 65:6 Who established the mountains by His strength, *Being* clothed with power;

Ps 66:7 He rules by His power forever; His eyes observe the nations; Do not let the rebellious exalt themselves. Selah

The miracles of Christ.

Luke 11:20 But if I cast out demons with the finger of God, surely the kingdom of God has come upon you.

The resurrection of Christ.

2 Cor 13:4 For though He was crucified in weakness, yet He lives by the power of God. For we also are weak in Him, but we shall live with Him by the power of God toward you.

Col 2:12 buried with Him in baptism, in which you also were raised with *Him* through faith in the working of God, who raised Him from the dead.

The resurrection of saints.

1 Cor 6:14 And God both raised up the Lord and will also raise us up by His power.

The work of the gospel.

Rom 1:16 For I am not ashamed of the gospel of Christ, for it is the power of God to salvation for everyone who believes, for the Jew first and also for the Greek.

1 Cor 1:18 For the message of the cross is foolishness to those who are perishing, but to us who are being saved it is the power of God.

1 Cor 1:24 but to those who are called, both Jews and Greeks, Christ the power of God and the wisdom of God.

Delivering His people.

Ps 106:8 Nevertheless He saved them for His name's sake, That He might make His mighty power known.

The destruction of the wicked.

Ex 9:16 But indeed for this *purpose* I have raised you up, that I may show My power *in* you, and that My name may be declared in all the earth.

Rom 9:22 *What* if God, wanting to show *His* wrath and to make His power known, endured with much longsuffering the vessels of wrath prepared for destruction,

Believers

Long for exhibitions of.

Ps 63:1–2 O God, You *are* my God; Early will I seek You; My soul thirsts for You; My flesh longs for You In a dry and thirsty land Where there is no water. 2 So I have looked for You in the sanctuary, To see Your power and Your glory.

Have confidence in.

Jer 20:11 But the LORD *is* with me as a mighty, awesome One. Therefore my persecutors will stumble, and will not prevail. They will be greatly ashamed, for they will not prosper. *Their* everlasting confusion will never be forgotten.

Receive increase of grace by.

2 Cor 9:8 And God *is* able to make all grace abound toward you, that you, always having all sufficiency in all *things,* may have an abundance for every good work.

Strengthened by.

Eph 6:10 Finally, my brethren, be strong in the Lord and in the power of His might.

Col 1:11 strengthened with all might, according to His glorious power, for all patience and longsuffering with joy;

Upheld by.

Ps 37:17 For the arms of the wicked shall be broken, But the LORD upholds the righteous.

Is 41:10 Fear not, for I *am* with you; Be not dismayed, for I *am* your God. I will strengthen you, Yes, I will help you, I will uphold you with My righteous right hand.'

Supported in affliction by.

2 Cor 6:7 by the word of truth, by the power of God, by the armor of righteousness on the right hand and on the left,

2 Tim 1:8 Therefore do not be ashamed of the testimony of our Lord, nor of me His prisoner, but share with me in the sufferings for the gospel according to the power of God,

Delivered by.

Neh 1:10 Now these *are* Your servants and Your people, whom You have redeemed by Your great power, and by Your strong hand.

Dan 3:17 If that *is the case,* our God whom we serve is able to deliver us from the burning fiery furnace, and He will deliver *us* from your hand, O king.

Exalted by.

Job 36:22 "Behold, God is exalted by His power; Who teaches like Him?

Kept by, to salvation.

1 Pet 1:5 who are kept by the power of God through faith for salvation ready to be revealed in the last time.

Exerted on their behalf.

2 Chr 16:9 For the eyes of the LORD run to and fro throughout the whole earth, to show Himself strong on behalf of *those* whose heart *is* loyal to Him. In this you have done foolishly; therefore from now on you shall have wars."

2 Cor 13:4 For though He was crucified in weakness, yet He lives by the power of God. For we also are weak in Him, but we shall live with Him by the power of God toward you.

Eph 1:19 and what *is* the exceeding greatness of His power toward us who believe, according to the working of His mighty power

Eph 3:20 Now to Him who is able to do exceedingly abundantly above all that we ask or think, according to the power that works in us,

Their faith rests in.

1 Cor 2:5 that your faith should not be in the wisdom of men but in the power of God.

Should be

Acknowledged.

1 Chr 29:11 Yours, O LORD, *is* the greatness, The power and the glory, The victory and the majesty; For all *that is* in heaven and in earth *is Yours;* Yours *is* the kingdom, O LORD, And You are exalted as head over all.

Is 33:13 Hear, you *who are* afar off, what I have done; And you *who are* near, acknowledge My might."

Pleaded in prayer.

Ps 79:11 Let the groaning of the prisoner come before You; According to the greatness of Your power Preserve those who are appointed to die;

Matt 6:13 And do not lead us into temptation, But deliver us from the evil one. For Yours is the kingdom and the power and the glory forever. Amen.

Feared.

Jer 5:22 Do you not fear Me?' says the LORD. 'Will you not tremble at My presence, Who have placed the sand as the bound of the sea, By a perpetual decree, that it cannot pass beyond it? And though its waves toss to and fro, Yet they cannot prevail; Though they roar, yet they cannot pass over it.

Matt 10:28 And do not fear those who kill the body but cannot kill the soul. But rather fear Him who is able to destroy both soul and body in hell.

Magnified.

Ps 21:13 Be exalted, O LORD, in Your own strength! We will sing and praise Your power.

Jude 1:25 To God our Savior, Who alone is wise, *Be* glory and majesty, Dominion and power, Both now and forever. Amen.

Efficiency of ministers is through.

1 Cor 3:6–8 I planted, Apollos watered, but God gave the increase. 7 So then neither he who plants is anything, nor he who waters, but God who gives the increase. 8 Now he who plants and he who waters are one, and each one will receive his own reward according to his own labor.

Gal 2:8 (for He who worked effectively in Peter for the apostleship to the circumcised also worked effectively in me toward the Gentiles),

Eph 3:7 of which I became a minister according to the gift of the grace of God given to me by the effective working of His power.

The wicked

Do not recognize.

Matt 22:29 Jesus answered and said to them, "You are mistaken, not knowing the Scriptures nor the power of God.

It is against them.

Ezra 8:22 For I was ashamed to request of the king an escort of soldiers and horsemen to help us against the enemy on the road, because we had spoken to the king, saying, "The hand of our God *is* upon all those for good who seek Him, but His power and His wrath *are* against all those who forsake Him."

Will be destroyed by.

Luke 12:5 But I will show you whom you should fear: Fear Him who, after He has killed, has power to cast into hell; yes, I say to you, fear Him!

The heavenly host magnify.

Rev 4:11 "You are worthy, O Lord, To receive glory and honor and power; For You created all things, And by Your will they exist and were created."

Rev 5:13 And every creature which is in heaven and on the earth and under the earth and such as are in the sea, and all that are in them, I heard saying: "Blessing and honor and glory and power *Be* to Him who sits on the throne, And to the Lamb, forever and ever!"

Rev 11:17 saying: "We give You thanks, O Lord God Almighty, The One who is and who was and who is to come, Because You have taken Your great power and reigned.

GOD, THE PROMISES OF

Contained in the Scriptures.

Rom 1:2 which He promised before through His prophets in the Holy Scriptures,

Made in Christ.

Eph 3:6 that the Gentiles should be fellow heirs, of the same body, and partakers of His promise in Christ through the gospel,

2 Tim 1:1 Paul, an apostle of Jesus Christ by the will of God, according to the promise of life which is in Christ Jesus,

Made to

Christ.

Gal 3:16 Now to Abraham and his Seed were the promises made. He does not say, "And to seeds," as of many, but as of one, *"And to your Seed,"* who is Christ.

Gal 3:19 What purpose then *does* the law *serve?* It was added because of transgressions, till the Seed should come to whom the promise was made; *and it was* appointed through angels by the hand of a mediator.

Abraham.

Gen 12:3 I will bless those who bless you, And I will curse him who curses you; And in you all the families of the earth shall be blessed."

Gen 12:7 Then the Lord appeared to Abram and said, "To your descendants I will give this land." And there he built an altar to the Lord, who had appeared to him.

Gal 3:16 Now to Abraham and his Seed were the promises made. He does not say, "And to seeds," as of many, but as of one, *"And to your Seed,"* who is Christ.

Isaac.

Gen 26:3–4 Dwell in this land, and I will be with you and bless you; for to you and your descendants I give all these lands, and I will perform the oath which I swore to Abraham your father. 4 And I will make your descendants multiply as the stars of heaven; I will give to your descendants all these lands; and in your seed all the nations of the earth shall be blessed;

Jacob.

Gen 28:14 Also your descendants shall be as the dust of the earth; you shall spread abroad to the west and the east, to the north and the south; and in you and in your seed all the families of the earth shall be blessed.

David.

2 Sam 7:12 "When your days are fulfilled and you rest with your fathers, I will set up your seed after you, who will come from your body, and I will establish his kingdom.

Ps 89:3 "I have made a covenant with My chosen, I have sworn to My servant David:

Ps 89:4 'Your seed I will establish forever, And build up your throne to all generations.' " Selah

Ps 89:35–36 Once I have sworn by My holiness; I will not lie to David: 36 His seed shall endure forever, And his throne as the sun before Me;

The Israelites.

Rom 9:4 who are Israelites, to whom *pertain* the adoption, the glory, the covenants, the giving of the law, the service *of God,* and the promises;

The fathers.

Acts 13:32 And we declare to you glad tidings—that promise which was made to the fathers.

Acts 26:6–7 And now I stand and am judged for the hope of the promise made by God to our fathers. 7 To this *promise* our twelve tribes, earnestly serving *God* night and day, hope to attain. For this hope's sake, King Agrippa, I am accused by the Jews.

All who are called of Him.

Acts 2:39 For the promise is to you and to your children, and to all who are afar off, as many as the Lord our God will call."

Those who love Him.

James 1:12 Blessed *is* the man who endures temptation; for when he has been approved, he will receive the crown of life which the Lord has promised to those who love Him.

James 2:5 Listen, my beloved brethren: Has God not chosen the poor of this world *to be* rich in faith and heirs of the kingdom which He promised to those who love Him?

Confirmed by an oath.

Ps 89:3–4 "I have made a covenant with My chosen, I have sworn to My servant David: 4 'Your seed I will establish forever, And build up your throne to all generations.' " Selah

Heb 8:6 But now He has obtained a more excellent ministry, inasmuch as He is also Mediator of a better covenant, which was established on better promises.

Covenant established upon.

Heb 8:6 But now He has obtained a more excellent ministry, inasmuch as He is also Mediator of a better covenant, which was established on better promises.

God is faithful to and remembers.

Ps 105:42 For He remembered His holy promise, *And* Abraham His servant.

Luke 1:54–55 He has helped His servant Israel, In remembrance of *His* mercy, 55 As He spoke to our fathers, To Abraham and to his seed forever."

Titus 1:2 in hope of eternal life which God, who cannot lie, promised before time began,

Heb 10:23 Let us hold fast the confession of *our* hope without wavering, for He who promised *is* faithful.

Characteristics of,

Good.

1 Kin 8:56 "Blessed *be* the Lord, who has given rest to His people Israel, according to all that He promised. There has not failed one word of all His good promise, which He promised through His servant Moses.

Holy.

Ps 105:42 For He remembered His holy promise, *And* Abraham His servant.

Exceedingly great and precious.

2 Pet 1:4 by which have been given to us exceedingly great and precious promises, that through these you may be partakers of the divine nature, having escaped the corruption *that is* in the world through lust.

Confirmed in Christ.

Rom 15:8 Now I say that Jesus Christ has become a servant to the circumcision for the truth of God, to confirm the promises *made* to the fathers,

Certain in Christ.

2 Cor 1:20 For all the promises of God in Him *are* Yes, and in Him Amen, to the glory of God through us.

Fulfilled in Christ.

Luke 1:69–73 And has raised up a horn of salvation for us In the house of His servant David, 70 As He spoke by the mouth of His holy prophets, Who *have been*

since the world began, **71** That we should be saved from our enemies And from the hand of all who hate us, **72** To perform the mercy *promised* to our fathers And to remember His holy covenant, **73** The oath which He swore to our father Abraham:

Acts 13:23 From this man's seed, according to *the* promise, God raised up for Israel a Savior—Jesus—

Obtained through faith and patience.

Rom 4:13 For the promise that he would be the heir of the world *was* not to Abraham or to his seed through the law, but through the righteousness of faith.

Rom 4:16 Therefore *it is* of faith that *it might be* according to grace, so that the promise might be sure to all the seed, not only to those who are of the law, but also to those who are of the faith of Abraham, who is the father of us all

Heb 6:12 that you do not become sluggish, but imitate those who through faith and patience inherit the promises.

Heb 6:15 And so, after he had patiently endured, he obtained the promise.

Heb 10:36 For you have need of endurance, so that after you have done the will of God, you may receive the promise:

Heb 11:33 who through faith subdued kingdoms, worked righteousness, obtained promises, stopped the mouths of lions,

Given to those who believe.

Gal 3:22 But the Scripture has confined all under sin, that the promise by faith in Jesus Christ might be given to those who believe.

Performed in due season.

Jer 33:14 'Behold, the days are coming,' says the LORD, 'that I will perform that good thing which I have promised to the house of Israel and to the house of Judah:

Acts 7:17 "But when the time of the promise drew near which God had sworn to Abraham, the people grew and multiplied in Egypt

Gal 4:4 But when the fullness of the time had come, God sent forth His Son, born of a woman, born under the law,

Not one shall fail.

Josh 23:14 "Behold, this day I *am* going the way of all the earth. And you know in all your hearts and in all your souls that not one thing has failed of all the good things which the LORD your God spoke concerning you. All have come to pass for you; not one word of them has failed.

1 Kin 8:56 "Blessed *be* the LORD, who has given rest to His people Israel, according to all that He promised. There has not failed one word of all His good promise, which He promised through His servant Moses.

The law not against.

Gal 3:21 *Is* the law then against the promises of God? Certainly not! For if there had been a law given which could have given life, truly righteousness would have been by the law.

The law could not annul.

Gal 3:17 And this I say, *that* the law, which was four hundred and thirty years later, cannot annul the cov-

enant that was confirmed before by God in Christ, that it should make the promise of no effect.

Subjects of,

Christ.

2 Sam 7:12–13 "When your days are fulfilled and you rest with your fathers, I will set up your seed after you, who will come from your body, and I will establish his kingdom. **13** He shall build a house for My name, and I will establish the throne of his kingdom forever.

Acts 13:22–23 And when He had removed him, He raised up for them David as king, to whom also He gave testimony and said, '*I have found David* the *son* of Jesse, *a man after My own heart,* who will do all My will.' **23** From this man's seed, according to *the* promise, God raised up for Israel a Savior—Jesus—

The Holy Spirit.

Acts 2:33 Therefore being exalted to the right hand of God, and having received from the Father the promise of the Holy Spirit, He poured out this which you now see and hear.

Eph 1:13 In Him you also *trusted,* after you heard the word of truth, the gospel of your salvation; in whom also, having believed, you were sealed with the Holy Spirit of promise,

The gospel.

Rom 1:1–2 Paul, a bondservant of Jesus Christ, called *to be* an apostle, separated to the gospel of God **2** which He promised before through His prophets in the Holy Scriptures,

Life in Christ.

2 Tim 1:1 Paul, an apostle of Jesus Christ by the will of God, according to the promise of life which is in Christ Jesus,

A crown of life.

James 1:12 Blessed *is* the man who endures temptation; for when he has been approved, he will receive the crown of life which the Lord has promised to those who love Him.

Eternal life.

Titus 1:2 in hope of eternal life which God, who cannot lie, promised before time began,

1 John 2:25 And this is the promise that He has promised us—eternal life.

Present and future life.

1 Tim 4:8 For bodily exercise profits a little, but godliness is profitable for all things, having promise of the life that now is and of that which is to come.

Adoption.

2 Cor 6:18 "*I will be a Father to you, And you shall be My sons and daughters, Says the LORD Almighty.*"

2 Cor 7:1 Therefore, having these promises, beloved, let us cleanse ourselves from all filthiness of the flesh and spirit, perfecting holiness in the fear of God.

Preservation in affliction.

Is 43:2 When you pass through the waters, I *will be* with you; And through the rivers, they shall not overflow you. When you walk through the fire, you shall not be burned, Nor shall the flame scorch you.

Blessing.

Deut 1:11 May the LORD God of your fathers make you a thousand times more numerous than you are, and bless you as He has promised you!

Forgiveness of sins.

Is 1:18 "Come now, and let us reason together," Says the LORD, "Though your sins are like scarlet, They shall be as white as snow; Though they are red like crimson, They shall be as wool.

Heb 8:12 *For I will be merciful to their unrighteousness, and their sins and their lawless deeds I will remember no more."*

Putting the law into the heart.

Jer 31:33 But this *is* the covenant that I will make with the house of Israel after those days, says the LORD: I will put My law in their minds, and write it on their hearts; and I will be their God, and they shall be My people.

Heb 8:10 *For this is the covenant that I will make with the house of Israel after those days, says the LORD: I will put My laws in their mind and write them on their hearts; and I will be their God, and they shall be My people.*

Second coming of Christ.

2 Pet 3:4 and saying, "Where is the promise of His coming? For since the fathers fell asleep, all things continue as *they were* from the beginning of creation."

New heavens and earth.

2 Pet 3:13 Nevertheless we, according to His promise, look for new heavens and a new earth in which righteousness dwells.

Entering into rest.

Josh 22:4 And now the LORD your God has given rest to your brethren, as He promised them; now therefore, return and go to your tents *and* to the land of your possession, which Moses the servant of the LORD gave you on the other side of the Jordan.

Heb 4:1 Therefore, since a promise remains of entering His rest, let us fear lest any of you seem to have come short of it.

Should lead to perfecting holiness.

2 Cor 7:1 Therefore, having these promises, beloved, let us cleanse ourselves from all filthiness of the flesh and spirit, perfecting holiness in the fear of God.

Believers

Are children of.

Rom 9:8 That is, those who *are* the children of the flesh, these *are* not the children of God; but the children of the promise are counted as the seed.

Gal 4:28 Now we, brethren, as Isaac *was*, are children of promise.

Are heirs of.

Rom 4:13 For the promise that he would be the heir of the world *was* not to Abraham or to his seed through the law, but through the righteousness of faith.

Gal 3:18 For if the inheritance *is* of the law, *it is* no longer of promise; but God gave *it* to Abraham by promise.

Gal 3:29 And if you *are* Christ's, then you are Abraham's seed, and heirs according to the promise.

Heb 6:17 Thus God, determining to show more abundantly to the heirs of promise the immutability of His counsel, confirmed *it* by an oath,

Heb 11:9 By faith he dwelt in the land of promise as *in* a foreign country, dwelling in tents with Isaac and Jacob, the heirs with him of the same promise;

Do not waver at.

Rom 4:20 He did not waver at the promise of God through unbelief, but was strengthened in faith, giving glory to God,

Have implicit confidence in.

Heb 11:11 By faith Sarah herself also received strength to conceive seed, and she bore a child when she was past the age, because she judged Him faithful who had promised.

Expect the performance of.

Luke 1:38 Then Mary said, "Behold the maidservant of the Lord! Let it be to me according to your word." And the angel departed from her.

Luke 1:45 Blessed *is* she who believed, for there will be a fulfillment of those things which were told her from the Lord."

2 Pet 3:13 Nevertheless we, according to His promise, look for new heavens and a new earth in which righteousness dwells.

Sometimes, through infirmity, tempted to doubt.

Ps 77:8 Has His mercy ceased forever? Has *His* promise failed forevermore?

Ps 77:10 And I said, "This *is* my anguish; *But I will remember* the years of the right hand of the Most High."

Plead in prayer.

Gen 32:9 Then Jacob said, "O God of my father Abraham and God of my father Isaac, the LORD who said to me, 'Return to your country and to your family, and I will deal well with you':

Gen 32:12 For You said, 'I will surely treat you well, and make your descendants as the sand of the sea, which cannot be numbered for multitude.' "

1 Chr 17:23 "And now, O LORD, the word which You have spoken concerning Your servant and concerning his house, *let it* be established forever, and do as You have said.

1 Chr 17:26 And now, LORD, You are God, and have promised this goodness to Your servant.

Is 43:26 Put Me in remembrance; Let us contend together; State your *case*, that you may be acquitted.

Wait for the performance of.

Acts 1:4 And being assembled together with *them*, He commanded them not to depart from Jerusalem, but to wait for the Promise of the Father, "which," He said, "you have heard from Me;

Fear, lest they come short of.

Heb 4:1 Therefore, since a promise remains of entering His rest, let us fear lest any of you seem to have come short of it.

Gentiles shall be partakers of.

Eph 3:6 that the Gentiles should be fellow heirs, of the same body, and partakers of His promise in Christ through the gospel,

Man, by nature, has no interest in.

Eph 2:12 that at that time you were without Christ, being aliens from the commonwealth of Israel and strangers from the covenants of promise, having no hope and without God in the world.

Scoffers despise.

2 Pet 3:3–4 knowing this first: that scoffers will come in the last days, walking according to their own lusts, **4** and saying, "Where is the promise of His coming? For since the fathers fell asleep, all things continue as *they were* from the beginning of creation."

GOD, THE PROVIDENCE OF

Is His care over His works.

Ps 145:9 The LORD *is* good to all, And His tender mercies *are* over all His works.

Is exercised in

Preserving His creatures.

Neh 9:6 You alone *are* the LORD; You have made heaven, The heaven of heavens, with all their host, The earth and everything on it, The seas and all that is in them, And You preserve them all. The host of heaven worships You.

Ps 36:6 Your righteousness *is* like the great mountains; Your judgments *are* a great deep; O LORD, You preserve man and beast.

Matt 10:29 Are not two sparrows sold for a copper coin? And not one of them falls to the ground apart from your Father's will.

Providing for His creatures.

Ps 104:27–28 These all wait for You, That You may give *them* their food in due season. **28** *What* You give them they gather in; You open Your hand, they are filled with good.

Ps 136:25 Who gives food to all flesh, For His mercy *endures* forever.

Ps 147:9 He gives to the beast its food, *And* to the young ravens that cry.

Matt 6:26 Look at the birds of the air, for they neither sow nor reap nor gather into barns; yet your heavenly Father feeds them. Are you not of more value than they?

Special preservation and protection of believers.

Ps 37:28 For the LORD loves justice, And does not forsake His saints; They are preserved forever, But the descendants of the wicked shall be cut off.

Ps 91:3–4 Surely He shall deliver you from the snare of the fowler *And* from the perilous pestilence. **4** He shall cover you with His feathers, And under His wings you shall take refuge; His truth *shall be your* shield and buckler.

Ps 91:11 For He shall give His angels charge over you, To keep you in all your ways.

Ps 140:7 O GOD the Lord, the strength of my salvation, You have covered my head in the day of battle.

Is 31:5 Like birds flying about, So will the LORD of hosts defend Jerusalem. Defending, He will also deliver *it*; Passing over, He will preserve *it*."

Matt 10:30 But the very hairs of your head are all numbered.

Prospering believers.

Gen 24:48 And I bowed my head and worshiped the LORD, and blessed the LORD God of my master Abraham, who had led me in the way of truth to take the daughter of my master's brother for his son.

Gen 24:56 And he said to them, "Do not hinder me, since the LORD has prospered my way; send me away so that I may go to my master."

Leading believers.

Deut 8:2 And you shall remember that the LORD your God led you all the way these forty years in the wilderness, to humble you *and* test you, to know what *was* in your heart, whether you would keep His commandments or not.

Deut 8:15 who led you through that great and terrible wilderness, *in which were* fiery serpents and scorpions and thirsty land where there was no water; who brought water for you out of the flinty rock;

Is 31:5 Like birds flying about, So will the LORD of hosts defend Jerusalem. Defending, He will also deliver *it*; Passing over, He will preserve *it*."

Is 63:12 Who led *them* by the right hand of Moses, With His glorious arm, Dividing the water before them To make for Himself an everlasting name,

Bringing His words to pass.

Num 26:65 For the LORD had said of them, "They shall surely die in the wilderness." So there was not left a man of them, except Caleb the son of Jephunneh and Joshua the son of Nun.

Josh 21:45 Not a word failed of any good thing which the LORD had spoken to the house of Israel. All came to pass.

Luke 21:32–33 Assuredly, I say to you, this generation will by no means pass away till all things take place. **33** Heaven and earth will pass away, but My words will by no means pass away.

Ordaining the lives of men.

1 Sam 2:7–8 The LORD makes poor and makes rich; He brings low and lifts up. **8** He raises the poor from the dust *And* lifts the beggar from the ash heap, To set *them* among princes And make them inherit the throne of glory. "For the pillars of the earth *are* the LORD's, And He has set the world upon them.

Ps 75:6–7 For exaltation *comes* neither from the east Nor from the west nor from the south. **7** But God *is* the Judge: He puts down one, And exalts another.

Prov 16:9 A man's heart plans his way, But the LORD directs his steps.

Prov 19:21 There are many plans in a man's heart, Nevertheless the LORD's counsel—that will stand.

Prov 20:24 A man's steps *are* of the LORD; How then can a man understand his own way?

Determining the period of human life.

Ps 31:15 My times *are* in Your hand; Deliver me from the hand of my enemies, And from those who persecute me.

Ps 39:5 Indeed, You have made my days *as* handbreadths, And my age *is* as nothing before You; Certainly every man at his best state *is* but vapor. Selah

Acts 17:26 And He has made from one blood every nation of men to dwell on all the face of the earth, and has determined their preappointed times and the boundaries of their dwellings,

Defeating wicked designs.

Ex 15:9–19 The enemy said, 'I will pursue, I will overtake, I will divide the spoil; My desire shall be satisfied on them. I will draw my sword, My hand shall destroy them.' **10** You blew with Your wind, The sea covered them; They sank like lead in the mighty waters. **11** "Who *is* like You, O LORD, among the gods? Who *is* like You, glorious in holiness, Fearful in praises, doing wonders? **12** You stretched out Your right hand; The earth swallowed them. **13** You in Your mercy have led forth The people whom You have redeemed; You have guided *them* in Your strength To Your holy habitation. **14** "The people will hear *and* be afraid; Sorrow will take hold of the inhabitants of Philistia. **15** Then the chiefs of Edom will be dismayed; The mighty men of Moab, Trembling will take hold of them; All the inhabitants of Canaan will melt away. **16** Fear and dread will fall on them; By the greatness of Your arm They will be *as* still as a stone, Till Your people pass over, O LORD, Till the people pass over Whom You have purchased. **17** You will bring them in and plant them In the mountain of Your inheritance, *In* the place, O LORD, *which* You have made For Your own dwelling, The sanctuary, O LORD, *which* Your hands have established. **18** "The LORD shall reign forever and ever." **19** For the horses of Pharaoh went with his chariots and his horsemen into the sea, and the LORD brought back the waters of the sea upon them. But the children of Israel went on dry *land* in the midst of the sea.

2 Sam 17:14–15 So Absalom and all the men of Israel said, "The advice of Hushai the Archite *is* better than the advice of Ahithophel." For the LORD had purposed to defeat the good advice of Ahithophel, to the intent that the LORD might bring disaster on Absalom. **15** Then Hushai said to Zadok and Abiathar the priests, "Thus and so Ahithophel advised Absalom and the elders of Israel, and thus and so I have advised.

Ps 33:10 The LORD brings the counsel of the nations to nothing; He makes the plans of the peoples of no effect.

Overruling wicked designs for good.

Gen 45:5–7 But now, do not therefore be grieved or angry with yourselves because you sold me here; for God sent me before you to preserve life. **6** For these two years the famine *has been* in the land, and *there are* still five years in which *there will be* neither plowing nor harvesting. **7** And God sent me before you to preserve a posterity for you in the earth, and to save your lives by a great deliverance.

Gen 50:20 But as for you, you meant evil against me; *but* God meant it for good, in order to bring it about as *it is* this day, to save many people alive.

Phil 1:12 But I want you to know, brethren, that the things *which happened* to me have actually turned out for the furtherance of the gospel,

Preserving the course of nature.

Gen 8:22 "While the earth remains, Seedtime and harvest, Cold and heat, Winter and summer, And day and night Shall not cease."

Job 26:10 He drew a circular horizon on the face of the waters, At the boundary of light and darkness.

Ps 104:5–9 *You who* laid the foundations of the earth, So *that* it should not be moved forever, **6** You covered it with the deep as *with* a garment; The waters stood above the mountains. **7** At Your rebuke they fled; At the voice of Your thunder they hastened away. **8** They went up over the mountains; They went down into the valleys, To the place which You founded for them. **9** You have set a boundary that they may not pass over, That they may not return to cover the earth.

Directing all events.

Josh 7:14 In the morning therefore you shall be brought according to your tribes. And it shall be *that* the tribe which the LORD takes shall come according to families; and the family which the LORD takes shall come by households; and the household which the LORD takes shall come man by man.

1 Sam 6:7–10 Now therefore, make a new cart, take two milk cows which have never been yoked, and hitch the cows to the cart; and take their calves home, away from them. **8** Then take the ark of the LORD and set it on the cart; and put the articles of gold which you are returning to Him *as* a trespass offering in a chest by its side. Then send it away, and let it go. **9** And watch: if it goes up the road to its own territory, to Beth Shemesh, *then* He has done us this great evil. But if not, then we shall know that *it is* not His hand *that* struck us—it happened to us by chance." **10** Then the men did so; they took two milk cows and hitched them to the cart, and shut up their calves at home.

1 Sam 6:12 Then the cows headed straight for the road to Beth Shemesh, *and* went along the highway, lowing as they went, and did not turn aside to the right hand or the left. And the lords of the Philistines went after them to the border of Beth Shemesh.

Prov 16:33 The lot is cast into the lap, But its every decision *is* from the LORD.

Is 44:7 And who can proclaim as I do? Then let him declare it and set it in order for Me, Since I appointed the ancient people. And the things that are coming and shall come, Let them show these to them.

Acts 1:26 And they cast their lots, and the lot fell on Matthias. And he was numbered with the eleven apostles.

Ruling the elements.

Job 37:9–13 From the chamber *of the south* comes the whirlwind, And cold from the scattering winds *of the north*. **10** By the breath of God ice is given, And the broad waters are frozen. **11** Also with moisture He saturates the thick clouds; He scatters His bright clouds. **12** And they swirl about, being turned by His guidance, That they may do whatever He commands them On the face of the whole earth. **13** He causes it to come, Whether for correction, Or for His land, Or for mercy.

Is 50:2 Why, when I came, *was there* no man? *Why,* when I called, *was there* none to answer? Is My hand shortened at all that it cannot redeem? Or have I no power to deliver? Indeed with My rebuke I dry up the sea, I make the rivers a wilderness; Their fish stink because *there is* no water, And die of thirst.

Jon 1:4 But the LORD sent out a great wind on the sea,

and there was a mighty tempest on the sea, so that the ship was about to be broken up.

Jon 1:15 So they picked up Jonah and threw him into the sea, and the sea ceased from its raging.

Nah 1:4 He rebukes the sea and makes it dry, And dries up all the rivers. Bashan and Carmel wither, And the flower of Lebanon wilts.

Ordering the minutest matters.

Matt 10:29–30 Are not two sparrows sold for a copper coin? And not one of them falls to the ground apart from your Father's will. **30** But the very hairs of your head are all numbered.

Luke 21:18 But not a hair of your head shall be lost.

Is righteous.

Ps 145:17 The LORD *is* righteous in all His ways, Gracious in all His works.

Dan 4:37 Now I, Nebuchadnezzar, praise and extol and honor the King of heaven, all of whose works *are* truth, and His ways justice. And those who walk in pride He is able to put down.

Is ever watchful.

Ps 121:4 Behold, He who keeps Israel Shall neither slumber nor sleep.

Is 27:3 I, the LORD, keep it, I water it every moment; Lest any hurt it, I keep it night and day.

Is all pervading.

Ps 139:1–5 O LORD, You have searched me and known *me.* **2** You know my sitting down and my rising up; You understand my thought afar off. **3** You comprehend my path and my lying down, And are acquainted with all my ways. **4** For *there is* not a word on my tongue, *But* behold, O LORD, You know it altogether. **5** You have hedged me behind and before, And laid Your hand upon me.

Sometimes dark and mysterious.

Ps 36:6 Your righteousness *is* like the great mountains; Your judgments *are* a great deep; O LORD, You preserve man and beast.

Ps 73:16 When I thought *how* to understand this, It *was* too painful for me—

Ps 77:19 Your way *was* in the sea, Your path in the great waters, And Your footsteps were not known.

Rom 11:33 Oh, the depth of the riches both of the wisdom and knowledge of God! How unsearchable *are* His judgments and His ways past finding out!

All things are ordered by,

For His glory.

Is 63:14 As a beast goes down into the valley, *And* the Spirit of the LORD causes him to rest, So You lead Your people, To make Yourself a glorious name.

For good to believers.

Rom 8:28 And we know that all things work together for good to those who love God, to those who are the called according to *His* purpose.

The wicked sometimes made to further.

Is 10:5–12 "Woe to Assyria, the rod of My anger And the staff in whose hand is My indignation. **6** I will send him against an ungodly nation, And against the people of My wrath I will give him charge, To seize the spoil, to take the prey, And to tread them down

like the mire of the streets. **7** Yet he does not mean so, Nor does his heart think so; But *it is* in his heart to destroy, And cut off not a few nations. **8** For he says, '*Are* not my princes altogether kings? **9** *Is* not Calno like Carchemish? *Is* not Hamath like Arpad? *Is* not Samaria like Damascus? **10** As my hand has found the kingdoms of the idols, Whose carved images excelled those of Jerusalem and Samaria, **11** As I have done to Samaria and her idols, Shall I not do also to Jerusalem and her idols?' " **12** Therefore it shall come to pass, when the Lord has performed all His work on Mount Zion and on Jerusalem, *that He will say,* "I will punish the fruit of the arrogant heart of the king of Assyria, and the glory of his haughty looks."

Acts 3:17–18 "Yet now, brethren, I know that you did *it* in ignorance, as *did* also your rulers. **18** But those things which God foretold by the mouth of all His prophets, that the Christ would suffer, He has thus fulfilled.

To be acknowledged

In prosperity.

Deut 8:18 "And you shall remember the LORD your God, for *it is* He who gives you power to get wealth, that He may establish His covenant which He swore to your fathers, as *it is* this day.

1 Chr 29:12 Both riches and honor *come* from You, And You reign over all. In Your hand *is* power and might; In Your hand *it is* to make great And to give strength to all.

In adversity.

Job 1:21 And he said: "Naked I came from my mother's womb, And naked shall I return there. The LORD gave, and the LORD has taken away; Blessed be the name of the LORD."

Ps 119:15 I will meditate on Your precepts, And contemplate Your ways.

In public calamities.

Amos 3:6 If a trumpet is blown in a city, will not the people be afraid? If there is calamity in a city, will not the LORD have done *it?*

In our daily support.

Gen 48:15 And he blessed Joseph, and said: "God, before whom my fathers Abraham and Isaac walked, The God who has fed me all my life long to this day,

In all things.

Prov 3:6 In all your ways acknowledge Him, And He shall direct your paths.

Cannot be defeated.

1 Kin 22:30 And the king of Israel said to Jehoshaphat, "I will disguise myself and go into battle; but you put on your robes." So the king of Israel disguised himself and went into battle.

1 Kin 22:34 Now a *certain* man drew a bow at random, and struck the king of Israel between the joints of his armor. So he said to the driver of his chariot, "Turn around and take me out of the battle, for I am wounded."

Prov 21:30 *There is* no wisdom or understanding Or counsel against the LORD.

Man's efforts are useless without.

Ps 127:1–2 Unless the LORD builds the house, They labor in vain who build it; Unless the LORD guards the city,

The watchman stays awake in vain. **2** *It is* vain for you to rise up early, To sit up late, To eat the bread of sorrows; *For* so He gives His beloved sleep.

Prov 21:31 The horse *is* prepared for the day of battle, But deliverance *is* of the LORD.

Believers should

Trust in.

Matt 6:33–34 But seek first the kingdom of God and His righteousness, and all these things shall be added to you. **34** Therefore do not worry about tomorrow, for tomorrow will worry about its own things. Sufficient for the day *is* its own trouble.

Matt 10:9 Provide neither gold nor silver nor copper in your money belts,

Matt 10:29–31 Are not two sparrows sold for a copper coin? And not one of them falls to the ground apart from your Father's will. **30** But the very hairs of your head are all numbered. **31** Do not fear therefore; you are of more value than many sparrows.

Have full confidence in.

Ps 16:8 I have set the LORD always before me; Because He *is* at my right hand I shall not be moved.

Ps 139:10 Even there Your hand shall lead me, And Your right hand shall hold me.

Commit their works to.

Prov 16:3 Commit your works to the LORD, And your thoughts will be established.

Encourage themselves with.

1 Sam 30:6 Now David was greatly distressed, for the people spoke of stoning him, because the soul of all the people was grieved, every man for his sons and his daughters. But David strengthened himself in the LORD his God.

Pray in dependence upon.

Acts 12:5 Peter was therefore kept in prison, but constant prayer was offered to God for him by the church.

Pray to be guided by.

Gen 24:12–14 Then he said, "O LORD God of my master Abraham, please give me success this day, and show kindness to my master Abraham. **13** Behold, *here* I stand by the well of water, and the daughters of the men of the city are coming out to draw water. **14** Now let it be that the young woman to whom I say, 'Please let down your pitcher that I may drink,' and she says, 'Drink, and I will also give your camels a drink'—*let* her *be the one* You have appointed for Your servant Isaac. And by this I will know that You have shown kindness to my master."

Gen 28:20–21 Then Jacob made a vow, saying, "If God will be with me, and keep me in this way that I am going, and give me bread to eat and clothing to put on, **21** so that I come back to my father's house in peace, then the LORD shall be my God.

Acts 1:24 And they prayed and said, "You, O Lord, who know the hearts of all, show which of these two You have chosen

Result of depending upon.

Luke 22:35 And He said to them, "When I sent you without money bag, knapsack, and sandals, did you lack anything?" So they said, "Nothing."

Connected with the use of means.

1 Kin 21:19 You shall speak to him, saying, 'Thus says the LORD: "Have you murdered and also taken possession?" ' And you shall speak to him, saying, 'Thus says the LORD: "In the place where dogs licked the blood of Naboth, dogs shall lick your blood, even yours." ' "

1 Kin 22:37–38 So the king died, and was brought to Samaria. And they buried the king in Samaria. **38** Then *someone* washed the chariot at a pool in Samaria, and the dogs licked up his blood while the harlots bathed, according to the word of the LORD which He had spoken.

Mic 5:2 "But you, Bethlehem Ephrathah, *Though* you are little among the thousands of Judah, *Yet* out of you shall come forth to Me The One to be Ruler in Israel, Whose goings forth *are* from of old, From everlasting."

Luke 2:1–4 And it came to pass in those days *that* a decree went out from Caesar Augustus that all the world should be registered. **2** This census first took place while Quirinius was governing Syria. **3** So all went to be registered, everyone to his own city. **4** Joseph also went up from Galilee, out of the city of Nazareth, into Judea, to the city of David, which is called Bethlehem, because he was of the house and lineage of David,

Acts 27:22 And now I urge you to take heart, for there will be no loss of life among you, but only of the ship.

Acts 27:31–32 Paul said to the centurion and the soldiers, "Unless these men stay in the ship, you cannot be saved." **32** Then the soldiers cut away the ropes of the skiff and let it fall off.

Danger of denying.

Is 10:13–17 For he says: "By the strength of my hand I have done *it*, And by my wisdom, for I am prudent; Also I have removed the boundaries of the people, And have robbed their treasuries; So I have put down the inhabitants like a valiant *man*. **14** My hand has found like a nest the riches of the people, And as one gathers eggs *that are* left, I have gathered all the earth; And there was no one who moved *his* wing, Nor opened *his* mouth with even a peep." **15** Shall the ax boast itself against him who chops with it? Or shall the saw exalt itself against him who saws with it? As if a rod could wield *itself* against those who lift it up, Or as if a staff could lift up, *as if it were* not wood! **16** Therefore the Lord, the Lord of hosts, Will send leanness among his fat ones; And under his glory He will kindle a burning Like the burning of a fire. **17** So the Light of Israel will be for a fire, And his Holy One for a flame; It will burn and devour His thorns and his briers in one day.

Ezek 28:2–10 "Son of man, say to the prince of Tyre, 'Thus says the Lord GOD: "Because your heart *is* lifted up, And you say, 'I *am* a god, I sit *in* the seat of gods, In the midst of the seas,' Yet you *are* a man, and not a god, Though you set your heart as the heart of a god **3** (Behold, you *are* wiser than Daniel! There is no secret that can be hidden from you! **4** With your wisdom and your understanding You have gained riches for yourself, And gathered gold and silver into your treasuries; **5** By your great wisdom in trade you have increased your riches, And your heart is lifted up because of your riches)," **6** 'Therefore thus says the Lord GOD: "Because you have set your heart as the heart of a god, **7** Behold, therefore, I will bring strangers against you, The most terrible of the nations; And they shall draw their swords against the beauty of your wisdom, And defile your splendor. **8** They shall throw you down into the Pit, And you shall die the death of the slain In the midst of the seas. **9** "Will you still say before him who slays you, 'I *am* a god'? But you *shall be* a man, and not a god, In the hand of him who slays you. **10** You shall die the death of the uncircumcised By the hand of aliens; For I have spoken," says the Lord GOD.' "

Dan 4:29–31 At the end of the twelve months he was walking about the royal palace of Babylon. **30** The king spoke, saying, "Is not this great Babylon, that I have built for a royal dwelling by my mighty power and for the honor of my majesty?" **31** While the word *was still* in the king's mouth, a voice fell from heaven: "King Nebuchadnezzar, to you it is spoken: the kingdom has departed from you!

Hos 2:8–9 For she did not know That I gave her grain, new wine, and oil, And multiplied her silver and gold— Which they prepared for Baal. **9** "Therefore I will return and take away My grain in its time And My new wine in its season, And will take back My wool and My linen, *Given* to cover her nakedness.

GOD, THE RIGHTEOUSNESS OF

Is part of His character.

Ps 7:9 Oh, let the wickedness of the wicked come to an end, But establish the just; For the righteous God tests the hearts and minds.

Ps 11:7 For the LORD *is* righteous, He loves righteousness; His countenance beholds the upright.

Ps 116:5 Gracious *is* the LORD, and righteous; Yes, our God *is* merciful.

Ps 119:137 Righteous *are* You, O LORD, And upright *are* Your judgments.

Described as

Very high.

Ps 71:19 Also Your righteousness, O God, *is* very high, You who have done great things; O God, who *is* like You?

Abundant.

Ps 48:10 According to Your name, O God, So *is* Your praise to the ends of the earth; Your right hand is full of righteousness.

Beyond computation.

Ps 71:15 My mouth shall tell of Your righteousness *And* Your salvation all the day, For I do not know *their* limits.

Everlasting.

Ps 119:142 Your righteousness *is* an everlasting righteousness, And Your law *is* truth.

Enduring forever.

Ps 111:3 His work *is* honorable and glorious, And His righteousness endures forever.

The habitation of his throne.

Ps 97:2 Clouds and darkness surround Him; Righteousness and justice *are* the foundation of His throne.

Christ acknowledged.

John 17:25 O righteous Father! The world has not known You, but I have known You; and these have known that You sent Me.

Christ committed His cause to.

1 Pet 2:23 who, when He was reviled, did not revile in return; when He suffered, He did not threaten, but committed *Himself* to Him who judges righteously;

Angels acknowledge.

Rev 16:5 And I heard the angel of the waters saying: "You are righteous, O Lord, The One who is and who was and who is to be, Because You have judged these things.

Exhibited in

His testimonies.

Ps 119:138 Your testimonies, *which* You have commanded, *Are* righteous and very faithful.

Ps 119:144 The righteousness of Your testimonies *is* everlasting; Give me understanding, and I shall live.

His commandments.

Deut 4:8 And what great nation *is there* that has *such* statutes and righteous judgments as are in all this law which I set before you this day?

Ps 119:172 My tongue shall speak of Your word, For all Your commandments *are* righteousness.

His judgments.

Ps 19:9 The fear of the LORD *is* clean, enduring forever; The judgments of the LORD *are* true *and* righteous altogether.

Ps 119:7 I will praise You with uprightness of heart, When I learn Your righteous judgments.

Ps 119:62 At midnight I will rise to give thanks to You, Because of Your righteous judgments.

His word.

Ps 119:123 My eyes fail *from seeking* Your salvation And Your righteous word.

His ways.

Ps 145:17 The LORD *is* righteous in all His ways, Gracious in all His works.

His acts.

Judg 5:11 Far from the noise of the archers, among the watering places, There they shall recount the righteous acts of the LORD, The righteous acts *for* His villagers in Israel; Then the people of the LORD shall go down to the gates.

1 Sam 12:7 Now therefore, stand still, that I may reason with you before the LORD concerning all the righteous acts of the LORD which He did to you and your fathers:

His government.

Ps 96:13 For He is coming, for He is coming to judge the earth. He shall judge the world with righteousness, And the peoples with His truth.

Ps 98:9 For He is coming to judge the earth. With righteousness He shall judge the world, And the peoples with equity.

The gospel.

Ps 85:10 Mercy and truth have met together; Righteousness and peace have kissed.

Rom 3:25–26 whom God set forth *as* a propitiation by His blood, through faith, to demonstrate His righteousness, because in His forbearance God had passed over the sins that were previously committed, **26** to demonstrate at the present time His righteousness, that He might be just and the justifier of the one who has faith in Jesus.

The final judgment.

Acts 17:31 because He has appointed a day on which He will judge the world in righteousness by the Man whom He has ordained. He has given assurance of this to all by raising Him from the dead."

The punishment of the wicked.

Rom 2:5 But in accordance with your hardness and your impenitent heart you are treasuring up for yourself wrath in the day of wrath and revelation of the righteous judgment of God,

2 Thess 1:6 since *it is* a righteous thing with God to repay with tribulation those who trouble you,

Rev 16:7 And I heard another from the altar saying, "Even so, Lord God Almighty, true and righteous *are* Your judgments."

Rev 19:2 For true and righteous *are* His judgments, because He has judged the great harlot who corrupted the earth with her fornication; and He has avenged on her the blood of His servants *shed* by her."

Shown to believers' posterity.

Ps 103:17 But the mercy of the LORD *is* from everlasting to everlasting On those who fear Him, And His righteousness to children's children,

Shown openly before the heathen.

Ps 98:2 The LORD has made known His salvation; His righteousness He has revealed in the sight of the nations.

He delights in the exercise of.

Jer 9:24 But let him who glories glory in this, That he understands and knows Me, That I *am* the LORD, exercising lovingkindness, judgment, and righteousness in the earth. For in these I delight," says the LORD.

The heavens shall declare.

Ps 50:6 Let the heavens declare His righteousness, For God Himself *is* Judge. Selah

Ps 97:6 The heavens declare His righteousness, And all the peoples see His glory.

Believers

Ascribe, to Him.

Job 36:3 I will fetch my knowledge from afar; I will ascribe righteousness to my Maker.

Dan 9:7 O Lord, righteousness *belongs* to You, but to us shame of face, as *it is* this day—to the men of Judah, to the inhabitants of Jerusalem and all Israel, those near and those far off in all the countries to which You have driven them, because of the unfaithfulness which they have committed against You.

Acknowledge, in His dealings.

Ezra 9:15 O LORD God of Israel, You *are* righteous, for we are left as a remnant, as *it is* this day. Here we are

before You, in our guilt, though no one can stand before You because of this!"

Acknowledge, though the wicked prosper.

Jer 12:1 Righteous *are* You, O LORD, when I plead with You; Yet let me talk with You about *Your* judgments. Why does the way of the wicked prosper? *Why* are those happy who deal so treacherously?

Ps 73:12–17 Behold, these *are* the ungodly, Who are always at ease; They increase *in* riches. **13** Surely I have cleansed my heart *in* vain, And washed my hands in innocence. **14** For all day long I have been plagued, And chastened every morning. **15** If I had said, "I will speak thus," Behold, I would have been untrue to the generation of Your children. **16** When I thought *how* to understand this, It *was* too painful for me— **17** Until I went into the sanctuary of God; *Then* I understood their end.

Recognize, in the fulfillment of His promises.

Neh 9:8 You found his heart faithful before You, And made a covenant with him To give the land of the Canaanites, The Hittites, the Amorites, The Perizzites, the Jebusites, And the Girgashites— To give *it* to his descendants. You have performed Your words, For You *are* righteous.

Confident of beholding.

Mic 7:9 I will bear the indignation of the LORD, Because I have sinned against Him, Until He pleads my case And executes justice for me. He will bring me forth to the light; I will see His righteousness.

Upheld by.

Is 41:10 Fear not, for I *am* with you; Be not dismayed, for I *am* your God. I will strengthen you, Yes, I will help you, I will uphold you with My righteous right hand.'

Do not conceal.

Ps 40:10 I have not hidden Your righteousness within my heart; I have declared Your faithfulness and Your salvation; I have not concealed Your lovingkindness and Your truth From the great assembly.

Talk of.

Ps 35:28 And my tongue shall speak of Your righteousness *And* of Your praise all the day long.

Ps 71:15–16 My mouth shall tell of Your righteousness *And* Your salvation all the day, For I do not know *their* limits. **16** I will go in the strength of the Lord GOD; I will make mention of Your righteousness, of Yours only.

Ps 71:24 My tongue also shall talk of Your righteousness all the day long; For they are confounded, For they are brought to shame Who seek my hurt.

Declare to others.

Ps 22:31 They will come and declare His righteousness to a people who will be born, That He has done *this*.

Magnify.

Ps 7:17 I will praise the LORD according to His righteousness, And will sing praise to the name of the LORD Most High.

Ps 51:14 Deliver me from the guilt of bloodshed, O God, The God of my salvation, *And* my tongue shall sing aloud of Your righteousness.

Ps 145:7 They shall utter the memory of Your great goodness, And shall sing of Your righteousness.

Plead in prayer.

Ps 143:11 Revive me, O LORD, for Your name's sake! For Your righteousness' sake bring my soul out of trouble.

Dan 9:16 "O Lord, according to all Your righteousness, I pray, let Your anger and Your fury be turned away from Your city Jerusalem, Your holy mountain; because for our sins, and for the iniquities of our fathers, Jerusalem and Your people *are* a reproach to all *those* around us.

We should pray

To be led in.

Ps 5:8 Lead me, O LORD, in Your righteousness because of my enemies; Make Your way straight before my face.

To be revived in.

Ps 119:40 Behold, I long for Your precepts; Revive me in Your righteousness.

To be delivered in.

Ps 31:1 In You, O LORD, I put my trust; Let me never be ashamed; Deliver me in Your righteousness.

Ps 71:2 Deliver me in Your righteousness, and cause me to escape; Incline Your ear to me, and save me.

To be answered in.

Ps 143:1 Hear my prayer, O LORD, Give ear to my supplications! In Your faithfulness answer me, *And* in Your righteousness.

To be judged according to.

Ps 35:24 Vindicate me, O LORD my God, according to Your righteousness; And let them not rejoice over me.

For its continued manifestation.

Ps 36:10 Oh, continue Your lovingkindness to those who know You, And Your righteousness to the upright in heart.

Redemption of His people designed to teach.

Mic 6:4–5 For I brought you up from the land of Egypt, I redeemed you from the house of bondage; And I sent before you Moses, Aaron, and Miriam. 5 O My people, remember now What Balak king of Moab counseled, And what Balaam the son of Beor answered him, From Acacia Grove to Gilgal, That you may know the righteousness of the LORD."

The wicked have no interest in.

Ps 69:27 Add iniquity to their iniquity, And let them not come into Your righteousness.

Illustrated.

Ps 36:6 Your righteousness *is* like the great mountains; Your judgments *are* a great deep; O LORD, You preserve man and beast.

GOD, THE TRUTH OF

Is one of His attributes.

Deut 32:4 *He is* the Rock, His work *is* perfect; For all His ways *are* justice, A God of truth and without injustice; Righteous and upright *is* He.

Ps 89:14 Righteousness and justice *are* the foundation of Your throne; Mercy and truth go before Your face.

Ps 146:6 Who made heaven and earth, The sea, and all that *is* in them; Who keeps truth forever,

Is 65:16 So that he who blesses himself in the earth Shall bless himself in the God of truth; And he who swears in the earth Shall swear by the God of truth; Because the former troubles are forgotten, And because they are hidden from My eyes.

Described as

Great and endless.

Ps 57:10 For Your mercy reaches unto the heavens, And Your truth unto the clouds.

Abundant.

Ex 34:6 And the LORD passed before him and proclaimed, "The LORD, the LORD God, merciful and gracious, longsuffering, and abounding in goodness and truth,

Ps 86:15 But You, O Lord, *are* a God full of compassion, and gracious, Longsuffering and abundant in mercy and truth.

Inviolable.

Num 23:19 "God *is* not a man, that He should lie, Nor a son of man, that He should repent. Has He said, and will He not do? Or has He spoken, and will He not make it good?

Titus 1:2 in hope of eternal life which God, who cannot lie, promised before time began,

Enduring to all generations.

Ps 100:5 For the LORD *is* good; His mercy *is* everlasting, And His truth *endures* to all generations.

United with mercy in redemption.

Ps 85:10 Mercy and truth have met together; Righteousness and peace have kissed.

Exhibited in His

Counsels of old.

Is 25:1 O LORD, You *are* my God. I will exalt You, I will praise Your name, For You have done wonderful *things; Your* counsels of old *are* faithfulness *and* truth.

Ways.

Rev 15:3 They sing the song of Moses, the servant of God, and the song of the Lamb, saying: "Great and marvelous *are* Your works, Lord God Almighty! Just and true *are* Your ways, O King of the saints!

Works.

Ps 11:7 For the LORD *is* righteous, He loves righteousness; His countenance beholds the upright.

Ps 33:4 For the word of the LORD *is* right, And all His work *is done* in truth.

Dan 4:37 Now I, Nebuchadnezzar, praise and extol and honor the King of heaven, all of whose works *are* truth, and His ways justice. And those who walk in pride He is able to put down.

Judgments.

Ps 19:9 The fear of the LORD *is* clean, enduring forever; The judgments of the LORD *are* true *and* righteous altogether.

Ps 96:13 For He is coming, for He is coming to judge the earth. He shall judge the world with righteousness, And the peoples with His truth.

Word.

Ps 119:160 The entirety of Your word *is* truth, And every one of Your righteous judgments *endures* forever.

John 17:17 Sanctify them by Your truth. Your word is truth.

Fulfillment of promises in Christ.

2 Cor 1:20 For all the promises of God in Him *are* Yes, and in Him Amen, to the glory of God through us.

Fulfillment of His covenant.

Mic 7:20 You will give truth to Jacob *And* mercy to Abraham, Which You have sworn to our fathers From days of old.

Preservation of believers.

Ps 9:14 That I may tell of all Your praise In the gates of the daughter of Zion. I will rejoice in Your salvation.

Ps 25:10 All the paths of the LORD *are* mercy and truth, To such as keep His covenant and His testimonies.

Ps 57:3 He shall send from heaven and save me; He reproaches the one who would swallow me up. Selah God shall send forth His mercy and His truth.

Ps 98:3 He has remembered His mercy and His faithfulness to the house of Israel; All the ends of the earth have seen the salvation of our God.

Punishment of the wicked.

Rev 16:7 And I heard another from the altar saying, "Even so, Lord God Almighty, true and righteous *are* Your judgments."

Believers should

Confide in.

Ps 31:5 Into Your hand I commit my spirit; You have redeemed me, O LORD God of truth.

Titus 1:2 in hope of eternal life which God, who cannot lie, promised before time began,

Plead, in prayer.

Ps 89:49 Lord, where *are* Your former lovingkindnesses, Which You swore to David in Your truth?

Pray for its manifestation to themselves.

2 Chr 6:17 And now, O LORD God of Israel, let Your word come true, which You have spoken to Your servant David.

Pray for its exhibition to others.

2 Sam 2:6 And now may the LORD show kindness and truth to you. I also will repay you this kindness, because you have done this thing.

Make known to others.

Is 38:19 The living, the living man, he shall praise You, As I *do* this day; The father shall make known Your truth to the children.

Magnify.

Ps 71:22 Also with the lute I will praise You— *And* Your faithfulness, O my God! To You I will sing with the harp, O Holy One of Israel.

Ps 138:2 I will worship toward Your holy temple, And praise Your name For Your lovingkindness and Your truth; For You have magnified Your word above all Your name.

Is denied by

The devil.

Gen 3:4–5 Then the serpent said to the woman, "You will not surely die. 5 For God knows that in the day you eat of it your eyes will be opened, and you will be like God, knowing good and evil."

The self-righteous.

1 John 1:10 If we say that we have not sinned, we make Him a liar, and His word is not in us.

Unbelievers.

1 John 5:10 He who believes in the Son of God has the witness in himself; he who does not believe God has made Him a liar, because he has not believed the testimony that God has given of His Son.

Exemplified toward

Abraham.

Gen 24:27 And he said, "Blessed *be* the LORD God of my master Abraham, who has not forsaken His mercy and His truth toward my master. As for me, being on the way, the LORD led me to the house of my master's brethren."

Jacob.

Gen 32:10 I am not worthy of the least of all the mercies and of all the truth which You have shown Your servant; for I crossed over this Jordan with my staff, and now I have become two companies.

Israel.

Ps 98:3 He has remembered His mercy and His faithfulness to the house of Israel; All the ends of the earth have seen the salvation of our God.

GOD, THE UNITY OF

A ground for obeying Him exclusively.

Deut 4:39–40 Therefore know this day, and consider *it* in your heart, that the LORD Himself *is* God in heaven above and on the earth beneath; *there is* no other. 40 You shall therefore keep His statutes and His commandments which I command you today, that it may go well with you and with your children after you, and that you may prolong *your* days in the land which the LORD your God is giving you for all time."

A ground for loving Him supremely.

Deut 6:4–5 "Hear, O Israel: The LORD our God, the LORD *is* one! 5 You shall love the LORD your God with all your heart, with all your soul, and with all your strength.

Mark 12:29–30 Jesus answered him, "The first of all the commandments *is*: 'Hear, O Israel, the LORD our God, the LORD is one. 30 And you shall love the LORD your God with all your heart, with all your soul, with all your mind, and with all your strength.' This *is* the first commandment.

Asserted by

God Himself.

Is 44:6 "Thus says the LORD, the King of Israel, And his Redeemer, the LORD of hosts: 'I *am* the First and I *am* the Last; Besides Me *there is* no God.

Is 44:8 Do not fear, nor be afraid; Have I not told you from that time, and declared *it*? You *are* My witnesses. Is there a God besides Me? Indeed *there is* no other Rock; I know not *one.*' "

Is 45:18 For thus says the LORD, Who created the heavens, Who is God, Who formed the earth and made it, Who has established it, Who did not create it in vain, Who formed it to be inhabited: "I *am* the LORD, and *there is* no other.

Is 45:21 Tell and bring forth *your* case; Yes, let them take counsel together. Who has declared this from ancient time? *Who* has told it from that time? *Have* not I, the LORD? And *there is* no other God besides Me, A just God and a Savior; *There is* none besides Me.

Christ.

Mark 12:29 Jesus answered him, "The first of all the commandments *is: 'Hear, O Israel, the LORD our God, the LORD is one.*

John 17:3 And this is eternal life, that they may know You, the only true God, and Jesus Christ whom You have sent.

Moses.

Deut 4:39 Therefore know this day, and consider *it* in your heart, that the LORD Himself *is* God in heaven above and on the earth beneath; *there is* no other.

Deut 6:4 "Hear, O Israel: The LORD our God, the LORD *is* one!

The apostles.

1 Cor 8:4 Therefore concerning the eating of things offered to idols, we know that an idol *is* nothing in the world, and that *there is* no other God but one.

1 Cor 8:6 yet for us *there is* one God, the Father, of whom *are* all things, and we for Him; and one Lord Jesus Christ, through whom *are* all things, and through whom we *live.*

Eph 4:6 one God and Father of all, who *is* above all, and through all, and in you all.

1 Tim 2:5 For *there is* one God and one Mediator between God and men, *the* Man Christ Jesus,

Consistent with the deity of Christ and of the Holy Spirit.

John 10:30 I and *My* Father are one."

John 14:9–11 Jesus said to him, "Have I been with you so long, and yet you have not known Me, Philip? He who has seen Me has seen the Father; so how can you say, 'Show us the Father'? 10 Do you not believe that I am in the Father, and the Father in Me? The words that I speak to you I do not speak on My own *authority;* but the Father who dwells in Me does the works. 11 Believe Me that I *am* in the Father and the Father in Me, or else believe Me for the sake of the works themselves.

1 John 5:7 For there are three that bear witness in heaven: the Father, the Word, and the Holy Spirit; and these three are one.

Exhibited in

His greatness and wonderful works.

2 Sam 7:22 Therefore You are great, O Lord GOD. For *there is* none like You, nor *is there any* God besides You, according to all that we have heard with our ears.

Ps 86:10 For You *are* great, and do wondrous things; You alone *are* God.

His works of creation and providence.

Is 44:24 Thus says the LORD, your Redeemer, And He who formed you from the womb: "I *am* the LORD, who makes all *things,* Who stretches out the heavens all alone, Who spreads abroad the earth by Myself;

Is 45:5–8 I *am* the LORD, and *there is* no other; *There is* no God besides Me. I will gird you, though you have not known Me, 6 That they may know from the rising of the sun to its setting That *there is* none besides Me. I *am* the LORD, and *there is* no other; 7 I form the light and create darkness, I make peace and create calamity; I, the LORD, do all these *things.'* 8 "Rain down, you heavens, from above, And let the skies pour down righteousness; Let the earth open, let them bring forth salvation, And let righteousness spring up together. I, the LORD, have created it.

His exclusive foreknowledge.

Is 46:9–11 Remember the former things of old, For I *am* God, and *there is* no other; *I am* God, and *there is* none like Me, 10 Declaring the end from the beginning, And from ancient times *things* that are not *yet* done, Saying, 'My counsel shall stand, And I will do all My pleasure,' 11 Calling a bird of prey from the east, The man who executes My counsel, from a far country. Indeed I have spoken *it;* I will also bring it to pass. I have purposed *it;* I will also do it.

His exercise of uncontrolled sovereignty.

Deut 32:39 'Now see that I, *even* I, *am* He, And *there is* no God besides Me; I kill and I make alive; I wound and I heal; Nor *is there any* who can deliver from My hand.

His being the sole object of worship in heaven and earth.

Neh 9:6 You alone *are* the LORD; You have made heaven, The heaven of heavens, with all their host, The earth and everything on it, The seas and all that is in them, And You preserve them all. The host of heaven worships You.

Matt 4:10 Then Jesus said to him, "Away with you, Satan! For it is written, '*You shall worship the LORD your God, and Him only you shall serve.'* "

His being alone good.

Matt 19:17 So He said to him, "Why do you call Me good? No one *is* good but One, *that is,* God. But if you want to enter into life, keep the commandments."

His being the only Savior.

Is 45:21–22 Tell and bring forth *your case;* Yes, let them take counsel together. Who has declared this from ancient time? *Who* has told it from that time? *Have* not I, the LORD? And *there is* no other God besides Me, A just God and a Savior; *There is* none besides Me. 22 "Look to Me, and be saved, All you ends of the earth! For I *am* God, and *there is* no other.

His being the only source of pardon.

Mic 7:18 Who *is* a God like You, Pardoning iniquity And passing over the transgression of the remnant of His heritage? He does not retain His anger forever, Because He delights *in* mercy.

Mark 2:7 "Why does this *Man* speak blasphemies like this? Who can forgive sins but God alone?"

His unparalleled election and care of His people.

Deut 4:32–35 "For ask now concerning the days that are past, which were before you, since the day that God created man on the earth, and *ask* from one end of heaven to the other, whether *any* great *thing* like this has happened, or *anything* like it has been heard. 33 Did *any* people *ever* hear the voice of God speaking out of the midst of the fire, as you have heard, and live? 34 Or did God *ever* try to go *and* take for Himself a nation from the midst of *another* nation, by trials, by signs, by wonders, by war, by a mighty hand and an outstretched arm, and by great terrors, according to all that the LORD your God did for you in Egypt before your eyes? **35** To you it was shown, that you might know that the LORD Himself *is* God; *there is* none other besides Him.

The knowledge of, necessary to eternal life.

John 17:3 And this is eternal life, that they may know You, the only true God, and Jesus Christ whom You have sent.

All believers acknowledge, in worshiping Him.

2 Sam 7:22 Therefore You are great, O Lord GOD. For *there is* none like You, nor *is there any* God besides You, according to all that we have heard with our ears.

2 Kin 19:15 Then Hezekiah prayed before the LORD, and said: "O LORD God of Israel, *the One* who dwells *between* the cherubim, You are God, You alone, of all the kingdoms of the earth. You have made heaven and earth.

1 Chr 17:20 O LORD, *there is* none like You, nor *is there any* God besides You, according to all that we have heard with our ears.

All should know and acknowledge.

Deut 4:35 To you it was shown, that you might know that the LORD Himself *is* God; *there is* none other besides Him.

Ps 83:18 That they may know that You, whose name alone *is* the LORD, *Are* the Most High over all the earth.

May be acknowledged without saving faith.

James 2:19–20 You believe that there is one God. You do well. Even the demons believe—and tremble! **20** But do you want to know, O foolish man, that faith without works is dead?

GOD, THE WISDOM OF

One of His attributes.

1 Sam 2:3 "Talk no more so very proudly; Let no arrogance come from your mouth, For the LORD *is* the God of knowledge; And by Him actions are weighed.

Job 9:4 *God is* wise in heart and mighty in strength. Who has hardened *himself* against Him and prospered?

Described as

Perfect.

Job 36:4 For truly my words *are* not false; One who is perfect in knowledge *is* with you.

Job 37:16 Do you know how the clouds are balanced, Those wondrous works of Him who is perfect in knowledge?

Mighty.

Job 36:5 "Behold, God *is* mighty, but despises *no one; He is* mighty in strength of understanding.

Universal.

Job 28:24 For He looks to the ends of the earth, *And* sees under the whole heavens,

Dan 2:22 He reveals deep and secret things; He knows what *is* in the darkness, And light dwells with Him.

Acts 15:18 "Known to God from eternity are all His works.

Infinite.

Ps 147:5 Great *is* our Lord, and mighty in power; His understanding *is* infinite.

Rom 11:33 Oh, the depth of the riches both of the wisdom and knowledge of God! How unsearchable *are* His judgments and His ways past finding out!

Unsearchable.

Is 40:28 Have you not known? Have you not heard? The everlasting God, the LORD, The Creator of the ends of the earth, Neither faints nor is weary. His understanding is unsearchable.

Rom 11:33 Oh, the depth of the riches both of the wisdom and knowledge of God! How unsearchable *are* His judgments and His ways past finding out!

Beyond human comprehension.

Ps 139:6 *Such* knowledge *is* too wonderful for me; It is high, I cannot *attain* it.

Incomparable.

Is 44:7 And who can proclaim as I do? Then let him declare it and set it in order for Me, Since I appointed the ancient people. And the things that are coming and shall come, Let them show these to them.

Jer 10:7 Who would not fear You, O King of the nations? For this is Your rightful due. For among all the wise *men* of the nations, And in all their kingdoms, *There is* none like You.

Underived.

Job 21:22 "Can *anyone* teach God knowledge, Since He judges those on high?

Is 40:14 With whom did He take counsel, and *who* instructed Him, And taught Him in the path of justice? Who taught Him knowledge, And showed Him the way of understanding?

The gospel contains treasures of.

1 Cor 2:7 But we speak the wisdom of God in a mystery, the hidden *wisdom* which God ordained before the ages for our glory,

Wisdom of believers is derived from.

Ezra 7:25 And you, Ezra, according to your God-given wisdom, set magistrates and judges who may judge all the people who *are in the region* beyond the River, all such as know the laws of your God; and teach those who do not know *them.*

All human wisdom derived from.

Dan 2:21 And He changes the times and the seasons; He removes kings and raises up kings; He gives wisdom to the wise And knowledge to those who have understanding.

Believers ascribe to Him.

Dan 2:20 Daniel answered and said: "Blessed be the name of God forever and ever, For wisdom and might are His.

Exhibited in

His works.

Job 37:16 Do you know how the clouds are balanced, Those wondrous works of Him who is perfect in knowledge?

Ps 104:24 O LORD, how manifold are Your works! In wisdom You have made them all. The earth is full of Your possessions—

Ps 136:5 To Him who by wisdom made the heavens, For His mercy *endures* forever;

Prov 3:19 The LORD by wisdom founded the earth; By understanding He established the heavens;

Jer 10:12 He has made the earth by His power, He has established the world by His wisdom, And has stretched out the heavens at His discretion.

His counsels.

Is 28:29 This also comes from the LORD of hosts, *Who* is wonderful in counsel *and* excellent in guidance.

Jer 32:19 *You are* great in counsel and mighty in work, for your eyes *are* open to all the ways of the sons of men, to give everyone according to his ways and according to the fruit of his doings.

His foreshadowing events.

Is 42:9 Behold, the former things have come to pass, And new things I declare; Before they spring forth I tell you of them."

Is 46:10 Declaring the end from the beginning, And from ancient times *things* that are not *yet* done, Saying, 'My counsel shall stand, And I will do all My pleasure,'

Redemption.

1 Cor 1:24 but to those who are called, both Jews and Greeks, Christ the power of God and the wisdom of God.

Eph 1:8 which He made to abound toward us in all wisdom and prudence,

Eph 3:10 to the intent that now the manifold wisdom of God might be made known by the church to the principalities and powers in the heavenly *places,*

Searching the heart.

1 Chr 28:9 "As for you, my son Solomon, know the God of your father, and serve Him with a loyal heart and with a willing mind; for the LORD searches all hearts and understands all the intent of the thoughts. If you seek Him, He will be found by you; but if you forsake Him, He will cast you off forever.

Rev 2:23 I will kill her children with death, and all the churches shall know that I am He who searches the minds and hearts. And I will give to each one of you according to your works.

Understanding the thoughts.

1 Chr 28:9 "As for you, my son Solomon, know the God of your father, and serve Him with a loyal heart and with a willing mind; for the LORD searches all hearts and understands all the intent of the thoughts. If you seek Him, He will be found by you; but if you forsake Him, He will cast you off forever.

Ps 139:2 You know my sitting down and my rising up; You understand my thought afar off.

Exhibited in knowing

The heart.

Ps 44:21 Would not God search this out? For He knows the secrets of the heart.

Prov 15:11 Hell and Destruction *are* before the LORD; So how much more the hearts of the sons of men.

Luke 16:15 And He said to them, "You are those who justify yourselves before men, but God knows your hearts. For what is highly esteemed among men is an abomination in the sight of God.

The actions.

Job 34:21 "For His eyes *are* on the ways of man, And He sees all his steps.

Ps 139:2–3 You know my sitting down and my rising up; You understand my thought afar off. **3** You comprehend my path and my lying down, And are acquainted with all my ways.

The words.

Ps 139:4 For *there is* not a word on my tongue, *But* behold, O LORD, You know it altogether.

Those who are His.

2 Sam 7:20 Now what more can David say to You? For You, Lord GOD, know Your servant.

2 Tim 2:19 Nevertheless the solid foundation of God stands, having this seal: "The Lord knows those who are His," and, "Let everyone who names the name of Christ depart from iniquity."

The way of believers.

Job 23:10 But He knows the way that I take; *When* He has tested me, I shall come forth as gold.

Ps 1:6 For the LORD knows the way of the righteous, But the way of the ungodly shall perish.

The needs of believers.

Deut 2:7 "For the LORD your God has blessed you in all the work of your hand. He knows your trudging through this great wilderness. These forty years the LORD your God *has been* with you; you have lacked nothing." '

Matt 6:8 "Therefore do not be like them. For your Father knows the things you have need of before you ask Him.

The afflictions of believers.

Ex 3:7 And the LORD said: "I have surely seen the oppression of My people who *are* in Egypt, and have heard their cry because of their taskmasters, for I know their sorrows.

Ps 142:3 When my spirit was overwhelmed within me, Then You knew my path. In the way in which I walk They have secretly set a snare for me.

The frailties of believers.

Ps 103:14 For He knows our frame; He remembers that we *are* dust.

The minutest matters.

Matt 10:29–30 Are not two sparrows sold for a copper coin? And not one of them falls to the ground apart from your Father's will. **30** But the very hairs of your head are all numbered.

The most secret things.

Matt 6:18 so that you do not appear to men to be fasting, but to your Father who *is* in the secret *place;* and your Father who sees in secret will reward you openly.

The time of judgment.

Matt 24:36 "But of that day and hour no one knows, not even the angels of heaven, but My Father only.

The wicked and their works.

Neh 9:10 You showed signs and wonders against Pharaoh, Against all his servants, And against all the people of his land. For You knew that they acted proudly against them. So You made a name for Yourself, as *it is* this day.

Job 11:11 For He knows deceitful men; He sees wickedness also. Will He not then consider *it*?

Is 66:18 "For I *know* their works and their thoughts. It shall be that I will gather all nations and tongues; and they shall come and see My glory.

Nothing is concealed from.

Ps 139:12 Indeed, the darkness shall not hide from You, But the night shines as the day; The darkness and the light *are* both alike *to* You.

The wicked question.

Ps 73:11 And they say, "How does God know? And is there knowledge in the Most High?"

Is 47:10 "For you have trusted in your wickedness; You have said, 'No one sees me'; Your wisdom and your knowledge have warped you; And you have said in your heart, 'I *am*, and *there is* no one else besides me.'

Should be magnified.

Rom 16:27 to God, alone wise, *be* glory through Jesus Christ forever. Amen.

Jude 1:25 To God our Savior, Who alone is wise, *Be* glory and majesty, Dominion and power, Both now and forever. Amen.

GOD, THE WRATH OF

Is averted by Christ.

Luke 2:11 For there is born to you this day in the city of David a Savior, who is Christ the Lord.

Luke 2:14 "Glory to God in the highest, And on earth peace, goodwill toward men!"

Rom 5:9 Much more then, having now been justified by His blood, we shall be saved from wrath through Him.

2 Cor 5:18–19 Now all things *are* of God, who has reconciled us to Himself through Jesus Christ, and has given us the ministry of reconciliation, **19** that is, that God was in Christ reconciling the world to Himself, not imputing their trespasses to them, and has committed to us the word of reconciliation.

Eph 2:14 For He Himself is our peace, who has made both one, and has broken down the middle wall of separation,

Eph 2:17 And He came and preached peace to you who were afar off and to those who were near.

Col 1:20 and by Him to reconcile all things to Himself, by Him, whether things on earth or things in heaven, having made peace through the blood of His cross.

1 Thess 1:10 and to wait for His Son from heaven, whom He raised from the dead, *even* Jesus who delivers us from the wrath to come.

Is averted from them that believe.

John 3:14–18 And as Moses lifted up the serpent in the wilderness, even so must the Son of Man be lifted up, **15** that whoever believes in Him should not perish but have eternal life. **16** For God so loved the world that He gave His only begotten Son, that whoever believes in Him should not perish but have everlasting life. **17** For God did not send His Son into the world to condemn the world, but that the world through Him might be saved. **18** "He who believes in Him is not condemned; but he who does not believe is condemned already, because he has not believed in the name of the only begotten Son of God.

Rom 3:25 whom God set forth *as* a propitiation by His blood, through faith, to demonstrate His righteousness, because in His forbearance God had passed over the sins that were previously committed,

Rom 5:1 Therefore, having been justified by faith, we have peace with God through our Lord Jesus Christ,

Is averted upon confession of sin and repentance.

Job 33:27–28 Then he looks at men and says, 'I have sinned, and perverted *what was* right, And it did not profit me.' **28** He will redeem his soul from going down to the Pit, And his life shall see the light.

Ps 106:43–45 Many times He delivered them; But they rebelled in their counsel, And were brought low for their iniquity. **44** Nevertheless He regarded their affliction, When He heard their cry; **45** And for their sake He remembered His covenant, And relented according to the multitude of His mercies.

Jer 3:12–13 Go and proclaim these words toward the north, and say: 'Return, backsliding Israel,' says the LORD; 'I will not cause My anger to fall on you. For I *am* merciful,' says the LORD; 'I will not remain angry forever. **13** Only acknowledge your iniquity, That you have transgressed against the LORD your God, And have scattered your charms To alien deities under every green tree, And you have not obeyed My voice,' says the LORD.

Jer 18:7–8 The instant I speak concerning a nation and concerning a kingdom, to pluck up, to pull down, and to destroy *it*, **8** if that nation against whom I have spoken turns from its evil, I will relent of the disaster that I thought to bring upon it.

Jer 31:18–20 "I have surely heard Ephraim bemoaning himself: 'You have chastised me, and I was chastised, Like an untrained bull; Restore me, and I will return, For You *are* the LORD my God. **19** Surely, after my turning, I repented; And after I was instructed, I struck myself on the thigh; I was ashamed, yes, even humiliated, Because I bore the reproach of my youth.' **20** *Is* Ephraim My dear son? *Is he* a pleasant child? For though I spoke against him, I earnestly remember him still; Therefore My heart yearns for him; I will surely have mercy on him, says the LORD.

Joel 2:12–14 "Now, therefore," says the LORD, "Turn to Me with all your heart, With fasting, with weeping, and with mourning." **13** So rend your heart, and not your garments; Return to the LORD your God, For He *is* gracious and merciful, Slow to anger, and of great kindness; And He relents from doing harm. **14** Who knows *if* He will turn and relent, And leave a blessing behind Him— A grain offering and a drink offering For the LORD your God?

Is slow.

Ps 103:8 The LORD *is* merciful and gracious, Slow to anger, and abounding in mercy.

Is 48:9 "For My name's sake I will defer My anger, And *for* My praise I will restrain it from you, So that I do not cut you off.

Jon 4:2 So he prayed to the LORD, and said, "Ah, LORD, was not this what I said when I was still in my country? Therefore I fled previously to Tarshish; for I know that You *are* a gracious and merciful God, slow to anger and abundant in lovingkindness, One who relents from doing harm.

Nah 1:3 The LORD *is* slow to anger and great in power, And will not at all acquit *the wicked*. The LORD has His way In the whirlwind and in the storm, And the clouds *are* the dust of His feet.

Is righteous.

Ps 58:10–11 The righteous shall rejoice when he sees the vengeance; He shall wash his feet in the blood of the wicked, **11** So that men will say, "Surely *there is* a reward for the righteous; Surely He is God who judges in the earth."

Lam 1:18 "The LORD is righteous, For I rebelled against His commandment. Hear now, all peoples, And behold my sorrow; My virgins and my young men Have gone into captivity.

Rom 2:6 who *"will render to each one according to his deeds"*:

Rom 2:8 but to those who are self-seeking and do not obey the truth, but obey unrighteousness—indignation and wrath,

Rom 3:5–6 But if our unrighteousness demonstrates the righteousness of God, what shall we say? *Is* God unjust who inflicts wrath? (I speak as a man.) **6** Certainly not! For then how will God judge the world?

Rev 16:6–7 For they have shed the blood of saints and prophets, And You have given them blood to drink. For it is their just due." **7** And I heard another from the altar saying, "Even so, Lord God Almighty, true and righteous *are* Your judgments."

The justice of, not to be questioned.

Rom 9:18 Therefore He has mercy on whom He wills, and whom He wills He hardens.

Rom 9:20 But indeed, O man, who are you to reply against God? Will the thing formed say to him who formed *it*, "Why have you made me like this?"

Rom 9:22 *What* if God, wanting to show *His* wrath and to make His power known, endured with much longsuffering the vessels of wrath prepared for destruction,

Manifested in terrors.

Ex 14:24 Now it came to pass, in the morning watch, that the LORD looked down upon the army of the Egyptians through the pillar of fire and cloud, and He troubled the army of the Egyptians.

Ps 76:6–8 At Your rebuke, O God of Jacob, Both the chariot and horse were cast into a dead sleep. **7** You, Yourself, *are* to be feared; And who may stand in Your presence When once You are angry? **8** You caused judgment to be heard from heaven; The earth feared and was still,

Jer 10:10 But the LORD *is* the true God; He *is* the living God and the everlasting King. At His wrath the earth will tremble, And the nations will not be able to endure His indignation.

Lam 2:20–22 "See, O LORD, and consider! To whom have You done this? Should the women eat their offspring, The children they have cuddled? Should the priest and prophet be slain In the sanctuary of the Lord? **21** "Young and old lie On the ground in the streets; My virgins and my young men Have fall-

en by the sword; You have slain *them* in the day of Your anger, You have slaughtered *and* not pitied. **22** "You have invited as to a feast day The terrors that surround me. In the day of the LORD's anger There was no refugee or survivor. Those whom I have borne and brought up My enemies have destroyed."

Manifested in judgments and afflictions.

Job 21:17 "How often is the lamp of the wicked put out? *How often* does their destruction come upon them, The sorrows *God* distributes in His anger?

Ps 78:49–51 He cast on them the fierceness of His anger, Wrath, indignation, and trouble, By sending angels of destruction *among them*. **50** He made a path for His anger; He did not spare their soul from death, But gave their life over to the plague, **51** And destroyed all the firstborn in Egypt, The first of *their* strength in the tents of Ham.

Ps 90:7 For we have been consumed by Your anger, And by Your wrath we are terrified.

Is 9:19 Through the wrath of the LORD of hosts The land is burned up, And the people shall be as fuel for the fire; No man shall spare his brother.

Jer 7:20 Therefore thus says the Lord GOD: "Behold, My anger and My fury will be poured out on this place—on man and on beast, on the trees of the field and on the fruit of the ground. And it will burn and not be quenched."

Ezek 7:19 'They will throw their silver into the streets, And their gold will be like refuse; Their silver and their gold will not be able to deliver them In the day of the wrath of the LORD; They will not satisfy their souls, Nor fill their stomachs, Because it became their stumbling block of iniquity.

Heb 3:17 Now with whom was He angry forty years? *Was it* not with those who sinned, whose corpses fell in the wilderness?

Cannot be resisted.

Job 9:13 God will not withdraw His anger, The allies of the proud lie prostrate beneath Him.

Job 14:13 "Oh, that You would hide me in the grave, That You would conceal me until Your wrath is past, That You would appoint me a set time, and remember me!

Ps 76:7 You, Yourself, *are* to be feared; And who may stand in Your presence When once You are angry?

Nah 1:6 Who can stand before His indignation? And who can endure the fierceness of His anger? His fury is poured out like fire, And the rocks are thrown down by Him.

Aggravated by continual provocation.

Num 32:14 And look! You have risen in your fathers' place, a brood of sinful men, to increase still more the fierce anger of the LORD against Israel.

Specially reserved for the day of wrath.

Zeph 1:14–18 The great day of the LORD *is* near; *It is* near and hastens quickly. The noise of the day of the LORD is bitter; There the mighty men shall cry out. **15** That day *is* a day of wrath, A day of trouble and distress, A day of devastation and desolation, A day of darkness and gloominess, A day of clouds and thick darkness, **16** A day of trumpet and alarm Against the fortified cities And against the high towers. **17** "I will bring distress upon men, And they shall walk like blind men, Because they have sinned against the LORD; Their blood shall be poured out like dust, And their flesh like refuse." **18** Neither their silver nor their gold Shall be able to deliver them In the day of the LORD's wrath; But the whole land shall be devoured By the fire of His jealousy, For He will make speedy riddance Of all those who dwell in the land.

Matt 25:41 "Then He will also say to those on the left hand, 'Depart from Me, you cursed, into the everlasting fire prepared for the devil and his angels:

Rom 2:5 But in accordance with your hardness and your impenitent heart you are treasuring up for yourself wrath in the day of wrath and revelation of the righteous judgment of God,

2 Thess 1:8 in flaming fire taking vengeance on those who do not know God, and on those who do not obey the gospel of our Lord Jesus Christ.

Rev 6:17 For the great day of His wrath has come, and who is able to stand?"

Rev 11:18 The nations were angry, and Your wrath has come, And the time of the dead, that they should be judged, And that You should reward Your servants the prophets and the saints, And those who fear Your name, small and great, And should destroy those who destroy the earth."

Rev 19:15 Now out of His mouth goes a sharp sword, that with it He should strike the nations. And He Himself will rule them with a rod of iron. He Himself treads the winepress of the fierceness and wrath of Almighty God.

Is against

The wicked.

Ps 7:11 God *is* a just judge, And God is angry *with the wicked* every day.

Ps 21:8–9 Your hand will find all Your enemies; Your right hand will find those who hate You. **9** You shall make them as a fiery oven in the time of Your anger; The LORD shall swallow them up in His wrath, And the fire shall devour them.

Is 3:8 For Jerusalem stumbled, And Judah is fallen, Because their tongue and their doings *Are* against the LORD, To provoke the eyes of His glory.

Is 13:9 Behold, the day of the LORD comes, Cruel, with both wrath and fierce anger, To lay the land desolate; And He will destroy its sinners from it.

Nah 1:2–3 God *is* jealous, and the LORD avenges; The LORD avenges and *is* furious. The LORD will take vengeance on His adversaries, And He reserves *wrath* for His enemies; **3** The LORD *is* slow to anger and great in power, And will not at all acquit *the wicked.* The LORD has His way In the whirlwind and in the storm, And the clouds *are* the dust of His feet.

Rom 1:18 For the wrath of God is revealed from heaven against all ungodliness and unrighteousness of men, who suppress the truth in unrighteousness,

Rom 2:8 but to those who are self-seeking and do not obey the truth, but obey unrighteousness—indignation and wrath,

Eph 5:6 Let no one deceive you with empty words, for because of these things the wrath of God comes upon the sons of disobedience.

Col 3:6 Because of these things the wrath of God is coming upon the sons of disobedience,

Those who forsake Him.

Ezra 8:22 For I was ashamed to request of the king an escort of soldiers and horsemen to help us against the enemy on the road, because we had spoken to the king, saying, "The hand of our God *is* upon all those for good who seek Him, but His power and His wrath *are* against all those who forsake Him."

Is 1:4 Alas, sinful nation, A people laden with iniquity, A brood of evildoers, Children who are corrupters! They have forsaken the LORD, They have provoked to anger The Holy One of Israel, They have turned away backward.

Unbelief.

Ps 78:21–22 Therefore the LORD heard *this* and was furious; So a fire was kindled against Jacob, And anger also came up against Israel, **22** Because they did not believe in God, And did not trust in His salvation.

Heb 3:18–19 And to whom did He swear that they would not enter His rest, but to those who did not obey? **19** So we see that they could not enter in because of unbelief.

John 3:36 He who believes in the Son has everlasting life; and he who does not believe the Son shall not see life, but the wrath of God abides on him."

Impenitence.

Ps 7:12 If he does not turn back, He will sharpen His sword; He bends His bow and makes it ready.

Prov 1:30–31 They would have none of my counsel *And* despised my every rebuke. **31** Therefore they shall eat the fruit of their own way, And be filled to the full with their own fancies.

Is 9:13–14 For the people do not turn to Him who strikes them, Nor do they seek the LORD of hosts. **14** Therefore the LORD will cut off head and tail from Israel, Palm branch and bulrush in one day.

Rom 2:5 But in accordance with your hardness and your impenitent heart you are treasuring up for yourself wrath in the day of wrath and revelation of the righteous judgment of God,

Apostasy.

Heb 10:26–27 For if we sin willfully after we have received the knowledge of the truth, there no longer remains a sacrifice for sins, **27** but a certain fearful expectation of judgment, and fiery indignation which will devour the adversaries.

Idolatry.

Deut 29:20 "The LORD would not spare him; for then the anger of the LORD and His jealousy would burn against that man, and every curse that is written in this book would settle on him, and the LORD would blot out his name from under heaven.

Deut 29:27–28 Then the anger of the LORD was aroused against this land, to bring on it every curse that is written in this book. **28** And the LORD uprooted them from their land in anger, in wrath, and in great indignation, and cast them into another land, as *it is* this day.'

Deut 32:19–22 "And when the LORD saw *it,* He spurned *them,* Because of the provocation of His sons and His daughters. **20** And He said: 'I will hide My face from them, I will see what their end *will be,* For they *are* a perverse generation, Children in whom *is* no faith. **21** They have provoked Me to jealousy by *what* is not God; They have moved Me to anger by their foolish idols. But I will provoke them to jealousy by *those who are* not a nation; I will move them to anger by a foolish nation. **22** For a fire is kindled in My anger, And shall burn to the lowest hell; It shall consume the earth with her increase, And set on fire the foundations of the mountains.

Josh 23:16 When you have transgressed the covenant of the LORD your God, which He commanded you, and have gone and served other gods, and bowed down to them, then the anger of the LORD will burn against you, and you shall perish quickly from the good land which He has given you."

2 Kin 22:17 because they have forsaken Me and burned incense to other gods, that they might provoke Me to anger with all the works of their hands. Therefore My wrath shall be aroused against this place and shall not be quenched.' " '

Ps 78:58–59 For they provoked Him to anger with their high places, And moved Him to jealousy with their carved images. **59** When God heard *this,* He was furious, And greatly abhorred Israel,

Jer 44:3 because of their wickedness which they have committed to provoke Me to anger, in that they went to burn incense *and* to serve other gods whom they did not know, they nor you nor your fathers.

Sin, in believers.

Ps 89:30–32 "If his sons forsake My law And do not walk in My judgments, **31** If they break My statutes And do not keep My commandments, **32** Then I will punish their transgression with the rod, And their iniquity with stripes.

Ps 90:7–9 For we have been consumed by Your anger, And by Your wrath we are terrified. **8** You have set our iniquities before You, Our secret *sins* in the light of Your countenance. **9** For all our days have passed away in Your wrath; We finish our years like a sigh.

Ps 99:8 You answered them, O LORD our God; You were to them God-Who-Forgives, Though You took vengeance on their deeds.

Ps 102:9–10 For I have eaten ashes like bread, And mingled my drink with weeping, **10** Because of Your indignation and Your wrath; For You have lifted me up and cast me away.

Is 47:6 I was angry with My people; I have profaned My inheritance, And given them into your hand. You showed them no mercy; On the elderly you laid your yoke very heavily.

Extreme, against those who oppose the gospel.

Ps 2:2–5 The kings of the earth set themselves, And the rulers take counsel together, Against the LORD and against His Anointed, *saying,* **3** "Let us break Their bonds in pieces And cast away Their cords from us." **4** He who sits in the heavens shall laugh; The LORD shall hold them in derision. **5** Then He shall speak to them in His wrath, And distress them in His deep displeasure:

1 Thess 2:16 forbidding us to speak to the Gentiles that they may be saved, so as always to fill up *the measure* *of* their sins; but wrath has come upon them to the uttermost.

Folly of provoking.

Jer 7:19 Do they provoke Me to anger?" says the LORD. "*Do they* not *provoke* themselves, to the shame of their own faces?"

1 Cor 10:22 Or do we provoke the Lord to jealousy? Are we stronger than He?

To be dreaded.

Ps 2:12 Kiss the Son, lest He be angry, And you perish *in* the way, When His wrath is kindled but a little. Blessed *are* all those who put their trust in Him.

Ps 76:7 You, Yourself, *are* to be feared; And who may stand in Your presence When once You are angry?

Ps 90:11 Who knows the power of Your anger? For as the fear of You, *so is* Your wrath.

Matt 10:28 And do not fear those who kill the body but cannot kill the soul. But rather fear Him who is able to destroy both soul and body in hell.

Removal of, should be prayed for.

Ex 32:11 Then Moses pleaded with the LORD his God, and said: "LORD, why does Your wrath burn hot against Your people whom You have brought out of the land of Egypt with great power and with a mighty hand?

Ps 6:1 O LORD, do not rebuke me in Your anger, Nor chasten me in Your hot displeasure.

Ps 38:1 O LORD, do not rebuke me in Your wrath, Nor chasten me in Your hot displeasure!

Ps 39:10 Remove Your plague from me; I am consumed by the blow of Your hand.

Ps 74:1–2 O God, why have You cast *us* off forever? *Why* does Your anger smoke against the sheep of Your pasture? **2** Remember Your congregation, *which* You have purchased of old, The tribe of Your inheritance, *which* You have redeemed— This Mount Zion where You have dwelt.

Ps 79:5 How long, LORD? Will You be angry forever? Will Your jealousy burn like fire?

Ps 80:4 O LORD God of hosts, How long will You be angry Against the prayer of Your people?

Is 64:9 Do not be furious, O LORD, Nor remember iniquity forever; Indeed, please look—we all *are* Your people!

Dan 9:16 "O Lord, according to all Your righteousness, I pray, let Your anger and Your fury be turned away from Your city Jerusalem, Your holy mountain; because for our sins, and for the iniquities of our fathers, Jerusalem and Your people *are* a reproach to all *those* around us.

Hab 3:2 O LORD, I have heard Your speech *and* was afraid; O LORD, revive Your work in the midst of the years! In the midst of the years make *it* known; In wrath remember mercy.

Tempered with mercy to saints.

Ps 30:5 For His anger *is but for* a moment, His favor *is for* life; Weeping may endure for a night, But joy *comes* in the morning.

Is 26:20 Come, my people, enter your chambers, And shut your doors behind you; Hide yourself, as it were, for a little moment, Until the indignation is past.

Is 54:8 With a little wrath I hid My face from you for a moment; But with everlasting kindness I will have mercy on you," Says the LORD, your Redeemer.

Is 57:15–16 For thus says the High and Lofty One Who inhabits eternity, whose name is Holy: "I dwell in the high and holy place, With him who has a contrite and humble spirit, To revive the spirit of the humble, And to revive the heart of the contrite ones. **16** For I will not contend forever, Nor will I always be angry; For the spirit would fail before Me, And the souls which I have made.

Jer 30:11 For I am with you,' says the LORD, 'to save you; Though I make a full end of all nations where I have scattered you, Yet I will not make a complete end of you. But I will correct you in justice, And will not let you go altogether unpunished.'

Mic 7:11 In the day when your walls are to be built, In that day the decree shall go far and wide.

To be borne with submission.

2 Sam 24:17 Then David spoke to the LORD when he saw the angel who was striking the people, and said, "Surely I have sinned, and I have done wickedly; but these sheep, what have they done? Let Your hand, I pray, be against me and against my father's house."

Lam 3:39 Why should a living man complain, A man for the punishment of his sins?

Mic 7:9 I will bear the indignation of the LORD, Because I have sinned against Him, Until He pleads my case And executes justice for me. He will bring me forth to the light; I will see His righteousness.

Should lead to repentance.

Is 42:24–25 Who gave Jacob for plunder, and Israel to the robbers? Was it not the LORD, He against whom we have sinned? For they would not walk in His ways, Nor were they obedient to His law. **25** Therefore He has poured on him the fury of His anger And the strength of battle; It has set him on fire all around, Yet he did not know; And it burned him, Yet he did not take it to heart.

Jer 4:8 For this, clothe yourself with sackcloth, Lament and wail. For the fierce anger of the LORD Has not turned back from us.

Exemplified against

The old world.

Gen 7:21–23 And all flesh died that moved on the earth: birds and cattle and beasts and every creeping thing that creeps on the earth, and every man. **22** All in whose nostrils was the breath of the spirit of life, all that was on the dry land, died. **23** So He destroyed all living things which were on the face of the ground: both man and cattle, creeping thing and bird of the air. They were destroyed from the earth. Only Noah and those who were with him in the ark remained alive.

The builders of Babel.

Gen 11:8 So the LORD scattered them abroad from there over the face of all the earth, and they ceased building the city.

Cities of the plain.

Gen 19:24–25 Then the LORD rained brimstone and fire on Sodom and Gomorrah, from the LORD out of the heavens. **25** So He overthrew those cities, all the plain, all the inhabitants of the cities, and what grew on the ground.

The Egyptians.

Ex 7:20 And Moses and Aaron did so, just as the LORD commanded. So he lifted up the rod and struck the waters that were in the river, in the sight of Pharaoh and in the sight of his servants. And all the waters that were in the river were turned to blood.

Ex 8:6 So Aaron stretched out his hand over the waters of Egypt, and the frogs came up and covered the land of Egypt.

Ex 8:16 So the LORD said to Moses, "Say to Aaron, 'Stretch out your rod, and strike the dust of the land, so that it may become lice throughout all the land of Egypt.' "

Ex 8:24 And the LORD did so. Thick swarms of flies came into the house of Pharaoh, into his servants' houses, and into all the land of Egypt. The land was corrupted because of the swarms of flies.

Ex 9:3 behold, the hand of the LORD will be on your cattle in the field, on the horses, on the donkeys, on the camels, on the oxen, and on the sheep—a very severe pestilence.

Ex 9:9 And it will become fine dust in all the land of Egypt, and it will cause boils that break out in sores on man and beast throughout all the land of Egypt."

Ex 9:23 And Moses stretched out his rod toward heaven; and the LORD sent thunder and hail, and fire darted to the ground. And the LORD rained hail on the land of Egypt.

Ex 10:13 So Moses stretched out his rod over the land of Egypt, and the LORD brought an east wind on the land all that day and all that night. When it was morning, the east wind brought the locusts.

Ex 10:22 So Moses stretched out his hand toward heaven, and there was thick darkness in all the land of Egypt three days.

Ex 12:29 And it came to pass at midnight that the LORD struck all the firstborn in the land of Egypt, from the firstborn of Pharaoh who sat on his throne to the firstborn of the captive who was in the dungeon, and all the firstborn of livestock.

Ex 14:27 And Moses stretched out his hand over the sea; and when the morning appeared, the sea returned to its full depth, while the Egyptians were fleeing into it. So the LORD overthrew the Egyptians in the midst of the sea.

The Israelites.

Ex 32:35 So the LORD plagued the people because of what they did with the calf which Aaron made.

Num 11:1 Now when the people complained, it displeased the LORD; for the LORD heard it, and His anger was aroused. So the fire of the LORD burned among them, and consumed some in the outskirts of the camp.

Num 11:33 But while the meat was still between their teeth, before it was chewed, the wrath of the LORD was aroused against the people, and the LORD struck the people with a very great plague.

Num 14:40–45 And they rose early in the morning and went up to the top of the mountain, saying, "Here we are, and we will go up to the place which the LORD has promised, for we have sinned!" **41** And Moses said, "Now why do you transgress the command of the LORD? For this will not succeed. **42** Do not go up, lest you be defeated by your enemies, for the LORD *is* not among you. **43** For the Amalekites and the Canaanites *are* there before you, and you shall fall by the sword; because you have turned away from the LORD, the LORD will not be with you." **44** But they presumed to go up to the mountaintop. Nevertheless, neither the ark of the covenant of the LORD nor Moses departed from the camp. **45** Then the Amalekites and the Canaanites who dwelt in that mountain came down and attacked them, and drove them back as far as Hormah.

Num 21:6 So the LORD sent fiery serpents among the people, and they bit the people; and many of the people of Israel died.

Num 25:9 And those who died in the plague were twenty-four thousand.

2 Sam 24:1 Again the anger of the LORD was aroused against Israel, and He moved David against them to say, "Go, number Israel and Judah."

2 Sam 24:15 So the LORD sent a plague upon Israel from the morning till the appointed time. From Dan to Beersheba seventy thousand men of the people died.

The enemies of Israel.

1 Sam 5:6 But the hand of the LORD was heavy on the people of Ashdod, and He ravaged them and struck them with tumors, *both* Ashdod and its territory.

1 Sam 7:10 Now as Samuel was offering up the burnt offering, the Philistines drew near to battle against Israel. But the LORD thundered with a loud thunder upon the Philistines that day, and so confused them that they were overcome before Israel.

Nadab and Abihu.

Lev 10:2 So fire went out from the LORD and devoured them, and they died before the LORD.

The spies.

Num 14:37 those very men who brought the evil report about the land, died by the plague before the LORD.

Korah, etc.

Num 16:31 Now it came to pass, as he finished speaking all these words, that the ground split apart under them,

Num 16:35 And a fire came out from the LORD and consumed the two hundred and fifty men who were offering incense.

Aaron and Miriam.

Num 12:9–10 So the anger of the LORD was aroused against them, and He departed. **10** And when the cloud departed from above the tabernacle, suddenly Miriam *became* leprous, as *white as* snow. Then Aaron turned toward Miriam, and there she was, a leper.

Five kings.

Josh 10:25 Then Joshua said to them, "Do not be afraid, nor be dismayed; be strong and of good courage, for thus the LORD will do to all your enemies against whom you fight."

Abimelech.

Judg 9:56 Thus God repaid the wickedness of Abime-

lech, which he had done to his father by killing his seventy brothers.

The men of Beth Shemesh.

1 Sam 6:19 Then He struck the men of Beth Shemesh, because they had looked into the ark of the LORD. He struck fifty thousand and seventy men of the people, and the people lamented because the LORD had struck the people with a great slaughter.

Saul.

1 Sam 31:6 So Saul, his three sons, his armorbearer, and all his men died together that same day.

Uzzah.

2 Sam 6:7 Then the anger of the LORD was aroused against Uzzah, and God struck him there for *his* error; and he died there by the ark of God.

Saul's family.

2 Sam 21:1 Now there was a famine in the days of David for three years, year after year; and David inquired of the LORD. And the LORD answered, "*It is* because of Saul and *his* bloodthirsty house, because he killed the Gibeonites."

Sennacherib.

2 Kin 19:28 Because your rage against Me and your tumult Have come up to My ears, Therefore I will put My hook in your nose And My bridle in your lips, And I will turn you back By the way which you came.

2 Kin 19:35 And it came to pass on a certain night that the angel of the LORD went out, and killed in the camp of the Assyrians one hundred and eighty-five thousand; and when *people* arose early in the morning, there were the corpses—all dead.

2 Kin 19:37 Now it came to pass, as he was worshiping in the temple of Nisroch his god, that his sons Adrammelech and Sharezer struck him down with the sword; and they escaped into the land of Ararat. Then Esarhaddon his son reigned in his place.

GODLINESS

Believers are to imitate.

Eph 5:1 Therefore be imitators of God as dear children.

Leads to a quiet and peaceable life.

1 Tim 2:2 for kings and all who are in authority, that we may lead a quiet and peaceable life in all godliness and reverence.

The mystery of, described.

1 Tim 3:16 And without controversy great is the mystery of godliness: God was manifested in the flesh, Justified in the Spirit, Seen by angels, Preached among the Gentiles, Believed on in the world, Received up in glory.

The prerequisite of all effective ministry.

1 Tim 4:7–8 But reject profane and old wives' fables, and exercise yourself toward godliness. **8** For bodily exercise profits a little, but godliness is profitable for all things, having promise of the life that now is and of that which is to come.

Results in great gain, when accompanied with contentment.

1 Tim 6:6 Now godliness with contentment is great gain.

Misunderstanding of, by false teachers.

1 Tim 6:3–5 If anyone teaches otherwise and does not consent to wholesome words, *even* the words of our Lord Jesus Christ, and to the doctrine which accords with godliness, **4** he is proud, knowing nothing, but is obsessed with disputes and arguments over words, from which come envy, strife, reviling, evil suspicions, **5** useless wranglings of men of corrupt minds and destitute of the truth, who suppose that godliness is a *means of* gain. From such withdraw yourself.

Man of God should pursue.

1 Tim 6:11 But you, O man of God, flee these things and pursue righteousness, godliness, faith, love, patience, gentleness.

Believer

Has divine resources leading to.

2 Pet 1:3 as His divine power has given to us all things that *pertain* to life and godliness, through the knowledge of Him who called us by glory and virtue,

Should add, to faith.

2 Pet 1:6 to knowledge self-control, to self-control perseverance, to perseverance godliness,

Should exemplify, in light of return of Christ.

2 Pet 3:11–12 Therefore, since all these things will be dissolved, what manner *of persons* ought you to be in holy conduct and godliness, **12** looking for and hastening the coming of the day of God, because of which the heavens will be dissolved, being on fire, and the elements will melt with fervent heat?

GOLD

Found in the earth.

Job 28:1 "Surely there is a mine for silver, And a place *where* gold is refined.

Job 28:6 Its stones *are* the source of sapphires, And it contains gold dust.

Plentiful in

Havilah.

Gen 2:11 The name of the first *is* Pishon; it *is* the one which skirts the whole land of Havilah, where *there is* gold.

Ophir.

1 Kin 9:28 And they went to Ophir, and acquired four hundred and twenty talents of gold from there, and brought *it* to King Solomon.

Ps 45:9 Kings' daughters *are* among Your honorable women; At Your right hand stands the queen in gold from Ophir.

Sheba.

Ps 72:15 And He shall live; And the gold of Sheba will be given to Him; Prayer also will be made for Him continually, *And* daily He shall be praised.

Is 60:6 The multitude of camels shall cover your *land,* The dromedaries of Midian and Ephah; All those from Sheba shall come; They shall bring gold and incense, And they shall proclaim the praises of the LORD.

Parvaim.

2 Chr 3:6 And he decorated the house with precious stones for beauty, and the gold *was* gold from Parvaim.

Belongs to God.

Joel 3:5 Because you have taken My silver and My gold, And have carried into your temples My prized possessions.

Hag 2:8 'The silver *is* Mine, and the gold *is* Mine,' says the LORD of hosts.

Described as

Yellow.

Ps 68:13 Though you lie down among the sheepfolds, *You will be* like the wings of a dove covered with silver, And her feathers with yellow gold."

Malleable.

Ex 39:3 And they beat the gold into thin sheets and cut *it into* threads, to work *it* in *with* the blue, purple, and scarlet *thread,* and the fine linen, *into* artistic designs.

1 Kin 10:16–17 And King Solomon made two hundred large shields *of* hammered gold; six hundred *shekels* of gold went into each shield. **17** He also *made* three hundred shields *of* hammered gold; three minas of gold went into each shield. The king put them in the House of the Forest of Lebanon.

Precious.

Ezra 8:27 twenty gold basins *worth* a thousand drachmas, and two vessels of fine polished bronze, precious as gold.

Is 13:12 I will make a mortal more rare than fine gold, A man more than the golden wedge of Ophir.

Valuable.

Job 28:15–16 It cannot be purchased for gold, Nor can silver be weighed *for* its price. **16** It cannot be valued in the gold of Ophir, In precious onyx or sapphire.

Most valuable when pure and fine.

Job 28:19 The topaz of Ethiopia cannot equal it, Nor can it be valued in pure gold.

Ps 19:10 More to be desired *are they* than gold, Yea, than much fine gold; Sweeter also than honey and the honeycomb.

Ps 21:3 For You meet him with the blessings of goodness; You set a crown of pure gold upon his head.

Prov 3:14 For her proceeds *are* better than the profits of silver, And her gain than fine gold.

Refined and tried by fire.

Zech 13:9 I will bring the *one*-third through the fire, Will refine them as silver is refined, And test them as gold is tested. They will call on My name, And I will answer them. I will say, 'This *is* My people'; And each one will say, 'The LORD *is* my God.' "

1 Pet 1:7 that the genuineness of your faith, *being* much more precious than gold that perishes, though it is tested by fire, may be found to praise, honor, and glory at the revelation of Jesus Christ,

Working in, a trade.

Neh 3:8 Next to him Uzziel the son of Harhaiah, one of the goldsmiths, made repairs. Also next to him Hananiah, one of the perfumers, made repairs; and they fortified Jerusalem as far as the Broad Wall.

Is 40:19 The workman molds an image, The goldsmith overspreads it with gold, And the silversmith casts silver chains.

An article of commerce.

Ezek 27:22 The merchants of Sheba and Raamah *were* your merchants. They traded for your wares the choicest spices, all kinds of precious stones, and gold.

The patriarchs were rich in.

Gen 13:2 Abram *was* very rich in livestock, in silver, and in gold.

Imported by Solomon.

1 Kin 9:11 (Hiram the king of Tyre had supplied Solomon with cedar and cypress and gold, as much as he desired), *that* King Solomon then gave Hiram twenty cities in the land of Galilee.

1 Kin 9:28 And they went to Ophir, and acquired four hundred and twenty talents of gold from there, and brought *it* to King Solomon.

1 Kin 10:11 Also, the ships of Hiram, which brought gold from Ophir, brought great *quantities* of almug wood and precious stones from Ophir.

Abundance of, in Solomon's reign.

2 Chr 1:15 Also the king made silver and gold as common in Jerusalem as stones, and he made cedars as abundant as the sycamores which *are* in the lowland.

Offerings of, for the tabernacle.

Ex 35:22 They came, both men and women, as many as had a willing heart, *and* brought earrings and nose rings, rings and necklaces, all jewelry of gold, that is, every man who *made* an offering of gold to the LORD.

Offerings of, for the temple.

1 Chr 22:14 Indeed I have taken much trouble to prepare for the house of the LORD one hundred thousand talents of gold and one million talents of silver, and bronze and iron beyond measure, for it is so abundant. I have prepared timber and stone also, and you may add to them.

1 Chr 29:4 three thousand talents of gold, of the gold of Ophir, and seven thousand talents of refined silver, to overlay the walls of the houses;

1 Chr 29:7 They gave for the work of the house of God five thousand talents and ten thousand darics of gold, ten thousand talents of silver, eighteen thousand talents of bronze, and one hundred thousand talents of iron.

Used as money.

Matt 10:9 Provide neither gold nor silver nor copper in your money belts,

Acts 3:6 Then Peter said, "Silver and gold I do not have, but what I do have I give you: In the name of Jesus Christ of Nazareth, rise up and walk."

Priestly and royal garments adorned with.

Ex 28:4–6 And these *are* the garments which they shall make: a breastplate, an ephod, a robe, a skillfully woven tunic, a turban, and a sash. So they shall make holy garments for Aaron your brother and his sons, that he may minister to Me as priest. **5** "They shall take the gold, blue, purple, and scarlet *thread*, and the fine linen, **6** and they shall make the ephod of gold, blue, purple, *and* scarlet *thread*, and fine woven linen, artistically worked.

Ps 45:9 Kings' daughters *are* among Your honorable women; At Your right hand stands the queen in gold from Ophir.

Ps 45:13 The royal daughter *is* all glorious within *the palace;* Her clothing *is* woven with gold.

Was used for

Overlaying the tabernacle.

Ex 36:34 He overlaid the boards with gold, made their rings of gold *to be* holders for the bars, and overlaid the bars with gold.

Ex 36:38 and its five pillars with their hooks. And he overlaid their capitals and their rings with gold, but their five sockets *were* bronze.

Overlaying the temple.

1 Kin 6:21–22 So Solomon overlaid the inside of the temple with pure gold. He stretched gold chains across the front of the inner sanctuary, and overlaid it with gold. **22** The whole temple he overlaid with gold, until he had finished all the temple; also he overlaid with gold the entire altar that *was* by the inner sanctuary.

Overlaying cherubims in the temple.

2 Chr 3:10 In the Most Holy Place he made two cherubim, fashioned by carving, and overlaid them with gold.

Overlaying the ark, etc.

Ex 25:11–13 And you shall overlay it with pure gold, inside and out you shall overlay it, and shall make on it a molding of gold all around. **12** You shall cast four rings of gold for it, and put *them* in its four corners; two rings *shall be* on one side, and two rings on the other side. **13** And you shall make poles *of* acacia wood, and overlay them with gold.

Overlaying floor of the temple.

1 Kin 6:30 And the floor of the temple he overlaid with gold, both the inner and outer *sanctuaries.*

Overlaying the throne of Solomon.

1 Kin 10:18 Moreover the king made a great throne of ivory, and overlaid it with pure gold.

Mercy seat and cherubims.

Ex 25:17–18 "You shall make a mercy seat of pure gold; two and a half cubits *shall be* its length and a cubit and a half its width. **18** And you shall make two cherubim of gold; of hammered work you shall make them at the two ends of the mercy seat.

Sacred lampstands.

Ex 25:31 "You shall also make a lampstand of pure gold; the lampstand shall be of hammered work. Its shaft, its branches, its bowls, its *ornamental* knobs, and flowers shall be *of one piece.*

2 Chr 4:7 And he made ten lampstands of gold according to their design, and set *them* in the temple, five on the right side and five on the left.

2 Chr 4:20 the lampstands with their lamps of pure gold, to burn in the prescribed manner in front of the inner sanctuary,

Sacred utensils.

Ex 25:29 You shall make its dishes, its pans, its pitchers, and its bowls for pouring. You shall make them of pure gold.

Ex 25:38 And its wick-trimmers and their trays *shall be* of pure gold.

2 Chr 4:19–22 Thus Solomon had all the furnishings

made for the house of God: the altar of gold and the tables on which *was* the showbread; **20** the lampstands with their lamps of pure gold, to burn in the prescribed manner in front of the inner sanctuary, **21** with the flowers and the lamps and the wick-trimmers of gold, of purest gold; **22** the trimmers, the bowls, the ladles, and the censers of pure gold. As for the entry of the sanctuary, its inner doors to the Most Holy *Place*, and the doors of the main hall of the temple, *were* gold.

Crowns.

2 Sam 12:30 Then he took their king's crown from his head. Its weight *was* a talent of gold, with precious stones. And it was *set* on David's head. Also he brought out the spoil of the city in great abundance.

Ps 21:3 For You meet him with the blessings of goodness; You set a crown of pure gold upon his head.

Scepters.

Esth 4:11 "All the king's servants and the people of the king's provinces know that any man or woman who goes into the inner court to the king, who has not been called, *he has* but one law: put *all* to death, except the one to whom the king holds out the golden scepter, that he may live. Yet I myself have not been called to go in to the king these thirty days."

Chains.

Gen 41:42 Then Pharaoh took his signet ring off his hand and put it on Joseph's hand; and he clothed him in garments of fine linen and put a gold chain around his neck.

Dan 5:29 Then Belshazzar gave the command, and they clothed Daniel with purple and *put* a chain of gold around his neck, and made a proclamation concerning him that he should be the third ruler in the kingdom.

Rings.

Song 5:14 His hands *are* rods of gold Set with beryl. His body *is* carved ivory Inlaid *with* sapphires.

James 2:2 For if there should come into your assembly a man with gold rings, in fine apparel, and there should also come in a poor man in filthy clothes,

Earrings.

Judg 8:24 Then Gideon said to them, "I would like to make a request of you, that each of you would give me the earrings from his plunder." For they had golden earrings, because they *were* Ishmaelites.

Judg 8:26 Now the weight of the gold earrings that he requested was one thousand seven hundred *shekels* of gold, besides the crescent ornaments, pendants, and purple robes which *were* on the kings of Midian, and besides the chains that *were* around their camels' necks.

Ornaments.

Jer 4:30 "And *when* you *are* plundered, What will you do? Though you clothe yourself with crimson, Though you adorn *yourself* with ornaments of gold, Though you enlarge your eyes with paint, In vain you will make yourself fair; *Your* lovers will despise you; They will seek your life.

Shields.

2 Sam 8:7 And David took the shields of gold that had belonged to the servants of Hadadezer, and brought them to Jerusalem.

1 Kin 10:16–17 And King Solomon made two hundred large shields *of* hammered gold; six hundred *shekels* of gold went into each shield. **17** He also *made* three hundred shields *of* hammered gold; three minas of gold went into each shield. The king put them in the House of the Forest of Lebanon.

Vessels.

1 Kin 10:21 All King Solomon's drinking vessels *were* gold, and all the vessels of the House of the Forest of Lebanon *were* pure gold. Not *one was* silver, for this was accounted as nothing in the days of Solomon.

Esth 1:7 And they served drinks in golden vessels, each vessel being different from the other, with royal wine in abundance, according to the generosity of the king.

Idols.

Ex 20:23 You shall not make *anything to be* with Me— gods of silver or gods of gold you shall not make for yourselves.

Ps 115:4 Their idols *are* silver and gold, The work of men's hands.

Dan 5:4 They drank wine, and praised the gods of gold and silver, bronze and iron, wood and stone.

Couches.

Esth 1:6 *There were* white and blue linen *curtains* fastened with cords of fine linen and purple on silver rods and marble pillars; *and the* couches *were* of gold and silver on a *mosaic* pavement of alabaster, turquoise, and white and black marble.

Footstools.

2 Chr 9:18 The throne *had* six steps, with a footstool of gold, *which were* fastened to the throne; there were armrests on either side of the place of the seat, and two lions stood beside the armrests.

Estimated by weight.

1 Chr 28:14 He gave gold by weight for *things* of gold, for all articles used in every kind of service; also *silver* for all articles of silver by weight, for all articles used in every kind of service;

Given as presents.

1 Kin 15:19 "*Let there be* a treaty between you and me, as there was between my father and your father. See, I have sent you a present of silver and gold. Come and break your treaty with Baasha king of Israel, so that he will withdraw from me."

Matt 2:11 And when they had come into the house, they saw the young Child with Mary His mother, and fell down and worshiped Him. And when they had opened their treasures, they presented gifts to Him: gold, frankincense, and myrrh.

Exacted as tribute.

1 Kin 20:3 'Your silver and your gold *are* mine; your loveliest wives and children are mine.' "

1 Kin 20:5 Then the messengers came back and said, "Thus speaks Ben-Hadad, saying, 'Indeed I have sent to you, saying, "You shall deliver to me your silver and your gold, your wives and your children";

2 Kin 23:33 Now Pharaoh Necho put him in prison at Riblah in the land of Hamath, that he might not reign in Jerusalem; and he imposed on the land a tribute of one hundred talents of silver and a talent of gold.

2 Kin 23:35 So Jehoiakim gave the silver and gold to Pharaoh; but he taxed the land to give money according to the command of Pharaoh; he exacted the silver and gold from the people of the land, from every one according to his assessment, to give *it* to Pharaoh Necho.

Taken in war, dedicated to God.

Josh 6:19 But all the silver and gold, and vessels of bronze and iron, *are* consecrated to the LORD; they shall come into the treasury of the LORD."

2 Sam 8:11 King David also dedicated these to the LORD, along with the silver and gold that he had dedicated from all the nations which he had subdued—

1 Kin 15:15 He also brought into the house of the LORD the things which his father had dedicated, and the things which he himself had dedicated: silver and gold and utensils.

Kings of Israel not to multiply.

Deut 17:17 Neither shall he multiply wives for himself, lest his heart turn away; nor shall he greatly multiply silver and gold for himself.

Jews condemned for multiplying.

Is 2:7 Their land is also full of silver and gold, And there is no end to their treasures; Their land is also full of horses, And there is no end to their chariots.

Vanity of heaping up.

Eccl 2:8 I also gathered for myself silver and gold and the special treasures of kings and of the provinces. I acquired male and female singers, the delights of the sons of men, *and* musical instruments of all kinds.

Eccl 2:11 Then I looked on all the works that my hands had done And on the labor in which I had toiled; And indeed all *was* vanity and grasping for the wind. *There was* no profit under the sun.

Liable to

Grow dim.

Lam 4:1 How the gold has become dim! *How* changed the fine gold! The stones of the sanctuary are scattered At the head of every street.

Corrode and rust.

James 5:3 Your gold and silver are corroded, and their corrosion will be a witness against you and will eat your flesh like fire. You have heaped up treasure in the last days.

Illustrative of

Believers after affliction.

Job 23:10 But He knows the way that I take; *When* He has tested me, I shall come forth as gold.

Tested faith.

1 Pet 1:7 that the genuineness of your faith, *being* much more precious than gold that perishes, though it is tested by fire, may be found to praise, honor, and glory at the revelation of Jesus Christ,

The doctrines of grace.

Rev 3:18 I counsel you to buy from Me gold refined in the fire, that you may be rich; and white garments, that you may be clothed, *that* the shame of your nakedness may not be revealed; and anoint your eyes with eye salve, that you may see.

True converts.

1 Cor 3:12 Now if anyone builds on this foundation *with* gold, silver, precious stones, wood, hay, straw,

Babylonian empire.

Dan 2:38 and wherever the children of men dwell, or the beasts of the field and the birds of the heaven, He has given *them* into your hand, and has made you ruler over them all—you *are* this head of gold.

GOOD WORKS

Christ, an example of.

John 10:32 Jesus answered them, "Many good works I have shown you from My Father. For which of those works do you stone Me?"

Acts 10:38 how God anointed Jesus of Nazareth with the Holy Spirit and with power, who went about doing good and healing all who were oppressed by the devil, for God was with Him.

Other names for,

Good fruits.

James 3:17 But the wisdom that is from above is first pure, then peaceable, gentle, willing to yield, full of mercy and good fruits, without partiality and without hypocrisy.

Fruits worthy of repentance.

Matt 3:8 Therefore bear fruits worthy of repentance,

Fruits of righteousness.

Phil 1:11 being filled with the fruits of righteousness which *are* by Jesus Christ, to the glory and praise of God.

Works and labors of love.

Heb 6:10 For God *is* not unjust to forget your work and labor of love which you have shown toward His name, *in that* you have ministered to the saints, and do minister.

The Scripture designed to lead us to.

2 Tim 3:16–17 All Scripture *is* given by inspiration of God, and *is* profitable for doctrine, for reproof, for correction, for instruction in righteousness, **17** that the man of God may be complete, thoroughly equipped for every good work.

James 1:25 But he who looks into the perfect law of liberty and continues *in it*, and is not a forgetful hearer but a doer of the work, this one will be blessed in what he does.

To be performed in Christ's name.

Col 3:17 And *whatever* you do in word or deed, *do* all in the name of the Lord Jesus, giving thanks to God the Father through Him.

Heavenly wisdom is full of.

James 3:17 But the wisdom that is from above is first pure, then peaceable, gentle, willing to yield, full of mercy and good fruits, without partiality and without hypocrisy.

Salvation unattainable by.

Rom 3:20 Therefore by the deeds of the law no flesh will be justified in His sight, for by the law *is* the knowledge of sin.

Gal 2:16 knowing that a man is not justified by the works of the law but by faith in Jesus Christ, even we have believed in Christ Jesus, that we might be justified by faith in Christ and not by the works of the law; for by the works of the law no flesh shall be justified.

Eph 2:8–9 For by grace you have been saved through faith, and that not of yourselves; *it is* the gift of God, **9** not of works, lest anyone should boast.

2 Tim 1:9 who has saved us and called *us* with a holy calling, not according to our works, but according to His own purpose and grace which was given to us in Christ Jesus before time began,

Titus 3:5 not by works of righteousness which we have done, but according to His mercy He saved us, through the washing of regeneration and renewing of the Holy Spirit,

Believers

Will have, if they abide in Christ.

John 15:4–5 Abide in Me, and I in you. As the branch cannot bear fruit of itself, unless it abides in the vine, neither can you, unless you abide in Me. **5** "I am the vine, you *are* the branches. He who abides in Me, and I in him, bears much fruit; for without Me you can do nothing.

Wrought by God in them.

Is 26:12 LORD, You will establish peace for us, For You have also done all our works in us.

Phil 2:13 for it is God who works in you both to will and to do for *His* good pleasure.

Created in Christ to.

Eph 2:10 For we are His workmanship, created in Christ Jesus for good works, which God prepared beforehand that we should walk in them.

Exhorted to put on.

Col 3:12–14 Therefore, as *the* elect of God, holy and beloved, put on tender mercies, kindness, humility, meekness, longsuffering; **13** bearing with one another, and forgiving one another, if anyone has a complaint against another; even as Christ forgave you, so you also *must do.* **14** But above all these things put on love, which is the bond of perfection.

Should be equipped for.

2 Tim 3:17 that the man of God may be complete, thoroughly equipped for every good work.

Should be careful to maintain.

Titus 3:8 This is a faithful saying, and these things I want you to affirm constantly, that those who have believed in God should be careful to maintain good works. These things are good and profitable to men.

Titus 3:14 And let our *people* also learn to maintain good works, to *meet* urgent needs, that they may not be unfruitful.

Should be ready to engage frequently in.

Acts 9:36 At Joppa there was a certain disciple named Tabitha, which is translated Dorcas. This woman was full of good works and charitable deeds which she did.

2 Cor 9:8 And God *is* able to make all grace abound toward you, that you, always having all sufficiency in all *things,* may have an abundance for every good work.

Col 1:10 that you may walk worthy of the Lord, fully pleasing *Him,* being fruitful in every good work and increasing in the knowledge of God;

2 Thess 2:17 comfort your hearts and establish you in every good word and work.

1 Tim 6:18 *Let them* do good, that they be rich in good works, ready to give, willing to share,

2 Tim 2:21 Therefore if anyone cleanses himself from the latter, he will be a vessel for honor, sanctified and useful for the Master, prepared for every good work.

Titus 2:14 who gave Himself for us, that He might redeem us from every lawless deed and purify for Himself *His* own special people, zealous for good works.

Titus 3:1 Remind them to be subject to rulers and authorities, to obey, to be ready for every good work,

Heb 13:21 make you complete in every good work to do His will, working in you what is well pleasing in His sight, through Jesus Christ, to whom *be* glory forever and ever. Amen.

Should encourage each other to.

Heb 10:24 And let us consider one another in order to stir up love and good works,

Should avoid ostentation in.

Matt 6:1–18 "Take heed that you do not do your charitable deeds before men, to be seen by them. Otherwise you have no reward from your Father in heaven. **2** Therefore, when you do a charitable deed, do not sound a trumpet before you as the hypocrites do in the synagogues and in the streets, that they may have glory from men. Assuredly, I say to you, they have their reward. **3** But when you do a charitable deed, do not let your left hand know what your right hand is doing, **4** that your charitable deed may be in secret; and your Father who sees in secret will Himself reward you openly. **5** "And when you pray, you shall not be like the hypocrites. For they love to pray standing in the synagogues and on the corners of the streets, that they may be seen by men. Assuredly, I say to you, they have their reward. **6** But you, when you pray, go into your room, and when you have shut your door, pray to your Father who *is* in the secret *place;* and your Father who sees in secret will reward you openly. **7** And when you pray, do not use vain repetitions as the heathen *do.* For they think that they will be heard for their many words. **8** "Therefore do not be like them. For your Father knows the things you have need of before you ask Him. **9** In this manner, therefore, pray: Our Father in heaven, Hallowed be Your name. **10** Your kingdom come. Your will be done On earth as *it is* in heaven. **11** Give us this day our daily bread. **12** And forgive us our debts, As we forgive our debtors. **13** And do not lead us into temptation, But deliver us from the evil one. For Yours is the kingdom and the power and the glory forever. Amen. **14** "For if you forgive men their trespasses, your heavenly Father will also forgive you. **15** But if you do not forgive men their trespasses, neither will your Father forgive your trespasses. **16** "Moreover, when you fast, do not be like the hypocrites, with a sad countenance. For they disfigure their faces that they may appear to men to be fasting. Assuredly, I say to you, they have their reward. **17** But you, when you fast, anoint your head and wash your face, 18 so that you do not appear to men to be fasting, but to your Father who *is* in the secret *place;* and your Father who sees in secret will reward you openly.

James 3:13 Who *is* wise and understanding among you? Let him show by good conduct *that* his works *are done* in the meekness of wisdom.

Deeds are seen in light of the truth.

John 3:21 But he who does the truth comes to the light, that his deeds may be clearly seen, that they have been done in God."

Follow them when they die.

Rev 14:13 Then I heard a voice from heaven saying to me, "Write: 'Blessed *are* the dead who die in the Lord from now on.' " "Yes," says the Spirit, "that they may rest from their labors, and their works follow them."

Godly women should manifest.

1 Tim 2:10 but, which is proper for women professing godliness, with good works.

1 Tim 5:10 well reported for good works: if she has brought up children, if she has lodged strangers, if she has washed the saints' feet, if she has relieved the afflicted, if she has diligently followed every good work.

God remembers.

Neh 13:14 Remember me, O my God, concerning this, and do not wipe out my good deeds that I have done for the house of my God, and for its services!

Heb 6:9–10 But, beloved, we are confident of better things concerning you, yes, things that accompany salvation, though we speak in this manner. 10 For God *is* not unjust to forget your work and labor of love which you have shown toward His name, *in that* you have ministered to the saints, and do minister.

Shall be brought into the judgment.

Eccl 12:14 For God will bring every work into judgment, Including every secret thing, Whether good or evil.

2 Cor 5:10 For we must all appear before the judgment seat of Christ, that each one may receive the things *done* in the body, according to what he has done, whether good or bad.

In the judgment, will be an evidence of faith.

Matt 25:34–40 Then the King will say to those on His right hand, 'Come, you blessed of My Father, inherit the kingdom prepared for you from the foundation of the world: 35 for I was hungry and you gave Me food; I was thirsty and you gave Me drink; I was a stranger and you took Me in; 36 I *was* naked and you clothed Me; I was sick and you visited Me; I was in prison and you came to Me.' 37 "Then the righteous will answer Him, saying, 'Lord, when did we see You hungry and feed *You,* or thirsty and give *You* drink? 38 When did we see You a stranger and take *You* in, or naked and clothe *You? 39* Or when did we see You sick, or in prison, and come to You?' 40 And the King will answer and say to them, 'Assuredly, I say to you, inasmuch as you did *it* to one of the least of these My brethren, you did *it* to Me.'

James 2:14–20 What *does it* profit, my brethren, if someone says he has faith but does not have works? Can faith save him? 15 If a brother or sister is naked and

destitute of daily food, 16 and one of you says to them, "Depart in peace, be warmed and filled," but you do not give them the things which are needed for the body, what *does it* profit? 17 Thus also faith by itself, if it does not have works, is dead. 18 But someone will say, "You have faith, and I have works." Show me your faith without your works, and I will show you my faith by my works. 19 You believe that there is one God. You do well. Even the demons believe—and tremble! 20 But do you want to know, O foolish man, that faith without works is dead?

Ministers should

Be patterns of.

Titus 2:7 in all things showing yourself *to be* a pattern of good works; in doctrine *showing* integrity, reverence, incorruptibility,

Exhort to.

1 Tim 6:17–18 Command those who are rich in this present age not to be haughty, nor to trust in uncertain riches but in the living God, who gives us richly all things to enjoy. 18 *Let them* do good, that they be rich in good works, ready to give, willing to share,

Titus 3:1 Remind them to be subject to rulers and authorities, to obey, to be ready for every good work,

Titus 3:8 This is a faithful saying, and these things I want you to affirm constantly, that those who have believed in God should be careful to maintain good works. These things are good and profitable to men.

Titus 3:14 And let our *people* also learn to maintain good works, to *meet* urgent needs, that they may not be unfruitful.

God is glorified by.

John 15:8 By this My Father is glorified, that you bear much fruit; so you will be My disciples.

Designed to lead others to glorify God.

Matt 5:16 Let your light so shine before men, that they may see your good works and glorify your Father in heaven.

1 Pet 2:12 having your conduct honorable among the Gentiles, that when they speak against you as evildoers, they may, by *your* good works which they observe, glorify God in the day of visitation.

A blessing attends.

James 1:25 But he who looks into the perfect law of liberty and continues *in it,* and is not a forgetful hearer but a doer of the work, this one will be blessed in what he does.

The reprobate disqualified from.

Titus 1:16 They profess to know God, but in works they deny Him, being abominable, disobedient, and disqualified for every good work.

Illustrated.

John 15:5 "I am the vine, you *are* the branches. He who abides in Me, and I in him, bears much fruit; for without Me you can do nothing.

GOSPEL, THE
Is good tidings of great joy for all people.

Luke 2:10–11 Then the angel said to them, "Do not be afraid, for behold, I bring you good tidings of great joy which will be to all people. 11 For there is born to you this day in the city of David a Savior, who is Christ the Lord.

Luke 2:31–32 Which You have prepared before the face of all peoples, **32** A light to *bring* revelation to the Gentiles, And the glory of Your people Israel."

Foretold.

Is 41:27 The first time *I said* to Zion, 'Look, there they are!' And I will give to Jerusalem one who brings good tidings.

Is 52:7 How beautiful upon the mountains Are the feet of him who brings good news, Who proclaims peace, Who brings glad tidings of good *things*, Who proclaims salvation, Who says to Zion, "Your God reigns!"

Is 61:1–3 "The Spirit of the Lord GOD *is* upon Me, Because the LORD has anointed Me To preach good tidings to the poor; He has sent Me to heal the brokenhearted, To proclaim liberty to the captives, And the opening of the prison to *those who are* bound; **2** To proclaim the acceptable year of the LORD, And the day of vengeance of our God; To comfort all who mourn, **3** To console those who mourn in Zion, To give them beauty for ashes, The oil of joy for mourning, The garment of praise for the spirit of heaviness; That they may be called trees of righteousness, The planting of the LORD, that He may be glorified."

Mark 1:15 and saying, "The time is fulfilled, and the kingdom of God is at hand. Repent, and believe in the gospel."

Preached under the Old Testament.

Heb 4:2 For indeed the gospel was preached to us as well as to them; but the word which they heard did not profit them, not being mixed with faith in those who heard *it*.

Exhibits the grace of God.

Acts 14:3 Therefore they stayed there a long time, speaking boldly in the Lord, who was bearing witness to the word of His grace, granting signs and wonders to be done by their hands.

Acts 20:32 "So now, brethren, I commend you to God and to the word of His grace, which is able to build you up and give you an inheritance among all those who are sanctified.

Reveals the glory of God.

2 Cor 4:4 whose minds the god of this age has blinded, who do not believe, lest the light of the gospel of the glory of Christ, who is the image of God, should shine on them.

2 Cor 4:6 For it is the God who commanded light to shine out of darkness, who has shone in our hearts to *give* the light of the knowledge of the glory of God in the face of Jesus Christ.

Brings life and immortality.

2 Tim 1:10 but has now been revealed by the appearing of our Savior Jesus Christ, *who* has abolished death and brought life and immortality to light through the gospel,

Is the power of God to salvation.

Rom 1:16 For I am not ashamed of the gospel of Christ, for it is the power of God to salvation for everyone who believes, for the Jew first and also for the Greek.

1 Cor 1:18 For the message of the cross is foolishness to those who are perishing, but to us who are being saved it is the power of God.

1 Thess 1:5 For our gospel did not come to you in word only, but also in power, and in the Holy Spirit and in much assurance, as you know what kind of men we were among you for your sake.

Is glorious.

2 Cor 4:4 whose minds the god of this age has blinded, who do not believe, lest the light of the gospel of the glory of Christ, who is the image of God, should shine on them.

Is everlasting.

1 Pet 1:25 *But the word of the LORD endures forever."* Now this is the word which by the gospel was preached to you.

Rev 14:6 Then I saw another angel flying in the midst of heaven, having the everlasting gospel to preach to those who dwell on the earth—to every nation, tribe, tongue, and people—

Preached by Christ.

Matt 4:23 And Jesus went about all Galilee, teaching in their synagogues, preaching the gospel of the kingdom, and healing all kinds of sickness and all kinds of disease among the people.

Mark 1:14 Now after John was put in prison, Jesus came to Galilee, preaching the gospel of the kingdom of God,

Ministers have a stewardship to preach.

1 Cor 9:17 For if I do this willingly, I have a reward; but if against my will, I have been entrusted with a stewardship.

Preached to

Abraham beforehand.

Gen 22:18 In your seed all the nations of the earth shall be blessed, because you have obeyed My voice."

Gal 3:8 And the Scripture, foreseeing that God would justify the Gentiles by faith, preached the gospel to Abraham beforehand, *saying, "In you all the nations shall be blessed."*

The Jews first.

Luke 24:47 and that repentance and remission of sins should be preached in His name to all nations, beginning at Jerusalem.

Acts 13:46 Then Paul and Barnabas grew bold and said, "It was necessary that the word of God should be spoken to you first; but since you reject it, and judge yourselves unworthy of everlasting life, behold, we turn to the Gentiles.

The Gentiles.

Mark 13:10 And the gospel must first be preached to all the nations.

Gal 2:2 And I went up by revelation, and communicated to them that gospel which I preach among the Gentiles, but privately to those who were of reputation, lest by any means I might run, or had run, in vain.

Gal 2:9 and when James, Cephas, and John, who seemed to be pillars, perceived the grace that had been given to me, they gave me and Barnabas the right hand of fellowship, that we *should go* to the Gentiles and they to the circumcised.

The poor.

Matt 11:5 *The* blind see and *the* lame walk; *the* lepers are cleansed and *the* deaf hear; *the* dead are raised up and *the* poor have the gospel preached to them.

Luke 4:18 *"The Spirit of the* LORD *is upon Me, Because He has anointed Me To preach the gospel to the poor; He has sent Me to heal the brokenhearted, To proclaim liberty to the captives And recovery of sight to the blind, To set at liberty those who are oppressed;*

Every creature.

Mark 16:15 And He said to them, "Go into all the world and preach the gospel to every creature.

Col 1:23 if indeed you continue in the faith, grounded and steadfast, and are not moved away from the hope of the gospel which you heard, which was preached to every creature under heaven, of which I, Paul, became a minister.

Must be believed.

Mark 1:15 and saying, "The time is fulfilled, and the kingdom of God is at hand. Repent, and believe in the gospel."

Heb 4:2 For indeed the gospel was preached to us as well as to them; but the word which they heard did not profit them, not being mixed with faith in those who heard *it.*

Brings peace.

Luke 2:10 Then the angel said to them, "Do not be afraid, for behold, I bring you good tidings of great joy which will be to all people.

Luke 2:14 "Glory to God in the highest, And on earth peace, goodwill toward men!"

Eph 6:15 and having shod your feet with the preparation of the gospel of peace;

Produces hope.

Col 1:23 if indeed you continue in the faith, grounded and steadfast, and are not moved away from the hope of the gospel which you heard, which was preached to every creature under heaven, of which I, Paul, became a minister.

Believers have fellowship in.

Phil 1:5 for your fellowship in the gospel from the first day until now,

There is fullness of blessing in.

Rom 15:29 But I know that when I come to you, I shall come in the fullness of the blessing of the gospel of Christ.

Those who receive, should

Adhere to the truth of.

Gal 1:6–7 I marvel that you are turning away so soon from Him who called you in the grace of Christ, to a different gospel, **7** which is not another; but there are some who trouble you and want to pervert the gospel of Christ.

Gal 2:14 But when I saw that they were not straightforward about the truth of the gospel, I said to Peter before *them* all, "If you, being a Jew, live in the manner of Gentiles and not as the Jews, why do you compel Gentiles to live as Jews?

2 Tim 1:13 Hold fast the pattern of sound words which you have heard from me, in faith and love which are in Christ Jesus.

Not be ashamed of.

Rom 1:16 For I am not ashamed of the gospel of Christ, for it is the power of God to salvation for everyone who believes, for the Jew first and also for the Greek.

2 Tim 1:8 Therefore do not be ashamed of the testimony of our Lord, nor of me His prisoner, but share with me in the sufferings for the gospel according to the power of God,

Live in subjection to.

2 Cor 9:13 while, through the proof of this ministry, they glorify God for the obedience of your confession to the gospel of Christ, and for *your* liberal sharing with them and all *men,*

Conform their conduct to.

Phil 1:27 Only let your conduct be worthy of the gospel of Christ, so that whether I come and see you or am absent, I may hear of your affairs, that you stand fast in one spirit, with one mind striving together for the faith of the gospel,

Earnestly contend for the faith of.

Phil 1:17 but the latter out of love, knowing that I am appointed for the defense of the gospel.

Phil 1:27 Only let your conduct be worthy of the gospel of Christ, so that whether I come and see you or am absent, I may hear of your affairs, that you stand fast in one spirit, with one mind striving together for the faith of the gospel,

Jude 1:3 Beloved, while I was very diligent to write to you concerning our common salvation, I found it necessary to write to you exhorting you to contend earnestly for the faith which was once for all delivered to the saints.

Sacrifice everything for.

Matt 10:37 He who loves father or mother more than Me is not worthy of Me. And he who loves son or daughter more than Me is not worthy of Me.

Mark 8:35 For whoever desires to save his life will lose it, but whoever loses his life for My sake and the gospel's will save it.

Expect afflictions.

2 Tim 3:12 Yes, and all who desire to live godly in Christ Jesus will suffer persecution.

The promises to those who suffer for it.

Mark 8:35 For whoever desires to save his life will lose it, but whoever loses his life for My sake and the gospel's will save it.

Mark 10:29–30 So Jesus answered and said, "Assuredly, I say to you, there is no one who has left house or brothers or sisters or father or mother or wife or children or lands, for My sake and the gospel's, **30** who shall not receive a hundredfold now in this time—houses and brothers and sisters and mothers and children and lands, with persecutions—and in the age to come, eternal life.

Be careful not to hinder.

1 Cor 9:12 If others are partakers of *this* right over you, *are* we not even more? Nevertheless we have not used this right, but endure all things lest we hinder the gospel of Christ.

Is hidden to the lost.

2 Cor 4:3 But even if our gospel is veiled, it is veiled to those who are perishing,

Testifies to the final judgment.

Rom 2:16 in the day when God will judge the secrets of men by Jesus Christ, according to my gospel.

Let him who preaches another, be accursed.

Gal 1:8 But even if we, or an angel from heaven, preach any other gospel to you than what we have preached to you, let him be accursed.

Awful consequences of not obeying.

2 Thess 1:8–9 in flaming fire taking vengeance on those who do not know God, and on those who do not obey the gospel of our Lord Jesus Christ. 9 These shall be punished with everlasting destruction from the presence of the Lord and from the glory of His power,

Other terms for,

Dispensation of the grace of God.

Eph 3:2 if indeed you have heard of the dispensation of the grace of God which was given to me for you,

Gospel of peace.

Eph 6:15 and having shod your feet with the preparation of the gospel of peace;

Gospel of God.

Rom 1:1 Paul, a bondservant of Jesus Christ, called *to be* an apostle, separated to the gospel of God

1 Thess 2:8 So, affectionately longing for you, we were well pleased to impart to you not only the gospel of God, but also our own lives, because you had become dear to us.

1 Pet 4:17 For the time *has come* for judgment to begin at the house of God; and if *it begins* with us first, what will *be* the end of those who do not obey the gospel of God?

Gospel of Christ.

Rom 1:9 For God is my witness, whom I serve with my spirit in the gospel of His Son, that without ceasing I make mention of you always in my prayers,

Rom 1:16 For I am not ashamed of the gospel of Christ, for it is the power of God to salvation for everyone who believes, for the Jew first and also for the Greek.

2 Cor 2:12 Furthermore, when I came to Troas to *preach* Christ's gospel, and a door was opened to me by the Lord,

1 Thess 3:2 and sent Timothy, our brother and minister of God, and our fellow laborer in the gospel of Christ, to establish you and encourage you concerning your faith,

Gospel of the grace of God.

Acts 20:24 But none of these things move me; nor do I count my life dear to myself, so that I may finish my race with joy, and the ministry which I received from the Lord Jesus, to testify to the gospel of the grace of God.

Gospel of the kingdom.

Matt 24:14 And this gospel of the kingdom will be preached in all the world as a witness to all the nations, and then the end will come.

Gospel of salvation.

Eph 1:13 In Him you also *trusted,* after you heard the

word of truth, the gospel of your salvation; in whom also, having believed, you were sealed with the Holy Spirit of promise,

Gospel of the glory of Jesus Christ.

2 Cor 4:4 whose minds the god of this age has blinded, who do not believe, lest the light of the gospel of the glory of Christ, who is the image of God, should shine on them.

Preaching of Jesus Christ.

Rom 16:25 Now to Him who is able to establish you according to my gospel and the preaching of Jesus Christ, according to the revelation of the mystery kept secret since the world began

Mystery of the gospel.

Eph 6:19 and for me, that utterance may be given to me, that I may open my mouth boldly to make known the mystery of the gospel,

Word of God.

1 Thess 2:13 For this reason we also thank God without ceasing, because when you received the word of God which you heard from us, you welcomed *it* not *as* the word of men, but as it is in truth, the word of God, which also effectively works in you who believe.

Word of Christ.

Col 3:16 Let the word of Christ dwell in you richly in all wisdom, teaching and admonishing one another in psalms and hymns and spiritual songs, singing with grace in your hearts to the Lord.

Word of His grace.

Acts 14:3 Therefore they stayed there a long time, speaking boldly in the Lord, who was bearing witness to the word of His grace, granting signs and wonders to be done by their hands.

Acts 20:32 "So now, brethren, I commend you to God and to the word of His grace, which is able to build you up and give you an inheritance among all those who are sanctified.

Word of salvation.

Acts 13:26 "Men *and* brethren, sons of the family of Abraham, and those among you who fear God, to you the word of this salvation has been sent.

Word of reconciliation.

2 Cor 5:19 that is, that God was in Christ reconciling the world to Himself, not imputing their trespasses to them, and has committed to us the word of reconciliation.

Word of truth.

Eph 1:13 In Him you also *trusted,* after you heard the word of truth, the gospel of your salvation; in whom also, having believed, you were sealed with the Holy Spirit of promise,

James 1:18 Of His own will He brought us forth by the word of truth, that we might be a kind of firstfruits of His creatures.

Word of faith.

Rom 10:8 But what does it say? *"The word is near you, in your mouth and in your heart"* (that is, the word of faith which we preach):

Word of life.

Phil 2:16 holding fast the word of life, so that I may rejoice in the day of Christ that I have not run in vain or labored in vain.

Ministration of the Spirit.

2 Cor 3:8 how will the ministry of the Spirit not be more glorious?

Doctrine which accords godliness.

1 Tim 6:3 If anyone teaches otherwise and does not consent to wholesome words, *even* the words of our Lord Jesus Christ, and to the doctrine which accords with godliness,

Pattern of sound words.

2 Tim 1:13 Hold fast the pattern of sound words which you have heard from me, in faith and love which are in Christ Jesus.

Rejection of, by many, foretold.

Is 53:1 Who has believed our report? And to whom has the arm of the LORD been revealed?

Rom 10:15–16 And how shall they preach unless they are sent? As it is written: *"How beautiful are the feet of those who preach the gospel of peace, Who bring glad tidings of good things!"* **16** But they have not all obeyed the gospel. For Isaiah says, *"LORD, who has believed our report?"*

Rejection of, by the Jews, a means of blessing to the Gentiles.

Rom 11:28 Concerning the gospel *they are* enemies for your sake, but concerning the election *they are* beloved for the sake of the fathers.

GOSPEL, DOCTRINES OF THE

Are from God.

John 7:16 Jesus answered them and said, "My doctrine is not Mine, but His who sent Me.

Acts 13:12 Then the proconsul believed, when he saw what had been done, being astonished at the teaching of the Lord.

Are taught by Scripture.

2 Tim 3:16 All Scripture *is* given by inspiration of God, and *is* profitable for doctrine, for reproof, for correction, for instruction in righteousness,

Are godly.

1 Tim 6:3 If anyone teaches otherwise and does not consent to wholesome words, *even* the words of our Lord Jesus Christ, and to the doctrine which accords with godliness,

Titus 1:1 Paul, a bondservant of God and an apostle of Jesus Christ, according to the faith of God's elect and the acknowledgment of the truth which accords with godliness,

Immorality condemned by.

1 Tim 1:9–11 knowing this: that the law is not made for a righteous person, but for *the* lawless and insubordinate, for *the* ungodly and for sinners, for *the* unholy and profane, for murderers of fathers and murderers of mothers, for manslayers, **10** for fornicators, for sodomites, for kidnappers, for liars, for perjurers, and if there is any other thing that is contrary to sound doctrine, **11** according to the glorious gospel of the blessed God which was committed to my trust.

Lead to fellowship with the Father and with the Son.

1 John 1:3 that which we have seen and heard we declare to you, that you also may have fellowship with us; and truly our fellowship *is* with the Father and with His Son Jesus Christ.

2 John 1:9 Whoever transgresses and does not abide in the doctrine of Christ does not have God. He who abides in the doctrine of Christ has both the Father and the Son.

Lead to holiness.

Rom 6:17–22 But God be thanked that *though* you were slaves of sin, yet you obeyed from the heart that form of doctrine to which you were delivered. **18** And having been set free from sin, you became slaves of righteousness. **19** I speak in human *terms* because of the weakness of your flesh. For just as you presented your members *as* slaves of uncleanness, and of lawlessness *leading* to *more* lawlessness, so now present your members *as* slaves *of* righteousness for holiness. **20** For when you were slaves of sin, you were free in regard to righteousness. **21** What fruit did you have then in the things of which you are now ashamed? For the end of those things *is* death. **22** But now having been set free from sin, and having become slaves of God, you have your fruit to holiness, and the end, everlasting life.

Titus 2:12 teaching us that, denying ungodliness and worldly lusts, we should live soberly, righteously, and godly in the present age,

Bring no reproach on.

1 Tim 6:1 Let as many bondservants as are under the yoke count their own masters worthy of all honor, so that the name of God and *His* doctrine may not be blasphemed.

Titus 2:5 to be discreet, chaste, homemakers, good, obedient to their own husbands, that the word of God may not be blasphemed.

Ministers should

Be nourished up in.

1 Tim 4:6 If you instruct the brethren in these things, you will be a good minister of Jesus Christ, nourished in the words of faith and of the good doctrine which you have carefully followed.

Attend to and continue in.

1 Tim 4:13 Till I come, give attention to reading, to exhortation, to doctrine.

1 Tim 4:16 Take heed to yourself and to the doctrine. Continue in them, for in doing this you will save both yourself and those who hear you.

Titus 2:1 But as for you, speak the things which are proper for sound doctrine:

Hold, in sincerity.

2 Cor 2:17 For we are not, as so many, peddling the word of God; but as of sincerity, but as from God, we speak in the sight of God in Christ.

Titus 2:7 in all things showing yourself *to be* a pattern of good works; in doctrine *showing* integrity, reverence, incorruptibility,

Hold steadfastly.

2 Tim 1:13 Hold fast the pattern of sound words which

you have heard from me, in faith and love which are in Christ Jesus.

Titus 1:9 holding fast the faithful word as he has been taught, that he may be able, by sound doctrine, both to exhort and convict those who contradict.

Believers must adhere to, sincerely.

Acts 2:42 And they continued steadfastly in the apostles' doctrine and fellowship, in the breaking of bread, and in prayers.

Rom 6:17 But God be thanked that *though* you were slaves of sin, yet you obeyed from the heart that form of doctrine to which you were delivered.

A faithful walk adorns.

Titus 2:10 not pilfering, but showing all good fidelity, that they may adorn the doctrine of God our Savior in all things.

The obedience of believers leads to surer knowledge of.

John 7:17 If anyone wills to do His will, he shall know concerning the doctrine, whether it is from God or *whether* I speak on My own *authority.*

Those who oppose, are

Proud.

1 Tim 6:3–4 If anyone teaches otherwise and does not consent to wholesome words, *even* the words of our Lord Jesus Christ, and to the doctrine which accords with godliness, 4 he is proud, knowing nothing, but is obsessed with disputes and arguments over words, from which come envy, strife, reviling, evil suspicions,

Ignorant.

1 Tim 6:4 he is proud, knowing nothing, but is obsessed with disputes and arguments over words, from which come envy, strife, reviling, evil suspicions,

Obsessed with disputes.

1 Tim 6:4 he is proud, knowing nothing, but is obsessed with disputes and arguments over words, from which come envy, strife, reviling, evil suspicions,

Not to be received.

2 John 1:10 If anyone comes to you and does not bring this doctrine, do not receive him into your house nor greet him;

To be avoided.

Rom 16:17 Now I urge you, brethren, note those who cause divisions and offenses, contrary to the doctrine which you learned, and avoid them.

Not endured by the wicked.

2 Tim 4:3 For the time will come when they will not endure sound doctrine, but according to their own desires, *because* they have itching ears, they will heap up for themselves teachers;

GOVERNMENT

Local officials of.

Ex 18:13–26 And so it was, on the next day, that Moses sat to judge the people; and the people stood before Moses from morning until evening. 14 So when Moses' father-in-law saw all that he did for the people, he said, "What *is* this thing that you are doing for the people? Why do you alone sit, and all the people stand before you from morning until evening?"

15 And Moses said to his father-in-law, "Because the people come to me to inquire of God. 16 When they have a difficulty, they come to me, and I judge between one and another; and I make known the statutes of God and His laws." 17 So Moses' father-in-law said to him, "The thing that you do *is* not good. 18 Both you and these people who *are* with you will surely wear yourselves out. For this thing *is* too much for you; you are not able to perform it by yourself. 19 Listen now to my voice; I will give you counsel, and God will be with you: Stand before God for the people, so that you may bring the difficulties to God. 20 And you shall teach them the statutes and the laws, and show them the way in which they must walk and the work they must do. 21 Moreover you shall select from all the people able men, such as fear God, men of truth, hating covetousness; and place *such* over them *to be* rulers of thousands, rulers of hundreds, rulers of fifties, and rulers of tens. 22 And let them judge the people at all times. Then it will be *that* every great matter they shall bring to you, but every small matter they themselves shall judge. So it will be easier for you, for they will bear *the burden* with you. 23 If you do this thing, and God *so* commands you, then you will be able to endure, and all this people will also go to their place in peace." 24 So Moses heeded the voice of his father-in-law and did all that he had said. 25 And Moses chose able men out of all Israel, and made them heads over the people: rulers of thousands, rulers of hundreds, rulers of fifties, and rulers of tens. 26 So they judged the people at all times; the hard cases they brought to Moses, but they judged every small case themselves.

1 Sam 8:10–12 So Samuel told all the words of the LORD to the people who asked him for a king. 11 And he said, "This will be the behavior of the king who will reign over you: He will take your sons and appoint *them* for his own chariots and *to be* his horsemen, and *some* will run before his chariots. 12 He will appoint captains over his thousands and captains over his fifties, *will set some* to plow his ground and reap his harvest, and *some* to make his weapons of war and equipment for his chariots.

1 Kin 8:1 Now Solomon assembled the elders of Israel and all the heads of the tribes, the chief fathers of the children of Israel, to King Solomon in Jerusalem, that they might bring up the ark of the covenant of the LORD from the City of David, which *is* Zion.

Dan 3:2 And King Nebuchadnezzar sent *word* to gather together the satraps, the administrators, the governors, the counselors, the treasurers, the judges, the magistrates, and all the officials of the provinces, to come to the dedication of the image which King Nebuchadnezzar had set up.

Cf. Num 11:16–30; 1 Sam 15:30; 2 Sam 17:15; 1 Kin 12:6–11

Of Christ, will be perfect and peaceful.

Is 2:4 He shall judge between the nations, And rebuke many people; They shall beat their swords into plowshares, And their spears into pruning hooks; Nation shall not lift up sword against nation, Neither shall they learn war anymore.

Is 9:6–7 For unto us a Child is born, Unto us a Son is given; And the government will be upon His shoulder. And His name will be called Wonderful, Counselor, Mighty God, Everlasting Father, Prince of Peace. **7** Of the increase of *His* government and peace *There will be* no end, Upon the throne of David and over His kingdom, To order it and establish it with judgment and justice From that time forward, even forever. The zeal of the Lord of hosts will perform this.

Is 11:6–9 "The wolf also shall dwell with the lamb, The leopard shall lie down with the young goat, The calf and the young lion and the fatling together; And a little child shall lead them. **7** The cow and the bear shall graze; Their young ones shall lie down together; And the lion shall eat straw like the ox. **8** The nursing child shall play by the cobra's hole, And the weaned child shall put his hand in the viper's den. **9** They shall not hurt nor destroy in all My holy mountain, For the earth shall be full of the knowledge of the LORD As the waters cover the sea.

Mic 4:3 He shall judge between many peoples, And rebuke strong nations afar off; They shall beat their swords into plowshares, And their spears into pruning hooks; Nation shall not lift up sword against nation, Neither shall they learn war anymore.

Cf. Rev 2:27; 19:15

Citizens, including believers, obligated to support.

Matt 22:15–21 Then the Pharisees went and plotted how they might entangle Him in *His* talk. **16** And they sent to Him their disciples with the Herodians, saying, "Teacher, we know that You are true, and teach the way of God in truth; nor do You care about anyone, for You do not regard the person of men. **17** Tell us, therefore, what do You think? Is it lawful to pay taxes to Caesar, or not?" **18** But Jesus perceived their wickedness, and said, "Why do you test Me, *you* hypocrites? **19** Show Me the tax money." So they brought Him a denarius. **20** And He said to them, "Whose image and inscription *is* this?" **21** They said to Him, "Caesar's." And He said to them, "Render therefore to Caesar the things that are Caesar's, and to God the things that are God's."

Mark 12:13–17 Then they sent to Him some of the Pharisees and the Herodians, to catch Him in *His* words. **14** When they had come, they said to Him, "Teacher, we know that You are true, and care about no one; for You do not regard the person of men, but teach the way of God in truth. Is it lawful to pay taxes to Caesar, or not? **15** Shall we pay, or shall we not pay?" But He, knowing their hypocrisy, said to them, "Why do you test Me? Bring Me a denarius that I may see *it*." **16** So they brought *it*. And He said to them, "Whose image and inscription *is* this?" They said to Him, "Caesar's." **17** And Jesus answered and said to them, "Render to Caesar the things that are Caesar's, and to God the things that are God's." And they marveled at Him.

Luke 20:20–26 So they watched *Him*, and sent spies who pretended to be righteous, that they might seize on His words, in order to deliver Him to the power and the authority of the governor. **21** Then they asked Him, saying, "Teacher, we know that You say and teach rightly, and You do not show personal favoritism, but teach the way of God in truth: **22** Is it lawful for us to pay taxes to Caesar or not?" **23** But He perceived their craftiness, and said to them,

"Why do you test Me? **24** Show Me a denarius. Whose image and inscription does it have?" They answered and said, "Caesar's." **25** And He said to them, "Render therefore to Caesar the things that are Caesar's, and to God the things that are God's." **26** But they could not catch Him in His words in the presence of the people. And they marveled at His answer and kept silent.

Rom 13:1–7 Let every soul be subject to the governing authorities. For there is no authority except from God, and the authorities that exist are appointed by God. **2** Therefore whoever resists the authority resists the ordinance of God, and those who resist will bring judgment on themselves. **3** For rulers are not a terror to good works, but to evil. Do you want to be unafraid of the authority? Do what is good, and you will have praise from the same. **4** For he is God's minister to you for good. But if you do evil, be afraid; for he does not bear the sword in vain; for he is God's minister, an avenger to *execute* wrath on him who practices evil. **5** Therefore *you* must be subject, not only because of wrath but also for conscience' sake. **6** For because of this you also pay taxes, for they are God's ministers attending continually to this very thing. **7** Render therefore to all their due: taxes to whom taxes *are due*, customs to whom customs, fear to whom fear, honor to whom honor.

1 Tim 2:1–4 Therefore I exhort first of all that supplications, prayers, intercessions, *and* giving of thanks be made for all men, **2** for kings and all who are in authority, that we may lead a quiet and peaceable life in all godliness and reverence. **3** For this *is* good and acceptable in the sight of God our Savior, **4** who desires all men to be saved and to come to the knowledge of the truth.

Titus 3:1 Remind them to be subject to rulers and authorities, to obey, to be ready for every good work,

1 Pet 2:13–17 Therefore submit yourselves to every ordinance of man for the Lord's sake, whether to the king as supreme, **14** or to governors, as to those who are sent by him for the punishment of evildoers and *for the* praise of those who do good. **15** For this is the will of God, that by doing good you may put to silence the ignorance of foolish men— **16** as free, yet not using liberty as a cloak for vice, but as bondservants of God. **17** Honor all *people*. Love the brotherhood. Fear God. Honor the king.

Cf. Matt 17:24–27

Census ordered by, at time of Christ.

Luke 2:1–3 And it came to pass in those days *that* a decree went out from Caesar Augustus that all the world should be registered. **2** This census first took place while Quirinius was governing Syria. **3** So all went to be registered, everyone to his own city.

Sometimes believers must obey God instead of.

Ex 1:15–17 Then the king of Egypt spoke to the Hebrew midwives, of whom the name of one *was* Shiphrah and the name of the other Puah; **16** and he said, "When you do the duties of a midwife for the Hebrew women, and see *them* on the birthstools, if it *is* a son, then you shall kill him; but if it *is* a daughter, then she shall live." **17** But the midwives feared God, and did not do as the king of Egypt commanded them, but saved the male children alive.

Dan 6:4–10 So the governors and satraps sought to find *some* charge against Daniel concerning the kingdom; but they could find no charge or fault, because he *was* faithful; nor was there any error or fault found in him. **5** Then these men said, "We shall not find any charge against this Daniel unless we find *it* against him concerning the law of his God." **6** So these governors and satraps thronged before the king, and said thus to him: "King Darius, live forever! **7** All the governors of the kingdom, the administrators and satraps, the counselors and advisors, have consulted together to establish a royal statute and to make a firm decree, that whoever petitions any god or man for thirty days, except you, O king, shall be cast into the den of lions. **8** Now, O king, establish the decree and sign the writing, so that it cannot be changed, according to the law of the Medes and Persians, which does not alter." **9** Therefore King Darius signed the written decree. **10** Now when Daniel knew that the writing was signed, he went home. And in his upper room, with his windows open toward Jerusalem, he knelt down on his knees three times that day, and prayed and gave thanks before his God, as was his custom since early days.

Acts 4:18–20 So they called them and commanded them not to speak at all nor teach in the name of Jesus. **19** But Peter and John answered and said to them, "Whether it is right in the sight of God to listen to you more than to God, you judge. **20** For we cannot but speak the things which we have seen and heard."

Paul exercised privileges granted by.

Acts 16:37 But Paul said to them, "They have beaten us openly, uncondemned Romans, *and* have thrown *us* into prison. And now do they put us out secretly? No indeed! Let them come themselves and get us out."

Acts 22:25 And as they bound him with thongs, Paul said to the centurion who stood by, "Is it lawful for you to scourge a man who is a Roman, and uncondemned?"

Acts 22:29 Then immediately those who were about to examine him withdrew from him; and the commander was also afraid after he found out that he was a Roman, and because he had bound him.

Acts 25:11 For if I am an offender, or have committed anything deserving of death, I do not object to dying; but if there is nothing in these things of which these men accuse me, no one can deliver me to them. I appeal to Caesar."

Of Antichrist, figuratively depicted.

Dan 2:32–45 This image's head *was* of fine gold, its chest and arms of silver, its belly and thighs of bronze, **33** its legs of iron, its feet partly of iron and partly of clay. **34** You watched while a stone was cut out without hands, which struck the image on its feet of iron and clay, and broke them in pieces. **35** Then the iron, the clay, the bronze, the silver, and the gold were crushed together, and became like chaff from the summer threshing floors; the wind carried them away so that no trace of them was found. And the stone that struck the image became a great mountain and filled the whole earth. **36** "This *is* the dream. Now we will tell the interpretation of it before the king. **37** You, O king, *are* a king of kings. For the God of heaven has given you a kingdom, power, strength,

and glory; **38** and wherever the children of men dwell, or the beasts of the field and the birds of the heaven, He has given *them* into your hand, and has made you ruler over them all—you *are* this head of gold. **39** But after you shall arise another kingdom inferior to yours; then another, a third kingdom of bronze, which shall rule over all the earth. **40** And the fourth kingdom shall be as strong as iron, inasmuch as iron breaks in pieces and shatters everything; and like iron that crushes, *that kingdom* will break in pieces and crush all the others. **41** Whereas you saw the feet and toes, partly of potter's clay and partly of iron, the kingdom shall be divided; yet the strength of the iron shall be in it, just as you saw the iron mixed with ceramic clay. **42** And *as* the toes of the feet *were* partly of iron and partly of clay, *so* the kingdom shall be partly strong and partly fragile. **43** As you saw iron mixed with ceramic clay, they will mingle with the seed of men; but they will not adhere to one another, just as iron does not mix with clay. **44** And in the days of these kings the God of heaven will set up a kingdom which shall never be destroyed; and the kingdom shall not be left to other people; it shall break in pieces and consume all these kingdoms, and it shall stand forever. **45** Inasmuch as you saw that the stone was cut out of the mountain without hands, and that it broke in pieces the iron, the bronze, the clay, the silver, and the gold—the great God has made known to the king what will come to pass after this. The dream is certain, and its interpretation is sure."

Dan 7:7–8 "After this I saw in the night visions, and behold, a fourth beast, dreadful and terrible, exceedingly strong. It had huge iron teeth; it was devouring, breaking in pieces, and trampling the residue with its feet. It *was* different from all the beasts that *were* before it, and it had ten horns. **8** I was considering the horns, and there was another horn, a little one, coming up among them, before whom three of the first horns were plucked out by the roots. And there, in this horn, *were* eyes like the eyes of a man, and a mouth speaking pompous words.

Dan 7:19–25 "Then I wished to know the truth about the fourth beast, which was different from all the others, exceedingly dreadful, *with* its teeth of iron and its nails of bronze, *which* devoured, broke in pieces, and trampled the residue with its feet; **20** and the ten horns that *were* on its head, and the other *horn* which came up, before which three fell, namely, that horn which had eyes and a mouth which spoke pompous words, whose appearance *was* greater than his fellows. **21** "I was watching; and the same horn was making war against the saints, and prevailing against them, **22** until the Ancient of Days came, and a judgment was made *in favor* of the saints of the Most High, and the time came for the saints to possess the kingdom. **23** "Thus he said: 'The fourth beast shall be A fourth kingdom on earth, Which shall be different from all *other* kingdoms, And shall devour the whole earth, Trample it and break it in pieces. **24** The ten horns *are* ten kings *Who* shall arise from this kingdom. And another shall rise after them; He shall be different from the first *ones*, And shall subdue three kings. **25** ·He shall speak *pompous* words against the Most High, Shall persecute the saints of the Most High, And shall intend to change times and law. Then *the saints* shall be given into his hand For a time and times and half a time.

Rev 12:3 And another sign appeared in heaven: behold, a great, fiery red dragon having seven heads and ten horns, and seven diadems on his heads.

Rev 13:1–2 Then I stood on the sand of the sea. And I saw a beast rising up out of the sea, having seven heads and ten horns, and on his horns ten crowns, and on his heads a blasphemous name. **2** Now the beast which I saw was like a leopard, his feet were like *the feet of* a bear, and his mouth like the mouth of a lion. The dragon gave him his power, his throne, and great authority.

GOVERNMENT, PATRIARCHAL
Vested in the heads of families.

Gen 18:19 For I have known him, in order that he may command his children and his household after him, that they keep the way of the LORD, to do righteousness and justice, that the LORD may bring to Abraham what He has spoken to him."

Exercised in

Training servants for war.

Gen 14:14 Now when Abram heard that his brother was taken captive, he armed his three hundred and eighteen trained *servants* who were born in his own house, and went in pursuit as far as Dan.

Vindicating wrongs.

Gen 14:12 They also took Lot, Abram's brother's son who dwelt in Sodom, and his goods, and departed.

Gen 14:15–16 He divided his forces against them by night, and he and his servants attacked them and pursued them as far as Hobah, which *is* north of Damascus. **16** So he brought back all the goods, and also brought back his brother Lot and his goods, as well as the women and the people.

Forming treaties and alliances.

Gen 14:13 Then one who had escaped came and told Abram the Hebrew, for he dwelt by the terebinth trees of Mamre the Amorite, brother of Eshcol and brother of Aner; and they *were* allies with Abram.

Gen 21:22–32 And it came to pass at that time that Abimelech and Phichol, the commander of his army, spoke to Abraham, saying, "God *is* with you in all that you do. **23** Now therefore, swear to me by God that you will not deal falsely with me, with my offspring, or with my posterity; but that according to the kindness that I have done to you, you will do to me and to the land in which you have dwelt." **24** And Abraham said, "I will swear." **25** Then Abraham rebuked Abimelech because of a well of water which Abimelech's servants had seized. **26** And Abimelech said, "I do not know who has done this thing; you did not tell me, nor had I heard *of it* until today." **27** So Abraham took sheep and oxen and gave them to Abimelech, and the two of them made a covenant. **28** And Abraham set seven ewe lambs of the flock by themselves. **29** Then Abimelech asked Abraham, "What *is the meaning of* these seven ewe lambs which you have set by themselves?" **30** And he said, "You will take *these* seven ewe lambs from my hand, that they may be my witness that I have dug this well." **31** Therefore he called that place Be-

ersheba, because the two of them swore an oath there. **32** Thus they made a covenant at Beersheba. So Abimelech rose with Phichol, the commander of his army, and they returned to the land of the Philistines.

Gen 26:28–33 But they said, "We have certainly seen that the LORD is with you. So we said, 'Let there now be an oath between us, between you and us; and let us make a covenant with you, **29** that you will do us no harm, since we have not touched you, and since we have done nothing to you but good and have sent you away in peace. You *are* now the blessed of the LORD.' " **30** So he made them a feast, and they ate and drank. **31** Then they arose early in the morning and swore an oath with one another; and Isaac sent them away, and they departed from him in peace. **32** It came to pass the same day that Isaac's servants came and told him about the well which they had dug, and said to him, "We have found water." **33** So he called it Shebah. Therefore the name of the city *is* Beersheba to this day.

Acting as priests.

Gen 8:20 Then Noah built an altar to the LORD, and took of every clean animal and of every clean bird, and offered burnt offerings on the altar.

Gen 12:7–8 Then the LORD appeared to Abram and said, "To your descendants I will give this land." And there he built an altar to the LORD, who had appeared to him. **8** And he moved from there to the mountain east of Bethel, and he pitched his tent *with* Bethel on the west and Ai on the east; there he built an altar to the LORD and called on the name of the LORD.

Gen 35:1–7 Then God said to Jacob, "Arise, go up to Bethel and dwell there; and make an altar there to God, who appeared to you when you fled from the face of Esau your brother." **2** And Jacob said to his household and to all who *were* with him, "Put away the foreign gods that *are* among you, purify yourselves, and change your garments. **3** Then let us arise and go up to Bethel; and I will make an altar there to God, who answered me in the day of my distress and has been with me in the way which I have gone." **4** So they gave Jacob all the foreign gods which *were* in their hands, and the earrings which *were* in their ears; and Jacob hid them under the terebinth tree which *was* by Shechem. **5** And they journeyed, and the terror of God was upon the cities that *were* all around them, and they did not pursue the sons of Jacob. **6** So Jacob came to Luz (that *is,* Bethel), which *is* in the land of Canaan, he and all the people who *were* with him. **7** And he built an altar there and called the place El Bethel, because there God appeared to him when he fled from the face of his brother.

Job 1:5 So it was, when the days of feasting had run their course, that Job would send and sanctify them, and he would rise early in the morning and offer burnt offerings *according* to the number of them all. For Job said, "It may be that my sons have sinned and cursed God in their hearts." Thus Job did regularly.

Acting as judges.

Gen 38:24 And it came to pass, about three months after, that Judah was told, saying, "Tamar your daughter-in-law has played the harlot; furthermore she *is* with child by harlotry." So Judah said, "Bring her out and let her be burned!"

Arbitrarily disinheriting and putting away servants and children.

Gen 21:14 So Abraham rose early in the morning, and took bread and a skin of water; and putting *it* on her shoulder, he gave *it* and the boy to Hagar, and sent her away. Then she departed and wandered in the Wilderness of Beersheba.

1 Chr 5:1 Now the sons of Reuben the firstborn of Israel—he *was* indeed the firstborn, but because he defiled his father's bed, his birthright was given to the sons of Joseph, the son of Israel, so that the genealogy is not listed according to the birthright;

Blessing and cursing children.

Gen 9:25–26 Then he said: "Cursed *be* Canaan; A servant of servants He shall be to his brethren." **26** And he said: "Blessed *be* the LORD, The God of Shem, And may Canaan be his servant.

Gen 27:28–29 Therefore may God give you Of the dew of heaven, Of the fatness of the earth, And plenty of grain and wine. **29** Let peoples serve you, And nations bow down to you. Be master over your brethren, And let your mother's sons bow down to you. Cursed *be* everyone who curses you, And blessed *be* those who bless you!"

Cf. Gen 49:1–33

Burying the dead.

Gen 23:6 "Hear us, my lord: You *are* a mighty prince among us; bury your dead in the choicest of our burial places. None of us will withhold from you his burial place, that you may bury your dead."

GRACE

God is the source of.

Ps 84:11 For the LORD God *is* a sun and shield; The LORD will give grace and glory; No good *thing* will He withhold From those who walk uprightly.

James 1:17 Every good gift and every perfect gift is from above, and comes down from the Father of lights, with whom there is no variation or shadow of turning.

1 Pet 5:10 But may the God of all grace, who called us to His eternal glory by Christ Jesus, after you have suffered a while, perfect, establish, strengthen, and settle *you.*

God's throne, the throne of.

Heb 4:16 Let us therefore come boldly to the throne of grace, that we may obtain mercy and find grace to help in time of need.

The Holy Spirit is the Spirit of.

Zech 12:10 "And I will pour on the house of David and on the inhabitants of Jerusalem the Spirit of grace and supplication; then they will look on Me whom they pierced. Yes, they will mourn for Him as one mourns for *his* only *son,* and grieve for Him as one grieves for a firstborn.

Heb 10:29 Of how much worse punishment, do you suppose, will he be thought worthy who has trampled the Son of God underfoot, counted the blood of the covenant by which he was sanctified a common thing, and insulted the Spirit of grace?

Christ received it from God.

Luke 2:40 And the Child grew and became strong in spirit, filled with wisdom; and the grace of God was upon Him.

John 1:14 And the Word became flesh and dwelt among us, and we beheld His glory, the glory as of the only begotten of the Father, full of grace and truth.

John 3:35 The Father loves the Son, and has given all things into His hand.

Christ spoke with.

Ps 45:2 You are fairer than the sons of men; Grace is poured upon Your lips; Therefore God has blessed You forever.

Luke 4:22 So all bore witness to Him, and marveled at the gracious words which proceeded out of His mouth. And they said, "Is this not Joseph's son?"

Came by Christ.

John 1:17 For the law was given through Moses, *but* grace and truth came through Jesus Christ.

Rom 5:15 But the free gift *is* not like the offense. For if by the one man's offense many died, much more the grace of God and the gift by the grace of the one Man, Jesus Christ, abounded to many.

1 Cor 1:4 I thank my God always concerning you for the grace of God which was given to you by Christ Jesus,

Foretold by the prophets.

1 Pet 1:10 Of this salvation the prophets have inquired and searched carefully, who prophesied of the grace *that would come* to you,

Riches of, exhibited in God's kindness through Christ.

Eph 2:7 that in the ages to come He might show the exceeding riches of His grace in *His* kindness toward us in Christ Jesus.

Glory of, exhibited in our acceptance in Christ.

Eph 1:6 to the praise of the glory of His grace, by which He made us accepted in the Beloved.

Descriptions of,

Great.

Acts 4:33 And with great power the apostles gave witness to the resurrection of the Lord Jesus. And great grace was upon them all.

Sovereign.

Rom 5:21 so that as sin reigned in death, even so grace might reign through righteousness to eternal life through Jesus Christ our Lord.

Rich.

Eph 1:7 In Him we have redemption through His blood, the forgiveness of sins, according to the riches of His grace

Eph 2:7 that in the ages to come He might show the exceeding riches of His grace in *His* kindness toward us in Christ Jesus.

Exceeding.

2 Cor 9:14 and by their prayer for you, who long for you because of the exceeding grace of God in you.

Manifold.

1 Pet 4:10 As each one has received a gift, minister it to one another, as good stewards of the manifold grace of God.

All-sufficient.

2 Cor 12:9 And He said to me, "My grace is sufficient for you, for My strength is made perfect in weakness." Therefore most gladly I will rather boast in my infirmities, that the power of Christ may rest upon me.

All-abundant.

Rom 5:15 But the free gift *is* not like the offense. For if by the one man's offense many died, much more the grace of God and the gift by the grace of the one Man, Jesus Christ, abounded to many.

Rom 5:17 For if by the one man's offense death reigned through the one, much more those who receive abundance of grace and of the gift of righteousness will reign in life through the One, Jesus Christ.)

Rom 5:20 Moreover the law entered that the offense might abound. But where sin abounded, grace abounded much more,

Glorious.

Eph 1:6 to the praise of the glory of His grace, by which He made us accepted in the Beloved.

The gospel, a declaration of.

Acts 20:24 But none of these things move me; nor do I count my life dear to myself, so that I may finish my race with joy, and the ministry which I received from the Lord Jesus, to testify to the gospel of the grace of God.

Acts 20:32 "So now, brethren, I commend you to God and to the word of His grace, which is able to build you up and give you an inheritance among all those who are sanctified.

Is the source of

Election.

Rom 11:5 Even so then, at this present time there is a remnant according to the election of grace.

The call of God.

Gal 1:15 But when it pleased God, who separated me from my mother's womb and called *me* through His grace,

Justification.

Rom 3:24 being justified freely by His grace through the redemption that is in Christ Jesus,

Titus 3:7 that having been justified by His grace we should become heirs according to the hope of eternal life.

Faith.

Acts 18:27 And when he desired to cross to Achaia, the brethren wrote, exhorting the disciples to receive him; and when he arrived, he greatly helped those who had believed through grace;

Forgiveness of sins.

Eph 1:7 In Him we have redemption through His blood, the forgiveness of sins, according to the riches of His grace

Salvation.

Acts 15:11 But we believe that through the grace of the Lord Jesus Christ we shall be saved in the same manner as they."

Eph 2:5 even when we were dead in trespasses, made us alive together with Christ (by grace you have been saved),

Eph 2:8 For by grace you have been saved through faith, and that not of yourselves; *it is* the gift of God,

Consolation.

2 Thess 2:16 Now may our Lord Jesus Christ Himself, and our God and Father, who has loved us and given *us* everlasting consolation and good hope by grace,

Hope.

2 Thess 2:16 Now may our Lord Jesus Christ Himself, and our God and Father, who has loved us and given *us* everlasting consolation and good hope by grace,

Necessary to the service of God.

Heb 12:28 Therefore, since we are receiving a kingdom which cannot be shaken, let us have grace, by which we may serve God acceptably with reverence and godly fear.

God's work completed in believers by.

2 Thess 1:11–12 Therefore we also pray always for you that our God would count you worthy of *this* calling, and fulfill all the good pleasure of *His* goodness and the work of faith with power, **12** that the name of our Lord Jesus Christ may be glorified in you, and you in Him, according to the grace of our God and the Lord Jesus Christ.

The success and completion of the work of God to be attributed to.

Zech 4:7 'Who *are* you, O great mountain? Before Zerubbabel *you shall become* a plain! And he shall bring forth the capstone With shouts of "Grace, grace to it!" ' "

Inheritance of the promises is by.

Rom 4:16 Therefore *it is* of faith that *it might be* according to grace, so that the promise might be sure to all the seed, not only to those who are of the law, but also to those who are of the faith of Abraham, who is the father of us all

Justification by, opposed to that by works.

Rom 4:4–5 Now to him who works, the wages are not counted as grace but as debt. **5** But to him who does not work but believes on Him who justifies the ungodly, his faith is accounted for righteousness,

Rom 11:6 And if by grace, then *it is* no longer of works; otherwise grace is no longer grace. But if *it is* of works, it is no longer grace; otherwise work is no longer work.

Gal 5:4 You have become estranged from Christ, you who *attempt to* be justified by law; you have fallen from grace.

Believers

Are heirs of.

1 Pet 3:7 Husbands, likewise, dwell with *them* with understanding, giving honor to the wife, as to the weaker vessel, and as *being* heirs together of the grace of life, that your prayers may not be hindered.

Are under.

Rom 6:14 For sin shall not have dominion over you, for you are not under law but under grace.

Receive, from Christ.

John 1:16 And of His fullness we have all received, and grace for grace.

Are what they are by.

1 Cor 15:10 But by the grace of God I am what I am, and His grace toward me was not in vain; but I labored more abundantly than they all, yet not I, but the grace of God *which was* with me.

2 Cor 1:12 For our boasting is this: the testimony of our conscience that we conducted ourselves in the world in simplicity and godly sincerity, not with fleshly wisdom but by the grace of God, and more abundantly toward you.

Abound in gifts of.

Acts 4:33 And with great power the apostles gave witness to the resurrection of the Lord Jesus. And great grace was upon them all.

2 Cor 8:1 Moreover, brethren, we make known to you the grace of God bestowed on the churches of Macedonia:

2 Cor 9:8 And God *is* able to make all grace abound toward you, that you, always having all sufficiency in all *things*, may have an abundance for every good work.

2 Cor 9:14 and by their prayer for you, who long for you because of the exceeding grace of God in you.

Should mature in.

2 Tim 2:1 You therefore, my son, be strong in the grace that is in Christ Jesus.

Heb 13:9 Do not be carried about with various and strange doctrines. For *it is* good that the heart be established by grace, not with foods which have not profited those who have been occupied with them.

2 Pet 3:18 but grow in the grace and knowledge of our Lord and Savior Jesus Christ. To Him *be* the glory both now and forever. Amen.

Should speak with.

Eph 4:29 Let no corrupt word proceed out of your mouth, but what is good for necessary edification, that it may impart grace to the hearers.

Col 4:6 *Let* your speech always *be* with grace, seasoned with salt, that you may know how you ought to answer each one.

Is especially given

To ministers.

Rom 12:3 For I say, through the grace given to me, to everyone who is among you, not to think *of himself* more highly than he ought to think, but to think soberly, as God has dealt to each one a measure of faith.

Rom 12:6 Having then gifts differing according to the grace that is given to us, *let us use them:* if prophecy, *let us prophesy* in proportion to our faith;

Rom 15:15 Nevertheless, brethren, I have written more boldly to you on *some* points, as reminding you, because of the grace given to me by God,

1 Cor 3:10 According to the grace of God which was given to me, as a wise master builder I have laid the foundation, and another builds on it. But let each one take heed how he builds on it.

Gal 2:9 and when James, Cephas, and John, who seemed to be pillars, perceived the grace that had been given to me, they gave me and Barnabas the right hand of fellowship, that we *should go* to the Gentiles and they to the circumcised.

Eph 3:7 of which I became a minister according to the gift of the grace of God given to me by the effective working of His power.

To the humble.

Prov 3:34 Surely He scorns the scornful, But gives grace to the humble.

James 4:6 But He gives more grace. Therefore He says: *"God resists the proud, But gives grace to the humble."*

To those who walk uprightly.

Ps 84:11 For the LORD God *is* a sun and shield; The LORD will give grace and glory; No good *thing* will He withhold From those who walk uprightly.

Not to be received in vain.

2 Cor 6:1 We then, *as* workers together *with Him* also plead with *you* not to receive the grace of God in vain.

Pray for it

For yourselves.

Heb 4:16 Let us therefore come boldly to the throne of grace, that we may obtain mercy and find grace to help in time of need.

For others.

2 Cor 13:14 The grace of the Lord Jesus Christ, and the love of God, and the communion of the Holy Spirit *be* with you all. Amen.

Eph 6:24 Grace *be* with all those who love our Lord Jesus Christ in sincerity. Amen.

Be careful not to fall short of.

Heb 12:15 looking carefully lest anyone fall short of the grace of God; lest any root of bitterness springing up cause trouble, and by this many become defiled;

Manifestation of, in others, a cause of gladness.

Acts 11:23 When he came and had seen the grace of God, he was glad, and encouraged them all that with purpose of heart they should continue with the Lord.

1 John 1:3–4 that which we have seen and heard we declare to you, that you also may have fellowship with us; and truly our fellowship *is* with the Father and with His Son Jesus Christ. **4** And these things we write to you that your joy may be full.

Special manifestation of, at the second coming of Christ.

1 Pet 1:13 Therefore gird up the loins of your mind, be sober, and rest *your* hope fully upon the grace that is to be brought to you at the revelation of Jesus Christ;

Not to be abused.

Rom 3:8 And *why* not *say,* "Let us do evil that good may come"?—as we are slanderously reported and as some affirm that we say. Their condemnation is just.

Rom 6:1 What shall we say then? Shall we continue in sin that grace may abound?

Rom 6:15 What then? Shall we sin because we are not under law but under grace? Certainly not!

Lawless men will abuse.

Jude 1:4 For certain men have crept in unnoticed, who long ago were marked out for this condemnation, ungodly men, who turn the grace of our God into lewdness and deny the only Lord God and our Lord Jesus Christ.

GRASS

A green plant.

Mark 6:39 Then He commanded them to make them all sit down in groups on the green grass.

Called

Grass of the earth.

Rev 9:4 They were commanded not to harm the grass of the earth, or any green thing, or any tree, but only those men who do not have the seal of God on their foreheads.

Grass of the field.

Num 22:4 So Moab said to the elders of Midian, "Now this company will lick up everything around us, as an ox licks up the grass of the field." And Balak the son of Zippor *was* king of the Moabites at that time.

Springs out of the earth.

2 Sam 23:4 And *he shall be* like the light of the morning *when* the sun rises, A morning without clouds, *Like* the tender grass *springing* out of the earth, By clear shining after rain.'

God

Originally created.

Gen 1:11–12 Then God said, "Let the earth bring forth grass, the herb *that* yields seed, *and* the fruit tree *that* yields fruit according to its kind, whose seed *is* in itself, on the earth"; and it was so. **12** And the earth brought forth grass, the herb *that* yields seed according to its kind, and the tree *that* yields fruit, whose seed *is* in itself according to its kind. And God saw that *it was* good.

Is the giver of.

Deut 11:15 And I will send grass in your fields for your livestock, that you may eat and be filled.'

Causes it to grow.

Ps 104:14 He causes the grass to grow for the cattle, And vegetation for the service of man, That he may bring forth food from the earth,

Ps 147:8 Who covers the heavens with clouds, Who prepares rain for the earth, Who makes grass to grow on the mountains.

Adorns and clothes.

Matt 6:30 Now if God so clothes the grass of the field, which today is, and tomorrow is thrown into the oven, *will He* not much more *clothe* you, O you of little faith?

Often grew on the tops of houses.

Ps 129:6 Let them be as the grass *on* the housetops, Which withers before it grows up,

When young, soft and tender.

Prov 27:25 *When* the hay is removed, and the tender grass shows itself, And the herbs of the mountains are gathered in,

Refreshed by rain and dew.

Deut 32:2 Let my teaching drop as the rain, My speech distill as the dew, As raindrops on the tender herb, And as showers on the grass.

Prov 19:12 The king's wrath *is* like the roaring of a lion, But his favor *is* like dew on the grass.

Livestock fed on.

Job 6:5 Does the wild donkey bray when it has grass, Or does the ox low over its fodder?

Jer 50:11 "Because you were glad, because you rejoiced, You destroyers of My heritage, Because you have grown fat like a heifer threshing grain, And you bellow like bulls,

Often burned in ovens.

Matt 6:30 Now if God so clothes the grass of the field, which today is, and tomorrow is thrown into the oven, *will He* not much more *clothe* you, O you of little faith?

Destroyed by

Locusts.

Rev 9:4 They were commanded not to harm the grass of the earth, or any green thing, or any tree, but only those men who do not have the seal of God on their foreheads.

Hail and lightning.

Rev 8:7 The first angel sounded: And hail and fire followed, mingled with blood, and they were thrown to the earth. And a third of the trees were burned up, and all green grass was burned up.

Drought.

1 Kin 17:1 And Elijah the Tishbite, of the inhabitants of Gilead, said to Ahab, "*As* the LORD God of Israel lives, before whom I stand, there shall not be dew nor rain these years, except at my word."

1 Kin 18:5 And Ahab had said to Obadiah, "Go into the land to all the springs of water and to all the brooks; perhaps we may find grass to keep the horses and mules alive, so that we will not have to kill any livestock."

Failure of, a great calamity.

Is 15:5–6 "My heart will cry out for Moab; His fugitives *shall flee* to Zoar, *Like* a three-year-old heifer. For by the Ascent of Luhith They will go up with weeping; For in the way of Horonaim They will raise up a cry of destruction, **6** For the waters of Nimrim will be desolate, For the green grass has withered away; The grass fails, there is nothing green.

Jer 14:5–6 Yes, the deer also gave birth in the field, But left because there was no grass. **6** And the wild donkeys stood in the desolate heights; They sniffed at the wind like jackals; Their eyes failed because *there was* no grass."

Illustrative of

Shortness and uncertainty of life.

Ps 90:5–6 You carry them away *like* a flood; *They are* like a sleep. In the morning they are like grass *which* grows up: **6** In the morning it flourishes and grows up; In the evening it is cut down and withers.

Ps 103:15 *As for* man, his days *are* like grass; As a flower of the field, so he flourishes.

Is 40:6–7 The voice said, "Cry out!" And he said, "What shall I cry?" "All flesh *is* grass, And all its loveliness *is* like the flower of the field. **7** The grass withers, the flower fades, Because the breath of the LORD blows upon it; Surely the people *are* grass.

1 Pet 1:24 because *"All flesh is as grass, And all the*

glory of man as the flower of the grass. The grass withers, And its flower falls away,

Prosperity of the wicked.

Ps 92:7 When the wicked spring up like grass, And when all the workers of iniquity flourish, *It is* that they may be destroyed forever.

(Refreshed by dew and showers) believers refreshed by grace.

Ps 72:6 He shall come down like rain upon the grass before mowing, Like showers *that* water the earth.

Mic 5:7 Then the remnant of Jacob Shall be in the midst of many peoples, Like dew from the LORD, Like showers on the grass, That tarry for no man Nor wait for the sons of men.

(On tops of houses) the wicked.

2 Kin 19:26 Therefore their inhabitants had little power; They were dismayed and confounded; They were *as* the grass of the field And the green herb, *As* the grass on the housetops And *grain* blighted before it is grown.

Is 37:27 Therefore their inhabitants *had* little power; They were dismayed and confounded; They were *as* the grass of the field And the green herb, *As* the grass on the housetops And grain blighted before it is grown.

GREED

Natural symbols of.

Prov 30:16 The grave, The barren womb, The earth *that* is not satisfied with water— And the fire never says, "Enough!"

Defined as vanity.

Eccl 5:10 He who loves silver will not be satisfied with silver; Nor he who loves abundance, with increase. This also *is* vanity.

Can result in desperate, unjust measures.

Amos 2:6–7 Thus says the LORD: "For three transgressions of Israel, and for four, I will not turn away its *punishment*, Because they sell the righteous for silver, And the poor for a pair of sandals. 7 They pant after the dust of the earth *which is* on the head of the poor, And pervert the way of the humble. A man and his father go in to the *same* girl, To defile My holy name.

Amos 8:5–6 Saying: "When will the New Moon be past, That we may sell grain? And the Sabbath, That we may trade wheat? Making the ephah small and the shekel large, Falsifying the scales by deceit, 6 That we may buy the poor for silver, And the needy for a pair of sandals— Even sell the bad wheat?"

Cf. Matt 18:23–35

Jesus' warning against.

Luke 12:13–34 Then one from the crowd said to Him, "Teacher, tell my brother to divide the inheritance with me." 14 But He said to him, "Man, who made Me a judge or an arbitrator over you?" 15 And He said to them, "Take heed and beware of covetousness, for one's life does not consist in the abundance of the things he possesses." 16 Then He spoke a parable to them, saying: "The ground of a certain rich man yielded plentifully. 17 And he thought within himself, saying, 'What shall I do, since I have no room to store my crops?' 18 So he said, 'I will do this: I will pull down my barns and build greater, and there I will store all my crops and my goods. 19 And I will say to my soul, "Soul, you have many goods laid up for many years; take your ease; eat, drink, *and* be merry." ' 20 But God said to him, 'Fool! This night your soul will be required of you; then whose will those things be which you have provided?' 21 "So *is* he who lays up treasure for himself, and is not rich toward God." 22 Then He said to His disciples, "Therefore I say to you, do not worry about your life, what you will eat; nor about the body, what you will put on. 23 Life is more than food, and the body *is more* than clothing. 24 Consider the ravens, for they neither sow nor reap, which have neither storehouse nor barn; and God feeds them. Of how much more value are you than the birds? 25 And which of you by worrying can add one cubit to his stature? 26 If you then are not able to do *the* least, why are you anxious for the rest? 27 Consider the lilies, how they grow: they neither toil nor spin; and yet I say to you, even Solomon in all his glory was not arrayed like one of these. 28 If then God so clothes the grass, which today is in the field and tomorrow is thrown into the oven, how much more *will He clothe* you, O *you* of little faith? 29 "And do not seek what you should eat or what you should drink, nor have an anxious mind. 30 For all these things the nations of the world seek after, and your Father knows that you need these things. 31 But seek the kingdom of God, and all these things shall be added to you. 32 "Do not fear, little flock, for it is your Father's good pleasure to give you the kingdom. 33 Sell what you have and give alms; provide yourselves money bags which do not grow old, a treasure in the heavens that does not fail, where no thief approaches nor moth destroys. 34 For where your treasure is, there your heart will be also.

Characterized the Pharisees.

Luke 11:39 Then the Lord said to him, "Now you Pharisees make the outside of the cup and dish clean, but your inward part is full of greed and wickedness.

Should never characterize believers.

Ps 10:3 For the wicked boasts of his heart's desire; He blesses the greedy *and* renounces the LORD.

Eccl 5:10 He who loves silver will not be satisfied with silver; Nor he who loves abundance, with increase. This also *is* vanity.

Mic 2:2 They covet fields and take *them* by violence, Also houses, and seize *them*. So they oppress a man and his house, A man and his inheritance.

Mark 7:22 thefts, covetousness, wickedness, deceit, lewdness, an evil eye, blasphemy, pride, foolishness.

Rom 1:29 being filled with all unrighteousness, sexual immorality, wickedness, covetousness, maliciousness; full of envy, murder, strife, deceit, evil-mindedness; *they are* whisperers,

1 Cor 5:11 But now I have written to you not to keep company with anyone named a brother, who is sexually immoral, or covetous, or an idolater, or a reviler, or a drunkard, or an extortioner—not even to eat with such a person.

1 Cor 6:9–10 Do you not know that the unrighteous will not inherit the kingdom of God? Do not be deceived. Neither fornicators, nor idolaters, nor adulterers, nor homosexuals, nor sodomites, **10** nor thieves, nor covetous, nor drunkards, nor revilers, nor extortioners will inherit the kingdom of God.

2 Cor 9:5 Therefore I thought it necessary to exhort the brethren to go to you ahead of time, and prepare your generous gift beforehand, which *you had* previously promised, that it may be ready as *a matter of* generosity and not as a grudging obligation.

Eph 5:3–5 But fornication and all uncleanness or covetousness, let it not even be named among you, as is fitting for saints; **4** neither filthiness, nor foolish talking, nor coarse jesting, which are not fitting, but rather giving of thanks. **5** For this you know, that no fornicator, unclean person, nor covetous man, who is an idolater, has any inheritance in the kingdom of Christ and God.

Col 3:5 Therefore put to death your members which are on the earth: fornication, uncleanness, passion, evil desire, and covetousness, which is idolatry.

1 Tim 6:9–10 But those who desire to be rich fall into temptation and a snare, and *into* many foolish and harmful lusts which drown men in destruction and perdition. **10** For the love of money is a root of all *kinds of* evil, for which some have strayed from the faith in their greediness, and pierced themselves through with many sorrows.

2 Pet 2:14 having eyes full of adultery and that cannot cease from sin, enticing unstable souls. *They have* a heart trained in covetous practices, *and are* accursed children.

GRIEF

The Savior acquainted with.

Is 53:3 He is despised and rejected by men, A Man of sorrows and acquainted with grief. And we hid, as it were, *our* faces from Him; He was despised, and we did not esteem Him.

Jesus', for Jerusalem.

Luke 19:41–44 Now as He drew near, He saw the city and wept over it, **42** saying, "If you had known, even you, especially in this your day, the things *that make* for your peace! But now they are hidden from your eyes. **43** For days will come upon you when your enemies will build an embankment around you, surround you and close you in on every side, **44** and level you, and your children within you, to the ground; and they will not leave in you one stone upon another, because you did not know the time of your visitation."

Believers should not cause, in the Holy Spirit.

Eph 4:30 And do not grieve the Holy Spirit of God, by whom you were sealed for the day of redemption.

Caused by trials.

1 Pet 1:6 In this you greatly rejoice, though now for a little while, if need be, you have been grieved by various trials,

Exemplified by

Samuel.

1 Sam 15:11 "I greatly regret that I have set up Saul *as* king, for he has turned back from following Me, and has not performed My commandments." And it grieved Samuel, and he cried out to the LORD all night.

David.

2 Sam 1:12 And they mourned and wept and fasted until evening for Saul and for Jonathan his son, for the people of the LORD and for the house of Israel, because they had fallen by the sword.

Daniel.

Dan 7:15 "I, Daniel, was grieved in my spirit within *my* body, and the visions of my head troubled me.

Jesus.

John 11:35 Jesus wept.

H

HAIR, THE

The natural covering of the head.

Ps 68:21 But God will wound the head of His enemies, The hairy scalp of the one who still goes on in his trespasses.

Innumerable.

Ps 40:12 For innumerable evils have surrounded me; My iniquities have overtaken me, so that I am not able to look up; They are more than the hairs of my head; Therefore my heart fails me.

Ps 69:4 Those who hate me without a cause Are more than the hairs of my head; They are mighty who would destroy me, *Being* my enemies wrongfully; Though I have stolen nothing, I *still* must restore *it.*

Growth of.

Judg 16:22 However, the hair of his head began to grow again after it had been shaven.

God

Numbers.

Matt 10:30 But the very hairs of your head are all numbered.

Takes care of.

Dan 3:27 And the satraps, administrators, governors, and the king's counselors gathered together, and they saw these men on whose bodies the fire had no power; the hair of their head was not singed nor were their garments affected, and the smell of fire was not on them.

Luke 21:18 But not a hair of your head shall be lost.

Black, particularly esteemed.

Song 5:11 His head *is like* the finest gold; His locks *are* wavy, *And* black as a raven.

White or gray,

A token of age.

1 Sam 12:2 And now here is the king, walking before you; and I am old and grayheaded, and look, my sons *are* with you. I have walked before you from my childhood to this day.

Ps 71:18 Now also when *I am* old and grayheaded, O God, do not forsake me, Until I declare Your strength to *this* generation, Your power to everyone *who is to* come.

A token of weakness and decay.

Hos 7:9 Aliens have devoured his strength, But he does not know *it;* Yes, gray hairs are here and there on him, Yet he does not know *it.*

An emblem of wisdom.

Job 12:12 Wisdom *is* with aged men, And with length of days, understanding.

Dan 7:9 "I watched till thrones were put in place, And the Ancient of Days was seated; His garment *was* white as snow, And the hair of His head *was* like pure wool. His throne *was* a fiery flame, Its wheels a burning fire;

With righteousness, a crown of glory.

Prov 16:31 The silver-haired head *is* a crown of glory, *If* it is found in the way of righteousness.

To be reverenced.

Lev 19:32 'You shall rise before the gray headed and honor the presence of an old man, and fear your God: I *am* the LORD.

Man cannot even change the color of.

Matt 5:36 Nor shall you swear by your head, because you cannot make one hair white or black.

Of women,

Worn long for a covering.

1 Cor 11:15 But if a woman has long hair, it is a glory to her; for *her* hair is given to her for a covering.

Braided and arranged.

1 Tim 2:9 in like manner also, that the women adorn themselves in modest apparel, with propriety and moderation, not with braided hair or gold or pearls or costly clothing,

1 Pet 3:3 Do not let your adornment be *merely* outward—arranging the hair, wearing gold, or putting on *fine* apparel—

Well-set.

Is 3:24 And so it shall be: Instead of a sweet smell there will be a stench; Instead of a sash, a rope; Instead of well-set hair, baldness; Instead of a rich robe, a girding of sackcloth; And branding instead of beauty.

Neglected in grief.

Luke 7:38 and stood at His feet behind *Him* weeping; and she began to wash His feet with her tears, and wiped *them* with the hair of her head; and she kissed His feet and anointed *them* with the fragrant oil.

John 12:3 Then Mary took a pound of very costly oil of spikenard, anointed the feet of Jesus, and wiped His feet with her hair. And the house was filled with the fragrance of the oil.

Sometimes worn long by men.

2 Sam 14:26 And when he cut the hair of his head—at the end of every year he cut *it* because it was heavy on him—when he cut it, he weighed the hair of his head at two hundred shekels according to the king's standard.

Men condemned for wearing long.

1 Cor 11:14 Does not even nature itself teach you that if a man has long hair, it is a dishonor to him?

Often expensively anointed.

Eccl 9:8 Let your garments always be white, And let your head lack no oil.

Of Nazirites

Not to be cut or shaved during their vow.

Num 6:5 'All the days of the vow of his separation no razor shall come upon his head; until the days are fulfilled for which he separated himself to the Lord, he shall be holy. *Then* he shall let the locks of the hair of his head grow.

Judg 16:17 that he told her all his heart, and said to her, "No razor has ever come upon my head, for I *have been* a Nazirite to God from my mother's womb. If I am shaven, then my strength will leave me, and I shall become weak, and be like any *other* man."

Judg 16:19–20 Then she lulled him to sleep on her knees, and called for a man and had him shave off the seven locks of his head. Then she began to torment him, and his strength left him. **20** And she said, "The Philistines *are* upon you, Samson!" So he awoke from his sleep, and said, "I will go out as before, at other times, and shake myself free!" But he did not know that the Lord had departed from him.

Shaved after completion of vow.

Num 6:18 Then the Nazirite shall shave his consecrated head *at* the door of the tabernacle of meeting, and shall take the hair from his consecrated head and put *it* on the fire which is under the sacrifice of the peace offering.

Of the healed leper, to be shaved.

Lev 14:9 But on the seventh day he shall shave all the hair off his head and his beard and his eyebrows—all his hair he shall shave off. He shall wash his clothes and wash his body in water, and he shall be clean.

Color of, changed by leprosy.

Lev 13:3 The priest shall examine the sore on the skin of the body; and if the hair on the sore has turned white, and the sore appears *to be* deeper than the skin of his body, it *is* a leprous sore. Then the priest shall examine him, and pronounce him unclean.

Lev 13:10 And the priest shall examine *him;* and indeed *if* the swelling on the skin *is* white, and it has turned the hair white, and *there is* a spot of raw flesh in the swelling,

Cut off in affliction.

Jer 7:29 Cut off your hair and cast *it* away, and take up a lamentation on the desolate heights; for the Lord has rejected and forsaken the generation of His wrath.'

Plucking out of, a reproach and sign of grief.

Ezra 9:3 So when I heard this thing, I tore my garment and my robe, and plucked out some of the hair of my head and beard, and sat down astonished.

Neh 13:25 So I contended with them and cursed them, struck some of them and pulled out their hair, and made them swear by God, *saying,* "You shall not give your daughters as wives to their sons, nor take their daughters for your sons or yourselves.

Is 50:6 I gave My back to those who struck *Me,* And My cheeks to those who plucked out the beard; I did not hide My face from shame and spitting.

Judgments involving,

Becoming bald.

Is 3:24 And so it shall be: Instead of a sweet smell there will be a stench; Instead of a sash, a rope; Instead of well-set hair, baldness; Instead of a rich robe, a girding of sackcloth; And branding instead of beauty.

Jer 47:5 Baldness has come upon Gaza, Ashkelon is cut off *With* the remnant of their valley. How long will you cut yourself?

Being shaved.

Is 7:20 In the same day the Lord will shave with a hired razor, With those from beyond the River, with the king of Assyria, The head and the hair of the legs, And will also remove the beard.

HANDS, THE

Necessary members of the body.

1 Cor 12:21 And the eye cannot say to the hand, "I have no need of you"; nor again the head to the feet, "I have no need of you."

Parts of, mentioned

The palm.

Is 49:16 See, I have inscribed you on the palms *of My hands;* Your walls *are* continually before Me.

Matt 26:67 Then they spat in His face and beat Him; and others struck *Him* with the palms of their hands,

The thumb.

Ex 29:20 Then you shall kill the ram, and take some of its blood and put *it* on the tip of the right ear of Aaron and on the tip of the right ear of his sons, on the thumb of their right hand and on the big toe of their right foot, and sprinkle the blood all around on the altar.

Lev 14:14 The priest shall take *some* of the blood of the trespass offering, and the priest shall put *it* on the tip of the right ear of him who is to be cleansed, on the thumb of his right hand, and on the big toe of his right foot.

Lev 14:17 And of the rest of the oil in his hand, the priest shall put *some* on the tip of the right ear of him who is to be cleansed, on the thumb of his right hand, and on the big toe of his right foot, on the blood of the trespass offering.

The fingers.

2 Sam 21:20 Yet again there was war at Gath, where there was a man of *great* stature, who had six fingers on each hand and six toes on each foot, twenty-four in number; and he also was born to the giant.

Dan 5:5 In the same hour the fingers of a man's hand appeared and wrote opposite the lampstand on the plaster of the wall of the king's palace; and the king saw the part of the hand that wrote.

God strengthens.

Gen 49:24 But his bow remained in strength, And the arms of his hands were made strong By the hands of the Mighty *God* of Jacob (From there *is* the Shepherd, the Stone of Israel),

God makes impotent.

Job 5:12 He frustrates the devices of the crafty, So that their hands cannot carry out their plans.

Operations of, mentioned

Feeling.

Ps 115:7 They have hands, but they do not handle; Feet they have, but they do not walk; Nor do they mutter through their throat.

1 John 1:1 That which was from the beginning, which we have heard, which we have seen with our eyes, which we have looked upon, and our hands have handled, concerning the Word of life—

Taking.

Gen 3:22 Then the LORD God said, "Behold, the man has become like one of Us, to know good and evil. And now, lest he put out his hand and take also of the tree of life, and eat, and live forever"—

Ex 4:4 Then the LORD said to Moses, "Reach out your hand and take *it* by the tail" (and he reached out his hand and caught it, and it became a rod in his hand),

Holding.

Judg 7:20 Then the three companies blew the trumpets and broke the pitchers—they held the torches in their left hands and the trumpets in their right hands for blowing—and they cried, "The sword of the LORD and of Gideon!"

Rev 10:2 He had a little book open in his hand. And he set his right foot on the sea and *his* left *foot* on the land,

Working.

Prov 31:19 She stretches out her hands to the distaff, And her hand holds the spindle.

1 Thess 4:11 that you also aspire to lead a quiet life, to mind your own business, and to work with your own hands, as we commanded you,

Writing.

Is 44:5 One will say, 'I *am* the LORD's'; Another will call *himself* by the name of Jacob; Another will write *with* his hand, 'The LORD's,' And name *himself* by the name of Israel.

Gal 6:11 See with what large letters I have written to you with my own hand!

Making signs.

Is 13:2 "Lift up a banner on the high mountain, Raise your voice to them; Wave your hand, that they may enter the gates of the nobles.

Acts 12:17 But motioning to them with his hand to keep silent, he declared to them how the Lord had brought him out of the prison. And he said, "Go, tell these things to James and to the brethren." And he departed and went to another place.

Striking.

Mark 14:65 Then some began to spit on Him, and to blindfold Him, and to beat Him, and to say to Him, "Prophesy!" And the officers struck Him with the palms of their hands.

John 19:3 Then they said, "Hail, King of the Jews!" And they struck Him with their hands.

Distinguished as

The right.

Acts 3:7 And he took him by the right hand and lifted *him* up, and immediately his feet and ankle bones received strength.

The left.

Judg 3:21 Then Ehud reached with his left hand, took the dagger from his right thigh, and thrust it into his belly.

Some were expert with both.

1 Chr 12:2 armed with bows, using both the right hand and the left in *hurling* stones and *shooting* arrows with the bow. *They were* of Benjamin, Saul's brethren.

Many had more command of the left.

Judg 3:15 But when the children of Israel cried out to the LORD, the LORD raised up a deliverer for them: Ehud the son of Gera, the Benjamite, a left-handed man. By him the children of Israel sent tribute to Eglon king of Moab.

Judg 3:21 Then Ehud reached with his left hand, took the dagger from his right thigh, and thrust it into his belly.

Judg 20:16 Among all this people *were* seven hundred select men *who were* left-handed; every one could sling a stone at a hair's *breadth* and not miss.

Significance of the right,

Place of honor.

1 Kin 2:19 Bathsheba therefore went to King Solomon, to speak to him for Adonijah. And the king rose up to meet her and bowed down to her, and sat down on his throne and had a throne set for the king's mother; so she sat at his right hand.

Ps 45:9 Kings' daughters *are* among Your honorable women; At Your right hand stands the queen in gold from Ophir.

Place of power.

Ps 110:1 The LORD said to my Lord, "Sit at My right hand, Till I make Your enemies Your footstool."

Mark 14:62 Jesus said, "I am. And you will see the Son of Man sitting at the right hand of the Power, and coming with the clouds of heaven."

Signet worn on.

Jer 22:24 "*As* I live," says the LORD, "though Coniah the son of Jehoiakim, king of Judah, were the signet on My right hand, yet I would pluck you off;

Given in token of friendship.

Gal 2:9 and when James, Cephas, and John, who seemed to be pillars, perceived the grace that had been given to me, they gave me and Barnabas the right hand of fellowship, that we *should go* to the Gentiles and they to the circumcised.

Used in embracing.

2 Sam 20:9 Then Joab said to Amasa, "*Are* you in health, my brother?" And Joab took Amasa by the beard with his right hand to kiss him.

Song 2:6 His left hand *is* under my head, And his right hand embraces me.

Cf. Song 8:3

Sworn by.

Is 62:8 The LORD has sworn by His right hand And by the arm of His strength: "Surely I will no longer give your grain *As* food for your enemies; And the sons of the foreigner shall not drink your new wine, For which you have labored.

The accuser stood at, of the accused.

Ps 109:6 Set a wicked man over him, And let an accuser stand at his right hand.

Zech 3:1 Then he showed me Joshua the high priest standing before the Angel of the LORD, and Satan standing at his right hand to oppose him.

Of priests, touched with blood, of consecration ram.

Ex 29:20 Then you shall kill the ram, and take some of its blood and put *it* on the tip of the right ear of Aaron and on the tip of the right ear of his sons, on the thumb of their right hand and on the big toe of their right foot, and sprinkle the blood all around on the altar.

Lev 8:23–24 and Moses killed *it.* Also he took *some* of its blood and put it on the tip of Aaron's right ear, on the thumb of his right hand, and on the big toe of his right foot. **24** Then he brought Aaron's sons. And Moses put *some* of the blood on the tips of their right ears, on the thumbs of their right hands, and on the big toes of their right feet. And Moses sprinkled the blood all around on the altar.

Of healed leper, touched with blood of his sacrifice and with oil.

Lev 14:14 The priest shall take *some* of the blood of the trespass offering, and the priest shall put *it* on the tip of the right ear of him who is to be cleansed, on the thumb of his right hand, and on the big toe of his right foot.

Lev 14:17 And of the rest of the oil in his hand, the priest shall put *some* on the tip of the right ear of him who is to be cleansed, on the thumb of his right hand, and on the big toe of his right foot, on the blood of the trespass offering.

Lev 14:25 Then he shall kill the lamb of the trespass offering, and the priest shall take *some* of the blood of the trespass offering and put *it* on the tip of the right ear of him who is to be cleansed, on the thumb of his right hand, and on the big toe of his right foot.

Lev 14:28 And the priest shall put *some* of the oil that *is* in his hand on the tip of the right ear of him who is to be cleansed, on the thumb of the right hand, and on the big toe of his right foot, on the place of the blood of the trespass offering.

The Jews carried a staff in, when walking.

Ex 12:11 And thus you shall eat it: *with* a belt on your waist, your sandals on your feet, and your staff in your hand. So you shall eat it in haste. It *is* the LORD's Passover.

2 Kin 4:29 Then he said to Gehazi, "Get yourself ready, and take my staff in your hand, and be on your way. If you meet anyone, do not greet him; and if anyone greets you, do not answer him; but lay my staff on the face of the child."

The Jews eat with.

Matt 26:23 He answered and said, "He who dipped *his* hand with Me in the dish will betray Me.

Were washed

Before eating.

Matt 15:2 "Why do Your disciples transgress the tradition of the elders? For they do not wash their hands when they eat bread."

Mark 7:3 For the Pharisees and all the Jews do not eat unless they wash *their* hands in a special way, holding the tradition of the elders.

After touching an unclean person.

Lev 15:11 And whomever the one who has the discharge touches, and has not rinsed his hands in water, he shall wash his clothes and bathe in water, and be unclean until evening.

In token of innocency.

Deut 21:6–7 And all the elders of that city nearest to the slain *man* shall wash their hands over the heifer whose neck was broken in the valley. **7** Then they shall answer and say, 'Our hands have not shed this blood, nor have our eyes seen *it.*

Matt 27:24 When Pilate saw that he could not prevail at all, but rather *that* a tumult was rising, he took water and washed *his* hands before the multitude, saying, "I am innocent of the blood of this just Person. You see *to it.*"

Custom of domestics pouring water upon, alluded to.

2 Kin 3:11 But Jehoshaphat said, "*Is there* no prophet of the LORD here, that we may inquire of the LORD by him?" So one of the servants of the king of Israel answered and said, "Elisha the son of Shaphat *is* here, who poured water on the hands of Elijah."

Servants directed by movements of.

Ps 123:2 Behold, as the eyes of servants *look* to the hand of their masters, As the eyes of a maid to the hand of her mistress, So our eyes *look* to the LORD our God, Until He has mercy on us.

Kissed in idolatrous worship.

Job 31:27 So that my heart has been secretly enticed, And my mouth has kissed my hand;

Treaties made by joining.

2 Kin 10:15 Now when he departed from there, he met Jehonadab the son of Rechab, *coming* to meet him; and he greeted him and said to him, "Is your heart right, as my heart *is* toward your heart?" And Jehonadab answered, "It is." *Jehu said,* "If it is, give *me* your hand." So he gave *him* his hand, and he took him up to him into the chariot.

Ezek 17:18 Since he despised the oath by breaking the covenant, and in fact gave his hand and still did all these *things,* he shall not escape.' "

A surety entered into by shaking hands.

Job 17:3 "Now put down a pledge for me with Yourself. Who *is* he *who* will shake hands with me?

Prov 6:1 My son, if you become surety for your friend, *If* you have shaken hands in pledge for a stranger,

Prov 17:18 A man devoid of understanding shakes hands in a pledge, *And* becomes surety for his friend.

Prov 22:26 Do not be one of those who shakes hands in a pledge, One of those who is surety for debts;

Were lifted up

In prayer.

Ps 141:2 Let my prayer be set before You *as* incense, The lifting up of my hands *as* the evening sacrifice.

Lam 3:41 Let us lift our hearts and hands To God in heaven.

In praise.

Ps 134:2 Lift up your hands *in* the sanctuary, And bless the LORD.

In taking an oath.

Gen 14:22 But Abram said to the king of Sodom, "I have raised my hand to the LORD, God Most High, the Possessor of heaven and earth,

Rev 10:5 The angel whom I saw standing on the sea and on the land raised up his hand to heaven

In blessing.

Lev 9:22 Then Aaron lifted his hand toward the people, blessed them, and came down from offering the sin offering, the burnt offering, and peace offerings.

Often spread out in prayer.

Ps 68:31 Envoys will come out of Egypt; Ethiopia will quickly stretch out her hands to God.

Is 1:15 When you spread out your hands, I will hide My eyes from you; Even though you make many prayers, I will not hear. Your hands are full of blood.

Placed under the thigh of a person to whom an oath was made.

Gen 24:2–3 So Abraham said to the oldest servant of his house, who ruled over all that he had, "Please, put your hand under my thigh, **3** and I will make you swear by the LORD, the God of heaven and the God of the earth, that you will not take a wife for my son from the daughters of the Canaanites, among whom I dwell;

Gen 47:29 When the time drew near that Israel must die, he called his son Joseph and said to him, "Now if I have found favor in your sight, please put your hand under my thigh, and deal kindly and truly with me. Please do not bury me in Egypt,

Gen 47:31 Then he said, "Swear to me." And he swore to him. So Israel bowed himself on the head of the bed.

Clapped together in joy.

2 Kin 11:12 And he brought out the king's son, put the crown on him, and *gave him* the Testimony; they made him king and anointed him, and they clapped their hands and said, "Long live the king!"

Ps 47:1 Oh, clap your hands, all you peoples! Shout to God with the voice of triumph!

Struck together in extreme anger.

Num 24:10 Then Balak's anger was aroused against Balaam, and he struck his hands together; and Balak said to Balaam, "I called you to curse my enemies, and look, you have bountifully blessed *them* these three times!

Ezek 21:14 "You therefore, son of man, prophesy, And strike *your* hands together. The third time let the sword do double *damage.* It *is* the sword *that* slays, The sword that slays the great *men,* That enters their private chambers.

Ezek 21:17 "I also will beat My fists together, And I will cause My fury to rest; I, the LORD, have spoken."

Stretched out in derision.

Hos 7:5 In the day of our king Princes have made *him* sick, inflamed with wine; He stretched out his hand with scoffers.

Zeph 2:15 This is the rejoicing city That dwelt securely, That said in her heart, "I *am it,* and *there is* none be-

sides me." How has she become a desolation, A place for beasts to lie down! Everyone who passes by her Shall hiss and shake his fist.

Imposition of, used in

Transferring guilt of sacrifices.

Lev 1:4 Then he shall put his hand on the head of the burnt offering, and it will be accepted on his behalf to make atonement for him.

Lev 3:2 And he shall lay his hand on the head of his offering, and kill it *at* the door of the tabernacle of meeting; and Aaron's sons, the priests, shall sprinkle the blood all around on the altar.

Lev 16:21–22 Aaron shall lay both his hands on the head of the live goat, confess over it all the iniquities of the children of Israel, and all their transgressions, concerning all their sins, putting them on the head of the goat, and shall send *it* away into the wilderness by the hand of a suitable man. **22** The goat shall bear on itself all their iniquities to an uninhabited land; and he shall release the goat in the wilderness.

Setting apart the Levites.

Num 8:10 So you shall bring the Levites before the LORD, and the children of Israel shall lay their hands on the Levites;

Conferring civil power.

Num 27:18 And the LORD said to Moses: "Take Joshua the son of Nun with you, a man in whom *is* the Spirit, and lay your hand on him;

Deut 34:9 Now Joshua the son of Nun was full of the spirit of wisdom, for Moses had laid his hands on him; so the children of Israel heeded him, and did as the LORD had commanded Moses.

Blessing.

Gen 48:14 Then Israel stretched out his right hand and laid *it* on Ephraim's head, who *was* the younger, and his left hand on Manasseh's head, guiding his hands knowingly, for Manasseh *was* the firstborn.

Mark 10:16 And He took them up in His arms, laid *His* hands on them, and blessed them.

Ordaining ministers.

Acts 6:6 whom they set before the apostles; and when they had prayed, they laid hands on them.

1 Tim 4:14 Do not neglect the gift that is in you, which was given to you by prophecy with the laying on of the hands of the eldership.

Imparting the gifts of the Holy Spirit.

Acts 8:17 Then they laid hands on them, and they received the Holy Spirit.

Acts 19:6 And when Paul had laid hands on them, the Holy Spirit came upon them, and they spoke with tongues and prophesied.

Imposition of, a first principle of the doctrine of Christ.

Heb 6:1–2 Therefore, leaving the discussion of the elementary *principles* of Christ, let us go on to perfection, not laying again the foundation of repentance from dead works and of faith toward God, **2** of the doctrine of baptisms, of laying on of hands, of resurrection of the dead, and of eternal judgment.

Should be employed

Industriously.

Eph 4:28 Let him who stole steal no longer, but rather let him labor, working with *his* hands what is good, that he may have something to give him who has need.

1 Thess 4:11 that you also aspire to lead a quiet life, to mind your own business, and to work with your own hands, as we commanded you,

In God's service.

Neh 2:18 And I told them of the hand of my God which had been good upon me, and also of the king's words that he had spoken to me. So they said, "Let us rise up and build." Then they set their hands to *this* good *work.*

Zech 8:9 "Thus says the LORD of hosts: 'Let your hands be strong, You who have been hearing in these days These words by the mouth of the prophets, Who *spoke* in the day the foundation was laid For the house of the LORD of hosts, That the temple might be built.

Zech 8:13 And it shall come to pass *That* just as you were a curse among the nations, O house of Judah and house of Israel, So I will save you, and you shall be a blessing. Do not fear, Let your hands be strong.'

In acts of benevolence.

Prov 3:27 Do not withhold good from those to whom it is due, When it is in the power of your hand to do *so.*

Prov 31:20 She extends her hand to the poor, Yes, she reaches out her hands to the needy.

Of the wicked, described as

Bloody.

Is 1:15 When you spread out your hands, I will hide My eyes from you; Even though you make many prayers, I will not hear. Your hands are full of blood.

Is 59:3 For your hands are defiled with blood, And your fingers with iniquity; Your lips have spoken lies, Your tongue has muttered perversity.

Violent.

Ps 58:2 No, in heart you work wickedness; You weigh out the violence of your hands in the earth.

Is 59:6 Their webs will not become garments, Nor will they cover themselves with their works; Their works *are* works of iniquity, And the act of violence *is* in their hands.

Mischievous.

Ps 26:10 In whose hands *is* a sinister scheme, And whose right hand is full of bribes.

Mic 7:3 That they may successfully do evil with both hands— The prince asks *for gifts,* The judge *seeks* a bribe, And the great *man* utters his evil desire; So they scheme together.

Lazy.

Prov 6:10 A little sleep, a little slumber, A little folding of the hands to sleep—

Prov 21:25 The desire of the lazy *man* kills him, For his hands refuse to labor.

Ensnaring to themselves.

Ps 9:16 The LORD is known *by* the judgment He executes; The wicked is snared in the work of his own hands. Meditation. Selah

The wicked recompensed for the work of.

Ps 28:4 Give them according to their deeds, And according to the wickedness of their endeavors; Give them according to the work of their hands; Render to them what they deserve.

Prov 12:14 A man will be satisfied with good by the fruit of *his* mouth, And the recompense of a man's hands will be rendered to him.

Is 3:11 Woe to the wicked! *It shall be* ill *with him,* For the reward of his hands shall be given him.

Believers blessed in the work of.

Deut 2:7 "For the LORD your God has blessed you in all the work of your hand. He knows your trudging through this great wilderness. These forty years the LORD your God *has been* with you; you have lacked nothing." '

Deut 30:9 The LORD your God will make you abound in all the work of your hand, in the fruit of your body, in the increase of your livestock, and in the produce of your land for good. For the LORD will again rejoice over you for good as He rejoiced over your fathers,

Job 1:10 Have You not made a hedge around him, around his household, and around all that he has on every side? You have blessed the work of his hands, and his possessions have increased in the land.

Ps 90:17 And let the beauty of the LORD our God be upon us, And establish the work of our hands for us; Yes, establish the work of our hands.

Criminals often

Bound by.

Matt 22:13 Then the king said to the servants, 'Bind him hand and foot, take him away, and cast *him* into outer darkness; there will be weeping and gnashing of teeth.'

Deprived of.

Deut 25:12 then you shall cut off her hand; your eye shall not pity *her.*

2 Sam 4:12 So David commanded his young men, and they executed them, cut off their hands and feet, and hanged *them* by the pool in Hebron. But they took the head of Ishbosheth and buried *it* in the tomb of Abner in Hebron.

Mutilated in.

Judg 1:6–7 Then Adoni-Bezek fled, and they pursued him and caught him and cut off his thumbs and big toes. 7 And Adoni-Bezek said, "Seventy kings with their thumbs and big toes cut off used to gather *scraps* under my table; as I have done, so God has repaid me." Then they brought him to Jerusalem, and there he died.

Hung by.

Lam 5:12 Princes were hung up by their hands, And elders were not respected.

Illustrative of

Power.

1 Kin 18:46 Then the hand of the LORD came upon Elijah; and he girded up his loins and ran ahead of Ahab to the entrance of Jezreel.

2 Kin 13:5 Then the LORD gave Israel a deliverer, so that they escaped from under the hand of the Syrians; and the children of Israel dwelt in their tents as before.

(Raised up against another) rebellion.

2 Sam 20:21 That *is* not so. But a man from the mountains of Ephraim, Sheba the son of Bichri by name, has raised his hand against the king, against David. Deliver him only, and I will depart from the city." So the woman said to Joab, "Watch, his head will be thrown to you over the wall."

(Opened) generosity.

Deut 15:8 but you shall open your hand wide to him and willingly lend him sufficient for his need, whatever he needs.

Ps 104:28 *What* You give them they gather in; You open Your hand, they are filled with good.

(Shut) lack of generosity.

Deut 15:7 "If there is among you a poor man of your brethren, within any of the gates in your land which the LORD your God is giving you, you shall not harden your heart nor shut your hand from your poor brother,

Right hand, illustrative of

Strength and power.

Ex 15:6 "Your right hand, O LORD, has become glorious in power; Your right hand, O LORD, has dashed the enemy in pieces.

Ps 17:7 Show Your marvelous lovingkindness by Your right hand, O You who save those who trust *in You* From those who rise up *against them.*

(Holding by) support.

Ps 73:23 Nevertheless I *am* continually with You; You hold *me* by my right hand.

Is 41:13 For I, the LORD your God, will hold your right hand, Saying to you, 'Fear not, I will help you.'

(Standing at) protection.

Ps 16:8 I have set the LORD always before me; Because *He is* at my right hand I shall not be moved.

Ps 109:31 For He shall stand at the right hand of the poor, To save *him* from those who condemn him.

Ps 110:5 The Lord *is* at Your right hand; He shall execute kings in the day of His wrath.

(Full of bribes) corruption.

Ps 26:10 In whose hands *is* a sinister scheme, And whose right hand is full of bribes.

(Full of falsehood) deceitfulness.

Ps 144:8 Whose mouth speaks lying words, And whose right hand *is* a right hand of falsehood.

Ps 144:11 Rescue me and deliver me from the hand of foreigners, Whose mouth speaks lying words, And whose right hand *is* a right hand of falsehood—

Is 44:20 He feeds on ashes; A deceived heart has turned him aside; And he cannot deliver his soul, Nor say, "Is *there* not a lie in my right hand?"

(Withdrawn) support withheld.

Ps 74:11 Why do You withdraw Your hand, even Your right hand? *Take it* out of Your bosom and destroy *them.*

(Cutting off) extreme self-denial.

Matt 5:30 And if your right hand causes you to sin, cut it off and cast *it* from you; for it is more profitable for you that one of your members perish, than for your whole body to be cast into hell.

HARVEST, THE

Ingathering of grains of the fields.

Mark 4:29 But when the grain ripens, immediately he puts in the sickle, because the harvest has come."

To continue without intermission.

Gen 8:22 "While the earth remains, Seedtime and harvest, Cold and heat, Winter and summer, And day and night Shall not cease."

Names for,

Appointed weeks of harvest.

Jer 5:24 They do not say in their heart, "Let us now fear the LORD our God, Who gives rain, both the former and the latter, in its season. He reserves for us the appointed weeks of the harvest."

Harvest time.

2 Sam 23:13 Then three of the thirty chief men went down at harvest time and came to David at the cave of Adullam. And the troop of Philistines encamped in the Valley of Rephaim.

Jer 50:16 Cut off the sower from Babylon, And him who handles the sickle at harvest time. For fear of the oppressing sword Everyone shall turn to his own people, And everyone shall flee to his own land.

Fields appeared white before.

John 4:35 Do you not say, 'There are still four months and *then* comes the harvest'? Behold, I say to you, lift up your eyes and look at the fields, for they are already white for harvest!

Of barley at the Passover.

Ex 9:31 Now the flax and the barley were struck, for the barley *was* in the head and the flax *was* in bud.

1 Sam 21:9 and he delivered them into the hands of the Gibeonites, and they hanged them on the hill before the LORD. So they fell, all seven together, and were put to death in the days of harvest, in the first days, in the beginning of barley harvest.

Ruth 1:22 So Naomi returned, and Ruth the Moabitess her daughter-in-law with her, who returned from the country of Moab. Now they came to Bethlehem at the beginning of barley harvest.

Of wheat at Pentecost.

Ex 34:22 "And you shall observe the Feast of Weeks, of the firstfruits of wheat harvest, and the Feast of Ingathering at the year's end.

1 Sam 12:17 Is today not the wheat harvest? I will call to the LORD, and He will send thunder and rain, that you may perceive and see that your wickedness *is* great, which you have done in the sight of the LORD, in asking a king for yourselves."

Men and women engaged in.

Ruth 2:8–9 Then Boaz said to Ruth, "You will listen, my daughter, will you not? Do not go to glean in another field, nor go from here, but stay close by my young women. 9 Let your eyes *be* on the field which they reap, and go after them. Have I not commanded the young men not to touch you? And when you are thirsty, go to the vessels and drink from what the young men have drawn."

Persons engaged in,

Reapers.

Ruth 2:4 Now behold, Boaz came from Bethlehem, and said to the reapers, "The LORD *be* with you!" And they answered him, "The LORD bless you!"

Binders.

Gen 37:7 There we were, binding sheaves in the field. Then behold, my sheaf arose and also stood upright; and indeed your sheaves stood all around and bowed down to my sheaf."

Ps 129:7 With which the reaper does not fill his hand, Nor he who binds sheaves, his arms.

Called harvesters.

Is 17:5 It shall be as when the harvester gathers the grain, And reaps the heads with his arm; It shall be as he who gathers heads of grain In the Valley of Rephaim.

Called laborers.

Matt 9:37 Then He said to His disciples, "The harvest truly *is* plentiful, but the laborers *are* few.

Fed by the harvest manager during.

Ruth 2:14 Now Boaz said to her at mealtime, "Come here, and eat of the bread, and dip your piece of bread in the vinegar." So she sat beside the reapers, and he passed parched *grain* to her; and she ate and was satisfied, and kept some back.

Received wages.

John 4:35–36 Do you not say, 'There are still four months and *then* comes the harvest'? Behold, I say to you, lift up your eyes and look at the fields, for they are already white for harvest! **36** And he who reaps receives wages, and gathers fruit for eternal life, that both he who sows and he who reaps may rejoice together.

Often defrauded of their wages.

James 5:4 Indeed the wages of the laborers who mowed your fields, which you kept back by fraud, cry out; and the cries of the reapers have reached the ears of the Lord of Sabaoth.

Former and latter rain necessary to abundance of.

Jer 5:24 They do not say in their heart, "Let us now fear the LORD our God, Who gives rain, both the former and the latter, in its season. He reserves for us the appointed weeks of the harvest."

Amos 4:7 "I also withheld rain from you, When *there were* still three months to the harvest. I made it rain on one city, I withheld rain from another city. One part was rained upon, And where it did not rain the part withered.

Patience required in waiting for.

James 5:7 Therefore be patient, brethren, until the coming of the Lord. See *how* the farmer waits for the precious fruit of the earth, waiting patiently for it until it receives the early and latter rain.

Not to be started until after offering the firstfruits.

Lev 23:10 "Speak to the children of Israel, and say to them: 'When you come into the land which I give to you, and reap its harvest, then you shall bring a sheaf of the firstfruits of your harvest to the priest.

Lev 23:14 You shall eat neither bread nor parched grain nor fresh grain until the same day that you have brought an offering to your God; *it shall be* a statute forever throughout your generations in all your dwellings.

A time of great joy.

Ps 126:6 He who continually goes forth weeping, Bearing seed for sowing, Shall doubtless come again with rejoicing, Bringing his sheaves *with him.*

Is 9:3 You have multiplied the nation *And* increased its joy; They rejoice before You According to the joy of harvest, As *men* rejoice when they divide the spoil.

Omitted in the sabbatical year.

Lev 25:5 What grows of its own accord of your harvest you shall not reap, nor gather the grapes of your untended vine, *for* it is a year of rest for the land.

Omitted in year of Jubilee.

Lev 25:11–12 That fiftieth year shall be a Jubilee to you; in it you shall neither sow nor reap what grows of its own accord, nor gather *the grapes* of your untended vine. **12** For it *is* the Jubilee; it shall be holy to you; you shall eat its produce from the field.

The Sabbath to be observed during.

Ex 34:21 "Six days you shall work, but on the seventh day you shall rest; in plowing time and in harvest you shall rest.

Legal provision for the poor during.

Lev 19:9–10 'When you reap the harvest of your land, you shall not wholly reap the corners of your field, nor shall you gather the gleanings of your harvest. **10** And you shall not glean your vineyard, nor shall you gather *every* grape of your vineyard; you shall leave them for the poor and the stranger: I *am* the LORD your God.

Lev 23:22 'When you reap the harvest of your land, you shall not wholly reap the corners of your field when you reap, nor shall you gather any gleaning from your harvest. You shall leave them for the poor and for the stranger: I *am* the LORD your God.' "

Deut 24:19 "When you reap your harvest in your field, and forget a sheaf in the field, you shall not go back to get it; it shall be for the stranger, the fatherless, and the widow, that the LORD your God may bless you in all the work of your hands.

Failure of,

Caused by drought.

Amos 4:7 "I also withheld rain from you, When *there were* still three months to the harvest. I made it rain on one city, I withheld rain from another city. One part was rained upon, And where it did not rain the part withered.

Caused by locusts.

Joel 1:4 What the chewing locust left, the swarming locust has eaten; What the swarming locust left, the crawling locust has eaten; And what the crawling locust left, the consuming locust has eaten.

Sometimes continued for years.

Gen 45:6 For these two years the famine *has been* in the land, and *there are* still five years in which *there will be* neither plowing nor harvesting.

A cause of great grief.

Is 16:9 Therefore I will bewail the vine of Sibmah, With the weeping of Jazer; I will drench you with my tears, O Heshbon and Elealeh; For battle cries have fallen Over your summer fruits and your harvest.

Joel 1:11 Be ashamed, you farmers, Wail, you vinedressers, For the wheat and the barley; Because the harvest of the field has perished.

A punishment for sin.

Is 17:10–11 Because you have forgotten the God of your salvation, And have not been mindful of the Rock of your stronghold, Therefore you will plant pleasant plants And set out foreign seedlings; **11** In the day you will make your plant to grow, And in the morning you will make your seed to flourish; *But* the harvest *will be* a heap of ruins In the day of grief and desperate sorrow.

Laziness during, shameful.

Prov 10:5 He who gathers in summer *is* a wise son; He who sleeps in harvest *is* a son who causes shame.

Miraculous thunder, etc., in.

1 Sam 12:17–18 *Is* today not the wheat harvest? I will call to the LORD, and He will send thunder and rain, that you may perceive and see that your wickedness *is* great, which you have done in the sight of the LORD, in asking a king for yourselves." **18** So Samuel called to the LORD, and the LORD sent thunder and rain that day; and all the people greatly feared the LORD and Samuel.

Illustrative of

Seasons of grace.

Jer 8:20 "The harvest is past, The summer is ended, And we are not saved!"

The end of the world.

Matt 13:30 Let both grow together until the harvest, and at the time of harvest I will say to the reapers, "First gather together the tares and bind them in bundles to burn them, but gather the wheat into my barn." ' "

Matt 13:39 The enemy who sowed them is the devil, the harvest is the end of the age, and the reapers are the angels.

A time when many are ready to receive the gospel.

Matt 9:37–38 Then He said to His disciples, "The harvest truly *is* plentiful, but the laborers *are* few. **38** Therefore pray the Lord of the harvest to send out laborers into His harvest."

John 4:35 Do you not say, 'There are still four months and *then* comes the harvest'? Behold, I say to you, lift up your eyes and look at the fields, for they are already white for harvest!

A time of judgment.

Jer 51:33 For thus says the LORD of hosts, the God of Israel: "The daughter of Babylon *is* like a threshing floor *When it is* time to thresh her; Yet a little while And the time of her harvest will come."

Hos 6:11 Also, O Judah, a harvest is appointed for you, When I return the captives of My people.

Ripeness for wrath.

Joel 3:13 Put in the sickle, for the harvest is ripe. Come, go down; For the winepress is full, The vats overflow— For their wickedness *is* great."

Rev 14:15 And another angel came out of the temple, crying with a loud voice to Him who sat on the cloud, "Thrust in Your sickle and reap, for the time has come for You to reap, for the harvest of the earth is ripe."

(Dew in) God's protection.

Is 18:4 For so the LORD said to me, "I will take My rest, And I will look from My dwelling place Like clear heat in sunshine, Like a cloud of dew in the heat of harvest."

(Cold in) a refreshing message.

Prov 25:13 Like the cold of snow in time of harvest *Is* a faithful messenger to those who send him, For he refreshes the soul of his masters.

(Rain in) honor given to fools.

Prov 26:1 As snow in summer and rain in harvest, So honor is not fitting for a fool.

HATRED. *SEE ALSO* JESUS CHRIST, HATRED OF

Forbidden.

Lev 19:17 'You shall not hate your brother in your heart. You shall surely rebuke your neighbor, and not bear sin because of him.

Col 3:8 But now you yourselves are to put off all these: anger, wrath, malice, blasphemy, filthy language out of your mouth.

Is murder.

1 John 3:15 Whoever hates his brother is a murderer, and you know that no murderer has eternal life abiding in him.

A work of the flesh.

Gal 5:20 idolatry, sorcery, hatred, contentions, jealousies, outbursts of wrath, selfish ambitions, dissensions, heresies,

Leads to deceit.

Prov 10:18 Whoever hides hatred *has* lying lips, And whoever spreads slander *is* a fool.

Prov 26:24–26 He who hates, disguises *it* with his lips, And lays up deceit within himself; **25** When he speaks kindly, do not believe him, For *there are* seven abominations in his heart; **26** *Though his* hatred is covered by deceit, His wickedness will be revealed before the assembly.

Stirs up strife.

Prov 10:12 Hatred stirs up strife, But love covers all sins.

Embitters life.

Prov 15:17 Better *is* a dinner of herbs where love is, Than a fatted calf with hatred.

Inconsistent with

The knowledge of God.

1 John 2:9 He who says he is in the light, and hates his brother, is in darkness until now.

1 John 2:11 But he who hates his brother is in darkness and walks in darkness, and does not know where he is going, because the darkness has blinded his eyes.

The love of God.

1 John 4:20 If someone says, "I love God," and hates his brother, he is a liar; for he who does not love his brother whom he has seen, how can he love God whom he has not seen?

Liars prone to.

Prov 26:28 A lying tongue hates *those who are* crushed by it, And a flattering mouth works ruin.

The wicked exhibit,

Toward God.

Rom 1:30 backbiters, haters of God, violent, proud, boasters, inventors of evil things, disobedient to parents,

Toward believers.

Ps 25:19 Consider my enemies, for they are many; And they hate me with cruel hatred.

Prov 29:10 The bloodthirsty hate the blameless, But the upright seek his well-being.

Toward each other.

Titus 3:3 For we ourselves were also once foolish, disobedient, deceived, serving various lusts and pleasures, living in malice and envy, hateful and hating one another.

Christ experienced.

Ps 35:19 Let them not rejoice over me who are wrongfully my enemies; Nor let them wink with the eye who hate me without a cause.

John 7:7 The world cannot hate you, but it hates Me because I testify of it that its works are evil.

John 15:18 "If the world hates you, you know that it hated Me before *it hated* you.

John 15:24–25 If I had not done among them the works which no one else did, they would have no sin; but now they have seen and also hated both Me and My Father. **25** But *this happened* that the word might be fulfilled which is written in their law, *'They hated Me without a cause.'*

Believers should

Expect.

Matt 10:22 And you will be hated by all for My name's sake. But he who endures to the end will be saved.

John 15:18–19 "If the world hates you, you know that it hated Me before *it hated* you. **19** If you were of the world, the world would love its own. Yet because you are not of the world, but I chose you out of the world, therefore the world hates you.

Not marvel at.

1 John 3:13 Do not marvel, my brethren, if the world hates you.

Return good for.

Ex 23:5 If you see the donkey of one who hates you lying under its burden, and you would refrain from helping it, you shall surely help him with it.

Matt 5:44 But I say to you, love your enemies, bless those who curse you, do good to those who hate you, and pray for those who spitefully use you and persecute you,

Not rejoice in the calamities of those who exhibit.

Job 31:29–30 "If I have rejoiced at the destruction of him who hated me, Or lifted myself up when evil found him **30** (Indeed I have not allowed my mouth to sin By asking for a curse on his soul);

Ps 35:13–14 But as for me, when they were sick, My clothing *was* sackcloth; I humbled myself with fasting; And my prayer would return to my own heart. **14** I paced about as though *he were* my friend *or* brother; I bowed down heavily, as one who mourns *for his* mother.

Give no cause for.

Prov 25:17 Seldom set foot in your neighbor's house, Lest he become weary of you and hate you.

Punishment of.

Ps 34:21 Evil shall slay the wicked, And those who hate the righteous shall be condemned.

Ps 44:7 But You have saved us from our enemies, And have put to shame those who hated us.

Ps 89:23 I will beat down his foes before his face, And plague those who hate him.

Amos 1:11 Thus says the LORD: "For three transgressions of Edom, and for four, I will not turn away its *punishment,* Because he pursued his brother with the sword, And cast off all pity; His anger tore perpetually, And he kept his wrath forever.

We should exhibit, against

False ways.

Ps 119:104 Through Your precepts I get understanding; Therefore I hate every false way.

Ps 119:128 Therefore all *Your* precepts *concerning* all *things* I consider *to be* right; I hate every false way.

Lying.

Ps 119:163 I hate and abhor lying, *But* I love Your law.

Evil.

Ps 97:10 You who love the LORD, hate evil! He preserves the souls of His saints; He delivers them out of the hand of the wicked.

Prov 8:13 The fear of the LORD *is* to hate evil; Pride and arrogance and the evil way And the perverse mouth I hate.

Backsliding.

Ps 101:3 I will set nothing wicked before my eyes; I hate the work of those who fall away; It shall not cling to me.

Those who oppose God.

Ps 139:21–22 Do I not hate them, O LORD, who hate You? And do I not loathe those who rise up against You? **22** I hate them with perfect hatred; I count them my enemies.

Illustrated by

Cain.

Gen 4:5 but He did not respect Cain and his offering. And Cain was very angry, and his countenance fell.

Gen 4:8 Now Cain talked with Abel his brother; and it came to pass, when they were in the field, that Cain rose up against Abel his brother and killed him.

Esau.

Gen 27:41 So Esau hated Jacob because of the blessing with which his father blessed him, and Esau said in his heart, "The days of mourning for my father are at hand; then I will kill my brother Jacob."

Joseph's brothers.

Gen 37:4 But when his brothers saw that their father loved him more than all his brothers, they hated him and could not speak peaceably to him.

The elders of Gilead.

Judg 11:7 So Jephthah said to the elders of Gilead, "Did you not hate me, and expel me from my father's house? Why have you come to me now when you are in distress?"

Saul.

1 Sam 18:8–9 Then Saul was very angry, and the saying displeased him; and he said, "They have ascribed to David ten thousands, and to me they have ascribed *only* thousands. Now *what* more can he have but the kingdom?" **9** So Saul eyed David from that day forward.

Ahab.

1 Kin 22:8 So the king of Israel said to Jehoshaphat, "*There is* still one man, Micaiah the son of Imlah, by whom we may inquire of the LORD; but I hate him, because he does not prophesy good concerning me, but evil." And Jehoshaphat said, "Let not the king say such things!"

Haman.

Esth 3:5–6 When Haman saw that Mordecai did not bow or pay him homage, Haman was filled with wrath. **6** But he disdained to lay hands on Mordecai alone, for they had told him of the people of Mordecai. Instead, Haman sought to destroy all the Jews who *were* throughout the whole kingdom of Ahasuerus—the people of Mordecai.

The enemies of the Jews.

Esth 9:1 Now in the twelfth month, that *is,* the month of Adar, on the thirteenth day, *the time* came for the king's command and his decree to be executed. On the day that the enemies of the Jews had hoped to overpower them, the opposite occurred, in that the Jews themselves overpowered those who hated them.

Esth 9:5 Thus the Jews defeated all their enemies with the stroke of the sword, with slaughter and destruction, and did what they pleased with those who hated them.

Ezek 35:5–6 "Because you have had an ancient hatred, and have shed *the blood of* the children of Israel by the power of the sword at the time of their calamity, *when* their iniquity *came to an* end, **6** therefore, *as* I live," says the Lord GOD, "I will prepare you for blood, and blood shall pursue you; since you have not hated blood, therefore blood shall pursue you."

The Chaldeans.

Dan 3:12 There are certain Jews whom you have set over the affairs of the province of Babylon: Shadrach, Meshach, and Abed-Nego; these men, O king, have not paid due regard to you. They do not serve your gods or worship the gold image which you have set up."

The enemies of Daniel.

Dan 6:4–15 So the governors and satraps sought to find *some* charge against Daniel concerning the kingdom; but they could find no charge or fault, because he *was* faithful; nor was there any error or fault found in him. **5** Then these men said, "We shall not find any charge against this Daniel unless we find *it* against him concerning the law of his God." **6** So these governors and satraps thronged before the king, and said thus to him: "King Darius, live forever! **7** All the governors of the kingdom, the administrators and satraps, the counselors and advisors, have consulted together to establish a royal statute and to make a firm decree, that whoever petitions any god or man for thirty days, except you, O king, shall be cast into

the den of lions. **8** Now, O king, establish the decree and sign the writing, so that it cannot be changed, according to the law of the Medes and Persians, which does not alter." **9** Therefore King Darius signed the written decree. **10** Now when Daniel knew that the writing was signed, he went home. And in his upper room, with his windows open toward Jerusalem, he knelt down on his knees three times that day, and prayed and gave thanks before his God, as was his custom since early days. **11** Then these men assembled and found Daniel praying and making supplication before his God. **12** And they went before the king, and spoke concerning the king's decree: "Have you not signed a decree that every man who petitions any god or man within thirty days, except you, O king, shall be cast into the den of lions?" The king answered and said, "The thing *is* true, according to the law of the Medes and Persians, which does not alter." **13** So they answered and said before the king, "That Daniel, who is one of the captives from Judah, does not show due regard for you, O king, or for the decree that you have signed, but makes his petition three times a day." **14** And the king, when he heard *these* words, was greatly displeased with himself, and set *his* heart on Daniel to deliver him; and he labored till the going down of the sun to deliver him. **15** Then these men approached the king, and said to the king, "Know, O king, that *it is* the law of the Medes and Persians that no decree or statute which the king establishes may be changed."

Herodias.

Matt 14:3 For Herod had laid hold of John and bound him, and put *him* in prison for the sake of Herodias, his brother Philip's wife.

Matt 14:8 So she, having been prompted by her mother, said, "Give me John the Baptist's head here on a platter."

The Jews.

Acts 23:12 And when it was day, some of the Jews banded together and bound themselves under an oath, saying that they would neither eat nor drink till they had killed Paul.

Acts 23:14 They came to the chief priests and elders, and said, "We have bound ourselves under a great oath that we will eat nothing until we have killed Paul.

HEAD, THE

The uppermost and chief member of the body.

2 Kin 6:31 Then he said, "God do so to me and more also, if the head of Elisha the son of Shaphat remains on him today!"

Is 1:6 From the sole of the foot even to the head, *There is* no soundness in it, *But* wounds and bruises and putrefying sores; They have not been closed or bound up, Or soothed with ointment.

All the other members related to.

1 Cor 12:21 And the eye cannot say to the hand, "I have no need of you"; nor again the head to the feet, "I have no need of you."

The body supported and supplied by.

Eph 4:16 from whom the whole body, joined and knit together by what every joint supplies, according to the effective working by which every part does its share, causes growth of the body for the edifying of itself in love.

Expression for the whole person.

Gen 49:26 The blessings of your father Have excelled the blessings of my ancestors, Up to the utmost bound of the everlasting hills. They shall be on the head of Joseph, And on the crown of the head of him who was separate from his brothers.

Prov 10:6 Blessings *are* on the head of the righteous, But violence covers the mouth of the wicked.

Expression for the life.

Dan 1:10 And the chief of the eunuchs said to Daniel, "I fear my lord the king, who has appointed your food and drink. For why should he see your faces looking worse than the young men who *are* your age? Then you would endanger my head before the king."

Parts of, mentioned

The skull.

2 Kin 9:35 So they went to bury her, but they found no more of her than the skull and the feet and the palms of *her* hands.

Matt 27:33 And when they had come to a place called Golgotha, that is to say, Place of a Skull,

The crown.

Gen 49:26 The blessings of your father Have excelled the blessings of my ancestors, Up to the utmost bound of the everlasting hills. They shall be on the head of Joseph, And on the crown of the head of him who was separate from his brothers.

Is 3:17 Therefore the Lord will strike with a scab The crown of the head of the daughters of Zion, And the LORD will uncover their secret parts."

The forehead.

1 Sam 17:49 Then David put his hand in his bag and took out a stone; and he slung *it* and struck the Philistine in his forehead, so that the stone sank into his forehead, and he fell on his face to the earth.

Ezek 9:4 and the LORD said to him, "Go through the midst of the city, through the midst of Jerusalem, and put a mark on the foreheads of the men who sigh and cry over all the abominations that are done within it."

The temples.

Judg 4:21–22 Then Jael, Heber's wife, took a tent peg and took a hammer in her hand, and went softly to him and drove the peg into his temple, and it went down into the ground; for he was fast asleep and weary. So he died. **22** And then, as Barak pursued Sisera, Jael came out to meet him, and said to him, "Come, I will show you the man whom you seek." And when he went into her *tent*, there lay Sisera, dead with the peg in his temple.

Song 4:3 Your lips *are* like a strand of scarlet, And your mouth is lovely. Your temples behind your veil *Are* like a piece of pomegranate.

The face.

Gen 48:12 So Joseph brought them from beside his knees, and he bowed down with his face to the earth.

2 Kin 9:30 Now when Jehu had come to Jezreel, Jezebel heard *of it;* and she put paint on her eyes and adorned her head, and looked through a window.

The hair.

Judg 16:22 However, the hair of his head began to grow again after it had been shaven.

Ps 40:12 For innumerable evils have surrounded me; My iniquities have overtaken me, so that I am not able to look up; They are more than the hairs of my head; Therefore my heart fails me.

The scalp.

Ps 68:21 But God will wound the head of His enemies, The hairy scalp of the one who still goes on in his trespasses.

Often anointed.

Eccl 9:8 Let your garments always be white, And let your head lack no oil.

Matt 6:17 But you, when you fast, anoint your head and wash your face,

Bowed down

In worshiping God.

Gen 24:26 Then the man bowed down his head and worshiped the LORD.

Ex 4:31 So the people believed; and when they heard that the LORD had visited the children of Israel and that He had looked on their affliction, then they bowed their heads and worshiped.

As a token of respect.

Gen 43:23 But he said, "Peace *be* with you, do not be afraid. Your God and the God of your father has given you treasure in your sacks; I had your money." Then he brought Simeon out to them.

In grief

Was covered up.

2 Sam 15:30 So David went up by the Ascent of the *Mount of* Olives, and wept as he went up; and he had his head covered and went barefoot. And all the people who *were* with him covered their heads and went up, weeping as they went up.

Esth 6:12 Afterward Mordecai went back to the king's gate. But Haman hurried to his house, mourning and with his head covered.

Was shaved.

Job 1:20 Then Job arose, tore his robe, and shaved his head; and he fell to the ground and worshiped.

Sprinkled with dust.

Josh 7:6 Then Joshua tore his clothes, and fell to the earth on his face before the ark of the LORD until evening, he and the elders of Israel; and they put dust on their heads.

The hands placed on.

2 Sam 13:19 Then Tamar put ashes on her head, and tore her robe of many colors that *was* on her, and laid her hand on her head and went away crying bitterly.

Jer 2:37 Indeed you will go forth from him With your hands on your head; For the LORD has rejected your trusted allies, And you will not prosper by them.

Priests forbidden to shave.

Lev 21:5 'They shall not make any bald *place* on their heads, nor shall they shave the edges of their beards nor make any cuttings in their flesh.

Lev 21:10 'He who is the high priest among his brethren, on whose head the anointing oil was poured and who is consecrated to wear the garments, shall not uncover his head nor tear his clothes;

Nazirites forbidden to shave.

Num 6:5 'All the days of the vow of his separation no razor shall come upon his head; until the days are fulfilled for which he separated himself to the LORD, he shall be holy. *Then* he shall let the locks of the hair of his head grow.

Derision expressed by shaking.

2 Kin 19:21 This *is* the word which the LORD has spoken concerning him: 'The virgin, the daughter of Zion, Has despised you, laughed you to scorn; The daughter of Jerusalem Has shaken *her* head behind your back!

Ps 22:7 All those who see Me ridicule Me; They shoot out the lip, they shake the head, *saying,*

Ps 109:25 I also have become a reproach to them; *When* they look at me, they shake their heads.

Matt 27:39 And those who passed by blasphemed Him, wagging their heads

The Jews censured for swearing by.

Matt 5:36 Nor shall you swear by your head, because you cannot make one hair white or black.

When gray with age, to be respected.

Lev 19:32 'You shall rise before the gray headed and honor the presence of an old man, and fear your God: I *am* the LORD.

Liable to

Leprosy.

Lev 13:42–44 And if there is on the bald head or bald forehead a reddish-white sore, it *is* leprosy breaking out on his bald head or his bald forehead. **43** Then the priest shall examine it; and indeed *if* the swelling of the sore *is* reddish-white on his bald head or on his bald forehead, as the appearance of leprosy on the skin of the body, **44** he is a leprous man. He *is* unclean. The priest shall surely pronounce him unclean; his sore *is* on his head.

Scab.

Is 3:17 Therefore the Lord will strike with a scab The crown of the head of the daughters of Zion, And the LORD will uncover their secret parts."

Internal disease.

2 Kin 4:19 And he said to his father, "My head, my head!" So he said to a servant, "Carry him to his mother."

Is 1:5 Why should you be stricken again? You will revolt more and more. The whole head is sick, And the whole heart faints.

Baldness.

Lev 13:40–41 "As for the man whose hair has fallen from his head, he *is* bald, *but* he *is* clean. **41** He whose hair has fallen from his forehead, he *is* bald on the forehead, *but* he *is* clean.

Is 15:2 He has gone up to the temple and Dibon, To the high places to weep. Moab will wail over Nebo and over Medeba; On all their heads *will be* baldness, And every beard cut off.

Of the leper, always uncovered.

Lev 13:45 "Now the leper on whom the sore *is,* his

clothes shall be torn and his head bare; and he shall cover his mustache, and cry, 'Unclean! Unclean!'

Of women, generally covered in public.

Gen 24:65 for she had said to the servant, "Who *is* this man walking in the field to meet us?" The servant said, "It *is* my master." So she took a veil and covered herself.

1 Cor 11:5 But every woman who prays or prophesies with *her* head uncovered dishonors her head, for that is one and the same as if her head were shaved.

Of criminals, often cut off.

Matt 14:10 So he sent and had John beheaded in prison.

Of enemies slain in war, often cut off.

1 Sam 17:51 Therefore David ran and stood over the Philistine, took his sword and drew it out of its sheath and killed him, and cut off his head with it. And when the Philistines saw that their champion was dead, they fled.

1 Sam 17:57 Then, as David returned from the slaughter of the Philistine, Abner took him and brought him before Saul with the head of the Philistine in his hand.

1 Sam 31:9 And they cut off his head and stripped off his armor, and sent *word* throughout the land of the Philistines, to proclaim *it in* the temple of their idols and among the people.

Illustrative of

God.

1 Cor 11:3 But I want you to know that the head of every man is Christ, the head of woman *is* man, and the head of Christ *is* God.

Christ.

1 Cor 11:3 But I want you to know that the head of every man is Christ, the head of woman *is* man, and the head of Christ *is* God.

Eph 1:22 And He put all *things* under His feet, and gave Him *to be* head over all *things* to the church,

Col 2:19 and not holding fast to the Head, from whom all the body, nourished and knit together by joints and ligaments, grows with the increase *that is* from God.

Rulers.

1 Sam 15:17 So Samuel said, "When you *were* little in your own eyes, *were* you not head of the tribes of Israel? And did not the LORD anoint you king over Israel?

Dan 2:38 and wherever the children of men dwell, or the beasts of the field and the birds of the heaven, He has given *them* into your hand, and has made you ruler over them all—you *are* this head of gold.

Chief men.

Is 9:14–15 Therefore the LORD will cut off head and tail from Israel, Palm branch and bulrush in one day. **15** The elder and honorable, he *is* the head; The prophet who teaches lies, he *is* the tail.

The chief city of a kingdom.

Is 7:8 For the head of Syria *is* Damascus, And the head of Damascus *is* Rezin. Within sixty-five years Ephraim will be broken, *So that it will* not *be* a people.

(Covered) defense and protection.

Ps 140:7 O GOD the Lord, the strength of my salvation, You have covered my head in the day of battle.

(Covered) subjection.

1 Cor 11:5 But every woman who prays or prophesies with *her* head uncovered dishonors her head, for that is one and the same as if her head were shaved.

1 Cor 11:10 For this reason the woman ought to have *a symbol of* authority on *her* head, because of the angels.

(Made bald) heavy judgments.

Is 3:24 And so it shall be: Instead of a sweet smell there will be a stench; Instead of a sash, a rope; Instead of well-set hair, baldness; Instead of a rich robe, a girding of sackcloth; And branding instead of beauty.

Is 15:2 He has gone up to the temple and Dibon, To the high places to weep. Moab will wail over Nebo and over Medeba; On all their heads *will be* baldness, *And* every beard cut off.

Is 22:12 And in that day the Lord GOD of hosts Called for weeping and for mourning, For baldness and for girding with sackcloth.

Mic 1:16 Make yourself bald and cut off your hair, Because of your precious children; Enlarge your baldness like an eagle, For they shall go from you into captivity.

(Lifted up) joy and confidence.

Ps 3:3 But You, O LORD, *are* a shield for me, My glory and the One who lifts up my head.

Luke 21:28 Now when these things begin to happen, look up and lift up your heads, because your redemption draws near."

(Lifted up) pride, etc.

Ps 83:2 For behold, Your enemies make a tumult; And those who hate You have lifted up their head.

(Lifted up) exaltation.

Gen 40:13 Now within three days Pharaoh will lift up your head and restore you to your place, and you will put Pharaoh's cup in his hand according to the former manner, when you were his butler.

Ps 27:6 And now my head shall be lifted up above my enemies all around me; Therefore I will offer sacrifices of joy in His tabernacle; I will sing, yes, I will sing praises to the LORD.

(Anointed) joy and prosperity.

Ps 23:5 You prepare a table before me in the presence of my enemies; You anoint my head with oil; My cup runs over.

Ps 92:10 But my horn You have exalted like a wild ox; I have been anointed with fresh oil.

HEART, GENERAL CHARACTER OF THE
Issues of life are out of.

Prov 4:23 Keep your heart with all diligence, For out of it *spring* the issues of life.

God
Tries.

1 Chr 29:17 I know also, my God, that You test the heart and have pleasure in uprightness. As for me, in the uprightness of my heart I have willingly offered all these *things*; and now with joy I have seen Your people, who are present here to offer willingly to You.

Jer 12:3 But You, O LORD, know me; You have seen me, And You have tested my heart toward You. Pull

them out like sheep for the slaughter, And prepare them for the day of slaughter.

Knows.

2 Chr 6:30 then hear from heaven Your dwelling place, and forgive, and give to everyone according to all his ways, whose heart You know (for You alone know the hearts of the sons of men),

Ps 44:21 Would not God search this out? For He knows the secrets of the heart.

Jer 20:12 But, O LORD of hosts, You who test the righteous, *And* see the mind and heart, Let me see Your vengeance on them; For I have pleaded my cause before You.

Searches.

1 Chr 28:9 "As for you, my son Solomon, know the God of your father, and serve Him with a loyal heart and with a willing mind; for the LORD searches all hearts and understands all the intent of the thoughts. If you seek Him, He will be found by you; but if you forsake Him, He will cast you off forever.

Jer 17:10 I, the LORD, search the heart, *I* test the mind, Even to give every man according to his ways, According to the fruit of his doings.

Looks at.

1 Sam 16:7 But the LORD said to Samuel, "Do not look at his appearance or at his physical stature, because I have refused him. For *the LORD does* not *see* as man sees; for man looks at the outward appearance, but the LORD looks at the heart."

Understands the thoughts of.

1 Chr 28:9 "As for you, my son Solomon, know the God of your father, and serve Him with a loyal heart and with a willing mind; for the LORD searches all hearts and understands all the intent of the thoughts. If you seek Him, He will be found by you; but if you forsake Him, He will cast you off forever.

Ps 139:2 You know my sitting down and my rising up; You understand my thought afar off.

Weighs.

Prov 21:2 Every way of a man *is* right in his own eyes, But the LORD weighs the hearts.

Prov 24:12 If you say, "Surely we did not know this," Does not He who weighs the hearts consider *it*? He who keeps your soul, does He *not* know *it*? And will He *not* render to *each* man according to his deeds?

Influences.

1 Sam 10:26 And Saul also went home to Gibeah; and valiant *men* went with him, whose hearts God had touched.

Ezra 6:22 And they kept the Feast of Unleavened Bread seven days with joy; for the LORD made them joyful, and turned the heart of the king of Assyria toward them, to strengthen their hands in the work of the house of God, the God of Israel.

Ezra 7:27 Blessed *be* the LORD God of our fathers, who has put *such a thing* as this in the king's heart, to beautify the house of the LORD which *is* in Jerusalem,

Prov 21:1 The king's heart *is* in the hand of the LORD, *Like* the rivers of water; He turns it wherever He wishes.

Jer 20:9 Then I said, "I will not make mention of Him,

Nor speak anymore in His name." But *His word* was in my heart like a burning fire Shut up in my bones; I was weary of holding *it* back, And I could not.

Creates a new.

Ps 51:10 Create in me a clean heart, O God, And renew a steadfast spirit within me.

Ezek 36:26 I will give you a new heart and put a new spirit within you; I will take the heart of stone out of your flesh and give you a heart of flesh.

Prepares.

1 Chr 29:18 O LORD God of Abraham, Isaac, and Israel, our fathers, keep this forever in the intent of the thoughts of the heart of Your people, and fix their heart toward You.

Prov 16:1 The preparations of the heart *belong* to man, But the answer of the tongue *is* from the LORD.

Opens.

Acts 16:14 Now a certain woman named Lydia heard *us.* She was a seller of purple from the city of Thyatira, who worshiped God. The Lord opened her heart to heed the things spoken by Paul.

Enlightens.

2 Cor 4:6 For it is the God who commanded light to shine out of darkness, who has shone in our hearts to *give* the light of the knowledge of the glory of God in the face of Jesus Christ.

Eph 1:18 the eyes of your understanding being enlightened; that you may know what is the hope of His calling, what are the riches of the glory of His inheritance in the saints,

Strengthens.

Ps 27:14 Wait on the LORD; Be of good courage, And He shall strengthen your heart; Wait, I say, on the LORD!

Establishes.

Ps 112:8 His heart *is* established; He will not be afraid, Until he sees *his desire* upon his enemies.

1 Thess 3:13 so that He may establish your hearts blameless in holiness before our God and Father at the coming of our Lord Jesus Christ with all His saints.

Should be

Dedicated to God.

1 Sam 7:3 Then Samuel spoke to all the house of Israel, saying, "If you return to the LORD with all your hearts, *then* put away the foreign gods and the Ashtoreths from among you, and prepare your hearts for the LORD, and serve Him only; and He will deliver you from the hand of the Philistines."

Prov 23:26 My son, give me your heart, And let your eyes observe my ways.

Perfect with God.

1 Kin 8:61 Let your heart therefore be loyal to the LORD our God, to walk in His statutes and keep His commandments, as at this day."

Applied to wisdom.

Ps 90:12 So teach *us* to number our days, That we may gain a heart of wisdom.

Prov 2:2 So that you incline your ear to wisdom, *And* apply your heart to understanding;

Guided in the way of wisdom.

Prov 23:19 Hear, my son, and be wise; And guide your heart in the way.

Purified.

James 4:8 Draw near to God and He will draw near to you. Cleanse *your* hands, *you* sinners; and purify *your* hearts, *you* double-minded.

Sincere.

Eph 6:5 Bondservants, be obedient to those who are your masters according to the flesh, with fear and trembling, in sincerity of heart, as to Christ;

Col 3:22 Bondservants, obey in all things your masters according to the flesh, not with eyeservice, as menpleasers, but in sincerity of heart, fearing God.

Tender.

Eph 4:32 And be kind to one another, tenderhearted, forgiving one another, even as God in Christ forgave you.

Kept with diligence.

Prov 4:23 Keep your heart with all diligence, For out of it *spring* the issues of life.

Believers should

Believe with.

Acts 8:37 Then Philip said, "If you believe with all your heart, you may." And he answered and said, "I believe that Jesus Christ is the Son of God."

Rom 10:10 For with the heart one believes unto righteousness, and with the mouth confession is made unto salvation.

Obey God with all.

Deut 11:13 'And it shall be that if you earnestly obey My commandments which I command you today, to love the LORD your God and serve Him with all your heart and with all your soul,

Deut 26:16 "This day the LORD your God commands you to observe these statutes and judgments; therefore you shall be careful to observe them with all your heart and with all your soul.

1 Kin 2:4 that the LORD may fulfill His word which He spoke concerning me, saying, 'If your sons take heed to their way, to walk before Me in truth with all their heart and with all their soul,' He said, 'you shall not lack a man on the throne of Israel.'

Eph 6:6 not with eyeservice, as men-pleasers, but as bondservants of Christ, doing the will of God from the heart,

Trust in God with all.

Prov 3:5 Trust in the LORD with all your heart, And lean not on your own understanding;

Love God with all.

Matt 22:37 Jesus said to him, " 'You shall love the LORD your God with all your heart, with all your soul, and with all your mind.'

Return to God with all.

Deut 30:2 and you return to the LORD your God and obey His voice, according to all that I command you today, you and your children, with all your heart and with all your soul,

Sanctify God in.

1 Pet 3:15 But sanctify the Lord God in your hearts, and always *be* ready to *give* a defense to everyone who asks you a reason for the hope that is in you, with meekness and fear;

Love one another with a pure.

1 Pet 1:22 Since you have purified your souls in obeying the truth through the Spirit in sincere love of the brethren, love one another fervently with a pure heart,

No man can cleanse.

Prov 20:9 Who can say, "I have made my heart clean, I am pure from my sin"?

Evidence of a man's treasure.

Matt 6:21 For where your treasure is, there your heart will be also.

The Word of God discerns the thoughts and intents of.

Heb 4:12 For the word of God *is* living and powerful, and sharper than any two-edged sword, piercing even to the division of soul and spirit, and of joints and marrow, and is a discerner of the thoughts and intents of the heart.

Faith, the means of purifying.

Acts 15:9 and made no distinction between us and them, purifying their hearts by faith.

Renewal of, promised under the gospel.

Ezek 11:19 Then I will give them one heart, and I will put a new spirit within them, and take the stony heart out of their flesh, and give them a heart of flesh,

Ezek 36:26 I will give you a new heart and put a new spirit within you; I will take the heart of stone out of your flesh and give you a heart of flesh.

Heb 3:10 *Therefore I was angry with that generation, And said, 'They always go astray in their heart, And they have not known My ways.'*

When broken and contrite, not despised by God.

Ps 51:17 The sacrifices of God *are* a broken spirit, A broken and a contrite heart— These, O God, You will not despise.

The pure in, shall see God.

Matt 5:8 Blessed *are* the pure in heart, For they shall see God.

Pray that it may be

Cleansed.

Ps 51:10 Create in me a clean heart, O God, And renew a steadfast spirit within me.

Inclined to God's testimonies.

Ps 119:36 Incline my heart to Your testimonies, And not to covetousness.

United to fear God.

Ps 86:11 Teach me Your way, O LORD; I will walk in Your truth; Unite my heart to fear Your name.

Directed into the love of God.

2 Thess 3:5 Now may the Lord direct your hearts into the love of God and into the patience of Christ.

Should not harden

Against God.

Ps 95:8 "Do not harden your hearts, as in the rebellion, As *in* the day of trial in the wilderness,

Heb 4:7 again He designates a certain day, saying in David, *"Today,"* after such a long time, as it has been said: *"Today, if you will hear His voice, Do not harden your hearts."*

Against the poor.

Deut 15:7 "If there is among you a poor man of your brethren, within any of the gates in your land which the LORD your God is giving you, you shall not harden your heart nor shut your hand from your poor brother,

Do not regard iniquity in.

Ps 66:18 If I regard iniquity in my heart, The Lord will not hear.

Take heed lest it be deceived.

Deut 11:16 Take heed to yourselves, lest your heart be deceived, and you turn aside and serve other gods and worship them,

Know the plague of.

1 Kin 8:38 whatever prayer, whatever supplication is made by anyone, *or* by all Your people Israel, when each one knows the plague of his own heart, and spreads out his hands toward this temple:

He that trusts in, is a fool.

Prov 28:26 He who trusts in his own heart is a fool, But whoever walks wisely will be delivered.

HEART, CHARACTER OF THE RENEWED

Prepared to seek God.

2 Chr 19:3 Nevertheless good things are found in you, in that you have removed the wooden images from the land, and have prepared your heart to seek God."

Ezra 7:10 For Ezra had prepared his heart to seek the Law of the LORD, and to do *it*, and to teach statutes and ordinances in Israel.

Ps 10:17 LORD, You have heard the desire of the humble; You will prepare their heart; You will cause Your ear to hear,

Fixed on God.

Ps 57:7 My heart is steadfast, O God, my heart is steadfast; I will sing and give praise.

Ps 112:7 He will not be afraid of evil tidings; His heart is steadfast, trusting in the LORD.

Joyful in God.

1 Sam 2:1 And Hannah prayed and said: "My heart rejoices in the LORD; My horn is exalted in the LORD. I smile at my enemies, Because I rejoice in Your salvation.

Zech 10:7 *Those of* Ephraim shall be like a mighty man, And their heart shall rejoice as if with wine. Yes, their children shall see *it* and be glad; Their heart shall rejoice in the LORD.

Perfect with God.

1 Kin 8:61 Let your heart therefore be loyal to the LORD our God, to walk in His statutes and keep His commandments, as at this day."

Ps 101:2 I will behave wisely in a perfect way. Oh, when will You come to me? I will walk within my house with a perfect heart.

Upright.

Ps 97:11 Light is sown for the righteous, And gladness for the upright in heart.

Ps 125:4 Do good, O LORD, to *those who are* good, And to *those who are* upright in their hearts.

Pure.

Ps 24:4 He who has clean hands and a pure heart, Who has not lifted up his soul to an idol, Nor sworn deceitfully.

Ps 73:1 Truly God *is* good to Israel, To such as are pure in heart.

Matt 5:8 Blessed *are* the pure in heart, For they shall see God.

Tender.

1 Sam 24:5 Now it happened afterward that David's heart troubled him because he had cut Saul's *robe.*

2 Kin 22:19 because your heart was tender, and you humbled yourself before the LORD when you heard what I spoke against this place and against its inhabitants, that they would become a desolation and a curse, and you tore your clothes and wept before Me, I also have heard *you,*" says the LORD.

Simple and sincere.

Acts 2:46 So continuing daily with one accord in the temple, and breaking bread from house to house, they ate their food with gladness and simplicity of heart,

Heb 10:22 let us draw near with a true heart in full assurance of faith, having our hearts sprinkled from an evil conscience and our bodies washed with pure water.

Honest and good.

Luke 8:15 But the ones *that* fell on the good ground are those who, having heard the word with a noble and good heart, keep *it* and bear fruit with patience.

Broken and contrite.

Ps 34:18 The LORD *is* near to those who have a broken heart, And saves such as have a contrite spirit.

Ps 51:17 The sacrifices of God *are* a broken spirit, A broken and a contrite heart— These, O God, You will not despise.

Obedient.

Ps 119:112 I have inclined my heart to perform Your statutes Forever, to the very end.

Rom 6:17 But God be thanked that *though* you were slaves of sin, yet you obeyed from the heart that form of doctrine to which you were delivered.

God's law is within.

Ps 40:8 I delight to do Your will, O my God, And Your law *is* within my heart."

Ps 119:11 Your word I have hidden in my heart, That I might not sin against You.

Awed by the Word of God.

Ps 119:161 Princes persecute me without a cause, But my heart stands in awe of Your word.

Filled with the fear of God.

Jer 32:40 And I will make an everlasting covenant with them, that I will not turn away from doing them good; but I will put My fear in their hearts so that they will not depart from Me.

Meditative.

Ps 4:4 Be angry, and do not sin. Meditate within your heart on your bed, and be still. Selah

Ps 77:6 I call to remembrance my song in the night; I meditate within my heart, And my spirit makes diligent search.

Circumcised.

Deut 30:6 And the LORD your God will circumcise your heart and the heart of your descendants, to love the LORD your God with all your heart and with all your soul, that you may live.

Rom 2:29 but *he is* a Jew who *is one* inwardly; and circumcision *is that* of the heart, in the Spirit, not in the letter; whose praise *is* not from men but from God.

Without fear.

Ps 27:3 Though an army may encamp against me, My heart shall not fear; Though war may rise against me, In this I *will be* confident.

Desirous of God.

Ps 84:2 My soul longs, yes, even faints For the courts of the LORD; My heart and my flesh cry out for the living God.

Enlarged.

Ps 119:32 I will run the course of Your commandments, For You shall enlarge my heart.

2 Cor 6:11 O Corinthians! We have spoken openly to you, our heart is wide open.

Confident in God.

Ps 112:7 He will not be afraid of evil tidings; His heart is steadfast, trusting in the LORD.

Sympathizing.

Jer 4:19 O my soul, my soul! I am pained in my very heart! My heart makes a noise in me; I cannot hold my peace, Because you have heard, O my soul, The sound of the trumpet, The alarm of war.

Lam 3:51 My eyes bring suffering to my soul Because of all the daughters of my city.

Prayerful.

1 Sam 1:13 Now Hannah spoke in her heart; only her lips moved, but her voice was not heard. Therefore Eli thought she was drunk.

Ps 27:8 *When You said,* "Seek My face," My heart said to You, "Your face, LORD, I will seek."

Wholly devoted to God.

Neh 9:8 You found his heart faithful before You, And made a covenant with him To give the land of the Canaanites, The Hittites, the Amorites, The Perizzites, the Jebusites, And the Girgashites— To give *it* to his descendants. You have performed Your words, For You *are* righteous.

Ps 9:1 I will praise *You,* O LORD, with my whole heart; I will tell of all Your marvelous works.

Ps 119:10 With my whole heart I have sought You; Oh, let me not wander from Your commandments!

Ps 119:69 The proud have forged a lie against me, *But* I will keep Your precepts with *my* whole heart.

Ps 119:145 I cry out with *my* whole heart; Hear me, O LORD! I will keep Your statutes.

Zealous.

2 Chr 17:6 And his heart took delight in the ways of the LORD; moreover he removed the high places and wooden images from Judah.

Jer 20:9 Then I said, "I will not make mention of Him,

Nor speak anymore in His name." But *His word* was in my heart like a burning fire Shut up in my bones; I was weary of holding *it* back, And I could not.

Wise.

Prov 10:8 The wise in heart will receive commands, But a prating fool will fall.

Prov 14:33 Wisdom rests in the heart of him who has understanding, But *what is* in the heart of fools is made known.

Prov 23:15 My son, if your heart is wise, My heart will rejoice—indeed, I myself;

A treasury of good.

Matt 12:35 A good man out of the good treasure of his heart brings forth good things, and an evil man out of the evil treasure brings forth evil things.

HEART, CHARACTER OF THE UNRENEWED

Hateful to God.

Prov 6:16 These six *things* the LORD hates, Yes, seven *are* an abomination to Him:

Prov 6:18 A heart that devises wicked plans, Feet that are swift in running to evil,

Prov 11:20 Those who are of a perverse heart *are* an abomination to the LORD, But *the* blameless in their ways *are* His delight.

Full of evil.

Gen 6:5 Then the LORD saw that the wickedness of man *was* great in the earth, and *that* every intent of the thoughts of his heart *was* only evil continually.

Gen 8:21 And the LORD smelled a soothing aroma. Then the LORD said in His heart, "I will never again curse the ground for man's sake, although the imagination of man's heart *is* evil from his youth; nor will I again destroy every living thing as I have done.

Prov 6:18 A heart that devises wicked plans, Feet that are swift in running to evil,

Eccl 9:3 This *is* an evil in all that is done under the sun: that one thing *happens* to all. Truly the hearts of the sons of men are full of evil; madness *is* in their hearts while they live, and after that *they go* to the dead.

Jer 4:14 O Jerusalem, wash your heart from wickedness, That you may be saved. How long shall your evil thoughts lodge within you?

Matt 12:35 A good man out of the good treasure of his heart brings forth good things, and an evil man out of the evil treasure brings forth evil things.

Mark 7:21 For from within, out of the heart of men, proceed evil thoughts, adulteries, fornications, murders,

Fully set to do evil.

Eccl 8:11 Because the sentence against an evil work is not executed speedily, therefore the heart of the sons of men is fully set in them to do evil.

Desperately wicked.

Jer 17:9 "The heart *is* deceitful above all *things*, And desperately wicked; Who can know it?

Far from God.

1 Kin 15:3 And he walked in all the sins of his father, which he had done before him; his heart was not loyal to the LORD his God, as was the heart of his father David.

2 Chr 12:14 And he did evil, because he did not prepare his heart to seek the LORD.

Prov 6:18 A heart that devises wicked plans, Feet that are swift in running to evil,

Is 29:13 Therefore the Lord said: "Inasmuch as these people draw near with their mouths And honor Me with their lips, But have removed their hearts far from Me, And their fear toward Me is taught by the commandment of men,

Matt 15:8 '*These people draw near to Me with their mouth, And honor Me with their lips, But their heart is far from Me.*

Acts 8:21 You have neither part nor portion in this matter, for your heart is not right in the sight of God.

Prone to depart from God.

Deut 29:18 so that there may not be among you man or woman or family or tribe, whose heart turns away today from the LORD our God, to go *and* serve the gods of these nations, and that there may not be among you a root bearing bitterness or wormwood;

Ps 95:10 For forty years I was grieved with *that* generation, And said, 'It *is* a people who go astray in their hearts, And they do not know My ways.'

Jer 17:5 Thus says the LORD: "Cursed *is* the man who trusts in man And makes flesh his strength, Whose heart departs from the LORD.

Impenitent.

Rom 2:5 But in accordance with your hardness and your impenitent heart you are treasuring up for yourself wrath in the day of wrath and revelation of the righteous judgment of God,

Unbelieving.

Rom 1:21 because, although they knew God, they did not glorify *Him* as God, nor were thankful, but became futile in their thoughts, and their foolish hearts were darkened.

Eph 4:18 having their understanding darkened, being alienated from the life of God, because of the ignorance that is in them, because of the blindness of their heart;

Heb 3:12 Beware, brethren, lest there be in any of you an evil heart of unbelief in departing from the living God;

Uncircumcised.

Lev 26:41 and *that* I also have walked contrary to them and have brought them into the land of their enemies; if their uncircumcised hearts are humbled, and they accept their guilt—

Acts 7:51 "*You* stiff-necked and uncircumcised in heart and ears! You always resist the Holy Spirit; as your fathers *did,* so *do* you.

Of little worth.

Prov 10:20 The tongue of the righteous *is* choice silver; The heart of the wicked *is worth* little.

Deceitful.

Jer 17:9 "The heart *is* deceitful above all *things*, And desperately wicked; Who can know it?

Deceived.

Is 44:20 He feeds on ashes; A deceived heart has turned him aside; And he cannot deliver his soul, Nor say, "*Is there* not a lie in my right hand?"

James 1:26 If anyone among you thinks he is religious, and does not bridle his tongue but deceives his own heart, this one's religion *is* useless.

Prone to division.

1 Chr 12:33 of Zebulun there were fifty thousand who went out to battle, expert in war with all weapons of war, stouthearted men who could keep ranks;

Ps 12:2 They speak idly everyone with his neighbor; *With* flattering lips *and* a double heart they speak.

Hos 10:2 Their heart is divided; Now they are held guilty. He will break down their altars; He will ruin their sacred pillars.

Hard.

Ezek 3:7 But the house of Israel will not listen to you, because they will not listen to Me; for all the house of Israel *are* impudent and hard-hearted.

Mark 10:5 And Jesus answered and said to them, "Because of the hardness of your heart he wrote you this precept.

Rom 2:5 But in accordance with your hardness and your impenitent heart you are treasuring up for yourself wrath in the day of wrath and revelation of the righteous judgment of God,

Haughty.

Prov 18:12 Before destruction the heart of a man is haughty, And before honor *is* humility.

Is 10:12 Therefore it shall come to pass, when the Lord has performed all His work on Mount Zion and on Jerusalem, *that He will say*, "I will punish the fruit of the arrogant heart of the king of Assyria, and the glory of his haughty looks."

Jer 48:29 "We have heard the pride of Moab (He *is* exceedingly proud), Of his loftiness and arrogance and pride, And of the haughtiness of his heart."

Influenced by the devil.

John 13:2 And supper being ended, the devil having already put it into the heart of Judas Iscariot, Simon's *son*, to betray Him,

Carnal.

Rom 8:7 Because the carnal mind *is* enmity against God; for it is not subject to the law of God, nor indeed can be.

Covetous.

Jer 22:17 "Yet your eyes and your heart *are* for nothing but your covetousness, For shedding innocent blood, And practicing oppression and violence."

2 Pet 2:14 having eyes full of adultery and that cannot cease from sin, enticing unstable souls. *They have* a heart trained in covetous practices, *and are* accursed children.

Despiteful.

Ezek 25:15 'Thus says the Lord GOD: "Because the Philistines dealt vengefully and took vengeance with a spiteful heart, to destroy because of the old hatred,"

Ensnaring.

Eccl 7:26 And I find more bitter than death The woman whose heart *is* snares and nets, Whose hands *are* fetters. He who pleases God shall escape from her, But the sinner shall be trapped by her.

Foolish.

Prov 12:23 A prudent man conceals knowledge, But the heart of fools proclaims foolishness.

Prov 22:15 Foolishness *is* bound up in the heart of a child; The rod of correction will drive it far from him.

Fretful against the Lord.

Prov 19:3 The foolishness of a man twists his way, And his heart frets against the LORD.

Idolatrous.

Ezek 14:3–4 "Son of man, these men have set up their idols in their hearts, and put before them that which causes them to stumble into iniquity. Should I let Myself be inquired of at all by them? 4 "Therefore speak to them, and say to them, 'Thus says the Lord GOD: "Everyone of the house of Israel who sets up his idols in his heart, and puts before him what causes him to stumble into iniquity, and then comes to the prophet, I the LORD will answer him who comes, according to the multitude of his idols,

Mad.

Eccl 9:3 This *is* an evil in all that is done under the sun: that one thing *happens* to all. Truly the hearts of the sons of men are full of evil; madness *is* in their hearts while they live, and after that *they go* to the dead.

Mischievous.

Ps 28:3 Do not take me away with the wicked And with the workers of iniquity, Who speak peace to their neighbors, But evil *is* in their hearts.

Ps 140:2 Who plan evil things in *their* hearts; They continually gather together *for* war.

Proud.

2 Chr 26:16 But when he was strong his heart was lifted up, to *his* destruction, for he transgressed against the LORD his God by entering the temple of the LORD to burn incense on the altar of incense.

Ps 101:5 Whoever secretly slanders his neighbor, Him I will destroy; The one who has a haughty look and a proud heart, Him I will not endure.

Jer 49:16 Your fierceness has deceived you, The pride of your heart, O you who dwell in the clefts of the rock, Who hold the height of the hill! Though you make your nest as high as the eagle, I will bring you down from there," says the LORD.

Dan 5:20 But when his heart was lifted up, and his spirit was hardened in pride, he was deposed from his kingly throne, and they took his glory from him.

Rebellious.

Jer 5:23 But this people has a defiant and rebellious heart; They have revolted and departed.

Perverse.

Ps 101:4 A perverse heart shall depart from me; I will not know wickedness.

Prov 6:14 Perversity *is* in his heart, He devises evil continually, He sows discord.

Prov 12:8 A man will be commended according to his wisdom, But he who is of a perverse heart will be despised.

Prov 17:20 He who has a deceitful heart finds no good, And he who has a perverse tongue falls into evil.

Stubborn.

Is 46:12 "Listen to Me, you stubborn-hearted, Who *are* far from righteousness:

Ezek 2:4 For *they are* impudent and stubborn children. I am sending you to them, and you shall say to them, 'Thus says the Lord GOD.'

Stony.

Ezek 11:19 Then I will give them one heart, and I will put a new spirit within them, and take the stony heart out of their flesh, and give them a heart of flesh,

Ezek 36:26 I will give you a new heart and put a new spirit within you; I will take the heart of stone out of your flesh and give you a heart of flesh.

Elated by sensual indulgence.

Hos 13:3 Therefore they shall be like the morning cloud And like the early dew that passes away, Like chaff blown off from a threshing floor And like smoke from a chimney.

Devises violence.

Prov 24:2 For their heart devises violence, And their lips talk of troublemaking.

Often judicially insensitive.

Ex 4:21 And the LORD said to Moses, "When you go back to Egypt, see that you do all those wonders before Pharaoh which I have put in your hand. But I will harden his heart, so that he will not let the people go.

Josh 11:20 For it was of the LORD to harden their hearts, that they should come against Israel in battle, that He might utterly destroy them, *and* that they might receive no mercy, but that He might destroy them, as the LORD had commanded Moses.

Is 6:10 "Make the heart of this people dull, And their ears heavy, And shut their eyes; Lest they see with their eyes, And hear with their ears, And understand with their heart, And return and be healed."

Acts 28:26–27 saying, *'Go to this people and say: "Hearing you will hear, and shall not understand; And seeing you will see, and not perceive; 27 For the hearts of this people have grown dull. Their ears are hard of hearing, And their eyes they have closed, Lest they should see with their eyes and hear with their ears, Lest they should understand with their hearts and turn, So that I should heal them." '*

HEAVEN

Created by God.

Gen 1:1 In the beginning God created the heavens and the earth.

Rev 10:6 and swore by Him who lives forever and ever, who created heaven and the things that are in it, the earth and the things that are in it, and the sea and the things that are in it, that there should be delay no longer,

Everlasting.

Ps 89:29 His seed also I will make *to endure* forever, And his throne as the days of heaven.

2 Cor 5:1 For we know that if our earthly house, *this* tent, is destroyed, we have a building from God, a house not made with hands, eternal in the heavens.

Immeasurable.

Jer 31:37 Thus says the LORD: "If heaven above can be measured, And the foundations of the earth searched out beneath, I will also cast off all the seed of Israel For all that they have done, says the LORD.

High.

Ps 103:11 For as the heavens are high above the earth, *So* great is His mercy toward those who fear Him;

Is 57:15 For thus says the High and Lofty One Who inhabits eternity, whose name *is* Holy: "I dwell in the high and holy *place,* With him *who* has a contrite and humble spirit, To revive the spirit of the humble, And to revive the heart of the contrite ones.

Holy.

Deut 26:15 Look down from Your holy habitation, from heaven, and bless Your people Israel and the land which You have given us, just as You swore to our fathers, "a land flowing with milk and honey." '

Ps 20:6 Now I know that the LORD saves His anointed; He will answer him from His holy heaven With the saving strength of His right hand.

Is 57:15 For thus says the High and Lofty One Who inhabits eternity, whose name *is* Holy: "I dwell in the high and holy *place,* With him *who* has a contrite and humble spirit, To revive the spirit of the humble, And to revive the heart of the contrite ones.

God

Is the Lord of.

Dan 5:23 And you have lifted yourself up against the Lord of heaven. They have brought the vessels of His house before you, and you and your lords, your wives and your concubines, have drunk wine from them. And you have praised the gods of silver and gold, bronze and iron, wood and stone, which do not see or hear or know; and the God who *holds* your breath in His hand and owns all your ways, you have not glorified.

Matt 11:25 At that time Jesus answered and said, "I thank You, Father, Lord of heaven and earth, that You have hidden these things from *the* wise and prudent and have revealed them to babes.

Reigns in.

Ps 11:4 The LORD *is* in His holy temple, The LORD's throne *is* in heaven; His eyes behold, His eyelids test the sons of men.

Ps 135:6 Whatever the LORD pleases He does, In heaven and in earth, In the seas and in all deep places.

Dan 4:35 All the inhabitants of the earth *are* reputed as nothing; He does according to His will in the army of heaven And *among* the inhabitants of the earth. No one can restrain His hand Or say to Him, "What have You done?"

Dwells in.

1 Kin 8:30 And may You hear the supplication of Your servant and of Your people Israel, when they pray toward this place. Hear in heaven Your dwelling place; and when You hear, forgive.

Matt 6:9 In this manner, therefore, pray: Our Father in heaven, Hallowed be Your name.

It is His throne.

Is 66:1 Thus says the LORD: "Heaven *is* My throne, And earth *is* My footstool. Where *is* the house that you will build Me? And where *is* the place of My rest?

Acts 7:49 'Heaven is My throne, And earth is My footstool. What house will you build for Me? says the LORD, Or what is the place of My rest?

Fills.

1 Kin 8:27 "But will God indeed dwell on the earth? Behold, heaven and the heaven of heavens cannot contain You. How much less this temple which I have built!

Jer 23:24 Can anyone hide himself in secret places, So I shall not see him?" says the LORD; "Do I not fill heaven and earth?" says the LORD.

Answers His people from.

1 Chr 21:26 And David built there an altar to the LORD, and offered burnt offerings and peace offerings, and called on the LORD; and He answered him from heaven by fire on the altar of burnt offering.

2 Chr 7:14 if My people who are called by My name will humble themselves, and pray and seek My face, and turn from their wicked ways, then I will hear from heaven, and will forgive their sin and heal their land.

Neh 9:27 Therefore You delivered them into the hand of their enemies, Who oppressed them; And in the time of their trouble, When they cried to You, You heard from heaven; And according to Your abundant mercies You gave them deliverers who saved them From the hand of their enemies.

Ps 20:6 Now I know that the LORD saves His anointed; He will answer him from His holy heaven With the saving strength of His right hand.

Sends His judgments from.

Gen 19:24 Then the LORD rained brimstone and fire on Sodom and Gomorrah, from the LORD out of the heavens.

1 Sam 2:10 The adversaries of the LORD shall be broken in pieces; From heaven He will thunder against them. The LORD will judge the ends of the earth. "He will give strength to His king, And exalt the horn of His anointed."

Dan 4:13–14 "I saw in the visions of my head *while* on my bed, and there was a watcher, a holy one, coming down from heaven. **14** He cried aloud and said thus: 'Chop down the tree and cut off its branches, Strip off its leaves and scatter its fruit. Let the beasts get out from under it, And the birds from its branches.

Rom 1:18 For the wrath of God is revealed from heaven against all ungodliness and unrighteousness of men, who suppress the truth in unrighteousness,

Christ

As Mediator, entered into.

Acts 3:21 whom heaven must receive until the times of restoration of all things, which God has spoken by the mouth of all His holy prophets since the world began.

Heb 6:20 where the forerunner has entered for us, *even* Jesus, having become High Priest forever according to the order of Melchizedek.

Heb 9:12 Not with the blood of goats and calves, but with His own blood He entered the Most Holy Place once for all, having obtained eternal redemption.

Heb 9:24 For Christ has not entered the holy places made with hands, *which are* copies of the true, but

into heaven itself, now to appear in the presence of God for us;

Is all-powerful in.

Matt 28:18 And Jesus came and spoke to them, saying, "All authority has been given to Me in heaven and on earth.

1 Pet 3:22 who has gone into heaven and is at the right hand of God, angels and authorities and powers having been made subject to Him.

Contains a place of rest, Abraham's bosom.

Luke 16:23 And being in torments in Hades, he lifted up his eyes and saw Abraham afar off, and Lazarus in his bosom.

Angels are in.

Matt 18:10 "Take heed that you do not despise one of these little ones, for I say to you that in heaven their angels always see the face of My Father who is in heaven.

Matt 24:36 "But of that day and hour no one knows, not even the angels of heaven, but My Father only.

Believers rewarded in.

Matt 5:12 Rejoice and be exceedingly glad, for great *is* your reward in heaven, for so they persecuted the prophets who were before you.

Luke 10:20 Nevertheless do not rejoice in this, that the spirits are subject to you, but rather rejoice because your names are written in heaven."

Heb 12:23 to the general assembly and church of the firstborn *who are* registered in heaven, to God the Judge of all, to the spirits of just men made perfect,

1 Pet 1:4 to an inheritance incorruptible and undefiled and that does not fade away, reserved in heaven for you,

Repentance causes joy in.

Luke 15:7 I say to you that likewise there will be more joy in heaven over one sinner who repents than over ninety-nine just persons who need no repentance.

Believers should lay up treasure in.

Matt 6:20 but lay up for yourselves treasures in heaven, where neither moth nor rust destroys and where thieves do not break in and steal.

Luke 12:33 Sell what you have and give alms; provide yourselves money bags which do not grow old, a treasure in the heavens that does not fail, where no thief approaches nor moth destroys.

Flesh and blood cannot inherit.

1 Cor 15:50 Now this I say, brethren, that flesh and blood cannot inherit the kingdom of God; nor does corruption inherit incorruption.

Happiness of, described.

Rev 7:16–17 They shall neither hunger anymore nor thirst anymore; the sun shall not strike them, nor any heat; **17** for the Lamb who is in the midst of the throne will shepherd them and lead them to living fountains of waters. And God will wipe away every tear from their eyes."

Is called

A barn.

Matt 3:12 His winnowing fan *is* in His hand, and He will thoroughly clean out His threshing floor, and gather His wheat into the barn; but He will burn up the chaff with unquenchable fire."

The kingdom of Christ and of God.

Eph 5:5 For this you know, that no fornicator, unclean person, nor covetous man, who is an idolater, has any inheritance in the kingdom of Christ and God.

The Father's house.

John 14:2 In My Father's house are many mansions; if *it were* not *so,* I would have told you. I go to prepare a place for you.

A heavenly country.

Heb 11:16 But now they desire a better, that is, a heavenly *country.* Therefore God is not ashamed to be called their God, for He has prepared a city for them.

A rest.

Heb 4:9 There remains therefore a rest for the people of God.

Paradise.

Luke 23:43 And Jesus said to him, "Assuredly, I say to you, today you will be with Me in Paradise."

2 Cor 12:2 I know a man in Christ who fourteen years ago—whether in the body I do not know, or whether out of the body I do not know, God knows—such a one was caught up to the third heaven.

2 Cor 12:4 how he was caught up into Paradise and heard inexpressible words, which it is not lawful for a man to utter.

The wicked excluded from.

Gal 5:21 envy, murders, drunkenness, revelries, and the like; of which I tell you beforehand, just as I also told *you* in time past, that those who practice such things will not inherit the kingdom of God.

Eph 5:5 For this you know, that no fornicator, unclean person, nor covetous man, who is an idolater, has any inheritance in the kingdom of Christ and God.

Rev 22:15 But outside *are* dogs and sorcerers and sexually immoral and murderers and idolaters, and whoever loves and practices a lie.

Enoch and Elijah were translated into.

Gen 5:24 And Enoch walked with God; and he *was* not, for God took him.

2 Kin 2:11 Then it happened, as they continued on and talked, that suddenly a chariot of fire *appeared* with horses of fire, and separated the two of them; and Elijah went up by a whirlwind into heaven.

Heb 11:5 By faith Enoch was taken away so that he did not see death, *"and was not found, because God had taken him";* for before he was taken he had this testimony, that he pleased God.

HEDGES (WALLS)

Often made of thorns.

Mic 7:4 The best of them *is* like a brier; The most upright *is sharper* than a thorn hedge; The day of your watchman and your punishment comes; Now shall be their perplexity.

Placed around

Gardens.

Song 4:12 A garden enclosed *Is* my sister, *my* spouse, A spring shut up, A fountain sealed.

Vineyards.

Matt 21:33 "Hear another parable: There was a certain landowner who planted a vineyard and set a hedge around it, dug a winepress in it and built a tower. And he leased it to vinedressers and went into a far country.

Mark 12:1 Then He began to speak to them in parables: "A man planted a vineyard and set a hedge around *it,* dug *a place for* the wine vat and built a tower. And he leased it to vinedressers and went into a far country.

Difficulty of breaking through.

Prov 15:19 The way of the lazy *man is* like a hedge of thorns, But the way of the upright *is* a highway.

Danger of breaking through.

Eccl 10:8 He who digs a pit will fall into it, And whoever breaks through a wall will be bitten by a serpent.

Desolation caused by removing.

Ps 80:12–13 Why have You broken down her hedges, So that all who pass by the way pluck her *fruit?* **13** The boar out of the woods uproots it, And the wild beast of the field devours it.

Filled with grasshoppers.

Nah 3:17 Your commanders *are* like *swarming* locusts, And your generals like great grasshoppers, Which camp in the hedges on a cold day; When the sun rises they flee away, And the place where they *are* is not known.

Poor travelers sought rest under.

Luke 14:23 Then the master said to the servant, 'Go out into the highways and hedges, and compel *them* to come in, that my house may be filled.

Afforded protection in danger.

Jer 49:3 "Wail, O Heshbon, for Ai is plundered! Cry, you daughters of Rabbah, Gird yourselves with sackcloth! Lament and run to and fro by the walls; For Milcom shall go into captivity With his priests and his princes together.

Making up gaps in, alluded to.

Ezek 13:5 You have not gone up into the gaps to build a wall for the house of Israel to stand in battle on the day of the LORD.

Ezek 22:30 So I sought for a man among them who would make a wall, and stand in the gap before Me on behalf of the land, that I should not destroy it; but I found no one.

Illustrative of

God's protection.

Job 1:10 Have You not made a hedge around him, around his household, and around all that he has on every side? You have blessed the work of his hands, and his possessions have increased in the land.

Numerous afflictions.

Job 3:23 *Why is light given* to a man whose way is hidden, And whom God has hedged in?

Job 19:8 He has fenced up my way, so that I cannot pass; And He has set darkness in my paths.

Heavy judgments.

Lam 3:7 He has hedged me in so that I cannot get out; He has made my chain heavy.

Hos 2:6 "Therefore, behold, I will hedge up your way

with thorns, And wall her in, So that she cannot find her paths.

God's concern for Israel.

Matt 21:33 "Hear another parable: There was a certain landowner who planted a vineyard and set a hedge around it, dug a winepress in it and built a tower. And he leased it to vinedressers and went into a far country.

The way of the lazy.

Prov 15:19 The way of the lazy *man is* like a hedge of thorns, But the way of the upright *is* a highway.

(Broken down) the taking away of protection.

Ps 80:12 Why have You broken down her hedges, So that all who pass by the way pluck her *fruit?*

Is 5:5 And now, please let Me tell you what I will do to My vineyard: I will take away its hedge, and it shall be burned; *And* break down its wall, and it shall be trampled down.

HEEDFULNESS

Commanded.

Ex 23:13 "And in all that I have said to you, be circumspect and make no mention of the name of other gods, nor let it be heard from your mouth.

Prov 4:25–27 Let your eyes look straight ahead, And your eyelids look right before you. **26** Ponder the path of your feet, And let all your ways be established. **27** Do not turn to the right or the left; Remove your foot from evil.

Necessary

In the care of the soul.

Deut 4:9 Only take heed to yourself, and diligently keep yourself, lest you forget the things your eyes have seen, and lest they depart from your heart all the days of your life. And teach them to your children and your grandchildren,

In the house and worship of God.

Eccl 5:1 Walk prudently when you go to the house of God; and draw near to hear rather than to give the sacrifice of fools, for they do not know that they do evil.

In what we hear.

Mark 4:24 Then He said to them, "Take heed what you hear. With the same measure you use, it will be measured to you; and to you who hear, more will be given.

In how we hear.

Luke 8:18 Therefore take heed how you hear. For whoever has, to him *more* will be given; and whoever does not have, even what he seems to have will be taken from him."

In keeping God's commandments.

Josh 22:5 But take careful heed to do the commandment and the law which Moses the servant of the LORD commanded you, to love the LORD your God, to walk in all His ways, to keep His commandments, to hold fast to Him, and to serve Him with all your heart and with all your soul."

In conduct.

Eph 5:15 See then that you walk circumspectly, not as fools but as wise,

In speech.

Prov 13:3 He who guards his mouth preserves his life, *But* he who opens wide his lips shall have destruction.

James 1:19 So then, my beloved brethren, let every man be swift to hear, slow to speak, slow to wrath;

In worldly company.

Ps 39:1 I said, "I will guard my ways, Lest I sin with my tongue; I will restrain my mouth with a muzzle, While the wicked are before me."

Col 4:5 Walk in wisdom toward those *who are* outside, redeeming the time.

In giving judgment.

1 Chr 19:6–7 When the people of Ammon saw that they had made themselves repulsive to David, Hanun and the people of Ammon sent a thousand talents of silver to hire for themselves chariots and horsemen from Mesopotamia, from Syrian Maacah, and from Zobah. **7** So they hired for themselves thirty-two thousand chariots, with the king of Maacah and his people, who came and encamped before Medeba. Also the people of Ammon gathered together from their cities, and came to battle.

Against sin.

Heb 12:15–16 looking carefully lest anyone fall short of the grace of God; lest any root of bitterness springing up cause trouble, and by this many become defiled; **16** lest there *be* any fornicator or profane person like Esau, who for one morsel of food sold his birthright.

Against unbelief.

Heb 3:12 Beware, brethren, lest there be in any of you an evil heart of unbelief in departing from the living God;

Against idolatry.

Deut 4:15–16 "Take careful heed to yourselves, for you saw no form when the LORD spoke to you at Horeb out of the midst of the fire, **16** lest you act corruptly and make for yourselves a carved image in the form of any figure: the likeness of male or female,

Against false Christs and false prophets.

Matt 24:4 And Jesus answered and said to them: "Take heed that no one deceives you.

Matt 24:5 For many will come in My name, saying, 'I am the Christ,' and will deceive many.

Matt 24:23–24 "Then if anyone says to you, 'Look, here *is* the Christ!' or 'There!' do not believe *it*. **24** For false christs and false prophets will rise and show great signs and wonders to deceive, if possible, even the elect.

Against false teachers.

Phil 3:2 Beware of dogs, beware of evil workers, beware of the mutilation!

Col 2:8 Beware lest anyone cheat you through philosophy and empty deceit, according to the tradition of men, according to the basic principles of the world, and not according to Christ.

2 Pet 3:16–17 as also in all his epistles, speaking in them of these things, in which are some things hard to understand, which untaught and unstable *people* twist to their own destruction, as *they do* also the rest of the Scriptures. **17** You therefore, beloved, since you know *this* beforehand, beware lest you also fall from your own steadfastness, being led away with the error of the wicked;

Against presumption.

1 Cor 10:12 Therefore let him who thinks he stands take heed lest he fall.

Promises to those who exhibit.

1 Kin 2:4 that the LORD may fulfill His word which He spoke concerning me, saying, 'If your sons take heed to their way, to walk before Me in truth with all their heart and with all their soul,' He said, 'you shall not lack a man on the throne of Israel.'

1 Chr 22:13 Then you will prosper, if you take care to fulfill the statutes and judgments with which the LORD charged Moses concerning Israel. Be strong and of good courage; do not fear nor be dismayed.

HEIRS

All believers become, through Christ.

Rom 4:13 For the promise that he would be the heir of the world *was* not to Abraham or to his seed through the law, but through the righteousness of faith.

Rom 8:17 and if children, then heirs—heirs of God and joint heirs with Christ, if indeed we suffer with *Him,* that we may also be glorified together.

Gal 3:29 And if you *are* Christ's, then you are Abraham's seed, and heirs according to the promise.

Eph 1:11 In Him also we have obtained an inheritance, being predestined according to the purpose of Him who works all things according to the counsel of His will,

Col 1:12 giving thanks to the Father who has qualified us to be partakers of the inheritance of the saints in the light.

Believers are joint, with Christ.

Rom 8:17 and if children, then heirs—heirs of God and joint heirs with Christ, if indeed we suffer with *Him,* that we may also be glorified together.

Will inherit eternal salvation.

Titus 3:7 that having been justified by His grace we should become heirs according to the hope of eternal life.

Receive promise of eternal inheritance.

Heb 6:12 that you do not become sluggish, but imitate those who through faith and patience inherit the promises.

Heb 9:15 And for this reason He is the Mediator of the new covenant, by means of death, for the redemption of the transgressions under the first covenant, that those who are called may receive the promise of the eternal inheritance.

1 Pet 1:4 to an inheritance incorruptible and undefiled and that does not fade away, reserved in heaven for you,

Of the spiritual blessing accompanying the Abrahamic covenant.

Gal 3:29 And if you *are* Christ's, then you are Abraham's seed, and heirs according to the promise.

Gal 4:28 Now we, brethren, as Isaac *was,* are children of promise.

Gentiles are fellow.

Eph 3:6 that the Gentiles should be fellow heirs, of the same body, and partakers of His promise in Christ through the gospel,

HELL (HADES)

The place of disembodied spirits

Which Christ visited.

Acts 2:31 he, foreseeing this, spoke concerning the resurrection of the Christ, that His soul was not left in Hades, nor did His flesh see corruption.

1 Pet 3:19 by whom also He went and preached to the spirits in prison,

A place of torment.

Luke 16:23 And being in torments in Hades, he lifted up his eyes and saw Abraham afar off, and Lazarus in his bosom.

2 Thess 1:9 These shall be punished with everlasting destruction from the presence of the Lord and from the glory of His power,

Described as

Everlasting punishment.

Matt 25:46 And these will go away into everlasting punishment, but the righteous into eternal life."

Everlasting fire.

Matt 25:41 "Then He will also say to those on the left hand, 'Depart from Me, you cursed, into the everlasting fire prepared for the devil and his angels:

Everlasting burnings.

Is 33:14 The sinners in Zion are afraid; Fearfulness has seized the hypocrites: "Who among us shall dwell with the devouring fire? Who among us shall dwell with everlasting burnings?"

A furnace of fire.

Matt 13:42 and will cast them into the furnace of fire. There will be wailing and gnashing of teeth.

Cf. Matt 13:50

A lake of fire.

Rev 20:15 And anyone not found written in the Book of Life was cast into the lake of fire.

Fire and brimstone.

Rev 14:10 he himself shall also drink of the wine of the wrath of God, which is poured out full strength into the cup of His indignation. He shall be tormented with fire and brimstone in the presence of the holy angels and in the presence of the Lamb.

Unquenchable fire.

Matt 3:12 His winnowing fan *is* in His hand, and He will thoroughly clean out His threshing floor, and gather His wheat into the barn; but He will burn up the chaff with unquenchable fire."

Outer darkness.

Matt 8:12 But the sons of the kingdom will be cast out into outer darkness. There will be weeping and gnashing of teeth."

Devouring fire.

Is 33:14 The sinners in Zion are afraid; Fearfulness has seized the hypocrites: "Who among us shall dwell with the devouring fire? Who among us shall dwell with everlasting burnings?"

Prepared for the devil, etc.

Matt 25:41 "Then He will also say to those on the left hand, 'Depart from Me, you cursed, into the everlasting fire prepared for the devil and his angels:

Demons are confined in, until the judgment day.

2 Pet 2:4 For if God did not spare the angels who sinned, but cast *them* down to hell and delivered *them* into chains of darkness, to be reserved for judgment;

Jude 1:6 And the angels who did not keep their proper domain, but left their own abode, He has reserved in everlasting chains under darkness for the judgment of the great day;

Punishment of, is eternal.

Is 33:14 The sinners in Zion are afraid; Fearfulness has seized the hypocrites: "Who among us shall dwell with the devouring fire? Who among us shall dwell with everlasting burnings?"

Rev 20:10 The devil, who deceived them, was cast into the lake of fire and brimstone where the beast and the false prophet *are*. And they will be tormented day and night forever and ever.

The wicked shall be turned into.

Ps 9:17 The wicked shall be turned into hell, *And* all the nations that forget God.

Human power cannot preserve from.

Ezek 32:27 They do not lie with the mighty *Who are* fallen of the uncircumcised, Who have gone down to hell with their weapons of war; They have laid their swords under their heads, But their iniquities will be on their bones, Because of the terror of the mighty in the land of the living.

Body and soul suffer in.

Matt 5:29 If your right eye causes you to sin, pluck it out and cast *it* from you; for it is more profitable for you that one of your members perish, than for your whole body to be cast into hell.

Matt 10:28 And do not fear those who kill the body but cannot kill the soul. But rather fear Him who is able to destroy both soul and body in hell.

The wise avoid.

Prov 15:24 The way of life *winds* upward for the wise, That he may turn away from hell below.

Believers endeavor to keep others from.

Prov 23:14 You shall beat him with a rod, And deliver his soul from hell.

Jude 1:23 but others save with fear, pulling *them* out of the fire, hating even the garment defiled by the flesh.

The society of the wicked leads to.

Prov 5:5 Her feet go down to death, Her steps lay hold of hell.

Prov 9:18 But he does not know that the dead *are* there, *That* her guests *are* in the depths of hell.

The beast, false prophets, and the devil shall be cast into.

Rev 19:20 Then the beast was captured, and with him the false prophet who worked signs in his presence, by which he deceived those who received the mark of the beast and those who worshiped his image.

These two were cast alive into the lake of fire burning with brimstone.

Rev 20:10 The devil, who deceived them, was cast into the lake of fire and brimstone where the beast and the false prophet *are*. And they will be tormented day and night forever and ever.

The powers of, cannot prevail against the church.

Matt 16:18 And I also say to you that you are Peter, and on this rock I will build My church, and the gates of Hades shall not prevail against it.

Described.

Is 30:33 For Tophet *was* established of old, Yes, for the king it is prepared. He has made *it* deep and large; Its pyre *is* fire with much wood; The breath of the LORD, like a stream of brimstone, Kindles it.

HERBS, ETC.

Called the grass of the field and the green.

2 Kin 19:26 Therefore their inhabitants had little power; They were dismayed and confounded; They were *as* the grass of the field And the green herb, *As* the grass on the housetops And *grain* blighted before it is grown.

God

Created.

Gen 1:11–12 Then God said, "Let the earth bring forth grass, the herb *that* yields seed, *and* the fruit tree *that* yields fruit according to its kind, whose seed *is* in itself, on the earth"; and it was so. **12** And the earth brought forth grass, the herb *that* yields seed according to its kind, and the tree *that* yields fruit, whose seed *is* in itself according to its kind. And God saw that *it was* good.

Gen 2:5 before any plant of the field was in the earth and before any herb of the field had grown. For the LORD God had not caused it to rain on the earth, and *there was* no man to till the ground;

Causes them to grow.

Job 38:27 To satisfy the desolate waste, And cause to spring forth the growth of tender grass?

Ps 104:14 He causes the grass to grow for the cattle, And vegetation for the service of man, That he may bring forth food from the earth,

Each kind of, contains its own seed.

Gen 1:11–12 Then God said, "Let the earth bring forth grass, the herb *that* yields seed, *and* the fruit tree *that* yields fruit according to its kind, whose seed *is* in itself, on the earth"; and it was so. **12** And the earth brought forth grass, the herb *that* yields seed according to its kind, and the tree *that* yields fruit, whose seed *is* in itself according to its kind. And God saw that *it was* good.

Given as food to man.

Gen 1:28–29 Then God blessed them, and God said to them, "Be fruitful and multiply; fill the earth and subdue it; have dominion over the fish of the sea, over the birds of the air, and over every living thing that moves on the earth." **29** And God said, "See, I have given you every herb *that* yields seed which *is* on the face of all the earth, and every tree whose fruit yields seed; to you it shall be for food.

Gen 9:3 Every moving thing that lives shall be food for you. I have given you all things, even as the green herbs.

Found in

The fields.

Jer 12:4 How long will the land mourn, And the herbs of every field wither? The beasts and birds are consumed, For the wickedness of those who dwell there, Because they said, "He will not see our final end."

The mountains.

Prov 27:25 *When* the hay is removed, and the tender grass shows itself, And the herbs of the mountains are gathered in,

The marshes.

Job 8:11 "Can the papyrus grow up without a marsh? Can the reeds flourish without water?

The deserts.

Job 24:5 Indeed, *like* wild donkeys in the desert, They go out to their work, searching for food. The wilderness *yields* food for them *and* for *their* children.

Jer 17:6 For he shall be like a shrub in the desert, And shall not see when good comes, But shall inhabit the parched places in the wilderness, *In* a salt land *which is* not inhabited.

Cultivated in gardens.

Deut 11:10 For the land which you go to possess *is* not like the land of Egypt from which you have come, where you sowed your seed and watered *it* by foot, as a vegetable garden;

1 Kin 21:2 So Ahab spoke to Naboth, saying, "Give me your vineyard, that I may have it for a vegetable garden, because it *is* near, next to my house; and for it I will give you a vineyard better than it. *Or,* if it seems good to you, I will give you its worth in money."

Cultivated for food.

Prov 15:17 Better *is* a dinner of herbs where love is, Than a fatted calf with hatred.

Heb 6:7 For the earth which drinks in the rain that often comes upon it, and bears herbs useful for those by whom it is cultivated, receives blessing from God;

Require rain to grow.

Deut 32:2 Let my teaching drop as the rain, My speech distill as the dew, As raindrops on the tender herb, And as showers on the grass.

Job 38:26–27 To cause it to rain on a land *where there is* no one, A wilderness in which *there is* no man; **27** To satisfy the desolate waste, And cause to spring forth the growth of tender grass?

Mode of watering, alluded to.

Deut 11:10 For the land which you go to possess *is* not like the land of Egypt from which you have come, where you sowed your seed and watered *it* by foot, as a vegetable garden;

Those mentioned in Scripture

Aloe.

Song 4:14 Spikenard and saffron, Calamus and cinnamon, With all trees of frankincense, Myrrh and aloes, With all the chief spices—

Anise.

Matt 23:23 "Woe to you, scribes and Pharisees, hypo-

crites! For you pay tithe of mint and anise and cummin, and have neglected the weightier *matters* of the law: justice and mercy and faith. These you ought to have done, without leaving the others undone.

Barley.

Ex 9:31 Now the flax and the barley were struck, for the barley *was* in the head and the flax *was* in bud.

2 Sam 14:30 So he said to his servants, "See, Joab's field is near mine, and he has barley there; go and set it on fire." And Absalom's servants set the field on fire.

Beans.

2 Sam 17:28 brought beds and basins, earthen vessels and wheat, barley and flour, parched *grain* and beans, lentils and parched *seeds,*

Bulrushes.

Ex 2:3 But when she could no longer hide him, she took an ark of bulrushes for him, daubed it with asphalt and pitch, put the child in it, and laid *it* in the reeds by the river's bank.

Is 58:5 Is it a fast that I have chosen, A day for a man to afflict his soul? *Is it* to bow down his head like a bulrush, And to spread out sackcloth and ashes? Would you call this a fast, And an acceptable day to the LORD?

Calamus.

Song 4:14 Spikenard and saffron, Calamus and cinnamon, With all trees of frankincense, Myrrh and aloes, With all the chief spices—

Cummin.

Is 28:27 For the black cummin is not threshed with a threshing sledge, Nor is a cartwheel rolled over the cummin; But the black cummin is beaten out with a stick, And the cummin with a rod.

Matt 23:23 "Woe to you, scribes and Pharisees, hypocrites! For you pay tithe of mint and anise and cummin, and have neglected the weightier *matters* of the law: justice and mercy and faith. These you ought to have done, without leaving the others undone.

Cucumber.

Num 11:5 We remember the fish which we ate freely in Egypt, the cucumbers, the melons, the leeks, the onions, and the garlic;

Is 1:8 So the daughter of Zion is left as a booth in a vineyard, As a hut in a garden of cucumbers, As a besieged city.

Black cummin.

Is 28:25 When he has leveled its surface, Does he not sow the black cummin And scatter the cummin, Plant the wheat in rows, The barley in the appointed place, And the spelt in its place?

Is 28:27 For the black cummin is not threshed with a threshing sledge, Nor is a cartwheel rolled over the cummin; But the black cummin is beaten out with a stick, And the cummin with a rod.

Flax.

Ex 9:31 Now the flax and the barley were struck, for the barley *was* in the head and the flax *was* in bud.

Garlic.

Num 11:5 We remember the fish which we ate freely in Egypt, the cucumbers, the melons, the leeks, the onions, and the garlic;

Gourds.

2 Kin 4:39 So one went out into the field to gather herbs, and found a wild vine, and gathered from it a lapful of wild gourds, and came and sliced *them* into the pot of stew, though they did not know *what they were.*

Grass.

Num 22:4 So Moab said to the elders of Midian, "Now this company will lick up everything around us, as an ox licks up the grass of the field." And Balak the son of Zippor *was* king of the Moabites at that time.

Shrub.

Jer 17:6 For he shall be like a shrub in the desert, And shall not see when good comes, But shall inhabit the parched places in the wilderness, *In* a salt land *which is* not inhabited.

Juniper.

Jer 48:6 "Flee, save your lives! And be like the juniper in the wilderness.

Hyssop.

Ex 12:22 And you shall take a bunch of hyssop, dip *it* in the blood that *is* in the basin, and strike the lintel and the two doorposts with the blood that *is* in the basin. And none of you shall go out of the door of his house until morning.

1 Kin 4:33 Also he spoke of trees, from the cedar tree of Lebanon even to the hyssop that springs out of the wall; he spoke also of animals, of birds, of creeping things, and of fish.

Leeks.

Num 11:5 We remember the fish which we ate freely in Egypt, the cucumbers, the melons, the leeks, the onions, and the garlic;

Lentils.

Gen 25:34 And Jacob gave Esau bread and stew of lentils; then he ate and drank, arose, and went his way. Thus Esau despised *his* birthright.

Mandrakes.

Gen 30:14 Now Reuben went in the days of wheat harvest and found mandrakes in the field, and brought them to his mother Leah. Then Rachel said to Leah, "Please give me *some* of your son's mandrakes."

Song 7:13 The mandrakes give off a fragrance, And at our gates *are* pleasant *fruits,* All manner, new and old, Which I have laid up for you, my beloved.

Mallow.

Job 30:4 Who pluck mallow by the bushes, And broom tree roots *for* their food.

Millet.

Ezek 4:9 "Also take for yourself wheat, barley, beans, lentils, millet, and spelt; put them into one vessel, and make bread of them for yourself. *During* the number of days that you lie on your side, three hundred and ninety days, you shall eat it.

Melons.

Num 11:5 We remember the fish which we ate freely in Egypt, the cucumbers, the melons, the leeks, the onions, and the garlic;

Mint.

Matt 23:23 "Woe to you, scribes and Pharisees, hypocrites! For you pay tithe of mint and anise and cummin, and have neglected the weightier *matters* of the law: justice and mercy and faith. These you ought to have done, without leaving the others undone.

Myrrh.

Song 4:14 Spikenard and saffron, Calamus and cinnamon, With all trees of frankincense, Myrrh and aloes, With all the chief spices—

Onions.

Num 11:5 We remember the fish which we ate freely in Egypt, the cucumbers, the melons, the leeks, the onions, and the garlic;

Reeds.

Ex 2:3 But when she could no longer hide him, she took an ark of bulrushes for him, daubed it with asphalt and pitch, put the child in it, and laid *it* in the reeds by the river's bank.

Job 8:11 "Can the papyrus grow up without a marsh? Can the reeds flourish without water?

Job 40:21 He lies under the lotus trees, In a covert of reeds and marsh.

Is 19:6 The rivers will turn foul; The brooks of defense will be emptied and dried up; The reeds and rushes will wither.

Spelt.

Ex 9:32 But the wheat and the spelt were not struck, for they *are* late crops.

Saffron.

Song 4:14 Spikenard and saffron, Calamus and cinnamon, With all trees of frankincense, Myrrh and aloes, With all the chief spices—

Spikenard.

Song 4:14 Spikenard and saffron, Calamus and cinnamon, With all trees of frankincense, Myrrh and aloes, With all the chief spices—

Tares.

Matt 13:30 Let both grow together until the harvest, and at the time of harvest I will say to the reapers, "First gather together the tares and bind them in bundles to burn them, but gather the wheat into my barn." ' "

Wheat.

Ex 9:32 But the wheat and the spelt were not struck, for they *are* late crops.

Jer 12:13 They have sown wheat but reaped thorns; They have put themselves to pain *but* do not profit. But be ashamed of your harvest Because of the fierce anger of the LORD."

Bitter, used at Passover.

Ex 12:8 Then they shall eat the flesh on that night; roasted in fire, with unleavened bread *and* with bitter *herbs* they shall eat it.

Num 9:11 On the fourteenth day of the second month, at twilight, they may keep it. They shall eat it with unleavened bread and bitter herbs.

Poisonous, not fit for man's use.

2 Kin 4:39–40 So one went out into the field to gather herbs, and found a wild vine, and gathered from it a lapful of wild gourds, and came and sliced *them* into the pot of stew, though they did not know *what they were.* **40** Then they served it to the men to eat. Now it happened, as they were eating the stew, that they cried out and said, "Man of God, *there is* death in the pot!" And they could not eat *it.*

Destroyed by

Hail and lightning.

Ex 9:22–25 Then the LORD said to Moses, "Stretch out your hand toward heaven, that there may be hail in all the land of Egypt—on man, on beast, and on every herb of the field, throughout the land of Egypt." **23** And Moses stretched out his rod toward heaven; and the LORD sent thunder and hail, and fire darted to the ground. And the LORD rained hail on the land of Egypt. **24** So there was hail, and fire mingled with the hail, so very heavy that there was none like it in all the land of Egypt since it became a nation. **25** And the hail struck throughout the whole land of Egypt, all that *was* in the field, both man and beast; and the hail struck every herb of the field and broke every tree of the field.

Locusts, etc.

Ex 10:12 Then the LORD said to Moses, "Stretch out your hand over the land of Egypt for the locusts, that they may come upon the land of Egypt, and eat every herb of the land—all that the hail has left."

Ex 10:15 For they covered the face of the whole earth, so that the land was darkened; and they ate every herb of the land and all the fruit of the trees which the hail had left. So there remained nothing green on the trees or on the plants of the field throughout all the land of Egypt.

Ps 105:34–35 He spoke, and locusts came, Young locusts without number, **35** And ate up all the vegetation in their land, And devoured the fruit of their ground.

Drought.

Is 42:15 I will lay waste the mountains and hills, And dry up all their vegetation; I will make the rivers coastlands, And I will dry up the pools.

The Jews can tithe.

Luke 11:42 "But woe to you Pharisees! For you tithe mint and rue and all manner of herbs, and pass by justice and the love of God. These you ought to have done, without leaving the others undone.

Were sometimes used instead of animal food by some believers.

Rom 14:2 For one believes he may eat all things, but he who is weak eats *only* vegetables.

Illustrative of

The wicked.

2 Kin 19:26 Therefore their inhabitants had little power; They were dismayed and confounded; They were *as* the grass of the field And the green herb, *As* the grass on the housetops And *grain* blighted before it is grown.

Ps 37:2 For they shall soon be cut down like the grass, And wither as the green herb.

(Dew on) grace given to believers.

Is 18:4 For so the LORD said to me, "I will take My rest, And I will look from My dwelling place Like clear heat in sunshine, Like a cloud of dew in the heat of harvest."

HERESY

Described as another gospel.

Gal 1:8–9 But even if we, or an angel from heaven, preach any other gospel to you than what we have preached to you, let him be accursed. **9** As we have said before, so now I say again, if anyone preaches any other gospel to you than what you have received, let him be accursed.

By nature is destructive.

2 Pet 2:1 But there were also false prophets among the people, even as there will be false teachers among you, who will secretly bring in destructive heresies, even denying the Lord who bought them, *and* bring on themselves swift destruction.

Spreads like cancer.

2 Tim 2:17 And their message will spread like cancer. Hymenaeus and Philetus are of this sort,

Believers should disassociate themselves from those who teach.

2 John 1:10 If anyone comes to you and does not bring this doctrine, do not receive him into your house nor greet him;

Types of,

Worship of angels.

Col 2:18 Let no one cheat you of your reward, taking delight in *false* humility and worship of angels, intruding into those things which he has not seen, vainly puffed up by his fleshly mind,

Profane and idle babblings.

2 Tim 2:16 But shun profane *and* idle babblings, for they will increase to more ungodliness.

Denial of believers' bodily resurrection.

2 Tim 2:18 who have strayed concerning the truth, saying that the resurrection is already past; and they overthrow the faith of some.

Denial of the Lord.

2 Pet 2:1 But there were also false prophets among the people, even as there will be false teachers among you, who will secretly bring in destructive heresies, even denying the Lord who bought them, *and* bring on themselves swift destruction.

Teachers of,

Hymenaeus and Philetus.

2 Tim 2:17 And their message will spread like cancer. Hymenaeus and Philetus are of this sort,

Nicolaitans.

Rev 2:6 But this you have, that you hate the deeds of the Nicolaitans, which I also hate.

Balaam.

Rev 2:14 But I have a few things against you, because you have there those who hold the doctrine of Balaam, who taught Balak to put a stumbling block before the children of Israel, to eat things sacrificed to idols, and to commit sexual immorality.

Cf. Num 22–25

HIGH PLACES, THE

Used for idolatrous worship.

1 Kin 11:7–8 Then Solomon built a high place for Chemosh the abomination of Moab, on the hill that *is* east of Jerusalem, and for Molech the abomination of the people of Ammon. **8** And he did likewise for all his foreign wives, who burned incense and sacrificed to their gods.

God sometimes worshiped on.

1 Sam 9:12 And they answered them and said, "Yes, there he is, just ahead of you. Hurry now; for today he came to this city, because there is a sacrifice of the people today on the high place.

1 Kin 3:2 Meanwhile the people sacrificed at the high places, because there was no house built for the name of the LORD until those days.

1 Kin 3:4 Now the king went to Gibeon to sacrifice there, for that *was* the great high place: Solomon offered a thousand burnt offerings on that altar.

2 Chr 33:17 Nevertheless the people still sacrificed on the high places, *but* only to the LORD their God.

Those mentioned in Scripture

Gibeon.

1 Kin 3:4 Now the king went to Gibeon to sacrifice there, for that *was* the great high place: Solomon offered a thousand burnt offerings on that altar.

Arnon.

Num 21:28 "For fire went out from Heshbon, A flame from the city of Sihon; It consumed Ar of Moab, The lords of the heights of the Arnon.

Baal.

Num 22:41 So it was, the next day, that Balak took Balaam and brought him up to the high places of Baal, that from there he might observe the extent of the people.

Tophet.

Jer 7:31 And they have built the high places of Tophet, which *is* in the Valley of the Son of Hinnom, to burn their sons and their daughters in the fire, which I did not command, nor did it come into My heart.

Bamah.

Ezek 20:29 Then I said to them, 'What *is* this high place to which you go?' So its name is called Bamah to this day." '

Aven.

Hos 10:8 Also the high places of Aven, the sin of Israel, Shall be destroyed. The thorn and thistle shall grow on their altars; They shall say to the mountains, "Cover us!" And to the hills, "Fall on us!"

Adorned with tapestry.

Ezek 16:16 You took some of your garments and adorned multicolored high places for yourself, and played the harlot on them. *Such things* should not happen, nor be.

Surrounded with groves of trees.

1 Kin 14:23 For they also built for themselves high places, *sacred* pillars, and wooden images on every high hill and under every green tree.

Built by

Solomon.

1 Kin 11:7 Then Solomon built a high place for Chemosh the abomination of Moab, on the hill that *is*

east of Jerusalem, and for Molech the abomination of the people of Ammon.

Jeroboam.

1 Kin 12:31 He made shrines on the high places, and made priests from every class of people, who were not of the sons of Levi.

Jehoram.

2 Chr 21:11 Moreover he made high places in the mountains of Judah, and caused the inhabitants of Jerusalem to commit harlotry, and led Judah astray.

Ahaz.

2 Chr 28:25 And in every single city of Judah he made high places to burn incense to other gods, and provoked to anger the LORD God of his fathers.

Manasseh.

2 Kin 21:3 For he rebuilt the high places which Hezekiah his father had destroyed; he raised up altars for Baal, and made a wooden image, as Ahab king of Israel had done; and he worshiped all the host of heaven and served them.

2 Chr 33:3 For he rebuilt the high places which Hezekiah his father had broken down; he raised up altars for the Baals, and made wooden images; and he worshiped all the host of heaven and served them.

People of Judah.

1 Kin 14:23 For they also built for themselves high places, *sacred* pillars, and wooden images on every high hill and under every green tree.

People of Israel.

2 Kin 17:9 Also the children of Israel secretly did against the LORD their God things that *were* not right, and they built for themselves high places in all their cities, from watchtower to fortified city.

Priests ordained for.

1 Kin 12:32 Jeroboam ordained a feast on the fifteenth day of the eighth month, like the feast that *was* in Judah, and offered sacrifices on the altar. So he did at Bethel, sacrificing to the calves that he had made. And at Bethel he installed the priests of the high places which he had made.

1 Kin 13:33 After this event Jeroboam did not turn from his evil way, but again he made priests from every class of people for the high places; whoever wished, he consecrated him, and he became *one* of the priests of the high places.

Sacrifices and incense offered to idols upon.

2 Kin 12:3 But the high places were not taken away; the people still sacrificed and burned incense on the high places.

2 Kin 16:4 And he sacrificed and burned incense on the high places, on the hills, and under every green tree.

Enchantments used upon.

Num 23:3 Then Balaam said to Balak, "Stand by your burnt offering, and I will go; perhaps the LORD will come to meet me, and whatever He shows me I will tell you." So he went to a desolate height.

Num 24:1 Now when Balaam saw that it pleased the LORD to bless Israel, he did not go as at other times, to seek to use sorcery, but he set his face toward the wilderness.

Of the Canaanites to be destroyed.

Num 33:52 then you shall drive out all the inhabitants of the land from before you, destroy all their engraved stones, destroy all their molded images, and demolish all their high places;

The Jews

Built, in their cities.

2 Kin 17:9 Also the children of Israel secretly did against the LORD their God things that *were* not right, and they built for themselves high places in all their cities, from watchtower to fortified city.

Built, in all their streets.

Ezek 16:24 *that* you also built for yourself a shrine, and made a high place for yourself in every street.

Ezek 16:31 "You erected your shrine at the head of every road, and built your high place in every street. Yet you were not like a harlot, because you scorned payment.

Condemned for building.

Ezek 16:23–35 "Then it was so, after all your wickedness—'Woe, woe to you!' says the Lord GOD— **24** *that* you also built for yourself a shrine, and made a high place for yourself in every street. **25** You built your high places at the head of every road, and made your beauty to be abhorred. You offered yourself to everyone who passed by, and multiplied your acts of harlotry. **26** You also committed harlotry with the Egyptians, your very fleshly neighbors, and increased your acts of harlotry to provoke Me to anger. **27** "Behold, therefore, I stretched out My hand against you, diminished your allotment, and gave you up to the will of those who hate you, the daughters of the Philistines, who were ashamed of your lewd behavior. **28** You also played the harlot with the Assyrians, because you were insatiable; indeed you played the harlot with them and still were not satisfied. **29** Moreover you multiplied your acts of harlotry as far as the land of the trader, Chaldea; and even then you were not satisfied. **30** "How degenerate is your heart!" says the Lord GOD, "seeing you do all these *things,* the deeds of a brazen harlot. **31** "You erected your shrine at the head of every road, and built your high place in every street. Yet you were not like a harlot, because you scorned payment. **32** *You are* an adulterous wife, *who* takes strangers instead of her husband. **33** Men make payment to all harlots, but you made your payments to all your lovers, and hired them to come to you from all around for your harlotry. **34** You are the opposite of *other* women in your harlotry, because no one solicited you to be a harlot. In that you gave payment but no payment was given you, therefore you are the opposite." **35** 'Now then, O harlot, hear the word of the LORD!

Provoked God with.

1 Kin 14:22–23 Now Judah did evil in the sight of the LORD, and they provoked Him to jealousy with their sins which they committed, more than all that their fathers had done. **23** For they also built for themselves high places, *sacred* pillars, and wooden images on every high hill and under every green tree.

Ps 78:58 For they provoked Him to anger with their high places, And moved Him to jealousy with their carved images.

Threatened with destruction of.

Lev 26:30 I will destroy your high places, cut down your incense altars, and cast your carcasses on the lifeless forms of your idols; and My soul shall abhor you.

Punished for.

2 Kin 17:11 There they burned incense on all the high places, like the nations whom the LORD had carried away before them; and they did wicked things to provoke the LORD to anger,

2 Kin 17:18 Therefore the LORD was very angry with Israel, and removed them from His sight; there was none left but the tribe of Judah alone.

Destroyed by

Asa, partially.

2 Chr 14:3 for he removed the altars of the foreign *gods* and the high places, and broke down the *sacred* pillars and cut down the wooden images.

2 Chr 14:5 He also removed the high places and the incense altars from all the cities of Judah, and the kingdom was quiet under him.

2 Chr 15:17 But the high places were not removed from Israel. Nevertheless the heart of Asa was loyal all his days.

Jehoshaphat.

2 Chr 17:6 And his heart took delight in the ways of the LORD; moreover he removed the high places and wooden images from Judah.

Hezekiah.

2 Kin 18:4 He removed the high places and broke the *sacred* pillars, cut down the wooden image and broke in pieces the bronze serpent that Moses had made; for until those days the children of Israel burned incense to it, and called it Nehushtan.

2 Chr 31:1 Now when all this was finished, all Israel who were present went out to the cities of Judah and broke the sacred pillars in pieces, cut down the wooden images, and threw down the high places and the altars—from all Judah, Benjamin, Ephraim, and Manasseh—until they had utterly destroyed them all. Then all the children of Israel returned to their own cities, every man to his possession.

Josiah.

2 Kin 23:8 And he brought all the priests from the cities of Judah, and defiled the high places where the priests had burned incense, from Geba to Beersheba; also he broke down the high places at the gates which *were* at the entrance of the Gate of Joshua the governor of the city, which *were* to the left of the city gate.

2 Chr 34:3 For in the eighth year of his reign, while he was still young, he began to seek the God of his father David; and in the twelfth year he began to purge Judah and Jerusalem of the high places, the wooden images, the carved images, and the molded images.

Not removed by

Jehoash.

2 Kin 12:3 But the high places were not taken away; the people still sacrificed and burned incense on the high places.

Amaziah.

2 Kin 14:4 However the high places were not taken

away, and the people still sacrificed and burned incense on the high places.

Azariah.

2 Kin 15:4 except that the high places were not removed; the people still sacrificed and burned incense on the high places.

Jotham.

2 Kin 15:35 However the high places were not removed; the people still sacrificed and burned incense on the high places. He built the Upper Gate of the house of the LORD.

HIGH PRIEST, THE

Specially called of God.

Ex 28:1–2 "Now take Aaron your brother, and his sons with him, from among the children of Israel, that he may minister to Me as priest, Aaron *and* Aaron's sons: Nadab, Abihu, Eleazar, and Ithamar. **2** And you shall make holy garments for Aaron your brother, for glory and for beauty.

Heb 5:4 And no man takes this honor to himself, but he who is called by God, just as Aaron *was.*

Consecrated to his office.

Ex 40:13 You shall put the holy garments on Aaron, and anoint him and consecrate him, that he may minister to Me as priest.

Lev 8:12 And he poured some of the anointing oil on Aaron's head and anointed him, to consecrate him.

Was called

The priest.

Ex 29:30 That son who becomes priest in his place shall put them on for seven days, when he enters the tabernacle of meeting to minister in the holy *place.*

Neh 7:65 And the governor said to them that they should not eat of the most holy things till a priest could consult with the Urim and Thummim.

God's high priest.

Acts 23:4 And those who stood by said, "Do you revile God's high priest?"

Ruler of the people.

Ex 22:28 "You shall not revile God, nor curse a ruler of your people.

Acts 23:5 Then Paul said, "I did not know, brethren, that he was the high priest; for it is written, *'You shall not speak evil of a ruler of your people.' "*

The office of, hereditary.

Ex 29:29 "And the holy garments of Aaron shall be his sons' after him, to be anointed in them and to be consecrated in them.

Next in rank to the king.

Lam 2:6 He has done violence to His tabernacle, *As if it were* a garden; He has destroyed His place of assembly; The LORD has caused The appointed feasts and Sabbaths to be forgotten in Zion. In His burning indignation He has spurned the king and the priest.

Often exercised chief civil power.

1 Sam 4:18 Then it happened, when he made mention of the ark of God, that Eli fell off the seat backward by the side of the gate; and his neck was broken and

he died, for the man was old and heavy. And he had judged Israel forty years.

Duties of,

Offering gifts and sacrifices.

Heb 5:1 For every high priest taken from among men is appointed for men in things *pertaining* to God, that he may offer both gifts and sacrifices for sins.

Lighting the sacred lamps.

Ex 30:8 And when Aaron lights the lamps at twilight, he shall burn incense on it, a perpetual incense before the LORD throughout your generations.

Num 8:3 And Aaron did so; he arranged the lamps to face toward the front of the lampstand, as the LORD commanded Moses.

Making atonement in the most holy place once a year.

Heb 9:7 But into the second part the high priest *went* alone once a year, not without blood, which he offered for himself and *for* the people's sins *committed* in ignorance;

Cf. Lev 16:1–34

Bearing before the Lord the names of Israel for a memorial.

Ex 28:12 And you shall put the two stones on the shoulders of the ephod *as* memorial stones for the sons of Israel. So Aaron shall bear their names before the LORD on his two shoulders as a memorial.

Ex 28:29 "So Aaron shall bear the names of the sons of Israel on the breastplate of judgment over his heart, when he goes into the holy *place,* as a memorial before the LORD continually.

Inquiring of God by Urim and Thummim.

1 Sam 23:9–12 When David knew that Saul plotted evil against him, he said to Abiathar the priest, "Bring the ephod here." **10** Then David said, "O LORD God of Israel, Your servant has certainly heard that Saul seeks to come to Keilah to destroy the city for my sake. **11** Will the men of Keilah deliver me into his hand? Will Saul come down, as Your servant has heard? O LORD God of Israel, I pray, tell Your servant." And the LORD said, "He will come down." **12** Then David said, "Will the men of Keilah deliver me and my men into the hand of Saul?" And the LORD said, "They will deliver *you.*"

1 Sam 30:7–8 Then David said to Abiathar the priest, Ahimelech's son, "Please bring the ephod here to me." And Abiathar brought the ephod to David. **8** So David inquired of the LORD, saying, "Shall I pursue this troop? Shall I overtake them?" And He answered him, "Pursue, for you shall surely overtake *them* and without fail recover *all.*"

Consecrating the Levites. **Num 8:5–20**

Appointing priests to offices.

1 Sam 2:36 And it shall come to pass that everyone who is left in your house will come *and* bow down to him for a piece of silver and a morsel of bread, and say, 'Please, put me in one of the priestly positions, that I may eat a piece of bread.' ' "

Taking charge of money collected in the sacred treasury.

2 Kin 12:10 So it was, whenever they saw that *there was* much money in the chest, that the king's scribe and the high priest came up and put it in bags, and counted the money that was found in the house of the LORD.

2 Kin 22:4 "Go up to Hilkiah the high priest, that he may count the money which has been brought into the house of the LORD, which the doorkeepers have gathered from the people.

Presiding in the superior court.

Matt 26:3 Then the chief priests, the scribes, and the elders of the people assembled at the palace of the high priest, who was called Caiaphas,

Matt 26:57–62 And those who had laid hold of Jesus led *Him* away to Caiaphas the high priest, where the scribes and the elders were assembled. **58** But Peter followed Him at a distance to the high priest's courtyard. And he went in and sat with the servants to see the end. **59** Now the chief priests, the elders, and all the council sought false testimony against Jesus to put Him to death, **60** but found none. Even though many false witnesses came forward, they found none. But at last two false witnesses came forward **61** and said, "This *fellow* said, 'I am able to destroy the temple of God and to build it in three days.' " **62** And the high priest arose and said to Him, "Do You answer nothing? What *is it* these men testify against You?"

Acts 5:21–28 And when they heard *that*, they entered the temple early in the morning and taught. But the high priest and those with him came and called the council together, with all the elders of the children of Israel, and sent to the prison to have them brought. **22** But when the officers came and did not find them in the prison, they returned and reported, **23** saying, "Indeed we found the prison shut securely, and the guards standing outside before the doors; but when we opened them, we found no one inside!" **24** Now when the high priest, the captain of the temple, and the chief priests heard these things, they wondered what the outcome would be. **25** So one came and told them, saying, "Look, the men whom you put in prison are standing in the temple and teaching the people!" **26** Then the captain went with the officers and brought them without violence, for they feared the people, lest they should be stoned. **27** And when they had brought them, they set *them* before the council. And the high priest asked them, **28** saying, "Did we not strictly command you not to teach in this name? And look, you have filled Jerusalem with your doctrine, and intend to bring this Man's blood on us!"

Acts 23:1–5 Then Paul, looking earnestly at the council, said, "Men *and* brethren, I have lived in all good conscience before God until this day." **2** And the high priest Ananias commanded those who stood by him to strike him on the mouth. **3** Then Paul said to him, "God will strike you, *you* whitewashed wall! For you sit to judge me according to the law, and do you command me to be struck contrary to the law?" **4** And those who stood by said, "Do you revile God's high priest?" **5** Then Paul said, "I did not know, brethren, that he was the high priest; for it is written, 'You shall not speak evil of a ruler of your people.' "

Taking the census of the people.

Num 1:3 from twenty years old and above—all who *are able to* go to war in Israel. You and Aaron shall number them by their armies.

Blessing the people.

Lev 9:22–23 Then Aaron lifted his hand toward the people, blessed them, and came down from offering the sin offering, the burnt offering, and peace offerings. **23** And Moses and Aaron went into the tabernacle of meeting, and came out and blessed the people. Then the glory of the LORD appeared to all the people,

Sometimes enabled to prophesy.

John 11:49–52 And one of them, Caiaphas, being high priest that year, said to them, "You know nothing at all, **50** nor do you consider that it is expedient for us that one man should die for the people, and not that the whole nation should perish." **51** Now this he did not say on his own *authority;* but being high priest that year he prophesied that Jesus would die for the nation, **52** and not for that nation only, but also that He would gather together in one the children of God who were scattered abroad.

Assisted by a deputy.

2 Sam 15:24 There was Zadok also, and all the Levites with him, bearing the ark of the covenant of God. And they set down the ark of God, and Abiathar went up until all the people had finished crossing over from the city.

Luke 3:2 while Annas and Caiaphas were high priests, the word of God came to John the son of Zacharias in the wilderness.

The deputy of,

Called the second priest.

2 Kin 25:18 And the captain of the guard took Seraiah the chief priest, Zephaniah the second priest, and the three doorkeepers.

Had oversight of the tabernacle.

Num 4:16 "The appointed duty of Eleazar the son of Aaron the priest *is* the oil for the light, the sweet incense, the daily grain offering, the anointing oil, the oversight of all the tabernacle, of all that *is* in it, with the sanctuary and its furnishings."

Had oversight of the Levites.

Num 3:32 And Eleazar the son of Aaron the priest *was to be* chief over the leaders of the Levites, *with* oversight of those who kept charge of the sanctuary.

Was to marry a virgin of Aaron's family.

Lev 21:13–14 And he shall take a wife in her virginity. **14** A widow or a divorced woman or a defiled woman *or* a harlot—these he shall not marry; but he shall take a virgin of his own people as wife.

Forbidden to mourn for anyone.

Lev 21:10–12 'He who *is* the high priest among his brethren, on whose head the anointing oil was poured and who is consecrated to wear the garments, shall not uncover his head nor tear his clothes; **11** nor shall he go near any dead body, nor defile himself for his father or his mother; **12** nor shall he go out of the sanctuary, nor profane the sanctuary of his God; for the consecration of the anointing oil of his God *is* upon him: I *am* the LORD.

To be tender and compassionate.

Heb 5:2 He can have compassion on those who are ignorant and going astray, since he himself is also subject to weakness.

Needed to sacrifice for himself.

Heb 5:1–3 For every high priest taken from among men is appointed for men in things *pertaining* to God, that he may offer both gifts and sacrifices for sins. **2** He can have compassion on those who are ignorant and going astray, since he himself is also subject to weakness. **3** Because of this he is required as for the people, so also for himself, to offer *sacrifices* for sins.

Special garments of,

Ephod with its fancy straps.

Ex 28:6–7 and they shall make the ephod of gold, blue, purple, *and* scarlet *thread,* and fine woven linen, artistically worked. **7** It shall have two shoulder straps joined at its two edges, and *so* it shall be joined together.

Sash.

Ex 28:4 And these *are* the garments which they shall make: a breastplate, an ephod, a robe, a skillfully woven tunic, a turban, and a sash. So they shall make holy garments for Aaron your brother and his sons, that he may minister to Me as priest.

Ex 28:39 "You shall skillfully weave the tunic of fine linen *thread,* you shall make the turban of fine linen, and you shall make the sash of woven work.

Woven tunic.

Ex 28:4 And these *are* the garments which they shall make: a breastplate, an ephod, a robe, a skillfully woven tunic, a turban, and a sash. So they shall make holy garments for Aaron your brother and his sons, that he may minister to Me as priest.

Ex 28:39 "You shall skillfully weave the tunic of fine linen *thread,* you shall make the turban of fine linen, and you shall make the sash of woven work.

Robe of the ephod.

Ex 28:31–35 "You shall make the robe of the ephod all of blue. **32** There shall be an opening for his head in the middle of it; it shall have a woven binding all around its opening, like the opening in a coat of mail, so that it does not tear. **33** And upon its hem you shall make pomegranates of blue, purple, and scarlet, all around its hem, and bells of gold between them all around: **34** a golden bell and a pomegranate, a golden bell and a pomegranate, upon the hem of the robe all around. **35** And it shall be upon Aaron when he ministers, and its sound will be heard when he goes into the holy *place* before the LORD and when he comes out, that he may not die.

Breastplate.

Ex 28:15–29 "You shall make the breastplate of judgment. Artistically woven according to the workmanship of the ephod you shall make it: of gold, blue, purple, and scarlet *thread,* and fine woven linen, you shall make it. **16** It shall be doubled into a square: a span *shall be* its length, and a span *shall be* its width. **17** And you shall put settings of stones in it, four rows of stones: *The first* row *shall be* a sardius, a topaz, and an emerald; *this shall be* the first row; **18** the second row *shall be* a turquoise, a sapphire, and a diamond; **19** the third row, a jacinth, an agate, and an amethyst; **20** and the fourth row, a beryl, an onyx, and a jasper. They shall be set in gold settings. **21** And the stones shall have the names of the sons of Israel, twelve according to their names, *like* the engravings of a signet,

each one with its own name; they shall be according to the twelve tribes. **22** "You shall make chains for the breastplate at the end, like braided cords of pure gold. **23** And you shall make two rings of gold for the breastplate, and put the two rings on the two ends of the breastplate. **24** Then you shall put the two braided *chains* of gold in the two rings which are on the ends of the breastplate; **25** and the *other* two ends of the two braided *chains* you shall fasten to the two settings, and put them on the shoulder straps of the ephod in the front. **26** "You shall make two rings of gold, and put them on the two ends of the breastplate, on the edge of it, which is on the inner side of the ephod. **27** And two *other* rings of gold you shall make, and put them on the two shoulder straps, underneath the ephod toward its front, right at the seam above the intricately woven band of the ephod. **28** They shall bind the breastplate by means of its rings to the rings of the ephod, using a blue cord, so that it is above the intricately woven band of the ephod, and so that the breastplate does not come loose from the ephod. **29** "So Aaron shall bear the names of the sons of Israel on the breastplate of judgment over his heart, when he goes into the holy *place,* as a memorial before the LORD continually.

Linen turban.

Ex 28:4 And these *are* the garments which they shall make: a breastplate, an ephod, a robe, a skillfully woven tunic, a turban, and a sash. So they shall make holy garments for Aaron your brother and his sons, that he may minister to Me as priest.

Ex 28:39 "You shall skillfully weave the tunic of fine linen *thread,* you shall make the turban of fine linen, and you shall make the sash of woven work.

Plate or crown of gold, etc.

Ex 28:36–38 "You shall also make a plate of pure gold and engrave on it, *like* the engraving of a signet: HOLINESS TO THE LORD. **37** And you shall put it on a blue cord, that it may be on the turban; it shall be on the front of the turban. **38** So it shall be on Aaron's forehead, that Aaron may bear the iniquity of the holy things which the children of Israel hallow in all their holy gifts; and it shall always be on his forehead, that they may be accepted before the LORD.

Made by divine wisdom given to Bezalel, etc.

Ex 28:3 So you shall speak to all *who are* gifted artisans, whom I have filled with the spirit of wisdom, that they may make Aaron's garments, to consecrate him, that he may minister to Me as priest.

Ex 36:1 "And Bezalel and Aholiab, and every gifted artisan in whom the LORD has put wisdom and understanding, to know how to do all manner of work for the service of the sanctuary, shall do according to all that the LORD has commanded."

Ex 39:1 Of the blue, purple, and scarlet *thread* they made garments of ministry, for ministering in the holy *place,* and made the holy garments for Aaron, as the LORD had commanded Moses.

Were for beauty and ornament.

Ex 28:2 And you shall make holy garments for Aaron your brother, for glory and for beauty.

Worn at his consecration.

Lev 8:7 And he put the tunic on him, girded him with the sash, clothed him with the robe, and put the ephod on him; and he girded him with the intricately woven band of the ephod, and with it tied *the ephod* on him.

Lev 8:9 And he put the turban on his head. Also on the turban, on its front, he put the golden plate, the holy crown, as the LORD had commanded Moses.

Worn seven days after consecration.

Ex 29:30 That son who becomes priest in his place shall put them on for seven days, when he enters the tabernacle of meeting to minister in the holy *place.*

Descended to his successors.

Ex 29:29 "And the holy garments of Aaron shall be his sons' after him, to be anointed in them and to be consecrated in them.

Wore the ordinary priest's garments when making atonement in the holy place.

Lev 16:4 He shall put the holy linen tunic and the linen trousers on his body; he shall be girded with a linen sash, and with the linen turban he shall be attired. These *are* holy garments. Therefore he shall wash his body in water, and put them on.

Office of, promised to the posterity of Phinehas for his zeal.

Num 25:12–13 Therefore say, 'Behold, I give to him My covenant of peace; 13 and it shall be to him and his descendants after him a covenant of an everlasting priesthood, because he was zealous for his God, and made atonement for the children of Israel.' "

Family of Eli disqualified from office of, for bad conduct.

1 Sam 2:27–36 Then a man of God came to Eli and said to him, "Thus says the LORD: 'Did I not clearly reveal Myself to the house of your father when they were in Egypt in Pharaoh's house? 28 Did I not choose him out of all the tribes of Israel *to be* My priest, to offer upon My altar, to burn incense, and to wear an ephod before Me? And did I not give to the house of your father all the offerings of the children of Israel made by fire? 29 Why do you kick at My sacrifice and My offering which I have commanded *in My* dwelling place, and honor your sons more than Me, to make yourselves fat with the best of all the offerings of Israel My people?' 30 Therefore the LORD God of Israel says: 'I said indeed *that* your house and the house of your father would walk before Me forever.' But now the LORD says: 'Far be it from Me; for those who honor Me I will honor, and those who despise Me shall be lightly esteemed. 31 Behold, the days are coming that I will cut off your arm and the arm of your father's house, so that there will not be an old man in your house. 32 And you will see an enemy *in* My dwelling place, *despite* all the good which God does for Israel. And there shall not be an old man in your house forever. 33 But any of your men *whom* I do not cut off from My altar shall consume your eyes and grieve your heart. And all the descendants of your house shall die in the flower of their age. 34 Now this *shall be* a sign to you that will come upon your two sons, on Hophni and Phinehas: in one day they shall die, both of them. 35 Then I will raise up for Myself a faithful priest *who* shall do according to what *is* in My heart and in My mind. I will build him a sure house, and he shall walk before My anointed

forever. 36 And it shall come to pass that everyone who is left in your house will come *and* bow down to him for a piece of silver and a morsel of bread, and say, "Please, put me in one of the priestly positions, that I may eat a piece of bread." ' "

Sometimes deposed by the kings.

1 Kin 2:27 So Solomon removed Abiathar from being priest to the LORD, that he might fulfill the word of the LORD which He spoke concerning the house of Eli at Shiloh.

Office of, made annual by the Romans.

John 11:49–51 And one of them, Caiaphas, being high priest that year, said to them, "You know nothing at all, 50 nor do you consider that it is expedient for us that one man should die for the people, and not that the whole nation should perish." 51 Now this he did not say on his own *authority;* but being high priest that year he prophesied that Jesus would die for the nation,

Acts 4:6 as well as Annas the high priest, Caiaphas, John, and Alexander, and as many as were of the family of the high priest, were gathered together at Jerusalem.

Typified Christ in

Being called of God.

Heb 5:4–5 And no man takes this honor to himself, but he who is called by God, just as Aaron *was.* 5 So also Christ did not glorify Himself to become High Priest, *but it* was He who said to Him: *"You are My Son, Today I have begotten You."*

His title.

Heb 3:1 Therefore, holy brethren, partakers of the heavenly calling, consider the Apostle and High Priest of our confession, Christ Jesus,

His appointment.

Is 61:1 "The Spirit of the Lord GOD *is* upon Me, Because the LORD has anointed Me To preach good tidings to the poor; He has sent Me to heal the brokenhearted, To proclaim liberty to the captives, And the opening of the prison to *those who are* bound;

John 1:32–34 And John bore witness, saying, "I saw the Spirit descending from heaven like a dove, and He remained upon Him. 33 I did not know Him, but He who sent me to baptize with water said to me, 'Upon whom you see the Spirit descending, and remaining on Him, this is He who baptizes with the Holy Spirit.' 34 And I have seen and testified that this is the Son of God."

Making atonement.

Lev 16:33 then he shall make atonement for the Holy Sanctuary, and he shall make atonement for the tabernacle of meeting and for the altar, and he shall make atonement for the priests and for all the people of the assembly.

Heb 2:17 Therefore, in all things He had to be made like *His* brethren, that He might be a merciful and faithful High Priest in things *pertaining* to God, to make propitiation for the sins of the people.

The splendid dress.

Ex 28:2 And you shall make holy garments for Aaron your brother, for glory and for beauty.

John 1:14 And the Word became flesh and dwelt among

us, and we beheld His glory, the glory as of the only begotten of the Father, full of grace and truth.

Being liable to temptation.

Heb 2:18 For in that He Himself has suffered, being tempted, He is able to aid those who are tempted.

Compassion and sympathy for the weak and ignorant.

Heb 4:15 For we do not have a High Priest who cannot sympathize with our weaknesses, but was in all *points* tempted as *we are, yet* without sin.

Heb 5:1–2 For every high priest taken from among men is appointed for men in things *pertaining* to God, that he may offer both gifts and sacrifices for sins. **2** He can have compassion on those who are ignorant and going astray, since he himself is also subject to weakness.

Marrying a virgin.

Lev 21:13–14 And he shall take a wife in her virginity. **14** A widow or a divorced woman or a defiled woman *or* a harlot—these he shall not marry; but he shall take a virgin of his own people as wife.

2 Cor 11:2 For I am jealous for you with godly jealousy. For I have betrothed you to one husband, that I may present *you as* a chaste virgin to Christ.

Holiness of office.

Lev 21:15 Nor shall he profane his posterity among his people, for I the LORD sanctify him.' "

Heb 7:26 For such a High Priest was fitting for us, *who is* holy, harmless, undefiled, separate from sinners, and has become higher than the heavens;

Performing by himself all the services on Day of Atonement.

Heb 1:3 who being the brightness of *His* glory and the express image of His person, and upholding all things by the word of His power, when He had by Himself purged our sins, sat down at the right hand of the Majesty on high,

Cf. Lev 16:1–34

Bearing the names of Israel upon his heart.

Ex 28:29 "So Aaron shall bear the names of the sons of Israel on the breastplate of judgment over his heart, when he goes into the holy *place,* as a memorial before the LORD continually.

Alone entering into the Most Holy Place.

Heb 4:14 Seeing then that we have a great High Priest who has passed through the heavens, Jesus the Son of God, let us hold fast *our* confession.

Heb 9:7 But into the second part the high priest *went* alone once a year, not without blood, which he offered for himself and *for* the people's sins *committed* in ignorance;

Heb 9:12 Not with the blood of goats and calves, but with His own blood He entered the Most Holy Place once for all, having obtained eternal redemption.

Heb 9:24 For Christ has not entered the holy places made with hands, *which are* copies of the true, but into heaven itself, now to appear in the presence of God for us;

Interceding.

Num 16:43–48 Then Moses and Aaron came before the tabernacle of meeting. **44** And the LORD spoke to Moses, saying, **45** "Get away from among this congre-

gation, that I may consume them in a moment." And they fell on their faces. **46** So Moses said to Aaron, "Take a censer and put fire in it from the altar, put incense *on it,* and take it quickly to the congregation and make atonement for them; for wrath has gone out from the LORD. The plague has begun." **47** Then Aaron took *it* as Moses commanded, and ran into the midst of the assembly; and already the plague had begun among the people. So he put in the incense and made atonement for the people. **48** And he stood between the dead and the living; so the plague was stopped.

Heb 7:25 Therefore He is also able to save to the uttermost those who come to God through Him, since He always lives to make intercession for them.

Blessing.

Lev 9:22–23 Then Aaron lifted his hand toward the people, blessed them, and came down from offering the sin offering, the burnt offering, and peace offerings. **23** And Moses and Aaron went into the tabernacle of meeting, and came out and blessed the people. Then the glory of the LORD appeared to all the people,

Acts 3:26 To you first, God, having raised up His Servant Jesus, sent Him to bless you, in turning away every one *of you* from your iniquities."

Inferior to Christ in

Needing to make atonement for his own sins.

Heb 5:2–3 He can have compassion on those who are ignorant and going astray, since he himself is also subject to weakness. **3** Because of this he is required as for the people, so also for himself, to offer *sacrifices* for sins.

Heb 7:26–28 For such a High Priest was fitting for us, *who is* holy, harmless, undefiled, separate from sinners, and has become higher than the heavens; **27** who does not need daily, as those high priests, to offer up sacrifices, first for His own sins and then for the people's, for this He did once for all when He offered up Himself. **28** For the law appoints as high priests men who have weakness, but the word of the oath, which came after the law, *appoints* the Son who has been perfected forever.

Heb 9:7 But into the second part the high priest *went* alone once a year, not without blood, which he offered for himself and *for* the people's sins *committed* in ignorance;

Being of the order of Aaron.

Heb 6:20 where the forerunner has entered for us, *even* Jesus, having become High Priest forever according to the order of Melchizedek.

Heb 7:11–17 Therefore, if perfection were through the Levitical priesthood (for under it the people received the law), what further need *was there* that another priest should rise according to the order of Melchizedek, and not be called according to the order of Aaron? **12** For the priesthood being changed, of necessity there is also a change of the law. **13** For He of whom these things are spoken belongs to another tribe, from which no man has officiated at the altar. **14** For *it is* evident that our Lord arose from Judah, of which tribe Moses spoke nothing concerning priesthood. **15** And it is yet far more evident if, in the likeness of Melchizedek, there arises another priest

16 who has come, not according to the law of a fleshly commandment, but according to the power of an endless life. 17 For He testifies: *"You are a priest forever According to the order of Melchizedek."*

Heb 8:1–6 Now *this is* the main point of the things we are saying: We have such a High Priest, who is seated at the right hand of the throne of the Majesty in the heavens, **2** a Minister of the sanctuary and of the true tabernacle which the Lord erected, and not man. **3** For every high priest is appointed to offer both gifts and sacrifices. Therefore *it is* necessary that this One also have something to offer. **4** For if He were on earth, He would not be a priest, since there are priests who offer the gifts according to the law; **5** who serve the copy and shadow of the heavenly things, as Moses was divinely instructed when he was about to make the tabernacle. For He said, *"See that you make all things according to the pattern shown you on the mountain."* **6** But now He has obtained a more excellent ministry, inasmuch as He is also Mediator of a better covenant, which was established on better promises.

Being made priest without an oath.

Heb 7:20–22 And inasmuch as *He was* not *made priest* without an oath **21** (for they have become priests without an oath, but He with an oath by Him who said to Him: *"The LORD has sworn And will not relent, 'You are a priest forever According to the order of Melchizedek' "*), **22** by so much more Jesus has become a surety of a better covenant.

Not being able to continue.

Heb 7:23–24 Also there were many priests, because they were prevented by death from continuing. **24** But He, because He continues forever, has an unchangeable priesthood.

Offering oftentimes the same sacrifices.

Heb 9:25–26 not that He should offer Himself often, as the high priest enters the Most Holy Place every year with blood of another— **26** He then would have had to suffer often since the foundation of the world; but now, once at the end of the ages, He has appeared to put away sin by the sacrifice of Himself.

Heb 9:28 so Christ was offered once to bear the sins of many. To those who eagerly wait for Him He will appear a second time, apart from sin, for salvation.

Heb 10:11–12 And every priest stands ministering daily and offering repeatedly the same sacrifices, which can never take away sins. **12** But this Man, after He had offered one sacrifice for sins forever, sat down at the right hand of God,

Heb 10:14 For by one offering He has perfected forever those who are being sanctified.

Entering into Most Holy Place every year.

Heb 9:7 But into the second part the high priest *went* alone once a year, not without blood, which he offered for himself and *for* the people's sins *committed* in ignorance.

Heb 9:12 Not with the blood of goats and calves, but with His own blood He entered the Most Holy Place once for all, having obtained eternal redemption.

Heb 9:25 not that He should offer Himself often, as the high priest enters the Most Holy Place every year with blood of another—

HIGHWAYS

Roads for public use.

Num 20:19 So the children of Israel said to him, "We will go by the Highway, and if I or my livestock drink any of your water, then I will pay for it; let me only pass through on foot, nothing *more*."

Deut 2:27 'Let me pass through your land; I will keep strictly to the road, and I will turn neither to the right nor to the left.

One called the King's Highway.

Num 20:17 Please let us pass through your country. We will not pass through fields or vineyards, nor will we drink water from wells; we will go along the King's Highway; we will not turn aside to the right hand or to the left until we have passed through your territory.' "

Marked out by heaps of stones.

Jer 31:21 "Set up signposts, Make landmarks; Set your heart toward the highway, The way in *which* you went. Turn back, O virgin of Israel, Turn back to these your cities.

Generally broad.

Judg 20:32 And the children of Benjamin said, "They *are* defeated before us, as at first." But the children of Israel said, "Let us flee and draw them away from the city to the highways."

Judg 20:45 Then they turned and fled toward the wilderness to the rock of Rimmon; and they cut down five thousand of them on the highways. Then they pursued them relentlessly up to Gidom, and killed two thousand of them.

Matt 7:13 "Enter by the narrow gate; for wide *is* the gate and broad *is* the way that leads to destruction, and there are many who go in by it.

Generally straight.

1 Sam 6:12 Then the cows headed straight for the road to Beth Shemesh, *and* went along the highway, lowing as they went, and did not turn aside to the right hand or the left. And the lords of the Philistines went after them to the border of Beth Shemesh.

Is 40:3 The voice of one crying in the wilderness: "Prepare the way of the LORD; Make straight in the desert A highway for our God.

Made to all cities of refuge.

Deut 19:2–3 you shall separate three cities for yourself in the midst of your land which the LORD your God is giving you to possess. **3** You shall prepare roads for yourself, and divide into three parts the territory of your land which the LORD your God is giving you to inherit, that any manslayer may flee there.

Often made in deserts.

Is 40:3 The voice of one crying in the wilderness: "Prepare the way of the LORD; Make straight in the desert A highway for our God.

Infested with

Serpents.

Gen 49:17 Dan shall be a serpent by the way, A viper by the path, That bites the horse's heels So that its rider shall fall backward.

Wild beasts.

1 Kin 13:24 When he was gone, a lion met him on the road and killed him. And his corpse was thrown on the road, and the donkey stood by it. The lion also stood by the corpse.

Is 35:9 No lion shall be there, Nor shall *any* ravenous beast go up on it; It shall not be found there. But the redeemed shall walk *there,*

Robbers.

Jer 3:2 "Lift up your eyes to the desolate heights and see: Where have you not lain *with men?* By the road you have sat for them Like an Arabian in the wilderness; And you have polluted the land With your harlotries and your wickedness.

Luke 10:30–33 Then Jesus answered and said: "A certain *man* went down from Jerusalem to Jericho, and fell among thieves, who stripped him of his clothing, wounded *him,* and departed, leaving *him* half dead. **31** Now by chance a certain priest came down that road. And when he saw him, he passed by on the other side. **32** Likewise a Levite, when he arrived at the place, came and looked, and passed by on the other side. **33** But a certain Samaritan, as he journeyed, came where he was. And when he saw him, he had compassion.

Beggars sat by sides of.

Matt 20:30 And behold, two blind men sitting by the road, when they heard that Jesus was passing by, cried out, saying, "Have mercy on us, O Lord, Son of David!"

Mark 10:46 Now they came to Jericho. As He went out of Jericho with His disciples and a great multitude, blind Bartimaeus, the son of Timaeus, sat by the road begging.

Often obstructed.

Jer 18:15 "Because My people have forgotten Me, They have burned incense to worthless idols. And they have caused themselves to stumble in their ways, *From* the ancient paths, To walk in pathways and not on a highway,

All obstructions removed from, before persons of distinction.

Is 40:3–4 The voice of one crying in the wilderness: "Prepare the way of the LORD; Make straight in the desert A highway for our God. **4** Every valley shall be exalted And every mountain and hill brought low; The crooked places shall be made straight And the rough places smooth;

Matt 3:3 For this is he who was spoken of by the prophet Isaiah, saying: *"The voice of one crying in the wilderness: 'Prepare the way of the LORD; Make His paths straight.' "*

Byways more secure in times of danger.

Judg 5:6 "In the days of Shamgar, son of Anath, In the days of Jael, The highways were deserted, And the travelers walked along the byways.

Desolation of, threatened as a punishment.

Lev 26:22 I will also send wild beasts among you, which shall rob you of your children, destroy your livestock, and make you few in number; and your highways shall be desolate.

Is 33:8 The highways lie waste, The traveling man ceas-

es. He has broken the covenant, He has despised the cities, He regards no man.

Illustrative of

Christ.

John 14:6 Jesus said to him, "I am the way, the truth, and the life. No one comes to the Father except through Me.

The way of holiness.

Is 35:8 A highway shall be there, and a road, And it shall be called the Highway of Holiness. The unclean shall not pass over it, But it *shall be* for others. Whoever walks the road, although a fool, Shall not go astray.

Facilities for the restoration of the Jews.

Is 11:16 There will be a highway for the remnant of His people Who will be left from Assyria, As it was for Israel In the day that he came up from the land of Egypt.

Is 62:10 Go through, Go through the gates! Prepare the way for the people; Build up, Build up the highway! Take out the stones, Lift up a banner for the peoples!

(Made in the deserts) facilities for the spread of the gospel.

Is 40:3 The voice of one crying in the wilderness: "Prepare the way of the LORD; Make straight in the desert A highway for our God.

Is 43:19 Behold, I will do a new thing, Now it shall spring forth; Shall you not know it? I will even make a road in the wilderness *And* rivers in the desert.

(Narrow) the way of life.

Matt 7:14 Because narrow *is* the gate and difficult *is* the way which leads to life, and there are few who find it.

(Broad) the way to destruction.

Matt 7:13 "Enter by the narrow gate; for wide *is* the gate and broad *is* the way that leads to destruction, and there are many who go in by it.

HITTITES, THE

Descended from Canaan's son Heth.

Gen 10:15 Canaan begot Sidon his firstborn, and Heth;

Other names for,

Sons of Heth.

Gen 23:3 Then Abraham stood up from before his dead, and spoke to the sons of Heth, saying,

Gen 23:20 So the field and the cave that *is* in it were deeded to Abraham by the sons of Heth as property for a burial place.

Children of Heth.

Gen 23:5 And the sons of Heth answered Abraham, saying to him,

One of the seven nations of Canaan.

Deut 7:1 "When the LORD your God brings you into the land which you go to possess, and has cast out many nations before you, the Hittites and the Girgashites and the Amorites and the Canaanites and the Perizzites and the Hivites and the Jebusites, seven nations greater and mightier than you,

Dwelt in Hebron.

Gen 23:2–3 So Sarah died in Kirjath Arba (that *is,* Hebron) in the land of Canaan, and Abraham came to mourn for Sarah and to weep for her. 3 Then Abraham stood up from before his dead, and spoke to the sons of Heth, saying,

Gen 23:10 Now Ephron dwelt among the sons of Heth; and Ephron the Hittite answered Abraham in the presence of the sons of Heth, all who entered at the gate of his city, saying,

Governed by kings.

1 Kin 10:29 Now a chariot that was imported from Egypt cost six hundred *shekels* of silver, and a horse one hundred and fifty; and thus, through their agents, they exported *them* to all the kings of the Hittites and the kings of Syria.

2 Kin 7:6 For the LORD had caused the army of the Syrians to hear the noise of chariots and the noise of horses—the noise of a great army; so they said to one another, "Look, the king of Israel has hired against us the kings of the Hittites and the kings of the Egyptians to attack us!"

Land of, promised to Israel.

Gen 15:20 the Hittites, the Perizzites, the Rephaim,

Ex 3:8 So I have come down to deliver them out of the hand of the Egyptians, and to bring them up from that land to a good and large land, to a land flowing with milk and honey, to the place of the Canaanites and the Hittites and the Amorites and the Perizzites and the Hivites and the Jebusites.

Israel commanded to destroy.

Deut 7:1–2 "When the LORD your God brings you into the land which you go to possess, and has cast out many nations before you, the Hittites and the Girgashites and the Amorites and the Canaanites and the Perizzites and the Hivites and the Jebusites, seven nations greater and mightier than you, **2** and when the LORD your God delivers them over to you, you shall conquer them *and* utterly destroy them. You shall make no covenant with them nor show mercy to them.

Deut 7:24 And He will deliver their kings into your hand, and you will destroy their name from under heaven; no one shall be able to stand against you until you have destroyed them.

Part of their land given to Caleb.

Josh 14:13 And Joshua blessed him, and gave Hebron to Caleb the son of Jephunneh as an inheritance.

Not entirely destroyed by Israel.

Judg 3:5 Thus the children of Israel dwelt among the Canaanites, the Hittites, the Amorites, the Perizzites, the Hivites, and the Jebusites.

The remnant of, performed forced labor in the reign of Solomon.

1 Kin 9:20–21 All the people *who were* left of the Amorites, Hittites, Perizzites, Hivites, and Jebusites, who *were* not of the children of Israel— **21** that is, their descendants who were left in the land after them, whom the children of Israel had not been able to destroy completely—from these Solomon raised forced labor, as it is to this day.

Luz built in the country of.

Judg 1:26 And the man went to the land of the Hittites, built a city, and called its name Luz, which *is* its name to this day.

Intermarriages with, by

Esau.

Gen 36:2 Esau took his wives from the daughters of Canaan: Adah the daughter of Elon the Hittite; Aholibamah the daughter of Anah, the daughter of Zibeon the Hivite;

Solomon.

1 Kin 11:1–2 But King Solomon loved many foreign women, as well as the daughter of Pharaoh: women of the Moabites, Ammonites, Edomites, Sidonians, *and* Hittites— **2** from the nations of whom the LORD had said to the children of Israel, "You shall not intermarry with them, nor they with you. Surely they will turn away your hearts after their gods." Solomon clung to these in love.

Israel after conquest of Canaan.

Judg 3:5–6 Thus the children of Israel dwelt among the Canaanites, the Hittites, the Amorites, the Perizzites, the Hivites, and the Jebusites. **6** And they took their daughters to be their wives, and gave their daughters to their sons; and they served their gods.

Israelites after the captivity.

Ezra 9:1 When these things were done, the leaders came to me, saying, "The people of Israel and the priests and the Levites have not separated themselves from the peoples of the lands, with respect to the abominations of the Canaanites, the Hittites, the Perizzites, the Jebusites, the Ammonites, the Moabites, the Egyptians, and the Amorites.

Descent from, illustrative of the degradation of the Jews.

Ezek 16:3 and say, 'Thus says the Lord GOD to Jerusalem: "Your birth and your nativity *are* from the land of Canaan; your father *was* an Amorite and your mother a Hittite.

Remarkable persons of,

Ephron.

Gen 49:30 in the cave that *is* in the field of Machpelah, which *is* before Mamre in the land of Canaan, which Abraham bought with the field of Ephron the Hittite as a possession for a burial place.

Ahimelech.

1 Sam 26:6 Then David answered, and said to Ahimelech the Hittite and to Abishai the son of Zeruiah, brother of Joab, saying, "Who will go down with me to Saul in the camp?" And Abishai said, "I will go down with you."

Uriah.

2 Sam 11:6 Then David sent to Joab, *saying*, "Send me Uriah the Hittite." And Joab sent Uriah to David.

2 Sam 11:21 Who struck Abimelech the son of Jerubbesheth? Was it not a woman who cast a piece of a millstone on him from the wall, so that he died in Thebez? Why did you go near the wall?'—then you shall say, 'Your servant Uriah the Hittite is dead also.' "

HIVITES, THE

Descended from Canaan.

Gen 10:15 Canaan begot Sidon his firstborn, and Heth;

Gen 10:17 the Hivite, the Arkite, and the Sinite;

Supposed to be the ancient Avim, or Avites.

Deut 2:23 And the Avim, who dwelt in villages as far as Gaza—the Caphtorim, who came from Caphtor, destroyed them and dwelt in their place.)

Josh 13:3 from Sihor, which *is* east of Egypt, as far as the border of Ekron northward (*which* is counted as Canaanite); the five lords of the Philistines—the Gazites, the Ashdodites, the Ashkelonites, the Gittites, and the Ekronites; also the Avites;

One of the seven nations of Canaan.

Deut 7:1 "When the LORD your God brings you into the land which you go to possess, and has cast out many nations before you, the Hittites and the Girgashites and the Amorites and the Canaanites and the Perizzites and the Hivites and the Jebusites, seven nations greater and mightier than you,

Dwelt near Lebanon.

Judg 3:3 *namely,* five lords of the Philistines, all the Canaanites, the Sidonians, and the Hivites who dwelt in Mount Lebanon, from Mount Baal Hermon to the entrance of Hamath.

The Shechemites a people of.

Gen 34:2 And when Shechem the son of Hamor the Hivite, prince of the country, saw her, he took her and lay with her, and violated her.

The Gibeonites a people of.

Josh 9:3 But when the inhabitants of Gibeon heard what Joshua had done to Jericho and Ai,

Josh 9:7 Then the men of Israel said to the Hivites, "Perhaps you dwell among us; so how can we make a covenant with you?"

Esau intermarried with.

Gen 36:2 Esau took his wives from the daughters of Canaan: Adah the daughter of Elon the Hittite; Aholibamah the daughter of Anah, the daughter of Zibeon the Hivite;

Land of, promised to Israel.

Ex 3:8 So I have come down to deliver them out of the hand of the Egyptians, and to bring them up from that land to a good and large land, to a land flowing with milk and honey, to the place of the Canaanites and the Hittites and the Amorites and the Perizzites and the Hivites and the Jebusites.

Ex 23:23 For My Angel will go before you and bring you in to the Amorites and the Hittites and the Perizzites and the Canaanites and the Hivites and the Jebusites; and I will cut them off.

Israel commanded to destroy.

Deut 7:1–2 "When the LORD your God brings you into the land which you go to possess, and has cast out many nations before you, the Hittites and the Girgashites and the Amorites and the Canaanites and the Perizzites and the Hivites and the Jebusites, seven nations greater and mightier than you, **2** and when the LORD your God delivers them over to you, you shall conquer them *and* utterly destroy them. You shall make no covenant with them nor show mercy to them.

Deut 7:24 And He will deliver their kings into your hand, and you will destroy their name from under heaven; no one shall be able to stand against you until you have destroyed them.

A part of, left to test Israel.

Judg 3:3 *namely,* five lords of the Philistines, all the Canaanites, the Sidonians, and the Hivites who dwelt in Mount Lebanon, from Mount Baal Hermon to the entrance of Hamath.

Remnant of, performed forced labor in the reign of Solomon.

1 Kin 9:20–21 All the people *who were* left of the Amorites, Hittites, Perizzites, Hivites, and Jebusites, who *were* not of the children of Israel— **21** that is, their descendants who were left in the land after them, whom the children of Israel had not been able to destroy completely—from these Solomon raised forced labor, as it is to this day.

HOLINESS

Commanded.

Lev 11:45 For I *am* the LORD who brings you up out of the land of Egypt, to be your God. You shall therefore be holy, for I *am* holy.

Lev 20:7 Consecrate yourselves therefore, and be holy, for I *am* the LORD your God.

Rom 12:1 I beseech you therefore, brethren, by the mercies of God, that you present your bodies a living sacrifice, holy, acceptable to God, *which is* your reasonable service.

Eph 5:8 For you were once darkness, but now *you are* light in the Lord. Walk as children of light

Col 3:12 Therefore, as *the* elect of God, holy and beloved, put on tender mercies, kindness, humility, meekness, longsuffering;

Christ

Desires, for His people.

John 17:17 Sanctify them by Your truth. Your word is truth.

Effects, in His people.

Eph 5:25–27 Husbands, love your wives, just as Christ also loved the church and gave Himself for her, **26** that He might sanctify and cleanse her with the washing of water by the word, **27** that He might present her to Himself a glorious church, not having spot or wrinkle or any such thing, but that she should be holy and without blemish.

An example of.

Heb 7:26 For such a High Priest was fitting for us, *who is* holy, harmless, undefiled, separate from sinners, and has become higher than the heavens;

1 Pet 2:21–22 For to this you were called, because Christ also suffered for us, leaving us an example, that you should follow His steps: **22** *"Who committed no sin, Nor was deceit found in His mouth";*

The character of God is the standard of.

Lev 19:2 "Speak to all the congregation of the children of Israel, and say to them: 'You shall be holy, for I the LORD your God *am* holy.

Eph 5:1 Therefore be imitators of God as dear children.

1 Pet 1:15–16 but as He who called you *is* holy, you also be holy in all *your* conduct, **16** because it is written, *"Be holy, for I am holy."*

The character of Christ is the standard of.

Rom 8:29 For whom He foreknew, He also predestined

to be conformed to the image of His Son, that He might be the firstborn among many brethren.

Phil 2:5 Let this mind be in you which was also in Christ Jesus,

1 John 2:6 He who says he abides in Him ought himself also to walk just as He walked.

The gospel the way of.

Is 35:8 A highway shall be there, and a road, And it shall be called the Highway of Holiness. The unclean shall not pass over it, But it *shall be* for others. Whoever walks the road, although a fool, Shall not go astray.

None shall see God without.

Ps 24:3–4 Who may ascend into the hill of the LORD? Or who may stand in His holy place? 4 He who has clean hands and a pure heart, Who has not lifted up his soul to an idol, Nor sworn deceitfully.

Eph 5:5 For this you know, that no fornicator, unclean person, nor covetous man, who is an idolater, has any inheritance in the kingdom of Christ and God.

Heb 12:14 Pursue peace with all *people,* and holiness, without which no one will see the Lord:

Believers

Elected to.

Rom 8:29 For whom He foreknew, He also predestined *to be* conformed to the image of His Son, that He might be the firstborn among many brethren.

Eph 1:4 just as He chose us in Him before the foundation of the world, that we should be holy and without blame before Him in love,

Called to.

1 Thess 4:7 For God did not call us to uncleanness, but in holiness.

2 Tim 1:9 who has saved us and called *us* with a holy calling, not according to our works, but according to His own purpose and grace which was given to us in Christ Jesus before time began,

New man created in.

Eph 4:24 and that you put on the new man which was created according to God, in true righteousness and holiness.

Possess.

1 Cor 3:17 If anyone defiles the temple of God, God will destroy him. For the temple of God is holy, which *temple* you are.

Heb 3:1 Therefore, holy brethren, partakers of the heavenly calling, consider the Apostle and High Priest of our confession, Christ Jesus,

Should follow after.

Heb 12:14 Pursue peace with all *people,* and holiness, without which no one will see the Lord:

Should serve God in.

Luke 1:74–75 To grant us that we, Being delivered from the hand of our enemies, Might serve Him without fear, 75 In holiness and righteousness before Him all the days of our life.

Should present their members as instruments of.

Rom 6:13 And do not present your members *as* instruments of unrighteousness to sin, but present yourselves to God as being alive from the dead, and your members *as* instruments of righteousness to God.

Rom 6:19 I speak in human *terms* because of the weakness of your flesh. For just as you presented your members *as* slaves of uncleanness, and of lawlessness *leading* to *more* lawlessness, so now present your members *as* slaves *of* righteousness for holiness.

Rom 12:1 I beseech you therefore, brethren, by the mercies of God, that you present your bodies a living sacrifice, holy, acceptable to God, *which is* your reasonable service.

Should conduct themselves in.

1 Pet 1:15 but as He who called you *is* holy, you also be holy in all *your* conduct,

2 Pet 3:11 Therefore, since all these things will be dissolved, what manner *of persons* ought you to be in holy conduct and godliness,

Should seek perfection in.

2 Cor 7:1 Therefore, having these promises, beloved, let us cleanse ourselves from all filthiness of the flesh and spirit, perfecting holiness in the fear of God.

Shall be presented to God in.

Col 1:22 in the body of His flesh through death, to present you holy, and blameless, and above reproach in His sight—

1 Thess 3:13 so that He may establish your hearts blameless in holiness before our God and Father at the coming of our Lord Jesus Christ with all His saints.

Shall continue in, forever.

Luke 1:75 In holiness and righteousness before Him all the days of our life.

Rev 22:11 He who is unjust, let him be unjust still; he who is filthy, let him be filthy still; he who is righteous, let him be righteous still; he who is holy, let him be holy still."

Behavior of aged women should reflect.

Titus 2:3 the older women likewise, that they be reverent in behavior, not slanderers, not given to much wine, teachers of good things—

Promise to women who continue in.

1 Tim 2:15 Nevertheless she will be saved in childbearing if they continue in faith, love, and holiness, with self-control.

Promised to God's people.

Is 35:8 A highway shall be there, and a road, And it shall be called the Highway of Holiness. The unclean shall not pass over it, But it *shall be* for others. Whoever walks the road, although a fool, Shall not go astray.

Obad 1:17 "But on Mount Zion there shall be deliverance, And there shall be holiness; The house of Jacob shall possess their possessions.

Zech 14:20–21 In that day "HOLINESS TO THE LORD" shall be *engraved* on the bells of the horses. The pots in the LORD's house shall be like the bowls before the altar. 21 Yes, every pot in Jerusalem and Judah shall be holiness to the LORD of hosts. Everyone who sacrifices shall come and take them and cook in them. In that day there shall no longer be a Canaanite in the house of the LORD of hosts.

Characteristic of the true church.

1 Chr 16:29 Give to the LORD the glory *due* His name; Bring an offering, and come before Him. Oh, worship the LORD in the beauty of holiness!

Ps 29:2 Give unto the LORD the glory due to His name; Worship the LORD in the beauty of holiness.

Ps 93:5 Your testimonies are very sure; Holiness adorns Your house, O LORD, forever.

The Word of God the means of producing.

John 17:17 Sanctify them by Your truth. Your word is truth.

2 Tim 3:16–17 All Scripture *is* given by inspiration of God, and *is* profitable for doctrine, for reproof, for correction, for instruction in righteousness, 17 that the man of God may be complete, thoroughly equipped for every good work.

Is the result of

The manifestation of God's grace.

Titus 2:3 the older women likewise, that they be reverent in behavior, not slanderers, not given to much wine, teachers of good things—

Titus 2:11–12 For the grace of God that brings salvation has appeared to all men, 12 teaching us that, denying ungodliness and worldly lusts, we should live soberly, righteously, and godly in the present age,

Subjection to God.

Rom 6:22 But now having been set free from sin, and having become slaves of God, you have your fruit to holiness, and the end, everlasting life.

God's keeping.

John 17:15 I do not pray that You should take them out of the world, but that You should keep them from the evil one.

Union with Christ.

John 15:4–5 Abide in Me, and I in you. As the branch cannot bear fruit of itself, unless it abides in the vine, neither can you, unless you abide in Me. 5 "I am the vine, you *are* the branches. He who abides in Me, and I in him, bears much fruit; for without Me you can do nothing.

John 17:9 "I pray for them. I do not pray for the world but for those whom You have given Me, for they are Yours.

Required in prayer.

1 Tim 2:8 I desire therefore that the men pray everywhere, lifting up holy hands, without wrath and doubting;

Ministers should

Possess.

Titus 1:8 but hospitable, a lover of what is good, soberminded, just, holy, self-controlled,

Avoid everything inconsistent with.

Lev 21:6 They shall be holy to their God and not profane the name of their God, for they offer the offerings of the LORD made by fire, *and* the bread of their God; therefore they shall be holy.

Is 52:11 Depart! Depart! Go out from there, Touch no unclean *thing*; Go out from the midst of her, Be clean, You who bear the vessels of the LORD.

Be examples of.

1 Tim 4:12 Let no one despise your youth, but be an example to the believers in word, in conduct, in love, in spirit, in faith, in purity.

Exhort others to.

Heb 12:14 Pursue peace with all *people*, and holiness, without which no one will see the Lord:

1 Pet 1:14–16 as obedient children, not conforming yourselves to the former lusts, *as* in your ignorance; 15 but as He who called you *is* holy, you also be holy in all *your* conduct, 16 because it is written, *"Be holy, for I am holy."*

Motives to,

The glory of God.

John 15:8 By this My Father is glorified, that you bear much fruit; so you will be My disciples.

Phil 1:11 being filled with the fruits of righteousness which *are* by Jesus Christ, to the glory and praise of God.

The love of Christ.

2 Cor 5:14–15 For the love of Christ compels us, because we judge thus: that if One died for all, then all died; 15 and He died for all, that those who live should live no longer for themselves, but for Him who died for them and rose again.

The mercies of God.

Rom 12:1–2 I beseech you therefore, brethren, by the mercies of God, that you present your bodies a living sacrifice, holy, acceptable to God, *which is* your reasonable service. 2 And do not be conformed to this world, but be transformed by the renewing of your mind, that you may prove what *is* that good and acceptable and perfect will of God.

The dissolution of all things.

2 Pet 3:11 Therefore, since all these things will be dissolved, what manner *of persons* ought you to be in holy conduct and godliness,

Chastisements are intended to produce, in believers.

Heb 12:10 For they indeed for a few days chastened *us* as seemed *best* to them, but He for *our* profit, that *we* may be partakers of His holiness.

James 1:2–3 My brethren, count it all joy when you fall into various trials, 3 knowing that the testing of your faith produces patience.

Should lead to separation from the wicked.

Num 16:21 "Separate yourselves from among this congregation, that I may consume them in a moment."

Num 16:26 And he spoke to the congregation, saying, "Depart now from the tents of these wicked men! Touch nothing of theirs, lest you be consumed in all their sins."

2 Cor 6:17–18 Therefore *"Come out from among them And be separate, says the Lord. Do not touch what is unclean, And I will receive you."* 18 *"I will be a Father to you, And you shall be My sons and daughters, Says the LORD Almighty."*

2 Cor 7:1 Therefore, having these promises, beloved, let us cleanse ourselves from all filthiness of the flesh and spirit, perfecting holiness in the fear of God.

The wicked are without.

1 Tim 1:9 knowing this: that the law is not made for a righteous person, but for *the* lawless and insubordinate, for *the* ungodly and for sinners, for *the* unholy

and profane, for murderers of fathers and murderers of mothers, for manslayers,

2 Tim 3:2 For men will be lovers of themselves, lovers of money, boasters, proud, blasphemers, disobedient to parents, unthankful, unholy,

Exemplified by

David.

Ps 86:2 Preserve my life, for I *am* holy; You are my God; Save Your servant who trusts in You!

Israel.

Jer 2:3 Israel *was* holiness to the LORD, The firstfruits of His increase. All that devour him will offend; Disaster will come upon them," says the LORD.' "

John the Baptist.

Mark 6:20 for Herod feared John, knowing that he *was* a just and holy man, and he protected him. And when he heard him, he did many things, and heard him gladly.

Prophets.

Luke 1:70 As He spoke by the mouth of His holy prophets, Who *have been* since the world began,

Paul.

1 Thess 2:10 You *are* witnesses, and God *also*, how devoutly and justly and blamelessly we behaved ourselves among you who believe;

Wives of the patriarchs.

1 Pet 3:5 For in this manner, in former times, the holy women who trusted in God also adorned themselves, being submissive to their own husbands,

HOLY LAND, THE

Extremely fruitful.

Ex 3:8 So I have come down to deliver them out of the hand of the Egyptians, and to bring them up from that land to a good and large land, to a land flowing with milk and honey, to the place of the Canaanites and the Hittites and the Amorites and the Perizzites and the Hivites and the Jebusites.

Num 13:27 Then they told him, and said: "We went to the land where you sent us. It truly flows with milk and honey, and this *is* its fruit.

Deut 8:7–9 For the LORD your God is bringing you into a good land, a land of brooks of water, of fountains and springs, that flow out of valleys and hills; **8** a land of wheat and barley, of vines and fig trees and pomegranates, a land of olive oil and honey; **9** a land in which you will eat bread without scarcity, in which you will lack nothing; a land whose stones *are* iron and out of whose hills you can dig copper.

Deut 11:10–12 For the land which you go to possess *is* not like the land of Egypt from which you have come, where you sowed your seed and watered *it* by foot, as a vegetable garden; **11** but the land which you cross over to possess *is* a land of hills and valleys, which drinks water from the rain of heaven, **12** a land for which the LORD your God cares; the eyes of the LORD your God *are* always on it, from the beginning of the year to the very end of the year.

Abounded in minerals.

Deut 8:9 a land in which you will eat bread without scarcity, in which you will lack nothing; a land whose stones *are* iron and out of whose hills you can dig copper.

Deut 33:25 Your sandals *shall be* iron and bronze; As your days, *so shall* your strength *be*.

Biblical names for,

The land.

Lev 26:42 then I will remember My covenant with Jacob, and My covenant with Isaac and My covenant with Abraham I will remember; I will remember the land.

Luke 4:25 But I tell you truly, many widows were in Israel in the days of Elijah, when the heaven was shut up three years and six months, and there was a great famine throughout all the land;

The Lord's land.

Hos 9:3 They shall not dwell in the LORD's land, But Ephraim shall return to Egypt, And shall eat unclean *things* in Assyria.

Land of Canaan.

Gen 11:31 And Terah took his son Abram and his grandson Lot, the son of Haran, and his daughter-in-law Sarai, his son Abram's wife, and they went out with them from Ur of the Chaldeans to go to the land of Canaan; and they came to Haran and dwelt there.

Lev 14:34 "When you have come into the land of Canaan, which I give you as a possession, and I put the leprous plague in a house in the land of your possession,

Land of Israel.

1 Sam 13:19 Now there was no blacksmith to be found throughout all the land of Israel, for the Philistines said, "Lest the Hebrews make swords or spears."

Matt 2:20–21 saying, "Arise, take the young Child and His mother, and go to the land of Israel, for those who sought the young Child's life are dead." **21** Then he arose, took the young Child and His mother, and came into the land of Israel.

Land of Judah.

Is 26:1 In that day this song will be sung in the land of Judah: "We have a strong city; *God* will appoint salvation *for* walls and bulwarks.

Land of the Hebrews.

Gen 40:15 For indeed I was stolen away from the land of the Hebrews; and also I have done nothing here that they should put me into the dungeon."

Land of promise.

Heb 11:9 By faith he dwelt in the land of promise as *in* a foreign country, dwelling in tents with Isaac and Jacob, the heirs with him of the same promise;

Land of Immanuel.

Is 8:8 He will pass through Judah, He will overflow and pass over, He will reach up to the neck; And the stretching out of his wings Will fill the breadth of Your land, O Immanuel.

Pleasant land.

Ps 106:24 Then they despised the pleasant land; They did not believe His word,

Good land.

Num 14:7 and they spoke to all the congregation of the children of Israel, saying: "The land we passed through to spy out *is* an exceedingly good land.

Deut 3:25 I pray, let me cross over and see the good land beyond the Jordan, those pleasant mountains, and Lebanon.'

Glorious land.

Dan 8:9 And out of one of them came a little horn which grew exceedingly great toward the south, toward the east, and toward the Glorious *Land.*

Dan 11:16 But he who comes against him shall do according to his own will, and no one shall stand against him. He shall stand in the Glorious Land with destruction in his power.

Original inhabitants of, expelled for wickedness.

Gen 15:16 But in the fourth generation they shall return here, for the iniquity of the Amorites *is* not yet complete."

Ex 23:23 For My Angel will go before you and bring you in to the Amorites and the Hittites and the Perizzites and the Canaanites and the Hivites and the Jebusites; and I will cut them off.

Lev 18:25 For the land is defiled; therefore I visit the punishment of its iniquity upon it, and the land vomits out its inhabitants.

Deut 18:12 For all who do these things *are* an abomination to the LORD, and because of these abominations the LORD your God drives them out from before you.

Promised to

Abraham.

Gen 12:7 Then the LORD appeared to Abram and said, "To your descendants I will give this land." And there he built an altar to the LORD, who had appeared to him.

Gen 13:15 for all the land which you see I give to you and your descendants forever.

Gen 17:8 Also I give to you and your descendants after you the land in which you are a stranger, all the land of Canaan, as an everlasting possession; and I will be their God."

Isaac.

Gen 26:3 Dwell in this land, and I will be with you and bless you; for to you and your descendants I give all these lands, and I will perform the oath which I swore to Abraham your father.

Jacob.

Gen 28:13 And behold, the LORD stood above it and said: "I *am* the LORD God of Abraham your father and the God of Isaac; the land on which you lie I will give to you and your descendants.

Gen 28:15 Behold, I *am* with you and will keep you wherever you go, and will bring you back to this land; for I will not leave you until I have done what I have spoken to you."

Gen 35:12 The land which I gave Abraham and Isaac I give to you; and to your descendants after you I give this land."

Israel.

Ex 6:4 I have also established My covenant with them, to give them the land of Canaan, the land of their pilgrimage, in which they were strangers.

Extent of,

As promised.

Gen 15:18 On the same day the LORD made a covenant with Abram, saying: "To your descendants I have given this land, from the river of Egypt to the great river, the River Euphrates—

Deut 1:7 Turn and take your journey, and go to the mountains of the Amorites, to all the neighboring *places* in the plain, in the mountains and in the lowland, in the South and on the seacoast, to the land of the Canaanites and to Lebanon, as far as the great river, the River Euphrates.

Josh 1:4 From the wilderness and this Lebanon as far as the great river, the River Euphrates, all the land of the Hittites, and to the Great Sea toward the going down of the sun, shall be your territory.

As at first divided.

Num 34:1–12 Then the LORD spoke to Moses, saying, **2** "Command the children of Israel, and say to them: 'When you come into the land of Canaan, this *is* the land that shall fall to you as an inheritance—the land of Canaan to its boundaries. **3** Your southern border shall be from the Wilderness of Zin along the border of Edom; then your southern border shall extend eastward to the end of the Salt Sea; **4** your border shall turn from the southern side of the Ascent of Akrabbim, continue to Zin, and be on the south of Kadesh Barnea; then it shall go on to Hazar Addar, and continue to Azmon; **5** the border shall turn from Azmon to the Brook of Egypt, and it shall end at the Sea. **6** 'As for the western border, you shall have the Great Sea for a border; this shall be your western border. **7** 'And this shall be your northern border: From the Great Sea you shall mark out your *border* line to Mount Hor; **8** from Mount Hor you shall mark out *your border* to the entrance of Hamath; then the direction of the border shall be toward Zedad; **9** the border shall proceed to Ziphron, and it shall end at Hazar Enan. This shall be your northern border. **10** 'You shall mark out your eastern border from Hazar Enan to Shepham; **11** the border shall go down from Shepham to Riblah on the east side of Ain; the border shall go down and reach to the eastern side of the Sea of Chinnereth; **12** the border shall go down along the Jordan, and it shall end at the Salt Sea. This shall be your land with its surrounding boundaries.' "

Under Solomon.

1 Kin 4:21 So Solomon reigned over all kingdoms from the River *to* the land of the Philistines, as far as the border of Egypt. *They* brought tribute and served Solomon all the days of his life.

1 Kin 4:24 For he had dominion over all *the region* on this side of the River from Tiphsah even to Gaza, namely over all the kings on this side of the River; and he had peace on every side all around him.

2 Chr 9:26 So he reigned over all the kings from the River to the land of the Philistines, as far as the border of Egypt.

Twelve men sent to spy in it. Num 13:1–33

Conquered by Joshua. Josh 6:1—12:24

Divided by lot. Num 34:16–29; Josh 13:7–14

Allotment of, specified. Josh 14:1—19:51

All inheritances in, inalienable.

Lev 25:10 And you shall consecrate the fiftieth year, and proclaim liberty throughout *all* the land to all its inhabitants. It shall be a Jubilee for you; and each of you shall return to his possession, and each of you shall return to his family.

Lev 25:23 'The land shall not be sold permanently, for the land *is* Mine; for you *are* strangers and sojourners with Me.

A sabbath of rest was appointed for.

Lev 25:2–5 "Speak to the children of Israel, and say to them: 'When you come into the land which I give you, then the land shall keep a sabbath for the LORD. 3 Six years you shall sow your field, and six years you shall prune your vineyard, and gather its fruit; 4 but in the seventh year there shall be a sabbath of solemn rest for the land, a sabbath to the LORD. You shall neither sow your field nor prune your vineyard. 5 What grows of its own accord of your harvest you shall not reap, nor gather the grapes of your untended vine, *for* it is a year of rest for the land.

Obedience, the condition of continuing in.

Lev 26:3 'If you walk in My statutes and keep My commandments, and perform them,

Deut 5:33 You shall walk in all the ways which the LORD your God has commanded you, that you may live and *that it may be* well with you, and *that* you may prolong *your* days in the land which you shall possess.

Deut 11:16–17 Take heed to yourselves, lest your heart be deceived, and you turn aside and serve other gods and worship them, 17 lest the LORD's anger be aroused against you, and He shut up the heavens so that there be no rain, and the land yield no produce, and you perish quickly from the good land which the LORD is giving you.

Deut 11:22–25 "For if you carefully keep all these commandments which I command you to do—to love the LORD your God, to walk in all His ways, and to hold fast to Him— 23 then the LORD will drive out all these nations from before you, and you will dispossess greater and mightier nations than yourselves. 24 Every place on which the sole of your foot treads shall be yours: from the wilderness and Lebanon, from the river, the River Euphrates, even to the Western Sea, shall be your territory. 25 No man shall be able to stand against you; the LORD your God will put the dread of you and the fear of you upon all the land where you tread, just as He has said to you.

Divided into

Twelve provinces by Solomon.

1 Kin 4:7–19 And Solomon had twelve governors over all Israel, who provided food for the king and his household; each one made provision for one month of the year. 8 These *are* their names: Ben-Hur, in the mountains of Ephraim; 9 Ben-Deker, in Makaz, Shaalbim, Beth Shemesh, and Elon Beth Hanan; 10 Ben-Hesed, in Arubboth; to him *belonged* Sochoh and all

the land of Hepher; 11 Ben-Abinadab, *in* all the regions of Dor; he had Taphath the daughter of Solomon as wife; 12 Baana the son of Ahilud, *in* Taanach, Megiddo, and all Beth Shean, which *is* beside Zaretan below Jezreel, from Beth Shean to Abel Meholah, as far as the other side of Jokneam; 13 Ben-Geber, in Ramoth Gilead; to him *belonged* the towns of Jair the son of Manasseh, in Gilead; to him *also belonged* the region of Argob in Bashan—sixty large cities with walls and bronze gate-bars; 14 Ahinadab the son of Iddo, *in* Mahanaim; 15 Ahimaaz, in Naphtali; he also took Basemath the daughter of Solomon as wife; 16 Baanah the son of Hushai, in Asher and Aloth; 17 Jehoshaphat the son of Paruah, in Issachar; 18 Shimei the son of Elah, in Benjamin; 19 Geber the son of Uri, in the land of Gilead, *in* the country of Sihon king of the Amorites, and of Og king of Bashan. *He was* the only governor who *was* in the land.

Two kingdoms in the time of Rehoboam.

1 Kin 11:35–36 But I will take the kingdom out of his son's hand and give it to you—ten tribes. 36 And to his son I will give one tribe, that My servant David may always have a lamp before Me in Jerusalem, the city which I have chosen for Myself, to put My name there.

1 Kin 12:19–20 So Israel has been in rebellion against the house of David to this day. 20 Now it came to pass when all Israel heard that Jeroboam had come back, they sent for him and called him to the congregation, and made him king over all Israel. There was none who followed the house of David, but the tribe of Judah only.

Four provinces by the Romans.

Luke 3:1 Now in the fifteenth year of the reign of Tiberius Caesar, Pontius Pilate being governor of Judea, Herod being tetrarch of Galilee, his brother Philip tetrarch of Iturea and the region of Trachonitis, and Lysanias tetrarch of Abilene,

Numerous population of, in Solomon's reign.

1 Kin 3:8 And Your servant *is* in the midst of Your people whom You have chosen, a great people, too numerous to be numbered or counted.

2 Chr 1:9 Now, O LORD God, let Your promise to David my father be established, for You have made me king over a people like the dust of the earth in multitude.

Extensive commerce of, in Solomon's reign.

1 Kin 9:26–28 King Solomon also built a fleet of ships at Ezion Geber, which *is* near Elath on the shore of the Red Sea, in the land of Edom. 27 Then Hiram sent his servants with the fleet, seamen who knew the sea, to work with the servants of Solomon. 28 And they went to Ophir, and acquired four hundred and twenty talents of gold from there, and brought *it* to King Solomon.

1 Kin 10:22–29 For the king had merchant ships at sea with the fleet of Hiram. Once every three years the merchant ships came bringing gold, silver, ivory, apes, and monkeys. 23 So King Solomon surpassed all the kings of the earth in riches and wisdom. 24 Now all the earth sought the presence of Solomon to hear his wisdom, which God had put in his heart. 25 Each man brought his present: articles of silver and gold, garments, armor, spices, horses, and mules, at a

set rate year by year. **26** And Solomon gathered chariots and horsemen; he had one thousand four hundred chariots and twelve thousand horsemen, whom he stationed in the chariot cities and with the king at Jerusalem. **27** The king made silver *as common* in Jerusalem as stones, and he made cedar trees as abundant as the sycamores which *are* in the lowland. **28** Also Solomon had horses imported from Egypt and Keveh; the king's merchants bought them in Keveh at the *current* price. **29** Now a chariot that was imported from Egypt cost six hundred *shekels* of silver, and a horse one hundred and fifty; and thus, through their agents, they exported *them* to all the kings of the Hittites and the kings of Syria.

Prosperity of, in Solomon's reign.

1 Kin 4:20 Judah and Israel *were* as numerous as the sand by the sea in multitude, eating and drinking and rejoicing.

Was the burial place of the patriarchs.

Gen 49:29–31 Then he charged them and said to them: "I am to be gathered to my people; bury me with my fathers in the cave that *is* in the field of Ephron the Hittite, **30** in the cave that *is* in the field of Machpelah, which *is* before Mamre in the land of Canaan, which Abraham bought with the field of Ephron the Hittite as a possession for a burial place. **31** There they buried Abraham and Sarah his wife, there they buried Isaac and Rebekah his wife, and there I buried Leah.

Gen 50:13 For his sons carried him to the land of Canaan, and buried him in the cave of the field of Machpelah, before Mamre, which Abraham bought with the field from Ephron the Hittite as property for a burial place.

Gen 50:25 Then Joseph took an oath from the children of Israel, saying, "God will surely visit you, and you shall carry up my bones from here."

Josh 24:32 The bones of Joseph, which the children of Israel had brought up out of Egypt, they buried at Shechem, in the plot of ground which Jacob had bought from the sons of Hamor the father of Shechem for one hundred pieces of silver, and which had become an inheritance of the children of Joseph.

Typical of the rest that remains for believers.

Heb 4:1–2 Therefore, since a promise remains of entering His rest, let us fear lest any of you seem to have come short of it. **2** For indeed the gospel was preached to us as well as to them; but the word which they heard did not profit them, not being mixed with faith in those who heard *it*.

Heb 4:9 There remains therefore a rest for the people of God.

1 Pet 1:4 to an inheritance incorruptible and undefiled and that does not fade away, reserved in heaven for you,

HOLY OF HOLIES (MOST HOLY PLACE), THE

Divided from the holy place by a veil.

Ex 26:31–33 "You shall make a veil woven of blue, purple, and scarlet *thread*, and fine woven linen. It shall be woven with an artistic design of cherubim. **32** You shall hang it upon the four pillars of acacia *wood* overlaid with gold. Their hooks *shall be* gold, upon four sockets of silver. **33** And you shall hang the veil from the clasps. Then you shall bring the ark of the Testimony in there, behind the veil. The veil shall be a divider for you between the holy *place* and the Most Holy.

Other names for

Sanctuary.

Lev 4:6 The priest shall dip his finger in the blood and sprinkle some of the blood seven times before the LORD, in front of the veil of the sanctuary.

1 Kin 6:5 Against the wall of the temple he built chambers all around, *against* the walls of the temple, all around the sanctuary and the inner sanctuary. Thus he made side chambers all around it.

1 Kin 6:20 The inner sanctuary *was* twenty cubits long, twenty cubits wide, and twenty cubits high. He overlaid it with pure gold, and overlaid the altar of cedar.

Ps 20:2 May He send you help from the sanctuary, And strengthen you out of Zion;

Holy Sanctuary.

Lev 16:33 then he shall make atonement for the Holy Sanctuary, and he shall make atonement for the tabernacle of meeting and for the altar, and he shall make atonement for the priests and for all the people of the assembly.

Holy Place.

Ex 28:29 "So Aaron shall bear the names of the sons of Israel on the breastplate of judgment over his heart, when he goes into the holy *place*, as a memorial before the LORD continually.

Lev 16:2–3 and the LORD said to Moses: "Tell Aaron your brother not to come at *just* any time into the Holy *Place* inside the veil, before the mercy seat which *is* on the ark, lest he die; for I will appear in the cloud above the mercy seat. **3** "Thus Aaron shall come into the Holy *Place*: with *the blood of* a young bull as a sin offering, and *of* a ram as a burnt offering.

Most Holy Place.

Ex 26:31–33 "You shall make a veil woven of blue, purple, and scarlet *thread*, and fine woven linen. It shall be woven with an artistic design of cherubim. **32** You shall hang it upon the four pillars of acacia *wood* overlaid with gold. Their hooks *shall be* gold, upon four sockets of silver. **33** And you shall hang the veil from the clasps. Then you shall bring the ark of the Testimony in there, behind the veil. The veil shall be a divider for you between the holy *place* and the Most Holy.

1 Kin 6:16 Then he built the twenty-cubit room at the rear of the temple, from floor to ceiling, with cedar boards; he built *it* inside as the inner sanctuary, as the Most Holy *Place*.

Holiest of All.

Heb 9:3 and behind the second veil, the part of the tabernacle which is called the Holiest of All,

Contained

Ark of the Testimony.

Ex 26:33 And you shall hang the veil from the clasps. Then you shall bring the ark of the Testimony in there, behind the veil. The veil shall be a divider for you between the holy *place* and the Most Holy.

Ex 40:3 You shall put in it the ark of the Testimony, and partition off the ark with the veil.

Ex 40:21 And he brought the ark into the tabernacle, hung up the veil of the covering, and partitioned off the ark of the Testimony, as the Lord had commanded Moses.

Mercy seat.

Ex 26:34 You shall put the mercy seat upon the ark of the Testimony in the Most Holy.

Cherubim.

Ex 25:18–22 And you shall make two cherubim of gold; of hammered work you shall make them at the two ends of the mercy seat. **19** Make one cherub at one end, and the other cherub at the other end; you shall make the cherubim at the two ends of it *of one piece* with the mercy seat. **20** And the cherubim shall stretch out *their* wings above, covering the mercy seat with their wings, and they shall face one another; the faces of the cherubim *shall be* toward the mercy seat. **21** You shall put the mercy seat on top of the ark, and in the ark you shall put the Testimony that I will give you. **22** And there I will meet with you, and I will speak with you from above the mercy seat, from between the two cherubim which *are* on the ark of the Testimony, about everything which I will give you in commandment to the children of Israel.

1 Kin 6:23–28 Inside the inner sanctuary he made two cherubim *of* olive wood, *each* ten cubits high. **24** One wing of the cherub *was* five cubits, and the other wing of the cherub five cubits: ten cubits from the tip of one wing to the tip of the other. **25** And the other cherub *was* ten cubits; both cherubim *were* of the same size and shape. **26** The height of one cherub *was* ten cubits, and so *was* the other cherub. **27** Then he set the cherubim inside the inner room; and they stretched out the wings of the cherubim so that the wing of the one touched *one* wall, and the wing of the other cherub touched the other wall. And their wings touched each other in the middle of the room. **28** Also he overlaid the cherubim with gold.

Golden censer.

Heb 9:4 which had the golden censer and the ark of the covenant overlaid on all sides with gold, in which *were* the golden pot that had the manna, Aaron's rod that budded, and the tablets of the covenant;

Pot of manna.

Ex 16:33 And Moses said to Aaron, "Take a pot and put an omer of manna in it, and lay it up before the Lord, to be kept for your generations."

Heb 9:4 which had the golden censer and the ark of the covenant overlaid on all sides with gold, in which *were* the golden pot that had the manna, Aaron's rod that budded, and the tablets of the covenant;

Aaron's rod.

Num 17:10 And the Lord said to Moses, "Bring Aaron's rod back before the Testimony, to be kept as a sign against the rebels, that you may put their complaints away from Me, lest they die."

Heb 9:4 which had the golden censer and the ark of the covenant overlaid on all sides with gold, in which *were* the golden pot that had the manna, Aaron's rod that budded, and the tablets of the covenant;

Book of the Law.

Deut 31:26 "Take this Book of the Law, and put it beside the ark of the covenant of the Lord your God, that it may be there as a witness against you;

2 Kin 22:8 Then Hilkiah the high priest said to Shaphan the scribe, "I have found the Book of the Law in the house of the Lord." And Hilkiah gave the book to Shaphan, and he read it.

God appeared in.

Ex 25:22 And there I will meet with you, and I will speak with you from above the mercy seat, from between the two cherubim which *are* on the ark of the Testimony, about everything which I will give you in commandment to the children of Israel.

Lev 16:2 and the Lord said to Moses: "Tell Aaron your brother not to come at *just* any time into the Holy *Place* inside the veil, before the mercy seat which *is* on the ark, lest he die; for I will appear in the cloud above the mercy seat.

The high priest

To enter only at certain times.

Lev 16:2 and the Lord said to Moses: "Tell Aaron your brother not to come at *just* any time into the Holy *Place* inside the veil, before the mercy seat which *is* on the ark, lest he die; for I will appear in the cloud above the mercy seat.

The only one to enter, once a year.

Heb 9:7 But into the second part the high priest *went* alone once a year, not without blood, which he offered for himself and *for* the people's sins *committed* in ignorance;

Entered, in ordinary priest's dress.

Lev 16:4 He shall put the holy linen tunic and the linen trousers on his body; he shall be girded with a linen sash, and with the linen turban he shall be attired. These *are* holy garments. Therefore he shall wash his body in water, and put them on.

Entered, not without blood of atonement.

Lev 16:14–15 He shall take some of the blood of the bull and sprinkle *it* with his finger on the mercy seat on the east *side;* and before the mercy seat he shall sprinkle some of the blood with his finger seven times. **15** "Then he shall kill the goat of the sin offering, which *is* for the people, bring its blood inside the veil, do with that blood as he did with the blood of the bull, and sprinkle it on the mercy seat and before the mercy seat.

Heb 9:7 But into the second part the high priest *went* alone once a year, not without blood, which he offered for himself and *for* the people's sins *committed* in ignorance;

Offered incense in.

Lev 16:12 Then he shall take a censer full of burning coals of fire from the altar before the Lord, with his hands full of sweet incense beaten fine, and bring *it* inside the veil.

Made atonement for.

Lev 16:15–16 "Then he shall kill the goat of the sin offering, which *is* for the people, bring its blood inside the veil, do with that blood as he did with the blood of the bull, and sprinkle it on the mercy seat and before the mercy seat. **16** So he shall make atonement for the Holy *Place*, because of the uncleanness of the children of Israel, and because of their transgressions, for all their sins; and so he shall do for the tabernacle of meeting which remains among them in the midst of their uncleanness.

Lev 16:20 "And when he has made an end of atoning for the Holy *Place*, the tabernacle of meeting, and the altar, he shall bring the live goat.

Lev 16:33 then he shall make atonement for the Holy Sanctuary, and he shall make atonement for the tabernacle of meeting and for the altar, and he shall make atonement for the priests and for all the people of the assembly.

The priests allowed to enter, and prepare the holy things for removal.

Num 4:5 When the camp prepares to journey, Aaron and his sons shall come, and they shall take down the covering veil and cover the ark of the Testimony with it.

Made public at Christ's death.

Matt 27:51 Then, behold, the veil of the temple was torn in two from top to bottom; and the earth quaked, and the rocks were split,

A type of heaven.

Ps 102:19 For He looked down from the height of His sanctuary; From heaven the Lord viewed the earth,

Heb 9:12–13 Not with the blood of goats and calves, but with His own blood He entered the Most Holy Place once for all, having obtained eternal redemption. **13** For if the blood of bulls and goats and the ashes of a heifer, sprinkling the unclean, sanctifies for the purifying of the flesh,

Heb 9:24 For Christ has not entered the holy places made with hands, *which are* copies of the true, but into heaven itself, now to appear in the presence of God for us;

Believers have boldness to enter the true.

Heb 10:19 Therefore, brethren, having boldness to enter the Holiest by the blood of Jesus,

Holy Spirit, Anointing of the

Is from God.

2 Cor 1:21 Now He who establishes us with you in Christ and has anointed us *is* God,

That Christ should receive, is

Foretold.

Is 61:1 "The Spirit of the Lord God *is* upon Me, Because the Lord has anointed Me To preach good tidings to the poor; He has sent Me to heal the brokenhearted, To proclaim liberty to the captives, And the opening of the prison to *those who are* bound;

Dan 9:24 "Seventy weeks are determined For your people and for your holy city, To finish the transgression, To make an end of sins, To make reconciliation for iniquity, To bring in everlasting righteousness, To seal up vision and prophecy, And to anoint the Most Holy.

Fulfilled.

Luke 4:18 *"The Spirit of the Lord is upon Me, Because He has anointed Me To preach the gospel to the poor; He has sent Me to heal the brokenhearted, To*

proclaim liberty to the captives And recovery of sight to the blind, To set at liberty those who are oppressed;

Luke 4:21 And He began to say to them, "Today this Scripture is fulfilled in your hearing."

Acts 4:27 "For truly against Your holy Servant Jesus, whom You anointed, both Herod and Pontius Pilate, with the Gentiles and the people of Israel, were gathered together

Acts 10:38 how God anointed Jesus of Nazareth with the Holy Spirit and with power, who went about doing good and healing all who were oppressed by the devil, for God was with Him.

Heb 1:9 *You have loved righteousness and hated lawlessness; Therefore God, Your God, has anointed You With the oil of gladness more than Your companions."*

God preserves those who receive.

Ps 18:50 Great deliverance He gives to His king, And shows mercy to His anointed, To David and his descendants forevermore.

Ps 20:6 Now I know that the Lord saves His anointed; He will answer him from His holy heaven With the saving strength of His right hand.

Ps 89:20–23 I have found My servant David; With My holy oil I have anointed him, **21** With whom My hand shall be established; Also My arm shall strengthen him. **22** The enemy shall not outwit him, Nor the son of wickedness afflict him. **23** I will beat down his foes before his face, And plague those who hate him.

Saints receive.

1 John 2:20 But you have an anointing from the Holy One, and you know all things.

1 John 2:27 But the anointing which you have received from Him abides in you, and you do not need that anyone teach you; but as the same anointing teaches you concerning all things, and is true, and is not a lie, and just as it has taught you, you will abide in Him.

Guides into all truth.

1 John 2:27 But the anointing which you have received from Him abides in you, and you do not need that anyone teach you; but as the same anointing teaches you concerning all things, and is true, and is not a lie, and just as it has taught you, you will abide in Him.

Holy Spirit, Baptism with the

Is through Christ.

Titus 3:6 whom He poured out on us abundantly through Jesus Christ our Savior,

Christ administered.

Matt 3:11 I indeed baptize you with water unto repentance, but He who is coming after me is mightier than I, whose sandals I am not worthy to carry. He will baptize you with the Holy Spirit and fire.

John 1:33 I did not know Him, but He who sent me to baptize with water said to me, 'Upon whom you see the Spirit descending, and remaining on Him, this is He who baptizes with the Holy Spirit.'

Promised to saints.

Acts 1:5 for John truly baptized with water, but you shall be baptized with the Holy Spirit not many days from now."

Acts 2:38–39 Then Peter said to them, "Repent, and let every one of you be baptized in the name of Jesus Christ for the remission of sins; and you shall receive the gift of the Holy Spirit. **39** For the promise is to you and to your children, and to all who are afar off, as many as the Lord our God will call."

Acts 11:16 Then I remembered the word of the Lord, how He said, 'John indeed baptized with water, but you shall be baptized with the Holy Spirit.'

All saints partake of.

1 Cor 12:13 For by one Spirit we were all baptized into one body—whether Jews or Greeks, whether slaves or free—and have all been made to drink into one Spirit.

Necessity for.

John 3:5 Jesus answered, "Most assuredly, I say to you, unless one is born of water and the Spirit, he cannot enter the kingdom of God.

Acts 19:2–6 he said to them, "Did you receive the Holy Spirit when you believed?" So they said to him, "We have not so much as heard whether there is a Holy Spirit." **3** And he said to them, "Into what then were you baptized?" So they said, "Into John's baptism." **4** Then Paul said, "John indeed baptized with a baptism of repentance, saying to the people that they should believe on Him who would come after him, that is, on Christ Jesus." **5** When they heard *this*, they were baptized in the name of the Lord Jesus. **6** And when Paul had laid hands on them, the Holy Spirit came upon them, and they spoke with tongues and prophesied.

Renews and cleanses the soul.

Titus 3:5 not by works of righteousness which we have done, but according to His mercy He saved us, through the washing of regeneration and renewing of the Holy Spirit,

1 Pet 3:20–21 who formerly were disobedient, when once the Divine longsuffering waited in the days of Noah, while *the* ark was being prepared, in which a few, that is, eight souls, were saved through water. **21** There is also an antitype which now saves us— baptism (not the removal of the filth of the flesh, but the answer of a good conscience toward God), through the resurrection of Jesus Christ,

The Word of God instrumental to.

Acts 10:44 While Peter was still speaking these words, the Holy Spirit fell upon all those who heard the word.

Eph 5:26 that He might sanctify and cleanse her with the washing of water by the word,

Typified.

Acts 2:1–4 When the Day of Pentecost had fully come, they were all with one accord in one place. **2** And suddenly there came a sound from heaven, as of a rushing mighty wind, and it filled the whole house where they were sitting. **3** Then there appeared to them divided tongues, as of fire, and *one* sat upon each of them. **4** And they were all filled with the Holy Spirit and began to speak with other tongues, as the Spirit gave them utterance.

HOLY SPIRIT, THE DEITY OF THE

As Lord.

Ex 17:7 So he called the name of the place Massah and Meribah, because of the contention of the children of Israel, and because they tempted the LORD, saying, "Is the LORD among us or not?"

Num 12:6 Then He said, "Hear now My words: If there is a prophet among you, *I*, the LORD, make Myself known to him in a vision; I speak to him in a dream.

Heb 3:7–9 Therefore, as the Holy Spirit says: *"Today, if you will hear His voice, 8 Do not harden your hearts as in the rebellion, In the day of trial in the wilderness, 9 Where your fathers tested Me, tried Me, And saw My works forty years.*

2 Pet 1:21 for prophecy never came by the will of man, but holy men of God spoke *as they were* moved by the Holy Spirit.

As Lord of hosts.

Is 6:3 And one cried to another and said: "Holy, holy, holy *is* the LORD of hosts; The whole earth *is* full of His glory!"

Is 6:8–10 Also I heard the voice of the Lord, saying: "Whom shall I send, And who will go for Us?" Then I said, "Here *am* I! Send me." **9** And He said, "Go, and tell this people: 'Keep on hearing, but do not understand; Keep on seeing, but do not perceive.' **10** "Make the heart of this people dull, And their ears heavy, And shut their eyes; Lest they see with their eyes, And hear with their ears, And understand with their heart, And return and be healed."

Acts 28:25 So when they did not agree among themselves, they departed after Paul had said one word: "The Holy Spirit spoke rightly through Isaiah the prophet to our fathers,

As Lord, Most High.

Ps 78:17 But they sinned even more against Him By rebelling against the Most High in the wilderness.

Ps 78:21 Therefore the LORD heard *this* and was furious; So a fire was kindled against Jacob, And anger also came up against Israel,

Acts 7:51 *"You* stiff-necked and uncircumcised in heart and ears! You always resist the Holy Spirit; as your fathers *did*, so *do* you.

Being invoked as Lord.

Luke 2:26–29 And it had been revealed to him by the Holy Spirit that he would not see death before he had seen the Lord's Christ. **27** So he came by the Spirit into the temple. And when the parents brought in the Child Jesus, to do for Him according to the custom of the law, **28** he took Him up in his arms and blessed God and said: **29** "Lord, now You are letting Your servant depart in peace, According to Your word;

Acts 1:16 "Men *and* brethren, this Scripture had to be fulfilled, which the Holy Spirit spoke before by the mouth of David concerning Judas, who became a guide to those who arrested Jesus;

Acts 1:20 "For it is written in the Book of Psalms: 'Let his dwelling place be desolate, And let no one live in it'; and, 'Let another take his office.'

Acts 4:23–25 And being let go, they went to their own *companions* and reported all that the chief priests and elders had said to them. **24** So when they heard that, they raised their voice to God with one accord and said: "Lord, You *are* God, who made heaven and earth and the sea, and all that is in them, **25** who by the mouth of Your servant David have said: *'Why did the nations rage, And the people plot vain things?*

2 Thess 3:5 Now may the Lord direct your hearts into the love of God and into the patience of Christ.

Was called God.

Acts 5:3–4 But Peter said, "Ananias, why has Satan filled your heart to lie to the Holy Spirit and keep back *part* of the price of the land for yourself? **4** While it remained, was it not your own? And after it was sold, was it not in your own control? Why have you conceived this thing in your heart? You have not lied to men but to God."

Part of the divine baptismal formula.

Matt 28:19 Go therefore and make disciples of all the nations, baptizing them in the name of the Father and of the Son and of the Holy Spirit,

As eternal.

Heb 9:14 how much more shall the blood of Christ, who through the eternal Spirit offered Himself without spot to God, cleanse your conscience from dead works to serve the living God?

As omnipresent.

Ps 139:7–13 Where can I go from Your Spirit? Or where can I flee from Your presence? **8** If I ascend into heaven, You *are* there; If I make my bed in hell, behold, You *are there.* **9** *If* I take the wings of the morning, *And* dwell in the uttermost parts of the sea, **10** Even there Your hand shall lead me, And Your right hand shall hold me. **11** If I say, "Surely the darkness shall fall on me," Even the night shall be light about me; **12** Indeed, the darkness shall not hide from You, But the night shines as the day; The darkness and the light *are* both alike *to* You. **13** For You formed my inward parts; You covered me in my mother's womb.

As omniscient.

1 Cor 2:10 But God has revealed *them* to us through His Spirit. For the Spirit searches all things, yes, the deep things of God.

As omnipotent.

Luke 1:35 And the angel answered and said to her, "*The* Holy Spirit will come upon you, and the power of the Highest will overshadow you; therefore, also, that Holy One who is to be born will be called the Son of God.

Rom 15:19 in mighty signs and wonders, by the power of the Spirit of God, so that from Jerusalem and round about to Illyricum I have fully preached the gospel of Christ.

As the Spirit of glory and of God.

1 Pet 4:14 If you are reproached for the name of Christ, blessed *are* you, for the Spirit of glory and of God rests upon you. On their part He is blasphemed, but on your part He is glorified.

As Creator.

Gen 1:26–27 Then God said, "Let Us make man in Our image, according to Our likeness; let them have dominion over the fish of the sea, over the birds of the air, and over the cattle, over all the earth and over every creeping thing that creeps on the earth." **27** So God created man in His *own* image; in the image of God He created him; male and female He created them.

Job 33:4 The Spirit of God has made me, And the breath of the Almighty gives me life.

As equal to and one with the Father.

Matt 28:19 Go therefore and make disciples of all the nations, baptizing them in the name of the Father and of the Son and of the Holy Spirit,

2 Cor 13:14 The grace of the Lord Jesus Christ, and the love of God, and the communion of the Holy Spirit *be* with you all. Amen.

As sovereign worker of all things.

Dan 4:35 All the inhabitants of the earth *are* reputed as nothing; He does according to His will in the army of heaven And *among* the inhabitants of the earth. No one can restrain His hand Or say to Him, "What have You done?"

1 Cor 12:6 And there are diversities of activities, but it is the same God who works all in all.

1 Cor 12:11 But one and the same Spirit works all these things, distributing to each one individually as He wills.

As author of the new birth.

John 3:5–6 Jesus answered, "Most assuredly, I say to you, unless one is born of water and the Spirit, he cannot enter the kingdom of God. **6** That which is born of the flesh is flesh, and that which is born of the Spirit is spirit.

1 John 5:4 For whatever is born of God overcomes the world. And this is the victory that has overcome the world—our faith.

As raising Christ from the dead.

Acts 2:24 whom God raised up, having loosed the pains of death, because it was not possible that He should be held by it.

Rom 1:4 *and* declared *to be* the Son of God with power according to the Spirit of holiness, by the resurrection from the dead.

Heb 13:20 Now may the God of peace who brought up our Lord Jesus from the dead, that great Shepherd of the sheep, through the blood of the everlasting covenant,

1 Pet 3:18 For Christ also suffered once for sins, the just for the unjust, that He might bring us to God, being put to death in the flesh but made alive by the Spirit,

As inspiring Scripture.

2 Tim 3:16 All Scripture *is* given by inspiration of God, and *is* profitable for doctrine, for reproof, for correction, for instruction in righteousness,

2 Pet 1:21 for prophecy never came by the will of man, but holy men of God spoke *as they were* moved by the Holy Spirit.

As the source of wisdom.

Is 11:2 The Spirit of the LORD shall rest upon Him, The Spirit of wisdom and understanding, The Spirit of counsel and might, The Spirit of knowledge and of the fear of the LORD.

John 14:26 But the Helper, the Holy Spirit, whom the Father will send in My name, He will teach you all things, and bring to your remembrance all things that I said to you.

John 16:13 However, when He, the Spirit of truth, has come, He will guide you into all truth; for He will not speak on His own *authority*, but whatever He hears He will speak; and He will tell you things to come.

1 Cor 12:8 for to one is given the word of wisdom through the Spirit, to another the word of knowledge through the same Spirit,

As the source of miraculous power.

Matt 12:28 But if I cast out demons by the Spirit of God, surely the kingdom of God has come upon you.

Luke 11:20 But if I cast out demons with the finger of God, surely the kingdom of God has come upon you.

Acts 19:11 Now God worked unusual miracles by the hands of Paul,

Rom 15:19 in mighty signs and wonders, by the power of the Spirit of God, so that from Jerusalem and round about to Illyricum I have fully preached the gospel of Christ.

As appointing and sending ministers.

Acts 13:2 As they ministered to the Lord and fasted, the Holy Spirit said, "Now separate to Me Barnabas and Saul for the work to which I have called them."

Acts 9:38 And since Lydda was near Joppa, and the disciples had heard that Peter was there, they sent two men to him, imploring *him* not to delay in coming to them.

Acts 13:4 So, being sent out by the Holy Spirit, they went down to Seleucia, and from there they sailed to Cyprus.

Acts 20:28 Therefore take heed to yourselves and to all the flock, among which the Holy Spirit has made you overseers, to shepherd the church of God which He purchased with His own blood.

As directing where the gospel should be preached.

Acts 16:6–7 Now when they had gone through Phrygia and the region of Galatia, they were forbidden by the Holy Spirit to preach the word in Asia. **7** After they had come to Mysia, they tried to go into Bithynia, but the Spirit did not permit them.

Acts 16:10 Now after he had seen the vision, immediately we sought to go to Macedonia, concluding that the Lord had called us to preach the gospel to them.

As dwelling in believers.

John 14:17 the Spirit of truth, whom the world cannot receive, because it neither sees Him nor knows Him; but you know Him, for He dwells with you and will be in you.

1 Cor 3:16 Do you not know that you are the temple of God and *that* the Spirit of God dwells in you?

1 Cor 6:19 Or do you not know that your body is the temple of the Holy Spirit *who is* in you, whom you have from God, and you are not your own?

1 Cor 14:25 And thus the secrets of his heart are revealed; and so, falling down on *his* face, he will worship God and report that God is truly among you.

As Comforter of the church.

Acts 9:31 Then the churches throughout all Judea, Galilee, and Samaria had peace and were edified. And

walking in the fear of the Lord and in the comfort of the Holy Spirit, they were multiplied.

2 Cor 1:3 Blessed *be* the God and Father of our Lord Jesus Christ, the Father of mercies and God of all comfort,

As sanctifying God's people.

Ezek 37:28 The nations also will know that I, the LORD, sanctify Israel, when My sanctuary is in their midst forevermore." ' "

Rom 15:16 that I might be a minister of Jesus Christ to the Gentiles, ministering the gospel of God, that the offering of the Gentiles might be acceptable, sanctified by the Holy Spirit.

As the witness.

Heb 10:15 But the Holy Spirit also witnesses to us; for after He had said before,

1 John 5:9 If we receive the witness of men, the witness of God is greater; for this is the witness of God which He has testified of His Son.

As convincing of sin, righteousness, and judgment.

John 16:8–11 And when He has come, He will convict the world of sin, and of righteousness, and of judgment: **9** of sin, because they do not believe in Me; **10** of righteousness, because I go to My Father and you see Me no more; **11** of judgment, because the ruler of this world is judged.

HOLY SPIRIT, THE EMBLEMS OF THE

Water,

John 3:5 Jesus answered, "Most assuredly, I say to you, unless one is born of water and the Spirit, he cannot enter the kingdom of God.

John 7:38–39 He who believes in Me, as the Scripture has said, out of his heart will flow rivers of living water." **39** But this He spoke concerning the Spirit, whom those believing in Him would receive; for the Holy Spirit was not yet *given,* because Jesus was not yet glorified.

Cleansing.

Ezek 16:9 "Then I washed you in water; yes, I thoroughly washed off your blood, and I anointed you with oil.

Ezek 36:25 Then I will sprinkle clean water on you, and you shall be clean; I will cleanse you from all your filthiness and from all your idols.

Eph 5:26 that He might sanctify and cleanse her with the washing of water by the word,

Heb 10:22 let us draw near with a true heart in full assurance of faith, having our hearts sprinkled from an evil conscience and our bodies washed with pure water.

Nourishing.

Ps 1:3 He shall be like a tree Planted by the rivers of water, That brings forth its fruit in its season, Whose leaf also shall not wither; And whatever he does shall prosper.

Is 27:3 I, the LORD, keep it, I water it every moment; Lest any hurt it, I keep it night and day.

Is 27:6 Those who come He shall cause to take root in

Jacob; Israel shall blossom and bud, And fill the face of the world with fruit.

Is 44:3–4 For I will pour water on him who is thirsty, And floods on the dry ground; I will pour My Spirit on your descendants, And My blessing on your offspring; **4** They will spring up among the grass Like willows by the watercourses.'

Is 58:11 The LORD will guide you continually, And satisfy your soul in drought, And strengthen your bones; You shall be like a watered garden, And like a spring of water, whose waters do not fail.

Refreshing.

Ps 46:4 *There is* a river whose streams shall make glad the city of God, The holy *place* of the tabernacle of the Most High.

Is 41:17–18 "The poor and needy seek water, but *there is* none, Their tongues fail for thirst. I, the LORD, will hear them; I, the God of Israel, will not forsake them. **18** I will open rivers in desolate heights, And fountains in the midst of the valleys; I will make the wilderness a pool of water, And the dry land springs of water.

Abundant.

John 7:37–38 On the last day, that great *day* of the feast, Jesus stood and cried out, saying, "If anyone thirsts, let him come to Me and drink. **38** He who believes in Me, as the Scripture has said, out of his heart will flow rivers of living water."

Freely given.

Is 55:1 "Ho! Everyone who thirsts, Come to the waters; And you who have no money, Come, buy and eat. Yes, come, buy wine and milk Without money and without price.

John 4:14 but whoever drinks of the water that I shall give him will never thirst. But the water that I shall give him will become in him a fountain of water springing up into everlasting life."

Rev 22:17 And the Spirit and the bride say, "Come!" And let him who hears say, "Come!" And let him who thirsts come. Whoever desires, let him take the water of life freely.

Fire,

Purifying.

Is 4:4 When the Lord has washed away the filth of the daughters of Zion, and purged the blood of Jerusalem from her midst, by the spirit of judgment and by the spirit of burning,

Mal 3:2–3 "But who can endure the day of His coming? And who can stand when He appears? For He *is* like a refiner's fire And like launderers' soap. **3** He will sit as a refiner and a purifier of silver; He will purify the sons of Levi, And purge them as gold and silver, That they may offer to the LORD An offering in righteousness.

Illuminating.

Ex 13:21 And the LORD went before them by day in a pillar of cloud to lead the way, and by night in a pillar of fire to give them light, so as to go by day and night.

Ps 78:14 In the daytime also He led them with the cloud, And all the night with a light of fire.

Searching.

Zeph 1:12 "And it shall come to pass at that time That I will search Jerusalem with lamps, And punish the men Who are settled in complacency, Who say in their heart, 'The LORD will not do good, Nor will He do evil.'

1 Cor 2:10 But God has revealed *them* to us through His Spirit. For the Spirit searches all things, yes, the deep things of God.

Wind,

Independent.

John 3:8 The wind blows where it wishes, and you hear the sound of it, but cannot tell where it comes from and where it goes. So is everyone who is born of the Spirit."

1 Cor 12:11 But one and the same Spirit works all these things, distributing to each one individually as He wills.

Powerful.

1 Kin 19:11 Then He said, "Go out, and stand on the mountain before the LORD." And behold, the LORD passed by, and a great and strong wind tore into the mountains and broke the rocks in pieces before the LORD, *but* the LORD *was* not in the wind; and after the wind an earthquake, *but* the LORD *was* not in the earthquake;

Acts 2:2 And suddenly there came a sound from heaven, as of a rushing mighty wind, and it filled the whole house where they were sitting.

Sensible in its effects.

John 3:8 The wind blows where it wishes, and you hear the sound of it, but cannot tell where it comes from and where it goes. So is everyone who is born of the Spirit."

Reviving.

Ezek 37:9–10 Also He said to me, "Prophesy to the breath, prophesy, son of man, and say to the breath, 'Thus says the Lord GOD: "Come from the four winds, O breath, and breathe on these slain, that they may live." ' " **10** So I prophesied as He commanded me, and breath came into them, and they lived, and stood upon their feet, an exceedingly great army.

Ezek 37:14 I will put My Spirit in you, and you shall live, and I will place you in your own land. Then you shall know that I, the LORD, have spoken *it* and performed *it*," says the LORD.' "

Oil,

Of gladness.

Ps 45:7 You love righteousness and hate wickedness; Therefore God, Your God, has anointed You With the oil of gladness more than Your companions.

Comforting.

Is 61:3 To console those who mourn in Zion, To give them beauty for ashes, The oil of joy for mourning, The garment of praise for the spirit of heaviness; That they may be called trees of righteousness, The planting of the LORD, that He may be glorified."

Heb 1:9 *You have loved righteousness and hated lawlessness; Therefore God, Your God, has anointed You With the oil of gladness more than Your companions."*

Illuminating.

Matt 25:3–4 Those who *were* foolish took their lamps and took no oil with them, **4** but the wise took oil in their vessels with their lamps.

1 John 2:20 But you have an anointing from the Holy One, and you know all things.

1 John 2:27 But the anointing which you have received from Him abides in you, and you do not need that anyone teach you; but as the same anointing teaches you concerning all things, and is true, and is not a lie, and just as it has taught you, you will abide in Him.

Consecrating.

Ex 29:7 And you shall take the anointing oil, pour *it* on his head, and anoint him.

Ex 30:30 And you shall anoint Aaron and his sons, and consecrate them, that *they* may minister to Me as priests.

Is 61:1 "The Spirit of the Lord God *is* upon Me, Because the Lord has anointed Me To preach good tidings to the poor; He has sent Me to heal the brokenhearted, To proclaim liberty to the captives, And the opening of the prison to *those who are* bound;

Rain and dew,

Ps 72:6 He shall come down like rain upon the grass before mowing, Like showers *that* water the earth.

Fertilizing.

Ezek 34:26–27 I will make them and the places all around My hill a blessing; and I will cause showers to come down in their season; there shall be showers of blessing. **27** Then the trees of the field shall yield their fruit, and the earth shall yield her increase. They shall be safe in their land; and they shall know that I *am* the Lord, when I have broken the bands of their yoke and delivered them from the hand of those who enslaved them.

Hos 6:3 Let us know, Let us pursue the knowledge of the Lord. His going forth is established as the morning; He will come to us like the rain, Like the latter *and* former rain to the earth.

Hos 10:12 Sow for yourselves righteousness; Reap in mercy; Break up your fallow ground, For *it is* time to seek the Lord, Till He comes and rains righteousness on you.

Hos 14:5 I will be like the dew to Israel; He shall grow like the lily, And lengthen his roots like Lebanon.

Refreshing.

Ps 68:9 You, O God, sent a plentiful rain, Whereby You confirmed Your inheritance, When it was weary.

Is 18:5 For before the harvest, when the bud is perfect And the sour grape is ripening in the flower, He will both cut off the sprigs with pruning hooks And take away *and* cut down the branches.

Abundant.

Ps 133:3 *It is* like the dew of Hermon, Descending upon the mountains of Zion; For there the Lord commanded the blessing— Life forevermore.

Imperceptible.

2 Sam 17:12 So we will come upon him in some place where he may be found, and we will fall on him as the dew falls on the ground. And of him and all the men who *are* with him there shall not be left so much as one.

Mark 4:26–28 And He said, "The kingdom of God is as if a man should scatter seed on the ground, **27** and should sleep by night and rise by day, and the seed should sprout and grow, he himself does not know how. **28** For the earth yields crops by itself: first the blade, then the head, after that the full grain in the head.

A dove,

Matt 3:16 When He had been baptized, Jesus came up immediately from the water; and behold, the heavens were opened to Him, and He saw the Spirit of God descending like a dove and alighting upon Him.

Gentle.

Matt 10:16 "Behold, I send you out as sheep in the midst of wolves. Therefore be wise as serpents and harmless as doves.

Gal 5:22 But the fruit of the Spirit is love, joy, peace, longsuffering, kindness, goodness, faithfulness,

A voice,

Is 6:8 Also I heard the voice of the Lord, saying: "Whom shall I send, And who will go for Us?" Then I said, "Here *am* I! Send me."

Speaking.

Matt 10:20 for it is not you who speak, but the Spirit of your Father who speaks in you.

Guiding.

Is 30:21 Your ears shall hear a word behind you, saying, "This *is* the way, walk in it," Whenever you turn to the right hand Or whenever you turn to the left.

John 16:13 However, when He, the Spirit of truth, has come, He will guide you into all truth; for He will not speak on His own *authority,* but whatever He hears He will speak; and He will tell you things to come.

Warning.

Heb 3:7–11 Therefore, as the Holy Spirit says: *"Today, if you will hear His voice,* **8** *Do not harden your hearts as in the rebellion, In the day of trial in the wilderness,* **9** *Where your fathers tested Me, tried Me, And saw My works forty years.* **10** *Therefore I was angry with that generation, And said, 'They always go astray in their heart, And they have not known My ways.'* **11** *So I swore in My wrath, 'They shall not enter My rest.' "*

A seal,

Rev 7:2 Then I saw another angel ascending from the east, having the seal of the living God. And he cried with a loud voice to the four angels to whom it was granted to harm the earth and the sea,

Securing.

Eph 1:13–14 In Him you also *trusted,* after you heard the word of truth, the gospel of your salvation; in whom also, having believed, you were sealed with the Holy Spirit of promise, **14** who is the guarantee of our inheritance until the redemption of the purchased possession, to the praise of His glory.

Eph 4:30 And do not grieve the Holy Spirit of God, by whom you were sealed for the day of redemption.

Authenticating.

John 6:27 Do not labor for the food which perishes, but

for the food which endures to everlasting life, which the Son of Man will give you, because God the Father has set His seal on Him."

2 Cor 1:22 who also has sealed us and given us the Spirit in our hearts as a guarantee.

Divided tongues.

Acts 2:3 Then there appeared to them divided tongues, as of fire, and *one* sat upon each of them.

Acts 2:6–11 And when this sound occurred, the multitude came together, and were confused, because everyone heard them speak in his own language. **7** Then they were all amazed and marveled, saying to one another, "Look, are not all these who speak Galileans? **8** And how *is it that* we hear, each in our own language in which we were born? **9** Parthians and Medes and Elamites, those dwelling in Mesopotamia, Judea and Cappadocia, Pontus and Asia, **10** Phrygia and Pamphylia, Egypt and the parts of Libya adjoining Cyrene, visitors from Rome, both Jews and proselytes, **11** Cretans and Arabs—we hear them speaking in our own tongues the wonderful works of God."

HOLY SPIRIT, THE GIFT OF THE

By the Father.

Neh 9:20 You also gave Your good Spirit to instruct them, And did not withhold Your manna from their mouth, And gave them water for their thirst.

Luke 11:13 If you then, being evil, know how to give good gifts to your children, how much more will *your* heavenly Father give the Holy Spirit to those who ask Him!"

By the Son.

John 20:22 And when He had said this, He breathed on *them,* and said to them, "Receive the Holy Spirit."

To Christ without measure.

John 3:34 For He whom God has sent speaks the words of God, for God does not give the Spirit by measure.

Given

According to promise.

Acts 2:38–39 Then Peter said to them, "Repent, and let every one of you be baptized in the name of Jesus Christ for the remission of sins; and you shall receive the gift of the Holy Spirit. **39** For the promise is to you and to your children, and to all who are afar off, as many as the Lord our God will call."

Upon the exaltation of Christ.

Ps 68:18 You have ascended on high, You have led captivity captive; You have received gifts among men, Even *from* the rebellious, That the LORD God might dwell *there.*

John 7:39 But this He spoke concerning the Spirit, whom those believing in Him would receive; for the Holy Spirit was not yet *given,* because Jesus was not yet glorified.

Through the intercession of Christ.

John 14:16 And I will pray the Father, and He will give you another Helper, that He may abide with you forever—

In answer to prayer.

Luke 11:13 If you then, being evil, know how to give good gifts to your children, how much more will *your* heavenly Father give the Holy Spirit to those who ask Him!"

Eph 1:16–17 do not cease to give thanks for you, making mention of you in my prayers: **17** that the God of our Lord Jesus Christ, the Father of glory, may give to you the spirit of wisdom and revelation in the knowledge of Him,

For instruction.

Neh 9:20 You also gave Your good Spirit to instruct them, And did not withhold Your manna from their mouth, And gave them water for their thirst.

To help believers.

John 14:16 And I will pray the Father, and He will give you another Helper, that He may abide with you forever—

To those who repent and believe.

Acts 2:38 Then Peter said to them, "Repent, and let every one of you be baptized in the name of Jesus Christ for the remission of sins; and you shall receive the gift of the Holy Spirit.

To those who obey God.

Acts 5:32 And we are His witnesses to these things, and *so* also *is* the Holy Spirit whom God has given to those who obey Him."

To the Gentiles.

Acts 10:44–45 While Peter was still speaking these words, the Holy Spirit fell upon all those who heard the word. **45** And those of the circumcision who believed were astonished, as many as came with Peter, because the gift of the Holy Spirit had been poured out on the Gentiles also.

Acts 11:17 If therefore God gave them the same gift as *He gave* us when we believed on the Lord Jesus Christ, who was I that I could withstand God?"

Acts 15:8 So God, who knows the heart, acknowledged them by giving them the Holy Spirit, just as *He did* to us,

Is abundant.

Ps 68:9 You, O God, sent a plentiful rain, Whereby You confirmed Your inheritance, When it was weary.

John 7:38–39 He who believes in Me, as the Scripture has said, out of his heart will flow rivers of living water." **39** But this He spoke concerning the Spirit, whom those believing in Him would receive; for the Holy Spirit was not yet *given,* because Jesus was not yet glorified.

Is permanent.

Is 59:21 "As for Me," says the LORD, "this *is* My covenant with them: My Spirit who *is* upon you, and My words which I have put in your mouth, shall not depart from your mouth, nor from the mouth of your descendants, nor from the mouth of your descendants' descendants," says the LORD, "from this time and forevermore."

Hag 2:5 '*According to* the word that I covenanted with you when you came out of Egypt, so My Spirit remains among you; do not fear!'

1 Pet 4:14 If you are reproached for the name of Christ, blessed *are you,* for the Spirit of glory and of God rests upon you. On their part He is blasphemed, but on your part He is glorified.

Is fruit bearing.

Is 32:15 Until the Spirit is poured upon us from on high, And the wilderness becomes a fruitful field, And the fruitful field is counted as a forest.

Received through faith.

Gal 3:14 that the blessing of Abraham might come upon the Gentiles in Christ Jesus, that we might receive the promise of the Spirit through faith.

An evidence of union with Christ.

1 John 3:24 Now he who keeps His commandments abides in Him, and He in him. And by this we know that He abides in us, by the Spirit whom He has given us.

1 John 4:13 By this we know that we abide in Him, and He in us, because He has given us of His Spirit.

A guarantee of the inheritance of believers.

2 Cor 1:22 who also has sealed us and given us the Spirit in our hearts as a guarantee.

2 Cor 5:5 Now He who has prepared us for this very thing *is* God, who also has given us the Spirit as a guarantee.

Eph 1:14 who is the guarantee of our inheritance until the redemption of the purchased possession, to the praise of His glory.

A pledge of the continued favor of God.

Ezek 39:29 And I will not hide My face from them anymore; for I shall have poured out My Spirit on the house of Israel,' says the Lord GOD."

HOLY SPIRIT, THE—HIS ROLE AS HELPER
Proceeds from the Father.

John 15:26 "But when the Helper comes, whom I shall send to you from the Father, the Spirit of truth who proceeds from the Father, He will testify of Me.

Given by
The Father.

John 14:16 And I will pray the Father, and He will give you another Helper, that He may abide with you forever—

Christ.

Is 61:3 To console those who mourn in Zion, To give them beauty for ashes, The oil of joy for mourning, The garment of praise for the spirit of heaviness; That they may be called trees of righteousness, The planting of the LORD, that He may be glorified."

Christ's intercession.

John 14:16 And I will pray the Father, and He will give you another Helper, that He may abide with you forever—

John 14:26 But the Helper, the Holy Spirit, whom the Father will send in My name, He will teach you all things, and bring to your remembrance all things that I said to you.

Sent by Christ from the Father.

John 15:26 "But when the Helper comes, whom I shall send to you from the Father, the Spirit of truth who proceeds from the Father, He will testify of Me.

John 16:7 Nevertheless I tell you the truth. It is to your advantage that I go away; for if I do not go away, the

Helper will not come to you; but if I depart, I will send Him to you.

Purposes of,
Communicates joy to believers.

Rom 14:17 for the kingdom of God is not eating and drinking, but righteousness and peace and joy in the Holy Spirit.

Gal 5:22 But the fruit of the Spirit is love, joy, peace, longsuffering, kindness, goodness, faithfulness,

1 Thess 1:6 And you became followers of us and of the Lord, having received the word in much affliction, with joy of the Holy Spirit,

Edifies the church.

Acts 9:31 Then the churches throughout all Judea, Galilee, and Samaria had peace and were edified. And walking in the fear of the Lord and in the comfort of the Holy Spirit, they were multiplied.

Testifies of Christ.

John 15:26 "But when the Helper comes, whom I shall send to you from the Father, the Spirit of truth who proceeds from the Father, He will testify of Me.

Imparts the love of God.

Rom 5:3–5 And not only *that,* but we also glory in tribulations, knowing that tribulation produces perseverance; **4** and perseverance, character; and character, hope. **5** Now hope does not disappoint, because the love of God has been poured out in our hearts by the Holy Spirit who was given to us.

Imparts hope.

Rom 15:13 Now may the God of hope fill you with all joy and peace in believing, that you may abound in hope by the power of the Holy Spirit.

Gal 5:5 For we through the Spirit eagerly wait for the hope of righteousness by faith.

Teaches believers.

John 14:26 But the Helper, the Holy Spirit, whom the Father will send in My name, He will teach you all things, and bring to your remembrance all things that I said to you.

Dwells with and in believers.

John 14:16–17 And I will pray the Father, and He will give you another Helper, that He may abide with you forever— **17** the Spirit of truth, whom the world cannot receive, because it neither sees Him nor knows Him; but you know Him, for He dwells with you and will be in you.

The world cannot receive.

John 14:17 the Spirit of truth, whom the world cannot receive, because it neither sees Him nor knows Him; but you know Him, for He dwells with you and will be in you.

HOLY SPIRIT, THE—HIS ROLE AS TEACHER
Promised.

Prov 1:23 Turn at my rebuke; Surely I will pour out my spirit on you; I will make my words known to you.

Is the Spirit of wisdom.

Is 11:2 The Spirit of the LORD shall rest upon Him, The Spirit of wisdom and understanding, The Spirit of counsel and might, The Spirit of knowledge and of the fear of the LORD.

Is 40:13–14 Who has directed the Spirit of the LORD, Or *as* His counselor has taught Him? **14** With whom did He take counsel, and *who* instructed Him, And taught Him in the path of justice? Who taught Him knowledge, And showed Him the way of understanding?

Given

In answer to prayer.

Eph 1:16–17 do not cease to give thanks for you, making mention of you in my prayers: **17** that the God of our Lord Jesus Christ, the Father of glory, may give to you the spirit of wisdom and revelation in the knowledge of Him,

To believers.

Neh 9:20 You also gave Your good Spirit to instruct them, And did not withhold Your manna from their mouth, And gave them water for their thirst.

1 Cor 2:12–13 Now we have received, not the spirit of the world, but the Spirit who is from God, that we might know the things that have been freely given to us by God. **13** These things we also speak, not in words which man's wisdom teaches but which the Holy Spirit teaches, comparing spiritual things with spiritual.

Necessity for.

1 Cor 2:9–10 But as it is written: *"Eye has not seen, nor ear heard, Nor have entered into the heart of man The things which God has prepared for those who love Him."* **10** But God has revealed *them* to us through His Spirit. For the Spirit searches all things, yes, the deep things of God.

Activities in that role

Reveals the things of God.

1 Cor 2:10 But God has revealed *them* to us through His Spirit. For the Spirit searches all things, yes, the deep things of God.

1 Cor 2:13 These things we also speak, not in words which man's wisdom teaches but which the Holy Spirit teaches, comparing spiritual things with spiritual.

Reveals the things of Christ.

John 16:14 He will glorify Me, for He will take of what is Mine and declare *it* to you.

Reveals the future.

Luke 2:26 And it had been revealed to him by the Holy Spirit that he would not see death before he had seen the Lord's Christ.

Acts 21:11 When he had come to us, he took Paul's belt, bound his *own* hands and feet, and said, "Thus says the Holy Spirit, 'So shall the Jews at Jerusalem bind the man who owns this belt, and deliver *him* into the hands of the Gentiles.' "

Brings the words of Christ to remembrance.

John 14:26 But the Helper, the Holy Spirit, whom the Father will send in My name, He will teach you all things, and bring to your remembrance all things that I said to you.

Directs in the way of godliness.

Is 30:21 Your ears shall hear a word behind you, saying,

"This *is* the way, walk in it," Whenever you turn to the right hand Or whenever you turn to the left.

Ezek 36:27 I will put My Spirit within you and cause you to walk in My statutes, and you will keep My judgments and do *them*.

Teaches believers to answer persecutors.

Mark 13:11 But when they arrest *you* and deliver you up, do not worry beforehand, or premeditate what you will speak. But whatever is given you in that hour, speak that; for it is not you who speak, but the Holy Spirit.

Luke 12:12 For the Holy Spirit will teach you in that very hour what you ought to say."

Enables ministers to teach.

1 Cor 12:8 for to one is given the word of wisdom through the Spirit, to another the word of knowledge through the same Spirit,

Guides into all truth.

John 14:26 But the Helper, the Holy Spirit, whom the Father will send in My name, He will teach you all things, and bring to your remembrance all things that I said to you.

John 16:13 However, when He, the Spirit of truth, has come, He will guide you into all truth; for He will not speak on His own *authority*, but whatever He hears He will speak; and He will tell you things to come.

Directs the decisions of the church.

Acts 15:28 For it seemed good to the Holy Spirit, and to us, to lay upon you no greater burden than these necessary things:

Should listen to His instruction.

Rev 2:7 "He who has an ear, let him hear what the Spirit says to the churches. To him who overcomes I will give to eat from the tree of life, which is in the midst of the Paradise of God." '

Rev 2:11 "He who has an ear, let him hear what the Spirit says to the churches. He who overcomes shall not be hurt by the second death." '

Rev 2:29 "He who has an ear, let him hear what the Spirit says to the churches." '

The natural man will not receive the things of.

1 Cor 2:14 But the natural man does not receive the things of the Spirit of God, for they are foolishness to him; nor can he know *them*, because they are spiritually discerned.

HOLY SPIRIT, THE INDWELLING OF THE

In His church, as His temple.

1 Cor 3:16 Do you not know that you are the temple of God and *that* the Spirit of God dwells in you?

In the body of believers, as His temple.

1 Cor 6:19 Or do you not know that your body is the temple of the Holy Spirit *who is* in you, whom you have from God, and you are not your own?

2 Cor 6:16 And what agreement has the temple of God with idols? For you are the temple of the living God. As God has said: *"I will dwell in them And walk among them. I will be their God, And they shall be My people."*

Promised to believers.

Ezek 36:27 I will put My Spirit within you and cause you to walk in My statutes, and you will keep My judgments and do *them.*

Acts 1:8 But you shall receive power when the Holy Spirit has come upon you; and you shall be witnesses to Me in Jerusalem, and in all Judea and Samaria, and to the end of the earth."

As a helper to believers.

John 14:16–17 And I will pray the Father, and He will give you another Helper, that He may abide with you forever— **17** the Spirit of truth, whom the world cannot receive, because it neither sees Him nor knows Him; but you know Him, for He dwells with you and will be in you.

A guarantee of eternal salvation.

Eph 1:13–14 In Him you also *trusted,* after you heard the word of truth, the gospel of your salvation; in whom also, having believed, you were sealed with the Holy Spirit of promise, **14** who is the guarantee of our inheritance until the redemption of the purchased possession, to the praise of His glory.

Believers filled with.

Is 63:11 Then he remembered the days of old, Moses *and* his people, *saying:* "Where *is* He who brought them up out of the sea With the shepherd of His flock? Where *is* He who put His Holy Spirit within them,

Acts 6:5 And the saying pleased the whole multitude. And they chose Stephen, a man full of faith and the Holy Spirit, and Philip, Prochorus, Nicanor, Timon, Parmenas, and Nicolas, a proselyte from Antioch,

Eph 5:18 And do not be drunk with wine, in which is dissipation; but be filled with the Spirit,

2 Tim 1:14 That good thing which was committed to you, keep by the Holy Spirit who dwells in us.

1 John 2:27 But the anointing which you have received from Him abides in you, and you do not need that anyone teach you; but as the same anointing teaches you concerning all things, and is true, and is not a lie, and just as it has taught you, you will abide in Him.

Is the means of

Receiving life.

Rom 8:11 But if the Spirit of Him who raised Jesus from the dead dwells in you, He who raised Christ from the dead will also give life to your mortal bodies through His Spirit who dwells in you.

Guiding.

John 16:13 However, when He, the Spirit of truth, has come, He will guide you into all truth; for He will not speak on His own *authority,* but whatever He hears He will speak; and He will tell you things to come.

Gal 5:18 But if you are led by the Spirit, you are not under the law.

Fruit bearing.

Gal 5:22 But the fruit of the Spirit is love, joy, peace, longsuffering, kindness, goodness, faithfulness,

A proof of being Christ's child.

Rom 8:9 But you are not in the flesh but in the Spirit, if indeed the Spirit of God dwells in you. Now if anyone does not have the Spirit of Christ, he is not His.

Rom 8:15 For you did not receive the spirit of bondage again to fear, but you received the Spirit of adoption by whom we cry out, "Abba, Father."

Gal 4:5 to redeem those who were under the law, that we might receive the adoption as sons.

1 John 4:13 By this we know that we abide in Him, and He in us, because He has given us of His Spirit.

Those who do not have,

Are sensual.

Jude 1:19 These are sensual persons, who cause divisions, not having the Spirit.

Are without Christ.

Rom 8:9 But you are not in the flesh but in the Spirit, if indeed the Spirit of God dwells in you. Now if anyone does not have the Spirit of Christ, he is not His.

Opposed by the carnal nature.

Gal 5:17 For the flesh lusts against the Spirit, and the Spirit against the flesh; and these are contrary to one another, so that you do not do the things that you wish.

HOLY SPIRIT, THE INSPIRATION OF THE

Foretold.

Joel 2:28 "And it shall come to pass afterward That I will pour out My Spirit on all flesh; Your sons and your daughters shall prophesy, Your old men shall dream dreams, Your young men shall see visions.

Acts 2:16–18 But this is what was spoken by the prophet Joel: **17** *'And it shall come to pass in the last days, says God, That I will pour out of My Spirit on all flesh; Your sons and your daughters shall prophesy, Your young men shall see visions, Your old men shall dream dreams.* **18** *And on My menservants and on My maidservants I will pour out My Spirit in those days; And they shall prophesy.*

All Scripture given by.

2 Sam 23:2 "The Spirit of the LORD spoke by me, And His word *was* on my tongue.

2 Tim 3:16 All Scripture *is* given by inspiration of God, and *is* profitable for doctrine, for reproof, for correction, for instruction in righteousness,

2 Pet 1:21 for prophecy never came by the will of man, but holy men of God spoke *as they were* moved by the Holy Spirit.

Purpose of,

To reveal future events.

Acts 1:16 "Men *and* brethren, this Scripture had to be fulfilled, which the Holy Spirit spoke before by the mouth of David concerning Judas, who became a guide to those who arrested Jesus;

Acts 28:25 So when they did not agree among themselves, they departed after Paul had said one word: "The Holy Spirit spoke rightly through Isaiah the prophet to our fathers,

1 Pet 1:11 searching what, or what manner of time, the Spirit of Christ who was in them was indicating when He testified beforehand the sufferings of Christ and the glories that would follow.

To reveal the mysteries of God.

Amos 3:7 Surely the Lord GOD does nothing, Unless He reveals His secret to His servants the prophets.

1 Cor 2:10 But God has revealed *them* to us through His Spirit. For the Spirit searches all things, yes, the deep things of God.

To give power to ministers.

Mic 3:8 But truly I am full of power by the Spirit of the LORD, And of justice and might, To declare to Jacob his transgression And to Israel his sin.

Acts 1:8 But you shall receive power when the Holy Spirit has come upon you; and you shall be witnesses to Me in Jerusalem, and in all Judea and Samaria, and to the end of the earth."

To direct ministers.

Ezek 3:24–27 Then the Spirit entered me and set me on my feet, and spoke with me and said to me: "Go, shut yourself inside your house. **25** And you, O son of man, surely they will put ropes on you and bind you with them, so that you cannot go out among them. **26** I will make your tongue cling to the roof of your mouth, so that you shall be mute and not be one to rebuke them, for they *are* a rebellious house. **27** But when I speak with you, I will open your mouth, and you shall say to them, 'Thus says the Lord GOD.' He who hears, let him hear; and he who refuses, let him refuse; for they *are* a rebellious house.

Acts 11:12 Then the Spirit told me to go with them, doubting nothing. Moreover these six brethren accompanied me, and we entered the man's house.

Acts 13:2 As they ministered to the Lord and fasted, the Holy Spirit said, "Now separate to Me Barnabas and Saul for the work to which I have called them."

Acts 16:6 Now when they had gone through Phrygia and the region of Galatia, they were forbidden by the Holy Spirit to preach the word in Asia.

To testify against sin.

2 Kin 17:13 Yet the LORD testified against Israel and against Judah, by all of His prophets, every seer, saying, "Turn from your evil ways, and keep My commandments *and* My statutes, according to all the law which I commanded your fathers, and which I sent to you by My servants the prophets."

Neh 9:30 Yet for many years You had patience with them, And testified against them by Your Spirit in Your prophets. Yet they would not listen; Therefore You gave them into the hand of the peoples of the lands.

Mic 3:8 But truly I am full of power by the Spirit of the LORD, And of justice and might, To declare to Jacob his transgression And to Israel his sin.

John 16:8–9 And when He has come, He will convict the world of sin, and of righteousness, and of judgment: **9** of sin, because they do not believe in Me;

Modes of,

Various.

Heb 1:1 God, who at various times and in various ways spoke in time past to the fathers by the prophets,

By secret impulse.

Judg 13:25 And the Spirit of the LORD began to move upon him at Mahaneh Dan between Zorah and Eshtaol.

2 Pet 1:21 for prophecy never came by the will of man, but holy men of God spoke *as they were* moved by the Holy Spirit.

By a voice.

Is 6:8 Also I heard the voice of the Lord, saying: "Whom shall I send, And who will go for Us?" Then I said, "Here *am* I! Send me."

Acts 8:29 Then the Spirit said to Philip, "Go near and overtake this chariot."

Rev 1:10 I was in the Spirit on the Lord's Day, and I heard behind me a loud voice, as of a trumpet,

By visions.

Num 12:6 Then He said, "Hear now My words: If there is a prophet among you, *I*, the LORD, make Myself known to him in a vision; I speak to him in a dream.

Ezek 11:24 Then the Spirit took me up and brought me in a vision by the Spirit of God into Chaldea, to those in captivity. And the vision that I had seen went up from me.

By dreams.

Num 12:6 Then He said, "Hear now My words: If there is a prophet among you, *I*, the LORD, make Myself known to him in a vision; I speak to him in a dream.

Dan 7:1 In the first year of Belshazzar king of Babylon, Daniel had a dream and visions of his head *while* on his bed. Then he wrote down the dream, telling the main facts.

Necessary to prophesying.

Num 11:25–27 Then the LORD came down in the cloud, and spoke to him, and took of the Spirit that *was* upon him, and placed *the same* upon the seventy elders; and it happened, when the Spirit rested upon them, that they prophesied, although they never did so again. **26** But two men had remained in the camp: the name of one *was* Eldad, and the name of the other Medad. And the Spirit rested upon them. Now they *were* among those listed, but who had not gone out to the tabernacle; yet they prophesied in the camp. **27** And a young man ran and told Moses, and said, "Eldad and Medad are prophesying in the camp."

2 Chr 20:14–17 Then the Spirit of the LORD came upon Jahaziel the son of Zechariah, the son of Benaiah, the son of Jeiel, the son of Mattaniah, a Levite of the sons of Asaph, in the midst of the assembly. **15** And he said, "Listen, all you of Judah and you inhabitants of Jerusalem, and you, King Jehoshaphat! Thus says the LORD to you: 'Do not be afraid nor dismayed because of this great multitude, for the battle *is* not yours, but God's. **16** Tomorrow go down against them. They will surely come up by the Ascent of Ziz, and you will find them at the end of the brook before the Wilderness of Jeruel. **17** You will not *need* to fight in this *battle.* Position yourselves, stand still and see the salvation of the LORD, who is with you, O Judah and Jerusalem!' Do not fear or be dismayed; tomorrow go out against them, for the LORD *is* with you."

Is irresistible.

Amos 3:8 A lion has roared! Who will not fear? The Lord GOD has spoken! Who can but prophesy?

Despisers of, punished.

2 Chr 36:15–16 And the LORD God of their fathers sent *warnings* to them by His messengers, rising up early and sending *them,* because He had compassion on His people and on His dwelling place. **16** But they mocked the messengers of God, despised His words, and scoffed at His prophets, until the wrath of the LORD arose against His people, till *there was* no remedy.

Zech 7:12 Yes, they made their hearts like flint, refusing to hear the law and the words which the LORD of hosts had sent by His Spirit through the former prophets. Thus great wrath came from the LORD of hosts.

HOLY SPIRIT, OFFENSES AGAINST THE
Exhortations against.

Eph 4:30 And do not grieve the Holy Spirit of God, by whom you were sealed for the day of redemption.

1 Thess 5:19 Do not quench the Spirit.

Exhibited in

Tempting Him.

Acts 5:9 Then Peter said to her, "How is it that you have agreed together to test the Spirit of the Lord? Look, the feet of those who have buried your husband *are* at the door, and they will carry you out."

Grieving Him.

Is 63:10 But they rebelled and grieved His Holy Spirit; So He turned Himself against them as an enemy, *And* He fought against them.

Eph 4:30 And do not grieve the Holy Spirit of God, by whom you were sealed for the day of redemption.

Quenching Him.

1 Thess 5:19 Do not quench the Spirit.

Lying to Him.

Acts 5:3–4 But Peter said, "Ananias, why has Satan filled your heart to lie to the Holy Spirit and keep back *part* of the price of the land for yourself? 4 While it remained, was it not your own? And after it was sold, was it not in your own control? Why have you conceived this thing in your heart? You have not lied to men but to God."

Resisting Him.

Acts 7:51 "*You* stiff-necked and uncircumcised in heart and ears! You always resist the Holy Spirit; as your fathers *did*, so *do* you.

Undervaluing His gifts.

Acts 8:19–20 saying, "Give me this power also, that anyone on whom I lay hands may receive the Holy Spirit." 20 But Peter said to him, "Your money perish with you, because you thought that the gift of God could be purchased with money!

Trifling with Him.

Heb 6:4–6 For *it is* impossible for those who were once enlightened, and have tasted the heavenly gift, and have become partakers of the Holy Spirit, 5 and have tasted the good word of God and the powers of the age to come, 6 if they fall away, to renew them again to repentance, since they crucify again for themselves the Son of God, and put *Him* to an open shame.

Insulting Him.

Heb 10:29 Of how much worse punishment, do you suppose, will he be thought worthy who has trampled the Son of God underfoot, counted the blood of the covenant by which he was sanctified a common thing, and insulted the Spirit of grace?

Disregarding His testimony.

Neh 9:30 Yet for many years You had patience with them, And testified against them by Your Spirit in Your prophets. Yet they would not listen; Therefore You gave them into the hand of the peoples of the lands.

Blasphemy against Him, unpardonable.

Matt 12:31–32 "Therefore I say to you, every sin and blasphemy will be forgiven men, but the blasphemy *against* the Spirit will not be forgiven men. 32 Anyone who speaks a word against the Son of Man, it will be forgiven him; but whoever speaks against the Holy Spirit, it will not be forgiven him, either in this age or in the *age* to come.

1 John 5:16 If anyone sees his brother sinning a sin *which does* not *lead* to death, he will ask, and He will give him life for those who commit sin not *leading* to death. There is sin *leading* to death. I do not say that he should pray about that.

HOLY SPIRIT, THE PERSONALITY OF THE
He creates and gives life.

Job 33:4 The Spirit of God has made me, And the breath of the Almighty gives me life.

He appoints and commissions ministers.

Is 48:16 "Come near to Me, hear this: I have not spoken in secret from the beginning; From the time that it was, I *was* there. And now the Lord GOD and His Spirit Have sent Me."

Acts 13:2 As they ministered to the Lord and fasted, the Holy Spirit said, "Now separate to Me Barnabas and Saul for the work to which I have called them."

Acts 20:28 Therefore take heed to yourselves and to all the flock, among which the Holy Spirit has made you overseers, to shepherd the church of God which He purchased with His own blood.

He directs ministers where to preach.

Acts 8:29 Then the Spirit said to Philip, "Go near and overtake this chariot."

Acts 10:19–20 While Peter thought about the vision, the Spirit said to him, "Behold, three men are seeking you. 20 Arise therefore, go down and go with them, doubting nothing; for I have sent them."

He directs ministers where not to preach.

Acts 16:6–7 Now when they had gone through Phrygia and the region of Galatia, they were forbidden by the Holy Spirit to preach the word in Asia. 7 After they had come to Mysia, they tried to go into Bithynia, but the Spirit did not permit them.

He instructs ministers what to preach.

1 Cor 2:13 These things we also speak, not in words which man's wisdom teaches but which the Holy Spirit teaches, comparing spiritual things with spiritual.

He spoke in, and by, the prophets.

Acts 1:16 "Men *and* brethren, this Scripture had to be fulfilled, which the Holy Spirit spoke before by the mouth of David concerning Judas, who became a guide to those who arrested Jesus;

1 Pet 1:11–12 searching what, or what manner of time, the Spirit of Christ who was in them was indicating when He testified beforehand the sufferings of Christ and the glories that would follow. **12** To them it was revealed that, not to themselves, but to us they were ministering the things which now have been reported to you through those who have preached the gospel to you by the Holy Spirit sent from heaven— things which angels desire to look into.

2 Pet 1:21 for prophecy never came by the will of man, but holy men of God spoke *as they were* moved by the Holy Spirit.

He strives with sinners.

Gen 6:3 And the LORD said, "My Spirit shall not strive with man forever, for he *is* indeed flesh; yet his days shall be one hundred and twenty years."

He reproves.

John 16:8 And when He has come, He will convict the world of sin, and of righteousness, and of judgment:

He comforts.

Acts 9:31 Then the churches throughout all Judea, Galilee, and Samaria had peace and were edified. And walking in the fear of the Lord and in the comfort of the Holy Spirit, they were multiplied.

He helps our weaknesses.

Rom 8:26 Likewise the Spirit also helps in our weaknesses. For we do not know what we should pray for as we ought, but the Spirit Himself makes intercession for us with groanings which cannot be uttered.

He teaches.

John 14:26 But the Helper, the Holy Spirit, whom the Father will send in My name, He will teach you all things, and bring to your remembrance all things that I said to you.

1 Cor 12:3 Therefore I make known to you that no one speaking by the Spirit of God calls Jesus accursed, and no one can say that Jesus is Lord except by the Holy Spirit.

He guides.

John 16:13 However, when He, the Spirit of truth, has come, He will guide you into all truth; for He will not speak on His own *authority*, but whatever He hears He will speak; and He will tell you things to come.

He sanctifies.

Rom 15:16 that I might be a minister of Jesus Christ to the Gentiles, ministering the gospel of God, that the offering of the Gentiles might be acceptable, sanctified by the Holy Spirit.

1 Cor 6:11 And such were some of you. But you were washed, but you were sanctified, but you were justified in the name of the Lord Jesus and by the Spirit of our God.

He testifies of Christ.

John 15:26 "But when the Helper comes, whom I shall send to you from the Father, the Spirit of truth who proceeds from the Father, He will testify of Me.

He glorifies Christ.

John 16:14 He will glorify Me, for He will take of what is Mine and declare *it* to you.

He has a power of His own.

Rom 15:13 Now may the God of hope fill you with all joy and peace in believing, that you may abound in hope by the power of the Holy Spirit.

He searches all things.

Rom 11:33–34 Oh, the depth of the riches both of the wisdom and knowledge of God! How unsearchable *are* His judgments and His ways past finding out! **34** *"For who has known the mind of the LORD? Or who has become His counselor?"*

1 Cor 2:10–11 But God has revealed *them* to us through His Spirit. For the Spirit searches all things, yes, the deep things of God. **11** For what man knows the things of a man except the spirit of the man which is in him? Even so no one knows the things of God except the Spirit of God.

He works according to His own will.

1 Cor 12:11 But one and the same Spirit works all these things, distributing to each one individually as He wills.

He dwells with believers.

John 14:17 the Spirit of truth, whom the world cannot receive, because it neither sees Him nor knows Him; but you know Him, for He dwells with you and will be in you.

He can be grieved.

Is 63:10 But they rebelled and grieved His Holy Spirit; So He turned Himself against them as an enemy, *And* He fought against them.

Eph 4:30 And do not grieve the Holy Spirit of God, by whom you were sealed for the day of redemption.

He can be resisted.

Acts 7:51 *"You* stiff-necked and uncircumcised in heart and ears! You always resist the Holy Spirit; as your fathers *did,* so *do* you.

He can be tested.

Acts 5:9 Then Peter said to her, "How is it that you have agreed together to test the Spirit of the Lord? Look, the feet of those who have buried your husband *are* at the door, and they will carry you out."

HOLY SPIRIT, THE POWER OF THE

Is the power of God.

Matt 12:28 But if I cast out demons by the Spirit of God, surely the kingdom of God has come upon you.

Luke 11:20 But if I cast out demons with the finger of God, surely the kingdom of God has come upon you.

Christ

Began His ministry in.

Luke 4:14 Then Jesus returned in the power of the Spirit to Galilee, and news of Him went out through all the surrounding region.

Worked His miracles by.

Matt 12:28 But if I cast out demons by the Spirit of God, surely the kingdom of God has come upon you.

Promised its coming.

Luke 24:49 Behold, I send the Promise of My Father upon you; but tarry in the city of Jerusalem until you are endued with power from on high."

Acts 1:8 But you shall receive power when the Holy Spirit has come upon you; and you shall be witnesses to Me in Jerusalem, and in all Judea and Samaria, and to the end of the earth."

Exhibited in

Creation.

Gen 1:2 The earth was without form, and void; and darkness *was* on the face of the deep. And the Spirit of God was hovering over the face of the waters.

Job 26:13 By His Spirit He adorned the heavens; His hand pierced the fleeing serpent.

Ps 104:30 You send forth Your Spirit, they are created; And You renew the face of the earth.

The conception of Christ.

Luke 1:35 And the angel answered and said to her, "The Holy Spirit will come upon you, and the power of the Highest will overshadow you; therefore, also, that Holy One who is to be born will be called the Son of God.

Raising Christ from the dead.

1 Pet 3:18 For Christ also suffered once for sins, the just for the unjust, that He might bring us to God, being put to death in the flesh but made alive by the Spirit,

Giving spiritual life.

Ezek 37:11–14 Then He said to me, "Son of man, these bones are the whole house of Israel. They indeed say, 'Our bones are dry, our hope is lost, and we ourselves are cut off!' **12** Therefore prophesy and say to them, 'Thus says the Lord GOD: "Behold, O My people, I will open your graves and cause you to come up from your graves, and bring you into the land of Israel. **13** Then you shall know that I *am* the LORD, when I have opened your graves, O My people, and brought you up from your graves. **14** I will put My Spirit in you, and you shall live, and I will place you in your own land. Then you shall know that I, the LORD, have spoken *it* and performed *it*," says the LORD.' "

Rom 8:11 But if the Spirit of Him who raised Jesus from the dead dwells in you, He who raised Christ from the dead will also give life to your mortal bodies through His Spirit who dwells in you.

Working of miracles.

Rom 15:19 in mighty signs and wonders, by the power of the Spirit of God, so that from Jerusalem and round about to Illyricum I have fully preached the gospel of Christ.

Making the gospel efficacious.

1 Cor 2:4 And my speech and my preaching *were* not with persuasive words of human wisdom, but in demonstration of the Spirit and of power,

1 Thess 1:5 For our gospel did not come to you in word only, but also in power, and in the Holy Spirit and in much assurance, as you know what kind of men we were among you for your sake.

Overcoming all difficulties.

Zech 4:6–7 So he answered and said to me: "This *is* the word of the LORD to Zerubbabel: 'Not by might nor by power, but by My Spirit,' Says the LORD of hosts. **7** 'Who *are* you, O great mountain? Before Zerubbabel *you shall become* a plain! And he shall bring forth the capstone With shouts of "Grace, grace to it!" ' "

Believers

Upheld by.

Ps 51:12 Restore to me the joy of Your salvation, And uphold me *by Your* generous Spirit.

Strengthened by.

Eph 3:16 that He would grant you, according to the riches of His glory, to be strengthened with might through His Spirit in the inner man,

Given boldness by.

Mic 3:8 But truly I am full of power by the Spirit of the LORD, And of justice and might, To declare to Jacob his transgression And to Israel his sin.

Acts 6:5 And the saying pleased the whole multitude. And they chose Stephen, a man full of faith and the Holy Spirit, and Philip, Prochorus, Nicanor, Timon, Parmenas, and Nicolas, a proselyte from Antioch,

Acts 6:10 And they were not able to resist the wisdom and the Spirit by which he spoke.

2 Tim 1:7–8 For God has not given us a spirit of fear, but of power and of love and of a sound mind. **8** Therefore do not be ashamed of the testimony of our Lord, nor of me His prisoner, but share with me in the sufferings for the gospel according to the power of God,

Helped in prayer by.

Rom 8:26 Likewise the Spirit also helps in our weaknesses. For we do not know what we should pray for as we ought, but the Spirit Himself makes intercession for us with groanings which cannot be uttered.

Abound in hope by.

Rom 15:13 Now may the God of hope fill you with all joy and peace in believing, that you may abound in hope by the power of the Holy Spirit.

Qualifies them for ministry.

Luke 24:49 Behold, I send the Promise of My Father upon you; but tarry in the city of Jerusalem until you are endued with power from on high."

Acts 1:8 But you shall receive power when the Holy Spirit has come upon you; and you shall be witnesses to Me in Jerusalem, and in all Judea and Samaria, and to the end of the earth."

God's Word the instrument of.

Eph 6:17 And take the helmet of salvation, and the sword of the Spirit, which is the word of God;

HOLY SPIRIT, SEALING OF THE

Christ received.

John 6:27 Do not labor for the food which perishes, but for the food which endures to everlasting life, which the Son of Man will give you, because God the Father has set His seal on Him."

Believers receive.

2 Cor 1:22 who also has sealed us and given us the Spirit in our hearts as a guarantee.

Eph 1:13 In Him you also *trusted,* after you heard the word of truth, the gospel of your salvation; in whom also, having believed, you were sealed with the Holy Spirit of promise,

Is to the day of redemption.

Eph 4:30 And do not grieve the Holy Spirit of God, by whom you were sealed for the day of redemption.

The wicked do not receive.

Rev 9:4 They were commanded not to harm the grass of the earth, or any green thing, or any tree, but only those men who do not have the seal of God on their foreheads.

Judgment suspended until all believers receive.

Rev 7:3 saying, "Do not harm the earth, the sea, or the trees till we have sealed the servants of our God on their foreheads."

Typified.

Rom 4:11 And he received the sign of circumcision, a seal of the righteousness of the faith which *he had while still* uncircumcised, that he might be the father of all those who believe, though they are uncircumcised, that righteousness might be imputed to them also,

Holy Spirit, Titles and Names of the

Breath of the Almighty.

Job 33:4 The Spirit of God has made me, And the breath of the Almighty gives me life.

Eternal Spirit.

Heb 9:14 how much more shall the blood of Christ, who through the eternal Spirit offered Himself without spot to God, cleanse your conscience from dead works to serve the living God?

Generous Spirit.

Ps 51:12 Restore to me the joy of Your salvation, And uphold me *by Your* generous Spirit.

God.

Acts 5:3–4 But Peter said, "Ananias, why has Satan filled your heart to lie to the Holy Spirit and keep back *part* of the price of the land for yourself? 4 While it remained, was it not your own? And after it was sold, was it not in your own control? Why have you conceived this thing in your heart? You have not lied to men but to God."

Good Spirit.

Neh 9:20 You also gave Your good Spirit to instruct them, And did not withhold Your manna from their mouth, And gave them water for their thirst.

Ps 143:10 Teach me to do Your will, For You *are* my God; Your Spirit *is* good. Lead me in the land of uprightness.

Helper.

John 14:16 And I will pray the Father, and He will give you another Helper, that He may abide with you forever—

John 14:26 But the Helper, the Holy Spirit, whom the Father will send in My name, He will teach you all things, and bring to your remembrance all things that I said to you.

John 15:26 "But when the Helper comes, whom I shall send to you from the Father, the Spirit of truth who proceeds from the Father, He will testify of Me.

Holy Spirit.

Ps 51:11 Do not cast me away from Your presence, And do not take Your Holy Spirit from me.

Luke 11:13 If you then, being evil, know how to give good gifts to your children, how much more will *your* heavenly Father give the Holy Spirit to those who ask Him!"

Eph 1:13 In Him you also *trusted*, after you heard the word of truth, the gospel of your salvation; in whom

also, having believed, you were sealed with the Holy Spirit of promise,

Eph 4:30 And do not grieve the Holy Spirit of God, by whom you were sealed for the day of redemption.

Lord.

2 Thess 3:5 Now may the Lord direct your hearts into the love of God and into the patience of Christ.

Power of the Highest.

Luke 1:35 And the angel answered and said to her, "*The* Holy Spirit will come upon you, and the power of the Highest will overshadow you; therefore, also, that Holy One who is to be born will be called the Son of God.

Spirit, the.

Matt 4:1 Then Jesus was led up by the Spirit into the wilderness to be tempted by the devil.

John 3:6 That which is born of the flesh is flesh, and that which is born of the Spirit is spirit.

1 Tim 4:1 Now the Spirit expressly says that in latter times some will depart from the faith, giving heed to deceiving spirits and doctrines of demons,

Spirit of the Lord God.

Is 61:1 "The Spirit of the Lord GOD *is* upon Me, Because the LORD has anointed Me To preach good tidings to the poor; He has sent Me to heal the brokenhearted, To proclaim liberty to the captives, And the opening of the prison to *those who are* bound;

Spirit of the Lord.

Is 11:2 The Spirit of the LORD shall rest upon Him, The Spirit of wisdom and understanding, The Spirit of counsel and might, The Spirit of knowledge and of the fear of the LORD.

Acts 5:9 Then Peter said to her, "How is it that you have agreed together to test the Spirit of the Lord? Look, the feet of those who have buried your husband *are* at the door, and they will carry you out."

Spirit of God.

Gen 1:2 The earth was without form, and void; and darkness *was* on the face of the deep. And the Spirit of God was hovering over the face of the waters.

Job 33:4 The Spirit of God has made me, And the breath of the Almighty gives me life.

Rom 8:9 But you are not in the flesh but in the Spirit, if indeed the Spirit of God dwells in you. Now if anyone does not have the Spirit of Christ, he is not His.

1 Cor 2:11 For what man knows the things of a man except the spirit of the man which is in him? Even so no one knows the things of God except the Spirit of God.

Spirit of the Father.

Matt 10:20 for it is not you who speak, but the Spirit of your Father who speaks in you.

Spirit of Christ.

Rom 8:9 But you are not in the flesh but in the Spirit, if indeed the Spirit of God dwells in you. Now if anyone does not have the Spirit of Christ, he is not His.

1 Pet 1:11 searching what, or what manner of time, the Spirit of Christ who was in them was indicating when He testified beforehand the sufferings of Christ and the glories that would follow.

Spirit of the Son.

Gal 4:6 And because you are sons, God has sent forth the Spirit of His Son into your hearts, crying out, "Abba, Father!"

Spirit of life.

Rom 8:2 For the law of the Spirit of life in Christ Jesus has made me free from the law of sin and death.

Rev 11:11 Now after the three-and-a-half days the breath of life from God entered them, and they stood on their feet, and great fear fell on those who saw them.

Spirit of grace.

Zech 12:10 "And I will pour on the house of David and on the inhabitants of Jerusalem the Spirit of grace and supplication; then they will look on Me whom they pierced. Yes, they will mourn for Him as one mourns for *his* only *son,* and grieve for Him as one grieves for a firstborn.

Heb 10:29 Of how much worse punishment, do you suppose, will he be thought worthy who has trampled the Son of God underfoot, counted the blood of the covenant by which he was sanctified a common thing, and insulted the Spirit of grace?

Spirit of prophecy.

Rev 19:10 And I fell at his feet to worship him. But he said to me, "See *that you do* not *do that!* I am your fellow servant, and of your brethren who have the testimony of Jesus. Worship God! For the testimony of Jesus is the spirit of prophecy."

Spirit of adoption.

Rom 8:15 For you did not receive the spirit of bondage again to fear, but you received the Spirit of adoption by whom we cry out, "Abba, Father."

Spirit of wisdom.

Is 11:2 The Spirit of the LORD shall rest upon Him, The Spirit of wisdom and understanding, The Spirit of counsel and might, The Spirit of knowledge and of the fear of the LORD.

Eph 1:17 that the God of our Lord Jesus Christ, the Father of glory, may give to you the spirit of wisdom and revelation in the knowledge of Him,

Spirit of counsel.

Is 11:2 The Spirit of the LORD shall rest upon Him, The Spirit of wisdom and understanding, The Spirit of counsel and might, The Spirit of knowledge and of the fear of the LORD.

Spirit of might.

Is 11:2 The Spirit of the LORD shall rest upon Him, The Spirit of wisdom and understanding, The Spirit of counsel and might, The Spirit of knowledge and of the fear of the LORD.

Spirit of understanding.

Is 11:2 The Spirit of the LORD shall rest upon Him, The Spirit of wisdom and understanding, The Spirit of counsel and might, The Spirit of knowledge and of the fear of the LORD.

Spirit of knowledge.

Is 11:2 The Spirit of the LORD shall rest upon Him, The Spirit of wisdom and understanding, The Spirit of counsel and might, The Spirit of knowledge and of the fear of the LORD.

Spirit of the fear of the Lord.

Is 11:2 The Spirit of the LORD shall rest upon Him, The Spirit of wisdom and understanding, The Spirit of counsel and might, The Spirit of knowledge and of the fear of the LORD.

Spirit of truth.

John 14:17 the Spirit of truth, whom the world cannot receive, because it neither sees Him nor knows Him; but you know Him, for He dwells with you and will be in you.

John 15:26 "But when the Helper comes, whom I shall send to you from the Father, the Spirit of truth who proceeds from the Father, He will testify of Me.

Spirit of holiness.

Rom 1:4 *and* declared *to be* the Son of God with power according to the Spirit of holiness, by the resurrection from the dead.

Spirit of revelation.

Eph 1:17 that the God of our Lord Jesus Christ, the Father of glory, may give to you the spirit of wisdom and revelation in the knowledge of Him,

Spirit of judgment.

Is 4:4 When the Lord has washed away the filth of the daughters of Zion, and purged the blood of Jerusalem from her midst, by the spirit of judgment and by the spirit of burning,

Is 28:6 For a spirit of justice to him who sits in judgment, And for strength to those who turn back the battle at the gate.

Spirit of burning.

Is 4:4 When the Lord has washed away the filth of the daughters of Zion, and purged the blood of Jerusalem from her midst, by the spirit of judgment and by the spirit of burning,

Spirit of glory.

1 Pet 4:14 If you are reproached for the name of Christ, blessed *are you,* for the Spirit of glory and of God rests upon you. On their part He is blasphemed, but on your part He is glorified.

Seven Spirits of God.

Rev 1:4 John, to the seven churches which are in Asia: Grace to you and peace from Him who is and who was and who is to come, and from the seven Spirits who are before His throne,

HOLY SPIRIT, WITNESS OF THE

Is truth.

1 John 5:6 This is He who came by water and blood—Jesus Christ; not only by water, but by water and blood. And it is the Spirit who bears witness, because the Spirit is truth.

To be implicitly received.

1 John 5:6 This is He who came by water and blood—Jesus Christ; not only by water, but by water and blood. And it is the Spirit who bears witness, because the Spirit is truth.

1 John 5:9 If we receive the witness of men, the witness of God is greater; for this is the witness of God which He has testified of His Son.

Borne to Christ

As Messiah.

Luke 3:22 And the Holy Spirit descended in bodily form like a dove upon Him, and a voice came from heaven which said, "You are My beloved Son; in You I am well pleased."

John 1:32–33 And John bore witness, saying, "I saw the Spirit descending from heaven like a dove, and He remained upon Him. **33** I did not know Him, but He who sent me to baptize with water said to me, 'Upon whom you see the Spirit descending, and remaining on Him, this is He who baptizes with the Holy Spirit.'

As coming to redeem and sanctify.

1 John 5:6 This is He who came by water and blood— Jesus Christ; not only by water, but by water and blood. And it is the Spirit who bears witness, because the Spirit is truth.

As exalted to be a Prince and Savior.

Acts 5:31–32 Him God has exalted to His right hand *to be* Prince and Savior, to give repentance to Israel and forgiveness of sins. **32** And we are His witnesses to these things, and *so* also *is* the Holy Spirit whom God has given to those who obey Him."

As perfecting believers.

Heb 10:14–15 For by one offering He has perfected forever those who are being sanctified. **15** But the Holy Spirit also witnesses to us; for after He had said before,

As foretold by Himself.

John 15:26 "But when the Helper comes, whom I shall send to you from the Father, the Spirit of truth who proceeds from the Father, He will testify of Me.

In heaven.

1 John 5:7 For there are three that bear witness in heaven: the Father, the Word, and the Holy Spirit; and these three are one.

1 John 5:11 And this is the testimony: that God has given us eternal life, and this life is in His Son.

On earth.

1 John 5:8 And there are three that bear witness on earth: the Spirit, the water, and the blood; and these three agree as one.

The first preaching of the gospel confirmed by.

Acts 14:3 Therefore they stayed there a long time, speaking boldly in the Lord, who was bearing witness to the word of His grace, granting signs and wonders to be done by their hands.

Heb 2:4 God also bearing witness both with signs and wonders, with various miracles, and gifts of the Holy Spirit, according to His own will?

The faithful preaching of the apostles accompanied by.

1 Cor 2:4 And my speech and my preaching *were* not with persuasive words of human wisdom, but in demonstration of the Spirit and of power,

1 Thess 1:5 For our gospel did not come to you in word only, but also in power, and in the Holy Spirit and in much assurance, as you know what kind of men we were among you for your sake.

Given to believers

At salvation.

Acts 15:8 So God, who knows the heart, acknowledged them by giving them the Holy Spirit, just as *He did* to us,

1 John 5:10 He who believes in the Son of God has the witness in himself; he who does not believe God has made Him a liar, because he has not believed the testimony that God has given of His Son.

To testify to them of Christ.

John 15:26 "But when the Helper comes, whom I shall send to you from the Father, the Spirit of truth who proceeds from the Father, He will testify of Me.

1 John 3:24 Now he who keeps His commandments abides in Him, and He in him. And by this we know that He abides in us, by the Spirit whom He has given us.

1 John 4:13 By this we know that we abide in Him, and He in us, because He has given us of His Spirit.

As an evidence of adoption.

Rom 8:16 The Spirit Himself bears witness with our spirit that we are children of God,

Borne against all unbelievers.

Neh 9:30 Yet for many years You had patience with them, And testified against them by Your Spirit in Your prophets. Yet they would not listen; Therefore You gave them into the hand of the peoples of the lands.

Acts 28:25–27 So when they did not agree among themselves, they departed after Paul had said one word: "The Holy Spirit spoke rightly through Isaiah the prophet to our fathers, **26** saying, *'Go to this people and say:* "*Hearing you will hear, and shall not understand; And seeing you will see, and not perceive;* **27** *For the hearts of this people have grown dull. Their ears are hard of hearing, And their eyes they have closed, Lest they should see with their eyes and hear with their ears, Lest they should understand with their hearts and turn, So that I should heal them."* '

HOMICIDE

Distinguished from murder.

Ex 21:13–14 However, if he did not lie in wait, but God delivered *him* into his hand, then I will appoint for you a place where he may flee. **14** "But if a man acts with premeditation against his neighbor, to kill him by treachery, you shall take him from My altar, that he may die.

Num 35:16–21 'But if he strikes him with an iron implement, so that he dies, he *is* a murderer; the murderer shall surely be put to death. **17** And if he strikes him with a stone in the hand, by which one could die, and he does die, he *is* a murderer; the murderer shall surely be put to death. **18** Or *if* he strikes him with a wooden hand weapon, by which one could die, and he does die, he *is* a murderer; the murderer shall surely be put to death. **19** The avenger of blood himself shall put the murderer to death; when he meets him, he shall put him to death. **20** If he pushes him out of hatred or, while lying in wait, hurls something at him so that he dies, **21** or in enmity he strikes him with his hand so that he dies, the one who struck *him* shall surely be put to death. He *is* a murderer. The avenger of blood shall put the murderer to death when he meets him.

Num 35:25 So the congregation shall deliver the manslayer from the hand of the avenger of blood, and the congregation shall return him to the city of refuge where he had fled, and he shall remain there until the death of the high priest who was anointed with the holy oil.

Justifiable, described as

Killing persons condemned by law.

Gen 9:6 "Whoever sheds man's blood, By man his blood shall be shed; For in the image of God He made man.

Ex 35:2 Work shall be done for six days, but the seventh day shall be a holy day for you, a Sabbath of rest to the LORD. Whoever does any work on it shall be put to death.

Lev 24:16 And whoever blasphemes the name of the LORD shall surely be put to death. All the congregation shall certainly stone him, the stranger as well as him who is born in the land. When he blasphemes the name *of the LORD*, he shall be put to death.

Killing a thief in the night.

Ex 22:2 If the thief is found breaking in, and he is struck so that he dies, *there shall be* no guilt for his bloodshed.

Killing enemies in battle.

Num 31:7–8 And they warred against the Midianites, just as the LORD commanded Moses, and they killed all the males. 8 They killed the kings of Midian with *the rest of* those who were killed—Evi, Rekem, Zur, Hur, and Reba, the five kings of Midian. Balaam the son of Beor they also killed with the sword.

Killing a manslayer by next of kin.

Num 35:27 and the avenger of blood finds him outside the limits of his city of refuge, and the avenger of blood kills the manslayer, he shall not be guilty of blood,

Unjustifiable, described as

Killing without enmity.

Num 35:22 'However, if he pushes him suddenly without enmity, or throws anything at him without lying in wait,

Killing without lying in wait.

Ex 21:13 However, if he did not lie in wait, but God delivered *him* into his hand, then I will appoint for you a place where he may flee.

Num 35:22 'However, if he pushes him suddenly without enmity, or throws anything at him without lying in wait,

Killing by accident.

Num 35:23 or uses a stone, by which a man could die, throwing *it* at him without seeing *him,* so that he dies, while he was not his enemy or seeking his harm,

Deut 19:5 as when *a man* goes to the woods with his neighbor to cut timber, and his hand swings a stroke with the ax to cut down the tree, and the head slips from the handle and strikes his neighbor so that he dies—he shall flee to one of these cities and live;

The avenger of blood might kill those guilty of unjustifiable.

Num 35:19 The avenger of blood himself shall put the murderer to death; when he meets him, he shall put him to death.

Num 35:27 and the avenger of blood finds him outside the limits of his city of refuge, and the avenger of blood kills the manslayer, he shall not be guilty of blood,

Protection afforded in the cities of refuge to those guilty of unjustifiable.

Num 35:11 then you shall appoint cities to be cities of refuge for you, that the manslayer who kills any person accidentally may flee there.

Num 35:15 These six cities shall be for refuge for the children of Israel, for the stranger, and for the sojourner among them, that anyone who kills a person accidentally may flee there.

Confinement in the city of refuge, the punishment for unjustifiable.

Num 35:25 So the congregation shall deliver the manslayer from the hand of the avenger of blood, and the congregation shall return him to the city of refuge where he had fled, and he shall remain there until the death of the high priest who was anointed with the holy oil.

Num 35:28 because he should have remained in his city of refuge until the death of the high priest. But after the death of the high priest the manslayer may return to the land of his possession.

HOMOSEXUALITY

Sinfulness of, in Sodom and Gomorrah.

Gen 18:20–21 And the LORD said, "Because the outcry against Sodom and Gomorrah is great, and because their sin is very grave, 21 I will go down now and see whether they have done altogether according to the outcry against it that has come to Me; and if not, I will know."

Gen 19:1–11 Now the two angels came to Sodom in the evening, and Lot was sitting in the gate of Sodom. When Lot saw *them,* he rose to meet them, and he bowed himself with his face toward the ground. 2 And he said, "Here now, my lords, please turn in to your servant's house and spend the night, and wash your feet; then you may rise early and go on your way." And they said, "No, but we will spend the night in the open square." 3 But he insisted strongly; so they turned in to him and entered his house. Then he made them a feast, and baked unleavened bread, and they ate. 4 Now before they lay down, the men of the city, the men of Sodom, both old and young, all the people from every quarter, surrounded the house. 5 And they called to Lot and said to him, "Where are the men who came to you tonight? Bring them out to us that we may know them *carnally.*" 6 So Lot went out to them through the doorway, shut the door behind him, 7 and said, "Please, my brethren, do not do so wickedly! 8 See now, I have two daughters who have not known a man; please, let me bring them out to you, and you may do to them as you wish; only do nothing to these men, since this is the reason they have come under the shadow of my roof." **9** And they said, "Stand back!" Then they said, "This one came in to stay *here*, and he keeps acting as a judge; now we will deal worse with you than with them." So they pressed hard against the man Lot, and came near to break down the door. **10** But the men reached out their hands and pulled Lot into the house with them, and shut the door. **11** And they struck the men who *were* at the doorway of the house with blindness, both small and great, so that they became weary *trying* to find the door.

Cf. Lam 4:6

Forbidden by God.

Lev 18:22 You shall not lie with a male as with a woman. It *is* an abomination.

Lev 20:13 If a man lies with a male as he lies with a woman, both of them have committed an abomination. They shall surely be put to death. Their blood *shall be* upon them.

Rom 1:26–27 For this reason God gave them up to vile passions. For even their women exchanged the natural use for what is against nature. **27** Likewise also the men, leaving the natural use of the woman, burned in their lust for one another, men with men committing what is shameful, and receiving in themselves the penalty of their error which was due.

1 Cor 6:9 Do you not know that the unrighteous will not inherit the kingdom of God? Do not be deceived. Neither fornicators, nor idolaters, nor adulterers, nor homosexuals, nor sodomites,

1 Tim 1:9–10 knowing this: that the law is not made for a righteous person, but for *the* lawless and insubordinate, for *the* ungodly and for sinners, for *the* unholy and profane, for murderers of fathers and murderers of mothers, for manslayers, **10** for fornicators, for sodomites, for kidnappers, for liars, for perjurers, and if there is any other thing that is contrary to sound doctrine,

Cf. Deut 22:5; Gal 5:19–21; Eph 5:3–5; Jude 1:7

HONEY

God the giver of.

Ps 81:16 He would have fed them also with the finest of wheat; And with honey from the rock I would have satisfied you."

Ezek 16:19 Also My food which I gave you—the pastry of fine flour, oil, and honey *which* I fed you—you set it before them as sweet incense; and *so* it was," says the Lord GOD.

Gathered and prepared by bees.

Judg 14:18 So the men of the city said to him on the seventh day before the sun went down: "What *is* sweeter than honey? And what *is* stronger than a lion?" And he said to them: "If you had not plowed with my heifer, You would not have solved my riddle!"

Found in

Rocks.

Deut 32:13 "He made him ride in the heights of the earth, That he might eat the produce of the fields; He made him draw honey from the rock, And oil from the flinty rock;

Ps 81:16 He would have fed them also with the finest of

wheat; And with honey from the rock I would have satisfied you."

Woods.

1 Sam 14:25–26 Now all *the people* of the land came to a forest; and there was honey on the ground. **26** And when the people had come into the woods, there was the honey, dripping; but no one put his hand to his mouth, for the people feared the oath.

Jer 41:8 But ten men were found among them who said to Ishmael, "Do not kill us, for we have treasures of wheat, barley, oil, and honey in the field." So he desisted and did not kill them among their brethren.

Carcasses of dead animals.

Judg 14:8 After some time, when he returned to get her, he turned aside to see the carcass of the lion. And behold, a swarm of bees and honey *were* in the carcass of the lion.

Sweetness of.

Judg 14:18 So the men of the city said to him on the seventh day before the sun went down: "What *is* sweeter than honey? And what *is* stronger than a lion?" And he said to them: "If you had not plowed with my heifer, You would not have solved my riddle!"

In the honeycomb, sweetest and most valuable.

Prov 16:24 Pleasant words *are like* a honeycomb, Sweetness to the soul and health to the bones.

Prov 24:13 My son, eat honey because *it is* good, And the honeycomb *which is* sweet to your taste;

Abounded in

Egypt.

Num 16:13 *Is it* a small thing that you have brought us up out of a land flowing with milk and honey, to kill us in the wilderness, that you should keep acting like a prince over us?

Assyria.

2 Kin 18:32 until I come and take you away to a land like your own land, a land of grain and new wine, a land of bread and vineyards, a land of olive groves and honey, that you may live and not die. But do not listen to Hezekiah, lest he persuade you, saying, "The LORD will deliver us."

Canaan.

Ex 3:8 So I have come down to deliver them out of the hand of the Egyptians, and to bring them up from that land to a good and large land, to a land flowing with milk and honey, to the place of the Canaanites and the Hittites and the Amorites and the Perizzites and the Hivites and the Jebusites.

Lev 20:24 But I have said to you, "You shall inherit their land, and I will give it to you to possess, a land flowing with milk and honey." I *am* the LORD your God, who has separated you from the peoples.

Deut 8:8 a land of wheat and barley, of vines and fig trees and pomegranates, a land of olive oil and honey;

Esteemed a wholesome food.

Prov 24:13 My son, eat honey because *it is* good, And the honeycomb *which is* sweet to your taste;

Moderation needful in the use of.

Prov 25:16 Have you found honey? Eat only as much as you need, Lest you be filled with it and vomit.

Prov 25:27 *It is* not good to eat much honey; So to seek one's own glory *is not* glory.

Loathed by those who are full.

Prov 27:7 A satisfied soul loathes the honeycomb, But to a hungry soul every bitter thing *is* sweet.

Was eaten

Plain.

1 Sam 14:25–26 Now all *the people* of the land came to a forest; and there was honey on the ground. 26 And when the people had come into the woods, there was the honey, dripping; but no one put his hand to his mouth, for the people feared the oath.

1 Sam 14:29 But Jonathan said, "My father has troubled the land. Look now, how my countenance has brightened because I tasted a little of this honey.

With the honeycomb.

Song 5:1 I have come to my garden, my sister, *my* spouse; I have gathered my myrrh with my spice; I have eaten my honeycomb with my honey; I have drunk my wine with my milk. Eat, O friends! Drink, yes, drink deeply, O beloved ones!

Luke 24:42 So they gave Him a piece of a broiled fish and some honeycomb.

With milk.

Song 4:11 Your lips, O *my* spouse, Drip as the honeycomb; Honey and milk *are* under your tongue; And the fragrance of your garments *Is* like the fragrance of Lebanon.

With curds.

Is 7:15 Curds and honey He shall eat, that He may know to refuse the evil and choose the good.

Is 7:22 So it shall be, from the abundance of milk they give, That he will eat curds; For curds and honey everyone will eat who is left in the land.

With locusts.

Matt 3:4 Now John himself was clothed in camel's hair, with a leather belt around his waist; and his food was locusts and wild honey.

Mark 1:6 Now John was clothed with camel's hair and with a leather belt around his waist, and he ate locusts and wild honey.

Mixed with flour.

Ex 16:31 And the house of Israel called its name Manna. And it *was* like white coriander seed, and the taste of it *was* like wafers *made* with honey.

Ezek 16:13 Thus you were adorned with gold and silver, and your clothing *was of* fine linen, silk, and embroidered cloth. You ate *pastry of* fine flour, honey, and oil. You were exceedingly beautiful, and succeeded to royalty.

Not to be offered with any sacrifice.

Lev 2:11 'No grain offering which you bring to the LORD shall be made with leaven, for you shall burn no leaven nor any honey in any offering to the LORD made by fire.

Firstfruits of, offered to God.

2 Chr 31:5 As soon as the commandment was circulated, the children of Israel brought in abundance the firstfruits of grain and wine, oil and honey, and of all the produce of the field; and they brought in abundantly the tithe of everything.

Often sent as a present.

Gen 43:11 And their father Israel said to them, "If *it must be* so, then do this: Take some of the best fruits of the land in your vessels and carry down a present for the man—a little balm and a little honey, spices and myrrh, pistachio nuts and almonds.

1 Kin 14:3 Also take with you ten loaves, *some* cakes, and a jar of honey, and go to him; he will tell you what will become of the child."

Exported from Canaan.

Ezek 27:17 Judah and the land of Israel *were* your traders. They traded for your merchandise wheat of Minnith, millet, honey, oil, and balm.

Illustrative of

The Word of God.

Ps 19:10 More to be desired *are they* than gold, Yea, than much fine gold; Sweeter also than honey and the honeycomb.

Ps 119:103 How sweet are Your words to my taste, *Sweeter* than honey to my mouth!

Wisdom.

Prov 24:13–14 My son, eat honey because *it is* good, And the honeycomb *which is* sweet to your taste; 14 So *shall* the knowledge of wisdom *be* to your soul; If you have found *it*, there is a prospect, And your hope will not be cut off.

Holy speech of believers.

Song 4:11 Your lips, O *my* spouse, Drip as the honeycomb; Honey and milk *are* under your tongue; And the fragrance of your garments *Is* like the fragrance of Lebanon.

Pleasant words.

Prov 16:24 Pleasant words *are like* a honeycomb, Sweetness to the soul and health to the bones.

Lips of a strange woman.

Prov 5:3 For the lips of an immoral woman drip honey, And her mouth *is* smoother than oil;

HOPE

In God.

Ps 39:7 "And now, Lord, what do I wait for? My hope *is* in You.

1 Pet 1:21 who through Him believe in God, who raised Him from the dead and gave Him glory, so that your faith and hope are in God.

In Christ.

1 Cor 15:19 If in this life only we have hope in Christ, we are of all men the most pitiable.

1 Tim 1:1 Paul, an apostle of Jesus Christ, by the commandment of God our Savior and the Lord Jesus Christ, our hope,

In God's promises.

Acts 26:6–7 And now I stand and am judged for the hope of the promise made by God to our fathers. 7 To this *promise* our twelve tribes, earnestly serving *God* night and day, hope to attain. For this hope's sake, King Agrippa, I am accused by the Jews.

Titus 1:2 in hope of eternal life which God, who cannot lie, promised before time began,

In the mercy of God.

Ps 33:18 Behold, the eye of the LORD *is* on those who fear Him, On those who hope in His mercy,

Is the work of the Holy Spirit.

Rom 15:13 Now may the God of hope fill you with all joy and peace in believing, that you may abound in hope by the power of the Holy Spirit.

Gal 5:5 For we through the Spirit eagerly wait for the hope of righteousness by faith.

Obtained through

Grace.

2 Thess 2:16 Now may our Lord Jesus Christ Himself, and our God and Father, who has loved us and given *us* everlasting consolation and good hope by grace,

Patience and comfort of the Scriptures.

Ps 119:81 My soul faints for Your salvation, But I hope in Your word.

Rom 15:4 For whatever things were written before were written for our learning, that we through the patience and comfort of the Scriptures might have hope.

The gospel.

Col 1:5 because of the hope which is laid up for you in heaven, of which you heard before in the word of the truth of the gospel,

Col 1:23 if indeed you continue in the faith, grounded and steadfast, and are not moved away from the hope of the gospel which you heard, which was preached to every creature under heaven, of which I, Paul, became a minister.

Faith.

Rom 5:1–2 Therefore, having been justified by faith, we have peace with God through our Lord Jesus Christ, 2 through whom also we have access by faith into this grace in which we stand, and rejoice in hope of the glory of God.

Gal 5:5 For we through the Spirit eagerly wait for the hope of righteousness by faith.

The result of character.

Rom 5:4 and perseverance, character; and character, hope.

The best, brought in by Christ.

Heb 7:19 for the law made nothing perfect; on the other hand, *there is the* bringing in of a better hope, through which we draw near to God.

Described as

Good.

2 Thess 2:16 Now may our Lord Jesus Christ Himself, and our God and Father, who has loved us and given *us* everlasting consolation and good hope by grace,

Living.

1 Pet 1:3 Blessed *be* the God and Father of our Lord Jesus Christ, who according to His abundant mercy has begotten us again to a living hope through the resurrection of Jesus Christ from the dead,

Sure and steadfast.

Heb 6:19 This *hope* we have as an anchor of the soul, both sure and steadfast, and which enters the Presence *behind* the veil,

Gladdening.

Prov 10:28 The hope of the righteous *will be* gladness, But the expectation of the wicked will perish.

Blessed.

Titus 2:13 looking for the blessed hope and glorious appearing of our great God and Savior Jesus Christ,

Does not disappoint.

Rom 5:5 Now hope does not disappoint, because the love of God has been poured out in our hearts by the Holy Spirit who was given to us.

Triumphs over difficulties.

Rom 4:18 who, contrary to hope, in hope believed, so that he became the father of many nations, according to what was spoken, *"So shall your descendants be."*

Is an encouragement to boldness in preaching.

2 Cor 3:12 Therefore, since we have such hope, we use great boldness of speech—

Believers

Are called to.

Eph 4:4 *There is* one body and one Spirit, just as you were called in one hope of your calling;

Will rejoice in.

Rom 5:2 through whom also we have access by faith into this grace in which we stand, and rejoice in hope of the glory of God.

Rom 12:12 rejoicing in hope, patient in tribulation, continuing steadfastly in prayer;

All have the same.

Eph 4:4 *There is* one body and one Spirit, just as you were called in one hope of your calling;

Have, in death.

Prov 14:32 The wicked is banished in his wickedness, But the righteous has a refuge in his death.

Should abound in.

Rom 15:13 Now may the God of hope fill you with all joy and peace in believing, that you may abound in hope by the power of the Holy Spirit.

Should look for the object of.

Titus 2:13 looking for the blessed hope and glorious appearing of our great God and Savior Jesus Christ,

Should not be ashamed of.

Ps 119:16 I will delight myself in Your statutes; I will not forget Your word.

Should hold fast.

Heb 3:6 but Christ as a Son over His own house, whose house we are if we hold fast the confidence and the rejoicing of the hope firm to the end.

Should not be moved from.

Col 1:23 if indeed you continue in the faith, grounded and steadfast, and are not moved away from the hope of the gospel which you heard, which was preached to every creature under heaven, of which I, Paul, became a minister.

Should continue in.

Ps 71:14 But I will hope continually, And will praise You yet more and more.

1 Pet 1:13 Therefore gird up the loins of your mind, be sober, and rest *your* hope fully upon the grace that is to be brought to you at the revelation of Jesus Christ;

Connected with faith and love.

1 Cor 13:13 And now abide faith, hope, love, these three; but the greatest of these *is* love.

Objects of,

Salvation.

1 Thess 5:8 But let us who are of the day be sober, putting on the breastplate of faith and love, and *as a* helmet the hope of salvation.

Righteousness.

Gal 5:5 For we through the Spirit eagerly wait for the hope of righteousness by faith.

Christ's glorious appearing.

Titus 2:13 looking for the blessed hope and glorious appearing of our great God and Savior Jesus Christ,

A resurrection.

Acts 23:6 But when Paul perceived that one part were Sadducees and the other Pharisees, he cried out in the council, "Men *and* brethren, I am a Pharisee, the son of a Pharisee; concerning the hope and resurrection of the dead I am being judged!"

Acts 24:15 I have hope in God, which they themselves also accept, that there will be a resurrection of *the* dead, both of *the* just and *the* unjust.

Eternal life.

Titus 1:2 in hope of eternal life which God, who cannot lie, promised before time began,

Titus 3:7 that having been justified by His grace we should become heirs according to the hope of eternal life.

Glory.

Rom 5:2 through whom also we have access by faith into this grace in which we stand, and rejoice in hope of the glory of God.

Col 1:27 To them God willed to make known what are the riches of the glory of this mystery among the Gentiles: which is Christ in you, the hope of glory.

Leads to purity.

1 John 3:3 And everyone who has this hope in Him purifies himself, just as He is pure.

Leads to patience.

Rom 8:25 But if we hope for what we do not see, we eagerly wait for *it* with perseverance.

1 Thess 1:3 remembering without ceasing your work of faith, labor of love, and patience of hope in our Lord Jesus Christ in the sight of our God and Father,

Seek for full assurance of.

Heb 6:11 And we desire that each one of you show the same diligence to the full assurance of hope until the end,

Be ready to give an answer concerning.

1 Pet 3:15 But sanctify the Lord God in your hearts, and always *be* ready to *give* a defense to everyone who asks you a reason for the hope that is in you, with meekness and fear;

Encouragement to.

Ps 130:7 O Israel, hope in the LORD; For with the LORD *there is* mercy, And with Him *is* abundant redemption.

Hos 2:15 I will give her her vineyards from there, And the Valley of Achor as a door of hope; She shall sing there, As in the days of her youth, As in the day when she came up from the land of Egypt.

Zech 9:12 Return to the stronghold, You prisoners of hope. Even today I declare *That* I will restore double to you.

Happiness of.

Ps 146:5 Happy *is he* who *has* the God of Jacob for his help, Whose hope *is* in the LORD his God,

Life is the season of.

Eccl 9:4 But for him who is joined to all the living there is hope, for a living dog is better than a dead lion.

Is 38:18 For Sheol cannot thank You, Death cannot praise You; Those who go down to the pit cannot hope for Your truth.

Of the wicked

There is no ground for.

Eph 2:12 that at that time you were without Christ, being aliens from the commonwealth of Israel and strangers from the covenants of promise, having no hope and without God in the world.

Is in their worldly possessions.

Job 31:24 "If I have made gold my hope, Or said to fine gold, '*You are* my confidence';

Shall make them ashamed.

Is 20:5–6 Then they shall be afraid and ashamed of Ethiopia their expectation and Egypt their glory. 6 And the inhabitant of this territory will say in that day, 'Surely such *is* our expectation, wherever we flee for help to be delivered from the king of Assyria; and how shall we escape?' "

Zech 9:5 Ashkelon shall see *it* and fear; Gaza also shall be very sorrowful; And Ekron, for He dried up her expectation. The king shall perish from Gaza, And Ashkelon shall not be inhabited.

Shall perish.

Job 8:13 So *are* the paths of all who forget God; And the hope of the hypocrite shall perish,

Job 11:20 But the eyes of the wicked will fail, And they shall not escape, And their hope—loss of life!"

Prov 10:28 The hope of the righteous *will be* gladness, But the expectation of the wicked will perish.

Shall be extinguished in death.

Job 27:8 For what is the hope of the hypocrite, Though he may gain *much,* If God takes away his life?

Illustrated by

An anchor.

Heb 6:19 This *hope* we have as an anchor of the soul, both sure and steadfast, and which enters the Presence *behind* the veil,

A helmet.

1 Thess 5:8 But let us who are of the day be sober, putting on the breastplate of faith and love, and *as a* helmet the hope of salvation.

Exemplified by

David.

Ps 39:7 "And now, Lord, what do I wait for? My hope *is* in You.

Paul.

Acts 24:15 I have hope in God, which they themselves also accept, that there will be a resurrection of *the* dead, both of *the* just and *the* unjust.

Abraham.

Rom 4:18 who, contrary to hope, in hope believed, so that he became the father of many nations, according to what was spoken, *"So shall your descendants be."*

The Thessalonians.

1 Thess 1:3 remembering without ceasing your work of faith, labor of love, and patience of hope in our Lord Jesus Christ in the sight of our God and Father,

HORNS

Animals with, mentioned

The ox.

Ps 22:21 Save Me from the lion's mouth And from the horns of the wild oxen! You have answered Me.

Ps 69:31 *This* also shall please the LORD better than an ox *or* bull, Which has horns and hooves.

Ps 92:10 But my horn You have exalted like a wild ox; I have been anointed with fresh oil.

The ram.

Gen 22:13 Then Abraham lifted his eyes and looked, and there behind *him was* a ram caught in a thicket by its horns. So Abraham went and took the ram, and offered it up for a burnt offering instead of his son.

The goat.

Dan 8:5 And as I was considering, suddenly a male goat came from the west, across the surface of the whole earth, without touching the ground; and the goat *had* a notable horn between his eyes.

Used offensively.

Ex 21:29 But if the ox tended to thrust with its horn in times past, and it has been made known to his owner, and he has not kept it confined, so that it has killed a man or a woman, the ox shall be stoned and its owner also shall be put to death.

Ezek 34:21 Because you have pushed with side and shoulder, butted all the weak ones with your horns, and scattered them abroad,

Practical uses

For holding oil.

1 Sam 16:1 Now the LORD said to Samuel, "How long will you mourn for Saul, seeing I have rejected him from reigning over Israel? Fill your horn with oil, and go; I am sending you to Jesse the Bethlehemite. For I have provided Myself a king among his sons."

1 Kin 1:39 Then Zadok the priest took a horn of oil from the tabernacle and anointed Solomon. And they blew the horn, and all the people said, *"Long* live King Solomon!"

As musical instruments.

Josh 6:4–5 And seven priests shall bear seven trumpets of rams' horns before the ark. But the seventh day you shall march around the city seven times, and the priests shall blow the trumpets. 5 It shall come to pass, when they make a long *blast* with the ram's horn, *and* when you hear the sound of the trumpet, that all the people shall shout with a great shout;

then the wall of the city will fall down flat. And the people shall go up every man straight before him."

1 Chr 25:5 All these *were* the sons of Heman the king's seer in the words of God, to exalt his horn. For God gave Heman fourteen sons and three daughters.

Representations of, placed at the four corners of the altars.

Ex 27:2 You shall make its horns on its four corners; its horns shall be of one piece with it. And you shall overlay it with bronze.

Ex 30:2 A cubit *shall be* its length and a cubit its width— it shall be square—and two cubits *shall be* its height. Its horns *shall be* of one piece with it.

Wearing of, alluded to.

Ps 75:5 Do not lift up your horn on high; Do *not* speak with a stiff neck.' "

Ps 75:10 "All the horns of the wicked I will also cut off, *But* the horns of the righteous shall be exalted."

Illustrative of

The power of God.

Ps 18:2 The LORD is my rock and my fortress and my deliverer; My God, my strength, in whom I will trust; My shield and the horn of my salvation, my stronghold.

2 Sam 22:3 The God of my strength, in whom I will trust; My shield and the horn of my salvation, My stronghold and my refuge; My Savior, You save me from violence.

The power of Christ.

Luke 1:69 And has raised up a horn of salvation for us In the house of His servant David,

Rev 5:6 And I looked, and behold, in the midst of the throne and of the four living creatures, and in the midst of the elders, stood a Lamb as though it had been slain, having seven horns and seven eyes, which are the seven Spirits of God sent out into all the earth.

The power of Ephraim, etc.

Deut 33:17 His glory *is like* a firstborn bull, And his horns *like* the horns of the wild ox; Together with them He shall push the peoples To the ends of the earth; They *are* the ten thousands of Ephraim, And they *are* the thousands of Manasseh."

The power of the wicked.

Ps 22:21 Save Me from the lion's mouth And from the horns of the wild oxen! You have answered Me.

Ps 75:10 "All the horns of the wicked I will also cut off, *But* the horns of the righteous shall be exalted."

Kings.

Dan 7:4 The first *was* like a lion, and had eagle's wings. I watched till its wings were plucked off; and it was lifted up from the earth and made to stand on two feet like a man, and a man's heart was given to it.

Dan 7:7–8 "After this I saw in the night visions, and behold, a fourth beast, dreadful and terrible, exceedingly strong. It had huge iron teeth; it was devouring, breaking in pieces, and trampling the residue with its feet. It *was* different from all the beasts that *were* before it, and it had ten horns. 8 I was considering the horns, and there was another horn, a little one, coming up among them, before whom three of the first horns were plucked out by the roots. And there, in this horn, *were* eyes like the eyes of a man, and a mouth speaking pompous words.

Dan 7:20 and the ten horns that *were* on its head, and the other *horn* which came up, before which three fell, namely, that horn which had eyes and a mouth which spoke pompous words, whose appearance *was* greater than his fellows.

Dan 8:3 Then I lifted my eyes and saw, and there, standing beside the river, was a ram which had two horns, and the two horns *were* high; but one *was* higher than the other, and the higher *one* came up last.

Dan 8:5 And as I was considering, suddenly a male goat came from the west, across the surface of the whole earth, without touching the ground; and the goat *had* a notable horn between his eyes.

Dan 8:20 The ram which you saw, having the two horns—*they are* the kings of Media and Persia.

Powers of the Antichrist.

Rev 13:1 Then I stood on the sand of the sea. And I saw a beast rising up out of the sea, having seven heads and ten horns, and on his horns ten crowns, and on his heads a blasphemous name.

Rev 17:3 So he carried me away in the Spirit into the wilderness. And I saw a woman sitting on a scarlet beast *which was* full of names of blasphemy, having seven heads and ten horns.

Rev 17:7 But the angel said to me, "Why did you marvel? I will tell you the mystery of the woman and of the beast that carries her, which has the seven heads and the ten horns.

(Springing forth) the commencement or revival of a nation.

Ps 132:17 There I will make the horn of David grow; I will prepare a lamp for My Anointed.

Ezek 29:21 'In that day I will cause the horn of the house of Israel to spring forth, and I will open your mouth to speak in their midst. Then they shall know that I *am* the LORD.' "

(Lifting up) arrogance.

Ps 75:4–5 "I said to the boastful, 'Do not deal boastfully,' And to the wicked, 'Do not lift up the horn. 5 Do not lift up your horn on high; Do *not* speak with a stiff neck.' "

(Exalting) increase of power and glory.

1 Sam 2:1 And Hannah prayed and said: "My heart rejoices in the LORD; My horn is exalted in the LORD. I smile at my enemies, Because I rejoice in Your salvation.

1 Sam 2:10 The adversaries of the LORD shall be broken in pieces; From heaven He will thunder against them. The LORD will judge the ends of the earth. "He will give strength to His king, And exalt the horn of His anointed."

Ps 89:17 For You *are* the glory of their strength, And in Your favor our horn is exalted.

Ps 89:24 "But My faithfulness and My mercy *shall be* with him, And in My name his horn shall be exalted.

Ps 92:10 But my horn You have exalted like a wild ox; I have been anointed with fresh oil.

Ps 112:9 He has dispersed abroad, He has given to the poor; His righteousness endures forever; His horn will be exalted with honor.

(Pushing with) conquests.

Deut 33:17 His glory *is like* a firstborn bull, And his horns *like* the horns of the wild ox; Together with them He shall push the peoples To the ends of the earth; They *are* the ten thousands of Ephraim, And they *are* the thousands of Manasseh."

1 Kin 22:11 Now Zedekiah the son of Chenaanah had made horns of iron for himself; and he said, "Thus says the LORD: 'With these you shall gore the Syrians until they are destroyed.' "

Mic 4:13 "Arise and thresh, O daughter of Zion; For I will make your horn iron, And I will make your hooves bronze; You shall beat in pieces many peoples; I will consecrate their gain to the LORD, And their substance to the Lord of the whole earth."

(Cutting off) destruction of power.

Ps 75:10 "All the horns of the wicked I will also cut off, *But* the horns of the righteous shall be exalted."

Jer 48:25 The horn of Moab is cut off, And his arm is broken," says the LORD.

Lam 2:3 He has cut off in fierce anger Every horn of Israel; He has drawn back His right hand From before the enemy. He has blazed against Jacob like a flaming fire Devouring all around.

HORSE, THE

Endued with strength by God.

Job 39:19 "Have you given the horse strength? Have you clothed his neck with thunder?

Described as

Strong.

Ps 33:17 A horse *is* a vain hope for safety; Neither shall it deliver *any* by its great strength.

Ps 147:10 He does not delight in the strength of the horse; He takes no pleasure in the legs of a man.

Swift.

Is 30:16 And you said, "No, for we will flee on horses"— Therefore you shall flee! And, "We will ride on swift *horses*"— Therefore those who pursue you shall be swift!

Jer 4:13 "Behold, he shall come up like clouds, And his chariots like a whirlwind. His horses are swifter than eagles. Woe to us, for we are plundered!"

Hab 1:8 Their horses also are swifter than leopards, And more fierce than evening wolves. Their chargers charge ahead; Their cavalry comes from afar; They fly as the eagle *that* hastens to eat.

Fearless.

Job 39:20 Can you frighten him like a locust? His majestic snorting strikes terror.

Job 39:22 He mocks at fear, and is not frightened; Nor does he turn back from the sword.

Fierce and impetuous.

Job 39:21 He paws in the valley, and rejoices in *his* strength; He gallops into the clash of arms.

Job 39:24 He devours the distance with fierceness and rage; Nor does he come to a halt because the trumpet *has* sounded.

Warlike in disposition.

Job 39:21 He paws in the valley, and rejoices in *his* strength; He gallops into the clash of arms.

Jer 8:6 I listened and heard, *But* they do not speak aright. No man repented of his wickedness, Saying, 'What have I done?' Everyone turned to his own course, As the horse rushes into the battle.

Having pounding hooves.

Judg 5:22 Then the horses' hooves pounded, The galloping, galloping of his steeds.

Sure footed.

Is 63:13 Who led them through the deep, As a horse in the wilderness, *That* they might not stumble?"

Has no understanding.

Ps 32:9 Do not be like the horse *or* like the mule, Which have no understanding, Which must be harnessed with bit and bridle, Else they will not come near you.

Hard hooves of, alluded to.

Is 5:28 Whose arrows *are* sharp, And all their bows bent; Their horses' hooves will seem like flint, And their wheels like a whirlwind.

Loud snorting of, alluded to.

Job 39:20 Can you frighten him like a locust? His majestic snorting strikes terror.

Jer 8:16 The snorting of His horses was heard from Dan. The whole land trembled at the sound of the neighing of His strong ones; For they have come and devoured the land and all that is in it, The city and those who dwell in it."

Colors of, mentioned

White.

Zech 1:8 I saw by night, and behold, a man riding on a red horse, and it stood among the myrtle trees in the hollow; and behind him *were* horses: red, sorrel, and white.

Zech 6:3 with the third chariot white horses, and with the fourth chariot dappled horses—strong *steeds*.

Rev 6:2 And I looked, and behold, a white horse. He who sat on it had a bow; and a crown was given to him, and he went out conquering and to conquer.

Black.

Zech 6:2 With the first chariot *were* red horses, with the second chariot black horses,

Zech 6:6 The one with the black horses is going to the north country, the white are going after them, and the dappled are going toward the south country."

Rev 6:5 When He opened the third seal, I heard the third living creature say, "Come and see." So I looked, and behold, a black horse, and he who sat on it had a pair of scales in his hand.

Red.

Zech 1:8 I saw by night, and behold, a man riding on a red horse, and it stood among the myrtle trees in the hollow; and behind him *were* horses: red, sorrel, and white.

Zech 6:2 With the first chariot *were* red horses, with the second chariot black horses,

Rev 6:4 Another horse, fiery red, went out. And it was granted to the one who sat on it to take peace from the earth, and that *people* should kill one another; and there was given to him a great sword.

Sorrel.

Zech 1:8 I saw by night, and behold, a man riding on a red horse, and it stood among the myrtle trees in the hollow; and behind him *were* horses: red, sorrel, and white.

Dappled.

Zech 6:3 with the third chariot white horses, and with the fourth chariot dappled horses—strong *steeds*.

Zech 6:6–7 The one with the black horses is going to the north country, the white are going after them, and the dappled are going toward the south country." **7** Then the strong *steeds* went out, eager to go, that they might walk to and fro throughout the earth. And He said, "Go, walk to and fro throughout the earth." So they walked to and fro throughout the earth.

Pale.

Rev 6:8 So I looked, and behold, a pale horse. And the name of him who sat on it was Death, and Hades followed with him. And power was given to them over a fourth of the earth, to kill with sword, with hunger, with death, and by the beasts of the earth.

Fed on grain and herbs.

1 Kin 18:5 And Ahab had said to Obadiah, "Go into the land to all the springs of water and to all the brooks; perhaps we may find grass to keep the horses and mules alive, so that we will not have to kill any livestock."

Used for

Mounting cavalry.

Ex 14:9 So the Egyptians pursued them, all the horses *and* chariots of Pharaoh, his horsemen and his army, and overtook them camping by the sea beside Pi Hahiroth, before Baal Zephon.

1 Sam 13:5 Then the Philistines gathered together to fight with Israel, thirty thousand chariots and six thousand horsemen, and people as the sand which *is* on the seashore in multitude. And they came up and encamped in Michmash, to the east of Beth Aven.

Drawing chariots.

Mic 1:13 O inhabitant of Lachish, Harness the chariot to the swift steeds (She *was* the beginning of sin to the daughter of Zion), For the transgressions of Israel were found in you.

Zech 6:2 With the first chariot *were* red horses, with the second chariot black horses,

Bearing burdens.

Ezra 2:66 Their horses *were* seven hundred and thirty-six, their mules two hundred and forty-five,

Neh 7:68 Their horses were seven hundred and thirty-six, their mules two hundred and forty-five,

Hunting.

Job 39:18 When she lifts herself on high, She scorns the horse and its rider.

Carrying letters, etc.

2 Kin 9:17–19 Now a watchman stood on the tower in Jezreel, and he saw the company of Jehu as he came, and said, "I see a company of men." And Joram said, "Get a horseman and send him to meet them, and let him say, *'Is it* peace?'" **18** So the horseman went to meet him, and said, "Thus says the king: 'Is it peace?'" And Jehu said, "What have you to do with peace? Turn around and follow me." So the watchman reported, saying, "The messenger went to them, but is not coming back." **19** Then he sent out a second horseman who came to them, and said, "Thus says the king: 'Is it peace?'" And Jehu answered, "What have you to do with peace? Turn around and follow me."

Esth 8:10 And he wrote in the name of King Ahasuerus, sealed *it* with the king's signet ring, and sent letters by couriers on horseback, riding on royal horses bred from swift steeds.

Kings and princes rode on.

Esth 6:8–11 let a royal robe be brought which the king has worn, and a horse on which the king has ridden, which has a royal crest placed on its head. **9** Then let this robe and horse be delivered to the hand of one of the king's most noble princes, that he may array the man whom the king delights to honor. Then parade him on horseback through the city square, and proclaim before him: 'Thus shall it be done to the man whom the king delights to honor!'" **10** Then the king said to Haman, "Hurry, take the robe and the horse, as you have suggested, and do so for Mordecai the Jew who sits within the king's gate! Leave nothing undone of all that you have spoken." **11** So Haman took the robe and the horse, arrayed Mordecai and led him on horseback through the city square, and proclaimed before him, "Thus shall it be done to the man whom the king delights to honor!"

Ezek 23:23 The Babylonians, All the Chaldeans, Pekod, Shoa, Koa, All the Assyrians with them, All of them desirable young men, Governors and rulers, Captains and men of renown, All of them riding on horses.

Governed by bit and bridle.

Ps 32:9 Do not be like the horse *or* like the mule, *Which* have no understanding, Which must be harnessed with bit and bridle, Else they will not come near you.

James 3:3 Indeed, we put bits in horses' mouths that they may obey us, and we turn their whole body.

Urged on by whips.

Prov 26:3 A whip for the horse, A bridle for the donkey, And a rod for the fool's back.

Adorned with bells on the neck.

Zech 14:20 In that day "HOLINESS TO THE LORD" shall be *engraved* on the bells of the horses. The pots in the LORD's house shall be like the bowls before the altar.

Numbers of, kept for war.

Prov 21:31 The horse *is* prepared for the day of battle, But deliverance *is* of the LORD.

Jer 51:27 Set up a banner in the land, Blow the trumpet among the nations! Prepare the nations against her, Call the kingdoms together against her: Ararat, Minni, and Ashkenaz. Appoint a general against her; Cause the horses to come up like the bristling locusts.

Ezek 26:10 Because of the abundance of his horses, their dust will cover you; your walls will shake at the noise of the horsemen, the wagons, and the chariots,

when he enters your gates, as men enter a city that has been breached.

In battle, protected by armor.

Jer 46:4 Harness the horses, And mount up, you horsemen! Stand forth with *your* helmets, Polish the spears, Put on the armor!

Vanity of trusting in.

Ps 33:17 A horse *is* a vain hope for safety; Neither shall it deliver *any* by its great strength.

Amos 2:15 He shall not stand who handles the bow, The swift of foot shall not escape, Nor shall he who rides a horse deliver himself.

The Jews

Forbidden to multiply them.

Deut 17:16 But he shall not multiply horses for himself, nor cause the people to return to Egypt to multiply horses, for the LORD has said to you, 'You shall not return that way again.'

Imported them from Egypt.

1 Kin 10:28–29 Also Solomon had horses imported from Egypt and Keveh; the king's merchants bought them in Keveh at the *current* price. **29** Now a chariot that was imported from Egypt cost six hundred *shekels* of silver, and a horse one hundred and fifty; and thus, through their agents, they exported *them* to all the kings of the Hittites and the kings of Syria.

Multiplied them in Solomon's reign.

1 Kin 4:26 Solomon had forty thousand stalls of horses for his chariots, and twelve thousand horsemen.

Condemned for multiplying them.

Is 2:7 Their land is also full of silver and gold, And there is no end to their treasures; Their land is also full of horses, And there is no end to their chariots.

Not to trust in them.

Hos 14:3 Assyria shall not save us, We will not ride on horses, Nor will we say anymore to the work of our hands, 'You are our gods.' For in You the fatherless finds mercy."

Condemned for trusting in.

Is 30:16 And you said, "No, for we will flee on horses"— Therefore you shall flee! And, "We will ride on swift *horses*"— Therefore those who pursue you shall be swift!

Is 31:3 Now the Egyptians *are* men, and not God; And their horses are flesh, and not spirit. When the LORD stretches out His hand, Both he who helps will fall, And he who is helped will fall down; They all will perish together.

Brought back many, from Babylon.

Ezra 2:66 Their horses *were* seven hundred and thirty-six, their mules two hundred and forty-five,

Notice of early trading in.

Gen 47:17 So they brought their livestock to Joseph, and Joseph gave them bread *in exchange* for the horses, the flocks, the cattle of the herds, and for the donkeys. Thus he fed them with bread *in exchange* for all their livestock that year.

Sold in fairs and markets.

Ezek 27:14 Those from the house of Togarmah traded for your wares with horses, steeds, and mules.

Rev 18:13 and cinnamon and incense, fragrant oil and frankincense, wine and oil, fine flour and wheat, cattle and sheep, horses and chariots, and bodies and souls of men.

Often suffered

From blindness.

Zech 12:4 In that day," says the LORD, "I will strike every horse with confusion, and its rider with madness; I will open My eyes on the house of Judah, and will strike every horse of the peoples with blindness.

From plague.

Zech 14:15 Such also shall be the plague On the horse *and* the mule, On the camel and the donkey, And on all the cattle that will be in those camps. So *shall* this plague *be.*

From pestilence.

Ex 9:3 behold, the hand of the LORD will be on your cattle in the field, on the horses, on the donkeys, on the camels, on the oxen, and on the sheep—a very severe pestilence.

From bites of serpents.

Gen 49:17 Dan shall be a serpent by the way, A viper by the path, That bites the horse's heels So that its rider shall fall backward.

In battle.

Jer 51:21 With you I will break in pieces the horse and its rider; With you I will break in pieces the chariot and its rider;

Hag 2:22 I will overthrow the throne of kingdoms; I will destroy the strength of the Gentile kingdoms. I will overthrow the chariots And those who ride in them; The horses and their riders shall come down, Every one by the sword of his brother.

Dedicated to the sun by idolaters.

2 Kin 23:11 Then he removed the horses that the kings of Judah had dedicated to the sun, at the entrance to the house of the LORD, by the chamber of Nathan-Melech, the officer who *was* in the court; and he burned the chariots of the sun with fire.

Illustrative of

Victory of God's people.

Is 63:13 Who led them through the deep, As a horse in the wilderness, *That* they might not stumble?"

Zech 10:3 "My anger is kindled against the shepherds, And I will punish the goatherds. For the LORD of hosts will visit His flock, The house of Judah, And will make them as His royal horse in the battle.

A dull, headstrong disposition.

Ps 32:9 Do not be like the horse *or* like the mule, *Which* have no understanding, Which must be harnessed with bit and bridle, Else they will not come near you.

Impetuosity of the wicked in sin.

Jer 8:6 I listened and heard, *But* they do not speak aright. No man repented of his wickedness, Saying, 'What have I done?' Everyone turned to his own course, As the horse rushes into the battle.

HOSPITALITY

Commanded.

Rom 12:13 distributing to the needs of the saints, given to hospitality.

1 Pet 4:9 *Be* hospitable to one another without grumbling.

Required in ministers.

1 Tim 3:2 A bishop then must be blameless, the husband of one wife, temperate, sober-minded, of good behavior, hospitable, able to teach;

Titus 1:8 but hospitable, a lover of what is good, sober-minded, just, holy, self-controlled,

A test of Christian character.

1 Tim 5:10 well reported for good works: if she has brought up children, if she has lodged strangers, if she has washed the saints' feet, if she has relieved the afflicted, if she has diligently followed every good work.

Specially to be shown to

Strangers.

Heb 13:2 Do not forget to entertain strangers, for by so *doing* some have unwittingly entertained angels.

The poor.

Is 58:7 *Is it* not to share your bread with the hungry, And that you bring to your house the poor who are cast out; When you see the naked, that you cover him, And not hide yourself from your own flesh?

Luke 14:13 But when you give a feast, invite *the* poor, *the* maimed, *the* lame, *the* blind.

Enemies.

2 Kin 6:22–23 But he answered, "You shall not kill *them.* Would you kill those whom you have taken captive with your sword and your bow? Set food and water before them, that they may eat and drink and go to their master." **23** Then he prepared a great feast for them; and after they ate and drank, he sent them away and they went to their master. So the bands of Syrian *raiders* came no more into the land of Israel.

Rom 12:20 Therefore *"If your enemy is hungry, feed him; If he is thirsty, give him a drink; For in so doing you will heap coals of fire on his head."*

Encouragement to.

Luke 14:14 And you will be blessed, because they cannot repay you; for you shall be repaid at the resurrection of the just."

Heb 13:2 Do not forget to entertain strangers, for by so *doing* some have unwittingly entertained angels.

Exemplified by

Melchizedek.

Gen 14:18 Then Melchizedek king of Salem brought out bread and wine; he *was* the priest of God Most High.

Abraham.

Gen 18:3–8 and said, "My Lord, if I have now found favor in Your sight, do not pass on by Your servant. **4** Please let a little water be brought, and wash your feet, and rest yourselves under the tree. **5** And I will bring a morsel of bread, that you may refresh your hearts. After that you may pass by, inasmuch as you have come to your servant." They said, "Do as you have said." **6** So Abraham hurried into the tent to Sarah and said, "Quickly, make ready three measures of fine meal; knead *it* and make cakes." **7** And Abraham ran to the herd, took a tender and good calf, gave *it* to a young man, and he hastened to prepare it. **8** So he took butter and milk and the calf which he had prepared, and set *it* before them; and he stood by them under the tree as they ate.

Lot.

Gen 19:2–3 And he said, "Here now, my lords, please turn in to your servant's house and spend the night, and wash your feet; then you may rise early and go on your way." And they said, "No, but we will spend the night in the open square." **3** But he insisted strongly; so they turned in to him and entered his house. Then he made them a feast, and baked unleavened bread, and they ate.

Laban.

Gen 24:31 And he said, "Come in, O blessed of the Lord! Why do you stand outside? For I have prepared the house, and a place for the camels."

Jethro.

Ex 2:20 So he said to his daughters, "And where *is* he? Why *is* it *that* you have left the man? Call him, that he may eat bread."

Manoah.

Judg 13:15 Then Manoah said to the Angel of the Lord, "Please let us detain You, and we will prepare a young goat for You."

Samuel.

1 Sam 9:22 Now Samuel took Saul and his servant and brought them into the hall, and had them sit in the place of honor among those who were invited; there *were* about thirty persons.

David.

2 Sam 6:19 Then he distributed among all the people, among the whole multitude of Israel, both the women and the men, to everyone a loaf of bread, a piece *of meat,* and a cake of raisins. So all the people departed, everyone to his house.

Barzillai.

2 Sam 19:32 Now Barzillai was a very aged man, eighty years old. And he had provided the king with supplies while he stayed at Mahanaim, for he *was* a very rich man.

A Shunammite woman.

2 Kin 4:8 Now it happened one day that Elisha went to Shunem, where there *was* a notable woman, and she persuaded him to eat some food. So it was, as often as he passed by, he would turn in there to eat some food.

Nehemiah.

Neh 5:17 And at my table *were* one hundred and fifty Jews and rulers, besides those who came to us from the nations around us.

Job.

Job 31:17 Or eaten my morsel by myself, So that the fatherless could not eat of it

Job 31:32 (*But* no sojourner had to lodge in the street, *For* I have opened my doors to the traveler);

Zacchaeus.

Luke 19:6 So he made haste and came down, and received Him joyfully.

The Samaritans.

John 4:40 So when the Samaritans had come to Him, they urged Him to stay with them; and He stayed there two days.

Lydia.

Acts 16:15 And when she and her household were baptized, she begged *us,* saying, "If you have judged me to be faithful to the Lord, come to my house and stay." So she persuaded us.

Jason.

Acts 17:7 Jason has harbored them, and these are all acting contrary to the decrees of Caesar, saying there is another king—Jesus."

Mnason.

Acts 21:16 Also some of the disciples from Caesarea went with us and brought with them a certain Mnason of Cyprus, an early disciple, with whom we were to lodge.

The people of Malta.

Acts 28:2 And the natives showed us unusual kindness; for they kindled a fire and made us all welcome, because of the rain that was falling and because of the cold.

Publius.

Acts 28:7 In that region there was an estate of the leading citizen of the island, whose name was Publius, who received us and entertained us courteously for three days.

Gaius.

3 John 1:5–6 Beloved, you do faithfully whatever you do for the brethren and for strangers, **6** who have borne witness of your love before the church. *If* you send them forward on their journey in a manner worthy of God, you will do well,

HOUSES

Antiquity of.

Gen 12:1 Now the Lord had said to Abram: "Get out of your country, From your family And from your father's house, To a land that I will show you.

Gen 19:3 But he insisted strongly; so they turned in to him and entered his house. Then he made them a feast, and baked unleavened bread, and they ate.

Deep and solid foundations required for.

Matt 7:24 "Therefore whoever hears these sayings of Mine, and does them, I will liken him to a wise man who built his house on the rock:

Luke 6:48 He is like a man building a house, who dug deep and laid the foundation on the rock. And when the flood arose, the stream beat vehemently against that house, and could not shake it, for it was founded on the rock.

Sometimes built without foundation.

Matt 7:26 "But everyone who hears these sayings of Mine, and does not do them, will be like a foolish man who built his house on the sand:

Luke 6:49 But he who heard and did nothing is like a

man who built a house on the earth without a foundation, against which the stream beat vehemently; and immediately it fell. And the ruin of that house was great."

Built of

Clay.

Job 4:19 How much more those who dwell in houses of clay, Whose foundation is in the dust, *Who* are crushed before a moth?

Bricks.

Ex 1:11–14 Therefore they set taskmasters over them to afflict them with their burdens. And they built for Pharaoh supply cities, Pithom and Raamses. **12** But the more they afflicted them, the more they multiplied and grew. And they were in dread of the children of Israel. **13** So the Egyptians made the children of Israel serve with rigor. **14** And they made their lives bitter with hard bondage—in mortar, in brick, and in all manner of service in the field. All their service in which they made them serve *was* with rigor.

Is 9:10 "The bricks have fallen down, But we will rebuild with hewn stones; The sycamores are cut down, But we will replace *them* with cedars."

Stone and wood.

Lev 14:40 then the priest shall command that they take away the stones in which *is* the plague, and they shall cast them into an unclean place outside the city.

Lev 14:42 Then they shall take other stones and put *them* in the place of *those* stones, and he shall take other mortar and plaster the house.

Hab 2:11 For the stone will cry out from the wall, And the beam from the timbers will answer it.

Hewn or cut stone.

Amos 5:11 Therefore, because you tread down the poor And take grain taxes from him, Though you have built houses of hewn stone, Yet you shall not dwell in them; You have planted pleasant vineyards, But you shall not drink wine from them.

In cities, built in streets.

Gen 19:2 And he said, "Here now, my lords, please turn in to your servant's house and spend the night, and wash your feet; then you may rise early and go on your way." And they said, "No, but we will spend the night in the open square."

Josh 2:19 So it shall be *that* whoever goes outside the doors of your house into the street, his blood *shall be* on his own head, and we *will be* guiltless. And whoever is with you in the house, his blood *shall be* on our head if a hand is laid on him.

Often built on city walls.

Josh 2:15 Then she let them down by a rope through the window, for her house *was* on the city wall; she dwelt on the wall.

2 Cor 11:33 but I was let down in a basket through a window in the wall, and escaped from his hands.

The flat roofs of,

Surrounded with parapets.

Deut 22:8 "When you build a new house, then you shall make a parapet for your roof, that you may not bring guilt of bloodshed on your household if anyone falls from it.

Often had booths or tents on them.

2 Sam 16:22 So they pitched a tent for Absalom on the top of the house, and Absalom went in to his father's concubines in the sight of all Israel.

Neh 8:16 Then the people went out and brought *them* and made themselves booths, each one on the roof of his house, or in their courtyards or the courts of the house of God, and in the open square of the Water Gate and in the open square of the Gate of Ephraim.

Prov 21:9 Better to dwell in a corner of a housetop, Than in a house shared with a contentious woman.

Often had idolatrous altars on them.

2 Kin 23:12 The altars that *were* on the roof, the upper chamber of Ahaz, which the kings of Judah had made, and the altars which Manasseh had made in the two courts of the house of the LORD, the king broke down and pulverized there, and threw their dust into the Brook Kidron.

Jer 19:13 And the houses of Jerusalem and the houses of the kings of Judah shall be defiled like the place of Tophet, because of all the houses on whose roofs they have burned incense to all the host of heaven, and poured out drink offerings to other gods." ' "

Zeph 1:5 Those who worship the host of heaven on the housetops; Those who worship and swear *oaths* by the LORD, But who *also* swear by Milcom;

Used for drying flax.

Josh 2:6 (But she had brought them up to the roof and hidden them with the stalks of flax, which she had laid in order on the roof.)

Used for exercise.

2 Sam 11:2 Then it happened one evening that David arose from his bed and walked on the roof of the king's house. And from the roof he saw a woman bathing, and the woman *was* very beautiful to behold.

Dan 4:29 At the end of the twelve months he was walking about the royal palace of Babylon.

Used for devotion.

Acts 10:9 The next day, as they went on their journey and drew near the city, Peter went up on the housetop to pray, about the sixth hour.

Used for making proclamations.

Luke 12:3 Therefore whatever you have spoken in the dark will be heard in the light, and what you have spoken in the ear in inner rooms will be proclaimed on the housetops.

Used for secret conferences.

1 Sam 9:25–26 When they had come down from the high place into the city, *Samuel* spoke with Saul on the top of the house. **26** They arose early; and it was about the dawning of the day that Samuel called to Saul on the top of the house, saying, "Get up, that I may send you on your way." And Saul arose, and both of them went outside, he and Samuel.

Resorted to in grief.

Is 15:3 In their streets they will clothe themselves with sackcloth; On the tops of their houses And in their streets Everyone will wail, weeping bitterly.

Jer 48:38 A general lamentation On all the housetops of Moab, And in its streets; For I have broken Moab like a vessel in which *is* no pleasure," says the LORD.

Often covered with grass.

Ps 129:6–7 Let them be as the grass *on* the housetops, Which withers before it grows up, **7** With which the reaper does not fill his hand, Nor he who binds sheaves, his arms.

Accessible from the outside.

Matt 24:17 Let him who is on the housetop not go down to take anything out of his house.

Luke 5:19 And when they could not find how they might bring him in, because of the crowd, they went up on the housetop and let him down with *his* bed through the tiling into the midst before Jesus.

The courts of, large and used as apartments.

Esth 1:5 And when these days were completed, the king made a feast lasting seven days for all the people who were present in Shushan the citadel, from great to small, in the court of the garden of the king's palace.

Entered by a gate or door.

Gen 43:19 When they drew near to the steward of Joseph's house, they talked with him at the door of the house,

Ex 12:22 And you shall take a bunch of hyssop, dip *it* in the blood that *is* in the basin, and strike the lintel and the two doorposts with the blood that *is* in the basin. And none of you shall go out of the door of his house until morning.

Luke 16:20 But there was a certain beggar named Lazarus, full of sores, who was laid at his gate,

Acts 10:17 Now while Peter wondered within himself what this vision which he had seen meant, behold, the men who had been sent from Cornelius had made inquiry for Simon's house, and stood before the gate.

Doors of, low and small for safety.

Prov 17:19 He who loves transgression loves strife, And he who exalts his gate seeks destruction.

Doors of, how fastened.

2 Sam 13:18 Now she had on a robe of many colors, for the king's virgin daughters wore such apparel. And his servant put her out and bolted the door behind her.

Song 5:5 I arose to open for my beloved, And my hands dripped *with* myrrh, My fingers with liquid myrrh, On the handles of the lock.

Luke 11:7 and he will answer from within and say, 'Do not trouble me; the door is now shut, and my children are with me in bed; I cannot rise and give to you'?

Admission to, gained by knocking at the door.

Acts 12:13 And as Peter knocked at the door of the gate, a girl named Rhoda came to answer.

Rev 3:20 Behold, I stand at the door and knock. If anyone hears My voice and opens the door, I will come in to him and dine with him, and he with Me.

Walls of, plastered.

Lev 14:42–43 Then they shall take other stones and put *them* in the place of *those* stones, and he shall take other mortar and plaster the house. **43** "Now if the plague comes back and breaks out in the house, after

he has taken away the stones, after he has scraped the house, and after it is plastered,

Serpents often lodged in walls of.

Amos 5:19 It *will be* as though a man fled from a lion, And a bear met him! Or *as though* he went into the house, Leaned his hand on the wall, And a serpent bit him!

Nails often driven in walls of.

Eccl 12:11 The words of the wise are like goads, and the words of scholars are like well-driven nails, given by one Shepherd.

Is 22:23 I will fasten him *as* a peg in a secure place, And he will become a glorious throne to his father's house.

Often had several stories.

Ezek 41:16 their doorposts and the beveled window frames. And the galleries all around their three stories opposite the threshold were paneled with wood from the ground to the windows—the windows were covered—

Acts 20:9 And in a window sat a certain young man named Eutychus, who was sinking into a deep sleep. He was overcome by sleep; and as Paul continued speaking, he fell down from the third story and was taken up dead.

Divided into apartments.

Gen 43:30 Now his heart yearned for his brother; so Joseph made haste and sought *somewhere* to weep. And he went into *his* chamber and wept there.

Is 26:20 Come, my people, enter your chambers, And shut your doors behind you; Hide yourself, as it were, for a little moment, Until the indignation is past.

Characteristics of their apartments

Large and airy.

Jer 22:14 Who says, 'I will build myself a wide house with spacious chambers, And cut out windows for it, Paneling *it* with cedar And painting *it* with vermilion.'

Paneled and painted.

Jer 22:14 Who says, 'I will build myself a wide house with spacious chambers, And cut out windows for it, Paneling *it* with cedar And painting *it* with vermilion.'

Hag 1:4 "Is it time for you yourselves to dwell in your paneled houses, and this temple *to lie* in ruins?"

Inlaid with ivory.

1 Kin 22:39 Now the rest of the acts of Ahab, and all that he did, the ivory house which he built and all the cities that he built, *are* they not written in the book of the chronicles of the kings of Israel?

Amos 3:15 I will destroy the winter house along with the summer house; The houses of ivory shall perish, And the great houses shall have an end," Says the LORD.

Hung with fine curtains.

Esth 1:6 *There were* white and blue linen *curtains* fastened with cords of fine linen and purple on silver rods and marble pillars; *and the* couches *were* of gold and silver on a *mosaic* pavement of alabaster, turquoise, and white and black marble.

Warmed with fires.

Jer 36:22 Now the king was sitting in the winter house in the ninth month, with *a fire* burning on the hearth before him.

John 18:18 Now the servants and officers who had made a fire of coals stood there, for it was cold, and they warmed themselves. And Peter stood with them and warmed himself.

Upper apartments of, the best and used for celebrations.

Mark 14:15 Then he will show you a large upper room, furnished *and* prepared; there make ready for us."

Often had detached apartments for secrecy and for strangers.

Judg 3:20–23 So Ehud came to him (now he was sitting upstairs in his cool private chamber). Then Ehud said, "I have a message from God for you." So he arose from *his* seat. **21** Then Ehud reached with his left hand, took the dagger from his right thigh, and thrust it into his belly. **22** Even the hilt went in after the blade, and the fat closed over the blade, for he did not draw the dagger out of his belly; and his entrails came out. **23** Then Ehud went out through the porch and shut the doors of the upper room behind him and locked them.

2 Kin 4:10–11 Please, let us make a small upper room on the wall; and let us put a bed for him there, and a table and a chair and a lampstand; so it will be, whenever he comes to us, he can turn in there." **11** And it happened one day that he came there, and he turned in to the upper room and lay down there.

2 Kin 9:2–3 Now when you arrive at that place, look there for Jehu the son of Jehoshaphat, the son of Nimshi, and go in and make him rise up from among his associates, and take him to an inner room. **3** Then take the flask of oil, and pour *it* on his head, and say, 'Thus says the LORD: "I have anointed you king over Israel." ' Then open the door and flee, and do not delay."

Lighted by windows.

1 Kin 7:4 *There were* windows *with beveled frames in* three rows, and window *was* opposite window *in* three tiers.

Street windows of, high and dangerous.

2 Kin 1:2 Now Ahaziah fell through the lattice of his upper room in Samaria, and was injured; so he sent messengers and said to them, "Go, inquire of Baal-Zebub, the god of Ekron, whether I shall recover from this injury."

2 Kin 9:30 Now when Jehu had come to Jezreel, Jezebel heard *of it;* and she put paint on her eyes and adorned her head, and looked through a window.

2 Kin 9:33 Then he said, "Throw her down." So they threw her down, and *some* of her blood spattered on the wall and on the horses; and he trampled her underfoot.

Acts 20:9 And in a window sat a certain young man named Eutychus, who was sinking into a deep sleep. He was overcome by sleep; and as Paul continued speaking, he fell down from the third story and was taken up dead.

Of the rich

Great.

Is 5:9 In my hearing the LORD of hosts *said,* "Truly, many houses shall be desolate, Great and beautiful ones, without inhabitant.

Amos 6:11 For behold, the LORD gives a command: He will break the great house into bits, And the little house into pieces.

2 Tim 2:20 But in a great house there are not only vessels of gold and silver, but also of wood and clay, some for honor and some for dishonor.

Beautiful.

Deut 8:12 lest—*when* you have eaten and are full, and have built beautiful houses and dwell *in them;*

Pleasant.

Ezek 26:12 They will plunder your riches and pillage your merchandise; they will break down your walls and destroy your pleasant houses; they will lay your stones, your timber, and your soil in the midst of the water.

Mic 2:9 The women of My people you cast out From their pleasant houses; From their children You have taken away My glory forever.

Of brick or clay

Plastered.

Ezek 13:10–11 "Because, indeed, because they have seduced My people, saying, 'Peace!' when *there is* no peace—and one builds a wall, and they plaster it with untempered *mortar*— **11** say to those who plaster *it* with untempered *mortar,* that it will fall. There will be flooding rain, and you, O great hailstones, shall fall; and a stormy wind shall tear *it* down.

Easily broken through.

Job 24:16 In the dark they break into houses Which they marked for themselves in the daytime; They do not know the light.

Ezek 12:5 Dig through the wall in their sight, and carry your belongings out through it.

Often swept away by torrents.

Ezek 13:13–14 Therefore thus says the Lord GOD: "I will cause a stormy wind to break forth in My fury; and there shall be a flooding rain in My anger, and great hailstones in fury to consume *it.* **14** So I will break down the wall you have plastered with untempered *mortar,* and bring it down to the ground, so that its foundation will be uncovered; it will fall, and you shall be consumed in the midst of it. Then you shall know that I *am* the LORD.

When finished, were usually dedicated.

Deut 20:5 "Then the officers shall speak to the people, saying: 'What man *is there* who has built a new house and has not dedicated it? Let him go and return to his house, lest he die in the battle and another man dedicate it.

Ps 30:title A Psalm. A Song at the dedication of the house of David.

For summer residence.

Amos 3:15 I will destroy the winter house along with the summer house; The houses of ivory shall perish, And the great houses shall have an end," Says the LORD.

Liable to leprosy. Lev 14:34–53

Not to be coveted.

Ex 20:17 "You shall not covet your neighbor's house; you shall not covet your neighbor's wife, nor his male servant, nor his female servant, nor his ox, nor his donkey, nor anything that *is* your neighbor's."

Mic 2:2 They covet fields and take *them* by violence, Also houses, and seize *them*. So they oppress a man and his house, A man and his inheritance.

Were rented.

Acts 28:30 Then Paul dwelt two whole years in his own rented house, and received all who came to him,

Were mortgaged.

Neh 5:3 There were also *some* who said, "We have mortgaged our lands and vineyards and houses, that we might buy grain because of the famine."

Were sold.

Acts 4:34 Nor was there anyone among them who lacked; for all who were possessors of lands or houses sold them, and brought the proceeds of the things that were sold,

Law respecting the sale of.

Lev 25:29–33 'If a man sells a house in a walled city, then he may redeem it within a whole year after it is sold; *within* a full year he may redeem it. **30** But if it is not redeemed within the space of a full year, then the house in the walled city shall belong permanently to him who bought it, throughout his generations. It shall not be released in the Jubilee. **31** However the houses of villages which have no wall around them shall be counted as the fields of the country. They may be redeemed, and they shall be released in the Jubilee. **32** Nevertheless the cities of the Levites, *and* the houses in the cities of their possession, the Levites may redeem at any time. **33** And if a man purchases a house from the Levites, then the house that was sold in the city of his possession shall be released in the Jubilee; for the houses in the cities of the Levites *are* their possession among the children of Israel.

Of criminals, desolated.

Dan 2:5 The king answered and said to the Chaldeans, "My decision is firm: if you do not make known the dream to me, and its interpretation, you shall be cut in pieces, and your houses shall be made an ash heap.

Dan 3:29 Therefore I make a decree that any people, nation, or language which speaks anything amiss against the God of Shadrach, Meshach, and Abed-Nego shall be cut in pieces, and their houses shall be made an ash heap; because there is no other God who can deliver like this."

Desolation of, threatened as a punishment.

Is 5:9 In my hearing the LORD of hosts *said*, "Truly, many houses shall be desolate, Great and beautiful ones, without inhabitant.

Is 13:16 Their children also will be dashed to pieces before their eyes; Their houses will be plundered And their wives ravished.

Is 13:21–22 But wild beasts of the desert will lie there, And their houses will be full of owls; Ostriches will dwell there, And wild goats will caper there. **22** The hyenas will howl in their citadels, And jackals in their pleasant palaces. Her time *is* near to come, And her days will not be prolonged."

Ezek 16:41 They shall burn your houses with fire, and execute judgments on you in the sight of many women; and I will make you cease playing the harlot, and you shall no longer hire lovers.

Ezek 26:12 They will plunder your riches and pillage your merchandise; they will break down your walls and destroy your pleasant houses; they will lay your stones, your timber, and your soil in the midst of the water.

Often broken down to repair city walls before sieges.

Is 22:10 You numbered the houses of Jerusalem, And the houses you broke down To fortify the wall.

Illustrative of

The body.

Job 4:19 How much more those who dwell in houses of clay, Whose foundation is in the dust, *Who* are crushed before a moth?

2 Cor 5:1 For we know that if our earthly house, *this* tent, is destroyed, we have a building from God, a house not made with hands, eternal in the heavens.

The grave.

Job 30:23 For I know *that* You will bring me *to* death, And *to* the house appointed for all living.

The church.

Heb 3:6 but Christ as a Son over His own house, whose house we are if we hold fast the confidence and the rejoicing of the hope firm to the end.

1 Pet 2:5 you also, as living stones, are being built up a spiritual house, a holy priesthood, to offer up spiritual sacrifices acceptable to God through Jesus Christ.

Believers' inheritance.

John 14:2 In My Father's house are many mansions; if *it were* not *so*, I would have told you. I go to prepare a place for you.

2 Cor 5:1 For we know that if our earthly house, *this* tent, is destroyed, we have a building from God, a house not made with hands, eternal in the heavens.

(On sand) the delusive hope of hypocrites.

Matt 7:26–27 "But everyone who hears these sayings of Mine, and does not do them, will be like a foolish man who built his house on the sand: **27** and the rain descended, the floods came, and the winds blew and beat on that house; and it fell. And great was its fall."

(On a rock) the hope of believers.

Matt 7:24–25 "Therefore whoever hears these sayings of Mine, and does them, I will liken him to a wise man who built his house on the rock: **25** and the rain descended, the floods came, and the winds blew and beat on that house; and it did not fall, for it was founded on the rock.

(Insecurity of) earthly trust.

Matt 6:19–20 "Do not lay up for yourselves treasures on earth, where moth and rust destroy and where thieves break in and steal; **20** but lay up for yourselves treasures in heaven, where neither moth nor rust destroys and where thieves do not break in and steal.

(Building of) great prosperity.

Is 65:21 They shall build houses and inhabit *them*; They shall plant vineyards and eat their fruit.

Ezek 28:26 And they will dwell safely there, build houses, and plant vineyards; yes, they will dwell securely, when I execute judgments on all those around them who despise them. Then they shall know that I *am* the LORD their God." ' "

(Built and not inhabited) calamity.

Deut 28:30 "You shall betroth a wife, but another man shall lie with her; you shall build a house, but you shall not dwell in it; you shall plant a vineyard, but shall not gather its grapes.

Amos 5:11 Therefore, because you tread down the poor And take grain taxes from him, Though you have built houses of hewn stone, Yet you shall not dwell in them; You have planted pleasant vineyards, But you shall not drink wine from them.

Zeph 1:13 Therefore their goods shall become booty, And their houses a desolation; They shall build houses, but not inhabit *them;* They shall plant vineyards, but not drink their wine."

(To inhabit those, built by others) feelings of abundance.

Deut 6:10–11 "So it shall be, when the LORD your God brings you into the land of which He swore to your fathers, to Abraham, Isaac, and Jacob, to give you large and beautiful cities which you did not build, **11** houses full of all good things, which you did not fill, hewn-out wells which you did not dig, vineyards and olive trees which you did not plant—when you have eaten and are full—

HUMILITY

Defined.

Phil 2:3–4 *Let* nothing *be done* through selfish ambition or conceit, but in lowliness of mind let each esteem others better than himself. **4** Let each of you look out not only for his own interests, but also for the interests of others.

Necessary to the service of God.

Mic 6:8 He has shown you, O man, what *is* good; And what does the LORD require of you But to do justly, To love mercy, And to walk humbly with your God?

Christ an example of.

Matt 11:29 Take My yoke upon you and learn from Me, for I am gentle and lowly in heart, and you will find rest for your souls.

John 13:14–15 If I then, *your* Lord and Teacher, have washed your feet, you also ought to wash one another's feet. **15** For I have given you an example, that you should do as I have done to you.

Phil 2:5–8 Let this mind be in you which was also in Christ Jesus, **6** who, being in the form of God, did not consider it robbery to be equal with God, **7** but made Himself of no reputation, taking the form of a bondservant, *and* coming in the likeness of men. **8** And being found in appearance as a man, He humbled Himself and became obedient to *the point of* death, even the death of the cross.

A characteristic of believers.

Ps 34:2 My soul shall make its boast in the LORD; The humble shall hear *of it* and be glad.

Those who have, are

Regarded by God.

Ps 138:6 Though the LORD *is* on high, Yet He regards the lowly; But the proud He knows from afar.

Is 66:2 For all those *things* My hand has made, And all those *things* exist," Says the LORD. "But on this *one* will I look: On *him who is* poor and of a contrite spirit, And who trembles at My word.

Heard by God.

Ps 9:12 When He avenges blood, He remembers them; He does not forget the cry of the humble.

Joyful in God's presence.

Is 57:15 For thus says the High and Lofty One Who inhabits eternity, whose name *is* Holy: "I dwell in the high and holy *place*, With him *who* has a contrite and humble spirit, To revive the spirit of the humble, And to revive the heart of the contrite ones.

Delivered by God.

Job 22:29 When they cast *you* down, and you say, 'Exaltation *will come!*' Then He will save the humble *person.*

Lifted up by God.

James 4:10 Humble yourselves in the sight of the Lord, and He will lift you up.

Exalted by God.

Luke 14:11 For whoever exalts himself will be humbled, and he who humbles himself will be exalted."

Luke 18:14 I tell you, this man went down to his house justified *rather* than the other; for everyone who exalts himself will be humbled, and he who humbles himself will be exalted."

Greatest in Christ's kingdom.

Matt 18:4 Therefore whoever humbles himself as this little child is the greatest in the kingdom of heaven.

Matt 20:26–28 Yet it shall not be so among you; but whoever desires to become great among you, let him be your servant. **27** And whoever desires to be first among you, let him be your slave— **28** just as the Son of Man did not come to be served, but to serve, and to give His life a ransom for many."

To receive more grace.

Prov 3:34 Surely He scorns the scornful, But gives grace to the humble.

James 4:6 But He gives more grace. Therefore He says: "God resists the proud, But gives grace to the humble."

Upheld by honor.

Prov 18:12 Before destruction the heart of a man is haughty, And before honor *is* humility.

Prov 29:23 A man's pride will bring him low, But the humble in spirit will retain honor.

Is before honor.

Prov 15:33 The fear of the LORD *is* the instruction of wisdom, And before honor *is* humility.

Leads to riches, honor, and life.

Prov 22:4 By humility *and* the fear of the LORD *Are* riches and honor and life.

Believers should

Live by.

Eph 4:1–2 I, therefore, the prisoner of the Lord, beseech you to walk worthy of the calling with which you were called, **2** with all lowliness and gentleness, with longsuffering, bearing with one another in love,

Col 3:12 Therefore, as *the* elect of God, holy and beloved, put on tender mercies, kindness, humility, meekness, longsuffering;

1 Pet 5:5 Likewise you younger people, submit yourselves to *your* elders. Yes, all of *you* be submissive to one another, and be clothed with humility, for *"God resists the proud, But gives grace to the humble."*

Beware of false.

Col 2:18 Let no one cheat you of your reward, taking delight in *false* humility and worship of angels, intruding into those things which he has not seen, vainly puffed up by his fleshly mind,

Col 2:23 These things indeed have an appearance of wisdom in self-imposed religion, *false* humility, and neglect of the body, *but are* of no value against the indulgence of the flesh.

Afflictions intended to produce.

Lev 26:41 and *that* I also have walked contrary to them and have brought them into the land of their enemies; if their uncircumcised hearts are humbled, and they accept their guilt—

Deut 8:3 So He humbled you, allowed you to hunger, and fed you with manna which you did not know nor did your fathers know, that He might make you know that man shall not live by bread alone; but man lives by every *word* that proceeds from the mouth of the LORD.

Lam 3:20 My soul still remembers And sinks within me.

Lack of, condemned.

2 Chr 33:23 And he did not humble himself before the LORD, as his father Manasseh had humbled himself; but Amon trespassed more and more.

2 Chr 36:12 He did evil in the sight of the LORD his God, *and* did not humble himself before Jeremiah the prophet, *who spoke* from the mouth of the LORD.

Jer 44:10 They have not been humbled, to this day, nor have they feared; they have not walked in My law or in My statutes that I set before you and your fathers.'

Dan 5:22 "But you his son, Belshazzar, have not humbled your heart, although you knew all this.

Temporal judgments averted by.

2 Chr 7:14 if My people who are called by My name will humble themselves, and pray and seek My face, and turn from their wicked ways, then I will hear from heaven, and will forgive their sin and heal their land.

2 Chr 12:6–7 So the leaders of Israel and the king humbled themselves; and they said, "The LORD *is* righteous." **7** Now when the LORD saw that they humbled themselves, the word of the LORD came to Shemaiah, saying, "They have humbled themselves; *therefore* I will not destroy them, but I will grant them some deliverance. My wrath shall not be poured out on Jerusalem by the hand of Shishak.

Virtue and reward for.

Prov 16:19 Better *to be* of a humble spirit with the lowly, Than to divide the spoil with the proud.

Matt 5:3 "Blessed *are* the poor in spirit, For theirs is the kingdom of heaven.

Exemplified by

Abraham.

Gen 18:27 Then Abraham answered and said, "Indeed now, I who *am but* dust and ashes have taken it upon myself to speak to the Lord:

Jacob.

Gen 32:10 I am not worthy of the least of all the mercies and of all the truth which You have shown Your servant; for I crossed over this Jordan with my staff, and now I have become two companies.

Moses.

Ex 3:11 But Moses said to God, "Who *am* I that I should go to Pharaoh, and that I should bring the children of Israel out of Egypt?"

Ex 4:10 Then Moses said to the LORD, "O my Lord, I *am* not eloquent, neither before nor since You have spoken to Your servant; but I *am* slow of speech and slow of tongue."

Joshua.

Josh 7:6 Then Joshua tore his clothes, and fell to the earth on his face before the ark of the LORD until evening, he and the elders of Israel; and they put dust on their heads.

Gideon.

Judg 6:15 So he said to Him, "O my Lord, how can I save Israel? Indeed my clan *is* the weakest in Manasseh, and I *am* the least in my father's house."

David.

1 Chr 29:14 But who *am* I, and who *are* my people, That we should be able to offer so willingly as this? For all things *come* from You, And of Your own we have given You.

Hezekiah.

2 Chr 32:26 Then Hezekiah humbled himself for the pride of his heart, he and the inhabitants of Jerusalem, so that the wrath of the LORD did not come upon them in the days of Hezekiah.

Manasseh.

2 Chr 33:12 Now when he was in affliction, he implored the LORD his God, and humbled himself greatly before the God of his fathers,

Josiah.

2 Chr 34:27 because your heart was tender, and you humbled yourself before God when you heard His words against this place and against its inhabitants, and you humbled yourself before Me, and you tore your clothes and wept before Me, I also have heard *you,*" says the LORD.

Job.

Job 40:4 "Behold, I am vile; What shall I answer You? I lay my hand over my mouth.

Job 42:6 Therefore I abhor *myself,* And repent in dust and ashes."

Isaiah.

Is 6:5 So I said: "Woe *is* me, for I am undone! Because I *am* a man of unclean lips, And I dwell in the midst of a people of unclean lips; For my eyes have seen the King, The LORD of hosts."

Jeremiah.

Jer 1:6 Then said I: "Ah, Lord GOD! Behold, I cannot speak, for I *am* a youth."

John the Baptist.

Matt 3:14 And John *tried to* prevent Him, saying, "I need to be baptized by You, and are You coming to me?"

A centurion.

Matt 8:8 The centurion answered and said, "Lord, I am not worthy that You should come under my roof. But only speak a word, and my servant will be healed.

A woman of Canaan.

Matt 15:27 And she said, "Yes, Lord, yet even the little dogs eat the crumbs which fall from their masters' table."

Elizabeth.

Luke 1:43 But why *is* this *granted* to me, that the mother of my Lord should come to me?

Peter.

Luke 5:8 When Simon Peter saw *it,* he fell down at Jesus' knees, saying, "Depart from me, for I am a sinful man, O Lord!"

Paul.

Acts 20:19 serving the Lord with all humility, with many tears and trials which happened to me by the plotting of the Jews;

HUSBANDS

Should have but one wife.

Gen 2:24 Therefore a man shall leave his father and mother and be joined to his wife, and they shall become one flesh.

Mark 10:6–8 But from the beginning of the creation, God 'made them male and female.' 7 'For this reason a man shall leave his father and mother and be joined to his wife, 8 and the two shall become one flesh'; so then they are no longer two, but one flesh.

1 Cor 7:2–4 Nevertheless, because of sexual immorality, let each man have his own wife, and let each woman have her own husband. 3 Let the husband render to his wife the affection due her, and likewise also the wife to her husband. 4 The wife does not have authority over her own body, but the husband *does.* And likewise the husband does not have authority over his own body, but the wife *does.*

Have authority over their wives.

Gen 3:16 To the woman He said: "I will greatly multiply your sorrow and your conception; In pain you shall bring forth children; Your desire *shall be* for your husband, And he shall rule over you."

1 Cor 11:3 But I want you to know that the head of every man is Christ, the head of woman *is* man, and the head of Christ *is* God.

Eph 5:23 For the husband is head of the wife, as also Christ is head of the church; and He is the Savior of the body.

Duty of, to wives

To respect them.

1 Pet 3:7 Husbands, likewise, dwell with *them* with understanding, giving honor to the wife, as to the weaker vessel, and as *being* heirs together of the grace of life, that your prayers may not be hindered.

To love them.

Eph 5:25–33 Husbands, love your wives, just as Christ also loved the church and gave Himself for her, 26 that He might sanctify and cleanse her with the washing of water by the word, 27 that He might present her to Himself a glorious church, not having spot or wrinkle or any such thing, but that she should be holy and without blemish. 28 So husbands ought to love their own wives as their own bodies; he who loves his wife loves himself. 29 For no one ever hated his own flesh, but nourishes and cherishes it, just as the Lord *does* the church. 30 For we are members of His body, of His flesh and of His bones. 31 *"For this reason a man shall leave his father and mother and be joined to his wife, and the two shall become one flesh."* 32 This is a great mystery, but I speak concerning Christ and the church. 33 Nevertheless let each one of you in particular so love his own wife as himself, and let the wife *see* that she respects *her* husband.

Col 3:19 Husbands, love your wives and do not be bitter toward them.

To regard them as themselves.

Gen 2:23 And Adam said: "This *is* now bone of my bones And flesh of my flesh; She shall be called Woman, Because she was taken out of Man."

Matt 19:5 and said, 'For this reason a man shall leave his father and mother and be joined to his wife, and the two shall become one flesh'?

To be faithful to them.

Prov 5:19 *As a* loving deer and a graceful doe, Let her breasts satisfy you at all times; And always be enraptured with her love.

Mal 2:14–15 Yet you say, "For what reason?" Because the LORD has been witness Between you and the wife of your youth, With whom you have dealt treacherously; Yet she is your companion And your wife by covenant. 15 But did He not make *them* one, Having a remnant of the Spirit? And why one? He seeks godly offspring. Therefore take heed to your spirit, And let none deal treacherously with the wife of his youth.

To dwell with them for life.

Gen 2:24 Therefore a man shall leave his father and mother and be joined to his wife, and they shall become one flesh.

Matt 19:3–9 The Pharisees also came to Him, testing Him, and saying to Him, "Is it lawful for a man to divorce his wife for *just* any reason?" 4 And He answered and said to them, "Have you not read that He who made *them* at the beginning 'made them male and female,' 5 and said, 'For this reason a man shall leave his father and mother and be joined to his wife, and the two shall become one flesh'? 6 So then, they are no longer two but one flesh. Therefore what God has joined together, let not man separate." 7 They said to Him, "Why then did Moses command to give a certificate of divorce, and to put her away?" 8 He said to them, "Moses, because of the hardness of your hearts, permitted you to divorce your wives, but from the beginning it was not so. 9 And I say to you, whoever divorces his wife, except for sexual immorality, and marries another, commits adultery; and whoever marries her who is divorced commits adultery."

To live with them with understanding.

1 Pet 3:7 Husbands, likewise, dwell with *them* with understanding, giving honor to the wife, as to the weaker vessel, and as *being* heirs together of the grace of life, that your prayers may not be hindered.

To comfort them.

1 Sam 1:8 Then Elkanah her husband said to her, "Hannah, why do you weep? Why do you not eat? And why is your heart grieved? *Am* I not better to you than ten sons?"

To consult with them.

Gen 31:4–7 So Jacob sent and called Rachel and Leah to the field, to his flock, **5** and said to them, "I see your father's countenance, that it *is* not *favorable* toward me as before; but the God of my father has been with me. **6** And you know that with all my might I have served your father. **7** Yet your father has deceived me and changed my wages ten times, but God did not allow him to hurt me.

Not to leave them, though unbelieving.

1 Cor 7:11–12 But even if she does depart, let her remain unmarried or be reconciled to *her* husband. And a husband is not to divorce *his* wife. **12** But to the rest I, not the Lord, say: If any brother has a wife who does not believe, and she is willing to live with him, let him not divorce her.

1 Cor 7:14 For the unbelieving husband is sanctified by the wife, and the unbelieving wife is sanctified by the husband; otherwise your children would be unclean, but now they are holy.

1 Cor 7:16 For how do you know, O wife, whether you will save *your* husband? Or how do you know, O husband, whether you will save *your* wife?

Duties of, not to interfere with duties to Christ.

Matt 19:29 And everyone who has left houses or brothers or sisters or father or mother or wife or children or lands, for My name's sake, shall receive a hundredfold, and inherit eternal life.

Luke 14:26 "If anyone comes to Me and does not hate his father and mother, wife and children, brothers and sisters, yes, and his own life also, he cannot be My disciple.

Good—exemplified by

Isaac.

Gen 24:67 Then Isaac brought her into his mother Sarah's tent; and he took Rebekah and she became his wife, and he loved her. So Isaac was comforted after his mother's *death.*

Elkanah.

1 Sam 1:4–5 And whenever the time came for Elkanah to make an offering, he would give portions to Peninnah his wife and to all her sons and daughters. **5** But to Hannah he would give a double portion, for he loved Hannah, although the LORD had closed her womb.

Bad—exemplified by

Solomon.

1 Kin 11:1 But King Solomon loved many foreign women, as well as the daughter of Pharaoh: women

of the Moabites, Ammonites, Edomites, Sidonians, *and* Hittites—

Ahasuerus.

Esth 1:10–11 On the seventh day, when the heart of the king was merry with wine, he commanded Mehuman, Biztha, Harbona, Bigtha, Abagtha, Zethar, and Carcas, seven eunuchs who served in the presence of King Ahasuerus, **11** to bring Queen Vashti before the king, *wearing* her royal crown, in order to show her beauty to the people and the officials, for she *was* beautiful to behold.

HYPOCRITES

God knows and detects.

Is 29:15–16 Woe to those who seek deep to hide their counsel far from the LORD, And their works are in the dark; They say, "Who sees us?" and, "Who knows us?" **16** Surely you have things turned around! Shall the potter be esteemed as the clay; For shall the thing made say of him who made it, "He did not make me"? Or shall the thing formed say of him who formed it, "He has no understanding"?

Christ knew and detected.

Matt 22:18 But Jesus perceived their wickedness, and said, "Why do you test Me, *you* hypocrites?

God has no pleasure in.

Is 9:17 Therefore the Lord will have no joy in their young men, Nor have mercy on their fatherless and widows; For everyone *is* a hypocrite and an evildoer, And every mouth speaks folly. For all this His anger is not turned away, But His hand *is* stretched out still.

Shall not come before God.

Job 13:16 He also *shall* be my salvation, For a hypocrite could not come before Him.

Described as

Willfully blind.

Matt 23:17 Fools and blind! For which is greater, the gold or the temple that sanctifies the gold?

Matt 23:19 Fools and blind! For which is greater, the gift or the altar that sanctifies the gift?

Matt 23:26 Blind Pharisee, first cleanse the inside of the cup and dish, that the outside of them may be clean also.

Foolish.

Is 32:6 For the foolish person will speak foolishness, And his heart will work iniquity: To practice ungodliness, To utter error against the LORD, To keep the hungry unsatisfied, And he will cause the drink of the thirsty to fail.

Self-righteous.

Is 65:5 Who say, 'Keep to yourself, Do not come near me, For I am holier than you!' These *are* smoke in My nostrils, A fire that burns all the day.

Luke 18:11 The Pharisee stood and prayed thus with himself, 'God, I thank You that I am not like other men—extortioners, unjust, adulterers, or even as this tax collector.

Covetous.

Ezek 33:31 So they come to you as people do, they sit before you *as* My people, and they hear your words, but they do not do them; for with their mouth they show much love, *but* their hearts pursue their *own* gain.

2 Pet 2:3 By covetousness they will exploit you with deceptive words; for a long time their judgment has not been idle, and their destruction does not slumber.

Ostentatious.

Matt 15:2 "Why do Your disciples transgress the tradition of the elders? For they do not wash their hands when they eat bread."

Matt 15:7–9 Hypocrites! Well did Isaiah prophesy about you, saying: **8** *'These people draw near to Me with their mouth, And honor Me with their lips, But their heart is far from Me.* **9** *And in vain they worship Me, Teaching as doctrines the commandments of men.'"*

Matt 15:12 Then His disciples came and said to Him, "Do You know that the Pharisees were offended when they heard this saying?"

Matt 23:5 But all their works they do to be seen by men. They make their phylacteries broad and enlarge the borders of their garments.

Censorious.

Matt 7:3–5 And why do you look at the speck in your brother's eye, but do not consider the plank in your own eye? **4** Or how can you say to your brother, 'Let me remove the speck from your eye'; and look, a plank *is* in your own eye? **5** Hypocrite! First remove the plank from your own eye, and then you will see clearly to remove the speck from your brother's eye.

Luke 13:14–15 But the ruler of the synagogue answered with indignation, because Jesus had healed on the Sabbath; and he said to the crowd, "There are six days on which men ought to work; therefore come and be healed on them, and not on the Sabbath day." **15** The Lord then answered him and said, "Hypocrite! Does not each one of you on the Sabbath loose his ox or donkey from the stall, and lead *it* away to water it?

Regarding tradition more than the Word of God.

Matt 15:1–3 Then the scribes and Pharisees who were from Jerusalem came to Jesus, saying, **2** "Why do Your disciples transgress the tradition of the elders? For they do not wash their hands when they eat bread." **3** He answered and said to them, "Why do you also transgress the commandment of God because of your tradition?

Exact in minor, but neglecting important duties.

Matt 23:23–24 "Woe to you, scribes and Pharisees, hypocrites! For you pay tithe of mint and anise and cummin, and have neglected the weightier *matters* of the law: justice and mercy and faith. These you ought to have done, without leaving the others undone. **24** Blind guides, who strain out a gnat and swallow a camel!

Having but a form of godliness.

2 Tim 3:5 having a form of godliness but denying its power. And from such people turn away!

Seeking only outward purity.

Luke 11:39 Then the Lord said to him, "Now you Pharisees make the outside of the cup and dish clean, but your inward part is full of greed and wickedness.

Professing but not practicing.

Ezek 33:31–32 So they come to you as people do, they sit before you *as* My people, and they hear your words, but they do not do them; for with their mouth they show much love, *but* their hearts pursue their *own* gain. **32** Indeed you *are* to them as a very lovely song of one who has a pleasant voice and can play well on an instrument; for they hear your words, but they do not do them.

Matt 23:3 Therefore whatever they tell you to observe, *that* observe and do, but do not do according to their works; for they say, and do not do.

Rom 2:17–23 Indeed you are called a Jew, and rest on the law, and make your boast in God, **18** and know His will, and approve the things that are excellent, being instructed out of the law, **19** and are confident that you yourself are a guide to the blind, a light to those who are in darkness, **20** an instructor of the foolish, a teacher of babes, having the form of knowledge and truth in the law. **21** You, therefore, who teach another, do you not teach yourself? You who preach that a man should not steal, do you steal? **22** You who say, "Do not commit adultery," do you commit adultery? You who abhor idols, do you rob temples? **23** You who make your boast in the law, do you dishonor God through breaking the law?

Using mere lip service.

Is 29:13 Therefore the Lord said: "Inasmuch as these people draw near with their mouths And honor Me with their lips, But have removed their hearts far from Me, And their fear toward Me is taught by the commandment of men,

Matt 15:8 *'These people draw near to Me with their mouth, And honor Me with their lips, But their heart is far from Me.*

Glorying in appearance only.

2 Cor 5:12 For we do not commend ourselves again to you, but give you opportunity to boast on our behalf, that you may have *an answer* for those who boast in appearance and not in heart.

Seeking glory from men.

Matt 6:2 Therefore, when you do a charitable deed, do not sound a trumpet before you as the hypocrites do in the synagogues and in the streets, that they may have glory from men. Assuredly, I say to you, they have their reward.

Trusting in privileges.

Jer 7:4 Do not trust in these lying words, saying, 'The temple of the LORD, the temple of the LORD, the temple of the LORD *are* these.'

Matt 3:9 and do not think to say to yourselves, 'We have Abraham as *our* father.' For I say to you that God is able to raise up children to Abraham from these stones.

Apparently zealous in the things of God.

Is 58:2 Yet they seek Me daily, And delight to know My ways, As a nation that did righteousness, And did not forsake the ordinance of their God. They ask of Me the ordinances of justice; They take delight in approaching God.

Zealous in making proselytes.

Matt 23:15 "Woe to you, scribes and Pharisees, hypocrites! For you travel land and sea to win one proselyte, and when he is won, you make him twice as much a son of hell as yourselves.

Devouring widows' houses.

Matt 23:14 Woe to you, scribes and Pharisees, hypocrites! For you devour widows' houses, and for a pretense make long prayers. Therefore you will receive greater condemnation.

Loving pre-eminence.

Matt 23:6–7 They love the best places at feasts, the best seats in the synagogues, **7** greetings in the marketplaces, and to be called by men, 'Rabbi, Rabbi.'

Characterized by double-mindedness.

James 1:8 *he is* a double-minded man, unstable in all his ways.

Worship of, not acceptable to God.

Is 1:11–15 "To what purpose *is* the multitude of your sacrifices to Me?" Says the LORD. "I have had enough of burnt offerings of rams And the fat of fed cattle. I do not delight in the blood of bulls, Or of lambs or goats. **12** "When you come to appear before Me, Who has required this from your hand, To trample My courts? **13** Bring no more futile sacrifices; Incense is an abomination to Me. The New Moons, the Sabbaths, and the calling of assemblies— I cannot endure iniquity and the sacred meeting. **14** Your New Moons and your appointed feasts My soul hates; They are a trouble to Me, I am weary of bearing *them.* **15** When you spread out your hands, I will hide My eyes from you; Even though you make many prayers, I will not hear. Your hands are full of blood.

Is 58:3–5 'Why have we fasted,' *they say,* 'and You have not seen? *Why* have we afflicted our souls, and You take no notice?' "In fact, in the day of your fast you find pleasure, And exploit all your laborers. **4** Indeed you fast for strife and debate, And to strike with the fist of wickedness. You will not fast as *you do* this day, To make your voice heard on high. **5** Is it a fast that I have chosen, A day for a man to afflict his soul? *Is it* to bow down his head like a bulrush, And to spread out sackcloth and ashes? Would you call this a fast, And an acceptable day to the LORD?

Matt 15:9 *And in vain they worship Me, Teaching as doctrines the commandments of men.'* "

Joy of, but for a moment.

Job 20:5 That the triumphing of the wicked is short, And the joy of the hypocrite is *but* for a moment?

Hope of, perishes.

Job 8:13 So *are* the paths of all who forget God; And the hope of the hypocrite shall perish,

Job 27:8–9 For what is the hope of the hypocrite, Though he may gain *much,* If God takes away his life? **9** Will God hear his cry When trouble comes upon him?

Heap up wrath.

Job 36:13 "But the hypocrites in heart store up wrath; They do not cry for help when He binds them.

Fearfulness shall surprise.

Is 33:14 The sinners in Zion are afraid; Fearfulness has seized the hypocrites: "Who among us shall dwell with the devouring fire? Who among us shall dwell with everlasting burnings?"

Destroy others by slander.

Prov 11:9 The hypocrite with *his* mouth destroys his neighbor, But through knowledge the righteous will be delivered.

In power, are a snare.

Job 34:30 That the hypocrite should not reign, Lest the people be ensnared.

The last days to abound with.

1 Tim 4:2 speaking lies in hypocrisy, having their own conscience seared with a hot iron,

Beware the principles of.

Luke 12:1 In the meantime, when an innumerable multitude of people had gathered together, so that they trampled one another, He began to say to His disciples first *of all,* "Beware of the leaven of the Pharisees, which is hypocrisy.

Spirit of, hinders growth in grace.

1 Pet 2:1 Therefore, laying aside all malice, all deceit, hypocrisy, envy, and all evil speaking,

Woe to.

Is 29:15 Woe to those who seek deep to hide their counsel far from the LORD, And their works are in the dark; They say, "Who sees us?" and, "Who knows us?"

Matt 23:13 "But woe to you, scribes and Pharisees, hypocrites! For you shut up the kingdom of heaven against men; for you neither go in *yourselves,* nor do you allow those who are entering to go in.

Punishment of.

Job 15:34 For the company of hypocrites *will be* barren, And fire will consume the tents of bribery.

Is 10:6 I will send him against an ungodly nation, And against the people of My wrath I will give him charge, To seize the spoil, to take the prey, And to tread them down like the mire of the streets.

Jer 42:20 For you were hypocrites in your hearts when you sent me to the LORD your God, saying, 'Pray for us to the LORD our God, and according to all that the LORD your God says, so declare to us and we will do *it.'*

Jer 42:22 Now therefore, know certainly that you shall die by the sword, by famine, and by pestilence in the place where you desire to go to dwell."

Matt 24:51 and will cut him in two and appoint *him* his portion with the hypocrites. There shall be weeping and gnashing of teeth.

Peter played the part of one.

Gal 2:11–13 Now when Peter had come to Antioch, I withstood him to his face, because he was to be blamed; **12** for before certain men came from James, he would eat with the Gentiles; but when they came, he withdrew and separated himself, fearing those who were of the circumcision. **13** And the rest of the Jews also played the hypocrite with him, so that even Barnabas was carried away with their hypocrisy.

Illustrated.

Matt 23:27–28 "Woe to you, scribes and Pharisees, hypocrites! For you are like whitewashed tombs which indeed appear beautiful outwardly, but inside are full of dead *men's* bones and all uncleanness. **28** Even so you also outwardly appear righteous to men, but inside you are full of hypocrisy and lawlessness.

Luke 11:44 Woe to you, scribes and Pharisees, hypocrites! For you are like graves which are not seen, and the men who walk over *them* are not aware *of them.*"

Examples of,

Cain.

Gen 4:3 And in the process of time it came to pass that Cain brought an offering of the fruit of the ground to the LORD.

Absalom.

2 Sam 15:7–8 Now it came to pass after forty years that Absalom said to the king, "Please, let me go to Hebron and pay the vow which I made to the LORD. 8 For your servant took a vow while I dwelt at Geshur in Syria, saying, 'If the LORD indeed brings me back to Jerusalem, then I will serve the LORD.'"

The Jews.

Jer 3:10 And yet for all this her treacherous sister Judah has not turned to Me with her whole heart, but in pretense," says the LORD.

The Pharisees, etc.

Matt 16:3 and in the morning, *'It will be* foul weather today, for the sky is red and threatening.' Hypocrites! You know how to discern the face of the sky, but you cannot *discern* the signs of the times.

Judas Iscariot.

Matt 26:49 Immediately he went up to Jesus and said, "Greetings, Rabbi!" and kissed Him.

The Herodians.

Mark 12:13 Then they sent to Him some of the Pharisees and the Herodians, to catch Him in *His* words.

Mark 12:15 Shall we pay, or shall we not pay?" But He, knowing their hypocrisy, said to them, "Why do you test Me? Bring Me a denarius that I may see *it.*"

Ananias and Sapphira.

Acts 5:1–11 But a certain man named Ananias, with Sapphira his wife, sold a possession. 2 And he kept back *part* of the proceeds, his wife also being aware *of it,* and brought a certain part and laid *it* at the apostles' feet. 3 But Peter said, "Ananias, why has Satan filled your heart to lie to the Holy Spirit and keep back *part* of the price of the land for yourself?

4 While it remained, was it not your own? And after it was sold, was it not in your own control? Why have you conceived this thing in your heart? You have not lied to men but to God." 5 Then Ananias, hearing these words, fell down and breathed his last. So great fear came upon all those who heard these things. 6 And the young men arose and wrapped him up, carried *him* out, and buried *him.* 7 Now it was about three hours later when his wife came in, not knowing what had happened. 8 And Peter answered her, "Tell me whether you sold the land for so much?" She said, "Yes, for so much." 9 Then Peter said to her, "How is it that you have agreed together to test the Spirit of the Lord? Look, the feet of those who have buried your husband *are* at the door, and they will carry you out." 10 Then immediately she fell down at his feet and breathed her last. And the young men came in and found her dead, and carrying *her* out, buried *her* by her husband. 11 So great fear came upon all the church and upon all who heard these things.

Simon the magician.

Acts 8:13–23 Then Simon himself also believed; and when he was baptized he continued with Philip, and was amazed, seeing the miracles and signs which were done. 14 Now when the apostles who were at Jerusalem heard that Samaria had received the word of God, they sent Peter and John to them, 15 who, when they had come down, prayed for them that they might receive the Holy Spirit. 16 For as yet He had fallen upon none of them. They had only been baptized in the name of the Lord Jesus. 17 Then they laid hands on them, and they received the Holy Spirit. 18 And when Simon saw that through the laying on of the apostles' hands the Holy Spirit was given, he offered them money, 19 saying, "Give me this power also, that anyone on whom I lay hands may receive the Holy Spirit." 20 But Peter said to him, "Your money perish with you, because you thought that the gift of God could be purchased with money! 21 You have neither part nor portion in this matter, for your heart is not right in the sight of God. 22 Repent therefore of this your wickedness, and pray God if perhaps the thought of your heart may be forgiven you. 23 For I see that you are poisoned by bitterness and bound by iniquity."

IDLENESS

Forbidden.

Rom 12:11 not lagging in diligence, fervent in spirit, serving the Lord;

Heb 6:12 that you do not become sluggish, but imitate those who through faith and patience inherit the promises.

Produces apathy.

Prov 12:27 The lazy *man* does not roast what he took in hunting, But diligence *is* man's precious possession.

Prov 26:15 The lazy *man* buries his hand in the bowl; It wearies him to bring it back to his mouth.

Akin to extravagance.

Prov 18:9 He who is slothful in his work Is a brother to him who is a great destroyer.

Accompanied by conceit.

Prov 26:16 The lazy *man is* wiser in his own eyes Than seven men who can answer sensibly.

Leads to

Poverty.

Prov 10:4 He who has a slack hand becomes poor, But the hand of the diligent makes rich.

Prov 20:13 Do not love sleep, lest you come to poverty; Open your eyes, *and* you will be satisfied with bread.

Want.

Prov 20:4 The lazy *man* will not plow because of winter; He will beg during harvest and *have* nothing.

Prov 24:34 So shall your poverty come *like* a prowler, And your need like an armed man.

Hunger.

Prov 19:15 Laziness casts *one* into a deep sleep, And an idle person will suffer hunger.

Prov 20:13 Do not love sleep, lest you come to poverty; Open your eyes, *and* you will be satisfied with bread.

Bondage.

Prov 12:24 The hand of the diligent will rule, But the lazy *man* will be put to forced labor.

Disappointment.

Prov 13:4 The soul of a lazy *man* desires, and *has* nothing; But the soul of the diligent shall be made rich.

Prov 21:25 The desire of the lazy *man* kills him, For his hands refuse to labor.

Ruin.

Prov 24:30–31 I went by the field of the lazy *man*, And by the vineyard of the man devoid of understanding; **31** And there it was, all overgrown with thorns; Its surface was covered with nettles; Its stone wall was broken down.

Eccl 10:18 Because of laziness the building decays, And through idleness of hands the house leaks.

Tattling and meddling.

1 Tim 5:13 And besides they learn *to be* idle, wandering about from house to house, and not only idle but also gossips and busybodies, saying things which they ought not.

Effects of, afford instruction to others.

Prov 24:30–32 I went by the field of the lazy *man*, And by the vineyard of the man devoid of understanding; **31** And there it was, all overgrown with thorns; Its surface was covered with nettles; Its stone wall was broken down. **32** When I saw *it*, I considered *it* well; I looked on *it and* received instruction:

Remonstrance against.

Prov 6:6 Go to the ant, you sluggard! Consider her ways and be wise,

Prov 6:9 How long will you slumber, O sluggard? When will you rise from your sleep?

False excuses for.

Prov 20:4 The lazy *man* will not plow because of winter; He will beg during harvest and *have* nothing.

Prov 22:13 The lazy *man* says, "*There is* a lion outside! I shall be slain in the streets!"

Illustrated.

Prov 26:14 *As* a door turns on its hinges, So *does* the lazy *man* on his bed.

Matt 25:18 But he who had received one went and dug in the ground, and hid his lord's money.

Matt 25:26 "But his lord answered and said to him, 'You wicked and lazy servant, you knew that I reap where I have not sown, and gather where I have not scattered seed.

Examples of,

Watchmen.

Is 56:10 His watchmen *are* blind, They are all ignorant; They *are* all dumb dogs, They cannot bark; Sleeping, lying down, loving to slumber.

The Athenians.

Acts 17:21 For all the Athenians and the foreigners who were there spent their time in nothing else but either to tell or to hear some new thing.

The Thessalonians.

2 Thess 3:11 For we hear that there are some who walk among you in a disorderly manner, not working at all, but are busybodies.

IDOLATRY

Forbidden.

Ex 20:2–3 "I *am* the LORD your God, who brought you

out of the land of Egypt, out of the house of bondage. 3 "You shall have no other gods before Me.

Deut 5:7 'You shall have no other gods before Me.

Elements of,

Bowing down to images.

Ex 20:5 you shall not bow down to them nor serve them. For I, the LORD your God, *am* a jealous God, visiting the iniquity of the fathers upon the children to the third and fourth *generations* of those who hate Me,

Deut 5:9 you shall not bow down to them nor serve them. For I, the LORD your God, *am* a jealous God, visiting the iniquity of the fathers upon the children to the third and fourth *generations* of those who hate Me,

Worshiping images.

Is 44:17 And the rest of it he makes into a god, His carved image. He falls down before it and worships *it*, Prays to it and says, "Deliver me, for you *are* my god!"

Dan 3:5 *that* at the time you hear the sound of the horn, flute, harp, lyre, *and* psaltery, in symphony with all kinds of music, you shall fall down and worship the gold image that King Nebuchadnezzar has set up;

Dan 3:10 You, O king, have made a decree that everyone who hears the sound of the horn, flute, harp, lyre, *and* psaltery, in symphony with all kinds of music, shall fall down and worship the gold image;

Dan 3:15 Now if you are ready at the time you hear the sound of the horn, flute, harp, lyre, *and* psaltery, in symphony with all kinds of music, and you fall down and worship the image which I have made, *good!* But if you do not worship, you shall be cast immediately into the midst of a burning fiery furnace. And who *is* the god who will deliver you from my hands?"

Sacrificing to images.

Ps 106:38 And shed innocent blood, The blood of their sons and daughters, Whom they sacrificed to the idols of Canaan; And the land was polluted with blood.

Acts 7:41 And they made a calf in those days, offered sacrifices to the idol, and rejoiced in the works of their own hands.

Worshiping other gods.

Ex 22:20 "He who sacrifices to *any* god, except to the LORD only, he shall be utterly destroyed.

Deut 8:19 Then it shall be, if you by any means forget the LORD your God, and follow other gods, and serve them and worship them, I testify against you this day that you shall surely perish.

Deut 30:17 But if your heart turns away so that you do not hear, and are drawn away, and worship other gods and serve them,

2 Kin 17:35 with whom the LORD had made a covenant and charged them, saying: "You shall not fear other gods, nor bow down to them nor serve them nor sacrifice to them;

Ps 81:9 There shall be no foreign god among you; Nor shall you worship any foreign god.

Swearing by other gods.

Ex 23:13 "And in all that I have said to you, be circumspect and make no mention of the name of other gods, nor let it be heard from your mouth.

Josh 23:7 *and* lest you go among these nations, these who remain among you. You shall not make mention of the name of their gods, nor cause *anyone* to swear *by them*; you shall not serve them nor bow down to them,

Speaking in the name of other gods.

Deut 18:20 But the prophet who presumes to speak a word in My name, which I have not commanded him to speak, or who speaks in the name of other gods, that prophet shall die.'

Looking to other gods.

Hos 3:1 Then the LORD said to me, "Go again, love a woman *who is* loved by a lover and is committing adultery, just like the love of the LORD for the children of Israel, who look to other gods and love *the* raisin cakes *of the pagans.*"

Serving other gods.

Deut 7:4 For they will turn your sons away from following Me, to serve other gods; so the anger of the LORD will be aroused against you and destroy you suddenly.

Jer 5:19 And it will be when you say, 'Why does the LORD our God do all these *things* to us?' then you shall answer them, 'Just as you have forsaken Me and served foreign gods in your land, so you shall serve aliens in a land *that is* not yours.'

Worshiping the true God by an image, etc.

Ex 32:4–6 And he received *the* gold from their hand, and he fashioned it with an engraving tool, and made a molded calf. Then they said, "This *is* your god, O Israel, that brought you out of the land of Egypt!" 5 So when Aaron saw *it*, he built an altar before it. And Aaron made a proclamation and said, "Tomorrow *is* a feast to the LORD." 6 Then they rose early on the next day, offered burnt offerings, and brought peace offerings; and the people sat down to eat and drink, and rose up to play.

Ps 106:19–20 They made a calf in Horeb, And worshiped the molded image. 20 Thus they changed their glory Into the image of an ox that eats grass.

Worshiping angels.

Col 2:18 Let no one cheat you of your reward, taking delight in *false* humility and worship of angels, intruding into those things which he has not seen, vainly puffed up by his fleshly mind,

Worshiping celestial objects.

Deut 4:19 And *take heed*, lest you lift your eyes to heaven, and *when* you see the sun, the moon, and the stars, all the host of heaven, you feel driven to worship them and serve them, which the LORD your God has given to all the peoples under the whole heaven as a heritage.

Deut 17:3 who has gone and served other gods and worshiped them, either the sun or moon or any of the host of heaven, which I have not commanded,

Worshiping demons.

Matt 4:9–10 And he said to Him, "All these things I will give You if You will fall down and worship me." 10 Then Jesus said to him, "Away with you, Satan! For it is written, 'You shall worship the LORD your God, and Him only you shall serve.'"

Rev 9:20 But the rest of mankind, who were not killed by these plagues, did not repent of the works of their hands, that they should not worship demons, and idols of gold, silver, brass, stone, and wood, which can neither see nor hear nor walk.

Worshiping dead men.

Ps 106:28 They joined themselves also to Baal of Peor, And ate sacrifices made to the dead.

Setting up idols in the heart.

Ezek 14:3–4 "Son of man, these men have set up their idols in their hearts, and put before them that which causes them to stumble into iniquity. Should I let Myself be inquired of at all by them? 4 "Therefore speak to them, and say to them, 'Thus says the Lord God: "Everyone of the house of Israel who sets up his idols in his heart, and puts before him what causes him to stumble into iniquity, and then comes to the prophet, I the Lord will answer him who comes, according to the multitude of his idols,

Covetousness.

Eph 5:5 For this you know, that no fornicator, unclean person, nor covetous man, who is an idolater, has any inheritance in the kingdom of Christ and God.

Col 3:5 Therefore put to death your members which are on the earth: fornication, uncleanness, passion, evil desire, and covetousness, which is idolatry.

Sensuality.

Phil 3:19 whose end is destruction, whose god is their belly, and whose glory is in their shame—who set their mind on earthly things.

Is changing the glory of God into an image.

Rom 1:23 and changed the glory of the incorruptible God into an image made like corruptible man—and birds and four-footed animals and creeping things.

Acts 17:29 Therefore, since we are the offspring of God, we ought not to think that the Divine Nature is like gold or silver or stone, something shaped by art and man's devising.

Is changing the truth of God into a lie.

Is 44:20 He feeds on ashes; A deceived heart has turned him aside; And he cannot deliver his soul, Nor say, "Is there not a lie in my right hand?"

Rom 1:25 who exchanged the truth of God for the lie, and worshiped and served the creature rather than the Creator, who is blessed forever. Amen.

Is a work of the flesh.

Gal 5:19–20 Now the works of the flesh are evident, which are: adultery, fornication, uncleanness, lewdness, 20 idolatry, sorcery, hatred, contentions, jealousies, outbursts of wrath, selfish ambitions, dissensions, heresies,

Incompatible with the service of God.

Gen 35:2–3 And Jacob said to his household and to all who were with him, "Put away the foreign gods that are among you, purify yourselves, and change your garments. 3 Then let us arise and go up to Bethel; and I will make an altar there to God, who answered me in the day of my distress and has been with me in the way which I have gone."

Josh 24:23 "Now therefore," he said, "put away the foreign gods which are among you, and incline your heart to the Lord God of Israel."

1 Sam 7:3 Then Samuel spoke to all the house of Israel, saying, "If you return to the Lord with all your

hearts, then put away the foreign gods and the Ashtoreths from among you, and prepare your hearts for the Lord, and serve Him only; and He will deliver you from the hand of the Philistines."

1 Kin 18:21 And Elijah came to all the people, and said, "How long will you falter between two opinions? If the Lord is God, follow Him; but if Baal, follow him." But the people answered him not a word.

2 Cor 6:15–16 And what accord has Christ with Belial? Or what part has a believer with an unbeliever? 16 And what agreement has the temple of God with idols? For you are the temple of the living God. As God has said: "I will dwell in them And walk among them. I will be their God, And they shall be My people."

Described as

Hateful abomination to God.

Deut 7:25 You shall burn the carved images of their gods with fire; you shall not covet the silver or gold that is on them, nor take it for yourselves, lest you be snared by it; for it is an abomination to the Lord your God.

Deut 16:22 You shall not set up a sacred pillar, which the Lord your God hates.

Jer 44:4 However I have sent to you all My servants the prophets, rising early and sending them, saying, "Oh, do not do this abominable thing that I hate!"

1 Pet 4:3 For we have spent enough of our past lifetime in doing the will of the Gentiles—when we walked in lewdness, lusts, drunkenness, revelries, drinking parties, and abominable idolatries.

Vain and foolish.

Ps 115:4–8 Their idols are silver and gold, The work of men's hands. 5 They have mouths, but they do not speak; Eyes they have, but they do not see; 6 They have ears, but they do not hear; Noses they have, but they do not smell; 7 They have hands, but they do not handle; Feet they have, but they do not walk; Nor do they mutter through their throat. 8 Those who make them are like them; So is everyone who trusts in them.

Is 44:19 And no one considers in his heart, Nor is there knowledge nor understanding to say, "I have burned half of it in the fire, Yes, I have also baked bread on its coals; I have roasted meat and eaten it; And shall I make the rest of it an abomination? Shall I fall down before a block of wood?"

Jer 10:3 For the customs of the peoples are futile; For one cuts a tree from the forest, The work of the hands of the workman, with the ax.

Bloody.

Ezek 23:39 For after they had slain their children for their idols, on the same day they came into My sanctuary to profane it; and indeed thus they have done in the midst of My house.

Unprofitable.

Judg 10:14 Go and cry out to the gods which you have chosen; let them deliver you in your time of distress."

Is 46:7 They bear it on the shoulder, they carry it And set it in its place, and it stands; From its place it shall not move. Though *one* cries out to it, yet it cannot answer Nor save him out of his trouble.

Irrational.

Acts 17:29 Therefore, since we are the offspring of God, we ought not to think that the Divine Nature is like gold or silver or stone, something shaped by art and man's devising.

Rom 1:21–23 because, although they knew God, they did not glorify *Him* as God, nor were thankful, but became futile in their thoughts, and their foolish hearts were darkened. **22** Professing to be wise, they became fools, **23** and changed the glory of the incorruptible God into an image made like corruptible man—and birds and four-footed animals and creeping things.

Defiling.

Ezek 20:7 Then I said to them, 'Each of you, throw away the abominations which are before his eyes, and do not defile yourselves with the idols of Egypt. I *am* the LORD your God.'

Ezek 36:18 Therefore I poured out My fury on them for the blood they had shed on the land, and for their idols *with which* they had defiled it.

They who practice,

Forget God.

Deut 8:19 Then it shall be, if you by any means forget the LORD your God, and follow other gods, and serve them and worship them, I testify against you this day that you shall surely perish.

Jer 18:15 "Because My people have forgotten Me, They have burned incense to worthless idols. And they have caused themselves to stumble in their ways, *From* the ancient paths, To walk in pathways and not on a highway,

Profane God's name and sanctuary.

Ezek 5:11 'Therefore, *as* I live,' says the Lord GOD, 'surely, because you have defiled My sanctuary with all your detestable things and with all your abominations, therefore I will also diminish *you;* My eye will not spare, nor will I have any pity.

Ezek 20:39 "As for you, O house of Israel," thus says the Lord GOD: "Go, serve every one of you his idols—and hereafter—if you will not obey Me; but profane My holy name no more with your gifts and your idols.

Forsake God.

2 Kin 22:17 because they have forsaken Me and burned incense to other gods, that they might provoke Me to anger with all the works of their hands. Therefore My wrath shall be aroused against this place and shall not be quenched.' " '

Jer 16:11 then you shall say to them, 'Because your fathers have forsaken Me,' says the LORD; 'they have walked after other gods and have served them and worshiped them, and have forsaken Me and not kept My law.

Ezek 14:5 that I may seize the house of Israel by their heart, because they are all estranged from Me by their idols." '

Ezek 44:10 "And the Levites who went far from Me, when Israel went astray, who strayed away from Me after their idols, they shall bear their iniquity.

Hate God.

2 Chr 19:2–3 And Jehu the son of Hanani the seer went out to meet him, and said to King Jehoshaphat, "Should you help the wicked and love those who hate the LORD? Therefore the wrath of the LORD *is* upon you. **3** Nevertheless good things are found in you, in that you have removed the wooden images from the land, and have prepared your heart to seek God."

Provoke God.

Deut 31:20 When I have brought them to the land flowing with milk and honey, of which I swore to their fathers, and they have eaten and filled themselves and grown fat, then they will turn to other gods and serve them; and they will provoke Me and break My covenant.

Is 65:3 A people who provoke Me to anger continually to My face; Who sacrifice in gardens, And burn incense on altars of brick;

Jer 25:6 Do not go after other gods to serve them and worship them, and do not provoke Me to anger with the works of your hands; and I will not harm you.'

Are ignorant and foolish.

Rom 1:21–22 because, although they knew God, they did not glorify *Him* as God, nor were thankful, but became futile in their thoughts, and their foolish hearts were darkened. **22** Professing to be wise, they became fools,

Inflame themselves.

Is 57:5 Inflaming yourselves with gods under every green tree, Slaying the children in the valleys, Under the clefts of the rocks?

Hold fast their deceit.

Jer 8:5 Why has this people slidden back, Jerusalem, in a perpetual backsliding? They hold fast to deceit, They refuse to return.

Are carried away by it.

1 Cor 12:2 You know that you were Gentiles, carried away to these dumb idols, however you were led.

Go after it in heart.

Ezek 20:16 because they despised My judgments and did not walk in My statutes, but profaned My Sabbaths; for their heart went after their idols.

Are insane about it.

Jer 50:38 A drought *is* against her waters, and they will be dried up. For it *is* the land of carved images, And they are insane with *their* idols.

Boast of it.

Ps 97:7 Let all be put to shame who serve carved images, Who boast of idols. Worship Him, all *you* gods.

Have fellowship with devils.

Hos 4:12 My people ask counsel from their wooden *idols*, And their staff informs them. For the spirit of harlotry has caused *them* to stray, And they have played the harlot against their God.

Look to idols for deliverance.

Is 44:17 And the rest of it he makes into a god, His carved image. He falls down before it and worships *it*, Prays to it and says, "Deliver me, for you *are* my god!"

Is 45:20 "Assemble yourselves and come; Draw near together, You *who have* escaped from the nations. They have no knowledge, Who carry the wood of their carved image, And pray to a god *that* cannot save.

Hos 4:12 My people ask counsel from their wooden *idols*, And their staff informs them. For the spirit of harlotry has caused *them* to stray, And they have played the harlot against their God.

Swear by their idols.

Amos 8:14 Those who swear by the sin of Samaria, Who say, 'As your god lives, O Dan!' And, 'As the way of Beersheba lives!' They shall fall and never rise again."

Objects of,

Numerous.

1 Cor 8:5 For even if there are so-called gods, whether in heaven or on earth (as there are many gods and many lords),

The heavenly bodies.

2 Kin 23:5 Then he removed the idolatrous priests whom the kings of Judah had ordained to burn incense on the high places in the cities of Judah and in the places all around Jerusalem, and those who burned incense to Baal, to the sun, to the moon, to the constellations, and to all the host of heaven.

Acts 7:42 Then God turned and gave them up to worship the host of heaven, as it is written in the book of the Prophets: *'Did you offer Me slaughtered animals and sacrifices during forty years in the wilderness, O house of Israel?*

Angels.

Col 2:18 Let no one cheat you of your reward, taking delight in *false* humility and worship of angels, intruding into those things which he has not seen, vainly puffed up by his fleshly mind,

Departed spirits.

1 Sam 28:14–15 So he said to her, "What *is* his form?" And she said, "An old man is coming up, and he *is* covered with a mantle." And Saul perceived that it *was* Samuel, and he stooped with *his* face to the ground and bowed down. **15** Now Samuel said to Saul, "Why have you disturbed me by bringing me up?" And Saul answered, "I am deeply distressed; for the Philistines make war against me, and God has departed from me and does not answer me anymore, neither by prophets nor by dreams. Therefore I have called you, that you may reveal to me what I should do."

Earthly creatures.

Rom 1:23 and changed the glory of the incorruptible God into an image made like corruptible man—and birds and four-footed animals and creeping things.

Images.

Deut 29:17 and you saw their abominations and their idols which *were* among them—wood and stone and silver and gold);

Ps 115:4 Their idols *are* silver and gold, The work of men's hands.

Is 44:17 And the rest of it he makes into a god, His carved image. He falls down before it and worships *it*, Prays to it and says, "Deliver me, for you *are* my god!"

Strange gods.

Gen 35:2 And Jacob said to his household and to all who *were* with him, "Put away the foreign gods that *are* among you, purify yourselves, and change your garments.

Gen 35:4 So they gave Jacob all the foreign gods which *were* in their hands, and the earrings which *were* in their ears; and Jacob hid them under the terebinth tree which *was* by Shechem.

Josh 24:20 If you forsake the LORD and serve foreign gods, then He will turn and do you harm and consume you, after He has done you good."

Other gods.

Judg 2:12 and they forsook the LORD God of their fathers, who had brought them out of the land of Egypt; and they followed other gods from *among* the gods of the people who *were* all around them, and they bowed down to them; and they provoked the LORD to anger.

Judg 2:17 Yet they would not listen to their judges, but they played the harlot with other gods, and bowed down to them. They turned quickly from the way in which their fathers walked, in obeying the commandments of the LORD; they did not do so.

1 Kin 14:9 but you have done more evil than all who were before you, for you have gone and made for yourself other gods and molded images to provoke Me to anger, and have cast Me behind your back—

New gods.

Deut 32:17 They sacrificed to demons, not to God, *To* gods they did not know, To new *gods*, new arrivals That your fathers did not fear.

Judg 5:8 They chose new gods; Then *there was* war in the gates; Not a shield or spear was seen among forty thousand in Israel.

Gods that cannot save.

Is 45:20 "Assemble yourselves and come; Draw near together, You *who have* escaped from the nations. They have no knowledge, Who carry the wood of their carved image, And pray to a god *that* cannot save.

Gods that have not made the heavens.

Jer 10:11 Thus you shall say to them: "The gods that have not made the heavens and the earth shall perish from the earth and from under these heavens."

No gods.

Jer 5:7 "How shall I pardon you for this? Your children have forsaken Me And sworn by *those* that are *not* gods. When I had fed them to the full, Then they committed adultery And assembled themselves by troops in the harlots' houses.

Gal 4:8 But then, indeed, when you did not know God, you served those which by nature are not gods.

Molten gods and images.

Ex 34:17 "You shall make no molded gods for yourselves.

Lev 19:4 'Do not turn to idols, nor make for yourselves molded gods: I *am* the LORD your God.

Deut 27:15 'Cursed *is* the one who makes a carved or molded image, an abomination to the LORD, the work of the hands of the craftsman, and sets *it* up in secret.' "And all the people shall answer and say, 'Amen!'

Hab 2:18 "What profit is the image, that its maker should carve it, The molded image, a teacher of lies, That the maker of its mold should trust in it, To make mute idols?

Carved images.

Is 45:20 "Assemble yourselves and come; Draw near together, You *who have* escaped from the nations. They have no knowledge, Who carry the wood of their carved image, And pray to a god *that* cannot save.

Hos 11:2 *As* they called them, So they went from them; They sacrificed to the Baals, And burned incense to carved images.

Senseless idols.

Deut 4:28 And there you will serve gods, the work of men's hands, wood and stone, which neither see nor hear nor eat nor smell.

Ps 115:5 They have mouths, but they do not speak; Eyes they have, but they do not see;

Ps 115:7 They have hands, but they do not handle; Feet they have, but they do not walk; Nor do they mutter through their throat.

Hab 2:18 "What profit is the image, that its maker should carve it, The molded image, a teacher of lies, That the maker of its mold should trust in it, To make mute idols?

Wood and stone.

Jer 3:9 So it came to pass, through her casual harlotry, that she defiled the land and committed adultery with stones and trees.

Hos 4:12 My people ask counsel from their wooden *idols*, And their staff informs them. For the spirit of harlotry has caused *them* to stray, And they have played the harlot against their God.

Hab 2:19 Woe to him who says to wood, 'Awake!' To silent stone, 'Arise! It shall teach!' Behold, it is overlaid with gold and silver, Yet in it there is no breath at all.

Abominations.

Is 44:19 And no one considers in his heart, Nor *is there* knowledge nor understanding to say, "I have burned half of it in the fire, Yes, I have also baked bread on its coals; I have roasted meat and eaten *it*; And shall I make the rest of it an abomination? Shall I fall down before a block of wood?"

Jer 32:34 But they set their abominations in the house which is called by My name, to defile it.

Ezek 7:20 'As for the beauty of his ornaments, He set it in majesty; But they made from it The images of their abominations— Their detestable things; Therefore I have made it Like refuse to them.

Ezek 16:36 Thus says the Lord GOD: "Because your filthiness was poured out and your nakedness uncovered in your harlotry with your lovers, and with all your abominable idols, and because of the blood of your children which you gave to them,

Stumbling blocks.

Ezek 14:3 "Son of man, these men have set up their idols in their hearts, and put before them that which causes them to stumble into iniquity. Should I let Myself be inquired of at all by them?

Teachers of lies.

Hab 2:18 "What profit is the image, that its maker should carve it, The molded image, a teacher of lies, That the maker of its mold should trust in it, To make mute idols?

Wind and confusion.

Is 41:29 Indeed they *are* all worthless; Their works *are* nothing; Their molded images *are* wind and confusion.

Nothing.

Is 41:24 Indeed you *are* nothing, And your work *is* nothing; *He who* chooses you *is* an abomination.

1 Cor 8:4 Therefore concerning the eating of things offered to idols, we know that an idol *is* nothing in the world, and that *there is* no other God but one.

Worthless and helpless.

Jer 10:5 They *are* upright, like a palm tree, And they cannot speak; They must be carried, Because they cannot go *by themselves*. Do not be afraid of them, For they cannot do evil, Nor can they do any good."

Jer 14:22 Are there any among the idols of the nations that can cause rain? Or can the heavens give showers? *Are* You not He, O LORD our God? Therefore we will wait for You, Since You have made all these.

Jer 18:15 "Because My people have forgotten Me, They have burned incense to worthless idols. And they have caused themselves to stumble in their ways, *From* the ancient paths, To walk in pathways and not on a highway,

Making idols for the purpose of, described and ridiculed.

Is 44:10–20 Who would form a god or mold an image *That* profits him nothing? **11** Surely all his companions would be ashamed; And the workmen, they *are* mere men. Let them all be gathered together, Let them stand up; Yet they shall fear, They shall be ashamed together. **12** The blacksmith with the tongs works one in the coals, Fashions it with hammers, And works it with the strength of his arms. Even so, he is hungry, and his strength fails; He drinks no water and is faint. **13** The craftsman stretches out *his* rule, He marks one out with chalk; He fashions it with a plane, He marks it out with the compass, And makes it like the figure of a man, According to the beauty of a man, that it may remain in the house. **14** He cuts down cedars for himself, And takes the cypress and the oak; He secures *it* for himself among the trees of the forest. He plants a pine, and the rain nourishes *it*. **15** Then it shall be for a man to burn, For he will take some of it and warm himself; Yes, he kindles *it* and bakes bread; Indeed he makes a god and worships *it*; He makes it a carved image, and falls down to it. **16** He burns half of it in the fire; With this half he eats meat; He roasts a roast, and is satisfied. He even warms *himself* and says, "Ah! I am warm, I have seen the fire." **17** And the rest of it he makes into a god, His carved image. He falls down before it and worships *it*, Prays to it and says, "Deliver me, for you *are* my god!" **18** They do not know nor understand; For He has shut their eyes, so that they cannot see, *And* their hearts, so that they cannot understand. **19** And no one considers in his heart, Nor *is there* knowledge nor understanding to say, "I have burned half of it in the fire, Yes, I have also baked bread on its coals; I have roasted meat and eaten *it;* And shall I make the rest of it an abomination? Shall I fall down before a block of wood?" **20** He feeds on ashes; A deceived heart has turned him aside; And he cannot deliver his soul, Nor say, "*Is there* not a lie in my right hand?"

Obstinate sinners judicially given up to.

Deut 4:28 And there you will serve gods, the work of men's hands, wood and stone, which neither see nor hear nor eat nor smell.

Deut 28:64 "Then the Lord will scatter you among all peoples, from one end of the earth to the other, and there you shall serve other gods, which neither you nor your fathers have known—wood and stone.

Hos 4:17 "Ephraim *is* joined to idols, Let him alone.

Warnings against.

Deut 4:15–19 "Take careful heed to yourselves, for you saw no form when the Lord spoke to you at Horeb out of the midst of the fire, **16** lest you act corruptly and make for yourselves a carved image in the form of any figure: the likeness of male or female, **17** the likeness of any animal that *is* on the earth or the likeness of any winged bird that flies in the air, **18** the likeness of anything that creeps on the ground or the likeness of any fish that *is* in the water beneath the earth. **19** And *take heed,* lest you lift your eyes to heaven, and *when* you see the sun, the moon, and the stars, all the host of heaven, you feel driven to worship them and serve them, which the Lord your God has given to all the peoples under the whole heaven as a heritage.

Exhortations to turn from.

Ezek 14:6 "Therefore say to the house of Israel, 'Thus says the Lord God: "Repent, turn away from your idols, and turn your faces away from all your abominations.

Ezek 20:7 Then I said to them, 'Each of you, throw away the abominations which are before his eyes, and do not defile yourselves with the idols of Egypt. I *am* the Lord your God.'

Acts 14:15 and saying, "Men, why are you doing these things? We also are men with the same nature as you, and preach to you that you should turn from these useless things to the living God, who made the heaven, the earth, the sea, and all things that are in them,

Renounced on conversion.

1 Thess 1:9 For they themselves declare concerning us what manner of entry we had to you, and how you turned to God from idols to serve the living and true God,

Led to abominable sins.

Rom 1:26–32 For this reason God gave them up to vile passions. For even their women exchanged the natural use for what is against nature. **27** Likewise also the men, leaving the natural use of the woman, burned in their lust for one another, men with men committing what is shameful, and receiving in themselves the penalty of their error which was due. **28** And even as they did not like to retain God in *their* knowledge, God gave them over to a debased mind, to do those things which are not fitting; **29** being filled with all unrighteousness, sexual immorality, wickedness, covetousness, maliciousness; full of

envy, murder, strife, deceit, evil-mindedness; *they are* whisperers, **30** backbiters, haters of God, violent, proud, boasters, inventors of evil things, disobedient to parents, **31** undiscerning, untrustworthy, unloving, unforgiving, unmerciful; **32** who, knowing the righteous judgment of God, that those who practice such things are deserving of death, not only do the same but also approve of those who practice them.

Acts 15:20 but that we write to them to abstain from things polluted by idols, *from* sexual immorality, *from* things strangled, and *from* blood.

Believers should

Keep from.

Josh 23:7 *and* lest you go among these nations, these who remain among you. You shall not make mention of the name of their gods, nor cause *anyone* to swear *by them;* you shall not serve them nor bow down to them,

1 Cor 10:14 Therefore, my beloved, flee from idolatry.

1 John 5:21 Little children, keep yourselves from idols. Amen.

Not have anything connected with.

Deut 7:26 Nor shall you bring an abomination into your house, lest you be doomed to destruction like it. You shall utterly detest it and utterly abhor it, for it *is* an accursed thing.

1 Cor 10:19–20 What am I saying then? That an idol is anything, or what is offered to idols is anything? **20** Rather, that the things which the Gentiles sacrifice they sacrifice to demons and not to God, and I do not want you to have fellowship with demons.

Not have close relationship with those who practice.

Ex 34:12 Take heed to yourself, lest you make a covenant with the inhabitants of the land where you are going, lest it be a snare in your midst.

Ex 34:15 lest you make a covenant with the inhabitants of the land, and they play the harlot with their gods and make sacrifice to their gods, and *one of them* invites you and you eat of his sacrifice,

Deut 7:2 and when the Lord your God delivers them over to you, you shall conquer them *and* utterly destroy them. You shall make no covenant with them nor show mercy to them.

Josh 23:7 *and* lest you go among these nations, these who remain among you. You shall not make mention of the name of their gods, nor cause *anyone* to swear *by them;* you shall not serve them nor bow down to them,

1 Cor 5:11 But now I have written to you not to keep company with anyone named a brother, who is sexually immoral, or covetous, or an idolater, or a reviler, or a drunkard, or an extortioner—not even to eat with such a person.

Not intermarry with those who practice.

Ex 34:16 and you take of his daughters for your sons, and his daughters play the harlot with their gods and make your sons play the harlot with their gods.

Deut 7:3 Nor shall you make marriages with them. You shall not give your daughter to their son, nor take their daughter for your son.

Testify against.

Acts 14:15 and saying, "Men, why are you doing these things? We also are men with the same nature as you, and preach to you that you should turn from these useless things to the living God, who made the heaven, the earth, the sea, and all things that are in them,

Acts 19:26 Moreover you see and hear that not only at Ephesus, but throughout almost all Asia, this Paul has persuaded and turned away many people, saying that they are not gods which are made with hands.

Refuse to engage in, though threatened with death.

Dan 3:18 But if not, let it be known to you, O king, that we do not serve your gods, nor will we worship the gold image which you have set up."

Realize God has preserved them from.

1 Kin 19:18 Yet I have reserved seven thousand in Israel, all whose knees have not bowed to Baal, and every mouth that has not kissed him."

Rom 11:4 But what does the divine response say to him? *"I have reserved for Myself seven thousand men who have not bowed the knee to Baal."*

Refuse to receive such worship.

Acts 10:25–26 As Peter was coming in, Cornelius met him and fell down at his feet and worshiped *him*. **26** But Peter lifted him up, saying, "Stand up; I myself am also a man."

Acts 14:11–15 Now when the people saw what Paul had done, they raised their voices, saying in the Lycaonian *language*, "The gods have come down to us in the likeness of men!" **12** And Barnabas they called Zeus, and Paul, Hermes, because he was the chief speaker. **13** Then the priest of Zeus, whose temple was in front of their city, brought oxen and garlands to the gates, intending to sacrifice with the multitudes. **14** But when the apostles Barnabas and Paul heard this, they tore their clothes and ran in among the multitude, crying out **15** and saying, "Men, why are you doing these things? We also are men with the same nature as you, and preach to you that you should turn from these useless things to the living God, who made the heaven, the earth, the sea, and all things that are in them,

Angels refuse to receive the worship of.

Rev 22:8–9 Now I, John, saw and heard these things. And when I heard and saw, I fell down to worship before the feet of the angel who showed me these things. **9** Then he said to me, "See *that you do* not *do that*. For I am your fellow servant, and of your brethren the prophets, and of those who keep the words of this book. Worship God."

Destruction of, promised.

Ezek 36:25 Then I will sprinkle clean water on you, and you shall be clean; I will cleanse you from all your filthiness and from all your idols.

Zech 13:2 "It shall be in that day," says the LORD of hosts, "*that* I will cut off the names of the idols from the land, and they shall no longer be remembered. I will also cause the prophets and the unclean spirit to depart from the land.

Everything connected with, should be destroyed.

Ex 34:13 But you shall destroy their altars, break their *sacred* pillars, and cut down their wooden images

Deut 7:5 But thus you shall deal with them: you shall destroy their altars, and break down their *sacred* pillars, and cut down their wooden images, and burn their carved images with fire.

2 Sam 5:21 And they left their images there, and David and his men carried them away.

2 Kin 23:14 And he broke in pieces the *sacred* pillars and cut down the wooden images, and filled their places with the bones of men.

God condemns.

Deut 27:15 'Cursed *is* the one who makes a carved or molded image, an abomination to the LORD, the work of the hands of the craftsman, and sets *it* up in secret.' "And all the people shall answer and say, 'Amen!'

Hab 2:19 Woe to him who says to wood, 'Awake!' To silent stone, 'Arise! It shall teach!' Behold, it is overlaid with gold and silver, Yet in it there is no breath at all.

Punishment of

Judicial death.

Deut 17:2–5 "If there is found among you, within any of your gates which the LORD your God gives you, a man or a woman who has been wicked in the sight of the LORD your God, in transgressing His covenant, **3** who has gone and served other gods and worshiped them, either the sun or moon or any of the host of heaven, which I have not commanded, **4** and it is told you, and you hear *of it*, then you shall inquire diligently. And if *it is* indeed true *and* certain that such an abomination has been committed in Israel, **5** then you shall bring out to your gates that man or woman who has committed that wicked thing, and shall stone to death that man or woman with stones.

Fatal judgments.

Jer 8:2 They shall spread them before the sun and the moon and all the host of heaven, which they have loved and which they have served and after which they have walked, which they have sought and which they have worshiped. They shall not be gathered nor buried; they shall be like refuse on the face of the earth.

Cf. Jer 16:1–11

Banishment.

Jer 8:3 Then death shall be chosen rather than life by all the residue of those who remain of this evil family, who remain in all the places where I have driven them," says the LORD of hosts.

Hos 8:5–8 Your calf is rejected, O Samaria! My anger is aroused against them— How long until they attain to innocence? **6** For from Israel *is* even this: A workman made it, and it *is* not God; But the calf of Samaria shall be broken to pieces. **7** "They sow the wind, And reap the whirlwind. The stalk has no bud; It shall never produce meal. If it should produce, Aliens would swallow it up. **8** Israel is swallowed up; Now they are among the Gentiles Like a vessel in which *is* no pleasure.

Amos 5:26–27 You also carried Sikkuth your king And Chiun, your idols, The star of your gods, Which you made for yourselves. **27** Therefore I will send you into captivity beyond Damascus," Says the LORD, whose name *is* the God of hosts.

Exclusion from heaven.

1 Cor 6:9–10 Do you not know that the unrighteous will not inherit the kingdom of God? Do not be deceived. Neither fornicators, nor idolaters, nor adulterers, nor homosexuals, nor sodomites, **10** nor thieves, nor covetous, nor drunkards, nor revilers, nor extortioners will inherit the kingdom of God.

Eph 5:5 For this you know, that no fornicator, unclean person, nor covetous man, who is an idolater, has any inheritance in the kingdom of Christ and God.

Rev 22:15 But outside *are* dogs and sorcerers and sexually immoral and murderers and idolaters, and whoever loves and practices a lie.

Eternal torments.

Rev 14:9–11 Then a third angel followed them, saying with a loud voice, "If anyone worships the beast and his image, and receives *his* mark on his forehead or on his hand, **10** he himself shall also drink of the wine of the wrath of God, which is poured out full strength into the cup of His indignation. He shall be tormented with fire and brimstone in the presence of the holy angels and in the presence of the Lamb. **11** And the smoke of their torment ascends forever and ever; and they have no rest day or night, who worship the beast and his image, and whoever receives the mark of his name."

Rev 21:8 But the cowardly, unbelieving, abominable, murderers, sexually immoral, sorcerers, idolaters, and all liars shall have their part in the lake which burns with fire and brimstone, which is the second death."

Examples of those who practiced,

Israel.

Ex 32:1 Now when the people saw that Moses delayed coming down from the mountain, the people gathered together to Aaron, and said to him, "Come, make us gods that shall go before us; for *as for* this Moses, the man who brought us up out of the land of Egypt, we do not know what has become of him."

2 Kin 17:12 for they served idols, of which the LORD had said to them, "You shall not do this thing."

The Philistines.

Judg 16:23 Now the lords of the Philistines gathered together to offer a great sacrifice to Dagon their god, and to rejoice. And they said: "Our god has delivered into our hands Samson our enemy!"

Micah.

Judg 17:4–5 Thus he returned the silver to his mother. Then his mother took two hundred *shekels* of silver and gave them to the silversmith, and he made it into a carved image and a molded image; and they were in the house of Micah. **5** The man Micah had a shrine, and made an ephod and household idols; and he consecrated one of his sons, who became his priest.

Jeroboam.

1 Kin 12:28 Therefore the king asked advice, made two calves of gold, and said to the people, "It is too much

for you to go up to Jerusalem. Here are your gods, O Israel, which brought you up from the land of Egypt!"

Maachah.

1 Kin 15:13 Also he removed Maachah his grandmother from *being* queen mother, because she had made an obscene image of Asherah. And Asa cut down her obscene image and burned *it* by the Brook Kidron.

Ahab.

1 Kin 16:31 And it came to pass, as though it had been a trivial thing for him to walk in the sins of Jeroboam the son of Nebat, that he took as wife Jezebel the daughter of Ethbaal, king of the Sidonians; and he went and served Baal and worshiped him.

Jezebel.

1 Kin 18:19 Now therefore, send *and* gather all Israel to me on Mount Carmel, the four hundred and fifty prophets of Baal, and the four hundred prophets of Asherah, who eat at Jezebel's table."

Sennacherib.

2 Kin 19:37 Now it came to pass, as he was worshiping in the temple of Nisroch his god, that his sons Adrammelech and Sharezer struck him down with the sword; and they escaped into the land of Ararat. Then Esarhaddon his son reigned in his place.

Manasseh.

2 Kin 21:4–7 He also built altars in the house of the LORD, of which the LORD had said, "In Jerusalem I will put My name." **5** And he built altars for all the host of heaven in the two courts of the house of the LORD. **6** Also he made his son pass through the fire, practiced soothsaying, used witchcraft, and consulted spiritists and mediums. He did much evil in the sight of the LORD, to provoke *Him* to anger. **7** He even set a carved image of Asherah that he had made, in the house of which the LORD had said to David and to Solomon his son, "In this house and in Jerusalem, which I have chosen out of all the tribes of Israel, I will put My name forever;

Amon.

2 Kin 21:21 So he walked in all the ways that his father had walked; and he served the idols that his father had served, and worshiped them.

Ahaz.

2 Chr 28:3 He burned incense in the Valley of the Son of Hinnom, and burned his children in the fire, according to the abominations of the nations whom the LORD had cast out before the children of Israel.

Judah.

Jer 11:13 For *according to* the number of your cities were your gods, O Judah; and *according to* the number of the streets of Jerusalem you have set up altars to *that* shameful thing, altars to burn incense to Baal.

Nebuchadnezzar.

Dan 3:1 Nebuchadnezzar the king made an image of gold, whose height *was* sixty cubits *and* its width six cubits. He set it up in the plain of Dura, in the province of Babylon.

Belshazzar.

Dan 5:23 And you have lifted yourself up against the Lord of heaven. They have brought the vessels of His house before you, and you and your lords, your wives and your concubines, have drunk wine from them. And you have praised the gods of silver and gold, bronze and iron, wood and stone, which do not see or hear or know; and the God who *holds* your breath in His hand and owns all your ways, you have not glorified.

The people of Lystra.

Acts 14:11–12 Now when the people saw what Paul had done, they raised their voices, saying in the Lycaonian *language,* "The gods have come down to us in the likeness of men!" **12** And Barnabas they called Zeus, and Paul, Hermes, because he was the chief speaker.

The Athenians.

Acts 17:16 Now while Paul waited for them at Athens, his spirit was provoked within him when he saw that the city was given over to idols.

The Ephesians.

Acts 19:28 Now when they heard *this,* they were full of wrath and cried out, saying, "Great *is* Diana of the Ephesians!"

Zeal against—exemplified by,

Asa.

1 Kin 15:12 And he banished the perverted persons from the land, and removed all the idols that his fathers had made.

Josiah.

2 Kin 23:5 Then he removed the idolatrous priests whom the kings of Judah had ordained to burn incense on the high places in the cities of Judah and in the places all around Jerusalem, and those who burned incense to Baal, to the sun, to the moon, to the constellations, and to all the host of heaven.

Jehoshaphat.

2 Chr 17:6 And his heart took delight in the ways of the LORD; moreover he removed the high places and wooden images from Judah.

Israel.

2 Chr 31:1 Now when all this was finished, all Israel who were present went out to the cities of Judah and broke the sacred pillars in pieces, cut down the wooden images, and threw down the high places and the altars—from all Judah, Benjamin, Ephraim, and Manasseh—until they had utterly destroyed them all. Then all the children of Israel returned to their own cities, every man to his possession.

Manasseh.

2 Chr 33:15 He took away the foreign gods and the idol from the house of the LORD, and all the altars that he had built in the mount of the house of the LORD and in Jerusalem; and he cast *them* out of the city.

All forms of, forbidden by the law of Moses.

Ex 20:4–5 "You shall not make for yourself a carved image—any likeness *of anything* that *is* in heaven above, or that *is* in the earth beneath, or that *is* in the water under the earth; **5** you shall not bow down to them nor serve them. For I, the LORD your God, *am* a jealous God, visiting the iniquity of the fathers upon the children to the third and fourth *generations* of those who hate Me,

All unbelieving nations given up to.

1 Kin 20:23 Then the servants of the king of Syria said to

him, "Their gods *are* gods of the hills. Therefore they were stronger than we; but if we fight against them in the plain, surely we will be stronger than they.

2 Kin 17:26 So they spoke to the king of Assyria, saying, "The nations whom you have removed and placed in the cities of Samaria do not know the rituals of the God of the land; therefore He has sent lions among them, and indeed, they are killing them because they do not know the rituals of the God of the land."

Ps 96:5 For all the gods of the peoples *are* idols, But the LORD made the heavens.

Acts 14:11 Now when the people saw what Paul had done, they raised their voices, saying in the Lycaonian *language,* "The gods have come down to us in the likeness of men!"

Rom 1:23 and changed the glory of the incorruptible God into an image made like corruptible man—and birds and four-footed animals and creeping things.

Rom 1:25 who exchanged the truth of God for the lie, and worshiped and served the creature rather than the Creator, who is blessed forever. Amen.

1 Cor 12:2 You know that you were Gentiles, carried away to these dumb idols, however you were led.

Temples built for.

Hos 8:14 "For Israel has forgotten his Maker, And has built temples; Judah also has multiplied fortified cities; But I will send fire upon his cities, And it shall devour his palaces."

Altars raised for.

1 Kin 18:26 So they took the bull which was given them, and they prepared *it,* and called on the name of Baal from morning even till noon, saying, "O Baal, hear us!" But *there was* no voice; no one answered. Then they leaped about the altar which they had made.

Hos 8:11 "Because Ephraim has made many altars for sin, They have become for him altars for sinning.

Accompanied by feasts.

2 Kin 10:20 And Jehu said, "Proclaim a solemn assembly for Baal." So they proclaimed *it.*

1 Cor 10:27–28 If any of those who do not believe invites you *to dinner,* and you desire to go, eat whatever is set before you, asking no question for conscience' sake. **28** But if anyone says to you, "This was offered to idols," do not eat it for the sake of the one who told you, and for conscience' sake; for *"the earth is the LORD's, and all its fullness."*

Objects of, worshiped

With sacrifices.

Num 22:40 Then Balak offered oxen and sheep, and he sent *some* to Balaam and to the princes who *were* with him.

2 Kin 10:24 So they went in to offer sacrifices and burnt offerings. Now Jehu had appointed for himself eighty men on the outside, and had said, "*If* any of the men whom I have brought into your hands escapes, *whoever lets him escape, it shall be* his life for the life of the other."

With drink offerings.

Is 57:6 Among the smooth *stones* of the stream *Is* your portion; They, they, *are* your lot! Even to them you have poured a drink offering, You have offered a grain offering. Should I receive comfort in these?

Jer 19:13 And the houses of Jerusalem and the houses of the kings of Judah shall be defiled like the place of Tophet, because of all the houses on whose roofs they have burned incense to all the host of heaven, and poured out drink offerings to other gods." ' "

With incense.

Jer 48:35 "Moreover," says the LORD, "I will cause to cease in Moab The one who offers *sacrifices* in the high places And burns incense to his gods.

With prayer.

1 Kin 18:26 So they took the bull which was given them, and they prepared *it,* and called on the name of Baal from morning even till noon, saying, "O Baal, hear us!" But *there was* no voice; no one answered. Then they leaped about the altar which they had made.

Is 44:17 And the rest of it he makes into a god, His carved image. He falls down before it and worships *it,* Prays to it and says, "Deliver me, for you *are* my god!"

With singing and dancing.

Ex 32:18–19 But he said: "*It is* not the noise of the shout of victory, Nor the noise of the cry of defeat, *But* the sound of singing I hear." **19** So it was, as soon as he came near the camp, that he saw the calf *and* the dancing. So Moses' anger became hot, and he cast the tablets out of his hands and broke them at the foot of the mountain.

1 Kin 18:26 So they took the bull which was given them, and they prepared *it,* and called on the name of Baal from morning even till noon, saying, "O Baal, hear us!" But *there was* no voice; no one answered. Then they leaped about the altar which they had made.

1 Cor 10:7 And do not become idolaters as *were* some of them. As it is written, *"The people sat down to eat and drink, and rose up to play."*

By bowing to them.

1 Kin 19:18 Yet I have reserved seven thousand in Israel, all whose knees have not bowed to Baal, and every mouth that has not kissed him."

2 Kin 5:18 Yet in this thing may the LORD pardon your servant: when my master goes into the temple of Rimmon to worship there, and he leans on my hand, and I bow down in the temple of Rimmon—when I bow down in the temple of Rimmon, may the LORD please pardon your servant in this thing."

By kissing them.

1 Kin 19:18 Yet I have reserved seven thousand in Israel, all whose knees have not bowed to Baal, and every mouth that has not kissed him."

Hos 13:2 Now they sin more and more, And have made for themselves molded images, Idols of their silver, according to their skill; All of it *is* the work of craftsmen. They say of them, "Let the men who sacrifice kiss the calves!"

By kissing the hand to them.

Job 31:26–27 If I have observed the sun when it shines, Or the moon moving *in* brightness, **27** So that my heart has been secretly enticed, And my mouth has kissed my hand;

By cutting the flesh.

1 Kin 18:28 So they cried aloud, and cut themselves, as was their custom, with knives and lances, until the blood gushed out on them.

By burning children.

Deut 12:31 You shall not worship the LORD your God in that way; for every abomination to the LORD which He hates they have done to their gods; for they burn even their sons and daughters in the fire to their gods.

2 Chr 33:6 Also he caused his sons to pass through the fire in the Valley of the Son of Hinnom; he practiced soothsaying, used witchcraft and sorcery, and consulted mediums and spiritists. He did much evil in the sight of the LORD, to provoke Him to anger.

Jer 19:4–5 "Because they have forsaken Me and made this an alien place, because they have burned incense in it to other gods whom neither they, their fathers, nor the kings of Judah have known, and have filled this place with the blood of the innocents **5** (they have also built the high places of Baal, to burn their sons with fire *for* burnt offerings to Baal, which I did not command or speak, nor did it come into My mind),

Ezek 16:21 that you have slain My children and offered them up to them by causing them to pass through *the fire?*

In temples.

2 Kin 5:18 Yet in this thing may the LORD pardon your servant: when my master goes into the temple of Rimmon to worship there, and he leans on my hand, and I bow down in the temple of Rimmon—when I bow down in the temple of Rimmon, may the LORD please pardon your servant in this thing."

On high places.

Num 22:41 So it was, the next day, that Balak took Balaam and brought him up to the high places of Baal, that from there he might observe the extent of the people.

Jer 2:20 "For of old I have broken your yoke *and* burst your bonds; And you said, 'I will not transgress,' When on every high hill and under every green tree You lay down, playing the harlot.

Under trees.

Is 57:5 Inflaming yourselves with gods under every green tree, Slaying the children in the valleys, Under the clefts of the rocks?

Jer 2:20 "For of old I have broken your yoke *and* burst your bonds; And you said, 'I will not transgress,' When on every high hill and under every green tree You lay down, playing the harlot.

In and on the tops of private houses.

Judg 17:4–5 Thus he returned the silver to his mother. Then his mother took two hundred *shekels* of silver and gave them to the silversmith, and he made it into a carved image and a molded image; and they were in the house of Micah. **5** The man Micah had a shrine, and made an ephod and household idols; and he consecrated one of his sons, who became his priest.

2 Kin 23:12 The altars that *were* on the roof, the upper chamber of Ahaz, which the kings of Judah had made, and the altars which Manasseh had made in the two courts of the house of the LORD, the king broke down and pulverized there, and threw their dust into the Brook Kidron.

Zeph 1:5 Those who worship the host of heaven on the housetops; Those who worship and swear *oaths* by the LORD, But who *also* swear by Milcom;

In secret places.

Is 57:8 Also behind the doors and their posts You have set up your remembrance; For you have uncovered yourself *to those other* than Me, And have gone up to them; You have enlarged your bed And made *a covenant* with them; You have loved their bed, Where you saw *their* nudity.

Rites of, obscene and impure.

Ex 32:25 Now when Moses saw that the people *were* unrestrained (for Aaron had not restrained them, to *their* shame among their enemies),

Num 25:1–3 Now Israel remained in Acacia Grove, and the people began to commit harlotry with the women of Moab. 2 They invited the people to the sacrifices of their gods, and the people ate and bowed down to their gods. 3 So Israel was joined to Baal of Peor, and the anger of the LORD was aroused against Israel.

2 Kin 17:9 Also the children of Israel secretly did against the LORD their God things that *were* not right, and they built for themselves high places in all their cities, from watchtower to fortified city.

Is 57:6 Among the smooth *stones* of the stream *Is* your portion; They, they, *are* your lot! Even to them you have poured a drink offering, You have offered a grain offering. Should I receive comfort in these?

Is 57:8–9 Also behind the doors and their posts You have set up your remembrance; For you have uncovered yourself *to those other* than Me, And have gone up to them; You have enlarged your bed And made *a covenant* with them; You have loved their bed, Where you saw *their* nudity. 9 You went to the king with ointment, And increased your perfumes; You sent your messengers far off, And *even* descended to Sheol.

1 Pet 4:3 For we *have spent* enough of our past lifetime in doing the will of the Gentiles—when we walked in lewdness, lusts, drunkenness, revelries, drinking parties, and abominable idolatries.

Divination connected with.

2 Chr 33:6 Also he caused his sons to pass through the fire in the Valley of the Son of Hinnom; he practiced soothsaying, used witchcraft and sorcery, and consulted mediums and spiritists. He did much evil in the sight of the LORD, to provoke Him to anger.

Victims sacrificed in, often adorned with garlands.

Acts 14:13 Then the priest of Zeus, whose temple was in front of their city, brought oxen and garlands to the gates, intending to sacrifice with the multitudes.

Idols, mentioned in Scripture

Adrammelech and Anammelech.

2 Kin 17:31 and the Avites made Nibhaz and Tartak; and the Sepharvites burned their children in fire to Adrammelech and Anammelech, the gods of Sepharvaim.

Ashima.

2 Kin 17:30 The men of Babylon made Succoth Benoth, the men of Cuth made Nergal, the men of Hamath made Ashima,

Ashtoreth.

Judg 2:13 They forsook the LORD and served Baal and the Ashtoreths.

1 Kin 11:33 because they have forsaken Me, and worshiped Ashtoreth the goddess of the Sidonians, Chemosh the god of the Moabites, and Milcom the god of the people of Ammon, and have not walked in My ways to do *what is* right in My eyes and *keep* My statutes and My judgments, as *did* his father David.

Baal.

Judg 2:11–13 Then the children of Israel did evil in the sight of the LORD, and served the Baals; 12 and they forsook the LORD God of their fathers, who had brought them out of the land of Egypt; and they followed other gods from *among* the gods of the people who *were* all around them, and they bowed down to them; and they provoked the LORD to anger. 13 They forsook the LORD and served Baal and the Ashtoreths.

Judg 6:25 Now it came to pass the same night that the LORD said to him, "Take your father's young bull, the second bull of seven years old, and tear down the altar of Baal that your father has, and cut down the wooden image that *is* beside it;

Baal-Berith.

Judg 8:33 So it was, as soon as Gideon was dead, that the children of Israel again played the harlot with the Baals, and made Baal-Berith their god.

Judg 9:4 So they gave him seventy *shekels* of silver from the temple of Baal-Berith, with which Abimelech hired worthless and reckless men; and they followed him.

Judg 9:46 Now when all the men of the tower of Shechem had heard *that*, they entered the stronghold of the temple of the god Berith.

Baal-Peor.

Num 25:1–3 Now Israel remained in Acacia Grove, and the people began to commit harlotry with the women of Moab. 2 They invited the people to the sacrifices of their gods, and the people ate and bowed down to their gods. 3 So Israel was joined to Baal of Peor, and the anger of the LORD was aroused against Israel.

Baal-Zebub.

2 Kin 1:2 Now Ahaziah fell through the lattice of his upper room in Samaria, and was injured; so he sent messengers and said to them, "Go, inquire of Baal-Zebub, the god of Ekron, whether I shall recover from this injury."

2 Kin 1:16 Then he said to him, "Thus says the LORD: 'Because you have sent messengers to inquire of Baal-Zebub, the god of Ekron, *is it* because *there is* no God in Israel to inquire of His word? Therefore you shall not come down from the bed to which you have gone up, but you shall surely die.' "

Baal Zephon.

Ex 14:2 "Speak to the children of Israel, that they turn and camp before Pi Hahiroth, between Migdol and the sea, opposite Baal Zephon; you shall camp before it by the sea.

Bel.

Jer 50:2 "Declare among the nations, Proclaim, and set

up a standard; Proclaim—do not conceal *it*— Say, 'Babylon is taken, Bel is shamed. Merodach is broken in pieces; Her idols are humiliated, Her images are broken in pieces.'

Jer 51:44 I will punish Bel in Babylon, And I will bring out of his mouth what he has swallowed; And the nations shall not stream to him anymore. Yes, the wall of Babylon shall fall.

Chemosh.

Num 21:29 Woe to you, Moab! You have perished, O people of Chemosh! He has given his sons as fugitives, And his daughters into captivity, To Sihon king of the Amorites.

1 Kin 11:33 because they have forsaken Me, and worshiped Ashtoreth the goddess of the Sidonians, Chemosh the god of the Moabites, and Milcom the god of the people of Ammon, and have not walked in My ways to do *what is* right in My eyes and *keep* My statutes and My judgments, as *did* his father David.

Chiun.

Amos 5:26 You also carried Sikkuth your king And Chiun, your idols, The star of your gods, Which you made for yourselves.

Dagon.

Judg 16:23 Now the lords of the Philistines gathered together to offer a great sacrifice to Dagon their god, and to rejoice. And they said: "Our god has delivered into our hands Samson our enemy!"

1 Sam 5:1–3 Then the Philistines took the ark of God and brought it from Ebenezer to Ashdod. **2** When the Philistines took the ark of God, they brought it into the house of Dagon and set it by Dagon. **3** And when the people of Ashdod arose early in the morning, there was Dagon, fallen on its face to the earth before the ark of the LORD. So they took Dagon and set it in its place again.

Diana.

Acts 19:24 For a certain man named Demetrius, a silversmith, who made silver shrines of Diana, brought no small profit to the craftsmen.

Acts 19:27 So not only is this trade of ours in danger of falling into disrepute, but also the temple of the great goddess Diana may be despised and her magnificence destroyed, whom all Asia and the world worship."

Molech or Milcom.

Lev 18:21 And you shall not let any of your descendants pass through *the fire* to Molech, nor shall you profane the name of your God: I *am* the LORD.

1 Kin 11:5 For Solomon went after Ashtoreth the goddess of the Sidonians, and after Milcom the abomination of the Ammonites.

1 Kin 11:33 because they have forsaken Me, and worshiped Ashtoreth the goddess of the Sidonians, Chemosh the god of the Moabites, and Milcom the god of the people of Ammon, and have not walked in My ways to do *what is* right in My eyes and *keep* My statutes and My judgments, as *did* his father David.

Merodach.

Jer 50:2 "Declare among the nations, Proclaim, and set up a standard; Proclaim—do not conceal *it*— Say, 'Babylon is taken, Bel is shamed. Merodach is broken in pieces; Her idols are humiliated, Her images are broken in pieces.'

Nergal.

2 Kin 17:30 The men of Babylon made Succoth Benoth, the men of Cuth made Nergal, the men of Hamath made Ashima,

Nebo.

Is 46:1 Bel bows down, Nebo stoops; Their idols were on the beasts and on the cattle. Your carriages *were* heavily loaded, A burden to the weary *beast*.

Nibhaz and Tartak.

2 Kin 17:31 and the Avites made Nibhaz and Tartak; and the Sepharvites burned their children in fire to Adrammelech and Anammelech, the gods of Sepharvaim.

Nisroch.

2 Kin 19:37 Now it came to pass, as he was worshiping in the temple of Nisroch his god, that his sons Adrammelech and Sharezer struck him down with the sword; and they escaped into the land of Ararat. Then Esarhaddon his son reigned in his place.

Queen of heaven.

Jer 44:17 But we will certainly do whatever has gone out of our own mouth, to burn incense to the queen of heaven and pour out drink offerings to her, as we have done, we and our fathers, our kings and our princes, in the cities of Judah and in the streets of Jerusalem. For *then* we had plenty of food, were well-off, and saw no trouble.

Jer 44:25 Thus says the LORD of hosts, the God of Israel, saying: 'You and your wives have spoken with your mouths and fulfilled with your hands, saying, "We will surely keep our vows that we have made, to burn incense to the queen of heaven and pour out drink offerings to her." You will surely keep your vows and perform your vows!'

Remphan.

Acts 7:43 *You also took up the tabernacle of Moloch, And the star of your god Remphan, Images which you made to worship; And I will carry you away beyond Babylon.'*

Rimmon.

2 Kin 5:18 Yet in this thing may the LORD pardon your servant: when my master goes into the temple of Rimmon to worship there, and he leans on my hand, and I bow down in the temple of Rimmon—when I bow down in the temple of Rimmon, may the LORD please pardon your servant in this thing."

Succoth Benoth.

2 Kin 17:30 The men of Babylon made Succoth Benoth, the men of Cuth made Nergal, the men of Hamath made Ashima,

Tammuz.

Ezek 8:14 So He brought me to the door of the north gate of the LORD's house; and to my dismay, women were sitting there weeping for Tammuz.

Zeus and Hermes.

Acts 14:12 And Barnabas they called Zeus, and Paul, Hermes, because he was the chief speaker.

Objects of, carried in procession.

Is 46:7 They bear it on the shoulder, they carry it And

set it in its place, and it stands; From its place it shall not move. Though *one* cries out to it, yet it cannot answer Nor save him out of his trouble.

Amos 5:26 You also carried Sikkuth your king And Chiun, your idols, The star of your gods, Which you made for yourselves.

Acts 7:43 *You also took up the tabernacle of Moloch, And the star of your god Remphan, Images which you made to worship; And I will carry you away beyond Babylon.'*

The Jews,

Early notice of.

Gen 31:19 Now Laban had gone to shear his sheep, and Rachel had stolen the household idols that were her father's.

Gen 31:30 And now you have surely gone because you greatly long for your father's house, *but* why did you steal my gods?"

Gen 35:1–4 Then God said to Jacob, "Arise, go up to Bethel and dwell there; and make an altar there to God, who appeared to you when you fled from the face of Esau your brother." 2 And Jacob said to his household and to all who *were* with him, "Put away the foreign gods that *are* among you, purify yourselves, and change your garments. 3 Then let us arise and go up to Bethel; and I will make an altar there to God, who answered me in the day of my distress and has been with me in the way which I have gone." 4 So they gave Jacob all the foreign gods which *were* in their hands, and the earrings which *were* in their ears; and Jacob hid them under the terebinth tree which *was* by Shechem.

Josh 24:2 And Joshua said to all the people, "Thus says the LORD God of Israel: 'Your fathers, *including* Terah, the father of Abraham and the father of Nahor, dwelt on the other side of the River in old times; and they served other gods.

Practiced, in Egypt.

Josh 24:14 "Now therefore, fear the LORD, serve Him in sincerity and in truth, and put away the gods which your fathers served on the other side of the River and in Egypt. Serve the LORD!

Ezek 23:3 They committed harlotry in Egypt, They committed harlotry in their youth; Their breasts were there embraced, Their virgin bosom was there pressed.

Ezek 23:19 "Yet she multiplied her harlotry In calling to remembrance the days of her youth, When she had played the harlot in the land of Egypt.

Brought, out of Egypt with them.

Ezek 23:8 She has never given up her harlotry *brought* from Egypt, For in her youth they had lain with her, Pressed her virgin bosom, And poured out their immorality upon her.

Acts 7:39–41 whom our fathers would not obey, but rejected. And in their hearts they turned back to Egypt, 40 saying to Aaron, 'Make us gods to go before us; as for this Moses who brought us out of the land of Egypt, we do not know what has become of him.' 41 And they made a calf in those days, offered sacrifices to the idol, and rejoiced in the works of their own hands.

Forbidden to practice.

Ex 20:1–5 And God spoke all these words, saying: 2 "I *am* the LORD your God, who brought you out of the land of Egypt, out of the house of bondage. 3 "You shall have no other gods before Me. 4 "You shall not make for yourself a carved image—any likeness *of anything* that *is* in heaven above, or that *is* in the earth beneath, or that *is* in the water under the earth; 5 you shall not bow down to them nor serve them. For I, the LORD your God, *am* a jealous God, visiting the iniquity of the fathers upon the children to the third and fourth *generations* of those who hate Me,

Ex 23:24 You shall not bow down to their gods, nor serve them, nor do according to their works; but you shall utterly overthrow them and completely break down their *sacred* pillars.

Often mixed in with true worship.

Ex 32:1–5 Now when the people saw that Moses delayed coming down from the mountain, the people gathered together to Aaron, and said to him, "Come, make us gods that shall go before us; for *as for* this Moses, the man who brought us up out of the land of Egypt, we do not know what has become of him." 2 And Aaron said to them, "Break off the golden earrings which *are* in the ears of your wives, your sons, and your daughters, and bring *them* to me." 3 So all the people broke off the golden earrings which *were* in their ears, and brought *them* to Aaron. 4 And he received *the* gold from their hand, and he fashioned it with an engraving tool, and made a molded calf. Then they said, "This *is* your god, O Israel, that brought you out of the land of Egypt!" 5 So when Aaron saw *it,* he built an altar before it. And Aaron made a proclamation and said, "Tomorrow *is* a feast to the LORD."

1 Kin 12:27–28 If these people go up to offer sacrifices in the house of the LORD at Jerusalem, then the heart of this people will turn back to their lord, Rehoboam king of Judah, and they will kill me and go back to Rehoboam king of Judah." 28 Therefore the king asked advice, made two calves of gold, and said to the people, "It is too much for you to go up to Jerusalem. Here are your gods, O Israel, which brought you up from the land of Egypt!"

Followed the Canaanites in.

Judg 2:11–13 Then the children of Israel did evil in the sight of the LORD, and served the Baals; 12 and they forsook the LORD God of their fathers, who had brought them out of the land of Egypt; and they followed other gods from *among* the gods of the people who *were* all around them, and they bowed down to them; and they provoked the LORD to anger. 13 They forsook the LORD and served Baal and the Ashtoreths.

1 Chr 5:25 And they were unfaithful to the God of their fathers, and played the harlot after the gods of the peoples of the land, whom God had destroyed before them.

Followed the Moabites in.

Num 25:1–3 Now Israel remained in Acacia Grove, and the people began to commit harlotry with the women of Moab. 2 They invited the people to the sacrifices of their gods, and the people ate and bowed down to their gods. 3 So Israel was joined to

Baal of Peor, and the anger of the LORD was aroused against Israel.

Followed the Assyrians in.

Ezek 16:28–30 You also played the harlot with the Assyrians, because you were insatiable; indeed you played the harlot with them and still were not satisfied. **29** Moreover you multiplied your acts of harlotry as far as the land of the trader, Chaldea; and even then you were not satisfied. **30** "How degenerate is your heart!" says the Lord GOD, "seeing you do all these *things*, the deeds of a brazen harlot.

Ezek 23:5–7 "Oholah played the harlot even though she was Mine; And she lusted for her lovers, the neighboring Assyrians, **6** *Who were* clothed in purple, Captains and rulers, All of them desirable young men, Horsemen riding on horses. **7** Thus she committed her harlotry with them, All of them choice men of Assyria; And with all for whom she lusted, With all their idols, she defiled herself.

Followed the Syrians in.

Judg 10:6 Then the children of Israel again did evil in the sight of the LORD, and served the Baals and the Ashtoreths, the gods of Syria, the gods of Sidon, the gods of Moab, the gods of the people of Ammon, and the gods of the Philistines; and they forsook the LORD and did not serve Him.

Solomon embraced it.

1 Kin 11:5–8 For Solomon went after Ashtoreth the goddess of the Sidonians, and after Milcom the abomination of the Ammonites. **6** Solomon did evil in the sight of the LORD, and did not fully follow the LORD, as *did* his father David. **7** Then Solomon built a high place for Chemosh the abomination of Moab, on the hill that *is* east of Jerusalem, and for Molech the abomination of the people of Ammon. **8** And he did likewise for all his foreign wives, who burned incense and sacrificed to their gods.

Wicked kings adopted it.

1 Kin 21:26 And he behaved very abominably in following idols, according to all *that* the Amorites had done, whom the LORD had cast out before the children of Israel.

2 Kin 21:21 So he walked in all the ways that his father had walked; and he served the idols that his father had served, and worshiped them.

2 Chr 28:2–4 For he walked in the ways of the kings of Israel, and made molded images for the Baals. **3** He burned incense in the Valley of the Son of Hinnom, and burned his children in the fire, according to the abominations of the nations whom the LORD had cast out before the children of Israel. **4** And he sacrificed and burned incense on the high places, on the hills, and under every green tree.

2 Chr 33:3 For he rebuilt the high places which Hezekiah his father had broken down; he raised up altars for the Baals, and made wooden images; and he worshiped all the host of heaven and served them.

2 Chr 33:7 He even set a carved image, the idol which he had made, in the house of God, of which God had said to David and to Solomon his son, "In this house and in Jerusalem, which I have chosen out of all the tribes of Israel, I will put My name forever;

Example of the kings encouraged Israel in.

1 Kin 12:30 Now this thing became a sin, for the people went *to worship* before the one as far as Dan.

2 Kin 21:11 "Because Manasseh king of Judah has done these abominations (he has acted more wickedly than all the Amorites who *were* before him, and has also made Judah sin with his idols),

2 Chr 33:9 So Manasseh seduced Judah and the inhabitants of Jerusalem to do more evil than the nations whom the LORD had destroyed before the children of Israel.

Great prevalence among them.

Is 2:8 Their land is also full of idols; They worship the work of their own hands, That which their own fingers have made.

Jer 2:28 But where *are* your gods that you have made for yourselves? Let them arise, If they can save you in the time of your trouble; For *according to* the number of your cities Are your gods, O Judah.

Ezek 8:10 So I went in and saw, and there—every sort of creeping thing, abominable beasts, and all the idols of the house of Israel, portrayed all around on the walls.

Meant they forsook God.

Jer 2:9–13 "Therefore I will yet bring charges against you," says the LORD, "And against your children's children I will bring charges. **10** For pass beyond the coasts of Cyprus and see, Send to Kedar and consider diligently, And see if there has been such *a thing*. **11** Has a nation changed *its* gods, Which *are* not gods? But My people have changed their Glory For *what* does not profit. **12** Be astonished, O heavens, at this, And be horribly afraid; Be very desolate," says the LORD. **13** "For My people have committed two evils: They have forsaken Me, the fountain of living waters, *And* hewn themselves cisterns—broken cisterns that can hold no water.

Good kings endeavored to destroy it.

2 Chr 15:16 Also he removed Maachah, the mother of Asa the king, from *being* queen mother, because she had made an obscene image of Asherah; and Asa cut down her obscene image, then crushed and burned *it* by the Brook Kidron.

2 Chr 34:7 When he had broken down the altars and the wooden images, had beaten the carved images into powder, and cut down all the incense altars throughout all the land of Israel, he returned to Jerusalem.

Captivity of Israel because of. 2 Kin 17:6–18
Captivity of Judah because of. 2 Kin 17:19–23

IGNORANCE OF GOD

Ignorance of Christ is.

John 8:19 Then they said to Him, "Where is Your Father?" Jesus answered, "You know neither Me nor My Father. If you had known Me, you would have known My Father also."

Darkness symbolizes.

Ps 82:5 They do not know, nor do they understand; They walk about in darkness; All the foundations of the earth are unstable.

Evidenced by

Lack of love.

1 John 4:8 He who does not love does not know God, for God is love.

Not keeping His commands.

1 John 2:4 He who says, "I know Him," and does not keep His commandments, is a liar, and the truth is not in him.

Living in sin.

Titus 1:16 They profess to know God, but in works they deny Him, being abominable, disobedient, and disqualified for every good work.

1 John 3:6 Whoever abides in Him does not sin. Whoever sins has neither seen Him nor known Him.

Leads to

Error.

Matt 22:29 Jesus answered and said to them, "You are mistaken, not knowing the Scriptures nor the power of God.

Idolatry.

Is 44:19 And no one considers in his heart, Nor *is there* knowledge nor understanding to say, "I have burned half of it in the fire, Yes, I have also baked bread on its coals; I have roasted meat and eaten *it*; And shall I make the rest of it an abomination? Shall I fall down before a block of wood?"

Acts 17:29–30 Therefore, since we are the offspring of God, we ought not to think that the Divine Nature is like gold or silver or stone, something shaped by art and man's devising. **30** Truly, these times of ignorance God overlooked, but now commands all men everywhere to repent,

Alienation from God.

Eph 4:18 having their understanding darkened, being alienated from the life of God, because of the ignorance that is in them, because of the blindness of their heart;

Sinful lusts.

1 Thess 4:5 not in passion of lust, like the Gentiles who do not know God;

1 Pet 1:14 as obedient children, not conforming yourselves to the former lusts, *as* in your ignorance;

Persecution of believers.

John 15:21 But all these things they will do to you for My name's sake, because they do not know Him who sent Me.

John 16:3 And these things they will do to you because they have not known the Father nor Me.

Is no excuse for sin.

Lev 4:2 "Speak to the children of Israel, saying: 'If a person sins unintentionally against any of the commandments of the LORD *in anything* which ought not to be done, and does any of them,

Luke 12:48 But he who did not know, yet committed things deserving of stripes, shall be beaten with few. For everyone to whom much is given, from him much will be required; and to whom much has been committed, of him they will ask the more.

The wicked, in a state of.

Jer 9:3 "And *like* their bow they have bent their tongues *for* lies. They are not valiant for the truth on the earth. For they proceed from evil to evil, And they do not know Me," says the LORD.

John 15:21 But all these things they will do to you for My name's sake, because they do not know Him who sent Me.

John 17:25 O righteous Father! The world has not known You, but I have known You; and these have known that You sent Me.

Acts 17:30 Truly, these times of ignorance God overlooked, but now commands all men everywhere to repent,

Rom 3:11 *There is none who understands; There is none who seeks after God.*

The wicked choose.

Job 21:14 Yet they say to God, 'Depart from us, For we do not desire the knowledge of Your ways.

Rom 1:28 And even as they did not like to retain God in *their* knowledge, God gave them over to a debased mind, to do those things which are not fitting;

Punishment of.

Ps 79:6 Pour out Your wrath on the nations that do not know You, And on the kingdoms that do not call on Your name.

2 Thess 1:8 in flaming fire taking vengeance on those who do not know God, and on those who do not obey the gospel of our Lord Jesus Christ.

Ministers should

Be compassionate to those in.

Heb 5:2 He can have compassion on those who are ignorant and going astray, since he himself is also subject to weakness.

2 Tim 2:24–25 And a servant of the Lord must not quarrel but be gentle to all, able to teach, patient, **25** in humility correcting those who are in opposition, if God perhaps will grant them repentance, so that they may know the truth,

Labor to remove.

Acts 17:23 for as I was passing through and considering the objects of your worship, I even found an altar with this inscription: TO THE UNKNOWN GOD. Therefore, the One whom you worship without knowing, Him I proclaim to you:

Illustrated by

Pharaoh.

Ex 5:2 And Pharaoh said, "Who *is* the LORD, that I should obey His voice to let Israel go? I do not know the LORD, nor will I let Israel go."

The Israelites.

Ps 95:10 For forty years I was grieved with *that* generation, And said, 'It *is* a people who go astray in their hearts, And they do not know My ways.'

Is 1:3 The ox knows its owner And the donkey its master's crib; *But* Israel does not know, My people do not consider."

The false prophets.

Is 56:10–11 His watchmen *are* blind, They are all ignorant; They *are* all dumb dogs, They cannot bark; Sleeping, lying down, loving to slumber. **11** Yes, *they are* greedy dogs *Which* never have enough. And they *are* shepherds Who cannot understand; They all look to their own way, Every one for his own gain, From his *own* territory.

The Jews.

Luke 23:34 Then Jesus said, "Father, forgive them, for they do not know what they do." And they divided His garments and cast lots.

Rom 10:3 For they being ignorant of God's righteousness, and seeking to establish their own righteousness, have not submitted to the righteousness of God.

Nicodemus.

John 3:10 Jesus answered and said to him, "Are you the teacher of Israel, and do not know these things?

The Gentiles.

Gal 4:8 But then, indeed, when you did not know God, you served those which by nature are not gods.

Paul.

1 Tim 1:13 although I was formerly a blasphemer, a persecutor, and an insolent man; but I obtained mercy because I did *it* ignorantly in unbelief.

INCENSE

Brought from Sheba.

Jer 6:20 For what purpose to Me Comes frankincense from Sheba, And sweet cane from a far country? Your burnt offerings *are* not acceptable, Nor your sacrifices sweet to Me."

Called frankincense.

Song 4:6 Until the day breaks And the shadows flee away, I will go my way to the mountain of myrrh And to the hill of frankincense.

Song 4:14 Spikenard and saffron, Calamus and cinnamon, With all trees of frankincense, Myrrh and aloes, With all the chief spices—

An article of extensive commerce.

Rev 18:13 and cinnamon and incense, fragrant oil and frankincense, wine and oil, fine flour and wheat, cattle and sheep, horses and chariots, and bodies and souls of men.

Common, not to be offered to God.

Ex 30:9 You shall not offer strange incense on it, or a burnt offering, or a grain offering; nor shall you pour a drink offering on it.

For God's service, mixed with sweet spices.

Ex 25:6 oil for the light, and spices for the anointing oil and for the sweet incense;

Ex 37:29 He also made the holy anointing oil and the pure incense of sweet spices, according to the work of the perfumer.

Recipe for mixing.

Ex 30:34–36 And the LORD said to Moses: "Take sweet spices, stacte and onycha and galbanum, and pure frankincense with *these* sweet spices; there shall be equal amounts of each. 35 You shall make of these an incense, a compound according to the art of the perfumer, salted, pure, *and* holy. 36 And you shall beat *some* of it very fine, and put some of it before the Testimony in the tabernacle of meeting where I will meet with you. It shall be most holy to you.

Offered

By the priests.

Num 16:40 *to be* a memorial to the children of Israel that no outsider, who *is* not a descendant of Aaron, should come near to offer incense before the LORD, that he might not become like Korah and his companions, just as the LORD had said to him through Moses.

Deut 33:10 They shall teach Jacob Your judgments, And Israel Your law. They shall put incense before You, And a whole burnt sacrifice on Your altar.

Luke 1:9 according to the custom of the priesthood, his lot fell to burn incense when he went into the temple of the Lord.

In censers.

Lev 10:1 Then Nadab and Abihu, the sons of Aaron, each took his censer and put fire in it, put incense on it, and offered profane fire before the LORD, which He had not commanded them.

Num 16:17 Let each take his censer and put incense in it, and each of you bring his censer before the LORD, two hundred and fifty censers; both you and Aaron, each *with* his censer."

Num 16:46 So Moses said to Aaron, "Take a censer and put fire in it from the altar, put incense *on it*, and take it quickly to the congregation and make atonement for them; for wrath has gone out from the LORD. The plague has begun."

On the altar of gold.

Ex 30:1 "You shall make an altar to burn incense on; you shall make it of acacia wood.

Ex 30:6 And you shall put it before the veil that *is* before the ark of the Testimony, before the mercy seat that *is* over the Testimony, where I will meet with you.

Ex 40:5 You shall also set the altar of gold for the incense before the ark of the Testimony, and put up the screen for the door of the tabernacle.

Morning and evening.

Ex 30:7–8 "Aaron shall burn on it sweet incense every morning; when he tends the lamps, he shall burn incense on it. 8 And when Aaron lights the lamps at twilight, he shall burn incense on it, a perpetual incense before the LORD throughout your generations.

Perpetually.

Ex 30:8 And when Aaron lights the lamps at twilight, he shall burn incense on it, a perpetual incense before the LORD throughout your generations.

By the high priest on the day of atonement.

Lev 16:12–13 Then he shall take a censer full of burning coals of fire from the altar before the LORD, with his hands full of sweet incense beaten fine, and bring *it* inside the veil. 13 And he shall put the incense on the fire before the LORD, that the cloud of incense may cover the mercy seat that *is* on the Testimony, lest he die.

With fire from the altar of burnt offering.

Lev 16:12 Then he shall take a censer full of burning coals of fire from the altar before the LORD, with his hands full of sweet incense beaten fine, and bring *it* inside the veil.

Num 16:46 So Moses said to Aaron, "Take a censer and put fire in it from the altar, put incense *on it*, and take it quickly to the congregation and make atonement for them; for wrath has gone out from the LORD. The plague has begun."

The Jews prayed at time of offering.

Luke 1:10 And the whole multitude of the people was praying outside at the hour of incense.

Designed for atonement.

Num 16:46–47 So Moses said to Aaron, "Take a censer and put fire in it from the altar, put incense *on it,* and take it quickly to the congregation and make atonement for them; for wrath has gone out from the LORD. The plague has begun." **47** Then Aaron took *it* as Moses commanded, and ran into the midst of the assembly; and already the plague had begun among the people. So he put in the incense and made atonement for the people.

Put on grain offerings.

Lev 2:1–2 'When anyone offers a grain offering to the LORD, his offering shall be *of* fine flour. And he shall pour oil on it, and put frankincense on it. **2** He shall bring it to Aaron's sons, the priests, one of whom shall take from it his handful of fine flour and oil with all the frankincense. And the priest shall burn *it* *as* a memorial on the altar, an offering made by fire, a sweet aroma to the LORD.

Lev 2:15–16 And you shall put oil on it, and lay frankincense on it. It *is* a grain offering. **16** Then the priest shall burn the memorial portion: *part* of its beaten grain and *part* of its oil, with all the frankincense, as an offering made by fire to the LORD.

Lev 6:15 He shall take from it his handful of the fine flour of the grain offering, with its oil, and all the frankincense which *is* on the grain offering, and shall burn *it* on the altar *for* a sweet aroma, as a memorial to the LORD.

Levites had charge of.

1 Chr 9:29 *Some* of them *were* appointed over the furnishings and over all the implements of the sanctuary, and over the fine flour and the wine and the oil and the incense and the spices.

Form of, used in idolatrous worship.

Jer 48:35 "Moreover," says the LORD, "I will cause to cease in Moab The one who offers *sacrifices* in the high places And burns incense to his gods.

The Jews

Not accepted in offering, because of sin.

Is 1:13 Bring no more futile sacrifices; Incense is an abomination to Me. The New Moons, the Sabbaths, and the calling of assemblies— I cannot endure iniquity and the sacred meeting.

Is 66:3 "He who kills a bull *is as if* he slays a man; He who sacrifices a lamb, *as if* he breaks a dog's neck; He who offers a grain offering, *as if he offers* swine's blood; He who burns incense, *as if* he blesses an idol. Just as they have chosen their own ways, And their soul delights in their abominations,

Offered, to idols on altars of brick.

Is 65:3 A people who provoke Me to anger continually to My face; Who sacrifice in gardens, And burn incense on altars of brick;

Punished for offering, to idols.

2 Chr 34:25 because they have forsaken Me and burned incense to other gods, that they might provoke Me to anger with all the works of their hands. Therefore My wrath will be poured out on this place, and not be quenched.' " '

Nadab and Abihu destroyed for offering, with profane fire.

Lev 10:1–2 Then Nadab and Abihu, the sons of Aaron, each took his censer and put fire in it, put incense on it, and offered profane fire before the LORD, which He had not commanded them. **2** So fire went out from the LORD and devoured them, and they died before the LORD.

Korah and his company punished for offering.

Num 16:16–35 And Moses said to Korah, "Tomorrow, you and all your company be present before the LORD—you and they, as well as Aaron. **17** Let each take his censer and put incense in it, and each of you bring his censer before the LORD, two hundred and fifty censers; both you and Aaron, each *with* his censer." **18** So every man took his censer, put fire in it, laid incense on it, and stood at the door of the tabernacle of meeting with Moses and Aaron. **19** And Korah gathered all the congregation against them at the door of the tabernacle of meeting. Then the glory of the LORD appeared to all the congregation. **20** And the LORD spoke to Moses and Aaron, saying, **21** "Separate yourselves from among this congregation, that I may consume them in a moment." **22** Then they fell on their faces, and said, "O God, the God of the spirits of all flesh, shall one man sin, and You be angry with all the congregation?" **23** So the LORD spoke to Moses, saying, **24** "Speak to the congregation, saying, 'Get away from the tents of Korah, Dathan, and Abiram.' " **25** Then Moses rose and went to Dathan and Abiram, and the elders of Israel followed him. **26** And he spoke to the congregation, saying, "Depart now from the tents of these wicked men! Touch nothing of theirs, lest you be consumed in all their sins." **27** So they got away from around the tents of Korah, Dathan, and Abiram; and Dathan and Abiram came out and stood at the door of their tents, with their wives, their sons, and their little children. **28** And Moses said: "By this you shall know that the LORD has sent me to do all these works, for I *have* not *done them* of my own will. **29** If these men die naturally like all men, or if they are visited by the common fate of all men, *then* the LORD has not sent me. **30** But if the LORD creates a new thing, and the earth opens its mouth and swallows them up with all that belongs to them, and they go down alive into the pit, then you will understand that these men have rejected the LORD." **31** Now it came to pass, as he finished speaking all these words, that the ground split apart under them, **32** and the earth opened its mouth and swallowed them up, with their households and all the men with Korah, with all *their* goods. **33** So they and all those with them went down alive into the pit; the earth closed over them, and they perished from among the assembly. **34** Then all Israel who *were* around them fled at their cry, for they said, "Lest the earth swallow us up *also!*" **35** And a fire came out from the LORD and consumed the two hundred and fifty men who were offering incense.

Uzziah punished for offering.

2 Chr 26:16–21 But when he was strong his heart was lifted up, to *his* destruction, for he transgressed against the LORD his God by entering the temple of the LORD to burn incense on the altar of incense. 17 So Azariah the priest went in after him, and with him were eighty priests of the LORD—valiant men. 18 And they withstood King Uzziah, and said to him, "*It is* not for you, Uzziah, to burn incense to the LORD, but for the priests, the sons of Aaron, who are consecrated to burn incense. Get out of the sanctuary, for you have trespassed! You *shall have* no honor from the LORD God." 19 Then Uzziah became furious; and he *had* a censer in his hand to burn incense. And while he was angry with the priests, leprosy broke out on his forehead, before the priests in the house of the LORD, beside the incense altar. 20 And Azariah the chief priest and all the priests looked at him, and there, on his forehead, he *was* leprous; so they thrust him out of that place. Indeed he also hurried to get out, because the LORD had struck him. 21 King Uzziah was a leper until the day of his death. He dwelt in an isolated house, because he was a leper; for he was cut off from the house of the LORD. Then Jotham his son *was* over the king's house, judging the people of the land.

Presented to Christ by the wise men.

Matt 2:11 And when they had come into the house, they saw the young Child with Mary His mother, and fell down and worshiped Him. And when they had opened their treasures, they presented gifts to Him: gold, frankincense, and myrrh.

Illustrative of

The merits of Christ.

Rev 8:3–4 Then another angel, having a golden censer, came and stood at the altar. He was given much incense, that he should offer *it* with the prayers of all the saints upon the golden altar which was before the throne. 4 And the smoke of the incense, with the prayers of the saints, ascended before God from the angel's hand.

Prayer.

Ps 141:2 Let my prayer be set before You *as* incense, The lifting up of my hands *as* the evening sacrifice.

Mal 1:11 For from the rising of the sun, even to its going down, My name *shall be* great among the Gentiles; In every place incense *shall be* offered to My name, And a pure offering; For My name shall be great among the nations," Says the LORD of hosts.

Rev 5:8 Now when He had taken the scroll, the four living creatures and the twenty-four elders fell down before the Lamb, each having a harp, and golden bowls full of incense, which are the prayers of the saints.

INCEST

By Lot's daughters, against him. Gen 19:30–38
By Judah, unknowingly, with Tamar. Gen 38:12–26
By Amnon against Tamar. 2 Sam 13:1–20
Prohibited by God.

Lev 18:6–18 'None of you shall approach anyone who is near of kin to him, to uncover his nakedness: I *am* the LORD. 7 The nakedness of your father or the nakedness of your mother you shall not uncover. She *is*

your mother; you shall not uncover her nakedness. 8 The nakedness of your father's wife you shall not uncover; it *is* your father's nakedness. 9 The nakedness of your sister, the daughter of your father, or the daughter of your mother, *whether* born at home or elsewhere, their nakedness you shall not uncover. 10 The nakedness of your son's daughter or your daughter's daughter, their nakedness you shall not uncover; for theirs *is* your own nakedness. 11 The nakedness of your father's wife's daughter, begotten by your father—she *is* your sister—you shall not uncover her nakedness. 12 You shall not uncover the nakedness of your father's sister; she *is* near of kin to your father. 13 You shall not uncover the nakedness of your mother's sister, for she *is* near of kin to your mother. 14 You shall not uncover the nakedness of your father's brother. You shall not approach his wife; she *is* your aunt. 15 You shall not uncover the nakedness of your daughter-in-law—she *is* your son's wife—you shall not uncover her nakedness. 16 You shall not uncover the nakedness of your brother's wife; it *is* your brother's nakedness. 17 You shall not uncover the nakedness of a woman and her daughter, nor shall you take her son's daughter or her daughter's daughter, to uncover her nakedness. They *are* near of kin to her. It *is* wickedness. 18 Nor shall you take a woman as a rival to her sister, to uncover her nakedness while the other is alive.

Deut 22:30 "A man shall not take his father's wife, nor uncover his father's bed.

Deut 27:20 'Cursed *is* the one who lies with his father's wife, because he has uncovered his father's bed.' "And all the people shall say, 'Amen!'

Deut 27:22–23 'Cursed *is* the one who lies with his sister, the daughter of his father or the daughter of his mother.' "And all the people shall say, 'Amen!' 23 'Cursed *is* the one who lies with his mother-in-law.' "And all the people shall say, 'Amen!'

Cf. 1 Cor 5:1

Death penalty imposed for.

Lev 20:11–12 The man who lies with his father's wife has uncovered his father's nakedness; both of them shall surely be put to death. Their blood *shall be* upon them. 12 If a man lies with his daughter-in-law, both of them shall surely be put to death. They have committed perversion. Their blood *shall be* upon them.

Lev 20:14 If a man marries a woman and her mother, it *is* wickedness. They shall be burned with fire, both he and they, that there may be no wickedness among you.

Lev 21:9 The daughter of any priest, if she profanes herself by playing the harlot, she profanes her father. She shall be burned with fire.

Part of the sin of Herod Antipas and family.

Matt 14:3–4 For Herod had laid hold of John and bound him, and put *him* in prison for the sake of Herodias, his brother Philip's wife. 4 Because John had said to him, "It is not lawful for you to have her."

Mark 6:17–18 For Herod himself had sent and laid hold of John, and bound him in prison for the sake of Herodias, his brother Philip's wife; for he had married her. 18 Because John had said to Herod, "It is not lawful for you to have your brother's wife."

INFLUENCE

Of God's kingdom

Likened to leaven in bread.

Matt 13:33 Another parable He spoke to them: "The kingdom of heaven is like leaven, which a woman took and hid in three measures of meal till it was all leavened."

Luke 13:20–21 And again He said, "To what shall I liken the kingdom of God? **21** It is like leaven, which a woman took and hid in three measures of meal till it was all leavened."

Likened to a mustard tree.

Matt 13:31–32 Another parable He put forth to them, saying: "The kingdom of heaven is like a mustard seed, which a man took and sowed in his field, **32** which indeed is the least of all the seeds; but when it is grown it is greater than the herbs and becomes a tree, so that the birds of the air come and nest in its branches."

Mark 4:30–32 Then He said, "To what shall we liken the kingdom of God? Or with what parable shall we picture it? **31** *It is* like a mustard seed which, when it is sown on the ground, is smaller than all the seeds on earth; **32** but when it is sown, it grows up and becomes greater than all herbs, and shoots out large branches, so that the birds of the air may nest under its shade."

Of the Pharisees' bad doctrine.

Matt 16:6–12 Then Jesus said to them, "Take heed and beware of the leaven of the Pharisees and the Sadducees." **7** And they reasoned among themselves, saying, "*It is* because we have taken no bread." **8** But Jesus, being aware of *it,* said to them, "O you of little faith, why do you reason among yourselves because you have brought no bread? **9** Do you not yet understand, or remember the five loaves of the five thousand and how many baskets you took up? **10** Nor the seven loaves of the four thousand and how many large baskets you took up? **11** How is it you do not understand that I did not speak to you concerning bread?—*but* to beware of the leaven of the Pharisees and Sadducees." **12** Then they understood that He did not tell *them* to beware of the leaven of bread, but of the doctrine of the Pharisees and Sadducees.

Mark 8:15 Then He charged them, saying, "Take heed, beware of the leaven of the Pharisees and the leaven of Herod."

Luke 12:1–3 In the meantime, when an innumerable multitude of people had gathered together, so that they trampled one another, He began to say to His disciples first *of all,* "Beware of the leaven of the Pharisees, which is hypocrisy. **2** For there is nothing covered that will not be revealed, nor hidden that will not be known. **3** Therefore whatever you have spoken in the dark will be heard in the light, and what you have spoken in the ear in inner rooms will be proclaimed on the housetops.

Cf. Matt 23:25; 1 Cor 5:6–7; Gal 5:9

Of sinners.

1 Cor 15:33 Do not be deceived: "Evil company corrupts good habits."

Of the Holy Spirit.

Acts 2:4 And they were all filled with the Holy Spirit and began to speak with other tongues, as the Spirit gave them utterance.

Acts 4:8 Then Peter, filled with the Holy Spirit, said to them, "Rulers of the people and elders of Israel:

Acts 4:31 And when they had prayed, the place where they were assembled together was shaken; and they were all filled with the Holy Spirit, and they spoke the word of God with boldness.

Acts 6:3 Therefore, brethren, seek out from among you seven men of *good* reputation, full of the Holy Spirit and wisdom, whom we may appoint over this business;

Acts 7:55 But he, being full of the Holy Spirit, gazed into heaven and saw the glory of God, and Jesus standing at the right hand of God,

Rom 8:13–17 For if you live according to the flesh you will die; but if by the Spirit you put to death the deeds of the body, you will live. **14** For as many as are led by the Spirit of God, these are sons of God. **15** For you did not receive the spirit of bondage again to fear, but you received the Spirit of adoption by whom we cry out, "Abba, Father." **16** The Spirit Himself bears witness with our spirit that we are children of God, **17** and if children, then heirs—heirs of God and joint heirs with Christ, if indeed we suffer with *Him,* that we may also be glorified together.

Gal 5:16–23 I say then: Walk in the Spirit, and you shall not fulfill the lust of the flesh. **17** For the flesh lusts against the Spirit, and the Spirit against the flesh; and these are contrary to one another, so that you do not do the things that you wish. **18** But if you are led by the Spirit, you are not under the law. **19** Now the works of the flesh are evident, which are: adultery, fornication, uncleanness, lewdness, **20** idolatry, sorcery, hatred, contentions, jealousies, outbursts of wrath, selfish ambitions, dissensions, heresies, **21** envy, murders, drunkenness, revelries, and the like; of which I tell you beforehand, just as I also told *you* in time past, that those who practice such things will not inherit the kingdom of God. **22** But the fruit of the Spirit is love, joy, peace, longsuffering, kindness, goodness, faithfulness, **23** gentleness, self-control. Against such there is no law.

Eph 5:18 And do not be drunk with wine, in which is dissipation; but be filled with the Spirit,

Col 3:16 Let the word of Christ dwell in you richly in all wisdom, teaching and admonishing one another in psalms and hymns and spiritual songs, singing with grace in your hearts to the Lord.

Of Antichrist.

2 Thess 2:9–12 The coming of the *lawless one* is according to the working of Satan, with all power, signs, and lying wonders, **10** and with all unrighteous deception among those who perish, because they did not receive the love of the truth, that they might be saved. **11** And for this reason God will send them strong delusion, that they should believe the lie, **12** that they all may be condemned who did not believe the truth but had pleasure in unrighteousness.

Rev 9:2–11 And he opened the bottomless pit, and smoke arose out of the pit like the smoke of a great furnace. So the sun and the air were darkened because of the smoke of the pit. **3** Then out of the smoke locusts came upon the earth. And to them was given power, as the scorpions of the earth have power. **4** They were commanded not to harm the grass of the earth, or any green thing, or any tree, but only those men who do not have the seal of God on their foreheads. **5** And they were not given *authority* to kill them, but to torment them *for* five months. Their torment *was* like the torment of a scorpion when it strikes a man. **6** In those days men will seek death and will not find it; they will desire to die, and death will flee from them. **7** The shape of the locusts was like horses prepared for battle. On their heads were crowns of something like gold, and their faces *were* like the faces of men. **8** They had hair like women's hair, and their teeth were like lions' *teeth.* **9** And they had breastplates like breastplates of iron, and the sound of their wings *was* like the sound of chariots with many horses running into battle. **10** They had tails like scorpions, and there were stings in their tails. Their power *was* to hurt men five months. **11** And they had as king over them the angel of the bottomless pit, whose name in Hebrew *is* Abaddon, but in Greek he has the name Apollyon.

Rev 13:11–18 Then I saw another beast coming up out of the earth, and he had two horns like a lamb and spoke like a dragon. **12** And he exercises all the authority of the first beast in his presence, and causes the earth and those who dwell in it to worship the first beast, whose deadly wound was healed. **13** He performs great signs, so that he even makes fire come down from heaven on the earth in the sight of men. **14** And he deceives those who dwell on the earth by those signs which he was granted to do in the sight of the beast, telling those who dwell on the earth to make an image to the beast who was wounded by the sword and lived. **15** He was granted *power* to give breath to the image of the beast, that the image of the beast should both speak and cause as many as would not worship the image of the beast to be killed. **16** He causes all, both small and great, rich and poor, free and slave, to receive a mark on their right hand or on their foreheads, **17** and that no one may buy or sell except one who has the mark or the name of the beast, or the number of his name. **18** Here is wisdom. Let him who has understanding calculate the number of the beast, for it is the number of a man: His number *is* 666.

Rev 16:14 For they are spirits of demons, performing signs, *which* go out to the kings of the earth and of the whole world, to gather them to the battle of that great day of God Almighty.

Rev 20:2–3 He laid hold of the dragon, that serpent of old, who is *the* Devil and Satan, and bound him for a thousand years; **3** and he cast him into the bottomless pit, and shut him up, and set a seal on him, so that he should deceive the nations no more till the thousand years were finished. But after these things he must be released for a little while.

Rev 20:8 and will go out to deceive the nations which are in the four corners of the earth, Gog and Magog, to gather them together to battle, whose number *is* as the sand of the sea.

Rev 20:10 The devil, who deceived them, was cast into the lake of fire and brimstone where the beast and the false prophet *are.* And they will be tormented day and night forever and ever.

INGRATITUDE
A characteristic of the wicked.
Ps 38:20 Those also who render evil for good, They are my adversaries, because I follow *what is* good.

2 Tim 3:2 For men will be lovers of themselves, lovers of money, boasters, proud, blasphemers, disobedient to parents, unthankful, unholy,

Often exhibited
By relatives.
Job 19:14 My relatives have failed, And my close friends have forgotten me.

By servants.
Job 19:15–16 Those who dwell in my house, and my maidservants, Count me as a stranger; I am an alien in their sight. **16** I call my servant, but he gives no answer; I beg him with my mouth.

To benefactors.
Ps 109:5 Thus they have rewarded me evil for good, And hatred for my love.

Eccl 9:15 Now there was found in it a poor wise man, and he by his wisdom delivered the city. Yet no one remembered that same poor man.

To friends in distress.
Ps 38:11 My loved ones and my friends stand aloof from my plague, And my relatives stand afar off.

Believers should avoid the guilt of.
Ps 7:4–5 If I have repaid evil to him who was at peace with me, Or have plundered my enemy without cause, **5** Let the enemy pursue me and overtake *me;* Yes, let him trample my life to the earth, And lay my honor in the dust. Selah

Should be met with
Prayer.
Ps 35:12–13 They reward me evil for good, *To* the sorrow of my soul. **13** But as for me, when they were sick, My clothing *was* sackcloth; I humbled myself with fasting; And my prayer would return to my own heart.

Ps 109:4 In return for my love they are my accusers, But I *give myself to* prayer.

Faithfulness.
Gen 31:38–42 These twenty years I *have been* with you; your ewes and your female goats have not miscarried their young, and I have not eaten the rams of your flock. **39** That which was torn *by beasts* I did not bring to you; I bore the loss of it. You required it from my hand, *whether* stolen by day or stolen by night. **40** *There* I was! In the day the drought consumed me, and the frost by night, and my sleep departed from my eyes. **41** Thus I have been in your house twenty years; I served you fourteen years for your two daughters, and six years for your flock, and you have changed my wages ten times. **42** Unless the God of my father, the God of Abraham and the Fear of Isaac, had been with me, surely now you would have sent me away empty-handed. God has seen my affliction and the labor of my hands, and rebuked *you* last night."

Persevering love.

2 Cor 12:15 And I will very gladly spend and be spent for your souls; though the more abundantly I love you, the less I am loved.

Punishment of.

Prov 17:13 Whoever rewards evil for good, Evil will not depart from his house.

Jer 18:20–21 Shall evil be repaid for good? For they have dug a pit for my life. Remember that I stood before You To speak good for them, To turn away Your wrath from them. **21** Therefore deliver up their children to the famine, And pour out their *blood* By the force of the sword; Let their wives *become* widows And bereaved of their children. Let their men be put to death, Their young men *be* slain By the sword in battle.

Illustrated by

Laban.

Gen 31:6–7 And you know that with all my might I have served your father. **7** Yet your father has deceived me and changed my wages ten times, but God did not allow him to hurt me.

The chief butler.

Gen 40:23 Yet the chief butler did not remember Joseph, but forgot him.

Israel.

Ex 17:4 So Moses cried out to the LORD, saying, "What shall I do with this people? They are almost ready to stone me!"

The men of Keilah.

1 Sam 23:5 And David and his men went to Keilah and fought with the Philistines, struck them with a mighty blow, and took away their livestock. So David saved the inhabitants of Keilah.

1 Sam 23:12 Then David said, "Will the men of Keilah deliver me and my men into the hand of Saul?" And the LORD said, "They will deliver *you.*"

Saul.

1 Sam 24:17 Then he said to David: "You *are* more righteous than I; for you have rewarded me with good, whereas I have rewarded you with evil.

Nabal.

1 Sam 25:5–11 David sent ten young men; and David said to the young men, "Go up to Carmel, go to Nabal, and greet him in my name. **6** And thus you shall say to him who lives *in prosperity:* 'Peace *be* to you, peace to your house, and peace to all that you have! **7** Now I have heard that you have shearers. Your shepherds were with us, and we did not hurt them, nor was there anything missing from them all the while they were in Carmel. **8** Ask your young men, and they will tell you. Therefore let *my* young men find favor in your eyes, for we come on a feast day. Please give whatever comes to your hand to your servants and to your son David.' " **9** So when David's young men came, they spoke to Nabal according to all these words in the name of David, and waited. **10** Then Nabal answered David's servants, and said, "Who *is* David, and who *is* the son of Jesse? There are many servants nowadays who break away each one from his master. **11** Shall I then take my bread and my water and my meat that I have killed

for my shearers, and give *it* to men when I do not know where they *are* from?"

1 Sam 25:21 Now David had said, "Surely in vain I have protected all that this *fellow* has in the wilderness, so that nothing was missed of all that *belongs* to him. And he has repaid me evil for good.

Absalom.

2 Sam 15:6 In this manner Absalom acted toward all Israel who came to the king for judgment. So Absalom stole the hearts of the men of Israel.

Joash.

2 Chr 24:22 Thus Joash the king did not remember the kindness which Jehoiada his father had done to him, but killed his son; and as he died, he said, "The LORD look on *it,* and repay!"

INGRATITUDE TO GOD

A characteristic of the wicked.

Rom 1:21 because, although they knew God, they did not glorify *Him* as God, nor were thankful, but became futile in their thoughts, and their foolish hearts were darkened.

Inexcusable.

Is 1:2–3 Hear, O heavens, and give ear, O earth! For the LORD has spoken: "I have nourished and brought up children, And they have rebelled against Me; **3** The ox knows its owner And the donkey its master's crib; *But* Israel does not know, My people do not consider."

Rom 1:21 because, although they knew God, they did not glorify *Him* as God, nor were thankful, but became futile in their thoughts, and their foolish hearts were darkened.

Unreasonable.

Jer 2:5–6 Thus says the LORD: "What injustice have your fathers found in Me, That they have gone far from Me, Have followed idols, And have become idolaters? **6** Neither did they say, 'Where *is* the LORD, Who brought us up out of the land of Egypt, Who led us through the wilderness, Through a land of deserts and pits, Through a land of drought and the shadow of death, Through a land that no one crossed And where no one dwelt?'

Jer 2:31 "O generation, see the word of the LORD! Have I been a wilderness to Israel, Or a land of darkness? Why do My people say, 'We are lords; We will come no more to You'?

Mic 6:2–3 Hear, O you mountains, the LORD's complaint, And you strong foundations of the earth; For the LORD has a complaint against His people, And He will contend with Israel. **3** "O My people, what have I done to you? And how have I wearied you? Testify against Me.

Exceeding folly of.

Deut 32:6 Do you thus deal with the LORD, O foolish and unwise people? *Is* He not your Father, *who* bought you? Has He not made you and established you?

Guilt of.

Ps 106:7 Our fathers in Egypt did not understand Your wonders; They did not remember the multitude of Your mercies, But rebelled by the sea—the Red Sea.

Ps 106:21 They forgot God their Savior, Who had done great things in Egypt,

Jer 2:11–13 Has a nation changed *its* gods, Which *are* not gods? But My people have changed their Glory For *what* does not profit. **12** Be astonished, O heavens, at this, And be horribly afraid; Be very desolate," says the Lord. **13** "For My people have committed two evils: They have forsaken Me, the fountain of living waters, *And* hewn themselves cisterns—broken cisterns that can hold no water.

Prosperity likely to produce.

Deut 31:20 When I have brought them to the land flowing with milk and honey, of which I swore to their fathers, and they have eaten and filled themselves and grown fat, then they will turn to other gods and serve them; and they will provoke Me and break My covenant.

Deut 32:15 "But Jeshurun grew fat and kicked; You grew fat, you grew thick, You are obese! Then he forsook God *who* made him, And scornfully esteemed the Rock of his salvation.

Jer 5:7–11 "How shall I pardon you for this? Your children have forsaken Me And sworn by *those* that are *not gods*. When I had fed them to the full, Then they committed adultery And assembled themselves by troops in the harlots' houses. **8** They were *like* well-fed lusty stallions; Every one neighed after his neighbor's wife. **9** Shall I not punish *them* for these *things?*" says the Lord. "And shall I not avenge Myself on such a nation as this? **10** "Go up on her walls and destroy, But do not make a complete end. Take away her branches, For they *are* not the Lord's. **11** For the house of Israel and the house of Judah Have dealt very treacherously with Me," says the Lord.

Warnings against.

Deut 8:11–14 "Beware that you do not forget the Lord your God by not keeping His commandments, His judgments, and His statutes which I command you today, **12** lest—*when* you have eaten and are full, and have built beautiful houses and dwell *in them;* **13** and *when* your herds and your flocks multiply, and your silver and your gold are multiplied, and all that you have is multiplied; **14** when your heart is lifted up, and you forget the Lord your God who brought you out of the land of Egypt, from the house of bondage;

1 Sam 12:24–25 Only fear the Lord, and serve Him in truth with all your heart; for consider what great things He has done for you. **25** But if you still do wickedly, you shall be swept away, both you and your king."

Punishment of.

Hos 2:8–9 For she did not know That I gave her grain, new wine, and oil, And multiplied her silver and gold— *Which* they prepared for Baal. **9** "Therefore I will return and take away My grain in its time And My new wine in its season, And will take back My wool and My linen, *Given* to cover her nakedness.

Cf. Neh 9:20–27

Illustrated.

Is 5:1–7 Now let me sing to my Well-beloved A song of my Beloved regarding His vineyard: My Well-beloved has a vineyard On a very fruitful hill. **2** He dug it up and cleared out its stones, And planted it with the choicest vine. He built a tower in its midst, And also made a winepress in it; So He expected *it* to bring forth *good* grapes, But it brought forth wild grapes. **3** "And now, O inhabitants of Jerusalem and men of Judah, Judge, please, between Me and My vineyard. **4** What more could have been done to My vineyard That I have not done in it? Why then, when I expected *it* to bring forth *good* grapes, Did it bring forth wild grapes? **5** And now, please let Me tell you what I will do to My vineyard: I will take away its hedge, and it shall be burned; *And* break down its wall, and it shall be trampled down. **6** I will lay it waste; It shall not be pruned or dug, But there shall come up briers and thorns. I will also command the clouds That they rain no rain on it." **7** For the vineyard of the Lord of hosts *is* the house of Israel, And the men of Judah are His pleasant plant. He looked for justice, but behold, oppression; For righteousness, but behold, a cry *for help.*

Cf. Ezek 16:1–15

Examples of,

Israel.

Deut 32:18 Of the Rock *who* begot you, you are unmindful, And have forgotten the God who fathered you.

Saul.

1 Sam 15:17–19 So Samuel said, "When you *were* little in your own eyes, *were* you not head of the tribes of Israel? And did not the Lord anoint you king over Israel? **18** Now the Lord sent you on a mission, and said, 'Go, and utterly destroy the sinners, the Amalekites, and fight against them until they are consumed.' **19** Why then did you not obey the voice of the Lord? Why did you swoop down on the spoil, and do evil in the sight of the Lord?"

David.

2 Sam 12:7–9 Then Nathan said to David, "You *are* the man! Thus says the Lord God of Israel: 'I anointed you king over Israel, and I delivered you from the hand of Saul. **8** I gave you your master's house and your master's wives into your keeping, and gave you the house of Israel and Judah. And if *that had been* too little, I also would have given you much more! **9** Why have you despised the commandment of the Lord, to do evil in His sight? You have killed Uriah the Hittite with the sword; you have taken his wife *to be* your wife, and have killed him with the sword of the people of Ammon.

Nebuchadnezzar.

Dan 5:18–21 O king, the Most High God gave Nebuchadnezzar your father a kingdom and majesty, glory and honor. **19** And because of the majesty that He gave him, all peoples, nations, and languages trembled and feared before him. Whomever he wished, he executed; whomever he wished, he kept alive; whomever he wished, he set up; and whomever he wished, he put down. **20** But when his heart was lifted up, and his spirit was hardened in pride, he was deposed from his kingly throne, and they took his glory from him. **21** Then he was driven from the sons of men, his heart was made like the beasts, and his dwelling *was* with the wild donkeys. They fed him with grass like oxen, and his body was wet with the dew of heaven, till he knew that the Most

High God rules in the kingdom of men, and appoints over it whomever He chooses.

The lepers.

Luke 17:17–18 So Jesus answered and said, "Were there not ten cleansed? But where *are* the nine? **18** Were there not any found who returned to give glory to God except this foreigner?"

INJUSTICE

Inherently wrong.

Prov 17:15 He who justifies the wicked, and he who condemns the just, Both of them alike *are* an abomination to the LORD.

Prov 17:26 Also, to punish the righteous *is* not good, *Nor* to strike princes for *their* uprightness.

Prov 24:23–25 These *things* also *belong* to the wise: *It is* not good to show partiality in judgment. **24** He who says to the wicked, "You *are* righteous," Him the people will curse; Nations will abhor him. **25** But those who rebuke *the wicked* will have delight, And a good blessing will come upon them.

Mic 2:1–2 Woe to those who devise iniquity, And work out evil on their beds! At morning light they practice it, Because it is in the power of their hand. **2** They covet fields and take *them* by violence, Also houses, and seize *them.* So they oppress a man and his house, A man and his inheritance.

Cf. Ex 23:7; Is 5:23

Forbidden.

Lev 19:15 'You shall do no injustice in judgment. You shall not be partial to the poor, nor honor the person of the mighty. In righteousness you shall judge your neighbor.

Lev 19:35 'You shall do no injustice in judgment, in measurement of length, weight, or volume.

Deut 16:19 You shall not pervert justice; you shall not show partiality, nor take a bribe, for a bribe blinds the eyes of the wise and twists the words of the righteous.

Specially to be avoided toward

The poor.

Ex 23:6 "You shall not pervert the judgment of your poor in his dispute.

Prov 22:16 He who oppresses the poor to increase his *riches, And* he who gives to the rich, *will* surely *come* to poverty.

Prov 22:22–23 Do not rob the poor because he *is* poor, Nor oppress the afflicted at the gate; **23** For the LORD will plead their cause, And plunder the soul of those who plunder them.

The stranger and fatherless.

Ex 22:21–22 "You shall neither mistreat a stranger nor oppress him, for you were strangers in the land of Egypt. **22** "You shall not afflict any widow or fatherless child.

Deut 24:17 "You shall not pervert justice due the stranger or the fatherless, nor take a widow's garment as a pledge.

Jer 22:3 Thus says the LORD: "Execute judgment and righteousness, and deliver the plundered out of the hand of the oppressor. Do no wrong and do no vio-

lence to the stranger, the fatherless, or the widow, nor shed innocent blood in this place.

Servants.

Job 31:13–14 "If I have despised the cause of my male or female servant When they complained against me, **14** What then shall I do when God rises up? When He punishes, how shall I answer Him?

Deut 24:14 "You shall not oppress a hired servant *who is* poor and needy, *whether* one of your brethren or one of the aliens who *is* in your land within your gates.

Jer 22:13 "Woe to him who builds his house by unrighteousness And his chambers by injustice, *Who* uses his neighbor's service without wages And gives him nothing for his work,

Nehemiah rebukes it. Neh 5:1–13

Of the least kind, also condemned.

Luke 16:10 He who *is* faithful in *what is* least is faithful also in much; and he who is unjust in *what is* least is unjust also in much.

God

Regards.

Eccl 5:8 If you see the oppression of the poor, and the violent perversion of justice and righteousness in a province, do not marvel at the matter; for high official watches over high official, and higher officials are over them.

Does not approve.

Prov 17:15 He who justifies the wicked, and he who condemns the just, Both of them alike *are* an abomination to the LORD.

Prov 20:10 Diverse weights *and* diverse measures, They *are* both alike, an abomination to the LORD.

Lam 3:35–36 To turn aside the justice *due* a man Before the face of the Most High, **36** Or subvert a man in his cause— The Lord does not approve.

Hears the cry of those who suffer.

James 5:4 Indeed the wages of the laborers who mowed your fields, which you kept back by fraud, cry out; and the cries of the reapers have reached the ears of the Lord of Sabaoth.

Provoked to avenge.

Ps 12:5 "For the oppression of the poor, for the sighing of the needy, Now I will arise," says the LORD; "I will set *him* in the safety for which he yearns."

Ultimately defeats.

Ps 10:1–18 Why do You stand afar off, O LORD? *Why do* You hide in times of trouble? **2** The wicked in *his* pride persecutes the poor; Let them be caught in the plots which they have devised. **3** For the wicked boasts of his heart's desire; He blesses the greedy *and* renounces the LORD. **4** The wicked in his proud countenance does not seek *God; God is* in none of his thoughts. **5** His ways are always prospering; Your judgments *are* far above, out of his sight; *As for* all his enemies, he sneers at them. **6** He has said in his heart, "I shall not be moved; I shall never be in adversity." **7** His mouth is full of cursing and deceit and oppression; Under his tongue *is* trouble and iniquity. **8** He sits in the lurking places of the villages; In the secret places he murders the innocent; His eyes are secretly fixed on the helpless. **9** He lies in wait secretly, as a lion in his den; He lies in wait to catch the poor; He catches the poor when he draws him into his net. **10** So he crouches, he lies low, That the helpless may fall by his strength. **11** He has said in his heart, "God has forgotten; He hides His face; He will never see." **12** Arise, O LORD! O God, lift up Your hand! Do not forget the humble. **13** Why do the wicked renounce God? He has said in his heart, "You will not require *an account.*" **14** But You have seen, for You observe trouble and grief, To repay *it* by Your hand. The helpless commits himself to You; You are the helper of the fatherless. **15** Break the arm of the wicked and the evil *man;* Seek out his wickedness *until* You find none. **16** The LORD *is* King forever and ever; The nations have perished out of His land. **17** LORD, You have heard the desire of the humble; You will prepare their heart; You will cause Your ear to hear, **18** To do justice to the fatherless and the oppressed, That the man of the earth may oppress no more.

Those who practice, will suffer.

Prov 13:23 Much food *is in* the fallow *ground* of the poor, And for lack of justice there is waste.

Mic 3:1–4 And I said: "Hear now, O heads of Jacob, And you rulers of the house of Israel: *Is it* not for you to know justice? **2** You who hate good and love evil; Who strip the skin from *My* people, And the flesh from their bones; **3** Who also eat the flesh of My people, Flay their skin from them, Break their bones, And chop *them* in pieces Like *meat* for the pot, Like flesh in the caldron." **4** Then they will cry to the LORD, But He will not hear them; He will even hide His face from them at that time, Because they have been evil in their deeds.

Mic 6:9–16 The LORD's voice cries to the city— Wisdom shall see Your name: "Hear the rod! Who has appointed it? **10** Are there yet the treasures of wickedness In the house of the wicked, And the short measure *that is* an abomination? **11** Shall I count pure *those* with the wicked scales, And with the bag of deceitful weights? **12** For her rich men are full of violence, Her inhabitants have spoken lies, And their tongue is deceitful in their mouth. **13** "Therefore I will also make *you* sick by striking you, By making *you* desolate because of your sins. **14** You shall eat, but not be satisfied; Hunger *shall be* in your midst. You may carry *some* away, but shall not save *them;* And what you do rescue I will give over to the sword. **15** "You shall sow, but not reap; You shall tread the olives, but not anoint yourselves with oil; And *make* sweet wine, but not drink wine. **16** For the statutes of Omri are kept; All the works of Ahab's house *are done;* And you walk in their counsels, That I may make you a desolation, And your inhabitants a hissing. Therefore you shall bear the reproach of My people."

Mal 3:5 And I will come near you for judgment; I will be a swift witness Against sorcerers, Against adulterers, Against perjurers, Against those who exploit wage earners and widows and orphans, And against those who turn away an alien— Because they do not fear Me," Says the LORD of hosts.

James 5:1–6 Come now, *you* rich, weep and howl for your miseries that are coming upon *you!* **2** Your riches are corrupted, and your garments are moth-eaten.

3 Your gold and silver are corroded, and their corrosion will be a witness against you and will eat your flesh like fire. You have heaped up treasure in the last days. **4** Indeed the wages of the laborers who mowed your fields, which you kept back by fraud, cry out; and the cries of the reapers have reached the ears of the Lord of Sabaoth. **5** You have lived on the earth in pleasure and luxury; you have fattened your hearts as in a day of slaughter. **6** You have condemned, you have murdered the just; he does not resist you.

Cf. Matt 21:12; Mark 3:5; John 2:15

Brings a curse.

Deut 27:17 'Cursed *is* the one who moves his neighbor's landmark.' "And all the people shall say, 'Amen!'

Deut 27:19 'Cursed *is* the one who perverts the justice due the stranger, the fatherless, and widow.' "And all the people shall say, 'Amen!'

A bad example leads to.

Ex 23:2 You shall not follow a crowd to do evil; nor shall you testify in a dispute so as to turn aside after many to pervert *justice.*

Intemperance leads to.

Prov 31:5 Lest they drink and forget the law, And pervert the justice of all the afflicted.

Covetousness leads to.

Jer 6:13 "Because from the least of them even to the greatest of them, Everyone *is* given to covetousness; And from the prophet even to the priest, Everyone deals falsely.

Ezek 22:12 In you they take bribes to shed blood; you take usury and increase; you have made profit from your neighbors by extortion, and have forgotten Me," says the Lord GOD.

Mic 2:2 They covet fields and take *them* by violence, Also houses, and seize *them.* So they oppress a man and his house, A man and his inheritance.

Believers should

Hate.

Prov 29:27 An unjust man *is* an abomination to the righteous, And *he who is* upright in the way *is* an abomination to the wicked.

Testify against.

Ps 58:1–2 Do you indeed speak righteousness, you silent ones? Do you judge uprightly, you sons of men? **2** No, in heart you work wickedness; You weigh out the violence of your hands in the earth.

Mic 3:8–9 But truly I am full of power by the Spirit of the LORD, And of justice and might, To declare to Jacob his transgression And to Israel his sin. **9** Now hear this, You heads of the house of Jacob And rulers of the house of Israel, Who abhor justice And pervert all equity,

Bear, patiently.

1 Cor 6:7 Now therefore, it is already an utter failure for you that you go to law against one another. Why do you not rather accept wrong? Why do you not rather *let yourselves* be cheated?

Take no vengeance for.

Matt 5:39 But I tell you not to resist an evil person. But whoever slaps you on your right cheek, turn the other to him also.

The wicked,

Their dealings with.

Is 26:10 Let grace be shown to the wicked, *Yet* he will not learn righteousness; In the land of uprightness he will deal unjustly, And will not behold the majesty of the LORD.

Judge with.

Ps 82:2 How long will you judge unjustly, And show partiality to the wicked? Selah

Eccl 3:16 Moreover I saw under the sun: *In* the place of judgment, Wickedness *was* there; And *in* the place of righteousness, Iniquity *was* there.

Hab 1:4 Therefore the law is powerless, And justice never goes forth. For the wicked surround the righteous; Therefore perverse judgment proceeds.

Practice, without shame.

Jer 6:13 "Because from the least of them even to the greatest of them, Everyone *is* given to covetousness; And from the prophet even to the priest, Everyone deals falsely.

Jer 6:15 Were they ashamed when they had committed abomination? No! They were not at all ashamed; Nor did they know how to blush. Therefore they shall fall among those who fall; At the time I punish them, They shall be cast down," says the LORD.

Zeph 3:5 The LORD *is* righteous in her midst, He will do no unrighteousness. Every morning He brings His justice to light; He never fails, But the unjust knows no shame.

Punishment of.

Prov 11:7 When a wicked man dies, *his* expectation will perish, And the hope of the unjust perishes.

Prov 28:8 One who increases his possessions by usury and extortion Gathers it for him who will pity the poor.

Amos 5:11–12 Therefore, because you tread down the poor And take grain taxes from him, Though you have built houses of hewn stone, Yet you shall not dwell in them; You have planted pleasant vineyards, But you shall not drink wine from them. **12** For I know your manifold transgressions And your mighty sins: Afflicting the just *and* taking bribes; Diverting the poor *from justice* at the gate.

Amos 8:5 Saying: "When will the New Moon be past, That we may sell grain? And the Sabbath, That we may trade wheat? Making the ephah small and the shekel large, Falsifying the scales by deceit,

Amos 8:8 Shall the land not tremble for this, And everyone mourn who dwells in it? All of it shall swell like the River, Heave and subside Like the River of Egypt.

1 Thess 4:6 that no one should take advantage of and defraud his brother in this matter, because the Lord *is* the avenger of all such, as we also forewarned you and testified.

Illustrated by

Potiphar.

Gen 39:20 Then Joseph's master took him and put him into the prison, a place where the king's prisoners *were* confined. And he was there in the prison.

The sons of Samuel.

1 Sam 8:3 But his sons did not walk in his ways; they turned aside after dishonest gain, took bribes, and perverted justice.

Ahab.

1 Kin 21:10 and seat two men, scoundrels, before him to bear witness against him, saying, You have blasphemed God and the king. *Then* take him out, and stone him, that he may die.

1 Kin 21:15–16 And it came to pass, when Jezebel heard that Naboth had been stoned and was dead, that Jezebel said to Ahab, "Arise, take possession of the vineyard of Naboth the Jezreelite, which he refused to give you for money; for Naboth is not alive, but dead." **16** So it was, when Ahab heard that Naboth was dead, that Ahab got up and went down to take possession of the vineyard of Naboth the Jezreelite.

The Jews.

Is 59:14 Justice is turned back, And righteousness stands afar off; For truth is fallen in the street, And equity cannot enter.

The governors, etc., of Babylon.

Dan 6:4 So the governors and satraps sought to find *some* charge against Daniel concerning the kingdom; but they could find no charge or fault, because he *was* faithful; nor was there any error or fault found in him.

Judas Iscariot.

Matt 27:4 saying, "I have sinned by betraying innocent blood." And they said, "What *is that* to us? You see *to it!*"

Pilate.

Matt 27:24–26 When Pilate saw that he could not prevail at all, but rather *that* a tumult was rising, he took water and washed *his* hands before the multitude, saying, "I am innocent of the blood of this just Person. You see *to it.*" **25** And all the people answered and said, "His blood *be* on us and on our children." **26** Then he released Barabbas to them; and when he had scourged Jesus, he delivered *Him* to be crucified.

The priests, etc.

Acts 4:1–3 Now as they spoke to the people, the priests, the captain of the temple, and the Sadducees came upon them, **2** being greatly disturbed that they taught the people and preached in Jesus the resurrection from the dead. **3** And they laid hands on them, and put *them* in custody until the next day, for it was already evening.

Felix.

Acts 24:27 But after two years Porcius Festus succeeded Felix; and Felix, wanting to do the Jews a favor, left Paul bound.

INSECTS

Created by God.

Gen 1:24–25 Then God said, "Let the earth bring forth the living creature according to its kind: cattle and creeping thing and beast of the earth, *each* according to its kind"; and it was so. **25** And God made the beast of the earth according to its kind, cattle according to its kind, and everything that creeps on the earth according to its kind. And God saw that *it was* good.

Divided into

Clean and fit for food.

Lev 11:21–22 Yet these you may eat of every flying insect that creeps on *all* fours: those which have jointed legs above their feet with which to leap on the earth. **22** These you may eat: the locust after its kind, the destroying locust after its kind, the cricket after its kind, and the grasshopper after its kind.

Unclean and abominable.

Lev 11:23–24 But all *other* flying insects which have four feet *shall be* an abomination to you. **24** 'By these you shall become unclean; whoever touches the carcass of any of them shall be unclean until evening;

Those mentioned in Scripture,

Ant.

Prov 6:6 Go to the ant, you sluggard! Consider her ways and be wise,

Prov 30:25 The ants *are* a people not strong, Yet they prepare their food in the summer;

Bee.

Judg 14:8 After some time, when he returned to get her, he turned aside to see the carcass of the lion. And behold, a swarm of bees and honey *were* in the carcass of the lion.

Ps 118:12 They surrounded me like bees; They were quenched like a fire of thorns; For in the name of the LORD I will destroy them.

Is 7:18 And it shall come to pass in that day *That* the LORD will whistle for the fly That *is* in the farthest part of the rivers of Egypt, And for the bee that *is* in the land of Assyria.

Caterpillar.

Ps 78:46 He also gave their crops to the caterpillar, And their labor to the locust.

Is 33:4 And Your plunder shall be gathered *Like* the gathering of the caterpillar; As the running to and fro of locusts, He shall run upon them.

Swarming locust.

Joel 1:4 What the chewing locust left, the swarming locust has eaten; What the swarming locust left, the crawling locust has eaten; And what the crawling locust left, the consuming locust has eaten.

Nah 3:15–16 There the fire will devour you, The sword will cut you off; It will eat you up like a locust. Make yourself many—like the locust! Make yourself many— like the *swarming* locusts! **16** You have multiplied your merchants more than the stars of heaven. The locust plunders and flies away.

Cricket.

Lev 11:22 These you may eat: the locust after its kind, the destroying locust after its kind, the cricket after its kind, and the grasshopper after its kind.

Flea.

1 Sam 24:14 After whom has the king of Israel come out? Whom do you pursue? A dead dog? A flea?

Fly.

Ex 8:22 And in that day I will set apart the land of Goshen, in which My people dwell, that no swarms of *flies* shall be there, in order that you may know that I *am* the LORD in the midst of the land.

Eccl 10:1 Dead flies putrefy the perfumer's ointment And cause it to give off a foul odor; So does a little folly to one respected for wisdom *and* honor.

Is 7:18 And it shall come to pass in that day *That* the LORD will whistle for the fly That *is* in the farthest part of the rivers of Egypt, And for the bee that *is* in the land of Assyria.

Gnat.

Matt 23:24 Blind guides, who strain out a gnat and swallow a camel!

Grasshopper.

Lev 11:22 These you may eat: the locust after its kind, the destroying locust after its kind, the cricket after its kind, and the grasshopper after its kind.

Hornet.

Deut 7:20 Moreover the LORD your God will send the hornet among them until those who are left, who hide themselves from you, are destroyed.

Locust.

Ex 10:12–13 Then the LORD said to Moses, "Stretch out your hand over the land of Egypt for the locusts, that they may come upon the land of Egypt, and eat every herb of the land—all that the hail has left." **13** So Moses stretched out his rod over the land of Egypt, and the LORD brought an east wind on the land all that day and all *that* night. When it was morning, the east wind brought the locusts.

Judg 6:5 For they would come up with their livestock and their tents, coming in as numerous as locusts; both they and their camels were without number; and they would enter the land to destroy it.

Job 39:20 Can you frighten him like a locust? His majestic snorting strikes terror.

Chewing locust.

Joel 1:4 What the chewing locust left, the swarming locust has eaten; What the swarming locust left, the crawling locust has eaten; And what the crawling locust left, the consuming locust has eaten.

Amos 4:9 "I blasted you with blight and mildew. When your gardens increased, Your vineyards, Your fig trees, And your olive trees, The locust devoured *them*; Yet you have not returned to Me," Says the LORD.

Lice.

Ex 8:16 So the LORD said to Moses, "Say to Aaron, 'Stretch out your rod, and strike the dust of the land, so that it may become lice throughout all the land of Egypt.' "

Ps 105:31 He spoke, and there came swarms of flies, *And* lice in all their territory.

Maggot.

Ex 16:20 Notwithstanding they did not heed Moses. But some of them left part of it until morning, and it bred worms and stank. And Moses was angry with them.

Job 25:6 How much less man, *who is* a maggot, And a son of man, *who is* a worm?"

Moth.

Job 4:19 How much more those who dwell in houses of clay, Whose foundation is in the dust, *Who* are crushed before a moth?

Job 27:18 He builds his house like a moth, Like a booth *which* a watchman makes.

Is 50:9 Surely the Lord GOD will help Me; Who *is he who* will condemn Me? Indeed they will all grow old like a garment; The moth will eat them up.

Spider.

Job 8:14 Whose confidence shall be cut off, And whose trust *is* a spider's web.

Prov 30:28 The spider skillfully grasps with its hands, And it is in kings' palaces.

Fed by God.

Ps 104:25 This great and wide sea, In which *are* innumerable teeming things, Living things both small and great.

Ps 104:27 These all wait for You, That You may give *them* their food in due season.

Ps 145:9 The LORD *is* good to all, And His tender mercies *are* over all His works.

Ps 145:15 The eyes of all look expectantly to You, And You give them their food in due season.

INTEGRITY

Those who have it are secure.

Prov 10:9 He who walks with integrity walks securely, But he who perverts his ways will become known.

Characteristic of a righteous person.

Prov 20:7 The righteous *man* walks in his integrity; His children *are* blessed after him.

Reflects a commitment to doctrine.

Titus 2:7 in all things showing yourself *to be* a pattern of good works; in doctrine *showing* integrity, reverence, incorruptibility,

God upholds, in His people.

Ps 41:12 As for me, You uphold me in my integrity, And set me before Your face forever.

A claim of innocence.

Ps 7:8 The LORD shall judge the peoples; Judge me, O LORD, according to my righteousness, And according to my integrity within me.

Ps 26:1 Vindicate me, O LORD, For I have walked in my integrity. I have also trusted in the LORD; I shall not slip.

It is better than wealth.

Prov 19:1 Better *is* the poor who walks in his integrity Than *one who is* perverse in his lips, and is a fool.

Exemplified by Job.

Job 2:3 Then the LORD said to Satan, "Have you considered My servant Job, that *there is* none like him on the earth, a blameless and upright man, one who fears God and shuns evil? And still he holds fast to his integrity, although you incited Me against him, to destroy him without cause."

Job's wife could not understand his.

Job 2:9 Then his wife said to him, "Do you still hold fast to your integrity? Curse God and die!"

INTEREST

The lending of money or other property for increase.

Lev 25:37 You shall not lend him your money for usury, nor lend him your food at a profit.

Those enriched by unlawful, not allowed to enjoy their gain.

Prov 28:8 One who increases his possessions by usury and extortion Gathers it for him who will pity the poor.

The curse attending the giving or receiving of unlawful, alluded to.

Jer 15:10 Woe is me, my mother, That you have borne me, A man of strife and a man of contention to the whole earth! I have neither lent for interest, Nor have men lent to me for interest. Every one of them curses me.

The Jews

Forbidden to take, from their brothers.

Deut 23:19 "You shall not charge interest to your brother—interest on money *or* food *or* anything that is lent out at interest.

Ps 15:5 He *who* does not put out his money at usury, Nor does he take a bribe against the innocent. He who does these *things* shall never be moved.

Ezek 18:8–9 If he has not exacted usury Nor taken any increase, *But* has withdrawn his hand from iniquity *And* executed true judgment between man and man; 9 *If* he has walked in My statutes And kept My judgments faithfully— He *is* just; He shall surely live!" Says the Lord GOD.

Forbidden to take, from their brothers, especially when poor.

Ex 22:25 "If you lend money to *any of* My people *who are* poor among you, you shall not be like a moneylender to him; you shall not charge him interest.

Lev 25:35–37 'If one of your brethren becomes poor, and falls into poverty among you, then you shall help him, like a stranger or a sojourner, that he may live with you. 36 Take no usury or interest from him; but fear your God, that your brother may live with you. 37 You shall not lend him your money for usury, nor lend him your food at a profit.

Often guilty of taking.

Neh 5:6–7 And I became very angry when I heard their outcry and these words. 7 After serious thought, I rebuked the nobles and rulers, and said to them, "Each of you is exacting usury from his brother." So I called a great assembly against them.

Ezek 22:12 In you they take bribes to shed blood; you take usury and increase; you have made profit from your neighbors by extortion, and have forgotten Me," says the Lord GOD.

Required to restore.

Neh 5:9–13 Then I said, "What you are doing *is* not good. Should you not walk in the fear of our God because of the reproach of the nations, our enemies? 10 I also, *with* my brethren and my servants, am lending them money and grain. Please, let us stop this usury! 11 Restore now to them, even this day, their lands, their vineyards, their olive groves, and their houses, also a hundredth of the money and the grain, the new wine and the oil, that you have charged them." 12 So they said, "We will restore *it*, and will require nothing from them; we will do as you say." Then I called the priests, and required an oath from them that they would do according to this promise.

13 Then I shook out the fold of my garment and said, "So may God shake out each man from his house, and from his property, who does not perform this promise. Even thus may he be shaken out and emptied." And all the assembly said, "Amen!" and praised the LORD. Then the people did according to this promise.

Allowed to take, from strangers.

Deut 23:20 To a foreigner you may charge interest, but to your brother you shall not charge interest, that the LORD your God may bless you in all to which you set your hand in the land which you are entering to possess.

Judgments pronounced against those who exacted, unlawful.

Is 24:1–2 Behold, the LORD makes the earth empty and makes it waste, Distorts its surface And scatters abroad its inhabitants. **2** And it shall be: As with the people, so with the priest; As with the servant, so with his master; As with the maid, so with her mistress; As with the buyer, so with the seller; As with the lender, so with the borrower; As with the creditor, so with the debtor.

Ezek 18:13 If he has exacted usury Or taken increase—Shall he then live? He shall not live! If he has done any of these abominations, He shall surely die; His blood shall be upon him.

Illustrative of the improvement of God-given talents.

Matt 25:27 So you ought to have deposited my money with the bankers, and at my coming I would have received back my own with interest.

Luke 19:23 Why then did you not put my money in the bank, that at my coming I might have collected it with interest?'

IRON (MINERAL AND METAL)

Dug out of the earth.

Job 28:2 Iron is taken from the earth, And copper *is* smelted *from* ore.

Described as

Strong and durable.

Job 40:18 His bones *are like* beams of bronze, His ribs like bars of iron.

Dan 2:40 And the fourth kingdom shall be as strong as iron, inasmuch as iron breaks in pieces and shatters everything; and like iron that crushes, *that kingdom* will break in pieces and crush all the others.

Fusible.

Ezek 22:20 *As men* gather silver, bronze, iron, lead, and tin into the midst of a furnace, to blow fire on it, to melt *it;* so I will gather *you* in My anger and in My fury, and I will leave *you there* and melt you.

Malleable.

Is 2:4 He shall judge between the nations, And rebuke many people; They shall beat their swords into plowshares, And their spears into pruning hooks; Nation shall not lift up sword against nation, Neither shall they learn war anymore.

Of small comparative value.

Is 60:17 "Instead of bronze I will bring gold, Instead of iron I will bring silver, Instead of wood, bronze, And instead of stones, iron. I will also make your officers peace, And your magistrates righteousness.

The land of Canaan abounded with.

Deut 8:9 a land in which you will eat bread without scarcity, in which you will lack nothing; a land whose stones *are* iron and out of whose hills you can dig copper.

Deut 33:25 Your sandals *shall be* iron and bronze; As your days, *so shall* your strength *be.*

From the north, hardest and best.

Jer 15:12 Can anyone break iron, The northern iron and the bronze?

Used from the earliest age.

Gen 4:22 And as for Zillah, she also bore Tubal-Cain, an instructor of every craftsman in bronze and iron. And the sister of Tubal-Cain *was* Naamah.

Made into

Armor.

2 Sam 23:7 But the man *who* touches them Must be armed with iron and the shaft of a spear, And they shall be utterly burned with fire in *their* place."

Rev 9:9 And they had breastplates like breastplates of iron, and the sound of their wings *was* like the sound of chariots with many horses running into battle.

Weapons of war.

1 Sam 13:19 Now there was no blacksmith to be found throughout all the land of Israel, for the Philistines said, "Lest the Hebrews make swords or spears."

1 Sam 17:7 Now the staff of his spear *was* like a weaver's beam, and his iron spearhead *weighed* six hundred shekels; and a shield-bearer went before him.

Job 20:24 He will flee from the iron weapon; A bronze bow will pierce him through.

Chariots.

Judg 4:3 And the children of Israel cried out to the LORD; for Jabin had nine hundred chariots of iron, and for twenty years he had harshly oppressed the children of Israel.

Implements for farming and industry.

1 Sam 13:20–21 But all the Israelites would go down to the Philistines to sharpen each man's plowshare, his mattock, his ax, and his sickle; **21** and the charge for a sharpening was a pim for the plowshares, the mattocks, the forks, and the axes, and to set the points of the goads.

2 Sam 12:31 And he brought out the people who *were* in it, and put *them to work* with saws and iron picks and iron axes, and made them cross over to the brick works. So he did to all the cities of the people of Ammon. Then David and all the people returned to Jerusalem.

Tools for artificers.

Josh 8:31 as Moses the servant of the LORD had commanded the children of Israel, as it is written in the Book of the Law of Moses: "an altar of whole stones over which no man has wielded an iron *tool.*" And they offered on it burnt offerings to the LORD, and sacrificed peace offerings.

1 Kin 6:7 And the temple, when it was being built, was built with stone finished at the quarry, so that no hammer or chisel *or* any iron tool was heard in the temple while it was being built.

Engraving tools.

Job 19:24 That they were engraved on a rock With an iron pen and lead, forever!

Jer 17:1 "The sin of Judah *is* written with a pen of iron; With the point of a diamond *it is* engraved On the tablet of their heart, And on the horns of your altars,

Gates.

Acts 12:10 When they were past the first and the second guard posts, they came to the iron gate that leads to the city, which opened to them of its own accord; and they went out and went down one street, and immediately the angel departed from him.

Nails and hinges.

1 Chr 22:3 And David prepared iron in abundance for the nails of the doors of the gates and for the joints, and bronze in abundance beyond measure,

Bars.

Ps 107:16 For He has broken the gates of bronze, And cut the bars of iron in two.

Is 45:2 'I will go before you And make the crooked places straight; I will break in pieces the gates of bronze And cut the bars of iron.

Fetters.

Ps 105:18 They hurt his feet with fetters, He was laid in irons.

Ps 149:8 To bind their kings with chains, And their nobles with fetters of iron;

Yokes.

Deut 28:48 therefore you shall serve your enemies, whom the LORD will send against you, in hunger, in thirst, in nakedness, and in need of everything; and He will put a yoke of iron on your neck until He has destroyed you.

Jer 28:13–14 "Go and tell Hananiah, saying, 'Thus says the LORD: "You have broken the yokes of wood, but you have made in their place yokes of iron." **14** For thus says the LORD of hosts, the God of Israel: "I have put a yoke of iron on the neck of all these nations, that they may serve Nebuchadnezzar king of Babylon; and they shall serve him. I have given him the beasts of the field also." ' "

Idols.

Dan 5:4 They drank wine, and praised the gods of gold and silver, bronze and iron, wood and stone.

Dan 5:23 And you have lifted yourself up against the Lord of heaven. They have brought the vessels of His house before you, and you and your lords, your wives and your concubines, have drunk wine from them. And you have praised the gods of silver and gold, bronze and iron, wood and stone, which do not see or hear or know; and the God who *holds* your breath in His hand and owns all your ways, you have not glorified.

Bedsteads.

Deut 3:11 "For only Og king of Bashan remained of the remnant of the giants. Indeed his bedstead *was* an iron bedstead. (*Is* it not in Rabbah of the people of Ammon?) Nine cubits *is* its length and four cubits its width, according to the standard cubit.

Pillars.

Jer 1:18 For behold, I have made you this day A fortified city and an iron pillar, And bronze walls against the whole land— Against the kings of Judah, Against its princes, Against its priests, And against the people of the land.

Rods.

Ps 2:9 You shall break them with a rod of iron; You shall dash them to pieces like a potter's vessel.' "

Rev 2:27 '*He shall rule them with a rod of iron; They shall be dashed to pieces like the potter's vessels'*— as I also have received from My Father;

Sharpens itself.

Prov 27:17 *As* iron sharpens iron, So a man sharpens the countenance of his friend.

Working in, a trade.

1 Sam 13:19 Now there was no blacksmith to be found throughout all the land of Israel, for the Philistines said, "Lest the Hebrews make swords or spears."

2 Chr 2:7 Therefore send me at once a man skillful to work in gold and silver, in bronze and iron, in purple and crimson and blue, who has skill to engrave with the skillful men who are with me in Judah and Jerusalem, whom David my father provided.

2 Chr 2:14 (the son of a woman of the daughters of Dan, and his father was a man of Tyre), skilled to work in gold and silver, bronze and iron, stone and wood, purple and blue, fine linen and crimson, and to make any engraving and to accomplish any plan which may be given to him, with your skillful men and with the skillful men of my lord David your father.

An article of commerce.

Ezek 27:12 "Tarshish *was* your merchant because of your many luxury goods. They gave you silver, iron, tin, and lead for your goods.

Ezek 27:19 Dan and Javan paid for your wares, traversing back and forth. Wrought iron, cassia, and cane were among your merchandise.

Rev 18:12 merchandise of gold and silver, precious stones and pearls, fine linen and purple, silk and scarlet, every kind of citron wood, every kind of object of ivory, every kind of object of most precious wood, bronze, iron, and marble;

Great quantity of, provided for the temple.

1 Chr 22:3 And David prepared iron in abundance for the nails of the doors of the gates and for the joints, and bronze in abundance beyond measure,

1 Chr 22:14 Indeed I have taken much trouble to prepare for the house of the LORD one hundred thousand talents of gold and one million talents of silver, and bronze and iron beyond measure, for it is so abundant. I have prepared timber and stone also, and you may add to them.

1 Chr 22:16 Of gold and silver and bronze and iron *there* is no limit. Arise and begin working, and the LORD be with you."

1 Chr 29:2 Now for the house of my God I have prepared with all my might: gold for *things to be made of* gold, silver for *things of* silver, bronze for *things of* bronze, iron for *things of* iron, wood for *things of* wood, onyx stones, *stones* to be set, glistening stones of various colors, all kinds of precious stones, and marble slabs in abundance.

Taken in war, often dedicated to God.

Josh 6:19 But all the silver and gold, and vessels of bronze and iron, *are* consecrated to the LORD; they shall come into the treasury of the LORD."

Josh 6:24 But they burned the city and all that *was* in it with fire. Only the silver and gold, and the vessels of bronze and iron, they put into the treasury of the house of the LORD.

Mode of purifying, taken in war.

Num 31:21–23 Then Eleazar the priest said to the men of war who had gone to the battle, "This *is* the ordinance of the law which the LORD commanded Moses: **22** "Only the gold, the silver, the bronze, the iron, the tin, and the lead, **23** everything that can endure fire, you shall put through the fire, and it shall be clean; and it shall be purified with the water of purification. But all that cannot endure fire you shall put through water.

Miraculously made to float.

2 Kin 6:5–6 But as one was cutting down a tree, the iron *ax head* fell into the water; and he cried out and said, "Alas, master! For it was borrowed." **6** So the man of God said, "Where did it fall?" And he showed him the place. So he cut off a stick, and threw *it* in there; and he made the iron float.

Illustrative of

Strength.

Dan 2:33 its legs of iron, its feet partly of iron and partly of clay.

Dan 2:40 And the fourth kingdom shall be as strong as iron, inasmuch as iron breaks in pieces and shatters everything; and like iron that crushes, *that kingdom* will break in pieces and crush all the others.

Stubbornness.

Is 48:4 Because I knew that you *were* obstinate, And your neck *was* an iron sinew, And your brow bronze,

Severe affliction.

Deut 4:20 But the LORD has taken you and brought you out of the iron furnace, out of Egypt, to be His people, an inheritance, as you are this day.

Ps 107:10 Those who sat in darkness and in the shadow of death, Bound in affliction and irons—

Hard, barren soil.

Deut 28:23 And your heavens which *are* over your head shall be bronze, and the earth which is under you *shall be* iron.

Severe exercise of power.

Ps 2:9 You shall break them with a rod of iron; You shall dash them to pieces like a potter's vessel.' "

Rev 2:27 'He shall rule them *with a rod of iron; They shall be dashed to pieces like the potter's vessels'*— as I also have received from My Father;

(Seared with) insensibility of conscience.

1 Tim 4:2 speaking lies in hypocrisy, having their own conscience seared with a hot iron,

ISAAC. *SEE ALSO* ABRAHAM

Birth of, promised.

Gen 17:16–21 And I will bless her and also give you a son by her; then I will bless her, and she shall be *a mother of* nations; kings of peoples shall be from her." **17** Then Abraham fell on his face and laughed, and said in his heart, "Shall *a child* be born to a man who is one hundred years old? And shall Sarah, who is ninety years old, bear *a child?*" **18** And Abraham said to God, "Oh, that Ishmael might live before You!" **19** Then God said: "No, Sarah your wife shall bear you a son, and you shall call his name Isaac; I will establish My covenant with him for an everlasting covenant, *and* with his descendants after him. **20** And as for Ishmael, I have heard you. Behold, I have blessed him, and will make him fruitful, and will multiply him exceedingly. He shall beget twelve princes, and I will make him a great nation. **21** But My covenant I will establish with Isaac, whom Sarah shall bear to you at this set time next year."

Cf. Gal 4:22–23

His birth and circumcision.

Gen 21:1–8 And the LORD visited Sarah as He had said, and the LORD did for Sarah as He had spoken. **2** For Sarah conceived and bore Abraham a son in his old age, at the set time of which God had spoken to him. **3** And Abraham called the name of his son who was born to him—whom Sarah bore to him—Isaac. **4** Then Abraham circumcised his son Isaac when he was eight days old, as God had commanded him. **5** Now Abraham was one hundred years old when his son Isaac was born to him. **6** And Sarah said, "God has made me laugh, *and* all who hear will laugh with me." **7** She also said, "Who would have said to Abraham that Sarah would nurse children? For I have borne *him* a son in his old age." **8** So the child grew and was weaned. And Abraham made a great feast on the same day that Isaac was weaned.

Offered up as sacrifice, but spared by God.
Gen 22:1–19

Received Rebekah as his wife.

Gen 24:61–67 Then Rebekah and her maids arose, and they rode on the camels and followed the man. So the servant took Rebekah and departed. **62** Now Isaac came from the way of Beer Lahai Roi, for he dwelt in the South. **63** And Isaac went out to meditate in the field in the evening; and he lifted his eyes and looked, and there, the camels *were* coming. **64** Then Rebekah lifted her eyes, and when she saw Isaac she dismounted from her camel; **65** for she had said to the servant, "Who *is* this man walking in the field to meet us?" The servant said, "It *is* my master." So she took a veil and covered herself. **66** And the servant told Isaac all the things that he had done. **67** Then Isaac brought her into his mother Sarah's tent; and he took Rebekah and she became his wife, and he loved her. So Isaac was comforted after his mother's *death.*

Covenant confirmed to, by God.

Gen 26:2–5 Then the LORD appeared to him and said: "Do not go down to Egypt; live in the land of which I shall tell you. **3** Dwell in this land, and I will be with you and bless you; for to you and your descendants

I give all these lands, and I will perform the oath which I swore to Abraham your father. 4 And I will make your descendants multiply as the stars of heaven; I will give to your descendants all these lands; and in your seed all the nations of the earth shall be blessed; 5 because Abraham obeyed My voice and kept My charge, My commandments, My statutes, and My laws."

Father of Esau and Jacob.

Gen 25:19–26 This *is* the genealogy of Isaac, Abraham's son. Abraham begot Isaac. 20 Isaac was forty years old when he took Rebekah as wife, the daughter of Bethuel the Syrian of Padan Aram, the sister of Laban the Syrian. 21 Now Isaac pleaded with the LORD for his wife, because she *was* barren; and the LORD granted his plea, and Rebekah his wife conceived. 22 But the children struggled together within her; and she said, "If *all is* well, why *am I like* this? " So she went to inquire of the LORD. 23 And the LORD said to her: "Two nations *are* in your womb, Two peoples shall be separated from your body; One people shall be stronger than the other, And the older shall serve the younger." 24 So when her days were fulfilled *for her* to give birth, indeed *there were* twins in her womb. 25 And the first came out red. *He was* like a hairy garment all over; so they called his name Esau. 26 Afterward his brother came out, and his hand took hold of Esau's heel; so his name was called Jacob. Isaac *was* sixty years old when she bore them.

Lied about Rebekah.

Gen 26:7–11 And the men of the place asked about his wife. And he said, "She *is* my sister"; for he was afraid to say, "*She is* my wife," *because he thought*, "lest the men of the place kill me for Rebekah, because she *is* beautiful to behold." 8 Now it came to pass, when he had been there a long time, that Abimelech king of the Philistines looked through a window, and saw, and there was Isaac, showing endearment to Rebekah his wife. 9 Then Abimelech called Isaac and said, "Quite obviously she *is* your wife; so how could you say, 'She *is* my sister'?" Isaac said to him, "Because I said, 'Lest I die on account of her.' " 10 And Abimelech said, "What *is* this you have done to us? One of the people might soon have lain with your wife, and you would have brought guilt on us." 11 So Abimelech charged all *his* people, saying, "He who touches this man or his wife shall surely be put to death."

Made agreement with Abimelech.

Gen 26:26–31 Then Abimelech came to him from Gerar with Ahuzzath, one of his friends, and Phichol the commander of his army. 27 And Isaac said to them, "Why have you come to me, since you hate me and have sent me away from you?" 28 But they said, "We have certainly seen that the LORD is with you. So we said, 'Let there now be an oath between us, between you and us; and let us make a covenant with you, 29 that you will do us no harm, since we have not touched you, and since we have done nothing to you but good and have sent you away in peace. You *are* now the blessed of the LORD.' " 30 So he made them a feast, and they ate and drank. 31 Then they arose early in the morning and swore an oath with one another; and Isaac sent them away, and they departed from him in peace.

Deceived by Jacob. Gen 27:1–25
Blessed his sons. Gen 27:26–40
Pattern for all believers.

Gal 4:28–31 Now we, brethren, as Isaac *was,* are children of promise. 29 But, as he who was born according to the flesh then persecuted him *who was born* according to the Spirit, even so *it is* now. 30 Nevertheless what does the Scripture say? *"Cast out the bondwoman and her son, for the son of the bondwoman shall not be heir with the son of the freewoman."* 31 So then, brethren, we are not children of the bondwoman but of the free.

Hero of faith.

Heb 11:9 By faith he dwelt in the land of promise as *in* a foreign country, dwelling in tents with Isaac and Jacob, the heirs with him of the same promise;

Heb 11:20 By faith Isaac blessed Jacob and Esau concerning things to come.

ISHMAELITES, THE
Descended from Abraham's son, Ishmael.

Gen 16:15–16 So Hagar bore Abram a son; and Abram named his son, whom Hagar bore, Ishmael. 16 Abram *was* eighty-six years old when Hagar bore Ishmael to Abram.

1 Chr 1:28 The sons of Abraham *were* Isaac and Ishmael.

Divided into twelve tribes.

Gen 25:16 These *were* the sons of Ishmael and these *were* their names, by their towns and their settlements, twelve princes according to their nations.

Heads of tribes.

Gen 25:13–15 And these *were* the names of the sons of Ishmael, by their names, according to their generations: The firstborn of Ishmael, Nebajoth; then Kedar, Adbeel, Mibsam, 14 Mishma, Dumah, Massa, 15 Hadar, Tema, Jetur, Naphish, and Kedemah.

1 Chr 1:29–31 These *are* their genealogies: The firstborn of Ishmael *was* Nebajoth; then Kedar, Adbeel, Mibsam, 30 Mishma, Dumah, Massa, Hadad, Tema, 31 Jetur, Naphish, and Kedemah. These *were* the sons of Ishmael.

Other names for
Hagrites.

1 Chr 5:10 Now in the days of Saul they made war with the Hagrites, who fell by their hand; and they dwelt in their tents throughout the entire *area* east of Gilead.

Ps 83:6 The tents of Edom and the Ishmaelites; Moab and the Hagrites;

Arabians.

Is 13:20 It will never be inhabited, Nor will it be settled from generation to generation; Nor will the Arabian pitch tents there, Nor will the shepherds make their sheepfolds there.

Original possessions of.

Gen 25:18 (They dwelt from Havilah as far as Shur, which *is* east of Egypt as you go toward Assyria.) He died in the presence of all his brethren.

Governed by kings.

Jer 25:24 all the kings of Arabia and all the kings of the mixed multitude who dwell in the desert;

Dwelt in tents.

Is 13:20 It will never be inhabited, Nor will it be settled from generation to generation; Nor will the Arabian pitch tents there, Nor will the shepherds make their sheepfolds there.

Rich in livestock.

1 Chr 5:21 Then they took away their livestock—fifty thousand of their camels, two hundred and fifty thousand of their sheep, and two thousand of their donkeys—also one hundred thousand of their men;

Wore ornaments of gold.

Judg 8:24 Then Gideon said to them, "I would like to make a request of you, that each of you would give me the earrings from his plunder." For they had golden earrings, because they *were* Ishmaelites.

Were the merchants of the east.

Gen 37:25 And they sat down to eat a meal. Then they lifted their eyes and looked, and there was a company of Ishmaelites, coming from Gilead with their camels, bearing spices, balm, and myrrh, on their way to carry *them* down to Egypt.

Ezek 27:20–21 Dedan *was* your merchant in saddlecloths for riding. **21** Arabia and all the princes of Kedar *were* your regular merchants. They traded with you in lambs, rams, and goats.

Traveled in large companies or caravans.

Gen 37:25 And they sat down to eat a meal. Then they lifted their eyes and looked, and there was a company of Ishmaelites, coming from Gilead with their camels, bearing spices, balm, and myrrh, on their way to carry *them* down to Egypt.

Job 6:19 The caravans of Tema look, The travelers of Sheba hope for them.

Waylaid and plundered travelers.

Jer 3:2 "Lift up your eyes to the desolate heights and see: Where have you not lain *with men?* By the road you have sat for them Like an Arabian in the wilderness; And you have polluted the land With your harlotries and your wickedness.

Often confederate against Israel.

Ps 83:6 The tents of Edom and the Ishmaelites; Moab and the Hagrites;

Overcome by

Gideon. **Judg 8:10–24**

Reubenites and Gadites.

1 Chr 5:10 Now in the days of Saul they made war with the Hagrites, who fell by their hand; and they dwelt in their tents throughout the entire *area* east of Gilead.

1 Chr 5:18–20 The sons of Reuben, the Gadites, and half the tribe of Manasseh *had* forty-four thousand seven hundred and sixty valiant men, men able to bear shield and sword, to shoot with the bow, and skillful in war, who went to war. **19** They made war with the Hagrites, Jetur, Naphish, and Nodab. **20** And they were helped against them, and the Hagrites were delivered into their hand, and all who *were* with them, for they cried out to God in the battle. He heeded their prayer, because they put their trust in Him.

Uzziah.

2 Chr 26:7 God helped him against the Philistines, against the Arabians who lived in Gur Baal, and against the Meunites.

Sent presents to Solomon.

1 Kin 10:15 besides *that* from the traveling merchants, from the income of traders, from all the kings of Arabia, and from the governors of the country.

2 Chr 9:14 besides *what* the traveling merchants and traders brought. And all the kings of Arabia and governors of the country brought gold and silver to Solomon.

Sent flocks to Jehoshaphat.

2 Chr 17:11 Also *some* of the Philistines brought Jehoshaphat presents and silver as tribute; and the Arabians brought him flocks, seven thousand seven hundred rams and seven thousand seven hundred male goats.

Predictions respecting

To be numerous.

Gen 16:10 Then the Angel of the LORD said to her, "I will multiply your descendants exceedingly, so that they shall not be counted for multitude."

Gen 17:20 And as for Ishmael, I have heard you. Behold, I have blessed him, and will make him fruitful, and will multiply him exceedingly. He shall beget twelve princes, and I will make him a great nation.

To be wild and warlike.

Gen 16:12 He shall be a wild man; His hand *shall be* against every man, And every man's hand against him. And he shall dwell in the presence of all his brethren."

To be divided into twelve tribes.

Gen 17:20 And as for Ishmael, I have heard you. Behold, I have blessed him, and will make him fruitful, and will multiply him exceedingly. He shall beget twelve princes, and I will make him a great nation.

To be a great nation.

Gen 21:13 Yet I will also make a nation of the son of the bondwoman, because he *is* your seed."

Gen 21:18 Arise, lift up the lad and hold him with your hand, for I will make him a great nation."

To be judged with the nations.

Jer 25:23–25 Dedan, Tema, Buz, and all *who are* in the farthest corners; **24** all the kings of Arabia and all the kings of the mixed multitude who dwell in the desert; **25** all the kings of Zimri, all the kings of Elam, and all the kings of the Medes;

Their glory, etc., to be diminished.

Is 21:13–17 The burden against Arabia. In the forest in Arabia you will lodge, O you traveling companies of Dedanites. **14** O inhabitants of the land of Tema, Bring water to him who is thirsty; With their bread they met him who fled. **15** For they fled from the swords, from the drawn sword, From the bent bow, and from the distress of war. **16** For thus the LORD has said to me: "Within a year, according to the year of a hired man, all the glory of Kedar will fail; **17** and the remainder of the number of archers, the mighty men of the people of Kedar, will be diminished; for the LORD God of Israel has spoken *it*."

Their submission to Christ.

Ps 72:10 The kings of Tarshish and of the isles Will bring presents; The kings of Sheba and Seba Will offer gifts.

Ps 72:15 And He shall live; And the gold of Sheba will be given to Him; Prayer also will be made for Him continually, *And* daily He shall be praised.

Probably preached to by Paul.

Gal 1:17 nor did I go up to Jerusalem to those *who were* apostles before me; but I went to Arabia, and returned again to Damascus.

ISRAEL, THE ARMIES OF

First mention of.

Ex 7:4 But Pharaoh will not heed you, so that I may lay My hand on Egypt and bring My armies *and* My people, the children of Israel, out of the land of Egypt by great judgments.

Called together by

Sound of trumpets.

Judg 3:27 And it happened, when he arrived, that he blew the trumpet in the mountains of Ephraim, and the children of Israel went down with him from the mountains; and he led them.

Judg 6:34 But the Spirit of the LORD came upon Gideon; then he blew the trumpet, and the Abiezrites gathered behind him.

Special messengers.

Judg 6:35 And he sent messengers throughout all Manasseh, who also gathered behind him. He also sent messengers to Asher, Zebulun, and Naphtali; and they came up to meet them.

2 Sam 20:14 And he went through all the tribes of Israel to Abel and Beth Maachah and all the Berites. So they were gathered together and also went after *Sheba.*

Extraordinary means.

Judg 19:29 When he entered his house he took a knife, laid hold of his concubine, and divided her into twelve pieces, limb by limb, and sent her throughout all the territory of Israel.

Judg 20:1 So all the children of Israel came out, from Dan to Beersheba, as well as from the land of Gilead, and the congregation gathered together as one man before the LORD at Mizpah.

1 Sam 11:7 So he took a yoke of oxen and cut them in pieces, and sent *them* throughout all the territory of Israel by the hands of messengers, saying, "Whoever does not go out with Saul and Samuel to battle, so it shall be done to his oxen." And the fear of the LORD fell on the people, and they came out with one consent.

Enrolled by the chief recruiting officer.

2 Kin 25:19 He also took out of the city an officer who had charge of the men of war, five men of the king's close associates who were found in the city, the chief recruiting officer of the army, who mustered the people of the land, and sixty men of the people of the land *who were* found in the city.

Called the armies of the living God.

1 Sam 17:26 Then David spoke to the men who stood by him, saying, "What shall be done for the man who kills this Philistine and takes away the reproach from Israel? For who *is* this uncircumcised Philistine, that he should defy the armies of the living God?"

Composed of infantry.

Num 11:21 And Moses said, "The people whom I *am* among *are* six hundred thousand men on foot; yet You have said, 'I will give them meat, that they may eat *for* a whole month.'

Judg 5:15 And the princes of Issachar *were* with Deborah; As Issachar, so *was* Barak Sent into the valley under his command; Among the divisions of Reuben *There were* great resolves of heart.

Horsemen and chariots introduced into, after David's reign.

1 Kin 1:5 Then Adonijah the son of Haggith exalted himself, saying, "I will be king"; and he prepared for himself chariots and horsemen, and fifty men to run before him.

1 Kin 4:26 Solomon had forty thousand stalls of horses for his chariots, and twelve thousand horsemen.

Divided into

Three divisions.

Judg 7:16 Then he divided the three hundred men *into* three companies, and he put a trumpet into every man's hand, with empty pitchers, and torches inside the pitchers.

1 Sam 11:11 So it was, on the next day, that Saul put the people in three companies; and they came into the midst of the camp in the morning watch, and killed Ammonites until the heat of the day. And it happened that those who survived were scattered, so that no two of them were left together.

Front and rear.

Josh 6:9 The armed men went before the priests who blew the trumpets, and the rear guard came after the ark, while *the priests* continued blowing the trumpets.

Companies of thousands, etc.

Num 31:14 But Moses was angry with the officers of the army, *with* the captains over thousands and captains over hundreds, who had come from the battle.

2 Kin 1:9 Then the king sent to him a captain of fifty with his fifty men. So he went up to him; and there he was, sitting on the top of a hill. And he spoke to him: "Man of God, the king has said, 'Come down!' "

2 Kin 1:11 Then he sent to him another captain of fifty with his fifty men. And he answered and said to him: "Man of God, thus has the king said, 'Come down quickly!' "

1 Chr 13:1 Then David consulted with the captains of thousands and hundreds, *and* with every leader.

1 Chr 27:1 And the children of Israel, according to their number, the heads of fathers' *houses,* the captains of thousands and hundreds and their officers, served the king in every matter of the *military* divisions. *These divisions* came in and went out month by month throughout all the months of the year, each division *having* twenty-four thousand.

Often led by the king in person.

1 Sam 8:20 that we also may be like all the nations, and that our king may judge us and go out before us and fight our battles."

1 Sam 15:4–5 So Saul gathered the people together and numbered them in Telaim, two hundred thousand foot soldiers and ten thousand men of Judah. **5** And Saul came to a city of Amalek, and lay in wait in the valley.

2 Sam 12:29 So David gathered all the people together and went to Rabbah, fought against it, and took it.

2 Kin 18:13 And in the fourteenth year of King Hezekiah, Sennacherib king of Assyria came up against all the fortified cities of Judah and took them.

2 Kin 25:1 Now it came to pass in the ninth year of his reign, in the tenth month, on the tenth *day* of the month, *that* Nebuchadnezzar king of Babylon and all his army came against Jerusalem and encamped against it; and they built a siege wall against it all around.

Cf. 1 Kin 22:1–53

Inferior officers of, appointed by

The chief officers.

Deut 20:9 And so it shall be, when the officers have finished speaking to the people, that they shall make captains of the armies to lead the people.

The king.

2 Sam 18:1 And David numbered the people who *were* with him, and set captains of thousands and captains of hundreds over them.

2 Chr 25:5 Moreover Amaziah gathered Judah together and set over them captains of thousands and captains of hundreds, according to *their* fathers' houses, throughout all Judah and Benjamin; and he numbered them from twenty years old and above, and found them to be three hundred thousand choice *men, able* to go to war, who could handle spear and shield.

The commander of the army.

2 Sam 24:2 So the king said to Joab the commander of the army who was with him, "Now go throughout all the tribes of Israel, from Dan to Beersheba, and count the people, that I may know the number of the people."

2 Kin 4:13 And he said to him, "Say now to her, 'Look, you have been concerned for us with all this care. What *can* I do for you? Do you want me to speak on your behalf to the king or to the commander of the army?' " She answered, "I dwell among my own people."

Persons eligible to serve in.

Num 1:2–3 "Take a census of all the congregation of the children of Israel, by their families, by their fathers' houses, according to the number of names, every male individually, **3** from twenty years old and above—all who *are able to* go to war in Israel. You and Aaron shall number them by their armies.

Persons exempted from serving in, those

Who had built a house.

Deut 20:5 "Then the officers shall speak to the people, saying: 'What man *is there* who has built a new house and has not dedicated it? Let him go and return to his house, lest he die in the battle and another man dedicate it.

Who had planted a vineyard.

Deut 20:6 Also what man *is there* who has planted a vineyard and has not eaten of it? Let him go and return to his house, lest he die in the battle and another man eat of it.

Who were lately betrothed.

Deut 20:7 And what man *is there* who is betrothed to a woman and has not married her? Let him go and return to his house, lest he die in the battle and another man marry her.'

Who were newly married.

Deut 24:5 "When a man has taken a new wife, he shall not go out to war or be charged with any business; he shall be free at home one year, and bring happiness to his wife whom he has taken.

Refusing to join, stigmatized.

Judg 5:15–17 And the princes of Issachar *were* with Deborah; As Issachar, so *was* Barak Sent into the valley under his command; Among the divisions of Reuben *There were* great resolves of heart. **16** Why did you sit among the sheepfolds, To hear the pipings for the flocks? The divisions of Reuben have great searchings of heart. **17** Gilead stayed beyond the Jordan, And why did Dan remain on ships? Asher continued at the seashore, And stayed by his inlets.

Refusing to join, often punished.

Judg 21:5 The children of Israel said, "Who *is there* among all the tribes of Israel who did not come up with the assembly to the LORD?" For they had made a great oath concerning anyone who had not come up to the LORD at Mizpah, saying, "He shall surely be put to death."

Judg 21:8–11 And they said, "What one *is there* from the tribes of Israel who did not come up to Mizpah to the LORD?" And, in fact, no one had come to the camp from Jabesh Gilead to the assembly. **9** For when the people were counted, indeed, not one of the inhabitants of Jabesh Gilead *was* there. **10** So the congregation sent out there twelve thousand of their most valiant men, and commanded them, saying, "Go and strike the inhabitants of Jabesh Gilead with the edge of the sword, including the women and children. **11** And this *is* the thing that you shall do: You shall utterly destroy every male, and every woman who has known a man intimately."

1 Sam 11:7 So he took a yoke of oxen and cut them in pieces, and sent *them* throughout all the territory of Israel by the hands of messengers, saying, "Whoever does not go out with Saul and Samuel to battle, so it shall be done to his oxen." And the fear of the LORD fell on the people, and they came out with one consent.

The fearful allowed to leave.

Deut 20:8 "The officers shall speak further to the people, and say, 'What man *is there who is* fearful and fainthearted? Let him go and return to his house, lest the heart of his brethren faint like his heart.'

Judg 7:3 Now therefore, proclaim in the hearing of the people, saying, 'Whoever *is* fearful and afraid, let him turn and depart at once from Mount Gilead.' " And twenty-two thousand of the people returned, and ten thousand remained.

Sometimes consisted of the whole nation.

Judg 20:11 So all the men of Israel were gathered against the city, united together as one man.

1 Sam 11:7 So he took a yoke of oxen and cut them in pieces, and sent *them* throughout all the territory of

Israel by the hands of messengers, saying, "Whoever does not go out with Saul and Samuel to battle, so it shall be done to his oxen." And the fear of the LORD fell on the people, and they came out with one consent.

Educated in the art of war.

Is 2:4 He shall judge between the nations, And rebuke many people; They shall beat their swords into plowshares, And their spears into pruning hooks; Nation shall not lift up sword against nation, Neither shall they learn war anymore.

Mic 4:3 He shall judge between many peoples, And rebuke strong nations afar off; They shall beat their swords into plowshares, And their spears into pruning hooks; Nation shall not lift up sword against nation, Neither shall they learn war anymore.

Often supplied with arms from public armories.

2 Chr 11:12 Also in every city *he put* shields and spears, and made them very strong, having Judah and Benjamin on his side.

2 Chr 26:14 Then Uzziah prepared for them, for the entire army, shields, spears, helmets, body armor, bows, and slings *to cast* stones.

Before going to war,

Were numbered and reviewed.

2 Sam 18:1–2 And David numbered the people who *were* with him, and set captains of thousands and captains of hundreds over them. **2** Then David sent out one third of the people under the hand of Joab, one third under the hand of Abishai the son of Zeruiah, Joab's brother, and one third under the hand of Ittai the Gittite. And the king said to the people, "I also will surely go out with you myself."

2 Sam 18:4 Then the king said to them, "Whatever seems best to you I will do." So the king stood beside the gate, and all the people went out by hundreds and by thousands.

Required to keep from iniquity.

Deut 23:9 "When the army goes out against your enemies, then keep yourself from every wicked thing.

Consulted the Lord.

Judg 1:1 Now after the death of Joshua it came to pass that the children of Israel asked the LORD, saying, "Who shall be first to go up for us against the Canaanites to fight against them?"

Judg 20:27–28 So the children of Israel inquired of the LORD (the ark of the covenant of God *was* there in those days, **28** and Phinehas the son of Eleazar, the son of Aaron, stood before it in those days), saying, "Shall I yet again go out to battle against the children of my brother Benjamin, or shall I cease?" And the LORD said, "Go up, for tomorrow I will deliver them into your hand."

Encouraged by their commanders.

2 Chr 20:20 So they rose early in the morning and went out into the Wilderness of Tekoa; and as they went out, Jehoshaphat stood and said, "Hear me, O Judah and you inhabitants of Jerusalem: Believe in the LORD your God, and you shall be established; believe His prophets, and you shall prosper."

Ark of God frequently brought with.

Josh 6:6–7 Then Joshua the son of Nun called the priests and said to them, "Take up the ark of the covenant, and let seven priests bear seven trumpets of rams' horns before the ark of the LORD." **7** And he said to the people, "Proceed, and march around the city, and let him who is armed advance before the ark of the LORD."

1 Sam 4:4–5 So the people sent to Shiloh, that they might bring from there the ark of the covenant of the LORD of hosts, who dwells *between* the cherubim. And the two sons of Eli, Hophni and Phinehas, *were* there with the ark of the covenant of God. **5** And when the ark of the covenant of the LORD came into the camp, all Israel shouted so loudly that the earth shook.

2 Sam 11:11 And Uriah said to David, "The ark and Israel and Judah are dwelling in tents, and my lord Joab and the servants of my lord are encamped in the open fields. Shall I then go to my house to eat and drink, and to lie with my wife? *As* you live, and *as* your soul lives, I will not do this thing."

2 Sam 15:24 There was Zadok also, and all the Levites with him, bearing the ark of the covenant of God. And they set down the ark of God, and Abiathar went up until all the people had finished crossing over from the city.

Attended by priests with trumpets.

Num 10:9 "When you go to war in your land against the enemy who oppresses you, then you shall sound an alarm with the trumpets, and you will be remembered before the LORD your God, and you will be saved from your enemies.

Num 31:6 Then Moses sent them to the war, one thousand from *each* tribe; he sent them to the war with Phinehas the son of Eleazar the priest, with the holy articles and the signal trumpets in his hand.

2 Chr 13:13–14 But Jeroboam caused an ambush to go around behind them; so they were in front of Judah, and the ambush *was* behind them. **14** And when Judah looked around, to their surprise the battle line *was* at both front and rear; and they cried out to the LORD, and the priests sounded the trumpets.

Praises of God often sung before.

2 Chr 20:21–22 And when he had consulted with the people, he appointed those who should sing to the LORD, and who should praise the beauty of holiness, as they went out before the army and were saying: "Praise the LORD, For His mercy *endures* forever." **22** Now when they began to sing and to praise, the LORD set ambushes against the people of Ammon, Moab, and Mount Seir, who had come against Judah; and they were defeated.

Often disposed to battle with judgment, etc.

2 Sam 10:9 When Joab saw that the battle line was against him before and behind, he chose some of Israel's best and put *them* in battle array against the Syrians.

Bravery and fidelity in, rewarded.

Josh 15:16 And Caleb said, "He who attacks Kirjath Sepher and takes it, to him I will give Achsah my daughter as wife."

1 Sam 17:25 So the men of Israel said, "Have you seen this man who has come up? Surely he has come up to defy Israel; and it shall be *that* the man who kills him the king will enrich with great riches, will give him his daughter, and give his father's house exemption *from taxes* in Israel."

1 Sam 18:17 Then Saul said to David, "Here is my older daughter Merab; I will give her to you as a wife. Only be valiant for me, and fight the LORD's battles." For Saul thought, "Let my hand not be against him, but let the hand of the Philistines be against him."

2 Sam 18:11 So Joab said to the man who told him, "You just saw *him!* And why did you not strike him there to the ground? I would have given you ten *shekels* of silver and a belt."

1 Chr 11:6 Now David said, "Whoever attacks the Jebusites first shall be chief and captain." And Joab the son of Zeruiah went up first, and became chief.

Men selected from, for difficult enterprises.

Ex 17:9 And Moses said to Joshua, "Choose us some men and go out, fight with Amalek. Tomorrow I will stand on the top of the hill with the rod of God in my hand."

Num 31:5–6 So there were recruited from the divisions of Israel one thousand from *each* tribe, twelve thousand armed for war. 6 Then Moses sent them to the war, one thousand from *each* tribe; he sent them to the war with Phinehas the son of Eleazar the priest, with the holy articles and the signal trumpets in his hand.

Josh 7:4 So about three thousand men went up there from the people, but they fled before the men of Ai.

Josh 8:3 So Joshua arose, and all the people of war, to go up against Ai; and Joshua chose thirty thousand mighty men of valor and sent them away by night.

Judg 7:5–6 So he brought the people down to the water. And the LORD said to Gideon, "Everyone who laps from the water with his tongue, as a dog laps, you shall set apart by himself; likewise everyone who gets down on his knees to drink." 6 And the number of those who lapped, *putting* their hand to their mouth, was three hundred men; but all the rest of the people got down on their knees to drink water.

2 Sam 17:1 Moreover Ahithophel said to Absalom, "Now let me choose twelve thousand men, and I will arise and pursue David tonight.

Directed in their movements by God.

Josh 8:1–2 Now the LORD said to Joshua: "Do not be afraid, nor be dismayed; take all the people of war with you, and arise, go up to Ai. See, I have given into your hand the king of Ai, his people, his city, and his land. 2 And you shall do to Ai and its king as you did to Jericho and its king. Only its spoil and its cattle you shall take as booty for yourselves. Lay an ambush for the city behind it."

Judg 1:2 And the LORD said, "Judah shall go up. Indeed I have delivered the land into his hand."

2 Sam 5:25 And David did so, as the LORD commanded him; and he drove back the Philistines from Geba as far as Gezer.

1 Chr 14:16 So David did as God commanded him, and they drove back the army of the Philistines from Gibeon as far as Gezer.

With the aid of God, all-powerful.

Lev 26:3 'If you walk in My statutes and keep My commandments, and perform them,

Lev 26:7–8 You will chase your enemies, and they shall fall by the sword before you. 8 Five of you shall chase a hundred, and a hundred of you shall put ten thousand to flight; your enemies shall fall by the sword before you.

Deut 7:24 And He will deliver their kings into your hand, and you will destroy their name from under heaven; no one shall be able to stand against you until you have destroyed them.

Deut 32:30 How could one chase a thousand, And two put ten thousand to flight, Unless their Rock had sold them, And the LORD had surrendered them?

Josh 1:5 No man shall *be able to* stand before you all the days of your life; as I was with Moses, *so* I will be with you. I will not leave you nor forsake you.

Without God, easily overcome.

Lev 26:17 I will set My face against you, and you shall be defeated by your enemies. Those who hate you shall reign over you, and you shall flee when no one pursues you.

Num 14:42 Do not go up, lest you be defeated by your enemies, for the LORD *is* not among you.

Num 14:45 Then the Amalekites and the Canaanites who dwelt in that mountain came down and attacked them, and drove them back as far as Hormah.

Mode of supplying,

Food brought by themselves.

Josh 1:11 "Pass through the camp and command the people, saying, 'Prepare provisions for yourselves, for within three days you will cross over this Jordan, to go in to possess the land which the LORD your God is giving you to possess.' "

Food sent by their families.

1 Sam 17:17 Then Jesse said to his son David, "Take now for your brothers an ephah of this dried *grain* and these ten loaves, and run to your brothers at the camp.

Contribution levied.

Judg 8:5 Then he said to the men of Succoth, "Please give loaves of bread to the people who follow me, for they are exhausted, and I am pursuing Zebah and Zalmunna, kings of Midian."

1 Sam 25:4–8 When David heard in the wilderness that Nabal was shearing his sheep, 5 David sent ten young men; and David said to the young men, "Go up to Carmel, go to Nabal, and greet him in my name. 6 And thus you shall say to him who lives *in prosperity:* 'Peace *be* to you, peace to your house, and peace to all that you have! 7 Now I have heard that you have shearers. Your shepherds were with us, and we did not hurt them, nor was there anything missing from them all the while they were in Carmel. 8 Ask your young men, and they will tell you. Therefore let *my* young men find favor in your eyes, for we come on a feast day. Please give whatever comes to your hand to your servants and to your son David.' "

By presents.

2 Sam 17:27–29 Now it happened, when David had come to Mahanaim, that Shobi the son of Nahash from Rabbah of the people of Ammon, Machir the son of Ammiel from Lo Debar, and Barzillai the Gileadite from Rogelim, 28 brought beds and basins, earthen vessels and wheat, barley and flour, parched *grain* and beans, lentils and parched *seeds,* **29** honey and curds, sheep and cheese of the herd, for David and the people who *were* with him to eat. For they said, "The people are hungry and weary and thirsty in the wilderness."

Congratulated on returning victorious.

1 Sam 18:6–7 Now it had happened as they were coming *home,* when David was returning from the slaughter of the Philistine, that the women had come out of all the cities of Israel, singing and dancing, to meet King Saul, with tambourines, with joy, and with musical instruments. **7** So the women sang as they danced, and said: "Saul has slain his thousands, And David his ten thousands."

Cf. Ex 15:1–21

Purified on returning from war.

Num 31:19–24 And as for you, remain outside the camp seven days; whoever has killed any person, and whoever has touched any slain, purify yourselves and your captives on the third day and on the seventh day. **20** Purify every garment, everything made of leather, everything woven of goats' *hair,* and everything made of wood." **21** Then Eleazar the priest said to the men of war who had gone to the battle, "This *is* the ordinance of the law which the LORD commanded Moses: **22** "Only the gold, the silver, the bronze, the iron, the tin, and the lead, **23** everything that can endure fire, you shall put through the fire, and it shall be clean; and it shall be purified with the water of purification. But all that cannot endure fire you shall put through water. **24** And you shall wash your clothes on the seventh day and be clean, and afterward you may come into the camp."

Disbanded after war.

1 Sam 13:2 Saul chose for himself three thousand *men* of Israel. Two thousand were with Saul in Michmash and in the mountains of Bethel, and a thousand were with Jonathan in Gibeah of Benjamin. The rest of the people he sent away, every man to his tent.

1 Kin 22:36 Then, as the sun was going down, a shout went throughout the army, saying, "Every man to his city, and every man to his own country!"

Part of, retained in times of peace by the kings.

1 Sam 13:1–2 Saul reigned one year; and when he had reigned two years over Israel, **2** Saul chose for himself three thousand *men* of Israel. Two thousand were with Saul in Michmash and in the mountains of Bethel, and a thousand were with Jonathan in Gibeah of Benjamin. The rest of the people he sent away, every man to his tent.

1 Chr 27:1 And the children of Israel, according to their number, the heads of fathers' *houses,* the captains of thousands and hundreds and their officers, served the king in every matter of the *military* divisions. *These divisions* came in and went out month by month throughout all the months of the year, each division *having* twenty-four thousand.

ISRAEL, DESERT JOURNEY OF

Date of its commencement.

Ex 12:41–42 And it came to pass at the end of the four

hundred and thirty years—on that very same day— it came to pass that all the armies of the LORD went out from the land of Egypt. **42** It *is* a night of solemn observance to the LORD for bringing them out of the land of Egypt. This *is* that night of the LORD, a solemn observance for all the children of Israel throughout their generations.

Her number and strength at the start.

Ex 12:37 Then the children of Israel journeyed from Rameses to Succoth, about six hundred thousand men on foot, besides children.

Ex 13:18 So God led the people around *by* way of the wilderness of the Red Sea. And the children of Israel went up in orderly ranks out of the land of Egypt.

Ps 105:37 He also brought them out with silver and gold, And *there was* none feeble among His tribes.

Accompanied by mixed multitude.

Ex 12:38 A mixed multitude went up with them also, and flocks and herds—a great deal of livestock.

Num 11:4 Now the mixed multitude who were among them yielded to intense craving; so the children of Israel also wept again and said: "Who will give us meat to eat?

Commenced in haste.

Ex 12:39 And they baked unleavened cakes of the dough which they had brought out of Egypt; for it was not leavened, because they were driven out of Egypt and could not wait, nor had they prepared provisions for themselves.

Under Moses as leader.

Ex 3:10–12 Come now, therefore, and I will send you to Pharaoh that you may bring My people, the children of Israel, out of Egypt." **11** But Moses said to God, "Who *am* I that I should go to Pharaoh, and that I should bring the children of Israel out of Egypt?" **12** So He said, "I will certainly be with you. And this *shall be* a sign to you that I have sent you: When you have brought the people out of Egypt, you shall serve God on this mountain."

Acts 7:36 He brought them out, after he had shown wonders and signs in the land of Egypt, and in the Red Sea, and in the wilderness forty years.

Acts 7:38 "This is he who was in the congregation in the wilderness with the Angel who spoke to him on Mount Sinai, and *with* our fathers, the one who received the living oracles to give to us,

By a circuitous route.

Ex 13:17–18 Then it came to pass, when Pharaoh had let the people go, that God did not lead them *by* way of the land of the Philistines, although that *was* near; for God said, "Lest perhaps the people change their minds when they see war, and return to Egypt." **18** So God led the people around *by* way of the wilderness of the Red Sea. And the children of Israel went up in orderly ranks out of the land of Egypt.

Order of marching during. Num 10:14–29

Order of encamping during. Num 2:1–34

Difficulty and danger of.

Deut 8:15 who led you through that great and terrible wilderness, *in which were* fiery serpents and scorpions and thirsty land where there was no water; who brought water for you out of the flinty rock;

Continued forty years

As a punishment.

Num 14:33–34 And your sons shall be shepherds in the wilderness forty years, and bear the brunt of your infidelity, until your carcasses are consumed in the wilderness. **34** According to the number of the days in which you spied out the land, forty days, for each day you shall bear your guilt one year, *namely* forty years, and you shall know My rejection.

To test and humble them.

Deut 8:2 And you shall remember that the LORD your God led you all the way these forty years in the wilderness, to humble you *and* test you, to know what *was* in your heart, whether you would keep His commandments or not.

To teach them to live on God's Word.

Deut 8:3 So He humbled you, allowed you to hunger, and fed you with manna which you did not know nor did your fathers know, that He might make you know that man shall not live by bread alone; but man lives by every *word* that proceeds from the mouth of the LORD.

Under God's guidance.

Ex 13:21–22 And the LORD went before them by day in a pillar of cloud to lead the way, and by night in a pillar of fire to give them light, so as to go by day and night. **22** He did not take away the pillar of cloud by day or the pillar of fire by night *from* before the people.

Ex 15:13 You in Your mercy have led forth The people whom You have redeemed; You have guided *them* in Your strength To Your holy habitation.

Neh 9:12 Moreover You led them by day with a cloudy pillar, And by night with a pillar of fire, To give them light on the road Which they should travel.

Ps 78:52 But He made His own people go forth like sheep, And guided them in the wilderness like a flock;

Is 63:11–14 Then he remembered the days of old, Moses *and* his people, *saying:* "Where *is* He who brought them up out of the sea With the shepherd of His flock? Where *is* He who put His Holy Spirit within them, **12** Who led *them* by the right hand of Moses, With His glorious arm, Dividing the water before them To make for Himself an everlasting name, **13** Who led them through the deep, As a horse in the wilderness, *That* they might not stumble?" **14** As a beast goes down into the valley, *And* the Spirit of the LORD causes him to rest, So You lead Your people, To make Yourself a glorious name.

Under God's protection.

Ex 14:19–20 And the Angel of God, who went before the camp of Israel, moved and went behind them; and the pillar of cloud went from before them and stood behind them. **20** So it came between the camp of the Egyptians and the camp of Israel. Thus it was a cloud and darkness *to the one,* and it gave light by night *to the other,* so that the one did not come near the other all that night.

Ex 23:20 "Behold, I send an Angel before you to keep you in the way and to bring you into the place which I have prepared.

Ps 78:53 And He led them on safely, so that they did not fear; But the sea overwhelmed their enemies.

Ps 105:39 He spread a cloud for a covering, And fire to give light in the night.

With miraculous provision.

Ex 16:35 And the children of Israel ate manna forty years, until they came to an inhabited land; they ate manna until they came to the border of the land of Canaan.

Deut 8:3 So He humbled you, allowed you to hunger, and fed you with manna which you did not know nor did your fathers know, that He might make you know that man shall not live by bread alone; but man lives by every *word* that proceeds from the mouth of the LORD.

Their clothing preserved during.

Deut 8:4 Your garments did not wear out on you, nor did your foot swell these forty years.

Deut 29:5 And I have led you forty years in the wilderness. Your clothes have not worn out on you, and your sandals have not worn out on your feet.

Neh 9:21 Forty years You sustained them in the wilderness; They lacked nothing; Their clothes did not wear out And their feet did not swell.

Worship of God celebrated during.

Ex 24:5–8 Then he sent young men of the children of Israel, who offered burnt offerings and sacrificed peace offerings of oxen to the LORD. **6** And Moses took half the blood and put *it* in basins, and half the blood he sprinkled on the altar. **7** Then he took the Book of the Covenant and read in the hearing of the people. And they said, "All that the LORD has said we will do, and be obedient." **8** And Moses took the blood, sprinkled *it* on the people, and said, "This is the blood of the covenant which the LORD has made with you according to all these words."

Ex 29:38–42 "Now this *is* what you shall offer on the altar: two lambs of the first year, day by day continually. **39** One lamb you shall offer in the morning, and the other lamb you shall offer at twilight. **40** With the one lamb shall be one-tenth *of an ephah* of flour mixed with one-fourth of a hin of pressed oil, and one-fourth of a hin of wine *as* a drink offering. **41** And the other lamb you shall offer at twilight; and you shall offer with it the grain offering and the drink offering, as in the morning, for a sweet aroma, an offering made by fire to the LORD. **42** *This shall be* a continual burnt offering throughout your generations *at* the door of the tabernacle of meeting before the LORD, where I will meet you to speak with you.

Ex 40:24–29 He put the lampstand in the tabernacle of meeting, across from the table, on the south side of the tabernacle; **25** and he lit the lamps before the LORD, as the LORD had commanded Moses. **26** He put the gold altar in the tabernacle of meeting in front of the veil; **27** and he burned sweet incense on it, as the LORD had commanded Moses. **28** He hung up the screen *at* the door of the tabernacle. **29** And he put the altar of burnt offering *before* the door of the tabernacle of the tent of meeting, and offered upon it the burnt offering and the grain offering, as the LORD had commanded Moses.

Justice administered during.

Ex 18:13 And so it was, on the next day, that Moses sat to judge the people; and the people stood before Moses from morning until evening.

Ex 18:26 So they judged the people at all times; the hard cases they brought to Moses, but they judged every small case themselves.

Circumcision omitted during.

Josh 5:5 For all the people who came out had been circumcised, but all the people born in the wilderness, on the way as they came out of Egypt, had not been circumcised.

Caused terror and dismay for neighbors.

Ex 15:14–16 "The people will hear *and* be afraid; Sorrow will take hold of the inhabitants of Philistia. **15** Then the chiefs of Edom will be dismayed; The mighty men of Moab, Trembling will take hold of them; All the inhabitants of Canaan will melt away. **16** Fear and dread will fall on them; By the greatness of Your arm They will be *as* still as a stone, Till Your people pass over, O LORD, Till the people pass over Whom You have purchased.

Num 22:3–4 And Moab was exceedingly afraid of the people because they *were* many, and Moab was sick with dread because of the children of Israel. **4** So Moab said to the elders of Midian, "Now this company will lick up everything around us, as an ox licks up the grass of the field." And Balak the son of Zippor *was* king of the Moabites at that time.

Obstructed, etc., by the surrounding nations.

Ex 17:8 Now Amalek came and fought with Israel in Rephidim.

Num 20:21 Thus Edom refused to give Israel passage through his territory; so Israel turned away from him.

Territory acquired during.

Deut 29:7–8 And when you came to this place, Sihon king of Heshbon and Og king of Bashan came out against us to battle, and we conquered them. **8** We took their land and gave it as an inheritance to the Reubenites, to the Gadites, and to half the tribe of Manasseh.

Marked by constant complaining and rebellion.

Ps 78:40 How often they provoked Him in the wilderness, *And* grieved Him in the desert!

Ps 95:10 For forty years I was grieved with *that* generation, And said, 'It *is* a people who go astray in their hearts, And they do not know My ways.'

Cf. Ps 106:7–39

Constant goodness and mercy of God to them during.

Ps 106:10 He saved them from the hand of him who hated *them,* And redeemed them from the hand of the enemy.

Ps 106:43–46 Many times He delivered them; But they rebelled in their counsel, And were brought low for their iniquity. **44** Nevertheless He regarded their affliction, When He heard their cry; **45** And for their sake He remembered His covenant, And relented according to the multitude of His mercies. **46** He also made them to be pitied By all those who carried them away captive.

Ps 107:6 Then they cried out to the LORD in their trouble, *And* He delivered them out of their distresses.

Ps 107:13 Then they cried out to the LORD in their trouble, *And* He saved them out of their distresses.

Commenced from Rameses in Egypt.

Ex 12:37 Then the children of Israel journeyed from Rameses to Succoth, about six hundred thousand men on foot, besides children.

To Succoth.

Ex 12:37 Then the children of Israel journeyed from Rameses to Succoth, about six hundred thousand men on foot, besides children.

Num 33:5 Then the children of Israel moved from Rameses and camped at Succoth.

To Etham.

Ex 13:20 So they took their journey from Succoth and camped in Etham at the edge of the wilderness.

Num 33:6 They departed from Succoth and camped at Etham, which *is* on the edge of the wilderness.

Between Baal Zephon and Pi Hahiroth.

Ex 14:2 "Speak to the children of Israel, that they turn and camp before Pi Hahiroth, between Migdol and the sea, opposite Baal Zephon; you shall camp before it by the sea.

Num 33:7 They moved from Etham and turned back to Pi Hahiroth, which *is* east of Baal Zephon; and they camped near Migdol.

Overtaken by Pharaoh.

Ex 14:9 So the Egyptians pursued them, all the horses *and* chariots of Pharaoh, his horsemen and his army, and overtook them camping by the sea beside Pi Hahiroth, before Baal Zephon.

Exhorted to look to God.

Ex 14:13–14 And Moses said to the people, "Do not be afraid. Stand still, and see the salvation of the LORD, which He will accomplish for you today. For the Egyptians whom you see today, you shall see again no more forever. **14** The LORD will fight for you, and you shall hold your peace."

The cloud removed to the rear.

Ex 14:19–20 And the Angel of God, who went before the camp of Israel, moved and went behind them; and the pillar of cloud went from before them and stood behind them. **20** So it came between the camp of the Egyptians and the camp of Israel. Thus it was a cloud and darkness *to the one,* and it gave light by night *to the other,* so that the one did not come near the other all that night.

Red Sea divided.

Ex 14:16 But lift up your rod, and stretch out your hand over the sea and divide it. And the children of Israel shall go on dry *ground* through the midst of the sea.

Ex 14:21 Then Moses stretched out his hand over the sea; and the LORD caused the sea to go *back* by a strong east wind all that night, and made the sea into dry *land,* and the waters were divided.

Through the Red Sea.

Ex 14:22 So the children of Israel went into the midst of the sea on the dry *ground,* and the waters *were* a wall to them on their right hand and on their left.

Ex 14:29 But the children of Israel had walked on dry *land* in the midst of the sea, and the waters *were* a wall to them on their right hand and on their left.

Faith exhibited in passing.

Heb 11:29 By faith they passed through the Red Sea as by dry *land, whereas* the Egyptians, attempting *to do* so, were drowned.

Pharaoh and his host destroyed.

Ps 106:11 The waters covered their enemies; There was not one of them left.

Cf. Ex 14:23–28

Israel's song of praise.

Ps 106:12 Then they believed His words; They sang His praise.

Cf. Ex 15:1–21

Through the Wilderness of Shur or Etham.

Ex 15:22 So Moses brought Israel from the Red Sea; then they went out into the Wilderness of Shur. And they went three days in the wilderness and found no water.

Num 33:8 They departed from before Hahiroth and passed through the midst of the sea into the wilderness, went three days' journey in the Wilderness of Etham, and camped at Marah.

To Marah.

Ex 15:23 Now when they came to Marah, they could not drink the waters of Marah, for they *were* bitter. Therefore the name of it was called Marah.

Num 33:8 They departed from before Hahiroth and passed through the midst of the sea into the wilderness, went three days' journey in the Wilderness of Etham, and camped at Marah.

Complaining of the people because of bitter water.

Ex 15:24 And the people complained against Moses, saying, "What shall we drink?"

Water sweetened.

Ex 15:25 So he cried out to the LORD, and the LORD showed him a tree. When he cast *it* into the waters, the waters were made sweet. There He made a statute and an ordinance for them, and there He tested them,

To Elim.

Ex 15:27 Then they came to Elim, where there *were* twelve wells of water and seventy palm trees; so they camped there by the waters.

Num 33:9 They moved from Marah and came to Elim. At Elim *were* twelve springs of water and seventy palm trees; so they camped there.

By the Red Sea.

Num 33:10 They moved from Elim and camped by the Red Sea.

Through the Wilderness of Sin.

Ex 16:1 And they journeyed from Elim, and all the congregation of the children of Israel came to the Wilderness of Sin, which is between Elim and Sinai, on the fifteenth day of the second month after they departed from the land of Egypt.

Num 33:11 They moved from the Red Sea and camped in the Wilderness of Sin.

Complaining for bread.

Ex 16:2–3 Then the whole congregation of the children of Israel complained against Moses and Aaron in the wilderness. 3 And the children of Israel said to them, "Oh, that we had died by the hand of the LORD in the land of Egypt, when we sat by the pots of meat *and* when we ate bread to the full! For you have brought us out into this wilderness to kill this whole assembly with hunger."

Quails given for one night.

Ex 16:8 Also Moses said, "*This shall be seen* when the LORD gives you meat to eat in the evening, and in the morning bread to the full; for the LORD hears your complaints which you make against Him. And what *are* we? Your complaints *are* not against us but against the LORD."

Ex 16:12–13 "I have heard the complaints of the children of Israel. Speak to them, saying, 'At twilight you shall eat meat, and in the morning you shall be filled with bread. And you shall know that I *am* the LORD your God.' " 13 So it was that quails came up at evening and covered the camp, and in the morning the dew lay all around the camp.

Manna sent.

Ex 16:4 Then the LORD said to Moses, "Behold, I will rain bread from heaven for you. And the people shall go out and gather a certain quota every day, that I may test them, whether they will walk in My law or not.

Ex 16:8 Also Moses said, "*This shall be seen* when the LORD gives you meat to eat in the evening, and in the morning bread to the full; for the LORD hears your complaints which you make against Him. And what *are* we? Your complaints *are* not against us but against the LORD."

Cf. Ex 16:16–31

To Dophkah.

Num 33:12 They journeyed from the Wilderness of Sin and camped at Dophkah.

To Alush.

Num 33:13 They departed from Dophkah and camped at Alush.

To Rephidim.

Ex 17:1 Then all the congregation of the children of Israel set out on their journey from the Wilderness of Sin, according to the commandment of the LORD, and camped in Rephidim; but *there was* no water for the people to drink.

Num 33:14 They moved from Alush and camped at Rephidim, where there was no water for the people to drink.

Complaining for water.

Ex 17:2–3 Therefore the people contended with Moses, and said, "Give us water, that we may drink." So Moses said to them, "Why do you contend with me? Why do you tempt the LORD?" 3 And the people thirsted there for water, and the people complained against Moses, and said, "Why *is* it you have brought us up out of Egypt, to kill us and our children and our livestock with thirst?"

Water brought from the rock.

Ex 17:5–6 And the LORD said to Moses, "Go on before the people, and take with you some of the elders of

Israel. Also take in your hand your rod with which you struck the river, and go. 6 Behold, I will stand before you there on the rock in Horeb; and you shall strike the rock, and water will come out of it, that the people may drink." And Moses did so in the sight of the elders of Israel.

Called Massah and Meribah.

Ex 17:7 So he called the name of the place Massah and Meribah, because of the contention of the children of Israel, and because they tempted the LORD, saying, "Is the LORD among us or not?"

Amalek opposes Israel.

Ex 17:8 Now Amalek came and fought with Israel in Rephidim.

Amalek overcome.

Ex 17:9–13 And Moses said to Joshua, "Choose us some men and go out, fight with Amalek. Tomorrow I will stand on the top of the hill with the rod of God in my hand." 10 So Joshua did as Moses said to him, and fought with Amalek. And Moses, Aaron, and Hur went up to the top of the hill. 11 And so it was, when Moses held up his hand, that Israel prevailed; and when he let down his hand, Amalek prevailed. 12 But Moses' hands *became* heavy; so they took a stone and put *it* under him, and he sat on it. And Aaron and Hur supported his hands, one on one side, and the other on the other side; and his hands were steady until the going down of the sun. 13 So Joshua defeated Amalek and his people with the edge of the sword.

To Mount Sinai.

Ex 19:1–2 In the third month after the children of Israel had gone out of the land of Egypt, on the same day, they came *to* the Wilderness of Sinai. 2 For they had departed from Rephidim, had come *to* the Wilderness of Sinai, and camped in the wilderness. So Israel camped there before the mountain.

Num 33:15 They departed from Rephidim and camped in the Wilderness of Sinai.

Jethro's visit.

Ex 18:1–6 And Jethro, the priest of Midian, Moses' father-in-law, heard of all that God had done for Moses and for Israel His people—that the LORD had brought Israel out of Egypt. 2 Then Jethro, Moses' father-in-law, took Zipporah, Moses' wife, after he had sent her back, 3 with her two sons, of whom the name of one *was* Gershom (for he said, "I have been a stranger in a foreign land") 4 and the name of the other *was* Eliezer (for *he said*, "The God of my father *was* my help, and delivered me from the sword of Pharaoh"); 5 and Jethro, Moses' father-in-law, came with his sons and his wife to Moses in the wilderness, where he was encamped at the mountain of God. 6 Now he had said to Moses, "I, your father-in-law Jethro, am coming to you with your wife and her two sons with her."

Judges appointed. Ex 18:14–26; Deut 1:9–15

Moral law given. Ex 19:3; 20:1–26

Covenant made.

Ex 24:3–8 So Moses came and told the people all the words of the LORD and all the judgments. And all the people answered with one voice and said, "All

the words which the LORD has said we will do." 4 And Moses wrote all the words of the LORD. And he rose early in the morning, and built an altar at the foot of the mountain, and twelve pillars according to the twelve tribes of Israel. 5 Then he sent young men of the children of Israel, who offered burnt offerings and sacrificed peace offerings of oxen to the LORD. 6 And Moses took half the blood and put *it* in basins, and half the blood he sprinkled on the altar. 7 Then he took the Book of the Covenant and read in the hearing of the people. And they said, "All that the LORD has said we will do, and be obedient." 8 And Moses took the blood, sprinkled *it* on the people, and said, "This is the blood of the covenant which the LORD has made with you according to all these words."

Moral law written on tablets.

Ex 31:18 And when He had made an end of speaking with him on Mount Sinai, He gave Moses two tablets of the Testimony, tablets of stone, written with the finger of God.

Order for making the tabernacle, etc. Ex 24:1—27:21

Tribe of Levi taken instead of the firstborn.

Num 3:11–13 Then the LORD spoke to Moses, saying: 12 "Now behold, I Myself have taken the Levites from among the children of Israel instead of every firstborn who opens the womb among the children of Israel. Therefore the Levites shall be Mine, 13 because all the firstborn *are* Mine. On the day that I struck all the firstborn in the land of Egypt, I sanctified to Myself all the firstborn in Israel, both man and beast. They shall be Mine: I *am* the LORD."

Aaron and his sons selected for priesthood.

Ex 28:1 "Now take Aaron your brother, and his sons with him, from among the children of Israel, that he may minister to Me as priest, Aaron *and* Aaron's sons: Nadab, Abihu, Eleazar, and Ithamar.

Num 3:1–3 Now these *are* the records of Aaron and Moses when the LORD spoke with Moses on Mount Sinai. 2 And these *are* the names of the sons of Aaron: Nadab, the firstborn, and Abihu, Eleazar, and Ithamar. 3 These *are* the names of the sons of Aaron, the anointed priests, whom he consecrated to minister as priests.

Num 3:10 So you shall appoint Aaron and his sons, and they shall attend to their priesthood; but the outsider who comes near shall be put to death."

Cf. Ex 28:2–43; 29:1–46

Levites set apart.

Num 3:5–9 And the LORD spoke to Moses, saying: 6 "Bring the tribe of Levi near, and present them before Aaron the priest, that they may serve him. 7 And they shall attend to his needs and the needs of the whole congregation before the tabernacle of meeting, to do the work of the tabernacle. 8 Also they shall attend to all the furnishings of the tabernacle of meeting, and to the needs of the children of Israel, to do the work of the tabernacle. 9 And you shall give the Levites to Aaron and his sons; they *are* given entirely to him from among the children of Israel.

Golden calf made.

Ex 32:1 Now when the people saw that Moses delayed coming down from the mountain, the people gathered together to Aaron, and said to him, "Come, make us gods that shall go before us; for *as for* this Moses, the man who brought us up out of the land of Egypt, we do not know what has become of him."

Ex 32:4 And he received *the gold* from their hand, and he fashioned it with an engraving tool, and made a molded calf. Then they said, "This *is* your god, O Israel, that brought you out of the land of Egypt!"

Tablets of the Testimony broken.

Ex 32:19 So it was, as soon as he came near the camp, that he saw the calf *and* the dancing. So Moses' anger became hot, and he cast the tablets out of his hands and broke them at the foot of the mountain.

People punished for idolatry.

Ex 32:25–29 Now when Moses saw that the people *were* unrestrained (for Aaron had not restrained them, to *their* shame among their enemies), **26** then Moses stood in the entrance of the camp, and said, "Whoever *is* on the LORD's side—*come* to me!" And all the sons of Levi gathered themselves together to him. **27** And he said to them, "Thus says the LORD God of Israel: 'Let every man put his sword on his side, and go in and out from entrance to entrance throughout the camp, and let every man kill his brother, every man his companion, and every man his neighbor.' " **28** So the sons of Levi did according to the word of Moses. And about three thousand men of the people fell that day. **29** Then Moses said, "Consecrate yourselves today to the LORD, that He may bestow on you a blessing this day, for every man has opposed his son and his brother."

Ex 32:35 So the LORD plagued the people because of what they did with the calf which Aaron made.

God's glory shown to Moses.

Ex 33:18–23 And he said, "Please, show me Your glory." **19** Then He said, "I will make all My goodness pass before you, and I will proclaim the name of the LORD before you. I will be gracious to whom I will be gracious, and I will have compassion on whom I will have compassion." **20** But He said, "You cannot see My face; for no man shall see Me, and live." **21** And the LORD said, "Here is a place by Me, and you shall stand on the rock. **22** So it shall be, while My glory passes by, that I will put you in the cleft of the rock, and will cover you with My hand while I pass by. **23** Then I will take away My hand, and you shall see My back; but My face shall not be seen."

Ex 34:5–8 Now the LORD descended in the cloud and stood with him there, and proclaimed the name of the LORD. **6** And the LORD passed before him and proclaimed, "The LORD, the LORD God, merciful and gracious, longsuffering, and abounding in goodness and truth, **7** keeping mercy for thousands, forgiving iniquity and transgression and sin, by no means clearing *the guilty*, visiting the iniquity of the fathers upon the children and the children's children to the third and the fourth generation." **8** So Moses made haste and bowed his head toward the earth, and worshiped.

The tablets of the Testimony renewed.

Ex 34:1–4 And the LORD said to Moses, "Cut two tablets of stone like the first *ones*, and I will write on *these* tablets the words that were on the first tablets which you broke. **2** So be ready in the morning, and come up in the morning to Mount Sinai, and present yourself to Me there on the top of the mountain. **3** And no man shall come up with you, and let no man be seen throughout all the mountain; let neither flocks nor herds feed before that mountain." **4** So he cut two tablets of stone like the first *ones*. Then Moses rose early in the morning and went up Mount Sinai, as the LORD had commanded him; and he took in his hand the two tablets of stone.

Ex 34:27–29 Then the LORD said to Moses, "Write these words, for according to the tenor of these words I have made a covenant with you and with Israel." **28** So he was there with the LORD forty days and forty nights; he neither ate bread nor drank water. And He wrote on the tablets the words of the covenant, the Ten Commandments. **29** Now it was so, when Moses came down from Mount Sinai (and the two tablets of the Testimony *were* in Moses' hand when he came down from the mountain), that Moses did not know that the skin of his face shone while he talked with Him.

Deut 10:1–5 "At that time the LORD said to me, 'Hew for yourself two tablets of stone like the first, and come up to Me on the mountain and make yourself an ark of wood. **2** And I will write on the tablets the words that were on the first tablets, which you broke; and you shall put them in the ark.' **3** "So I made an ark of acacia wood, hewed two tablets of stone like the first, and went up the mountain, having the two tablets in my hand. **4** And He wrote on the tablets according to the first writing, the Ten Commandments, which the LORD had spoken to you in the mountain from the midst of the fire in the day of the assembly; and the LORD gave them to me. **5** Then I turned and came down from the mountain, and put the tablets in the ark which I had made; and there they are, just as the LORD commanded me."

The tabernacle first set up. Ex 40:1–38

Nadab and Abihu destroyed for offering profane fire.

Lev 10:1–2 Then Nadab and Abihu, the sons of Aaron, each took his censer and put fire in it, put incense on it, and offered profane fire before the LORD, which He had not commanded them. **2** So fire went out from the LORD and devoured them, and they died before the LORD.

Num 3:4 Nadab and Abihu had died before the LORD when they offered profane fire before the LORD in the Wilderness of Sinai; and they had no children. So Eleazar and Ithamar ministered as priests in the presence of Aaron their father.

The Passover first commemorated.

Num 9:1–5 Now the LORD spoke to Moses in the Wilderness of Sinai, in the first month of the second year after they had come out of the land of Egypt, saying: **2** "Let the children of Israel keep the Passover at its appointed time. **3** On the fourteenth day of this month, at twilight, you shall keep it at its appointed time. According to all its rites and ceremonies you shall keep it." **4** So Moses told the children of Israel that they should keep the Passover. **5** And they kept the Passover on the fourteenth day of the first month, at twilight, in the Wilderness of Sinai; according to all that the LORD commanded Moses, so the children of Israel did.

Second numbering of the people.

Num 1:1–4 Now the LORD spoke to Moses in the Wilderness of Sinai, in the tabernacle of meeting, on the first *day* of the second month, in the second year after they had come out of the land of Egypt, saying: **2** "Take a census of all the congregation of the children of Israel, by their families, by their fathers' houses, according to the number of names, every male individually, **3** from twenty years old and above—all who *are able to* go to war in Israel. You and Aaron shall number them by their armies. **4** And with you there shall be a man from every tribe, each one the head of his father's house.

Ex 38:25–26 And the silver from those who were numbered of the congregation *was* one hundred talents and one thousand seven hundred and seventy-five shekels, according to the shekel of the sanctuary: **26** a bekah for each man (*that is,* half a shekel, according to the shekel of the sanctuary), for everyone included in the numbering from twenty years old and above, for six hundred and three thousand, five hundred and fifty *men.*

Cf. Num 1:5–38

To Kibroth Hattaavah.

Num 33:16 They moved from the Wilderness of Sinai and camped at Kibroth Hattaavah.

Complaining punished by fire.

Num 11:1–3 Now *when* the people complained, it displeased the LORD; for the LORD heard *it,* and His anger was aroused. So the fire of the LORD burned among them, and consumed *some* in the outskirts of the camp. **2** Then the people cried out to Moses, and when Moses prayed to the LORD, the fire was quenched. **3** So he called the name of the place Taberah, because the fire of the LORD had burned among them.

Called Taberah.

Num 11:3 So he called the name of the place Taberah, because the fire of the LORD had burned among them.

Complaining of the mixed multitude and of Israel, for meat.

Num 11:4–9 Now the mixed multitude who were among them yielded to intense craving; so the children of Israel also wept again and said: "Who will give us meat to eat? **5** We remember the fish which we ate freely in Egypt, the cucumbers, the melons, the leeks, the onions, and the garlic; **6** but now our whole being *is* dried up; *there is* nothing at all except this manna *before* our eyes!" **7** Now the manna *was* like coriander seed, and its color like the color of bdellium. **8** The people went about and gathered *it,* ground *it* on millstones or beat *it* in the mortar, cooked *it* in pans, and made cakes of it; and its taste was like the taste of pastry prepared with oil. **9** And when the dew fell on the camp in the night, the manna fell on it.

Meat promised.

Num 11:10–15 Then Moses heard the people weeping throughout their families, everyone at the door of his tent; and the anger of the LORD was greatly aroused;

Moses also was displeased. **11** So Moses said to the LORD, "Why have You afflicted Your servant? And why have I not found favor in Your sight, that You have laid the burden of all these people on me? **12** Did I conceive all these people? Did I beget them, that You should say to me, 'Carry them in your bosom, as a guardian carries a nursing child,' to the land which You swore to their fathers? **13** Where am I to get meat to give to all these people? For they weep all over me, saying, 'Give us meat, that we may eat.' **14** I am not able to bear all these people alone, because the burden *is* too heavy for me. **15** If You treat me like this, please kill me here and now—if I have found favor in Your sight—and do not let me see my wretchedness!"

Num 11:18–23 Then you shall say to the people, 'Consecrate yourselves for tomorrow, and you shall eat meat; for you have wept in the hearing of the LORD, saying, "Who will give us meat to eat? For *it was* well with us in Egypt." Therefore the LORD will give you meat, and you shall eat. **19** You shall eat, not one day, nor two days, nor five days, nor ten days, nor twenty days, **20** but *for* a whole month, until it comes out of your nostrils and becomes loathsome to you, because you have despised the LORD who is among you, and have wept before Him, saying, "Why did we ever come up out of Egypt?" ' " **21** And Moses said, "The people whom I *am* among *are* six hundred thousand men on foot; yet You have said, 'I will give them meat, that they may eat *for* a whole month.' **22** Shall flocks and herds be slaughtered for them, to provide enough for them? Or shall all the fish of the sea be gathered together for them, to provide enough for them?" **23** And the LORD said to Moses, "Has the LORD's arm been shortened? Now you shall see whether what I say will happen to you or not."

Seventy elders appointed to assist Moses.

Num 11:16–17 So the LORD said to Moses: "Gather to Me seventy men of the elders of Israel, whom you know to be the elders of the people and officers over them; bring them to the tabernacle of meeting, that they may stand there with you. **17** Then I will come down and talk with you there. I will take of the Spirit that *is* upon you and will put *the same* upon them; and they shall bear the burden of the people with you, that you may not bear *it* yourself alone.

Num 11:24–30 So Moses went out and told the people the words of the LORD, and he gathered the seventy men of the elders of the people and placed them around the tabernacle. **25** Then the LORD came down in the cloud, and spoke to him, and took of the Spirit that *was* upon him, and placed *the same* upon the seventy elders; and it happened, when the Spirit rested upon them, that they prophesied, although they never did *so* again. **26** But two men had remained in the camp: the name of one *was* Eldad, and the name of the other Medad. And the Spirit rested upon them. Now they *were* among those listed, but who had not gone out to the tabernacle; yet they prophesied in the camp. **27** And a young man ran and told Moses, and said, "Eldad and Medad are prophesying in the camp." **28** So Joshua the son of Nun, Moses' assistant, *one* of his choice men, answered and said, "Moses my lord, forbid them!" **29** Then Moses said to him, "Are you zealous for my sake? Oh, that all the

LORD's people were prophets *and* that the LORD would put His Spirit upon them!" **30** And Moses returned to the camp, he and the elders of Israel.

Quail sent for a month.

Num 11:19–20 You shall eat, not one day, nor two days, nor five days, nor ten days, nor twenty days, **20** but *for* a whole month, until it comes out of your nostrils and becomes loathsome to you, because you have despised the LORD who is among you, and have wept before Him, saying, "Why did we ever come up out of Egypt?" ' "

Num 11:31–32 Now a wind went out from the LORD, and it brought quail from the sea and left *them* fluttering near the camp, about a day's journey on this side and about a day's journey on the other side, all around the camp, and about two cubits above the surface of the ground. **32** And the people stayed up all that day, all night, and all the next day, and gathered the quail (he who gathered least gathered ten homers); and they spread *them* out for themselves all around the camp.

Their complaining punished.

Num 11:33 But while the meat *was* still between their teeth, before it was chewed, the wrath of the LORD was aroused against the people, and the LORD struck the people with a very great plague.

Ps 78:30–31 They were not deprived of their craving; But while their food *was* still in their mouths, **31** The wrath of God came against them, And slew the stoutest of them, And struck down the choice *men* of Israel.

Why called Kibroth Hattaavah.

Num 11:34 So he called the name of that place Kibroth Hattaavah, because there they buried the people who had yielded to craving.

To Hazeroth.

Num 11:35 From Kibroth Hattaavah the people moved to Hazeroth, and camped at Hazeroth.

Num 33:17 They departed from Kibroth Hattaavah and camped at Hazeroth.

Aaron and Miriam envy Moses.

Num 12:1–2 Then Miriam and Aaron spoke against Moses because of the Ethiopian woman whom he had married; for he had married an Ethiopian woman. **2** So they said, "Has the LORD indeed spoken only through Moses? Has He not spoken through us also?" And the LORD heard *it.*

Miriam punished by leprosy.

Num 12:10 And when the cloud departed from above the tabernacle, suddenly Miriam *became* leprous, as *white as* snow. Then Aaron turned toward Miriam, and there she was, a leper.

Delayed seven days for Miriam.

Num 12:14–15 Then the LORD said to Moses, "If her father had but spit in her face, would she not be shamed seven days? Let her be shut out of the camp seven days, and afterward she may be received *again.*" **15** So Miriam was shut out of the camp seven days, and the people did not journey till Miriam was brought in *again.*

To Kadesh Barnea in Wilderness of Rithmah or Paran.

Num 32:8 Thus your fathers did when I sent them away from Kadesh Barnea to see the land.

Num 12:16 And afterward the people moved from Hazeroth and camped in the Wilderness of Paran.

Num 33:18 They departed from Hazeroth and camped at Rithmah.

Deut 1:19 "So we departed from Horeb, and went through all that great and terrible wilderness which you saw on the way to the mountains of the Amorites, as the LORD our God had commanded us. Then we came to Kadesh Barnea.

The people anxious to have the land of Canaan searched.

Deut 1:22 "And every one of you came near to me and said, 'Let us send men before us, and let them search out the land for us, and bring back word to us of the way by which we should go up, and of the cities into which we shall come.'

Moses commanded to send spies.

Num 13:1–2 And the LORD spoke to Moses, saying, **2** "Send men to spy out the land of Canaan, which I am giving to the children of Israel; from each tribe of their fathers you shall send a man, every one a leader among them."

Persons selected as spies.

Num 13:3–16 So Moses sent them from the Wilderness of Paran according to the command of the LORD, all of them men who *were* heads of the children of Israel. **4** Now these *were* their names: from the tribe of Reuben, Shammua the son of Zaccur; **5** from the tribe of Simeon, Shaphat the son of Hori; **6** from the tribe of Judah, Caleb the son of Jephunneh; **7** from the tribe of Issachar, Igal the son of Joseph; **8** from the tribe of Ephraim, Hoshea the son of Nun; **9** from the tribe of Benjamin, Palti the son of Raphu; **10** from the tribe of Zebulun, Gaddiel the son of Sodi; **11** from the tribe of Joseph, *that is,* from the tribe of Manasseh, Gaddi the son of Susi; **12** from the tribe of Dan, Ammiel the son of Gemalli; **13** from the tribe of Asher, Sethur the son of Michael; **14** from the tribe of Naphtali, Nahbi the son of Vophsi; **15** from the tribe of Gad, Geuel the son of Machi. **16** These *are* the names of the men whom Moses sent to spy out the land. And Moses called Hoshea the son of Nun, Joshua.

Spies sent.

Josh 14:7 I *was* forty years old when Moses the servant of the LORD sent me from Kadesh Barnea to spy out the land, and I brought back word to him as *it was* in my heart.

Num 13:17–20 Then Moses sent them to spy out the land of Canaan, and said to them, "Go up this *way* into the South, and go up to the mountains, **18** and see what the land is like: whether the people who dwell in it *are* strong or weak, few or many; **19** whether the land they dwell in *is* good or bad; whether the cities they inhabit *are* like camps or strongholds; **20** whether the land *is* rich or poor; and whether there are forests there or not. Be of good courage. And bring some of the fruit of the land." Now the time *was* the season of the first ripe grapes.

Spies bring back evil report.

Num 13:26–33 Now they departed and came back to Moses and Aaron and all the congregation of the children of Israel in the Wilderness of Paran, at Kadesh; they brought back word to them and to all the congregation, and showed them the fruit of the land. **27** Then they told him, and said: "We went to the land where you sent us. It truly flows with milk and honey, and this *is* its fruit. **28** Nevertheless the people who dwell in the land *are* strong; the cities *are* fortified *and* very large; moreover we saw the descendants of Anak there. **29** The Amalekites dwell in the land of the South; the Hittites, the Jebusites, and the Amorites dwell in the mountains; and the Canaanites dwell by the sea and along the banks of the Jordan." **30** Then Caleb quieted the people before Moses, and said, "Let us go up at once and take possession, for we are well able to overcome it." **31** But the men who had gone up with him said, "We are not able to go up against the people, for they *are* stronger than we." **32** And they gave the children of Israel a bad report of the land which they had spied out, saying, "The land through which we have gone as spies *is* a land that devours its inhabitants, and all the people whom we saw in it *are* men of *great* stature. **33** There we saw the giants (the descendants of Anak came from the giants); and we were like grasshoppers in our own sight, and so we were in their sight."

The people terrified and rebel.

Num 14:1–4 So all the congregation lifted up their voices and cried, and the people wept that night. **2** And all the children of Israel complained against Moses and Aaron, and the whole congregation said to them, "If only we had died in the land of Egypt! Or if only we had died in this wilderness! **3** Why has the LORD brought us to this land to fall by the sword, that our wives and children should become victims? Would it not be better for us to return to Egypt?" **4** So they said to one another, "Let us select a leader and return to Egypt."

Punishment for rebellion.

Num 14:29 The carcasses of you who have complained against Me shall fall in this wilderness, all of you who were numbered, according to your entire number, from twenty years old and above.

Num 14:35 I the LORD have spoken this. I will surely do so to all this evil congregation who are gathered together against Me. In this wilderness they shall be consumed, and there they shall die.' "

Num 32:11–13 'Surely none of the men who came up from Egypt, from twenty years old and above, shall see the land of which I swore to Abraham, Isaac, and Jacob, because they have not wholly followed Me, **12** except Caleb the son of Jephunneh, the Kenizzite, and Joshua the son of Nun, for they have wholly followed the LORD.' **13** So the LORD's anger was aroused against Israel, and He made them wander in the wilderness forty years, until all the generation that had done evil in the sight of the LORD was gone.

Deut 1:35–36 'Surely not one of these men of this evil generation shall see that good land of which I swore to give to your fathers, **36** except Caleb the son of Jephunneh; he shall see it, and to him and his children

I am giving the land on which he walked, because he wholly followed the LORD.'

Deut 1:40 But *as for* you, turn and take your journey into the wilderness by the Way of the Red Sea.'

Guilty spies slain by plague.

Num 14:36–37 Now the men whom Moses sent to spy out the land, who returned and made all the congregation complain against him by bringing a bad report of the land, **37** those very men who brought the evil report about the land, died by the plague before the LORD.

People smitten by Amalek for going up without the Lord.

Num 14:40–45 And they rose early in the morning and went up to the top of the mountain, saying, "Here we are, and we will go up to the place which the LORD has promised, for we have sinned!" **41** And Moses said, "Now why do you transgress the command of the LORD? For this will not succeed. **42** Do not go up, lest you be defeated by your enemies, for the LORD *is* not among you. **43** For the Amalekites and the Canaanites *are* there before you, and you shall fall by the sword; because you have turned away from the LORD, the LORD will not be with you." **44** But they presumed to go up to the mountaintop. Nevertheless, neither the ark of the covenant of the LORD nor Moses departed from the camp. **45** Then the Amalekites and the Canaanites who dwelt in that mountain came down and attacked them, and drove them back as far as Hormah.

Deut 1:41–44 "Then you answered and said to me, 'We have sinned against the LORD; we will go up and fight, just as the LORD our God commanded us.' And when everyone of you had girded on his weapons of war, you were ready to go up into the mountain. **42** "And the LORD said to me, 'Tell them, "Do not go up nor fight, for I *am* not among you; lest you be defeated before your enemies." ' **43** So I spoke to you; yet you would not listen, but rebelled against the command of the LORD, and presumptuously went up into the mountain. **44** And the Amorites who dwelt in that mountain came out against you and chased you as bees do, and drove you back from Seir to Hormah.

Returned by the way to the Red Sea.

Num 14:25 Now the Amalekites and the Canaanites dwell in the valley; tomorrow turn and move out into the wilderness by the Way of the Red Sea."

Deut 1:40 But *as for* you, turn and take your journey into the wilderness by the Way of the Red Sea.'

Deut 2:1 "Then we turned and journeyed into the wilderness of the Way of the Red Sea, as the LORD spoke to me, and we skirted Mount Seir for many days.

Sabbath-breaker stoned.

Num 15:32–36 Now while the children of Israel were in the wilderness, they found a man gathering sticks on the Sabbath day. **33** And those who found him gathering sticks brought him to Moses and Aaron, and to all the congregation. **34** They put him under guard, because it had not been explained what should be done to him. **35** Then the LORD said to Moses, "The man must surely be put to death; all the congregation shall stone him with stones outside the camp."

36 So, as the LORD commanded Moses, all the congregation brought him outside the camp and stoned him with stones, and he died.

Rebellion of Korah. Num 16:1–19

Korah, etc., punished.

Num 16:30–35 But if the LORD creates a new thing, and the earth opens its mouth and swallows them up with all that belongs to them, and they go down alive into the pit, then you will understand that these men have rejected the LORD." 31 Now it came to pass, as he finished speaking all these words, that the ground split apart under them, 32 and the earth opened its mouth and swallowed them up, with their households and all the men with Korah, with all *their* goods. 33 So they and all those with them went down alive into the pit; the earth closed over them, and they perished from among the assembly. 34 Then all Israel who *were* around them fled at their cry, for they said, "Lest the earth swallow us up *also!*" 35 And a fire came out from the LORD and consumed the two hundred and fifty men who were offering incense.

Plague sent.

Num 16:41–46 On the next day all the congregation of the children of Israel complained against Moses and Aaron, saying, "You have killed the people of the LORD." 42 Now it happened, when the congregation had gathered against Moses and Aaron, that they turned toward the tabernacle of meeting; and suddenly the cloud covered it, and the glory of the LORD appeared. 43 Then Moses and Aaron came before the tabernacle of meeting. 44 And the LORD spoke to Moses, saying, 45 "Get away from among this congregation, that I may consume them in a moment." And they fell on their faces. 46 So Moses said to Aaron, "Take a censer and put fire in it from the altar, put incense *on it*, and take it quickly to the congregation and make atonement for them; for wrath has gone out from the LORD. The plague has begun."

Plague stopped.

Num 16:47–50 Then Aaron took *it* as Moses commanded, and ran into the midst of the assembly; and already the plague had begun among the people. So he put in the incense and made atonement for the people. 48 And he stood between the dead and the living; so the plague was stopped. 49 Now those who died in the plague were fourteen thousand seven hundred, besides those who died in the Korah incident. 50 So Aaron returned to Moses at the door of the tabernacle of meeting, for the plague had stopped.

God's choice of Aaron confirmed.

Num 17:1–13 And the LORD spoke to Moses, saying: 2 "Speak to the children of Israel, and get from them a rod from each father's house, all their leaders according to their fathers' houses—twelve rods. Write each man's name on his rod. 3 And you shall write Aaron's name on the rod of Levi. For there shall be one rod for the head of *each* father's house. 4 Then you shall place them in the tabernacle of meeting before the Testimony, where I meet with you. 5 And it shall be *that* the rod of the man whom I choose will blossom; thus I will rid Myself of the complaints of the children of Israel, which they make against you." 6 So Moses spoke to the children of Israel, and each

of their leaders gave him a rod apiece, for each leader according to their fathers' houses, twelve rods; and the rod of Aaron *was* among their rods. 7 And Moses placed the rods before the LORD in the tabernacle of witness. 8 Now it came to pass on the next day that Moses went into the tabernacle of witness, and behold, the rod of Aaron, of the house of Levi, had sprouted and put forth buds, had produced blossoms and yielded ripe almonds. 9 Then Moses brought out all the rods from before the LORD to all the children of Israel; and they looked, and each man took his rod. 10 And the LORD said to Moses, "Bring Aaron's rod back before the Testimony, to be kept as a sign against the rebels, that you may put their complaints away from Me, lest they die." 11 Thus did Moses; just as the LORD had commanded him, so he did. 12 So the children of Israel spoke to Moses, saying, "Surely we die, we perish, we all perish! 13 Whoever even comes near the tabernacle of the LORD must die. Shall we all utterly die?"

To Rimmon Perez.

Num 33:19 They departed from Rithmah and camped at Rimmon Perez.

To Libnah or Laban.

Num 33:20 They departed from Rimmon Perez and camped at Libnah.

Deut 1:1 These *are* the words which Moses spoke to all Israel on this side of the Jordan in the wilderness, in the plain opposite Suph, between Paran, Tophel, Laban, Hazeroth, and Dizahab.

To Rissah.

Num 33:21 They moved from Libnah and camped at Rissah.

To Kehelathah.

Num 33:22 They journeyed from Rissah and camped at Kehelathah.

To Mount Shepher.

Num 33:23 They went from Kehelathah and camped at Mount Shepher.

To Haradah.

Num 33:24 They moved from Mount Shepher and camped at Haradah.

To Makheloth.

Num 33:25 They moved from Haradah and camped at Makheloth.

To Tahath.

Num 33:26 They moved from Makheloth and camped at Tahath.

To Terah.

Num 33:27 They departed from Tahath and camped at Terah.

To Mithkah.

Num 33:28 They moved from Terah and camped at Mithkah.

To Hashmonah.

Num 33:29 They went from Mithkah and camped at Hashmonah.

To Moseroth or Mosera.

Num 33:30 They departed from Hashmonah and camped at Moseroth.

To Bene Jaakan.

Num 33:31 They departed from Moseroth and camped at Bene Jaakan.

To Hor Hagidgad or Gudgodah.

Num 33:32 They moved from Bene Jaakan and camped at Hor Hagidgad.

Deut 10:7 From there they journeyed to Gudgodah, and from Gudgodah to Jotbathah, a land of rivers of water.

To Jotbathah or land of rivers.

Num 33:33 They went from Hor Hagidgad and camped at Jotbathah.

Deut 10:7 From there they journeyed to Gudgodah, and from Gudgodah to Jotbathah, a land of rivers of water.

Several of the stations probably revisited.

Num 33:30–32 They departed from Hashmonah and camped at Moseroth. 31 They departed from Moseroth and camped at Bene Jaakan. 32 They moved from Bene Jaakan and camped at Hor Hagidgad.

Deut 10:6–7 (Now the children of Israel journeyed from the wells of Bene Jaakan to Moserah, where Aaron died, and where he was buried; and Eleazar his son ministered as priest in his stead. 7 From there they journeyed to Gudgodah, and from Gudgodah to Jotbathah, a land of rivers of water.

To Abronah.

Num 33:34 They moved from Jotbathah and camped at Abronah.

To Ezion Geber.

Num 33:35 They departed from Abronah and camped at Ezion Geber.

To Kadesh in the Wilderness of Zin.

Num 20:1 Then the children of Israel, the whole congregation, came into the Wilderness of Zin in the first month, and the people stayed in Kadesh; and Miriam died there and was buried there.

Num 33:36 They moved from Ezion Geber and camped in the Wilderness of Zin, which is Kadesh.

Judg 11:16 for when Israel came up from Egypt, they walked through the wilderness as far as the Red Sea and came to Kadesh.

Second complaining for water.

Num 20:2–6 Now there was no water for the congregation; so they gathered together against Moses and Aaron. 3 And the people contended with Moses and spoke, saying: "If only we had died when our brethren died before the LORD! 4 Why have you brought up the assembly of the LORD into this wilderness, that we and our animals should die here? 5 And why have you made us come up out of Egypt, to bring us to this evil place? It is not a place of grain or figs or vines or pomegranates; nor is there any water to drink." 6 So Moses and Aaron went from the presence of the assembly to the door of the tabernacle of meeting, and they fell on their faces. And the glory of the LORD appeared to them.

Moses, striking the rock instead of speaking to it, disobeys God.

Num 20:7–11 Then the LORD spoke to Moses, saying, 8 "Take the rod; you and your brother Aaron gather the congregation together. Speak to the rock before their eyes, and it will yield its water; thus you shall bring water for them out of the rock, and give drink to the congregation and their animals." 9 So Moses took the rod from before the LORD as He commanded him. 10 And Moses and Aaron gathered the assembly together before the rock; and he said to them, "Hear now, you rebels! Must we bring water for you out of this rock?" 11 Then Moses lifted his hand and struck the rock twice with his rod; and water came out abundantly, and the congregation and their animals drank.

Moses and Aaron punished.

Num 20:12 Then the LORD spoke to Moses and Aaron, "Because you did not believe Me, to hallow Me in the eyes of the children of Israel, therefore you shall not bring this assembly into the land which I have given them."

Called Meribah to commemorate the complaining.

Num 20:13 This was the water of Meribah, because the children of Israel contended with the LORD, and He was hallowed among them.

Num 27:14 For in the Wilderness of Zin, during the strife of the congregation, you rebelled against My command to hallow Me at the waters before their eyes." (These are the waters of Meribah, at Kadesh in the Wilderness of Zin.)

Orders given respecting the descendants of Esau.

Deut 2:3–6 'You have skirted this mountain long enough; turn northward. 4 And command the people, saying, "You are about to pass through the territory of your brethren, the descendants of Esau, who live in Seir; and they will be afraid of you. Therefore watch yourselves carefully. 5 Do not meddle with them, for I will not give you any of their land, no, not so much as one footstep, because I have given Mount Seir to Esau as a possession. 6 You shall buy food from them with money, that you may eat; and you shall also buy water from them with money, that you may drink.

The king of Edom refuses a passage.

Num 20:14–21 Now Moses sent messengers from Kadesh to the king of Edom. "Thus says your brother Israel: 'You know all the hardship that has befallen us, 15 how our fathers went down to Egypt, and we dwelt in Egypt a long time, and the Egyptians afflicted us and our fathers. 16 When we cried out to the LORD, He heard our voice and sent the Angel and brought us up out of Egypt; now here we are in Kadesh, a city on the edge of your border. 17 Please let us pass through your country. We will not pass through fields or vineyards, nor will we drink water from wells; we will go along the King's Highway; we will not turn aside to the right hand or to the left until we have passed through your territory.' " 18 Then Edom said to him, "You shall not pass through my land, lest I come out against you with the sword." 19 So the children of Israel said to him, "We will go by the Highway, and if I or my livestock drink any of your water, then I will pay for it; let me only pass through on foot, nothing more." 20 Then he said, "You shall not pass through." So Edom came out against them with many men and with a strong hand. 21 Thus Edom refused to give Israel passage through his territory; so Israel turned away from him.

To Mount Hor.

Num 20:22 Now the children of Israel, the whole congregation, journeyed from Kadesh and came to Mount Hor.

Num 33:37 They moved from Kadesh and camped at Mount Hor, on the boundary of the land of Edom.

Aaron dies.

Num 20:28–29 Moses stripped Aaron of his garments and put them on Eleazar his son; and Aaron died there on the top of the mountain. Then Moses and Eleazar came down from the mountain. **29** Now when all the congregation saw that Aaron was dead, all the house of Israel mourned for Aaron thirty days.

Num 33:38–39 Then Aaron the priest went up to Mount Hor at the command of the LORD, and died there in the fortieth year after the children of Israel had come out of the land of Egypt, on the first *day* of the fifth month. **39** Aaron *was* one hundred and twenty-three years old when he died on Mount Hor.

Arad conquered.

Num 21:1–3 The king of Arad, the Canaanite, who dwelt in the South, heard that Israel was coming on the road to Atharim. Then he fought against Israel and took *some* of them prisoners. **2** So Israel made a vow to the LORD, and said, "If You will indeed deliver this people into my hand, then I will utterly destroy their cities." **3** And the LORD listened to the voice of Israel and delivered up the Canaanites, and they utterly destroyed them and their cities. So the name of that place was called Hormah.

Num 33:40 Now the king of Arad, the Canaanite, who dwelt in the South in the land of Canaan, heard of the coming of the children of Israel.

Called Hormah.

Num 21:2–3 So Israel made a vow to the LORD, and said, "If You will indeed deliver this people into my hand, then I will utterly destroy their cities." **3** And the LORD listened to the voice of Israel and delivered up the Canaanites, and they utterly destroyed them and their cities. So the name of that place was called Hormah.

To Zalmonah.

Num 33:41 So they departed from Mount Hor and camped at Zalmonah.

Complaining of the people.

Num 21:4–5 Then they journeyed from Mount Hor by the Way of the Red Sea, to go around the land of Edom; and the soul of the people became very discouraged on the way. **5** And the people spoke against God and against Moses: "Why have you brought us up out of Egypt to die in the wilderness? For *there is* no food and no water, and our soul loathes this worthless bread."

Fiery serpents sent.

Num 21:6 So the LORD sent fiery serpents among the people, and they bit the people; and many of the people of Israel died.

Bronze serpent raised up.

Num 21:7–9 Therefore the people came to Moses, and said, "We have sinned, for we have spoken against the LORD and against you; pray to the LORD that He take away the serpents from us." So Moses prayed for the people. **8** Then the LORD said to Moses, "Make a fiery *serpent,* and set it on a pole; and it shall be that everyone who is bitten, when he looks at it, shall live." **9** So Moses made a bronze serpent, and put it on a pole; and so it was, if a serpent had bitten anyone, when he looked at the bronze serpent, he lived.

To Punon.

Num 33:42 They departed from Zalmonah and camped at Punon.

To Oboth.

Num 21:10 Now the children of Israel moved on and camped in Oboth.

Num 33:43 They departed from Punon and camped at Oboth.

To Ije Abarim before Moab.

Num 21:11 And they journeyed from Oboth and camped at Ije Abarim, in the wilderness which *is* east of Moab, toward the sunrise.

Num 33:44 They departed from Oboth and camped at Ije Abarim, at the border of Moab.

Orders given respecting Moab.

Deut 2:8–9 "And when we passed beyond our brethren, the descendants of Esau who dwell in Seir, away from the road of the plain, away from Elath and Ezion Geber, we turned and passed by way of the Wilderness of Moab. **9** Then the LORD said to me, 'Do not harass Moab, nor contend with them in battle, for I will not give you *any* of their land *as* a possession, because I have given Ar to the descendants of Lot *as* a possession.' "

To Zered or Dibon Gad.

Num 21:12 From there they moved and camped in the Valley of Zered.

Num 33:45 They departed from Ijim and camped at Dibon Gad.

To Almon Diblathaim.

Num 33:46 They moved from Dibon Gad and camped at Almon Diblathaim.

Across the Valley of the Zered.

Deut 2:13 " 'Now rise and cross over the Valley of the Zered.' So we crossed over the Valley of the Zered.

Time occupied in going from Kadesh Barnea to this station.

Deut 2:14 And the time we took to come from Kadesh Barnea until we crossed over the Valley of the Zered *was* thirty-eight years, until all the generation of the men of war was consumed from the midst of the camp, just as the LORD had sworn to them.

Order to pass through Ar.

Deut 2:18 'This day you are to cross over at Ar, the boundary of Moab.

Orders given respecting Ammon.

Deut 2:19 And *when* you come near the people of Ammon, do not harass them or meddle with them, for I will not give you *any* of the land of the people of Ammon *as* a possession, because I have given it to the descendants of Lot *as* a possession.' "

Across the Arnon.

Num 21:13–15 From there they moved and camped on the other side of the Arnon, which *is* in the wilderness that extends from the border of the Amorites; for the Arnon *is* the border of Moab, between Moab and the Amorites. **14** Therefore it is said in the Book of the Wars of the LORD: "Waheb in Suphah, The brooks of the Arnon, **15** And the slope of the brooks That reaches to the dwelling of Ar, And lies on the border of Moab."

Deut 2:24 " 'Rise, take your journey, and cross over the River Arnon. Look, I have given into your hand Sihon the Amorite, king of Heshbon, and his land. Begin to possess *it*, and engage him in battle.

To Beer.

Num 21:16 From there *they went* to Beer, which *is* the well where the LORD said to Moses, "Gather the people together, and I will give them water."

To Mattanah.

Num 21:18 The well the leaders sank, Dug by the nation's nobles, By the lawgiver, with their staves." And from the wilderness *they went* to Mattanah,

To Nahaliel.

Num 21:19 from Mattanah to Nahaliel, from Nahaliel to Bamoth,

To Bamoth.

Num 21:19 from Mattanah to Nahaliel, from Nahaliel to Bamoth,

To the mountains of Abarim.

Num 21:20 and from Bamoth, *in* the valley that *is* in the country of Moab, to the top of Pisgah which looks down on the wasteland.

Num 33:47 They moved from Almon Diblathaim and camped in the mountains of Abarim, before Nebo.

The Amorites refuse a passage to Israel.

Num 21:21–23 Then Israel sent messengers to Sihon king of the Amorites, saying, **22** "Let me pass through your land. We will not turn aside into fields or vineyards; we will not drink water from wells. We will go by the King's Highway until we have passed through your territory." **23** But Sihon would not allow Israel to pass through his territory. So Sihon gathered all his people together and went out against Israel in the wilderness, and he came to Jahaz and fought against Israel.

Deut 2:26–30 "And I sent messengers from the Wilderness of Kedemoth to Sihon king of Heshbon, with words of peace, saying, **27** 'Let me pass through your land; I will keep strictly to the road, and I will turn neither to the right nor to the left. **28** You shall sell me food for money, that I may eat, and give me water for money, that I may drink; only let me pass through on foot, **29** just as the descendants of Esau who dwell in Seir and the Moabites who dwell in Ar did for me, until I cross the Jordan to the land which the LORD our God is giving us.' **30** "But Sihon king of Heshbon would not let us pass through, for the LORD your God hardened his spirit and made his heart obstinate, that He might deliver him into your hand, as *it is* this day.

Sihon conquered.

Num 21:23–32 But Sihon would not allow Israel to pass through his territory. So Sihon gathered all his people together and went out against Israel in the wilderness, and he came to Jahaz and fought against Israel. **24** Then Israel defeated him with the edge of

the sword, and took possession of his land from the Arnon to the Jabbok, as far as the people of Ammon; for the border of the people of Ammon *was* fortified. **25** So Israel took all these cities, and Israel dwelt in all the cities of the Amorites, in Heshbon and in all its villages. **26** For Heshbon *was* the city of Sihon king of the Amorites, who had fought against the former king of Moab, and had taken all his land from his hand as far as the Arnon. **27** Therefore those who speak in proverbs say: "Come to Heshbon, let it be built; Let the city of Sihon be repaired. **28** "For fire went out from Heshbon, A flame from the city of Sihon; It consumed Ar of Moab, The lords of the heights of the Arnon. **29** Woe to you, Moab! You have perished, O people of Chemosh! He has given his sons as fugitives, And his daughters into captivity, To Sihon king of the Amorites. **30** "But we have shot at them; Heshbon has perished as far as Dibon. Then we laid waste as far as Nophah, Which *reaches* to Medeba." **31** Thus Israel dwelt in the land of the Amorites. **32** Then Moses sent to spy out Jazer; and they took its villages and drove out the Amorites who *were* there.

Cf. Deut 2:32–36

Og conquered.

Num 21:33–35 And they turned and went up by the way to Bashan. So Og king of Bashan went out against them, he and all his people, to battle at Edrei. **34** Then the LORD said to Moses, "Do not fear him, for I have delivered him into your hand, with all his people and his land; and you shall do to him as you did to Sihon king of the Amorites, who dwelt at Heshbon." **35** So they defeated him, his sons, and all his people, until there was no survivor left him; and they took possession of his land.

Cf. Deut 3:1–11

Reubenites, etc., obtained the land taken from the Amorites. **Num 32:1–42; Deut 3:12–17**

Return to the plains of Moab.

Num 22:1 Then the children of Israel moved, and camped in the plains of Moab on the side of the Jordan *across from* Jericho.

Num 33:48–49 They departed from the mountains of Abarim and camped in the plains of Moab by the Jordan, *across from* Jericho. **49** They camped by the Jordan, from Beth Jesimoth as far as the Abel Acacia Grove in the plains of Moab.

Balak sends for Balaam.

Num 22:5 Then he sent messengers to Balaam the son of Beor at Pethor, which *is* near the River in the land of the sons of his people, to call him, saying: "Look, a people has come from Egypt. See, they cover the face of the earth, and are settling next to me!

Num 22:6 Therefore please come at once, curse this people for me, for they *are* too mighty for me. Perhaps I shall be able to defeat them and drive them out of the land, for I know that he whom you bless *is* blessed, and he whom you curse is cursed."

Num 22:15–17 Then Balak again sent princes, more numerous and more honorable than they. **16** And they came to Balaam and said to him, "Thus says Balak the son of Zippor: 'Please let nothing hinder you from coming to me; **17** for I will certainly honor you

greatly, and I will do whatever you say to me. Therefore please come, curse this people for me.' "

Balaam not permitted to curse Israel.

Num 22:9–12 Then God came to Balaam and said,
"Who *are* these men with you?" **10** So Balaam said to
God, "Balak the son of Zippor, king of Moab, has
sent to me, *saying,* **11** 'Look, a people has come out of
Egypt, and they cover the face of the earth. Come
now, curse them for me; perhaps I shall be able to
overpower them and drive them out.' " **12** And God
said to Balaam, "You shall not go with them; you
shall not curse the people, for they *are* blessed."

Cf. Num 22:13–41; 23:1–30; 24:1–25

Israel seduced to idolatry, etc., by advice of Balaam.

Num 25:1–3 Now Israel remained in Acacia Grove, and
the people began to commit harlotry with the
women of Moab. **2** They invited the people to the
sacrifices of their gods, and the people ate and
bowed down to their gods. **3** So Israel was joined to
Baal of Peor, and the anger of the LORD was aroused
against Israel.

Rev 2:14 But I have a few things against you, because
you have there those who hold the doctrine of Balaam, who taught Balak to put a stumbling block before the children of Israel, to eat things sacrificed to
idols, and to commit sexual immorality.

Israel punished.

Num 25:5 So Moses said to the judges of Israel, "Every
one of you kill his men who were joined to Baal of
Peor."

Num 25:9 And those who died in the plague were
twenty-four thousand.

Third numbering.

Num 26:1–4 And it came to pass, after the plague, that
the LORD spoke to Moses and Eleazar the son of
Aaron the priest, saying: **2** "Take a census of all the
congregation of the children of Israel from twenty
years old and above, by their fathers' houses, all who
are able to go to war in Israel." **3** So Moses and Eleazar the priest spoke with them in the plains of Moab
by the Jordan, *across from* Jericho, saying: **4** *"Take a
census of the people* from twenty years old and above,
just as the LORD commanded Moses and the children
of Israel who came out of the land of Egypt."

All formerly numbered over twenty years old, except Caleb and Joshua, dead.

Num 14:29 The carcasses of you who have complained
against Me shall fall in this wilderness, all of you
who were numbered, according to your entire number, from twenty years old and above.

Num 26:63–65 These *are* those who were numbered by
Moses and Eleazar the priest, who numbered the
children of Israel in the plains of Moab by the Jordan,
across from Jericho. **64** But among these there was not
a man of those who were numbered by Moses and
Aaron the priest when they numbered the children
of Israel in the Wilderness of Sinai. **65** For the LORD
had said of them, "They shall surely die in the
wilderness." So there was not left a man of them, except Caleb the son of Jephunneh and Joshua the son
of Nun.

The law of female inheritance settled.

Num 27:1–11 Then came the daughters of Zelophehad
the son of Hepher, the son of Gilead, the son of
Machir, the son of Manasseh, from the families of Manasseh the son of Joseph; and these *were* the names of
his daughters: Mahlah, Noah, Hoglah, Milcah, and
Tirzah. **2** And they stood before Moses, before Eleazar
the priest, and before the leaders and all the congregation, *by* the doorway of the tabernacle of meeting,
saying: **3** "Our father died in the wilderness; but he
was not in the company of those who gathered together against the LORD, in company with Korah, but
he died in his own sin; and he had no sons. **4** Why
should the name of our father be removed from
among his family because he had no son? Give us a
possession among our father's brothers." **5** So Moses
brought their case before the LORD. **6** And the LORD
spoke to Moses, saying: **7** "The daughters of Zelophehad speak *what is* right; you shall surely give them a
possession of inheritance among their father's brothers, and cause the inheritance of their father to pass to
them. **8** And you shall speak to the children of Israel,
saying: 'If a man dies and has no son, then you shall
cause his inheritance to pass to his daughter. **9** If he
has no daughter, then you shall give his inheritance to
his brothers. **10** If he has no brothers, then you shall
give his inheritance to his father's brothers. **11** And if
his father has no brothers, then you shall give his inheritance to the relative closest to him in his family,
and he shall possess it.' " And it shall be to the children of Israel a statute of judgment, just as the LORD
commanded Moses.

Cf. Num 36:1–9

Appointment of Joshua.

Num 27:15–23 Then Moses spoke to the LORD, saying:
16 "Let the LORD, the God of the spirits of all flesh, set
a man over the congregation, **17** who may go out before them and go in before them, who may lead them
out and bring them in, that the congregation of the
LORD may not be like sheep which have no shepherd."
18 And the LORD said to Moses: "Take Joshua the son
of Nun with you, a man in whom *is* the Spirit, and lay
your hand on him; **19** set him before Eleazar the priest
and before all the congregation, and inaugurate him
in their sight. **20** And you shall give *some* of your authority to him, that all the congregation of the children
of Israel may be obedient. **21** He shall stand before Eleazar the priest, who shall inquire before the LORD for
him by the judgment of the Urim. At his word they
shall go out, and at his word they shall come in, he
and all the children of Israel with him—all the congregation." **22** So Moses did as the LORD commanded
him. He took Joshua and set him before Eleazar the
priest and before all the congregation. **23** And he laid
his hands on him and inaugurated him, just as the
LORD commanded by the hand of Moses.

Midianites destroyed and Balaam slain.

Num 25:17–18 "Harass the Midianites, and attack them;
18 for they harassed you with their schemes by
which they seduced you in the matter of Peor and in
the matter of Cozbi, the daughter of a leader of Midian, their sister, who was killed in the day of the
plague because of Peor."

Cf. Num 31:1–54

The law rehearsed.

Deut 1:3 Now it came to pass in the fortieth year, in the eleventh month, on the first *day* of the month, *that* Moses spoke to the children of Israel according to all that the LORD had given him as commandments to them,

The law written by Moses.

Deut 31:9 So Moses wrote this law and delivered it to the priests, the sons of Levi, who bore the ark of the covenant of the LORD, and to all the elders of Israel.

Moses beholds Canaan.

Deut 34:1–4 Then Moses went up from the plains of Moab to Mount Nebo, to the top of Pisgah, which is across from Jericho. And the LORD showed him all the land of Gilead as far as Dan, **2** all Naphtali and the land of Ephraim and Manasseh, all the land of Judah as far as the Western Sea, **3** the South, and the plain of the Valley of Jericho, the city of palm trees, as far as Zoar. **4** Then the LORD said to him, "This *is* the land of which I swore to give Abraham, Isaac, and Jacob, saying, 'I will give it to your descendants.' I have caused you to see *it* with your eyes, but you shall not cross over there."

Moses dies and is buried.

Deut 34:5–6 So Moses the servant of the LORD died there in the land of Moab, according to the word of the LORD. **6** And He buried him in a valley in the land of Moab, opposite Beth Peor; but no one knows his grave to this day.

Joshua ordered to cross the Jordan.

Josh 1:2 "Moses My servant is dead. Now therefore, arise, go over this Jordan, you and all this people, to the land which I am giving to them—the children of Israel.

Two spies sent to Jericho.

Josh 2:1 Now Joshua the son of Nun sent out two men from Acacia Grove to spy secretly, saying, "Go, view the land, especially Jericho." So they went, and came to the house of a harlot named Rahab, and lodged there.

Across the river Jordan.

Josh 4:10 So the priests who bore the ark stood in the midst of the Jordan until everything was finished that the LORD had commanded Joshua to speak to the people, according to all that Moses had commanded Joshua; and the people hurried and crossed over.

ISRAEL, DISPERSION OF

Because of disobedience.

Hos 9:17 My God will cast them away, Because they did not obey Him; And they shall be wanderers among the nations.

Judgment for idolatry.

Deut 4:27 And the LORD will scatter you among the peoples, and you will be left few in number among the nations where the LORD will drive you.

To serve other gods.

Deut 28:64 "Then the LORD will scatter you among all peoples, from one end of the earth to the other, and there you shall serve other gods, which neither you nor your fathers have known—wood and stone.

Like a whirlwind.

Zech 7:14 "But I scattered them with a whirlwind among all the nations which they had not known. Thus the land became desolate after them, so that no one passed through or returned; for they made the pleasant land desolate."

James wrote to Jewish believers who were part of.

James 1:1 James, a bondservant of God and of the Lord Jesus Christ, To the twelve tribes which are scattered abroad: Greetings.

Regathering from.

Is 11:11–12 It shall come to pass in that day *That* the Lord shall set His hand again the second time To recover the remnant of His people who are left, From Assyria and Egypt, From Pathros and Cush, From Elam and Shinar, From Hamath and the islands of the sea. **12** He will set up a banner for the nations, And will assemble the outcasts of Israel, And gather together the dispersed of Judah From the four corners of the earth.

Is 41:9 *You* whom I have taken from the ends of the earth, And called from its farthest regions, And said to you, 'You *are* My servant, I have chosen you and have not cast you away:

Cf. Is 43:5–6

ISRAEL, RESTORATION OF

The goal of God's judgment.

Is 1:25–26 I will turn My hand against you, And thoroughly purge away your dross, And take away all your alloy. **26** I will restore your judges as at the first, And your counselors as at the beginning. Afterward you shall be called the city of righteousness, the faithful city."

Is yet future.

Jer 23:3–4 "But I will gather the remnant of My flock out of all countries where I have driven them, and bring them back to their folds; and they shall be fruitful and increase. **4** I will set up shepherds over them who will feed them; and they shall fear no more, nor be dismayed, nor shall they be lacking," says the LORD.

Jer 30:3 For behold, the days are coming,' says the LORD, 'that I will bring back from captivity My people Israel and Judah,' says the LORD. 'And I will cause them to return to the land that I gave to their fathers, and they shall possess it.' "

Cf. Is 1:25–26

From the Babylonian captivity.

Jer 23:3–4 "But I will gather the remnant of My flock out of all countries where I have driven them, and bring them back to their folds; and they shall be fruitful and increase. **4** I will set up shepherds over them who will feed them; and they shall fear no more, nor be dismayed, nor shall they be lacking," says the LORD.

From the dispersion among the nations.

Ezek 34:12–14 As a shepherd seeks out his flock on the day he is among his scattered sheep, so will I seek out My sheep and deliver them from all the places where they were scattered on a cloudy and dark day. **13** And I will bring them out from the peoples and gather them from the countries, and will bring them to their own land; I will feed them on the mountains of Israel, in the valleys and in all the inhabited places of the country. **14** I will feed them in good pasture, and their fold shall be on the high mountains of Israel. There they shall lie down in a good fold and feed in rich pasture on the mountains of Israel.

What the future will encompass.

Ezek 36:25–31 Then I will sprinkle clean water on you, and you shall be clean; I will cleanse you from all your filthiness and from all your idols. **26** I will give you a new heart and put a new spirit within you; I will take the heart of stone out of your flesh and give you a heart of flesh. **27** I will put My Spirit within you and cause you to walk in My statutes, and you will keep My judgments and do *them.* **28** Then you shall dwell in the land that I gave to your fathers; you shall be My people, and I will be your God. **29** I will deliver you from all your uncleannesses. I will call for the grain and multiply it, and bring no famine upon you. **30** And I will multiply the fruit of your trees and the increase of your fields, so that you need never again bear the reproach of famine among the nations. **31** Then you will remember your evil ways and your deeds that *were* not good; and you will loathe yourselves in your own sight, for your iniquities and your abominations.

ISRAEL, THE TRIBES OF
Were twelve in number.

Gen 49:28 All these *are* the twelve tribes of Israel, and this *is* what their father spoke to them. And he blessed them; he blessed each one according to his own blessing.

Acts 26:12 "While thus occupied, as I journeyed to Damascus with authority and commission from the chief priests,

James 1:1 James, a bondservant of God and of the Lord Jesus Christ, To the twelve tribes which are scattered abroad: Greetings.

Descended from Jacob's sons.

Gen 35:22–26 And it happened, when Israel dwelt in that land, that Reuben went and lay with Bilhah his father's concubine; and Israel heard *about it.* Now the sons of Jacob were twelve: **23** the sons of Leah *were* Reuben, Jacob's firstborn, and Simeon, Levi, Judah, Issachar, and Zebulun; **24** the sons of Rachel *were* Joseph and Benjamin; **25** the sons of Bilhah, Rachel's maidservant, *were* Dan and Naphtali; **26** and the sons of Zilpah, Leah's maidservant, *were* Gad and Asher. These *were* the sons of Jacob who were born to him in Padan Aram.

Manasseh and Ephraim numbered among, instead of Joseph and Levi.

Gen 48:5 And now your two sons, Ephraim and Manasseh, who were born to you in the land of Egypt before I came to you in Egypt, *are* mine; as Reuben and Simeon, they shall be mine.

Josh 14:3–4 For Moses had given the inheritance of the

two tribes and the half-tribe on the other side of the Jordan; but to the Levites he had given no inheritance among them. **4** For the children of Joseph were two tribes: Manasseh and Ephraim. And they gave no part to the Levites in the land, except cities to dwell *in,* with their common-lands for their livestock and their property.

Predictions respecting each of. Gen 49:3–27; Deut 33:6–29
Characteristics of each.

Num 1:2–16 "Take a census of all the congregation of the children of Israel, by their families, by their fathers' houses, according to the number of names, every male individually, **3** from twenty years old and above—all who *are able to* go to war in Israel. You and Aaron shall number them by their armies. **4** And with you there shall be a man from every tribe, each one the head of his father's house. **5** "These are the names of the men who shall stand with you: from Reuben, Elizur the son of Shedeur; **6** from Simeon, Shelumiel the son of Zurishaddai; **7** from Judah, Nahshon the son of Amminadab; **8** from Issachar, Nethanel the son of Zuar; **9** from Zebulun, Eliab the son of Helon; **10** from the sons of Joseph: from Ephraim, Elishama the son of Ammihud; from Manasseh, Gamaliel the son of Pedahzur; **11** from Benjamin, Abidan the son of Gideoni; **12** from Dan, Ahiezer the son of Ammishaddai; **13** from Asher, Pagiel the son of Ocran; **14** from Gad, Eliasaph the son of Deuel; **15** from Naphtali, Ahira the son of Enan." **16** These *were* chosen from the congregation, leaders of their fathers' tribes, heads of the divisions in Israel.

Num 31:4 A thousand from each tribe of all the tribes of Israel you shall send to the war."

Num 36:1 Now the chief fathers of the families of the children of Gilead the son of Machir, the son of Manasseh, of the families of the sons of Joseph, came near and spoke before Moses and before the leaders, the chief fathers of the children of Israel.

1 Chr 4:38 these mentioned by name *were* leaders in their families, and their father's house increased greatly.

Cf. Num 26:5–50; Josh 7:14

Total strength of, on leaving Egypt.

Ex 12:37 Then the children of Israel journeyed from Rameses to Succoth, about six hundred thousand men on foot, besides children.

Num 1:44–46 These are the ones who were numbered, whom Moses and Aaron numbered, with the leaders of Israel, twelve men, each one representing his father's house. **45** So all who were numbered of the children of Israel, by their fathers' houses, from twenty years old and above, all who *were able to* go to war in Israel— **46** all who were numbered were six hundred and three thousand five hundred and fifty.

Num 2:32 These *are* the ones who were numbered of the children of Israel by their fathers' houses. All who were numbered according to their armies of the forces *were* six hundred and three thousand five hundred and fifty.

Divided into four divisions while in the wilderness. Num 10:14–28

Encamped in their divisions and by their standards around the tabernacle. Num 2:2–31

Canaan to be divided among according to their numbers.

Num 33:54 And you shall divide the land by lot as an inheritance among your families; to the larger you shall give a larger inheritance, and to the smaller you shall give a smaller inheritance; there everyone's *inheritance* shall be whatever falls to him by lot. You shall inherit according to the tribes of your fathers.

Reuben, Gad, and half of Manasseh

Settled on east side of Jordan.

Deut 3:12–17 "And this land, *which* we possessed at that time, from Aroer, which *is* by the River Arnon, and half the mountains of Gilead and its cities, I gave to the Reubenites and the Gadites. **13** The rest of Gilead, and all Bashan, the kingdom of Og, I gave to half the tribe of Manasseh. (All the region of Argob, with all Bashan, was called the land of the giants. **14** Jair the son of Manasseh took all the region of Argob, as far as the border of the Geshurites and the Maachathites, and called Bashan after his own name, Havoth Jair, to this day.) **15** "Also I gave Gilead to Machir. **16** And to the Reubenites and the Gadites I gave from Gilead as far as the River Arnon, the middle of the river as *the* border, as far as the River Jabbok, the border of the people of Ammon; **17** the plain also, with the Jordan as *the* border, from Chinnereth as far as the east side of the Sea of the Arabah (the Salt Sea), below the slopes of Pisgah.

Cf. Josh 13:23–32

Were required to assist in subduing Canaan.

Deut 3:18–20 "Then I commanded you at that time, saying: 'The LORD your God has given you this land to possess. All you men of valor shall cross over armed before your brethren, the children of Israel. **19** But your wives, your little ones, and your livestock (I know that you have much livestock) shall stay in your cities which I have given you, **20** until the LORD has given rest to your brethren as to you, and they also possess the land which the LORD your God is giving them beyond the Jordan. Then each of you may return to his possession which I have given you.'

Cf. Num 32:6–32

Total strength of, on entering the land of Canaan.

Num 26:51 These *are* those who were numbered of the children of Israel: six hundred and one thousand seven hundred and thirty.

Canaan divided among nine and a half of, by lot.

Josh 14:1–5 These *are the areas* which the children of Israel inherited in the land of Canaan, which Eleazar the priest, Joshua the son of Nun, and the heads of the fathers of the tribes of the children of Israel distributed as an inheritance to them. **2** Their inheritance *was* by lot, as the LORD had commanded by the hand of Moses, for the nine tribes and the half-tribe. **3** For Moses had given the inheritance of the two tribes and the half-tribe on the other side of the Jordan; but to the Levites he had given no inheritance among them. **4** For the children of Joseph were two tribes: Manasseh and Ephraim. And they gave no part to the Levites in the land, except cities to dwell *in*, with their common-lands for their livestock and their property. **5** As the LORD had commanded Moses, so the children of Israel did; and they divided the land.

Situation of, and borders of the inheritance of each. Josh 15:1—17:18

All inheritance to remain in the tribe and family to which allotted.

Num 36:3–9 Now if they are married to any of the sons of the *other* tribes of the children of Israel, then their inheritance will be taken from the inheritance of our fathers, and it will be added to the inheritance of the tribe into which they marry; so it will be taken from the lot of our inheritance. **4** And when the Jubilee of the children of Israel comes, then their inheritance will be added to the inheritance of the tribe into which they marry; so their inheritance will be taken away from the inheritance of the tribe of our fathers." **5** Then Moses commanded the children of Israel according to the word of the LORD, saying: "What the tribe of the sons of Joseph speaks is right. **6** This *is* what the LORD commands concerning the daughters of Zelophehad, saying, 'Let them marry whom they think best, but they may marry only within the family of their father's tribe.' **7** So the inheritance of the children of Israel shall not change hands from tribe to tribe, for every one of the children of Israel shall keep the inheritance of the tribe of his fathers. **8** And every daughter who possesses an inheritance in any tribe of the children of Israel shall be the wife of one of the family of her father's tribe, so that the children of Israel each may possess the inheritance of his fathers. **9** Thus no inheritance shall change hands from *one* tribe to another, but every tribe of the children of Israel shall keep its own inheritance."

Names of, engraved on the breastplate of the high priest.

Ex 28:21 And the stones shall have the names of the sons of Israel, twelve according to their names, *like* the engravings of a signet, each one with its own name; they shall be according to the twelve tribes.

Ex 39:14 *There were* twelve stones according to the names of the sons of Israel: according to their names, *engraved like* a signet, each one with its own name according to the twelve tribes.

Divided on mounts Ebal and Gerizim to hear the law.

Deut 27:12–13 "These shall stand on Mount Gerizim to bless the people, when you have crossed over the Jordan: Simeon, Levi, Judah, Issachar, Joseph, and Benjamin; **13** and these shall stand on Mount Ebal to curse: Reuben, Gad, Asher, Zebulun, Dan, and Naphtali.

Remained as one people until the reign of Rehoboam.

1 Kin 12:16–20 Now when all Israel saw that the king did not listen to them, the people answered the king, saying: "What share have we in David? *We have* no inheritance in the son of Jesse. To your tents, O Israel! Now, see to your own house, O David!" So Israel departed to their tents. 17 But Rehoboam reigned over the children of Israel who dwelt in the cities of Judah. 18 Then King Rehoboam sent Adoram, who *was* in charge of the revenue; but all Israel stoned him with stones, and he died. Therefore King Rehoboam mounted his chariot in haste to flee to Jerusalem. 19 So Israel has been in rebellion against the house of David to this day. 20 Now it came to pass when all Israel heard that Jeroboam had come back, they sent for him and called him to the congregation, and made him king over all Israel. There was none who followed the house of David, but the tribe of Judah only.

ISSACHAR, THE TRIBE OF

Descended from Jacob's fifth son.

Gen 30:17–18 And God listened to Leah, and she conceived and bore Jacob a fifth son. 18 Leah said, "God has given me my wages, because I have given my maid to my husband." So she called his name Issachar.

Predictions respecting.

Gen 49:14–15 "Issachar is a strong donkey, Lying down between two burdens; 15 He saw that rest *was* good, And that the land *was* pleasant; He bowed his shoulder to bear *a burden*, And became a band of slaves.

Deut 33:18–19 And of Zebulun he said: "Rejoice, Zebulun, in your going out, And Issachar in your tents! 19 They shall call the peoples *to* the mountain; There they shall offer sacrifices of righteousness; For they shall partake *of* the abundance of the seas And *of* treasures hidden in the sand."

Persons selected from,

To number the people.

Num 1:8 from Issachar, Nethanel the son of Zuar;

To spy out the land.

Num 13:7 from the tribe of Issachar, Igal the son of Joseph;

To divide the land.

Num 34:26 a leader from the tribe of the children of Issachar, Paltiel the son of Azzan;

Strength of, on leaving Egypt.

Num 1:28–29 From the children of Issachar, their genealogies by their families, by their fathers' house, according to the number of names, from twenty years old and above, all who *were able to* go to war: 29 those who were numbered of the tribe of Issachar *were* fifty-four thousand four hundred.

Num 2:6 And his army was numbered at fifty-four thousand four hundred.

Encamped under the standard of Judah east of the tabernacle.

Num 2:5 "Those who camp next to him *shall be* the tribe of Issachar, and Nethanel the son of Zuar *shall be* the leader of the children of Issachar."

Next to and under standard of Judah in the journeys of Israel.

Num 10:14–15 The standard of the camp of the children of Judah set out first according to their armies;

over their army was Nahshon the son of Amminadab. 15 Over the army of the tribe of the children of Issachar *was* Nethanel the son of Zuar.

Offering of, at the dedication.

Num 7:18–23 On the second day Nethanel the son of Zuar, leader of Issachar, presented *an offering*. 19 *For* his offering he offered one silver platter, the weight of which *was* one hundred and thirty *shekels*, and one silver bowl of seventy shekels, according to the shekel of the sanctuary, both of them full of fine flour mixed with oil as a grain offering; 20 one gold pan of ten *shekels*, full of incense; 21 one young bull, one ram, and one male lamb in its first year, as a burnt offering; 22 one kid of the goats as a sin offering; 23 and as the sacrifice of peace offerings: two oxen, five rams, five male goats, and five male lambs in their first year. This *was* the offering of Nethanel the son of Zuar.

Families of.

Num 26:23–24 The sons of Issachar according to their families *were: of* Tola, the family of the Tolaites; of Puah, the family of the Punites; 24 of Jashub, the family of the Jashubites; of Shimron, the family of the Shimronites.

Strength of, on entering Canaan.

Num 26:25 These *are* the families of Issachar according to those who were numbered of them: sixty-four thousand three hundred.

On Gerizim, said amen to the blessings.

Deut 27:12 "These shall stand on Mount Gerizim to bless the people, when you have crossed over the Jordan: Simeon, Levi, Judah, Issachar, Joseph, and Benjamin;

Borders of their inheritance.

Josh 19:17–23 The fourth lot came out to Issachar, for the children of Issachar according to their families. 18 And their territory went to Jezreel, and *included* Chesulloth, Shunem, 19 Haphraim, Shion, Anaharath, 20 Rabbith, Kishion, Abez, 21 Remeth, En Gannim, En Haddah, and Beth Pazzez. 22 And the border reached to Tabor, Shahazimah, and Beth Shemesh; their border ended at the Jordan: sixteen cities with their villages. 23 This *was* the inheritance of the tribe of the children of Issachar according to their families, the cities and their villages.

Assisted Deborah against Sisera.

Judg 5:15 And the princes of Issachar *were* with Deborah; As Issachar, so *was* Barak Sent into the valley under his command; Among the divisions of Reuben *There were* great resolves of heart.

Officers of, appointed by David.

1 Chr 27:18 *over* Judah, Elihu, *one* of David's brothers; *over* Issachar, Omri the son of Michael;

Officers of, appointed by Solomon.

1 Kin 4:17 Jehoshaphat the son of Paruah, in Issachar;

Some of, at David's coronation.

1 Chr 12:32 of the sons of Issachar who had understanding of the times, to know what Israel ought to do, their chiefs were two hundred; and all their brethren were at their command;

Number of warriors belonging to, in David's time.

1 Chr 7:2 The sons of Tola *were* Uzzi, Rephaiah, Jeriel, Jahmai, Jibsam, and Shemuel, heads of their father's house. *The sons* of Tola *were* mighty men of valor in their generations; their number in the days of David *was* twenty-two thousand six hundred.

1 Chr 7:5 Now their brethren among all the families of Issachar *were* mighty men of valor, listed by their genealogies, eighty-seven thousand in all.

Many of, at Hezekiah's Passover.

2 Chr 30:18 For a multitude of the people, many from Ephraim, Manasseh, Issachar, and Zebulun, had not cleansed themselves, yet they ate the Passover contrary to what was written. But Hezekiah prayed for them, saying, "May the good LORD provide atonement for everyone

Remarkable persons of.

Judg 10:1 After Abimelech there arose to save Israel Tola the son of Puah, the son of Dodo, a man of Issachar; and he dwelt in Shamir in the mountains of Ephraim.

1 Kin 15:27 Then Baasha the son of Ahijah, of the house of Issachar, conspired against him. And Baasha killed him at Gibbethon, which *belonged* to the Philistines, while Nadab and all Israel laid siege to Gibbethon.

J

JACOB

Son of Isaac.

Gen 25:20–26 Isaac was forty years old when he took Rebekah as wife, the daughter of Bethuel the Syrian of Padan Aram, the sister of Laban the Syrian. **21** Now Isaac pleaded with the LORD for his wife, because she *was* barren; and the LORD granted his plea, and Rebekah his wife conceived. **22** But the children struggled together within her; and she said, "If *all is* well, why *am I like* this?" So she went to inquire of the LORD. **23** And the LORD said to her: "Two nations *are* in your womb, Two peoples shall be separated from your body; *One* people shall be stronger than the other, And the older shall serve the younger." **24** So when her days were fulfilled *for her* to give birth, indeed *there were* twins in her womb. **25** And the first came out red. *He was* like a hairy garment all over; so they called his name Esau. **26** Afterward his brother came out, and his hand took hold of Esau's heel; so his name was called Jacob. Isaac *was* sixty years old when she bore them.

Obtained Esau's birthright.

Gen 25:27–34 So the boys grew. And Esau was a skillful hunter, a man of the field; but Jacob was a mild man, dwelling in tents. **28** And Isaac loved Esau because he ate *of his* game, but Rebekah loved Jacob. **29** Now Jacob cooked a stew; and Esau came in from the field, and he *was* weary. **30** And Esau said to Jacob, "Please feed me with that same red *stew,* for I *am* weary." Therefore his name was called Edom. **31** But Jacob said, "Sell me your birthright as of this day." **32** And Esau said, "Look, I *am* about to die; so what *is* this birthright to me?" **33** Then Jacob said, "Swear to me as of this day." So he swore to him, and sold his birthright to Jacob. **34** And Jacob gave Esau bread and stew of lentils; then he ate and drank, arose, and went his way. Thus Esau despised *his* birthright.

Heb 12:16 lest there *be* any fornicator or profane person like Esau, who for one morsel of food sold his birthright.

Received Isaac's blessing, ahead of Esau.

Gen 27:1–38

Saw heavenly ladder.

Gen 28:10–22 Now Jacob went out from Beersheba and went toward Haran. **11** So he came to a certain place and stayed there all night, because the sun had set. And he took one of the stones of that place and put it at his head, and he lay down in that place to sleep. **12** Then he dreamed, and behold, a ladder *was* set up on the earth, and its top reached to heaven; and there the angels of God were ascending and descending on it. **13** And behold, the LORD stood above it and said: "I *am* the LORD God of Abraham your father and the God of Isaac; the land on which you lie I will give to you and your descendants. **14** Also your descendants shall be as the dust of the earth; you shall spread abroad to the west and the east, to the north and the south; and in you and in your seed all the families of the earth shall be blessed. **15** Behold, I *am* with you and will keep you wherever you go, and will bring you back to this land; for I will not leave you until I have done what I have spoken to you." **16** Then Jacob awoke from his sleep and said, "Surely the LORD is in this place, and I did not know *it.*" **17** And he was afraid and said, "How awesome *is* this place! This *is* none other than the house of God, and this *is* the gate of heaven!" **18** Then Jacob rose early in the morning, and took the stone that he had put at his head, set it up as a pillar, and poured oil on top of it. **19** And he called the name of that place Bethel; but the name of that city had been Luz previously. **20** Then Jacob made a vow, saying, "If God will be with me, and keep me in this way that I am going, and give me bread to eat and clothing to put on, **21** so that I come back to my father's house in peace, then the LORD shall be my God. **22** And this stone which I have set as a pillar shall be God's house, and of all that You give me I will surely give a tenth to You."

Met Rachel and served Laban. Gen 29:1–30

Asked departure from Laban.

Gen 30:25–43 And it came to pass, when Rachel had borne Joseph, that Jacob said to Laban, "Send me away, that I may go to my own place and to my country. **26** Give *me* my wives and my children for whom I have served you, and let me go; for you know my service which I have done for you." **27** And Laban said to him, "Please *stay,* if I have found favor in your eyes, *for* I have learned by experience that the LORD has blessed me for your sake." **28** Then he said, "Name me your wages, and I will give *it.*" **29** So Jacob said to him, "You know how I have served you and how your livestock has been with me. **30** For what you had before I *came was* little, and it has increased to a great amount; the LORD has blessed you since my coming. And now, when shall I also provide for my own house?" **31** So he said, "What shall I give you?" And Jacob said, "You shall not give me anything. If you will do this thing for me, I will again feed and keep your flocks: **32** Let me pass through all your flock today, removing from there all the speckled and spotted sheep, and all the brown ones among the lambs, and the spotted and speckled among the goats; and *these* shall be my wages. **33** So my righteousness will answer for me in time to come, when the subject of my wages comes before you: every one that *is* not speckled and spotted among the goats, and brown among the lambs, will be considered stolen, if *it is* with me." **34** And Laban said, "Oh, that it were according to your word!" **35** So he removed that day the male goats that were speckled and spotted, all the female goats that were speckled and spotted, every one that had *some* white in it, and all the brown ones among the lambs, and gave *them* into the hand of his sons. **36** Then he put three days' journey between himself and Jacob, and Jacob fed the rest of Laban's flocks. **37** Now Jacob took for himself rods of green poplar and of the almond and chestnut trees, peeled white strips in them, and exposed the white which *was* in the rods. **38** And the rods which he had peeled, he set before the flocks in the gutters, in the watering troughs where the flocks came to drink, so that they should conceive when they came to drink. **39** So the flocks conceived before the rods, and the flocks brought forth streaked, speckled, and spotted. **40** Then Jacob separated the lambs, and made the flocks face toward the streaked and all the brown in the flock of Laban; but he put his own flocks by themselves and did not put them with Laban's flock. **41** And it came to pass, whenever the stronger livestock conceived, that Jacob placed the rods before the eyes of the livestock in the gutters, that they might conceive among the rods. **42** But when the flocks were feeble, he did not put *them* in; so the feebler were Laban's and the stronger Jacob's. **43** Thus the man became exceedingly prosperous, and had large flocks, female and male servants, and camels and donkeys.

His covenant with Laban.

Gen 31:44–55 Now therefore, come, let us make a covenant, you and I, and let it be a witness between you and me." **45** So Jacob took a stone and set it up *as* a pillar. **46** Then Jacob said to his brethren, "Gather stones." And they took stones and made a heap, and they ate there on the heap. **47** Laban called it Jegar Sahadutha, but Jacob called it Galeed. **48** And Laban said, "This heap *is* a witness between you and me this day." Therefore its name was called Galeed, **49** also Mizpah, because he said, "May the LORD watch between you and me when we are absent one from another. **50** If you afflict my daughters, or if you take *other* wives besides my daughters, *although* no man *is* with us—see, God *is* witness between you and me!" **51** Then Laban said to Jacob, "Here is this heap and here is *this* pillar, which I have placed between you and me. **52** This heap *is* a witness, and *this* pillar *is* a witness, that I will not pass beyond this heap to you, and you will not pass beyond this heap and this pillar to me, for harm. **53** The God of Abraham, the God of Nahor, and the God of their father judge between us." And Jacob swore by the Fear of his father Isaac. **54** Then Jacob offered a sacrifice on the mountain, and called his brethren to eat bread. And they ate bread and stayed all night on the mountain. **55** And early in the morning Laban arose, and kissed his sons and daughters and blessed them. Then Laban departed and returned to his place.

Wrestled with an angel.

Gen 32:22–32 And he arose that night and took his two wives, his two female servants, and his eleven sons, and crossed over the ford of Jabbok. **23** He took them, sent them over the brook, and sent over what he had. **24** Then Jacob was left alone; and a Man wrestled with him until the breaking of day. **25** Now when He saw that He did not prevail against him, He touched the socket of his hip; and the socket of Jacob's hip was out of joint as He wrestled with him. **26** And He said, "Let Me go, for the day breaks." But he said, "I will not let You go unless You bless me!" **27** So He said to him, "What *is* your name?" He said, "Jacob." **28** And He said, "Your name shall no longer be called Jacob, but Israel; for you have struggled with God and with men, and have prevailed." **29** Then Jacob asked, saying, "Tell *me* Your name, I pray." And He said, "Why *is* it *that* you ask about My name?" And He blessed him there. **30** So Jacob called the name of the place Peniel: "For I have seen God face to face, and my life is preserved." **31** Just as he crossed over Penuel the sun rose on him, and he limped on his hip. **32** Therefore to this day the children of Israel do not eat the muscle that shrank, which *is* on the hip socket, because He touched the socket of Jacob's hip in the muscle that shrank.

Hos 12:3–4 He took his brother by the heel in the womb, And in his strength he struggled with God. **4** Yes, he struggled with the Angel and prevailed; He wept, and sought favor from Him. He found Him *in* Bethel, And there He spoke to us—

Name changed to Israel.

Gen 32:28 And He said, "Your name shall no longer be called Jacob, but Israel; for you have struggled with God and with men, and have prevailed."

Reconciled to Esau.

Gen 33:1–16 Now Jacob lifted his eyes and looked, and there, Esau was coming, and with him were four hundred men. So he divided the children among Leah, Rachel, and the two maidservants. **2** And he put the maidservants and their children in front, Leah and her children behind, and Rachel and Joseph last. **3** Then he crossed over before them and bowed himself to the ground seven times, until he came near to his brother. **4** But Esau ran to meet him, and embraced him, and fell on his neck and kissed him, and they wept. **5** And he lifted his eyes and saw the women and children, and said, "Who *are* these with you?" So he said, "The children whom God has graciously given your servant." **6** Then the maidservants came near, they and their children, and bowed down. **7** And Leah also came near with her children, and they bowed down. Afterward Joseph and Rachel came near, and they bowed down. **8** Then Esau said, "What *do* you *mean by* all this company which I met?" And he said, "*These are* to find favor in the sight of my lord." **9** But Esau said, "I have enough, my brother; keep what you have for yourself." **10** And Jacob said, "No, please, if I have now found favor in your sight, then receive my present from my hand, inasmuch as I have seen your face as though I had seen the face of God, and you were pleased with me. **11** Please, take my blessing that is brought to you, because God has dealt graciously with me, and because I have enough." So he urged him, and he took *it.* **12** Then Esau said, "Let us take our journey; let us go, and I will go before you." **13** But Jacob said to him, "My lord knows that the children *are* weak, and the flocks and herds which are nursing *are* with me. And if the men should drive them hard one day, all the flock will die. **14** Please let my lord go on ahead before his servant. I will lead on slowly at a pace which the livestock that go before me, and the children, are able to endure, until I come to my lord in Seir." **15** And Esau said, "Now let me leave with you *some* of the people who *are* with me." But he said, "What need is there? Let me find favor in the sight of my lord." **16** So Esau returned that day on his way to Seir.

His renewal at Bethel.

Gen 35:1–15 Then God said to Jacob, "Arise, go up to Bethel and dwell there; and make an altar there to God, who appeared to you when you fled from the face of Esau your brother." **2** And Jacob said to his household and to all who *were* with him, "Put away the foreign gods that *are* among you, purify yourselves, and change your garments. **3** Then let us arise and go up to Bethel; and I will make an altar there to God, who answered me in the day of my distress and has been with me in the way which I have gone." **4** So they gave Jacob all the foreign gods which *were* in their hands, and the earrings which *were* in their ears; and Jacob hid them under the terebinth tree which *was* by Shechem. **5** And they journeyed, and the terror of God was upon the cities that *were* all around them, and they did not pursue the sons of Jacob. **6** So Jacob came to Luz (that *is*, Bethel), which *is* in the land of Canaan, he and all the people who *were* with him. **7** And he built an altar there and called the place El Bethel, because there God appeared to him when he fled from the face of his brother. **8** Now Deborah, Rebekah's nurse, died, and she was buried below Bethel under the terebinth tree. So the name of it was called Allon Bachuth. **9** Then God appeared to Jacob again, when he came from Padan Aram, and blessed him. **10** And God said to him, "Your name *is* Jacob; your name shall not be called Jacob anymore, but Israel shall be your name." So He called his name Israel. **11** Also God said to him: "I *am* God Almighty. Be fruitful and multiply; a nation and a company of nations shall proceed from you, and kings shall come from your body. **12** The land which I gave Abraham and Isaac I give to you; and to your descendants after you I give this land." **13** Then God went up from him in the place where He talked with him. **14** So Jacob set up a pillar in the place where He talked with him, a pillar of stone; and he poured a drink offering on it, and he poured oil on it. **15** And Jacob called the name of the place where God spoke with him, Bethel.

His twelve sons listed.

Gen 35:22–26 And it happened, when Israel dwelt in that land, that Reuben went and lay with Bilhah his father's concubine; and Israel heard *about it*. Now the sons of Jacob were twelve: **23** the sons of Leah *were* Reuben, Jacob's firstborn, and Simeon, Levi, Judah, Issachar, and Zebulun; **24** the sons of Rachel *were* Joseph and Benjamin; **25** the sons of Bilhah, Rachel's maidservant, *were* Dan and Naphtali; **26** and the sons of Zilpah, Leah's maidservant, *were* Gad and Asher. These *were* the sons of Jacob who were born to him in Padan Aram.

Displayed favoritism toward son Joseph.
Gen 37:1–31

Sent sons to Egypt for food.

Gen 42:1–5 When Jacob saw that there was grain in Egypt, Jacob said to his sons, "Why do you look at one another?" **2** And he said, "Indeed I have heard that there is grain in Egypt; go down to that place and buy for us there, that we may live and not die." **3** So Joseph's ten brothers went down to buy grain in Egypt. **4** But Jacob did not send Joseph's brother Benjamin with his brothers, for he said, "Lest some calamity befall him." **5** And the sons of Israel went to buy *grain* among those who journeyed, for the famine was in the land of Canaan.

Went with family to Egypt.

Gen 46:1–27 So Israel took his journey with all that he had, and came to Beersheba, and offered sacrifices to the God of his father Isaac. **2** Then God spoke to Israel in the visions of the night, saying, "Jacob, Jacob!" And he said, "Here I am." **3** So He said, "I *am* God, the God of your father; do not fear to go down to Egypt, for I will make of you a great nation there. **4** I will go down with you to Egypt, and I will also surely bring you up *again;* and Joseph will put his hand on your eyes." **5** Then Jacob arose from Beersheba; and the sons of Israel carried their father Jacob, their little ones, and their wives, in the carts which Pharaoh had sent to carry him. **6** So they took their livestock and their goods, which they had acquired in the land of Canaan, and went to Egypt, Jacob and all his descendants with him. **7** His sons and his sons' sons, his daughters and his sons' daughters, and all his descendants he brought with him to Egypt. **8** Now these *were* the names of the children of Israel, Jacob and his sons, who went to Egypt: Reuben *was* Jacob's firstborn. **9** The sons of Reuben *were* Hanoch, Pallu, Hezron, and Carmi. **10** The sons of Simeon *were* Jemuel, Jamin, Ohad, Jachin, Zohar, and Shaul, the son of a Canaanite woman. **11** The sons of Levi *were* Gershon, Kohath, and Merari. **12** The sons of Judah *were* Er, Onan, Shelah, Perez, and Zerah (but Er and Onan died in the land of Canaan). The sons of Perez were Hezron and Hamul. **13** The sons of Issachar *were* Tola, Puvah, Job, and Shimron. **14** The sons of Zebulun *were* Sered, Elon, and Jahleel. **15** These *were* the sons of Leah, whom she bore to Jacob in Padan Aram, with his daughter Dinah. All the persons, his sons and his daughters, *were* thirty-three. **16** The sons of Gad *were* Ziphion, Haggi, Shuni, Ezbon, Eri, Arodi, and Areli. **17** The sons of Asher *were* Jimnah, Ishuah, Isui, Beriah, and Serah, their sister. And the sons of Beriah *were* Heber and Malchiel. **18** These *were* the sons of Zilpah, whom Laban gave to Leah his daughter; and these she bore to Jacob: sixteen persons. **19** The sons of Rachel, Jacob's wife, *were* Joseph and Benjamin. **20** And to Joseph in the land of Egypt were born Manasseh and Ephraim, whom Asenath, the daughter of Poti-Pherah priest of On, bore to him. **21** The sons of Benjamin *were* Belah, Becher, Ashbel, Gera, Naaman, Ehi, Rosh, Muppim, Huppim, and Ard. **22** These *were* the sons of Rachel, who were born to Jacob: fourteen persons in all. **23** The son of Dan *was* Hushim. **24** The sons of Naphtali *were* Jahzeel, Guni, Jezer, and Shillem. **25** These *were* the sons of Bilhah, whom Laban gave to Rachel his daughter, and she bore these to Jacob: seven persons in all. **26** All the persons who went with Jacob to Egypt, who came from his body, besides Jacob's sons' wives, *were* sixty-six persons in all. **27** And the sons of Joseph who were born to him in Egypt *were* two persons. All the persons of the house of Jacob who went to Egypt were seventy.

Reunited with Joseph.

Gen 46:28–34 Then he sent Judah before him to Joseph, to point out before him *the way* to Goshen. And they came to the land of Goshen. **29** So Joseph made ready his chariot and went up to Goshen to meet his father Israel; and he presented himself to him, and fell on his neck and wept on his neck a good while. **30** And Israel said to Joseph, "Now let me die, since I have seen your face, because you *are* still alive." **31** Then Joseph said to his brothers and to his father's household, "I will go up and tell Pharaoh, and say to him, 'My brothers and those of my father's house, who *were* in the land of Canaan, have come to me. **32** And the men *are* shepherds, for their occupation has been to feed livestock; and they have brought their flocks, their herds, and all that they have.' **33** So it shall be, when Pharaoh calls you and says, 'What is your occupation?' **34** that you shall say, 'Your servants' occupation has been with livestock from our youth even till now, both we *and* also our fathers,' that you may dwell in the land of Goshen; for every shepherd *is* an abomination to the Egyptians."

Blessed Joseph's sons. Gen 48:1–22

Blessed his own sons. Gen 49:1–28

Buried in Canaan.

Gen 50:1–14 Then Joseph fell on his father's face and wept over him, and kissed him. **2** And Joseph commanded his servants the physicians to embalm his father. So the physicians embalmed Israel. **3** Forty days were required for him, for such are the days required for those who are embalmed; and the Egyptians mourned for him seventy days. **4** Now when the days of his mourning were past, Joseph spoke to the household of Pharaoh, saying, "If now I have found favor in your eyes, please speak in the hearing of Pharaoh, saying, **5** 'My father made me swear, saying, "Behold, I am dying; in my grave which I dug for myself in the land of Canaan, there you shall bury me." Now therefore, please let me go up and bury my father, and I will come back.' " **6** And Pharaoh said, "Go up and bury your father, as he made you swear." **7** So Joseph went up to bury his father; and with him went up all the servants of Pharaoh, the elders of his house, and all the elders of the land of Egypt, **8** as well as all the house of Joseph, his brothers, and his father's house. Only their little ones, their flocks, and their herds they left in the land of Goshen. **9** And there went up with him both chariots and horsemen, and it was a very great gathering. **10** Then they came to the threshing floor of Atad, which *is* beyond the Jordan, and they mourned there with a great and very solemn lamentation. He observed seven days of mourning for his father. **11** And when the inhabitants of the land, the Canaanites, saw the mourning at the threshing floor of Atad, they said, "This *is* a deep mourning of the Egyptians." Therefore its name was called Abel Mizraim, which *is* beyond the Jordan. **12** So his sons did for him just as he had commanded them. **13** For his sons carried him to the land of Canaan, and buried him in the cave of the field of Machpelah, before Mamre, which Abraham bought with the field from Ephron

the Hittite as property for a burial place. **14** And after he had buried his father, Joseph returned to Egypt, he and his brothers and all who went up with him to bury his father.

JEALOUSY

Of God

Against those who don't follow Him.

Josh 24:19 But Joshua said to the people, "You cannot serve the LORD, for He *is* a holy God. He *is* a jealous God; He will not forgive your transgressions nor your sins.

Nah 1:2 God *is* jealous, and the LORD avenges; The LORD avenges and *is* furious. The LORD will take vengeance on His adversaries, And He reserves *wrath* for His enemies;

Cf. Deut 29:18–28; Ezek 5:13; 1 Cor 10:21–22

For those who do obey Him.

Ex 20:5 you shall not bow down to them nor serve them. For I, the LORD your God, *am* a jealous God, visiting the iniquity of the fathers upon the children to the third and fourth *generations* of those who hate Me,

Ex 34:14 (for you shall worship no other god, for the LORD, whose name *is* Jealous, *is* a jealous God),

Zech 1:14 So the angel who spoke with me said to me, "Proclaim, saying, 'Thus says the LORD of hosts: "I am zealous for Jerusalem And for Zion with great zeal.

As legitimate motivation for Jews to repent.

Rom 11:11–15 I say then, have they stumbled that they should fall? Certainly not! But through their fall, to provoke them to jealousy, salvation *has come* to the Gentiles. **12** Now if their fall *is* riches for the world, and their failure riches for the Gentiles, how much more their fullness! **13** For I speak to you Gentiles; inasmuch as I am an apostle to the Gentiles, I magnify my ministry, **14** if by any means I may provoke to jealousy *those who are* my flesh and save some of them. **15** For if their being cast away *is* the reconciling of the world, what *will* their acceptance *be* but life from the dead?

Of Paul, for converts' spiritual well-being.

2 Cor 11:1–3 Oh, that you would bear with me in a little folly—and indeed you do bear with me. **2** For I am jealous for you with godly jealousy. For I have betrothed you to one husband, that I may present *you as* a chaste virgin to Christ. **3** But I fear, lest somehow, as the serpent deceived Eve by his craftiness, so your minds may be corrupted from the simplicity that is in Christ.

JEHU

The king

Anointed to be king.

2 Kin 9:2–6 Now when you arrive at that place, look there for Jehu the son of Jehoshaphat, the son of Nimshi, and go in and make him rise up from among his associates, and take him to an inner room. **3** Then take the flask of oil, and pour *it* on his head, and say, 'Thus says the LORD: "I have anointed you king over Israel." ' Then open the door and flee, and do not delay." **4** So the young man, the servant of the prophet, went to Ramoth Gilead. **5** And when he arrived, there *were* the captains of the army sitting; and he said, "I have a message for you, Commander." Jehu said, "For which *one* of us?" And he said, "For you, Commander." **6** Then he arose and went into the house. And he poured the oil on his head, and said to him, "Thus says the LORD God of Israel: 'I have anointed you king over the people of the LORD, over Israel.

Led a revolt.

2 Kin 9:14–26 So Jehu the son of Jehoshaphat, the son of Nimshi, conspired against Joram. (Now Joram had been defending Ramoth Gilead, he and all Israel, against Hazael king of Syria. **15** But King Joram had returned to Jezreel to recover from the wounds which the Syrians had inflicted on him when he fought with Hazael king of Syria.) And Jehu said, "If you are so minded, let no one leave *or* escape from the city to go and tell *it* in Jezreel." **16** So Jehu rode in a chariot and went to Jezreel, for Joram was laid up there; and Ahaziah king of Judah had come down to see Joram. **17** Now a watchman stood on the tower in Jezreel, and he saw the company of Jehu as he came, and said, "I see a company of men." And Joram said, "Get a horseman and send him to meet them, and let him say, 'Is it peace?' " **18** So the horseman went to meet him, and said, "Thus says the king: 'Is it peace?' " And Jehu said, "What have you to do with peace? Turn around and follow me." So the watchman reported, saying, "The messenger went to them, but is not coming back." **19** Then he sent out a second horseman who came to them, and said, "Thus says the king: 'Is it peace?' " And Jehu answered, "What have you to do with peace? Turn around and follow me." **20** So the watchman reported, saying, "He went up to them and is not coming back; and the driving *is* like the driving of Jehu the son of Nimshi, for he drives furiously!" **21** Then Joram said, "Make ready." And his chariot was made ready. Then Joram king of Israel and Ahaziah king of Judah went out, each in his chariot; and they went out to meet Jehu, and met him on the property of Naboth the Jezreelite. **22** Now it happened, when Joram saw Jehu, that he said, "Is it peace, Jehu?" So he answered, "What peace, as long as the harlotries of your mother Jezebel and her witchcraft *are so* many?" **23** Then Joram turned around and fled, and said to Ahaziah, "Treachery, Ahaziah!" **24** Now Jehu drew his bow with full strength and shot Jehoram between his arms; and the arrow came out at his heart, and he sank down in his chariot. **25** Then *Jehu* said to Bidkar his captain, "Pick *him* up, *and* throw him into the tract of the field of Naboth the Jezreelite; for remember, when you and I were riding together behind Ahab his father, that the LORD laid this burden upon him: **26** 'Surely I saw yesterday the blood of Naboth and the blood of his sons,' says the LORD, 'and I will repay you in this plot,' says the LORD. Now therefore, take *and* throw him on the plot *of ground*, according to the word of the LORD."

Served as king of Israel.

2 Kin 9:30–37 Now when Jehu had come to Jezreel, Jezebel heard *of it;* and she put paint on her eyes and adorned her head, and looked through a window. **31** Then, as Jehu entered at the gate, she said, "Is it peace, Zimri, murderer of your master?" **32** And he

looked up at the window, and said, "Who *is* on my side? Who?" So two *or* three eunuchs looked out at him. **33** Then he said, "Throw her down." So they threw her down, and *some* of her blood spattered on the wall and on the horses; and he trampled her underfoot. **34** And when he had gone in, he ate and drank. Then he said, "Go now, see to this accursed *woman*, and bury her, for she was a king's daughter." **35** So they went to bury her, but they found no more of her than the skull and the feet and the palms of *her* hands. **36** Therefore they came back and told him. And he said, "This *is* the word of the LORD, which He spoke by His servant Elijah the Tishbite, saying, 'On the plot *of ground* at Jezreel dogs shall eat the flesh of Jezebel; **37** and the corpse of Jezebel shall be as refuse on the surface of the field, in the plot at Jezreel, so that they shall not say, "Here *lies* Jezebel." ' "

2 Chr 22:7–12 His going to Joram was God's occasion for Ahaziah's downfall; for when he arrived, he went out with Jehoram against Jehu the son of Nimshi, whom the LORD had anointed to cut off the house of Ahab. **8** And it happened, when Jehu was executing judgment on the house of Ahab, and found the princes of Judah and the sons of Ahaziah's brothers who served Ahaziah, that he killed them. **9** Then he searched for Ahaziah; and they caught him (he was hiding in Samaria), and brought him to Jehu. When they had killed him, they buried him, "because," they said, "he is the son of Jehoshaphat, who sought the LORD with all his heart." So the house of Ahaziah had no one to assume power over the kingdom. **10** Now when Athaliah the mother of Ahaziah saw that her son was dead, she arose and destroyed all the royal heirs of the house of Judah. **11** But Jehoshabeath, the daughter of the king, took Joash the son of Ahaziah, and stole him away from among the king's sons who were being murdered, and put him and his nurse in a bedroom. So Jehoshabeath, the daughter of King Jehoram, the wife of Jehoiada the priest (for she was the sister of Ahaziah), hid him from Athaliah so that she did not kill him. **12** And he was hidden with them in the house of God for six years, while Athaliah reigned over the land.

Cf. 2 Kin 10:1–36

Son of Hanani and a prophet.

1 Kin 16:1 Then the word of the LORD came to Jehu the son of Hanani, against Baasha, saying:

2 Chr 19:2 And Jehu the son of Hanani the seer went out to meet him, and said to King Jehoshaphat, "Should you help the wicked and love those who hate the LORD? Therefore the wrath of the LORD *is* upon you.

Cf. 2 Chr 20:34

JERICHO

Two spies visit there.

Josh 2:1–21 Now Joshua the son of Nun sent out two men from Acacia Grove to spy secretly, saying, "Go, view the land, especially Jericho." So they went, and came to the house of a harlot named Rahab, and lodged there. **2** And it was told the king of Jericho, saying, "Behold, men have come here tonight from the children of Israel to search out the country." **3** So the king of Jericho sent to Rahab, saying, "Bring out the men who have come to you, who have entered your house, for they have come to search out all the country." 4 Then the woman took the two men and hid them. So she said, "Yes, the men came to me, but I did not know where they were from. 5 And it happened as the gate was being shut, when it was dark, that the men went out. Where the men went I do not know; pursue them quickly, for you may overtake them." 6 (But she had brought them up to the roof and hidden them with the stalks of flax, which she had laid in order on the roof.) 7 Then the men pursued them by the road to the Jordan, to the fords. And as soon as those who pursued them had gone out, they shut the gate. 8 Now before they lay down, she came up to them on the roof, 9 and said to the men: "I know that the LORD has given you the land, that the terror of you has fallen on us, and that all the inhabitants of the land are fainthearted because of you. 10 For we have heard how the LORD dried up the water of the Red Sea for you when you came out of Egypt, and what you did to the two kings of the Amorites who were on the other side of the Jordan, Sihon and Og, whom you utterly destroyed. 11 And as soon as we heard these things, our hearts melted; neither did there remain any more courage in anyone because of you, for the LORD your God, He is God in heaven above and on earth beneath. 12 Now therefore, I beg you, swear to me by the LORD, since I have shown you kindness, that you also will show kindness to my father's house, and give me a true token, 13 and spare my father, my mother, my brothers, my sisters, and all that they have, and deliver our lives from death." 14 So the men answered her, "Our lives for yours, if none of you tell this business of ours. And it shall be, when the LORD has given us the land, that we will deal kindly and truly with you." 15 Then she let them down by a rope through the window, for her house was on the city wall; she dwelt on the wall. 16 And she said to them, "Get to the mountain, lest the pursuers meet you. Hide there three days, until the pursuers have returned. Afterward you may go your way." 17 So the men said to her: "We will be blameless of this oath of yours which you have made us swear, 18 unless, when we come into the land, you bind this line of scarlet cord in the window through which you let us down, and unless you bring your father, your mother, your brothers, and all your father's household to your own home. 19 So it shall be that whoever goes outside the doors of your house into the street, his blood shall be on his own head, and we will be guiltless. And whoever is with you in the house, his blood shall be on our head if a hand is laid on him. 20 And if you tell this business of ours, then we will be free from your oath which you made us swear." 21 Then she said, "According to your words, so be it." And she sent them away, and they departed. And she bound the scarlet cord in the window.

Destruction of.

Heb 11:30 By faith the walls of Jericho fell down after they were encircled for seven days.

Cf. Josh 6:1–26

Eventually rebuilt.

1 Kin 16:34 In his days Hiel of Bethel built Jericho. He laid its foundation with Abiram his firstborn, and with his youngest son Segub he set up its gates, according to the word of the LORD, which He had spoken through Joshua the son of Nun.

Near the place of Elijah's departure to heaven.

2 Kin 2:4–6 Then Elijah said to him, "Elisha, stay here, please, for the LORD has sent me on to Jericho." But he said, "As the LORD lives, and as your soul lives, I will not leave you!" So they came to Jericho. 5 Now the sons of the prophets who were at Jericho came to Elisha and said to him, "Do you know that the LORD will take away your master from over you today?" So he answered, "Yes, I know; keep silent!" 6 Then Elijah said to him, "Stay here, please, for the LORD has sent me on to the Jordan." But he said, "As the LORD lives, and as your soul lives, I will not leave you!" So the two of them went on.

2 Kin 2:15–17 Now when the sons of the prophets who were from Jericho saw him, they said, "The spirit of Elijah rests on Elisha." And they came to meet him, and bowed to the ground before him. 16 Then they said to him, "Look now, there are fifty strong men with your servants. Please let them go and search for your master, lest perhaps the Spirit of the LORD has taken him up and cast him upon some mountain or into some valley." And he said, "You shall not send anyone." 17 But when they urged him till he was ashamed, he said, "Send them!" Therefore they sent fifty men, and they searched for three days but did not find him.

Jesus encounters and heals the blind near there.

Matt 20:29–33 Now as they went out of Jericho, a great multitude followed Him. 30 And behold, two blind men sitting by the road, when they heard that Jesus was passing by, cried out, saying, "Have mercy on us, O Lord, Son of David!" 31 Then the multitude warned them that they should be quiet; but they cried out all the more, saying, "Have mercy on us, O Lord, Son of David!" 32 So Jesus stood still and called them, and said, "What do you want Me to do for you?" 33 They said to Him, "Lord, that our eyes may be opened."

Mark 10:46–52 Now they came to Jericho. As He went out of Jericho with His disciples and a great multitude, blind Bartimaeus, the son of Timaeus, sat by the road begging. 47 And when he heard that it was Jesus of Nazareth, he began to cry out and say, "Jesus, Son of David, have mercy on me!" 48 Then many warned him to be quiet; but he cried out all the more, "Son of David, have mercy on me!" 49 So Jesus stood still and commanded him to be called. Then they called the blind man, saying to him, "Be of good cheer. Rise, He is calling you." 50 And throwing aside his garment, he rose and came to Jesus. 51 So Jesus answered and said to him, "What do you want Me to do for you?" The blind man said to Him, "Rabboni, that I may receive my sight." 52 Then Jesus said to him, "Go your way; your faith has made you well." And immediately he received his sight and followed Jesus on the road.

Luke 18:35–43 Then it happened, as He was coming near Jericho, that a certain blind man sat by the road begging. 36 And hearing a multitude passing by, he asked what it meant. 37 So they told him that Jesus of Nazareth was passing by. 38 And he cried out, saying, "Jesus, Son of David, have mercy on me!" **39** Then those who went before warned him that he should be quiet; but he cried out all the more, "Son of David, have mercy on me!" **40** So Jesus stood still and commanded him to be brought to Him. And when he had come near, He asked him, **41** saying, "What do you want Me to do for you?" He said, "Lord, that I may receive my sight." **42** Then Jesus said to him, "Receive your sight; your faith has made you well." **43** And immediately he received his sight, and followed Him, glorifying God. And all the people, when they saw *it*, gave praise to God.

Between there and Jerusalem, setting for story of the Good Samaritan.

Luke 10:30 Then Jesus answered and said: "A certain *man* went down from Jerusalem to Jericho, and fell among thieves, who stripped him of his clothing, wounded *him*, and departed, leaving *him* half dead."

JEROBOAM

Son of Nebat

Rebelled against Solomon.

1 Kin 11:26–40 Then Solomon's servant, Jeroboam the son of Nebat, an Ephraimite from Zereda, whose mother's name *was* Zeruah, a widow, also rebelled against the king. **27** And this *is* what caused him to rebel against the king: Solomon had built the Millo *and* repaired the damages to the City of David his father. **28** The man Jeroboam *was* a mighty man of valor; and Solomon, seeing that the young man was industrious, made him the officer over all the labor force of the house of Joseph. **29** Now it happened at that time, when Jeroboam went out of Jerusalem, that the prophet Ahijah the Shilonite met him on the way; and he had clothed himself with a new garment, and the two *were* alone in the field. **30** Then Ahijah took hold of the new garment that *was* on him, and tore it *into* twelve pieces. **31** And he said to Jeroboam, "Take for yourself ten pieces, for thus says the LORD, the God of Israel: 'Behold, I will tear the kingdom out of the hand of Solomon and will give ten tribes to you **32** (but he shall have one tribe for the sake of My servant David, and for the sake of Jerusalem, the city which I have chosen out of all the tribes of Israel), **33** because they have forsaken Me, and worshiped Ashtoreth the goddess of the Sidonians, Chemosh the god of the Moabites, and Milcom the god of the people of Ammon, and have not walked in My ways to do *what is* right in My eyes and *keep* My statutes and My judgments, as *did* his father David. **34** However I will not take the whole kingdom out of his hand, because I have made him ruler all the days of his life for the sake of My servant David, whom I chose because he kept My commandments and My statutes. **35** But I will take the kingdom out of his son's hand and give it to you— ten tribes. **36** And to his son I will give one tribe, that My servant David may always have a lamp before Me in Jerusalem, the city which I have chosen for Myself, to put My name there. **37** So I will take you, and you shall reign over all your heart desires, and you shall be king over Israel. **38** Then it shall be, if you heed all that I command you, walk in My ways, and do *what is* right in My sight, to keep My statutes and My commandments, as My servant David did,

then I will be with you and build for you an enduring house, as I built for David, and will give Israel to you. **39** And I will afflict the descendants of David because of this, but not forever.' " **40** Solomon therefore sought to kill Jeroboam. But Jeroboam arose and fled to Egypt, to Shishak king of Egypt, and was in Egypt until the death of Solomon.

Made king over northern kingdom.

1 Kin 12:2–20 So it happened, when Jeroboam the son of Nebat heard *it* (he was still in Egypt, for he had fled from the presence of King Solomon and had been dwelling in Egypt), **3** that they sent and called him. Then Jeroboam and the whole assembly of Israel came and spoke to Rehoboam, saying, **4** "Your father made our yoke heavy; now therefore, lighten the burdensome service of your father, and his heavy yoke which he put on us, and we will serve you." **5** So he said to them, "Depart *for* three days, then come back to me." And the people departed. **6** Then King Rehoboam consulted the elders who stood before his father Solomon while he still lived, and he said, "How do you advise *me* to answer these people?" **7** And they spoke to him, saying, "If you will be a servant to these people today, and serve them, and answer them, and speak good words to them, then they will be your servants forever." **8** But he rejected the advice which the elders had given him, and consulted the young men who had grown up with him, who stood before him. **9** And he said to them, "What advice do you give? How should we answer this people who have spoken to me, saying, 'Lighten the yoke which your father put on us'?" **10** Then the young men who had grown up with him spoke to him, saying, "Thus you should speak to this people who have spoken to you, saying, 'Your father made our yoke heavy, but you make it lighter on us'—thus you shall say to them: 'My little *finger* shall be thicker than my father's waist! **11** And now, whereas my father put a heavy yoke on you, I will add to your yoke; my father chastised you with whips, but I will chastise you with scourges!' " **12** So Jeroboam and all the people came to Rehoboam the third day, as the king had directed, saying, "Come back to me the third day." **13** Then the king answered the people roughly, and rejected the advice which the elders had given him; **14** and he spoke to them according to the advice of the young men, saying, "My father made your yoke heavy, but I will add to your yoke; my father chastised you with whips, but I will chastise you with scourges!" **15** So the king did not listen to the people; for the turn of *events* was from the LORD, that He might fulfill His word, which the LORD had spoken by Ahijah the Shilonite to Jeroboam the son of Nebat. **16** Now when all Israel saw that the king did not listen to them, the people answered the king, saying: "What share have we in David? *We have* no inheritance in the son of Jesse. To your tents, O Israel! Now, see to your own house, O David!" So Israel departed to their tents. **17** But Rehoboam reigned over the children of Israel who dwelt in the cities of Judah. **18** Then King Rehoboam sent Adoram, who *was* in charge of the revenue; but all Israel stoned him with stones, and he died. Therefore King Rehoboam mounted his chariot in haste to flee to Jerusalem. **19** So Israel has been in rebellion against the house of David to this day. **20** Now it came to pass when all Israel heard that Jeroboam had come back, they sent for him and called him to the congregation, and made him king over all Israel. There was none who followed the house of David, but the tribe of Judah only.

Cf. 2 Chr 10:2–16

Promoted idolatry.

1 Kin 12:25–33 Then Jeroboam built Shechem in the mountains of Ephraim, and dwelt there. Also he went out from there and built Penuel. **26** And Jeroboam said in his heart, "Now the kingdom may return to the house of David: **27** If these people go up to offer sacrifices in the house of the LORD at Jerusalem, then the heart of this people will turn back to their lord, Rehoboam king of Judah, and they will kill me and go back to Rehoboam king of Judah." **28** Therefore the king asked advice, made two calves of gold, and said to the people, "It is too much for you to go up to Jerusalem. Here are your gods, O Israel, which brought you up from the land of Egypt!" **29** And he set up one in Bethel, and the other he put in Dan. **30** Now this thing became a sin, for the people went *to worship* before the one as far as Dan. **31** He made shrines on the high places, and made priests from every class of people, who were not of the sons of Levi. **32** Jeroboam ordained a feast on the fifteenth day of the eighth month, like the feast that *was* in Judah, and offered sacrifices on the altar. So he did at Bethel, sacrificing to the calves that he had made. And at Bethel he installed the priests of the high places which he had made. **33** So he made offerings on the altar which he had made at Bethel on the fifteenth day of the eighth month, in the month which he had devised in his own heart. And he ordained a feast for the children of Israel, and offered sacrifices on the altar and burned incense.

Judged by God.

1 Kin 14:6–20 And so it was, when Ahijah heard the sound of her footsteps as she came through the door, he said, "Come in, wife of Jeroboam. Why do you pretend *to be* another *person?* For I *have been* sent to you *with* bad *news.* **7** Go, tell Jeroboam, 'Thus says the LORD God of Israel: "Because I exalted you from among the people, and made you ruler over My people Israel, **8** and tore the kingdom away from the house of David, and gave it to you; and *yet* you have not been as My servant David, who kept My commandments and who followed Me with all his heart, to do only *what was* right in My eyes; **9** but you have done more evil than all who were before you, for you have gone and made for yourself other gods and molded images to provoke Me to anger, and have cast Me behind your back— **10** therefore behold! I will bring disaster on the house of Jeroboam, and will cut off from Jeroboam every male in Israel, bond and free; I will take away the remnant of the house of Jeroboam, as one takes away refuse until it is all gone. **11** The dogs shall eat whoever belongs to Jeroboam and dies in the city, and the birds of the air shall eat whoever dies in the field; for the LORD has spoken!" ' **12** Arise therefore, go to your own house. When your feet enter the city, the child shall die. **13** And all Israel shall mourn for him and bury him, for he is the only one of Jeroboam who shall come to

the grave, because in him there is found something good toward the LORD God of Israel in the house of Jeroboam. **14** "Moreover the LORD will raise up for Himself a king over Israel who shall cut off the house of Jeroboam; this is the day. What? Even now! **15** For the LORD will strike Israel, as a reed is shaken in the water. He will uproot Israel from this good land which He gave to their fathers, and will scatter them beyond the River, because they have made their wooden images, provoking the LORD to anger. **16** And He will give Israel up because of the sins of Jeroboam, who sinned and who made Israel sin." **17** Then Jeroboam's wife arose and departed, and came to Tirzah. When she came to the threshold of the house, the child died. **18** And they buried him; and all Israel mourned for him, according to the word of the LORD which He spoke through His servant Ahijah the prophet. **19** Now the rest of the acts of Jeroboam, how he made war and how he reigned, indeed they *are* written in the book of the chronicles of the kings of Israel. **20** The period that Jeroboam reigned *was* twenty-two years. So he rested with his fathers. Then Nadab his son reigned in his place.

Cf. 1 Kin 15:29–30

Defeated by Abijah.

2 Chr 13:2–20 He reigned three years in Jerusalem. His mother's name *was* Michaiah the daughter of Uriel of Gibeah. And there was war between Abijah and Jeroboam. **3** Abijah set the battle in order with an army of valiant warriors, four hundred thousand choice men. Jeroboam also drew up in battle formation against him with eight hundred thousand choice men, mighty men of valor. **4** Then Abijah stood on Mount Zemaraim, which *is* in the mountains of Ephraim, and said, "Hear me, Jeroboam and all Israel: **5** Should you not know that the LORD God of Israel gave the dominion over Israel to David forever, to him and his sons, by a covenant of salt? **6** Yet Jeroboam the son of Nebat, the servant of Solomon the son of David, rose up and rebelled against his lord. **7** Then worthless rogues gathered to him, and strengthened themselves against Rehoboam the son of Solomon, when Rehoboam was young and inexperienced and could not withstand them. **8** And now you think to withstand the kingdom of the LORD, which is in the hand of the sons of David; and you *are* a great multitude, and with you are the gold calves which Jeroboam made for you as gods. **9** Have you not cast out the priests of the LORD, the sons of Aaron, and the Levites, and made for yourselves priests, like the peoples of *other* lands, so that whoever comes to consecrate himself with a young bull and seven rams may be a priest of *things that are* not gods? **10** But as for us, the LORD *is* our God, and we have not forsaken Him; and the priests who minister to the LORD *are* the sons of Aaron, and the Levites *attend* to *their* duties. **11** And they burn to the LORD every morning and every evening burnt sacrifices and sweet incense; *they* also *set* the showbread *in order on* the pure *gold* table, and the lampstand of gold with its lamps to burn every evening; for we keep the command of the LORD our God, but you have forsaken Him. **12** Now look, God Himself is with us as *our* head, and His priests with sounding trumpets to sound the alarm against you. O children of Israel, do not fight against the LORD God of your fathers, for you shall not prosper!" 13 But Jeroboam caused an ambush to go around behind them; so they were in front of Judah, and the ambush *was* behind them. 14 And when Judah looked around, to their surprise the battle line *was* at both front and rear; and they cried out to the LORD, and the priests sounded the trumpets. 15 Then the men of Judah gave a shout; and as the men of Judah shouted, it happened that God struck Jeroboam and all Israel before Abijah and Judah. 16 And the children of Israel fled before Judah, and God delivered them into their hand. 17 Then Abijah and his people struck them with a great slaughter; so five hundred thousand choice men of Israel fell slain. 18 Thus the children of Israel were subdued at that time; and the children of Judah prevailed, because they relied on the LORD God of their fathers. 19 And Abijah pursued Jeroboam and took cities from him: Bethel with its villages, Jeshanah with its villages, and Ephrain with its villages. 20 So Jeroboam did not recover strength again in the days of Abijah; and the LORD struck him, and he died.

Son of Joash, ruled Israel forty-one years.

2 Kin 14:23–29 In the fifteenth year of Amaziah the son of Joash, king of Judah, Jeroboam the son of Joash, king of Israel, became king in Samaria, *and reigned* forty-one years. 24 And he did evil in the sight of the LORD; he did not depart from all the sins of Jeroboam the son of Nebat, who had made Israel sin. 25 He restored the territory of Israel from the entrance of Hamath to the Sea of the Arabah, according to the word of the LORD God of Israel, which He had spoken through His servant Jonah the son of Amittai, the prophet who *was* from Gath Hepher. 26 For the LORD saw *that* the affliction of Israel *was* very bitter; for whether bond or free, there was no helper for Israel. 27 And the LORD did not say that He would blot out the name of Israel from under heaven; but He saved them by the hand of Jeroboam the son of Joash. 28 Now the rest of the acts of Jeroboam, and all that he did—his might, how he made war, and how he recaptured for Israel, from Damascus and Hamath, *what had belonged* to Judah—*are* they not written in the book of the chronicles of the kings of Israel? 29 So Jeroboam rested with his fathers, the kings of Israel. Then Zechariah his son reigned in his place.

JERUSALEM

The ancient Salem.

Gen 14:18 Then Melchizedek king of Salem brought out bread and wine; he *was* the priest of God Most High.

Ps 76:2 In Salem also is His tabernacle, And His dwelling place in Zion.

The ancient Jebus.

Josh 15:8 And the border went up by the Valley of the Son of Hinnom to the southern slope of the Jebusite *city* (which *is* Jerusalem). The border went up to the top of the mountain that *lies* before the Valley of Hinnom westward, which *is* at the end of the Valley of Rephaim northward.

Josh 18:28 Zelah, Eleph, Jebus (which *is* Jerusalem), Gibeath, *and* Kirjath: fourteen cities with their villages. This was the inheritance of the children of Benjamin according to their families.

Judg 19:10 However, the man was not willing to spend that night; so he rose and departed, and came opposite Jebus (that *is,* Jerusalem). With him were the two saddled donkeys; his concubine *was* also with him.

The king of, defeated and slain by Joshua.

Josh 10:5–23 Therefore the five kings of the Amorites, the king of Jerusalem, the king of Hebron, the king of Jarmuth, the king of Lachish, *and* the king of Eglon, gathered together and went up, they and all their armies, and camped before Gibeon and made war against it. 6 And the men of Gibeon sent to Joshua at the camp at Gilgal, saying, "Do not forsake your servants; come up to us quickly, save us and help us, for all the kings of the Amorites who dwell in the mountains have gathered together against us." 7 So Joshua ascended from Gilgal, he and all the people of war with him, and all the mighty men of valor. 8 And the LORD said to Joshua, "Do not fear them, for I have delivered them into your hand; not a man of them shall stand before you." 9 Joshua therefore came upon them suddenly, having marched all night from Gilgal. 10 So the LORD routed them before Israel, killed them with a great slaughter at Gibeon, chased them along the road that goes to Beth Horon, and struck them down as far as Azekah and Makkedah. 11 And it happened, as they fled before Israel *and* were on the descent of Beth Horon, that the LORD cast down large hailstones from heaven on them as far as Azekah, and they died. *There were* more who died from the hailstones than the children of Israel killed with the sword. 12 Then Joshua spoke to the LORD in the day when the LORD delivered up the Amorites before the children of Israel, and he said in the sight of Israel: "Sun, stand still over Gibeon; And Moon, in the Valley of Aijalon." 13 So the sun stood still, And the moon stopped, Till the people had revenge Upon their enemies. *Is* this not written in the Book of Jasher? So the sun stood still in the midst of heaven, and did not hasten to go *down* for about a whole day. 14 And there has been no day like that, before it or after it, that the LORD heeded the voice of a man; for the LORD fought for Israel. 15 Then Joshua returned, and all Israel with him, to the camp at Gilgal. 16 But these five kings had fled and hidden themselves in a cave at Makkedah. 17 And it was told Joshua, saying, "The five kings have been found hidden in the cave at Makkedah." 18 So Joshua said, "Roll large stones against the mouth of the cave, and set men by it to guard them. 19 And do not stay *there* yourselves, *but* pursue your enemies, and attack their rear *guard*. Do not allow them to enter their cities, for the LORD your God has delivered them into your hand." 20 Then it happened, while Joshua and the children of Israel made an end of slaying them with a very great slaughter, till they had finished, that those who escaped entered fortified cities. 21 And all the people returned to the camp, to Joshua at Makkedah, in peace. No one moved his tongue against any of the children of Israel. 22 Then Joshua said, "Open the mouth of the cave, and bring out those five kings to me from the cave." 23 And they did so, and brought out those five kings to him from the cave: the king of Jerusalem, the king of Hebron, the king of Jarmuth, the king of Lachish, *and* the king of Eglon.

Allotted to the tribe of Benjamin.

Josh 18:28 Zelah, Eleph, Jebus (which *is* Jerusalem), Gibeath, *and* Kirjath: fourteen cities with their villages. This was the inheritance of the children of Benjamin according to their families.

Partly taken and burned by Judah.

Judg 1:8 Now the children of Judah fought against Jerusalem and took it; they struck it with the edge of the sword and set the city on fire.

The Jebusites

Formerly dwelt in.

Judg 19:10–11 However, the man was not willing to spend that night; so he rose and departed, and came opposite Jebus (that *is,* Jerusalem). With him were the two saddled donkeys; his concubine *was* also with him. **11** They *were* near Jebus, and the day was far spent; and the servant said to his master, "Come, please, and let us turn aside into this city of the Jebusites and lodge in it."

Held possession of, with Judah and Benjamin.

Josh 15:63 As for the Jebusites, the inhabitants of Jerusalem, the children of Judah could not drive them out; but the Jebusites dwell with the children of Judah at Jerusalem to this day.

Judg 1:21 But the children of Benjamin did not drive out the Jebusites who inhabited Jerusalem; so the Jebusites dwell with the children of Benjamin in Jerusalem to this day.

Finally dispossessed of, by David.

2 Sam 5:6–8 And the king and his men went to Jerusalem against the Jebusites, the inhabitants of the land, who spoke to David, saying, "You shall not come in here; but the blind and the lame will repel you," thinking, "David cannot come in here." **7** Nevertheless David took the stronghold of Zion (that *is,* the City of David). **8** Now David said on that day, "Whoever climbs up by way of the water shaft and defeats the Jebusites (the lame and the blind, *who are* hated by David's soul), *he shall be chief and captain.*" Therefore they say, "The blind and the lame shall not come into the house."

Made the royal city.

2 Sam 5:9 Then David dwelt in the stronghold, and called it the City of David. And David built all around from the Millo and inward.

2 Sam 20:3 Now David came to his house at Jerusalem. And the king took the ten women, his concubines whom he had left to keep the house, and put them in seclusion and supported them, but did not go in to them. So they were shut up to the day of their death, living in widowhood.

Specially chosen by God.

2 Chr 6:6 Yet I have chosen Jerusalem, that My name may be there, and I have chosen David to be over My people Israel.'

Ps 135:21 Blessed be the LORD out of Zion, Who dwells in Jerusalem! Praise the LORD!

The seat of government under the Romans for a time.

Matt 27:2 And when they had bound Him, they led Him away and delivered Him to Pontius Pilate the governor.

Matt 27:19 While he was sitting on the judgment seat, his wife sent to him, saying, "Have nothing to do with that just Man, for I have suffered many things today in a dream because of Him."

Roman government transferred from, to Caesarea.

Acts 23:23–24 And he called for two centurions, saying, "Prepare two hundred soldiers, seventy horsemen, and two hundred spearmen to go to Caesarea at the third hour of the night; **24** and provide mounts to set Paul on, and bring *him* safely to Felix the governor."

Acts 25:1–13 Now when Festus had come to the province, after three days he went up from Caesarea to Jerusalem. **2** Then the high priest and the chief men of the Jews informed him against Paul; and they petitioned him, **3** asking a favor against him, that he would summon him to Jerusalem—while *they* lay in ambush along the road to kill him. **4** But Festus answered that Paul should be kept at Caesarea, and that he himself was going *there* shortly. **5** "Therefore," he said, "let those who have authority among you go down with *me* and accuse this man, to see if there is any fault in him." **6** And when he had remained among them more than ten days, he went down to Caesarea. And the next day, sitting on the judgment seat, he commanded Paul to be brought. **7** When he had come, the Jews who had come down from Jerusalem stood about and laid many serious complaints against Paul, which they could not prove, **8** while he answered for himself, "Neither against the law of the Jews, nor against the temple, nor against Caesar have I offended in anything at all." **9** But Festus, wanting to do the Jews a favor, answered Paul and said, "Are you willing to go up to Jerusalem and there be judged before me concerning these things?" **10** So Paul said, "I stand at Caesar's judgment seat, where I ought to be judged. To the Jews I have done no wrong, as you very well know. **11** For if I am an offender, or have committed anything deserving of death, I do not object to dying; but if there is nothing in these things of which these men accuse me, no one can deliver me to them. I appeal to Caesar." **12** Then Festus, when he had conferred with the council, answered, "You have appealed to Caesar? To Caesar you shall go!" **13** And after some days King Agrippa and Bernice came to Caesarea to greet Festus.

Other names for,

City of God.

Ps 46:4 *There is* a river whose streams shall make glad the city of God, The holy *place* of the tabernacle of the Most High.

Ps 48:1 Great *is* the LORD, and greatly to be praised In the city of our God, *In* His holy mountain.

City of the Lord.

Is 60:14 Also the sons of those who afflicted you Shall come bowing to you, And all those who despised you shall fall prostrate at the soles of your feet; And they shall call you The City of the LORD, Zion of the Holy One of Israel.

City of Judah.

2 Chr 25:28 Then they brought him on horses and buried him with his fathers in the City of Judah.

City of the great King.

Ps 48:2 Beautiful in elevation, The joy of the whole

earth, *Is* Mount Zion *on* the sides of the north, The city of the great King.

Matt 5:5 Blessed *are* the meek, For they shall inherit the earth.

City of our appointed feasts.

Is 33:20 Look upon Zion, the city of our appointed feasts; Your eyes will see Jerusalem, a quiet home, A tabernacle *that* will not be taken down; Not one of its stakes will ever be removed, Nor will any of its cords be broken.

City of righteousness.

Is 1:26 I will restore your judges as at the first, And your counselors as at the beginning. Afterward you shall be called the city of righteousness, the faithful city."

City of Truth.

Zech 8:3 "Thus says the LORD: 'I will return to Zion, And dwell in the midst of Jerusalem. Jerusalem shall be called the City of Truth, The Mountain of the LORD of hosts, The Holy Mountain.'

A City Not Forsaken.

Is 62:12 And they shall call them The Holy People, The Redeemed of the LORD; And you shall be called Sought Out, A City Not Forsaken.

Faithful city.

Is 1:21 How the faithful city has become a harlot! It was full of justice; Righteousness lodged in it, But now murderers.

Is 1:26 I will restore your judges as at the first, And your counselors as at the beginning. Afterward you shall be called the city of righteousness, the faithful city."

Holy city.

Neh 11:1 Now the leaders of the people dwelt at Jerusalem; the rest of the people cast lots to bring one out of ten to dwell in Jerusalem, the holy city, and nine-tenths *were to dwell* in *other* cities.

Is 48:2 For they call themselves after the holy city, And lean on the God of Israel; The LORD of hosts *is* His name:

Matt 4:5 Then the devil took Him up into the holy city, set Him on the pinnacle of the temple,

Throne of the Lord.

Jer 3:17 "At that time Jerusalem shall be called The Throne of the LORD, and all the nations shall be gathered to it, to the name of the LORD, to Jerusalem. No more shall they follow the dictates of their evil hearts.

Zion.

Ps 48:12 Walk about Zion, And go all around her. Count her towers;

Is 33:20 Look upon Zion, the city of our appointed feasts; Your eyes will see Jerusalem, a quiet home, A tabernacle *that* will not be taken down; Not one of its stakes will ever be removed, Nor will any of its cords be broken.

Zion of the Holy One of Israel.

Is 60:14 Also the sons of those who afflicted you shall come bowing to you, And all those who despised you shall fall prostrate at the soles of your feet; And they shall call you The City of the LORD, Zion of the Holy One of Israel.

Surrounded by mountains.

Ps 125:2 As the mountains surround Jerusalem, So the LORD surrounds His people From this time forth and forever.

Surrounded by a wall.

1 Kin 3:1 Now Solomon made a treaty with Pharaoh king of Egypt, and married Pharaoh's daughter; then he brought her to the City of David until he had finished building his own house, and the house of the LORD, and the wall all around Jerusalem.

Protected by forts and bulwarks.

Ps 48:12–13 Walk about Zion, And go all around her. Count her towers; **13** Mark well her bulwarks; Consider her palaces; That you may tell *it* to the generation following.

Entered by gates.

Ps 122:2 Our feet have been standing Within your gates, O Jerusalem!

Jer 17:19–21 Thus the LORD said to me: "Go and stand in the gate of the children of the people, by which the kings of Judah come in and by which they go out, and in all the gates of Jerusalem; **20** and say to them, 'Hear the word of the LORD, you kings of Judah, and all Judah, and all the inhabitants of Jerusalem, who enter by these gates. **21** Thus says the LORD: "Take heed to yourselves, and bear no burden on the Sabbath day, nor bring *it* in by the gates of Jerusalem;

Hezekiah made an aqueduct for.

2 Kin 20:20 Now the rest of the acts of Hezekiah—all his might, and how he made a pool and a tunnel and brought water into the city—*are* they not written in the book of the chronicles of the kings of Judah?

Spoils of war placed in.

1 Sam 17:54 And David took the head of the Philistine and brought it to Jerusalem, but he put his armor in his tent.

2 Sam 8:7 And David took the shields of gold that had belonged to the servants of Hadadezer, and brought them to Jerusalem.

Described as

Beautiful in elevation.

Ps 48:2 Beautiful in elevation, The joy of the whole earth, *Is* Mount Zion *on* the sides of the north, The city of the great King.

Compact.

Ps 122:3 Jerusalem is built As a city that is compact together,

Lovely.

Song 6:4 O my love, you *are as* beautiful as Tirzah, Lovely as Jerusalem, Awesome as *an army* with banners!

The perfection of beauty.

Lam 2:15 All who pass by clap *their* hands at you; They hiss and shake their heads At the daughter of Jerusalem: "Is this the city that is called 'The perfection of beauty, The joy of the whole earth'?"

Joy of the whole earth.

Ps 48:2 Beautiful in elevation, The joy of the whole earth, *Is* Mount Zion *on* the sides of the north, The city of the great King.

Lam 2:15 All who pass by clap *their* hands at you; They hiss and shake their heads At the daughter of Jerusalem: "*Is* this the city that is called 'The perfection of beauty, The joy of the whole earth'?"

Princess among the provinces.

Lam 1:1 How lonely sits the city *That was* full of people! *How* like a widow is she, Who *was* great among the nations! The princess among the provinces Has become a slave!

Great.

Jer 22:8 And many nations will pass by this city; and everyone will say to his neighbor, 'Why has the LORD done so to this great city?'

Populous.

Lam 1:1 How lonely sits the city *That was* full of people! *How* like a widow is she, Who *was* great among the nations! The princess among the provinces Has become a slave!

Wealth, etc., in the time of Solomon.

1 Kin 10:26–27 And Solomon gathered chariots and horsemen; he had one thousand four hundred chariots and twelve thousand horsemen, whom he stationed in the chariot cities and with the king at Jerusalem. 27 The king made silver *as common* in Jerusalem as stones, and he made cedar trees as abundant as the sycamores which *are* in the lowland.

Protected by God.

Is 31:5 Like birds flying about, So will the LORD of hosts defend Jerusalem. Defending, He will also deliver *it*; Passing over, He will preserve *it*."

Instances of God's care and protection of.

2 Sam 24:16 And when the angel stretched out His hand over Jerusalem to destroy it, the LORD relented from the destruction, and said to the angel who was destroying the people, "It is enough; now restrain your hand." And the angel of the LORD was by the threshing floor of Araunah the Jebusite.

2 Kin 19:32–34 "Therefore thus says the LORD concerning the king of Assyria: 'He shall not come into this city, Nor shoot an arrow there, Nor come before it with shield, Nor build a siege mound against it. 33 By the way that he came, By the same shall he return; And he shall not come into this city,' Says the LORD. 34 'For I will defend this city, to save it For My own sake and for My servant David's sake.' "

2 Chr 12:7 Now when the LORD saw that they humbled themselves, the word of the LORD came to Shemaiah, saying, "They have humbled themselves; *therefore* I will not destroy them, but I will grant them some deliverance. My wrath shall not be poured out on Jerusalem by the hand of Shishak.

The temple built in.

2 Chr 3:1 Now Solomon began to build the house of the LORD at Jerusalem on Mount Moriah, where *the LORD* had appeared to his father David, at the place that David had prepared on the threshing floor of Ornan the Jebusite.

Ps 68:29 Because of Your temple at Jerusalem, Kings will bring presents to You.

The Jews

Went up to, at the feasts.

Ps 122:4 Where the tribes go up, The tribes of the LORD, To the Testimony of Israel, To give thanks to the name of the LORD.

Luke 2:42 And when He was twelve years old, they went up to Jerusalem according to the custom of the feast.

Loved.

Ps 137:5–6 If I forget you, O Jerusalem, Let my right hand forget *its skill!* 6 If I do not remember you, Let my tongue cling to the roof of my mouth— If I do not exalt Jerusalem Above my chief joy.

Lamented the affliction of.

Neh 1:2–4 that Hanani one of my brethren came with men from Judah; and I asked them concerning the Jews who had escaped, who had survived the captivity, and concerning Jerusalem. 3 And they said to me, "The survivors who are left from the captivity in the province *are* there in great distress and reproach. The wall of Jerusalem *is* also broken down, and its gates *are* burned with fire." 4 So it was, when I heard these words, that I sat down and wept, and mourned *for many* days; I was fasting and praying before the God of heaven.

Prayed for the prosperity of.

Ps 51:18 Do good in Your good pleasure to Zion; Build the walls of Jerusalem.

Ps 122:6 Pray for the peace of Jerusalem: "May they prosper who love you.

Prayed toward.

1 Kin 8:41 "Moreover, concerning a foreigner, who *is* not of Your people Israel, but has come from a far country for Your name's sake

Dan 6:10 Now when Daniel knew that the writing was signed, he went home. And in his upper room, with his windows open toward Jerusalem, he knelt down on his knees three times that day, and prayed and gave thanks before his God, as was his custom since early days.

Wickedness and idolatry of.

2 Chr 28:4 And he sacrificed and burned incense on the high places, on the hills, and under every green tree.

Is 1:1–4 The vision of Isaiah the son of Amoz, which he saw concerning Judah and Jerusalem in the days of Uzziah, Jotham, Ahaz, *and* Hezekiah, kings of Judah. 2 Hear, O heavens, and give ear, O earth! For the LORD has spoken: "I have nourished and brought up children, And they have rebelled against Me; 3 The ox knows its owner And the donkey its master's crib; *But* Israel does not know, My people do not consider." 4 Alas, sinful nation, A people laden with iniquity, A brood of evildoers, Children who are corrupters! They have forsaken the LORD, They have provoked to anger The Holy One of Israel, They have turned away backward.

Jer 5:1–5 "Run to and fro through the streets of Jerusalem; See now and know; And seek in her open places If you can find a man, If there is *anyone* who executes judgment, Who seeks the truth, And I will pardon her. 2 Though they say, 'As the LORD lives,' Surely they swear falsely." 3 O LORD, *are* not Your eyes on the truth? You have stricken them, But they have not grieved; You have consumed them, But they have refused to receive correction. They have made their faces harder than rock; They have refused to return. 4 Therefore I said, "Surely these *are* poor. They are foolish; For they do not know the way of the LORD, The judgment of their God. 5 I will go to the great men and speak to them, For they have known the way of the LORD, The judgment of their God." But these have altogether broken the yoke *And* burst the bonds.

Ezek 8:7–10 So He brought me to the door of the court; and when I looked, there was a hole in the wall. 8 Then He said to me, "Son of man, dig into the wall"; and when I dug into the wall, there was a door. 9 And He said to me, "Go in, and see the wicked abominations which they are doing there." 10 So I went in and saw, and there—every sort of creeping thing, abominable beasts, and all the idols of the house of Israel, portrayed all around on the walls.

Mic 3:10 Who build up Zion with bloodshed And Jerusalem with iniquity:

Wickedness of, the cause of its calamities.

2 Kin 21:12–15 therefore thus says the LORD God of Israel: 'Behold, *I* am bringing *such* calamity upon Jerusalem and Judah, that whoever hears of it, both his ears will tingle. 13 And I will stretch over Jerusalem the measuring line of Samaria and the plummet of the house of Ahab; I will wipe Jerusalem as *one* wipes a dish, wiping *it* and turning *it* upside down. 14 So I will forsake the remnant of My inheritance and deliver them into the hand of their enemies; and they shall become victims of plunder to all their enemies, 15 because they have done evil in My sight, and have provoked Me to anger since the day their fathers came out of Egypt, even to this day.' "

2 Chr 24:18 Therefore they left the house of the LORD God of their fathers, and served wooden images and idols; and wrath came upon Judah and Jerusalem because of their trespass.

Lam 1:8 Jerusalem has sinned gravely, Therefore she has become vile. All who honored her despise her Because they have seen her nakedness; Yes, she sighs and turns away.

Ezek 5:5–8 "Thus says the Lord GOD: 'This *is* Jerusalem; I have set her in the midst of the nations and the countries all around her. 6 She has rebelled against My judgments by doing wickedness more than the nations, and against My statutes more than the countries that *are* all around her; for they have refused My judgments, and they have not walked in My statutes.' 7 Therefore thus says the Lord GOD: 'Because you have multiplied *disobedience* more than the nations that *are* all around you, have not walked in My statutes nor kept My judgments, nor even done according to the judgments of the nations that *are* all around you'— 8 therefore thus says the Lord GOD: 'Indeed I, even I, *am* against you and will execute judgments in your midst in the sight of the nations.

Was the tomb of the prophets.

Luke 13:33–34 Nevertheless I must journey today, tomorrow, and the *day* following; for it cannot be that a prophet should perish outside of Jerusalem. 34 "O Jerusalem, Jerusalem, the one who kills the prophets

and stones those who are sent to her! How often I wanted to gather your children together, as a hen *gathers* her brood under *her* wings, but you were not willing!

Christ

Preached in.

Luke 21:37–38 And in the daytime He was teaching in the temple, but at night He went out and stayed on the mountain called Olivet. 38 Then early in the morning all the people came to Him in the temple to hear Him.

John 18:20 Jesus answered him, "I spoke openly to the world. I always taught in synagogues and in the temple, where the Jews always meet, and in secret I have said nothing.

Did many miracles in.

John 4:45 So when He came to Galilee, the Galileans received Him, having seen all the things He did in Jerusalem at the feast; for they also had gone to the feast.

Publicly entered, as king.

Matt 21:9–10 Then the multitudes who went before and those who followed cried out, saying: "Hosanna to the Son of David! *'Blessed is He who comes in the name of the LORD!'* Hosanna in the highest!" 10 And when He had come into Jerusalem, all the city was moved, saying, "Who is this?"

Lamented over.

Matt 23:37 "O Jerusalem, Jerusalem, the one who kills the prophets and stones those who are sent to her! How often I wanted to gather your children together, as a hen gathers her chicks under *her* wings, but you were not willing!

Luke 19:41 Now as He drew near, He saw the city and wept over it,

Was put to death at.

Luke 9:31 who appeared in glory and spoke of His decease which He was about to accomplish at Jerusalem.

Acts 13:27 For those who dwell in Jerusalem, and their rulers, because they did not know Him, nor even the voices of the Prophets which are read every Sabbath, have fulfilled *them* in condemning *Him.*

Acts 13:29 Now when they had fulfilled all that was written concerning Him, they took *Him* down from the tree and laid *Him* in a tomb.

Gospel first preached at.

Luke 24:47 and that repentance and remission of sins should be preached in His name to all nations, beginning at Jerusalem.

Acts 2:14 But Peter, standing up with the eleven, raised his voice and said to them, "Men of Judea and all who dwell in Jerusalem, let this be known to you, and heed my words.

Miraculous gift of the Holy Spirit first given at.

Acts 1:4 And being assembled together with *them,* He commanded them not to depart from Jerusalem, but to wait for the Promise of the Father, "which," *He* said, "you have heard from Me;

Acts 2:1–5 When the Day of Pentecost had fully come, they were all with one accord in one place. 2 And suddenly there came a sound from heaven, as of a rushing mighty wind, and it filled the whole house where they were sitting. 3 Then there appeared to them divided tongues, as of fire, and *one* sat upon each of them. 4 And they were all filled with the Holy Spirit and began to speak with other tongues, as the Spirit gave them utterance. 5 And there were dwelling in Jerusalem Jews, devout men, from every nation under heaven.

Persecution of the Christian church commenced at.

Acts 4:1 Now as they spoke to the people, the priests, the captain of the temple, and the Sadducees came upon them,

Acts 8:1 Now Saul was consenting to his death. At that time a great persecution arose against the church which was at Jerusalem; and they were all scattered throughout the regions of Judea and Samaria, except the apostles.

First Christian council held at.

Acts 15:4 And when they had come to Jerusalem, they were received by the church and the apostles and the elders; and they reported all things that God had done with them.

Acts 15:6 Now the apostles and elders came together to consider this matter.

Calamities of, mentioned

Taken and plundered by Shishak.

1 Kin 14:25–26 It happened in the fifth year of King Rehoboam *that* Shishak king of Egypt came up against Jerusalem. 26 And he took away the treasures of the house of the LORD and the treasures of the king's house; he took away everything. He also took away all the gold shields which Solomon had made.

2 Chr 12:1–4 Now it came to pass, when Rehoboam had established the kingdom and had strengthened himself, that he forsook the law of the LORD, and all Israel along with him. 2 And it happened in the fifth year of King Rehoboam *that* Shishak king of Egypt came up against Jerusalem, because they had transgressed against the LORD, 3 with twelve hundred chariots, sixty thousand horsemen, and people without number who came with him out of Egypt—the Lubim and the Sukkiim and the Ethiopians. 4 And he took the fortified cities of Judah and came to Jerusalem.

Taken and plundered by Jehoash king of Israel.

2 Kin 14:13–14 Then Jehoash king of Israel captured Amaziah king of Judah, the son of Jehoash, the son of Ahaziah, at Beth Shemesh; and he went to Jerusalem, and broke down the wall of Jerusalem from the Gate of Ephraim to the Corner Gate—four hundred cubits. 14 And he took all the gold and silver, all the articles that were found in the house of the LORD and in the treasuries of the king's house, and hostages, and returned to Samaria.

Besieged but not taken by Rezin and Pekah.

Is 7:1 Now it came to pass in the days of Ahaz the son of Jotham, the son of Uzziah, king of Judah, *that* Rezin king of Syria and Pekah the son of Remaliah, king of Israel, went up to Jerusalem to *make* war against it, but could not prevail against it.

2 Kin 16:5 Then Rezin king of Syria and Pekah the son

of Remaliah, king of Israel, came up to Jerusalem to *make* war; and they besieged Ahaz but could not overcome *him*.

Besieged but not taken by Sennacherib. **2 Kin 18:17; 19:1–37**

Taken and made tributary by Pharaoh Necho.

2 Kin 23:33–35 Now Pharaoh Necho put him in prison at Riblah in the land of Hamath, that he might not reign in Jerusalem; and he imposed on the land a tribute of one hundred talents of silver and a talent of gold. 34 Then Pharaoh Necho made Eliakim the son of Josiah king in place of his father Josiah, and changed his name to Jehoiakim. And *Pharaoh* took Jehoahaz and went to Egypt, and he died there. 35 So Jehoiakim gave the silver and gold to Pharaoh; but he taxed the land to give money according to the command of Pharaoh; he exacted the silver and gold from the people of the land, from every one according to his assessment, to give *it* to Pharaoh Necho.

Besieged by Nebuchadnezzar.

2 Kin 24:10–11 At that time the servants of Nebuchadnezzar king of Babylon came up against Jerusalem, and the city was besieged. 11 And Nebuchadnezzar king of Babylon came against the city, as his servants were besieging it.

Taken and burned by Nebuchadnezzar.

Jer 39:1–8 In the ninth year of Zedekiah king of Judah, in the tenth month, Nebuchadnezzar king of Babylon and all his army came against Jerusalem, and besieged it. 2 In the eleventh year of Zedekiah, in the fourth month, on the ninth *day* of the month, the city was penetrated. 3 Then all the princes of the king of Babylon came in and sat in the Middle Gate: Nergal-Sharezer, Samgar-Nebo, Sarsechim, Rabsaris, Nergal-Sarezer, Rabmag, with the rest of the princes of the king of Babylon. 4 So it was, when Zedekiah the king of Judah and all the men of war saw them, that they fled and went out of the city by night, by way of the king's garden, by the gate between the two walls. And he went out by way of the plain. 5 But the Chaldean army pursued them and overtook Zedekiah in the plains of Jericho. And when they had captured him, they brought him up to Nebuchadnezzar king of Babylon, to Riblah in the land of Hamath, where he pronounced judgment on him. 6 Then the king of Babylon killed the sons of Zedekiah before his eyes in Riblah; the king of Babylon also killed all the nobles of Judah. 7 Moreover he put out Zedekiah's eyes, and bound him with bronze fetters to carry him off to Babylon. 8 And the Chaldeans burned the king's house and the houses of the people with fire, and broke down the walls of Jerusalem.

Cf. 2 Kin 25:1–30

Threatened by Sanballat.

Neh 4:7–8 Now it happened, when Sanballat, Tobiah, the Arabs, the Ammonites, and the Ashdodites heard that the walls of Jerusalem were being restored and the gaps were beginning to be closed, that they became very angry, 8 and all of them conspired together to come *and* attack Jerusalem and create confusion.

Rebuilt after the captivity by order of Cyrus.

Ezra 1:1–4 Now in the first year of Cyrus king of Persia, that the word of the LORD by the mouth of Jeremiah might be fulfilled, the LORD stirred up the spirit of Cyrus king of Persia, so that he made a proclamation throughout all his kingdom, and also *put it* in writing, saying, **2** Thus says Cyrus king of Persia: All the kingdoms of the earth the LORD God of heaven has given me. And He has commanded me to build Him a house at Jerusalem which *is* in Judah. **3** Who *is* among you of all His people? May his God be with him, and let him go up to Jerusalem which *is* in Judah, and build the house of the LORD God of Israel (He *is* God), which *is* in Jerusalem. **4** And whoever is left in any place where he dwells, let the men of his place help him with silver and gold, with goods and livestock, besides the freewill offerings for the house of God which *is* in Jerusalem.

Prophecies respecting,

To be taken by king of Babylon.

Jer 20:5 Moreover I will deliver all the wealth of this city, all its produce, and all its precious things; all the treasures of the kings of Judah I will give into the hand of their enemies, who will plunder them, seize them, and carry them to Babylon.

To be made a heap of ruins.

Jer 9:11 "I will make Jerusalem a heap of ruins, a den of jackals. I will make the cities of Judah desolate, without an inhabitant."

Jer 26:18 "Micah of Moresheth prophesied in the days of Hezekiah king of Judah, and spoke to all the people of Judah, saying, 'Thus says the LORD of hosts: "Zion shall be plowed *like* a field, Jerusalem shall become heaps of ruins, And the mountain of the temple Like the bare hills of the forest."' '

To be a wilderness.

Is 64:10 Your holy cities are a wilderness, Zion is a wilderness, Jerusalem a desolation.

To be rebuilt by Cyrus.

Is 44:26–28 Who confirms the word of His servant, And performs the counsel of His messengers; Who says to Jerusalem, 'You shall be inhabited,' To the cities of Judah, 'You shall be built,' And I will raise up her waste places; **27** Who says to the deep, 'Be dry! And I will dry up your rivers'; **28** Who says of Cyrus, '*He is* My shepherd, And he shall perform all My pleasure, Saying to Jerusalem, "You shall be built," And to the temple, "Your foundation shall be laid." '

To be a quiet habitation.

Is 33:20 Look upon Zion, the city of our appointed feasts; Your eyes will see Jerusalem, a quiet home, A tabernacle *that* will not be taken down; Not one of its stakes will ever be removed, Nor will any of its cords be broken.

To be a terror to her enemies.

Zech 12:2–3 "Behold, I will make Jerusalem a cup of drunkenness to all the surrounding peoples, when they lay siege against Judah and Jerusalem. **3** And it shall happen in that day that I will make Jerusalem a very heavy stone for all peoples; all who would heave it away will surely be cut in pieces, though all nations of the earth are gathered against it.

Christ to enter, as king.

Zech 9:9 "Rejoice greatly, O daughter of Zion! Shout, O daughter of Jerusalem! Behold, your King is coming to you; He *is* just and having salvation, Lowly and riding on a donkey, A colt, the foal of a donkey.

The gospel to go forth from.

Is 2:3 Many people shall come and say, "Come, and let us go up to the mountain of the LORD, To the house of the God of Jacob; He will teach us His ways, And we shall walk in His paths." For out of Zion shall go forth the law, And the word of the LORD from Jerusalem.

Is 40:9 O Zion, You who bring good tidings, Get up into the high mountain; O Jerusalem, You who bring good tidings, Lift up your voice with strength, Lift *it* up, be not afraid; Say to the cities of Judah, "Behold your God!"

To be destroyed by the Romans.

Luke 19:42–44 saying, "If you had known, even you, especially in this your day, the things *that make* for your peace! But now they are hidden from your eyes. **43** For days will come upon you when your enemies will build an embankment around you, surround you and close you in on every side, **44** and level you, and your children within you, to the ground; and they will not leave in you one stone upon another, because you did not know the time of your visitation."

Its destruction accompanied by severe calamities.

Matt 24:21 For then there will be great tribulation, such as has not been since the beginning of the world until this time, no, nor ever shall be.

Matt 24:29 "Immediately after the tribulation of those days the sun will be darkened, and the moon will not give its light; the stars will fall from heaven, and the powers of the heavens will be shaken.

Luke 21:23–24 But woe to those who are pregnant and to those who are nursing babies in those days! For there will be great distress in the land and wrath upon this people. **24** And they will fall by the edge of the sword, and be led away captive into all nations. And Jerusalem will be trampled by Gentiles until the times of the Gentiles are fulfilled.

Signs preceding its destruction.

Matt 24:6–15 And you will hear of wars and rumors of wars. See that you are not troubled; for all *these things* must come to pass, but the end is not yet. **7** For nation will rise against nation, and kingdom against kingdom. And there will be famines, pestilences, and earthquakes in various places. **8** All these *are* the beginning of sorrows. **9** "Then they will deliver you up to tribulation and kill you, and you will be hated by all nations for My name's sake. **10** And then many will be offended, will betray one another, and will hate one another. **11** Then many false prophets will rise up and deceive many. **12** And because lawlessness will abound, the love of many will grow cold. **13** But he who endures to the end shall be saved. **14** And this gospel of the kingdom will be preached in all the world as a witness to all the nations, and then the end will come. **15** "Therefore when you see the *'abomination of desolation,'* spoken of by Daniel the prophet, standing in the holy place" (whoever reads, let him understand),

Luke 21:7–11 So they asked Him, saying, "Teacher, but when will these things be? And what sign *will there*

be when these things are about to take place?" **8** And He said: "Take heed that you not be deceived. For many will come in My name, saying, 'I am *He*,' and, 'The time has drawn near.' Therefore do not go after them. **9** But when you hear of wars and commotions, do not be terrified; for these things must come to pass first, but the end *will not come* immediately." **10** Then He said to them, "Nation will rise against nation, and kingdom against kingdom. **11** And there will be great earthquakes in various places, and famines and pestilences; and there will be fearful sights and great signs from heaven.

Luke 21:25 "And there will be signs in the sun, in the moon, and in the stars; and on the earth distress of nations, with perplexity, the sea and the waves roaring;

Luke 21:28 Now when these things begin to happen, look up and lift up your heads, because your redemption draws near."

Illustrative of

The church.

Gal 4:25–26 for this Hagar is Mount Sinai in Arabia, and corresponds to Jerusalem which now is, and is in bondage with her children— **26** but the Jerusalem above is free, which is the mother of us all.

Heb 12:22 But you have come to Mount Zion and to the city of the living God, the heavenly Jerusalem, to an innumerable company of angels,

The church glorified.

Rev 3:12 He who overcomes, I will make him a pillar in the temple of My God, and he shall go out no more. I will write on him the name of My God and the name of the city of My God, the New Jerusalem, which comes down out of heaven from My God. And *I will write on him* My new name.

Rev 21:2 Then I, John, saw the holy city, New Jerusalem, coming down out of heaven from God, prepared as a bride adorned for her husband.

Rev 21:10 And he carried me away in the Spirit to a great and high mountain, and showed me the great city, the holy Jerusalem, descending out of heaven from God,

(Its strong position) believers under God's protection.

Ps 125:2 As the mountains surround Jerusalem, So the LORD surrounds His people From this time forth and forever.

JESUS CHRIST, THE ASCENSION OF

Prophecies respecting.

Ps 68:18 You have ascended on high, You have led captivity captive; You have received gifts among men, Even *from* the rebellious, That the LORD God might dwell *there*.

Eph 4:7–8 But to each one of us grace was given according to the measure of Christ's gift. **8** Therefore He says: *"When He ascended on high, He led captivity captive, And gave gifts to men."*

Foretold by Himself.

John 6:62 *What* then if you should see the Son of Man ascend where He was before?

John 7:33 Then Jesus said to them, "I shall be with you a little while longer, and *then* I go to Him who sent Me.

John 14:28 You have heard Me say to you, 'I am going away and coming *back* to you.' If you loved Me, you would rejoice because I said, 'I am going to the Father,' for My Father is greater than I.

John 16:5 "But now I go away to Him who sent Me, and none of you asks Me, 'Where are You going?'

John 20:17 Jesus said to her, "Do not cling to Me, for I have not yet ascended to My Father; but go to My brethren and say to them, 'I am ascending to My Father and your Father, and *to* My God and your God.' "

Forty days after His resurrection.

Acts 1:3 to whom He also presented Himself alive after His suffering by many infallible proofs, being seen by them during forty days and speaking of the things pertaining to the kingdom of God.

Described.

Acts 1:9 Now when He had spoken these things, while they watched, He was taken up, and a cloud received Him out of their sight.

From Mount Olivet.

Mark 11:1 Now when they drew near Jerusalem, to Bethphage and Bethany, at the Mount of Olives, He sent two of His disciples;

Luke 24:50 And He led them out as far as Bethany, and He lifted up His hands and blessed them.

Acts 1:12 Then they returned to Jerusalem from the mount called Olivet, which is near Jerusalem, a Sabbath day's journey.

While blessing His disciples.

Luke 24:50 And He led them out as far as Bethany, and He lifted up His hands and blessed them.

When He had atoned for sin.

Heb 9:12 Not with the blood of goats and calves, but with His own blood He entered the Most Holy Place once for all, having obtained eternal redemption.

Heb 10:12 But this Man, after He had offered one sacrifice for sins forever, sat down at the right hand of God,

Was triumphant.

Ps 68:18 You have ascended on high, You have led captivity captive; You have received gifts among men, Even *from* the rebellious, That the LORD God might dwell *there*.

Was to supreme power and dignity.

Luke 24:26 Ought not the Christ to have suffered these things and to enter into His glory?"

Eph 1:20–21 which He worked in Christ when He raised Him from the dead and seated *Him* at His right hand in the heavenly *places*, **21** far above all principality and power and might and dominion, and every name that is named, not only in this age but also in that which is to come.

1 Pet 3:22 who has gone into heaven and is at the right hand of God, angels and authorities and powers having been made subject to Him.

As the forerunner of His people.

Heb 6:20 where the forerunner has entered for us, *even*

Jesus, having become High Priest forever according to the order of Melchizedek.

To intercede.

Rom 8:34 Who *is* he who condemns? *It is* Christ who died, and furthermore is also risen, who is even at the right hand of God, who also makes intercession for us.

Heb 9:24 For Christ has not entered the holy places made with hands, *which are* copies of the true, but into heaven itself, now to appear in the presence of God for us;

To send the Holy Spirit.

John 16:7 Nevertheless I tell you the truth. It is to your advantage that I go away; for if I do not go away, the Helper will not come to you; but if I depart, I will send Him to you.

Acts 2:33 Therefore being exalted to the right hand of God, and having received from the Father the promise of the Holy Spirit, He poured out this which you now see and hear.

To receive gifts for men.

Ps 68:18 You have ascended on high, You have led captivity captive; You have received gifts among men, Even *from* the rebellious, That the LORD God might dwell *there*.

Eph 4:8 Therefore He says: *"When He ascended on high, He led captivity captive, And gave gifts to men."*

Eph 4:11 And He Himself gave some *to be* apostles, some prophets, some evangelists, and some pastors and teachers,

To prepare a place for His people.

John 14:2 In My Father's house are many mansions; if *it were* not *so*, I would have told you. I go to prepare a place for you.

His second coming shall be in like manner as.

Acts 1:10–11 And while they looked steadfastly toward heaven as He went up, behold, two men stood by them in white apparel, **11** who also said, "Men of Galilee, why do you stand gazing up into heaven? This *same* Jesus, who was taken up from you into heaven, will so come in like manner as you saw Him go into heaven."

Typified.

Lev 16:15 "Then he shall kill the goat of the sin offering, which *is* for the people, bring its blood inside the veil, do with that blood as he did with the blood of the bull, and sprinkle it on the mercy seat and before the mercy seat.

Heb 6:20 where the forerunner has entered for us, *even* Jesus, having become High Priest forever according to the order of Melchizedek.

Heb 9:7 But into the second part the high priest *went* alone once a year, not without blood, which he offered for himself and *for* the people's sins *committed* in ignorance;

Heb 9:9 It *was* symbolic for the present time in which both gifts and sacrifices are offered which cannot make him who performed the service perfect in regard to the conscience—

Heb 9:12 Not with the blood of goats and calves, but with His own blood He entered the Most Holy Place once for all, having obtained eternal redemption.

JESUS CHRIST, THE CHARACTER AND ATTRIBUTES OF

Holy.

Luke 1:35 And the angel answered and said to her, *"The* Holy Spirit will come upon you, and the power of the Highest will overshadow you; therefore, also, that Holy One who is to be born will be called the Son of God.

Acts 3:14 But you denied the Holy One and the Just, and asked for a murderer to be granted to you,

Acts 4:27 "For truly against Your holy Servant Jesus, whom You anointed, both Herod and Pontius Pilate, with the Gentiles and the people of Israel, were gathered together

Rev 3:7 "And to the angel of the church in Philadelphia write, 'These things says He who is holy, He who is true, *'He who has the key of David, He who opens and no one shuts, and shuts and no one opens"*:

Righteous.

Is 53:11 He shall see the labor of His soul, *and* be satisfied. By His knowledge My righteous Servant shall justify many, For He shall bear their iniquities.

Heb 1:9 *You have loved righteousness and hated lawlessness; Therefore God, Your God, has anointed You With the oil of gladness more than Your companions."*

Good.

Matt 19:16 Now behold, one came and said to Him, "Good Teacher, what good thing shall I do that I may have eternal life?"

Faithful.

Is 11:5 Righteousness shall be the belt of His loins, And faithfulness the belt of His waist.

1 Thess 5:24 He who calls you *is* faithful, who also will do *it*.

True.

John 1:14 And the Word became flesh and dwelt among us, and we beheld His glory, the glory as of the only begotten of the Father, full of grace and truth.

John 7:18 He who speaks from himself seeks his own glory; but He who seeks the glory of the One who sent Him is true, and no unrighteousness is in Him.

1 John 5:20 And we know that the Son of God has come and has given us an understanding, that we may know Him who is true; and we are in Him who is true, in His Son Jesus Christ. This is the true God and eternal life.

Just.

Zech 9:9 "Rejoice greatly, O daughter of Zion! Shout, O daughter of Jerusalem! Behold, your King is coming to you; He *is* just and having salvation, Lowly and riding on a donkey, A colt, the foal of a donkey.

John 5:30 I can of Myself do nothing. As I hear, I judge; and My judgment is righteous, because I do not seek My own will but the will of the Father who sent Me.

Acts 22:14 Then he said, 'The God of our fathers has chosen you that you should know His will, and see the Just One, and hear the voice of His mouth.

Sinless.

Is 53:9 And they made His grave with the wicked— But with the rich at His death, Because He had done no violence, Nor *was any* deceit in His mouth.

Matt 4:1–10 Then Jesus was led up by the Spirit into the wilderness to be tempted by the devil. **2** And when He had fasted forty days and forty nights, afterward He was hungry. **3** Now when the tempter came to Him, he said, "If You are the Son of God, command that these stones become bread." **4** But He answered and said, "It is written, *'Man shall not live by bread alone, but by every word that proceeds from the mouth of God.'"* **5** Then the devil took Him up into the holy city, set Him on the pinnacle of the temple, **6** and said to Him, "If You are the Son of God, throw Yourself down. For it is written: *'He shall give His angels charge over you,'* and, *'In their hands they shall bear you up, Lest you dash your foot against a stone.'"* **7** Jesus said to him, "It is written again, *'You shall not tempt the LORD your God.'"* **8** Again, the devil took Him up on an exceedingly high mountain, and showed Him all the kingdoms of the world and their glory. **9** And he said to Him, "All these things I will give You if You will fall down and worship me." **10** Then Jesus said to him, "Away with you, Satan! For it is written, *'You shall worship the LORD your God, and Him only you shall serve.'"*

Matt 27:4 saying, "I have sinned by betraying innocent blood." And they said, "What *is that* to us? You see *to it!*"

John 8:46 Which of you convicts Me of sin? And if I tell the truth, why do you not believe Me?

2 Cor 5:21 For He made Him who knew no sin *to be* sin for us, that we might become the righteousness of God in Him.

Heb 7:26 For such a High Priest was fitting for us, *who is* holy, harmless, undefiled, separate from sinners, and has become higher than the heavens;

1 Pet 1:19 but with the precious blood of Christ, as of a lamb without blemish and without spot.

1 Pet 2:22 *"Who committed no sin, Nor was deceit found in His mouth";*

Obedient to God the Father.

Ps 40:8 I delight to do Your will, O my God, And Your law *is* within my heart."

Luke 22:42 saying, "Father, if it is Your will, take this cup away from Me; nevertheless not My will, but Yours, be done."

John 4:34 Jesus said to them, "My food is to do the will of Him who sent Me, and to finish His work.

John 15:10 If you keep My commandments, you will abide in My love, just as I have kept My Father's commandments and abide in His love.

Zealous.

Luke 2:49 And He said to them, "Why did you seek Me? Did you not know that I must be about My Father's business?"

John 2:17 Then His disciples remembered that it was written, *"Zeal for Your house has eaten Me up."*

John 8:29 And He who sent Me is with Me. The Father has not left Me alone, for I always do those things that please Him."

Humble.

Is 53:7 He was oppressed and He was afflicted, Yet He opened not His mouth; He was led as a lamb to the slaughter, And as a sheep before its shearers is silent, So He opened not His mouth.

Zech 9:9 "Rejoice greatly, O daughter of Zion! Shout, O daughter of Jerusalem! Behold, your King is coming to you; He *is* just and having salvation, Lowly and riding on a donkey, A colt, the foal of a donkey.

Matt 11:29 Take My yoke upon you and learn from Me, for I am gentle and lowly in heart, and you will find rest for your souls.

Luke 22:27 For who *is* greater, he who sits at the table, or he who serves? *Is* it not he who sits at the table? Yet I am among you as the One who serves.

Phil 2:8 And being found in appearance as a man, He humbled Himself and became obedient to *the point of* death, even the death of the cross.

Merciful.

Heb 2:17 Therefore, in all things He had to be made like *His* brethren, that He might be a merciful and faithful High Priest in things *pertaining* to God, to make propitiation for the sins of the people.

Patient.

Is 53:7 He was oppressed and He was afflicted, Yet He opened not His mouth; He was led as a lamb to the slaughter, And as a sheep before its shearers is silent, So He opened not His mouth.

Matt 27:14 But He answered him not one word, so that the governor marveled greatly.

1 Tim 1:16 However, for this reason I obtained mercy, that in me first Jesus Christ might show all long-suffering, as a pattern to those who are going to believe on Him for everlasting life.

Compassionate.

Is 40:11 He will feed His flock like a shepherd; He will gather the lambs with His arm, And carry *them* in His bosom, *And* gently lead those who are with young.

Matt 4:23–24 And Jesus went about all Galilee, teaching in their synagogues, preaching the gospel of the kingdom, and healing all kinds of sickness and all kinds of disease among the people. **24** Then His fame went throughout all Syria; and they brought to Him all sick people who were afflicted with various diseases and torments, and those who were demon-possessed, epileptics, and paralytics; and He healed them.

Luke 19:41 Now as He drew near, He saw the city and wept over it,

Acts 10:38 how God anointed Jesus of Nazareth with the Holy Spirit and with power, who went about doing good and healing all who were oppressed by the devil, for God was with Him.

Loving.

John 13:1 Now before the Feast of the Passover, when Jesus knew that His hour had come that He should depart from this world to the Father, having loved His own who were in the world, He loved them to the end.

John 15:13 Greater love has no one than this, than to lay down one's life for his friends.

Self-denying.

Matt 8:20 And Jesus said to him, "Foxes have holes and birds of the air *have* nests, but the Son of Man has nowhere to lay *His* head."

2 Cor 8:9 For you know the grace of our Lord Jesus Christ, that though He was rich, yet for your sakes He became poor, that you through His poverty might become rich.

Forgiving.

Luke 23:34 Then Jesus said, "Father, forgive them, for they do not know what they do." And they divided His garments and cast lots.

Eternal.

Is 9:6 For unto us a Child is born, Unto us a Son is given; And the government will be upon His shoulder. And His name will be called Wonderful, Counselor, Mighty God, Everlasting Father, Prince of Peace.

Mic 5:2 "But you, Bethlehem Ephrathah, *Though* you are little among the thousands of Judah, *Yet* out of you shall come forth to Me The One to be Ruler in Israel, Whose goings forth *are* from of old, From everlasting."

John 1:1 In the beginning was the Word, and the Word was with God, and the Word was God.

Col 1:17 And He is before all things, and in Him all things consist.

Heb 1:8–10 But to the Son He says: "Your throne, O God, is forever and ever; A scepter of righteousness is the scepter of Your kingdom. **9** You have loved righteousness and hated lawlessness; Therefore God, Your God, has anointed You With the oil of gladness more than Your companions." **10** And: "You, LORD, in the beginning laid the foundation of the earth, And the heavens are the work of Your hands.

Rev 1:8 "I am the Alpha and the Omega, *the* Beginning and *the* End," says the Lord, "who is and who was and who is to come, the Almighty."

Omnipresent.

Matt 18:20 For where two or three are gathered together in My name, I am there in the midst of them."

Matt 28:20 teaching them to observe all things that I have commanded you; and lo, I am with you always, *even* to the end of the age." Amen.

John 3:13 No one has ascended to heaven but He who came down from heaven, *that is*, the Son of Man who is in heaven.

Omnipotent.

Ps 45:3 Gird Your sword upon *Your* thigh, O Mighty One, With Your glory and Your majesty.

Phil 3:21 who will transform our lowly body that it may be conformed to His glorious body, according to the working by which He is able even to subdue all things to Himself.

Rev 1:8 "I am the Alpha and the Omega, *the* Beginning and *the* End," says the Lord, "who is and who was and who is to come, the Almighty."

Omniscient.

1 Kin 8:39 then hear in heaven Your dwelling place, and forgive, and act, and give to everyone according to all his ways, whose heart You know (for You alone know the hearts of all the sons of men),

Luke 5:22 But when Jesus perceived their thoughts, He answered and said to them, "Why are you reasoning in your hearts?

Ezek 11:5 Then the Spirit of the LORD fell upon me, and said to me, "Speak! 'Thus says the LORD: "Thus you have said, O house of Israel; for I know the things that come into your mind.

John 2:24–25 But Jesus did not commit Himself to them, because He knew all *men*, **25** and had no need that anyone should testify of man, for He knew what was in man.

John 16:30 Now we are sure that You know all things, and have no need that anyone should question You. By this we believe that You came forth from God."

John 21:17 He said to him the third time, "Simon, *son* of Jonah, do you love Me?" Peter was grieved because He said to him the third time, "Do you love Me?" And he said to Him, "Lord, You know all things; You know that I love You." Jesus said to him, "Feed My sheep.

Rev 2:23 I will kill her children with death, and all the churches shall know that I am He who searches the minds and hearts. And I will give to each one of you according to your works.

Unchangeable.

Mal 3:6 "For I *am* the LORD, I do not change; Therefore you are not consumed, O sons of Jacob.

Heb 1:12 Like a cloak You will fold them up, And they will be changed. But You are the same, And Your years will not fail."

Heb 13:8 Jesus Christ *is* the same yesterday, today, and forever.

The object of divine worship.

Acts 7:59 And they stoned Stephen as he was calling on *God* and saying, "Lord Jesus, receive my spirit."

Heb 1:6 But when He again brings the firstborn into the world, He says: *"Let all the angels of God worship Him."*

Rev 5:12 saying with a loud voice: "Worthy is the Lamb who was slain To receive power and riches and wisdom, And strength and honor and glory and blessing!"

The object of faith.

Ps 2:12 Kiss the Son, lest He be angry, And you perish *in* the way, When His wrath is kindled but a little. Blessed *are* all those who put their trust in Him.

Jer 17:5 Thus says the LORD: "Cursed *is* the man who trusts in man And makes flesh his strength, Whose heart departs from the LORD.

Jer 17:7 "Blessed *is* the man who trusts in the LORD, And whose hope is the LORD.

John 14:1 "Let not your heart be troubled; you believe in God, believe also in Me.

1 Pet 2:6 Therefore it is also contained in the Scripture, *"Behold, I lay in Zion A chief cornerstone, elect, precious, And he who believes on Him will by no means be put to shame."*

Subject to His parents.

Luke 2:51 Then He went down with them and came to Nazareth, and was subject to them, but His mother kept all these things in her heart.

Saints are conformed to.

Rom 8:29 For whom He foreknew, He also predestined *to be* conformed to the image of His Son, that He might be the firstborn among many brethren.

JESUS CHRIST, THE COMPASSION AND SYMPATHY OF

Necessary to His priestly office.

Heb 5:2 He can have compassion on those who are ignorant and going astray, since he himself is also subject to weakness.

Heb 5:7 who, in the days of His flesh, when He had offered up prayers and supplications, with vehement cries and tears to Him who was able to save Him from death, and was heard because of His godly fear,

Manifested for the

Weary and heavy laden.

Matt 11:28–30 Come to Me, all *you* who labor and are heavy laden, and I will give you rest. **29** Take My yoke upon you and learn from Me, for I am gentle and lowly in heart, and you will find rest for your souls. **30** For My yoke *is* easy and My burden is light."

Weak in faith.

Is 40:11 He will feed His flock like a shepherd; He will gather the lambs with His arm, And carry *them* in His bosom, *And* gently lead those who are with young.

Is 42:3 A bruised reed He will not break, And smoking flax He will not quench; He will bring forth justice for truth.

Matt 12:20 *A bruised reed He will not break, And smoking flax He will not quench, Till He sends forth justice to victory;*

Tempted.

Heb 2:18 For in that He Himself has suffered, being tempted, He is able to aid those who are tempted.

Afflicted.

Luke 7:13 When the Lord saw her, He had compassion on her and said to her, "Do not weep."

John 11:33 Therefore, when Jesus saw her weeping, and the Jews who came with her weeping, He groaned in the spirit and was troubled.

John 11:35 Jesus wept.

Diseased.

Matt 14:14 And when Jesus went out He saw a great multitude; and He was moved with compassion for them, and healed their sick.

Mark 1:41 Then Jesus, moved with compassion, stretched out *His* hand and touched him, and said to him, "I am willing; be cleansed."

Poor.

Mark 8:2 "I have compassion on the multitude, because they have now continued with Me three days and have nothing to eat.

Perishing sinners.

Matt 9:36 But when He saw the multitudes, He was moved with compassion for them, because they were weary and scattered, like sheep having no shepherd.

Luke 19:41 Now as He drew near, He saw the city and wept over it,

John 3:16 For God so loved the world that He gave His only begotten Son, that whoever believes in Him should not perish but have everlasting life.

An encouragement to prayer.

Heb 4:15 For we do not have a High Priest who cannot sympathize with our weaknesses, but was in all *points* tempted as *we are, yet* without sin.

JESUS CHRIST, THE CRUCIFIXION OF

Predictions of.

Ps 22:1 My God, My God, why have You forsaken Me? *Why are You so* far from helping Me, *And from* the words of My groaning?

Ps 22:14–18 I am poured out like water, And all My bones are out of joint; My heart is like wax; It has melted within Me. **15** My strength is dried up like a potsherd, And My tongue clings to My jaws; You have brought Me to the dust of death. **16** For dogs have surrounded Me; The congregation of the wicked has enclosed Me. They pierced My hands and My feet; **17** I can count all My bones. They look *and* stare at Me. **18** They divide My garments among them, And for My clothing they cast lots.

Ps 69:20–21 Reproach has broken my heart, And I am full of heaviness; I looked *for someone* to take pity, but *there was* none; And for comforters, but I found none. **21** They also gave me gall for my food, And for my thirst they gave me vinegar to drink.

Ps 69:25 Let their dwelling place be desolate; Let no one live in their tents.

Zech 13:7 "Awake, O sword, against My Shepherd, Against the Man who is My Companion," Says the LORD of hosts. "Strike the Shepherd, And the sheep will be scattered; Then I will turn My hand against the little ones.

Mark 2:20 But the days will come when the bridegroom will be taken away from them, and then they will fast in those days.

Mark 14:1 After two days it was the Passover and *the Feast* of Unleavened Bread. And the chief priests and the scribes sought how they might take Him by trickery and put *Him* to death.

Events surrounding the.

Matt 27:32–56 Now as they came out, they found a man of Cyrene, Simon by name. Him they compelled to bear His cross. **33** And when they had come to a place called Golgotha, that is to say, Place of a Skull, **34** they gave Him sour wine mingled with gall to drink. But when He had tasted *it*, He would not drink. **35** Then they crucified Him, and divided His garments, casting lots, that it might be fulfilled which was spoken by the prophet: *"They divided My garments among them, And for My clothing they cast lots."* **36** Sitting down, they kept watch over Him there. **37** And they put up over His head the accusation written against Him: THIS IS JESUS THE KING OF THE JEWS. **38** Then two robbers were crucified with Him, one on the right and another on the left. **39** And those who passed by blasphemed Him, wagging their heads **40** and saying, "You who destroy the temple and build *it* in three days, save Yourself! If You are the Son of God, come down from the cross." **41** Likewise the chief priests also, mocking with the scribes and elders, said, **42** "He saved others; Himself He cannot save. If He is the King of Israel, let Him now come down from the cross, and we will believe Him. **43** He trusted in God; let Him deliver Him now if He will have Him; for He said, 'I am the Son of God.' " **44** Even the robbers who were crucified with Him reviled Him with the same thing. **45** Now from the sixth hour until the ninth hour there was darkness over all the land. **46** And about the ninth hour Jesus cried out with a loud voice, saying, "Eli, Eli, lama sabachthani?" that is, *My God, My God, why have You forsaken Me?"* **47** Some of those who stood there, when they heard *that,* said, "This Man is calling for Elijah!" **48** Immediately one of them ran and took a sponge, filled *it* with sour wine and put *it* on a reed, and offered it to Him to drink. **49** The rest said, "Let Him alone; let us see if Elijah will come to save Him." **50** And Jesus cried out again with a loud voice, and yielded up His spirit. **51** Then, behold, the veil of the temple was torn in two from top to bottom; and the earth quaked, and the rocks were split, **52** and the graves were opened; and many bodies of the saints who had fallen asleep were raised; **53** and coming out of the graves after His resurrection, they went into the holy city and appeared to many. **54** So when the centurion and those with him, who were guarding Jesus, saw the earthquake and the things that had happened, they feared greatly, saying, "Truly this was the Son of God!" **55** And many women who followed Jesus from Galilee, ministering to Him, were there looking on from afar, **56** among whom were Mary Magdalene, Mary the mother of James and Joses, and the mother of Zebedee's sons.

Cf. Mark 15:21–41; Luke 23:26–49

The desire of the people.

Luke 23:23–25 But they were insistent, demanding with loud voices that He be crucified. And the voices of these men and of the chief priests prevailed. **24** So Pilate gave sentence that it should be as they requested. **25** And he released to them the one they requested, who for rebellion and murder had been thrown into prison; but he delivered Jesus to their will.

References to, the rejected stone.

Matt 21:42 Jesus said to them, "Have you never read in the Scriptures: *'The stone which the builders rejected Has become the chief cornerstone. This was the LORD's doing, And it is marvelous in our eyes'* ?

Mary's preparation for.

Mark 14:3–9 And being in Bethany at the house of Simon the leper, as He sat at the table, a woman came having an alabaster flask of very costly oil of spikenard. Then she broke the flask and poured *it* on His head. **4** But there were some who were indignant among themselves, and said, "Why was this fragrant oil wasted? **5** For it might have been sold for more than three hundred denarii and given to the poor." And they criticized her sharply. **6** But Jesus said, "Let her alone. Why do you trouble her? She has done a good work for Me. **7** For you have the poor with you always, and whenever you wish you may do them good; but Me you do not have always. **8** She has done what she could. She has come beforehand to anoint My body for burial. **9** Assuredly, I say to you, wherever this gospel is preached in the whole world,

what this woman has done will also be told as a memorial to her."

Led to, after being mocked.

Matt 27:31 And when they had mocked Him, they took the robe off Him, put His *own* clothes on Him, and led Him away to be crucified.

The place of.

Matt 27:33 And when they had come to a place called Golgotha, that is to say, Place of a Skull,

The time of.

Matt 27:45 Now from the sixth hour until the ninth hour there was darkness over all the land.

Given gall to drink during.

Matt 27:34 they gave Him sour wine mingled with gall to drink. But when He had tasted *it,* He would not drink.

Mark 15:23 Then they gave Him wine mingled with myrrh to drink, but He did not take *it.*

Soldiers dividing His garments during.

Mark 15:24 And when they crucified Him, they divided His garments, casting lots for them to determine what every man should take.

Cried out to God.

Matt 27:46 And about the ninth hour Jesus cried out with a loud voice, saying, "Eli, Eli, lama sabachthani?" that is, *My God, My God, why have You forsaken Me?"*

He endured it in spite of the disgrace attached to.

Gal 3:13 Christ has redeemed us from the curse of the law, having become a curse for us (for it is written, *"Cursed is everyone who hangs on a tree"*),

Gal 5:11 And I, brethren, if I still preach circumcision, why do I still suffer persecution? Then the offense of the cross has ceased.

Heb 12:2 looking unto Jesus, the author and finisher of *our* faith, who for the joy that was set before Him endured the cross, despising the shame, and has sat down at the right hand of the throne of God.

Proved His humility.

Phil 2:8 And being found in appearance as a man, He humbled Himself and became obedient to *the point of* death, even the death of the cross.

Paul proclaimed, as essential to the gospel message.

1 Cor 2:2 For I determined not to know anything among you except Jesus Christ and Him crucified.

Gal 3:1 O foolish Galatians! Who has bewitched you that you should not obey the truth, before whose eyes Jesus Christ was clearly portrayed among you as crucified?

JESUS CHRIST, THE DEATH OF
Foretold.

Is 53:8 He was taken from prison and from judgment, And who will declare His generation? For He was cut off from the land of the living; For the transgressions of My people He was stricken.

Dan 9:26 "And after the sixty-two weeks Messiah shall be cut off, but not for Himself; And the people of the prince who is to come Shall destroy the city and the sanctuary. The end of it *shall be* with a flood, And till the end of the war desolations are determined.

Zech 13:7 "Awake, O sword, against My Shepherd, Against the Man who is My Companion," Says the LORD of hosts. "Strike the Shepherd, And the sheep will be scattered; Then I will turn My hand against the little ones.

Appointed by God.

Is 53:6 All we like sheep have gone astray; We have turned, every one, to his own way; And the LORD has laid on Him the iniquity of us all.

Is 53:10 Yet it pleased the LORD to bruise Him; He has put *Him* to grief. When You make His soul an offering for sin, He shall see *His* seed, He shall prolong *His* days, And the pleasure of the LORD shall prosper in His hand.

Acts 2:23 Him, being delivered by the determined purpose and foreknowledge of God, you have taken by lawless hands, have crucified, and put to death;

Necessary for the redemption of man.

Luke 24:46 Then He said to them, "Thus it is written, and thus it was necessary for the Christ to suffer and to rise from the dead the third day,

Acts 17:3 explaining and demonstrating that the Christ had to suffer and rise again from the dead, and *saying*, "This Jesus whom I preach to you is the Christ."

Acceptable, as a sacrifice to God.

Matt 20:28 just as the Son of Man did not come to be served, but to serve, and to give His life a ransom for many."

Eph 5:2 And walk in love, as Christ also has loved us and given Himself for us, an offering and a sacrifice to God for a sweet-smelling aroma.

1 Thess 5:10 who died for us, that whether we wake or sleep, we should live together with Him.

Was voluntary.

Is 53:12 Therefore I will divide Him a portion with the great, And He shall divide the spoil with the strong, Because He poured out His soul unto death, And He was numbered with the transgressors, And He bore the sin of many, And made intercession for the transgressors.

Matt 26:53 Or do you think that I cannot now pray to My Father, and He will provide Me with more than twelve legions of angels?

John 10:17–18 "Therefore My Father loves Me, because I lay down My life that I may take it again. 18 No one takes it from Me, but I lay it down of Myself. I have power to lay it down, and I have power to take it again. This command I have received from My Father."

Was undeserved.

Is 53:9 And they made His grave with the wicked— But with the rich at His death, Because He had done no violence, Nor *was any* deceit in His mouth.

Mode of,

Foretold by Himself.

Matt 20:18–19 "Behold, we are going up to Jerusalem, and the Son of Man will be betrayed to the chief priests and to the scribes; and they will condemn

Him to death, 19 and deliver Him to the Gentiles to mock and to scourge and to crucify. And the third day He will rise again."

John 12:32–33 And I, if I am lifted up from the earth, will draw all *peoples* to Myself." 33 This He said, signifying by what death He would die.

Prefigured.

Num 21:8 Then the LORD said to Moses, "Make a fiery *serpent*, and set it on a pole; and it shall be that everyone who is bitten, when he looks at it, shall live."

John 3:14 And as Moses lifted up the serpent in the wilderness, even so must the Son of Man be lifted up,

Ignominious.

Heb 12:2 looking unto Jesus, the author and finisher of *our* faith, who for the joy that was set before Him endured the cross, despising the shame, and has sat down at the right hand of the throne of God.

Accursed.

Gal 3:13 Christ has redeemed us from the curse of the law, having become a curse for us (for it is written, "*Cursed is everyone who hangs on a tree*"),

Exhibited His humility.

Phil 2:8 And being found in appearance as a man, He humbled Himself and became obedient to *the point of* death, even the death of the cross.

A stumbling block to Jews.

1 Cor 1:23 but we preach Christ crucified, to the Jews a stumbling block and to the Greeks foolishness,

Foolishness to Gentiles.

1 Cor 1:18 For the message of the cross is foolishness to those who are perishing, but to us who are being saved it is the power of God.

1 Cor 1:23 but we preach Christ crucified, to the Jews a stumbling block and to the Greeks foolishness,

Demanded by the Jews.

Matt 27:22–23 Pilate said to them, "What then shall I do with Jesus who is called Christ?" *They* all said to him, "Let Him be crucified!" 23 Then the governor said, "Why, what evil has He done?" But they cried out all the more, saying, "Let Him be crucified!"

Inflicted by the Gentiles.

Matt 27:26–35 Then he released Barabbas to them; and when he had scourged Jesus, he delivered *Him* to be crucified. 27 Then the soldiers of the governor took Jesus into the Praetorium and gathered the whole garrison around Him. 28 And they stripped Him and put a scarlet robe on Him. 29 When they had twisted a crown of thorns, they put *it* on His head, and a reed in His right hand. And they bowed the knee before Him and mocked Him, saying, "Hail, King of the Jews!" 30 Then they spat on Him, and took the reed and struck Him on the head. 31 And when they had mocked Him, they took the robe off Him, put His *own* clothes on Him, and led Him away to be crucified. 32 Now as they came out, they found a man of Cyrene, Simon by name. Him they compelled to bear His cross. 33 And when they had come to a place called Golgotha, that is to say, Place of a Skull, 34 they gave Him sour wine mingled with gall to drink. But when He had tasted *it*, He would not drink. 35 Then they crucified Him, and divided His garments, casting lots, that it might be fulfilled which was spoken by the prophet: *"They divided My garments among them, And for My clothing they cast lots."*

In the company of transgressors.

Is 53:12 Therefore I will divide Him a portion with the great, And He shall divide the spoil with the strong, Because He poured out His soul unto death, And He was numbered with the transgressors, And He bore the sin of many, And made intercession for the transgressors.

Matt 27:38 Then two robbers were crucified with Him, one on the right and another on the left.

Accompanied by supernatural signs.

Matt 27:45 Now from the sixth hour until the ninth hour there was darkness over all the land.

Matt 27:51–53 Then, behold, the veil of the temple was torn in two from top to bottom; and the earth quaked, and the rocks were split, **52** and the graves were opened; and many bodies of the saints who had fallen asleep were raised; **53** and coming out of the graves after His resurrection, they went into the holy city and appeared to many.

Signified death to sin.

Rom 6:3–8 Or do you not know that as many of us as were baptized into Christ Jesus were baptized into His death? **4** Therefore we were buried with Him through baptism into death, that just as Christ was raised from the dead by the glory of the Father, even so we also should walk in newness of life. **5** For if we have been united together in the likeness of His death, certainly we also shall be *in the likeness of His* resurrection, **6** knowing this, that our old man was crucified with *Him,* that the body of sin might be done away with, that we should no longer be slaves of sin. **7** For he who has died has been freed from sin. **8** Now if we died with Christ, we believe that we shall also live with Him,

Gal 2:20 I have been crucified with Christ; it is no longer I who live, but Christ lives in me; and the *life* which I now live in the flesh I live by faith in the Son of God, who loved me and gave Himself for me.

Commemorated in the Lord's Supper.

Luke 22:19–20 And He took bread, gave thanks and broke *it,* and gave *it* to them, saying, "This is My body which is given for you; do this in remembrance of Me." **20** Likewise He also *took* the cup after supper, saying, "This cup *is* the new covenant in My blood, which is shed for you.

1 Cor 11:26–29 For as often as you eat this bread and drink this cup, you proclaim the Lord's death till He comes. **27** Therefore whoever eats this bread or drinks *this* cup of the Lord in an unworthy manner will be guilty of the body and blood of the Lord. **28** But let a man examine himself, and so let him eat of the bread and drink of the cup. **29** For he who eats and drinks in an unworthy manner eats and drinks judgment to himself, not discerning the Lord's body.

JESUS CHRIST, THE DEITY OF

As Messiah.

Ps 24:7 Lift up your heads, O you gates! And be lifted up, you everlasting doors! And the King of glory shall come in.

Ps 24:10 Who is this King of glory? The LORD of hosts, He *is* the King of glory. Selah

Ps 45:6–7 Your throne, O God, *is* forever and ever; A scepter of righteousness *is* the scepter of Your kingdom. **7** You love righteousness and hate wickedness; Therefore God, Your God, has anointed You With the oil of gladness more than Your companions.

Is 8:13–14 The LORD of hosts, Him you shall hallow; *Let* Him *be* your fear, And *let* Him *be* your dread. **14** He will be as a sanctuary, But a stone of stumbling and a rock of offense To both the houses of Israel, As a trap and a snare to the inhabitants of Jerusalem.

Is 40:3 The voice of one crying in the wilderness: "Prepare the way of the LORD; Make straight in the desert A highway for our God.

Is 40:11 He will feed His flock like a shepherd; He will gather the lambs with His arm, And carry *them* in His bosom, *And* gently lead those who are with young.

Jer 23:5–6 "Behold, *the* days are coming," says the LORD, "That I will raise to David a Branch of righteousness; A King shall reign and prosper, And execute judgment and righteousness in the earth. **6** In His days Judah will be saved, And Israel will dwell safely; Now this *is* His name by which He will be called: THE LORD OUR RIGHTEOUSNESS.

Zech 13:7 "Awake, O sword, against My Shepherd, Against the Man who is My Companion," Says the LORD of hosts. "Strike the Shepherd, And the sheep will be scattered; Then I will turn My hand against the little ones.

Matt 3:3 For this is he who was spoken of by the prophet Isaiah, saying: *"The voice of one crying in the wilderness: 'Prepare the way of the LORD; Make His paths straight.' "*

Mark 2:7 "Why does this *Man* speak blasphemies like this? Who can forgive sins but God alone?"

Mark 2:10 But that you may know that the Son of Man has power on earth to forgive sins"—He said to the paralytic,

Rom 9:5 of whom *are* the fathers and from whom, according to the flesh, Christ *came,* who is over all, *the* eternally blessed God. Amen.

Col 3:13 bearing with one another, and forgiving one another, if anyone has a complaint against another; even as Christ forgave you, so you also *must do.*

Titus 2:13 looking for the blessed hope and glorious appearing of our great God and Savior Jesus Christ,

Heb 13:20 Now may the God of peace who brought up our Lord Jesus from the dead, that great Shepherd of the sheep, through the blood of the everlasting covenant,

1 Pet 2:8 and *"A stone of stumbling And a rock of offense."* They stumble, being disobedient to the word, to which they also were appointed.

As God.

Gen 2:3 Then God blessed the seventh day and sanctified it, because in it He rested from all His work which God had created and made.

Is 7:14 Therefore the Lord Himself will give you a sign: Behold, the virgin shall conceive and bear a Son, and shall call His name Immanuel.

Is 9:6 For unto us a Child is born, Unto us a Son is given;

And the government will be upon His shoulder. And His name will be called Wonderful, Counselor, Mighty God, Everlasting Father, Prince of Peace.

Is 44:6 "Thus says the LORD, the King of Israel, And his Redeemer, the LORD of hosts: 'I *am* the First and I *am* the Last; Besides Me *there is* no God.

Is 48:12–16 "Listen to Me, O Jacob, And Israel, My called: I *am* He, I *am* the First, I *am* also the Last. **13** Indeed My hand has laid the foundation of the earth, And My right hand has stretched out the heavens; *When* I call to them, They stand up together. **14** "All of you, assemble yourselves, and hear! Who among them has declared these *things?* The LORD loves him; He shall do His pleasure on Babylon, And His arm *shall be against* the Chaldeans. **15** I, *even* I, have spoken; Yes, I have called him, I have brought him, and his way will prosper. **16** "Come near to Me, hear this: I have not spoken in secret from the beginning; From the time that it was, I *was* there. And now the Lord GOD and His Spirit Have sent Me."

Matt 1:23 *"Behold, the virgin shall be with child, and bear a Son, and they shall call His name Immanuel,"* which is translated, "God with us."

Matt 12:8 For the Son of Man is Lord even of the Sabbath."

Matt 26:63–67 But Jesus kept silent. And the high priest answered and said to Him, "I put You under oath by the living God: Tell us if You are the Christ, the Son of God!" **64** Jesus said to him, *"It is as* you said. Nevertheless, I say to you, hereafter you will see the Son of Man sitting at the right hand of the Power, and coming on the clouds of heaven." **65** Then the high priest tore his clothes, saying, "He has spoken blasphemy! What further need do we have of witnesses? Look, now you have heard His blasphemy! **66** What do you think?" They answered and said, "He is deserving of death." **67** Then they spat in His face and beat Him; and others struck *Him* with the palms of their hands,

John 1:1 In the beginning was the Word, and the Word was with God, and the Word was God.

John 1:14 And the Word became flesh and dwelt among us, and we beheld His glory, the glory as of the only begotten of the Father, full of grace and truth.

John 1:18 No one has seen God at any time. The only begotten Son, who is in the bosom of the Father, He has declared *Him.*

John 3:16 For God so loved the world that He gave His only begotten Son, that whoever believes in Him should not perish but have everlasting life.

John 3:18 "He who believes in Him is not condemned; but he who does not believe is condemned already, because he has not believed in the name of the only begotten Son of God.

John 3:31 He who comes from above is above all; he who is of the earth is earthly and speaks of the earth. He who comes from heaven is above all.

Acts 10:36 The word which *God* sent to the children of Israel, preaching peace through Jesus Christ—He is Lord of all—

Rom 10:11–13 For the Scripture says, *"Whoever believes on Him will not be put to shame."* **12** For there is no distinction between Jew and Greek, for the same Lord over all is rich to all who call upon Him. **13** For *"whoever calls on the name of the LORD shall be saved."*

1 Cor 1:30 But of Him you are in Christ Jesus, who became for us wisdom from God—and righteousness and sanctification and redemption—

1 Cor 2:8 which none of the rulers of this age knew; for had they known, they would not have crucified the Lord of glory.

1 Cor 4:5 Therefore judge nothing before the time, until the Lord comes, who will both bring to light the hidden things of darkness and reveal the counsels of the hearts. Then each one's praise will come from God.

1 Cor 15:47 The first man *was* of the earth, *made* of dust; the second Man *is* the Lord from heaven.

2 Cor 5:10 For we must all appear before the judgment seat of Christ, that each one may receive the things *done* in the body, according to what he has done, whether good or bad.

Phil 2:6 who, being in the form of God, did not consider it robbery to be equal with God,

Col 1:16 For by Him all things were created that are in heaven and that are on earth, visible and invisible, whether thrones or dominions or principalities or powers. All things were created through Him and for Him.

Col 2:9 For in Him dwells all the fullness of the Godhead bodily;

2 Tim 4:1 I charge *you* therefore before God and the Lord Jesus Christ, who will judge the living and the dead at His appearing and His kingdom:

Heb 1:3 who being the brightness of *His* glory and the express image of His person, and upholding all things by the word of His power, when He had by Himself purged our sins, sat down at the right hand of the Majesty on high,

Heb 1:8 But to the Son *He says:* *"Your throne, O God, is forever and ever; A scepter of righteousness is the scepter of Your kingdom.*

Heb 1:10–12 And: *"You, LORD, in the beginning laid the foundation of the earth, And the heavens are the work of Your hands.* **11** *They will perish, but You remain; And they will all grow old like a garment;* **12** *Like a cloak You will fold them up, And they will be changed. But You are the same, And Your years will not fail."*

James 2:1 My brethren, do not hold the faith of our Lord Jesus Christ, *the Lord* of glory, with partiality.

1 John 4:9 In this the love of God was manifested toward us, that God has sent His only begotten Son into the world, that we might live through Him.

1 John 5:20 And we know that the Son of God has come and has given us an understanding, that we may know Him who is true; and we are in Him who is true, in His Son Jesus Christ. This is the true God and eternal life.

Rev 1:5 and from Jesus Christ, the faithful witness, the firstborn from the dead, and the ruler over the kings of the earth. To Him who loved us and washed us from our sins in His own blood,

Rev 1:17 And when I saw Him, I fell at His feet as dead.

But He laid His right hand on me, saying to me, "Do not be afraid; I am the First and the Last.

Rev 17:14 These will make war with the Lamb, and the Lamb will overcome them, for He is Lord of lords and King of kings; and those *who are* with Him *are* called, chosen, and faithful."

Rev 22:13 I am the Alpha and the Omega, *the* Beginning and *the* End, the First and the Last."

As one with the Father.

Prov 30:4 Who has ascended into heaven, or descended? Who has gathered the wind in His fists? Who has bound the waters in a garment? Who has established all the ends of the earth? What *is* His name, and what *is* His Son's name, If you know?

Matt 11:27 All things have been delivered to Me by My Father, and no one knows the Son except the Father. Nor does anyone know the Father except the Son, and *the one* to whom the Son wills to reveal *Him.*

John 5:17 But Jesus answered them, "My Father has been working until now, and I have been working."

John 5:23 that all should honor the Son just as they honor the Father. He who does not honor the Son does not honor the Father who sent Him.

John 10:30 I and *My* Father are one."

John 10:38 but if I do, though you do not believe Me, believe the works, that you may know and believe that the Father *is* in Me, and I in Him."

John 12:45 And he who sees Me sees Him who sent Me.

John 14:7–10 "If you had known Me, you would have known My Father also; and from now on you know Him and have seen Him." **8** Philip said to Him, "Lord, show us the Father, and it is sufficient for us." **9** Jesus said to him, "Have I been with you so long, and yet you have not known Me, Philip? He who has seen Me has seen the Father; so how can you say, 'Show us the Father'? **10** Do you not believe that I am in the Father, and the Father in Me? The words that I speak to you I do not speak on My own *authority;* but the Father who dwells in Me does the works.

John 16:15 All things that the Father has are Mine. Therefore I said that He will take of Mine and declare *it* to you.

John 17:10 And all Mine are Yours, and Yours are Mine, and I am glorified in them.

1 Thess 3:11 Now may our God and Father Himself, and our Lord Jesus Christ, direct our way to you.

2 Thess 2:16–17 Now may our Lord Jesus Christ Himself, and our God and Father, who has loved us and given *us* everlasting consolation and good hope by grace, **17** comfort your hearts and establish you in every good word and work.

As sending the Spirit.

John 14:16 And I will pray the Father, and He will give you another Helper, that He may abide with you forever—

John 15:26 "But when the Helper comes, whom I shall send to you from the Father, the Spirit of truth who proceeds from the Father, He will testify of Me.

As Creator of all things.

Neh 9:6 You alone *are* the Lord; You have made heaven, The heaven of heavens, with all their host, The earth and everything on it, The seas and all that is in them, And You preserve them all. The host of heaven worships You.

John 1:3 All things were made through Him, and without Him nothing was made that was made.

Col 1:16–17 For by Him all things were created that are in heaven and that are on earth, visible and invisible, whether thrones or dominions or principalities or powers. All things were created through Him and for Him. **17** And He is before all things, and in Him all things consist.

Heb 1:2–3 has in these last days spoken to us by *His* Son, whom He has appointed heir of all things, through whom also He made the worlds; **3** who being the brightness of *His* glory and the express image of His person, and upholding all things by the word of His power, when He had by Himself purged our sins, sat down at the right hand of the Majesty on high,

Raises the dead.

John 5:21 For as the Father raises the dead and gives life to *them,* even so the Son gives life to whom He will.

John 6:40 And this is the will of Him who sent Me, that everyone who sees the Son and believes in Him may have everlasting life; and I will raise him up at the last day."

John 6:54 Whoever eats My flesh and drinks My blood has eternal life, and I will raise him up at the last day.

Raises Himself from the dead.

John 2:19 Jesus answered and said to them, "Destroy this temple, and in three days I will raise it up."

John 2:21 But He was speaking of the temple of His body.

John 10:18 No one takes it from Me, but I lay it down of Myself. I have power to lay it down, and I have power to take it again. This command I have received from My Father."

Acknowledged by the Old Testament saints.

Job 19:25–27 For I know *that* my Redeemer lives, And He shall stand at last on the earth; **26** And after my skin is destroyed, this *I know,* That in my flesh I shall see God, **27** Whom I shall see for myself, And my eyes shall behold, and not another. *How* my heart yearns within me!

JESUS CHRIST, THE EXALTATION OF

To right hand of God.

Mark 14:62 Jesus said, "I am. And you will see the Son of Man sitting at the right hand of the Power, and coming with the clouds of heaven."

Acts 5:31 Him God has exalted to His right hand *to be* Prince and Savior, to give repentance to Israel and forgiveness of sins.

Heb 1:3 who being the brightness of *His* glory and the express image of His person, and upholding all things by the word of His power, when He had by Himself purged our sins, sat down at the right hand of the Majesty on high,

He was received up in glory.

1 Tim 3:16 And without controversy great is the mystery of godliness: God was manifested in the flesh,

Justified in the Spirit, Seen by angels, Preached among the Gentiles, Believed on in the world, Received up in glory.

Purpose of.

Acts 5:31 Him God has exalted to His right hand *to be* Prince and Savior, to give repentance to Israel and forgiveness of sins.

A result of

His humble obedience.

Phil 2:5–9 Let this mind be in you which was also in Christ Jesus, **6** who, being in the form of God, did not consider it robbery to be equal with God, **7** but made Himself of no reputation, taking the form of a bondservant, *and* coming in the likeness of men. **8** And being found in appearance as a man, He humbled Himself and became obedient to *the point of* death, even the death of the cross. **9** Therefore God also has highly exalted Him and given Him the name which is above every name,

Enduring the shame of the cross.

Heb 12:2 looking unto Jesus, the author and finisher of *our* faith, who for the joy that was set before Him endured the cross, despising the shame, and has sat down at the right hand of the throne of God.

Purging sins.

Heb 1:3 who being the brightness of *His* glory and the express image of His person, and upholding all things by the word of His power, when He had by Himself purged our sins, sat down at the right hand of the Majesty on high,

Proper response to.

Phil 2:9–11 Therefore God also has highly exalted Him and given Him the name which is above every name, **10** that at the name of Jesus every knee should bow, of those in heaven, and of those on earth, and of those under the earth, **11** and *that* every tongue should confess that Jesus Christ *is* Lord, to the glory of God the Father.

JESUS CHRIST, THE EXAMPLE OF

Is perfect.

Heb 7:26 For such a High Priest was fitting for us, *who is* holy, harmless, undefiled, separate from sinners, and has become higher than the heavens;

Conformity to, required in

Holiness.

Rom 1:6 among whom you also are the called of Jesus Christ;

1 Pet 1:15–16 but as He who called you *is* holy, you also be holy in all *your* conduct, **16** because it is written, "Be holy, for I am holy."

Righteousness.

1 John 2:6 He who says he abides in Him ought himself also to walk just as He walked.

Purity.

1 John 3:3 And everyone who has this hope in Him purifies himself, just as He is pure.

Love.

John 13:34 A new commandment I give to you, that you love one another; as I have loved you, that you also love one another.

Eph 5:2 And walk in love, as Christ also has loved us and given Himself for us, an offering and a sacrifice to God for a sweet-smelling aroma.

1 John 3:16 By this we know love, because He laid down His life for us. And we also ought to lay down *our* lives for the brethren.

Humility.

Luke 22:27 For who *is* greater, he who sits at the table, or he who serves? *Is* it not he who sits at the table? Yet I am among you as the One who serves.

Phil 2:5 Let this mind be in you which was also in Christ Jesus,

Phil 2:7 but made Himself of no reputation, taking the form of a bondservant, *and* coming in the likeness of men.

Meekness.

Matt 11:29 Take My yoke upon Me and learn from Me, for I am gentle and lowly in heart, and you will find rest for your souls.

Obedience.

John 15:10 If you keep My commandments, you will abide in My love, just as I have kept My Father's commandments and abide in His love.

Self-denial.

Matt 16:24 Then Jesus said to His disciples, "If anyone desires to come after Me, let him deny himself, and take up his cross, and follow Me.

Rom 15:3 For even Christ did not please Himself; but as it is written, *"The reproaches of those who reproached You fell on Me."*

Ministering to others.

Matt 20:28 just as the Son of Man did not come to be served, but to serve, and to give His life a ransom for many."

John 13:14–15 If I then, *your* Lord and Teacher, have washed your feet, you also ought to wash one another's feet. **15** For I have given you an example, that you should do as I have done to you.

Benevolence.

Acts 20:35 I have shown you in every way, by laboring like this, that you must support the weak. And remember the words of the Lord Jesus, that He said, 'It is more blessed to give than to receive.' "

2 Cor 8:7 But as you abound in everything—in faith, in speech, in knowledge, in all diligence, and in your love for us—*see* that you abound in this grace also.

2 Cor 8:9 For you know the grace of our Lord Jesus Christ, that though He was rich, yet for your sakes He became poor, that you through His poverty might become rich.

Forgiving complaints.

Col 3:13 bearing with one another, and forgiving one another, if anyone has a complaint against another; even as Christ forgave you, so you also *must do.*

Overcoming the world.

John 16:33 These things I have spoken to you, that in Me you may have peace. In the world you will have tribulation; but be of good cheer, I have overcome the world."

1 John 5:4 For whatever is born of God overcomes the

world. And this is the victory that has overcome the world—our faith.

Being not of the world.

John 17:16 They are not of the world, just as I am not of the world.

Being without deceit.

1 Pet 2:21–22 For to this you were called, because Christ also suffered for us, leaving us an example, that you should follow His steps: **22** *"Who committed no sin, Nor was deceit found in His mouth";*

Suffering wrongfully.

1 Pet 2:21–23 For to this you were called, because Christ also suffered for us, leaving us an example, that you should follow His steps: **22** *"Who committed no sin, Nor was deceit found in His mouth";* **23** who, when He was reviled, did not revile in return; when He suffered, He did not threaten, but committed *Himself* to Him who judges righteously;

Suffering for righteousness.

Heb 12:3–4 For consider Him who endured such hostility from sinners against Himself, lest you become weary and discouraged in your souls. **4** You have not yet resisted to bloodshed, striving against sin.

Believers predestined to follow.

Rom 8:29 For whom He foreknew, He also predestined *to be* conformed to the image of His Son, that He might be the firstborn among many brethren.

Conformity to, progressive.

2 Cor 3:18 But we all, with unveiled face, beholding as in a mirror the glory of the Lord, are being transformed into the same image from glory to glory, just as by the Spirit of the Lord.

JESUS CHRIST, THE EXCELLENCY AND GLORY OF

As God.

John 1:1–5 In the beginning was the Word, and the Word was with God, and the Word was God. **2** He was in the beginning with God. **3** All things were made through Him, and without Him nothing was made that was made. **4** In Him was life, and the life was the light of men. **5** And the light shines in the darkness, and the darkness did not comprehend it.

Phil 2:6 who, being in the form of God, did not consider it robbery to be equal with God,

Phil 2:9–10 Therefore God also has highly exalted Him and given Him the name which is above every name, **10** that at the name of Jesus every knee should bow, of those in heaven, and of those on earth, and of those under the earth,

As the Son of God.

Matt 3:17 And suddenly a voice *came* from heaven, saying, "This is My beloved Son, in whom I am well pleased."

Heb 1:6 But when He again brings the firstborn into the world, He says: *"Let all the angels of God worship Him."*

Heb 1:8 But to the Son *He says: "Your throne, O God, is forever and ever; A scepter of righteousness is the scepter of Your kingdom."*

As one with the Father.

John 10:30 I and *My* Father are one."

John 10:38 but if I do, though you do not believe Me, believe the works, that you may know and believe that the Father *is* in Me, and I in Him."

As the firstborn.

Col 1:15 He is the image of the invisible God, the firstborn over all creation.

Col 1:18 And He is the head of the body, the church, who is the beginning, the firstborn from the dead, that in all things He may have the preeminence.

Heb 1:6 But when He again brings the firstborn into the world, He says: *"Let all the angels of God worship Him."*

As Lord of lords, etc.

Rev 17:14 These will make war with the Lamb, and the Lamb will overcome them, for He is Lord of lords and King of kings; and those *who are* with Him *are* called, chosen, and faithful."

As the image of God.

Col 1:15 He is the image of the invisible God, the firstborn over all creation.

Heb 1:3 who being the brightness of *His* glory and the express image of His person, and upholding all things by the word of His power, when He had by Himself purged our sins, sat down at the right hand of the Majesty on high,

As Creator.

John 1:3 All things were made through Him, and without Him nothing was made that was made.

Col 1:16 For by Him all things were created that are in heaven and that are on earth, visible and invisible, whether thrones or dominions or principalities or powers. All things were created through Him and for Him.

Heb 1:2 has in these last days spoken to us by *His* Son, whom He has appointed heir of all things, through whom also He made the worlds;

As the Blessed of God.

Ps 45:2 You are fairer than the sons of men; Grace is poured upon Your lips; Therefore God has blessed You forever.

As Mediator.

1 Tim 2:5 For *there is* one God and one Mediator between God and men, *the* Man Christ Jesus,

Heb 8:6 But now He has obtained a more excellent ministry, inasmuch as He is also Mediator of a better covenant, which was established on better promises.

As Prophet.

Deut 18:15–16 "The LORD your God will raise up for you a Prophet like me from your midst, from your brethren. Him you shall hear, **16** according to all you desired of the LORD your God in Horeb in the day of the assembly, saying, 'Let me not hear again the voice of the LORD my God, nor let me see this great fire anymore, lest I die.'

Acts 3:22 For Moses truly said to the fathers, 'The LORD your God will raise up for you a Prophet like me from your brethren. Him you shall hear in all things, whatever He says to you.

As Priest.

Ps 110:4 The LORD has sworn And will not relent, "You *are* a priest forever According to the order of Melchizedek."

Heb 4:15 For we do not have a High Priest who cannot sympathize with our weaknesses, but was in all *points* tempted as *we are, yet* without sin.

As King.

Is 6:1–5 In the year that King Uzziah died, I saw the Lord sitting on a throne, high and lifted up, and the train of His *robe* filled the temple. **2** Above it stood seraphim; each one had six wings: with two he covered his face, with two he covered his feet, and with two he flew. **3** And one cried to another and said: "Holy, holy, holy *is* the LORD of hosts; The whole earth *is* full of His glory!" **4** And the posts of the door were shaken by the voice of him who cried out, and the house was filled with smoke. **5** So I said: "Woe *is* me, for I am undone! Because I *am* a man of unclean lips, And I dwell in the midst of a people of unclean lips; For my eyes have seen the King, The LORD of hosts."

John 12:41 These things Isaiah said when he saw His glory and spoke of Him.

As Judge.

Matt 16:27 For the Son of Man will come in the glory of His Father with His angels, and then He will reward each according to his works.

Matt 25:31 "When the Son of Man comes in His glory, and all the holy angels with Him, then He will sit on the throne of His glory.

Matt 25:33 And He will set the sheep on His right hand, but the goats on the left.

As Shepherd.

Is 40:10–11 Behold, the Lord GOD shall come with a strong *hand,* And His arm shall rule for Him; Behold, His reward *is* with Him, And His work before Him. **11** He will feed His flock like a shepherd; He will gather the lambs with His arm, And carry *them* in His bosom, *And* gently lead those who are with young.

John 10:11 "I am the good shepherd. The good shepherd gives His life for the sheep.

John 10:14 I am the good shepherd; and I know My *sheep,* and am known by My own.

As Head of the church.

Eph 1:22 And He put all *things* under His feet, and gave Him *to be* head over all *things* to the church,

As the true Light.

Luke 1:78–79 Through the tender mercy of our God, With which the Dayspring from on high has visited us; **79** To give light to those who sit in darkness and the shadow of death, To guide our feet into the way of peace."

John 1:4 In Him was life, and the life was the light of men.

John 1:9 That was the true Light which gives light to every man coming into the world.

As the Foundation of the church.

1 Pet 2:6 Therefore it is also contained in the Scripture, "Behold, I lay in Zion A chief cornerstone, elect, pre-

cious, And he who believes on Him will by no means be put to shame."

Cf. Is 28:16

As the way.

John 14:6 Jesus said to him, "I am the way, the truth, and the life. No one comes to the Father except through Me.

Heb 10:19–20 Therefore, brethren, having boldness to enter the Holiest by the blood of Jesus, **20** by a new and living way which He consecrated for us, through the veil, that is, His flesh,

As the truth.

1 John 5:20 And we know that the Son of God has come and has given us an understanding, that we may know Him who is true; and we are in Him who is true, in His Son Jesus Christ. This is the true God and eternal life.

Rev 3:7 "And to the angel of the church in Philadelphia write, 'These things says He who is holy, He who is true, *"He who has the key of David, He who opens and no one shuts, and shuts and no one opens"*:

As the life.

John 11:25 Jesus said to her, "I am the resurrection and the life. He who believes in Me, though he may die, he shall live.

Col 3:4 When Christ *who is* our life appears, then you also will appear with Him in glory.

1 John 5:11 And this is the testimony: that God has given us eternal life, and this life is in His Son.

As incarnate.

John 1:14 And the Word became flesh and dwelt among us, and we beheld His glory, the glory as of the only begotten of the Father, full of grace and truth.

In His words.

Luke 4:22 So all bore witness to Him, and marveled at the gracious words which proceeded out of His mouth. And they said, "Is this not Joseph's son?"

John 7:46 The officers answered, "No man ever spoke like this Man!"

In His works.

Matt 13:54 When He had come to His own country, He taught them in their synagogue, so that they were astonished and said, "Where did this *Man* get this wisdom and *these* mighty works?

John 2:11 This beginning of signs Jesus did in Cana of Galilee, and manifested His glory; and His disciples believed in Him.

In His sinless perfection.

Heb 7:26–28 For such a High Priest was fitting for us, *who is* holy, harmless, undefiled, separate from sinners, and has become higher than the heavens; **27** who does not need daily, as those high priests, to offer up sacrifices, first for His own sins and then for the people's, for this He did once for all when He offered up Himself. **28** For the law appoints as high priests men who have weakness, but the word of the oath, which came after the law, *appoints* the Son who has been perfected forever.

In the fullness of His grace and truth.

Ps 45:2 You are fairer than the sons of men; Grace is

poured upon Your lips; Therefore God has blessed You forever.

John 1:14 And the Word became flesh and dwelt among us, and we beheld His glory, the glory as of the only begotten of the Father, full of grace and truth.

In His transfiguration.

Matt 17:2 and He was transfigured before them. His face shone like the sun, and His clothes became as white as the light.

2 Pet 1:16–18 For we did not follow cunningly devised fables when we made known to you the power and coming of our Lord Jesus Christ, but were eyewitnesses of His majesty. **17** For He received from God the Father honor and glory when such a voice came to Him from the Excellent Glory: "This is My beloved Son, in whom I am well pleased." **18** And we heard this voice which came from heaven when we were with Him on the holy mountain.

In His exaltation.

Acts 7:55–56 But he, being full of the Holy Spirit, gazed into heaven and saw the glory of God, and Jesus standing at the right hand of God, **56** and said, "Look! I see the heavens opened and the Son of Man standing at the right hand of God!"

Eph 1:21 far above all principality and power and might and dominion, and every name that is named, not only in this age but also in that which is to come.

In the calling of the Gentiles.

Ps 72:17 His name shall endure forever; His name shall continue as long as the sun. And *men* shall be blessed in Him; All nations shall call Him blessed.

John 12:21 Then they came to Philip, who was from Bethsaida of Galilee, and asked him, saying, "Sir, we wish to see Jesus."

John 12:23 But Jesus answered them, saying, "The hour has come that the Son of Man should be glorified.

In the restoration of the Jews.

Ps 102:16 For the LORD shall build up Zion; He shall appear in His glory.

In His triumph.

Is 63:1–3 Who *is* this who comes from Edom, With dyed garments from Bozrah, This *One who is* glorious in His apparel, Traveling in the greatness of His strength?— "I who speak in righteousness, mighty to save." **2** Why *is* Your apparel red, And Your garments like one who treads in the winepress? **3** "I have trodden the winepress alone, And from the peoples no one *was* with Me. For I have trodden them in My anger, And trampled them in My fury; Their blood is sprinkled upon My garments, And I have stained all My robes.

Rev 19:11 Now I saw heaven opened, and behold, a white horse. And He who sat on him *was* called Faithful and True, and in righteousness He judges and makes war.

Rev 19:16 And He has on *His* robe and on His thigh a name written: KING OF KINGS AND LORD OF LORDS.

Followed His sufferings.

1 Pet 1:10–11 Of this salvation the prophets have inquired and searched carefully, who prophesied of the grace *that would come* to you, **11** searching what, or what manner of time, the Spirit of Christ who was in them was indicating when He testified beforehand the sufferings of Christ and the glories that would follow.

Followed His resurrection.

1 Pet 1:21 who through Him believe in God, who raised Him from the dead and gave Him glory, so that your faith and hope are in God.

Is unchangeable.

Heb 1:10–12 And: *"You,* LORD, *in the beginning laid the foundation of the earth, And the heavens are the work of Your hands.* **11** *They will perish, but You remain; And they will all grow old like a garment;* **12** *Like a cloak You will fold them up, And they will be changed. But You are the same, And Your years will not fail."*

Is incomparable.

Song 5:10 My beloved *is* white and ruddy, Chief among ten thousand.

Phil 2:9 Therefore God also has highly exalted Him and given Him the name which is above every name,

Imparted to believers.

John 17:22 And the glory which You gave Me I have given them, that they may be one just as We are one:

2 Cor 3:18 But we all, with unveiled face, beholding as in a mirror the glory of the Lord, are being transformed into the same image from glory to glory, just as by the Spirit of the Lord.

Celebrated by the redeemed.

Rev 5:8–14 Now when He had taken the scroll, the four living creatures and the twenty-four elders fell down before the Lamb, each having a harp, and golden bowls full of incense, which are the prayers of the saints. **9** And they sang a new song, saying: "You are worthy to take the scroll, And to open its seals; For You were slain, And have redeemed us to God by Your blood Out of every tribe and tongue and people and nation, **10** And have made us kings and priests to our God; And we shall reign on the earth." **11** Then I looked, and I heard the voice of many angels around the throne, the living creatures, and the elders; and the number of them was ten thousand times ten thousand, and thousands of thousands, **12** saying with a loud voice: "Worthy is the Lamb who was slain To receive power and riches and wisdom, And strength and honor and glory and blessing!" **13** And every creature which is in heaven and on the earth and under the earth and such as are in the sea, and all that are in them, I heard saying: "Blessing and honor and glory and power *Be* to Him who sits on the throne, And to the Lamb, forever and ever!" **14** Then the four living creatures said, "Amen!" And the twenty-four elders fell down and worshiped Him who lives forever and ever.

Rev 7:9–12 After these things I looked, and behold, a great multitude which no one could number, of all nations, tribes, peoples, and tongues, standing before the throne and before the Lamb, clothed with white robes, with palm branches in their hands, **10** and crying out with a loud voice, saying, "Salvation *belongs* to our God who sits on the throne, and to the Lamb!" **11** All the angels stood around the throne and the elders and the four living creatures, and fell on their faces before the throne and worshiped God, **12** saying: "Amen! Blessing and glory and wisdom, Thanksgiving and honor and power and might, *Be* to our God forever and ever. Amen."

Revealed in the gospel.

Is 40:5 The glory of the LORD shall be revealed, And all flesh shall see *it* together; For the mouth of the LORD has spoken."

Believers will see and rejoice.

John 17:24 "Father, I desire that they also whom You gave Me may be with Me where I am, that they may behold My glory which You have given Me; for You loved Me before the foundation of the world.

1 Pet 4:13 but rejoice to the extent that you partake of Christ's sufferings, that when His glory is revealed, you may also be glad with exceeding joy.

JESUS CHRIST, HATRED OF

Is without cause.

Ps 69:4 Those who hate me without a cause Are more than the hairs of my head; They are mighty who would destroy me, *Being* my enemies wrongfully; Though I have stolen nothing, I *still* must restore *it*.

John 15:25 But *this happened* that the word might be fulfilled which is written in their law, 'They hated Me without a cause.'

Is because of His testimony against the world.

John 7:7 The world cannot hate you, but it hates Me because I testify of it that its works are evil.

Involves

Hatred of His Father.

John 15:23–24 He who hates Me hates My Father also. **24** If I had not done among them the works which no one else did, they would have no sin; but now they have seen and also hated both Me and My Father.

Hatred of His people.

John 15:18 "If the world hates you, you know that it hated Me before *it hated* you.

Punishment for.

Ps 2:2 The kings of the earth set themselves, And the rulers take counsel together, Against the LORD and against His Anointed, *saying,*

Ps 2:9 You shall break them with a rod of iron; You shall dash them to pieces like a potter's vessel.' "

Ps 21:8 Your hand will find all Your enemies; Your right hand will find those who hate You.

1 Cor 15:25 For He must reign till He has put all enemies under His feet.

Heb 10:29–31 Of how much worse punishment, do you suppose, will he be thought worthy who has trampled the Son of God underfoot, counted the blood of the covenant by which he was sanctified a common thing, and insulted the Spirit of grace? **30** For we know Him who said, *"Vengeance is Mine, I will repay,"* says the Lord. And again, *"The LORD will judge His people."* **31** It is a fearful thing to fall into the hands of the living God.

Illustrated.

Luke 19:12–14 Therefore He said: "A certain nobleman went into a far country to receive for himself a kingdom and to return. **13** So he called ten of his servants,

delivered to them ten minas, and said to them, 'Do business till I come.' **14** But his citizens hated him, and sent a delegation after him, saying, 'We will not have this *man* to reign over us.'

Luke 19:17 And he said to him, 'Well *done,* good servant; because you were faithful in a very little, have authority over ten cities.'

Those who practiced,

Chief priests, etc.

Matt 27:1–2 When morning came, all the chief priests and elders of the people plotted against Jesus to put Him to death. **2** And when they had bound Him, they led Him away and delivered Him to Pontius Pilate the governor.

Luke 22:5 And they were glad, and agreed to give him money.

The Jews.

Matt 27:22–23 Pilate said to them, "What then shall I do with Jesus who is called Christ?" *They* all said to him, "Let Him be crucified!" **23** Then the governor said, "Why, what evil has He done?" But they cried out all the more, saying, "Let Him be crucified!"

The scribes, etc.

Mark 11:18 And the scribes and chief priests heard it and sought how they might destroy Him; for they feared Him, because all the people were astonished at His teaching.

Luke 11:53–54 And as He said these things to them, the scribes and the Pharisees began to assail *Him* vehemently, and to cross-examine Him about many things, **54** lying in wait for Him, and seeking to catch Him in something He might say, that they might accuse Him.

JESUS CHRIST, THE HEAD OF THE CHURCH

Predicted.

Ps 118:22 The stone *which* the builders rejected Has become the chief cornerstone.

Matt 21:42 Jesus said to them, "Have you never read in the Scriptures: *'The stone which the builders rejected Has become the chief cornerstone. This was the LORD's doing, And it is marvelous in our eyes'*?

Appointed by God.

Eph 1:22 And He put all *things* under His feet, and gave Him *to be* head over all *things* to the church,

Over the body of believers.

Eph 4:12 for the equipping of the saints for the work of ministry, for the edifying of the body of Christ,

Eph 4:15 but, speaking the truth in love, may grow up in all things into Him who is the head—Christ—

Eph 5:23 For the husband is head of the wife, as also Christ is head of the church; and He is the Savior of the body.

Col 2:10 and you are complete in Him, who is the head of all principality and power.

The church is His body.

Eph 1:23 which is His body, the fullness of Him who fills all in all.

Col 1:24 I now rejoice in my sufferings for you, and fill up in my flesh what is lacking in the afflictions of Christ, for the sake of His body, which is the church,

The foundation of.

1 Cor 3:11 For no other foundation can anyone lay than that which is laid, which is Jesus Christ.

Eph 2:20 having been built on the foundation of the apostles and prophets, Jesus Christ Himself being the chief corner*stone*,

1 Pet 2:4–5 Coming to Him *as to* a living stone, rejected indeed by men, but chosen by God *and* precious, **5** you also, as living stones, are being built up a spiritual house, a holy priesthood, to offer up spiritual sacrifices acceptable to God through Jesus Christ.

Purchases the church by His death.

Acts 20:28 Therefore take heed to yourselves and to all the flock, among which the Holy Spirit has made you overseers, to shepherd the church of God which He purchased with His own blood.

Eph 5:25 Husbands, love your wives, just as Christ also loved the church and gave Himself for her,

Heb 9:12 Not with the blood of goats and calves, but with His own blood He entered the Most Holy Place once for all, having obtained eternal redemption.

Sanctifies and cleanses the church.

1 Cor 6:11 And such were some of you. But you were washed, but you were sanctified, but you were justified in the name of the Lord Jesus and by the Spirit of our God.

Eph 5:26–27 that He might sanctify and cleanse her with the washing of water by the word, **27** that He might present her to Himself a glorious church, not having spot or wrinkle or any such thing, but that she should be holy and without blemish.

Subjects the church to Himself.

Rom 7:4 Therefore, my brethren, you also have become dead to the law through the body of Christ, that you may be married to another—to Him who was raised from the dead, that we should bear fruit to God.

Eph 5:24 Therefore, just as the church is subject to Christ, so *let* the wives *be* to their own husbands in everything.

Has the preeminence in all things.

1 Cor 11:3 But I want you to know that the head of every man is Christ, the head of woman *is* man, and the head of Christ *is* God.

Eph 1:22 And He put all *things* under His feet, and gave Him *to be* head over all *things* to the church,

Col 1:18 And He is the head of the body, the church, who is the beginning, the firstborn from the dead, that in all things He may have the preeminence.

Called His apostles.

Matt 10:1 And when He had called His twelve disciples to *Him*, He gave them power *over* unclean spirits, to cast them out, and to heal all kinds of sickness and all kinds of disease.

Matt 10:7 And as you go, preach, saying, 'The kingdom of heaven is at hand.'

Matt 28:19 Go therefore and make disciples of all the nations, baptizing them in the name of the Father and of the Son and of the Holy Spirit,

John 20:21 So Jesus said to them again, "Peace to you! As the Father has sent Me, I also send you."

Giver of pastors to the church.

Jer 3:15 And I will give you shepherds according to My heart, who will feed you with knowledge and understanding.

Eph 4:11–13 And He Himself gave some *to be* apostles, some prophets, some evangelists, and some pastors and teachers, **12** for the equipping of the saints for the work of ministry, for the edifying of the body of Christ, **13** till we all come to the unity of the faith and of the knowledge of the Son of God, to a perfect man, to the measure of the stature of the fullness of Christ;

As Husband of the church.

Is 54:5 For your Maker *is* your husband, The LORD of hosts *is* His name; And your Redeemer *is* the Holy One of Israel; He is called the God of the whole earth.

Is 62:5 For *as* a young man marries a virgin, So shall your sons marry you; And *as* the bridegroom rejoices over the bride, So shall your God rejoice over you.

Eph 5:25–32 Husbands, love your wives, just as Christ also loved the church and gave Himself for her, **26** that He might sanctify and cleanse her with the washing of water by the word, **27** that He might present her to Himself a glorious church, not having spot or wrinkle or any such thing, but that she should be holy and without blemish. **28** So husbands ought to love their own wives as their own bodies; he who loves his wife loves himself. **29** For no one ever hated his own flesh, but nourishes and cherishes it, just as the Lord *does* the church. **30** For we are members of His body, of His flesh and of His bones. **31** *"For this reason a man shall leave his father and mother and be joined to his wife, and the two shall become one flesh."* **32** This is a great mystery, but I speak concerning Christ and the church.

Rev 21:2 Then I, John, saw the holy city, New Jerusalem, coming down out of heaven from God, prepared as a bride adorned for her husband.

Rev 21:9 Then one of the seven angels who had the seven bowls filled with the seven last plagues came to me and talked with me, saying, "Come, I will show you the bride, the Lamb's wife."

As God, He redeems and purifies the church to Himself.

Titus 2:14 who gave Himself for us, that He might redeem us from every lawless deed and purify for Himself His own special people, zealous for good works.

Rev 5:9 And they sang a new song, saying: "You are worthy to take the scroll, And to open its seals; For You were slain, And have redeemed us to God by Your blood Out of every tribe and tongue and people and nation,

As God, He presents the church to Himself.

Eph 5:27 that He might present her to Himself a glorious church, not having spot or wrinkle or any such thing, but that she should be holy and without blemish.

Jude 1:24–25 Now to Him who is able to keep you from stumbling, And to present *you* faultless Before the presence of His glory with exceeding joy, **25** To God our Savior, Who alone is wise, *Be* glory and majesty, Dominion and power, Both now and forever. Amen.

Instituted the ordinances.

Matt 28:19 Go therefore and make disciples of all the nations, baptizing them in the name of the Father and of the Son and of the Holy Spirit,

Luke 22:19–20 And He took bread, gave thanks and broke *it*, and gave *it* to them, saying, "This is My body which is given for you; do this in remembrance of Me." 20 Likewise He also *took* the cup after supper, saying, "This cup *is* the new covenant in My blood, which is shed for you.

Imparts gifts.

Ps 68:18 You have ascended on high, You have led captivity captive; You have received gifts among men, Even *from* the rebellious, That the LORD God might dwell *there*.

Eph 4:8 Therefore He says: *"When He ascended on high, He led captivity captive, And gave gifts to men."*

JESUS CHRIST, THE HIGH PRIEST

Appointed and called by God.

Heb 3:1–2 Therefore, holy brethren, partakers of the heavenly calling, consider the Apostle and High Priest of our confession, Christ Jesus, 2 who was faithful to Him who appointed Him, as Moses also *was faithful* in all His house.

Heb 5:4–5 And no man takes this honor to himself, but he who is called by God, just as Aaron *was*. 5 So also Christ did not glorify Himself to become High Priest, *but it* was He who said to Him: *"You are My Son, Today I have begotten You."*

After the order of Melchizedek.

Ps 110:4 The LORD has sworn And will not relent, "You *are* a priest forever According to the order of Melchizedek."

Heb 5:6 As He also *says* in another *place:* *"You are a priest forever According to the order of Melchizedek";*

Heb 6:20 where the forerunner has entered for us, *even* Jesus, having become High Priest forever according to the order of Melchizedek.

Heb 7:15 And it is yet far more evident if, in the likeness of Melchizedek, there arises another priest

Heb 7:17 For He testifies: *"You are a priest forever According to the order of Melchizedek."*

Superior to Aaron and the Levitical priests.

Heb 7:11 Therefore, if perfection were through the Levitical priesthood (for under it the people received the law), what further need *was there* that another priest should rise according to the order of Melchizedek, and not be called according to the order of Aaron?

Heb 7:16 who has come, not according to the law of a fleshly commandment, but according to the power of an endless life.

Heb 7:22 by so much more Jesus has become a surety of a better covenant.

Heb 8:1–2 Now *this is* the main point of the things we are saying: We have such a High Priest, who is seated at the right hand of the throne of the Majesty in the heavens, 2 a Minister of the sanctuary and of the true tabernacle which the Lord erected, and not man.

Heb 8:6 But now He has obtained a more excellent ministry, inasmuch as He is also Mediator of a better covenant, which was established on better promises.

Consecrated with an oath.

Heb 7:20–21 And inasmuch as *He was* not *made priest* without an oath 21 (for they have become priests without an oath, but He with an oath by Him who said to Him: *"The LORD has sworn And will not relent, 'You are a priest forever According to the order of Melchizedek' "),*

Unchangeable.

Heb 7:23 Also there were many priests, because they were prevented by death from continuing.

Heb 7:28 For the law appoints as high priests men who have weakness, but the word of the oath, which came after the law, *appoints* the Son who has been perfected forever.

Is of unblemished purity.

Heb 7:26 For such a High Priest was fitting for us, *who is* holy, harmless, undefiled, separate from sinners, and has become higher than the heavens;

Heb 7:28 For the law appoints as high priests men who have weakness, but the word of the oath, which came after the law, *appoints* the Son who has been perfected forever.

Faithful.

Heb 3:2 who was faithful to Him who appointed Him, as Moses also *was faithful* in all His house.

As a sacrifice.

Offered Himself once.

Heb 7:27 who does not need daily, as those high priests, to offer up sacrifices, first for His own sins and then for the people's, for this He did once for all when He offered up Himself.

Heb 9:14 how much more shall the blood of Christ, who through the eternal Spirit offered Himself without spot to God, cleanse your conscience from dead works to serve the living God?

Heb 9:25–26 not that He should offer Himself often, as the high priest enters the Most Holy Place every year with blood of another— 26 He then would have had to suffer often since the foundation of the world; but now, once at the end of the ages, He has appeared to put away sin by the sacrifice of Himself.

Superior to all others.

Heb 9:13–14 For if the blood of bulls and goats and the ashes of a heifer, sprinkling the unclean, sanctifies for the purifying of the flesh, 14 how much more shall the blood of Christ, who through the eternal Spirit offered Himself without spot to God, cleanse your conscience from dead works to serve the living God?

Heb 9:23 Therefore *it was* necessary that the copies of the things in the heavens should be purified with these, but the heavenly things themselves with better sacrifices than these.

Obtained redemption.

Heb 2:17 Therefore, in all things He had to be made like *His* brethren, that He might be a merciful and faithful High Priest in things *pertaining* to God, to make propitiation for the sins of the people.

Heb 9:12 Not with the blood of goats and calves, but with His own blood He entered the Most Holy Place once for all, having obtained eternal redemption.

Entered into heaven.

Heb 4:14 Seeing then that we have a great High Priest who has passed through the heavens, Jesus the Son of God, let us hold fast *our* confession.

Heb 10:12 But this Man, after He had offered one sacrifice for sins forever, sat down at the right hand of God,

Intercedes for those who are tempted.

Heb 2:18 For in that He Himself has suffered, being tempted, He is able to aid those who are tempted.

Heb 4:15 For we do not have a High Priest who cannot sympathize with our weaknesses, but was in all *points* tempted as *we are, yet* without sin.

Heb 7:25 Therefore He is also able to save to the uttermost those who come to God through Him, since He always lives to make intercession for them.

Heb 9:24 For Christ has not entered the holy places made with hands, *which are* copies of the true, but into heaven itself, now to appear in the presence of God for us;

On His throne.

Zech 6:13 Yes, He shall build the temple of the LORD. He shall bear the glory, And shall sit and rule on His throne; So He shall be a priest on His throne, And the counsel of peace shall be between them both." '

Encouragement to steadfastness.

Heb 4:14 Seeing then that we have a great High Priest who has passed through the heavens, Jesus the Son of God, let us hold fast *our* confession.

Typified by

Melchizedek.

Gen 14:18–20 Then Melchizedek king of Salem brought out bread and wine; he *was* the priest of God Most High. **19** And he blessed him and said: "Blessed be Abram of God Most High, Possessor of heaven and earth; **20** And blessed be God Most High, Who has delivered your enemies into your hand." And he gave him a tithe of all.

Aaron, etc.

Ex 40:12–15 "Then you shall bring Aaron and his sons to the door of the tabernacle of meeting and wash them with water. **13** You shall put the holy garments on Aaron, and anoint him and consecrate him, that he may minister to Me as priest. **14** And you shall bring his sons and clothe them with tunics. **15** You shall anoint them, as you anointed their father, that they may minister to Me as priests; for their anointing shall surely be an everlasting priesthood throughout their generations."

JESUS CHRIST, THE HUMAN NATURE OF

Was necessary to His mediatorial office.

Gal 4:4–5 But when the fullness of the time had come, God sent forth His Son, born of a woman, born under the law, **5** to redeem those who were under the law, that we might receive the adoption as sons.

1 Cor 15:21 For since by man *came* death, by Man also *came* the resurrection of the dead.

Rom 6:15 What then? Shall we sin because we are not under law but under grace? Certainly not!

Rom 6:19 I speak in human *terms* because of the weakness of your flesh. For just as you presented your members *as* slaves of uncleanness, and of lawlessness *leading* to *more* lawlessness, so now present your members *as* slaves *of* righteousness for holiness.

1 Tim 2:5 For *there is* one God and one Mediator between God and men, *the* Man Christ Jesus,

Heb 2:17 Therefore, in all things He had to be made like *His* brethren, that He might be a merciful and faithful High Priest in things *pertaining* to God, to make propitiation for the sins of the people.

Is proved by His

Conception in the virgin's womb.

Matt 1:18 Now the birth of Jesus Christ was as follows: After His mother Mary was betrothed to Joseph, before they came together, she was found with child of the Holy Spirit.

Luke 1:31 And behold, you will conceive in your womb and bring forth a Son, and shall call His name JESUS.

Birth.

Matt 1:16 And Jacob begot Joseph the husband of Mary, of whom was born Jesus who is called Christ.

Matt 1:25 and did not know her till she had brought forth her firstborn Son. And he called His name JESUS.

Matt 2:2 saying, "Where is He who has been born King of the Jews? For we have seen His star in the East and have come to worship Him."

Luke 2:7 And she brought forth her firstborn Son, and wrapped Him in swaddling cloths, and laid Him in a manger, because there was no room for them in the inn.

Luke 2:11 For there is born to you this day in the city of David a Savior, who is Christ the Lord.

Partaking of flesh and blood.

John 1:14 And the Word became flesh and dwelt among us, and we beheld His glory, the glory as of the only begotten of the Father, full of grace and truth.

Heb 2:14 Inasmuch then as the children have partaken of flesh and blood, He Himself likewise shared in the same, that through death He might destroy him who had the power of death, that is, the devil,

Having a human soul.

Matt 26:38 Then He said to them, "My soul is exceedingly sorrowful, even to death. Stay here and watch with Me."

Luke 23:46 And when Jesus had cried out with a loud voice, He said, "Father, *'into Your hands I commit My spirit.'* " Having said this, He breathed His last.

Acts 2:31 he, foreseeing this, spoke concerning the resurrection of the Christ, that His soul was not left in Hades, nor did His flesh see corruption.

Circumcision.

Luke 2:21 And when eight days were completed for the circumcision of the Child, His name was called JESUS, the name given by the angel before He was conceived in the womb.

Increase in wisdom and stature.

Luke 2:52 And Jesus increased in wisdom and stature, and in favor with God and men.

Weeping.

Luke 19:41 Now as He drew near, He saw the city and wept over it,

John 11:35 Jesus wept.

Hungering.

Matt 4:2 And when He had fasted forty days and forty nights, afterward He was hungry.

Matt 21:18 Now in the morning, as He returned to the city, He was hungry.

Thirsting.

John 4:7 A woman of Samaria came to draw water. Jesus said to her, "Give Me a drink."

John 19:28 After this, Jesus, knowing that all things were now accomplished, that the Scripture might be fulfilled, said, "I thirst!"

Sleeping.

Matt 8:24 And suddenly a great tempest arose on the sea, so that the boat was covered with the waves. But He was asleep.

Mark 4:38 But He was in the stern, asleep on a pillow. And they awoke Him and said to Him, "Teacher, do You not care that we are perishing?"

Being subject to weariness.

John 4:6 Now Jacob's well was there. Jesus therefore, being wearied from *His* journey, sat thus by the well. It was about the sixth hour.

Being a man of sorrows.

Is 53:3–4 He is despised and rejected by men, A Man of sorrows and acquainted with grief. And we hid, as it were, *our* faces from Him; He was despised, and we did not esteem Him. 4 Surely He has borne our griefs And carried our sorrows; Yet we esteemed Him stricken, Smitten by God, and afflicted.

Luke 22:44 And being in agony, He prayed more earnestly. Then His sweat became like great drops of blood falling down to the ground.

John 11:33 Therefore, when Jesus saw her weeping, and the Jews who came with her weeping, He groaned in the spirit and was troubled.

John 12:27 "Now My soul is troubled, and what shall I say? 'Father, save Me from this hour'? But for this purpose I came to this hour.

Enduring indignities.

Matt 26:67 Then they spat in His face and beat Him; and others struck *Him* with the palms of their hands,

Luke 22:64 And having blindfolded Him, they struck Him on the face and asked Him, saying, "Prophesy! Who is the one who struck You?"

Luke 23:11 Then Herod, with his men of war, treated Him with contempt and mocked *Him,* arrayed Him in a gorgeous robe, and sent Him back to Pilate.

Being scourged.

Matt 27:26 Then he released Barabbas to them; and when he had scourged Jesus, he delivered *Him* to be crucified.

Mark 15:15 So Pilate, wanting to gratify the crowd, re-

leased Barabbas to them; and he delivered Jesus, after he had scourged *Him,* to be crucified.

Being nailed to the cross.

Ps 22:16 For dogs have surrounded Me; The congregation of the wicked has enclosed Me. They pierced My hands and My feet;

Luke 23:33 And when they had come to the place called Calvary, there they crucified Him, and the criminals, one on the right hand and the other on the left.

Death.

John 19:30 So when Jesus had received the sour wine, He said, "It is finished!" And bowing His head, He gave up His spirit.

Side being pierced.

John 19:34 But one of the soldiers pierced His side with a spear, and immediately blood and water came out.

Burial.

Matt 27:59–60 When Joseph had taken the body, he wrapped it in a clean linen cloth, 60 and laid it in his new tomb which he had hewn out of the rock; and he rolled a large stone against the door of the tomb, and departed.

Mark 15:46 Then he bought fine linen, took Him down, and wrapped Him in the linen. And he laid Him in a tomb which had been hewn out of the rock, and rolled a stone against the door of the tomb.

Resurrection.

Acts 3:15 and killed the Prince of life, whom God raised from the dead, of which we are witnesses.

2 Tim 2:8 Remember that Jesus Christ, of the seed of David, was raised from the dead according to my gospel,

Was like our own, in all things except sin.

Acts 3:22 For Moses truly said to the fathers, 'The LORD your God will raise up for you a Prophet like me from your brethren. Him you shall hear in all things, whatever He says to you.

Phil 2:7–8 but made Himself of no reputation, taking the form of a bondservant, *and* coming in the likeness of men. 8 And being found in appearance as a man, He humbled Himself and became obedient to *the point of* death, even the death of the cross.

Heb 2:17 Therefore, in all things He had to be made like His brethren, that He might be a merciful and faithful High Priest in things *pertaining* to God, to make propitiation for the sins of the people.

Was without sin.

John 8:46 Which of you convicts Me of sin? And if I tell the truth, why do you not believe Me?

John 18:38 Pilate said to Him, "What is truth?" And when he had said this, he went out again to the Jews, and said to them, "I find no fault in Him at all.

Heb 4:15 For we do not have a High Priest who cannot sympathize with our weaknesses, but was in all *points* tempted as *we are,* yet without sin.

Heb 7:26 For such a High Priest was fitting for us, *who is* holy, harmless, undefiled, separate from sinners, and has become higher than the heavens;

Heb 7:28 For the law appoints as high priests men who have weakness, but the word of the oath, which came after the law, *appoints* the Son who has been perfected forever.

1 Pet 2:22 *"Who committed no sin, Nor was deceit found in His mouth"*;

1 John 3:5 And you know that He was manifested to take away our sins, and in Him there is no sin.

Verified by senses.

Luke 24:39 Behold My hands and My feet, that it is I Myself. Handle Me and see, for a spirit does not have flesh and bones as you see I have."

John 20:27 Then He said to Thomas, "Reach your finger here, and look at My hands; and reach your hand *here*, and put *it* into My side. Do not be unbelieving, but believing."

1 John 1:1–2 That which was from the beginning, which we have heard, which we have seen with our eyes, which we have looked upon, and our hands have handled, concerning the Word of life— **2** the life was manifested, and we have seen, and bear witness, and declare to you that eternal life which was with the Father and was manifested to us—

Was of the seed of

The woman.

Gen 3:15 And I will put enmity Between you and the woman, And between your seed and her Seed; He shall bruise your head, And you shall bruise His heel."

Is 7:4 and say to him: 'Take heed, and be quiet; do not fear or be fainthearted for these two stubs of smoking firebrands, for the fierce anger of Rezin and Syria, and the son of Remaliah.

Jer 31:22 How long will you gad about, O you backsliding daughter? For the LORD has created a new thing in the earth— A woman shall encompass a man."

Luke 1:31 And behold, you will conceive in your womb and bring forth a Son, and shall call His name JESUS.

Gal 4:4 But when the fullness of the time had come, God sent forth His Son, born of a woman, born under the law,

Abraham.

Gen 22:18 In your seed all the nations of the earth shall be blessed, because you have obeyed My voice."

Gal 3:16 Now to Abraham and his Seed were the promises made. He does not say, "And to seeds," as of many, but as of one, *"And to your Seed,"* who is Christ.

Heb 2:16 For indeed He does not give aid to angels, but He does give aid to the seed of Abraham.

David.

2 Sam 7:12 "When your days are fulfilled and you rest with your fathers, I will set up your seed after you, who will come from your body, and I will establish his kingdom.

2 Sam 7:16 And your house and your kingdom shall be established forever before you. Your throne shall be established forever." ' "

Ps 89:35–36 Once I have sworn by My holiness; I will not lie to David: **36** His seed shall endure forever, And his throne as the sun before Me;

Jer 23:5 "Behold, *the* days are coming," says the LORD,

"That I will raise to David a Branch of righteousness; A King shall reign and prosper, And execute judgment and righteousness in the earth.

Matt 22:42 saying, "What do you think about the Christ? Whose Son is He?" They said to Him, *"The Son* of David."

Mark 10:47 And when he heard that it was Jesus of Nazareth, he began to cry out and say, "Jesus, Son of David, have mercy on me!"

Acts 2:30 Therefore, being a prophet, and knowing that God had sworn with an oath to him that of the fruit of his body, according to the flesh, He would raise up the Christ to sit on his throne,

Acts 13:23 From this man's seed, according to *the* promise, God raised up for Israel a Savior—Jesus—

Rom 1:3 concerning His Son Jesus Christ our Lord, who was born of the seed of David according to the flesh,

Genealogy of.

Matt 1:1–17 The book of the genealogy of Jesus Christ, the Son of David, the Son of Abraham: **2** Abraham begot Isaac, Isaac begot Jacob, and Jacob begot Judah and his brothers. **3** Judah begot Perez and Zerah by Tamar, Perez begot Hezron, and Hezron begot Ram. **4** Ram begot Amminadab, Amminadab begot Nahshon, and Nahshon begot Salmon. **5** Salmon begot Boaz by Rahab, Boaz begot Obed by Ruth, Obed begot Jesse, **6** and Jesse begot David the king. David the king begot Solomon by her *who had been the wife* of Uriah. **7** Solomon begot Rehoboam, Rehoboam begot Abijah, and Abijah begot Asa. **8** Asa begot Jehoshaphat, Jehoshaphat begot Joram, and Joram begot Uzziah. **9** Uzziah begot Jotham, Jotham begot Ahaz, and Ahaz begot Hezekiah. **10** Hezekiah begot Manasseh, Manasseh begot Amon, and Amon begot Josiah. **11** Josiah begot Jeconiah and his brothers about the time they were carried away to Babylon. **12** And after they were brought to Babylon, Jeconiah begot Shealtiel, and Shealtiel begot Zerubbabel. **13** Zerubbabel begot Abiud, Abiud begot Eliakim, and Eliakim begot Azor. **14** Azor begot Zadok, Zadok begot Achim, and Achim begot Eliud. **15** Eliud begot Eleazar, Eleazar begot Matthan, and Matthan begot Jacob. **16** And Jacob begot Joseph the husband of Mary, of whom was born Jesus who is called Christ. **17** So all the generations from Abraham to David *are* fourteen generations, from David until the captivity in Babylon *are* fourteen generations, and from the captivity in Babylon until the Christ *are* fourteen generations.

Luke 3:23–38 Now Jesus Himself began *His ministry at* about thirty years of age, being (as was supposed) *the* son of Joseph, *the son* of Heli, **24** *the son* of Matthat, *the son* of Levi, *the son* of Melchi, *the son* of Janna, *the son* of Joseph, **25** *the son* of Mattathiah, *the son* of Amos, *the son* of Nahum, *the son* of Esli, *the son* of Naggai, **26** *the son* of Maath, *the son* of Mattathiah, *the son* of Semei, *the son* of Joseph, *the son* of Judah, **27** *the son* of Joannas, *the son* of Rhesa, *the son* of Zerubbabel, *the son* of Shealtiel, *the son* of Neri, **28** *the son* of Melchi, *the son* of Addi, *the son* of Cosam, *the son* of Elmodam, *the son* of Er, **29** *the son* of Jose, *the son* of Eliezer, *the son* of Jorim, *the son* of Matthat, *the son* of Levi, **30** *the son* of Simeon, *the son* of Judah, *the son* of Joseph, *the son* of Jonan, *the son* of Eliakim, **31** *the son* of Melea, *the son* of Menan, *the son* of Mattathah, *the son* of Nathan, *the son* of David, **32** *the son* of Jesse, *the son* of Obed, *the son* of Boaz, *the son* of Salmon, *the son* of Nahshon, **33** *the son* of Amminadab, *the son* of Ram, *the son* of Hezron, *the son* of Perez, *the son* of Judah, **34** *the son* of Jacob, *the son* of Isaac, *the son* of Abraham, *the son* of Terah, *the son* of Nahor, **35** *the son* of Serug, *the son* of Reu, *the son* of Peleg, *the son* of Eber, *the son* of Shelah, **36** *the son* of Cainan, *the son* of Arphaxad, *the son* of Shem, *the son* of Noah, *the son* of Lamech, **37** *the son* of Methuselah, *the son* of Enoch, *the son* of Jared, *the son* of Mahalalel, *the son* of Cainan, **38** *the son* of Enosh, *the son* of Seth, *the son* of Adam, *the son* of God.

Attested by Himself.

Matt 8:20 And Jesus said to him, "Foxes have holes and birds of the air *have* nests, but the Son of Man has nowhere to lay *His* head."

Matt 16:13 When Jesus came into the region of Caesarea Philippi, He asked His disciples, saying, "Who do men say that I, the Son of Man, am?"

Confession of, a test of belonging to God.

1 John 4:2 By this you know the Spirit of God: Every spirit that confesses that Jesus Christ has come in the flesh is of God,

Acknowledged by men.

Mark 6:3 Is this not the carpenter, the Son of Mary, and brother of James, Joses, Judas, and Simon? And are not His sisters here with us?" So they were offended at Him.

John 7:27 However, we know where this Man is from; but when the Christ comes, no one knows where He is from."

John 19:5 Then Jesus came out, wearing the crown of thorns and the purple robe. And *Pilate* said to them, "Behold the Man!"

Acts 2:22 "Men of Israel, hear these words: Jesus of Nazareth, a Man attested by God to you by miracles, wonders, and signs which God did through Him in your midst, as you yourselves also know—

Denied by Antichrist.

1 John 4:3 and every spirit that does not confess that Jesus Christ has come in the flesh is not of God. And this is the *spirit* of the Antichrist, which you have heard was coming, and is now already in the world.

2 John 1:7 For many deceivers have gone out into the world who do not confess Jesus Christ *as* coming in the flesh. This is a deceiver and an antichrist.

JESUS CHRIST, THE HUMILITY OF
Declared by Himself.

Matt 11:29 Take My yoke upon you and learn from Me, for I am gentle and lowly in heart, and you will find rest for your souls.

Exhibited in His
Taking our nature.

Phil 2:7 but made Himself of no reputation, taking the form of a bondservant, *and* coming in the likeness of men.

Heb 2:16 For indeed He does not give aid to angels, but He does give aid to the seed of Abraham.

Birth.

Luke 2:4–7 Joseph also went up from Galilee, out of the city of Nazareth, into Judea, to the city of David, which is called Bethlehem, because he was of the house and lineage of David, **5** to be registered with Mary, his betrothed wife, who was with child. **6** So it was, that while they were there, the days were completed for her to be delivered. **7** And she brought forth her firstborn Son, and wrapped Him in swaddling cloths, and laid Him in a manger, because there was no room for them in the inn.

Subjection to His parents.

Luke 2:51 Then He went down with them and came to Nazareth, and was subject to them, but His mother kept all these things in her heart.

Station in life.

Matt 13:55 Is this not the carpenter's son? Is not His mother called Mary? And His brothers James, Joses, Simon, and Judas?

John 9:29 We know that God spoke to Moses; *as for* this *fellow,* we do not know where He is from."

Poverty.

Luke 9:58 And Jesus said to him, "Foxes have holes and birds of the air *have* nests, but the Son of Man has nowhere to lay *His* head."

2 Cor 8:9 For you know the grace of our Lord Jesus Christ, that though He was rich, yet for your sakes He became poor, that you through His poverty might become rich.

Partaking of our weaknesses.

Heb 4:15 For we do not have a High Priest who cannot sympathize with our weaknesses, but was in all *points* tempted as *we are, yet* without sin.

Heb 5:7 who, in the days of His flesh, when He had offered up prayers and supplications, with vehement cries and tears to Him who was able to save Him from death, and was heard because of His godly fear,

Submitting to ordinances.

Matt 3:13–15 Then Jesus came from Galilee to John at the Jordan to be baptized by him. **14** And John *tried to* prevent Him, saying, "I need to be baptized by You, and are You coming to me?" **15** But Jesus answered and said to him, "Permit *it to be so* now, for thus it is fitting for us to fulfill all righteousness." Then he allowed Him.

Becoming a servant.

Matt 20:28 just as the Son of Man did not come to be served, but to serve, and to give His life a ransom for many."

Luke 22:27 For who *is* greater, he who sits at the table, or he who serves? *Is* it not he who sits at the table? Yet I am among you as the One who serves.

Phil 2:7 but made Himself of no reputation, taking the form of a bondservant, *and* coming in the likeness of men.

Associating with the despised.

Matt 9:10–11 Now it happened, as Jesus sat at the table in the house, *that* behold, many tax collectors and sinners came and sat down with Him and His disciples. **11** And when the Pharisees saw *it,* they said to

His disciples, "Why does your Teacher eat with tax collectors and sinners?"

Luke 15:1–2 Then all the tax collectors and the sinners drew near to Him to hear Him. **2** And the Pharisees and scribes complained, saying, "This Man receives sinners and eats with them."

Refusing honors.

John 5:41 "I do not receive honor from men.

John 6:15 Therefore when Jesus perceived that they were about to come and take Him by force to make Him king, He departed again to the mountain by Himself alone.

Entry into Jerusalem.

Zech 9:9 "Rejoice greatly, O daughter of Zion! Shout, O daughter of Jerusalem! Behold, your King is coming to you; He *is* just and having salvation, Lowly and riding on a donkey, A colt, the foal of a donkey.

Matt 21:5 *"Tell the daughter of Zion, 'Behold, your King is coming to you, Lowly, and sitting on a donkey, A colt, the foal of a donkey.' "*

Matt 21:7 They brought the donkey and the colt, laid their clothes on them, and set *Him* on them.

Washing His disciples' feet.

John 13:5 After that, He poured water into a basin and began to wash the disciples' feet, and to wipe *them* with the towel with which He was girded.

Obedience.

John 6:38 For I have come down from heaven, not to do My own will, but the will of Him who sent Me.

Heb 10:9 then He said, *"Behold, I have come to do Your will, O God."* He takes away the first that He may establish the second.

Submitting to sufferings.

Is 50:6 I gave My back to those who struck *Me,* And My cheeks to those who plucked out the beard; I did not hide My face from shame and spitting.

Is 53:7 He was oppressed and He was afflicted, Yet He opened not His mouth; He was led as a lamb to the slaughter, And as a sheep before its shearers is silent, So He opened not His mouth.

Matt 26:37–39 And He took with Him Peter and the two sons of Zebedee, and He began to be sorrowful and deeply distressed. **38** Then He said to them, "My soul is exceedingly sorrowful, even to death. Stay here and watch with Me." **39** He went a little farther and fell on His face, and prayed, saying, "O My Father, if it is possible, let this cup pass from Me; nevertheless, not as I will, but as You *will."*

Acts 8:32 The place in the Scripture which he read was this: *"He was led as a sheep to the slaughter; And as a lamb before its shearer is silent, So He opened not His mouth.*

Exposing Himself to reproach and contempt.

Ps 22:6 But I *am* a worm, and no man; A reproach of men, and despised by the people.

Ps 69:9 Because zeal for Your house has eaten me up, And the reproaches of those who reproach You have fallen on me.

Is 53:3 He is despised and rejected by men, A Man of sorrows and acquainted with grief. And we hid, as it were, *our* faces from Him; He was despised, and we did not esteem Him.

Mark 6:3 Is this not the carpenter, the Son of Mary, and brother of James, Joses, Judas, and Simon? And are not His sisters here with us?" So they were offended at Him.

John 9:29 We know that God spoke to Moses; *as for* this *fellow,* we do not know where He is from."

Rom 15:3 For even Christ did not please Himself; but as it is written, *"The reproaches of those who reproached You fell on Me."*

Being obedient to death.

John 10:15 As the Father knows Me, even so I know the Father; and I lay down My life for the sheep.

John 10:17–18 "Therefore My Father loves Me, because I lay down My life that I may take it again. **18** No one takes it from Me, but I lay it down of Myself. I have power to lay it down, and I have power to take it again. This command I have received from My Father."

Phil 2:8 And being found in appearance as a man, He humbled Himself and became obedient to *the point of* death, even the death of the cross.

Heb 12:2 looking unto Jesus, the author and finisher of *our* faith, who for the joy that was set before Him endured the cross, despising the shame, and has sat down at the right hand of the throne of God.

Believers should imitate.

Phil 2:5–8 Let this mind be in you which was also in Christ Jesus, **6** who, being in the form of God, did not consider it robbery to be equal with God, **7** but made Himself of no reputation, taking the form of a bondservant, *and* coming in the likeness of men. **8** And being found in appearance as a man, He humbled Himself and became obedient to *the point of* death, even the death of the cross.

His exaltation, the result of.

Phil 2:9 Therefore God also has highly exalted Him and given Him the name which is above every name,

JESUS CHRIST, THE INCARNATION OF

Defined as

God coming into the world.

John 1:9 That was the true Light which gives light to every man coming into the world.

The Word became flesh.

John 1:14 And the Word became flesh and dwelt among us, and we beheld His glory, the glory as of the only begotten of the Father, full of grace and truth.

Descending to earth.

Eph 4:9 (Now this, *"He ascended"*—what does it mean but that He also first descended into the lower parts of the earth?

He possessed the fullness of the divine nature in a human body.

Col 2:9 For in Him dwells all the fullness of the Godhead bodily;

Described as self-emptying (made Himself of no reputation). *See* Jesus Christ, Human Nature of.

Phil 2:6–11 who, being in the form of God, did not consider it robbery to be equal with God, **7** but made

Himself of no reputation, taking the form of a bondservant, *and* coming in the likeness of men. 8 And being found in appearance as a man, He humbled Himself and became obedient to *the point of* death, even the death of the cross. 9 Therefore God also has highly exalted Him and given Him the name which is above every name, 10 that at the name of Jesus every knee should bow, of those in heaven, and of those on earth, and of those under the earth, 11 and *that* every tongue should confess that Jesus Christ *is* Lord, to the glory of God the Father.

He was born according to the flesh.

Rom 1:3–4 concerning His Son Jesus Christ our Lord, who was born of the seed of David according to the flesh, 4 *and* declared *to be* the Son of God with power according to the Spirit of holiness, by the resurrection from the dead.

Rom 8:3 For what the law could not do in that it was weak through the flesh, God *did* by sending His own Son in the likeness of sinful flesh, on account of sin: He condemned sin in the flesh,

Became poor, a reference to.

2 Cor 8:9 For you know the grace of our Lord Jesus Christ, that though He was rich, yet for your sakes He became poor, that you through His poverty might become rich.

Prophecy of.

Mic 5:2 "But you, Bethlehem Ephrathah, *Though* you are little among the thousands of Judah, *Yet* out of you shall come forth to Me The One to be Ruler in Israel, Whose goings forth *are* from of old, From everlasting."

JESUS CHRIST, THE KING

Foretold.

Num 24:17 "I see Him, but not now; I behold Him, but not near; A Star shall come out of Jacob; A Scepter shall rise out of Israel, And batter the brow of Moab, And destroy all the sons of tumult.

Ps 2:6 "Yet I have set My King On My holy hill of Zion."

Is 9:7 Of the increase of *His* government and peace *There will be* no end, Upon the throne of David and over His kingdom, To order it and establish it with judgment and justice From that time forward, even forever. The zeal of the Lord of hosts will perform this.

Jer 23:5 "Behold, *the* days are coming," says the LORD, "That I will raise to David a Branch of righteousness; A King shall reign and prosper, And execute judgment and righteousness in the earth.

Mic 5:2 "But you, Bethlehem Ephrathah, *Though* you are little among the thousands of Judah, *Yet* out of you shall come forth to Me The One to be Ruler in Israel, Whose goings forth *are* from of old, From everlasting."

Cf. Ps 45:1–17

Glorious.

Ps 24:7–10 Lift up your heads, O you gates! And be lifted up, you everlasting doors! And the King of glory shall come in. 8 Who *is* this King of glory? The LORD strong and mighty, The LORD mighty in battle. 9 Lift up your heads, O you gates! Lift up, you everlasting

doors! And the King of glory shall come in. 10 Who is this King of glory? The LORD of hosts, He *is* the King of glory. Selah

1 Cor 2:8 which none of the rulers of this age knew; for had they known, they would not have crucified the Lord of glory.

James 2:1 My brethren, do not hold the faith of our Lord Jesus Christ, *the Lord* of glory, with partiality.

Supreme.

Ps 89:27 Also I will make him *My* firstborn, The highest of the kings of the earth.

Rev 1:5 and from Jesus Christ, the faithful witness, the firstborn from the dead, and the ruler over the kings of the earth. To Him who loved us and washed us from our sins in His own blood,

Rev 19:16 And He has on *His* robe and on His thigh a name written: KING OF KINGS AND LORD OF LORDS.

His throne,

From God.

Rev 3:21 To him who overcomes I will grant to sit with Me on My throne, as I also overcame and sat down with My Father on His throne.

In the line of David.

Is 9:7 Of the increase of *His* government and peace *There will be* no end, Upon the throne of David and over His kingdom, To order it and establish it with judgment and justice From that time forward, even forever. The zeal of the Lord of hosts will perform this.

Ezek 37:24–25 "David My servant *shall be* king over them, and they shall all have one shepherd; they shall also walk in My judgments and observe My statutes, and do them. 25 Then they shall dwell in the land that I have given to Jacob My servant, where your fathers dwelt; and they shall dwell there, they, their children, and their children's children, forever; and My servant David *shall be* their prince forever.

Luke 1:32 He will be great, and will be called the Son of the Highest; and the Lord God will give Him the throne of His father David.

Acts 2:30 Therefore, being a prophet, and knowing that God had sworn with an oath to him that of the fruit of his body, according to the flesh, He would raise up the Christ to sit on his throne,

Rules Zion.

Ps 2:6 "Yet I have set My King On My holy hill of Zion."

Is 52:7 How beautiful upon the mountains Are the feet of him who brings good news, Who proclaims peace, Who brings glad tidings of good *things*, Who proclaims salvation, Who says to Zion, "Your God reigns!"

Zech 9:9 "Rejoice greatly, O daughter of Zion! Shout, O daughter of Jerusalem! Behold, your King is coming to you; He *is* just and having salvation, Lowly and riding on a donkey, A colt, the foal of a donkey.

Matt 21:5 *"Tell the daughter of Zion, 'Behold, your King is coming to you, Lowly, and sitting on a donkey, A colt, the foal of a donkey.' "*

John 12:12–15 The next day a great multitude that had come to the feast, when they heard that Jesus was coming to Jerusalem, **13** took branches of palm trees and went out to meet Him, and cried out: "Hosanna! *'Blessed is He who comes in the name of the LORD!'* The King of Israel!" **14** Then Jesus, when He had found a young donkey, sat on it; as it is written: **15** *"Fear not, daughter of Zion; Behold, your King is coming, Sitting on a donkey's colt."*

Has a righteous kingdom.

Ps 45:6 Your throne, O God, *is* forever and ever; A scepter of righteousness *is* the scepter of Your kingdom.

Is 32:1 Behold, a king will reign in righteousness, And princes will rule with justice.

Jer 23:5 "Behold, *the* days are coming," says the LORD, "That I will raise to David a Branch of righteousness; A King shall reign and prosper, And execute judgment and righteousness in the earth.

Heb 1:8–9 But to the Son *He says:* *"Your throne, O God, is forever and ever; A scepter of righteousness is the scepter of Your kingdom.* **9** *You have loved righteousness and hated lawlessness; Therefore God, Your God, has anointed You With the oil of gladness more than Your companions."*

Has an everlasting kingdom.

Dan 2:44 And in the days of these kings the God of heaven will set up a kingdom which shall never be destroyed; and the kingdom shall not be left to other people; it shall break in pieces and consume all these kingdoms, and it shall stand forever.

Dan 7:14 Then to Him was given dominion and glory and a kingdom, That all peoples, nations, and languages should serve Him. His dominion *is* an everlasting dominion, Which shall not pass away, And His kingdom *the one* Which shall not be destroyed.

Luke 1:33 And He will reign over the house of Jacob forever, and of His kingdom there will be no end."

Has a universal kingdom.

Ps 2:8 Ask of Me, and I will give *You* The nations *for* Your inheritance, And the ends of the earth *for* Your possession.

Ps 72:8 He shall have dominion also from sea to sea, And from the River to the ends of the earth.

Zech 14:9 And the LORD shall be King over all the earth. In that day it shall be— "The LORD *is* one," And His name one.

Rev 11:15 Then the seventh angel sounded: And there were loud voices in heaven, saying, "The kingdoms of this world have become *the kingdoms* of our Lord and of His Christ, and He shall reign forever and ever!"

Has a spiritual kingdom.

John 18:36 Jesus answered, "My kingdom is not of this world. If My kingdom were of this world, My servants would fight, so that I should not be delivered to the Jews; but now My kingdom is not from here."

Believers are the subjects of His kingdom.

Is 33:17 Your eyes will see the King in His beauty; They will see the land that is very far off.

Luke 22:29–30 And I bestow upon you a kingdom, just as My Father bestowed *one* upon Me, **30** that you may eat and drink at My table in My kingdom, and sit on thrones judging the twelve tribes of Israel."

Col 1:13 He has delivered us from the power of darkness and conveyed *us* into the kingdom of the Son of His love,

Heb 12:28 Therefore, since we are receiving a kingdom which cannot be shaken, let us have grace, by which we may serve God acceptably with reverence and godly fear.

Rev 15:3 They sing the song of Moses, the servant of God, and the song of the Lamb, saying: "Great and marvelous *are* Your works, Lord God Almighty! Just and true *are* Your ways, O King of the saints!

Rev 22:3–4 And there shall be no more curse, but the throne of God and of the Lamb shall be in it, and His servants shall serve Him. **4** They shall see His face, and His name *shall be* on their foreheads.

Acknowledged by

The wise men from the East.

Matt 2:2 saying, "Where is He who has been born King of the Jews? For we have seen His star in the East and have come to worship Him."

Nathanael.

John 1:49 Nathanael answered and said to Him, "Rabbi, You are the Son of God! You are the King of Israel!"

His followers.

Luke 19:38 saying: " *'Blessed is the King who comes in the name of the LORD!'* Peace in heaven and glory in the highest!"

John 12:13 took branches of palm trees and went out to meet Him, and cried out: "Hosanna! *'Blessed is He who comes in the name of the LORD!'* The King of Israel!"

Declared by Himself.

Matt 25:34 Then the King will say to those on His right hand, 'Come, you blessed of My Father, inherit the kingdom prepared for you from the foundation of the world:

John 18:37 Pilate therefore said to Him, "Are You a king then?" Jesus answered, "You say *rightly* that I am a king. For this cause I was born, and for this cause I have come into the world, that I should bear witness to the truth. Everyone who is of the truth hears My voice."

Written on His cross.

John 19:19 Now Pilate wrote a title and put *it* on the cross. And the writing was: JESUS OF NAZARETH, THE KING OF THE JEWS.

The Jews shall turn to.

Hos 3:5 Afterward the children of Israel shall return and seek the LORD their God and David their king. They shall fear the LORD and His goodness in the latter days.

Earthly kings shall pay homage to.

Ps 72:10 The kings of Tarshish and of the isles Will bring presents; The kings of Sheba and Seba Will offer gifts.

Is 49:7 Thus says the LORD, The Redeemer of Israel, their Holy One, To Him whom man despises, To Him whom the nation abhors, To the Servant of rulers: "Kings shall see and arise, Princes also shall worship, Because of the LORD who is faithful, The Holy One of Israel; And He has chosen You."

Shall overcome all His enemies.

Ps 110:1 The LORD said to my Lord, "Sit at My right hand, Till I make Your enemies Your footstool."

Mark 12:36 For David himself said by the Holy Spirit: *'The LORD said to my Lord, "Sit at My right hand, Till I make Your enemies Your footstool." '*

1 Cor 15:25 For He must reign till He has put all enemies under His feet.

Rev 17:14 These will make war with the Lamb, and the Lamb will overcome them, for He is Lord of lords and King of kings; and those *who are* with Him *are* called, chosen, and faithful."

Typified by

Melchizedek.

Gen 14:18 Then Melchizedek king of Salem brought out bread and wine; he *was* the priest of God Most High.

David.

1 Sam 16:1 Now the LORD said to Samuel, "How long will you mourn for Saul, seeing I have rejected him from reigning over Israel? Fill your horn with oil, and go; I am sending you to Jesse the Bethlehemite. For I have provided Myself a king among his sons."

1 Sam 16:12–13 So he sent and brought him in. Now he *was* ruddy, with bright eyes, and good-looking. And the LORD said, "Arise, anoint him; for this *is* the one!" **13** Then Samuel took the horn of oil and anointed him in the midst of his brothers; and the Spirit of the LORD came upon David from that day forward. So Samuel arose and went to Ramah.

Luke 1:32 He will be great, and will be called the Son of the Highest; and the Lord God will give Him the throne of His father David.

Solomon.

1 Chr 28:6–7 Now He said to me, 'It is your son Solomon *who* shall build My house and My courts; for I have chosen him *to be* My son, and I will be his Father. **7** Moreover I will establish his kingdom forever, if he is steadfast to observe My commandments and My judgments, as it is this day.'

JESUS CHRIST, THE LOVE OF

To the Father.

Ps 91:14 "Because he has set his love upon Me, therefore I will deliver him; I will set him on high, because he has known My name.

John 14:31 But that the world may know that I love the Father, and as the Father gave Me commandment, so I do. Arise, let us go from here.

To His church.

John 15:9 "As the Father loved Me, I also have loved you; abide in My love.

Eph 5:24 Therefore, just as the church is subject to Christ, so *let* the wives *be* to their own husbands in everything.

To those who love Him.

Prov 8:17 I love those who love me, And those who seek me diligently will find me.

John 14:21 He who has My commandments and keeps them, it is he who loves Me. And he who loves Me will be loved by My Father, and I will love him and manifest Myself to him."

Manifested in His

Praying for His enemies.

Luke 23:34 Then Jesus said, "Father, forgive them, for they do not know what they do." And they divided His garments and cast lots.

Dying for us.

Luke 19:10 for the Son of Man has come to seek and to save that which was lost."

John 15:13 Greater love has no one than this, than to lay down one's life for his friends.

Gal 2:20 I have been crucified with Christ; it is no longer I who live, but Christ lives in me; and the *life* which I now live in the flesh I live by faith in the Son of God, who loved me and gave Himself for me.

1 John 3:16 By this we know love, because He laid down His life for us. And we also ought to lay down *our* lives for the brethren.

Rev 1:5 and from Jesus Christ, the faithful witness, the firstborn from the dead, and the ruler over the kings of the earth. To Him who loved us and washed us from our sins in His own blood,

Interceding for us.

Heb 7:25 Therefore He is also able to save to the uttermost those who come to God through Him, since He always lives to make intercession for them.

Heb 9:24 For Christ has not entered the holy places made with hands, *which are* copies of the true, but into heaven itself, now to appear in the presence of God for us;

Sending the Spirit.

Ps 68:18 You have ascended on high, You have led captivity captive; You have received gifts among men, Even *from* the rebellious, That the LORD God might dwell *there.*

John 16:7 Nevertheless I tell you the truth. It is to your advantage that I go away; for if I do not go away, the Helper will not come to you; but if I depart, I will send Him to you.

Rebukes and chastisements.

Rev 3:19 As many as I love, I rebuke and chasten. Therefore be zealous and repent.

Passes knowledge.

Eph 3:19 to know the love of Christ which passes knowledge; that you may be filled with all the fullness of God.

Regarding believers,

They should imitate.

John 13:34 A new commandment I give to you, that you love one another; as I have loved you, that you also love one another.

John 15:10 If you keep My commandments, you will abide in My love, just as I have kept My Father's commandments and abide in His love.

John 15:12 This is My commandment, that you love one another as I have loved you.

Eph 5:2 And walk in love, as Christ also has loved us and given Himself for us, an offering and a sacrifice to God for a sweet-smelling aroma.

1 John 3:16 By this we know love, because He laid

down His life for us. And we also ought to lay down *our* lives for the brethren.

Is compelling.

2 Cor 5:14 For the love of Christ compels us, because we judge thus: that if One died for all, then all died;

Is unchangeable.

John 13:1 Now before the Feast of the Passover, when Jesus knew that His hour had come that He should depart from this world to the Father, having loved His own who were in the world, He loved them to the end.

Is indissoluble.

Rom 8:35 Who shall separate us from the love of Christ? *Shall* tribulation, or distress, or persecution, or famine, or nakedness, or peril, or sword?

They obtain victory through.

Rom 8:37 Yet in all these things we are more than conquerors through Him who loved us.

Is the ground of their love to Him.

Luke 7:47 Therefore I say to you, her sins, *which are* many, are forgiven, for she loved much. But to whom little is forgiven, *the same* loves little."

Shall be acknowledged even by His enemies.

Rev 3:9 Indeed I will make *those* of the synagogue of Satan, who say they are Jews and are not, but lie—indeed I will make them come and worship before your feet, and to know that I have loved you.

Illustrated.

Matt 18:11–13 For the Son of Man has come to save that which was lost. 12 "What do you think? If a man has a hundred sheep, and one of them goes astray, does he not leave the ninety-nine and go to the mountains to seek the one that is straying? 13 And if he should find it, assuredly, I say to you, he rejoices more over that *sheep* than over the ninety-nine that did not go astray.

Exemplified toward

Peter.

Luke 22:32 But I have prayed for you, that your faith should not fail; and when you have returned to *Me*, strengthen your brethren."

Luke 22:61 And the Lord turned and looked at Peter. Then Peter remembered the word of the Lord, how He had said to him, "Before the rooster crows, you will deny Me three times."

Lazarus, etc.

John 11:5 Now Jesus loved Martha and her sister and Lazarus.

John 11:36 Then the Jews said, "See how He loved him!"

His apostles.

John 13:1 Now before the Feast of the Passover, when Jesus knew that His hour had come that He should depart from this world to the Father, having loved His own who were in the world, He loved them to the end.

John 13:34 A new commandment I give to you, that you love one another; as I have loved you, that you also love one another.

John.

John 13:23 Now there was leaning on Jesus' bosom one of His disciples, whom Jesus loved.

JESUS CHRIST, THE MEDIATOR
Through His death.

Eph 2:13–18 But now in Christ Jesus you who once were far off have been brought near by the blood of Christ. 14 For He Himself is our peace, who has made both one, and has broken down the middle wall of separation, 15 having abolished in His flesh the enmity, *that is*, the law of commandments *contained* in ordinances, so as to create in Himself one new man *from* the two, *thus* making peace, 16 and that He might reconcile them both to God in one body through the cross, thereby putting to death the enmity. 17 And He came and preached peace to you who were afar off and to those who were near. 18 For through Him we both have access by one Spirit to the Father.

Heb 9:15 And for this reason He is the Mediator of the new covenant, by means of death, for the redemption of the transgressions under the first covenant, that those who are called may receive the promise of the eternal inheritance.

The only one between God and man.

1 Tim 2:5 For *there is* one God and one Mediator between God and men, *the* Man Christ Jesus,

Of the gospel covenant.

Heb 8:6 But now He has obtained a more excellent ministry, inasmuch as He is also Mediator of a better covenant, which was established on better promises.

Heb 12:24 to Jesus the Mediator of the new covenant, and to the blood of sprinkling that speaks better things than *that of* Abel.

Typified by

Moses.

Deut 5:5 I stood between the LORD and you at that time, to declare to you the word of the LORD; for you were afraid because of the fire, and you did not go up the mountain. *He* said:

Gal 3:19 What purpose then *does* the law *serve?* It was added because of transgressions, till the Seed should come to whom the promise was made; *and it was* appointed through angels by the hand of a mediator.

Aaron.

Num 16:48 And he stood between the dead and the living; so the plague was stopped.

JESUS CHRIST, THE MIRACLES OF
Water turned to wine.

John 2:6–10 Now there were set there six waterpots of stone, according to the manner of purification of the Jews, containing twenty or thirty gallons apiece. 7 Jesus said to them, "Fill the waterpots with water." And they filled them up to the brim. 8 And He said to them, "Draw *some* out now, and take *it* to the master of the feast." And they took *it*. 9 When the master of the feast had tasted the water that was made wine, and did not know where it came from (but the servants who had drawn the water knew), the master of the feast called the bridegroom. 10 And he said to him, "Every man at the beginning sets out the good wine, and when the *guests* have well drunk, then the inferior. You have kept the good wine until now!"

Nobleman's son healed.

John 4:46–53 So Jesus came again to Cana of Galilee where He had made the water wine. And there was a certain nobleman whose son was sick at Capernaum. **47** When he heard that Jesus had come out of Judea into Galilee, he went to Him and implored Him to come down and heal his son, for he was at the point of death. **48** Then Jesus said to him, "Unless you *people* see signs and wonders, you will by no means believe." **49** The nobleman said to Him, "Sir, come down before my child dies!" **50** Jesus said to him, "Go your way; your son lives." So the man believed the word that Jesus spoke to him, and he went his way. **51** And as he was now going down, his servants met him and told *him*, saying, "Your son lives!" **52** Then he inquired of them the hour when he got better. And they said to him, "Yesterday at the seventh hour the fever left him." **53** So the father knew that *it was* at the same hour in which Jesus said to him, "Your son lives." And he himself believed, and his whole household.

Centurion's servant healed.

Matt 9:5–13 For which is easier, to say, *'Your* sins are forgiven you,' or to say, 'Arise and walk'? **6** But that you may know that the Son of Man has power on earth to forgive sins"—then He said to the paralytic, "Arise, take up your bed, and go to your house." **7** And he arose and departed to his house. **8** Now when the multitudes saw *it,* they marveled and glorified God, who had given such power to men. **9** As Jesus passed on from there, He saw a man named Matthew sitting at the tax office. And He said to him, "Follow Me." So he arose and followed Him. **10** Now it happened, as Jesus sat at the table in the house, *that* behold, many tax collectors and sinners came and sat down with Him and His disciples. **11** And when the Pharisees saw *it,* they said to His disciples, "Why does your Teacher eat with tax collectors and sinners?" **12** When Jesus heard *that,* He said to them, "Those who are well have no need of a physician, but those who are sick. **13** But go and learn what *this* means: *'I desire mercy and not sacrifice.'* For I did not come to call the righteous, but sinners, to repentance."

Catch of fish.

Luke 5:4–6 When He had stopped speaking, He said to Simon, "Launch out into the deep and let down your nets for a catch." **5** But Simon answered and said to Him, "Master, we have toiled all night and caught nothing; nevertheless at Your word I will let down the net." **6** And when they had done this, they caught a great number of fish, and their net was breaking.

John 21:6 And He said to them, "Cast the net on the right side of the boat, and you will find *some.*" So they cast, and now they were not able to draw it in because of the multitude of fish.

Demons cast out.

Matt 8:28–32 When He had come to the other side, to the country of the Gergesenes, there met Him two demon-possessed *men,* coming out of the tombs, exceedingly fierce, so that no one could pass that way. **29** And suddenly they cried out, saying, "What have

we to do with You, Jesus, You Son of God? Have You come here to torment us before the time?" **30** Now a good way off from them there was a herd of many swine feeding. **31** So the demons begged Him, saying, "If You cast us out, permit us to go away into the herd of swine." **32** And He said to them, "Go." So when they had come out, they went into the herd of swine. And suddenly the whole herd of swine ran violently down the steep place into the sea, and perished in the water.

Matt 9:32–33 As they went out, behold, they brought to Him a man, mute and demon-possessed. **33** And when the demon was cast out, the mute spoke. And the multitudes marveled, saying, "It was never seen like this in Israel!"

Matt 15:22–28 And behold, a woman of Canaan came from that region and cried out to Him, saying, "Have mercy on me, O Lord, Son of David! My daughter is severely demon-possessed." **23** But He answered her not a word. And His disciples came and urged Him, saying, "Send her away, for she cries out after us." **24** But He answered and said, "I was not sent except to the lost sheep of the house of Israel." **25** Then she came and worshiped Him, saying, "Lord, help me!" **26** But He answered and said, "It is not good to take the children's bread and throw *it* to the little dogs." **27** And she said, "Yes, Lord, yet even the little dogs eat the crumbs which fall from their masters' table." **28** Then Jesus answered and said to her, "O woman, great *is* your faith! Let it be to you as you desire." And her daughter was healed from that very hour.

Matt 17:14–18 And when they had come to the multitude, a man came to Him, kneeling down to Him and saying, **15** "Lord, have mercy on my son, for he is an epileptic and suffers severely; for he often falls into the fire and often into the water. **16** So I brought him to Your disciples, but they could not cure him." **17** Then Jesus answered and said, "O faithless and perverse generation, how long shall I be with you? How long shall I bear with you? Bring him here to Me." **18** And Jesus rebuked the demon, and it came out of him; and the child was cured from that very hour.

Mark 1:23–27 Now there was a man in their synagogue with an unclean spirit. And he cried out, **24** saying, "Let *us* alone! What have we to do with You, Jesus of Nazareth? Did You come to destroy us? I know who You are—the Holy One of God!" **25** But Jesus rebuked him, saying, "Be quiet, and come out of him!" **26** And when the unclean spirit had convulsed him and cried out with a loud voice, he came out of him. **27** Then they were all amazed, so that they questioned among themselves, saying, "What is this? What new doctrine *is* this? For with authority He commands even the unclean spirits, and they obey Him."

Peter's mother-in-law healed.

Matt 8:14–15 Now when Jesus had come into Peter's house, He saw his wife's mother lying sick with a fever. **15** So He touched her hand, and the fever left her. And she arose and served them.

Lepers cleansed.

Matt 8:3 Then Jesus put out *His* hand and touched him,

saying, "I am willing; be cleansed." Immediately his leprosy was cleansed.

Luke 17:14 So when He saw *them,* He said to them, "Go, show yourselves to the priests." And so it was that as they went, they were cleansed.

Paralytic healed.

Mark 2:3–12 Then they came to Him, bringing a paralytic who was carried by four *men.* 4 And when they could not come near Him because of the crowd, they uncovered the roof where He was. So when they had broken through, they let down the bed on which the paralytic was lying. 5 When Jesus saw their faith, He said to the paralytic, "Son, your sins are forgiven you." 6 And some of the scribes were sitting there and reasoning in their hearts, 7 "Why does this *Man* speak blasphemies like this? Who can forgive sins but God alone?" 8 But immediately, when Jesus perceived in His spirit that they reasoned thus within themselves, He said to them, "Why do you reason about these things in your hearts? 9 Which is easier, to say to the paralytic, '*Your* sins are forgiven you,' or to say, 'Arise, take up your bed and walk'? 10 But that you may know that the Son of Man has power on earth to forgive sins"—He said to the paralytic, 11 "I say to you, arise, take up your bed, and go to your house." 12 Immediately he arose, took up the bed, and went out in the presence of them all, so that all were amazed and glorified God, saying, "We never saw *anything* like this!"

Withered hand restored.

Matt 12:10–13 And behold, there was a man who had a withered hand. And they asked Him, saying, "Is it lawful to heal on the Sabbath?"—that they might accuse Him. 11 Then He said to them, "What man is there among you who has one sheep, and if it falls into a pit on the Sabbath, will not lay hold of it and lift *it* out? 12 Of how much more value then is a man than a sheep? Therefore it is lawful to do good on the Sabbath." 13 Then He said to the man, "Stretch out your hand." And he stretched *it* out, and it was restored as whole as the other.

Handicapped man healed.

John 5:5–9 Now a certain man was there who had an infirmity thirty-eight years. 6 When Jesus saw him lying there, and knew that he already had been *in that condition* a long time, He said to him, "Do you want to be made well?" 7 The sick man answered Him, "Sir, I have no man to put me into the pool when the water is stirred up; but while I am coming, another steps down before me." 8 Jesus said to him, "Rise, take up your bed and walk." 9 And immediately the man was made well, took up his bed, and walked. And that day was the Sabbath.

The dead raised to life.

Matt 9:18 While He spoke these things to them, behold, a ruler came and worshiped Him, saying, "My daughter has just died, but come and lay Your hand on her and she will live."

Matt 19:23–25 Then Jesus said to His disciples, "Assuredly, I say to you that it is hard for a rich man to enter the kingdom of heaven. 24 And again I say to you, it is easier for a camel to go through the eye of a needle than for a rich man to enter the kingdom of God." 25 When His disciples heard *it,* they were

greatly astonished, saying, "Who then can be saved?"

Luke 7:12–15 And when He came near the gate of the city, behold, a dead man was being carried out, the only son of his mother; and she was a widow. And a large crowd from the city was with her. 13 When the Lord saw her, He had compassion on her and said to her, "Do not weep." 14 Then He came and touched the open coffin, and those who carried *him* stood still. And He said, "Young man, I say to you, arise." 15 So he who was dead sat up and began to speak. And He presented him to his mother.

Cf. John 11:11–44

Flow of blood stopped.

Matt 9:20–22 And suddenly, a woman who had a flow of blood for twelve years came from behind and touched the hem of His garment. 21 For she said to herself, "If only I may touch His garment, I shall be made well." 22 But Jesus turned around, and when He saw her He said, "Be of good cheer, daughter; your faith has made you well." And the woman was made well from that hour.

The blind restored to sight.

Matt 9:27–30 When Jesus departed from there, two blind men followed Him, crying out and saying, "Son of David, have mercy on us!" 28 And when He had come into the house, the blind men came to Him. And Jesus said to them, "Do you believe that I am able to do this?" They said to Him, "Yes, Lord." 29 Then He touched their eyes, saying, "According to your faith let it be to you." 30 And their eyes were opened. And Jesus sternly warned them, saying, "See *that* no one knows *it.*"

Mark 8:22–25 Then He came to Bethsaida; and they brought a blind man to Him, and begged Him to touch him. 23 So He took the blind man by the hand and led him out of the town. And when He had spit on his eyes and put His hands on him, He asked him if he saw anything. 24 And he looked up and said, "I see men like trees, walking." 25 Then He put *His* hands on his eyes again and made him look up. And he was restored and saw everyone clearly.

John 9:1–7 Now as *Jesus* passed by, He saw a man who was blind from birth. 2 And His disciples asked Him, saying, "Rabbi, who sinned, this man or his parents, that he was born blind?" 3 Jesus answered, "Neither this man nor his parents sinned, but that the works of God should be revealed in him. 4 I must work the works of Him who sent Me while it is day; *the* night is coming when no one can work. 5 As long as I am in the world, I am the light of the world." 6 When He had said these things, He spat on the ground and made clay with the saliva; and He anointed the eyes of the blind man with the clay. 7 And He said to him, "Go, wash in the pool of Siloam" (which is translated, Sent). So he went and washed, and came back seeing.

The deaf and mute cured.

Mark 7:32–35 Then they brought to Him one who was deaf and had an impediment in his speech, and they begged Him to put His hand on him. 33 And He took him aside from the multitude, and put His fingers in his ears, and He spat and touched his tongue. 34 Then, looking up to heaven, He sighed, and said to him, "Ephphatha," that is, "Be opened." 35 Immediately his ears were opened, and the impediment of his tongue was loosed, and he spoke plainly.

The multitudes fed.

Matt 14:15–21 When it was evening, His disciples came to Him, saying, "This is a deserted place, and the hour is already late. Send the multitudes away, that they may go into the villages and buy themselves food." 16 But Jesus said to them, "They do not need to go away. You give them something to eat." 17 And they said to Him, "We have here only five loaves and two fish." 18 He said, "Bring them here to Me." 19 Then He commanded the multitudes to sit down on the grass. And He took the five loaves and the two fish, and looking up to heaven, He blessed and broke and gave the loaves to the disciples; and the disciples gave to the multitudes. 20 So they all ate and were filled, and they took up twelve baskets full of the fragments that remained. 21 Now those who had eaten were about five thousand men, besides women and children.

Matt 15:32–38 Now Jesus called His disciples to *Himself* and said, "I have compassion on the multitude, because they have now continued with Me three days and have nothing to eat. And I do not want to send them away hungry, lest they faint on the way." 33 Then His disciples said to Him, "Where could we get enough bread in the wilderness to fill such a great multitude?" 34 Jesus said to them, "How many loaves do you have?" And they said, "Seven, and a few little fish." 35 So He commanded the multitude to sit down on the ground. 36 And He took the seven loaves and the fish and gave thanks, broke *them* and gave *them* to His disciples; and the disciples *gave* to the multitude. 37 So they all ate and were filled, and they took up seven large baskets full of the fragments that were left. 38 Now those who ate were four thousand men, besides women and children.

His walking on the sea.

Matt 14:25–27 Now in the fourth watch of the night Jesus went to them, walking on the sea. 26 And when the disciples saw Him walking on the sea, they were troubled, saying, "It is a ghost!" And they cried out for fear. 27 But immediately Jesus spoke to them, saying, "Be of good cheer! It is I; do not be afraid."

His allowing Peter to walk on the water.

Matt 14:29 So He said, "Come." And when Peter had come down out of the boat, he walked on the water to go to Jesus.

Storm stilled.

Matt 8:23–26 Now when He got into a boat, His disciples followed Him. 24 And suddenly a great tempest arose on the sea, so that the boat was covered with the waves. But He was asleep. 25 Then His disciples came to *Him* and awoke Him, saying, "Lord, save us! We are perishing!" 26 But He said to them, "Why are you fearful, O you of little faith?" Then He arose and rebuked the winds and the sea, and there was a great calm.

Matt 14:32 And when they got into the boat, the wind ceased.

Sudden arrival of the boat.

John 6:21 Then they willingly received Him into the boat, and immediately the boat was at the land where they were going.

Tribute money.

Matt 17:27 Nevertheless, lest we offend them, go to the sea, cast in a hook, and take the fish that comes up first. And when you have opened its mouth, you will find a piece of money; take that and give it to them for Me and you."

Woman healed of infirmity.

Luke 13:11–13 And behold, there was a woman who had a spirit of infirmity eighteen years, and was bent over and could in no way raise *herself* up. 12 But when Jesus saw her, He called *her* to *Him* and said to her, "Woman, you are loosed from your infirmity." 13 And He laid *His* hands on her, and immediately she was made straight, and glorified God.

Dropsy cured.

Luke 14:2–4 And behold, there was a certain man before Him who had dropsy. 3 And Jesus, answering, spoke to the lawyers and Pharisees, saying, "Is it lawful to heal on the Sabbath?" 4 But they kept silent. And He took *him* and healed him, and let him go.

Fig tree blighted.

Matt 21:19 And seeing a fig tree by the road, He came to it and found nothing on it but leaves, and said to it, "Let no fruit grow on you ever again." Immediately the fig tree withered away.

Malchus healed.

Luke 22:50–51 And one of them struck the servant of the high priest and cut off his right ear. 51 But Jesus answered and said, "Permit even this." And He touched his ear and healed him.

Performed for messengers of John the Baptist.

Luke 7:21–22 And that very hour He cured many of infirmities, afflictions, and evil spirits; and to many blind He gave sight. 22 Jesus answered and said to them, "Go and tell John the things you have seen and heard: that *the* blind see, *the* lame walk, *the* lepers are cleansed, *the* deaf hear, *the* dead are raised, *the* poor have the gospel preached to them.

Many different diseases healed.

Matt 4:23–24 And Jesus went about all Galilee, teaching in their synagogues, preaching the gospel of the kingdom, and healing all kinds of sickness and all kinds of disease among the people. 24 Then His fame went throughout all Syria; and they brought to Him all sick people who were afflicted with various diseases and torments, and those who were demon-possessed, epileptics, and paralytics; and He healed them.

Matt 14:14 And when Jesus went out He saw a great multitude; and He was moved with compassion for them, and healed their sick.

Matt 15:30 Then great multitudes came to Him, having with them *the* lame, blind, mute, maimed, and many others; and they laid them down at Jesus' feet, and He healed them.

Mark 1:34 Then He healed many who were sick with various diseases, and cast out many demons; and He did not allow the demons to speak, because they knew Him.

Luke 6:17–19 And He came down with them and stood on a level place with a crowd of His disciples and a great multitude of people from all Judea and Jerusalem, and from the seacoast of Tyre and Sidon, who came to hear Him and be healed of their diseases, **18** as well as those who were tormented with unclean spirits. And they were healed. **19** And the whole multitude sought to touch Him, for power went out from Him and healed *them* all.

His transfiguration.

Matt 17:1–8 Now after six days Jesus took Peter, James, and John his brother, led them up on a high mountain by themselves; **2** and He was transfigured before them. His face shone like the sun, and His clothes became as white as the light. **3** And behold, Moses and Elijah appeared to them, talking with Him. **4** Then Peter answered and said to Jesus, "Lord, it is good for us to be here; if You wish, let us make here three tabernacles: one for You, one for Moses, and one for Elijah." **5** While he was still speaking, behold, a bright cloud overshadowed them; and suddenly a voice came out of the cloud, saying, "This is My beloved Son, in whom I am well pleased. Hear Him!" **6** And when the disciples heard *it,* they fell on their faces and were greatly afraid. **7** But Jesus came and touched them and said, "Arise, and do not be afraid." **8** When they had lifted up their eyes, they saw no one but Jesus only.

His resurrection.

Matt 28:1–6 Now after the Sabbath, as the first *day* of the week began to dawn, Mary Magdalene and the other Mary came to see the tomb. **2** And behold, there was a great earthquake; for an angel of the Lord descended from heaven, and came and rolled back the stone from the door, and sat on it. **3** His countenance was like lightning, and his clothing as white as snow. **4** And the guards shook for fear of him, and became like dead *men.* **5** But the angel answered and said to the women, "Do not be afraid, for I know that you seek Jesus who was crucified. **6** He is not here; for He is risen, as He said. Come, see the place where the Lord lay.

Mark 16:6 But he said to them, "Do not be alarmed. You seek Jesus of Nazareth, who was crucified. He is risen! He is not here. See the place where they laid Him.

Luke 24:5–6 Then, as they were afraid and bowed *their* faces to the earth, they said to them, "Why do you seek the living among the dead? **6** He is not here, but is risen! Remember how He spoke to you when He was still in Galilee,

John 10:18 No one takes it from Me, but I lay it down of Myself. I have power to lay it down, and I have power to take it again. This command I have received from My Father."

John 20:1–14 Now the first *day* of the week Mary Magdalene went to the tomb early, while it was still dark, and saw *that* the stone had been taken away from the tomb. **2** Then she ran and came to Simon Peter, and to the other disciple, whom Jesus loved, and said to them, "They have taken away the Lord out of the tomb, and we do not know where they have laid Him." **3** Peter therefore went out, and the other disciple, and were going to the tomb. **4** So they both ran together, and the other disciple outran Peter and came to the tomb first. **5** And he, stooping down and

looking in, saw the linen cloths lying *there;* yet he di| not go in. **6** Then Simon Peter came, following him and went into the tomb; and he saw the linen cloth| lying *there,* **7** and the handkerchief that had beer around His head, not lying with the linen cloths, bu folded together in a place by itself. **8** Then the othe: disciple, who came to the tomb first, went in also and he saw and believed. **9** For as yet they did no| know the Scripture, that He must rise again from the dead. **10** Then the disciples went away again to thei| own homes. **11** But Mary stood outside by the tomb weeping, and as she wept she stooped down *and looked* into the tomb. **12** And she saw two angels ir white sitting, one at the head and the other at the feet, where the body of Jesus had lain. **13** Then they said to her, "Woman, why are you weeping?" She said to them, "Because they have taken away my Lord, and I do not know where they have laid Him."| **14** Now when she had said this, she turned around| and saw Jesus standing *there,* and did not know that it was Jesus.

His appearance to His disciples, the doors being shut.

John 20:19 Then, the same day at evening, being the first *day* of the week, when the doors were shut where the disciples were assembled, for fear of the Jews, Jesus came and stood in the midst, and said to them, "Peace *be* with you."

His ascension.

Acts 1:9 Now when He had spoken these things, while they watched, He was taken up, and a cloud received Him out of their sight.

JESUS CHRIST, THE POWER OF
As the Son of God, is the power of God.

John 5:17–19 But Jesus answered them, "My Father has been working until now, and I have been working." **18** Therefore the Jews sought all the more to kill Him, because He not only broke the Sabbath, but also said that God was His Father, making Himself equal with God. **19** Then Jesus answered and said to them, "Most assuredly, I say to you, the Son can do nothing of Himself, but what He sees the Father do; for whatever He does, the Son also does in like manner.

John 10:28–30 And I give them eternal life, and they shall never perish; neither shall anyone snatch them out of My hand. **29** My Father, who has given *them* to Me, is greater than all; and no one is able to snatch *them* out of My Father's hand. **30** I and *My* Father are one."

As man, is from the Father.

Acts 10:38 how God anointed Jesus of Nazareth with the Holy Spirit and with power, who went about doing good and healing all who were oppressed by the devil, for God was with Him.

Described as
Supreme.

Eph 1:20–21 which He worked in Christ when He raised Him from the dead and seated *Him* at His right hand in the heavenly *places,* **21** far above all principality and power and might and dominion, and every name that is named, not only in this age but also in that which is to come.

1 Pet 3:22 who has gone into heaven and is at the right hand of God, angels and authorities and powers having been made subject to Him.

Unlimited.

Matt 28:18 And Jesus came and spoke to them, saying, "All authority has been given to Me in heaven and on earth.

Over all flesh.

John 17:2 as You have given Him authority over all flesh, that He should give eternal life to as many as You have given Him.

Over all things.

John 3:35 The Father loves the Son, and has given all things into His hand.

Eph 1:22 And He put all *things* under His feet, and gave Him *to be* head over all *things* to the church,

Glorious.

2 Thess 1:9 These shall be punished with everlasting destruction from the presence of the Lord and from the glory of His power,

Everlasting.

1 Tim 6:16 who alone has immortality, dwelling in unapproachable light, whom no man has seen or can see, to whom *be* honor and everlasting power. Amen.

Is able to subdue all things.

Phil 3:21 who will transform our lowly body that it may be conformed to His glorious body, according to the working by which He is able even to subdue all things to Himself.

Exhibited in

Creation.

John 1:3 All things were made through Him, and without Him nothing was made that was made.

John 1:10 He was in the world, and the world was made through Him, and the world did not know Him.

Col 1:16 For by Him all things were created that are in heaven and that are on earth, visible and invisible, whether thrones or dominions or principalities or powers. All things were created through Him and for Him.

Upholding all things.

Col 1:17 And He is before all things, and in Him all things consist.

Heb 1:3 who being the brightness of *His* glory and the express image of His person, and upholding all things by the word of His power, when He had by Himself purged our sins, sat down at the right hand of the Majesty on high,

Salvation.

Is 63:1 Who *is* this who comes from Edom, With dyed garments from Bozrah, This *One who is* glorious in His apparel, Traveling in the greatness of His strength?— "I who speak in righteousness, mighty to save."

Heb 7:25 Therefore He is also able to save to the uttermost those who come to God through Him, since He always lives to make intercession for them.

His teaching.

Matt 7:28–29 And so it was, when Jesus had ended these sayings, that the people were astonished at His teaching, **29** for He taught them as one having authority, and not as the scribes.

Luke 4:32 And they were astonished at His teaching, for His word was with authority.

Working of miracles.

Matt 8:27 So the men marveled, saying, "Who can this be, that even the winds and the sea obey Him?"

Luke 5:17 Now it happened on a certain day, as He was teaching, that there were Pharisees and teachers of the law sitting by, who had come out of every town of Galilee, Judea, and Jerusalem. And the power of the Lord was *present* to heal them.

Enabling others to work miracles.

Matt 10:1 And when He had called His twelve disciples to *Him,* He gave them power *over* unclean spirits, to cast them out, and to heal all kinds of sickness and all kinds of disease.

Mark 16:17–18 And these signs will follow those who believe: In My name they will cast out demons; they will speak with new tongues; **18** they will take up serpents; and if they drink anything deadly, it will by no means hurt them; they will lay hands on the sick, and they will recover."

Luke 10:17 Then the seventy returned with joy, saying, "Lord, even the demons are subject to us in Your name."

Forgiving sins.

Matt 9:6 But that you may know that the Son of Man has power on earth to forgive sins"—then He said to the paralytic, "Arise, take up your bed, and go to your house."

Acts 5:31 Him God has exalted to His right hand *to be* Prince and Savior, to give repentance to Israel and forgiveness of sins.

Giving spiritual life.

John 5:21 For as the Father raises the dead and gives life to *them,* even so the Son gives life to whom He will.

John 5:25–26 Most assuredly, I say to you, the hour is coming, and now is, when the dead will hear the voice of the Son of God; and those who hear will live. **26** For as the Father has life in Himself, so He has granted the Son to have life in Himself,

Giving eternal life.

John 17:2 as You have given Him authority over all flesh, that He should give eternal life to as many as You have given Him.

Raising the dead.

John 5:28–29 Do not marvel at this; for the hour is coming in which all who are in the graves will hear His voice **29** and come forth—those who have done good, to the resurrection of life, and those who have done evil, to the resurrection of condemnation.

Raising Himself from the dead.

John 2:19–21 Jesus answered and said to them, "Destroy this temple, and in three days I will raise it up." **20** Then the Jews said, "It has taken forty-six years to build this temple, and will You raise it up in three days?" **21** But He was speaking of the temple of His body.

John 10:18 No one takes it from Me, but I lay it down of Myself. I have power to lay it down, and I have power to take it again. This command I have received from My Father."

Overcoming the world.

John 16:33 These things I have spoken to you, that in Me you may have peace. In the world you will have tribulation; but be of good cheer, I have overcome the world."

Overcoming the devil.

Col 2:15 Having disarmed principalities and powers, He made a public spectacle of them, triumphing over them in it.

Heb 2:14 Inasmuch then as the children have partaken of flesh and blood, He Himself likewise shared in the same, that through death He might destroy him who had the power of death, that is, the devil,

Destroying the works of the devil.

1 John 3:8 He who sins is of the devil, for the devil has sinned from the beginning. For this purpose the Son of God was manifested, that He might destroy the works of the devil.

Ministers should make known.

2 Pet 1:16 For we did not follow cunningly devised fables when we made known to you the power and coming of our Lord Jesus Christ, but were eyewitnesses of His majesty.

Believers

Made willing by.

Ps 110:3 Your people *shall be* volunteers In the day of Your power; In the beauties of holiness, from the womb of the morning, You have the dew of Your youth.

Aided by.

Heb 2:18 For in that He Himself has suffered, being tempted, He is able to aid those who are tempted.

Strengthened by.

Phil 4:13 I can do all things through Christ who strengthens me.

2 Tim 4:17 But the Lord stood with me and strengthened me, so that the message might be preached fully through me, and *that* all the Gentiles might hear. Also I was delivered out of the mouth of the lion.

Preserved by.

2 Tim 1:12 For this reason I also suffer these things; nevertheless I am not ashamed, for I know whom I have believed and am persuaded that He is able to keep what I have committed to Him until that Day.

2 Tim 4:18 And the Lord will deliver me from every evil work and preserve *me* for His heavenly kingdom. To Him *be* glory forever and ever. Amen!

Bodies of, shall be changed by.

Phil 3:21 who will transform our lowly body that it may be conformed to His glorious body, according to the working by which He is able even to subdue all things to Himself.

It rests upon them.

2 Cor 12:9 And He said to me, "My grace is sufficient for you, for My strength is made perfect in weakness." Therefore most gladly I will rather boast in my infirmities, that the power of Christ may rest upon me.

Is present in the assembly of.

1 Cor 5:4 In the name of our Lord Jesus Christ, when you are gathered together, along with my spirit, with the power of our Lord Jesus Christ,

Shall be specially manifested at His second coming.

Mark 13:26 Then they will see the Son of Man coming in the clouds with great power and glory.

2 Pet 1:16 For we did not follow cunningly devised fables when we made known to you the power and coming of our Lord Jesus Christ, but were eyewitnesses of His majesty.

Shall subdue all other power.

1 Cor 15:24 Then *comes* the end, when He delivers the kingdom to God the Father, when He puts an end to all rule and all authority and power.

The wicked shall be destroyed by.

Ps 2:9 You shall break them with a rod of iron; You shall dash them to pieces like a potter's vessel.' "

Is 11:4 But with righteousness He shall judge the poor, And decide with equity for the meek of the earth; He shall strike the earth with the rod of His mouth, And with the breath of His lips He shall slay the wicked.

Is 63:3 "I have trodden the winepress alone, And from the peoples no one *was* with Me. For I have trodden them in My anger, And trampled them in My fury; Their blood is sprinkled upon My garments, And I have stained all My robes.

2 Thess 1:9 These shall be punished with everlasting destruction from the presence of the Lord and from the glory of His power,

JESUS CHRIST, PRECIOUSNESS OF

To God.

Matt 3:17 And suddenly a voice *came* from heaven, saying, "This is My beloved Son, in whom I am well pleased."

1 Pet 2:4 Coming to Him *as to* a living stone, rejected indeed by men, but chosen by God *and* precious,

To believers.

Phil 3:8 Yet indeed I also count all things loss for the excellence of the knowledge of Christ Jesus my Lord, for whom I have suffered the loss of all things, and count them as rubbish, that I may gain Christ

1 Pet 2:7 Therefore, to you who believe, *He is* precious; but to those who are disobedient, *"The stone which the builders rejected Has become the chief cornerstone,"*

Because of His

Goodness and beauty.

Zech 9:17 For how great is its goodness And how great its beauty! Grain shall make the young men thrive, And new wine the young women.

Excellence and grace.

Ps 45:2 You are fairer than the sons of men; Grace is poured upon Your lips; Therefore God has blessed You forever.

Name.

Heb 1:4 having become so much better than the angels,

as He has by inheritance obtained a more excellent name than they.

Atonement.

Heb 12:24 to Jesus the Mediator of the new covenant, and to the blood of sprinkling that speaks better things than *that of* Abel.

1 Pet 1:19 but with the precious blood of Christ, as of a lamb without blemish and without spot.

Words.

John 6:68 But Simon Peter answered Him, "Lord, to whom shall we go? You have the words of eternal life.

Promises.

2 Pet 1:4 by which have been given to us exceedingly great and precious promises, that through these you may be partakers of the divine nature, having escaped the corruption *that is* in the world through lust.

Care and tenderness.

Is 40:11 He will feed His flock like a shepherd; He will gather the lambs with His arm, And carry *them* in His bosom, *And* gently lead those who are with young.

As the cornerstone of the church.

Is 28:16 Therefore thus says the Lord GOD: "Behold, I lay in Zion a stone for a foundation, A tried stone, a precious cornerstone, a sure foundation; Whoever believes will not act hastily.

1 Pet 2:6 Therefore it is also contained in the Scripture, *"Behold, I lay in Zion A chief cornerstone, elect, precious, And he who believes on Him will by no means be put to shame."*

As the source of all grace.

John 1:14 And the Word became flesh and dwelt among us, and we beheld His glory, the glory as of the only begotten of the Father, full of grace and truth.

Col 1:19 For it pleased *the Father that* in Him all the fullness should dwell,

Unsearchable.

Eph 3:8 To me, who am less than the least of all the saints, this grace was given, that I should preach among the Gentiles the unsearchable riches of Christ,

Illustrated.

Matt 13:44–46 "Again, the kingdom of heaven is like treasure hidden in a field, which a man found and hid; and for joy over it he goes and sells all that he has and buys that field. **45** "Again, the kingdom of heaven is like a merchant seeking beautiful pearls, **46** who, when he had found one pearl of great price, went and sold all that he had and bought it.

JESUS CHRIST, PROPHECIES FULFILLED IN

As the Son of God.

Ps 2:7 "I will declare the decree: The LORD has said to Me, 'You *are* My Son, Today I have begotten You.

Fulfilled.

Luke 1:32 He will be great, and will be called the Son of the Highest; and the Lord God will give Him the throne of His father David.

Luke 1:35 And the angel answered and said to her, "The Holy Spirit will come upon you, and the power of the Highest will overshadow you; therefore, also, that Holy One who is to be born will be called the Son of God.

As the seed of the woman.

Gen 3:15 And I will put enmity Between you and the woman, And between your seed and her Seed; He shall bruise your head, And you shall bruise His heel."

Fulfilled.

Gal 4:4 But when the fullness of the time had come, God sent forth His Son, born of a woman, born under the law,

As the seed of Abraham.

Gen 17:7 And I will establish My covenant between Me and you and your descendants after you in their generations, for an everlasting covenant, to be God to you and your descendants after you.

Gen 22:18 In your seed all the nations of the earth shall be blessed, because you have obeyed My voice."

Fulfilled.

Gal 3:16 Now to Abraham and his Seed were the promises made. He does not say, "And to seeds," as of many, but as of one, *"And to your Seed,"* who is Christ.

As the seed of Isaac.

Gen 21:12 But God said to Abraham, "Do not let it be displeasing in your sight because of the lad or because of your bondwoman. Whatever Sarah has said to you, listen to her voice; for in Isaac your seed shall be called.

Fulfilled.

Heb 11:17–19 By faith Abraham, when he was tested, offered up Isaac, and he who had received the promises offered up his only begotten *son,* **18** of whom it was said, *"In Isaac your seed shall be called,"* **19** concluding that God *was* able to raise *him* up, even from the dead, from which he also received him in a figurative sense.

As the seed of David.

Ps 132:11 The LORD has sworn *in* truth to David; He will not turn from it: "I will set upon your throne the fruit of your body.

Jer 23:5 "Behold, *the* days are coming," says the LORD, "That I will raise to David a Branch of righteousness; A King shall reign and prosper, And execute judgment and righteousness in the earth.

Fulfilled.

Acts 13:23 From this man's seed, according to *the* promise, God raised up for Israel a Savior—Jesus—

Rom 1:3 concerning His Son Jesus Christ our Lord, who was born of the seed of David according to the flesh,

His coming at a set time.

Gen 49:10 The scepter shall not depart from Judah, Nor a lawgiver from between his feet, Until Shiloh comes; And to Him *shall be* the obedience of the people.

Dan 9:24–25 "Seventy weeks are determined For your people and for your holy city, To finish the transgression, To make an end of sins, To make reconciliation for iniquity, To bring in everlasting righteousness, To seal up vision and prophecy, And to anoint the Most Holy. **25** "Know therefore and understand,

That from the going forth of the command To restore and build Jerusalem Until Messiah the Prince, *There shall be* seven weeks and sixty-two weeks; The street shall be built again, and the wall, Even in troublesome times.

Fulfilled.

Luke 2:1 And it came to pass in those days *that* a decree went out from Caesar Augustus that all the world should be registered.

His being born of a virgin.

Is 7:14 Therefore the Lord Himself will give you a sign: Behold, the virgin shall conceive and bear a Son, and shall call His name Immanuel.

Fulfilled.

Matt 1:22–23 So all this was done that it might be fulfilled which was spoken by the Lord through the prophet, saying: 23 *"Behold, the virgin shall be with child, and bear a Son, and they shall call His name Immanuel,"* which is translated, "God with us."

Luke 2:7 And she brought forth her firstborn Son, and wrapped Him in swaddling cloths, and laid Him in a manger, because there was no room for them in the inn.

His being called Immanuel.

Is 7:14 Therefore the Lord Himself will give you a sign: Behold, the virgin shall conceive and bear a Son, and shall call His name Immanuel.

Fulfilled.

Matt 1:22–23 So all this was done that it might be fulfilled which was spoken by the Lord through the prophet, saying: 23 *"Behold, the virgin shall be with child, and bear a Son, and they shall call His name Immanuel,"* which is translated, "God with us."

His being born in Bethlehem Ephrathah of Judea.

Mic 5:2 "But you, Bethlehem Ephrathah, *Though* you are little among the thousands of Judah, *Yet* out of you shall come forth to Me The One to be Ruler in Israel, Whose goings forth *are* from of old, From everlasting."

Fulfilled.

Matt 2:1 Now after Jesus was born in Bethlehem of Judea in the days of Herod the king, behold, wise men from the East came to Jerusalem,

Luke 2:4–6 Joseph also went up from Galilee, out of the city of Nazareth, into Judea, to the city of David, which is called Bethlehem, because he was of the house and lineage of David, 5 to be registered with Mary, his betrothed wife, who was with child. 6 So it was, that while they were there, the days were completed for her to be delivered.

Great persons coming to adore him.

Ps 72:10 The kings of Tarshish and of the isles Will bring presents; The kings of Sheba and Seba Will offer gifts.

Fulfilled.

Matt 2:1–11 Now after Jesus was born in Bethlehem of Judea in the days of Herod the king, behold, wise men from the East came to Jerusalem, 2 saying, "Where is He who has been born King of the Jews? For we have seen His star in the East and have come to worship Him." 3 When Herod the king heard *this,* he was troubled, and all Jerusalem with him. 4 And

when he had gathered all the chief priests and scribes of the people together, he inquired of them where the Christ was to be born. 5 So they said to him, "In Bethlehem of Judea, for thus it is written by the prophet: 6 *'But you, Bethlehem, in the land of Judah, Are not the least among the rulers of Judah; For out of you shall come a Ruler Who will shepherd My people Israel.'"* 7 Then Herod, when he had secretly called the wise men, determined from them what time the star appeared. 8 And he sent them to Bethlehem and said, "Go and search carefully for the young Child, and when you have found *Him,* bring back word to me, that I may come and worship Him also." 9 When they heard the king, they departed; and behold, the star which they had seen in the East went before them, till it came and stood over where the young Child was. 10 When they saw the star, they rejoiced with exceedingly great joy. 11 And when they had come into the house, they saw the young Child with Mary His mother, and fell down and worshiped Him. And when they had opened their treasures, they presented gifts to Him: gold, frankincense, and myrrh.

The killing of the children of Bethlehem.

Jer 31:15 Thus says the LORD: "A voice was heard in Ramah, Lamentation *and* bitter weeping, Rachel weeping for her children, Refusing to be comforted for her children, Because they *are* no more."

Fulfilled.

Matt 2:16–18 Then Herod, when he saw that he was deceived by the wise men, was exceedingly angry; and he sent forth and put to death all the male children who were in Bethlehem and in all its districts, from two years old and under, according to the time which he had determined from the wise men. 17 Then was fulfilled what was spoken by Jeremiah the prophet, saying: 18 *"A voice was heard in Ramah, Lamentation, weeping, and great mourning, Rachel weeping for her children, Refusing to be comforted, Because they are no more."*

His being called out of Egypt.

Hos 11:1 "When Israel *was* a child, I loved him, And out of Egypt I called My son.

Fulfilled.

Matt 2:15 and was there until the death of Herod, that it might be fulfilled which was spoken by the Lord through the prophet, saying, *"Out of Egypt I called My Son."*

His being preceded by John the Baptist.

Is 40:3 The voice of one crying in the wilderness: "Prepare the way of the LORD; Make straight in the desert A highway for our God.

Mal 3:1 "Behold, I send My messenger, And he will prepare the way before Me. And the Lord, whom you seek, Will suddenly come to His temple, Even the Messenger of the covenant, In whom you delight. Behold, He is coming," Says the LORD of hosts.

Fulfilled.

Matt 3:1 In those days John the Baptist came preaching in the wilderness of Judea,

Matt 3:3 For this is he who was spoken of by the prophet Isaiah, saying: *"The voice of one crying in the*

wilderness: 'Prepare the way of the LORD; Make His paths straight.' "

Luke 1:17 He will also go before Him in the spirit and power of Elijah, 'to turn the hearts of the fathers to the children,' and the disobedient to the wisdom of the just, to make ready a people prepared for the Lord."

His being anointed with the Spirit.

Ps 45:7 You love righteousness and hate wickedness; Therefore God, Your God, has anointed You With the oil of gladness more than Your companions.

Is 11:2 The Spirit of the LORD shall rest upon Him, The Spirit of wisdom and understanding, The Spirit of counsel and might, The Spirit of knowledge and of the fear of the LORD.

Is 61:1 "The Spirit of the Lord GOD is upon Me, Because the LORD has anointed Me To preach good tidings to the poor; He has sent Me to heal the brokenhearted, To proclaim liberty to the captives, And the opening of the prison to those who are bound;

Fulfilled.

Matt 3:16 When He had been baptized, Jesus came up immediately from the water; and behold, the heavens were opened to Him, and He saw the Spirit of God descending like a dove and alighting upon Him.

John 3:34 For He whom God has sent speaks the words of God, for God does not give the Spirit by measure.

Acts 10:38 how God anointed Jesus of Nazareth with the Holy Spirit and with power, who went about doing good and healing all who were oppressed by the devil, for God was with Him.

His being a prophet like Moses.

Deut 18:15–18 "The LORD your God will raise up for you a Prophet like me from your midst, from your brethren. Him you shall hear, **16** according to all you desired of the LORD your God in Horeb in the day of the assembly, saying, 'Let me not hear again the voice of the LORD my God, nor let me see this great fire anymore, lest I die.' **17** "And the LORD said to me: 'What they have spoken is good. **18** I will raise up for them a Prophet like you from among their brethren, and will put My words in His mouth, and He shall speak to them all that I command Him.

Fulfilled.

Acts 3:20–22 and that He may send Jesus Christ, who was preached to you before, **21** whom heaven must receive until the times of restoration of all things, which God has spoken by the mouth of all His holy prophets since the world began. **22** For Moses truly said to the fathers, 'The LORD your God will raise up for you a Prophet like me from your brethren. Him you shall hear in all things, whatever He says to you.

His being a priest after the order of Melchizedek.

Ps 110:4 The LORD has sworn And will not relent, "You are a priest forever According to the order of Melchizedek."

Fulfilled.

Heb 5:5–6 So also Christ did not glorify Himself to become High Priest, but it was He who said to Him: "You are My Son, Today I have begotten You." **6** As He also says in another place: "You are a priest forever According to the order of Melchizedek";

His entering on His public ministry.

Is 61:1–2 "The Spirit of the Lord GOD is upon Me, Because the LORD has anointed Me To preach good tidings to the poor; He has sent Me to heal the brokenhearted, To proclaim liberty to the captives, And the opening of the prison to those who are bound; **2** To proclaim the acceptable year of the LORD, And the day of vengeance of our God; To comfort all who mourn,

Fulfilled.

Luke 4:16–21 So He came to Nazareth, where He had been brought up. And as His custom was, He went into the synagogue on the Sabbath day, and stood up to read. **17** And He was handed the book of the prophet Isaiah. And when He had opened the book, He found the place where it was written: **18** *"The Spirit of the LORD is upon Me, Because He has anointed Me To preach the gospel to the poor; He has sent Me to heal the brokenhearted, To proclaim liberty to the captives And recovery of sight to the blind, To set at liberty those who are oppressed;* **19** *To proclaim the acceptable year of the LORD."* **20** Then He closed the book, and gave it back to the attendant and sat down. And the eyes of all who were in the synagogue were fixed on Him. **21** And He began to say to them, "Today this Scripture is fulfilled in your hearing."

Luke 4:43 but He said to them, "I must preach the kingdom of God to the other cities also, because for this purpose I have been sent."

His ministry commencing in Galilee.

Is 9:1–2 Nevertheless the gloom will not be upon her who is distressed, As when at first He lightly esteemed The land of Zebulun and the land of Naphtali, And afterward more heavily oppressed her, By the way of the sea, beyond the Jordan, In Galilee of the Gentiles. **2** The people who walked in darkness Have seen a great light; Those who dwelt in the land of the shadow of death, Upon them a light has shined.

Fulfilled.

Matt 4:12–16 Now when Jesus heard that John had been put in prison, He departed to Galilee. **13** And leaving Nazareth, He came and dwelt in Capernaum, which is by the sea, in the regions of Zebulun and Naphtali, **14** that it might be fulfilled which was spoken by Isaiah the prophet, saying: **15** *"The land of Zebulun and the land of Naphtali, By the way of the sea, beyond the Jordan, Galilee of the Gentiles:* **16** *The people who sat in darkness have seen a great light, And upon those who sat in the region and shadow of death Light has dawned."*

Matt 4:23 And Jesus went about all Galilee, teaching in their synagogues, preaching the gospel of the kingdom, and healing all kinds of sickness and all kinds of disease among the people.

His entering publicly into Jerusalem.

Zech 9:9 "Rejoice greatly, O daughter of Zion! Shout, O daughter of Jerusalem! Behold, your King is coming to you; He is just and having salvation, Lowly and riding on a donkey, A colt, the foal of a donkey.

Fulfilled.

Matt 21:1–5 Now when they drew near Jerusalem, and

came to Bethphage, at the Mount of Olives, then Jesus sent two disciples, **2** saying to them, "Go into the village opposite you, and immediately you will find a donkey tied, and a colt with her. Loose *them* and bring *them* to Me. **3** And if anyone says anything to you, you shall say, 'The Lord has need of them,' and immediately he will send them." **4** All this was done that it might be fulfilled which was spoken by the prophet, saying: **5** *"Tell the daughter of Zion, 'Behold, your King is coming to you, Lowly, and sitting on a donkey, A colt, the foal of a donkey.' "*

His coming into the temple.

Hag 2:7 and I will shake all nations, and they shall come to the Desire of All Nations, and I will fill this temple with glory,' says the LORD of hosts.

Hag 2:9 'The glory of this latter temple shall be greater than the former,' says the LORD of hosts. 'And in this place I will give peace,' says the LORD of hosts."

Mal 3:1 "Behold, I send My messenger, And he will prepare the way before Me. And the Lord, whom you seek, Will suddenly come to His temple, Even the Messenger of the covenant, In whom you delight. Behold, He is coming," Says the LORD of hosts.

Fulfilled.

Matt 21:12 Then Jesus went into the temple of God and drove out all those who bought and sold in the temple, and overturned the tables of the money changers and the seats of those who sold doves.

Luke 2:27–32 So he came by the Spirit into the temple. And when the parents brought in the Child Jesus, to do for Him according to the custom of the law, **28** he took Him up in his arms and blessed God and said: **29** "Lord, now You are letting Your servant depart in peace, According to Your word; **30** For my eyes have seen Your salvation **31** Which You have prepared before the face of all peoples, **32** A light to *bring* revelation to the Gentiles, And the glory of Your people Israel."

John 2:13–16 Now the Passover of the Jews was at hand, and Jesus went up to Jerusalem. **14** And He found in the temple those who sold oxen and sheep and doves, and the money changers doing business. **15** When He had made a whip of cords, He drove them all out of the temple, with the sheep and the oxen, and poured out the changers' money and overturned the tables. **16** And He said to those who sold doves, "Take these things away! Do not make My Father's house a house of merchandise!"

His poverty.

Is 53:2 For He shall grow up before Him as a tender plant, And as a root out of dry ground. He has no form or comeliness; And when we see Him, *There is* no beauty that we should desire Him.

Fulfilled.

Mark 6:3 Is this not the carpenter, the Son of Mary, and brother of James, Joses, Judas, and Simon? And are not His sisters here with us?" So they were offended at Him.

Luke 9:58 And Jesus said to him, "Foxes have holes and birds of the air *have* nests, but the Son of Man has nowhere to lay His head."

His meekness.

Is 42:2 He will not cry out, nor raise *His voice*, Nor cause His voice to be heard in the street.

Fulfilled.

Matt 12:15–16 But when Jesus knew *it*, He withdrew from there. And great multitudes followed Him, and He healed them all. **16** Yet He warned them not to make Him known,

Matt 12:19 *He will not quarrel nor cry out, Nor will anyone hear His voice in the streets.*

His tenderness and compassion.

Is 40:11 He will feed His flock like a shepherd; He will gather the lambs with His arm, And carry *them* in His bosom, *And* gently lead those who are with young.

Is 42:3 A bruised reed He will not break, And smoking flax He will not quench; He will bring forth justice for truth.

Fulfilled.

Matt 12:15 But when Jesus knew *it*, He withdrew from there. And great multitudes followed Him, and He healed them all.

Matt 12:20 *A bruised reed He will not break, And smoking flax He will not quench, Till He sends forth justice to victory;*

Heb 4:15 For we do not have a High Priest who cannot sympathize with our weaknesses, but was in all *points* tempted as *we are, yet* without sin.

His being without deceit.

Is 53:9 And they made His grave with the wicked— But with the rich at His death, Because He had done no violence, Nor *was any* deceit in His mouth.

Fulfilled.

1 Pet 2:22 *"Who committed no sin, Nor was deceit found in His mouth";*

His zeal.

Ps 69:9 Because zeal for Your house has eaten me up, And the reproaches of those who reproach You have fallen on me.

Fulfilled.

John 2:17 Then His disciples remembered that it was written, *"Zeal for Your house has eaten Me up."*

His preaching by parables.

Ps 78:2 I will open my mouth in a parable; I will utter dark sayings of old,

Fulfilled.

Matt 13:34–35 All these things Jesus spoke to the multitude in parables; and without a parable He did not speak to them, **35** that it might be fulfilled which was spoken by the prophet, saying: *"I will open My mouth in parables; I will utter things kept secret from the foundation of the world."*

His working miracles.

Is 35:5–6 Then the eyes of the blind shall be opened, And the ears of the deaf shall be unstopped. **6** Then the lame shall leap like a deer, And the tongue of the dumb sing. For waters shall burst forth in the wilderness, And streams in the desert.

Fulfilled.

Matt 11:4–6 Jesus answered and said to them, "Go and tell John the things which you hear and see: **5** The blind see and *the* lame walk; *the* lepers are cleansed and *the* deaf hear; *the* dead are raised up and *the* poor have the gospel preached to them. 6 And blessed is he who is not offended because of Me."

John 11:47 Then the chief priests and the Pharisees gathered a council and said, "What shall we do? For this Man works many signs.

His bearing reproach.

Ps 22:6 But I *am* a worm, and no man; A reproach of men, and despised by the people.

Ps 69:7 Because for Your sake I have borne reproach; Shame has covered my face.

Ps 69:9 Because zeal for Your house has eaten me up, And the reproaches of those who reproach You have fallen on me.

Ps 69:20 Reproach has broken my heart, And I am full of heaviness; I looked *for someone* to take pity, but *there was* none; And for comforters, but I found none.

Fulfilled.

Rom 15:3 For even Christ did not please Himself; but as it is written, *"The reproaches of those who reproached You fell on Me."*

His being rejected by His brethren.

Ps 69:8 I have become a stranger to my brothers, And an alien to my mother's children;

Is 63:3 "I have trodden the winepress alone, And from the peoples no one *was* with Me. For I have trodden them in My anger, And trampled them in My fury; Their blood is sprinkled upon My garments, And I have stained all My robes.

Fulfilled.

John 1:11 He came to His own, and His own did not receive Him.

John 7:3 His brothers therefore said to Him, "Depart from here and go into Judea, that Your disciples also may see the works that You are doing.

His being a stone of stumbling to the Jews.

Is 8:14 He will be as a sanctuary, But a stone of stumbling and a rock of offense To both the houses of Israel, As a trap and a snare to the inhabitants of Jerusalem.

Fulfilled.

Rom 9:32 Why? Because *they did* not *seek it* by faith, but as it were, by the works of the law. For they stumbled at that stumbling stone.

1 Pet 2:8 and *"A stone of stumbling And a rock of offense."* They stumble, being disobedient to the word, to which they also were appointed.

His being hated by the Jews.

Ps 69:4 Those who hate me without a cause Are more than the hairs of my head; They are mighty who would destroy me, *Being* my enemies wrongfully; Though I have stolen nothing, I *still* must restore *it.*

Is 49:7 Thus says the LORD, The Redeemer of Israel, their Holy One, To Him whom man despises, To Him whom the nation abhors, To the Servant of rulers: "Kings shall see and arise, Princes also shall worship, Because of the LORD who is faithful, The Holy One of Israel; And He has chosen You."

Fulfilled.

John 15:24–25 If I had not done among them the works which no one else did, they would have no sin; but now they have seen and also hated both Me and My Father. 25 But *this happened* that the word might be fulfilled which is written in their law, *'They hated Me without a cause.'*

His being rejected by the Jewish rulers.

Ps 118:22 The stone *which* the builders rejected Has become the chief cornerstone.

Fulfilled.

Matt 21:42 Jesus said to them, "Have you never read in the Scriptures: *'The stone which the builders rejected Has become the chief cornerstone. This was the LORD's doing, And it is marvelous in our eyes'*?

John 7:48 Have any of the rulers or the Pharisees believed in Him?

That the Jews and Gentiles should combine against Him.

Ps 2:1–2 Why do the nations rage, And the people plot a vain thing? 2 The kings of the earth set themselves, And the rulers take counsel together, Against the LORD and against His Anointed, *saying,*

Fulfilled.

Luke 23:12 That very day Pilate and Herod became friends with each other, for previously they had been at enmity with each other.

Acts 4:27 "For truly against Your holy Servant Jesus, whom You anointed, both Herod and Pontius Pilate, with the Gentiles and the people of Israel, were gathered together

His being betrayed by a friend.

Ps 41:9 Even my own familiar friend in whom I trusted, Who ate my bread, Has lifted up *his* heel against me.

Ps 55:12–14 For *it is* not an enemy *who* reproaches me; Then I could bear *it.* Nor *is it* one *who* hates me who has exalted *himself* against me; Then I could hide from him. 13 But *it was* you, a man my equal, My companion and my acquaintance. 14 We took sweet counsel together, *And* walked to the house of God in the throng.

Fulfilled.

John 13:18 "I do not speak concerning all of you. I know whom I have chosen; but that the Scripture may be fulfilled, *'He who eats bread with Me has lifted up his heel against Me.'*

John 13:21 When Jesus had said these things, He was troubled in spirit, and testified and said, "Most assuredly, I say to you, one of you will betray Me."

His disciples forsaking Him.

Zech 13:7 "Awake, O sword, against My Shepherd, Against the Man who is My Companion," Says the LORD of hosts. "Strike the Shepherd, And the sheep will be scattered; Then I will turn My hand against the little ones.

Fulfilled.

Matt 26:31 Then Jesus said to them, "All of you will be made to stumble because of Me this night, for it is written: *'I will strike the Shepherd, And the sheep of the flock will be scattered.'*

Matt 26:56 But all this was done that the Scriptures of

the prophets might be fulfilled." Then all the disciples forsook Him and fled.

His being sold for thirty pieces of silver.

Zech 11:12 Then I said to them, "If it is agreeable to you, give *me* my wages; and if not, refrain." So they weighed out for my wages thirty *pieces* of silver.

Fulfilled.

Matt 26:15 and said, "What are you willing to give me if I deliver Him to you?" And they counted out to him thirty pieces of silver.

His price being given for the potter's field.

Zech 11:13 And the LORD said to me, "Throw it to the potter"—that princely price they set on me. So I took the thirty *pieces* of silver and threw them into the house of the LORD for the potter.

Fulfilled.

Matt 27:7 And they consulted together and bought with them the potter's field, to bury strangers in.

The intensity of His sufferings.

Ps 22:14–15 I am poured out like water, And all My bones are out of joint; My heart is like wax; It has melted within Me. **15** My strength is dried up like a potsherd, And My tongue clings to My jaws; You have brought Me to the dust of death.

Fulfilled.

Luke 22:42 saying, "Father, if it is Your will, take this cup away from Me; nevertheless not My will, but Yours, be done."

Luke 22:44 And being in agony, He prayed more earnestly. Then His sweat became like great drops of blood falling down to the ground.

His sufferings being for others.

Is 53:4–6 Surely He has borne our griefs And carried our sorrows; Yet we esteemed Him stricken, Smitten by God, and afflicted. **5** But He *was* wounded for our transgressions, *He was* bruised for our iniquities; The chastisement for our peace *was* upon Him, And by His stripes we are healed. **6** All we like sheep have gone astray; We have turned, every one, to his own way; And the LORD has laid on Him the iniquity of us all.

Is 53:12 Therefore I will divide Him a portion with the great, And He shall divide the spoil with the strong, Because He poured out His soul unto death, And He was numbered with the transgressors, And He bore the sin of many, And made intercession for the transgressors.

Dan 9:26 "And after the sixty-two weeks Messiah shall be cut off, but not for Himself; And the people of the prince who is to come Shall destroy the city and the sanctuary. The end of it *shall be* with a flood, And till the end of the war desolations are determined.

Fulfilled.

Matt 20:28 just as the Son of Man did not come to be served, but to serve, and to give His life a ransom for many."

His patience and silence under suffering.

Is 53:7 He was oppressed and He was afflicted, Yet He opened not His mouth; He was led as a lamb to the slaughter, And as a sheep before its shearers is silent, So He opened not His mouth.

Fulfilled.

Matt 26:63 But Jesus kept silent. And the high priest answered and said to Him, "I put You under oath by the living God: Tell us if You are the Christ, the Son of God!"

Matt 27:12–14 And while He was being accused by the chief priests and elders, He answered nothing. **13** Then Pilate said to Him, "Do You not hear how many things they testify against You?" **14** But He answered him not one word, so that the governor marveled greatly.

His being struck on the cheek.

Mic 5:1 Now gather yourself in troops, O daughter of troops; He has laid siege against us; They will strike the judge of Israel with a rod on the cheek.

Fulfilled.

Matt 27:30 Then they spat on Him, and took the reed and struck Him on the head.

His visage being marred.

Is 52:14 Just as many were astonished at you, So His visage was marred more than any man, And His form more than the sons of men;

Is 53:3 He is despised and rejected by men, A Man of sorrows and acquainted with grief. And we hid, as it were, *our* faces from Him; He was despised, and we did not esteem Him.

Fulfilled.

John 19:5 Then Jesus came out, wearing the crown of thorns and the purple robe. And *Pilate* said to them, "Behold the Man!"

His being spit on and scourged.

Is 50:6 I gave My back to those who struck *Me,* And My cheeks to those who plucked out the beard; I did not hide My face from shame and spitting.

Fulfilled.

Mark 14:65 Then some began to spit on Him, and to blindfold Him, and to beat Him, and to say to Him, "Prophesy!" And the officers struck Him with the palms of their hands.

John 19:1 So then Pilate took Jesus and scourged *Him.*

His hands and feet being nailed to the cross.

Ps 22:16 For dogs have surrounded Me; The congregation of the wicked has enclosed Me. They pierced My hands and My feet;

Fulfilled.

John 19:18 where they crucified Him, and two others with Him, one on either side, and Jesus in the center.

John 20:25 The other disciples therefore said to him, "We have seen the Lord." So he said to them, "Unless I see in His hands the print of the nails, and put my finger into the print of the nails, and put my hand into His side, I will not believe."

His being forsaken by God.

Ps 22:1 My God, My God, why have You forsaken Me? *Why are You so* far from helping Me, *And from* the words of My groaning?

Fulfilled.

Matt 27:46 And about the ninth hour Jesus cried out with a loud voice, saying, "Eli, Eli, lama sabachthani?" that is, *"My God, My God, why have You forsaken Me?"*

His being mocked.

Ps 22:7–8 All those who see Me ridicule Me; They shoot out the lip, they shake the head, *saying,* **8** "He trusted in the LORD, let Him rescue Him; Let Him deliver Him, since He delights in Him!"

Fulfilled.

Matt 27:39–44 And those who passed by blasphemed Him, wagging their heads **40** and saying, "You who destroy the temple and build *it* in three days, save Yourself! If You are the Son of God, come down from the cross." **41** Likewise the chief priests also, mocking with the scribes and elders, said, **42** "He saved others; Himself He cannot save. If He is the King of Israel, let Him now come down from the cross, and we will believe Him. **43** He trusted in God; let Him deliver Him now if He will have Him; for He said, 'I am the Son of God.'" **44** Even the robbers who were crucified with Him reviled Him with the same thing.

Gall and vinegar being given Him to drink.

Ps 69:21 They also gave me gall for my food, And for my thirst they gave me vinegar to drink.

Fulfilled.

Matt 27:34 they gave Him sour wine mingled with gall to drink. But when He had tasted *it,* He would not drink.

His garments being parted, and lots cast for His clothing.

Ps 22:18 They divide My garments among them, And for My clothing they cast lots.

Fulfilled.

Matt 27:35 Then they crucified Him, and divided His garments, casting lots, that it might be fulfilled which was spoken by the prophet: *"They divided My garments among them, And for My clothing they cast lots."*

His being numbered with the transgressors.

Is 53:12 Therefore I will divide Him a portion with the great, And He shall divide the spoil with the strong, Because He poured out His soul unto death, And He was numbered with the transgressors, And He bore the sin of many, And made intercession for the transgressors.

Fulfilled.

Mark 15:28 So the Scripture was fulfilled which says, *"And He was numbered with the transgressors."*

His intercession for His murderers.

Is 53:12 Therefore I will divide Him a portion with the great, And He shall divide the spoil with the strong, Because He poured out His soul unto death, And He was numbered with the transgressors, And He bore the sin of many, And made intercession for the transgressors.

Fulfilled.

Luke 23:34 Then Jesus said, "Father, forgive them, for they do not know what they do." And they divided His garments and cast lots.

His death.

Is 53:12 Therefore I will divide Him a portion with the great, And He shall divide the spoil with the strong,

Because He poured out His soul unto death, And He was numbered with the transgressors, And He bore the sin of many, And made intercession for the transgressors.

Fulfilled.

Matt 27:50 And Jesus cried out again with a loud voice, and yielded up His spirit.

That not a bone of His should be broken.

Ex 12:46 In one house it shall be eaten; you shall not carry any of the flesh outside the house, nor shall you break one of its bones.

Ps 34:20 He guards all his bones; Not one of them is broken.

Fulfilled.

John 19:33 But when they came to Jesus and saw that He was already dead, they did not break His legs.

John 19:36 For these things were done that the Scripture should be fulfilled, *"Not one of His bones shall be broken."*

His being pierced.

Zech 12:10 "And I will pour on the house of David and on the inhabitants of Jerusalem the Spirit of grace and supplication; then they will look on Me whom they pierced. Yes, they will mourn for Him as one mourns for *his* only *son,* and grieve for Him as one grieves for a firstborn.

Fulfilled.

John 19:34 But one of the soldiers pierced His side with a spear, and immediately blood and water came out.

John 19:37 And again another Scripture says, *"They shall look on Him whom they pierced."*

His being buried with the rich.

Is 53:9 And they made His grave with the wicked— But with the rich at His death, Because He had done no violence, Nor *was any* deceit in His mouth.

Fulfilled.

Matt 27:57–60 Now when evening had come, there came a rich man from Arimathea, named Joseph, who himself had also become a disciple of Jesus. **58** This man went to Pilate and asked for the body of Jesus. Then Pilate commanded the body to be given to him. **59** When Joseph had taken the body, he wrapped it in a clean linen cloth, **60** and laid it in his new tomb which he had hewn out of the rock; and he rolled a large stone against the door of the tomb, and departed.

His flesh not seeing corruption.

Ps 16:10 For You will not leave my soul in Sheol, Nor will You allow Your Holy One to see corruption.

Fulfilled.

Acts 2:31 he, foreseeing this, spoke concerning the resurrection of the Christ, that His soul was not left in Hades, nor did His flesh see corruption.

His resurrection.

Ps 16:10 For You will not leave my soul in Sheol, Nor will You allow Your Holy One to see corruption.

Is 26:19 Your dead shall live; *Together with* my dead body they shall arise. Awake and sing, you who dwell in dust; For your dew *is like* the dew of herbs, And the earth shall cast out the dead.

Fulfilled.

Luke 24:6 He is not here, but is risen! Remember how He spoke to you when He was still in Galilee,

Luke 24:31 Then their eyes were opened and they knew Him; and He vanished from their sight.

Luke 24:34 saying, "The Lord is risen indeed, and has appeared to Simon!"

His ascension.

Ps 68:18 You have ascended on high, You have led captivity captive; You have received gifts among men, Even *from* the rebellious, That the LORD God might dwell *there.*

Fulfilled.

Luke 24:51 Now it came to pass, while He blessed them, that He was parted from them and carried up into heaven.

Acts 1:9 Now when He had spoken these things, while they watched, He was taken up, and a cloud received Him out of their sight.

His sitting on the right hand of God.

Ps 110:1 The LORD said to my Lord, "Sit at My right hand, Till I make Your enemies Your footstool."

Fulfilled.

Heb 1:3 who being the brightness of *His* glory and the express image of His person, and upholding all things by the word of His power, when He had by Himself purged our sins, sat down at the right hand of the Majesty on high,

His exercising the priestly office in heaven.

Zech 6:13 Yes, He shall build the temple of the LORD. He shall bear the glory, And shall sit and rule on His throne; So He shall be a priest on His throne, And the counsel of peace shall be between them both." '

Fulfilled.

Rom 8:34 Who *is* he who condemns? *It is* Christ who died, and furthermore is also risen, who is even at the right hand of God, who also makes intercession for us.

His being the chief cornerstone of the church.

Is 28:16 Therefore thus says the Lord GOD: "Behold, I lay in Zion a stone for a foundation, A tried stone, a precious cornerstone, a sure foundation; Whoever believes will not act hastily.

Fulfilled.

1 Pet 2:6–7 Therefore it is also contained in the Scripture, *"Behold, I lay in Zion A chief cornerstone, elect, precious, And he who believes on Him will by no means be put to shame."* 7 Therefore, to you who believe, *He is* precious; but to those who are disobedient, *"The stone which the builders rejected Has become the chief cornerstone,"*

His being king in Zion.

Ps 2:6 "Yet I have set My King On My holy hill of Zion."

Fulfilled.

Luke 1:32 He will be great, and will be called the Son of the Highest; and the Lord God will give Him the throne of His father David.

John 18:33–37 Then Pilate entered the Praetorium again, called Jesus, and said to Him, "Are You the King of the Jews?" 34 Jesus answered him, "Are you speaking for yourself about this, or did others tell you this concerning Me?" 35 Pilate answered, "Am I a Jew? Your own nation and the chief priests have delivered You to me. What have You done?" 36 Jesus answered, "My kingdom is not of this world. If My kingdom were of this world, My servants would fight, so that I should not be delivered to the Jews; but now My kingdom is not from here." 37 Pilate therefore said to Him, "Are You a king then?" Jesus answered, "You say *rightly* that I am a king. For this cause I was born, and for this cause I have come into the world, that I should bear witness to the truth. Everyone who is of the truth hears My voice."

The conversion of the Gentiles to Him.

Is 11:10 "And in that day there shall be a Root of Jesse, Who shall stand as a banner to the people; For the Gentiles shall seek Him, And His resting place shall be glorious."

Is 42:1 "Behold! My Servant whom I uphold, My Elect One *in whom* My soul delights! I have put My Spirit upon Him; He will bring forth justice to the Gentiles.

Fulfilled.

Matt 1:17 So all the generations from Abraham to David *are* fourteen generations, from David until the captivity in Babylon *are* fourteen generations, and from the captivity in Babylon until the Christ *are* fourteen generations.

Matt 1:21 And she will bring forth a Son, and you shall call His name JESUS, for He will save His people from their sins."

John 10:16 And other sheep I have which are not of this fold; them also I must bring, and they will hear My voice; and there will be one flock *and* one shepherd.

Acts 10:45 And those of the circumcision who believed were astonished, as many as came with Peter, because the gift of the Holy Spirit had been poured out on the Gentiles also.

Acts 10:47 "Can anyone forbid water, that these should not be baptized who have received the Holy Spirit just as we *have?"*

His righteous government.

Ps 45:6–7 Your throne, O God, *is* forever and ever; A scepter of righteousness *is* the scepter of Your kingdom. 7 You love righteousness and hate wickedness; Therefore God, Your God, has anointed You With the oil of gladness more than Your companions.

Fulfilled.

John 5:30 I can of Myself do nothing. As I hear, I judge; and My judgment is righteous, because I do not seek My own will but the will of the Father who sent Me.

Rev 19:11 Now I saw heaven opened, and behold, a white horse. And He who sat on him *was* called Faithful and True, and in righteousness He judges and makes war.

His universal dominion.

Ps 72:8 He shall have dominion also from sea to sea, And from the River to the ends of the earth.

Dan 7:14 Then to Him was given dominion and glory and a kingdom, That all peoples, nations, and languages should serve Him. His dominion *is* an everlasting dominion, Which shall not pass away, And His kingdom the one Which shall not be destroyed.

Fulfilled.

Phil 2:9 Therefore God also has highly exalted Him and given Him the name which is above every name,

Phil 2:11 and *that* every tongue should confess that Jesus Christ *is* Lord, to the glory of God the Father.

The perpetuity of His kingdom.

Is 9:7 Of the increase of *His* government and peace *There will be* no end, Upon the throne of David and over His kingdom, To order it and establish it with judgment and justice From that time forward, even forever. The zeal of the Lord of hosts will perform this.

Dan 7:14 Then to Him was given dominion and glory and a kingdom, That all peoples, nations, and languages should serve Him. His dominion *is* an everlasting dominion, Which shall not pass away, And His kingdom *the one* Which shall not be destroyed.

Fulfilled.

Luke 1:32–33 He will be great, and will be called the Son of the Highest; and the Lord God will give Him the throne of His father David. **33** And He will reign over the house of Jacob forever, and of His kingdom there will be no end."

JESUS CHRIST, THE PROPHET

Foretold.

Deut 18:15 "The LORD your God will raise up for you a Prophet like me from your midst, from your brethren. Him you shall hear,

Deut 18:18 I will raise up for them a Prophet like you from among their brethren, and will put My words in His mouth, and He shall speak to them all that I command Him.

Is 52:7 How beautiful upon the mountains Are the feet of him who brings good news, Who proclaims peace, Who brings glad tidings of good *things*, Who proclaims salvation, Who says to Zion, "Your God reigns!"

Anointed with the Holy Spirit.

Is 42:1 "Behold! My Servant whom I uphold, My Elect One *in whom* My soul delights! I have put My Spirit upon Him; He will bring forth justice to the Gentiles.

Is 61:1 "The Spirit of the Lord GOD *is* upon Me, Because the LORD has anointed Me To preach good tidings to the poor; He has sent Me to heal the brokenhearted, To proclaim liberty to the captives, And the opening of the prison to *those who are* bound;

Luke 4:18 *"The Spirit of the LORD is upon Me, Because He has anointed Me To preach the gospel to the poor; He has sent Me to heal the brokenhearted, To proclaim liberty to the captives And recovery of sight to the blind, To set at liberty those who are oppressed;*

John 3:34 For He whom God has sent speaks the words of God, for God does not give the Spirit by measure.

Alone knows and reveals God.

Matt 11:27 All things have been delivered to Me by My Father, and no one knows the Son except the Father. Nor does anyone know the Father except the Son, and *the one* to whom the Son wills to reveal *Him*.

John 3:2 This man came to Jesus by night and said to Him, "Rabbi, we know that You are a teacher come

from God; for no one can do these signs that You do unless God is with him."

John 3:13 No one has ascended to heaven but He who came down from heaven, *that is,* the Son of Man who is in heaven.

John 3:34 For He whom God has sent speaks the words of God, for God does not give the Spirit by measure.

John 17:6 "I have manifested Your name to the men whom You have given Me out of the world. They were Yours, You gave them to Me, and they have kept Your word.

John 17:14 I have given them Your word; and the world has hated them because they are not of the world, just as I am not of the world.

John 17:26 And I have declared to them Your name, and will declare *it*, that the love with which You loved Me may be in them, and I in them."

Heb 1:1–2 God, who at various times and in various ways spoke in time past to the fathers by the prophets, **2** has in these last days spoken to us by *His* Son, whom He has appointed heir of all things, through whom also He made the worlds;

Same doctrine as the Father's.

John 8:26 I have many things to say and to judge concerning you, but He who sent Me is true; and I speak to the world those things which I heard from Him."

John 8:28 Then Jesus said to them, "When you lift up the Son of Man, then you will know that I am *He,* and *that* I do nothing of Myself; but as My Father taught Me, I speak these things.

John 12:49–50 For I have not spoken on My own *authority;* but the Father who sent Me gave Me a command, what I should say and what I should speak. **50** And I know that His command is everlasting life. Therefore, whatever I speak, just as the Father has told Me, so I speak."

John 14:10 Do you not believe that I am in the Father, and the Father in Me? The words that I speak to you I do not speak on My own *authority;* but the Father who dwells in Me does the works.

John 14:24 He who does not love Me does not keep My words; and the word which you hear is not Mine but the Father's who sent Me.

John 15:15 No longer do I call you servants, for a servant does not know what his master is doing; but I have called you friends, for all things that I heard from My Father I have made known to you.

John 17:8 For I have given to them the words which You have given Me; and they have received *them*, and have known surely that I came forth from You; and they have believed that You sent Me.

John 17:16 They are not of the world, just as I am not of the world.

Preached the gospel, worked miracles.

Matt 4:23 And Jesus went about all Galilee, teaching in their synagogues, preaching the gospel of the kingdom, and healing all kinds of sickness and all kinds of disease among the people.

Matt 11:5 *The* blind see and *the* lame walk; *the* lepers are cleansed and *the* deaf hear; *the* dead are raised up and *the* poor have the gospel preached to them.

Luke 4:43 but He said to them, "I must preach the kingdom of God to the other cities also, because for this purpose I have been sent."

Foretold things to come.

Matt 24:3–35 Now as He sat on the Mount of Olives, the disciples came to Him privately, saying, "Tell us, when will these things be? And what *will be* the sign of Your coming, and of the end of the age?" **4** And Jesus answered and said to them: "Take heed that no one deceives you. **5** For many will come in My name, saying, 'I am the Christ,' and will deceive many. **6** And you will hear of wars and rumors of wars. See that you are not troubled; for all *these things* must come to pass, but the end is not yet. **7** For nation will rise against nation, and kingdom against kingdom. And there will be famines, pestilences, and earthquakes in various places. **8** All these *are* the beginning of sorrows. **9** "Then they will deliver you up to tribulation and kill you, and you will be hated by all nations for My name's sake. **10** And then many will be offended, will betray one another, and will hate one another. **11** Then many false prophets will rise up and deceive many. **12** And because lawlessness will abound, the love of many will grow cold. **13** But he who endures to the end shall be saved. **14** And this gospel of the kingdom will be preached in all the world as a witness to all the nations, and then the end will come. **15** "Therefore when you see the *'abomination of desolation,'* spoken of by Daniel the prophet, standing in the holy place" (whoever reads, let him understand), **16** "then let those who are in Judea flee to the mountains. **17** Let him who is on the housetop not go down to take anything out of his house. **18** And let him who is in the field not go back to get his clothes. **19** But woe to those who are pregnant and to those who are nursing babies in those days! **20** And pray that your flight may not be in winter or on the Sabbath. **21** For then there will be great tribulation, such as has not been since the beginning of the world until this time, no, nor ever shall be. **22** And unless those days were shortened, no flesh would be saved; but for the elect's sake those days will be shortened. **23** "Then if anyone says to you, 'Look, here *is* the Christ!' or 'There!' do not believe *it*. **24** For false christs and false prophets will rise and show great signs and wonders to deceive, if possible, even the elect. **25** See, I have told you beforehand. **26** "Therefore if they say to you, 'Look, He is in the desert!' do not go out; *or* 'Look, *He is* in the inner rooms!' do not believe *it*. **27** For as the lightning comes from the east and flashes to the west, so also will the coming of the Son of Man be. **28** For wherever the carcass is, there the eagles will be gathered together. **29** "Immediately after the tribulation of those days the sun will be darkened, and the moon will not give its light; the stars will fall from heaven, and the powers of the heavens will be shaken. **30** Then the sign of the Son of Man will appear in heaven, and then all the tribes of the earth will mourn, and they will see the Son of Man coming on the clouds of heaven with power and great glory. **31** And He will send His angels with a great sound of a trumpet, and they will gather together His elect from the four winds, from one end of heaven to the other. **32** "Now learn this parable from the fig tree: When its branch has already become tender and puts

forth leaves, you know that summer *is* near. **33** So you also, when you see all these things, know that it is near—at the doors! **34** Assuredly, I say to you, this generation will by no means pass away till all these things take place. **35** Heaven and earth will pass away, but My words will by no means pass away.

Luke 19:41 Now as He drew near, He saw the city and wept over it,

Luke 19:44 and level you, and your children within you, to the ground; and they will not leave in you one stone upon another, because you did not know the time of your visitation."

Faithful to His trust.

Luke 4:43 but He said to them, "I must preach the kingdom of God to the other cities also, because for this purpose I have been sent."

John 17:8 For I have given to them the words which You have given Me; and they have received *them*, and have known surely that I came forth from You; and they have believed that You sent Me.

Heb 3:2 who was faithful to Him who appointed Him, as Moses also *was faithful* in all His house.

Rev 1:5 and from Jesus Christ, the faithful witness, the firstborn from the dead, and the ruler over the kings of the earth. To Him who loved us and washed us from our sins in His own blood,

Rev 3:14 "And to the angel of the church of the Laodiceans write, 'These things says the Amen, the Faithful and True Witness, the Beginning of the creation of God:

Full of wisdom.

Luke 2:40 And the Child grew and became strong in spirit, filled with wisdom; and the grace of God was upon Him.

Luke 2:47 And all who heard Him were astonished at His understanding and answers.

Luke 2:52 And Jesus increased in wisdom and stature, and in favor with God and men.

Col 2:3 in whom are hidden all the treasures of wisdom and knowledge.

Mighty in word and deed.

Matt 13:54 When He had come to His own country, He taught them in their synagogue, so that they were astonished and said, "Where did this *Man* get this wisdom and *these* mighty works?

Mark 1:27 Then they were all amazed, so that they questioned among themselves, saying, "What is this? What new doctrine *is* this? For with authority He commands even the unclean spirits, and they obey Him."

Luke 4:32 And they were astonished at His teaching, for His word was with authority.

John 7:46 The officers answered, "No man ever spoke like this Man!"

Humble.

Is 42:2 He will not cry out, nor raise *His voice,* Nor cause His voice to be heard in the street.

Matt 12:17–20 that it might be fulfilled which was spoken by Isaiah the prophet, saying: **18** *"Behold! My Servant whom I have chosen, My Beloved in whom My soul is well pleased! I will put My Spirit upon*

Him, And He will declare justice to the Gentiles.
19 He will not quarrel nor cry out, Nor will anyone
hear His voice in the streets. 20 A bruised reed He
will not break, And smoking flax He will not quench,
Till He sends forth justice to victory;

God commands us to hear.

Deut 18:15 "The LORD your God will raise up for you a Prophet like me from your midst, from your brethren. Him you shall hear,

Matt 17:25 He said, "Yes." And when he had come into the house, Jesus anticipated him, saying, "What do you think, Simon? From whom do the kings of the earth take customs or taxes, from their sons or from strangers?"

Acts 3:22–23 For Moses truly said to the fathers, 'The LORD your God will raise up for you a Prophet like me from your brethren. Him you shall hear in all things, whatever He says to you. 23 And it shall be that every soul who will not hear that Prophet shall be utterly destroyed from among the people.'

Acts 7:37 "This is that Moses who said to the children of Israel, 'The LORD your God will raise up for you a Prophet like me from your brethren. Him you shall hear.'

Heb 2:3 how shall we escape if we neglect so great a salvation, which at the first began to be spoken by the Lord, and was confirmed to us by those who heard Him,

Typified by Moses.

Deut 18:15 "The LORD your God will raise up for you a Prophet like me from your midst, from your brethren. Him you shall hear,

JESUS CHRIST, THE RESURRECTION OF

Foretold by the prophets.

Ps 16:10 For You will not leave my soul in Sheol, Nor will You allow Your Holy One to see corruption.

Acts 13:34–35 And that He raised Him from the dead, no more to return to corruption, He has spoken thus: 'I will give you the sure mercies of David.' 35 Therefore He also says in another *Psalm*: 'You will not allow Your Holy One to see corruption.'

Is 26:19 Your dead shall live; *Together with* my dead body they shall arise. Awake and sing, you who dwell in dust; For your dew is *like* the dew of herbs, And the earth shall cast out the dead.

Foretold by Himself.

Matt 20:19 and deliver Him to the Gentiles to mock and to scourge and to crucify. And the third day He will rise again."

Mark 9:9 Now as they came down from the mountain, He commanded them that they should tell no one the things they had seen, till the Son of Man had risen from the dead.

Mark 14:28 "But after I have been raised, I will go before you to Galilee."

John 2:19–22 Jesus answered and said to them, "Destroy this temple, and in three days I will raise it up." 20 Then the Jews said, "It has taken forty-six years to build this temple, and will You raise it up in three days?" 21 But He was speaking of the temple of His body. 22 Therefore, when He had risen from the

dead, His disciples remembered that He had said this to them; and they believed the Scripture and the word which Jesus had said.

Was necessary for

The fulfillment of Scripture.

Luke 24:45–46 And He opened their understanding, that they might comprehend the Scriptures. 46 Then He said to them, "Thus it is written, and thus it was necessary for the Christ to suffer and to rise from the dead the third day,

Forgiveness of sins.

1 Cor 15:17 And if Christ is not risen, your faith *is* futile; you are still in your sins!

Justification.

Rom 4:25 who was delivered up because of our offenses, and was raised because of our justification.

Rom 8:34 Who *is* he who condemns? *It is* Christ who died, and furthermore is also risen, who is even at the right hand of God, who also makes intercession for us.

Hope.

1 Cor 15:19 If in this life only we have hope in Christ, we are of all men the most pitiable.

The efficacy of preaching.

1 Cor 15:14 And if Christ is not risen, then our preaching *is* empty and your faith *is* also empty.

The efficacy of faith.

1 Cor 15:14 And if Christ is not risen, then our preaching *is* empty and your faith *is* also empty.

1 Cor 15:17 And if Christ is not risen, your faith *is* futile; you are still in your sins!

The truth of the gospel.

1 Cor 15:14–15 And if Christ is not risen, then our preaching *is* empty and your faith *is* also empty. 15 Yes, and we are found false witnesses of God, because we have testified of God that He raised up Christ, whom He did not raise up—if in fact the dead do not rise.

A proof of His being the Son of God.

Ps 2:7 "I will declare the decree: The LORD has said to Me, 'You *are* My Son, Today I have begotten You.

Acts 13:33 God has fulfilled this for us their children, in that He has raised up Jesus. As it is also written in the second Psalm: 'You are My Son, Today I have begotten You.'

Rom 1:4 *and* declared *to be* the Son of God with power according to the Spirit of holiness, by the resurrection from the dead.

Effected by

The power of God.

Acts 2:24 whom God raised up, having loosed the pains of death, because it was not possible that He should be held by it.

Acts 3:15 and killed the Prince of life, whom God raised from the dead, of which we are witnesses.

Rom 8:11 But if the Spirit of Him who raised Jesus from the dead dwells in you, He who raised Christ from the dead will also give life to your mortal bodies through His Spirit who dwells in you.

Eph 1:20 which He worked in Christ when He raised

Him from the dead and seated *Him* at His right hand in the heavenly *places,*

Col 2:12 buried with Him in baptism, in which you also were raised with *Him* through faith in the working of God, who raised Him from the dead.

His own power.

John 2:19 Jesus answered and said to them, "Destroy this temple, and in three days I will raise it up."

John 10:18 No one takes it from Me, but I lay it down of Myself. I have power to lay it down, and I have power to take it again. This command I have received from My Father."

The power of the Holy Spirit.

1 Pet 3:18 For Christ also suffered once for sins, the just for the unjust, that He might bring us to God, being put to death in the flesh but made alive by the Spirit,

On the first day of the week.

Mark 16:9 Now when *He* rose early on the first *day* of the week, He appeared first to Mary Magdalene, out of whom He had cast seven demons.

On the third day after His death.

Luke 24:46 Then He said to them, "Thus it is written, and thus it was necessary for the Christ to suffer and to rise from the dead the third day,

Acts 10:40 Him God raised up on the third day, and showed Him openly,

1 Cor 15:4 and that He was buried, and that He rose again the third day according to the Scriptures,

The apostles

At first did not understand the predictions respecting.

Mark 9:10 So they kept this word to themselves, questioning what the rising from the dead meant.

John 20:9 For as yet they did not know the Scripture, that He must rise again from the dead.

Very slow to believe.

Mark 16:13 And they went and told *it* to the rest, *but* they did not believe them either.

Luke 24:9 Then they returned from the tomb and told all these things to the eleven and to all the rest.

Luke 24:11 And their words seemed to them like idle tales, and they did not believe them.

Luke 24:37–38 But they were terrified and frightened, and supposed they had seen a spirit. 38 And He said to them, "Why are you troubled? And why do doubts arise in your hearts?

Rebuked for their unbelief of.

Mark 16:14 Later He appeared to the eleven as they sat at the table; and He rebuked their unbelief and hardness of heart, because they did not believe those who had seen Him after He had risen.

He appeared after, to

Mary Magdalene.

Mark 16:9 Now when *He* rose early on the first *day* of the week, He appeared first to Mary Magdalene, out of whom He had cast seven demons.

John 20:18 Mary Magdalene came and told the disciples that she had seen the Lord, and *that* He had spoken these things to her.

The women.

Matt 28:9 And as they went to tell His disciples, behold, Jesus met them, saying, "Rejoice!" So they came and held Him by the feet and worshiped Him.

Simon.

Luke 24:34 saying, "The Lord is risen indeed, and has appeared to Simon!"

Two disciples.

Luke 24:13–31 Now behold, two of them were traveling that same day to a village called Emmaus, which was seven miles from Jerusalem. 14 And they talked together of all these things which had happened. 15 So it was, while they conversed and reasoned, that Jesus Himself drew near and went with them. 16 But their eyes were restrained, so that they did not know Him. 17 And He said to them, "What kind of conversation *is* this that you have with one another as you walk and are sad?" 18 Then the one whose name was Cleopas answered and said to Him, "Are You the only stranger in Jerusalem, and have You not known the things which happened there in these days?" 19 And He said to them, "What things?" So they said to Him, "The things concerning Jesus of Nazareth, who was a Prophet mighty in deed and word before God and all the people, 20 and how the chief priests and our rulers delivered Him to be condemned to death, and crucified Him. 21 But we were hoping that it was He who was going to redeem Israel. Indeed, besides all this, today is the third day since these things happened. 22 Yes, and certain women of our company, who arrived at the tomb early, astonished us. 23 When they did not find His body, they came saying that they had also seen a vision of angels who said He was alive. 24 And certain of those *who were* with us went to the tomb and found *it* just as the women had said; but Him they did not see." 25 Then He said to them, "O foolish ones, and slow of heart to believe in all that the prophets have spoken! 26 Ought not the Christ to have suffered these things and to enter into His glory?" 27 And beginning at Moses and all the Prophets, He expounded to them in all the Scriptures the things concerning Himself. 28 Then they drew near to the village where they were going, and He indicated that He would have gone farther. 29 But they constrained Him, saying, "Abide with us, for it is toward evening, and the day is far spent." And He went in to stay with them. 30 Now it came to pass, as He sat at the table with them, that He took bread, blessed and broke *it,* and gave it to them. 31 Then their eyes were opened and they knew Him; and He vanished from their sight.

The apostles, except Thomas.

John 20:19 Then, the same day at evening, being the first *day* of the week, when the doors were shut where the disciples were assembled, for fear of the Jews, Jesus came and stood in the midst, and said to them, "Peace *be* with you."

John 20:24 Now Thomas, called the Twin, one of the twelve, was not with them when Jesus came.

The apostles, including Thomas.

John 20:26 And after eight days His disciples were again inside, and Thomas with them. Jesus came, the doors being shut, and stood in the midst, and said, "Peace to you!"

The apostles (disciples) at the Sea of Tiberias.

John 21:1 After these things Jesus showed Himself again to the disciples at the Sea of Tiberias, and in this way He showed *Himself:*

The apostles in Galilee.

Matt 28:16–17 Then the eleven disciples went away into Galilee, to the mountain which Jesus had appointed for them. **17** When they saw Him, they worshiped Him; but some doubted.

About five hundred brethren.

1 Cor 15:6 After that He was seen by over five hundred brethren at once, of whom the greater part remain to the present, but some have fallen asleep.

James.

1 Cor 15:7 After that He was seen by James, then by all the apostles.

All the apostles.

Luke 24:51 Now it came to pass, while He blessed them, that He was parted from them and carried up into heaven.

Acts 1:9 Now when He had spoken these things, while they watched, He was taken up, and a cloud received Him out of their sight.

1 Cor 15:7 After that He was seen by James, then by all the apostles.

Paul.

1 Cor 15:8 Then last of all He was seen by me also, as by one born out of due time.

Fraud impossible in.

Matt 27:63–66 saying, "Sir, we remember, while He was still alive, how that deceiver said, 'After three days I will rise.' **64** Therefore command that the tomb be made secure until the third day, lest His disciples come by night and steal Him *away,* and say to the people, 'He has risen from the dead.' So the last deception will be worse than the first." **65** Pilate said to them, "You have a guard; go your way, make *it* as secure as you know how." **66** So they went and made the tomb secure, sealing the stone and setting the guard.

He gave many infallible proofs of.

Luke 24:35 And they told about the things *that had happened* on the road, and how He was known to them in the breaking of bread.

Luke 24:39 Behold My hands and My feet, that it is I Myself. Handle Me and see, for a spirit does not have flesh and bones as you see I have."

Luke 24:43 And He took *it* and ate in their presence.

John 20:20 When He had said this, He showed them *His* hands and His side. Then the disciples were glad when they saw the Lord.

John 20:27 Then He said to Thomas, "Reach your finger here, and look at My hands; and reach your hand *here,* and put *it* into My side. Do not be unbelieving, but believing."

Acts 1:3 to whom He also presented Himself alive after His suffering by many infallible proofs, being seen by them during forty days and speaking of the things pertaining to the kingdom of God.

Was attested by

Angels.

Matt 28:5–7 But the angel answered and said to the women, "Do not be afraid, for I know that you seek Jesus who was crucified. **6** He is not here; for He is risen, as He said. Come, see the place where the Lord lay. **7** And go quickly and tell His disciples that He is risen from the dead, and indeed He is going before you into Galilee; there you will see Him. Behold, I have told you."

Luke 24:4–7 And it happened, as they were greatly perplexed about this, that behold, two men stood by them in shining garments. **5** Then, as they were afraid and bowed *their* faces to the earth, they said to them, "Why do you seek the living among the dead? **6** He is not here, but is risen! Remember how He spoke to you when He was still in Galilee, **7** saying, 'The Son of Man must be delivered into the hands of sinful men, and be crucified, and the third day rise again.' "

Luke 24:23 When they did not find His body, they came saying that they had also seen a vision of angels who said He was alive.

Apostles.

Acts 1:22 beginning from the baptism of John to that day when He was taken up from us, one of these must become a witness with us of His resurrection."

Acts 2:32 This Jesus God has raised up, of which we are all witnesses.

Acts 3:15 and killed the Prince of life, whom God raised from the dead, of which we are witnesses.

Acts 4:33 And with great power the apostles gave witness to the resurrection of the Lord Jesus. And great grace was upon them all.

His enemies.

Matt 28:11–15 Now while they were going, behold, some of the guard came into the city and reported to the chief priests all the things that had happened. **12** When they had assembled with the elders and consulted together, they gave a large sum of money to the soldiers, **13** saying, "Tell them, 'His disciples came at night and stole Him *away* while we slept.' **14** And if this comes to the governor's ears, we will appease him and make you secure." **15** So they took the money and did as they were instructed; and this saying is commonly reported among the Jews until this day.

Asserted and preached by the apostles.

Acts 25:19 but had some questions against him about their own religion and about a certain Jesus, who had died, whom Paul affirmed to be alive.

Acts 26:23 that the Christ would suffer, that He would be the first to rise from the dead, and would proclaim light to the *Jewish* people and to the Gentiles."

Believers

Begotten to a living hope by.

1 Pet 1:3 Blessed *be* the God and Father of our Lord Jesus Christ, who according to His abundant mercy has begotten us again to a living hope through the resurrection of Jesus Christ from the dead,

1 Pet 1:21 who through Him believe in God, who raised

Him from the dead and gave Him glory, so that your faith and hope are in God.

Desire to know the power of.

Phil 3:10 that I may know Him and the power of His resurrection, and the fellowship of His sufferings, being conformed to His death,

Should keep, in remembrance.

2 Tim 2:8 Remember that Jesus Christ, of the seed of David, was raised from the dead according to my gospel,

Shall rise in the likeness of.

Rom 6:5 For if we have been united together in the likeness of His death, certainly we also shall be *in the likeness of His* resurrection,

1 Cor 15:49 And as we have borne the image of the *man* of dust, we shall also bear the image of the heavenly *Man.*

Phil 3:21 who will transform our lowly body that it may be conformed to His glorious body, according to the working by which He is able even to subdue all things to Himself.

Is an emblem of the new birth.

Rom 6:4 Therefore we were buried with Him through baptism into death, that just as Christ was raised from the dead by the glory of the Father, even so we also should walk in newness of life.

Col 2:12 buried with Him in baptism, in which you also were raised with *Him* through faith in the working of God, who raised Him from the dead.

The firstfruits of our resurrection.

Acts 26:23 that the Christ would suffer, that He would be the first to rise from the dead, and would proclaim light to the *Jewish* people and to the Gentiles."

1 Cor 15:20 But now Christ is risen from the dead, *and* has become the firstfruits of those who have fallen asleep.

1 Cor 15:23 But each one in his own order: Christ the firstfruits, afterward those *who are* Christ's at His coming.

Followed by His exaltation.

Acts 4:10–11 let it be known to you all, and to all the people of Israel, that by the name of Jesus Christ of Nazareth, whom you crucified, whom God raised from the dead, by Him this man stands here before you whole. **11** This is the 'stone which was rejected by you builders, which has become the chief cornerstone.'

Rom 8:34 Who *is* he who condemns? *It is* Christ who died, and furthermore is also risen, who is even at the right hand of God, who also makes intercession for us.

Eph 1:20 which He worked in Christ when He raised Him from the dead and seated *Him* at His right hand in the heavenly *places,*

Phil 2:9–10 Therefore God also has highly exalted Him and given Him the name which is above every name, **10** that at the name of Jesus every knee should bow, of those in heaven, and of those on earth, and of those under the earth,

Rev 1:18 I *am* He who lives, and was dead, and behold,

I am alive forevermore. Amen. And I have the key of Hades and of Death.

An assurance of the judgment.

Acts 17:31 because He has appointed a day on which He will judge the world in righteousness by the Man whom He has ordained. He has given assurance o this to all by raising Him from the dead."

Typified by

Isaac.

Gen 22:13 Then Abraham lifted his eyes and looked, and there behind *him was* a ram caught in a thicket by its horns. So Abraham went and took the ram, and offered it up for a burnt offering instead of his son.

Heb 11:19 concluding that God *was* able to raise *him up,* even from the dead, from which he also received him in a figurative sense.

Jonah.

Jon 2:10 So the LORD spoke to the fish, and it vomited Jonah onto dry *land.*

Matt 12:40 For as Jonah was three days and three nights in the belly of the great fish, so will the Son of Man be three days and three nights in the heart of the earth.

JESUS CHRIST, THE SECOND COMING OF

Time of, unknown.

Matt 24:36 "But of that day and hour no one knows, not even the angels of heaven, but My Father only.

Mark 13:32 "But of that day and hour no one knows, not even the angels in heaven, nor the Son, but only the Father.

Other names for,

Times of restoration of all things.

Acts 3:21 whom heaven must receive until the times of restoration of all things, which God has spoken by the mouth of all His holy prophets since the world began.

Rom 8:21 because the creation itself also will be delivered from the bondage of corruption into the glorious liberty of the children of God.

Last time.

1 Pet 1:5 who are kept by the power of God through faith for salvation ready to be revealed in the last time.

Revelation of Jesus Christ.

1 Pet 1:7 that the genuineness of your faith, *being* much more precious than gold that perishes, though it is tested by fire, may be found to praise, honor, and glory at the revelation of Jesus Christ,

1 Pet 1:13 Therefore gird up the loins of your mind, be sober, and rest *your* hope fully upon the grace that is to be brought to you at the revelation of Jesus Christ;

Glorious appearing of our great God and Savior.

Titus 2:13 looking for the blessed hope and glorious appearing of our great God and Savior Jesus Christ,

Coming of the day of God.

2 Pet 3:12 looking for and hastening the coming of the day of God, because of which the heavens will be dissolved, being on fire, and the elements will melt with fervent heat?

Day of our Lord Jesus Christ.

1 Cor 1:8 who will also confirm you to the end, *that you may be* blameless in the day of our Lord Jesus Christ.

oretold by

Prophets.

Dan 7:13 "I was watching in the night visions, And behold, *One* like the Son of Man, Coming with the clouds of heaven! He came to the Ancient of Days, And they brought Him near before Him.

Jude 1:14 Now Enoch, the seventh from Adam, prophesied about these men also, saying, "Behold, the Lord comes with ten thousands of His saints,

Himself.

Matt 25:31 "When the Son of Man comes in His glory, and all the holy angels with Him, then He will sit on the throne of His glory.

John 14:3 And if I go and prepare a place for you, I will come again and receive you to Myself; that where I am, *there* you may be also.

Apostles.

Acts 3:20 and that He may send Jesus Christ, who was preached to you before,

1 Tim 6:14 that you keep *this* commandment without spot, blameless until our Lord Jesus Christ's appearing,

Angels.

Acts 1:10–11 And while they looked steadfastly toward heaven as He went up, behold, two men stood by them in white apparel, **11** who also said, "Men of Galilee, why do you stand gazing up into heaven? This *same* Jesus, who was taken up from you into heaven, will so come in like manner as you saw Him go into heaven."

Signs preceding. Matt 24:3–51

The manner of,

In clouds.

Matt 24:30 Then the sign of the Son of Man will appear in heaven, and then all the tribes of the earth will mourn, and they will see the Son of Man coming on the clouds of heaven with power and great glory.

Matt 26:64 Jesus said to him, "*It is as* you said. Nevertheless, I say to you, hereafter you will see the Son of Man sitting at the right hand of the Power, and coming on the clouds of heaven."

Rev 1:7 Behold, He is coming with clouds, and every eye will see Him, even they who pierced Him. And all the tribes of the earth will mourn because of Him. Even so, Amen.

In the glory of His Father.

Matt 16:27 For the Son of Man will come in the glory of His Father with His angels, and then He will reward each according to his works.

In His own glory.

Matt 25:31 "When the Son of Man comes in His glory, and all the holy angels with Him, then He will sit on the throne of His glory.

In flaming fire.

2 Thess 1:8 in flaming fire taking vengeance on those who do not know God, and on those who do not obey the gospel of our Lord Jesus Christ.

With power and great glory.

Matt 24:30 Then the sign of the Son of Man will appear in heaven, and then all the tribes of the earth will mourn, and then they will see the Son of Man coming on the clouds of heaven with power and great glory.

Same as He ascended.

Acts 1:9 Now when He had spoken these things, while they watched, He was taken up, and a cloud received Him out of their sight.

Acts 1:11 who also said, "Men of Galilee, why do you stand gazing up into heaven? This *same* Jesus, who was taken up from you into heaven, will so come in like manner as you saw Him go into heaven."

With a shout and the voice of an archangel.

1 Thess 4:16 For the Lord Himself will descend from heaven with a shout, with the voice of an archangel, and with the trumpet of God. And the dead in Christ will rise first.

Accompanied by angels.

Matt 16:27 For the Son of Man will come in the glory of His Father with His angels, and then He will reward each according to his works.

Matt 25:31 "When the Son of Man comes in His glory, and all the holy angels with Him, then He will sit on the throne of His glory.

Mark 8:38 For whoever is ashamed of Me and My words in this adulterous and sinful generation, of him the Son of Man also will be ashamed when He comes in the glory of His Father with the holy angels."

2 Thess 1:7 and to *give* you who are troubled rest with us when the Lord Jesus is revealed from heaven with His mighty angels,

With His saints.

1 Thess 3:13 so that He may establish your hearts blameless in holiness before our God and Father at the coming of our Lord Jesus Christ with all His saints.

Jude 1:14 Now Enoch, the seventh from Adam, prophesied about these men also, saying, "Behold, the Lord comes with ten thousands of His saints,

Suddenly.

Mark 13:36 lest, coming suddenly, he find you sleeping.

Unexpectedly.

Matt 24:44 Therefore you also be ready, for the Son of Man is coming at an hour you do not expect.

Luke 12:40 Therefore you also be ready, for the Son of Man is coming at an hour you do not expect."

As a thief in the night.

1 Thess 5:2 For you yourselves know perfectly that the day of the Lord so comes as a thief in the night.

2 Pet 3:10 But the day of the Lord will come as a thief in the night, in which the heavens will pass away with a great noise, and the elements will melt with fervent heat; both the earth and the works that are in it will be burned up.

Rev 16:15 "Behold, I am coming as a thief. Blessed *is* he who watches, and keeps his garments, lest he walk naked and they see his shame."

As the lightning.

Matt 24:27 For as the lightning comes from the east and flashes to the west, so also will the coming of the Son of Man be.

The heavens and earth shall be dissolved, etc., at.

2 Pet 3:10 But the day of the Lord will come as a thief in the night, in which the heavens will pass away with a great noise, and the elements will melt with fervent heat; both the earth and the works that are in it will be burned up.

2 Pet 3:12 looking for and hastening the coming of the day of God, because of which the heavens will be dissolved, being on fire, and the elements will melt with fervent heat?

Dead in Christ will rise first at.

1 Thess 4:16 For the Lord Himself will descend from heaven with a shout, with the voice of an archangel, and with the trumpet of God. And the dead in Christ will rise first.

Believers alive at, shall be caught up to meet Him.

1 Thess 4:17 Then we who are alive *and* remain shall be caught up together with them in the clouds to meet the Lord in the air. And thus we shall always be with the Lord.

Is not to make atonement.

Heb 9:28 so Christ was offered once to bear the sins of many. To those who eagerly wait for Him He will appear a second time, apart from sin, for salvation.

Rom 6:9–10 knowing that Christ, having been raised from the dead, dies no more. Death no longer has dominion over Him. 10 For *the death* that He died, He died to sin once for all; but *the life* that He lives, He lives to God.

Heb 10:14 For by one offering He has perfected forever those who are being sanctified.

The purposes of, are to

Complete the salvation of believers.

Heb 9:28 so Christ was offered once to bear the sins of many. To those who eagerly wait for Him He will appear a second time, apart from sin, for salvation.

1 Pet 1:5 who are kept by the power of God through faith for salvation ready to be revealed in the last time.

Be glorified in His saints.

2 Thess 1:10 when He comes, in that Day, to be glorified in His saints and to be admired among all those who believe, because our testimony among you was believed.

Bring to light the hidden things of darkness.

1 Cor 4:5 Therefore judge nothing before the time, until the Lord comes, who will both bring to light the hidden things of darkness and reveal the counsels of the hearts. Then each one's praise will come from God.

Judge.

Ps 50:3–4 Our God shall come, and shall not keep silent; A fire shall devour before Him, And it shall be very tempestuous all around Him. 4 He shall call to the heavens from above, And to the earth, that He may judge His people:

John 5:22 For the Father judges no one, but has committed all judgment to the Son,

2 Tim 4:1 I charge *you* therefore before God and the Lord Jesus Christ, who will judge the living and the dead at His appearing and His kingdom:

Jude 1:15 to execute judgment on all, to convict all who are ungodly among them of all their ungodly deeds which they have committed in an ungodly way, and of all the harsh things which ungodly sinners have spoken against Him."

Rev 20:11–13 Then I saw a great white throne and Him who sat on it, from whose face the earth and the heaven fled away. And there was found no place for them. 12 And I saw the dead, small and great, standing before God, and books were opened. And another book was opened, which is *the Book* of Life. And the dead were judged according to their works, by the things which were written in the books. 13 The sea gave up the dead who were in it, and Death and Hades delivered up the dead who were in them. And they were judged, each one according to his works.

Reign.

Is 24:23 Then the moon will be disgraced And the sun ashamed; For the LORD of hosts will reign On Mount Zion and in Jerusalem And before His elders, gloriously.

Dan 7:14 Then to Him was given dominion and glory and a kingdom, That all peoples, nations, and languages should serve Him. His dominion *is* an everlasting dominion, Which shall not pass away, And His kingdom *the one* Which shall not be destroyed.

Rev 11:15 Then the seventh angel sounded: And there were loud voices in heaven, saying, "The kingdoms of this world have become *the kingdoms* of our Lord and of His Christ, and He shall reign forever and ever!"

Destroy death.

1 Cor 15:25–26 For He must reign till He has put all enemies under His feet. 26 The last enemy *that* will be destroyed *is* death.

Every eye shall see Him at.

Rev 1:7 Behold, He is coming with clouds, and every eye will see Him, even they who pierced Him. And all the tribes of the earth will mourn because of Him. Even so, Amen.

Should be always considered as at hand.

Rom 13:12 The night is far spent, the day is at hand. Therefore let us cast off the works of darkness, and let us put on the armor of light.

Phil 4:5 Let your gentleness be known to all men. The Lord *is* at hand.

1 Pet 4:7 But the end of all things is at hand; therefore be serious and watchful in your prayers.

Blessedness of being prepared for.

Matt 24:46 Blessed *is* that servant whom his master, when he comes, will find so doing.

Luke 12:37–38 Blessed *are* those servants whom the master, when he comes, will find watching. Assuredly, I say to you that he will gird himself and have them sit down *to eat*, and will come and serve them. 38 And if he should come in the second watch, or come in the third watch, and find *them* so, blessed are those servants.

Believers

Assured of.

Job 19:25–26 For I know *that* my Redeemer lives, And He shall stand at last on the earth; 26 And after my skin is destroyed, this *I know*, That in my flesh I shall see God,

Love.

2 Tim 4:8 Finally, there is laid up for me the crown of righteousness, which the Lord, the righteous Judge, will give to me on that Day, and not to me only but also to all who have loved His appearing.

Look for.

Phil 3:20 For our citizenship is in heaven, from which we also eagerly wait for the Savior, the Lord Jesus Christ,

Titus 2:13 looking for the blessed hope and glorious appearing of our great God and Savior Jesus Christ,

Wait for.

1 Cor 1:7 so that you come short in no gift, eagerly waiting for the revelation of our Lord Jesus Christ,

1 Thess 1:10 and to wait for His Son from heaven, whom He raised from the dead, *even* Jesus who delivers us from the wrath to come.

Are eager for.

2 Pet 3:12 looking for and hastening the coming of the day of God, because of which the heavens will be dissolved, being on fire, and the elements will melt with fervent heat?

Pray for.

Rev 22:20 He who testifies to these things says, "Surely I am coming quickly." Amen. Even so, come, Lord Jesus!

Should watch and be ready for.

Matt 24:42 Watch therefore, for you do not know what hour your Lord is coming.

Matt 24:44 Therefore you also be ready, for the Son of Man is coming at an hour you do not expect.

Mark 13:35–37 Watch therefore, for you do not know when the master of the house is coming—in the evening, at midnight, at the crowing of the rooster, or in the morning— 36 lest, coming suddenly, he find you sleeping. 37 And what I say to you, I say to all: Watch!"

Luke 12:40 Therefore you also be ready, for the Son of Man is coming at an hour you do not expect."

Luke 21:36 Watch therefore, and pray always that you may be counted worthy to escape all these things that will come to pass, and to stand before the Son of Man."

Should be patient until.

2 Thess 3:5 Now may the Lord direct your hearts into the love of God and into the patience of Christ.

James 5:7–8 Therefore be patient, brethren, until the coming of the Lord. See *how* the farmer waits for the precious fruit of the earth, waiting patiently for it until it receives the early and latter rain. 8 You also be patient. Establish your hearts, for the coming of the Lord is at hand.

Shall be preserved until.

Phil 1:6 being confident of this very thing, that He who has begun a good work in you will complete *it* until the day of Jesus Christ;

2 Tim 4:18 And the Lord will deliver me from every evil work and preserve *me* for His heavenly kingdom. To Him *be* glory forever and ever. Amen!

1 Pet 1:5 who are kept by the power of God through faith for salvation ready to be revealed in the last time.

Jude 1:24 Now to Him who is able to keep you from stumbling, And to present *you* faultless Before the presence of His glory with exceeding joy,

Shall not be ashamed at.

1 John 2:28 And now, little children, abide in Him, that when He appears, we may have confidence and not be ashamed before Him at His coming.

1 John 4:17 Love has been perfected among us in this: that we may have boldness in the day of judgment; because as He is, so are we in this world.

Shall be blameless at.

1 Cor 1:8 who will also confirm you to the end, *that you may be* blameless in the day of our Lord Jesus Christ.

1 Thess 3:13 so that He may establish your hearts blameless in holiness before our God and Father at the coming of our Lord Jesus Christ with all His saints.

1 Thess 5:23 Now may the God of peace Himself sanctify you completely; and may your whole spirit, soul, and body be preserved blameless at the coming of our Lord Jesus Christ.

Jude 1:24 Now to Him who is able to keep you from stumbling, And to present *you* faultless Before the presence of His glory with exceeding joy,

Shall be like Him at.

Phil 3:21 who will transform our lowly body that it may be conformed to His glorious body, according to the working by which He is able even to subdue all things to Himself.

1 John 3:2 Beloved, now we are children of God; and it has not yet been revealed what we shall be, but we know that when He is revealed, we shall be like Him, for we shall see Him as He is.

Shall see Him as He is, at.

1 John 3:2 Beloved, now we are children of God; and it has not yet been revealed what we shall be, but we know that when He is revealed, we shall be like Him, for we shall see Him as He is.

Shall appear with Him in glory at.

Col 3:4 When Christ *who is* our life appears, then you also will appear with Him in glory.

Shall receive a crown of glory at.

2 Tim 4:8 Finally, there is laid up for me the crown of righteousness, which the Lord, the righteous Judge, will give to me on that Day, and not to me only but also to all who have loved His appearing.

1 Pet 5:4 and when the Chief Shepherd appears, you will receive the crown of glory that does not fade away.

Shall reign with Him at.

Dan 7:27 Then the kingdom and dominion, And the greatness of the kingdoms under the whole heaven, Shall be given to the people, the saints of the Most

High. His kingdom *is* an everlasting kingdom, And all dominions shall serve and obey Him.'

2 Tim 2:12 If we endure, We shall also reign with *Him.* If we deny *Him,* He also will deny us.

Rev 5:10 And have made us kings and priests to our God; And we shall reign on the earth."

Rev 20:6 Blessed and holy *is* he who has part in the first resurrection. Over such the second death has no power, but they shall be priests of God and of Christ, and shall reign with Him a thousand years.

Rev 22:5 There shall be no night there: They need no lamp nor light of the sun, for the Lord God gives them light. And they shall reign forever and ever.

Faith of, shall be found to praise at.

1 Pet 1:7 that the genuineness of your faith, *being* much more precious than gold that perishes, though it is tested by fire, may be found to praise, honor, and glory at the revelation of Jesus Christ,

The wicked

Scoff at.

2 Pet 3:3–4 knowing this first: that scoffers will come in the last days, walking according to their own lusts, **4** and saying, "Where is the promise of His coming? For since the fathers fell asleep, all things continue as *they were* from the beginning of creation."

Presume upon the delay of.

Matt 24:48 But if that evil servant says in his heart, 'My master is delaying his coming,'

Shall be surprised by.

Matt 24:37–39 But as the days of Noah *were,* so also will the coming of the Son of Man be. **38** For as in the days before the flood, they were eating and drinking, marrying and giving in marriage, until the day that Noah entered the ark, **39** and did not know until the flood came and took them all away, so also will the coming of the Son of Man be.

1 Thess 5:3 For when they say, "Peace and safety!" then sudden destruction comes upon them, as labor pains upon a pregnant woman. And they shall not escape.

2 Pet 3:10 But the day of the Lord will come as a thief in the night, in which the heavens will pass away with a great noise, and the elements will melt with fervent heat; both the earth and the works that are in it will be burned up.

Shall be punished at.

2 Thess 1:8–9 in flaming fire taking vengeance on those who do not know God, and on those who do not obey the gospel of our Lord Jesus Christ. **9** These shall be punished with everlasting destruction from the presence of the Lord and from the glory of His power,

The lawless one to be destroyed at.

2 Thess 2:8 And then the lawless one will be revealed, whom the Lord will consume with the breath of His mouth and destroy with the brightness of His coming.

Illustrated.

Matt 25:6 "And at midnight a cry was *heard:* 'Behold, the bridegroom is coming; go out to meet him!'

Luke 12:36 and you yourselves be like men who wait for their master, when he will return from the wedding, that when he comes and knocks they may open to him immediately.

Luke 12:39 But know this, that if the master of the house had known what hour the thief would come, he would have watched and not allowed his house to be broken into.

Luke 19:12 Therefore He said: "A certain nobleman went into a far country to receive for himself a kingdom and to return.

Luke 19:15 "And so it was that when he returned, having received the kingdom, he then commanded these servants, to whom he had given the money, to be called to him, that he might know how much every man had gained by trading.

JESUS CHRIST, THE SHEPHERD

Foretold.

Gen 49:24 But his bow remained in strength, And the arms of his hands were made strong By the hands of the Mighty *God* of Jacob (From there *is* the Shepherd, the Stone of Israel),

Is 40:11 He will feed His flock like a shepherd; He will gather the lambs with His arm, And carry *them* in His bosom, *And* gently lead those who are with young.

Ezek 34:23 I will establish one shepherd over them, and he shall feed them—My servant David. He shall feed them and be their shepherd.

Ezek 37:24 "David My servant *shall be* king over them, and they shall all have one shepherd; they shall also walk in My judgments and observe My statutes, and do them.

The chief.

1 Pet 5:4 and when the Chief Shepherd appears, you will receive the crown of glory that does not fade away.

The good.

John 10:11 "I am the good shepherd. The good shepherd gives His life for the sheep.

John 10:14 I am the good shepherd; and I know My *sheep,* and am known by My own.

The great.

Mic 5:4 And He shall stand and feed *His flock* In the strength of the LORD, In the majesty of the name of the LORD His God; And they shall abide, For now He shall be great To the ends of the earth;

Heb 13:20 Now may the God of peace who brought up our Lord Jesus from the dead, that great Shepherd of the sheep, through the blood of the everlasting covenant,

His sheep

He knows.

John 10:3 To him the doorkeeper opens, and the sheep hear his voice; and he calls his own sheep by name and leads them out.

John 10:14 I am the good shepherd; and I know My *sheep,* and am known by My own.

John 10:16 And other sheep I have which are not of this fold; them also I must bring, and they will hear My voice; and there will be one flock *and* one shepherd.

John 10:27 My sheep hear My voice, and I know them, and they follow Me.

He guides.

John 10:3–4 To him the doorkeeper opens, and the sheep hear his voice; and he calls his own sheep by name and leads them out. **4** And when he brings out his own sheep, he goes before them; and the sheep follow him, for they know his voice.

He feeds.

John 10:9 I am the door. If anyone enters by Me, he will be saved, and will go in and out and find pasture.

He leads.

1 Pet 2:25 For you were like sheep going astray, but have now returned to the Shepherd and Overseer of your souls.

He protects and preserves.

John 10:28 And I give them eternal life, and they shall never perish; neither shall anyone snatch them out of My hand.

He laid down his life for.

Zech 13:7 "Awake, O sword, against My Shepherd, Against the Man who is My Companion," Says the LORD of hosts. "Strike the Shepherd, And the sheep will be scattered; Then I will turn My hand against the little ones.

Matt 26:31 Then Jesus said to them, "All of you will be made to stumble because of Me this night, for it is written: *'I will strike the Shepherd, And the sheep of the flock will be scattered.'*

John 10:11 "I am the good shepherd. The good shepherd gives His life for the sheep.

John 10:15 As the Father knows Me, even so I know the Father; and I lay down My life for the sheep.

Acts 20:28 Therefore take heed to yourselves and to all the flock, among which the Holy Spirit has made you overseers, to shepherd the church of God which He purchased with His own blood.

He gives eternal life to.

John 10:28 And I give them eternal life, and they shall never perish; neither shall anyone snatch them out of My hand.

Typified by David.

1 Sam 16:11 And Samuel said to Jesse, "Are all the young men here?" Then he said, "There remains yet the youngest, and there he is, keeping the sheep." And Samuel said to Jesse, "Send and bring him. For we will not sit down till he comes here."

JESUS CHRIST, TITLES AND NAMES OF

Almighty.

Rev 1:8 "I am the Alpha and the Omega, *the* Beginning and *the* End," says the Lord, "who is and who was and who is to come, the Almighty."

Amen.

Rev 3:14 "And to the angel of the church of the Laodiceans write, 'These things says the Amen, the Faithful and True Witness, the Beginning of the creation of God:

Alpha and Omega.

Rev 1:8 "I am the Alpha and the Omega, *the* Beginning and *the* End," says the Lord, "who is and who was and who is to come, the Almighty."

Rev 22:13 I am the Alpha and the Omega, *the* Beginning and *the* End, the First and the Last."

Advocate.

1 John 2:1 My little children, these things I write to you, so that you may not sin. And if anyone sins, we have an Advocate with the Father, Jesus Christ the righteous.

Angel.

Gen 48:16 The Angel who has redeemed me from all evil, Bless the lads; Let my name be named upon them, And the name of my fathers Abraham and Isaac; And let them grow into a multitude in the midst of the earth."

Ex 23:20–21 "Behold, I send an Angel before you to keep you in the way and to bring you into the place which I have prepared. **21** Beware of Him and obey His voice; do not provoke Him, for He will not pardon your transgressions; for My name *is* in Him.

Angel of the Lord.

Ex 3:2 And the Angel of the LORD appeared to him in a flame of fire from the midst of a bush. So he looked, and behold, the bush was burning with fire, but the bush *was* not consumed.

Judg 13:15–18 Then Manoah said to the Angel of the LORD, "Please let us detain You, and we will prepare a young goat for You." **16** And the Angel of the LORD said to Manoah, "Though you detain Me, I will not eat your food. But if you offer a burnt offering, you must offer it to the LORD." (For Manoah did not know He *was* the Angel of the LORD.) **17** Then Manoah said to the Angel of the LORD, "What *is* Your name, that when Your words come *to pass* we may honor You?" **18** And the Angel of the LORD said to him, "Why do you ask My name, seeing it *is* wonderful?"

Angel of God's Presence.

Is 63:9 In all their affliction He was afflicted, And the Angel of His Presence saved them; In His love and in His pity He redeemed them; And He bore them and carried them All the days of old.

Apostle.

Heb 3:1 Therefore, holy brethren, partakers of the heavenly calling, consider the Apostle and High Priest of our confession, Christ Jesus,

Arm of the Lord.

Is 51:9 Awake, awake, put on strength, O arm of the LORD! Awake as in the ancient days, In the generations of old. *Are* You not *the arm* that cut Rahab apart, *And* wounded the serpent?

Is 53:1 Who has believed our report? And to whom has the arm of the LORD been revealed?

Author and Finisher or our faith.

Heb 12:2 looking unto Jesus, the author and finisher of *our* faith, who for the joy that was set before Him endured the cross, despising the shame, and has sat down at the right hand of the throne of God.

Blessed and only Potentate.

1 Tim 6:15 which He will manifest in His own time, *He who is* the blessed and only Potentate, the King of kings and Lord of lords,

Beginning of the creation of God.

Rev 3:14 "And to the angel of the church of the Laodiceans write, 'These things says the Amen, the Faithful and True Witness, the Beginning of the creation of God:

Branch.

Jer 23:5 "Behold, *the* days are coming," says the LORD, "That I will raise to David a Branch of righteousness; A King shall reign and prosper, And execute judgment and righteousness in the earth.

Zech 3:8 'Hear, O Joshua, the high priest, You and your companions who sit before you, For they are a wondrous sign; For behold, I am bringing forth My Servant the BRANCH.

Zech 6:12 Then speak to him, saying, 'Thus says the LORD of hosts, saying: "Behold, the Man whose name *is* the BRANCH! From His place He shall branch out, And He shall build the temple of the LORD;

Bread of Life.

John 6:35 And Jesus said to them, "I am the bread of life. He who comes to Me shall never hunger, and he who believes in Me shall never thirst.

John 6:48 I am the bread of life.

Commander of the army of the Lord.

Josh 5:14–15 So He said, "No, but *as* Commander of the army of the LORD I have now come." And Joshua fell on his face to the earth and worshiped, and said to Him, "What does my Lord say to His servant?" 15 Then the Commander of the LORD's army said to Joshua, "Take your sandal off your foot, for the place where you stand *is* holy." And Joshua did so.

Captain of salvation.

Heb 2:10 For it was fitting for Him, for whom *are* all things and by whom *are* all things, in bringing many sons to glory, to make the captain of their salvation perfect through sufferings.

Chief Cornerstone.

Eph 2:20 having been built on the foundation of the apostles and prophets, Jesus Christ Himself being the chief cornerstone,

1 Pet 2:6 Therefore it is also contained in the Scripture, *"Behold, I lay in Zion A chief cornerstone, elect, precious, And he who believes on Him will by no means be put to shame."*

Chief Shepherd.

1 Pet 5:4 and when the Chief Shepherd appears, you will receive the crown of glory that does not fade away.

Christ of God.

Luke 9:20 He said to them, "But who do you say that I am?" Peter answered and said, "The Christ of God."

Consolation of Israel.

Luke 2:25 And behold, there was a man in Jerusalem whose name was Simeon, and this man was just and devout, waiting for the Consolation of Israel, and the Holy Spirit was upon him.

Commander.

Is 55:4 Indeed I have given him *as* a witness to the people, A leader and commander for the people.

Counselor.

Is 9:6 For unto us a Child is born, Unto us a Son is given; And the government will be upon His shoulder. And His name will be called Wonderful, Counselor, Mighty God, Everlasting Father, Prince of Peace.

David.

Jer 30:9 But they shall serve the LORD their God, And David their king, Whom I will raise up for them.

Ezek 34:23 I will establish one shepherd over them, and he shall feed them—My servant David. He shall feed them and be their shepherd.

Dayspring.

Luke 1:78 Through the tender mercy of our God, With which the Dayspring from on high has visited us;

Deliverer.

Rom 11:26 And so all Israel will be saved, as it is written: *"The Deliverer will come out of Zion, And He will turn away ungodliness from Jacob;*

Desire of all nations.

Hag 2:7 and I will shake all nations, and they shall come to the Desire of All Nations, and I will fill this temple with glory,' says the LORD of hosts.

Door.

John 10:7 Then Jesus said to them again, "Most assuredly, I say to you, I am the door of the sheep.

Elect One.

Is 42:1 "Behold! My Servant whom I uphold, My Elect One *in whom* My soul delights! I have put My Spirit upon Him; He will bring forth justice to the Gentiles.

Eternal life.

1 John 1:2 the life was manifested, and we have seen, and bear witness, and declare to you that eternal life which was with the Father and was manifested to us—

1 John 5:20 And we know that the Son of God has come and has given us an understanding, that we may know Him who is true; and we are in Him who is true, in His Son Jesus Christ. This is the true God and eternal life.

Eternally blessed God.

Rom 9:5 of whom *are* the fathers and from whom, according to the flesh, Christ *came,* who is over all, *the* eternally blessed God. Amen.

Everlasting Father.

Is 9:6 For unto us a Child is born, Unto us a Son is given; And the government will be upon His shoulder. And His name will be called Wonderful, Counselor, Mighty God, Everlasting Father, Prince of Peace.

Faithful witness.

Rev 1:5 and from Jesus Christ, the faithful witness, the firstborn from the dead, and the ruler over the kings of the earth. To Him who loved us and washed us from our sins in His own blood,

Rev 3:14 "And to the angel of the church of the Laodiceans write, 'These things says the Amen, the Faithful and True Witness, the Beginning of the creation of God:

First and Last.

Rev 1:17 And when I saw Him, I fell at His feet as dead. But He laid His right hand on me, saying to me, "Do not be afraid; I am the First and the Last.

Rev 2:8 "And to the angel of the church in Smyrna write, 'These things says the First and the Last, who was dead, and came to life:

Firstborn over all creation.

Col 1:15 He is the image of the invisible God, the firstborn over all creation.

Firstborn from the dead.

Rev 1:5 and from Jesus Christ, the faithful witness, the firstborn from the dead, and the ruler over the kings of the earth. To Him who loved us and washed us from our sins in His own blood,

Forerunner.

Heb 6:20 where the forerunner has entered for us, *even* Jesus, having become High Priest forever according to the order of Melchizedek.

God.

Is 40:9 O Zion, You who bring good tidings, Get up into the high mountain; O Jerusalem, You who bring good tidings, Lift up your voice with strength, Lift *it* up, be not afraid; Say to the cities of Judah, "Behold your God!"

John 20:28 And Thomas answered and said to Him, "My Lord and my God!"

God's Companion.

Zech 13:7 "Awake, O sword, against My Shepherd, Against the Man who is My Companion," Says the LORD of hosts. "Strike the Shepherd, And the sheep will be scattered; Then I will turn My hand against the little ones.

Glory of the Lord.

Is 40:5 The glory of the LORD shall be revealed, And all flesh shall see *it* together; For the mouth of the LORD has spoken."

Good Shepherd.

John 10:14 I am the good shepherd; and I know My *sheep*, and am known by My own.

Great High Priest.

Heb 4:14 Seeing then that we have a great High Priest who has passed through the heavens, Jesus the Son of God, let us hold fast *our* confession.

Head of the church.

Eph 5:23 For the husband is head of the wife, as also Christ is head of the church; and He is the Savior of the body.

Col 1:18 And He is the head of the body, the church, who is the beginning, the firstborn from the dead, that in all things He may have the preeminence.

Heir of all things.

Heb 1:2 has in these last days spoken to us by *His* Son, whom He has appointed heir of all things, through whom also He made the worlds;

Holy One.

Ps 16:10 For You will not leave my soul in Sheol, Nor will You allow Your Holy One to see corruption.

Acts 2:27 *For You will not leave my soul in Hades, Nor will You allow Your Holy One to see corruption.*

Acts 2:31 he, foreseeing this, spoke concerning the resurrection of the Christ, that His soul was not left in Hades, nor did His flesh see corruption.

Holy One of God.

Mark 1:24 saying, "Let *us* alone! What have we to do with You, Jesus of Nazareth? Did You come to destroy us? I know who You are—the Holy One of God!"

Holy One of Israel.

Is 41:14 "Fear not, you worm Jacob, You men of Israel! I will help you," says the LORD And your Redeemer, the Holy One of Israel.

Horn of salvation.

Luke 1:69 And has raised up a horn of salvation for us In the house of His servant David,

I AM.

Ex 3:14 And God said to Moses, "I AM WHO I AM." And He said, "Thus you shall say to the children of Israel, 'I AM has sent me to you.' "

John 8:58 Jesus said to them, "Most assuredly, I say to you, before Abraham was, I AM."

Immanuel.

Is 7:14 Therefore the Lord Himself will give you a sign: Behold, the virgin shall conceive and bear a Son, and shall call His name Immanuel.

Matt 1:23 *"Behold, the virgin shall be with child, and bear a Son, and they shall call His name Immanuel,"* which is translated, "God with us."

Jesus.

Matt 1:21 And she will bring forth a Son, and you shall call His name JESUS, for He will save His people from their sins."

1 Thess 1:10 and to wait for His Son from heaven, whom He raised from the dead, *even* Jesus who delivers us from the wrath to come.

Judge of Israel.

Mic 5:1 Now gather yourself in troops, O daughter of troops; He has laid siege against us; They will strike the judge of Israel with a rod on the cheek.

Just One.

Acts 7:52 Which of the prophets did your fathers not persecute? And they killed those who foretold the coming of the Just One, of whom you now have become the betrayers and murderers,

King.

Zech 9:9 "Rejoice greatly, O daughter of Zion! Shout, O daughter of Jerusalem! Behold, your King is coming to you; He *is* just and having salvation, Lowly and riding on a donkey, A colt, the foal of a donkey.

Matt 21:5 *"Tell the daughter of Zion, 'Behold, your King is coming to you, Lowly, and sitting on a donkey, A colt, the foal of a donkey.' "*

King of Israel.

John 1:49 Nathanael answered and said to Him, "Rabbi, You are the Son of God! You are the King of Israel!"

King of the Jews.

Matt 2:2 saying, "Where is He who has been born King of the Jews? For we have seen His star in the East and have come to worship Him."

King of the saints.

Rev 15:3 They sing the song of Moses, the servant of God, and the song of the Lamb, saying: "Great and marvelous *are* Your works, Lord God Almighty! Just and true *are* Your ways, O King of the saints!

King of kings.

1 Tim 6:15 which He will manifest in His own time, *He who is* the blessed and only Potentate, the King of kings and Lord of lords,

Rev 17:14 These will make war with the Lamb, and the Lamb will overcome them, for He is Lord of lords and King of kings; and those *who are* with Him *are* called, chosen, and faithful."

Last Adam.

1 Cor 15:45 And so it is written, *"The first man Adam became a living being."* The last Adam *became* a life-giving spirit.

Lawgiver.

Is 33:22 (For the LORD *is* our Judge, The LORD *is* our Lawgiver, The LORD *is* our King; He will save us);

Lamb.

Rev 5:6 And I looked, and behold, in the midst of the throne and of the four living creatures, and in the midst of the elders, stood a Lamb as though it had been slain, having seven horns and seven eyes, which are the seven Spirits of God sent out into all the earth.

Rev 5:12 saying with a loud voice: "Worthy is the Lamb who was slain To receive power and riches and wisdom, And strength and honor and glory and blessing!"

Rev 13:8 All who dwell on the earth will worship him, whose names have not been written in the Book of Life of the Lamb slain from the foundation of the world.

Rev 21:22 But I saw no temple in it, for the Lord God Almighty and the Lamb are its temple.

Rev 22:3 And there shall be no more curse, but the throne of God and of the Lamb shall be in it, and His servants shall serve Him.

Lamb of God.

John 1:29 The next day John saw Jesus coming toward him, and said, "Behold! The Lamb of God who takes away the sin of the world!

John 1:36 And looking at Jesus as He walked, he said, "Behold the Lamb of God!"

Leader.

Is 55:4 Indeed I have given him *as* a witness to the people, A leader and commander for the people.

Life.

John 14:6 Jesus said to him, "I am the way, the truth, and the life. No one comes to the Father except through Me.

Col 3:4 When Christ *who is* our life appears, then you also will appear with Him in glory.

1 John 1:2 the life was manifested, and we have seen, and bear witness, and declare to you that eternal life which was with the Father and was manifested to us—

Light of the world.

John 8:12 Then Jesus spoke to them again, saying, "I am the light of the world. He who follows Me shall not walk in darkness, but have the light of life."

Lion of the tribe of Judah.

Rev 5:5 But one of the elders said to me, "Do not weep. Behold, the Lion of the tribe of Judah, the Root of David, has prevailed to open the scroll and to loose its seven seals."

Lord of glory.

1 Cor 2:8 which none of the rulers of this age knew; for had they known, they would not have crucified the Lord of glory.

Lord of all.

Acts 10:36 The word which *God* sent to the children of Israel, preaching peace through Jesus Christ—He is Lord of all—

Lord our righteousness.

Jer 23:6 In His days Judah will be saved, And Israel will dwell safely; Now this *is* His name by which He will be called: THE LORD OUR RIGHTEOUSNESS.

Lord God of the holy prophets.

Rev 22:6 Then he said to me, "These words *are* faithful and true." And the Lord God of the holy prophets sent His angel to show His servants the things which must shortly take place.

Lord God Almighty.

Rev 15:3 They sing the song of Moses, the servant of God, and the song of the Lamb, saying: "Great and marvelous *are* Your works, Lord God Almighty! Just and true *are* Your ways, O King of the saints!

Mediator.

1 Tim 2:5 For *there is* one God and one Mediator between God and men, *the* Man Christ Jesus,

Messenger of the covenant.

Mal 3:1 "Behold, I send My messenger, And he will prepare the way before Me. And the Lord, whom you seek, Will suddenly come to His temple, Even the Messenger of the covenant, In whom you delight. Behold, He is coming," Says the LORD of hosts.

Messiah.

Dan 9:25 "Know therefore and understand, *That* from the going forth of the command To restore and build Jerusalem Until Messiah the Prince, *There shall be* seven weeks and sixty-two weeks; The street shall be built again, and the wall, Even in troublesome times.

John 1:41 He first found his own brother Simon, and said to him, "We have found the Messiah" (which is translated, the Christ).

Mighty God.

Is 9:6 For unto us a Child is born, Unto us a Son is given; And the government will be upon His shoulder. And His name will be called Wonderful, Counselor, Mighty God, Everlasting Father, Prince of Peace.

Mighty One of Jacob.

Is 60:16 You shall drink the milk of the Gentiles, And milk the breast of kings; You shall know that I, the LORD, *am* your Savior And your Redeemer, the Mighty One of Jacob.

Morning Star.

Rev 22:16 "I, Jesus, have sent My angel to testify to you these things in the churches. I am the Root and the Offspring of David, the Bright and Morning Star."

Nazarene.

Matt 2:23 And he came and dwelt in a city called Nazareth, that it might be fulfilled which was spoken by the prophets, "He shall be called a Nazarene."

Offspring of David.

Rev 22:16 "I, Jesus, have sent My angel to testify to you these things in the churches. I am the Root and the Offspring of David, the Bright and Morning Star."

Only begotten.

John 1:14 And the Word became flesh and dwelt among us, and we beheld His glory, the glory as of the only begotten of the Father, full of grace and truth.

Our Passover.

1 Cor 5:7 Therefore purge out the old leaven, that you may be a new lump, since you truly are unleavened. For indeed Christ, our Passover, was sacrificed for us.

Prince of life.

Acts 3:15 and killed the Prince of life, whom God raised from the dead, of which we are witnesses.

Prince of Peace.

Is 9:6 For unto us a Child is born, Unto us a Son is given; And the government will be upon His shoulder. And His name will be called Wonderful, Counselor, Mighty God, Everlasting Father, Prince of Peace.

Prophet.

Luke 24:19 And He said to them, "What things?" So they said to Him, "The things concerning Jesus of Nazareth, who was a Prophet mighty in deed and word before God and all the people,

John 7:40 Therefore many from the crowd, when they heard this saying, said, "Truly this is the Prophet."

Ransom.

1 Tim 2:6 who gave Himself a ransom for all, to be testified in due time,

Redeemer.

Job 19:25 For I know *that* my Redeemer lives, And He shall stand at last on the earth;

Is 59:20 "The Redeemer will come to Zion, And to those who turn from transgression in Jacob," Says the LORD.

Is 60:16 You shall drink the milk of the Gentiles, And milk the breast of kings; You shall know that I, the LORD, *am* your Savior And your Redeemer, the Mighty One of Jacob.

Resurrection and the life.

John 11:25 Jesus said to her, "I am the resurrection and the life. He who believes in Me, though he may die, he shall live.

Rock.

1 Cor 10:4 and all drank the same spiritual drink. For they drank of that spiritual Rock that followed them, and that Rock was Christ.

Root of David.

Rev 22:16 "I, Jesus, have sent My angel to testify to you these things in the churches. I am the Root and the Offspring of David, the Bright and Morning Star."

Root of Jesse.

Is 11:10 "And in that day there shall be a Root of Jesse, Who shall stand as a banner to the people; For the Gentiles shall seek Him, And His resting place shall be glorious."

Ruler.

Matt 2:6 *'But you, Bethlehem, in the land of Judah, Are not the least among the rulers of Judah; For out of you shall come a Ruler Who will shepherd My people Israel.'"*

Ruler in Israel.

Mic 5:2 "But you, Bethlehem Ephrathah, *Though* you are little among the thousands of Judah, *Yet* out of you shall come forth to Me The One to be Ruler in Israel, Whose goings forth *are* from of old, From everlasting."

Ruler over the kings of the earth.

Rev 1:5 and from Jesus Christ, the faithful witness, the firstborn from the dead, and the ruler over the kings of the earth. To Him who loved us and washed us from our sins in His own blood,

Savior.

2 Pet 2:20 For if, after they have escaped the pollutions of the world through the knowledge of the Lord and Savior Jesus Christ, they are again entangled in them and overcome, the latter end is worse for them than the beginning.

2 Pet 3:18 but grow in the grace and knowledge of our Lord and Savior Jesus Christ. To Him *be* the glory both now and forever. Amen.

Servant.

Is 42:1 "Behold! My Servant whom I uphold, My Elect One *in whom* My soul delights! I have put My Spirit upon Him; He will bring forth justice to the Gentiles.

Is 52:13 Behold, My Servant shall deal prudently; He shall be exalted and extolled and be very high.

Shepherd and Overseer of souls.

1 Pet 2:25 For you were like sheep going astray, but have now returned to the Shepherd and Overseer of your souls.

Shiloh.

Gen 49:10 The scepter shall not depart from Judah, Nor a lawgiver from between his feet, Until Shiloh comes; And to Him *shall be* the obedience of the people.

Son of the Blessed.

Mark 14:61 But He kept silent and answered nothing. Again the high priest asked Him, saying to Him, "Are You the Christ, the Son of the Blessed?"

Son of God.

Luke 1:35 And the angel answered and said to her, "*The* Holy Spirit will come upon you, and the power of the Highest will overshadow you; therefore, also, that Holy One who is to be born will be called the Son of God.

John 1:49 Nathanael answered and said to Him, "Rabbi, You are the Son of God! You are the King of Israel!"

Son of the Highest.

Luke 1:32 He will be great, and will be called the Son of the Highest; and the Lord God will give Him the throne of His father David.

Son of David.

Matt 9:27 When Jesus departed from there, two blind men followed Him, crying out and saying, "Son of David, have mercy on us!"

Son of Man.

John 5:27 and has given Him authority to execute judgment also, because He is the Son of Man.

John 6:37 All that the Father gives Me will come to Me, and the one who comes to Me I will by no means cast out.

Star.

Num 24:17 "I see Him, but not now; I behold Him, but not near; A Star shall come out of Jacob; A Scepter shall rise out of Israel, And batter the brow of Moab, And destroy all the sons of tumult.

Sun of Righteousness.

Mal 4:2 But to you who fear My name The Sun of Righteousness shall arise With healing in His wings; And you shall go out And grow fat like stall-fed calves.

Surety.

Heb 7:22 by so much more Jesus has become a surety of a better covenant.

True God.

1 John 5:20 And we know that the Son of God has come and has given us an understanding, that we may know Him who is true; and we are in Him who is true, in His Son Jesus Christ. This is the true God and eternal life.

True Light.

John 1:9 That was the true Light which gives light to every man coming into the world.

True vine.

John 15:1 "I am the true vine, and My Father is the vinedresser.

Truth.

John 14:6 Jesus said to him, "I am the way, the truth, and the life. No one comes to the Father except through Me.

Way.

John 14:6 Jesus said to him, "I am the way, the truth, and the life. No one comes to the Father except through Me.

Wisdom.

Prov 8:12 "I, wisdom, dwell with prudence, And find out knowledge *and* discretion.

Witness.

Is 55:4 Indeed I have given him *as* a witness to the people, A leader and commander for the people.

Wonderful.

Is 9:6 For unto us a Child is born, Unto us a Son is given; And the government will be upon His shoulder. And His name will be called Wonderful, Counselor, Mighty God, Everlasting Father, Prince of Peace.

Word.

John 1:1 In the beginning was the Word, and the Word was with God, and the Word was God.

John 1:14 And the Word became flesh and dwelt among us, and we beheld His glory, the glory as of the only begotten of the Father, full of grace and truth.

Word of God.

Rev 19:13 He *was* clothed with a robe dipped in blood, and His name is called The Word of God.

Word of life.

1 John 1:1 That which was from the beginning, which we have heard, which we have seen with our eyes, which we have looked upon, and our hands have handled, concerning the Word of life—

Yah.

Is 26:4 Trust in the LORD forever, For in YAH, the LORD, *is* everlasting strength.

JESUS CHRIST, TYPES OF

Adam.

Rom 5:14 Nevertheless death reigned from Adam to Moses, even over those who had not sinned according to the likeness of the transgression of Adam, who is a type of Him who was to come.

1 Cor 15:45 And so it is written, *"The first man Adam became a living being."* The last Adam *became* a life-giving spirit.

Abel.

Gen 4:8 Now Cain talked with Abel his brother; and it came to pass, when they were in the field, that Cain rose up against Abel his brother and killed him.

Gen 4:10 And He said, "What have you done? The voice of your brother's blood cries out to Me from the ground.

Heb 12:24 to Jesus the Mediator of the new covenant, and to the blood of sprinkling that speaks better things than *that of* Abel.

Abraham.

Gen 17:5 No longer shall your name be called Abram, but your name shall be Abraham; for I have made you a father of many nations.

Eph 3:15 from whom the whole family in heaven and earth is named,

Aaron.

Ex 28:1 "Now take Aaron your brother, and his sons with him, from among the children of Israel, that he may minister to Me as priest, Aaron *and* Aaron's sons: Nadab, Abihu, Eleazar, and Ithamar.

Heb 5:4–5 And no man takes this honor to himself, but he who is called by God, just as Aaron *was*. 5 So also Christ did not glorify Himself to become High Priest, *but it* was He who said to Him: *"You are My Son, Today I have begotten You."*

Cf. Lev 16:15; Heb 9:7,24

Ark (Noah's).

Gen 7:16 So those that entered, male and female of all flesh, went in as God had commanded him; and the LORD shut him in.

1 Pet 3:20–21 who formerly were disobedient, when once the Divine longsuffering waited in the days of

Noah, while *the* ark was being prepared, in which a few, that is, eight souls, were saved through water. 21 There is also an antitype which now saves us—baptism (not the removal of the filth of the flesh, but the answer of a good conscience toward God), through the resurrection of Jesus Christ,

Ark of the Covenant.

Ex 25:16 And you shall put into the ark the Testimony which I will give you.

Ps 40:8 I delight to do Your will, O my God, And Your law *is* within my heart."

Is 42:6 "I, the LORD, have called You in righteousness, And will hold Your hand; I will keep You and give You as a covenant to the people, As a light to the Gentiles,

Bronze serpent.

Num 21:9 So Moses made a bronze serpent, and put it on a pole; and so it was, if a serpent had bitten anyone, when he looked at the bronze serpent, he lived.

John 3:14–15 And as Moses lifted up the serpent in the wilderness, even so must the Son of Man be lifted up, **15** that whoever believes in Him should not perish but have eternal life.

Bronze altar.

Ex 27:1–2 "You shall make an altar of acacia wood, five cubits long and five cubits wide—the altar shall be square—and its height *shall be* three cubits. **2** You shall make its horns on its four corners; its horns shall be of one piece with it. And you shall overlay it with bronze.

Heb 13:10 We have an altar from which those who serve the tabernacle have no right to eat.

Burnt offering.

Lev 1:2 "Speak to the children of Israel, and say to them: 'When any one of you brings an offering to the LORD, you shall bring your offering of the livestock—of the herd and of the flock.

Lev 1:4 Then he shall put his hand on the head of the burnt offering, and it will be accepted on his behalf to make atonement for him.

Heb 10:10 By that will we have been sanctified through the offering of the body of Jesus Christ once *for all.*

Cities of refuge.

Num 35:6 "Now among the cities which you will give to the Levites *you shall appoint* six cities of refuge, to which a manslayer may flee. And to these you shall add forty-two cities.

Heb 6:18 that by two immutable things, in which it *is* impossible for God to lie, we might have strong consolation, who have fled for refuge to lay hold of the hope set before *us.*

David.

2 Sam 8:15 So David reigned over all Israel; and David administered judgment and justice to all his people.

Ezek 37:24 "David My servant *shall be* king over them, and they shall all have one shepherd; they shall also walk in My judgments and observe My statutes, and do them.

Ps 89:19–20 Then You spoke in a vision to Your holy one, And said: "I have given help to *one who is* mighty; I have exalted one chosen from the people.

20 I have found My servant David; With My holy oil I have anointed him,

Phil 2:9 Therefore God also has highly exalted Him and given Him the name which is above every name,

Eliakim.

Is 22:20–22 'Then it shall be in that day, That I will call My servant Eliakim the son of Hilkiah; **21** I will clothe him with your robe And strengthen him with your belt; I will commit your responsibility into his hand. He shall be a father to the inhabitants of Jerusalem And to the house of Judah. **22** The key of the house of David I will lay on his shoulder; So he shall open, and no one shall shut; And he shall shut, and no one shall open.

Rev 3:7 "And to the angel of the church in Philadelphia write, 'These things says He who is holy, He who is true, *"He who has the key of David, He who opens and no one shuts, and shuts and no one opens"*:

Firstfruits.

Ex 22:29 "You shall not delay *to offer* the first of your ripe produce and your juices. The firstborn of your sons you shall give to Me.

1 Cor 15:20 But now Christ is risen from the dead, *and* has become the firstfruits of those who have fallen asleep.

Gold lampstand.

Ex 25:31 "You shall also make a lampstand of pure gold; the lampstand shall be of hammered work. Its shaft, its branches, its bowls, its *ornamental* knobs, and flowers shall be *of one piece.*

John 8:12 Then Jesus spoke to them again, saying, "I am the light of the world. He who follows Me shall not walk in darkness, but have the light of life."

Golden altar.

Ex 40:5 You shall also set the altar of gold for the incense before the ark of the Testimony, and put up the screen for the door of the tabernacle.

Ex 40:26–27 He put the gold altar in the tabernacle of meeting in front of the veil; **27** and he burned sweet incense on it, as the LORD had commanded Moses.

Heb 13:15 Therefore by Him let us continually offer the sacrifice of praise to God, that is, the fruit of *our* lips, giving thanks to His name.

Rev 8:3 Then another angel, having a golden censer, came and stood at the altar. He was given much incense, that he should offer *it* with the prayers of all the saints upon the golden altar which was before the throne.

Isaac.

Gen 22:1–2 Now it came to pass after these things that God tested Abraham, and said to him, "Abraham!" And he said, "Here I am." **2** Then He said, "Take now your son, your only *son* Isaac, whom you love, and go to the land of Moriah, and offer him there as a burnt offering on one of the mountains of which I shall tell you."

Heb 11:17–19 By faith Abraham, when he was tested, offered up Isaac, and he who had received the promises offered up his only begotten *son,* **18** of whom it was said, *"In Isaac your seed shall be called,"* **19** concluding that God *was* able to raise *him* up, even from the dead, from which he also received him in a figurative sense.

Jacob.

Gen 32:28 And He said, "Your name shall no longer be called Jacob, but Israel; for you have struggled with God and with men, and have prevailed."

John 11:42 And I know that You always hear Me, but because of the people who are standing by I said *this,* that they may believe that You sent Me."

Heb 7:25 Therefore He is also able to save to the uttermost those who come to God through Him, since He always lives to make intercession for them.

Jacob's ladder.

Gen 28:12 Then he dreamed, and behold, a ladder *was* set up on the earth, and its top reached to heaven; and there the angels of God were ascending and descending on it.

John 1:51 And He said to him, "Most assuredly, I say to you, hereafter you shall see heaven open, and the angels of God ascending and descending upon the Son of Man."

Joseph.

Gen 50:19–20 Joseph said to them, "Do not be afraid, for *am* I in the place of God? 20 But as for you, you meant evil against me; *but* God meant it for good, in order to bring it about as *it is* this day, to save many people alive.

Joshua.

Josh 1:5–6 No man shall *be able to* stand before you all the days of your life; as I was with Moses, *so* I will be with you. I will not leave you nor forsake you. 6 Be strong and of good courage, for to this people you shall divide as an inheritance the land which I swore to their fathers to give them.

Josh 11:23 So Joshua took the whole land, according to all that the LORD had said to Moses; and Joshua gave it as an inheritance to Israel according to their divisions by their tribes. Then the land rested from war.

Acts 20:32 "So now, brethren, I commend you to God and to the word of His grace, which is able to build you up and give you an inheritance among all those who are sanctified.

Heb 4:8–9 For if Joshua had given them rest, then He would not afterward have spoken of another day. 9 There remains therefore a rest for the people of God.

Jonah.

Jon 1:17 Now the LORD had prepared a great fish to swallow Jonah. And Jonah was in the belly of the fish three days and three nights.

Matt 12:40 For as Jonah was three days and three nights in the belly of the great fish, so will the Son of Man be three days and three nights in the heart of the earth.

Laver of bronze.

Ex 30:18–20 "You shall also make a laver of bronze, with its base also of bronze, for washing. You shall put it between the tabernacle of meeting and the altar. And you shall put water in it, 19 for Aaron and his sons shall wash their hands and their feet in water from it. 20 When they go into the tabernacle of meeting, or when they come near the altar to minister, to burn an

offering made by fire to the LORD, they shall wash with water, lest they die.

Zech 13:1 "In that day a fountain shall be opened for the house of David and for the inhabitants of Jerusalem, for sin and for uncleanness.

Eph 5:26–27 that He might sanctify and cleanse her with the washing of water by the word, 27 that He might present her to Himself a glorious church, not having spot or wrinkle or any such thing, but that she should be holy and without blemish.

Leper's offering.

Lev 14:4–7 then the priest shall command to take for him who is to be cleansed two living *and* clean birds, cedar wood, scarlet, and hyssop. 5 And the priest shall command that one of the birds be killed in an earthen vessel over running water. 6 As for the living bird, he shall take it, the cedar wood and the scarlet and the hyssop, and dip them and the living bird in the blood of the bird *that was* killed over the running water. 7 And he shall sprinkle it seven times on him who is to be cleansed from the leprosy, and shall pronounce him clean, and shall let the living bird loose in the open field.

Rom 4:25 who was delivered up because of our offenses, and was raised because of our justification.

Manna (Bread from heaven).

Ex 16:11–15 And the LORD spoke to Moses, saying, 12 "I have heard the complaints of the children of Israel. Speak to them, saying, 'At twilight you shall eat meat, and in the morning you shall be filled with bread. And you shall know that I *am* the LORD your God.' " 13 So it was that quails came up at evening and covered the camp, and in the morning the dew lay all around the camp. 14 And when the layer of dew lifted, there, on the surface of the wilderness, was a small round substance, *as* fine as frost on the ground. 15 So when the children of Israel saw *it*, they said to one another, "What is it?" For they did not know what it *was*. And Moses said to them, "This *is* the bread which the LORD has given you to eat.

John 6:32–35 Then Jesus said to them, "Most assuredly, I say to you, Moses did not give you the bread from heaven, but My Father gives you the true bread from heaven. 33 For the bread of God is He who comes down from heaven and gives life to the world." 34 Then they said to Him, "Lord, give us this bread always." 35 And Jesus said to them, "I am the bread of life. He who comes to Me shall never hunger, and he who believes in Me shall never thirst.

Melchizedek.

Gen 14:18–20 Then Melchizedek king of Salem brought out bread and wine; he *was* the priest of God Most High. 19 And he blessed him and said: "Blessed be Abram of God Most High, Possessor of heaven and earth; 20 And blessed be God Most High, Who has delivered your enemies into your hand." And he gave him a tithe of all.

Heb 7:1–17 For this Melchizedek, king of Salem, priest of the Most High God, who met Abraham returning from the slaughter of the kings and blessed him, 2 to whom also Abraham gave a tenth part of all, first being translated "king of righteousness," and then also king of Salem, meaning "king of peace," 3 without father, without mother, without genealogy, having neither beginning of days nor end of life, but made like the Son of God, remains a priest continually. **4** Now consider how great this man *was,* to whom even the patriarch Abraham gave a tenth of the spoils. **5** And indeed those who are of the sons of Levi, who receive the priesthood, have a commandment to receive tithes from the people according to the law, that is, from their brethren, though they have come from the loins of Abraham; **6** but he whose genealogy is not derived from them received tithes from Abraham and blessed him who had the promises. **7** Now beyond all contradiction the lesser is blessed by the better. **8** Here mortal men receive tithes, but there he *receives them,* of whom it is witnessed that he lives. **9** Even Levi, who receives tithes, paid tithes through Abraham, so to speak, **10** for he was still in the loins of his father when Melchizedek met him. **11** Therefore, if perfection were through the Levitical priesthood (for under it the people received the law), what further need *was there* that another priest should rise according to the order of Melchizedek, and not be called according to the order of Aaron? **12** For the priesthood being changed, of necessity there is also a change of the law. **13** For He of whom these things are spoken belongs to another tribe, from which no man has officiated at the altar. **14** For *it is* evident that our Lord arose from Judah, of which tribe Moses spoke nothing concerning priesthood. **15** And it is yet far more evident if, in the likeness of Melchizedek, there arises another priest **16** who has come, not according to the law of a fleshly commandment, but according to the power of an endless life. **17** For He testifies: *"You are a priest forever According to the order of Melchizedek."*

Mercy seat.

Ex 25:17–22 "You shall make a mercy seat of pure gold; two and a half cubits *shall be* its length and a cubit and a half its width. **18** And you shall make two cherubim of gold; of hammered work you shall make them at the two ends of the mercy seat. **19** Make one cherub at one end, and the other cherub at the other end; you shall make the cherubim at the two ends of it *of one piece* with the mercy seat. **20** And the cherubim shall stretch out *their* wings above, covering the mercy seat with their wings, and they shall face one another; the faces of the cherubim *shall be* toward the mercy seat. **21** You shall put the mercy seat on top of the ark, and in the ark you shall put the Testimony that I will give you. **22** And there I will meet with you, and I will speak with you from above the mercy seat, from between the two cherubim which *are* on the ark of the Testimony, about everything which I will give you in commandment to the children of Israel.

Rom 3:25 whom God set forth *as* a propitiation by His blood, through faith, to demonstrate His righteousness, because in His forbearance God had passed over the sins that were previously committed,

Heb 4:16 Let us therefore come boldly to the throne of grace, that we may obtain mercy and find grace to help in time of need.

Morning and evening offerings.

Ex 29:38–41 "Now this *is* what you shall offer on the altar: two lambs of the first year, day by day contin-

ually. **39** One lamb you shall offer in the morning, and the other lamb you shall offer at twilight. **40** With the one lamb shall be one-tenth *of an ephah* of flour mixed with one-fourth of a hin of pressed oil, and one-fourth of a hin of wine *as* a drink offering. **41** And the other lamb you shall offer at twilight; and you shall offer with it the grain offering and the drink offering, as in the morning, for a sweet aroma, an offering made by fire to the LORD.

John 1:29 The next day John saw Jesus coming toward him, and said, "Behold! The Lamb of God who takes away the sin of the world!

John 1:36 And looking at Jesus as He walked, he said, "Behold the Lamb of God!"

Moses.

Num 12:7 Not so with My servant Moses; He *is* faithful in all My house.

Heb 3:2 who was faithful to Him who appointed Him, as Moses also *was faithful* in all His house.

Deut 18:15 "The LORD your God will raise up for you a Prophet like me from your midst, from your brethren. Him you shall hear,

Acts 3:20–22 and that He may send Jesus Christ, who was preached to you before, **21** whom heaven must receive until the times of restoration of all things, which God has spoken by the mouth of all His holy prophets since the world began. **22** For Moses truly said to the fathers, 'The LORD *your God will raise up for you a Prophet like me from your brethren. Him you shall hear in all things, whatever He says to you.*

Noah.

Gen 5:29 And he called his name Noah, saying, "This *one* will comfort us concerning our work and the toil of our hands, because of the ground which the LORD has cursed."

2 Cor 1:5 For as the sufferings of Christ abound in us, so our consolation also abounds through Christ.

Passover lamb.

Ex 12:3–6 Speak to all the congregation of Israel, saying: 'On the tenth of this month every man shall take for himself a lamb, according to the house of *his* father, a lamb for a household. **4** And if the household is too small for the lamb, let him and his neighbor next to his house take *it* according to the number of the persons; according to each man's need you shall make your count for the lamb. **5** Your lamb shall be without blemish, a male of the first year. You may take *it* from the sheep or from the goats. **6** Now you shall keep it until the fourteenth day of the same month. Then the whole assembly of the congregation of Israel shall kill it at twilight.

Ex 12:46 In one house it shall be eaten; you shall not carry any of the flesh outside the house, nor shall you break one of its bones.

John 19:36 For these things were done that the Scripture should be fulfilled, *"Not one of His bones shall be broken."*

1 Cor 5:7 Therefore purge out the old leaven, that you may be a new lump, since you truly are unleavened. For indeed Christ, our Passover, was sacrificed for us.

Peace offerings.

Lev 3:1 'When his offering *is* a sacrifice of a peace offering, if he offers *it* of the herd, whether male or female, he shall offer it without blemish before the LORD.

Eph 2:14 For He Himself is our peace, who has made both one, and has broken down the middle wall of separation,

Eph 2:16 and that He might reconcile them both to God in one body through the cross, thereby putting to death the enmity.

Red heifer.

Num 19:2–6 "This *is* the ordinance of the law which the LORD has commanded, saying: 'Speak to the children of Israel, that they bring you a red heifer without blemish, in which there *is* no defect *and* on which a yoke has never come. **3** You shall give it to Eleazar the priest, that he may take it outside the camp, and it shall be slaughtered before him; **4** and Eleazar the priest shall take some of its blood with his finger, and sprinkle some of its blood seven times directly in front of the tabernacle of meeting. **5** Then the heifer shall be burned in his sight: its hide, its flesh, its blood, and its offal shall be burned. **6** And the priest shall take cedar wood and hyssop and scarlet, and cast *them* into the midst of the fire burning the heifer.

Heb 9:13–14 For if the blood of bulls and goats and the ashes of a heifer, sprinkling the unclean, sanctifies for the purifying of the flesh, **14** how much more shall the blood of Christ, who through the eternal Spirit offered Himself without spot to God, cleanse your conscience from dead works to serve the living God?

Rock in Horeb.

Ex 17:6 Behold, I will stand before you there on the rock in Horeb; and you shall strike the rock, and water will come out of it, that the people may drink." And Moses did so in the sight of the elders of Israel.

1 Cor 10:4 and all drank the same spiritual drink. For they drank of that spiritual Rock that followed them, and that Rock was Christ.

Sacrifices offered on the day of Atonement.

Lev 16:15–16 "Then he shall kill the goat of the sin offering, which *is* for the people, bring its blood inside the veil, do with that blood as he did with the blood of the bull, and sprinkle it on the mercy seat and before the mercy seat. **16** So he shall make atonement for the Holy *Place*, because of the uncleanness of the children of Israel, and because of their transgressions, for all their sins; and so he shall do for the tabernacle of meeting which remains among them in the midst of their uncleanness.

Heb 9:12 Not with the blood of goats and calves, but with His own blood He entered the Most Holy Place once for all, having obtained eternal redemption.

Heb 9:24 For Christ has not entered the holy places made with hands, *which are* copies of the true, but into heaven itself, now to appear in the presence of God for us;

Samson.

Judg 16:30 Then Samson said, "Let me die with the Philistines!" And he pushed with *all his* might, and the temple fell on the lords and all the people who *were* in it. So the dead that he killed at his death were more than he had killed in his life.

Col 2:14–15 having wiped out the handwriting of requirements that was against us, which was contrary to us. And He has taken it out of the way, having nailed it to the cross. **15** Having disarmed principalities and powers, He made a public spectacle of them, triumphing over them in it.

Scapegoat.

Lev 16:20–22 "And when he has made an end of atoning for the Holy *Place*, the tabernacle of meeting, and the altar, he shall bring the live goat. **21** Aaron shall lay both his hands on the head of the live goat, confess over it all the iniquities of the children of Israel, and all their transgressions, concerning all their sins, putting them on the head of the goat, and shall send *it* away into the wilderness by the hand of a suitable man. **22** The goat shall bear on itself all their iniquities to an uninhabited land; and he shall release the goat in the wilderness.

Is 53:6 All we like sheep have gone astray; We have turned, every one, to his own way; And the LORD has laid on Him the iniquity of us all.

Is 53:12 Therefore I will divide Him a portion with the great, And He shall divide the spoil with the strong, Because He poured out His soul unto death, And He was numbered with the transgressors, And He bore the sin of many, And made intercession for the transgressors.

Sin offering.

Lev 4:2–3 "Speak to the children of Israel, saying: 'If a person sins unintentionally against any of the commandments of the LORD *in anything* which ought not to be done, and does any of them, **3** if the anointed priest sins, bringing guilt on the people, then let him offer to the LORD for his sin which he has sinned a young bull without blemish as a sin offering.

Lev 4:12 the whole bull he shall carry outside the camp to a clean place, where the ashes are poured out, and burn it on wood with fire; where the ashes are poured out it shall be burned.

Heb 13:11–12 For the bodies of those animals, whose blood is brought into the sanctuary by the high priest for sin, are burned outside the camp. **12** Therefore Jesus also, that He might sanctify the people with His own blood, suffered outside the gate.

Solomon.

2 Sam 7:12–13 "When your days are fulfilled and you rest with your fathers, I will set up your seed after you, who will come from your body, and I will establish his kingdom. **13** He shall build a house for My name, and I will establish the throne of his kingdom forever.

Tabernacle.

Ex 40:2 "On the first day of the first month you shall set up the tabernacle of the tent of meeting.

Ex 40:34 Then the cloud covered the tabernacle of meeting, and the glory of the LORD filled the tabernacle.

Col 2:9 For in Him dwells all the fullness of the Godhead bodily;

Heb 9:11 But Christ came *as* High Priest of the good things to come, with the greater and more perfect tabernacle not made with hands, that is, not of this creation.

Table and showbread.

Ex 25:23–30 "You shall also make a table of acacia wood; two cubits *shall be* its length, a cubit its width, and a cubit and a half its height. **24** And you shall overlay it with pure gold, and make a molding of gold all around. **25** You shall make for it a frame of a handbreadth all around, and you shall make a gold molding for the frame all around. **26** And you shall make for it four rings of gold, and put the rings on the four corners that *are* at its four legs. **27** The rings shall be close to the frame, as holders for the poles to bear the table. **28** And you shall make the poles of acacia wood, and overlay them with gold, that the table may be carried with them. **29** You shall make its dishes, its pans, its pitchers, and its bowls for pouring. You shall make them of pure gold. **30** And you shall set the showbread on the table before Me always.

John 1:16 And of His fullness we have all received, and grace for grace.

John 6:48 I am the bread of life.

Temple.

1 Kin 6:1 And it came to pass in the four hundred and eightieth year after the children of Israel had come out of the land of Egypt, in the fourth year of Solomon's reign over Israel, in the month of Ziv, which *is* the second month, that he began to build the house of the LORD.

1 Kin 6:38 And in the eleventh year, in the month of Bul, which is the eighth month, the house was finished in all its details and according to all its plans. So he was seven years in building it.

John 2:19 Jesus answered and said to them, "Destroy this temple, and in three days I will raise it up."

John 2:21 But He was speaking of the temple of His body.

Tree of life.

Gen 2:9 And out of the ground the LORD God made every tree grow that is pleasant to the sight and good for food. The tree of life *was* also in the midst of the garden, and the tree of the knowledge of good and evil.

John 1:4 In Him was life, and the life was the light of men.

Rev 22:2 In the middle of its street, and on either side of the river, *was* the tree of life, which bore twelve fruits, each *tree* yielding its fruit every month. The leaves of the tree *were* for the healing of the nations.

Trespass offering.

Lev 6:1–7 And the LORD spoke to Moses, saying: **2** "If a person sins and commits a trespass against the LORD by lying to his neighbor about what was delivered to him for safekeeping, or about a pledge, or about a robbery, or if he has extorted from his neighbor, **3** or if he has found what was lost and lies concerning it, and swears falsely—in any one of these things that a man may do in which he sins: **4** then it shall be, because he has sinned and is guilty, that he shall restore what he has stolen, or the thing which he has extorted, or what was delivered to him for safekeeping, or the lost thing which he found, **5** or all that about which he has sworn falsely. He shall restore its full value, add one-fifth more to it, *and* give it to whomever it belongs, on the day of his trespass offering.

6 And he shall bring his trespass offering to the LORD, a ram without blemish from the flock, with your valuation, as a trespass offering, to the priest. **7** So the priest shall make atonement for him before the LORD, and he shall be forgiven for any one of these things that he may have done in which he trespasses."

Is 53:10 Yet it pleased the LORD to bruise Him; He has put *Him* to grief. When You make His soul an offering for sin, He shall see *His* seed, He shall prolong *His* days, And the pleasure of the LORD shall prosper in His hand.

Veil of the tabernacle and temple.

Ex 40:21 And he brought the ark into the tabernacle, hung up the veil of the covering, and partitioned off the ark of the Testimony, as the LORD had commanded Moses.

2 Chr 3:14 And he made the veil of blue, purple, crimson, and fine linen, and wove cherubim into it.

Heb 10:20 by a new and living way which He consecrated for us, through the veil, that is, His flesh,

Zerubbabel.

Zech 4:7–9 'Who *are* you, O great mountain? Before Zerubbabel *you shall become* a plain! And he shall bring forth the capstone With shouts of "Grace, grace to it!" ' " **8** Moreover the word of the LORD came to me, saying: **9** "The hands of Zerubbabel Have laid the foundation of this temple; His hands shall also finish *it*. Then you will know That the LORD of hosts has sent Me to you.

Heb 12:2–3 looking unto Jesus, the author and finisher of *our* faith, who for the joy that was set before Him endured the cross, despising the shame, and has sat down at the right hand of the throne of God. **3** For consider Him who endured such hostility from sinners against Himself, lest you become weary and discouraged in your souls.

JESUS CHRIST, UNION WITH

As head of the church.

Eph 1:22–23 And He put all *things* under His feet, and gave Him *to be* head over all *things* to the church, **23** which is His body, the fullness of Him who fills all in all.

Eph 4:15–16 but, speaking the truth in love, may grow up in all things into Him who is the head—Christ—**16** from whom the whole body, joined and knit together by what every joint supplies, according to the effective working by which every part does its share, causes growth of the body for the edifying of itself in love.

Col 1:18 And He is the head of the body, the church, who is the beginning, the firstborn from the dead, that in all things He may have the preeminence.

Christ prayed that all believers might have.

John 17:21 that they all may be one, as You, Father, *are* in Me, and I in You; that they also may be one in Us, that the world may believe that You sent Me.

John 17:23 I in them, and You in Me; that they may be made perfect in one, and that the world may know that You have sent Me, and have loved them as You have loved Me.

Described as

Christ being in believers.

Eph 3:17 that Christ may dwell in your hearts through faith; that you, being rooted and grounded in love,

Col 1:27 To them God willed to make known what are the riches of the glory of this mystery among the Gentiles: which is Christ in you, the hope of glory.

Believers being in Christ.

2 Cor 12:2 I know a man in Christ who fourteen years ago—whether in the body I do not know, or whether out of the body I do not know, God knows—such a one was caught up to the third heaven.

1 John 5:20 And we know that the Son of God has come and has given us an understanding, that we may know Him who is true; and we are in Him who is true, in His Son Jesus Christ. This is the true God and eternal life.

Includes union with the Father.

John 17:21 that they all may be one, as You, Father, *are* in Me, and I in You; that they also may be one in Us, that the world may believe that You sent Me.

1 John 2:24 Therefore let that abide in you which you heard from the beginning. If what you heard from the beginning abides in you, you also will abide in the Son and in the Father.

Is of God.

1 Cor 1:30 But of Him you are in Christ Jesus, who became for us wisdom from God—and righteousness and sanctification and redemption—

Maintained by

Faith.

Gal 2:20 I have been crucified with Christ; it is no longer I who live, but Christ lives in me; and the *life* which I now live in the flesh I live by faith in the Son of God, who loved me and gave Himself for me.

Eph 3:17 that Christ may dwell in your hearts through faith; that you, being rooted and grounded in love,

Abiding in Him.

John 15:4 Abide in Me, and I in you. As the branch cannot bear fruit of itself, unless it abides in the vine, neither can you, unless you abide in Me.

John 15:7 If you abide in Me, and My words abide in you, you will ask what you desire, and it shall be done for you.

His Word abiding in us.

John 15:7 If you abide in Me, and My words abide in you, you will ask what you desire, and it shall be done for you.

1 John 2:24 Therefore let that abide in you which you heard from the beginning. If what you heard from the beginning abides in you, you also will abide in the Son and in the Father.

2 John 1:9 Whoever transgresses and does not abide in the doctrine of Christ does not have God. He who abides in the doctrine of Christ has both the Father and the Son.

Feeding on Him.

John 6:56 He who eats My flesh and drinks My blood abides in Me, and I in him.

Obeying Him.

1 John 3:24 Now he who keeps His commandments abides in Him, and He in him. And by this we know that He abides in us, by the Spirit whom He has given us.

The Holy Spirit witnesses.

1 John 3:24 Now he who keeps His commandments abides in Him, and He in him. And by this we know that He abides in us, by the Spirit whom He has given us.

The gift of the Holy Spirit is an evidence of.

1 John 4:13 By this we know that we abide in Him, and He in us, because He has given us of His Spirit.

Believers

Have, in mind.

1 Cor 2:16 For *"who has known the mind of the Lord that he may instruct Him?"* But we have the mind of Christ.

Phil 2:5 Let this mind be in you which was also in Christ Jesus,

Have, in spirit.

1 Cor 6:17 But he who is joined to the Lord is one spirit *with Him.*

Have, in love.

Song 2:16 My beloved *is* mine, and I *am* his. He feeds *his* flock among the lilies.

Song 7:10 I *am* my beloved's, And his desire *is* toward me.

Have, in sufferings.

Phil 3:10 that I may know Him and the power of His resurrection, and the fellowship of His sufferings, being conformed to His death,

2 Tim 2:12 If we endure, We shall also reign with *Him.* If we deny *Him,* He also will deny us.

Have, in His death.

Rom 6:3–8 Or do you not know that as many of us as were baptized into Christ Jesus were baptized into His death? **4** Therefore we were buried with Him through baptism into death, that just as Christ was raised from the dead by the glory of the Father, even so we also should walk in newness of life. **5** For if we have been united together in the likeness of His death, certainly we also shall be *in the likeness* of His resurrection, **6** knowing this, that our old man was crucified with *Him,* that the body of sin might be done away with, that we should no longer be slaves of sin. **7** For he who has died has been freed from sin. **8** Now if we died with Christ, we believe that we shall also live with Him,

Gal 2:20 I have been crucified with Christ; it is no longer I who live, but Christ lives in me; and the *life* which I now live in the flesh I live by faith in the Son of God, who loved me and gave Himself for me.

Have assurance of.

John 14:20 At that day you will know that I *am* in My Father, and you in Me, and I in you.

Enjoy, in the Lord's Supper.

1 Cor 10:16–17 The cup of blessing which we bless, is it not the communion of the blood of Christ? The bread which we break, is it not the communion of the body of Christ? **17** For we, *though* many, are one bread *and* one body; for we all partake of that one bread.

Identified with Him by.

Matt 25:40 And the King will answer and say to them, 'Assuredly, I say to you, inasmuch as you did *it* to one of the least of these My brethren, you did *it* to Me.'

Matt 25:45 Then He will answer them, saying, 'Assuredly, I say to you, inasmuch as you did not do *it* to one of the least of these, you did not do *it* to Me.'

Acts 8:1 Now Saul was consenting to his death. At that time a great persecution arose against the church which was at Jerusalem; and they were all scattered throughout the regions of Judea and Samaria, except the apostles.

Acts 9:4 Then he fell to the ground, and heard a voice saying to him, "Saul, Saul, why are you persecuting Me?"

Are complete through.

Col 2:10 and you are complete in Him, who is the head of all principality and power.

Exhorted to maintain.

John 15:4 Abide in Me, and I in you. As the branch cannot bear fruit of itself, unless it abides in the vine, neither can you, unless you abide in Me.

Acts 11:23 When he came and had seen the grace of God, he was glad, and encouraged them all that with purpose of heart they should continue with the Lord.

Col 2:7 rooted and built up in Him and established in the faith, as you have been taught, abounding in it with thanksgiving.

Necessary to growth in grace.

Eph 4:15–16 but, speaking the truth in love, may grow up in all things into Him who is the head—Christ— **16** from whom the whole body, joined and knit together by what every joint supplies, according to the effective working by which every part does its share, causes growth of the body for the edifying of itself in love.

Col 2:19 and not holding fast to the Head, from whom all the body, nourished and knit together by joints and ligaments, grows with the increase *that is* from God.

Necessary for fruitfulness.

John 15:4–5 Abide in Me, and I in you. As the branch cannot bear fruit of itself, unless it abides in the vine, neither can you, unless you abide in Me. **5** "I am the vine, you *are* the branches. He who abides in Me, and I in him, bears much fruit; for without Me you can do nothing.

Beneficial results of,

Righteousness imputed.

2 Cor 5:21 For He made Him who knew no sin *to be* sin for us, that we might become the righteousness of God in Him.

Phil 3:9 and be found in Him, not having my own righteousness, which *is* from the law, but that which *is* through faith in Christ, the righteousness which is from God by faith;

Freedom from condemnation.

Rom 8:1 *There is* therefore now no condemnation to those who are in Christ Jesus, who do not walk according to the flesh, but according to the Spirit.

Freedom from dominion of sin.

1 John 3:6 Whoever abides in Him does not sin. Whoever sins has neither seen Him nor known Him.

Being created anew.

2 Cor 5:17 Therefore, if anyone is in Christ, *he is* a new creation; old things have passed away; behold, all things have become new.

The spirit alive to righteousness.

Rom 8:10 And if Christ *is* in you, the body *is* dead because of sin, but the Spirit *is* life because of righteousness.

Confidence at His coming.

1 John 2:28 And now, little children, abide in Him, that when He appears, we may have confidence and not be ashamed before Him at His coming.

Abundant fruitfulness.

John 15:5 "I am the vine, you *are* the branches. He who abides in Me, and I in him, bears much fruit; for without Me you can do nothing.

Answers to prayer.

John 15:7 If you abide in Me, and My words abide in you, you will ask what you desire, and it shall be done for you.

Those who have, ought to walk as He walked.

1 John 2:6 He who says he abides in Him ought himself also to walk just as He walked.

False teachers do not have.

Col 2:18–19 Let no one cheat you of your reward, taking delight in *false* humility and worship of angels, intruding into those things which he has not seen, vainly puffed up by his fleshly mind, **19** and not holding fast to the Head, from whom all the body, nourished and knit together by joints and ligaments, grows with the increase *that is* from God.

Is indissoluble.

Rom 8:35 Who shall separate us from the love of Christ? *Shall* tribulation, or distress, or persecution, or famine, or nakedness, or peril, or sword?

Punishment of those without.

John 15:6 If anyone does not abide in Me, he is cast out as a branch and is withered; and they gather them and throw *them* into the fire, and they are burned.

Illustrated by

Vine and branches.

John 15:1 "I am the true vine, and My Father is the vinedresser.

John 15:5 "I am the vine, you *are* the branches. He who abides in Me, and I in him, bears much fruit; for without Me you can do nothing.

Foundation and building.

1 Cor 3:10–11 According to the grace of God which was given to me, as a wise master builder I have laid the foundation, and another builds on it. But let each one take heed how he builds on it. **11** For no other foundation can anyone lay than that which is laid, which is Jesus Christ.

Eph 2:20–21 having been built on the foundation of the apostles and prophets, Jesus Christ Himself being the chief cornerstone, **21** in whom the whole building, being fitted together, grows into a holy temple in the Lord,

1 Pet 2:4–6 Coming to Him *as to* a living stone, rejected indeed by men, but chosen by God *and* precious, **5** you also, as living stones, are being built up a spiritual house, a holy priesthood, to offer up spiritual sacrifices acceptable to God through Jesus Christ. **6** Therefore it is also contained in the Scripture, *"Behold, I lay in Zion A chief cornerstone, elect, precious, And he who believes on Him will by no means be put to shame."*

Body and members.

1 Cor 12:12 For as the body is one and has many members, but all the members of that one body, being many, are one body, so also *is* Christ.

1 Cor 12:27 Now you are the body of Christ, and members individually.

Eph 5:30 For we are members of His body, of His flesh and of His bones.

Husband and wife.

Eph 5:25–32 Husbands, love your wives, just as Christ also loved the church and gave Himself for her, **26** that He might sanctify and cleanse her with the washing of water by the word, **27** that He might present her to Himself a glorious church, not having spot or wrinkle or any such thing, but that she should be holy and without blemish. **28** So husbands ought to love their own wives as their own bodies; he who loves his wife loves himself. **29** For no one ever hated his own flesh, but nourishes and cherishes it, just as the Lord *does* the church. **30** For we are members of His body, of His flesh and of His bones. **31** *"For this reason a man shall leave his father and mother and be joined to his wife, and the two shall become one flesh."* **32** This is a great mystery, but I speak concerning Christ and the church.

JEWS, THE

Divided into twelve tribes.

Gen 35:22 And it happened, when Israel dwelt in that land, that Reuben went and lay with Bilhah his father's concubine; and Israel heard *about it*. Now the sons of Jacob were twelve:

Gen 49:28 All these *are* the twelve tribes of Israel, and this *is* what their father spoke to them. And he blessed them; he blessed each one according to his own blessing.

Other names for

Hebrews.

Gen 14:13 Then one who had escaped came and told Abram the Hebrew, for he dwelt by the terebinth trees of Mamre the Amorite, brother of Eshcol and brother of Aner; and they *were* allies with Abram.

Gen 40:15 For indeed I was stolen away from the land of the Hebrews; and also I have done nothing here that they should put me into the dungeon."

2 Cor 11:22 Are they Hebrews? So *am* I. Are they Israelites? So *am* I. Are they the seed of Abraham? So *am* I.

Israelites.

Ex 9:7 Then Pharaoh sent, and indeed, not even one of the livestock of the Israelites was dead. But the heart

of Pharaoh became hard, and he did not let the people go.

Josh 3:17 Then the priests who bore the ark of the covenant of the LORD stood firm on dry ground in the midst of the Jordan; and all Israel crossed over on dry ground, until all the people had crossed completely over the Jordan.

Seed of Abraham.

Ps 105:6 O seed of Abraham His servant, You children of Jacob, His chosen ones!

Is 41:8 "But you, Israel, *are* My servant, Jacob whom I have chosen, The descendants of Abraham My friend.

Descendants of Jacob.

Jer 33:26 then I will cast away the descendants of Jacob and David My servant, *so* that I will not take *any* of his descendants *to be* rulers over the descendants of Abraham, Isaac, and Jacob. For I will cause their captives to return, and will have mercy on them.' "

Seed of Israel.

1 Chr 16:13 O seed of Israel His servant, You children of Jacob, His chosen ones!

Children of Jacob.

1 Chr 16:13 O seed of Israel His servant, You children of Jacob, His chosen ones!

Children of Israel.

Gen 50:25 Then Joseph took an oath from the children of Israel, saying, "God will surely visit you, and you shall carry up my bones from here."

Is 27:12 And it shall come to pass in that day *That* the LORD will thresh, From the channel of the River to the Brook of Egypt; And you will be gathered one by one, O you children of Israel.

Jeshurun.

Deut 32:15 "But Jeshurun grew fat and kicked; You grew fat, you grew thick, You are obese! Then he forsook God *who* made him, And scornfully esteemed the Rock of his salvation.

Chosen and loved by God.

Deut 7:6–7 "For you *are* a holy people to the LORD your God; the LORD your God has chosen you to be a people for Himself, a special treasure above all the peoples on the face of the earth. **7** The LORD did not set His love on you nor choose you because you were more in number than any other people, for you were the least of all peoples;

Circumcised as a sign of their covenant relation.

Gen 17:10–11 This *is* My covenant which you shall keep, between Me and you and your descendants after you: Every male child among you shall be circumcised; **11** and you shall be circumcised in the flesh of your foreskins, and it shall be a sign of the covenant between Me and you.

Acts 7:8 Then He gave him the covenant of circumcision; and so *Abraham* begot Isaac and circumcised him on the eighth day; and Isaac *begot* Jacob, and Jacob *begot* the twelve patriarchs.

Separated from all other nations.

Ex 33:16 For how then will it be known that Your people and I have found grace in Your sight, except You go with us? So we shall be separate, Your people and

I, from all the people who *are* upon the face of the earth."

Lev 20:24 But I have said to you, "You shall inherit their land, and I will give it to you to possess, a land flowing with milk and honey." I *am* the LORD your God, who has separated you from the peoples.

1 Kin 8:53 For You separated them from among all the peoples of the earth *to be* Your inheritance, as You spoke by Your servant Moses, when You brought our fathers out of Egypt, O Lord GOD."

Described as

A special treasure.

Ex 19:5 Now therefore, if you will indeed obey My voice and keep My covenant, then you shall be a special treasure to Me above all people; for all the earth *is* Mine.

Deut 7:6 "For you *are* a holy people to the LORD your God; the LORD your God has chosen you to be a people for Himself, a special treasure above all the peoples on the face of the earth.

Deut 14:2 For you *are* a holy people to the LORD your God, and the LORD has chosen you to be a people for Himself, a special treasure above all the peoples who *are* on the face of the earth.

Ps 135:4 For the LORD has chosen Jacob for Himself, Israel for His special treasure.

A holy nation.

Ex 19:6 And you shall be to Me a kingdom of priests and a holy nation.' These *are* the words which you shall speak to the children of Israel."

A holy people.

Deut 7:6 "For you *are* a holy people to the LORD your God; the LORD your God has chosen you to be a people for Himself, a special treasure above all the peoples on the face of the earth.

Deut 14:21 "You shall not eat anything that dies *of itself*; you may give it to the alien who *is* within your gates, that he may eat it, or you may sell it to a foreigner; for you *are* a holy people to the LORD your God. "You shall not boil a young goat in its mother's milk.

A kingdom of priests.

Ex 19:6 And you shall be to Me a kingdom of priests and a holy nation.' These *are* the words which you shall speak to the children of Israel."

The Lord's portion.

Deut 32:9 For the LORD's portion *is* His people; Jacob *is* the place of His inheritance.

Sojourned in Egypt.

Ex 12:40–41 Now the sojourn of the children of Israel who lived in Egypt *was* four hundred and thirty years. **41** And it came to pass at the end of the four hundred and thirty years—on that very same day—it came to pass that all the armies of the LORD went out from the land of Egypt.

Brought out of Egypt by God.

Ex 12:42 It *is* a night of solemn observance to the LORD for bringing them out of the land of Egypt. This *is* that night of the LORD, a solemn observance for all the children of Israel throughout their generations.

Deut 5:15 And remember that you were a slave in the land of Egypt, and the LORD your God brought you out from there by a mighty hand and by an outstretched arm; therefore the LORD your God commanded you to keep the Sabbath day.

Deut 6:12 *then* beware, lest you forget the LORD who brought you out of the land of Egypt, from the house of bondage.

In the wilderness forty years.

Num 14:33 And your sons shall be shepherds in the wilderness forty years, and bear the brunt of your infidelity, until your carcasses are consumed in the wilderness.

Josh 5:6 For the children of Israel walked forty years in the wilderness, till all the people *who were* men of war, who came out of Egypt, were consumed, because they did not obey the voice of the LORD—to whom the LORD swore that He would not show them the land which the LORD had sworn to their fathers that He would give us, "a land flowing with milk and honey."

Settled in Canaan.

Num 32:18 We will not return to our homes until every one of the children of Israel has received his inheritance.

Josh 14:1–5 These *are the areas* which the children of Israel inherited in the land of Canaan, which Eleazar the priest, Joshua the son of Nun, and the heads of the fathers of the tribes of the children of Israel distributed as an inheritance to them. **2** Their inheritance *was* by lot, as the LORD had commanded by the hand of Moses, for the nine tribes and the half-tribe. **3** For Moses had given the inheritance of the two tribes and the half-tribe on the other side of the Jordan; but to the Levites he had given no inheritance among them. **4** For the children of Joseph were two tribes: Manasseh and Ephraim. And they gave no part to the Levites in the land, except cities to dwell *in*, with their common-lands for their livestock and their property. **5** As the LORD had commanded Moses, so the children of Israel did; and they divided the land.

Under the theocracy until the time of Samuel.

Ex 19:4–6 'You have seen what I did to the Egyptians, and *how* I bore you on eagles' wings and brought you to Myself. **5** Now therefore, if you will indeed obey My voice and keep My covenant, then you shall be a special treasure to Me above all people; for all the earth *is* Mine. **6** And you shall be to Me a kingdom of priests and a holy nation.' These *are* the words which you shall speak to the children of Israel."

1 Sam 8:7 And the LORD said to Samuel, "Heed the voice of the people in all that they say to you; for they have not rejected you, but they have rejected Me, that I should not reign over them.

Desired and obtained kings.

1 Sam 8:5 and said to him, "Look, you are old, and your sons do not walk in your ways. Now make us a king to judge us like all the nations."

1 Sam 8:22 So the LORD said to Samuel, "Heed their voice, and make them a king." And Samuel said to the men of Israel, "Every man go to his city."

Divided into two kingdoms after Solomon.

1 Kin 11:31–32 And he said to Jeroboam, "Take for

yourself ten pieces, for thus says the LORD, the God of Israel: 'Behold, I will tear the kingdom out of the hand of Solomon and will give ten tribes to you 32 (but he shall have one tribe for the sake of My servant David, and for the sake of Jerusalem, the city which I have chosen out of all the tribes of Israel),

1 Kin 12:19–20 So Israel has been in rebellion against the house of David to this day. 20 Now it came to pass when all Israel heard that Jeroboam had come back, they sent for him and called him to the congregation, and made him king over all Israel. There was none who followed the house of David, but the tribe of Judah only.

Often subdued and made tributary.

Judg 2:13–14 They forsook the LORD and served Baal and the Ashtoreths. 14 And the anger of the LORD was hot against Israel. So He delivered them into the hands of plunderers who despoiled them; and He sold them into the hands of their enemies all around, so that they could no longer stand before their enemies.

Judg 4:2 So the LORD sold them into the hand of Jabin king of Canaan, who reigned in Hazor. The commander of his army *was* Sisera, who dwelt in Harosheth Hagoyim.

Judg 6:2 and the hand of Midian prevailed against Israel. Because of the Midianites, the children of Israel made for themselves the dens, the caves, and the strongholds which *are* in the mountains.

Judg 6:6 So Israel was greatly impoverished because of the Midianites, and the children of Israel cried out to the LORD.

2 Kin 23:33 Now Pharaoh Necho put him in prison at Riblah in the land of Hamath, that he might not reign in Jerusalem; and he imposed on the land a tribute of one hundred talents of silver and a talent of gold.

Taken captive to Assyria and Babylon.

2 Kin 17:32 So they feared the LORD, and from every class they appointed for themselves priests of the high places, who sacrificed for them in the shrines of the high places.

2 Kin 18:11 Then the king of Assyria carried Israel away captive to Assyria, and put them in Halah and by the Habor, the River of Gozan, and in the cities of the Medes,

2 Kin 24:16 All the valiant men, seven thousand, and craftsmen and smiths, one thousand, all *who were* strong *and* fit for war, these the king of Babylon brought captive to Babylon.

2 Kin 25:11 Then Nebuzaradan the captain of the guard carried away captive the rest of the people *who* remained in the city and the defectors who had deserted to the king of Babylon, with the rest of the multitude.

Restored to their own land by Cyrus.

Ezra 1:1–4 Now in the first year of Cyrus king of Persia, that the word of the LORD by the mouth of Jeremiah might be fulfilled, the LORD stirred up the spirit of Cyrus king of Persia, so that he made a proclamation throughout all his kingdom, and also *put it* in writing, saying, 2 Thus says Cyrus king of Persia: All the kingdoms of the earth the LORD God of heaven has given me. And He has commanded me to build Him

a house at Jerusalem which *is* in Judah. 3 Who *is* among you of all His people? May his God be with him, and let him go up to Jerusalem which *is* in Judah, and build the house of the LORD God of Israel (He *is* God), which *is* in Jerusalem. 4 And whoever is left in any place where he dwells, let the men of his place help him with silver and gold, with goods and livestock, besides the freewill offerings for the house of God which *is* in Jerusalem.

Had courts of justice.

Deut 16:18 "You shall appoint judges and officers in all your gates, which the LORD your God gives you, according to your tribes, and they shall judge the people with just judgment.

Had an ecclesiastical establishment.

Ex 28:1 "Now take Aaron your brother, and his sons with him, from among the children of Israel, that he may minister to Me as priest, Aaron *and* Aaron's sons: Nadab, Abihu, Eleazar, and Ithamar.

Num 18:6 Behold, I Myself have taken your brethren the Levites from among the children of Israel; *they are* a gift to you, given by the LORD, to do the work of the tabernacle of meeting.

Mal 2:4–7 Then you shall know that I have sent this commandment to you, That My covenant with Levi may continue," Says the LORD of hosts. 5 "My covenant was with him, *one* of life and peace, And I gave them to him *that he might* fear *Me;* So he feared Me And was reverent before My name. 6 The law of truth was in his mouth, And injustice was not found on his lips. He walked with Me in peace and equity, And turned many away from iniquity. 7 "For the lips of a priest should keep knowledge, And *people* should seek the law from his mouth; For he is the messenger of the LORD of hosts.

Had a series of prophets.

Jer 7:25 Since the day that your fathers came out of the land of Egypt until this day, I have even sent to you all My servants the prophets, daily rising up early and sending *them.*

Jer 26:4–5 And you shall say to them, 'Thus says the LORD: "If you will not listen to Me, to walk in My law which I have set before you, 5 to heed the words of My servants the prophets whom I sent to you, both rising up early and sending *them* (but you have not heeded),

Jer 35:15 I have also sent to you all My servants the prophets, rising up early and sending *them,* saying, 'Turn now everyone from his evil way, amend your doings, and do not go after other gods to serve them; then you will dwell in the land which I have given you and your fathers.' But you have not inclined your ear, nor obeyed Me.

Jer 44:4 However I have sent to you all My servants the prophets, rising early and sending *them,* saying, "Oh, do not do this abominable thing that I hate!"

Ezek 38:17 Thus says the Lord GOD: "Are *you* he of whom I have spoken in former days by My servants the prophets of Israel, who prophesied for years in those days that I would bring you against them?

The only people who knew and worshiped God.

Ex 5:17 But he said, "You *are* idle! Idle! Therefore you say, 'Let us go *and* sacrifice to the LORD.'

Ps 48:3 God *is* in her palaces; He is known as her refuge.

Ps 76:1 In Judah God *is* known; His name *is* great in Israel.

Ps 96:5 For all the gods of the peoples *are* idols, But the LORD made the heavens.

Ps 115:3–4 But our God *is* in heaven; He does whatever He pleases. 4 Their idols *are* silver and gold, The work of men's hands.

John 4:22 You worship what you do not know; we know what we worship, for salvation is of the Jews.

Rom 1:28 And even as they did not like to retain God in *their* knowledge, God gave them over to a debased mind, to do those things which are not fitting;

1 Thess 4:5 not in passion of lust, like the Gentiles who do not know God;

Religion of, according to rites prescribed by God.

Lev 18:4 You shall observe My judgments and keep My ordinances, to walk in them: I *am* the LORD your God.

Deut 12:8–11 "You shall not at all do as we are doing here today—every man doing whatever *is* right in his own eyes— 9 for as yet you have not come to the rest and the inheritance which the LORD your God is giving you. 10 But *when* you cross over the Jordan and dwell in the land which the LORD your God is giving you to inherit, and He gives you rest from all your enemies round about, so that you dwell in safety, 11 then there will be the place where the LORD your God chooses to make His name abide. There you shall bring all that I command you: your burnt offerings, your sacrifices, your tithes, the heave offerings of your hand, and all your choice offerings which you vow to the LORD.

Heb 9:1 Then indeed, even the first *covenant* had ordinances of divine service and the earthly sanctuary.

Religion of, typical of greater works.

Heb 9:8–11 the Holy Spirit indicating this, that the way into the Holiest of All was not yet made manifest while the first tabernacle was still standing. 9 It *was* symbolic for the present time in which both gifts and sacrifices are offered which cannot make him who performed the service perfect in regard to the conscience— 10 *concerned* only with foods and drinks, various washings, and fleshly ordinances imposed until the time of reformation. 11 But Christ came *as* High Priest of the good things to come, with the greater and more perfect tabernacle not made with hands, that is, not of this creation.

Heb 10:1 For the law, having a shadow of the good things to come, *and* not the very image of the things, can never with these same sacrifices, which they offer continually year by year, make those who approach perfect.

Great national privileges.

Gen 12:2 I will make you a great nation; I will bless you And make your name great; And you shall be a blessing.

Deut 33:29 Happy *are* you, O Israel! Who *is* like you, a people saved by the LORD, The shield of your help And the sword of your majesty! Your enemies shall submit to you, And you shall tread down their high places."

Rom 3:2 Much in every way! Chiefly because to them were committed the oracles of God.

Rom 9:4–5 who are Israelites, to whom *pertain* the adoption, the glory, the covenants, the giving of the law, the service *of God,* and the promises; 5 of whom *are* the fathers and from whom, according to the flesh, Christ *came,* who is over all, *the* eternally blessed God. Amen.

Their vast numbers.

Gen 22:17 blessing I will bless you, and multiplying I will multiply your descendants as the stars of the heaven and as the sand which *is* on the seashore; and your descendants shall possess the gate of their enemies.

Num 10:36 And when it rested, he said: "Return, O LORD, *To* the many thousands of Israel."

National character of,

Pride of heritage.

Jer 13:9 "Thus says the LORD: 'In this manner I will ruin the pride of Judah and the great pride of Jerusalem.

John 8:33 They answered Him, "We are Abraham's descendants, and have never been in bondage to anyone. How *can* You say, 'You will be made free'?"

John 8:41 You do the deeds of your father." Then they said to Him, "We were not born of fornication; we have one Father—God."

Love of country.

Ps 137:6 If I do not remember you, Let my tongue cling to the roof of my mouth— If I do not exalt Jerusalem Above my chief joy.

Fondness for their brethren.

Ex 2:11–12 Now it came to pass in those days, when Moses was grown, that he went out to his brethren and looked at their burdens. And he saw an Egyptian beating a Hebrew, one of his brethren. 12 So he looked this way and that way, and when he saw no one, he killed the Egyptian and hid him in the sand.

Rom 9:1–3 I tell the truth in Christ, I am not lying, my conscience also bearing me witness in the Holy Spirit, 2 that I have great sorrow and continual grief in my heart. 3 For I could wish that I myself were accursed from Christ for my brethren, my countrymen according to the flesh,

Attachment to Moses.

John 9:28–29 Then they reviled him and said, "You are His disciple, but we are Moses' disciples. 29 We know that God spoke to Moses; *as for* this *fellow,* we do not know where He is from."

Acts 6:11 Then they secretly induced men to say, "We have heard him speak blasphemous words against Moses and God."

Attachment to customs of the law.

Acts 6:14 for we have heard him say that this Jesus of Nazareth will destroy this place and change the customs which Moses delivered to us."

Acts 21:21 but they have been informed about you that you teach all the Jews who are among the Gentiles to forsake Moses, saying that they ought not to circumcise *their* children nor to walk according to the customs.

Acts 22:3 "I am indeed a Jew, born in Tarsus of Cilicia, but brought up in this city at the feet of Gamaliel, taught according to the strictness of our fathers' law, and was zealous toward God as you all are today.

Fondness for traditional customs.

Jer 44:17 But we will certainly do whatever has gone out of our own mouth, to burn incense to the queen of heaven and pour out drink offerings to her, as we have done, we and our fathers, our kings and our princes, in the cities of Judah and in the streets of Jerusalem. For *then* we had plenty of food, were well-off, and saw no trouble.

Ezek 20:18 "But I said to their children in the wilderness, 'Do not walk in the statutes of your fathers, nor observe their judgments, nor defile yourselves with their idols.

Ezek 20:30 Therefore say to the house of Israel, 'Thus says the Lord GOD: "Are you defiling yourselves in the manner of your fathers, and committing harlotry according to their abominations?

Ezek 20:21 "Notwithstanding, the children rebelled against Me; they did not walk in My statutes, and were not careful to observe My judgments, 'which, *if* a man does, he shall live by them'; but they profaned My Sabbaths. Then I said I would pour out My fury on them and fulfill My anger against them in the wilderness.

Mark 7:3–4 For the Pharisees and all the Jews do not eat unless they wash *their* hands in a special way, holding the tradition of the elders. 4 *When they come* from the marketplace, they do not eat unless they wash. And there are many other things which they have received and hold, *like* the washing of cups, pitchers, copper vessels, and couches.

Prone to rebellion.

Ex 32:9 And the LORD said to Moses, "I have seen this people, and indeed it *is* a stiff-necked people!

Deut 9:7 "Remember! Do not forget how you provoked the LORD your God to wrath in the wilderness. From the day that you departed from the land of Egypt until you came to this place, you have been rebellious against the LORD.

Deut 9:24 You have been rebellious against the LORD from the day that I knew you.

Is 1:2 Hear, O heavens, and give ear, O earth! For the LORD has spoken: "I have nourished and brought up children, And they have rebelled against Me;

Acts 7:51 "You stiff-necked and uncircumcised in heart and ears! You always resist the Holy Spirit; as your fathers *did*, so *do* you.

Prone to backsliding and idolatry.

Is 2:8 Their land is also full of idols; They worship the work of their own hands, That which their own fingers have made.

Is 57:5 Inflaming yourselves with gods under every green tree, Slaying the children in the valleys, Under the clefts of the rocks?

Jer 2:11–13 Has a nation changed *its* gods, Which *are* not gods? But My people have changed their Glory For *what* does not profit. 12 Be astonished, O heavens, at this, And be horribly afraid; Be very desolate," says the LORD. 13 "For My people have committed two evils: They have forsaken Me, the fountain of living

waters, *And* hewn themselves cisterns—broken cisterns that can hold no water.

Jer 8:5 Why has this people slidden back, Jerusalem, in a perpetual backsliding? They hold fast to deceit, They refuse to return.

Prone to formality in religion.

Is 29:13 Therefore the Lord said: "Inasmuch as these people draw near with their mouths And honor Me with their lips, But have removed their hearts far from Me, And their fear toward Me is taught by the commandment of men,

Ezek 33:31 So they come to you as people do, they sit before you *as* My people, and they hear your words, but they do not do them; for with their mouth they show much love, *but* their hearts pursue their *own* gain.

Matt 15:7–9 Hypocrites! Well did Isaiah prophesy about you, saying: 8 *'These people draw near to Me with their mouth, And honor Me with their lips, But their heart is far from Me. 9 And in vain they worship Me, Teaching as doctrines the commandments of men.'"*

Self-righteous.

Is 65:5 Who say, 'Keep to yourself, Do not come near me, For I am holier than you!' These *are* smoke in My nostrils, A fire that burns all the day.

Rom 10:3 For they being ignorant of God's righteousness, and seeking to establish their own righteousness, have not submitted to the righteousness of God.

Unfaithful to covenant engagements.

Jer 3:6–8 The LORD said also to me in the days of Josiah the king: "Have you seen what backsliding Israel has done? She has gone up on every high mountain and under every green tree, and there played the harlot. 7 And I said, after she had done all these *things*, 'Return to Me.' But she did not return. And her treacherous sister Judah saw it. 8 Then I saw that for all the causes for which backsliding Israel had committed adultery, I had put her away and given her a certificate of divorce; yet her treacherous sister Judah did not fear, but went and played the harlot also.

Jer 31:32 not according to the covenant that I made with their fathers in the day *that* I took them by the hand to lead them out of the land of Egypt, My covenant which they broke, though I was a husband to them, says the LORD.

Ezek 16:59 For thus says the Lord GOD: "I will deal with you as you have done, who despised the oath by breaking the covenant.

Ungrateful to God.

Deut 32:15 "But Jeshurun grew fat and kicked; You grew fat, you grew thick, You are obese! Then he forsook God *who* made him, And scornfully esteemed the Rock of his salvation.

Is 1:2 Hear, O heavens, and give ear, O earth! For the LORD has spoken: "I have nourished and brought up children, And they have rebelled against Me;

Ignorant of the true sense of Scripture.

Acts 13:27 For those who dwell in Jerusalem, and their rulers, because they did not know Him, nor even the voices of the Prophets which are read every Sabbath, have fulfilled *them* in condemning *Him.*

2 Cor 3:13–15 unlike Moses, *who* put a veil over his face so that the children of Israel could not look steadily at the end of what was passing away. **14** But their minds were blinded. For until this day the same veil remains unlifted in the reading of the Old Testament, because the *veil* is taken away in Christ. **15** But even to this day, when Moses is read, a veil lies on their heart.

Distrustful of God.

Num 14:11 Then the Lord said to Moses: "How long will these people reject Me? And how long will they not believe Me, with all the signs which I have performed among them?

Ps 78:22 Because they did not believe in God, And did not trust in His salvation.

Sometimes covetous.

Jer 6:13 "Because from the least of them even to the greatest of them, Everyone *is* given to covetousness; And from the prophet even to the priest, Everyone deals falsely.

Ezek 33:31 So they come to you as people do, they sit before you *as* My people, and they hear your words, but they do not do them; for with their mouth they show much love, *but* their hearts pursue their *own* gain.

Mic 2:2 They covet fields and take *them* by violence, Also houses, and seize *them*. So they oppress a man and his house, A man and his inheritance.

Sometimes cowardly.

Ex 14:10 And when Pharaoh drew near, the children of Israel lifted their eyes, and behold, the Egyptians marched after them. So they were very afraid, and the children of Israel cried out to the Lord.

Num 14:3 Why has the Lord brought us to this land to fall by the sword, that our wives and children should become victims? Would it not be better for us to return to Egypt?"

Is 51:12 "I, *even* I, *am* He who comforts you. Who *are* you that you should be afraid Of a man *who* will die, And of the son of a man *who* will be made like grass?

Trusted to their privileges for salvation.

Jer 7:4 Do not trust in these lying words, saying, 'The temple of the Lord, the temple of the Lord, the temple of the Lord *are* these.'

Matt 3:9 and do not think to say to yourselves, 'We have Abraham as *our* father.' For I say to you that God is able to raise up children to Abraham from these stones.

Distinction among classes noticed.

Is 65:5 Who say, 'Keep to yourself, Do not come near me, For I am holier than you!' These *are* smoke in My nostrils, A fire that burns all the day.

Luke 7:39 Now when the Pharisee who had invited Him saw *this*, he spoke to himself, saying, "This Man, if He were a prophet, would know who and what manner of woman *this is* who is touching Him, for she is a sinner."

Luke 15:2 And the Pharisees and scribes complained, saying, "This Man receives sinners and eats with them."

Acts 26:5 They knew me from the first, if they were willing to testify, that according to the strictest sect of our religion I lived a Pharisee.

Degenerated as they increased in national greatness.

Amos 6:4 Who lie on beds of ivory, Stretch out on your couches, Eat lambs from the flock And calves from the midst of the stall;

Often displeased God by their sins.

Num 25:3 So Israel was joined to Baal of Peor, and the anger of the Lord was aroused against Israel.

Deut 32:16 They provoked Him to jealousy with foreign *gods;* With abominations they provoked Him to anger.

1 Kin 16:2 "Inasmuch as I lifted you out of the dust and made you ruler over My people Israel, and you have walked in the way of Jeroboam, and have made My people Israel sin, to provoke Me to anger with their sins,

Is 1:4 Alas, sinful nation, A people laden with iniquity, A brood of evildoers, Children who are corrupters! They have forsaken the Lord, They have provoked to anger The Holy One of Israel, They have turned away backward.

Is 5:24–25 Therefore, as the fire devours the stubble, And the flame consumes the chaff, *So* their root will be as rottenness, And their blossom will ascend like dust; Because they have rejected the law of the Lord of hosts, And despised the word of the Holy One of Israel. **25** Therefore the anger of the Lord is aroused against His people; He has stretched out His hand against them And stricken them, And the hills trembled. Their carcasses *were* as refuse in the midst of the streets. For all this His anger is not turned away, But His hand *is* stretched out still.

A spiritual seed of true believers always among.

1 Kin 19:18 Yet I have reserved seven thousand in Israel, all whose knees have not bowed to Baal, and every mouth that has not kissed him."

Is 6:13 But yet a tenth *will be* in it, And will return and be for consuming, As a terebinth tree or as an oak, Whose stump *remains* when it is cut down. So the holy seed *shall be* its stump."

Rom 9:6–7 But it is not that the word of God has taken no effect. For they *are* not all Israel who *are* of Israel, **7** nor *are they* all children because they are the seed of Abraham; but, *"In Isaac your seed shall be called."*

Rom 11:1 I say then, has God cast away His people? Certainly not! For I also am an Israelite, of the seed of Abraham, *of* the tribe of Benjamin.

Rom 11:5 Even so then, at this present time there is a remnant according to the election of grace.

New Testament, divided into

Hebrews or pure Jews.

Acts 6:1 Now in those days, when *the number of* the disciples was multiplying, there arose a complaint against the Hebrews by the Hellenists, because their widows were neglected in the daily distribution.

Phil 3:5 circumcised the eighth day, of the stock of Israel, *of* the tribe of Benjamin, a Hebrew of the Hebrews; concerning the law, a Pharisee;

Hellenists or Greek Jews.

Acts 6:1 Now in those days, when *the number of* the disciples was multiplying, there arose a complaint against the Hebrews by the Hellenists, because their widows were neglected in the daily distribution.

Acts 9:29 And he spoke boldly in the name of the Lord Jesus and disputed against the Hellenists, but they attempted to kill him.

Many sects and parties.

Matt 16:6 Then Jesus said to them, "Take heed and beware of the leaven of the Pharisees and the Sadducees."

Mark 8:15 Then He charged them, saying, "Take heed, beware of the leaven of the Pharisees and the leaven of Herod."

Engaged in both agriculture and commerce.

Gen 46:32 And the men *are* shepherds, for their occupation has been to feed livestock; and they have brought their flocks, their herds, and all that they have.'

Ezek 27:17 Judah and the land of Israel *were* your traders. They traded for your merchandise wheat of Minnith, millet, honey, oil, and balm.

Obliged to unite against enemies.

Num 32:20–22 Then Moses said to them: "If you do this thing, if you arm yourselves before the LORD for the war, 21 and all your armed men cross over the Jordan before the LORD until He has driven out His enemies from before Him, 22 and the land is subdued before the LORD, then afterward you may return and be blameless before the LORD and before Israel; and this land shall be your possession before the LORD.

1 Sam 11:7–8 So he took a yoke of oxen and cut them in pieces, and sent *them* throughout all the territory of Israel by the hands of messengers, saying, "Whoever does not go out with Saul and Samuel to battle, so it shall be done to his oxen." And the fear of the LORD fell on the people, and they came out with one consent. 8 When he numbered them in Bezek, the children of Israel were three hundred thousand, and the men of Judah thirty thousand.

Cf. Judg 19:29; 20:1–48

Often distinguished in war.

Judg 7:19–23 So Gideon and the hundred men who *were* with him came to the outpost of the camp at the beginning of the middle watch, just as they had posted the watch; and they blew the trumpets and broke the pitchers that *were* in their hands. 20 Then the three companies blew the trumpets and broke the pitchers—they held the torches in their left hands and the trumpets in their right hands for blowing—and they cried, "The sword of the LORD and of Gideon!" 21 And every man stood in his place all around the camp; and the whole army ran and cried out and fled. 22 When the three hundred blew the trumpets, the LORD set every man's sword against his companion throughout the whole camp; and the army fled to Beth Acacia, toward Zererah, as far as the border of Abel Meholah, by Tabbath. 23 And the men of Israel gathered together from Naphtali, Asher, and all Manasseh, and pursued the Midianites.

1 Sam 14:6–13 Then Jonathan said to the young man who bore his armor, "Come, let us go over to the garrison of these uncircumcised; it may be that the LORD will work for us. For nothing restrains the LORD from saving by many or by few." 7 So his armorbearer said to him, "Do all that is in your heart. Go then; here I am with you, according to your heart." 8 Then Jona-

than said, "Very well, let us cross over to *these* men, and we will show ourselves to them. 9 If they say thus to us, 'Wait until we come to you,' then we will stand still in our place and not go up to them. 10 But if they say thus, 'Come up to us,' then we will go up. For the LORD has delivered them into our hand, and this *will be* a sign to us." 11 So both of them showed themselves to the garrison of the Philistines. And the Philistines said, "Look, the Hebrews are coming out of the holes where they have hidden." 12 Then the men of the garrison called to Jonathan and his armorbearer, and said, "Come up to us, and we will show you something." Jonathan said to his armorbearer, "Come up after me, for the LORD has delivered them into the hand of Israel." 13 And Jonathan climbed up on his hands and knees with his armorbearer after him; and they fell before Jonathan. And as he came after him, his armorbearer killed them.

1 Sam 17:32–33 Then David said to Saul, "Let no man's heart fail because of him; your servant will go and fight with this Philistine." 33 And Saul said to David, "You are not able to go against this Philistine to fight with him; for you *are* a youth, and he a man of war from his youth."

Neh 4:16–22 So it was, from that time on, *that* half of my servants worked at construction, while the other half held the spears, the shields, the bows, and *wore* armor; and the leaders *were* behind all the house of Judah. 17 Those who built on the wall, and those who carried burdens, loaded themselves so that with one hand they worked at construction, and with the other held a weapon. 18 Every one of the builders had his sword girded at his side as he built. And the one who sounded the trumpet *was* beside me. 19 Then I said to the nobles, the rulers, and the rest of the people, "The work is great and extensive, and we are separated far from one another on the wall. 20 Wherever you hear the sound of the trumpet, rally to us there. Our God will fight for us." 21 So we labored in the work, and half of *the* men held the spears from daybreak until the stars appeared. 22 At the same time I also said to the people, "Let each man and his servant stay at night in Jerusalem, that they may be our guard by night and a working party by day."

Strengthened by God in war.

Lev 26:7–8 You will chase your enemies, and they shall fall by the sword before you. 8 Five of you shall chase a hundred, and a hundred of you shall put ten thousand to flight; your enemies shall fall by the sword before you.

Josh 5:13–14 And it came to pass, when Joshua was by Jericho, that he lifted his eyes and looked, and behold, a Man stood opposite him with His sword drawn in His hand. And Joshua went to Him and said to Him, "*Are* You for us or for our adversaries?" 14 So He said, "No, but *as* Commander of the army of the LORD I have now come." And Joshua fell on his face to the earth and worshiped, and said to Him, "What does my Lord say to His servant?"

Josh 8:1–2 Now the LORD said to Joshua: "Do not be afraid, nor be dismayed; take all the people of war with you, and arise, go up to Ai. See, I have given into your hand the king of Ai, his people, his city, and his land. **2** And you shall do to Ai and its king as you did to Jericho and its king. Only its spoil and its cattle you shall take as booty for yourselves. Lay an ambush for the city behind it."

Under God's special protection.

Deut 32:10–11 "He found him in a desert land And in the wasteland, a howling wilderness; He encircled him, He instructed him, He kept him as the apple of His eye. **11** As an eagle stirs up its nest, Hovers over its young, Spreading out its wings, taking them up, Carrying them on its wings,

Deut 33:27–29 The eternal God *is your* refuge, And underneath *are* the everlasting arms; He will thrust out the enemy from before you, And will say, 'Destroy!' **28** Then Israel shall dwell in safety, The fountain of Jacob alone, In a land of grain and new wine; His heavens shall also drop dew. **29** Happy *are* you, O Israel! Who *is* like you, a people saved by the LORD, The shield of your help And the sword of your majesty! Your enemies shall submit to you, And you shall tread down their high places."

Ps 105:13–15 When they went from one nation to another, From *one* kingdom to another people, **14** He permitted no one to do them wrong; Yes, He rebuked kings for their sakes, **15** *Saying,* "Do not touch My anointed ones, And do My prophets no harm."

Ps 121:3–5 He will not allow your foot to be moved; He who keeps you will not slumber. **4** Behold, He who keeps Israel Shall neither slumber nor sleep. **5** The LORD *is* your keeper; The LORD *is* your shade at your right hand.

Enemies of, obliged to acknowledge them as divinely protected.

Josh 2:9–11 and said to the men: "I know that the LORD has given you the land, that the terror of you has fallen on us, and that all the inhabitants of the land are fainthearted because of you. **10** For we have heard how the LORD dried up the water of the Red Sea for you when you came out of Egypt, and what you did to the two kings of the Amorites who *were* on the other side of the Jordan, Sihon and Og, whom you utterly destroyed. **11** And as soon as we heard *these things,* our hearts melted; neither did there remain any more courage in anyone because of you, for the LORD your God, He *is* God in heaven above and on earth beneath.

Esth 6:13 When Haman told his wife Zeresh and all his friends everything that had happened to him, his wise men and his wife Zeresh said to him, "If Mordecai, before whom you have begun to fall, is of Jewish descent, you will not prevail against him but will surely fall before him."

Prohibited from

Associating with other peoples.

Acts 10:28 Then he said to them, "You know how unlawful it is for a Jewish man to keep company with or go to one of another nation. But God has shown me that I should not call any man common or unclean.

Covenanting with others.

Ex 23:32 You shall make no covenant with them, nor with their gods.

Deut 7:2 and when the LORD your God delivers them

over to you, you shall conquer them *and* utterly destroy them. You shall make no covenant with them nor show mercy to them.

Intermarrying with others.

Deut 7:3 Nor shall you make marriages with them. You shall not give your daughter to their son, nor take their daughter for your son.

Josh 23:12 Or else, if indeed you do go back, and cling to the remnant of these nations—these that remain among you—and make marriages with them, and go in to them and they to you,

Following practices of others.

Deut 12:29–31 "When the LORD your God cuts off from before you the nations which you go to dispossess, and you displace them and dwell in their land, **30** take heed to yourself that you are not ensnared to follow them, after they are destroyed from before you, and that you do not inquire after their gods, saying, 'How did these nations serve their gods? I also will do likewise.' **31** You shall not worship the LORD your God in that way; for every abomination to the LORD which He hates they have done to their gods; for they burn even their sons and daughters in the fire to their gods.

Deut 18:9–14 "When you come into the land which the LORD your God is giving you, you shall not learn to follow the abominations of those nations. **10** There shall not be found among you *anyone* who makes his son or his daughter pass through the fire, *or one* who practices witchcraft, *or* a soothsayer, or one who interprets omens, or a sorcerer, **11** or one who conjures spells, or a medium, or a spiritist, or one who calls up the dead. **12** For all who do these things *are* an abomination to the LORD, and because of these abominations the LORD your God drives them out from before you. **13** You shall be blameless before the LORD your God. **14** For these nations which you will dispossess listened to soothsayers and diviners; but as for you, the LORD your God has not appointed such for you.

Despised and avoided all foreigners.

1 Sam 17:36 Your servant has killed both lion and bear; and this uncircumcised Philistine will be like one of them, seeing he has defied the armies of the living God."

Matt 16:26–27 For what profit is it to a man if he gains the whole world, and loses his own soul? Or what will a man give in exchange for his soul? **27** For the Son of Man will come in the glory of His Father with His angels, and then He will reward each according to his works.

John 4:9 Then the woman of Samaria said to Him, "How is it that You, being a Jew, ask a drink from me, a Samaritan woman?" For Jews have no dealings with Samaritans.

Acts 11:2–3 And when Peter came up to Jerusalem, those of the circumcision contended with him, **3** saying, "You went in to uncircumcised men and ate with them!"

Eph 2:11 Therefore remember that you, once Gentiles in the flesh—who are called Uncircumcision by what is called the Circumcision made in the flesh by hands—

Condemned for associating with other nations.

Judg 2:1–3 Then the Angel of the LORD came up from Gilgal to Bochim, and said: "I led you up from Egypt and brought you to the land of which I swore to your fathers; and I said, 'I will never break My covenant with you. **2** And you shall make no covenant with the inhabitants of this land; you shall tear down their altars.' But you have not obeyed My voice. Why have you done this? **3** Therefore I also said, 'I will not drive them out before you; but they shall be *thorns* in your side, and their gods shall be a snare to you.' "

Jer 2:18 And now why take the road to Egypt, To drink the waters of Sihor? Or why take the road to Assyria, To drink the waters of the River?

Received proselytes from other nations.

Ex 12:44 But every man's servant who is bought for money, when you have circumcised him, then he may eat it.

Ex 12:48 And when a stranger dwells with you *and wants* to keep the Passover to the LORD, let all his males be circumcised, and then let him come near and keep it; and he shall be as a native of the land. For no uncircumcised person shall eat it.

Acts 2:10 Phrygia and Pamphylia, Egypt and the parts of Libya adjoining Cyrene, visitors from Rome, both Jews and proselytes,

Gentiles made one with, under the gospel.

Acts 10:15 And a voice *spoke* to him again the second time, "What God has cleansed you must not call common."

Acts 10:28 Then he said to them, "You know how unlawful it is for a Jewish man to keep company with or go to one of another nation. But God has shown me that I should not call any man common or unclean.

Acts 15:8–9 So God, who knows the heart, acknowledged them by giving them the Holy Spirit, just as *He did* to us, **9** and made no distinction between us and them, purifying their hearts by faith.

Gal 3:28 There is neither Jew nor Greek, there is neither slave nor free, there is neither male nor female; for you are all one in Christ Jesus.

Eph 2:14–16 For He Himself is our peace, who has made both one, and has broken down the middle wall of separation, **15** having abolished in His flesh the enmity, *that is,* the law of commandments *contained* in ordinances, so as to create in Himself one new man *from* the two, *thus* making peace, **16** and that He might reconcile them both to God in one body through the cross, thereby putting to death the enmity.

All other nations

Envied.

Neh 4:1 But it so happened, when Sanballat heard that we were rebuilding the wall, that he was furious and very indignant, and mocked the Jews.

Is 26:11 LORD, *when* Your hand is lifted up, they will not see. But they will see and be ashamed For *their* envy of people; Yes, the fire of Your enemies shall devour them.

Ezek 35:11 therefore, *as* I live," says the Lord GOD, "I will do according to your anger and according to the envy which you showed in your hatred against them; and I will make Myself known among them when I judge you.

Hated.

Ps 44:10 You make us turn back from the enemy, And those who hate us have taken spoil for themselves.

Ezek 35:5 "Because you have had an ancient hatred, and have shed *the blood of* the children of Israel by the power of the sword at the time of their calamity, *when* their iniquity *came to an* end,

Oppressed.

Ex 3:9 Now therefore, behold, the cry of the children of Israel has come to Me, and I have also seen the oppression with which the Egyptians oppress them.

Judg 2:18 And when the LORD raised up judges for them, the LORD was with the judge and delivered them out of the hand of their enemies all the days of the judge; for the LORD was moved to pity by their groaning because of those who oppressed them and harassed them.

Judg 4:3 And the children of Israel cried out to the LORD; for Jabin had nine hundred chariots of iron, and for twenty years he had harshly oppressed the children of Israel.

Persecuted.

Lam 1:3 Judah has gone into captivity, Under affliction and hard servitude; She dwells among the nations, She finds no rest; All her persecutors overtake her in dire straits.

Lam 5:5 *They* pursue at our heels; We labor *and* have no rest.

Rejoiced at calamities of.

Ps 44:13–14 You make us a reproach to our neighbors, A scorn and a derision to those all around us. **14** You make us a byword among the nations, A shaking of the head among the peoples.

Ps 80:5–6 You have fed them with the bread of tears, And given them tears to drink in great measure. **6** You have made us a strife to our neighbors, And our enemies laugh among themselves.

Ezek 36:4 therefore, O mountains of Israel, hear the word of the Lord GOD! Thus says the Lord GOD to the mountains, the hills, the rivers, the valleys, the desolate wastes, and the cities that have been forsaken, which became plunder and mockery to the rest of the nations all around—

Were punished for oppression of.

Ps 137:8–9 O daughter of Babylon, who are to be destroyed, Happy the one who repays you as you have served us! **9** Happy the one who takes and dashes Your little ones against the rock!

Ezek 25:15–16 'Thus says the Lord GOD: "Because the Philistines dealt vengefully and took vengeance with a spiteful heart, to destroy because of the old hatred," **16** therefore thus says the Lord GOD: "I will stretch out My hand against the Philistines, and I will cut off the Cherethites and destroy the remnant of the seacoast.

Ezek 35:6 therefore, *as* I live," says the Lord GOD, "I will prepare you for blood, and blood shall pursue you; since you have not hated blood, therefore blood shall pursue you.

Obad 1:10–16 "For violence against your brother Jacob, Shame shall cover you, And you shall be cut off forever. **11** In the day that you stood on the other side— In the day that strangers carried captive his forces, When foreigners entered his gates And cast lots for Jerusalem— Even you *were* as one of them. **12** "But you should not have gazed on the day of your brother In the day of his captivity; Nor should you have rejoiced over the children of Judah In the day of their destruction; Nor should you have spoken proudly In the day of distress. **13** You should not have entered the gate of My people In the day of their calamity. Indeed, you should not have gazed on their affliction In the day of their calamity, Nor laid *hands* on their substance In the day of their calamity. **14** You should not have stood at the crossroads To cut off those among them who escaped; Nor should you have delivered up those among them who remained In the day of distress. **15** "For the day of the LORD upon all the nations *is* near; As you have done, it shall be done to you; Your reprisal shall return upon your own head. **16** For as you drank on My holy mountain, *So* shall all the nations drink continually; Yes, they shall drink, and swallow, And they shall be as though they had never been.

Christ was

Promised to.

Gen 49:10 The scepter shall not depart from Judah, Nor a lawgiver from between his feet, Until Shiloh comes; And to Him *shall be* the obedience of the people.

Dan 9:25 "Know therefore and understand, *That* from the going forth of the command To restore and build Jerusalem Until Messiah the Prince, *There shall be* seven weeks and sixty-two weeks; The street shall be built again, and the wall, Even in troublesome times.

Expected by.

Ps 14:7 Oh, that the salvation of Israel *would come* out of Zion! When the LORD brings back the captivity of His people, Let Jacob rejoice *and* Israel be glad.

Matt 11:3 and said to Him, "Are You the Coming One, or do we look for another?"

Luke 2:25 And behold, there was a man in Jerusalem whose name was Simeon, and this man was just and devout, waiting for the Consolation of Israel, and the Holy Spirit was upon him.

Luke 2:38 And coming in that instant she gave thanks to the Lord, and spoke of Him to all those who looked for redemption in Jerusalem.

John 4:22 You worship what you do not know; we know what we worship, for salvation is of the Jews.

John 8:56 Your father Abraham rejoiced to see My day, and he saw *it* and was glad."

Was sent to.

Matt 15:24 But He answered and said, "I was not sent except to the lost sheep of the house of Israel."

Matt 21:37 Then last of all he sent his son to them, saying, 'They will respect my son.'

Acts 3:20 and that He may send Jesus Christ, who was preached to you before,

Acts 3:22 For Moses truly said to the fathers, 'The LORD your God will raise up for you a Prophet like me

from your brethren. Him you shall hear in all things, whatever He says to you.

Acts 3:26 To you first, God, having raised up His Servant Jesus, sent Him to bless you, in turning away every one *of you* from your iniquities."

Regarded as the restorer of national greatness.

Matt 20:21 And He said to her, "What do you wish?" She said to Him, "Grant that these two sons of mine may sit, one on Your right hand and the other on the left, in Your kingdom."

Luke 24:21 But we were hoping that it was He who was going to redeem Israel. Indeed, besides all this, today is the third day since these things happened.

Acts 1:6 Therefore, when they had come together, they asked Him, saying, "Lord, will You at this time restore the kingdom to Israel?"

One of.

Rom 9:5 of whom *are* the fathers and from whom, according to the flesh, Christ *came*, who is over all, *the* eternally blessed God. Amen.

Heb 7:14 For *it is* evident that our Lord arose from Judah, of which tribe Moses spoke nothing concerning priesthood.

Rejected by.

Is 53:3 He is despised and rejected by men, A Man of sorrows and acquainted with grief. And we hid, as it were, *our* faces from Him; He was despised, and we did not esteem Him.

Mark 6:3 Is this not the carpenter, the Son of Mary, and brother of James, Joses, Judas, and Simon? And are not His sisters here with us?" So they were offended at Him.

John 1:11 He came to His own, and His own did not receive Him.

Compassionate for.

Matt 23:37 "O Jerusalem, Jerusalem, the one who kills the prophets and stones those who are sent to her! How often I wanted to gather your children together, as a hen gathers her chicks under *her* wings, but you were not willing!

Luke 19:41 Now as He drew near, He saw the city and wept over it,

Took responsibility for Christ's death.

Matt 27:25 And all the people answered and said, "His blood *be* on us and on our children."

Acts 7:52 Which of the prophets did your fathers not persecute? And they killed those who foretold the coming of the Just One, of whom you now have become the betrayers and murderers,

1 Thess 2:15 who killed both the Lord Jesus and their own prophets, and have persecuted us; and they do not please God and are contrary to all men,

Many of, believed the gospel.

Acts 21:20 And when they heard *it*, they glorified the Lord. And they said to him, "You see, brother, how many myriads of Jews there are who have believed, and they are all zealous for the law;

Unbelieving, persecuted the Christians.

Acts 17:5 But the Jews who were not persuaded, becoming envious, took some of the evil men from the marketplace, and gathering a mob, set all the city in an uproar and attacked the house of Jason, and sought to bring them out to the people.

Acts 17:13 But when the Jews from Thessalonica learned that the word of God was preached by Paul at Berea, they came there also and stirred up the crowds.

1 Thess 2:14–16 For you, brethren, became imitators of the churches of God which are in Judea in Christ Jesus. For you also suffered the same things from your own countrymen, just as they *did* from the Judeans, **15** who killed both the Lord Jesus and their own prophets, and have persecuted us; and they do not please God and are contrary to all men, **16** forbidding us to speak to the Gentiles that they may be saved, so as always to fill up *the measure of* their sins; but wrath has come upon them to the uttermost.

Broken off for unbelief.

Rom 11:17 And if some of the branches were broken off, and you, being a wild olive tree, were grafted in among them, and with them became a partaker of the root and fatness of the olive tree,

Rom 11:20 Well *said*. Because of unbelief they were broken off, and you stand by faith. Do not be haughty, but fear.

Dispersed abroad.

Deut 28:64 "Then the LORD will scatter you among all peoples, from one end of the earth to the other, and there you shall serve other gods, which neither you nor your fathers have known—wood and stone.

Is 18:2 Which sends ambassadors by sea, Even in vessels of reed on the waters, *saying*, "Go, swift messengers, to a nation tall and smooth *of skin*, To a people terrible from their beginning onward, A nation powerful and treading down, Whose land the rivers divide."

Is 18:7 In that time a present will be brought to the LORD of hosts From a people tall and smooth *of skin*, And from a people terrible from their beginning onward, A nation powerful and treading down, Whose land the rivers divide— To the place of the name of the LORD of hosts, To Mount Zion.

Ezek 6:8 "Yet I will leave a remnant, so that you may have *some* who escape the sword among the nations, when you are scattered through the countries.

Ezek 36:19 So I scattered them among the nations, and they were dispersed throughout the countries; I judged them according to their ways and their deeds.

James 1:1 James, a bondservant of God and of the Lord Jesus Christ, To the twelve tribes which are scattered abroad: Greetings.

Shall finally be saved.

Rom 11:26–27 And so all Israel will be saved, as it is written: *"The Deliverer will come out of Zion, And He will turn away ungodliness from Jacob; 27 For this is My covenant with them, When I take away their sins."*

Punishment of, for rejecting and killing Christ, illustrated.

Matt 21:37–43 Then last of all he sent his son to them, saying, 'They will respect my son.' **38** But when the vinedressers saw the son, they said among themselves, 'This is the heir. Come, let us kill him and seize his inheritance.' **39** So they took him and cast *him* out of the vineyard and killed *him.* **40** "Therefore, when the owner of the vineyard comes, what will he do to those vinedressers?" **41** They said to Him, "He will destroy those wicked men miserably, and lease *his* vineyard to other vinedressers who will render to him the fruits in their seasons." **42** Jesus said to them, "Have you never read in the Scriptures: *'The stone which the builders rejected Has become the chief cornerstone. This was the LORD's doing, And it is marvelous in our eyes'* ? **43** "Therefore I say to you, the kingdom of God will be taken from you and given to a nation bearing the fruits of it.

Descendants of Abraham.

Ps 105:6 O seed of Abraham His servant, You children of Jacob, His chosen ones!

Is 51:2 Look to Abraham your father, And to Sarah *who* bore you; For I called him alone, And blessed him and increased him."

John 8:33 They answered Him, "We are Abraham's descendants, and have never been in bondage to anyone. How *can* You say, 'You will be made free'?"

John 8:39 They answered and said to Him, "Abraham is our father." Jesus said to them, "If you were Abraham's children, you would do the works of Abraham.

Rom 9:7 nor *are they* all children because they are the seed of Abraham; but, *"In Isaac your seed shall be called."*

Separated to God.

Ex 33:16 For how then will it be known that Your people and I have found grace in Your sight, except You go with us? So we shall be separate, Your people and I, from all the people who *are* upon the face of the earth."

Num 23:9 For from the top of the rocks I see him, And from the hills I behold him; There! A people dwelling alone, Not reckoning itself among the nations.

Deut 4:34 Or did God *ever* try to go *and* take for Himself a nation from the midst of *another* nation, by trials, by signs, by wonders, by war, by a mighty hand and an outstretched arm, and by great terrors, according to all that the LORD your God did for you in Egypt before your eyes?

Deut 32:9 For the LORD's portion *is* His people; Jacob *is* the place of His inheritance.

2 Sam 7:24 For You have made Your people Israel Your very own people forever; and You, LORD, have become their God.

Is 51:16 And I have put My words in your mouth; I have covered you with the shadow of My hand, That I may plant the heavens, Lay the foundations of the earth, And say to Zion, 'You *are* My people.' "

Beloved for their fathers' sake.

Deut 4:37 And because He loved your fathers, therefore He chose their descendants after them; and He brought you out of Egypt with His Presence, with His mighty power,

Deut 10:15 The LORD delighted only in your fathers, to love them; and He chose their descendants after them, you above all peoples, as *it is* this day.

Rom 11:28 Concerning the gospel *they are* enemies for your sake, but concerning the election *they are* beloved for the sake of the fathers.

Were the objects of

God's love.

Deut 7:8 but because the LORD loves you, and because He would keep the oath which He swore to your fathers, the LORD has brought you out with a mighty hand, and redeemed you from the house of bondage, from the hand of Pharaoh king of Egypt.

Deut 23:5 Nevertheless the LORD your God would not listen to Balaam, but the LORD your God turned the curse into a blessing for you, because the LORD your God loves you.

Jer 31:3 The LORD has appeared of old to me, *saying:* "Yes, I have loved you with an everlasting love; Therefore with lovingkindness I have drawn you.

God's choice.

Deut 7:6 "For you *are* a holy people to the LORD your God; the LORD your God has chosen you to be a people for Himself, a special treasure above all the peoples on the face of the earth.

God's protection.

Ps 105:15 *Saying*, "Do not touch My anointed ones, And do My prophets no harm."

Zech 2:8 For thus says the LORD of hosts: "He sent Me after glory, to the nations which plunder you; for he who touches you touches the apple of His eye.

The covenant established with.

Ex 6:4 I have also established My covenant with them, to give them the land of Canaan, the land of their pilgrimage, in which they were strangers.

Ex 24:6–8 And Moses took half the blood and put *it* in basins, and half the blood he sprinkled on the altar. 7 Then he took the Book of the Covenant and read in the hearing of the people. And they said, "All that the LORD has said we will do, and be obedient." 8 And Moses took the blood, sprinkled *it* on the people, and said, "This is the blood of the covenant which the LORD has made with you according to all these words."

Ex 34:27 Then the LORD said to Moses, "Write these words, for according to the tenor of these words I have made a covenant with you and with Israel."

Promises respecting, made to

Abraham.

Gen 12:1–3 Now the LORD had said to Abram: "Get out of your country, From your family And from your father's house, To a land that I will show you. 2 I will make you a great nation; I will bless you And make your name great; And you shall be a blessing. 3 I will bless those who bless you, And I will curse him who curses you; And in you all the families of the earth shall be blessed."

Gen 13:14–17 And the LORD said to Abram, after Lot had separated from him: "Lift your eyes now and look from the place where you are—northward, southward, eastward, and westward; 15 for all the land which you see I give to you and your descendants forever. 16 And I will make your descendants as the dust of the earth; so that if a man could number the dust of the earth, *then* your descendants also

could be numbered. 17 Arise, walk in the land through its length and its width, for I give it to you."

Gen 15:18 On the same day the LORD made a covenant with Abram, saying: "To your descendants I have given this land, from the river of Egypt to the great river, the River Euphrates—

Gen 17:7–8 And I will establish My covenant between Me and you and your descendants after you in their generations, for an everlasting covenant, to be God to you and your descendants after you. 8 Also I give to you and your descendants after you the land in which you are a stranger, all the land of Canaan, as an everlasting possession; and I will be their God."

Isaac.

Gen 26:2–5 Then the LORD appeared to him and said: "Do not go down to Egypt; live in the land of which I shall tell you. 3 Dwell in this land, and I will be with you and bless you; for to you and your descendants I give all these lands, and I will perform the oath which I swore to Abraham your father. 4 And I will make your descendants multiply as the stars of heaven; I will give to your descendants all these lands; and in your seed all the nations of the earth shall be blessed; 5 because Abraham obeyed My voice and kept My charge, My commandments, My statutes, and My laws."

Gen 26:24 And the LORD appeared to him the same night and said, "I *am* the God of your father Abraham; do not fear, for I *am* with you. I will bless you and multiply your descendants for My servant Abraham's sake."

Jacob.

Gen 28:12–15 Then he dreamed, and behold, a ladder *was* set up on the earth, and its top reached to heaven; and there the angels of God were ascending and descending on it. 13 And behold, the LORD stood above it and said: "I *am* the LORD God of Abraham your father and the God of Isaac; the land on which you lie I will give to you and your descendants. 14 Also your descendants shall be as the dust of the earth; you shall spread abroad to the west and the east, to the north and the south; and in you and in your seed all the families of the earth shall be blessed. 15 Behold, I *am* with you and will keep you wherever you go, and will bring you back to this land; for I will not leave you until I have done what I have spoken to you."

Gen 35:9–12 Then God appeared to Jacob again, when he came from Padan Aram, and blessed him. 10 And God said to him, "Your name *is* Jacob; your name shall not be called Jacob anymore, but Israel shall be your name." So He called his name Israel. 11 Also God said to him: "I *am* God Almighty. Be fruitful and multiply; a nation and a company of nations shall proceed from you, and kings shall come from your body. 12 The land which I gave Abraham and Isaac I give to you; and to your descendants after you I give this land."

Themselves.

Ex 6:7–8 I will take you as My people, and I will be your God. Then you shall know that I *am* the LORD your God who brings you out from under the burdens of the Egyptians. 8 And I will bring you into the land which I swore to give to Abraham, Isaac, and Jacob; and I will give it to you *as* a heritage: I *am* the LORD.' "

Ex 19:5–6 Now therefore, if you will indeed obey My voice and keep My covenant, then you shall be a special treasure to Me above all people; for all the earth *is* Mine. **6** And you shall be to Me a kingdom of priests and a holy nation.' These *are* the words which you shall speak to the children of Israel."

Deut 26:18–19 Also today the LORD has proclaimed you to be His special people, just as He promised you, that *you* should keep all His commandments, **19** and that He will set you high above all nations which He has made, in praise, in name, and in honor, and that you may be a holy people to the LORD your God, just as He has spoken."

Privileges of.

Ps 76:1–2 In Judah God *is* known; His name *is* great in Israel. **2** In Salem also is His tabernacle, And His dwelling place in Zion.

Rom 3:1–2 What advantage then has the Jew, or what *is* the profit of circumcision? **2** Much in every way! Chiefly because to them were committed the oracles of God.

Rom 9:4–5 who are Israelites, to whom *pertain* the adoption, the glory, the covenants, the giving of the law, the service *of God,* and the promises; **5** of whom *are* the fathers and from whom, according to the flesh, Christ *came,* who is over all, *the* eternally blessed God. Amen.

Punished for

Idolatry.

Ps 78:58–64 For they provoked Him to anger with their high places, And moved Him to jealousy with their carved images. **59** When God heard *this,* He was furious, And greatly abhorred Israel, **60** So that He forsook the tabernacle of Shiloh, The tent He had placed among men, **61** And delivered His strength into captivity, And His glory into the enemy's hand. **62** He also gave His people over to the sword, And was furious with His inheritance. **63** The fire consumed their young men, And their maidens were not given in marriage. **64** Their priests fell by the sword, And their widows made no lamentation.

Is 65:3–7 A people who provoke Me to anger continually to My face; Who sacrifice in gardens, And burn incense on altars of brick; **4** Who sit among the graves, And spend the night in the tombs; Who eat swine's flesh, And the broth of abominable things is *in* their vessels; **5** Who say, 'Keep to yourself, Do not come near me, For I am holier than you!' These *are* smoke in My nostrils, A fire that burns all the day. **6** "Behold, *it is* written before Me: I will not keep silence, but will repay— Even repay into their bosom— **7** Your iniquities and the iniquities of your fathers together," Says the LORD, "Who have burned incense on the mountains And blasphemed Me on the hills; Therefore I will measure their former work into their bosom."

Unbelief.

Rom 11:20 Well *said.* Because of unbelief they were broken off, and you stand by faith. Do not be haughty, but fear.

Breaking the covenant.

Is 24:5 The earth is also defiled under its inhabitants, Because they have transgressed the laws, Changed the ordinance, Broken the everlasting covenant.

Jer 11:10 They have turned back to the iniquities of their forefathers who refused to hear My words, and they have gone after other gods to serve them; the house of Israel and the house of Judah have broken My covenant which I made with their fathers."

Transgressing the law.

Is 1:4 Alas, sinful nation, A people laden with iniquity, A brood of evildoers, Children who are corrupters! They have forsaken the LORD, They have provoked to anger The Holy One of Israel, They have turned away backward.

Is 1:7 Your country *is* desolate, Your cities *are* burned with fire; Strangers devour your land in your presence; And *it is* desolate, as overthrown by strangers.

Is 24:5–6 The earth is also defiled under its inhabitants, Because they have transgressed the laws, Changed the ordinance, Broken the everlasting covenant. **6** Therefore the curse has devoured the earth, And those who dwell in it are desolate. Therefore the inhabitants of the earth are burned, And few men *are* left.

Changing the ordinances.

Is 24:5 The earth is also defiled under its inhabitants, Because they have transgressed the laws, Changed the ordinance, Broken the everlasting covenant.

Killing the prophets.

Matt 23:37–38 "O Jerusalem, Jerusalem, the one who kills the prophets and stones those who are sent to her! How often I wanted to gather your children together, as a hen gathers her chicks under *her* wings, but you were not willing! **38** See! Your house is left to you desolate;

Oppressed by the nations.

Deut 28:49–52 The LORD will bring a nation against you from afar, from the end of the earth, *as swift* as the eagle flies, a nation whose language you will not understand, **50** a nation of fierce countenance, which does not respect the elderly nor show favor to the young. **51** And they shall eat the increase of your livestock and the produce of your land, until you are destroyed; they shall not leave you grain or new wine or oil, *or* the increase of your cattle or the offspring of your flocks, until they have destroyed you. **52** "They shall besiege you at all your gates until your high and fortified walls, in which you trust, come down throughout all your land; and they shall besiege you at all your gates throughout all your land which the LORD your God has given you.

Ezek 36:3 therefore prophesy, and say, 'Thus says the Lord GOD: "Because they made *you* desolate and swallowed you up on every side, so that you became the possession of the rest of the nations, and you are taken up by the lips of talkers and slandered by the people"—

Luke 21:24 And they will fall by the edge of the sword, and be led away captive into all nations. And Jerusalem will be trampled by Gentiles until the times of the Gentiles are fulfilled.

Deprived of civil and religious privileges.

Hos 3:4 For the children of Israel shall abide many days without king or prince, without sacrifice or sacred pillar, without ephod or teraphim.

Denunciations against those who

Cursed.

Gen 27:29 Let peoples serve you, And nations bow down to you. Be master over your brethren, And let your mother's sons bow down to you. Cursed *be* everyone who curses you, And blessed *be* those who bless you!"

Num 24:9 'He bows down, he lies down as a lion; And as a lion, who shall rouse him?' "Blessed *is* he who blesses you, And cursed *is* he who curses you."

Contended with.

Is 41:11 "Behold, all those who were incensed against you Shall be ashamed and disgraced; They shall be as nothing, And those who strive with you shall perish.

Is 49:25 But thus says the LORD: "Even the captives of the mighty shall be taken away, And the prey of the terrible be delivered; For I will contend with him who contends with you, And I will save your children.

Oppressed.

Is 49:26 I will feed those who oppress you with their own flesh, And they shall be drunk with their own blood as with sweet wine. All flesh shall know That I, the LORD, *am* your Savior, And your Redeemer, the Mighty One of Jacob."

Is 51:21–23 Therefore please hear this, you afflicted, And drunk but not with wine. **22** Thus says your Lord, The LORD and your God, *Who* pleads the cause of His people: "See, I have taken out of your hand The cup of trembling, The dregs of the cup of My fury; You shall no longer drink it. **23** But I will put it into the hand of those who afflict you, Who have said to you, 'Lie down, that we may walk over you.' And you have laid your body like the ground, And as the street, for those who walk over."

Hated.

Ps 129:5 Let all those who hate Zion Be put to shame and turned back.

Ezek 35:5–6 "Because you have had an ancient hatred, and have shed *the blood of* the children of Israel by the power of the sword at the time of their calamity, *when* their iniquity *came to an* end, **6** therefore, *as* I live," says the Lord GOD, "I will prepare you for blood, and blood shall pursue you; since you have not hated blood, therefore blood shall pursue you.

Aggravated the afflictions of.

Zech 1:14–15 So the angel who spoke with me said to me, "Proclaim, saying, 'Thus says the LORD of hosts: "I am zealous for Jerusalem And for Zion with great zeal. **15** I am exceedingly angry with the nations at ease; For I was a little angry, And they helped—*but* with evil *intent*."

Slaughtered.

Ps 79:1–7 O God, the nations have come into Your inheritance; Your holy temple they have defiled; They have laid Jerusalem in heaps. **2** The dead bodies of Your servants They have given *as* food for the birds of the heavens, The flesh of Your saints to the beasts of the earth. **3** Their blood they have shed like water all around Jerusalem, And *there was* no one to bury *them*. **4** We have become a reproach to our neighbors, A scorn and derision to those who are around us. **5** How long, LORD? Will You be angry forever? Will Your jealousy burn like fire? **6** Pour out Your wrath on the nations that do not know You, And on the kingdoms that do not call on Your name. **7** For they have devoured Jacob, And laid waste his dwelling place.

Ezek 35:5–6 "Because you have had an ancient hatred, and have shed *the blood of* the children of Israel by the power of the sword at the time of their calamity, *when* their iniquity *came to an* end, **6** therefore, *as* I live," says the Lord GOD, "I will prepare you for blood, and blood shall pursue you; since you have not hated blood, therefore blood shall pursue you.

God, mindful of.

Ps 98:3 He has remembered His mercy and His faithfulness to the house of Israel; All the ends of the earth have seen the salvation of our God.

Is 49:15–16 "Can a woman forget her nursing child, And not have compassion on the son of her womb? Surely they may forget, Yet I will not forget you. **16** See, I have inscribed you on the palms *of My hands;* Your walls *are* continually before Me.

The gospel preached to, first.

Matt 10:6 But go rather to the lost sheep of the house of Israel.

Luke 24:47 and that repentance and remission of sins should be preached in His name to all nations, beginning at Jerusalem.

Acts 1:8 But you shall receive power when the Holy Spirit has come upon you; and you shall be witnesses to Me in Jerusalem, and in all Judea and Samaria, and to the end of the earth."

Blessedness of blessing.

Gen 27:29 Let peoples serve you, And nations bow down to you. Be master over your brethren, And let your mother's sons bow down to you. Cursed *be* everyone who curses you, And blessed *be* those who bless you!"

Blessedness of favoring.

Gen 12:3 I will bless those who bless you, And I will curse him who curses you; And in you all the families of the earth shall be blessed."

Ps 122:6 Pray for the peace of Jerusalem: "May they prosper who love you.

Believers should,

Pray earnestly for.

Ps 122:6 Pray for the peace of Jerusalem: "May they prosper who love you.

Is 62:1 For Zion's sake I will not hold My peace, And for Jerusalem's sake I will not rest, Until her righteousness goes forth as brightness, And her salvation as a lamp *that* burns.

Is 62:6–7 I have set watchmen on your walls, O Jerusalem; They shall never hold their peace day or night. You who make mention of the LORD, do not keep silent, **7** And give Him no rest till He establishes And till He makes Jerusalem a praise in the earth.

Jer 31:7 For thus says the LORD: "Sing with gladness for Jacob, And shout among the chief of the nations; Proclaim, give praise, and say, 'O LORD, save Your people, The remnant of Israel!'

Rom 10:1 Brethren, my heart's desire and prayer to God for Israel is that they may be saved.

Remember.

Ps 102:14 For Your servants take pleasure in her stones, And show favor to her dust.

Ps 137:5 If I forget you, O Jerusalem, Let my right hand forget *its skill!*

Jer 51:50 You who have escaped the sword, Get away! Do not stand still! Remember the LORD afar off, And let Jerusalem come to your mind.

Promises respecting,

The pouring out of the Spirit upon them.

Ezek 39:29 And I will not hide My face from them anymore; for I shall have poured out My Spirit on the house of Israel,' says the Lord GOD."

Zech 12:10 "And I will pour on the house of David and on the inhabitants of Jerusalem the Spirit of grace and supplication; then they will look on Me whom they pierced. Yes, they will mourn for Him as one mourns for *his* only *son*, and grieve for Him as one grieves for a firstborn.

The removal of their blindness.

Rom 11:25 For I do not desire, brethren, that you should be ignorant of this mystery, lest you should be wise in your own opinion, that blindness in part has happened to Israel until the fullness of the Gentiles has come in.

2 Cor 3:14–16 But their minds were blinded. For until this day the same veil remains unlifted in the reading of the Old Testament, because the *veil* is taken away in Christ. 15 But even to this day, when Moses is read, a veil lies on their heart. 16 Nevertheless when one turns to the Lord, the veil is taken away.

Their return and seeking after God.

Hos 3:5 Afterward the children of Israel shall return and seek the LORD their God and David their king. They shall fear the LORD and His goodness in the latter days.

Their humiliation for the rejection of Christ.

Zech 12:10 "And I will pour on the house of David and on the inhabitants of Jerusalem the Spirit of grace and supplication; then they will look on Me whom they pierced. Yes, they will mourn for Him as one mourns for *his* only *son*, and grieve for Him as one grieves for a firstborn.

Pardon of sin.

Is 44:22 I have blotted out, like a thick cloud, your transgressions, And like a cloud, your sins. Return to Me, for I have redeemed you."

Rom 11:27 *For this is My covenant with them, When I take away their sins."*

Salvation.

Is 59:20 "The Redeemer will come to Zion, And to those who turn from transgression in Jacob," Says the LORD.

Rom 11:26 And so all Israel will be saved, as it is writ-

ten: *"The Deliverer will come out of Zion, And He will turn away ungodliness from Jacob;*

Sanctification.

Jer 33:8 I will cleanse them from all their iniquity by which they have sinned against Me, and I will pardon all their iniquities by which they have sinned and by which they have transgressed against Me.

Ezek 36:25 Then I will sprinkle clean water on you, and you shall be clean; I will cleanse you from all your filthiness and from all your idols.

Zech 12:1 The burden of the word of the LORD against Israel. Thus says the LORD, who stretches out the heavens, lays the foundation of the earth, and forms the spirit of man within him:

Zech 12:8–9 In that day the LORD will defend the inhabitants of Jerusalem; the one who is feeble among them in that day shall be like David, and the house of David *shall be* like God, like the Angel of the LORD before them. 9 It shall be in that day *that* I will seek to destroy all the nations that come against Jerusalem.

Joy experienced by conversion of.

Is 44:23 Sing, O heavens, for the LORD has done *it!* Shout, you lower parts of the earth; Break forth into singing, you mountains, O forest, and every tree in it! For the LORD has redeemed Jacob, And glorified Himself in Israel.

Is 49:13 Sing, O heavens! Be joyful, O earth! And break out in singing, O mountains! For the LORD has comforted His people, And will have mercy on His afflicted.

Is 52:8–9 Your watchmen shall lift up *their* voices, With their voices they shall sing together; For they shall see eye to eye When the LORD brings back Zion. 9 Break forth into joy, sing together, You waste places of Jerusalem! For the LORD has comforted His people, He has redeemed Jerusalem.

Is 66:10 "Rejoice with Jerusalem, And be glad with her, all you who love her; Rejoice for joy with her, all you who mourn for her;

Blessing to the Gentiles by conversion of.

Is 2:1–5 The word that Isaiah the son of Amoz saw concerning Judah and Jerusalem. 2 Now it shall come to pass in the latter days *That* the mountain of the LORD's house Shall be established on the top of the mountains, And shall be exalted above the hills; And all nations shall flow to it. 3 Many people shall come and say, "Come, and let us go up to the mountain of the LORD, To the house of the God of Jacob; He will teach us His ways, And we shall walk in His paths." For out of Zion shall go forth the law, And the word of the LORD from Jerusalem. 4 He shall judge between the nations, And rebuke many people; They shall beat their swords into plowshares, And their spears into pruning hooks; Nation shall not lift up sword against nation, Neither shall they learn war anymore. 5 O house of Jacob, come and let us walk In the light of the LORD.

Is 60:5 Then you shall see and become radiant, And your heart shall swell with joy; Because the abundance of the sea shall be turned to you, The wealth of the Gentiles shall come to you.

Is 66:19 I will set a sign among them; and those among

them who escape I will send to the nations: *to* Tarshish and Pul and Lud, who draw the bow, and Tubal and Javan, *to* the coastlands afar off who have not heard My fame nor seen My glory. And they shall declare My glory among the Gentiles.

Rom 11:12 Now if their fall *is* riches for the world, and their failure riches for the Gentiles, how much more their fullness!

Rom 11:15 For if their being cast away *is* the reconciling of the world, what *will* their acceptance *be* but life from the dead?

Reunion of, in their own land.

Is 11:15–16 The LORD will utterly destroy the tongue of the Sea of Egypt; With His mighty wind He will shake His fist over the River, And strike it in the seven streams, And make *men* cross over dryshod. **16** There will be a highway for the remnant of His people Who will be left from Assyria, As it was for Israel In the day that he came up from the land of Egypt.

Is 14:1–3 For the LORD will have mercy on Jacob, and will still choose Israel, and settle them in their own land. The strangers will be joined with them, and they will cling to the house of Jacob. **2** Then people will take them and bring them to their place, and the house of Israel will possess them for servants and maids in the land of the LORD; they will take them captive whose captives they were, and rule over their oppressors. **3** It shall come to pass in the day the LORD gives you rest from your sorrow, and from your fear and the hard bondage in which you were made to serve,

Is 27:12–13 And it shall come to pass in that day *That* the LORD will thresh, From the channel of the River to the Brook of Egypt; And you will be gathered one by one, O you children of Israel. **13** So it shall be in that day: The great trumpet will be blown; They will come, who are about to perish in the land of Assyria, And they who are outcasts in the land of Egypt, And shall worship the LORD in the holy mount at Jerusalem.

Jer 3:18 "In those days the house of Judah shall walk with the house of Israel, and they shall come together out of the land of the north to the land that I have given as an inheritance to your fathers.

Jer 16:14–15 "Therefore behold, the days are coming," says the LORD, "that it shall no more be said, 'The LORD lives who brought up the children of Israel from the land of Egypt,' **15** but, 'The LORD lives who brought up the children of Israel from the land of the north and from all the lands where He had driven them.' For I will bring them back into their land which I gave to their fathers.

Ezek 36:24 For I will take you from among the nations, gather you out of all countries, and bring you into your own land.

Ezek 37:16–17 "As for you, son of man, take a stick for yourself and write on it: 'For Judah and for the children of Israel, his companions.' Then take another stick and write on it, 'For Joseph, the stick of Ephraim, and *for* all the house of Israel, his companions.' **17** Then join them one to another for yourself into one stick, and they will become one in your hand.

Ezek 37:20–22 And the sticks on which you write will be in your hand before their eyes. **21** "Then say to them, Thus says the Lord GOD: "Surely I will take the children of Israel from among the nations, wherever they have gone, and will gather them from every side and bring them into their own land; **22** and I will make them one nation in the land, on the mountains of Israel; and one king shall be king over them all; they shall no longer be two nations, nor shall they ever be divided into two kingdoms again.

Ezek 37:25 Then they shall dwell in the land that I have given to Jacob My servant, where your fathers dwelt; and they shall dwell there, they, their children, and their children's children, forever; and My servant David *shall be* their prince forever.

Ezek 39:25 "Therefore thus says the Lord GOD: 'Now I will bring back the captives of Jacob, and have mercy on the whole house of Israel; and I will be jealous for My holy name—

Ezek 39:28 then they shall know that I *am* the LORD their God, who sent them into captivity among the nations, but also brought them back to their land, and left none of them captive any longer.

Hos 1:11 Then the children of Judah and the children of Israel Shall be gathered together, And appoint for themselves one head; And they shall come up out of the land, For great *will be* the day of Jezreel!

Mic 2:12 "I will surely assemble all of you, O Jacob, I will surely gather the remnant of Israel; I will put them together like sheep of the fold, Like a flock in the midst of their pasture; They shall make a loud noise because of *so many* people.

Luke 21:24 And they will fall by the edge of the sword, and be led away captive into all nations. And Jerusalem will be trampled by Gentiles until the times of the Gentiles are fulfilled.

Gentiles assisting in their restoration.

Is 49:22–23 Thus says the Lord GOD: "Behold, I will lift My hand in an oath to the nations, And set up My standard for the peoples; They shall bring your sons in *their* arms, And your daughters shall be carried on *their* shoulders; **23** Kings shall be your foster fathers, And their queens your nursing mothers; They shall bow down to you with *their* faces to the earth, And lick up the dust of your feet. Then you will know that I *am* the LORD, For they shall not be ashamed who wait for Me."

Is 60:10 "The sons of foreigners shall build up your walls, And their kings shall minister to you; For in My wrath I struck you, But in My favor I have had mercy on you.

Is 60:14 Also the sons of those who afflicted you Shall come bowing to you, And all those who despised you shall fall prostrate at the soles of your feet; And they shall call you The City of the LORD, Zion of the Holy One of Israel.

Is 61:4–6 And they shall rebuild the old ruins, They shall raise up the former desolations, And they shall repair the ruined cities, The desolations of many generations. **5** Strangers shall stand and feed your flocks, And the sons of the foreigner *Shall be* your plowmen and your vinedressers. **6** But you shall be named the priests of the LORD, They shall call you the servants of our God. You shall eat the riches of the Gentiles, And in their glory you shall boast.

Subjection of Gentiles to.

Is 60:11–12 Therefore your gates shall be open continually; They shall not be shut day or night, That *men* may bring to you the wealth of the Gentiles, And their kings in procession. **12** For the nation and kingdom which will not serve you shall perish, And *those* nations shall be utterly ruined.

Is 60:14 Also the sons of those who afflicted you Shall come bowing to you, And all those who despised you shall fall prostrate at the soles of your feet; And they shall call you The City of the LORD, Zion of the Holy One of Israel.

Future glory of.

Is 60:19 "The sun shall no longer be your light by day, Nor for brightness shall the moon give light to you; But the LORD will be to you an everlasting light, And your God your glory.

Is 62:3–4 You shall also be a crown of glory In the hand of the LORD, And a royal diadem In the hand of your God. **4** You shall no longer be termed Forsaken, Nor shall your land any more be termed Desolate; But you shall be called Hephzibah, and your land Beulah; For the LORD delights in you, And your land shall be married.

Zeph 3:19–20 Behold, at that time I will deal with all who afflict you; I will save the lame, And gather those who were driven out; I will appoint them for praise and fame In every land where they were put to shame. **20** At that time I will bring you back, Even at the time I gather you; For I will give you fame and praise Among all the peoples of the earth, When I return your captives before your eyes," Says the LORD.

Zech 2:5 For I,' says the LORD, 'will be a wall of fire all around her, and I will be the glory in her midst.' "

Future prosperity of.

Is 60:6–7 The multitude of camels shall cover your *land,* The dromedaries of Midian and Ephah; All those from Sheba shall come; They shall bring gold and incense, And they shall proclaim the praises of the LORD. **7** All the flocks of Kedar shall be gathered together to you, The rams of Nebaioth shall minister to you; They shall ascend with acceptance on My altar, And I will glorify the house of My glory.

Is 60:9 Surely the coastlands shall wait for Me; And the ships of Tarshish *will come* first, To bring your sons from afar, Their silver and their gold with them, To the name of the LORD your God, And to the Holy One of Israel, Because He has glorified you.

Is 60:17 "Instead of bronze I will bring gold, Instead of iron I will bring silver, Instead of wood, bronze, And instead of stones, iron. I will also make your officers peace, And your magistrates righteousness.

Is 61:4–6 And they shall rebuild the old ruins, They shall raise up the former desolations, And they shall repair the ruined cities, The desolations of many generations. **5** Strangers shall stand and feed your flocks, And the sons of the foreigner *Shall be* your plowmen and your vinedressers. **6** But you shall be named the priests of the LORD, They shall call you the servants

of our God. You shall eat the riches of the Gentiles, And in their glory you shall boast.

Hos 14:5–6 I will be like the dew to Israel; He shall grow like the lily, And lengthen his roots like Lebanon. **6** His branches shall spread; His beauty shall be like an olive tree, And his fragrance like Lebanon.

That Christ shall appear among.

Is 59:20 "The Redeemer will come to Zion, And to those who turn from transgression in Jacob," Says the LORD.

Zech 14:4 And in that day His feet will stand on the Mount of Olives, Which faces Jerusalem on the east. And the Mount of Olives shall be split in two, From east to west, *Making* a very large valley; Half of the mountain shall move toward the north And half of it toward the south.

That Christ shall dwell among.

Ezek 43:7 And He said to me, "Son of man, *this is* the place of My throne and the place of the soles of My feet, where I will dwell in the midst of the children of Israel forever. No more shall the house of Israel defile My holy name, they nor their kings, by their harlotry or with the carcasses of their kings on their high places.

Ezek 43:9 Now let them put their harlotry and the carcasses of their kings far away from Me, and I will dwell in their midst forever.

Zech 2:11 "Many nations shall be joined to the LORD in that day, and they shall become My people. And I will dwell in your midst. Then you will know that the LORD of hosts has sent Me to you.

That Christ shall reign over.

Ezek 34:23–24 I will establish one shepherd over them, and he shall feed them—My servant David. He shall feed them and be their shepherd. **24** And I, the LORD, will be their God, and My servant David a prince among them; I, the LORD, have spoken.

Ezek 37:24–25 "David My servant *shall be* king over them, and they shall all have one shepherd; they shall also walk in My judgments and observe My statutes, and do them. **25** Then they shall dwell in the land that I have given to Jacob My servant, where your fathers dwelt; and they shall dwell there, they, their children, and their children's children, forever; and My servant David *shall be* their prince forever.

Conversion of, illustrated.

Ezek 37:1–14 The hand of the LORD came upon me and brought me out in the Spirit of the LORD, and set me down in the midst of the valley; and it *was* full of bones. **2** Then He caused me to pass by them all around, and behold, *there were* very many in the open valley; and indeed *they were* very dry. **3** And He said to me, "Son of man, can these bones live?" So I answered, "O Lord GOD, You know." **4** Again He said to me, "Prophesy to these bones, and say to them, 'O dry bones, hear the word of the LORD! **5** Thus says the Lord GOD to these bones: "Surely I will cause breath to enter into you, and you shall live. **6** I will put sinews on you and bring flesh upon you, cover you with skin and put breath in you; and you shall live. Then you shall know that I *am* the LORD." ' " **7** So I prophesied as I was commanded; and as I prophesied, there was a noise, and suddenly a rattling; and the bones came together, bone to bone. **8** Indeed, as I looked, the sinews and the flesh came upon them, and the skin covered them over; but *there was* no breath in them. **9** Also He said to me, "Prophesy to the breath, prophesy, son of man, and say to the breath, 'Thus says the Lord GOD: "Come from the four winds, O breath, and breathe on these slain, that they may live." ' " **10** So I prophesied as He commanded me, and breath came into them, and they lived, and stood upon their feet, an exceedingly great army. **11** Then He said to me, "Son of man, these bones are the whole house of Israel. They indeed say, 'Our bones are dry, our hope is lost, and we ourselves are cut off!' **12** Therefore prophesy and say to them, 'Thus says the Lord GOD: "Behold, O My people, I will open your graves and cause you to come up from your graves, and bring you into the land of Israel. **13** Then you shall know that I *am* the LORD, when I have opened your graves, O My people, and brought you up from your graves. **14** I will put My Spirit in you, and you shall live, and I will place you in your own land. Then you shall know that I, the LORD, have spoken *it* and performed *it*," says the LORD.' "

Rom 11:24 For if you were cut out of the olive tree which is wild by nature, and were grafted contrary to nature into a cultivated olive tree, how much more will these, who *are* natural *branches,* be grafted into their own olive tree?

JEWS, DIETARY CUSTOMS OF THE

In patriarchal age.

Gen 18:7–8 And Abraham ran to the herd, took a tender and good calf, gave *it* to a young man, and he hastened to prepare it. **8** So he took butter and milk and the calf which he had prepared, and set *it* before them; and he stood by them under the tree as they ate.

Gen 27:4 And make me savory food, such as I love, and bring *it* to me that I may eat, that my soul may bless you before I die."

In Egypt.

Ex 16:3 And the children of Israel said to them, "Oh, that we had died by the hand of the LORD in the land of Egypt, when we sat by the pots of meat *and* when we ate bread to the full! For you have brought us out into this wilderness to kill this whole assembly with hunger."

Num 11:5 We remember the fish which we ate freely in Egypt, the cucumbers, the melons, the leeks, the onions, and the garlic;

In the desert.

Ex 16:4–12 Then the LORD said to Moses, "Behold, I will rain bread from heaven for you. And the people shall go out and gather a certain quota every day, that I may test them, whether they will walk in My law or not. **5** And it shall be on the sixth day that they shall prepare what they bring in, and it shall be twice as much as they gather daily." **6** Then Moses and Aaron said to all the children of Israel, "At evening you shall know that the LORD has brought you out of the land of Egypt. **7** And in the morning you shall see the glory of the LORD; for He hears your complaints against the LORD. But what *are* we, that you complain against us?" **8** Also Moses said, "*This shall be seen*

when the LORD gives you meat to eat in the evening, and in the morning bread to the full; for the LORD hears your complaints which you make against Him. And what *are* we? Your complaints *are* not against us but against the LORD." **9** Then Moses spoke to Aaron, "Say to all the congregation of the children of Israel, 'Come near before the LORD, for He has heard your complaints.' " **10** Now it came to pass, as Aaron spoke to the whole congregation of the children of Israel, that they looked toward the wilderness, and behold, the glory of the LORD appeared in the cloud. **11** And the LORD spoke to Moses, saying, **12** "I have heard the complaints of the children of Israel. Speak to them, saying, 'At twilight you shall eat meat, and in the morning you shall be filled with bread. And you shall know that I *am* the LORD your God.' "

Of the poor, frugal.

Ruth 2:14 Now Boaz said to her at mealtime, "Come here, and eat of the bread, and dip your piece of bread in the vinegar." So she sat beside the reapers, and he passed parched *grain* to her; and she ate and was satisfied, and kept some back.

Prov 15:17 Better *is* a dinner of herbs where love is, Than a fatted calf with hatred.

Of the rich, luxurious.

Prov 23:1–3 When you sit down to eat with a ruler, Consider carefully what *is* before you; **2** And put a knife to your throat If you *are* a man given to appetite. **3** Do not desire his delicacies, For they *are* deceptive food.

Lam 4:5 Those who ate delicacies Are desolate in the streets; Those who were brought up in scarlet Embrace ash heaps.

Amos 6:4–5 Who lie on beds of ivory, Stretch out on your couches, Eat lambs from the flock And calves from the midst of the stall; **5** Who sing idly to the sound of stringed instruments, *And* invent for yourselves musical instruments like David;

Luke 16:19 "There was a certain rich man who was clothed in purple and fine linen and fared sumptuously every day.

Articles used for,

Milk.

Gen 49:12 His eyes *are* darker than wine, And his teeth whiter than milk.

Prov 27:27 *You shall have* enough goats' milk for your food, For the food of your household, And the nourishment of your maidservants.

Butter.

Deut 32:14 Curds from the cattle, and milk of the flock, With fat of lambs; And rams of the breed of Bashan, and goats, With the choicest wheat; And you drank wine, the blood of the grapes.

2 Sam 17:29 honey and curds, sheep and cheese of the herd, for David and the people who *were* with him to eat. For they said, "The people are hungry and weary and thirsty in the wilderness."

Cheese.

1 Sam 17:18 And carry these ten cheeses to the captain of *their* thousand, and see how your brothers fare, and bring back news of them."

Job 10:10 Did You not pour me out like milk, And curdle me like cheese,

Bread.

Gen 18:5 And I will bring a morsel of bread, that you may refresh your hearts. After that you may pass by, inasmuch as you have come to your servant." They said, "Do as you have said."

1 Sam 17:17 Then Jesse said to his son David, "Take now for your brothers an ephah of this dried *grain* and these ten loaves, and run to your brothers at the camp.

Parched grain.

Ruth 2:14 Now Boaz said to her at mealtime, "Come here, and eat of the bread, and dip your piece of bread in the vinegar." So she sat beside the reapers, and he passed parched *grain* to her; and she ate and was satisfied, and kept some back.

1 Sam 17:17 Then Jesse said to his son David, "Take now for your brothers an ephah of this dried *grain* and these ten loaves, and run to your brothers at the camp.

Meat.

2 Sam 6:19 Then he distributed among all the people, among the whole multitude of Israel, both the women and the men, to everyone a loaf of bread, a piece *of meat*, and a cake of raisins. So all the people departed, everyone to his house.

Prov 9:2 She has slaughtered her meat, She has mixed her wine, She has also furnished her table.

Fish.

Matt 7:10 Or if he asks for a fish, will he give him a serpent?

Luke 24:42 So they gave Him a piece of a broiled fish and some honeycomb.

Herbs (vegetables).

Prov 15:17 Better *is* a dinner of herbs where love is, Than a fatted calf with hatred.

Rom 14:2 For one believes he may eat all things, but he who is weak eats *only* vegetables.

Heb 6:7 For the earth which drinks in the rain that often comes upon it, and bears herbs useful for those by whom it is cultivated, receives blessing from God;

Fruit.

2 Sam 16:2 And the king said to Ziba, "What do you mean to do with these?" So Ziba said, "The donkeys *are* for the king's household to ride on, the bread and summer fruit for the young men to eat, and the wine for those who are faint in the wilderness to drink."

Dried fruit (raisins and figs).

1 Sam 25:18 Then Abigail made haste and took two hundred *loaves* of bread, two skins of wine, five sheep already dressed, five seahs of roasted *grain,* one hundred clusters of raisins, and two hundred cakes of figs, and loaded *them* on donkeys.

1 Sam 30:12 And they gave him a piece of a cake of figs and two clusters of raisins. So when he had eaten, his strength came back to him; for he had eaten no bread nor drunk water for three days and three nights.

2 Sam 6:19 Then he distributed among all the people, among the whole multitude of Israel, both the women and the men, to everyone a loaf of bread, a piece *of meat*, and a cake of raisins. So all the people departed, everyone to his house.

Honey.

Song 5:1 I have come to my garden, my sister, *my* spouse; I have gathered my myrrh with my spice; I have eaten my honeycomb with my honey; I have drunk my wine with my milk. Eat, O friends! Drink, yes, drink deeply, O beloved ones!

Is 7:15 Curds and honey He shall eat, that He may know to refuse the evil and choose the good.

Oil (olive).

Deut 12:17 You may not eat within your gates the tithe of your grain or your new wine or your oil, of the firstborn of your herd or your flock, of any of your offerings which you vow, of your freewill offerings, or of the heave offering of your hand.

Prov 21:17 He who loves pleasure *will be* a poor man; He who loves wine and oil will not be rich.

Ezek 16:13 Thus you were adorned with gold and silver, and your clothing *was of* fine linen, silk, and embroidered cloth. You ate *pastry of* fine flour, honey, and oil. You were exceedingly beautiful, and succeeded to royalty.

Vinegar.

Num 6:3 he shall separate himself from wine and *similar* drink; he shall drink neither vinegar made from wine nor vinegar made from *similar* drink; neither shall he drink any grape juice, nor eat fresh grapes or raisins.

Ruth 2:14 Now Boaz said to her at mealtime, "Come here, and eat of the bread, and dip your piece of bread in the vinegar." So she sat beside the reapers, and he passed parched *grain* to her; and she ate and was satisfied, and kept some back.

Wine.

John 2:3 And when they ran out of wine, the mother of Jesus said to Him, "They have no wine."

John 2:10 And he said to him, "Every man at the beginning sets out the good wine, and when the *guests* have well drunk, then the inferior. You have kept the good wine until now!"

Water.

Gen 21:14 So Abraham rose early in the morning, and took bread and a skin of water; and putting *it* on her shoulder, he gave *it* and the boy to Hagar, and sent her away. Then she departed and wandered in the Wilderness of Beersheba.

Matt 10:42 And whoever gives one of these little ones only a cup of cold *water* in the name of a disciple, assuredly, I say to you, he shall by no means lose his reward."

Expressed by the term bread and water.

1 Kin 13:9 For so it was commanded me by the word of the LORD, saying, 'You shall not eat bread, nor drink water, nor return by the same way you came.' "

1 Kin 13:16 And he said, "I cannot return with you nor go in with you; neither can I eat bread nor drink water with you in this place.

Generally prepared by women.

Gen 27:9 Go now to the flock and bring me from there two choice kids of the goats, and I will make savory food from them for your father, such as he loves.

1 Sam 8:13 He will take your daughters *to be* perfumers, cooks, and bakers.

Prov 31:15 She also rises while it is yet night, And provides food for her household, And a portion for her maidservants.

Meals

Morning ones were sparing.

Judg 19:5 Then it came to pass on the fourth day that they arose early in the morning, and he stood to depart; but the young woman's father said to his son-in-law, "Refresh your heart with a morsel of bread, and afterward go your way."

Eccl 10:16–17 Woe to you, O land, when your king *is* a child, And your princes feast in the morning! **17** Blessed *are* you, O land, when your king *is* the son of nobles, And your princes feast at the proper time— For strength and not for drunkenness!

At noon.

Gen 43:16 When Joseph saw Benjamin with them, he said to the steward of his house, "Take *these* men to my home, and slaughter an animal and make ready; for *these* men will dine with me at noon."

John 4:6 Now Jacob's well was there. Jesus therefore, being wearied from *His* journey, sat thus by the well. It was about the sixth hour.

John 4:8 For His disciples had gone away into the city to buy food.

In the evening.

Gen 24:11 And he made his camels kneel down outside the city by a well of water at evening time, the time when women go out to draw *water.*

Gen 24:33 *Food* was set before him to eat, but he said, "I will not eat until I have told about my errand." And he said, "Speak on."

Luke 24:29–30 But they constrained Him, saying, "Abide with us, for it is toward evening, and the day is far spent." And He went in to stay with them. **30** Now it came to pass, as He sat at the table with them, that He took bread, blessed and broke *it,* and gave it to them.

Sometimes served sitting.

Gen 27:19 Jacob said to his father, "I *am* Esau your firstborn; I have done just as you told me; please arise, sit and eat of my game, that your soul may bless me."

Gen 43:33 And they sat before him, the firstborn according to his birthright and the youngest according to his youth; and the men looked in astonishment at one another.

Often served reclining.

Amos 6:4 Who lie on beds of ivory, Stretch out on your couches, Eat lambs from the flock And calves from the midst of the stall;

John 13:23 Now there was leaning on Jesus' bosom one of His disciples, whom Jesus loved.

Eaten with the hand.

Matt 26:23 He answered and said, "He who dipped *his* hand with Me in the dish will betray Me.

Luke 22:21 But behold, the hand of My betrayer *is* with Me on the table.

Thanks given before.

Mark 8:6 So He commanded the multitude to sit down on the ground. And He took the seven loaves and gave thanks, broke *them* and gave *them* to His disciples to set before *them;* and they set *them* before the multitude.

Acts 27:35 And when he had said these things, he took bread and gave thanks to God in the presence of them all; and when he had broken *it* he began to eat.

Purification before.

2 Kin 3:11 But Jehoshaphat said, "*Is there* no prophet of the LORD here, that we may inquire of the LORD by him?" So one of the servants of the king of Israel answered and said, "Elisha the son of Shaphat *is* here, who poured water on the hands of Elijah."

Matt 15:2 "Why do Your disciples transgress the tradition of the elders? For they do not wash their hands when they eat bread."

A hymn sung after.

Matt 26:30 And when they had sung a hymn, they went out to the Mount of Olives.

Men and women did not partake of together.

Gen 18:8–9 So he took butter and milk and the calf which he had prepared, and set *it* before them; and he stood by them under the tree as they ate. **9** Then they said to him, "Where *is* Sarah your wife?" So he said, "Here, in the tent."

Esth 1:3 *that* in the third year of his reign he made a feast for all his officials and servants—the powers of Persia and Media, the nobles, and the princes of the provinces *being* before him—

Esth 1:9 Queen Vashti also made a feast for the women *in* the royal palace which *belonged* to King Ahasuerus.

Articles of, often sent as presents.

1 Sam 17:18 And carry these ten cheeses to the captain of *their* thousand, and see how your brothers fare, and bring back news of them."

1 Sam 25:18 Then Abigail made haste and took two hundred *loaves* of bread, two skins of wine, five sheep already dressed, five seahs of roasted *grain,* one hundred clusters of raisins, and two hundred cakes of figs, and loaded *them* on donkeys.

1 Sam 25:27 And now this present which your maidservant has brought to my lord, let it be given to the young men who follow my lord.

2 Sam 16:1–2 When David was a little past the top *of the mountain,* there was Ziba the servant of Mephibosheth, who met him with a couple of saddled donkeys, and on them two hundred *loaves* of bread, one hundred clusters of raisins, one hundred summer fruits, and a skin of wine. **2** And the king said to Ziba, "What do you mean to do with these?" So Ziba said, "The donkeys *are* for the king's household to ride on, the bread and summer fruit for the young men to eat, and the wine for those who are faint in the wilderness to drink."

JEZREEL

Staging area for armies.

1 Sam 29:1–2 Then the Philistines gathered together all their armies at Aphek, and the Israelites encamped by a fountain which *is* in Jezreel. **2** And the lords of the Philistines passed in review by hundreds and by thousands, but David and his men passed in review at the rear with Achish.

Elijah ran to, ahead of Ahab.

1 Kin 18:45–46 Now it happened in the meantime that the sky became black with clouds and wind, and there was a heavy rain. So Ahab rode away and went to Jezreel. **46** Then the hand of the LORD came upon Elijah; and he girded up his loins and ran ahead of Ahab to the entrance of Jezreel.

Home of Naboth.

1 Kin 21:1 And it came to pass after these things *that* Naboth the Jezreelite had a vineyard which *was* in Jezreel, next to the palace of Ahab king of Samaria.

Where Jezebel died.

2 Kin 9:10 The dogs shall eat Jezebel on the plot *of ground* at Jezreel, and *there shall be* none to bury *her.'* " And he opened the door and fled.

Son of Hosea.

Hos 1:3–5 So he went and took Gomer the daughter of Diblaim, and she conceived and bore him a son. **4** Then the LORD said to him: "Call his name Jezreel, For in a little *while* I will avenge the bloodshed of Jezreel on the house of Jehu, And bring an end to the kingdom of the house of Israel. **5** It shall come to pass in that day That I will break the bow of Israel in the Valley of Jezreel."

Equated with blessing.

Hos 1:11 Then the children of Judah and the children of Israel Shall be gathered together, And appoint for themselves one head; And they shall come up out of the land, For great *will be* the day of Jezreel!

Cf. Hos 2:22

JOAB

Head of David's army.

2 Sam 2:13–17 And Joab the son of Zeruiah, and the servants of David, went out and met them by the pool of Gibeon. So they sat down, one on one side of the pool and the other on the other side of the pool. **14** Then Abner said to Joab, "Let the young men now arise and compete before us." And Joab said, "Let them arise." **15** So they arose and went over by number, twelve from Benjamin, *followers* of Ishbosheth the son of Saul, and twelve from the servants of David. **16** And each one grasped his opponent by the head and *thrust* his sword in his opponent's side; so they fell down together. Therefore that place was called the Field of Sharp Swords, which *is* in Gibeon. **17** So there was a very fierce battle that day, and Abner and the men of Israel were beaten before the servants of David.

2 Sam 2:28 So Joab blew a trumpet; and all the people stood still and did not pursue Israel anymore, nor did they fight anymore.

2 Sam 20:23 And Joab *was* over all the army of Israel; Benaiah the son of Jehoiada *was* over the Cherethites and the Pelethites;

Murdered Abner.

2 Sam 3:22–30 At that moment the servants of David and Joab came from a raid and brought much spoil with them. But Abner *was* not with David in Hebron, for he had sent him away, and he had gone in peace. **23** When Joab and all the troops that *were* with him had come, they told Joab, saying, "Abner the son of Ner came to the king, and he sent him away, and he has gone in peace." **24** Then Joab came to the king and said, "What have you done? Look, Abner came to you; why *is it that* you sent him away, and he has already gone? **25** Surely you realize that Abner the son of Ner came to deceive you, to know your going out and your coming in, and to know all that you are doing." **26** And when Joab had gone from David's presence, he sent messengers after Abner, who brought him back from the well of Sirah. But David did not know *it.* **27** Now when Abner had returned to Hebron, Joab took him aside in the gate to speak with him privately, and there stabbed him in the stomach, so that he died for the blood of Asahel his brother. **28** Afterward, when David heard *it,* he said, "My kingdom and I *are* guiltless before the LORD forever of the blood of Abner the son of Ner. **29** Let it rest on the head of Joab and on all his father's house; and let there never fail to be in the house of Joab one who has a discharge or is a leper, who leans on a staff or falls by the sword, or who lacks bread." **30** So Joab and Abishai his brother killed Abner, because he had killed their brother Asahel at Gibeon in the battle.

Killed in the tabernacle.

1 Kin 2:28–35 Then news came to Joab, for Joab had defected to Adonijah, though he had not defected to Absalom. So Joab fled to the tabernacle of the LORD, and took hold of the horns of the altar. **29** And King Solomon was told, "Joab has fled to the tabernacle of the LORD; there *he is,* by the altar." Then Solomon sent Benaiah the son of Jehoiada, saying, "Go, strike him down." **30** So Benaiah went to the tabernacle of the LORD, and said to him, "Thus says the king, 'Come out!' " And he said, "No, but I will die here." And Benaiah brought back word to the king, saying, "Thus said Joab, and thus he answered me." **31** Then the king said to him, "Do as he has said, and strike him down and bury him, that you may take away from me and from the house of my father the innocent blood which Joab shed. **32** So the LORD will return his blood on his head, because he struck down two men more righteous and better than he, and killed them with the sword—Abner the son of Ner, the commander of the army of Israel, and Amasa the son of Jether, the commander of the army of Judah—though my father David did not know *it.* **33** Their blood shall therefore return upon the head of Joab and upon the head of his descendants forever. But upon David and his descendants, upon his house and his throne, there shall be peace forever from the LORD." **34** So Benaiah the son of Jehoiada went up and struck and killed him; and he was buried in his own house in the wilderness. **35** The king put Benaiah the son of Jehoiada in his place over the army, and the king put Zadok the priest in the place of Abiathar.

Defeated Syria and Ammon.

2 Sam 10:13–19 So Joab and the people who *were* with him drew near for the battle against the Syrians, and they fled before him. **14** When the people of Ammon saw that the Syrians were fleeing, they also fled before Abishai, and entered the city. So Joab returned from the people of Ammon and went to Jerusalem. **15** When the Syrians saw that they had been defeated by Israel, they gathered together. **16** Then Hadadezer sent and brought out the Syrians who *were* beyond the River, and they came to Helam. And Shobach the commander of Hadadezer's army *went* before them. **17** When it was told David, he gathered all Israel, crossed over the Jordan, and came to Helam. And the Syrians set themselves in battle array against David and fought with him. **18** Then the Syrians fled before Israel; and David killed seven hundred charioteers and forty thousand horsemen of the Syrians, and struck Shobach the commander of their army, who died there. **19** And when all the kings *who were* servants to Hadadezer saw that they were defeated by Israel, they made peace with Israel and served them. So the Syrians were afraid to help the people of Ammon anymore.

2 Sam 11:1 It happened in the spring of the year, at the time when kings go out *to battle*, that David sent Joab and his servants with him, and all Israel; and they destroyed the people of Ammon and besieged Rabbah. But David remained at Jerusalem.

2 Sam 11:18 Then Joab sent and told David all the things concerning the war,

Mediated between David and Absalom.

2 Sam 14:1–4 So Joab the son of Zeruiah perceived that the king's heart *was* concerned about Absalom. **2** And Joab sent to Tekoa and brought from there a wise woman, and said to her, "Please pretend to be a mourner, and put on mourning apparel; do not anoint yourself with oil, but act like a woman who has been mourning a long time for the dead. **3** Go to the king and speak to him in this manner." So Joab put the words in her mouth. **4** And when the woman of Tekoa spoke to the king, she fell on her face to the ground and prostrated herself, and said, "Help, O king!"

2 Sam 14:29–33 Therefore Absalom sent for Joab, to send him to the king, but he would not come to him. And when he sent again the second time, he would not come. **30** So he said to his servants, "See, Joab's field is near mine, and he has barley there; go and set it on fire." And Absalom's servants set the field on fire. **31** Then Joab arose and came to Absalom's house, and said to him, "Why have your servants set my field on fire?" **32** And Absalom answered Joab, "Look, I sent to you, saying, 'Come here, so that I may send you to the king, to say, "Why have I come from Geshur? *It would be* better for me *to be* there still." ' Now therefore, let me see the king's face; but if there is iniquity in me, let him execute me." **33** So Joab went to the king and told him. And when he had called for Absalom, he came to the king and bowed himself on his face to the ground before the king. Then the king kissed Absalom.

Killed Absalom.

2 Sam 18:14–17 Then Joab said, "I cannot linger with you." And he took three spears in his hand and thrust them through Absalom's heart, while he was *still* alive in the midst of the terebinth tree. **15** And ten young men who bore Joab's armor surrounded Absalom, and struck and killed him. **16** So Joab blew the trumpet, and the people returned from pursuing Israel. For Joab held back the people. **17** And they took Absalom and cast him into a large pit in the

woods, and laid a very large heap of stones over him. Then all Israel fled, everyone to his tent.

Rebuked David.

2 Sam 19:5–8 Then Joab came into the house to the king, and said, "Today you have disgraced all your servants who today have saved your life, the lives of your sons and daughters, the lives of your wives and the lives of your concubines, **6** in that you love your enemies and hate your friends. For you have declared today that you regard neither princes nor servants; for today I perceive that if Absalom had lived and all of us had died today, then it would have pleased you well. **7** Now therefore, arise, go out and speak comfort to your servants. For I swear by the LORD, if you do not go out, not one will stay with you this night. And that will be worse for you than all the evil that has befallen you from your youth until now." **8** Then the king arose and sat in the gate. And they told all the people, saying, "There is the king, sitting in the gate." So all the people came before the king. For everyone of Israel had fled to his tent.

Replaced as commander by Amasa.

2 Sam 19:13 And say to Amasa, '*Are* you not my bone and my flesh? God do so to me, and more also, if you are not commander of the army before me continually in place of Joab.' "

Opposed the rebellion of Sheba, son of Bichri.
2 Sam 20:7–22

David's nephew.

1 Chr 2:16 Now their sisters *were* Zeruiah and Abigail. And the sons of Zeruiah *were* Abishai, Joab, and Asahel—three.

Reluctantly helped David with census.

1 Chr 21:1–6 Now Satan stood up against Israel, and moved David to number Israel. **2** So David said to Joab and to the leaders of the people, "Go, number Israel from Beersheba to Dan, and bring the number of them to me that I may know *it*." **3** And Joab answered, "May the LORD make His people a hundred times more than they are. But, my lord the king, *are* they not all my lord's servants? Why then does my lord require this thing? Why should he be a cause of guilt in Israel?" **4** Nevertheless the king's word prevailed against Joab. Therefore Joab departed and went throughout all Israel and came to Jerusalem. **5** Then Joab gave the sum of the number of the people to David. All Israel *had* one million one hundred thousand men who drew the sword, and Judah *had* four hundred and seventy thousand men who drew the sword. **6** But he did not count Levi and Benjamin among them, for the king's word was abominable to Joab.

JOHN THE BAPTIST

Coming was prophesied.

Is 40:3–5 The voice of one crying in the wilderness: "Prepare the way of the LORD; Make straight in the desert A highway for our God. **4** Every valley shall be exalted And every mountain and hill brought low; The crooked places shall be made straight And the rough places smooth; **5** The glory of the LORD shall be revealed, And all flesh shall see *it* together; For the mouth of the LORD has spoken."

Angel announced birth of.

Luke 1:11–20 Then an angel of the Lord appeared to him, standing on the right side of the altar of incense. **12** And when Zacharias saw *him*, he was troubled, and fear fell upon him. **13** But the angel said to him, "Do not be afraid, Zacharias, for your prayer is heard; and your wife Elizabeth will bear you a son, and you shall call his name John. **14** And you will have joy and gladness, and many will rejoice at his birth. **15** For he will be great in the sight of the Lord, and shall drink neither wine nor strong drink. He will also be filled with the Holy Spirit, even from his mother's womb. **16** And he will turn many of the children of Israel to the Lord their God. **17** He will also go before Him in the spirit and power of Elijah, *'to turn the hearts of the fathers to the children,'* and the disobedient to the wisdom of the just, to make ready a people prepared for the Lord." **18** And Zacharias said to the angel, "How shall I know this? For I am an old man, and my wife is well advanced in years." **19** And the angel answered and said to him, "I am Gabriel, who stands in the presence of God, and was sent to speak to you and bring you these glad tidings. **20** But behold, you will be mute and not able to speak until the day these things take place, because you did not believe my words which will be fulfilled in their own time."

Ministry of.

Matt 3:1–12 In those days John the Baptist came preaching in the wilderness of Judea, **2** and saying, "Repent, for the kingdom of heaven is at hand!" **3** For this is he who was spoken of by the prophet Isaiah, saying: *"The voice of one crying in the wilderness: 'Prepare the way of the LORD; Make His paths straight.'"* **4** Now John himself was clothed in camel's hair, with a leather belt around his waist; and his food was locusts and wild honey. **5** Then Jerusalem, all Judea, and all the region around the Jordan went out to him **6** and were baptized by him in the Jordan, confessing their sins. **7** But when he saw many of the Pharisees and Sadducees coming to his baptism, he said to them, "Brood of vipers! Who warned you to flee from the wrath to come? **8** Therefore bear fruits worthy of repentance, **9** and do not think to say to yourselves, 'We have Abraham as *our* father.' For I say to you that God is able to raise up children to Abraham from these stones. **10** And even now the ax is laid to the root of the trees. Therefore every tree which does not bear good fruit is cut down and thrown into the fire. **11** I indeed baptize you with water unto repentance, but He who is coming after me is mightier than I, whose sandals I am not worthy to carry. He will baptize you with the Holy Spirit and fire. **12** His winnowing fan *is* in His hand, and He will thoroughly clean out His threshing floor, and gather His wheat into the barn; but He will burn up the chaff with unquenchable fire."

Mark 1:2–8 As it is written in the Prophets: *"Behold, I send My messenger before Your face, Who will prepare Your way before You."* **3** *"The voice of one crying in the wilderness: 'Prepare the way of the LORD; Make His paths straight.'"* **4** John came baptizing in the wilderness and preaching a baptism of repentance for the remission of sins. **5** Then all the land of Judea, and those from Jerusalem, went out to him and were all baptized by him in the Jordan River, confessing their sins. **6** Now John was clothed with camel's hair and with a leather belt around his waist, and he ate locusts and wild honey. **7** And he preached, saying, "There comes One after me who is mightier than I, whose sandal strap I am not worthy to stoop down and loose. **8** I indeed baptized you with water, but He will baptize you with the Holy Spirit."

John 1:19–31 Now this is the testimony of John, when the Jews sent priests and Levites from Jerusalem to ask him, "Who are you?" **20** He confessed, and did not deny, but confessed, "I am not the Christ." **21** And they asked him, "What then? Are you Elijah?" He said, "I am not." "Are you the Prophet?" And he answered, "No." **22** Then they said to him, "Who are you, that we may give an answer to those who sent us? What do you say about yourself?" **23** He said: "I am 'The voice of one crying in the wilderness: "Make straight the way of the LORD,"' as the prophet Isaiah said." **24** Now those who were sent were from the Pharisees. **25** And they asked him, saying, "Why then do you baptize if you are not the Christ, nor Elijah, nor the Prophet?" **26** John answered them, saying, "I baptize with water, but there stands One among you whom you do not know. **27** It is He who, coming after me, is preferred before me, whose sandal strap I am not worthy to loose." **28** These things were done in Bethabara beyond the Jordan, where John was baptizing. **29** The next day John saw Jesus coming toward him, and said, "Behold! The Lamb of God who takes away the sin of the world! **30** This is He of whom I said, 'After me comes a Man who is preferred before me, for He was before me.' **31** I did not know Him; but that He should be revealed to Israel, therefore I came baptizing with water."

Cf. Luke 3:1–20

Called Jesus the Messiah.

John 1:29–36 The next day John saw Jesus coming toward him, and said, "Behold! The Lamb of God who takes away the sin of the world! **30** This is He of whom I said, 'After me comes a Man who is preferred before me, for He was before me.' **31** I did not know Him; but that He should be revealed to Israel, therefore I came baptizing with water." **32** And John bore witness, saying, "I saw the Spirit descending from heaven like a dove, and He remained upon Him. **33** I did not know Him, but He who sent me to baptize with water said to me, 'Upon whom you see the Spirit descending, and remaining on Him, this is He who baptizes with the Holy Spirit.' **34** And I have seen and testified that this is the Son of God." **35** Again, the next day, John stood with two of his disciples. **36** And looking at Jesus as He walked, he said, "Behold the Lamb of God!"

Cf. John 3:25–36; 5:33

Baptized Jesus.

Matt 3:13–16 Then Jesus came from Galilee to John at the Jordan to be baptized by him. **14** And John *tried to* prevent Him, saying, "I need to be baptized by You, and are You coming to me?" **15** But Jesus answered and said to him, "Permit *it to be so* now, for thus it is fitting for us to fulfill all righteousness." Then he allowed Him. **16** When He had been baptized, Jesus came up immediately from the water; and behold, the heavens were opened to Him, and He saw the Spirit of God descending like a dove and alighting upon Him.

Mark 1:9–11 It came to pass in those days *that* Jesus came from Nazareth of Galilee, and was baptized by John in the Jordan. **10** And immediately, coming up from the water, He saw the heavens parting and the Spirit descending upon Him like a dove. **11** Then a voice came from heaven, "You are My beloved Son, in whom I am well pleased."

Luke 3:21–23 When all the people were baptized, it came to pass that Jesus also was baptized; and while He prayed, the heaven was opened. **22** And the Holy Spirit descended in bodily form like a dove upon Him, and a voice came from heaven which said, "You are My beloved Son; in You I am well pleased." **23** Now Jesus Himself began *His ministry at* about thirty years of age, being (as was supposed) *the* son of Joseph, *the son* of Heli,

Jesus' testimony concerning.

Matt 11:9–13 But what did you go out to see? A prophet? Yes, I say to you, and more than a prophet. **10** For this is *he* of whom it is written: *'Behold, I send My messenger before Your face, Who will prepare Your way before You.'* **11** "Assuredly, I say to you, among those born of women there has not risen one greater than John the Baptist; but he who is least in the kingdom of heaven is greater than he. **12** And from the days of John the Baptist until now the kingdom of heaven suffers violence, and the violent take it by force. **13** For all the prophets and the law prophesied until John.

Luke 7:24–28 When the messengers of John had departed, He began to speak to the multitudes concerning John: "What did you go out into the wilderness to see? A reed shaken by the wind? **25** But what did you go out to see? A man clothed in soft garments? Indeed those who are gorgeously appareled and live in luxury are in kings' courts. **26** But what did you go out to see? A prophet? Yes, I say to you, and more than a prophet. **27** This is *he* of whom it is written: *'Behold, I send My messenger before Your face, Who will prepare Your way before You.'* **28** For I say to you, among those born of women there is not a greater prophet than John the Baptist; but he who is least in the kingdom of God is greater than he."

Murdered by Herod.

Matt 14:1–12 At that time Herod the tetrarch heard the report about Jesus **2** and said to his servants, "This is John the Baptist; he is risen from the dead, and therefore these powers are at work in him." **3** For Herod had laid hold of John and bound him, and put *him* in prison for the sake of Herodias, his brother Philip's wife. **4** Because John had said to him, "It is not lawful for you to have her." **5** And although he wanted to put him to death, he feared the multitude, because they counted him as a prophet. **6** But when Herod's birthday was celebrated, the daughter of Herodias danced before them and pleased Herod. **7** Therefore he promised with an oath to give her whatever she might ask. **8** So she, having been prompted by her mother, said, "Give me John the Baptist's head here on a platter." **9** And the king was sorry; nevertheless,

because of the oaths and because of those who sat with him, he commanded *it* to be given to *her.* **10** So he sent and had John beheaded in prison. **11** And his head was brought on a platter and given to the girl, and she brought *it* to her mother. **12** Then his disciples came and took away the body and buried it, and went and told Jesus.

Mark 6:14–29 Now King Herod heard *of Him,* for His name had become well known. And he said, "John the Baptist is risen from the dead, and therefore these powers are at work in him." **15** Others said, "It is Elijah." And others said, "It is the Prophet, or like one of the prophets." **16** But when Herod heard, he said, "This is John, whom I beheaded; he has been raised from the dead!" **17** For Herod himself had sent and laid hold of John, and bound him in prison for the sake of Herodias, his brother Philip's wife; for he had married her. **18** Because John had said to Herod, "It is not lawful for you to have your brother's wife." **19** Therefore Herodias held it against him and wanted to kill him, but she could not; **20** for Herod feared John, knowing that he *was* a just and holy man, and he protected him. And when he heard him, he did many things, and heard him gladly. **21** Then an opportune day came when Herod on his birthday gave a feast for his nobles, the high officers, and the chief *men* of Galilee. **22** And when Herodias' daughter herself came in and danced, and pleased Herod and those who sat with him, the king said to the girl, "Ask me whatever you want, and I will give *it* to you." **23** He also swore to her, "Whatever you ask me, I will give you, up to half my kingdom." **24** So she went out and said to her mother, "What shall I ask?" And she said, "The head of John the Baptist!" **25** Immediately she came in with haste to the king and asked, saying, "I want you to give me at once the head of John the Baptist on a platter." **26** And the king was exceedingly sorry; *yet,* because of the oaths and because of those who sat with him, he did not want to refuse her. **27** Immediately the king sent an executioner and commanded his head to be brought. And he went and beheaded him in prison, **28** brought his head on a platter, and gave it to the girl; and the girl gave it to her mother. **29** When his disciples heard *of it,* they came and took away his corpse and laid it in a tomb.

Luke 9:7–9 Now Herod the tetrarch heard of all that was done by Him; and he was perplexed, because it was said by some that John had risen from the dead, **8** and by some that Elijah had appeared, and by others that one of the old prophets had risen again. **9** Herod said, "John I have beheaded, but who is this of whom I hear such things?" So he sought to see Him.

JONAH

Prophesied during time of Jeroboam II.

2 Kin 14:23–25 In the fifteenth year of Amaziah the son of Joash, king of Judah, Jeroboam the son of Joash, king of Israel, became king in Samaria, *and reigned* forty-one years. **24** And he did evil in the sight of the LORD; he did not depart from all the sins of Jeroboam the son of Nebat, who had made Israel sin. **25** He restored the territory of Israel from the entrance of Hamath to the Sea of the Arabah, according to the word of the LORD God of Israel, which He had spoken through His servant Jonah the son of Amittai, the prophet who *was* from Gath Hepher.

Used by Christ as illustration of repentance.

Matt 12:38–41 Then some of the scribes and Pharisees answered, saying, "Teacher, we want to see a sign from You." **39** But He answered and said to them, "An evil and adulterous generation seeks after a sign, and no sign will be given to it except the sign of the prophet Jonah. **40** For as Jonah was three days and three nights in the belly of the great fish, so will the Son of Man be three days and three nights in the heart of the earth. **41** The men of Nineveh will rise up in the judgment with this generation and condemn it, because they repented at the preaching of Jonah; and indeed a greater than Jonah *is* here.

Luke 11:29–32 And while the crowds were thickly gathered together, He began to say, "This is an evil generation. It seeks a sign, and no sign will be given to it except the sign of Jonah the prophet. **30** For as Jonah became a sign to the Ninevites, so also the Son of Man will be to this generation. **31** The queen of the South will rise up in the judgment with the men of this generation and condemn them, for she came from the ends of the earth to hear the wisdom of Solomon; and indeed a greater than Solomon *is* here. **32** The men of Nineveh will rise up in the judgment with this generation and condemn it, for they repented at the preaching of Jonah; and indeed a greater than Jonah *is* here.

Cf. Matt 16:4

Song of.

Jon 2:1–9 Then Jonah prayed to the LORD his God from the fish's belly. **2** And he said: "I cried out to the LORD because of my affliction, And He answered me. "Out of the belly of Sheol I cried, *And* You heard my voice. **3** For You cast me into the deep, Into the heart of the seas, And the floods surrounded me; All Your billows and Your waves passed over me. **4** Then I said, 'I have been cast out of Your sight; Yet I will look again toward Your holy temple.' **5** The waters surrounded me, *even* to my soul; The deep closed around me; Weeds were wrapped around my head. **6** I went down to the moorings of the mountains; The earth with its bars *closed* behind me forever; Yet You have brought up my life from the pit, O LORD, my God. **7** "When my soul fainted within me, I remembered the LORD; And my prayer went *up* to You, Into Your holy temple. **8** "Those who regard worthless idols Forsake their own Mercy. **9** But I will sacrifice to You With the voice of thanksgiving; I will pay what I have vowed. Salvation *is* of the LORD."

JONATHAN

Saul's son.

1 Sam 13:16 Saul, Jonathan his son, and the people present with them remained in Gibeah of Benjamin. But the Philistines encamped in Michmash.

1 Sam 14:49 The sons of Saul were Jonathan, Jishui, and Malchishua. And the names of his two daughters *were these:* the name of the firstborn Merab, and the name of the younger Michal.

1 Sam 31:2 Then the Philistines followed hard after Saul

and his sons. And the Philistines killed Jonathan, Abinadab, and Malchishua, Saul's sons.

Defeated the Philistines. 1 Sam 14:1–23

Love for David.

1 Sam 18:1–4 Now when he had finished speaking to Saul, the soul of Jonathan was knit to the soul of David, and Jonathan loved him as his own soul. **2** Saul took him that day, and would not let him go home to his father's house anymore. **3** Then Jonathan and David made a covenant, because he loved him as his own soul. **4** And Jonathan took off the robe that *was* on him and gave it to David, with his armor, even to his sword and his bow and his belt.

1 Sam 19:1–5 Now Saul spoke to Jonathan his son and to all his servants, that they should kill David; but Jonathan, Saul's son, delighted greatly in David. **2** So Jonathan told David, saying, "My father Saul seeks to kill you. Therefore please be on your guard until morning, and stay in a secret *place* and hide. **3** And I will go out and stand beside my father in the field where you *are,* and I will speak with my father about you. Then what I observe, I will tell you." **4** Thus Jonathan spoke well of David to Saul his father, and said to him, "Let not the king sin against his servant, against David, because he has not sinned against you, and because his works *have been* very good toward you. **5** For he took his life in his hands and killed the Philistine, and the LORD brought about a great deliverance for all Israel. You saw *it* and rejoiced. Why then will you sin against innocent blood, to kill David without a cause?"

Cf. 2 Sam 21:7

Loyalty to David.

1 Sam 20:1–23 Then David fled from Naioth in Ramah, and went and said to Jonathan, "What have I done? What *is* my iniquity, and what *is* my sin before your father, that he seeks my life?" **2** So Jonathan said to him, "By no means! You shall not die! Indeed, my father will do nothing either great or small without first telling me. And why should my father hide this thing from me? It *is* not *so!*" **3** Then David took an oath again, and said, "Your father certainly knows that I have found favor in your eyes, and he has said, 'Do not let Jonathan know this, lest he be grieved.' But truly, *as* the LORD lives and *as* your soul lives, *there is* but a step between me and death." **4** So Jonathan said to David, "Whatever you yourself desire, I will do *it* for you." **5** And David said to Jonathan, "Indeed tomorrow *is* the New Moon, and I should not fail to sit with the king to eat. But let me go, that I may hide in the field until the third *day* at evening. **6** If your father misses me at all, then say, 'David earnestly asked *permission* of me that he might run over to Bethlehem, his city, for *there is* a yearly sacrifice there for all the family.' **7** If he says thus: '*It is* well,' your servant will be safe. But if he is very angry, be sure that evil is determined by him. **8** Therefore you shall deal kindly with your servant, for you have brought your servant into a covenant of the LORD with you. Nevertheless, if there is iniquity in me, kill me yourself, for why should you bring me to your father?" **9** But Jonathan said, "Far be it from you! For if I knew certainly that evil was determined by my father to come upon you, then would I not tell you?" **10** Then David said to Jonathan, "Who will tell me, or what *if* your father answers you roughly?" **11** And Jonathan said to David, "Come, let us go out into the field." So both of them went out into the field. **12** Then Jonathan said to David: "The LORD God of Israel *is witness!* When I have sounded out my father sometime tomorrow, *or* the third *day*, and indeed *there is* good toward David, and I do not send to you and tell you, **13** may the LORD do so and much more to Jonathan. But if it pleases my father *to do* you evil, then I will report it to you and send you away, that you may go in safety. And the LORD be with you as He has been with my father. **14** And you shall not only show me the kindness of the LORD while I still live, that I may not die; **15** but you shall not cut off your kindness from my house forever, no, not when the LORD has cut off every one of the enemies of David from the face of the earth." **16** So Jonathan made *a covenant* with the house of David, *saying*, "Let the LORD require *it* at the hand of David's enemies." **17** Now Jonathan again caused David to vow, because he loved him; for he loved him as he loved his own soul. **18** Then Jonathan said to David, "Tomorrow *is* the New Moon; and you will be missed, because your seat will be empty. **19** And *when* you have stayed three days, go down quickly and come to the place where you hid on the day of the deed; and remain by the stone Ezel. **20** Then I will shoot three arrows to the side, as though I shot at a target; **21** and there I will send a lad, *saying*, 'Go, find the arrows.' If I expressly say to the lad, 'Look, the arrows *are* on this side of you; get them and come'—then, as the LORD lives, *there is* safety for you and no harm. **22** But if I say thus to the young man, 'Look, the arrows *are* beyond you'—go your way, for the LORD has sent you away. **23** And as for the matter which you and I have spoken of, indeed the LORD *be* between you and me forever."

1 Sam 20:34–42 So Jonathan arose from the table in fierce anger, and ate no food the second day of the month, for he was grieved for David, because his father had treated him shamefully. **35** And so it was, in the morning, that Jonathan went out into the field at the time appointed with David, and a little lad *was* with him. **36** Then he said to his lad, "Now run, find the arrows which I shoot." As the lad ran, he shot an arrow beyond him. **37** When the lad had come to the place where the arrow was which Jonathan had shot, Jonathan cried out after the lad and said, "*Is* not the arrow beyond you?" **38** And Jonathan cried out after the lad, "Make haste, hurry, do not delay!" So Jonathan's lad gathered up the arrows and came back to his master. **39** But the lad did not know anything. Only Jonathan and David knew of the matter. **40** Then Jonathan gave his weapons to his lad, and said to him, "Go, carry *them* to the city." **41** As soon as the lad had gone, David arose from *a place* toward the south, fell on his face to the ground, and bowed down three times. And they kissed one another; and they wept together, but David more so. **42** Then Jonathan said to David, "Go in peace, since we have both sworn in the name of the LORD, saying, 'May the LORD be between you and me, and between your descendants and my descendants, forever.' " So he arose and departed, and Jonathan went into the city.

Last meeting with David.

1 Sam 23:14–18 And David stayed in strongholds in the wilderness, and remained in the mountains in the Wilderness of Ziph. Saul sought him every day, but God did not deliver him into his hand. **15** So David saw that Saul had come out to seek his life. And David *was* in the Wilderness of Ziph in a forest. **16** Then Jonathan, Saul's son, arose and went to David in the woods and strengthened his hand in God. **17** And he said to him, "Do not fear, for the hand of Saul my father shall not find you. You shall be king over Israel, and I shall be next to you. Even my father Saul knows that." **18** So the two of them made a covenant before the LORD. And David stayed in the woods, and Jonathan went to his own house.

With father when Saul was killed.

2 Sam 1:1–12 Now it came to pass after the death of Saul, when David had returned from the slaughter of the Amalekites, and David had stayed two days in Ziklag, **2** on the third day, behold, it happened that a man came from Saul's camp with his clothes torn and dust on his head. So it was, when he came to David, that he fell to the ground and prostrated himself. **3** And David said to him, "Where have you come from?" So he said to him, "I have escaped from the camp of Israel." **4** Then David said to him, "How did the matter go? Please tell me." And he answered, "The people have fled from the battle, many of the people are fallen and dead, and Saul and Jonathan his son are dead also." **5** So David said to the young man who told him, "How do you know that Saul and Jonathan his son are dead?" **6** Then the young man who told him said, "As I happened by chance *to be* on Mount Gilboa, there was Saul, leaning on his spear; and indeed the chariots and horsemen followed hard after him. **7** Now when he looked behind him, he saw me and called to me. And I answered, 'Here I am.' **8** And he said to me, 'Who *are* you?' So I answered him, 'I *am* an Amalekite.' **9** He said to me again, 'Please stand over me and kill me, for anguish has come upon me, but my life still *remains* in me.' **10** So I stood over him and killed him, because I was sure that he could not live after he had fallen. And I took the crown that *was* on his head and the bracelet that *was* on his arm, and have brought them here to my lord." **11** Therefore David took hold of his own clothes and tore them, and *so did* all the men who *were* with him. **12** And they mourned and wept and fasted until evening for Saul and for Jonathan his son, for the people of the LORD and for the house of Israel, because they had fallen by the sword.

David mourned for.

2 Sam 1:17 Then David lamented with this lamentation over Saul and over Jonathan his son,

2 Sam 1:22–27 From the blood of the slain, From the fat of the mighty, The bow of Jonathan did not turn back, And the sword of Saul did not return empty. **23** "Saul and Jonathan *were* beloved and pleasant in their lives, And in their death they were not divided; They were swifter than eagles, They were stronger than lions. **24** "O daughters of Israel, weep over Saul, Who clothed you in scarlet, with luxury; Who put ornaments of gold on your apparel. **25** "How the mighty have fallen in the midst of the battle! Jonathan *was* slain in your high places. **26** I am distressed for you, my brother Jonathan; You have been very pleasant to me; Your love to me was wonderful, Surpassing the love of women. **27** "How the mighty have fallen, And the weapons of war perished!"

JORDAN, THE RIVER

Eastern boundary of Canaan.

Num 34:12 the border shall go down along the Jordan, and it shall end at the Salt Sea. This shall be your land with its surrounding boundaries.' "

Often overflowed.

Josh 3:15 and as those who bore the ark came to the Jordan, and the feet of the priests who bore the ark dipped in the edge of the water (for the Jordan overflows all its banks during the whole time of harvest),

1 Chr 12:15 These *are* the ones who crossed the Jordan in the first month, when it had overflowed all its banks; and they put to flight all *those* in the valleys, to the east and to the west.

Overflowing of, called the floodplain of.

Jer 12:5 "If you have run with the footmen, and they have wearied you, Then how can you contend with horses? And *if* in the land of peace, *In which* you trusted, *they wearied you,* Then how will you do in the floodplain of the Jordan?

Jer 49:19 "Behold, he shall come up like a lion from the floodplain of the Jordan Against the dwelling place of the strong; But I will suddenly make him run away from her. And who *is* a chosen *man that* I may appoint over her? For who *is* like Me? Who will arraign Me? And who *is* that shepherd Who will withstand Me?"

Empties itself into the Dead (Salt) Sea.

Num 34:12 the border shall go down along the Jordan, and it shall end at the Salt Sea. This shall be your land with its surrounding boundaries.' "

The plains of,

Thickly wooded.

2 Kin 6:2 Please, let us go to the Jordan, and let every man take a beam from there, and let us make there a place where we may dwell." So he answered, "Go."

Extremely fertile.

Gen 13:10 And Lot lifted his eyes and saw all the plain of Jordan, that it *was* well watered everywhere (before the LORD destroyed Sodom and Gomorrah) like the garden of the LORD, like the land of Egypt as you go toward Zoar.

Contained many lions.

Jer 49:19 "Behold, he shall come up like a lion from the floodplain of the Jordan Against the dwelling place of the strong; But I will suddenly make him run away from her. And who *is* a chosen *man that* I may appoint over her? For who *is* like Me? Who will arraign Me? And who *is* that shepherd Who will withstand Me?"

Jer 50:44 "Behold, he shall come up like a lion from the floodplain of the Jordan Against the dwelling place of the strong; But I will make him suddenly run away from her. And who *is* a chosen *man that* I may appoint over her? For who *is* like Me? Who will ar-

raign Me? And who *is* that shepherd Who will withstand Me?"

Provided clay for molding metals.

1 Kin 7:46 In the plain of Jordan the king had them cast in clay molds, between Succoth and Zaretan.

2 Chr 4:17 In the plain of Jordan the king had them cast in clay molds, between Succoth and Zeredah.

Chosen by Lot for a residence.

Gen 13:11 Then Lot chose for himself all the plain of Jordan, and Lot journeyed east. And they separated from each other.

Fordable in some places.

Josh 2:7 Then the men pursued them by the road to the Jordan, to the fords. And as soon as those who pursued them had gone out, they shut the gate.

Judg 12:5–6 The Gileadites seized the fords of the Jordan before the Ephraimites *arrived.* And when *any* Ephraimite who escaped said, "Let me cross over," the men of Gilead would say to him, "*Are* you an Ephraimite?" If he said, "No," **6** then they would say to him, "Then say, 'Shibboleth'!" And he would say, "Sibboleth," for he could not pronounce *it* right. Then they would take him and kill him at the fords of the Jordan. There fell at that time forty-two thousand Ephraimites.

Ferryboats often used on.

2 Sam 19:18 Then a ferryboat went across to carry over the king's household, and to do what he thought good. Now Shimei the son of Gera fell down before the king when he had crossed the Jordan.

Remarkable events connected with,

Division of its waters to let Israel pass over.

Josh 3:12–16 Now therefore, take for yourselves twelve men from the tribes of Israel, one man from every tribe. **13** And it shall come to pass, as soon as the soles of the feet of the priests who bear the ark of the LORD, the Lord of all the earth, shall rest in the waters of the Jordan, *that* the waters of the Jordan shall be cut off, the waters that come down from upstream, and they shall stand as a heap." **14** So it was, when the people set out from their camp to cross over the Jordan, with the priests bearing the ark of the covenant before the people, **15** and as those who bore the ark came to the Jordan, and the feet of the priests who bore the ark dipped in the edge of the water (for the Jordan overflows all its banks during the whole time of harvest), **16** that the waters which came down from upstream stood *still, and* rose in a heap very far away at Adam, the city that *is* beside Zaretan. So the waters that went down into the Sea of the Arabah, the Salt Sea, failed, *and* were cut off; and the people crossed over opposite Jericho.

Josh 5:1 So it was, when all the kings of the Amorites who *were* on the west side of the Jordan, and all the kings of the Canaanites who *were* by the sea, heard that the LORD had dried up the waters of the Jordan from before the children of Israel until we had crossed over, that their heart melted; and there was no spirit in them any longer because of the children of Israel.

Return of its waters to their place.

Josh 4:18 And it came to pass, when the priests who

bore the ark of the covenant of the LORD had come from the midst of the Jordan, *and* the soles of the priests' feet touched the dry land, that the waters of the Jordan returned to their place and overflowed all its banks as before.

Slaughter of Moabites.

Judg 3:28–29 Then he said to them, "Follow *me*, for the LORD has delivered your enemies the Moabites into your hand." So they went down after him, seized the fords of the Jordan leading to Moab, and did not allow anyone to cross over. **29** And at that time they killed about ten thousand men of Moab, all stout men of valor; not a man escaped.

Slaughter of the Ephraimites.

Judg 12:4–6 Now Jephthah gathered together all the men of Gilead and fought against Ephraim. And the men of Gilead defeated Ephraim, because they said, "You Gileadites *are* fugitives of Ephraim among the Ephraimites *and* among the Manassites." **5** The Gileadites seized the fords of the Jordan before the Ephraimites *arrived*. And when *any* Ephraimite who escaped said, "Let me cross over," the men of Gilead would say to him, "*Are* you an Ephraimite?" If he said, "No," **6** then they would say to him, "Then say, 'Shibboleth'!" And he would say, "Sibboleth," for he could not pronounce *it* right. Then they would take him and kill him at the fords of the Jordan. There fell at that time forty-two thousand Ephraimites.

Its division by Elijah.

2 Kin 2:8 Now Elijah took his mantle, rolled *it* up, and struck the water; and it was divided this way and that, so that the two of them crossed over on dry ground.

Its division by Elisha.

2 Kin 2:14 Then he took the mantle of Elijah that had fallen from him, and struck the water, and said, "Where *is* the LORD God of Elijah?" And when he also had struck the water, it was divided this way and that; and Elisha crossed over.

Healing of Naaman the leper.

2 Kin 5:10 And Elisha sent a messenger to him, saying, "Go and wash in the Jordan seven times, and your flesh shall be restored to you, and *you shall* be clean."

2 Kin 5:14 So he went down and dipped seven times in the Jordan, according to the saying of the man of God; and his flesh was restored like the flesh of a little child, and he was clean.

Baptism of multitudes by John the Baptist.

Matt 3:6 and were baptized by him in the Jordan, confessing their sins.

Mark 1:5 Then all the land of Judea, and those from Jerusalem, went out to him and were all baptized by him in the Jordan River, confessing their sins.

John 1:28 These things were done in Bethabara beyond the Jordan, where John was baptizing.

Baptism of our Lord.

Matt 3:13 Then Jesus came from Galilee to John at the Jordan to be baptized by him.

Matt 3:15 But Jesus answered and said to him, "Permit *it to be so* now, for thus it is fitting for us to fulfill all righteousness." Then he allowed Him.

Mark 1:9 It came to pass in those days *that* Jesus came

from Nazareth of Galilee, and was baptized by John in the Jordan.

Passage of Israel over.

Promised.

Deut 4:22 But I must die in this land, I must not cross over the Jordan; but you shall cross over and possess that good land.

Deut 9:1 "Hear, O Israel: You *are* to cross over the Jordan today, and go in to dispossess nations greater and mightier than yourself, cities great and fortified up to heaven,

Deut 11:31 For you will cross over the Jordan and go in to possess the land which the LORD your God is giving you, and you will possess it and dwell in it.

Cf. Josh 3:12-16; 5:1

In an appointed order.

Josh 3:1–8 Then Joshua rose early in the morning; and they set out from Acacia Grove and came to the Jordan, he and all the children of Israel, and lodged there before they crossed over. **2** So it was, after three days, that the officers went through the camp; **3** and they commanded the people, saying, "When you see the ark of the covenant of the LORD your God, and the priests, the Levites, bearing it, then you shall set out from your place and go after it. **4** Yet there shall be a space between you and it, about two thousand cubits by measure. Do not come near it, that you may know the way by which you must go, for you have not passed *this* way before." **5** And Joshua said to the people, "Sanctify yourselves, for tomorrow the LORD will do wonders among you." **6** Then Joshua spoke to the priests, saying, "Take up the ark of the covenant and cross over before the people." So they took up the ark of the covenant and went before the people. **7** And the LORD said to Joshua, "This day I will begin to exalt you in the sight of all Israel, that they may know that, as I was with Moses, *so* I will be with you. **8** You shall command the priests who bear the ark of the covenant, saying, 'When you have come to the edge of the water of the Jordan, you shall stand in the Jordan.' "

Preceded by priests with the ark.

Josh 3:6 Then Joshua spoke to the priests, saying, "Take up the ark of the covenant and cross over before the people." So they took up the ark of the covenant and went before the people.

Josh 3:11 Behold, the ark of the covenant of the Lord of all the earth is crossing over before you into the Jordan.

Josh 3:14 So it was, when the people set out from their camp to cross over the Jordan, with the priests bearing the ark of the covenant before the people,

Successfully effected.

Josh 3:17 Then the priests who bore the ark of the covenant of the LORD stood firm on dry ground in the midst of the Jordan; and all Israel crossed over on dry ground, until all the people had crossed completely over the Jordan.

Josh 4:1 And it came to pass, when all the people had completely crossed over the Jordan, that the LORD spoke to Joshua, saying:

Josh 4:10–11 So the priests who bore the ark stood in the midst of the Jordan until everything was finished that the LORD had commanded Joshua to speak to the people, according to all that Moses had commanded Joshua; and the people hurried and crossed over. **11** Then it came to pass, when all the people had completely crossed over, that the ark of the LORD and the priests crossed over in the presence of the people.

Commemorated by a pillar of stones raised in it.

Josh 4:2–9 "Take for yourselves twelve men from the people, one man from every tribe, **3** and command them, saying, 'Take for yourselves twelve stones from here, out of the midst of the Jordan, from the place where the priests' feet stood firm. You shall carry them over with you and leave them in the lodging place where you lodge tonight.' " **4** Then Joshua called the twelve men whom he had appointed from the children of Israel, one man from every tribe; **5** and Joshua said to them: "Cross over before the ark of the LORD your God into the midst of the Jordan, and each one of you take up a stone on his shoulder, according to the number of the tribes of the children of Israel, **6** that this may be a sign among you when your children ask in time to come, saying, 'What do these stones *mean* to you?' **7** Then you shall answer them that the waters of the Jordan were cut off before the ark of the covenant of the LORD; when it crossed over the Jordan, the waters of the Jordan were cut off. And these stones shall be for a memorial to the children of Israel forever." **8** And the children of Israel did so, just as Joshua commanded, and took up twelve stones from the midst of the Jordan, as the LORD had spoken to Joshua, according to the number of the tribes of the children of Israel, and carried them over with them to the place where they lodged, and laid them down there. **9** Then Joshua set up twelve stones in the midst of the Jordan, in the place where the feet of the priests who bore the ark of the covenant stood; and they are there to this day.

Commemorated by a pillar of stones in Gilgal.

Josh 4:20–24 And those twelve stones which they took out of the Jordan, Joshua set up in Gilgal. **21** Then he spoke to the children of Israel, saying: "When your children ask their fathers in time to come, saying, 'What *are* these stones?' **22** then you shall let your children know, saying, 'Israel crossed over this Jordan on dry land'; **23** for the LORD your God dried up the waters of the Jordan before you until you had crossed over, as the LORD your God did to the Red Sea, which He dried up before us until we had crossed over, **24** that all the peoples of the earth may know the hand of the LORD, that it *is* mighty, that you may fear the LORD your God forever."

Alluded to.

Ps 74:15 You broke open the fountain and the flood; You dried up mighty rivers.

Ps 114:3 The sea saw *it* and fled; Jordan turned back.

Ps 114:5 What ails you, O sea, that you fled? O Jordan, *that* you turned back?

A pledge that God would drive the Canaanites, etc. out of their land.

Josh 3:10 And Joshua said, "By this you shall know that the living God *is* among you, and *that* He will without fail drive out from before you the Canaanites and the Hittites and the Hivites and the Perizzites and the Girgashites and the Amorites and the Jebusites:

The Jews had great pride in.

Zech 11:3 *There is* the sound of wailing shepherds! For their glory is in ruins! *There is* the sound of roaring lions! For the pride of the Jordan is in ruins!

Despised by foreigners.

2 Kin 5:12 *Are* not the Abanah and the Pharpar, the rivers of Damascus, better than all the waters of Israel? Could I not wash in them and be clean?" So he turned and went away in a rage.

Moses not allowed to cross.

Deut 3:27 Go up to the top of Pisgah, and lift your eyes toward the west, the north, the south, and the east; behold *it* with your eyes, for you shall not cross over this Jordan.

Deut 31:2 And he said to them: "I *am* one hundred and twenty years old today. I can no longer go out and come in. Also the LORD has said to me, 'You shall not cross over this Jordan.'

JOSEPH

Son of Jacob and Rachel.

Gen 30:22–25 Then God remembered Rachel, and God listened to her and opened her womb. **23** And she conceived and bore a son, and said, "God has taken away my reproach." **24** So she called his name Joseph, and said, "The LORD shall add to me another son." **25** And it came to pass, when Rachel had borne Joseph, that Jacob said to Laban, "Send me away, that I may go to my own place and to my country.

Sold into Egypt by his brothers.

Gen 37:25–28 And they sat down to eat a meal. Then they lifted their eyes and looked, and there was a company of Ishmaelites, coming from Gilead with their camels, bearing spices, balm, and myrrh, on their way to carry *them* down to Egypt. **26** So Judah said to his brothers, "What profit *is there* if we kill our brother and conceal his blood? **27** Come and let us sell him to the Ishmaelites, and let not our hand be upon him, for he *is* our brother *and* our flesh." And his brothers listened. **28** Then Midianite traders passed by; so *the brothers* pulled Joseph up and lifted him out of the pit, and sold him to the Ishmaelites for twenty *shekels* of silver. And they took Joseph to Egypt.

Interpreted Pharaoh's dream.

Gen 41:1–37 Then it came to pass, at the end of two full years, that Pharaoh had a dream; and behold, he stood by the river. **2** Suddenly there came up out of the river seven cows, fine looking and fat; and they fed in the meadow. **3** Then behold, seven other cows came up after them out of the river, ugly and gaunt, and stood by the *other* cows on the bank of the river. **4** And the ugly and gaunt cows ate up the seven fine looking and fat cows. So Pharaoh awoke. **5** He slept and dreamed a second time; and suddenly seven heads of grain came up on one stalk, plump and good. **6** Then behold, seven thin heads, blighted by the east wind, sprang up after them. **7** And the seven thin heads devoured the seven plump and full heads. So Pharaoh awoke, and indeed, *it was* a dream. **8** Now it came to pass in the morning that his spirit was troubled, and he sent and called for all the magicians of Egypt and all its wise men. And Pharaoh told them his dreams, but *there was* no one who could interpret them for Pharaoh. **9** Then the chief butler spoke to Pharaoh, saying: "I remember my faults this day. **10** When Pharaoh was angry with his servants, and put me in custody in the house of the captain of the guard, *both* me and the chief baker, **11** we each had a dream in one night, he and I. Each of us dreamed according to the interpretation of his *own* dream. **12** Now there *was* a young Hebrew man with us there, a servant of the captain of the guard. And we told him, and he interpreted our dreams for us; to each man he interpreted according to his *own* dream. **13** And it came to pass, just as he interpreted for us, so it happened. He restored me to my office, and he hanged him." **14** Then Pharaoh sent and called Joseph, and they brought him quickly out of the dungeon; and he shaved, changed his clothing, and came to Pharaoh. **15** And Pharaoh said to Joseph, "I have had a dream, and *there is* no one who can interpret it. But I have heard it said of you *that* you can understand a dream, to interpret it." **16** So Joseph answered Pharaoh, saying, "*It is* not in me; God will give Pharaoh an answer of peace." **17** Then Pharaoh said to Joseph: "Behold, in my dream I stood on the bank of the river. **18** Suddenly seven cows came up out of the river, fine looking and fat; and they fed in the meadow. **19** Then behold, seven other cows came up after them, poor and very ugly and gaunt, such ugliness as I have never seen in all the land of Egypt. **20** And the gaunt and ugly cows ate up the first seven, the fat cows. **21** When they had eaten them up, no one would have known that they had eaten them, for they *were* just as ugly as at the beginning. So I awoke. **22** Also I saw in my dream, and suddenly seven heads came up on one stalk, full and good. **23** Then behold, seven heads, withered, thin, *and* blighted by the east wind, sprang up after them. **24** And the thin heads devoured the seven good heads. So I told *this* to the magicians, but *there was* no one who could explain *it* to me." **25** Then Joseph said to Pharaoh, "The dreams of Pharaoh *are* one; God has shown Pharaoh what He *is* about to do: **26** The seven good cows *are* seven years, and the seven good heads *are* seven years; the dreams *are* one. **27** And the seven thin and ugly cows which came up after them *are* seven years, and the seven empty heads blighted by the east wind *are* seven years of famine. **28** This *is* the thing which I have spoken to Pharaoh. God has shown Pharaoh what He *is* about to do. **29** Indeed seven years of great plenty will come throughout all the land of Egypt; **30** but after them seven years of famine will arise, and all the plenty will be forgotten in the land of Egypt; and the famine will deplete the land. **31** So the plenty will not be known in the land because of the famine following, for it *will be* very severe. **32** And the dream was repeated to Pharaoh twice because the thing *is* established by God, and God will shortly bring it to pass. **33** "Now therefore, let Pharaoh select a discerning and wise man, and set him over the land of Egypt. **34** Let Pharaoh do *this*, and let him appoint officers over the land, to collect one-fifth *of the produce* of the land of Egypt in the seven plentiful years. **35** And let them gather all the food of those good years that are coming, and store up grain under the authority of Pharaoh, and let them keep food in the cities. **36** Then that food shall be as a reserve for the land for the seven years of famine which shall be in the land of Egypt, that the land may not perish during the famine." **37** So the advice was good in the eyes of Pharaoh and in the eyes of all his servants.

Became Egyptian prime minister.

Gen 41:38–46 And Pharaoh said to his servants, "Can we find *such a one* as this, a man in whom *is* the Spirit of God?" **39** Then Pharaoh said to Joseph, "Inasmuch as God has shown you all this, *there is* no one as discerning and wise as you. **40** You shall be over my house, and all my people shall be ruled according to your word; only in regard to the throne will I be greater than you." **41** And Pharaoh said to Joseph, "See, I have set you over all the land of Egypt." **42** Then Pharaoh took his signet ring off his hand and put it on Joseph's hand; and he clothed him in garments of fine linen and put a gold chain around his neck. **43** And he had him ride in the second chariot which he had; and they cried out before him, "Bow the knee!" So he set him over all the land of Egypt. **44** Pharaoh also said to Joseph, "I *am* Pharaoh, and without your consent no man may lift his hand or foot in all the land of Egypt." **45** And Pharaoh called Joseph's name Zaphnath-Paaneah. And he gave him as a wife Asenath, the daughter of Poti-Pherah priest of On. So Joseph went out over *all* the land of Egypt. **46** Joseph was thirty years old when he stood before Pharaoh king of Egypt. And Joseph went out from the presence of Pharaoh, and went throughout all the land of Egypt.

His leadership during the famine.

Gen 41:53–57 Then the seven years of plenty which were in the land of Egypt ended, **54** and the seven years of famine began to come, as Joseph had said. The famine was in all lands, but in all the land of Egypt there was bread. **55** So when all the land of Egypt was famished, the people cried to Pharaoh for bread. Then Pharaoh said to all the Egyptians, "Go to Joseph; whatever he says to you, do." **56** The famine was over all the face of the earth, and Joseph opened all the storehouses and sold to the Egyptians. And the famine became severe in the land of Egypt. **57** So all countries came to Joseph in Egypt to buy *grain*, because the famine was severe in all lands.

Disclosed his identity to his brothers.

Gen 45:1–16 Then Joseph could not restrain himself before all those who stood by him, and he cried out, "Make everyone go out from me!" So no one stood with him while Joseph made himself known to his brothers. **2** And he wept aloud, and the Egyptians and the house of Pharaoh heard *it*. **3** Then Joseph said to his brothers, "I *am* Joseph; does my father still live?" But his brothers could not answer him, for they were dismayed in his presence. **4** And Joseph said to his brothers, "Please come near to me." So they came near. Then he said: "I *am* Joseph your brother, whom you sold into Egypt. **5** But now, do not therefore be grieved or angry with yourselves because you sold me here; for God sent me before you to preserve life. **6** For these two years the famine *has been* in the land, and *there are* still five years in which *there will be* neither plowing nor harvesting. **7** And God sent me before you to preserve a posterity for you in the earth, and to save your lives by a great deliverance. **8** So now *it was* not you *who* sent me here, but God; and He has made me a father to Pharaoh, and lord of all his house, and a ruler throughout all the land of Egypt. **9** "Hurry and go up to my father, and say to him, 'Thus says your son Joseph: "God has made me lord of all Egypt; come down to me, do not tarry. **10** You shall dwell in the land of Goshen, and you shall be near to me, you and your children, your children's children, your flocks and your herds, and all that you have. **11** There I will provide for you, lest you and your household, and all that you have, come to poverty; for *there are* still five years of famine." ' **12** "And behold, your eyes and the eyes of my brother Benjamin see that *it is* my mouth that speaks to you. **13** So you shall tell my father of all my glory in Egypt, and of all that you have seen; and you shall hurry and bring my father down here." **14** Then he fell on his brother Benjamin's neck and wept, and Benjamin wept on his neck. **15** Moreover he kissed all his brothers and wept over them, and after that his brothers talked with him. **16** Now the report of it was heard in Pharaoh's house, saying, "Joseph's brothers have come." So it pleased Pharaoh and his servants well.

Invited Jacob to Egypt.

Gen 45:17–28 And Pharaoh said to Joseph, "Say to your brothers, 'Do this: Load your animals and depart; go to the land of Canaan. **18** Bring your father and your households and come to me; I will give you the best of the land of Egypt, and you will eat the fat of the land. **19** Now you are commanded—do this: Take carts out of the land of Egypt for your little ones and your wives; bring your father and come. **20** Also do not be concerned about your goods, for the best of all the land of Egypt *is* yours.' " **21** Then the sons of Israel did so; and Joseph gave them carts, according to the command of Pharaoh, and he gave them provisions for the journey. **22** He gave to all of them, to each man, changes of garments; but to Benjamin he gave three hundred *pieces* of silver and five changes of garments. **23** And he sent to his father these *things:* ten donkeys loaded with the good things of Egypt, and ten female donkeys loaded with grain, bread, and food for his father for the journey. **24** So he sent his brothers away, and they departed; and he said to them, "See that you do not become troubled along the way." **25** Then they went up out of Egypt, and came to the land of Canaan to Jacob their father. **26** And they told him, saying, "Joseph *is* still alive, and he *is* governor over all the land of Egypt." And Jacob's heart stood still, because he did not believe them. **27** But when they told him all the words which Joseph had said to them, and when he saw the carts which Joseph had sent to carry him, the spirit of Jacob their father revived. **28** Then Israel said, "*It is* enough. Joseph my son *is* still alive. I will go and see him before I die."

Exercised complete authority over Egypt.

Gen 47:13–26 Now *there was* no bread in all the land; for the famine *was* very severe, so that the land of Egypt and the land of Canaan languished because of the famine. **14** And Joseph gathered up all the money that was found in the land of Egypt and in the land of Canaan, for the grain which they bought; and Jo-

seph brought the money into Pharaoh's house. **15** So when the money failed in the land of Egypt and in the land of Canaan, all the Egyptians came to Joseph and said, "Give us bread, for why should we die in your presence? For the money has failed." **16** Then Joseph said, "Give your livestock, and I will give you *bread* for your livestock, if the money is gone." **17** So they brought their livestock to Joseph, and Joseph gave them bread *in exchange* for the horses, the flocks, the cattle of the herds, and for the donkeys. Thus he fed them with bread *in exchange* for all their livestock that year. **18** When that year had ended, they came to him the next year and said to him, "We will not hide from my lord that our money is gone; my lord also has our herds of livestock. There is nothing left in the sight of my lord but our bodies and our lands. **19** Why should we die before your eyes, both we and our land? Buy us and our land for bread, and we and our land will be servants of Pharaoh; give *us* seed, that we may live and not die, that the land may not be desolate." **20** Then Joseph bought all the land of Egypt for Pharaoh; for every man of the Egyptians sold his field, because the famine was severe upon them. So the land became Pharaoh's. **21** And as for the people, he moved them into the cities, from *one* end of the borders of Egypt to the *other* end. **22** Only the land of the priests he did not buy; for the priests had rations *allotted to them* by Pharaoh, and they ate their rations which Pharaoh gave them; therefore they did not sell their lands. **23** Then Joseph said to the people, "Indeed I have bought you and your land this day for Pharaoh. Look, *here is* seed for you, and you shall sow the land. **24** And it shall come to pass in the harvest that you shall give one-fifth to Pharaoh. Four-fifths shall be your own, as seed for the field and for your food, for those of your households and as food for your little ones." **25** So they said, "You have saved our lives; let us find favor in the sight of my lord, and we will be Pharaoh's servants." **26** And Joseph made it a law over the land of Egypt to this day, *that* Pharaoh should have one-fifth, except for the land of the priests only, *which* did not become Pharaoh's.

Forgave his brothers.

Gen 50:15–21 When Joseph's brothers saw that their father was dead, they said, "Perhaps Joseph will hate us, and may actually repay us for all the evil which we did to him." **16** So they sent *messengers* to Joseph, saying, "Before your father died he commanded, saying, **17** 'Thus you shall say to Joseph: "I beg you, please forgive the trespass of your brothers and their sin; for they did evil to you." ' Now, please, forgive the trespass of the servants of the God of your father." And Joseph wept when they spoke to him. **18** Then his brothers also went and fell down before his face, and they said, "Behold, we *are* your servants." **19** Joseph said to them, "Do not be afraid, for *am* I in the place of God? **20** But as for you, you meant evil against me; *but* God meant it for good, in order to bring it about as *it is* this day, to save many people alive. **21** Now therefore, do not be afraid; I will provide for you and your little ones." And he comforted them and spoke kindly to them.

Death of.

Gen 50:22–26 So Joseph dwelt in Egypt, he and his father's household. And Joseph lived one hundred and ten years. 23 Joseph saw Ephraim's children to the third *generation.* The children of Machir, the son of Manasseh, were also brought up on Joseph's knees. 24 And Joseph said to his brethren, "I am dying; but God will surely visit you, and bring you out of this land to the land of which He swore to Abraham, to Isaac, and to Jacob." 25 Then Joseph took an oath from the children of Israel, saying, "God will surely visit you, and you shall carry up my bones from here." 26 So Joseph died, *being* one hundred and ten years old; and they embalmed him, and he was put in a coffin in Egypt.

Descendants of.

Num 26:28–37 The sons of Joseph according to their families, by Manasseh and Ephraim, *were:* 29 The sons of Manasseh: of Machir, the family of the Machirites; and Machir begot Gilead; of Gilead, the family of the Gileadites. 30 These *are* the sons of Gilead: *of* Jeezer, the family of the Jeezerites; of Helek, the family of the Helekites; 31 *of* Asriel, the family of the Asrielites; *of* Shechem, the family of the Shechemites; 32 *of* Shemida, the family of the Shemidaites; *of* Hepher, the family of the Hepherites. 33 Now Zelophehad the son of Hepher had no sons, but daughters; and the names of the daughters of Zelophehad *were* Mahlah, Noah, Hoglah, Milcah, and Tirzah. 34 These *are* the families of Manasseh; and those who were numbered of them *were* fifty-two thousand seven hundred. 35 These *are* the sons of Ephraim according to their families: of Shuthelah, the family of the Shuthalhites; of Becher, the family of the Bachrites; of Tahan, the family of the Tahanites. 36 And these *are* the sons of Shuthelah: of Eran, the family of the Eranites. 37 These *are* the families of the sons of Ephraim according to those who were numbered of them: thirty-two thousand five hundred. These *are* the sons of Joseph according to their families.

Hero of faith.

Heb 11:22 By faith Joseph, when he was dying, made mention of the departure of the children of Israel, and gave instructions concerning his bones.

JOSHUA (HOSHEA)

Son of Nun.

Num 13:8 from the tribe of Ephraim, Hoshea the son of Nun;

Num 13:16 These *are* the names of the men whom Moses sent to spy out the land. And Moses called Hoshea the son of Nun, Joshua.

As a spy, presented favorable report.

Num 13:1–3 And the LORD spoke to Moses, saying, 2 "Send men to spy out the land of Canaan, which I am giving to the children of Israel; from each tribe of their fathers you shall send a man, every one a leader among them." 3 So Moses sent them from the Wilderness of Paran according to the command of the LORD, all of them men who *were* heads of the children of Israel.

Num 13:16 These *are* the names of the men whom Moses sent to spy out the land. And Moses called Hoshea the son of Nun, Joshua.

Num 14:6–10 But Joshua the son of Nun and Caleb the son of Jephunneh, *who were* among those who had spied out the land, tore their clothes; 7 and they spoke to all the congregation of the children of Israel, saying: "The land we passed through to spy out *is* an exceedingly good land. 8 If the LORD delights in us, then He will bring us into this land and give it to us, 'a land which flows with milk and honey.' 9 Only do not rebel against the LORD, nor fear the people of the land, for they *are* our bread; their protection has departed from them, and the LORD *is* with us. Do not fear them." 10 And all the congregation said to stone them with stones. Now the glory of the LORD appeared in the tabernacle of meeting before all the children of Israel.

Succeeded Moses as leader.

Num 27:18–23 And the LORD said to Moses: "Take Joshua the son of Nun with you, a man in whom *is* the Spirit, and lay your hand on him; 19 set him before Eleazar the priest and before all the congregation, and inaugurate him in their sight. 20 And you shall give *some* of your authority to him, that all the congregation of the children of Israel may be obedient. 21 He shall stand before Eleazar the priest, who shall inquire before the LORD for him by the judgment of the Urim. At his word they shall go out, and at his word they shall come in, he and all the children of Israel with him—all the congregation." 22 So Moses did as the LORD commanded him. He took Joshua and set him before Eleazar the priest and before all the congregation. 23 And he laid his hands on him and inaugurated him, just as the LORD commanded by the hand of Moses.

Unified the Israelites.

Josh 1:10–18 Then Joshua commanded the officers of the people, saying, 11 "Pass through the camp and command the people, saying, 'Prepare provisions for yourselves, for within three days you will cross over this Jordan, to go in to possess the land which the LORD your God is giving you to possess.'" 12 And to the Reubenites, the Gadites, and half the tribe of Manasseh Joshua spoke, saying, 13 "Remember the word which Moses the ·servant of the LORD commanded you, saying, 'The LORD your God is giving you rest and is giving you this land.' 14 Your wives, your little ones, and your livestock shall remain in the land which Moses gave you on this side of the Jordan. But you shall pass before your brethren armed, all your mighty men of valor, and help them, 15 until the LORD has given your brethren rest, as He *gave* you, and they also have taken possession of the land which the LORD your God is giving them. Then you shall return to the land of your possession and enjoy it, which Moses the LORD's servant gave you on this side of the Jordan toward the sunrise." 16 So they answered Joshua, saying, "All that you command us we will do, and wherever you send us we will go. 17 Just as we heeded Moses in all things, so we will heed you. Only the LORD your God be with you, as He was with Moses. 18 Whoever rebels against your command and does not heed your words, in all that you command him, shall be put to death. Only be strong and of good courage."

Sent spies to Jericho. Josh 2:1–24

Crossed Jordan River. Josh 3:1–17

Destroyed Jericho. Josh 6:1–27
Final address to Israel.

Josh 24:1–28 Then Joshua gathered all the tribes of Israel to Shechem and called for the elders of Israel, for their heads, for their judges, and for their officers; and they presented themselves before God. **2** And Joshua said to all the people, "Thus says the LORD God of Israel: 'Your fathers, *including* Terah, the father of Abraham and the father of Nahor, dwelt on the other side of the River in old times; and they served other gods. **3** Then I took your father Abraham from the other side of the River, led him throughout all the land of Canaan, and multiplied his descendants and gave him Isaac. **4** To Isaac I gave Jacob and Esau. To Esau I gave the mountains of Seir to possess, but Jacob and his children went down to Egypt. **5** Also I sent Moses and Aaron, and I plagued Egypt, according to what I did among them. Afterward I brought you out. **6** 'Then I brought your fathers out of Egypt, and you came to the sea; and the Egyptians pursued your fathers with chariots and horsemen to the Red Sea. **7** So they cried out to the LORD; and He put darkness between you and the Egyptians, brought the sea upon them, and covered them. And your eyes saw what I did in Egypt. Then you dwelt in the wilderness a long time. **8** And I brought you into the land of the Amorites, who dwelt on the other side of the Jordan, and they fought with you. But I gave them into your hand, that you might possess their land, and I destroyed them from before you. **9** Then Balak the son of Zippor, king of Moab, arose to make war against Israel, and sent and called Balaam the son of Beor to curse you. **10** But I would not listen to Balaam; therefore he continued to bless you. So I delivered you out of his hand. **11** Then you went over the Jordan and came to Jericho. And the men of Jericho fought against you— *also* the Amorites, the Perizzites, the Canaanites, the Hittites, the Girgashites, the Hivites, and the Jebusites. But I delivered them into your hand. **12** I sent the hornet before you which drove them out from before you, *also* the two kings of the Amorites, *but* not with your sword or with your bow. **13** I have given you a land for which you did not labor, and cities which you did not build, and you dwell in them; you eat of the vineyards and olive groves which you did not plant.' **14** "Now therefore, fear the LORD, serve Him in sincerity and in truth, and put away the gods which your fathers served on the other side of the River and in Egypt. Serve the LORD! **15** And if it seems evil to you to serve the LORD, choose for yourselves this day whom you will serve, whether the gods which your fathers served that *were* on the other side of the River, or the gods of the Amorites, in whose land you dwell. But as for me and my house, we will serve the LORD." **16** So the people answered and said: "Far be it from us that we should forsake the LORD to serve other gods; **17** for the LORD our God *is* He who brought us and our fathers up out of the land of Egypt, from the house of bondage, who did those great signs in our sight, and preserved us in all the way that we went and among all the people through whom we passed. **18** And the LORD drove out from before us all the people, including the Amorites who dwelt in the land. We also will serve

the LORD, for He *is* our God." **19** But Joshua said to the people, "You cannot serve the LORD, for He *is* a holy God. He *is* a jealous God; He will not forgive your transgressions nor your sins. **20** If you forsake the LORD and serve foreign gods, then He will turn and do you harm and consume you, after He has done you good." **21** And the people said to Joshua, "No, but we will serve the LORD!" **22** So Joshua said to the people, "You *are* witnesses against yourselves that you have chosen the LORD for yourselves, to serve Him." And they said, "*We are* witnesses!" **23** "Now therefore," *he said*, "put away the foreign gods which *are* among you, and incline your heart to the LORD God of Israel." **24** And the people said to Joshua, "The LORD our God we will serve, and His voice we will obey!" **25** So Joshua made a covenant with the people that day, and made for them a statute and an ordinance in Shechem. **26** Then Joshua wrote these words in the Book of the Law of God. And he took a large stone, and set it up there under the oak that *was* by the sanctuary of the LORD. **27** And Joshua said to all the people, "Behold, this stone shall be a witness to us, for it has heard all the words of the LORD which He spoke to us. It shall therefore be a witness to you, lest you deny your God." **28** So Joshua let the people depart, each to his own inheritance.

Saw the Commander of the Lord's army.

Josh 5:13–15 And it came to pass, when Joshua was by Jericho, that he lifted his eyes and looked, and behold, a Man stood opposite him with His sword drawn in His hand. And Joshua went to Him and said to Him, "*Are* You for us or for our adversaries?" **14** So He said, "No, but *as* Commander of the army of the LORD I have now come." And Joshua fell on his face to the earth and worshiped, and said to Him, "What does my Lord say to His servant?" **15** Then the Commander of the LORD's army said to Joshua, "Take your sandal off your foot, for the place where you stand *is* holy." And Joshua did so.

Death of.

Josh 24:29–30 Now it came to pass after these things that Joshua the son of Nun, the servant of the LORD, died, *being* one hundred and ten years old. **30** And they buried him within the border of his inheritance at Timnath Serah, which *is* in the mountains of Ephraim, on the north side of Mount Gaash.

Favorable remembrance of.

Judg 2:7 So the people served the LORD all the days of Joshua, and all the days of the elders who outlived Joshua, who had seen all the great works of the LORD which He had done for Israel.

JOSIAH
King of Judah.

2 Kin 22:1–20 Josiah *was* eight years old when he became king, and he reigned thirty-one years in Jerusalem. His mother's name *was* Jedidah the daughter of Adaiah of Bozkath. **2** And he did *what was* right in the sight of the LORD, and walked in all the ways of his father David; he did not turn aside to the right hand or to the left. **3** Now it came to pass, in the eighteenth year of King Josiah, *that* the king sent Shaphan the scribe, the son of Azaliah, the son of Meshullam, to the house of the LORD, saying: **4** "Go up to Hilkiah the high priest, that he may count the money which has been brought into the house of the LORD, which the doorkeepers have gathered from the people. 5 And let them deliver it into the hand of those doing the work, who are the overseers in the house of the LORD; let them give it to those who *are* in the house of the LORD doing the work, to repair the damages of the house— 6 to carpenters and builders and masons—and to buy timber and hewn stone to repair the house. 7 However there need be no accounting made with them of the money delivered into their hand, because they deal faithfully." 8 Then Hilkiah the high priest said to Shaphan the scribe, "I have found the Book of the Law in the house of the LORD." And Hilkiah gave the book to Shaphan, and he read it. 9 So Shaphan the scribe went to the king, bringing the king word, saying, "Your servants have gathered the money that was found in the house, and have delivered it into the hand of those who do the work, who oversee the house of the LORD." 10 Then Shaphan the scribe showed the king, saying, "Hilkiah the priest has given me a book." And Shaphan read it before the king. 11 Now it happened, when the king heard the words of the Book of the Law, that he tore his clothes. 12 Then the king commanded Hilkiah the priest, Ahikam the son of Shaphan, Achbor the son of Michaiah, Shaphan the scribe, and Asaiah a servant of the king, saying, 13 "Go, inquire of the LORD for me, for the people and for all Judah, concerning the words of this book that has been found; for great *is* the wrath of the LORD that is aroused against us, because our fathers have not obeyed the words of this book, to do according to all that is written concerning us." 14 So Hilkiah the priest, Ahikam, Achbor, Shaphan, and Asaiah went to Huldah the prophetess, the wife of Shallum the son of Tikvah, the son of Harhas, keeper of the wardrobe. (She dwelt in Jerusalem in the Second Quarter.) And they spoke with her. 15 Then she said to them, "Thus says the LORD God of Israel, 'Tell the man who sent you to Me, 16 "Thus says the LORD: 'Behold, I will bring calamity on this place and on its inhabitants—all the words of the book which the king of Judah has read— 17 because they have forsaken Me and burned incense to other gods, that they might provoke Me to anger with all the works of their hands. Therefore My wrath shall be aroused against this place and shall not be quenched.' " ' 18 But as for the king of Judah, who sent you to inquire of the LORD, in this manner you shall speak to him, 'Thus says the LORD God of Israel: "*Concerning* the words which you have heard— 19 because your heart was tender, and you humbled yourself before the LORD when you heard what I spoke against this place and against its inhabitants, that they would become a desolation and a curse, and you tore your clothes and wept before Me, I also have heard *you*," says the LORD. 20 Surely, therefore, I will gather you to your fathers, and you shall be gathered to your grave in peace; and your eyes shall not see all the calamity which I will bring on this place." ' " So they brought back word to the king.

2 Kin 23:1–30 Now the king sent them to gather all the elders of Judah and Jerusalem to him. 2 The king went up to the house of the LORD with all the men of Judah, and with him all the inhabitants of Jerusa-

lem—the priests and the prophets and all the people, both small and great. And he read in their hearing all the words of the Book of the Covenant which had been found in the house of the LORD. 3 Then the king stood by a pillar and made a covenant before the LORD, to follow the LORD and to keep His commandments and His testimonies and His statutes, with all *his* heart and all *his* soul, to perform the words of this covenant that were written in this book. And all the people took a stand for the covenant. 4 And the king commanded Hilkiah the high priest, the priests of the second order, and the doorkeepers, to bring out of the temple of the LORD all the articles that were made for Baal, for Asherah, and for all the host of heaven; and he burned them outside Jerusalem in the fields of Kidron, and carried their ashes to Bethel. 5 Then he removed the idolatrous priests whom the kings of Judah had ordained to burn incense on the high places in the cities of Judah and in the places all around Jerusalem, and those who burned incense to Baal, to the sun, to the moon, to the constellations, and to all the host of heaven. 6 And he brought out the wooden image from the house of the LORD, to the Brook Kidron outside Jerusalem, burned it at the Brook Kidron and ground *it* to ashes, and threw its ashes on the graves of the common people. 7 Then he tore down the *ritual* booths of the perverted persons that *were* in the house of the LORD, where the women wove hangings for the wooden image. 8 And he brought all the priests from the cities of Judah, and defiled the high places where the priests had burned incense, from Geba to Beersheba; also he broke down the high places at the gates which *were* at the entrance of the Gate of Joshua the governor of the city, which *were* to the left of the city gate. 9 Nevertheless the priests of the high places did not come up to the altar of the LORD in Jerusalem, but they ate unleavened bread among their brethren. 10 And he defiled Topheth, which *is* in the Valley of the Son of Hinnom, that no man might make his son or his daughter pass through the fire to Molech. 11 Then he removed the horses that the kings of Judah had dedicated to the sun, at the entrance to the house of the LORD, by the chamber of Nathan-Melech, the officer who *was* in the court; and he burned the chariots of the sun with fire. 12 The altars that *were* on the roof, the upper chamber of Ahaz, which the kings of Judah had made, and the altars which Manasseh had made in the two courts of the house of the LORD, the king broke down and pulverized there, and threw their dust into the Brook Kidron. 13 Then the king defiled the high places that *were* east of Jerusalem, which *were* on the south of the Mount of Corruption, which Solomon king of Israel had built for Ashtoreth the abomination of the Sidonians, for Chemosh the abomination of the Moabites, and for Milcom the abomination of the people of Ammon. 14 And he broke in pieces the *sacred* pillars and cut down the wooden images, and filled their places with the bones of men. 15 Moreover the altar that *was* at Bethel, *and* the high place which Jeroboam the son of Nebat, who made Israel sin, had made, both that altar and the high place he broke down; and he burned the high place *and* crushed *it* to powder, and burned the wooden image. 16 As Josiah turned, he saw the tombs that *were* there on the mountain. And he sent and took the bones out of the tombs and burned *them* on the altar, and defiled it according to the word of the LORD which the man of God proclaimed, who proclaimed these words. **17** Then he said, "What gravestone *is* this that I see?" So the men of the city told him, "*It is* the tomb of the man of God who came from Judah and proclaimed these things which you have done against the altar of Bethel." **18** And he said, "Let him alone; let no one move his bones." So they let his bones alone, with the bones of the prophet who came from Samaria. **19** Now Josiah also took away all the shrines of the high places that *were* in the cities of Samaria, which the kings of Israel had made to provoke the LORD to anger; and he did to them according to all the deeds he had done in Bethel. **20** He executed all the priests of the high places who *were* there, on the altars, and burned men's bones on them; and he returned to Jerusalem. **21** Then the king commanded all the people, saying, "Keep the Passover to the LORD your God, as *it is* written in this Book of the Covenant." **22** Such a Passover surely had never been held since the days of the judges who judged Israel, nor in all the days of the kings of Israel and the kings of Judah. **23** But in the eighteenth year of King Josiah this Passover was held before the LORD in Jerusalem. **24** Moreover Josiah put away those who consulted mediums and spiritists, the household gods and idols, all the abominations that were seen in the land of Judah and in Jerusalem, that he might perform the words of the law which were written in the book that Hilkiah the priest found in the house of the LORD. **25** Now before him there was no king like him, who turned to the LORD with all his heart, with all his soul, and with all his might, according to all the Law of Moses; nor after him did *any* arise like him. **26** Nevertheless the LORD did not turn from the fierceness of His great wrath, with which His anger was aroused against Judah, because of all the provocations with which Manasseh had provoked Him. **27** And the LORD said, "I will also remove Judah from My sight, as I have removed Israel, and will cast off this city Jerusalem which I have chosen, and the house of which I said, 'My name shall be there.' " **28** Now the rest of the acts of Josiah, and all that he did, *are* they not written in the book of the chronicles of the kings of Judah? **29** In his days Pharaoh Necho king of Egypt went to the aid of the king of Assyria, to the River Euphrates; and King Josiah went against him. And *Pharaoh Necho* killed him at Megiddo when he confronted him. **30** Then his servants moved his body in a chariot from Megiddo, brought him to Jerusalem, and buried him in his own tomb. And the people of the land took Jehoahaz the son of Josiah, anointed him, and made him king in his father's place.

Cf. 2 Chr 34:1–33; 35:1–27

His role prophesied.

1 Kin 13:2–3 Then he cried out against the altar by the word of the LORD, and said, "O altar, altar! Thus says the LORD: 'Behold, a child, Josiah by name, shall be born to the house of David; and on you he shall sacrifice the priests of the high places who burn incense on you, and men's bones shall be burned on you.' " **3** And he gave a sign the same day, saying, "This *is* the sign which the LORD has spoken: Surely the altar shall split apart, and the ashes on it shall be poured out."

Led a revival of obedience to the Law.

2 Kin 22:11–13 Now it happened, when the king heard the words of the Book of the Law, that he tore his clothes. **12** Then the king commanded Hilkiah the priest, Ahikam the son of Shaphan, Achbor the son of Michaiah, Shaphan the scribe, and Asaiah a servant of the king, saying, **13** "Go, inquire of the LORD for me, for the people and for all Judah, concerning the words of this book that has been found; for great *is* the wrath of the LORD that is aroused against us, because our fathers have not obeyed the words of this book, to do according to all that is written concerning us."

2 Kin 23:1–3 Now the king sent them to gather all the elders of Judah and Jerusalem to him. **2** The king went up to the house of the LORD with all the men of Judah, and with him all the inhabitants of Jerusalem—the priests and the prophets and all the people, both small and great. And he read in their hearing all the words of the Book of the Covenant which had been found in the house of the LORD. **3** Then the king stood by a pillar and made a covenant before the LORD, to follow the LORD and to keep His commandments and His testimonies and His statutes, with all *his* heart and all *his* soul, to perform the words of this covenant that were written in this book. And all the people took a stand for the covenant.

2 Kin 23:21–25 Then the king commanded all the people, saying, "Keep the Passover to the LORD your God, as *it is* written in this Book of the Covenant." **22** Such a Passover surely had never been held since the days of the judges who judged Israel, nor in all the days of the kings of Israel and the kings of Judah. **23** But in the eighteenth year of King Josiah this Passover was held before the LORD in Jerusalem. **24** Moreover Josiah put away those who consulted mediums and spiritists, the household gods and idols, all the abominations that were seen in the land of Judah and in Jerusalem, that he might perform the words of the law which were written in the book that Hilkiah the priest found in the house of the LORD. **25** Now before him there was no king like him, who turned to the LORD with all his heart, with all his soul, and with all his might, according to all the Law of Moses; nor after him did *any* arise like him.

2 Chr 34:19–21 Thus it happened, when the king heard the words of the Law, that he tore his clothes. **20** Then the king commanded Hilkiah, Ahikam the son of Shaphan, Abdon the son of Micah, Shaphan the scribe, and Asaiah a servant of the king, saying, **21** "Go, inquire of the LORD for me, and for those who are left in Israel and Judah, concerning the words of the book that is found; for great *is* the wrath of the LORD that is poured out on us, because our fathers have not kept the word of the LORD, to do according to all that is written in this book."

2 Chr 34:29–33 Then the king sent and gathered all the elders of Judah and Jerusalem. **30** The king went up to the house of the LORD, with all the men of Judah and the inhabitants of Jerusalem—the priests and the Levites, and all the people, great and small. And he read in their hearing all the words of the Book of the

Covenant which had been found in the house of the LORD. **31** Then the king stood in his place and made a covenant before the LORD, to follow the LORD, and to keep His commandments and His testimonies and His statutes with all his heart and all his soul, to perform the words of the covenant that were written in this book. **32** And he made all who were present in Jerusalem and Benjamin take a stand. So the inhabitants of Jerusalem did according to the covenant of God, the God of their fathers. **33** Thus Josiah removed all the abominations from all the country that *belonged* to the children of Israel, and made all who were present in Israel diligently serve the LORD their God. All his days they did not depart from following the LORD God of their fathers.

2 Chr 35:1–10 Now Josiah kept a Passover to the LORD in Jerusalem, and they slaughtered the Passover *lambs* on the fourteenth *day* of the first month. **2** And he set the priests in their duties and encouraged them for the service of the house of the LORD. **3** Then he said to the Levites who taught all Israel, who were holy to the LORD: "Put the holy ark in the house which Solomon the son of David, king of Israel, built. *It shall* no longer *be* a burden on *your* shoulders. Now serve the LORD your God and His people Israel. **4** Prepare *yourselves* according to your fathers' houses, according to your divisions, following the written instruction of David king of Israel and the written instruction of Solomon his son. **5** And stand in the holy *place* according to the divisions of the fathers' houses of your brethren the *lay* people, and *according to* the division of the father's house of the Levites. **6** So slaughter the Passover *offerings*, consecrate yourselves, and prepare *them* for your brethren, that *they* may do according to the word of the LORD by the hand of Moses." **7** Then Josiah gave the *lay* people lambs and young goats from the flock, all for Passover *offerings* for all who were present, to the number of thirty thousand, as well as three thousand cattle; these *were* from the king's possessions. **8** And his leaders gave willingly to the people, to the priests, and to the Levites. Hilkiah, Zechariah, and Jehiel, rulers of the house of God, gave to the priests for the Passover *offerings* two thousand six hundred *from the flock,* and three hundred cattle. **9** Also Conaniah, his brothers Shemaiah and Nethanel, and Hashabiah and Jeiel and Jozabad, chief of the Levites, gave to the Levites for Passover *offerings* five thousand *from the flock* and five hundred cattle. **10** So the service was prepared, and the priests stood in their places, and the Levites in their divisions, according to the king's command.

2 Chr 35:16 So all the service of the LORD was prepared the same day, to keep the Passover and to offer burnt offerings on the altar of the LORD, according to the command of King Josiah.

Killed in battle.

2 Kin 23:28–30 Now the rest of the acts of Josiah, and all that he did, *are* they not written in the book of the chronicles of the kings of Judah? **29** In his days Pharaoh Necho king of Egypt went to the aid of the king of Assyria, to the River Euphrates; and King Josiah went against him. And *Pharaoh Necho* killed him at Megiddo when he confronted him. **30** Then his servants moved his body in a chariot from Megiddo,

brought him to Jerusalem, and buried him in his own tomb. And the people of the land took Jehoahaz the son of Josiah, anointed him, and made him king in his father's place.

2 Chr 35:20–25 After all this, when Josiah had prepared the temple, Necho king of Egypt came up to fight against Carchemish by the Euphrates; and Josiah went out against him. **21** But he sent messengers to him, saying, "What have I to do with you, king of Judah? *I have* not *come* against you this day, but against the house with which I have war; for God commanded me to make haste. Refrain *from meddling with* God, who *is* with me, lest He destroy you." **22** Nevertheless Josiah would not turn his face from him, but disguised himself so that he might fight with him, and did not heed the words of Necho from the mouth of God. So he came to fight in the Valley of Megiddo. **23** And the archers shot King Josiah; and the king said to his servants, "Take me away, for I am severely wounded." **24** His servants therefore took him out of that chariot and put him in the second chariot that he had, and they brought him to Jerusalem. So he died, and was buried in *one of* the tombs of his fathers. And all Judah and Jerusalem mourned for Josiah. **25** Jeremiah also lamented for Josiah. And to this day all the singing men and the singing women speak of Josiah in their lamentations. They made it a custom in Israel; and indeed they *are* written in the Laments.

JOY

God gives.

Eccl 2:26 For *God* gives wisdom and knowledge and joy to a man who *is* good in His sight; but to the sinner He gives the work of gathering and collecting, that he may give to *him who is* good before God. This also *is* vanity and grasping for the wind.

Ps 4:7 You have put gladness in my heart, More than in the season that their grain and wine increased.

Christ appointed to give.

Is 61:3 To console those who mourn in Zion, To give them beauty for ashes, The oil of joy for mourning, The garment of praise for the spirit of heaviness; That they may be called trees of righteousness, The planting of the LORD, that He may be glorified."

Is a fruit of the Spirit.

Gal 5:22 But the fruit of the Spirit is love, joy, peace, longsuffering, kindness, goodness, faithfulness,

The gospel, good tidings of.

Luke 2:10–11 Then the angel said to them, "Do not be afraid, for behold, I bring you good tidings of great joy which will be to all people. **11** For there is born to you this day in the city of David a Savior, who is Christ the Lord.

God's Word affords.

Neh 8:12 And all the people went their way to eat and drink, to send portions and rejoice greatly, because they understood the words that were declared to them.

Jer 15:16 Your words were found, and I ate them, And Your word was to me the joy and rejoicing of my heart; For I am called by Your name, O LORD God of hosts.

The gospel to be received with.

1 Thess 1:6 And you became followers of us and of the Lord, having received the word in much affliction, with joy of the Holy Spirit,

Promised to believers.

Ps 132:16 I will also clothe her priests with salvation, And her saints shall shout aloud for joy.

Is 35:10 And the ransomed of the LORD shall return, And come to Zion with singing, With everlasting joy on their heads. They shall obtain joy and gladness, And sorrow and sighing shall flee away.

Is 55:12 "For you shall go out with joy, And be led out with peace; The mountains and the hills Shall break forth into singing before you, And all the trees of the field shall clap *their* hands.

Is 56:7 Even them I will bring to My holy mountain, And make them joyful in My house of prayer. Their burnt offerings and their sacrifices *Will be* accepted on My altar; For My house shall be called a house of prayer for all nations."

Commanded of believers.

Ps 32:11 Be glad in the LORD and rejoice, you righteous; And shout for joy, all *you* upright in heart!

Ps 100:2 Serve the LORD with gladness; Come before His presence with singing.

Phil 3:1 Finally, my brethren, rejoice in the Lord. For me to write the same things to you *is* not tedious, but for you *it is* safe.

Fullness of, in God's presence.

Ps 16:11 You will show me the path of life; In Your presence *is* fullness of joy; At Your right hand *are* pleasures forevermore.

Vanity of seeking, from earthly things.

Eccl 2:10–11 Whatever my eyes desired I did not keep from them. I did not withhold my heart from any pleasure, For my heart rejoiced in all my labor; And this was my reward from all my labor. **11** Then I looked on all the works that my hands had done And on the labor in which I had toiled; And indeed all *was* vanity and grasping for the wind. *There was* no profit under the sun.

Eccl 11:8 But if a man lives many years *And* rejoices in them all, Yet let him remember the days of darkness, For they will be many. All that is coming *is* vanity.

Experienced by

Believers.

Ps 97:11 Light is sown for the righteous, And gladness for the upright in heart.

Luke 24:52 And they worshiped Him, and returned to Jerusalem with great joy,

Acts 16:34 Now when he had brought them into his house, he set food before them; and he rejoiced, having believed in God with all his household.

Peacemakers.

Prov 12:20 Deceit is in the heart of those who devise evil, But counselors of peace have joy.

The just.

Prov 21:15 *It is* a joy for the just to do justice, But destruction *will come* to the workers of iniquity.

The wise and discreet.

Prov 15:23 A man has joy by the answer of his mouth, And a word *spoken* in due season, how good *it is!*

Parents of wise children.

Prov 23:24 The father of the righteous will greatly rejoice, And he who begets a wise *child* will delight in him.

Increased to the humble.

Is 29:19 The humble also shall increase *their* joy in the LORD, And the poor among men shall rejoice In the Holy One of Israel.

Of believers, is

In God.

Ps 89:16 In Your name they rejoice all day long, And in Your righteousness they are exalted.

Ps 149:2 Let Israel rejoice in their Maker; Let the children of Zion be joyful in their King.

Hab 3:18 Yet I will rejoice in the LORD, I will joy in the God of my salvation.

Rom 5:11 And not only *that*, but we also rejoice in God through our Lord Jesus Christ, through whom we have now received the reconciliation.

In Christ.

Luke 1:47 And my spirit has rejoiced in God my Savior.

Phil 3:3 For we are the circumcision, who worship God in the Spirit, rejoice in Christ Jesus, and have no confidence in the flesh,

In the Holy Spirit.

Rom 14:17 for the kingdom of God is not eating and drinking, but righteousness and peace and joy in the Holy Spirit.

For election.

Luke 10:20 Nevertheless do not rejoice in this, that the spirits are subject to you, but rather rejoice because your names are written in heaven."

For salvation.

Ps 21:1 The king shall have joy in Your strength, O LORD; And in Your salvation how greatly shall he rejoice!

Is 61:10 I will greatly rejoice in the LORD, My soul shall be joyful in my God; For He has clothed me with the garments of salvation, He has covered me with the robe of righteousness, As a bridegroom decks *himself* with ornaments, And as a bride adorns *herself* with her jewels.

For deliverance from bondage.

Ps 105:43 He brought out His people with joy, His chosen ones with gladness.

Jer 31:10–13 "Hear the word of the LORD, O nations, And declare *it* in the isles afar off, and say, 'He who scattered Israel will gather him, And keep him as a shepherd *does* his flock.' **11** For the LORD has redeemed Jacob, And ransomed him from the hand of one stronger than he. **12** Therefore they shall come and sing in the height of Zion, Streaming to the goodness of the LORD— For wheat and new wine and oil, For the young of the flock and the herd; Their souls shall be like a well-watered garden, And they shall sorrow no more at all. **13** "Then shall the virgin rejoice in the dance, And the young men and the old, together; For I will turn their mourning to joy, Will comfort them, And make them rejoice rather than sorrow.

For manifestation of goodness.

2 Chr 7:10 On the twenty-third day of the seventh month he sent the people away to their tents, joyful and glad of heart for the good that the LORD had done for David, for Solomon, and for His people Israel.

For temporal blessings.

Joel 2:23–24 Be glad then, you children of Zion, And rejoice in the LORD your God; For He has given you the former rain faithfully, And He will cause the rain to come down for you— The former rain, And the latter rain in the first *month.* **24** The threshing floors shall be full of wheat, And the vats shall overflow with new wine and oil.

For supplies of grace.

Is 12:3 Therefore with joy you will draw water From the wells of salvation.

For divine protection and support.

Neh 8:10 Then he said to them, "Go your way, eat the fat, drink the sweet, and send portions to those for whom nothing is prepared; for *this* day *is* holy to our Lord. Do not sorrow, for the joy of the LORD is your strength."

Ps 5:11 But let all those rejoice who put their trust in You; Let them ever shout for joy, because You defend them; Let those also who love Your name Be joyful in You.

Ps 16:8–9 I have set the LORD always before me; Because *He is* at my right hand I shall not be moved. **9** Therefore my heart is glad, and my glory rejoices; My flesh also will rest in hope.

Ps 28:7 The LORD *is* my strength and my shield; My heart trusted in Him, and I am helped; Therefore my heart greatly rejoices, And with my song I will praise Him.

Ps 63:7 Because You have been my help, Therefore in the shadow of Your wings I will rejoice.

For the victory of Christ.

John 16:33 These things I have spoken to you, that in Me you may have peace. In the world you will have tribulation; but be of good cheer, I have overcome the world."

For the hope of glory.

Rom 5:2 through whom also we have access by faith into this grace in which we stand, and rejoice in hope of the glory of God.

For the success of the gospel.

Acts 15:3 So, being sent on their way by the church, they passed through Phoenicia and Samaria, describing the conversion of the Gentiles; and they caused great joy to all the brethren.

Of believers, should be

In all their undertakings.

Deut 12:18 But you must eat them before the LORD your God in the place which the LORD your God chooses, you and your son and your daughter, your male servant and your female servant, and the Levite who *is*

within your gates; and you shall rejoice before the LORD your God in all to which you put your hands.

Great.

Zech 9:9 "Rejoice greatly, O daughter of Zion! Shout, O daughter of Jerusalem! Behold, your King is coming to you; He *is* just and having salvation, Lowly and riding on a donkey, A colt, the foal of a donkey.

Acts 8:8 And there was great joy in that city.

Abundant.

2 Cor 8:2 that in a great trial of affliction the abundance of their joy and their deep poverty abounded in the riches of their liberality.

Exceeding.

Ps 21:6 For You have made him most blessed forever; You have made him exceedingly glad with Your presence.

Ps 68:3 But let the righteous be glad; Let them rejoice before God; Yes, let them rejoice exceedingly.

Animated.

Ps 32:11 Be glad in the LORD and rejoice, you righteous; And shout for joy, all *you* upright in heart!

Luke 6:23 Rejoice in that day and leap for joy! For indeed your reward *is* great in heaven, For in like manner their fathers did to the prophets.

Unspeakable.

1 Pet 1:8 whom having not seen you love. Though now you do not see *Him,* yet believing, you rejoice with joy inexpressible and full of glory,

Full of glory.

1 Pet 1:8 whom having not seen you love. Though now you do not see *Him,* yet believing, you rejoice with joy inexpressible and full of glory,

Constant.

2 Cor 6:10 as sorrowful, yet always rejoicing; as poor, yet making many rich; as having nothing, and *yet* possessing all things.

Phil 4:4 Rejoice in the Lord always. Again I will say, rejoice!

1 Thess 5:16 Rejoice always,

With awe.

Ps 2:11 Serve the LORD with fear, And rejoice with trembling.

In hope.

Rom 12:12 rejoicing in hope, patient in tribulation, continuing steadfastly in prayer;

In sorrow.

2 Cor 6:10 as sorrowful, yet always rejoicing; as poor, yet making many rich; as having nothing, and *yet* possessing all things.

Under persecutions.

Matt 5:11–12 "Blessed are you when they revile and persecute you, and say all kinds of evil against you falsely for My sake. **12** Rejoice and be exceedingly glad, for great *is* your reward in heaven, for so they persecuted the prophets who were before you.

Luke 6:22–23 Blessed are you when men hate you, And when they exclude you, And revile *you,* and cast out your name as evil, For the Son of Man's sake. **23** Rejoice in that day and leap for joy! For indeed your reward *is* great in heaven, For in like manner their fathers did to the prophets.

Heb 10:34 for you had compassion on me in my chains, and joyfully accepted the plundering of your goods, knowing that you have a better and an enduring possession for yourselves in heaven.

Under trials and calamities.

Hab 3:17–18 Though the fig tree may not blossom, Nor fruit be on the vines; Though the labor of the olive may fail, And the fields yield no food; Though the flock may be cut off from the fold, And there be no herd in the stalls— **18** Yet I will rejoice in the Lord, I will joy in the God of my salvation.

James 1:2 My brethren, count it all joy when you fall into various trials,

1 Pet 1:6 In this you greatly rejoice, though now for a little while, if need be, you have been grieved by various trials,

Expressed in hymns.

Eph 5:19 speaking to one another in psalms and hymns and spiritual songs, singing and making melody in your heart to the Lord,

James 5:13 Is anyone among you suffering? Let him pray. Is anyone cheerful? Let him sing psalms.

Afflictions of believers followed by.

Ps 30:5 For His anger *is but for* a moment, His favor *is for* life; Weeping may endure for a night, But joy *comes* in the morning.

Ps 126:5 Those who sow in tears Shall reap in joy.

Is 35:10 And the ransomed of the Lord shall return, And come to Zion with singing, With everlasting joy on their heads. They shall obtain joy and gladness, And sorrow and sighing shall flee away.

John 16:20 Most assuredly, I say to you that you will weep and lament, but the world will rejoice; and you will be sorrowful, but your sorrow will be turned into joy.

Believers should pray for restoration of.

Ps 51:8 Make me hear joy and gladness, *That* the bones You have broken may rejoice.

Ps 51:12 Restore to me the joy of Your salvation, And uphold me *by Your* generous Spirit.

Ps 85:6 Will You not revive us again, That Your people may rejoice in You?

Friends should promote, in the afflicted.

Job 29:13 The blessing of a perishing *man* came upon me, And I caused the widow's heart to sing for joy.

Of believers, made full by

The favor of God.

Acts 2:28 *You have made known to me the ways of life; You will make me full of joy in Your presence.'*

Faith in Christ.

Rom 15:13 Now may the God of hope fill you with all joy and peace in believing, that you may abound in hope by the power of the Holy Spirit.

Abiding in Christ.

John 15:10–11 If you keep My commandments, you will abide in My love, just as I have kept My Father's commandments and abide in His love. **11** "These things I have spoken to you, that My joy may remain in you, and *that* your joy may be full.

The word of Christ.

John 17:13 But now I come to You, and these things I speak in the world, that they may have My joy fulfilled in themselves.

Answers to prayer.

John 16:24 Until now you have asked nothing in My name. Ask, and you will receive, that your joy may be full.

Fellowship with others.

2 Tim 1:4 greatly desiring to see you, being mindful of your tears, that I may be filled with joy,

1 John 1:3–4 that which we have seen and heard we declare to you, that you also may have fellowship with us; and truly our fellowship *is* with the Father and with His Son Jesus Christ. **4** And these things we write to you that your joy may be full.

2 John 1:12 Having many things to write to you, I did not wish *to do so* with paper and ink; but I hope to come to you and speak face to face, that our joy may be full.

Believers should afford, to their ministers.

Phil 2:2 fulfill my joy by being like-minded, having the same love, *being* of one accord, of one mind.

Philem 1:20 Yes, brother, let me have joy from you in the Lord; refresh my heart in the Lord.

Ministers should

Esteem their people as their.

Phil 4:1 Therefore, my beloved and longed-for brethren, my joy and crown, so stand fast in the Lord, beloved.

1 Thess 2:20 For you are our glory and joy.

Promote, in their people.

2 Cor 1:24 Not that we have dominion over your faith, but are fellow workers for your joy; for by faith you stand.

Phil 1:25 And being confident of this, I know that I shall remain and continue with you all for your progress and joy of faith,

Pray for, for their people.

Rom 15:13 Now may the God of hope fill you with all joy and peace in believing, that you may abound in hope by the power of the Holy Spirit.

Have, in the faith and holiness of their people.

2 Cor 7:4 Great *is* my boldness of speech toward you, great *is* my boasting on your behalf. I am filled with comfort. I am exceedingly joyful in all our tribulation.

1 Thess 3:9 For what thanks can we render to God for you, for all the joy with which we rejoice for your sake before our God,

3 John 1:4 I have no greater joy than to hear that my children walk in truth.

Come to their people with.

Rom 15:32 that I may come to you with joy by the will of God, and may be refreshed together with you.

Finish their course with.

Acts 20:24 But none of these things move me; nor do I count my life dear to myself, so that I may finish my race with joy, and the ministry which I received from the Lord Jesus, to testify to the gospel of the grace of God.

Desire to render an account with.

Phil 2:16 holding fast the word of life, so that I may rejoice in the day of Christ that I have not run in vain or labored in vain.

Heb 13:17 Obey those who rule over you, and be submissive, for they watch out for your souls, as those who must give account. Let them do so with joy and not with grief, for that would be unprofitable for you.

Generosity in God's service should cause.

1 Chr 29:9 Then the people rejoiced, for they had offered willingly, because with a loyal heart they had offered willingly to the LORD; and King David also rejoiced greatly.

1 Chr 29:17 I know also, my God, that You test the heart and have pleasure in uprightness. As for me, in the uprightness of my heart I have willingly offered all these *things;* and now with joy I have seen Your people, who are present here to offer willingly to You.

Believers should worship with.

Ezra 6:22 And they kept the Feast of Unleavened Bread seven days with joy; for the LORD made them joyful, and turned the heart of the king of Assyria toward them, to strengthen their hands in the work of the house of God, the God of Israel.

Ps 42:4 When I remember these *things,* I pour out my soul within me. For I used to go with the multitude; I went with them to the house of God, With the voice of joy and praise, With a multitude that kept a pilgrim feast.

The coming of Christ will afford to believers, exceeding.

1 Pet 4:13 but rejoice to the extent that you partake of Christ's sufferings, that when His glory is revealed, you may also be glad with exceeding joy.

Jude 1:24 Now to Him who is able to keep you from stumbling, And to present *you* faultless Before the presence of His glory with exceeding joy,

Shall be the final reward of believers at the judgment day.

Matt 25:21 His lord said to him, 'Well *done,* good and faithful servant; you were faithful over a few things, I will make you ruler over many things. Enter into the joy of your lord.'

Of the wicked

Is derived from earthly pleasures.

Eccl 2:10 Whatever my eyes desired I did not keep from them. I did not withhold my heart from any pleasure, For my heart rejoiced in all my labor; And this was my reward from all my labor.

Eccl 11:9 Rejoice, O young man, in your youth, And let your heart cheer you in the days of your youth; Walk in the ways of your heart, And in the sight of your eyes; But know that for all these God will bring you into judgment.

Is derived from folly.

Prov 15:21 Folly *is* joy *to him who is* destitute of discernment, But a man of understanding walks uprightly.

Is delusive.

Prov 14:13 Even in laughter the heart may sorrow, And the end of mirth *may be* grief.

Is short-lived.

Job 20:5 That the triumphing of the wicked is short, And the joy of the hypocrite is *but* for a moment?

Eccl 7:6 For like the crackling of thorns under a pot, So *is* the laughter of the fool. This also is vanity.

Should be turned into mourning.

James 4:9 Lament and mourn and weep! Let your laughter be turned to mourning and *your* joy to gloom.

Shall be taken away.

Is 16:10 Gladness is taken away, And joy from the plentiful field; In the vineyards there will be no singing, Nor will there be shouting; No treaders will tread out wine in the presses; I have made their shouting cease.

Holy—illustrated.

Is 9:3 You have multiplied the nation *And* increased its joy; They rejoice before You According to the joy of harvest, As *men* rejoice when they divide the spoil.

Matt 13:44 "Again, the kingdom of heaven is like treasure hidden in a field, which a man found and hid; and for joy over it he goes and sells all that he has and buys that field.

Holy—exemplified by

Hannah.

1 Sam 2:1 And Hannah prayed and said: "My heart rejoices in the LORD; My horn is exalted in the LORD. I smile at my enemies, Because I rejoice in Your salvation.

David.

1 Chr 29:9 Then the people rejoiced, for they had offered willingly, because with a loyal heart they had offered willingly to the LORD; and King David also rejoiced greatly.

The wise men.

Matt 2:10 When they saw the star, they rejoiced with exceedingly great joy.

Mary.

Luke 1:47 And my spirit has rejoiced in God my Savior.

Zacchaeus.

Luke 19:6 So he made haste and came down, and received Him joyfully.

Converts.

Acts 2:46 So continuing daily with one accord in the temple, and breaking bread from house to house, they ate their food with gladness and simplicity of heart,

Acts 13:52 And the disciples were filled with joy and with the Holy Spirit.

Peter, etc.

Acts 5:41 So they departed from the presence of the council, rejoicing that they were counted worthy to suffer shame for His name.

The Samaritans.

Acts 8:8 And there was great joy in that city.

The jailer.

Acts 16:34 Now when he had brought them into his house, he set food before them; and he rejoiced, having believed in God with all his household.

JOY OF GOD OVER HIS PEOPLE, THE
Greatness of, described.

Zeph 3:17 The LORD your God in your midst, The Mighty One, will save; He will rejoice over you with gladness, He will quiet *you* with His love, He will rejoice over you with singing."

Because of their
Repentance.

Luke 15:7 I say to you that likewise there will be more joy in heaven over one sinner who repents than over ninety-nine just persons who need no repentance.

Luke 15:10 Likewise, I say to you, there is joy in the presence of the angels of God over one sinner who repents."

Faith.

Heb 11:5–6 By faith Enoch was taken away so that he did not see death, *"and was not found, because God had taken him"*; for before he was taken he had this testimony, that he pleased God. **6** But without faith *it is* impossible to please *Him,* for he who comes to God must believe that He is, and *that* He is a rewarder of those who diligently seek Him.

Fear of Him.

Ps 147:11 The LORD takes pleasure in those who fear Him, In those who hope in His mercy.

Praying to Him.

Prov 15:8 The sacrifice of the wicked *is* an abomination to the LORD, But the prayer of the upright *is* His delight.

Hope in His mercy.

Ps 147:11 The LORD takes pleasure in those who fear Him, In those who hope in His mercy.

Meekness.

Ps 149:4 For the LORD takes pleasure in His people; He will beautify the humble with salvation.

Uprightness.

1 Chr 29:17 I know also, my God, that You test the heart and have pleasure in uprightness. As for me, in the uprightness of my heart I have willingly offered all these *things;* and now with joy I have seen Your people, who are present here to offer willingly to You.

Prov 11:20 Those who are of a perverse heart *are* an abomination to the LORD, But *the* blameless in their ways *are* His delight.

Causes Him to
Prosper them.

Deut 30:9 The LORD your God will make you abound in all the work of your hand, in the fruit of your body, in the increase of your livestock, and in the produce of your land for good. For the LORD will again rejoice over you for good as He rejoiced over your fathers,

Do them good.

Deut 28:63 And it shall be, *that* just as the LORD rejoiced over you to do you good and multiply you, so the LORD will rejoice over you to destroy you and bring you to nothing; and you shall be plucked from off the land which you go to possess.

Jer 32:41 Yes, I will rejoice over them to do them good, and I will assuredly plant them in this land, with all My heart and with all My soul.'

Deliver them.

2 Sam 22:20 He also brought me out into a broad place; He delivered me because He delighted in me.

Comfort them.

Is 65:19 I will rejoice in Jerusalem, And joy in My people; The voice of weeping shall no longer be heard in her, Nor the voice of crying.

Give them the inheritance.

Num 14:8 If the LORD delights in us, then He will bring us into this land and give it to us, 'a land which flows with milk and honey.'

Illustrated.

Is 62:5 For *as* a young man marries a virgin, *So* shall your sons marry you; And *as* the bridegroom rejoices over the bride, *So* shall your God rejoice over you.

Luke 15:23–24 And bring the fatted calf here and kill *it,* and let us eat and be merry; **24** for this my son was dead and is alive again; he was lost and is found.' And they began to be merry.

Exemplified by Solomon.

1 Kin 10:9 Blessed be the LORD your God, who delighted in you, setting you on the throne of Israel! Because the LORD has loved Israel forever, therefore He made you king, to do justice and righteousness."

JUDAH, THE TRIBE OF
Descended from Jacob's fourth son.

Gen 29:35 And she conceived again and bore a son, and said, "Now I will praise the LORD." Therefore she called his name Judah. Then she stopped bearing.

Predictions respecting.

Gen 49:8–12 "Judah, you *are he* whom your brothers shall praise; Your hand *shall be* on the neck of your enemies; Your father's children shall bow down before you. **9** Judah *is* a lion's whelp; From the prey, my son, you have gone up. He bows down, he lies down as a lion; And as a lion, who shall rouse him? **10** The scepter shall not depart from Judah, Nor a lawgiver from between his feet, Until Shiloh comes; And to Him *shall be* the obedience of the people. **11** Binding his donkey to the vine, And his donkey's colt to the choice vine, He washed his garments in wine, And his clothes in the blood of grapes. **12** His eyes *are* darker than wine, And his teeth whiter than milk.

Deut 33:7 And this he said of Judah: "Hear, LORD, the voice of Judah, And bring him to his people; Let his hands be sufficient for him, And may You be a help against his enemies."

Persons selected from,
To number the people.

Num 1:7 from Judah, Nahshon the son of Amminadab;

To spy out the land.

Num 13:6 from the tribe of Judah, Caleb the son of Jephunneh;

To divide the land.

Num 34:19 These *are* the names of the men: from the tribe of Judah, Caleb the son of Jephunneh;

Strength of, on leaving Egypt.

Num 1:26–27 From the children of Judah, their genealogies by their families, by their fathers' house, according to the number of names, from twenty years old and above, all who *were able to* go to war: **27** those who were numbered of the tribe of Judah *were* seventy-four thousand six hundred.

Num 2:4 And his army was numbered at seventy-four thousand six hundred.

Encamped with its standard east of the tabernacle.

Num 2:3 On the east side, toward the rising of the sun, those of the standard of the forces with Judah shall camp according to their armies; and Nahshon the son of Amminadab *shall be* the leader of the children of Judah."

Led the first division of Israel in their journeys.

Num 10:14 The standard of the camp of the children of Judah set out first according to their armies; over their army was Nahshon the son of Amminadab.

Offering of, at dedication.

Num 7:12–17 And the one who offered his offering on the first day *was* Nahshon the son of Amminadab, from the tribe of Judah. **13** His offering *was* one silver platter, the weight of which *was* one hundred and thirty *shekels*, and one silver bowl of seventy shekels, according to the shekel of the sanctuary, both of them full of fine flour mixed with oil as a grain offering; **14** one gold pan of ten *shekels*, full of incense; **15** one young bull, one ram, and one male lamb in its first year, as a burnt offering; **16** one kid of the goats as a sin offering; **17** and for the sacrifice of peace offerings: two oxen, five rams, five male goats, and five male lambs in their first year. This *was* the offering of Nahshon the son of Amminadab.

Families of.

Num 26:19–21 The sons of Judah *were* Er and Onan; and Er and Onan died in the land of Canaan. **20** And the sons of Judah according to their families were: *of* Shelah, the family of the Shelanites; *of* Perez, the family of the Parzites; *of* Zerah, the family of the Zarhites. **21** And the sons of Perez were: *of* Hezron, the family of the Hezronites; *of* Hamul, the family of the Hamulites.

Strength of, on entering Canaan.

Num 26:22 These *are* the families of Judah according to those who were numbered of them: seventy-six thousand five hundred.

On Gerizim, said amen to the blessings.

Deut 27:12 "These shall stand on Mount Gerizim to bless the people, when you have crossed over the Jordan: Simeon, Levi, Judah, Issachar, Joseph, and Benjamin;

Borders of inheritance.

Josh 15:1–12 So *this* was the lot of the tribe of the children of Judah according to their families: The border of Edom at the Wilderness of Zin southward *was* the extreme southern boundary. **2** And their southern border began at the shore of the Salt Sea, from the bay that faces southward. **3** Then it went out to the southern side of the Ascent of Akrabbim, passed along to Zin, ascended on the south side of Kadesh Barnea, passed along to Hezron, went up to Adar, and went around to Karkaa. **4** *From there* it passed toward Azmon and went out to the Brook of Egypt; and the border ended at the sea. This shall be your southern border. **5** The east border *was* the Salt Sea as far as the mouth of the Jordan. And the border on the northern quarter *began* at the bay of the sea at the mouth of the Jordan. **6** The border went up to Beth Hoglah and passed north of Beth Arabah; and the border went up to the stone of Bohan the son of Reuben. **7** Then the border went up toward Debir from the Valley of Achor, and it turned northward toward Gilgal, which *is* before the Ascent of Adummim, which *is* on the south side of the valley. The border continued toward the waters of En Shemesh and ended at En Rogel. **8** And the border went up by the Valley of the Son of Hinnom to the southern slope of the Jebusite *city* (which *is* Jerusalem). The border went up to the top of the mountain that *lies* before the Valley of Hinnom westward, which *is* at the end of the Valley of Rephaim northward. **9** Then the border went around from the top of the hill to the fountain of the water of Nephtoah, and extended to the cities of Mount Ephron. And the border went around to Baalah (which *is* Kirjath Jearim). **10** Then the border turned westward from Baalah to Mount Seir, passed along to the side of Mount Jearim on the north (which *is* Chesalon), went down to Beth Shemesh, and passed on to Timnah. **11** And the border went out to the side of Ekron northward. Then the border went around to Shicron, passed along to Mount Baalah, and extended to Jabneel; and the border ended at the sea. **12** The west border *was* the coastline of the Great Sea. This *is* the boundary of the children of Judah all around according to their families.

First and most vigorous in driving out the Canaanites.

Judg 1:3–20 So Judah said to Simeon his brother, "Come up with me to my allotted territory, that we may fight against the Canaanites; and I will likewise go with you to your allotted territory." And Simeon went with him. **4** Then Judah went up, and the LORD delivered the Canaanites and the Perizzites into their hand; and they killed ten thousand men at Bezek. **5** And they found Adoni-Bezek in Bezek, and fought against him; and they defeated the Canaanites and the Perizzites. **6** Then Adoni-Bezek fled, and they pursued him and caught him and cut off his thumbs and big toes. **7** And Adoni-Bezek said, "Seventy kings with their thumbs and big toes cut off used to gather *scraps* under my table; as I have done, so God has repaid me." Then they brought him to Jerusalem, and there he died. **8** Now the children of Judah fought against Jerusalem and took it; they struck it with the edge of the sword and set the city on fire. **9** And afterward the children of Judah went down to fight against the Canaanites who dwelt in the mountains, in the South, and in the lowland. **10** Then Judah went against the Canaanites who dwelt in Hebron. (Now the name of Hebron *was* formerly Kirjath Arba.) And they killed Sheshai, Ahiman, and Talmai. **11** From there they went against the inhabitants of

Debir. (The name of Debir *was* formerly Kirjath Se-pher.) **12** Then Caleb said, "Whoever attacks Kirjath Sepher and takes it, to him I will give my daughter Achsah as wife." **13** And Othniel the son of Kenaz, Caleb's younger brother, took it; so he gave him his daughter Achsah as wife. **14** Now it happened, when she came *to him*, that she urged him to ask her father for a field. And she dismounted from *her* donkey, and Caleb said to her, "What do you wish?" **15** So she said to him, "Give me a blessing; since you have given me land in the South, give me also springs of water." And Caleb gave her the upper springs and the lower springs. **16** Now the children of the Kenite, Moses' father-in-law, went up from the City of Palms with the children of Judah into the Wilderness of Judah, which *lies* in the South *near* Arad; and they went and dwelt among the people. **17** And Judah went with his brother Simeon, and they attacked the Canaanites who inhabited Zephath, and utterly destroyed it. So the name of the city was called Hormah. **18** Also Judah took Gaza with its territory, Ashkelon with its territory, and Ekron with its territory. **19** So the LORD was with Judah. And they drove out the mountaineers, but they could not drive out the inhabitants of the lowland, because they had chariots of iron. **20** And they gave Hebron to Caleb, as Moses had said. Then he expelled from there the three sons of Anak.

Went first against Gibeah.

Judg 20:18 Then the children of Israel arose and went up to the house of God to inquire of God. They said, "Which of us shall go up first to battle against the children of Benjamin?" The LORD said, "Judah first!"

Furnished to Israel the first judge.

Judg 3:9 When the children of Israel cried out to the LORD, the LORD raised up a deliverer for the children of Israel, who delivered them: Othniel the son of Kenaz, Caleb's younger brother.

Aided Saul in his wars.

1 Sam 11:8 When he numbered them in Bezek, the children of Israel were three hundred thousand, and the men of Judah thirty thousand.

1 Sam 15:4 So Saul gathered the people together and numbered them in Telaim, two hundred thousand foot soldiers and ten thousand men of Judah.

After Saul's rebellion, appointed to furnish kings to Israel.

1 Sam 13:14 But now your kingdom shall not continue. The LORD has sought for Himself a man after His own heart, and the LORD has commanded him *to be* commander over His people, because you have not kept what the LORD commanded you."

1 Sam 15:28 So Samuel said to him, "The LORD has torn the kingdom of Israel from you today, and has given it to a neighbor of yours, *who is* better than you.

1 Sam 16:6 So it was, when they came, that he looked at Eliab and said, "Surely the LORD's anointed *is* before Him!"

1 Sam 16:13 Then Samuel took the horn of oil and anointed him in the midst of his brothers; and the Spirit of the LORD came upon David from that day forward. So Samuel arose and went to Ramah.

2 Sam 2:4 Then the men of Judah came, and there they anointed David king over the house of Judah. And they told David, saying, "The men of Jabesh Gilead *were the ones* who buried Saul."

2 Sam 7:16–17 And your house and your kingdom shall be established forever before you. Your throne shall be established forever." ' " **17** According to all these words and according to all this vision, so Nathan spoke to David.

The first to submit to David.

2 Sam 2:10 Ishbosheth, Saul's son, *was* forty years old when he began to reign over Israel, and he reigned two years. Only the house of Judah followed David.

Reigned over alone over David for seven years and six months.

2 Sam 2:11 And the time that David was king in Hebron over the house of Judah was seven years and six months.

2 Sam 5:5 In Hebron he reigned over Judah seven years and six months, and in Jerusalem he reigned thirty-three years over all Israel and Judah.

Officer placed over, by David.

1 Chr 27:18 *over* Judah, Elihu, *one* of David's brothers; *over* Issachar, Omri the son of Michael;

Reproved for tardiness in bringing back David after Absalom's rebellion.

2 Sam 19:11–15 So King David sent to Zadok and Abiathar the priests, saying, "Speak to the elders of Judah, saying, 'Why are you the last to bring the king back to his house, since the words of all Israel have come to the king, to his *very* house? **12** You *are* my brethren, you *are* my bone and my flesh. Why then are you the last to bring back the king?' **13** And say to Amasa, '*Are* you not my bone and my flesh? God do so to me, and more also, if you are not commander of the army before me continually in place of Joab.' " **14** So he swayed the hearts of all the men of Judah, just as *the heart of* one man, so that they sent *this word* to the king: "Return, you and all your servants!" **15** Then the king returned and came to the Jordan. And Judah came to Gilgal, to go to meet the king, to escort the king across the Jordan.

Other tribes jealous of, on account of David.

2 Sam 19:41–42 Just then all the men of Israel came to the king, and said to the king, "Why have our brethren, the men of Judah, stolen you away and brought the king, his household, and all David's men with him across the Jordan?" **42** So all the men of Judah answered the men of Israel, "Because the king *is* a close relative of ours. Why then are you angry over this matter? Have we ever eaten at the king's *expense*? Or has he given us any gift?"

2 Sam 20:1–2 And there happened to be there a rebel, whose name *was* Sheba the son of Bichri, a Benjamite. And he blew a trumpet, and said: "We have no share in David, Nor do we have inheritance in the son of Jesse; Every man to his tents, O Israel!" **2** So every man of Israel deserted David, *and* followed Sheba the son of Bichri. But the men of Judah, from the Jordan as far as Jerusalem, remained loyal to their king.

With Benjamin alone, adhered to the house of David.

1 Kin 12:21 And when Rehoboam came to Jerusalem,

he assembled all the house of Judah with the tribe of Benjamin, one hundred and eighty thousand chosen *men* who were warriors, to fight against the house of Israel, that he might restore the kingdom to Rehoboam the son of Solomon.

The last tribe carried into captivity.

2 Kin 17:18 Therefore the LORD was very angry with Israel, and removed them from His sight; there was none left but the tribe of Judah alone.

2 Kin 17:20 And the LORD rejected all the descendants of Israel, afflicted them, and delivered them into the hand of plunderers, until He had cast them from His sight.

2 Kin 25:21 Then the king of Babylon struck them and put them to death at Riblah in the land of Hamath. Thus Judah was carried away captive from its own land.

Christ descended from.

Heb 7:14 For *it is* evident that our Lord arose from Judah, of which tribe Moses spoke nothing concerning priesthood.

Cf. Matt 1:3–16; Luke 3:23–33

Remarkable persons of,

Achan.

Josh 7:18 Then he brought his household man by man, and Achan the son of Carmi, the son of Zabdi, the son of Zerah, of the tribe of Judah, was taken.

Elimelech.

Ruth 1:1–2 Now it came to pass, in the days when the judges ruled, that there was a famine in the land. And a certain man of Bethlehem, Judah, went to dwell in the country of Moab, he and his wife and his two sons. **2** The name of the man *was* Elimelech, the name of his wife *was* Naomi, and the names of his two sons *were* Mahlon and Chilion—Ephrathites of Bethlehem, Judah. And they went to the country of Moab and remained there.

Boaz.

Ruth 2:1 There was a relative of Naomi's husband, a man of great wealth, of the family of Elimelech. His name *was* Boaz.

Obed.

Ruth 4:21 Salmon begot Boaz, and Boaz begot Obed;

Jesse.

Ruth 4:22 Obed begot Jesse, and Jesse begot David.

1 Sam 16:1 Now the LORD said to Samuel, "How long will you mourn for Saul, seeing I have rejected him from reigning over Israel? Fill your horn with oil, and go; I am sending you to Jesse the Bethlehemite. For I have provided Myself a king among his sons."

David.

1 Sam 16:1 Now the LORD said to Samuel, "How long will you mourn for Saul, seeing I have rejected him from reigning over Israel? Fill your horn with oil, and go; I am sending you to Jesse the Bethlehemite. For I have provided Myself a king among his sons."

1 Sam 16:13 Then Samuel took the horn of oil and anointed him in the midst of his brothers; and the Spirit of the LORD came upon David from that day forward. So Samuel arose and went to Ramah.

Solomon.

1 Kin 1:32–39 And King David said, "Call to me Zadok the priest, Nathan the prophet, and Benaiah the son of Jehoiada." So they came before the king. **33** The king also said to them, "Take with you the servants of your lord, and have Solomon my son ride on my own mule, and take him down to Gihon. **34** There let Zadok the priest and Nathan the prophet anoint him king over Israel; and blow the horn, and say, *'Long live King Solomon!'* **35** Then you shall come up after him, and he shall come and sit on my throne, and he shall be king in my place. For I have appointed him to be ruler over Israel and Judah." **36** Benaiah the son of Jehoiada answered the king and said, "Amen! May the LORD God of my lord the king say so *too.* **37** As the LORD has been with my lord the king, even so may He be with Solomon, and make his throne greater than the throne of my lord King David." **38** So Zadok the priest, Nathan the prophet, Benaiah the son of Jehoiada, the Cherethites, and the Pelethites went down and had Solomon ride on King David's mule, and took him to Gihon. **39** Then Zadok the priest took a horn of oil from the tabernacle and anointed Solomon. And they blew the horn, and all the people said, *"Long* live King Solomon!"

Elihu.

1 Chr 27:18 *over* Judah, Elihu, *one* of David's brothers; *over* Issachar, Omri the son of Michael;

Pethahiah.

Neh 11:24 Pethahiah the son of Meshezabel, of the children of Zerah the son of Judah, *was* the king's deputy in all matters concerning the people.

Bezalel.

Ex 31:2 "See, I have called by name Bezalel the son of Uri, the son of Hur, of the tribe of Judah.

Ex 35:30 And Moses said to the children of Israel, "See, the LORD has called by name Bezalel the son of Uri, the son of Hur, of the tribe of Judah;

Nahshon.

Num 7:12 And the one who offered his offering on the first day *was* Nahshon the son of Amminadab, from the tribe of Judah.

Caleb.

Num 14:24 But My servant Caleb, because he has a different spirit in him and has followed Me fully, I will bring into the land where he went, and his descendants shall inherit it.

Absalom.

2 Sam 15:1 After this it happened that Absalom provided himself with chariots and horses, and fifty men to run before him.

Elhanan.

2 Sam 21:19 Again there was war at Gob with the Philistines, where Elhanan the son of Jaare-Oregim the Bethlehemite killed *the brother of* Goliath the Gittite, the shaft of whose spear *was* like a weaver's beam.

2 Sam 23:24 Asahel the brother of Joab *was* one of the thirty; Elhanan the son of Dodo of Bethlehem,

Adonijah.

1 Kin 1:5–6 Then Adonijah the son of Haggith exalted himself, saying, "I will be king"; and he prepared for himself chariots and horsemen, and fifty men to run before him. **6** (And his father had not rebuked him at any time by saying, "Why have you done so?" He *was* also very good-looking. *His mother* had borne him after Absalom.)

Jonathan.

2 Sam 21:21 So when he defied Israel, Jonathan the son of Shimea, David's brother, killed him.

See also Kings, Those who reigned over Judah.

JUDAIZERS

First mentioned.

Acts 15:1 And certain *men* came down from Judea and taught the brethren, "Unless you are circumcised according to the custom of Moses, you cannot be saved."

Effect of their teaching.

Acts 15:24 Since we have heard that some who went out from us have troubled you with words, unsettling your souls, saying, "*You must* be circumcised and keep the law"—to whom we gave no *such* commandment—

Gal 1:6–9 I marvel that you are turning away so soon from Him who called you in the grace of Christ, to a different gospel, **7** which is not another; but there are some who trouble you and want to pervert the gospel of Christ. **8** But even if we, or an angel from heaven, preach any other gospel to you than what we have preached to you, let him be accursed. **9** As we have said before, so now I say again, if anyone preaches any other gospel to you than what you have received, let him be accursed.

Gal 2:1–5 Then after fourteen years I went up again to Jerusalem with Barnabas, and also took Titus with *me.* **2** And I went up by revelation, and communicated to them that gospel which I preach among the Gentiles, but privately to those who were of reputation, lest by any means I might run, or had run, in vain. **3** Yet not even Titus who *was* with me, being a Greek, was compelled to be circumcised. **4** And *this occurred* because of false brethren secretly brought in (who came in by stealth to spy out our liberty which we have in Christ Jesus, that they might bring us into bondage), **5** to whom we did not yield submission even for an hour, that the truth of the gospel might continue with you.

Gal 4:17–20 They zealously court you, *but* for no good; yes, they want to exclude you, that you may be zealous for them. **18** But it is good to be zealous in a good thing always, and not only when I am present with you. **19** My little children, for whom I labor in birth again until Christ is formed in you, **20** I would like to be present with you now and to change my tone; for I have doubts about you.

Misrepresented Paul.

Acts 21:20–21 And when they heard *it,* they glorified the Lord. And they said to him, "You see, brother, how many myriads of Jews there are who have believed, and they are all zealous for the law; **21** but they have been informed about you that you teach all the Jews who are among the Gentiles to forsake Moses, saying that they ought not to circumcise *their* children nor to walk according to the customs.

Cf. Gal 5:11–12

Fallacy of their teaching.

Gal 5:1–6 Stand fast therefore in the liberty by which Christ has made us free, and do not be entangled again with a yoke of bondage. **2** Indeed I, Paul, say to you that if you become circumcised, Christ will profit you nothing. **3** And I testify again to every man who becomes circumcised that he is a debtor to keep the whole law. **4** You have become estranged from Christ, you who *attempt to* be justified by law; you have fallen from grace. **5** For we through the Spirit eagerly wait for the hope of righteousness by faith. **6** For in Christ Jesus neither circumcision nor uncircumcision avails anything, but faith working through love.

Temporarily influenced Peter.

Gal 2:11–21 Now when Peter had come to Antioch, I withstood him to his face, because he was to be blamed; **12** for before certain men came from James, he would eat with the Gentiles; but when they came, he withdrew and separated himself, fearing those who were of the circumcision. **13** And the rest of the Jews also played the hypocrite with him, so that even Barnabas was carried away with their hypocrisy. **14** But when I saw that they were not straightforward about the truth of the gospel, I said to Peter before *them* all, "If you, being a Jew, live in the manner of Gentiles and not as the Jews, why do you compel Gentiles to live as Jews? **15** We *who are* Jews by nature, and not sinners of the Gentiles, **16** knowing that a man is not justified by the works of the law but by faith in Jesus Christ, even we have believed in Christ Jesus, that we might be justified by faith in Christ and not by the works of the law; for by the works of the law no flesh shall be justified. **17** "But if, while we seek to be justified by Christ, we ourselves also are found sinners, *is* Christ therefore a minister of sin? Certainly not! **18** For if I build again those things which I destroyed, I make myself a transgressor. **19** For I through the law died to the law that I might live to God. **20** I have been crucified with Christ; it is no longer I who live, but Christ lives in me; and the *life* which I now live in the flesh I live by faith in the Son of God, who loved me and gave Himself for me. **21** I do not set aside the grace of God; for if righteousness *comes* through the law, then Christ died in vain."

Their wrong motives.

Gal 6:12–13 As many as desire to make a good showing in the flesh, these *would* compel you to be circumcised, only that they may not suffer persecution for the cross of Christ. **13** For not even those who are circumcised keep the law, but they desire to have you circumcised that they may boast in your flesh.

Paul warned against them.

Phil 3:2–3 Beware of dogs, beware of evil workers, beware of the mutilation! **3** For we are the circumcision, who worship God in the Spirit, rejoice in Christ Jesus, and have no confidence in the flesh,

Cf. Phil 3:18–19

JUDEA (NEW TESTAMENT)

One of the divisions of the Holy Land under the Romans.

Luke 3:1 Now in the fifteenth year of the reign of Tiberius Caesar, Pontius Pilate being governor of Judea,

Herod being tetrarch of Galilee, his brother Philip tetrarch of Iturea and the region of Trachonitis, and Lysanias tetrarch of Abilene,

Was the Old Testament kingdom of Judah.

1 Kin 12:21–24 And when Rehoboam came to Jerusalem, he assembled all the house of Judah with the tribe of Benjamin, one hundred and eighty thousand chosen *men* who were warriors, to fight against the house of Israel, that he might restore the kingdom to Rehoboam the son of Solomon. **22** But the word of God came to Shemaiah the man of God, saying, **23** "Speak to Rehoboam the son of Solomon, king of Judah, to all the house of Judah and Benjamin, and to the rest of the people, saying, **24** 'Thus says the LORD: "You shall not go up nor fight against your brethren the children of Israel. Let every man return to his house, for this thing is from Me." ' " Therefore they obeyed the word of the LORD, and turned back, according to the word of the LORD.

Also called the land of Judah.

Dan 5:13 Then Daniel was brought in before the king. The king spoke, and said to Daniel, "*Are* you that Daniel who is one of the captives from Judah, whom my father the king brought from Judah?

Matt 2:6 '*But you, Bethlehem, in the land of Judah, Are not the least among the rulers of Judah; For out of you shall come a Ruler Who will shepherd My people Israel.'* "

A mountainous district.

Luke 1:39 Now Mary arose in those days and went into the hill country with haste, to a city of Judah,

Luke 1:65 Then fear came on all who dwelt around them; and all these sayings were discussed throughout all the hill country of Judea.

Parts of, desert.

Matt 3:1 In those days John the Baptist came preaching in the wilderness of Judea,

Acts 8:26 Now an angel of the Lord spoke to Philip, saying, "Arise and go toward the south along the road which goes down from Jerusalem to Gaza." This is desert.

Jerusalem the capital of.

Matt 4:25 Great multitudes followed Him—from Galilee, and *from* Decapolis, Jerusalem, Judea, and beyond the Jordan.

Towns of,

Arimathea.

Matt 27:57 Now when evening had come, there came a rich man from Arimathea, named Joseph, who himself had also become a disciple of Jesus.

John 19:38 After this, Joseph of Arimathea, being a disciple of Jesus, but secretly, for fear of the Jews, asked Pilate that he might take away the body of Jesus; and Pilate gave *him* permission. So he came and took the body of Jesus.

Azotus (Ashdod).

Acts 8:40 But Philip was found at Azotus. And passing through, he preached in all the cities till he came to Caesarea.

Bethany.

John 11:1 Now a certain *man* was sick, Lazarus of Bethany, the town of Mary and her sister Martha.

John 11:18 Now Bethany was near Jerusalem, about two miles away.

Bethlehem.

Matt 2:1 Now after Jesus was born in Bethlehem of Judea in the days of Herod the king, behold, wise men from the East came to Jerusalem,

Matt 2:6 '*But you, Bethlehem, in the land of Judah, Are not the least among the rulers of Judah; For out of you shall come a Ruler Who will shepherd My people Israel.'* "

Matt 2:16 Then Herod, when he saw that he was deceived by the wise men, was exceedingly angry; and he sent forth and put to death all the male children who were in Bethlehem and in all its districts, from two years old and under, according to the time which he had determined from the wise men.

Bethphage.

Matt 21:1 Now when they drew near Jerusalem, and came to Bethphage, at the Mount of Olives, then Jesus sent two disciples,

Emmaus.

Luke 24:13 Now behold, two of them were traveling that same day to a village called Emmaus, which was seven miles from Jerusalem.

Ephraim.

John 11:54 Therefore Jesus no longer walked openly among the Jews, but went from there into the country near the wilderness, to a city called Ephraim, and there remained with His disciples.

Gaza.

Acts 8:26 Now an angel of the Lord spoke to Philip, saying, "Arise and go toward the south along the road which goes down from Jerusalem to Gaza." This is desert.

Jericho.

Luke 10:30 Then Jesus answered and said: "A certain *man* went down from Jerusalem to Jericho, and fell among thieves, who stripped him of his clothing, wounded *him*, and departed, leaving *him* half dead.

Luke 19:1 Then *Jesus* entered and passed through Jericho.

Joppa.

Acts 9:36 At Joppa there was a certain disciple named Tabitha, which is translated Dorcas. This woman was full of good works and charitable deeds which she did.

Acts 10:5 Now send men to Joppa, and send for Simon whose surname is Peter.

Acts 10:8 So when he had explained all *these* things to them, he sent them to Joppa.

Lydda.

Acts 9:32 Now it came to pass, as Peter went through all *parts of the country*, that he also came down to the saints who dwelt in Lydda.

Acts 9:35 So all who dwelt at Lydda and Sharon saw him and turned to the Lord.

Acts 9:38 And since Lydda was near Joppa, and the disciples had heard that Peter was there, they sent two men to him, imploring *him* not to delay in coming to them.

John the Baptist preached in.

Matt 3:1 In those days John the Baptist came preaching in the wilderness of Judea,

Christ

Was born in.

Matt 2:1 Now after Jesus was born in Bethlehem of Judea in the days of Herod the king, behold, wise men from the East came to Jerusalem,

Matt 2:5–6 So they said to him, "In Bethlehem of Judea, for thus it is written by the prophet: **6** *'But you, Bethlehem, in the land of Judah, Are not the least among the rulers of Judah; For out of you shall come a Ruler Who will shepherd My people Israel.'*"

Was tempted in the wilderness of.

Matt 4:1 Then Jesus was led up by the Spirit into the wilderness to be tempted by the devil.

Frequently visited.

John 11:7 Then after this He said to *the* disciples, "Let us go to Judea again."

Often left, to escape persecution.

John 4:1–3 Therefore, when the Lord knew that the Pharisees had heard that Jesus made and baptized more disciples than John **2** (though Jesus Himself did not baptize, but His disciples), **3** He left Judea and departed again to Galilee.

Several early churches in.

Acts 9:31 Then the churches throughout all Judea, Galilee, and Samaria had peace and were edified. And walking in the fear of the Lord and in the comfort of the Holy Spirit, they were multiplied.

1 Thess 2:14 For you, brethren, became imitators of the churches of God which are in Judea in Christ Jesus. For you also suffered the same things from your own countrymen, just as they *did* from the Judeans,

JUDGES (EXTRAORDINARY LEADERS)
Raised up to deliver Israel.

Judg 2:16 Nevertheless, the LORD raised up judges who delivered them out of the hand of those who plundered them.

Upheld and strengthened by God.

Judg 2:18 And when the LORD raised up judges for them, the LORD was with the judge and delivered them out of the hand of their enemies all the days of the judge; for the LORD was moved to pity by their groaning because of those who oppressed them and harassed them.

Remarkable for their faith.

Heb 11:32 And what more shall I say? For the time would fail me to tell of Gideon and Barak and Samson and Jephthah, also *of* David and Samuel and the prophets:

Names of,

Othniel.

Judg 3:9–10 When the children of Israel cried out to the LORD, the LORD raised up a deliverer for the children of Israel, who delivered them: Othniel the son of Kenaz, Caleb's younger brother. **10** The Spirit of the LORD came upon him, and he judged Israel. He went out to war, and the LORD delivered Cushan-Rishathaim king of Mesopotamia into his hand; and his hand prevailed over Cushan-Rishathaim.

Ehud.

Judg 3:15 But when the children of Israel cried out to the LORD, the LORD raised up a deliverer for them: Ehud the son of Gera, the Benjamite, a left-handed man. By him the children of Israel sent tribute to Eglon king of Moab.

Shamgar.

Judg 3:31 After him was Shamgar the son of Anath, who killed six hundred men of the Philistines with an ox goad; and he also delivered Israel.

Deborah.

Judg 4:4 Now Deborah, a prophetess, the wife of Lapidoth, was judging Israel at that time.

Gideon.

Judg 6:11 Now the Angel of the LORD came and sat under the terebinth tree which *was* in Ophrah, which *belonged* to Joash the Abiezrite, while his son Gideon threshed wheat in the winepress, in order to hide *it* from the Midianites.

Abimelech.

Judg 9:6 And all the men of Shechem gathered together, all of Beth Millo, and they went and made Abimelech king beside the terebinth tree at the pillar that *was* in Shechem.

Tola.

Judg 10:1 After Abimelech there arose to save Israel Tola the son of Puah, the son of Dodo, a man of Issachar; and he dwelt in Shamir in the mountains of Ephraim.

Jair.

Judg 10:3 After him arose Jair, a Gileadite; and he judged Israel twenty-two years.

Jephthah.

Judg 11:1 Now Jephthah the Gileadite was a mighty man of valor, but he *was* the son of a harlot; and Gilead begot Jephthah.

Ibzan.

Judg 12:8 After him, Ibzan of Bethlehem judged Israel.

Elon.

Judg 12:11 After him, Elon the Zebulunite judged Israel. He judged Israel ten years.

Abdon.

Judg 12:13 After him, Abdon the son of Hillel the Pirathonite judged Israel.

Samson.

Judg 13:24–25 So the woman bore a son and called his name Samson; and the child grew, and the LORD blessed him. **25** And the Spirit of the LORD began to move upon him at Mahaneh Dan between Zorah and Eshtaol.

Judg 16:31 And his brothers and all his father's household came down and took him, and brought *him* up and buried him between Zorah and Eshtaol in the tomb of his father Manoah. He had judged Israel twenty years.

JUDGES

Eli.

1 Sam 4:18 Then it happened, when he made mention of the ark of God, that Eli fell off the seat backward by the side of the gate; and his neck was broken and he died, for the man was old and heavy. And he had judged Israel forty years.

Samuel.

1 Sam 7:6 So they gathered together at Mizpah, drew water, and poured *it* out before the LORD. And they fasted that day, and said there, "We have sinned against the LORD." And Samuel judged the children of Israel at Mizpah.

1 Sam 7:15–17 And Samuel judged Israel all the days of his life. **16** He went from year to year on a circuit to Bethel, Gilgal, and Mizpah, and judged Israel in all those places. **17** But he always returned to Ramah, for his home *was* there. There he judged Israel, and there he built an altar to the LORD.

During four hundred and fifty years.

Acts 13:20 "After that He gave *them* judges for about four hundred and fifty years, until Samuel the prophet.

Not without intermission.

Judg 17:6 In those days *there was* no king in Israel; everyone did *what was* right in his own eyes.

Judg 18:1 In those days *there was* no king in Israel. And in those days the tribe of the Danites was seeking an inheritance for itself to dwell in; for until that day *their* inheritance among the tribes of Israel had not fallen to them.

Judg 19:1 And it came to pass in those days, when *there was* no king in Israel, that there was a certain Levite staying in the remote mountains of Ephraim. He took for himself a concubine from Bethlehem in Judah.

Judg 21:25 In those days *there was* no king in Israel; everyone did *what was* right in his own eyes.

The office of, not always for life, or hereditary.

Judg 8:23 But Gideon said to them, "I will not rule over you, nor shall my son rule over you; the LORD shall rule over you."

Judg 8:29 Then Jerubbaal the son of Joash went and dwelt in his own house.

Israel not permanently or spiritually benefited by.

Judg 2:17–19 Yet they would not listen to their judges, but they played the harlot with other gods, and bowed down to them. They turned quickly from the way in which their fathers walked, in obeying the commandments of the LORD; they did not do so. **18** And when the LORD raised up judges for them, the LORD was with the judge and delivered them out of the hand of their enemies all the days of the judge; for the LORD was moved to pity by their groaning because of those who oppressed them and harassed them. **19** And it came to pass, when the judge was dead, that they reverted and behaved more corruptly than their fathers, by following other gods, to serve them and bow down to them. They did not cease from their own doings nor from their stubborn way.

JUDGMENTS

Are from God.

Deut 32:39 'Now see that I, *even* I, *am* He, And *there is* no God besides Me; I kill and I make alive; I wound and I heal; Nor *is there any* who can deliver from My hand.

Job 12:23 He makes nations great, and destroys them; He enlarges nations, and guides them.

Amos 3:6 If a trumpet is blown in a city, will not the people be afraid? If there is calamity in a city, will not the LORD have done *it*?

Mic 6:9 The LORD's voice cries to the city— Wisdom shall see Your name: "Hear the rod! Who has appointed it?

Different kinds of,

Blotting out the name.

Deut 29:20 "The LORD would not spare him; for then the anger of the LORD and His jealousy would burn against that man, and every curse that is written in this book would settle on him, and the LORD would blot out his name from under heaven.

Abandonment by God.

Hos 4:17 "Ephraim *is* joined to idols, Let him alone.

Cursing men's blessings.

Mal 2:2 If you will not hear, And if you will not take *it* to heart, To give glory to My name," Says the LORD of hosts, "I will send a curse upon you, And I will curse your blessings. Yes, I have cursed them already, Because you do not take *it* to heart.

Plague.

Deut 28:21–22 The LORD will make the plague cling to you until He has consumed you from the land which you are going to possess. **22** The LORD will strike you with consumption, with fever, with inflammation, with severe burning fever, with the sword, with scorching, and with mildew; they shall pursue you until you perish.

Amos 4:10 "I sent among you a plague after the manner of Egypt; Your young men I killed with a sword, Along with your captive horses; I made the stench of your camps come up into your nostrils; Yet you have not returned to Me," Says the LORD.

Enemies.

2 Sam 24:13 So Gad came to David and told him; and he said to him, "Shall seven years of famine come to you in your land? Or shall you flee three months before your enemies, while they pursue you? Or shall there be three days' plague in your land? Now consider and see what answer I should take back to Him who sent me."

Famine.

Deut 28:38–40 "You shall carry much seed out to the field but gather little in, for the locust shall consume it. **39** You shall plant vineyards and tend *them*, but you shall neither drink *of* the wine nor gather the *grapes*; for the worms shall eat them. **40** You shall have olive trees throughout all your territory, but you shall not anoint *yourself* with the oil; for your olives shall drop off.

Amos 4:7–9 "I also withheld rain from you, When *there were* still three months to the harvest. I made it rain on one city, I withheld rain from another city. One part was rained upon, And where it did not rain the part withered. 8 So two *or* three cities wandered to another city to drink water, But they were not satisfied; Yet you have not returned to Me," Says the LORD. 9 "I blasted you with blight and mildew. When your gardens increased, Your vineyards, Your fig trees, And your olive trees, The locust devoured *them;* Yet you have not returned to Me," Says the LORD.

Famine of hearing the Word.

Amos 8:11 "Behold, the days are coming," says the Lord GOD, "That I will send a famine on the land, Not a famine of bread, Nor a thirst for water, But of hearing the words of the LORD.

The sword.

Ex 22:24 and My wrath will become hot, and I will kill you with the sword; your wives shall be widows, and your children fatherless.

Jer 19:7 And I will make void the counsel of Judah and Jerusalem in this place, and I will cause them to fall by the sword before their enemies and by the hands of those who seek their lives; their corpses I will give as meat for the birds of the heaven and for the beasts of the earth.

Captivity.

Deut 28:41 You shall beget sons and daughters, but they shall not be yours; for they shall go into captivity.

Ezek 39:23 The Gentiles shall know that the house of Israel went into captivity for their iniquity; because they were unfaithful to Me, therefore I hid My face from them. I gave them into the hand of their enemies, and they all fell by the sword.

Continued sorrows.

Ps 32:10 Many sorrows *shall be* to the wicked; But he who trusts in the LORD, mercy shall surround him.

Ps 78:32–33 In spite of this they still sinned, And did not believe in His wondrous works. 33 Therefore their days He consumed in futility, And their years in fear.

Ezek 24:23 Your turbans shall be on your heads and your sandals on your feet; you shall neither mourn nor weep, but you shall pine away in your iniquities and mourn with one another.

Desolation.

Ezek 33:29 Then they shall know that I *am* the LORD, when I have made the land most desolate because of all their abominations which they have committed." '

Joel 3:19 "Egypt shall be a desolation, And Edom a desolate wilderness, Because of violence *against* the people of Judah, For they have shed innocent blood in their land.

Destruction.

Job 31:3 *Is* it not destruction for the wicked, And disaster for the workers of iniquity?

Ps 34:16 The face of the LORD *is* against those who do evil, To cut off the remembrance of them from the earth.

Prov 2:22 But the wicked will be cut off from the earth, And the unfaithful will be uprooted from it.

Is 11:4 But with righteousness He shall judge the poor, And decide with equity for the meek of the earth; He

shall strike the earth with the rod of His mouth, And with the breath of His lips He shall slay the wicked.

Inflicted upon

Nations.

Gen 15:14 And also the nation whom they serve I will judge; afterward they shall come out with great possessions.

Jer 51:20–21 "You *are* My battle-ax *and* weapons of war: For with you I will break the nation in pieces; With you I will destroy kingdoms; 21 With you I will break in pieces the horse and its rider; With you I will break in pieces the chariot and its rider;

Individuals.

Deut 29:20 "The LORD would not spare him; for then the anger of the LORD and His jealousy would burn against that man, and every curse that is written in this book would settle on him, and the LORD would blot out his name from under heaven.

Jer 23:34 "And *as for* the prophet and the priest and the people who say, 'The oracle of the LORD!' I will even punish that man and his house.

False gods.

Ex 12:12 'For I will pass through the land of Egypt on that night, and will strike all the firstborn in the land of Egypt, both man and beast; and against all the gods of Egypt I will execute judgment: I *am* the LORD.

Num 33:4 For the Egyptians were burying all *their* firstborn, whom the LORD had killed among them. Also on their gods the LORD had executed judgments.

Posterity of sinners.

Ex 20:5 you shall not bow down to them nor serve them. For I, the LORD your God, *am* a jealous God, visiting the iniquity of the fathers upon the children to the third and fourth *generations* of those who hate Me,

Ps 37:28 For the LORD loves justice, And does not forsake His saints; They are preserved forever, But the descendants of the wicked shall be cut off.

Lam 5:7 Our fathers sinned *and are* no more, But we bear their iniquities.

All enemies of believers.

Jer 30:16 'Therefore all those who devour you shall be devoured; And all your adversaries, every one of them, shall go into captivity; Those who plunder you shall become plunder, And all who prey upon you I will make a prey.

Sent for correction.

Job 37:13 He causes it to come, Whether for correction, Or for His land, Or for mercy.

Jer 30:11 For I *am* with you,' says the LORD, 'to save you; Though I make a full end of all nations where I have scattered you, Yet I will not make a complete end of you. But I will correct you in justice, And will not let you go altogether unpunished.'

Sent for the deliverance of saints.

Ex 6:6 Therefore say to the children of Israel: 'I *am* the LORD; I will bring you out from under the burdens of the Egyptians, I will rescue you from their bondage, and I will redeem you with an outstretched arm and with great judgments.

Are sent, as punishment for

Disobedience to God.

Lev 26:14–16 'But if you do not obey Me, and do not observe all these commandments, **15** and if you despise My statutes, or if your soul abhors My judgments, so that you do not perform all My commandments, *but* break My covenant, **16** I also will do this to you: I will even appoint terror over you, wasting disease and fever which shall consume the eyes and cause sorrow of heart. And you shall sow your seed in vain, for your enemies shall eat it.

2 Chr 7:19–20 "But if you turn away and forsake My statutes and My commandments which I have set before you, and go and serve other gods, and worship them, **20** then I will uproot them from My land which I have given them; and this house which I have sanctified for My name I will cast out of My sight, and will make it a proverb and a byword among all peoples.

Despising the warnings of God.

2 Chr 36:16 But they mocked the messengers of God, despised His words, and scoffed at His prophets, until the wrath of the LORD arose against His people, till *there was* no remedy.

Prov 1:24–31 Because I have called and you refused, I have stretched out my hand and no one regarded, **25** Because you disdained all my counsel, And would have none of my rebuke, **26** I also will laugh at your calamity; I will mock when your terror comes, **27** When your terror comes like a storm, And your destruction comes like a whirlwind, When distress and anguish come upon you. **28** "Then they will call on me, but I will not answer; They will seek me diligently, but they will not find me. **29** Because they hated knowledge And did not choose the fear of the LORD, **30** They would have none of my counsel *And* despised my every rebuke. **31** Therefore they shall eat the fruit of their own way, And be filled to the full with their own fancies.

Jer 44:4–6 However I have sent to you all My servants the prophets, rising early and sending *them,* saying, "Oh, do not do this abominable thing that I hate!" **5** But they did not listen or incline their ear to turn from their wickedness, to burn no incense to other gods. **6** So My fury and My anger were poured out and kindled in the cities of Judah and in the streets of Jerusalem; and they are wasted *and* desolate, as it is this day.'

Complaining against God.

Num 14:29 The carcasses of you who have complained against Me shall fall in this wilderness, all of you who were numbered, according to your entire number, from twenty years old and above.

Idolatry.

2 Kin 22:17 because they have forsaken Me and burned incense to other gods, that they might provoke Me to anger with all the works of their hands. Therefore My wrath shall be aroused against this place and shall not be quenched.' " '

Jer 16:18 And first I will repay double for their iniquity and their sin, because they have defiled My land; they have filled My inheritance with the carcasses of their detestable and abominable idols."

Great sin.

Is 26:21 For behold, the LORD comes out of His place To punish the inhabitants of the earth for their iniquity; The earth will also disclose her blood, And will no more cover her slain.

Ezek 24:13–14 In your filthiness *is* lewdness. Because I have cleansed you, and you were not cleansed, You will not be cleansed of your filthiness anymore, Till I have caused My fury to rest upon you. **14** I, the LORD, have spoken *it;* It shall come to pass, and I will do *it;* I will not hold back, Nor will I spare, Nor will I relent; According to your ways And according to your deeds They will judge you," Says the Lord GOD.' "

Persecuting believers.

Deut 32:43 "Rejoice, O Gentiles, *with* His people; For He will avenge the blood of His servants, And render vengeance to His adversaries; He will provide atonement for His land *and* His people."

Sins of Leaders.

1 Chr 21:2 So David said to Joab and to the leaders of the people, "Go, number Israel from Beersheba to Dan, and bring the number of them to me that I may know *it."*

1 Chr 21:12 either three years of famine, or three months to be defeated by your foes with the sword of your enemies overtaking *you,* or else for three days the sword of the LORD—the plague in the land, with the angel of the LORD destroying throughout all the territory of Israel.' Now consider what answer I should take back to Him who sent me."

Manifest the righteous character of God.

Ex 9:14–16 for at this time I will send all My plagues to your very heart, and on your servants and on your people, that you may know that *there is* none like Me in all the earth. **15** Now if I had stretched out My hand and struck you and your people with pestilence, then you would have been cut off from the earth. **16** But indeed for this *purpose* I have raised you up, that I may show My power *in* you, and that My name may be declared in all the earth.

Ezek 39:21 "I will set My glory among the nations; all the nations shall see My judgment which I have executed, and My hand which I have laid on them.

Dan 9:14 Therefore the LORD has kept the disaster in mind, and brought it upon us; for the LORD our God *is* righteous in all the works which He does, though we have not obeyed His voice.

Are in all the earth.

1 Chr 16:14 He *is* the LORD our God; His judgments *are* in all the earth.

Are frequently tempered with mercy.

Jer 4:27 For thus says the LORD: "The whole land shall be desolate; Yet I will not make a full end.

Jer 5:10 "Go up on her walls and destroy, But do not make a complete end. Take away her branches, For they *are* not the LORD's.

Jer 5:15–18 Behold, I will bring a nation against you from afar, O house of Israel," says the LORD. "It *is* a mighty nation, It *is* an ancient nation, A nation whose language you do not know, Nor can you understand what they say. **16** Their quiver *is* like an open tomb; They *are* all mighty men. **17** And they shall eat up your harvest and your bread, *Which* your sons and daughters should eat. They shall eat up your flocks and your herds; They shall eat up your vines and your fig trees; They shall destroy your fortified cities, In which you trust, with the sword. **18** "Nevertheless in those days," says the LORD, "I will not make a complete end of you.

Amos 9:8 "Behold, the eyes of the Lord GOD *are* on the sinful kingdom, And I will destroy it from the face of the earth; Yet I will not utterly destroy the house of Jacob," Says the LORD.

Should lead to

Humiliation.

Josh 7:6 Then Joshua tore his clothes, and fell to the earth on his face before the ark of the LORD until evening, he and the elders of Israel; and they put dust on their heads.

2 Chr 12:6 So the leaders of Israel and the king humbled themselves; and they said, "The LORD *is* righteous."

Lam 3:1–20 I *am* the man *who* has seen affliction by the rod of His wrath. **2** He has led me and made *me* walk *In* darkness and not *in* light. **3** Surely He has turned His hand against me Time and time again throughout the day. **4** He has aged my flesh and my skin, And broken my bones. **5** He has besieged me And surrounded *me* with bitterness and woe. **6** He has set me in dark places Like the dead of long ago. **7** He has hedged me in so that I cannot get out; He has made my chain heavy. **8** Even when I cry and shout, He shuts out my prayer. **9** He has blocked my ways with hewn stone; He has made my paths crooked. **10** He *has been* to me a bear lying in wait, *Like* a lion in ambush. **11** He has turned aside my ways and torn me in pieces; He has made me desolate. **12** He has bent His bow And set me up as a target for the arrow. **13** He has caused the arrows of His quiver To pierce my loins. **14** I have become the ridicule of all my people— Their taunting song all the day. **15** He has filled me with bitterness, He has made me drink wormwood. **16** He has also broken my teeth with gravel, And covered me with ashes. **17** You have moved my soul far from peace; I have forgotten prosperity. **18** And I said, "My strength and my hope Have perished from the LORD." **19** Remember my affliction and roaming, The wormwood and the gall. **20** My soul still remembers And sinks within me.

Joel 1:13 Gird yourselves and lament, you priests; Wail, you who minister before the altar; Come, lie all night in sackcloth, You who minister to my God; For the grain offering and the drink offering Are withheld from the house of your God.

Jon 3:5–6 So the people of Nineveh believed God, proclaimed a fast, and put on sackcloth, from the greatest to the least of them. **6** Then word came to the king of Nineveh; and he arose from his throne and laid aside his robe, covered *himself* with sackcloth and sat in ashes.

Prayer.

2 Chr 20:9 'If disaster comes upon us—sword, judgment, pestilence, or famine—we will stand before this temple and in Your presence (for Your name *is* in this temple), and cry out to You in our affliction, and You will hear and save.'

Contrition.

Neh 1:4 So it was, when I heard these words, that I sat down and wept, and mourned *for many* days; I was fasting and praying before the God of heaven.

Esth 4:3 And in every province where the king's command and decree arrived, *there was* great mourning among the Jews, with fasting, weeping, and wailing; and many lay in sackcloth and ashes.

Is 22:12 And in that day the Lord GOD of hosts Called for weeping and for mourning, For baldness and for girding with sackcloth.

Learning righteousness.

Is 26:9 With my soul I have desired You in the night, Yes, by my spirit within me I will seek You early; For when Your judgments *are* in the earth, The inhabitants of the world will learn righteousness.

Should be a warning to others.

Luke 13:3 I tell you, no; but unless you repent you will all likewise perish.

May be averted by

Humiliation.

Ex 33:3–4 *Go up* to a land flowing with milk and honey; for I will not go up in your midst, lest I consume you on the way, for you *are* a stiff-necked people." **4** And when the people heard this bad news, they mourned, and no one put on his ornaments.

Ex 33:14 And He said, "My Presence will go *with you,* and I will give you rest."

2 Chr 7:14 if My people who are called by My name will humble themselves, and pray and seek My face, and turn from their wicked ways, then I will hear from heaven, and will forgive their sin and heal their land.

Prayer.

Judg 3:9–11 When the children of Israel cried out to the LORD, the LORD raised up a deliverer for the children of Israel, who delivered them: Othniel the son of Kenaz, Caleb's younger brother. **10** The Spirit of the LORD came upon him, and he judged Israel. He went out to war, and the LORD delivered Cushan-Rishathaim king of Mesopotamia into his hand; and his hand prevailed over Cushan-Rishathaim. **11** So the land had rest for forty years. Then Othniel the son of Kenaz died.

2 Chr 7:13–14 When I shut up heaven and there is no rain, or command the locusts to devour the land, or send pestilence among My people, **14** if My people who are called by My name will humble themselves, and pray and seek My face, and turn from their wicked ways, then I will hear from heaven, and will forgive their sin and heal their land.

Forsaking iniquity.

Jer 18:7–8 The instant I speak concerning a nation and concerning a kingdom, to pluck up, to pull down, and to destroy *it,* **8** if that nation against whom I have spoken turns from its evil, I will relent of the disaster that I thought to bring upon it.

Turning to God.

Deut 30:1–3 "Now it shall come to pass, when all these things come upon you, the blessing and the curse which I have set before you, and you call *them* to mind among all the nations where the LORD your God drives you, **2** and you return to the LORD your

God and obey His voice, according to all that I command you today, you and your children, with all your heart and with all your soul, **3** that the LORD your God will bring you back from captivity, and have compassion on you, and gather you again from all the nations where the LORD your God has scattered you.

Believers,

Preserved during.

Job 5:19–20 He shall deliver you in six troubles, Yes, in seven no evil shall touch you. **20** In famine He shall redeem you from death, And in war from the power of the sword.

Ps 91:7 A thousand may fall at your side, And ten thousand at your right hand; *But* it shall not come near you.

Is 26:20 Come, my people, enter your chambers, And shut your doors behind you; Hide yourself, as it were, for a little moment, Until the indignation is past.

Ezek 9:6 Utterly slay old *and* young men, maidens and little children and women; but do not come near anyone on whom *is* the mark; and begin at My sanctuary." So they began with the elders who *were* before the temple.

Rev 7:3 saying, "Do not harm the earth, the sea, or the trees till we have sealed the servants of our God on their foreheads."

Provided for, during.

Gen 47:12 Then Joseph provided his father, his brothers, and all his father's household with bread, according to the number in *their* families.

Ps 33:19 To deliver their soul from death, And to keep them alive in famine.

Ps 37:19 They shall not be ashamed in the evil time, And in the days of famine they shall be satisfied.

Should pray for those under.

Ex 32:11–13 Then Moses pleaded with the LORD his God, and said: "LORD, why does Your wrath burn hot against Your people whom You have brought out of the land of Egypt with great power and with a mighty hand? **12** Why should the Egyptians speak, and say, 'He brought them out to harm them, to kill them in the mountains, and to consume them from the face of the earth'? Turn from Your fierce wrath, and relent from this harm to Your people. **13** Remember Abraham, Isaac, and Israel, Your servants, to whom You swore by Your own self, and said to them, 'I will multiply your descendants as the stars of heaven; and all this land that I have spoken of I give to your descendants, and they shall inherit *it* forever.' "

Num 11:2 Then the people cried out to Moses, and when Moses prayed to the LORD, the fire was quenched.

Dan 9:3 Then I set my face toward the Lord God to make request by prayer and supplications, with fasting, sackcloth, and ashes.

Should sympathize with those under.

Jer 9:1 Oh, that my head were waters, And my eyes a fountain of tears, That I might weep day and night For the slain of the daughter of my people!

Jer 13:17 But if you will not hear it, My soul will weep in secret for *your* pride; My eyes will weep bitterly And run down with tears, Because the LORD's flock has been taken captive.

Lam 3:48 My eyes overflow with rivers of water For the destruction of the daughter of my people.

Should acknowledge the justice of.

2 Sam 24:17 Then David spoke to the LORD when he saw the angel who was striking the people, and said, "Surely I have sinned, and I have done wickedly; but these sheep, what have they done? Let Your hand, I pray, be against me and against my father's house."

Ezra 9:13 And after all that has come upon us for our evil deeds and for our great guilt, since You our God have punished us less than our iniquities *deserve,* and have given us *such* deliverance as this,

Neh 9:33 However You *are* just in all that has befallen us; For You have dealt faithfully, But we have done wickedly.

Jer 14:17 "Therefore you shall say this word to them: 'Let my eyes flow with tears night and day, And let them not cease; For the virgin daughter of my people Has been broken with a mighty stroke, with a very severe blow.

Upon nations—illustrated by

The ancient world.

Gen 6:7 So the LORD said, "I will destroy man whom I have created from the face of the earth, both man and beast, creeping thing and birds of the air, for I am sorry that I have made them."

Gen 6:17 And behold, I Myself am bringing floodwaters on the earth, to destroy from under heaven all flesh in which *is* the breath of life; everything that *is* on the earth shall die.

Sodom and Gomorrah.

Gen 19:24 Then the LORD rained brimstone and fire on Sodom and Gomorrah, from the LORD out of the heavens.

Egypt.

Ex 9:14 for at this time I will send all My plagues to your very heart, and on your servants and on your people, that you may know that *there is* none like Me in all the earth.

Israel.

Num 14:29 The carcasses of you who have complained against Me shall fall in this wilderness, all of you who were numbered, according to your entire number, from twenty years old and above.

Num 14:35 I the LORD have spoken this. I will surely do so to all this evil congregation who are gathered together against Me. In this wilderness they shall be consumed, and there they shall die.' "

Num 21:6 So the LORD sent fiery serpents among the people, and they bit the people; and many of the people of Israel died.

The people of Ashdod.

1 Sam 5:6 But the hand of the LORD was heavy on the people of Ashdod, and He ravaged them and struck them with tumors, *both* Ashdod and its territory.

The people of Beth Shemesh.

1 Sam 6:19 Then He struck the men of Beth Shemesh,

because they had looked into the ark of the LORD. He struck fifty thousand and seventy men of the people, and the people lamented because the LORD had struck the people with a great slaughter.

The Amalekites.

1 Sam 15:3 Now go and attack Amalek, and utterly destroy all that they have, and do not spare them. But kill both man and woman, infant and nursing child, ox and sheep, camel and donkey.' "

Upon individuals—illustrated by

Cain.

Gen 4:11–12 So now you *are* cursed from the earth, which has opened its mouth to receive your brother's blood from your hand. **12** When you till the ground, it shall no longer yield its strength to you. A fugitive and a vagabond you shall be on the earth."

Canaan.

Gen 9:25 Then he said: "Cursed *be* Canaan; A servant of servants He shall be to his brethren."

Korah, etc.

Num 16:33–35 So they and all those with them went down alive into the pit; the earth closed over them, and they perished from among the assembly. **34** Then all Israel who *were* around them fled at their cry, for they said, "Lest the earth swallow us up *also!*" **35** And a fire came out from the LORD and consumed the two hundred and fifty men who were offering incense.

Achan.

Josh 7:25 And Joshua said, "Why have you troubled us? The LORD will trouble you this day." So all Israel stoned him with stones; and they burned them with fire after they had stoned them with stones.

Hophni, etc.

1 Sam 2:34 Now this *shall be* a sign to you that will come upon your two sons, on Hophni and Phinehas: in one day they shall die, both of them.

Saul.

1 Sam 15:23 For rebellion *is as* the sin of witchcraft, And stubbornness *is as* iniquity and idolatry. Because you have rejected the word of the LORD, He also has rejected you from *being* king."

Uzzah.

2 Sam 6:7 Then the anger of the LORD was aroused against Uzzah, and God struck him there for *his* error; and he died there by the ark of God.

Jeroboam.

1 Kin 13:4 So it came to pass when King Jeroboam heard the saying of the man of God, who cried out against the altar in Bethel, that he stretched out his hand from the altar, saying, "Arrest him!" Then his hand, which he stretched out toward him, withered, so that he could not pull it back to himself.

Ahab.

1 Kin 22:38 Then *someone* washed the chariot at a pool in Samaria, and the dogs licked up his blood while the harlots bathed, according to the word of the LORD which He had spoken.

Gehazi.

2 Kin 5:27 Therefore the leprosy of Naaman shall cling to you and your descendants forever." And he went out from his presence leprous, *as white* as snow.

Jezebel.

2 Kin 9:35 So they went to bury her, but they found no more of her than the skull and the feet and the palms of *her* hands.

Nebuchadnezzar.

Dan 4:31 While the word *was still* in the king's mouth, a voice fell from heaven: "King Nebuchadnezzar, to you it is spoken: the kingdom has departed from you!

Belshazzar.

Dan 5:30 That very night Belshazzar, king of the Chaldeans, was slain.

Zacharias.

Luke 1:20 But behold, you will be mute and not able to speak until the day these things take place, because you did not believe my words which will be fulfilled in their own time."

Ananias and Sapphira.

Acts 5:1–10 But a certain man named Ananias, with Sapphira his wife, sold a possession. **2** And he kept back *part* of the proceeds, his wife also being aware *of it,* and brought a certain part and laid *it* at the apostles' feet. **3** But Peter said, "Ananias, why has Satan filled your heart to lie to the Holy Spirit and keep back *part* of the price of the land for yourself? **4** While it remained, was it not your own? And after it was sold, was it not in your own control? Why have you conceived this thing in your heart? You have not lied to men but to God." **5** Then Ananias, hearing these words, fell down and breathed his last. So great fear came upon all those who heard these things. **6** And the young men arose and wrapped him up, carried *him* out, and buried *him.* **7** Now it was about three hours later when his wife came in, not knowing what had happened. **8** And Peter answered her, "Tell me whether you sold the land for so much?" She said, "Yes, for so much." **9** Then Peter said to her, "How is it that you have agreed together to test the Spirit of the Lord? Look, the feet of those who have buried your husband *are* at the door, and they will carry you out." **10** Then immediately she fell down at his feet and breathed her last. And the young men came in and found her dead, and carrying *her* out, buried *her* by her husband.

Herod.

Acts 12:23 Then immediately an angel of the Lord struck him, because he did not give glory to God. And he was eaten by worms and died.

Elymas.

Acts 13:11 And now, indeed, the hand of the Lord *is* upon you, and you shall be blind, not seeing the sun for a time." And immediately a dark mist fell on him, and he went around seeking someone to lead him by the hand.

Preservation during—illustrated by

Noah.

Gen 7:1 Then the LORD said to Noah, "Come into the ark, you and all your household, because I have seen *that* you *are* righteous before Me in this generation.

Gen 7:16 So those that entered, male and female of all

flesh, went in as God had commanded him; and the LORD shut him in.

Lot.

Gen 19:15–17 When the morning dawned, the angels urged Lot to hurry, saying, "Arise, take your wife and your two daughters who are here, lest you be consumed in the punishment of the city." **16** And while he lingered, the men took hold of his hand, his wife's hand, and the hands of his two daughters, the LORD being merciful to him, and they brought him out and set him outside the city. **17** So it came to pass, when they had brought them outside, that he said, "Escape for your life! Do not look behind you nor stay anywhere in the plain. Escape to the mountains, lest you be destroyed."

Joseph, etc.

Gen 45:7 And God sent me before you to preserve a posterity for you in the earth, and to save your lives by a great deliverance.

Elijah.

1 Kin 17:9 "Arise, go to Zarephath, which *belongs* to Sidon, and dwell there. See, I have commanded a widow there to provide for you."

Elisha, etc.

2 Kin 4:38–41 And Elisha returned to Gilgal, and *there was* a famine in the land. Now the sons of the prophets *were* sitting before him; and he said to his servant, "Put on the large pot, and boil stew for the sons of the prophets." **39** So one went out into the field to gather herbs, and found a wild vine, and gathered from it a lapful of wild gourds, and came and sliced *them* into the pot of stew, though they did not know *what they were.* **40** Then they served it to the men to eat. Now it happened, as they were eating the stew, that they cried out and said, "Man of God, *there is* death in the pot!" And they could not eat *it.* **41** So he said, "Then bring some flour." And he put *it* into the pot, and said, "Serve *it* to the people, that they may eat." And there was nothing harmful in the pot.

A Shunammite.

2 Kin 8:1–2 Then Elisha spoke to the woman whose son he had restored to life, saying, "Arise and go, you and your household, and stay wherever you can; for the LORD has called for a famine, and furthermore, it will come upon the land for seven years." **2** So the woman arose and did according to the saying of the man of God, and she went with her household and dwelt in the land of the Philistines seven years.

JUDGMENT, THE

Predicted in the Old Testament.

1 Chr 16:33 Then the trees of the woods shall rejoice before the LORD, For He is coming to judge the earth.

Ps 9:7 But the LORD shall endure forever; He has prepared His throne for judgment.

Ps 96:13 For He is coming, for He is coming to judge the earth. He shall judge the world with righteousness, And the peoples with His truth.

Eccl 3:17 I said in my heart, "God shall judge the righteous and the wicked, For *there is* a time there for every purpose and for every work."

A first principle of the gospel.

Heb 6:2 of the doctrine of baptisms, of laying on of hands, of resurrection of the dead, and of eternal judgment.

A day appointed for.

Acts 17:31 because He has appointed a day on which He will judge the world in righteousness by the Man whom He has ordained. He has given assurance of this to all by raising Him from the dead."

Rom 2:16 in the day when God will judge the secrets of men by Jesus Christ, according to my gospel.

Time of, unknown to us.

Mark 13:32 "But of that day and hour no one knows, not even the angels in heaven, nor the Son, but only the Father.

Other names for,

Day of wrath.

Job 21:30 For the wicked are reserved for the day of doom; They shall be brought out on the day of wrath.

Rom 2:5 But in accordance with your hardness and your impenitent heart you are treasuring up for yourself wrath in the day of wrath and revelation of the righteous judgment of God,

Rev 6:17 For the great day of His wrath has come, and who is able to stand?"

Revelation of the righteous judgment of God.

Rom 2:5 But in accordance with your hardness and your impenitent heart you are treasuring up for yourself wrath in the day of wrath and revelation of the righteous judgment of God,

Day of judgment and perdition of ungodly men.

2 Pet 3:7 But the heavens and the earth *which* are now preserved by the same word, are reserved for fire until the day of judgment and perdition of ungodly men.

Day of doom.

Job 21:30 For the wicked are reserved for the day of doom; They shall be brought out on the day of wrath.

Judgment of the great day.

Jude 1:6 And the angels who did not keep their proper domain, but left their own abode, He has reserved in everlasting chains under darkness for the judgment of the great day;

Shall be administered by Christ.

John 5:22 For the Father judges no one, but has committed all judgment to the Son,

John 5:27 and has given Him authority to execute judgment also, because He is the Son of Man.

Acts 10:42 And He commanded us to preach to the people, and to testify that it is He who was ordained by God *to be* Judge of the living and the dead.

Rom 14:10 But why do you judge your brother? Or why do you show contempt for your brother? For we shall all stand before the judgment seat of Christ.

2 Cor 5:10 For we must all appear before the judgment seat of Christ, that each one may receive the things *done* in the body, according to what he has done, whether good or bad.

Believers shall sit with Christ in.

1 Cor 6:2 Do you not know that the saints will judge the world? And if the world will be judged by you, are you unworthy to judge the smallest matters?

Rev 20:4 And I saw thrones, and they sat on them, and judgment was committed to them. Then *I saw* the souls of those who had been beheaded for their witness to Jesus and for the word of God, who had not worshiped the beast or his image, and had not received *his* mark on their foreheads or on their hands. And they lived and reigned with Christ for a thousand years.

Shall take place at the coming of Christ.

Matt 25:31 "When the Son of Man comes in His glory, and all the holy angels with Him, then He will sit on the throne of His glory.

2 Tim 4:1 I charge *you* therefore before God and the Lord Jesus Christ, who will judge the living and the dead at His appearing and His kingdom:

Of unbelievers, by the law of conscience.

Rom 2:12 For as many as have sinned without law will also perish without law, and as many as have sinned in the law will be judged by the law

Rom 2:14–15 for when Gentiles, who do not have the law, by nature do the things in the law, these, although not having the law, are a law to themselves, **15** who show the work of the law written in their hearts, their conscience also bearing witness, and between themselves *their* thoughts accusing or else excusing *them*)

Of Jews, by the law of Moses.

Rom 2:12 For as many as have sinned without law will also perish without law, and as many as have sinned in the law will be judged by the law

Of Christians, by the gospel.

James 2:12 So speak and so do as those who will be judged by the law of liberty.

Shall involve

All nations.

Matt 25:32 All the nations will be gathered before Him, and He will separate them one from another, as a shepherd divides *his* sheep from the goats.

All men.

Heb 9:27 And as it is appointed for men to die once, but after this the judgment,

Heb 12:23 to the general assembly and church of the firstborn *who are* registered in heaven, to God the Judge of all, to the spirits of just men made perfect,

Small and great.

Rev 20:12 And I saw the dead, small and great, standing before God, and books were opened. And another book was opened, which is *the Book* of Life. And the dead were judged according to their works, by the things which were written in the books.

The righteous and wicked.

Eccl 3:17 I said in my heart, "God shall judge the righteous and the wicked, For *there is* a time there for every purpose and for every work."

The living and the dead.

2 Tim 4:1 I charge *you* therefore before God and the Lord Jesus Christ, who will judge the living and the dead at His appearing and His kingdom:

1 Pet 4:5 They will give an account to Him who is ready to judge the living and the dead.

Shall be in righteousness.

Ps 98:9 For He is coming to judge the earth. With righteousness He shall judge the world, And the peoples with equity.

Acts 17:31 because He has appointed a day on which He will judge the world in righteousness by the Man whom He has ordained. He has given assurance of this to all by raising Him from the dead."

The books shall be opened at.

Dan 7:10 A fiery stream issued And came forth from before Him. A thousand thousands ministered to Him; Ten thousand times ten thousand stood before Him. The court was seated, And the books were opened.

Shall encompass all

Actions.

Eccl 11:9 Rejoice, O young man, in your youth, And let your heart cheer you in the days of your youth; Walk in the ways of your heart, And in the sight of your eyes; But know that for all these God will bring you into judgment.

Eccl 12:14 For God will bring every work into judgment, Including every secret thing, Whether good or evil.

Rev 20:13 The sea gave up the dead who were in it, and Death and Hades delivered up the dead who were in them. And they were judged, each one according to his works.

Words.

Matt 12:36–37 But I say to you that for every idle word men may speak, they will give account of it in the day of judgment. **37** For by your words you will be justified, and by your words you will be condemned."

Jude 1:15 to execute judgment on all, to convict all who are ungodly among them of all their ungodly deeds which they have committed in an ungodly way, and of all the harsh things which ungodly sinners have spoken against Him."

Thoughts.

Eccl 12:14 For God will bring every work into judgment, Including every secret thing, Whether good or evil.

1 Cor 4:5 Therefore judge nothing before the time, until the Lord comes, who will both bring to light the hidden things of darkness and reveal the counsels of the hearts. Then each one's praise will come from God.

None, by nature, can stand in.

Ps 130:3 If You, LORD, should mark iniquities, O Lord, who could stand?

Ps 143:2 Do not enter into judgment with Your servant, For in Your sight no one living is righteous.

Rom 3:19 Now we know that whatever the law says, it says to those who are under the law, that every mouth may be stopped, and all the world may become guilty before God.

Believers shall, through Christ, be enabled to stand in.

Rom 8:33–34 Who shall bring a charge against God's elect? *It is* God who justifies. **34** Who *is* he who condemns? *It is* Christ who died, and furthermore is also risen, who is even at the right hand of God, who also makes intercession for us.

Christ will acknowledge believers at.

Matt 25:34–40 Then the King will say to those on His right hand, 'Come, you blessed of My Father, inherit the kingdom prepared for you from the foundation of the world: **35** for I was hungry and you gave Me food; I was thirsty and you gave Me drink; I was a stranger and you took Me in; **36** I *was* naked and you clothed Me; I was sick and you visited Me; I was in prison and you came to Me.' **37** "Then the righteous will answer Him, saying, 'Lord, when did we see You hungry and feed *You*, or thirsty and give *You* drink? **38** When did we see You a stranger and take *You* in, or naked and clothe *You*? **39** Or when did we see You sick, or in prison, and come to You?' **40** And the King will answer and say to them, 'Assuredly, I say to you, inasmuch as you did *it* to one of the least of these My brethren, you did *it* to Me.'

Rev 3:5 He who overcomes shall be clothed in white garments, and I will not blot out his name from the Book of Life; but I will confess his name before My Father and before His angels.

Perfect love will give boldness in.

1 John 4:17 Love has been perfected among us in this: that we may have boldness in the day of judgment; because as He is, so are we in this world.

Believers shall be rewarded at.

2 Tim 4:8 Finally, there is laid up for me the crown of righteousness, which the Lord, the righteous Judge, will give to me on that Day, and not to me only but also to all who have loved His appearing.

Rev 11:18 The nations were angry, and Your wrath has come, And the time of the dead, that they should be judged, And that You should reward Your servants the prophets and the saints, And those who fear Your name, small and great, And should destroy those who destroy the earth."

The wicked shall be condemned in.

Matt 7:22–23 Many will say to Me in that day, 'Lord, Lord, have we not prophesied in Your name, cast out demons in Your name, and done many wonders in Your name?' **23** And then I will declare to them, 'I never knew you; depart from Me, you who practice lawlessness!'

Matt 13:40–42 Therefore as the tares are gathered and burned in the fire, so it will be at the end of this age. **41** The Son of Man will send out His angels, and they will gather out of His kingdom all things that offend, and those who practice lawlessness, **42** and will cast them into the furnace of fire. There will be wailing and gnashing of teeth.

Matt 25:41 "Then He will also say to those on the left hand, 'Depart from Me, you cursed, into the everlasting fire prepared for the devil and his angels:

Matt 25:46 And these will go away into everlasting punishment, but the righteous into eternal life."

The word of Christ shall be a witness against the wicked in.

John 12:48 He who rejects Me, and does not receive My words, has that which judges him—the word that I have spoken will judge him in the last day.

The certainty of, a motive to

Repentance.

Acts 17:30–31 Truly, these times of ignorance God overlooked, but now commands all men everywhere to repent, **31** because He has appointed a day on which He will judge the world in righteousness by the Man whom He has ordained. He has given assurance of this to all by raising Him from the dead."

Faith.

Is 28:16–17 Therefore thus says the Lord GOD: "Behold, I lay in Zion a stone for a foundation, A tried stone, a precious cornerstone, a sure foundation; Whoever believes will not act hastily. **17** Also I will make justice the measuring line, And righteousness the plummet; The hail will sweep away the refuge of lies, And the waters will overflow the hiding place.

Holiness.

2 Cor 5:9–10 Therefore we make it our aim, whether present or absent, to be well pleasing to Him. **10** For we must all appear before the judgment seat of Christ, that each one may receive the things *done* in the body, according to what he has done, whether good or bad.

2 Pet 3:11 Therefore, since all these things will be dissolved, what manner *of persons* ought you to be in holy conduct and godliness,

2 Pet 3:14 Therefore, beloved, looking forward to these things, be diligent to be found by Him in peace, without spot and blameless;

Prayer and watchfulness.

Mark 13:33 Take heed, watch and pray; for you do not know when the time is.

The wicked dread.

Acts 24:25 Now as he reasoned about righteousness, self-control, and the judgment to come, Felix was afraid and answered, "Go away for now; when I have a convenient time I will call for you."

2 Cor 5:11 Knowing, therefore, the terror of the Lord, we persuade men; but we are well known to God, and I also trust are well known in your consciences.

Heb 10:27 but a certain fearful expectation of judgment, and fiery indignation which will devour the adversaries.

Neglected blessings increase condemnation at.

Matt 11:20–24 Then He began to rebuke the cities in which most of His mighty works had been done, because they did not repent: **21** "Woe to you, Chorazin! Woe to you, Bethsaida! For if the mighty works which were done in you had been done in Tyre and Sidon, they would have repented long ago in sackcloth and ashes. **22** But I say to you, it will be more tolerable for Tyre and Sidon in the day of judgment than for you. **23** And you, Capernaum, who are exalted to heaven, will be brought down to Hades; for if the mighty works which were done in you had been done in Sodom, it would have remained until this day. **24** But I say to you that it shall be more tolerable for the land of Sodom in the day of judgment than for you."

Luke 11:31–32 The queen of the South will rise up in the judgment with the men of this generation and condemn them, for she came from the ends of the earth to hear the wisdom of Solomon; and indeed a greater than Solomon *is* here. **32** The men of Nineveh will rise up in the judgment with this generation and condemn it, for they repented at the preaching of Jonah; and indeed a greater than Jonah *is* here.

Demons shall be condemned at.

2 Pet 2:4 For if God did not spare the angels who sinned, but cast *them* down to hell and delivered *them* into chains of darkness, to be reserved for judgment;

Jude 1:6 And the angels who did not keep their proper domain, but left their own abode, He has reserved in everlasting chains under darkness for the judgment of the great day;

JUSTICE
Commanded.

Deut 16:20 You shall follow what is altogether just, that you may live and inherit the land which the LORD your God is giving you.

Is 56:1 Thus says the LORD: "Keep justice, and do righteousness, For My salvation *is* about to come, And My righteousness to be revealed.

Christ, an example of.

Ps 98:9 For He is coming to judge the earth. With righteousness He shall judge the world, And the peoples with equity.

Is 11:4 But with righteousness He shall judge the poor, And decide with equity for the meek of the earth; He shall strike the earth with the rod of His mouth, And with the breath of His lips He shall slay the wicked.

Jer 23:5 "Behold, *the* days are coming," says the LORD, "That I will raise to David a Branch of righteousness; A King shall reign and prosper, And execute judgment and righteousness in the earth.

Specially required in rulers.

2 Sam 23:3 The God of Israel said, The Rock of Israel spoke to me: 'He who rules over men *must be* just, Ruling in the fear of God.

Ezek 45:9 Thus says the Lord GOD: "Enough, O princes of Israel! Remove violence and plundering, execute justice and righteousness, and stop dispossessing My people," says the Lord GOD.

To be done
In executing judgment.

Deut 16:18 "You shall appoint judges and officers in all your gates, which the LORD your God gives you, according to your tribes, and they shall judge the people with just judgment.

Jer 21:12 O house of David! Thus says the LORD: "Execute judgment in the morning; And deliver *him who is* plundered Out of the hand of the oppressor, Lest My fury go forth like fire And burn so that no one can quench *it*, Because of the evil of your doings.

In buying and selling.

Lev 19:36 You shall have honest scales, honest weights,

an honest ephah, and an honest hin: I *am* the LORD your God, who brought you out of the land of Egypt.

Deut 25:15 You shall have a perfect and just weight, a perfect and just measure, that your days may be lengthened in the land which the LORD your God is giving you.

To the poor.

Prov 29:14 The king who judges the poor with truth, His throne will be established forever.

Prov 31:9 Open your mouth, judge righteously, And plead the cause of the poor and needy.

To the fatherless and widows.

Is 1:17 Learn to do good; Seek justice, Rebuke the oppressor; Defend the fatherless, Plead for the widow.

To bondservants.

Col 4:1 Masters, give your bondservants what is just and fair, knowing that you also have a Master in heaven.

Bribes impede.

Ex 23:8 And you shall take no bribe, for a bribe blinds the discerning and perverts the words of the righteous.

God
Requires.

Mic 6:8 He has shown you, O man, what *is* good; And what does the LORD require of you But to do justly, To love mercy, And to walk humbly with your God?

Sets the highest value on.

Prov 2:13 From those who leave the paths of uprightness To walk in the ways of darkness;

Delights in.

Prov 11:1 Dishonest scales *are* an abomination to the LORD, But a just weight *is* His delight.

Gives wisdom to execute.

1 Kin 3:11–12 Then God said to him: "Because you have asked this thing, and have not asked long life for yourself, nor have asked riches for yourself, nor have asked the life of your enemies, but have asked for yourself understanding to discern justice, **12** behold, I have done according to your words; see, I have given you a wise and understanding heart, so that there has not been anyone like you before you, nor shall any like you arise after you.

Prov 2:6 For the LORD gives wisdom; From His mouth *come* knowledge and understanding;

Prov 2:9 Then you will understand righteousness and justice, Equity *and* every good path.

Displeased with the lack of.

Eccl 5:8 If you see the oppression of the poor, and the violent perversion of justice and righteousness in a province, do not marvel at the matter; for high official watches over high official, and higher officials are over them.

Brings its own reward.

Jer 22:15 "Shall you reign because you enclose *yourself* in cedar? Did not your father eat and drink, And do justice and righteousness? Then *it was* well with him.

Believers should
Study the principles of.

Phil 4:8 Finally, brethren, whatever things are true,

whatever things *are* noble, whatever things *are* just, whatever things *are* pure, whatever things *are* lovely, whatever things *are* of good report, if *there is* any virtue and if *there is* anything praiseworthy— meditate on these things.

Receive instruction in.

Prov 1:3 To receive the instruction of wisdom, Justice, judgment, and equity;

Pray for wisdom to execute.

1 Kin 3:9 Therefore give to Your servant an understanding heart to judge Your people, that I may discern between good and evil. For who is able to judge this great people of Yours?"

Always do.

Ps 119:121 I have done justice and righteousness; Do not leave me to my oppressors.

Ezek 18:8–9 If he has not exacted usury Nor taken any increase, *But* has withdrawn his hand from iniquity *And* executed true judgment between man and man; **9** *If* he has walked in My statutes And kept My judgments faithfully— He *is* just; He shall surely live!" Says the Lord GOD.

Take pleasure in doing.

Prov 21:15 *It is* a joy for the just to do justice, But destruction *will come* to the workers of iniquity.

Teach others to do.

Gen 18:19 For I have known him, in order that he may command his children and his household after him, that they keep the way of the LORD, to do righteousness and justice, that the LORD may bring to Abraham what He has spoken to him."

Promises concerning.

Is 33:15–16 He who walks righteously and speaks uprightly, He who despises the gain of oppressions, Who gestures with his hands, refusing bribes, Who stops his ears from hearing of bloodshed, And shuts his eyes from seeing evil: **16** He will dwell on high; His place of defense *will be* the fortress of rocks; Bread will be given him, His water *will be* sure.

Jer 7:5 "For if you thoroughly amend your ways and your doings, if you thoroughly execute judgment between a man and his neighbor,

Jer 7:7 then I will cause you to dwell in this place, in the land that I gave to your fathers forever and ever.

The wicked

Scorn.

Prov 19:28 A disreputable witness scorns justice, And the mouth of the wicked devours iniquity.

Is 59:14 Justice is turned back, And righteousness stands afar off; For truth is fallen in the street, And equity cannot enter.

Abhor.

Mic 3:9 Now hear this, You heads of the house of Jacob And rulers of the house of Israel, Who abhor justice And pervert all equity,

Do not call for.

Is 59:4 No one calls for justice, Nor does *any* plead for truth. They trust in empty words and speak lies; They conceive evil and bring forth iniquity.

Pass by.

Luke 11:42 "But woe to you Pharisees! For you tithe mint and rue and all manner of herbs, and pass by justice and the love of God. These you ought to have done, without leaving the others undone.

Afflict those who act with.

Job 12:4 "I am one mocked by his friends, Who called on God, and He answered him, The just and blameless *who is* ridiculed.

Amos 5:12 For I know your manifold transgressions And your mighty sins: Afflicting the just *and* taking bribes; Diverting the poor *from justice* at the gate.

Exemplified by

Moses.

Num 16:15 Then Moses was very angry, and said to the LORD, "Do not respect their offering. I have not taken one donkey from them, nor have I hurt one of them."

Samuel.

1 Sam 12:4 And they said, "You have not cheated us or oppressed us, nor have you taken anything from any man's hand."

David.

2 Sam 8:15 So David reigned over all Israel; and David administered judgment and justice to all his people.

Solomon.

1 Kin 3:16–27 Now two women *who were* harlots came to the king, and stood before him. **17** And one woman said, "O my lord, this woman and I dwell in the same house; and I gave birth while she *was* in the house. **18** Then it happened, the third day after I had given birth, that this woman also gave birth. And we *were* together; no one *was* with us in the house, except the two of us in the house. **19** And this woman's son died in the night, because she lay on him. **20** So she arose in the middle of the night and took my son from my side, while your maidservant slept, and laid him in her bosom, and laid her dead child in my bosom. **21** And when I rose in the morning to nurse my son, there he was, dead. But when I had examined him in the morning, indeed, he was not my son whom I had borne." **22** Then the other woman said, "No! But the living one *is* my son, and the dead one *is* your son." And the first woman said, "No! But the dead one *is* your son, and the living one *is* my son." Thus they spoke before the king. **23** And the king said, "The one says, 'This *is* my son, who lives, and your son *is* the dead one'; and the other says, 'No! But your son *is* the dead one, and my son *is* the living one.'" **24** Then the king said, "Bring me a sword." So they brought a sword before the king. **25** And the king said, "Divide the living child in two, and give half to one, and half to the other." **26** Then the woman whose son *was* living spoke to the king, for she yearned with compassion for her son; and she said, "O my lord, give her the living child, and by no means kill him!" But the other said, "Let him be neither mine nor yours, *but* divide *him.*" **27** So the king answered and said, "Give the first woman the living child, and by no means kill him; she *is* his mother."

Josiah.

Jer 22:15 "Shall you reign because you enclose *yourself*

in cedar? Did not your father eat and drink, And do justice and righteousness? Then *it was* well with him.

Joseph.

Luke 23:50–51 Now behold, *there was* a man named Joseph, a council member, a good and just man. **51** He had not consented to their decision and deed. *He was* from Arimathea, a city of the Jews, who himself was also waiting for the kingdom of God.

The apostles.

1 Thess 2:10 You *are* witnesses, and God *also*, how devoutly and justly and blamelessly we behaved ourselves among you who believe;

JUSTIFICATION

Promised in Christ.

Is 45:25 In the LORD all the descendants of Israel Shall be justified, and shall glory.' "

Is 53:11 He shall see the labor of His soul, *and* be satisfied. By His knowledge My righteous Servant shall justify many, For He shall bear their iniquities.

Is the act of God.

Is 50:8 *He is* near who justifies Me; Who will contend with Me? Let us stand together. Who *is* My adversary? Let him come near Me.

Rom 8:33 Who shall bring a charge against God's elect? *It is* God who justifies.

Under law,

Requires perfect obedience.

Lev 18:5 You shall therefore keep My statutes and My judgments, which if a man does, he shall live by them: I *am* the LORD.

Rom 2:13 (for not the hearers of the law *are* just in the sight of God, but the doers of the law will be justified;

Rom 10:5 For Moses writes about the righteousness which is of the law, *"The man who does those things shall live by them."*

James 2:10 For whoever shall keep the whole law, and yet stumble in one *point*, he is guilty of all.

Man cannot attain to.

Job 9:2–3 "Truly I know *it is* so, But how can a man be righteous before God? **3** If one wished to contend with Him, He could not answer Him one time out of a thousand.

Job 9:20 Though I were righteous, my own mouth would condemn me; Though I *were* blameless, it would prove me perverse.

Job 25:4 How then can man be righteous before God? Or how can he be pure *who is* born of a woman?

Ps 130:3 If You, LORD, should mark iniquities, O Lord, who could stand?

Ps 143:2 Do not enter into judgment with Your servant, For in Your sight no one living is righteous.

Rom 3:20 Therefore by the deeds of the law no flesh will be justified in His sight, for by the law *is* the knowledge of sin.

Rom 9:31–32 but Israel, pursuing the law of righteousness, has not attained to the law of righteousness. **32** Why? Because *they did* not *seek it* by faith, but as it

were, by the works of the law. For they stumbled at that stumbling stone.

Under the gospel,

Is not of works.

Acts 13:39 and by Him everyone who believes is justified from all things from which you could not be justified by the law of Moses.

Rom 8:3 For what the law could not do in that it was weak through the flesh, God *did* by sending His own Son in the likeness of sinful flesh, on account of sin: He condemned sin in the flesh,

Gal 2:16 knowing that a man is not justified by the works of the law but by faith in Jesus Christ, even we have believed in Christ Jesus, that we might be justified by faith in Christ and not by the works of the law; for by the works of the law no flesh shall be justified.

Gal 3:11 But that no one is justified by the law in the sight of God *is* evident, for *"the just shall live by faith."*

Is not of faith and works united.

Rom 3:28 Therefore we conclude that a man is justified by faith apart from the deeds of the law.

Rom 11:6 And if by grace, then *it is* no longer of works; otherwise grace is no longer grace. But if *it is* of works, it is no longer grace; otherwise work is no longer work.

Gal 2:14–21 But when I saw that they were not straightforward about the truth of the gospel, I said to Peter before *them* all, "If you, being a Jew, live in the manner of Gentiles and not as the Jews, why do you compel Gentiles to live as Jews? **15** We *who are* Jews by nature, and not sinners of the Gentiles, **16** knowing that a man is not justified by the works of the law but by faith in Jesus Christ, even we have believed in Christ Jesus, that we might be justified by faith in Christ and not by the works of the law; for by the works of the law no flesh shall be justified. **17** "But if, while we seek to be justified by Christ, we ourselves also are found sinners, *is* Christ therefore a minister of sin? Certainly not! **18** For if I build again those things which I destroyed, I make myself a transgressor. **19** For I through the law died to the law that I might live to God. **20** I have been crucified with Christ; it is no longer I who live, but Christ lives in me; and the *life* which I now live in the flesh I live by faith in the Son of God, who loved me and gave Himself for me. **21** I do not set aside the grace of God; for if righteousness *comes* through the law, then Christ died in vain."

Gal 5:4 You have become estranged from Christ, you who *attempt to* be justified by law; you have fallen from grace.

Cf. Acts 15:1–29

Is by faith alone.

John 5:24 "Most assuredly, I say to you, he who hears My word and believes in Him who sent Me has everlasting life, and shall not come into judgment, but has passed from death into life.

Acts 13:39 and by Him everyone who believes is justified from all things from which you could not be justified by the law of Moses.

Rom 3:30 since *there is* one God who will justify the circumcised by faith and the uncircumcised through faith.

Rom 5:1 Therefore, having been justified by faith, we have peace with God through our Lord Jesus Christ,

Gal 2:16 knowing that a man is not justified by the works of the law but by faith in Jesus Christ, even we have believed in Christ Jesus, that we might be justified by faith in Christ and not by the works of the law; for by the works of the law no flesh shall be justified.

Is of grace.

Rom 3:24 being justified freely by His grace through the redemption that is in Christ Jesus,

Rom 4:16 Therefore *it is* of faith that *it might be* according to grace, so that the promise might be sure to all the seed, not only to those who are of the law, but also to those who are of the faith of Abraham, who is the father of us all

Rom 5:17–21 For if by the one man's offense death reigned through the one, much more those who receive abundance of grace and of the gift of righteousness will reign in life through the One, Jesus Christ.) 18 Therefore, as through one man's offense *judgment* came to all men, resulting in condemnation, even so through one Man's righteous act *the free gift came* to all men, resulting in justification of life. 19 For as by one man's disobedience many were made sinners, so also by one Man's obedience many will be made righteous. 20 Moreover the law entered that the offense might abound. But where sin abounded, grace abounded much more, 21 so that as sin reigned in death, even so grace might reign through righteousness to eternal life through Jesus Christ our Lord.

In the name of Christ.

1 Cor 6:11 And such were some of you. But you were washed, but you were sanctified, but you were justified in the name of the Lord Jesus and by the Spirit of our God.

By imputation of Christ's righteousness.

Is 61:10 I will greatly rejoice in the LORD, My soul shall be joyful in my God; For He has clothed me with the garments of salvation, He has covered me with the robe of righteousness, As a bridegroom decks *himself* with ornaments, And as a bride adorns *herself* with her jewels.

Jer 23:6 In His days Judah will be saved, And Israel will dwell safely; Now this *is* His name by which He will be called: THE LORD OUR RIGHTEOUSNESS.

Rom 3:22 even the righteousness of God, through faith in Jesus Christ, to all and on all who believe. For there is no difference;

Rom 5:18 Therefore, as through one man's offense *judgment* came to all men, resulting in condemnation, even so through one Man's righteous act *the free gift came* to all men, resulting in justification of life.

1 Cor 1:30 But of Him you are in Christ Jesus, who became for us wisdom from God—and righteousness and sanctification and redemption—

2 Cor 5:21 For He made Him who knew no sin *to be* sin for us, that we might become the righteousness of God in Him.

By the blood of Christ.

Rom 5:9 Much more then, having now been justified by His blood, we shall be saved from wrath through Him.

By the resurrection of Christ.

Rom 4:25 who was delivered up because of our offenses, and was raised because of our justification.

1 Cor 15:17 And if Christ is not risen, your faith *is* futile; you are still in your sins!

Blessedness of.

Ps 32:1–2 Blessed *is he whose* transgression *is* forgiven, *Whose* sin *is* covered. 2 Blessed *is* the man to whom the LORD does not impute iniquity, And in whose spirit *there is* no deceit.

Rom 4:6–8 just as David also describes the blessedness of the man to whom God imputes righteousness apart from works: 7 *"Blessed are those whose lawless deeds are forgiven, And whose sins are covered; 8 Blessed is the man to whom the LORD shall not impute sin."*

Frees from condemnation.

Is 50:8–9 *He is* near who justifies Me; Who will contend with Me? Let us stand together. Who *is* My adversary? Let him come near Me. 9 Surely the Lord GOD will help Me; Who *is* he *who* will condemn Me? Indeed they will all grow old like a garment; The moth will eat them up.

Is 54:17 No weapon formed against you shall prosper, And every tongue *which* rises against you in judgment You shall condemn. This *is* the heritage of the servants of the LORD, And their righteousness *is* from Me," Says the LORD.

Rom 8:33–34 Who shall bring a charge against God's elect? *It is* God who justifies. 34 Who *is* he who condemns? *It is* Christ who died, and furthermore is also risen, who is even at the right hand of God, who also makes intercession for us.

Entitles to an inheritance.

Titus 3:7 that having been justified by His grace we should become heirs according to the hope of eternal life.

Ensures glorification.

Rom 8:30 Moreover whom He predestined, these He also called; whom He called, these He also justified; and whom He justified, these He also glorified.

The wicked shall not attain to.

Ex 23:7 Keep yourself far from a false matter; do not kill the innocent and righteous. For I will not justify the wicked.

By faith,

Revealed under the Old Testament age.

Hab 2:4 "Behold the proud, His soul is not upright in him; But the just shall live by his faith.

Rom 1:17 For in it the righteousness of God is revealed from faith to faith; as it is written, *"The just shall live by faith."*

Excludes boasting.

Rom 3:27 Where *is* boasting then? It is excluded. By what law? Of works? No, but by the law of faith.

Rom 4:2 For if Abraham was justified by works, he has *something* to boast about, but not before God.

1 Cor 1:29 that no flesh should glory in His presence.

1 Cor 1:31 that, as it is written, *"He who glories, let him glory in the* LORD.*"*

Does not make void the law.

Rom 3:30–31 since *there is* one God who will justify the circumcised by faith and the uncircumcised through faith. **31** Do we then make void the law through faith? Certainly not! On the contrary, we establish the law.

1 Cor 9:21 to those *who are* without law, as without law (not being without law toward God, but under law toward Christ), that I might win those *who are* without law;

Typified.

Zech 3:4–5 Then He answered and spoke to those who stood before Him, saying, "Take away the filthy garments from him." And to him He said, "See, I have removed your iniquity from you, and I will clothe you with rich robes." **5** And I said, "Let them put a clean turban on his head." So they put a clean turban on his head, and they put the clothes on him. And the Angel of the LORD stood by.

Illustrated.

Luke 18:14 I tell you, this man went down to his house justified *rather* than the other; for everyone who exalts himself will be humbled, and he who humbles himself will be exalted."

Exemplified in

Abraham.

Gen 15:6 And he believed in the LORD, and He accounted it to him for righteousness.

Paul.

Phil 3:8–9 Yet indeed I also count all things loss for the excellence of the knowledge of Christ Jesus my Lord, for whom I have suffered the loss of all things, and count them as rubbish, that I may gain Christ **9** and be found in Him, not having my own righteousness, which *is* from the law, but that which *is* through faith in Christ, the righteousness which is from God by faith;

KENITES, THE

Originally a people of Canaan.

Gen 15:19 the Kenites, the Kenezzites, the Kadmonites,

Connected with the Midianites.

Num 10:29 Now Moses said to Hobab the son of Reuel the Midianite, Moses' father-in-law, "We are setting out for the place of which the LORD said, 'I will give it to you.' Come with us, and we will treat you well; for the LORD has promised good things to Israel."

Judg 4:11 Now Heber the Kenite, of the children of Hobab the father-in-law of Moses, had separated himself from the Kenites and pitched his tent near the terebinth tree at Zaanaim, which *is* beside Kedesh.

Dwelt in strongholds.

Num 24:21 Then he looked on the Kenites, and he took up his oracle and said: "Firm is your dwelling place, And your nest is set in the rock;

Had many cities.

1 Sam 30:29 *those* who *were* in Rachal, *those* who *were* in the cities of the Jerahmeelites, *those* who *were* in the cities of the Kenites,

Moses

Intermarried with.

Ex 2:21 Then Moses was content to live with the man, and he gave Zipporah his daughter to Moses.

Judg 1:16 Now the children of the Kenite, Moses' father-in-law, went up from the City of Palms with the children of Judah into the Wilderness of Judah, which *lies* in the South *near* Arad; and they went and dwelt among the people.

Invited, to accompany Israel.

Num 10:29–32 Now Moses said to Hobab the son of Reuel the Midianite, Moses' father-in-law, "We are setting out for the place of which the LORD said, 'I will give it to you.' Come with us, and we will treat you well; for the LORD has promised good things to Israel." **30** And he said to him, "I will not go, but I will depart to my *own* land and to my relatives." **31** So *Moses* said, "Please do not leave, inasmuch as you know how we are to camp in the wilderness, and you can be our eyes. **32** And it shall be, if you go with us—indeed it shall be—that whatever good the LORD will do to us, the same we will do to you."

Part of, dwelt with Israel.

Judg 1:16 Now the children of the Kenite, Moses' father-in-law, went up from the City of Palms with the children of Judah into the Wilderness of Judah, which *lies* in the South *near* Arad; and they went and dwelt among the people.

Judg 4:11 Now Heber the Kenite, of the children of Hobab the father-in-law of Moses, had separated himself from the Kenites and pitched his tent near the terebinth tree at Zaanaim, which *is* beside Kedesh.

Part of, dwelt with the Amalekites.

1 Sam 15:6 Then Saul said to the Kenites, "Go, depart, get down from among the Amalekites, lest I destroy you with them. For you showed kindness to all the children of Israel when they came up out of Egypt." So the Kenites departed from among the Amalekites.

Showed kindness to Israel in the desert. Ex 18:1–27

Not destroyed with the Amalekites.

1 Sam 15:6 Then Saul said to the Kenites, "Go, depart, get down from among the Amalekites, lest I destroy you with them. For you showed kindness to all the children of Israel when they came up out of Egypt." So the Kenites departed from among the Amalekites.

The Rechabites descended from.

1 Chr 2:55 And the families of the scribes who dwelt at Jabez *were* the Tirathites, the Shimeathites, *and* the Suchathites. These *were* the Kenites who came from Hammath, the father of the house of Rechab.

Sisera slain by Jael, one of.

Judg 4:22 And then, as Barak pursued Sisera, Jael came out to meet him, and said to him, "Come, I will show you the man whom you seek." And when he went into her *tent,* there lay Sisera, dead with the peg in his temple.

Judg 5:24 "Most blessed among women is Jael, The wife of Heber the Kenite; Blessed is she among women in tents.

David

Pretended that he invaded.

1 Sam 27:10 Then Achish would say, "Where have you made a raid today?" And David would say, "Against the southern *area* of Judah, or against the southern *area* of the Jerahmeelites, or against the southern *area* of the Kenites."

Sent part of the spoil of war to.

1 Sam 30:29 *those* who *were* in Rachal, *those* who *were* in the cities of the Jerahmeelites, *those* who *were* in the cities of the Kenites,

Ruin of, predicted.

Num 24:21–22 Then he looked on the Kenites, and he took up his oracle and said: "Firm is your dwelling place, And your nest is set in the rock; **22** Nevertheless Kain shall be burned. How long until Asshur carries you away captive?"

KINDNESS

Of God

Conveyed to the people.

Num 6:22–27 And the LORD spoke to Moses, saying:

23 "Speak to Aaron and his sons, saying, 'This is the way you shall bless the children of Israel. Say to them: 24 "The LORD bless you and keep you; 25 The LORD make His face shine upon you, And be gracious to you; 26 The LORD lift up His countenance upon you, And give you peace." ' 27 "So they shall put My name on the children of Israel, and I will bless them."

Cf. Matt 11:28–29; 19:13–14; 2 Tim 2:24; Titus 3:4

Toward Ruth.

Ruth 2:13–20 Then she said, "Let me find favor in your sight, my lord; for you have comforted me, and have spoken kindly to your maidservant, though I am not like one of your maidservants." 14 Now Boaz said to her at mealtime, "Come here, and eat of the bread, and dip your piece of bread in the vinegar." So she sat beside the reapers, and he passed parched *grain* to her; and she ate and was satisfied, and kept some back. 15 And when she rose up to glean, Boaz commanded his young men, saying, "Let her glean even among the sheaves, and do not reproach her. 16 Also let *grain* from the bundles fall purposely for her; leave *it* that she may glean, and do not rebuke her." 17 So she gleaned in the field until evening, and beat out what she had gleaned, and it was about an ephah of barley. 18 Then she took *it* up and went into the city, and her mother-in-law saw what she had gleaned. So she brought out and gave to her what she had kept back after she had been satisfied. 19 And her mother-in-law said to her, "Where have you gleaned today? And where did you work? Blessed be the one who took notice of you." So she told her mother-in-law with whom she had worked, and said, "The man's name with whom I worked today *is* Boaz." 20 Then Naomi said to her daughter-in-law, "Blessed *be* he of the LORD, who has not forsaken His kindness to the living and the dead!" And Naomi said to her, "This man *is* a relation of ours, one of our close relatives."

Acknowledged by Solomon.

1 Kin 3:6–9 And Solomon said: "You have shown great mercy to Your servant David my father, because he walked before You in truth, in righteousness, and in uprightness of heart with You; You have continued this great kindness for him, and You have given him a son to sit on his throne, as *it is* this day. 7 Now, O LORD my God, You have made Your servant king instead of my father David, but I *am* a little child; I do not know *how* to go out or come in. 8 And Your servant *is* in the midst of Your people whom You have chosen, a great people, too numerous to be numbered or counted. 9 Therefore give to Your servant an understanding heart to judge Your people, that I may discern between good and evil. For who is able to judge this great people of Yours?"

Remains for His people.

Is 54:10 For the mountains shall depart And the hills be removed, But My kindness shall not depart from you, Nor shall My covenant of peace be removed," Says the LORD, who has mercy on you.

Is 55:3 Incline your ear, and come to Me. Hear, and your soul shall live; And I will make an everlasting covenant with you— The sure mercies of David.

Is 59:21 "As for Me," says the LORD, "this *is* My covenant with them: My Spirit who *is* upon you, and My words which I have put in your mouth, shall not de-

part from your mouth, nor from the mouth of your descendants, nor from the mouth of your descendants' descendants," says the LORD, "from this time and forevermore."

Is 61:8 "For I, the LORD, love justice; I hate robbery for burnt offering; I will direct their work in truth, And will make with them an everlasting covenant.

Requested by Jonathan of David.

1 Sam 20:11–16 And Jonathan said to David, "Come, let us go out into the field." So both of them went out into the field. 12 Then Jonathan said to David: "The LORD God of Israel *is witness!* When I have sounded out my father sometime tomorrow, *or* the third *day,* and indeed *there is* good toward David, and I do not send to you and tell you, 13 may the LORD do so and much more to Jonathan. But if it pleases my father *to do* you evil, then I will report it to you and send you away, that you may go in safety. And the LORD be with you as He has been with my father. 14 And you shall not only show me the kindness of the LORD while I still live, that I may not die; 15 but you shall not cut off your kindness from my house forever, no, not when the LORD has cut off every one of the enemies of David from the face of the earth." 16 So Jonathan made *a covenant* with the house of David, *saying,* "Let the LORD require *it* at the hand of David's enemies."

Of David to Mephibosheth.

2 Sam 9:1–13 Now David said, "Is there still anyone who is left of the house of Saul, that I may show him kindness for Jonathan's sake?" 2 And *there was* a servant of the house of Saul whose name *was* Ziba. So when they had called him to David, the king said to him, "*Are* you Ziba?" He said, "At your service!" 3 Then the king said, "*Is* there not still someone of the house of Saul, to whom I may show the kindness of God?" And Ziba said to the king, "There is still a son of Jonathan *who is* lame in *his* feet." 4 So the king said to him, "Where *is* he?" And Ziba said to the king, "Indeed he *is* in the house of Machir the son of Ammiel, in Lo Debar." 5 Then King David sent and brought him out of the house of Machir the son of Ammiel, from Lo Debar. 6 Now when Mephibosheth the son of Jonathan, the son of Saul, had come to David, he fell on his face and prostrated himself. Then David said, "Mephibosheth?" And he answered, "Here is your servant!" 7 So David said to him, "Do not fear, for I will surely show you kindness for Jonathan your father's sake, and will restore to you all the land of Saul your grandfather; and you shall eat bread at my table continually." 8 Then he bowed himself, and said, "What *is* your servant, that you should look upon such a dead dog as I?" 9 And the king called to Ziba, Saul's servant, and said to him, "I have given to your master's son all that belonged to Saul and to all his house. 10 You therefore, and your sons and your servants, shall work the land for him, and you shall bring in *the harvest,* that your master's son may have food to eat. But Mephibosheth your master's son shall eat bread at my table always." Now Ziba had fifteen sons and twenty servants. 11 Then Ziba said to the king, "According to all that my lord the king has commanded his servant, so will your servant do." "As for Mephibosheth," *said the king,* "he shall eat at my table like one of the king's sons." **12** Mephibosheth had a young son whose name *was* Micha. And all who dwelt in the house of Ziba *were* servants of Mephibosheth. **13** So Mephibosheth dwelt in Jerusalem, for he ate continually at the king's table. And he was lame in both his feet.

Job responded to Eliphaz for lack of.

Job 6:14 "To him who is afflicted, kindness *should be shown* by his friend, Even though he forsakes the fear of the Almighty.

To be shown toward enemies.

Prov 25:21–22 If your enemy is hungry, give him bread to eat; And if he is thirsty, give him water to drink; **22** For *so* you will heap coals of fire on his head, And the LORD will reward you.

Matt 5:43–48 "You have heard that it was said, '*You shall love your neighbor* and hate your enemy.' **44** But I say to you, love your enemies, bless those who curse you, do good to those who hate you, and pray for those who spitefully use you and persecute you, **45** that you may be sons of your Father in heaven; for He makes His sun rise on the evil and on the good, and sends rain on the just and on the unjust. **46** For if you love those who love you, what reward have you? Do not even the tax collectors do the same? **47** And if you greet your brethren only, what do you do more *than others?* Do not even the tax collectors do so? **48** Therefore you shall be perfect, just as your Father in heaven is perfect.

Rom 12:20 Therefore *"If your enemy is hungry, feed him; If he is thirsty, give him a drink; For in so doing you will heap coals of fire on his head."*

Characterizes a virtuous wife.

Prov 31:26 She opens her mouth with wisdom, And on her tongue *is* the law of kindness.

Part of the fruit of the Spirit.

Gal 5:22 But the fruit of the Spirit is love, joy, peace, longsuffering, kindness, goodness, faithfulness,

Col 3:12 Therefore, as *the* elect of God, holy and beloved, put on tender mercies, kindness, humility, meekness, longsuffering;

2 Pet 1:7 to godliness brotherly kindness, and to brotherly kindness love.

Cf. Luke 10:25–37

KINGDOM, SPIRITUAL

Parables of.

Matt 13:24–30 Another parable He put forth to them, saying: "The kingdom of heaven is like a man who sowed good seed in his field; **25** but while men slept, his enemy came and sowed tares among the wheat and went his way. **26** But when the grain had sprouted and produced a crop, then the tares also appeared. **27** So the servants of the owner came and said to him, 'Sir, did you not sow good seed in your field? How then does it have tares?' **28** He said to them, 'An enemy has done this.' The servants said to him, 'Do you want us then to go and gather them up?' **29** But he said, 'No, lest while you gather up the tares you also uproot the wheat with them. **30** Let both grow together until the harvest, and at the time of harvest I will say to the reapers, "First gather together the tares and bind them in bundles to burn them, but gather the wheat into my barn." ' "

Matt 13:31–32 Another parable He put forth to them, saying: "The kingdom of heaven is like a mustard seed, which a man took and sowed in his field, **32** which indeed is the least of all the seeds; but when it is grown it is greater than the herbs and becomes a tree, so that the birds of the air come and nest in its branches."

Matt 13:38–43 The field is the world, the good seeds are the sons of the kingdom, but the tares are the sons of the wicked *one*. **39** The enemy who sowed them is the devil, the harvest is the end of the age, and the reapers are the angels. **40** Therefore as the tares are gathered and burned in the fire, so it will be at the end of this age. **41** The Son of Man will send out His angels, and they will gather out of His kingdom all things that offend, and those who practice lawlessness, **42** and will cast them into the furnace of fire. There will be wailing and gnashing of teeth. **43** Then the righteous will shine forth as the sun in the kingdom of their Father. He who has ears to hear, let him hear!

Matt 13:47–50 "Again, the kingdom of heaven is like a dragnet that was cast into the sea and gathered some of every kind, **48** which, when it was full, they drew to shore; and they sat down and gathered the good into vessels, but threw the bad away. **49** So it will be at the end of the age. The angels will come forth, separate the wicked from among the just, **50** and cast them into the furnace of fire. There will be wailing and gnashing of teeth."

Matt 20:1–16 "For the kingdom of heaven is like a landowner who went out early in the morning to hire laborers for his vineyard. **2** Now when he had agreed with the laborers for a denarius a day, he sent them into his vineyard. **3** And he went out about the third hour and saw others standing idle in the marketplace, **4** and said to them, 'You also go into the vineyard, and whatever is right I will give you.' So they went. **5** Again he went out about the sixth and the ninth hour, and did likewise. **6** And about the eleventh hour he went out and found others standing idle, and said to them, 'Why have you been standing here idle all day?' **7** They said to him, 'Because no one hired us.' He said to them, 'You also go into the vineyard, and whatever is right you will receive.' **8** "So when evening had come, the owner of the vineyard said to his steward, 'Call the laborers and give them *their* wages, beginning with the last to the first.' **9** And when those came who *were* hired about the eleventh hour, they each received a denarius. **10** But when the first came, they supposed that they would receive more; and they likewise received each a denarius. **11** And when they had received *it*, they complained against the landowner, **12** saying, 'These last *men* have worked *only* one hour, and you made them equal to us who have borne the burden and the heat of the day.' **13** But he answered one of them and said, 'Friend, I am doing you no wrong. Did you not agree with me for a denarius? **14** Take *what is* yours and go your way. I wish to give to this last man *the same* as to you. **15** Is it not lawful for me to do what I wish with my own things? Or is your eye evil because I am good?' **16** So the last will be first, and the first last. For many are called, but few chosen."

Matt 22:2–14 "The kingdom of heaven is like a certain king who arranged a marriage for his son, **3** and sent out his servants to call those who were invited to the wedding; and they were not willing to come. **4** Again, he sent out other servants, saying, 'Tell those who are invited, "See, I have prepared my dinner; my oxen and fatted cattle *are* killed, and all things *are* ready. Come to the wedding." ' **5** But they made light of it and went their ways, one to his own farm, another to his business. **6** And the rest seized his servants, treated *them* spitefully, and killed *them.* **7** But when the king heard *about it,* he was furious. And he sent out his armies, destroyed those murderers, and burned up their city. **8** Then he said to his servants, 'The wedding is ready, but those who were invited were not worthy. **9** Therefore go into the highways, and as many as you find, invite to the wedding.' **10** So those servants went out into the highways and gathered together all whom they found, both bad and good. And the wedding *hall* was filled with guests. **11** "But when the king came in to see the guests, he saw a man there who did not have on a wedding garment. **12** So he said to him, 'Friend, how did you come in here without a wedding garment?' And he was speechless. **13** Then the king said to the servants, 'Bind him hand and foot, take him away, and cast *him* into outer darkness; there will be weeping and gnashing of teeth.' **14** "For many are called, but few *are* chosen."

Cf. Matt 21:28–45; 25:1–30; Mark 4:26–32; 12:1–12; Luke 1:32–33; 13:18–19; 14:16–24; 19:11–27; 20:9–19; 22:29

Greatness and extent of.

Ps 22:27–28 All the ends of the world Shall remember and turn to the LORD, And all the families of the nations Shall worship before You. **28** For the kingdom *is* the LORD's, And He rules over the nations.

Ps 72:5 They shall fear You As long as the sun and moon endure, Throughout all generations.

Ps 72:8–17 He shall have dominion also from sea to sea, And from the River to the ends of the earth. **9** Those who dwell in the wilderness will bow before Him, And His enemies will lick the dust. **10** The kings of Tarshish and of the isles Will bring presents; The kings of Sheba and Seba Will offer gifts. **11** Yes, all kings shall fall down before Him; All nations shall serve Him. **12** For He will deliver the needy when he cries, The poor also, and *him* who has no helper. **13** He will spare the poor and needy, And will save the souls of the needy. **14** He will redeem their life from oppression and violence; And precious shall be their blood in His sight. **15** And He shall live; And the gold of Sheba will be given to Him; Prayer also will be made for Him continually, *And* daily He shall be praised. **16** There will be an abundance of grain in the earth, On the top of the mountains; Its fruit shall wave like Lebanon; And *those* of the city shall flourish like grass of the earth. **17** His name shall endure forever; His name shall continue as long as the sun. And *men* shall be blessed in Him; All nations shall call Him blessed.

Ps 138:4–5 All the kings of the earth shall praise You, O LORD, When they hear the words of Your mouth. **5** Yes, they shall sing of the ways of the LORD, For great *is* the glory of the LORD.

Is 2:2–4 Now it shall come to pass in the latter days *That* the mountain of the LORD's house Shall be established on the top of the mountains, And shall be exalted above the hills; And all nations shall flow to it. **3** Many people shall come and say, "Come, and let us go up to the mountain of the LORD, To the house of the God of Jacob; He will teach us His ways, And we shall walk in His paths." For out of Zion shall go forth the law, And the word of the LORD from Jerusalem. **4** He shall judge between the nations, And rebuke many people; They shall beat their swords into plowshares, And their spears into pruning hooks; Nation shall not lift up sword against nation, Neither shall they learn war anymore.

Is 9:7 Of the increase of *His* government and peace *There will be* no end, Upon the throne of David and over His kingdom, To order it and establish it with judgment and justice From that time forward, even forever. The zeal of the Lord of hosts will perform this.

Is 59:19 So shall they fear The name of the LORD from the west, And His glory from the rising of the sun; When the enemy comes in like a flood, The Spirit of the LORD will lift up a standard against him.

Is 60:1–4 Arise, shine; For your light has come! And the glory of the LORD is risen upon you. **2** For behold, the darkness shall cover the earth, And deep darkness the people; But the LORD will arise over you, And His glory will be seen upon you. **3** The Gentiles shall come to your light, And kings to the brightness of your rising. **4** "Lift up your eyes all around, and see: They all gather together, they come to you; Your sons shall come from afar, And your daughters shall be nursed at *your* side.

Dan 2:44 And in the days of these kings the God of heaven will set up a kingdom which shall never be destroyed; and the kingdom shall not be left to other people; it shall break in pieces and consume all these kingdoms, and it shall stand forever.

Dan 7:9–14 "I watched till thrones were put in place, And the Ancient of Days was seated; His garment *was* white as snow, And the hair of His head *was* like pure wool. His throne *was* a fiery flame, Its wheels a burning fire; **10** A fiery stream issued And came forth from before Him. A thousand thousands ministered to Him; Ten thousand times ten thousand stood before Him. The court was seated, And the books were opened. **11** "I watched then because of the sound of the pompous words which the horn was speaking; I watched till the beast was slain, and its body destroyed and given to the burning flame. **12** As for the rest of the beasts, they had their dominion taken away, yet their lives were prolonged for a season and a time. **13** "I was watching in the night visions, And behold, *One* like the Son of Man, Coming with the clouds of heaven! He came to the Ancient of Days, And they brought Him near before Him. **14** Then to Him was given dominion and glory and a kingdom, That all peoples, nations, and languages should serve Him. His dominion *is* an everlasting dominion, Which shall not pass away, And His kingdom *the one* Which shall not be destroyed.

Dan 7:27 Then the kingdom and dominion, And the greatness of the kingdoms under the whole heaven,

Shall be given to the people, the saints of the Most High. His kingdom *is* an everlasting kingdom, And all dominions shall serve and obey Him.'

Mic 4:1–3 Now it shall come to pass in the latter days *That* the mountain of the LORD's house Shall be established on the top of the mountains, And shall be exalted above the hills; And peoples shall flow to it. **2** Many nations shall come and say, "Come, and let us go up to the mountain of the LORD, To the house of the God of Jacob; He will teach us His ways, And we shall walk in His paths." For out of Zion the law shall go forth, And the word of the LORD from Jerusalem. **3** He shall judge between many peoples, And rebuke strong nations afar off; They shall beat their swords into plowshares, And their spears into pruning hooks; Nation shall not lift up sword against nation, Neither shall they learn war anymore.

Heb 1:8 But to the Son *He says: "Your throne, O God, is forever and ever; A scepter of righteousness is the scepter of Your kingdom.*

2 Pet 1:11 for so an entrance will be supplied to you abundantly into the everlasting kingdom of our Lord and Savior Jesus Christ.

Rev 5:9 And they sang a new song, saying: "You are worthy to take the scroll, And to open its seals; For You were slain, And have redeemed us to God by Your blood Out of every tribe and tongue and people and nation,

Rev 5:13–14 And every creature which is in heaven and on the earth and under the earth and such as are in the sea, and all that are in them, I heard saying: "Blessing and honor and glory and power *Be* to Him who sits on the throne, And to the Lamb, forever and ever!" **14** Then the four living creatures said, "Amen!" And the twenty-four elders fell down and worshiped Him who lives forever and ever.

Rev 11:15 Then the seventh angel sounded: And there were loud voices in heaven, saying, "The kingdoms of this world have become *the kingdoms* of our Lord and of His Christ, and He shall reign forever and ever!"

Rev 19:6 And I heard, as it were, the voice of a great multitude, as the sound of many waters and as the sound of mighty thunderings, saying, "Alleluia! For the Lord God Omnipotent reigns!

Nature of.

Mark 1:15 and saying, "The time is fulfilled, and the kingdom of God is at hand. Repent, and believe in the gospel."

Luke 17:21 nor will they say, 'See here!' or 'See there!' For indeed, the kingdom of God is within you."

John 18:36 Jesus answered, "My kingdom is not of this world. If My kingdom were of this world, My servants would fight, so that I should not be delivered to the Jews; but now My kingdom is not from here."

Rom 14:17 for the kingdom of God is not eating and drinking, but righteousness and peace and joy in the Holy Spirit.

Eph 5:5 For this you know, that no fornicator, unclean person, nor covetous man, who is an idolater, has any inheritance in the kingdom of Christ and God.

Col 1:13 He has delivered us from the power of darkness and conveyed *us* into the kingdom of the Son of His love,

Entrance to, means of.

Matt 3:2 and saying, "Repent, for the kingdom of heaven is at hand!"

Matt 18:3 and said, "Assuredly, I say to you, unless you are converted and become as little children, you will by no means enter the kingdom of heaven.

Mark 10:15 Assuredly, I say to you, whoever does not receive the kingdom of God as a little child will by no means enter it."

Luke 18:17 Assuredly, I say to you, whoever does not receive the kingdom of God as a little child will by no means enter it."

John 3:1–8 There was a man of the Pharisees named Nicodemus, a ruler of the Jews. **2** This man came to Jesus by night and said to Him, "Rabbi, we know that You are a teacher come from God; for no one can do these signs that You do unless God is with him." **3** Jesus answered and said to him, "Most assuredly, I say to you, unless one is born again, he cannot see the kingdom of God." **4** Nicodemus said to Him, "How can a man be born when he is old? Can he enter a second time into his mother's womb and be born?" **5** Jesus answered, "Most assuredly, I say to you, unless one is born of water and the Spirit, he cannot enter the kingdom of God. **6** That which is born of the flesh is flesh, and that which is born of the Spirit is spirit. **7** Do not marvel that I said to you, 'You must be born again.' **8** The wind blows where it wishes, and you hear the sound of it, but cannot tell where it comes from and where it goes. So is everyone who is born of the Spirit."

1 Thess 2:12 that you would walk worthy of God who calls you into His own kingdom and glory.

And the rich.

Matt 19:23–24 Then Jesus said to His disciples, "Assuredly, I say to you that it is hard for a rich man to enter the kingdom of heaven. **24** And again I say to you, it is easier for a camel to go through the eye of a needle than for a rich man to enter the kingdom of God."

Mark 10:23–25 Then Jesus looked around and said to His disciples, "How hard it is for those who have riches to enter the kingdom of God!" **24** And the disciples were astonished at His words. But Jesus answered again and said to them, "Children, how hard it is for those who trust in riches to enter the kingdom of God! **25** It is easier for a camel to go through the eye of a needle than for a rich man to enter the kingdom of God."

Luke 18:24–25 And when Jesus saw that he became very sorrowful, He said, "How hard it is for those who have riches to enter the kingdom of God! **25** For it is easier for a camel to go through the eye of a needle than for a rich man to enter the kingdom of God."

Luke 18:29–30 So He said to them, "Assuredly, I say to you, there is no one who has left house or parents or brothers or wife or children, for the sake of the kingdom of God, **30** who shall not receive many times more in this present time, and in the age to come eternal life."

Members of

Pray for it.

Matt 6:10 Your kingdom come. Your will be done On earth as *it is* in heaven.

Seek it first.

Matt 6:33 But seek first the kingdom of God and His righteousness, and all these things shall be added to you.

Work in it.

Col 4:11 and Jesus who is called Justus. These *are my* only fellow workers for the kingdom of God who are of the circumcision; they have proved to be a comfort to me.

KINGS

Israel warned against seeking.

1 Sam 8:9–18 Now therefore, heed their voice. However, you shall solemnly forewarn them, and show them the behavior of the king who will reign over them." **10** So Samuel told all the words of the LORD to the people who asked him for a king. **11** And he said, "This will be the behavior of the king who will reign over you: He will take your sons and appoint *them* for his own chariots and *to be* his horsemen, and *some* will run before his chariots. **12** He will appoint captains over his thousands and captains over his fifties, *will set some* to plow his ground and reap his harvest, and *some* to make his weapons of war and equipment for his chariots. **13** He will take your daughters *to be* perfumers, cooks, and bakers. **14** And he will take the best of your fields, your vineyards, and your olive groves, and give *them* to his servants. **15** He will take a tenth of your grain and your vintage, and give it to his officers and servants. **16** And he will take your male servants, your female servants, your finest young men, and your donkeys, and put *them* to his work. **17** He will take a tenth of your sheep. And you will be his servants. **18** And you will cry out in that day because of your king whom you have chosen for yourselves, and the LORD will not hear you in that day."

Sin of Israel in seeking.

1 Sam 12:17–20 *Is* today not the wheat harvest? I will call to the LORD, and He will send thunder and rain, that you may perceive and see that your wickedness *is* great, which you have done in the sight of the LORD, in asking a king for yourselves." **18** So Samuel called to the LORD, and the LORD sent thunder and rain that day; and all the people greatly feared the LORD and Samuel. **19** And all the people said to Samuel, "Pray for your servants to the LORD your God, that we may not die; for we have added to all our sins the evil of asking a king for ourselves." **20** Then Samuel said to the people, "Do not fear. You have done all this wickedness; yet do not turn aside from following the LORD, but serve the LORD with all your heart.

Israel in seeking, rejected God as their king.

1 Sam 8:7 And the LORD said to Samuel, "Heed the voice of the people in all that they say to you; for they have not rejected you, but they have rejected Me, that I should not reign over them.

1 Sam 10:19 But you have today rejected your God, who Himself saved you from all your adversities

and your tribulations; and you have said to Him, 'No, set a king over us!' Now therefore, present yourselves before the LORD by your tribes and by your clans."

Israel asked for, that they might be like the nations.

1 Sam 8:5 and said to him, "Look, you are old, and your sons do not walk in your ways. Now make us a king to judge us like all the nations."

1 Sam 8:19–20 Nevertheless the people refused to obey the voice of Samuel; and they said, "No, but we will have a king over us, **20** that we also may be like all the nations, and that our king may judge us and go out before us and fight our battles."

First given to Israel in divine anger.

Hos 13:11 I gave you a king in My anger, And took *him* away in My wrath.

God reserved to Himself the choice of.

Deut 17:14–15 "When you come to the land which the LORD your God is giving you, and possess it and dwell in it, and say, 'I will set a king over me like all the nations that *are* around me,' **15** you shall surely set a king over you whom the LORD your God chooses; *one* from among your brethren you shall set as king over you; you may not set a foreigner over you, who *is* not your brother.

1 Sam 9:16–17 "Tomorrow about this time I will send you a man from the land of Benjamin, and you shall anoint him commander over My people Israel, that he may save My people from the hand of the Philistines; for I have looked upon My people, because their cry has come to Me." **17** So when Samuel saw Saul, the LORD said to him, "There he is, the man of whom I spoke to you. This one shall reign over My people."

1 Sam 16:12 So he sent and brought him in. Now he *was* ruddy, with bright eyes, and good-looking. And the LORD said, "Arise, anoint him; for this *is* the one!"

When first established in Israel, not hereditary.

Deut 17:20 that his heart may not be lifted above his brethren, that he may not turn aside from the commandment *to* the right hand or *to* the left, and that he may prolong *his* days in his kingdom, he and his children in the midst of Israel.

1 Sam 13:13–14 And Samuel said to Saul, "You have done foolishly. You have not kept the commandment of the LORD your God, which He commanded you. For now the LORD would have established your kingdom over Israel forever. **14** But now your kingdom shall not continue. The LORD has sought for Himself a man after His own heart, and the LORD has commanded him *to be* commander over His people, because you have not kept what the LORD commanded you."

1 Sam 15:28–29 So Samuel said to him, "The LORD has torn the kingdom of Israel from you today, and has given it to a neighbor of yours, *who is* better than you. **29** And also the Strength of Israel will not lie nor relent. For He *is* not a man, that He should relent."

Rendered hereditary in the family of David.

2 Sam 7:12–16 "When your days are fulfilled and you rest with your fathers, I will set up your seed after you, who will come from your body, and I will establish his kingdom. 13 He shall build a house for My name, and I will establish the throne of his kingdom forever. 14 I will be his Father, and he shall be My son. If he commits iniquity, I will chasten him with the rod of men and with the blows of the sons of men. 15 But My mercy shall not depart from him, as I took *it* from Saul, whom I removed from before you. 16 And your house and your kingdom shall be established forever before you. Your throne shall be established forever." ' "

Ps 89:35–37 Once I have sworn by My holiness; I will not lie to David: 36 His seed shall endure forever, And his throne as the sun before Me; 37 It shall be established forever like the moon, Even *like* the faithful witness in the sky." Selah

Of Israel not to be foreigners.

Deut 17:15 you shall surely set a king over you whom the LORD your God chooses; *one* from among your brethren you shall set as king over you; you may not set a foreigner over you, who *is* not your brother.

Laws for the government of the kingdom by, written by Samuel.

1 Sam 10:25 Then Samuel explained to the people the behavior of royalty, and wrote *it* in a book and laid *it* up before the LORD. And Samuel sent all the people away, every man to his house.

Things they were forbidden to multiply

Horses.

Deut 17:16 But he shall not multiply horses for himself, nor cause the people to return to Egypt to multiply horses, for the LORD has said to you, 'You shall not return that way again.'

Wives.

Deut 17:17 Neither shall he multiply wives for himself, lest his heart turn away; nor shall he greatly multiply silver and gold for himself.

Treasure.

Deut 17:17 Neither shall he multiply wives for himself, lest his heart turn away; nor shall he greatly multiply silver and gold for himself.

Required to write and keep by them a copy of the divine law.

Deut 17:18–20 "Also it shall be, when he sits on the throne of his kingdom, that he shall write for himself a copy of this law in a book, from *the one* before the priests, the Levites. 19 And it shall be with him, and he shall read it all the days of his life, that he may learn to fear the LORD his God and be careful to observe all the words of this law and these statutes, 20 that his heart may not be lifted above his brethren, that he may not turn aside from the commandment *to* the right hand or *to* the left, and that he may prolong *his* days in his kingdom, he and his children in the midst of Israel.

Had power to make war and peace.

1 Sam 11:5–7 Now there was Saul, coming behind the herd from the field; and Saul said, "What *troubles* the people, that they weep?" And they told him the words of the men of Jabesh. 6 Then the Spirit of God came upon Saul when he heard this news, and his anger was greatly aroused. 7 So he took a yoke of

oxen and cut them in pieces, and sent *them* throughout all the territory of Israel by the hands of messengers, saying, "Whoever does not go out with Saul and Samuel to battle, so it shall be done to his oxen." And the fear of the LORD fell on the people, and they came out with one consent.

Often exercised power arbitrarily.

1 Sam 22:17–18 Then the king said to the guards who stood about him, "Turn and kill the priests of the LORD, because their hand also *is* with David, and because they knew when he fled and did not tell it to me." But the servants of the king would not lift their hands to strike the priests of the LORD. 18 And the king said to Doeg, "You turn and kill the priests!" So Doeg the Edomite turned and struck the priests, and killed on that day eighty-five men who wore a linen ephod.

2 Sam 1:15 Then David called one of the young men and said, "Go near, *and* execute him!" And he struck him so that he died.

2 Sam 4:9–12 But David answered Rechab and Baanah his brother, the sons of Rimmon the Beerothite, and said to them, "*As* the LORD lives, who has redeemed my life from all adversity, 10 when someone told me, saying, 'Look, Saul is dead,' thinking to have brought good news, I arrested him and had him executed in Ziklag—the one who *thought* I would give him a reward for *his* news. 11 How much more, when wicked men have killed a righteous person in his own house on his bed? Therefore, shall I not now require his blood at your hand and remove you from the earth?" 12 So David commanded his young men, and they executed them, cut off their hands and feet, and hanged *them* by the pool in Hebron. But they took the head of Ishbosheth and buried *it* in the tomb of Abner in Hebron.

1 Kin 2:23 Then King Solomon swore by the LORD, saying, "May God do so to me, and more also, if Adonijah has not spoken this word against his own life!

1 Kin 2:25 So King Solomon sent by the hand of Benaiah the son of Jehoiada; and he struck him down, and he died.

1 Kin 2:31 Then the king said to him, "Do as he has said, and strike him down and bury him, that you may take away from me and from the house of my father the innocent blood which Joab shed.

Ceremonies at inauguration of,

Anointing.

1 Sam 10:1 Then Samuel took a flask of oil and poured *it* on his head, and kissed him and said: "*Is it* not because the LORD has anointed you commander over His inheritance?

1 Sam 16:13 Then Samuel took the horn of oil and anointed him in the midst of his brothers; and the Spirit of the LORD came upon David from that day forward. So Samuel arose and went to Ramah.

Ps 89:20 I have found My servant David; With My holy oil I have anointed him,

Crowning.

2 Kin 11:12 And he brought out the king's son, put the crown on him, and *gave him* the Testimony; they made him king and anointed him, and they clapped their hands and said, "Long live the king!"

2 Chr 23:11 And they brought out the king's son, put the crown on him, *gave him* the Testimony, and made him king. Then Jehoiada and his sons anointed him, and said, "*Long* live the king!"

Ps 21:3 For You meet him with the blessings of goodness; You set a crown of pure gold upon his head.

Proclaiming with trumpets.

2 Sam 15:10 Then Absalom sent spies throughout all the tribes of Israel, saying, "As soon as you hear the sound of the trumpet, then you shall say, 'Absalom reigns in Hebron!' "

1 Kin 1:34 There let Zadok the priest and Nathan the prophet anoint him king over Israel; and blow the horn, and say, 'Long live King Solomon!'

2 Kin 9:13 Then each man hastened to take his garment and put *it* under him on the top of the steps; and they blew trumpets, saying, "Jehu is king!"

2 Kin 11:14 When she looked, there was the king standing by a pillar according to custom; and the leaders and the trumpeters were by the king. All the people of the land were rejoicing and blowing trumpets. So Athaliah tore her clothes and cried out, "Treason! Treason!"

Enthroning.

1 Kin 1:35 Then you shall come up after him, and he shall come and sit on my throne, and he shall be king in my place. For I have appointed him to be ruler over Israel and Judah."

1 Kin 1:46 Also Solomon sits on the throne of the kingdom.

2 Kin 11:19 Then he took the captains of hundreds, the bodyguards, the escorts, and all the people of the land; and they brought the king down from the house of the LORD, and went by way of the gate of the escorts to the king's house. Then he sat on the throne of the kings.

Girding on the sword.

Ps 45:3 Gird Your sword upon *Your* thigh, O Mighty One, With Your glory and Your majesty.

Putting into their hands the Testimony.

2 Kin 11:12 And he brought out the king's son, put the crown on him, and *gave him* the Testimony; they made him king and anointed him, and they clapped their hands and said, "Long live the king!"

2 Chr 23:11 And they brought out the king's son, put the crown on him, *gave him* the Testimony, and made him king. Then Jehoiada and his sons anointed him, and said, "*Long* live the king!"

Covenanting to govern lawfully.

2 Sam 5:3 Therefore all the elders of Israel came to the king at Hebron, and King David made a covenant with them at Hebron before the LORD. And they anointed David king over Israel.

Receiving homage.

1 Sam 10:1 Then Samuel took a flask of oil and poured *it* on his head, and kissed him and said: "*Is it* not because the LORD has anointed you commander over His inheritance?

1 Chr 29:24 All the leaders and the mighty men, and also all the sons of King David, submitted themselves to King Solomon.

Shouting "Long live the king."

1 Sam 10:24 And Samuel said to all the people, "Do you see him whom the LORD has chosen, that *there is* no one like him among all the people?" So all the people shouted and said, "Long live the king!"

2 Sam 16:16 And so it was, when Hushai the Archite, David's friend, came to Absalom, that Hushai said to Absalom, "*Long* live the king! *Long* live the king!"

2 Kin 11:12 And he brought out the king's son, put the crown on him, and *gave him* the Testimony; they made him king and anointed him, and they clapped their hands and said, "Long live the king!"

Offering sacrifice.

1 Sam 11:15 So all the people went to Gilgal, and there they made Saul king before the LORD in Gilgal. There they made sacrifices of peace offerings before the LORD, and there Saul and all the men of Israel rejoiced greatly.

Feasting.

1 Chr 12:38–39 All these men of war, who could keep ranks, came to Hebron with a loyal heart, to make David king over all Israel; and all the rest of Israel *were* of one mind to make David king. **39** And they were there with David three days, eating and drinking, for their brethren had prepared for them.

1 Chr 29:22 So they ate and drank before the LORD with great gladness on that day. And they made Solomon the son of David king the second time, and anointed *him* before the LORD *to be* the leader, and Zadok *to be* priest.

Attended by a bodyguard.

1 Sam 13:2 Saul chose for himself three thousand *men* of Israel. Two thousand were with Saul in Michmash and in the mountains of Bethel, and a thousand were with Jonathan in Gibeah of Benjamin. The rest of the people he sent away, every man to his tent.

2 Sam 8:18 Benaiah the son of Jehoiada *was over* both the Cherethites and the Pelethites; and David's sons were chief ministers.

1 Chr 11:25 Indeed he was more honored than the thirty, but he did not attain to the *first* three. And David appointed him over his guard.

2 Chr 12:10 Then King Rehoboam made bronze shields in their place, and committed *them* to the hands of the captains of the guard, who guarded the doorway of the king's house.

Dwelt in royal palaces.

2 Chr 9:11 And the king made walkways *of* the algum wood for the house of the LORD and for the king's house, also harps and stringed instruments for singers; and there were none such *as these* seen before in the land of Judah.

Ps 45:15 With gladness and rejoicing they shall be brought; They shall enter the King's palace.

Arrayed in royal apparel.

1 Kin 22:30 And the king of Israel said to Jehoshaphat, "I will disguise myself and go into battle; but you put on your robes." So the king of Israel disguised himself and went into battle.

Matt 6:29 and yet I say to you that even Solomon in all his glory was not arrayed like one of these.

Names of, often changed at their accession.

2 Kin 23:34 Then Pharaoh Necho made Eliakim the son of Josiah king in place of his father Josiah, and changed his name to Jehoiakim. And *Pharaoh* took Jehoahaz and went to Egypt, and he died there.

2 Kin 24:17 Then the king of Babylon made Mattaniah, *Jehoiachin's* uncle, king in his place, and changed his name to Zedekiah.

Officers of,

Prime minister.

2 Chr 19:11 And take notice: Amariah the chief priest *is* over you in all matters of the LORD; and Zebadiah the son of Ishmael, the ruler of the house of Judah, for all the king's matters; also the Levites *will be* officials before you. Behave courageously, and the LORD will be with the good."

2 Chr 28:7 Zichri, a mighty man of Ephraim, killed Maaseiah the king's son, Azrikam the officer over the house, and Elkanah *who was* second to the king.

First counselor.

1 Chr 27:33 Ahithophel *was* the king's counselor, and Hushai the Archite *was* the king's companion.

Confidant or king's special friend.

1 Kin 4:5 Azariah the son of Nathan, over the officers; Zabud the son of Nathan, a priest *and* the king's friend;

1 Chr 27:33 Ahithophel *was* the king's counselor, and Hushai the Archite *was* the king's companion.

Controller of the household.

1 Kin 4:6 Ahishar, over the household; and Adoniram the son of Abda, over the labor force.

2 Chr 28:7 Zichri, a mighty man of Ephraim, killed Maaseiah the king's son, Azrikam the officer over the house, and Elkanah *who was* second to the king.

Scribe or recorder.

2 Sam 8:17 Zadok the son of Ahitub and Ahimelech the son of Abiathar *were* the priests; Seraiah *was* the scribe;

1 Kin 4:3 Elihoreph and Ahijah, the sons of Shisha, scribes; Jehoshaphat the son of Ahilud, the recorder;

Captain of the army.

2 Sam 8:16 Joab the son of Zeruiah *was* over the army; Jehoshaphat the son of Ahilud *was* recorder;

1 Kin 4:4 Benaiah the son of Jehoiada, over the army; Zadok and Abiathar, the priests;

Captain of the guard.

2 Sam 8:18 Benaiah the son of Jehoiada *was over* both the Cherethites and the Pelethites; and David's sons were chief ministers.

2 Sam 20:23 And Joab *was* over all the army of Israel; Benaiah the son of Jehoiada *was* over the Cherethites and the Pelethites;

Recorder.

2 Sam 8:16 Joab the son of Zeruiah *was* over the army; Jehoshaphat the son of Ahilud *was* recorder;

1 Kin 4:3 Elihoreph and Ahijah, the sons of Shisha, scribes; Jehoshaphat the son of Ahilud, the recorder;

Providers for the king's table.

1 Kin 4:7–19 And Solomon had twelve governors over all Israel, who provided food for the king and his household; each one made provision for one month of the year. **8** These *are* their names: Ben-Hur, in the mountains of Ephraim; **9** Ben-Deker, in Makaz, Shaalbim, Beth Shemesh, and Elon Beth Hanan; **10** Ben-Hesed, in Arubboth; to him *belonged* Sochoh and all the land of Hepher; **11** Ben-Abinadab, *in* all the regions of Dor; he had Taphath the daughter of Solomon as wife; **12** Baana the son of Ahilud, *in* Taanach, Megiddo, and all Beth Shean, which *is* beside Zaretan below Jezreel, from Beth Shean to Abel Meholah, as far as the other side of Jokneam; **13** Ben-Geber, in Ramoth Gilead; to him *belonged* the towns of Jair the son of Manasseh, in Gilead; to him *also belonged* the region of Argob in Bashan—sixty large cities with walls and bronze gate-bars; **14** Ahinadab the son of Iddo, *in* Mahanaim; **15** Ahimaaz, in Naphtali; he also took Basemath the daughter of Solomon as wife; **16** Baanah the son of Hushai, in Asher and Aloth; **17** Jehoshaphat the son of Paruah, in Issachar; **18** Shimei the son of Elah, in Benjamin; **19** Geber the son of Uri, in the land of Gilead, *in* the country of Sihon king of the Amorites, and of Og king of Bashan. *He was* the only governor who *was* in the land.

Keeper of the wardrobe.

2 Kin 22:14 So Hilkiah the priest, Ahikam, Achbor, Shaphan, and Asaiah went to Huldah the prophetess, the wife of Shallum the son of Tikvah, the son of Harhas, keeper of the wardrobe. (She dwelt in Jerusalem in the Second Quarter.) And they spoke with her.

2 Chr 34:22 So Hilkiah and those the king *had appointed* went to Huldah the prophetess, the wife of Shallum the son of Tokhath, the son of Hasrah, keeper of the wardrobe. (She dwelt in Jerusalem in the Second Quarter.) And they spoke to her to that *effect.*

Treasurer.

1 Chr 27:25 And Azmaveth the son of Adiel *was* over the king's treasuries; and Jehonathan the son of Uzziah was over the storehouses in the field, in the cities, in the villages, and in the fortresses.

Storekeeper.

1 Chr 27:25 And Azmaveth the son of Adiel *was* over the king's treasuries; and Jehonathan the son of Uzziah was over the storehouses in the field, in the cities, in the villages, and in the fortresses.

Overseer of the tribute.

1 Kin 4:6 Ahishar, over the household; and Adoniram the son of Abda, over the labor force.

1 Kin 12:18 Then King Rehoboam sent Adoram, who *was* in charge of the revenue; but all Israel stoned him with stones, and he died. Therefore King Rehoboam mounted his chariot in haste to flee to Jerusalem.

Overseer of royal farms.

1 Chr 27:26 Ezri the son of Chelub was over those who did the work of the field for tilling the ground.

Overseer of royal vineyards.

1 Chr 27:27 And Shimei the Ramathite *was* over the vineyards, and Zabdi the Shiphmite was over the produce of the vineyards for the supply of wine.

Overseer of royal plantations.

1 Chr 27:28 Baal-Hanan the Gederite was over the olive trees and the sycamore trees that *were* in the lowlands, and Joash *was* over the store of oil.

Overseer of royal herds.

1 Sam 21:7 Now a certain man of the servants of Saul *was* there that day, detained before the LORD. And his name *was* Doeg, an Edomite, the chief of the herdsmen who *belonged* to Saul.

1 Chr 27:29 And Shitrai the Sharonite *was* over the herds that fed in Sharon, and Shaphat the son of Adlai was over the herds *that were* in the valleys.

Overseer of royal camels.

1 Chr 27:30 Obil the Ishmaelite *was* over the camels, Jehdeiah the Meronothite *was* over the donkeys,

Overseer of royal flocks.

1 Chr 27:31 and Jaziz the Hagrite *was* over the flocks. All these *were* the officials over King David's property.

Armorbearer.

1 Sam 16:21 So David came to Saul and stood before him. And he loved him greatly, and he became his armorbearer.

Cupbearer.

1 Kin 10:5 the food on his table, the seating of his servants, the service of his waiters and their apparel, his cupbearers, and his entryway by which he went up to the house of the LORD, there was no more spirit in her.

2 Chr 9:4–5 the food on his table, the seating of his servants, the service of his waiters and their apparel, his cupbearers and their apparel, and his entryway by which he went up to the house of the LORD, there was no more spirit in her. **5** Then she said to the king: "*It was* a true report which I heard in my own land about your words and your wisdom.

Approached with greatest reverence.

1 Sam 24:8 David also arose afterward, went out of the cave, and called out to Saul, saying, "My lord the king!" And when Saul looked behind him, David stooped with his face to the earth, and bowed down.

2 Sam 9:8 Then he bowed himself, and said, "What *is* your servant, that you should look upon such a dead dog as I?"

2 Sam 14:22 Then Joab fell to the ground on his face and bowed himself, and thanked the king. And Joab said, "Today your servant knows that I have found favor in your sight, my lord, O king, in that the king has fulfilled the request of his servant."

1 Kin 1:23 So they told the king, saying, "Here is Nathan the prophet." And when he came in before the king, he bowed down before the king with his face to the ground.

Presented with gifts by strangers.

1 Kin 10:2 She came to Jerusalem with a very great retinue, with camels that bore spices, very much gold, and precious stones; and when she came to Solomon, she spoke with him about all that was in her heart.

1 Kin 10:10 Then she gave the king one hundred and twenty talents of gold, spices in great quantity, and precious stones. There never again came such abundance of spices as the queen of Sheba gave to King Solomon.

1 Kin 10:25 Each man brought his present: articles of

silver and gold, garments, armor, spices, horses, and mules, at a set rate year by year.

2 Kin 5:5 Then the king of Syria said, "Go now, and I will send a letter to the king of Israel." So he departed and took with him ten talents of silver, six thousand *shekels* of gold, and ten changes of clothing.

Matt 2:11 And when they had come into the house, they saw the young Child with Mary His mother, and fell down and worshiped Him. And when they had opened their treasures, they presented gifts to Him: gold, frankincense, and myrrh.

Right hand of, the place of honor.

1 Kin 2:19 Bathsheba therefore went to King Solomon, to speak to him for Adonijah. And the king rose up to meet her and bowed down to her, and sat down on his throne and had a throne set for the king's mother; so she sat at his right hand.

Ps 45:9 Kings' daughters *are* among Your honorable women; At Your right hand stands the queen in gold from Ophir.

Ps 110:1 The LORD said to my Lord, "Sit at My right hand, Till I make Your enemies Your footstool."

Attendants of, stood in their presence.

1 Kin 10:8 Happy *are* your men and happy *are* these your servants, who stand continually before you *and* hear your wisdom!

2 Kin 25:19 He also took out of the city an officer who had charge of the men of war, five men of the king's close associates who were found in the city, the chief recruiting officer of the army, who mustered the people of the land, and sixty men of the people of the land *who were* found in the city.

Exercised great hospitality.

1 Sam 20:25–27 Now the king sat on his seat, as at other times, on a seat by the wall. And Jonathan arose, and Abner sat by Saul's side, but David's place was empty. **26** Nevertheless Saul did not say anything that day, for he thought, "Something has happened to him; he *is* unclean, surely he *is* unclean." **27** And it happened the next day, the second *day* of the month, that David's place was empty. And Saul said to Jonathan his son, "Why has the son of Jesse not come to eat, either yesterday or today?"

2 Sam 9:7–13 So David said to him, "Do not fear, for I will surely show you kindness for Jonathan your father's sake, and will restore to you all the land of Saul your grandfather; and you shall eat bread at my table continually." **8** Then he bowed himself, and said, "What *is* your servant, that you should look upon such a dead dog as I?" **9** And the king called to Ziba, Saul's servant, and said to him, "I have given to your master's son all that belonged to Saul and to all his house. **10** You therefore, and your sons and your servants, shall work the land for him, and you shall bring in *the harvest*, that your master's son may have food to eat. But Mephibosheth your master's son shall eat bread at my table always." Now Ziba had fifteen sons and twenty servants. **11** Then Ziba said to the king, "According to all that my lord the king has commanded his servant, so will your servant do." "As for Mephibosheth," *said the king*, "he shall eat at my table like one of the king's sons." **12** Mephibosheth had a young son whose name *was* Micha.

And all who dwelt in the house of Ziba *were* servants of Mephibosheth. **13** So Mephibosheth dwelt in Jerusalem, for he ate continually at the king's table. And he was lame in both his feet.

2 Sam 19:33 And the king said to Barzillai, "Come across with me, and I will provide for you while you are with me in Jerusalem."

1 Kin 4:22–23 Now Solomon's provision for one day was thirty kors of fine flour, sixty kors of meal, **23** ten fatted oxen, twenty oxen from the pastures, and one hundred sheep, besides deer, gazelles, roebucks, and fatted fowl.

1 Kin 4:28 They also brought barley and straw to the proper place, for the horses and steeds, each man according to his charge.

Sources of their revenues,

Voluntary contributions.

1 Sam 10:27 But some rebels said, "How can this man save us?" So they despised him, and brought him no presents. But he held his peace.

1 Sam 16:20 And Jesse took a donkey *loaded with* bread, a skin of wine, and a young goat, and sent *them* by his son David to Saul.

1 Chr 12:39–40 And they were there with David three days, eating and drinking, for their brethren had prepared for them. **40** Moreover those who were near to them, from as far away as Issachar and Zebulun and Naphtali, were bringing food on donkeys and camels, on mules and oxen—provisions of flour and cakes of figs and cakes of raisins, wine and oil and oxen and sheep abundantly, for *there was* joy in Israel.

Tribute from foreign nations.

1 Kin 4:21 So Solomon reigned over all kingdoms from the River *to* the land of the Philistines, as far as the border of Egypt. *They* brought tribute and served Solomon all the days of his life.

1 Kin 4:24–25 For he had dominion over all *the region* on this side of the River from Tiphsah even to Gaza, namely over all the kings on this side of the River; and he had peace on every side all around him. **25** And Judah and Israel dwelt safely, each man under his vine and his fig tree, from Dan as far as Beersheba, all the days of Solomon.

2 Chr 8:8 that is, their descendants who were left in the land after them, whom the children of Israel did not destroy—from these Solomon raised forced labor, as it is to this day.

2 Chr 17:11 Also *some* of the Philistines brought Jehoshaphat presents and silver as tribute; and the Arabians brought him flocks, seven thousand seven hundred rams and seven thousand seven hundred male goats.

Taxes on produce of the land.

1 Kin 4:7–19 And Solomon had twelve governors over all Israel, who provided food for the king and his household; each one made provision for one month of the year. **8** These *are* their names: Ben-Hur, in the mountains of Ephraim; **9** Ben-Deker, in Makaz, Shaalbim, Beth Shemesh, and Elon Beth Hanan; **10** Ben-Hesed, in Arubboth; to him *belonged* Sochoh and all the land of Hepher; **11** Ben-Abinadab, *in* all the regions of Dor; he had Taphath the daughter of Sol-

omon as wife; **12** Baana the son of Ahilud, *in* Taanach, Megiddo, and all Beth Shean, which *is* beside Zaretan below Jezreel, from Beth Shean to Abel Meholah, as far as the other side of Jokneam; **13** Ben-Geber, in Ramoth Gilead; to him *belonged* the towns of Jair the son of Manasseh, in Gilead; to him *also belonged* the region of Argob in Bashan—sixty large cities with walls and bronze gate-bars; **14** Ahinadab the son of Iddo, *in* Mahanaim; **15** Ahimaaz, in Naphtali; he also took Basemath the daughter of Solomon as wife; **16** Baanah the son of Hushai, in Asher and Aloth; **17** Jehoshaphat the son of Paruah, in Issachar; **18** Shimei the son of Elah, in Benjamin; **19** Geber the son of Uri, in the land of Gilead, *in* the country of Sihon king of the Amorites, and of Og king of Bashan. *He was* the only governor who *was* in the land.

Taxes on foreign merchandise.

1 Kin 10:15 besides *that* from the traveling merchants, from the income of traders, from all the kings of Arabia, and from the governors of the country.

Their own flocks and herds.

2 Chr 32:29 Moreover he provided cities for himself, and possessions of flocks and herds in abundance; for God had given him very much property.

Produce of their own lands.

2 Chr 26:10 Also he built towers in the desert. He dug many wells, for he had much livestock, both in the lowlands and in the plains; *he also had* farmers and vinedressers in the mountains and in Carmel, for he loved the soil.

Sometimes nominated their successors.

1 Kin 1:33–34 The king also said to them, "Take with you the servants of your lord, and have Solomon my son ride on my own mule, and take him down to Gihon. **34** There let Zadok the priest and Nathan the prophet anoint him king over Israel; and blow the horn, and say, 'Long live King Solomon!'

2 Chr 11:22–23 And Rehoboam appointed Abijah the son of Maachah as chief, *to be* leader among his brothers; for he *intended* to make him king. **23** He dealt wisely, and dispersed some of his sons throughout all the territories of Judah and Benjamin, to every fortified city; and he gave them provisions in abundance. He also sought many wives *for them*.

Punished for transgressing the divine law.

2 Sam 12:7–12 Then Nathan said to David, "You *are* the man! Thus says the LORD God of Israel: 'I anointed you king over Israel, and I delivered you from the hand of Saul. **8** I gave you your master's house and your master's wives into your keeping, and gave you the house of Israel and Judah. And if *that had been* too little, I also would have given you much more! **9** Why have you despised the commandment of the LORD, to do evil in His sight? You have killed Uriah the Hittite with the sword; you have taken his wife *to be* your wife, and have killed him with the sword of the people of Ammon. **10** Now therefore, the sword shall never depart from your house, because you have despised Me, and have taken the wife of Uriah the Hittite to be your wife.' **11** Thus says the LORD: 'Behold, I will raise up adversity against you from your own house; and I will take your wives before your eyes and give *them* to your neighbor, and he shall lie with your wives in the sight of this sun. 12 For you did *it* secretly, but I will do this thing before all Israel, before the sun.' "

1 Kin 21:18–24 "Arise, go down to meet Ahab king of Israel, who *lives* in Samaria. There *he is*, in the vineyard of Naboth, where he has gone down to take possession of it. 19 You shall speak to him, saying, 'Thus says the LORD: "Have you murdered and also taken possession?" ' And you shall speak to him, saying, 'Thus says the LORD: "In the place where dogs licked the blood of Naboth, dogs shall lick your blood, even yours." ' " 20 So Ahab said to Elijah, "Have you found me, O my enemy?" And he answered, "I have found *you*, because you have sold yourself to do evil in the sight of the LORD: 21 'Behold, I will bring calamity on you. I will take away your posterity, and will cut off from Ahab every male in Israel, both bond and free. 22 I will make your house like the house of Jeroboam the son of Nebat, and like the house of Baasha the son of Ahijah, because of the provocation with which you have provoked *Me* to anger, and made Israel sin.' 23 And concerning Jezebel the LORD also spoke, saying, 'The dogs shall eat Jezebel by the wall of Jezreel.' 24 The dogs shall eat whoever belongs to Ahab and dies in the city, and the birds of the air shall eat whoever dies in the field."

Those who reigned over all Israel,

Saul. **1 Sam 11:15—31:13; 1 Chr 10:1—10:14**

David. **2 Sam 2:4—1 Kin 2:11; 1 Chr 11:1—29:30**

Solomon. **1 Kin 1:39—11:43; 2 Chr 1:1—9:31**

Rehoboam (first part of his reign). **1 Kin 12:1–20; 2 Chr 10:1–16**

Those who reigned over Judah,

Rehoboam (latter part of his reign). **1 Kin 12:21–24; 14:21–31; 2 Chr 10:17—12:16**

Abijam or Abijah. **1 Kin 15:1–8; 2 Chr 13:1–22**

Asa. **1 Kin 15:9–24; 2 Chr 14:1—16:14**

Jehoshaphat. **1 Kin 22:41–50; 2 Chr 17:1—21:1**

Jehoram or Joram. **2 Kin 8:16–24; 2 Chr 21:1–20**

Ahaziah. **2 Kin 8:25–29; 9:16–29; 2 Chr 22:1–9**

Athaliah, mother of Ahaziah (usurper). **2 Kin 11:1–3; 2 Chr 22:10–12**

Joash or Jehoash. **2 Kin 11:4—12:21; 2 Chr 23:1—24:27**

Amaziah. **2 Kin 14:1–20; 2 Chr 25:1–28**

Azariah or Uzziah. **2 Kin 14:21–22; 15:1–7; 2 Chr 26:1–23**

Jotham. **2 Kin 15:32–38; 2 Chr 27:1–9**

Ahaz. **2 Kin 16:1–20; 2 Chr 28:1–27**

Hezekiah. **2 Kin 18:1—20:21; 2 Chr 29:1—32:33**

Manasseh. **2 Kin 21:1–18; 2 Chr 33:1–20**

Amon. **2 Kin 21:19–26; 2 Chr 33:21–25**

Josiah. **2 Kin 22:1—23:30; 2 Chr 34:1—35:27**

Jehoahaz. **2 Kin 23:31–33; 2 Chr 36:1–4**

Jehoiakim. **2 Kin 23:34—24:6; 2 Chr 36:5–8**

Jehoiachin. **2 Kin 24:8–16; 2 Chr 36:9,10**

Zedekiah. **2 Kin 24:17—25:7; 2 Chr 36:11–21**

Those who reigned over Israel,

Jeroboam. **1 Kin 12:20; 12:25—14:20**

Nadab. **1 Kin 15:25–27,32**

Baasha. **1 Kin 15:28—16:7**

Elah. **1 Kin 16:8–14**

Zimri. **1 Kin 16:11–12,15,20**

Omri. **1 Kin 16:23–28**

Ahab. **1 Kin 16:29—22:40**

Ahaziah. **1 Kin 22:51–53; 2 Kin 1:18**

Jehoram or Joram. **2 Kin 3:1—9:26**

Jehu. **2 Kin 9:3—10:36**

Jehoahaz. **2 Kin 13:1–9**

Jehoash or Joash. **2 Kin 13:10–25; 14:8–16**

Jeroboam the Second. **2 Kin 14:23–29**

Zachariah. **2 Kin 15:8–12**

Shallum. **2 Kin 15:13–15**

Menahem. **2 Kin 15:16–22**

Pekahiah. **2 Kin 15:23–26**

Pekah. **2 Kin 15:27–31; 16:5**

Hoshea. **2 Kin 17:1–6**

Called the Lord's anointed.

1 Sam 16:6 So it was, when they came, that he looked at Eliab and said, "Surely the LORD's anointed *is* before Him!"

1 Sam 24:6 And he said to his men, "The LORD forbid that I should do this thing to my master, the LORD's anointed, to stretch out my hand against him, seeing he *is* the anointed of the LORD."

2 Sam 19:21 But Abishai the son of Zeruiah answered and said, "Shall not Shimei be put to death for this, because he cursed the LORD's anointed?"

Conspiracies against,

Absalom against David.

2 Sam 15:10 Then Absalom sent spies throughout all the tribes of Israel, saying, "As soon as you hear the sound of the trumpet, then you shall say, 'Absalom reigns in Hebron!' "

Adonijah against Solomon.

1 Kin 1:5–7 Then Adonijah the son of Haggith exalted himself, saying, "I will be king"; and he prepared for himself chariots and horsemen, and fifty men to run before him. 6 (And his father had not rebuked him at any time by saying, "Why have you done so?" He *was* also very good-looking. *His mother* had borne him after Absalom.) 7 Then he conferred with Joab the son of Zeruiah and with Abiathar the priest, and they followed and helped Adonijah.

Jeroboam against Rehoboam.

1 Kin 12:12 So Jeroboam and all the people came to Rehoboam the third day, as the king had directed, saying, "Come back to me the third day."

1 Kin 12:16 Now when all Israel saw that the king did not listen to them, the people answered the king, saying: "What share have we in David? *We have* no inheritance in the son of Jesse. To your tents, O Israel! Now, see to your own house, O David!" So Israel departed to their tents.

Baasha against Nadab.

1 Kin 15:27 Then Baasha the son of Ahijah, of the house of Issachar, conspired against him. And Baasha killed him at Gibbethon, which *belonged* to the Philistines, while Nadab and all Israel laid siege to Gibbethon.

Zimri against Elah.

1 Kin 16:9–10 Now his servant Zimri, commander of half *his* chariots, conspired against him as he was in Tirzah drinking himself drunk in the house of Arza, steward of *his* house in Tirzah. **10** And Zimri went in and struck him and killed him in the twenty-seventh year of Asa king of Judah, and reigned in his place.

Omri against Zimri.

1 Kin 16:17 Then Omri and all Israel with him went up from Gibbethon, and they besieged Tirzah.

Jehu against Joram.

2 Kin 9:14 So Jehu the son of Jehoshaphat, the son of Nimshi, conspired against Joram. (Now Joram had been defending Ramoth Gilead, he and all Israel, against Hazael king of Syria.

Shallum against Zechariah.

2 Kin 15:10 Then Shallum the son of Jabesh conspired against him, and struck and killed him in front of the people; and he reigned in his place.

Menahem against Shallum.

2 Kin 15:14 For Menahem the son of Gadi went up from Tirzah, came to Samaria, and struck Shallum the son of Jabesh in Samaria and killed him; and he reigned in his place.

Pekah against Menahem.

2 Kin 15:25 Then Pekah the son of Remaliah, an officer of his, conspired against him and killed him in Samaria, in the citadel of the king's house, along with Argob and Arieh; and with him were fifty men of Gilead. He killed him and reigned in his place.

God chooses.

Deut 17:15 you shall surely set a king over you whom the LORD your God chooses; *one* from among your brethren you shall set as king over you; you may not set a foreigner over you, who *is* not your brother.

1 Chr 28:4–6 However the LORD God of Israel chose me above all the house of my father to be king over Israel forever, for He has chosen Judah *to be* the ruler. And of the house of Judah, the house of my father, and among the sons of my father, He was pleased with me to make *me* king over all Israel. **5** And of all my sons (for the LORD has given me many sons) He has chosen my son Solomon to sit on the throne of the kingdom of the LORD over Israel. **6** Now He said to me, 'It is your son Solomon *who* shall build My house and My courts; for I have chosen him *to be* My son, and I will be his Father.

God ordains.

Rom 13:1 Let every soul be subject to the governing authorities. For there is no authority except from God, and the authorities that exist are appointed by God.

God anoints.

1 Sam 16:12 So he sent and brought him in. Now he *was* ruddy, with bright eyes, and good-looking. And the LORD said, "Arise, anoint him; for this *is* the one!"

2 Sam 12:7 Then Nathan said to David, "You *are* the man! Thus says the LORD God of Israel: 'I anointed you king over Israel, and I delivered you from the hand of Saul.

Set up by God.

1 Sam 12:13 "Now therefore, here is the king whom you have chosen *and* whom you have desired. And take note, the LORD has set a king over you.

Dan 2:21 And He changes the times and the seasons; He removes kings and raises up kings; He gives wisdom to the wise And knowledge to those who have understanding.

Removed by God.

1 Kin 11:11 Therefore the LORD said to Solomon, "Because you have done this, and have not kept My covenant and My statutes, which I have commanded you, I will surely tear the kingdom away from you and give it to your servant.

Dan 2:21 And He changes the times and the seasons; He removes kings and raises up kings; He gives wisdom to the wise And knowledge to those who have understanding.

Christ is the ruler of.

Rev 1:5 and from Jesus Christ, the faithful witness, the firstborn from the dead, and the ruler over the kings of the earth. To Him who loved us and washed us from our sins in His own blood,

Christ is the King of.

Rev 17:14 These will make war with the Lamb, and the Lamb will overcome them, for He is Lord of lords and King of kings; and those *who are* with Him *are* called, chosen, and faithful."

Their reign directed by wisdom.

Prov 8:15 By me kings reign, And rulers decree justice.

Supreme judges of nations.

1 Sam 8:5 and said to him, "Look, you are old, and your sons do not walk in your ways. Now make us a king to judge us like all the nations."

Resistance to, is resistance to the ordinance of God.

Rom 13:2 Therefore whoever resists the authority resists the ordinance of God, and those who resist will bring judgment on themselves.

Are able to enforce their commands.

Eccl 8:4 Where the word of a king *is*, *there is* power; And who may say to him, "What are you doing?"

Numerous subjects the honor of.

Prov 14:28 In a multitude of people *is* a king's honor, But in the lack of people *is* the downfall of a prince.

Are not saved by their armies.

Ps 33:16 No king *is* saved by the multitude of an army; A mighty man is not delivered by great strength.

Are dependent on the earth.

Eccl 5:9 Moreover the profit of the land is for all; *even* the king is served from the field.

Instructions for,

Fear God.

Deut 17:19 And it shall be with him, and he shall read it all the days of his life, that he may learn to fear the LORD his God and be careful to observe all the words of this law and these statutes,

Serve Christ.

Ps 2:10–12 Now therefore, be wise, O kings; Be instructed, you judges of the earth. **11** Serve the LORD with fear, And rejoice with trembling. **12** Kiss the Son, lest He be angry, And you perish *in* the way, When His wrath is kindled but a little. Blessed *are* all those who put their trust in Him.

Keep the Law of God.

1 Kin 2:3 And keep the charge of the LORD your God: to walk in His ways, to keep His statutes, His commandments, His judgments, and His testimonies, as it is written in the Law of Moses, that you may prosper in all that you do and wherever you turn;

Study the Scriptures.

Deut 17:19 And it shall be with him, and he shall read it all the days of his life, that he may learn to fear the LORD his God and be careful to observe all the words of this law and these statutes,

Promote the interests of God's people.

Ezra 1:2–4 Thus says Cyrus king of Persia: All the kingdoms of the earth the LORD God of heaven has given me. And He has commanded me to build Him a house at Jerusalem which *is* in Judah. **3** Who *is* among you of all His people? May his God be with him, and let him go up to Jerusalem which *is* in Judah, and build the house of the LORD God of Israel (He *is* God), which *is* in Jerusalem. **4** And whoever is left in any place where he dwells, let the men of his place help him with silver and gold, with goods and livestock, besides the freewill offerings for the house of God which *is* in Jerusalem.

Ezra 6:1–12 Then King Darius issued a decree, and a search was made in the archives, where the treasures were stored in Babylon. **2** And at Achmetha, in the palace that *is* in the province of Media, a scroll was found, and in it a record *was* written thus: **3** In the first year of King Cyrus, King Cyrus issued a decree *concerning* the house of God at Jerusalem: "Let the house be rebuilt, the place where they offered sacrifices; and let the foundations of it be firmly laid, its height sixty cubits *and* its width sixty cubits, **4** *with* three rows of heavy stones and one row of new timber. Let the expenses be paid from the king's treasury. **5** Also let the gold and silver articles of the house of God, which Nebuchadnezzar took from the temple which *is* in Jerusalem and brought to Babylon, be restored and taken back to the temple which *is* in Jerusalem, *each* to its place; and deposit *them* in the house of God"— **6** Now *therefore,* Tattenai, governor of *the region* beyond the River, and Shethar-Boznai, and your companions the Persians who *are* beyond the River, keep yourselves far from there. **7** Let the work of this house of God alone; let the governor of the Jews and the elders of the Jews build this house of God on its site. **8** Moreover I issue a decree *as to* what you shall do for the elders of these Jews, for the building of this house of God: Let the cost be paid at the king's expense from taxes *on the region* beyond the River; this is to be given immediately to these men, so that they are not hindered. **9** And whatever they need—young bulls, rams, and lambs for the burnt offerings of the God of heaven, wheat, salt, wine, and oil, according to the request of the priests who *are* in Jerusalem—let it be given them day by day without fail, **10** that they may offer sacrifices of sweet aroma to the God of heaven, and pray for the life of the king and his sons. **11** Also I issue a decree that whoever alters this edict, let a timber be pulled from his house and erected, and let him be hanged on it; and let his house be made a refuse heap because of this. **12** And may the God who causes His name to dwell there destroy any king or people who put their hand to alter it, or to destroy this house of God which is in Jerusalem. I Darius issue a decree; let it be done diligently.

Is 49:23 Kings shall be your foster fathers, And their queens your nursing mothers; They shall bow down to you with *their* faces to the earth, And lick up the dust of your feet. Then you will know that I *am* the LORD, For they shall not be ashamed who wait for Me."

Rule in the fear of God.

2 Sam 23:3 The God of Israel said, The Rock of Israel spoke to me: 'He who rules over men *must be* just, Ruling in the fear of God.

Maintain the cause of the poor and oppressed.

Prov 31:8–9 Open your mouth for the speechless, In the cause of all *who are* appointed to die. **9** Open your mouth, judge righteously, And plead the cause of the poor and needy.

Investigate all matters.

Prov 25:2 *It is* the glory of God to conceal a matter, But the glory of kings *is* to search out a matter.

Do not pervert judgment.

Prov 31:5 Lest they drink and forget the law, And pervert the justice of all the afflicted.

Prolong their reign by hating covetousness.

Prov 28:16 A ruler who lacks understanding *is* a great oppressor, *But* he who hates covetousness will prolong *his* days.

Throne of, established by righteousness and justice.

Prov 16:12 *It is* an abomination for kings to commit wickedness, For a throne is established by righteousness.

Prov 29:14 The king who judges the poor with truth, His throne will be established forever.

Specially warned against

Impurity.

Prov 31:3 Do not give your strength to women, Nor your ways to that which destroys kings.

Lying.

Prov 17:7 Excellent speech is not becoming to a fool, Much less lying lips to a prince.

Paying attention to lies.

Prov 29:12 If a ruler pays attention to lies, All his servants *become* wicked.

Intemperance.

Prov 31:4–5 *It is* not for kings, O Lemuel, *It is* not for kings to drink wine, Nor for princes intoxicating drink; **5** Lest they drink and forget the law, And pervert the justice of all the afflicted.

The gospel to be preached to.

Acts 9:15 But the Lord said to him, "Go, for he is a chosen vessel of Mine to bear My name before Gentiles, kings, and the children of Israel.

Acts 26:27–28 King Agrippa, do you believe the prophets? I know that you do believe." **28** Then Agrippa said to Paul, "You almost persuade me to become a Christian."

Without understanding, are oppressors.

Prov 28:16 A ruler who lacks understanding *is* a great oppressor, *But* he who hates covetousness will prolong *his* days.

Often rebuked by God.

1 Chr 16:21 He permitted no man to do them wrong; Yes, He rebuked kings for their sakes,

Judgments upon, when opposed to God and Christ.

Ps 2:2 The kings of the earth set themselves, And the rulers take counsel together, Against the LORD and against His Anointed, *saying,*

Ps 2:5 Then He shall speak to them in His wrath, And distress them in His deep displeasure:

Ps 2:9 You shall break them with a rod of iron; You shall dash them to pieces like a potter's vessel.' "

When good,

Regard God as their strength.

Ps 99:4 The King's strength also loves justice; You have established equity; You have executed justice and righteousness in Jacob.

Speak righteously.

Prov 16:10 Divination *is* on the lips of the king; His mouth must not transgress in judgment.

Love righteous lips.

Prov 16:13 Righteous lips *are* the delight of kings, And they love him who speaks *what is* right.

Abhor wickedness.

Prov 16:12 *It is* an abomination for kings to commit wickedness, For a throne is established by righteousness.

Do not tolerate evil.

Prov 20:8 A king who sits on the throne of judgment Scatters all evil with his eyes.

Punish the wicked.

Prov 20:8 A king who sits on the throne of judgment Scatters all evil with his eyes.

Favor the wise.

Prov 14:35 The king's favor *is* toward a wise servant, But his wrath *is against* him who causes shame.

Honor the diligent.

Prov 22:29 Do you see a man *who* excels in his work? He will stand before kings; He will not stand before unknown *men.*

Befriend the good.

Prov 22:14 The mouth of an immoral woman *is* a deep pit; He who is abhorred by the LORD will fall there.

Are pacified by submission.

Prov 16:14 As messengers of death *is* the king's wrath, But a wise man will appease it.

Prov 25:15 By long forbearance a ruler is persuaded, And a gentle tongue breaks a bone.

Evil counselors should be removed from.

2 Chr 22:3–4 He also walked in the ways of the house of Ahab, for his mother advised him to do wickedly. **4** Therefore he did evil in the sight of the LORD, like the house of Ahab; for they were his counselors after the death of his father, to his destruction.

Prov 25:5 Take away the wicked from before the king, And his throne will be established in righteousness.

Do not curse, even in thought.

Ex 22:28 "You shall not revile God, nor curse a ruler of your people.

Eccl 10:20 Do not curse the king, even in your thought; Do not curse the rich, even in your bedroom; For a bird of the air may carry your voice, And a bird in flight may tell the matter.

Speak no evil of.

Job 34:18 *Is it fitting* to say to a king, *'You are* worthless,' *And* to nobles, *'You are* wicked'?

2 Pet 2:10 and especially those who walk according to the flesh in the lust of uncleanness and despise authority. *They are* presumptuous, self-willed. They are not afraid to speak evil of dignitaries,

Pay tribute to.

Matt 22:21 They said to Him, "Caesar's." And He said to them, "Render therefore to Caesar the things that are Caesar's, and to God the things that are God's."

Rom 13:6–7 For because of this you also pay taxes, for they are God's ministers attending continually to this very thing. **7** Render therefore to all their due: taxes to whom taxes *are due,* customs to whom customs, fear to whom fear, honor to whom honor.

Be not presumptuous before.

Prov 25:6 Do not exalt yourself in the presence of the king, And do not stand in the place of the great;

Should be

Honored.

Rom 13:7 Render therefore to all their due: taxes to whom taxes *are due,* customs to whom customs, fear to whom fear, honor to whom honor.

1 Pet 2:17 Honor all *people.* Love the brotherhood. Fear God. Honor the king.

Feared.

Prov 24:21 My son, fear the LORD and the king; Do not associate with those given to change;

Reverenced.

1 Sam 24:8 David also arose afterward, went out of the cave, and called out to Saul, saying, "My lord the king!" And when Saul looked behind him, David stooped with his face to the earth, and bowed down.

1 Kin 1:21 Otherwise it will happen, when my lord the king rests with his fathers, that I and my son Solomon will be counted as offenders."

1 Kin 1:23 So they told the king, saying, "Here is Nathan the prophet." And when he came in before the king, he bowed down before the king with his face to the ground.

Obeyed.

Rom 13:1 Let every soul be subject to the governing authorities. For there is no authority except from God, and the authorities that exist are appointed by God.

Rom 13:5 Therefore *you* must be subject, not only because of wrath but also for conscience' sake.

1 Pet 2:13 Therefore submit yourselves to every ordinance of man for the Lord's sake, whether to the king as supreme,

Prayed for.

1 Tim 2:1–2 Therefore I exhort first of all that supplications, prayers, intercessions, *and* giving of thanks be made for all men, **2** for kings and all who are in authority, that we may lead a quiet and peaceable life in all godliness and reverence.

Folly and punishment for resisting.

Prov 19:12 The king's wrath *is* like the roaring of a lion, But his favor *is* like dew on the grass.

Prov 20:2 The wrath of a king *is* like the roaring of a lion; *Whoever* provokes him to anger sins *against* his own life.

Rom 13:2 Therefore whoever resists the authority resists the ordinance of God, and those who resist will bring judgment on themselves.

Guilt and danger of stretching out the hand against.

1 Sam 26:9 But David said to Abishai, "Do not destroy him; for who can stretch out his hand against the LORD's anointed, and be guiltless?"

2 Sam 1:14 So David said to him, "How was it you were not afraid to put forth your hand to destroy the LORD's anointed?"

They that walk after the flesh despise.

2 Pet 2:10 and especially those who walk according to the flesh in the lust of uncleanness and despise authority. *They are* presumptuous, self-willed. They are not afraid to speak evil of dignitaries,

Jude 1:8 Likewise also these dreamers defile the flesh, reject authority, and speak evil of dignitaries.

Good, exemplified by

David.

2 Sam 8:15 So David reigned over all Israel; and David administered judgment and justice to all his people.

Asa.

1 Kin 15:11 Asa did *what was* right in the eyes of the LORD, as *did* his father David.

Jehoshaphat.

1 Kin 22:43 And he walked in all the ways of his father Asa. He did not turn aside from them, doing *what was* right in the eyes of the LORD. Nevertheless the high places were not taken away, *for* the people offered sacrifices and burned incense on the high places.

Amaziah.

2 Kin 15:3 And he did *what was* right in the sight of the LORD, according to all that his father Amaziah had done,

Uzziah.

2 Kin 15:34 And he did *what was* right in the sight of the LORD; he did according to all that his father Uzziah had done.

Hezekiah.

2 Kin 18:3 And he did *what was* right in the sight of the LORD, according to all that his father David had done.

Josiah.

2 Kin 22:2 And he did *what was* right in the sight of the LORD, and walked in all the ways of his father David; he did not turn aside to the right hand or to the left.

KNOWLEDGE

Tree of.

Gen 2:9 And out of the ground the LORD God made every tree grow that is pleasant to the sight and good for food. The tree of life *was* also in the midst of the garden, and the tree of the knowledge of good and evil.

Gen 2:16–17 And the LORD God commanded the man, saying, "Of every tree of the garden you may freely eat; **17** but of the tree of the knowledge of good and evil you shall not eat, for in the day that you eat of it you shall surely die."

Gen 3:1–6 Now the serpent was more cunning than any beast of the field which the LORD God had made. And he said to the woman, "Has God indeed said, 'You shall not eat of every tree of the garden'?" **2** And the woman said to the serpent, "We may eat the fruit of the trees of the garden; **3** but of the fruit of the tree which *is* in the midst of the garden, God has said, 'You shall not eat it, nor shall you touch it, lest you die.' " **4** Then the serpent said to the woman, "You will not surely die. **5** For God knows that in the day you eat of it your eyes will be opened, and you will be like God, knowing good and evil." **6** So when the woman saw that the tree *was* good for food, that it *was* pleasant to the eyes, and a tree desirable to make *one* wise, she took of its fruit and ate. She also gave to her husband with her, and he ate.

Gen 3:11 And He said, "Who told you that you *were* naked? Have you eaten from the tree of which I commanded you that you should not eat?"

Cf. Gen 3:22

Of the Law commanded.

Deut 4:1–14 "Now, O Israel, listen to the statutes and the judgments which I teach you to observe, that you may live, and go in and possess the land which the LORD God of your fathers is giving you. **2** You shall not add to the word which I command you, nor take from it, that you may keep the commandments of the LORD your God which I command you. **3** Your eyes have seen what the LORD did at Baal Peor; for the LORD your God has destroyed from among you all the men who followed Baal of Peor. **4** But you who held fast to the LORD your God *are* alive today, every one of you. **5** "Surely I have taught you statutes and judgments, just as the LORD my God commanded me, that you should act according *to them* in the land which you go to possess. **6** Therefore be careful to observe *them;* for this *is* your wisdom and your understanding in the sight of the peoples who will hear all these statutes, and say, 'Surely this great nation *is* a wise and understanding people.' **7** "For what great nation *is there* that has God so near to it, as the LORD our God *is* to us, for whatever *reason* we may call upon Him? **8** And what great nation *is there* that has *such* statutes and righteous judgments as are in all this law which I set before you this day? **9** Only take heed to yourself, and diligently keep yourself, lest you forget the things your eyes have seen, and lest they depart from your heart all the days of your life. And teach them to your children and your grandchildren, **10** *especially concerning* the day you stood before the LORD your God in Horeb, when the LORD said to me, 'Gather the people to Me, and I will let them hear My words, that they may learn to fear Me all the days they live on the earth, and *that* they may teach their children.' 11 "Then you came near and stood at the foot of the mountain, and the mountain burned with fire to the midst of heaven, with darkness, cloud, and thick darkness. 12 And the LORD spoke to you out of the midst of the fire. You heard the sound of the words, but saw no form; *you* only *heard* a voice. 13 So He declared to you His covenant which He commanded you to perform, the Ten Commandments; and He wrote them on two tablets of stone. 14 And the LORD commanded me at that time to teach you statutes and judgments, that you might observe them in the land which you cross over to possess.

Hos 6:3 Let us know, Let us pursue the knowledge of the LORD. His going forth is established as the morning; He will come to us like the rain, Like the latter *and* former rain to the earth.

Some belongs only to God.

Deut 29:29 "The secret *things belong* to the LORD our God, but those *things which are* revealed *belong* to us and to our children forever, that *we* may do all the words of this law.

Job 36:26 "Behold, God *is* great, and we do not know *Him;* Nor can the number of His years *be* discovered.

Can come only from God.

Job 28:12–28 "But where can wisdom be found? And where *is* the place of understanding? 13 Man does not know its value, Nor is it found in the land of the living. 14 The deep says, '*It is* not in me'; And the sea says, '*It is* not with me.' 15 It cannot be purchased for gold, Nor can silver be weighed *for* its price. 16 It cannot be valued in the gold of Ophir, In precious onyx or sapphire. 17 Neither gold nor crystal can equal it, Nor can it be exchanged for jewelry of fine gold. 18 No mention shall be made of coral or quartz, For the price of wisdom *is* above rubies. 19 The topaz of Ethiopia cannot equal it, Nor can it be valued in pure gold. 20 "From where then does wisdom come? And where *is* the place of understanding? 21 It is hidden from the eyes of all living, And concealed from the birds of the air. 22 Destruction and Death say, 'We have heard a report about it with our ears.' 23 God understands its way, And He knows its place. 24 For He looks to the ends of the earth, *And* sees under the whole heavens, 25 To establish a weight for the wind, And apportion the waters by measure. 26 When He made a law for the rain, And a path for the thunderbolt, 27 Then He saw *wisdom* and declared it; He prepared it, indeed, He searched it out. 28 And to man He said, 'Behold, the fear of the Lord, that *is* wisdom, And to depart from evil *is* understanding.' "

Cf. Job 38:1–3; Ps 73:11

Derives from the proverbs.

Prov 1:1–6 The proverbs of Solomon the son of David, king of Israel: 2 To know wisdom and instruction, To perceive the words of understanding, 3 To receive the instruction of wisdom, Justice, judgment, and equity; 4 To give prudence to the simple, To the young man knowledge and discretion— 5 A wise *man* will hear and increase learning, And a man of understanding will attain wise counsel, 6 To understand a proverb and an enigma, The words of the wise and their riddles.

Fear of God, the beginning of.

Job 28:28 And to man He said, 'Behold, the fear of the Lord, that *is* wisdom, And to depart from evil *is* understanding.' "

Ps 111:10 The fear of the LORD *is* the beginning of wisdom; A good understanding have all those who do *His commandments.* His praise endures forever.

Prov 1:7 The fear of the LORD *is* the beginning of knowledge, *But* fools despise wisdom and instruction.

Prov 2:4–6 If you seek her as silver, And search for her as *for* hidden treasures; 5 Then you will understand the fear of the LORD, And find the knowledge of God. 6 For the LORD gives wisdom; From His mouth *come* knowledge and understanding;

Prov 9:10 "The fear of the LORD *is* the beginning of wisdom, And the knowledge of the Holy One *is* understanding.

Prov 15:33 The fear of the LORD *is* the instruction of wisdom, And before honor *is* humility.

Eccl 12:13 Let us hear the conclusion of the whole matter: Fear God and keep His commandments, For this is man's all.

God's is higher than man's.

Job 5:9 Who does great things, and unsearchable, Marvelous things without number.

Ps 92:5 O LORD, how great are Your works! Your thoughts are very deep.

Ps 145:3 Great *is* the LORD, and greatly to be praised; And His greatness *is* unsearchable.

Eccl 3:11 He has made everything beautiful in its time. Also He has put eternity in their hearts, except that no one can find out the work that God does from beginning to end.

Is 40:28 Have you not known? Have you not heard? The everlasting God, the LORD, The Creator of the ends of the earth, Neither faints nor is weary. His understanding is unsearchable.

Is 46:10 Declaring the end from the beginning, And from ancient times *things* that are not *yet* done, Saying, 'My counsel shall stand, And I will do all My pleasure,'

Is 55:8–9 "For My thoughts *are* not your thoughts, Nor *are* your ways My ways," says the LORD. 9 "For *as* the heavens are higher than the earth, So are My ways higher than your ways, And My thoughts than your thoughts.

Acts 15:18 "Known to God from eternity are all His works.

Rom 11:33–36 Oh, the depth of the riches both of the wisdom and knowledge of God! How unsearchable *are* His judgments and His ways past finding out! 34 *"For who has known the mind of the LORD? Or who has become His counselor?"* 35 *"Or who has first given to Him And it shall be repaid to him?"* 36 For of Him and through Him and to Him *are* all things, to whom *be* glory forever. Amen.

Heb 4:13 And there is no creature hidden from His sight, but all things *are* naked and open to the eyes of Him to whom we *must give* account.

Cf. Prov 30:2–4; Eccl 6:12; 8:17

Spirit of, rests upon Christ.

Is 11:2 The Spirit of the LORD shall rest upon Him, The Spirit of wisdom and understanding, The Spirit of counsel and might, The Spirit of knowledge and of the fear of the LORD.

Cf. Is 53:11

Of the Lord

Will fill the earth during the Millennium.

Is 11:9 They shall not hurt nor destroy in all My holy mountain, For the earth shall be full of the knowledge of the LORD As the waters cover the sea.

Is 19:21 Then the LORD will be known to Egypt, and the Egyptians will know the LORD in that day, and will make sacrifice and offering; yes, they will make a vow to the LORD and perform *it.*

Is 33:13 Hear, you *who are* afar off, what I have done; And you *who are* near, acknowledge My might."

Is 40:5 The glory of the LORD shall be revealed, And all flesh shall see *it* together; For the mouth of the LORD has spoken."

Is 41:20 That they may see and know, And consider and understand together, That the hand of the LORD has done this, And the Holy One of Israel has created it.

Is 45:6 That they may know from the rising of the sun to its setting That *there is* none besides Me. I *am* the LORD, and *there is* no other;

Is 45:14 Thus says the LORD: "The labor of Egypt and merchandise of Cush And of the Sabeans, men of stature, Shall come over to you, and they shall be yours; They shall walk behind you, They shall come over in chains; And they shall bow down to you. They will make supplication to you, *saying,* 'Surely God *is* in you, And *there is* no other; *There is* no other God.' "

Is 49:26 I will feed those who oppress you with their own flesh, And they shall be drunk with their own blood as with sweet wine. All flesh shall know That I, the LORD, *am* your Savior, And your Redeemer, the Mighty One of Jacob."

Is 52:10 The LORD has made bare His holy arm In the eyes of all the nations; And all the ends of the earth shall see The salvation of our God.

Is 52:13 Behold, My Servant shall deal prudently; He shall be exalted and extolled and be very high.

Is 52:15 So shall He sprinkle many nations. Kings shall shut their mouths at Him; For what had not been told them they shall see, And what they had not heard they shall consider.

Is 54:13 All your children *shall be* taught by the LORD, And great *shall be* the peace of your children.

Is 66:23 And it shall come to pass *That* from one New Moon to another, And from one Sabbath to another, All flesh shall come to worship before Me," says the LORD.

Is available to all.

Rom 1:18–20 For the wrath of God is revealed from heaven against all ungodliness and unrighteousness of men, who suppress the truth in unrighteousness, **19** because what may be known of God is manifest in them, for God has shown *it* to them. **20** For since the creation of the world His invisible *attributes* are clearly seen, being understood by the things that are

made, *even* His eternal power and Godhead, so that they are without excuse,

Rom 2:1–2 Therefore you are inexcusable, O man, whoever you are who judge, for in whatever you judge another you condemn yourself; for you who judge practice the same things. **2** But we know that the judgment of God is according to truth against those who practice such things.

Rom 2:14–16 for when Gentiles, who do not have the law, by nature do the things in the law, these, although not having the law, are a law to themselves, **15** who show the work of the law written in their hearts, their conscience also bearing witness, and between themselves *their* thoughts accusing or else excusing *them*) **16** in the day when God will judge the secrets of men by Jesus Christ, according to my gospel.

1 Tim 2:4 who desires all men to be saved and to come to the knowledge of the truth.

Cf. Heb 10:26; 2 Pet 2:20–21

Of the day of Christ's return.

Matt 24:36 "But of that day and hour no one knows, not even the angels of heaven, but My Father only.

Mark 13:32 "But of that day and hour no one knows, not even the angels in heaven, nor the Son, but only the Father.

Of truth, prevented by teachers of the Law.

Matt 23:13 "But woe to you, scribes and Pharisees, hypocrites! For you shut up the kingdom of heaven against men; for you neither go in *yourselves,* nor do you allow those who are entering to go in.

Luke 11:52 "Woe to you lawyers! For you have taken away the key of knowledge. You did not enter in yourselves, and those who were entering in you hindered."

Of sin is from the law.

Rom 3:19–20 Now we know that whatever the law says, it says to those who are under the law, that every mouth may be stopped, and all the world may become guilty before God. **20** Therefore by the deeds of the law no flesh will be justified in His sight, for by the law *is* the knowledge of sin.

Rom 7:7 What shall we say then? *Is* the law sin? Certainly not! On the contrary, I would not have known sin except through the law. For I would not have known covetousness unless the law had said, *"You shall not covet."*

Possessed by believers.

Jer 31:34 No more shall every man teach his neighbor, and every man his brother, saying, 'Know the LORD,' for they all shall know Me, from the least of them to the greatest of them, says the LORD. For I will forgive their iniquity, and their sin I will remember no more."

Rom 15:14 Now I myself am confident concerning you, my brethren, that you also are full of goodness, filled with all knowledge, able also to admonish one another.

1 Cor 1:5–7 that you were enriched in everything by Him in all utterance and all knowledge, **6** even as the testimony of Christ was confirmed in you, **7** so that you come short in no gift, eagerly waiting for the revelation of our Lord Jesus Christ,

1 Cor 8:1 Now concerning things offered to idols: We know that we all have knowledge. Knowledge puffs up, but love edifies.

2 Cor 2:14 Now thanks *be* to God who always leads us in triumph in Christ, and through us diffuses the fragrance of His knowledge in every place.

2 Cor 4:6 For it is the God who commanded light to shine out of darkness, who has shone in our hearts to *give* the light of the knowledge of the glory of God in the face of Jesus Christ.

2 Cor 8:7 But as you abound in everything—in faith, in speech, in knowledge, in all diligence, and in your love for us—*see* that you abound in this grace also.

Eph 4:13 till we all come to the unity of the faith and of the knowledge of the Son of God, to a perfect man, to the measure of the stature of the fullness of Christ;

Phil 1:9 And this I pray, that your love may abound still more and more in knowledge and all discernment,

Col 1:9–10 For this reason we also, since the day we heard it, do not cease to pray for you, and to ask that you may be filled with the knowledge of His will in all wisdom and spiritual understanding; **10** that you may walk worthy of the Lord, fully pleasing *Him*, being fruitful in every good work and increasing in the knowledge of God;

Col 2:2 that their hearts may be encouraged, being knit together in love, and *attaining* to all riches of the full assurance of understanding, to the knowledge of the mystery of God, both of the Father and of Christ,

Col 3:10 and have put on the new *man* who is renewed in knowledge according to the image of Him who created him,

2 Pet 1:2–9 Grace and peace be multiplied to you in the knowledge of God and of Jesus our Lord, **3** as His divine power has given to us all things that *pertain* to life and godliness, through the knowledge of Him who called us by glory and virtue, **4** by which have been given to us exceedingly great and precious promises, that through these you may be partakers of the divine nature, having escaped the corruption *that is* in the world through lust. **5** But also for this very reason, giving all diligence, add to your faith virtue, to virtue knowledge, **6** to knowledge self-control, to self-control perseverance, to perseverance godliness, **7** to godliness brotherly kindness, and to brotherly kindness love. **8** For if these things are yours and abound, *you will be* neither barren nor unfruitful in the knowledge of our Lord Jesus Christ. **9** For he who lacks these things is shortsighted, even to blindness, and has forgotten that he was cleansed from his old sins.

2 Pet 3:18 but grow in the grace and knowledge of our Lord and Savior Jesus Christ. To Him *be* the glory both now and forever. Amen.

Word of, a spiritual gift.

1 Cor 12:8 for to one is given the word of wisdom through the Spirit, to another the word of knowledge through the same Spirit,

Cf. 1 Cor 13:2

Man's, cannot grasp Christ's love.

Eph 3:19 to know the love of Christ which passes knowledge; that you may be filled with all the fullness of God.

Of Jesus Christ, more valuable than anything.

Phil 3:7–11 But what things were gain to me, these I have counted loss for Christ. **8** Yet indeed I also count all things loss for the excellence of the knowledge of Christ Jesus my Lord, for whom I have suffered the loss of all things, and count them as rubbish, that I may gain Christ **9** and be found in Him, not having my own righteousness, which *is* from the law, but that which *is* through faith in Christ, the righteousness which is from God by faith; **10** that I may know Him and the power of His resurrection, and the fellowship of His sufferings, being conformed to His death, **11** if, by any means, I may attain to the resurrection from the dead.

Warning against that of false teachers.

1 Tim 6:20 O Timothy! Guard what was committed to your trust, avoiding the profane *and* idle babblings and contradictions of what is falsely called knowledge—

2 Tim 3:1–9 But know this, that in the last days perilous times will come: **2** For men will be lovers of themselves, lovers of money, boasters, proud, blasphemers, disobedient to parents, unthankful, unholy, **3** unloving, unforgiving, slanderers, without self-control, brutal, despisers of good, **4** traitors, headstrong, haughty, lovers of pleasure rather than lovers of God, **5** having a form of godliness but denying its power. And from such people turn away! **6** For of this sort are those who creep into households and make captives of gullible women loaded down with sins, led away by various lusts, **7** always learning and never able to come to the knowledge of the truth. **8** Now as Jannes and Jambres resisted Moses, so do these also resist the truth: men of corrupt minds, disapproved concerning the faith; **9** but they will progress no further, for their folly will be manifest to all, as theirs also was.

L

LABOR (WORK)
Object of man's, cursed after the Fall.

Gen 3:17–19 Then to Adam He said, "Because you have heeded the voice of your wife, and have eaten from the tree of which I commanded you, saying, 'You shall not eat of it': "Cursed *is* the ground for your sake; In toil you shall eat *of* it All the days of your life. **18** Both thorns and thistles it shall bring forth for you, And you shall eat the herb of the field. **19** In the sweat of your face you shall eat bread Till you return to the ground, For out of it you were taken; For dust you *are*, And to dust you shall return."

Jacob's agreement of, with Laban.

Gen 29:18–30 Now Jacob loved Rachel; so he said, "I will serve you seven years for Rachel your younger daughter." **19** And Laban said, "*It is* better that I give her to you than that I should give her to another man. Stay with me." **20** So Jacob served seven years for Rachel, and they seemed *only* a few days to him because of the love he had for her. **21** Then Jacob said to Laban, "Give *me* my wife, for my days are fulfilled, that I may go in to her." **22** And Laban gathered together all the men of the place and made a feast. **23** Now it came to pass in the evening, that he took Leah his daughter and brought her to Jacob; and he went in to her. **24** And Laban gave his maid Zilpah to his daughter Leah *as* a maid. **25** So it came to pass in the morning, that behold, it *was* Leah. And he said to Laban, "What is this you have done to me? Was it not for Rachel that I served you? Why then have you deceived me?" **26** And Laban said, "It must not be done so in our country, to give the younger before the firstborn. **27** Fulfill her week, and we will give you this one also for the service which you will serve with me still another seven years." **28** Then Jacob did so and fulfilled her week. So he gave him his daughter Rachel as wife also. **29** And Laban gave his maid Bilhah to his daughter Rachel as a maid. **30** Then *Jacob* also went in to Rachel, and he also loved Rachel more than Leah. And he served with Laban still another seven years.

Prohibited on the Sabbath.

Ex 20:8–11 "Remember the Sabbath day, to keep it holy. **9** Six days you shall labor and do all your work, **10** but the seventh day *is* the Sabbath of the Lord your God. *In it* you shall do no work: you, nor your son, nor your daughter, nor your male servant, nor your female servant, nor your cattle, nor your stranger who *is* within your gates. **11** For *in* six days the Lord made the heavens and the earth, the sea, and all that *is* in them, and rested the seventh day. Therefore the Lord blessed the Sabbath day and hallowed it.

Ex 31:12–17 And the Lord spoke to Moses, saying,

13 "Speak also to the children of Israel, saying: 'Surely My Sabbaths you shall keep, for it *is* a sign between Me and you throughout your generations, that *you* may know that I *am* the Lord who sanctifies you. **14** You shall keep the Sabbath, therefore, for *it is* holy to you. Everyone who profanes it shall surely be put to death; for whoever does *any* work on it, that person shall be cut off from among his people. **15** Work shall be done for six days, but the seventh *is* the Sabbath of rest, holy to the Lord. Whoever does *any* work on the Sabbath day, he shall surely be put to death. **16** Therefore the children of Israel shall keep the Sabbath, to observe the Sabbath throughout their generations *as* a perpetual covenant. **17** It *is* a sign between Me and the children of Israel forever; for *in* six days the Lord made the heavens and the earth, and on the seventh day He rested and was refreshed.' "

Deut 5:12–15 'Observe the Sabbath day, to keep it holy, as the Lord your God commanded you. **13** Six days you shall labor and do all your work, **14** but the seventh day *is* the Sabbath of the Lord your God. *In it* you shall do no work: you, nor your son, nor your daughter, nor your male servant, nor your female servant, nor your ox, nor your donkey, nor any of your cattle, nor your stranger who *is* within your gates, that your male servant and your female servant may rest as well as you. **15** And remember that you were a slave in the land of Egypt, and the Lord your God brought you out from there by a mighty hand and by an outstretched arm; therefore the Lord your God commanded you to keep the Sabbath day.

Fruit of, to be fairly paid.

Deut 25:4 "You shall not muzzle an ox while it treads out *the* grain.

Matt 20:2 Now when he had agreed with the laborers for a denarius a day, he sent them into his vineyard.

1 Cor 9:9 For it is written in the law of Moses, *"You shall not muzzle an ox while it treads out the grain."* Is it oxen God is concerned about?

1 Tim 5:18 For the Scripture says, *"You shall not muzzle an ox while it treads out the grain,"* and, "The laborer *is* worthy of his wages."

2 Tim 2:6 The hardworking farmer must be first to partake of the crops.

Performed by special forces under Solomon.

1 Kin 5:13–18 Then King Solomon raised up a labor force out of all Israel; and the labor force was thirty thousand men. **14** And he sent them to Lebanon, ten thousand a month in shifts: they were one month in Lebanon *and* two months at home; Adoniram *was* in charge of the labor force. **15** Solomon had seventy thousand who carried burdens, and eighty thousand who quarried *stone* in the mountains, **16** besides three thousand three hundred from the chiefs of Solomon's deputies, who supervised the people who labored in the work. **17** And the king commanded them to quarry large stones, costly stones, *and* hewn stones, to lay the foundation of the temple. **18** So Solomon's builders, Hiram's builders, and the Gebalites quarried *them;* and they prepared timber and stones to build the temple.

1 Kin 9:20–22 All the people *who were* left of the Amorites, Hittites, Perizzites, Hivites, and Jebusites, who *were* not of the children of Israel— **21** that is, their descendants who were left in the land after them, whom the children of Israel had not been able to destroy completely—from these Solomon raised forced labor, as it is to this day. **22** But of the children of Israel Solomon made no forced laborers, because they *were* men of war and his servants: his officers, his captains, commanders of his chariots, and his cavalry.

1 Kin 11:28 The man Jeroboam *was* a mighty man of valor; and Solomon, seeing that the young man was industrious, made him the officer over all the labor force of the house of Joseph.

Division of, under David.

1 Chr 23:1–6 So when David was old and full of days, he made his son Solomon king over Israel. **2** And he gathered together all the leaders of Israel, with the priests and the Levites. **3** Now the Levites were numbered from the age of thirty years and above; and the number of individual males was thirty-eight thousand. **4** Of these, twenty-four thousand *were* to look after the work of the house of the LORD, six thousand *were* officers and judges, **5** four thousand *were* gatekeepers, and four thousand praised the LORD with *musical* instruments, "which I made," *said David,* "for giving praise." **6** Also David separated them into divisions among the sons of Levi: Gershon, Kohath, and Merari.

1 Chr 24:1–3 Now *these are* the divisions of the sons of Aaron. The sons of Aaron *were* Nadab, Abihu, Eleazar, and Ithamar. **2** And Nadab and Abihu died before their father, and had no children; therefore Eleazar and Ithamar ministered as priests. **3** Then David with Zadok of the sons of Eleazar, and Ahimelech of the sons of Ithamar, divided them according to the schedule of their service.

1 Chr 24:19 This *was* the schedule of their service for coming into the house of the LORD according to their ordinance by the hand of Aaron their father, as the LORD God of Israel had commanded him.

1 Chr 25:1 Moreover David and the captains of the army separated for the service *some* of the sons of Asaph, of Heman, and of Jeduthun, who *should* prophesy with harps, stringed instruments, and cymbals. And the number of the skilled men performing their service was:

1 Chr 25:6–8 All these *were* under the direction of their father for the music *in* the house of the LORD, with cymbals, stringed instruments, and harps, for the service of the house of God. Asaph, Jeduthun, and Heman *were* under the authority of the king. **7** So the number of them, with their brethren who were instructed in the songs of the LORD, all who were skillful, *was* two hundred and eighty-eight. **8** And they cast lots for their duty, the small as well as the great, the teacher with the student.

1 Chr 26:1–3 Concerning the divisions of the gatekeepers: of the Korahites, Meshelemiah the son of Kore, of the sons of Asaph. **2** And the sons of Meshelemiah *were* Zechariah the firstborn, Jediael the second, Zebadiah the third, Jathniel the fourth, **3** Elam the fifth, Jehohanan the sixth, Eliehoenai the seventh.

1 Chr 26:12–20 Among these *were* the divisions of the gatekeepers, among the chief men, *having* duties just like their brethren, to serve in the house of the LORD. **13** And they cast lots for each gate, the small as well as the great, according to their father's house. **14** The lot for the East *Gate* fell to Shelemiah. Then they cast lots *for* his son Zechariah, a wise counselor, and his lot came out for the North Gate; **15** to Obed-Edom the South Gate, and to his sons the storehouse. **16** To Shuppim and Hosah *the lot came out* for the West Gate, with the Shallecheth Gate on the ascending highway—watchman opposite watchman. **17** On the east were *six* Levites, on the north four each day, on the south four each day, and for the storehouse two by two. **18** As for the Parbar on the west, *there were* four on the highway *and* two at the Parbar. **19** These were the divisions of the gatekeepers among the sons of Korah and among the sons of Merari. **20** Of the Levites, Ahijah *was* over the treasuries of the house of God and over the treasuries of the dedicated things.

1 Chr 26:26–32 This Shelomith and his brethren *were* over all the treasuries of the dedicated things which King David and the heads of fathers' *houses,* the captains over thousands and hundreds, and the captains of the army, had dedicated. **27** Some of the spoils won in battles they dedicated to maintain the house of the LORD. **28** And all that Samuel the seer, Saul the son of Kish, Abner the son of Ner, and Joab the son of Zeruiah had dedicated, every dedicated *thing,* was under the hand of Shelomith and his brethren. **29** Of the Izharites, Chenaniah and his sons *performed* duties as officials and judges over Israel outside Jerusalem. **30** Of the Hebronites, Hashabiah and his brethren, one thousand seven hundred able men, had the oversight of Israel on the west side of the Jordan for all the business of the LORD, and in the service of the king. **31** Among the Hebronites, Jerijah *was* head of the Hebronites according to his genealogy of the fathers. In the fortieth year of the reign of David they were sought, and there were found among them capable men at Jazer of Gilead. **32** And his brethren *were* two thousand seven hundred able men, heads of fathers' *houses,* whom King David made officials over the Reubenites, the Gadites, and the half-tribe of Manasseh, for every matter pertaining to God and the affairs of the king.

1 Chr 27:1 And the children of Israel, according to their number, the heads of fathers' *houses,* the captains of thousands and hundreds and their officers, served the king in every matter of the *military* divisions. *These divisions* came in and went out month by month throughout all the months of the year, each division *having* twenty-four thousand.

1 Chr 27:25–34 And Azmaveth the son of Adiel *was* over the king's treasuries; and Jehonathan the son of Uzziah was over the storehouses in the field, in the cities, in the villages, and in the fortresses. **26** Ezri the son of

Chelub was over those who did the work of the field for tilling the ground. **27** And Shimei the Ramathite *was* over the vineyards, and Zabdi the Shiphmite was over the produce of the vineyards for the supply of wine. **28** Baal-Hanan the Gederite was over the olive trees and the sycamore trees that *were* in the lowlands, and Joash *was* over the store of oil. **29** And Shitrai the Sharonite *was* over the herds that fed in Sharon, and Shaphat the son of Adlai was over the herds *that were* in the valleys. **30** Obil the Ishmaelite *was* over the camels, Jehdeiah the Meronothite *was* over the donkeys, **31** and Jaziz the Hagrite *was* over the flocks. All these *were* the officials over King David's property. **32** Also Jehonathan, David's uncle, *was* a counselor, a wise man, and a scribe; and Jehiel the son of Hachmoni *was* with the king's sons. **33** Ahithophel *was* the king's counselor, and Hushai the Archite *was* the king's companion. **34** After Ahithophel *was* Jehoiada the son of Benaiah, then Abiathar. And the general of the king's army *was* Joab.

And the lazy man.

Prov 12:24 The hand of the diligent will rule, But the lazy *man* will be put to forced labor.

Necessity of.

Prov 16:26 The person who labors, labors for himself, For his *hungry* mouth drives him *on*.

Eccl 6:7 All the labor of man *is* for his mouth, And yet the soul is not satisfied.

Eph 4:28 Let him who stole steal no longer, but rather let him labor, working with *his* hands what is good, that he may have something to give him who has need.

Eph 6:7 with goodwill doing service, as to the Lord, and not to men,

2 Thess 3:10–12 For even when we were with you, we commanded you this: If anyone will not work, neither shall he eat. **11** For we hear that there are some who walk among you in a disorderly manner, not working at all, but are busybodies. **12** Now those who are such we command and exhort through our Lord Jesus Christ that they work in quietness and eat their own bread.

Diligent, will be rewarded.

Prov 27:23–27 Be diligent to know the state of your flocks, *And* attend to your herds; **24** For riches *are* not forever, Nor does a crown *endure* to all generations. **25** *When* the hay is removed, and the tender grass shows itself, And the herbs of the mountains are gathered in, **26** The lambs *will provide* your clothing, And the goats the price of a field; **27** *You shall have* enough goats' milk for your food, For the food of your household, And the nourishment of your maidservants.

Cf. Prov 10:22; 11:24–26; 28:20; Heb 6:10

Refers to all of life's activities.

Eccl 1:3 What profit has a man from all his labor In which he toils under the sun?

Sometimes related to futility.

Eccl 2:11 Then I looked on all the works that my hands had done And on the labor in which I had toiled; And indeed all *was* vanity and grasping for the wind. *There was* no profit under the sun.

Eccl 2:17–23 Therefore I hated life because the work that was done under the sun *was* distressing to me, for all *is* vanity and grasping for the wind. **18** Then I hated all my labor in which I had toiled under the sun, because I must leave it to the man who will come after me. **19** And who knows whether he will be wise or a fool? Yet he will rule over all my labor in which I toiled and in which I have shown myself wise under the sun. This also *is* vanity. **20** Therefore I turned my heart and despaired of all the labor in which I had toiled under the sun. **21** For there is a man whose labor *is* with wisdom, knowledge, and skill; yet he must leave his heritage to a man who has not labored for it. This also *is* vanity and a great evil. **22** For what has man for all his labor, and for the striving of his heart with which he has toiled under the sun? **23** For all his days *are* sorrowful, and his work burdensome; even in the night his heart takes no rest. This also is vanity.

Eccl 3:9 What profit has the worker from that in which he labors?

Eccl 4:8 There is one alone, without companion: He has neither son nor brother. Yet *there is* no end to all his labors, Nor is his eye satisfied with riches. *But he never asks*, "For whom do I toil and deprive myself of good?" This also *is* vanity and a grave misfortune.

Cf. Jer 51:58

As a gift of God.

Eccl 3:13 and also that every man should eat and drink and enjoy the good of all his labor—it *is* the gift of God.

Eccl 5:19 As for every man to whom God has given riches and wealth, and given him power to eat of it, to receive his heritage and rejoice in his labor—this *is* the gift of God.

Concerning spiritual struggle.

Matt 11:28–30 Come to Me, all *you* who labor and are heavy laden, and I will give you rest. **29** Take My yoke upon you and learn from Me, for I am gentle and lowly in heart, and you will find rest for your souls. **30** For My yoke *is* easy and My burden is light."

Cf. John 6:29

By Paul.

Acts 18:3 So, because he was of the same trade, he stayed with them and worked; for by occupation they were tentmakers.

Acts 20:34 Yes, you yourselves know that these hands have provided for my necessities, and for those who were with me.

1 Cor 4:12 And we labor, working with our own hands. Being reviled, we bless; being persecuted, we endure;

1 Cor 9:1–12 Am I not an apostle? Am I not free? Have I not seen Jesus Christ our Lord? Are you not my work in the Lord? **2** If I am not an apostle to others, yet doubtless I am to you. For you are the seal of my apostleship in the Lord. **3** My defense to those who examine me is this: **4** Do we have no right to eat and drink? **5** Do we have no right to take along a believing wife, as *do* also the other apostles, the brothers of the Lord, and Cephas? **6** Or *is it* only Barnabas and I *who* have no right to refrain from working? **7** Who ever goes to war at his own expense? Who plants a vineyard and does not eat of its fruit? Or who tends a flock and does not drink of the milk of the flock?

8 Do I say these things as a *mere* man? Or does not the law say the same also? **9** For it is written in the law of Moses, *"You shall not muzzle an ox while it treads out the grain."* Is it oxen God is concerned about? **10** Or does He say *it* altogether for our sakes? For our sakes, no doubt, *this* is written, that he who plows should plow in hope, and he who threshes in hope should be partaker of his hope. **11** If we have sown spiritual things for you, *is it* a great thing if we reap your material things? **12** If others are partakers of *this* right over you, *are* we not even more? Nevertheless we have not used this right, but endure all things lest we hinder the gospel of Christ.

2 Cor 11:27 in weariness and toil, in sleeplessness often, in hunger and thirst, in fastings often, in cold and nakedness—

Col 1:29 To this *end* I also labor, striving according to His working which works in me mightily.

1 Thess 2:9 For you remember, brethren, our labor and toil; for laboring night and day, that we might not be a burden to any of you, we preached to you the gospel of God.

2 Thess 3:8 nor did we eat anyone's bread free of charge, but worked with labor and toil night and day, that we might not be a burden to any of you,

2 Tim 3:12 Yes, and all who desire to live godly in Christ Jesus will suffer persecution.

Cf. 2 Cor 11:7–9

Concerning elders.

1 Tim 5:17–18 Let the elders who rule well be counted worthy of double honor, especially those who labor in the word and doctrine. **18** For the Scripture says, *"You shall not muzzle an ox while it treads out the grain,"* and, "The laborer *is* worthy of his wages."

By believers, should be diligent.

Eph 6:5–9 Bondservants, be obedient to those who are your masters according to the flesh, with fear and trembling, in sincerity of heart, as to Christ; **6** not with eyeservice, as men-pleasers, but as bondservants of Christ, doing the will of God from the heart, **7** with goodwill doing service, as to the Lord, and not to men, **8** knowing that whatever good anyone does, he will receive the same from the Lord, whether *he is* a slave or free. **9** And you, masters, do the same things to them, giving up threatening, knowing that your own Master also is in heaven, and there is no partiality with Him.

Col 3:22–25 Bondservants, obey in all things your masters according to the flesh, not with eyeservice, as men-pleasers, but in sincerity of heart, fearing God. **23** And whatever you do, do it heartily, as to the Lord and not to men, **24** knowing that from the Lord you will receive the reward of the inheritance; for you serve the Lord Christ. **25** But he who does wrong will be repaid for what he has done, and there is no partiality.

1 Tim 6:1–2 Let as many bondservants as are under the yoke count their own masters worthy of all honor, so that the name of God and *His* doctrine may not be blasphemed. **2** And those who have believing masters, let them not despise *them* because they are brethren, but rather serve *them* because those who are benefited are believers and beloved. Teach and exhort these things.

LABOR (IN CHILDBIRTH)

Symbolic of suffering before a deliverance.

Is 13:8 And they will be afraid. Pangs and sorrows will take hold of *them;* They will be in pain as a woman in childbirth; They will be amazed at one another; Their faces *will be like* flames.

Is 21:3 Therefore my loins are filled with pain; Pangs have taken hold of me, like the pangs of a woman in labor. I was distressed when *I* heard *it;* I was dismayed when *I* saw *it.*

Is 26:17–18 As a woman with child Is in pain and cries out in her pangs, *When* she draws near the time of her delivery, So have we been in Your sight, O LORD. **18** We have been with child, we have been in pain; We have, as it were, brought forth wind; We have not accomplished any deliverance in the earth, Nor have the inhabitants of the world fallen.

Is 66:7–9 "Before she was in labor, she gave birth; Before her pain came, She delivered a male child. **8** Who has heard such a thing? Who has seen such things? Shall the earth be made to give birth in one day? *Or* shall a nation be born at once? For as soon as Zion was in labor, She gave birth to her children. **9** Shall I bring to the time of birth, and not cause delivery?" says the LORD. "Shall I who cause delivery shut up *the womb?*" says your God.

Jer 4:31 "For I have heard a voice as of a woman in labor, The anguish as of her who brings forth her first child, The voice of the daughter of Zion bewailing herself; She spreads her hands, *saying,* 'Woe *is* me now, for my soul is weary Because of murderers!'

Jer 13:21 What will you say when He punishes you? For you have taught them *To be* chieftains, to be head over you. Will not pangs seize you, Like a woman in labor?

Jer 22:23 O inhabitant of Lebanon, Making your nest in the cedars, How gracious will you be when pangs come upon you, Like the pain of a woman in labor?

Hos 13:13 The sorrows of a woman in childbirth shall come upon him. He *is* an unwise son, For he should not stay long where children are born.

Mic 4:10 Be in pain, and labor to bring forth, O daughter of Zion, Like a woman in birth pangs. For now you shall go forth from the city, You shall dwell in the field, And to Babylon you shall go. There you shall be delivered; There the LORD will redeem you From the hand of your enemies.

Mic 5:2–3 "But you, Bethlehem Ephrathah, *Though* you are little among the thousands of Judah, *Yet* out of you shall come forth to Me The One to be Ruler in Israel, Whose goings forth *are* from of old, From everlasting." **3** Therefore He shall give them up, Until the time *that* she who is in labor has given birth; Then the remnant of His brethren Shall return to the children of Israel.

Matt 24:8 All these *are* the beginning of sorrows.

1 Thess 5:3 For when they say, "Peace and safety!" then sudden destruction comes upon them, as labor pains upon a pregnant woman. And they shall not escape.

Lack of, means desolation.

Is 23:4 Be ashamed, O Sidon; For the sea has spoken, The strength of the sea, saying, "I do not labor, nor bring forth children; Neither do I rear young men, *Nor* bring up virgins."

LAKE

Of fire.

2 Thess 1:7–9 and to *give* you who are troubled rest with us when the Lord Jesus is revealed from heaven with His mighty angels, **8** in flaming fire taking vengeance on those who do not know God, and on those who do not obey the gospel of our Lord Jesus Christ. **9** These shall be punished with everlasting destruction from the presence of the Lord and from the glory of His power,

Rev 19:20 Then the beast was captured, and with him the false prophet who worked signs in his presence, by which he deceived those who received the mark of the beast and those who worshiped his image. These two were cast alive into the lake of fire burning with brimstone.

Rev 20:10 The devil, who deceived them, was cast into the lake of fire and brimstone where the beast and the false prophet *are*. And they will be tormented day and night forever and ever.

Rev 20:14–15 Then Death and Hades were cast into the lake of fire. This is the second death. **15** And anyone not found written in the Book of Life was cast into the lake of fire.

Rev 21:8 But the cowardly, unbelieving, abominable, murderers, sexually immoral, sorcerers, idolaters, and all liars shall have their part in the lake which burns with fire and brimstone, which is the second death."

Cf. Dan 7:11; Matt 13:38–42,49–50; 25:41; Heb 10:27; 2 Pet 3:7; Jude 6–7

Of Gennesaret (Sea of Galilee), where disciples fished.

Mark 1:16 And as He walked by the Sea of Galilee, He saw Simon and Andrew his brother casting a net into the sea; for they were fishermen.

Luke 5:1–11 So it was, as the multitude pressed about Him to hear the word of God, that He stood by the Lake of Gennesaret, **2** and saw two boats standing by the lake; but the fishermen had gone from them and were washing *their* nets. **3** Then He got into one of the boats, which was Simon's, and asked him to put out a little from the land. And He sat down and taught the multitudes from the boat. **4** When He had stopped speaking, He said to Simon, "Launch out into the deep and let down your nets for a catch." **5** But Simon answered and said to Him, "Master, we have toiled all night and caught nothing; nevertheless at Your word I will let down the net." **6** And when they had done this, they caught a great number of fish, and their net was breaking. **7** So they signaled to *their* partners in the other boat to come and help them. And they came and filled both the boats, so that they began to sink. **8** When Simon Peter saw *it,* he fell down at Jesus' knees, saying, "Depart from me, for I am a sinful man, O Lord!" **9** For he and all who were with him were astonished at the catch of fish which they had taken; **10** and so also *were* James and John, the sons of Zebedee, who were partners with Simon. And Jesus said to Simon, "Do not be afraid. From now on you will catch men." **11** So when they had brought their boats to land, they forsook all and followed Him.

LAMB, THE

Described as

The young of the flock.

Ex 12:5 Your lamb shall be without blemish, a male of the first year. You may take *it* from the sheep or from the goats.

Ezek 45:15 And one lamb shall be given from a flock of two hundred, from the rich pastures of Israel. These shall be for grain offerings, burnt offerings, and peace offerings, to make atonement for them," says the Lord GOD.

Patient.

Is 53:7 He was oppressed and He was afflicted, Yet He opened not His mouth; He was led as a lamb to the slaughter, And as a sheep before its shearers is silent, So He opened not His mouth.

Playful.

Ps 114:4 The mountains skipped like rams, The little hills like lambs.

Ps 114:6 O mountains, *that* you skipped like rams? O little hills, like lambs?

Vulnerable to wild beasts.

1 Sam 17:34 But David said to Saul, "Your servant used to keep his father's sheep, and when a lion or a bear came and took a lamb out of the flock,

Cared for by shepherds.

Is 40:11 He will feed His flock like a shepherd; He will gather the lambs with His arm, And carry *them* in His bosom, *And* gently lead those who are with young.

Used for

Food.

Deut 32:14 Curds from the cattle, and milk of the flock, With fat of lambs; And rams of the breed of Bashan, and goats, With the choicest wheat; And you drank wine, the blood of the grapes.

2 Sam 12:4 And a traveler came to the rich man, who refused to take from his own flock and from his own herd to prepare one for the wayfaring man who had come to him; but he took the poor man's lamb and prepared it for the man who had come to him."

Amos 6:4 Who lie on beds of ivory, Stretch out on your couches, Eat lambs from the flock And calves from the midst of the stall;

Clothing.

Prov 27:26 The lambs *will provide* your clothing, And the goats the price of a field;

Sacrifice.

1 Chr 29:21 And they made sacrifices to the LORD and offered burnt offerings to the LORD on the next day: a thousand bulls, a thousand rams, a thousand lambs, with their drink offerings, and sacrifices in abundance for all Israel.

2 Chr 29:32 And the number of the burnt offerings which the assembly brought was seventy bulls, one hundred rams, *and* two hundred lambs; all these *were* for a burnt offering to the LORD.

Offered in sacrifice

Males.

Ex 12:5 Your lamb shall be without blemish, a male of

the first year. You may take *it* from the sheep or from the goats.

Females.

Num 6:14 And he shall present his offering to the LORD: one male lamb in its first year without blemish as a burnt offering, one ewe lamb in its first year without blemish as a sin offering, one ram without blemish as a peace offering,

While a suckling.

1 Sam 7:9 And Samuel took a suckling lamb and offered *it as* a whole burnt offering to the LORD. Then Samuel cried out to the LORD for Israel, and the LORD answered him.

At a year old.

Ex 12:5 Your lamb shall be without blemish, a male of the first year. You may take *it* from the sheep or from the goats.

Num 6:14 And he shall present his offering to the LORD: one male lamb in its first year without blemish as a burnt offering, one ewe lamb in its first year without blemish as a sin offering, one ram without blemish as a peace offering,

From the earliest times.

Gen 4:4 Abel also brought of the firstborn of his flock and of their fat. And the LORD respected Abel and his offering,

Gen 22:7–8 But Isaac spoke to Abraham his father and said, "My father!" And he said, "Here I am, my son." Then he said, "Look, the fire and the wood, but where *is* the lamb for a burnt offering?" **8** And Abraham said, "My son, God will provide for Himself the lamb for a burnt offering." So the two of them went together.

Every morning and evening.

Ex 29:38–39 "Now this *is* what you shall offer on the altar: two lambs of the first year, day by day continually. **39** One lamb you shall offer in the morning, and the other lamb you shall offer at twilight.

Num 28:3–4 "And you shall say to them, 'This *is* the offering made by fire which you shall offer to the LORD: two male lambs in their first year without blemish, day by day, as a regular burnt offering. **4** The one lamb you shall offer in the morning, the other lamb you shall offer in the evening,

At the Passover.

Ex 12:3 Speak to all the congregation of Israel, saying: 'On the tenth of this month every man shall take for himself a lamb, according to the house of *his* father, a lamb for a household.

Ex 12:6–7 Now you shall keep it until the fourteenth day of the same month. Then the whole assembly of the congregation of Israel shall kill it at twilight. **7** And they shall take *some* of the blood and put *it* on the two doorposts and on the lintel of the houses where they eat it.

By Josiah.

2 Chr 35:7 Then Josiah gave the *lay* people lambs and young goats from the flock, all for Passover *offerings* for all who were present, to the number of thirty thousand, as well as three thousand cattle; these *were* from the king's possessions.

The firstborn of a donkey to be redeemed with.

Ex 13:13 But every firstborn of a donkey you shall redeem with a lamb; and if you will not redeem *it*, then you shall break its neck. And all the firstborn of man among your sons you shall redeem.

Ex 34:20 But the firstborn of a donkey you shall redeem with a lamb. And if you will not redeem *him*, then you shall break his neck. All the firstborn of your sons you shall redeem. "And none shall appear before Me empty-handed.

An extensive commerce in.

Ezra 7:17 now therefore, be careful to buy with this money bulls, rams, and lambs, with their grain offerings and their drink offerings, and offer them on the altar of the house of your God in Jerusalem.

Ezek 27:21 Arabia and all the princes of Kedar *were* your regular merchants. They traded with you in lambs, rams, and goats.

Tribute often paid in.

2 Kin 3:4 Now Mesha king of Moab was a sheep-breeder, and he regularly paid the king of Israel one hundred thousand lambs and the wool of one hundred thousand rams.

Is 16:1 Send the lamb to the ruler of the land, From Sela to the wilderness, To the mount of the daughter of Zion.

Covenants confirmed by gift of.

Gen 21:28–30 And Abraham set seven ewe lambs of the flock by themselves. **29** Then Abimelech asked Abraham, "What *is the meaning of* these seven ewe lambs which you have set by themselves?" **30** And he said, "You will take *these* seven ewe lambs from my hand, that they may be my witness that I have dug this well."

The image of, was on money.

Gen 33:19 And he bought the parcel of land, where he had pitched his tent, from the children of Hamor, Shechem's father, for one hundred pieces of money.

Josh 24:32 The bones of Joseph, which the children of Israel had brought up out of Egypt, they buried at Shechem, in the plot of ground which Jacob had bought from the sons of Hamor the father of Shechem for one hundred pieces of silver, and which had become an inheritance of the children of Joseph.

Illustrative of

Christ as a perfect sacrifice.

John 1:29 The next day John saw Jesus coming toward him, and said, "Behold! The Lamb of God who takes away the sin of the world!

1 Pet 1:19 but with the precious blood of Christ, as of a lamb without blemish and without spot.

Rev 5:6 And I looked, and behold, in the midst of the throne and of the four living creatures, and in the midst of the elders, stood a Lamb as though it had been slain, having seven horns and seven eyes, which are the seven Spirits of God sent out into all the earth.

Anything dear or cherished.

2 Sam 12:3 But the poor *man* had nothing, except one little ewe lamb which he had bought and nourished; and it grew up together with him and with his children. It ate of his own food and drank from his own cup and lay in his bosom; and it was like a daughter to him.

2 Sam 12:9 Why have you despised the commandment of the LORD, to do evil in His sight? You have killed Uriah the Hittite with the sword; you have taken his wife *to be* your wife, and have killed him with the sword of the people of Ammon.

The Lord's people.

Is 5:17 Then the lambs shall feed in their pasture, And in the waste places of the fat ones strangers shall eat.

Is 11:6 "The wolf also shall dwell with the lamb, The leopard shall lie down with the young goat, The calf and the young lion and the fatling together; And a little child shall lead them.

Is 40:11 He will feed His flock like a shepherd; He will gather the lambs with His arm, And carry *them* in His bosom, *And* gently lead those who are with young.

John 21:15 So when they had eaten breakfast, Jesus said to Simon Peter, "Simon, *son* of Jonah, do you love Me more than these?" He said to Him, "Yes, Lord; You know that I love You." He said to him, "Feed My lambs."

The patience of Christ.

Is 53:7 He was oppressed and He was afflicted, Yet He opened not His mouth; He was led as a lamb to the slaughter, And as a sheep before its shearers is silent, So He opened not His mouth.

Acts 8:32 The place in the Scripture which he read was this: *"He was led as a sheep to the slaughter; And as a lamb before its shearer is silent, So He opened not His mouth.*

Ministers among the ungodly.

Luke 10:3 Go your way; behold, I send you out as lambs among wolves.

Israel deprived of God's protection.

Hos 4:16 "For Israel is stubborn Like a stubborn calf; Now the LORD will let them forage Like a lamb in open country.

The wicked under judgments.

Jer 51:40 "I will bring them down Like lambs to the slaughter, Like rams with male goats.

LAMPS

Described as

Burning.

Gen 15:17 And it came to pass, when the sun went down and it was dark, that behold, there appeared a smoking oven and a burning torch that passed between those pieces.

Shining.

John 5:35 He was the burning and shining lamp, and you were willing for a time to rejoice in his light.

Lighted with oil.

Zech 4:2 And he said to me, "What do you see?" So I said, "I am looking, and there *is* a lampstand of solid gold with a bowl on top of it, and on the *stand* seven lamps with seven pipes to the seven lamps.

Matt 25:3 Those who *were* foolish took their lamps and took no oil with them,

Matt 25:4 but the wise took oil in their vessels with their lamps.

Matt 25:7–8 Then all those virgins arose and trimmed their lamps. 8 And the foolish said to the wise, 'Give us *some* of your oil, for our lamps are going out.'

Used for lighting

The tabernacle.

Ex 25:37 You shall make seven lamps for it, and they shall arrange its lamps so that they give light in front of it.

Houses.

Matt 5:15 Nor do they light a lamp and put it under a basket, but on a lampstand, and it gives light to all *who are* in the house.

Acts 20:8 There were many lamps in the upper room where they were gathered together.

Chariots of war by night.

Nah 2:3–4 The shields of his mighty men *are* made red, The valiant men *are* in scarlet. The chariots *come* with flaming torches In the day of his preparation, And the spears are brandished. 4 The chariots rage in the streets, They jostle one another in the broad roads; They seem like torches, They run like lightning.

Marriage processions.

Matt 25:1 "Then the kingdom of heaven shall be likened to ten virgins who took their lamps and went out to meet the bridegroom.

Persons going out at night.

John 18:3 Then Judas, having received a detachment of troops, and officers from the chief priests and Pharisees, came there with lanterns, torches, and weapons.

All night.

Prov 31:18 She perceives that her merchandise *is* good, And her lamp does not go out by night.

Illustrative of

The Word of God.

Ps 119:105 Your word *is* a lamp to my feet And a light to my path.

Prov 6:23 For the commandment *is* a lamp, And the law a light; Reproofs of instruction *are* the way of life,

2 Pet 1:19 And so we have the prophetic word confirmed, which you do well to heed as a light that shines in a dark place, until the day dawns and the morning star rises in your hearts;

Omniscience of Christ.

Dan 10:6 His body *was* like beryl, his face like the appearance of lightning, his eyes like torches of fire, his arms and feet like burnished bronze in color, and the sound of his words like the voice of a multitude.

Rev 1:14 His head and hair *were* white like wool, as white as snow, and His eyes like a flame of fire;

Graces of the Holy Spirit.

Rev 4:5 And from the throne proceeded lightnings, thunderings, and voices. Seven lamps of fire *were* burning before the throne, which are the seven Spirits of God.

Salvation of God.

Gen 15:17 And it came to pass, when the sun went down and it was dark, that behold, there appeared a smoking oven and a burning torch that passed between those pieces.

Is 62:1 For Zion's sake I will not hold My peace, And for Jerusalem's sake I will not rest, Until her righteousness goes forth as brightness, And her salvation as a lamp *that* burns.

God's guidance.

2 Sam 22:29 "For You *are* my lamp, O Lᴏʀᴅ; The Lᴏʀᴅ shall enlighten my darkness.

Job 29:3–4 When His lamp shone upon my head, *And when* by His light I walked *through* darkness; **4** Just as I was in the days of my prime, When the friendly counsel of God *was* over my tent;

Ps 18:28 For You will light my lamp; The Lᴏʀᴅ my God will enlighten my darkness.

Glory of the cherubim.

Ezek 1:13 As for the likeness of the living creatures, their appearance *was* like burning coals of fire, like the appearance of torches going back and forth among the living creatures. The fire was bright, and out of the fire went lightning.

Spirit of man.

Prov 20:27 The spirit of a man *is* the lamp of the Lᴏʀᴅ, Searching all the inner depths of his heart.

Ministers.

John 5:35 He was the burning and shining lamp, and you were willing for a time to rejoice in his light.

Severe judgments.

Rev 8:10 Then the third angel sounded: And a great star fell from heaven, burning like a torch, and it fell on a third of the rivers and on the springs of water.

A succession of heirs.

1 Kin 11:36 And to his son I will give one tribe, that My servant David may always have a lamp before Me in Jerusalem, the city which I have chosen for Myself, to put My name there.

1 Kin 15:4 Nevertheless for David's sake the Lᴏʀᴅ his God gave him a lamp in Jerusalem, by setting up his son after him and by establishing Jerusalem;

(Put out) destruction of the wicked.

Job 18:5–6 "The light of the wicked indeed goes out, And the flame of his fire does not shine. **6** The light is dark in his tent, And his lamp beside him is put out.

Job 13:9 Will it be well when He searches you out? Or can you mock Him as one mocks a man?

Job 21:17 "How often is the lamp of the wicked put out? *How often* does their destruction come upon them, The sorrows God distributes in His anger?

(Totally quenched) complete destruction of those who curse parents.

Prov 20:20 Whoever curses his father or his mother, His lamp will be put out in deep darkness.

LAMPSTAND

A part of household furniture.

2 Kin 4:10 Please, let us make a small upper room on the wall; and let us put a bed for him there, and a table and a chair and a lampstand; so it will be, whenever he comes to us, he can turn in there."

Used for holding

Candles or torches.

Matt 5:15 Nor do they light a lamp and put it under a basket, but on a lampstand, and it gives light to all *who are* in the house.

Lamps.

Ex 25:31 "You shall also make a lampstand of pure gold; the lampstand shall be of hammered work. Its shaft, its branches, its bowls, its *ornamental* knobs, and flowers shall be *of one piece.*

Ex 25:37 You shall make seven lamps for it, and they shall arrange its lamps so that they give light in front of it.

Zech 4:2 And he said to me, "What do you see?" So I said, "I am looking, and there *is* a lampstand of solid gold with a bowl on top of it, and on the *stand* seven lamps with seven pipes to the seven lamps.

For the tabernacle,

Form, etc., of.

Ex 25:31–36 "You shall also make a lampstand of pure gold; the lampstand shall be of hammered work. Its shaft, its branches, its bowls, its *ornamental* knobs, and flowers shall be *of one piece.* **32** And six branches shall come out of its sides: three branches of the lampstand out of one side, and three branches of the lampstand out of the other side. **33** Three bowls *shall be* made like almond *blossoms* on one branch, *with an ornamental* knob and a flower, and three bowls made like almond *blossoms* on the other branch, *with an ornamental* knob and a flower—and so for the six branches that come out of the lampstand. **34** On the lampstand itself four bowls *shall be* made like almond *blossoms, each with* its *ornamental* knob and flower. **35** And *there shall be* a knob under the *first* two branches of the same, a knob under the *second* two branches of the same, and a knob under the *third* two branches of the same, according to the six branches that extend from the lampstand. **36** Their knobs and their branches *shall be of one piece;* all of it *shall be* one hammered piece of pure gold.

Ex 37:17–22 He also made the lampstand of pure gold; of hammered work he made the lampstand. Its shaft, its branches, its bowls, its *ornamental* knobs, and its flowers were of the same piece. **18** And six branches came out of its sides: three branches of the lampstand out of one side, and three branches of the lampstand out of the other side. **19** There were three bowls made like almond *blossoms* on one branch, with an *ornamental* knob and a flower, and three bowls made like almond *blossoms* on the other branch, with an *ornamental* knob and a flower—and so for the six branches coming out of the lampstand. **20** And on the lampstand itself *were* four bowls made like almond *blossoms, each with* its *ornamental* knob and flower. **21** *There was* a knob under the *first* two branches of the same, a knob under the *second* two branches of the same, and a knob under the *third* two branches of the same, according to the six branches extending from it. **22** Their knobs and their branches were of one piece; all of it *was* one hammered piece of pure gold.

Held seven golden lamps.

Ex 25:37 You shall make seven lamps for it, and they shall arrange its lamps so that they give light in front of it.

Ex 37:23 And he made its seven lamps, its wick-trimmers, and its trays of pure gold.

Had snuffers, etc., of gold.

Ex 25:38 And its wick-trimmers and their trays *shall be* of pure gold.

Ex 37:23 And he made its seven lamps, its wick-trimmers, and its trays of pure gold.

Weighed a talent of gold.

Ex 25:39 It shall be made of a talent of pure gold, with all these utensils.

Made after a divine pattern.

Ex 25:40 And see to it that you make *them* according to the pattern which was shown you on the mountain.

Num 8:4 Now this workmanship of the lampstand *was* hammered gold; from its shaft to its flowers it *was* hammered work. According to the pattern which the LORD had shown Moses, so he made the lampstand.

Called the lamp of God.

1 Sam 3:3 and before the lamp of God went out in the tabernacle of the LORD where the ark of God *was,* and while Samuel was lying down,

Called the pure lampstand.

Lev 24:4 He shall be in charge of the lamps on the pure *gold* lampstand before the LORD continually.

Placed in the outer sanctuary over against the table.

Ex 40:24 He put the lampstand in the tabernacle of meeting, across from the table, on the south side of the tabernacle;

Heb 9:2 For a tabernacle was prepared: the first *part,* in which *was* the lampstand, the table, and the showbread, which is called the sanctuary;

Lighted with olive oil.

Ex 27:20 "And you shall command the children of Israel that they bring you pure oil of pressed olives for the light, to cause the lamp to burn continually.

Lev 24:2 "Command the children of Israel that they bring to you pure oil of pressed olives for the light, to make the lamps burn continually.

Lighted, etc., by priests.

Ex 27:21 In the tabernacle of meeting, outside the veil which *is* before the Testimony, Aaron and his sons shall tend it from evening until morning before the LORD. *It shall be* a statute forever to their generations on behalf of the children of Israel.

Lev 24:3–4 Outside the veil of the Testimony, in the tabernacle of meeting, Aaron shall be in charge of it from evening until morning before the LORD continually; *it shall be* a statute forever in your generations. 4 He shall be in charge of the lamps on the pure *gold* lampstand before the LORD continually.

Directions for removing.

Num 4:9–10 And they shall take a blue cloth and cover the lampstand of the light, with its lamps, its wick-trimmers, its trays, and all its oil vessels, with which they service it. 10 Then they shall put it with all its utensils in a covering of badger skins, and put *it* on a carrying beam.

Illustrative of

Christ.

Zech 4:2 And he said to me, "What do you see?" So I

said, "I am looking, and there *is* a lampstand of solid gold with a bowl on top of it, and on the *stand* seven lamps with seven pipes to the seven lamps.

John 8:12 Then Jesus spoke to them again, saying, "I am the light of the world. He who follows Me shall not walk in darkness, but have the light of life."

Heb 9:2 For a tabernacle was prepared: the first *part,* in which *was* the lampstand, the table, and the showbread, which is called the sanctuary;

The church.

Rev 1:13 and in the midst of the seven lampstands One like the Son of Man, clothed with a garment down to the feet and girded about the chest with a golden band.

Rev 1:20 The mystery of the seven stars which you saw in My right hand, and the seven golden lampstands: The seven stars are the angels of the seven churches, and the seven lampstands which you saw are the seven churches.

Believers.

Matt 5:14–16 "You are the light of the world. A city that is set on a hill cannot be hidden. 15 Nor do they light a lamp and put it under a basket, but on a lampstand, and it gives light to all *who are* in the house. 16 Let your light so shine before men, that they may see your good works and glorify your Father in heaven.

LANGUAGES

Universal at first.

Gen 11:1 Now the whole earth had one language and one speech.

Gen 11:6 And the LORD said, "Indeed the people *are* one and they all have one language, and this is what they begin to do; now nothing that they propose to do will be withheld from them.

Called

Speech.

Mark 14:70 But he denied it again. And a little later those who stood by said to Peter again, "Surely you are *one* of them; for you are a Galilean, and your speech shows *it.*"

Tongue.

Rev 5:9 And they sang a new song, saying: "You are worthy to take the scroll, And to open its seals; For You were slain, And have redeemed us to God by Your blood Out of every tribe and tongue and people and nation,

Confusion of,

A punishment for presumption, etc.

Gen 11:2–7 And it came to pass, as they journeyed from the east, that they found a plain in the land of Shinar, and they dwelt there. 3 Then they said to one another, "Come, let us make bricks and bake *them* thoroughly." They had brick for stone, and they had asphalt for mortar. 4 And they said, "Come, let us build ourselves a city, and a tower whose top *is* in the heavens; let us make a name for ourselves, lest we be scattered abroad over the face of the whole earth." 5 But the LORD came down to see the city and the tower which the sons of men had built. 6 And the LORD said, "Indeed the people *are* one and they all have one language, and this is what they begin to do; now nothing that they propose to do will be withheld from them. **7** Come, let Us go down and there confuse their language, that they may not understand one another's speech."

Scattered men over the earth.

Gen 11:8–9 So the LORD scattered them abroad from there over the face of all the earth, and they ceased building the city. **9** Therefore its name is called Babel, because there the LORD confused the language of all the earth; and from there the LORD scattered them abroad over the face of all the earth.

Divided men into separate nations.

Gen 10:5 From these the coastland *peoples* of the Gentiles were separated into their lands, everyone according to his language, according to their families, into their nations.

Gen 10:20 These *were* the sons of Ham, according to their families, according to their languages, in their lands *and* in their nations.

Gen 10:31 These *were* the sons of Shem, according to their families, according to their languages, in their lands, according to their nations.

Dialects.

Esth 1:22 Then he sent letters to all the king's provinces, to each province in its own script, and to every people in their own language, that each man should be master in his own house, and speak in the language of his own people.

Dan 3:4 Then a herald cried aloud: "To you it is commanded, O peoples, nations, and languages,

Dan 6:25 Then King Darius wrote: To all peoples, nations, and languages that dwell in all the earth: Peace be multiplied to you.

Acts 1:19 And it became known to all those dwelling in Jerusalem; so that field is called in their own language, Akel Dama, that is, Field of Blood.)

1 Cor 14:10 There are, it may be, so many kinds of languages in the world, and none of them *is* without significance.

Variety of,

Hebrew.

2 Kin 18:28 Then *the* Rabshakeh stood and called out with a loud voice in Hebrew, and spoke, saying, "Hear the word of the great king, the king of Assyria!

Acts 26:14 And when we all had fallen to the ground, I heard a voice speaking to me and saying in the Hebrew language, 'Saul, Saul, why are you persecuting Me? *It is* hard for you to kick against the goads.'

Chaldean.

Dan 1:4 young men in whom *there was* no blemish, but good-looking, gifted in all wisdom, possessing knowledge and quick to understand, who *had* ability to serve in the king's palace, and whom they might teach the language and literature of the Chaldeans.

Aramaic.

2 Kin 18:26 Then Eliakim the son of Hilkiah, Shebna, and Joah said to *the* Rabshakeh, "Please speak to your servants in Aramaic, for we understand *it*; and do not speak to us in Hebrew in the hearing of the people who *are* on the wall."

Ezra 4:7 In the days of Artaxerxes also, Bishlam, Mithredath, Tabel, and the rest of their companions wrote to Artaxerxes king of Persia; and the letter *was* written in Aramaic script, and translated into the Aramaic language.

Greek.

Acts 21:37 Then as Paul was about to be led into the barracks, he said to the commander, "May I speak to you?" He replied, "Can you speak Greek?

Latin.

Luke 23:38 And an inscription also was written over Him in letters of Greek, Latin, and Hebrew: THIS IS THE KING OF THE JEWS.

Lycaonian.

Acts 14:11 Now when the people saw what Paul had done, they raised their voices, saying in the Lycaonian *language,* "The gods have come down to us in the likeness of men!"

Arabic, etc.

Acts 2:11 Cretans and Arabs—we hear them speaking in our own tongues the wonderful works of God."

Egyptian.

Ps 81:5 This He established in Joseph *as* a testimony, When He went throughout the land of Egypt, *Where* I heard a language I did not understand.

Ps 114:1 When Israel went out of Egypt, The house of Jacob from a people of strange language,

Acts 2:10 Phrygia and Pamphylia, Egypt and the parts of Libya adjoining Cyrene, visitors from Rome, both Jews and proselytes,

Some unfamiliar.

Ezek 3:5–6 For you *are* not sent to a people of unfamiliar speech and of hard language, *but* to the house of Israel, **6** not to many people of unfamiliar speech and of hard language, whose words you cannot understand. Surely, had I sent you to them, they would have listened to you.

1 Cor 14:11 Therefore, if I do not know the meaning of the language, I shall be a foreigner to him who speaks, and he who speaks *will be* a foreigner to me.

Power of speaking different,

A gift of the Holy Spirit.

1 Cor 12:10 to another the working of miracles, to another prophecy, to another discerning of spirits, to another *different* kinds of tongues, to another the interpretation of tongues.

Promised.

Mark 16:17 And these signs will follow those who believe: In My name they will cast out demons; they will speak with new tongues;

Given on the day of Pentecost.

Acts 2:3–4 Then there appeared to them divided tongues, as of fire, and *one* sat upon each of them. **4** And they were all filled with the Holy Spirit and began to speak with other tongues, as the Spirit gave them utterance.

Followed receiving the gospel.

Acts 10:44–46 While Peter was still speaking these words, the Holy Spirit fell upon all those who heard the word. **45** And those of the circumcision who believed were astonished, as many as came with Peter, because the gift of the Holy Spirit had been poured out on the Gentiles also. **46** For they heard them speak with tongues and magnify God. Then Peter answered,

Conferred by laying on of the apostles' hands.

Acts 19:6 And when Paul had laid hands on them, the Holy Spirit came upon them, and they spoke with tongues and prophesied.

Necessary to spread of the gospel.

Acts 2:7–11 Then they were all amazed and marveled, saying to one another, "Look, are not all these who speak Galileans? **8** And how *is it that* we hear, each in our own language in which we were born? **9** Parthians and Medes and Elamites, those dwelling in Mesopotamia, Judea and Cappadocia, Pontus and Asia, **10** Phrygia and Pamphylia, Egypt and the parts of Libya adjoining Cyrene, visitors from Rome, both Jews and proselytes, **11** Cretans and Arabs—we hear them speaking in our own tongues the wonderful works of God."

A sign to unbelievers.

1 Cor 14:22 Therefore tongues are for a sign, not to those who believe but to unbelievers; but prophesying is not for unbelievers but for those who believe.

Sometimes abused.

1 Cor 14:2–12 For he who speaks in a tongue does not speak to men but to God, for no one understands *him;* however, in the spirit he speaks mysteries. **3** But he who prophesies speaks edification and exhortation and comfort to men. **4** He who speaks in a tongue edifies himself, but he who prophesies edifies the church. **5** I wish you all spoke with tongues, but even more that you prophesied; for he who prophesies *is* greater than he who speaks with tongues, unless indeed he interprets, that the church may receive edification. **6** But now, brethren, if I come to you speaking with tongues, what shall I profit you unless I speak to you either by revelation, by knowledge, by prophesying, or by teaching? **7** Even things without life, whether flute or harp, when they make a sound, unless they make a distinction in the sounds, how will it be known what is piped or played? **8** For if the trumpet makes an uncertain sound, who will prepare for battle? **9** So likewise you, unless you utter by the tongue words easy to understand, how will it be known what is spoken? For you will be speaking into the air. **10** There are, it may be, so many kinds of languages in the world, and none of them *is* without significance. **11** Therefore, if I do not know the meaning of the language, I shall be a foreigner to him who speaks, and he who speaks *will be* a foreigner to me. **12** Even so you, since you are zealous for spiritual *gifts, let it be* for the edification of the church *that* you seek to excel.

1 Cor 14:23 Therefore if the whole church comes together in one place, and all speak with tongues, and there come in *those who are* uninformed or unbelievers, will they not say that you are out of your mind?

Ceased when Scripture completed.

1 Cor 13:8–10 Love never fails. But whether *there are* prophecies, they will fail; whether *there are* tongues,

they will cease; whether *there is* knowledge, it will vanish away. **9** For we know in part and we prophesy in part. **10** But when that which is perfect has come, then that which is in part will be done away.

Interpretation of,

A gift of the Holy Spirit.

1 Cor 12:10 to another the working of miracles, to another prophecy, to another discerning of spirits, to another *different* kinds of tongues, to another the interpretation of tongues.

Most important in the early church.

1 Cor 14:5 I wish you all spoke with tongues, but even more that you prophesied; for he who prophesies *is* greater than he who speaks with tongues, unless indeed he interprets, that the church may receive edification.

1 Cor 14:13 Therefore let him who speaks in a tongue pray that he may interpret.

1 Cor 14:27–28 If anyone speaks in a tongue, *let there be* two or at the most three, *each* in turn, and let one interpret. **28** But if there is no interpreter, let him keep silent in church, and let him speak to himself and to God.

Lack of, was punishment.

Deut 28:49 The LORD will bring a nation against you from afar, from the end of the earth, *as swift* as the eagle flies, a nation whose language you will not understand,

Is 28:11 For with stammering lips and another tongue He will speak to this people,

Jer 5:15 Behold, I will bring a nation against you from afar, O house of Israel," says the LORD. "It *is* a mighty nation, It *is* an ancient nation, A nation whose language you do not know, Nor can you understand what they say.

LAVER OF BRONZE

Moses was commanded to make.

Ex 30:18 "You shall also make a laver of bronze, with its base also of bronze, for washing. You shall put it between the tabernacle of meeting and the altar. And you shall put water in it,

Wisdom was given to Bezalel to make.

Ex 31:2 "See, I have called by name Bezalel the son of Uri, the son of Hur, of the tribe of Judah.

Ex 31:9 the altar of burnt offering with all its utensils, and the laver and its base—

Ex 38:8 He made the laver of bronze and its base of bronze, from the bronze mirrors of the serving women who assembled at the door of the tabernacle of meeting.

Was placed in the court between the altar and the tabernacle.

Ex 30:18 "You shall also make a laver of bronze, with its base also of bronze, for washing. You shall put it between the tabernacle of meeting and the altar. And you shall put water in it,

Ex 40:7 And you shall set the laver between the tabernacle of meeting and the altar, and put water in it.

Ex 40:30 He set the laver between the tabernacle of

meeting and the altar, and put water there for washing;

Was anointed with holy oil.

Ex 40:11 And you shall anoint the laver and its base, and consecrate it.

Lev 8:11 He sprinkled some of it on the altar seven times, anointed the altar and all its utensils, and the laver and its base, to consecrate them.

The priests washed in,

Before consecration.

Ex 40:12 "Then you shall bring Aaron and his sons to the door of the tabernacle of meeting and wash them with water.

Before entering the tabernacle.

Ex 30:19–20 for Aaron and his sons shall wash their hands and their feet in water from it. **20** When they go into the tabernacle of meeting, or when they come near the altar to minister, to burn an offering made by fire to the LORD, they shall wash with water, lest they die.

Before approaching the altar.

Ex 30:20 When they go into the tabernacle of meeting, or when they come near the altar to minister, to burn an offering made by fire to the LORD, they shall wash with water, lest they die.

One made by Solomon for the temple.

1 Kin 7:23–26 And he made the Sea of cast bronze, ten cubits from one brim to the other; *it was* completely round. Its height *was* five cubits, and a line of thirty cubits measured its circumference. **24** Below its brim *were* ornamental buds encircling it all around, ten to a cubit, all the way around the Sea. The ornamental buds *were* cast in two rows when it was cast. **25** It stood on twelve oxen: three looking toward the north, three looking toward the west, three looking toward the south, and three looking toward the east; the Sea *was set* upon them, and all their back parts *pointed* inward. **26** It *was* a handbreadth thick; and its brim was shaped like the brim of a cup, *like* a lily blossom. It contained two thousand baths.

Called the bronze Sea.

2 Kin 25:13 The bronze pillars that *were* in the house of the LORD, and the carts and the bronze Sea that *were* in the house of the LORD, the Chaldeans broke in pieces, and carried their bronze to Babylon.

Jer 52:17 The bronze pillars that *were* in the house of the LORD, and the carts and the bronze Sea that *were* in the house of the LORD, the Chaldeans broke in pieces, and carried all their bronze to Babylon.

Illustrative of

Christ the fountain for sin.

Zech 13:1 "In that day a fountain shall be opened for the house of David and for the inhabitants of Jerusalem, for sin and for uncleanness.

Rev 1:5 and from Jesus Christ, the faithful witness, the firstborn from the dead, and the ruler over the kings of the earth. To Him who loved us and washed us from our sins in His own blood,

Regeneration.

Eph 5:26 that He might sanctify and cleanse her with the washing of water by the word,

Titus 3:5 not by works of righteousness which we have done, but according to His mercy He saved us, through the washing of regeneration and renewing of the Holy Spirit,

LAW OF GOD, THE

Given

To Adam.

Gen 2:16–17 And the LORD God commanded the man, saying, "Of every tree of the garden you may freely eat; **17** but of the tree of the knowledge of good and evil you shall not eat, for in the day that you eat of it you shall surely die."

To Noah.

Gen 9:6 "Whoever sheds man's blood, By man his blood shall be shed; For in the image of God He made man.

To Moses. See Law of Moses, The.

To the Israelites.

Ex 20:2–17 "I *am* the LORD your God, who brought you out of the land of Egypt, out of the house of bondage. **3** "You shall have no other gods before Me. **4** "You shall not make for yourself a carved image—any likeness *of anything* that *is* in heaven above, or that *is* in the earth beneath, or that *is* in the water under the earth; **5** you shall not bow down to them nor serve them. For I, the LORD your God, *am* a jealous God, visiting the iniquity of the fathers upon the children to the third and fourth *generations* of those who hate Me, **6** but showing mercy to thousands, to those who love Me and keep My commandments. **7** "You shall not take the name of the LORD your God in vain, for the LORD will not hold *him* guiltless who takes His name in vain. **8** "Remember the Sabbath day, to keep it holy. **9** Six days you shall labor and do all your work, **10** but the seventh day *is* the Sabbath of the LORD your God. *In it* you shall do no work: you, nor your son, nor your daughter, nor your male servant, nor your female servant, nor your cattle, nor your stranger who *is* within your gates. **11** For *in* six days the LORD made the heavens and the earth, the sea, and all that *is* in them, and rested the seventh day. Therefore the LORD blessed the Sabbath day and hallowed it. **12** "Honor your father and your mother, that your days may be long upon the land which the LORD your God is giving you. **13** "You shall not murder. **14** "You shall not commit adultery. **15** "You shall not steal. **16** "You shall not bear false witness against your neighbor. **17** "You shall not covet your neighbor's house; you shall not covet your neighbor's wife, nor his male servant, nor his female servant, nor his ox, nor his donkey, nor anything that *is* your neighbor's."

Ps 78:5 For He established a testimony in Jacob, And appointed a law in Israel, Which He commanded our fathers, That they should make them known to their children;

Described as

Absolute and perpetual.

Matt 5:18 For assuredly, I say to you, till heaven and earth pass away, one jot or one tittle will by no means pass from the law till all is fulfilled.

Pure.

Ps 19:8 The statutes of the L ORD *are* right, rejoicing the heart; The commandment of the L ORD *is* pure, enlightening the eyes;

Spiritual.

Rom 7:14 For we know that the law is spiritual, but I am carnal, sold under sin.

Holy, just, and good.

Rom 7:12 Therefore the law *is* holy, and the commandment holy and just and good.

1 Tim 1:8 But we know that the law *is* good if one uses it lawfully,

Exceedingly broad.

Ps 119:96 I have seen the consummation of all perfection, *But* Your commandment *is* exceedingly broad.

Perfect.

Ps 19:7 The law of the L ORD *is* perfect, converting the soul; The testimony of the L ORD *is* sure, making wise the simple;

Rom 12:2 And do not be conformed to this world, but be transformed by the renewing of your mind, that you may prove what *is* that good and acceptable and perfect will of God.

Truth.

Ps 119:142 Your righteousness *is* an everlasting righteousness, And Your law *is* truth.

Tutor.

Gal 3:24 Therefore the law was our tutor *to bring us* to Christ, that we might be justified by faith.

Not burdensome.

1 John 5:3 For this is the love of God, that we keep His commandments. And His commandments are not burdensome.

Requires obedience of the heart.

Deut 27:26 'Cursed *is* the one who does not confirm *all* the words of this law.' "And all the people shall say, 'Amen!' "

Ps 51:6 Behold, You desire truth in the inward parts, And in the hidden *part* You will make me to know wisdom.

Eccl 12:13 Let us hear the conclusion of the whole matter: Fear God and keep His commandments, For this is man's all.

Matt 5:28 But I say to you that whoever looks at a woman to lust for her has already committed adultery with her in his heart.

Matt 22:37 Jesus said to him, " 'You shall love the L ORD your God with all your heart, with all your soul, and with all your mind.'

Gal 3:10 For as many as are of the works of the law are under the curse; for it is written, *"Cursed is everyone who does not continue in all things which are written in the book of the law, to do them."*

James 2:10 For whoever shall keep the whole law, and yet stumble in one *point,* he is guilty of all.

Love is the fulfilling of.

Rom 13:8 Owe no one anything except to love one another, for he who loves another has fulfilled the law.

Rom 13:10 Love does no harm to a neighbor; therefore love *is* the fulfillment of the law.

Man, by nature, not in subjection to.

1 Kin 8:46 "When they sin against You (for *there is* no one who does not sin), and You become angry with them and deliver them to the enemy, and they take them captive to the land of the enemy, far or near;

Eccl 7:20 For *there is* not a just man on earth who does good And does not sin.

Rom 3:9–10 What then? Are we better *than they?* Not at all. For we have previously charged both Jews and Greeks that they are all under sin. **10** As it is written: *"There is none righteous, no, not one;*

Rom 3:19 Now we know that whatever the law says, it says to those who are under the law, that every mouth may be stopped, and all the world may become guilty before God.

Rom 7:5 For when we were in the flesh, the sinful passions which were aroused by the law were at work in our members to bear fruit to death.

Rom 8:7 Because the carnal mind *is* enmity against God; for it is not subject to the law of God, nor indeed can be.

Sin is a transgression of.

Rom 2:12 For as many as have sinned without law will also perish without law, and as many as have sinned in the law will be judged by the law

James 2:10 For whoever shall keep the whole law, and yet stumble in one *point,* he is guilty of all.

1 John 3:4 Whoever commits sin also commits lawlessness, and sin is lawlessness.

Man cannot be justified by.

Acts 13:39 and by Him everyone who believes is justified from all things from which you could not be justified by the law of Moses.

Rom 3:20 Therefore by the deeds of the law no flesh will be justified in His sight, for by the law *is* the knowledge of sin.

Rom 3:28 Therefore we conclude that a man is justified by faith apart from the deeds of the law.

Gal 2:16 knowing that a man is not justified by the works of the law but by faith in Jesus Christ, even we have believed in Christ Jesus, that we might be justified by faith in Christ and not by the works of the law; for by the works of the law no flesh shall be justified.

Gal 3:11 But that no one is justified by the law in the sight of God *is* evident, for *"the just shall live by faith."*

Gives the knowledge of sin.

Rom 2:15 who show the work of the law written in their hearts, their conscience also bearing witness, and between themselves *their* thoughts accusing or else excusing *them)*

Rom 3:20 Therefore by the deeds of the law no flesh will be justified in His sight, for by the law *is* the knowledge of sin.

Rom 4:15 because the law brings about wrath; for where there is no law *there is* no transgression.

Rom 5:12–14 Therefore, just as through one man sin entered the world, and death through sin, and thus death spread to all men, because all sinned— **13** (For until the law sin was in the world, but sin is not imputed when there is no law. **14** Nevertheless death reigned from Adam to Moses, even over those who had not sinned according to the likeness of the transgression of Adam, who is a type of Him who was to come.

Rom 7:7 What shall we say then? *Is* the law sin? Certainly not! On the contrary, I would not have known sin except through the law. For I would not have known covetousness unless the law had said, *"You shall not covet."*

Blessedness of keeping.

Ps 119:1 Blessed *are* the undefiled in the way, Who walk in the law of the LORD!

Matt 5:19 Whoever therefore breaks one of the least of these commandments, and teaches men so, shall be called least in the kingdom of heaven; but whoever does and teaches *them*, he shall be called great in the kingdom of heaven.

1 John 3:22 And whatever we ask we receive from Him, because we keep His commandments and do those things that are pleasing in His sight.

1 John 3:24 Now he who keeps His commandments abides in Him, and He in him. And by this we know that He abides in us, by the Spirit whom He has given us.

Rev 22:14 Blessed *are* those who do His commandments, that they may have the right to the tree of life, and may enter through the gates into the city.

Christ and, *See* The Law of Moses
Believers

Are freed from the bondage of.

Rom 6:14 For sin shall not have dominion over you, for you are not under law but under grace.

Rom 7:4 Therefore, my brethren, you also have become dead to the law through the body of Christ, that you may be married to another—to Him who was raised from the dead, that we should bear fruit to God.

Rom 7:6 But now we have been delivered from the law, having died to what we were held by, so that we should serve in the newness of the Spirit and not *in* the oldness of the letter.

Gal 3:10 For as many as are of the works of the law are under the curse; for it is written, *"Cursed is everyone who does not continue in all things which are written in the book of the law, to do them."*

Gal 3:13 Christ has redeemed us from the curse of the law, having become a curse for us (for it is written, *"Cursed is everyone who hangs on a tree"*),

Have, written on their hearts.

Jer 31:33 But this *is* the covenant that I will make with the house of Israel after those days, says the LORD: I will put My law in their minds, and write it on their hearts; and I will be their God, and they shall be My people.

Heb 8:10 *For this is the covenant that I will make with the house of Israel after those days, says the LORD: I will put My laws in their mind and write them on their hearts; and I will be their God, and they shall be My people.*

Love.

Ps 119:97 Oh, how I love Your law! It *is* my meditation all the day.

Ps 119:113 I hate the double-minded, But I love Your law.

Ps 119:165 Great peace have those who love Your law, And nothing causes them to stumble.

Delight in and establish.

Ps 119:77 Let Your tender mercies come to me, that I may live; For Your law *is* my delight.

Rom 3:31 Do we then make void the law through faith? Certainly not! On the contrary, we establish the law.

Rom 7:22 For I delight in the law of God according to the inward man.

Prepare their hearts to seek.

Ezra 7:10 For Ezra had prepared his heart to seek the Law of the LORD, and to do *it*, and to teach statutes and ordinances in Israel.

Obey.

Ps 119:18 Open my eyes, that I may see Wondrous things from Your law.

Ps 119:34 Give me understanding, and I shall keep Your law; Indeed, I shall observe it with *my* whole heart.

Ps 119:55 I remember Your name in the night, O LORD, And I keep Your law.

Neh 10:29 these joined with their brethren, their nobles, and entered into a curse and an oath to walk in God's Law, which was given by Moses the servant of God, and to observe and do all the commandments of the LORD our Lord, and His ordinances and His statutes:

Mal 4:4 "Remember the Law of Moses, My servant, Which I commanded him in Horeb for all Israel, *With the* statutes and judgments.

1 Cor 7:19 Circumcision is nothing and uncircumcision is nothing, but keeping the commandments of God *is what matters.*

1 Cor 9:21 to those *who are* without law, as without law (not being without law toward God, but under law toward Christ), that I might win those *who are* without law;

Gal 5:13–14 For you, brethren, have been called to liberty; only do not *use* liberty as an opportunity for the flesh, but through love serve one another. **14** For all the law is fulfilled in one word, *even* in this: *"You shall love your neighbor as yourself."*

1 John 5:3 For this is the love of God, that we keep His commandments. And His commandments are not burdensome.

Rev 12:17 And the dragon was enraged with the woman, and he went to make war with the rest of her offspring, who keep the commandments of God and have the testimony of Jesus Christ.

Should make, the subject of their conversation.

Ex 13:9 It shall be as a sign to you on your hand and as a memorial between your eyes, that the LORD's law may be in your mouth; for with a strong hand the LORD has brought you out of Egypt.

Lament over the violation of, by others.

Ps 119:136 Rivers of water run down from my eyes, Because *men* do not keep Your law.

The wicked disregard.

2 Chr 12:1 Now it came to pass, when Rehoboam had established the kingdom and had strengthened himself, that he forsook the law of the LORD, and all Israel along with him.

Ps 78:10 They did not keep the covenant of God; They refused to walk in His law,

Is 5:24 Therefore, as the fire devours the stubble, And the flame consumes the chaff, *So* their root will be as rottenness, And their blossom will ascend like dust; Because they have rejected the law of the LORD of hosts, And despised the word of the Holy One of Israel.

Is 30:9 That this *is* a rebellious people, Lying children, Children *who* will not hear the law of the LORD;

Jer 6:19 Hear, O earth! Behold, I will certainly bring calamity on this people— The fruit of their thoughts, Because they have not heeded My words Nor My law, but rejected it.

Jer 9:13 And the LORD said, "Because they have forsaken My law which I set before them, and have not obeyed My voice, nor walked according to it,

Amos 2:4 Thus says the LORD: "For three transgressions of Judah, and for four, I will not turn away its *punishment*, Because they have despised the law of the LORD, And have not kept His commandments. Their lies lead them astray, *Lies* which their fathers followed.

Hos 4:6 My people are destroyed for lack of knowledge. Because you have rejected knowledge, I also will reject you from being priest for Me; Because you have forgotten the law of your God, I also will forget your children.

Punishment for disobeying.

Neh 9:26–27 "Nevertheless they were disobedient And rebelled against You, Cast Your law behind their backs And killed Your prophets, who testified against them To turn them to Yourself; And they worked great provocations. **27** Therefore You delivered them into the hand of their enemies, Who oppressed them; And in the time of their trouble, When they cried to You, You heard from heaven; And according to Your abundant mercies You gave them deliverers who saved them From the hand of their enemies.

Is 65:11–13 "But you *are* those who forsake the LORD, Who forget My holy mountain, Who prepare a table for Gad, And who furnish a drink offering for Meni. **12** Therefore I will number you for the sword, And you shall all bow down to the slaughter; Because, when I called, you did not answer; When I spoke, you did not hear, But did evil before My eyes, And chose *that* in which I do not delight." **13** Therefore thus says the Lord GOD: "Behold, My servants shall eat, But you shall be hungry; Behold, My servants shall drink, But you shall be thirsty; Behold, My servants shall rejoice, But you shall be ashamed;

Jer 9:13–16 And the LORD said, "Because they have forsaken My law which I set before them, and have not obeyed My voice, nor walked according to it, **14** but they have walked according to the dictates of their own hearts and after the Baals, which their fathers taught them," **15** therefore thus says the LORD of hosts, the God of Israel: "Behold, I will feed them, this people, with wormwood, and give them water of gall to drink. **16** I will scatter them also among the Gentiles, whom neither they nor their fathers have

known. And I will send a sword after them until I have consumed them."

LAW OF MOSES, THE

Is from God.

Lev 26:46 These *are* the statutes and judgments and laws which the LORD made between Himself and the children of Israel on Mount Sinai by the hand of Moses.

Given

In the desert.

Ezek 20:10–11 "Therefore I made them go out of the land of Egypt and brought them into the wilderness. **11** And I gave them My statutes and showed them My judgments, 'which, *if* a man does, he shall live by them.'

At Horeb.

Deut 4:10 *especially concerning* the day you stood before the LORD your God in Horeb, when the LORD said to me, 'Gather the people to Me, and I will let them hear My words, that they may learn to fear Me all the days they live on the earth, and *that* they may teach their children.'

Deut 4:15 "Take careful heed to yourselves, for you saw no form when the LORD spoke to you at Horeb out of the midst of the fire,

Deut 5:2 The LORD our God made a covenant with us in Horeb.

From Mount Sinai.

Ex 19:11 And let them be ready for the third day. For on the third day the LORD will come down upon Mount Sinai in the sight of all the people.

Ex 19:20 Then the LORD came down upon Mount Sinai, on the top of the mountain. And the LORD called Moses to the top of the mountain, and Moses went up.

Through Moses as mediator.

Ex 31:18 And when He had made an end of speaking with him on Mount Sinai, He gave Moses two tablets of the Testimony, tablets of stone, written with the finger of God.

Deut 1:1–3 These *are* the words which Moses spoke to all Israel on this side of the Jordan in the wilderness, in the plain opposite Suph, between Paran, Tophel, Laban, Hazeroth, and Dizahab. **2** *It is* eleven days' *journey* from Horeb by way of Mount Seir to Kadesh Barnea. **3** Now it came to pass in the fortieth year, in the eleventh month, on the first *day* of the month, *that* Moses spoke to the children of Israel according to all that the LORD had given him as commandments to them,

Deut 5:5 I stood between the LORD and you at that time, to declare to you the word of the LORD; for you were afraid because of the fire, and you did not go up the mountain. *He* said:

Deut 5:27–28 You go near and hear all that the LORD our God may say, and tell us all that the LORD our God says to you, and we will hear and do *it*.' **28** "Then the LORD heard the voice of your words when you spoke to me, and the LORD said to me: 'I have heard the voice of the words of this people which they have spoken to you. They are right *in* all that they have spoken.

John 1:17 For the law was given through Moses, *but* grace and truth came through Jesus Christ.

John 7:19 Did not Moses give you the law, yet none of you keeps the law? Why do you seek to kill Me?"

Gal 3:19 What purpose then *does* the law *serve*? It was added because of transgressions, till the Seed should come to whom the promise was made; *and it was* appointed through angels by the hand of a mediator.

Through the ministration of angels.

Acts 7:53 who have received the law by the direction of angels and have not kept *it*."

Gal 3:19 What purpose then *does* the law *serve*? It was added because of transgressions, till the Seed should come to whom the promise was made; *and it was* appointed through angels by the hand of a mediator.

Heb 2:2 For if the word spoken through angels proved steadfast, and every transgression and disobedience received a just reward,

To the Jews.

Lev 26:46 These *are* the statutes and judgments and laws which the LORD made between Himself and the children of Israel on Mount Sinai by the hand of Moses.

Deut 4:8 And what great nation *is there* that has *such* statutes and righteous judgments as are in all this law which I set before you this day?

Ps 78:5 For He established a testimony in Jacob, And appointed a law in Israel, Which He commanded our fathers, That they should make them known to their children;

Ps 147:20 He has not dealt thus with any nation; And *as for His* judgments, they have not known them. Praise the LORD!

After the exodus.

Deut 4:45 These *are* the testimonies, the statutes, and the judgments which Moses spoke to the children of Israel after they came out of Egypt,

Ps 81:4–5 For this *is* a statute for Israel, A law of the God of Jacob. 5 This He established in Joseph *as* a testimony, When He went throughout the land of Egypt, *Where* I heard a language I did not understand.

Sacredness of.

Ex 19:13 Not a hand shall touch him, but he shall surely be stoned or shot *with an arrow;* whether man or beast, he shall not live.' When the trumpet sounds long, they shall come near the mountain."

Ex 19:21–24 And the LORD said to Moses, "Go down and warn the people, lest they break through to gaze at the LORD, and many of them perish. 22 Also let the priests who come near the LORD consecrate themselves, lest the LORD break out against them." 23 But Moses said to the LORD, "The people cannot come up to Mount Sinai; for You warned us, saying, 'Set bounds around the mountain and consecrate it.' " 24 Then the LORD said to him, "Away! Get down and then come up, you and Aaron with you. But do not let the priests and the people break through to come up to the LORD, lest He break out against them."

Heb 12:20 (For they could not endure what was commanded: *"And if so much as a beast touches the mountain, it shall be stoned or shot with an arrow."*

Terror of Israel at receiving.

Ex 19:16–19 Then it came to pass on the third day, in the morning, that there were thunderings and lightnings, and a thick cloud on the mountain; and the sound of the trumpet was very loud, so that all the people who *were* in the camp trembled. 17 And Moses brought the people out of the camp to meet with God, and they stood at the foot of the mountain. 18 Now Mount Sinai *was* completely in smoke, because the LORD descended upon it in fire. Its smoke ascended like the smoke of a furnace, and the whole mountain quaked greatly. 19 And when the blast of the trumpet sounded long and became louder and louder, Moses spoke, and God answered him by voice.

Ex 20:18–20 Now all the people witnessed the thunderings, the lightning flashes, the sound of the trumpet, and the mountain smoking; and when the people saw *it*, they trembled and stood afar off. 19 Then they said to Moses, "You speak with us, and we will hear; but let not God speak with us, lest we die." 20 And Moses said to the people, "Do not fear; for God has come to test you, and that His fear may be before you, so that you may not sin."

Deut 5:5 I stood between the LORD and you at that time, to declare to you the word of the LORD; for you were afraid because of the fire, and you did not go up the mountain. *He* said:

Deut 5:23–25 "So it was, when you heard the voice from the midst of the darkness, while the mountain was burning with fire, that you came near to me, all the heads of your tribes and your elders. 24 And you said: 'Surely the LORD our God has shown us His glory and His greatness, and we have heard His voice from the midst of the fire. We have seen this day that God speaks with man; yet he *still* lives. 25 Now therefore, why should we die? For this great fire will consume us; if we hear the voice of the LORD our God anymore, then we shall die.

Called

A fiery law.

Deut 33:2 And he said: "The LORD came from Sinai, And dawned on them from Seir; He shone forth from Mount Paran, And He came with ten thousands of saints; From His right hand *Came* a fiery law for them.

Ministry of death and condemnation.

2 Cor 3:7 But if the ministry of death, written *and* engraved on stones, was glorious, so that the children of Israel could not look steadily at the face of Moses because of the glory of his countenance, which *glory* was passing away,

2 Cor 3:9 For if the ministry of condemnation *had* glory, the ministry of righteousness exceeds much more in glory.

Living oracles.

Acts 7:38 "This is he who was in the congregation in the wilderness with the Angel who spoke to him on Mount Sinai, and *with* our fathers, the one who received the living oracles to give to us,

Royal law.

James 2:8 If you really fulfill *the* royal law according to the Scripture, *"You shall love your neighbor as yourself,"* you do well;

Book of the Law.

Deut 30:10 if you obey the voice of the LORD your God, to keep His commandments and His statutes which are written in this Book of the Law, *and* if you turn to the LORD your God with all your heart and with all your soul.

Josh 1:8 This Book of the Law shall not depart from your mouth, but you shall meditate in it day and night, that you may observe to do according to all that is written in it. For then you will make your way prosperous, and then you will have good success.

Book of Moses.

2 Chr 25:4 However he did not execute their children, but *did* as *it is* written in the Law in the Book of Moses, where the LORD commanded, saying, "The fathers shall not be put to death for their children, nor shall the children be put to death for their fathers; but a person shall die for his own sin."

2 Chr 35:12 Then they removed the burnt offerings that *they* might give them to the divisions of the fathers' houses of the *lay* people, to offer to the LORD, as *it is* written in the Book of Moses. And so *they did* with the cattle.

Written.

Deut 10:5 Then I turned and came down from the mountain, and put the tablets in the ark which I had made; and there they are, just as the LORD commanded me."

Deut 31:9 So Moses wrote this law and delivered it to the priests, the sons of Levi, who bore the ark of the covenant of the LORD, and to all the elders of Israel.

Deut 31:26 "Take this Book of the Law, and put it beside the ark of the covenant of the LORD your God, that it may be there as a witness against you;

Divided into

Moral, embodied in the Ten Commandments.

Deut 5:22 "These words the LORD spoke to all your assembly, in the mountain from the midst of the fire, the cloud, and the thick darkness, with a loud voice; and He added no more. And He wrote them on two tablets of stone and gave them to me.

Deut 10:4 And He wrote on the tablets according to the first writing, the Ten Commandments, which the LORD had spoken to you in the mountain from the midst of the fire in the day of the assembly; and the LORD gave them to me.

Ceremonial, relating to manner of worshiping God.

Lev 7:37–38 This *is* the law of the burnt offering, the grain offering, the sin offering, the trespass offering, the consecrations, and the sacrifice of the peace offering, 38 which the LORD commanded Moses on Mount Sinai, on the day when He commanded the children of Israel to offer their offerings to the LORD in the Wilderness of Sinai.

Heb 9:1–7 Then indeed, even the first *covenant* had ordinances of divine service and the earthly sanctuary. 2 For a tabernacle was prepared: the first *part*, in which *was* the lampstand, the table, and the showbread, which is called the sanctuary; 3 and behind the second veil, the part of the tabernacle which is called the Holiest of All, 4 which had the golden censer and the ark of the covenant overlaid on all sides with gold, in which *were* the golden pot that had the manna, Aaron's rod that budded, and the tablets of the covenant; 5 and above it were the cherubim of glory overshadowing the mercy seat. Of these things we cannot now speak in detail. 6 Now when these things had been thus prepared, the priests always went into the first part of the tabernacle, performing *the services.* 7 But into the second part the high priest *went* alone once a year, not without blood, which he offered for himself and *for* the people's sins *committed* in ignorance;

Civil, relating to administration of justice.

Deut 17:9–11 And you shall come to the priests, the Levites, and to the judge *there* in those days, and inquire *of them;* they shall pronounce upon you the sentence of judgment. 10 You shall do according to the sentence which they pronounce upon you in that place which the LORD chooses. And you shall be careful to do according to all that they order you. 11 According to the sentence of the law in which they instruct you, according to the judgment which they tell you, you shall do; you shall not turn aside *to* the right hand or *to* the left from the sentence which they pronounce upon you.

Acts 23:3 Then Paul said to him, "God will strike you, *you* whitewashed wall! For you sit to judge me according to the law, and do you command me to be struck contrary to the law?"

Acts 24:6 He even tried to profane the temple, and we seized him, and wanted to judge him according to our law.

A covenant with Israel.

Deut 28:1 "Now it shall come to pass, if you diligently obey the voice of the LORD your God, to observe carefully all His commandments which I command you today, that the LORD your God will set you high above all nations of the earth.

Deut 28:15 "But it shall come to pass, if you do not obey the voice of the LORD your God, to observe carefully all His commandments and His statutes which I command you today, that all these curses will come upon you and overtake you:

Jer 31:32 not according to the covenant that I made with their fathers in the day *that* I took them by the hand to lead them out of the land of Egypt, My covenant which they broke, though I was a husband to them, says the LORD.

Taught the Jews

To love and fear God.

Deut 6:5 You shall love the LORD your God with all your heart, with all your soul, and with all your strength.

Deut 10:12–13 "And now, Israel, what does the LORD your God require of you, but to fear the LORD your God, to walk in all His ways and to love Him, to serve the LORD your God with all your heart and with all your soul, 13 *and* to keep the commandments of the LORD and His statutes which I command you today for your good?

Matt 22:36 "Teacher, which *is* the great commandment in the law?"

Matt 22:38 This is *the* first and great commandment.

To love their neighbor.

Lev 19:18 You shall not take vengeance, nor bear any grudge against the children of your people, but you shall love your neighbor as yourself: I *am* the LORD.

Matt 22:39 And *the* second *is* like it: *'You shall love your neighbor as yourself.'*

Strict justice and impartiality.

Lev 19:35–36 'You shall do no injustice in judgment, in measurement of length, weight, or volume. **36** You shall have honest scales, honest weights, an honest ephah, and an honest hin: I *am* the LORD your God, who brought you out of the land of Egypt.

All punishments awarded according to.

John 8:5 Now Moses, in the law, commanded us that such should be stoned. But what do You say?"

John 19:7 The Jews answered him, "We have a law, and according to our law He ought to die, because He made Himself the Son of God."

Heb 10:28 Anyone who has rejected Moses' law dies without mercy on the testimony of two or three witnesses.

All Israelites required

To know.

Ex 18:16 When they have a difficulty, they come to me, and I judge between one and another; and I make known the statutes of God and His laws."

To observe.

Deut 4:6 Therefore be careful to observe *them*; for this *is* your wisdom and your understanding in the sight of the peoples who will hear all these statutes, and say, 'Surely this great nation *is* a wise and understanding people.'

Deut 6:2 that you may fear the LORD your God, to keep all His statutes and His commandments which I command you, you and your son and your grandson, all the days of your life, and that your days may be prolonged.

To remember.

Deut 6:6 "And these words which I command you today shall be in your heart.

Deut 11:18 "Therefore you shall lay up these words of mine in your heart and in your soul, and bind them as a sign on your hand, and they shall be as frontlets between your eyes.

Mal 4:4 "Remember the Law of Moses, My servant, Which I commanded him in Horeb for all Israel, *With the* statutes and judgments.

To teach their children.

Deut 6:7 You shall teach them diligently to your children, and shall talk of them when you sit in your house, when you walk by the way, when you lie down, and when you rise up.

Deut 11:19 You shall teach them to your children, speaking of them when you sit in your house, when you walk by the way, when you lie down, and when you rise up.

Kings to write and study.

Deut 17:18–19 "Also it shall be, when he sits on the throne of his kingdom, that he shall write for himself a copy of this law in a book, from *the one* before the priests, the Levites. **19** And it shall be with him, and

he shall read it all the days of his life, that he may learn to fear the LORD his God and be careful to observe all the words of this law and these statutes,

Good kings enforced.

2 Kin 23:24–25 Moreover Josiah put away those who consulted mediums and spiritists, the household gods and idols, all the abominations that were seen in the land of Judah and in Jerusalem, that he might perform the words of the law which were written in the book that Hilkiah the priest found in the house of the LORD. **25** Now before him there was no king like him, who turned to the LORD with all his heart, with all his soul, and with all his might, according to all the Law of Moses; nor after him did *any* arise like him.

2 Chr 31:21 And in every work that he began in the service of the house of God, in the law and in the commandment, to seek his God, he did *it* with all his heart. So he prospered.

Priests and Levites to teach.

Deut 33:8–10 And of Levi he said: "*Let* Your Thummim and Your Urim *be* with Your holy one, Whom You tested at Massah, And with whom You contended at the waters of Meribah, **9** Who says of his father and mother, 'I have not seen them'; Nor did he acknowledge his brothers, Or know his own children; For they have observed Your word And kept Your covenant. **10** They shall teach Jacob Your judgments, And Israel Your law. They shall put incense before You, And a whole burnt sacrifice on Your altar.

Neh 8:7 Also Jeshua, Bani, Sherebiah, Jamin, Akkub, Shabbethai, Hodijah, Maaseiah, Kelita, Azariah, Jozabad, Hanan, Pelaiah, and the Levites, helped the people to understand the Law; and the people *stood* in their place.

Mal 2:7 "For the lips of a priest should keep knowledge, And *people* should seek the law from his mouth; For he is the messenger of the LORD of hosts.

The scribes were learned in, and expounded.

Ezra 7:6 this Ezra came up from Babylon; and he *was* a skilled scribe in the Law of Moses, which the LORD God of Israel had given. The king granted him all his request, according to the hand of the LORD his God upon him.

Matt 23:2 saying: "The scribes and the Pharisees sit in Moses' seat.

Public instruction given to youth in.

Luke 2:46 Now so it was *that* after three days they found Him in the temple, sitting in the midst of the teachers, both listening to them and asking them questions.

Acts 22:3 "I am indeed a Jew, born in Tarsus of Cilicia, but brought up in this city at the feet of Gamaliel, taught according to the strictness of our fathers' law, and was zealous toward God as you all are today.

Publicly read

At the Feast of Tabernacles in the sabbatical year.

Deut 31:10–13 And Moses commanded them, saying: "At the end of *every* seven years, at the appointed time in the year of release, at the Feast of Tabernacles, **11** when all Israel comes to appear before the LORD your God in the place which He chooses, you shall read this law before all Israel in their hearing.

12 Gather the people together, men and women and little ones, and the stranger who *is* within your gates, that they may hear and that they may learn to fear the LORD your God and carefully observe all the words of this law, **13** and *that* their children, who have not known it, may hear and learn to fear the LORD your God as long as you live in the land which you cross the Jordan to possess."

By Joshua.

Josh 8:34–35 And afterward he read all the words of the law, the blessings and the cursings, according to all that is written in the Book of the Law. **35** There was not a word of all that Moses had commanded which Joshua did not read before all the assembly of Israel, with the women, the little ones, and the strangers who were living among them.

By Ezra.

Neh 8:2–3 So Ezra the priest brought the Law before the assembly of men and women and all who *could* hear with understanding on the first day of the seventh month. **3** Then he read from it in the open square that *was* in front of the Water Gate from morning until midday, before the men and women and those who could understand; and the ears of all the people *were attentive* to the Book of the Law.

In the synagogues every Sabbath day.

Acts 13:15 And after the reading of the Law and the Prophets, the rulers of the synagogue sent to them, saying, "Men *and* brethren, if you have any word of exhortation for the people, say on."

Acts 15:21 For Moses has had throughout many generations those who preach him in every city, being read in the synagogues every Sabbath."

A means of national reformation.

2 Chr 34:19–21 Thus it happened, when the king heard the words of the Law, that he tore his clothes. **20** Then the king commanded Hilkiah, Ahikam the son of Shaphan, Abdon the son of Micah, Shaphan the scribe, and Asaiah a servant of the king, saying, **21** "Go, inquire of the LORD for me, and for those who are left in Israel and Judah, concerning the words of the book that is found; for great *is* the wrath of the LORD that is poured out on us, because our fathers have not kept the word of the LORD, to do according to all that is written in this book."

Neh 8:13–18 Now on the second day the heads of the fathers' *houses* of all the people, with the priests and Levites, were gathered to Ezra the scribe, in order to understand the words of the Law. **14** And they found written in the Law, which the LORD had commanded by Moses, that the children of Israel should dwell in booths during the feast of the seventh month, **15** and that they should announce and proclaim in all their cities and in Jerusalem, saying, "Go out to the mountain, and bring olive branches, branches of oil trees, myrtle branches, palm branches, and branches of leafy trees, to make booths, as *it is* written." **16** Then the people went out and brought *them* and made themselves booths, each one on the roof of his house, or in their courtyards or the courts of the house of God, and in the open square of the Water Gate and in the open square of the Gate of Ephraim. **17** So the whole assembly of those who had returned from the captivity made booths and sat under the booths; for

since the days of Joshua the son of Nun until that day the children of Israel had not done so. And there was very great gladness. **18** Also day by day, from the first day until the last day, he read from the Book of the Law of God. And they kept the feast seven days; and on the eighth day *there was* a sacred assembly, according to the *prescribed* manner.

Could not give righteousness and spiritual life.

Rom 8:3–4 For what the law could not do in that it was weak through the flesh, God *did* by sending His own Son in the likeness of sinful flesh, on account of sin: He condemned sin in the flesh, **4** that the righteous requirement of the law might be fulfilled in us who do not walk according to the flesh but according to the Spirit.

Gal 3:21 *Is* the law then against the promises of God? Certainly not! For if there had been a law given which could have given life, truly righteousness would have been by the law.

Heb 10:1 For the law, having a shadow of the good things to come, *and* not the very image of the things, can never with these same sacrifices, which they offer continually year by year, make those who approach perfect.

Christ

Explained.

Matt 7:12 Therefore, whatever you want men to do to you, do also to them, for this is the Law and the Prophets.

Matt 22:37–40 Jesus said to him, " *'You shall love the LORD your God with all your heart, with all your soul, and with all your mind.'* **38** This is *the* first and great commandment. **39** And *the* second *is* like it: *'You shall love your neighbor as yourself.'* **40** On these two commandments hang all the Law and the Prophets."

Born under.

Gal 4:4 But when the fullness of the time had come, God sent forth His Son, born of a woman, born under the law,

Circumcised according to.

Luke 2:21 And when eight days were completed for the circumcision of the Child, His name was called JESUS, the name given by the angel before He was conceived in the womb.

Rom 15:8 Now I say that Jesus Christ has become a servant to the circumcision for the truth of God, to confirm the promises *made* to the fathers,

Came not to destroy but to fulfill.

Matt 5:17–18 "Do not think that I came to destroy the Law or the Prophets. I did not come to destroy but to fulfill. **18** For assuredly, I say to you, till heaven and earth pass away, one jot or one tittle will by no means pass from the law till all is fulfilled.

Attended all feasts of.

John 2:23 Now when He was in Jerusalem at the Passover, during the feast, many believed in His name when they saw the signs which He did.

John 7:2 Now the Jews' Feast of Tabernacles was at hand.

John 7:10 But when His brothers had gone up, then He also went up to the feast, not openly, but as it were in secret.

John 7:37 On the last day, that great *day* of the feast, Jesus stood and cried out, saying, "If anyone thirsts, let him come to Me and drink.

Fulfilled all aspects of.

Ps 40:7–8 Then I said, "Behold, I come; In the scroll of the book *it is* written of me. **8** I delight to do Your will, O my God, And Your law *is* within my heart."

Heb 9:8 the Holy Spirit indicating this, that the way into the Holiest of All was not yet made manifest while the first tabernacle was still standing.

Heb 9:11–14 But Christ came *as* High Priest of the good things to come, with the greater and more perfect tabernacle not made with hands, that is, not of this creation. **12** Not with the blood of goats and calves, but with His own blood He entered the Most Holy Place once for all, having obtained eternal redemption. **13** For if the blood of bulls and goats and the ashes of a heifer, sprinkling the unclean, sanctifies for the purifying of the flesh, **14** how much more shall the blood of Christ, who through the eternal Spirit offered Himself without spot to God, cleanse your conscience from dead works to serve the living God?

Heb 10:1 For the law, having a shadow of the good things to come, *and* not the very image of the things, can never with these same sacrifices, which they offer continually year by year, make those who approach perfect.

Heb 10:11–14 And every priest stands ministering daily and offering repeatedly the same sacrifices, which can never take away sins. **12** But this Man, after He had offered one sacrifice for sins forever, sat down at the right hand of God, **13** from that time waiting till His enemies are made His footstool. **14** For by one offering He has perfected forever those who are being sanctified.

Magnified and made honorable.

Is 42:21 The LORD is well pleased for His righteousness' sake; He will exalt the law and make *it* honorable.

Bore the curse of.

Deut 21:23 his body shall not remain overnight on the tree, but you shall surely bury him that day, so that you do not defile the land which the LORD your God is giving you *as* an inheritance; for he who is hanged *is* accursed of God.

Gal 3:13 Christ has redeemed us from the curse of the law, having become a curse for us (for it is written, *"Cursed is everyone who hangs on a tree"*),

Was not the manifestation of the grace of God.

John 1:17 For the law was given through Moses, *but* grace and truth came through Jesus Christ.

Rom 8:3–4 For what the law could not do in that it was weak through the flesh, God *did* by sending His own Son in the likeness of sinful flesh, on account of sin: He condemned sin in the flesh, **4** that the righteous requirement of the law might be fulfilled in us who do not walk according to the flesh but according to the Spirit.

Gal 3:17 And this I say, *that* the law, which was four hundred and thirty years later, cannot annul the covenant that was confirmed before by God in Christ, that it should make the promise of no effect.

The Jews

Zealous for.

John 9:28–29 Then they reviled him and said, "You are His disciple, but we are Moses' disciples. **29** We know that God spoke to Moses; *as for* this *fellow*, we do not know where He is from."

Acts 21:20 And when they heard *it*, they glorified the Lord. And they said to him, "You see, brother, how many myriads of Jews there are who have believed, and they are all zealous for the law;

Held those ignorant of, accursed.

John 7:49 But this crowd that does not know the law is accursed."

From regard to, rejected Christ.

Rom 9:31–33 but Israel, pursuing the law of righteousness, has not attained to the law of righteousness. **32** Why? Because *they did* not *seek it* by faith, but as it were, by the works of the law. For they stumbled at that stumbling stone. **33** As it is written: *"Behold, I lay in Zion a stumbling stone and rock of offense, And whoever believes on Him will not be put to shame."*

Accused Christ of breaking.

John 19:7 The Jews answered him, "We have a law, and according to our law He ought to die, because He made Himself the Son of God."

Accused Christians of speaking against.

Acts 6:11–14 Then they secretly induced men to say, "We have heard him speak blasphemous words against Moses and God." **12** And they stirred up the people, the elders, and the scribes; and they came upon *him*, seized him, and brought *him* to the council. **13** They also set up false witnesses who said, "This man does not cease to speak blasphemous words against this holy place and the law; **14** for we have heard him say that this Jesus of Nazareth will destroy this place and change the customs which Moses delivered to us."

Acts 21:28 crying out, "Men of Israel, help! This is the man who teaches all *men* everywhere against the people, the law, and this place; and furthermore he also brought Greeks into the temple and has defiled this holy place."

Dishonored God by breaking.

John 7:19 Did not Moses give you the law, yet none of you keeps the law? Why do you seek to kill Me?"

Rom 2:23 You who make your boast in the law, do you dishonor God through breaking the law?

Shall be judged by.

John 5:45 Do not think that I shall accuse you to the Father; there is *one* who accuses you—Moses, in whom you trust.

Rom 2:12 For as many as have sinned without law will also perish without law, and as many as have sinned in the law will be judged by the law

Was a burdensome yoke.

Acts 15:10 Now therefore, why do you test God by putting a yoke on the neck of the disciples which neither our fathers nor we were able to bear?

Contrasted with new covenant.

Heb 12:18–24 For you have not come to the mountain

that may be touched and that burned with fire, and to blackness and darkness and tempest, **19** and the sound of a trumpet and the voice of words, so that those who heard *it* begged that the word should not be spoken to them anymore. **20** (For they could not endure what was commanded: *"And if so much as a beast touches the mountain, it shall be stoned or shot with an arrow."* **21** And so terrifying was the sight *that* Moses said, *"I am exceedingly afraid and trembling."*) **22** But you have come to Mount Zion and to the city of the living God, the heavenly Jerusalem, to an innumerable company of angels, **23** to the general assembly and church of the firstborn *who are* registered in heaven, to God the Judge of all, to the spirits of just men made perfect, **24** to Jesus the Mediator of the new covenant, and to the blood of sprinkling that speaks better things than *that of* Abel.

LEADERSHIP

Of Abraham.

Gen 14:14–16 Now when Abram heard that his brother was taken captive, he armed his three hundred and eighteen trained *servants* who were born in his own house, and went in pursuit as far as Dan. **15** He divided his forces against them by night, and he and his servants attacked them and pursued them as far as Hobah, which *is* north of Damascus. **16** So he brought back all the goods, and also brought back his brother Lot and his goods, as well as the women and the people.

Gen 23:5–6 And the sons of Heth answered Abraham, saying to him, **6** "Hear us, my lord: You *are* a mighty prince among us; bury your dead in the choicest of our burial places. None of us will withhold from you his burial place, that you may bury your dead."

Gen 24:1–9 Now Abraham was old, well advanced in age; and the LORD had blessed Abraham in all things. **2** So Abraham said to the oldest servant of his house, who ruled over all that he had, "Please, put your hand under my thigh, **3** and I will make you swear by the LORD, the God of heaven and the God of the earth, that you will not take a wife for my son from the daughters of the Canaanites, among whom I dwell; **4** but you shall go to my country and to my family, and take a wife for my son Isaac." **5** And the servant said to him, "Perhaps the woman will not be willing to follow me to this land. Must I take your son back to the land from which you came?" **6** But Abraham said to him, "Beware that you do not take my son back there. **7** The LORD God of heaven, who took me from my father's house and from the land of my family, and who spoke to me and swore to me, saying, 'To your descendants I give this land,' He will send His angel before you, and you shall take a wife for my son from there. **8** And if the woman is not willing to follow you, then you will be released from this oath; only do not take my son back there." **9** So the servant put his hand under the thigh of Abraham his master, and swore to him concerning this matter.

Of Joseph in Egypt.

Gen 41:37–45 So the advice was good in the eyes of Pharaoh and in the eyes of all his servants. **38** And Pharaoh said to his servants, "Can we find *such a one* as this, a man in whom *is* the Spirit of God?" **39** Then Pharaoh said to Joseph, "Inasmuch as God has shown you all this, *there is* no one as discerning and wise as you. **40** You shall be over my house, and all my people shall be ruled according to your word; only in regard to the throne will I be greater than you." **41** And Pharaoh said to Joseph, "See, I have set you over all the land of Egypt." **42** Then Pharaoh took his signet ring off his hand and put it on Joseph's hand; and he clothed him in garments of fine linen and put a gold chain around his neck. **43** And he had him ride in the second chariot which he had; and they cried out before him, "Bow the knee!" So he set him over all the land of Egypt. **44** Pharaoh also said to Joseph, "I *am* Pharaoh, and without your consent no man may lift his hand or foot in all the land of Egypt." **45** And Pharaoh called Joseph's name Zaphnath-Paaneah. And he gave him as a wife Asenath, the daughter of Poti-Pherah priest of On. So Joseph went out over *all* the land of Egypt.

Of Moses.

Ex 3:7–10 And the LORD said: "I have surely seen the oppression of My people who *are* in Egypt, and have heard their cry because of their taskmasters, for I know their sorrows. **8** So I have come down to deliver them out of the hand of the Egyptians, and to bring them up from that land to a good and large land, to a land flowing with milk and honey, to the place of the Canaanites and the Hittites and the Amorites and the Perizzites and the Hivites and the Jebusites. **9** Now therefore, behold, the cry of the children of Israel has come to Me, and I have also seen the oppression with which the Egyptians oppress them. **10** Come now, therefore, and I will send you to Pharaoh that you may bring My people, the children of Israel, out of Egypt."

Ex 4:10–17 Then Moses said to the LORD, "O my Lord, I *am* not eloquent, neither before nor since You have spoken to Your servant; but I *am* slow of speech and slow of tongue." **11** So the LORD said to him, "Who has made man's mouth? Or who makes the mute, the deaf, the seeing, or the blind? *Have* not I, the LORD? **12** Now therefore, go, and I will be with your mouth and teach you what you shall say." **13** But he said, "O my Lord, please send by the hand of whomever *else* You may send." **14** So the anger of the LORD was kindled against Moses, and He said: "Is not Aaron the Levite your brother? I know that he can speak well. And look, he is also coming out to meet you. When he sees you, he will be glad in his heart. **15** Now you shall speak to him and put the words in his mouth. And I will be with your mouth and with his mouth, and I will teach you what you shall do. **16** So he shall be your spokesman to the people. And he himself shall be as a mouth for you, and you shall be to him as God. **17** And you shall take this rod in your hand, with which you shall do the signs."

Ex 18:17–26 So Moses' father-in-law said to him, "The thing that you do *is* not good. **18** Both you and these people who *are* with you will surely wear yourselves out. For this thing *is* too much for you; you are not able to perform it by yourself. **19** Listen now to my voice; I will give you counsel, and God will be with you: Stand before God for the people, so that you may bring the difficulties to God. **20** And you shall teach them the statutes and the laws, and show them the way in which they must walk and the work they must do. **21** Moreover you shall select from all the people able men, such as fear God, men of truth, hating covetousness; and place *such* over them *to be* rulers of thousands, rulers of hundreds, rulers of fifties, and rulers of tens. **22** And let them judge the people at all times. Then it will be *that* every great matter they shall bring to you, but every small matter they themselves shall judge. So it will be easier for you, for they will bear *the burden* with you. **23** If you do this thing, and God *so* commands you, then you will be able to endure, and all this people will also go to their place in peace." **24** So Moses heeded the voice of his father-in-law and did all that he had said. **25** And Moses chose able men out of all Israel, and made them heads over the people: rulers of thousands, rulers of hundreds, rulers of fifties, and rulers of tens. **26** So they judged the people at all times; the hard cases they brought to Moses, but they judged every small case themselves.

Num 12:1–8 Then Miriam and Aaron spoke against Moses because of the Ethiopian woman whom he had married; for he had married an Ethiopian woman. **2** So they said, "Has the LORD indeed spoken only through Moses? Has He not spoken through us also?" And the LORD heard *it*. **3** (Now the man Moses *was* very humble, more than all men who *were* on the face of the earth.) **4** Suddenly the LORD said to Moses, Aaron, and Miriam, "Come out, you three, to the tabernacle of meeting!" So the three came out. **5** Then the LORD came down in the pillar of cloud and stood *in* the door of the tabernacle, and called Aaron and Miriam. And they both went forward. **6** Then He said, "Hear now My words: If there is a prophet among you, I, the LORD, make Myself known to him in a vision; I speak to him in a dream. **7** Not so with My servant Moses; He *is* faithful in all My house. **8** I speak with him face to face, Even plainly, and not in dark sayings; And he sees the form of the LORD. Why then were you not afraid To speak against My servant Moses?"

Ps 105:26–36 He sent Moses His servant, *And* Aaron whom He had chosen. **27** They performed His signs among them, And wonders in the land of Ham. **28** He sent darkness, and made *it* dark; And they did not rebel against His word. **29** He turned their waters into blood, And killed their fish. **30** Their land abounded with frogs, *Even* in the chambers of their kings. **31** He spoke, and there came swarms of flies, *And* lice in all their territory. **32** He gave them hail for rain, *And* flaming fire in their land. **33** He struck their vines also, and their fig trees, And splintered the trees of their territory. **34** He spoke, and locusts came, Young locusts without number, **35** And ate up all the vegetation in their land, And devoured the fruit of their ground. **36** He also destroyed all the firstborn in their land, The first of all their strength.

Heb 11:23–29 By faith Moses, when he was born, was hidden three months by his parents, because they saw *he was* a beautiful child; and they were not afraid of the king's command. **24** By faith Moses, when he became of age, refused to be called the son of Pharaoh's daughter, **25** choosing rather to suffer affliction with the people of God than to enjoy the passing pleasures of sin, **26** esteeming the reproach of Christ

greater riches than the treasures in Egypt; for he looked to the reward. **27** By faith he forsook Egypt, not fearing the wrath of the king; for he endured as seeing Him who is invisible. **28** By faith he kept the Passover and the sprinkling of blood, lest he who destroyed the firstborn should touch them. **29** By faith they passed through the Red Sea as by dry *land*, *whereas* the Egyptians, attempting *to do* so, were drowned.

And sins of leaders.

Lev 4:22–26 'When a ruler has sinned, and done *something* unintentionally *against* any of the commandments of the LORD his God *in anything* which should not be done, and is guilty, **23** or if his sin which he has committed comes to his knowledge, he shall bring as his offering a kid of the goats, a male without blemish. **24** And he shall lay his hand on the head of the goat, and kill it at the place where they kill the burnt offering before the LORD. It *is* a sin offering. **25** The priest shall take some of the blood of the sin offering with his finger, put *it* on the horns of the altar of burnt offering, and pour its blood at the base of the altar of burnt offering. **26** And he shall burn all its fat on the altar, like the fat of the sacrifice of the peace offering. So the priest shall make atonement for him concerning his sin, and it shall be forgiven him.

Of the tribes of Israel.

Num 1:4–16 And with you there shall be a man from every tribe, each one the head of his father's house. **5** "These are the names of the men who shall stand with you: from Reuben, Elizur the son of Shedeur; **6** from Simeon, Shelumiel the son of Zurishaddai; **7** from Judah, Nahshon the son of Amminadab; **8** from Issachar, Nethanel the son of Zuar; **9** from Zebulun, Eliab the son of Helon; **10** from the sons of Joseph: from Ephraim, Elishama the son of Ammihud; from Manasseh, Gamaliel the son of Pedahzur; **11** from Benjamin, Abidan the son of Gideoni; **12** from Dan, Ahiezer the son of Ammishaddai; **13** from Asher, Pagiel the son of Ocran; **14** from Gad, Eliasaph the son of Deuel; **15** from Naphtali, Ahira the son of Enan." **16** These *were* chosen from the congregation, leaders of their fathers' tribes, heads of the divisions in Israel.

Of Joshua.

Ex 17:9–10 And Moses said to Joshua, "Choose us some men and go out, fight with Amalek. Tomorrow I will stand on the top of the hill with the rod of God in my hand." **10** So Joshua did as Moses said to him, and fought with Amalek. And Moses, Aaron, and Hur went up to the top of the hill.

Num 27:15–23 Then Moses spoke to the LORD, saying: **16** "Let the LORD, the God of the spirits of all flesh, set a man over the congregation, **17** who may go out before them and go in before them, who may lead them out and bring them in, that the congregation of the LORD may not be like sheep which have no shepherd." **18** And the LORD said to Moses: "Take Joshua the son of Nun with you, a man in whom *is* the Spirit, and lay your hand on him; **19** set him before Eleazar the priest and before all the congregation, and inaugurate him in their sight. **20** And you shall give *some* of your authority to him, that all the congregation of the children of Israel may be obedient. **21** He shall stand before Eleazar the priest, who shall inquire before the Lord for him by the judgment of the Urim. At his word they shall go out, and at his word they shall come in, he and all the children of Israel with him—all the congregation." 22 So Moses did as the Lord commanded him. He took Joshua and set him before Eleazar the priest and before all the congregation. 23 And he laid his hands on him and inaugurated him, just as the Lord commanded by the hand of Moses.

Cf. Deut 31:1–29; Josh 1:1–18

Of the judges.

Judg 2:16 Nevertheless, the Lord raised up judges who delivered them out of the hand of those who plundered them.

Judg 3:1–11 Now these *are* the nations which the Lord left, that He might test Israel by them, *that is,* all who had not known any of the wars in Canaan 2 (*this was* only so that the generations of the children of Israel might be taught to know war, at least those who had not formerly known it), 3 *namely,* five lords of the Philistines, all the Canaanites, the Sidonians, and the Hivites who dwelt in Mount Lebanon, from Mount Baal Hermon to the entrance of Hamath. 4 And they were *left, that He might* test Israel by them, to know whether they would obey the commandments of the Lord, which He had commanded their fathers by the hand of Moses. 5 Thus the children of Israel dwelt among the Canaanites, the Hittites, the Amorites, the Perizzites, the Hivites, and the Jebusites. 6 And they took their daughters to be their wives, and gave their daughters to their sons; and they served their gods. 7 So the children of Israel did evil in the sight of the Lord. They forgot the Lord their God, and served the Baals and Asherahs. 8 Therefore the anger of the Lord was hot against Israel, and He sold them into the hand of Cushan-Rishathaim king of Mesopotamia; and the children of Israel served Cushan-Rishathaim eight years. 9 When the children of Israel cried out to the Lord, the Lord raised up a deliverer for the children of Israel, who delivered them: Othniel the son of Kenaz, Caleb's younger brother. 10 The Spirit of the Lord came upon him, and he judged Israel. He went out to war, and the Lord delivered Cushan-Rishathaim king of Mesopotamia into his hand; and his hand prevailed over Cushan-Rishathaim. 11 So the land had rest for forty years. Then Othniel the son of Kenaz died.

Judg 4:4–9 Now Deborah, a prophetess, the wife of Lapidoth, was judging Israel at that time. 5 And she would sit under the palm tree of Deborah between Ramah and Bethel in the mountains of Ephraim. And the children of Israel came up to her for judgment. 6 Then she sent and called for Barak the son of Abinoam from Kedesh in Naphtali, and said to him, "Has not the Lord God of Israel commanded, 'Go and deploy *troops* at Mount Tabor; take with you ten thousand men of the sons of Naphtali and of the sons of Zebulun; 7 and against you I will deploy Sisera, the commander of Jabin's army, with his chariots and his multitude at the River Kishon; and I will deliver him into your hand'?" 8 And Barak said to her, "If you will go with me, then I will go; but if you will not go with me, I will not go!" 9 So she said, "I will surely go with you; nevertheless there will be no glory

for you in the journey you are taking, for the Lord will sell Sisera into the hand of a woman." Then Deborah arose and went with Barak to Kedesh.

Judg 6:11–18 Now the Angel of the Lord came and sat under the terebinth tree which *was* in Ophrah, which *belonged* to Joash the Abiezrite, while his son Gideon threshed wheat in the winepress, in order to hide *it* from the Midianites. 12 And the Angel of the Lord appeared to him, and said to him, "The Lord *is* with you, you mighty man of valor!" 13 Gideon said to Him, "O my lord, if the Lord is with us, why then has all this happened to us? And where *are* all His miracles which our fathers told us about, saying, 'Did not the Lord bring us up from Egypt?' But now the Lord has forsaken us and delivered us into the hands of the Midianites." 14 Then the Lord turned to him and said, "Go in this might of yours, and you shall save Israel from the hand of the Midianites. Have I not sent you?" 15 So he said to Him, "O my Lord, how can I save Israel? Indeed my clan *is* the weakest in Manasseh, and I *am* the least in my father's house." 16 And the Lord said to him, "Surely I will be with you, and you shall defeat the Midianites as one man." 17 Then he said to Him, "If now I have found favor in Your sight, then show me a sign that it is You who talk with me. 18 Do not depart from here, I pray, until I come to You and bring out my offering and set *it* before You." And He said, "I will wait until you come back."

Judg 8:22–28 Then the men of Israel said to Gideon, "Rule over us, both you and your son, and your grandson also; for you have delivered us from the hand of Midian." 23 But Gideon said to them, "I will not rule over you, nor shall my son rule over you; the Lord shall rule over you." 24 Then Gideon said to them, "I would like to make a request of you, that each of you would give me the earrings from his plunder." For they had golden earrings, because they *were* Ishmaelites. 25 So they answered, "We will gladly give *them.*" And they spread out a garment, and each man threw into it the earrings from his plunder. 26 Now the weight of the gold earrings that he requested was one thousand seven hundred *shekels* of gold, besides the crescent ornaments, pendants, and purple robes which *were* on the kings of Midian, and besides the chains that *were* around their camels' necks. 27 Then Gideon made it into an ephod and set it up in his city, Ophrah. And all Israel played the harlot with it there. It became a snare to Gideon and to his house. 28 Thus Midian was subdued before the children of Israel, so that they lifted their heads no more. And the country was quiet for forty years in the days of Gideon.

Judg 9:1–6 Then Abimelech the son of Jerubbaal went to Shechem, to his mother's brothers, and spoke with them and with all the family of the house of his mother's father, saying, 2 "Please speak in the hearing of all the men of Shechem: 'Which is better for you, that all seventy of the sons of Jerubbaal reign over you, or that one reign over you?' Remember that I *am* your own flesh and bone." 3 And his mother's brothers spoke all these words concerning him in the hearing of all the men of Shechem; and their heart was inclined to follow Abimelech, for they said, "He is our brother." 4 So they gave him seventy *shekels* of silver from the temple of Baal-Berith, with which Abimelech hired worthless and reckless men; and they followed him. 5 Then he went to his father's house at Ophrah and killed his brothers, the seventy sons of Jerubbaal, on one stone. But Jotham the youngest son of Jerubbaal was left, because he hid himself. 6 And all the men of Shechem gathered together, all of Beth Millo, and they went and made Abimelech king beside the terebinth tree at the pillar that *was* in Shechem.

Judg 10:1–5 After Abimelech there arose to save Israel Tola the son of Puah, the son of Dodo, a man of Issachar; and he dwelt in Shamir in the mountains of Ephraim. 2 He judged Israel twenty-three years; and he died and was buried in Shamir. 3 After him arose Jair, a Gileadite; and he judged Israel twenty-two years. 4 Now he had thirty sons who rode on thirty donkeys; they also had thirty towns, which are called "Havoth Jair" to this day, which *are* in the land of Gilead. 5 And Jair died and was buried in Camon.

Judg 11:1–11 Now Jephthah the Gileadite was a mighty man of valor, but he *was* the son of a harlot; and Gilead begot Jephthah. 2 Gilead's wife bore sons; and when his wife's sons grew up, they drove Jephthah out, and said to him, "You shall have no inheritance in our father's house, for you *are* the son of another woman." 3 Then Jephthah fled from his brothers and dwelt in the land of Tob; and worthless men banded together with Jephthah and went out *raiding* with him. 4 It came to pass after a time that the people of Ammon made war against Israel. 5 And so it was, when the people of Ammon made war against Israel, that the elders of Gilead went to get Jephthah from the land of Tob. 6 Then they said to Jephthah, "Come and be our commander, that we may fight against the people of Ammon." 7 So Jephthah said to the elders of Gilead, "Did you not hate me, and expel me from my father's house? Why have you come to me now when you are in distress?" 8 And the elders of Gilead said to Jephthah, "That is why we have turned again to you now, that you may go with us and fight against the people of Ammon, and be our head over all the inhabitants of Gilead." 9 So Jephthah said to the elders of Gilead, "If you take me back home to fight against the people of Ammon, and the LORD delivers them to me, shall I be your head?" 10 And the elders of Gilead said to Jephthah, "The LORD will be a witness between us, if we do not do according to your words." 11 Then Jephthah went with the elders of Gilead, and the people made him head and commander over them; and Jephthah spoke all his words before the LORD in Mizpah.

Judg 12:8–15 After him, Ibzan of Bethlehem judged Israel. 9 He had thirty sons. And he gave away thirty daughters in marriage, and brought in thirty daughters from elsewhere for his sons. He judged Israel seven years. 10 Then Ibzan died and was buried at Bethlehem. 11 After him, Elon the Zebulunite judged Israel. He judged Israel ten years. 12 And Elon the Zebulunite died and was buried at Aijalon in the country of Zebulun. 13 After him, Abdon the son of Hillel the Pirathonite judged Israel. 14 He had forty sons and thirty grandsons, who rode on seventy young donkeys. He judged Israel eight years. 15 Then Abdon the son of Hillel the Pirathonite died

and was buried in Pirathon in the land of Ephraim, in the mountains of the Amalekites.

Judg 13:24–25 So the woman bore a son and called his name Samson; and the child grew, and the LORD blessed him. 25 And the Spirit of the LORD began to move upon him at Mahaneh Dan between Zorah and Eshtaol.

Judg 16:28–31 Then Samson called to the LORD, saying, "O Lord GOD, remember me, I pray! Strengthen me, I pray, just this once, O God, that I may with one *blow* take vengeance on the Philistines for my two eyes!" 29 And Samson took hold of the two middle pillars which supported the temple, and he braced himself against them, one on his right and the other on his left. 30 Then Samson said, "Let me die with the Philistines!" And he pushed with *all his* might, and the temple fell on the lords and all the people who *were* in it. So the dead that he killed at his death were more than he had killed in his life. 31 And his brothers and all his father's household came down and took him, and brought *him* up and buried him between Zorah and Eshtaol in the tomb of his father Manoah. He had judged Israel twenty years.

Heb 11:32–34 And what more shall I say? For the time would fail me to tell of Gideon and Barak and Samson and Jephthah, also *of* David and Samuel and the prophets: 33 who through faith subdued kingdoms, worked righteousness, obtained promises, stopped the mouths of lions, 34 quenched the violence of fire, escaped the edge of the sword, out of weakness were made strong, became valiant in battle, turned to flight the armies of the aliens.

Cf. Judg 3:15–31

Of Samuel.

1 Sam 3:19–21 So Samuel grew, and the LORD was with him and let none of his words fall to the ground. 20 And all Israel from Dan to Beersheba knew that Samuel *had been* established as a prophet of the LORD. 21 Then the LORD appeared again in Shiloh. For the LORD revealed Himself to Samuel in Shiloh by the word of the LORD.

1 Sam 7:2–6 So it was that the ark remained in Kirjath Jearim a long time; it was there twenty years. And all the house of Israel lamented after the LORD. 3 Then Samuel spoke to all the house of Israel, saying, "If you return to the LORD with all your hearts, *then* put away the foreign gods and the Ashtoreths from among you, and prepare your hearts for the LORD, and serve Him only; and He will deliver you from the hand of the Philistines." 4 So the children of Israel put away the Baals and the Ashtoreths, and served the LORD only. 5 And Samuel said, "Gather all Israel to Mizpah, and I will pray to the LORD for you." 6 So they gathered together at Mizpah, drew water, and poured *it* out before the LORD. And they fasted that day, and said there, "We have sinned against the LORD." And Samuel judged the children of Israel at Mizpah.

Cf. 1 Sam 8:4–22; 12:1–18

Of King Saul.

1 Sam 9:27 As they were going down to the outskirts of the city, Samuel said to Saul, "Tell the servant to go on ahead of us." And he went on. "But you stand here awhile, that I may announce to you the word of God."

1 Sam 10:1 Then Samuel took a flask of oil and poured *it* on his head, and kissed him and said: *"Is it* not because the LORD has anointed you commander over His inheritance?

1 Sam 10:17–24 Then Samuel called the people together to the LORD at Mizpah, **18** and said to the children of Israel, "Thus says the LORD God of Israel: 'I brought up Israel out of Egypt, and delivered you from the hand of the Egyptians *and* from the hand of all kingdoms and from those who oppressed you.' **19** But you have today rejected your God, who Himself saved you from all your adversities and your tribulations; and you have said to Him, 'No, set a king over us!' Now therefore, present yourselves before the LORD by your tribes and by your clans." **20** And when Samuel had caused all the tribes of Israel to come near, the tribe of Benjamin was chosen. **21** When he had caused the tribe of Benjamin to come near by their families, the family of Matri was chosen. And Saul the son of Kish was chosen. But when they sought him, he could not be found. **22** Therefore they inquired of the LORD further, "Has the man come here yet?" And the LORD answered, "There he is, hidden among the equipment." **23** So they ran and brought him from there; and when he stood among the people, he was taller than any of the people from his shoulders upward. **24** And Samuel said to all the people, "Do you see him whom the LORD has chosen, that *there is* no one like him among all the people?" So all the people shouted and said, "Long live the king!"

1 Sam 13:13–14 And Samuel said to Saul, "You have done foolishly. You have not kept the commandment of the LORD your God, which He commanded you. For now the LORD would have established your kingdom over Israel forever. **14** But now your kingdom shall not continue. The LORD has sought for Himself a man after His own heart, and the LORD has commanded him *to be* commander over His people, because you have not kept what the LORD commanded you."

1 Sam 15:24–35 Then Saul said to Samuel, "I have sinned, for I have transgressed the commandment of the LORD and your words, because I feared the people and obeyed their voice. **25** Now therefore, please pardon my sin, and return with me, that I may worship the LORD." **26** But Samuel said to Saul, "I will not return with you, for you have rejected the word of the LORD, and the LORD has rejected you from being king over Israel." **27** And as Samuel turned around to go away, *Saul* seized the edge of his robe, and it tore. **28** So Samuel said to him, "The LORD has torn the kingdom of Israel from you today, and has given it to a neighbor of yours, *who is* better than you. **29** And also the Strength of Israel will not lie nor relent. For He *is* not a man, that He should relent." **30** Then he said, "I have sinned; *yet* honor me now, please, before the elders of my people and before Israel, and return with me, that I may worship the LORD your God." **31** So Samuel turned back after Saul, and Saul worshiped the LORD. **32** Then Samuel said, "Bring Agag king of the Amalekites here to me." So Agag came to him cautiously. And Agag said, "Surely the bitterness of death is past." **33** But Samuel said, "As your sword has made women childless, so shall your mother be childless among women." And Samuel hacked Agag in pieces before the LORD in Gilgal. **34** Then Samuel went to Ramah, and Saul went up to his house at Gibeah of Saul. **35** And Samuel went no more to see Saul until the day of his death. Nevertheless Samuel mourned for Saul, and the LORD regretted that He had made Saul king over Israel.

Of David.

1 Sam 16:1 Now the LORD said to Samuel, "How long will you mourn for Saul, seeing I have rejected him from reigning over Israel? Fill your horn with oil, and go; I am sending you to Jesse the Bethlehemite. For I have provided Myself a king among his sons.

1 Sam 16:7–13 But the LORD said to Samuel, "Do not look at his appearance or at his physical stature, because I have refused him. For *the LORD does* not *see* as man sees; for man looks at the outward appearance, but the LORD looks at the heart." **8** So Jesse called Abinadab, and made him pass before Samuel. And he said, "Neither has the LORD chosen this one." **9** Then Jesse made Shammah pass by. And he said, "Neither has the LORD chosen this one." **10** Thus Jesse made seven of his sons pass before Samuel. And Samuel said to Jesse, "The LORD has not chosen these." **11** And Samuel said to Jesse, "Are all the young men here?" Then he said, "There remains yet the youngest, and there he is, keeping the sheep." And Samuel said to Jesse, "Send and bring him. For we will not sit down till he comes here." **12** So he sent and brought him in. Now he *was* ruddy, with bright eyes, and good-looking. And the LORD said, "Arise, anoint him; for this *is* the one!" **13** Then Samuel took the horn of oil and anointed him in the midst of his brothers; and the Spirit of the LORD came upon David from that day forward. So Samuel arose and went to Ramah.

1 Sam 22:1–2 David therefore departed from there and escaped to the cave of Adullam. So when his brothers and all his father's house heard *it,* they went down there to him. **2** And everyone *who was* in distress, everyone who *was* in debt, and everyone *who was* discontented gathered to him. So he became captain over them. And there were about four hundred men with him.

2 Sam 2:1–7 It happened after this that David inquired of the LORD, saying, "Shall I go up to any of the cities of Judah?" And the LORD said to him, "Go up." David said, "Where shall I go up?" And He said, "To Hebron." **2** So David went up there, and his two wives also, Ahinoam the Jezreelitess, and Abigail the widow of Nabal the Carmelite. **3** And David brought up the men who *were* with him, every man with his household. So they dwelt in the cities of Hebron. **4** Then the men of Judah came, and there they anointed David king over the house of Judah. And they told David, saying, "The men of Jabesh Gilead *were the ones* who buried Saul." **5** So David sent messengers to the men of Jabesh Gilead, and said to them, "You *are* blessed of the LORD, for you have shown this kindness to your lord, to Saul, and have buried him. **6** And now may the LORD show kindness and truth to you. I also will repay you this kindness, because you have done this thing. **7** Now therefore, let your hands be strengthened, and be valiant; for your master Saul is dead, and also the house of Judah has anointed me king over them."

2 Sam 5:1–10 Then all the tribes of Israel came to David at Hebron and spoke, saying, "Indeed we *are* your bone and your flesh. **2** Also, in time past, when Saul was king over us, you were the one who led Israel out and brought them in; and the LORD said to you, 'You shall shepherd My people Israel, and be ruler over Israel.'" **3** Therefore all the elders of Israel came to the king at Hebron, and King David made a covenant with them at Hebron before the LORD. And they anointed David king over Israel. **4** David *was* thirty years old when he began to reign, *and* he reigned forty years. **5** In Hebron he reigned over Judah seven years and six months, and in Jerusalem he reigned thirty-three years over all Israel and Judah. **6** And the king and his men went to Jerusalem against the Jebusites, the inhabitants of the land, who spoke to David, saying, "You shall not come in here; but the blind and the lame will repel you," thinking, "David cannot come in here." **7** Nevertheless David took the stronghold of Zion (that *is*, the City of David). **8** Now David said on that day, "Whoever climbs up by way of the water shaft and defeats the Jebusites (the lame and the blind, *who are* hated by David's soul), *he shall be chief and captain.*" Therefore they say, "The blind and the lame shall not come into the house." **9** Then David dwelt in the stronghold, and called it the City of David. And David built all around from the Millo and inward. **10** So David went on and became great, and the LORD God of hosts *was* with him.

2 Sam 8:15–18 So David reigned over all Israel; and David administered judgment and justice to all his people. **16** Joab the son of Zeruiah *was* over the army; Jehoshaphat the son of Ahilud *was* recorder; **17** Zadok the son of Ahitub and Ahimelech the son of Abiathar *were* the priests; Seraiah *was* the scribe; **18** Benaiah the son of Jehoiada *was over* both the Cherethites and the Pelethites; and David's sons were chief ministers.

2 Sam 18:1–8 And David numbered the people who *were* with him, and set captains of thousands and captains of hundreds over them. **2** Then David sent out one third of the people under the hand of Joab, one third under the hand of Abishai the son of Zeruiah, Joab's brother, and one third under the hand of Ittai the Gittite. And the king said to the people, "I also will surely go out with you myself." **3** But the people answered, "You shall not go out! For if we flee away, they will not care about us; nor if half of us die, will they care about us. But *you are* worth ten thousand of us now. For you are now more help to us in the city." **4** Then the king said to them, "Whatever seems best to you I will do." So the king stood beside the gate, and all the people went out by hundreds and by thousands. **5** Now the king had commanded Joab, Abishai, and Ittai, saying, "*Deal* gently for my sake with the young man Absalom." And all the people heard when the king gave all the captains orders concerning Absalom. **6** So the people went out into the field of battle against Israel. And the battle was in the woods of Ephraim. **7** The people of Israel were overthrown there before the servants of David, and a great slaughter of twenty thousand took place there that day. **8** For the battle there was scattered over the face of the whole countryside, and the woods devoured more people that day than the sword devoured.

2 Sam 19:11–18 So King David sent to Zadok and Abiathar the priests, saying, "Speak to the elders of Judah, saying, 'Why are you the last to bring the king back to his house, since the words of all Israel have come to the king, to his *very* house? **12** You *are* my brethren, you *are* my bone and my flesh. Why then are you the last to bring back the king?' **13** And say to Amasa, '*Are* you not my bone and my flesh? God do so to me, and more also, if you are not commander of the army before me continually in place of Joab.'" **14** So he swayed the hearts of all the men of Judah, just as *the heart of* one man, so that they sent *this word* to the king: "Return, you and all your servants!" **15** Then the king returned and came to the Jordan. And Judah came to Gilgal, to go to meet the king, to escort the king across the Jordan. **16** And Shimei the son of Gera, a Benjamite, who *was* from Bahurim, hurried and came down with the men of Judah to meet King David. **17** *There were* a thousand men of Benjamin with him, and Ziba the servant of the house of Saul, and his fifteen sons and his twenty servants with him; and they went over the Jordan before the king. **18** Then a ferryboat went across to carry over the king's household, and to do what he thought good. Now Shimei the son of Gera fell down before the king when he had crossed the Jordan.

1 Kin 2:1–4 Now the days of David drew near that he should die, and he charged Solomon his son, saying: **2** "I go the way of all the earth; be strong, therefore, and prove yourself a man. **3** And keep the charge of the LORD your God: to walk in His ways, to keep His statutes, His commandments, His judgments, and His testimonies, as it is written in the Law of Moses, that you may prosper in all that you do and wherever you turn; **4** that the LORD may fulfill His word which He spoke concerning me, saying, 'If your sons take heed to their way, to walk before Me in truth with all their heart and with all their soul,' He said, 'you shall not lack a man on the throne of Israel.'

Cf. 2 Sam 23:8–23; 1 Chr 11:1–3; 14:1–2; 18:14–17; 22:17–19; Ps 18:29–45

Of Solomon.

1 Kin 1:32–40 And King David said, "Call to me Zadok the priest, Nathan the prophet, and Benaiah the son of Jehoiada." So they came before the king. **33** The king also said to them, "Take with you the servants of your lord, and have Solomon my son ride on my own mule, and take him down to Gihon. **34** There let Zadok the priest and Nathan the prophet anoint him king over Israel; and blow the horn, and say, '*Long live King Solomon!*' **35** Then you shall come up after him, and he shall come and sit on my throne, and he shall be king in my place. For I have appointed him to be ruler over Israel and Judah." **36** Benaiah the son of Jehoiada answered the king and said, "Amen! May the LORD God of my lord the king say so *too*. **37** As the LORD has been with my lord the king, even so may He be with Solomon, and make his throne greater than the throne of my lord King David." **38** So Zadok the priest, Nathan the prophet, Benaiah the son of Jehoiada, the Cherethites, and the Pelethites went down and had Solomon ride on King David's mule, and took him to Gihon. **39** Then Zadok the priest took a horn of oil from the tabernacle and anointed Solomon. And they blew the horn, and all the people said, "Long live King Solomon!" 40 And all the people went up after him; and the people played the flutes and rejoiced with great joy, so that the earth *seemed to* split with their sound.

1 Kin 3:5–15 At Gibeon the LORD appeared to Solomon in a dream by night; and God said, "Ask! What shall I give you?" 6 And Solomon said: "You have shown great mercy to Your servant David my father, because he walked before You in truth, in righteousness, and in uprightness of heart with You; You have continued this great kindness for him, and You have given him a son to sit on his throne, as *it is* this day. 7 Now, O LORD my God, You have made Your servant king instead of my father David, but I *am* a little child; I do not know *how* to go out or come in. 8 And Your servant *is* in the midst of Your people whom You have chosen, a great people, too numerous to be numbered or counted. 9 Therefore give to Your servant an understanding heart to judge Your people, that I may discern between good and evil. For who is able to judge this great people of Yours?" 10 The speech pleased the LORD, that Solomon had asked this thing. 11 Then God said to him: "Because you have asked this thing, and have not asked long life for yourself, nor have asked riches for yourself, nor have asked the life of your enemies, but have asked for yourself understanding to discern justice, 12 behold, I have done according to your words; see, I have given you a wise and understanding heart, so that there has not been anyone like you before you, nor shall any like you arise after you. 13 And I have also given you what you have not asked: both riches and honor, so that there shall not be anyone like you among the kings all your days. 14 So if you walk in My ways, to keep My statutes and My commandments, as your father David walked, then I will lengthen your days." 15 Then Solomon awoke; and indeed it had been a dream. And he came to Jerusalem and stood before the ark of the covenant of the LORD, offered up burnt offerings, offered peace offerings, and made a feast for all his servants.

1 Kin 5:13–18 Then King Solomon raised up a labor force out of all Israel; and the labor force was thirty thousand men. 14 And he sent them to Lebanon, ten thousand a month in shifts: they were one month in Lebanon *and* two months at home; Adoniram *was* in charge of the labor force. 15 Solomon had seventy thousand who carried burdens, and eighty thousand who quarried *stone* in the mountains, 16 besides three thousand three hundred from the chiefs of Solomon's deputies, who supervised the people who labored in the work. 17 And the king commanded them to quarry large stones, costly stones, *and* hewn stones, to lay the foundation of the temple. 18 So Solomon's builders, Hiram's builders, and the Gebalites quarried *them;* and they prepared timber and stones to build the temple.

1 Kin 8:54–66 And so it was, when Solomon had finished praying all this prayer and supplication to the LORD, that he arose from before the altar of the LORD, from kneeling on his knees with his hands spread up to heaven. 55 Then he stood and blessed all the assembly of Israel with a loud voice, saying:

56 "Blessed *be* the LORD, who has given rest to His people Israel, according to all that He promised. There has not failed one word of all His good promise, which He promised through His servant Moses. 57 May the LORD our God be with us, as He was with our fathers. May He not leave us nor forsake us, 58 that He may incline our hearts to Himself, to walk in all His ways, and to keep His commandments and His statutes and His judgments, which He commanded our fathers. 59 And may these words of mine, with which I have made supplication before the LORD, be near the LORD our God day and night, that He may maintain the cause of His servant and the cause of His people Israel, as each day may require, 60 that all the peoples of the earth may know that the LORD *is* God; *there is* no other. 61 Let your heart therefore be loyal to the LORD our God, to walk in His statutes and keep His commandments, as at this day." 62 Then the king and all Israel with him offered sacrifices before the LORD. 63 And Solomon offered a sacrifice of peace offerings, which he offered to the LORD, twenty-two thousand bulls and one hundred and twenty thousand sheep. So the king and all the children of Israel dedicated the house of the LORD. 64 On the same day the king consecrated the middle of the court that *was* in front of the house of the LORD; for there he offered burnt offerings, grain offerings, and the fat of the peace offerings, because the bronze altar that *was* before the LORD *was* too small to receive the burnt offerings, the grain offerings, and the fat of the peace offerings. 65 At that time Solomon held a feast, and all Israel with him, a great assembly from the entrance of Hamath to the Brook of Egypt, before the LORD our God, seven days and seven *more* days—fourteen days. 66 On the eighth day he sent the people away; and they blessed the king, and went to their tents joyful and glad of heart for all the good that the LORD had done for His servant David, and for Israel His people.

1 Kin 9:15–28 And this *is* the reason for the labor force which King Solomon raised: to build the house of the LORD, his own house, the Millo, the wall of Jerusalem, Hazor, Megiddo, and Gezer. 16 (Pharaoh king of Egypt had gone up and taken Gezer and burned it with fire, had killed the Canaanites who dwelt in the city, and had given it *as* a dowry to his daughter, Solomon's wife.) 17 And Solomon built Gezer, Lower Beth Horon, 18 Baalath, and Tadmor in the wilderness, in the land *of Judah,* 19 all the storage cities that Solomon had, cities for his chariots and cities for his cavalry, and whatever Solomon desired to build in Jerusalem, in Lebanon, and in all the land of his dominion. 20 All the people *who were* left of the Amorites, Hittites, Perizzites, Hivites, and Jebusites, who *were* not of the children of Israel— 21 that is, their descendants who were left in the land after them, whom the children of Israel had not been able to destroy completely—from these Solomon raised forced labor, as it is to this day. 22 But of the children of Israel Solomon made no forced laborers, because they *were* men of war and his servants: his officers, his captains, commanders of his chariots, and his cavalry. 23 Others *were* chiefs of the officials who *were* over Solomon's work: five hundred and fifty, who ruled over the people who did the work. 24 But Pharaoh's daughter came up from the City of David to her house which *Solomon* had built for her. Then he built the Millo. 25 Now three times a year Solomon offered burnt offerings and peace offerings on the altar which he had built for the LORD, and he burned incense with them *on the altar* that *was* before the LORD. So he finished the temple. 26 King Solomon also built a fleet of ships at Ezion Geber, which *is* near Elath on the shore of the Red Sea, in the land of Edom. 27 Then Hiram sent his servants with the fleet, seamen who knew the sea, to work with the servants of Solomon. 28 And they went to Ophir, and acquired four hundred and twenty talents of gold from there, and brought *it* to King Solomon.

Cf. 1 Kin 4:20–34; 1 Chr 29:21–25; 2 Chr 1:13–17; 2:17–18; 3:1–2; 6:3–11; 7:1–6; 8:1–6,16

Of Zerubbabel.

Ezra 3:2 Then Jeshua the son of Jozadak and his brethren the priests, and Zerubbabel the son of Shealtiel and his brethren, arose and built the altar of the God of Israel, to offer burnt offerings on it, as *it is* written in the Law of Moses the man of God.

Ezra 3:8–11 Now in the second month of the second year of their coming to the house of God at Jerusalem, Zerubbabel the son of Shealtiel, Jeshua the son of Jozadak, and the rest of their brethren the priests and the Levites, and all those who had come out of the captivity to Jerusalem, began *work* and appointed the Levites from twenty years old and above to oversee the work of the house of the LORD. 9 Then Jeshua *with* his sons and brothers, Kadmiel *with* his sons, and the sons of Judah, arose as one to oversee those working on the house of God: the sons of Henadad *with* their sons and their brethren the Levites. 10 When the builders laid the foundation of the temple of the LORD, the priests stood in their apparel with trumpets, and the Levites, the sons of Asaph, with cymbals, to praise the LORD, according to the ordinance of David king of Israel. 11 And they sang responsively, praising and giving thanks to the LORD: "For *He* is good, For His mercy *endures* forever toward Israel." Then all the people shouted with a great shout, when they praised the LORD, because the foundation of the house of the LORD was laid.

Of Ezra.

Ezra 7:1–10 Now after these things, in the reign of Artaxerxes king of Persia, Ezra the son of Seraiah, the son of Azariah, the son of Hilkiah, 2 the son of Shallum, the son of Zadok, the son of Ahitub, 3 the son of Amariah, the son of Azariah, the son of Meraioth, 4 the son of Zerahiah, the son of Uzzi, the son of Bukki, 5 the son of Abishua, the son of Phinehas, the son of Eleazar, the son of Aaron the chief priest— 6 this Ezra came up from Babylon; and he *was* a skilled scribe in the Law of Moses, which the LORD God of Israel had given. The king granted him all his request, according to the hand of the LORD his God upon him. 7 *Some* of the children of Israel, the priests, the Levites, the singers, the gatekeepers, and the Nethinim came up to Jerusalem in the seventh year of King Artaxerxes. 8 And Ezra came to Jerusalem in the fifth month, which *was* in the seventh year of the king. 9 On the first *day* of the first month he began *his* journey from Babylon, and on the first *day* of the fifth month he came to Jerusalem, according to the good

hand of his God upon him. 10 For Ezra had prepared his heart to seek the Law of the LORD, and to do *it*, and to teach statutes and ordinances in Israel.

Neh 8:4–6 So Ezra the scribe stood on a platform of wood which they had made for the purpose; and beside him, at his right hand, stood Mattithiah, Shema, Anaiah, Urijah, Hilkiah, and Maaseiah; and at his left hand Pedaiah, Mishael, Malchijah, Hashum, Hashbadana, Zechariah, *and* Meshullam. 5 And Ezra opened the book in the sight of all the people, for he was *standing* above all the people; and when he opened it, all the people stood up. 6 And Ezra blessed the LORD, the great God. Then all the people answered, "Amen, Amen!" while lifting up their hands. And they bowed their heads and worshiped the LORD with *their* faces to the ground.

Cf. Ezra 8:15–32; 10:5–17

Of Nehemiah.

Neh 4:13–14 Therefore I positioned *men* behind the lower parts of the wall, at the openings; and I set the people according to their families, with their swords, their spears, and their bows. 14 And I looked, and arose and said to the nobles, to the leaders, and to the rest of the people, "Do not be afraid of them. Remember the Lord, great and awesome, and fight for your brethren, your sons, your daughters, your wives, and your houses."

Neh 4:19–23 Then I said to the nobles, the rulers, and the rest of the people, "The work *is* great and extensive, and we are separated far from one another on the wall. 20 Wherever you hear the sound of the trumpet, rally to us there. Our God will fight for us." 21 So we labored in the work, and half of *the men* held the spears from daybreak until the stars appeared. 22 At the same time I also said to the people, "Let each man and his servant stay at night in Jerusalem, that they may be our guard by night and a working party by day." 23 So neither I, my brethren, my servants, nor the men of the guard who followed me took off our clothes, *except* that everyone took them off for washing.

Neh 5:6–13 And I became very angry when I heard their outcry and these words. 7 After serious thought, I rebuked the nobles and rulers, and said to them, "Each of you is exacting usury from his brother." So I called a great assembly against them. 8 And I said to them, "According to our ability we have redeemed our Jewish brethren who were sold to the nations. Now indeed, will you even sell your brethren? Or should they be sold to us?" Then they were silenced and found nothing *to say.* 9 Then I said, "What you are doing *is* not good. Should you not walk in the fear of our God because of the reproach of the nations, our enemies? 10 I also, *with* my brethren and my servants, am lending them money and grain. Please, let us stop this usury! 11 Restore now to them, even this day, their lands, their vineyards, their olive groves, and their houses, also a hundredth of the money and the grain, the new wine and the oil, that you have charged them." 12 So they said, "We will restore *it,* and will require nothing from them; we will do as you say." Then I called the priests, and required an oath from them that they would do according to this promise. 13 Then I shook out the fold of my garment and said, "So may God shake out each man from his house, and from his property, who does not perform this promise. Even thus may he be shaken out and emptied." And all the assembly said, "Amen!" and praised the LORD. Then the people did according to this promise.

Neh 7:1–3 Then it was, when the wall was built and I had hung the doors, when the gatekeepers, the singers, and the Levites had been appointed, **2** that I gave the charge of Jerusalem to my brother Hanani, and Hananiah the leader of the citadel, for he *was* a faithful man and feared God more than many. **3** And I said to them, "Do not let the gates of Jerusalem be opened until the sun is hot; and while they stand *guard,* let them shut and bar the doors; and appoint guards from among the inhabitants of Jerusalem, one at his watch station and another in front of his own house."

Neh 8:9 And Nehemiah, who *was* the governor, Ezra the priest *and* scribe, and the Levites who taught the people said to all the people, "This day *is* holy to the LORD your God; do not mourn nor weep." For all the people wept, when they heard the words of the Law.

Neh 12:31–43 So I brought the leaders of Judah up on the wall, and appointed two large thanksgiving choirs. *One* went to the right hand on the wall toward the Refuse Gate. **32** After them went Hoshaiah and half of the leaders of Judah, **33** and Azariah, Ezra, Meshullam, **34** Judah, Benjamin, Shemaiah, Jeremiah, **35** and some of the priests' sons with trumpets—Zechariah the son of Jonathan, the son of Shemaiah, the son of Mattaniah, the son of Michaiah, the son of Zaccur, the son of Asaph, **36** and his brethren, Shemaiah, Azarel, Milalai, Gilalai, Maai, Nethanel, Judah, *and* Hanani, with the musical instruments of David the man of God. And Ezra the scribe *went* before them. **37** By the Fountain Gate, in front of them, they went up the stairs of the City of David, on the stairway of the wall, beyond the house of David, as far as the Water Gate eastward. **38** The other thanksgiving choir went the opposite *way,* and I *was* behind them with half of the people on the wall, going past the Tower of the Ovens as far as the Broad Wall, **39** and above the Gate of Ephraim, above the Old Gate, above the Fish Gate, the Tower of Hananel, the Tower of the Hundred, as far as the Sheep Gate; and they stopped by the Gate of the Prison. **40** So the two thanksgiving choirs stood in the house of God, likewise I and the half of the rulers with me; **41** and the priests, Eliakim, Maaseiah, Minjamin, Michaiah, Elioenai, Zechariah, *and* Hananiah, with trumpets; **42** also Maaseiah, Shemaiah, Eleazar, Uzzi, Jehohanan, Malchijah, Elam, and Ezer. The singers sang loudly with Jezrahiah the director. **43** Also that day they offered great sacrifices, and rejoiced, for God had made them rejoice with great joy; the women and the children also rejoiced, so that the joy of Jerusalem was heard afar off.

Neh 13:4–13 Now before this, Eliashib the priest, having authority over the storerooms of the house of our God, *was* allied with Tobiah. **5** And he had prepared for him a large room, where previously they had stored the grain offerings, the frankincense, the articles, the tithes of grain, the new wine and oil, which were commanded *to be given* to the Levites and

singers and gatekeepers, and the offerings for the priests. **6** But during all this I was not in Jerusalem, for in the thirty-second year of Artaxerxes king of Babylon I had returned to the king. Then after certain days I obtained leave from the king, **7** and I came to Jerusalem and discovered the evil that Eliashib had done for Tobiah, in preparing a room for him in the courts of the house of God. **8** And it grieved me bitterly; therefore I threw all the household goods of Tobiah out of the room. **9** Then I commanded them to cleanse the rooms; and I brought back into them the articles of the house of God, with the grain offering and the frankincense. **10** I also realized that the portions for the Levites had not been given *them;* for each of the Levites and the singers who did the work had gone back to his field. **11** So I contended with the rulers, and said, "Why is the house of God forsaken?" And I gathered them together and set them in their place. **12** Then all Judah brought the tithe of the grain and the new wine and the oil to the storehouse. **13** And I appointed as treasurers over the storehouse Shelemiah the priest and Zadok the scribe, and of the Levites, Pedaiah; and next to them *was* Hanan the son of Zaccur, the son of Mattaniah; for they were considered faithful, and their task *was* to distribute to their brethren.

Neh 13:17–31 Then I contended with the nobles of Judah, and said to them, "What evil thing *is* this that you do, by which you profane the Sabbath day? **18** Did not your fathers do thus, and did not our God bring all this disaster on us and on this city? Yet you bring added wrath on Israel by profaning the Sabbath." **19** So it was, at the gates of Jerusalem, as it began to be dark before the Sabbath, that I commanded the gates to be shut, and charged that they must not be opened till after the Sabbath. Then I posted *some* of my servants at the gates, *so that* no burdens would be brought in on the Sabbath day. **20** Now the merchants and sellers of all kinds of wares lodged outside Jerusalem once or twice. **21** Then I warned them, and said to them, "Why do you spend the night around the wall? If you do *so* again, I will lay hands on you!" From that time on they came no *more* on the Sabbath. **22** And I commanded the Levites that they should cleanse themselves, and that they should go and guard the gates, to sanctify the Sabbath day. Remember me, O my God, *concerning* this also, and spare me according to the greatness of Your mercy! **23** In those days I also saw Jews *who* had married women of Ashdod, Ammon, *and* Moab. **24** And half of their children spoke the language of Ashdod, and could not speak the language of Judah, but spoke according to the language of one or the other people. **25** So I contended with them and cursed them, struck some of them and pulled out their hair, and made them swear by God, *saying,* "You shall not give your daughters as wives to their sons, nor take their daughters for your sons or yourselves. **26** Did not Solomon king of Israel sin by these things? Yet among many nations there was no king like him, who was beloved of his God; and God made him king over all Israel. Nevertheless pagan women caused even him to sin. **27** Should we then hear of your doing all this great evil, transgressing against our God by marrying pagan women?" **28** And *one* of the sons of Joiada, the son of Eliashib the high priest, *was* a son-in-law of Sanballat the

Horonite; therefore I drove him from me. **29** Remember them, O my God, because they have defiled the priesthood and the covenant of the priesthood and the Levites. **30** Thus I cleansed them of everything pagan. I also assigned duties to the priests and the Levites, each to his service, **31** and *to bringing* the wood offering and the firstfruits at appointed times. Remember me, O my God, for good!

Cf. Neh 2:1–18

Of Job.

Job 29:21–24 "*Men* listened to me and waited, And kept silence for my counsel. **22** After my words they did not speak again, And my speech settled on them *as dew.* **23** They waited for me *as* for the rain, And they opened their mouth wide *as* for the spring rain. **24** *If* I mocked at them, they did not believe *it,* And the light of my countenance they did not cast down.

Of James.

Acts 12:17 But motioning to them with his hand to keep silent, he declared to them how the Lord had brought him out of the prison. And he said, "Go, tell these things to James and to the brethren." And he departed and went to another place.

Acts 15:13 And after they had become silent, James answered, saying, "Men *and* brethren, listen to me:

Acts 21:18 On the following *day* Paul went in with us to James, and all the elders were present.

1 Cor 15:7 After that He was seen by James, then by all the apostles.

Gal 1:19 But I saw none of the other apostles except James, the Lord's brother.

Gal 2:9 and when James, Cephas, and John, who seemed to be pillars, perceived the grace that had been given to me, they gave me and Barnabas the right hand of fellowship, that we *should go* to the Gentiles and they to the circumcised.

Gal 2:12 for before certain men came from James, he would eat with the Gentiles; but when they came, he withdrew and separated himself, fearing those who were of the circumcision.

Of the church, guidelines.

1 Tim 3:1–13 This *is* a faithful saying: If a man desires the position of a bishop, he desires a good work. **2** A bishop then must be blameless, the husband of one wife, temperate, sober-minded, of good behavior, hospitable, able to teach; **3** not given to wine, not violent, not greedy for money, but gentle, not quarrelsome, not covetous; **4** one who rules his own house well, having *his* children in submission with all reverence **5** (for if a man does not know how to rule his own house, how will he take care of the church of God?); **6** not a novice, lest being puffed up with pride he fall into the *same* condemnation as the devil. **7** Moreover he must have a good testimony among those who are outside, lest he fall into reproach and the snare of the devil. **8** Likewise deacons *must be* reverent, not double-tongued, not given to much wine, not greedy for money, **9** holding the mystery of the faith with a pure conscience. **10** But let these also first be tested; then let them serve as deacons, being *found* blameless. **11** Likewise, *their* wives *must be* reverent, not slanderers, temperate, faithful in all things. **12** Let deacons be the husbands of one wife, ruling *their* children and their own houses well. **13** For those who have served well as deacons obtain for themselves a good standing and great boldness in the faith which is in Christ Jesus.

Titus 1:5–9 For this reason I left you in Crete, that you should set in order the things that are lacking, and appoint elders in every city as I commanded you— **6** if a man is blameless, the husband of one wife, having faithful children not accused of dissipation or insubordination. **7** For a bishop must be blameless, as a steward of God, not self-willed, not quick-tempered, not given to wine, not violent, not greedy for money, **8** but hospitable, a lover of what is good, sober-minded, just, holy, self-controlled, **9** holding fast the faithful word as he has been taught, that he may be able, by sound doctrine, both to exhort and convict those who contradict.

Cf. Acts 6:1–4; 20:28; 1 Pet 5:1–4

Of husbands.

Eph 5:22–29 Wives, submit to your own husbands, as to the Lord. **23** For the husband is head of the wife, as also Christ is head of the church; and He is the Savior of the body. **24** Therefore, just as the church is subject to Christ, so *let* the wives *be* to their own husbands in everything. **25** Husbands, love your wives, just as Christ also loved the church and gave Himself for her, **26** that He might sanctify and cleanse her with the washing of water by the word, **27** that He might present her to Himself a glorious church, not having spot or wrinkle or any such thing, but that she should be holy and without blemish. **28** So husbands ought to love their own wives as their own bodies; he who loves his wife loves himself. **29** For no one ever hated his own flesh, but nourishes and cherishes it, just as the Lord *does* the church.

1 Pet 3:1–7 Wives, likewise, *be* submissive to your own husbands, that even if some do not obey the word, they, without a word, may be won by the conduct of their wives, **2** when they observe your chaste conduct *accompanied* by fear. **3** Do not let your adornment be *merely* outward—arranging the hair, wearing gold, or putting on *fine* apparel— **4** rather *let it be* the hidden person of the heart, with the incorruptible *beauty* of a gentle and quiet spirit, which is very precious in the sight of God. **5** For in this manner, in former times, the holy women who trusted in God also adorned themselves, being submissive to their own husbands, **6** as Sarah obeyed Abraham, calling him lord, whose daughters you are if you do good and are not afraid with any terror. **7** Husbands, likewise, dwell with *them* with understanding, giving honor to the wife, as to the weaker vessel, and as *being* heirs together of the grace of life, that your prayers may not be hindered.

Of Messiah.

Is 9:6–7 For unto us a Child is born, Unto us a Son is given; And the government will be upon His shoulder. And His name will be called Wonderful, Counselor, Mighty God, Everlasting Father, Prince of Peace. **7** Of the increase of *His* government and peace *There will be* no end, Upon the throne of David and over His kingdom, To order it and establish it with judgment and justice From that time forward, even forever. The zeal of the Lord of hosts will perform this.

Is 11:2–3 The Spirit of the LORD shall rest upon Him, The Spirit of wisdom and understanding, The Spirit of counsel and might, The Spirit of knowledge and of the fear of the LORD. **3** His delight *is* in the fear of the LORD, And He shall not judge by the sight of His eyes, Nor decide by the hearing of His ears;

Is 16:5 In mercy the throne will be established; And One will sit on it in truth, in the tabernacle of David, Judging and seeking justice and hastening righteousness."

Is 24:23 Then the moon will be disgraced And the sun ashamed; For the LORD of hosts will reign On Mount Zion and in Jerusalem And before His elders, gloriously.

Is 25:3 Therefore the strong people will glorify You; The city of the terrible nations will fear You.

Is 32:1 Behold, a king will reign in righteousness, And princes will rule with justice.

Is 33:22 (For the LORD *is* our Judge, The LORD *is* our Lawgiver, The LORD *is* our King; He will save us);

Is 42:1 "Behold! My Servant whom I uphold, My Elect One *in whom* My soul delights! I have put My Spirit upon Him; He will bring forth justice to the Gentiles.

Is 42:4 He will not fail nor be discouraged, Till He has established justice in the earth; And the coastlands shall wait for His law."

Is 43:15 I *am* the LORD, your Holy One, The Creator of Israel, your King."

Is 52:13 Behold, My Servant shall deal prudently; He shall be exalted and extolled and be very high.

Is 53:12 Therefore I will divide Him a portion with the great, And He shall divide the spoil with the strong, Because He poured out His soul unto death, And He was numbered with the transgressors, And He bore the sin of many, And made intercession for the transgressors.

Is 55:3–5 Incline your ear, and come to Me. Hear, and your soul shall live; And I will make an everlasting covenant with you— The sure mercies of David. **4** Indeed I have given him *as* a witness to the people, A leader and commander for the people. **5** Surely you shall call a nation you do not know, And nations *who* do not know you shall run to you, Because of the LORD your God, And the Holy One of Israel; For He has glorified you."

Of Daniel.

Dan 1:8–17 But Daniel purposed in his heart that he would not defile himself with the portion of the king's delicacies, nor with the wine which he drank; therefore he requested of the chief of the eunuchs that he might not defile himself. **9** Now God had brought Daniel into the favor and goodwill of the chief of the eunuchs. **10** And the chief of the eunuchs said to Daniel, "I fear my lord the king, who has appointed your food and drink. For why should he see your faces looking worse than the young men who *are* your age? Then you would endanger my head before the king." **11** So Daniel said to the steward whom the chief of the eunuchs had set over Daniel, Hananiah, Mishael, and Azariah, **12** "Please test your servants for ten days, and let them give us vegetables to eat and water to drink. **13** Then let our appearance be examined before you, and the appearance of the

young men who eat the portion of the king's delicacies; and as you see fit, *so* deal with your servants." **14** So he consented with them in this matter, and tested them ten days. **15** And at the end of ten days their features appeared better and fatter in flesh than all the young men who ate the portion of the king's delicacies. **16** Thus the steward took away their portion of delicacies and the wine that they were to drink, and gave them vegetables. **17** As for these four young men, God gave them knowledge and skill in all literature and wisdom; and Daniel had understanding in all visions and dreams.

Dan 2:46–49 Then King Nebuchadnezzar fell on his face, prostrate before Daniel, and commanded that they should present an offering and incense to him. **47** The king answered Daniel, and said, "Truly your God *is* the God of gods, the Lord of kings, and a revealer of secrets, since you could reveal this secret." **48** Then the king promoted Daniel and gave him many great gifts; and he made him ruler over the whole province of Babylon, and chief administrator over all the wise *men* of Babylon. **49** Also Daniel petitioned the king, and he set Shadrach, Meshach, and Abed-Nego over the affairs of the province of Babylon; but Daniel *sat* in the gate of the king.

Dan 6:1–3 It pleased Darius to set over the kingdom one hundred and twenty satraps, to be over the whole kingdom; **2** and over these, three governors, of whom Daniel *was* one, that the satraps might give account to them, so that the king would suffer no loss. **3** Then this Daniel distinguished himself above the governors and satraps, because an excellent spirit *was* in him; and the king gave thought to setting him over the whole realm.

LEAVEN

Used in making bread.

Hos 7:4 "They *are* all adulterers. Like an oven heated by a baker— He ceases stirring *the fire* after kneading the dough, Until it is leavened.

Diffusive properties of.

1 Cor 5:6 Your glorying *is* not good. Do you not know that a little leaven leavens the whole lump?

Forbidden

During the Feast of the Passover.

Ex 12:15–20 Seven days you shall eat unleavened bread. On the first day you shall remove leaven from your houses. For whoever eats leavened bread from the first day until the seventh day, that person shall be cut off from Israel. **16** On the first day *there shall be* a holy convocation, and on the seventh day there shall be a holy convocation for you. No manner of work shall be done on them; but *that* which everyone must eat—that only may be prepared by you. **17** So you shall observe *the Feast of* Unleavened Bread, for on this same day I will have brought your armies out of the land of Egypt. Therefore you shall observe this day throughout your generations as an everlasting ordinance. **18** In the first *month*, on the fourteenth day of the month at evening, you shall eat unleavened bread, until the twenty-first day of the month at evening. **19** For seven days no leaven shall be found in your houses, since whoever eats what is leavened, that same person shall be cut off from the congregation of Israel, whether *he is* a stranger or a native of the land. **20** You shall eat nothing leavened; in all your dwellings you shall eat unleavened bread.' "

To be offered with blood.

Ex 34:25 "You shall not offer the blood of My sacrifice with leaven, nor shall the sacrifice of the Feast of the Passover be left until morning.

To be offered, etc. with grain offerings which were burned.

Lev 2:11 'No grain offering which you bring to the LORD shall be made with leaven, for you shall burn no leaven nor any honey in any offering to the LORD made by fire.

Lev 10:12 And Moses spoke to Aaron, and to Eleazar and Ithamar, his sons who were left: "Take the grain offering that remains of the offerings made by fire to the LORD, and eat it without leaven beside the altar; for it *is* most holy.

Used with thank offerings.

Lev 7:13 Besides the cakes, *as* his offering he shall offer leavened bread with the sacrifice of thanksgiving of his peace offering.

Amos 4:5 Offer a sacrifice of thanksgiving with leaven, Proclaim *and* announce the freewill offerings; For this you love, *You* children of Israel!" Says the Lord GOD.

Firstfruits of wheat offered with.

Lev 23:17 You shall bring from your dwellings two wave *loaves* of two-tenths *of an ephah.* They shall be of fine flour; they shall be baked with leaven. *They are* the firstfruits to the LORD.

Illustrative of

The rapid spread of the gospel.

Matt 13:33 Another parable He spoke to them: "The kingdom of heaven is like leaven, which a woman took and hid in three measures of meal till it was all leavened."

Luke 13:21 It is like leaven, which a woman took and hid in three measures of meal till it was all leavened."

Doctrines of Pharisees, etc.

Matt 16:6 Then Jesus said to them, "Take heed and beware of the leaven of the Pharisees and the Sadducees."

Matt 16:12 Then they understood that He did not tell *them* to beware of the leaven of bread, but of the doctrine of the Pharisees and Sadducees.

False teachers and believers.

1 Cor 5:6–7 Your glorying *is* not good. Do you not know that a little leaven leavens the whole lump? **7** Therefore purge out the old leaven, that you may be a new lump, since you truly are unleavened. For indeed Christ, our Passover, was sacrificed for us.

Gal 5:8–9 This persuasion does not *come* from Him who calls you. **9** A little leaven leavens the whole lump.

Malice and wickedness.

1 Cor 5:8 Therefore let us keep the feast, not with old leaven, nor with the leaven of malice and wickedness, but with the unleavened *bread* of sincerity and truth.

LEBANON

Location of.

Deut 1:7 Turn and take your journey, and go to the mountains of the Amorites, to all the neighboring *places* in the plain, in the mountains and in the lowland, in the South and on the seacoast, to the land of the Canaanites and to Lebanon, as far as the great river, the River Euphrates.

Deut 11:24 Every place on which the sole of your foot treads shall be yours: from the wilderness and Lebanon, from the river, the River Euphrates, even to the Western Sea, shall be your territory.

Given to Israel.

Josh 13:5–6 the land of the Gebalites, and all Lebanon, toward the sunrise, from Baal Gad below Mount Hermon as far as the entrance to Hamath; **6** all the inhabitants of the mountains from Lebanon as far as the Brook Misrephoth, *and* all the Sidonians—them I will drive out from before the children of Israel; only divide it by lot to Israel as an inheritance, as I have commanded you.

Celebrated for

Cedars.

Ps 29:5 The voice of the LORD breaks the cedars, Yes, the LORD splinters the cedars of Lebanon.

Ps 92:12 The righteous shall flourish like a palm tree, He shall grow like a cedar in Lebanon.

Is 14:8 Indeed the cypress trees rejoice over you, *And* the cedars of Lebanon, *Saying,* 'Since you were cut down, No woodsman has come up against us.'

Flowers.

Nah 1:4 He rebukes the sea and makes it dry, And dries up all the rivers. Bashan and Carmel wither, And the flower of Lebanon wilts.

Fragrances.

Song 4:11 Your lips, O *my* spouse, Drip as the honeycomb; Honey and milk *are* under your tongue; And the fragrance of your garments *Is* like the fragrance of Lebanon.

Hos 14:7 Those who dwell under his shadow shall return; They shall be revived *like* grain, And grow like a vine. Their scent *shall be* like the wine of Lebanon.

Glorious appearance.

Is 35:2 It shall blossom abundantly and rejoice, Even with joy and singing. The glory of Lebanon shall be given to it, The excellence of Carmel and Sharon. They shall see the glory of the LORD, The excellency of our God.

Great part of, not conquered by the Israelites.

Josh 13:2 This is the land that yet remains: all the territory of the Philistines and all *that of* the Geshurites,

Josh 13:5 the land of the Gebalites, and all Lebanon, toward the sunrise, from Baal Gad below Mount Hermon as far as the entrance to Hamath;

Judg 3:1–4 Now these *are* the nations which the LORD left, that He might test Israel by them, *that is,* all who had not known any of the wars in Canaan **2** (*this was* only so that the generations of the children of Israel might be taught to know war, at least those who had not formerly known it), **3** *namely,* five lords of the Philistines, all the Canaanites, the Sidonians, and the

Hivites who dwelt in Mount Lebanon, from Mount Baal Hermon to the entrance of Hamath. 4 And they were *left, that He might* test Israel by them, to know whether they would obey the commandments of the LORD, which He had commanded their fathers by the hand of Moses.

Called

The mountains.

2 Chr 2:2 Solomon selected seventy thousand men to bear burdens, eighty thousand to quarry *stone* in the mountains, and three thousand six hundred to oversee them.

Mount Lebanon.

Judg 3:3 *namely,* five lords of the Philistines, all the Canaanites, the Sidonians, and the Hivites who dwelt in Mount Lebanon, from Mount Baal Hermon to the entrance of Hamath.

Those pleasant mountains.

Deut 3:25 I pray, let me cross over and see the good land beyond the Jordan, those pleasant mountains, and Lebanon.'

Physical features,

Mountain tops covered with snow.

Jer 18:14 Will *a man* leave the snow water of Lebanon, Which comes from the rock of the field? Will the cold flowing waters be forsaken for strange waters?

Part of, is barren.

Is 29:17 *Is* it not yet a very little while Till Lebanon shall be turned into a fruitful field, And the fruitful field be esteemed as a forest?

Forests of, filled with wild beasts.

Song 4:8 Come with me from Lebanon, *my* spouse, With me from Lebanon. Look from the top of Amana, From the top of Senir and Hermon, From the lions' dens, From the mountains of the leopards.

Is 40:16 And Lebanon *is* not sufficient to burn, Nor its beasts sufficient for a burnt offering.

Hab 2:17 For the violence *done to* Lebanon will cover you, And the plunder of beasts *which* made them afraid, Because of men's blood And the violence of the land *and* the city, And of all who dwell in it.

Many streams came from.

Song 4:15 A fountain of gardens, A well of living waters, And streams from Lebanon.

Formerly inhabited by the Hivites.

Judg 3:3 *namely,* five lords of the Philistines, all the Canaanites, the Sidonians, and the Hivites who dwelt in Mount Lebanon, from Mount Baal Hermon to the entrance of Hamath.

Moses anxious to behold.

Deut 3:25 I pray, let me cross over and see the good land beyond the Jordan, those pleasant mountains, and Lebanon.'

Furnished

Wood for Solomon's temple.

1 Kin 5:5–6 And behold, I propose to build a house for the name of the LORD my God, as the LORD spoke to my father David, saying, "Your son, whom I will set on your throne in your place, he shall build the house for My name." **6** Now therefore, command

that they cut down cedars for me from Lebanon; and my servants will be with your servants, and I will pay you wages for your servants according to whatever you say. For you know *there is* none among us who has skill to cut timber like the Sidonians.

Stones for Solomon's temple.

1 Kin 5:14 And he sent them to Lebanon, ten thousand a month in shifts: they were one month in Lebanon *and* two months at home; Adoniram *was* in charge of the labor force.

1 Kin 5:18 So Solomon's builders, Hiram's builders, and the Gebalites quarried *them;* and they prepared timber and stones to build the temple.

Wood for second temple.

Ezra 3:7 They also gave money to the masons and the carpenters, and food, drink, and oil to the people of Sidon and Tyre to bring cedar logs from Lebanon to the sea, to Joppa, according to the permission which they had from Cyrus king of Persia.

Solomon built in.

1 Kin 9:19 all the storage cities that Solomon had, cities for his chariots and cities for his cavalry, and whatever Solomon desired to build in Jerusalem, in Lebanon, and in all the land of his dominion.

Difficulties of passing through, surmounted by Assyrian army.

2 Kin 19:23 By your messengers you have reproached the Lord, And said: "By the multitude of my chariots I have come up to the height of the mountains, To the limits of Lebanon; I will cut down its tall cedars *And* its choice cypress trees; I will enter the extremity of its borders, *To* its fruitful forest.

Illustrative of

Great and powerful monarchs.

Is 10:24 Therefore thus says the Lord GOD of hosts: "O My people, who dwell in Zion, do not be afraid of the Assyrian. He shall strike you with a rod and lift up his staff against you, in the manner of Egypt.

Is 10:34 He will cut down the thickets of the forest with iron, And Lebanon will fall by the Mighty One.

The Gentile world.

Is 29:17 *Is* it not yet a very little while Till Lebanon shall be turned into a fruitful field, And the fruitful field be esteemed as a forest?

The Jewish nation.

Jer 22:6 For thus says the LORD to the house of the king of Judah: "You *are* Gilead to Me, The head of Lebanon; *Yet* I surely will make you a wilderness, Cities *which* are not inhabited.

Jer 22:23 O inhabitant of Lebanon, Making your nest in the cedars, How gracious will you be when pangs come upon you, Like the pain of a woman in labor?

The temple.

Zech 11:1 Open your doors, O Lebanon, That fire may devour your cedars.

The glory of renewed Israel.

Is 35:2 It shall blossom abundantly and rejoice, Even with joy and singing. The glory of Lebanon shall be given to it, The excellence of Carmel and Sharon. They shall see the glory of the LORD, The excellency of our God.

Is 60:13 "The glory of Lebanon shall come to you, The cypress, the pine, and the box tree together, To beautify the place of My sanctuary; And I will make the place of My feet glorious.

Hos 14:6–7 His branches shall spread; His beauty shall be like an olive tree, And his fragrance like Lebanon. 7 Those who dwell under his shadow shall return; They shall be revived *like* grain, And grow like a vine. Their scent *shall be* like the wine of Lebanon.

Deep affliction.

Ezek 31:15 "Thus says the Lord GOD: 'In the day when it went down to hell, I caused mourning. I covered the deep because of it. I restrained its rivers, and the great waters were held back. I caused Lebanon to mourn for it, and all the trees of the field wilted because of it.

LEGALISM

Jesus condemned that of the Pharisees.

Matt 23:1–12 Then Jesus spoke to the multitudes and to His disciples, 2 saying: "The scribes and the Pharisees sit in Moses' seat. 3 Therefore whatever they tell you to observe, *that* observe and do, but do not do according to their works; for they say, and do not do. 4 For they bind heavy burdens, hard to bear, and lay *them* on men's shoulders; but they *themselves* will not move them with one of their fingers. 5 But all their works they do to be seen by men. They make their phylacteries broad and enlarge the borders of their garments. 6 They love the best places at feasts, the best seats in the synagogues, 7 greetings in the marketplaces, and to be called by men, 'Rabbi, Rabbi.' 8 But you, do not be called 'Rabbi'; for One is your Teacher, the Christ, and you are all brethren. 9 Do not call anyone on earth your father; for One is your Father, He who is in heaven. 10 And do not be called teachers; for One is your Teacher, the Christ. 11 But he who is greatest among you shall be your servant. 12 And whoever exalts himself will be humbled, and he who humbles himself will be exalted.

Illustrated by rich young ruler.

Matt 19:16–22 Now behold, one came and said to Him, "Good Teacher, what good thing shall I do that I may have eternal life?" 17 So He said to him, "Why do you call Me good? No one *is* good but One, *that is,* God. But if you want to enter into life, keep the commandments." 18 He said to Him, "Which ones?" Jesus said, "'You shall not murder,' 'You shall not commit adultery,' 'You shall not steal,' 'You shall not bear false witness,' 19 'Honor your father and your mother,' and, 'You shall love your neighbor as yourself.'" 20 The young man said to Him, "All these things I have kept from my youth. What do I still lack?" 21 Jesus said to him, "If you want to be perfect, go, sell what you have and give to the poor, and you will have treasure in heaven; and come, follow Me." 22 But when the young man heard that saying, he went away sorrowful, for he had great possessions.

Mark 10:17–22 Now as He was going out on the road, one came running, knelt before Him, and asked Him, "Good Teacher, what shall I do that I may inherit eternal life?" 18 So Jesus said to him, "Why do you call Me good? No one *is* good but One, *that is,* God.

19 You know the commandments: 'Do not commit adultery,' 'Do not murder,' 'Do not steal,' 'Do not bear false witness,' 'Do not defraud,' 'Honor your father and your mother.'" 20 And he answered and said to Him, "Teacher, all these things I have kept from my youth." 21 Then Jesus, looking at him, loved him, and said to him, "One thing you lack: Go your way, sell whatever you have and give to the poor, and you will have treasure in heaven; and come, take up the cross, and follow Me." 22 But he was sad at this word, and went away sorrowful, for he had great possessions.

Luke 18:18–23 Now a certain ruler asked Him, saying, "Good Teacher, what shall I do to inherit eternal life?" 19 So Jesus said to him, "Why do you call Me good? No one *is* good but One, *that is,* God. 20 You know the commandments: 'Do not commit adultery,' 'Do not murder,' 'Do not steal,' 'Do not bear false witness,' 'Honor your father and your mother.'" 21 And he said, "All these things I have kept from my youth." 22 So when Jesus heard these things, He said to him, "You still lack one thing. Sell all that you have and distribute to the poor, and you will have treasure in heaven; and come, follow Me." 23 But when he heard this, he became very sorrowful, for he was very rich.

Jesus provides freedom from.

John 8:31–36 Then Jesus said to those Jews who believed Him, "If you abide in My word, you are My disciples indeed. 32 And you shall know the truth, and the truth shall make you free." 33 They answered Him, "We are Abraham's descendants, and have never been in bondage to anyone. How *can* You say, 'You will be made free'?" 34 Jesus answered them, "Most assuredly, I say to you, whoever commits sin is a slave of sin. 35 And a slave does not abide in the house forever, *but* a son abides forever. 36 Therefore if the Son makes you free, you shall be free indeed.

Rom 8:2 For the law of the Spirit of life in Christ Jesus has made me free from the law of sin and death.

Gal 5:1 Stand fast therefore in the liberty by which Christ has made us free, and do not be entangled again with a yoke of bondage.

Propagated by the Judaizers.

Acts 15:1 And certain *men* came down from Judea and taught the brethren, "Unless you are circumcised according to the custom of Moses, you cannot be saved."

Gal 2:11–13 Now when Peter had come to Antioch, I withstood him to his face, because he was to be blamed; 12 for before certain men came from James, he would eat with the Gentiles; but when they came, he withdrew and separated himself, fearing those who were of the circumcision. 13 And the rest of the Jews also played the hypocrite with him, so that even Barnabas was carried away with their hypocrisy.

Paul testified against.

Col 2:11–23 In Him you were also circumcised with the circumcision made without hands, by putting off the body of the sins of the flesh, by the circumcision of Christ, 12 buried with Him in baptism, in which you also were raised with *Him* through faith in the working of God, who raised Him from the dead. 13 And you, being dead in your trespasses and the uncircumcision of your flesh, He has made alive together with Him, having forgiven you all trespasses, **14** having wiped out the handwriting of requirements that was against us, which was contrary to us. And He has taken it out of the way, having nailed it to the cross. **15** Having disarmed principalities and powers, He made a public spectacle of them, triumphing over them in it. **16** So let no one judge you in food or in drink, or regarding a festival or a new moon or sabbaths, **17** which are a shadow of things to come, but the substance is of Christ. **18** Let no one cheat you of your reward, taking delight in *false* humility and worship of angels, intruding into those things which he has not seen, vainly puffed up by his fleshly mind, **19** and not holding fast to the Head, from whom all the body, nourished and knit together by joints and ligaments, grows with the increase *that is* from God. **20** Therefore, if you died with Christ from the basic principles of the world, why, as *though* living in the world, do you subject yourselves to regulations— **21** "Do not touch, do not taste, do not handle," **22** which all concern things which perish with the using—according to the commandments and doctrines of men? **23** These things indeed have an appearance of wisdom in self-imposed religion, *false* humility, and neglect of the body, *but are* of no value against the indulgence of the flesh.

Cf. Phil 3:1–16

LEOPARD

Inhabited mountains of Canaan.

Song 4:8 Come with me from Lebanon, *my* spouse, With me from Lebanon. Look from the top of Amana, From the top of Senir and Hermon, From the lions' dens, From the mountains of the leopards.

Described as

Spotted.

Jer 13:23 Can the Ethiopian change his skin or the leopard its spots? *Then* may you also do good who are accustomed to do evil.

Fierce and cruel.

Jer 5:6 Therefore a lion from the forest shall slay them, A wolf of the deserts shall destroy them; A leopard will watch over their cities. Everyone who goes out from there shall be torn in pieces, Because their transgressions are many; Their backslidings have increased.

Swift.

Hab 1:8 Their horses also are swifter than leopards, And more fierce than evening wolves. Their chargers charge ahead; Their cavalry comes from afar; They fly as the eagle *that* hastens to eat.

Lies in wait for its prey.

Jer 5:6 Therefore a lion from the forest shall slay them, A wolf of the deserts shall destroy them; A leopard will watch over their cities. Everyone who goes out from there shall be torn in pieces, Because their transgressions are many; Their backslidings have increased.

Hos 13:7 "So I will be to them like a lion; Like a leopard by the road I will lurk;

Illustrative of

God in his judgments.

Hos 13:7 "So I will be to them like a lion; Like a leopard by the road I will lurk;

The Greek empire.

Dan 7:6 "After this I looked, and there was another, like a leopard, which had on its back four wings of a bird. The beast also had four heads, and dominion was given to it.

Antichrist.

Rev 13:2 Now the beast which I saw was like a leopard, his feet were like *the feet of* a bear, and his mouth like the mouth of a lion. The dragon gave him his power, his throne, and great authority.

(Tamed) the wicked subdued by the gospel.

Is 11:6 "The wolf also shall dwell with the lamb, The leopard shall lie down with the young goat, The calf and the young lion and the fatling together; And a little child shall lead them.

LEPROSY

A common disease among the Jews.

Luke 4:27 And many lepers were in Israel in the time of Elisha the prophet, and none of them was cleansed except Naaman the Syrian."

Infected

Men.

Luke 17:12 Then as He entered a certain village, there met Him ten men who were lepers, who stood afar off.

Women.

Num 12:10 And when the cloud departed from above the tabernacle, suddenly Miriam *became* leprous, as *white as* snow. Then Aaron turned toward Miriam, and there she was, a leper.

Houses.

Lev 14:34 "When you have come into the land of Canaan, which I give you as a possession, and I put the leprous plague in a house in the land of your possession,

Garments.

Lev 13:47 "Also, if a garment has a leprous plague in it, *whether it is* a woolen garment or a linen garment,

An incurable disease.

2 Kin 5:7 And it happened, when the king of Israel read the letter, that he tore his clothes and said, "*Am* I God, to kill and make alive, that this man sends a man to me to heal him of his leprosy? Therefore please consider, and see how he seeks a quarrel with me."

Sometimes sent as a punishment for sin.

Num 12:9–10 So the anger of the LORD was aroused against them, and He departed. **10** And when the cloud departed from above the tabernacle, suddenly Miriam *became* leprous, as *white as* snow. Then Aaron turned toward Miriam, and there she was, a leper.

2 Chr 26:19 Then Uzziah became furious; and he *had* a censer in his hand to burn incense. And while he was angry with the priests, leprosy broke out on his forehead, before the priests in the house of the LORD, beside the incense altar.

Often hereditary.

2 Sam 3:29 Let it rest on the head of Joab and on all his father's house; and let there never fail to be in the house of Joab one who has a discharge or is a leper, who leans on a staff or falls by the sword, or who lacks bread."

2 Kin 5:27 Therefore the leprosy of Naaman shall cling to you and your descendants forever." And he went out from his presence leprous, *as white* as snow.

Parts affected by,

The hand.

Ex 4:6 Furthermore the LORD said to him, "Now put your hand in your bosom." And he put his hand in his bosom, and when he took it out, behold, his hand *was* leprous, like snow.

The head.

Lev 13:44 he is a leprous man. He *is* unclean. The priest shall surely pronounce him unclean; his sore *is* on his head.

The forehead.

2 Chr 26:19 Then Uzziah became furious; and he *had* a censer in his hand to burn incense. And while he was angry with the priests, leprosy broke out on his forehead, before the priests in the house of the LORD, beside the incense altar.

The beard.

Lev 13:30 then the priest shall examine the sore; and indeed if it appears deeper than the skin, *and there is* in it thin yellow hair, then the priest shall pronounce him unclean. It *is* a scaly leprosy of the head or beard.

The whole body.

Luke 5:12 And it happened when He was in a certain city, that behold, a man who was full of leprosy saw Jesus; and he fell on *his* face and implored Him, saying, "Lord, if You are willing, You can make me clean."

Often began with a bright spot.

Lev 13:2 "When a man has on the skin of his body a swelling, a scab, or a bright spot, and it becomes on the skin of his body *like* a leprous sore, then he shall be brought to Aaron the priest or to one of his sons the priests.

Lev 13:24 "Or if the body receives a burn on its skin by fire, and the raw *flesh* of the burn becomes a bright spot, reddish-white or white,

Turned the skin white.

Ex 4:6 Furthermore the LORD said to him, "Now put your hand in your bosom." And he put his hand in his bosom, and when he took it out, behold, his hand *was* leprous, like snow.

2 Kin 5:27 Therefore the leprosy of Naaman shall cling to you and your descendants forever." And he went out from his presence leprous, *as white* as snow.

Turned the hair white or yellow.

Lev 13:3 The priest shall examine the sore on the skin of the body; and if the hair on the sore has turned white, and the sore appears *to be* deeper than the skin of his body, it *is* a leprous sore. Then the priest shall examine him, and pronounce him unclean.

Lev 13:10 And the priest shall examine *him*; and indeed

if the swelling on the skin *is* white, and it has turned the hair white, and *there is* a spot of raw flesh in the swelling,

Lev 13:30 then the priest shall examine the sore; and indeed if it appears deeper than the skin, *and there is* in it thin yellow hair, then the priest shall pronounce him unclean. It *is* a scaly leprosy of the head or beard.

The priests

Were judges and directors in cases of.

Deut 24:8 "Take heed in an outbreak of leprosy, that you carefully observe and do according to all that the priests, the Levites, shall teach you; just as I commanded them, *so* you shall be careful to do.

Examined persons suspected of.

Lev 13:2 "When a man has on the skin of his body a swelling, a scab, or a bright spot, and it becomes on the skin of his body *like* a leprous sore, then he shall be brought to Aaron the priest or to one of his sons the priests.

Lev 13:9 "When the leprous sore is on a person, then he shall be brought to the priest.

Shut up persons suspected of, seven days.

Lev 13:4 But if the bright spot *is* white on the skin of his body, and does not appear *to be* deeper than the skin, and its hair has not turned white, then the priest shall isolate *the one who has* the sore seven days.

Had rules for distinguishing. **Lev 13:5–44**

Examined all persons healed of.

Lev 14:2 "This shall be the law of the leper for the day of his cleansing: He shall be brought to the priest.

Matt 8:4 And Jesus said to him, "See that you tell no one; but go your way, show yourself to the priest, and offer the gift that Moses commanded, as a testimony to them."

Luke 17:14 So when He saw *them*, He said to them, "Go, show yourselves to the priests." And so it was that as they went, they were cleansed.

Ceremonies at cleansing of.

Lev 17:14 for *it is* the life of all flesh. Its blood sustains its life. Therefore I said to the children of Israel, 'You shall not eat the blood of any flesh, for the life of all flesh is its blood. Whoever eats it shall be cut off.'

Those afflicted with,

Ceremonially unclean.

Lev 13:8 And *if* the priest sees that the scab has indeed spread on the skin, then the priest shall pronounce him unclean. It *is* leprosy.

Lev 13:11 it *is* an old leprosy on the skin of his body. The priest shall pronounce him unclean, and shall not isolate him, for he *is* unclean.

Lev 13:22 and if it should at all spread over the skin, then the priest shall pronounce him unclean. It *is* a leprous sore.

Lev 13:44 he is a leprous man. He *is* unclean. The priest shall surely pronounce him unclean; his sore *is* on his head.

Separated from interaction with others.

Num 5:2 "Command the children of Israel that they put out of the camp every leper, everyone who has a discharge, and whoever becomes defiled by a corpse.

Num 12:14–15 Then the LORD said to Moses, "If her father had but spit in her face, would she not be shamed seven days? Let her be shut out of the camp seven days, and afterward she may be received *again*." **15** So Miriam was shut out of the camp seven days, and the people did not journey till Miriam was brought in *again*.

Associated together.

2 Kin 7:3 Now there were four leprous men at the entrance of the gate; and they said to one another, "Why are we sitting here until we die?

Luke 17:12 Then as He entered a certain village, there met Him ten men who were lepers, who stood afar off.

Dwelt in a separate house.

2 Kin 15:5 Then the LORD struck the king, so that he was a leper until the day of his death; so he dwelt in an isolated house. And Jotham the king's son *was* over the *royal* house, judging the people of the land.

Cut off from God's house.

2 Chr 26:21 King Uzziah was a leper until the day of his death. He dwelt in an isolated house, because he was a leper; for he was cut off from the house of the LORD. Then Jotham his son *was* over the king's house, judging the people of the land.

Excluded from priest's office.

Lev 22:2–4 "Speak to Aaron and his sons, that they separate themselves from the holy things of the children of Israel, and that they do not profane My holy name *by* what they dedicate to Me: I *am* the LORD. **3** Say to them: 'Whoever of all your descendants throughout your generations, who goes near the holy things which the children of Israel dedicate to the LORD, while he has uncleanness upon him, that person shall be cut off from My presence: I *am* the LORD. **4** 'Whatever man of the descendants of Aaron, who *is* a leper or has a discharge, shall not eat the holy offerings until he is clean. And whoever touches anything made unclean *by* a corpse, or a man who has had an emission of semen,

To cry unclean when approached.

Lev 13:45 "Now the leper on whom the sore *is*, his clothes shall be torn and his head bare; and he shall cover his mustache, and cry, 'Unclean! Unclean!'

Less persistent when it covered the whole body.

Lev 13:13 then the priest shall consider; and indeed *if* the leprosy has covered all his body, he shall pronounce *him* clean *who has* the sore. It has all turned white. He *is* clean.

Power of God manifested in curing.

Num 12:13–14 So Moses cried out to the LORD, saying, "Please heal her, O God, I pray!" **14** Then the LORD said to Moses, "If her father had but spit in her face, would she not be shamed seven days? Let her be shut out of the camp seven days, and afterward she may be received *again*."

2 Kin 5:8–14 So it was, when Elisha the man of God heard that the king of Israel had torn his clothes, that he sent to the king, saying, "Why have you torn your clothes? Please let him come to me, and he shall know that there is a prophet in Israel." **9** Then Naaman went with his horses and chariot, and he stood at the door of Elisha's house. **10** And Elisha sent a messenger to him, saying, "Go and wash in the Jordan seven times, and your flesh shall be restored to you, and *you shall* be clean." **11** But Naaman became furious, and went away and said, "Indeed, I said to myself, 'He will surely come out *to me*, and stand and call on the name of the LORD his God, and wave his hand over the place, and heal the leprosy.' **12** *Are* not the Abanah and the Pharpar, the rivers of Damascus, better than all the waters of Israel? Could I not wash in them and be clean?" So he turned and went away in a rage. **13** And his servants came near and spoke to him, and said, "My father, *if* the prophet had told you *to do* something great, would you not have done *it?* How much more then, when he says to you, 'Wash, and be clean'?" **14** So he went down and dipped seven times in the Jordan, according to the saying of the man of God; and his flesh was restored like the flesh of a little child, and he was clean.

Power of Christ manifested in curing.

Matt 8:3 Then Jesus put out *His* hand and touched him, saying, "I am willing; be cleansed." Immediately his leprosy was cleansed.

Luke 5:13 Then He put out *His* hand and touched him, saying, "I am willing; be cleansed." Immediately the leprosy left him.

Luke 17:13–14 And they lifted up *their* voices and said, "Jesus, Master, have mercy on us!" **14** So when He saw *them*, He said to them, "Go, show yourselves to the priests." And so it was that as they went, they were cleansed.

Garments

Suspected of, shown to priest.

Lev 13:49 and if the plague is greenish or reddish in the garment or in the leather, whether in the warp or in the woof, or in anything made of leather, it *is* a leprous plague and shall be shown to the priest.

Suspected of, shut up seven days.

Lev 13:50 The priest shall examine the plague and isolate *that which has* the plague seven days.

Infected with, to have the piece first torn out.

Lev 13:56 If the priest examines *it*, and indeed the plague has faded after washing it, then he shall tear it out of the garment, whether out of the warp or out of the woof, or out of the leather.

Infected with incurable, burned.

Lev 13:51–52 And he shall examine the plague on the seventh day. If the plague has spread in the garment, either in the warp or in the woof, in the leather *or* in anything made of leather, the plague *is* an active leprosy. It *is* unclean. **52** He shall therefore burn that garment in which is the plague, whether warp or woof, in wool or in linen, or anything of leather, for it *is* an active leprosy; *the garment* shall be burned in the fire.

Suspected of, but not having, washed and pronounced clean.

Lev 13:53–54 "But if the priest examines *it*, and indeed the plague has not spread in the garment, either in the warp or in the woof, or in anything made of leather, **54** then the priest shall command that they wash *the thing* in which *is* the plague; and he shall isolate it another seven days.

Lev 13:58–59 And if you wash the garment, either warp or woof, or whatever is made of leather, if the plague has disappeared from it, then it shall be washed a second time, and shall be clean. **59** "This *is* the law of the leprous plague in a garment of wool or linen, either in the warp or woof, or in anything made of leather, to pronounce it clean or to pronounce it unclean."

Houses
Suspected of, reported to priest.

Lev 14:35 and he who owns the house comes and tells the priest, saying, 'It seems to me that *there is* some plague in the house,'

Suspected of, emptied.

Lev 14:36 then the priest shall command that they empty the house, before the priest goes *into it* to examine the plague, that all that *is* in the house may not be made unclean; and afterward the priest shall go in to examine the house.

Suspected of, inspected by priest.

Lev 14:37 And he shall examine the plague; and indeed *if* the plague *is* on the walls of the house with in-grained streaks, greenish or reddish, which appear to be deep in the wall,

Suspected of, shut up seven days.

Lev 14:38 then the priest shall go out of the house, to the door of the house, and shut up the house seven days.

To have the part infected with, first removed, and the rest scraped, etc.

Lev 14:39 And the priest shall come again on the seventh day and look; and indeed *if* the plague has spread on the walls of the house,

Lev 14:42 Then they shall take other stones and put *them* in the place of *those* stones, and he shall take other mortar and plaster the house.

Incurably infected with, pulled down and removed.

Lev 14:43–45 "Now if the plague comes back and breaks out in the house, after he has taken away the stones, after he has scraped the house, and after it is plastered, **44** then the priest shall come and look; and indeed *if* the plague has spread in the house, it *is* an active leprosy in the house. It *is* unclean. **45** And he shall break down the house, its stones, its timber, and all the plaster of the house, and he shall carry *them* outside the city to an unclean place.

Infected with, communicated uncleanness.

Lev 14:46–47 Moreover he who goes into the house at all while it is shut up shall be unclean until evening. **47** And he who lies down in the house shall wash his clothes, and he who eats in the house shall wash his clothes.

Suspected of, but not infected, pronounced clean.

Lev 14:48 "But if the priest comes in and examines *it*, and indeed the plague has not spread in the house after the house was plastered, then the priest shall pronounce the house clean, because the plague is healed.

Ceremonies at cleansing of.

Lev 14:49–53 And he shall take, to cleanse the house, two birds, cedar wood, scarlet, and hyssop. **50** Then he shall kill one of the birds in an earthen vessel over running water; **51** and he shall take the cedar wood,

the hyssop, the scarlet, and the living bird, and dip them in the blood of the slain bird and in the running water, and sprinkle the house seven times. **52** And he shall cleanse the house with the blood of the bird and the running water and the living bird, with the cedar wood, the hyssop, and the scarlet. **53** Then he shall let the living bird loose outside the city in the open field, and make atonement for the house, and it shall be clean.

LEVIATHAN (MIGHTY SEA MONSTER)
Created by God.
Ps 104:26 There the ships sail about; *There is* that Leviathan Which You have made to play there.

Nature and habits of. Job 41:1–34
God's power, exhibited in destroying.
Ps 74:14 You broke the heads of Leviathan in pieces, *And* gave him *as* food to the people inhabiting the wilderness.

Illustrative of
Powerful and cruel kings.

Is 27:1 In that day the LORD with His severe sword, great and strong, Will punish Leviathan the fleeing serpent, Leviathan that twisted serpent; And He will slay the reptile that *is* in the sea.

Power and severity of God.

Job 41:10 No one *is so* fierce that he would dare stir him up. Who then is able to stand against Me?

LEVITES, THE
Descended from Jacob's third son.
Gen 29:34 She conceived again and bore a son, and said, "Now this time my husband will become attached to me, because I have borne him three sons." Therefore his name was called Levi.

Heb 7:9–10 Even Levi, who receives tithes, paid tithes through Abraham, so to speak, **10** for he was still in the loins of his father when Melchizedek met him.

Prophecies respecting.
Gen 49:5 "Simeon and Levi *are* brothers; Instruments of cruelty *are in* their dwelling place.

Gen 49:7 Cursed *be* their anger, for *it is* fierce; And their wrath, for it is cruel! I will divide them in Jacob And scatter them in Israel.

Deut 33:8–11 And of Levi he said: "*Let* Your Thummim and Your Urim *be* with Your holy one, Whom You tested at Massah, And with whom You contended at the waters of Meribah, **9** Who says of his father and mother, 'I have not seen them'; Nor did he acknowledge his brothers, Or know his own children; For they have observed Your word And kept Your covenant. **10** They shall teach Jacob Your judgments, And Israel Your law. They shall put incense before You, And a whole burnt sacrifice on Your altar. **11** Bless his substance, LORD, And accept the work of his hands; Strike the loins of those who rise against him, And of those who hate him, that they rise not again."

Originally consisted of three families or divisions.
Num 3:17 These were the sons of Levi by their names: Gershon, Kohath, and Merari.

Cf. 1 Chr 6:16–48

Numbered separately, not with Israel.

Num 1:47–49 But the Levites were not numbered among them by their fathers' tribe; **48** for the LORD had spoken to Moses, saying: **49** "Only the tribe of Levi you shall not number, nor take a census of them among the children of Israel;

Num 3:14–16 Then the LORD spoke to Moses in the Wilderness of Sinai, saying: **15** "Number the children of Levi by their fathers' houses, by their families; you shall number every male from a month old and above." **16** So Moses numbered them according to the word of the LORD, as he was commanded.

Num 3:39 All who were numbered of the Levites, whom Moses and Aaron numbered at the commandment of the LORD, by their families, all the males from a month old and above, *were* twenty-two thousand.

Families, as numbered

Of Gershon.

Num 3:18 And these *are* the names of the sons of Gershon by their families: Libni and Shimei.

Num 3:21–22 From Gershon *came* the family of the Libnites and the family of the Shimites; these *were* the families of the Gershonites. **22** Those who were numbered, according to the number of all the males from a month old and above—of those who were numbered *there were* seven thousand five hundred.

Of Kohath.

Num 3:19 And the sons of Kohath by their families: Amram, Izehar, Hebron, and Uzziel.

Num 3:27–28 From Kohath *came* the family of the Amramites, the family of the Izharites, the family of the Hebronites, and the family of the Uzzielites; these *were* the families of the Kohathites. **28** According to the number of all the males, from a month old and above, *there were* eight thousand six hundred keeping charge of the sanctuary.

Of Merari.

Num 3:20 And the sons of Merari by their families: Mahli and Mushi. These *are* the families of the Levites by their fathers' houses.

Num 3:33–34 From Merari *came* the family of the Mahlites and the family of the Mushites; these *were* the families of Merari. **34** And those who were numbered, according to the number of all the males from a month old and above, *were* six thousand two hundred.

Chosen by God for service of the sanctuary.

1 Chr 15:2 Then David said, "No one may carry the ark of God but the Levites, for the LORD has chosen them to carry the ark of God and to minister before Him forever."

Num 3:6 "Bring the tribe of Levi near, and present them before Aaron the priest, that they may serve him.

Num 8:6 "Take the Levites from among the children of Israel and cleanse them *ceremonially.*

Num 8:14 Thus you shall separate the Levites from among the children of Israel, and the Levites shall be Mine.

Taken instead of the firstborn of Israel.

Num 3:12–13 "Now behold, I Myself have taken the Le-vites from among the children of Israel instead of every firstborn who opens the womb among the children of Israel. Therefore the Levites shall be Mine, **13** because all the firstborn *are* Mine. On the day that I struck all the firstborn in the land of Egypt, I sanctified to Myself all the firstborn in Israel, both man and beast. They shall be Mine: I *am* the LORD."

Num 3:40–45 Then the LORD said to Moses: "Number all the firstborn males of the children of Israel from a month old and above, and take the number of their names. **41** And you shall take the Levites for Me—I *am* the LORD—instead of all the firstborn among the children of Israel, and the livestock of the Levites instead of all the firstborn among the livestock of the children of Israel." **42** So Moses numbered all the firstborn among the children of Israel, as the LORD commanded him. **43** And all the firstborn males, according to the number of names from a month old and above, of those who were numbered of them, were twenty-two thousand two hundred and seventy-three. **44** Then the LORD spoke to Moses, saying: **45** "Take the Levites instead of all the firstborn among the children of Israel, and the livestock of the Levites instead of their livestock. The Levites shall be Mine: I *am* the LORD.

Num 8:16–18 For they *are* wholly given to Me from among the children of Israel; I have taken them for Myself instead of all who open the womb, the firstborn of all the children of Israel. **17** For all the firstborn among the children of Israel *are* Mine, *both* man and beast; on the day that I struck all the firstborn in the land of Egypt I sanctified them to Myself. **18** I have taken the Levites instead of all the firstborn of the children of Israel.

Zeal against idolatry.

Ex 32:26–28 then Moses stood in the entrance of the camp, and said, "Whoever *is* on the LORD's side— *come* to me!" And all the sons of Levi gathered themselves together to him. **27** And he said to them, "Thus says the LORD God of Israel: 'Let every man put his sword on his side, and go in and out from entrance to entrance throughout the camp, and let every man kill his brother, every man his companion, and every man his neighbor.' " **28** So the sons of Levi did according to the word of Moses. And about three thousand men of the people fell that day.

Deut 33:9–10 Who says of his father and mother, 'I have not seen them'; Nor did he acknowledge his brothers, Or know his own children; For they have observed Your word And kept Your covenant. **10** They shall teach Jacob Your judgments, And Israel Your law. They shall put incense before You, And a whole burnt sacrifice on Your altar.

Entered their service at age twenty-five.

Num 8:24 "This *is* what *pertains* to the Levites: From twenty-five years old and above one may enter to perform service in the work of the tabernacle of meeting;

Numbered as ministers at age thirty.

Num 4:3 from thirty years old and above, even to fifty years old, all who enter the service to do the work in the tabernacle of meeting.

Cf. Num 4:23–49

Retired at age fifty.

Num 8:25–26 and at the age of fifty years they must cease performing this work, and shall work no more. **26** They may minister with their brethren in the tabernacle of meeting, to attend to needs, but they *themselves* shall do no work. Thus you shall do to the Levites regarding their duties."

Ceremonies at consecration of,

Cleansing and purifying.

Num 8:7 Thus you shall do to them to cleanse them: Sprinkle water of purification on them, and let them shave all their body, and let them wash their clothes, and *so* make themselves clean.

Making a sin offering for.

Num 8:8 Then let them take a young bull with its grain offering of fine flour mixed with oil, and you shall take another young bull as a sin offering.

Num 8:12 Then the Levites shall lay their hands on the heads of the young bulls, and you shall offer one as a sin offering and the other as a burnt offering to the LORD, to make atonement for the Levites.

Elders of Israel laying their hands on them.

Num 8:9–10 And you shall bring the Levites before the tabernacle of meeting, and you shall gather together the whole congregation of the children of Israel. **10** So you shall bring the Levites before the LORD, and the children of Israel shall lay their hands on the Levites;

Presenting them to God as an offering for the people.

Num 8:11 and Aaron shall offer the Levites before the LORD *like* a wave offering from the children of Israel, that they may perform the work of the LORD.

Num 8:15 After that the Levites shall go in to service the tabernacle of meeting. So you shall cleanse them and offer them *like* a wave offering.

Setting them before the priests and presenting them as their offering to God.

Num 8:13 "And you shall stand the Levites before Aaron and his sons, and then offer them *like* a wave offering to the LORD.

Given to Aaron and sons.

Num 3:9 And you shall give the Levites to Aaron and his sons; they *are* given entirely to him from among the children of Israel.

Num 8:19 And I have given the Levites as a gift to Aaron and his sons from among the children of Israel, to do the work for the children of Israel in the tabernacle of meeting, and to make atonement for the children of Israel, that there be no plague among the children of Israel when the children of Israel come near the sanctuary."

Encamped around the tabernacle.

Num 1:50 but you shall appoint the Levites over the tabernacle of the Testimony, over all its furnishings, and over all things that belong to it; they shall carry the tabernacle and all its furnishings; they shall attend to it and camp around the tabernacle.

Num 1:52–53 The children of Israel shall pitch their tents, everyone by his own camp, everyone by his own standard, according to their armies; **53** but the Levites shall camp around the tabernacle of the Tes-

timony, that there may be no wrath on the congregation of the children of Israel; and the Levites shall keep charge of the tabernacle of the Testimony."

Num 3:23 The families of the Gershonites were to camp behind the tabernacle westward.

Num 3:29 The families of the children of Kohath were to camp on the south side of the tabernacle.

Num 3:35 The leader of the fathers' house of the families of Merari *was* Zuriel the son of Abihail. These *were* to camp on the north side of the tabernacle.

Marched in the center of Israel.

Num 2:17 "And the tabernacle of meeting shall move out with the camp of the Levites in the middle of the camps; as they camp, so they shall move out, everyone in his place, by their standards.

Services of,

Ministering to the Lord.

Deut 10:8 At that time the LORD separated the tribe of Levi to bear the ark of the covenant of the LORD, to stand before the LORD to minister to Him and to bless in His name, to this day.

Ministering to priests.

Num 3:6–7 "Bring the tribe of Levi near, and present them before Aaron the priest, that they may serve him. **7** And they shall attend to his needs and the needs of the whole congregation before the tabernacle of meeting, to do the work of the tabernacle.

Num 18:2 Also bring with you your brethren of the tribe of Levi, the tribe of your father, that they may be joined with you and serve you while you and your sons *are* with you before the tabernacle of witness.

Ministering to the people.

2 Chr 35:3 Then he said to the Levites who taught all Israel, who were holy to the LORD: "Put the holy ark in the house which Solomon the son of David, king of Israel, built. *It shall* no longer *be* a burden on *your* shoulders. Now serve the LORD your God and His people Israel.

Caring for the sanctuary.

Num 18:3 They shall attend to your needs and all the needs of the tabernacle; but they shall not come near the articles of the sanctuary and the altar, lest they die—they and you also.

1 Chr 23:32 and that they should attend to the needs of the tabernacle of meeting, the needs of the holy *place*, and the needs of the sons of Aaron their brethren in the work of the house of the LORD.

Taking charge of the sacred instruments and vessels.

Num 3:8 Also they shall attend to all the furnishings of the tabernacle of meeting, and to the needs of the children of Israel, to do the work of the tabernacle.

1 Chr 9:28–29 Now *some* of them were in charge of the serving vessels, for they brought them in and took them out by count. **29** *Some* of them *were* appointed over the furnishings and over all the implements of the sanctuary, and over the fine flour and the wine and the oil and the incense and the spices.

Keeping sacred oil, flour, etc.

1 Chr 9:29–30 *Some* of them *were* appointed over the furnishings and over all the implements of the sanctuary, and over the fine flour and the wine and the oil and the incense and the spices. **30** And *some* of the sons of the priests made the ointment of the spices.

Overseeing sacred treasures.

1 Chr 26:20 Of the Levites, Ahijah *was* over the treasuries of the house of God and over the treasuries of the dedicated things.

Taking charge of the tithes, offerings, etc.

2 Chr 31:11–19 Now Hezekiah commanded *them* to prepare rooms in the house of the LORD, and they prepared them. **12** Then they faithfully brought in the offerings, the tithes, and the dedicated things; Cononiah the Levite had charge of them, and Shimei his brother *was* the next. **13** Jehiel, Azaziah, Nahath, Asahel, Jerimoth, Jozabad, Eliel, Ismachiah, Mahath, and Benaiah *were* overseers under the hand of Cononiah and Shimei his brother, at the commandment of Hezekiah the king and Azariah the ruler of the house of God. **14** Kore the son of Imnah the Levite, the keeper of the East Gate, *was* over the freewill offerings to God, to distribute the offerings of the LORD and the most holy things. **15** And under him *were* Eden, Miniamin, Jeshua, Shemaiah, Amariah, and Shecaniah, *his* faithful assistants in the cities of the priests, to distribute allotments to their brethren by divisions, to the great as well as the small. **16** Besides those males from three years old and up who were written in the genealogy, they distributed to everyone who entered the house of the LORD his daily portion for the work of his service, by his division, **17** and to the priests who were written in the genealogy according to their father's house, and to the Levites from twenty years old and up according to their work, by their divisions, **18** and to all who were written in the genealogy—their little ones and their wives, their sons and daughters, the whole company of them—for in their faithfulness they sanctified themselves in holiness. **19** Also for the sons of Aaron the priests, *who were* in the fields of the common-lands of their cities, in every single city, *there were* men who were designated by name to distribute portions to all the males among the priests and to all who were listed by genealogies among the Levites.

Neh 12:44 And at the same time some were appointed over the rooms of the storehouse for the offerings, the firstfruits, and the tithes, to gather into them from the fields of the cities the portions specified by the Law for the priests and Levites; for Judah rejoiced over the priests and Levites who ministered.

Doing the service of the tabernacle, etc.

Num 1:50–51 but you shall appoint the Levites over the tabernacle of the Testimony, over all its furnishings, and over all things that belong to it; they shall carry the tabernacle and all its furnishings; they shall attend to it and camp around the tabernacle. **51** And when the tabernacle is to go forward, the Levites shall take it down; and when the tabernacle is to be set up, the Levites shall set it up. The outsider who comes near shall be put to death.

Num 8:19 And I have given the Levites as a gift to Aaron and his sons from among the children of Israel, to do the work for the children of Israel in the tabernacle of meeting, and to make atonement for the children of Israel, that there be no plague among

the children of Israel when the children of Israel come near the sanctuary."

Num 8:22 After that the Levites went in to do their work in the tabernacle of meeting before Aaron and his sons; as the LORD commanded Moses concerning the Levites, so they did to them.

Cf. Num 4:5–33

Preparing the sacrifices for the priests.

1 Chr 23:31 and at every presentation of a burnt offering to the LORD on the Sabbaths and on the New Moons and on the set feasts, by number according to the ordinance governing them, regularly before the LORD;

2 Chr 35:11 And they slaughtered the Passover *offerings;* and the priests sprinkled *the blood* with their hands, while the Levites skinned *the animals.*

Preparing the showbread.

1 Chr 9:31–32 Mattithiah of the Levites, the firstborn of Shallum the Korahite, had the trusted office over the things that were baked in the pans. **32** And some of their brethren of the sons of the Kohathites *were* in charge of preparing the showbread for every Sabbath.

1 Chr 23:29 both with the showbread and the fine flour for the grain offering, with the unleavened cakes and *what is baked in* the pan, with what is mixed and with all kinds of measures and sizes;

Purifying the holy things.

1 Chr 23:28 because their duty *was* to help the sons of Aaron in the service of the house of the LORD, in the courts and in the chambers, in the purifying of all holy things and the work of the service of the house of God,

Regulating weights and measures.

1 Chr 23:29 both with the showbread and the fine flour for the grain offering, with the unleavened cakes and *what is baked in* the pan, with what is mixed and with all kinds of measures and sizes;

Teaching the people.

2 Chr 17:8–9 And with them *he sent* Levites: Shemaiah, Nethaniah, Zebadiah, Asahel, Shemiramoth, Jehonathan, Adonijah, Tobijah, and Tobadonijah—the Levites; and with them Elishama and Jehoram, the priests. **9** So they taught in Judah, and *had* the Book of the Law of the LORD with them; they went throughout all the cities of Judah and taught the people.

2 Chr 30:22 And Hezekiah gave encouragement to all the Levites who taught the good knowledge of the LORD; and they ate throughout the feast seven days, offering peace offerings and making confession to the LORD God of their fathers.

2 Chr 35:3 Then he said to the Levites who taught all Israel, who were holy to the LORD: "Put the holy ark in the house which Solomon the son of David, king of Israel, built. *It shall* no longer *be* a burden on *your* shoulders. Now serve the LORD your God and His people Israel.

Neh 8:7 Also Jeshua, Bani, Sherebiah, Jamin, Akkub, Shabbethai, Hodijah, Maaseiah, Kelita, Azariah, Jozabad, Hanan, Pelaiah, and the Levites, helped the people to understand the Law; and the people *stood* in their place.

Blessing the people.

Deut 10:8 At that time the LORD separated the tribe of Levi to bear the ark of the covenant of the LORD, to stand before the LORD to minister to Him and to bless in His name, to this day.

Keeping the gates of the temple.

1 Chr 9:17–26 And the gatekeepers *were* Shallum, Akkub, Talmon, Ahiman, and their brethren. Shallum *was* the chief. **18** Until then *they had been* gatekeepers for the camps of the children of Levi at the King's Gate on the east. **19** Shallum the son of Kore, the son of Ebiasaph, the son of Korah, and his brethren, from his father's house, the Korahites, *were* in charge of the work of the service, gatekeepers of the tabernacle. Their fathers had been keepers of the entrance to the camp of the LORD. **20** And Phinehas the son of Eleazar had been the officer over them in time past; the LORD *was* with him. **21** Zechariah the son of Meshelemiah *was* keeper of the door of the tabernacle of meeting. **22** All those chosen as gatekeepers *were* two hundred and twelve. They were recorded by their genealogy, in their villages. David and Samuel the seer had appointed them to their trusted office. **23** So they and their children *were* in charge of the gates of the house of the LORD, the house of the tabernacle, by assignment. **24** The gatekeepers were assigned to the four directions: the east, west, north, and south. **25** And their brethren in their villages *had* to come with them from time to time for seven days. **26** For in this trusted office *were* four chief gatekeepers; they were Levites. And they had charge over the chambers and treasuries of the house of God.

1 Chr 23:5 four thousand *were* gatekeepers, and four thousand praised the LORD with *musical* instruments, "which I made," *said David,* "for giving praise."

2 Chr 35:15 And the singers, the sons of Asaph, *were* in their places, according to the command of David, Asaph, Heman, and Jeduthun the king's seer. Also the gatekeepers were at each gate; they did not have to leave their position, because their brethren the Levites prepared portions for them.

Neh 12:25 Mattaniah, Bakbukiah, Obadiah, Meshullam, Talmon, and Akkub *were* gatekeepers keeping the watch at the storerooms of the gates.

Conducting the sacred music. **1 Chr 23:5–30; 2 Chr 5:12–13; Neh 12:24,27–43**

Singing praises before the army.

2 Chr 20:21–22 And when he had consulted with the people, he appointed those who should sing to the LORD, and who should praise the beauty of holiness, as they went out before the army and were saying: "Praise the LORD, For His mercy *endures* forever." **22** Now when they began to sing and to praise, the LORD set ambushes against the people of Ammon, Moab, and Mount Seir, who had come against Judah; and they were defeated.

Judging and deciding in controversies.

Deut 17:9 And you shall come to the priests, the Levites, and to the judge *there* in those days, and inquire *of them;* they shall pronounce upon you the sentence of judgment.

1 Chr 23:4 Of these, twenty-four thousand *were* to look

after the work of the house of the LORD, six thousand *were* officers and judges,

2 Chr 19:8 Moreover in Jerusalem, for the judgment of the LORD and for controversies, Jehoshaphat appointed some of the Levites and priests, and some of the chief fathers of Israel, when they returned to Jerusalem.

Guarding the king and his house.

2 Kin 11:5–9 Then he commanded them, saying, "This *is* what you shall do: One-third of you who come on duty on the Sabbath shall be keeping watch over the king's house, **6** one-third *shall be* at the gate of Sur, and one-third at the gate behind the escorts. You shall keep the watch of the house, lest it be broken down. **7** The two contingents of you who go off duty on the Sabbath shall keep the watch of the house of the LORD for the king. **8** But you shall surround the king on all sides, every man with his weapons in his hand; and whoever comes within range, let him be put to death. You are to be with the king as he goes out and as he comes in." **9** So the captains of the hundreds did according to all that Jehoiada the priest commanded. Each of them took his men who were to be on duty on the Sabbath, with those who were going off duty on the Sabbath, and came to Jehoiada the priest.

2 Chr 23:5–7 one-third *shall be* at the king's house; and one-third at the Gate of the Foundation. All the people *shall be* in the courts of the house of the LORD. **6** But let no one come into the house of the LORD except the priests and those of the Levites who serve. They may go in, for they *are* holy; but all the people shall keep the watch of the LORD. **7** And the Levites shall surround the king on all sides, every man with his weapons in his hand; and whoever comes into the house, let him be put to death. You are to be with the king when he comes in and when he goes out."

Had no inheritance in Israel.

Deut 10:9 Therefore Levi has no portion nor inheritance with his brethren; the LORD *is* his inheritance, just as the LORD your God promised him.)

Deut 18:1–2 "The priests, the Levites—all the tribe of Levi—shall have no part nor inheritance with Israel; they shall eat the offerings of the LORD made by fire, and His portion. **2** Therefore they shall have no inheritance among their brethren; the LORD is their inheritance, as He said to them.

Josh 13:33 But to the tribe of Levi Moses had given no inheritance; the LORD God of Israel *was* their inheritance, as He had said to them.

Josh 14:3 For Moses had given the inheritance of the two tribes and the half-tribe on the other side of the Jordan; but to the Levites he had given no inheritance among them.

The Jews to be kind and benevolent to.

Deut 12:12 And you shall rejoice before the LORD your God, you and your sons and your daughters, your male and female servants, and the Levite who *is* within your gates, since he has no portion nor inheritance with you.

Deut 12:18–19 But you must eat them before the LORD your God in the place which the LORD your God chooses, you and your son and your daughter, your male servant and your female servant, and the Levite who *is* within your gates; and you shall rejoice before the LORD your God in all to which you put your hands. 19 Take heed to yourself that you do not forsake the Levite as long as you live in your land.

Deut 14:29 And the Levite, because he has no portion nor inheritance with you, and the stranger and the fatherless and the widow who *are* within your gates, may come and eat and be satisfied, that the LORD your God may bless you in all the work of your hand which you do.

Deut 16:11 You shall rejoice before the LORD your God, you and your son and your daughter, your male servant and your female servant, the Levite who *is* within your gates, the stranger and the fatherless and the widow who *are* among you, at the place where the LORD your God chooses to make His name abide.

Deut 16:14 And you shall rejoice in your feast, you and your son and your daughter, your male servant and your female servant and the Levite, the stranger and the fatherless and the widow, who *are* within your gates.

Forty-eight cities, with extensive suburbs, appointed for.

Num 35:2–8 "Command the children of Israel that they give the Levites cities to dwell in from the inheritance of their possession, and you shall *also* give the Levites common-land around the cities. 3 They shall have the cities to dwell in; and their common-land shall be for their cattle, for their herds, and for all their animals. 4 The common-land of the cities which you will give the Levites *shall extend* from the wall of the city outward a thousand cubits all around. 5 And you shall measure outside the city on the east side two thousand cubits, on the south side two thousand cubits, on the west side two thousand cubits, and on the north side two thousand cubits. The city *shall be* in the middle. This shall belong to them as common-land for the cities. 6 "Now among the cities which you will give to the Levites *you shall appoint* six cities of refuge, to which a manslayer may flee. And to these you shall add forty-two cities. 7 So all the cities you will give to the Levites *shall be* forty-eight; these *you shall give* with their common-land. 8 And the cities which you will give *shall be* from the possession of the children of Israel; from the larger *tribe* you shall give many, from the smaller you shall give few. Each shall give some of its cities to the Levites, in proportion to the inheritance that each receives."

The tithes given to, for their support.

Num 18:21 "Behold, I have given the children of Levi all the tithes in Israel as an inheritance in return for the work which they perform, the work of the tabernacle of meeting.

Num 18:24 For the tithes of the children of Israel, which they offer up *as* a heave offering to the LORD, I have given to the Levites as an inheritance; therefore I have said to them, 'Among the children of Israel they shall have no inheritance.' "

2 Chr 31:4–5 Moreover he commanded the people who dwelt in Jerusalem to contribute support for the priests and the Levites, that they might devote themselves to the Law of the LORD. 5 As soon as the commandment was circulated, the children of Israel brought in abundance the firstfruits of grain and wine, oil and honey, and of all the produce of the field; and they brought in abundantly the tithe of everything.

Neh 12:44–45 And at the same time some were appointed over the rooms of the storehouse for the offerings, the firstfruits, and the tithes, to gather into them from the fields of the cities the portions specified by the Law for the priests and Levites; for Judah rejoiced over the priests and Levites who ministered. 45 Both the singers and the gatekeepers kept the charge of their God and the charge of the purification, according to the command of David *and* Solomon his son.

Heb 7:5 And indeed those who are of the sons of Levi, who receive the priesthood, have a commandment to receive tithes from the people according to the law, that is, from their brethren, though they have come from the loins of Abraham;

Bound to give a tenth of their tithes to the priests.

Num 18:26–32 "Speak thus to the Levites, and say to them: 'When you take from the children of Israel the tithes which I have given you from them as your inheritance, then you shall offer up a heave offering of it to the LORD, a tenth of the tithe. 27 And your heave offering shall be reckoned to you as though *it were* the grain of the threshing floor and as the fullness of the winepress. 28 Thus you shall also offer a heave offering to the LORD from all your tithes which you receive from the children of Israel, and you shall give the LORD's heave offering from it to Aaron the priest. 29 Of all your gifts you shall offer up every heave offering due to the LORD, from all the best of them, the consecrated part of them.' 30 Therefore you shall say to them: 'When you have lifted up the best of it, then *the rest* shall be accounted to the Levites as the produce of the threshing floor and as the produce of the winepress. 31 You may eat it in any place, you and your households, for it *is* your reward for your work in the tabernacle of meeting. 32 And you shall bear no sin because of it, when you have lifted up the best of it. But you shall not profane the holy gifts of the children of Israel, lest you die.' "

David

Numbered them first from thirty years old.

1 Chr 23:2–3 And he gathered together all the leaders of Israel, with the priests and the Levites. 3 Now the Levites were numbered from the age of thirty years and above; and the number of individual males was thirty-eight thousand.

Divided them into four classes.

1 Chr 23:4–6 Of these, twenty-four thousand *were* to look after the work of the house of the LORD, six thousand *were* officers and judges, 5 four thousand *were* gatekeepers, and four thousand praised the LORD with *musical* instruments, "which I made," *said David*, "for giving praise." 6 Also David separated them into divisions among the sons of Levi: Gershon, Kohath, and Merari.

By his last words had them numbered from twenty years old.

1 Chr 23:24 These *were* the sons of Levi by their fathers' houses—the heads of the fathers' *houses* as they were counted individually by the number of their names, who did the work for the service of the house of the LORD, from the age of twenty years and above.

1 Chr 23:27 For by the last words of David the Levites *were* numbered from twenty years old and above;

Made them serve because of the lightness of their duties.

1 Chr 23:26 and also to the Levites, "They shall no longer carry the tabernacle, or any of the articles for its service."

1 Chr 23:28–32 because their duty *was* to help the sons of Aaron in the service of the house of the LORD, in the courts and in the chambers, in the purifying of all holy things and the work of the service of the house of God, **29** both with the showbread and the fine flour for the grain offering, with the unleavened cakes and *what is baked in* the pan, with what is mixed and with all kinds of measures and sizes; **30** to stand every morning to thank and praise the LORD, and likewise at evening; **31** and at every presentation of a burnt offering to the LORD on the Sabbaths and on the New Moons and on the set feasts, by number according to the ordinance governing them, regularly before the LORD; **32** and that they should attend to the needs of the tabernacle of meeting, the needs of the holy *place*, and the needs of the sons of Aaron their brethren in the work of the house of the LORD.

Subdivided into twenty-four divisions.

1 Chr 23:6 Also David separated them into divisions among the sons of Levi: Gershon, Kohath, and Merari.

1 Chr 25:8–31 And they cast lots for their duty, the small as well as the great, the teacher with the student. **9** Now the first lot for Asaph came out for Joseph; the second for Gedaliah, him with his brethren and sons, twelve; **10** the third for Zaccur, his sons and his brethren, twelve; **11** the fourth for Jizri, his sons and his brethren, twelve; **12** the fifth for Nethaniah, his sons and his brethren, twelve; **13** the sixth for Bukkiah, his sons and his brethren, twelve; **14** the seventh for Jesharelah, his sons and his brethren, twelve; **15** the eighth for Jeshaiah, his sons and his brethren, twelve; **16** the ninth for Mattaniah, his sons and his brethren, twelve; **17** the tenth for Shimei, his sons and his brethren, twelve; **18** the eleventh for Azarel, his sons and his brethren, twelve; **19** the twelfth for Hashabiah, his sons and his brethren, twelve; **20** the thirteenth for Shubael, his sons and his brethren, twelve; **21** the fourteenth for Mattithiah, his sons and his brethren, twelve; **22** the fifteenth for Jeremoth, his sons and his brethren, twelve; **23** the sixteenth for Hananiah, his sons and his brethren, twelve; **24** the seventeenth for Joshbekashah, his sons and his brethren, twelve; **25** the eighteenth for Hanani, his sons and his brethren, twelve; **26** the nineteenth for Mallothi, his sons and his brethren, twelve; **27** the twentieth for Eliathah, his sons and his brethren, twelve; **28** the twenty-first for Hothir, his sons and his brethren, twelve; **29** the twenty-second for Giddalti, his sons and his brethren, twelve; **30** the twenty-third for Mahazioth, his sons and his brethren, twelve; **31** the twenty-fourth for Romamti-Ezer, his sons and his brethren, twelve.

Made them attend in divisions.

2 Chr 8:14 And, according to the order of David his fa-

ther, he appointed the divisions of the priests for their service, the Levites for their duties (to praise and serve before the priests) as the duty of each day required, and the gatekeepers by their divisions at each gate; for so David the man of God had commanded.

2 Chr 31:17 and to the priests who were written in the genealogy according to their father's house, and to the Levites from twenty years old and up according to their work, by their divisions,

Served in divisions after captivity.

Ezra 6:18 They assigned the priests to their divisions and the Levites to their divisions, over the service of God in Jerusalem, as it is written in the Book of Moses.

Had chiefs or officers over them.

Num 3:24 And the leader of the father's house of the Gershonites *was* Eliasaph the son of Lael.

Num 3:30 And the leader of the fathers' house of the families of the Kohathites *was* Elizaphan the son of Uzziel.

Num 3:32 And Eleazar the son of Aaron the priest *was to be* chief over the leaders of the Levites, *with* oversight of those who kept charge of the sanctuary.

Num 3:35 The leader of the fathers' house of the families of Merari *was* Zuriel the son of Abihail. These *were* to camp on the north side of the tabernacle.

1 Chr 9:20 And Phinehas the son of Eleazar had been the officer over them in time past; the LORD *was* with him.

1 Chr 15:4–10 Then David assembled the children of Aaron and the Levites: **5** of the sons of Kohath, Uriel the chief, and one hundred and twenty of his brethren; **6** of the sons of Merari, Asaiah the chief, and two hundred and twenty of his brethren; **7** of the sons of Gershom, Joel the chief, and one hundred and thirty of his brethren; **8** of the sons of Elizaphan, Shemaiah the chief, and two hundred of his brethren; **9** of the sons of Hebron, Eliel the chief, and eighty of his brethren; **10** of the sons of Uzziel, Amminadab the chief, and one hundred and twelve of his brethren.

2 Chr 35:9 Also Conaniah, his brothers Shemaiah and Nethanel, and Hashabiah and Jeiel and Jozabad, chief of the Levites, gave to the Levites for Passover *offerings* five thousand *from the flock* and five hundred cattle.

Ezra 8:29 Watch and keep *them* until you weigh *them* before the leaders of the priests and the Levites and heads of the fathers' *houses* of Israel in Jerusalem, *in* the chambers of the house of the LORD."

While in attendance lodged around the temple.

1 Chr 9:27 And they lodged *all* around the house of God because they *had* the responsibility, and they *were* in charge of opening *it* every morning.

Punished with death for encroaching on the priestly office.

Num 18:3 They shall attend to your needs and all the needs of the tabernacle; but they shall not come near the articles of the sanctuary and the altar, lest they die—they and you also.

Punishment of Korah and others of, for offering incense. Num 16:1–35

LIFE, NATURAL

God is the author of.

Gen 2:7 And the LORD God formed man *of* the dust of the ground, and breathed into his nostrils the breath of life; and man became a living being.

Acts 17:28 for in Him we live and move and have our being, as also some of your own poets have said, 'For we are also His offspring.'

God preserves.

Job 12:10 In whose hand *is* the life of every living thing, And the breath of all mankind?

Ps 36:6 Your righteousness *is* like the great mountains; Your judgments *are* a great deep; O LORD, You preserve man and beast.

Ps 66:9 Who keeps our soul among the living, And does not allow our feet to be moved.

Dan 5:23 And you have lifted yourself up against the Lord of heaven. They have brought the vessels of His house before you, and you and your lords, your wives and your concubines, have drunk wine from them. And you have praised the gods of silver and gold, bronze and iron, wood and stone, which do not see or hear or know; and the God who *holds* your breath in His hand and owns all your ways, you have not glorified.

Forfeited by sin.

Gen 2:17 but of the tree of the knowledge of good and evil you shall not eat, for in the day that you eat of it you shall surely die."

Gen 3:17–19 Then to Adam He said, "Because you have heeded the voice of your wife, and have eaten from the tree of which I commanded you, saying, 'You shall not eat of it': "Cursed *is* the ground for your sake; In toil you shall eat *of* it All the days of your life. **18** Both thorns and thistles it shall bring forth for you, And you shall eat the herb of the field. **19** In the sweat of your face you shall eat bread Till you return to the ground, For out of it you were taken; For dust you *are*, And to dust you shall return."

Not to be taken away unlawfully.

Ex 20:13 "You shall not murder.

Described as

Vain.

Eccl 6:12 For who knows what *is* good for man in life, all the days of his vain life which he passes like a shadow? Who can tell a man what will happen after him under the sun?

Limited.

Job 7:1 "*Is there* not a time of hard service for man on earth? *Are not* his days also like the days of a hired man?

Job 14:5 Since his days *are* determined, The number of his months *is* with You; You have appointed his limits, so that he cannot pass.

Short.

Job 14:1 "Man *who is* born of woman Is of few days and full of trouble.

Ps 89:47 Remember how short my time is; For what futility have You created all the children of men?

Uncertain.

James 4:13–15 Come now, you who say, "Today or tomorrow we will go to such and such a city, spend a year there, buy and sell, and make a profit"; **14** whereas you do not know what *will happen* tomorrow. For what *is* your life? It is even a vapor that appears for a little time and then vanishes away. **15** Instead you *ought* to say, "If the Lord wills, we shall live and do this or that."

Full of trouble.

Job 14:1 "Man *who is* born of woman Is of few days and full of trouble.

God's lovingkindness better than.

Ps 63:3 Because Your lovingkindness *is* better than life, My lips shall praise You.

The value of.

Job 2:4 So Satan answered the LORD and said, "Skin for skin! Yes, all that a man has he will give for his life.

Matt 6:25 "Therefore I say to you, do not worry about your life, what you will eat or what you will drink; nor about your body, what you will put on. Is not life more than food and the body more than clothing?

Preserved by discretion.

Prov 13:3 He who guards his mouth preserves his life, *But* he who opens wide his lips shall have destruction.

Prolonged

In answer to prayer.

Is 38:2–5 Then Hezekiah turned his face toward the wall, and prayed to the LORD, **3** and said, "Remember now, O LORD, I pray, how I have walked before You in truth and with a loyal heart, and have done *what is* good in Your sight." And Hezekiah wept bitterly. **4** And the word of the LORD came to Isaiah, saying, **5** "Go and tell Hezekiah, 'Thus says the LORD, the God of David your father: "I have heard your prayer, I have seen your tears; surely I will add to your days fifteen years.

James 5:15 And the prayer of faith will save the sick, and the Lord will raise him up. And if he has committed sins, he will be forgiven.

By obedience to God.

Deut 30:20 that you may love the LORD your God, that you may obey His voice, and that you may cling to Him, for He *is* your life and the length of your days; and that you may dwell in the land which the LORD swore to your fathers, to Abraham, Isaac, and Jacob, to give them."

By obedience to parents.

Ex 20:12 "Honor your father and your mother, that your days may be long upon the land which the LORD your God is giving you.

Prov 4:10 Hear, my son, and receive my sayings, And the years of your life will be many.

Cares and pleasures of, dangerous.

Luke 8:14 Now the ones *that* fell among thorns are those who, when they have heard, go out and are choked with cares, riches, and pleasures of life, and bring no fruit to maturity.

Luke 21:34 "But take heed to yourselves, lest your hearts be weighed down with carousing, drunkenness, and cares of this life, and that Day come on you unexpectedly.

2 Tim 2:4 No one engaged in warfare entangles himself with the affairs of *this* life, that he may please him who enlisted him as a soldier.

Believers

Have true enjoyment of.

Ps 128:2 When you eat the labor of your hands, You *shall be* happy, and *it shall be* well with you.

1 Tim 4:8 For bodily exercise profits a little, but godliness is profitable for all things, having promise of the life that now is and of that which is to come.

Lives of, specially protected by God.

Job 2:6 And the LORD said to Satan, "Behold, he *is* in your hand, but spare his life."

Acts 18:10 for I am with you, and no one will attack you to hurt you; for I have many people in this city."

1 Pet 3:13 And who *is* he who will harm you if you become followers of what is good?

Of the wicked,

Not specially protected by God.

Job 36:6 He does not preserve the life of the wicked, But gives justice to the oppressed.

Ps 78:50 He made a path for His anger; He did not spare their soul from death, But gave their life over to the plague,

Have their portion of good during.

Ps 17:14 With Your hand from men, O LORD, From men of the world *who have* their portion in *this* life, And whose belly You fill with Your hidden treasure. They are satisfied with children, And leave the rest of their *possession* for their babes.

Luke 6:24 "But woe to you who are rich, For you have received your consolation.

Luke 16:25 But Abraham said, 'Son, remember that in your lifetime you received your good things, and likewise Lazarus evil things; but now he is comforted and you are tormented.

Should be spent in

Obedience to God.

Luke 1:75 In holiness and righteousness before Him all the days of our life.

Rom 14:8 For if we live, we live to the Lord; and if we die, we die to the Lord. Therefore, whether we live or die, we are the Lord's.

Phil 1:21 For to me, to live *is* Christ, and to die *is* gain.

1 Pet 1:17 And if you call on the Father, who without partiality judges according to each one's work, conduct yourselves throughout the time of your stay *here* in fear;

Peace.

Rom 12:18 If it is possible, as much as depends on you, live peaceably with all men.

1 Tim 2:2 for kings and all who are in authority, that we may lead a quiet and peaceable life in all godliness and reverence.

Doing good.

Eccl 3:12 I know that nothing *is* better for them than to rejoice, and to do good in their lives,

Should be laid down, if necessary

For Christ.

Matt 10:39 He who finds his life will lose it, and he who loses his life for My sake will find it.

Luke 14:26 "If anyone comes to Me and does not hate his father and mother, wife and children, brothers and sisters, yes, and his own life also, he cannot be My disciple.

Acts 20:24 But none of these things move me; nor do I count my life dear to myself, so that I may finish my race with joy, and the ministry which I received from the Lord Jesus, to testify to the gospel of the grace of God.

For the brethren.

Rom 16:4 who risked their own necks for my life, to whom not only I give thanks, but also all the churches of the Gentiles.

1 John 3:16 By this we know love, because He laid down His life for us. And we also ought to lay down *our* lives for the brethren.

Be thankful for

The preservation of.

Ps 103:4 Who redeems your life from destruction, Who crowns you with lovingkindness and tender mercies,

John 2:6 Now there were set there six waterpots of stone, according to the manner of purification of the Jews, containing twenty or thirty gallons apiece.

The supply of its wants.

Gen 48:15 And he blessed Joseph, and said: "God, before whom my fathers Abraham and Isaac walked, The God who has fed me all my life long to this day,

Earthly cares often intrude.

Eccl 2:17 Therefore I hated life because the work that was done under the sun *was* distressing to me, for all *is* vanity and grasping for the wind.

Eccl 6:12 For who knows what *is* good for man in life, all the days of his vain life which he passes like a shadow? Who can tell a man what will happen after him under the sun?

Matt 6:25 "Therefore I say to you, do not worry about your life, what you will eat or what you will drink; nor about your body, what you will put on. Is not life more than food and the body more than clothing?

Luke 12:15 And He said to them, "Take heed and beware of covetousness, for one's life does not consist in the abundance of the things he possesses."

Is compared to

An eagle swooping on its prey.

Job 9:26 They pass by like swift ships, Like an eagle swooping on its prey.

A pilgrimage.

Gen 47:9 And Jacob said to Pharaoh, "The days of the years of my pilgrimage *are* one hundred and thirty years; few and evil have been the days of the years of my life, and they have not attained to the days of the years of the life of my fathers in the days of their pilgrimage."

A sigh.

Ps 90:9 For all our days have passed away in Your wrath; We finish our years like a sigh.

A swift runner.

Job 9:25 "Now my days are swifter than a runner; They flee away, they see no good.

A swift ship.

Job 9:26 They pass by like swift ships, Like an eagle swooping on its prey.

A handbreadth.

Ps 39:5 Indeed, You have made my days *as* handbreadths, And my age *is* as nothing before You; Certainly every man at his best state *is* but vapor. Selah

A shepherd's tent removed.

Is 38:12 My life span is gone, Taken from me like a shepherd's tent; I have cut off my life like a weaver. He cuts me off from the loom; From day until night You make an end of me.

A dream.

Ps 73:20 As a dream when *one* awakes, *So,* Lord, when You awake, You shall despise their image.

A sleep.

Ps 90:5 You carry them away *like* a flood; *They are* like a sleep. In the morning they are like grass *which* grows up:

A vapor.

James 4:14 whereas you do not know what *will happen* tomorrow. For what *is* your life? It is even a vapor that appears for a little time and then vanishes away.

A shadow.

Eccl 6:12 For who knows what *is* good for man in life, all the days of his vain life which he passes like a shadow? Who can tell a man what will happen after him under the sun?

A thread cut by the weaver.

Is 38:12 My life span is gone, Taken from me like a shepherd's tent; I have cut off my life like a weaver. He cuts me off from the loom; From day until night You make an end of me.

A weaver's shuttle.

Job 7:6 "My days are swifter than a weaver's shuttle, And are spent without hope.

A flower.

Job 14:2 He comes forth like a flower and fades away; He flees like a shadow and does not continue.

Breath.

Job 7:7 Oh, remember that my life *is* a breath! My eye will never again see good.

Grass.

1 Pet 1:24 because "All flesh *is* as grass, And all the glory of man as the flower of the grass. The grass withers, And its flower falls away,

Water spilled on the ground.

2 Sam 14:14 For we will surely die and *become* like water spilled on the ground, which cannot be gathered up again. Yet God does not take away a life; but He devises means, so that His banished ones are not expelled from Him.

Shortness of, should lead to spiritual improvement.

Deut 32:29 Oh, that they were wise, *that* they understood this, *That* they would consider their latter end!

Ps 90:12 So teach *us* to number our days, That we may gain a heart of wisdom.

Sometimes judicially shortened.

1 Sam 2:32–33 And you will see an enemy *in My* dwelling place, *despite* all the good which God does for Israel. And there shall not be an old man in your house forever. 33 But any of your men *whom* I do not cut off from My altar shall consume your eyes and grieve your heart. And all the descendants of your house shall die in the flower of their age.

Job 36:14 They die in youth, And their life *ends* among the perverted persons.

Miraculously restored by Christ.

Matt 9:18 While He spoke these things to them, behold, a ruler came and worshiped Him, saying, "My daughter has just died, but come and lay Your hand on her and she will live."

Matt 9:25 But when the crowd was put outside, He went in and took her by the hand, and the girl arose.

Luke 7:15 So he who was dead sat up and began to speak. And He presented him to his mother.

Luke 7:22 Jesus answered and said to them, "Go and tell John the things you have seen and heard: that *the* blind see, *the* lame walk, *the* lepers are cleansed, *the* deaf hear, *the* dead are raised, *the* poor have the gospel preached to them.

John 11:43 Now when He had said these things, He cried with a loud voice, "Lazarus, come forth!"

LIFE, SPIRITUAL

God is the author of.

Ps 36:9 For with You *is* the fountain of life; In Your light we see light.

Col 2:13 And you, being dead in your trespasses and the uncircumcision of your flesh, He has made alive together with Him, having forgiven you all trespasses,

Christ is the author of.

John 5:21 For as the Father raises the dead and gives life to *them,* even so the Son gives life to whom He will.

John 5:25 Most assuredly, I say to you, the hour is coming, and now is, when the dead will hear the voice of the Son of God; and those who hear will live.

John 6:33 For the bread of God is He who comes down from heaven and gives life to the world."

John 6:51–53 I am the living bread which came down from heaven. If anyone eats of this bread, he will live forever; and the bread that I shall give is My flesh, which I shall give for the life of the world." 52 The Jews therefore quarreled among themselves, saying, "How can this Man give us *His* flesh to eat?" 53 Then Jesus said to them, "Most assuredly, I say to you, unless you eat the flesh of the Son of Man and drink His blood, you have no life in you.

John 14:6 Jesus said to him, "I am the way, the truth, and the life. No one comes to the Father except through Me.

1 John 4:9 In this the love of God was manifested toward us, that God has sent His only begotten Son into the world, that we might live through Him.

The Holy Spirit is the author of.

Ezek 37:14 I will put My Spirit in you, and you shall

live, and I will place you in your own land. Then you shall know that I, the LORD, have spoken *it* and performed *it*," says the LORD.' "

Rom 8:9–13 But you are not in the flesh but in the Spirit, if indeed the Spirit of God dwells in you. Now if anyone does not have the Spirit of Christ, he is not His. **10** And if Christ *is* in you, the body *is* dead because of sin, but the Spirit *is* life because of righteousness. **11** But if the Spirit of Him who raised Jesus from the dead dwells in you, He who raised Christ from the dead will also give life to your mortal bodies through His Spirit who dwells in you. **12** Therefore, brethren, we are debtors—not to the flesh, to live according to the flesh. **13** For if you live according to the flesh you will die; but if by the Spirit you put to death the deeds of the body, you will live.

2 Cor 3:6 who also made us sufficient as ministers of the new covenant, not of the letter but of the Spirit; for the letter kills, but the Spirit gives life.

The Word of God is the instrument of.

Is 55:3 Incline your ear, and come to Me. Hear, and your soul shall live; And I will make an everlasting covenant with you— The sure mercies of David.

1 Pet 4:6 For this reason the gospel was preached also to those who are dead, that they might be judged according to men in the flesh, but live according to God in the spirit.

Defined as

Alive to God.

Rom 6:11 Likewise you also, reckon yourselves to be dead indeed to sin, but alive to God in Christ Jesus our Lord.

Gal 2:19 For I through the law died to the law that I might live to God.

Newness of life.

Rom 6:4 Therefore we were buried with Him through baptism into death, that just as Christ was raised from the dead by the glory of the Father, even so we also should walk in newness of life.

Living in the Spirit.

Gal 5:25 If we live in the Spirit, let us also walk in the Spirit.

Hidden with Christ.

Col 3:3 For you died, and your life is hidden with Christ in God.

The fear of God is.

Prov 14:27 The fear of the LORD *is* a fountain of life, To turn *one* away from the snares of death.

Prov 19:23 The fear of the LORD *leads* to life, And *he who has it* will abide in satisfaction; He will not be visited with evil.

Life and peace.

Rom 8:6 For to be carnally minded *is* death, but to be spiritually minded *is* life and peace.

Is maintained by

Christ.

John 6:57 As the living Father sent Me, and I live because of the Father, so he who feeds on Me will live because of Me.

1 Cor 10:3–4 all ate the same spiritual food, **4** and all drank the same spiritual drink. For they drank of that spiritual Rock that followed them, and that Rock was Christ.

Faith.

Gal 2:20 I have been crucified with Christ; it is no longer I who live, but Christ lives in me; and the *life* which I now live in the flesh I live by faith in the Son of God, who loved me and gave Himself for me.

The Word of God.

Deut 8:3 So He humbled you, allowed you to hunger, and fed you with manna which you did not know nor did your fathers know, that He might make you know that man shall not live by bread alone; but man lives by every *word* that proceeds from the mouth of the LORD.

Matt 4:4 But He answered and said, "It is written, '*Man shall not live by bread alone, but by every word that proceeds from the mouth of God.*'"

Prayer.

Ps 69:32 The humble shall see *this and* be glad; And you who seek God, your hearts shall live.

Has its origin in the new birth.

John 3:3–8 Jesus answered and said to him, "Most assuredly, I say to you, unless one is born again, he cannot see the kingdom of God." **4** Nicodemus said to Him, "How can a man be born when he is old? Can he enter a second time into his mother's womb and be born?" **5** Jesus answered, "Most assuredly, I say to you, unless one is born of water and the Spirit, he cannot enter the kingdom of God. **6** That which is born of the flesh is flesh, and that which is born of the Spirit is spirit. **7** Do not marvel that I said to you, 'You must be born again.' **8** The wind blows where it wishes, and you hear the sound of it, but cannot tell where it comes from and where it goes. So is everyone who is born of the Spirit."

Stages of,

Infancy.

Luke 10:21 In that hour Jesus rejoiced in the Spirit and said, "I thank You, Father, Lord of heaven and earth, that You have hidden these things from *the* wise and prudent and revealed them to babes. Even so, Father, for so it seemed good in Your sight.

1 Cor 3:1–2 And I, brethren, could not speak to you as to spiritual *people* but as to carnal, as to babes in Christ. **2** I fed you with milk and not with solid food; for until now you were not able *to receive it*, and even now you are still not able;

1 John 2:12 I write to you, little children, Because your sins are forgiven you for His name's sake.

Youth.

1 John 2:13–14 I write to you, fathers, Because you have known Him *who is* from the beginning. I write to you, young men, Because you have overcome the wicked one. I write to you, little children, Because you have known the Father. **14** I have written to you, fathers, Because you have known Him *who is* from the beginning. I have written to you, young men, Because you are strong, and the word of God abides in you, And you have overcome the wicked one.

Maturity.

Eph 4:13 till we all come to the unity of the faith and of the knowledge of the Son of God, to a perfect man, to the measure of the stature of the fullness of Christ;

1 John 2:13–14 I write to you, fathers, Because you have known Him *who is* from the beginning. I write to you, young men, Because you have overcome the wicked one. I write to you, little children, Because you have known the Father. **14** I have written to you, fathers, Because you have known Him *who is* from the beginning. I have written to you, young men, Because you are strong, and the word of God abides in you, And you have overcome the wicked one.

Revived by God.

Ps 85:6 Will You not revive us again, That Your people may rejoice in You?

Hos 6:2 After two days He will revive us; On the third day He will raise us up, That we may live in His sight.

Eph 2:1 And you *He made alive*, who were dead in trespasses and sins,

Eph 2:5 even when we were dead in trespasses, made us alive together with Christ (by grace you have been saved),

Col 2:13 And you, being dead in your trespasses and the uncircumcision of your flesh, He has made alive together with Him, having forgiven you all trespasses,

Should characterize all believers.

Ps 119:25 My soul clings to the dust; Revive me according to Your word.

Ps 119:175 Let my soul live, and it shall praise You; And let Your judgments help me.

Ps 143:11 Revive me, O LORD, for Your name's sake! For Your righteousness' sake bring my soul out of trouble.

Rom 12:1 I beseech you therefore, brethren, by the mercies of God, that you present your bodies a living sacrifice, holy, acceptable to God, *which is* your reasonable service.

1 Cor 14:15 What is *the conclusion* then? I will pray with the spirit, and I will also pray with the understanding. I will sing with the spirit, and I will also sing with the understanding.

Eph 4:15 but, speaking the truth in love, may grow up in all things into Him who is the head—Christ—

1 Pet 2:2 as newborn babes, desire the pure milk of the word, that you may grow thereby,

1 John 3:14 We know that we have passed from death to life, because we love the brethren. He who does not love *his* brother abides in death.

Unbelievers do not have.

Eph 4:18 having their understanding darkened, being alienated from the life of God, because of the ignorance that is in them, because of the blindness of their heart;

1 Tim 5:6 But she who lives in pleasure is dead while she lives.

Jude 1:12 These are spots in your love feasts, while they feast with you without fear, serving *only* themselves. *They are* clouds without water, carried about by the winds; late autumn trees without fruit, twice dead, pulled up by the roots;

Rev 3:1 "And to the angel of the church in Sardis write, 'These things says He who has the seven Spirits of God and the seven stars: "I know your works, that you have a name that you are alive, but you are dead.

Illustrated.

Ezek 37:9–10 Also He said to me, "Prophesy to the breath, prophesy, son of man, and say to the breath, 'Thus says the Lord GOD: "Come from the four winds, O breath, and breathe on these slain, that they may live." ' " **10** So I prophesied as He commanded me, and breath came into them, and they lived, and stood upon their feet, an exceedingly great army.

Luke 15:24 for this my son was dead and is alive again; he was lost and is found.' And they began to be merry.

LIGHT

Created by God.

Gen 1:3–4 Then God said, "Let there be light"; and there was light. **4** And God saw the light, that *it was* good; and God divided the light from the darkness.

Is 45:7 I form the light and create darkness, I make peace and create calamity; I, the LORD, do all these *things*.'

James 1:17 Every good gift and every perfect gift is from above, and comes down from the Father of lights, with whom there is no variation or shadow of turning.

Role of sun, moon, and stars.

Gen 1:14–17 Then God said, "Let there be lights in the firmament of the heavens to divide the day from the night; and let them be for signs and seasons, and for days and years; **15** and let them be for lights in the firmament of the heavens to give light on the earth"; and it was so. **16** Then God made two great lights: the greater light to rule the day, and the lesser light to rule the night. *He made* the stars also. **17** God set them in the firmament of the heavens to give light on the earth,

Jer 31:35 Thus says the LORD, Who gives the sun for a light by day, The ordinances of the moon and the stars for a light by night, Who disturbs the sea, And its waves roar (The LORD of hosts *is* His name):

Divided into

Natural.

Job 24:14 The murderer rises with the light; He kills the poor and needy; And in the night he is like a thief.

Is 5:30 In that day they will roar against them Like the roaring of the sea. And if *one* looks to the land, Behold, darkness *and* sorrow; And the light is darkened by the clouds.

Extraordinary or miraculous.

Ex 14:20 So it came between the camp of the Egyptians and the camp of Israel. Thus it was a cloud and darkness *to the one,* and it gave light by night *to the other,* so that the one did not come near the other all that night.

Ps 78:14 In the daytime also He led them with the cloud, And all the night with a light of fire.

Acts 9:3 As he journeyed he came near Damascus, and suddenly a light shone around him from heaven.

Acts 12:7 Now behold, an angel of the Lord stood by

him, and a light shone in the prison; and he struck Peter on the side and raised him up, saying, "Arise quickly!" And his chains fell off *his* hands.

Artificial.

Jer 25:10 Moreover I will take from them the voice of mirth and the voice of gladness, the voice of the bridegroom and the voice of the bride, the sound of the millstones and the light of the lamp.

Acts 16:29 Then he called for a light, ran in, and fell down trembling before Paul and Silas.

Communicated to the body through the eye.

Prov 15:30 The light of the eyes rejoices the heart, *And* a good report makes the bones healthy.

Matt 6:22 "The lamp of the body is the eye. If therefore your eye is good, your whole body will be full of light.

Described as

White and pure.

Matt 17:2 and He was transfigured before them. His face shone like the sun, and His clothes became as white as the light.

Bright.

Job 37:21 Even now *men* cannot look at the light *when it is* bright in the skies, When the wind has passed and cleared them.

Shining.

2 Sam 23:4 And *he shall be* like the light of the morning *when* the sun rises, A morning without clouds, *Like* the tender grass *springing* out of the earth, By clear shining after rain.'

Job 41:18 His sneezings flash forth light, And his eyes *are* like the eyelids of the morning.

Diffusive.

Job 25:3 Is there any number to His armies? Upon whom does His light not rise?

Job 36:30 Look, He scatters His light upon it, And covers the depths of the sea.

Useful and pleasant.

Eccl 2:13 Then I saw that wisdom excels folly As light excels darkness.

Eccl 11:7 Truly the light is sweet, And *it is* pleasant for the eyes to behold the sun;

Exposing good and bad.

John 3:20–21 For everyone practicing evil hates the light and does not come to the light, lest his deeds should be exposed. **21** But he who does the truth comes to the light, that his deeds may be clearly seen, that they have been done in God."

Eph 5:13 But all things that are exposed are made manifest by the light, for whatever makes manifest is light.

The theory of, beyond man's comprehension.

Job 38:19–20 "Where *is* the way *to* the dwelling of light? And darkness, where *is* its place, **20** That you may take it to its territory, That you may know the paths *to* its home?

Job 38:24 By what way is light diffused, *Or* the east wind scattered over the earth?

Illustrative of

The glory of God.

Ps 104:2 Who cover *Yourself* with light as *with* a garment, Who stretch out the heavens like a curtain.

1 Tim 6:16 who alone has immortality, dwelling in unapproachable light, whom no man has seen or can see, to whom *be* honor and everlasting power. Amen.

The purity of God.

1 John 1:5 This is the message which we have heard from Him and declare to you, that God is light and in Him is no darkness at all.

The wisdom of God.

Dan 2:22 He reveals deep and secret things; He knows what *is* in the darkness, And light dwells with Him.

The guidance of God.

Ps 27:1 The LORD *is* my light and my salvation; Whom shall I fear? The LORD *is* the strength of my life; Of whom shall I be afraid?

Ps 36:9 For with You *is* the fountain of life; In Your light we see light.

The favor of God.

Ps 4:6 *There are* many who say, "Who will show us *any* good?" LORD, lift up the light of Your countenance upon us.

Is 2:5 O house of Jacob, come and let us walk In the light of the LORD.

Christ the source of all wisdom.

Luke 2:32 A light to *bring* revelation to the Gentiles, And the glory of Your people Israel."

John 1:4 In Him was life, and the life was the light of men.

John 1:9 That was the true Light which gives light to every man coming into the world.

John 8:12 Then Jesus spoke to them again, saying, "I am the light of the world. He who follows Me shall not walk in darkness, but have the light of life."

John 12:46 I have come *as* a light into the world, that whoever believes in Me should not abide in darkness.

The glory of Christ.

Matt 17:2 and He was transfigured before them. His face shone like the sun, and His clothes became as white as the light.

Acts 9:3 As he journeyed he came near Damascus, and suddenly a light shone around him from heaven.

Acts 9:5 And he said, "Who are You, Lord?" Then the Lord said, "I am Jesus, whom you are persecuting. It *is* hard for you to kick against the goads."

Acts 26:13 at midday, O king, along the road I saw a light from heaven, brighter than the sun, shining around me and those who journeyed with me.

The word of God.

Ps 119:105 Your word *is* a lamp to my feet And a light to my path.

Ps 119:130 The entrance of Your words gives light; It gives understanding to the simple.

2 Pet 1:19 And so we have the prophetic word confirmed, which you do well to heed as a light that shines in a dark place, until the day dawns and the morning star rises in your hearts;

Gospel.

2 Cor 4:4 whose minds the god of this age has blinded, who do not believe, lest the light of the gospel of the glory of Christ, who is the image of God, should shine on them.

1 Pet 2:9 But you *are* a chosen generation, a royal priesthood, a holy nation, His own special people, that you may proclaim the praises of Him who called you out of darkness into His marvelous light;

Wise rulers.

2 Sam 21:17 But Abishai the son of Zeruiah came to his aid, and struck the Philistine and killed him. Then the men of David swore to him, saying, "You shall go out no more with us to battle, lest you quench the lamp of Israel."

2 Sam 23:4 And *he shall be* like the light of the morning *when* the sun rises, A morning without clouds, *Like* the tender grass *springing* out of the earth, By clear shining after rain.'

The soul of man.

Job 18:5–6 "The light of the wicked indeed goes out, And the flame of his fire does not shine. **6** The light is dark in his tent, And his lamp beside him is put out.

Believers.

Ps 97:11 Light is sown for the righteous, And gladness for the upright in heart.

Prov 4:18 But the path of the just *is* like the shining sun, That shines ever brighter unto the perfect day.

Matt 5:14 "You are the light of the world. A city that is set on a hill cannot be hidden.

Luke 16:8 So the master commended the unjust steward because he had dealt shrewdly. For the sons of this world are more shrewd in their generation than the sons of light.

John 5:35 He was the burning and shining lamp, and you were willing for a time to rejoice in his light.

Eph 5:8 For you were once darkness, but now *you are* light in the Lord. Walk as children of light

Phil 2:15 that you may become blameless and harmless, children of God without fault in the midst of a crooked and perverse generation, among whom you shine as lights in the world,

Col 1:12 giving thanks to the Father who has qualified us to be partakers of the inheritance of the saints in the light.

Whatever it makes manifest.

John 3:21 But he who does the truth comes to the light, that his deeds may be clearly seen, that they have been done in God."

Eph 5:13 But all things that are exposed are made manifest by the light, for whatever makes manifest is light.

LIKENESS

Man created in God's.

Gen 1:26–27 Then God said, "Let Us make man in Our image, according to Our likeness; let them have dominion over the fish of the sea, over the birds of the air, and over the cattle, over all the earth and over every creeping thing that creeps on the earth." **27** So God created man in His *own* image; in the image of God He created him; male and female He created them.

Gen 5:1–2 This is the book of the genealogy of Adam. In the day that God created man, He made him in the likeness of God. **2** He created them male and female, and blessed them and called them Mankind in the day they were created.

Cf. Ps 8:4–5

Children born in parents'.

Gen 5:3 And Adam lived one hundred and thirty years, and begot *a son* in his own likeness, after his image, and named him Seth.

Ezekiel saw God's.

Ezek 1:26–28 And above the firmament over their heads *was* the likeness of a throne, in appearance like a sapphire stone; on the likeness of the throne *was* a likeness with the appearance of a man high above it. **27** Also from the appearance of His waist and upward I saw, as it were, the color of amber with the appearance of fire all around within it; and from the appearance of His waist and downward I saw, as it were, the appearance of fire with brightness all around. **28** Like the appearance of a rainbow in a cloud on a rainy day, so *was* the appearance of the brightness all around it. This *was* the appearance of the likeness of the glory of the LORD. So when I saw *it*, I fell on my face, and I heard a voice of One speaking.

Ezek 8:1–4 And it came to pass in the sixth year, in the sixth *month*, on the fifth *day* of the month, as I sat in my house with the elders of Judah sitting before me, that the hand of the Lord GOD fell upon me there. **2** Then I looked, and there was a likeness, like the appearance of fire—from the appearance of His waist and downward, fire; and from His waist and upward, like the appearance of brightness, like the color of amber. **3** He stretched out the form of a hand, and took me by a lock of my hair; and the Spirit lifted me up between earth and heaven, and brought me in visions of God to Jerusalem, to the door of the north gate of the inner *court*, where the seat of the image of jealousy *was*, which provokes to jealousy. **4** And behold, the glory of the God of Israel *was* there, like the vision that I saw in the plain.

Christ was on earth in humanity's.

Rom 8:3–4 For what the law could not do in that it was weak through the flesh, God *did* by sending His own Son in the likeness of sinful flesh, on account of sin: He condemned sin in the flesh, **4** that the righteous requirement of the law might be fulfilled in us who do not walk according to the flesh but according to the Spirit.

Phil 2:5–8 Let this mind be in you which was also in Christ Jesus, **6** who, being in the form of God, did not consider it robbery to be equal with God, **7** but made Himself of no reputation, taking the form of a bondservant, *and* coming in the likeness of men. **8** And being found in appearance as a man, He humbled Himself and became obedient to *the point of* death, even the death of the cross.

Believers chosen to follow Christ's.

Rom 8:29 For whom He foreknew, He also predestined

to be conformed to the image of His Son, that He might be the firstborn among many brethren.

Cf. 2 Cor 3:18; Gal 4:19; Eph 1:4–5,11; Phil 3:13–14; Col 2:7; 1 John 3:2,3

Christ exists in God's.

Col 1:15 He is the image of the invisible God, the firstborn over all creation.

LION, THE

Canaan populated by.

2 Kin 17:25–26 And it was so, at the beginning of their dwelling there, *that* they did not fear the LORD; therefore the LORD sent lions among them, which killed *some* of them. **26** So they spoke to the king of Assyria, saying, "The nations whom you have removed and placed in the cities of Samaria do not know the rituals of the God of the land; therefore He has sent lions among them, and indeed, they are killing them because they do not know the rituals of the God of the land."

Described as

Superior in strength.

Judg 14:18 So the men of the city said to him on the seventh day before the sun went down: "What *is* sweeter than honey? And what *is* stronger than a lion?" And he said to them: "If you had not plowed with my heifer, You would not have solved my riddle!"

Prov 30:30 A lion, *which is* mighty among beasts And does not turn away from any;

Active.

Deut 33:22 And of Dan he said: "Dan *is* a lion's whelp; He shall leap from Bashan."

Courageous.

2 Sam 17:10 And even he *who is* valiant, whose heart *is* like the heart of a lion, will melt completely. For all Israel knows that your father *is* a mighty man, and *those* who *are* with him *are* valiant men.

Fearless even of man.

Is 31:4 For thus the LORD has spoken to me: "As a lion roars, And a young lion over his prey (When a multitude of shepherds is summoned against him, *He* will not be afraid of their voice Nor be disturbed by their noise), So the LORD of hosts will come down To fight for Mount Zion and for its hill.

Nah 2:11 Where *is* the dwelling of the lions, And the feeding place of the young lions, Where the lion walked, the lioness *and* lion's cub, And no one made *them* afraid?

Fierce.

Job 10:16 If *my head* is exalted, You hunt me like a fierce lion, And again You show Yourself awesome against me.

Job 28:8 The proud lions have not trodden it, Nor has the fierce lion passed over it.

Voracious.

Ps 17:12 As a lion is eager to tear his prey, And like a young lion lurking in secret places.

Majestic in movement.

Prov 30:29–30 There are three *things which* are majestic in pace, Yes, four *which* are stately in walk: **30** A lion,

which is mighty among beasts And does not turn away from any;

Having strong teeth.

Ps 58:6 Break their teeth in their mouth, O God! Break out the fangs of the young lions, O LORD!

Joel 1:6 For a nation has come up against My land, Strong, and without number; His teeth *are* the teeth of a lion, And he has the fangs of a fierce lion.

God's power exhibited in restraining.

1 Kin 13:28 Then he went and found his corpse thrown on the road, and the donkey and the lion standing by the corpse. The lion had not eaten the corpse nor torn the donkey.

Dan 6:22 My God sent His angel and shut the lions' mouths, so that they have not hurt me, because I was found innocent before Him; and also, O king, I have done no wrong before you."

Dan 6:27 He delivers and rescues, And He works signs and wonders In heaven and on earth, Who has delivered Daniel from the power of the lions.

God provides for.

Job 38:39 "Can you hunt the prey for the lion, Or satisfy the appetite of the young lions,

Ps 104:21 The young lions roar after their prey, And seek their food from God.

Ps 104:28 *What* You give them they gather in; You open Your hand, they are filled with good.

Hunts its prey.

Deut 33:20 And of Gad he said: "Blessed *is* he who enlarges Gad; He dwells as a lion, And tears the arm and the crown of his head.

Ps 7:2 Lest they tear me like a lion, Rending *me* in pieces, while *there is* none to deliver.

Ps 10:9 He lies in wait secretly, as a lion in his den; He lies in wait to catch the poor; He catches the poor when he draws him into his net.

Ps 104:21 The young lions roar after their prey, And seek their food from God.

Is 31:4 For thus the LORD has spoken to me: "As a lion roars, And a young lion over his prey (When a multitude of shepherds is summoned against him, *He* will not be afraid of their voice Nor be disturbed by their noise), So the LORD of hosts will come down To fight for Mount Zion and for its hill.

Nah 2:12 The lion tore in pieces enough for his cubs, Killed for his lionesses, Filled his caves with prey, And his dens with flesh.

Conceals itself by day.

Ps 104:22 *When* the sun rises, they gather together And lie down in their dens.

Sometimes perishes for lack of food.

Job 4:11 The old lion perishes for lack of prey, And the cubs of the lioness are scattered.

Inhabits

Forests.

Jer 5:6 Therefore a lion from the forest shall slay them, A wolf of the deserts shall destroy them; A leopard will watch over their cities. Everyone who goes out from there shall be torn in pieces, Because their transgressions are many; Their backslidings have increased.

Thickets.

Jer 4:7 The lion has come up from his thicket, And the destroyer of nations is on his way. He has gone forth from his place To make your land desolate. Your cities will be laid waste, Without inhabitant.

Mountains.

Song 4:8 Come with me from Lebanon, *my* spouse, With me from Lebanon. Look from the top of Amana, From the top of Senir and Hermon, From the lions' dens, From the mountains of the leopards.

Deserts.

Is 30:6 The burden against the beasts of the South. Through a land of trouble and anguish, From which *came* the lioness and lion, The viper and fiery flying serpent, They will carry their riches on the backs of young donkeys, And their treasures on the humps of camels, To a people *who* shall not profit;

Attacks the sheepfolds.

1 Sam 17:34 But David said to Saul, "Your servant used to keep his father's sheep, and when a lion or a bear came and took a lamb out of the flock,

Amos 3:12 Thus says the LORD: "As a shepherd takes from the mouth of a lion Two legs or a piece of an ear, So shall the children of Israel be taken out Who dwell in Samaria— In the corner of a bed and on the edge of a couch!

Mic 5:8 And the remnant of Jacob Shall be among the Gentiles, In the midst of many peoples, Like a lion among the beasts of the forest, Like a young lion among flocks of sheep, Who, if he passes through, Both treads down and tears in pieces, And none can deliver.

Attacks and destroys men.

1 Kin 13:24 When he was gone, a lion met him on the road and killed him. And his corpse was thrown on the road, and the donkey stood by it. The lion also stood by the corpse.

1 Kin 20:36 Then he said to him, "Because you have not obeyed the voice of the LORD, surely, as soon as you depart from me, a lion shall kill you." And as soon as he left him, a lion found him and killed him.

Universal terror caused by roaring of.

Jer 2:15 The young lions roared at him, *and* growled; They made his land waste; His cities are burned, without inhabitant.

Amos 3:8 A lion has roared! Who will not fear? The Lord GOD has spoken! Who can but prophesy?

Criminals often thrown to.

Dan 6:7 All the governors of the kingdom, the administrators and satraps, the counselors and advisors, have consulted together to establish a royal statute and to make a firm decree, that whoever petitions any god or man for thirty days, except you, O king, shall be cast into the den of lions.

Dan 6:16 So the king gave the command, and they brought Daniel and cast *him* into the den of lions. *But* the king spoke, saying to Daniel, "Your God, whom you serve continually, He will deliver you."

Dan 6:24 And the king gave the command, and they brought those men who had accused Daniel, and they cast *them* into the den of lions—them, their children, and their wives; and the lions overpowered

them, and broke all their bones in pieces before they ever came to the bottom of the den.

Hunting of, alluded to.

Job 10:16 If *my head* is exalted, You hunt me like a fierce lion, And again You show Yourself awesome against me.

Slain by

Samson.

Judg 14:5–6 So Samson went down to Timnah with his father and mother, and came to the vineyards of Timnah. Now *to his* surprise, a young lion *came* roaring against him. **6** And the Spirit of the LORD came mightily upon him, and he tore the lion apart as one would have torn apart a young goat, though *he had* nothing in his hand. But he did not tell his father or his mother what he had done.

Judg 14:8 After some time, when he returned to get her, he turned aside to see the carcass of the lion. And behold, a swarm of bees and honey *were* in the carcass of the lion.

David.

1 Sam 17:35–36 I went out after it and struck it, and delivered *the lamb* from its mouth; and when it arose against me, I caught *it* by its beard, and struck and killed it. **36** Your servant has killed both lion and bear; and this uncircumcised Philistine will be like one of them, seeing he has defied the armies of the living God."

Benaiah.

2 Sam 23:20 Benaiah *was* the son of Jehoiada, the son of a valiant man from Kabzeel, who had done many deeds. He had killed two lion-like heroes of Moab. He also had gone down and killed a lion in the midst of a pit on a snowy day.

Disobedient prophet slain by.

1 Kin 13:24 When he was gone, a lion met him on the road and killed him. And his corpse was thrown on the road, and the donkey stood by it. The lion also stood by the corpse.

1 Kin 13:26 Now when the prophet who had brought him back from the way heard *it*, he said, "It *is* the man of God who was disobedient to the word of the LORD. Therefore the LORD has delivered him to the lion, which has torn him and killed him, according to the word of the LORD which He spoke to him."

Illustrative of

Israel.

Num 24:9 'He bows down, he lies down as a lion; And as a lion, who shall rouse him?' "Blessed *is* he who blesses you, And cursed *is* he who curses you."

The tribe of Judah.

Gen 49:9 Judah *is* a lion's whelp; From the prey, my son, you have gone up. He bows down, he lies down as a lion; And as a lion, who shall rouse him?

The tribe of Gad.

Deut 33:20 And of Gad he said: "Blessed *is* he who enlarges Gad; He dwells as a lion, And tears the arm and the crown of his head.

Christ.

Rev 5:5 But one of the elders said to me, "Do not weep. Behold, the Lion of the tribe of Judah, the Root of

David, has prevailed to open the scroll and to loose its seven seals."

God in protecting His people.

Is 31:4 For thus the LORD has spoken to me: "As a lion roars, And a young lion over his prey (When a multitude of shepherds is summoned against him, *He* will not be afraid of their voice Nor be disturbed by their noise), So the LORD of hosts will come down To fight for Mount Zion and for its hill.

God in executing judgments.

Is 38:13 I have considered until morning— Like a lion, So He breaks all my bones; From day until night You make an end of me.

Lam 3:10 He *has been* to me a bear lying in wait, *Like* a lion in ambush.

Hos 5:14 For I *will be* like a lion to Ephraim, And like a young lion to the house of Judah. I, *even* I, will tear *them* and go away; I will take *them* away, and no one shall rescue.

Hos 13:8 I will meet them like a bear deprived *of her cubs;* I will tear open their rib cage, And there I will devour them like a lion. The wild beast shall tear them.

Boldness of saints.

Prov 28:1 The wicked flee when no one pursues, But the righteous are bold as a lion.

Brave men.

2 Sam 1:23 "Saul and Jonathan *were* beloved and pleasant in their lives, And in their death they were not divided; They were swifter than eagles, They were stronger than lions.

2 Sam 23:20 Benaiah *was* the son of Jehoiada, the son of a valiant man from Kabzeel, who had done many deeds. He had killed two lion-like heroes of Moab. He also had gone down and killed a lion in the midst of a pit on a snowy day.

Cruel and powerful enemies.

Is 5:29 Their roaring *will be* like a lion, They will roar like young lions; Yes, they will roar And lay hold of the prey; They will carry *it* away safely, And no one will deliver.

Jer 49:19 "Behold, he shall come up like a lion from the floodplain of the Jordan Against the dwelling place of the strong; But I will suddenly make him run away from her. And who *is* a chosen *man that* I may appoint over her? For who *is* like Me? Who will arraign Me? And who *is* that shepherd Who will withstand Me?"

Jer 51:38 They shall roar together like lions, They shall growl like lions' whelps.

Persecutors.

Ps 22:13 They gape at Me *with* their mouths, *Like* a raging and roaring lion.

2 Tim 4:17 But the Lord stood with me and strengthened me, so that the message might be preached fully through me, and *that* all the Gentiles might hear. Also I was delivered out of the mouth of the lion.

The devil.

1 Pet 5:8 Be sober, be vigilant; because your adversary the devil walks about like a roaring lion, seeking whom he may devour.

Imaginary fears of the slothful.

Prov 22:13 The lazy *man* says, "There is a lion outside! I shall be slain in the streets!"

Prov 26:13 The lazy *man* says, "There is a lion in the road! A fierce lion *is* in the streets!"

(Tamed) the natural man subdued by grace.

Is 11:7 The cow and the bear shall graze; Their young ones shall lie down together; And the lion shall eat straw like the ox.

Is 65:25 The wolf and the lamb shall feed together, The lion shall eat straw like the ox, And dust *shall be* the serpent's food. They shall not hurt nor destroy in all My holy mountain," Says the LORD.

(Roaring of) a king's wrath.

Prov 19:12 The king's wrath *is* like the roaring of a lion, But his favor *is* like dew on the grass.

Prov 20:2 The wrath of a king *is* like the roaring of a lion; *Whoever* provokes him to anger sins *against* his own life.

LOCUST, THE

Clean and fit for food.

Lev 11:21–22 Yet these you may eat of every flying insect that creeps on *all* fours: those which have jointed legs above their feet with which to leap on the earth. 22 These you may eat: the locust after its kind, the destroying locust after its kind, the cricket after its kind, and the grasshopper after its kind.

Described as

Wise and ordered.

Prov 30:24 There are four *things which* are little on the earth, But they *are* exceedingly wise:

Prov 30:27 The locusts have no king, Yet they all advance in ranks;

Voracious.

Ex 10:15 For they covered the face of the whole earth, so that the land was darkened; and they ate every herb of the land and all the fruit of the trees which the hail had left. So there remained nothing green on the trees or on the plants of the field throughout all the land of Egypt.

Rapid in movement.

Is 33:4 And Your plunder shall be gathered *Like* the gathering of the caterpillar; As the running to and fro of locusts, He shall run upon them.

Horses prepared for battle.

Joel 2:4 Their appearance is like the appearance of horses; And like swift steeds, so they run.

Rev 9:7 The shape of the locusts was like horses prepared for battle. On their heads were crowns of something like gold, and their faces *were* like the faces of men.

Coming by the wind.

Ex 10:13 So Moses stretched out his rod over the land of Egypt, and the LORD brought an east wind on the land all that day and all *that* night. When it was morning, the east wind brought the locusts.

Ex 10:19 And the LORD turned a very strong west wind, which took the locusts away and blew them into the

Red Sea. There remained not one locust in all the territory of Egypt.

Immensely numerous.

Ps 105:34 He spoke, and locusts came, Young locusts without number,

Nah 3:15 There the fire will devour you, The sword will cut you off; It will eat you up like a locust. Make yourself many—like the locust! Make yourself many— like the *swarming* locusts!

One of the plagues of Egypt.

Ex 10:4–15 Or else, if you refuse to let My people go, behold, tomorrow I will bring locusts into your territory. **5** And they shall cover the face of the earth, so that no one will be able to see the earth; and they shall eat the residue of what is left, which remains to you from the hail, and they shall eat every tree which grows up for you out of the field. **6** They shall fill your houses, the houses of all your servants, and the houses of all the Egyptians—which neither your fathers nor your fathers' fathers have seen, since the day that they were on the earth to this day.' " And he turned and went out from Pharaoh. **7** Then Pharaoh's servants said to him, "How long shall this man be a snare to us? Let the men go, that they may serve the LORD their God. Do you not yet know that Egypt is destroyed?" **8** So Moses and Aaron were brought again to Pharaoh, and he said to them, "Go, serve the LORD your God. Who *are* the ones that are going?" **9** And Moses said, "We will go with our young and our old; with our sons and our daughters, with our flocks and our herds we will go, for we must hold a feast to the LORD." **10** Then he said to them, "The LORD had better be with you when I let you and your little ones go! Beware, for evil is ahead of you. **11** Not so! Go now, you *who are* men, and serve the LORD, for that is what you desired." And they were driven out from Pharaoh's presence. **12** Then the LORD said to Moses, "Stretch out your hand over the land of Egypt for the locusts, that they may come upon the land of Egypt, and eat every herb of the land—all that the hail has left." **13** So Moses stretched out his rod over the land of Egypt, and the LORD brought an east wind on the land all that day and all *that* night. When it was morning, the east wind brought the locusts. **14** And the locusts went up over all the land of Egypt and rested on all the territory of Egypt. *They were* very severe; previously there had been no such locusts as they, nor shall there be such after them. **15** For they covered the face of the whole earth, so that the land was darkened; and they ate every herb of the land and all the fruit of the trees which the hail had left. So there remained nothing green on the trees or on the plants of the field throughout all the land of Egypt.

The Jews

Used, as food.

Matt 3:4 Now John himself was clothed in camel's hair, with a leather belt around his waist; and his food was locusts and wild honey.

Threatened with, as a punishment for sin.

Deut 28:38 "You shall carry much seed out to the field but gather little in, for the locust shall consume it.

Deut 28:42 Locusts shall consume all your trees and the produce of your land.

Often plagued by.

1 Kin 8:37–38 "When there is famine in the land, pestilence *or* blight *or* mildew, locusts *or* grasshoppers; when their enemy besieges them in the land of their cities; whatever plague or whatever sickness *there is;* **38** whatever prayer, whatever supplication is made by anyone, *or* by all Your people Israel, when each one knows the plague of his own heart, and spreads out his hands toward this temple:

Joel 1:4 What the chewing locust left, the swarming locust has eaten; What the swarming locust left, the crawling locust has eaten; And what the crawling locust left, the consuming locust has eaten.

Joel 2:25 "So I will restore to you the years that the swarming locust has eaten, The crawling locust, The consuming locust, And the chewing locust, My great army which I sent among you.

Promised deliverance from the plague of, if humble, etc.

2 Chr 7:13–14 When I shut up heaven and there is no rain, or command the locusts to devour the land, or send pestilence among My people, **14** if My people who are called by My name will humble themselves, and pray and seek My face, and turn from their wicked ways, then I will hear from heaven, and will forgive their sin and heal their land.

Illustrative of

Destructive enemies.

Joel 1:6–7 For a nation has come up against My land, Strong, and without number; His teeth *are* the teeth of a lion, And he has the fangs of a fierce lion. **7** He has laid waste My vine, And ruined My fig tree; He has stripped it bare and thrown *it* away; Its branches are made white.

Joel 2:2–9 A day of darkness and gloominess, A day of clouds and thick darkness, Like the morning *clouds* spread over the mountains. A people *come,* great and strong, The like of whom has never been; Nor will there ever be any *such* after them, Even for many successive generations. **3** A fire devours before them, And behind them a flame burns; The land *is* like the Garden of Eden before them, And behind them a desolate wilderness; Surely nothing shall escape them. **4** Their appearance is like the appearance of horses; And like swift steeds, so they run. **5** With a noise like chariots Over mountaintops they leap, Like the noise of a flaming fire that devours the stubble, Like a strong people set in battle array. **6** Before them the people writhe in pain; All faces are drained of color. **7** They run like mighty men, They climb the wall like men of war; Every one marches in formation, And they do not break ranks. **8** They do not push one another; Every one marches in his own column. Though they lunge between the weapons, They are not cut down. **9** They run to and fro in the city, They run on the wall; They climb into the houses, They enter at the windows like a thief.

False teachers of the apostasy.

Rev 9:3 Then out of the smoke locusts came upon the earth. And to them was given power, as the scorpions of the earth have power.

Ungodly rulers.

Nah 3:17 Your commanders *are* like *swarming* locusts, And your generals like great grasshoppers, Which camp in the hedges on a cold day; When the sun rises they flee away, And the place where they *are* is not known.

Destruction of God's enemies.

Nah 3:15 There the fire will devour you, The sword will cut you off; It will eat you up like a locust. Make yourself many—like the locust! Make yourself many— like the *swarming* locusts!

LORDSHIP

Christ's, over the Sabbath.

Matt 12:1–8 At that time Jesus went through the grainfields on the Sabbath. And His disciples were hungry, and began to pluck heads of grain and to eat. **2** And when the Pharisees saw *it,* they said to Him, "Look, Your disciples are doing what is not lawful to do on the Sabbath!" **3** But He said to them, "Have you not read what David did when he was hungry, he and those who were with him: **4** how he entered the house of God and ate the showbread which was not lawful for him to eat, nor for those who were with him, but only for the priests? **5** Or have you not read in the law that on the Sabbath the priests in the temple profane the Sabbath, and are blameless? **6** Yet I say to you that in this place there is *One* greater than the temple. **7** But if you had known what *this* means, *'I desire mercy and not sacrifice,'* you would not have condemned the guiltless. **8** For the Son of Man is Lord even of the Sabbath."

Mark 2:23–28 Now it happened that He went through the grainfields on the Sabbath; and as they went His disciples began to pluck the heads of grain. **24** And the Pharisees said to Him, "Look, why do they do what is not lawful on the Sabbath?" **25** But He said to them, "Have you never read what David did when he was in need and hungry, he and those with him: **26** how he went into the house of God *in the days* of Abiathar the high priest, and ate the showbread, which is not lawful to eat except for the priests, and also gave some to those who were with him?" **27** And He said to them, "The Sabbath was made for man, and not man for the Sabbath. **28** Therefore the Son of Man is also Lord of the Sabbath."

Luke 6:1–5 Now it happened on the second Sabbath after the first that He went through the grainfields. And His disciples plucked the heads of grain and ate *them,* rubbing *them* in *their* hands. **2** And some of the Pharisees said to them, "Why are you doing what is not lawful to do on the Sabbath?" **3** But Jesus answering them said, "Have you not even read this, what David did when he was hungry, he and those who were with him: **4** how he went into the house of God, took and ate the showbread, and also gave some to those with him, which is not lawful for any but the priests to eat?" **5** And He said to them, "The Son of Man is also Lord of the Sabbath."

Christ's, over the universe.

Matt 11:27 All things have been delivered to Me by My Father, and no one knows the Son except the Father. Nor does anyone know the Father except the Son, and *the one* to whom the Son wills to reveal *Him.*

Matt 28:18 And Jesus came and spoke to them, saying, "All authority has been given to Me in heaven and on earth.

John 3:35 The Father loves the Son, and has given all things into His hand.

Phil 2:9–11 Therefore God also has highly exalted Him and given Him the name which is above every name, **10** that at the name of Jesus every knee should bow, of those in heaven, and of those on earth, and of those under the earth, **11** and *that* every tongue should confess that Jesus Christ *is* Lord, to the glory of God the Father.

Heb 1:1–13 God, who at various times and in various ways spoke in time past to the fathers by the prophets, **2** has in these last days spoken to us by *His* Son, whom He has appointed heir of all things, through whom also He made the worlds; **3** who being the brightness of *His* glory and the express image of His person, and upholding all things by the word of His power, when He had by Himself purged our sins, sat down at the right hand of the Majesty on high, **4** having become so much better than the angels, as He has by inheritance obtained a more excellent name than they. **5** For to which of the angels did He ever say: *"You are My Son, Today I have begotten You"?* And again: *"I will be to Him a Father, And He shall be to Me a Son"?* **6** But when He again brings the firstborn into the world, He says: *"Let all the angels of God worship Him."* **7** And of the angels He says: *"Who makes His angels spirits And His ministers a flame of fire."* **8** But to the Son *He says: "Your throne, O God, is forever and ever; A scepter of righteousness is the scepter of Your kingdom.* **9** *You have loved righteousness and hated lawlessness; Therefore God, Your God, has anointed You With the oil of gladness more than Your companions."* **10** And: *"You, LORD, in the beginning laid the foundation of the earth, And the heavens are the work of Your hands.* **11** *They will perish, but You remain; And they will all grow old like a garment;* **12** *Like a cloak You will fold them up, And they will be changed. But You are the same, And Your years will not fail."* **13** But to which of the angels has He ever said: *"Sit at My right hand, Till I make Your enemies Your footstool"?*

Of Christ, over His followers.

Matt 7:21–23 "Not everyone who says to Me, 'Lord, Lord,' shall enter the kingdom of heaven, but he who does the will of My Father in heaven. **22** Many will say to Me in that day, 'Lord, Lord, have we not prophesied in Your name, cast out demons in Your name, and done many wonders in Your name?' **23** And then I will declare to them, 'I never knew you; depart from Me, you who practice lawlessness!'

Matt 16:24–27 Then Jesus said to His disciples, "If anyone desires to come after Me, let him deny himself, and take up his cross, and follow Me. **25** For whoever desires to save his life will lose it, but whoever loses his life for My sake will find it. **26** For what profit is it to a man if he gains the whole world, and loses his own soul? Or what will a man give in exchange for his soul? **27** For the Son of Man will come in the glory of His Father with His angels, and then He will reward each according to his works.

Mark 8:34–38 When He had called the people to *Him-*

self, with His disciples also, He said to them, "Whoever desires to come after Me, let him deny himself, and take up his cross, and follow Me. 35 For whoever desires to save his life will lose it, but whoever loses his life for My sake and the gospel's will save it. 36 For what will it profit a man if he gains the whole world, and loses his own soul? 37 Or what will a man give in exchange for his soul? 38 For whoever is ashamed of Me and My words in this adulterous and sinful generation, of him the Son of Man also will be ashamed when He comes in the glory of His Father with the holy angels."

Luke 6:46 "But why do you call Me 'Lord, Lord,' and not do the things which I say?

Luke 9:22–26 saying, "The Son of Man must suffer many things, and be rejected by the elders and chief priests and scribes, and be killed, and be raised the third day." 23 Then He said to *them* all, "If anyone desires to come after Me, let him deny himself, and take up his cross daily, and follow Me. 24 For whoever desires to save his life will lose it, but whoever loses his life for My sake will save it. 25 For what profit is it to a man if he gains the whole world, and is himself destroyed or lost? 26 For whoever is ashamed of Me and My words, of him the Son of Man will be ashamed when He comes in His *own* glory, and *in* His Father's, and of the holy angels.

Cf. John 15:26; 1 Cor 2:8–14; 12:3; 1 John 5:6–8

LORD'S SUPPER, THE
Prefigured.

Ex 12:21–28 Then Moses called for all the elders of Israel and said to them, "Pick out and take lambs for yourselves according to your families, and kill the Passover *lamb.* 22 And you shall take a bunch of hyssop, dip *it* in the blood that *is* in the basin, and strike the lintel and the two doorposts with the blood that *is* in the basin. And none of you shall go out of the door of his house until morning. 23 For the LORD will pass through to strike the Egyptians; and when He sees the blood on the lintel and on the two doorposts, the LORD will pass over the door and not allow the destroyer to come into your houses to strike *you.* 24 And you shall observe this thing as an ordinance for you and your sons forever. 25 It will come to pass when you come to the land which the LORD will give you, just as He promised, that you shall keep this service. 26 And it shall be, when your children say to you, 'What do you mean by this service?' 27 that you shall say, 'It *is* the Passover sacrifice of the LORD, who passed over the houses of the children of Israel in Egypt when He struck the Egyptians and delivered our households.' " So the people bowed their heads and worshiped. 28 Then the children of Israel went away and did *so;* just as the LORD had commanded Moses and Aaron, so they did.

1 Cor 5:7–8 Therefore purge out the old leaven, that you may be a new lump, since you truly are unleavened. For indeed Christ, our Passover, was sacrificed for us. 8 Therefore let us keep the feast, not with old leaven, nor with the leaven of malice and wickedness, but with the unleavened *bread* of sincerity and truth.

Instituted.

Matt 26:26 And as they were eating, Jesus took bread, blessed and broke *it,* and gave *it* to the disciples and said, "Take, eat; this is My body."

1 Cor 11:23 For I received from the Lord that which I also delivered to you: that the Lord Jesus on the *same* night in which He was betrayed took bread;

Purpose and character.

Matt 26:27 Then He took the cup, and gave thanks, and gave *it* to them, saying, "Drink from it, all of you.

Luke 22:19 And He took bread, gave thanks and broke *it,* and gave *it* to them, saying, "This is My body which is given for you; do this in remembrance of Me."

1 Cor 10:16 The cup of blessing which we bless, is it not the communion of the blood of Christ? The bread which we break, is it not the communion of the body of Christ?

1 Cor 11:24 and when He had given thanks, He broke *it* and said, "Take, eat; this is My body which is broken for you; do this in remembrance of Me."

1 Cor 11:26 For as often as you eat this bread and drink this cup, you proclaim the Lord's death till He comes.

Qualifications to partake.

1 Cor 5:7–8 Therefore purge out the old leaven, that you may be a new lump, since you truly are unleavened. For indeed Christ, our Passover, was sacrificed for us. 8 Therefore let us keep the feast, not with old leaven, nor with the leaven of malice and wickedness, but with the unleavened *bread* of sincerity and truth.

1 Cor 10:21 You cannot drink the cup of the Lord and the cup of demons; you cannot partake of the Lord's table and of the table of demons.

1 Cor 11:28 But let a man examine himself, and so let him eat of the bread and drink of the cup.

1 Cor 11:31 For if we would judge ourselves, we would not be judged.

Was continually observed by the early church.

Acts 2:42 And they continued steadfastly in the apostles' doctrine and fellowship, in the breaking of bread, and in prayers.

Acts 20:7 Now on the first *day* of the week, when the disciples came together to break bread, Paul, ready to depart the next day, spoke to them and continued his message until midnight.

Unworthy partakers of
Are guilty of the body and blood of Christ.

1 Cor 11:27 Therefore whoever eats this bread or drinks *this* cup of the Lord in an unworthy manner will be guilty of the body and blood of the Lord.

Discern not the Lord's body.

1 Cor 11:29 For he who eats and drinks in an unworthy manner eats and drinks judgment to himself, not discerning the Lord's body.

Are visited with judgments.

1 Cor 11:30 For this reason many *are* weak and sick among you, and many sleep.

LOST, THE

As the object of Christ's ministry.

Luke 9:56 For the Son of Man did not come to destroy men's lives but to save *them*." And they went to another village.

Luke 19:10 for the Son of Man has come to seek and to save that which was lost."

Pictured as,

Sheep.

Jer 50:6 "My people have been lost sheep. Their shepherds have led them astray; They have turned them away *on* the mountains. They have gone from mountain to hill; They have forgotten their resting place.

Matt 10:6 But go rather to the lost sheep of the house of Israel.

Matt 15:24 But He answered and said, "I was not sent except to the lost sheep of the house of Israel."

Matt 18:10–14 "Take heed that you do not despise one of these little ones, for I say to you that in heaven their angels always see the face of My Father who is in heaven. **11** For the Son of Man has come to save that which was lost. **12** "What do you think? If a man has a hundred sheep, and one of them goes astray, does he not leave the ninety-nine and go to the mountains to seek the one that is straying? **13** And if he should find it, assuredly, I say to you, he rejoices more over that *sheep* than over the ninety-nine that did not go astray. **14** Even so it is not the will of your Father who is in heaven that one of these little ones should perish.

Luke 15:4–7 "What man of you, having a hundred sheep, if he loses one of them, does not leave the ninety-nine in the wilderness, and go after the one which is lost until he finds it? **5** And when he has found *it*, he lays *it* on his shoulders, rejoicing. **6** And when he comes home, he calls together *his* friends and neighbors, saying to them, 'Rejoice with me, for I have found my sheep which was lost!' **7** I say to you that likewise there will be more joy in heaven over one sinner who repents than over ninety-nine just persons who need no repentance.

A lost coin.

Luke 15:8–10 "Or what woman, having ten silver coins, if she loses one coin, does not light a lamp, sweep the house, and search carefully until she finds *it*? **9** And when she has found *it*, she calls *her* friends and neighbors together, saying, 'Rejoice with me, for I have found the piece which I lost!' **10** Likewise, I say to you, there is joy in the presence of the angels of God over one sinner who repents."

A lost son.

Luke 15:11–32 Then He said: "A certain man had two sons. **12** And the younger of them said to *his* father, 'Father, give me the portion of goods that falls *to me*.' So he divided to them *his* livelihood. **13** And not many days after, the younger son gathered all together, journeyed to a far country, and there wasted his possessions with prodigal living. **14** But when he had spent all, there arose a severe famine in that land, and he began to be in want. **15** Then he went and joined himself to a citizen of that country, and he sent him into his fields to feed swine. **16** And he would gladly have filled his stomach with the pods that the swine ate, and no one gave him *anything*. **17** "But when he came to himself, he said, 'How many of my father's hired servants have bread enough and to spare, and I perish with hunger! **18** I will arise and go to my father, and will say to him, "Father, I have sinned against heaven and before you, **19** and I am no longer worthy to be called your son. Make me like one of your hired servants." ' **20** "And he arose and came to his father. But when he was still a great way off, his father saw him and had compassion, and ran and fell on his neck and kissed him. **21** And the son said to him, 'Father, I have sinned against heaven and in your sight, and am no longer worthy to be called your son.' **22** "But the father said to his servants, 'Bring out the best robe and put *it* on him, and put a ring on his hand and sandals on *his* feet. **23** And bring the fatted calf here and kill *it*, and let us eat and be merry; **24** for this my son was dead and is alive again; he was lost and is found.' And they began to be merry. **25** "Now his older son was in the field. And as he came and drew near to the house, he heard music and dancing. **26** So he called one of the servants and asked what these things meant. **27** And he said to him, 'Your brother has come, and because he has received him safe and sound, your father has killed the fatted calf.' **28** "But he was angry and would not go in. Therefore his father came out and pleaded with him. **29** So he answered and said to *his* father, 'Lo, these many years I have been serving you; I never transgressed your commandment at any time; and yet you never gave me a young goat, that I might make merry with my friends. **30** But as soon as this son of yours came, who has devoured your livelihood with harlots, you killed the fatted calf for him.' **31** "And he said to him, 'Son, you are always with me, and all that I have is yours. **32** It was right that we should make merry and be glad, for your brother was dead and is alive again, and was lost and is found.' "

Compared to the harvest.

Matt 9:36–38 But when He saw the multitudes, He was moved with compassion for them, because they were weary and scattered, like sheep having no shepherd. **37** Then He said to His disciples, "The harvest truly *is* plentiful, but the laborers *are* few. **38** Therefore pray the Lord of the harvest to send out laborers into His harvest."

Luke 10:2 Then He said to them, "The harvest truly *is* great, but the laborers *are* few; therefore pray the Lord of the harvest to send out laborers into His harvest.

John 4:34–38 Jesus said to them, "My food is to do the will of Him who sent Me, and to finish His work. **35** Do you not say, 'There are still four months and *then* comes the harvest'? Behold, I say to you, lift up your eyes and look at the fields, for they are already white for harvest! **36** And he who reaps receives wages, and gathers fruit for eternal life, that both he who sows and he who reaps may rejoice together. **37** For in this the saying is true: 'One sows and another reaps.' **38** I sent you to reap that for which you have not labored; others have labored, and you have entered into their labors."

Certainty that some will be saved.

John 6:37 All that the Father gives Me will come to Me, and the one who comes to Me I will by no means cast out.

John 10:28–29 And I give them eternal life, and they shall never perish; neither shall anyone snatch them out of My hand. **29** My Father, who has given *them* to Me, is greater than all; and no one is able to snatch *them* out of My Father's hand.

John 17:6 "I have manifested Your name to the men whom You have given Me out of the world. They were Yours, You gave them to Me, and they have kept Your word.

John 17:12 While I was with them in the world, I kept them in Your name. Those whom You gave Me I have kept; and none of them is lost except the son of perdition, that the Scripture might be fulfilled.

John 17:24 "Father, I desire that they also whom You gave Me may be with Me where I am, that they may behold My glory which You have given Me; for You loved Me before the foundation of the world.

John 18:9 that the saying might be fulfilled which He spoke, "Of those whom You gave Me I have lost none."

Acts 13:48 Now when the Gentiles heard this, they were glad and glorified the word of the Lord. And as many as had been appointed to eternal life believed.

Rom 8:28–39 And we know that all things work together for good to those who love God, to those who are the called according to *His* purpose. **29** For whom He foreknew, He also predestined *to be* conformed to the image of His Son, that He might be the firstborn among many brethren. **30** Moreover whom He predestined, these He also called; whom He called, these He also justified; and whom He justified, these He also glorified. **31** What then shall we say to these things? If God *is* for us, who *can be* against us? **32** He who did not spare His own Son, but delivered Him up for us all, how shall He not with Him also freely give us all things? **33** Who shall bring a charge against God's elect? *It is* God who justifies. **34** Who *is* he who condemns? *It is* Christ who died, and furthermore is also risen, who is even at the right hand of God, who also makes intercession for us. **35** Who shall separate us from the love of Christ? *Shall* tribulation, or distress, or persecution, or famine, or nakedness, or peril, or sword? **36** As it is written: *"For Your sake we are killed all day long; We are accounted as sheep for the slaughter."* **37** Yet in all these things we are more than conquerors through Him who loved us. **38** For I am persuaded that neither death nor life, nor angels nor principalities nor powers, nor things present nor things to come, **39** nor height nor depth, nor any other created thing, shall be able to separate us from the love of God which is in Christ Jesus our Lord.

Christ's and God's love for.

Matt 23:37–39 "O Jerusalem, Jerusalem, the one who kills the prophets and stones those who are sent to her! How often I wanted to gather your children together, as a hen gathers her chicks under *her* wings, but you were not willing! **38** See! Your house is left to you desolate; **39** for I say to you, you shall see Me no more till you say, *'Blessed is He who comes in the name of the Lord!'"*

Luke 13:34–35 "O Jerusalem, Jerusalem, the one who kills the prophets and stones those who are sent to her! How often I wanted to gather your children together, as a hen *gathers* her brood under *her* wings, but you were not willing! **35** See! Your house is left to you desolate; and assuredly, I say to you, you shall not see Me until *the time* comes when you say, *'Blessed is He who comes in the name of the Lord!'"*

John 3:16–17 For God so loved the world that He gave His only begotten Son, that whoever believes in Him should not perish but have everlasting life. **17** For God did not send His Son into the world to condemn the world, but that the world through Him might be saved.

1 Tim 2:3–6 For this *is* good and acceptable in the sight of God our Savior, **4** who desires all men to be saved and to come to the knowledge of the truth. **5** For *there is* one God and one Mediator between God and men, *the* Man Christ Jesus, **6** who gave Himself a ransom for all, to be testified in due time,

2 Pet 3:9 The Lord is not slack concerning *His* promise, as some count slackness, but is longsuffering toward us, not willing that any should perish but that all should come to repentance.

Cf. Ezek 18:23,32; 1 Tim 4:10; Titus 2:11

LOT

Abraham's relative (nephew).

Gen 11:31 And Terah took his son Abram and his grandson Lot, the son of Haran, and his daughter-in-law Sarai, his son Abram's wife, and they went out with them from Ur of the Chaldeans to go to the land of Canaan; and they came to Haran and dwelt there.

Gen 13:8 So Abram said to Lot, "Please let there be no strife between you and me, and between my herdsmen and your herdsmen; for we *are* brethren.

Gen 14:12 They also took Lot, Abram's brother's son who dwelt in Sodom, and his goods, and departed.

Separated from Abraham.

Gen 13:5–12 Lot also, who went with Abram, had flocks and herds and tents. **6** Now the land was not able to support them, that they might dwell together, for their possessions were so great that they could not dwell together. **7** And there was strife between the herdsmen of Abram's livestock and the herdsmen of Lot's livestock. The Canaanites and the Perizzites then dwelt in the land. **8** So Abram said to Lot, "Please let there be no strife between you and me, and between my herdsmen and your herdsmen; for we *are* brethren. **9** *Is* not the whole land before you? Please separate from me. If *you take* the left, then I will go to the right; or, if *you go* to the right, then I will go to the left." **10** And Lot lifted his eyes and saw all the plain of Jordan, that *it was* well watered everywhere (before the Lord destroyed Sodom and Gomorrah) like the garden of the Lord, like the land of Egypt as you go toward Zoar. **11** Then Lot chose for himself all the plain of Jordan, and Lot journeyed east. And they separated from each other. **12** Abram dwelt in the land of Canaan, and Lot dwelt in the cities of the plain and pitched *his* tent even as far as Sodom.

Rescued by Abraham.

Gen 14:8–16 And the king of Sodom, the king of Gomorrah, the king of Admah, the king of Zeboiim, and the king of Bela (that *is*, Zoar) went out and joined together in battle in the Valley of Siddim **9** against Chedorlaomer king of Elam, Tidal king of nations, Amraphel king of Shinar, and Arioch king of Ellasar—four kings against five. **10** Now the Valley of Siddim *was full of* asphalt pits; and the kings of Sodom and Gomorrah fled; *some* fell there, and the remainder fled to the mountains. **11** Then they took all the goods of Sodom and Gomorrah, and all their provisions, and went their way. **12** They also took Lot, Abram's brother's son who dwelt in Sodom, and his goods, and departed. **13** Then one who had escaped came and told Abram the Hebrew, for he dwelt by the terebinth trees of Mamre the Amorite, brother of Eshcol and brother of Aner; and they *were* allies with Abram. **14** Now when Abram heard that his brother was taken captive, he armed his three hundred and eighteen trained *servants* who were born in his own house, and went in pursuit as far as Dan. **15** He divided his forces against them by night, and he and his servants attacked them and pursued them as far as Hobah, which *is* north of Damascus. **16** So he brought back all the goods, and also brought back his brother Lot and his goods, as well as the women and the people.

Called righteous.

2 Pet 2:7–8 and delivered righteous Lot, *who was* oppressed by the filthy conduct of the wicked **8** (for that righteous man, dwelling among them, tormented *his* righteous soul from day to day by seeing and hearing *their* lawless deeds)—

Cf. Gen 18:26–32

Escaped the destruction of Sodom and Gomorrah.
Gen 19:1–29; Luke 17:28–29,32

Descendants of (Moab and Ammon).

Gen 19:30–38 Then Lot went up out of Zoar and dwelt in the mountains, and his two daughters were with him; for he was afraid to dwell in Zoar. And he and his two daughters dwelt in a cave. **31** Now the firstborn said to the younger, "Our father *is* old, and *there is* no man on the earth to come in to us as is the custom of all the earth. **32** Come, let us make our father drink wine, and we will lie with him, that we may preserve the lineage of our father." **33** So they made their father drink wine that night. And the firstborn went in and lay with her father, and he did not know when she lay down or when she arose. **34** It happened on the next day that the firstborn said to the younger, "Indeed I lay with my father last night; let us make him drink wine tonight also, and you go in *and* lie with him, that we may preserve the lineage of our father." **35** Then they made their father drink wine that night also. And the younger arose and lay with him, and he did not know when she lay down or when she arose. **36** Thus both the daughters of Lot were with child by their father. **37** The firstborn bore a son and called his name Moab; he *is* the father of the Moabites to this day. **38** And the younger, she also bore a son and called his name Ben-Ammi; he *is* the father of the people of Ammon to this day.

LOVE TO CHRIST

Exhibited by God.

Matt 17:5 While he was still speaking, behold, a bright cloud overshadowed them; and suddenly a voice came out of the cloud, saying, "This is My beloved Son, in whom I am well pleased. Hear Him!"

John 5:20 For the Father loves the Son, and shows Him all things that He Himself does; and He will show Him greater works than these, that you may marvel.

Exhibited by saints.

1 Pet 1:8 whom having not seen you love. Though now you do not see *Him*, yet believing, you rejoice with joy inexpressible and full of glory,

Manifested in
Obeying Him.

John 14:15 "If you love Me, keep My commandments.

John 14:21 He who has My commandments and keeps them, it is he who loves Me. And he who loves Me will be loved by My Father, and I will love him and manifest Myself to him."

John 14:23 Jesus answered and said to him, "If anyone loves Me, he will keep My word; and My Father will love him, and We will come to him and make Our home with him.

Ministering to Him.

Matt 25:40 And the King will answer and say to them, 'Assuredly, I say to you, inasmuch as you did *it* to one of the least of these My brethren, you did *it* to Me.'

Matt 27:55 And many women who followed Jesus from Galilee, ministering to Him, were there looking on from afar,

Preferring Him to all others.

Matt 10:37 He who loves father or mother more than Me is not worthy of Me. And he who loves son or daughter more than Me is not worthy of Me.

Taking up the cross for Him.

Matt 10:38 And he who does not take his cross and follow after Me is not worthy of Me.

2 Cor 5:14 For the love of Christ compels us, because we judge thus: that if One died for all, then all died;

An evidence of adoption.

John 8:42 Jesus said to them, "If God were your Father, you would love Me, for I proceeded forth and came from God; nor have I come of Myself, but He sent Me.

Should be
Sincere.

Eph 6:24 Grace *be* with all those who love our Lord Jesus Christ in sincerity. Amen.

In proportion to our mercies.

Luke 7:47 Therefore I say to you, her sins, *which are* many, are forgiven, for she loved much. But to whom little is forgiven, *the same* loves little."

Supreme.

Matt 10:37 He who loves father or mother more than Me is not worthy of Me. And he who loves son or daughter more than Me is not worthy of Me.

Even to death.

Acts 21:13 Then Paul answered, "What do you mean by weeping and breaking my heart? For I am ready not only to be bound, but also to die at Jerusalem for the name of the Lord Jesus."

Rev 12:11 And they overcame him by the blood of the Lamb and by the word of their testimony, and they did not love their lives to the death.

Promises regarding.

2 Tim 4:8 Finally, there is laid up for me the crown of righteousness, which the Lord, the righteous Judge, will give to me on that Day, and not to me only but also to all who have loved His appearing.

James 1:12 Blessed *is* the man who endures temptation; for when he has been approved, he will receive the crown of life which the Lord has promised to those who love Him.

Those who have,

Should be prayed for.

Eph 6:24 Grace *be* with all those who love our Lord Jesus Christ in sincerity. Amen.

Phil 1:9 And this I pray, that your love may abound still more and more in knowledge and all discernment,

Are loved by the Father.

John 14:21 He who has My commandments and keeps them, it is he who loves Me. And he who loves Me will be loved by My Father, and I will love him and manifest Myself to him."

John 14:23 Jesus answered and said to him, "If anyone loves Me, he will keep My word; and My Father will love him, and We will come to him and make Our home with him.

John 16:27 for the Father Himself loves you, because you have loved Me, and have believed that I came forth from God.

Are loved by Christ.

Prov 8:17 I love those who love me, And those who seek me diligently will find me.

John 14:21 He who has My commandments and keeps them, it is he who loves Me. And he who loves Me will be loved by My Father, and I will love him and manifest Myself to him."

Enjoy communion with God and Christ.

John 14:23 Jesus answered and said to him, "If anyone loves Me, he will keep My word; and My Father will love him, and We will come to him and make Our home with him.

Peril of not having.

1 Cor 16:22 If anyone does not love the Lord Jesus Christ, let him be accursed. O Lord, come!

Rev 2:4 Nevertheless I have *this* against you, that you have left your first love.

The wicked, destitute of.

John 15:18 "If the world hates you, you know that it hated Me before *it hated* you.

John 15:25 But *this happened* that the word might be fulfilled which is written in their law, *'They hated Me without a cause.'*

Exemplified by

Joseph of Arimathea.

Matt 27:57–60 Now when evening had come, there came a rich man from Arimathea, named Joseph, who himself had also become a disciple of Jesus.

58 This man went to Pilate and asked for the body of Jesus. Then Pilate commanded the body to be given to him. **59** When Joseph had taken the body, he wrapped it in a clean linen cloth, **60** and laid it in his new tomb which he had hewn out of the rock; and he rolled a large stone against the door of the tomb, and departed.

A penitent woman.

Luke 7:47 Therefore I say to you, her sins, *which are* many, are forgiven, for she loved much. But to whom little is forgiven, *the same* loves little."

Certain women.

Luke 23:28 But Jesus, turning to them, said, "Daughters of Jerusalem, do not weep for Me, but weep for yourselves and for your children.

Thomas.

John 11:16 Then Thomas, who is called the Twin, said to his fellow disciples, "Let us also go, that we may die with Him."

Mary Magdalene.

John 20:11 But Mary stood outside by the tomb weeping, and as she wept she stooped down *and looked* into the tomb.

Peter.

John 21:15–17 So when they had eaten breakfast, Jesus said to Simon Peter, "Simon, *son* of Jonah, do you love Me more than these?" He said to Him, "Yes, Lord; You know that I love You." He said to him, "Feed My lambs." **16** He said to him again a second time, "Simon, *son* of Jonah, do you love Me?" He said to Him, "Yes, Lord; You know that I love You." He said to him, "Tend My sheep." **17** He said to him the third time, "Simon, *son* of Jonah, do you love Me?" Peter was grieved because He said to him the third time, "Do you love Me?" And he said to Him, "Lord, You know all things; You know that I love You." Jesus said to him, "Feed My sheep.

Paul.

Acts 21:13 Then Paul answered, "What do you mean by weeping and breaking my heart? For I am ready not only to be bound, but also to die at Jerusalem for the name of the Lord Jesus."

LOVE FOR GOD

Commanded of believers.

Deut 6:5 You shall love the LORD your God with all your heart, with all your soul, and with all your strength.

Deut 11:1 "Therefore you shall love the LORD your God, and keep His charge, His statutes, His judgments, and His commandments always.

Josh 22:5 But take careful heed to do the commandment and the law which Moses the servant of the LORD commanded you, to love the LORD your God, to walk in all His ways, to keep His commandments, to hold fast to Him, and to serve Him with all your heart and with all your soul."

Ps 5:11 But let all those rejoice who put their trust in You; Let them ever shout for joy, because You defend them; Let those also who love Your name Be joyful in You.

Matt 22:37 Jesus said to him, " *'You shall love the LORD*

your God with all your heart, with all your soul, and with all your mind.'

The first great commandment.

Matt 22:37–38 Jesus said to him, " 'You shall love the LORD your God with all your heart, with all your soul, and with all your mind.' **38** This is *the* first and great commandment.

Better than all sacrifices.

Mark 12:33 And to love Him with all the heart, with all the understanding, with all the soul, and with all the strength, and to love one's neighbor as oneself, is more than all the whole burnt offerings and sacrifices."

Produced by

The Holy Spirit.

Gal 5:22 But the fruit of the Spirit is love, joy, peace, longsuffering, kindness, goodness, faithfulness,

2 Thess 3:5 Now may the Lord direct your hearts into the love of God and into the patience of Christ.

The love of God to us.

1 John 4:19 We love Him because He first loved us.

Answers to prayer.

Ps 116:1 I love the LORD, because He has heard My voice *and* my supplications.

Exhibited by Christ.

John 14:31 But that the world may know that I love the Father, and as the Father gave Me commandment, so I do. Arise, let us go from here.

Should produce

Joy.

Ps 5:11 But let all those rejoice who put their trust in You; Let them ever shout for joy, because You defend them; Let those also who love Your name Be joyful in You.

Love to believers.

1 John 5:1 Whoever believes that Jesus is the Christ is born of God, and everyone who loves Him who begot also loves him who is begotten of Him.

Hatred of sin.

Ps 97:10 You who love the LORD, hate evil! He preserves the souls of His saints; He delivers them out of the hand of the wicked.

Obedience to God.

Deut 30:20 that you may love the LORD your God, that you may obey His voice, and that you may cling to Him, for He *is* your life and the length of your days; and that you may dwell in the land which the LORD swore to your fathers, to Abraham, Isaac, and Jacob, to give them."

1 John 2:5 But whoever keeps His word, truly the love of God is perfected in him. By this we know that we are in Him.

1 John 5:3 For this is the love of God, that we keep His commandments. And His commandments are not burdensome.

Perfected, gives boldness.

1 John 4:17–18 Love has been perfected among us in this: that we may have boldness in the day of judgment; because as He is, so are we in this world. **18** There is no fear in love; but perfect love casts out

fear, because fear involves torment. But he who fears has not been made perfect in love.

Those who have,

Are known and preserved by Him.

Ps 145:20 The LORD preserves all who love Him, But all the wicked He will destroy.

1 Cor 8:3 But if anyone loves God, this one is known by Him.

Are delivered by Him.

Ps 91:14 "Because he has set his love upon Me, therefore I will deliver him; I will set him on high, because he has known My name.

Partake of His mercy.

Ex 20:6 but showing mercy to thousands, to those who love Me and keep My commandments.

Deut 7:9 "Therefore know that the LORD your God, He *is* God, the faithful God who keeps covenant and mercy for a thousand generations with those who love Him and keep His commandments;

Have all things working for their good.

Rom 8:28 And we know that all things work together for good to those who love God, to those who are the called according to *His* purpose.

Persevere in.

Jude 1:21 keep yourselves in the love of God, looking for the mercy of our Lord Jesus Christ unto eternal life.

Exhort one another to.

Ps 31:23 Oh, love the LORD, all you His saints! *For* the LORD preserves the faithful, And fully repays the proud person.

2 Thess 3:5 Now may the Lord direct your hearts into the love of God and into the patience of Christ.

Unbelievers do not have.

Luke 11:42 "But woe to you Pharisees! For you tithe mint and rue and all manner of herbs, and pass by justice and the love of God. These you ought to have done, without leaving the others undone.

John 5:42 But I know you, that you do not have the love of God in you.

1 John 2:15 Do not love the world or the things in the world. If anyone loves the world, the love of the Father is not in him.

1 John 3:17 But whoever has this world's goods, and sees his brother in need, and shuts up his heart from him, how does the love of God abide in him?

1 John 4:20 If someone says, "I love God," and hates his brother, he is a liar; for he who does not love his brother whom he has seen, how can he love God whom he has not seen?

God tries the sincerity of.

Deut 13:3 you shall not listen to the words of that prophet or that dreamer of dreams, for the LORD your God is testing you to know whether you love the LORD your God with all your heart and with all your soul.

Promises connected with.

Deut 11:13–15 'And it shall be that if you earnestly obey My commandments which I command you today, to love the LORD your God and serve Him with all your heart and with all your soul, **14** then I will give *you* the rain for your land in its season, the early rain and the latter rain, that you may gather in your grain, your new wine, and your oil. **15** And I will send grass in your fields for your livestock, that you may eat and be filled.'

Ps 69:36 Also, the descendants of His servants shall inherit it, And those who love His name shall dwell in it.

Is 56:6–7 "Also the sons of the foreigner Who join themselves to the LORD, to serve Him, And to love the name of the LORD, to be His servants— Everyone who keeps from defiling the Sabbath, And holds fast My covenant— **7** Even them I will bring to My holy mountain, And make them joyful in My house of prayer. Their burnt offerings and their sacrifices *Will be* accepted on My altar; For My house shall be called a house of prayer for all nations."

James 1:12 Blessed *is* the man who endures temptation; for when he has been approved, he will receive the crown of life which the Lord has promised to those who love Him.

LOVE FOR MAN

Explained.

1 Cor 13:4–7 Love suffers long *and* is kind; love does not envy; love does not parade itself, is not puffed up; **5** does not behave rudely, does not seek its own, is not provoked, thinks no evil; **6** does not rejoice in iniquity, but rejoices in the truth; **7** bears all things, believes all things, hopes all things, endures all things.

Commanded by God and Christ.

John 13:34 A new commandment I give to you, that you love one another; as I have loved you, that you also love one another.

John 15:12 This is My commandment, that you love one another as I have loved you.

1 Thess 4:9 But concerning brotherly love you have no need that I should write to you, for you yourselves are taught by God to love one another;

1 John 3:23 And this is His commandment: that we should believe on the name of His Son Jesus Christ and love one another, as He gave us commandment.

1 John 4:7 Beloved, let us love one another, for love is of God; and everyone who loves is born of God and knows God.

1 John 4:21 And this commandment we have from Him: that he who loves God *must* love his brother also.

After the example of Christ.

Eph 5:2 And walk in love, as Christ also has loved us and given Himself for us, an offering and a sacrifice to God for a sweet-smelling aroma.

Characteristics of,

Faith works by.

Gal 5:6 For in Christ Jesus neither circumcision nor uncircumcision avails anything, but faith working through love.

A fruit of the Spirit.

Gal 5:22 But the fruit of the Spirit is love, joy, peace, longsuffering, kindness, goodness, faithfulness,

Col 1:8 who also declared to us your love in the Spirit.

Purity of heart leads to.

1 Pet 1:22 Since you have purified your souls in obeying the truth through the Spirit in sincere love of the brethren, love one another fervently with a pure heart,

An active and abiding principle.

1 Cor 13:8 Love never fails. But whether *there are* prophecies, they will fail; whether *there are* tongues, they will cease; whether *there is* knowledge, it will vanish away.

1 Cor 13:13 And now abide faith, hope, love, these three; but the greatest of these *is* love.

1 Thess 1:3 remembering without ceasing your work of faith, labor of love, and patience of hope in our Lord Jesus Christ in the sight of our God and Father,

Heb 6:10 For God *is* not unjust to forget your work and labor of love which you have shown toward His name, *in that* you have ministered to the saints, and do minister.

Related to brotherly kindness.

Rom 12:10 *Be* kindly affectionate to one another with brotherly love, in honor giving preference to one another;

2 Pet 1:7 to godliness brotherly kindness, and to brotherly kindness love.

Necessary to true happiness.

Prov 15:17 Better *is* a dinner of herbs where love is, Than a fatted calf with hatred.

The second great commandment.

Matt 22:37–39 Jesus said to him, " 'You shall love the LORD your God with all your heart, with all your soul, and with all your mind.' **38** This is *the* first and great commandment. **39** And *the* second *is* like it: 'You shall love your neighbor as yourself.'

1 Tim 1:5 Now the purpose of the commandment is love from a pure heart, *from* a good conscience, and *from* sincere faith,

Is the fulfilling of the law.

Rom 13:8–10 Owe no one anything except to love one another, for he who loves another has fulfilled the law. **9** For the commandments, *"You shall not commit adultery," "You shall not murder," "You shall not steal," "You shall not bear false witness," "You shall not covet,"* and if *there is* any other commandment, *are all* summed up in this saying, namely, *"You shall love your neighbor as yourself."* **10** Love does no harm to a neighbor; therefore love *is* the fulfillment of the law.

Gal 5:14 For all the law is fulfilled in one word, *even* in this: *"You shall love your neighbor as yourself."*

James 2:8 If you really fulfill *the* royal law according to the Scripture, *"You shall love your neighbor as yourself,"* you do well;

Is good and pleasant.

Ps 133:1–2 Behold, how good and how pleasant *it is* For brethren to dwell together in unity! **2** *It is* like the precious oil upon the head, Running down on the beard, The beard of Aaron, Running down on the edge of his garments.

Is a bond of perfect union.

Col 2:2 that their hearts may be encouraged, being knit

together in love, and *attaining* to all riches of the full assurance of understanding, to the knowledge of the mystery of God, both of the Father and of Christ,

Col 3:14 But above all these things put on love, which is the bond of perfection.

Greatest gifts and sacrifices are nothing without.

1 Cor 13:1–3 Though I speak with the tongues of men and of angels, but have not love, I have become sounding brass or a clanging cymbal. **2** And though I have *the gift of* prophecy, and understand all mysteries and all knowledge, and though I have all faith, so that I could remove mountains, but have not love, I am nothing. **3** And though I bestow all my goods to feed *the poor,* and though I give my body to be burned, but have not love, it profits me nothing.

Especially enjoined upon ministers.

1 Tim 4:12 Let no one despise your youth, but be an example to the believers in word, in conduct, in love, in spirit, in faith, in purity.

2 Tim 2:22 Flee also youthful lusts; but pursue righteousness, faith, love, peace with those who call on the Lord out of a pure heart.

Believers should

Practice.

1 Cor 14:1 Pursue love, and desire spiritual *gifts,* but especially that you may prophesy.

1 Cor 16:14 Let all *that* you *do* be done with love.

Phil 1:9 And this I pray, that your love may abound still more and more in knowledge and all discernment,

Col 3:14 But above all these things put on love, which is the bond of perfection.

1 Thess 3:12 And may the Lord make you increase and abound in love to one another and to all, just as we *do* to you,

1 Tim 2:15 Nevertheless she will be saved in childbearing if they continue in faith, love, and holiness, with self-control.

Heb 13:1 Let brotherly love continue.

Encourage each other to.

2 Cor 8:7 But as you abound in everything—in faith, in speech, in knowledge, in all diligence, and in your love for us—*see* that you abound in this grace also.

2 Cor 9:2 for I know your willingness, about which I boast of you to the Macedonians, that Achaia was ready a year ago; and your zeal has stirred up the majority.

Heb 10:24 And let us consider one another in order to stir up love and good works,

Be sincere in.

Rom 12:9 *Let* love *be* without hypocrisy. Abhor what is evil. Cling to what is good.

2 Cor 6:6 by purity, by knowledge, by longsuffering, by kindness, by the Holy Spirit, by sincere love,

2 Cor 8:8 I speak not by commandment, but I am testing the sincerity of your love by the diligence of others.

1 John 3:18 My little children, let us not love in word or in tongue, but in deed and in truth.

Be unselfish in.

1 Cor 10:24 Let no one seek his own, but each one the other's *well-being.*

1 Cor 13:5 does not behave rudely, does not seek its own, is not provoked, thinks no evil;

Phil 2:4 Let each of you look out not only for his own interests, but also for the interests of others.

Be fervent in.

1 Pet 1:22 Since you have purified your souls in obeying the truth through the Spirit in sincere love of the brethren, love one another fervently with a pure heart,

1 Pet 4:8 And above all things have fervent love for one another, for *"love will cover a multitude of sins."*

Should be exhibited, toward

Believers.

1 Pet 2:17 Honor all *people.* Love the brotherhood. Fear God. Honor the king.

1 John 5:1 Whoever believes that Jesus is the Christ is born of God, and everyone who loves Him who begot also loves him who is begotten of Him.

Ministers.

1 Thess 5:13 and to esteem them very highly in love for their work's sake. Be at peace among yourselves.

Our families.

Eph 5:25 Husbands, love your wives, just as Christ also loved the church and gave Himself for her,

Titus 2:4 that they admonish the young women to love their husbands, to love their children,

Fellow-countrymen.

Ex 32:32 Yet now, if You will forgive their sin—but if not, I pray, blot me out of Your book which You have written."

Rom 9:2–3 that I have great sorrow and continual grief in my heart. **3** For I could wish that I myself were accursed from Christ for my brethren, my countrymen according to the flesh,

Rom 10:1 Brethren, my heart's desire and prayer to God for Israel is that they may be saved.

Strangers.

Lev 19:34 The stranger who dwells among you shall be to you as one born among you, and you shall love him as yourself; for you were strangers in the land of Egypt: I *am* the LORD your God.

Deut 10:19 Therefore love the stranger, for you were strangers in the land of Egypt.

Enemies.

Ex 23:4–5 "If you meet your enemy's ox or his donkey going astray, you shall surely bring it back to him again. **5** If you see the donkey of one who hates you lying under its burden, and you would refrain from helping it, you shall surely help him with it.

2 Kin 6:22 But he answered, "You shall not kill *them.* Would you kill those whom you have taken captive with your sword and your bow? Set food and water before them, that they may eat and drink and go to their master."

Matt 5:44 But I say to you, love your enemies, bless those who curse you, do good to those who hate you, and pray for those who spitefully use you and persecute you,

Rom 12:14 Bless those who persecute you; bless and do not curse.

Rom 12:20 Therefore *"If your enemy is hungry, feed*

him; If he is thirsty, give him a drink; For in so doing you will heap coals of fire on his head."

1 Pet 3:9 not returning evil for evil or reviling for reviling, but on the contrary blessing, knowing that you were called to this, that you may inherit a blessing.

All people.

Gal 6:10 Therefore, as we have opportunity, let us do good to all, especially to those who are of the household of faith.

Should be exhibited, in

Ministering to the wants of others.

Matt 25:35 for I was hungry and you gave Me food; I was thirsty and you gave Me drink; I was a stranger and you took Me in;

Heb 6:10 For God *is* not unjust to forget your work and labor of love which you have shown toward His name, *in that* you have ministered to the saints, and do minister.

Loving each other.

Gal 5:13 For you, brethren, have been called to liberty; only do not *use* liberty as an opportunity for the flesh, but through love serve one another.

Relieving strangers.

Lev 25:35 'If one of your brethren becomes poor, and falls into poverty among you, then you shall help him, like a stranger or a sojourner, that he may live with you.

Matt 25:36 I *was* naked and you clothed Me; I was sick and you visited Me; I was in prison and you came to Me.'

Clothing the naked.

Is 58:7 *Is it* not to share your bread with the hungry, And that you bring to your house the poor who are cast out; When you see the naked, that you cover him, And not hide yourself from your own flesh?

Matt 25:36 I *was* naked and you clothed Me; I was sick and you visited Me; I was in prison and you came to Me.'

Visiting the sick, etc.

Job 31:16–22 "If I have kept the poor from *their* desire, Or caused the eyes of the widow to fail, **17** Or eaten my morsel by myself, So that the fatherless could not eat of it **18** (But from my youth I reared him as a father, And from my mother's womb I guided *the widow*); **19** If I have seen anyone perish for lack of clothing, Or any poor *man* without covering; **20** If his heart has not blessed me, And *if* he was *not* warmed with the fleece of my sheep; **21** If I have raised my hand against the fatherless, When I saw I had help in the gate; **22** *Then* let my arm fall from my shoulder, Let my arm be torn from the socket.

James 1:27 Pure and undefiled religion before God and the Father is this: to visit orphans and widows in their trouble, *and* to keep oneself unspotted from the world.

Sympathizing.

Rom 12:15 Rejoice with those who rejoice, and weep with those who weep.

1 Cor 12:26 And if one member suffers, all the members suffer with *it;* or if one member is honored, all the members rejoice with *it.*

Supporting the weak.

Gal 6:2 Bear one another's burdens, and so fulfill the law of Christ.

1 Thess 5:14 Now we exhort you, brethren, warn those who are unruly, comfort the fainthearted, uphold the weak, be patient with all.

Covering the faults of others.

Prov 10:12 Hatred stirs up strife, But love covers all sins.

1 Pet 4:8 And above all things have fervent love for one another, for *"love will cover a multitude of sins."*

Forbearing.

Eph 4:2 with all lowliness and gentleness, with longsuffering, bearing with one another in love,

Eph 4:32 And be kind to one another, tenderhearted, forgiving one another, even as God in Christ forgave you.

Col 3:13 bearing with one another, and forgiving one another, if anyone has a complaint against another; even as Christ forgave you, so you also *must do.*

Rebuking.

Lev 19:17 'You shall not hate your brother in your heart. You shall surely rebuke your neighbor, and not bear sin because of him.

Matt 18:15 "Moreover if your brother sins against you, go and tell him his fault between you and him alone. If he hears you, you have gained your brother.

The love of God is a motive to.

John 13:34 A new commandment I give to you, that you love one another; as I have loved you, that you also love one another.

1 John 4:11 Beloved, if God so loved us, we also ought to love one another.

An evidence of

Selflessness.

Mark 12:33 And to love Him with all the heart, with all the understanding, with all the soul, and with all the strength, and to love one's neighbor as oneself, is more than all the whole burnt offerings and sacrifices.

Being in the light.

1 John 2:10 He who loves his brother abides in the light, and there is no cause for stumbling in him.

Discipleship with Christ.

John 13:35 By this all will know that you are My disciples, if you have love for one another."

Spiritual life.

1 John 3:14 We know that we have passed from death to life, because we love the brethren. He who does not love *his* brother abides in death.

Unbelievers, devoid of.

1 John 2:9 He who says he is in the light, and hates his brother, is in darkness until now.

1 John 2:11 But he who hates his brother is in darkness and walks in darkness, and does not know where he is going, because the darkness has blinded his eyes.

1 John 3:10 In this the children of God and the children of the devil are manifest: Whoever does not practice righteousness is not of God, nor *is* he who does not love his brother.

1 John 4:20 If someone says, "I love God," and hates his brother, he is a liar; for he who does not love his brother whom he has seen, how can he love God whom he has not seen?

Exemplified by

Joseph.

Gen 45:15 Moreover he kissed all his brothers and wept over them, and after that his brothers talked with him.

Ruth.

Ruth 1:16–17 But Ruth said: "Entreat me not to leave you, *Or to* turn back from following after you; For wherever you go, I will go; And wherever you lodge, I will lodge; Your people *shall be* my people, And your God, my God. **17** Where you die, I will die, And there will I be buried. The LORD do so to me, and more also, If *anything but* death parts you and me."

Jonathan and David.

1 Sam 20:17 Now Jonathan again caused David to vow, because he loved him; for he loved him as he loved his own soul.

1 Sam 20:41–42 As soon as the lad had gone, David arose from *a place* toward the south, fell on his face to the ground, and bowed down three times. And they kissed one another; and they wept together, but David more so. **42** Then Jonathan said to David, "Go in peace, since we have both sworn in the name of the LORD, saying, 'May the LORD be between you and me, and between your descendants and my descendants, forever.' " So he arose and departed, and Jonathan went into the city.

Obadiah.

1 Kin 18:4 For so it was, while Jezebel massacred the prophets of the LORD, that Obadiah had taken one hundred prophets and hidden them, fifty to a cave, and had fed them with bread and water.)

The centurion.

Luke 7:5 "for he loves our nation, and has built us a synagogue."

The early church.

Acts 2:46 So continuing daily with one accord in the temple, and breaking bread from house to house, they ate their food with gladness and simplicity of heart,

Heb 10:33–34 partly while you were made a spectacle both by reproaches and tribulations, and partly while you became companions of those who were so treated; **34** for you had compassion on me in my chains, and joyfully accepted the plundering of your goods, knowing that you have a better and an enduring possession for yourselves in heaven.

Lydia.

Acts 16:15 And when she and her household were baptized, she begged *us,* saying, "If you have judged me to be faithful to the Lord, come to my house and stay." So she persuaded us.

Aquila.

Rom 16:3–4 Greet Priscilla and Aquila, my fellow workers in Christ Jesus, **4** who risked their own necks for my life, to whom not only I give thanks, but also all the churches of the Gentiles.

Paul.

2 Cor 6:11–12 O Corinthians! We have spoken openly to you, our heart is wide open. **12** You are not restricted by us, but you are restricted by your *own* affections.

Epaphroditus.

Phil 2:25–26 Yet I considered it necessary to send to you Epaphroditus, my brother, fellow worker, and fellow soldier, but your messenger and the one who ministered to my need; **26** since he was longing for you all, and was distressed because you had heard that he was sick.

Phil 2:30 because for the work of Christ he came close to death, not regarding his life, to supply what was lacking in your service toward me.

The Philippians.

Phil 4:15–19 Now you Philippians know also that in the beginning of the gospel, when I departed from Macedonia, no church shared with me concerning giving and receiving but you only. **16** For even in Thessalonica you sent *aid* once and again for my necessities. **17** Not that I seek the gift, but I seek the fruit that abounds to your account. **18** Indeed I have all and abound. I am full, having received from Epaphroditus the things *sent* from you, a sweet-smelling aroma, an acceptable sacrifice, well pleasing to God. **19** And my God shall supply all your need according to His riches in glory by Christ Jesus.

The Colossians.

Col 1:4 since we heard of your faith in Christ Jesus and of your love for all the saints;

The Thessalonians.

1 Thess 3:6 But now that Timothy has come to us from you, and brought us good news of your faith and love, and that you always have good remembrance of us, greatly desiring to see us, as we also *to see* you—

Onesiphorus.

2 Tim 1:16–18 The Lord grant mercy to the household of Onesiphorus, for he often refreshed me, and was not ashamed of my chain; **17** but when he arrived in Rome, he sought me out very zealously and found *me.* **18** The Lord grant to him that he may find mercy from the Lord in that Day—and you know very well how many ways he ministered *to me* at Ephesus.

Philemon.

Philem 1:7–9 For we have great joy and consolation in your love, because the hearts of the saints have been refreshed by you, brother. **8** Therefore, though I might be very bold in Christ to command you what is fitting, **9** yet for love's sake I rather appeal *to you*—being such a one as Paul, the aged, and now also a prisoner of Jesus Christ—

Moses.

Heb 11:25 choosing rather to suffer affliction with the people of God than to enjoy the passing pleasures of sin,

LOYALTY

Joab's, to David.

2 Sam 12:26–31 Now Joab fought against Rabbah of the people of Ammon, and took the royal city. **27** And Joab sent messengers to David, and said, "I have fought against Rabbah, and I have taken the city's water *supply*. 28 Now therefore, gather the rest of the people together and encamp against the city and take it, lest I take the city and it be called after my name." 29 So David gathered all the people together and went to Rabbah, fought against it, and took it. 30 Then he took their king's crown from his head. Its weight *was* a talent of gold, with precious stones. And it was *set* on David's head. Also he brought out the spoil of the city in great abundance. 31 And he brought out the people who *were* in it, and put *them to work* with saws and iron picks and iron axes, and made them cross over to the brick works. So he did to all the cities of the people of Ammon. Then David and all the people returned to Jerusalem.

Caleb's, to Moses.

Num 13:30 Then Caleb quieted the people before Moses, and said, "Let us go up at once and take possession, for we are well able to overcome it."

Josh 14:6–15 Then the children of Judah came to Joshua in Gilgal. And Caleb the son of Jephunneh the Kenizzite said to him: "You know the word which the LORD said to Moses the man of God concerning you and me in Kadesh Barnea. 7 I *was* forty years old when Moses the servant of the LORD sent me from Kadesh Barnea to spy out the land, and I brought back word to him as *it was* in my heart. 8 Nevertheless my brethren who went up with me made the heart of the people melt, but I wholly followed the LORD my God. 9 So Moses swore on that day, saying, 'Surely the land where your foot has trodden shall be your inheritance and your children's forever, because you have wholly followed the LORD my God.' 10 And now, behold, the LORD has kept me alive, as He said, these forty-five years, ever since the LORD spoke this word to Moses while Israel wandered in the wilderness; and now, here I am this day, eighty-five years old. 11 As yet I *am* as strong this day as on the day that Moses sent me; just as my strength *was* then, so now *is* my strength for war, both for going out and for coming in. 12 Now therefore, give me this mountain of which the LORD spoke in that day; for you heard in that day how the Anakim *were* there, and *that* the cities *were* great *and* fortified. It may be that the LORD *will be* with me, and I shall be able to drive them out as the LORD said." 13 And Joshua blessed him, and gave Hebron to Caleb the son of Jephunneh as an inheritance. 14 Hebron therefore became the inheritance of Caleb the son of Jephunneh the Kenizzite to this day, because he wholly followed the LORD God of Israel. 15 And the name of Hebron formerly was Kirjath Arba (*Arba was* the greatest man among the Anakim). Then the land had rest from war.

Ruth's, to

Naomi.

Ruth 1:16–18 But Ruth said: "Entreat me not to leave you, *Or to* turn back from following after you; For wherever you go, I will go; And wherever you lodge, I will lodge; Your people *shall be* my people, And your God, my God. 17 Where you die, I will die, And there will I be buried. The LORD do so to me, and more also, If *anything but* death parts you and me." 18 When she saw that she was determined to go with her, she stopped speaking to her.

Boaz.

Ruth 2:14–22 Now Boaz said to her at mealtime, "Come here, and eat of the bread, and dip your piece of bread in the vinegar." So she sat beside the reapers, and he passed parched *grain* to her; and she ate and was satisfied, and kept some back. 15 And when she rose up to glean, Boaz commanded his young men, saying, "Let her glean even among the sheaves, and do not reproach her. 16 Also let *grain* from the bundles fall purposely for her; leave *it* that she may glean, and do not rebuke her." 17 So she gleaned in the field until evening, and beat out what she had gleaned, and it was about an ephah of barley. 18 Then she took *it* up and went into the city, and her mother-in-law saw what she had gleaned. So she brought out and gave to her what she had kept back after she had been satisfied. 19 And her mother-in-law said to her, "Where have you gleaned today? And where did you work? Blessed be the one who took notice of you." So she told her mother-in-law with whom she had worked, and said, "The man's name with whom I worked today *is* Boaz." 20 Then Naomi said to her daughter-in-law, "Blessed *be* he of the LORD, who has not forsaken His kindness to the living and the dead!" And Naomi said to her, "This man *is* a relation of ours, one of our close relatives." 21 Ruth the Moabitess said, "He also said to me, 'You shall stay close by my young men until they have finished all my harvest.' " 22 And Naomi said to Ruth her daughter-in-law, "*It is* good, my daughter, that you go out with his young women, and that people do not meet you in any other field."

Ruth 3:8–9 Now it happened at midnight that the man was startled, and turned himself; and there, a woman was lying at his feet. 9 And he said, "Who *are* you?" So she answered, "I *am* Ruth, your maidservant. Take your maidservant under your wing, for you are a close relative."

Between Jonathan and David.

1 Sam 18:1–3 Now when he had finished speaking to Saul, the soul of Jonathan was knit to the soul of David, and Jonathan loved him as his own soul. 2 Saul took him that day, and would not let him go home to his father's house anymore. 3 Then Jonathan and David made a covenant, because he loved him as his own soul.

1 Sam 19:4 Thus Jonathan spoke well of David to Saul his father, and said to him, "Let not the king sin against his servant, against David, because he has not sinned against you, and because his works *have been* very good toward you.

2 Sam 9:1 Now David said, "Is there still anyone who is left of the house of Saul, that I may show him kindness for Jonathan's sake?"

Of Judah and King Abijah to God.

2 Chr 13:4–12 Then Abijah stood on Mount Zemaraim, which *is* in the mountains of Ephraim, and said, "Hear me, Jeroboam and all Israel: 5 Should you not know that the LORD God of Israel gave the dominion over Israel to David forever, to him and his sons, by a covenant of salt? 6 Yet Jeroboam the son of Nebat, the servant of Solomon the son of David, rose up and rebelled against his lord. 7 Then worthless rogues gathered to him, and strengthened themselves against Rehoboam the son of Solomon, when Rehoboam was young and inexperienced and could not withstand them. **8** And now you think to withstand the kingdom of the LORD, which is in the hand of the sons of David; and you *are* a great multitude, and with you are the gold calves which Jeroboam made for you as gods. **9** Have you not cast out the priests of the LORD, the sons of Aaron, and the Levites, and made for yourselves priests, like the peoples of *other* lands, so that whoever comes to consecrate himself with a young bull and seven rams may be a priest of *things that are* not gods? **10** But as for us, the LORD *is* our God, and we have not forsaken Him; and the priests who minister to the LORD *are* the sons of Aaron, and the Levites *attend* to *their* duties. **11** And they burn to the LORD every morning and every evening burnt sacrifices and sweet incense; *they* also *set* the showbread *in order on* the pure *gold* table, and the lampstand of gold with its lamps to burn every evening; for we keep the command of the LORD our God, but you have forsaken Him. **12** Now look, God Himself is with us as *our* head, and His priests with sounding trumpets to sound the alarm against you. O children of Israel, do not fight against the LORD God of your fathers, for you shall not prosper!"

Of Mordecai to the king of Persia and Esther.

Esth 2:19–23 When virgins were gathered together a second time, Mordecai sat within the king's gate. **20** *Now* Esther had not revealed her family and her people, just as Mordecai had charged her, for Esther obeyed the command of Mordecai as when she was brought up by him. **21** In those days, while Mordecai sat within the king's gate, two of the king's eunuchs, Bigthan and Teresh, doorkeepers, became furious and sought to lay hands on King Ahasuerus. **22** So the matter became known to Mordecai, who told Queen Esther, and Esther informed the king in Mordecai's name. **23** And when an inquiry was made into the matter, it was confirmed, and both were hanged on a gallows; and it was written in the book of the chronicles in the presence of the king.

Esth 6:1–3 That night the king could not sleep. So one was commanded to bring the book of the records of the chronicles; and they were read before the king. **2** And it was found written that Mordecai had told of Bigthana and Teresh, two of the king's eunuchs, the doorkeepers who had sought to lay hands on King Ahasuerus. **3** Then the king said, "What honor or dignity has been bestowed on Mordecai for this?" And the king's servants who attended him said, "Nothing has been done for him."

Esth 8:2 So the king took off his signet ring, which he had taken from Haman, and gave it to Mordecai; and Esther appointed Mordecai over the house of Haman.

David's, to God.

Ps 26:3–8 For Your lovingkindness *is* before my eyes, And I have walked in Your truth. **4** I have not sat with idolatrous mortals, Nor will I go in with hypocrites. **5** I have hated the assembly of evildoers, And will not sit with the wicked. **6** I will wash my hands in innocence; So I will go about Your altar, O LORD, **7** That I may proclaim with the voice of thanksgiving, And tell of all Your wondrous works. **8** LORD, I have loved the habitation of Your house, And the place where Your glory dwells.

Of the virtuous wife.

Prov 31:10–12 Who can find a virtuous wife? For her worth *is* far above rubies. **11** The heart of her husband safely trusts her; So he will have no lack of gain. **12** She does him good and not evil All the days of her life.

LUST

Of the Sodomites.

Gen 19:4–9 Now before they lay down, the men of the city, the men of Sodom, both old and young, all the people from every quarter, surrounded the house. **5** And they called to Lot and said to him, "Where are the men who came to you tonight? Bring them out to us that we may know them *carnally.*" **6** So Lot went out to them through the doorway, shut the door behind him, **7** and said, "Please, my brethren, do not do so wickedly! **8** See now, I have two daughters who have not known a man; please, let me bring them out to you, and you may do to them as you wish; only do nothing to these men, since this is the reason they have come under the shadow of my roof." **9** And they said, "Stand back!" Then they said, "This one came in to stay *here,* and he keeps acting as a judge; now we will deal worse with you than with them." So they pressed hard against the man Lot, and came near to break down the door.

The dangers of.

Prov 6:25–29 Do not lust after her beauty in your heart, Nor let her allure you with her eyelids. **26** For by means of a harlot *A man is reduced* to a crust of bread; And an adulteress will prey upon his precious life. **27** Can a man take fire to his bosom, And his clothes not be burned? **28** Can one walk on hot coals, And his feet not be seared? **29** So *is* he who goes in to his neighbor's wife; Whoever touches her shall not be innocent.

Intensity of, compared to oven's heat.

Hos 7:4–7 "They *are* all adulterers. Like an oven heated by a baker— He ceases stirring *the fire* after kneading the dough, Until it is leavened. **5** In the day of our king Princes have made *him* sick, inflamed with wine; He stretched out his hand with scoffers. **6** They prepare their heart like an oven, While they lie in wait; Their baker sleeps all night; In the morning it burns like a flaming fire. **7** They are all hot, like an oven, And have devoured their judges; All their kings have fallen. None among them calls upon Me.

Jesus tempted to.

Matt 4:1–11 Then Jesus was led up by the Spirit into the wilderness to be tempted by the devil. **2** And when He had fasted forty days and forty nights, afterward He was hungry. **3** Now when the tempter came to Him, he said, "If You are the Son of God, command that these stones become bread." **4** But He answered and said, "It is written, *'Man shall not live by bread alone, but by every word that proceeds from the mouth of God.'"* **5** Then the devil took Him up into the holy city, set Him on the pinnacle of the temple, **6** and said to Him, "If You are the Son of God, throw Yourself down. For it is written: *'He shall give His angels charge over you,'* and, *'In their hands they shall bear you up, Lest you dash your foot against a stone.'"* **7** Jesus said to him, "It is written again, *'You shall not tempt the LORD your God.'"* **8** Again, the devil took Him up on an exceedingly high mountain, and showed Him all the kingdoms of the world and their glory. **9** And he said to Him, "All these things I will give You if You will fall down and worship me." **10** Then Jesus said to him, "Away with you, Satan! For it is written, *'You shall worship the* LORD *your God, and Him only you shall serve.'"* **11** Then the devil left Him, and behold, angels came and ministered to Him.

Mark 1:12–13 Immediately the Spirit drove Him into the wilderness. **13** And He was there in the wilderness forty days, tempted by Satan, and was with the wild beasts; and the angels ministered to Him.

Luke 4:1–4 Then Jesus, being filled with the Holy Spirit, returned from the Jordan and was led by the Spirit into the wilderness, **2** being tempted for forty days by the devil. And in those days He ate nothing, and afterward, when they had ended, He was hungry. **3** And the devil said to Him, "If You are the Son of God, command this stone to become bread." **4** But Jesus answered him, saying, "It is written, *'Man shall not live by bread alone, but by every word of God.'"*

Remedy for, drastically illustrated.

Matt 5:27–30 "You have heard that it was said to those of old, *'You shall not commit adultery.'* **28** But I say to you that whoever looks at a woman to lust for her has already committed adultery with her in his heart. **29** If your right eye causes you to sin, pluck it out and cast *it* from you; for it is more profitable for you that one of your members perish, than for your whole body to be cast into hell. **30** And if your right hand causes you to sin, cut it off and cast *it* from you; for it is more profitable for you that one of your members perish, than for your whole body to be cast into hell.

Believers must resist.

Rom 13:13–14 Let us walk properly, as in the day, not in revelry and drunkenness, not in lewdness and lust, not in strife and envy. **14** But put on the Lord Jesus Christ, and make no provision for the flesh, to *fulfill its* lusts.

1 Pet 2:11 Beloved, I beg *you* as sojourners and pilgrims, abstain from fleshly lusts which war against the soul,

1 Pet 4:2 that he no longer should live the rest of *his* time in the flesh for the lusts of men, but for the will of God.

1 John 2:15–16 Do not love the world or the things in the world. If anyone loves the world, the love of the Father is not in him. **16** For all that *is* in the world—the lust of the flesh, the lust of the eyes, and the pride of life—is not of the Father but is of the world.

Cf. 1 Cor 6:18; Eph 5:3; Col 3:5; 1 Thess 4:3; 2 Tim 2:22

Source of.

James 1:13–14 Let no one say when he is tempted, "I am tempted by God"; for God cannot be tempted by evil, nor does He Himself tempt anyone. **14** But each one is tempted when he is drawn away by his own desires and enticed.

Cf. Matt 15:18–20; James 4:1–4

Characteristic of false teachers.

2 Tim 3:1–7 But know this, that in the last days perilous times will come: **2** For men will be lovers of themselves, lovers of money, boasters, proud, blasphemers, disobedient to parents, unthankful, unholy, **3** unloving, unforgiving, slanderers, without self-control, brutal, despisers of good, **4** traitors, headstrong, haughty, lovers of pleasure rather than lovers of God, **5** having a form of godliness but denying its power. And from such people turn away! **6** For of this sort are those who creep into households and make captives of gullible women loaded down with sins, led away by various lusts, **7** always learning and never able to come to the knowledge of the truth.

2 Pet 2:12–14 But these, like natural brute beasts made to be caught and destroyed, speak evil of the things they do not understand, and will utterly perish in their own corruption, **13** *and* will receive the wages of unrighteousness, *as* those who count it pleasure to carouse in the daytime. *They are* spots and blemishes, carousing in their own deceptions while they feast with you, **14** having eyes full of adultery and that cannot cease from sin, enticing unstable souls. *They have* a heart trained in covetous practices, *and are* accursed children.

2 Pet 2:18 For when they speak great swelling *words* of emptiness, they allure through the lusts of the flesh, through lewdness, the ones who have actually escaped from those who live in error.

2 Pet 3:3 knowing this first: that scoffers will come in the last days, walking according to their own lusts,

Jude 1:16–19 These are grumblers, complainers, walking according to their own lusts; and they mouth great swelling *words,* flattering people to gain advantage. **17** But you, beloved, remember the words which were spoken before by the apostles of our Lord Jesus Christ: **18** how they told you that there would be mockers in the last time who would walk according to their own ungodly lusts. **19** These are sensual persons, who cause divisions, not having the Spirit.

Cf. 2 Tim 4:3; Jude 10

LYING

Forbidden.

Ex 20:15–16 "You shall not steal. **16** "You shall not bear false witness against your neighbor.

Lev 19:11 'You shall not steal, nor deal falsely, nor lie to one another.

Col 3:9 Do not lie to one another, since you have put off the old man with his deeds,

An abomination to God.

Prov 6:16–19 These six *things* the LORD hates, Yes, seven *are* an abomination to Him: **17** A proud look, A lying tongue, Hands that shed innocent blood, **18** A heart that devises wicked plans, Feet that are swift in running to evil, **19** A false witness *who* speaks lies, And one who sows discord among brethren.

Prov 12:22 Lying lips *are* an abomination to the LORD, But those who deal truthfully *are* His delight.

A hindrance to prayer.

Is 59:2–3 But your iniquities have separated you from your God; And your sins have hidden *His* face from you, So that He will not hear. **3** For your hands are defiled with blood, And your fingers with iniquity; Your lips have spoken lies, Your tongue has muttered perversity.

The devil prompts men to.

1 Kin 22:22 The LORD said to him, 'In what way?' So he said, 'I will go out and be a lying spirit in the mouth of all his prophets.' And the LORD said, 'You shall persuade *him,* and also prevail. Go out and do so.'

John 8:44 You are of *your* father the devil, and the desires of your father you want to do. He was a murderer from the beginning, and does not stand in the truth, because there is no truth in him. When he speaks a lie, he speaks from his own *resources,* for he is a liar and the father of it.

Acts 5:3 But Peter said, "Ananias, why has Satan filled your heart to lie to the Holy Spirit and keep back *part* of the price of the land for yourself?

Believers

Hate.

Ps 119:163 I hate and abhor lying, *But* I love Your law.

Prov 13:5 A righteous *man* hates lying, But a wicked *man* is loathsome and comes to shame.

Avoid.

Is 63:8 For He said, "Surely they *are* My people, Children *who* will not lie." So He became their Savior.

Zeph 3:13 The remnant of Israel shall do no unrighteousness And speak no lies, Nor shall a deceitful tongue be found in their mouth; For they shall feed *their* flocks and lie down, And no one shall make *them* afraid."

Reject those who practice.

Ps 40:4 Blessed *is* that man who makes the LORD his trust, And does not respect the proud, nor such as turn aside to lies.

Ps 101:7 He who works deceit shall not dwell within my house; He who tells lies shall not continue in my presence.

Pray to be preserved from.

Ps 119:29 Remove from me the way of lying, And grant me Your law graciously.

Prov 30:8 Remove falsehood and lies far from me; Give me neither poverty nor riches— Feed me with the food allotted to me;

Unbecoming in rulers.

Prov 17:7 Excellent speech is not becoming to a fool, Much less lying lips to a prince.

Prov 29:12 If a ruler pays attention to lies, All his servants *become* wicked.

False prophets addicted to.

Jer 23:14 Also I have seen a horrible thing in the prophets of Jerusalem: They commit adultery and walk in lies; They also strengthen the hands of evildoers, So that no one turns back from his wickedness. All of them are like Sodom to Me, And her inhabitants like Gomorrah.

Ezek 22:28 Her prophets plastered them with untempered *mortar,* seeing false visions, and divining lies for them, saying, 'Thus says the Lord GOD,' when the LORD had not spoken.

False witnesses addicted to.

Prov 14:5 A faithful witness does not lie, But a false witness will utter lies.

Prov 14:25 A true witness delivers souls, But a deceitful *witness* speaks lies.

Antinomians guilty of.

1 John 1:6 If we say that we have fellowship with Him, and walk in darkness, we lie and do not practice the truth.

1 John 2:4 He who says, "I know Him," and does not keep His commandments, is a liar, and the truth is not in him.

Hypocrites addicted to.

Is 57:4 Whom do you ridicule? Against whom do you make a wide mouth *And* stick out the tongue? *Are* you not children of transgression, Offspring of falsehood,

Hos 11:12 "Ephraim has encircled Me with lies, And the house of Israel with deceit; But Judah still walks with God, Even with the Holy One *who is* faithful.

The wicked

Addicted to, from their infancy.

Ps 58:3 The wicked are estranged from the womb; They go astray as soon as they are born, speaking lies.

Love.

Ps 52:3 You love evil more than good, Lying rather than speaking righteousness. Selah

Ps 62:4 They only consult to cast *him* down from his high position; They delight in lies; They bless with their mouth, But they curse inwardly. Selah

Seek after.

Ps 4:2 How long, O you sons of men, *Will you turn* my glory to shame? *How long* will you love worthlessness *And* seek falsehood? Selah

Prepare their tongues for.

Jer 9:3 "And *like* their bow they have bent their tongues *for* lies. They are not valiant for the truth on the earth. For they proceed from evil to evil, And they do not know Me," says the LORD.

Jer 9:5 Everyone will deceive his neighbor, And will not speak the truth; They have taught their tongue to speak lies; They weary themselves to commit iniquity.

Bring forth.

Ps 7:14 Behold, *the wicked* brings forth iniquity; Yes, he conceives trouble and brings forth falsehood.

Give heed to.

Prov 17:4 An evildoer gives heed to false lips; A liar listens eagerly to a spiteful tongue.

A characteristic of the end times.

2 Thess 2:9 The coming of the *lawless one* is according to the working of Satan, with all power, signs, and lying wonders,

1 Tim 4:2 speaking lies in hypocrisy, having their own conscience seared with a hot iron,

Leads to

Hatred.

Prov 26:28 A lying tongue hates *those who are* crushed by it, And a flattering mouth works ruin.

Love of impure conversation.

Prov 17:4 An evildoer gives heed to false lips; A liar listens eagerly to a spiteful tongue.

Often accompanied by gross crimes.

Hos 4:1–2 Hear the word of the LORD, You children of Israel, For the LORD *brings* a charge against the inhabitants of the land: "There is no truth or mercy Or knowledge of God in the land. **2** *By* swearing and lying, Killing and stealing and committing adultery, They break all restraint, With bloodshed upon bloodshed.

Folly of.

Prov 10:18 Whoever hides hatred *has* lying lips, And whoever spreads slander *is* a fool.

Prov 21:6 Getting treasures by a lying tongue. *Is* the fleeting fantasy of those who seek death.

Shall be detected.

Prov 12:19 The truthful lip shall be established forever, But a lying tongue *is* but for a moment.

Poverty preferable to.

Prov 19:22 What is desired in a man is kindness, And a poor man is better than a liar.

Excludes from heaven.

Rev 21:8 But the cowardly, unbelieving, abominable, murderers, sexually immoral, sorcerers, idolaters, and all liars shall have their part in the lake which burns with fire and brimstone, which is the second death."

Rev 21:27 But there shall by no means enter it anything that defiles, or causes an abomination or a lie, but only those who are written in the Lamb's Book of Life.

Rev 22:15 But outside *are* dogs and sorcerers and sexually immoral and murderers and idolaters, and whoever loves and practices a lie.

Punishment for.

Ps 5:6 You shall destroy those who speak falsehood; The Lord abhors the bloodthirsty and deceitful man.

Ps 120:3–4 What shall be given to you, Or what shall be done to you, You false tongue? **4** Sharp arrows of the warrior, With coals of the broom tree!

Prov 19:5 A false witness will not go unpunished, And *he who* speaks lies will not escape.

Jer 50:36 A sword *is* against the soothsayers, and they will be fools. A sword *is* against her mighty men, and they will be dismayed.

Illustrated by

The devil.

Gen 3:4 Then the serpent said to the woman, "You will not surely die.

Cain.

Gen 4:9 Then the Lord said to Cain, "Where *is* Abel your brother?" He said, "I do not know. *Am* I my brother's keeper?"

Sarah.

Gen 18:15 But Sarah denied *it,* saying, "I did not laugh," for she was afraid. And He said, "No, but you did laugh!"

Jacob.

Gen 27:19 Jacob said to his father, "I *am* Esau your firstborn; I have done just as you told me; please arise, sit and eat of my game, that your soul may bless me."

Joseph's brethren.

Gen 37:31–32 So they took Joseph's tunic, killed a kid of the goats, and dipped the tunic in the blood. **32** Then they sent the tunic of *many* colors, and they brought *it* to their father and said, "We have found this. Do you know whether it *is* your son's tunic or not?"

The Gibeonites.

Josh 9:9–13 So they said to him: "From a very far country your servants have come, because of the name of the Lord your God; for we have heard of His fame, and all that He did in Egypt, **10** and all that He did

to the two kings of the Amorites who *were* beyond the Jordan—to Sihon king of Heshbon, and Og king of Bashan, who was at Ashtaroth. **11** Therefore our elders and all the inhabitants of our country spoke to us, saying, 'Take provisions with you for the journey, and go to meet them, and say to them, "We *are* your servants; now therefore, make a covenant with us." ' **12** This bread of ours we took hot *for* our provision from our houses on the day we departed to come to you. But now look, it is dry and moldy. **13** And these wineskins which we filled *were* new, and see, they are torn; and these our garments and our sandals have become old because of the very long journey."

Samson.

Judg 16:10 Then Delilah said to Samson, "Look, you have mocked me and told me lies. Now, please tell me what you may be bound with."

Saul.

1 Sam 15:13 Then Samuel went to Saul, and Saul said to him, "Blessed *are* you of the Lord! I have performed the commandment of the Lord."

Michal.

1 Sam 19:14 So when Saul sent messengers to take David, she said, "He *is* sick."

David.

1 Sam 21:2 So David said to Ahimelech the priest, "The king has ordered me on some business, and said to me, 'Do not let anyone know anything about the business on which I send you, or what I have commanded you.' And I have directed *my* young men to such and such a place.

A prophet of Bethel.

1 Kin 13:18 He said to him, "I too *am* a prophet as you *are,* and an angel spoke to me by the word of the Lord, saying, 'Bring him back with you to your house, that he may eat bread and drink water.' " (He was lying to him.)

Gehazi.

2 Kin 5:22 And he said, "All *is* well. My master has sent me, saying, 'Indeed, just now two young men of the sons of the prophets have come to me from the mountains of Ephraim. Please give them a talent of silver and two changes of garments.' "

Job's friends.

Job 13:4 But you forgers of lies, You *are* all worthless physicians.

The Ninevites.

Nah 3:1 Woe to the bloody city! It *is* all full of lies *and* robbery. *Its* victim never departs.

Peter.

Matt 26:72 But again he denied with an oath, "I do not know the Man!"

Ananias.

Acts 5:5 Then Ananias, hearing these words, fell down and breathed his last. So great fear came upon all those who heard these things.

The Cretans.

Titus 1:12 One of them, a prophet of their own, said, "Cretans *are* always liars, evil beasts, lazy gluttons."

MACEDONIAN (GREEK) EMPIRE, THE
Called the kingdom of Greece.

Dan 11:2 And now I will tell you the truth: Behold, three more kings will arise in Persia, and the fourth shall be far richer than *them* all; by his strength, through his riches, he shall stir up all against the realm of Greece.

Illustrated by the

Bronze part of the image in Nebuchadnezzar's dream.

Dan 2:32 This image's head *was* of fine gold, its chest and arms of silver, its belly and thighs of bronze,

Dan 2:39 But after you shall arise another kingdom inferior to yours; then another, a third kingdom of bronze, which shall rule over all the earth.

Leopard with four wings and four heads.

Dan 7:16–17 I came near to one of those who stood by, and asked him the truth of all this. So he told me and made known to me the interpretation of these things: **17** 'Those great beasts, which are four, *are* four kings *which* arise out of the earth.

Rough goat with notable horn.

Dan 8:5 And as I was considering, suddenly a male goat came from the west, across the surface of the whole earth, without touching the ground; and the goat *had* a notable horn between his eyes.

Dan 8:21 And the male goat *is* the kingdom of Greece. The large horn that *is* between its eyes *is* the first king.

Philippi the chief city of.

Acts 16:12 and from there to Philippi, which is the foremost city of that part of Macedonia, a colony. And we were staying in that city for some days.

Predictions respecting,

Conquest of the Medo-Persian kingdom.

Dan 8:6–7 Then he came to the ram that had two horns, which I had seen standing beside the river, and ran at him with furious power. **7** And I saw him confronting the ram; he was moved with rage against him, attacked the ram, and broke his two horns. There was no power in the ram to withstand him, but he cast him down to the ground and trampled him; and there was no one that could deliver the ram from his hand.

Dan 11:2–3 And now I will tell you the truth: Behold, three more kings will arise in Persia, and the fourth shall be far richer than *them* all; by his strength, through his riches, he shall stir up all against the realm of Greece. **3** Then a mighty king shall arise, who shall rule with great dominion, and do according to his will.

Power and greatness of Alexander (the male goat) its last king.

Dan 8:8 Therefore the male goat grew very great; but when he became strong, the large horn was broken, and in place of it four notable ones came up toward the four winds of heaven.

Dan 11:3 Then a mighty king shall arise, who shall rule with great dominion, and do according to his will.

Division of it into four kingdoms.

Dan 8:8 Therefore the male goat grew very great; but when he became strong, the large horn was broken, and in place of it four notable ones came up toward the four winds of heaven.

Dan 8:22 As for the broken *horn* and the four that stood up in its place, four kingdoms shall arise out of that nation, but not with its power.

Divisions of it ruled by strangers.

Dan 11:4 And when he has arisen, his kingdom shall be broken up and divided toward the four winds of heaven, but not among his posterity nor according to his dominion with which he ruled; for his kingdom shall be uprooted, even for others besides these.

History of its four divisions. **Dan 11:4–29**

The little horn to arise out of one of its divisions.

Dan 8:8–12 Therefore the male goat grew very great; but when he became strong, the large horn was broken, and in place of it four notable ones came up toward the four winds of heaven. **9** And out of one of them came a little horn which grew exceedingly great toward the south, toward the east, and toward the Glorious *Land*. **10** And it grew up to the host of heaven; and it cast down *some* of the host and *some* of the stars to the ground, and trampled them. **11** He even exalted *himself* as high as the Prince of the host; and by him the daily *sacrifices* were taken away, and the place of His sanctuary was cast down. **12** Because of transgression, an army was given over *to the horn* to oppose the daily *sacrifices*; and he cast truth down to the ground. He did *all this* and prospered.

Dan 8:23–25 "And in the latter time of their kingdom, When the transgressors have reached their fullness, A king shall arise, Having fierce features, Who understands sinister schemes. **24** His power shall be mighty, but not by his own power; He shall destroy fearfully, And shall prosper and thrive; He shall destroy the mighty, and *also* the holy people. **25** "Through his cunning He shall cause deceit to prosper under his rule; And he shall exalt *himself* in his heart. He shall destroy many in *their* prosperity. He shall even rise against the Prince of princes; But he shall be broken without *human* means.

Gospel preached in, by God's desire.

Acts 16:9–10 And a vision appeared to Paul in the night. A man of Macedonia stood and pleaded with him, saying, "Come over to Macedonia and help us."

10 Now after he had seen the vision, immediately we sought to go to Macedonia, concluding that the Lord had called us to preach the gospel to them.

Generosity of the churches of.

2 Cor 8:1–5 Moreover, brethren, we make known to you the grace of God bestowed on the churches of Macedonia: **2** that in a great trial of affliction the abundance of their joy and their deep poverty abounded in the riches of their liberality. **3** For I bear witness that according to *their* ability, yes, and beyond *their* ability, *they were* freely willing, **4** imploring us with much urgency that we would receive the gift and the fellowship of the ministering to the saints. **5** And not *only* as we had hoped, but they first gave themselves to the Lord, and *then* to us by the will of God.

MAGISTRATES

Are appointed by God.

Rom 13:1 Let every soul be subject to the governing authorities. For there is no authority except from God, and the authorities that exist are appointed by God.

Purpose of their appointment.

Rom 13:3–4 For rulers are not a terror to good works, but to evil. Do you want to be unafraid of the authority? Do what is good, and you will have praise from the same. **4** For he is God's minister to you for good. But if you do evil, be afraid; for he does not bear the sword in vain; for he is God's minister, an avenger to *execute* wrath on him who practices evil.

1 Pet 2:14 or to governors, as to those who are sent by him for the punishment of evildoers and *for the* praise of those who do good.

Their office to be respected.

Acts 23:5 Then Paul said, "I did not know, brethren, that he was the high priest; for it is written, 'You shall not speak evil of a ruler of your people.'"

To be wisely selected and appointed.

Ex 18:21 Moreover you shall select from all the people able men, such as fear God, men of truth, hating covetousness; and place *such* over them *to be* rulers of thousands, rulers of hundreds, rulers of fifties, and rulers of tens.

Ezra 7:25 And you, Ezra, according to your God-given wisdom, set magistrates and judges who may judge all the people who *are in the region* beyond the River, all such as know the laws of your God; and teach those who do not know *them*.

To be prayed for.

1 Tim 2:1–2 Therefore I exhort first of all that supplications, prayers, intercessions, *and* giving of thanks be made for all men, **2** for kings and all who are in authority, that we may lead a quiet and peaceable life in all godliness and reverence.

Should

Seek wisdom from God.

1 Kin 3:9 Therefore give to Your servant an understanding heart to judge Your people, that I may discern between good and evil. For who is able to judge this great people of Yours?"

Rule in the fear of God.

2 Sam 23:3 The God of Israel said, The Rock of Israel spoke to me: 'He who rules over men *must be* just, Ruling in the fear of God.

2 Chr 19:7 Now therefore, let the fear of the LORD be upon you; take care and do *it*, for *there is* no iniquity with the LORD our God, no partiality, nor taking of bribes."

Know and enforce the law of God.

Ezra 7:25–26 And you, Ezra, according to your God-given wisdom, set magistrates and judges who may judge all the people who *are in the region* beyond the River, all such as know the laws of your God; and teach those who do not know *them*. **26** Whoever will not observe the law of your God and the law of the king, let judgment be executed speedily on him, whether *it be* death, or banishment, or confiscation of goods, or imprisonment.

Be faithful to God.

Dan 6:4 So the governors and satraps sought to find *some* charge against Daniel concerning the kingdom; but they could find no charge or fault, because he *was* faithful; nor was there any error or fault found in him.

Judge wisely.

1 Kin 3:16–28 Now two women *who were* harlots came to the king, and stood before him. **17** And one woman said, "O my lord, this woman and I dwell in the same house; and I gave birth while she *was* in the house. **18** Then it happened, the third day after I had given birth, that this woman also gave birth. And we *were* together; no one *was* with us in the house, except the two of us in the house. **19** And this woman's son died in the night, because she lay on him. **20** So she arose in the middle of the night and took my son from my side, while your maidservant slept, and laid him in her bosom, and laid her dead child in my bosom. **21** And when I rose in the morning to nurse my son, there he was, dead. But when I had examined him in the morning, indeed, he was not my son whom I had borne." **22** Then the other woman said, "No! But the living one *is* my son, and the dead one *is* your son." And the first woman said, "No! But the dead one *is* your son, and the living one *is* my son." Thus they spoke before the king. **23** And the king said, "The one says, 'This *is* my son, who lives, and your son *is* the dead one'; and the other says, 'No! But your son *is* the dead one, and my son *is* the living one.'" **24** Then the king said, "Bring me a sword." So they brought a sword before the king. **25** And the king said, "Divide the living child in two, and give half to one, and half to the other." **26** Then the woman whose son *was* living spoke to the king, for she yearned with compassion for her son; and she said, "O my lord, give her the living child, and by no means kill him!" But the other said, "Let him be neither mine nor yours, *but* divide *him*." **27** So the king answered and said, "Give the first woman the living child, and by no means kill him; she *is* his mother." **28** And all Israel heard of the judgment which the king had rendered; and they feared the king, for they saw that the wisdom of God *was* in him to administer justice.

Hate covetousness.

Ex 18:21 Moreover you shall select from all the people able men, such as fear God, men of truth, hating covetousness; and place *such* over them *to be* rulers of thousands, rulers of hundreds, rulers of fifties, and rulers of tens.

Not take bribes.

Ex 23:8 And you shall take no bribe, for a bribe blinds the discerning and perverts the words of the righteous.

Deut 16:19 You shall not pervert justice; you shall not show partiality, nor take a bribe, for a bribe blinds the eyes of the wise and twists the words of the righteous.

Defend the poor.

Ex 23:6 "You shall not pervert the judgment of your poor in his dispute.

Job 29:12 Because I delivered the poor who cried out, The fatherless and *the one who* had no helper.

Job 29:16 I *was* a father to the poor, And I searched out the case *that* I did not know.

Judge righteously.

Deut 1:16 "Then I commanded your judges at that time, saying, 'Hear *the cases* between your brethren, and judge righteously between a man and his brother or the stranger who is with him.

Deut 16:18 "You shall appoint judges and officers in all your gates, which the LORD your God gives you, according to your tribes, and they shall judge the people with just judgment.

Deut 25:1 "If there is a dispute between men, and they come to court, that *the judges* may judge them, and they justify the righteous and condemn the wicked,

2 Chr 19:6 and said to the judges, "Take heed to what you are doing, for you do not judge for man but for the LORD, who *is* with you in the judgment.

Be impartial.

Deut 1:17 You shall not show partiality in judgment; you shall hear the small as well as the great; you shall not be afraid in any man's presence, for the judgment *is* God's. The case that is too hard for you, bring to me, and I will hear it.'

Be diligent in ruling.

Rom 12:8 he who exhorts, in exhortation; he who gives, with liberality; he who leads, with diligence; he who shows mercy, with cheerfulness.

Subjection to their authority commanded.

Matt 23:2–3 saying: "The scribes and the Pharisees sit in Moses' seat. 3 Therefore whatever they tell you to observe, *that* observe and do, but do not do according to their works; for they say, and do not do.

Rom 13:1 Let every soul be subject to the governing authorities. For there is no authority except from God, and the authorities that exist are appointed by God.

1 Pet 2:13–14 Therefore submit yourselves to every ordinance of man for the Lord's sake, whether to the king as supreme, 14 or to governors, as to those who are sent by him for the punishment of evildoers and *for the* praise of those who do good.

Good—Exemplified by

Joseph.

Gen 41:46 Joseph was thirty years old when he stood before Pharaoh king of Egypt. And Joseph went out from the presence of Pharaoh, and went throughout all the land of Egypt.

Gideon.

Judg 8:35 nor did they show kindness to the house of Jerubbaal (Gideon) in accordance with the good he had done for Israel.

Samuel.

1 Sam 12:3–4 Here I am. Witness against me before the LORD and before His anointed: Whose ox have I taken, or whose donkey have I taken, or whom have I cheated? Whom have I oppressed, or from whose hand have I received *any* bribe with which to blind my eyes? I will restore *it* to you." 4 And they said, "You have not cheated us or oppressed us, nor have you taken anything from any man's hand."

Ezra.

Ezra 10:1–9 Now while Ezra was praying, and while he was confessing, weeping, and bowing down before the house of God, a very large assembly of men, women, and children gathered to him from Israel; for the people wept very bitterly. 2 And Shechaniah the son of Jehiel, *one* of the sons of Elam, spoke up and said to Ezra, "We have trespassed against our God, and have taken pagan wives from the peoples of the land; yet now there is hope in Israel in spite of this. 3 Now therefore, let us make a covenant with our God to put away all these wives and those who have been born to them, according to the advice of my master and of those who tremble at the commandment of our God; and let it be done according to the law. 4 Arise, for *this* matter *is* your *responsibility*. We also *are* with you. Be of good courage, and do *it.*" 5 Then Ezra arose, and made the leaders of the priests, the Levites, and all Israel swear an oath that they would do according to this word. So they swore an oath. 6 Then Ezra rose up from before the house of God, and went into the chamber of Jehohanan the son of Eliashib; and *when* he came there, he ate no bread and drank no water, for he mourned because of the guilt of those from the captivity. 7 And they issued a proclamation throughout Judah and Jerusalem to all the descendants of the captivity, that they must gather at Jerusalem, 8 and that whoever would not come within three days, according to the instructions of the leaders and elders, all his property would be confiscated, and he himself would be separated from the assembly of those from the captivity. 9 So all the men of Judah and Benjamin gathered at Jerusalem within three days. It *was* the ninth month, on the twentieth of the month; and all the people sat in the open square of the house of God, trembling because of *this* matter and because of heavy rain.

Nehemiah.

Neh 3:16 After him Nehemiah the son of Azbuk, leader of half the district of Beth Zur, made repairs as far as *the place* in front of the tombs of David, to the man-made pool, and as far as the House of the Mighty.

Job.

Job 29:16 I *was* a father to the poor, And I searched out the case *that* I did not know.

Daniel.

Dan 6:3 Then this Daniel distinguished himself above the governors and satraps, because an excellent spirit *was* in him; and the king gave thought to setting him over the whole realm.

Wicked—generally illustrated.

Prov 28:15 *Like* a roaring lion and a charging bear *Is* a wicked ruler over poor people.

Wicked—portrayed

The sons of Samuel.

1 Sam 8:3 But his sons did not walk in his ways; they turned aside after dishonest gain, took bribes, and perverted justice.

Pilate.

Matt 27:24 When Pilate saw that he could not prevail at all, but rather *that* a tumult was rising, he took water and washed *his* hands before the multitude, saying, "I am innocent of the blood of this just Person. You see *to it.*"

Matt 27:26 Then he released Barabbas to them; and when he had scourged Jesus, he delivered *Him* to be crucified.

The magistrates in Philippi.

Acts 16:22–23 Then the multitude rose up together against them; and the magistrates tore off their clothes and commanded *them* to be beaten with rods. **23** And when they had laid many stripes on them, they threw *them* into prison, commanding the jailer to keep them securely.

Gallio.

Acts 18:16–17 And he drove them from the judgment seat. **17** Then all the Greeks took Sosthenes, the ruler of the synagogue, and beat *him* before the judgment seat. But Gallio took no notice of these things.

Felix.

Acts 24:26 Meanwhile he also hoped that money would be given him by Paul, that he might release him. Therefore he sent for him more often and conversed with him.

MAJESTY

Of God.

Ex 3:1–6 Now Moses was tending the flock of Jethro his father-in-law, the priest of Midian. And he led the flock to the back of the desert, and came to Horeb, the mountain of God. **2** And the Angel of the LORD appeared to him in a flame of fire from the midst of a bush. So he looked, and behold, the bush was burning with fire, but the bush *was* not consumed. **3** Then Moses said, "I will now turn aside and see this great sight, why the bush does not burn." **4** So when the LORD saw that he turned aside to look, God called to him from the midst of the bush and said, "Moses, Moses!" And he said, "Here I am." **5** Then He said, "Do not draw near this place. Take your sandals off your feet, for the place where you stand *is* holy ground." **6** Moreover He said, "I *am* the God of your father—the God of Abraham, the God of Isaac, and the God of Jacob." And Moses hid his face, for he was afraid to look upon God.

Ex 19:16–20 Then it came to pass on the third day, in the morning, that there were thunderings and lightnings, and a thick cloud on the mountain; and the sound of the trumpet was very loud, so that all the people who *were* in the camp trembled. **17** And Moses brought the people out of the camp to meet with God, and they stood at the foot of the mountain. **18** Now Mount Sinai *was* completely in smoke, because the LORD descended upon it in fire. Its smoke ascended like the smoke of a furnace, and the whole mountain quaked greatly. **19** And when the blast of the trumpet sounded long and became louder and louder, Moses spoke, and God answered him by voice. **20** Then the LORD came down upon Mount Sinai, on the top of the mountain. And the LORD called Moses to the top of the mountain, and Moses went up.

Ex 20:18–21 Now all the people witnessed the thunderings, the lightning flashes, the sound of the trumpet, and the mountain smoking; and when the people saw *it,* they trembled and stood afar off. **19** Then they said to Moses, "You speak with us, and we will hear; but let not God speak with us, lest we die." **20** And Moses said to the people, "Do not fear; for God has come to test you, and that His fear may be before you, so that you may not sin." **21** So the people stood afar off, but Moses drew near the thick darkness where God *was.*

Ex 33:7–11 Moses took his tent and pitched it outside the camp, far from the camp, and called it the tabernacle of meeting. And it came to pass *that* everyone who sought the LORD went out to the tabernacle of meeting which *was* outside the camp. **8** So it was, whenever Moses went out to the tabernacle, *that* all the people rose, and each man stood at *his* tent door and watched Moses until he had gone into the tabernacle. **9** And it came to pass, when Moses entered the tabernacle, that the pillar of cloud descended and stood *at* the door of the tabernacle, and *the* LORD talked with Moses. **10** All the people saw the pillar of cloud standing *at* the tabernacle door, and all the people rose and worshiped, each man *in* his tent door. **11** So the LORD spoke to Moses face to face, as a man speaks to his friend. And he would return to the camp, but his servant Joshua the son of Nun, a young man, did not depart from the tabernacle.

Ex 33:18–23 And he said, "Please, show me Your glory." **19** Then He said, "I will make all My goodness pass before you, and I will proclaim the name of the LORD before you. I will be gracious to whom I will be gracious, and I will have compassion on whom I will have compassion." **20** But He said, "You cannot see My face; for no man shall see Me, and live." **21** And the LORD said, "Here is a place by Me, and you shall stand on the rock. **22** So it shall be, while My glory passes by, that I will put you in the cleft of the rock, and will cover you with My hand while I pass by. **23** Then I will take away My hand, and you shall see My back; but My face shall not be seen."

Ex 34:5–9 Now the LORD descended in the cloud and stood with him there, and proclaimed the name of the LORD. **6** And the LORD passed before him and proclaimed, "The LORD, the LORD God, merciful and gracious, longsuffering, and abounding in goodness and truth, **7** keeping mercy for thousands, forgiving iniquity and transgression and sin, by no means clearing *the guilty,* visiting the iniquity of the fathers upon the children and the children's children to the third and the fourth generation." **8** So Moses made haste and bowed his head toward the earth, and worshiped. **9** Then he said, "If now I have found grace in Your sight, O Lord, let my Lord, I pray, go among us, even though we *are* a stiff-necked people; and pardon our iniquity and our sin, and take us as Your inheritance."

Ex 40:34–38 Then the cloud covered the tabernacle of meeting, and the glory of the LORD filled the tabernacle. **35** And Moses was not able to enter the tabernacle of meeting, because the cloud rested above it, and the glory of the LORD filled the tabernacle. **36** Whenever the cloud was taken up from above the tabernacle, the children of Israel would go onward in all their journeys. **37** But if the cloud was not taken up, then they did not journey till the day that it was taken up. **38** For the cloud of the LORD *was* above the tabernacle by day, and fire was over it by night, in the sight of all the house of Israel, throughout all their journeys.

Deut 5:23–31 "So it was, when you heard the voice from the midst of the darkness, while the mountain was burning with fire, that you came near to me, all the heads of your tribes and your elders. **24** And you said: 'Surely the LORD our God has shown us His glory and His greatness, and we have heard His voice from the midst of the fire. We have seen this day that God speaks with man; yet he *still* lives. **25** Now therefore, why should we die? For this great fire will consume us; if we hear the voice of the LORD our God anymore, then we shall die. **26** For who *is there* of all flesh who has heard the voice of the living God speaking from the midst of the fire, as we *have,* and lived? **27** You go near and hear all that the LORD our God may say, and tell us all that the LORD our God says to you, and we will hear and do *it.*' **28** "Then the LORD heard the voice of your words when you spoke to me, and the LORD said to me: 'I have heard the voice of the words of this people which they have spoken to you. They are right *in* all that they have spoken. **29** Oh, that they had such a heart in them that they would fear Me and always keep all My commandments, that it might be well with them and with their children forever! **30** Go and say to them, "Return to your tents." **31** But as for you, stand here by Me, and I will speak to you all the commandments, the statutes, and the judgments which you shall teach them, that they may observe *them* in the land which I am giving them to possess.'

2 Sam 22:8–16 "Then the earth shook and trembled; The foundations of heaven quaked and were shaken, Because He was angry. **9** Smoke went up from His nostrils, And devouring fire from His mouth; Coals were kindled by it. **10** He bowed the heavens also, and came down With darkness under His feet. **11** He rode upon a cherub, and flew; And He was seen upon the wings of the wind. **12** He made darkness canopies around Him, Dark waters *and* thick clouds of the skies. **13** From the brightness before Him Coals of fire were kindled. **14** "The LORD thundered from heaven, And the Most High uttered His voice. **15** He sent out arrows and scattered them; Lightning bolts, and He vanquished them. **16** Then the channels of

the sea were seen, The foundations of the world were uncovered, At the rebuke of the LORD, At the blast of the breath of His nostrils.

1 Kin 8:10–13 And it came to pass, when the priests came out of the holy *place,* that the cloud filled the house of the LORD, **11** so that the priests could not continue ministering because of the cloud; for the glory of the LORD filled the house of the LORD. **12** Then Solomon spoke: "The LORD said He would dwell in the dark cloud. **13** I have surely built You an exalted house, And a place for You to dwell in forever."

2 Chr 7:1–3 When Solomon had finished praying, fire came down from heaven and consumed the burnt offering and the sacrifices; and the glory of the LORD filled the temple. **2** And the priests could not enter the house of the LORD, because the glory of the LORD had filled the LORD's house. **3** When all the children of Israel saw how the fire came down, and the glory of the LORD on the temple, they bowed their faces to the ground on the pavement, and worshiped and praised the LORD, *saying:* "For *He is* good, For His mercy *endures* forever."

Job 36:24–33 "Remember to magnify His work, Of which men have sung. **25** Everyone has seen it; Man looks on *it* from afar. **26** "Behold, God *is* great, and we do not know *Him;* Nor can the number of His years *be* discovered. **27** For He draws up drops of water, Which distill as rain from the mist, **28** Which the clouds drop down *And* pour abundantly on man. **29** Indeed, can *anyone* understand the spreading of clouds, The thunder from His canopy? **30** Look, He scatters His light upon it, And covers the depths of the sea. **31** For by these He judges the peoples; He gives food in abundance. **32** He covers *His* hands with lightning, And commands it to strike. **33** His thunder declares it, The cattle also, concerning the rising *storm.*

Job 40:6–14 Then the LORD answered Job out of the whirlwind, and said: **7** "Now prepare yourself like a man; I will question you, and you shall answer Me: **8** "Would you indeed annul My judgment? Would you condemn Me that you may be justified? **9** Have you an arm like God? Or can you thunder with a voice like His? **10** Then adorn yourself *with* majesty and splendor, And array yourself with glory and beauty. **11** Disperse the rage of your wrath; Look on everyone *who is* proud, and humble him. **12** Look on everyone *who is* proud, *and* bring him low; Tread down the wicked in their place. **13** Hide them in the dust together, Bind their faces in hidden *darkness.* **14** Then I will also confess to you That your own right hand can save you.

Ps 8:1 O LORD, our Lord, How excellent *is* Your name in all the earth, Who have set Your glory above the heavens!

Ps 8:9 O LORD, our Lord, How excellent *is* Your name in all the earth!

Ps 68:19–31 Blessed *be* the Lord, *Who* daily loads us *with benefits,* The God of our salvation! Selah **20** Our God *is* the God of salvation; And to GOD the Lord *belong* escapes from death. **21** But God will wound the head of His enemies, The hairy scalp of the one who still goes on in his trespasses. **22** The Lord said, "I will bring back from Bashan, I will bring *them* back from the depths of the sea, **23** That your foot may crush *them* in blood, And the tongues of your dogs *may have* their portion from *your* enemies." **24** They have seen Your procession, O God, The procession of my God, my King, into the sanctuary. **25** The singers went before, the players on instruments *followed* after; Among *them were* the maidens playing timbrels. **26** Bless God in the congregations, The Lord, from the fountain of Israel. **27** There *is* little Benjamin, their leader, The princes of Judah *and* their company, The princes of Zebulun *and* the princes of Naphtali. **28** Your God has commanded your strength; Strengthen, O God, what You have done for us. **29** Because of Your temple at Jerusalem, Kings will bring presents to You. **30** Rebuke the beasts of the reeds, The herd of bulls with the calves of the peoples, *Till everyone* submits himself with pieces of silver. Scatter the peoples *who* delight in war. **31** Envoys will come out of Egypt; Ethiopia will quickly stretch out her hands to God.

Ps 76:4–12 You *are* more glorious and excellent *Than* the mountains of prey. **5** The stouthearted were plundered; They have sunk into their sleep; And none of the mighty men have found the use of their hands. **6** At Your rebuke, O God of Jacob, Both the chariot and horse were cast into a dead sleep. **7** You, Yourself, *are* to be feared; And who may stand in Your presence When once You are angry? **8** You caused judgment to be heard from heaven; The earth feared and was still, **9** When God arose to judgment, To deliver all the oppressed of the earth. Selah **10** Surely the wrath of man shall praise You; With the remainder of wrath You shall gird Yourself. **11** Make vows to the LORD your God, and pay *them;* Let all who are around Him bring presents to Him who ought to be feared. **12** He shall cut off the spirit of princes; *He is* awesome to the kings of the earth.

Is 6:1–4 In the year that King Uzziah died, I saw the Lord sitting on a throne, high and lifted up, and the train of His *robe* filled the temple. **2** Above it stood seraphim; each one had six wings: with two he covered his face, with two he covered his feet, and with two he flew. **3** And one cried to another and said: "Holy, holy, holy *is* the LORD of hosts; The whole earth *is* full of His glory!" **4** And the posts of the door were shaken by the voice of him who cried out, and the house was filled with smoke.

Rev 4:1–11 After these things I looked, and behold, a door *standing* open in heaven. And the first voice which I heard *was* like a trumpet speaking with me, saying, "Come up here, and I will show you things which must take place after this." **2** Immediately I was in the Spirit; and behold, a throne set in heaven, and *One* sat on the throne. **3** And He who sat there was like a jasper and a sardius stone in appearance; and *there was* a rainbow around the throne, in appearance like an emerald. **4** Around the throne *were* twenty-four thrones, and on the thrones I saw twenty-four elders sitting, clothed in white robes; and they had crowns of gold on their heads. **5** And from the throne proceeded lightnings, thunderings, and voices. Seven lamps of fire *were* burning before the throne, which are the seven Spirits of God. **6** Before the throne *there was* a sea of glass, like crystal. And in the midst of the throne, and around the throne, *were* four living creatures full of eyes in front and in back. **7** The first living creature *was* like a lion, the second living creature like a calf, the third living creature had a face like a man, and the fourth living creature *was* like a flying eagle. **8** *The* four living creatures, each having six wings, were full of eyes around and within. And they do not rest day or night, saying: "Holy, holy, holy, Lord God Almighty, Who was and is and is to come!" **9** Whenever the living creatures give glory and honor and thanks to Him who sits on the throne, who lives forever and ever, **10** the twenty-four elders fall down before Him who sits on the throne and worship Him who lives forever and ever, and cast their crowns before the throne, saying: **11** "You are worthy, O Lord, To receive glory and honor and power; For You created all things, And by Your will they exist and were created."

Cf. Job 37:1–24; Ezek 1:4–28; Hab 3:3–15

Of Jesus Christ.

Ps 110:1 The LORD said to my Lord, "Sit at My right hand, Till I make Your enemies Your footstool."

Matt 17:1–8 Now after six days Jesus took Peter, James, and John his brother, led them up on a high mountain by themselves; **2** and He was transfigured before them. His face shone like the sun, and His clothes became as white as the light. **3** And behold, Moses and Elijah appeared to them, talking with Him. **4** Then Peter answered and said to Jesus, "Lord, it is good for us to be here; if You wish, let us make here three tabernacles: one for You, one for Moses, and one for Elijah." **5** While he was still speaking, behold, a bright cloud overshadowed them; and suddenly a voice came out of the cloud, saying, "This is My beloved Son, in whom I am well pleased. Hear Him!" **6** And when the disciples heard *it*, they fell on their faces and were greatly afraid. **7** But Jesus came and touched them and said, "Arise, and do not be afraid." **8** When they had lifted up their eyes, they saw no one but Jesus only.

Mark 9:2–8 Now after six days Jesus took Peter, James, and John, and led them up on a high mountain apart by themselves; and He was transfigured before them. **3** His clothes became shining, exceedingly white, like snow, such as no launderer on earth can whiten them. **4** And Elijah appeared to them with Moses, and they were talking with Jesus. **5** Then Peter answered and said to Jesus, "Rabbi, it is good for us to be here; and let us make three tabernacles: one for You, one for Moses, and one for Elijah"— **6** because he did not know what to say, for they were greatly afraid. **7** And a cloud came and overshadowed them; and a voice came out of the cloud, saying, "This is My beloved Son. Hear Him!" **8** Suddenly, when they had looked around, they saw no one anymore, but only Jesus with themselves.

Luke 9:28–36 Now it came to pass, about eight days after these sayings, that He took Peter, John, and James and went up on the mountain to pray. **29** As He prayed, the appearance of His face was altered, and His robe *became* white *and* glistening. **30** And behold, two men talked with Him, who were Moses and Elijah, **31** who appeared in glory and spoke of His decease which He was about to accomplish at Jerusalem. **32** But Peter and those with him were heavy with sleep; and when they were fully awake, they saw His glory and the two men who stood with Him. **33** Then it happened, as they were parting from Him, *that* Peter said to Jesus, "Master, it is good for us to be here; and let us make three tabernacles: one for You, one for Moses, and one for Elijah"—not knowing what he said. **34** While he was saying this, a cloud came and overshadowed them; and they were fearful as they entered the cloud. **35** And a voice came out of the cloud, saying, "This is My beloved Son. Hear Him!" **36** When the voice had ceased, Jesus was found alone. But they kept quiet, and told no one in those days any of the things they had seen.

John 1:14 And the Word became flesh and dwelt among us, and we beheld His glory, the glory as of the only begotten of the Father, full of grace and truth.

Acts 1:9–11 Now when He had spoken these things, while they watched, He was taken up, and a cloud received Him out of their sight. **10** And while they looked steadfastly toward heaven as He went up, behold, two men stood by them in white apparel, **11** who also said, "Men of Galilee, why do you stand gazing up into heaven? This *same* Jesus, who was taken up from you into heaven, will so come in like manner as you saw Him go into heaven."

Acts 2:33 Therefore being exalted to the right hand of God, and having received from the Father the promise of the Holy Spirit, He poured out this which you now see and hear.

Acts 5:31 Him God has exalted to His right hand *to be* Prince and Savior, to give repentance to Israel and forgiveness of sins.

Acts 7:55–56 But he, being full of the Holy Spirit, gazed into heaven and saw the glory of God, and Jesus standing at the right hand of God, **56** and said, "Look! I see the heavens opened and the Son of Man standing at the right hand of God!"

Eph 1:20 which He worked in Christ when He raised Him from the dead and seated *Him* at His right hand in the heavenly *places,*

Col 1:15–18 He is the image of the invisible God, the firstborn over all creation. **16** For by Him all things were created that are in heaven and that are on earth, visible and invisible, whether thrones or dominions or principalities or powers. All things were created through Him and for Him. **17** And He is before all things, and in Him all things consist. **18** And He is the head of the body, the church, who is the beginning, the firstborn from the dead, that in all things He may have the preeminence.

Col 2:9 For in Him dwells all the fullness of the Godhead bodily;

Heb 8:1–2 Now *this is* the main point of the things we are saying: We have such a High Priest, who is seated at the right hand of the throne of the Majesty in the heavens, **2** a Minister of the sanctuary and of the true tabernacle which the Lord erected, and not man.

1 Pet 3:22 who has gone into heaven and is at the right hand of God, angels and authorities and powers having been made subject to Him.

2 Pet 1:16–17 For we did not follow cunningly devised fables when we made known to you the power and coming of our Lord Jesus Christ, but were eye-witnesses of His majesty. **17** For He received from God the Father honor and glory when such a voice came to Him from the Excellent Glory: "This is My beloved Son, in whom I am well pleased."

Rev 14:14 Then I looked, and behold, a white cloud, and on the cloud sat *One* like the Son of Man, having on His head a golden crown, and in His hand a sharp sickle.

Rev 19:11–16 Now I saw heaven opened, and behold, a white horse. And He who sat on him *was* called Faithful and True, and in righteousness He judges and makes war. **12** His eyes *were* like a flame of fire, and on His head *were* many crowns. He had a name written that no one knew except Himself. **13** He *was* clothed with a robe dipped in blood, and His name is called The Word of God. **14** And the armies in heaven, clothed in fine linen, white and clean, followed Him on white horses. **15** Now out of His mouth goes a sharp sword, that with it He should strike the nations. And He Himself will rule them with a rod of iron. He Himself treads the winepress of the fierceness and wrath of Almighty God. **16** And He has on *His* robe and on His thigh a name written: KING OF KINGS AND LORD OF LORDS.

Rev 22:16 "I, Jesus, have sent My angel to testify to you these things in the churches. I am the Root and the Offspring of David, the Bright and Morning Star."

Cf. Heb 1:1–13; Rev 5:1–14

Of heaven. Rev 21:9–27

MALICE

Springs from an evil heart.

Matt 15:19–20 For out of the heart proceed evil thoughts, murders, adulteries, fornications, thefts, false witness, blasphemies. **20** These are *the things* which defile a man, but to eat with unwashed hands does not defile a man."

Gal 5:19 Now the works of the flesh are evident, which are: adultery, fornication, uncleanness, lewdness,

Forbidden.

1 Cor 14:20 Brethren, do not be children in understanding; however, in malice be babes, but in understanding be mature.

Eph 4:26–27 *"Be angry, and do not sin":* do not let the sun go down on your wrath, **27** nor give place to the devil.

Col 3:8 But now you yourselves are to put off all these: anger, wrath, malice, blasphemy, filthy language out of your mouth.

A hindrance to spiritual growth.

1 Cor 5:7–8 Therefore purge out the old leaven, that you may be a new lump, since you truly are unleavened. For indeed Christ, our Passover, was sacrificed for us. **8** Therefore let us keep the feast, not with old leaven, nor with the leaven of malice and wickedness, but with the unleavened *bread* of sincerity and truth.

1 Pet 2:1–2 Therefore, laying aside all malice, all deceit, hypocrisy, envy, and all evil speaking, **2** as newborn babes, desire the pure milk of the word, that you may grow thereby,

Christian liberty not to be a cloak for.

1 Pet 2:16 as free, yet not using liberty as a cloak for vice, but as bondservants of God.

Believers

Should avoid.

Job 31:29–30 "If I have rejoiced at the destruction of him who hated me, Or lifted myself up when evil found him **30** (Indeed I have not allowed my mouth to sin By asking for a curse on his soul);

Ps 35:12–14 They reward me evil for good, *To* the sorrow of my soul. **13** But as for me, when they were sick, My clothing *was* sackcloth; I humbled myself with fasting; And my prayer would return to my own heart. **14** I paced about as though *he were* my friend *or* brother; I bowed down heavily, as one who mourns *for his* mother.

Are sometimes targets of.

Ps 83:3 They have taken crafty counsel against Your people, And consulted together against Your sheltered ones.

Matt 22:6 And the rest seized his servants, treated *them* spitefully, and killed *them.*

Should pray for those who use it.

Matt 5:44 But I say to you, love your enemies, bless those who curse you, do good to those who hate you, and pray for those who spitefully use you and persecute you,

The wicked indulge in.

Ps 7:14 Behold, *the wicked* brings forth iniquity; Yes, he conceives trouble and brings forth falsehood.

Rom 1:29 being filled with all unrighteousness, sexual immorality, wickedness, covetousness, maliciousness; full of envy, murder, strife, deceit, evil-mindedness; *they are* whisperers,

Titus 3:3 For we ourselves were also once foolish, disobedient, deceived, serving various lusts and pleasures, living in malice and envy, hateful and hating one another.

3 John 1:10 Therefore, if I come, I will call to mind his deeds which he does, prating against us with malicious words. And not content with that, he himself does not receive the brethren, and forbids those who wish to, putting *them* out of the church.

God repays.

Ps 10:14 But You have seen, for You observe trouble and grief, To repay *it* by Your hand. The helpless commits himself to You; You are the helper of the fatherless.

Ezek 36:5 therefore thus says the Lord GOD: "Surely I have spoken in My burning jealousy against the rest of the nations and against all Edom, who gave My land to themselves as a possession, with wholehearted joy *and* spiteful minds, in order to plunder its open country." '

Punishment of.

Ps 7:15–16 He made a pit and dug it out, And has fallen into the ditch *which* he made. **16** His trouble shall return upon his own head, And his violent dealing shall come down on his own crown.

Amos 1:11–12 Thus says the LORD: "For three transgressions of Edom, and for four, I will not turn away its *punishment,* Because he pursued his brother with the sword, And cast off all pity; His anger tore perpetually, And he kept his wrath forever. **12** But I will send a fire upon Teman, Which shall devour the palaces of Bozrah."

Obad 1:10–15 "For violence against your brother Jacob, Shame shall cover you, And you shall be cut off forever. **11** In the day that you stood on the other side— In the day that strangers carried captive his forces, When foreigners entered his gates And cast lots for Jerusalem— Even you *were* as one of them. **12** "But you should not have gazed on the day of your brother In the day of his captivity; Nor should you have rejoiced over the children of Judah In the day of their destruction; Nor should you have spoken proudly In the day of distress. **13** You should not have entered the gate of My people In the day of their calamity. Indeed, you should not have gazed on their affliction In the day of their calamity, Nor laid *hands* on their substance In the day of their calamity. **14** You should not have stood at the crossroads To cut off those among them who escaped; Nor should you have delivered up those among them who remained In the day of distress. **15** "For the day of the LORD upon all the nations *is* near; As you have done, it shall be done to you; Your reprisal shall return upon your own head.

Illustrated by

Cain.

Gen 4:5 but He did not respect Cain and his offering. And Cain was very angry, and his countenance fell.

Esau.

Gen 27:41 So Esau hated Jacob because of the blessing with which his father blessed him, and Esau said in his heart, "The days of mourning for my father are at hand; then I will kill my brother Jacob."

Joseph's brethren.

Gen 37:19–20 Then they said to one another, "Look, this dreamer is coming! **20** Come therefore, let us now kill him and cast him into some pit; and we shall say, 'Some wild beast has devoured him.' We shall see what will become of his dreams!"

Saul.

1 Sam 18:9–11 So Saul eyed David from that day forward. **10** And it happened on the next day that the distressing spirit from God came upon Saul, and he prophesied inside the house. So David played *music* with his hand, as at other times; but *there was* a spear in Saul's hand. **11** And Saul cast the spear, for he said, "I will pin David to the wall!" But David escaped his presence twice.

Shimei.

2 Sam 16:5 Now when King David came to Bahurim, there was a man from the family of the house of Saul, whose name *was* Shimei the son of Gera, coming from there. He came out, cursing continuously as he came.

1 Kin 2:8–9 "And see, *you have* with you Shimei the son of Gera, a Benjamite from Bahurim, who cursed me with a malicious curse in the day when I went to Mahanaim. But he came down to meet me at the Jordan, and I swore to him by the LORD, saying, 'I will not put you to death with the sword.' **9** Now therefore, do not hold him guiltless, for you *are* a wise man and know what you ought to do to him; but bring his gray hair down to the grave with blood."

Joab.

2 Sam 3:27 Now when Abner had returned to Hebron, Joab took him aside in the gate to speak with him privately, and there stabbed him in the stomach, so that he died for the blood of Asahel his brother.

1 Kin 2:5 "Moreover you know also what Joab the son of Zeruiah did to me, *and* what he did to the two commanders of the armies of Israel, to Abner the son of Ner and Amasa the son of Jether, whom he killed. And he shed the blood of war in peacetime, and put the blood of war on his belt that *was* around his waist, and on his sandals that *were* on his feet.

1 Kin 2:28–33 Then news came to Joab, for Joab had defected to Adonijah, though he had not defected to Absalom. So Joab fled to the tabernacle of the LORD, and took hold of the horns of the altar. 29 And King Solomon was told, "Joab has fled to the tabernacle of the LORD; there *he is,* by the altar." Then Solomon sent Benaiah the son of Jehoiada, saying, "Go, strike him down." 30 So Benaiah went to the tabernacle of the LORD, and said to him, "Thus says the king, 'Come out!' " And he said, "No, but I will die here." And Benaiah brought back word to the king, saying, "Thus said Joab, and thus he answered me." 31 Then the king said to him, "Do as he has said, and strike him down and bury him, that you may take away from me and from the house of my father the innocent blood which Joab shed. 32 So the LORD will return his blood on his head, because he struck down two men more righteous and better than he, and killed them with the sword—Abner the son of Ner, the commander of the army of Israel, and Amasa the son of Jether, the commander of the army of Judah—though my father David did not know *it.* 33 Their blood shall therefore return upon the head of Joab and upon the head of his descendants forever. But upon David and his descendants, upon his house and his throne, there shall be peace forever from the LORD."

Sanballat.

Neh 2:10 When Sanballat the Horonite and Tobiah the Ammonite official heard *of it,* they were deeply disturbed that a man had come to seek the well-being of the children of Israel.

Haman.

Esth 3:5–6 When Haman saw that Mordecai did not bow or pay him homage, Haman was filled with wrath. 6 But he disdained to lay hands on Mordecai alone, for they had told him of the people of Mordecai. Instead, Haman sought to destroy all the Jews who *were* throughout the whole kingdom of Ahasuerus—the people of Mordecai.

The Edomites.

Ezek 35:5 "Because you have had an ancient hatred, and have shed *the blood of* the children of Israel by the power of the sword at the time of their calamity, *when* their iniquity *came to an* end,

The governors, etc.

Dan 6:4–9 So the governors and satraps sought to find *some* charge against Daniel concerning the kingdom; but they could find no charge or fault, because he *was* faithful; nor was there any error or fault found in him. 5 Then these men said, "We shall not find any charge against this Daniel unless we find *it* against him concerning the law of his God." 6 So these governors and satraps thronged before the king, and said thus to him: "King Darius, live forever! 7 All the governors of the kingdom, the administrators and satraps, the counselors and advisors, have consulted together to establish a royal statute and to make a firm decree, that whoever petitions any god or man for thirty days, except you, O king, shall be cast into the den of lions. 8 Now, O king, establish the decree and sign the writing, so that it cannot be changed, according to the law of the Medes and Persians, which does not alter." 9 Therefore King Darius signed the written decree.

Herodias.

Mark 6:19 Therefore Herodias held it against him and wanted to kill him, but she could not;

The scribes, etc.

Mark 11:18 And the scribes and chief priests heard it and sought how they might destroy Him; for they feared Him, because all the people were astonished at His teaching.

Luke 11:54 lying in wait for Him, and seeking to catch Him in something He might say, that they might accuse Him.

Diotrephes.

3 John 1:10 Therefore, if I come, I will call to mind his deeds which he does, prating against us with malicious words. And not content with that, he himself does not receive the brethren, and forbids those who wish to, putting *them* out of the church.

MANKIND

Made for God.

Prov 16:4 The LORD has made all for Himself, Yes, even the wicked for the day of doom.

Rev 4:11 "You are worthy, O Lord, To receive glory and honor and power; For You created all things, And by Your will they exist and were created."

Unworthy of God's favor.

Job 7:17 "What *is* man, that You should exalt him, *That* You should set Your heart on him,

Job 22:2 "Can a man be profitable to God, Though he who is wise may be profitable to himself?

Ps 8:4 What is man that You are mindful of him, And the son of man that You visit him?

Ps 16:2 *O my soul,* you have said to the LORD, "You *are* my Lord, My goodness is nothing apart from You."

Created

In successive generations.

Job 10:8–11 'Your hands have made me and fashioned me, An intricate unity; Yet You would destroy me. 9 Remember, I pray, that You have made me like clay. And will You turn me into dust again? 10 Did You not pour me out like milk, And curdle me like cheese, 11 Clothe me with skin and flesh, And knit me together with bones and sinews?

Job 31:15 Did not He who made me in the womb make them? Did not the same One fashion us in the womb?

Marvelously.

Ps 139:14 I will praise You, for I am fearfully *and* wonderfully made; Marvelous are Your works, And *that* my soul knows very well.

By God.

Gen 1:27 So God created man in His *own* image; in the image of God He created him; male and female He created them.

Gen 2:7 And the LORD God formed man *of* the dust of the ground, and breathed into his nostrils the breath of life; and man became a living being.

Is 45:12 I have made the earth, And created man on it. I—My hands—stretched out the heavens, And all their host I have commanded.

By Christ.

John 1:3 All things were made through Him, and without Him nothing was made that was made.

Col 1:16 For by Him all things were created that are in heaven and that are on earth, visible and invisible, whether thrones or dominions or principalities or powers. All things were created through Him and for Him.

By the Spirit of God.

Job 33:4 The Spirit of God has made me, And the breath of the Almighty gives me life.

After consultation, by the Trinity.

Gen 1:26 Then God said, "Let Us make man in Our image, according to Our likeness; let them have dominion over the fish of the sea, over the birds of the air, and over the cattle, over all the earth and over every creeping thing that creeps on the earth."

On the sixth day.

Gen 1:31 Then God saw everything that He had made, and indeed *it was* very good. So the evening and the morning were the sixth day.

Upon the earth.

Deut 4:32 "For ask now concerning the days that are past, which were before you, since the day that God created man on the earth, and *ask* from one end of heaven to the other, whether *any* great *thing* like this has happened, or *anything* like it has been heard.

Job 20:4 "Do you *not* know this of old, Since man was placed on earth,

From the dust.

Gen 2:7 And the LORD God formed man *of* the dust of the ground, and breathed into his nostrils the breath of life; and man became a living being.

Job 33:6 Truly I *am* as your spokesman before God; I also have been formed out of clay.

1 Cor 15:47 The first man *was* of the earth, *made* of dust; the second Man *is* the Lord from heaven.

In the image of God.

Gen 1:26–27 Then God said, "Let Us make man in Our image, according to Our likeness; let them have dominion over the fish of the sea, over the birds of the air, and over the cattle, over all the earth and over every creeping thing that creeps on the earth." **27** So God created man in His *own* image; in the image of God He created him; male and female He created them.

1 Cor 11:7 For a man indeed ought not to cover *his* head, since he is the image and glory of God; but woman is the glory of man.

James 3:9 With it we bless our God and Father, and with it we curse men, who have been made in the similitude of God.

Male and female.

Gen 1:27 So God created man in His *own* image; in the image of God He created him; male and female He created them.

Gen 2:25 And they were both naked, the man and his wife, and were not ashamed.

Gen 5:2 He created them male and female, and blessed them and called them Mankind in the day they were created.

A living being.

Gen 2:7 And the LORD God formed man *of* the dust of the ground, and breathed into his nostrils the breath of life; and man became a living being.

1 Cor 15:45 And so it is written, *"The first man Adam became a living being."* The last Adam *became* a life-giving spirit.

In uprightness.

Eccl 7:29 Truly, this only I have found: That God made man upright, But they have sought out many schemes."

In knowledge (implied).

Col 3:10 and have put on the new *man* who is renewed in knowledge according to the image of Him who created him,

Under obligations to obedience.

Gen 2:16–17 And the LORD God commanded the man, saying, "Of every tree of the garden you may freely eat; **17** but of the tree of the knowledge of good and evil you shall not eat, for in the day that you eat of it you shall surely die."

A type of Christ.

Rom 5:14 Nevertheless death reigned from Adam to Moses, even over those who had not sinned according to the likeness of the transgression of Adam, who is a type of Him who was to come.

With purpose.

Gen 2:5 before any plant of the field was in the earth and before any herb of the field had grown. For the LORD God had not caused it to rain on the earth, and *there was* no man to till the ground;

Gen 2:15 Then the LORD God took the man and put him in the garden of Eden to tend and keep it.

Blessed by God.

Gen 1:28 Then God blessed them, and God said to them, "Be fruitful and multiply; fill the earth and subdue it; have dominion over the fish of the sea, over the birds of the air, and over every living thing that moves on the earth."

Gen 1:31 Then God saw everything that He had made, and indeed *it was* very good. So the evening and the morning were the sixth day.

Gen 5:2 He created them male and female, and blessed them and called them Mankind in the day they were created.

Not good for, to be alone.

Gen 2:18 And the LORD God said, "*It is* not good that man should be alone; I will make him a helper comparable to him."

Described as having

A body.

Matt 6:25 "Therefore I say to you, do not worry about your life, what you will eat or what you will drink; nor about your body, what you will put on. Is not life more than food and the body more than clothing?

A soul.

Luke 12:20 But God said to him, 'Fool! This night your soul will be required of you; then whose will those things be which you have provided?'

Acts 14:22 strengthening the souls of the disciples, exhorting *them* to continue in the faith, and *saying*, "We must through many tribulations enter the kingdom of God."

1 Pet 4:19 Therefore let those who suffer according to the will of God commit their souls *to Him* in doing good, as to a faithful Creator.

A spirit.

Prov 18:14 The spirit of a man will sustain him in sickness, But who can bear a broken spirit?

1 Cor 2:11 For what man knows the things of a man except the spirit of the man which is in him? Even so no one knows the things of God except the Spirit of God.

Understanding.

Eph 1:18 the eyes of your understanding being enlightened; that you may know what is the hope of His calling, what are the riches of the glory of His inheritance in the saints,

Eph 4:18 having their understanding darkened, being alienated from the life of God, because of the ignorance that is in them, because of the blindness of their heart;

Will.

1 Cor 9:17 For if I do this willingly, I have a reward; but if against my will, I have been entrusted with a stewardship.

2 Pet 1:21 for prophecy never came by the will of man, but holy men of God spoke *as they were* moved by the Holy Spirit.

Affections.

1 Chr 29:3 Moreover, because I have set my affection on the house of my God, I have given to the house of my God, over and above all that I have prepared for the holy house, my own special treasure of gold and silver:

Col 3:2 Set your mind on things above, not on things on the earth.

Conscience.

Rom 2:15 who show the work of the law written in their hearts, their conscience also bearing witness, and between themselves *their* thoughts accusing or else excusing *them*)

1 Tim 4:2 speaking lies in hypocrisy, having their own conscience seared with a hot iron,

Memory.

Gen 41:9 Then the chief butler spoke to Pharaoh, saying: "I remember my faults this day.

1 Cor 15:2 by which also you are saved, if you hold fast that word which I preached to you—unless you believed in vain.

Of every nation, made of one blood.

Acts 17:26 And He has made from one blood every nation of men to dwell on all the face of the earth, and has determined their preappointed times and the boundaries of their dwellings,

Made wise by the inspiration of the Almighty.

Job 32:8–9 But *there is* a spirit in man, And the breath of the Almighty gives him understanding. 9 Great men are not *always* wise, Nor do the aged *always* understand justice.

Inferior to angels.

Ps 8:5 For You have made him a little lower than the angels, And You have crowned him with glory and honor.

Heb 2:7 *You have made him a little lower than the angels; You have crowned him with glory and honor, And set him over the works of Your hands.*

Set apart from animals

Different constitution.

1 Cor 15:39 All flesh *is* not the same flesh, but *there is* one *kind of* flesh of men, another flesh of animals, another of fish, *and* another of birds.

More valuable than.

Matt 6:26 Look at the birds of the air, for they neither sow nor reap nor gather into barns; yet your heavenly Father feeds them. Are you not of more value than they?

Matt 10:31 Do not fear therefore; you are of more value than many sparrows.

Matt 12:12 Of how much more value then is a man than a sheep? Therefore it is lawful to do good on the Sabbath."

Wiser than.

Job 35:11 Who teaches us more than the beasts of the earth, And makes us wiser than the birds of heaven?'

Received dominion over.

Gen 1:28 Then God blessed them, and God said to them, "Be fruitful and multiply; fill the earth and subdue it; have dominion over the fish of the sea, over the birds of the air, and over every living thing that moves on the earth."

Gen 2:19–20 Out of the ground the LORD God formed every beast of the field and every bird of the air, and brought *them* to Adam to see what he would call them. And whatever Adam called each living creature, that *was* its name. 20 So Adam gave names to all cattle, to the birds of the air, and to every beast of the field. But for Adam there was not found a helper comparable to him.

Ps 8:6–8 You have made him to have dominion over the works of Your hands; You have put all *things* under his feet, 7 All sheep and oxen— Even the beasts of the field, 8 The birds of the air, And the fish of the sea That pass through the paths of the seas.

Intellect of, matured by age.

1 Cor 13:11 When I was a child, I spoke as a child, I understood as a child, I thought as a child; but when I became a man, I put away childish things.

Likened to

The potsherd of the earth.

Is 45:9 "Woe to him who strives with his Maker! *Let the*

potsherd *strive* with the potsherds of the earth! Shall the clay say to him who forms it, 'What are you making?' Or shall your handiwork *say*, 'He has no hands'?

A worm.

Job 25:6 How much less man, *who is* a maggot, And a son of man, *who is* a worm?"

A vain man.

Job 11:12 For an empty-headed man will be wise, When a wild donkey's colt is born a man.

James 2:20 But do you want to know, O foolish man, that faith without works is dead?

Flesh.

Gen 6:12 So God looked upon the earth, and indeed it was corrupt; for all flesh had corrupted their way on the earth.

Joel 2:28 "And it shall come to pass afterward That I will pour out My Spirit on all flesh; Your sons and your daughters shall prophesy, Your old men shall dream dreams, Your young men shall see visions.

Grass.

Is 40:6–8 The voice said, "Cry out!" And he said, "What shall I cry?" "All flesh *is* grass, And all its loveliness *is* like the flower of the field. **7** The grass withers, the flower fades, Because the breath of the LORD blows upon it; Surely the people *are* grass. **8** The grass withers, the flower fades, But the word of our God stands forever."

1 Pet 1:24 because *"All flesh is as grass, And all the glory of man as the flower of the grass. The grass withers, And its flower falls away,*

Clay in the potter's hand.

Is 64:8 But now, O LORD, You *are* our Father; We *are* the clay, and You our potter; And all we *are* the work of Your hand.

Jer 18:2 "Arise and go down to the potter's house, and there I will cause you to hear My words."

Jer 18:6 "O house of Israel, can I not do with you as this potter?" says the LORD. "Look, as the clay *is* in the potter's hand, so *are* you in My hand, O house of Israel!

Vanity.

Ps 144:4 Man is like a breath; His days *are* like a passing shadow.

A sleep.

Ps 90:5 You carry them away *like* a flood; *They are* like a sleep. In the morning they are like grass *which* grows up:

The Fall of,

Disobeyed God by eating forbidden fruit.

Gen 3:1–12 Now the serpent was more cunning than any beast of the field which the LORD God had made. And he said to the woman, "Has God indeed said, 'You shall not eat of every tree of the garden'?" **2** And the woman said to the serpent, "We may eat the fruit of the trees of the garden; **3** but of the fruit of the tree which *is* in the midst of the garden, God has said, 'You shall not eat it, nor shall you touch it, lest you die.' " **4** Then the serpent said to the woman, "You will not surely die. **5** For God knows that in the day you eat of it your eyes will be opened, and you will be like God, knowing good and evil." **6** So when the woman saw that the tree *was* good for food, that it *was* pleasant to the eyes, and a tree desirable to make *one* wise, she took of its fruit and ate. She also gave to her husband with her, and he ate. **7** Then the eyes of both of them were opened, and they knew that they *were* naked; and they sewed fig leaves together and made themselves coverings. **8** And they heard the sound of the LORD God walking in the garden in the cool of the day, and Adam and his wife hid themselves from the presence of the LORD God among the trees of the garden. **9** Then the LORD God called to Adam and said to him, "Where *are* you?" **10** So he said, "I heard Your voice in the garden, and I was afraid because I was naked; and I hid myself." **11** And He said, "Who told you that you *were* naked? Have you eaten from the tree of which I commanded you that you should not eat?" **12** Then the man said, "The woman whom You gave *to be* with me, she gave me of the tree, and I ate."

Filled with shame after.

Gen 3:7 Then the eyes of both of them were opened, and they knew that they *were* naked; and they sewed fig leaves together and made themselves coverings.

Gen 3:10 So he said, "I heard Your voice in the garden, and I was afraid because I was naked; and I hid myself."

Gen 3:21 Also for Adam and his wife the LORD God made tunics of skin, and clothed them.

Punished for disobedience.

Gen 3:16–19 To the woman He said: "I will greatly multiply your sorrow and your conception; In pain you shall bring forth children; Your desire *shall be* for your husband, And he shall rule over you." **17** Then to Adam He said, "Because you have heeded the voice of your wife, and have eaten from the tree of which I commanded you, saying, 'You shall not eat of it': "Cursed *is* the ground for your sake; In toil you shall eat *of* it All the days of your life. **18** Both thorns and thistles it shall bring forth for you, And you shall eat the herb of the field. **19** In the sweat of your face you shall eat bread Till you return to the ground, For out of it you were taken; For dust you *are*, And to dust you shall return."

Gen 3:23–24 therefore the LORD God sent him out of the garden of Eden to till the ground from which he was taken. **24** So He drove out the man; and He placed cherubim at the east of the garden of Eden, and a flaming sword which turned every way, to guard the way to the tree of life.

Involved posterity.

Rom 5:12–19 Therefore, just as through one man sin entered the world, and death through sin, and thus death spread to all men, because all sinned— **13** (For until the law sin was in the world, but sin is not imputed when there is no law. **14** Nevertheless death reigned from Adam to Moses, even over those who had not sinned according to the likeness of the transgression of Adam, who is a type of Him who was to come. **15** But the free gift *is* not like the offense. For if by the one man's offense many died, much more the grace of God and the gift by the grace of the one Man, Jesus Christ, abounded to many. **16** And the gift *is* not like *that which came* through the one who sinned. For the judgment *which came* from one *offense* *resulted* in condemnation, but the free gift *which came* from many offenses *resulted* in justification. **17** For if by the one man's offense death reigned through the one, much more those who receive abundance of grace and of the gift of righteousness will reign in life through the One, Jesus Christ.) **18** Therefore, as through one man's offense *judgment* came to all men, resulting in condemnation, even so through one Man's righteous act *the free gift came* to all men, resulting in justification of life. **19** For as by one man's disobedience many were made sinners, so also by one Man's obedience many will be made righteous.

Born in sin after the Fall.

Job 5:7 Yet man is born to trouble, As the sparks fly upward.

Ps 51:5 Behold, I was brought forth in iniquity, And in sin my mother conceived me.

Days of, are limited.

1 Chr 29:15 For we *are* aliens and pilgrims before You, As *were* all our fathers; Our days on earth *are* as a shadow, And without hope.

Job 7:1 "*Is there* not a time of hard service for man on earth? *Are not* his days also like the days of a hired man?

Job 14:1 "Man *who is* born of woman Is of few days and full of trouble.

Ps 90:10 The days of our lives *are* seventy years; And if by reason of strength *they are* eighty years, Yet their boast *is* only labor and sorrow; For it is soon cut off, and we fly away.

Ignorant of what is best.

Ps 39:6 Surely every man walks about like a shadow; Surely they busy themselves in vain; He heaps up *riches*, And does not know who will gather them.

Prov 20:24 A man's steps *are* of the LORD; How then can a man understand his own way?

Eccl 2:22 For what has man for all his labor, and for the striving of his heart with which he has toiled under the sun?

Eccl 6:12 For who knows what *is* good for man in life, all the days of his vain life which he passes like a shadow? Who can tell a man what will happen after him under the sun?

Eccl 10:2 A wise man's heart *is* at his right hand, But a fool's heart at his left.

Eccl 10:14 A fool also multiplies words. No man knows what is to be; Who can tell him what will be after him?

Jer 10:23 O LORD, I know the way of man *is* not in himself; *It is* not in man who walks to direct his own steps.

Relationship to God

Instructed by Him.

Ps 94:10 He who instructs the nations, shall He not correct, He who teaches man knowledge?

Guided by Him.

Prov 5:21 For the ways of man *are* before the eyes of the LORD, And He ponders all his paths.

Prov 16:1 The preparations of the heart *belong* to man, But the answer of the tongue *is* from the LORD.

Prov 20:24 A man's steps *are* of the LORD; How then can a man understand his own way?

Cared for by Him.

Job 7:20 Have I sinned? What have I done to You, O watcher of men? Why have You set me as Your target, So that I am a burden to myself?

Ps 36:6 Your righteousness *is* like the great mountains; Your judgments *are* a great deep; O LORD, You preserve man and beast.

Ps 145:15–16 The eyes of all look expectantly to You, And You give them their food in due season. **16** You open Your hand And satisfy the desire of every living thing.

Life limited by Him.

Job 14:19 *As* water wears away stones, *And as* torrents wash away the soil of the earth; So You destroy the hope of man.

Made to praise Him.

Ps 39:11 When with rebukes You correct man for iniquity, You make his beauty melt away like a moth; Surely every man *is* vapor. Selah

Ps 76:10 Surely the wrath of man shall praise You; With the remainder of wrath You shall gird Yourself.

Ps 90:3 You turn man to destruction, And say, "Return, O children of men."

Made subordinate before Him.

Job 9:2 "Truly I know *it is* so, But how can a man be righteous before God?

Job 15:14 "What *is* man, that he could be pure? And *he who is* born of a woman, that he could be righteous?

Job 25:4 How then can man be righteous before God? Or how can he be pure *who is* born of a woman?

Ps 143:2 Do not enter into judgment with Your servant, For in Your sight no one living is righteous.

Prov 16:2 All the ways of a man *are* pure in his own eyes, But the LORD weighs the spirits.

Jer 2:22 For though you wash yourself with lye, and use much soap, *Yet* your iniquity is marked before Me," says the Lord GOD.

Rom 3:20 Therefore by the deeds of the law no flesh will be justified in His sight, for by the law *is* the knowledge of sin.

And Christ

Nature of, known by Him.

John 2:25 and had no need that anyone should testify of man, for He knew what was in man.

Nature of, taken by Him.

John 1:14 And the Word became flesh and dwelt among us, and we beheld His glory, the glory as of the only begotten of the Father, full of grace and truth.

Phil 2:7–8 but made Himself of no reputation, taking the form of a bondservant, *and* coming in the likeness of men. **8** And being found in appearance as a man, He humbled Himself and became obedient to *the point of* death, even the death of the cross.

Heb 2:14 Inasmuch then as the children have partaken of flesh and blood, He Himself likewise shared in the same, that through death He might destroy him who had the power of death, that is, the devil,

Heb 2:16 For indeed He does not give aid to angels, but He does give aid to the seed of Abraham.

Dependent on Him as refuge and head.

Is 32:2 A man will be as a hiding place from the wind, And a cover from the tempest, As rivers of water in a dry place, As the shadow of a great rock in a weary land.

1 Cor 11:3 But I want you to know that the head of every man is Christ, the head of woman *is* man, and the head of Christ *is* God.

Shall be recompensed according to his works.

Ps 62:12 Also to You, O Lord, *belongs* mercy; For You render to each one according to his work.

Rom 2:6 who *"will render to each one according to his deeds":*

Fragile existence.

Job 2:4 So Satan answered the LORD and said, "Skin for skin! Yes, all that a man has he will give for his life.

Prov 18:14 The spirit of a man will sustain him in sickness, But who can bear a broken spirit?

Eccl 8:8 No one has power over the spirit to retain the spirit, And no one has power in the day of death. *There is* no release from that war, And wickedness will not deliver those who are given to it.

No trust to be placed in.

Ps 60:11 Give us help from trouble, For the help of man *is* useless.

Ps 118:8 *It is* better to trust in the LORD Than to put confidence in man.

Is 2:22 Sever yourselves from such a man, Whose breath *is* in his nostrils; For of what account is he?

The whole duty of.

Eccl 12:13 Let us hear the conclusion of the whole matter: Fear God and keep His commandments, For this is man's all.

MANASSEH, THE TRIBE OF

Descended from Joseph's eldest son adopted by Jacob.

Gen 41:51 Joseph called the name of the firstborn Manasseh: "For God has made me forget all my toil and all my father's house."

Gen 48:5 And now your two sons, Ephraim and Manasseh, who were born to you in the land of Egypt before I came to you in Egypt, *are* mine; as Reuben and Simeon, they shall be mine.

Predictions respecting.

Gen 48:20 So he blessed them that day, saying, "By you Israel will bless, saying, 'May God make you as Ephraim and as Manasseh!' " And thus he set Ephraim before Manasseh.

Gen 49:22–26 "Joseph *is* a fruitful bough, A fruitful bough by a well; His branches run over the wall. **23** The archers have bitterly grieved him, Shot *at him* and hated him. **24** But his bow remained in strength, And the arms of his hands were made strong By the hands of the Mighty *God* of Jacob (From there *is* the Shepherd, the Stone of Israel), **25** By the God of your father who will help you, And by the Almighty who will bless you *With* blessings of heaven above, Blessings of the deep that lies beneath, Blessings of the breasts and of the womb. **26** The blessings of your father Have excelled the blessings of my ancestors, Up

to the utmost bound of the everlasting hills. They shall be on the head of Joseph, And on the crown of the head of him who was separate from his brothers.

Deut 33:13–17 And of Joseph he said: "Blessed of the LORD *is* his land, With the precious things of heaven, with the dew, And the deep lying beneath, **14** With the precious fruits of the sun, With the precious produce of the months, **15** With the best things of the ancient mountains, With the precious things of the everlasting hills, **16** With the precious things of the earth and its fullness, And the favor of Him who dwelt in the bush. Let *the blessing* come 'on the head of Joseph, And on the crown of the head of him *who was* separate from his brothers.' **17** His glory *is like* a firstborn bull, And his horns *like* the horns of the wild ox; Together with them He shall push the peoples To the ends of the earth; They *are* the ten thousands of Ephraim, And they *are* the thousands of Manasseh."

Persons selected from,

To number the people.

Num 1:10 from the sons of Joseph: from Ephraim, Elishama the son of Ammihud; from Manasseh, Gamaliel the son of Pedahzur;

To spy out the land.

Num 13:11 from the tribe of Joseph, *that is,* from the tribe of Manasseh, Gaddi the son of Susi;

To divide the land.

Num 34:23 from the sons of Joseph: a leader from the tribe of the children of Manasseh, Hanniel the son of Ephod,

Strength of,

On leaving Egypt.

Num 1:34–35 From the children of Manasseh, their genealogies by their families, by their fathers' house, according to the number of names, from twenty years old and above, all who *were able to* go to war: **35** those who were numbered of the tribe of Manasseh *were* thirty-two thousand two hundred.

On entering Canaan.

Num 26:34 These *are* the families of Manasseh; and those who were numbered of them *were* fifty-two thousand seven hundred.

Part of third division of Israel.

Num 10:22–23 And the standard of the camp of the children of Ephraim set out according to their armies; over their army *was* Elishama the son of Ammihud. **23** Over the army of the tribe of the children of Manasseh *was* Gamaliel the son of Pedahzur.

Encamped next to and under the standard of Ephraim, west of tabernacle.

Num 2:18 "On the west side *shall be* the standard of the forces with Ephraim according to their armies, and the leader of the children of Ephraim *shall be* Elishama the son of Ammihud."

Num 2:20 "Next to him *comes* the tribe of Manasseh, and the leader of the children of Manasseh *shall be* Gamaliel the son of Pedahzur."

Offering of, at dedication of tabernacle.

Num 7:54–59 On the eighth day Gamaliel the son of Pedahzur, leader of the children of Manasseh, *presented*

an offering. **55** His offering *was* one silver platter, the weight of which *was* one hundred and thirty *shekels,* and one silver bowl of seventy shekels, according to the shekel of the sanctuary, both of them full of fine flour mixed with oil as a grain offering; **56** one gold pan of ten *shekels,* full of incense; **57** one young bull, one ram, and one male lamb in its first year, as a burnt offering; **58** one kid of the goats as a sin offering; **59** and as the sacrifice of peace offerings: two oxen, five rams, five male goats, and five male lambs in their first year. This *was* the offering of Gamaliel the son of Pedahzur.

Families of.

Num 26:29–33 The sons of Manasseh: of Machir, the family of the Machirites; and Machir begot Gilead; of Gilead, the family of the Gileadites. **30** These *are* the sons of Gilead: *of* Jeezer, the family of the Jeezerites; of Helek, the family of the Helekites; **31** *of* Asriel, the family of the Asrielites; *of* Shechem, the family of the Shechemites; **32** *of* Shemida, the family of the Shemidaites; *of* Hepher, the family of the Hepherites. **33** Now Zelophehad the son of Hepher had no sons, but daughters; and the names of the daughters of Zelophehad *were* Mahlah, Noah, Hoglah, Milcah, and Tirzah.

On Gerizim, said amen to the blessing.

Deut 27:12 "These shall stand on Mount Gerizim to bless the people, when you have crossed over the Jordan: Simeon, Levi, Judah, Issachar, Joseph, and Benjamin;

Half of, obtained inheritance east of Jordan.

Num 32:33 So Moses gave to the children of Gad, to the children of Reuben, and to half the tribe of Manasseh the son of Joseph, the kingdom of Sihon king of the Amorites and the kingdom of Og king of Bashan, the land with its cities within the borders, the cities of the surrounding country.

Num 32:39–42 And the children of Machir the son of Manasseh went to Gilead and took it, and dispossessed the Amorites who *were* in it. **40** So Moses gave Gilead to Machir the son of Manasseh, and he dwelt in it. **41** Also Jair the son of Manasseh went and took its small towns, and called them Havoth Jair. **42** Then Nobah went and took Kenath and its villages, and he called it Nobah, after his own name.

Josh 13:29–31 Moses also had given *an inheritance* to half the tribe of Manasseh; it was for half the tribe of the children of Manasseh according to their families: **30** Their territory was from Mahanaim, all Bashan, all the kingdom of Og king of Bashan, and all the towns of Jair which are in Bashan, sixty cities; **31** half of Gilead, and Ashtaroth and Edrei, cities of the kingdom of Og in Bashan, *were* for the children of Machir the son of Manasseh, for half of the children of Machir according to their families.

Half of, obtained inheritance west of Jordan.

Josh 17:1–11 There was also a lot for the tribe of Manasseh, for he *was* the firstborn of Joseph: *namely* for Machir the firstborn of Manasseh, the father of Gilead, because he was a man of war; therefore he was given Gilead and Bashan. **2** And there was *a lot* for the rest of the children of Manasseh according to their families: for the children of Abiezer, the children of Helek, the children of Asriel, the children of Shechem,

the children of Hepher, and the children of Shemida; these *were* the male children of Manasseh the son of Joseph according to their families. **3** But Zelophehad the son of Hepher, the son of Gilead, the son of Machir, the son of Manasseh, had no sons, but only daughters. And these *are* the names of his daughters: Mahlah, Noah, Hoglah, Milcah, and Tirzah. **4** And they came near before Eleazar the priest, before Joshua the son of Nun, and before the rulers, saying, "The Lord commanded Moses to give us an inheritance among our brothers." Therefore, according to the commandment of the Lord, he gave them an inheritance among their father's brothers. **5** Ten shares fell to Manasseh, besides the land of Gilead and Bashan, which *were* on the other side of the Jordan, **6** because the daughters of Manasseh received an inheritance among his sons; and the rest of Manasseh's sons had the land of Gilead. **7** And the territory of Manasseh was from Asher to Michmethath, that *lies* east of Shechem; and the border went along south to the inhabitants of En Tappuah. **8** Manasseh had the land of Tappuah, but Tappuah on the border of Manasseh *belonged* to the children of Ephraim. **9** And the border descended to the Brook Kanah, southward to the brook. These cities of Ephraim *are* among the cities of Manasseh. The border of Manasseh *was* on the north side of the brook; and it ended at the sea. **10** Southward *it was* Ephraim's, northward *it was* Manasseh's, and the sea was its border. Manasseh's territory was adjoining Asher on the north and Issachar on the east. **11** And in Issachar and in Asher, Manasseh had Beth Shean and its towns, Ibleam and its towns, the inhabitants of Dor and its towns, the inhabitants of En Dor and its towns, the inhabitants of Taanach and its towns, and the inhabitants of Megiddo and its towns—three hilly regions.

Accomodated the Canaanites.

Josh 17:12–13 Yet the children of Manasseh could not drive out *the inhabitants of* those cities, but the Canaanites were determined to dwell in that land. **13** And it happened, when the children of Israel grew strong, that they put the Canaanites to forced labor, but did not utterly drive them out.

Judg 1:27–28 However, Manasseh did not drive out *the inhabitants of* Beth Shean and its villages, or Taanach and its villages, or the inhabitants of Dor and its villages, or the inhabitants of Ibleam and its villages, or the inhabitants of Megiddo and its villages; for the Canaanites were determined to dwell in that land. **28** And it came to pass, when Israel was strong, that they put the Canaanites under tribute, but did not completely drive them out.

Some of,

Aided David against Saul.

1 Chr 12:19–21 And *some* from Manasseh defected to David when he was going with the Philistines to battle against Saul; but they did not help them, for the lords of the Philistines sent him away by agreement, saying, "He may defect to his master Saul *and endanger* our heads." **20** When he went to Ziklag, those of Manasseh who defected to him were Adnah, Jozabad, Jediael, Michael, Jozabad, Elihu, and Zillethai, captains of the thousands who *were* from Manasseh. **21** And they helped David against the bands of raiders, for they *were* all mighty men of valor, and they were captains in the army.

Attended coronation of David.

1 Chr 12:31–37 of the half-tribe of Manasseh eighteen thousand, who were designated by name to come and make David king; **32** of the sons of Issachar who had understanding of the times, to know what Israel ought to do, their chiefs were two hundred; and all their brethren were at their command; **33** of Zebulun there were fifty thousand who went out to battle, expert in war with all weapons of war, stouthearted men who could keep ranks; **34** of Naphtali one thousand captains, and with them thirty-seven thousand with shield and spear; **35** of the Danites who could keep battle formation, twenty-eight thousand six hundred; **36** of Asher, those who could go out to war, able to keep battle formation, forty thousand; **37** of the Reubenites and the Gadites and the half-tribe of Manasseh, from the other side of the Jordan, one hundred and twenty thousand armed for battle with every *kind* of weapon of war.

Resumed their allegiance to the house of David during Asa's reign.

2 Chr 15:9 Then he gathered all Judah and Benjamin, and those who dwelt with them from Ephraim, Manasseh, and Simeon, for they came over to him in great numbers from Israel when they saw that the LORD his God was with him.

Attended Hezekiah's Passover.

2 Chr 30:1 And Hezekiah sent to all Israel and Judah, and also wrote letters to Ephraim and Manasseh, that they should come to the house of the LORD at Jerusalem, to keep the Passover to the LORD God of Israel.

2 Chr 30:11 Nevertheless some from Asher, Manasseh, and Zebulun humbled themselves and came to Jerusalem.

2 Chr 30:18 For a multitude of the people, many from Ephraim, Manasseh, Issachar, and Zebulun, had not cleansed themselves, yet they ate the Passover contrary to what was written. But Hezekiah prayed for them, saying, "May the good LORD provide atonement for everyone

David appointed rulers and captains over.

1 Chr 26:32 And his brethren *were* two thousand seven hundred able men, heads of fathers' *houses*, whom King David made officials over the Reubenites, the Gadites, and the half-tribe of Manasseh, for every matter pertaining to God and the affairs of the king.

1 Chr 27:20–21 *over* the children of Ephraim, Hoshea the son of Azaziah; *over* the half-tribe of Manasseh, Joel the son of Pedaiah; **21** *over* the half-*tribe* of Manasseh in Gilead, Iddo the son of Zechariah; *over* Benjamin, Jaasiel the son of Abner;

Often at war with Ephraim.

Judg 12:1 Then the men of Ephraim gathered together, crossed over toward Zaphon, and said to Jephthah, "Why did you cross over to fight against the people of Ammon, and did not call us to go with you? We will burn your house down on you with fire!"

Judg 12:6 then they would say to him, "Then say, 'Shibboleth'!" And he would say, "Sibboleth," for he could not pronounce *it* right. Then they would take

him and kill him at the fords of the Jordan. There fell at that time forty-two thousand Ephraimites.

Is 9:21 Manasseh *shall devour* Ephraim, and Ephraim Manasseh; Together they *shall be* against Judah. For all this His anger is not turned away, But His hand *is* stretched out still.

Country of, purified from idols by Hezekiah and Josiah.

2 Chr 31:1 Now when all this was finished, all Israel who were present went out to the cities of Judah and broke the sacred pillars in pieces, cut down the wooden images, and threw down the high places and the altars—from all Judah, Benjamin, Ephraim, and Manasseh—until they had utterly destroyed them all. Then all the children of Israel returned to their own cities, every man to his possession.

2 Chr 34:6 And *so he did* in the cities of Manasseh, Ephraim, and Simeon, as far as Naphtali and all around, with axes.

Remarkable persons of,

The daughters of Zelophehad.

Num 27:1–7 Then came the daughters of Zelophehad the son of Hepher, the son of Gilead, the son of Machir, the son of Manasseh, from the families of Manasseh the son of Joseph; and these *were* the names of his daughters: Mahlah, Noah, Hoglah, Milcah, and Tirzah. **2** And they stood before Moses, before Eleazar the priest, and before the leaders and all the congregation, *by* the doorway of the tabernacle of meeting, saying: **3** "Our father died in the wilderness; but he was not in the company of those who gathered together against the LORD, in company with Korah, but he died in his own sin; and he had no sons. **4** Why should the name of our father be removed from among his family because he had no son? Give us a possession among our father's brothers." **5** So Moses brought their case before the LORD. **6** And the LORD spoke to Moses, saying: **7** "The daughters of Zelophehad speak *what is* right; you shall surely give them a possession of inheritance among their father's brothers, and cause the inheritance of their father to pass to them.

Gideon.

Judg 6:15 So he said to Him, "O my Lord, how can I save Israel? Indeed my clan *is* the weakest in Manasseh, and I *am* the least in my father's house."

Abimelech.

Judg 9:1 Then Abimelech the son of Jerubbaal went to Shechem, to his mother's brothers, and spoke with them and with all the family of the house of his mother's father, saying,

Jotham.

Judg 9:5 Then he went to his father's house at Ophrah and killed his brothers, the seventy sons of Jerubbaal, on one stone. But Jotham the youngest son of Jerubbaal was left, because he hid himself.

Judg 9:7 Now when they told Jotham, he went and stood on top of Mount Gerizim, and lifted his voice and cried out. And he said to them: "Listen to me, you men of Shechem, That God may listen to you!

Judg 9:21 And Jotham ran away and fled; and he went

to Beer and dwelt there, for fear of Abimelech his brother.

Jair.

Judg 10:3 After him arose Jair, a Gileadite; and he judged Israel twenty-two years.

Jephthah.

Judg 11:1 Now Jephthah the Gileadite was a mighty man of valor, but he *was* the son of a harlot; and Gilead begot Jephthah.

Barzillai.

2 Sam 17:27 Now it happened, when David had come to Mahanaim, that Shobi the son of Nahash from Rabbah of the people of Ammon, Machir the son of Ammiel from Lo Debar, and Barzillai the Gileadite from Rogelim,

Elijah.

1 Kin 17:1 And Elijah the Tishbite, of the inhabitants of Gilead, said to Ahab, "As the LORD God of Israel lives, before whom I stand, there shall not be dew nor rain these years, except at my word."

MANNA

Miraculously given to Israel for food in the wilderness.

Ex 16:4 Then the LORD said to Moses, "Behold, I will rain bread from heaven for you. And the people shall go out and gather a certain quota every day, that I may test them, whether they will walk in My law or not.

Ex 16:15 So when the children of Israel saw *it*, they said to one another, "What is it?" For they did not know what it *was*. And Moses said to them, "This *is* the bread which the LORD has given you to eat.

Neh 9:15 You gave them bread from heaven for their hunger, And brought them water out of the rock for their thirst, And told them to go in to possess the land Which You had sworn to give them.

Other names for,

God's manna.

Neh 9:20 You also gave Your good Spirit to instruct them, And did not withhold Your manna from their mouth, And gave them water for their thirst.

Bread of and from heaven.

Ex 16:4 Then the LORD said to Moses, "Behold, I will rain bread from heaven for you. And the people shall go out and gather a certain quota every day, that I may test them, whether they will walk in My law or not.

Ps 78:24 Had rained down manna on them to eat, And given them of the bread of heaven.

Ps 105:40 *The people* asked, and He brought quail, And satisfied them with the bread of heaven.

John 6:31 Our fathers ate the manna in the desert; as it is written, *'He gave them bread from heaven to eat.'* "

Angel's food.

Ps 78:25 Men ate angels' food; He sent them food to the full.

Spiritual food.

1 Cor 10:3 all ate the same spiritual food,

Previously unknown.

Deut 8:3 So He humbled you, allowed you to hunger, and fed you with manna which you did not know nor did your fathers know, that He might make you know that man shall not live by bread alone; but man lives by every *word* that proceeds from the mouth of the LORD.

Deut 8:16 who fed you in the wilderness with manna, which your fathers did not know, that He might humble you and that He might test you, to do you good in the end—

Described as

Like white or bdellium coriander seed.

Ex 16:31 And the house of Israel called its name Manna. And it *was* like white coriander seed, and the taste of it *was* like wafers *made* with honey.

Num 11:7 Now the manna *was* like coriander seed, and its color like the color of bdellium.

Tasting like honey wafers.

Ex 16:31 And the house of Israel called its name Manna. And it *was* like white coriander seed, and the taste of it *was* like wafers *made* with honey.

Tasting like oil.

Num 11:8 The people went about and gathered *it*, ground *it* on millstones or beat *it* in the mortar, cooked *it* in pans, and made cakes of it; and its taste was like the taste of pastry prepared with oil.

Like frost.

Ex 16:14 And when the layer of dew lifted, there, on the surface of the wilderness, was a small round substance, *as* fine as frost on the ground.

Fell after the evening dew.

Num 11:9 And when the dew fell on the camp in the night, the manna fell on it.

Gathered every morning.

Ex 16:19–21 And Moses said, "Let no one leave any of it till morning." **20** Notwithstanding they did not heed Moses. But some of them left part of it until morning, and it bred worms and stank. And Moses was angry with them. **21** So they gathered it every morning, every man according to his need. And when the sun became hot, it melted.

An omer of, gathered for each person, was adequate.

Ex 16:16 This is the thing which the LORD has commanded: 'Let every man gather it according to each one's need, one omer for each person, *according to the* number of persons; let every man take for *those* who *are* in his tent.' "

Ex 16:18 So when they measured *it* by omers, he who gathered much had nothing left over, and he who gathered little had no lack. Every man had gathered according to each one's need.

Two portions of, gathered the sixth day because none could be gathered on the Sabbath.

Ex 16:5 And it shall be on the sixth day that they shall prepare what they bring in, and it shall be twice as much as they gather daily."

Ex 16:22–27 And so it was, on the sixth day, *that* they gathered twice as much bread, two omers for each one. And all the rulers of the congregation came and told Moses. **23** Then he said to them, "This *is what* the LORD has said: 'Tomorrow *is* a Sabbath rest, a holy Sabbath to the LORD. Bake what you will bake *today,* and boil what you will boil; and lay up for yourselves all that remains, to be kept until morning.' " **24** So they laid it up till morning, as Moses commanded; and it did not stink, nor were there any worms in it. **25** Then Moses said, "Eat that today, for today *is* a Sabbath to the LORD; today you will not find it in the field. **26** Six days you shall gather it, but on the seventh day, the Sabbath, there will be none." **27** Now it happened *that some* of the people went out on the seventh day to gather, but they found none.

Given

When Israel murmured for bread.

Ex 16:2–3 Then the whole congregation of the children of Israel complained against Moses and Aaron in the wilderness. **3** And the children of Israel said to them, "Oh, that we had died by the hand of the LORD in the land of Egypt, when we sat by the pots of meat *and* when we ate bread to the full! For you have brought us out into this wilderness to kill this whole assembly with hunger."

In answer to prayer.

Ps 105:40 *The people* asked, and He brought quail, And satisfied them with the bread of heaven.

To exhibit God's glory.

Ex 16:7 And in the morning you shall see the glory of the LORD; for He hears your complaints against the LORD. But what *are* we, that you complain against us?"

As a sign of Moses's divine mission.

John 6:30–32 Therefore they said to Him, "What sign will You perform then, that we may see it and believe You? What work will You do? **31** Our fathers ate the manna in the desert; as it is written, *'He gave them bread from heaven to eat.'* " **32** Then Jesus said to them, "Most assuredly, I say to you, Moses did not give you the bread from heaven, but My Father gives you the true bread from heaven.

For forty years.

Neh 9:21 Forty years You sustained them in the wilderness; They lacked nothing; Their clothes did not wear out And their feet did not swell.

As a test of obedience.

Ex 16:4 Then the LORD said to Moses, "Behold, I will rain bread from heaven for you. And the people shall go out and gather a certain quota every day, that I may test them, whether they will walk in My law or not.

Deut 8:16 who fed you in the wilderness with manna, which your fathers did not know, that He might humble you and that He might test you, to do you good in the end—

To teach that man does not live by bread alone.

Deut 8:3 So He humbled you, allowed you to hunger, and fed you with manna which you did not know nor did your fathers know, that He might make you know that man shall not live by bread alone; but man lives by every *word* that proceeds from the mouth of the LORD.

Matt 4:4 But He answered and said, "It is written, *'Man shall not live by bread alone, but by every word that proceeds from the mouth of God.'* "

The Israelites

At first covetous of it.

Ex 16:17 Then the children of Israel did so and gathered, some more, some less.

Made it into cakes.

Num 11:8 The people went about and gathered *it,* ground *it* on millstones or beat *it* in the mortar, cooked *it* in pans, and made cakes of it; and its taste was like the taste of pastry prepared with oil.

Counted it inferior to food of Egypt.

Num 11:4–6 Now the mixed multitude who were among them yielded to intense craving; so the children of Israel also wept again and said: "Who will give us meat to eat? **5** We remember the fish which we ate freely in Egypt, the cucumbers, the melons, the leeks, the onions, and the garlic; **6** but now our whole being *is* dried up; *there is* nothing at all except this manna *before* our eyes!"

Punished for despising it.

Num 11:10–20 Then Moses heard the people weeping throughout their families, everyone at the door of his tent; and the anger of the LORD was greatly aroused; Moses also was displeased. **11** So Moses said to the LORD, "Why have You afflicted Your servant? And why have I not found favor in Your sight, that You have laid the burden of all these people on me? **12** Did I conceive all these people? Did I beget them, that You should say to me, 'Carry them in your bosom, as a guardian carries a nursing child,' to the land which You swore to their fathers? **13** Where am I to get meat to give to all these people? For they weep all over me, saying, 'Give us meat, that we may eat.' **14** I am not able to bear all these people alone, because the burden *is* too heavy for me. **15** If You treat me like this, please kill me here and now—if I have found favor in Your sight—and do not let me see my wretchedness!" **16** So the LORD said to Moses: "Gather to Me seventy men of the elders of Israel, whom you know to be the elders of the people and officers over them; bring them to the tabernacle of meeting, that they may stand there with you. **17** Then I will come down and talk with you there. I will take of the Spirit that *is* upon you and will put *the same* upon them; and they shall bear the burden of the people with you, that you may not bear *it* yourself alone. **18** Then you shall say to the people, 'Consecrate yourselves for tomorrow, and you shall eat meat; for you have wept in the hearing of the LORD, saying, "Who will give us meat to eat? For *it was* well with us in Egypt." Therefore the LORD will give you meat, and you shall eat. **19** You shall eat, not one day, nor two days, nor five days, nor ten days, nor twenty days, **20** but *for* a whole month, until it comes out of your nostrils and becomes loathsome to you, because you have despised the LORD who is among you, and have wept before Him, saying, "Why did we ever come up out of Egypt?" ' "

Num 21:5–6 And the people spoke against God and against Moses: "Why have you brought us up out of Egypt to die in the wilderness? For *there is* no food and no water, and our soul loathes this worthless bread." **6** So the LORD sent fiery serpents among the people, and they bit the people; and many of the people of Israel died.

Ceased when Israel entered Canaan.

Ex 16:35 And the children of Israel ate manna forty years, until they came to an inhabited land; they ate manna until they came to the border of the land of Canaan.

Josh 5:12 Then the manna ceased on the day after they had eaten the produce of the land; and the children of Israel no longer had manna, but they ate the food of the land of Canaan that year.

Illustrative of

Christ.

John 6:32–35 Then Jesus said to them, "Most assuredly, I say to you, Moses did not give you the bread from heaven, but My Father gives you the true bread from heaven. **33** For the bread of God is He who comes down from heaven and gives life to the world." **34** Then they said to Him, "Lord, give us this bread always." **35** And Jesus said to them, "I am the bread of life. He who comes to Me shall never hunger, and he who believes in Me shall never thirst.

Blessedness given to believers.

Rev 2:17 "He who has an ear, let him hear what the Spirit says to the churches. To him who overcomes I will give some of the hidden manna to eat. And I will give him a white stone, and on the stone a new name written which no one knows except him who receives *it.*" '

A golden pot of, as a memorial.

Ex 16:32–34 Then Moses said, "This *is* the thing which the LORD has commanded: 'Fill an omer with it, to be kept for your generations, that they may see the bread with which I fed you in the wilderness, when I brought you out of the land of Egypt.' " **33** And Moses said to Aaron, "Take a pot and put an omer of manna in it, and lay it up before the LORD, to be kept for your generations." **34** As the LORD commanded Moses, so Aaron laid it up before the Testimony, to be kept.

Heb 9:4 which had the golden censer and the ark of the covenant overlaid on all sides with gold, in which *were* the golden pot that had the manna, Aaron's rod that budded, and the tablets of the covenant;

MARRIAGE

Divinely instituted.

Gen 2:24 Therefore a man shall leave his father and mother and be joined to his wife, and they shall become one flesh.

Designed for

The happiness of man.

Gen 2:18 And the LORD God said, "*It is* not good that man should be alone; I will make him a helper comparable to him."

Increasing the human population.

Gen 1:28 Then God blessed them, and God said to them, "Be fruitful and multiply; fill the earth and subdue it; have dominion over the fish of the sea, over the birds of the air, and over every living thing that moves on the earth."

Gen 9:1 So God blessed Noah and his sons, and said to them: "Be fruitful and multiply, and fill the earth.

Raising up godly offspring.

Mal 2:15 But did He not make *them* one, Having a remnant of the Spirit? And why one? He seeks godly offspring. Therefore take heed to your spirit, And let none deal treacherously with the wife of his youth.

Preventing fornication.

1 Cor 7:2 Nevertheless, because of sexual immorality, let each man have his own wife, and let each woman have her own husband.

Heb 13:4 Marriage *is* honorable among all, and the bed undefiled; but fornicators and adulterers God will judge.

Lawful in all.

1 Cor 7:2 Nevertheless, because of sexual immorality, let each man have his own wife, and let each woman have her own husband.

1 Cor 7:28 But even if you do marry, you have not sinned; and if a virgin marries, she has not sinned. Nevertheless such will have trouble in the flesh, but I would spare you.

1 Tim 5:14 Therefore I desire that *the* younger *widows* marry, bear children, manage the house, give no opportunity to the adversary to speak reproachfully.

Should be only in the Lord.

1 Cor 7:39 A wife is bound by law as long as her husband lives; but if her husband dies, she is at liberty to be married to whom she wishes, only in the Lord.

Expressed by

Joining together.

Matt 19:6 So then, they are no longer two but one flesh. Therefore what God has joined together, let not man separate."

Giving daughters to sons, and sons to daughters.

Deut 7:3 Nor shall you make marriages with them. You shall not give your daughter to their son, nor take their daughter for your son.

Ezra 9:12 Now therefore, do not give your daughters as wives for their sons, nor take their daughters to your sons; and never seek their peace or prosperity, that you may be strong and eat the good of the land, and leave *it* as an inheritance to your children forever.'

Indissoluble during the joint lives of the parties.

Matt 19:6 So then, they are no longer two but one flesh. Therefore what God has joined together, let not man separate."

Rom 7:2–3 For the woman who has a husband is bound by the law to *her* husband as long as he lives. But if the husband dies, she is released from the law of *her* husband. **3** So then if, while *her* husband lives, she marries another man, she will be called an adulteress; but if her husband dies, she is free from that law, so that she is no adulteress, though she has married another man.

1 Cor 7:39 A wife is bound by law as long as her husband lives; but if her husband dies, she is at liberty to be married to whom she wishes, only in the Lord.

Should be with consent.

Gen 24:57–58 So they said, "We will call the young woman and ask her personally." **58** Then they called Rebekah and said to her, "Will you go with this man?" And she said, "I will go."

Gen 28:8 Also Esau saw that the daughters of Canaan did not please his father Isaac.

Ex 22:17 If her father utterly refuses to give her to him, he shall pay money according to the bride-price of virgins.

Judg 14:2–3 So he went up and told his father and mother, saying, "I have seen a woman in Timnah of the daughters of the Philistines; now therefore, get her for me as a wife." **3** Then his father and mother said to him, "*Is there* no woman among the daughters of your brethren, or among all my people, that you must go and get a wife from the uncircumcised Philistines?" And Samson said to his father, "Get her for me, for she pleases me well."

1 Sam 18:20 Now Michal, Saul's daughter, loved David. And they told Saul, and the thing pleased him.

1 Sam 25:41 Then she arose, bowed her face to the earth, and said, "Here is your maidservant, a servant to wash the feet of the servants of my lord."

The Jews

Contracted in patriarchal age with near relatives, which was later forbidden.

Gen 20:12 But indeed *she is* truly my sister. She *is* the daughter of my father, but not the daughter of my mother; and she became my wife.

Gen 24:24 So she said to him, "I *am* the daughter of Bethuel, Milcah's son, whom she bore to Nahor."

Gen 28:2 Arise, go to Padan Aram, to the house of Bethuel your mother's father; and take yourself a wife from there of the daughters of Laban your mother's brother.

Lev 18:6 'None of you shall approach anyone who is near of kin to him, to uncover his nakedness: I *am* the LORD.

Sometimes contracted by parents for children.

Gen 24:2 So Abraham said to the oldest servant of his house, who ruled over all that he had, "Please, put your hand under my thigh,

Gen 24:3 and I will make you swear by the LORD, the God of heaven and the God of the earth, that you will not take a wife for my son from the daughters of the Canaanites, among whom I dwell;

Gen 24:49–51 Now if you will deal kindly and truly with my master, tell me. And if not, tell me, that I may turn to the right hand or to the left." **50** Then Laban and Bethuel answered and said, "The thing comes from the LORD; we cannot speak to you either bad or good. **51** Here *is* Rebekah before you; take *her* and go, and let her be your master's son's wife, as the LORD has spoken."

Gen 28:1–2 Then Isaac called Jacob and blessed him, and charged him, and said to him: "You shall not take a wife from the daughters of Canaan. **2** Arise, go to Padan Aram, to the house of Bethuel your mother's father; and take yourself a wife from there of the daughters of Laban your mother's brother.

Gen 34:6 Then Hamor the father of Shechem went out to Jacob to speak with him.

Gen 34:8 But Hamor spoke with them, saying, "The soul of my son Shechem longs for your daughter. Please give her to him as a wife.

Forbidden to contract with idolaters.

Deut 7:3–4 Nor shall you make marriages with them. You shall not give your daughter to their son, nor take their daughter for your son. **4** For they will turn your sons away from following Me, to serve other gods; so the anger of the LORD will be aroused against you and destroy you suddenly.

Josh 23:12 Or else, if indeed you do go back, and cling to the remnant of these nations—these that remain among you—and make marriages with them, and go in to them and they to you,

Ezra 9:11–12 which You commanded by Your servants the prophets, saying, 'The land which you are entering to possess is an unclean land, with the uncleanness of the peoples of the lands, with their abominations which have filled it from one end to another with their impurity. **12** Now therefore, do not give your daughters as wives for their sons, nor take their daughters to your sons; and never seek their peace or prosperity, that you may be strong and eat the good of the land, and leave *it* as an inheritance to your children forever.'

Often contracted with foreigners.

1 Kin 11:1 But King Solomon loved many foreign women, as well as the daughter of Pharaoh: women of the Moabites, Ammonites, Edomites, Sidonians, *and* Hittites—

Neh 13:23 In those days I also saw Jews *who* had married women of Ashdod, Ammon, *and* Moab.

Sometimes guilty of polygamy.

1 Kin 11:1 But King Solomon loved many foreign women, as well as the daughter of Pharaoh: women of the Moabites, Ammonites, Edomites, Sidonians, *and* Hittites—

1 Kin 11:3 And he had seven hundred wives, princesses, and three hundred concubines; and his wives turned away his heart.

Betrothed themselves some time before.

Deut 20:7 And what man *is there* who is betrothed to a woman and has not married her? Let him go and return to his house, lest he die in the battle and another man marry her.'

Judg 14:1–2 Now Samson went down to Timnah, and saw a woman in Timnah of the daughters of the Philistines. **2** So he went up and told his father and mother, saying, "I have seen a woman in Timnah of the daughters of the Philistines; now therefore, get her for me as a wife."

Judg 14:8 After some time, when he returned to get her, he turned aside to see the carcass of the lion. And behold, a swarm of bees and honey *were* in the carcass of the lion.

Matt 1:18 Now the birth of Jesus Christ was as follows: After His mother Mary was betrothed to Joseph, before they came together, she was found with child of the Holy Spirit.

Contracted when young.

Prov 2:17 Who forsakes the companion of her youth, And forgets the covenant of her God.

Joel 1:8 Lament like a virgin girded with sackcloth For the husband of her youth.

Often contracted in their own tribe.

Ex 2:1 And a man of the house of Levi went and took *as wife* a daughter of Levi.

Num 36:6–13 This *is* what the Lord commands concerning the daughters of Zelophehad, saying, 'Let them marry whom they think best, but they may marry only within the family of their father's tribe.' 7 So the inheritance of the children of Israel shall not change hands from tribe to tribe, for every one of the children of Israel shall keep the inheritance of the tribe of his fathers. 8 And every daughter who possesses an inheritance in any tribe of the children of Israel shall be the wife of one of the family of her father's tribe, so that the children of Israel each may possess the inheritance of his fathers. 9 Thus no inheritance shall change hands from *one* tribe to another, but every tribe of the children of Israel shall keep its own inheritance." 10 Just as the Lord commanded Moses, so did the daughters of Zelophehad; 11 for Mahlah, Tirzah, Hoglah, Milcah, and Noah, the daughters of Zelophehad, were married to the sons of their father's brothers. 12 They were married into the families of the children of Manasseh the son of Joseph, and their inheritance remained in the tribe of their father's family. 13 These *are* the commandments and the judgments which the Lord commanded the children of Israel by the hand of Moses in the plains of Moab by the Jordan, *across from* Jericho.

Luke 1:5 There was in the days of Herod, the king of Judea, a certain priest named Zacharias, of the division of Abijah. His wife *was* of the daughters of Aaron, and her name *was* Elizabeth.

Luke 1:27 to a virgin betrothed to a man whose name was Joseph, of the house of David. The virgin's name *was* Mary.

Obliged to contract with a brother's wife who died without offspring.

Deut 25:5 "If brothers dwell together, and one of them dies and has no son, the widow of the dead man shall not be *married* to a stranger outside *the family;* her husband's brother shall go in to her, take her as his wife, and perform the duty of a husband's brother to her.

Matt 22:24 saying: "Teacher, Moses said that if a man dies, having no children, his brother shall marry his wife and raise up offspring for his brother.

Often punished by being prevented from.

Judg 11:38 So he said, "Go." And he sent her away *for* two months; and she went with her friends, and bewailed her virginity on the mountains.

Is 4:1 And in that day seven women shall take hold of one man, saying, "We will eat our own food and wear our own apparel; Only let us be called by your name, To take away our reproach."

Jer 7:34 Then I will cause to cease from the cities of Judah and from the streets of Jerusalem the voice of mirth and the voice of gladness, the voice of the bridegroom and the voice of the bride. For the land shall be desolate.

Jer 16:9 For thus says the Lord of hosts, the God of Israel: "Behold, I will cause to cease from this place, before your eyes and in your days, the voice of mirth and the voice of gladness, the voice of the bridegroom and the voice of the bride.

Jer 25:10 Moreover I will take from them the voice of mirth and the voice of gladness, the voice of the bridegroom and the voice of the bride, the sound of the millstones and the light of the lamp.

Were allowed divorce, because of hardness of their hearts.

Deut 24:1 "When a man takes a wife and marries her, and it happens that she finds no favor in his eyes because he has found some uncleanness in her, and he writes her a certificate of divorce, puts *it* in her hand, and sends her out of his house,

Matt 19:7–8 They said to Him, "Why then did Moses command to give a certificate of divorce, and to put her away?" 8 He said to them, "Moses, because of the hardness of your hearts, permitted you to divorce your wives, but from the beginning it was not so.

Exempted from going to war immediately after.

Deut 20:7 And what man *is there* who is betrothed to a woman and has not married her? Let him go and return to his house, lest he die in the battle and another man marry her.'

Priest not to contract, with divorced or improper persons.

Lev 21:7 They shall not take a wife *who is* a harlot or a defiled woman, nor shall they take a woman divorced from her husband; for *the priest* is holy to his God.

Lev 21:14 A widow or a divorced woman or a defiled woman *or* a harlot—these he shall not marry; but he shall take a virgin of his own people as wife.

Contracted at the gate and before witnesses.

Ruth 4:1 Now Boaz went up to the gate and sat down there; and behold, the close relative of whom Boaz had spoken came by. So Boaz said, "Come aside, friend, sit down here." So he came aside and sat down.

Ruth 4:10–11 Moreover, Ruth the Moabitess, the widow of Mahlon, I have acquired as my wife, to perpetuate the name of the dead through his inheritance, that the name of the dead may not be cut off from among his brethren and from his position at the gate. You *are* witnesses this day." 11 And all the people who *were* at the gate, and the elders, said, "*We are* witnesses. The Lord make the woman who is coming to your house like Rachel and Leah, the two who built the house of Israel; and may you prosper in Ephrathah and be famous in Bethlehem.

Sometimes men demanded wives for.

Gen 24:3–4 and I will make you swear by the Lord, the God of heaven and the God of the earth, that you will not take a wife for my son from the daughters of the Canaanites, among whom I dwell; 4 but you shall go to my country and to my family, and take a wife for my son Isaac."

Gen 34:6 Then Hamor the father of Shechem went out to Jacob to speak with him.

Gen 34:8 But Hamor spoke with them, saying, "The soul of my son Shechem longs for your daughter. Please give her to him as a wife.

1 Sam 25:39–40 So when David heard that Nabal was dead, he said, "Blessed *be* the Lord, who has pleaded the cause of my reproach from the hand of Nabal, and has kept His servant from evil! For the LORD has returned the wickedness of Nabal on his own head." And David sent and proposed to Abigail, to take her as his wife. **40** When the servants of David had come to Abigail at Carmel, they spoke to her saying, "David sent us to you, to ask you to become his wife."

Elder daughters usually given in, before the younger.

Gen 29:26 And Laban said, "It must not be done so in our country, to give the younger before the firstborn.

A dowry given to the woman's parents before.

Gen 29:18 Now Jacob loved Rachel; so he said, "I will serve you seven years for Rachel your younger daughter."

Gen 34:12 Ask me ever so much dowry and gift, and I will give according to what you say to me; but give me the young woman as a wife."

1 Sam 18:27–28 therefore David arose and went, he and his men, and killed two hundred men of the Philistines. And David brought their foreskins, and they gave them in full count to the king, that he might become the king's son-in-law. Then Saul gave him Michal his daughter as a wife. **28** Thus Saul saw and knew that the LORD *was* with David, and *that* Michal, Saul's daughter, loved him;

Hos 3:2 So I bought her for myself for fifteen *shekels* of silver, and one and one-half homers of barley.

Celebrated

With great rejoicing.

Jer 33:11 the voice of joy and the voice of gladness, the voice of the bridegroom and the voice of the bride, the voice of those who will say: "Praise the LORD of hosts, For the LORD *is* good, For His mercy *endures* forever"— *and* of those *who will* bring the sacrifice of praise into the house of the LORD. For I will cause the captives of the land to return as at the first,' says the LORD.

John 3:29 He who has the bride is the bridegroom; but the friend of the bridegroom, who stands and hears him, rejoices greatly because of the bridegroom's voice. Therefore this joy of mine is fulfilled.

With feasting.

Gen 29:22 And Laban gathered together all the men of the place and made a feast.

Judg 14:10 So his father went down to the woman. And Samson gave a feast there, for young men used to do so.

Matt 22:2–3 "The kingdom of heaven is like a certain king who arranged a marriage for his son, **3** and sent out his servants to call those who were invited to the wedding; and they were not willing to come.

John 2:1–10 On the third day there was a wedding in Cana of Galilee, and the mother of Jesus was there. **2** Now both Jesus and His disciples were invited to the wedding. **3** And when they ran out of wine, the mother of Jesus said to Him, "They have no wine." **4** Jesus said to her, "Woman, what does your concern have to do with Me? My hour has not yet come." **5** His mother said to the servants, "Whatever He says to you, do *it*." **6** Now there were set there six waterpots of stone, according to the manner of purification of the Jews, containing twenty or thirty gallons

apiece. **7** Jesus said to them, "Fill the waterpots with water." And they filled them up to the brim. **8** And He said to them, "Draw *some* out now, and take *it* to the master of the feast." And they took *it*. **9** When the master of the feast had tasted the water that was made wine, and did not know where it came from (but the servants who had drawn the water knew), the master of the feast called the bridegroom. **10** And he said to him, "Every man at the beginning sets out the good wine, and when the *guests* have well drunk, then the inferior. You have kept the good wine until now!"

For seven days.

Judg 14:12 Then Samson said to them, "Let me pose a riddle to you. If you can correctly solve and explain it to me within the seven days of the feast, then I will give you thirty linen garments and thirty changes of clothing.

A benediction pronounced after.

Gen 24:60 And they blessed Rebekah and said to her: "Our sister, *may* you *become The mother of* thousands of ten thousands; And may your descendants possess The gates of those who hate them."

Ruth 4:11–12 And all the people who *were* at the gate, and the elders, said, "*We are* witnesses. The LORD make the woman who is coming to your house like Rachel and Leah, the two who built the house of Israel; and may you prosper in Ephrathah and be famous in Bethlehem. **12** May your house be like the house of Perez, whom Tamar bore to Judah, because of the offspring which the LORD will give you from this young woman."

The bride

Received presents before.

Gen 24:53 Then the servant brought out jewelry of silver, jewelry of gold, and clothing, and gave *them* to Rebekah. He also gave precious things to her brother and to her mother.

Given a maid at.

Gen 24:59 So they sent away Rebekah their sister and her nurse, and Abraham's servant and his men.

Gen 29:24 And Laban gave his maid Zilpah to his daughter Leah *as* a maid.

Gen 29:29 And Laban gave his maid Bilhah to his daughter Rachel as a maid.

Adorned with jewels for.

Is 49:18 Lift up your eyes, look around and see; All these gather together *and* come to you. As I live," says the LORD, "You shall surely clothe yourselves with them all as an ornament, And bind them *on you* as a bride *does*.

Is 61:10 I will greatly rejoice in the LORD, My soul shall be joyful in my God; For He has clothed me with the garments of salvation, He has covered me with the robe of righteousness, As a bridegroom decks *himself* with ornaments, And as a bride adorns *herself* with her jewels.

Gloriously apparelled.

Ps 45:13–14 The royal daughter *is* all glorious within *the palace;* Her clothing *is* woven with gold. **14** She shall be brought to the King in robes of many colors; The virgins, her companions who follow her, shall be brought to You.

Attended by bridesmaids.

Ps 45:9 Kings' daughters *are* among Your honorable women; At Your right hand stands the queen in gold from Ophir.

Stood on the right of bridegroom.

Ps 45:9 Kings' daughters *are* among Your honorable women; At Your right hand stands the queen in gold from Ophir.

Called to forget her father's house.

Ps 45:10 Listen, O daughter, Consider and incline your ear; Forget your own people also, and your father's house;

The bridegroom

Adorned with ornaments.

Is 61:10 I will greatly rejoice in the LORD, My soul shall be joyful in my God; For He has clothed me with the garments of salvation, He has covered me with the robe of righteousness, As a bridegroom decks *himself* with ornaments, And as a bride adorns *herself* with her jewels.

Attended by many friends.

Judg 14:11 And it happened, when they saw him, that they brought thirty companions to be with him.

John 3:29 He who has the bride is the bridegroom; but the friend of the bridegroom, who stands and hears him, rejoices greatly because of the bridegroom's voice. Therefore this joy of mine is fulfilled.

Crowned with garlands.

Song 3:11 Go forth, O daughters of Zion, And see King Solomon with the crown With which his mother crowned him On the day of his wedding, The day of the gladness of his heart.

Rejoiced over the bride.

Is 62:5 For *as* a young man marries a virgin, *So* shall your sons marry you; And *as* the bridegroom rejoices over the bride, *So* shall your God rejoice over you.

Returned with the bride to his house at night.

Matt 25:1–6 "Then the kingdom of heaven shall be likened to ten virgins who took their lamps and went out to meet the bridegroom. **2** Now five of them were wise, and five *were* foolish. **3** Those who *were* foolish took their lamps and took no oil with them, **4** but the wise took oil in their vessels with their lamps. **5** But while the bridegroom was delayed, they all slumbered and slept. **6** "And at midnight a cry was *heard:* 'Behold, the bridegroom is coming; go out to meet him!'

Infidelity of those engaged, punished as if married.

Deut 22:23–24 "If a young woman *who is* a virgin is betrothed to a husband, and a man finds her in the city and lies with her, **24** then you shall bring them both out to the gate of that city, and you shall stone them to death with stones, the young woman because she did not cry out in the city, and the man because he humbled his neighbor's wife; so you shall put away the evil from among you.

Matt 1:19 Then Joseph her husband, being a just *man,* and not wanting to make her a public example, was minded to put her away secretly.

Illustrative of

God's union with the Jewish nation.

Is 54:5 For your Maker *is* your husband, The LORD of hosts *is* His name; And your Redeemer *is* the Holy One of Israel; He is called the God of the whole earth.

Jer 3:14 "Return, O backsliding children," says the LORD; "for I am married to you. I will take you, one from a city and two from a family, and I will bring you to Zion.

Hos 2:19–20 "I will betroth you to Me forever; Yes, I will betroth you to Me In righteousness and justice, In lovingkindness and mercy; **20** I will betroth you to Me in faithfulness, And you shall know the LORD.

Christ's union with His church.

Eph 5:23–24 For the husband is head of the wife, as also Christ is head of the church; and He is the Savior of the body. **24** Therefore, just as the church is subject to Christ, so *let* the wives *be* to their own husbands in everything.

Eph 5:32 This is a great mystery, but I speak concerning Christ and the church.

MATERIALISM

Foolish and sinful to trust in.

Job 31:24–28 "If I have made gold my hope, Or said to fine gold, '*You are* my confidence'; **25** If I have rejoiced because my wealth *was* great, And because my hand had gained much; **26** If I have observed the sun when it shines, Or the moon moving *in* brightness, **27** So that my heart has been secretly enticed, And my mouth has kissed my hand; **28** This also *would be* an iniquity *deserving of* judgment, For I would have denied God *who is* above.

Matt 6:19–34 "Do not lay up for yourselves treasures on earth, where moth and rust destroy and where thieves break in and steal; **20** but lay up for yourselves treasures in heaven, where neither moth nor rust destroys and where thieves do not break in and steal. **21** For where your treasure is, there your heart will be also. **22** "The lamp of the body is the eye. If therefore your eye is good, your whole body will be full of light. **23** But if your eye is bad, your whole body will be full of darkness. If therefore the light that is in you is darkness, how great *is* that darkness! **24** "No one can serve two masters; for either he will hate the one and love the other, or else he will be loyal to the one and despise the other. You cannot serve God and mammon. **25** "Therefore I say to you, do not worry about your life, what you will eat or what you will drink; nor about your body, what you will put on. Is not life more than food and the body more than clothing? **26** Look at the birds of the air, for they neither sow nor reap nor gather into barns; yet your heavenly Father feeds them. Are you not of more value than they? **27** Which of you by worrying can add one cubit to his stature? **28** "So why do you worry about clothing? Consider the lilies of the field, how they grow: they neither toil nor spin; **29** and yet I say to you that even Solomon in all his glory was not arrayed like one of these. **30** Now if God so clothes the grass of the field, which today is, and tomorrow is thrown into the oven, *will He* not much more *clothe* you, O you of little faith? **31** "Therefore do not worry, saying, 'What shall we eat?' or 'What shall we drink?' or 'What shall we wear?' **32** For after all these things the Gentiles seek. For your heavenly Father knows that you need all these things. **33** But seek first the kingdom of God and His righteousness, and all these things shall be added to you. **34** Therefore do not worry about tomorrow, for tomorrow will worry about its own things. Sufficient for the day *is* its own trouble.

Luke 16:13 "No servant can serve two masters; for either he will hate the one and love the other, or else he will be loyal to the one and despise the other. You cannot serve God and mammon."

Warning against dangers of.

Luke 12:13–21 Then one from the crowd said to Him, "Teacher, tell my brother to divide the inheritance with me." **14** But He said to him, "Man, who made Me a judge or an arbitrator over you?" **15** And He said to them, "Take heed and beware of covetousness, for one's life does not consist in the abundance of the things he possesses." **16** Then He spoke a parable to them, saying: "The ground of a certain rich man yielded plentifully. **17** And he thought within himself, saying, 'What shall I do, since I have no room to store my crops?' **18** So he said, 'I will do this: I will pull down my barns and build greater, and there I will store all my crops and my goods. **19** And I will say to my soul, "Soul, you have many goods laid up for many years; take your ease; eat, drink, *and* be merry." ' **20** But God said to him, 'Fool! This night your soul will be required of you; then whose will those things be which you have provided?' **21** "So *is* he who lays up treasure for himself, and is not rich toward God."

1 Tim 6:6–10 Now godliness with contentment is great gain. **7** For we brought nothing into *this* world, *and it is* certain we can carry nothing out. **8** And having food and clothing, with these we shall be content. **9** But those who desire to be rich fall into temptation and a snare, and *into* many foolish and harmful lusts which drown men in destruction and perdition. **10** For the love of money is a root of all *kinds of* evil, for which some have strayed from the faith in their greediness, and pierced themselves through with many sorrows.

1 Tim 6:17–19 Command those who are rich in this present age not to be haughty, nor to trust in uncertain riches but in the living God, who gives us richly all things to enjoy. **18** *Let them* do good, that they be rich in good works, ready to give, willing to share, **19** storing up for themselves a good foundation for the time to come, that they may lay hold on eternal life.

Should be engaged in properly.

1 Cor 7:31 and those who use this world as not misusing *it.* For the form of this world is passing away.

MARTYRDOM

Is death endured for the Word of God and testimony of Christ.

Rev 6:9 When He opened the fifth seal, I saw under the altar the souls of those who had been slain for the word of God and for the testimony which they held.

Rev 20:4 And I saw thrones, and they sat on them, and judgment was committed to them. Then *I saw* the souls of those who had been beheaded for their witness to Jesus and for the word of God, who had not worshiped the beast or his image, and had not received *his* mark on their foreheads or on their hands. And they lived and reigned with Christ for a thousand years.

Believers

Forewarned of.

Matt 10:21 "Now brother will deliver up brother to death, and a father *his* child; and children will rise up against parents and cause them to be put to death.

Matt 24:9 "Then they will deliver you up to tribulation and kill you, and you will be hated by all nations for My name's sake.

John 16:2 They will put you out of the synagogues; yes, the time is coming that whoever kills you will think that he offers God service.

Should not fear.

Matt 10:28 And do not fear those who kill the body but cannot kill the soul. But rather fear Him who is able to destroy both soul and body in hell.

Rev 2:10 Do not fear any of those things which you are about to suffer. Indeed, the devil is about to throw *some* of you into prison, that you may be tested, and you will have tribulation ten days. Be faithful until death, and I will give you the crown of life.

Should be prepared for.

Matt 16:24–25 Then Jesus said to His disciples, "If anyone desires to come after Me, let him deny himself, and take up his cross, and follow Me. **25** For whoever desires to save his life will lose it, but whoever loses his life for My sake will find it.

Acts 21:13 Then Paul answered, "What do you mean by weeping and breaking my heart? For I am ready not only to be bound, but also to die at Jerusalem for the name of the Lord Jesus."

Resisting sin may lead to.

Heb 12:4 You have not yet resisted to bloodshed, striving against sin.

Will be avenged of.

Luke 11:50–51 that the blood of all the prophets which was shed from the foundation of the world may be required of this generation, **51** from the blood of Abel to the blood of Zechariah who perished between the altar and the temple. Yes, I say to you, it shall be required of this generation.

Rev 18:20–24 "Rejoice over her, O heaven, and *you* holy apostles and prophets, for God has avenged you on her!" **21** Then a mighty angel took up a stone like a great millstone and threw *it* into the sea, saying, "Thus with violence the great city Babylon shall be thrown down, and shall not be found anymore. **22** The sound of harpists, musicians, flutists, and trumpeters shall not be heard in you anymore. No craftsman of any craft shall be found in you anymore, and the sound of a millstone shall not be heard in you anymore. **23** The light of a lamp shall not shine in you anymore, and the voice of bridegroom and bride shall not be heard in you anymore. For your merchants were the great men of the earth, for by your sorcery all the nations were deceived. **24** And in her was found the blood of prophets and saints, and of all who were slain on the earth."

Reward of.

Rev 2:10 Do not fear any of those things which you are about to suffer. Indeed, the devil is about to throw *some* of you into prison, that you may be tested, and you will have tribulation ten days. Be faithful until death, and I will give you the crown of life.

Rev 6:11 Then a white robe was given to each of them; and it was said to them that they should rest a little while longer, until both *the number of* their fellow servants and their brethren, who would be killed as they *were*, was completed.

Inflicted at the instigation of the devil.

Rev 2:10 Do not fear any of those things which you are about to suffer. Indeed, the devil is about to throw *some* of you into prison, that you may be tested, and you will have tribulation ten days. Be faithful until death, and I will give you the crown of life.

Rev 2:13 "I know your works, and where you dwell, where Satan's throne *is*. And you hold fast to My name, and did not deny My faith even in the days in which Antipas *was* My faithful martyr, who was killed among you, where Satan dwells.

The apostate guilty of inflicting.

Rev 17:6 I saw the woman, drunk with the blood of the saints and with the blood of the martyrs of Jesus. And when I saw her, I marveled with great amazement.

Rev 18:24 And in her was found the blood of prophets and saints, and of all who were slain on the earth."

Exemplified by

Abel.

Gen 4:8 Now Cain talked with Abel his brother; and it came to pass, when they were in the field, that Cain rose up against Abel his brother and killed him.

1 John 3:12 not as Cain *who* was of the wicked one and murdered his brother. And why did he murder him? Because his works were evil and his brother's righteous.

Ahimelech and his fellow priests.

1 Sam 22:18–19 And the king said to Doeg, "You turn and kill the priests!" So Doeg the Edomite turned and struck the priests, and killed on that day eighty-five men who wore a linen ephod. **19** Also Nob, the city of the priests, he struck with the edge of the sword, both men and women, children and nursing infants, oxen and donkeys and sheep—with the edge of the sword.

Prophets and believers of old.

1 Kin 18:4 For so it was, while Jezebel massacred the prophets of the LORD, that Obadiah had taken one hundred prophets and hidden them, fifty to a cave, and had fed them with bread and water.)

1 Kin 19:10 So he said, "I have been very zealous for the LORD God of hosts; for the children of Israel have forsaken Your covenant, torn down Your altars, and killed Your prophets with the sword. I alone am left; and they seek to take my life."

Luke 11:50–51 that the blood of all the prophets which was shed from the foundation of the world may be required of this generation, **51** from the blood of Abel

to the blood of Zechariah who perished between the altar and the temple. Yes, I say to you, it shall be required of this generation.

Heb 11:37 They were stoned, they were sawn in two, were tempted, were slain with the sword. They wandered about in sheepskins and goatskins, being destitute, afflicted, tormented—

Urijah.

Jer 26:23 And they brought Urijah from Egypt and brought him to Jehoiakim the king, who killed him with the sword and cast his dead body into the graves of the common people.

John the Baptist.

Mark 6:27 Immediately the king sent an executioner and commanded his head to be brought. And he went and beheaded him in prison,

Peter.

John 21:18–19 Most assuredly, I say to you, when you were younger, you girded yourself and walked where you wished; but when you are old, you will stretch out your hands, and another will gird you and carry *you* where you do not wish." **19** This He spoke, signifying by what death he would glorify God. And when He had spoken this, He said to him, "Follow Me."

Stephen.

Acts 7:58 and they cast *him* out of the city and stoned *him*. And the witnesses laid down their clothes at the feet of a young man named Saul.

The early church.

Acts 9:1 Then Saul, still breathing threats and murder against the disciples of the Lord, went to the high priest

Acts 22:4 I persecuted this Way to the death, binding and delivering into prisons both men and women,

Acts 26:10 This I also did in Jerusalem, and many of the saints I shut up in prison, having received authority from the chief priests; and when they were put to death, I cast my vote against *them*.

James.

Acts 12:2 Then he killed James the brother of John with the sword.

Antipas.

Rev 2:13 "I know your works, and where you dwell, where Satan's throne *is*. And you hold fast to My name, and did not deny My faith even in the days in which Antipas *was* My faithful martyr, who was killed among you, where Satan dwells.

MASTERS

Authority of, established.

Col 3:22 Bondservants, obey in all things your masters according to the flesh, not with eyeservice, as menpleasers, but in sincerity of heart, fearing God.

1 Pet 2:18 Servants, *be* submissive to *your* masters with all fear, not only to the good and gentle, but also to the harsh.

Should, with their households,

Worship God.

Gen 35:3 Then let us arise and go up to Bethel; and I will make an altar there to God, who answered me in the day of my distress and has been with me in the way which I have gone."

Fear God.

Acts 10:2 a devout *man* and one who feared God with all his household, who gave alms generously to the people, and prayed to God always.

Serve God.

Josh 24:15 And if it seems evil to you to serve the LORD, choose for yourselves this day whom you will serve, whether the gods which your fathers served that *were* on the other side of the River, or the gods of the Amorites, in whose land you dwell. But as for me and my house, we will serve the LORD."

Observe the Sabbath.

Ex 20:10 but the seventh day *is* the Sabbath of the LORD your God. *In it* you shall do no work: you, nor your son, nor your daughter, nor your male servant, nor your female servant, nor your cattle, nor your stranger who *is* within your gates.

Deut 5:12–14 'Observe the Sabbath day, to keep it holy, as the LORD your God commanded you. **13** Six days you shall labor and do all your work, **14** but the seventh day *is* the Sabbath of the LORD your God. *In it* you shall do no work: you, nor your son, nor your daughter, nor your male servant, nor your female servant, nor your ox, nor your donkey, nor any of your cattle, nor your stranger who *is* within your gates, that your male servant and your female servant may rest as well as you.

Put away idols.

Gen 35:2 And Jacob said to his household and to all who *were* with him, "Put away the foreign gods that *are* among you, purify yourselves, and change your garments.

Should select faithful servants.

Gen 24:2 So Abraham said to the oldest servant of his house, who ruled over all that he had, "Please, put your hand under my thigh,

2 Kin 5:13–14 And his servants came near and spoke to him, and said, "My father, *if* the prophet had told you *to do* something great, would you not have done *it*? How much more then, when he says to you, 'Wash, and be clean'?" **14** So he went down and dipped seven times in the Jordan, according to the saying of the man of God; and his flesh was restored like the flesh of a little child, and he was clean.

Ps 101:6–7 My eyes *shall be* on the faithful of the land, That they may dwell with me; He who walks in a perfect way, He shall serve me. **7** He who works deceit shall not dwell within my house; He who tells lies shall not continue in my presence.

Duty of, toward servants,

To act justly.

Gen 31:7 Yet your father has deceived me and changed my wages ten times, but God did not allow him to hurt me.

Lev 19:13 'You shall not cheat your neighbor, nor rob *him*. The wages of him who is hired shall not remain with you all night until morning.

Deut 24:15 Each day you shall give *him* his wages, and not let the sun go down on it, for he *is* poor and has set his heart on it; lest he cry out against you to the LORD, and it be sin to you.

Job 31:13 "If I have despised the cause of my male or female servant When they complained against me,

Job 31:15 Did not He who made me in the womb make them? Did not the same One fashion us in the womb?

Col 4:1 Masters, give your bondservants what is just and fair, knowing that you also have a Master in heaven.

To deal with them in the fear of God.

Eph 6:9 And you, masters, do the same things to them, giving up threatening, knowing that your own Master also is in heaven, and there is no partiality with Him.

Col 4:1 Masters, give your bondservants what is just and fair, knowing that you also have a Master in heaven.

To esteem them highly, if believers.

Philem 1:16 no longer as a slave but more than a slave—a beloved brother, especially to me but how much more to you, both in the flesh and in the Lord.

To take care of them in sickness.

Luke 7:3 So when he heard about Jesus, he sent elders of the Jews to Him, pleading with Him to come and heal his servant.

Not to oppress them.

Lev 25:43 You shall not rule over him with rigor, but you shall fear your God.

Deut 24:14 "You shall not oppress a hired servant *who is* poor and needy, *whether* one of your brethren or one of the aliens who *is* in your land within your gates.

Benevolent, blessed.

Deut 15:18 It shall not seem hard to you when you send him away free from you; for he has been worth a double hired servant in serving you six years. Then the LORD your God will bless you in all that you do.

Unjust, denounced.

Jer 22:13 "Woe to him who builds his house by unrighteousness And his chambers by injustice, *Who* uses his neighbor's service without wages And gives him nothing for his work,

James 5:4 Indeed the wages of the laborers who mowed your fields, which you kept back by fraud, cry out; and the cries of the reapers have reached the ears of the Lord of Sabaoth.

Good—exemplified by

Abraham.

Gen 18:19 For I have known him, in order that he may command his children and his household after him, that they keep the way of the LORD, to do righteousness and justice, that the LORD may bring to Abraham what He has spoken to him."

Jacob.

Gen 35:2 And Jacob said to his household and to all who *were* with him, "Put away the foreign gods that *are* among you, purify yourselves, and change your garments.

Joshua.

Josh 24:15 And if it seems evil to you to serve the LORD, choose for yourselves this day whom you will serve, whether the gods which your fathers served that *were* on the other side of the River, or the gods of the Amorites, in whose land you dwell. But as for me and my house, we will serve the LORD."

A centurion.

Luke 7:2–3 And a certain centurion's servant, who was dear to him, was sick and ready to die. **3** So when he heard about Jesus, he sent elders of the Jews to Him, pleading with Him to come and heal his servant.

Cornelius.

Acts 10:2 a devout *man* and one who feared God with all his household, who gave alms generously to the people, and prayed to God always.

Bad—illustrated by

The Egyptians.

Ex 1:13–14 So the Egyptians made the children of Israel serve with rigor. **14** And they made their lives bitter with hard bondage—in mortar, in brick, and in all manner of service in the field. All their service in which they made them serve *was* with rigor.

Nabal.

1 Sam 25:17 Now therefore, know and consider what you will do, for harm is determined against our master and against all his household. For he *is such* a scoundrel that *one* cannot speak to him."

The Amalekite.

1 Sam 30:13 Then David said to him, "To whom do you *belong*, and where *are* you from?" And he said, "I *am* a young man from Egypt, servant of an Amalekite; and my master left me behind, because three days ago I fell sick.

MATURITY, SPIRITUAL

Expressed in freedom in Christ.

John 8:31–36 Then Jesus said to those Jews who believed Him, "If you abide in My word, you are My disciples indeed. **32** And you shall know the truth, and the truth shall make you free." **33** They answered Him, "We are Abraham's descendants, and have never been in bondage to anyone. How *can* You say, 'You will be made free'?" **34** Jesus answered them, "Most assuredly, I say to you, whoever commits sin is a slave of sin. **35** And a slave does not abide in the house forever, *but* a son abides forever. **36** Therefore if the Son makes you free, you shall be free indeed.

Christ the standard of.

Rom 8:29 For whom He foreknew, He also predestined *to be* conformed to the image of His Son, that He might be the firstborn among many brethren.

2 Cor 3:18 But we all, with unveiled face, beholding as in a mirror the glory of the Lord, are being transformed into the same image from glory to glory, just as by the Spirit of the Lord.

Eph 4:13–16 till we all come to the unity of the faith and of the knowledge of the Son of God, to a perfect man, to the measure of the stature of the fullness of Christ; **14** that we should no longer be children, tossed to and fro and carried about with every wind of doc-trine, by the trickery of men, in the cunning craftiness of deceitful plotting, **15** but, speaking the truth in love, may grow up in all things into Him who is the head—Christ— **16** from whom the whole body, joined and knit together by what every joint supplies, according to the effective working by which every part does its share, causes growth of the body for the edifying of itself in love.

Col 1:28–29 Him we preach, warning every man and teaching every man in all wisdom, that we may present every man perfect in Christ Jesus. **29** To this *end* I also labor, striving according to His working which works in me mightily.

Col 2:10 and you are complete in Him, who is the head of all principality and power.

Definition of.

1 Cor 11:1 Imitate me, just as I also *imitate* Christ.

Phil 3:12–14 Not that I have already attained, or am already perfected; but I press on, that I may lay hold of that for which Christ Jesus has also laid hold of me. **13** Brethren, I do not count myself to have apprehended; but one thing *I do*, forgetting those things which are behind and reaching forward to those things which are ahead, **14** I press toward the goal for the prize of the upward call of God in Christ Jesus.

Phil 3:19–20 whose end *is* destruction, whose god *is their* belly, and *whose* glory *is* in their shame—who set their mind on earthly things. **20** For our citizenship is in heaven, from which we also eagerly wait for the Savior, the Lord Jesus Christ,

1 John 2:6 He who says he abides in Him ought himself also to walk just as He walked.

1 John 3:2 Beloved, now we are children of God; and it has not yet been revealed what we shall be, but we know that when He is revealed, we shall be like Him, for we shall see Him as He is.

Cf. James 1:4; 1 Pet 5:10

Based on sound doctrine.

1 Tim 4:6 If you instruct the brethren in these things, you will be a good minister of Jesus Christ, nourished in the words of faith and of the good doctrine which you have carefully followed.

2 Tim 3:16–17 All Scripture *is* given by inspiration of God, and *is* profitable for doctrine, for reproof, for correction, for instruction in righteousness, **17** that the man of God may be complete, thoroughly equipped for every good work.

Titus 2:1 But as for you, speak the things which are proper for sound doctrine:

Reflected in submission to leaders.

1 Cor 16:15 I urge you, brethren—you know the household of Stephanas, that it is the firstfruits of Achaia, and *that* they have devoted themselves to the ministry of the saints—

1 Thess 5:12–14 And we urge you, brethren, to recognize those who labor among you, and are over you in the Lord and admonish you, **13** and to esteem them very highly in love for their work's sake. Be at peace among yourselves. **14** Now we exhort you, brethren, warn those who are unruly, comfort the fainthearted, uphold the weak, be patient with all.

Titus 3:1–2 Remind them to be subject to rulers and authorities, to obey, to be ready for every good work, **2** to speak evil of no one, to be peaceable, gentle, showing all humility to all men.

Heb 13:7 Remember those who rule over you, who have spoken the word of God to you, whose faith follow, considering the outcome of *their* conduct.

Heb 13:17 Obey those who rule over you, and be submissive, for they watch out for your souls, as those who must give account. Let them do so with joy and not with grief, for that would be unprofitable for you.

1 Pet 5:5–7 Likewise you younger people, submit yourselves to *your* elders. Yes, all of *you* be submissive to one another, and be clothed with humility, for *"God resists the proud, But gives grace to the humble."* **6** Therefore humble yourselves under the mighty hand of God, that He may exalt you in due time, **7** casting all your care upon Him, for He cares for you.

MEASUREMENTS

Unjust, an abomination to God.

Prov 20:10 Diverse weights *and* diverse measures, They *are* both alike, an abomination to the LORD.

Mic 6:10 Are there yet the treasures of wickedness In the house of the wicked, And the short measure *that is* an abomination?

The Jews not to be unjust in.

Lev 19:35 'You shall do no injustice in judgment, in measurement of length, weight, or volume.

Deut 25:14–15 You shall not have in your house differing measures, a large and a small. **15** You shall have a perfect and just weight, a perfect and just measure, that your days may be lengthened in the land which the LORD your God is giving you.

Of liquids and solids

Log.

Lev 14:10 "And on the eighth day he shall take two male lambs without blemish, one ewe lamb of the first year without blemish, three-tenths *of an ephah* of fine flour mixed with oil as a grain offering, and one log of oil.

Lev 14:15 And the priest shall take *some* of the log of oil, and pour *it* into the palm of his own left hand.

Kab.

2 Kin 6:25 And there was a great famine in Samaria; and indeed they besieged it until a donkey's head was *sold* for eighty *shekels* of silver, and one-fourth of a kab of dove droppings for five *shekels* of silver.

Omer (one-tenth of an ephah).

Ex 16:36 Now an omer *is* one-tenth of an ephah.

Lev 5:11 'But if he is not able to bring two turtledoves or two young pigeons, then he who sinned shall bring for his offering one-tenth of an ephah of fine flour as a sin offering. He shall put no oil on it, nor shall he put frankincense on it, for it *is* a sin offering.

Lev 14:10 "And on the eighth day he shall take two male lambs without blemish, one ewe lamb of the first year without blemish, three-tenths *of an ephah* of fine flour mixed with oil as a grain offering, and one log of oil.

Hin.

Ex 29:40 With the one lamb shall be one-tenth *of an ephah* of flour mixed with one-fourth of a hin of pressed oil, and one-fourth of a hin of wine *as* a drink offering.

Bath or ephah.

Is 5:10 For ten acres of vineyard shall yield one bath, And a homer of seed shall yield one ephah."

Ezek 45:11 The ephah and the bath shall be of the same measure, so that the bath contains one-tenth of a homer, and the ephah one-tenth of a homer; their measure shall be according to the homer.

Homer or kor.

Is 5:10 For ten acres of vineyard shall yield one bath, And a homer of seed shall yield one ephah."

Ezek 45:14 The ordinance concerning oil, the bath of oil, *is* one-tenth of a bath from a kor. A kor *is* a homer or ten baths, for ten baths *are* a homer.

Gallon.

John 2:6 Now there were set there six waterpots of stone, according to the manner of purification of the Jews, containing twenty or thirty gallons apiece.

Of length

Handbreadth.

Ex 25:25 You shall make for it a frame of a handbreadth all around, and you shall make a gold molding for the frame all around.

Ps 39:5 Indeed, You have made my days *as* handbreadths, And my age *is* as nothing before You; Certainly every man at his best state *is* but vapor. Selah

Span.

Ex 28:16 It shall be doubled into a square: a span *shall be* its length, and a span *shall be* its width.

1 Sam 17:4 And a champion went out from the camp of the Philistines, named Goliath, from Gath, whose height *was* six cubits and a span.

Cubit.

Gen 6:15–16 And this is how you shall make it: The length of the ark *shall be* three hundred cubits, its width fifty cubits, and its height thirty cubits. **16** You shall make a window for the ark, and you shall finish it to a cubit from above; and set the door of the ark in its side. You shall make it *with* lower, second, and third *decks.*

Deut 3:11 "For only Og king of Bashan remained of the remnant of the giants. Indeed his bedstead *was* an iron bedstead. (*Is* it not in Rabbah of the people of Ammon?) Nine cubits *is* its length and four cubits its width, according to the standard cubit.

Fathom.

Acts 27:28 And they took soundings and found *it* to be twenty fathoms; and when they had gone a little farther, they took soundings again and found *it* to be fifteen fathoms.

Mile.

Matt 5:41 And whoever compels you to go one mile, go with him two.

Luke 24:13 Now behold, two of them were traveling that same day to a village called Emmaus, which was seven miles from Jerusalem.

John 11:18 Now Bethany was near Jerusalem, about two miles away.

Rods and lines.

2 Sam 8:2 Then he defeated Moab. Forcing them down to the ground, he measured them off with a line. With two lines he measured off those to be put to death, and with one full line those to be kept alive. So the Moabites became David's servants, *and* brought tribute.

Jer 31:39 The surveyor's line shall again extend straight forward over the hill Gareb; then it shall turn toward Goath.

Ezek 40:3 He took me there, and behold, *there was* a man whose appearance *was* like the appearance of bronze. He had a line of flax and a measuring rod in his hand, and he stood in the gateway.

Rev 21:16 The city is laid out as a square; its length is as great as its breadth. And he measured the city with the reed: twelve thousand furlongs. Its length, breadth, and height are equal.

Were regulated by the standard of the sanctuary.

1 Chr 23:29 both with the showbread and the fine flour for the grain offering, with the unleavened cakes and *what is baked in* the pan, with what is mixed and with all kinds of measures and sizes;

Illustrative of

(Drinking tears in great measure) severe afflictions.

Ps 80:5 You have fed them with the bread of tears, And given them tears to drink in great measure.

(Weighing the waters by measure) God's infinite wisdom.

Job 28:23 God understands its way, And He knows its place.

Job 28:25 To establish a weight for the wind, And apportion the waters by measure.

(Measuring the dust of the earth) God's greatness.

Is 40:12 Who has measured the waters in the hollow of His hand, Measured heaven with a span And calculated the dust of the earth in a measure? Weighed the mountains in scales And the hills in a balance?

(The measure of our days) the shortness of life.

Ps 39:4 "LORD, make me to know my end, And what *is* the measure of my days, *That* I may know how frail I *am.*

(Drinking water, by measure) severe famine.

Ezek 4:11 You shall also drink water by measure, one-sixth of a hin; from time to time you shall drink.

Ezek 4:16 Moreover He said to me, "Son of man, surely I will cut off the supply of bread in Jerusalem; they shall eat bread by weight and with anxiety, and shall drink water by measure and with dread,

(The measure of the stature of Christ) perfection.

Eph 4:13 till we all come to the unity of the faith and of the knowledge of the Son of God, to a perfect man, to the measure of the stature of the fullness of Christ;

(Opening the mouth without measure) the insatiableness of hell.

Is 5:14 Therefore Sheol has enlarged itself And opened its mouth beyond measure; Their glory and their multitude and their pomp, And he who is jubilant, shall descend into it.

MEDO-PERSIAN KINGDOM

Extended from India to Ethiopia.

Esth 1:1 Now it came to pass in the days of Ahasuerus (this *was* the Ahasuerus who reigned over one hundred and twenty-seven provinces, from India to Ethiopia),

Peopled by descendants of Elam.

Gen 10:22 The sons of Shem *were* Elam, Asshur, Arphaxad, Lud, and Aram.

Illustrated by

Silver part of image in Nebuchadnezzar's dream.

Dan 2:32 This image's head *was* of fine gold, its chest and arms of silver, its belly and thighs of bronze,

Cf. Dan 2:39,45

A bear.

Dan 7:5 "And suddenly another beast, a second, like a bear. It was raised up on one side, and *had* three ribs in its mouth between its teeth. And they said thus to it: 'Arise, devour much flesh!'

A ram with two horns.

Dan 8:3 Then I lifted my eyes and saw, and there, standing beside the river, was a ram which had two horns, and the two horns *were* high; but one *was* higher than the other, and the higher *one* came up last.

Dan 8:20 The ram which you saw, having the two horns—*they are* the kings of Media and Persia.

Shushan a chief city of.

Esth 1:2 in those days when King Ahasuerus sat on the throne of his kingdom, which *was* in Shushan the citadel,

Esth 8:15 So Mordecai went out from the presence of the king in royal apparel of blue and white, with a great crown of gold and a garment of fine linen and purple; and the city of Shushan rejoiced and was glad.

Achmetha, or Ecbatana, a chief city of.

Ezra 6:2 And at Achmetha, in the palace that *is* in the province of Media, a scroll was found, and in it a record *was* written thus:

Divided into many provinces.

Esth 1:1 Now it came to pass in the days of Ahasuerus (this *was* the Ahasuerus who reigned over one hundred and twenty-seven provinces, from India to Ethiopia),

Dan 6:1 It pleased Darius to set over the kingdom one hundred and twenty satraps, to be over the whole kingdom;

Laws of, unalterable.

Dan 6:12 And they went before the king, and spoke concerning the king's decree: "Have you not signed a decree that every man who petitions any god or man within thirty days, except you, O king, shall be cast into the den of lions?" The king answered and said, "The thing *is* true, according to the law of the Medes and Persians, which does not alter."

Dan 6:15 Then these men approached the king, and said to the king, "Know, O king, that *it is* the law of the Medes and Persians that no decree or statute which the king establishes may be changed."

Ruled by absolute kings.

Esth 3:8 Then Haman said to King Ahasuerus, "There is a certain people scattered and dispersed among the people in all the provinces of your kingdom; their laws *are* different from all *other* people's, and they do not keep the king's laws. Therefore it *is* not fitting for the king to let them remain.

Esth 3:11 And the king said to Haman, "The money and the people *are* given to you, to do with them as seems good to you."

Esth 7:9 Now Harbonah, one of the eunuchs, said to the king, "Look! The gallows, fifty cubits high, which Haman made for Mordecai, who spoke good on the king's behalf, is standing at the house of Haman." Then the king said, "Hang him on it!"

Kings of, mentioned in Scripture

Cyrus.

Ezra 1:1 Now in the first year of Cyrus king of Persia, that the word of the LORD by the mouth of Jeremiah might be fulfilled, the LORD stirred up the spirit of Cyrus king of Persia, so that he made a proclamation throughout all his kingdom, and also *put it* in writing, saying,

Ahasuerus.

Ezra 4:6 In the reign of Ahasuerus, in the beginning of his reign, they wrote an accusation against the inhabitants of Judah and Jerusalem.

Artaxerxes (a usurper).

Ezra 4:7 In the days of Artaxerxes also, Bishlam, Mithredath, Tabel, and the rest of their companions wrote to Artaxerxes king of Persia; and the letter *was* written in Aramaic script, and translated into the Aramaic language.

Darius.

Ezra 6:1 Then King Darius issued a decree, and a search was made in the archives, where the treasures were stored in Babylon.

Dan 5:31 And Darius the Mede received the kingdom, *being* about sixty-two years old.

Xerxes.

Dan 11:2 And now I will tell you the truth: Behold, three more kings will arise in Persia, and the fourth shall be far richer than *them* all; by his strength, through his riches, he shall stir up all against the realm of Greece.

Artaxerxes or Ahasuerus.

Ezra 6:14 So the elders of the Jews built, and they prospered through the prophesying of Haggai the prophet and Zechariah the son of Iddo. And they built and finished *it*, according to the commandment of the God of Israel, and according to the command of Cyrus, Darius, and Artaxerxes king of Persia.

Ezra 7:1 Now after these things, in the reign of Artaxerxes king of Persia, Ezra the son of Seraiah, the son of Azariah, the son of Hilkiah,

Esth 1:1 Now it came to pass in the days of Ahasuerus (this *was* the Ahasuerus who reigned over one hundred and twenty-seven provinces, from India to Ethiopia),

Kings of

Called kings of Assyria.

Ezra 6:22 And they kept the Feast of Unleavened Bread seven days with joy; for the LORD made them joyful, and turned the heart of the king of Assyria toward them, to strengthen their hands in the work of the house of God, the God of Israel.

Called kings of Babylon.

Neh 13:6 But during all this I was not in Jerusalem, for in the thirty-second year of Artaxerxes king of Babylon I had returned to the king. Then after certain days I obtained leave from the king,

Styled themselves king of kings.

Ezra 7:12 Artaxerxes, king of kings, To Ezra the priest, a scribe of the Law of the God of heaven: Perfect *peace*, and so forth.

Dwelt in citadels.

Esth 1:2 in those days when King Ahasuerus sat on the throne of his kingdom, which *was* in Shushan the citadel,

Esth 8:14 The couriers who rode on royal horses went out, hastened and pressed on by the king's command. And the decree was issued in Shushan the citadel.

Were very rich.

Esth 1:4 when he showed the riches of his glorious kingdom and the splendor of his excellent majesty for many days, one hundred and eighty days *in all*.

Entertained magnificently.

Esth 1:3 *that* in the third year of his reign he made a feast for all his officials and servants—the powers of Persia and Media, the nobles, and the princes of the provinces *being* before him—

Esth 1:5 And when these days were completed, the king made a feast lasting seven days for all the people who were present in Shushan the citadel, from great to small, in the court of the garden of the king's palace.

Esth 1:7 And they served drinks in golden vessels, each vessel being different from the other, with royal wine in abundance, according to the generosity of the king.

Held in their hand a golden scepter.

Esth 5:2 So it was, when the king saw Queen Esther standing in the court, *that* she found favor in his sight, and the king held out to Esther the golden scepter that *was* in his hand. Then Esther went near and touched the top of the scepter.

Put to death all who approached without permission.

Esth 4:11 "All the king's servants and the people of the king's provinces know that any man or woman who goes into the inner court to the king, who has not been called, *he has* but one law: put *all* to death, except the one to whom the king holds out the golden scepter, that he may live. Yet I myself have not been called to go in to the king these thirty days."

Esth 4:16 "Go, gather all the Jews who are present in Shushan, and fast for me; neither eat nor drink for three days, night or day. My maids and I will fast likewise. And so I will go to the king, which *is* against the law; and if I perish, I perish!"

Celebrated for wise men.

Esth 1:13 Then the king said to the wise men who understood the times (for this *was* the king's manner toward all who knew law and justice,

Matt 2:1 Now after Jesus was born in Bethlehem of Judea in the days of Herod the king, behold, wise men from the East came to Jerusalem,

People of, warlike.

Ezek 27:10 "Those from Persia, Lydia, and Libya Were in your army as men of war; They hung shield and helmet in you; They gave splendor to you.

Ezek 38:5 Persia, Ethiopia, and Libya are with them, all of them *with* shield and helmet;

Peculiar customs in.

Esth 1:8 In accordance with the law, the drinking was not compulsory; for so the king had ordered all the officers of his household, that they should do according to each man's pleasure.

Esth 2:12–13 Each young woman's turn came to go in to King Ahasuerus after she had completed twelve months' preparation, according to the regulations for the women, for thus were the days of their preparation apportioned: six months with oil of myrrh, and six months with perfumes and preparations for beautifying women. **13** Thus *prepared, each* young woman went to the king, and she was given whatever she desired to take with her from the women's quarters to the king's palace.

Babylon conquered by.

Dan 5:20 But when his heart was lifted up, and his spirit was hardened in pride, he was deposed from his kingly throne, and they took his glory from him.

Dan 5:31 And Darius the Mede received the kingdom, *being* about sixty-two years old.

The Jews delivered from captivity by means of.

2 Chr 36:20 And those who escaped from the sword he carried away to Babylon, where they became servants to him and his sons until the rule of the kingdom of Persia,

2 Chr 36:22–23 Now in the first year of Cyrus king of Persia, that the word of the LORD by the mouth of Jeremiah might be fulfilled, the LORD stirred up the spirit of Cyrus king of Persia, so that he made a proclamation throughout all his kingdom, and also *put it* in writing, saying, **23** Thus says Cyrus king of Persia: All the kingdoms of the earth the LORD God of heaven has given me. And He has commanded me to build Him a house at Jerusalem which is in Judah. Who *is* among you of all His people? May the LORD his God *be* with him, and let him go up!

Ezra 1:1–4 Now in the first year of Cyrus king of Persia, that the word of the LORD by the mouth of Jeremiah might be fulfilled, the LORD stirred up the spirit of Cyrus king of Persia, so that he made a proclamation throughout all his kingdom, and also *put it* in writing, saying, **2** Thus says Cyrus king of Persia: All the kingdoms of the earth the LORD God of heaven has given me. And He has commanded me to build Him a house at Jerusalem which *is* in Judah. **3** Who *is* among you of all His people? May his God be with him, and let him go up to Jerusalem which *is* in Judah, and build the house of the LORD God of Israel

(He *is* God), which *is* in Jerusalem. **4** And whoever is left in any place where he dwells, let the men of his place help him with silver and gold, with goods and livestock, besides the freewill offerings for the house of God which *is* in Jerusalem.

Predictions respecting,

Extensive conquest.

Dan 8:4 I saw the ram pushing westward, northward, and southward, so that no animal could withstand him; nor *was there any* that could deliver from his hand, but he did according to his will and became great.

Conquest of Babylon.

Is 21:1–2 The burden against the Wilderness of the Sea. As whirlwinds in the South pass through, *So* it comes from the desert, from a terrible land. **2** A distressing vision is declared to me; The treacherous dealer deals treacherously, And the plunderer plunders. Go up, O Elam! Besiege, O Media! All its sighing I have made to cease.

Dan 5:28 PERES: Your kingdom has been divided, and given to the Medes and Persians."

Deliverance of the Jews.

Is 44:28 Who says of Cyrus, '*He is* My shepherd, And he shall perform all My pleasure, Saying to Jerusalem, "You shall be built," And to the temple, "Your foundation shall be laid." '

Is 45:1–4 "Thus says the LORD to His anointed, To Cyrus, whose right hand I have held—To subdue nations before him And loose the armor of kings, To open before him the double doors, So that the gates will not be shut: **2** 'I will go before you And make the crooked places straight; I will break in pieces the gates of bronze And cut the bars of iron. **3** I will give you the treasures of darkness And hidden riches of secret places, That you may know that I, the LORD, Who call *you* by your name, *Am* the God of Israel. **4** For Jacob My servant's sake, And Israel My elect, I have even called you by your name; I have named you, though you have not known Me.

Invasion of Greece under Xerxes.

Dan 11:2 And now I will tell you the truth: Behold, three more kings will arise in Persia, and the fourth shall be far richer than *them* all; by his strength, through his riches, he shall stir up all against the realm of Greece.

Downfall by Alexander.

Dan 8:6–7 Then he came to the ram that had two horns, which I had seen standing beside the river, and ran at him with furious power. **7** And I saw him confronting the ram; he was moved with rage against him, attacked the ram, and broke his two horns. There was no power in the ram to withstand him, but he cast him down to the ground and trampled him; and there was no one that could deliver the ram from his hand.

Dan 11:3 Then a mighty king shall arise, who shall rule with great dominion, and do according to his will.

MEEKNESS (GENTLENESS)
Christ: His example and teaching of.

Ps 45:4 And in Your majesty ride prosperously because

of truth, humility, *and* righteousness; And Your right hand shall teach You awesome things.

Is 53:7 He was oppressed and He was afflicted, Yet He opened not His mouth; He was led as a lamb to the slaughter, And as a sheep before its shearers is silent, So He opened not His mouth.

Is 61:1 "The Spirit of the Lord GOD *is* upon Me, Because the LORD has anointed Me To preach good tidings to the poor; He has sent Me to heal the brokenhearted, To proclaim liberty to the captives, And the opening of the prison to *those who are* bound;

Matt 5:38–45 "You have heard that it was said, *'An eye for an eye and a tooth for a tooth.'* **39** But I tell you not to resist an evil person. But whoever slaps you on your right cheek, turn the other to him also. **40** If anyone wants to sue you and take away your tunic, let him have *your* cloak also. **41** And whoever compels you to go one mile, go with him two. **42** Give to him who asks you, and from him who wants to borrow from you do not turn away. **43** "You have heard that it was said, *'You shall love your neighbor* and hate your enemy.' **44** But I say to you, love your enemies, bless those who curse you, do good to those who hate you, and pray for those who spitefully use you and persecute you, **45** that you may be sons of your Father in heaven; for He makes His sun rise on the evil and on the good, and sends rain on the just and on the unjust.

Matt 11:29 Take My yoke upon you and learn from Me, for I am gentle and lowly in heart, and you will find rest for your souls.

Matt 21:5 *"Tell the daughter of Zion, 'Behold, your King is coming to you, Lowly, and sitting on a donkey, A colt, the foal of a donkey.' "*

2 Cor 10:1 Now I, Paul, myself am pleading with you by the meekness and gentleness of Christ—who in presence *am* lowly among you, but being absent am bold toward you.

1 Pet 2:21–23 For to this you were called, because Christ also suffered for us, leaving us an example, that you should follow His steps: **22** *"Who committed no sin, Nor was deceit found in His mouth"*; **23** who, when He was reviled, did not revile in return; when He suffered, He did not threaten, but committed *Himself* to Him who judges righteously;

A fruit of the Spirit.

Gal 5:22–23 But the fruit of the Spirit is love, joy, peace, longsuffering, kindness, goodness, faithfulness, **23** gentleness, self-control. Against such there is no law.

Believers should

Exhibit.

Zeph 2:3 Seek the LORD, all you meek of the earth, Who have upheld His justice. Seek righteousness, seek humility. It may be that you will be hidden In the day of the LORD's anger.

Col 3:12–13 Therefore, as *the* elect of God, holy and beloved, put on tender mercies, kindness, humility, meekness, longsuffering; **13** bearing with one another, and forgiving one another, if anyone has a complaint against another; even as Christ forgave you, so you also *must do.*

Titus 3:2 to speak evil of no one, to be peaceable, gentle, showing all humility to all men.

James 3:13 Who *is* wise and understanding among you? Let him show by good conduct *that* his works *are done* in the meekness of wisdom.

1 Pet 3:4 rather *let it be* the hidden person of the heart, with the incorruptible *beauty* of a gentle and quiet spirit, which is very precious in the sight of God.

Receive the Word of God with.

James 1:21 Therefore lay aside all filthiness and overflow of wickedness, and receive with meekness the implanted word, which is able to save your souls.

Defend their hope with.

1 Pet 3:15 But sanctify the Lord God in your hearts, and always *be* ready to *give* a defense to everyone who asks you a reason for the hope that is in you, with meekness and fear;

Restore the erring with.

Gal 6:1 Brethren, if a man is overtaken in any trespass, you who *are* spiritual restore such a one in a spirit of gentleness, considering yourself lest you also be tempted.

Ministers should

Follow after.

1 Tim 6:11 But you, O man of God, flee these things and pursue righteousness, godliness, faith, love, patience, gentleness.

Instruct opposers with.

2 Tim 2:24–25 And a servant of the Lord must not quarrel but be gentle to all, able to teach, patient, **25** in humility correcting those who are in opposition, if God perhaps will grant them repentance, so that they may know the truth,

Urge, on their people.

Titus 3:1–2 Remind them to be subject to rulers and authorities, to obey, to be ready for every good work, **2** to speak evil of no one, to be peaceable, gentle, showing all humility to all men.

A characteristic of divine wisdom.

James 3:17 But the wisdom that is from above is first pure, then peaceable, gentle, willing to yield, full of mercy and good fruits, without partiality and without hypocrisy.

Necessary to a Christian walk.

1 Cor 6:7 Now therefore, it is already an utter failure for you that you go to law against one another. Why do you not rather accept wrong? Why do you not rather *let yourselves* be cheated?

Eph 4:1–2 I, therefore, the prisoner of the Lord, beseech you to walk worthy of the calling with which you were called, **2** with all lowliness and gentleness, with longsuffering, bearing with one another in love,

Blessedness of.

Ps 22:26 The poor shall eat and be satisfied; Those who seek Him will praise the LORD. Let your heart live forever!

Ps 25:9 The humble He guides in justice, And the humble He teaches His way.

Ps 37:11 But the meek shall inherit the earth, And shall delight themselves in the abundance of peace.

Ps 76:9 When God arose to judgment, To deliver all the oppressed of the earth. Selah

Ps 147:6 The LORD lifts up the humble; He casts the wicked down to the ground.

Ps 149:4 For the LORD takes pleasure in His people; He will beautify the humble with salvation.

Is 29:19 The humble also shall increase *their* joy in the LORD, And the poor among men shall rejoice In the Holy One of Israel.

Matt 5:5 Blessed *are* the meek, For they shall inherit the earth.

Matt 23:12 And whoever exalts himself will be humbled, and he who humbles himself will be exalted.

Exemplified by

Moses.

Num 12:3 (Now the man Moses *was* very humble, more than all men who *were* on the face of the earth.)

David.

1 Sam 30:6 Now David was greatly distressed, for the people spoke of stoning him, because the soul of all the people was grieved, every man for his sons and his daughters. But David strengthened himself in the LORD his God.

2 Sam 16:9–12 Then Abishai the son of Zeruiah said to the king, "Why should this dead dog curse my lord the king? Please, let me go over and take off his head!" **10** But the king said, "What have I to do with you, you sons of Zeruiah? So let him curse, because the LORD has said to him, 'Curse David.' Who then shall say, 'Why have you done so?' " **11** And David said to Abishai and all his servants, "See how my son who came from my own body seeks my life. How much more now *may this* Benjamite? Let him alone, and let him curse; for so the LORD has ordered him. **12** It may be that the LORD will look on my affliction, and that the LORD will repay me with good for his cursing this day."

Paul.

1 Cor 4:12 And we labor, working with our own hands. Being reviled, we bless; being persecuted, we endure;

1 Thess 2:7 But we were gentle among you, just as a nursing *mother* cherishes her own children.

MERCY

Commanded.

2 Kin 6:21–23 Now when the king of Israel saw them, he said to Elisha, "My father, shall I kill *them?* Shall I kill *them?*" **22** But he answered, "You shall not kill *them.* Would you kill those whom you have taken captive with your sword and your bow? Set food and water before them, that they may eat and drink and go to their master." **23** Then he prepared a great feast for them; and after they ate and drank, he sent them away and they went to their master. So the bands of Syrian *raiders* came no more into the land of Israel.

Prov 3:3 Let not mercy and truth forsake you; Bind them around your neck, Write them on the tablet of your heart,

Hos 12:6 So you, by *the help of* your God, return; Observe mercy and justice, And wait on your God continually.

Luke 6:36 Therefore be merciful, just as your Father also is merciful.

Rom 12:20–21 Therefore *"If your enemy is hungry, feed him; If he is thirsty, give him a drink; For in so doing you will heap coals of fire on his head."* **21** Do not be overcome by evil, but overcome evil with good.

Col 3:12 Therefore, as *the* elect of God, holy and beloved, put on tender mercies, kindness, humility, meekness, longsuffering;

Characteristic of believers.

Ps 37:26 *He is* ever merciful, and lends; And his descendants *are* blessed.

Is 57:1 The righteous perishes, And no man takes *it* to heart; Merciful men *are* taken away, While no one considers That the righteous is taken away from evil.

Should be shown

With cheerfulness.

Rom 12:8 he who exhorts, in exhortation; he who gives, with liberality; he who leads, with diligence; he who shows mercy, with cheerfulness.

To our brethren.

Zech 7:9 "Thus says the LORD of hosts: 'Execute true justice, Show mercy and compassion Everyone to his brother.

To those in distress.

Luke 10:37 And he said, "He who showed mercy on him." Then Jesus said to him, "Go and do likewise."

To the poor.

Prov 14:31 He who oppresses the poor reproaches his Maker, But he who honors Him has mercy on the needy.

Dan 4:27 Therefore, O king, let my advice be acceptable to you; break off your sins by *being* righteous, and your iniquities by showing mercy to *the* poor. Perhaps there may be a lengthening of your prosperity."

To backsliders.

Luke 15:18–20 I will arise and go to my father, and will say to him, "Father, I have sinned against heaven and before you, **19** and I am no longer worthy to be called your son. Make me like one of your hired servants." ' **20** "And he arose and came to his father. But when he was still a great way off, his father saw him and had compassion, and ran and fell on his neck and kissed him.

2 Cor 2:6–8 This punishment which *was inflicted* by the majority *is* sufficient for such a man, **7** so that, on the contrary, you *ought* rather to forgive and comfort *him,* lest perhaps such a one be swallowed up with too much sorrow. **8** Therefore I urge you to reaffirm *your* love to him.

To animals.

Prov 12:10 A righteous *man* regards the life of his animal, But the tender mercies of the wicked *are* cruel.

Upholds the throne of kings.

Prov 20:28 Mercy and truth preserve the king, And by lovingkindness he upholds his throne.

Blessedness of showing.

Prov 11:17 The merciful man does good for his own soul, But *he who is* cruel troubles his own flesh.

Prov 14:21 He who despises his neighbor sins; But he who has mercy on the poor, happy *is* he.

Matt 5:7 Blessed *are* the merciful, For they shall obtain mercy.

Denunciations against those devoid of.

Hos 4:1 Hear the word of the LORD, You children of Israel, For the LORD *brings* a charge against the inhabitants of the land: "There is no truth or mercy Or knowledge of God in the land.

Hos 4:3 Therefore the land will mourn; And everyone who dwells there will waste away With the beasts of the field And the birds of the air; Even the fish of the sea will be taken away.

Matt 18:23–25 Therefore the kingdom of heaven is like a certain king who wanted to settle accounts with his servants. **24** And when he had begun to settle accounts, one was brought to him who owed him ten thousand talents. **25** But as he was not able to pay, his master commanded that he be sold, with his wife and children and all that he had, and that payment be made.

Matt 23:23 "Woe to you, scribes and Pharisees, hypocrites! For you pay tithe of mint and anise and cummin, and have neglected the weightier *matters* of the law: justice and mercy and faith. These you ought to have done, without leaving the others undone.

James 2:13 For judgment is without mercy to the one who has shown no mercy. Mercy triumphs over judgment.

MERCY SEAT

Moses commanded to make.

Ex 25:17 "You shall make a mercy seat of pure gold; two and a half cubits *shall be* its length and a cubit and a half its width.

Bezalel given wisdom to make.

Ex 31:2–3 "See, I have called by name Bezalel the son of Uri, the son of Hur, of the tribe of Judah. **3** And I have filled him with the Spirit of God, in wisdom, in understanding, in knowledge, and in all *manner of* workmanship,

Ex 31:7 the tabernacle of meeting, the ark of the Testimony and the mercy seat that *is* on it, and all the furniture of the tabernacle—

Made of pure gold.

Ex 25:17 "You shall make a mercy seat of pure gold; two and a half cubits *shall be* its length and a cubit and a half its width.

Ex 37:6 He also made the mercy seat of pure gold; two and a half cubits *was* its length and a cubit and a half its width.

Cherubim at each end of.

Ex 25:18–20 And you shall make two cherubim of gold; of hammered work you shall make them at the two ends of the mercy seat. **19** Make one cherub at one end, and the other cherub at the other end; you shall make the cherubim at the two ends of it *of one piece* with the mercy seat. **20** And the cherubim shall stretch out *their* wings above, covering the mercy seat with their wings, and they shall face one another; the faces of the cherubim *shall be* toward the mercy seat.

Heb 9:5 and above it were the cherubim of glory overshadowing the mercy seat. Of these things we cannot now speak in detail.

Placed upon the ark of Testimony.

Ex 25:21 You shall put the mercy seat on top of the ark, and in the ark you shall put the Testimony that I will give you.

Ex 26:34 You shall put the mercy seat upon the ark of the Testimony in the Most Holy.

Ex 40:20 He took the Testimony and put *it* into the ark, inserted the poles through the rings of the ark, and put the mercy seat on top of the ark.

God

Appeared over it in the cloud.

Lev 16:2 and the LORD said to Moses: "Tell Aaron your brother not to come at *just* any time into the Holy *Place* inside the veil, before the mercy seat which *is* on the ark, lest he die; for I will appear in the cloud above the mercy seat.

Dwelt over.

Ps 80:1 Give ear, O Shepherd of Israel, You who lead Joseph like a flock; You who dwell *between* the cherubim, shine forth!

Spoke from above.

Ex 25:22 And there I will meet with you, and I will speak with you from above the mercy seat, from between the two cherubim which *are* on the ark of the Testimony, about everything which I will give you in commandment to the children of Israel.

Num 7:89 Now when Moses went into the tabernacle of meeting to speak with Him, he heard the voice of One speaking to him from above the mercy seat that *was* on the ark of the Testimony, from between the two cherubim; thus He spoke to him.

On the day of atonement.

Lev 16:13–15 And he shall put the incense on the fire before the LORD, that the cloud of incense may cover the mercy seat that *is* on the Testimony, lest he die. **14** He shall take some of the blood of the bull and sprinkle *it* with his finger on the mercy seat on the east *side;* and before the mercy seat he shall sprinkle some of the blood with his finger seven times. **15** "Then he shall kill the goat of the sin offering, which *is* for the people, bring its blood inside the veil, do with that blood as he did with the blood of the bull, and sprinkle it on the mercy seat and before the mercy seat.

Illustrative of

Christ.

Rom 3:25 whom God set forth *as* a propitiation by His blood, through faith, to demonstrate His righteousness, because in His forbearance God had passed over the sins that were previously committed,

Heb 9:3 and behind the second veil, the part of the tabernacle which is called the Holiest of All,

The throne of grace.

Heb 4:16 Let us therefore come boldly to the throne of grace, that we may obtain mercy and find grace to help in time of need.

MESSENGER

Divine,

To Joshua.

Josh 5:13–15 And it came to pass, when Joshua was by Jericho, that he lifted his eyes and looked, and behold, a Man stood opposite him with His sword drawn in His hand. And Joshua went to Him and said to Him, "*Are* You for us or for our adversaries?" **14** So He said, "No, but *as* Commander of the army of the LORD I have now come." And Joshua fell on his face to the earth and worshiped, and said to Him, "What does my Lord say to His servant?" **15** Then the Commander of the LORD's army said to Joshua, "Take your sandal off your foot, for the place where you stand *is* holy." And Joshua did so.

To the Israelites.

Judg 2:1–4 Then the Angel of the LORD came up from Gilgal to Bochim, and said: "I led you up from Egypt and brought you to the land of which I swore to your fathers; and I said, 'I will never break My covenant with you. **2** And you shall make no covenant with the inhabitants of this land; you shall tear down their altars.' But you have not obeyed My voice. Why have you done this? **3** Therefore I also said, 'I will not drive them out before you; but they shall be *thorns* in your side, and their gods shall be a snare to you.' " **4** So it was, when the Angel of the LORD spoke these words to all the children of Israel, that the people lifted up their voices and wept.

To Gideon. **Judg 6:11–24**

To Manoah and wife. **Judg 13:3–23**

To Elijah.

1 Kin 19:7 And the angel of the LORD came back the second time, and touched him, and said, "Arise *and* eat, because the journey *is* too great for you."

2 Kin 1:3–4 But the angel of the LORD said to Elijah the Tishbite, "Arise, go up to meet the messengers of the king of Samaria, and say to them, '*Is it* because *there is* no God in Israel *that* you are going to inquire of Baal-Zebub, the god of Ekron?' **4** Now therefore, thus says the LORD: 'You shall not come down from the bed to which you have gone up, but you shall surely die.' " So Elijah departed.

To Daniel.

Dan 10:4–6 Now on the twenty-fourth day of the first month, as I was by the side of the great river, that *is,* the Tigris, **5** I lifted my eyes and looked, and behold, a certain man clothed in linen, whose waist *was* girded with gold of Uphaz! **6** His body *was* like beryl, his face like the appearance of lightning, his eyes like torches of fire, his arms and feet like burnished bronze in color, and the sound of his words like the voice of a multitude.

Dan 10:10–21 Suddenly, a hand touched me, which made me tremble on my knees and *on* the palms of my hands. **11** And he said to me, "O Daniel, man greatly beloved, understand the words that I speak to you, and stand upright, for I have now been sent to you." While he was speaking this word to me, I stood trembling. **12** Then he said to me, "Do not fear, Daniel, for from the first day that you set your heart to understand, and to humble yourself before your God, your words were heard; and I have come because of your words. **13** But the prince of the kingdom of Persia withstood me twenty-one days; and behold, Michael, one of the chief princes, came to help me, for I had been left alone there with the kings of Persia. **14** Now I have come to make you understand what will happen to your people in the latter days, for the vision *refers* to *many* days yet *to come*." **15** When he had spoken such words to me, I turned my face toward the ground and became speechless. **16** And suddenly, *one* having the likeness of the sons of men touched my lips; then I opened my mouth and spoke, saying to him who stood before me, "My lord, because of the vision my sorrows have overwhelmed me, and I have retained no strength. **17** For how can this servant of my lord talk with you, my lord? As for me, no strength remains in me now, nor is any breath left in me." **18** Then again, *the one* having the likeness of a man touched me and strengthened me. **19** And he said, "O man greatly beloved, fear not! Peace *be* to you; be strong, yes, be strong!" So when he spoke to me I was strengthened, and said, "Let my lord speak, for you have strengthened me." **20** Then he said, "Do you know why I have come to you? And now I must return to fight with the prince of Persia; and when I have gone forth, indeed the prince of Greece will come. **21** But I will tell you what is noted in the Scripture of Truth. (No one upholds me against these, except Michael your prince.

To Zechariah.

Zech 3:1–2 Then he showed me Joshua the high priest standing before the Angel of the LORD, and Satan standing at his right hand to oppose him. **2** And the LORD said to Satan, "The LORD rebuke you, Satan! The LORD who has chosen Jerusalem rebuke you! *Is* this not a brand plucked from the fire?"

Zech 3:6–7 Then the Angel of the LORD admonished Joshua, saying, **7** "Thus says the LORD of hosts: 'If you will walk in My ways, And if you will keep My command, Then you shall also judge My house, And likewise have charge of My courts; I will give you places to walk Among these who stand here.

Zech 4:1–2 Now the angel who talked with me came back and wakened me, as a man who is wakened out of his sleep. **2** And he said to me, "What do you see?" So I said, "I am looking, and there *is* a lampstand of solid gold with a bowl on top of it, and on the *stand* seven lamps with seven pipes to the seven lamps.

Zech 4:5–6 Then the angel who talked with me answered and said to me, "Do you not know what these are?" And I said, "No, my lord." **6** So he answered and said to me: "This *is* the word of the LORD to Zerubbabel: 'Not by might nor by power, but by My Spirit,' Says the LORD of hosts.

Ones sent by Nehemiah.

Neh 6:3 So I sent messengers to them, saying, "I *am* doing a great work, so that I cannot come down. Why should the work cease while I leave it and go down to you?"

Applied to Israel.

Is 42:19 Who *is* blind but My servant, Or deaf as My messenger *whom* I send? Who *is* blind as *he who is* perfect, And blind as the LORD's servant?

Applied to John the Baptist.

Mal 3:1–3 "Behold, I send My messenger, And he will prepare the way before Me. And the Lord, whom you seek, Will suddenly come to His temple, Even the Messenger of the covenant, In whom you delight. Behold, He is coming," Says the LORD of hosts. 2 "But who can endure the day of His coming? And who can stand when He appears? For He *is* like a refiner's fire And like launderers' soap. 3 He will sit as a refiner and a purifier of silver; He will purify the sons of Levi, And purge them as gold and silver, That they may offer to the LORD An offering in righteousness.

Matt 3:3 For this is he who was spoken of by the prophet Isaiah, saying: *"The voice of one crying in the wilderness: 'Prepare the way of the LORD; Make His paths straight.' "*

Matt 11:10 For this is *he* of whom it is written: *'Behold, I send My messenger before Your face, Who will prepare Your way before You.'*

Matt 11:14 And if you are willing to receive *it*, he is Elijah who is to come.

Matt 17:12–13 But I say to you that Elijah has come already, and they did not know him but did to him whatever they wished. Likewise the Son of Man is also about to suffer at their hands." 13 Then the disciples understood that He spoke to them of John the Baptist.

Mark 1:2 As it is written in the Prophets: *"Behold, I send My messenger before Your face, Who will prepare Your way before You."*

Luke 1:17 He will also go before Him in the spirit and power of Elijah, *'to turn the hearts of the fathers to the children,'* and the disobedient to the wisdom of the just, to make ready a people prepared for the Lord."

Luke 7:26–27 But what did you go out to see? A prophet? Yes, I say to you, and more than a prophet. 27 This is *he* of whom it is written: *'Behold, I send My messenger before Your face, Who will prepare Your way before You.'*

John 1:23 He said: "I *am* 'The voice of one crying in the wilderness: "Make straight the way of the LORD," ' as the prophet Isaiah said."

Cf. Is 40:3; Mal 4:5

Demonic ones.

2 Cor 11:14–15 And no wonder! For Satan himself transforms himself into an angel of light. 15 Therefore *it is* no great thing if his ministers also transform themselves into ministers of righteousness, whose end will be according to their works.

2 Cor 12:7 And lest I should be exalted above measure by the abundance of the revelations, a thorn in the flesh was given to me, a messenger of Satan to buffet me, lest I be exalted above measure.

Applies to all believers.

2 Cor 5:20 Now then, we are ambassadors for Christ, as though God were pleading through us: we implore *you* on Christ's behalf, be reconciled to God.

Must be discerning toward.

Gal 1:8–9 But even if we, or an angel from heaven, preach any other gospel to you than what we have preached to you, let him be accursed. 9 As we have said before, so now I say again, if anyone preaches any other gospel to you than what you have received, let him be accursed.

Applied to Epaphroditus.

Phil 2:25 Yet I considered it necessary to send to you Epaphroditus, my brother, fellow worker, and fellow soldier, but your messenger and the one who ministered to my need;

Applied to ones in the seven churches of Asia.

Rev 1:20 The mystery of the seven stars which you saw in My right hand, and the seven golden lampstands: The seven stars are the angels of the seven churches, and the seven lampstands which you saw are the seven churches.

MESSIAH, THE

He was foreseen

As coming out of Judah.

Gen 49:10 The scepter shall not depart from Judah, Nor a lawgiver from between his feet, Until Shiloh comes; And to Him *shall be* the obedience of the people.

Mic 5:2–5 "But you, Bethlehem Ephrathah, *Though* you are little among the thousands of Judah, *Yet* out of you shall come forth to Me The One to be Ruler in Israel, Whose goings forth *are* from of old, From everlasting." 3 Therefore He shall give them up, Until the time *that* she who is in labor has given birth; Then the remnant of His brethren Shall return to the children of Israel. 4 And He shall stand and feed *His flock* In the strength of the LORD, In the majesty of the name of the LORD His God; And they shall abide, For now He shall be great To the ends of the earth; 5 And this *One* shall be peace. When the Assyrian comes into our land, And when he treads in our palaces, Then we will raise against him Seven shepherds and eight princely men.

Cf. Num 24:8–9; Rev 5:5

By Moses.

Deut 18:15–18 "The LORD your God will raise up for you a Prophet like me from your midst, from your brethren. Him you shall hear, 16 according to all you desired of the LORD your God in Horeb in the day of the assembly, saying, 'Let me not hear again the voice of the LORD my God, nor let me see this great fire anymore, lest I die.' 17 "And the LORD said to me: 'What they have spoken is good. 18 I will raise up for them a Prophet like you from among their brethren, and will put My words in His mouth, and He shall speak to them all that I command Him.

Cf. 1 Sam 2:35

By David.

2 Sam 7:12–14 "When your days are fulfilled and you rest with your fathers, I will set up your seed after you, who will come from your body, and I will establish his kingdom. 13 He shall build a house for My name, and I will establish the throne of his kingdom forever. 14 I will be his Father, and he shall be My son. If he commits iniquity, I will chasten him with the rod of men and with the blows of the sons of men.

Cf. 2 Sam 22:51

By the psalmist.

Ps 2:1–12 Why do the nations rage, And the people plot a vain thing? **2** The kings of the earth set themselves, And the rulers take counsel together, Against the LORD and against His Anointed, *saying,* **3** "Let us break Their bonds in pieces And cast away Their cords from us." **4** He who sits in the heavens shall laugh; The LORD shall hold them in derision. **5** Then He shall speak to them in His wrath, And distress them in His deep displeasure: **6** "Yet I have set My King On My holy hill of Zion." **7** "I will declare the decree: The LORD has said to Me, 'You *are* My Son, Today I have begotten You. **8** Ask of Me, and I will give *You* The nations *for* Your inheritance, And the ends of the earth *for* Your possession. **9** You shall break them with a rod of iron; You shall dash them to pieces like a potter's vessel.' " **10** Now therefore, be wise, O kings; Be instructed, you judges of the earth. **11** Serve the LORD with fear, And rejoice with trembling. **12** Kiss the Son, lest He be angry, And you perish *in* the way, When His wrath is kindled but a little. Blessed *are* all those who put their trust in Him.

Suffering was predicted.

Ps 22:1–18 My God, My God, why have You forsaken Me? *Why are You so* far from helping Me, *And from* the words of My groaning? **2** O My God, I cry in the daytime, but You do not hear; And in the night season, and am not silent. **3** But You *are* holy, Enthroned in the praises of Israel. **4** Our fathers trusted in You; They trusted, and You delivered them. **5** They cried to You, and were delivered; They trusted in You, and were not ashamed. **6** But I *am* a worm, and no man; A reproach of men, and despised by the people. **7** All those who see Me ridicule Me; They shoot out the lip, they shake the head, *saying,* **8** "He trusted in the LORD, let Him rescue Him; Let Him deliver Him, since He delights in Him!" **9** But You *are* He who took Me out of the womb; You made Me trust *while* on My mother's breasts. **10** I was cast upon You from birth. From My mother's womb You *have been* My God. **11** Be not far from Me, For trouble *is* near; For *there is* none to help. **12** Many bulls have surrounded Me; Strong *bulls* of Bashan have encircled Me. **13** They gape at Me *with* their mouths, *Like* a raging and roaring lion. **14** I am poured out like water, And all My bones are out of joint; My heart is like wax; It has melted within Me. **15** My strength is dried up like a potsherd, And My tongue clings to My jaws; You have brought Me to the dust of death. **16** For dogs have surrounded Me; The congregation of the wicked has enclosed Me. They pierced My hands and My feet; **17** I can count all My bones. They look *and* stare at Me. **18** They divide My garments among them, And for My clothing they cast lots.

Is 52:13–15 Behold, My Servant shall deal prudently; He shall be exalted and extolled and be very high. **14** Just as many were astonished at you, So His visage was marred more than any man, And His form more than the sons of men; **15** So shall He sprinkle many nations. Kings shall shut their mouths at Him; For what had not been told them they shall see, And what they had not heard they shall consider.

Is 53:1–12 Who has believed our report? And to whom has the arm of the LORD been revealed? **2** For He shall grow up before Him as a tender plant, And as a root out of dry ground. He has no form or comeliness; And when we see Him, *There is* no beauty that we should desire Him. **3** He is despised and rejected by men, A Man of sorrows and acquainted with grief. And we hid, as it were, *our* faces from Him; He was despised, and we did not esteem Him. **4** Surely He has borne our griefs And carried our sorrows; Yet we esteemed Him stricken, Smitten by God, and afflicted. **5** But He *was* wounded for our transgressions, *He was* bruised for our iniquities; The chastisement for our peace *was* upon Him, And by His stripes we are healed. **6** All we like sheep have gone astray; We have turned, every one, to his own way; And the LORD has laid on Him the iniquity of us all. **7** He was oppressed and He was afflicted, Yet He opened not His mouth; He was led as a lamb to the slaughter, And as a sheep before its shearers is silent, So He opened not His mouth. **8** He was taken from prison and from judgment, And who will declare His generation? For He was cut off from the land of the living; For the transgressions of My people He was stricken. **9** And they made His grave with the wicked— But with the rich at His death, Because He had done no violence, Nor *was any* deceit in His mouth. **10** Yet it pleased the LORD to bruise Him; He has put *Him* to grief. When You make His soul an offering for sin, He shall see *His* seed, He shall prolong *His* days, And the pleasure of the LORD shall prosper in His hand. **11** He shall see the labor of His soul, *and* be satisfied. By His knowledge My righteous Servant shall justify many, For He shall bear their iniquities. **12** Therefore I will divide Him a portion with the great, And He shall divide the spoil with the strong, Because He poured out His soul unto death, And He was numbered with the transgressors, And He bore the sin of many, And made intercession for the transgressors.

Zech 13:7–9 "Awake, O sword, against My Shepherd, Against the Man who is My Companion," Says the LORD of hosts. "Strike the Shepherd, And the sheep will be scattered; Then I will turn My hand against the little ones. **8** And it shall come to pass in all the land," Says the LORD, "*That* two-thirds in it shall be cut off *and* die, But *one*-third shall be left in it: **9** I will bring the *one*-third through the fire, Will refine them as silver is refined, And test them as gold is tested. They will call on My name, And I will answer them. I will say, 'This *is* My people'; And each one will say, 'The LORD *is* my God.' "

Birth and ministry of, anticipated by Isaiah.

Is 7:14 Therefore the Lord Himself will give you a sign: Behold, the virgin shall conceive and bear a Son, and shall call His name Immanuel.

Is 9:6 For unto us a Child is born, Unto us a Son is given; And the government will be upon His shoulder. And His name will be called Wonderful, Counselor, Mighty God, Everlasting Father, Prince of Peace.

Is 11:1–5 There shall come forth a Rod from the stem of Jesse, And a Branch shall grow out of his roots. **2** The Spirit of the LORD shall rest upon Him, The Spirit of wisdom and understanding, The Spirit of counsel and might, The Spirit of knowledge and of the fear of the LORD. **3** His delight *is* in the fear of the LORD, And He shall not judge by the sight of His eyes, Nor decide by the hearing of His ears; **4** But with righteousness He shall judge the poor, And decide with equity for the meek of the earth; He shall strike the earth with the rod of His mouth, And with the breath of His lips He shall slay the wicked. **5** Righteousness shall be the belt of His loins, And faithfulness the belt of His waist.

Is 28:16 Therefore thus says the Lord GOD: "Behold, I lay in Zion a stone for a foundation, A tried stone, a precious cornerstone, a sure foundation; Whoever believes will not act hastily.

Is 42:1–3 "Behold! My Servant whom I uphold, My Elect One *in whom* My soul delights! I have put My Spirit upon Him; He will bring forth justice to the Gentiles. **2** He will not cry out, nor raise *His voice*, Nor cause His voice to be heard in the street. **3** A bruised reed He will not break, And smoking flax He will not quench; He will bring forth justice for truth.

Is 42:6–7 "I, the LORD, have called You in righteousness, And will hold Your hand; I will keep You and give You as a covenant to the people, As a light to the Gentiles, **7** To open blind eyes, To bring out prisoners from the prison, Those who sit in darkness from the prison house.

Is 61:1–2 "The Spirit of the Lord GOD *is* upon Me, Because the LORD has anointed Me To preach good tidings to the poor; He has sent Me to heal the brokenhearted, To proclaim liberty to the captives, And the opening of the prison to *those who are* bound; **2** To proclaim the acceptable year of the LORD, And the day of vengeance of our God; To comfort all who mourn,

Cf. Is 49:1–13; 50:4–11; 59:16–21

Anticipated by Jeremiah.

Jer 23:1–8 "Woe to the shepherds who destroy and scatter the sheep of My pasture!" says the LORD. **2** Therefore thus says the LORD God of Israel against the shepherds who feed My people: "You have scattered My flock, driven them away, and not attended to them. Behold, I will attend to you for the evil of your doings," says the LORD. **3** "But I will gather the remnant of My flock out of all countries where I have driven them, and bring them back to their folds; and they shall be fruitful and increase. **4** I will set up shepherds over them who will feed them; and they shall fear no more, nor be dismayed, nor shall they be lacking," says the LORD. **5** "Behold, *the* days are coming," says the LORD, "That I will raise to David a Branch of righteousness; A King shall reign and prosper, And execute judgment and righteousness in the earth. **6** In His days Judah will be saved, And Israel will dwell safely; Now this *is* His name by which He will be called: THE LORD OUR RIGHTEOUSNESS. **7** "Therefore, behold, *the* days are coming," says the LORD, "that they shall no longer say, 'As the LORD lives who brought up the children of Israel from the land of Egypt,' **8** but, 'As the LORD lives who brought up and led the descendants of the house of Israel from the north country and from all the countries where I had driven them.' And they shall dwell in their own land."

Jer 33:14–18 'Behold, the days are coming,' says the LORD, 'that I will perform that good thing which I have promised to the house of Israel and to the house of Judah: **15** 'In those days and at that time I will

cause to grow up to David A Branch of righteousness; He shall execute judgment and righteousness in the earth. **16** In those days Judah will be saved, And Jerusalem will dwell safely. And this *is the* name by which she will be called: THE LORD OUR RIGHTEOUSNESS.' **17** "For thus says the LORD: 'David shall never lack a man to sit on the throne of the house of Israel; **18** nor shall the priests, the Levites, lack a man to offer burnt offerings before Me, to kindle grain offerings, and to sacrifice continually.' "

Anticipated by Ezekiel.

Ezek 18:22–24 None of the transgressions which he has committed shall be remembered against him; because of the righteousness which he has done, he shall live. **23** Do I have any pleasure at all that the wicked should die?" says the Lord GOD, "*and* not that he should turn from his ways and live? **24** "But when a righteous man turns away from his righteousness and commits iniquity, and does according to all the abominations that the wicked *man* does, shall he live? All the righteousness which he has done shall not be remembered; because of the unfaithfulness of which he is guilty and the sin which he has committed, because of them he shall die.

Ezek 34:23–24 I will establish one shepherd over them, and he shall feed them—My servant David. He shall feed them and be their shepherd. **24** And I, the LORD, will be their God, and My servant David a prince among them; I, the LORD, have spoken.

Ezek 37:24–25 "David My servant *shall be* king over them, and they shall all have one shepherd; they shall also walk in My judgments and observe My statutes, and do them. **25** Then they shall dwell in the land that I have given to Jacob My servant, where your fathers dwelt; and they shall dwell there, they, their children, and their children's children, forever; and My servant David *shall be* their prince forever.

Foreseen by Daniel.

Dan 2:35 Then the iron, the clay, the bronze, the silver, and the gold were crushed together, and became like chaff from the summer threshing floors; the wind carried them away so that no trace of them was found. And the stone that struck the image became a great mountain and filled the whole earth.

Dan 2:45 Inasmuch as you saw that the stone was cut out of the mountain without hands, and that it broke in pieces the iron, the bronze, the clay, the silver, and the gold—the great God has made known to the king what will come to pass after this. The dream is certain, and its interpretation is sure."

Dan 7:13–14 "I was watching in the night visions, And behold, *One* like the Son of Man, Coming with the clouds of heaven! He came to the Ancient of Days, And they brought Him near before Him. **14** Then to Him was given dominion and glory and a kingdom, That all peoples, nations, and languages should serve Him. His dominion *is* an everlasting dominion, Which shall not pass away, And His kingdom *the one* Which shall not be destroyed.

Dan 7:27 Then the kingdom and dominion, And the greatness of the kingdoms under the whole heaven, Shall be given to the people, the saints of the Most High. His kingdom *is* an everlasting kingdom, And all dominions shall serve and obey Him.'

Dan 9:26 "And after the sixty-two weeks Messiah shall be cut off, but not for Himself; And the people of the prince who is to come Shall destroy the city and the sanctuary. The end of it *shall be* with a flood, And till the end of the war desolations are determined.

Foreseen by Haggai.

Hag 2:7 and I will shake all nations, and they shall come to the Desire of All Nations, and I will fill this temple with glory,' says the LORD of hosts.

Presence during Millennium described.

Is 32:1–8 Behold, a king will reign in righteousness, And princes will rule with justice. 2 A man will be as a hiding place from the wind, And a cover from the tempest, As rivers of water in a dry place, As the shadow of a great rock in a weary land. 3 The eyes of those who see will not be dim, And the ears of those who hear will listen. 4 Also the heart of the rash will understand knowledge, And the tongue of the stammerers will be ready to speak plainly. 5 The foolish person will no longer be called generous, Nor the miser said *to be* bountiful; 6 For the foolish person will speak foolishness, And his heart will work iniquity: To practice ungodliness, To utter error against the LORD, To keep the hungry unsatisfied, And he will cause the drink of the thirsty to fail. 7 Also the schemes of the schemer *are* evil; He devises wicked plans To destroy the poor with lying words, Even when the needy speaks justice. 8 But a generous man devises generous things, And by generosity he shall stand.

Is 33:17–24 Your eyes will see the King in His beauty; They will see the land that is very far off. 18 Your heart will meditate on terror: "Where *is* the scribe? Where *is* he who weighs? Where *is* he who counts the towers?" 19 You will not see a fierce people, A people of obscure speech, beyond perception, Of a stammering tongue *that you* cannot understand. 20 Look upon Zion, the city of our appointed feasts; Your eyes will see Jerusalem, a quiet home, A tabernacle *that* will not be taken down; Not one of its stakes will ever be removed, Nor will any of its cords be broken. 21 But there the majestic LORD *will be* for us A place of broad rivers *and* streams, In which no galley with oars will sail, Nor majestic ships pass by 22 (For the LORD *is* our Judge, The LORD *is* our Lawgiver, The LORD *is* our King; He will save us); 23 Your tackle is loosed, They could not strengthen their mast, They could not spread the sail. Then the prey of great plunder is divided; The lame take the prey. 24 And the inhabitant will not say, "I am sick"; The people who dwell in it *will be* forgiven *their* iniquity.

Is 42:4–9 He will not fail nor be discouraged, Till He has established justice in the earth; And the coastlands shall wait for His law." 5 Thus says God the LORD, Who created the heavens and stretched them out, Who spread forth the earth and that which comes from it, Who gives breath to the people on it, And spirit to those who walk on it: 6 "I, the LORD, have called You in righteousness, And will hold Your hand; I will keep You and give You as a covenant to the people, As a light to the Gentiles, 7 To open blind eyes, To bring out prisoners from the prison, Those who sit in darkness from the prison house. 8 I *am* the LORD, that *is* My name; And My glory I will not give

to another, Nor My praise to carved images. 9 Behold, the former things have come to pass, And new things I declare; Before they spring forth I tell you of them."

Is 45:22 "Look to Me, and be saved, All you ends of the earth! For I *am* God, and *there is* no other.

Is 61:1–7 "The Spirit of the Lord GOD *is* upon Me, Because the LORD has anointed Me To preach good tidings to the poor; He has sent Me to heal the brokenhearted, To proclaim liberty to the captives, And the opening of the prison to *those who are* bound; 2 To proclaim the acceptable year of the LORD, And the day of vengeance of our God; To comfort all who mourn, 3 To console those who mourn in Zion, To give them beauty for ashes, The oil of joy for mourning, The garment of praise for the spirit of heaviness; That they may be called trees of righteousness, The planting of the LORD, that He may be glorified." 4 And they shall rebuild the old ruins, They shall raise up the former desolations, And they shall repair the ruined cities, The desolations of many generations. 5 Strangers shall stand and feed your flocks, And the sons of the foreigner *Shall be* your plowmen and your vinedressers. 6 But you shall be named the priests of the LORD, They shall call you the servants of our God. You shall eat the riches of the Gentiles, And in their glory you shall boast. 7 Instead of your shame *you shall have* double *honor,* And *instead of* confusion they shall rejoice in their portion. Therefore in their land they shall possess double; Everlasting joy shall be theirs.

Zech 2:10–13 "Sing and rejoice, O daughter of Zion! For behold, I am coming and I will dwell in your midst," says the LORD. 11 "Many nations shall be joined to the LORD in that day, and they shall become My people. And I will dwell in your midst. Then you will know that the LORD of hosts has sent Me to you. 12 And the LORD will take possession of Judah as His inheritance in the Holy Land, and will again choose Jerusalem. 13 Be silent, all flesh, before the LORD, for He is aroused from His holy habitation!"

Zech 3:6–10 Then the Angel of the LORD admonished Joshua, saying, 7 "Thus says the LORD of hosts: 'If you will walk in My ways, And if you will keep My command, Then you shall also judge My house, And likewise have charge of My courts; I will give you places to walk Among these who stand here. 8 'Hear, O Joshua, the high priest, You and your companions who sit before you, For they are a wondrous sign; For behold, I am bringing forth My Servant the BRANCH. 9 For behold, the stone That I have laid before Joshua: Upon the stone *are* seven eyes. Behold, I will engrave its inscription,' Says the LORD of hosts, 'And I will remove the iniquity of that land in one day. 10 In that day,' says the LORD of hosts, 'Everyone will invite his neighbor Under his vine and under his fig tree.' "

Cf. Is 55:3–5; Zech 6:9–15

Two advents foreseen.

Zech 9:9–17 "Rejoice greatly, O daughter of Zion! Shout, O daughter of Jerusalem! Behold, your King is coming to you; He *is* just and having salvation, Lowly and riding on a donkey, A colt, the foal of a donkey. 10 I will cut off the chariot from Ephraim And the horse from Jerusalem; The battle bow shall be cut off. He shall speak peace to the nations; His dominion *shall be* 'from sea to sea, And from the River to the ends of the earth.' 11 "As for you also, Because of the blood of your covenant, I will set your prisoners free from the waterless pit. 12 Return to the stronghold, You prisoners of hope. Even today I declare *That* I will restore double to you. 13 For I have bent Judah, My *bow,* Fitted the bow with Ephraim, And raised up your sons, O Zion, Against your sons, O Greece, And made you like the sword of a mighty man." 14 Then the LORD will be seen over them, And His arrow will go forth like lightning. The Lord GOD will blow the trumpet, And go with whirlwinds from the south. 15 The LORD of hosts will defend them; They shall devour and subdue with slingstones. They shall drink *and* roar as if with wine; They shall be filled *with blood* like basins, Like the corners of the altar. 16 The LORD their God will save them in that day, As the flock of His people. For they *shall be like* the jewels of a crown, Lifted like a banner over His land— 17 For how great is its goodness And how great its beauty! Grain shall make the young men thrive, And new wine the young women.

Prophesied by Malachi.

Mal 4:2 But to you who fear My name The Sun of Righteousness shall arise With healing in His wings; And you shall go out And grow fat like stall-fed calves.

Promises to be, fulfilled by Jesus.

Matt 2:4–6 And when he had gathered all the chief priests and scribes of the people together, he inquired of them where the Christ was to be born. 5 So they said to him, "In Bethlehem of Judea, for thus it is written by the prophet: 6 *'But you, Bethlehem, in the land of Judah, Are not the least among the rulers of Judah; For out of you shall come a Ruler Who will shepherd My people Israel.'"*

Matt 2:17–18 Then was fulfilled what was spoken by Jeremiah the prophet, saying: 18 *"A voice was heard in Ramah, Lamentation, weeping, and great mourning, Rachel weeping for her children, Refusing to be comforted, Because they are no more."*

Matt 4:13–16 And leaving Nazareth, He came and dwelt in Capernaum, which is by the sea, in the regions of Zebulun and Naphtali, 14 that it might be fulfilled which was spoken by Isaiah the prophet, saying: 15 *"The land of Zebulun and the land of Naphtali, By the way of the sea, beyond the Jordan, Galilee of the Gentiles: 16 The people who sat in darkness have seen a great light, And upon those who sat in the region and shadow of death Light has dawned."*

Matt 12:16–21 Yet He warned them not to make Him known, 17 that it might be fulfilled which was spoken by Isaiah the prophet, saying: 18 *"Behold! My Servant whom I have chosen, My Beloved in whom My soul is well pleased! I will put My Spirit upon Him, And He will declare justice to the Gentiles. 19 He will not quarrel nor cry out, Nor will anyone hear His voice in the streets. 20 A bruised reed He will not break, And smoking flax He will not quench, Till He sends forth justice to victory; 21 And in His name Gentiles will trust."*

Matt 13:35 that it might be fulfilled which was spoken by the prophet, saying: *"I will open My mouth in parables; I will utter things kept secret from the foundation of the world."*

Matt 21:1–11 Now when they drew near Jerusalem, and came to Bethphage, at the Mount of Olives, then Jesus sent two disciples, 2 saying to them, "Go into the village opposite you, and immediately you will find a donkey tied, and a colt with her. Loose *them* and bring *them* to Me. 3 And if anyone says anything to you, you shall say, 'The Lord has need of them,' and immediately he will send them." 4 All this was done that it might be fulfilled which was spoken by the prophet, saying: 5 *"Tell the daughter of Zion, 'Behold, your King is coming to you, Lowly, and sitting on a donkey, A colt, the foal of a donkey.'"* 6 So the disciples went and did as Jesus commanded them. 7 They brought the donkey and the colt, laid their clothes on them, and set *Him* on them. 8 And a very great multitude spread their clothes on the road; others cut down branches from the trees and spread *them* on the road. 9 Then the multitudes who went before and those who followed cried out, saying: "Hosanna to the Son of David! *'Blessed is He who comes in the name of the LORD!'* Hosanna in the highest!" 10 And when He had come into Jerusalem, all the city was moved, saying, "Who is this?" 11 So the multitudes said, "This is Jesus, the prophet from Nazareth of Galilee."

Matt 22:41–46 While the Pharisees were gathered together, Jesus asked them, 42 saying, "What do you think about the Christ? Whose Son is He?" They said to Him, *"The Son* of David." 43 He said to them, "How then does David in the Spirit call Him 'Lord,' saying: 44 *'The LORD said to my Lord, "Sit at My right hand, Till I make Your enemies Your footstool"'*? 45 If David then calls Him 'Lord,' how is He his Son?" 46 And no one was able to answer Him a word, nor from that day on did anyone dare question Him anymore.

Matt 27:9–10 Then was fulfilled what was spoken by Jeremiah the prophet, saying, *"And they took the thirty pieces of silver, the value of Him who was priced,* whom they of the children of Israel priced, 10 *and gave them for the potter's field, as the LORD directed me."*

Mark 11:1–10 Now when they drew near Jerusalem, to Bethphage and Bethany, at the Mount of Olives, He sent two of His disciples; 2 and He said to them, "Go into the village opposite you; and as soon as you have entered it you will find a colt tied, on which no one has sat. Loose it and bring *it.* 3 And if anyone says to you, 'Why are you doing this?' say, 'The Lord has need of it,' and immediately he will send it here." 4 So they went their way, and found the colt tied by the door outside on the street, and they loosed it. 5 But some of those who stood there said to them, "What are you doing, loosing the colt?" 6 And they spoke to them just as Jesus had commanded. So they let them go. 7 Then they brought the colt to Jesus and threw their clothes on it, and He sat on it. 8 And many spread their clothes on the road, and others cut down leafy branches from the trees and spread *them* on the road. 9 Then those who went before and those who followed cried out, saying: "Hosanna! *'Blessed is He who comes in the name of the LORD!'* 10 Blessed *is* the kingdom of our father David That comes in the name of the Lord! Hosanna in the highest!"

Mark 12:35–37 Then Jesus answered and said, while He taught in the temple, "How *is it* that the scribes say that the Christ is the Son of David? **36** For David himself said by the Holy Spirit: *'The LORD said to my Lord, "Sit at My right hand, Till I make Your enemies Your footstool."'* **37** Therefore David himself calls Him *'Lord';* how is He *then* his Son?" And the common people heard Him gladly.

Luke 4:16–22 So He came to Nazareth, where He had been brought up. And as His custom was, He went into the synagogue on the Sabbath day, and stood up to read. **17** And He was handed the book of the prophet Isaiah. And when He had opened the book, He found the place where it was written: **18** *"The Spirit of the LORD is upon Me, Because He has anointed Me To preach the gospel to the poor; He has sent Me to heal the brokenhearted, To proclaim liberty to the captives And recovery of sight to the blind, To set at liberty those who are oppressed;* **19** *To proclaim the acceptable year of the LORD."* **20** Then He closed the book, and gave *it* back to the attendant and sat down. And the eyes of all who were in the synagogue were fixed on Him. **21** And He began to say to them, "Today this Scripture is fulfilled in your hearing." **22** So all bore witness to Him, and marveled at the gracious words which proceeded out of His mouth. And they said, "Is this not Joseph's son?"

Luke 7:22–23 Jesus answered and said to them, "Go and tell John the things you have seen and heard: that *the* blind see, *the* lame walk, *the* lepers are cleansed, *the* deaf hear, *the* dead are raised, *the* poor have the gospel preached to them. **23** And blessed is *he* who is not offended because of Me."

Luke 19:29–38 And it came to pass, when He drew near to Bethphage and Bethany, at the mountain called Olivet, *that* He sent two of His disciples, **30** saying, "Go into the village opposite *you,* where as you enter you will find a colt tied, on which no one has ever sat. Loose it and bring *it here.* **31** And if anyone asks you, 'Why are you loosing *it?'* thus you shall say to him, 'Because the Lord has need of it.'" **32** So those who were sent their way and found *it* just as He had said to them. **33** But as they were loosing the colt, the owners of it said to them, "Why are you loosing the colt?" **34** And they said, "The Lord has need of him." **35** Then they brought him to Jesus. And they threw their own clothes on the colt, and they set Jesus on him. **36** And as He went, *many* spread their clothes on the road. **37** Then, as He was now drawing near the descent of the Mount of Olives, the whole multitude of the disciples began to rejoice and praise God with a loud voice for all the mighty works they had seen, **38** saying: "'Blessed is the King who comes in the name of the LORD!' Peace in heaven and glory in the highest!"

Luke 20:41–44 And He said to them, "How can they say that the Christ is the Son of David? **42** Now David himself said in the Book of Psalms: *'The LORD said to my Lord, "Sit at My right hand,* **43** *Till I make Your enemies Your footstool."'* **44** Therefore David calls Him *'Lord';* how is He then his Son?"

John 12:12–15 The next day a great multitude that had come to the feast, when they heard that Jesus was coming to Jerusalem, **13** took branches of palm trees and went out to meet Him, and cried out: "Hosanna! *'Blessed is He who comes in the name of the LORD!'* The King of Israel!" **14** Then Jesus, when He had found a young donkey, sat on it; as it is written: **15** *"Fear not, daughter of Zion; Behold, your King is coming, Sitting on a donkey's colt."*

Cf. Matt 11:3–6; John 2:16–17; Heb 1:1–13; 10:5–10

Presence of, attested by Peter.

Matt 16:13–17 When Jesus came into the region of Caesarea Philippi, He asked His disciples, saying, "Who do men say that I, the Son of Man, am?" **14** So they said, "Some *say* John the Baptist, some Elijah, and others Jeremiah or one of the prophets." **15** He said to them, "But who do you say that I am?" **16** Simon Peter answered and said, "You are the Christ, the Son of the living God." **17** Jesus answered and said to him, "Blessed are you, Simon Bar-Jonah, for flesh and blood has not revealed *this* to you, but My Father who is in heaven.

Mark 8:27–29 Now Jesus and His disciples went out to the towns of Caesarea Philippi; and on the road He asked His disciples, saying to them, "Who do men say that I am?" **28** So they answered, "John the Baptist; but some *say,* Elijah; and others, one of the prophets." **29** He said to them, "But who do you say that I am?" Peter answered and said to Him, "You are the Christ."

Luke 9:18–22 And it happened, as He was alone praying, *that* His disciples joined Him, and He asked them, saying, "Who do the crowds say that I am?" **19** So they answered and said, "John the Baptist, but some *say* Elijah; and others *say* that one of the old prophets has risen again." **20** He said to them, "But who do you say that I am?" Peter answered and said, "The Christ of God." **21** And He strictly warned and commanded them to tell this to no one, **22** saying, "The Son of Man must suffer many things, and be rejected by the elders and chief priests and scribes, and be killed, and be raised the third day."

Cf. Acts 2:14–36; 3:12–26

Death of, predicted by Jesus.

Matt 17:22–23 Now while they were staying in Galilee, Jesus said to them, "The Son of Man is about to be betrayed into the hands of men, **23** and they will kill Him, and the third day He will be raised up." And they were exceedingly sorrowful.

Matt 20:17–19 Now Jesus, going up to Jerusalem, took the twelve disciples aside on the road and said to them, **18** "Behold, we are going up to Jerusalem, and the Son of Man will be betrayed to the chief priests and to the scribes; and they will condemn Him to death, **19** and deliver Him to the Gentiles to mock and to scourge and to crucify. And the third day He will rise again."

Mark 8:31 And He began to teach them that the Son of Man must suffer many things, and be rejected by the elders and chief priests and scribes, and be killed, and after three days rise again.

Mark 9:30–32 Then they departed from there and passed through Galilee, and He did not want anyone to know *it.* **31** For He taught His disciples and said to them, "The Son of Man is being betrayed into the hands of men, and they will kill Him. And after He is killed, He will rise the third day." **32** But they did not understand this saying, and were afraid to ask Him.

Mark 10:32–34 Now they were on the road, going up to Jerusalem, and Jesus was going before them; and they were amazed. And as they followed they were afraid. Then He took the twelve aside again and began to tell them the things that would happen to Him: **33** "Behold, we are going up to Jerusalem, and the Son of Man will be betrayed to the chief priests and to the scribes; and they will condemn Him to death and deliver Him to the Gentiles; **34** and they will mock Him, and scourge Him, and spit on Him, and kill Him. And the third day He will rise again."

Luke 9:30–32 And behold, two men talked with Him, who were Moses and Elijah, **31** who appeared in glory and spoke of His decease which He was about to accomplish at Jerusalem. **32** But Peter and those with him were heavy with sleep; and when they were fully awake, they saw His glory and the two men who stood with Him.

Luke 18:31–34 Then He took the twelve aside and said to them, "Behold, we are going up to Jerusalem, and all things that are written by the prophets concerning the Son of Man will be accomplished. **32** For He will be delivered to the Gentiles and will be mocked and insulted and spit upon. **33** They will scourge *Him* and kill Him. And the third day He will rise again." **34** But they understood none of these things; this saying was hidden from them, and they did not know the things which were spoken.

Angels' announcement of.

Luke 2:8–14 Now there were in the same country shepherds living out in the fields, keeping watch over their flock by night. **9** And behold, an angel of the Lord stood before them, and the glory of the Lord shone around them, and they were greatly afraid. **10** Then the angel said to them, "Do not be afraid, for behold, I bring you good tidings of great joy which will be to all people. **11** For there is born to you this day in the city of David a Savior, who is Christ the Lord. **12** And this *will be* the sign to you: You will find a Babe wrapped in swaddling cloths, lying in a manger." **13** And suddenly there was with the angel a multitude of the heavenly host praising God and saying: **14** "Glory to God in the highest, And on earth peace, goodwill toward men!"

Simeon's testimony of.

Luke 2:25–35 And behold, there was a man in Jerusalem whose name was Simeon, and this man was just and devout, waiting for the Consolation of Israel, and the Holy Spirit was upon him. **26** And it had been revealed to him by the Holy Spirit that he would not see death before he had seen the Lord's Christ. **27** So he came by the Spirit into the temple. And when the parents brought in the Child Jesus, to do for Him according to the custom of the law, **28** he took Him up in his arms and blessed God and said: **29** "Lord, now You are letting Your servant depart in peace, According to Your word; **30** For my eyes have seen Your salvation **31** Which You have prepared before the face of all peoples, **32** A light to *bring* revelation to the Gentiles, And the glory of Your people Is-

rael." **33** And Joseph and His mother marveled at those things which were spoken of Him. **34** Then Simeon blessed them, and said to Mary His mother, "Behold, this *Child* is destined for the fall and rising of many in Israel, and for a sign which will be spoken against **35** (yes, a sword will pierce through your own soul also), that the thoughts of many hearts may be revealed."

John the Baptist pointed toward.

Matt 3:1–12 In those days John the Baptist came preaching in the wilderness of Judea, **2** and saying, "Repent, for the kingdom of heaven is at hand!" **3** For this is he who was spoken of by the prophet Isaiah, saying: *"The voice of one crying in the wilderness: 'Prepare the way of the LORD; Make His paths straight.' "* **4** Now John himself was clothed in camel's hair, with a leather belt around his waist; and his food was locusts and wild honey. **5** Then Jerusalem, all Judea, and all the region around the Jordan went out to him **6** and were baptized by him in the Jordan, confessing their sins. **7** But when he saw many of the Pharisees and Sadducees coming to his baptism, he said to them, "Brood of vipers! Who warned you to flee from the wrath to come? **8** Therefore bear fruits worthy of repentance, **9** and do not think to say to yourselves, 'We have Abraham as *our* father.' For I say to you that God is able to raise up children to Abraham from these stones. **10** And even now the ax is laid to the root of the trees. Therefore every tree which does not bear good fruit is cut down and thrown into the fire. **11** I indeed baptize you with water unto repentance, but He who is coming after me is mightier than I, whose sandals I am not worthy to carry. He will baptize you with the Holy Spirit and fire. **12** His winnowing fan *is* in His hand, and He will thoroughly clean out His threshing floor, and gather His wheat into the barn; but He will burn up the chaff with unquenchable fire."

Mark 1:2–8 As it is written in the Prophets: *"Behold, I send My messenger before Your face, Who will prepare Your way before You." 3 "The voice of one crying in the wilderness: 'Prepare the way of the LORD; Make His paths straight.' "* **4** John came baptizing in the wilderness and preaching a baptism of repentance for the remission of sins. **5** Then all the land of Judea, and those from Jerusalem, went out to him and were all baptized by him in the Jordan River, confessing their sins. **6** Now John was clothed with camel's hair and with a leather belt around his waist, and he ate locusts and wild honey. **7** And he preached, saying, "There comes One after me who is mightier than I, whose sandal strap I am not worthy to stoop down and loose. **8** I indeed baptized you with water, but He will baptize you with the Holy Spirit."

Cf. Luke 3:3–16; John 1:19–34

Andrew's testimony of.

John 1:40–42 One of the two who heard John *speak,* and followed Him, was Andrew, Simon Peter's brother. **41** He first found his own brother Simon, and said to him, "We have found the Messiah" (which is translated, the Christ). **42** And he brought him to Jesus. Now when Jesus looked at him, He said, "You are

Simon the son of Jonah. You shall be called Cephas" (which is translated, A Stone).

Jesus confirms

Nathanael's testimony of.

John 1:49–51 Nathanael answered and said to Him, "Rabbi, You are the Son of God! You are the King of Israel!" **50** Jesus answered and said to him, "Because I said to you, 'I saw you under the fig tree,' do you believe? You will see greater things than these." **51** And He said to him, "Most assuredly, I say to you, hereafter you shall see heaven open, and the angels of God ascending and descending upon the Son of Man."

A woman's testimony of.

John 4:25–26 The woman said to Him, "I know that Messiah is coming" (who is called Christ). "When He comes, He will tell us all things." **26** Jesus said to her, "I who speak to you am *He*."

Stephen's testimony of.

Acts 7:37 "This is that Moses who said to the children of Israel, *'The LORD your God will raise up for you a Prophet like me from your brethren. Him you shall hear.'*

Acts 7:48–52 "However, the Most High does not dwell in temples made with hands, as the prophet says: **49** *'Heaven is My throne, And earth is My footstool. What house will you build for Me? says the LORD, Or what is the place of My rest? 50 Has My hand not made all these things?'* **51** *"You* stiff-necked and uncircumcised in heart and ears! You always resist the Holy Spirit; as your fathers *did,* so *do* you. **52** Which of the prophets did your fathers not persecute? And they killed those who foretold the coming of the Just One, of whom you now have become the betrayers and murderers,

Paul's testimony of. Acts 13:20–39

Israel will yet turn to.

Rom 11:26–27 And so all Israel will be saved, as it is written: *"The Deliverer will come out of Zion, And He will turn away ungodliness from Jacob; 27 For this is My covenant with them, When I take away their sins."*

METALS

Taken from the earth.

Job 28:1–2 "Surely there is a mine for silver, And a place *where* gold is refined. **2** Iron is taken from the earth, And copper *is* smelted *from* ore.

Job 28:6 Its stones *are* the source of sapphires, And it contains gold dust.

Mentioned in Scripture

Gold.

Gen 2:11–12 The name of the first *is* Pishon; it *is* the one which skirts the whole land of Havilah, where *there is* gold. **12** And the gold of that land *is* good. Bdellium and the onyx stone *are* there.

Silver.

Gen 44:2 Also put my cup, the silver cup, in the mouth of the sack of the youngest, and his grain money." So he did according to the word that Joseph had spoken.

Bronze.

Ex 27:2 You shall make its horns on its four corners; its horns shall be of one piece with it. And you shall overlay it with bronze.

Ex 27:4 You shall make a grate for it, a network of bronze; and on the network you shall make four bronze rings at its four corners.

2 Chr 12:10 Then King Rehoboam made bronze shields in their place, and committed *them* to the hands of the captains of the guard, who guarded the doorway of the king's house.

Ezra 8:27 twenty gold basins *worth* a thousand drachmas, and two vessels of fine polished bronze, precious as gold.

Copper.

2 Tim 4:14 Alexander the coppersmith did me much harm. May the Lord repay him according to his works.

Iron.

Num 35:16 'But if he strikes him with an iron implement, so that he dies, he *is* a murderer; the murderer shall surely be put to death.

Prov 27:17 *As* iron sharpens iron, So a man sharpens the countenance of his friend.

Lead.

Ex 15:10 You blew with Your wind, The sea covered them; They sank like lead in the mighty waters.

Jer 6:29 The bellows blow fiercely, The lead is consumed by the fire; The smelter refines in vain, For the wicked are not drawn off.

Tin.

Num 31:22 "Only the gold, the silver, the bronze, the iron, the tin, and the lead,

Comparative value of.

Is 60:17 "Instead of bronze I will bring gold, Instead of iron I will bring silver, Instead of wood, bronze, And instead of stones, iron. I will also make your officers peace, And your magistrates righteousness.

Cf. Dan 2:32–45

Mixed with dross.

Is 1:25 I will turn My hand against you, And thoroughly purge away your dross, And take away all your alloy.

Abundant in Canaan.

Deut 8:9 a land in which you will eat bread without scarcity, in which you will lack nothing; a land whose stones *are* iron and out of whose hills you can dig copper.

Object of ancient craftsmanship.

Gen 4:22 And as for Zillah, she also bore Tubal-Cain, an instructor of every craftsman in bronze and iron. And the sister of Tubal-Cain *was* Naamah.

Fire used to

Free dross from.

Ezek 22:18 "Son of man, the house of Israel has become dross to Me; they *are* all bronze, tin, iron, and lead, in the midst of a furnace; they have become dross from silver.

Ezek 22:20 *As men* gather silver, bronze, iron, lead, and tin into the midst of a furnace, to blow fire on it, to melt *it;* so I will gather *you* in My anger and in My fury, and I will leave *you there* and melt you.

Ceremonially cleanse.

Num 31:21–23 Then Eleazar the priest said to the men of war who had gone to the battle, "This *is* the ordinance of the law which the LORD commanded Moses: **22** "Only the gold, the silver, the bronze, the iron, the tin, and the lead, **23** everything that can endure fire, you shall put through the fire, and it shall be clean; and it shall be purified with the water of purification. But all that cannot endure fire you shall put through water.

Cast in molds.

Judg 17:4 Thus he returned the silver to his mother. Then his mother took two hundred *shekels* of silver and gave them to the silversmith, and he made it into a carved image and a molded image; and they were in the house of Micah.

1 Kin 7:46 In the plain of Jordan the king had them cast in clay molds, between Succoth and Zaretan.

Jer 6:29 The bellows blow fiercely, The lead is consumed by the fire; The smelter refines in vain, For the wicked are not drawn off.

An extensive commerce in.

Ezek 27:12 "Tarshish *was* your merchant because of your many luxury goods. They gave you silver, iron, tin, and lead for your goods.

MIDIANITES, THE

Descended from Midian, son of Abraham by Keturah.

Gen 25:1–2 Abraham again took a wife, and her name *was* Keturah. **2** And she bore him Zimran, Jokshan, Medan, Midian, Ishbak, and Shuah.

1 Chr 1:32 Now the sons born to Keturah, Abraham's concubine, *were* Zimran, Jokshan, Medan, Midian, Ishbak, and Shuah. The sons of Jokshan *were* Sheba and Dedan.

Dwelt east of Jordan, beside Moab.

Num 22:1 Then the children of Israel moved, and camped in the plains of Moab on the side of the Jordan *across from* Jericho.

Num 22:4 So Moab said to the elders of Midian, "Now this company will lick up everything around us, as an ox licks up the grass of the field." And Balak the son of Zippor *was* king of the Moabites at that time.

A small part of,

Dwelt near Horeb.

Ex 2:15 When Pharaoh heard of this matter, he sought to kill Moses. But Moses fled from the face of Pharaoh and dwelt in the land of Midian; and he sat down by a well.

Ex 3:1 Now Moses was tending the flock of Jethro his father-in-law, the priest of Midian. And he led the flock to the back of the desert, and came to Horeb, the mountain of God.

Retained the knowledge and worship of God.

Ex 2:16 Now the priest of Midian had seven daughters. And they came and drew water, and they filled the troughs to water their father's flock.

Ex 18:9–12 Then Jethro rejoiced for all the good which the LORD had done for Israel, whom He had delivered out of the hand of the Egyptians. **10** And Jethro said, "Blessed *be* the LORD, who has delivered you out of the hand of the Egyptians and out of the hand of Pharaoh, *and* who has delivered the people from under the hand of the Egyptians. **11** Now I know that the LORD *is* greater than all the gods; for in the very thing in which they behaved proudly, *He was* above them." **12** Then Jethro, Moses' father-in-law, took a burnt offering and *other* sacrifices *to offer* to God. And Aaron came with all the elders of Israel to eat bread with Moses' father-in-law before God.

Governed by kings.

Num 31:8 They killed the kings of Midian with *the rest of* those who were killed—Evi, Rekem, Zur, Hur, and Reba, the five kings of Midian. Balaam the son of Beor they also killed with the sword.

Judg 8:5 Then he said to the men of Succoth, "Please give loaves of bread to the people who follow me, for they are exhausted, and I am pursuing Zebah and Zalmunna, kings of Midian."

Dwelt in tents.

Hab 3:7 I saw the tents of Cushan in affliction; The curtains of the land of Midian trembled.

Engaged in commerce.

Gen 37:28 Then Midianite traders passed by; so *the brothers* pulled Joseph up and lifted him out of the pit, and sold him to the Ishmaelites for twenty *shekels* of silver. And they took Joseph to Egypt.

Gen 37:36 Now the Midianites had sold him in Egypt to Potiphar, an officer of Pharaoh *and* captain of the guard.

Conquered by Hadad.

1 Chr 1:46 And when Husham died, Hadad the son of Bedad, who attacked Midian in the field of Moab, reigned in his place. The name of his city *was* Avith.

Terrified at the approach of Israel.

Hab 3:3–7 God came from Teman, The Holy One from Mount Paran. Selah His glory covered the heavens, And the earth was full of His praise. **4** *His* brightness was like the light; He had rays *flashing* from His hand, And there His power *was* hidden. **5** Before Him went pestilence, And fever followed at His feet. **6** He stood and measured the earth; He looked and startled the nations. And the everlasting mountains were scattered, The perpetual hills bowed. His ways *are* everlasting. **7** I saw the tents of Cushan in affliction; The curtains of the land of Midian trembled.

With Moab

Opposed Israel.

Num 22:4 So Moab said to the elders of Midian, "Now this company will lick up everything around us, as an ox licks up the grass of the field." And Balak the son of Zippor *was* king of the Moabites at that time.

Sent for Balaam to curse Israel.

Num 22:5–7 Then he sent messengers to Balaam the son of Beor at Pethor, which *is* near the River in the land of the sons of his people, to call him, saying: "Look, a people has come from Egypt. See, they cover the face of the earth, and are settling next to me! **6** Therefore please come at once, curse this people for me, for they *are* too mighty for me. Perhaps I shall be able to defeat them and drive them out of the land, for I know that he whom you bless *is* blessed, and he whom you curse is cursed." 7 So the elders of Moab and the elders of Midian departed with the diviner's fee in their hand, and they came to Balaam and spoke to him the words of Balak.

Seduced Israel to idolatry.

Num 25:1–6 Now Israel remained in Acacia Grove, and the people began to commit harlotry with the women of Moab. 2 They invited the people to the sacrifices of their gods, and the people ate and bowed down to their gods. 3 So Israel was joined to Baal of Peor, and the anger of the LORD was aroused against Israel. 4 Then the LORD said to Moses, "Take all the leaders of the people and hang the offenders before the LORD, out in the sun, that the fierce anger of the LORD may turn away from Israel." 5 So Moses said to the judges of Israel, "Every one of you kill his men who were joined to Baal of Peor." 6 And indeed, one of the children of Israel came and presented to his brethren a Midianite woman in the sight of Moses and in the sight of all the congregation of the children of Israel, who *were* weeping at the door of the tabernacle of meeting.

Were punished for seducing Israel.

Num 25:16–18 Then the LORD spoke to Moses, saying: 17 "Harass the Midianites, and attack them; 18 for they harassed you with their schemes by which they seduced you in the matter of Peor and in the matter of Cozbi, the daughter of a leader of Midian, their sister, who was killed in the day of the plague because of Peor."

Num 31:1–12 And the LORD spoke to Moses, saying: 2 "Take vengeance on the Midianites for the children of Israel. Afterward you shall be gathered to your people." 3 So Moses spoke to the people, saying, "Arm some of yourselves for war, and let them go against the Midianites to take vengeance for the LORD on Midian. 4 A thousand from each tribe of all the tribes of Israel you shall send to the war." 5 So there were recruited from the divisions of Israel one thousand from *each* tribe, twelve thousand armed for war. 6 Then Moses sent them to the war, one thousand from *each* tribe; he sent them to the war with Phinehas the son of Eleazar the priest, with the holy articles and the signal trumpets in his hand. 7 And they warred against the Midianites, just as the LORD commanded Moses, and they killed all the males. 8 They killed the kings of Midian with *the rest of* those who were killed—Evi, Rekem, Zur, Hur, and Reba, the five kings of Midian. Balaam the son of Beor they also killed with the sword. 9 And the children of Israel took the women of Midian captive, with their little ones, and took as spoil all their cattle, all their flocks, and all their goods. 10 They also burned with fire all the cities where they dwelt, and all their forts. 11 And they took all the spoil and all the booty—of man and beast. 12 Then they brought the captives, the booty, and the spoil to Moses, to Eleazar the priest, and to the congregation of the children of Israel, to the camp in the plains of Moab by the Jordan, *across from* Jericho.

Allowed to oppress Israel.

Judg 6:1–6 Then the children of Israel did evil in the sight of the LORD. So the LORD delivered them into the hand of Midian for seven years, 2 and the hand of Midian prevailed against Israel. Because of the Midianites, the children of Israel made for themselves the dens, the caves, and the strongholds which *are* in the mountains. 3 So it was, whenever Israel had sown, Midianites would come up; also Amalekites and the people of the East would come up against them. 4 Then they would encamp against them and destroy the produce of the earth as far as Gaza, and leave no sustenance for Israel, neither sheep nor ox nor donkey. 5 For they would come up with their livestock and their tents, coming in as numerous as locusts; both they and their camels were without number; and they would enter the land to destroy it. 6 So Israel was greatly impoverished because of the Midianites, and the children of Israel cried out to the LORD.

Judg 6:33 Then all the Midianites and Amalekites, the people of the East, gathered together; and they crossed over and encamped in the Valley of Jezreel.

Gideon's role against,

Called by God.

Judg 6:11–14 Now the Angel of the LORD came and sat under the terebinth tree which *was* in Ophrah, which *belonged* to Joash the Abiezrite, while his son Gideon threshed wheat in the winepress, in order to hide *it* from the Midianites. 12 And the Angel of the LORD appeared to him, and said to him, "The LORD *is* with you, you mighty man of valor!" 13 Gideon said to Him, "O my lord, if the LORD is with us, why then has all this happened to us? And where *are* all His miracles which our fathers told us about, saying, 'Did not the LORD bring us up from Egypt?' But now the LORD has forsaken us and delivered us into the hands of the Midianites." 14 Then the LORD turned to him and said, "Go in this might of yours, and you shall save Israel from the hand of the Midianites. Have I not sent you?"

Destroy nation and leaders.

Judg 7:16–22 Then he divided the three hundred men *into* three companies, and he put a trumpet into every man's hand, with empty pitchers, and torches inside the pitchers. 17 And he said to them, "Look at me and do likewise; watch, and when I come to the edge of the camp you shall do as I do: 18 When I blow the trumpet, I and all who *are* with me, then you also blow the trumpets on every side of the whole camp, and say, 'The sword of the LORD and of Gideon!' " 19 So Gideon and the hundred men who *were* with him came to the outpost of the camp at the beginning of the middle watch, just as they had posted the watch; and they blew the trumpets and broke the pitchers that *were* in their hands. 20 Then the three companies blew the trumpets and broke the pitchers—they held the torches in their left hands and the trumpets in their right hands for blowing—and they cried, "The sword of the LORD and of Gideon!" 21 And every man stood in his place all around the camp; and the whole army ran and cried out and fled. 22 When the three hundred blew the trumpets, the LORD set every man's sword against his companion throughout the whole camp; and the army fled to Beth Acacia, toward Zererah, as far as the border of Abel Meholah, by Tabbath.

Judg 7:24–25 Then Gideon sent messengers throughout all the mountains of Ephraim, saying, "Come down against the Midianites, and seize from them the watering places as far as Beth Barah and the Jordan." Then all the men of Ephraim gathered together and seized the watering places as far as Beth Barah and the Jordan. **25** And they captured two princes of the Midianites, Oreb and Zeeb. They killed Oreb at the rock of Oreb, and Zeeb they killed at the winepress of Zeeb. They pursued Midian and brought the heads of Oreb and Zeeb to Gideon on the other side of the Jordan.

Judg 8:10–12 Now Zebah and Zalmunna were at Karkor, and their armies with them, about fifteen thousand, all who were left of all the army of the people of the East; for one hundred and twenty thousand men who drew the sword had fallen. **11** Then Gideon went up by the road of those who dwell in tents on the east of Nobah and Jogbehah; and he attacked the army while the camp felt secure. **12** When Zebah and Zalmunna fled, he pursued them; and he took the two kings of Midian, Zebah and Zalmunna, and routed the whole army.

Judg 8:21 So Zebah and Zalmunna said, "Rise yourself, and kill us; for as a man is, so is his strength." So Gideon arose and killed Zebah and Zalmunna, and took the crescent ornaments that were on their camels' necks.

Completeness of their destruction, alluded to.

Ps 83:9–11 Deal with them as with Midian, As with Sisera, As with Jabin at the Brook Kishon, **10** Who perished at En Dor, Who became as refuse on the earth. **11** Make their nobles like Oreb and like Zeeb, Yes, all their princes like Zebah and Zalmunna,

Is 9:4 For You have broken the yoke of his burden And the staff of his shoulder, The rod of his oppressor, As in the day of Midian.

Is 10:26 And the LORD of hosts will stir up a scourge for him like the slaughter of Midian at the rock of Oreb; as His rod was on the sea, so will He lift it up in the manner of Egypt.

Shall minister in Millennium.

Is 60:6 The multitude of camels shall cover your land, The dromedaries of Midian and Ephah; All those from Sheba shall come; They shall bring gold and incense, And they shall proclaim the praises of the LORD.

MILK

An animal secretion, of a white color.

Lam 4:7 Her Nazirites were brighter than snow And whiter than milk; They were more ruddy in body than rubies, Like sapphire in their appearance.

Used as food by the Jews.

Gen 18:8 So he took butter and milk and the calf which he had prepared, and set it before them; and he stood by them under the tree as they ate.

Judg 5:25 He asked for water, she gave milk; She brought out cream in a lordly bowl.

Job 10:10 Did You not pour me out like milk, And curdle me like cheese,

Prov 30:33 For as the churning of milk produces butter,

And wringing the nose produces blood, So the forcing of wrath produces strife.

Different kinds, mentioned

Of cows.

Deut 32:14 Curds from the cattle, and milk of the flock, With fat of lambs; And rams of the breed of Bashan, and goats, With the choicest wheat; And you drank wine, the blood of the grapes.

1 Sam 6:7 Now therefore, make a new cart, take two milk cows which have never been yoked, and hitch the cows to the cart; and take their calves home, away from them.

Of camels.

Gen 32:15 thirty milk camels with their colts, forty cows and ten bulls, twenty female donkeys and ten foals.

Of goats.

Prov 27:27 You shall have enough goats' milk for your food, For the food of your household, And the nourishment of your maidservants.

Of sheep.

Deut 32:14 Curds from the cattle, and milk of the flock, With fat of lambs; And rams of the breed of Bashan, and goats, With the choicest wheat; And you drank wine, the blood of the grapes.

Of jackals.

Lam 4:3 Even the jackals present their breasts To nurse their young; But the daughter of my people is cruel, Like ostriches in the wilderness.

Flocks and herds fed for supply of.

Prov 27:23 Be diligent to know the state of your flocks, And attend to your herds;

Prov 27:27 You shall have enough goats' milk for your food, For the food of your household, And the nourishment of your maidservants.

Is 7:21–22 It shall be in that day That a man will keep alive a young cow and two sheep; **22** So it shall be, from the abundance of milk they give, That he will eat curds; For curds and honey everyone will eat who is left in the land.

1 Cor 9:7 Who ever goes to war at his own expense? Who plants a vineyard and does not eat of its fruit? Or who tends a flock and does not drink of the milk of the flock?

Canaan abounded with.

Ex 3:8 So I have come down to deliver them out of the hand of the Egyptians, and to bring them up from that land to a good and large land, to a land flowing with milk and honey, to the place of the Canaanites and the Hittites and the Amorites and the Perizzites and the Hivites and the Jebusites.

Ex 3:17 and I have said I will bring you up out of the affliction of Egypt to the land of the Canaanites and the Hittites and the Amorites and the Perizzites and the Hivites and the Jebusites, to a land flowing with milk and honey." '

Josh 5:6 For the children of Israel walked forty years in the wilderness, till all the people who were men of war, who came out of Egypt, were consumed, because they did not obey the voice of the LORD—to whom the LORD swore that He would not show them the land which the LORD had sworn to their fathers that He would give us, "a land flowing with milk and honey."

Kept by the Jews in bottles.

Judg 4:19 Then he said to her, "Please give me a little water to drink, for I am thirsty." So she opened a jug of milk, gave him a drink, and covered him.

Young animals not to be boiled in that of the mother.

Ex 23:19 The first of the firstfruits of your land you shall bring into the house of the LORD your God. You shall not boil a young goat in its mother's milk.

Illustrative of

Temporal blessings.

Gen 49:12 His eyes *are* darker than wine, And his teeth whiter than milk.

Blessings of the gospel.

Is 55:1 "Ho! Everyone who thirsts, Come to the waters; And you who have no money, Come, buy and eat. Yes, come, buy wine and milk Without money and without price.

Joel 3:18 And it will come to pass in that day *That* the mountains shall drip with new wine, The hills shall flow with milk, And all the brooks of Judah shall be flooded with water; A fountain shall flow from the house of the LORD And water the Valley of Acacias.

First principles of God's Word.

1 Cor 3:2 I fed you with milk and not with solid food; for until now you were not able *to receive it,* and even now you are still not able;

Heb 5:12 For though by this time you ought to be teachers, you need *someone* to teach you again the first principles of the oracles of God; and you have come to need milk and not solid food.

1 Pet 2:2 as newborn babes, desire the pure milk of the word, that you may grow thereby,

Godly and edifying discourses.

Song 4:11 Your lips, O *my* spouse, Drip as the honeycomb; Honey and milk *are* under your tongue; And the fragrance of your garments *Is* like the fragrance of Lebanon.

Wealth of the Gentiles.

Is 60:16 You shall drink the milk of the Gentiles, And milk the breast of kings; You shall know that I, the LORD, *am* your Savior And your Redeemer, the Mighty One of Jacob.

MILLS

Antiquity of.

Ex 11:5 and all the firstborn in the land of Egypt shall die, from the firstborn of Pharaoh who sits on his throne, even to the firstborn of the female servant who *is* behind the handmill, and all the firstborn of the animals.

Used for grinding

Manna in the wilderness.

Num 11:8 The people went about and gathered *it,* ground *it* on millstones or beat *it* in the mortar, cooked *it* in pans, and made cakes of it; and its taste was like the taste of pastry prepared with oil.

Meal.

Is 47:2 Take the millstones and grind meal. Remove your veil, Take off the skirt, Uncover the thigh, Pass through the rivers.

Female servants and male captives often employed at.

Ex 11:5 and all the firstborn in the land of Egypt shall die, from the firstborn of Pharaoh who sits on his throne, even to the firstborn of the female servant who *is* behind the handmill, and all the firstborn of the animals.

Judg 16:21 Then the Philistines took him and put out his eyes, and brought him down to Gaza. They bound him with bronze fetters, and he became a grinder in the prison.

Lam 5:13 Young men ground at the millstones; Boys staggered under *loads of* wood.

Matt 24:41 Two *women will be* grinding at the mill: one will be taken and the other left.

Stones were

Sturdy.

Job 41:24 His heart is as hard as stone, Even as hard as the lower *millstone.*

Matt 18:6 "Whoever causes one of these little ones who believe in Me to sin, it would be better for him if a millstone were hung around his neck, and he were drowned in the depth of the sea.

Large.

Rev 18:21 Then a mighty angel took up a stone like a great millstone and threw *it* into the sea, saying, "Thus with violence the great city Babylon shall be thrown down, and shall not be found anymore.

Not to be taken in pledge.

Deut 24:6 "No man shall take the lower or the upper millstone in pledge, for he takes *one's* living in pledge.

Often thrown down on enemies during sieges.

Judg 9:53 But a certain woman dropped an upper millstone on Abimelech's head and crushed his skull.

2 Sam 11:21 Who struck Abimelech the son of Jerubbesheth? Was it not a woman who cast a piece of a millstone on him from the wall, so that he died in Thebez? Why did you go near the wall?'—then you shall say, 'Your servant Uriah the Hittite is dead also.' "

Illustrative of

(Grinding at) degradation.

Is 47:1–2 "Come down and sit in the dust, O virgin daughter of Babylon; Sit on the ground without a throne, O daughter of the Chaldeans! For you shall no more be called Tender and delicate. **2** Take the millstones and grind meal. Remove your veil, Take off the skirt, Uncover the thigh, Pass through the rivers.

(Ceasing) desolation.

Jer 25:10 Moreover I will take from them the voice of mirth and the voice of gladness, the voice of the bridegroom and the voice of the bride, the sound of the millstones and the light of the lamp.

Rev 18:22 The sound of harpists, musicians, flutists, and trumpeters shall not be heard in you anymore. No craftsman of any craft shall be found in you anymore, and the sound of a millstone shall not be heard in you anymore.

MIND

Should remember what God has done.

Deut 30:1–3 "Now it shall come to pass, when all these things come upon you, the blessing and the curse which I have set before you, and you call *them* to mind among all the nations where the LORD your God drives you, **2** and you return to the LORD your God and obey His voice, according to all that I command you today, you and your children, with all your heart and with all your soul, **3** that the LORD your God will bring you back from captivity, and have compassion on you, and gather you again from all the nations where the LORD your God has scattered you.

Ps 77:10–15 And I said, "This *is* my anguish; *But I will remember* the years of the right hand of the Most High." **11** I will remember the works of the LORD; Surely I will remember Your wonders of old. **12** I will also meditate on all Your work, And talk of Your deeds. **13** Your way, O God, *is* in the sanctuary; Who *is* so great a God as *our* God? **14** You *are* the God who does wonders; You have declared Your strength among the peoples. **15** You have with *Your* arm redeemed Your people, The sons of Jacob and Joseph. Selah

Cf. Luke 2:51; Heb 10:32

God will test it.

Ps 7:9 Oh, let the wickedness of the wicked come to an end, But establish the just; For the righteous God tests the hearts and minds.

Cf. Jer 17:10; Acts 1:24; 15:8

Should be fully engaged in love for God.

Deut 6:5 You shall love the LORD your God with all your heart, with all your soul, and with all your strength.

Matt 22:37 Jesus said to him, " 'You shall love the LORD your God with all your heart, with all your soul, and with all your mind.'

Mark 12:30 And you shall love the LORD your God with all your heart, with all your soul, with all your mind, and with all your strength.' This *is* the first commandment.

Cf. Ps 111:1

Should believe the gospel.

Rom 10:10–11 For with the heart one believes unto righteousness, and with the mouth confession is made unto salvation. **11** For the Scripture says, "*Whoever believes on Him will not be put to shame."*

Cf. Rom 1:16

Is necessary to serve Christ.

Rom 7:25 I thank God—through Jesus Christ our Lord! So then, with the mind I myself serve the law of God, but with the flesh the law of sin.

Sin wars against.

Rom 7:23 But I see another law in my members, warring against the law of my mind, and bringing me into captivity to the law of sin which is in my members.

Rom 8:6–8 For to be carnally minded *is* death, but to be spiritually minded *is* life and peace. **7** Because the carnal mind *is* enmity against God; for it is not subject to the law of God, nor indeed can be. **8** So then, those who are in the flesh cannot please God.

Of the Spirit, agrees with God.

Rom 8:27 Now He who searches the hearts knows what the mind of the Spirit *is*, because He makes intercession for the saints according to *the will of* God.

Of believers,

Must be renewed.

Rom 12:2 And do not be conformed to this world, but be transformed by the renewing of your mind, that you may prove what *is* that good and acceptable and perfect will of God.

Eph 4:23–24 and be renewed in the spirit of your mind, **24** and that you put on the new man which was created according to God, in true righteousness and holiness.

Cf. 2 Cor 3:18; Eph 1:18; 5:17; 1 Pet 1:13

Must be unified and humble.

Rom 12:16 Be of the same mind toward one another. Do not set your mind on high things, but associate with the humble. Do not be wise in your own opinion.

Phil 1:27 Only let your conduct be worthy of the gospel of Christ, so that whether I come and see you or am absent, I may hear of your affairs, that you stand fast in one spirit, with one mind striving together for the faith of the gospel,

Phil 2:2–3 fulfill my joy by being like-minded, having the same love, *being* of one accord, of one mind. **3** *Let* nothing *be done* through selfish ambition or conceit, but in lowliness of mind let each esteem others better than himself.

Cf. Phil 4:2; 1 Pet 3:8; 4:1

Must be willing to give.

2 Cor 8:12 For if there is first a willing mind, *it is* accepted according to what one has, *and* not according to what he does not have.

Should be fixed on spiritual things.

Col 3:2 Set your mind on things above, not on things on the earth.

Is important part of Christian unity.

Rom 15:6 that you may with one mind *and* one mouth glorify the God and Father of our Lord Jesus Christ.

1 Cor 1:10 Now I plead with you, brethren, by the name of our Lord Jesus Christ, that you all speak the same thing, and *that* there be no divisions among you, but *that* you be perfectly joined together in the same mind and in the same judgment.

Believers can know that of Christ.

1 Cor 2:16 For *"who has known the mind of the LORD that he may instruct Him?"* But we have the mind of Christ.

Cf. Is 40:13; Luke 24:45; 2 Tim 1:7

Of unbelievers, spiritually ignorant.

Eph 4:17 This I say, therefore, and testify in the Lord, that you should no longer walk as the rest of the Gentiles walk, in the futility of their mind,

Cf. 1 Cor 2:14; Col 2:18; Titus 1:15

MINISTERS. *SEE ALSO* ELDERS; PREACHERS, PREACHING

Divinely called and protected.

Ex 28:1 "Now take Aaron your brother, and his sons with him, from among the children of Israel, that he may minister to Me as priest, Aaron *and* Aaron's sons: Nadab, Abihu, Eleazar, and Ithamar.

Is 6:5–7 So I said: "Woe *is* me, for I am undone! Because I *am* a man of unclean lips, And I dwell in the midst of a people of unclean lips; For my eyes have seen the King, The LORD of hosts." **6** Then one of the seraphim flew to me, having in his hand a live coal *which* he had taken with the tongs from the altar. **7** And he touched my mouth *with it*, and said: "Behold, this has touched your lips; Your iniquity is taken away, And your sin purged."

Matt 28:19 Go therefore and make disciples of all the nations, baptizing them in the name of the Father and of the Son and of the Holy Spirit,

Acts 13:2 As they ministered to the Lord and fasted, the Holy Spirit said, "Now separate to Me Barnabas and Saul for the work to which I have called them."

Acts 13:4 So, being sent out by the Holy Spirit, they went down to Seleucia, and from there they sailed to Cyprus.

Rom 1:1 Paul, a bondservant of Jesus Christ, called *to be* an apostle, separated to the gospel of God

2 Cor 1:10 who delivered us from so great a death, and does deliver us; in whom we trust that He will still deliver *us*,

2 Cor 3:5–6 Not that we are sufficient of ourselves to think of anything as *being* from ourselves, but our sufficiency *is* from God, **6** who also made us sufficient as ministers of the new covenant, not of the letter but of the Spirit; for the letter kills, but the Spirit gives life.

1 Thess 2:4 But as we have been approved by God to be entrusted with the gospel, even so we speak, not as pleasing men, but God who tests our hearts.

Heb 5:4 And no man takes this honor to himself, but he who is called by God, just as Aaron *was*.

Have authority from God.

2 Cor 10:8 For even if I should boast somewhat more about our authority, which the Lord gave us for edification and not for your destruction, I shall not be ashamed—

2 Cor 13:10 Therefore I write these things being absent, lest being present I should use sharpness, according to the authority which the Lord has given me for edification and not for destruction.

Described as

Ambassadors for Christ.

2 Cor 5:20 Now then, we are ambassadors for Christ, as though God were pleading through us: we implore *you* on Christ's behalf, be reconciled to God.

Servants of Christ.

1 Cor 4:1 Let a man so consider us, as servants of Christ and stewards of the mysteries of God.

Stewards of the mysteries of God.

1 Cor 4:1 Let a man so consider us, as servants of Christ and stewards of the mysteries of God.

Defenders of the faith.

Phil 1:7 just as it is right for me to think this of you all, because I have you in my heart, inasmuch as both in my chains and in the defense and confirmation of the gospel, you all are partakers with me of grace.

The bondservants of Christ's people.

2 Cor 4:5 For we do not preach ourselves, but Christ Jesus the Lord, and ourselves your bondservants for Jesus' sake.

Necessity for.

Matt 9:37–38 Then He said to His disciples, "The harvest truly *is* plentiful, but the laborers *are* few. **38** Therefore pray the Lord of the harvest to send out laborers into His harvest."

Rom 10:14 How then shall they call on Him in whom they have not believed? And how shall they believe in Him of whom they have not heard? And how shall they hear without a preacher?

Excellency of.

Rom 10:15 And how shall they preach unless they are sent? As it is written: *"How beautiful are the feet of those who preach the gospel of peace, Who bring glad tidings of good things!"*

Labors of, vain, without God's blessing.

1 Cor 3:7 So then neither he who plants is anything, nor he who waters, but God who gives the increase.

1 Cor 15:10 But by the grace of God I am what I am, and His grace toward me was not in vain; but I labored more abundantly than they all, yet not I, but the grace of God *which was* with me.

Should be

Pure.

Is 52:11 Depart! Depart! Go out from there, Touch no unclean *thing;* Go out from the midst of her, Be clean, You who bear the vessels of the LORD.

1 Tim 3:9 holding the mystery of the faith with a pure conscience.

Holy.

Ex 28:36 "You shall also make a plate of pure gold and engrave on it, *like* the engraving of a signet: HOLINESS TO THE LORD.

Lev 21:6 They shall be holy to their God and not profane the name of their God, for they offer the offerings of the LORD made by fire, *and* the bread of their God; therefore they shall be holy.

Titus 1:8 but hospitable, a lover of what is good, sober-minded, just, holy, self-controlled,

Humble.

Acts 20:19 serving the Lord with all humility, with many tears and trials which happened to me by the plotting of the Jews;

Patient.

2 Cor 6:4 But in all *things* we commend ourselves as ministers of God: in much patience, in tribulations, in needs, in distresses,

2 Tim 2:24 And a servant of the Lord must not quarrel but be gentle to all, able to teach, patient,

Blameless.

1 Tim 3:2 A bishop then must be blameless, the husband of one wife, temperate, sober-minded, of good behavior, hospitable, able to teach;

Titus 1:7 For a bishop must be blameless, as a steward of God, not self-willed, not quick-tempered, not given to wine, not violent, not greedy for money,

Willing.

Is 6:8 Also I heard the voice of the Lord, saying: "Whom shall I send, And who will go for Us?" Then I said, "Here *am* I! Send me."

1 Pet 5:2 Shepherd the flock of God which is among you, serving as overseers, not by compulsion but willingly, not for dishonest gain but eagerly;

Unselfish.

2 Cor 12:14 Now *for* the third time I am ready to come to you. And I will not be burdensome to you; for I do not seek yours, but you. For the children ought not to lay up for the parents, but the parents for the children.

1 Thess 2:6 Nor did we seek glory from men, either from you or from others, when we might have made demands as apostles of Christ.

Impartial.

1 Tim 5:21 I charge *you* before God and the Lord Jesus Christ and the elect angels that you observe these things without prejudice, doing nothing with partiality.

Gentle.

1 Thess 2:7 But we were gentle among you, just as a nursing *mother* cherishes her own children.

2 Tim 2:24 And a servant of the Lord must not quarrel but be gentle to all, able to teach, patient,

Devoted.

Acts 20:24 But none of these things move me; nor do I count my life dear to myself, so that I may finish my race with joy, and the ministry which I received from the Lord Jesus, to testify to the gospel of the grace of God.

Phil 1:20–21 according to my earnest expectation and hope that in nothing I shall be ashamed, but with all boldness, as always, so now also Christ will be magnified in my body, whether by life or by death. 21 For to me, to live *is* Christ, and to die *is* gain.

Strong in grace.

2 Tim 2:1 You therefore, my son, be strong in the grace that is in Christ Jesus.

Self-denying.

1 Cor 9:27 But I discipline my body and bring *it* into subjection, lest, when I have preached to others, I myself should become disqualified.

Sober, just, and self-controlled.

Lev 10:9 "Do not drink wine or intoxicating drink, you, nor your sons with you, when you go into the tabernacle of meeting, lest you die. *It shall be* a statute forever throughout your generations,

Titus 1:8 but hospitable, a lover of what is good, sober-minded, just, holy, self-controlled,

Hospitable.

1 Tim 3:2 A bishop then must be blameless, the husband of one wife, temperate, sober-minded, of good behavior, hospitable, able to teach;

Titus 1:8 but hospitable, a lover of what is good, sober-minded, just, holy, self-controlled,

Able to teach.

1 Tim 3:2 A bishop then must be blameless, the husband of one wife, temperate, sober-minded, of good behavior, hospitable, able to teach;

2 Tim 2:24 And a servant of the Lord must not quarrel but be gentle to all, able to teach, patient,

Studious, meditative and prayerful.

Eph 3:14 For this reason I bow my knees to the Father of our Lord Jesus Christ,

Phil 1:4 always in every prayer of mine making request for you all with joy,

1 Tim 4:13 Till I come, give attention to reading, to exhortation, to doctrine.

1 Tim 4:15 Meditate on these things; give yourself entirely to them, that your progress may be evident to all.

2 Tim 4:5 But you be watchful in all things, endure afflictions, do the work of an evangelist, fulfill your ministry.

Diligent in ruling their own families.

1 Tim 3:4 one who rules his own house well, having *his* children in submission with all reverence

1 Tim 3:12 Let deacons be the husbands of one wife, ruling *their* children and their own houses well.

Affectionate to their people.

Phil 1:7 just as it is right for me to think this of you all, because I have you in my heart, inasmuch as both in my chains and in the defense and confirmation of the gospel, you all are partakers with me of grace.

1 Thess 2:8 So, affectionately longing for you, we were well pleased to impart to you not only the gospel of God, but also our own lives, because you had become dear to us.

1 Thess 2:11 as you know how we exhorted, and comforted, and charged every one of you, as a father *does* his own children,

Examples to the flock.

Phil 3:17 Brethren, join in following my example, and note those who so walk, as you have us for a pattern.

2 Thess 3:9 not because we do not have authority, but to make ourselves an example of how you should follow us.

1 Tim 4:12 Let no one despise your youth, but be an example to the believers in word, in conduct, in love, in spirit, in faith, in purity.

1 Pet 5:3 nor as being lords over those entrusted to you, but being examples to the flock;

Should not be

Lords over God's heritage.

1 Pet 5:3 nor as being lords over those entrusted to you, but being examples to the flock;

Greedy for money.

Acts 20:33 I have coveted no one's silver or gold or apparel.

1 Tim 3:3 not given to wine, not violent, not greedy for money, but gentle, not quarrelsome, not covetous;

1 Tim 3:8 Likewise deacons *must be* reverent, not double-tongued, not given to much wine, not greedy for money,

1 Pet 5:2 Shepherd the flock of God which is among you, serving as overseers, not by compulsion but willingly, not for dishonest gain but eagerly;

Quarrelsome.

1 Tim 3:3 not given to wine, not violent, not greedy for money, but gentle, not quarrelsome, not covetous;

Titus 1:7 For a bishop must be blameless, as a steward of God, not self-willed, not quick-tempered, not given to wine, not violent, not greedy for money,

Crafty.

2 Cor 4:2 But we have renounced the hidden things of shame, not walking in craftiness nor handling the word of God deceitfully, but by manifestation of the truth commending ourselves to every man's conscience in the sight of God.

Men-pleasers.

Gal 1:10 For do I now persuade men, or God? Or do I seek to please men? For if I still pleased men, I would not be a bondservant of Christ.

1 Thess 2:4 But as we have been approved by God to be entrusted with the gospel, even so we speak, not as pleasing men, but God who tests our hearts.

Easily dispirited.

2 Cor 4:8–9 *We are* hard-pressed on every side, yet not crushed; *we are* perplexed, but not in despair; **9** persecuted, but not forsaken; struck down, but not destroyed—

2 Cor 6:10 as sorrowful, yet always rejoicing; as poor, yet making many rich; as having nothing, and *yet* possessing all things.

Entangled by cares.

Luke 9:60 Jesus said to him, "Let the dead bury their own dead, but you go and preach the kingdom of God."

2 Tim 2:4 No one engaged in warfare entangles himself with the affairs of *this* life, that he may please him who enlisted him as a soldier.

Given to wine.

1 Tim 3:3 not given to wine, not violent, not greedy for money, but gentle, not quarrelsome, not covetous;

Titus 1:7 For a bishop must be blameless, as a steward of God, not self-willed, not quick-tempered, not given to wine, not violent, not greedy for money,

Are responsible to

Avoid giving unnecessary offense.

1 Cor 10:32–33 Give no offense, either to the Jews or to the Greeks or to the church of God, **33** just as I also please all *men* in all *things,* not seeking my own profit, but the *profit* of many, that they may be saved.

2 Cor 6:3 We give no offense in anything, that our ministry may not be blamed.

Make full proof of their ministry.

2 Tim 4:5 But you be watchful in all things, endure afflictions, do the work of an evangelist, fulfill your ministry.

Preach the gospel to all.

Mark 16:16 He who believes and is baptized will be saved; but he who does not believe will be condemned.

1 Cor 1:17 For Christ did not send me to baptize, but to preach the gospel, not with wisdom of words, lest the cross of Christ should be made of no effect.

1 Cor 9:16 For if I preach the gospel, I have nothing to boast of, for necessity is laid upon me; yes, woe is me if I do not preach the gospel!

1 Cor 10:33 just as I also please all *men* in all *things,* not seeking my own profit, but the *profit* of many, that they may be saved.

Feed the church.

John 21:15–17 So when they had eaten breakfast, Jesus said to Simon Peter, "Simon, *son* of Jonah, do you love Me more than these?" He said to Him, "Yes, Lord; You know that I love You." He said to him, "Feed My lambs." **16** He said to him again a second time, "Simon, *son* of Jonah, do you love Me?" He said to Him, "Yes, Lord; You know that I love You." He said to him, "Tend My sheep." **17** He said to him the third time, "Simon, *son* of Jonah, do you love Me?" Peter was grieved because He said to him the third time, "Do you love Me?" And he said to Him, "Lord, You know all things; You know that I love You." Jesus said to him, "Feed My sheep.

Acts 20:28 Therefore take heed to yourselves and to all the flock, among which the Holy Spirit has made you overseers, to shepherd the church of God which He purchased with His own blood.

1 Pet 5:2 Shepherd the flock of God which is among you, serving as overseers, not by compulsion but willingly, not for dishonest gain but eagerly;

Build up the church.

2 Cor 12:19 Again, do you think that we excuse ourselves to you? We speak before God in Christ. But *we do* all things, beloved, for your edification.

Eph 4:12 for the equipping of the saints for the work of ministry, for the edifying of the body of Christ,

Have concern for their people.

Joel 2:17 Let the priests, who minister to the LORD, Weep between the porch and the altar; Let them say, "Spare Your people, O LORD, And do not give Your heritage to reproach, That the nations should rule over them. Why should they say among the peoples, 'Where *is* their God?' "

Luke 22:32 But I have prayed for you, that your faith should not fail; and when you have returned to *Me,* strengthen your brethren."

Acts 14:22 strengthening the souls of the disciples, exhorting *them* to continue in the faith, and *saying,* "We must through many tribulations enter the kingdom of God."

Col 1:9 For this reason we also, since the day we heard it, do not cease to pray for you, and to ask that you may be filled with the knowledge of His will in all wisdom and spiritual understanding;

Heb 13:17 Obey those who rule over you, and be submissive, for they watch out for your souls, as those who must give account. Let them do so with joy and not with grief, for that would be unprofitable for you.

Teach.

2 Tim 2:2 And the things that you have heard from me among many witnesses, commit these to faithful men who will be able to teach others also.

Exhort.

Acts 20:31 Therefore watch, and remember that for three years I did not cease to warn everyone night and day with tears.

Titus 1:9 holding fast the faithful word as he has been taught, that he may be able, by sound doctrine, both to exhort and convict those who contradict.

Titus 2:15 Speak these things, exhort, and rebuke with all authority. Let no one despise you.

Rebuke.

Titus 1:13 This testimony is true. Therefore rebuke them sharply, that they may be sound in the faith,

Titus 2:15 Speak these things, exhort, and rebuke with all authority. Let no one despise you.

Comfort.

2 Cor 1:4–6 who comforts us in all our tribulation, that we may be able to comfort those who are in any trouble, with the comfort with which we ourselves are comforted by God. **5** For as the sufferings of Christ abound in us, so our consolation also abounds through Christ. **6** Now if we are afflicted, *it is* for your consolation and salvation, which is effective for enduring the same sufferings which we also suffer. Or if we are comforted, *it is* for your consolation and salvation.

Convince opponents of truth.

Titus 1:9 holding fast the faithful word as he has been taught, that he may be able, by sound doctrine, both to exhort and convict those who contradict.

Wage a good warfare.

1 Tim 1:18 This charge I commit to you, son Timothy, according to the prophecies previously made concerning you, that by them you may wage the good warfare,

2 Tim 2:3 You therefore must endure hardship as a good soldier of Jesus Christ.

2 Tim 4:7 I have fought the good fight, I have finished the race, I have kept the faith.

Should preach

Christ only.

Acts 8:5 Then Philip went down to the city of Samaria and preached Christ to them.

Acts 8:35 Then Philip opened his mouth, and beginning at this Scripture, preached Jesus to him.

1 Cor 2:2 For I determined not to know anything among you except Jesus Christ and Him crucified.

2 Cor 4:5 For we do not preach ourselves, but Christ Jesus the Lord, and ourselves your bondservants for Jesus' sake.

Repentance and faith.

Acts 20:21 testifying to Jews, and also to Greeks, repentance toward God and faith toward our Lord Jesus Christ.

As spokesmen of God.

1 Pet 4:11 If anyone speaks, *let him speak* as the oracles of God. If anyone ministers, *let him do it* as with the ability which God supplies, that in all things God may be glorified through Jesus Christ, to whom belong the glory and the dominion forever and ever. Amen.

Everywhere.

Mark 16:20 And they went out and preached everywhere, the Lord working with *them* and confirming the word through the accompanying signs. Amen.

Acts 8:4 Therefore those who were scattered went everywhere preaching the word.

Not with enticing words of man's wisdom.

1 Cor 1:17 For Christ did not send me to baptize, but to preach the gospel, not with wisdom of words, lest the cross of Christ should be made of no effect.

1 Cor 2:1 And I, brethren, when I came to you, did not come with excellence of speech or of wisdom declaring to you the testimony of God.

1 Cor 2:4 And my speech and my preaching *were* not with persuasive words of human wisdom, but in demonstration of the Spirit and of power,

Without deceitfulness.

2 Cor 2:17 For we are not, as so many, peddling the word of God; but as of sincerity, but as from God, we speak in the sight of God in Christ.

2 Cor 4:2 But we have renounced the hidden things of shame, not walking in craftiness nor handling the word of God deceitfully, but by manifestation of the truth commending ourselves to every man's conscience in the sight of God.

1 Thess 2:3 For our exhortation *did* not *come* from error or uncleanness, nor *was it* in deceit.

1 Thess 2:5 For neither at any time did we use flattering words, as you know, nor a cloak for covetousness—God *is* witness.

Fully and boldly.

Is 58:1 "Cry aloud, spare not; Lift up your voice like a trumpet; Tell My people their transgression, And the house of Jacob their sins.

Ezek 2:6 "And you, son of man, do not be afraid of them nor be afraid of their words, though briers and thorns *are* with you and you dwell among scorpions; do not be afraid of their words or dismayed by their looks, though they *are* a rebellious house.

Matt 10:27–28 "Whatever I tell you in the dark, speak in the light; and what you hear in the ear, preach on the housetops. **28** And do not fear those who kill the body but cannot kill the soul. But rather fear Him who is able to destroy both soul and body in hell.

Acts 5:20 "Go, stand in the temple and speak to the people all the words of this life."

Acts 20:20 how I kept back nothing that was helpful, but proclaimed it to you, and taught you publicly and from house to house,

Acts 20:27 For I have not shunned to declare to you the whole counsel of God.

Rom 15:19 in mighty signs and wonders, by the power of the Spirit of God, so that from Jerusalem and round about to Illyricum I have fully preached the gospel of Christ.

2 Cor 3:12 Therefore, since we have such hope, we use great boldness of speech—

1 Thess 2:8 So, affectionately longing for you, we were well pleased to impart to you not only the gospel of God, but also our own lives, because you had become dear to us.

With care and faithfulness.

Ezek 3:17–18 "Son of man, I have made you a watchman for the house of Israel; therefore hear a word from My mouth, and give them warning from Me: **18** When I say to the wicked, 'You shall surely die,' and you give him no warning, nor speak to warn the wicked from his wicked way, to save his life, that same wicked *man* shall die in his iniquity; but his blood I will require at your hand.

Acts 6:4 but we will give ourselves continually to prayer and to the ministry of the word."

2 Cor 1:18–19 But *as* God *is* faithful, our word to you was not Yes and No. **19** For the Son of God, Jesus Christ, who was preached among you by us—by me, Silvanus, and Timothy—was not Yes and No, but in Him was Yes.

Phil 1:15–17 Some indeed preach Christ even from envy and strife, and some also from goodwill: **16** The former preach Christ from selfish ambition, not sincerely, supposing to add affliction to my chains; **17** but the latter out of love, knowing that I am appointed for the defense of the gospel.

1 Tim 4:16 Take heed to yourself and to the doctrine. Continue in them, for in doing this you will save both yourself and those who hear you.

2 Tim 4:2 Preach the word! Be ready in season *and* out of season. Convince, rebuke, exhort, with all long-suffering and teaching.

Without charge, if possible.

1 Cor 9:18 What is my reward then? That when I preach the gospel, I may present the gospel of Christ without charge, that I may not abuse my authority in the gospel.

1 Thess 2:9 For you remember, brethren, our labor and toil; for laboring night and day, that we might not be a burden to any of you, we preached to you the gospel of God.

When faithful,

Approve themselves as God's ministers.

2 Cor 6:4 But in all *things* we commend ourselves as ministers of God: in much patience, in tribulations, in needs, in distresses,

Thank God for His gifts to their people.

1 Cor 1:4 I thank my God always concerning you for the grace of God which was given to you by Christ Jesus,

Phil 1:3 I thank my God upon every remembrance of you,

1 Thess 3:9 For what thanks can we render to God for you, for all the joy with which we rejoice for your sake before our God,

Glory in their people.

2 Cor 7:4 Great *is* my boldness of speech toward you, great *is* my boasting on your behalf. I am filled with comfort. I am exceedingly joyful in all our tribulation.

Rejoice in the faith and holiness of their people.

1 Thess 3:6–9 But now that Timothy has come to us from you, and brought us good news of your faith and love, and that you always have good remembrance of us, greatly desiring to see us, as we also *to see* you— **7** therefore, brethren, in all our affliction

and distress we were comforted concerning you by your faith. **8** For now we live, if you stand fast in the Lord. **9** For what thanks can we render to God for you, for all the joy with which we rejoice for your sake before our God,

Commend themselves to people's consciences.

2 Cor 4:2 But we have renounced the hidden things of shame, not walking in craftiness nor handling the word of God deceitfully, but by manifestation of the truth commending ourselves to every man's conscience in the sight of God.

Are rewarded.

Matt 24:47 Assuredly, I say to you that he will make him ruler over all his goods.

1 Cor 3:14 If anyone's work which he has built on *it* endures, he will receive a reward.

1 Cor 9:17–18 For if I do this willingly, I have a reward; but if against my will, I have been entrusted with a stewardship. **18** What is my reward then? That when I preach the gospel, I may present the gospel of Christ without charge, that I may not abuse my authority in the gospel.

1 Pet 5:4 and when the Chief Shepherd appears, you will receive the crown of glory that does not fade away.

False,

Described.

Is 56:10–12 His watchmen *are* blind, They are all ignorant; They *are* all dumb dogs, They cannot bark; Sleeping, lying down, loving to slumber. **11** Yes, *they are* greedy dogs *Which* never have enough. And they *are* shepherds Who cannot understand; They all look to their own way, Every one for his own gain, From his *own* territory. **12** "Come," *one says,* "I will bring wine, And we will fill ourselves with intoxicating drink; Tomorrow will be as today, *And* much more abundant."

Titus 1:10–11 For there are many insubordinate, both idle talkers and deceivers, especially those of the circumcision, **11** whose mouths must be stopped, who subvert whole households, teaching things which they ought not, for the sake of dishonest gain.

Deal treacherously with their people.

John 10:12 But a hireling, *he who is* not the shepherd, one who does not own the sheep, sees the wolf coming and leaves the sheep and flees; and the wolf catches the sheep and scatters them.

Delude men.

Jer 6:14 They have also healed the hurt of My people slightly, Saying, 'Peace, peace!' When *there is* no peace.

Matt 15:14 Let them alone. They are blind leaders of the blind. And if the blind leads the blind, both will fall into a ditch."

Seek gain.

Mic 3:11 Her heads judge for a bribe, Her priests teach for pay, And her prophets divine for money. Yet they lean on the Lord, and say, "Is not the Lord among us? No harm can come upon us."

2 Pet 2:3 By covetousness they will exploit you with deceptive words; for a long time their judgment has not been idle, and their destruction does not slumber.

Shall be punished.

Ezek 33:6–8 But if the watchman sees the sword coming and does not blow the trumpet, and the people are not warned, and the sword comes and takes *any* person from among them, he is taken away in his iniquity; but his blood I will require at the watchman's hand.' **7** "So you, son of man: I have made you a watchman for the house of Israel; therefore you shall hear a word from My mouth and warn them for Me. **8** When I say to the wicked, 'O wicked *man*, you shall surely die!' and you do not speak to warn the wicked from his way, that wicked *man* shall die in his iniquity; but his blood I will require at your hand.

Matt 24:48–51 But if that evil servant says in his heart, 'My master is delaying his coming,' **49** and begins to beat *his* fellow servants, and to eat and drink with the drunkards, **50** the master of that servant will come on a day when he is not looking for *him* and at an hour that he is not aware of, **51** and will cut him in two and appoint *him* his portion with the hypocrites. There shall be weeping and gnashing of teeth.

Flock responsible to,

Regard them as God's messengers.

1 Cor 4:1 Let a man so consider us, as servants of Christ and stewards of the mysteries of God.

Gal 4:14 And my trial which was in my flesh you did not despise or reject, but you received me as an angel of God, *even* as Christ Jesus.

Not to despise them.

Luke 10:16 He who hears you hears Me, he who rejects you rejects Me, and he who rejects Me rejects Him who sent Me."

1 Tim 4:12 Let no one despise your youth, but be an example to the believers in word, in conduct, in love, in spirit, in faith, in purity.

Attend to their instructions.

Mal 2:7 "For the lips of a priest should keep knowledge, And *people* should seek the law from his mouth; For he is the messenger of the LORD of hosts.

Matt 23:3 Therefore whatever they tell you to observe, *that* observe and do, but do not do according to their works; for they say, and do not do.

Follow their holy example.

1 Cor 11:1 Imitate me, just as I also *imitate* Christ.

Phil 3:17 Brethren, join in following my example, and note those who so walk, as you have us for a pattern.

Heb 13:7 Remember those who rule over you, who have spoken the word of God to you, whose faith follow, considering the outcome of *their* conduct.

Respect them.

Phil 2:29 Receive him therefore in the Lord with all gladness, and hold such men in esteem;

1 Thess 5:13 and to esteem them very highly in love for their work's sake. Be at peace among yourselves.

1 Tim 5:17 Let the elders who rule well be counted worthy of double honor, especially those who labor in the word and doctrine.

Love them.

2 Cor 8:7 But as you abound in everything—in faith, in speech, in knowledge, in all diligence, and in your love for us—*see* that you abound in this grace also.

1 Thess 3:6 But now that Timothy has come to us from you, and brought us good news of your faith and love, and that you always have good remembrance of us, greatly desiring to see us, as we also *to see* you—

Pray for them.

Rom 15:30 Now I beg you, brethren, through the Lord Jesus Christ, and through the love of the Spirit, that you strive together with me in prayers to God for me,

2 Cor 1:11 you also helping together in prayer for us, that thanks may be given by many persons on our behalf for the gift *granted* to us through many.

Eph 6:19 and for me, that utterance may be given to me, that I may open my mouth boldly to make known the mystery of the gospel,

Heb 13:18 Pray for us; for we are confident that we have a good conscience, in all things desiring to live honorably.

Obey them.

1 Cor 16:16 that you also submit to such, and to everyone who works and labors with *us*.

Heb 13:17 Obey those who rule over you, and be submissive, for they watch out for your souls, as those who must give account. Let them do so with joy and not with grief, for that would be unprofitable for you.

Give them joy.

2 Cor 1:14 (as also you have understood us in part), that we are your boast as you also *are* ours, in the day of the Lord Jesus.

2 Cor 2:3 And I wrote this very thing to you, lest, when I came, I should have sorrow over those from whom I ought to have joy, having confidence in you all that my joy is *the joy* of you all.

Help and support them.

2 Chr 31:4 Moreover he commanded the people who dwelt in Jerusalem to contribute support for the priests and the Levites, that they might devote themselves to the Law of the LORD.

Rom 16:9 Greet Urbanus, our fellow worker in Christ, and Stachys, my beloved.

1 Cor 9:7–11 Who ever goes to war at his own expense? Who plants a vineyard and does not eat of its fruit? Or who tends a flock and does not drink of the milk of the flock? **8** Do I say these things as a *mere* man? Or does not the law say the same also? **9** For it is written in the law of Moses, *"You shall not muzzle an ox while it treads out the grain."* Is it oxen God is concerned about? **10** Or does He say *it* altogether for our sakes? For our sakes, no doubt, *this* is written, that he who plows should plow in hope, and he who threshes in hope should be partaker of his hope. **11** If we have sown spiritual things for you, *is it* a great thing if we reap your material things?

Gal 6:6 Let him who is taught the word share in all good things with him who teaches.

Phil 4:3 And I urge you also, true companion, help these women who labored with me in the gospel, with Clement also, and the rest of my fellow workers, whose names *are* in the Book of Life.

Pray for the increase of.

Matt 9:38 Therefore pray the Lord of the harvest to send out laborers into His harvest."

Faithful—exemplified by

The eleven disciples.

Matt 28:16–19 Then the eleven disciples went away into Galilee, to the mountain which Jesus had appointed for them. **17** When they saw Him, they worshiped Him; but some doubted. **18** And Jesus came and spoke to them, saying, "All authority has been given to Me in heaven and on earth. **19** Go therefore and make disciples of all the nations, baptizing them in the name of the Father and of the Son and of the Holy Spirit,

The seventy.

Luke 10:1 After these things the Lord appointed seventy others also, and sent them two by two before His face into every city and place where He Himself was about to go.

Luke 10:17 Then the seventy returned with joy, saying, "Lord, even the demons are subject to us in Your name."

Matthias.

Acts 1:26 And they cast their lots, and the lot fell on Matthias. And he was numbered with the eleven apostles.

Philip.

Acts 8:5 Then Philip went down to the city of Samaria and preached Christ to them.

Barnabas.

Acts 11:23 When he came and had seen the grace of God, he was glad, and encouraged them all that with purpose of heart they should continue with the Lord.

Simeon, etc.

Acts 13:1 Now in the church that was at Antioch there were certain prophets and teachers: Barnabas, Simeon who was called Niger, Lucius of Cyrene, Manaen who had been brought up with Herod the tetrarch, and Saul.

Paul.

Acts 28:31 preaching the kingdom of God and teaching the things which concern the Lord Jesus Christ with all confidence, no one forbidding him.

Tychicus.

Eph 6:21 But that you also may know my affairs *and* how I am doing, Tychicus, a beloved brother and faithful minister in the Lord, will make all things known to you;

Timothy.

Phil 2:22 But you know his proven character, that as a son with *his* father he served with me in the gospel.

Epaphroditus.

Phil 2:24 But I trust in the Lord that I myself shall also come shortly.

Archippus.

Col 4:17 And say to Archippus, "Take heed to the ministry which you have received in the Lord, that you may fulfill it."

Titus.

Titus 1:5 For this reason I left you in Crete, that you should set in order the things that are lacking, and appoint elders in every city as I commanded you—

MINISTERS, TITLES AND NAMES OF

Ambassadors for Christ.

2 Cor 5:20 Now then, we are ambassadors for Christ, as though God were pleading through us: we implore *you* on Christ's behalf, be reconciled to God.

Angels of the church.

Rev 1:20 The mystery of the seven stars which you saw in My right hand, and the seven golden lampstands: The seven stars are the angels of the seven churches, and the seven lampstands which you saw are the seven churches.

Rev 2:1 "To the angel of the church of Ephesus write, 'These things says He who holds the seven stars in His right hand, who walks in the midst of the seven golden lampstands:

Apostles.

Luke 6:13 And when it was day, He called His disciples to *Himself;* and from them He chose twelve whom He also named apostles:

Eph 4:11 And He Himself gave some *to be* apostles, some prophets, some evangelists, and some pastors and teachers,

Rev 18:20 "Rejoice over her, O heaven, and *you* holy apostles and prophets, for God has avenged you on her!"

Apostles of Jesus Christ.

Titus 1:1 Paul, a bondservant of God and an apostle of Jesus Christ, according to the faith of God's elect and the acknowledgment of the truth which accords with godliness,

Bishops.

Phil 1:1 Paul and Timothy, bondservants of Jesus Christ, To all the saints in Christ Jesus who are in Philippi, with the bishops and deacons:

1 Tim 3:1 This *is* a faithful saying: If a man desires the position of a bishop, he desires a good work.

Titus 1:7 For a bishop must be blameless, as a steward of God, not self-willed, not quick-tempered, not given to wine, not violent, not greedy for money,

Bondservants of God.

Titus 1:1 Paul, a bondservant of God and an apostle of Jesus Christ, according to the faith of God's elect and the acknowledgment of the truth which accords with godliness,

James 1:1 James, a bondservant of God and of the Lord Jesus Christ, To the twelve tribes which are scattered abroad: Greetings.

Bondservants of Jesus Christ.

2 Cor 4:5 For we do not preach ourselves, but Christ Jesus the Lord, and ourselves your bondservants for Jesus' sake.

Phil 1:1 Paul and Timothy, bondservants of Jesus Christ, To all the saints in Christ Jesus who are in Philippi, with the bishops and deacons:

Jude 1:1 Jude, a bondservant of Jesus Christ, and brother of James, To those who are called, sanctified by God the Father, and preserved in Jesus Christ:

Deacons.

Phil 1:1 Paul and Timothy, bondservants of Jesus Christ, To all the saints in Christ Jesus who are in Philippi, with the bishops and deacons:

1 Tim 3:8 Likewise deacons *must be* reverent, not double-tongued, not given to much wine, not greedy for money,

Elders.

1 Tim 5:17 Let the elders who rule well be counted worthy of double honor, especially those who labor in the word and doctrine.

1 Pet 5:1 The elders who are among you I exhort, I who am a fellow elder and a witness of the sufferings of Christ, and also a partaker of the glory that will be revealed:

Evangelists.

Eph 4:11 And He Himself gave some *to be* apostles, some prophets, some evangelists, and some pastors and teachers,

2 Tim 4:5 But you be watchful in all things, endure afflictions, do the work of an evangelist, fulfill your ministry.

Fishers of men.

Matt 4:19 Then He said to them, "Follow Me, and I will make you fishers of men."

Mark 1:17 Then Jesus said to them, "Follow Me, and I will make you become fishers of men."

Laborers.

Matt 9:38 Therefore pray the Lord of the harvest to send out laborers into His harvest."

Philem 1:1 Paul, a prisoner of Christ Jesus, and Timothy *our* brother, To Philemon our beloved *friend* and fellow laborer,

Messengers of the church.

2 Cor 8:23 If *anyone inquires* about Titus, *he is* my partner and fellow worker concerning you. Or if our brethren *are inquired about, they are* messengers of the churches, the glory of Christ.

Messengers of the Lord of hosts.

Mal 2:7 "For the lips of a priest should keep knowledge, And *people* should seek the law from his mouth; For he is the messenger of the LORD of hosts.

Ministers of God.

2 Cor 6:4 But in all *things* we commend ourselves as ministers of God: in much patience, in tribulations, in needs, in distresses,

Ministers of Christ.

Rom 15:16 that I might be a minister of Jesus Christ to the Gentiles, ministering the gospel of God, that the offering of the Gentiles might be acceptable, sanctified by the Holy Spirit.

Ministers of the sanctuary.

Ezek 45:4 It shall be a holy *section* of the land, belonging to the priests, the ministers of the sanctuary, who come near to minister to the LORD; it shall be a place for their houses and a holy place for the sanctuary.

Ministers of the gospel.

Eph 3:7 of which I became a minister according to the gift of the grace of God given to me by the effective working of His power.

Col 1:23 if indeed you continue in the faith, grounded and steadfast, and are not moved away from the hope of the gospel which you heard, which was preached to every creature under heaven, of which I, Paul, became a minister.

Ministers of the Word.

Luke 1:2 just as those who from the beginning were eyewitnesses and ministers of the word delivered them to us,

Ministers of the new covenant.

2 Cor 3:6 who also made us sufficient as ministers of the new covenant, not of the letter but of the Spirit; for the letter kills, but the Spirit gives life.

Ministers of the church.

Col 1:24–25 I now rejoice in my sufferings for you, and fill up in my flesh what is lacking in the afflictions of Christ, for the sake of His body, which is the church, **25** of which I became a minister according to the stewardship from God which was given to me for you, to fulfill the word of God,

Ministers of righteousness.

2 Cor 11:15 Therefore *it is* no great thing if his ministers also transform themselves into ministers of righteousness, whose end will be according to their works.

Ministers to the Lord.

Joel 2:17 Let the priests, who minister to the LORD, Weep between the porch and the altar; Let them say, "Spare Your people, O LORD, And do not give Your heritage to reproach, That the nations should rule over them. Why should they say among the peoples, 'Where *is* their God?' "

Overseers.

Acts 20:28 Therefore take heed to yourselves and to all the flock, among which the Holy Spirit has made you overseers, to shepherd the church of God which He purchased with His own blood.

Pastors.

Eph 4:11 And He Himself gave some *to be* apostles, some prophets, some evangelists, and some pastors and teachers,

Preachers.

Rom 10:14 How then shall they call on Him in whom they have not believed? And how shall they believe in Him of whom they have not heard? And how shall they hear without a preacher?

1 Tim 2:7 for which I was appointed a preacher and an apostle—I am speaking the truth in Christ *and* not lying—a teacher of the Gentiles in faith and truth.

Servants of the Lord.

2 Tim 2:24 And a servant of the Lord must not quarrel but be gentle to all, able to teach, patient,

Servants of Jesus Christ.

1 Cor 4:1 Let a man so consider us, as servants of Christ and stewards of the mysteries of God.

Shepherds.

Jer 3:15 And I will give you shepherds according to My heart, who will feed you with knowledge and understanding.

Jer 23:4 I will set up shepherds over them who will feed them; and they shall fear no more, nor be dismayed, nor shall they be lacking," says the LORD.

Soldiers of Jesus Christ.

Phil 2:25 Yet I considered it necessary to send to you Epaphroditus, my brother, fellow worker, and fellow soldier, but your messenger and the one who ministered to my need;

2 Tim 2:3 You therefore must endure hardship as a good soldier of Jesus Christ.

Stars.

Rev 1:20 The mystery of the seven stars which you saw in My right hand, and the seven golden lampstands: The seven stars are the angels of the seven churches, and the seven lampstands which you saw are the seven churches.

Rev 2:1 "To the angel of the church of Ephesus write, 'These things says He who holds the seven stars in His right hand, who walks in the midst of the seven golden lampstands:

Stewards of God.

Titus 1:7 For a bishop must be blameless, as a steward of God, not self-willed, not quick-tempered, not given to wine, not violent, not greedy for money,

Stewards of the grace of God.

1 Pet 4:10 As each one has received a gift, minister it to one another, as good stewards of the manifold grace of God.

Stewards of the mysteries of God.

1 Cor 4:1 Let a man so consider us, as servants of Christ and stewards of the mysteries of God.

Teachers.

Is 30:20 And *though* the Lord gives you The bread of adversity and the water of affliction, Yet your teachers will not be moved into a corner anymore, But your eyes shall see your teachers.

Eph 4:11 And He Himself gave some *to be* apostles, some prophets, some evangelists, and some pastors and teachers,

Watchmen.

Is 62:6 I have set watchmen on your walls, O Jerusalem; They shall never hold their peace day or night. You who make mention of the LORD, do not keep silent,

Ezek 33:7 "So you, son of man: I have made you a watchman for the house of Israel; therefore you shall hear a word from My mouth and warn them for Me.

Witnesses.

Acts 1:8 But you shall receive power when the Holy Spirit has come upon you; and you shall be witnesses to Me in Jerusalem, and in all Judea and Samaria, and to the end of the earth."

Acts 5:32 And we are His witnesses to these things, and *so* also *is* the Holy Spirit whom God has given to those who obey Him."

Acts 26:16 But rise and stand on your feet; for I have appeared to you for this purpose, to make you a minister and a witness both of the things which you have seen and of the things which I will yet reveal to you.

Workers together with God.

2 Cor 6:1 We then, *as* workers together *with Him* also plead with *you* not to receive the grace of God in vain.

MIRACLES

Described as

Marvelous.

Ps 78:12 Marvelous things He did in the sight of their fathers, In the land of Egypt, *in* the field of Zoan.

Ps 105:5 Remember His marvelous works which He has done, His wonders, and the judgments of His mouth,

Is 29:14 Therefore, behold, I will again do a marvelous work Among this people, A marvelous work and a wonder; For the wisdom of their wise *men* shall perish, And the understanding of their prudent *men* shall be hidden."

Signs and wonders.

Jer 32:21 You have brought Your people Israel out of the land of Egypt with signs and wonders, with a strong hand and an outstretched arm, and with great terror;

John 4:48 Then Jesus said to him, "Unless you *people* see signs and wonders, you will by no means believe."

2 Cor 12:12 Truly the signs of an apostle were accomplished among you with all perseverance, in signs and wonders and mighty deeds.

Demonstrate

The glory of God.

John 11:4 When Jesus heard *that*, He said, "This sickness is not unto death, but for the glory of God, that the Son of God may be glorified through it."

The glory of Christ.

John 2:11 This beginning of signs Jesus did in Cana of Galilee, and manifested His glory; and His disciples believed in Him.

John 11:4 When Jesus heard *that*, He said, "This sickness is not unto death, but for the glory of God, that the Son of God may be glorified through it."

The works of God.

John 9:3 Jesus answered, "Neither this man nor his parents sinned, but that the works of God should be revealed in him.

Were evidences of a divine commission.

Ex 4:1–5 Then Moses answered and said, "But suppose they will not believe me or listen to my voice; suppose they say, 'The LORD has not appeared to you.' " **2** So the LORD said to him, "What *is* that in your hand?" He said, "A rod." **3** And He said, "Cast it on the ground." So he cast it on the ground, and it became a serpent; and Moses fled from it. **4** Then the LORD said to Moses, "Reach out your hand and take *it* by the tail" (and he reached out his hand and caught it, and it became a rod in his hand), **5** "that they may believe that the LORD God of their fathers, the God of Abraham, the God of Isaac, and the God of Jacob, has appeared to you."

Mark 16:20 And they went out and preached everywhere, the Lord working with *them* and confirming the word through the accompanying signs. Amen.

John 3:2 This man came to Jesus by night and said to Him, "Rabbi, we know that You are a teacher come from God; for no one can do these signs that You do unless God is with him."

Performed by Christ.

Matt 4:23–25 And Jesus went about all Galilee, teaching

in their synagogues, preaching the gospel of the kingdom, and healing all kinds of sickness and all kinds of disease among the people. **24** Then His fame went throughout all Syria; and they brought to Him all sick people who were afflicted with various diseases and torments, and those who were demon-possessed, epileptics, and paralytics; and He healed them. **25** Great multitudes followed Him—from Galilee, and *from* Decapolis, Jerusalem, Judea, and beyond the Jordan.

Matt 11:2–6 And when John had heard in prison about the works of Christ, he sent two of his disciples **3** and said to Him, "Are You the Coming One, or do we look for another?" **4** Jesus answered and said to them, "Go and tell John the things which you hear and see: **5** *The* blind see and *the* lame walk; *the* lepers are cleansed and *the* deaf hear; *the* dead are raised up and *the* poor have the gospel preached to them. **6** And blessed is he who is not offended because of Me."

Matt 14:35–36 And when the men of that place recognized Him, they sent out into all that surrounding region, brought to Him all who were sick, **36** and begged Him that they might only touch the hem of His garment. And as many as touched *it* were made perfectly well.

Luke 7:20–22 When the men had come to Him, they said, "John the Baptist has sent us to You, saying, 'Are You the Coming One, or do we look for another?' " **21** And that very hour He cured many of infirmities, afflictions, and evil spirits; and to many blind He gave sight. **22** Jesus answered and said to them, "Go and tell John the things you have seen and heard: that *the* blind see, *the* lame walk, *the* lepers are cleansed, *the* deaf hear, *the* dead are raised, *the* poor have the gospel preached to them.

John 5:36 But I have a greater witness than John's; for the works which the Father has given Me to finish— the very works that I do—bear witness of Me, that the Father has sent Me.

John 6:2 Then a great multitude followed Him, because they saw His signs which He performed on those who were diseased.

John 6:26 Jesus answered them and said, "Most assuredly, I say to you, you seek Me, not because you saw the signs, but because you ate of the loaves and were filled.

John 7:31 And many of the people believed in Him, and said, "When the Christ comes, will He do more signs than these which this *Man* has done?"

John 12:18 For this reason the people also met Him, because they heard that He had done this sign.

Acts 2:22 "Men of Israel, hear these words: Jesus of Nazareth, a Man attested by God to you by miracles, wonders, and signs which God did through Him in your midst, as you yourselves also know—

A gift of the Holy Spirit.

1 Cor 12:10 to another the working of miracles, to another prophecy, to another discerning of spirits, to another *different* kinds of tongues, to another the interpretation of tongues.

Controlled by

The power of God.

Ex 8:19 Then the magicians said to Pharaoh, "This *is* the finger of God." But Pharaoh's heart grew hard, and he did not heed them, just as the Lord had said.

Acts 14:3 Therefore they stayed there a long time, speaking boldly in the Lord, who was bearing witness to the word of His grace, granting signs and wonders to be done by their hands.

Acts 15:12 Then all the multitude kept silent and listened to Barnabas and Paul declaring how many miracles and wonders God had worked through them among the Gentiles.

Acts 19:11 Now God worked unusual miracles by the hands of Paul,

The power and name of Christ.

Matt 10:1 And when He had called His twelve disciples to *Him,* He gave them power *over* unclean spirits, to cast them out, and to heal all kinds of sickness and all kinds of disease.

Acts 3:16 And His name, through faith in His name, has made this man strong, whom you see and know. Yes, the faith which *comes* through Him has given him this perfect soundness in the presence of you all.

Acts 4:30 by stretching out Your hand to heal, and that signs and wonders may be done through the name of Your holy Servant Jesus."

The power of the Spirit of God.

Matt 12:28 But if I cast out demons by the Spirit of God, surely the kingdom of God has come upon you.

Rom 15:19 in mighty signs and wonders, by the power of the Spirit of God, so that from Jerusalem and round about to Illyricum I have fully preached the gospel of Christ.

First preaching of the gospel confirmed by.

Mark 16:20 And they went out and preached everywhere, the Lord working with *them* and confirming the word through the accompanying signs. Amen.

Acts 8:6 And the multitudes with one accord heeded the things spoken by Philip, hearing and seeing the miracles which he did.

Acts 14:3 Therefore they stayed there a long time, speaking boldly in the Lord, who was bearing witness to the word of His grace, granting signs and wonders to be done by their hands.

Rom 15:18–19 For I will not dare to speak of any of those things which Christ has not accomplished through me, in word and deed, to make the Gentiles obedient— **19** in mighty signs and wonders, by the power of the Spirit of God, so that from Jerusalem and round about to Illyricum I have fully preached the gospel of Christ.

Heb 2:4 God also bearing witness both with signs and wonders, with various miracles, and gifts of the Holy Spirit, according to His own will?

Should produce obedience.

Deut 11:1–3 "Therefore you shall love the Lord your God, and keep His charge, His statutes, His judgments, and His commandments always. **2** Know today that *I do* not *speak* with your children, who have not known and who have not seen the chastening of the LORD your God, His greatness and His mighty hand and His outstretched arm— **3** His signs and His acts which He did in the midst of Egypt, to Pharaoh king of Egypt, and to all his land;

Deut 29:2–3 Now Moses called all Israel and said to them: "You have seen all that the LORD did before your eyes in the land of Egypt, to Pharaoh and to all his servants and to all his land— **3** the great trials which your eyes have seen, the signs, and those great wonders.

Deut 29:9 Therefore keep the words of this covenant, and do them, that you may prosper in all that you do.

Faith required by

Those who performed.

Matt 17:20 So Jesus said to them, "Because of your unbelief; for assuredly, I say to you, if you have faith as a mustard seed, you will say to this mountain, 'Move from here to there,' and it will move; and nothing will be impossible for you.

Matt 21:21 So Jesus answered and said to them, "Assuredly, I say to you, if you have faith and do not doubt, you will not only do what was done to the fig tree, but also if you say to this mountain, 'Be removed and be cast into the sea,' it will be done.

John 14:12 "Most assuredly, I say to you, he who believes in Me, the works that I do he will do also; and greater *works* than these he will do, because I go to My Father.

Acts 3:16 And His name, through faith in His name, has made this man strong, whom you see and know. Yes, the faith which *comes* through Him has given him this perfect soundness in the presence of you all.

Acts 6:8 And Stephen, full of faith and power, did great wonders and signs among the people.

Those who observed.

Matt 9:28 And when He had come into the house, the blind men came to Him. And Jesus said to them, "Do you believe that I am able to do this?" They said to Him, "Yes, Lord."

Matt 13:58 Now He did not do many mighty works there because of their unbelief.

Mark 9:22–24 And often he has thrown him both into the fire and into the water to destroy him. But if You can do anything, have compassion on us and help us." **23** Jesus said to him, "If you can believe, all things *are* possible to him who believes." **24** Immediately the father of the child cried out and said with tears, "Lord, I believe; help my unbelief!"

John 2:23 Now when He was in Jerusalem at the Passover, during the feast, many believed in His name when they saw the signs which He did.

John 20:30–31 And truly Jesus did many other signs in the presence of His disciples, which are not written in this book; **31** but these are written that you may believe that Jesus is the Christ, the Son of God, and that believing you may have life in His name.

Acts 14:9 *This* man heard Paul speaking. Paul, observing him intently and seeing that he had faith to be healed,

Should be remembered and recounted.

Ex 10:2 and that you may tell in the hearing of your son and your son's son the mighty things I have done in Egypt, and My signs which I have done among them, that you may know that I *am* the LORD."

Judg 6:13 Gideon said to Him, "O my lord, if the LORD is with us, why then has all this happened to us? And where *are* all His miracles which our fathers told us about, saying, 'Did not the LORD bring us up from Egypt?' But now the LORD has forsaken us and delivered us into the hands of the Midianites."

1 Chr 16:12 Remember His marvelous works which He has done, His wonders, and the judgments of His mouth,

Ps 105:5 Remember His marvelous works which He has done, His wonders, and the judgments of His mouth,

Insufficient of themselves, to produce conversion.

Luke 16:31 But he said to him, 'If they do not hear Moses and the prophets, neither will they be persuaded though one rise from the dead.' "

The wicked

Desire to see.

Matt 27:42 "He saved others; Himself He cannot save. If He is the King of Israel, let Him now come down from the cross, and we will believe Him.

Luke 11:29 And while the crowds were thickly gathered together, He began to say, "This is an evil generation. It seeks a sign, and no sign will be given to it except the sign of Jonah the prophet.

Luke 23:8 Now when Herod saw Jesus, he was exceedingly glad; for he had desired for a long *time* to see Him, because he had heard many things about Him, and he hoped to see some miracle done by Him.

Often acknowledge.

John 11:47 Then the chief priests and the Pharisees gathered a council and said, "What shall we do? For this Man works many signs.

Acts 4:16 saying, "What shall we do to these men? For, indeed, that a notable miracle has been done through them *is* evident to all who dwell in Jerusalem, and we cannot deny *it.*

Do not understand.

Ps 106:7 Our fathers in Egypt did not understand Your wonders; They did not remember the multitude of Your mercies, But rebelled by the sea—the Red Sea.

Mark 6:52 For they had not understood about the loaves, because their heart was hardened.

Forget.

Neh 9:17 They refused to obey, And they were not mindful of Your wonders That You did among them. But they hardened their necks, And in their rebellion They appointed a leader To return to their bondage. But You *are* God, Ready to pardon, Gracious and merciful, Slow to anger, Abundant in kindness, And did not forsake them.

Ps 78:1 Give ear, O my people, *to* my law; Incline your ears to the words of my mouth.

Ps 78:11 And forgot His works And His wonders that He had shown them.

Identity proved by.

Num 14:22 because all these men who have seen My glory and the signs which I did in Egypt and in the wilderness, and have put Me to the test now these ten times, and have not heeded My voice,

Matt 11:20–24 Then He began to rebuke the cities in which most of His mighty works had been done, because they did not repent: **21** "Woe to you, Chorazin! Woe to you, Bethsaida! For if the mighty works which were done in you had been done in Tyre and Sidon, they would have repented long ago in sackcloth and ashes. **22** But I say to you, it will be more tolerable for Tyre and Sidon in the day of judgment than for you. **23** And you, Capernaum, who are exalted to heaven, will be brought down to Hades; for if the mighty works which were done in you had been done in Sodom, it would have remained until this day. **24** But I say to you that it shall be more tolerable for the land of Sodom in the day of judgment than for you."

John 12:37 But although He had done so many signs before them, they did not believe in Him,

John 15:24 If I had not done among them the works which no one else did, they would have no sin; but now they have seen and also hated both Me and My Father.

MIRACLES THROUGH EVIL AGENTS

Performed

Through the power of Satan.

2 Thess 2:9 The coming of the *lawless one* is according to the working of Satan, with all power, signs, and lying wonders,

Rev 16:14 For they are spirits of demons, performing signs, *which* go out to the kings of the earth and of the whole world, to gather them to the battle of that great day of God Almighty.

In support of false religions.

Deut 13:1–2 "If there arises among you a prophet or a dreamer of dreams, and he gives you a sign or a wonder, **2** and the sign or the wonder comes to pass, of which he spoke to you, saying, 'Let us go after other gods'—which you have not known—'and let us serve them,'

By false prophets.

Matt 24:24 For false christs and false prophets will rise and show great signs and wonders to deceive, if possible, even the elect.

Rev 19:20 Then the beast was captured, and with him the false prophet who worked signs in his presence, by which he deceived those who received the mark of the beast and those who worshiped his image. These two were cast alive into the lake of fire burning with brimstone.

A mark of the end times.

2 Thess 2:3 Let no one deceive you by any means; for *that Day will not come* unless the falling away comes first, and the man of sin is revealed, the son of perdition,

2 Thess 2:9 The coming of the *lawless one* is according to the working of Satan, with all power, signs, and lying wonders,

Rev 13:13 He performs great signs, so that he even makes fire come down from heaven on the earth in the sight of men.

Not to be regarded.

Deut 13:3 you shall not listen to the words of that proph-

et or that dreamer of dreams, for the LORD your God is testing you to know whether you love the LORD your God with all your heart and with all your soul.

Deceive the ungodly.

2 Thess 2:10–12 and with all unrighteous deception among those who perish, because they did not receive the love of the truth, that they might be saved. **11** And for this reason God will send them strong delusion, that they should believe the lie, **12** that they all may be condemned who did not believe the truth but had pleasure in unrighteousness.

Rev 13:14 And he deceives those who dwell on the earth by those signs which he was granted to do in the sight of the beast, telling those who dwell on the earth to make an image to the beast who was wounded by the sword and lived.

Rev 19:20 Then the beast was captured, and with him the false prophet who worked signs in his presence, by which he deceived those who received the mark of the beast and those who worshiped his image. These two were cast alive into the lake of fire burning with brimstone.

Illustrated by

The magicians of Egypt.

Ex 7:11 But Pharaoh also called the wise men and the sorcerers; so the magicians of Egypt, they also did in like manner with their enchantments.

Ex 7:22 Then the magicians of Egypt did so with their enchantments; and Pharaoh's heart grew hard, and he did not heed them, as the LORD had said.

Ex 8:7 And the magicians did so with their enchantments, and brought up frogs on the land of Egypt.

The medium of En Dor.

1 Sam 28:7–14 Then Saul said to his servants, "Find me a woman who is a medium, that I may go to her and inquire of her." And his servants said to him, "In fact, *there is* a woman who is a medium at En Dor." **8** So Saul disguised himself and put on other clothes, and he went, and two men with him; and they came to the woman by night. And he said, "Please conduct a séance for me, and bring up for me the one I shall name to you." **9** Then the woman said to him, "Look, you know what Saul has done, how he has cut off the mediums and the spiritists from the land. Why then do you lay a snare for my life, to cause me to die?" **10** And Saul swore to her by the LORD, saying, "*As* the LORD lives, no punishment shall come upon you for this thing." **11** Then the woman said, "Whom shall I bring up for you?" And he said, "Bring up Samuel for me." **12** When the woman saw Samuel, she cried out with a loud voice. And the woman spoke to Saul, saying, "Why have you deceived me? For you *are* Saul!" **13** And the king said to her, "Do not be afraid. What did you see?" And the woman said to Saul, "I saw a spirit ascending out of the earth." **14** So he said to her, "What *is* his form?" And she said, "An old man is coming up, and he *is* covered with a mantle." And Saul perceived that it *was* Samuel, and he stooped with *his* face to the ground and bowed down.

Simon the sorceror.

Acts 8:9–11 But there was a certain man called Simon, who previously practiced sorcery in the city and astonished the people of Samaria, claiming that he was someone great, **10** to whom they all gave heed, from the least to the greatest, saying, "This man is the great power of God." **11** And they heeded him because he had astonished them with his sorceries for a long time.

Miracles Through God's Servants

Moses and Aaron

Rod turned into a serpent.

Ex 4:3 And He said, "Cast it on the ground." So he cast it on the ground, and it became a serpent; and Moses fled from it.

Ex 7:10 So Moses and Aaron went in to Pharaoh, and they did so, just as the LORD commanded. And Aaron cast down his rod before Pharaoh and before his servants, and it became a serpent.

Rod restored.

Ex 4:4 Then the LORD said to Moses, "Reach out your hand and take *it* by the tail" (and he reached out his hand and caught it, and it became a rod in his hand),

Hand made leprous.

Ex 4:6 Furthermore the LORD said to him, "Now put your hand in your bosom." And he put his hand in his bosom, and when he took it out, behold, his hand *was* leprous, like snow.

Hand restored.

Ex 4:7 And He said, "Put your hand in your bosom again." So he put his hand in his bosom again, and drew it out of his bosom, and behold, it was restored like his *other* flesh.

Water turned into blood.

Ex 4:9 And it shall be, if they do not believe even these two signs, or listen to your voice, that you shall take water from the river and pour *it* on the dry *land*. The water which you take from the river will become blood on the dry *land*."

Ex 4:30 And Aaron spoke all the words which the LORD had spoken to Moses. Then he did the signs in the sight of the people.

River turned into blood.

Ex 7:20 And Moses and Aaron did so, just as the LORD commanded. So he lifted up the rod and struck the waters that *were* in the river, in the sight of Pharaoh and in the sight of his servants. And all the waters that *were* in the river were turned to blood.

Frogs came up.

Ex 8:6 So Aaron stretched out his hand over the waters of Egypt, and the frogs came up and covered the land of Egypt.

Frogs died.

Ex 8:13 So the LORD did according to the word of Moses. And the frogs died out of the houses, out of the courtyards, and out of the fields.

Lice brought.

Ex 8:17 And they did so. For Aaron stretched out his hand with his rod and struck the dust of the earth, and it became lice on man and beast. All the dust of the land became lice throughout all the land of Egypt.

Flies brought.

Ex 8:21–24 Or else, if you will not let My people go, behold, I will send swarms *of flies* on you and your servants, on your people and into your houses. The houses of the Egyptians shall be full of swarms *of flies*, and also the ground on which they *stand*. **22** And in that day I will set apart the land of Goshen, in which My people dwell, that no swarms *of flies* shall be there, in order that you may know that I *am* the LORD in the midst of the land. **23** I will make a difference between My people and your people. Tomorrow this sign shall be." ' " **24** And the LORD did so. Thick swarms *of flies* came into the house of Pharaoh, *into* his servants' houses, and into all the land of Egypt. The land was corrupted because of the swarms *of flies*.

Flies removed.

Ex 8:31 And the LORD did according to the word of Moses; He removed the swarms *of flies* from Pharaoh, from his servants, and from his people. Not one remained.

Pestilence of livestock.

Ex 9:3–6 behold, the hand of the LORD will be on your cattle in the field, on the horses, on the donkeys, on the camels, on the oxen, and on the sheep—a very severe pestilence. **4** And the LORD will make a difference between the livestock of Israel and the livestock of Egypt. So nothing shall die of all *that* belongs to the children of Israel." ' " **5** Then the LORD appointed a set time, saying, "Tomorrow the LORD will do this thing in the land." **6** So the LORD did this thing on the next day, and all the livestock of Egypt died; but of the livestock of the children of Israel, not one died.

Boils and sores brought.

Ex 9:10–11 Then they took ashes from the furnace and stood before Pharaoh, and Moses scattered *them* toward heaven. And *they* caused boils that break out in sores on man and beast. **11** And the magicians could not stand before Moses because of the boils, for the boils were on the magicians and on all the Egyptians.

Hail brought.

Ex 9:23 And Moses stretched out his rod toward heaven; and the LORD sent thunder and hail, and fire darted to the ground. And the LORD rained hail on the land of Egypt.

Hail removed.

Ex 9:33 So Moses went out of the city from Pharaoh and spread out his hands to the LORD; then the thunder and the hail ceased, and the rain was not poured on the earth.

Locusts brought.

Ex 10:13 So Moses stretched out his rod over the land of Egypt, and the LORD brought an east wind on the land all that day and all *that* night. When it was morning, the east wind brought the locusts.

Locust removed.

Ex 10:19 And the LORD turned a very strong west wind, which took the locusts away and blew them into the Red Sea. There remained not one locust in all the territory of Egypt.

Darkness brought.

Ex 10:22 So Moses stretched out his hand toward heaven, and there was thick darkness in all the land of Egypt three days.

The firstborn destroyed.

Ex 12:29 And it came to pass at midnight that the LORD struck all the firstborn in the land of Egypt, from the firstborn of Pharaoh who sat on his throne to the firstborn of the captive who *was* in the dungeon, and all the firstborn of livestock.

The Red Sea divided.

Ex 14:21–22 Then Moses stretched out his hand over the sea; and the LORD caused the sea to go *back* by a strong east wind all that night, and made the sea into dry *land,* and the waters were divided. **22** So the children of Israel went into the midst of the sea on the dry *ground,* and the waters *were* a wall to them on their right hand and on their left.

Egyptians overwhelmed.

Ex 14:26–28 Then the LORD said to Moses, "Stretch out your hand over the sea, that the waters may come back upon the Egyptians, on their chariots, and on their horsemen." **27** And Moses stretched out his hand over the sea; and when the morning appeared, the sea returned to its full depth, while the Egyptians were fleeing into it. So the LORD overthrew the Egyptians in the midst of the sea. **28** Then the waters returned and covered the chariots, the horsemen, *and* all the army of Pharaoh that came into the sea after them. Not so much as one of them remained.

Water sweetened.

Ex 15:25 So he cried out to the LORD, and the LORD showed him a tree. When he cast *it* into the waters, the waters were made sweet. There He made a statute and an ordinance for them, and there He tested them,

Water from rock in Horeb.

Ex 17:6 Behold, I will stand before you there on the rock in Horeb; and you shall strike the rock, and water will come out of it, that the people may drink." And Moses did so in the sight of the elders of Israel.

Amalek defeated.

Ex 17:11–13 And so it was, when Moses held up his hand, that Israel prevailed; and when he let down his hand, Amalek prevailed. **12** But Moses' hands *became* heavy; so they took a stone and put *it* under him, and he sat on it. And Aaron and Hur supported his hands, one on one side, and the other on the other side; and his hands were steady until the going down of the sun. **13** So Joshua defeated Amalek and his people with the edge of the sword.

Destruction of Korah.

Num 16:28–32 And Moses said: "By this you shall know that the LORD has sent me to do all these works, for *I have* not *done them* of my own will. **29** If these men die naturally like all men, or if they are visited by the common fate of all men, *then* the LORD has not sent me. **30** But if the LORD creates a new thing, and the earth opens its mouth and swallows them up with all that belongs to them, and they go down alive into the pit, then you will understand that these men have rejected the LORD." **31** Now it came to pass, as he finished speaking all these words, that the ground split apart under them, **32** and the earth opened its mouth and swallowed them up, with their households and all the men with Korah, with all *their* goods.

Water from rock in Kadesh.

Num 20:11 Then Moses lifted his hand and struck the rock twice with his rod; and water came out abundantly, and the congregation and their animals drank.

Healing by bronze serpent.

Num 21:8–9 Then the LORD said to Moses, "Make a fiery *serpent,* and set it on a pole; and it shall be that everyone who is bitten, when he looks at it, shall live." **9** So Moses made a bronze serpent, and put it on a pole; and so it was, if a serpent had bitten anyone, when he looked at the bronze serpent, he lived.

Joshua

Waters of Jordan divided.

Josh 3:10–17 And Joshua said, "By this you shall know that the living God *is* among you, and *that* He will without fail drive out from before you the Canaanites and the Hittites and the Hivites and the Perizzites and the Girgashites and the Amorites and the Jebusites: **11** Behold, the ark of the covenant of the Lord of all the earth is crossing over before you into the Jordan. **12** Now therefore, take for yourselves twelve men from the tribes of Israel, one man from every tribe. **13** And it shall come to pass, as soon as the soles of the feet of the priests who bear the ark of the LORD, the Lord of all the earth, shall rest in the waters of the Jordan, *that* the waters of the Jordan shall be cut off, the waters that come down from upstream, and they shall stand as a heap." **14** So it was, when the people set out from their camp to cross over the Jordan, with the priests bearing the ark of the covenant before the people, **15** and as those who bore the ark came to the Jordan, and the feet of the priests who bore the ark dipped in the edge of the water (for the Jordan overflows all its banks during the whole time of harvest), **16** that the waters which came down from upstream stood *still, and* rose in a heap very far away at Adam, the city that *is* beside Zaretan. So the waters that went down into the Sea of the Arabah, the Salt Sea, failed, *and* were cut off; and the people crossed over opposite Jericho. **17** Then the priests who bore the ark of the covenant of the LORD stood firm on dry ground in the midst of the Jordan; and all Israel crossed over on dry ground, until all the people had crossed completely over the Jordan.

Jordan returned to its place.

Josh 4:18 And it came to pass, when the priests who bore the ark of the covenant of the LORD had come from the midst of the Jordan, *and* the soles of the priests' feet touched the dry land, that the waters of the Jordan returned to their place and overflowed all its banks as before.

Jericho taken. **Josh 6:6–20**

The sun and moon stopped.

Josh 10:12–14 Then Joshua spoke to the LORD in the day when the LORD delivered up the Amorites before the children of Israel, and he said in the sight of Israel: "Sun, stand still over Gibeon; And Moon, in the Valley of Aijalon." **13** So the sun stood still, And the moon stopped, Till the people had revenge Upon their enemies. *Is* this not written in the Book of Jasher? So the sun stood still in the midst of heaven, and did not hasten to go *down* for about a whole day.

14 And there has been no day like that, before it or after it, that the LORD heeded the voice of a man; for the LORD fought for Israel.

Gideon

Midianites destroyed.

Judg 7:16–22 Then he divided the three hundred men *into* three companies, and he put a trumpet into every man's hand, with empty pitchers, and torches inside the pitchers. **17** And he said to them, "Look at me and do likewise; watch, and when I come to the edge of the camp you shall do as I do: **18** When I blow the trumpet, I and all who *are* with me, then you also blow the trumpets on every side of the whole camp, and say, 'The sword of the LORD and of Gideon!' " **19** So Gideon and the hundred men who *were* with him came to the outpost of the camp at the beginning of the middle watch, just as they had posted the watch; and they blew the trumpets and broke the pitchers that *were* in their hands. **20** Then the three companies blew the trumpets and broke the pitchers—they held the torches in their left hands and the trumpets in their right hands for blowing—and they cried, "The sword of the LORD and of Gideon!" **21** And every man stood in his place all around the camp; and the whole army ran and cried out and fled. **22** When the three hundred blew the trumpets, the LORD set every man's sword against his companion throughout the whole camp; and the army fled to Beth Acacia, toward Zererah, as far as the border of Abel Meholah, by Tabbath.

Samson

A lion killed.

Judg 14:6 And the Spirit of the LORD came mightily upon him, and he tore the lion apart as one would have torn apart a young goat, though *he had* nothing in his hand. But he did not tell his father or his mother what he had done.

Philistines killed.

Judg 14:19 Then the Spirit of the LORD came upon him mightily, and he went down to Ashkelon and killed thirty of their men, took their apparel, and gave the changes *of clothing* to those who had explained the riddle. So his anger was aroused, and he went back up to his father's house.

Judg 15:15 He found a fresh jawbone of a donkey, reached out his hand and took it, and killed a thousand men with it.

The gates of Gaza carried away.

Judg 16:3 And Samson lay *low* till midnight; then he arose at midnight, took hold of the doors of the gate of the city and the two gateposts, pulled them up, bar and all, put *them* on his shoulders, and carried them to the top of the hill that faces Hebron.

Dagon's house pulled down.

Judg 16:30 Then Samson said, "Let me die with the Philistines!" And he pushed with *all his* might, and the temple fell on the lords and all the people who *were* in it. So the dead that he killed at his death were more than he had killed in his life.

Samuel

Thunder and rain in harvest.

1 Sam 12:18 So Samuel called to the LORD, and the LORD sent thunder and rain that day; and all the people greatly feared the LORD and Samuel.

The prophet of Judah

Jeroboam's hand withered.

1 Kin 13:4 So it came to pass when King Jeroboam heard the saying of the man of God, who cried out against the altar in Bethel, that he stretched out his hand from the altar, saying, "Arrest him!" Then his hand, which he stretched out toward him, withered, so that he could not pull it back to himself.

The altar split.

1 Kin 13:5 The altar also was split apart, and the ashes poured out from the altar, according to the sign which the man of God had given by the word of the LORD.

The withered hand restored.

1 Kin 13:6 Then the king answered and said to the man of God, "Please entreat the favor of the LORD your God, and pray for me, that my hand may be restored to me." So the man of God entreated the LORD, and the king's hand was restored to him, and became as before.

Elijah

Drought caused.

1 Kin 17:1 And Elijah the Tishbite, of the inhabitants of Gilead, said to Ahab, "*As* the LORD God of Israel lives, before whom I stand, there shall not be dew nor rain these years, except at my word."

James 5:17 Elijah was a man with a nature like ours, and he prayed earnestly that it would not rain; and it did not rain on the land for three years and six months.

Meal and oil multiplied.

1 Kin 17:14–16 For thus says the LORD God of Israel: 'The bin of flour shall not be used up, nor shall the jar of oil run dry, until the day the LORD sends rain on the earth.' " **15** So she went away and did according to the word of Elijah; and she and he and her household ate for *many* days. **16** The bin of flour was not used up, nor did the jar of oil run dry, according to the word of the LORD which He spoke by Elijah.

A child restored to life.

1 Kin 17:22–23 Then the LORD heard the voice of Elijah; and the soul of the child came back to him, and he revived. **23** And Elijah took the child and brought him down from the upper room into the house, and gave him to his mother. And Elijah said, "See, your son lives!"

Sacrifice consumed by fire.

1 Kin 18:36 And it came to pass, at *the time of* the offering of the *evening* sacrifice, that Elijah the prophet came near and said, "LORD God of Abraham, Isaac, and Israel, let it be known this day that You *are* God in Israel and I *am* Your servant, and *that* I have done all these things at Your word.

1 Kin 18:38 Then the fire of the LORD fell and consumed the burnt sacrifice, and the wood and the stones and the dust, and it licked up the water that *was* in the trench.

Men destroyed by fire.

2 Kin 1:10–12 So Elijah answered and said to the captain of fifty, "If I *am* a man of God, then let fire come down from heaven and consume you and your fifty men." And fire came down from heaven and consumed him and his fifty. **11** Then he sent to him another captain of fifty with his fifty men. And he answered and said to him: "Man of God, thus has the king said, 'Come down quickly!'" **12** So Elijah answered and said to them, "If I *am* a man of God, let fire come down from heaven and consume you and your fifty men." And the fire of God came down from heaven and consumed him and his fifty.

Rain brought.

1 Kin 18:41–45 Then Elijah said to Ahab, "Go up, eat and drink; for *there is* the sound of abundance of rain." **42** So Ahab went up to eat and drink. And Elijah went up to the top of Carmel; then he bowed down on the ground, and put his face between his knees, **43** and said to his servant, "Go up now, look toward the sea." So he went up and looked, and said, "*There is* nothing." And seven times he said, "Go again." **44** Then it came to pass the seventh *time*, that he said, "There is a cloud, as small as a man's hand, rising out of the sea!" So he said, "Go up, say to Ahab, 'Prepare *your chariot*, and go down before the rain stops you.'" **45** Now it happened in the meantime that the sky became black with clouds and wind, and there was a heavy rain. So Ahab rode away and went to Jezreel.

James 5:18 And he prayed again, and the heaven gave rain, and the earth produced its fruit.

Waters of Jordan divided.

2 Kin 2:8 Now Elijah took his mantle, rolled *it* up, and struck the water; and it was divided this way and that, so that the two of them crossed over on dry ground.

Taken to heaven.

2 Kin 2:11 Then it happened, as they continued on and talked, that suddenly a chariot of fire *appeared* with horses of fire, and separated the two of them; and Elijah went up by a whirlwind into heaven.

Elisha

Waters of Jordan divided.

2 Kin 2:14 Then he took the mantle of Elijah that had fallen from him, and struck the water, and said, "Where *is* the LORD God of Elijah?" And when he also had struck the water, it was divided this way and that; and Elisha crossed over.

Waters healed.

2 Kin 2:21–22 Then he went out to the source of the water, and cast in the salt there, and said, "Thus says the LORD: 'I have healed this water; from it there shall be no more death or barrenness.'" **22** So the water remains healed to this day, according to the word of Elisha which he spoke.

Children torn by bears.

2 Kin 2:24 So he turned around and looked at them, and pronounced a curse on them in the name of the LORD. And two female bears came out of the woods and mauled forty-two of the youths.

Oil multiplied.

2 Kin 4:1–7 A certain woman of the wives of the sons of the prophets cried out to Elisha, saying, "Your servant my husband is dead, and you know that your servant feared the LORD. And the creditor is coming to take my two sons to be his slaves." **2** So Elisha said to her, "What shall I do for you? Tell me, what do you have in the house?" And she said, "Your maidservant has nothing in the house but a jar of oil." **3** Then he said, "Go, borrow vessels from everywhere, from all your neighbors—empty vessels; do not gather just a few. **4** And when you have come in, you shall shut the door behind you and your sons; then pour it into all those vessels, and set aside the full ones." **5** So she went from him and shut the door behind her and her sons, who brought *the vessels* to her; and she poured *it* out. **6** Now it came to pass, when the vessels were full, that she said to her son, "Bring me another vessel." And he said to her, "*There is* not another vessel." So the oil ceased. **7** Then she came and told the man of God. And he said, "Go, sell the oil and pay your debt; and you *and* your sons live on the rest."

A child restored to life.

2 Kin 4:32–35 When Elisha came into the house, there was the child, lying dead on his bed. **33** He went in therefore, shut the door behind the two of them, and prayed to the LORD. **34** And he went up and lay on the child, and put his mouth on his mouth, his eyes on his eyes, and his hands on his hands; and he stretched himself out on the child, and the flesh of the child became warm. **35** He returned and walked back and forth in the house, and again went up and stretched himself out on him; then the child sneezed seven times, and the child opened his eyes.

Naaman healed.

2 Kin 5:10 And Elisha sent a messenger to him, saying, "Go and wash in the Jordan seven times, and your flesh shall be restored to you, and *you shall* be clean."

2 Kin 5:14 So he went down and dipped seven times in the Jordan, according to the saying of the man of God; and his flesh was restored like the flesh of a little child, and he was clean.

Gehazi struck with leprosy.

2 Kin 5:27 Therefore the leprosy of Naaman shall cling to you and your descendants forever." And he went out from his presence leprous, *as white* as snow.

Iron caused to swim.

2 Kin 6:6 So the man of God said, "Where did it fall?" And he showed him the place. So he cut off a stick, and threw *it* in there; and he made the iron float.

The Syrians smitten with blindness.

2 Kin 6:20 So it was, when they had come to Samaria, that Elisha said, "LORD, open the eyes of these *men*, that they may see." And the LORD opened their eyes, and they saw; and there *they were*, inside Samaria!

The Syrians restored to sight.

2 Kin 6:20 So it was, when they had come to Samaria, that Elisha said, "LORD, open the eyes of these *men*, that they may see." And the LORD opened their eyes, and they saw; and there *they were*, inside Samaria!

A man restored to life.

2 Kin 13:21 So it was, as they were burying a man, that suddenly they spied a band *of raiders;* and they put the man in the tomb of Elisha; and when the man was let down and touched the bones of Elisha, he revived and stood on his feet.

Isaiah

Hezekiah healed.

2 Kin 20:7 Then Isaiah said, "Take a lump of figs." So they took and laid *it* on the boil, and he recovered.

Shadow put back on the dial.

2 Kin 20:11 So Isaiah the prophet cried out to the LORD, and He brought the shadow ten degrees backward, by which it had gone down on the sundial of Ahaz.

The seventy disciples.

Luke 10:9 And heal the sick there, and say to them, 'The kingdom of God has come near to you.'

Luke 10:17 Then the seventy returned with joy, saying, "Lord, even the demons are subject to us in Your name."

The apostles.

Acts 2:43 Then fear came upon every soul, and many wonders and signs were done through the apostles.

Acts 5:12 And through the hands of the apostles many signs and wonders were done among the people. And they were all with one accord in Solomon's Porch.

Peter

Lame man cured.

Acts 3:7 And he took him by the right hand and lifted *him* up, and immediately his feet and ankle bones received strength.

Death of Ananias.

Acts 5:5 Then Ananias, hearing these words, fell down and breathed his last. So great fear came upon all those who heard these things.

Death of Sapphira.

Acts 5:10 Then immediately she fell down at his feet and breathed her last. And the young men came in and found her dead, and carrying *her* out, buried *her* by her husband.

The sick healed.

Acts 5:15–16 so that they brought the sick out into the streets and laid *them* on beds and couches, that at least the shadow of Peter passing by might fall on some of them. 16 Also a multitude gathered from the surrounding cities to Jerusalem, bringing sick people and those who were tormented by unclean spirits, and they were all healed.

Aeneas made whole.

Acts 9:34 And Peter said to him, "Aeneas, Jesus the Christ heals you. Arise and make your bed." Then he arose immediately.

Tabitha restored to life.

Acts 9:40 But Peter put them all out, and knelt down and prayed. And turning to the body he said, "Tabitha, arise." And she opened her eyes, and when she saw Peter she sat up.

Stephen.

Acts 6:8 And Stephen, full of faith and power, did great wonders and signs among the people.

Philip.

Acts 8:6–7 And the multitudes with one accord heeded the things spoken by Philip, hearing and seeing the miracles which he did. 7 For unclean spirits, crying with a loud voice, came out of many who were possessed; and many who were paralyzed and lame were healed.

Acts 8:13 Then Simon himself also believed; and when he was baptized he continued with Philip, and was amazed, seeing the miracles and signs which were done.

Paul

Elymas smitten with blindness.

Acts 13:11 And now, indeed, the hand of the Lord *is* upon you, and you shall be blind, not seeing the sun for a time." And immediately a dark mist fell on him, and he went around seeking someone to lead him by the hand.

Lame man cured.

Acts 14:10 said with a loud voice, "Stand up straight on your feet!" And he leaped and walked.

An unclean spirit cast out.

Acts 16:18 And this she did for many days. But Paul, greatly annoyed, turned and said to the spirit, "I command you in the name of Jesus Christ to come out of her." And he came out that very hour.

Special miracles.

Acts 19:11–12 Now God worked unusual miracles by the hands of Paul, 12 so that even handkerchiefs or aprons were brought from his body to the sick, and the diseases left them and the evil spirits went out of them.

Eutychus restored to life.

Acts 20:10–12 But Paul went down, fell on him, and embracing *him* said, "Do not trouble yourselves, for his life is in him." 11 Now when he had come up, had broken bread and eaten, and talked a long while, even till daybreak, he departed. 12 And they brought the young man in alive, and they were not a little comforted.

Viper's bite made harmless.

Acts 28:5 But he shook off the creature into the fire and suffered no harm.

Father of Publius healed.

Acts 28:8 And it happened that the father of Publius lay sick of a fever and dysentery. Paul went in to him and prayed, and he laid his hands on him and healed him.

Paul and Barnabas.

Acts 14:3 Therefore they stayed there a long time, speaking boldly in the Lord, who was bearing witness to the word of His grace, granting signs and wonders to be done by their hands.

MISSIONS

Commanded.

Matt 28:19 Go therefore and make disciples of all the nations, baptizing them in the name of the Father and of the Son and of the Holy Spirit,

Mark 16:15 And He said to them, "Go into all the world and preach the gospel to every creature.

Luke 10:2 Then He said to them, "The harvest truly *is* great, but the laborers *are* few; therefore pray the Lord of the harvest to send out laborers into His harvest.

Rom 10:14–15 How then shall they call on Him in whom they have not believed? And how shall they believe in Him of whom they have not heard? And how shall they hear without a preacher? **15** And how shall they preach unless they are sent? As it is written: *"How beautiful are the feet of those who preach the gospel of peace, Who bring glad tidings of good things!"*

Warranted by predictions concerning the heathen, etc.

Is 42:10–12 Sing to the LORD a new song, *And* His praise from the ends of the earth, You who go down to the sea, and all that is in it, You coastlands and you inhabitants of them! **11** Let the wilderness and its cities lift up *their voice*, The villages *that* Kedar inhabits. Let the inhabitants of Sela sing, Let them shout from the top of the mountains. **12** Let them give glory to the LORD, And declare His praise in the coastlands.

Is 66:19 I will set a sign among them; and those among them who escape I will send to the nations: *to* Tarshish and Pul and Lud, who draw the bow, and Tubal and Javan, *to* the coastlands afar off who have not heard My fame nor seen My glory. And they shall declare My glory among the Gentiles.

Is according to the purpose of God.

Luke 24:46–47 Then He said to them, "Thus it is written, and thus it was necessary for the Christ to suffer and to rise from the dead the third day, **47** and that repentance and remission of sins should be preached in His name to all nations, beginning at Jerusalem.

Acts 13:2 As they ministered to the Lord and fasted, the Holy Spirit said, "Now separate to Me Barnabas and Saul for the work to which I have called them."

Gal 1:15–16 But when it pleased God, who separated me from my mother's womb and called *me* through His grace, **16** to reveal His Son in me, that I might preach Him among the Gentiles, I did not immediately confer with flesh and blood,

Col 1:25–27 of which I became a minister according to the stewardship from God which was given to me for you, to fulfill the word of God, **26** the mystery which has been hidden from ages and from generations, but now has been revealed to His saints. **27** To them God willed to make known what are the riches of the glory of this mystery among the Gentiles: which is Christ in you, the hope of glory.

Christ engaged in.

Matt 4:17 From that time Jesus began to preach and to say, "Repent, for the kingdom of heaven is at hand."

Matt 4:23 And Jesus went about all Galilee, teaching in their synagogues, preaching the gospel of the kingdom, and healing all kinds of sickness and all kinds of disease among the people.

Matt 11:1 Now it came to pass, when Jesus finished commanding His twelve disciples, that He departed from there to teach and to preach in their cities.

Mark 1:38–39 But He said to them, "Let us go into the next towns, that I may preach there also, because for this purpose I have come forth." **39** And He was preaching in their synagogues throughout all Galilee, and casting out demons.

Luke 8:1 Now it came to pass, afterward, that He went through every city and village, preaching and bringing the glad tidings of the kingdom of God. And the twelve *were* with Him,

Apostles constrained to engage in.

Mark 3:14 Then He appointed twelve, that they might be with Him and that He might send them out to preach,

Mark 6:7 And He called the twelve to *Himself*, and began to send them out two *by* two, and gave them power over unclean spirits.

Luke 10:1–11 After these things the Lord appointed seventy others also, and sent them two by two before His face into every city and place where He Himself was about to go. **2** Then He said to them, "The harvest truly *is* great, but the laborers *are* few; therefore pray the Lord of the harvest to send out laborers into His harvest. **3** Go your way; behold, I send you out as lambs among wolves. **4** Carry neither money bag, knapsack, nor sandals; and greet no one along the road. **5** But whatever house you enter, first say, 'Peace to this house.' **6** And if a son of peace is there, your peace will rest on it; if not, it will return to you. **7** And remain in the same house, eating and drinking such things as they give, for the laborer is worthy of his wages. Do not go from house to house. **8** Whatever city you enter, and they receive you, eat such things as are set before you. **9** And heal the sick there, and say to them, 'The kingdom of God has come near to you.' **10** But whatever city you enter, and they do not receive you, go out into its streets and say, **11** 'The very dust of your city which clings to us we wipe off against you. Nevertheless know this, that the kingdom of God has come near you.'

Acts 4:19–20 But Peter and John answered and said to them, "Whether it is right in the sight of God to listen to you more than to God, you judge. **20** For we cannot but speak the things which we have seen and heard."

Rom 1:13–15 Now I do not want you to be unaware, brethren, that I often planned to come to you (but was hindered until now), that I might have some fruit among you also, just as among the other Gentiles. **14** I am a debtor both to Greeks and to barbarians, both to wise and to unwise. **15** So, as much as is in me, *I am* ready to preach the gospel to you who are in Rome also.

1 Cor 9:16 For if I preach the gospel, I have nothing to boast of, for necessity is laid upon me; yes, woe is me if I do not preach the gospel!

Excellency of.

Is 52:7 How beautiful upon the mountains Are the feet of him who brings good news, Who proclaims peace, Who brings glad tidings of good *things*, Who proclaims salvation, Who says to Zion, "Your God reigns!"

Rom 10:15 And how shall they preach unless they are sent? As it is written: *"How beautiful are the feet of those who preach the gospel of peace, Who bring glad tidings of good things!"*

God qualifies people for.

Ex 3:11 But Moses said to God, "Who *am* I that I should go to Pharaoh, and that I should bring the children of Israel out of Egypt?"

Ex 3:18 Then they will heed your voice; and you shall come, you and the elders of Israel, to the king of Egypt; and you shall say to him, 'The LORD God of the Hebrews has met with us; and now, please, let us go three days' journey into the wilderness, that we may sacrifice to the LORD our God.'

Ex 4:11–12 So the LORD said to him, "Who has made man's mouth? Or who makes the mute, the deaf, the seeing, or the blind? *Have* not I, the LORD? **12** Now therefore, go, and I will be with your mouth and teach you what you shall say."

Ex 4:15 Now you shall speak to him and put the words in his mouth. And I will be with your mouth and with his mouth, and I will teach you what you shall do.

Is 6:5–9 So I said: "Woe *is* me, for I am undone! Because I *am* a man of unclean lips, And I dwell in the midst of a people of unclean lips; For my eyes have seen the King, The LORD of hosts." **6** Then one of the seraphim flew to me, having in his hand a live coal *which* he had taken with the tongs from the altar. **7** And he touched my mouth *with it,* and said: "Behold, this has touched your lips; Your iniquity is taken away, And your sin purged." **8** Also I heard the voice of the Lord, saying: "Whom shall I send, And who will go for Us?" Then I said, "Here *am* I! Send me." **9** And He said, "Go, and tell this people: 'Keep on hearing, but do not understand; Keep on seeing, but do not perceive.'

Jer 1:7–9 But the LORD said to me: "Do not say, 'I *am* a youth,' For you shall go to all to whom I send you, And whatever I command you, you shall speak. **8** Do not be afraid of their faces, For I *am* with you to deliver you," says the LORD. **9** Then the LORD put forth His hand and touched my mouth, and the LORD said to me: "Behold, I have put My words in your mouth.

Danger of shrinking from.

Jon 1:3–4 But Jonah arose to flee to Tarshish from the presence of the LORD. He went down to Joppa, and found a ship going to Tarshish; so he paid the fare, and went down into it, to go with them to Tarshish from the presence of the LORD. **4** But the LORD sent out a great wind on the sea, and there was a mighty tempest on the sea, so that the ship was about to be broken up.

Requirements for,

Wisdom and meekness.

Matt 10:16 "Behold, I send you out as sheep in the midst of wolves. Therefore be wise as serpents and harmless as doves.

Willingness.

Is 6:8 Also I heard the voice of the Lord, saying: "Whom shall I send, And who will go for Us?" Then I said, "Here *am* I! Send me."

Aid others engaged in.

Rom 16:1–2 I commend to you Phoebe our sister, who is a servant of the church in Cenchrea, **2** that you may receive her in the Lord in a manner worthy of the saints, and assist her in whatever business she has need of you; for indeed she has been a helper of many and of myself also.

2 Cor 11:9 And when I was present with you, and in need, I was a burden to no one, for what I lacked the brethren who came from Macedonia supplied. And in everything I kept myself from being burdensome to you, and so I will keep *myself.*

3 John 1:5–8 Beloved, you do faithfully whatever you do for the brethren and for strangers, **6** who have borne witness of your love before the church. *If* you send them forward on their journey in a manner worthy of God, you will do well, **7** because they went forth for His name's sake, taking nothing from the Gentiles. **8** We therefore ought to receive such, that we may become fellow workers for the truth.

Harmony of effort.

Gal 2:9 and when James, Cephas, and John, who seemed to be pillars, perceived the grace that had been given to me, they gave me and Barnabas the right hand of fellowship, that we *should go* to the Gentiles and they to the circumcised.

Worldly concerns should not delay.

Luke 9:59–62 Then He said to another, "Follow Me." But he said, "Lord, let me first go and bury my father." **60** Jesus said to him, "Let the dead bury their own dead, but you go and preach the kingdom of God." **61** And another also said, "Lord, I will follow You, but let me first go *and* bid them farewell who are at my house." **62** But Jesus said to him, "No one, having put his hand to the plow, and looking back, is fit for the kingdom of God."

Success of,

To be prayed for.

Eph 6:18–19 praying always with all prayer and supplication in the Spirit, being watchful to this end with all perseverance and supplication for all the saints— **19** and for me, that utterance may be given to me, that I may open my mouth boldly to make known the mystery of the gospel,

Col 4:3 meanwhile praying also for us, that God would open to us a door for the word, to speak the mystery of Christ, for which I am also in chains,

A cause of joy and praise.

Acts 11:18 When they heard these things they became silent; and they glorified God, saying, "Then God has also granted to the Gentiles repentance to life."

Acts 15:3 So, being sent on their way by the church, they passed through Phoenicia and Samaria, describing the conversion of the Gentiles; and they caused great joy to all the brethren.

Acts 21:19–20 When he had greeted them, he told in detail those things which God had done among the Gentiles through his ministry. **20** And when they heard *it,* they glorified the Lord. And they said to him, "You see, brother, how many myriads of Jews there are who have believed, and they are all zealous for the law;

People should not limit.

Is 11:9 They shall not hurt nor destroy in all My holy mountain, For the earth shall be full of the knowledge of the LORD As the waters cover the sea.

Mark 16:15 And He said to them, "Go into all the world and preach the gospel to every creature.

1 Cor 16:9 For a great and effective door has opened to me, and *there are* many adversaries.

Rev 14:6 Then I saw another angel flying in the midst of heaven, having the everlasting gospel to preach to those who dwell on the earth—to every nation, tribe, tongue, and people—

Exemplified by

The Levites.

2 Chr 17:8–9 And with them *he sent* Levites: Shemaiah, Nethaniah, Zebadiah, Asahel, Shemiramoth, Jehonathan, Adonijah, Tobijah, and Tobadonijah—the Levites; and with them Elishama and Jehoram, the priests. **9** So they taught in Judah, and *had* the Book of the Law of the LORD with them; they went throughout all the cities of Judah and taught the people.

Jonah.

Jon 3:2 "Arise, go to Nineveh, that great city, and preach to it the message that I tell you."

The Seventy.

Luke 10:1 After these things the Lord appointed seventy others also, and sent them two by two before His face into every city and place where He Himself was about to go.

Luke 10:17 Then the seventy returned with joy, saying, "Lord, even the demons are subject to us in Your name."

The apostles.

Mark 6:12 So they went out and preached that *people* should repent.

Acts 13:2–5 As they ministered to the Lord and fasted, the Holy Spirit said, "Now separate to Me Barnabas and Saul for the work to which I have called them." **3** Then, having fasted and prayed, and laid hands on them, they sent *them* away. **4** So, being sent out by the Holy Spirit, they went down to Seleucia, and from there they sailed to Cyprus. **5** And when they arrived in Salamis, they preached the word of God in the synagogues of the Jews. They also had John as *their* assistant.

Philip.

Acts 8:5 Then Philip went down to the city of Samaria and preached Christ to them.

Paul, etc.

Acts 13:2–4 As they ministered to the Lord and fasted, the Holy Spirit said, "Now separate to Me Barnabas and Saul for the work to which I have called them." **3** Then, having fasted and prayed, and laid hands on them, they sent *them* away. **4** So, being sent out by the Holy Spirit, they went down to Seleucia, and from there they sailed to Cyprus.

Silas.

Acts 15:40–41 but Paul chose Silas and departed, being commended by the brethren to the grace of God. **41** And he went through Syria and Cilicia, strengthening the churches.

Timothy.

Acts 16:3 Paul wanted to have him go on with him. And he took *him* and circumcised him because of the Jews who were in that region, for they all knew that his father was Greek.

Noah.

2 Pet 2:5 and did not spare the ancient world, but saved Noah, *one of* eight *people*, a preacher of righteousness, bringing in the flood on the world of the ungodly;

MOABITES, THE

Descended from Lot.

Gen 19:37 The firstborn bore a son and called his name Moab; he *is* the father of the Moabites to this day.

Called

Children of Lot.

Deut 2:9 Then the LORD said to me, 'Do not harass Moab, nor contend with them in battle, for I will not give you *any* of their land *as* a possession, because I have given Ar to the descendants of Lot *as* a possession.' "

People of Chemosh.

Num 21:29 Woe to you, Moab! You have perished, O people of Chemosh! He has given his sons as fugitives, And his daughters into captivity, To Sihon king of the Amorites.

Jer 48:46 Woe to you, O Moab! The people of Chemosh perish; For your sons have been taken captive, And your daughters captive.

Separated from the Amorites by the river Arnon.

Num 21:13 From there they moved and camped on the other side of the Arnon, which *is* in the wilderness that extends from the border of the Amorites; for the Arnon *is* the border of Moab, between Moab and the Amorites.

Expelled the ancient Emims.

Deut 2:9–11 Then the LORD said to me, 'Do not harass Moab, nor contend with them in battle, for I will not give you *any* of their land *as* a possession, because I have given Ar to the descendants of Lot *as* a possession.' " **10** (The Emim had dwelt there in times past, a people as great and numerous and tall as the Anakim. **11** They were also regarded as giants, like the Anakim, but the Moabites call them Emim.

Possessed many cities.

Num 21:28 "For fire went out from Heshbon, A flame from the city of Sihon; It consumed Ar of Moab, The lords of the heights of the Arnon.

Num 21:30 "But we have shot at them; Heshbon has perished as far as Dibon. Then we laid waste as far as Nophah, Which *reaches* to Medeba."

Is 15:1–4 The burden against Moab. Because in the night Ar of Moab is laid waste *And* destroyed, Because in the night Kir of Moab is laid waste *And* destroyed, **2** He has gone up to the temple and Dibon, To the high places to weep. Moab will wail over Nebo and over Medeba; On all their heads *will be* baldness, *And* every beard cut off. **3** In their streets they will clothe themselves with sackcloth; On the tops of their houses And in their streets Everyone will wail, weeping bitterly. **4** Heshbon and Elealeh will cry out, Their voice shall be heard as far as Jahaz; Therefore the armed soldiers of Moab will cry out; His life will be burdensome to him.

Jer 48:21–24 "And judgment has come on the plain country: On Holon and Jahzah and Mephaath, **22** On Dibon and Nebo and Beth Diblathaim, **23** On Kirjathaim and Beth Gamul and Beth Meon, **24** On Kerioth and Bozrah, On all the cities of the land of Moab, Far or near.

Governed by kings.

Num 23:7 And he took up his oracle and said: "Balak the king of Moab has brought me from Aram, From the mountains of the east. 'Come, curse Jacob for me, And come, denounce Israel!'

Josh 24:9 Then Balak the son of Zippor, king of Moab, arose to make war against Israel, and sent and called Balaam the son of Beor to curse you.

Described as

Proud and arrogant.

Is 16:6 We have heard of the pride of Moab— *He is* very proud— Of his haughtiness and his pride and his wrath; *But* his lies *shall* not *be* so.

Jer 48:29 "We have heard the pride of Moab (He *is* exceedingly proud), Of his loftiness and arrogance and pride, And of the haughtiness of his heart."

Idolatrous.

1 Kin 11:7 Then Solomon built a high place for Chemosh the abomination of Moab, on the hill that *is* east of Jerusalem, and for Molech the abomination of the people of Ammon.

Superstitious.

Jer 27:3 and send them to the king of Edom, the king of Moab, the king of the Ammonites, the king of Tyre, and the king of Sidon, by the hand of the messengers who come to Jerusalem to Zedekiah king of Judah.

Jer 27:9 Therefore do not listen to your prophets, your diviners, your dreamers, your soothsayers, or your sorcerers, who speak to you, saying, "You shall not serve the king of Babylon."

Rich and confident.

Jer 48:7 For because you have trusted in your works and your treasures, You also shall be taken. And Chemosh shall go forth into captivity, His priests and his princes together.

Jer 48:11 "Moab has been at ease from his youth; He has settled on his dregs, And has not been emptied from vessel to vessel, Nor has he gone into captivity. Therefore his taste remained in him, And his scent has not changed.

Mighty men of war.

Jer 48:14 "How can you say, 'We *are* mighty And strong men for the war'?

Amorites captured much of their land.

Num 21:26 For Heshbon *was* the city of Sihon king of the Amorites, who had fought against the former king of Moab, and had taken all his land from his hand as far as the Arnon.

Alarmed at the number, etc. of Israel.

Num 22:3 And Moab was exceedingly afraid of the people because they *were* many, and Moab was sick with dread because of the children of Israel.

Relationship to Israel

Opposed Israel.

Judg 11:17–18 Then Israel sent messengers to the king of Edom, saying, "Please let me pass through your land." But the king of Edom would not heed. And in like manner they sent to the king of Moab, but he would not *consent*. So Israel remained in Kadesh. **18** And they went along through the wilderness and bypassed the land of Edom and the land of Moab, came to the east side of the land of Moab, and encamped on the other side of the Arnon. But they did not enter the border of Moab, for the Arnon *was* the border of Moab.

Ezek 25:8 'Thus says the Lord GOD: "Because Moab and Seir say, 'Look! The house of Judah *is* like all the nations,'

Jews enticed to idolatry by.

Num 25:1–3 Now Israel remained in Acacia Grove, and the people began to commit harlotry with the women of Moab. **2** They invited the people to the sacrifices of their gods, and the people ate and bowed down to their gods. **3** So Israel was joined to Baal of Peor, and the anger of the LORD was aroused against Israel.

Israel forbidden to harass.

Deut 2:9 Then the LORD said to me, 'Do not harass Moab, nor contend with them in battle, for I will not give you *any* of their land *as* a possession, because I have given Ar to the descendants of Lot *as* a possession.' "

Judg 11:15 and said to him, "Thus says Jephthah: 'Israel did not take away the land of Moab, nor the land of the people of Ammon;

Israel forbidden to seek peace with.

Deut 23:6 You shall not seek their peace nor their prosperity all your days forever.

Israel sometimes intermarried with.

Ruth 1:4 Now they took wives of the women of Moab: the name of the one *was* Orpah, and the name of the other Ruth. And they dwelt there about ten years.

1 Kin 11:1 But King Solomon loved many foreign women, as well as the daughter of Pharaoh: women of the Moabites, Ammonites, Edomites, Sidonians, *and* Hittites—

1 Chr 8:8 Also Shaharaim had children in the country of Moab, after he had sent away Hushim and Baara his wives.

Neh 13:23 In those days I also saw Jews *who* had married women of Ashdod, Ammon, *and* Moab.

Excluded from Israel's congregation forever.

Deut 23:3–4 "An Ammonite or Moabite shall not enter the assembly of the LORD; even to the tenth generation none of his *descendants* shall enter the assembly of the LORD forever, **4** because they did not meet you with bread and water on the road when you came out of Egypt, and because they hired against you Balaam the son of Beor from Pethor of Mesopotamia, to curse you.

Neh 13:1–2 On that day they read from the Book of Moses in the hearing of the people, and in it was found written that no Ammonite or Moabite should ever come into the assembly of God, **2** because they had not met the children of Israel with bread and water, but hired Balaam against them to curse them. However, our God turned the curse into a blessing.

Harassed and subdued by Saul.

1 Sam 14:47 So Saul established his sovereignty over Israel, and fought against all his enemies on every side, against Moab, against the people of Ammon, against Edom, against the kings of Zobah, and against the Philistines. Wherever he turned, he harassed *them*.

Cooperated with David.

1 Sam 22:4 So he brought them before the king of Moab, and they dwelt with him all the time that David was in the stronghold.

2 Sam 8:2 Then he defeated Moab. Forcing them down to the ground, he measured them off with a line. With two lines he measured off those to be put to death, and with one full line those to be kept alive. So the Moabites became David's servants, *and* brought tribute.

2 Sam 8:12 from Syria, from Moab, from the people of Ammon, from the Philistines, from Amalek, and from the spoil of Hadadezer the son of Rehob, king of Zobah.

Benaiah slew two heroes of.

2 Sam 23:20 Benaiah *was* the son of Jehoiada, the son of a valiant man from Kabzeel, who had done many deeds. He had killed two lion-like heroes of Moab. He also had gone down and killed a lion in the midst of a pit on a snowy day.

Paid tribute of sheep and wool to the king of Israel.

2 Kin 3:4 Now Mesha king of Moab was a sheep-breeder, and he regularly paid the king of Israel one hundred thousand lambs and the wool of one hundred thousand rams.

Is 16:1 Send the lamb to the ruler of the land, From Sela to the wilderness, To the mount of the daughter of Zion.

Revolted from Israel after the death of Ahab.

2 Kin 1:1 Moab rebelled against Israel after the death of Ahab.

2 Kin 3:5 But it happened, when Ahab died, that the king of Moab rebelled against the king of Israel.

Israel and Judah joined against.

2 Kin 3:6 So King Jehoram went out of Samaria at that time and mustered all Israel.

2 Kin 3:7 Then he went and sent to Jehoshaphat king of Judah, saying, "The king of Moab has rebelled against me. Will you go up with me to fight against Moab?" And he said, "I will go up; I *am* as you *are*, my people as your people, my horses as your horses."

2 Kin 3:21–27 And when all the Moabites heard that the kings had come up to fight against them, all who were able to bear arms and older were gathered; and they stood at the border. **22** Then they rose up early in the morning, and the sun was shining on the water; and the Moabites saw the water on the other side *as* red as blood. **23** And they said, "This is blood; the kings have surely struck swords and have killed one another; now therefore, Moab, to the spoil!" **24** So when they came to the camp of Israel, Israel rose up and attacked the Moabites, so that they fled before them; and they entered *their* land, killing the Moabites. **25** Then they destroyed the cities, and each man threw a stone on every good piece of land and filled it; and they stopped up all the springs of water and cut down all the good trees. But they left the stones of Kir Haraseth *intact.* However the slingers surrounded and attacked it. **26** And when the king of Moab saw that the battle was too fierce for him, he took with him seven hundred men who drew swords, to break through to the king of Edom, but

they could not. **27** Then he took his eldest son who would have reigned in his place, and offered him *as* a burnt offering upon the wall; and there was great indignation against Israel. So they departed from him and returned to *their own* land.

Joined Babylon against Judah.

2 Kin 24:2 And the LORD sent against him *raiding* bands of Chaldeans, bands of Syrians, bands of Moabites, and bands of the people of Ammon; He sent them against Judah to destroy it, according to the word of the LORD which He had spoken by His servants the prophets.

Prophecies respecting,

Terror on account of Israel.

Ex 15:15 Then the chiefs of Edom will be dismayed; The mighty men of Moab, Trembling will take hold of them; All the inhabitants of Canaan will melt away.

Desolation and grief.

Is 15:1–9 The burden against Moab. Because in the night Ar of Moab is laid waste *And* destroyed, Because in the night Kir of Moab is laid waste *And* destroyed, **2** He has gone up to the temple and Dibon, To the high places to weep. Moab will wail over Nebo and over Medeba; On all their heads *will be* baldness, *And* every beard cut off. **3** In their streets they will clothe themselves with sackcloth; On the tops of their houses And in their streets Everyone will wail, weeping bitterly. **4** Heshbon and Elealeh will cry out, Their voice shall be heard as far as Jahaz; Therefore the armed soldiers of Moab will cry out; His life will be burdensome to him. **5** "My heart will cry out for Moab; His fugitives *shall flee* to Zoar, *Like* a three-year-old heifer. For by the Ascent of Luhith They will go up with weeping; For in the way of Horonaim They will raise up a cry of destruction, **6** For the waters of Nimrim will be desolate, For the green grass has withered away; The grass fails, there is nothing green. **7** Therefore the abundance they have gained, And what they have laid up, They will carry away to the Brook of the Willows. **8** For the cry has gone all around the borders of Moab, Its wailing to Eglaim And its wailing to Beer Elim. **9** For the waters of Dimon will be full of blood; Because I will bring more upon Dimon, Lions upon him who escapes from Moab, And on the remnant of the land."

Cf. Is 16:2–11

Inability to avert destruction.

Is 16:12 And it shall come to pass, When it is seen that Moab is weary on the high place, That he will come to his sanctuary to pray; But he will not prevail.

To be destroyed in three years.

Is 16:13–14 This *is* the word which the LORD has spoken concerning Moab since that time. **14** But now the LORD has spoken, saying, "Within three years, as the years of a hired man, the glory of Moab will be despised with all that great multitude, and the remnant *will be* very small *and* feeble."

To be captives in Babylon.

Jer 27:3 and send them to the king of Edom, the king of Moab, the king of the Ammonites, the king of Tyre, and the king of Sidon, by the hand of the messengers who come to Jerusalem to Zedekiah king of Judah.

Jer 27:8 And it shall be, *that* the nation and kingdom which will not serve Nebuchadnezzar the king of Babylon, and which will not put its neck under the yoke of the king of Babylon, that nation I will punish,' says the LORD, 'with the sword, the famine, and the pestilence, until I have consumed them by his hand.

Jer 48:7 For because you have trusted in your works and your treasures, You also shall be taken. And Chemosh shall go forth into captivity, His priests and his princes together.

Their desolation as a punishment for their hatred of Israel.

Jer 48:26–27 "Make him drunk, Because he exalted *himself* against the LORD. Moab shall wallow in his vomit, And he shall also be in derision. **27** For was not Israel a derision to you? Was he found among thieves? For whenever you speak of him, You shake *your head in scorn.*

Ezek 25:8–9 Thus says the Lord GOD: "Because Moab and Seir say, 'Look! The house of Judah *is* like all the nations,' **9** therefore, behold, I will clear the territory of Moab of cities, of the cities on its frontier, the glory of the country, Beth Jeshimoth, Baal Meon, and Kirjathaim.

Restoration from captivity.

Jer 48:47 "Yet I will bring back the captives of Moab In the latter days," says the LORD. Thus far *is* the judgment of Moab.

Subjugation to Messiah.

Num 24:17 "I see Him, but not now; I behold Him, but not near; A Star shall come out of Jacob; A Scepter shall rise out of Israel, And batter the brow of Moab, And destroy all the sons of tumult.

Is 25:10 For on this mountain the hand of the LORD will rest, And Moab shall be trampled down under Him, As straw is trampled down for the refuse heap.

Subjugation to Israel.

Is 11:14 But they shall fly down upon the shoulder of the Philistines toward the west; Together they shall plunder the people of the East; They shall lay their hand on Edom and Moab; And the people of Ammon shall obey them.

MOCKERY

Of Nehemiah.

Neh 4:1–3 But it so happened, when Sanballat heard that we were rebuilding the wall, that he was furious and very indignant, and mocked the Jews. **2** And he spoke before his brethren and the army of Samaria, and said, "What are these feeble Jews doing? Will they fortify themselves? Will they offer sacrifices? Will they complete it in a day? Will they revive the stones from the heaps of rubbish—*stones* that are burned?" **3** Now Tobiah the Ammonite *was* beside him, and he said, "Whatever they build, if even a fox goes up *on it,* he will break down their stone wall."

Anticipated by David.

Ps 35:19–28 Let them not rejoice over me who are wrongfully my enemies; Nor let them wink with the eye who hate me without a cause. **20** For they do not speak peace, But they devise deceitful matters Against *the* quiet *ones* in the land. **21** They also

opened their mouth wide against me, And said, "Aha, aha! Our eyes have seen *it.*" **22** *This* You have seen, O LORD; Do not keep silence. O Lord, do not be far from me. **23** Stir up Yourself, and awake to my vindication, To my cause, my God and my Lord. **24** Vindicate me, O LORD my God, according to Your righteousness; And let them not rejoice over me. **25** Let them not say in their hearts, "Ah, so we would have it!" Let them not say, "We have swallowed him up." **26** Let them be ashamed and brought to mutual confusion Who rejoice at my hurt; Let them be clothed with shame and dishonor Who exalt themselves against me. **27** Let them shout for joy and be glad, Who favor my righteous cause; And let them say continually, "Let the LORD be magnified, Who has pleasure in the prosperity of His servant." **28** And my tongue shall speak of Your righteousness *And* of Your praise all the day long.

Of God, toward the rebellious and stubborn.

Prov 1:24–26 Because I have called and you refused, I have stretched out my hand and no one regarded, **25** Because you disdained all my counsel, And would have none of my rebuke, **26** I also will laugh at your calamity; I will mock when your terror comes,

Against Jeremiah.

Jer 23:33 "So when these people or the prophet or the priest ask you, saying, 'What is the oracle of the LORD?' you shall then say to them, 'What oracle?' I will even forsake you," says the LORD.

Of Christ,

By soldiers.

Matt 27:27–30 Then the soldiers of the governor took Jesus into the Praetorium and gathered the whole garrison around Him. **28** And they stripped Him and put a scarlet robe on Him. **29** When they had twisted a crown of thorns, they put *it* on His head, and a reed in His right hand. And they bowed the knee before Him and mocked Him, saying, "Hail, King of the Jews!" **30** Then they spat on Him, and took the reed and struck Him on the head.

Mark 15:16–19 Then the soldiers led Him away into the hall called Praetorium, and they called together the whole garrison. **17** And they clothed Him with purple; and they twisted a crown of thorns, put it on His *head,* **18** and began to salute Him, "Hail, King of the Jews!" **19** Then they struck Him on the head with a reed and spat on Him; and bowing the knee, they worshiped Him.

By people at the cross.

Mark 15:35 Some of those who stood by, when they heard *that,* said, "Look, He is calling for Elijah!"

By the Jews.

John 8:22 So the Jews said, "Will He kill Himself, because He says, 'Where I go you cannot come'?"

By Pontius Pilate.

John 19:14 Now it was the Preparation Day of the Passover, and about the sixth hour. And he said to the Jews, "Behold your King!"

By the Corinthians, of the Lord's Supper.

1 Cor 11:17–22 Now in giving these instructions I do not praise *you,* since you come together not for the better but for the worse. **18** For first of all, when you come together as a church, I hear that there are divisions among you, and in part I believe it. **19** For there must also be factions among you, that those who are approved may be recognized among you. **20** Therefore when you come together in one place, it is not to eat the Lord's Supper. **21** For in eating, each one takes his own supper ahead of *others;* and one is hungry and another is drunk. **22** What! Do you not have houses to eat and drink in? Or do you despise the church of God and shame those who have nothing? What shall I say to you? Shall I praise you in this? I do not praise *you.*

MONEY

Gold and silver used as.

Gen 13:2 Abram *was* very rich in livestock, in silver, and in gold.

Num 22:18 Then Balaam answered and said to the servants of Balak, "Though Balak were to give me his house full of silver and gold, I could not go beyond the word of the LORD my God, to do less or more.

Copper introduced as, by the Romans.

Matt 10:9 Provide neither gold nor silver nor copper in your money belts,

Units of, referred to by weight or piece.

Gen 23:15 "My lord, listen to me; the land *is worth* four hundred shekels of silver. What *is* that between you and me? So bury your dead."

Gen 33:19 And he bought the parcel of land, where he had pitched his tent, from the children of Hamor, Shechem's father, for one hundred pieces of money.

Of the Romans, stamped with the image of Caesar.

Matt 22:20–21 And He said to them, "Whose image and inscription *is* this?" **21** They said to Him, "Caesar's." And He said to them, "Render therefore to Caesar the things that are Caesar's, and to God the things that are God's."

Usually taken by weight.

Gen 23:16 And Abraham listened to Ephron; and Abraham weighed out the silver for Ephron which he had named in the hearing of the sons of Heth, four hundred shekels of silver, currency of the merchants.

Jer 32:10 And I signed the deed and sealed *it,* took witnesses, and weighed the money on the scales.

Pieces of, mentioned

Talent of gold.

1 Kin 9:14 Then Hiram sent the king one hundred and twenty talents of gold.

Talent of silver.

1 Kin 16:24 And he bought the hill of Samaria from Shemer for two talents of silver; then he built on the hill, and called the name of the city which he built, Samaria, after the name of Shemer, owner of the hill.

2 Kin 5:22–23 And he said, "All *is* well. My master has sent me, saying, 'Indeed, just now two young men of the sons of the prophets have come to me from the mountains of Ephraim. Please give them a talent of silver and two changes of garments.' " **23** So Naaman said, "Please, take two talents." And he urged him, and bound two talents of silver in two bags,

with two changes of garments, and handed *them* to two of his servants; and they carried *them* on ahead of him.

Shekel of silver.

Judg 17:10 Micah said to him, "Dwell with me, and be a father and a priest to me, and I will give you ten *shekels* of silver per year, a suit of clothes, and your sustenance." So the Levite went in.

2 Kin 15:20 And Menahem exacted the money from Israel, from all the very wealthy, from each man fifty shekels of silver, to give to the king of Assyria. So the king of Assyria turned back, and did not stay there in the land.

Half a shekel or bekah.

Ex 30:15 The rich shall not give more and the poor shall not give less than half a shekel, when *you* give an offering to the LORD, to make atonement for yourselves.

One-third of a shekel.

Neh 10:32 Also we made ordinances for ourselves, to exact from ourselves yearly one-third of a shekel for the service of the house of our God:

One-fourth of a shekel.

1 Sam 9:8 And the servant answered Saul again and said, "Look, I have here at hand one-fourth of a shekel of silver. I will give *that* to the man of God, to tell us our way."

Gerah the twentieth of a shekel.

Num 3:47 you shall take five shekels for each one individually; you shall take *them* in the currency of the shekel of the sanctuary, the shekel of twenty gerahs.

Minah.

Luke 19:13 So he called ten of his servants, delivered to them ten minas, and said to them, 'Do business till I come.'

Denarius.

Matt 20:2 Now when he had agreed with the laborers for a denarius a day, he sent them into his vineyard.

Mark 6:37 But He answered and said to them, "You give them something to eat." And they said to Him, "Shall we go and buy two hundred denarii worth of bread and give them *something* to eat?"

Penny.

Matt 5:26 Assuredly, I say to you, you will by no means get out of there till you have paid the last penny.

Luke 12:6 "Are not five sparrows sold for two copper coins? And not one of them is forgotten before God.

Mite.

Mark 12:42 Then one poor widow came and threw in two mites, which make a quadrans.

Luke 21:2 and He saw also a certain poor widow putting in two mites.

Of the Jews, regulated by the shekel of the sanctuary.

Lev 5:15 "If a person commits a trespass, and sins unintentionally in regard to the holy things of the LORD, then he shall bring to the LORD as his trespass offering a ram without blemish from the flocks, with your valuation in shekels of silver according to the shekel of the sanctuary, as a trespass offering.

Num 3:47 you shall take five shekels for each one individually; you shall take *them* in the currency of the shekel of the sanctuary, the shekel of twenty gerahs.

Jews forbidden to take usury for.

Lev 25:37 You shall not lend him your money for usury, nor lend him your food at a profit.

Changing of, a trade.

Matt 21:12 Then Jesus went into the temple of God and drove out all those who bought and sold in the temple, and overturned the tables of the money changers and the seats of those who sold doves.

John 2:15 When He had made a whip of cords, He drove them all out of the temple, with the sheep and the oxen, and poured out the changers' money and overturned the tables.

Uses of,

Currency with merchants.

Gen 23:16 And Abraham listened to Ephron; and Abraham weighed out the silver for Ephron which he had named in the hearing of the sons of Heth, four hundred shekels of silver, currency of the merchants.

Payment for lands.

Gen 23:9 that he may give me the cave of Machpelah which he has, which *is* at the end of his field. Let him give it to me at the full price, as property for a burial place among you."

Acts 4:37 having land, sold *it*, and brought the money and laid *it* at the apostles' feet.

Payment for slaves.

Gen 37:28 Then Midianite traders passed by; so *the brothers* pulled Joseph up and lifted him out of the pit, and sold him to the Ishmaelites for twenty *shekels* of silver. And they took Joseph to Egypt.

Ex 21:21 Notwithstanding, if he remains alive a day or two, he shall not be punished; for he *is* his property.

Payment for merchandise.

Gen 43:12 Take double money in your hand, and take back in your hand the money that was returned in the mouth of your sacks; perhaps it was an oversight.

Deut 2:6 You shall buy food from them with money, that you may eat; and you shall also buy water from them with money, that you may drink.

For tribute.

2 Kin 23:33 Now Pharaoh Necho put him in prison at Riblah in the land of Hamath, that he might not reign in Jerusalem; and he imposed on the land a tribute of one hundred talents of silver and a talent of gold.

Matt 22:19 Show Me the tax money." So they brought Him a denarius.

As wages.

Ezra 3:7 They also gave money to the masons and the carpenters, and food, drink, and oil to the people of Sidon and Tyre to bring cedar logs from Lebanon to the sea, to Joppa, according to the permission which they had from Cyrus king of Persia.

Matt 20:2 Now when he had agreed with the laborers for a denarius a day, he sent them into his vineyard.

James 5:4 Indeed the wages of the laborers who mowed your fields, which you kept back by fraud, cry out;

and the cries of the reapers have reached the ears of the Lord of Sabaoth.

As offerings.

2 Kin 12:7–9 So King Jehoash called Jehoiada the priest and the *other* priests, and said to them, "Why have you not repaired the damages of the temple? Now therefore, do not take *more* money from your constituency, but deliver it for repairing the damages of the temple." **8** And the priests agreed that they would neither receive *more* money from the people, nor repair the damages of the temple. **9** Then Jehoiada the priest took a chest, bored a hole in its lid, and set it beside the altar, on the right side as one comes into the house of the Lord; and the priests who kept the door put there all the money brought into the house of the Lord.

Neh 10:32 Also we made ordinances for ourselves, to exact from ourselves yearly one-third of a shekel for the service of the house of our God:

As alms.

1 Sam 2:36 And it shall come to pass that everyone who is left in your house will come *and* bow down to him for a piece of silver and a morsel of bread, and say, "Please, put me in one of the priestly positions, that I may eat a piece of bread." ' "

Acts 3:3 who, seeing Peter and John about to go into the temple, asked for alms.

Acts 3:6 Then Peter said, "Silver and gold I do not have, but what I do have I give you: In the name of Jesus Christ of Nazareth, rise up and walk."

As gifts within families.

Job 42:11 Then all his brothers, all his sisters, and all those who had been his acquaintances before, came to him and ate food with him in his house; and they consoled him and comforted him for all the adversity that the Lord had brought upon him. Each one gave him a piece of silver and each a ring of gold.

Power and usefulness of.

Eccl 7:12 For wisdom *is* a defense *as* money *is* a defense, But the excellence of knowledge *is that* wisdom gives life to those who have it.

Eccl 10:19 A feast is made for laughter, And wine makes merry; But money answers everything.

Love of, the root of all kinds of evil.

1 Tim 6:10 For the love of money is a root of all *kinds of* evil, for which some have strayed from the faith in their greediness, and pierced themselves through with many sorrows.

MONTHS

Sun and new moon designed to mark out.

Gen 1:14 Then God said, "Let there be lights in the firmament of the heavens to divide the day from the night; and let them be for signs and seasons, and for days and years;

Num 10:10 Also in the day of your gladness, in your appointed feasts, and at the beginning of your months, you shall blow the trumpets over your burnt offerings and over the sacrifices of your peace offerings; and they shall be a memorial for you before your God: I *am* the Lord your God."

Ps 81:3 Blow the trumpet at the time of the New Moon, At the full moon, on our solemn feast day.

The patriarchs and Jews computed time by.

Gen 29:14 And Laban said to him, "Surely you *are* my bone and my flesh." And he stayed with him for a month.

Judg 11:37 Then she said to her father, "Let this thing be done for me: let me alone for two months, that I may go and wander on the mountains and bewail my virginity, my friends and I."

1 Sam 6:1 Now the ark of the LORD was in the country of the Philistines seven months.

1 Kin 4:7 And Solomon had twelve governors over all Israel, who provided food for the king and his household; each one made provision for one month of the year.

Originally had no names.

Gen 7:11 In the six hundredth year of Noah's life, in the second month, the seventeenth day of the month, on that day all the fountains of the great deep were broken up, and the windows of heaven were opened.

Gen 8:4 Then the ark rested in the seventh month, the seventeenth day of the month, on the mountains of Ararat.

The year composed of twelve.

1 Chr 27:2–15 Over the first division for the first month *was* Jashobeam the son of Zabdiel, and in his division *were* twenty-four thousand; **3** *he was* of the children of Perez, and the chief of all the captains of the army for the first month. **4** Over the division of the second month *was* Dodai an Ahohite, and of his division Mikloth also *was* the leader; in his division *were* twenty-four thousand. **5** The third captain of the army for the third month *was* Benaiah, the son of Jehoiada the priest, who was chief; in his division *were* twenty-four thousand. **6** This was the Benaiah *who was* mighty *among* the thirty, and was over the thirty; in his division *was* Ammizabad his son. **7** The fourth *captain* for the fourth month *was* Asahel the brother of Joab, and Zebadiah his son after him; in his division *were* twenty-four thousand. **8** The fifth *captain* for the fifth month *was* Shamhuth the Izrahite; in his division were twenty-four thousand. **9** The sixth *captain* for the sixth month *was* Ira the son of Ikkesh the Tekoite; in his division *were* twenty-four thousand. **10** The seventh *captain* for the seventh month *was* Helez the Pelonite, of the children of Ephraim; in his division *were* twenty-four thousand. **11** The eighth *captain* for the eighth month *was* Sibbechai the Hushathite, of the Zarhites; in his division *were* twenty-four thousand. **12** The ninth *captain* for the ninth month *was* Abiezer the Anathothite, of the Benjamites; in his division *were* twenty-four thousand. **13** The tenth *captain* for the tenth month *was* Maharai the Netophathite, of the Zarhites; in his division *were* twenty-four thousand. **14** The eleventh *captain* for the eleventh month *was* Benaiah the Pirathonite, of the children of Ephraim; in his division *were* twenty-four thousand. **15** The twelfth *captain* for the twelfth month *was* Heldai the Netophathite, of Othniel; in his division *were* twenty-four thousand.

Esth 2:12 Each young woman's turn came to go in to King Ahasuerus after she had completed twelve months' preparation, according to the regulations for the women, for thus were the days of their preparation apportioned: six months with oil of myrrh, and six months with perfumes and preparations for beautifying women.

Rev 22:2 In the middle of its street, and on either side of the river, *was* the tree of life, which bore twelve fruits, each *tree* yielding its fruit every month. The leaves of the tree *were* for the healing of the nations.

Hebrew names of the twelve months

First, Nisan or Abib.

Ex 13:4 On this day you are going out, in the month Abib.

Neh 2:1 And it came to pass in the month of Nisan, in the twentieth year of King Artaxerxes, *when* wine *was* before him, that I took the wine and gave it to the king. Now I had never been sad in his presence before.

Second, Ziv.

1 Kin 6:1 And it came to pass in the four hundred and eightieth year after the children of Israel had come out of the land of Egypt, in the fourth year of Solomon's reign over Israel, in the month of Ziv, which *is* the second month, that he began to build the house of the LORD.

1 Kin 6:37 In the fourth year the foundation of the house of the LORD was laid, in the month of Ziv.

Third, Sivan.

Esth 8:9 So the king's scribes were called at that time, in the third month, which *is* the month of Sivan, on the twenty-third *day;* and it was written, according to all that Mordecai commanded, to the Jews, the satraps, the governors, and the princes of the provinces from India to Ethiopia, one hundred and twenty-seven provinces *in all,* to every province in its own script, to every people in their own language, and to the Jews in their own script and language.

Fourth, Tammuz.

Zech 8:19 "Thus says the LORD of hosts: 'The fast of the fourth *month,* The fast of the fifth, The fast of the seventh, And the fast of the tenth, Shall be joy and gladness and cheerful feasts For the house of Judah. Therefore love truth and peace.'

Fifth, Av.

Zech 7:3 *and* to ask the priests who *were* in the house of the LORD of hosts, and the prophets, saying, "Should I weep in the fifth month and fast as I have done for so many years?"

Sixth, Elul.

Neh 6:15 So the wall was finished on the twenty-fifth *day* of Elul, in fifty-two days.

Seventh, Ethanim.

1 Kin 8:2 Therefore all the men of Israel assembled with King Solomon at the feast in the month of Ethanim, which *is* the seventh month.

Eighth, Bul.

1 Kin 6:38 And in the eleventh year, in the month of Bul, which is the eighth month, the house was finished in all its details and according to all its plans. So he was seven years in building it.

Ninth, Chislev.

Zech 7:1 Now in the fourth year of King Darius it came to pass *that* the word of the LORD came to Zechariah, on the fourth day of the ninth month, Chislev,

Tenth, Tebeth.

Esth 2:16 So Esther was taken to King Ahasuerus, into his royal palace, in the tenth month, which *is* the month of Tebeth, in the seventh year of his reign.

Eleventh, Shebat.

Zech 1:7 On the twenty-fourth day of the eleventh month, which is the month Shebat, in the second year of Darius, the word of the LORD came to Zechariah the son of Berechiah, the son of Iddo the prophet:

Twelfth, Adar.

Ezra 6:15 Now the temple was finished on the third day of the month of Adar, which was in the sixth year of the reign of King Darius.

Esth 3:7 In the first month, which is the month of Nisan, in the twelfth year of King Ahasuerus, they cast Pur (that *is*, the lot), before Haman to determine the day and the month, until *it fell on the* twelfth *month,* which *is* the month of Adar.

Idolaters prognosticated by.

Is 47:13 You are wearied in the multitude of your counsels; Let now the astrologers, the stargazers, *And* the monthly prognosticators Stand up and save you From what shall come upon you.

Legalistic observance of, condemned.

Gal 4:10 You observe days and months and seasons and years.

MOON, THE

Created by God to glorify Him.

Gen 1:14 Then God said, "Let there be lights in the firmament of the heavens to divide the day from the night; and let them be for signs and seasons, and for days and years;

Ps 8:3 When I consider Your heavens, the work of Your fingers, The moon and the stars, which You have ordained,

Ps 148:3 Praise Him, sun and moon; Praise Him, all you stars of light!

Described as

The lesser light.

Gen 1:16 Then God made two great lights: the greater light to rule the day, and the lesser light to rule the night. *He made* the stars also.

Fair.

Song 6:10 Who is she who looks forth as the morning, Fair as the moon, Clear as the sun, Awesome as *an army* with banners?

Bright.

Job 31:26 If I have observed the sun when it shines, Or the moon moving *in* brightness,

Having glory.

1 Cor 15:41 *There is* one glory of the sun, another glory of the moon, and another glory of the stars; for *one* star differs from *another* star in glory.

Appointed

To divide day from night.

Gen 1:14 Then God said, "Let there be lights in the firmament of the heavens to divide the day from the night; and let them be for signs and seasons, and for days and years;

For signs and seasons.

Gen 1:14 Then God said, "Let there be lights in the firmament of the heavens to divide the day from the night; and let them be for signs and seasons, and for days and years;

Ps 104:19 He appointed the moon for seasons; The sun knows its going down.

For a light in the firmament.

Gen 1:15 and let them be for lights in the firmament of the heavens to give light on the earth"; and it was so.

To rule the night.

Gen 1:16 Then God made two great lights: the greater light to rule the day, and the lesser light to rule the night. *He made* the stars also.

Ps 136:9 The moon and stars to rule by night, For His mercy *endures* forever.

Jer 31:35 Thus says the LORD, Who gives the sun for a light by day, The ordinances of the moon and the stars for a light by night, Who disturbs the sea, And its waves roar (The LORD of hosts *is* His name):

By an ordinance forever.

Ps 72:5 They shall fear You As long as the sun and moon endure, Throughout all generations.

Ps 72:7 In His days the righteous shall flourish, And abundance of peace, Until the moon is no more.

Ps 89:37 It shall be established forever like the moon, Even *like* the faithful witness in the sky." Selah

Jer 31:36 "If those ordinances depart From before Me, says the LORD, *Then* the seed of Israel shall also cease From being a nation before Me forever."

For the benefit of all.

Deut 4:19 And *take heed,* lest you lift your eyes to heaven, and *when* you see the sun, the moon, and the stars, all the host of heaven, you feel driven to worship them and serve them, which the LORD your God has given to all the peoples under the whole heaven as a heritage.

Influences vegetation.

Deut 33:14 With the precious fruits of the sun, With the precious produce of the months,

First appearance of, a time of festivity.

1 Sam 20:5–6 And David said to Jonathan, "Indeed tomorrow *is* the New Moon, and I should not fail to sit with the king to eat. But let me go, that I may hide in the field until the third *day* at evening. 6 If your father misses me at all, then say, 'David earnestly asked *permission* of me that he might run over to Bethlehem, his city, for *there is* a yearly sacrifice there for all the family.'

Ps 81:3 Blow the trumpet at the time of the New Moon, At the full moon, on our solemn feast day.

Miracles connected with,

Standing still in Aijalon.

Josh 10:12–13 Then Joshua spoke to the LORD in the day

when the Lord delivered up the Amorites before the children of Israel, and he said in the sight of Israel: "Sun, stand still over Gibeon; And Moon, in the Valley of Aijalon." **13** So the sun stood still, And the moon stopped, Till the people had revenge Upon their enemies. *Is* this not written in the Book of Jasher? So the sun stood still in the midst of heaven, and did not hasten to go *down* for about a whole day.

Signs in, before the destruction of Jerusalem.

Luke 21:25 "And there will be signs in the sun, in the moon, and in the stars; and on the earth distress of nations, with perplexity, the sea and the waves roaring;

Worshiping of,

As the queen of heaven.

Jer 7:18 The children gather wood, the fathers kindle the fire, and the women knead dough, to make cakes for the queen of heaven; and *they* pour out drink offerings to other gods, that they may provoke Me to anger.

Jer 44:17–19 But we will certainly do whatever has gone out of our own mouth, to burn incense to the queen of heaven and pour out drink offerings to her, as we have done, we and our fathers, our kings and our princes, in the cities of Judah and in the streets of Jerusalem. For *then* we had plenty of food, were well-off, and saw no trouble. **18** But since we stopped burning incense to the queen of heaven and pouring out drink offerings to her, we have lacked everything and have been consumed by the sword and by famine." **19** *The women also said,* "And when we burned incense to the queen of heaven and poured out drink offerings to her, did we make cakes for her, to worship her, and pour out drink offerings to her without our husbands' *permission?*"

Jer 44:25 Thus says the Lord of hosts, the God of Israel, saying: 'You and your wives have spoken with your mouths and fulfilled with your hands, saying, "We will surely keep our vows that we have made, to burn incense to the queen of heaven and pour out drink offerings to her." You will surely keep your vows and perform your vows!'

Forbidden to the Jews.

Deut 4:19 And *take heed,* lest you lift your eyes to heaven, and *when* you see the sun, the moon, and the stars, all the host of heaven, you feel driven to worship them and serve them, which the Lord your God has given to all the peoples under the whole heaven as a heritage.

Condemned as atheism.

Job 31:26 If I have observed the sun when it shines, Or the moon moving *in* brightness,

Job 31:28 This also *would be* an iniquity *deserving of* judgment, For I would have denied God *who is* above.

Jews often guilty of.

2 Kin 23:5 Then he removed the idolatrous priests whom the kings of Judah had ordained to burn incense on the high places in the cities of Judah and in the places all around Jerusalem, and those who burned incense to Baal, to the sun, to the moon, to the constellations, and to all the host of heaven.

Jer 8:2 They shall spread them before the sun and the moon and all the host of heaven, which they have loved and which they have served and after which they have walked, which they have sought and which they have worshiped. They shall not be gathered nor buried; they shall be like refuse on the face of the earth.

Jews punished for.

Deut 17:3–6 who has gone and served other gods and worshiped them, either the sun or moon or any of the host of heaven, which I have not commanded, **4** and it is told you, and you hear *of it,* then you shall inquire diligently. And if *it is* indeed true *and* certain that such an abomination has been committed in Israel, **5** then you shall bring out to your gates that man or woman who has committed that wicked thing, and shall stone to death that man or woman with stones. **6** Whoever is deserving of death shall be put to death on the testimony of two or three witnesses; he shall not be put to death on the testimony of one witness.

Jer 8:1–3 "At that time," says the Lord, "they shall bring out the bones of the kings of Judah, and the bones of its princes, and the bones of the priests, and the bones of the prophets, and the bones of the inhabitants of Jerusalem, out of their graves. **2** They shall spread them before the sun and the moon and all the host of heaven, which they have loved and which they have served and after which they have walked, which they have sought and which they have worshiped. They shall not be gathered nor buried; they shall be like refuse on the face of the earth. **3** Then death shall be chosen rather than life by all the residue of those who remain of this evil family, who remain in all the places where I have driven them," says the Lord of hosts.

Illustrative of

Glory of God.

Is 60:20 Your sun shall no longer go down, Nor shall your moon withdraw itself; For the Lord will be your everlasting light, And the days of your mourning shall be ended.

Beauty of the Shulamite.

Song 6:10 Who is she who looks forth as the morning, Fair as the moon, Clear as the sun, Awesome as *an army* with banners?

Changeableness of the world.

Rev 12:1 Now a great sign appeared in heaven: a woman clothed with the sun, with the moon under her feet, and on her head a garland of twelve stars.

(Becoming blood) judgments.

Rev 6:12 I looked when He opened the sixth seal, and behold, there was a great earthquake; and the sun became black as sackcloth of hair, and the moon became like blood.

(Withdrawing her light) deep calamities.

Is 13:10 For the stars of heaven and their constellations Will not give their light; The sun will be darkened in its going forth, And the moon will not cause its light to shine.

Joel 2:10 The earth quakes before them, The heavens tremble; The sun and moon grow dark, And the stars diminish their brightness.

Joel 3:15 The sun and moon will grow dark, And the stars will diminish their brightness.

Matt 24:29 "Immediately after the tribulation of those days the sun will be darkened, and the moon will not give its light; the stars will fall from heaven, and the powers of the heavens will be shaken.

MORALITY

Amnon's lack of. 2 Sam 13:1–22

Reversal of (confusing good and evil).

Is 5:20–23 Woe to those who call evil good, and good evil; Who put darkness for light, and light for darkness; Who put bitter for sweet, and sweet for bitter! **21** Woe to *those who are* wise in their own eyes, And prudent in their own sight! **22** Woe to men mighty at drinking wine, Woe to men valiant for mixing intoxicating drink, **23** Who justify the wicked for a bribe, And take away justice from the righteous man!

Jesus' standard of.

Luke 6:27–38 "But I say to you who hear: Love your enemies, do good to those who hate you, **28** bless those who curse you, and pray for those who spitefully use you. **29** To him who strikes you on the *one* cheek, offer the other also. And from him who takes away your cloak, do not withhold *your* tunic either. **30** Give to everyone who asks of you. And from him who takes away your goods do not ask *them* back. **31** And just as you want men to do to you, you also do to them likewise. **32** "But if you love those who love you, what credit is that to you? For even sinners love those who love them. **33** And if you do good to those who do good to you, what credit is that to you? For even sinners do the same. **34** And if you lend *to those* from whom you hope to receive back, what credit is that to you? For even sinners lend to sinners to receive as much back. **35** But love your enemies, do good, and lend, hoping for nothing in return; and your reward will be great, and you will be sons of the Most High. For He is kind to the unthankful and evil. **36** Therefore be merciful, just as your Father also is merciful. **37** "Judge not, and you shall not be judged. Condemn not, and you shall not be condemned. Forgive, and you will be forgiven. **38** Give, and it will be given to you: good measure, pressed down, shaken together, and running over will be put into your bosom. For with the same measure that you use, it will be measured back to you."

Cf. Matt 5:21–48

Should be more than outward.

Matt 23:27–28 "Woe to you, scribes and Pharisees, hypocrites! For you are like whitewashed tombs which indeed appear beautiful outwardly, but inside are full of dead *men's* bones and all uncleanness. **28** Even so you also outwardly appear righteous to men, but inside you are full of hypocrisy and lawlessness.

Cf. 1 John 2:3–17

MORNING

The second part of the day at the creation.

Gen 1:5 God called the light Day, and the darkness He called Night. So the evening and the morning were the first day.

Gen 1:8 And God called the firmament Heaven. So the evening and the morning were the second day.

Gen 1:13 So the evening and the morning were the third day.

Gen 1:19 So the evening and the morning were the fourth day.

Gen 1:23 So the evening and the morning were the fifth day.

Gen 1:31 Then God saw everything that He had made, and indeed *it was* very good. So the evening and the morning were the sixth day.

The first part of the natural day.

Mark 16:2 Very early in the morning, on the first *day* of the week, they came to the tomb when the sun had risen.

Ordained by God.

Job 38:12 "Have you commanded the morning since your days *began, And* caused the dawn to know its place,

Began with first dawn.

Josh 6:15 But it came to pass on the seventh day that they rose early, about the dawning of the day, and marched around the city seven times in the same manner. On that day only they marched around the city seven times.

Ps 119:147 I rise before the dawning of the morning, And cry for help; I hope in Your word.

Continued until noon.

1 Kin 18:26 So they took the bull which was given them, and they prepared *it*, and called on the name of Baal from morning even till noon, saying, "O Baal, hear us!" But *there was* no voice; no one answered. Then they leaped about the altar which they had made.

Neh 8:3 Then he read from it in the open square that *was* in front of the Water Gate from morning until midday, before the men and women and those who could understand; and the ears of all the people *were* attentive to the Book of the Law.

First dawning of, called the eyelids of the morning.

Job 3:9 May the stars of its morning be dark; May it look for light, but *have* none, And not see the dawning of the day;

Job 41:18 His sneezings flash forth light, And his eyes *are* like the eyelids of the morning.

The outgoings of, made to rejoice.

Ps 65:8 They also who dwell in the farthest parts are afraid of Your signs; You make the outgoings of the morning and evening rejoice.

The Jews

Generally rose early in.

Gen 28:18 Then Jacob rose early in the morning, and took the stone that he had put at his head, set it up as a pillar, and poured oil on top of it.

Judg 6:28 And when the men of the city arose early in the morning, there was the altar of Baal, torn down; and the wooden image that *was* beside it was cut down, and the second bull was being offered on the altar *which had been* built.

Went to the temple in.

Luke 21:38 Then early in the morning all the people came to Him in the temple to hear Him.

John 8:2 Now early in the morning He came again into the temple, and all the people came to Him; and He sat down and taught them.

Offered a part of the daily sacrifice in.

Ex 29:38–39 "Now this *is* what you shall offer on the altar: two lambs of the first year, day by day continually. **39** One lamb you shall offer in the morning, and the other lamb you shall offer at twilight.

Num 28:4–7 The one lamb you shall offer in the morning, the other lamb you shall offer in the evening, **5** and one-tenth of an ephah of fine flour as a grain offering mixed with one-fourth of a hin of pressed oil. **6** *It is* a regular burnt offering which was ordained at Mount Sinai for a sweet aroma, an offering made by fire to the LORD. **7** And its drink offering *shall be* one-fourth of a hin for each lamb; in a holy place you shall pour out the drink to the LORD as an offering.

Devoted a part of, to prayer and praise.

Ps 5:3 My voice You shall hear in the morning, O LORD; In the morning I will direct *it* to You, And I will look up.

Ps 59:16 But I will sing of Your power; Yes, I will sing aloud of Your mercy in the morning; For You have been my defense And refuge in the day of my trouble.

Ps 88:13 But to You I have cried out, O LORD, And in the morning my prayer comes before You.

Gathered the manna in.

Ex 16:21 So they gathered it every morning, every man according to his need. And when the sun became hot, it melted.

Began their journeys in.

Gen 22:3 So Abraham rose early in the morning and saddled his donkey, and took two of his young men with him, and Isaac his son; and he split the wood for the burnt offering, and arose and went to the place of which God had told him.

Held courts of justice in.

Jer 21:12 O house of David! Thus says the LORD: "Execute judgment in the morning; And deliver *him who is* plundered Out of the hand of the oppressor, Lest My fury go forth like fire And burn so that no one can quench *it,* Because of the evil of your doings.

Matt 27:1 When morning came, all the chief priests and elders of the people plotted against Jesus to put Him to death.

Contracted covenants in.

Gen 26:31 Then they arose early in the morning and swore an oath with one another; and Isaac sent them away, and they departed from him in peace.

Transacted business in.

Eccl 11:6 In the morning sow your seed, And in the evening do not withhold your hand; For you do not know which will prosper, Either this or that, Or whether both alike *will be* good.

Matt 20:1 "For the kingdom of heaven is like a landowner who went out early in the morning to hire laborers for his vineyard.

Was frequently cloudless.

2 Sam 23:4 And *he shall be* like the light of the morning *when* the sun rises, A morning without clouds, *Like* the tender grass *springing* out of the earth, By clear shining after rain.'

A red sky in, a sign of foul weather.

Matt 16:3 and in the morning, '*It will be* foul weather today, for the sky is red and threatening.' Hypocrites! You know how to discern the face of the sky, but you cannot *discern* the signs of the times.

Ushered in by the morning star.

Job 38:7 When the morning stars sang together, And all the sons of God shouted for joy?

Illustrative of

The resurrection day.

Ps 49:14 Like sheep they are laid in the grave; Death shall feed on them; The upright shall have dominion over them in the morning; And their beauty shall be consumed in the grave, far from their dwelling.

(Star of) the glory of Christ.

Rev 22:16 "I, Jesus, have sent My angel to testify to you these things in the churches. I am the Root and the Offspring of David, the Bright and Morning Star."

(Star of) reward for believers.

Rev 2:28 and I will give him the morning star.

(Clouds in) the short lived profession of hypocrites.

Hos 6:4 "O Ephraim, what shall I do to you? O Judah, what shall I do to you? For your faithfulness is like a morning cloud, And like the early dew it goes away.

(Wings of) rapid movements.

Ps 139:9 *If* I take the wings of the morning, *And* dwell in the uttermost parts of the sea,

(Spread upon the mountains) heavy calamities.

Joel 2:2 A day of darkness and gloominess, A day of clouds and thick darkness, Like the morning *clouds* spread over the mountains. A people *come,* great and strong, The like of whom has never been; Nor will there ever be any *such* after them, Even for many successive generations.

MOSES

Parents of.

Ex 6:16–20 These *are* the names of the sons of Levi according to their generations: Gershon, Kohath, and Merari. And the years of the life of Levi *were* one hundred and thirty-seven. **17** The sons of Gershon *were* Libni and Shimi according to their families. **18** And the sons of Kohath *were* Amram, Izhar, Hebron, and Uzziel. And the years of the life of Kohath *were* one hundred and thirty-three. **19** The sons of Merari *were* Mahli and Mushi. These *are* the families of Levi according to their generations. **20** Now Amram took for himself Jochebed, his father's sister, as wife; and she bore him Aaron and Moses. And the years of the life of Amram *were* one hundred and thirty-seven.

Born under slavery in Egypt.

Ex 2:1–10 And a man of the house of Levi went and took *as wife* a daughter of Levi. **2** So the woman conceived and bore a son. And when she saw that he *was* a beautiful *child*, she hid him three months. 3 But when she could no longer hide him, she took an ark of bulrushes for him, daubed it with asphalt and pitch, put the child in it, and laid *it* in the reeds by the river's bank. 4 And his sister stood afar off, to know what would be done to him. 5 Then the daughter of Pharaoh came down to bathe at the river. And her maidens walked along the riverside; and when she saw the ark among the reeds, she sent her maid to get it. 6 And when she opened *it*, she saw the child, and behold, the baby wept. So she had compassion on him, and said, "This is one of the Hebrews' children." 7 Then his sister said to Pharaoh's daughter, "Shall I go and call a nurse for you from the Hebrew women, that she may nurse the child for you?" 8 And Pharaoh's daughter said to her, "Go." So the maiden went and called the child's mother. 9 Then Pharaoh's daughter said to her, "Take this child away and nurse him for me, and I will give *you* your wages." So the woman took the child and nursed him. 10 And the child grew, and she brought him to Pharaoh's daughter, and he became her son. So she called his name Moses, saying, "Because I drew him out of the water."

Refused privileges of Egypt.

Heb 11:23–27 By faith Moses, when he was born, was hidden three months by his parents, because they saw *he was* a beautiful child; and they were not afraid of the king's command. 24 By faith Moses, when he became of age, refused to be called the son of Pharaoh's daughter, 25 choosing rather to suffer affliction with the people of God than to enjoy the passing pleasures of sin, 26 esteeming the reproach of Christ greater riches than the treasures in Egypt; for he looked to the reward. 27 By faith he forsook Egypt, not fearing the wrath of the king; for he endured as seeing Him who is invisible.

Hears God's plan for him.

Ex 3:2–10 And the Angel of the LORD appeared to him in a flame of fire from the midst of a bush. So he looked, and behold, the bush was burning with fire, but the bush *was* not consumed. 3 Then Moses said, "I will now turn aside and see this great sight, why the bush does not burn." 4 So when the LORD saw that he turned aside to look, God called to him from the midst of the bush and said, "Moses, Moses!" And he said, "Here I am." 5 Then He said, "Do not draw near this place. Take your sandals off your feet, for the place where you stand *is* holy ground." 6 Moreover He said, "I *am* the God of your father—the God of Abraham, the God of Isaac, and the God of Jacob." And Moses hid his face, for he was afraid to look upon God. 7 And the LORD said: "I have surely seen the oppression of My people who *are* in Egypt, and have heard their cry because of their taskmasters, for I know their sorrows. 8 So I have come down to deliver them out of the hand of the Egyptians, and to bring them up from that land to a good and large land, to a land flowing with milk and honey, to the place of the Canaanites and the Hittites and the Amorites and the Perizzites and the Hivites and the Jebusites. 9 Now therefore, behold, the cry of the children of Israel has come to Me, and I have also seen the oppression with which the Egyptians op-

press them. 10 Come now, therefore, and I will send you to Pharaoh that you may bring My people, the children of Israel, out of Egypt."

Argued with God. Ex 4:1–17

Received first Passover instructions and observed them.

Heb 11:28 By faith he kept the Passover and the sprinkling of blood, lest he who destroyed the firstborn should touch them.

Cf. Ex 12:1–29,39–51

Song of. Ex 15:1–18

Arrived at Mt. Sinai.

Ex 19:1–2 In the third month after the children of Israel had gone out of the land of Egypt, on the same day, they came *to* the Wilderness of Sinai. 2 For they had departed from Rephidim, had come *to* the Wilderness of Sinai, and camped in the wilderness. So Israel camped there before the mountain.

Received covenant and the Law.

Ex 19:3 And Moses went up to God, and the LORD called to him from the mountain, saying, "Thus you shall say to the house of Jacob, and tell the children of Israel:

Ex 19:20 Then the LORD came down upon Mount Sinai, on the top of the mountain. And the LORD called Moses to the top of the mountain, and Moses went up.

Ex 20:1 And God spoke all these words, saying:

Ex 24:2–4 And Moses alone shall come near the LORD, but they shall not come near; nor shall the people go up with him." 3 So Moses came and told the people all the words of the LORD and all the judgments. And all the people answered with one voice and said, "All the words which the LORD has said we will do." 4 And Moses wrote all the words of the LORD. And he rose early in the morning, and built an altar at the foot of the mountain, and twelve pillars according to the twelve tribes of Israel.

Cf. Deut 5:1–21

Received blueprint for the tabernacle.

Ex 25:1–9 Then the LORD spoke to Moses, saying: 2 "Speak to the children of Israel, that they bring Me an offering. From everyone who gives it willingly with his heart you shall take My offering. 3 And this *is* the offering which you shall take from them: gold, silver, and bronze; 4 blue, purple, and scarlet *thread,* fine linen, and goats' *hair;* 5 ram skins dyed red, badger skins, and acacia wood; 6 oil for the light, and spices for the anointing oil and for the sweet incense; 7 onyx stones, and stones to be set in the ephod and in the breastplate. 8 And let them make Me a sanctuary, that I may dwell among them. 9 According to all that I show you, *that is,* the pattern of the tabernacle and the pattern of all its furnishings, just so you shall make *it.*

Consecrated Aaron and sons to priesthood.

Lev 8:1–5 And the LORD spoke to Moses, saying: 2 "Take Aaron and his sons with him, and the garments, the anointing oil, a bull as the sin offering, two rams, and a basket of unleavened bread; 3 and gather all the congregation together at the door of the tabernacle of meeting." 4 So Moses did as the LORD commanded him. And the congregation was gathered together at the door of the tabernacle of meeting. **5** And Moses said to the congregation, "This *is* what the LORD commanded to be done."

Miriam and Aaron rebelled against.

Num 12:1–6 Then Miriam and Aaron spoke against Moses because of the Ethiopian woman whom he had married; for he had married an Ethiopian woman. **2** So they said, "Has the LORD indeed spoken only through Moses? Has He not spoken through us also?" And the LORD heard *it.* **3** (Now the man Moses *was* very humble, more than all men who *were* on the face of the earth.) **4** Suddenly the LORD said to Moses, Aaron, and Miriam, "Come out, you three, to the tabernacle of meeting!" So the three came out. **5** Then the LORD came down in the pillar of cloud and stood *in* the door of the tabernacle, and called Aaron and Miriam. And they both went forward. **6** Then He said, "Hear now My words: If there is a prophet among you, I, the LORD, make Myself known to him in a vision; I speak to him in a dream.

Sinned in anger at the rock.

Num 20:2–13 Now there was no water for the congregation; so they gathered together against Moses and Aaron. **3** And the people contended with Moses and spoke, saying: "If only we had died when our brethren died before the LORD! **4** Why have you brought up the assembly of the LORD into this wilderness, that we and our animals should die here? **5** And why have you made us come up out of Egypt, to bring us to this evil place? It *is* not a place of grain or figs or vines or pomegranates; nor *is* there any water to drink." **6** So Moses and Aaron went from the presence of the assembly to the door of the tabernacle of meeting, and they fell on their faces. And the glory of the LORD appeared to them. **7** Then the LORD spoke to Moses, saying, **8** "Take the rod; you and your brother Aaron gather the congregation together. Speak to the rock before their eyes, and it will yield its water; thus you shall bring water for them out of the rock, and give drink to the congregation and their animals." **9** So Moses took the rod from before the LORD as He commanded him. **10** And Moses and Aaron gathered the assembly together before the rock; and he said to them, "Hear now, you rebels! Must we bring water for you out of this rock?" **11** Then Moses lifted his hand and struck the rock twice with his rod; and water came out abundantly, and the congregation and their animals drank. **12** Then the LORD spoke to Moses and Aaron, "Because you did not believe Me, to hallow Me in the eyes of the children of Israel, therefore you shall not bring this assembly into the land which I have given them." **13** This *was* the water of Meribah, because the children of Israel contended with the LORD, and He was hallowed among them.

Sent spies to Canaan. Num 13:1–20
Made bronze serpent.

Num 21:4–9 Then they journeyed from Mount Hor by the Way of the Red Sea, to go around the land of Edom; and the soul of the people became very discouraged on the way. **5** And the people spoke against God and against Moses: "Why have you brought us up out of Egypt to die in the wilderness? For *there is* no food and no water, and our soul loathes this

worthless bread." **6** So the LORD sent fiery serpents among the people, and they bit the people; and many of the people of Israel died. **7** Therefore the people came to Moses, and said, "We have sinned, for we have spoken against the LORD and against you; pray to the LORD that He take away the serpents from us." So Moses prayed for the people. **8** Then the LORD said to Moses, "Make a fiery *serpent,* and set it on a pole; and it shall be that everyone who is bitten, when he looks at it, shall live." **9** So Moses made a bronze serpent, and put it on a pole; and so it was, if a serpent had bitten anyone, when he looked at the bronze serpent, he lived.

John 3:14 And as Moses lifted up the serpent in the wilderness, even so must the Son of Man be lifted up,

Forbidden to enter Promised Land.

Num 20:12 Then the LORD spoke to Moses and Aaron, "Because you did not believe Me, to hallow Me in the eyes of the children of Israel, therefore you shall not bring this assembly into the land which I have given them."

Deut 3:23–29 "Then I pleaded with the LORD at that time, saying: **24** 'O Lord GOD, You have begun to show Your servant Your greatness and Your mighty hand, for what god *is there* in heaven or on earth who can do *anything* like Your works and Your mighty *deeds?* **25** I pray, let me cross over and see the good land beyond the Jordan, those pleasant mountains, and Lebanon.' **26** "But the LORD was angry with me on your account, and would not listen to me. So the LORD said to me: 'Enough of that! Speak no more to Me of this matter. **27** Go up to the top of Pisgah, and lift your eyes toward the west, the north, the south, and the east; behold *it* with your eyes, for you shall not cross over this Jordan. **28** But command Joshua, and encourage him and strengthen him; for he shall go over before this people, and he shall cause them to inherit the land which you will see.' **29** "So we stayed in the valley opposite Beth Peor.

Deut 4:21–22 Furthermore the LORD was angry with me for your sakes, and swore that I would not cross over the Jordan, and that I would not enter the good land which the LORD your God is giving you as an inheritance. **22** But I must die in this land, I must not cross over the Jordan; but you shall cross over and possess that good land.

His blessings on the twelve tribes. Deut 33:1–29
Saw the Promised Land.

Deut 34:1–4 Then Moses went up from the plains of Moab to Mount Nebo, to the top of Pisgah, which is across from Jericho. And the LORD showed him all the land of Gilead as far as Dan, **2** all Naphtali and the land of Ephraim and Manasseh, all the land of Judah as far as the Western Sea, **3** the South, and the plain of the Valley of Jericho, the city of palm trees, as far as Zoar. **4** Then the LORD said to him, "This *is* the land of which I swore to give Abraham, Isaac, and Jacob, saying, 'I will give it to your descendants.' I have caused you to see *it* with your eyes, but you shall not cross over there."

Death of.

Deut 34:5–8 So Moses the servant of the LORD died there in the land of Moab, according to the word of the LORD. **6** And He buried him in a valley in the land of Moab, opposite Beth Peor; but no one knows his grave to this day. 7 Moses *was* one hundred and twenty years old when he died. His eyes were not dim nor his natural vigor diminished. 8 And the children of Israel wept for Moses in the plains of Moab thirty days. So the days of weeping *and* mourning for Moses ended.

MOTH, THE

Destructive to garments.

Matt 6:19 "Do not lay up for yourselves treasures on earth, where moth and rust destroy and where thieves break in and steal;

James 5:2 Your riches are corrupted, and your garments are moth-eaten.

Destroyed by the slightest touch.

Job 4:19 How much more those who dwell in houses of clay, Whose foundation is in the dust, *Who* are crushed before a moth?

Illustrative of

God in the execution of his judgments.

Hos 5:12 Therefore I *will be* to Ephraim like a moth, And to the house of Judah like rottenness.

(Eating a garment) God's judgments.

Is 50:9 Surely the Lord GOD will help Me; Who *is he who* will condemn Me? Indeed they will all grow old like a garment; The moth will eat them up.

Is 51:8 For the moth will eat them up like a garment, And the worm will eat them like wool; But My righteousness will be forever, And My salvation from generation to generation."

(Garments eaten by) those who have suffered severe judgments.

Job 13:28 "Man decays like a rotten thing, Like a garment that is moth-eaten.

(Making its house in garments) man's folly in providing earthly things.

Job 27:18 He builds his house like a moth, Like a booth *which* a watchman makes.

MOTHER

General designation of,

For Eve.

Gen 3:20 And Adam called his wife's name Eve, because she was the mother of all living.

For Sarah.

Gen 17:15–16 Then God said to Abraham, "As for Sarai your wife, you shall not call her name Sarai, but Sarah *shall be* her name. 16 And I will bless her and also give you a son by her; then I will bless her, and she shall be *a mother of* nations; kings of peoples shall be from her."

Must be honored.

Ex 20:12 "Honor your father and your mother, that your days may be long upon the land which the LORD your God is giving you.

Lev 19:3 'Every one of you shall revere his mother and his father, and keep My Sabbaths: I *am* the LORD your God.

Lev 20:9 'For everyone who curses his father or his

mother shall surely be put to death. He has cursed his father or his mother. His blood *shall be* upon him.

Deut 5:16 'Honor your father and your mother, as the LORD your God has commanded you, that your days may be long, and that it may be well with you in the land which the LORD your God is giving you.

Deut 27:16 'Cursed *is* the one who treats his father or his mother with contempt.' "And all the people shall say, 'Amen!'

Matt 15:4 For God commanded, saying, 'Honor your father and your mother'; and, 'He who curses father or mother, let him be put to death.'

Matt 19:19 'Honor your father and your mother,' and, 'You shall love your neighbor as yourself.' "

Mark 7:10 For Moses said, 'Honor your father and your mother'; and, 'He who curses father or mother, let him be put to death.'

Mark 10:19 You know the commandments: 'Do not commit adultery,' 'Do not murder,' 'Do not steal,' 'Do not bear false witness,' 'Do not defraud,' 'Honor your father and your mother.' "

Luke 18:20 You know the commandments: 'Do not commit adultery,' 'Do not murder,' 'Do not steal,' 'Do not bear false witness,' 'Honor your father and your mother.' "

Eph 6:2 "Honor your father and mother," which is the first commandment with promise:

Cf. Prov 23:25

As synonym for a city.

2 Sam 20:19 I *am among the* peaceable *and* faithful in Israel. You seek to destroy a city and a mother in Israel. Why would you swallow up the inheritance of the LORD?"

Gal 4:26 but the Jerusalem above is free, which is the mother of us all.

Of the kings of the Davidic line.

1 Kin 2:13 Now Adonijah the son of Haggith came to Bathsheba the mother of Solomon. So she said, "Do you come peaceably?" And he said, "Peaceably."

1 Kin 2:19 Bathsheba therefore went to King Solomon, to speak to him for Adonijah. And the king rose up to meet her and bowed down to her, and sat down on his throne and had a throne set for the king's mother; so she sat at his right hand.

1 Kin 14:21 And Rehoboam the son of Solomon reigned in Judah. Rehoboam *was* forty-one years old when he became king. He reigned seventeen years in Jerusalem, the city which the LORD had chosen out of all the tribes of Israel, to put His name there. His mother's name *was* Naamah, an Ammonitess.

1 Kin 15:2 He reigned three years in Jerusalem. His mother's name *was* Maachah the granddaughter of Abishalom.

2 Kin 8:26 Ahaziah *was* twenty-two years old when he became king, and he reigned one year in Jerusalem. His mother's name *was* Athaliah the granddaughter of Omri, king of Israel.

2 Kin 12:1 In the seventh year of Jehu, Jehoash became king, and he reigned forty years in Jerusalem. His mother's name *was* Zibiah of Beersheba.

2 Kin 14:2 He was twenty-five years old when he became king, and he reigned twenty-nine years in Jerusalem. His mother's name was Jehoaddan of Jerusalem.

2 Kin 15:2 He was sixteen years old when he became king, and he reigned fifty-two years in Jerusalem. His mother's name *was* Jecholiah of Jerusalem.

2 Kin 15:33 He was twenty-five years old when he became king, and he reigned sixteen years in Jerusalem. His mother's name *was* Jerusha the daughter of Zadok.

2 Kin 18:2 He was twenty-five years old when he became king, and he reigned twenty-nine years in Jerusalem. His mother's name *was* Abi the daughter of Zechariah.

2 Kin 21:1 Manasseh *was* twelve years old when he became king, and he reigned fifty-five years in Jerusalem. His mother's name *was* Hephzibah.

2 Kin 21:19 Amon *was* twenty-two years old when he became king, and he reigned two years in Jerusalem. His mother's name *was* Meshullemeth the daughter of Haruz of Jotbah.

2 Kin 22:1 Josiah *was* eight years old when he became king, and he reigned thirty-one years in Jerusalem. His mother's name *was* Jedidah the daughter of Adaiah of Bozkath.

2 Kin 23:31 Jehoahaz *was* twenty-three years old when he became king, and he reigned three months in Jerusalem. His mother's name *was* Hamutal the daughter of Jeremiah of Libnah.

2 Kin 23:36 Jehoiakim *was* twenty-five years old when he became king, and he reigned eleven years in Jerusalem. His mother's name *was* Zebudah the daughter of Pedaiah of Rumah.

2 Kin 24:8 Jehoiachin *was* eighteen years old when he became king, and he reigned in Jerusalem three months. His mother's name *was* Nehushta the daughter of Elnathan of Jerusalem.

Picture of the ideal one.

Prov 31:10–31 Who can find a virtuous wife? For her worth *is* far above rubies. **11** The heart of her husband safely trusts her; So he will have no lack of gain. **12** She does him good and not evil All the days of her life. **13** She seeks wool and flax, And willingly works with her hands. **14** She is like the merchant ships, She brings her food from afar. **15** She also rises while it is yet night, And provides food for her household, And a portion for her maidservants. **16** She considers a field and buys it; From her profits she plants a vineyard. **17** She girds herself with strength, And strengthens her arms. **18** She perceives that her merchandise *is* good, And her lamp does not go out by night. **19** She stretches out her hands to the distaff, And her hand holds the spindle. **20** She extends her hand to the poor, Yes, she reaches out her hands to the needy. **21** She is not afraid of snow for her household, For all her household *is* clothed with scarlet. **22** She makes tapestry for herself; Her clothing *is* fine linen and purple. **23** Her husband is known in the gates, When he sits among the elders of the land. **24** She makes linen garments and sells *them,* And supplies sashes for the merchants. **25** Strength and honor *are* her clothing; She shall rejoice in time to come. **26** She opens her mouth with wisdom, And on

her tongue *is* the law of kindness. **27** She watches over the ways of her household, And does not eat the bread of idleness. **28** Her children rise up and call her blessed; Her husband *also*, and he praises her: **29** "Many daughters have done well, But you excel them all." **30** Charm *is* deceitful and beauty *is* passing, But a woman *who* fears the LORD, she shall be praised. **31** Give her of the fruit of her hands, And let her own works praise her in the gates.

Cares about son's well-being.

Prov 10:1 The proverbs of Solomon: A wise son makes a glad father, But a foolish son *is* the grief of his mother.

Cf. Prov 1:8; 29:17; 31:1; Zech 13:3

As synonym for a nation.

Ezek 16:44–45 "Indeed everyone who quotes proverbs will use *this* proverb against you: 'Like mother, like daughter!' **45** You *are* your mother's daughter, loathing husband and children; and you *are* the sister of your sisters, who loathed their husbands and children; your mother *was* a Hittite and your father an Amorite.

Hos 2:2 "Bring charges against your mother, bring charges; For she *is* not My wife, nor *am* I her Husband! Let her put away her harlotries from her sight, And her adulteries from between her breasts;

Hos 4:5 Therefore you shall stumble in the day; The prophet also shall stumble with you in the night; And I will destroy your mother.

Cf. Ezek 19:1–14

Of Jesus Christ.

Matt 1:16 And Jacob begot Joseph the husband of Mary, of whom was born Jesus who is called Christ.

Matt 1:18–25 Now the birth of Jesus Christ was as follows: After His mother Mary was betrothed to Joseph, before they came together, she was found with child of the Holy Spirit. **19** Then Joseph her husband, being a just *man,* and not wanting to make her a public example, was minded to put her away secretly. **20** But while he thought about these things, behold, an angel of the Lord appeared to him in a dream, saying, "Joseph, son of David, do not be afraid to take to you Mary your wife, for that which is conceived in her is of the Holy Spirit. **21** And she will bring forth a Son, and you shall call His name JESUS, for He will save His people from their sins." **22** So all this was done that it might be fulfilled which was spoken by the Lord through the prophet, saying: **23** *"Behold, the virgin shall be with child, and bear a Son, and they shall call His name Immanuel,"* which is translated, "God with us." **24** Then Joseph, being aroused from sleep, did as the angel of the Lord commanded him and took to him his wife, **25** and did not know her till she had brought forth her firstborn Son. And he called His name JESUS.

Matt 2:11 And when they had come into the house, they saw the young Child with Mary His mother, and fell down and worshiped Him. And when they had opened their treasures, they presented gifts to Him: gold, frankincense, and myrrh.

Matt 2:13–14 Now when they had departed, behold, an angel of the Lord appeared to Joseph in a dream, saying, "Arise, take the young Child and His mother, flee to Egypt, and stay there until I bring you word; for Herod will seek the young Child to destroy Him." **14** When he arose, he took the young Child and His mother by night and departed for Egypt,

Matt 2:20–21 saying, "Arise, take the young Child and His mother, and go to the land of Israel, for those who sought the young Child's life are dead." **21** Then he arose, took the young Child and His mother, and came into the land of Israel.

Matt 12:46–50 While He was still talking to the multitudes, behold, His mother and brothers stood outside, seeking to speak with Him. **47** Then one said to Him, "Look, Your mother and Your brothers are standing outside, seeking to speak with You." **48** But He answered and said to the one who told Him, "Who is My mother and who are My brothers?" **49** And He stretched out His hand toward His disciples and said, "Here are My mother and My brothers! **50** For whoever does the will of My Father in heaven is My brother and sister and mother."

Mark 3:31–35 Then His brothers and His mother came, and standing outside they sent to Him, calling Him. **32** And a multitude was sitting around Him; and they said to Him, "Look, Your mother and Your brothers are outside seeking You." **33** But He answered them, saying, "Who is My mother, or My brothers?" **34** And He looked around in a circle at those who sat about Him, and said, "Here are My mother and My brothers! **35** For whoever does the will of God is My brother and My sister and mother."

Mark 6:3 Is this not the carpenter, the Son of Mary, and brother of James, Joses, Judas, and Simon? And are not His sisters here with us?" So they were offended at Him.

Luke 2:4–7 Joseph also went up from Galilee, out of the city of Nazareth, into Judea, to the city of David, which is called Bethlehem, because he was of the house and lineage of David, **5** to be registered with Mary, his betrothed wife, who was with child. **6** So it was, that while they were there, the days were completed for her to be delivered. **7** And she brought forth her firstborn Son, and wrapped Him in swaddling cloths, and laid Him in a manger, because there was no room for them in the inn.

Luke 2:16–19 And they came with haste and found Mary and Joseph, and the Babe lying in a manger. **17** Now when they had seen *Him*, they made widely known the saying which was told them concerning this Child. **18** And all those who heard *it* marveled at those things which were told them by the shepherds. **19** But Mary kept all these things and pondered *them* in her heart.

Luke 2:33–35 And Joseph and His mother marveled at those things which were spoken of Him. **34** Then Simeon blessed them, and said to Mary His mother, "Behold, this *Child* is destined for the fall and rising of many in Israel, and for a sign which will be spoken against **35** (yes, a sword will pierce through your own soul also), that the thoughts of many hearts may be revealed."

Luke 2:51 Then He went down with them and came to Nazareth, and was subject to them, but His mother kept all these things in her heart.

Luke 8:19–21 Then His mother and brothers came to Him, and could not approach Him because of the crowd. **20** And it was told Him *by some*, who said, "Your mother and Your brothers are standing outside, desiring to see You." **21** But He answered and said to them, "My mother and My brothers are these who hear the word of God and do it."

John 2:1–5 On the third day there was a wedding in Cana of Galilee, and the mother of Jesus was there. **2** Now both Jesus and His disciples were invited to the wedding. **3** And when they ran out of wine, the mother of Jesus said to Him, "They have no wine." **4** Jesus said to her, "Woman, what does your concern have to do with Me? My hour has not yet come." **5** His mother said to the servants, "Whatever He says to you, do *it*."

John 6:42 And they said, "Is not this Jesus, the son of Joseph, whose father and mother we know? How is it then that He says, 'I have come down from heaven'?"

John 19:25–27 Now there stood by the cross of Jesus His mother, and His mother's sister, Mary the *wife* of Clopas, and Mary Magdalene. **26** When Jesus therefore saw His mother, and the disciple whom He loved standing by, He said to His mother, "Woman, behold your son!" **27** Then He said to the disciple, "Behold your mother!" And from that hour that disciple took her to his own *home*.

Acts 1:14 These all continued with one accord in prayer and supplication, with the women and Mary the mother of Jesus, and with His brothers.

Cf. Luke 1:26–56

Of Zebedee's sons.

Matt 20:20–21 Then the mother of Zebedee's sons came to Him with her sons, kneeling down and asking something from Him. **21** And He said to her, "What do you wish?" She said to Him, "Grant that these two sons of mine may sit, one on Your right hand and the other on the left, in Your kingdom."

Matt 27:56 among whom were Mary Magdalene, Mary the mother of James and Joses, and the mother of Zebedee's sons.

Of John Mark.

Acts 12:12 So, when he had considered *this*, he came to the house of Mary, the mother of John whose surname was Mark, where many were gathered together praying.

Of Peter's wife.

Matt 8:14–15 Now when Jesus had come into Peter's house, He saw his wife's mother lying sick with a fever. **15** So He touched her hand, and the fever left her. And she arose and served them.

Mark 1:29–31 Now as soon as they had come out of the synagogue, they entered the house of Simon and Andrew, with James and John. **30** But Simon's wife's mother lay sick with a fever, and they told Him about her at once. **31** So He came and took her by the hand and lifted her up, and immediately the fever left her. And she served them.

Luke 4:38–39 Now He arose from the synagogue and entered Simon's house. But Simon's wife's mother was sick with a high fever, and they made request of Him concerning her. **39** So He stood over her and rebuked the fever, and it left her. And immediately she arose and served them.

Of James the Less and of Joses.

Mark 15:40 There were also women looking on from afar, among whom were Mary Magdalene, Mary the mother of James the Less and of Joses, and Salome,

Mark 16:1 Now when the Sabbath was past, Mary Magdalene, Mary *the mother* of James, and Salome bought spices, that they might come and anoint Him.

Luke 24:10 It was Mary Magdalene, Joanna, Mary *the mother* of James, and the other *women* with them, who told these things to the apostles.

Of John the Baptist.

Luke 1:13 But the angel said to him, "Do not be afraid, Zacharias, for your prayer is heard; and your wife Elizabeth will bear you a son, and you shall call his name John.

Luke 1:24–25 Now after those days his wife Elizabeth conceived; and she hid herself five months, saying, 25 "Thus the Lord has dealt with me, in the days when He looked on *me*, to take away my reproach among people."

Luke 1:39–44 Now Mary arose in those days and went into the hill country with haste, to a city of Judah, 40 and entered the house of Zacharias and greeted Elizabeth. 41 And it happened, when Elizabeth heard the greeting of Mary, that the babe leaped in her womb; and Elizabeth was filled with the Holy Spirit. 42 Then she spoke out with a loud voice and said, "Blessed *are* you among women, and blessed *is* the fruit of your womb! 43 But why *is* this *granted* to me, that the mother of my Lord should come to me? 44 For indeed, as soon as the voice of your greeting sounded in my ears, the babe leaped in my womb for joy.

Luke 1:57–60 Now Elizabeth's full time came for her to be delivered, and she brought forth a son. 58 When her neighbors and relatives heard how the Lord had shown great mercy to her, they rejoiced with her. 59 So it was, on the eighth day, that they came to circumcise the child; and they would have called him by the name of his father, Zacharias. 60 His mother answered and said, "No; he shall be called John."

Of Timothy.

2 Tim 1:5 when I call to remembrance the genuine faith that is in you, which dwelt first in your grandmother Lois and your mother Eunice, and I am persuaded is in you also.

Of Rufus (and "by adoption, " Paul).

Rom 16:13 Greet Rufus, chosen in the Lord, and his mother and mine.

As Paul's symbol of spiritual care.

1 Thess 2:7 But we were gentle among you, just as a nursing *mother* cherishes her own children.

Cf. Num 11:12; 2 Cor 12:14–15; Gal 4:19

Role as, not lessened by widowhood.

1 Tim 5:4 But if any widow has children or grandchildren, let them first learn to show piety at home and to repay their parents; for this is good and acceptable before God.

1 Tim 5:14 Therefore I desire that *the* younger *widows*

marry, bear children, manage the house, give no opportunity to the adversary to speak reproachfully.

Part of designation for source of all false religion.

Rev 17:5 And on her forehead a name *was* written: MYSTERY, BABYLON THE GREAT, THE MOTHER OF HARLOTS AND OF THE ABOMINATIONS OF THE EARTH.

MOUNTAINS

The elevated parts of the earth.

Gen 7:19–20 And the waters prevailed exceedingly on the earth, and all the high hills under the whole heaven were covered. 20 The waters prevailed fifteen cubits upward, and the mountains were covered.

God

Formed and established them.

Ps 65:6 Who established the mountains by His strength, *Being* clothed with power;

Amos 4:13 For behold, He who forms mountains, And creates the wind, Who declares to man what his thought *is*, And makes the morning darkness, Who treads the high places of the earth— The LORD God of hosts *is* His name.

Gives strength to.

Ps 95:4 In His hand *are* the deep places of the earth; The heights of the hills *are* His also.

Weighs, in a balance.

Is 40:12 Who has measured the waters in the hollow of His hand, Measured heaven with a span And calculated the dust of the earth in a measure? Weighed the mountains in scales And the hills in a balance?

Waters, from His chambers.

Ps 104:13 He waters the hills from His upper chambers; The earth is satisfied with the fruit of Your works.

Parches, with drought.

Hag 1:11 For I called for a drought on the land and the mountains, on the grain and the new wine and the oil, on whatever the ground brings forth, on men and livestock, and on all the labor of *your* hands."

Sets on fire and causes to smoke.

Deut 32:22 For a fire is kindled in My anger, And shall burn to the lowest hell; It shall consume the earth with her increase, And set on fire the foundations of the mountains.

Ps 104:32 He looks on the earth, and it trembles; He touches the hills, and they smoke.

Ps 144:5 Bow down Your heavens, O LORD, and come down; Touch the mountains, and they shall smoke.

Makes waste.

Is 42:15 I will lay waste the mountains and hills, And dry up all their vegetation; I will make the rivers coastlands, And I will dry up the pools.

Causes to tremble.

Nah 1:5 The mountains quake before Him, The hills melt, And the earth heaves at His presence, Yes, the world and all who dwell in it.

Hab 3:10 The mountains saw You *and* trembled; The overflowing of the water passed by. The deep uttered its voice, *And* lifted its hands on high.

Causes to skip.

Ps 114:4 The mountains skipped like rams, The little hills like lambs.

Ps 114:6 O mountains, *that* you skipped like rams? O little hills, like lambs?

Causes to melt.

Judg 5:5 The mountains gushed before the LORD, This Sinai, before the LORD God of Israel.

Ps 97:5 The mountains melt like wax at the presence of the LORD, At the presence of the Lord of the whole earth.

Is 64:1 Oh, that You would rend the heavens! That You would come down! That the mountains might shake at Your presence—

Is 64:3 When You did awesome things *for which* we did not look, You came down, The mountains shook at Your presence.

Removes.

Job 9:5 He removes the mountains, and they do not know When He overturns them in His anger;

Overturns.

Job 9:5 He removes the mountains, and they do not know When He overturns them in His anger;

Job 28:9 He puts his hand on the flint; He overturns the mountains at the roots.

Scatters.

Hab 3:6 He stood and measured the earth; He looked and startled the nations. And the everlasting mountains were scattered, The perpetual hills bowed. His ways *are* everlasting.

Made to glorify God.

Ps 148:9 Mountains and all hills; Fruitful trees and all cedars;

Called

God's mountains.

Is 49:11 I will make each of My mountains a road, And My highways shall be elevated.

The ancient mountains.

Deut 33:15 With the best things of the ancient mountains, With the precious things of the everlasting hills,

Perpetual hills and everlasting mountains.

Hab 3:6 He stood and measured the earth; He looked and startled the nations. And the everlasting mountains were scattered, The perpetual hills bowed. His ways *are* everlasting.

Everlasting hills.

Gen 49:26 The blessings of your father Have excelled the blessings of my ancestors, Up to the utmost bound of the everlasting hills. They shall be on the head of Joseph, And on the crown of the head of him who was separate from his brothers.

Pillars of heaven.

Job 26:11 The pillars of heaven tremble, And are astonished at His rebuke.

High hills and mountains.

Ps 104:18 The high hills *are* for the wild goats; The cliffs are a refuge for the rock badgers.

Is 2:14 Upon all the high mountains, And upon all the hills *that are* lifted up;

Collect the vapors which ascend from the earth.

Ps 104:6 You covered it with the deep as *with* a garment; The waters stood above the mountains.

Ps 104:8 They went up over the mountains; They went down into the valleys, To the place which You founded for them.

Are the sources of springs and rivers.

Deut 8:7 For the LORD your God is bringing you into a good land, a land of brooks of water, of fountains and springs, that flow out of valleys and hills;

Ps 104:8–10 They went up over the mountains; They went down into the valleys, To the place which You founded for them. **9** You have set a boundary that they may not pass over, That they may not return to cover the earth. **10** He sends the springs into the valleys; They flow among the hills.

Many in Canaan.

Deut 11:11 but the land which you cross over to possess *is* a land of hills and valleys, which drinks water from the rain of heaven,

Volcanic fires of, alluded to.

Is 64:1–2 Oh, that You would rend the heavens! That You would come down! That the mountains might shake at Your presence— **2** As fire burns brushwood, As fire causes water to boil— To make Your name known to Your adversaries, *That* the nations may tremble at Your presence!

Jer 51:25 "Behold, I *am* against you, O destroying mountain, Who destroys all the earth," says the LORD. "And I will stretch out My hand against you, Roll you down from the rocks, And make you a burnt mountain.

Nah 1:5–6 The mountains quake before Him, The hills melt, And the earth heaves at His presence, Yes, the world and all who dwell in it. **6** Who can stand before His indignation? And who can endure the fierceness of His anger? His fury is poured out like fire, And the rocks are thrown down by Him.

Mentioned in Scripture

Ararat.

Gen 8:4 Then the ark rested in the seventh month, the seventeenth day of the month, on the mountains of Ararat.

Abarim.

Num 33:47–48 They moved from Almon Diblathaim and camped in the mountains of Abarim, before Nebo. **48** They departed from the mountains of Abarim and camped in the plains of Moab by the Jordan, *across from* Jericho.

Amalek.

Judg 12:15 Then Abdon the son of Hillel the Pirathonite died and was buried in Pirathon in the land of Ephraim, in the mountains of the Amalekites.

Bashan.

Ps 68:15 A mountain of God *is* the mountain of Bashan; A mountain *of many* peaks *is* the mountain of Bashan.

Bethel.

1 Sam 13:2 Saul chose for himself three thousand *men* of Israel. Two thousand were with Saul in Michmash and in the mountains of Bethel, and a thousand were with Jonathan in Gibeah of Benjamin. The rest of the people he sent away, every man to his tent.

Carmel.

Josh 15:55 Maon, Carmel, Ziph, Juttah,

Josh 19:26 Alammelech, Amad, and Mishal; it reached to Mount Carmel westward, along *the Brook* Shihor Libnath.

2 Kin 18:19–20 Now therefore, send *and* gather all Israel to me on Mount Carmel, the four hundred and fifty prophets of Baal, and the four hundred prophets of Asherah, who eat at Jezebel's table." **20** So Ahab sent for all the children of Israel, and gathered the prophets together on Mount Carmel.

Ebal.

Deut 11:29 Now it shall be, when the LORD your God has brought you into the land which you go to possess, that you shall put the blessing on Mount Gerizim and the curse on Mount Ebal.

Deut 27:13 and these shall stand on Mount Ebal to curse: Reuben, Gad, Asher, Zebulun, Dan, and Naphtali.

Ephraim.

Josh 17:15 So Joshua answered them, "If you *are* a great people, *then* go up to the forest *country* and clear a place for yourself there in the land of the Perizzites and the giants, since the mountains of Ephraim are too confined for you."

Judg 2:9 And they buried him within the border of his inheritance at Timnath Heres, in the mountains of Ephraim, on the north side of Mount Gaash.

Gerizim.

Deut 11:29 Now it shall be, when the LORD your God has brought you into the land which you go to possess, that you shall put the blessing on Mount Gerizim and the curse on Mount Ebal.

Judg 9:7 Now when they told Jotham, he went and stood on top of Mount Gerizim, and lifted his voice and cried out. And he said to them: "Listen to me, you men of Shechem, That God may listen to you!

Gilboa.

1 Sam 31:1 Now the Philistines fought against Israel; and the men of Israel fled from before the Philistines, and fell slain on Mount Gilboa.

2 Sam 1:6 Then the young man who told him said, "As I happened by chance *to be* on Mount Gilboa, there was Saul, leaning on his spear; and indeed the chariots and horsemen followed hard after him.

2 Sam 1:21 "O mountains of Gilboa, *Let there be* no dew nor rain upon you, Nor fields of offerings. For the shield of the mighty is cast away there! The shield of Saul, not anointed with oil.

Gilead.

Gen 31:21 So he fled with all that he had. He arose and crossed the river, and headed toward the mountains of Gilead.

Gen 31:25 So Laban overtook Jacob. Now Jacob had pitched his tent in the mountains, and Laban with his brethren pitched in the mountains of Gilead.

Song 4:1 Behold, you *are* fair, my love! Behold, you *are* fair! You *have* dove's eyes behind your veil. Your hair

is like a flock of goats, Going down from Mount Gilead.

Hachilah.

1 Sam 23:19 Then the Ziphites came up to Saul at Gibeah, saying, "Is David not hiding with us in strongholds in the woods, in the hill of Hachilah, which *is* on the south of Jeshimon?

Hermon.

Josh 13:11 Gilead, and the border of the Geshurites and Maachathites, all Mount Hermon, and all Bashan as far as Salcah;

Hor.

Num 20:22 Now the children of Israel, the whole congregation, journeyed from Kadesh and came to Mount Hor.

Num 34:7–8 'And this shall be your northern border: From the Great Sea you shall mark out your *border* line to Mount Hor; **8** from Mount Hor you shall mark out *your border* to the entrance of Hamath; then the direction of the border shall be toward Zedad;

Horeb.

Ex 3:1 Now Moses was tending the flock of Jethro his father-in-law, the priest of Midian. And he led the flock to the back of the desert, and came to Horeb, the mountain of God.

Lebanon.

Deut 3:25 I pray, let me cross over and see the good land beyond the Jordan, those pleasant mountains, and Lebanon.'

Mizar.

Ps 42:6 O my God, my soul is cast down within me; Therefore I will remember You from the land of the Jordan, And from the heights of Hermon, From the Hill Mizar.

Moreh.

Judg 7:1 Then Jerubbaal (that *is*, Gideon) and all the people who *were* with him rose early and encamped beside the well of Harod, so that the camp of the Midianites was on the north side of them by the hill of Moreh in the valley.

Moriah.

Gen 22:2 Then He said, "Take now your son, your only *son* Isaac, whom you love, and go to the land of Moriah, and offer him there as a burnt offering on one of the mountains of which I shall tell you."

2 Chr 3:1 Now Solomon began to build the house of the LORD at Jerusalem on Mount Moriah, where *the LORD* had appeared to his father David, at the place that David had prepared on the threshing floor of Ornan the Jebusite.

Nebo (part of Abarim).

Num 32:3 "Ataroth, Dibon, Jazer, Nimrah, Heshbon, Elealeh, Shebam, Nebo, and Beon,

Deut 34:1 Then Moses went up from the plains of Moab to Mount Nebo, to the top of Pisgah, which is across from Jericho. And the LORD showed him all the land of Gilead as far as Dan,

Olivet or Mount of Corruption.

1 Kin 11:7 Then Solomon built a high place for Chemosh the abomination of Moab, on the hill that *is*

east of Jerusalem, and for Molech the abomination of the people of Ammon.

2 Kin 23:13 Then the king defiled the high places that *were* east of Jerusalem, which *were* on the south of the Mount of Corruption, which Solomon king of Israel had built for Ashtoreth the abomination of the Sidonians, for Chemosh the abomination of the Moabites, and for Milcom the abomination of the people of Ammon.

Luke 21:37 And in the daytime He was teaching in the temple, but at night He went out and stayed on the mountain called Olivet.

Pisgah (part of Abarim).

Num 21:20 and from Bamoth, *in* the valley that *is* in the country of Moab, to the top of Pisgah which looks down on the wasteland.

Deut 34:1 Then Moses went up from the plains of Moab to Mount Nebo, to the top of Pisgah, which is across from Jericho. And the LORD showed him all the land of Gilead as far as Dan,

Seir.

Gen 14:6 and the Horites in their mountain of Seir, as far as El Paran, which *is* by the wilderness.

Gen 36:8 So Esau dwelt in Mount Seir. Esau *is* Edom.

Sinai.

Ex 18:20 And you shall teach them the statutes and the laws, and show them the way in which they must walk and the work they must do.

Ex 18:23 If you do this thing, and God *so* commands you, then you will be able to endure, and all this people will also go to their place in peace."

Ex 19:2 For they had departed from Rephidim, had come *to* the Wilderness of Sinai, and camped in the wilderness. So Israel camped there before the mountain.

Ex 31:18 And when He had made an end of speaking with him on Mount Sinai, He gave Moses two tablets of the Testimony, tablets of stone, written with the finger of God.

Tabor.

Judg 4:6 Then she sent and called for Barak the son of Abinoam from Kedesh in Naphtali, and said to him, "Has not the LORD God of Israel commanded, 'Go and deploy *troops* at Mount Tabor; take with you ten thousand men of the sons of Naphtali and of the sons of Zebulun;

Judg 4:12 And they reported to Sisera that Barak the son of Abinoam had gone up to Mount Tabor.

Judg 4:14 Then Deborah said to Barak, "Up! For this *is* the day in which the LORD has delivered Sisera into your hand. Has not the LORD gone out before you?" So Barak went down from Mount Tabor with ten thousand men following him.

Zion.

2 Sam 5:7 Nevertheless David took the stronghold of Zion (that *is*, the City of David).

Provided defense to Jerusalem.

Ps 125:2 As the mountains surround Jerusalem, So the LORD surrounds His people From this time forth and forever.

Afforded refuge in time of danger.

Gen 14:10 Now the Valley of Siddim *was full of* asphalt pits; and the kings of Sodom and Gomorrah fled; *some* fell there, and the remainder fled to the mountains.

Judg 6:2 and the hand of Midian prevailed against Israel. Because of the Midianites, the children of Israel made for themselves the dens, the caves, and the strongholds which *are* in the mountains.

Matt 24:16 "then let those who are in Judea flee to the mountains.

Heb 11:38 of whom the world was not worthy. They wandered in deserts and mountains, *in* dens and caves of the earth.

Afforded pasturage.

Ex 3:1 Now Moses was tending the flock of Jethro his father-in-law, the priest of Midian. And he led the flock to the back of the desert, and came to Horeb, the mountain of God.

1 Sam 25:7 Now I have heard that you have shearers. Your shepherds were with us, and we did not hurt them, nor was there anything missing from them all the while they were in Carmel.

1 Kin 22:17 Then he said, "I saw all Israel scattered on the mountains, as sheep that have no shepherd. And the LORD said, 'These have no master. Let each return to his house in peace.' "

Ps 147:8 Who covers the heavens with clouds, Who prepares rain for the earth, Who makes grass to grow on the mountains.

Amos 4:1 Hear this word, you cows of Bashan, who *are* on the mountain of Samaria, Who oppress the poor, Who crush the needy, Who say to your husbands, "Bring *wine*, let us drink!"

Abounded with

Herbs.

Prov 27:25 *When* the hay is removed, and the tender grass shows itself, And the herbs of the mountains are gathered in,

Minerals.

Deut 8:9 a land in which you will eat bread without scarcity, in which you will lack nothing; a land whose stones *are* iron and out of whose hills you can dig copper.

Precious things.

Deut 33:15 With the best things of the ancient mountains, With the precious things of the everlasting hills,

Stone for building.

1 Kin 5:14 And he sent them to Lebanon, ten thousand a month in shifts: they were one month in Lebanon *and* two months at home; Adoniram *was* in charge of the labor force.

1 Kin 5:17 And the king commanded them to quarry large stones, costly stones, *and* hewn stones, to lay the foundation of the temple.

Dan 2:45 Inasmuch as you saw that the stone was cut out of the mountain without hands, and that it broke in pieces the iron, the bronze, the clay, the silver, and the gold—the great God has made known to the king what will come to pass after this. The dream is certain, and its interpretation is sure."

Forests.

2 Kin 19:23 By your messengers you have reproached the Lord, And said: "By the multitude of my chariots I have come up to the height of the mountains, To the limits of Lebanon; I will cut down its tall cedars *And* its choice cypress trees; I will enter the extremity of its borders, *To* its fruitful forest.

2 Chr 2:2 Solomon selected seventy thousand men to bear burdens, eighty thousand to quarry *stone* in the mountains, and three thousand six hundred to oversee them.

2 Chr 2:8–10 Also send me cedar and cypress and algum logs from Lebanon, for I know that your servants have skill to cut timber in Lebanon; and indeed my servants *will be* with your servants, **9** to prepare timber for me in abundance, for the temple which I am about to build *shall be* great and wonderful. **10** And indeed I will give to your servants, the woodsmen who cut timber, twenty thousand kors of ground wheat, twenty thousand kors of barley, twenty thousand baths of wine, and twenty thousand baths of oil.

Vineyards.

2 Chr 26:10 Also he built towers in the desert. He dug many wells, for he had much livestock, both in the lowlands and in the plains; *he also had* farmers and vinedressers in the mountains and in Carmel, for he loved the soil.

Jer 31:5 You shall yet plant vines on the mountains of Samaria; The planters shall plant and eat *them* as ordinary food.

Spices (implied).

Song 4:6 Until the day breaks And the shadows flee away, I will go my way to the mountain of myrrh And to the hill of frankincense.

Song 8:14 Make haste, my beloved, And be like a gazelle Or a young stag On the mountains of spices.

Gazelles.

1 Chr 12:8 *Some* Gadites joined David at the stronghold in the wilderness, mighty men of valor, men trained for battle, who could handle shield and spear, whose faces *were like* the faces of lions, and *were* as swift as gazelles on the mountains:

Song 2:9 My beloved is like a gazelle or a young stag. Behold, he stands behind our wall; He is looking through the windows, Gazing through the lattice.

Wild game.

1 Sam 26:20 So now, do not let my blood fall to the earth before the face of the LORD. For the king of Israel has come out to seek a flea, as when one hunts a partridge in the mountains."

Wild beasts.

Song 4:8 Come with me from Lebanon, *my* spouse, With me from Lebanon. Look from the top of Amana, From the top of Senir and Hermon, From the lions' dens, From the mountains of the leopards.

Hab 2:17 For the violence *done to* Lebanon will cover you, And the plunder of beasts *which* made them afraid, Because of men's blood And the violence of the land *and* the city, And of all who dwell in it.

Often inhabited.

Gen 36:8 So Esau dwelt in Mount Seir. Esau *is* Edom.

Josh 11:21 And at that time Joshua came and cut off the Anakim from the mountains: from Hebron, from Debir, from Anab, from all the mountains of Judah, and from all the mountains of Israel; Joshua utterly destroyed them with their cities.

Sometimes selected as places for divine worship.

Gen 22:2 Then He said, "Take now your son, your only *son* Isaac, whom you love, and go to the land of Moriah, and offer him there as a burnt offering on one of the mountains of which I shall tell you."

Gen 22:5 And Abraham said to his young men, "Stay here with the donkey; the lad and I will go yonder and worship, and we will come back to you."

Ex 3:12 So He said, "I will certainly be with you. And this *shall be* a sign to you that I have sent you: When you have brought the people out of Egypt, you shall serve God on this mountain."

Is 2:2 Now it shall come to pass in the latter days *That* the mountain of the LORD's house Shall be established on the top of the mountains, And shall be exalted above the hills; And all nations shall flow to it.

Often selected as places for idolatrous worship.

Deut 12:2 You shall utterly destroy all the places where the nations which you shall dispossess served their gods, on the high mountains and on the hills and under every green tree.

2 Chr 21:11 Moreover he made high places in the mountains of Judah, and caused the inhabitants of Jerusalem to commit harlotry, and led Judah astray.

Proclamations often made from.

Is 40:9 O Zion, You who bring good tidings, Get up into the high mountain; O Jerusalem, You who bring good tidings, Lift up your voice with strength, Lift *it* up, be not afraid; Say to the cities of Judah, "Behold your God!"

Beacons or ensigns often raised upon.

Is 13:2 "Lift up a banner on the high mountain, Raise your voice to them; Wave your hand, that they may enter the gates of the nobles.

Is 30:17 One thousand *shall flee* at the threat of one, At the threat of five you shall flee, Till you are left as a pole on top of a mountain And as a banner on a hill.

Illustrative of

Difficulties.

Is 40:4 Every valley shall be exalted And every mountain and hill brought low; The crooked places shall be made straight And the rough places smooth;

Zech 4:7 'Who *are* you, O great mountain? Before Zerubbabel *you shall become* a plain! And he shall bring forth the capstone With shouts of "Grace, grace to it!" ' "

Matt 17:20 So Jesus said to them, "Because of your unbelief; for assuredly, I say to you, if you have faith as a mustard seed, you will say to this mountain, 'Move from here to there,' and it will move; and nothing will be impossible for you.

Persons in authority.

Ps 72:3 The mountains will bring peace to the people, And the little hills, by righteousness.

Is 44:23 Sing, O heavens, for the LORD has done *it!* Shout, you lower parts of the earth; Break forth into singing, you mountains, O forest, and every tree in it! For the LORD has redeemed Jacob, And glorified Himself in Israel.

The people of God.

Is 2:2 Now it shall come to pass in the latter days *That* the mountain of the LORD's house Shall be established on the top of the mountains, And shall be exalted above the hills; And all nations shall flow to it.

Dan 2:35 Then the iron, the clay, the bronze, the silver, and the gold were crushed together, and became like chaff from the summer threshing floors; the wind carried them away so that no trace of them was found. And the stone that struck the image became a great mountain and filled the whole earth.

Dan 2:44–45 And in the days of these kings the God of heaven will set up a kingdom which shall never be destroyed; and the kingdom shall not be left to other people; it shall break in pieces and consume all these kingdoms, and it shall stand forever. **45** Inasmuch as you saw that the stone was cut out of the mountain without hands, and that it broke in pieces the iron, the bronze, the clay, the silver, and the gold—the great God has made known to the king what will come to pass after this. The dream is certain, and its interpretation is sure."

God's righteousness.

Ps 36:6 Your righteousness *is* like the great mountains; Your judgments *are* a great deep; O LORD, You preserve man and beast.

Proud and haughty persons.

Is 2:14 Upon all the high mountains, And upon all the hills *that are* lifted up;

(Burning) destructive enemies.

Jer 51:25 "Behold, I *am* against you, O destroying mountain, Who destroys all the earth," says the LORD. "And I will stretch out My hand against you, Roll you down from the rocks, And make you a burnt mountain.

Rev 8:8 Then the second angel sounded: And *something* like a great mountain burning with fire was thrown into the sea, and a third of the sea became blood.

(Breaking forth into singing) exceeding joy.

Is 44:23 Sing, O heavens, for the LORD has done *it!* Shout, you lower parts of the earth; Break forth into singing, you mountains, O forest, and every tree in it! For the LORD has redeemed Jacob, And glorified Himself in Israel.

Is 55:12 "For you shall go out with joy, And be led out with peace; The mountains and the hills Shall break forth into singing before you, And all the trees of the field shall clap *their* hands.

(Threshing of) heavy judgments.

Is 41:15 "Behold, I will make you into a new threshing sledge with sharp teeth; You shall thresh the mountains and beat *them* small, And make the hills like chaff.

(Made waste) desolation.

Is 42:15 I will lay waste the mountains and hills, And dry up all their vegetation; I will make the rivers coastlands, And I will dry up the pools.

Mal 1:3 But Esau I have hated, And laid waste his mountains and his heritage For the jackals of the wilderness."

(Dropping new wine) abundance.

Amos 9:13 "Behold, the days are coming," says the LORD, "When the plowman shall overtake the reaper, And the treader of grapes him who sows seed; The mountains shall drip with sweet wine, And all the hills shall flow *with it.*

MOURNING

Is proper, concerning sin.

Matt 5:4 Blessed *are* those who mourn, For they shall be comforted.

Cf. 2 Cor 7:10; James 4:9

Sinners will engage in, when Christ returns.

Matt 24:30 Then the sign of the Son of Man will appear in heaven, and then all the tribes of the earth will mourn, and they will see the Son of Man coming on the clouds of heaven with power and great glory.

Rev 1:7 Behold, He is coming with clouds, and every eye will see Him, even they who pierced Him. And all the tribes of the earth will mourn because of Him. Even so, Amen.

Cf. Zech 12:12

For the dead, was loud and emotional.

Matt 9:23 When Jesus came into the ruler's house, and saw the flute players and the noisy crowd wailing,

Mark 5:38–39 Then He came to the house of the ruler of the synagogue, and saw a tumult and those who wept and wailed loudly. **39** When He came in, He said to them, "Why make this commotion and weep? The child is not dead, but sleeping."

Luke 8:52 Now all wept and mourned for her; but He said, "Do not weep; she is not dead, but sleeping."

John 11:33 Therefore, when Jesus saw her weeping, and the Jews who came with her weeping, He groaned in the spirit and was troubled.

Cf. Luke 23:27

Results from judgment.

Is 32:11–12 Tremble, you *women* who are at ease; Be troubled, you complacent ones; Strip yourselves, make yourselves bare, And gird *sackcloth* on *your* waists. **12** People shall mourn upon their breasts For the pleasant fields, for the fruitful vine.

Prohibited for Ezekiel, at death of his wife.

Ezek 24:15–24 Also the word of the LORD came to me, saying, **16** "Son of man, behold, I take away from you the desire of your eyes with one stroke; yet you shall neither mourn nor weep, nor shall your tears run down. **17** Sigh in silence, make no mourning for the dead; bind your turban on your head, and put your sandals on your feet; do not cover *your* lips, and do not eat man's bread *of sorrow.*" **18** So I spoke to the people in the morning, and at evening my wife died; and the next morning I did as I was commanded. **19** And the people said to me, "Will you not tell us what these *things signify* to us, that you behave so?" **20** Then I answered them, "The word of the LORD came to me, saying, **21** 'Speak to the house of Israel, "Thus says the Lord GOD: 'Behold, I will profane My sanctuary, your arrogant boast, the desire of your eyes, the delight of your soul; and your sons and daughters whom you left behind shall fall by the sword. **22** And you shall do as I have done; you shall not cover *your* lips nor eat man's bread *of sorrow.* **23** Your turbans shall be on your heads and your sandals on your feet; you shall neither mourn nor weep, but you shall pine away in your iniquities and mourn with one another. **24** Thus Ezekiel is a sign to you; according to all that he has done you shall do; and when this comes, you shall know that I *am* the Lord God.' "

MOUTH

God's, as source of Scripture.

Deut 8:3 So He humbled you, allowed you to hunger, and fed you with manna which you did not know nor did your fathers know, that He might make you know that man shall not live by bread alone; but man lives by every *word* that proceeds from the mouth of the LORD.

Job 23:12 I have not departed from the commandment of His lips; I have treasured the words of His mouth More than my necessary *food.*

Prov 2:6 For the LORD gives wisdom; From His mouth *come* knowledge and understanding;

Is 55:11 So shall My word be that goes forth from My mouth; It shall not return to Me void, But it shall accomplish what I please, And it shall prosper *in the thing* for which I sent it.

Cf. Is 34:16; 40:6; Matt 4:4; Heb 1:1–2; 2 Pet 1:20–21

With God's help, controls speech.

Ex 4:11–12 So the LORD said to him, "Who has made man's mouth? Or who makes the mute, the deaf, the seeing, or the blind? *Have* not I, the LORD? **12** Now therefore, go, and I will be with your mouth and teach you what you shall say."

Num 22:28 Then the LORD opened the mouth of the donkey, and she said to Balaam, "What have I done to you, that you have struck me these three times?"

Num 22:30 So the donkey said to Balaam, "*Am* I not your donkey on which you have ridden, ever since *I became* yours, to this day? Was I ever disposed to do this to you?" And he said, "No."

Num 23:5 Then the LORD put a word in Balaam's mouth, and said, "Return to Balak, and thus you shall speak."

Ezra 1:1 Now in the first year of Cyrus king of Persia, that the word of the LORD by the mouth of Jeremiah might be fulfilled, the LORD stirred up the spirit of Cyrus king of Persia, so that he made a proclamation throughout all his kingdom, and also *put it* in writing, saying,

Is 51:16 And I have put My words in your mouth; I have covered you with the shadow of My hand, That I may plant the heavens, Lay the foundations of the earth, And say to Zion, 'You *are* My people.' "

Jer 1:9 Then the LORD put forth His hand and touched my mouth, and the LORD said to me: "Behold, I have put My words in your mouth.

Jer 15:16 Your words were found, and I ate them, And Your word was to me the joy and rejoicing of my heart; For I am called by Your name, O LORD God of hosts.

Ezek 2:8 But you, son of man, hear what I say to you. Do not be rebellious like that rebellious house; open your mouth and eat what I give you."

Ezek 3:1–3 Moreover He said to me, "Son of man, eat what you find; eat this scroll, and go, speak to the house of Israel." **2** So I opened my mouth, and He caused me to eat that scroll. **3** And He said to me, "Son of man, feed your belly, and fill your stomach with this scroll that I give you." So I ate, and it was in my mouth like honey in sweetness.

Ezek 3:10 Moreover He said to me: "Son of man, receive into your heart all My words that I speak to you, and hear with your ears.

Ezek 29:21 'In that day I will cause the horn of the house of Israel to spring forth, and I will open your mouth to speak in their midst. Then they shall know that I *am* the LORD.' "

Ezek 33:22 Now the hand of the LORD had been upon me the evening before the man came who had escaped. And He had opened my mouth; so when he came to me in the morning, my mouth was opened, and I was no longer mute.

Acts 1:16 "Men *and* brethren, this Scripture had to be fulfilled, which the Holy Spirit spoke before by the mouth of David concerning Judas, who became a guide to those who arrested Jesus;

Acts 3:18 But those things which God foretold by the mouth of all His prophets, that the Christ would suffer, He has thus fulfilled.

Acts 4:25 who by the mouth of Your servant David have said: 'Why did the nations rage, And the people plot vain things?

Acts 15:7 And when there had been much dispute, Peter rose up and said to them: "Men and brethren, you know that a good while ago God chose among us, that by my mouth the Gentiles should hear the word of the gospel and believe.

Of the adulteress, deceptive.

Prov 5:3 For the lips of an immoral woman drip honey, And her mouth *is* smoother than oil;

Of the wicked, perverse.

Prov 6:12 A worthless person, a wicked man, Walks with a perverse mouth;

Cf. Prov 10:6,11,14; 15:28; Eph 4:29; Jude 16

Is the source of good words.

Prov 10:11 The mouth of the righteous *is* a well of life, But violence covers the mouth of the wicked.

Prov 12:14 A man will be satisfied with good by the fruit of *his* mouth, And the recompense of a man's hands will be rendered to him.

Prov 15:4 A wholesome tongue *is* a tree of life, But perverseness in it breaks the spirit.

Prov 18:4 The words of a man's mouth *are* deep waters; The wellspring of wisdom *is* a flowing brook.

Prov 31:26 She opens her mouth with wisdom, And on her tongue *is* the law of kindness.

As the source of sin.

Eccl 5:6 Do not let your mouth cause your flesh to sin, nor say before the messenger *of God* that it *was* an error. Why should God be angry at your excuse and destroy the work of your hands?

Matt 15:11 Not what goes into the mouth defiles a man; but what comes out of the mouth, this defiles a man."

Cf. James 3:6

Words from Christ's, always effective.

Is 11:4 But with righteousness He shall judge the poor, And decide with equity for the meek of the earth; He shall strike the earth with the rod of His mouth, And with the breath of His lips He shall slay the wicked.

Is 49:2 And He has made My mouth like a sharp sword; In the shadow of His hand He has hidden Me, And made Me a polished shaft; In His quiver He has hidden Me."

Is 55:11 So shall My word be that goes forth from My mouth; It shall not return to Me void, But it shall accomplish what I please, And it shall prosper *in the thing* for which I sent it.

Eph 6:17 And take the helmet of salvation, and the sword of the Spirit, which is the word of God;

Heb 4:12 For the word of God *is* living and powerful, and sharper than any two-edged sword, piercing even to the division of soul and spirit, and of joints and marrow, and is a discerner of the thoughts and intents of the heart.

Cf. Ps 2:9; Rev 1:16; 2:12,16; 19:15

Should not hinder practical Christian unity.

Rom 15:6 that you may with one mind *and* one mouth glorify the God and Father of our Lord Jesus Christ.

MULE, THE

Stupid and intractable.

Ps 32:9 Do not be like the horse *or* like the mule, *Which* have no understanding, Which must be harnessed with bit and bridle, Else they will not come near you.

Used for

Riding, by persons of distinction.

2 Sam 13:29 So the servants of Absalom did to Amnon as Absalom had commanded. Then all the king's sons arose, and each one got on his mule and fled.

2 Sam 18:9 Then Absalom met the servants of David. Absalom rode on a mule. The mule went under the thick boughs of a great terebinth tree, and his head caught in the terebinth; so he was left hanging between heaven and earth. And the mule which *was* under him went on.

1 Kin 1:33 The king also said to them, "Take with you the servants of your lord, and have Solomon my son ride on my own mule, and take him down to Gihon.

1 Kin 1:38 So Zadok the priest, and Nathan the prophet, and Benaiah the son of Jehoiada, and the Cherethites, and the Pelethites, went down, and caused Solomon to ride upon king David's mule, and brought him to Gihon.

Carrying burdens.

2 Kin 5:17 So Naaman said, "Then, if not, please let your servant be given two mule-loads of earth; for

your servant will no longer offer either burnt offering or sacrifice to other gods, but to the LORD.

1 Chr 12:40 Moreover those who were near to them, from as far away as Issachar and Zebulun and Naphtali, were bringing food on donkeys and camels, on mules and oxen—provisions of flour and cakes of figs and cakes of raisins, wine and oil and oxen and sheep abundantly, for *there was* joy in Israel.

Target of the plague.

Zech 14:15 Such also shall be the plague On the horse *and* the mule, On the camel and the donkey, And on all the cattle that will be in those camps. So *shall* this plague *be.*

Food of.

1 Kin 4:28 They also brought barley and straw to the proper place, for the horses and steeds, each man according to his charge.

1 Kin 18:5 And Ahab had said to Obadiah, "Go into the land to all the springs of water and to all the brooks; perhaps we may find grass to keep the horses and mules alive, so that we will not have to kill any livestock."

The Jews

Forbidden to breed.

Lev 19:19 'You shall keep My statutes. You shall not let your livestock breed with another kind. You shall not sow your field with mixed seed. Nor shall a garment of mixed linen and wool come upon you.

Set a great value upon.

1 Kin 18:5 And Ahab had said to Obadiah, "Go into the land to all the springs of water and to all the brooks; perhaps we may find grass to keep the horses and mules alive, so that we will not have to kill any livestock."

Brought many, from Babylon.

Ezra 2:66 Their horses *were* seven hundred and thirty-six, their mules two hundred and forty-five,

Neh 7:68 Their horses were seven hundred and thirty-six, their mules two hundred and forty-five,

Shall be used, at the restoration.

Is 66:20 Then they shall bring all your brethren for an offering to the LORD out of all nations, on horses and in chariots and in litters, on mules and on camels, to My holy mountain Jerusalem," says the LORD, "as the children of Israel bring an offering in a clean vessel into the house of the LORD.

Of Togarmah, sold in fairs of Tyre.

Ezek 27:14 Those from the house of Togarmah traded for your wares with horses, steeds, and mules.

Often given as tribute.

1 Kin 10:25 Each man brought his present: articles of silver and gold, garments, armor, spices, horses, and mules, at a set rate year by year.

2 Chr 9:24 Each man brought his present: articles of silver and gold, garments, armor, spices, horses, and mules, at a set rate year by year.

MURDER

Forbidden and restrained by Mosaic law.

Ex 20:13 "You shall not murder.

Deut 5:17 'You shall not murder.

1 Tim 1:9 knowing this: that the law is not made for a righteous person, but for *the* lawless and insubordinate, for *the* ungodly and for sinners, for *the* unholy and profane, for murderers of fathers and murderers of mothers, for manslayers,

Described as killing

With premeditation.

Ex 21:14 "But if a man acts with premeditation against his neighbor, to kill him by treachery, you shall take him from My altar, that he may die.

From hatred.

Num 35:20–21 If he pushes him out of hatred or, while lying in wait, hurls something at him so that he dies, **21** or in enmity he strikes him with his hand so that he dies, the one who struck *him* shall surely be put to death. He *is* a murderer. The avenger of blood shall put the murderer to death when he meets him.

Deut 19:11 "But if anyone hates his neighbor, lies in wait for him, rises against him and strikes him mortally, so that he dies, and he flees to one of these cities,

By lying in wait.

Num 35:20 If he pushes him out of hatred or, while lying in wait, hurls something at him so that he dies,

Deut 19:11 "But if anyone hates his neighbor, lies in wait for him, rises against him and strikes him mortally, so that he dies, and he flees to one of these cities,

By an instrument of iron.

Num 35:16 'But if he strikes him with an iron implement, so that he dies, he *is* a murderer; the murderer shall surely be put to death.

By the blow of a stone.

Num 35:17 And if he strikes him with a stone in the hand, by which one could die, and he does die, he *is* a murderer; the murderer shall surely be put to death.

By a hand weapon of wood.

Num 35:18 Or *if* he strikes him with a wooden hand weapon, by which one could die, and he does die, he *is* a murderer; the murderer shall surely be put to death.

First mention of.

Gen 4:8 Now Cain talked with Abel his brother; and it came to pass, when they were in the field, that Cain rose up against Abel his brother and killed him.

Represented as a sin crying to heaven.

Gen 4:10 And He said, "What have you done? The voice of your brother's blood cries out to Me from the ground.

Heb 12:24 to Jesus the Mediator of the new covenant, and to the blood of sprinkling that speaks better things than *that of* Abel.

Rev 6:10 And they cried with a loud voice, saying, "How long, O Lord, holy and true, until You judge and avenge our blood on those who dwell on the earth?"

Those guilty of,

Nation of Israel.

Is 1:21 How the faithful city has become a harlot! It was full of justice; Righteousness lodged in it, But now murderers.

Fearful and cowardly.

Gen 4:14 Surely You have driven me out this day from the face of the ground; I shall be hidden from Your face; I shall be a fugitive and a vagabond on the earth, and it will happen *that* anyone who finds me will kill me."

Wanderers and vagabonds.

Gen 4:14 Surely You have driven me out this day from the face of the ground; I shall be hidden from Your face; I shall be a fugitive and a vagabond on the earth, and it will happen *that* anyone who finds me will kill me."

Flee from God's presence.

Gen 4:16 Then Cain went out from the presence of the Lord and dwelt in the land of Nod on the east of Eden.

Not protected in refuge cities.

Deut 19:11–12 "But if anyone hates his neighbor, lies in wait for him, rises against him and strikes him mortally, so that he dies, and he flees to one of these cities, **12** then the elders of his city shall send and bring him from there, and deliver him over to the hand of the avenger of blood, that he may die.

Had no protection from altars.

Ex 21:14 "But if a man acts with premeditation against his neighbor, to kill him by treachery, you shall take him from My altar, that he may die.

Not to be pitied or spared.

Deut 19:13 Your eye shall not pity him, but you shall put away *the guilt of* innocent blood from Israel, that it may go well with you.

Often committed at night.

Neh 6:10 Afterward I came to the house of Shemaiah the son of Delaiah, the son of Mehetabel, who *was* a secret informer; and he said, "Let us meet together in the house of God, within the temple, and let us close the doors of the temple, for they are coming to kill you; indeed, at night they will come to kill you."

Job 24:14 The murderer rises with the light; He kills the poor and needy; And in the night he is like a thief.

Imputed to nearest city when murderer was unknown.

Deut 21:1–9 "If *anyone* is found slain, lying in the field in the land which the Lord your God is giving you to possess, *and* it is not known who killed him, **2** then your elders and your judges shall go out and measure *the distance* from the slain man to the surrounding cities. **3** And it shall be *that* the elders of the city nearest to the slain man will take a heifer which has not been worked *and* which has not pulled with a yoke. **4** The elders of that city shall bring the heifer down to a valley with flowing water, which is neither plowed nor sown, and they shall break the heifer's neck there in the valley. **5** Then the priests, the sons of Levi, shall come near, for the Lord your God has chosen them to minister to Him and to bless in the name of the Lord; by their word every controversy and every assault shall be *settled*. **6** And all the elders of that city nearest to the slain *man* shall wash their hands over the heifer whose neck was broken in the valley. **7** Then they shall answer and say, 'Our hands have not shed this blood, nor have our eyes seen *it*. **8** Provide atonement, O LORD, for Your people Israel, whom You have redeemed, and do not lay innocent blood to the charge of Your people Israel.' And atonement shall be provided on their behalf for the blood. **9** So you shall put away the *guilt of* innocent blood from among you when you do *what is* right in the sight of the LORD.

Matt 27:24 When Pilate saw that he could not prevail at all, but rather *that* a tumult was rising, he took water and washed *his* hands before the multitude, saying, "I am innocent of the blood of this just Person. You see *to it*."

To be proved by at least two witnesses.

Num 35:30 Whoever kills a person, the murderer shall be put to death on the testimony of witnesses; but one witness is not *sufficient* testimony against a person for the death *penalty*.

Deut 19:11 "But if anyone hates his neighbor, lies in wait for him, rises against him and strikes him mortally, so that he dies, and he flees to one of these cities,

Deut 19:15 "One witness shall not rise against a man concerning any iniquity or any sin that he commits; by the mouth of two or three witnesses the matter shall be established.

Punishment for,

Explained and illustrated.

Gen 4:12–15 When you till the ground, it shall no longer yield its strength to you. A fugitive and a vagabond you shall be on the earth." **13** And Cain said to the LORD, "My punishment *is* greater than I can bear! **14** Surely You have driven me out this day from the face of the ground; I shall be hidden from Your face; I shall be a fugitive and a vagabond on the earth, and it will happen *that* anyone who finds me will kill me." **15** And the LORD said to him, "Therefore, whoever kills Cain, vengeance shall be taken on him sevenfold." And the LORD set a mark on Cain, lest anyone finding him should kill him.

Gen 9:6 "Whoever sheds man's blood, By man his blood shall be shed; For in the image of God He made man.

Num 35:30 Whoever kills a person, the murderer shall be put to death on the testimony of witnesses; but one witness is not *sufficient* testimony against a person for the death *penalty*.

2 Kin 9:36–37 Therefore they came back and told him. And he said, "This *is* the word of the LORD, which He spoke by His servant Elijah the Tishbite, saying, 'On the plot *of ground* at Jezreel dogs shall eat the flesh of Jezebel; **37** and the corpse of Jezebel shall be as refuse on the surface of the field, in the plot at Jezreel, so that they shall not say, "Here *lies* Jezebel." ' "

Jer 19:4–9 "Because they have forsaken Me and made this an alien place, because they have burned incense in it to other gods whom neither they, their fathers, nor the kings of Judah have known, and have filled this place with the blood of the innocents **5** (they

have also built the high places of Baal, to burn their sons with fire *for* burnt offerings to Baal, which I did not command or speak, nor did it come into My mind), **6** therefore behold, the days are coming," says the LORD, "that this place shall no more be called Tophet or the Valley of the Son of Hinnom, but the Valley of Slaughter. **7** And I will make void the counsel of Judah and Jerusalem in this place, and I will cause them to fall by the sword before their enemies and by the hands of those who seek their lives; their corpses I will give as meat for the birds of the heaven and for the beasts of the earth. **8** I will make this city desolate and a hissing; everyone who passes by it will be astonished and hiss because of all its plagues. **9** And I will cause them to eat the flesh of their sons and the flesh of their daughters, and everyone shall eat the flesh of his friend in the siege and in the desperation with which their enemies and those who seek their lives shall drive them to despair." '

Was death.

Gen 9:5–6 Surely for your lifeblood I will demand *a reckoning;* from the hand of every beast I will require it, and from the hand of man. From the hand of every man's brother I will require the life of man. **6** "Whoever sheds man's blood, By man his blood shall be shed; For in the image of God He made man.

Ex 21:12 "He who strikes a man so that he dies shall surely be put to death.

Num 35:16 'But if he strikes him with an iron implement, so that he dies, he *is* a murderer; the murderer shall surely be put to death.

Not to be commuted.

Num 35:31–32 Moreover you shall take no ransom for the life of a murderer who *is* guilty of death, but he shall surely be put to death. **32** And you shall take no ransom for him who has fled to his city of refuge, that he may return to dwell in the land before the death of the priest.

Inflicted by the avenger of blood.

Num 35:19 The avenger of blood himself shall put the murderer to death; when he meets him, he shall put him to death.

Num 35:21 or in enmity he strikes him with his hand so that he dies, the one who struck *him* shall surely be put to death. He *is* a murderer. The avenger of blood shall put the murderer to death when he meets him.

Forbidden.

Gen 9:6 "Whoever sheds man's blood, By man his blood shall be shed; For in the image of God He made man.

Ex 20:13 "You shall not murder.

Deut 5:17 'You shall not murder.

Rom 13:9 For the commandments, *"You shall not commit adultery," "You shall not murder," "You shall not steal," "You shall not bear false witness," "You shall not covet,"* and if *there is* any other commandment, *are all* summed up in this saying, namely, *"You shall love your neighbor as yourself."*

Explained as

Anger.

Matt 5:21–22 "You have heard that it was said to those

of old, 'You shall not murder, and whoever murders will be in danger of the judgment.' **22** But I say to you that whoever is angry with his brother without a cause shall be in danger of the judgment. And whoever says to his brother, 'Raca!' shall be in danger of the council. But whoever says, 'You fool!' shall be in danger of hell fire.

Hatred.

1 John 3:15 Whoever hates his brother is a murderer, and you know that no murderer has eternal life abiding in him.

Work of the flesh.

Gal 5:21 envy, murders, drunkenness, revelries, and the like; of which I tell you beforehand, just as I also told *you* in time past, that those who practice such things will not inherit the kingdom of God.

Coming from the heart.

Matt 15:19 For out of the heart proceed evil thoughts, murders, adulteries, fornications, thefts, false witness, blasphemies.

Defiles the

Hands.

Is 59:3 For your hands are defiled with blood, And your fingers with iniquity; Your lips have spoken lies, Your tongue has muttered perversity.

Person and garments.

Lam 4:13–14 Because of the sins of her prophets *And* the iniquities of her priests, Who shed in her midst The blood of the just. **14** They wandered blind in the streets; They have defiled themselves with blood, So that no one would touch their garments.

Land.

Num 35:33 So you shall not pollute the land where you *are;* for blood defiles the land, and no atonement can be made for the land, for the blood that is shed on it, except by the blood of him who shed it.

Ps 106:38 And shed innocent blood, The blood of their sons and daughters, Whom they sacrificed to the idols of Canaan; And the land was polluted with blood.

Cries for vengeance.

Gen 4:10 And He said, "What have you done? The voice of your brother's blood cries out to Me from the ground.

God

Is aware of.

Is 26:21 For behold, the LORD comes out of His place To punish the inhabitants of the earth for their iniquity; The earth will also disclose her blood, And will no more cover her slain.

Jer 2:34 Also on your skirts is found The blood of the lives of the poor innocents. I have not found it by secret search, But plainly on all these things.

Abominates.

Prov 6:16–17 These six *things* the LORD hates, Yes, seven *are* an abomination to Him: **17** A proud look, A lying tongue, Hands that shed innocent blood,

Will avenge.

Deut 32:43 "Rejoice, O Gentiles, *with* His people; For He will avenge the blood of His servants, And render

vengeance to His adversaries; He will provide atonement for His land *and* His people."

1 Kin 21:19 You shall speak to him, saying, 'Thus says the LORD: "Have you murdered and also taken possession?" ' And you shall speak to him, saying, 'Thus says the LORD: "In the place where dogs licked the blood of Naboth, dogs shall lick your blood, even yours." ' "

Ps 9:12 When He avenges blood, He remembers them; He does not forget the cry of the humble.

Hos 1:4 Then the LORD said to him: "Call his name Jezreel, For in a little *while* I will avenge the bloodshed of Jezreel on the house of Jehu, And bring an end to the kingdom of the house of Israel.

Requires blood for.

Gen 9:5 Surely for your lifeblood I will demand *a reckoning;* from the hand of every beast I will require it, and from the hand of man. From the hand of every man's brother I will require the life of man.

Num 35:33 So you shall not pollute the land where you *are;* for blood defiles the land, and no atonement can be made for the land, for the blood that is shed on it, except by the blood of him who shed it.

1 Kin 2:32 So the LORD will return his blood on his head, because he struck down two men more righteous and better than he, and killed them with the sword—Abner the son of Ner, the commander of the army of Israel, and Amasa the son of Jether, the commander of the army of Judah—though my father David did not know *it.*

Rejects the prayers of those guilty of.

Is 1:15 When you spread out your hands, I will hide My eyes from you; Even though you make many prayers, I will not hear. Your hands are full of blood.

Is 59:2–3 But your iniquities have separated you from your God; And your sins have hidden *His* face from you, So that He will not hear. **3** For your hands are defiled with blood, And your fingers with iniquity; Your lips have spoken lies, Your tongue has muttered perversity.

Curses those guilty of.

Gen 4:11 So now you *are* cursed from the earth, which has opened its mouth to receive your brother's blood from your hand.

Believers

Specially warned against.

1 Pet 4:15 But let none of you suffer as a murderer, a thief, an evildoer, or as a busybody in other people's matters.

Want to avoid.

Ps 51:14 Deliver me from the guilt of bloodshed, O God, The God of my salvation, *And* my tongue shall sing aloud of Your righteousness.

Should warn others against.

Gen 37:22 And Reuben said to them, "Shed no blood, *but* cast him into this pit which *is* in the wilderness, and do not lay a hand on him"—that he might deliver him out of their hands, and bring him back to his father.

Jer 26:15 But know for certain that if you put me to death, you will surely bring innocent blood on yourselves, on this city, and on its inhabitants; for truly the LORD has sent me to you to speak all these words in your hearing."

Connected with idolatry.

2 Kin 3:27 Then he took his eldest son who would have reigned in his place, and offered him *as* a burnt offering upon the wall; and there was great indignation against Israel. So they departed from him and returned to *their own* land.

Ezek 22:3–4 Then say, 'Thus says the Lord GOD: "The city sheds blood in her own midst, that her time may come; and she makes idols within herself to defile herself. **4** You have become guilty by the blood which you have shed, and have defiled yourself with the idols which you have made. You have caused your days to draw near, and have come to *the end of* your years; therefore I have made you a reproach to the nations, and a mockery to all countries.

The wicked

Filled with.

Is 1:15 When you spread out your hands, I will hide My eyes from you; Even though you make many prayers, I will not hear. Your hands are full of blood.

Rom 1:29 being filled with all unrighteousness, sexual immorality, wickedness, covetousness, maliciousness; full of envy, murder, strife, deceit, evil-mindedness; *they are* whisperers,

Conspire.

Gen 27:41 So Esau hated Jacob because of the blessing with which his father blessed him, and Esau said in his heart, "The days of mourning for my father are at hand; then I will kill my brother Jacob."

Gen 37:18 Now when they saw him afar off, even before he came near them, they conspired against him to kill him.

Intent on.

Job 24:14 The murderer rises with the light; He kills the poor and needy; And in the night he is like a thief.

Ps 10:8–10 He sits in the lurking places of the villages; In the secret places he murders the innocent; His eyes are secretly fixed on the helpless. **9** He lies in wait secretly, as a lion in his den; He lies in wait to catch the poor; He catches the poor when he draws him into his net. **10** So he crouches, he lies low, That the helpless may fall by his strength.

Prov 1:16 For their feet run to evil, And they make haste to shed blood.

Jer 22:17 "Yet your eyes and your heart *are* for nothing but your covetousness, For shedding innocent blood, And practicing oppression and violence."

Ezek 22:3 Then say, 'Thus says the Lord GOD: "The city sheds blood in her own midst, that her time may come; and she makes idols within herself to defile herself.

Rom 3:15 *"Their feet are swift to shed blood;*

Encourage others to commit.

1 Kin 21:8–10 And she wrote letters in Ahab's name, sealed *them* with his seal, and sent the letters to the elders and the nobles who *were* dwelling in the city with Naboth. **9** She wrote in the letters, saying, Proclaim a fast, and seat Naboth with high honor among the people; **10** and seat two men, scoundrels, before

him to bear witness against him, saying, You have blasphemed God and the king. *Then* take him out, and stone him, that he may die.

Prov 1:11 If they say, "Come with us, Let us lie in wait to *shed* blood; Let us lurk secretly for the innocent without cause;

Of believers, specially avenged.

Deut 32:43 "Rejoice, O Gentiles, *with* His people; For He will avenge the blood of His servants, And render vengeance to His adversaries; He will provide atonement for His land *and* His people."

Matt 23:35 that on you may come all the righteous blood shed on the earth, from the blood of righteous Abel to the blood of Zechariah, son of Berechiah, whom you murdered between the temple and the altar.

Rev 18:20 "Rejoice over her, O heaven, and *you* holy apostles and prophets, for God has avenged you on her!"

Rev 18:24 And in her was found the blood of prophets and saints, and of all who were slain on the earth."

Excludes from heaven.

Gal 5:21 envy, murders, drunkenness, revelries, and the like; of which I tell you beforehand, just as I also told *you* in time past, that those who practice such things will not inherit the kingdom of God.

Rev 22:15 But outside *are* dogs and sorcerers and sexually immoral and murderers and idolaters, and whoever loves and practices a lie.

Characterized by

The devil.

John 8:44 You are of *your* father the devil, and the desires of your father you want to do. He was a murderer from the beginning, and does not stand in the truth, because there is no truth in him. When he speaks a lie, he speaks from his own *resources,* for he is a liar and the father of it.

Cain.

Gen 4:8 Now Cain talked with Abel his brother; and it came to pass, when they were in the field, that Cain rose up against Abel his brother and killed him.

Esau.

Gen 27:41 So Esau hated Jacob because of the blessing with which his father blessed him, and Esau said in his heart, "The days of mourning for my father are at hand; then I will kill my brother Jacob."

Joseph's brethren.

Gen 37:20 Come therefore, let us now kill him and cast him into some pit; and we shall say, 'Some wild beast has devoured him.' We shall see what will become of his dreams!"

Pharaoh.

Ex 1:22 So Pharaoh commanded all his people, saying, "Every son who is born you shall cast into the river, and every daughter you shall save alive."

Abimelech.

Judg 9:5 Then he went to his father's house at Ophrah and killed his brothers, the seventy sons of Jerubbaal, on one stone. But Jotham the youngest son of Jerubbaal was left, because he hid himself.

The men of Shechem.

Judg 9:24 that the crime *done* to the seventy sons of Jerubbaal might be settled and their blood be laid on Abimelech their brother, who killed them, and on the men of Shechem, who aided him in the killing of his brothers.

Amalekite.

2 Sam 1:16 So David said to him, "Your blood *is* on your own head, for your own mouth has testified against you, saying, 'I have killed the LORD's anointed.' "

Rechab.

2 Sam 4:5–7 Then the sons of Rimmon the Beerothite, Rechab and Baanah, set out and came at about the heat of the day to the house of Ishbosheth, who was lying on his bed at noon. **6** And they came there, all the way into the house, *as though* to get wheat, and they stabbed him in the stomach. Then Rechab and Baanah his brother escaped. **7** For when they came into the house, he was lying on his bed in his bedroom; then they struck him and killed him, beheaded him and took his head, and were all night escaping through the plain.

David.

2 Sam 12:9 Why have you despised the commandment of the LORD, to do evil in His sight? You have killed Uriah the Hittite with the sword; you have taken his wife *to be* your wife, and have killed him with the sword of the people of Ammon.

Absalom.

2 Sam 13:29 So the servants of Absalom did to Amnon as Absalom had commanded. Then all the king's sons arose, and each one got on his mule and fled.

Joab.

1 Kin 2:31–32 Then the king said to him, "Do as he has said, and strike him down and bury him, that you may take away from me and from the house of my father the innocent blood which Joab shed. **32** So the LORD will return his blood on his head, because he struck down two men more righteous and better than he, and killed them with the sword—Abner the son of Ner, the commander of the army of Israel, and Amasa the son of Jether, the commander of the army of Judah—though my father David did not know *it*.

Baasha.

1 Kin 15:27 Then Baasha the son of Ahijah, of the house of Issachar, conspired against him. And Baasha killed him at Gibbethon, which *belonged* to the Philistines, while Nadab and all Israel laid siege to Gibbethon.

Zimri.

1 Kin 16:10 And Zimri went in and struck him and killed him in the twenty-seventh year of Asa king of Judah, and reigned in his place.

Jezebel.

1 Kin 21:10 and seat two men, scoundrels, before him to bear witness against him, saying, You have blasphemed God and the king. *Then* take him out, and stone him, that he may die.

The elders of Jezreel.

1 Kin 21:13 And two men, scoundrels, came in and sat before him; and the scoundrels witnessed against him, against Naboth, in the presence of the people, saying, "Naboth has blasphemed God and the king!"

Then they took him outside the city and stoned him with stones, so that he died.

Ahab.

1 Kin 21:19 You shall speak to him, saying, 'Thus says the LORD: "Have you murdered and also taken possession?" ' And you shall speak to him, saying, 'Thus says the LORD: "In the place where dogs licked the blood of Naboth, dogs shall lick your blood, even yours." ' "

Hazael.

2 Kin 8:12 And Hazael said, "Why is my lord weeping?" He answered, "Because I know the evil that you will do to the children of Israel: Their strongholds you will set on fire, and their young men you will kill with the sword; and you will dash their children, and rip open their women with child."

2 Kin 8:15 But it happened on the next day that he took a thick cloth and dipped *it* in water, and spread *it* over his face so that he died; and Hazael reigned in his place.

Adrammelech, etc.

2 Kin 19:37 Now it came to pass, as he was worshiping in the temple of Nisroch his god, that his sons Adrammelech and Sharezer struck him down with the sword; and they escaped into the land of Ararat. Then Esarhaddon his son reigned in his place.

Manasseh.

2 Kin 21:16 Moreover Manasseh shed very much innocent blood, till he had filled Jerusalem from one end to another, besides his sin by which he made Judah sin, in doing evil in the sight of the LORD.

Ishmael.

Jer 41:7 So it was, when they came into the midst of the city, that Ishmael the son of Nethaniah killed them *and cast them* into the midst of a pit, he and the men who were with him.

The princes of Israel.

Ezek 11:6 You have multiplied your slain in this city, and you have filled its streets with the slain."

The people of Gilead.

Hos 6:8 Gilead *is* a city of evildoers *And* defiled with blood.

The Herods.

Matt 2:16 Then Herod, when he saw that he was deceived by the wise men, was exceedingly angry; and he sent forth and put to death all the male children who were in Bethlehem and in all its districts, from two years old and under, according to the time which he had determined from the wise men.

Matt 14:10 So he sent and had John beheaded in prison.

Acts 12:2 Then he killed James the brother of John with the sword.

Herodias and her daughter.

Matt 14:8–11 So she, having been prompted by her mother, said, "Give me John the Baptist's head here on a platter." **9** And the king was sorry; nevertheless, because of the oaths and because of those who sat with him, he commanded *it* to be given to *her*. **10** So he sent and had John beheaded in prison. **11** And his head was brought on a platter and given to the girl, and she brought *it* to her mother.

The chief priests.

Matt 27:1 When morning came, all the chief priests and elders of the people plotted against Jesus to put Him to death.

Judas.

Matt 27:4 saying, "I have sinned by betraying innocent blood." And they said, "What *is that* to us? You see *to it!*"

Barabbas.

Mark 15:7 And there was one named Barabbas, *who was* chained with his fellow rebels; they had committed murder in the rebellion.

The Jewish leaders.

Acts 7:52 Which of the prophets did your fathers not persecute? And they killed those who foretold the coming of the Just One, of whom you now have become the betrayers and murderers,

1 Thess 2:15 who killed both the Lord Jesus and their own prophets, and have persecuted us; and they do not please God and are contrary to all men,

MUSIC

Divided into

Vocal.

2 Sam 19:35 I *am* today eighty years old. Can I discern between the good and bad? Can your servant taste what I eat or what I drink? Can I hear any longer the voice of singing men and singing women? Why then should your servant be a further burden to my lord the king?

Acts 16:25 But at midnight Paul and Silas were praying and singing hymns to God, and the prisoners were listening to them.

Instrumental.

Dan 6:18 Now the king went to his palace and spent the night fasting; and no musicians were brought before him. Also his sleep went from him.

Designed to promote joy.

Eccl 2:8 I also gathered for myself silver and gold and the special treasures of kings and of the provinces. I acquired male and female singers, the delights of the sons of men, *and* musical instruments of all kinds.

Eccl 2:10 Whatever my eyes desired I did not keep from them. I did not withhold my heart from any pleasure, For my heart rejoiced in all my labor; And this was my reward from all my labor.

Secular is vanity.

Eccl 2:8 I also gathered for myself silver and gold and the special treasures of kings and of the provinces. I acquired male and female singers, the delights of the sons of men, *and* musical instruments of all kinds.

Eccl 2:11 Then I looked on all the works that my hands had done And on the labor in which I had toiled; And indeed all *was* vanity and grasping for the wind. *There was* no profit under the sun.

Considered emotionally soothing.

1 Sam 16:14–17 But the Spirit of the LORD departed from Saul, and a distressing spirit from the LORD troubled him. **15** And Saul's servants said to him, "Surely, a distressing spirit from God is troubling you. **16** Let our master now command your servants,

who are before you, to seek out a man *who is* a skillful player on the harp. And it shall be that he will play it with his hand when the distressing spirit from God is upon you, and you shall be well." **17** So Saul said to his servants, "Provide me now a man who can play well, and bring *him* to me."

1 Sam 16:23 And so it was, whenever the spirit from God was upon Saul, that David would take a harp and play *it* with his hand. Then Saul would become refreshed and well, and the distressing spirit would depart from him.

Effects produced on the prophets of old by.

1 Sam 10:5–6 After that you shall come to the hill of God where the Philistine garrison *is.* And it will happen, when you have come there to the city, that you will meet a group of prophets coming down from the high place with a stringed instrument, a tambourine, a flute, and a harp before them; and they will be prophesying. **6** Then the Spirit of the LORD will come upon you, and you will prophesy with them and be turned into another man.

2 Kin 3:15 But now bring me a musician." Then it happened, when the musician played, that the hand of the LORD came upon him.

Instruments of,

Cymbals.

1 Chr 16:5 Asaph the chief, and next to him Zechariah, *then* Jeiel, Shemiramoth, Jehiel, Mattithiah, Eliab, Benaiah, and Obed-Edom: Jeiel with stringed instruments and harps, but Asaph made music with cymbals;

Ps 150:5 Praise Him with loud cymbals; Praise Him with clashing cymbals!

Flute.

Gen 4:21 His brother's name *was* Jubal. He was the father of all those who play the harp and flute.

1 Kin 1:40 And all the people went up after him; and the people played the flutes and rejoiced with great joy, so that the earth *seemed to* split with their sound.

Job 21:12 They sing to the tambourine and harp, And rejoice to the sound of the flute.

Ps 150:4 Praise Him with the timbrel and dance; Praise Him with stringed instruments and flutes!

Is 5:12 The harp and the strings, The tambourine and flute, And wine are in their feasts; But they do not regard the work of the LORD, Nor consider the operation of His hands.

Jer 48:36 Therefore My heart shall wail like flutes for Moab, And like flutes My heart shall wail For the men of Kir Heres. Therefore the riches they have acquired have perished.

Dan 3:5 *that* at the time you hear the sound of the horn, flute, harp, lyre, *and* psaltery, in symphony with all kinds of music, you shall fall down and worship the gold image that King Nebuchadnezzar has set up;

Harp.

Ps 137:2 We hung our harps Upon the willows in the midst of it.

Ezek 26:13 I will put an end to the sound of your songs, and the sound of your harps shall be heard no more.

Lyre.

Dan 3:5 *that* at the time you hear the sound of the horn, flute, harp, lyre, *and* psaltery, in symphony with all kinds of music, you shall fall down and worship the gold image that King Nebuchadnezzar has set up;

Psaltery.

Ps 33:2 Praise the LORD with the harp; Make melody to Him with an instrument of ten strings.

Ps 71:22 Also with the lute I will praise You— *And* Your faithfulness, O my God! To You I will sing with the harp, O Holy One of Israel.

Dan 3:5 *that* at the time you hear the sound of the horn, flute, harp, lyre, *and* psaltery, in symphony with all kinds of music, you shall fall down and worship the gold image that King Nebuchadnezzar has set up;

Stringed instruments.

Ps 33:2 Praise the LORD with the harp; Make melody to Him with an instrument of ten strings.

Ps 150:4 Praise Him with the timbrel and dance; Praise Him with stringed instruments and flutes!

Is 14:11 Your pomp is brought down to Sheol, *And* the sound of your stringed instruments; The maggot is spread under you, And worms cover you.'

Amos 5:23 Take away from Me the noise of your songs, For I will not hear the melody of your stringed instruments.

Tambourine.

1 Sam 10:5 After that you shall come to the hill of God where the Philistine garrison *is*. And it will happen, when you have come there to the city, that you will meet a group of prophets coming down from the high place with a stringed instrument, a tambourine, a flute, and a harp before them; and they will be prophesying.

Is 24:8 The mirth of the tambourine ceases, The noise of the jubilant ends, The joy of the harp ceases.

Timbrel.

Ex 15:20 Then Miriam the prophetess, the sister of Aaron, took the timbrel in her hand; and all the women went out after her with timbrels and with dances.

Ps 68:25 The singers went before, the players on instruments *followed* after; Among *them were* the maidens playing timbrels.

Ps 150:4 Praise Him with the timbrel and dance; Praise Him with stringed instruments and flutes!

Trumpet.

2 Kin 11:14 When she looked, there was the king standing by a pillar according to custom; and the leaders and the trumpeters were by the king. All the people of the land were rejoicing and blowing trumpets. So Athaliah tore her clothes and cried out, "Treason! Treason!"

2 Chr 29:27 Then Hezekiah commanded *them* to offer the burnt offering on the altar. And when the burnt offering began, the song of the LORD *also* began, with the trumpets and with the instruments of David king of Israel.

Ps 98:6 With trumpets and the sound of a horn; Shout joyfully before the LORD, the King.

Hos 5:8 "Blow the ram's horn in Gibeah, The trumpet in Ramah! Cry aloud *at* Beth Aven, '*Look* behind you, O Benjamin!'

Made of fir wood.

2 Sam 6:5 Then David and all the house of Israel played *music* before the LORD on all kinds of *instruments of* fir wood, on harps, on stringed instruments, on tambourines, on sistrums, and on cymbals.

Made of almug wood.

1 Kin 10:12 And the king made steps of the almug wood for the house of the LORD and for the king's house, also harps and stringed instruments for singers. There never again came such almug wood, nor has the like been seen to this day.

Made of brass.

1 Cor 13:1 Though I speak with the tongues of men and of angels, but have not love, I have become sounding brass or a clanging cymbal.

Made of silver.

Num 10:2 "Make two silver trumpets for yourself; you shall make them of hammered work; you shall use them for calling the congregation and for directing the movement of the camps.

Made of horns of animals.

Josh 6:8 So it was, when Joshua had spoken to the people, that the seven priests bearing the seven trumpets of rams' horns before the LORD advanced and blew the trumpets, and the ark of the covenant of the LORD followed them.

Early invention of.

Gen 4:21 His brother's name *was* Jubal. He was the father of all those who play the harp and flute.

Invented by David.

1 Chr 23:5 four thousand *were* gatekeepers, and four thousand praised the LORD with *musical* instruments, "which I made," *said* David, "for giving praise."

2 Chr 7:6 And the priests attended to their services; the Levites also with instruments of the music of the LORD, which King David had made to praise the LORD, saying, "For His mercy *endures* forever," whenever David offered praise by their ministry. The priests sounded trumpets opposite them, while all Israel stood.

The Jews celebrated for inventing.

Amos 6:5 Who sing idly to the sound of stringed instruments, *And* invent for yourselves musical instruments like David;

Often expensively ornamented.

Ezek 28:13 You were in Eden, the garden of God; Every precious stone *was* your covering: The sardius, topaz, and diamond, Beryl, onyx, and jasper, Sapphire, turquoise, and emerald with gold. The workmanship of your timbrels and pipes Was prepared for you on the day you were created.

Great diversity of.

Eccl 2:8 I also gathered for myself silver and gold and the special treasures of kings and of the provinces. I acquired male and female singers, the delights of the sons of men, *and* musical instruments of all kinds.

Appointed to be played in the temple.

1 Chr 16:4–6 And he appointed some of the Levites to minister before the ark of the LORD, to commemorate, to thank, and to praise the LORD God of Israel: **5** Asaph the chief, and next to him Zechariah, *then* Jeiel, Shemiramoth, Jehiel, Mattithiah, Eliab, Benaiah, and Obed-Edom: Jeiel with stringed instruments and harps, but Asaph made music with cymbals; **6** Benaiah and Jahaziel the priests regularly *blew* the trumpets before the ark of the covenant of God.

1 Chr 23:5–6 four thousand *were* gatekeepers, and four thousand praised the LORD with *musical* instruments, "which I made," *said David,* "for giving praise." **6** Also David separated them into divisions among the sons of Levi: Gershon, Kohath, and Merari.

1 Chr 25:1 Moreover David and the captains of the army separated for the service *some* of the sons of Asaph, of Heman, and of Jeduthun, who *should* prophesy with harps, stringed instruments, and cymbals. And the number of the skilled men performing their service was:

2 Chr 29:25 And he stationed the Levites in the house of the LORD with cymbals, with stringed instruments, and with harps, according to the commandment of David, of Gad the king's seer, and of Nathan the prophet; for thus *was* the commandment of the LORD by his prophets.

Custom of sending away friends with.

Gen 31:27 Why did you flee away secretly, and steal away from me, and not tell me; for I might have sent you away with joy and songs, with timbrel and harp?

The Jews used,

In sacred processions.

2 Sam 6:4–5 And they brought it out of the house of Abinadab, which *was* on the hill, accompanying the ark of God; and Ahio went before the ark. **5** Then David and all the house of Israel played *music* before the LORD on all kinds of *instruments* of fir wood, on harps, on stringed instruments, on tambourines, on sistrums, and on cymbals.

2 Sam 6:15 So David and all the house of Israel brought up the ark of the LORD with shouting and with the sound of the trumpet.

1 Chr 13:6–8 And David and all Israel went up to Baalah, to Kirjath Jearim, which belonged to Judah, to bring up from there the ark of God the LORD, who dwells *between* the cherubim, where *His* name is proclaimed. **7** So they carried the ark of God on a new cart from the house of Abinadab, and Uzza and Ahio drove the cart. **8** Then David and all Israel played *music* before God with all *their* might, with singing, on harps, on stringed instruments, on tambourines, on cymbals, and with trumpets.

1 Chr 15:27–28 David was clothed with a robe of fine linen, as were all the Levites who bore the ark, the singers, and Chenaniah the music master *with* the singers. David also wore a linen ephod. **28** Thus all Israel brought up the ark of the covenant of the LORD with shouting and with the sound of the horn, with trumpets and with cymbals, making music with stringed instruments and harps.

At laying foundation of the temple.

Ezra 3:9–10 Then Jeshua *with* his sons and brothers, Kadmiel *with* his sons, and the sons of Judah, arose as one to oversee those working on the house of God:

the sons of Henadad *with* their sons and their brethren the Levites. **10** When the builders laid the foundation of the temple of the LORD, the priests stood in their apparel with trumpets, and the Levites, the sons of Asaph, with cymbals, to praise the LORD, according to the ordinance of David king of Israel.

At consecration of the temple.

2 Chr 5:11–13 And it came to pass when the priests came out of the *Most* Holy *Place* (for all the priests who *were* present had sanctified themselves, without keeping to their divisions), **12** and the Levites *who were* the singers, all those of Asaph and Heman and Jeduthun, with their sons and their brethren, stood at the east end of the altar, clothed in white linen, having cymbals, stringed instruments and harps, and with them one hundred and twenty priests sounding with trumpets— **13** indeed it came to pass, when the trumpeters and singers *were* as one, to make one sound to be heard in praising and thanking the LORD, and when they lifted up their voice with the trumpets and cymbals and instruments of music, and praised the LORD, *saying:* "For He is good, For His mercy *endures* forever," that the house, the house of the LORD, was filled with a cloud,

At coronation of kings.

2 Chr 23:11 And they brought out the king's son, put the crown on him, *gave him* the Testimony, and made him king. Then Jehoiada and his sons anointed him, and said, "Long live the king!"

2 Chr 23:13 *When* she looked, there was the king standing by his pillar at the entrance; and the leaders and the trumpeters *were* by the king. All the people of the land were rejoicing and blowing trumpets, also the singers with musical instruments, and those who led in praise. So Athaliah tore her clothes and said, "Treason! Treason!"

At dedication of city walls.

Neh 12:27–28 Now at the dedication of the wall of Jerusalem they sought out the Levites in all their places, to bring them to Jerusalem to celebrate the dedication with gladness, both with thanksgivings and singing, *with* cymbals and stringed instruments and harps. **28** And the sons of the singers gathered together from the countryside around Jerusalem, from the villages of the Netophathites,

To celebrate victories.

Ex 15:20 Then Miriam the prophetess, the sister of Aaron, took the timbrel in her hand; and all the women went out after her with timbrels and with dances.

1 Sam 18:6–7 Now it had happened as they were coming *home,* when David was returning from the slaughter of the Philistine, that the women had come out of all the cities of Israel, singing and dancing, to meet King Saul, with tambourines, with joy, and with musical instruments. **7** So the women sang as they danced, and said: "Saul has slain his thousands, And David his ten thousands."

In religious feasts.

2 Chr 30:21 So the children of Israel who were present at Jerusalem kept the Feast of Unleavened Bread seven days with great gladness; and the Levites and the priests praised the LORD day by day, *singing* to the LORD, accompanied by loud instruments.

In private entertainments.

Is 5:12 The harp and the strings, The tambourine and flute, And wine are in their feasts; But they do not regard the work of the LORD, Nor consider the operation of His hands.

Amos 6:5 Who sing idly to the sound of stringed instruments, *And* invent for yourselves musical instruments like David;

In dances.

Matt 11:17 and saying: 'We played the flute for you, And you did not dance; We mourned to you, And you did not lament.'

Luke 15:25 "Now his older son was in the field. And as he came and drew near to the house, he heard music and dancing.

In funeral ceremonies.

Matt 9:23 When Jesus came into the ruler's house, and saw the flute players and the noisy crowd wailing,

In commemorating great men.

2 Chr 35:25 Jeremiah also lamented for Josiah. And to this day all the singing men and the singing women speak of Josiah in their lamentations. They made it a custom in Israel; and indeed they *are* written in the Laments.

Used in idol worship.

Dan 3:5 *that* at the time you hear the sound of the horn, flute, harp, lyre, *and* psaltery, in symphony with all kinds of music, you shall fall down and worship the gold image that King Nebuchadnezzar has set up;

The movements of armies regulated by.

Josh 6:8 So it was, when Joshua had spoken to the people, that the seven priests bearing the seven trumpets of rams' horns before the LORD advanced and blew the trumpets, and the ark of the covenant of the LORD followed them.

1 Cor 14:8 For if the trumpet makes an uncertain sound, who will prepare for battle?

Generally put aside in times of affliction.

Ps 137:2–4 We hung our harps Upon the willows in the midst of it. **3** For there those who carried us away captive asked of us a song, And those who plundered us *requested* mirth, *Saying,* "Sing us *one* of the songs of Zion!" **4** How shall we sing the LORD's song In a foreign land?

Dan 6:18 Now the king went to his palace and spent the night fasting; and no musicians were brought before him. Also his sleep went from him.

Illustrative of

Joy and gladness.

Zeph 3:17 The LORD your God in your midst, The Mighty One, will save; He will rejoice over you with gladness, He will quiet *you* with His love, He will rejoice over you with singing."

Eph 5:19 speaking to one another in psalms and hymns and spiritual songs, singing and making melody in your heart to the Lord,

Heavenly happiness.

Rev 5:8–9 Now when He had taken the scroll, the four living creatures and the twenty-four elders fell down before the Lamb, each having a harp, and golden bowls full of incense, which are the prayers of the saints. **9** And they sang a new song, saying: "You are worthy to take the scroll, And to open its seals; For You were slain, And have redeemed us to God by Your blood Out of every tribe and tongue and people and nation,

(Ceasing of) calamities.

Is 24:8–9 The mirth of the tambourine ceases, The noise of the jubilant ends, The joy of the harp ceases. **9** They shall not drink wine with a song; Strong drink is bitter to those who drink it.

Rev 18:22 The sound of harpists, musicians, flutists, and trumpeters shall not be heard in you anymore. No craftsman of any craft shall be found in you anymore, and the sound of a millstone shall not be heard in you anymore.

MYSTERY

Of God's kingdom, in parables.

Matt 13:11–17 He answered and said to them, "Because it has been given to you to know the mysteries of the kingdom of heaven, but to them it has not been given. **12** For whoever has, to him more will be given, and he will have abundance; but whoever does not have, even what he has will be taken away from him. **13** Therefore I speak to them in parables, because seeing they do not see, and hearing they do not hear, nor do they understand. **14** And in them the prophecy of Isaiah is fulfilled, which says: *'Hearing you will hear and shall not understand, And seeing you will see and not perceive;* **15** *For the hearts of this people have grown dull. Their ears are hard of hearing, And their eyes they have closed, Lest they should see with their eyes and hear with their ears, Lest they should understand with their hearts and turn, So that I should heal them.'* **16** But blessed *are* your eyes for they see, and your ears for they hear; **17** for assuredly, I say to you that many prophets and righteous *men* desired to see what you see, and did not see *it*, and to hear what you hear, and did not hear *it*.

Mark 4:10–20 But when He was alone, those around Him with the twelve asked Him about the parable. **11** And He said to them, "To you it has been given to know the mystery of the kingdom of God; but to those who are outside, all things come in parables, **12** so that *'Seeing they may see and not perceive, And hearing they may hear and not understand; Lest they should turn, And their sins be forgiven them.'"* **13** And He said to them, "Do you not understand this parable? How then will you understand all the parables? **14** The sower sows the word. **15** And these are the ones by the wayside where the word is sown. When they hear, Satan comes immediately and takes away the word that was sown in their hearts. **16** These likewise are the ones sown on stony ground who, when they hear the word, immediately receive it with gladness; **17** and they have no root in themselves, and so endure only for a time. Afterward, when tribulation or persecution arises for the word's sake, immediately they stumble. **18** Now these are the ones sown among thorns; *they are* the ones who hear the word, **19** and the cares of this world, the deceitfulness of riches, and the desires for other things entering in choke the word, and it becomes unfruitful. **20** But these are the ones sown on good ground, those who hear the word, accept *it*, and bear fruit: some thirtyfold, some sixty, and some a hundred."

Cf. 1 Tim 3:9,16

As previously hidden truth, now revealed.

1 Cor 2:7 But we speak the wisdom of God in a mystery, the hidden *wisdom* which God ordained before the ages for our glory,

1 Cor 4:1 Let a man so consider us, as servants of Christ and stewards of the mysteries of God.

1 Cor 15:51 Behold, I tell you a mystery: We shall not all sleep, but we shall all be changed—

Eph 3:4–6 by which, when you read, you may understand my knowledge in the mystery of Christ), **5** which in other ages was not made known to the sons of men, as it has now been revealed by the Spirit to His holy apostles and prophets: **6** that the Gentiles should be fellow heirs, of the same body, and partakers of His promise in Christ through the gospel,

Eph 3:8–12 To me, who am less than the least of all the saints, this grace was given, that I should preach among the Gentiles the unsearchable riches of Christ, **9** and to make all see what *is* the fellowship of the mystery, which from the beginning of the ages has been hidden in God who created all things through Jesus Christ; **10** to the intent that now the manifold wisdom of God might be made known by the church to the principalities and powers in the heavenly *places*, **11** according to the eternal purpose which He accomplished in Christ Jesus our Lord, **12** in whom we have boldness and access with confidence through faith in Him.

Eph 6:19 and for me, that utterance may be given to me, that I may open my mouth boldly to make known the mystery of the gospel,

Col 1:25–27 of which I became a minister according to the stewardship from God which was given to me for you, to fulfill the word of God, **26** the mystery which has been hidden from ages and from generations, but now has been revealed to His saints. **27** To them God willed to make known what are the riches of the glory of this mystery among the Gentiles: which is Christ in you, the hope of glory.

Col 2:2 that their hearts may be encouraged, being knit together in love, and *attaining* to all riches of the full assurance of understanding, to the knowledge of the mystery of God, both of the Father and of Christ,

Col 4:3 meanwhile praying also for us, that God would open to us a door for the word, to speak the mystery of Christ, for which I am also in chains,

Rev 10:7 but in the days of the sounding of the seventh angel, when he is about to sound, the mystery of God would be finished, as He declared to His servants the prophets.

Concerning Israel's final salvation. Rom 11:1–27
Of Christ and the church and analogy of marriage.

Eph 5:22–33 Wives, submit to your own husbands, as to the Lord. **23** For the husband is head of the wife, as also Christ is head of the church; and He is the Savior of the body. **24** Therefore, just as the church is subject to Christ, so *let* the wives *be* to their own husbands in everything. **25** Husbands, love your wives, just as Christ also loved the church and gave Himself for her, **26** that He might sanctify and cleanse her with the washing of water by the word, **27** that He might present her to Himself a glorious church, not having spot or wrinkle or any such thing, but that she should be holy and without blemish. **28** So husbands ought to love their own wives as their own bodies; he who loves his wife loves himself. **29** For no one ever hated his own flesh, but nourishes and cherishes it, just as the Lord *does* the church. **30** For we are members of His body, of His flesh and of His bones. **31** *"For this reason a man shall leave his father and mother and be joined to his wife, and the two shall become one flesh."* **32** This is a great mystery, but I speak concerning Christ and the church. **33** Nevertheless let each one of you in particular so love his own wife as himself, and let the wife *see* that she respects *her* husband.

Concerning end-times lawlessness (Antichrist).

2 Thess 2:5–12 Do you not remember that when I was still with you I told you these things? **6** And now you know what is restraining, that he may be revealed in his own time. **7** For the mystery of lawlessness is already at work; only He who now restrains *will do so* until He is taken out of the way. **8** And then the lawless one will be revealed, whom the Lord will consume with the breath of His mouth and destroy with the brightness of His coming. **9** The coming of the *lawless one* is according to the working of Satan, with all power, signs, and lying wonders, **10** and with all unrighteous deception among those who perish, because they did not receive the love of the truth, that they might be saved. **11** And for this reason God will send them strong delusion, that they should believe the lie, **12** that they all may be condemned who did not believe the truth but had pleasure in unrighteousness.

Concerning figure of harlot and end-times Babylon.

Rev 17:5–7 And on her forehead a name *was* written: MYSTERY, BABYLON THE GREAT, THE MOTHER OF HARLOTS AND OF THE ABOMINATIONS OF THE EARTH. **6** I saw the woman, drunk with the blood of the saints and with the blood of the martyrs of Jesus. And when I saw her, I marveled with great amazement. **7** But the angel said to me, "Why did you marvel? I will tell you the mystery of the woman and of the beast that carries her, which has the seven heads and the ten horns.

N

NAPHTALI, THE TRIBE OF

Descended from Jacob's sixth son.

Gen 30:7–8 And Rachel's maid Bilhah conceived again and bore Jacob a second son. **8** Then Rachel said, "With great wrestlings I have wrestled with my sister, *and* indeed I have prevailed." So she called his name Naphtali.

Predictions respecting.

Gen 49:21 "Naphtali *is* a deer let loose; He uses beautiful words.

Deut 33:23 And of Naphtali he said: "O Naphtali, satisfied with favor, And full of the blessing of the LORD, Possess the west and the south."

Persons selected from,

To number the people.

Num 1:15 from Naphtali, Ahira the son of Enan."

To spy out the land.

Num 13:14 from the tribe of Naphtali, Nahbi the son of Vophsi;

To divide the land.

Num 34:28 and a leader from the tribe of the children of Naphtali, Pedahel the son of Ammihud."

Strength of,

On leaving Egypt.

Num 1:42–43 From the children of Naphtali, their genealogies by their families, by their fathers' house, according to the number of names, from twenty years old and above, all who *were able to* go to war: **43** those who were numbered of the tribe of Naphtali *were* fifty-three thousand four hundred.

On entering Canaan.

Num 26:50 These *are* the families of Naphtali according to their families; and those who were numbered of them *were* forty-five thousand four hundred.

The rear of the fourth division of Israel.

Num 10:25 Then the standard of the camp of the children of Dan (the rear guard of all the camps) set out according to their armies; over their army *was* Ahiezer the son of Ammishaddai.

Num 10:27 And over the army of the tribe of the children of Naphtali *was* Ahira the son of Enan.

Encamped under the standard of Dan north of the tabernacle.

Num 2:25 "The standard of the forces with Dan *shall be* on the north side according to their armies, and the leader of the children of Dan *shall be* Ahiezer the son of Ammishaddai."

Num 2:29 "Then *comes* the tribe of Naphtali, and the leader of the children of Naphtali *shall be* Ahira the son of Enan."

Offering of, at the dedication.

Num 7:78–83 On the twelfth day Ahira the son of Enan, leader of the children of Naphtali, *presented an offering.* **79** His offering *was* one silver platter, the weight of which *was* one hundred and thirty *shekels,* and one silver bowl of seventy shekels, according to the shekel of the sanctuary, both of them full of fine flour mixed with oil as a grain offering; **80** one gold pan of ten *shekels,* full of incense; **81** one young bull, one ram, and one male lamb in its first year, as a burnt offering; **82** one kid of the goats as a sin offering; **83** and as the sacrifice of peace offerings: two oxen, five rams, five male goats, and five male lambs in their first year. This *was* the offering of Ahira the son of Enan.

Families of.

Num 26:48–49 The sons of Naphtali according to their families *were:* of Jahzeel, the family of the Jahzeelites; of Guni, the family of the Gunites; **49** of Jezer, the family of the Jezerites; of Shillem, the family of the Shillemites.

On Ebal, said Amen to the curses.

Deut 27:13 and these shall stand on Mount Ebal to curse: Reuben, Gad, Asher, Zebulun, Dan, and Naphtali.

Boundaries of its inheritance.

Josh 19:32–39 The sixth lot came out to the children of Naphtali, for the children of Naphtali according to their families. **33** And their border began at Heleph, enclosing the territory from the terebinth tree in Zaanannim, Adami Nekeb, and Jabneel, as far as Lakkum; it ended at the Jordan. **34** From Heleph the border extended westward to Aznoth Tabor, and went out from there toward Hukkok; it adjoined Zebulun on the south side and Asher on the west side, and ended at Judah by the Jordan toward the sunrise. **35** And the fortified cities *are* Ziddim, Zer, Hammath, Rakkath, Chinnereth, **36** Adamah, Ramah, Hazor, **37** Kedesh, Edrei, En Hazor, **38** Iron, Migdal El, Horem, Beth Anath, and Beth Shemesh: nineteen cities with their villages. **39** This *was* the inheritance of the tribe of the children of Naphtali according to their families, the cities and their villages.

Did not drive out the Canaanites, but made them tributary.

Judg 1:33 Nor did Naphtali drive out the inhabitants of Beth Shemesh or the inhabitants of Beth Anath; but they dwelt among the Canaanites, the inhabitants of the land. Nevertheless the inhabitants of Beth Shemesh and Beth Anath were put under tribute to them.

Chosen from Zebulun to go with Barak against Sisera.

Judg 4:6 Then she sent and called for Barak the son of Abinoam from Kedesh in Naphtali, and said to him, "Has not the LORD God of Israel commanded, 'Go and deploy *troops* at Mount Tabor; take with you ten thousand men of the sons of Naphtali and of the sons of Zebulun;

Judg 4:10 And Barak called Zebulun and Naphtali to Kedesh; he went up with ten thousand men under his command, and Deborah went up with him.

Praised for aiding against Sisera.

Judg 5:18 Zebulun *is* a people *who* jeopardized their lives to the point of death, Naphtali also, on the heights of the battlefield.

Joined Gideon in the pursuit and overthrow of the Midianites.

Judg 7:23 And the men of Israel gathered together from Naphtali, Asher, and all Manasseh, and pursued the Midianites.

Some of, at David's coronation.

1 Chr 12:34 of Naphtali one thousand captains, and with them thirty-seven thousand with shield and spear;

Officer placed over,

By David.

1 Chr 27:19 *over* Zebulun, Ishmaiah the son of Obadiah; *over* Naphtali, Jerimoth the son of Azriel;

By Solomon.

1 Kin 4:15 Ahimaaz, in Naphtali; he also took Basemath the daughter of Solomon as wife;

Land of,

Ravaged by Ben-Hadad.

1 Kin 15:20 So Ben-Hadad heeded King Asa, and sent the captains of his armies against the cities of Israel. He attacked Ijon, Dan, Abel Beth Maachah, and all Chinneroth, with all the land of Naphtali.

Purged of idols by Josiah.

2 Chr 34:6 And *so he did* in the cities of Manasseh, Ephraim, and Simeon, as far as Naphtali and all around, with axes.

Captured by Tiglath-Pileser.

2 Kin 15:29 In the days of Pekah king of Israel, Tiglath-Pileser king of Assyria came and took Ijon, Abel Beth Maachah, Janoah, Kedesh, Hazor, Gilead, and Galilee, all the land of Naphtali; and he carried them captive to Assyria.

Specially favored by our Lord's ministry.

Is 9:1–2 Nevertheless the gloom *will* not *be* upon her who *is* distressed, As when at first He lightly esteemed The land of Zebulun and the land of Naphtali, And afterward more heavily oppressed *her*, By the way of the sea, beyond the Jordan, In Galilee of the Gentiles. 2 The people who walked in darkness Have seen a great light; Those who dwelt in the land of the shadow of death, Upon them a light has shined.

Matt 4:13–15 And leaving Nazareth, He came and dwelt in Capernaum, which is by the sea, in the regions of Zebulun and Naphtali, 14 that it might be fulfilled which was spoken by Isaiah the prophet, saying: 15 "The land of Zebulun and the land of Naphtali, By the way of the sea, beyond the Jordan, Galilee of the Gentiles:

Remarkable persons of,

Barak.

Judg 4:6 Then she sent and called for Barak the son of Abinoam from Kedesh in Naphtali, and said to him, "Has not the LORD God of Israel commanded, 'Go and deploy *troops* at Mount Tabor; take with you ten thousand men of the sons of Naphtali and of the sons of Zebulun;

Hiram.

1 Kin 7:14 He *was* the son of a widow from the tribe of Naphtali, and his father *was* a man of Tyre, a bronze worker; he was filled with wisdom and understanding and skill in working with all kinds of bronze work. So he came to King Solomon and did all his work.

NAZIRITES

Persons separated to the holy service of God.

Num 6:2 "Speak to the children of Israel, and say to them: 'When either a man or woman consecrates an offering to take the vow of a Nazirite, to separate himself to the LORD,

Num 6:8 All the days of his separation he shall be holy to the LORD.

Different kinds of,

From the womb.

Judg 13:5 For behold, you shall conceive and bear a son. And no razor shall come upon his head, for the child shall be a Nazirite to God from the womb; and he shall begin to deliver Israel out of the hand of the Philistines."

Luke 1:15 For he will be great in the sight of the Lord, and shall drink neither wine nor strong drink. He will also be filled with the Holy Spirit, even from his mother's womb.

By a particular vow.

Num 6:2 "Speak to the children of Israel, and say to them: 'When either a man or woman consecrates an offering to take the vow of a Nazirite, to separate himself to the LORD,

Esteemed pure.

Lam 4:7 Her Nazirites were brighter than snow And whiter than milk; They were more ruddy in body than rubies, *Like* sapphire in their appearance.

Prohibited from

Wine or strong drink.

Num 6:3–4 he shall separate himself from wine and *similar* drink; he shall drink neither vinegar made from wine nor vinegar made from *similar* drink; neither shall he drink any grape juice, nor eat fresh grapes or raisins. 4 All the days of his separation he shall eat nothing that is produced by the grapevine, from seed to skin.

Judg 13:14 She may not eat anything that comes from the vine, nor may she drink wine or *similar* drink, nor eat anything unclean. All that I commanded her let her observe."

Luke 1:15 For he will be great in the sight of the Lord, and shall drink neither wine nor strong drink. He will also be filled with the Holy Spirit, even from his mother's womb.

Cutting or shaving the head.

Num 6:5 'All the days of the vow of his separation no razor shall come upon his head; until the days are fulfilled for which he separated himself to the LORD, he shall be holy. *Then* he shall let the locks of the hair of his head grow.

Judg 13:5 For behold, you shall conceive and bear a son. And no razor shall come upon his head, for the child shall be a Nazirite to God from the womb; and he shall begin to deliver Israel out of the hand of the Philistines."

Judg 16:17 that he told her all his heart, and said to her, "No razor has ever come upon my head, for I *have been* a Nazirite to God from my mother's womb. If I am shaven, then my strength will leave me, and I shall become weak, and be like any *other* man."

Defiling themselves by the dead.

Num 6:6–7 All the days that he separates himself to the LORD he shall not go near a dead body. 7 He shall not make himself unclean even for his father or his mother, for his brother or his sister, when they die, because his separation to God *is* on his head.

Raised up for good of the nation.

Amos 2:11 I raised up some of your sons as prophets, And some of your young men as Nazirites. *Is it* not so, O you children of Israel?" Says the LORD.

Ungodly Jews tried to corrupt.

Amos 2:12 "But you gave the Nazirites wine to drink, And commanded the prophets saying, 'Do not prophesy!'

If defiled during vow

Must shave head the seventh day.

Num 6:9 'And if anyone dies very suddenly beside him, and he defiles his consecrated head, then he shall shave his head on the day of his cleansing; on the seventh day he shall shave it.

Must bring two turtledoves for a burnt offering.

Num 6:10–11 Then on the eighth day he shall bring two turtledoves or two young pigeons to the priest, to the door of the tabernacle of meeting; 11 and the priest shall offer one as a sin offering and *the* other as a burnt offering, and make atonement for him, because he sinned in regard to the corpse; and he shall sanctify his head that same day.

Must recompense vow with a trespass offering.

Num 6:12 He shall consecrate to the LORD the days of his separation, and bring a male lamb in its first year as a trespass offering; but the former days shall be lost, because his separation was defiled.

On completion of vow

To be brought to tabernacle door.

Num 6:13 'Now this *is* the law of the Nazirite: When the days of his separation are fulfilled, he shall be brought to the door of the tabernacle of meeting.

To offer sacrifices.

Num 6:14–17 And he shall present his offering to the LORD: one male lamb in its first year without blemish as a burnt offering, one ewe lamb in its first year

without blemish as a sin offering, one ram without blemish as a peace offering, **15** a basket of unleavened bread, cakes of fine flour mixed with oil, unleavened wafers anointed with oil, and their grain offering with their drink offerings. **16** 'Then the priest shall bring *them* before the LORD and offer his sin offering and his burnt offering; **17** and he shall offer the ram as a sacrifice of a peace offering to the LORD, with the basket of unleavened bread; the priest shall also offer its grain offering and its drink offering.

To shave their heads.

Num 6:18 Then the Nazirite shall shave his consecrated head *at* the door of the tabernacle of meeting, and shall take the hair from his consecrated head and put *it* on the fire which is under the sacrifice of the peace offering.

Acts 18:18 So Paul still remained a good while. Then he took leave of the brethren and sailed for Syria, and Priscilla and Aquila *were* with him. He had *his* hair cut off at Cenchrea, for he had taken a vow.

Acts 21:24 Take them and be purified with them, and pay their expenses so that they may shave *their* heads, and that all may know that those things of which they were informed concerning you are nothing, but *that* you yourself also walk orderly and keep the law.

To receive wave offering from the priest.

Lev 7:32 Also the right thigh you shall give to the priest *as* a heave offering from the sacrifices of your peace offerings.

Num 6:19–20 'And the priest shall take the boiled shoulder of the ram, one unleavened cake from the basket, and one unleavened wafer, and put *them* upon the hands of the Nazirite after he has shaved his consecrated *hair,* **20** and the priest shall wave them as a wave offering before the LORD; they *are* holy for the priest, together with the breast of the wave offering and the thigh of the heave offering. After that the Nazirite may drink wine.'

Illustrative of

Christ.

Heb 7:26 For such a High Priest was fitting for us, *who is* holy, harmless, undefiled, separate from sinners, and has become higher than the heavens;

Believers.

2 Cor 6:17 Therefore *"Come out from among them And be separate, says the Lord. Do not touch what is unclean, And I will receive you."*

James 1:27 Pure and undefiled religion before God and the Father is this: to visit orphans and widows in their trouble, *and* to keep oneself unspotted from the world.

NEBUCHADNEZZAR

Took Daniel and his friends captive.

Dan 1:1–3 In the third year of the reign of Jehoiakim king of Judah, Nebuchadnezzar king of Babylon came to Jerusalem and besieged it. **2** And the Lord gave Jehoiakim king of Judah into his hand, with some of the articles of the house of God, which he carried into the land of Shinar to the house of his god; and he brought the articles into the treasure house of his god. **3** Then the king instructed Ashpenaz, the master of his eunuchs, to bring some of the children of Israel and some of the king's descendants and some of the nobles,

Carried sacred vessels to Babylon.

2 Kin 24:13 And he carried out from there all the treasures of the house of the LORD and the treasures of the king's house, and he cut in pieces all the articles of gold which Solomon king of Israel had made in the temple of the LORD, as the LORD had said.

Instrument of God's judgment.

Jer 25:8–9 "Therefore thus says the LORD of hosts: 'Because you have not heard My words, **9** behold, I will send and take all the families of the north,' says the LORD, 'and Nebuchadnezzar the king of Babylon, My servant, and will bring them against this land, against its inhabitants, and against these nations all around, and will utterly destroy them, and make them an astonishment, a hissing, and perpetual desolations.

Jer 27:8 And it shall be, *that* the nation and kingdom which will not serve Nebuchadnezzar the king of Babylon, and which will not put its neck under the yoke of the king of Babylon, that nation I will punish,' says the LORD, 'with the sword, the famine, and the pestilence, until I have consumed them by his hand.

Insanity of.

Dan 4:28–37 All *this* came upon King Nebuchadnezzar. **29** At the end of the twelve months he was walking about the royal palace of Babylon. **30** The king spoke, saying, "Is not this great Babylon, that I have built for a royal dwelling by my mighty power and for the honor of my majesty?" **31** While the word *was still* in the king's mouth, a voice fell from heaven: "King Nebuchadnezzar, to you it is spoken: the kingdom has departed from you! **32** And they shall drive you from men, and your dwelling *shall be* with the beasts of the field. They shall make you eat grass like oxen; and seven times shall pass over you, until you know that the Most High rules in the kingdom of men, and gives it to whomever He chooses." **33** That very hour the word was fulfilled concerning Nebuchadnezzar; he was driven from men and ate grass like oxen; his body was wet with the dew of heaven till his hair had grown like eagles' *feathers* and his nails like birds' *claws*. **34** And at the end of the time I, Nebuchadnezzar, lifted my eyes to heaven, and my understanding returned to me; and I blessed the Most High and praised and honored Him who lives forever: For His dominion *is* an everlasting dominion, And His kingdom *is* from generation to generation. **35** All the inhabitants of the earth *are* reputed as nothing; He does according to His will in the army of heaven And *among* the inhabitants of the earth. No one can restrain His hand Or say to Him, "What have You done?" **36** At the same time my reason returned to me, and for the glory of my kingdom, my honor and splendor returned to me. My counselors and nobles resorted to me, I was restored to my kingdom, and excellent majesty was added to me. **37** Now I, Nebuchadnezzar, praise and extol and honor the King of heaven, all of whose works *are* truth, and His ways justice. And those who walk in pride He is able to put down.

NEED

Physical

God's concern for.

Neh 9:19 Yet in Your manifold mercies You did not forsake them in the wilderness. The pillar of the cloud did not depart from them by day, To lead them on the road; Nor the pillar of fire by night, To show them light, And the way they should go.

Ps 146:7–9 Who executes justice for the oppressed, Who gives food to the hungry. The LORD gives freedom to the prisoners. **8** The LORD opens *the eyes of* the blind; The LORD raises those who are bowed down; The LORD loves the righteous. **9** The LORD watches over the strangers; He relieves the fatherless and widow; But the way of the wicked He turns upside down.

Phil 4:19 And my God shall supply all your need according to His riches in glory by Christ Jesus.

Looking out for others'.

Is 1:17 Learn to do good; Seek justice, Rebuke the oppressor; Defend the fatherless, Plead for the widow.

Acts 2:45 and sold their possessions and goods, and divided them among all, as anyone had need.

Acts 4:32–35 Now the multitude of those who believed were of one heart and one soul; neither did anyone say that any of the things he possessed was his own, but they had all things in common. **33** And with great power the apostles gave witness to the resurrection of the Lord Jesus. And great grace was upon them all. **34** Nor was there anyone among them who lacked; for all who were possessors of lands or houses sold them, and brought the proceeds of the things that were sold, **35** and laid *them* at the apostles' feet; and they distributed to each as anyone had need.

Eph 4:28 Let him who stole steal no longer, but rather let him labor, working with *his* hands what is good, that he may have something to give him who has need.

Of the poor.

Deut 15:8 but you shall open your hand wide to him and willingly lend him sufficient for his need, whatever he needs.

Spiritual

A recognition of.

John 7:37 On the last day, that great *day* of the feast, Jesus stood and cried out, saying, "If anyone thirsts, let him come to Me and drink.

For salvation.

Is 64:5 You meet him who rejoices and does righteousness, *Who* remembers You in Your ways. You are indeed angry, for we have sinned— In these ways we continue; And we need to be saved.

Matt 9:36 But when He saw the multitudes, He was moved with compassion for them, because they were weary and scattered, like sheep having no shepherd.

John 3:3 Jesus answered and said to him, "Most assuredly, I say to you, unless one is born again, he cannot see the kingdom of God."

For repentance.

1 Sam 6:3 So they said, "If you send away the ark of the God of Israel, do not send it empty; but by all means return *it* to Him *with* a trespass offering. Then you will be healed, and it will be known to you why His hand is not removed from you."

For wisdom.

1 Kin 3:9 Therefore give to Your servant an understanding heart to judge Your people, that I may discern between good and evil. For who is able to judge this great people of Yours?"

For sanctification.

John 13:10 Jesus said to him, "He who is bathed needs only to wash *his* feet, but is completely clean; and you are clean, but not all of you."

Christ's identification with man's.

Heb 2:17–18 Therefore, in all things He had to be made like *His* brethren, that He might be a merciful and faithful High Priest in things *pertaining* to God, to make propitiation for the sins of the people. **18** For in that He Himself has suffered, being tempted, He is able to aid those who are tempted.

Seeking God in time of.

Heb 4:16 Let us therefore come boldly to the throne of grace, that we may obtain mercy and find grace to help in time of need.

NEIGHBOR

The command to love your.

Lev 19:18 You shall not take vengeance, nor bear any grudge against the children of your people, but you shall love your neighbor as yourself: I *am* the LORD.

Matt 22:37–40 Jesus said to him, " 'You shall love the LORD your God with all your heart, with all your soul, and with all your mind.' **38** This is *the* first and great commandment. **39** And *the* second *is* like it: 'You shall love your neighbor as yourself.' **40** On these two commandments hang all the Law and the Prophets."

Rom 13:9–10 For the commandments, *"You shall not commit adultery," "You shall not murder," "You shall not steal," "You shall not bear false witness," "You shall not covet,"* and if *there is* any other commandment, are *all* summed up in this saying, namely, *"You shall love your neighbor as yourself."* **10** Love does no harm to a neighbor; therefore love *is* the fulfillment of the law.

Gal 5:14 For all the law is fulfilled in one word, *even* in this: *"You shall love your neighbor as yourself."*

Importance in helping your.

Prov 3:28–29 Do not say to your neighbor, "Go, and come back, And tomorrow I will give *it*," When *you have* it with you. **29** Do not devise evil against your neighbor, For he dwells by you for safety's sake.

Working out problems with your.

Prov 25:8–10 Do not go hastily to court; For what will you do in the end, When your neighbor has put you to shame? **9** Debate your case with your neighbor, And do not disclose the secret to another; **10** Lest he who hears *it* expose your shame, And your reputation be ruined.

Jesus' description of a.

Luke 10:29–37 But he, wanting to justify himself, said to Jesus, "And who is my neighbor?" **30** Then Jesus an-

swered and said: "A certain *man* went down from Jerusalem to Jericho, and fell among thieves, who stripped him of his clothing, wounded *him*, and departed, leaving *him* half dead. **31** Now by chance a certain priest came down that road. And when he saw him, he passed by on the other side. **32** Likewise a Levite, when he arrived at the place, came and looked, and passed by on the other side. **33** But a certain Samaritan, as he journeyed, came where he was. And when he saw him, he had compassion. **34** So he went to *him* and bandaged his wounds, pouring on oil and wine; and he set him on his own animal, brought him to an inn, and took care of him. **35** On the next day, when he departed, he took out two denarii, gave *them* to the innkeeper, and said to him, 'Take care of him; and whatever more you spend, when I come again, I will repay you.' **36** So which of these three do you think was neighbor to him who fell among the thieves?" **37** And he said, "He who showed mercy on him." Then Jesus said to him, "Go and do likewise."

Being honest with your.

Eph 4:25 Therefore, putting away lying, *"Let each one of you speak truth with his neighbor,"* for we are members of one another.

NEW BIRTH, THE

The corruption of human nature requires.

John 3:6 That which is born of the flesh is flesh, and that which is born of the Spirit is spirit.

Rom 8:7–8 Because the carnal mind *is* enmity against God; for it is not subject to the law of God, nor indeed can be. **8** So then, those who are in the flesh cannot please God.

None can enter heaven without.

John 3:3 Jesus answered and said to him, "Most assuredly, I say to you, unless one is born again, he cannot see the kingdom of God."

Effected by

God.

John 1:13 who were born, not of blood, nor of the will of the flesh, nor of the will of man, but of God.

1 Pet 1:3 Blessed *be* the God and Father of our Lord Jesus Christ, who according to His abundant mercy has begotten us again to a living hope through the resurrection of Jesus Christ from the dead,

Christ.

1 John 2:29 If you know that He is righteous, you know that everyone who practices righteousness is born of Him.

The Holy Spirit.

John 3:6 That which is born of the flesh is flesh, and that which is born of the Spirit is spirit.

John 3:8 The wind blows where it wishes, and you hear the sound of it, but cannot tell where it comes from and where it goes. So is everyone who is born of the Spirit."

Titus 3:5 not by works of righteousness which we have done, but according to His mercy He saved us, through the washing of regeneration and renewing of the Holy Spirit,

Through the instrumentality of

The word of God.

James 1:18 Of His own will He brought us forth by the word of truth, that we might be a kind of firstfruits of His creatures.

1 Pet 1:23 having been born again, not of corruptible seed but incorruptible, through the word of God which lives and abides forever,

The resurrection of Christ.

1 Pet 1:3 Blessed *be* the God and Father of our Lord Jesus Christ, who according to His abundant mercy has begotten us again to a living hope through the resurrection of Jesus Christ from the dead,

The ministry of the gospel.

1 Cor 4:15 For though you might have ten thousand instructors in Christ, yet *you do* not *have* many fathers; for in Christ Jesus I have begotten you through the gospel.

God and,

Is His will.

James 1:18 Of His own will He brought us forth by the word of truth, that we might be a kind of firstfruits of His creatures.

Is by His mercy.

Titus 3:5 not by works of righteousness which we have done, but according to His mercy He saved us, through the washing of regeneration and renewing of the Holy Spirit,

Is for His glory.

Is 43:7 Everyone who is called by My name, Whom I have created for My glory; I have formed him, yes, I have made him."

Described as

A new creation.

2 Cor 5:17 Therefore, if anyone *is* in Christ, *he is* a new creation; old things have passed away; behold, all things have become new.

Gal 6:15 For in Christ Jesus neither circumcision nor uncircumcision avails anything, but a new creation.

Eph 2:10 For we are His workmanship, created in Christ Jesus for good works, which God prepared beforehand that we should walk in them.

Newness of life.

Rom 6:4 Therefore we were buried with Him through baptism into death, that just as Christ was raised from the dead by the glory of the Father, even so we also should walk in newness of life.

A spiritual resurrection.

Rom 6:4–6 Therefore we were buried with Him through baptism into death, that just as Christ was raised from the dead by the glory of the Father, even so we also should walk in newness of life. **5** For if we have been united together in the likeness of His death, certainly we also shall be *in the likeness* of His resurrection, **6** knowing this, that our old man was crucified with *Him*, that the body of sin might be done away with, that we should no longer be slaves of sin.

Eph 2:1 And you He *made alive*, who were dead in trespasses and sins,

Eph 2:5 even when we were dead in trespasses, made

us alive together with Christ (by grace you have been saved),

Col 2:12 buried with Him in baptism, in which you also were raised with *Him* through faith in the working of God, who raised Him from the dead.

Col 3:1 If then you were raised with Christ, seek those things which are above, where Christ is, sitting at the right hand of God.

A new heart.

Ezek 36:26 I will give you a new heart and put a new spirit within you; I will take the heart of stone out of your flesh and give you a heart of flesh.

A new spirit.

Ezek 11:19 Then I will give them one heart, and I will put a new spirit within them, and take the stony heart out of their flesh, and give them a heart of flesh,

Rom 7:6 But now we have been delivered from the law, having died to what we were held by, so that we should serve in the newness of the Spirit and not *in* the oldness of the letter.

Putting on the new man.

Eph 4:24 and that you put on the new man which was created according to God, in true righteousness and holiness.

The inward man.

Rom 7:22 For I delight in the law of God according to the inward man.

2 Cor 4:16 Therefore we do not lose heart. Even though our outward man is perishing, yet the inward *man* is being renewed day by day.

Circumcision of the heart.

Deut 30:6 And the LORD your God will circumcise your heart and the heart of your descendants, to love the LORD your God with all your heart and with all your soul, that you may live.

Rom 2:29 but *he is* a Jew who *is one* inwardly; and circumcision *is that* of the heart, in the Spirit, not in the letter; whose praise *is* not from men but from God.

Col 2:11 In Him you were also circumcised with the circumcision made without hands, by putting off the body of the sins of the flesh, by the circumcision of Christ,

Partaking of the divine nature.

2 Pet 1:4 by which have been given to us exceedingly great and precious promises, that through these you may be partakers of the divine nature, having escaped the corruption *that is* in the world through lust.

The washing of regeneration.

Titus 3:5 not by works of righteousness which we have done, but according to His mercy He saved us, through the washing of regeneration and renewing of the Holy Spirit,

True for all believers.

Rom 8:16–17 The Spirit Himself bears witness with our spirit that we are children of God, **17** and if children, then heirs—heirs of God and joint heirs with Christ, if indeed we suffer with *Him*, that we may also be glorified together.

1 Pet 2:2 as newborn babes, desire the pure milk of the word, that you may grow thereby,

1 John 5:1 Whoever believes that Jesus is the Christ is born of God, and everyone who loves Him who begot also loves him who is begotten of Him.

Produces

Likeness to God.

Eph 4:24 and that you put on the new man which was created according to God, in true righteousness and holiness.

Col 3:10 and have put on the new *man* who is renewed in knowledge according to the image of Him who created him,

Likeness to Christ.

Rom 8:29 For whom He foreknew, He also predestined *to be* conformed to the image of His Son, that He might be the firstborn among many brethren.

2 Cor 3:18 But we all, with unveiled face, beholding as in a mirror the glory of the Lord, are being transformed into the same image from glory to glory, just as by the Spirit of the Lord.

1 John 3:2 Beloved, now we are children of God; and it has not yet been revealed what we shall be, but we know that when He is revealed, we shall be like Him, for we shall see Him as He is.

Knowledge of God.

Jer 24:7 Then I will give them a heart to know Me, that I *am* the LORD; and they shall be My people, and I will be their God, for they shall return to Me with their whole heart.

Col 3:10 and have put on the new *man* who is renewed in knowledge according to the image of Him who created him,

Hatred of sin.

1 John 3:9 Whoever has been born of God does not sin, for His seed remains in him; and he cannot sin, because he has been born of God.

1 John 5:18 We know that whoever is born of God does not sin; but he who has been born of God keeps himself, and the wicked one does not touch him.

Victory over the world.

1 John 5:4 For whatever is born of God overcomes the world. And this is the victory that has overcome the world—our faith.

Delight in God's law.

Rom 7:22 For I delight in the law of God according to the inward man.

Evidenced by

Faith in Christ.

1 John 5:1 Whoever believes that Jesus is the Christ is born of God, and everyone who loves Him who begot also loves him who is begotten of Him.

Righteousness.

1 John 2:29 If you know that He is righteous, you know that everyone who practices righteousness is born of Him.

1 John 5:18 We know that whoever is born of God does not sin; but he who has been born of God keeps himself, and the wicked one does not touch him.

Brotherly love.

1 John 4:7 Beloved, let us love one another, for love is of God; and everyone who loves is born of God and knows God.

Connected with adoption.

Is 43:6–7 I will say to the north, 'Give them up!' And to the south, 'Do not keep them back!' Bring My sons from afar, And My daughters from the ends of the earth— **7** Everyone who is called by My name, Whom I have created for My glory; I have formed him, yes, I have made him."

John 1:12–13 But as many as received Him, to them He gave the right to become children of God, to those who believe in His name: **13** who were born, not of blood, nor of the will of the flesh, nor of the will of man, but of God.

The natural man does not understand.

John 3:4 Nicodemus said to Him, "How can a man be born when he is old? Can he enter a second time into his mother's womb and be born?"

NEW COVENANT, THE

Christ

The substance of.

Is 42:6 "I, the LORD, have called You in righteousness, And will hold Your hand; I will keep You and give You as a covenant to the people, As a light to the Gentiles,

Is 49:8 Thus says the LORD: "In an acceptable time I have heard You, And in the day of salvation I have helped You; I will preserve You and give You As a covenant to the people, To restore the earth, To cause them to inherit the desolate heritages;

The Mediator of.

Heb 8:6 But now He has obtained a more excellent ministry, inasmuch as He is also Mediator of a better covenant, which was established on better promises.

Heb 9:15 And for this reason He is the Mediator of the new covenant, by means of death, for the redemption of the transgressions under the first covenant, that those who are called may receive the promise of the eternal inheritance.

Heb 12:24 to Jesus the Mediator of the new covenant, and to the blood of sprinkling that speaks better things than *that of* Abel.

The Messenger of.

Mal 3:1 "Behold, I send My messenger, And he will prepare the way before Me. And the Lord, whom you seek, Will suddenly come to His temple, Even the Messenger of the covenant, In whom you delight. Behold, He is coming," Says the LORD of hosts.

God's making of.

Jer 31:31–33 "Behold, the days are coming, says the LORD, when I will make a new covenant with the house of Israel and with the house of Judah— **32** not according to the covenant that I made with their fathers in the day *that* I took them by the hand to lead them out of the land of Egypt, My covenant which they broke, though I was a husband to them, says the LORD. **33** But this *is* the covenant that I will make with the house of Israel after those days, says the LORD: I will put My law in their minds, and write it on their hearts; and I will be their God, and they shall be My people.

Rom 11:27 *For this is My covenant with them, When I take away their sins."*

Heb 8:8–10 Because finding fault with them, He says: *"Behold, the days are coming, says the LORD, when I will make a new covenant with the house of Israel and with the house of Judah— 9 not according to the covenant that I made with their fathers in the day when I took them by the hand to lead them out of the land of Egypt; because they did not continue in My covenant, and I disregarded them, says the LORD. 10 For this is the covenant that I will make with the house of Israel after those days, says the LORD: I will put My laws in their mind and write them on their hearts; and I will be their God, and they shall be My people.*

Heb 8:13 In that He says, *"A new covenant,"* He has made the first obsolete. Now what is becoming obsolete and growing old is ready to vanish away.

Fulfilled in Christ.

Luke 1:68–79 *"Blessed is the Lord God of Israel, For He has visited and redeemed His people, 69 And has raised up a horn of salvation for us In the house of His servant David, 70 As He spoke by the mouth of His holy prophets, Who have been since the world began, 71 That we should be saved from our enemies And from the hand of all who hate us, 72 To perform the mercy promised to our fathers And to remember His holy covenant, 73 The oath which He swore to our father Abraham: 74 To grant us that we, Being delivered from the hand of our enemies, Might serve Him without fear, 75 In holiness and righteousness before Him all the days of our life. 76 "And you, child, will be called the prophet of the Highest; For you will go before the face of the Lord to prepare His ways, 77 To give knowledge of salvation to His people By the remission of their sins, 78 Through the tender mercy of our God, With which the Dayspring from on high has visited us; 79 To give light to those who sit in darkness and the shadow of death, To guide our feet into the way of peace."*

Ratified by the blood of Christ.

Heb 9:11–14 But Christ came as High Priest of the good things to come, with the greater and more perfect tabernacle not made with hands, that is, not of this creation. 12 Not with the blood of goats and calves, but with His own blood He entered the Most Holy Place once for all, having obtained eternal redemption. 13 For if the blood of bulls and goats and the ashes of a heifer, sprinkling the unclean, sanctifies for the purifying of the flesh, 14 how much more shall the blood of Christ, who through the eternal Spirit offered Himself without spot to God, cleanse your conscience from dead works to serve the living God?

Heb 9:16–23 For where there is a testament, there must also of necessity be the death of the testator. 17 For a testament is in force after men are dead, since it has no power at all while the testator lives. 18 Therefore not even the first covenant was dedicated without blood. 19 For when Moses had spoken every precept to all the people according to the law, he took the blood of calves and goats, with water, scarlet wool, and hyssop, and sprinkled both the book itself and all the people, 20 saying, *"This is the blood of the covenant which God has commanded you."* 21 Then

likewise he sprinkled with blood both the tabernacle and all the vessels of the ministry. 22 And according to the law almost all things are purified with blood, and without shedding of blood there is no remission. 23 Therefore it was necessary that the copies of the things in the heavens should be purified with these, but the heavenly things themselves with better sacrifices than these.

Is a covenant of peace.

Is 54:9–10 "For this is like the waters of Noah to Me; For as I have sworn That the waters of Noah would no longer cover the earth, So have I sworn That I would not be angry with you, nor rebuke you. 10 For the mountains shall depart And the hills be removed, But My kindness shall not depart from you, Nor shall My covenant of peace be removed," Says the LORD, who has mercy on you.

Ezek 34:25 "I will make a covenant of peace with them, and cause wild beasts to cease from the land; and they will dwell safely in the wilderness and sleep in the woods.

Ezek 37:26 Moreover I will make a covenant of peace with them, and it shall be an everlasting covenant with them; I will establish them and multiply them, and I will set My sanctuary in their midst forevermore.

Is unalterable.

Is 54:10 For the mountains shall depart And the hills be removed, But My kindness shall not depart from you, Nor shall My covenant of peace be removed," Says the LORD, who has mercy on you.

Is 59:21 "As for Me," says the LORD, "this is My covenant with them: My Spirit who is upon you, and My words which I have put in your mouth, shall not depart from your mouth, nor from the mouth of your descendants, nor from the mouth of your descendants' descendants," says the LORD, "from this time and forevermore."

Is everlasting.

Is 55:3 Incline your ear, and come to Me. Hear, and your soul shall live; And I will make an everlasting covenant with you— The sure mercies of David.

Is 61:8 "For I, the LORD, love justice; I hate robbery for burnt offering; I will direct their work in truth, And will make with them an everlasting covenant.

Ezek 16:60 "Nevertheless I will remember My covenant with you in the days of your youth, and I will establish an everlasting covenant with you.

Heb 13:20 Now may the God of peace who brought up our Lord Jesus from the dead, that great Shepherd of the sheep, through the blood of the everlasting covenant,

All saints have an interest in.

Heb 8:10 *For this is the covenant that I will make with the house of Israel after those days, says the LORD: I will put My laws in their mind and write them on their hearts; and I will be their God, and they shall be My people.*

The wicked have no interest in.

Eph 2:12 that at that time you were without Christ, being aliens from the commonwealth of Israel and strangers from the covenants of promise, having no hope and without God in the world.

Blessings connected with.

Heb 8:10–12 *For this is the covenant that I will make with the house of Israel after those days, says the* L*ORD*: *I will put My laws in their mind and write them on their hearts; and I will be their God, and they shall be My people.* 11 *None of them shall teach his neighbor, and none his brother, saying, 'Know the* L*ORD*,' *for all shall know Me, from the least of them to the greatest of them.* 12 *For I will be merciful to their unrighteousness, and their sins and their lawless deeds I will remember no more."*

Punishment for despising.

Heb 10:29–30 Of how much worse punishment, do you suppose, will he be thought worthy who has trampled the Son of God underfoot, counted the blood of the covenant by which he was sanctified a common thing, and insulted the Spirit of grace? 30 For we know Him who said, *"Vengeance is Mine, I will repay,"* says the Lord. And again, *"The* L*ORD* *will judge His people."*

NIGHT

Created by God.

Gen 1:5 God called the light Day, and the darkness He called Night. So the evening and the morning were the first day.

Gen 1:14 Then God said, "Let there be lights in the firmament of the heavens to divide the day from the night; and let them be for signs and seasons, and for days and years;

Ps 74:16 The day *is* Yours, the night also *is* Yours; You have prepared the light and the sun.

Ps 104:20 You make darkness, and it is night, In which all the beasts of the forest creep about.

The moon and stars designed to rule and give light by.

Gen 1:16–18 Then God made two great lights: the greater light to rule the day, and the lesser light to rule the night. *He made* the stars also. 17 God set them in the firmament of the heavens to give light on the earth, 18 and to rule over the day and over the night, and to divide the light from the darkness. And God saw that *it was* good.

Jer 31:35 Thus says the L*ORD*, Who gives the sun for a light by day, The ordinances of the moon and the stars for a light by night, Who disturbs the sea, And its waves roar (The L*ORD* of hosts *is* His name):

Commenced at sunset.

Gen 28:11 So he came to a certain place and stayed there all night, because the sun had set. And he took one of the stones of that place and put it at his head, and he lay down in that place to sleep.

Continued until sunrise.

Ps 104:22 *When* the sun rises, they gather together And lie down in their dens.

Matt 28:1 Now after the Sabbath, as the first *day* of the week began to dawn, Mary Magdalene and the other Mary came to see the tomb.

Mark 16:2 Very early in the morning, on the first *day* of the week, they came to the tomb when the sun had risen,

Regular succession of,

Established by covenant.

Gen 8:22 "While the earth remains, Seedtime and harvest, Cold and heat, Winter and summer, And day and night Shall not cease."

Jer 33:20 "Thus says the L*ORD*: 'If you can break My covenant with the day and My covenant with the night, so that there will not be day and night in their season,

Ordained for the glory of God.

Ps 19:2 Day unto day utters speech, And night unto night reveals knowledge.

Originally divided into three watches.

Ex 14:24 Now it came to pass, in the morning watch, that the L*ORD* looked down upon the army of the Egyptians through the pillar of fire and cloud, and He troubled the army of the Egyptians.

Judg 7:19 So Gideon and the hundred men who *were* with him came to the outpost of the camp at the beginning of the middle watch, just as they had posted the watch; and they blew the trumpets and broke the pitchers that *were* in their hands.

Lam 2:19 "Arise, cry out in the night, At the beginning of the watches; Pour out your heart like water before the face of the Lord. Lift your hands toward Him For the life of your young children, Who faint from hunger at the head of every street."

Divided into four watches by the Romans.

Matt 14:25 Now in the fourth watch of the night Jesus went to them, walking on the sea.

Mark 13:35 Watch therefore, for you do not know when the master of the house is coming—in the evening, at midnight, at the crowing of the rooster, or in the morning—

Luke 12:38 And if he should come in the second watch, or come in the third watch, and find *them* so, blessed are those servants.

Common characteristics,

Exceedingly dark.

Prov 7:9 In the twilight, in the evening, In the black and dark night.

Cold and frosty.

Gen 31:40 *There* I was! In the day the drought consumed me, and the frost by night, and my sleep departed from my eyes.

Jer 36:30 Therefore thus says the L*ORD* concerning Jehoiakim king of Judah: "He shall have no one to sit on the throne of David, and his dead body shall be cast out to the heat of the day and the frost of the night.

Accompanied by heavy dew.

Num 11:9 And when the dew fell on the camp in the night, the manna fell on it.

Judg 6:38 And it was so. When he rose early the next morning and squeezed the fleece together, he wrung the dew out of the fleece, a bowlful of water.

Judg 6:40 And God did so that night. It was dry on the fleece only, but there was dew on all the ground.

Job 29:19 My root *is* spread out to the waters, And the dew lies all night on my branch.

Song 5:2 I sleep, but my heart is awake; *It is* the voice of my beloved! He knocks, *saying,* "Open for me, my sister, my love, My dove, my perfect one; For my head is covered with dew, My locks with the drops of the night."

Designed for rest.

Ps 104:23 Man goes out to his work And to his labor until the evening.

Wearisome to the afflicted.

Job 7:3–4 So I have been allotted months of futility, And wearisome nights have been appointed to me. 4 When I lie down, I say, 'When shall I arise, And the night be ended?' For I have had my fill of tossing till dawn.

Favorable to the purposes of the wicked.

Gen 31:39 That which was torn *by beasts* I did not bring to you; I bore the loss of it. You required it from my hand, *whether* stolen by day or stolen by night.

Job 24:14–15 The murderer rises with the light; He kills the poor and needy; And in the night he is like a thief. 15 The eye of the adulterer waits for the twilight, Saying, 'No eye will see me'; And he disguises *his* face.

Obad 1:5 "If thieves had come to you, If robbers by night— Oh, how you will be cut off!— Would they not have stolen till they had enough? If grape-gatherers had come to you, Would they not have left *some* gleanings?

1 Thess 5:2 For you yourselves know perfectly that the day of the Lord so comes as a thief in the night.

Wild beasts hunt during.

2 Sam 21:10 Now Rizpah the daughter of Aiah took sackcloth and spread it for herself on the rock, from the beginning of harvest until the late rains poured on them from heaven. And she did not allow the birds of the air to rest on them by day nor the beasts of the field by night.

Ps 104:21–22 The young lions roar after their prey, And seek their food from God. 22 *When* the sun rises, they gather together And lie down in their dens.

The Jews

Required to pay wages prior to.

Lev 19:13 'You shall not cheat your neighbor, nor rob *him.* The wages of him who is hired shall not remain with you all night until morning.

Required to bury bodies of the executed before.

Deut 21:23 his body shall not remain overnight on the tree, but you shall surely bury him that day, so that you do not defile the land which the LORD your God is giving you *as* an inheritance; for he who is hanged *is* accursed of God.

Sometimes equated with sorrow, etc.

Ps 6:6 I am weary with my groaning; All night I make my bed swim; I drench my couch with my tears.

Ps 30:5 For His anger *is but for* a moment, His favor *is for* life; Weeping may endure for a night, But joy *comes* in the morning.

Joel 1:13 Gird yourselves and lament, you priests; Wail, you who minister before the altar; Come, lie all night

in sackcloth, You who minister to my God; For the grain offering and the drink offering Are withheld from the house of your God.

Sometimes spent in prayer.

Ps 22:2 O My God, I cry in the daytime, but You do not hear; And in the night season, and am not silent.

Often kept lamps burning during.

Prov 31:18 She perceives that her merchandise *is* good, And her lamp does not go out by night.

Eastern shepherds watched over their flocks during.

Gen 31:40 *There* I was! In the day the drought consumed me, and the frost by night; and my sleep departed from my eyes.

Luke 2:8 Now there were in the same country shepherds living out in the fields, keeping watch over their flock by night.

Eastern fishermen continued their employment during.

Luke 5:5 But Simon answered and said to Him, "Master, we have toiled all night and caught nothing; nevertheless at Your word I will let down the net."

John 21:3 Simon Peter said to them, "I am going fishing." They said to him, "We are going with you also." They went out and immediately got into the boat, and that night they caught nothing.

God frequently

Revealed his will in.

Gen 31:24 But God had come to Laban the Syrian in a dream by night, and said to him, "Be careful that you speak to Jacob neither good nor bad."

Gen 46:2 Then God spoke to Israel in the visions of the night, and said, "Jacob, Jacob!" And he said, "Here I am."

Num 22:30 So the donkey said to Balaam, "*Am* I not your donkey on which you have ridden, ever since *I* became yours, to this day? Was I ever disposed to do this to you?" And he said, "No."

Dan 7:2 Daniel spoke, saying, "I saw in my vision by night, and behold, the four winds of heaven were stirring up the Great Sea.

Visited his people in.

1 Kin 3:5 At Gibeon the LORD appeared to Solomon in a dream by night; and God said, "Ask! What shall I give you?"

Ps 17:3 You have tested my heart; You have visited *me* in the night; You have tried me and have found nothing; I have purposed that my mouth shall not transgress.

Executed his judgments in.

Ex 12:12 'For I will pass through the land of Egypt on that night, and will strike all the firstborn in the land of Egypt, both man and beast; and against all the gods of Egypt I will execute judgment: I *am* the LORD.

2 Kin 19:35 And it came to pass on a certain night that the angel of the LORD went out, and killed in the camp of the Assyrians one hundred and eighty-five thousand; and when *people* arose early in the morning, there were the corpses—all dead.

Job 27:20 Terrors overtake him like a flood; A tempest steals him away in the night.

Dan 5:30 That very night Belshazzar, king of the Chaldeans, was slain.

Illustrative of

Spiritual darkness.

John 11:10 But if one walks in the night, he stumbles, because the light is not in him."

Rom 13:12 The night is far spent, the day is at hand. Therefore let us cast off the works of darkness, and let us put on the armor of light.

Seasons of severe calamities.

Is 21:12 The watchman said, "The morning comes, and also the night. If you will inquire, inquire; Return! Come back!"

Amos 5:8 He made the Pleiades and Orion; He turns the shadow of death into morning And makes the day dark as night; He calls for the waters of the sea And pours them out on the face of the earth; The LORD *is* His name.

Death.

John 9:4 I must work the works of Him who sent Me while it is day; *the* night is coming when no one can work.

NILE RIVER, THE

Empties into the Mediterranean by seven streams.

Is 11:15 The LORD will utterly destroy the tongue of the Sea of Egypt; With His mighty wind He will shake His fist over the River, And strike it in the seven streams, And make *men* cross over dryshod.

Called

The river.

Gen 41:1 Then it came to pass, at the end of two full years, that Pharaoh had a dream; and behold, he stood by the river.

Gen 41:3 Then behold, seven other cows came up after them out of the river, ugly and gaunt, and stood by the *other* cows on the bank of the river.

The Sea of Egypt.

Is 11:15 The LORD will utterly destroy the tongue of the Sea of Egypt; With His mighty wind He will shake His fist over the River, And strike it in the seven streams, And make *men* cross over dryshod.

The Brook of Egypt.

Is 27:12 And it shall come to pass in that day *That* the LORD will thresh, From the channel of the River to the Brook of Egypt; And you will be gathered one by one, O you children of Israel.

Sihor.

Josh 13:3 from Sihor, which *is* east of Egypt, as far as the border of Ekron northward (*which* is counted as Canaanite); the five lords of the Philistines—the Gazites, the Ashdodites, the Ashkelonites, the Gittites, and the Ekronites; also the Avites;

Jer 2:18 And now why take the road to Egypt, To drink the waters of Sihor? Or why take the road to Assyria, To drink the waters of the River?

Abounded in

Great Monsters (crocodiles).

Ezek 29:3 Speak, and say, 'Thus says the Lord GOD: "Behold, I *am* against you, O Pharaoh king of Egypt, O great monster who lies in the midst of his rivers, Who has said, 'My River *is* my own; I have made *it* for myself.'

Fish.

Ex 7:21 The fish that *were* in the river died, the river stank, and the Egyptians could not drink the water of the river. So there was blood throughout all the land of Egypt.

Ezek 29:4 But I will put hooks in your jaws, And cause the fish of your rivers to stick to your scales; I will bring you up out of the midst of your rivers, And all the fish in your rivers will stick to your scales.

Reeds and rushes.

Is 19:6–7 The rivers will turn foul; The brooks of defense will be emptied and dried up; The reeds and rushes will wither. **7** The papyrus reeds by the River, by the mouth of the River, And everything sown by the River, Will wither, be driven away, and be no more.

Annual overflow of its banks alluded to.

Jer 46:8 Egypt rises up like a flood, And *its* waters move like the rivers; And he says, 'I will go up *and* cover the earth, I will destroy the city and its inhabitants.'

Amos 8:8 Shall the land not tremble for this, And everyone mourn who dwells in it? All of it shall swell like the River, Heave and subside Like the River of Egypt.

Amos 9:5 The Lord GOD of hosts, He who touches the earth and it melts, And all who dwell there mourn; All of it shall swell like the River, And subside like the River of Egypt.

The Egyptians

Took great pride in.

Ezek 29:9 And the land of Egypt shall become desolate and waste; then they will know that I *am* the LORD, because he said, 'The River *is* mine, and I have made it.'

Carried on extensive commerce by.

Is 23:3 And on great waters the grain of Shihor, The harvest of the River, *is* her revenue; And she is a marketplace for the nations.

Bathed in.

Ex 2:5 Then the daughter of Pharaoh came down to bathe at the river. And her maidens walked along the riverside; and when she saw the ark among the reeds, she sent her maid to get it.

Drank of.

Ex 7:21 The fish that *were* in the river died, the river stank, and the Egyptians could not drink the water of the river. So there was blood throughout all the land of Egypt.

Ex 7:24 So all the Egyptians dug all around the river for water to drink, because they could not drink the water of the river.

Punished by failure of its waters.

Is 19:5–6 The waters will fail from the sea, And the river will be wasted and dried up. **6** The rivers will turn foul; The brooks of defense will be emptied and dried up; The reeds and rushes will wither.

Punished by destruction of its fish.

Is 19:8 The fishermen also will mourn; All those will

lament who cast hooks into the River, And they will languish who spread nets on the waters.

Remarkable events connected with

Male children drowned in.

Ex 1:22 So Pharaoh commanded all his people, saying, "Every son who is born you shall cast into the river, and every daughter you shall save alive."

Moses found on its banks.

Ex 2:3 But when she could no longer hide him, she took an ark of bulrushes for him, daubed it with asphalt and pitch, put the child in it, and laid *it* in the reeds by the river's bank.

Its waters turned into blood.

Ex 7:15 Go to Pharaoh in the morning, when he goes out to the water, and you shall stand by the river's bank to meet him; and the rod which was turned to a serpent you shall take in your hand.

Ex 7:20 And Moses and Aaron did so, just as the LORD commanded. So he lifted up the rod and struck the waters that *were* in the river, in the sight of Pharaoh and in the sight of his servants. And all the waters that *were* in the river were turned to blood.

Miraculous generation of frogs.

Ex 8:3 So the river shall bring forth frogs abundantly, which shall go up and come into your house, into your bedroom, on your bed, into the houses of your servants, on your people, into your ovens, and into your kneading bowls.

NINEVEH

Origin and antiquity of.

Gen 10:11 From that land he went to Assyria and built Nineveh, Rehoboth Ir, Calah,

Situated on the river Tigris.

Nah 2:6 The gates of the rivers are opened, And the palace is dissolved.

Nah 2:8 Though Nineveh of old *was* like a pool of water, Now they flee away. "Halt! Halt!" *they* cry; But no one turns back.

The ancient capital of Assyria.

2 Kin 19:36 So Sennacherib king of Assyria departed and went away, returned *home*, and remained at Nineveh.

Is 37:37 So Sennacherib king of Assyria departed and went away, returned *home*, and remained at Nineveh.

Called the bloody city.

Nah 3:1 Woe to the bloody city! It *is* all full of lies *and* robbery. *Its* victim never departs.

Described as

Great.

Jon 1:2 "Arise, go to Nineveh, that great city, and cry out against it; for their wickedness has come up before Me."

Jon 3:2 "Arise, go to Nineveh, that great city, and preach to it the message that I tell you."

Extensive.

Jon 3:3 So Jonah arose and went to Nineveh, according to the word of the LORD. Now Nineveh was an exceedingly great city, a three-day journey *in extent.*

Rich.

Nah 2:9 Take spoil of silver! Take spoil of gold! *There is* no end of treasure, Or wealth of every desirable prize.

Strong.

Nah 3:12 All your strongholds *are* fig trees with ripened figs: If they are shaken, They fall into the mouth of the eater.

Commercial.

Nah 3:16 You have multiplied your merchants more than the stars of heaven. The locust plunders and flies away.

Populous.

Jon 4:11 And should I not pity Nineveh, that great city, in which are more than one hundred and twenty thousand persons who cannot discern between their right hand and their left—and much livestock?"

Vile.

Nah 1:14 The LORD has given a command concerning you: "Your name shall be perpetuated no longer. Out of the house of your gods I will cut off the carved image and the molded image. I will dig your grave, For you are vile."

Wicked.

Jon 1:2 "Arise, go to Nineveh, that great city, and cry out against it; for their wickedness has come up before Me."

Idolatrous.

Nah 1:14 The LORD has given a command concerning you: "Your name shall be perpetuated no longer. Out of the house of your gods I will cut off the carved image and the molded image. I will dig your grave, For you are vile."

Full of joy and carelessness.

Zeph 2:15 This is the rejoicing city That dwelt securely, That said in her heart, "I *am* it, and *there is* none besides me." How has she become a desolation, A place for beasts to lie down! Everyone who passes by her Shall hiss and shake his fist.

Full of lies and robbery.

Nah 3:1 Woe to the bloody city! It *is* all full of lies *and* robbery. *Its* victim never departs.

Full of witchcraft.

Nah 3:4 Because of the multitude of harlotries of the seductive harlot, The mistress of sorceries, Who sells nations through her harlotries, And families through her sorceries.

Jonah sent to proclaim the destruction of.

Jon 1:2 "Arise, go to Nineveh, that great city, and cry out against it; for their wickedness has come up before Me."

Jon 3:1–2 Now the word of the LORD came to Jonah the second time, saying, 2 "Arise, go to Nineveh, that great city, and preach to it the message that I tell you."

Jon 3:4 And Jonah began to enter the city on the first day's walk. Then he cried out and said, "Yet forty days, and Nineveh shall be overthrown!"

Repented at Jonah's preaching.

Jon 3:5–9 So the people of Nineveh believed God, proclaimed a fast, and put on sackcloth, from the greatest to the least of them. **6** Then word came to the king of Nineveh; and he arose from his throne and laid aside his robe, covered *himself* with sackcloth and sat in ashes. **7** And he caused *it* to be proclaimed and published throughout Nineveh by the decree of the king and his nobles, saying, Let neither man nor beast, herd nor flock, taste anything; do not let them eat, or drink water. **8** But let man and beast be covered with sackcloth, and cry mightily to God; yes, let every one turn from his evil way and from the violence that is in his hands. **9** Who can tell *if* God will turn and relent, and turn away from His fierce anger, so that we may not perish?

Matt 12:41 The men of Nineveh will rise up in the judgment with this generation and condemn it, because they repented at the preaching of Jonah; and indeed a greater than Jonah *is* here.

Luke 11:32 The men of Nineveh will rise up in the judgment with this generation and condemn it, for they repented at the preaching of Jonah; and indeed a greater than Jonah *is* here.

Jonah saw God spare.

Jon 3:10 Then God saw their works, that they turned from their evil way; and God relented from the disaster that He had said He would bring upon them, and He did not do it.

Jon 4:11 And should I not pity Nineveh, that great city, in which are more than one hundred and twenty thousand persons who cannot discern between their right hand and their left—and much livestock?"

Predictions respecting,

Coming up of the Babylonian armies against.

Nah 2:1–4 He who scatters has come up before your face. Man the fort! Watch the road! Strengthen *your* flanks! Fortify *your* power mightily. **2** For the LORD will restore the excellence of Jacob Like the excellence of Israel, For the emptiers have emptied them out And ruined their vine branches. **3** The shields of his mighty men *are* made red, The valiant men *are* in scarlet. The chariots *come* with flaming torches In the day of his preparation, And the spears are brandished. **4** The chariots rage in the streets, They jostle one another in the broad roads; They seem like torches, They run like lightning.

Nah 3:2 The noise of a whip And the noise of rattling wheels, Of galloping horses, Of clattering chariots!

Destruction of its people.

Nah 1:12 Thus says the LORD: "Though *they are* safe, and likewise many, Yet in this manner they will be cut down When he passes through. Though I have afflicted you, I will afflict you no more;

Nah 3:3 Horsemen charge with bright sword and glittering spear. *There is* a multitude of slain, A great number of bodies, Countless corpses— They stumble over the corpses—

Spoiling of its treasures.

Nah 2:9 Take spoil of silver! Take spoil of gold! *There is* no end of treasure, Or wealth of every desirable prize.

Destruction of its idols.

Nah 1:14 The LORD has given a command concerning

you: "Your name shall be perpetuated no longer. Out of the house of your gods I will cut off the carved image and the molded image. I will dig your grave, For you are vile."

Nah 2:7 It is decreed: She shall be led away captive, She shall be brought up; And her maidservants shall lead *her* as with the voice of doves, Beating their breasts.

Degradation and contempt put on.

Nah 3:5–7 "Behold, I *am* against you," says the LORD of hosts; "I will lift your skirts over your face, I will show the nations your nakedness, And the kingdoms your shame. **6** I will cast abominable filth upon you, Make you vile, And make you a spectacle. **7** It shall come to pass *that* all who look upon you Will flee from you, and say, 'Nineveh is laid waste! Who will bemoan her?' Where shall I seek comforters for you?"

Zeph 2:15 This is the rejoicing city That dwelt securely, That said in her heart, "I *am it*, and *there is* none besides me." How has she become a desolation, A place for beasts to lie down! Everyone who passes by her Shall hiss and shake his fist.

Destruction and desolation.

Nah 1:8–9 But with an overflowing flood He will make an utter end of its place, And darkness will pursue His enemies. **9** What do you conspire against the LORD? He will make an utter end *of it*. Affliction will not rise up a second time.

Zeph 2:13–15 And He will stretch out His hand against the north, Destroy Assyria, And make Nineveh a desolation, As dry as the wilderness. **14** The herds shall lie down in her midst, Every beast of the nation. Both the pelican and the bittern Shall lodge on the capitals *of* her *pillars;* Their voice shall sing in the windows; Desolation *shall be* at the threshold; For He will lay bare the cedar work. **15** This is the rejoicing city That dwelt securely, That said in her heart, "I *am it*, and *there is* none besides me." How has she become a desolation, A place for beasts to lie down! Everyone who passes by her Shall hiss and shake his fist.

Feebleness of its people.

Nah 3:13 Surely, your people in your midst *are* women! The gates of your land are wide open for your enemies; Fire shall devour the bars of your *gates.*

People captured in disgrace.

Nah 1:10 For while tangled *like* thorns, And while drunken *like* drunkards, They shall be devoured like stubble fully dried.

Nah 3:10–11 Yet she *was* carried away, She went into captivity; Her young children also were dashed to pieces At the head of every street; They cast lots for her honorable men, And all her great men were bound in chains. **11** You also will be drunk; You will be hidden; You also will seek refuge from the enemy.

NOAH

Son of Lamech.

Gen 5:28–29 Lamech lived one hundred and eighty-two years, and had a son. **29** And he called his name Noah, saying, "This *one* will comfort us concerning our work and the toil of our hands, because of the ground which the LORD has cursed."

Names of three sons.

Gen 5:32 And Noah was five hundred years old, and Noah begot Shem, Ham, and Japheth.

Gen 9:18–19 Now the sons of Noah who went out of the ark were Shem, Ham, and Japheth. And Ham *was* the father of Canaan. **19** These three *were* the sons of Noah, and from these the whole earth was populated.

Found favor with God in the midst of corrupt generation.

Gen 6:1–13 Now it came to pass, when men began to multiply on the face of the earth, and daughters were born to them, **2** that the sons of God saw the daughters of men, that they *were* beautiful; and they took wives for themselves of all whom they chose. **3** And the LORD said, "My Spirit shall not strive with man forever, for he *is* indeed flesh; yet his days shall be one hundred and twenty years." **4** There were giants on the earth in those days, and also afterward, when the sons of God came in to the daughters of men and they bore *children* to them. Those *were* the mighty men who *were* of old, men of renown. **5** Then the LORD saw that the wickedness of man *was* great in the earth, and *that* every intent of the thoughts of his heart *was* only evil continually. **6** And the LORD was sorry that He had made man on the earth, and He was grieved in His heart. **7** So the LORD said, "I will destroy man whom I have created from the face of the earth, both man and beast, creeping thing and birds of the air, for I am sorry that I have made them." **8** But Noah found grace in the eyes of the LORD. **9** This is the genealogy of Noah. Noah was a just man, perfect in his generations. Noah walked with God. **10** And Noah begot three sons: Shem, Ham, and Japheth. **11** The earth also was corrupt before God, and the earth was filled with violence. **12** So God looked upon the earth, and indeed it was corrupt; for all flesh had corrupted their way on the earth. **13** And God said to Noah, "The end of all flesh has come before Me, for the earth is filled with violence through them; and behold, I will destroy them with the earth.

Received instructions for the ark.

Gen 6:13–22 And God said to Noah, "The end of all flesh has come before Me, for the earth is filled with violence through them; and behold, I will destroy them with the earth. **14** Make yourself an ark of gopherwood; make rooms in the ark, and cover it inside and outside with pitch. **15** And this is how you shall make it: The length of the ark *shall be* three hundred cubits, its width fifty cubits, and its height thirty cubits. **16** You shall make a window for the ark, and you shall finish it to a cubit from above; and set the door of the ark in its side. You shall make it *with* lower, second, and third *decks*. **17** And behold, I Myself am bringing floodwaters on the earth, to destroy from under heaven all flesh in which *is* the breath of life; everything that *is* on the earth shall die. **18** But I will establish My covenant with you; and you shall go into the ark—you, your sons, your wife, and your sons' wives with you. **19** And of every living thing of all flesh you shall bring two of every *sort* into the ark, to keep *them* alive with you; they shall be male and female. **20** Of the birds after their kind, of animals after their kind, and of every creeping thing of the

earth after its kind, two of every *kind* will come to you to keep *them* alive. **21** And you shall take for yourself of all food that is eaten, and you shall gather *it* to yourself; and it shall be food for you and for them." **22** Thus Noah did; according to all that God commanded him, so he did.

Preached righteousness to his contemporaries.

2 Pet 2:5 and did not spare the ancient world, but saved Noah, *one of* eight *people,* a preacher of righteousness, bringing in the flood on the world of the ungodly;

Entered the ark.

Gen 7:6–10 Noah *was* six hundred years old when the floodwaters were on the earth. **7** So Noah, with his sons, his wife, and his sons' wives, went into the ark because of the waters of the flood. **8** Of clean animals, of animals that *are* unclean, of birds, and of everything that creeps on the earth, **9** two by two they went into the ark to Noah, male and female, as God had commanded Noah. **10** And it came to pass after seven days that the waters of the flood were on the earth.

Worshiped God and received covenant after the Flood.

Gen 8:13–22 And it came to pass in the six hundred and first year, in the first *month,* the first *day* of the month, that the waters were dried up from the earth; and Noah removed the covering of the ark and looked, and indeed the surface of the ground was dry. **14** And in the second month, on the twenty-seventh day of the month, the earth was dried. **15** Then God spoke to Noah, saying, **16** "Go out of the ark, you and your wife, and your sons and your sons' wives with you. **17** Bring out with you every living thing of all flesh that *is* with you: birds and cattle and every creeping thing that creeps on the earth, so that they may abound on the earth, and be fruitful and multiply on the earth." **18** So Noah went out, and his sons and his wife and his sons' wives with him. **19** Every animal, every creeping thing, every bird, *and* whatever creeps on the earth, according to their families, went out of the ark. **20** Then Noah built an altar to the LORD, and took of every clean animal and of every clean bird, and offered burnt offerings on the altar. **21** And the LORD smelled a soothing aroma. Then the LORD said in His heart, "I will never again curse the ground for man's sake, although the imagination of man's heart *is* evil from his youth; nor will I again destroy every living thing as I have done. **22** "While the earth remains, Seedtime and harvest, Cold and heat, Winter and summer, And day and night Shall not cease."

Gen 9:1–17 So God blessed Noah and his sons, and said to them: "Be fruitful and multiply, and fill the earth. **2** And the fear of you and the dread of you shall be on every beast of the earth, on every bird of the air, on all that move *on* the earth, and on all the fish of the sea. They are given into your hand. **3** Every moving thing that lives shall be food for you. I have given you all things, even as the green herbs. **4** But you shall not eat flesh with its life, *that is,* its blood. **5** Surely for your lifeblood I will demand *a reckoning;* from the hand of every beast I will require it, and from the hand of man. From the hand of every man's brother I will require the life of man. **6** "Whoever sheds man's blood, By man his blood shall be shed; For in the image of God He made man. **7** And as for you, be fruitful and multiply; Bring forth abundantly in the earth And multiply in it." **8** Then God spoke to Noah and to his sons with him, saying: **9** "And as for Me, behold, I establish My covenant with you and with your descendants after you, **10** and with every living creature that *is* with you: the birds, the cattle, and every beast of the earth with you, of all that go out of the ark, every beast of the earth. **11** Thus I establish My covenant with you: Never again shall all flesh be cut off by the waters of the flood; never again shall there be a flood to destroy the earth." **12** And God said: "This *is* the sign of the covenant which I make between Me and you, and every living creature that *is* with you, for perpetual generations: **13** I set My rainbow in the cloud, and it shall be for the sign of the covenant between Me and the earth. **14** It shall be, when I bring a cloud over the earth, that the rainbow shall be seen in the cloud; **15** and I will remember My covenant which *is* between Me and you and every living creature of all flesh; the waters shall never again become a flood to destroy all flesh. **16** The rainbow shall be in the cloud, and I will look on it to remember the everlasting covenant between God and every living creature of all flesh that *is* on the earth." **17** And God said to Noah, "This *is* the sign of the covenant which I have established between Me and all flesh that *is* on the earth."

Became drunk, pronounced curse and blessings.

Gen 9:20–27 And Noah began *to be* a farmer, and he planted a vineyard. **21** Then he drank of the wine and was drunk, and became uncovered in his tent.

22 And Ham, the father of Canaan, saw the nakedness of his father, and told his two brothers outside. **23** But Shem and Japheth took a garment, laid *it* on both their shoulders, and went backward and covered the nakedness of their father. Their faces *were* turned away, and they did not see their father's nakedness. **24** So Noah awoke from his wine, and knew what his younger son had done to him. **25** Then he said: "Cursed *be* Canaan; A servant of servants He shall be to his brethren." **26** And he said: "Blessed *be* the LORD, The God of Shem, And may Canaan be his servant. **27** May God enlarge Japheth, And may he dwell in the tents of Shem; And may Canaan be his servant."

Death of.

Gen 9:28–29 And Noah lived after the flood three hundred and fifty years. **29** So all the days of Noah were nine hundred and fifty years; and he died.

Was obedient man of faith.

Heb 11:7 By faith Noah, being divinely warned of things not yet seen, moved with godly fear, prepared an ark for the saving of his household, by which he condemned the world and became heir of the righteousness which is according to faith.

Was a righteous example.

Ezek 14:14 Even *if* these three men, Noah, Daniel, and Job, were in it, they would deliver *only* themselves by their righteousness," says the Lord GOD.

Ezek 14:20 even *though* Noah, Daniel, and Job *were* in it, *as* I live," says the Lord GOD, "they would deliver neither son nor daughter; they would deliver *only* themselves by their righteousness."

OAK TREE (TEREBINTH), THE

The hill of Bashan celebrated for.

Is 2:13 Upon all the cedars of Lebanon *that are* high and lifted up, And upon all the oaks of Bashan;

Described as

Strong.

Amos 2:9 "Yet *it was* I *who* destroyed the Amorite before them, Whose height *was* like the height of the cedars, And he *was as* strong as the oaks; Yet I destroyed his fruit above And his roots beneath.

Thick spreading.

2 Sam 18:9 Then Absalom met the servants of David. Absalom rode on a mule. The mule went under the thick boughs of a great terebinth tree, and his head caught in the terebinth; so he was left hanging between heaven and earth. And the mule which *was* under him went on.

Ezek 6:13 Then you shall know that I *am* the LORD, when their slain are among their idols all around their altars, on every high hill, on all the mountaintops, under every green tree, and under every thick oak, wherever they offered sweet incense to all their idols.

Casting its leaves in winter.

Is 6:13 But yet a tenth *will be* in it, And will return and be for consuming, As a terebinth tree or as an oak, Whose stump *remains* when it is cut down. So the holy seed *shall be* its stump."

The ancients

Made oars of.

Ezek 27:6 *Of* oaks from Bashan they made your oars; The company of Ashurites have inlaid your planks *With* ivory from the coasts of Cyprus.

Made idols of.

Is 44:14–15 He cuts down cedars for himself, And takes the cypress and the oak; He secures *it* for himself among the trees of the forest. He plants a pine, and the rain nourishes *it*. 15 Then it shall be for a man to burn, For he will take some of it and warm himself; Yes, he kindles *it* and bakes bread; Indeed he makes a god and worships *it*; He makes it a carved image, and falls down to it.

Rested under.

Judg 6:11 Now the Angel of the LORD came and sat under the terebinth tree which *was* in Ophrah, which *belonged* to Joash the Abiezrite, while his son Gideon threshed wheat in the winepress, in order to hide *it* from the Midianites.

Judg 6:19 So Gideon went in and prepared a young goat, and unleavened bread from an ephah of flour. The meat he put in a basket, and he put the broth in a pot; and he brought *them* out to Him under the terebinth tree and presented *them*.

1 Kin 13:14 and went after the man of God, and found him sitting under an oak. Then he said to him, "*Are* you the man of God who came from Judah?" And he said, "I *am*."

Buried their dead under.

Gen 35:8 Now Deborah, Rebekah's nurse, died, and she was buried below Bethel under the terebinth tree. So the name of it was called Allon Bachuth.

Erected monuments under.

Josh 24:26 Then Joshua wrote these words in the Book of the Law of God. And he took a large stone, and set it up there under the oak that *was* by the sanctuary of the LORD.

Performed idolatrous rites under.

Is 1:29 For they shall be ashamed of the terebinth trees Which you have desired; And you shall be embarrassed because of the gardens Which you have chosen.

Is 57:5 Inflaming yourselves with gods under every green tree, Slaying the children in the valleys, Under the clefts of the rocks?

Ezek 6:13 Then you shall know that I *am* the LORD, when their slain are among their idols all around their altars, on every high hill, on all the mountaintops, under every green tree, and under every thick oak, wherever they offered sweet incense to all their idols.

Hos 4:13 They offer sacrifices on the mountaintops, And burn incense on the hills, Under oaks, poplars, and terebinths, Because their shade *is* good. Therefore your daughters commit harlotry, And your brides commit adultery.

Absalom in his flight intercepted by, and suspended from.

2 Sam 18:9–10 Then Absalom met the servants of David. Absalom rode on a mule. The mule went under the thick boughs of a great terebinth tree, and his head caught in the terebinth; so he was left hanging between heaven and earth. And the mule which *was* under him went on. 10 Now a certain man saw *it* and told Joab, and said, "I just saw Absalom hanging in a terebinth tree!"

2 Sam 18:14 Then Joab said, "I cannot linger with you." And he took three spears in his hand and thrust them through Absalom's heart, while he was *still* alive in the midst of the terebinth tree.

Jacob buried his family idols under.

Gen 35:4 So they gave Jacob all the foreign gods which *were* in their hands, and the earrings which *were* in their ears; and Jacob hid them under the terebinth tree which *was* by Shechem.

Illustrative of

The people of God.

Is 6:13 But yet a tenth *will be* in it, And will return and be for consuming, As a terebinth tree or as an oak, Whose stump *remains* when it is cut down. So the holy seed *shall be* its stump."

Strong and powerful men.

Amos 2:9 "Yet *it was* I *who* destroyed the Amorite before them, Whose height *was* like the height of the cedars, And he *was as* strong as the oaks; Yet I destroyed his fruit above And his roots beneath.

Wicked rulers.

Is 2:13 Upon all the cedars of Lebanon *that are* high and lifted up, And upon all the oaks of Bashan;

Zech 11:2 Wail, O cypress, for the cedar has fallen, Because the mighty *trees* are ruined. Wail, O oaks of Bashan, For the thick forest has come down.

(Fading) the wicked under judgments.

Is 1:30 For you shall be as a terebinth whose leaf fades, And as a garden that has no water.

OATHS

The lawful purpose of, explained.

Heb 6:16 For men indeed swear by the greater, and an oath for confirmation *is* for them an end of all dispute.

Antiquity of.

Gen 14:22 But Abram said to the king of Sodom, "I have raised my hand to the LORD, God Most High, the Possessor of heaven and earth,

Gen 24:3 and I will make you swear by the LORD, the God of heaven and the God of the earth, that you will not take a wife for my son from the daughters of the Canaanites, among whom I dwell;

Gen 24:8 And if the woman is not willing to follow you, then you will be released from this oath; only do not take my son back there."

Used for

Confirming covenants.

Gen 26:28 But they said, "We have certainly seen that the LORD is with you. So we said, 'Let there now be an oath between us, between you and us; and let us make a covenant with you,

Gen 31:44 Now therefore, come, let us make a covenant, you and I, and let it be a witness between you and me."

Gen 31:53 The God of Abraham, the God of Nahor, and the God of their father judge between us." And Jacob swore by the Fear of his father Isaac.

1 Sam 20:16–17 So Jonathan made *a covenant* with the house of David, *saying,* "Let the LORD require *it* at the hand of David's enemies." **17** Now Jonathan again caused David to vow, because he loved him; for he loved him as he loved his own soul.

Deciding controversies in courts of law.

Ex 22:11 *then* an oath of the LORD shall be between them both, that he has not put his hand into his neighbor's

goods; and the owner of it shall accept *that,* and he shall not make *it* good.

Num 5:19 And the priest shall put her under oath, and say to the woman, "If no man has lain with you, and if you have not gone astray to uncleanness *while* under your husband's *authority,* be free from this bitter water that brings a curse.

1 Kin 8:31 "When anyone sins against his neighbor, and is forced to take an oath, and comes *and* takes an oath before Your altar in this temple,

Pledging allegiance to sovereigns.

2 Kin 11:4 In the seventh year Jehoiada sent and brought the captains of hundreds—of the bodyguards and the escorts—and brought them into the house of the LORD to him. And he made a covenant with them and took an oath from them in the house of the LORD, and showed them the king's son.

Eccl 8:2 I *say,* "Keep the king's commandment for the sake of your oath to God.

Binding to performance of sacred duties.

Num 30:2 If a man makes a vow to the LORD, or swears an oath to bind himself by some agreement, he shall not break his word; he shall do according to all that proceeds out of his mouth.

2 Chr 15:14–15 Then they took an oath before the LORD with a loud voice, with shouting and trumpets and rams' horns. **15** And all Judah rejoiced at the oath, for they had sworn with all their heart and sought Him with all their soul; and He was found by them, and the LORD gave them rest all around.

Neh 10:29 these joined with their brethren, their nobles, and entered into a curse and an oath to walk in God's Law, which was given by Moses the servant of God, and to observe and do all the commandments of the LORD our Lord, and His ordinances and His statutes:

Ps 132:2 How he swore to the LORD, *And* vowed to the Mighty One of Jacob:

Binding to performance of any particular act.

Gen 24:3–4 and I will make you swear by the LORD, the God of heaven and the God of the earth, that you will not take a wife for my son from the daughters of the Canaanites, among whom I dwell; **4** but you shall go to my country and to my family, and take a wife for my son Isaac."

Gen 50:25 Then Joseph took an oath from the children of Israel, saying, "God will surely visit you, and you shall carry up my bones from here."

Josh 2:12 Now therefore, I beg you, swear to me by the LORD, since I have shown you kindness, that you also will show kindness to my father's house, and give me a true token,

Judicial form of administering.

1 Kin 22:16 So the king said to him, "How many times shall I make you swear that you tell me nothing but the truth in the name of the LORD?"

Matt 26:63 But Jesus kept silent. And the high priest answered and said to Him, "I put You under oath by the living God: Tell us if You are the Christ, the Son of God!"

With raising up of the hand.

Gen 14:22 But Abram said to the king of Sodom, "I have

raised my hand to the LORD, God Most High, the Possessor of heaven and earth,

Dan 12:7 Then I heard the man clothed in linen, who *was* above the waters of the river, when he held up his right hand and his left hand to heaven, and swore by Him who lives forever, that *it shall be* for a time, times, and half *a time;* and when the power of the holy people has been completely shattered, all these *things* shall be finished.

Rev 10:5–6 The angel whom I saw standing on the sea and on the land raised up his hand to heaven **6** and swore by Him who lives forever and ever, who created heaven and the things that are in it, the earth and the things that are in it, and the sea and the things that are in it, that there should be delay no longer,

With placing the hand under the thigh of recipient.

Gen 24:2 So Abraham said to the oldest servant of his house, who ruled over all that he had, "Please, put your hand under my thigh,

Gen 24:9 So the servant put his hand under the thigh of Abraham his master, and swore to him concerning this matter.

Gen 47:29 When the time drew near that Israel must die, he called his son Joseph and said to him, "Now if I have found favor in your sight, please put your hand under my thigh, and deal kindly and truly with me. Please do not bury me in Egypt,

To be taken in fear and reverence.

Eccl 9:2 All things *come* alike to all: One event *happens* to the righteous and the wicked; To the good, the clean, and the unclean; To him who sacrifices and him who does not sacrifice. As is the good, so *is* the sinner; He who takes an oath as *he* who fears an oath.

The Jews

Forbidden to take, in name of idols.

Josh 23:7 *and* lest you go among these nations, these who remain among you. You shall not make mention of the name of their gods, nor cause *anyone* to swear *by them;* you shall not serve them nor bow down to them,

Forbidden to take, in the name of any created thing.

Matt 5:34–36 But I say to you, do not swear at all: neither by heaven, for it is God's throne; **35** nor by the earth, for it is His footstool; nor by Jerusalem, for it is the city of the great King. **36** Nor shall you swear by your head, because you cannot make one hair white or black.

James 5:12 But above all, my brethren, do not swear, either by heaven or by earth or with any other oath. But let your "Yes" be "Yes," and *your* "No," "No," lest you fall into judgment.

Forbidden to take false.

Lev 6:3 or if he has found what was lost and lies concerning it, and swears falsely—in any one of these things that a man may do in which he sins:

Zech 8:17 Let none of you think evil in your heart against your neighbor; And do not love a false oath. For all these *are things* that I hate,' Says the LORD."

Forbidden to take rash, or unholy.

Lev 5:4 'Or if a person swears, speaking thoughtlessly with *his* lips to do evil or to do good, whatever *it is* that a man may pronounce by an oath, and he is unaware of it—when he realizes *it,* then he shall be guilty in any of these *matters.*

To use God's name alone in.

Deut 6:13 You shall fear the LORD your God and serve Him, and shall take oaths in His name.

Deut 10:20 You shall fear the LORD your God; you shall serve Him, and to Him you shall hold fast, and take oaths in His name.

Is 65:16 So that he who blesses himself in the earth Shall bless himself in the God of truth; And he who swears in the earth Shall swear by the God of truth; Because the former troubles are forgotten, And because they are hidden from My eyes.

To take, in truth, judgment, etc.

Jer 4:2 And you shall swear, 'The LORD lives,' In truth, in judgment, and in righteousness; The nations shall bless themselves in Him, And in Him they shall glory."

Generally respected the obligation of.

Josh 9:19–20 Then all the rulers said to all the congregation, "We have sworn to them by the LORD God of Israel; now therefore, we may not touch them. **20** This we will do to them: We will let them live, lest wrath be upon us because of the oath which we swore to them."

2 Sam 21:7 But the king spared Mephibosheth the son of Jonathan, the son of Saul, because of the LORD's oath that *was* between them, between David and Jonathan the son of Saul.

Ps 15:4 In whose eyes a vile person is despised, But he honors those who fear the LORD; He *who* swears to his own hurt and does not change;

Matt 14:9 And the king was sorry; nevertheless, because of the oaths and because of those who sat with him, he commanded *it* to be given to *her.*

Fell into many errors respecting.

Matt 23:16–22 "Woe to you, blind guides, who say, 'Whoever swears by the temple, it is nothing; but whoever swears by the gold of the temple, he is obliged *to perform it.'* **17** Fools and blind! For which is greater, the gold or the temple that sanctifies the gold? **18** And, 'Whoever swears by the altar, it is nothing; but whoever swears by the gift that is on it, he is obliged *to perform it.'* **19** Fools and blind! For which is greater, the gift or the altar that sanctifies the gift? **20** Therefore he who swears by the altar, swears by it and by all things on it. **21** He who swears by the temple, swears by it and by Him who dwells in it. **22** And he who swears by heaven, swears by the throne of God and by Him who sits on it.

Often guilty of rashly taking.

Judg 21:7 What shall we do for wives for those who remain, seeing we have sworn by the LORD that we will not give them our daughters as wives?"

Matt 14:7 Therefore he promised with an oath to give her whatever she might ask.

Matt 26:72 But again he denied with an oath, "I do not know the Man!"

Often guilty of falsely taking.

Lev 6:3 or if he has found what was lost and lies concerning it, and swears falsely—in any one of these things that a man may do in which he sins:

Jer 5:2 Though they say, '*As* the LORD lives,' Surely they swear falsely."

Jer 7:9 Will you steal, murder, commit adultery, swear falsely, burn incense to Baal, and walk after other gods whom you do not know,

Condemned for false.

Zech 5:4 "I will send out *the curse*," says the LORD of hosts; "It shall enter the house of the thief And the house of the one who swears falsely by My name. It shall remain in the midst of his house And consume it, with its timber and stones."

Mal 3:5 And I will come near you for judgment; I will be a swift witness Against sorcerers, Against adulterers, Against perjurers, Against those who exploit wage earners and widows and orphans, And against those who turn away an alien— Because they do not fear Me," Says the LORD of hosts.

Condemned for profane.

Jer 23:10 For the land is full of adulterers; For because of a curse the land mourns. The pleasant places of the wilderness are dried up. Their course of life is evil, And their might *is* not right.

Hos 4:2 *By* swearing and lying, Killing and stealing and committing adultery, They break all restraint, With bloodshed upon bloodshed.

Instances of rash,

Joshua and rulers.

Josh 9:15–16 So Joshua made peace with them, and made a covenant with them to let them live; and the rulers of the congregation swore to them. 16 And it happened at the end of three days, after they had made a covenant with them, that they heard that they *were* their neighbors who dwelt near them.

Jephthah.

Judg 11:30–36 And Jephthah made a vow to the LORD, and said, "If You will indeed deliver the people of Ammon into my hands, 31 then it will be that whatever comes out of the doors of my house to meet me, when I return in peace from the people of Ammon, shall surely be the LORD's, and I will offer it up as a burnt offering." 32 So Jephthah advanced toward the people of Ammon to fight against them, and the LORD delivered them into his hands. 33 And he defeated them from Aroer as far as Minnith—twenty cities— and to Abel Keramim, with a very great slaughter. Thus the people of Ammon were subdued before the children of Israel. 34 When Jephthah came to his house at Mizpah, there was his daughter, coming out to meet him with timbrels and dancing; and she *was* his only child. Besides her he had neither son nor daughter. 35 And it came to pass, when he saw her, that he tore his clothes, and said, "Alas, my daughter! You have brought me very low! You are among those who trouble me! For I have given my word to the LORD, and I cannot go back on it." 36 So she said to him, "My father, *if* you have given your word to the LORD, do to me according to what has gone out of your mouth, because the LORD has avenged you of your enemies, the people of Ammon."

Saul.

1 Sam 14:27 But Jonathan had not heard his father charge the people with the oath; therefore he stretched out the end of the rod that *was* in his hand and dipped it in a honeycomb, and put his hand to his mouth; and his countenance brightened.

1 Sam 14:44 Saul answered, "God do so and more also; for you shall surely die, Jonathan."

Herod.

Matt 14:7–9 Therefore he promised with an oath to give her whatever she might ask. 8 So she, having been prompted by her mother, said, "Give me John the Baptist's head here on a platter." 9 And the king was sorry; nevertheless, because of the oaths and because of those who sat with him, he commanded *it* to be given to *her.*

The Jews who sought to kill Paul.

Acts 23:21 But do not yield to them, for more than forty of them lie in wait for him, men who have bound themselves by an oath that they will neither eat nor drink till they have killed him; and now they are ready, waiting for the promise from you."

Custom of swearing, by the life of the king.

Gen 42:15–16 In this *manner* you shall be tested: By the life of Pharaoh, you shall not leave this place unless your youngest brother comes here. 16 Send one of you, and let him bring your brother; and you shall be kept in prison, that your words may be tested to see whether *there is* any truth in you; or else, by the life of Pharaoh, surely you *are* spies!"

Expressions used as,

By the fear of Isaac.

Gen 31:53 The God of Abraham, the God of Nahor, and the God of their father judge between us." And Jacob swore by the Fear of his father Isaac.

As the Lord lives.

Judg 8:19 Then he said, "They *were* my brothers, the sons of my mother. *As* the LORD lives, if you had let them live, I would not kill you."

Ruth 3:13 Stay this night, and in the morning it shall be *that* if he will perform the duty of a close relative for you—good; let him do it. But if he does not want to perform the duty for you, then I will perform the duty for you, *as* the LORD lives! Lie down until morning."

The Lord do so to me, and more also.

Ruth 1:17 Where you die, I will die, And there will I be buried. The LORD do so to me, and more also, If *anything but* death parts you and me."

God do so to you, and more also.

1 Sam 3:17 And he said, "What *is* the word that *the* LORD spoke to you? Please do not hide *it* from me. God do so to you, and more also, if you hide anything from me of all the things that He said to you."

By the Lord.

2 Sam 19:7 Now therefore, arise, go out and speak comfort to your servants. For I swear by the LORD, if you do not go out, not one will stay with you this night. And that will be worse for you than all the evil that has befallen you from your youth until now."

1 Kin 2:42 Then the king sent and called for Shimei, and said to him, "Did I not make you swear by the LORD, and warn you, saying, 'Know for certain that on the day you go out and travel anywhere, you shall surely die'? And you said to me, 'The word I have heard *is* good.'

Before God I do not lie.

Gal 1:20 (Now *concerning* the things which I write to you, indeed, before God, I do not lie.)

I call God as witness.

2 Cor 1:23 Moreover I call God as witness against my soul, that to spare you I came no more to Corinth.

God is witness.

1 Thess 2:5 For neither at any time did we use flattering words, as you know, nor a cloak for covetousness— God *is* witness.

I charge you by the Lord.

1 Thess 5:27 I charge you by the Lord that this epistle be read to all the holy brethren.

As your soul lives.

1 Sam 1:26 And she said, "O my lord! As your soul lives, my lord, I *am* the woman who stood by you here, praying to the LORD.

1 Sam 25:26 Now therefore, my lord, *as* the LORD lives and *as* your soul lives, since the LORD has held you back from coming to bloodshed and from avenging yourself with your own hand, now then, let your enemies and those who seek harm for my lord be as Nabal.

God used, to show the immutability of His counsel.

Gen 22:16 and said: "By Myself I have sworn, says the LORD, because you have done this thing, and have not withheld your son, your only *son*—

Num 6:17 and he shall offer the ram as a sacrifice of a peace offering to the LORD, with the basket of unleavened bread; the priest shall also offer its grain offering and its drink offering.

Num 14:28 Say to them, 'As I live,' says the LORD, 'just as you have spoken in My hearing, so I will do to you:

OBEDIENCE TO GOD

Commanded.

Deut 13:4 You shall walk after the LORD your God and fear Him, and keep His commandments and obey His voice; you shall serve Him and hold fast to Him.

Without faith, is impossible.

Heb 11:6 But without faith *it is* impossible to please *Him*, for he who comes to God must believe that He is, and *that* He is a rewarder of those who diligently seek Him.

Includes

Obeying His voice.

Ex 19:5 Now therefore, if you will indeed obey My voice and keep My covenant, then you shall be a special treasure to Me above all people; for all the earth *is* Mine.

Jer 7:23 But this is what I commanded them, saying, 'Obey My voice, and I will be your God, and you shall be My people. And walk in all the ways that I have commanded you, that it may be well with you.'

Obeying His law.

Deut 11:27 the blessing, if you obey the commandments of the LORD your God which I command you today;

Is 42:24 Who gave Jacob for plunder, and Israel to the robbers? Was it not the LORD, He against whom we have sinned? For they would not walk in His ways, Nor were they obedient to His law.

Obeying Christ.

Ex 23:21 Beware of Him and obey His voice; do not provoke Him, for He will not pardon your transgressions; for My name *is* in Him.

2 Cor 10:5 casting down arguments and every high thing that exalts itself against the knowledge of God, bringing every thought into captivity to the obedience of Christ,

Obeying the gospel.

Rom 1:5 Through Him we have received grace and apostleship for obedience to the faith among all nations for His name,

Rom 6:17 But God be thanked that *though* you were slaves of sin, yet you obeyed from the heart that form of doctrine to which you were delivered.

Rom 10:16–17 But they have not all obeyed the gospel. For Isaiah says, *"LORD, who has believed our report?"* **17** So then faith *comes* by hearing, and hearing by the word of God.

Keeping His commandments.

Eccl 12:13 Let us hear the conclusion of the whole matter: Fear God and keep His commandments, For this is man's all.

Submission to higher powers.

Rom 13:1 Let every soul be subject to the governing authorities. For there is no authority except from God, and the authorities that exist are appointed by God.

Better than sacrifice.

1 Sam 15:22 So Samuel said: "Has the LORD *as great* delight in burnt offerings and sacrifices, As in obeying the voice of the LORD? Behold, to obey is better than sacrifice, *And* to heed than the fat of rams.

Justification obtained by that of Christ.

Rom 5:19 For as by one man's disobedience many were made sinners, so also by one Man's obedience many will be made righteous.

Christ, an example of.

Matt 3:15 But Jesus answered and said to him, "Permit *it to be so* now, for thus it is fitting for us to fulfill all righteousness." Then he allowed Him.

John 15:20 Remember the word that I said to you, 'A servant is not greater than his master.' If they persecuted Me, they will also persecute you. If they kept My word, they will keep yours also.

Phil 2:5–8 Let this mind be in you which was also in Christ Jesus, **6** who, being in the form of God, did not consider it robbery to be equal with God, **7** but made Himself of no reputation, taking the form of a bondservant, *and* coming in the likeness of men. **8** And being found in appearance as a man, He humbled Himself and became obedient to *the point of* death, even the death of the cross.

Heb 5:8 though He was a Son, *yet* He learned obedience by the things which He suffered.

Angels engaged in.

Ps 103:20 Bless the LORD, you His angels, Who excel in strength, who do His word, Heeding the voice of His word.

A characteristic of believers.

1 Pet 1:2 elect according to the foreknowledge of God the Father, in sanctification of the Spirit, for obedience and sprinkling of the blood of Jesus Christ: Grace to you and peace be multiplied.

1 Pet 1:14 as obedient children, not conforming yourselves to the former lusts, *as* in your ignorance;

Obligations to.

Acts 4:19–20 But Peter and John answered and said to them, "Whether it is right in the sight of God to listen to you more than to God, you judge. **20** For we cannot but speak the things which we have seen and heard."

Acts 5:29 But Peter and the *other* apostles answered and said: "We ought to obey God rather than men.

Exhortations to.

Jer 26:13 Now therefore, amend your ways and your doings, and obey the voice of the LORD your God; then the LORD will relent concerning the doom that He has pronounced against you.

Jer 38:20 But Jeremiah said, "They shall not deliver *you.* Please, obey the voice of the LORD which I speak to you. So it shall be well with you, and your soul shall live.

Should be

From the heart.

Deut 11:13 'And it shall be that if you earnestly obey My commandments which I command you today, to love the LORD your God and serve Him with all your heart and with all your soul,

1 Sam 7:3 Then Samuel spoke to all the house of Israel, saying, "If you return to the LORD with all your hearts, *then* put away the foreign gods and the Ashtoreths from among you, and prepare your hearts for the LORD, and serve Him only; and He will deliver you from the hand of the Philistines."

Ezra 7:10 For Ezra had prepared his heart to seek the Law of the LORD, and to do *it,* and to teach statutes and ordinances in Israel.

Rom 6:17 But God be thanked that *though* you were slaves of sin, yet you obeyed from the heart that form of doctrine to which you were delivered.

With willingness.

Ps 18:44 As soon as they hear of me they obey me; The foreigners submit to me.

Is 1:19 If you are willing and obedient, You shall eat the good of the land;

Unreserved.

Josh 22:2–3 and said to them: "You have kept all that Moses the servant of the LORD commanded you, and have obeyed my voice in all that I commanded you. **3** You have not left your brethren these many days, up to this day, but have kept the charge of the commandment of the LORD your God.

With resolve.

Ex 24:7 Then he took the Book of the Covenant and read

in the hearing of the people. And they said, "All that the LORD has said we will do, and be obedient."

Deut 28:14 So you shall not turn aside from any of the words which I command you this day, *to* the right or the left, to go after other gods to serve them.

Josh 24:24 And the people said to Joshua, "The LORD our God we will serve, and His voice we will obey!"

Phil 2:12 Therefore, my beloved, as you have always obeyed, not as in my presence only, but now much more in my absence, work out your own salvation with fear and trembling;

Confess your failure in.

Dan 9:10 We have not obeyed the voice of the LORD our God, to walk in His laws, which He set before us by His servants the prophets.

Pray to be taught.

Ps 119:35 Make me walk in the path of Your commandments, For I delight in it.

Ps 143:10 Teach me to do Your will, For You *are* my God; Your Spirit *is* good. Lead me in the land of uprightness.

Promises regarding.

Ex 23:22 But if you indeed obey His voice and do all that I speak, then I will be an enemy to your enemies and an adversary to your adversaries.

1 Sam 12:14 If you fear the LORD and serve Him and obey His voice, and do not rebel against the commandment of the LORD, then both you and the king who reigns over you will continue following the LORD your God.

Is 1:19 If you are willing and obedient, You shall eat the good of the land;

Jer 7:23 But this is what I commanded them, saying, 'Obey My voice, and I will be your God, and you shall be My people. And walk in all the ways that I have commanded you, that it may be well with you.'

To be universal in the latter days.

Dan 7:27 Then the kingdom and dominion, And the greatness of the kingdoms under the whole heaven, Shall be given to the people, the saints of the Most High. His kingdom *is* an everlasting kingdom, And all dominions shall serve and obey Him.'

Blessedness of.

Deut 11:27 the blessing, if you obey the commandments of the LORD your God which I command you today;

Luke 11:28 But He said, "More than that, blessed *are* those who hear the word of God and keep it!"

James 1:25 But he who looks into the perfect law of liberty and continues *in it,* and is not a forgetful hearer but a doer of the work, this one will be blessed in what he does.

Cf. Deut 28:1–13

The wicked refuse.

Ex 5:2 And Pharaoh said, "Who *is* the LORD, that I should obey His voice to let Israel go? I do not know the LORD, nor will I let Israel go."

Neh 9:17 They refused to obey, And they were not mindful of Your wonders That You did among them. But they hardened their necks, And in their rebellion They appointed a leader To return to their bondage. But You *are* God, Ready to pardon, Gracious and merciful, Slow to anger, Abundant in kindness, And did not forsake them.

Punishment for refusing.

Deut 11:28 and the curse, if you do not obey the commandments of the LORD your God, but turn aside from the way which I command you today, to go after other gods which you have not known.

Josh 5:6 For the children of Israel walked forty years in the wilderness, till all the people *who were* men of war, who came out of Egypt, were consumed, because they did not obey the voice of the LORD—to whom the LORD swore that He would not show them the land which the LORD had sworn to their fathers that He would give us, "a land flowing with milk and honey."

Is 1:20 But if you refuse and rebel, You shall be devoured by the sword"; For the mouth of the LORD has spoken.

Cf. Is 28:15–68

Exemplified by

Noah.

Gen 6:22 Thus Noah did; according to all that God commanded him, so he did.

Abraham (Abram).

Gen 12:1–4 Now the LORD had said to Abram: "Get out of your country, From your family And from your father's house, To a land that I will show you. 2 I will make you a great nation; I will bless you And make your name great; And you shall be a blessing. 3 I will bless those who bless you, And I will curse him who curses you; And in you all the families of the earth shall be blessed." 4 So Abram departed as the LORD had spoken to him, and Lot went with him. And Abram *was* seventy-five years old when he departed from Haran.

Gen 22:3 So Abraham rose early in the morning and saddled his donkey, and took two of his young men with him, and Isaac his son; and he split the wood for the burnt offering, and arose and went to the place of which God had told him.

Gen 22:12 And He said, "Do not lay your hand on the lad, or do anything to him; for now I know that you fear God, since you have not withheld your son, your only *son*, from Me."

Heb 11:8 By faith Abraham obeyed when he was called to go out to the place which he would receive as an inheritance. And he went out, not knowing where he was going.

Israelites.

Ex 12:28 Then the children of Israel went away and did *so;* just as the LORD had commanded Moses and Aaron, so they did.

Ex 24:7 Then he took the Book of the Covenant and read in the hearing of the people. And they said, "All that the LORD has said we will do, and be obedient."

Caleb, etc.

Num 32:12 except Caleb the son of Jephunneh, the Kenizzite, and Joshua the son of Nun, for they have wholly followed the LORD.'

Asa.

1 Kin 15:11 Asa did *what was* right in the eyes of the LORD, as *did* his father David.

Elijah.

1 Kin 17:5 So he went and did according to the word of the LORD, for he went and stayed by the Brook Cherith, which flows into the Jordan.

Hezekiah.

2 Kin 18:6 For he held fast to the LORD; he did not depart from following Him, but kept His commandments, which the LORD had commanded Moses.

Josiah.

2 Kin 22:2 And he did *what was* right in the sight of the LORD, and walked in all the ways of his father David; he did not turn aside to the right hand or to the left.

David.

Ps 119:106 I have sworn and confirmed That I will keep Your righteous judgments.

Zerubbabel.

Hag 1:12 Then Zerubbabel the son of Shealtiel, and Joshua the son of Jehozadak, the high priest, with all the remnant of the people, obeyed the voice of the LORD their God, and the words of Haggai the prophet, as the LORD their God had sent him; and the people feared the presence of the LORD.

Joseph.

Matt 1:24 Then Joseph, being aroused from sleep, did as the angel of the Lord commanded him and took to him his wife,

The wise men.

Matt 2:12 Then, being divinely warned in a dream that they should not return to Herod, they departed for their own country another way.

Zacharias, etc.

Luke 1:6 And they were both righteous before God, walking in all the commandments and ordinances of the Lord blameless.

Paul.

Acts 26:19 "Therefore, King Agrippa, I was not disobedient to the heavenly vision,

The believers of Rome.

Rom 16:19 For your obedience has become known to all. Therefore I am glad on your behalf; but I want you to be wise in what is good, and simple concerning evil.

OCCULT, THE

Forbidden by God.

Ex 22:18 "You shall not permit a sorceress to live.

Lev 19:31 'Give no regard to mediums and familiar spirits; do not seek after them, to be defiled by them: I *am* the LORD your God.

Lev 20:6 'And the person who turns to mediums and familiar spirits, to prostitute himself with them, I will set My face against that person and cut him off from his people.

Lev 20:27 'A man or a woman who is a medium, or who has familiar spirits, shall surely be put to death; they shall stone them with stones. Their blood *shall be* upon them.' "

Deut 18:10–12 There shall not be found among you *any-one* who makes his son or his daughter pass through the fire, *or one* who practices witchcraft, *or* a sooth-sayer, or one who interprets omens, or a sorcerer, **11** or one who conjures spells, or a medium, or a spiritist, or one who calls up the dead. **12** For all who do these things *are* an abomination to the LORD, and because of these abominations the LORD your God drives them out from before you.

Jer 27:9–10 Therefore do not listen to your prophets, your diviners, your dreamers, your soothsayers, or your sorcerers, who speak to you, saying, "You shall not serve the king of Babylon." **10** For they prophesy a lie to you, to remove you far from your land; and I will drive you out, and you will perish.

Cf. Mal 3:5; Gal 5:20; Rev 9:20–21

Practiced by

Simon of Samaria.

Acts 8:9–10 But there was a certain man called Simon, who previously practiced sorcery in the city and as-tonished the people of Samaria, claiming that he was someone great, **10** to whom they all gave heed, from the least to the greatest, saying, "This man is the great power of God."

Cf. Acts 13:6

King Saul. **1 Sam 28:3–15**

OFFENSE

Occasions of, will arise.

Matt 18:7 Woe to the world because of offenses! For of-fenses must come, but woe to that man by whom the offense comes!

Occasions of, forbidden.

1 Cor 10:32 Give no offense, either to the Jews or to the Greeks or to the church of God,

2 Cor 6:3 We give no offense in anything, that our min-istry may not be blamed.

Persecution is a cause of, to merely professing believers.

Matt 13:21 yet he has no root in himself, but endures only for a while. For when tribulation or persecution arises because of the word, immediately he stumbles.

Matt 24:10 And then many will be offended, will betray one another, and will hate one another.

Matt 26:31 Then Jesus said to them, "All of you will be made to stumble because of Me this night, for it is written: *'I will strike the Shepherd, And the sheep of the flock will be scattered.'*

Causes of, for unbelievers

The lowliness of Christ.

Is 53:1–3 Who has believed our report? And to whom has the arm of the LORD been revealed? **2** For He shall grow up before Him as a tender plant, And as a root out of dry ground. He has no form or comeli-ness; And when we see Him, *There is* no beauty that we should desire Him. **3** He is despised and rejected by men, A Man of sorrows and acquainted with grief. And we hid, as it were, *our* faces from Him; He was despised, and we did not esteem Him.

Matt 13:54–57 When He had come to His own country, He taught them in their synagogue, so that they were

astonished and said, "Where did this *Man* get this wisdom and *these* mighty works? **55** Is this not the carpenter's son? Is not His mother called Mary? And His brothers James, Joses, Simon, and Judas? **56** And His sisters, are they not all with us? Where then did this *Man* get all these things?" **57** So they were of-fended at Him. But Jesus said to them, "A prophet is not without honor except in his own country and in his own house."

Christ as a stumbling stone.

Is 8:14 He will be as a sanctuary, But a stone of stum-bling and a rock of offense To both the houses of Is-rael, As a trap and a snare to the inhabitants of Jerusalem.

Rom 9:33 As it is written: *"Behold, I lay in Zion a stum-bling stone and rock of offense, And whoever be-lieves on Him will not be put to shame."*

1 Pet 2:8 and *"A stone of stumbling And a rock of of-fense."* They stumble, being disobedient to the word, to which they also were appointed.

Christ as the bread of life.

John 6:58–61 This is the bread which came down from heaven—not as your fathers ate the manna, and are dead. He who eats this bread will live forever." **59** These things He said in the synagogue as He taught in Capernaum. **60** Therefore many of His dis-ciples, when they heard *this,* said, "This is a hard say-ing; who can understand it?" **61** When Jesus knew in Himself that His disciples complained about this, He said to them, "Does this offend you?

Christ crucified.

1 Cor 1:23 but we preach Christ crucified, to the Jews a stumbling block and to the Greeks foolishness,

Gal 5:11 And I, brethren, if I still preach circumcision, why do I still suffer persecution? Then the offense of the cross has ceased.

The righteousness of faith.

Rom 9:32 Why? Because *they did* not *seek it* by faith, but as it were, by the works of the law. For they stumbled at that stumbling stone.

The necessity of inward purity.

Matt 15:11–12 Not what goes into the mouth defiles a man; but what comes out of the mouth, this defiles a man." **12** Then His disciples came and said to Him, "Do You know that the Pharisees were offended when they heard this saying?"

Blessedness of not taking, at Christ.

Matt 11:6 And blessed is he who is not offended be-cause of Me."

Believers should

Be without.

John 16:1 "These things I have spoken to you, that you should not be made to stumble.

Phil 1:10 that you may approve the things that are ex-cellent, that you may be sincere and without offense till the day of Christ,

Be cautious of giving.

Ps 73:15 If I had said, "I will speak thus," Behold, I would have been untrue to the generation of Your children.

Rom 14:13 Therefore let us not judge one another anymore, but rather resolve this, not to put a stumbling block or a cause to fall in *our* brother's way.

1 Cor 8:9 But beware lest somehow this liberty of yours become a stumbling block to those who are weak.

Have a conscience void of.

Acts 24:16 This *being* so, I myself always strive to have a conscience without offense toward God and men.

Cut off what causes, to themselves.

Matt 5:29–30 If your right eye causes you to sin, pluck it out and cast *it* from you; for it is more profitable for you that one of your members perish, than for your whole body to be cast into hell. **30** And if your right hand causes you to sin, cut it off and cast *it* from you; for it is more profitable for you that one of your members perish, than for your whole body to be cast into hell.

Mark 9:43–47 If your hand causes you to sin, cut it off. It is better for you to enter into life maimed, rather than having two hands, to go to hell, into the fire that shall never be quenched— **44** where *'Their worm does not die And the fire is not quenched.'* **45** And if your foot causes you to sin, cut it off. It is better for you to enter life lame, rather than having two feet, to be cast into hell, into the fire that shall never be quenched— **46** where *'Their worm does not die And the fire is not quenched.'* **47** And if your eye causes you to sin, pluck it out. It is better for you to enter the kingdom of God with one eye, rather than having two eyes, to be cast into hell fire—

Not let their liberty cause for others.

1 Cor 8:9 But beware lest somehow this liberty of yours become a stumbling block to those who are weak.

Use self-denial rather than cause.

Rom 14:21 *It is* good neither to eat meat nor drink wine nor *do anything* by which your brother stumbles or is offended or is made weak.

1 Cor 8:13 Therefore, if food makes my brother stumble, I will never again eat meat, lest I make my brother stumble.

Avoid those who cause.

Rom 16:17 Now I urge you, brethren, note those who cause divisions and offenses, contrary to the doctrine which you learned, and avoid them.

Reprove those who cause.

Ex 32:21 And Moses said to Aaron, "What did this people do to you that you have brought *so* great a sin upon them?"

1 Sam 2:24 No, my sons! For *it is* not a good report that I hear. You make the LORD's people transgress.

Ministers should

Be cautious of giving.

2 Cor 6:3 We give no offense in anything, that our ministry may not be blamed.

Remove that which causes.

Is 57:14 And one shall say, "Heap it up! Heap it up! Prepare the way, Take the stumbling block out of the way of My people."

Punishment because of.

Ezek 44:12 Because they ministered to them before their idols and caused the house of Israel to fall into iniquity, therefore I have raised My hand in an oath

against them," says the Lord GOD, "that they shall bear their iniquity.

Mal 2:8–9 But you have departed from the way; You have caused many to stumble at the law. You have corrupted the covenant of Levi," Says the LORD of hosts. **9** "Therefore I also have made you contemptible and base Before all the people, Because you have not kept My ways But have shown partiality in the law."

Matt 13:41 The Son of Man will send out His angels, and they will gather out of His kingdom all things that offend, and those who practice lawlessness,

Matt 18:6–7 "Whoever causes one of these little ones who believe in Me to sin, it would be better for him if a millstone were hung around his neck, and he were drowned in the depth of the sea. **7** Woe to the world because of offenses! For offenses must come, but woe to that man by whom the offense comes!

Denunciation against those who cause.

Matt 18:7 Woe to the world because of offenses! For offenses must come, but woe to that man by whom the offense comes!

Mark 9:42 "But whoever causes one of these little ones who believe in Me to stumble, it would be better for him if a millstone were hung around his neck, and he were thrown into the sea.

Demonstrated by

Aaron.

Ex 32:2–6 And Aaron said to them, "Break off the golden earrings which *are* in the ears of your wives, your sons, and your daughters, and bring *them* to me." **3** So all the people broke off the golden earrings which *were* in their ears, and brought *them* to Aaron. **4** And he received *the gold* from their hand, and he fashioned it with an engraving tool, and made a molded calf. Then they said, "This *is* your god, O Israel, that brought you out of the land of Egypt!" **5** So when Aaron saw *it*, he built an altar before it. And Aaron made a proclamation and said, "Tomorrow *is* a feast to the LORD." **6** Then they rose early on the next day, offered burnt offerings, and brought peace offerings; and the people sat down to eat and drink, and rose up to play.

Balaam, etc.

Num 31:16 Look, these *women* caused the children of Israel, through the counsel of Balaam, to trespass against the LORD in the incident of Peor, and there was a plague among the congregation of the LORD.

Rev 2:14 But I have a few things against you, because you have there those who hold the doctrine of Balaam, who taught Balak to put a stumbling block before the children of Israel, to eat things sacrificed to idols, and to commit sexual immorality.

Gideon.

Judg 8:27 Then Gideon made it into an ephod and set it up in his city, Ophrah. And all Israel played the harlot with it there. It became a snare to Gideon and to his house.

Sons of Eli.

1 Sam 2:12–17 Now the sons of Eli *were* corrupt; they did not know the LORD. **13** And the priests' custom with the people *was that* when any man offered a sacrifice, the priest's servant would come with a three-pronged fleshhook in his hand while the meat was boiling. **14** Then he would thrust *it* into the pan, or kettle, or caldron, or pot; and the priest would take for himself all that the fleshhook brought up. So they did in Shiloh to all the Israelites who came there. **15** Also, before they burned the fat, the priest's servant would come and say to the man who sacrificed, "Give meat for roasting to the priest, for he will not take boiled meat from you, but raw." **16** And *if* the man said to him, "They should really burn the fat first; *then* you may take *as much* as your heart desires," he would then answer him, "*No,* but you must give *it* now; and if not, I will take *it* by force." **17** Therefore the sin of the young men was very great before the LORD, for men abhorred the offering of the LORD.

Jeroboam.

1 Kin 12:26–30 And Jeroboam said in his heart, "Now the kingdom may return to the house of David: **27** If these people go up to offer sacrifices in the house of the LORD at Jerusalem, then the heart of this people will turn back to their lord, Rehoboam king of Judah, and they will kill me and go back to Rehoboam king of Judah." **28** Therefore the king asked advice, made two calves of gold, and said to the people, "It is too much for you to go up to Jerusalem. Here are your gods, O Israel, which brought you up from the land of Egypt!" **29** And he set up one in Bethel, and the other he put in Dan. **30** Now this thing became a sin, for the people went *to worship* before the one as far as Dan.

A prophet.

1 Kin 13:18–26 He said to him, "I too *am* a prophet as you *are,* and an angel spoke to me by the word of the LORD, saying, 'Bring him back with you to your house, that he may eat bread and drink water.' " (He was lying to him.) **19** So he went back with him, and ate bread in his house, and drank water. **20** Now it happened, as they sat at the table, that the word of the LORD came to the prophet who had brought him back; **21** and he cried out to the man of God who came from Judah, saying, "Thus says the LORD: 'Because you have disobeyed the word of the LORD, and have not kept the commandment which the LORD your God commanded you, **22** but you came back, ate bread, and drank water in the place of which *the* LORD said to you, "Eat no bread and drink no water," your corpse shall not come to the tomb of your fathers.' " **23** So it was, after he had eaten bread and after he had drunk, that he saddled the donkey for him, the prophet whom he had brought back. **24** When he was gone, a lion met him on the road and killed him. And his corpse was thrown on the road, and the donkey stood by it. The lion also stood by the corpse. **25** And there, men passed by and saw the corpse thrown on the road, and the lion standing by the corpse. Then they went and told *it* in the city where the old prophet dwelt. **26** Now when the prophet who had brought him back from the way heard *it,* he said, "It *is* the man of God who was disobedient to the word of the LORD. Therefore the LORD has delivered him to the lion, which has torn him and killed him, according to the word of the LORD which He spoke to him."

Priests.

Mal 2:8 But you have departed from the way; You have caused many to stumble at the law. You have corrupted the covenant of Levi," Says the LORD of hosts.

Peter.

Matt 16:23 But He turned and said to Peter, "Get behind Me, Satan! You are an offense to Me, for you are not mindful of the things of God, but the things of men."

OFFERING

To be made to God alone.

Ex 22:20 "He who sacrifices to *any* god, except to the LORD only, he shall be utterly destroyed.

Judg 13:16 And the Angel of the LORD said to Manoah, "Though you detain Me, I will not eat your food. But if you offer a burnt offering, you must offer it to the LORD." (For Manoah did not know He *was* the Angel of the LORD.)

Antiquity of.

Gen 4:3–4 And in the process of time it came to pass that Cain brought an offering of the fruit of the ground to the LORD. **4** Abel also brought of the firstborn of his flock and of their fat. And the LORD respected Abel and his offering,

Different kinds of,

Burnt.

Ps 66:15 I will offer You burnt sacrifices of fat animals, With the sweet aroma of rams; I will offer bulls with goats. Selah

Cf. Lev 1:3–17

Sin.

Lev 6:25 "Speak to Aaron and to his sons, saying, 'This *is* the law of the sin offering: In the place where the burnt offering is killed, the sin offering shall be killed before the LORD. It *is* most holy.

Lev 10:17 "Why have you not eaten the sin offering in a holy place, since it *is* most holy, and *God* has given it to you to bear the guilt of the congregation, to make atonement for them before the LORD?

Cf. Lev 4:3–35

Trespass.

Lev 5:16–19 And he shall make restitution for the harm that he has done in regard to the holy thing, and shall add one-fifth to it and give it to the priest. So the priest shall make atonement for him with the ram of the trespass offering, and it shall be forgiven him. **17** "If a person sins, and commits any of these things which are forbidden to be done by the commandments of the LORD, though he does not know *it,* yet he is guilty and shall bear his iniquity. **18** And he shall bring to the priest a ram without blemish from the flock, with your valuation, as a trespass offering. So the priest shall make atonement for him regarding his ignorance in which he erred and did not know *it,* and it shall be forgiven him. **19** It is a trespass offering; he has certainly trespassed against the LORD."

Lev 6:6 And he shall bring his trespass offering to the LORD, a ram without blemish from the flock, with your valuation, as a trespass offering, to the priest.

Lev 7:1 'Likewise this *is* the law of the trespass offering (it *is* most holy):

Peace.

Lev 7:11 'This *is* the law of the sacrifice of peace offerings which he shall offer to the LORD:

Cf. Lev 3:1–17

Heave.

Ex 7:14 So the LORD said to Moses: "Pharaoh's heart *is* hard; he refuses to let the people go.

Ex 29:27–28 And from the ram of the consecration you shall consecrate the breast of the wave offering which is waved, and the thigh of the heave offering which is raised, of *that* which *is* for Aaron and of *that* which is for his sons. 28 It shall be from the children of Israel *for* Aaron and his sons by a statute forever. For it is a heave offering; it shall be a heave offering from the children of Israel from the sacrifices of their peace offerings, *that is,* their heave offering to the LORD.

Num 15:19 then it will be, when you eat of the bread of the land, that you shall offer up a heave offering to the LORD.

Wave.

Ex 29:26 "Then you shall take the breast of the ram of Aaron's consecration and wave it *as* a wave offering before the LORD; and it shall be your portion.

Lev 7:30 His own hands shall bring the offerings made by fire to the LORD. The fat with the breast he shall bring, that the breast may be waved *as* a wave offering before the LORD.

Grain.

Num 15:4 then he who presents his offering to the LORD shall bring a grain offering of one-tenth *of an ephah* of fine flour mixed with one-fourth of a hin of oil;

Cf. Lev 2:1–16

Drink.

Gen 35:14 So Jacob set up a pillar in the place where He talked with him, a pillar of stone; and he poured a drink offering on it, and he poured oil on it.

Ex 29:40 With the one lamb shall be one-tenth *of an ephah* of flour mixed with one-fourth of a hin of pressed oil, and one-fourth of a hin of wine *as* a drink offering.

Num 15:5 and one-fourth of a hin of wine as a drink offering you shall prepare with the burnt offering or the sacrifice, for each lamb.

Thanksgiving.

Lev 7:12 If he offers it for a thanksgiving, then he shall offer, with the sacrifice of thanksgiving, unleavened cakes mixed with oil, unleavened wafers anointed with oil, or cakes of blended flour mixed with oil.

Lev 22:29 And when you offer a sacrifice of thanksgiving to the LORD, offer *it* of your own free will.

Ps 50:14 Offer to God thanksgiving, And pay your vows to the Most High.

Freewill.

Lev 23:38 besides the Sabbaths of the LORD, besides your gifts, besides all your vows, and besides all your freewill offerings which you give to the LORD.

Deut 16:10 Then you shall keep the Feast of Weeks to the LORD your God with the tribute of a freewill offering from your hand, which you shall give as the LORD your God blesses you.

Deut 23:23 That which has gone from your lips you shall keep and perform, for you voluntarily vowed to the LORD your God what you have promised with your mouth.

Incense.

Ex 30:8 And when Aaron lights the lamps at twilight, he shall burn incense on it, a perpetual incense before the LORD throughout your generations.

Mal 1:11 For from the rising of the sun, even to its going down, My name *shall be* great among the Gentiles; In every place incense *shall be* offered to My name, And a pure offering; For My name shall be great among the nations," Says the LORD of hosts.

Luke 1:9 according to the custom of the priesthood, his lot fell to burn incense when he went into the temple of the Lord.

Firstfruits.

Ex 22:29 "You shall not delay *to offer* the first of your ripe produce and your juices. The firstborn of your sons you shall give to Me.

Deut 18:4 The firstfruits of your grain and your new wine and your oil, and the first of the fleece of your sheep, you shall give him.

Tithe.

Lev 27:30 And all the tithe of the land, *whether* of the seed of the land *or* of the fruit of the tree, *is* the LORD's. It *is* holy to the LORD.

Num 18:21 "Behold, I have given the children of Levi all the tithes in Israel as an inheritance in return for the work which they perform, the work of the tabernacle of meeting.

Deut 14:22 "You shall truly tithe all the increase of your grain that the field produces year by year.

Gifts for.

Ex 35:22 They came, both men and women, as many as had a willing heart, *and* brought earrings and nose rings, rings and necklaces, all jewelry of gold, that is, every man who *made* an offering of gold to the LORD.

Cf. Num 7:2–88

Jealousy.

Num 5:15 then the man shall bring his wife to the priest. He shall bring the offering required for her, one-tenth of an ephah of barley meal; he shall pour no oil on it and put no frankincense on it, because it *is* a grain offering of jealousy, an offering for remembering, for bringing iniquity to remembrance.

Personal, for redemption.

Ex 30:13 This is what everyone among those who are numbered shall give: half a shekel according to the shekel of the sanctuary (a shekel *is* twenty gerahs). The half-shekel *shall be* an offering to the LORD.

Ex 30:15 The rich shall not give more and the poor shall not give less than half a shekel, when *you* give an offering to the LORD, to make atonement for yourselves.

Declared to be most holy.

Num 18:9 This shall be yours of the most holy things *reserved* from the fire: every offering of theirs, every grain offering and every sin offering and every trespass offering which they render to Me, *shall be* most holy for you and your sons.

Required to be

Perfect.

Lev 22:21 And whoever offers a sacrifice of a peace offering to the LORD, to fulfill *his* vow, or a freewill offering from the cattle or the sheep, it must be perfect
to be accepted; there shall be no defect in it.

The best of their kind.

Mal 1:14 "But cursed *be* the deceiver Who has in his
flock a male, And takes a vow, But sacrifices to the
Lord what is blemished— For I *am* a great King,"
Says the LORD of hosts, "And My name *is to be* feared
among the nations.

Offered willingly.

Lev 22:19 *you shall offer* of your own free will a male
without blemish from the cattle, from the sheep, or
from the goats.

Offered in righteousness.

Mal 3:3 He will sit as a refiner and a purifier of silver;
He will purify the sons of Levi, And purge them as
gold and silver, That they may offer to the LORD An
offering in righteousness.

Offered with clear conscience.

Matt 5:23–24 Therefore if you bring your gift to the
altar, and there remember that your brother has
something against you, **24** leave your gift there before the altar, and go your way. First be reconciled to
your brother, and then come and offer your gift.

Brought in a clean vessel.

Is 66:20 Then they shall bring all your brethren for an
offering to the LORD out of all nations, on horses and
in chariots and in litters, on mules and on camels, to
My holy mountain Jerusalem," says the LORD, "as the
children of Israel bring an offering in a clean vessel
into the house of the LORD.

Brought to the place appointed of God.

Deut 12:6 There you shall take your burnt offerings,
your sacrifices, your tithes, the heave offerings of
your hand, your vowed offerings, your freewill offerings, and the firstborn of your herds and flocks.

Ps 27:6 And now my head shall be lifted up above my
enemies all around me; Therefore I will offer sacrifices of joy in His tabernacle; I will sing, yes, I will
sing praises to the LORD.

Heb 9:9 It *was* symbolic for the present time in which
both gifts and sacrifices are offered which cannot
make him who performed the service perfect in regard to the conscience—

Presented by the priest.

Heb 5:1 For every high priest taken from among men is
appointed for men in things *pertaining* to God, that
he may offer both gifts and sacrifices for sins.

Brought without delay.

Ex 22:29–30 "You shall not delay *to offer* the first of your
ripe produce and your juices. The firstborn of your
sons you shall give to Me. **30** Likewise you shall do
with your oxen *and* your sheep. It shall be with its
mother seven days; on the eighth day you shall give
it to Me.

Brought regularly.

Ps 50:8 I will not rebuke you for your sacrifices Or your
burnt offerings, *Which are* continually before Me.

Offered with gratitude.

Ps 50:14 Offer to God thanksgiving, And pay your
vows to the Most High.

Could not make the offerer perfect.

Heb 9:9 It *was* symbolic for the present time in which
both gifts and sacrifices are offered which cannot
make him who performed the service perfect in regard to the conscience—

Things forbidden as,

The wages of a harlot or price of a dog.

Deut 23:18 You shall not bring the wages of a harlot or
the price of a dog to the house of the LORD your God
for any vowed offering, for both of these *are* an
abomination to the LORD your God.

Whatever was defective.

Lev 22:20 Whatever has a defect, you shall not offer, for
it shall not be acceptable on your behalf.

Lev 22:24 'You shall not offer to the LORD what is
bruised or crushed, or torn or cut; nor shall you
make *any offering of them* in your land.

Whatever was unclean.

Lev 27:11 If *it is* an unclean animal which they do not
offer as a sacrifice to the LORD, then he shall present
the animal before the priest;

Lev 27:27 And if *it is* an unclean animal, then he shall
redeem *it* according to your valuation, and shall add
one-fifth to it; or if it is not redeemed, then it shall be
sold according to your valuation.

Laid up in the temple.

2 Chr 31:12 Then they faithfully brought in the offerings, the tithes, and the dedicated things; Cononiah
the Levite had charge of them, and Shimei his brother *was* the next.

Neh 10:37 to bring the firstfruits of our dough, our offerings, the fruit from all kinds of trees, *the* new wine
and oil, to the priests, to the storerooms of the house
of our God; and to bring the tithes of our land to the
Levites, for the Levites should receive the tithes in all
our farming communities.

Hezekiah prepared rooms for.

2 Chr 31:11 Now Hezekiah commanded *them* to prepare rooms in the house of the LORD, and they prepared them.

And the Jews

Slow in presenting.

Neh 13:10–12 I also realized that the portions for the Levites had not been given *them;* for each of the Levites
and the singers who did the work had gone back to
his field. **11** So I contended with the rulers, and said,
"Why is the house of God forsaken?" And I gathered
them together and set them in their place. **12** Then all
Judah brought the tithe of the grain and the new
wine and the oil to the storehouse.

Robbed God of.

Mal 3:8 "Will a man rob God? Yet you have robbed Me!
But you say, 'In what way have we robbed You?' In
tithes and offerings.

Gave the worst they had as.

Mal 1:8 And when you offer the blind as a sacrifice, *Is it*
not evil? And when you offer the lame and sick, *Is it*

not evil? Offer it then to your governor! Would he be pleased with you? Would he accept you favorably?" Says the LORD of hosts.

Mal 1:13 You also say, 'Oh, what a weariness!' And you sneer at it," Says the LORD of hosts. "And you bring the stolen, the lame, and the sick; Thus you bring an offering! Should I accept this from your hand?" Says the LORD.

Their sin caused rejection of.

Is 1:13 Bring no more futile sacrifices; Incense is an abomination to Me. The New Moons, the Sabbaths, and the calling of assemblies— I cannot endure iniquity and the sacred meeting.

Mal 1:10 "Who *is there* even among you who would shut the doors, So that you would not kindle fire *on* My altar in vain? I have no pleasure in you," Says the LORD of hosts, "Nor will I accept an offering from your hands.

Priests' sins caused abhorring of.

1 Sam 2:17 Therefore the sin of the young men was very great before the LORD, for men abhorred the offering of the LORD.

Presented, to idols.

Ezek 20:28 When I brought them into the land *concerning* which I had raised My hand in an oath to give them, and they saw all the high hills and all the thick trees, there they offered their sacrifices and provoked Me with their offerings. There they also sent up their sweet aroma and poured out their drink offerings.

Strangers' to be made the same as the Jews'.

Num 15:14–16 And if a stranger dwells with you, or whoever *is* among you throughout your generations, and would present an offering made by fire, a sweet aroma to the LORD, just as you do, so shall he do. **15** One ordinance *shall be* for you of the assembly and for the stranger who dwells *with you*, an ordinance forever throughout your generations; as you are, so shall the stranger be before the LORD. **16** One law and one custom shall be for you and for the stranger who dwells with you.' "

Same offenses under the law, beyond the efficacy of.

1 Sam 3:14 And therefore I have sworn to the house of Eli that the iniquity of Eli's house shall not be atoned for by sacrifice or offering forever."

Ps 51:16 For You do not desire sacrifice, or else I would give *it*; You do not delight in burnt offering.

Illustrative of

Christ's offering of Himself.

Eph 5:2 And walk in love, as Christ also has loved us and given Himself for us, an offering and a sacrifice to God for a sweet-smelling aroma.

The conversion of the Gentiles.

Rom 15:16 that I might be a minister of Jesus Christ to the Gentiles, ministering the gospel of God, that the offering of the Gentiles might be acceptable, sanctified by the Holy Spirit.

The conversion of the Jews.

Is 66:20 Then they shall bring all your brethren for an offering to the LORD out of all nations, on horses and in chariots and in litters, on mules and on camels, to My holy mountain Jerusalem," says the LORD, "as the children of Israel bring an offering in a clean vessel into the house of the LORD.

OFFERING, BURNT

To be offered only to the Lord.

Judg 13:16 And the Angel of the LORD said to Manoah, "Though you detain Me, I will not eat your food. But if you offer a burnt offering, you must offer it to the LORD." (For Manoah did not know He *was* the Angel of the LORD.)

Specially acceptable.

Gen 8:21 And the LORD smelled a soothing aroma. Then the LORD said in His heart, "I will never again curse the ground for man's sake, although the imagination of man's heart *is* evil from his youth; nor will I again destroy every living thing as I have done.

Lev 1:9 but he shall wash its entrails and its legs with water. And the priest shall burn all on the altar as a burnt sacrifice, an offering made by fire, a sweet aroma to the LORD.

Lev 1:13 but he shall wash the entrails and the legs with water. Then the priest shall bring *it* all and burn *it* on the altar; it *is* a burnt sacrifice, an offering made by fire, a sweet aroma to the LORD.

Lev 1:17 Then he shall split it at its wings, *but* shall not divide *it* completely; and the priest shall burn it on the altar, on the wood that *is* on the fire. It *is* a burnt sacrifice, an offering made by fire, a sweet aroma to the LORD.

The most ancient of all sacrifices.

Gen 4:4 Abel also brought of the firstborn of his flock and of their fat. And the LORD respected Abel and his offering,

Gen 8:20 Then Noah built an altar to the LORD, and took of every clean animal and of every clean bird, and offered burnt offerings on the altar.

Gen 22:2 Then He said, "Take now your son, your only *son* Isaac, whom you love, and go to the land of Moriah, and offer him there as a burnt offering on one of the mountains of which I shall tell you."

Gen 22:13 Then Abraham lifted his eyes and looked, and there behind *him was* a ram caught in a thicket by its horns. So Abraham went and took the ram, and offered it up for a burnt offering instead of his son.

Job 1:5 So it was, when the days of feasting had run their course, that Job would send and sanctify them, and he would rise early in the morning and offer burnt offerings *according to* the number of them all. For Job said, "It may be that my sons have sinned and cursed God in their hearts." Thus Job did regularly.

Offered by the Jews before the law.

Ex 10:25 But Moses said, "You must also give us sacrifices and burnt offerings, that we may sacrifice to the LORD our God.

Ex 24:5 Then he sent young men of the children of Israel, who offered burnt offerings and sacrificed peace offerings of oxen to the LORD.

To be taken from

The flock or herd.

Lev 1:2 "Speak to the children of Israel, and say to them: 'When any one of you brings an offering to the LORD, you shall bring your offering of the livestock—of the herd and of the flock.

The birds.

Lev 1:14 'And if the burnt sacrifice of his offering to the LORD *is* of birds, then he shall bring his offering of turtledoves or young pigeons.

Was an atonement for sin.

Lev 9:7 And Moses said to Aaron, "Go to the altar, offer your sin offering and your burnt offering, and make atonement for yourself and for the people. Offer the offering of the people, and make atonement for them, as the LORD commanded."

Guilt transferred to, by imposition of hands.

Lev 1:4 Then he shall put his hand on the head of the burnt offering, and it will be accepted on his behalf to make atonement for him.

Num 8:12 Then the Levites shall lay their hands on the heads of the young bulls, and you shall offer one as a sin offering and the other as a burnt offering to the LORD, to make atonement for the Levites.

Required to be

Killed, if a beast, by the person who brought it.

Lev 1:5 He shall kill the bull before the LORD; and the priests, Aaron's sons, shall bring the blood and sprinkle the blood all around on the altar that *is by* the door of the tabernacle of meeting.

Lev 1:11 He shall kill it on the north side of the altar before the LORD; and the priests, Aaron's sons, shall sprinkle its blood all around on the altar.

Killed, if a bird, by the priest.

Lev 1:15 The priest shall bring it to the altar, wring off its head, and burn *it* on the altar; its blood shall be drained out at the side of the altar.

For the people at large, killed and prepared by the Levites.

Ezek 44:11 Yet they shall be ministers in My sanctuary, *as* gatekeepers of the house and ministers of the house; they shall slay the burnt offering and the sacrifice for the people, and they shall stand before them to minister to them.

A male without blemish.

Lev 1:3 'If his offering *is* a burnt sacrifice of the herd, let him offer a male without blemish; he shall offer it of his own free will at the door of the tabernacle of meeting before the LORD.

Lev 22:19 *you shall offer* of your own free will a male without blemish from the cattle, from the sheep, or from the goats.

Voluntary.

Lev 1:3 'If his offering *is* a burnt sacrifice of the herd, let him offer a male without blemish; he shall offer it of his own free will at the door of the tabernacle of meeting before the LORD.

Lev 22:18–19 "Speak to Aaron and his sons, and to all the children of Israel, and say to them: 'Whatever man of the house of Israel, or of the strangers in Israel, who offers his sacrifice for any of his vows or for

any of his freewill offerings, which they offer to the LORD as a burnt offering— **19** *you shall offer* of your own free will a male without blemish from the cattle, from the sheep, or from the goats.

Presented at the door of the tabernacle.

Lev 1:3 'If his offering *is* a burnt sacrifice of the herd, let him offer a male without blemish; he shall offer it of his own free will at the door of the tabernacle of meeting before the LORD.

Deut 12:6 There you shall take your burnt offerings, your sacrifices, your tithes, the heave offerings of your hand, your vowed offerings, your freewill offerings, and the firstborn of your herds and flocks.

Deut 12:11 then there will be the place where the LORD your God chooses to make His name abide. There you shall bring all that I command you: your burnt offerings, your sacrifices, your tithes, the heave offerings of your hand, and all your choice offerings which you vow to the LORD.

Deut 12:14 but in the place which the LORD chooses, in one of your tribes, there you shall offer your burnt offerings, and there you shall do all that I command you.

Offered by priests only.

Lev 1:9 but he shall wash its entrails and its legs with water. And the priest shall burn all on the altar as a burnt sacrifice, an offering made by fire, a sweet aroma to the LORD.

Ezek 44:15 "But the priests, the Levites, the sons of Zadok, who kept charge of My sanctuary when the children of Israel went astray from Me, they shall come near Me to minister to Me; and they shall stand before Me to offer to Me the fat and the blood," says the Lord GOD.

Offered in righteousness.

Ps 51:19 Then You shall be pleased with the sacrifices of righteousness, With burnt offering and whole burnt offering; Then they shall offer bulls on Your altar.

Entirely burned.

Lev 1:8 Then the priests, Aaron's sons, shall lay the parts, the head, and the fat in order on the wood that *is* on the fire upon the altar;

Lev 1:9 but he shall wash its entrails and its legs with water. And the priest shall burn all on the altar as a burnt sacrifice, an offering made by fire, a sweet aroma to the LORD.

Lev 1:12–13 And he shall cut it into its pieces, with its head and its fat; and the priest shall lay them in order on the wood that *is* on the fire upon the altar; **13** but he shall wash the entrails and the legs with water. Then the priest shall bring *it* all and burn *it* on the altar; it *is* a burnt sacrifice, an offering made by fire, a sweet aroma to the LORD.

Lev 6:9 "Command Aaron and his sons, saying, 'This is the law of the burnt offering: The burnt offering *shall be* on the hearth upon the altar all night until morning, and the fire of the altar shall be kept burning on it.

Blood of, sprinkled all around on the altar.

Lev 1:5 He shall kill the bull before the LORD; and the priests, Aaron's sons, shall bring the blood and sprinkle the blood all around on the altar that *is by* the door of the tabernacle of meeting.

Lev 1:11 He shall kill it on the north side of the altar before the LORD; and the priests, Aaron's sons, shall sprinkle its blood all around on the altar.

If a bird, the blood was wrung out at the side of the altar.

Lev 1:15 The priest shall bring it to the altar, wring off its head, and burn *it* on the altar; its blood shall be drained out at the side of the altar.

Ashes of, collected at foot of the altar, and carried outside the camp.

Lev 6:11 Then he shall take off his garments, put on other garments, and carry the ashes outside the camp to a clean place.

Skin of, given to the priests for clothing.

Gen 3:21 Also for Adam and his wife the LORD God made tunics of skin, and clothed them.

Lev 7:8 And the priest who offers anyone's burnt offering, that priest shall have for himself the skin of the burnt offering which he has offered.

Was offered

Every morning and evening.

Ex 29:38–42 "Now this *is* what you shall offer on the altar: two lambs of the first year, day by day continually. **39** One lamb you shall offer in the morning, and the other lamb you shall offer at twilight. **40** With the one lamb shall be one-tenth *of an ephah* of flour mixed with one-fourth of a hin of pressed oil, and one-fourth of a hin of wine *as* a drink offering. **41** And the other lamb you shall offer at twilight; and you shall offer with it the grain offering and the drink offering, as in the morning, for a sweet aroma, an offering made by fire to the LORD. **42** *This shall be* a continual burnt offering throughout your generations *at* the door of the tabernacle of meeting before the LORD, where I will meet you to speak with you.

Every Sabbath day.

Num 28:9–10 'And on the Sabbath day two lambs in their first year, without blemish, and two-tenths *of an ephah* of fine flour as a grain offering, mixed with oil, with its drink offering— **10** *this is* the burnt offering for every Sabbath, besides the regular burnt offering with its drink offering.

The first day of every month.

Num 28:11 'At the beginnings of your months you shall present a burnt offering to the LORD: two young bulls, one ram, and seven lambs in their first year, without blemish;

The seven days of unleavened bread.

Num 28:19 And you shall present an offering made by fire as a burnt offering to the LORD: two young bulls, one ram, and seven lambs in their first year. Be sure they are without blemish.

Num 28:24 In this manner you shall offer the food of the offering made by fire daily for seven days, as a sweet aroma to the LORD; it shall be offered besides the regular burnt offering and its drink offering.

The Day of Atonement.

Lev 16:3 "Thus Aaron shall come into the Holy *Place:*

with *the blood of* a young bull as a sin offering, and *of* a ram as a burnt offering.

Lev 16:5 And he shall take from the congregation of the children of Israel two kids of the goats as a sin offering, and one ram as a burnt offering.

Num 29:8 You shall present a burnt offering to the LORD *as* a sweet aroma: one young bull, one ram, *and* seven lambs in their first year. Be sure they are without blemish.

At consecration of Levites.

Num 8:12 Then the Levites shall lay their hands on the heads of the young bulls, and you shall offer one as a sin offering and the other as a burnt offering to the LORD, to make atonement for the Levites.

At consecration of priests.

Lev 9:2 And he said to Aaron, "Take for yourself a young bull as a sin offering and a ram as a burnt offering, without blemish, and offer *them* before the LORD.

Lev 9:12–14 And he killed the burnt offering; and Aaron's sons presented to him the blood, which he sprinkled all around on the altar. **13** Then they presented the burnt offering to him, with its pieces and head, and he burned *them* on the altar. **14** And he washed the entrails and the legs, and burned *them* with the burnt offering on the altar.

At consecration of kings.

1 Chr 29:21–23 And they made sacrifices to the LORD and offered burnt offerings to the LORD on the next day: a thousand bulls, a thousand rams, a thousand lambs, with their drink offerings, and sacrifices in abundance for all Israel. **22** So they ate and drank before the LORD with great gladness on that day. And they made Solomon the son of David king the second time, and anointed *him* before the LORD *to be* the leader, and Zadok *to be* priest. **23** Then Solomon sat on the throne of the LORD as king instead of David his father, and prospered; and all Israel obeyed him.

At purification of women.

Lev 12:6 'When the days of her purification are fulfilled, whether for a son or a daughter, she shall bring to the priest a lamb of the first year as a burnt offering, and a young pigeon or a turtledove as a sin offering, to the door of the tabernacle of meeting.

For Nazirites after defilement, or at the end of their vow.

Num 6:11 and the priest shall offer one as a sin offering and *the* other as a burnt offering, and make atonement for him, because he sinned in regard to the corpse; and he shall sanctify his head that same day.

Num 6:14 And he shall present his offering to the LORD: one male lamb in its first year without blemish as a burnt offering, one ewe lamb in its first year without blemish as a sin offering, one ram without blemish as a peace offering,

For the healed leper.

Lev 14:13 Then he shall kill the lamb in the place where he kills the sin offering and the burnt offering, in a holy place; for as the sin offering *is* the priest's, so *is* the trespass offering. It *is* most holy.

Lev 14:19–20 "Then the priest shall offer the sin offering, and make atonement for him who is to be cleansed from his uncleanness. Afterward he shall kill the burnt offering. **20** And the priest shall offer the burnt offering and the grain offering on the altar. So the priest shall make atonement for him, and he shall be clean.

At dedication of sacred places.

Num 7:15 one young bull, one ram, and one male lamb in its first year, as a burnt offering;

1 Kin 8:64 On the same day the king consecrated the middle of the court that *was* in front of the house of the LORD; for there he offered burnt offerings, grain offerings, and the fat of the peace offerings, because the bronze altar that *was* before the LORD *was* too small to receive the burnt offerings, the grain offerings, and the fat of the peace offerings.

After great mercies.

1 Sam 6:14 Then the cart came into the field of Joshua of Beth Shemesh, and stood there; a large stone *was* there. So they split the wood of the cart and offered the cows as a burnt offering to the LORD.

2 Sam 24:22 Now Araunah said to David, "Let my lord the king take and offer up whatever *seems* good to him. Look, *here are* oxen for burnt sacrifice, and threshing implements and the yokes of the oxen for wood.

2 Sam 24:25 And David built there an altar to the LORD, and offered burnt offerings and peace offerings. So the LORD heeded the prayers for the land, and the plague was withdrawn from Israel.

Before going to war.

1 Sam 7:9 And Samuel took a suckling lamb and offered *it as* a whole burnt offering to the LORD. Then Samuel cried out to the LORD for Israel, and the LORD answered him.

With sounds of trumpets at feasts.

Num 10:10 Also in the day of your gladness, in your appointed feasts, and at the beginning of your months, you shall blow the trumpets over your burnt offerings and over the sacrifices of your peace offerings; and they shall be a memorial for you before your God: I *am* the LORD your God."

The fat, etc. of all peace offerings laid on, and consumed with the daily.

Lev 3:5 and Aaron's sons shall burn it on the altar upon the burnt sacrifice, which *is* on the wood that *is* on the fire, *as* an offering made by fire, a sweet aroma to the LORD.

Lev 6:12 And the fire on the altar shall be kept burning on it; it shall not be put out. And the priest shall burn wood on it every morning, and lay the burnt offering in order on it; and he shall burn on it the fat of the peace offerings.

Of the wicked, not accepted by God.

Is 1:10–11 Hear the word of the LORD, You rulers of Sodom; Give ear to the law of our God, You people of Gomorrah: **11** "To what purpose *is* the multitude of your sacrifices to Me?" Says the LORD. "I have had enough of burnt offerings of rams And the fat of fed cattle. I do not delight in the blood of bulls, Or of lambs or goats.

Jer 6:19–20 Hear, O earth! Behold, I will certainly bring calamity on this people— The fruit of their thoughts,

Because they have not heeded My words Nor My law, but rejected it. **20** For what purpose to Me Comes frankincense from Sheba, And sweet cane from a far country? Your burnt offerings *are* not acceptable, Nor your sacrifices sweet to Me."

Amos 5:22 Though you offer Me burnt offerings and your grain offerings, I will not accept *them*, Nor will I regard your fattened peace offerings.

Obedience better than.

1 Sam 15:22 So Samuel said: "Has the LORD *as great* delight in burnt offerings and sacrifices, As in obeying the voice of the LORD? Behold, to obey is better than sacrifice, *And* to heed than the fat of rams.

Jer 7:21–23 Thus says the LORD of hosts, the God of Israel: "Add your burnt offerings to your sacrifices and eat meat. **22** For I did not speak to your fathers, or command them in the day that I brought them out of the land of Egypt, concerning burnt offerings or sacrifices. **23** But this is what I commanded them, saying, 'Obey My voice, and I will be your God, and you shall be My people. And walk in all the ways that I have commanded you, that it may be well with you.'

Knowledge of God better than.

Hos 6:6 For I desire mercy and not sacrifice, And the knowledge of God more than burnt offerings.

Love of God better than.

Mark 12:33 And to love Him with all the heart, with all the understanding, with all the soul, and with all the strength, and to love one's neighbor as oneself, is more than all the whole burnt offerings and sacrifices."

Abraham tried by the command to offer Isaac as.

Gen 22:1–18 Now it came to pass after these things that God tested Abraham, and said to him, "Abraham!" And he said, "Here I am." **2** Then He said, "Take now your son, your only *son* Isaac, whom you love, and go to the land of Moriah, and offer him there as a burnt offering on one of the mountains of which I shall tell you." **3** So Abraham rose early in the morning and saddled his donkey, and took two of his young men with him, and Isaac his son; and he split the wood for the burnt offering, and arose and went to the place of which God had told him. **4** Then on the third day Abraham lifted his eyes and saw the place afar off. **5** And Abraham said to his young men, "Stay here with the donkey; the lad and I will go yonder and worship, and we will come back to you." **6** So Abraham took the wood of the burnt offering and laid *it* on Isaac his son; and he took the fire in his hand, and a knife, and the two of them went together. **7** But Isaac spoke to Abraham his father and said, "My father!" And he said, "Here I am, my son." Then he said, "Look, the fire and the wood, but where *is* the lamb for a burnt offering?" **8** And Abraham said, "My son, God will provide for Himself the lamb for a burnt offering." So the two of them went together. **9** Then they came to the place of which God had told him. And Abraham built an altar there and placed the wood in order; and he bound Isaac his son and laid him on the altar, upon the wood. **10** And Abraham stretched out his hand and took the knife to slay his son. **11** But the Angel of the LORD called to him from heaven and said, "Abraham, Abraham!" So he said, "Here I am." **12** And He said, "Do not lay your hand on the lad, or do anything to him; for now I know that you fear God, since you have not withheld your son, your only *son*, from Me." **13** Then Abraham lifted his eyes and looked, and there behind *him was* a ram caught in a thicket by its horns. So Abraham went and took the ram, and offered it up for a burnt offering instead of his son. **14** And Abraham called the name of the place, The-LORD-Will-Provide; as it is said *to* this day, "In the Mount of the LORD it shall be provided." **15** Then the Angel of the LORD called to Abraham a second time out of heaven, **16** and said: "By Myself I have sworn, says the LORD, because you have done this thing, and have not withheld your son, your only *son*— **17** blessing I will bless you, and multiplying I will multiply your descendants as the stars of the heaven and as the sand which *is* on the seashore; and your descendants shall possess the gate of their enemies. **18** In your seed all the nations of the earth shall be blessed, because you have obeyed My voice."

Incapable of removing sin, and reconciling to God.

Ps 40:6 Sacrifice and offering You did not desire; My ears You have opened. Burnt offering and sin offering You did not require.

Ps 50:8 I will not rebuke you for your sacrifices Or your burnt offerings, *Which are* continually before Me.

Heb 10:6 *In burnt offerings and sacrifices for sin You had no pleasure.*

The most costly, no adequate tribute to God.

Is 40:16 And Lebanon *is* not sufficient to burn, Nor its beasts sufficient for a burnt offering.

Ps 50:9–13 I will not take a bull from your house, *Nor* goats out of your folds. **10** For every beast of the forest *is* Mine, *And* the cattle on a thousand hills. **11** I know all the birds of the mountains, And the wild beasts of the field *are* Mine. **12** "If I were hungry, I would not tell you; For the world *is* Mine, and all its fullness. **13** Will I eat the flesh of bulls, Or drink the blood of goats?

Guilt of unauthorized persons offering.

1 Sam 13:12–13 then I said, 'The Philistines will now come down on me at Gilgal, and I have not made supplication to the LORD.' Therefore I felt compelled, and offered a burnt offering." **13** And Samuel said to Saul, "You have done foolishly. You have not kept the commandment of the LORD your God, which He commanded you. For now the LORD would have established your kingdom over Israel forever.

Guilt of offering, except in the place appointed.

Lev 17:8–9 "Also you shall say to them: 'Whatever man of the house of Israel, or of the strangers who dwell among you, who offers a burnt offering or sacrifice, **9** and does not bring it to the door of the tabernacle of meeting, to offer it to the LORD, that man shall be cut off from among his people.

Of human victims execrated.

Deut 12:31 You shall not worship the LORD your God in that way; for every abomination to the LORD which He hates they have done to their gods; for they burn even their sons and daughters in the fire to their gods.

2 Kin 3:27 Then he took his eldest son who would have reigned in his place, and offered him *as* a burnt offering upon the wall; and there was great indignation against Israel. So they departed from him and returned to *their own* land.

Jer 7:31 And they have built the high places of Tophet, which *is* in the Valley of the Son of Hinnom, to burn their sons and their daughters in the fire, which I did not command, nor did it come into My heart.

Jer 19:5 (they have also built the high places of Baal, to burn their sons with fire *for* burnt offerings to Baal, which I did not command or speak, nor did it come into My mind),

Illustrative of

The offering of Christ.

Eph 5:2 And walk in love, as Christ also has loved us and given Himself for us, an offering and a sacrifice to God for a sweet-smelling aroma.

Heb 10:8–10 Previously saying, *"Sacrifice and offering, burnt offerings, and offerings for sin You did not desire, nor had pleasure in them"* (which are offered according to the law), **9** then He said, *"Behold, I have come to do Your will, O God."* He takes away the first that He may establish the second. **10** By that will we have been sanctified through the offering of the body of Jesus Christ once *for all.*

Devotedness to God.

Rom 12:1 I beseech you therefore, brethren, by the mercies of God, that you present your bodies a living sacrifice, holy, acceptable to God, *which is* your reasonable service.

OFFERING, DRINK

Antiquity of.

Gen 35:14 So Jacob set up a pillar in the place where He talked with him, a pillar of stone; and he poured a drink offering on it, and he poured oil on it.

Sacrifices accompanied by.

Ex 29:40 With the one lamb shall be one-tenth *of an ephah* of flour mixed with one-fourth of a hin of pressed oil, and one-fourth of a hin of wine *as* a drink offering.

Lev 23:13 Its grain offering *shall be* two-tenths *of an ephah* of fine flour mixed with oil, an offering made by fire to the LORD, for a sweet aroma; and its drink offering *shall be* of wine, one-fourth of a hin.

Quantity appointed for use in each kind of sacrifice.

Num 15:3–10 and you make an offering by fire to the LORD, a burnt offering or a sacrifice, to fulfill a vow or as a freewill offering or in your appointed feasts, to make a sweet aroma to the LORD, from the herd or the flock, **4** then he who presents his offering to the LORD shall bring a grain offering of one-tenth *of an ephah* of fine flour mixed with one-fourth of a hin of oil; **5** and one-fourth of a hin of wine as a drink offering you shall prepare with the burnt offering or the sacrifice, for each lamb. **6** Or for a ram you shall prepare as a grain offering two-tenths *of an ephah* of fine flour mixed with one-third of a hin of oil; **7** and as a drink offering you shall offer one-third of a hin of wine as a sweet aroma to the LORD. **8** And when you prepare a young bull as a burnt offering, or as a sacrifice to fulfill a vow, or as a peace offering to the LORD, **9** then shall be offered with the young bull a grain offering of three-tenths *of an ephah* of fine flour mixed with half a hin of oil; **10** and you shall bring as the drink offering half a hin of wine as an offering made by fire, a sweet aroma to the LORD.

For public sacrifices provided by the state.

Ezra 7:17 now therefore, be careful to buy with this money bulls, rams, and lambs, with their grain offerings and their drink offerings, and offer them on the altar of the house of your God in Jerusalem.

Ezek 45:17 Then it shall be the prince's part *to give* burnt offerings, grain offerings, and drink offerings, at the feasts, the New Moons, the Sabbaths, and at all the appointed seasons of the house of Israel. He shall prepare the sin offering, the grain offering, the burnt offering, and the peace offerings to make atonement for the house of Israel."

Not poured on the altar of incense.

Ex 30:9 You shall not offer strange incense on it, or a burnt offering, or a grain offering; nor shall you pour a drink offering on it.

Omission of, caused by bad vintage.

Joel 1:9 The grain offering and the drink offering Have been cut off from the house of the LORD; The priests mourn, who minister to the LORD.

Joel 1:13 Gird yourselves and lament, you priests; Wail, you who minister before the altar; Come, lie all night in sackcloth, You who minister to my God; For the grain offering and the drink offering Are withheld from the house of your God.

Idolatrous Jews

Offered them to the queen of heaven.

Jer 7:18 The children gather wood, the fathers kindle the fire, and the women knead dough, to make cakes for the queen of heaven; and *they* pour out drink offerings to other gods, that they may provoke Me to anger.

Jer 44:17–19 But we will certainly do whatever has gone out of our own mouth, to burn incense to the queen of heaven and pour out drink offerings to her, as we have done, we and our fathers, our kings and our princes, in the cities of Judah and in the streets of Jerusalem. For *then* we had plenty of food, were well-off, and saw no trouble. **18** But since we stopped burning incense to the queen of heaven and pouring out drink offerings to her, we have lacked everything and have been consumed by the sword and by famine." **19** *The women also said,* "And when we burned incense to the queen of heaven and poured out drink offerings to her, did we make cakes for her, to worship her, and pour out drink offerings to her without our husbands' *permission?*"

Reproved for offering, to idols.

Is 57:5–6 Inflaming yourselves with gods under every green tree, Slaying the children in the valleys, Under the clefts of the rocks? **6** Among the smooth *stones* of the stream *Is* your portion; They, they, *are* your lot! Even to them you have poured a drink offering, You have offered a grain offering. Should I receive comfort in these?

Is 65:11 "But you *are* those who forsake the LORD, Who forget My holy mountain, Who prepare a table for Gad, And who furnish a drink offering for Meni.

Jer 19:13 And the houses of Jerusalem and the houses of the kings of Judah shall be defiled like the place of Tophet, because of all the houses on whose roofs they have burned incense to all the host of heaven, and poured out drink offerings to other gods." ' "

Ezek 20:28 When I brought them into the land *concerning* which I had raised My hand in an oath to give them, and they saw all the high hills and all the thick trees, there they offered their sacrifices and provoked Me with their offerings. There they also sent up their sweet aroma and poured out their drink offerings.

Often used blood for.

Ps 16:4 Their sorrows shall be multiplied who hasten *after* another *god;* Their drink offerings of blood I will not offer, Nor take up their names on my lips.

Futility of offering, to idols.

Deut 32:37–38 He will say: 'Where *are* their gods, The rock in which they sought refuge? **38** Who ate the fat of their sacrifices, *And* drank the wine of their drink offering? Let them rise and help you, *And* be your refuge.

Illustrative of the

Offering of Christ.

Is 53:12 Therefore I will divide Him a portion with the great, And He shall divide the spoil with the strong, Because He poured out His soul unto death, And He was numbered with the transgressors, And He bore the sin of many, And made intercession for the transgressors.

Pouring out of the Spirit.

Joel 2:28 "And it shall come to pass afterward That I will pour out My Spirit on all flesh; Your sons and your daughters shall prophesy, Your old men shall dream dreams, Your young men shall see visions.

Devotedness of ministers.

Phil 2:17 Yes, and if I am being poured out *as a drink offering* on the sacrifice and service of your faith, I am glad and rejoice with you all.

OFFERING, GRAIN

Was most holy.

Lev 6:17 It shall not be baked with leaven. I have given it *as* their portion of My offerings made by fire; it *is* most holy, like the sin offering and the trespass offering.

Consisted of

Fine flour.

Lev 2:1 'When anyone offers a grain offering to the LORD, his offering shall be *of* fine flour. And he shall pour oil on it, and put frankincense on it.

Lev 2:5 But if your offering *is* a grain offering *baked* in a pan, *it shall be of* fine flour, unleavened, mixed with oil.

Lev 2:7 'If your offering *is* a grain offering *baked* in a covered pan, it shall be made *of* fine flour with oil.

Unleavened cakes baked in the oven.

Lev 2:4 'And if you bring as an offering a grain offering baked in the oven, *it shall be* unleavened cakes of fine flour mixed with oil, or unleavened wafers anointed with oil.

Barley meal.

Num 5:15 then the man shall bring his wife to the priest. He shall bring the offering required for her, one-tenth of an ephah of barley meal; he shall pour no oil on it and put no frankincense on it, because it *is* a grain offering of jealousy, an offering for remembering, for bringing iniquity to remembrance.

Oil and frankincense used with.

Lev 2:1 'When anyone offers a grain offering to the LORD, his offering shall be *of* fine flour. And he shall pour oil on it, and put frankincense on it.

Lev 2:4 'And if you bring as an offering a grain offering baked in the oven, *it shall be* unleavened cakes of fine flour mixed with oil, or unleavened wafers anointed with oil.

Lev 2:15 And you shall put oil on it, and lay frankincense on it. It *is* a grain offering.

Of jealousy, without oil or frankincense.

Num 5:15 then the man shall bring his wife to the priest. He shall bring the offering required for her, one-tenth of an ephah of barley meal; he shall pour no oil on it and put no frankincense on it, because it *is* a grain offering of jealousy, an offering for remembering, for bringing iniquity to remembrance.

Always seasoned with salt.

Lev 2:13 And every offering of your grain offering you shall season with salt; you shall not allow the salt of the covenant of your God to be lacking from your grain offering. With all your offerings you shall offer salt.

No leaven used with.

Lev 2:11 'No grain offering which you bring to the LORD shall be made with leaven, for you shall burn no leaven nor any honey in any offering to the LORD made by fire.

Lev 6:17 It shall not be baked with leaven. I have given it *as* their portion of My offerings made by fire; it *is* most holy, like the sin offering and the trespass offering.

Not to be offered on altar of incense.

Ex 30:9 You shall not offer strange incense on it, or a burnt offering, or a grain offering; nor shall you pour a drink offering on it.

Offered

With the daily sacrifices.

Ex 29:40–42 With the one lamb shall be one-tenth *of an ephah* of flour mixed with one-fourth of a hin of pressed oil, and one-fourth of a hin of wine *as* a drink offering. **41** And the other lamb you shall offer at twilight; and you shall offer with it the grain offering and the drink offering, as in the morning, for a sweet aroma, an offering made by fire to the LORD. **42** *This shall be* a continual burnt offering throughout your generations *at* the door of the tabernacle of meeting before the LORD, where I will meet you to speak with you.

Lev 6:20–23 "This *is* the offering of Aaron and his sons, which they shall offer to the LORD, *beginning* on the day when he is anointed: one-tenth of an ephah of fine flour as a daily grain offering, half of it in the

morning and half of it at night. **21** It shall be made in a pan with oil. *When it is* mixed, you shall bring it in. The baked pieces of the grain offering you shall offer *for* a sweet aroma to the LORD. **22** The priest from among his sons, who is anointed in his place, shall offer it. *It is* a statute forever to the LORD. It shall be wholly burned. **23** For every grain offering for the priest shall be wholly burned. It shall not be eaten."

With all burnt offerings.

Ex 40:29 And he put the altar of burnt offering *before* the door of the tabernacle of the tent of meeting, and offered upon it the burnt offering and the grain offering, as the LORD had commanded Moses.

Num 15:3–12 and you make an offering by fire to the LORD, a burnt offering or a sacrifice, to fulfill a vow or as a freewill offering or in your appointed feasts, to make a sweet aroma to the LORD, from the herd or the flock, **4** then he who presents his offering to the LORD shall bring a grain offering of one-tenth *of an ephah* of fine flour mixed with one-fourth of a hin of oil; **5** and one-fourth of a hin of wine as a drink offering you shall prepare with the burnt offering or the sacrifice, for each lamb. **6** Or for a ram you shall prepare as a grain offering two-tenths *of an ephah* of fine flour mixed with one-third of a hin of oil; **7** and as a drink offering you shall offer one-third of a hin of wine as a sweet aroma to the LORD. **8** And when you prepare a young bull as a burnt offering, or as a sacrifice to fulfill a vow, or as a peace offering to the LORD, **9** then shall be offered with the young bull a grain offering of three-tenths *of an ephah* of fine flour mixed with half a hin of oil; **10** and you shall bring as the drink offering half a hin of wine as an offering made by fire, a sweet aroma to the LORD. **11** 'Thus it shall be done for each young bull, for each ram, or for each lamb or young goat. **12** According to the number that you prepare, so you shall do with everyone according to their number.

By the poor for a sin offering.

Lev 5:11 'But if he is not able to bring two turtledoves or two young pigeons, then he who sinned shall bring for his offering one-tenth of an ephah of fine flour as a sin offering. He shall put no oil on it, nor shall he put frankincense on it, for it *is* a sin offering.

A small part of, was consumed on the altar for a memorial.

Lev 2:2 He shall bring it to Aaron's sons, the priests, one of whom shall take from it his handful of fine flour and oil with all the frankincense. And the priest shall burn *it as* a memorial on the altar, an offering made by fire, a sweet aroma to the LORD.

Lev 2:9 Then the priest shall take from the grain offering a memorial portion, and burn *it* on the altar. *It is* an offering made by fire, a sweet aroma to the LORD.

Lev 2:16 Then the priest shall burn the memorial portion: *part* of its beaten grain and *part* of its oil, with all the frankincense, as an offering made by fire to the LORD.

Lev 6:15 He shall take from it his handful of the fine flour of the grain offering, with its oil, and all the frankincense which *is* on the grain offering, and shall burn *it* on the altar *for* a sweet aroma, as a memorial to the LORD.

High priest's deputy had care of.

Num 4:16 "The appointed duty of Eleazar the son of Aaron the priest *is* the oil for the light, the sweet incense, the daily grain offering, the anointing oil, the oversight of all the tabernacle, of all that *is* in it, with the sanctuary and its furnishings."

Laid up in a chamber of the temple.

Neh 10:39 For the children of Israel and the children of Levi shall bring the offering of the grain, of the new wine and the oil, to the storerooms where the articles of the sanctuary *are, where* the priests who minister and the gatekeepers and the singers *are;* and we will not neglect the house of our God.

Neh 13:5 And he had prepared for him a large room, where previously they had stored the grain offerings, the frankincense, the articles, the tithes of grain, the new wine and oil, which were commanded *to be given* to the Levites and singers and gatekeepers, and the offerings for the priests.

Ezek 42:13 Then he said to me, "The north chambers *and* the south chambers, which *are* opposite the separating courtyard, *are* the holy chambers where the priests who approach the LORD shall eat the most holy offerings. There they shall lay the most holy offerings—the grain offering, the sin offering, and the trespass offering—for the place *is* holy.

The priest's portion.

Lev 2:3 The rest of the grain offering *shall be* Aaron's and his sons'. *It is* most holy of the offerings to the LORD made by fire.

Lev 6:16–18 And the remainder of it Aaron and his sons shall eat; with unleavened bread it shall be eaten in a holy place; in the court of the tabernacle of meeting they shall eat it. **17** It shall not be baked with leaven. I have given it *as* their portion of My offerings made by fire; it *is* most holy, like the sin offering and the trespass offering. **18** All the males among the children of Aaron may eat it. *It shall be* a statute forever in your generations concerning the offerings made by fire to the LORD. Everyone who touches them must be holy.' "

The Jews

Often not accepted in.

Amos 5:22 Though you offer Me burnt offerings and your grain offerings, I will not accept *them,* Nor will I regard your fattened peace offerings.

Condemned for offering, to idols.

Is 57:6 Among the smooth *stones* of the stream *Is* your portion; They, they, *are* your lot! Even to them you have poured a drink offering, You have offered a grain offering. Should I receive comfort in these?

Often prevented from offering, by judgments.

Joel 1:9 The grain offering and the drink offering Have been cut off from the house of the LORD; The priests mourn, who minister to the LORD.

Joel 1:13 Gird yourselves and lament, you priests; Wail, you who minister before the altar; Come, lie all night in sackcloth, You who minister to my God; For the grain offering and the drink offering Are withheld from the house of your God.

Materials for public, often provided by the princes.

Num 7:13 His offering *was* one silver platter, the weight of which *was* one hundred and thirty *shekels,* and one silver bowl of seventy shekels, according to the shekel of the sanctuary, both of them full of fine flour mixed with oil as a grain offering;

Num 7:19 *For* his offering he offered one silver platter, the weight of which *was* one hundred and thirty *shekels,* and one silver bowl of seventy shekels, according to the shekel of the sanctuary, both of them full of fine flour mixed with oil as a grain offering;

Num 7:25 His offering *was* one silver platter, the weight of which *was* one hundred and thirty *shekels,* and one silver bowl of seventy shekels, according to the shekel of the sanctuary, both of them full of fine flour mixed with oil as a grain offering;

Ezek 45:16 "All the people of the land shall give this offering for the prince in Israel.

OFFERING, HEAVE

To be brought to God's house.

Deut 12:6 There you shall take your burnt offerings, your sacrifices, your tithes, the heave offerings of your hand, your vowed offerings, your freewill offerings, and the firstborn of your herds and flocks.

Consisted of

Firstfruits of bread.

Num 15:19–21 then it will be, when you eat of the bread of the land, that you shall offer up a heave offering to the LORD. **20** You shall offer up a cake of the first of your ground meal *as* a heave offering; as a heave offering of the threshing floor, so shall you offer it up. **21** Of the first of your ground meal you shall give to the LORD a heave offering throughout your generations.

Right thigh of peace offerings.

Lev 7:32 Also the right thigh you shall give to the priest *as* a heave offering from the sacrifices of your peace offerings.

Part of the grain offering of all peace offerings.

Lev 7:14 And from it he shall offer one cake from each offering *as* a heave offering to the LORD. It shall belong to the priest who sprinkles the blood of the peace offering.

Thigh of the priest's consecration ram.

Ex 29:27 And from the ram of the consecration you shall consecrate the breast of the wave offering which is waved, and the thigh of the heave offering which is raised, of *that* which *is* for Aaron and of *that* which is for his sons.

Tenth of all tithes.

Num 18:26 "Speak thus to the Levites, and say to them: 'When you take from the children of Israel the tithes which I have given you from them as your inheritance, then you shall offer up a heave offering of it to the LORD, a tenth of the tithe.

Part of all gifts.

Num 18:29 Of all your gifts you shall offer up every heave offering due to the LORD, from all the best of them, the consecrated part of them.'

Part of spoil taken in war. **Num 31:26–47**

To be the best of their kind.

Num 18:29 Of all your gifts you shall offer up every heave offering due to the LORD, from all the best of them, the consecrated part of them.'

To be heaved up by the priest.

Ex 29:27 And from the ram of the consecration you shall consecrate the breast of the wave offering which is waved, and the thigh of the heave offering which is raised, of *that* which *is* for Aaron and of *that* which is for his sons.

Sanctified the whole offering.

Num 18:27 And your heave offering shall be reckoned to you as though *it were* the grain of the threshing floor and as the fullness of the winepress.

Num 18:30 Therefore you shall say to them: 'When you have lifted up the best of it, then *the rest* shall be accounted to the Levites as the produce of the threshing floor and as the produce of the winepress.

Given to the priests.

Ex 29:28 It shall be from the children of Israel *for* Aaron and his sons by a statute forever. For it is a heave offering; it shall be a heave offering from the children of Israel from the sacrifices of their peace offerings, *that is,* their heave offering to the LORD.

Lev 7:34 For the breast of the wave offering and the thigh of the heave offering I have taken from the children of Israel, from the sacrifices of their peace offerings, and I have given them to Aaron the priest and to his sons from the children of Israel by a statute forever.' "

To be eaten in a holy place.

Lev 10:12–15 And Moses spoke to Aaron, and to Eleazar and Ithamar, his sons who were left: "Take the grain offering that remains of the offerings made by fire to the LORD, and eat it without leaven beside the altar; for it *is* most holy. **13** You shall eat it in a holy place, because it *is* your due and your sons' due, of the sacrifices made by fire to the LORD; for so I have been commanded. **14** The breast of the wave offering and the thigh of the heave offering you shall eat in a clean place, you, your sons, and your daughters with you; for *they are* your due and your sons' due, *which* are given from the sacrifices of peace offerings of the children of Israel. **15** The thigh of the heave offering and the breast of the wave offering they shall bring with the offerings of fat made by fire, to offer *as* a wave offering before the LORD. And it shall be yours and your sons' with you, by a statute forever, as the LORD has commanded."

OFFERING, PEACE

A male or female of herd or flock.

Lev 3:1 'When his offering *is* a sacrifice of a peace offering, if he offers *it* of the herd, whether male or female, he shall offer it without blemish before the LORD.

Lev 3:6 'If his offering as a sacrifice of a peace offering to the LORD *is* of the flock, *whether* male or female, he shall offer it without blemish.

Lev 3:12 'And if his offering *is* a goat, then he shall offer it before the LORD.

The offerer required

To give it freely.

Lev 19:5 'And if you offer a sacrifice of a peace offering to the LORD, you shall offer it of your own free will.

To bring it himself.

Lev 7:29–30 "Speak to the children of Israel, saying: 'He who offers the sacrifice of his peace offering to the LORD shall bring his offering to the LORD from the sacrifice of his peace offering. **30** His own hands shall bring the offerings made by fire to the LORD. The fat with the breast he shall bring, that the breast may be waved *as* a wave offering before the LORD.

To lay his hand upon its head.

Lev 3:2 And he shall lay his hand on the head of his offering, and kill it *at* the door of the tabernacle of meeting; and Aaron's sons, the priests, shall sprinkle the blood all around on the altar.

Lev 3:8 And he shall lay his hand on the head of his offering, and kill it before the tabernacle of meeting; and Aaron's sons shall sprinkle its blood all around on the altar.

Lev 3:13 He shall lay his hand on its head and kill it before the tabernacle of meeting; and the sons of Aaron shall sprinkle its blood all around on the altar.

To kill it at tabernacle door.

Lev 3:2 And he shall lay his hand on the head of his offering, and kill it *at* the door of the tabernacle of meeting; and Aaron's sons, the priests, shall sprinkle the blood all around on the altar.

Lev 8:13 Then Moses brought Aaron's sons and put tunics on them, girded them with sashes, and put hats on them, as the LORD had commanded Moses.

Required to be perfect and free from blemish.

Lev 3:1 'When his offering *is* a sacrifice of a peace offering, if he offers *it* of the herd, whether male or female, he shall offer it without blemish before the LORD.

Lev 3:6 'If his offering as a sacrifice of a peace offering to the LORD *is* of the flock, *whether* male or female, he shall offer it without blemish.

Lev 22:21 And whoever offers a sacrifice of a peace offering to the LORD, to fulfill *his* vow, or a freewill offering from the cattle or the sheep, it must be perfect to be accepted; there shall be no defect in it.

The priest

Prepared it.

Ezek 46:2 The prince shall enter by way of the vestibule of the gateway from the outside, and stand by the gatepost. The priests shall prepare his burnt offering and his peace offerings. He shall worship at the threshold of the gate. Then he shall go out, but the gate shall not be shut until evening.

Sprinkled the blood on the altar.

Lev 3:2 And he shall lay his hand on the head of his offering, and kill it *at* the door of the tabernacle of meeting; and Aaron's sons, the priests, shall sprinkle the blood all around on the altar.

Lev 3:8 And he shall lay his hand on the head of his offering, and kill it before the tabernacle of meeting; and Aaron's sons shall sprinkle its blood all around on the altar.

Lev 3:13 He shall lay his hand on its head and kill it before the tabernacle of meeting; and the sons of Aaron shall sprinkle its blood all around on the altar.

Offered the inside fat, etc. by fire.

Lev 3:3 Then he shall offer from the sacrifice of the peace offering an offering made by fire to the LORD. The fat that covers the entrails and all the fat that *is* on the entrails,

Lev 3:4 the two kidneys and the fat that *is* on them by the flanks, and the fatty lobe *attached* to the liver above the kidneys, he shall remove;

Lev 3:9–10 'Then he shall offer from the sacrifice of the peace offering, as an offering made by fire to the LORD, its fat *and* the whole fat tail which he shall remove close to the backbone. And the fat that covers the entrails and all the fat that *is* on the entrails, **10** the two kidneys and the fat that *is* on them by the flanks, and the fatty lobe *attached* to the liver above the kidneys, he shall remove;

Laid it upon the daily burnt offering.

Lev 3:5 and Aaron's sons shall burn it on the altar upon the burnt sacrifice, which *is* on the wood that *is* on the fire, *as* an offering made by fire, a sweet aroma to the LORD.

Lev 6:12–13 And the fire on the altar shall be kept burning on it; it shall not be put out. And the priest shall burn wood on it every morning, and lay the burnt offering in order on it; and he shall burn on it the fat of the peace offerings. **13** A fire shall always be burning on the altar; it shall never go out.

Waved the breast as a wave offering.

Ex 29:26 "Then you shall take the breast of the ram of Aaron's consecration and wave it *as* a wave offering before the LORD; and it shall be your portion.

Ex 29:28 It shall be from the children of Israel *for* Aaron and his sons by a statute forever. For it is a heave offering; it shall be a heave offering from the children of Israel from the sacrifices of their peace offerings, *that is,* their heave offering to the LORD.

Lev 7:29–30 "Speak to the children of Israel, saying: 'He who offers the sacrifice of his peace offering to the LORD shall bring his offering to the LORD from the sacrifice of his peace offering. **30** His own hands shall bring the offerings made by fire to the LORD. The fat with the breast he shall bring, that the breast may be waved *as* a wave offering before the LORD.

Heaved the right thigh as a heave offering.

Ex 29:22–27 "Also you shall take the fat of the ram, the fat tail, the fat that covers the entrails, the fatty lobe *attached to* the liver, the two kidneys and the fat on them, the right thigh (for it *is* a ram of consecration), **23** one loaf of bread, one cake *made with* oil, and one wafer from the basket of the unleavened bread that *is* before the LORD; **24** and you shall put all these in the hands of Aaron and in the hands of his sons, and you shall wave them *as* a wave offering before the LORD. **25** You shall receive them back from their hands and burn *them* on the altar as a burnt offering, as a sweet aroma before the LORD. It *is* an offering made by fire to the LORD. **26** "Then you shall take the breast of the ram of Aaron's consecration and wave it *as* a wave offering before the LORD; and it shall be your portion. **27** And from the ram of the consecration you shall

consecrate the breast of the wave offering which is waved, and the thigh of the heave offering which is raised, of *that* which *is* for Aaron and of *that* which is for his sons.

Had the thigh and breast as his part.

Ex 29:28 It shall be from the children of Israel *for* Aaron and his sons by a statute forever. For it is a heave offering; it shall be a heave offering from the children of Israel from the sacrifices of their peace offerings, *that is,* their heave offering to the LORD.

Lev 7:31–34 And the priest shall burn the fat on the altar, but the breast shall be Aaron's and his sons'. **32** Also the right thigh you shall give to the priest *as* a heave offering from the sacrifices of your peace offerings. **33** He among the sons of Aaron, who offers the blood of the peace offering and the fat, shall have the right thigh for *his* part. **34** For the breast of the wave offering and the thigh of the heave offering I have taken from the children of Israel, from the sacrifices of their peace offerings, and I have given them to Aaron the priest and to his sons from the children of Israel by a statute forever.' "

An offering most acceptable.

Lev 3:5 and Aaron's sons shall burn it on the altar upon the burnt sacrifice, which *is* on the wood that *is* on the fire, *as* an offering made by fire, a sweet aroma to the LORD.

Lev 3:16 and the priest shall burn them on the altar *as* food, an offering made by fire for a sweet aroma; all the fat *is* the LORD's.

Was offered

With a burnt offering.

Judg 21:4 So it was, on the next morning, that the people rose early and built an altar there, and offered burnt offerings and peace offerings.

1 Sam 10:8 You shall go down before me to Gilgal; and surely I will come down to you to offer burnt offerings *and* make sacrifices of peace offerings. Seven days you shall wait, till I come to you and show you what you should do."

1 Kin 3:15 Then Solomon awoke; and indeed it had been a dream. And he came to Jerusalem and stood before the ark of the covenant of the LORD, offered up burnt offerings, offered peace offerings, and made a feast for all his servants.

With a sin offering.

Lev 23:19 Then you shall sacrifice one kid of the goats as a sin offering, and two male lambs of the first year as a sacrifice of a peace offering.

As a thanksgiving offering.

Lev 7:12–13 If he offers it for a thanksgiving, then he shall offer, with the sacrifice of thanksgiving, unleavened cakes mixed with oil, unleavened wafers anointed with oil, or cakes of blended flour mixed with oil. **13** Besides the cakes, *as* his offering he shall offer leavened bread with the sacrifice of thanksgiving of his peace offering.

As a voluntary offering.

Lev 7:16 But if the sacrifice of his offering *is* a vow or a voluntary offering, it shall be eaten the same day that he offers his sacrifice; but on the next day the remainder of it also may be eaten;

For atonement.

Ezek 45:15 And one lamb shall be given from a flock of two hundred, from the rich pastures of Israel. These shall be for grain offerings, burnt offerings, and peace offerings, to make atonement for them," says the Lord GOD.

Eph 2:13–14 But now in Christ Jesus you who once were far off have been brought near by the blood of Christ. **14** For He Himself is our peace, who has made both one, and has broken down the middle wall of separation,

For confirming the legal covenant.

Ex 24:5 Then he sent young men of the children of Israel, who offered burnt offerings and sacrificed peace offerings of oxen to the LORD.

At consecration of priests.

Ex 29:22 "Also you shall take the fat of the ram, the fat tail, the fat that covers the entrails, the fatty lobe *attached to* the liver, the two kidneys and the fat on them, the right thigh (for it *is* a ram of consecration),

Ex 29:29 "And the holy garments of Aaron shall be his sons' after him, to be anointed in them and to be consecrated in them.

For the people at large.

Lev 9:4 also a bull and a ram as peace offerings, to sacrifice before the LORD, and a grain offering mixed with oil; for today the LORD will appear to you.' "

At expiration of Nazirite's vow.

Num 6:14 And he shall present his offering to the LORD: one male lamb in its first year without blemish as a burnt offering, one ewe lamb in its first year without blemish as a sin offering, one ram without blemish as a peace offering,

At all the festivals.

Num 10:10 Also in the day of your gladness, in your appointed feasts, and at the beginning of your months, you shall blow the trumpets over your burnt offerings and over the sacrifices of your peace offerings; and they shall be a memorial for you before your God: I *am* the LORD your God."

At dedication of tabernacle.

Num 7:17 and for the sacrifice of peace offerings: two oxen, five rams, five male goats, and five male lambs in their first year. This *was* the offering of Nahshon the son of Amminadab.

Num 7:23 and as the sacrifice of peace offerings: two oxen, five rams, five male goats, and five male lambs in their first year. This *was* the offering of Nethanel the son of Zuar.

At dedication of temple.

1 Kin 8:62–64 Then the king and all Israel with him offered sacrifices before the LORD. **63** And Solomon offered a sacrifice of peace offerings, which he offered to the LORD, twenty-two thousand bulls and one hundred and twenty thousand sheep. So the king and all the children of Israel dedicated the house of the LORD. **64** On the same day the king consecrated the middle of the court that *was* in front of the house of the LORD; for there he offered burnt offerings, grain offerings, and the fat of the peace offerings, because the bronze altar that *was* before the LORD *was*

too small to receive the burnt offerings, the grain offerings, and the fat of the peace offerings.

At coronation of kings.

1 Sam 11:15 So all the people went to Gilgal, and there they made Saul king before the LORD in Gilgal. There they made sacrifices of peace offerings before the LORD, and there Saul and all the men of Israel rejoiced greatly.

By Joshua after his victories.

Josh 8:31 as Moses the servant of the LORD had commanded the children of Israel, as it is written in the Book of the Law of Moses: "an altar of whole stones over which no man has wielded an iron *tool.*" And they offered on it burnt offerings to the LORD, and sacrificed peace offerings.

By Israel after their defeat.

Judg 20:26 Then all the children of Israel, that is, all the people, went up and came to the house of God and wept. They sat there before the LORD and fasted that day until evening; and they offered burnt offerings and peace offerings before the LORD.

By David on bringing up the ark.

2 Sam 6:17 So they brought the ark of the LORD, and set it in its place in the midst of the tabernacle that David had erected for it. Then David offered burnt offerings and peace offerings before the LORD.

By David after the plague.

2 Sam 24:25 And David built there an altar to the LORD, and offered burnt offerings and peace offerings. So the LORD heeded the prayers for the land, and the plague was withdrawn from Israel.

By Solomon three times a year.

1 Kin 9:25 Now three times a year Solomon offered burnt offerings and peace offerings on the altar which he had built for the LORD, and he burned incense with them *on the altar* that *was* before the LORD. So he finished the temple.

By Manasseh on repairing and restoring the altar.

2 Chr 33:15–16 He took away the foreign gods and the idol from the house of the LORD, and all the altars that he had built in the mount of the house of the LORD and in Jerusalem; and he cast *them* out of the city. **16** He also repaired the altar of the LORD, sacrificed peace offerings and thank offerings on it, and commanded Judah to serve the LORD God of Israel.

If a thanksgiving offering, to be eaten the day offered.

Lev 7:15 'The flesh of the sacrifice of his peace offering for thanksgiving shall be eaten the same day it is offered. He shall not leave any of it until morning.

If a voluntary offering to be eaten the same day or the next.

Lev 7:16–17 But if the sacrifice of his offering *is* a vow or a voluntary offering, it shall be eaten the same day that he offers his sacrifice; but on the next day the remainder of it also may be eaten; **17** the remainder of the flesh of the sacrifice on the third day must be burned with fire.

Lev 19:6–8 It shall be eaten the same day you offer *it*, and on the next day. And if any remains until the third day, it shall be burned in the fire. **7** And if it is eaten at all on the third day, it *is* an abomination. It shall not be accepted. **8** Therefore *everyone* who eats it shall bear his iniquity, because he has profaned the hallowed *offering* of the LORD; and that person shall be cut off from his people.

To be eaten before the Lord.

Deut 12:17–18 You may not eat within your gates the tithe of your grain or your new wine or your oil, of the firstborn of your herd or your flock, of any of your offerings which you vow, of your freewill offerings, or of the heave offering of your hand. **18** But you must eat them before the LORD your God in the place which the LORD your God chooses, you and your son and your daughter, your male servant and your female servant, and the Levite who *is* within your gates; and you shall rejoice before the LORD your God in all to which you put your hands.

No unclean person to eat of.

Lev 7:20–21 But the person who eats the flesh of the sacrifice of the peace offering that *belongs* to the LORD, while he is unclean, that person shall be cut off from his people. **21** Moreover the person who touches any unclean thing, *such as* human uncleanness, *an* unclean animal, or any abominable unclean thing, and who eats the flesh of the sacrifice of the peace offering that *belongs* to the LORD, that person shall be cut off from his people.' "

OFFERING, SIN

Probable origin of.

Gen 4:4 Abel also brought of the firstborn of his flock and of their fat. And the LORD respected Abel and his offering,

Gen 4:7 If you do well, will you not be accepted? And if you do not do well, sin lies at the door. And its desire *is* for you, but you should rule over it."

Was offered

For unintentional sins.

Lev 4:2 "Speak to the children of Israel, saying: 'If a person sins unintentionally against any of the commandments of the LORD *in anything* which ought not to be done, and does any of them,

Lev 4:13 'Now if the whole congregation of Israel sins unintentionally, and the thing is hidden from the eyes of the assembly, and they have done *something against* any of the commandments of the LORD *in anything* which should not be done, and are guilty;

Lev 4:22 'When a ruler has sinned, and done *something* unintentionally *against* any of the commandments of the LORD his God *in anything* which should not be done, and is guilty,

Lev 4:27 'If anyone of the common people sins unintentionally by doing *something against* any of the commandments of the LORD *in anything* which ought not to be done, and is guilty,

At the consecration of priests.

Ex 29:10 "You shall also have the bull brought before the tabernacle of meeting, and Aaron and his sons shall put their hands on the head of the bull.

Ex 29:14 But the flesh of the bull, with its skin and its offal, you shall burn with fire outside the camp. It *is* a sin offering.

Lev 8:14 And he brought the bull for the sin offering.

Then Aaron and his sons laid their hands on the head of the bull for the sin offering,

At the consecration of Levites.

Num 8:8 Then let them take a young bull with its grain offering of fine flour mixed with oil, and you shall take another young bull as a sin offering.

At the expiration of a Nazirite's vow.

Num 6:14 And he shall present his offering to the LORD: one male lamb in its first year without blemish as a burnt offering, one ewe lamb in its first year without blemish as a sin offering, one ram without blemish as a peace offering,

On the day of atonement.

Lev 16:3 "Thus Aaron shall come into the Holy *Place:* with *the blood of* a young bull as a sin offering, and *of* a ram as a burnt offering.

Lev 16:9 And Aaron shall bring the goat on which the LORD's lot fell, and offer it *as* a sin offering.

Was a most holy sacrifice.

Lev 6:25 "Speak to Aaron and to his sons, saying, 'This *is* the law of the sin offering: In the place where the burnt offering is killed, the sin offering shall be killed before the LORD. It *is* most holy.

Lev 6:29 All the males among the priests may eat it. It *is* most holy.

Consisted of

A young bull for the priests.

Lev 4:3 if the anointed priest sins, bringing guilt on the people, then let him offer to the LORD for his sin which he has sinned a young bull without blemish as a sin offering.

Lev 9:2 And he said to Aaron, "Take for yourself a young bull as a sin offering and a ram as a burnt offering, without blemish, and offer *them* before the LORD.

Lev 9:8 Aaron therefore went to the altar and killed the calf of the sin offering, which *was* for himself.

Lev 16:3 "Thus Aaron shall come into the Holy *Place:* with *the blood of* a young bull as a sin offering, and *of* a ram as a burnt offering.

Lev 16:6 "Aaron shall offer the bull as a sin offering, which *is* for himself, and make atonement for himself and for his house.

A young bull or male goat for the congregation.

Lev 4:14 when the sin which they have committed becomes known, then the assembly shall offer a young bull for the sin, and bring it before the tabernacle of meeting.

Lev 16:9 And Aaron shall bring the goat on which the LORD's lot fell, and offer it *as* a sin offering.

2 Chr 29:23 Then they brought out the male goats *for* the sin offering before the king and the assembly, and they laid their hands on them.

A male kid for a ruler.

Lev 4:23 or if his sin which he has committed comes to his knowledge, he shall bring as his offering a kid of the goats, a male without blemish.

A female kid or female lamb for a private person.

Lev 4:28 or if his sin which he has committed comes to his knowledge, then he shall bring as his offering a kid of the goats, a female without blemish, for his sin which he has committed.

Lev 4:32 'If he brings a lamb as his sin offering, he shall bring a female without blemish.

Sins of the offerer transferred to, by imposition of hands.

Lev 4:4 He shall bring the bull to the door of the tabernacle of meeting before the LORD, lay his hand on the bull's head, and kill the bull before the LORD.

Lev 4:15 And the elders of the congregation shall lay their hands on the head of the bull before the LORD. Then the bull shall be killed before the LORD.

Lev 4:24 And he shall lay his hand on the head of the goat, and kill it at the place where they kill the burnt offering before the LORD. It *is* a sin offering.

Lev 4:29 And he shall lay his hand on the head of the sin offering, and kill the sin offering at the place of the burnt offering.

2 Chr 29:23 Then they brought out the male goats *for* the sin offering before the king and the assembly, and they laid their hands on them.   .

Was killed in the same place as the burnt offering.

Lev 4:24 And he shall lay his hand on the head of the goat, and kill it at the place where they kill the burnt offering before the LORD. It *is* a sin offering.

Lev 6:25 "Speak to Aaron and to his sons, saying, 'This *is* the law of the sin offering: In the place where the burnt offering is killed, the sin offering shall be killed before the LORD. It *is* most holy.

The blood of,

Brought by the priest into the tabernacle.

Lev 4:5 Then the anointed priest shall take some of the bull's blood and bring it to the tabernacle of meeting.

Lev 4:16 The anointed priest shall bring some of the bull's blood to the tabernacle of meeting.

Sprinkled seven times before the Lord, outside the veil.

Lev 4:6 The priest shall dip his finger in the blood and sprinkle some of the blood seven times before the LORD, in front of the veil of the sanctuary.

Lev 4:17 Then the priest shall dip his finger in the blood and sprinkle *it* seven times before the LORD, in front of the veil.

Put upon the horns of the altar of burnt offering.

Lev 4:25 The priest shall take some of the blood of the sin offering with his finger, put *it* on the horns of the altar of burnt offering, and pour its blood at the base of the altar of burnt offering.

Lev 4:30 Then the priest shall take *some* of its blood with his finger, put *it* on the horns of the altar of burnt offering, and pour all *the remaining* blood at the base of the altar.

Poured at the base of the altar of burnt offering.

Lev 4:7 And the priest shall put some of the blood on the horns of the altar of sweet incense before the LORD, which is in the tabernacle of meeting; and he shall pour the remaining blood of the bull at the base of the altar of the burnt offering, which is at the door of the tabernacle of meeting.

Lev 4:18 And he shall put *some* of the blood on the horns

of the altar which *is* before the LORD, which *is* in the tabernacle of meeting; and he shall pour the remaining blood at the base of the altar of burnt offering, which is at the door of the tabernacle of meeting.

Lev 4:25 The priest shall take some of the blood of the sin offering with his finger, put *it* on the horns of the altar of burnt offering, and pour its blood at the base of the altar of burnt offering.

Lev 4:30 Then the priest shall take *some* of its blood with his finger, put *it* on the horns of the altar of burnt offering, and pour all *the remaining* blood at the base of the altar.

Lev 9:9 Then the sons of Aaron brought the blood to him. And he dipped his finger in the blood, put *it* on the horns of the altar, and poured the blood at the base of the altar.

Fat of the inside and kidneys, burned on the altar of burnt offering.

Lev 4:8–10 He shall take from it all the fat of the bull as the sin offering. The fat that covers the entrails and all the fat which *is* on the entrails, **9** the two kidneys and the fat that *is* on them by the flanks, and the fatty lobe *attached* to the liver above the kidneys, he shall remove, **10** as it was taken from the bull of the sacrifice of the peace offering; and the priest shall burn them on the altar of the burnt offering.

Lev 4:19 He shall take all the fat from it and burn *it* on the altar.

Lev 4:26 And he shall burn all its fat on the altar, like the fat of the sacrifice of the peace offering. So the priest shall make atonement for him concerning his sin, and it shall be forgiven him.

Lev 4:31 He shall remove all its fat, as fat is removed from the sacrifice of the peace offering; and the priest shall burn it on the altar for a sweet aroma to the LORD. So the priest shall make atonement for him, and it shall be forgiven him.

Lev 9:10 But the fat, the kidneys, and the fatty lobe from the liver of the sin offering he burned on the altar, as the LORD had commanded Moses.

When for priest or congregation, the flesh and hide burned outside the camp.

Lev 4:11–12 But the bull's hide and all its flesh, with its head and legs, its entrails and offal— **12** the whole bull he shall carry outside the camp to a clean place, where the ashes are poured out, and burn it on wood with fire; where the ashes are poured out it shall be burned.

Lev 4:21 Then he shall carry the bull outside the camp, and burn it as he burned the first bull. It *is* a sin offering for the assembly.

Lev 6:30 But no sin offering from which *any* of the blood is brought into the tabernacle of meeting, to make atonement in the holy *place*, shall be eaten. It shall be burned in the fire.

Lev 9:11 The flesh and the hide he burned with fire outside the camp.

Eaten by priests in a holy place, when its blood not brought into the tabernacle.

Lev 6:26 The priest who offers it for sin shall eat it. In a holy place it shall be eaten, in the court of the tabernacle of meeting.

Lev 6:29–30 All the males among the priests may eat it. It *is* most holy. **30** But no sin offering from which *any* of the blood is brought into the tabernacle of meeting, to make atonement in the holy *place,* shall be eaten. It shall be burned in the fire.

Aaron, etc. rebuked for burning and not eating that of the congregation.

Lev 9:9 Then the sons of Aaron brought the blood to him. And he dipped his finger in the blood, put *it* on the horns of the altar, and poured the blood at the base of the altar.

Lev 9:15 Then he brought the people's offering, and took the goat, which *was* the sin offering for the people, and killed it and offered it for sin, like the first one.

Lev 10:16–18 Then Moses made careful inquiry about the goat of the sin offering, and there it was—burned up. And he was angry with Eleazar and Ithamar, the sons of Aaron *who were* left, saying, **17** "Why have you not eaten the sin offering in a holy place, since it *is* most holy, and *God* has given it to you to bear the guilt of the congregation, to make atonement for them before the LORD? **18** See! Its blood was not brought inside the holy *place;* indeed you should have eaten it in a holy *place,* as I commanded."

Whatever touched the flesh of, was rendered holy.

Lev 6:27 Everyone who touches its flesh must be holy. And when its blood is sprinkled on any garment, you shall wash that on which it was sprinkled, in a holy place.

Garments sprinkled with the blood of, to be washed.

Lev 6:27 Everyone who touches its flesh must be holy. And when its blood is sprinkled on any garment, you shall wash that on which it was sprinkled, in a holy place.

Laws respecting the vessels used for boiling the flesh of.

Lev 6:28 But the earthen vessel in which it is boiled shall be broken. And if it is boiled in a bronze pot, it shall be both scoured and rinsed in water.

Was typical of Christ's sacrifice.

2 Cor 5:21 For He made Him who knew no sin *to be* sin for us, that we might become the righteousness of God in Him.

Heb 13:11–13 For the bodies of those animals, whose blood is brought into the sanctuary by the high priest for sin, are burned outside the camp. **12** Therefore Jesus also, that He might sanctify the people with His own blood, suffered outside the gate. **13** Therefore let us go forth to Him, outside the camp, bearing His reproach.

OFFERING, TRESPASS

Esteemed as a sin offering, and frequently so called.

Lev 5:6 and he shall bring his trespass offering to the LORD for his sin which he has committed, a female from the flock, a lamb or a kid of the goats as a sin offering. So the priest shall make atonement for him concerning his sin.

Lev 5:9 Then he shall sprinkle *some* of the blood of the sin offering on the side of the altar, and the rest of the blood shall be drained out at the base of the altar. It *is* a sin offering.

To be offered

For concealing knowledge of an oath.

Lev 5:1 'If a person sins in hearing the utterance of an oath, and *is* a witness, whether he has seen or known *of the matter*—if he does not tell *it,* he bears guilt.

For involuntarily touching unclean things.

Lev 5:2–3 'Or if a person touches any unclean thing, whether *it is* the carcass of an unclean beast, or the carcass of unclean livestock, or the carcass of unclean creeping things, and he is unaware of it, he also shall be unclean and guilty. **3** Or if he touches human uncleanness—whatever uncleanness with which a man may be defiled, and he is unaware of it—when he realizes *it,* then he shall be guilty.

For rash swearing.

Lev 5:4 'Or if a person swears, speaking thoughtlessly with *his* lips to do evil or to do good, whatever *it is* that a man may pronounce by an oath, and he is unaware of it—when he realizes *it,* then he shall be guilty in any of these *matters.*

For unintentional sins in regard to holy things.

Lev 5:15 "If a person commits a trespass, and sins unintentionally in regard to the holy things of the LORD, then he shall bring to the LORD as his trespass offering a ram without blemish from the flocks, with your valuation in shekels of silver according to the shekel of the sanctuary, as a trespass offering.

For any sin of ignorance.

Lev 5:17 "If a person sins, and commits any of these things which are forbidden to be done by the commandments of the LORD, though he does not know *it,* yet he is guilty and shall bear his iniquity.

For breach of trust or fraud.

Lev 6:2–5 "If a person sins and commits a trespass against the LORD by lying to his neighbor about what was delivered to him for safekeeping, or about a pledge, or about a robbery, or if he has extorted from his neighbor, **3** or if he has found what was lost and lies concerning it, and swears falsely—in any one of these things that a man may do in which he sins: **4** then it shall be, because he has sinned and is guilty, that he shall restore what he has stolen, or the thing which he has extorted, or what was delivered to him for safekeeping, or the lost thing which he found, **5** or all that about which he has sworn falsely. He shall restore its full value, add one-fifth more to it, *and* give it to whomever it belongs, on the day of his trespass offering.

Was a most holy offering.

Lev 14:13 Then he shall kill the lamb in the place where he kills the sin offering and the burnt offering, in a holy place; for as the sin offering *is* the priest's, so *is* the trespass offering. It *is* most holy.

Consisted of

A female lamb or kid.

Lev 5:6 and he shall bring his trespass offering to the LORD for his sin which he has committed, a female from the flock, a lamb or a kid of the goats as a sin offering. So the priest shall make atonement for him concerning his sin.

A ram without blemish.

Lev 5:15 "If a person commits a trespass, and sins unintentionally in regard to the holy things of the LORD, then he shall bring to the LORD as his trespass offering a ram without blemish from the flocks, with your valuation in shekels of silver according to the shekel of the sanctuary, as a trespass offering.

Lev 6:6 And he shall bring his trespass offering to the LORD, a ram without blemish from the flock, with your valuation, as a trespass offering, to the priest.

Two turtle doves by those unable to bring a lamb.

Lev 5:7–10 'If he is not able to bring a lamb, then he shall bring to the LORD, for his trespass which he has committed, two turtledoves or two young pigeons: one as a sin offering and the other as a burnt offering. 8 And he shall bring them to the priest, who shall offer *that* which *is* for the sin offering first, and wring off its head from its neck, but shall not divide *it* completely. 9 Then he shall sprinkle *some* of the blood of the sin offering on the side of the altar, and the rest of the blood shall be drained out at the base of the altar. It *is* a sin offering. 10 And he shall offer the second *as* a burnt offering according to the prescribed manner. So the priest shall make atonement on his behalf for his sin which he has committed, and it shall be forgiven him.

A grain offering by the very poor.

Lev 5:11–13 'But if he is not able to bring two turtledoves or two young pigeons, then he who sinned shall bring for his offering one-tenth of an ephah of fine flour as a sin offering. He shall put no oil on it, nor shall he put frankincense on it, for it *is* a sin offering. 12 Then he shall bring it to the priest, and the priest shall take his handful of it as a memorial portion, and burn *it* on the altar according to the offerings made by fire to the LORD. It *is* a sin offering. 13 The priest shall make atonement for him, for his sin that he has committed in any of these matters; and it shall be forgiven him. *The rest* shall be the priest's as a grain offering.' "

Instructions for ceremony of. Lev 4:1–35; 5:1–19
Atonement made by.

Lev 5:6 and he shall bring his trespass offering to the LORD for his sin which he has committed, a female from the flock, a lamb or a kid of the goats as a sin offering. So the priest shall make atonement for him concerning his sin.

Lev 5:10 And he shall offer the second *as* a burnt offering according to the prescribed manner. So the priest shall make atonement on his behalf for his sin which he has committed, and it shall be forgiven him.

Lev 5:13 The priest shall make atonement for him, for his sin that he has committed in any of these matters; and it shall be forgiven him. *The rest* shall be the priest's as a grain offering.' "

Lev 5:16 And he shall make restitution for the harm that he has done in regard to the holy thing, and shall add one-fifth to it and give it to the priest. So the priest shall make atonement for him with the ram of the trespass offering, and it shall be forgiven him.

Lev 5:18 And he shall bring to the priest a ram without blemish from the flock, with your valuation, as a trespass offering. So the priest shall make atonement for him regarding his ignorance in which he erred and did not know *it*, and it shall be forgiven him.

Lev 6:7 So the priest shall make atonement for him before the LORD, and he shall be forgiven for any one of these things that he may have done in which he trespasses."

Lev 19:22 The priest shall make atonement for him with the ram of the trespass offering before the LORD for his sin which he has committed. And the sin which he has committed shall be forgiven him.

Accompanied by confession.

Lev 5:5 'And it shall be, when he is guilty in any of these *matters,* that he shall confess that he has sinned in that *thing;*

Generally accompanied by restitution.

Lev 5:16 And he shall make restitution for the harm that he has done in regard to the holy thing, and shall add one-fifth to it and give it to the priest. So the priest shall make atonement for him with the ram of the trespass offering, and it shall be forgiven him.

Lev 6:5 or all that about which he has sworn falsely. He shall restore its full value, add one-fifth more to it, *and* give it to whomever it belongs, on the day of his trespass offering.

To be slain where the sin offering and burnt offering were slain.

Lev 14:13 Then he shall kill the lamb in the place where he kills the sin offering and the burnt offering, in a holy place; for as the sin offering *is* the priest's, so *is* the trespass offering. It *is* most holy.

Ezek 40:39 In the vestibule of the gateway *were* two tables on this side and two tables on that side, on which to slay the burnt offering, the sin offering, and the trespass offering.

Sometimes waved alive before the Lord.

Lev 14:12–13 And the priest shall take one male lamb and offer it as a trespass offering, and the log of oil, and wave them *as* a wave offering before the LORD. 13 Then he shall kill the lamb in the place where he kills the sin offering and the burnt offering, in a holy place; for as the sin offering *is* the priest's, so *is* the trespass offering. It *is* most holy.

Special occasions of offering,

Cleansing of a leper.

Lev 14:2 "This shall be the law of the leper for the day of his cleansing: He shall be brought to the priest.

Lev 14:12–14 And the priest shall take one male lamb and offer it as a trespass offering, and the log of oil, and wave them *as* a wave offering before the LORD. 13 Then he shall kill the lamb in the place where he kills the sin offering and the burnt offering, in a holy place; for as the sin offering *is* the priest's, so *is* the trespass offering. It *is* most holy. 14 The priest shall take *some* of the blood of the trespass offering, and the priest shall put *it* on the tip of the right ear of him who is to be cleansed, on the thumb of his right hand, and on the big toe of his right foot.

Lev 14:21–22 "But if he *is* poor and cannot afford it, then he shall take one male lamb *as* a trespass offering to be waved, to make atonement for him, one-tenth *of* *an ephah* of fine flour mixed with oil as a grain offering, a log of oil, **22** and two turtledoves or two young pigeons, such as he is able to afford: one shall be a sin offering and the other a burnt offering.

Purification of women.

Lev 12:6–8 'When the days of her purification are fulfilled, whether for a son or a daughter, she shall bring to the priest a lamb of the first year as a burnt offering, and a young pigeon or a turtledove as a sin offering, to the door of the tabernacle of meeting. **7** Then he shall offer it before the LORD, and make atonement for her. And she shall be clean from the flow of her blood. This *is* the law for her who has borne a male or a female. **8** 'And if she is not able to bring a lamb, then she may bring two turtledoves or two young pigeons—one as a burnt offering and the other as a sin offering. So the priest shall make atonement for her, and she will be clean.' "

Purification of those with discharge of fluids.

Lev 15:14–15 On the eighth day he shall take for himself two turtledoves or two young pigeons, and come before the LORD, to the door of the tabernacle of meeting, and give them to the priest. **15** Then the priest shall offer them, the one *as* a sin offering and the other *as* a burnt offering. So the priest shall make atonement for him before the LORD because of his discharge.

Purification of Nazirites who had broken their vow.

Num 6:12 He shall consecrate to the LORD the days of his separation, and bring a male lamb in its first year as a trespass offering; but the former days shall be lost, because his separation was defiled.

For fornication with a betrothed woman.

Lev 19:20–22 'Whoever lies carnally with a woman who *is* betrothed to a man as a concubine, and who has not at all been redeemed nor given her freedom, for this there shall be scourging; *but* they shall not be put to death, because she was not free. **21** And he shall bring his trespass offering to the LORD, to the door of the tabernacle of meeting, a ram as a trespass offering. **22** The priest shall make atonement for him with the ram of the trespass offering before the LORD for his sin which he has committed. And the sin which he has committed shall be forgiven him.

Was the perquisites of the priest.

Lev 14:13 Then he shall kill the lamb in the place where he kills the sin offering and the burnt offering, in a holy place; for as the sin offering *is* the priest's, so *is* the trespass offering. It *is* most holy.

Ezek 44:29 They shall eat the grain offering, the sin offering, and the trespass offering; every dedicated thing in Israel shall be theirs.

Illustrative of Christ.

Is 53:10 Yet it pleased the LORD to bruise Him; He has put *Him* to grief. When You make His soul an offering for sin, He shall see *His* seed, He shall prolong *His* days, And the pleasure of the LORD shall prosper in His hand.

Ezek 46:20 And he said to me, "This *is* the place where the priests shall boil the trespass offering and the sin offering, *and* where they shall bake the grain offering, so that they do not bring *them* out into the outer court to sanctify the people."

OFFERING, WAVE

Priest waved it before the Lord.

Ex 29:24 and you shall put all these in the hands of Aaron and in the hands of his sons, and you shall wave them *as* a wave offering before the LORD.

Lev 8:27 and he put all *these* in Aaron's hands and in his sons' hands, and waved them *as* a wave offering before the LORD.

Consisted of

The fat, right thigh, etc., of the priest's consecration ram.

Ex 29:22–23 "Also you shall take the fat of the ram, the fat tail, the fat that covers the entrails, the fatty lobe *attached to* the liver, the two kidneys and the fat on them, the right thigh (for it *is* a ram of consecration), **23** one loaf of bread, one cake *made with* oil, and one wafer from the basket of the unleavened bread that *is* before the LORD;

Lev 8:25–26 Then he took the fat and the fat tail, all the fat that *was* on the entrails, the fatty lobe *attached to* the liver, the two kidneys and their fat, and the right thigh; **26** and from the basket of unleavened bread that was before the LORD he took one unleavened cake, a cake of bread *anointed with* oil, and one wafer, and put *them* on the fat and on the right thigh;

The breast of the priest's consecration ram.

Ex 29:26 "Then you shall take the breast of the ram of Aaron's consecration and wave it *as* a wave offering before the LORD; and it shall be your portion.

Lev 8:29 And Moses took the breast and waved it *as* a wave offering before the LORD. It was Moses' part of the ram of consecration, as the LORD had commanded Moses.

The breast of all peace offerings.

Lev 7:30 His own hands shall bring the offerings made by fire to the LORD. The fat with the breast he shall bring, that the breast may be waved *as* a wave offering before the LORD.

Lev 9:18 He also killed the bull and the ram *as* sacrifices of peace offerings, which *were* for the people. And Aaron's sons presented to him the blood, which he sprinkled all around on the altar,

Lev 9:21 but the breasts and the right thigh Aaron waved *as* a wave offering before the LORD, as Moses had commanded.

Shoulder of Nazirite's peace offering.

Num 6:17 and he shall offer the ram as a sacrifice of a peace offering to the LORD, with the basket of unleavened bread; the priest shall also offer its grain offering and its drink offering.

Num 6:19 'And the priest shall take the boiled shoulder of the ram, one unleavened cake from the basket, and one unleavened wafer, and put *them* upon the hands of the Nazirite after he has shaved his consecrated *hair,*

The firstfruits of barley harvest.

Lev 23:10–11 "Speak to the children of Israel, and say to them: 'When you come into the land which I give to you, and reap its harvest, then you shall bring a sheaf of the firstfruits of your harvest to the priest. **11** He shall wave the sheaf before the LORD, to be accepted on your behalf; on the day after the Sabbath the priest shall wave it.

The firstfruits of wheat bread.

Lev 23:20 The priest shall wave them with the bread of the firstfruits *as* a wave offering before the LORD, with the two lambs. They shall be holy to the LORD for the priest.

The jealousy offering.

Num 5:25 Then the priest shall take the grain offering of jealousy from the woman's hand, shall wave the offering before the LORD, and bring it to the altar;

The leper's trespass offering.

Lev 14:12 And the priest shall take one male lamb and offer it as a trespass offering, and the log of oil, and wave them *as* a wave offering before the LORD.

Lev 14:24 And the priest shall take the lamb of the trespass offering and the log of oil, and the priest shall wave them *as* a wave offering before the LORD.

Of the fat, etc., of the consecration ram burnt on the altar.

Ex 29:25 You shall receive them back from their hands and burn *them* on the altar as a burnt offering, as a sweet aroma before the LORD. It *is* an offering made by fire to the LORD.

Lev 8:28 Then Moses took them from their hands and burned *them* on the altar, on the burnt offering. They *were* consecration offerings for a sweet aroma. That *was* an offering made by fire to the LORD.

Was given to the priest as his due.

Ex 29:26–28 "Then you shall take the breast of the ram of Aaron's consecration and wave it *as* a wave offering before the LORD; and it shall be your portion. 27 And from the ram of the consecration you shall consecrate the breast of the wave offering which is waved, and the thigh of the heave offering which is raised, of *that* which *is* for Aaron and of *that* which is for his sons. 28 It shall be from the children of Israel *for* Aaron and his sons by a statute forever. For it is a heave offering; it shall be a heave offering from the children of Israel from the sacrifices of their peace offerings, *that is,* their heave offering to the LORD.

Lev 7:31 And the priest shall burn the fat on the altar, but the breast shall be Aaron's and his sons'.

Lev 7:34 For the breast of the wave offering and the thigh of the heave offering I have taken from the children of Israel, from the sacrifices of their peace offerings, and I have given them to Aaron the priest and to his sons from the children of Israel by a statute forever.' "

Lev 8:29 And Moses took the breast and waved it *as* a wave offering before the LORD. It was Moses' part of the ram of consecration, as the LORD had commanded Moses.

Lev 10:15 The thigh of the heave offering and the breast of the wave offering they shall bring with the offerings of fat made by fire, to offer *as* a wave offering before the LORD. And it shall be yours and your sons' with you, by a statute forever, as the LORD has commanded."

Lev 23:20 The priest shall wave them with the bread of the firstfruits *as* a wave offering before the LORD,

with the two lambs. They shall be holy to the LORD for the priest.

Num 18:11 "This also *is* yours: the heave offering of their gift, with all the wave offerings of the children of Israel; I have given them to you, and your sons and daughters with you, as an ordinance forever. Everyone who is clean in your house may eat it.

Was to be eaten in a holy place by the priest's family.

Lev 10:14 The breast of the wave offering and the thigh of the heave offering you shall eat in a clean place, you, your sons, and your daughters with you; for *they are* your due and your sons' due, *which* are given from the sacrifices of peace offerings of the children of Israel.

OFFICE

Of king, anticipated.

Gen 17:16 And I will bless her and also give you a son by her; then I will bless her, and she shall be *a* mother *of* nations; kings of peoples shall be from her."

Gen 35:11 Also God said to him: "I *am* God Almighty. Be fruitful and multiply; a nation and a company of nations shall proceed from you, and kings shall come from your body.

Gen 49:9–12 Judah *is* a lion's whelp; From the prey, my son, you have gone up. He bows down, he lies down as a lion; And as a lion, who shall rouse him? 10 The scepter shall not depart from Judah, Nor a lawgiver from between his feet, Until Shiloh comes; And to Him *shall be* the obedience of the people. 11 Binding his donkey to the vine, And his donkey's colt to the choice vine, He washed his garments in wine, And his clothes in the blood of grapes. 12 His eyes *are* darker than wine, And his teeth whiter than milk.

Num 24:7 He shall pour water from his buckets, And his seed *shall be* in many waters. "His king shall be higher than Agag, And his kingdom shall be exalted.

Num 24:17 "I see Him, but not now; I behold Him, but not near; A Star shall come out of Jacob; A Scepter shall rise out of Israel, And batter the brow of Moab, And destroy all the sons of tumult.

Deut 17:14 "When you come to the land which the LORD your God is giving you, and possess it and dwell in it, and say, 'I will set a king over me like all the nations that *are* around me,'

Examples of,

Joseph in Egypt.

Gen 41:42 Then Pharaoh took his signet ring off his hand and put it on Joseph's hand; and he clothed him in garments of fine linen and put a gold chain around his neck.

Gen 44:2 Also put my cup, the silver cup, in the mouth of the sack of the youngest, and his grain money." So he did according to the word that Joseph had spoken.

Priesthood in Israel.

Ex 28:1–4 "Now take Aaron your brother, and his sons with him, from among the children of Israel, that he may minister to Me as priest, Aaron *and* Aaron's sons: Nadab, Abihu, Eleazar, and Ithamar. 2 And you shall make holy garments for Aaron your brother, for glory and for beauty. **3** So you shall speak to all *who are* gifted artisans, whom I have filled with the spirit of wisdom, that they may make Aaron's garments, to consecrate him, that he may minister to Me as priest. **4** And these *are* the garments which they shall make: a breastplate, an ephod, a robe, a skillfully woven tunic, a turban, and a sash. So they shall make holy garments for Aaron your brother and his sons, that he may minister to Me as priest.

Investiture ceremony for priesthood.

Ex 29:1–18 "And this is what you shall do to them to hallow them for ministering to Me as priests: Take one young bull and two rams without blemish, **2** and unleavened bread, unleavened cakes mixed with oil, and unleavened wafers anointed with oil (you shall make them of wheat flour). **3** You shall put them in one basket and bring them in the basket, with the bull and the two rams. **4** "And Aaron and his sons you shall bring to the door of the tabernacle of meeting, and you shall wash them with water. **5** Then you shall take the garments, put the tunic on Aaron, and the robe of the ephod, the ephod, and the breastplate, and gird him with the intricately woven band of the ephod. **6** You shall put the turban on his head, and put the holy crown on the turban. **7** And you shall take the anointing oil, pour *it* on his head, and anoint him. **8** Then you shall bring his sons and put tunics on them. **9** And you shall gird them with sashes, Aaron and his sons, and put the hats on them. The priesthood shall be theirs for a perpetual statute. So you shall consecrate Aaron and his sons. **10** "You shall also have the bull brought before the tabernacle of meeting, and Aaron and his sons shall put their hands on the head of the bull. **11** Then you shall kill the bull before the LORD, *by* the door of the tabernacle of meeting. **12** You shall take *some* of the blood of the bull and put *it* on the horns of the altar with your finger, and pour all the blood beside the base of the altar. **13** And you shall take all the fat that covers the entrails, the fatty lobe *attached* to the liver, and the two kidneys and the fat that *is* on them, and burn *them* on the altar. **14** But the flesh of the bull, with its skin and its offal, you shall burn with fire outside the camp. It *is* a sin offering. **15** "You shall also take one ram, and Aaron and his sons shall put their hands on the head of the ram; **16** and you shall kill the ram, and you shall take its blood and sprinkle *it* all around on the altar. **17** Then you shall cut the ram in pieces, wash its entrails and its legs, and put *them* with its pieces and with its head. **18** And you shall burn the whole ram on the altar. It *is* a burnt offering to the LORD; it *is* a sweet aroma, an offering made by fire to the LORD.

Num 8:10 So you shall bring the Levites before the LORD, and the children of Israel shall lay their hands on the Levites;

Cf. Num 27:18; Ezek 21:26

Of priesthood

Sanctioned by God.

1 Sam 2:35 Then I will raise up for Myself a faithful priest *who* shall do according to what *is* in My heart and in My mind. I will build him a sure house, and he shall walk before My anointed forever.

Zech 6:9–15 Then the word of the LORD came to me, saying: **10** "Receive *the gift* from the captives—from Heldai, Tobijah, and Jedaiah, who have come from Babylon—and go the same day and enter the house of Josiah the son of Zephaniah. **11** Take the silver and gold, make an elaborate crown, and set *it* on the head of Joshua the son of Jehozadak, the high priest. **12** Then speak to him, saying, 'Thus says the LORD of hosts, saying: "Behold, the Man whose name *is* the BRANCH! From His place He shall branch out, And He shall build the temple of the LORD; **13** Yes, He shall build the temple of the LORD. He shall bear the glory, And shall sit and rule on His throne; So He shall be a priest on His throne, And the counsel of peace shall be between them both." ' **14** "Now the elaborate crown shall be for a memorial in the temple of the LORD for Helem, Tobijah, Jedaiah, and Hen the son of Zephaniah. **15** Even those from afar shall come and build the temple of the LORD. Then you shall know that the LORD of hosts has sent Me to you. And *this* shall come to pass if you diligently obey the voice of the LORD your God."

Cf. Heb 7:11–19

Only for Levites.

Num 3:9–12 And you shall give the Levites to Aaron and his sons; they *are* given entirely to him from among the children of Israel. **10** So you shall appoint Aaron and his sons, and they shall attend to their priesthood; but the outsider who comes near shall be put to death." **11** Then the LORD spoke to Moses, saying: **12** "Now behold, I Myself have taken the Levites from among the children of Israel instead of every firstborn who opens the womb among the children of Israel. Therefore the Levites shall be Mine,

Of intercessory High-Priest (Jesus Christ).

Is 53:12 Therefore I will divide Him a portion with the great, And He shall divide the spoil with the strong, Because He poured out His soul unto death, And He was numbered with the transgressors, And He bore the sin of many, And made intercession for the transgressors.

Luke 23:34 Then Jesus said, "Father, forgive them, for they do not know what they do." And they divided His garments and cast lots.

Heb 7:25 Therefore He is also able to save to the uttermost those who come to God through Him, since He always lives to make intercession for them.

Heb 9:24 For Christ has not entered the holy places made with hands, *which are* copies of the true, but into heaven itself, now to appear in the presence of God for us;

As facility for tax collector.

Matt 9:9 As Jesus passed on from there, He saw a man named Matthew sitting at the tax office. And He said to him, "Follow Me." So he arose and followed Him.

Mark 2:14 As He passed by, He saw Levi the *son* of Alphaeus sitting at the tax office. And He said to him, "Follow Me." So he arose and followed Him.

Of deacon.

1 Tim 3:8–13 Likewise deacons *must be* reverent, not double-tongued, not given to much wine, not greedy for money, **9** holding the mystery of the faith with a pure conscience. **10** But let these also first be tested; then let them serve as deacons, being *found* blameless. **11** Likewise, *their* wives *must be* reverent, not slanderers, temperate, faithful in all things. **12** Let deacons be the husbands of one wife, ruling *their* children and their own houses well. **13** For those who have served well as deacons obtain for themselves a good standing and great boldness in the faith which is in Christ Jesus.

Cf. Acts 6:3

Of prophet, in the church.

Acts 11:21–28 And the hand of the Lord was with them, and a great number believed and turned to the Lord. **22** Then news of these things came to the ears of the church in Jerusalem, and they sent out Barnabas to go as far as Antioch. **23** When he came and had seen the grace of God, he was glad, and encouraged them all that with purpose of heart they should continue with the Lord. **24** For he was a good man, full of the Holy Spirit and of faith. And a great many people were added to the Lord. **25** Then Barnabas departed for Tarsus to seek Saul. **26** And when he had found him, he brought him to Antioch. So it was that for a whole year they assembled with the church and taught a great many people. And the disciples were first called Christians in Antioch. **27** And in these days prophets came from Jerusalem to Antioch. **28** Then one of them, named Agabus, stood up and showed by the Spirit that there was going to be a great famine throughout all the world, which also happened in the days of Claudius Caesar.

Acts 13:1 Now in the church that was at Antioch there were certain prophets and teachers: Barnabas, Simeon who was called Niger, Lucius of Cyrene, Manaen who had been brought up with Herod the tetrarch, and Saul.

1 Cor 12:28 And God has appointed these in the church: first apostles, second prophets, third teachers, after that miracles, then gifts of healings, helps, administrations, varieties of tongues.

Eph 2:20 having been built on the foundation of the apostles and prophets, Jesus Christ Himself being the chief corner*stone*,

Eph 4:11 And He Himself gave some *to be* apostles, some prophets, some evangelists, and some pastors and teachers,

Cf. Acts 21:10; 1 Cor 14:29–32

Of apostle.

Acts 1:20–22 "For it is written in the Book of Psalms: *'Let his dwelling place be desolate, And let no one live in it';* and, *'Let another take his office.'* **21** "Therefore, of these men who have accompanied us all the time that the Lord Jesus went in and out among us, **22** beginning from the baptism of John to that day when He was taken up from us, one of these must become a witness with us of His resurrection."

2 Cor 8:23 If *anyone inquires* about Titus, *he is* my partner and fellow worker concerning you. Or if our brethren *are inquired about, they are* messengers of the churches, the glory of Christ.

Eph 4:11 And He Himself gave some *to be* apostles, some prophets, some evangelists, and some pastors and teachers,

Cf. Rom 16:7; Phil 2:25

Of evangelist.

Acts 21:8 On the next *day* we who were Paul's companions departed and came to Caesarea, and entered the house of Philip the evangelist, who was *one* of the seven, and stayed with him.

Eph 4:11 And He Himself gave some *to be* apostles, some prophets, some evangelists, and some pastors and teachers,

Cf. 2 Tim 4:5

Of elder.

Acts 20:28 Therefore take heed to yourselves and to all the flock, among which the Holy Spirit has made you overseers, to shepherd the church of God which He purchased with His own blood.

1 Tim 3:1–7 This *is* a faithful saying: If a man desires the position of a bishop, he desires a good work. **2** A bishop then must be blameless, the husband of one wife, temperate, sober-minded, of good behavior, hospitable, able to teach; **3** not given to wine, not violent, not greedy for money, but gentle, not quarrelsome, not covetous; **4** one who rules his own house well, having *his* children in submission with all reverence **5** (for if a man does not know how to rule his own house, how will he take care of the church of God?); **6** not a novice, lest being puffed up with pride he fall into the *same* condemnation as the devil. **7** Moreover he must have a good testimony among those who are outside, lest he fall into reproach and the snare of the devil.

1 Tim 5:17–22 Let the elders who rule well be counted worthy of double honor, especially those who labor in the word and doctrine. **18** For the Scripture says, *"You shall not muzzle an ox while it treads out the grain,"* and, *"*The laborer *is* worthy of his wages.*"* **19** Do not receive an accusation against an elder except from two or three witnesses. **20** Those who are sinning rebuke in the presence of all, that the rest also may fear. **21** I charge *you* before God and the Lord Jesus Christ and the elect angels that you observe these things without prejudice, doing nothing with partiality. **22** Do not lay hands on anyone hastily, nor share in other people's sins; keep yourself pure.

Titus 1:5–9 For this reason I left you in Crete, that you should set in order the things that are lacking, and appoint elders in every city as I commanded you— **6** if a man is blameless, the husband of one wife, having faithful children not accused of dissipation or insubordination. **7** For a bishop must be blameless, as a steward of God, not self-willed, not quick-tempered, not given to wine, not violent, not greedy for money, **8** but hospitable, a lover of what is good, sober-minded, just, holy, self-controlled, **9** holding fast the faithful word as he has been taught, that he may be able, by sound doctrine, both to exhort and convict those who contradict.

1 Pet 5:1–2 The elders who are among you I exhort, I who am a fellow elder and a witness of the sufferings of Christ, and also a partaker of the glory that will be revealed: **2** Shepherd the flock of God which is among you, serving as overseers, not by compulsion but willingly, not for dishonest gain but eagerly;

Cf. Eph 4:11

Of Christ's sonship and priesthood.

Heb 1:5 For to which of the angels did He ever say: *"You are My Son, Today I have begotten You"*? And again: *"I will be to Him a Father, And He shall be to Me a Son"*?

Heb 5:5–6 So also Christ did not glorify Himself to become High Priest, *but it* was He who said to Him: *"You are My Son, Today I have begotten You."* **6** As He also *says* in another *place: "You are a priest forever According to the order of Melchizedek"*;

Heb 5:10 called by God as High Priest *"according to the order of Melchizedek,"*

Heb 7:20–28 And inasmuch as *He was* not *made priest* without an oath **21** (for they have become priests without an oath, but He with an oath by Him who said to Him: *"The LORD has sworn And will not relent, 'You are a priest forever According to the order of Melchizedek' "*), **22** by so much more Jesus has become a surety of a better covenant. **23** Also there were many priests, because they were prevented by death from continuing. **24** But He, because He continues forever, has an unchangeable priesthood. **25** Therefore He is also able to save to the uttermost those who come to God through Him, since He always lives to make intercession for them. **26** For such a High Priest was fitting for us, *who is* holy, harmless, undefiled, separate from sinners, and has become higher than the heavens; **27** who does not need daily, as those high priests, to offer up sacrifices, first for His own sins and then for the people's, for this He did once for all when He offered up Himself. **28** For the law appoints as high priests men who have weakness, but the word of the oath, which came after the law, *appoints* the Son who has been perfected forever.

Heb 8:1–6 Now *this is* the main point of the things we are saying: We have such a High Priest, who is seated at the right hand of the throne of the Majesty in the heavens, **2** a Minister of the sanctuary and of the true tabernacle which the Lord erected, and not man. **3** For every high priest is appointed to offer both gifts and sacrifices. Therefore *it is* necessary that this One also have something to offer. **4** For if He were on earth, He would not be a priest, since there are priests who offer the gifts according to the law; **5** who serve the copy and shadow of the heavenly things, as Moses was divinely instructed when he was about to make the tabernacle. For He said, *"See that you make all things according to the pattern shown you on the mountain."* **6** But now He has obtained a more excellent ministry, inasmuch as He is also Mediator of a better covenant, which was established on better promises.

OFFSPRING

Mandated by God.

Gen 1:28 Then God blessed them, and God said to them, "Be fruitful and multiply; fill the earth and subdue it; have dominion over the fish of the sea, over the birds of the air, and over every living thing that moves on the earth."

Promised to the patriarchs.

Gen 12:1–3 Now the LORD had said to Abram: "Get out of your country, From your family And from your fa-

ther's house, To a land that I will show you. **2** I will make you a great nation; I will bless you And make your name great; And you shall be a blessing. **3** I will bless those who bless you, And I will curse him who curses you; And in you all the families of the earth shall be blessed."

Gen 13:16 And I will make your descendants as the dust of the earth; so that if a man could number the dust of the earth, *then* your descendants also could be numbered.

Gen 15:5 Then He brought him outside and said, "Look now toward heaven, and count the stars if you are able to number them." And He said to him, "So shall your descendants be."

Gen 17:5–6 No longer shall your name be called Abram, but your name shall be Abraham; for I have made you a father of many nations. **6** I will make you exceedingly fruitful; and I will make nations of you, and kings shall come from you.

Gen 26:2–5 Then the LORD appeared to him and said: "Do not go down to Egypt; live in the land of which I shall tell you. **3** Dwell in this land, and I will be with you and bless you; for to you and your descendants I give all these lands, and I will perform the oath which I swore to Abraham your father. **4** And I will make your descendants multiply as the stars of heaven; I will give to your descendants all these lands; and in your seed all the nations of the earth shall be blessed; **5** because Abraham obeyed My voice and kept My charge, My commandments, My statutes, and My laws."

Gen 28:13–14 And behold, the LORD stood above it and said: "I *am* the LORD God of Abraham your father and the God of Isaac; the land on which you lie I will give to you and your descendants. **14** Also your descendants shall be as the dust of the earth; you shall spread abroad to the west and the east, to the north and the south; and in you and in your seed all the families of the earth shall be blessed."

Cf. Ex 1:1–7; Neh 9:23

As blessing from God.

Ps 127:3–5 Behold, children *are* a heritage from the LORD, The fruit of the womb *is* a reward. **4** Like arrows in the hand of a warrior, So *are* the children of one's youth. **5** Happy *is* the man who has his quiver full of them; They shall not be ashamed, But shall speak with their enemies in the gate.

Eaten during siege of Jerusalem.

Lam 2:20 "See, O LORD, and consider! To whom have You done this? Should the women eat their offspring, The children they have cuddled? Should the priest and prophet be slain In the sanctuary of the Lord?

Man is God's.

Acts 17:29 Therefore, since we are the offspring of God, we ought not to think that the Divine Nature is like gold or silver or stone, something shaped by art and man's devising.

Christians are Abraham's, spiritually.

Rom 4:11 And he received the sign of circumcision, a seal of the righteousness of the faith which *he had while still* uncircumcised, that he might be the father of all those who believe, though they are uncircumcised, that righteousness might be imputed to them also,

Rom 4:16 Therefore *it is* of faith that *it might be* according to grace, so that the promise might be sure to all the seed, not only to those who are of the law, but also to those who are of the faith of Abraham, who is the father of us all

Gal 3:29 And if you *are* Christ's, then you are Abraham's seed, and heirs according to the promise.

Of the woman, are followers of Christ.

Rev 12:17 And the dragon was enraged with the woman, and he went to make war with the rest of her offspring, who keep the commandments of God and have the testimony of Jesus Christ.

Jesus is David's.

Rev 22:16 "I, Jesus, have sent My angel to testify to you these things in the churches. I am the Root and the Offspring of David, the Bright and Morning Star."

Cf. Matt 9:27

OIL

Given by God.

Ps 104:14–15 He causes the grass to grow for the cattle, And vegetation for the service of man, That he may bring forth food from the earth, **15** And wine *that* makes glad the heart of man, Oil to make *his* face shine, And bread *which* strengthens man's heart.

Jer 31:12 Therefore they shall come and sing in the height of Zion, Streaming to the goodness of the LORD— For wheat and new wine and oil, For the young of the flock and the herd; Their souls shall be like a well-watered garden, And they shall sorrow no more at all.

Joel 2:19 The LORD will answer and say to His people, "Behold, I will send you grain and new wine and oil, And you will be satisfied by them; I will no longer make you a reproach among the nations.

Joel 2:24 The threshing floors shall be full of wheat, And the vats shall overflow with new wine and oil.

Earth provides.

Hos 2:22 The earth shall answer With grain, With new wine, And with oil; They shall answer Jezreel.

Kinds of, mentioned

Olive.

Ex 30:24 five hundred *shekels* of cassia, according to the shekel of the sanctuary, and a hin of olive oil.

Lev 24:2 "Command the children of Israel that they bring to you pure oil of pressed olives for the light, to make the lamps burn continually.

Myrrh.

Esth 2:12 Each young woman's turn came to go in to King Ahasuerus after she had completed twelve months' preparation, according to the regulations for the women, for thus were the days of their preparation apportioned: six months with oil of myrrh, and six months with perfumes and preparations for beautifying women.

Extracted with presses by the poor.

Job 24:11 They press out oil within their walls, And tread winepresses, yet suffer thirst.

Mic 6:15 "You shall sow, but not reap; You shall tread the olives, but not anoint yourselves with oil; And *make* sweet wine, but not drink wine.

Canaan abounded in.

Deut 8:8 a land of wheat and barley, of vines and fig trees and pomegranates, a land of olive oil and honey;

Described as

Soft.

Ps 55:21 *The words* of his mouth were smoother than butter, But war *was* in his heart; His words were softer than oil, Yet they *were* drawn swords.

Smooth.

Prov 5:3 For the lips of an immoral woman drip honey, And her mouth *is* smoother than oil;

Penetrating.

Ps 109:18 As he clothed himself with cursing as with his garment, So let it enter his body like water, And like oil into his bones.

Healing.

Is 1:6 From the sole of the foot even to the head, *There is* no soundness in it, *But* wounds and bruises and putrefying sores; They have not been closed or bound up, Or soothed with ointment.

Luke 10:34 So he went to *him* and bandaged his wounds, pouring on oil and wine; and he set him on his own animal, brought him to an inn, and took care of him.

Jews' ointments made of perfumes mixed with.

Ex 30:23–25 "Also take for yourself quality spices—five hundred *shekels* of liquid myrrh, half as much sweet-smelling cinnamon (two hundred and fifty *shekels*), two hundred and fifty *shekels* of sweet-smelling cane, **24** five hundred *shekels* of cassia, according to the shekel of the sanctuary, and a hin of olive oil. **25** And you shall make from these a holy anointing oil, an ointment compounded according to the art of the perfumer. It shall be a holy anointing oil.

John 12:3 Then Mary took a pound of very costly oil of spikenard, anointed the feet of Jesus, and wiped His feet with her hair. And the house was filled with the fragrance of the oil.

Jews often extravagant in the use of.

Prov 21:17 He who loves pleasure *will be* a poor man; He who loves wine and oil will not be rich.

Subject to tithe.

Deut 12:17 You may not eat within your gates the tithe of your grain or your new wine or your oil, of the firstborn of your herd or your flock, of any of your offerings which you vow, of your freewill offerings, or of the heave offering of your hand.

Firstfruits of, given to God.

Deut 18:4 The firstfruits of your grain and your new wine and your oil, and the first of the fleece of your sheep, you shall give him.

2 Chr 31:5 As soon as the commandment was circulated, the children of Israel brought in abundance the firstfruits of grain and wine, oil and honey, and of all the produce of the field; and they brought in abundantly the tithe of everything.

Neh 10:37 to bring the firstfruits of our dough, our offerings, the fruit from all kinds of trees, *the* new wine and oil, to the priests, to the storerooms of the house of our God; and to bring the tithes of our land to the Levites, for the Levites should receive the tithes in all our farming communities.

Used

For food.

1 Kin 17:12 So she said, "As the LORD your God lives, I do not have bread, only a handful of flour in a bin, and a little oil in a jar; and see, I *am* gathering a couple of sticks that I may go in and prepare it for myself and my son, that we may eat it, and die."

Ezek 16:13 Thus you were adorned with gold and silver, and your clothing *was of* fine linen, silk, and embroidered cloth. You ate *pastry of* fine flour, honey, and oil. You were exceedingly beautiful, and succeeded to royalty.

For anointing the person.

Ps 23:5 You prepare a table before me in the presence of my enemies; You anoint my head with oil; My cup runs over.

Ps 104:15 And wine *that* makes glad the heart of man, Oil to make *his* face shine, And bread *which* strengthens man's heart.

Luke 7:46 You did not anoint My head with oil, but this woman has anointed My feet with fragrant oil.

For anointing to offices of trust.

Ex 29:7 And you shall take the anointing oil, pour *it* on his head, and anoint him.

1 Sam 10:1 Then Samuel took a flask of oil and poured *it* on his head, and kissed him and said: "*Is it* not because the LORD has anointed you commander over His inheritance?

1 Kin 19:16 Also you shall anoint Jehu the son of Nimshi *as* king over Israel. And Elisha the son of Shaphat of Abel Meholah you shall anoint *as* prophet in your place.

For anointing the sick.

Mark 6:13 And they cast out many demons, and anointed with oil many who were sick, and healed *them.*

In God's worship.

Lev 7:10 Every grain offering, *whether* mixed with oil or dry, shall belong to all the sons of Aaron, to one *as much* as the other.

Num 15:4–10 then he who presents his offering to the LORD shall bring a grain offering of one-tenth *of an ephah* of fine flour mixed with one-fourth of a hin of oil; **5** and one-fourth of a hin of wine as a drink offering you shall prepare with the burnt offering or the sacrifice, for each lamb. **6** Or for a ram you shall prepare as a grain offering two-tenths *of an ephah* of fine flour mixed with one-third of a hin of oil; **7** and as a drink offering you shall offer one-third of a hin of wine as a sweet aroma to the LORD. **8** And when you prepare a young bull as a burnt offering, or as a sacrifice to fulfill a vow, or as a peace offering to the LORD, **9** then shall be offered with the young bull a grain offering of three-tenths *of an ephah* of fine flour mixed with half a hin of oil; **10** and you shall bring as the drink offering half a hin of wine as an offering made by fire, a sweet aroma to the LORD.

In idolatrous worship.

Hos 2:5 For their mother has played the harlot; She who conceived them has behaved shamefully. For she said, 'I will go after my lovers, Who give *me* my bread and my water, My wool and my linen, My oil and my drink.'

Hos 2:8 For she did not know That I gave her grain, new wine, and oil, And multiplied her silver and gold— *Which* they prepared for Baal.

For lamps.

Ex 25:6 oil for the light, and spices for the anointing oil and for the sweet incense;

Ex 27:20 "And you shall command the children of Israel that they bring you pure oil of pressed olives for the light, to cause the lamp to burn continually.

Matt 25:3 Those who *were* foolish took their lamps and took no oil with them,

When fresh, especially esteemed.

Ps 92:10 But my horn You have exalted like a wild ox; I have been anointed with fresh oil.

Dealing in, a trade.

2 Kin 4:7 Then she came and told the man of God. And he said, "Go, sell the oil and pay your debt; and you *and* your sons live on the rest."

Exported.

1 Kin 5:11 And Solomon gave Hiram twenty thousand kors of wheat *as* food for his household, and twenty kors of pressed oil. Thus Solomon gave to Hiram year by year.

Ezek 27:17 Judah and the land of Israel *were* your traders. They traded for your merchandise wheat of Minnith, millet, honey, oil, and balm.

Hos 12:1 "Ephraim feeds on the wind, And pursues the east wind; He daily increases lies and desolation. Also they make a covenant with the Assyrians, And oil is carried to Egypt.

Sold by measure.

1 Kin 5:11 And Solomon gave Hiram twenty thousand kors of wheat *as* food for his household, and twenty kors of pressed oil. Thus Solomon gave to Hiram year by year.

Luke 16:6 And he said, 'A hundred measures of oil.' So he said to him, 'Take your bill, and sit down quickly and write fifty.'

Kept in

Flasks.

2 Kin 9:1 And Elisha the prophet called one of the sons of the prophets, and said to him, "Get yourself ready, take this flask of oil in your hand, and go to Ramoth Gilead.

Horns.

1 Kin 1:39 Then Zadok the priest took a horn of oil from the tabernacle and anointed Solomon. And they blew the horn, and all the people said, "*Long* live King Solomon!"

Jars.

1 Kin 17:12 So she said, "As the LORD your God lives, I do not have bread, only a handful of flour in a bin, and a little oil in a jar; and see, I *am* gathering a couple of sticks that I may go in and prepare it for myself and my son, that we may eat it, and die."

2 Kin 4:2 So Elisha said to her, "What shall I do for you? Tell me, what do you have in the house?" And she said, "Your maidservant has nothing in the house but a jar of oil."

Stores of, laid up.

1 Chr 27:28 Baal-Hanan the Gederite was over the olive trees and the sycamore trees that *were* in the lowlands, and Joash *was* over the store of oil.

2 Chr 11:11 And he fortified the strongholds, and put captains in them, and stores of food, oil, and wine.

2 Chr 32:28 storehouses for the harvest of grain, wine, and oil; and stalls for all kinds of livestock, and folds for flocks.

Failure of, a severe calamity.

Hag 1:11 For I called for a drought on the land and the mountains, on the grain and the new wine and the oil, on whatever the ground brings forth, on men and livestock, and on all the labor of *your* hands."

Miraculous increase of.

2 Kin 4:2–6 So Elisha said to her, "What shall I do for you? Tell me, what do you have in the house?" And she said, "Your maidservant has nothing in the house but a jar of oil." 3 Then he said, "Go, borrow vessels from everywhere, from all your neighbors—empty vessels; do not gather just a few. 4 And when you have come in, you shall shut the door behind you and your sons; then pour it into all those vessels, and set aside the full ones." 5 So she went from him and shut the door behind her and her sons, who brought *the vessels* to her; and she poured *it* out. 6 Now it came to pass, when the vessels were full, that she said to her son, "Bring me another vessel." And he said to her, "*There is* not another vessel." So the oil ceased.

Illustrative of

The unction of the Holy Spirit.

Ps 45:7 You love righteousness and hate wickedness; Therefore God, Your God, has anointed You With the oil of gladness more than Your companions.

Ps 89:20 I have found My servant David; With My holy oil I have anointed him,

Zech 4:12 And I further answered and said to him, "What *are these* two olive branches that *drip* into the receptacles of the two gold pipes from which the golden *oil* drains?"

The consolation of the gospel.

Is 61:3 To console those who mourn in Zion, To give them beauty for ashes, The oil of joy for mourning, The garment of praise for the spirit of heaviness; That they may be called trees of righteousness, The planting of the LORD, that He may be glorified."

Kind reproof.

Ps 141:5 Let the righteous strike me; *It shall be* a kindness. And let him rebuke me; *It shall be* as excellent oil; Let my head not refuse it. For still my prayer *is* against the deeds of the wicked.

OLIVE TREE, THE

Often grew wild.

Rom 11:17 And if some of the branches were broken off, and you, being a wild olive tree, were grafted in among them, and with them became a partaker of the root and fatness of the olive tree,

Cultivated

In groves.

1 Sam 8:14 And he will take the best of your fields, your vineyards, and your olive groves, and give *them* to his servants.

Neh 5:11 Restore now to them, even this day, their lands, their vineyards, their olive groves, and their houses, also a hundredth of the money and the grain, the new wine and the oil, that you have charged them."

Among rocks.

Deut 32:13 "He made him ride in the heights of the earth, That he might eat the produce of the fields; He made him draw honey from the rock, And oil from the flinty rock;

Canaan abounded in.

Deut 6:11 houses full of all good things, which you did not fill, hewn-out wells which you did not dig, vineyards and olive trees which you did not plant—when you have eaten and are full—

Deut 8:8 a land of wheat and barley, of vines and fig trees and pomegranates, a land of olive oil and honey;

Assyria abounded in.

2 Kin 18:32 until I come and take you away to a land like your own land, a land of grain and new wine, a land of bread and vineyards, a land of olive groves and honey, that you may live and not die. But do not listen to Hezekiah, lest he persuade you, saying, "The LORD will deliver us."

Kings of Israel largely cultivated.

1 Chr 27:28 Baal-Hanan the Gederite was over the olive trees and the sycamore trees that *were* in the lowlands, and Joash *was* over the store of oil.

Described as

Green.

Jer 11:16 The LORD called your name, Green Olive Tree, Lovely *and* of Good Fruit. With the noise of a great tumult He has kindled fire on it, And its branches are broken.

Fair and beautiful.

Hos 14:6 His branches shall spread; His beauty shall be like an olive tree, And his fragrance like Lebanon.

Fat.

Judg 9:9 But the olive tree said to them, 'Should I cease giving my oil, With which they honor God and men, And go to sway over trees?'

Rom 11:17 And if some of the branches were broken off, and you, being a wild olive tree, were grafted in among them, and with them became a partaker of the root and fatness of the olive tree,

Bearing good fruit.

Jer 11:16 The LORD called your name, Green Olive Tree, Lovely *and* of Good Fruit. With the noise of a great tumult He has kindled fire on it, And its branches are broken.

James 3:12 Can a fig tree, my brethren, bear olives, or a grapevine bear figs? Thus no spring yields both salt water and fresh.

Grafting of, alluded to.

Rom 11:24 For if you were cut out of the olive tree which is wild by nature, and were grafted contrary to nature into a cultivated olive tree, how much more will these, who *are* natural *branches*, be grafted into their own olive tree?

Pruning of, alluded to.

Rom 11:18–19 do not boast against the branches. But if you do boast, *remember that* you do not support the root, but the root supports you. **19** You will say then, "Branches were broken off that I might be grafted in."

Often cast its flowers.

Job 15:33 He will shake off his unripe grape like a vine, And cast off his blossom like an olive tree.

Often cast its fruit.

Deut 28:40 You shall have olive trees throughout all your territory, but you shall not anoint *yourself* with the oil; for your olives shall drop off.

Often suffered from locusts.

Amos 4:9 "I blasted you with blight and mildew. When your gardens increased, Your vineyards, Your fig trees, And your olive trees, The locust devoured *them;* Yet you have not returned to Me," Says the LORD.

Good for the service of God and man.

Judg 9:9 But the olive tree said to them, 'Should I cease giving my oil, With which they honor God and men, And go to sway over trees?'

Oil procured from.

Ex 27:20 "And you shall command the children of Israel that they bring you pure oil of pressed olives for the light, to cause the lamp to burn continually.

Deut 8:8 a land of wheat and barley, of vines and fig trees and pomegranates, a land of olive oil and honey;

Used for making

The cherubim in the temple.

1 Kin 6:23 Inside the inner sanctuary he made two cherubim *of* olive wood, *each* ten cubits high.

The doors and posts of the temple.

1 Kin 6:31–33 For the entrance of the inner sanctuary he made doors *of* olive wood; the lintel *and* doorposts *were* one-fifth *of the wall.* **32** The two doors *were of* olive wood; and he carved on them figures of cherubim, palm trees, and open flowers, and overlaid *them* with gold; and he spread gold on the cherubim and on the palm trees. **33** So for the door of the sanctuary he also made doorposts *of* olive wood, one-fourth *of the wall.*

Booths at feast of tabernacles.

Neh 8:15 and that they should announce and proclaim in all their cities and in Jerusalem, saying, "Go out to the mountain, and bring olive branches, branches of oil trees, myrtle branches, palm branches, and

branches of leafy trees, to make booths, as *it is* written."

Beaten to remove the fruit.

Deut 24:20 When you beat your olive trees, you shall not go over the boughs again; it shall be for the stranger, the fatherless, and the widow.

Shaken when fully ripe.

Is 17:6 Yet gleaning grapes will be left in it, Like the shaking of an olive tree, Two *or* three olives at the top of the uppermost bough, Four *or* five in its most fruitful branches," Says the LORD God of Israel.

Gleaning of, left for the poor.

Deut 24:20 When you beat your olive trees, you shall not go over the boughs again; it shall be for the stranger, the fatherless, and the widow.

The fruit of,

During sabbatical year left for the poor, etc.

Ex 23:11 but the seventh *year* you shall let it rest and lie fallow, that the poor of your people may eat; and what they leave, the beasts of the field may eat. In like manner you shall do with your vineyard *and* your olive grove.

Trodden in presses to extract the oil.

Job 24:11 They press out oil within their walls, And tread winepresses, yet suffer thirst.

Mic 6:15 "You shall sow, but not reap; You shall tread the olives, but not anoint yourselves with oil; And *make* sweet wine, but not drink wine.

Failure of, a great calamity.

Hab 3:17–18 Though the fig tree may not blossom, Nor fruit be on the vines; Though the labor of the olive may fail, And the fields yield no food; Though the flock may be cut off from the fold, And there be no herd in the stalls— **18** Yet I will rejoice in the LORD, I will joy in the God of my salvation.

Illustrative of

Christ.

Rom 11:24 For if you were cut out of the olive tree which is wild by nature, and were grafted contrary to nature into a cultivated olive tree, how much more will these, who *are* natural *branches,* be grafted into their own olive tree?

Zech 4:3 Two olive trees *are* by it, one at the right of the bowl and the other at its left."

Zech 4:12 And I further answered and said to him, "What *are these* two olive branches that *drip* into the receptacles of the two gold pipes from which the golden *oil* drains?"

Rom 11:17 And if some of the branches were broken off, and you, being a wild olive tree, were grafted in among them, and with them became a partaker of the root and fatness of the olive tree,

The righteous.

Ps 52:8 But I *am* like a green olive tree in the house of God; I trust in the mercy of God forever and ever.

Hos 14:6 His branches shall spread; His beauty shall be like an olive tree, And his fragrance like Lebanon.

Believers' children.

Ps 128:3 Your wife *shall be* like a fruitful vine In the very heart of your house, Your children like olive plants All around your table.

The two witnesses.

Rev 11:3–4 And I will give *power* to my two witnesses, and they will prophesy one thousand two hundred and sixty days, clothed in sackcloth." **4** These are the two olive trees and the two lampstands standing before the God of the earth.

(When wild) the Gentiles.

Rom 11:17 And if some of the branches were broken off, and you, being a wild olive tree, were grafted in among them, and with them became a partaker of the root and fatness of the olive tree,

Rom 11:24 For if you were cut out of the olive tree which is wild by nature, and were grafted contrary to nature into a cultivated olive tree, how much more will these, who *are* natural *branches*, be grafted into their own olive tree?

(Gleaning of) the remnant of grace.

Is 17:6 Yet gleaning grapes will be left in it, Like the shaking of an olive tree, Two *or* three olives at the top of the uppermost bough, Four *or* five in its most fruitful branches," Says the Lord God of Israel.

Is 24:13 When it shall be thus in the midst of the land among the people, *It shall be* like the shaking of an olive tree, Like the gleaning of grapes when the vintage is done.

Peace (implied).

Gen 8:11 Then the dove came to him in the evening, and behold, a freshly plucked olive leaf *was* in her mouth; and Noah knew that the waters had receded from the earth.

OPPRESSION

Of the Jews,

Intensified in Egypt.

Ex 1:8–22 Now there arose a new king over Egypt, who did not know Joseph. **9** And he said to his people, "Look, the people of the children of Israel *are* more and mightier than we; **10** come, let us deal shrewdly with them, lest they multiply, and it happen, in the event of war, that they also join our enemies and fight against us, and *so* go up out of the land." **11** Therefore they set taskmasters over them to afflict them with their burdens. And they built for Pharaoh supply cities, Pithom and Raamses. **12** But the more they afflicted them, the more they multiplied and grew. And they were in dread of the children of Israel. **13** So the Egyptians made the children of Israel serve with rigor. **14** And they made their lives bitter with hard bondage—in mortar, in brick, and in all manner of service in the field. All their service in which they made them serve *was* with rigor. **15** Then the king of Egypt spoke to the Hebrew midwives, of whom the name of one *was* Shiphrah and the name of the other Puah; **16** and he said, "When you do the duties of a midwife for the Hebrew women, and see *them* on the birthstools, if it *is* a son, then you shall kill him; but if it *is* a daughter, then she shall live." **17** But the midwives feared God, and did not do as the king of Egypt commanded them, but saved the male children alive. **18** So the king of Egypt called for the midwives and said to them, "Why have you

done this thing, and saved the male children alive?" **19** And the midwives said to Pharaoh, "Because the Hebrew women *are* not like the Egyptian women; for they *are* lively and give birth before the midwives come to them." **20** Therefore God dealt well with the midwives, and the people multiplied and grew very mighty. **21** And so it was, because the midwives feared God, that He provided households for them. **22** So Pharaoh commanded all his people, saying, "Every son who is born you shall cast into the river, and every daughter you shall save alive."

By the Canaanites.

Judg 2:14–19 And the anger of the Lord was hot against Israel. So He delivered them into the hands of plunderers who despoiled them; and He sold them into the hands of their enemies all around, so that they could no longer stand before their enemies. **15** Wherever they went out, the hand of the Lord was against them for calamity, as the Lord had said, and as the Lord had sworn to them. And they were greatly distressed. **16** Nevertheless, the Lord raised up judges who delivered them out of the hand of those who plundered them. **17** Yet they would not listen to their judges, but they played the harlot with other gods, and bowed down to them. They turned quickly from the way in which their fathers walked, in obeying the commandments of the Lord; they did not do so. **18** And when the Lord raised up judges for them, the Lord was with the judge and delivered them out of the hand of their enemies all the days of the judge; for the Lord was moved to pity by their groaning because of those who oppressed them and harassed them. **19** And it came to pass, when the judge was dead, that they reverted and behaved more corruptly than their fathers, by following other gods, to serve them and bow down to them. They did not cease from their own doings nor from their stubborn way.

Judg 3:8 Therefore the anger of the Lord was hot against Israel, and He sold them into the hand of Cushan-Rishathaim king of Mesopotamia; and the children of Israel served Cushan-Rishathaim eight years.

Judg 3:14 So the children of Israel served Eglon king of Moab eighteen years.

Judg 4:2–3 So the Lord sold them into the hand of Jabin king of Canaan, who reigned in Hazor. The commander of his army *was* Sisera, who dwelt in Harosheth Hagoyim. **3** And the children of Israel cried out to the Lord; for Jabin had nine hundred chariots of iron, and for twenty years he had harshly oppressed the children of Israel.

Judg 6:1–6 Then the children of Israel did evil in the sight of the Lord. So the Lord delivered them into the hand of Midian for seven years, **2** and the hand of Midian prevailed against Israel. Because of the Midianites, the children of Israel made for themselves the dens, the caves, and the strongholds which *are* in the mountains. **3** So it was, whenever Israel had sown, Midianites would come up; also Amalekites and the people of the East would come up against them. **4** Then they would encamp against them and destroy the produce of the earth as far as Gaza, and leave no sustenance for Israel, neither sheep nor ox nor donkey. 5 For they would come up with their livestock and their tents, coming in as numerous as locusts; both they and their camels were without number; and they would enter the land to destroy it. 6 So Israel was greatly impoverished because of the Midianites, and the children of Israel cried out to the LORD.

Judg 10:6–14 Then the children of Israel again did evil in the sight of the LORD, and served the Baals and the Ashtoreths, the gods of Syria, the gods of Sidon, the gods of Moab, the gods of the people of Ammon, and the gods of the Philistines; and they forsook the LORD and did not serve Him. 7 So the anger of the LORD was hot against Israel; and He sold them into the hands of the Philistines and into the hands of the people of Ammon. 8 From that year they harassed and oppressed the children of Israel for eighteen years—all the children of Israel who *were* on the other side of the Jordan in the land of the Amorites, in Gilead. 9 Moreover the people of Ammon crossed over the Jordan to fight against Judah also, against Benjamin, and against the house of Ephraim, so that Israel was severely distressed. 10 And the children of Israel cried out to the LORD, saying, "We have sinned against You, because we have both forsaken our God and served the Baals!" 11 So the LORD said to the children of Israel, "*Did I* not *deliver you* from the Egyptians and from the Amorites and from the people of Ammon and from the Philistines? 12 Also the Sidonians and Amalekites and Maonites oppressed you; and you cried out to Me, and I delivered you from their hand. 13 Yet you have forsaken Me and served other gods. Therefore I will deliver you no more. 14 Go and cry out to the gods which you have chosen; let them deliver you in your time of distress."

Judg 13:1 Again the children of Israel did evil in the sight of the LORD, and the LORD delivered them into the hand of the Philistines for forty years.

By the Romans.

John 11:48 If we let Him alone like this, everyone will believe in Him, and the Romans will come and take away both our place and nation."

Used by God in bringing repentance.

Job 36:15 He delivers the poor in their affliction, And opens their ears in oppression.

ORDER, DIVINE

Of the days of the week. Gen 1:5—2:3; Ex 20:8–11

Concerning

Marriage.

Gen 2:24 Therefore a man shall leave his father and mother and be joined to his wife, and they shall become one flesh.

Matt 19:5 and said, '*For this reason a man shall leave his father and mother and be joined to his wife, and the two shall become one flesh'* ?

Mark 10:7–8 '*For this reason a man shall leave his father and mother and be joined to his wife, 8 and the two shall become one flesh'*; so then they are no longer two, but one flesh.

1 Cor 6:16 Or do you not know that he who is joined to

a harlot is one body *with her?* For *"the two,"* He says, *"shall become one flesh."*

Eph 5:31 *"For this reason a man shall leave his father and mother and be joined to his wife, and the two shall become one flesh."*

Man and his world. Ps 104:1–35; 148:1–4

Roles of men and women.

Gen 2:20–23 So Adam gave names to all cattle, to the birds of the air, and to every beast of the field. But for Adam there was not found a helper comparable to him. 21 And the LORD God caused a deep sleep to fall on Adam, and he slept; and He took one of his ribs, and closed up the flesh in its place. 22 Then the rib which the LORD God had taken from man He made into a woman, and He brought her to the man. 23 And Adam said: "This is now bone of my bones And flesh of my flesh; She shall be called Woman, Because she was taken out of Man."

1 Cor 11:2–15 Now I praise you, brethren, that you remember me in all things and keep the traditions just as I delivered *them* to you. 3 But I want you to know that the head of every man is Christ, the head of woman *is* man, and the head of Christ *is* God. 4 Every man praying or prophesying, having *his* head covered, dishonors his head. 5 But every woman who prays or prophesies with *her* head uncovered dishonors her head, for that is one and the same as if her head were shaved. 6 For if a woman is not covered, let her also be shorn. But if it is shameful for a woman to be shorn or shaved, let her be covered. 7 For a man indeed ought not to cover *his* head, since he is the image and glory of God; but woman is the glory of man. 8 For man is not from woman, but woman from man. 9 Nor was man created for the woman, but woman for the man. 10 For this reason the woman ought to have *a symbol of* authority on *her* head, because of the angels. 11 Nevertheless, neither *is* man independent of woman, nor woman independent of man, in the Lord. 12 For as woman *came* from man, even so man also *comes* through woman; but all things are from God. 13 Judge among yourselves. Is it proper for a woman to pray to God with her head uncovered? 14 Does not even nature itself teach you that if a man has long hair, it is a dishonor to him? 15 But if a woman has long hair, it is a glory to her; for *her* hair is given to her for a covering.

1 Cor 14:34–35 Let your women keep silent in the churches, for they are not permitted to speak; but *they are* to be submissive, as the law also says. 35 And if they want to learn something, let them ask their own husbands at home; for it is shameful for women to speak in church.

Eph 5:22–24 Wives, submit to your own husbands, as to the Lord. 23 For the husband is head of the wife, as also Christ is head of the church; and He is the Savior of the body. 24 Therefore, just as the church is subject to Christ, so *let* the wives *be* to their own husbands in everything.

1 Pet 3:1–7 Wives, likewise, *be* submissive to your own husbands, that even if some do not obey the word, they, without a word, may be won by the conduct of their wives, 2 when they observe your chaste conduct *accompanied* by fear. 3 Do not let your adornment be *merely* outward—arranging the hair, wearing gold, or putting on *fine* apparel— 4 rather *let it be* the hidden person of the heart, with the incorruptible *beauty* of a gentle and quiet spirit, which is very precious in the sight of God. 5 For in this manner, in former times, the holy women who trusted in God also adorned themselves, being submissive to their own husbands, 6 as Sarah obeyed Abraham, calling him lord, whose daughters you are if you do good and are not afraid with any terror. 7 Husbands, likewise, dwell with *them* with understanding, giving honor to the wife, as to the weaker vessel, and as *being* heirs together of the grace of life, that your prayers may not be hindered.

Cf. Gen 3:16–20

Life, death, and resurrection for the believer.

1 Cor 15:12–57

The world before and after the Flood.

Gen 2:4–6 This *is* the history of the heavens and the earth when they were created, in the day that the LORD God made the earth and the heavens, 5 before any plant of the field was in the earth and before any herb of the field had grown. For the LORD God had not caused it to rain on the earth, and *there was* no man to till the ground; 6 but a mist went up from the earth and watered the whole face of the ground.

Gen 9:8–17 Then God spoke to Noah and to his sons with him, saying: 9 "And as for Me, behold, I establish My covenant with you and with your descendants after you, 10 and with every living creature that *is* with you: the birds, the cattle, and every beast of the earth with you, of all that go out of the ark, every beast of the earth. 11 Thus I establish My covenant with you: Never again shall all flesh be cut off by the waters of the flood; never again shall there be a flood to destroy the earth." 12 And God said: "This *is* the sign of the covenant which I make between Me and you, and every living creature that *is* with you, for perpetual generations: 13 I set My rainbow in the cloud, and it shall be for the sign of the covenant between Me and the earth. 14 It shall be, when I bring a cloud over the earth, that the rainbow shall be seen in the cloud; 15 and I will remember My covenant which *is* between Me and you and every living creature of all flesh; the waters shall never again become a flood to destroy all flesh. 16 The rainbow shall be in the cloud, and I will look on it to remember the everlasting covenant between God and every living creature of all flesh that *is* on the earth." 17 And God said to Noah, "This *is* the sign of the covenant which I have established between Me and all flesh that *is* on the earth."

2 Pet 3:5–7 For this they willfully forget: that by the word of God the heavens were of old, and the earth standing out of water and in the water, 6 by which the world *that* then existed perished, being flooded with water. 7 But the heavens and the earth *which* are now preserved by the same word, are reserved for fire until the day of judgment and perdition of ungodly men.

Heaven.

Rev 19:6–10 And I heard, as it were, the voice of a great multitude, as the sound of many waters and as the sound of mighty thunderings, saying, "Alleluia! For the Lord God Omnipotent reigns! 7 Let us be glad and rejoice and give Him glory, for the marriage of the Lamb has come, and His wife has made herself ready." 8 And to her it was granted to be arrayed in fine linen, clean and bright, for the fine linen is the righteous acts of the saints. 9 Then he said to me, "Write: 'Blessed *are* those who are called to the marriage supper of the Lamb!' " And he said to me, "These are the true sayings of God." 10 And I fell at his feet to worship him. But he said to me, "See *that you do* not *do that!* I am your fellow servant, and of your brethren who have the testimony of Jesus. Worship God! For the testimony of Jesus is the spirit of prophecy."

Cf. Rev 21:1—22:5

Of birth, for Jacob's sons.

Gen 29:32–35 So Leah conceived and bore a son, and she called his name Reuben; for she said, "The LORD has surely looked on my affliction. Now therefore, my husband will love me." 33 Then she conceived again and bore a son, and said, "Because the LORD has heard that I *am* unloved, He has therefore given me this *son* also." And she called his name Simeon. 34 She conceived again and bore a son, and said, "Now this time my husband will become attached to me, because I have borne him three sons." Therefore his name was called Levi. 35 And she conceived again and bore a son, and said, "Now I will praise the LORD." Therefore she called his name Judah. Then she stopped bearing.

Gen 30:1–24 Now when Rachel saw that she bore Jacob no children, Rachel envied her sister, and said to Jacob, "Give me children, or else I die!" 2 And Jacob's anger was aroused against Rachel, and he said, "*Am* I in the place of God, who has withheld from you the fruit of the womb?" 3 So she said, "Here is my maid Bilhah; go in to her, and she will bear *a child* on my knees, that I also may have children by her." 4 Then she gave him Bilhah her maid as wife, and Jacob went in to her. 5 And Bilhah conceived and bore Jacob a son. 6 Then Rachel said, "God has judged my case; and He has also heard my voice and given me a son." Therefore she called his name Dan. 7 And Rachel's maid Bilhah conceived again and bore Jacob a second son. 8 Then Rachel said, "With great wrestlings I have wrestled with my sister, *and* indeed I have prevailed." So she called his name Naphtali. 9 When Leah saw that she had stopped bearing, she took Zilpah her maid and gave her to Jacob as wife. 10 And Leah's maid Zilpah bore Jacob a son. 11 Then Leah said, "A troop comes!" So she called his name Gad. 12 And Leah's maid Zilpah bore Jacob a second son. 13 Then Leah said, "I am happy, for the daughters will call me blessed." So she called his name Asher. 14 Now Reuben went in the days of wheat harvest and found mandrakes in the field, and brought them to his mother Leah. Then Rachel said to Leah, "Please give me *some* of your son's mandrakes." 15 But she said to her, "*Is it* a small matter that you have taken away my husband? Would you take away my son's mandrakes also?" And Rachel said, "Therefore he will lie with you tonight for your son's mandrakes." 16 When Jacob came out of the field in the evening, Leah went out to meet him and said, "You must come in to me, for I have surely hired you with my son's mandrakes." And he lay with her that night. **17** And God listened to Leah, and she conceived and bore Jacob a fifth son. **18** Leah said, "God has given me my wages, because I have given my maid to my husband." So she called his name Issachar. **19** Then Leah conceived again and bore Jacob a sixth son. **20** And Leah said, "God has endowed me *with* a good endowment; now my husband will dwell with me, because I have borne him six sons." So she called his name Zebulun. **21** Afterward she bore a daughter, and called her name Dinah. **22** Then God remembered Rachel, and God listened to her and opened her womb. **23** And she conceived and bore a son, and said, "God has taken away my reproach." **24** So she called his name Joseph, and said, "The LORD shall add to me another son."

Gen 35:18 And so it was, as her soul was departing (for she died), that she called his name Ben-Oni; but his father called him Benjamin.

Cf. Gen 49:2–27

Of Jewish festivals, according to calendar.
Lev 23:4–44

Of march, of 12 tribes. Num 2:3–32; 10:14–28

Of Jewish inheritance.

Lev 25:48–49 after he is sold he may be redeemed again. One of his brothers may redeem him; **49** or his uncle or his uncle's son may redeem him; or *anyone* who is near of kin to him in his family may redeem him; or if he is able he may redeem himself.

Num 27:8–11 And you shall speak to the children of Israel, saying: 'If a man dies and has no son, then you shall cause his inheritance to pass to his daughter. **9** If he has no daughter, then you shall give his inheritance to his brothers. **10** If he has no brothers, then you shall give his inheritance to his father's brothers. **11** And if his father has no brothers, then you shall give his inheritance to the relative closest to him in his family, and he shall possess it.' " And it shall be to the children of Israel a statute of judgment, just as the LORD commanded Moses.

Restored by Jehoshaphat.

2 Chr 19:4–11 So Jehoshaphat dwelt at Jerusalem; and he went out again among the people from Beersheba to the mountains of Ephraim, and brought them back to the LORD God of their fathers. **5** Then he set judges in the land throughout all the fortified cities of Judah, city by city, **6** and said to the judges, "Take heed to what you are doing, for you do not judge for man but for the LORD, who *is* with you in the judgment. **7** Now therefore, let the fear of the LORD be upon you; take care and do *it*, for *there is* no iniquity with the LORD our God, no partiality, nor taking of bribes." **8** Moreover in Jerusalem, for the judgment of the LORD and for controversies, Jehoshaphat appointed some of the Levites and priests, and some of the chief fathers of Israel, when they returned to Jerusalem. **9** And he commanded them, saying, "Thus you shall act in the fear of the LORD, faithfully and with a loyal heart: **10** Whatever case comes to you from your brethren who dwell in their cities, whether of bloodshed or offenses against law or commandment, against statutes or ordinances, you shall warn them, lest they trespass against the LORD

and wrath come upon you and your brethren. Do this, and you will not be guilty. **11** And take notice: Amariah the chief priest *is* over you in all matters of the LORD; and Zebadiah the son of Ishmael, the ruler of the house of Judah, for all the king's matters; also the Levites *will be* officials before you. Behave courageously, and the LORD will be with the good."

ORDER, ADMINISTRATIVE

Of King Darius, concerning temple rebuilding.

Ezra 6:1 Then King Darius issued a decree, and a search was made in the archives, where the treasures were stored in Babylon.

Ezra 6:14 So the elders of the Jews built, and they prospered through the prophesying of Haggai the prophet and Zechariah the son of Iddo. And they built and finished *it*, according to the commandment of the God of Israel, and according to the command of Cyrus, Darius, and Artaxerxes king of Persia.

Of Melchizedek.

Ps 110:4 The LORD has sworn And will not relent, "You *are* a priest forever According to the order of Melchizedek."

Heb 5:6 As *He* also *says* in another *place:* "You are a priest forever According to the order of Melchizedek";

Heb 5:10 called by God as High Priest *"according to the order of Melchizedek,"*

Heb 7:11–21 Therefore, if perfection were through the Levitical priesthood (for under it the people received the law), what further need *was there* that another priest should rise according to the order of Melchizedek, and not be called according to the order of Aaron? **12** For the priesthood being changed, of necessity there is also a change of the law. **13** For He of whom these things are spoken belongs to another tribe, from which no man has officiated at the altar. **14** For *it is* evident that our Lord arose from Judah, of which tribe Moses spoke nothing concerning priesthood. **15** And it is yet far more evident if, in the likeness of Melchizedek, there arises another priest **16** who has come, not according to the law of a fleshly commandment, but according to the power of an endless life. **17** For He testifies: *"You are a priest forever According to the order of Melchizedek."* **18** For on the one hand there is an annulling of the former commandment because of its weakness and unprofitableness, **19** for the law made nothing perfect; on the other hand, *there is the* bringing in of a better hope, through which we draw near to God. **20** And inasmuch as *He was* not *made priest* without an oath **21** (for they have become priests without an oath, but He with an oath by Him who said to Him: *"The LORD has sworn And will not relent, 'You are a priest forever According to the order of Melchizedek' "),*

Of angels.

Is 6:2–3 Above it stood seraphim; each one had six wings: with two he covered his face, with two he covered his feet, and with two he flew. **3** And one cried to another and said: "Holy, holy, holy *is* the LORD of hosts; The whole earth *is* full of His glory!"

Ezek 1:15–21 Now as I looked at the living creatures, behold, a wheel *was* on the earth beside each living creature with its four faces. **16** The appearance of the wheels and their workings *was* like the color of beryl, and all four had the same likeness. The appearance of their workings *was*, as it were, a wheel in the middle of a wheel. **17** When they moved, they went toward any one of four directions; they did not turn aside when they went. **18** As for their rims, they were so high they were awesome; and their rims *were* full of eyes, all around the four of them. **19** When the living creatures went, the wheels went beside them; and when the living creatures were lifted up from the earth, the wheels were lifted up. **20** Wherever the spirit wanted to go, they went, *because* there the spirit went; and the wheels were lifted together with them, for the spirit of the living creatures *was* in the wheels. **21** When those went, *these* went; when those stood, *these* stood; and when those were lifted up from the earth, the wheels were lifted up together with them, for the spirit of the living creatures *was* in the wheels.

Rev 4:6–8 Before the throne *there was* a sea of glass, like crystal. And in the midst of the throne, and around the throne, *were* four living creatures full of eyes in front and in back. **7** The first living creature *was* like a lion, the second living creature like a calf, the third living creature had a face like a man, and the fourth living creature *was* like a flying eagle. **8** *The* four living creatures, each having six wings, were full of eyes around and within. And they do not rest day or night, saying: "Holy, holy, holy, Lord God Almighty, Who was and is and is to come!"

Rev 19:4 And the twenty-four elders and the four living creatures fell down and worshiped God who sat on the throne, saying, "Amen! Alleluia!"

Cf. Ezek 10:1–22

Of the lists of the twelve.

Matt 10:2–4 Now the names of the twelve apostles are these: first, Simon, who is called Peter, and Andrew his brother; James the *son* of Zebedee, and John his brother; **3** Philip and Bartholomew; Thomas and Matthew the tax collector; James the *son* of Alphaeus, and Lebbaeus, whose surname was Thaddaeus; **4** Simon the Cananite, and Judas Iscariot, who also betrayed Him.

Mark 3:16–19 Simon, to whom He gave the name Peter; **17** James the *son* of Zebedee and John the brother of James, to whom He gave the name Boanerges, that is, "Sons of Thunder"; **18** Andrew, Philip, Bartholomew, Matthew, Thomas, James the *son* of Alphaeus, Thaddaeus, Simon the Cananite; **19** and Judas Iscariot, who also betrayed Him. And they went into a house.

Luke 6:13–16 And when it was day, He called His disciples to *Himself*; and from them He chose twelve whom He also named apostles: **14** Simon, whom He also named Peter, and Andrew his brother; James and John; Philip and Bartholomew; **15** Matthew and Thomas; James the *son* of Alphaeus, and Simon called the Zealot; **16** Judas *the son* of James, and Judas Iscariot who also became a traitor.

Acts 1:13 And when they had entered, they went up into the upper room where they were staying: Peter, James, John, and Andrew; Philip and Thomas; Bartholomew and Matthew; James *the son* of Alphaeus and Simon the Zealot; and Judas *the son* of James.

Of the signs of Christ's return.

Matt 24:3–31 Now as He sat on the Mount of Olives, the disciples came to Him privately, saying, "Tell us, when will these things be? And what *will be* the sign of Your coming, and of the end of the age?" **4** And Jesus answered and said to them: "Take heed that no one deceives you. **5** For many will come in My name, saying, 'I am the Christ,' and will deceive many. **6** And you will hear of wars and rumors of wars. See that you are not troubled; for all *these things* must come to pass, but the end is not yet. **7** For nation will rise against nation, and kingdom against kingdom. And there will be famines, pestilences, and earthquakes in various places. **8** All these *are* the beginning of sorrows. **9** "Then they will deliver you up to tribulation and kill you, and you will be hated by all nations for My name's sake. **10** And then many will be offended, will betray one another, and will hate one another. **11** Then many false prophets will rise up and deceive many. **12** And because lawlessness will abound, the love of many will grow cold. **13** But he who endures to the end shall be saved. **14** And this gospel of the kingdom will be preached in all the world as a witness to all the nations, and then the end will come. **15** "Therefore when you see the *'abomination of desolation,'* spoken of by Daniel the prophet, standing in the holy place" (whoever reads, let him understand), **16** "then let those who are in Judea flee to the mountains. **17** Let him who is on the housetop not go down to take anything out of his house. **18** And let him who is in the field not go back to get his clothes. **19** But woe to those who are pregnant and to those who are nursing babies in those days! **20** And pray that your flight may not be in winter or on the Sabbath. **21** For then there will be great tribulation, such as has not been since the beginning of the world until this time, no, nor ever shall be. **22** And unless those days were shortened, no flesh would be saved; but for the elect's sake those days will be shortened. **23** "Then if anyone says to you, 'Look, here *is* the Christ!' or 'There!' do not believe *it*. **24** For false christs and false prophets will rise and show great signs and wonders to deceive, if possible, even the elect. **25** See, I have told you beforehand. **26** "Therefore if they say to you, 'Look, He is in the desert!' do not go out; *or* 'Look, *He is* in the inner rooms!' do not believe *it*. **27** For as the lightning comes from the east and flashes to the west, so also will the coming of the Son of Man be. **28** For wherever the carcass is, there the eagles will be gathered together. **29** "Immediately after the tribulation of those days the sun will be darkened, and the moon will not give its light; the stars will fall from heaven, and the powers of the heavens will be shaken. **30** Then the sign of the Son of Man will appear in heaven, and then all the tribes of the earth will mourn, and they will see the Son of Man coming on the clouds of heaven with power and great glory. **31** And He will send His angels with a great sound of a trumpet, and they will gather together His elect from the four winds, from one end of heaven to the other.

Mark 13:3–4 Now as He sat on the Mount of Olives opposite the temple, Peter, James, John, and Andrew asked Him privately, **4** "Tell us, when will these things be? And what *will be* the sign when all these things will be fulfilled?"

Mark 13:24–27 "But in those days, after that tribulation, the sun will be darkened, and the moon will not give its light; **25** the stars of heaven will fall, and the powers in the heavens will be shaken. **26** Then they will see the Son of Man coming in the clouds with great power and glory. **27** And then He will send His angels, and gather together His elect from the four winds, from the farthest part of earth to the farthest part of heaven.

Luke 21:7 So they asked Him, saying, "Teacher, but when will these things be? And what sign *will there be* when these things are about to take place?"

Luke 21:25–28 "And there will be signs in the sun, in the moon, and in the stars; and on the earth distress of nations, with perplexity, the sea and the waves roaring; **26** men's hearts failing them from fear and the expectation of those things which are coming on the earth, for the powers of the heavens will be shaken. **27** Then they will see the Son of Man coming in a cloud with power and great glory. **28** Now when these things begin to happen, look up and lift up your heads, because your redemption draws near."

Of the resurrection events.

Matt 28:1–8 Now after the Sabbath, as the first *day* of the week began to dawn, Mary Magdalene and the other Mary came to see the tomb. **2** And behold, there was a great earthquake; for an angel of the Lord descended from heaven, and came and rolled back the stone from the door, and sat on it. **3** His countenance was like lightning, and his clothing as white as snow. **4** And the guards shook for fear of him, and became like dead *men.* **5** But the angel answered and said to the women, "Do not be afraid, for I know that you seek Jesus who was crucified. **6** He is not here; for He is risen, as He said. Come, see the place where the Lord lay. **7** And go quickly and tell His disciples that He is risen from the dead, and indeed He is going before you into Galilee; there you will see Him. Behold, I have told you." **8** So they went out quickly from the tomb with fear and great joy, and ran to bring His disciples word.

Mark 16:1–8 Now when the Sabbath was past, Mary Magdalene, Mary *the mother* of James, and Salome bought spices, that they might come and anoint Him. **2** Very early in the morning, on the first *day* of the week, they came to the tomb when the sun had risen. **3** And they said among themselves, "Who will roll away the stone from the door of the tomb for us?" **4** But when they looked up, they saw that the stone had been rolled away—for it was very large. **5** And entering the tomb, they saw a young man clothed in a long white robe sitting on the right side; and they were alarmed. **6** But he said to them, "Do not be alarmed. You seek Jesus of Nazareth, who was crucified. He is risen! He is not here. See the place where they laid Him. **7** But go, tell His disciples—and Peter—that He is going before you into Galilee; there you will see Him, as He said to you." **8** So they went out quickly and fled from the tomb, for they trembled and were amazed. And they said nothing to anyone, for they were afraid.

Luke 24:1–12 Now on the first *day* of the week, very

early in the morning, they, and certain *other women* with them, came to the tomb bringing the spices which they had prepared. **2** But they found the stone rolled away from the tomb. **3** Then they went in and did not find the body of the Lord Jesus. **4** And it happened, as they were greatly perplexed about this, that behold, two men stood by them in shining garments. **5** Then, as they were afraid and bowed *their* faces to the earth, they said to them, "Why do you seek the living among the dead? **6** He is not here, but is risen! Remember how He spoke to you when He was still in Galilee, **7** saying, 'The Son of Man must be delivered into the hands of sinful men, and be crucified, and the third day rise again.' " **8** And they remembered His words. **9** Then they returned from the tomb and told all these things to the eleven and to all the rest. **10** It was Mary Magdalene, Joanna, Mary *the mother* of James, and the other *women* with them, who told these things to the apostles. **11** And their words seemed to them like idle tales, and they did not believe them. **12** But Peter arose and ran to the tomb; and stooping down, he saw the linen cloths lying by themselves; and he departed, marveling to himself at what had happened.

John 20:1–10 Now the first *day* of the week Mary Magdalene went to the tomb early, while it was still dark, and saw *that* the stone had been taken away from the tomb. **2** Then she ran and came to Simon Peter, and to the other disciple, whom Jesus loved, and said to them, "They have taken away the Lord out of the tomb, and we do not know where they have laid Him." **3** Peter therefore went out, and the other disciple, and were going to the tomb. **4** So they both ran together, and the other disciple outran Peter and came to the tomb first. **5** And he, stooping down and looking in, saw the linen cloths lying *there;* yet he did not go in. **6** Then Simon Peter came, following him, and went into the tomb; and he saw the linen cloths lying *there,* **7** and the handkerchief that had been around His head, not lying with the linen cloths, but folded together in a place by itself. **8** Then the other disciple, who came to the tomb first, went in also; and he saw and believed. **9** For as yet they did not know the Scripture, that He must rise again from the dead. **10** Then the disciples went away again to their own homes.

Concerning Luke's writings.

Luke 1:1–4 Inasmuch as many have taken in hand to set in order a narrative of those things which have been fulfilled among us, **2** just as those who from the beginning were eyewitnesses and ministers of the word delivered them to us, **3** it seemed good to me also, having had perfect understanding of all things from the very first, to write to you an orderly account, most excellent Theophilus, **4** that you may know the certainty of those things in which you were instructed.

Cf. Acts 1:1–3

For church meetings.

1 Cor 14:26–40 How is it then, brethren? Whenever you come together, each of you has a psalm, has a teaching, has a tongue, has a revelation, has an interpretation. Let all things be done for edification. **27** If anyone speaks in a tongue, *let there be* two or at the most three, *each* in turn, and let one interpret. **28** But if there is no interpreter, let him keep silent in church, and let him speak to himself and to God. **29** Let two or three prophets speak, and let the others judge. **30** But if *anything* is revealed to another who sits by, let the first keep silent. **31** For you can all prophesy one by one, that all may learn and all may be encouraged. **32** And the spirits of the prophets are subject to the prophets. **33** For God is not *the author of* confusion but of peace, as in all the churches of the saints. **34** Let your women keep silent in the churches, for they are not permitted to speak; but *they are* to be submissive, as the law also says. **35** And if they want to learn something, let them ask their own husbands at home; for it is shameful for women to speak in church. **36** Or did the word of God come *originally* from you? Or *was it* you only that it reached? **37** If anyone thinks himself to be a prophet or spiritual, let him acknowledge that the things which I write to you are the commandments of the Lord. **38** But if anyone is ignorant, let him be ignorant. **39** Therefore, brethren, desire earnestly to prophesy, and do not forbid to speak with tongues. **40** Let all things be done decently and in order.

Cf. Titus 1:5

Of the world's system.

1 Cor 1:19–24 For it is written: *"I will destroy the wisdom of the wise, And bring to nothing the understanding of the prudent."* **20** Where *is* the wise? Where *is* the scribe? Where *is* the disputer of this age? Has not God made foolish the wisdom of this world? **21** For since, in the wisdom of God, the world through wisdom did not know God, it pleased God through the foolishness of the message preached to save those who believe. **22** For Jews request a sign, and Greeks seek after wisdom; **23** but we preach Christ crucified, to the Jews a stumbling block and to the Greeks foolishness, **24** but to those who are called, both Jews and Greeks, Christ the power of God and the wisdom of God.

Gal 1:4 who gave Himself for our sins, that He might deliver us from this present evil age, according to the will of our God and Father,

Eph 2:2 in which you once walked according to the course of this world, according to the prince of the power of the air, the spirit who now works in the sons of disobedience,

1 John 2:15–16 Do not love the world or the things in the world. If anyone loves the world, the love of the Father is not in him. **16** For all that *is* in the world— the lust of the flesh, the lust of the eyes, and the pride of life—is not of the Father but is of the world.

1 John 5:19 We know that we are of God, and the whole world lies *under the sway of* the wicked one.

Cf. 2 Cor 4:3–4; 10:3–5; Gal 6:12

For obedience to government.

Rom 13:1–7 Let every soul be subject to the governing authorities. For there is no authority except from God, and the authorities that exist are appointed by God. **2** Therefore whoever resists the authority resists the ordinance of God, and those who resist will bring judgment on themselves. **3** For rulers are not a terror to good works, but to evil. Do you want to be unafraid of the authority? Do what is good, and you

will have praise from the same. **4** For he is God's minister to you for good. But if you do evil, be afraid; for he does not bear the sword in vain; for he is God's minister, an avenger to *execute* wrath on him who practices evil. **5** Therefore *you* must be subject, not only because of wrath but also for conscience' sake. **6** For because of this you also pay taxes, for they are God's ministers attending continually to this very thing. **7** Render therefore to all their due: taxes to whom taxes *are due*, customs to whom customs, fear to whom fear, honor to whom honor.

1 Pet 2:13–17 Therefore submit yourselves to every ordinance of man for the Lord's sake, whether to the king as supreme, **14** or to governors, as to those who are sent by him for the punishment of evildoers and *for the* praise of those who do good. **15** For this is the will of God, that by doing good you may put to silence the ignorance of foolish men— **16** as free, yet not using liberty as a cloak for vice, but as bondservants of God. **17** Honor all *people*. Love the brotherhood. Fear God. Honor the king.

OSTRICH, THE

Furnished with wings and feathers.

Job 39:13 "The wings of the ostrich wave proudly, But are her wings and pinions *like the* kindly stork's?

Lays her eggs in the sand.

Job 39:14 For she leaves her eggs on the ground, And warms them in the dust;

Described as

Void of wisdom.

Job 39:17 Because God deprived her of wisdom, And did not endow her with understanding.

Imprudent.

Job 39:15 She forgets that a foot may crush them, Or that a wild beast may break them.

Harsh to her young.

Job 39:16 She treats her young harshly, as though *they were* not hers; Her labor is in vain, without concern,

Rapid in movement.

Job 39:18 When she lifts herself on high, She scorns the horse and its rider.

Illustrative of

The unnatural cruelty of the Jews in their calamities.

Lam 4:3 Even the jackals present their breasts To nurse their young; *But* the daughter of my people *is* cruel, Like ostriches in the wilderness.

(Companionship with) extreme desolation.

Job 30:29 I am a brother of jackals, And a companion of ostriches.

Is 13:21 But wild beasts of the desert will lie there, And their houses will be full of owls; Ostriches will dwell there, And wild goats will caper there.

OVERCOMER

Term applied to Christ.

John 16:33 These things I have spoken to you, that in Me you may have peace. In the world you will have tribulation; but be of good cheer, I have overcome the world."

Cf. John 1:5

Term applied to believers.

Rom 8:37 Yet in all these things we are more than conquerors through Him who loved us.

2 Cor 2:14 Now thanks *be* to God who always leads us in triumph in Christ, and through us diffuses the fragrance of His knowledge in every place.

1 John 2:13 I write to you, fathers, Because you have known Him *who is* from the beginning. I write to you, young men, Because you have overcome the wicked one. I write to you, little children, Because you have known the Father.

1 John 5:4–5 For whatever is born of God overcomes the world. And this is the victory that has overcome the world—our faith. **5** Who is he who overcomes the world, but he who believes that Jesus is the Son of God?

Rev 2:7 "He who has an ear, let him hear what the Spirit says to the churches. To him who overcomes I will give to eat from the tree of life, which is in the midst of the Paradise of God." '

Rev 2:11 "He who has an ear, let him hear what the Spirit says to the churches. He who overcomes shall not be hurt by the second death." '

Rev 2:17 "He who has an ear, let him hear what the Spirit says to the churches. To him who overcomes I will give some of the hidden manna to eat. And I will give him a white stone, and on the stone a new name written which no one knows except him who receives *it*." '

Rev 2:26 And he who overcomes, and keeps My works until the end, to him I will give power over the nations—

Rev 3:5 He who overcomes shall be clothed in white garments, and I will not blot out his name from the Book of Life; but I will confess his name before My Father and before His angels.

Rev 3:12 He who overcomes, I will make him a pillar in the temple of My God, and he shall go out no more. I will write on him the name of My God and the name of the city of My God, the New Jerusalem, which comes down out of heaven from My God. And *I will write on him* My new name.

Rev 3:21 To him who overcomes I will grant to sit with Me on My throne, as I also overcame and sat down with My Father on His throne.

OWL, THE

Varieties of.

Lev 11:16–17 the ostrich, the short-eared owl, the sea gull, and the hawk after its kind; **17** the little owl, the fisher owl, and the screech owl;

Deut 14:15–16 the ostrich, the short-eared owl, the sea gull, and the hawk after their kinds; **16** the little owl, the screech owl, the white owl,

Unclean and not to be eaten.

Lev 11:13 'And these you shall regard as an abomination among the birds; they shall not be eaten, they *are* an abomination: the eagle, the vulture, the buzzard,

Lev 11:16 the ostrich, the short-eared owl, the sea gull, and the hawk after its kind;

Solitary in disposition.

Ps 102:6 I am like a pelican of the wilderness; I am like an owl of the desert.

Inhabits deserted cities and houses.

Is 13:21 But wild beasts of the desert will lie there, And their houses will be full of owls; Ostriches will dwell there, And wild goats will caper there.

Is 34:11–14 But the pelican and the porcupine shall possess it, Also the owl and the raven shall dwell in it. And He shall stretch out over it The line of confusion and the stones of emptiness. **12** They shall call its nobles to the kingdom, But none *shall be* there, and all its princes shall be nothing. **13** And thorns shall come up in its palaces, Nettles and brambles in its fortresses; It shall be a habitation of jackals, A courtyard for ostriches. **14** The wild beasts of the desert shall also meet with the jackals, And the wild goat shall bleat to its companion; Also the night creature shall rest there, And find for herself a place of rest.

Jer 50:39 "Therefore the wild desert beasts shall dwell *there* with the jackals, And the ostriches shall dwell in it. It shall be inhabited no more forever, Nor shall it be dwelt in from generation to generation.

Illustrative of mourners.

Ps 102:6 I am like a pelican of the wilderness; I am like an owl of the desert.

OX, THE

Includes

The bull.

Gen 32:15 thirty milk camels with their colts, forty cows and ten bulls, twenty female donkeys and ten foals.

Job 21:10 Their bull breeds without failure; Their cow calves without miscarriage.

Ps 50:9 I will not take a bull from your house, *Nor* goats out of your folds.

Jer 46:21 Also her mercenaries are in her midst like fat bulls, For they also are turned back, They have fled away together. They did not stand, For the day of their calamity had come upon them, The time of their punishment.

The cow.

Num 18:17 But the firstborn of a cow, the firstborn of a sheep, or the firstborn of a goat you shall not redeem; they *are* holy. You shall sprinkle their blood on the altar, and burn their fat *as* an offering made by fire for a sweet aroma to the LORD.

Job 21:10 Their bull breeds without failure; Their cow calves without miscarriage.

The heifer.

Gen 15:9 So He said to him, "Bring Me a three-year-old heifer, a three-year-old female goat, a three-year-old ram, a turtledove, and a young pigeon."

Num 19:2 "This *is* the ordinance of the law which the LORD has commanded, saying: 'Speak to the children of Israel, that they bring you a red heifer without blemish, in which there *is* no defect *and* on which a yoke has never come.

Was clean and fit for food.

Deut 14:4 These *are* the animals which you may eat: the ox, the sheep, the goat,

Described as

Strong.

Ps 144:14 *That* our oxen *may be* well laden; *That there be* no breaking in or going out; *That there be* no outcry in our streets.

Prov 14:4 Where no oxen *are*, the trough *is* clean; But much increase *comes* by the strength of an ox.

Beautiful.

Jer 46:20 "Egypt *is* a very pretty heifer, *But* destruction comes, it comes from the north.

Hos 10:11 Ephraim *is* a trained heifer That loves to thresh *grain;* But I harnessed her fair neck, I will make Ephraim pull *a plow.* Judah shall plow; Jacob shall break his clods."

Intelligent.

Is 1:3 The ox knows its owner And the donkey its master's crib; *But* Israel does not know, My people do not consider."

Horns and hoofs of, alluded to.

Ps 69:31 *This* also shall please the LORD better than an ox *or* bull, Which has horns and hooves.

Lowing of, alluded to.

1 Sam 15:14 But Samuel said, "What then *is* this bleating of the sheep in my ears, and the lowing of the oxen which I hear?"

Job 6:5 Does the wild donkey bray when it has grass, Or does the ox low over its fodder?

Was fed

With grass.

Job 40:15 "Look now at the behemoth, which I made *along* with you; He eats grass like an ox.

Ps 106:20 Thus they changed their glory Into the image of an ox that eats grass.

Dan 4:25 They shall drive you from men, your dwelling shall be with the beasts of the field, and they shall make you eat grass like oxen. They shall wet you with the dew of heaven, and seven times shall pass over you, till you know that the Most High rules in the kingdom of men, and gives it to whomever He chooses.

With corn.

Is 30:24 Likewise the oxen and the young donkeys that work the ground Will eat cured fodder, Which has been winnowed with the shovel and fan.

With straw.

Is 11:7 The cow and the bear shall graze; Their young ones shall lie down together; And the lion shall eat straw like the ox.

On the hills.

Is 7:25 And to any hill which could be dug with the hoe, You will not go there for fear of briers and thorns; But it will become a range for oxen And a place for sheep to roam.

In the valleys.

1 Chr 27:29 And Shitrai the Sharonite *was* over the herds that fed in Sharon, and Shaphat the son of Adlai was over the herds *that were* in the valleys.

Is 65:10 Sharon shall be a fold of flocks, And the Valley of Achor a place for herds to lie down, For My people who have sought Me.

In stalls.

Hab 3:17 Though the fig tree may not blossom, Nor fruit be on the vines; Though the labor of the olive may fail, And the fields yield no food; Though the flock may be cut off from the fold, And there be no herd in the stalls—

For slaughter.

Prov 7:22 Immediately he went after her, as an ox goes to the slaughter, Or as a fool to the correction of the stocks,

Prov 15:17 Better *is* a dinner of herbs where love is, Than a fatted calf with hatred.

Rapid manner of collecting its food.

Num 22:4 So Moab said to the elders of Midian, "Now this company will lick up everything around us, as an ox licks up the grass of the field." And Balak the son of Zippor *was* king of the Moabites at that time.

Was a part of Jews' wealth

For patriarchs.

Gen 13:2 Abram *was* very rich in livestock, in silver, and in gold.

Gen 13:5 Lot also, who went with Abram, had flocks and herds and tents.

Gen 26:14 for he had possessions of flocks and possessions of herds and a great number of servants. So the Philistines envied him.

Job 1:3 Also, his possessions were seven thousand sheep, three thousand camels, five hundred yoke of oxen, five hundred female donkeys, and a very large household, so that this man was the greatest of all the people of the East.

While in Egypt.

Gen 50:8 as well as all the house of Joseph, his brothers, and his father's house. Only their little ones, their flocks, and their herds they left in the land of Goshen.

Ex 10:9 And Moses said, "We will go with our young and our old; with our sons and our daughters, with our flocks and our herds we will go, for we must hold a feast to the LORD."

Ex 12:32 Also take your flocks and your herds, as you have said, and be gone; and bless me also."

In Israel.

Num 32:4 the country which the LORD defeated before the congregation of Israel, *is* a land for livestock, and your servants have livestock."

Ps 144:14 *That* our oxen *may be* well laden; *That there be* no breaking in or going out; *That there be* no outcry in our streets.

Required great care and attention.

Prov 27:23 Be diligent to know the state of your flocks, *And* attend to your herds;

Herdmen appointed over.

Gen 13:7 And there was strife between the herdsmen of Abram's livestock and the herdsmen of Lot's livestock. The Canaanites and the Perizzites then dwelt in the land.

1 Sam 21:7 Now a certain man of the servants of Saul *was* there that day, detained before the LORD. And his name *was* Doeg, an Edomite, the chief of the herds-men who *belonged* to Saul.

Urged on by the goad.

Judg 3:31 After him was Shamgar the son of Anath, who killed six hundred men of the Philistines with an ox goad; and he also delivered Israel.

Used for

Drawing wagons, etc.

Num 7:3 And they brought their offering before the LORD, six covered carts and twelve oxen, a cart for *every* two of the leaders, and for each one an ox; and they presented them before the tabernacle.

1 Sam 6:7 Now therefore, make a new cart, take two milk cows which have never been yoked, and hitch the cows to the cart; and take their calves home, away from them.

Carrying burdens.

1 Chr 12:40 Moreover those who were near to them, from as far away as Issachar and Zebulun and Naphtali, were bringing food on donkeys and camels, on mules and oxen—provisions of flour and cakes of figs and cakes of raisins, wine and oil and oxen and sheep abundantly, for *there was* joy in Israel.

Plowing.

1 Kin 19:19 So he departed from there, and found Elisha the son of Shaphat, who *was* plowing *with* twelve yoke *of oxen* before him, and he was with the twelfth. Then Elijah passed by him and threw his mantle on him.

Job 1:14 and a messenger came to Job and said, "The oxen were plowing and the donkeys feeding beside them,

Amos 6:12 Do horses run on rocks? Does *one* plow *there* with oxen? Yet you have turned justice into gall, And the fruit of righteousness into wormwood,

Cultivating.

Is 30:24 Likewise the oxen and the young donkeys that work the ground Will eat cured fodder, Which has been winnowed with the shovel and fan.

Is 32:20 Blessed *are* you who sow beside all waters, Who send out freely the feet of the ox and the donkey.

Threshing out the grain.

Hos 10:11 Ephraim *is* a trained heifer That loves to thresh *grain;* But I harnessed her fair neck, I will make Ephraim pull *a plow.* Judah shall plow; Jacob shall break his clods."

Sacrifice.

Ex 20:24 An altar of earth you shall make for Me, and you shall sacrifice on it your burnt offerings and your peace offerings, your sheep and your oxen. In every place where I record My name I will come to you, and I will bless you.

2 Sam 24:22 Now Araunah said to David, "Let my lord the king take and offer up whatever *seems* good to him. Look, *here are* oxen for burnt sacrifice, and threshing implements and the yokes of the oxen for wood.

Food.

Gen 18:7 And Abraham ran to the herd, took a tender

and good calf, gave *it* to a young man, and he hastened to prepare it.

1 Kin 1:9 And Adonijah sacrificed sheep and oxen and fattened cattle by the stone of Zoheleth, which *is* by En Rogel; he also invited all his brothers, the king's sons, and all the men of Judah, the king's servants.

1 Kin 19:21 So *Elisha* turned back from him, and took a yoke of oxen and slaughtered them and boiled their flesh, using the oxen's equipment, and gave it to the people, and they ate. Then he arose and followed Elijah, and became his servant.

2 Chr 18:2 After some years he went down to *visit* Ahab in Samaria; and Ahab killed sheep and oxen in abundance for him and the people who were with him, and persuaded him to go up *with him* to Ramoth Gilead.

Amos 6:4 Who lie on beds of ivory, Stretch out on your couches, Eat lambs from the flock And calves from the midst of the stall;

Male firstlings of, belonged to God.

Ex 34:19 "All that open the womb *are* Mine, and every male firstborn among your livestock, *whether* ox or sheep.

Tithe of, given to the priests.

2 Chr 31:6 And the children of Israel and Judah, who dwelt in the cities of Judah, brought the tithe of oxen and sheep; also the tithe of holy things which were consecrated to the LORD their God they laid in heaps.

Laws respecting,

To rest on the Sabbath.

Ex 23:12 Six days you shall do your work, and on the seventh day you shall rest, that your ox and your donkey may rest, and the son of your female servant and the stranger may be refreshed.

Deut 5:14 but the seventh day *is* the Sabbath of the LORD your God. *In it* you shall do no work: you, nor your son, nor your daughter, nor your male servant, nor your female servant, nor your ox, nor your donkey, nor any of your cattle, nor your stranger who *is* within your gates, that your male servant and your female servant may rest as well as you.

Not to be yoked with a donkey in the same plow.

Deut 22:10 "You shall not plow with an ox and a donkey together.

Not to be muzzled when treading out the grain.

Deut 25:4 "You shall not muzzle an ox while it treads out *the grain.*

1 Cor 9:9 For it is written in the law of Moses, *"You shall not muzzle an ox while it treads out the grain."* Is it oxen God is concerned about?

If stolen, to be restored double.

Ex 22:4 If the theft is certainly found alive in his hand, whether it is an ox or donkey or sheep, he shall restore double.

Of others not to be coveted.

Ex 20:17 "You shall not covet your neighbor's house; you shall not covet your neighbor's wife, nor his male servant, nor his female servant, nor his ox, nor his donkey, nor anything that *is* your neighbor's."

Deut 5:21 'You shall not covet your neighbor's wife; and you shall not desire your neighbor's house, his field, his male servant, his female servant, his ox, his donkey, or anything that *is* your neighbor's.'

If others' lost or hurt through neglect, to be made good.

Ex 22:9–13 "For any kind of trespass, *whether it concerns* an ox, a donkey, a sheep, or clothing, *or* for any kind of lost thing which *another* claims to be his, the cause of both parties shall come before the judges; *and* whomever the judges condemn shall pay double to his neighbor. **10** If a man delivers to his neighbor a donkey, an ox, a sheep, or any animal to keep, and it dies, is hurt, or driven away, no one seeing *it*, **11** *then* an oath of the LORD shall be between them both, that he has not put his hand into his neighbor's goods; and the owner of it shall accept *that*, and he shall not make *it* good. **12** But if, in fact, it is stolen from him, he shall make restitution to the owner of it. **13** If it is torn to pieces *by a beast, then* he shall bring it as evidence, *and* he shall not make good what was torn.

Killing a man, to be stoned.

Ex 21:28–32 "If an ox gores a man or a woman to death, then the ox shall surely be stoned, and its flesh shall not be eaten; but the owner of the ox *shall be* acquitted. **29** But if the ox tended to thrust with its horn in times past, and it has been made known to his owner, and he has not kept it confined, so that it has killed a man or a woman, the ox shall be stoned and its owner also shall be put to death. **30** If there is imposed on him a sum of money, then he shall pay to redeem his life, whatever is imposed on him. **31** Whether it has gored a son or gored a daughter, according to this judgment it shall be done to him. **32** If the ox gores a male or female servant, he shall give to their master thirty shekels of silver, and the ox shall be stoned.

Mode of reparation for one ox that kills another.

Ex 21:35–36 "If one man's ox hurts another's, so that it dies, then they shall sell the live ox and divide the money from it; and the dead *ox* they shall also divide. **36** Or if it was known that the ox tended to thrust in time past, and its owner has not kept it confined, he shall surely pay ox for ox, and the dead animal shall be his own.

Strays to be returned to owners.

Ex 23:4 "If you meet your enemy's ox or his donkey going astray, you shall surely bring it back to him again.

Deut 22:1–2 "You shall not see your brother's ox or his sheep going astray, and hide yourself from them; you shall certainly bring them back to your brother. **2** And if your brother *is* not near you, or if you do not know him, then you shall bring it to your own house, and it shall remain with you until your brother seeks it; then you shall restore it to him.

Fallen ones to be raised up again.

Deut 22:4 "You shall not see your brother's donkey or his ox fall down along the road, and hide yourself from them; you shall surely help him lift *them* up again.

Fat of, not to be eaten.

Lev 7:23 "Speak to the children of Israel, saying: 'You shall not eat any fat, of ox or sheep or goat.

Increase of, promised.

Deut 7:13 And He will love you and bless you and multiply you; He will also bless the fruit of your womb and the fruit of your land, your grain and your new wine and your oil, the increase of your cattle and the offspring of your flock, in the land of which He swore to your fathers to give you.

Deut 28:4 "Blessed *shall be* the fruit of your body, the produce of your ground and the increase of your herds, the increase of your cattle and the offspring of your flocks.

Publicly sold.

2 Sam 24:24 Then the king said to Araunah, "No, but I will surely buy *it* from you for a price; nor will I offer burnt offerings to the LORD my God with that which costs me nothing." So David bought the threshing floor and the oxen for fifty shekels of silver.

Luke 14:19 And another said, 'I have bought five yoke of oxen, and I am going to test them. I ask you to have me excused.'

Often given as a present.

Gen 12:16 He treated Abram well for her sake. He had sheep, oxen, male donkeys, male and female servants, female donkeys, and camels.

Gen 20:14 Then Abimelech took sheep, oxen, and male and female servants, and gave *them* to Abraham; and he restored Sarah his wife to him.

The wicked often took, in pledge from the poor.

Job 24:3 They drive away the donkey of the fatherless; They take the widow's ox as a pledge.

Custom of sending the pieces of, to collect the people to war.

1 Sam 11:7 So he took a yoke of oxen and cut them in pieces, and sent *them* throughout all the territory of Israel by the hands of messengers, saying, "Whoever does not go out with Saul and Samuel to battle, so it shall be done to his oxen." And the fear of the LORD fell on the people, and they came out with one consent.

Sea of bronze rested on figures of.

1 Kin 7:25 It stood on twelve oxen: three looking toward the north, three looking toward the west, three looking toward the south, and three looking toward the east; the Sea *was set* upon them, and all their back parts *pointed* inward.

Illustrative of

(Engaged in work) ministers.

Is 30:24 Likewise the oxen and the young donkeys that work the ground Will eat cured fodder, Which has been winnowed with the shovel and fan.

Is 32:20 Blessed *are* you who sow beside all waters, Who send out freely the feet of the ox and the donkey.

(Not muzzled in treading grain) minister's right to support.

1 Cor 9:9–10 For it is written in the law of Moses, *"You shall not muzzle an ox while it treads out the grain."* Is it oxen God is concerned about? **10** Or does He say *it* altogether for our sakes? For our sakes, no doubt, *this* is written, that he who plows should plow in hope, and he who threshes in hope should be partaker of his hope.

(Prepared for a feast) the provision of the gospel.

Prov 9:2 She has slaughtered her meat, She has mixed her wine, She has also furnished her table.

Matt 22:4 Again, he sent out other servants, saying, 'Tell those who are invited, "See, I have prepared my dinner; my oxen and fatted cattle *are* killed, and all things *are* ready. Come to the wedding." '

(Led to slaughter) a rash youth.

Prov 7:22 Immediately he went after her, as an ox goes to the slaughter, Or as a fool to the correction of the stocks,

(Stall fed) luxurious living.

Prov 15:17 Better *is* a dinner of herbs where love is, Than a fatted calf with hatred.

Illustrative of bull

Fierce enemies.

Ps 22:12 Many bulls have surrounded Me; Strong *bulls* of Bashan have encircled Me.

Ps 68:30 Rebuke the beasts of the reeds, The herd of bulls with the calves of the peoples, *Till everyone* submits himself with pieces of silver. Scatter the peoples *who* delight in war.

(Firstling of) the glory of Joseph.

Deut 33:17 His glory *is like* a firstborn bull, And his horns *like* the horns of the wild ox; Together with them He shall push the peoples To the ends of the earth; They *are* the ten thousands of Ephraim, And they *are* the thousands of Manasseh."

(In a net) the impatient under judgment.

Is 51:20 Your sons have fainted, They lie at the head of all the streets, Like an antelope in a net; They are full of the fury of the LORD, The rebuke of your God.

(Fatted) greedy mercenaries.

Jer 46:21 Also her mercenaries are in her midst like fat bulls, For they also are turned back, They have fled away together. They did not stand, For the day of their calamity had come upon them, The time of their punishment.

(Unaccustomed to the yoke) intractable sinners.

Jer 31:18 "I have surely heard Ephraim bemoaning himself: 'You have chastised me, and I was chastised, Like an untrained bull; Restore me, and I will return, For You *are* the LORD my God.

Illustrative of cows

Proud and wealthy women rulers.

Amos 4:1 Hear this word, you cows of Bashan, who *are* on the mountain of Samaria, Who oppress the poor, Who crush the needy, Who say to your husbands, "Bring *wine*, let us drink!"

(Well favored) years of plenty.

Gen 41:2 Suddenly there came up out of the river seven cows, fine looking and fat; and they fed in the meadow.

Gen 41:26 The seven good cows *are* seven years, and the seven good heads *are* seven years; the dreams *are* one.

Gen 41:29 Indeed seven years of great plenty will come throughout all the land of Egypt;

(Lean) years of scarcity.

Gen 27:30 Now it happened, as soon as Isaac had finished blessing Jacob, and Jacob had scarcely gone out from the presence of Isaac his father, that Esau his brother came in from his hunting.

Gen 41:3 Then behold, seven other cows came up after them out of the river, ugly and gaunt, and stood by the *other* cows on the bank of the river.

Illustrative of heifers

A beloved wife.

Judg 14:18 So the men of the city said to him on the seventh day before the sun went down: "What *is* sweeter than honey? And what *is* stronger than a lion?" And he said to them: "If you had not plowed with my heifer, You would not have solved my riddle!"

(Sliding back) backsliding Israel.

Hos 4:16 "For Israel is stubborn Like a stubborn calf; Now the LORD will let them forage Like a lamb in open country.

(Taught, etc.) Israel's fondness for ease in preference to obedience.

Hos 10:11 Ephraim *is* a trained heifer That loves to thresh *grain*; But I harnessed her fair neck, I will make Ephraim pull *a plow*. Judah shall plow; Jacob shall break his clods."

(Of three years old) Moab in affliction.

Is 15:5 "My heart will cry out for Moab; His fugitives *shall flee* to Zoar, Like a three-year-old heifer. For by the Ascent of Luhith They will go up with weeping; For in the way of Horonaim They will raise up a cry of destruction,

Jer 48:34 "From the cry of Heshbon to Elealeh and to Jahaz They have uttered their voice, From Zoar to Horonaim, *Like* a three-year-old heifer; For the waters of Nimrim also shall be desolate.

(Fair) the beauty and wealth of Egypt.

Jer 46:20 "Egypt *is* a very pretty heifer, *But* destruction comes, it comes from the north.

(At grass) the wealthy Chaldees.

Jer 50:11 "Because you were glad, because you rejoiced, You destroyers of My heritage, Because you have grown fat like a heifer threshing grain, And you bellow like bulls,

P

PALACES

Jerusalem celebrated for.

Ps 48:3 God *is* in her palaces; He is known as her refuge.

Ps 48:13 Mark well her bulwarks; Consider her palaces; That you may tell *it* to the generation following.

The term applied to

Residences of kings.

Dan 4:4 I, Nebuchadnezzar, was at rest in my house, and flourishing in my palace.

Dan 6:18 Now the king went to his palace and spent the night fasting; and no musicians were brought before him. Also his sleep went from him.

Houses of great men.

Amos 3:9 "Proclaim in the palaces at Ashdod, And in the palaces in the land of Egypt, and say: 'Assemble on the mountains of Samaria; See great tumults in her midst, And the oppressed within her.

Mic 5:5 And this *One* shall be peace. When the Assyrian comes into our land, And when he treads in our palaces, Then we will raise against him Seven shepherds and eight princely men.

Described as

High.

Ps 78:69 And He built His sanctuary like the heights, Like the earth which He has established forever.

Polished.

Ps 144:12 That our sons *may be* as plants grown up in their youth; *That* our daughters *may be* as pillars, Sculptured in palace style;

Pleasant.

Is 13:22 The hyenas will howl in their citadels, And jackals in their pleasant palaces. Her time *is* near to come, And her days will not be prolonged."

Of kings and high officials

Called the high priest's courtyard.

Matt 26:58 But Peter followed Him at a distance to the high priest's courtyard. And he went in and sat with the servants to see the end.

Called the king's house.

2 Kin 25:9 He burned the house of the LORD and the king's house; all the houses of Jerusalem, that is, all the houses of the great, he burned with fire.

2 Chr 7:11 Thus Solomon finished the house of the LORD and the king's house; and Solomon successfully accomplished all that came into his heart to make in the house of the LORD and in his own house.

Called the temple (of God).

1 Chr 29:1 Furthermore King David said to all the assembly: "My son Solomon, whom alone God has chosen, *is* young and inexperienced; and the work *is* great, because the temple *is* not for man but for the LORD God.

1 Chr 29:19 And give my son Solomon a loyal heart to keep Your commandments and Your testimonies and Your statutes, to do all *these things*, and to build the temple for which I have made provision."

2 Chr 2:1 Then Solomon determined to build a temple for the name of the LORD, and a royal house for himself.

2 Chr 2:12 Hiram also said: Blessed *be* the LORD God of Israel, who made heaven and earth, for He has given King David a wise son, endowed with prudence and understanding, who will build a temple for the LORD and a royal house for himself!

Called the king's palace.

Esth 1:5 And when these days were completed, the king made a feast lasting seven days for all the people who were present in Shushan the citadel, from great to small, in the court of the garden of the king's palace.

Called the royal palace.

Esth 1:9 Queen Vashti also made a feast for the women *in* the royal palace which *belonged* to King Ahasuerus.

Splendidly furnished.

Esth 1:6 *There were* white and blue linen *curtains* fastened with cords of fine linen and purple on silver rods and marble pillars; *and the* couches *were* of gold and silver on a *mosaic* pavement of alabaster, turquoise, and white and black marble.

Surrounded with gardens and walkways.

2 Chr 9:11 And the king made walkways *of* the algum wood for the house of the LORD and for the king's house, also harps and stringed instruments for singers; and there were none such *as these* seen before in the land of Judah.

Esth 1:5 And when these days were completed, the king made a feast lasting seven days for all the people who were present in Shushan the citadel, from great to small, in the court of the garden of the king's palace.

Under governors.

1 Kin 4:6 Ahishar, over the household; and Adoniram the son of Abda, over the labor force.

Neh 7:2 that I gave the charge of Jerusalem to my brother Hanani, and Hananiah the leader of the citadel, for he *was* a faithful man and feared God more than many.

Often attended by eunuchs as servants.

2 Kin 20:18 'And they shall take away some of your sons who will descend from you, whom you will beget; and they shall be eunuchs in the palace of the king of Babylon.' "

Dan 1:3–4 Then the king instructed Ashpenaz, the master of his eunuchs, to bring some of the children of Israel and some of the king's descendants and some of the nobles, **4** young men in whom *there was* no blemish, but good-looking, gifted in all wisdom, possessing knowledge and quick to understand, who *had* ability to serve in the king's palace, and whom they might teach the language and literature of the Chaldeans.

Were strictly guarded.

2 Kin 11:5 Then he commanded them, saying, "This *is* what you shall do: One-third of you who come on duty on the Sabbath shall be keeping watch over the king's house,

Afforded support to all the king's retainers.

Ezra 4:14 Now because we receive support from the palace, it was not proper for us to see the king's dishonor; therefore we have sent and informed the king,

Dan 1:5 And the king appointed for them a daily provision of the king's delicacies and of the wine which he drank, and three years of training for them, so that at the end of *that time* they might serve before the king.

Royal decrees issued from and kept in.

Ezra 6:2 And at Achmetha, in the palace that *is* in the province of Media, a scroll was found, and in it a record *was* written thus:

Esth 3:15 The couriers went out, hastened by the king's command; and the decree was proclaimed in Shushan the citadel. So the king and Haman sat down to drink, but the city of Shushan was perplexed.

Esth 8:14 The couriers who rode on royal horses went out, hastened and pressed on by the king's command. And the decree was issued in Shushan the citadel.

Contained treasures of the king.

1 Kin 15:18 Then Asa took all the silver and gold *that was* left in the treasuries of the house of the Lord and the treasuries of the king's house, and delivered them into the hand of his servants. And King Asa sent them to Ben-Hadad the son of Tabrimmon, the son of Hezion, king of Syria, who dwelt in Damascus, saying,

2 Chr 12:9 So Shishak king of Egypt came up against Jerusalem, and took away the treasures of the house of the Lord and the treasures of the king's house; he took everything. He also carried away the gold shields which Solomon had made.

2 Chr 25:24 And *he took* all the gold and silver, all the articles that were found in the house of God with Obed-Edom, the treasures of the king's house, and hostages, and returned to Samaria.

Gorgeous apparel suited to, alone.

Luke 7:25 But what did you go out to see? A man clothed in soft garments? Indeed those who are gorgeously appareled and live in luxury are in kings' courts.

Even contain spiders.

Prov 30:28 The spider skillfully grasps with its hands, And it is in kings' palaces.

Were entered by gates.

Neh 2:8 and a letter to Asaph the keeper of the king's forest, that he must give me timber to make beams for the gates of the citadel which *pertains* to the temple, for the city wall, and for the house that I will occupy." And the king granted *them* to me according to the good hand of my God upon me.

Often as punishment were

Plundered.

Amos 3:11 Therefore thus says the Lord God: "An adversary *shall be* all around the land; He shall sap your strength from you, And your palaces shall be plundered."

Forsaken.

Is 32:14 Because the palaces will be forsaken, The bustling city will be deserted. The forts and towers will become lairs forever, A joy of wild donkeys, a pasture of flocks—

Desolate.

Ps 69:25 Let their dwelling place be desolate; Let no one live in their tents.

Ezek 19:7 He knew their desolate places, And laid waste their cities; The land with its fullness was desolated By the noise of his roaring.

Scenes of bloodshed.

Jer 9:21 For death has come through our windows, Has entered our palaces, To kill off the children—*no longer to be* outside! *And* the young men—*no longer* on the streets!

Burned with fire.

2 Chr 36:19 Then they burned the house of God, broke down the wall of Jerusalem, burned all its palaces with fire, and destroyed all its precious possessions.

Jer 17:27 "But if you will not heed Me to hallow the Sabbath day, such as not carrying a burden when entering the gates of Jerusalem on the Sabbath day, then I will kindle a fire in its gates, and it shall devour the palaces of Jerusalem, and it shall not be quenched." ' "

Overgrown with thorns, etc.

Is 34:13 And thorns shall come up in its palaces, Nettles and brambles in its fortresses; It shall be a habitation of jackals, A courtyard for ostriches.

The habitation of dragons, etc.

Is 13:22 The hyenas will howl in their citadels, And jackals in their pleasant palaces. Her time *is* near to come, And her days will not be prolonged."

Illustrative of

The godly children of believers.

Ps 144:12 That our sons *may be* as plants grown up in their youth; *That* our daughters *may be* as pillars, Sculptured in palace style;

Place of stored-up violence.

Amos 3:10 For they do not know to do right,' Says the Lord, 'Who store up violence and robbery in their palaces.' "

The place of Satan's dominion.

Luke 11:21 When a strong man, fully armed, guards his own palace, his goods are in peace.

PALM TREE, THE

First mention of, in Scripture.

Ex 15:27 Then they came to Elim, where there *were* twelve wells of water and seventy palm trees; so they camped there by the waters.

Jericho celebrated for.

Deut 34:3 the South, and the plain of the Valley of Jericho, the city of palm trees, as far as Zoar.

Judg 1:16 Now the children of the Kenite, Moses' father-in-law, went up from the City of Palms with the children of Judah into the Wilderness of Judah, which *lies* in the South *near* Arad; and they went and dwelt among the people.

Described as

Tall.

Song 7:7 This stature of yours is like a palm tree, And your breasts *like* its clusters.

Upright.

Jer 10:5 They *are* upright, like a palm tree, And they cannot speak; They must be carried, Because they cannot go *by themselves*. Do not be afraid of them, For they cannot do evil, Nor can they do any good."

Flourishing.

Ps 92:12 The righteous shall flourish like a palm tree, He shall grow like a cedar in Lebanon.

Fruitful to a great age.

Ps 92:14 They shall still bear fruit in old age; They shall be fresh and flourishing,

Requires a moist and fertile soil.

Ex 15:27 Then they came to Elim, where there *were* twelve wells of water and seventy palm trees; so they camped there by the waters.

Tents often pitched under the shade of.

Judg 4:5 And she would sit under the palm tree of Deborah between Ramah and Bethel in the mountains of Ephraim. And the children of Israel came up to her for judgment.

The branches of, were

The emblem of victory.

Rev 7:9 After these things I looked, and behold, a great multitude which no one could number, of all nations, tribes, peoples, and tongues, standing before the throne and before the Lamb, clothed with white robes, with palm branches in their hands,

Carried at feast of tabernacles.

Lev 23:40 And you shall take for yourselves on the first day the fruit of beautiful trees, branches of palm trees, the boughs of leafy trees, and willows of the brook; and you shall rejoice before the LORD your God for seven days.

Used for constructing booths.

Neh 8:15 and that they should announce and proclaim in all their cities and in Jerusalem, saying, "Go out to the mountain, and bring olive branches, branches of oil trees, myrtle branches, palm branches, and branches of leafy trees, to make booths, as *it is* written."

Spread before Christ.

John 12:13 took branches of palm trees and went out to meet Him, and cried out: "Hosanna! *'Blessed is He who comes in the name of the LORD!'* The King of Israel!"

Withered as a punishment.

Joel 1:12 The vine has dried up, And the fig tree has withered; The pomegranate tree, The palm tree also, And the apple tree— All the trees of the field are withered; Surely joy has withered away from the sons of men.

Represented in carved work on the walls and doors of the temple of Solomon.

1 Kin 6:29 Then he carved all the walls of the temple all around, both the inner and outer *sanctuaries*, with carved figures of cherubim, palm trees, and open flowers.

1 Kin 6:32 The two doors *were of* olive wood; and he carved on them figures of cherubim, palm trees, and open flowers, and overlaid *them* with gold; and he spread gold on the cherubim and on the palm trees.

1 Kin 6:35 Then he carved cherubim, palm trees, and open flowers *on them*, and overlaid *them* with gold applied evenly on the carved work.

2 Chr 3:5 The larger room he paneled with cypress which he overlaid with fine gold, and he carved palm trees and chainwork on it.

Illustrative of

The righteous.

Ps 92:12 The righteous shall flourish like a palm tree, He shall grow like a cedar in Lebanon.

The upright appearance of idols.

Jer 10:5 They *are* upright, like a palm tree, And they cannot speak; They must be carried, Because they cannot go *by themselves*. Do not be afraid of them, For they cannot do evil, Nor can they do any good."

PARABLES

Remarkable parables of the Old Testament.

Judg 9:8–15 "The trees once went forth to anoint a king over them. And they said to the olive tree, 'Reign over us!' 9 But the olive tree said to them, 'Should I cease giving my oil, With which they honor God and men, And go to sway over trees?' 10 "Then the trees said to the fig tree, 'You come *and* reign over us!' 11 But the fig tree said to them, 'Should I cease my sweetness and my good fruit, And go to sway over trees?' 12 "Then the trees said to the vine, 'You come *and* reign over us!' 13 But the vine said to them, 'Should I cease my new wine, Which cheers *both* God and men, And go to sway over trees?' 14 "Then all the trees said to the bramble, 'You come *and* reign over us!' 15 And the bramble said to the trees, 'If in truth you anoint me as king over you, *Then* come *and* take shelter in my shade; But if not, let fire come out of the bramble And devour the cedars of Lebanon!'

2 Sam 12:1–4 Then the LORD sent Nathan to David. And he came to him, and said to him: "There were two men in one city, one rich and the other poor. 2 The rich *man* had exceedingly many flocks and herds. 3 But the poor *man* had nothing, except one little ewe lamb which he had bought and nourished; and it grew up together with him and with his children. It ate of his own food and drank from his own cup and lay in his bosom; and it was like a daughter to him.

4 And a traveler came to the rich man, who refused to take from his own flock and from his own herd to prepare one for the wayfaring man who had come to him; but he took the poor man's lamb and prepared it for the man who had come to him."

2 Sam 14:5–7 Then the king said to her, "What troubles you?" And she answered, "Indeed I *am* a widow, my husband is dead. 6 Now your maidservant had two sons; and the two fought with each other in the field, and *there was* no one to part them, but the one struck the other and killed him. 7 And now the whole family has risen up against your maidservant, and they said, 'Deliver him who struck his brother, that we may execute him for the life of his brother whom he killed; and we will destroy the heir also.' So they would extinguish my ember that is left, and leave to my husband *neither* name nor remnant on the earth."

2 Kin 14:9 And Jehoash king of Israel sent to Amaziah king of Judah, saying, "The thistle that *was* in Lebanon sent to the cedar that *was* in Lebanon, saying, 'Give your daughter to my son as wife'; and a wild beast that *was* in Lebanon passed by and trampled the thistle.

Is 28:23–29 Give ear and hear my voice, Listen and hear my speech. 24 Does the plowman keep plowing all day to sow? Does he keep turning his soil and breaking the clods? 25 When he has leveled its surface, Does he not sow the black cummin And scatter the cummin, Plant the wheat in rows, The barley in the appointed place, And the spelt in its place? 26 For He instructs him in right judgment, His God teaches him. 27 For the black cummin is not threshed with a threshing sledge, Nor is a cartwheel rolled over the cummin; But the black cummin is beaten out with a stick, And the cummin with a rod. 28 Bread *flour* must be ground; Therefore he does not thresh it forever, Break *it with* his cartwheel, Or crush *it with* his horsemen. 29 This also comes from the LORD of hosts, *Who* is wonderful in counsel *and* excellent in guidance.

Ezek 17:1–10 And the word of the LORD came to me, saying, 2 "Son of man, pose a riddle, and speak a parable to the house of Israel, 3 and say, 'Thus says the Lord GOD: "A great eagle with large wings and long pinions, Full of feathers of various colors, Came to Lebanon And took from the cedar the highest branch. 4 He cropped off its topmost young twig And carried it to a land of trade; He set it in a city of merchants. 5 Then he took some of the seed of the land And planted it in a fertile field; He placed *it* by abundant waters *And* set it like a willow tree. 6 And it grew and became a spreading vine of low stature; Its branches turned toward him, But its roots were under it. So it became a vine, Brought forth branches, And put forth shoots. 7 "But there was another great eagle with large wings and many feathers; And behold, this vine bent its roots toward him, And stretched its branches toward him, From the garden terrace where it had been planted, That he might water it. 8 It was planted in good soil by many waters, To bring forth branches, bear fruit, *And* become a majestic vine." ' 9 "Say, 'Thus says the Lord GOD: "Will it thrive? Will he not pull up its roots, Cut off its fruit, And leave it to wither? All of its spring leaves will wither, And no great power or many people Will be needed to pluck it up by its roots. 10 Be-

hold, *it is* planted, Will it thrive? Will it not utterly wither when the east wind touches it? It will wither in the garden terrace where it grew." ' "

Ezek 24:3–5 And utter a parable to the rebellious house, and say to them, 'Thus says the Lord GOD: "Put on a pot, set *it* on, And also pour water into it. 4 Gather pieces *of meat* in it, Every good piece, The thigh and the shoulder. Fill *it* with choice cuts; 5 Take the choice of the flock. Also pile *fuel* bones under it, Make it boil well, And let the cuts simmer in it."

Parables of Christ

Wise and foolish builders.

Matt 7:24–27 "Therefore whoever hears these sayings of Mine, and does them, I will liken him to a wise man who built his house on the rock: 25 and the rain descended, the floods came, and the winds blew and beat on that house; and it did not fall, for it was founded on the rock. 26 "But everyone who hears these sayings of Mine, and does not do them, will be like a foolish man who built his house on the sand: 27 and the rain descended, the floods came, and the winds blew and beat on that house; and it fell. And great was its fall."

Friends of the bridegroom.

Matt 9:15 And Jesus said to them, "Can the friends of the bridegroom mourn as long as the bridegroom is with them? But the days will come when the bridegroom will be taken away from them, and then they will fast.

New cloth and old garment.

Matt 9:16 No one puts a piece of unshrunk cloth on an old garment; for the patch pulls away from the garment, and the tear is made worse.

New wine and old wineskins.

Matt 9:17 Nor do they put new wine into old wineskins, or else the wineskins break, the wine is spilled, and the wineskins are ruined. But they put new wine into new wineskins, and both are preserved."

Unclean spirit.

Matt 12:43 "When an unclean spirit goes out of a man, he goes through dry places, seeking rest, and finds none.

Sower.

Matt 13:3–23 Then He spoke many things to them in parables, saying: "Behold, a sower went out to sow. 4 And as he sowed, some *seed* fell by the wayside; and the birds came and devoured them. 5 Some fell on stony places, where they did not have much earth; and they immediately sprang up because they had no depth of earth. 6 But when the sun was up they were scorched, and because they had no root they withered away. 7 And some fell among thorns, and the thorns sprang up and choked them. 8 But others fell on good ground and yielded a crop: some a hundredfold, some sixty, some thirty. 9 He who has ears to hear, let him hear!" 10 And the disciples came and said to Him, "Why do You speak to them in parables?" 11 He answered and said to them, "Because it has been given to you to know the mysteries of the kingdom of heaven, but to them it has not been given. 12 For whoever has, to him more will be given, and he will have abundance; but whoever does not have, even what he has will be taken away from him. 13 Therefore I speak to them in parables, because seeing they do not see, and hearing they do not hear, nor do they understand. **14** And in them the prophecy of Isaiah is fulfilled, which says: *'Hearing you will hear and shall not understand, And seeing you will see and not perceive;* **15** *For the hearts of this people have grown dull. Their ears are hard of hearing, And their eyes they have closed, Lest they should see with their eyes and hear with their ears, Lest they should understand with their hearts and turn, So that I should heal them.'* **16** But blessed *are* your eyes for they see, and your ears for they hear; **17** for assuredly, I say to you that many prophets and righteous *men* desired to see what you see, and did not see *it*, and to hear what you hear, and did not hear *it*. **18** "Therefore hear the parable of the sower: **19** When anyone hears the word of the kingdom, and does not understand *it*, then the wicked *one* comes and snatches away what was sown in his heart. This is he who received seed by the wayside. **20** But he who received the seed on stony places, this is he who hears the word and immediately receives it with joy; **21** yet he has no root in himself, but endures only for a while. For when tribulation or persecution arises because of the word, immediately he stumbles. **22** Now he who received seed among the thorns is he who hears the word, and the cares of this world and the deceitfulness of riches choke the word, and he becomes unfruitful. **23** But he who received seed on the good ground is he who hears the word and understands *it*, who indeed bears fruit and produces: some a hundredfold, some sixty, some thirty."

Cf. Luke 8:5–15

Tares.

Matt 13:24–30 Another parable He put forth to them, saying: "The kingdom of heaven is like a man who sowed good seed in his field; **25** but while men slept, his enemy came and sowed tares among the wheat and went his way. **26** But when the grain had sprouted and produced a crop, then the tares also appeared. **27** So the servants of the owner came and said to him, 'Sir, did you not sow good seed in your field? How then does it have tares?' **28** He said to them, 'An enemy has done this.' The servants said to him, 'Do you want us then to go and gather them up?' **29** But he said, 'No, lest while you gather up the tares you also uproot the wheat with them. **30** Let both grow together until the harvest, and at the time of harvest I will say to the reapers, "First gather together the tares and bind them in bundles to burn them, but gather the wheat into my barn."' "

Matt 13:36–43 Then Jesus sent the multitude away and went into the house. And His disciples came to Him, saying, "Explain to us the parable of the tares of the field." **37** He answered and said to them: "He who sows the good seed is the Son of Man. **38** The field is the world, the good seeds are the sons of the kingdom, but the tares are the sons of the wicked *one*. **39** The enemy who sowed them is the devil, the harvest is the end of the age, and the reapers are the angels. **40** Therefore as the tares are gathered and burned in the fire, so it will be at the end of this age. **41** The Son of Man will send out His angels, and they will gather out of His kingdom all things that offend, and those who practice lawlessness, **42** and will cast them into the furnace of fire. There will be wailing

and gnashing of teeth. **43** Then the righteous will shine forth as the sun in the kingdom of their Father. He who has ears to hear, let him hear!

Mustard seed.

Matt 13:31–32 Another parable He put forth to them, saying: "The kingdom of heaven is like a mustard seed, which a man took and sowed in his field, **32** which indeed is the least of all the seeds; but when it is grown it is greater than the herbs and becomes a tree, so that the birds of the air come and nest in its branches."

Luke 13:19 It is like a mustard seed, which a man took and put in his garden; and it grew and became a large tree, and the birds of the air nested in its branches."

Leaven.

Matt 13:33 Another parable He spoke to them: "The kingdom of heaven is like leaven, which a woman took and hid in three measures of meal till it was all leavened."

Treasure hid in a field.

Matt 13:44 "Again, the kingdom of heaven is like treasure hidden in a field, which a man found and hid; and for joy over it he goes and sells all that he has and buys that field.

Pearl of great price.

Matt 13:45–46 "Again, the kingdom of heaven is like a merchant seeking beautiful pearls, **46** who, when he had found one pearl of great price, went and sold all that he had and bought it.

Net cast into the sea.

Matt 13:47–50 "Again, the kingdom of heaven is like a dragnet that was cast into the sea and gathered some of every kind, **48** which, when it was full, they drew to shore; and they sat down and gathered the good into vessels, but threw the bad away. **49** So it will be at the end of the age. The angels will come forth, separate the wicked from among the just, **50** and cast them into the furnace of fire. There will be wailing and gnashing of teeth."

What defiles a person.

Matt 15:10–15 When He had called the multitude to *Himself*, He said to them, "Hear and understand: **11** Not what goes into the mouth defiles a man; but what comes out of the mouth, this defiles a man." **12** Then His disciples came and said to Him, "Do You know that the Pharisees were offended when they heard this saying?" **13** But He answered and said, "Every plant which My heavenly Father has not planted will be uprooted. **14** Let them alone. They are blind leaders of the blind. And if the blind leads the blind, both will fall into a ditch." **15** Then Peter answered and said to Him, "Explain this parable to us."

Unmerciful servant.

Matt 18:23–35 Therefore the kingdom of heaven is like a certain king who wanted to settle accounts with his servants. **24** And when he had begun to settle accounts, one was brought to him who owed him ten thousand talents. **25** But as he was not able to pay, his master commanded that he be sold, with his wife and children and all that he had, and that payment be made. **26** The servant therefore fell down before him, saying, 'Master, have patience with me, and I will pay you all.' **27** Then the master of that servant was moved with compassion, released him, and forgave him the debt. **28** "But that servant went out and found one of his fellow servants who owed him a hundred denarii; and he laid hands on him and took *him* by the throat, saying, 'Pay me what you owe!' **29** So his fellow servant fell down at his feet and begged him, saying, 'Have patience with me, and I will pay you all.' **30** And he would not, but went and threw him into prison till he should pay the debt. **31** So when his fellow servants saw what had been done, they were very grieved, and came and told their master all that had been done. **32** Then his master, after he had called him, said to him, 'You wicked servant! I forgave you all that debt because you begged me. **33** Should you not also have had compassion on your fellow servant, just as I had pity on you?' **34** And his master was angry, and delivered him to the torturers until he should pay all that was due to him. **35** "So My heavenly Father also will do to you if each of you, from his heart, does not forgive his brother his trespasses."

Laborers hired.

Matt 20:1–16 "For the kingdom of heaven is like a landowner who went out early in the morning to hire laborers for his vineyard. **2** Now when he had agreed with the laborers for a denarius a day, he sent them into his vineyard. **3** And he went out about the third hour and saw others standing idle in the marketplace, **4** and said to them, 'You also go into the vineyard, and whatever is right I will give you.' So they went. **5** Again he went out about the sixth and the ninth hour, and did likewise. **6** And about the eleventh hour he went out and found others standing idle, and said to them, 'Why have you been standing here idle all day?' **7** They said to him, 'Because no one hired us.' He said to them, 'You also go into the vineyard, and whatever is right you will receive.' **8** "So when evening had come, the owner of the vineyard said to his steward, 'Call the laborers and give them *their* wages, beginning with the last to the first.' **9** And when those came who *were hired* about the eleventh hour, they each received a denarius. **10** But when the first came, they supposed that they would receive more; and they likewise received each a denarius. **11** And when they had received *it*, they complained against the landowner, **12** saying, 'These last *men* have worked *only* one hour, and you made them equal to us who have borne the burden and the heat of the day.' **13** But he answered one of them and said, 'Friend, I am doing you no wrong. Did you not agree with me for a denarius? **14** Take *what is* yours and go your way. I wish to give to this last man *the same* as to you. **15** Is it not lawful for me to do what I wish with my own things? Or is your eye evil because I am good?' **16** So the last will be first, and the first last. For many are called, but few chosen."

Two sons.

Matt 21:28–32 "But what do you think? A man had two sons, and he came to the first and said, 'Son, go, work today in my vineyard.' **29** He answered and said, 'I will not,' but afterward he regretted it and went. **30** Then he came to the second and said likewise. And he answered and said, 'I *go*, sir,' but he did

not go. **31** Which of the two did the will of *his* father?" They said to Him, "The first." Jesus said to them, "Assuredly, I say to you that tax collectors and harlots enter the kingdom of God before you. **32** For John came to you in the way of righteousness, and you did not believe him; but tax collectors and harlots believed him; and when you saw *it*, you did not afterward relent and believe him.

Wicked vinedressers.

Matt 21:33–45 "Hear another parable: There was a certain landowner who planted a vineyard and set a hedge around it, dug a winepress in it and built a tower. And he leased it to vinedressers and went into a far country. **34** Now when vintage-time drew near, he sent his servants to the vinedressers, that they might receive its fruit. **35** And the vinedressers took his servants, beat one, killed one, and stoned another. **36** Again he sent other servants, more than the first, and they did likewise to them. **37** Then last of all he sent his son to them, saying, 'They will respect my son.' **38** But when the vinedressers saw the son, they said among themselves, 'This is the heir. Come, let us kill him and seize his inheritance.' **39** So they took him and cast *him* out of the vineyard and killed *him*. **40** "Therefore, when the owner of the vineyard comes, what will he do to those vinedressers?" **41** They said to Him, "He will destroy those wicked men miserably, and lease *his* vineyard to other vinedressers who will render to him the fruits in their seasons." **42** Jesus said to them, "Have you never read in the Scriptures: *'The stone which the builders rejected Has become the chief cornerstone. This was the LORD's doing, And it is marvelous in our eyes'*? **43** "Therefore I say to you, the kingdom of God will be taken from you and given to a nation bearing the fruits of it. **44** And whoever falls on this stone will be broken; but on whomever it falls, it will grind him to powder." **45** Now when the chief priests and Pharisees heard His parables, they perceived that He was speaking of them.

Marriage feast.

Matt 22:2–14 "The kingdom of heaven is like a certain king who arranged a marriage for his son, **3** and sent out his servants to call those who were invited to the wedding; and they were not willing to come. **4** Again, he sent out other servants, saying, 'Tell those who are invited, "See, I have prepared my dinner; my oxen and fatted cattle *are* killed, and all things *are* ready. Come to the wedding." ' **5** But they made light of it and went their ways, one to his own farm, another to his business. **6** And the rest seized his servants, treated *them* spitefully, and killed *them*. **7** But when the king heard *about it*, he was furious. And he sent out his armies, destroyed those murderers, and burned up their city. **8** Then he said to his servants, 'The wedding is ready, but those who were invited were not worthy. **9** Therefore go into the highways, and as many as you find, invite to the wedding.' **10** So those servants went out into the highways and gathered together all whom they found, both bad and good. And the wedding *hall* was filled with guests. **11** "But when the king came in to see the guests, he saw a man there who did not have on a wedding garment. **12** So he said to him, 'Friend, how did you come in here without a wedding garment?' And he was speechless. **13** Then the king said to the servants, 'Bind him hand and foot, take him away, and cast *him* into outer darkness; there will be weeping and gnashing of teeth.' **14** "For many are called, but few *are* chosen."

Fig tree.

Matt 24:32–34 "Now learn this parable from the fig tree: When its branch has already become tender and puts forth leaves, you know that summer *is* near. **33** So you also, when you see all these things, know that it is near—at the doors! **34** Assuredly, I say to you, this generation will by no means pass away till all these things take place.

Master of the house watching.

Matt 24:43 But know this, that if the master of the house had known what hour the thief would come, he would have watched and not allowed his house to be broken into.

Faithful and evil servants.

Matt 24:45–51 "Who then is a faithful and wise servant, whom his master made ruler over his household, to give them food in due season? **46** Blessed *is* that servant whom his master, when he comes, will find so doing. **47** Assuredly, I say to you that he will make him ruler over all his goods. **48** But if that evil servant says in his heart, 'My master is delaying his coming,' **49** and begins to beat *his* fellow servants, and to eat and drink with the drunkards, **50** the master of that servant will come on a day when he is not looking for *him* and at an hour that he is not aware of, **51** and will cut him in two and appoint *him* his portion with the hypocrites. There shall be weeping and gnashing of teeth.

Ten virgins.

Matt 25:1–13 "Then the kingdom of heaven shall be likened to ten virgins who took their lamps and went out to meet the bridegroom. **2** Now five of them were wise, and five *were* foolish. **3** Those who *were* foolish took their lamps and took no oil with them, **4** but the wise took oil in their vessels with their lamps. **5** But while the bridegroom was delayed, they all slumbered and slept. **6** "And at midnight a cry was *heard:* 'Behold, the bridegroom is coming; go out to meet him!' **7** Then all those virgins arose and trimmed their lamps. **8** And the foolish said to the wise, 'Give us *some* of your oil, for our lamps are going out.' **9** But the wise answered, saying, 'No, lest there should not be enough for us and you; but go rather to those who sell, and buy for yourselves.' **10** And while they went to buy, the bridegroom came, and those who were ready went in with him to the wedding; and the door was shut. **11** "Afterward the other virgins came also, saying, 'Lord, Lord, open to us!' **12** But he answered and said, 'Assuredly, I say to you, I do not know you.' **13** "Watch therefore, for you know neither the day nor the hour in which the Son of Man is coming.

Talents.

Matt 25:14–30 "For *the kingdom of heaven is* like a man traveling to a far country, *who* called his own servants and delivered his goods to them. **15** And to one he gave five talents, to another two, and to another one, to each according to his own ability; and immediately he went on a journey. **16** Then he who had re-

ceived the five talents went and traded with them, and made another five talents. **17** And likewise he who *had received* two gained two more also. **18** But he who had received one went and dug in the ground, and hid his lord's money. **19** After a long time the lord of those servants came and settled accounts with them. **20** "So he who had received five talents came and brought five other talents, saying, 'Lord, you delivered to me five talents; look, I have gained five more talents besides them.' **21** His lord said to him, 'Well *done*, good and faithful servant; you were faithful over a few things, I will make you ruler over many things. Enter into the joy of your lord.' **22** He also who had received two talents came and said, 'Lord, you delivered to me two talents; look, I have gained two more talents besides them.' **23** His lord said to him, 'Well *done*, good and faithful servant; you have been faithful over a few things, I will make you ruler over many things. Enter into the joy of your lord.' **24** "Then he who had received the one talent came and said, 'Lord, I knew you to be a hard man, reaping where you have not sown, and gathering where you have not scattered seed. **25** And I was afraid, and went and hid your talent in the ground. Look, *there* you have *what is* yours.' **26** "But his lord answered and said to him, 'You wicked and lazy servant, you knew that I reap where I have not sown, and gather where I have not scattered seed. **27** So you ought to have deposited my money with the bankers, and at my coming I would have received back my own with interest. **28** So take the talent from him, and give *it* to him who has ten talents. **29** 'For to everyone who has, more will be given, and he will have abundance; but from him who does not have, even what he has will be taken away. **30** And cast the unprofitable servant into the outer darkness. There will be weeping and gnashing of teeth.'

Kingdom divided against itself.

Mark 3:24 If a kingdom is divided against itself, that kingdom cannot stand.

House divided against itself.

Mark 3:25 And if a house is divided against itself, that house cannot stand.

Strong man armed.

Mark 3:27 No one can enter a strong man's house and plunder his goods, unless he first binds the strong man. And then he will plunder his house.

Luke 11:21 When a strong man, fully armed, guards his own palace, his goods are in peace.

Seed growing secretly.

Mark 4:26–29 And He said, "The kingdom of God is as if a man should scatter seed on the ground, **27** and should sleep by night and rise by day, and the seed should sprout and grow, he himself does not know how. **28** For the earth yields crops by itself: first the blade, then the head, after that the full grain in the head. **29** But when the grain ripens, immediately he puts in the sickle, because the harvest has come."

Lighted lamp.

Mark 4:21 Also He said to them, "Is a lamp brought to be put under a basket or under a bed? Is it not to be set on a lampstand?

Luke 11:33–36 "No one, when he has lit a lamp, puts *it* in a secret place or under a basket, but on a lamp-stand, that those who come in may see the light. 34 The lamp of the body is the eye. Therefore, when your eye is good, your whole body also is full of light. But when *your eye* is bad, your body also *is* full of darkness. 35 Therefore take heed that the light which is in you is not darkness. 36 If then your whole body *is* full of light, having no part dark, *the* whole *body* will be full of light, as when the bright shining of a lamp gives you light."

Man going to a far country.

Mark 13:34–37 *It is* like a man going to a far country, who left his house and gave authority to his servants, and to each his work, and commanded the door-keeper to watch. 35 Watch therefore, for you do not know when the master of the house is coming—in the evening, at midnight, at the crowing of the rooster, or in the morning— 36 lest, coming suddenly, he find you sleeping. 37 And what I say to you, I say to all: Watch!"

Blind leading the blind.

Luke 6:39 And He spoke a parable to them: "Can the blind lead the blind? Will they not both fall into the ditch?

Plank and speck.

Luke 6:41–42 And why do you look at the speck in your brother's eye, but do not perceive the plank in your own eye? 42 Or how can you say to your brother, 'Brother, let me remove the speck that *is* in your eye,' when you yourself do not see the plank that *is* in your own eye? Hypocrite! First remove the plank from your own eye, and then you will see clearly to remove the speck that is in your brother's eye.

Tree and its fruit.

Luke 6:43–45 "For a good tree does not bear bad fruit, nor does a bad tree bear good fruit. 44 For every tree is known by its own fruit. For *men* do not gather figs from thorns, nor do they gather grapes from a bramble bush. 45 A good man out of the good treasure of his heart brings forth good; and an evil man out of the evil treasure of his heart brings forth evil. For out of the abundance of the heart his mouth speaks.

Creditor and debtors.

Luke 7:41–47 "There was a certain creditor who had two debtors. One owed five hundred denarii, and the other fifty. 42 And when they had nothing with which to repay, he freely forgave them both. Tell Me, therefore, which of them will love him more?" 43 Simon answered and said, "I suppose the *one* whom he forgave more." And He said to him, "You have rightly judged." 44 Then He turned to the woman and said to Simon, "Do you see this woman? I entered your house; you gave Me no water for My feet, but she has washed My feet with her tears and wiped *them* with the hair of her head. 45 You gave Me no kiss, but this woman has not ceased to kiss My feet since the time I came in. 46 You did not anoint My head with oil, but this woman has anointed My feet with fragrant oil. 47 Therefore I say to you, her sins, *which are* many, are forgiven, for she loved much. But to whom little is forgiven, *the same* loves little."

Good Samaritan.

Luke 10:30–37 Then Jesus answered and said: "A cer-

tain *man* went down from Jerusalem to Jericho, and fell among thieves, who stripped him of his clothing, wounded *him,* and departed, leaving *him* half dead. 31 Now by chance a certain priest came down that road. And when he saw him, he passed by on the other side. 32 Likewise a Levite, when he arrived at the place, came and looked, and passed by on the other side. 33 But a certain Samaritan, as he journeyed, came where he was. And when he saw him, he had compassion. 34 So he went to *him* and bandaged his wounds, pouring on oil and wine; and he set him on his own animal, brought him to an inn, and took care of him. 35 On the next day, when he departed, he took out two denarii, gave *them* to the innkeeper, and said to him, 'Take care of him; and whatever more you spend, when I come again, I will repay you.' 36 So which of these three do you think was neighbor to him who fell among the thieves?" 37 And he said, "He who showed mercy on him." Then Jesus said to him, "Go and do likewise."

Persistent friend.

Luke 11:5–9 And He said to them, "Which of you shall have a friend, and go to him at midnight and say to him, 'Friend, lend me three loaves; 6 for a friend of mine has come to me on his journey, and I have nothing to set before him'; 7 and he will answer from within and say, 'Do not trouble me; the door is now shut, and my children are with me in bed; I cannot rise and give to you'? 8 I say to you, though he will not rise and give to him because he is his friend, yet because of his persistence he will rise and give him as many as he needs. 9 "So I say to you, ask, and it will be given to you; seek, and you will find; knock, and it will be opened to you.

Rich fool.

Luke 12:16–21 Then He spoke a parable to them, saying: "The ground of a certain rich man yielded plentifully. 17 And he thought within himself, saying, 'What shall I do, since I have no room to store my crops?' 18 So he said, 'I will do this: I will pull down my barns and build greater, and there I will store all my crops and my goods. 19 And I will say to my soul, "Soul, you have many goods laid up for many years; take your ease; eat, drink, *and* be merry." ' 20 But God said to him, 'Fool! This night your soul will be required of you; then whose will those things be which you have provided?' 21 "So *is* he who lays up treasure for himself, and is not rich toward God."

Cloud and wind.

Luke 12:54–57 Then He also said to the multitudes, "Whenever *you see* a cloud rising out of the west, immediately you say, 'A shower is coming'; and so it is. 55 And when you see the south wind blow, you say, 'There will be hot weather'; and there is. 56 Hypocrites! You can discern the face of the sky and of the earth, but how *is it* you do not discern this time? 57 "Yes, and why, even of yourselves, do you not judge what is right?

Barren fig tree.

Luke 13:6–9 He also spoke this parable: "A certain *man* had a fig tree planted in his vineyard, and he came seeking fruit on it and found none. 7 Then he said to the keeper of his vineyard, 'Look, for three years I have come seeking fruit on this fig tree and find none. Cut it down; why does it use up the ground?' **8** But he answered and said to him, 'Sir, let it alone this year also, until I dig around it and fertilize *it.* **9** And if it bears fruit, *well.* But if not, after that you can cut it down.' "

Men invited to a feast.

Luke 14:7–11 So He told a parable to those who were invited, when He noted how they chose the best places, saying to them: **8** "When you are invited by anyone to a wedding feast, do not sit down in the best place, lest one more honorable than you be invited by him; **9** and he who invited you and him come and say to you, 'Give place to this man,' and then you begin with shame to take the lowest place. **10** But when you are invited, go and sit down in the lowest place, so that when he who invited you comes he may say to you, 'Friend, go up higher.' Then you will have glory in the presence of those who sit at the table with you. **11** For whoever exalts himself will be humbled, and he who humbles himself will be exalted."

Builder of a tower.

Luke 14:28–30 For which of you, intending to build a tower, does not sit down first and count the cost, whether he has *enough* to finish *it*— **29** lest, after he has laid the foundation, and is not able to finish, all who see *it* begin to mock him, **30** saying, 'This man began to build and was not able to finish.'

Luke 14:33 So likewise, whoever of you does not forsake all that he has cannot be My disciple.

King going to war.

Luke 14:31–33 Or what king, going to make war against another king, does not sit down first and consider whether he is able with ten thousand to meet him who comes against him with twenty thousand? **32** Or else, while the other is still a great way off, he sends a delegation and asks conditions of peace. **33** So likewise, whoever of you does not forsake all that he has cannot be My disciple.

Seasoning of salt.

Luke 14:34–35 "Salt *is* good; but if the salt has lost its flavor, how shall it be seasoned? **35** It is neither fit for the land nor for the dunghill, *but* men throw it out. He who has ears to hear, let him hear!"

Lost sheep.

Luke 15:3–7 So He spoke this parable to them, saying: **4** "What man of you, having a hundred sheep, if he loses one of them, does not leave the ninety-nine in the wilderness, and go after the one which is lost until he finds it? **5** And when he has found *it,* he lays *it* on his shoulders, rejoicing. **6** And when he comes home, he calls together *his* friends and neighbors, saying to them, 'Rejoice with me, for I have found my sheep which was lost!' **7** I say to you that likewise there will be more joy in heaven over one sinner who repents than over ninety-nine just persons who need no repentance.

Lost piece of silver.

Luke 15:8–10 "Or what woman, having ten silver coins, if she loses one coin, does not light a lamp, sweep the house, and search carefully until she finds *it?* **9** And when she has found *it,* she calls *her* friends and neighbors together, saying, 'Rejoice with me, for I

have found the piece which I lost!' **10** Likewise, I say to you, there is joy in the presence of the angels of God over one sinner who repents."

Prodigal son.

Luke 15:11–32 Then He said: "A certain man had two sons. **12** And the younger of them said to *his* father, 'Father, give me the portion of goods that falls *to me.*' So he divided to them *his* livelihood. **13** And not many days after, the younger son gathered all together, journeyed to a far country, and there wasted his possessions with prodigal living. **14** But when he had spent all, there arose a severe famine in that land, and he began to be in want. **15** Then he went and joined himself to a citizen of that country, and he sent him into his fields to feed swine. **16** And he would gladly have filled his stomach with the pods that the swine ate, and no one gave him *anything.* **17** "But when he came to himself, he said, 'How many of my father's hired servants have bread enough and to spare, and I perish with hunger! **18** I will arise and go to my father, and will say to him, "Father, I have sinned against heaven and before you, **19** and I am no longer worthy to be called your son. Make me like one of your hired servants." ' **20** "And he arose and came to his father. But when he was still a great way off, his father saw him and had compassion, and ran and fell on his neck and kissed him. **21** And the son said to him, 'Father, I have sinned against heaven and in your sight, and am no longer worthy to be called your son.' **22** "But the father said to his servants, 'Bring out the best robe and put *it* on him, and put a ring on his hand and sandals on *his* feet. **23** And bring the fatted calf here and kill *it,* and let us eat and be merry; **24** for this my son was dead and is alive again; he was lost and is found.' And they began to be merry. **25** "Now his older son was in the field. And as he came and drew near to the house, he heard music and dancing. **26** So he called one of the servants and asked what these things meant. **27** And he said to him, 'Your brother has come, and because he has received him safe and sound, your father has killed the fatted calf.' **28** "But he was angry and would not go in. Therefore his father came out and pleaded with him. **29** So he answered and said to *his* father, 'Lo, these many years I have been serving you; I never transgressed your commandment at any time; and yet you never gave me a young goat, that I might make merry with my friends. **30** But as soon as this son of yours came, who has devoured your livelihood with harlots, you killed the fatted calf for him.' **31** "And he said to him, 'Son, you are always with me, and all that I have is yours. **32** It was right that we should make merry and be glad, for your brother was dead and is alive again, and was lost and is found.' "

Unjust steward.

Luke 16:1–8 He also said to His disciples: "There was a certain rich man who had a steward, and an accusation was brought to him that this man was wasting his goods. **2** So he called him and said to him, 'What is this I hear about you? Give an account of your stewardship, for you can no longer be steward.' **3** "Then the steward said within himself, 'What shall I do? For my master is taking the stewardship away from me. I cannot dig; I am ashamed to beg. **4** I have resolved what to do, that when I am put out of the stewardship, they may receive me into their houses.' 5 "So he called every one of his master's debtors to *him*, and said to the first, 'How much do you owe my master?' 6 And he said, 'A hundred measures of oil.' So he said to him, 'Take your bill, and sit down quickly and write fifty.' 7 Then he said to another, 'And how much do you owe?' So he said, 'A hundred measures of wheat.' And he said to him, 'Take your bill, and write eighty.' 8 So the master commended the unjust steward because he had dealt shrewdly. For the sons of this world are more shrewd in their generation than the sons of light.

Rich man and Lazarus.

Luke 16:19–31 "There was a certain rich man who was clothed in purple and fine linen and fared sumptuously every day. 20 But there was a certain beggar named Lazarus, full of sores, who was laid at his gate, 21 desiring to be fed with the crumbs which fell from the rich man's table. Moreover the dogs came and licked his sores. 22 So it was that the beggar died, and was carried by the angels to Abraham's bosom. The rich man also died and was buried. 23 And being in torments in Hades, he lifted up his eyes and saw Abraham afar off, and Lazarus in his bosom. 24 "Then he cried and said, 'Father Abraham, have mercy on me, and send Lazarus that he may dip the tip of his finger in water and cool my tongue; for I am tormented in this flame.' 25 But Abraham said, 'Son, remember that in your lifetime you received your good things, and likewise Lazarus evil things; but now he is comforted and you are tormented. 26 And besides all this, between us and you there is a great gulf fixed, so that those who want to pass from here to you cannot, nor can those from there pass to us.' 27 "Then he said, 'I beg you therefore, father, that you would send him to my father's house, 28 for I have five brothers, that he may testify to them, lest they also come to this place of torment.' 29 Abraham said to him, 'They have Moses and the prophets; let them hear them.' 30 And he said, 'No, father Abraham; but if one goes to them from the dead, they will repent.' 31 But he said to him, 'If they do not hear Moses and the prophets, neither will they be persuaded though one rise from the dead.' "

Persistent widow.

Luke 18:1–8 Then He spoke a parable to them, that men always ought to pray and not lose heart, 2 saying: "There was in a certain city a judge who did not fear God nor regard man. 3 Now there was a widow in that city; and she came to him, saying, 'Get justice for me from my adversary.' 4 And he would not for a while; but afterward he said within himself, 'Though I do not fear God nor regard man, 5 yet because this widow troubles me I will avenge her, lest by her continual coming she weary me.' " 6 Then the Lord said, "Hear what the unjust judge said. 7 And shall God not avenge His own elect who cry out day and night to Him, though He bears long with them? 8 I tell you that He will avenge them speedily. Nevertheless, when the Son of Man comes, will He really find faith on the earth?"

Pharisee and tax collector.

Luke 18:9–14 Also He spoke this parable to some who trusted in themselves that they were righteous, and despised others: 10 "Two men went up to the temple to pray, one a Pharisee and the other a tax collector. 11 The Pharisee stood and prayed thus with himself, 'God, I thank You that I am not like other men—extortioners, unjust, adulterers, or even as this tax collector. 12 I fast twice a week; I give tithes of all that I possess.' 13 And the tax collector, standing afar off, would not so much as raise *his* eyes to heaven, but beat his breast, saying, 'God, be merciful to me a sinner!' 14 I tell you, this man went down to his house justified *rather* than the other; for everyone who exalts himself will be humbled, and he who humbles himself will be exalted."

Responsibility (minas).

Luke 19:12–27 Therefore He said: "A certain nobleman went into a far country to receive for himself a kingdom and to return. 13 So he called ten of his servants, delivered to them ten minas, and said to them, 'Do business till I come.' 14 But his citizens hated him, and sent a delegation after him, saying, 'We will not have this *man* to reign over us.' 15 "And so it was that when he returned, having received the kingdom, he then commanded these servants, to whom he had given the money, to be called to him, that he might know how much every man had gained by trading. 16 Then came the first, saying, 'Master, your mina has earned ten minas.' 17 And he said to him, 'Well *done*, good servant; because you were faithful in a very little, have authority over ten cities.' 18 And the second came, saying, 'Master, your mina has earned five minas.' 19 Likewise he said to him, 'You also be over five cities.' 20 "Then another came, saying, 'Master, here is your mina, which I have kept put away in a handkerchief. 21 For I feared you, because you are an austere man. You collect what you did not deposit, and reap what you did not sow.' 22 And he said to him, 'Out of your own mouth I will judge you, *you* wicked servant. You knew that I was an austere man, collecting what I did not deposit and reaping what I did not sow. 23 Why then did you not put my money in the bank, that at my coming I might have collected it with interest?' 24 "And he said to those who stood by, 'Take the mina from him, and give *it* to him who has ten minas.' 25 (But they said to him, 'Master, he has ten minas.') 26 'For I say to you, that to everyone who has will be given; and from him who does not have, even what he has will be taken away from him. 27 But bring here those enemies of mine, who did not want me to reign over them, and slay *them* before me.' "

Good Shepherd.

John 10:1–6 "Most assuredly, I say to you, he who does not enter the sheepfold by the door, but climbs up some other way, the same is a thief and a robber. 2 But he who enters by the door is the shepherd of the sheep. 3 To him the doorkeeper opens, and the sheep hear his voice; and he calls his own sheep by name and leads them out. 4 And when he brings out his own sheep, he goes before them; and the sheep follow him, for they know his voice. 5 Yet they will by no means follow a stranger, but will flee from him, for they do not know the voice of strangers." 6 Jesus used this illustration, but they did not understand the things which He spoke to them.

Vine and branches.

John 15:1–5 "I am the true vine, and My Father is the vinedresser. **2** Every branch in Me that does not bear fruit He takes away; and every *branch* that bears fruit He prunes, that it may bear more fruit. **3** You are already clean because of the word which I have spoken to you. **4** Abide in Me, and I in you. As the branch cannot bear fruit of itself, unless it abides in the vine, neither can you, unless you abide in Me. **5** "I am the vine, you *are* the branches. He who abides in Me, and I in him, bears much fruit; for without Me you can do nothing.

PARDON

Promised.

Is 1:18 "Come now, and let us reason together," Says the LORD, "Though your sins are like scarlet, They shall be as white as snow; Though they are red like crimson, They shall be as wool.

Jer 31:34 No more shall every man teach his neighbor, and every man his brother, saying, 'Know the LORD,' for they all shall know Me, from the least of them to the greatest of them, says the LORD. For I will forgive their iniquity, and their sin I will remember no more."

Jer 50:20 In those days and in that time," says the LORD, "The iniquity of Israel shall be sought, but *there shall be* none; And the sins of Judah, but they shall not be found; For I will pardon those whom I preserve.

Heb 8:12 *For I will be merciful to their unrighteousness, and their sins and their lawless deeds I will remember no more."*

None without shedding of blood.

Lev 17:11 For the life of the flesh *is* in the blood, and I have given it to you upon the altar to make atonement for your souls; for it *is* the blood *that* makes atonement for the soul.'

Heb 9:22 And according to the law almost all things are purified with blood, and without shedding of blood there is no remission.

Not possible by

Legal sacrifices.

Heb 10:4 For *it is* not possible that the blood of bulls and goats could take away sins.

Outward purifications.

Job 9:30–31 If I wash myself with snow water, And cleanse my hands with soap, **31** Yet You will plunge me into the pit, And my own clothes will abhor me.

Jer 2:22 For though you wash yourself with lye, and use much soap, *Yet* your iniquity is marked before Me," says the Lord GOD.

Is granted

By God alone.

Dan 9:9 To the Lord our God *belong* mercy and forgiveness, though we have rebelled against Him.

Mark 2:7 "Why does this *Man* speak blasphemies like this? Who can forgive sins but God alone?"

By Christ Himself.

Mark 2:5 When Jesus saw their faith, He said to the paralytic, "Son, your sins are forgiven you."

Luke 7:48 Then He said to her, "Your sins are forgiven."

Through Christ's work.

Luke 1:69 And has raised up a horn of salvation for us In the house of His servant David,

Luke 1:77 To give knowledge of salvation to His people By the remission of their sins,

Acts 5:31 Him God has exalted to His right hand *to be* Prince and Savior, to give repentance to Israel and forgiveness of sins.

Acts 13:38 Therefore let it be known to you, brethren, that through this Man is preached to you the forgiveness of sins;

Through the blood of Christ.

Matt 26:28 For this is My blood of the new covenant, which is shed for many for the remission of sins.

Rom 3:25 whom God set forth *as* a propitiation by His blood, through faith, to demonstrate His righteousness, because in His forbearance God had passed over the sins that were previously committed,

Col 1:14 in whom we have redemption through His blood, the forgiveness of sins.

1 John 1:7 But if we walk in the light as He is in the light, we have fellowship with one another, and the blood of Jesus Christ His Son cleanses us from all sin.

For Christ's name's sake.

1 John 2:12 I write to you, little children, Because your sins are forgiven you for His name's sake.

According to the riches of grace.

Eph 1:7 In Him we have redemption through His blood, the forgiveness of sins, according to the riches of His grace

By the exaltation of Christ.

Acts 5:31 Him God has exalted to His right hand *to be* Prince and Savior, to give repentance to Israel and forgiveness of sins.

Freely.

Is 43:25 "I, *even* I, *am* He who blots out your transgressions for My own sake; And I will not remember your sins.

Readily.

Neh 9:17 They refused to obey, And they were not mindful of Your wonders That You did among them. But they hardened their necks, And in their rebellion They appointed a leader To return to their bondage. But You *are* God, Ready to pardon, Gracious and merciful, Slow to anger, Abundant in kindness, And did not forsake them.

Ps 86:5 For You, Lord, *are* good, and ready to forgive, And abundant in mercy to all those who call upon You.

Abundantly.

Is 55:7 Let the wicked forsake his way, And the unrighteous man his thoughts; Let him return to the LORD, And He will have mercy on him; And to our God, For He will abundantly pardon.

Rom 5:20 Moreover the law entered that the offense might abound. But where sin abounded, grace abounded much more,

To those who confess their sins.

2 Sam 12:13 So David said to Nathan, "I have sinned

against the LORD." And Nathan said to David, "The LORD also has put away your sin; you shall not die.

Ps 32:5 I acknowledged my sin to You, And my iniquity I have not hidden. I said, "I will confess my transgressions to the LORD," And You forgave the iniquity of my sin. Selah

1 John 1:9 If we confess our sins, He is faithful and just to forgive us *our* sins and to cleanse us from all unrighteousness.

To those who repent.

Acts 2:38 Then Peter said to them, "Repent, and let every one of you be baptized in the name of Jesus Christ for the remission of sins; and you shall receive the gift of the Holy Spirit.

To those who believe.

Acts 10:43 To Him all the prophets witness that, through His name, whoever believes in Him will receive remission of sins."

Should be preached in the name of Christ.

Luke 24:47 and that repentance and remission of sins should be preached in His name to all nations, beginning at Jerusalem.

Exhibits the

Compassion of God.

Mic 7:18–19 Who *is* a God like You, Pardoning iniquity And passing over the transgression of the remnant of His heritage? He does not retain His anger forever, Because He delights *in* mercy. **19** He will again have compassion on us, And will subdue our iniquities. You will cast all our sins Into the depths of the sea.

Grace of God.

Rom 5:15–16 But the free gift *is* not like the offense. For if by the one man's offense many died, much more the grace of God and the gift by the grace of the one Man, Jesus Christ, abounded to many. **16** And the gift *is* not like *that which came* through the one who sinned. For the judgment *which came* from one *offense resulted* in condemnation, but the free gift *which came* from many offenses *resulted* in justification.

Mercy of God.

Ex 34:7 keeping mercy for thousands, forgiving iniquity and transgression and sin, by no means clearing *the guilty,* visiting the iniquity of the fathers upon the children and the children's children to the third and the fourth generation."

Ps 51:1 Have mercy upon me, O God, According to Your lovingkindness; According to the multitude of Your tender mercies, Blot out my transgressions.

Goodness of God.

2 Chr 30:18 For a multitude of the people, many from Ephraim, Manasseh, Issachar, and Zebulun, had not cleansed themselves, yet they ate the Passover contrary to what was written. But Hezekiah prayed for them, saying, "May the good LORD provide atonement for everyone

Ps 86:5 For You, Lord, *are* good, and ready to forgive, And abundant in mercy to all those who call upon You.

Forbearance of God.

Rom 3:25 whom God set forth *as* a propitiation by His blood, through faith, to demonstrate His righteous-

ness, because in His forbearance God had passed over the sins that were previously committed,

Lovingkindness of God.

Ps 51:1 Have mercy upon me, O God, According to Your lovingkindness; According to the multitude of Your tender mercies, Blot out my transgressions.

Justice of God.

1 John 1:9 If we confess our sins, He is faithful and just to forgive us *our* sins and to cleanse us from all unrighteousness.

Faithfulness of God.

1 John 1:9 If we confess our sins, He is faithful and just to forgive us *our* sins and to cleanse us from all unrighteousness.

Expressed by

Removing sin and transgression.

Ps 32:1 Blessed *is he whose* transgression *is* forgiven, *Whose* sin *is* covered.

Ps 103:12 As far as the east is from the west, *So* far has He removed our transgressions from us.

Is 44:22 I have blotted out, like a thick cloud, your transgressions, And like a cloud, your sins. Return to Me, for I have redeemed you."

Acts 3:19 Repent therefore and be converted, that your sins may be blotted out, so that times of refreshing may come from the presence of the Lord,

Casting sins into the sea.

Mic 7:19 He will again have compassion on us, And will subdue our iniquities. You will cast all our sins Into the depths of the sea.

Not imputing sin.

Rom 4:8 Blessed *is the man to whom the* LORD *shall not impute sin."*

Not remembering sin and transgression.

Ezek 18:22 None of the transgressions which he has committed shall be remembered against him; because of the righteousness which he has done, he shall live.

Heb 10:17 then He adds, *"Their sins and their lawless deeds I will remember no more."*

All believers enjoy.

Col 2:13 And you, being dead in your trespasses and the uncircumcision of your flesh, He has made alive together with Him, having forgiven you all trespasses,

1 John 2:12 I write to you, little children, Because your sins are forgiven you for His name's sake.

Blessedness of.

Ps 32:1 Blessed *is he whose* transgression *is* forgiven, *Whose* sin *is* covered.

Rom 4:7 *"Blessed are those whose lawless deeds are forgiven, And whose sins are covered;*

Should lead to

Returning to God.

Is 44:22 I have blotted out, like a thick cloud, your transgressions, And like a cloud, your sins. Return to Me, for I have redeemed you."

Loving God.

Luke 7:47 Therefore I say to you, her sins, *which are*

many, are forgiven, for she loved much. But to whom little is forgiven, *the same* loves little."

Fearing God.

Ps 130:4 But *there is* forgiveness with You, That You may be feared.

Praising God.

Ps 103:2–3 Bless the Lord, O my soul, And forget not all His benefits: 3 Who forgives all your iniquities, Who heals all your diseases,

Ministers are appointed to proclaim.

Is 40:1–2 "Comfort, yes, comfort My people!" Says your God. 2 "Speak comfort to Jerusalem, and cry out to her, That her warfare is ended, That her iniquity is pardoned; For she has received from the Lord's hand Double for all her sins."

2 Cor 5:19 that is, that God was in Christ reconciling the world to Himself, not imputing their trespasses to them, and has committed to us the word of reconciliation.

Pray for on behalf of,

Yourselves.

Ps 25:11 For Your name's sake, O Lord, Pardon my iniquity, for it *is* great.

Ps 25:18 Look on my affliction and my pain, And forgive all my sins.

Ps 51:1 Have mercy upon me, O God, According to Your lovingkindness; According to the multitude of Your tender mercies, Blot out my transgressions.

Matt 6:12 And forgive us our debts, As we forgive our debtors.

Luke 11:4 And forgive us our sins, For we also forgive everyone who is indebted to us. And do not lead us into temptation, But deliver us from the evil one."

Others.

James 5:15 And the prayer of faith will save the sick, and the Lord will raise him up. And if he has committed sins, he will be forgiven.

1 John 5:16 If anyone sees his brother sinning a sin *which does* not *lead* to death, he will ask, and He will give him life for those who commit sin not *leading* to death. There is sin *leading* to death. I do not say that he should pray about that.

Encouragement to pray for.

2 Chr 7:14 if My people who are called by My name will humble themselves, and pray and seek My face, and turn from their wicked ways, then I will hear from heaven, and will forgive their sin and heal their land.

Withheld from

The unforgiving.

Mark 11:26 But if you do not forgive, neither will your Father in heaven forgive your trespasses."

Luke 6:37 "Judge not, and you shall not be judged. Condemn not, and you shall not be condemned. Forgive, and you will be forgiven.

The unbelieving.

John 8:21 Then Jesus said to them again, "I am going away, and you will seek Me, and will die in your sin. Where I go you cannot come."

John 8:24 Therefore I said to you that you will die in your sins; for if you do not believe that I am *He*, you will die in your sins."

The impenitent.

Luke 13:2–5 And Jesus answered and said to them, "Do you suppose that these Galileans were worse sinners than all *other* Galileans, because they suffered such things? 3 I tell you, no; but unless you repent you will all likewise perish. 4 Or those eighteen on whom the tower in Siloam fell and killed them, do you think that they were worse sinners than all *other* men who dwelt in Jerusalem? 5 I tell you, no; but unless you repent you will all likewise perish."

Blasphemers against the Holy Spirit.

Matt 12:32 Anyone who speaks a word against the Son of Man, it will be forgiven him; but whoever speaks against the Holy Spirit, it will not be forgiven him, either in this age or in the *age* to come.

Mark 3:28–29 "Assuredly, I say to you, all sins will be forgiven the sons of men, and whatever blasphemies they may utter; 29 but he who blasphemes against the Holy Spirit never has forgiveness, but is subject to eternal condemnation"—

Apostates.

Heb 10:26–27 For if we sin willfully after we have received the knowledge of the truth, there no longer remains a sacrifice for sins, 27 but a certain fearful expectation of judgment, and fiery indignation which will devour the adversaries.

1 John 5:16 If anyone sees his brother sinning a sin *which does* not *lead* to death, he will ask, and He will give him life for those who commit sin not *leading* to death. There is sin *leading* to death. I do not say that he should pray about that.

Illustrated.

Luke 7:42 And when they had nothing with which to repay, he freely forgave them both. Tell Me, therefore, which of them will love him more?"

Luke 15:20–24 "And he arose and came to his father. But when he was still a great way off, his father saw him and had compassion, and ran and fell on his neck and kissed him. 21 And the son said to him, 'Father, I have sinned against heaven and in your sight, and am no longer worthy to be called your son.' 22 "But the father said to his servants, 'Bring out the best robe and put *it* on him, and put a ring on his hand and sandals on *his* feet. 23 And bring the fatted calf here and kill *it*, and let us eat and be merry; 24 for this my son was dead and is alive again; he was lost and is found.' And they began to be merry.

Exemplified for

The Israelites.

Num 14:20 Then the Lord said: "I have pardoned, according to your word;

David.

2 Sam 12:13 So David said to Nathan, "I have sinned against the Lord." And Nathan said to David, "The Lord also has put away your sin; you shall not die.

Manasseh.

2 Chr 33:13 and prayed to Him; and He received his entreaty, heard his supplication, and brought him back to Jerusalem into his kingdom. Then Manasseh knew that the Lord *was* God.

Hezekiah.

Is 38:17 Indeed *it was* for *my own* peace *That* I had great bitterness; But You have lovingly *delivered* my soul from the pit of corruption, For You have cast all my sins behind Your back.

The paralytic.

Matt 9:2 Then behold, they brought to Him a paralytic lying on a bed. When Jesus saw their faith, He said to the paralytic, "Son, be of good cheer; your sins are forgiven you."

The penitent.

Luke 7:47 Therefore I say to you, her sins, *which are* many, are forgiven, for she loved much. But to whom little is forgiven, *the same* loves little."

PARENTS

Receive their children from God.

Gen 33:5 And he lifted his eyes and saw the women and children, and said, "Who *are* these with you?" So he said, "The children whom God has graciously given your servant."

1 Sam 1:27 For this child I prayed, and the LORD has granted me my petition which I asked of Him.

Ps 127:3 Behold, children *are* a heritage from the LORD, The fruit of the womb *is* a reward.

Duties to children

To love them.

Titus 2:4 that they admonish the young women to love their husbands, to love their children,

To bring them to Christ.

Matt 19:13–14 Then little children were brought to Him that He might put *His* hands on them and pray, but the disciples rebuked them. **14** But Jesus said, "Let the little children come to Me, and do not forbid them; for of such is the kingdom of heaven."

Train them in God's way.

Deut 4:9 Only take heed to yourself, and diligently keep yourself, lest you forget the things your eyes have seen, and lest they depart from your heart all the days of your life. And teach them to your children and your grandchildren,

Deut 11:19 You shall teach them to your children, speaking of them when you sit in your house, when you walk by the way, when you lie down, and when you rise up.

Deut 32:46 and he said to them: "Set your hearts on all the words which I testify among you today, which you shall command your children to be careful to observe—all the words of this law.

1 Chr 28:9 "As for you, my son Solomon, know the God of your father, and serve Him with a loyal heart and with a willing mind; for the LORD searches all hearts and understands all the intent of the thoughts. If you seek Him, He will be found by you; but if you forsake Him, He will cast you off forever.

Prov 22:6 Train up a child in the way he should go, And when he is old he will not depart from it.

Is 38:19 The living, the living man, he shall praise You, As I *do* this day; The father shall make known Your truth to the children.

Joel 1:3 Tell your children about it, *Let* your children *tell* their children, And their children another generation.

Eph 6:4 And you, fathers, do not provoke your children to wrath, but bring them up in the training and admonition of the Lord.

To tell them of the miraculous works of God.

Ex 10:2 and that you may tell in the hearing of your son and your son's son the mighty things I have done in Egypt, and My signs which I have done among them, that you may know that I *am* the LORD."

Ex 12:26–27 And it shall be, when your children say to you, 'What do you mean by this service?' **27** that you shall say, 'It *is* the Passover sacrifice of the LORD, who passed over the houses of the children of Israel in Egypt when He struck the Egyptians and delivered our households.' " So the people bowed their heads and worshiped.

Ps 78:4 We will not hide *them* from their children, Telling to the generation to come the praises of the LORD, And His strength and His wonderful works that He has done.

To bless them.

Gen 48:15 And he blessed Joseph, and said: "God, before whom my fathers Abraham and Isaac walked, The God who has fed me all my life long to this day,

Heb 11:20 By faith Isaac blessed Jacob and Esau concerning things to come.

To pity them.

Ps 103:13 As a father pities *his* children, So the LORD pities those who fear Him.

To provide for them.

Job 42:15 In all the land were found no women *so* beautiful as the daughters of Job; and their father gave them an inheritance among their brothers.

2 Cor 12:14 Now *for* the third time I am ready to come to you. And I will not be burdensome to you; for I do not seek yours, but you. For the children ought not to lay up for the parents, but the parents for the children.

1 Tim 5:8 But if anyone does not provide for his own, and especially for those of his household, he has denied the faith and is worse than an unbeliever.

To rule them.

1 Tim 3:4 one who rules his own house well, having *his* children in submission with all reverence

1 Tim 3:12 Let deacons be the husbands of one wife, ruling *their* children and their own houses well.

To correct them.

Prov 13:24 He who spares his rod hates his son, But he who loves him disciplines him promptly.

Prov 19:18 Chasten your son while there is hope, And do not set your heart on his destruction.

Prov 23:13 Do not withhold correction from a child, For *if* you beat him with a rod, he will not die.

Prov 29:17 Correct your son, and he will give you rest; Yes, he will give delight to your soul.

Heb 12:7 If you endure chastening, God deals with you as with sons; for what son is there whom a father does not chasten?

Not to provoke them.

Eph 6:4 And you, fathers, do not provoke your children

to wrath, but bring them up in the training and admonition of the Lord.

Col 3:21 Fathers, do not provoke your children, lest they become discouraged.

Not to make unholy connections for them.

Gen 24:1–4 Now Abraham was old, well advanced in age; and the LORD had blessed Abraham in all things. 2 So Abraham said to the oldest servant of his house, who ruled over all that he had, "Please, put your hand under my thigh, 3 and I will make you swear by the LORD, the God of heaven and the God of the earth, that you will not take a wife for my son from the daughters of the Canaanites, among whom I dwell; 4 but you shall go to my country and to my family, and take a wife for my son Isaac."

Gen 28:1–2 Then Isaac called Jacob and blessed him, and charged him, and said to him: "You shall not take a wife from the daughters of Canaan. 2 Arise, go to Padan Aram, to the house of Bethuel your mother's father; and take yourself a wife from there of the daughters of Laban your mother's brother.

Wicked children, a cause of grief to.

Prov 10:1 The proverbs of Solomon: A wise son makes a glad father, But a foolish son *is* the grief of his mother.

Prov 17:25 A foolish son *is* a grief to his father, And bitterness to her who bore him.

Should pray for their children

For their spiritual welfare.

Gen 17:18 And Abraham said to God, "Oh, that Ishmael might live before You!"

1 Chr 29:19 And give my son Solomon a loyal heart to keep Your commandments and Your testimonies and Your statutes, to do all *these things,* and to build the temple for which I have made provision."

When in temptation.

Job 1:5 So it was, when the days of feasting had run their course, that Job would send and sanctify them, and he would rise early in the morning and offer burnt offerings *according to* the number of them all. For Job said, "It may be that my sons have sinned and cursed God in their hearts." Thus Job did regularly.

When in sickness.

2 Sam 12:16 David therefore pleaded with God for the child, and David fasted and went in and lay all night on the ground.

Mark 5:23 and begged Him earnestly, saying, "My little daughter lies at the point of death. Come and lay Your hands on her, that she may be healed, and she will live."

John 4:46 So Jesus came again to Cana of Galilee where He had made the water wine. And there was a certain nobleman whose son was sick at Capernaum.

John 4:49 The nobleman said to Him, "Sir, come down before my child dies!"

When faithful,

Are blessed by their children.

Prov 31:28 Her children rise up and call her blessed; Her husband *also,* and he praises her:

Leave a blessing to their children.

Ps 112:2 His descendants will be mighty on earth; The generation of the upright will be blessed.

Prov 11:21 *Though they join* forces, the wicked will not go unpunished; But the posterity of the righteous will be delivered.

Is 65:23 They shall not labor in vain, Nor bring forth children for trouble; For they *shall be* the descendants of the blessed of the LORD, And their offspring with them.

Their sins

Affect children.

Ex 20:5 you shall not bow down to them nor serve them. For I, the LORD your God, *am* a jealous God, visiting the iniquity of the fathers upon the children to the third and fourth *generations* of those who hate Me,

Is 14:20 You will not be joined with them in burial, Because you have destroyed your land *And* slain your people. The brood of evildoers shall never be named.

Jer 9:14 but they have walked according to the dictates of their own hearts and after the Baals, which their fathers taught them,"

Lam 5:7 Our fathers sinned *and are* no more, But we bear their iniquities.

Ezek 20:18 "But I said to their children in the wilderness, 'Do not walk in the statutes of your fathers, nor observe their judgments, nor defile yourselves with their idols.

Amos 2:4 Thus says the LORD: "For three transgressions of Judah, and for four, I will not turn away its *punishment,* Because they have despised the law of the LORD, And have not kept His commandments. Their lies lead them astray, *Lies* which their fathers followed.

1 Pet 1:18 knowing that you were not redeemed with corruptible things, *like* silver or gold, from your aimless conduct *received* by tradition from your fathers,

May be severely punished.

1 Sam 3:13 For I have told him that I will judge his house forever for the iniquity which he knows, because his sons made themselves vile, and he did not restrain them.

Examples of good,

Abraham.

Gen 18:19 For I have known him, in order that he may command his children and his household after him, that they keep the way of the LORD, to do righteousness and justice, that the LORD may bring to Abraham what He has spoken to him."

Jacob.

Gen 44:20 And we said to my lord, 'We have a father, an old man, and a child of *his* old age, *who is* young; his brother is dead, and he alone is left of his mother's children, and his father loves him.'

Gen 44:30 "Now therefore, when I come to your servant my father, and the lad *is* not with us, since his life is bound up in the lad's life,

Joseph.

Gen 48:13–20 And Joseph took them both, Ephraim with his right hand toward Israel's left hand, and Manasseh with his left hand toward Israel's right hand, and brought *them* near him. 14 Then Israel stretched out his right hand and laid *it* on Ephraim's head, who *was* the younger, and his left hand on Manasseh's head, guiding his hands knowingly, for Manasseh *was* the firstborn. **15** And he blessed Joseph, and said: "God, before whom my fathers Abraham and Isaac walked, The God who has fed me all my life long to this day, **16** The Angel who has redeemed me from all evil, Bless the lads; Let my name be named upon them, And the name of my fathers Abraham and Isaac; And let them grow into a multitude in the midst of the earth." **17** Now when Joseph saw that his father laid his right hand on the head of Ephraim, it displeased him; so he took hold of his father's hand to remove it from Ephraim's head to Manasseh's head. **18** And Joseph said to his father, "Not so, my father, for this *one is* the firstborn; put your right hand on his head." **19** But his father refused and said, "I know, my son, I know. He also shall become a people, and he also shall be great; but truly his younger brother shall be greater than he, and his descendants shall become a multitude of nations." **20** So he blessed them that day, saying, "By you Israel will bless, saying, 'May God make you as Ephraim and as Manasseh!' " And thus he set Ephraim before Manasseh.

The mother of Moses.

Ex 2:2–3 So the woman conceived and bore a son. And when she saw that he *was* a beautiful *child,* she hid him three months. **3** But when she could no longer hide him, she took an ark of bulrushes for him, daubed it with asphalt and pitch, put the child in it, and laid *it* in the reeds by the river's bank.

Manoah.

Judg 13:8 Then Manoah prayed to the Lord, and said, "O my Lord, please let the Man of God whom You sent come to us again and teach us what we shall do for the child who will be born."

Hannah.

1 Sam 1:28 Therefore I also have lent him to the Lord; as long as he lives he shall be lent to the Lord." So they worshiped the Lord there.

David.

2 Sam 18:5 Now the king had commanded Joab, Abishai, and Ittai, saying, "*Deal* gently for my sake with the young man Absalom." And all the people heard when the king gave all the captains orders concerning Absalom.

2 Sam 18:33 Then the king was deeply moved, and went up to the chamber over the gate, and wept. And as he went, he said thus: "O my son Absalom—my son, my son Absalom—if only I had died in your place! O Absalom my son, my son!"

The Shunammite.

2 Kin 4:19–20 And he said to his father, "My head, my head!" So he said to a servant, "Carry him to his mother." **20** When he had taken him and brought him to his mother, he sat on her knees till noon, and *then* died.

Job.

Job 1:5 So it was, when the days of feasting had run their course, that Job would send and sanctify them, and he would rise early in the morning and offer burnt offerings *according to* the number of them all. For Job said, "It may be that my sons have sinned and cursed God in their hearts." Thus Job did regularly.

The mother of Lemuel.

Prov 31:1 The words of King Lemuel, the utterance which his mother taught him:

A nobleman.

John 4:49 The nobleman said to Him, "Sir, come down before my child dies!"

Lois and Eunice.

2 Tim 1:5 when I call to remembrance the genuine faith that is in you, which dwelt first in your grandmother Lois and your mother Eunice, and I am persuaded is in you also.

Examples of bad,

The mother of Micah.

Judg 17:3 So when he had returned the eleven hundred *shekels* of silver to his mother, his mother said, "I had wholly dedicated the silver from my hand to the Lord for my son, to make a carved image and a molded image; now therefore, I will return it to you."

Eli.

1 Sam 3:13 For I have told him that I will judge his house forever for the iniquity which he knows, because his sons made themselves vile, and he did not restrain them.

Saul.

1 Sam 20:33 Then Saul cast a spear at him to kill him, by which Jonathan knew that it was determined by his father to kill David.

Athaliah.

2 Chr 22:3 He also walked in the ways of the house of Ahab, for his mother advised him to do wickedly.

Manasseh.

2 Chr 33:6 Also he caused his sons to pass through the fire in the Valley of the Son of Hinnom; he practiced soothsaying, used witchcraft and sorcery, and consulted mediums and spiritists. He did much evil in the sight of the Lord, to provoke Him to anger.

Herodias.

Mark 6:24 So she went out and said to her mother, "What shall I ask?" And she said, "The head of John the Baptist!"

PASCHAL LAMB, COMPARED WITH CHRIST AND THE GOSPEL

A type of Christ.

Ex 12:3 Speak to all the congregation of Israel, saying: 'On the tenth of this month every man shall take for himself a lamb, according to the house of *his* father, a lamb for a household.

1 Cor 5:7 Therefore purge out the old leaven, that you may be a new lump, since you truly are unleavened. For indeed Christ, our Passover, was sacrificed for us.

A male of the first year.

Ex 12:5 Your lamb shall be without blemish, a male of the first year. You may take *it* from the sheep or from the goats.

Is 9:6 For unto us a Child is born, Unto us a Son is given; And the government will be upon His shoulder. And His name will be called Wonderful, Counselor, Mighty God, Everlasting Father, Prince of Peace.

Without blemish.

Ex 12:5 Your lamb shall be without blemish, a male of the first year. You may take *it* from the sheep or from the goats.

1 Pet 1:19 but with the precious blood of Christ, as of a lamb without blemish and without spot.

Taken out of the flock.

Ex 12:5 Your lamb shall be without blemish, a male of the first year. You may take *it* from the sheep or from the goats.

Heb 2:14 Inasmuch then as the children have partaken of flesh and blood, He Himself likewise shared in the same, that through death He might destroy him who had the power of death, that is, the devil,

Heb 2:17 Therefore, in all things He had to be made like *His* brethren, that He might be a merciful and faithful High Priest in things *pertaining* to God, to make propitiation for the sins of the people.

Chosen beforehand.

Ex 12:3 Speak to all the congregation of Israel, saying: 'On the tenth of this month every man shall take for himself a lamb, according to the house of *his* father, a lamb for a household.

1 Pet 2:4 Coming to Him *as to* a living stone, rejected indeed by men, but chosen by God *and* precious,

Killed by the people.

Ex 12:6 Now you shall keep it until the fourteenth day of the same month. Then the whole assembly of the congregation of Israel shall kill it at twilight.

Acts 2:23 Him, being delivered by the determined purpose and foreknowledge of God, you have taken by lawless hands, have crucified, and put to death;

Killed at the place where the Lord put His name.

Deut 16:2 Therefore you shall sacrifice the Passover to the Lord your God, from the flock and the herd, in the place where the Lord chooses to put His name.

Deut 16:5–7 "You may not sacrifice the Passover within any of your gates which the Lord your God gives you; **6** but at the place where the Lord your God chooses to make His name abide, there you shall sacrifice the Passover at twilight, at the going down of the sun, at the time you came out of Egypt. **7** And you shall roast and eat *it* in the place which the Lord your God chooses, and in the morning you shall turn and go to your tents.

2 Chr 35:1 Now Josiah kept a Passover to the Lord in Jerusalem, and they slaughtered the Passover *lambs* on the fourteenth *day* of the first month.

Luke 13:33 Nevertheless I must journey today, tomorrow, and the *day* following; for it cannot be that a prophet should perish outside of Jerusalem.

Killed in the evening.

Ex 12:6 Now you shall keep it until the fourteenth day of the same month. Then the whole assembly of the congregation of Israel shall kill it at twilight.

Mark 15:34 And at the ninth hour Jesus cried out with a loud voice, saying, "Eloi, Eloi, lama sabachthani?" which is translated, *"My God, My God, why have You forsaken Me?"*

Mark 15:37 And Jesus cried out with a loud voice, and breathed His last.

Its blood to be shed.

Ex 12:7 And they shall take *some* of the blood and put *it* on the two doorposts and on the lintel of the houses where they eat it.

Luke 22:20 Likewise He also *took* the cup after supper, saying, "This cup *is* the new covenant in My blood, which is shed for you.

Blood of, sprinkled on lintel and doorposts.

Ex 12:22 And you shall take a bunch of hyssop, dip *it* in the blood that *is* in the basin, and strike the lintel and the two doorposts with the blood that *is* in the basin. And none of you shall go out of the door of his house until morning.

Heb 9:13–14 For if the blood of bulls and goats and the ashes of a heifer, sprinkling the unclean, sanctifies for the purifying of the flesh, **14** how much more shall the blood of Christ, who through the eternal Spirit offered Himself without spot to God, cleanse your conscience from dead works to serve the living God?

Heb 10:22 let us draw near with a true heart in full assurance of faith, having our hearts sprinkled from an evil conscience and our bodies washed with pure water.

1 Pet 1:2 elect according to the foreknowledge of God the Father, in sanctification of the Spirit, for obedience and sprinkling of the blood of Jesus Christ: Grace to you and peace be multiplied.

Blood of, not sprinkled on threshold.

Ex 12:7 And they shall take *some* of the blood and put *it* on the two doorposts and on the lintel of the houses where they eat it.

Heb 10:29 Of how much worse punishment, do you suppose, will he be thought worthy who has trampled the Son of God underfoot, counted the blood of the covenant by which he was sanctified a common thing, and insulted the Spirit of grace?

Not a bone of, broken.

Ex 12:46 In one house it shall be eaten; you shall not carry any of the flesh outside the house, nor shall you break one of its bones.

John 19:36 For these things were done that the Scripture should be fulfilled, *"Not one of His bones shall be broken."*

Not eaten raw.

Ex 12:9 Do not eat it raw, nor boiled at all with water, but roasted in fire—its head with its legs and its entrails.

1 Cor 11:28–29 But let a man examine himself, and so let him eat of the bread and drink of the cup. **29** For he who eats and drinks in an unworthy manner eats and drinks judgment to himself, not discerning the Lord's body.

Roasted with fire.

Ex 12:8 Then they shall eat the flesh on that night; roasted in fire, with unleavened bread *and* with bitter *herbs* they shall eat it.

Ps 22:14–15 I am poured out like water, And all My bones are out of joint; My heart is like wax; It has melted within Me. **15** My strength is dried up like a potsherd, And My tongue clings to My jaws; You have brought Me to the dust of death.

Eaten with bitter herbs.

Ex 12:8 Then they shall eat the flesh on that night; roasted in fire, with unleavened bread *and* with bitter *herbs* they shall eat it.

Zech 12:10 "And I will pour on the house of David and on the inhabitants of Jerusalem the Spirit of grace and supplication; then they will look on Me whom they pierced. Yes, they will mourn for Him as one mourns for *his* only *son,* and grieve for Him as one grieves for a firstborn.

Eaten with unleavened bread.

Ex 12:39 And they baked unleavened cakes of the dough which they had brought out of Egypt; for it was not leavened, because they were driven out of Egypt and could not wait, nor had they prepared provisions for themselves.

1 Cor 5:7–8 Therefore purge out the old leaven, that you may be a new lump, since you truly are unleavened. For indeed Christ, our Passover, was sacrificed for us. **8** Therefore let us keep the feast, not with old leaven, nor with the leaven of malice and wickedness, but with the unleavened *bread* of sincerity and truth.

2 Cor 1:12 For our boasting is this: the testimony of our conscience that we conducted ourselves in the world in simplicity and godly sincerity, not with fleshly wisdom but by the grace of God, and more abundantly toward you.

Eaten in haste.

Ex 12:11 And thus you shall eat it: *with* a belt on your waist, your sandals on your feet, and your staff in your hand. So you shall eat it in haste. It *is* the LORD's Passover.

Heb 6:18 that by two immutable things, in which it *is* impossible for God to lie, we might have strong consolation, who have fled for refuge to lay hold of the hope set before *us.*

Eaten with the loins girded.

Ex 12:11 And thus you shall eat it: *with* a belt on your waist, your sandals on your feet, and your staff in your hand. So you shall eat it in haste. It *is* the LORD's Passover.

Luke 12:35 "Let your waist be girded and *your* lamps burning;

Eph 6:14 Stand therefore, having girded your waist with truth, having put on the breastplate of righteousness,

1 Pet 1:13 Therefore gird up the loins of your mind, be sober, and rest *your* hope fully upon the grace that is to be brought to you at the revelation of Jesus Christ;

Eaten with staff in hand.

Ex 12:11 And thus you shall eat it: *with* a belt on your waist, your sandals on your feet, and your staff in your hand. So you shall eat it in haste. It *is* the LORD's Passover.

Ps 23:4 Yea, though I walk through the valley of the shadow of death, I will fear no evil; For You *are* with me; Your rod and Your staff, they comfort me.

Eaten with shoes on.

Ex 12:11 And thus you shall eat it: *with* a belt on your waist, your sandals on your feet, and your staff in your hand. So you shall eat it in haste. It *is* the LORD's Passover.

Eph 6:15 and having shod your feet with the preparation of the gospel of peace;

Not taken out of the house.

Ex 12:46 In one house it shall be eaten; you shall not carry any of the flesh outside the house, nor shall you break one of its bones.

Eph 3:17 that Christ may dwell in your hearts through faith; that you, being rooted and grounded in love,

What remained of it till morning to be burned.

Ex 12:10 You shall let none of it remain until morning, and what remains of it until morning you shall burn with fire.

Matt 7:6 "Do not give what is holy to the dogs; nor cast your pearls before swine, lest they trample them under their feet, and turn and tear you in pieces.

Luke 11:3 Give us day by day our daily bread.

PATIENCE

God, characterized by.

Rom 15:5 Now may the God of patience and comfort grant you to be like-minded toward one another, according to Christ Jesus,

Christ, an example of.

Is 53:7 He was oppressed and He was afflicted, Yet He opened not His mouth; He was led as a lamb to the slaughter, And as a sheep before its shearers is silent, So He opened not His mouth.

Matt 27:14 But He answered him not one word, so that the governor marveled greatly.

Acts 8:32 The place in the Scripture which he read was this: *"He was led as a sheep to the slaughter; And as a lamb before its shearer is silent, So He opened not His mouth.*

Commanded.

1 Thess 5:14 Now we exhort you, brethren, warn those who are unruly, comfort the fainthearted, uphold the weak, be patient with all.

Titus 2:2 that the older men be sober, reverent, temperate, sound in faith, in love, in patience;

James 1:4 But let patience have *its* perfect work, that you may be perfect and complete, lacking nothing.

2 Pet 1:6 to knowledge self-control, to self-control perseverance, to perseverance godliness,

Trials and sufferings of believers lead to.

Rom 5:3–4 And not only *that,* but we also glory in tribulations, knowing that tribulation produces perseverance; **4** and perseverance, character; and character, hope.

Rom 15:4 For whatever things were written before were written for our learning, that we through the patience and comfort of the Scriptures might have hope.

James 1:3 knowing that the testing of your faith produces patience.

1 Pet 2:20 For what credit *is it* if, when you are beaten for your faults, you take it patiently? But when you do good and suffer, if you take it patiently, this *is* commendable before God.

To be exercised

Running the race set before us.

Heb 12:1 Therefore we also, since we are surrounded by

so great a cloud of witnesses, let us lay aside every weight, and the sin which so easily ensnares *us*, and let us run with endurance the race that is set before us,

Bringing forth fruits.

Luke 8:15 But the ones *that* fell on the good ground are those who, having heard the word with a noble and good heart, keep *it* and bear fruit with patience.

Doing good.

Rom 2:7 eternal life to those who by patient continuance in doing good seek for glory, honor, and immortality;

Gal 6:9 And let us not grow weary while doing good, for in due season we shall reap if we do not lose heart.

Waiting for God.

Ps 37:7 Rest in the Lord, and wait patiently for Him; Do not fret because of him who prospers in his way, Because of the man who brings wicked schemes to pass.

Ps 40:1 I waited patiently for the Lord; And He inclined to me, And heard my cry.

Lam 3:26 It *is* good that *one* should hope and wait quietly For the salvation of the Lord.

Waiting for Christ.

1 Cor 1:7 so that you come short in no gift, eagerly waiting for the revelation of our Lord Jesus Christ,

2 Thess 3:5 Now may the Lord direct your hearts into the love of God and into the patience of Christ.

Waiting for the hope of the gospel.

Rom 8:25 But if we hope for what we do not see, we eagerly wait for *it* with perseverance.

Gal 5:5 For we through the Spirit eagerly wait for the hope of righteousness by faith.

Bearing the yoke.

Lam 3:27 It *is* good for a man to bear The yoke in his youth.

In tribulation.

Luke 21:19 By your patience possess your souls.

Rom 12:12 rejoicing in hope, patient in tribulation, continuing steadfastly in prayer;

Necessary to the inheritance of the promises.

Heb 6:12 that you do not become sluggish, but imitate those who through faith and patience inherit the promises.

Heb 10:36 For you have need of endurance, so that after you have done the will of God, you may receive the promise:

They who are in authority, should exercise.

Matt 18:26 The servant therefore fell down before him, saying, 'Master, have patience with me, and I will pay you all.'

Acts 26:3 especially because you are expert in all customs and questions which have to do with the Jews. Therefore I beg you to hear me patiently.

2 Cor 6:4 But in all *things* we commend ourselves as ministers of God: in much patience, in tribulations, in needs, in distresses,

1 Tim 6:11 But you, O man of God, flee these things and pursue righteousness, godliness, faith, love, patience, gentleness.

A fruit of the Spirit.

Gal 5:22 But the fruit of the Spirit is love, joy, peace, longsuffering, kindness, goodness, faithfulness,

Outgrowth of humility and gentleness.

Eph 4:2 with all lowliness and gentleness, with longsuffering, bearing with one another in love,

One of the tender mercies.

Col 3:12 Therefore, as *the* elect of God, holy and beloved, put on tender mercies, kindness, humility, meekness, longsuffering;

Should be accompanied by

Godliness.

2 Pet 1:6 to knowledge self-control, to self-control perseverance, to perseverance godliness,

Faith.

2 Thess 1:4 so that we ourselves boast of you among the churches of God for your patience and faith in all your persecutions and tribulations that you endure,

Heb 6:12 that you do not become sluggish, but imitate those who through faith and patience inherit the promises.

Rev 13:10 He who leads into captivity shall go into captivity; he who kills with the sword must be killed with the sword. Here is the patience and the faith of the saints.

Self-control.

2 Pet 1:6 to knowledge self-control, to self-control perseverance, to perseverance godliness,

Longsuffering.

Col 1:11 strengthened with all might, according to His glorious power, for all patience and longsuffering with joy;

Joyfulness.

Col 1:11 strengthened with all might, according to His glorious power, for all patience and longsuffering with joy;

Commended.

Eccl 7:8 The end of a thing *is* better than its beginning; The patient in spirit *is* better than the proud in spirit.

Rev 2:2–3 "I know your works, your labor, your patience, and that you cannot bear those who are evil. And you have tested those who say they are apostles and are not, and have found them liars; 3 and you have persevered and have patience, and have labored for My name's sake and have not become weary.

Illustrated.

James 5:7 Therefore be patient, brethren, until the coming of the Lord. See *how* the farmer waits for the precious fruit of the earth, waiting patiently for it until it receives the early and latter rain.

Examples of,

Job.

Job 1:21 And he said: "Naked I came from my mother's womb, And naked shall I return there. The Lord gave, and the Lord has taken away; Blessed be the name of the Lord."

James 5:11 Indeed we count them blessed who endure. You have heard of the perseverance of Job and seen the end *intended by* the Lord—that the Lord is very compassionate and merciful.

Simeon.

Luke 2:25 And behold, there was a man in Jerusalem whose name was Simeon, and this man was just and devout, waiting for the Consolation of Israel, and the Holy Spirit was upon him.

Paul.

2 Tim 3:10 But you have carefully followed my doctrine, manner of life, purpose, faith, longsuffering, love, perseverance,

Abraham.

Heb 6:15 And so, after he had patiently endured, he obtained the promise.

The prophets.

James 5:10 My brethren, take the prophets, who spoke in the name of the Lord, as an example of suffering and patience.

John.

Rev 1:9 I, John, both your brother and companion in the tribulation and kingdom and patience of Jesus Christ, was on the island that is called Patmos for the word of God and for the testimony of Jesus Christ.

PAUL

Was originally Saul of Tarsus.

Acts 9:11 So the Lord *said* to him, "Arise and go to the street called Straight, and inquire at the house of Judas for *one* called Saul of Tarsus, for behold, he is praying.

Acts 13:9 Then Saul, who also *is called* Paul, filled with the Holy Spirit, looked intently at him

Acts 21:39 But Paul said, "I am a Jew from Tarsus, in Cilicia, a citizen of no mean city; and I implore you, permit me to speak to the people."

Acts 22:3 "I am indeed a Jew, born in Tarsus of Cilicia, but brought up in this city at the feet of Gamaliel, taught according to the strictness of our fathers' law, and was zealous toward God as you all are today.

Worked as a tentmaker.

Acts 18:1–3 After these things Paul departed from Athens and went to Corinth. **2** And he found a certain Jew named Aquila, born in Pontus, who had recently come from Italy with his wife Priscilla (because Claudius had commanded all the Jews to depart from Rome); and he came to them. **3** So, because he was of the same trade, he stayed with them and worked; for by occupation they were tentmakers.

Zealous for the law.

Acts 23:6 But when Paul perceived that one part were Sadducees and the other Pharisees, he cried out in the council, "Men *and* brethren, I am a Pharisee, the son of a Pharisee; concerning the hope and resurrection of the dead I am being judged!"

Acts 26:4–5 "My manner of life from my youth, which was spent from the beginning among my own nation at Jerusalem, all the Jews know. **5** They knew me from the first, if they were willing to testify, that according to the strictest sect of our religion I lived a Pharisee.

Gal 1:14 And I advanced in Judaism beyond many of my contemporaries in my own nation, being more exceedingly zealous for the traditions of my fathers.

Phil 3:5–6 circumcised the eighth day, of the stock of Israel, *of* the tribe of Benjamin, a Hebrew of the Hebrews; concerning the law, a Pharisee; **6** concerning zeal, persecuting the church; concerning the righteousness which is in the law, blameless.

Agreed to Stephen's death.

Acts 7:58 and they cast *him* out of the city and stoned *him.* And the witnesses laid down their clothes at the feet of a young man named Saul.

Acts 8:1 Now Saul was consenting to his death. At that time a great persecution arose against the church which was at Jerusalem; and they were all scattered throughout the regions of Judea and Samaria, except the apostles.

Acts 22:20 And when the blood of Your martyr Stephen was shed, I also was standing by consenting to his death, and guarding the clothes of those who were killing him.'

Persecuted Christians.

Acts 9:1–3 Then Saul, still breathing threats and murder against the disciples of the Lord, went to the high priest **2** and asked letters from him to the synagogues of Damascus, so that if he found any who were of the Way, whether men or women, he might bring them bound to Jerusalem. **3** As he journeyed he came near Damascus, and suddenly a light shone around him from heaven.

Acts 22:3–5 "I am indeed a Jew, born in Tarsus of Cilicia, but brought up in this city at the feet of Gamaliel, taught according to the strictness of our fathers' law, and was zealous toward God as you all are today. **4** I persecuted this Way to the death, binding and delivering into prisons both men and women, **5** as also the high priest bears me witness, and all the council of the elders, from whom I also received letters to the brethren, and went to Damascus to bring in chains even those who were there to Jerusalem to be punished.

Acts 26:9–11 "Indeed, I myself thought I must do many things contrary to the name of Jesus of Nazareth. **10** This I also did in Jerusalem, and many of the saints I shut up in prison, having received authority from the chief priests; and when they were put to death, I cast my vote against *them.* **11** And I punished them often in every synagogue and compelled *them* to blaspheme; and being exceedingly enraged against them, I persecuted *them* even to foreign cities.

Gal 1:13 For you have heard of my former conduct in Judaism, how I persecuted the church of God beyond measure and *tried to* destroy it.

1 Tim 1:13 although I was formerly a blasphemer, a persecutor, and an insolent man; but I obtained mercy because I did *it* ignorantly in unbelief.

Conversion of.

Acts 9:1–9 Then Saul, still breathing threats and murder against the disciples of the Lord, went to the high priest **2** and asked letters from him to the synagogues of Damascus, so that if he found any who were of the Way, whether men or women, he might bring them bound to Jerusalem. **3** As he journeyed he came near Damascus, and suddenly a light shone around him from heaven. **4** Then he fell to the ground, and heard a voice saying to him, "Saul, Saul, why are you persecuting Me?" 5 And he said, "Who are You, Lord?" Then the Lord said, "I am Jesus, whom you are persecuting. It *is* hard for you to kick against the goads." 6 So he, trembling and astonished, said, "Lord, what do You want me to do?" Then the Lord *said* to him, "Arise and go into the city, and you will be told what you must do." 7 And the men who journeyed with him stood speechless, hearing a voice but seeing no one. 8 Then Saul arose from the ground, and when his eyes were opened he saw no one. But they led him by the hand and brought *him* into Damascus. 9 And he was three days without sight, and neither ate nor drank.

Cf. Acts 22:1–11; 26:12–18; Gal 1:12–16; Phil 3:4–10; 1 Tim 1:12–16

Persecuted by the Jews.

Acts 9:23–25 Now after many days were past, the Jews plotted to kill him. 24 But their plot became known to Saul. And they watched the gates day and night, to kill him. 25 Then the disciples took him by night and let *him* down through the wall in a large basket.

2 Cor 11:32–33 In Damascus the governor, under Aretas the king, was guarding the city of the Damascenes with a garrison, desiring to arrest me; 33 but I was let down in a basket through a window in the wall, and escaped from his hands.

2 Tim 3:11 persecutions, afflictions, which happened to me at Antioch, at Iconium, at Lystra—what persecutions I endured. And out of *them* all the Lord delivered me.

Given a divine commission.

Acts 9:6 So he, trembling and astonished, said, "Lord, what do You want me to do?" Then the Lord *said* to him, "Arise and go into the city, and you will be told what you must do."

Acts 9:10–18 Now there was a certain disciple at Damascus named Ananias; and to him the Lord said in a vision, "Ananias." And he said, "Here I am, Lord." 11 So the Lord *said* to him, "Arise and go to the street called Straight, and inquire at the house of Judas for *one* called Saul of Tarsus, for behold, he is praying. 12 And in a vision he has seen a man named Ananias coming in and putting *his* hand on him, so that he might receive his sight." 13 Then Ananias answered, "Lord, I have heard from many about this man, how much harm he has done to Your saints in Jerusalem. 14 And here he has authority from the chief priests to bind all who call on Your name." 15 But the Lord said to him, "Go, for he is a chosen vessel of Mine to bear My name before Gentiles, kings, and the children of Israel. 16 For I will show him how many things he must suffer for My name's sake." 17 And Ananias went his way and entered the house; and laying his hands on him he said, "Brother Saul, the Lord Jesus, who appeared to you on the road as you came, has sent me that you may receive your sight and be filled with the Holy Spirit." 18 Immediately there fell from his eyes *something* like scales, and he received his sight at once; and he arose and was baptized.

Acts 13:1–4 Now in the church that was at Antioch there were certain prophets and teachers: Barnabas, Simeon who was called Niger, Lucius of Cyrene, Manaen who had been brought up with Herod the tetrarch, and Saul. 2 As they ministered to the Lord and fasted, the Holy Spirit said, "Now separate to Me Barnabas and Saul for the work to which I have called them." 3 Then, having fasted and prayed, and laid hands on them, they sent *them* away. 4 So, being sent out by the Holy Spirit, they went down to Seleucia, and from there they sailed to Cyprus.

Acts 22:12–21 "Then a certain Ananias, a devout man according to the law, having a good testimony with all the Jews who dwelt *there,* 13 came to me; and he stood and said to me, 'Brother Saul, receive your sight.' And at that same hour I looked up at him. 14 Then he said, 'The God of our fathers has chosen you that you should know His will, and see the Just One, and hear the voice of His mouth. 15 For you will be His witness to all men of what you have seen and heard. 16 And now why are you waiting? Arise and be baptized, and wash away your sins, calling on the name of the Lord.' 17 "Now it happened, when I returned to Jerusalem and was praying in the temple, that I was in a trance 18 and saw Him saying to me, 'Make haste and get out of Jerusalem quickly, for they will not receive your testimony concerning Me.' 19 So I said, 'Lord, they know that in every synagogue I imprisoned and beat those who believe on You. 20 And when the blood of Your martyr Stephen was shed, I also was standing by consenting to his death, and guarding the clothes of those who were killing him.' 21 Then He said to me, 'Depart, for I will send you far from here to the Gentiles.' "

Acts 26:16–20 But rise and stand on your feet; for I have appeared to you for this purpose, to make you a minister and a witness both of the things which you have seen and of the things which I will yet reveal to you. 17 I will deliver you from the *Jewish* people, as well as *from* the Gentiles, to whom I now send you, 18 to open their eyes, *in order* to turn *them* from darkness to light, and *from* the power of Satan to God, that they may receive forgiveness of sins and an inheritance among those who are sanctified by faith in Me.' 19 "Therefore, King Agrippa, I was not disobedient to the heavenly vision, 20 but declared first to those in Damascus and in Jerusalem, and throughout all the region of Judea, and *then* to the Gentiles, that they should repent, turn to God, and do works befitting repentance.

1 Cor 9:1 Am I not an apostle? Am I not free? Have I not seen Jesus Christ our Lord? Are you not my work in the Lord?

1 Cor 9:16 For if I preach the gospel, I have nothing to boast of, for necessity is laid upon me; yes, woe is me if I do not preach the gospel!

1 Cor 15:8–10 Then last of all He was seen by me also, as by one born out of due time. 9 For I am the least of the apostles, who am not worthy to be called an apostle, because I persecuted the church of God. 10 But by the grace of God I am what I am, and His grace toward me was not in vain; but I labored more abundantly than they all, yet not I, but the grace of God *which was* with me.

Eph 3:1–8 For this reason I, Paul, the prisoner of Christ Jesus for you Gentiles— 2 if indeed you have heard of the dispensation of the grace of God which was given to me for you, 3 how that by revelation He made known to me the mystery (as I have briefly written already, **4** by which, when you read, you may understand my knowledge in the mystery of Christ), **5** which in other ages was not made known to the sons of men, as it has now been revealed by the Spirit to His holy apostles and prophets: **6** that the Gentiles should be fellow heirs, of the same body, and partakers of His promise in Christ through the gospel, **7** of which I became a minister according to the gift of the grace of God given to me by the effective working of His power. **8** To me, who am less than the least of all the saints, this grace was given, that I should preach among the Gentiles the unsearchable riches of Christ,

Rejected in Iconium, stoned at Lystra.

2 Tim 3:11 persecutions, afflictions, which happened to me at Antioch, at Iconium, at Lystra—what persecutions I endured. And out of *them* all the Lord delivered me.

Cf. Acts 14:1–20

Participated in Jerusalem Council.

Gal 2:1–10 Then after fourteen years I went up again to Jerusalem with Barnabas, and also took Titus with *me.* **2** And I went up by revelation, and communicated to them that gospel which I preach among the Gentiles, but privately to those who were of reputation, lest by any means I might run, or had run, in vain. **3** Yet not even Titus who *was* with me, being a Greek, was compelled to be circumcised. **4** And *this occurred* because of false brethren secretly brought in (who came in by stealth to spy out our liberty which we have in Christ Jesus, that they might bring us into bondage), **5** to whom we did not yield submission even for an hour, that the truth of the gospel might continue with you. **6** But from those who seemed to be something— whatever they were, it makes no difference to me; God shows personal favoritism to no man—for those who seemed *to be something* added nothing to me. **7** But on the contrary, when they saw that the gospel for the uncircumcised had been committed to me, as *the gospel* for the circumcised *was* to Peter **8** (for He who worked effectively in Peter for the apostleship to the circumcised also worked effectively in me toward the Gentiles), **9** and when James, Cephas, and John, who seemed to be pillars, perceived the grace that had been given to me, they gave me and Barnabas the right hand of fellowship, that we *should go* to the Gentiles and they to the circumcised. **10** *They desired* only that we should remember the poor, the very thing which I also was eager to do.

Cf. Acts 15:2–22

Rebuked Peter concerning hypocrisy and legalism.

Gal 2:11–21 Now when Peter had come to Antioch, I withstood him to his face, because he was to be blamed; **12** for before certain men came from James, he would eat with the Gentiles; but when they came, he withdrew and separated himself, fearing those who were of the circumcision. **13** And the rest of the Jews also played the hypocrite with him, so that even Barnabas was carried away with their hypocrisy. **14** But when I saw that they were not straightforward about the truth of the gospel, I said to Peter before *them* all, "If you, being a Jew, live in the manner of Gentiles and not as the Jews, why do you compel Gentiles to live as Jews? **15** We *who are* Jews by nature, and not sinners of the Gentiles, **16** knowing that a man is not justified by the works of the law but by faith in Jesus Christ, even we have believed in Christ Jesus, that we might be justified by faith in Christ and not by the works of the law; for by the works of the law no flesh shall be justified. **17** "But if, while we seek to be justified by Christ, we ourselves also are found sinners, *is* Christ therefore a minister of sin? Certainly not! **18** For if I build again those things which I destroyed, I make myself a transgressor. **19** For I through the law died to the law that I might live to God. **20** I have been crucified with Christ; it is no longer I who live, but Christ lives in me; and the *life* which I now live in the flesh I live by faith in the Son of God, who loved me and gave Himself for me. **21** I do not set aside the grace of God; for if righteousness *comes* through the law, then Christ died in vain."

Parted from Barnabas and John Mark.

Acts 15:36–40 Then after some days Paul said to Barnabas, "Let us now go back and visit our brethren in every city where we have preached the word of the Lord, *and see* how they are doing." **37** Now Barnabas was determined to take with them John called Mark. **38** But Paul insisted that they should not take with them the one who had departed from them in Pamphylia, and had not gone with them to the work. **39** Then the contention became so sharp that they parted from one another. And so Barnabas took Mark and sailed to Cyprus; **40** but Paul chose Silas and departed, being commended by the brethren to the grace of God.

Took Timothy as co-worker.

Acts 16:1–5 Then he came to Derbe and Lystra. And behold, a certain disciple was there, named Timothy, *the* son of a certain Jewish woman who believed, but his father *was* Greek. **2** He was well spoken of by the brethren who were at Lystra and Iconium. **3** Paul wanted to have him go on with him. And he took *him* and circumcised him because of the Jews who were in that region, for they all knew that his father was Greek. **4** And as they went through the cities, they delivered to them the decrees to keep, which were determined by the apostles and elders at Jerusalem. **5** So the churches were strengthened in the faith, and increased in number daily.

In jail at Philippi. Acts 16:16–34

Went to Athens, preached at Mars Hill (Areopagus). Acts 17:14–34

Saved from a mob at Ephesus. Acts 19:13–41

Farewell message to Ephesian elders. Acts 20:14–38

Defense before Jewish council.

Acts 23:1–10 Then Paul, looking earnestly at the council, said, "Men *and* brethren, I have lived in all good conscience before God until this day." **2** And the high priest Ananias commanded those who stood by him to strike him on the mouth. **3** Then Paul said to him, "God will strike you, *you* whitewashed wall! For you sit to judge me according to the law, and do you command me to be struck contrary to the law?" **4** And those who stood by said, "Do you revile God's high priest?" **5** Then Paul said, "I did not know, brethren, that he was the high priest; for it is written, *'You shall not speak evil of a ruler of your people.' "* **6** But when Paul perceived that one part were Sadducees and the other Pharisees, he cried out in the council, "Men *and* brethren, I am a Pharisee, the son of a Pharisee; concerning the hope and resurrection of the dead I am being judged!" **7** And when he had said this, a dissension arose between the Pharisees and the Sadducees; and the assembly was divided. **8** For Sadducees say that there is no resurrection—and no angel or spirit; but the Pharisees confess both. **9** Then there arose a loud outcry. And the scribes of the Pharisees' party arose and protested, saying, "We find no evil in this man; but if a spirit or an angel has spoken to him, let us not fight against God." **10** Now when there arose a great dissension, the commander, fearing lest Paul might be pulled to pieces by them, commanded the soldiers to go down and take him by force from among them, and bring *him* into the barracks.

Defense before Felix.

Acts 24:1–23 Now after five days Ananias the high priest came down with the elders and a certain orator *named* Tertullus. These gave evidence to the governor against Paul. **2** And when he was called upon, Tertullus began his accusation, saying: "Seeing that through you we enjoy great peace, and prosperity is being brought to this nation by your foresight, **3** we accept *it* always and in all places, most noble Felix, with all thankfulness. **4** Nevertheless, not to be tedious to you any further, I beg you to hear, by your courtesy, a few words from us. **5** For we have found this man a plague, a creator of dissension among all the Jews throughout the world, and a ringleader of the sect of the Nazarenes. **6** He even tried to profane the temple, and we seized him, and wanted to judge him according to our law. **7** But the commander Lysias came by and with great violence took *him* out of our hands, **8** commanding his accusers to come to you. By examining him yourself you may ascertain all these things of which we accuse him." **9** And the Jews also assented, maintaining that these things were so. **10** Then Paul, after the governor had nodded to him to speak, answered: "Inasmuch as I know that you have been for many years a judge of this nation, I do the more cheerfully answer for myself, **11** because you may ascertain that it is no more than twelve days since I went up to Jerusalem to worship. **12** And they neither found me in the temple disputing with anyone nor inciting the crowd, either in the synagogues or in the city. **13** Nor can they prove the things of which they now accuse me. **14** But this I confess to you, that according to the Way which they call a sect, so I worship the God of my fathers, believing all things which are written in the Law and in the Prophets. **15** I have hope in God, which they themselves also accept, that there will be a resurrection of *the* dead, both of *the* just and *the* unjust. **16** This *being* so, I myself always strive to have a conscience without offense toward God and men. **17** "Now after many years I came to bring alms and offerings to my nation, **18** in the midst of which some Jews from Asia found me purified in the temple, neither with a mob nor with tumult. **19** They ought to have been here before you to object if they had anything against me. **20** Or else let those who are *here*

themselves say if they found any wrongdoing in me while I stood before the council, **21** unless *it is* for this one statement which I cried out, standing among them, 'Concerning the resurrection of the dead I am being judged by you this day.' " **22** But when Felix heard these things, having more accurate knowledge of *the* Way, he adjourned the proceedings and said, "When Lysias the commander comes down, I will make a decision on your case." **23** So he commanded the centurion to keep Paul and to let *him* have liberty, and told him not to forbid any of his friends to provide for or visit him.

Defense before Agrippa.

Acts 26:1–32 Then Agrippa said to Paul, "You are permitted to speak for yourself." So Paul stretched out his hand and answered for himself: **2** "I think myself happy, King Agrippa, because today I shall answer for myself before you concerning all the things of which I am accused by the Jews, **3** especially because you are expert in all customs and questions which have to do with the Jews. Therefore I beg you to hear me patiently. **4** "My manner of life from my youth, which was spent from the beginning among my own nation at Jerusalem, all the Jews know. **5** They knew me from the first, if they were willing to testify, that according to the strictest sect of our religion I lived a Pharisee. **6** And now I stand and am judged for the hope of the promise made by God to our fathers. **7** To this *promise* our twelve tribes, earnestly serving *God* night and day, hope to attain. For this hope's sake, King Agrippa, I am accused by the Jews. **8** Why should it be thought incredible by you that God raises the dead? **9** "Indeed, I myself thought I must do many things contrary to the name of Jesus of Nazareth. **10** This I also did in Jerusalem, and many of the saints I shut up in prison, having received authority from the chief priests; and when they were put to death, I cast my vote against *them*. **11** And I punished them often in every synagogue and compelled *them* to blaspheme; and being exceedingly enraged against them, I persecuted *them* even to foreign cities. **12** "While thus occupied, as I journeyed to Damascus with authority and commission from the chief priests, **13** at midday, O king, along the road I saw a light from heaven, brighter than the sun, shining around me and those who journeyed with me. **14** And when we all had fallen to the ground, I heard a voice speaking to me and saying in the Hebrew language, 'Saul, Saul, why are you persecuting Me? *It is* hard for you to kick against the goads.' **15** So I said, 'Who are You, Lord?' And He said, 'I am Jesus, whom you are persecuting. **16** But rise and stand on your feet; for I have appeared to you for this purpose, to make you a minister and a witness both of the things which you have seen and of the things which I will yet reveal to you. **17** I will deliver you from the *Jewish* people, as well as *from* the Gentiles, to whom I now send you, **18** to open their eyes, *in order* to turn *them* from darkness to light, and *from* the power of Satan to God, that they may receive forgiveness of sins and an inheritance among those who are sanctified by faith in Me.' **19** "Therefore, King Agrippa, I was not disobedient to the heavenly vision, **20** but declared first to those in Damascus and in Jerusalem, and throughout all the region of Judea, and *then* to the Gentiles, that they should repent, turn to God, and do works befitting repentance. 21 For these reasons the Jews seized me in the temple and tried to kill *me*. 22 Therefore, having obtained help from God, to this day I stand, witnessing both to small and great, saying no other things than those which the prophets and Moses said would come— 23 that the Christ would suffer, that He would be the first to rise from the dead, and would proclaim light to the *Jewish* people and to the Gentiles." 24 Now as he thus made his defense, Festus said with a loud voice, "Paul, you are beside yourself! Much learning is driving you mad!" 25 But he said, "I am not mad, most noble Festus, but speak the words of truth and reason. 26 For the king, before whom I also speak freely, knows these things; for I am convinced that none of these things escapes his attention, since this thing was not done in a corner. 27 King Agrippa, do you believe the prophets? I know that you do believe." 28 Then Agrippa said to Paul, "You almost persuade me to become a Christian." 29 And Paul said, "I would to God that not only you, but also all who hear me today, might become both almost and altogether such as I am, except for these chains." 30 When he had said these things, the king stood up, as well as the governor and Bernice and those who sat with them; 31 and when they had gone aside, they talked among themselves, saying, "This man is doing nothing deserving of death or chains. 32 Then Agrippa said to Festus, "This man might have been set free if he had not appealed to Caesar."

Cf. Acts 25:13–27

Shipwrecked on Malta.

Acts 28:1–10 Now when they had escaped, they then found out that the island was called Malta. 2 And the natives showed us unusual kindness; for they kindled a fire and made us all welcome, because of the rain that was falling and because of the cold. 3 But when Paul had gathered a bundle of sticks and laid *them* on the fire, a viper came out because of the heat, and fastened on his hand. 4 So when the natives saw the creature hanging from his hand, they said to one another, "No doubt this man is a murderer, whom, though he has escaped the sea, yet justice does not allow to live." 5 But he shook off the creature into the fire and suffered no harm. 6 However, they were expecting that he would swell up or suddenly fall down dead. But after they had looked for a long time and saw no harm come to him, they changed their minds and said that he was a god. 7 In that region there was an estate of the leading citizen of the island, whose name was Publius, who received us and entertained us courteously for three days. 8 And it happened that the father of Publius lay sick of a fever and dysentery. Paul went in to him and prayed, and he laid his hands on him and healed him. 9 So when this was done, the rest of those on the island who had diseases also came and were healed. 10 They also honored us in many ways; and when we departed, they provided such things as were necessary.

Cf. Acts 27:26–44

Final news and greetings to Timothy.

2 Tim 4:9–22 Be diligent to come to me quickly; 10 for Demas has forsaken me, having loved this present world, and has departed for Thessalonica—Crescens for Galatia, Titus for Dalmatia. 11 Only Luke is with me. Get Mark and bring him with you, for he is useful to me for ministry. 12 And Tychicus I have sent to Ephesus. 13 Bring the cloak that I left with Carpus at Troas when you come—and the books, especially the parchments. 14 Alexander the coppersmith did me much harm. May the Lord repay him according to his works. 15 You also must beware of him, for he has greatly resisted our words. 16 At my first defense no one stood with me, but all forsook me. May it not be charged against them. 17 But the Lord stood with me and strengthened me, so that the message might be preached fully through me, and *that* all the Gentiles might hear. Also I was delivered out of the mouth of the lion. 18 And the Lord will deliver me from every evil work and preserve *me* for His heavenly kingdom. To Him *be* glory forever and ever. Amen! 19 Greet Prisca and Aquila, and the household of Onesiphorus. 20 Erastus stayed in Corinth, but Trophimus I have left in Miletus sick. 21 Do your utmost to come before winter. Eubulus greets you, as well as Pudens, Linus, Claudia, and all the brethren. 22 The Lord Jesus Christ be with your spirit. Grace be with you. Amen.

Missionary methods of,

Preached to Jews first.

Acts 13:46 Then Paul and Barnabas grew bold and said, "It was necessary that the word of God should be spoken to you first; but since you reject it, and judge yourselves unworthy of everlasting life, behold, we turn to the Gentiles.

Acts 17:1–5 Now when they had passed through Amphipolis and Apollonia, they came to Thessalonica, where there was a synagogue of the Jews. 2 Then Paul, as his custom was, went in to them, and for three Sabbaths reasoned with them from the Scriptures, 3 explaining and demonstrating that the Christ had to suffer and rise again from the dead, and *saying*, "This Jesus whom I preach to you is the Christ." 4 And some of them were persuaded; and a great multitude of the devout Greeks, and not a few of the leading women, joined Paul and Silas. 5 But the Jews who were not persuaded, becoming envious, took some of the evil men from the marketplace, and gathering a mob, set all the city in an uproar and attacked the house of Jason, and sought to bring them out to the people.

Ministered with others.

Acts 15:40 but Paul chose Silas and departed, being commended by the brethren to the grace of God.

Acts 20:4 And Sopater of Berea accompanied him to Asia—also Aristarchus and Secundus of the Thessalonians, and Gaius of Derbe, and Timothy, and Tychicus and Trophimus of Asia.

Col 4:14 Luke the beloved physician and Demas greet you.

Planted churches in large cities.

Acts 19:1–10 And it happened, while Apollos was at Corinth, that Paul, having passed through the upper regions, came to Ephesus. And finding some disciples 2 he said to them, "Did you receive the Holy Spirit when you believed?" So they said to him, "We have not so much as heard whether there is a Holy Spirit."

3 And he said to them, "Into what then were you baptized?" So they said, "Into John's baptism." 4 Then Paul said, "John indeed baptized with a baptism of repentance, saying to the people that they should believe on Him who would come after him, that is, on Christ Jesus." 5 When they heard *this*, they were baptized in the name of the Lord Jesus. 6 And when Paul had laid hands on them, the Holy Spirit came upon them, and they spoke with tongues and prophesied. 7 Now the men were about twelve in all. 8 And he went into the synagogue and spoke boldly for three months, reasoning and persuading concerning the things of the kingdom of God. 9 But when some were hardened and did not believe, but spoke evil of the Way before the multitude, he departed from them and withdrew the disciples, reasoning daily in the school of Tyrannus. 10 And this continued for two years, so that all who dwelt in Asia heard the word of the Lord Jesus, both Jews and Greeks.

Rom 1:7–15 To all who are in Rome, beloved of God, called *to be* saints: Grace to you and peace from God our Father and the Lord Jesus Christ. 8 First, I thank my God through Jesus Christ for you all, that your faith is spoken of throughout the whole world. 9 For God is my witness, whom I serve with my spirit in the gospel of His Son, that without ceasing I make mention of you always in my prayers, 10 making request if, by some means, now at last I may find a way in the will of God to come to you. 11 For I long to see you, that I may impart to you some spiritual gift, so that you may be established— 12 that is, that I may be encouraged together with you by the mutual faith both of you and me. 13 Now I do not want you to be unaware, brethren, that I often planned to come to you (but was hindered until now), that I might have some fruit among you also, just as among the other Gentiles. 14 I am a debtor both to Greeks and to barbarians, both to wise and to unwise. 15 So, as much as is in me, *I am* ready to preach the gospel to you who are in Rome also.

Was not a burden to others.

Acts 20:33–35 I have coveted no one's silver or gold or apparel. 34 Yes, you yourselves know that these hands have provided for my necessities, and for those who were with me. 35 I have shown you in every way, by laboring like this, that you must support the weak. And remember the words of the Lord Jesus, that He said, 'It is more blessed to give than to receive.' "

2 Cor 11:7 Did I commit sin in humbling myself that you might be exalted, because I preached the gospel of God to you free of charge?

2 Cor 11:9 And when I was present with you, and in need, I was a burden to no one, for what I lacked the brethren who came from Macedonia supplied. And in everything I kept myself from being burdensome to you, and so I will keep *myself*.

Reported to sending churches.

Acts 14:26–28 From there they sailed to Antioch, where they had been commended to the grace of God for the work which they had completed. 27 Now when they had come and gathered the church together, they reported all that God had done with them, and that He had opened the door of faith to the Gentiles. 28 So they stayed there a long time with the disciples.

Acts 21:17–20 And when we had come to Jerusalem, the brethren received us gladly. 18 On the following *day* Paul went in with us to James, and all the elders were present. 19 When he had greeted them, he told in detail those things which God had done among the Gentiles through his ministry. 20 And when they heard *it*, they glorified the Lord. And they said to him, "You see, brother, how many myriads of Jews there are who have believed, and they are all zealous for the law;

Goal was to reach everyone.

Col 1:23–29 if indeed you continue in the faith, grounded and steadfast, and are not moved away from the hope of the gospel which you heard, which was preached to every creature under heaven, of which I, Paul, became a minister. 24 I now rejoice in my sufferings for you, and fill up in my flesh what is lacking in the afflictions of Christ, for the sake of His body, which is the church, 25 of which I became a minister according to the stewardship from God which was given to me for you, to fulfill the word of God, 26 the mystery which has been hidden from ages and from generations, but now has been revealed to His saints. 27 To them God willed to make known what are the riches of the glory of this mystery among the Gentiles: which is Christ in you, the hope of glory. 28 Him we preach, warning every man and teaching every man in all wisdom, that we may present every man perfect in Christ Jesus. 29 To this *end* I also labor, striving according to His working which works in me mightily.

2 Tim 4:17 But the Lord stood with me and strengthened me, so that the message might be preached fully through me, and *that* all the Gentiles might hear. Also I was delivered out of the mouth of the lion.

Nature of his writings

Inspired by God.

2 Cor 13:3 since you seek a proof of Christ speaking in me, who is not weak toward you, but mighty in you.

1 Thess 2:13 For this reason we also thank God without ceasing, because when you received the word of God which you heard from us, you welcomed *it* not *as* the word of men, but as it is in truth, the word of God, which also effectively works in you who believe.

2 Tim 3:15–16 and that from childhood you have known the Holy Scriptures, which are able to make you wise for salvation through faith which is in Christ Jesus. 16 All Scripture *is* given by inspiration of God, and *is* profitable for doctrine, for reproof, for correction, for instruction in righteousness,

Had difficult and weighty content.

2 Cor 10:10 "For *his* letters," they say, "*are* weighty and powerful, but *his* bodily presence *is* weak, and *his* speech contemptible."

2 Pet 3:15–16 and consider *that* the longsuffering of our Lord *is* salvation—as also our beloved brother Paul, according to the wisdom given to him, has written to you, 16 as also in all his epistles, speaking in them of these things, in which are some things hard to understand, which untaught and unstable *people* twist to their own destruction, as *they do* also the rest of the Scriptures.

PEACE

God is the Author of.

Ps 147:14 He makes peace *in* your borders, *And* fills you with the finest wheat.

Is 45:7 I form the light and create darkness, I make peace and create calamity; I, the LORD, do all these *things.'*

1 Cor 14:33 For God is not *the author* of confusion but of peace, as in all the churches of the saints.

Results from

Heavenly wisdom.

James 3:17 But the wisdom that is from above is first pure, then peaceable, gentle, willing to yield, full of mercy and good fruits, without partiality and without hypocrisy.

The government of Christ.

Is 2:4 He shall judge between the nations, And rebuke many people; They shall beat their swords into plowshares, And their spears into pruning hooks; Nation shall not lift up sword against nation, Neither shall they learn war anymore.

Praying for rulers.

1 Tim 2:2 for kings and all who are in authority, that we may lead a quiet and peaceable life in all godliness and reverence.

Seeking the peace of those with whom we dwell.

Jer 29:7 And seek the peace of the city where I have caused you to be carried away captive, and pray to the LORD for it; for in its peace you will have peace.

Necessary to the enjoyment of life.

Ps 34:12 Who *is* the man *who* desires life, And loves *many* days, that he may see good?

Ps 34:14 Depart from evil and do good; Seek peace and pursue it.

1 Pet 3:10–11 For *"He who would love life And see good days, Let him refrain his tongue from evil, And his lips from speaking deceit. 11 Let him turn away from evil and do good; Let him seek peace and pursue it.*

God bestows, upon those who

Obey Him.

Lev 26:6 I will give peace in the land, and you shall lie down, and none will make *you* afraid; I will rid the land of evil beasts, and the sword will not go through your land.

Please Him.

Ps 16:7 I will bless the LORD who has given me counsel; My heart also instructs me in the night seasons.

Endure His chastisements.

Job 5:17 "Behold, happy *is* the man whom God corrects; Therefore do not despise the chastening of the Almighty.

Job 5:23–24 For you shall have a covenant with the stones of the field, And the beasts of the field shall be at peace with you. 24 You shall know that your tent *is* in peace; You shall visit your dwelling and find nothing amiss.

God's people shall enjoy.

Ps 125:5 As for such as turn aside to their crooked ways,

The LORD shall lead them away With the workers of iniquity. Peace *be* upon Israel!

Ps 128:6 Yes, may you see your children's children. Peace *be* upon Israel!

Is 2:4 He shall judge between the nations, And rebuke many people; They shall beat their swords into plowshares, And their spears into pruning hooks; Nation shall not lift up sword against nation, Neither shall they learn war anymore.

Hos 2:18 In that day I will make a covenant for them With the beasts of the field, With the birds of the air, And *with* the creeping things of the ground. Bow and sword of battle I will shatter from the earth, To make them lie down safely.

Believers should

Love.

Zech 8:19 "Thus says the LORD of hosts: 'The fast of the fourth *month*, The fast of the fifth, The fast of the seventh, And the fast of the tenth, Shall be joy and gladness and cheerful feasts For the house of Judah. Therefore love truth and peace.'

Seek.

Ps 34:14 Depart from evil and do good; Seek peace and pursue it.

1 Pet 3:11 *Let him turn away from evil and do good; Let him seek peace and pursue it.*

Follow.

2 Tim 2:22 Flee also youthful lusts; but pursue righteousness, faith, love, peace with those who call on the Lord out of a pure heart.

James 3:18 Now the fruit of righteousness is sown in peace by those who make peace.

Follow the things which make for.

Rom 14:19 Therefore let us pursue the things *which make* for peace and the things by which one may edify another.

Cultivate.

Ps 120:7 I *am for* peace; But when I speak, they *are* for war.

Speak.

Esth 10:3 For Mordecai the Jew *was* second to King Ahasuerus, and was great among the Jews and well received by the multitude of his brethren, seeking the good of his people and speaking peace to all his countrymen.

Live in.

2 Cor 13:11 Finally, brethren, farewell. Become complete. Be of good comfort, be of one mind, live in peace; and the God of love and peace will be with you.

Have, with each other.

Mark 9:50 Salt *is* good, but if the salt loses its flavor, how will you season it? Have salt in yourselves, and have peace with one another."

Eph 4:3 endeavoring to keep the unity of the Spirit in the bond of peace.

1 Thess 5:13 and to esteem them very highly in love for their work's sake. Be at peace among yourselves.

Endeavor to have with all men.

Rom 12:18 If it is possible, as much as depends on you, live peaceably with all men.

Heb 12:14 Pursue peace with all *people*, and holiness, without which no one will see the Lord:

Pray for it among believers.

Ps 122:6–8 Pray for the peace of Jerusalem: "May they prosper who love you. **7** Peace be within your walls, Prosperity within your palaces." **8** For the sake of my brethren and companions, I will now say, "Peace *be* within you."

Exhort others to.

Gen 45:24 So he sent his brothers away, and they departed; and he said to them, "See that you do not become troubled along the way."

2 Thess 3:12 Now those who are such we command and exhort through our Lord Jesus Christ that they work in quietness and eat their own bread.

Advantages of.

Ps 133:1 Behold, how good and how pleasant *it is* For brethren to dwell together in unity!

Prov 17:1 Better *is* a dry morsel with quietness, Than a house full of feasting *with* strife.

Eccl 4:6 Better a handful *with* quietness Than both hands full, *together with* toil and grasping for the wind.

Blessedness of promoting.

Matt 5:9 Blessed *are* the peacemakers, For they shall be called sons of God.

The wicked

Speak hypocritically of.

Ps 28:3 Do not take me away with the wicked And with the workers of iniquity, Who speak peace to their neighbors, But evil *is* in their hearts.

Do not enjoy.

Is 48:22 "*There is* no peace," says the LORD, "for the wicked."

Ezek 7:25 Destruction comes; They will seek peace, but *there shall be* none.

Opposed to.

Ps 35:20 For they do not speak peace, But they devise deceitful matters Against *the* quiet ones in the land.

Ps 120:6–7 My soul has dwelt too long With one who hates peace. **7** I *am for* peace; But when I speak, they *are* for war.

Shall abound in the latter days.

Is 2:4 He shall judge between the nations, And rebuke many people; They shall beat their swords into plowshares, And their spears into pruning hooks; Nation shall not lift up sword against nation, Neither shall they learn war anymore.

Is 11:13 Also the envy of Ephraim shall depart, And the adversaries of Judah shall be cut off; Ephraim shall not envy Judah, And Judah shall not harass Ephraim.

Is 32:18 My people will dwell in a peaceful habitation, In secure dwellings, and in quiet resting places,

Exemplified by

Abraham.

Gen 13:8–9 So Abram said to Lot, "Please let there be no strife between you and me, and between my herdsmen and your herdsmen; for we *are* brethren. **9** *Is* not the whole land before you? Please separate from me. If *you take* the left, then I will go to the right; or, if *you go* to the right, then I will go to the left."

Abimelech.

Gen 26:29 that you will do us no harm, since we have not touched you, and since we have done nothing to you but good and have sent you away in peace. You *are* now the blessed of the LORD.' "

Mordecai.

Esth 10:3 For Mordecai the Jew *was* second to King Ahasuerus, and was great among the Jews and well received by the multitude of his brethren, seeking the good of his people and speaking peace to all his countrymen.

David.

Ps 120:7 I *am for* peace; But when I speak, they *are* for war.

PEACE, SPIRITUAL

God

Is the God of.

Rom 15:33 Now the God of peace *be* with you all. Amen.

2 Cor 13:11 Finally, brethren, farewell. Become complete. Be of good comfort, be of one mind, live in peace; and the God of love and peace will be with you.

1 Thess 5:23 Now may the God of peace Himself sanctify you completely; and may your whole spirit, soul, and body be preserved blameless at the coming of our Lord Jesus Christ.

Heb 13:20 Now may the God of peace who brought up our Lord Jesus from the dead, that great Shepherd of the sheep, through the blood of the everlasting covenant,

Ordains, for believers.

Ps 85:8 I will hear what God the LORD will speak, For He will speak peace To His people and to His saints; But let them not turn back to folly.

Is 26:12 LORD, You will establish peace for us, For You have also done all our works in us.

Christ

Is the Lord of.

2 Thess 3:16 Now may the Lord of peace Himself give you peace always in every way. The Lord *be* with you all.

Is the Prince of.

Is 9:6 For unto us a Child is born, Unto us a Son is given; And the government will be upon His shoulder. And His name will be called Wonderful, Counselor, Mighty God, Everlasting Father, Prince of Peace.

Grants.

Luke 1:79 To give light to those who sit in darkness and the shadow of death, To guide our feet into the way of peace."

John 14:27 Peace I leave with you, My peace I give to you; not as the world gives do I give to you. Let not your heart be troubled, neither let it be afraid.

2 Thess 3:16 Now may the Lord of peace Himself give you peace always in every way. The Lord *be* with you all.

He is our.

Eph 2:14 For He Himself is our peace, who has made both one, and has broken down the middle wall of separation,

Comes through His atonement.

Is 53:5 But He *was* wounded for our transgressions, *He was* bruised for our iniquities; The chastisement for our peace *was* upon Him, And by His stripes we are healed.

Eph 2:14–15 For He Himself is our peace, who has made both one, and has broken down the middle wall of separation, **15** having abolished in His flesh the enmity, *that is,* the law of commandments *contained* in ordinances, so as to create in Himself one new man *from* the two, *thus* making peace,

Col 1:20 and by Him to reconcile all things to Himself, by Him, whether things on earth or things in heaven, having made peace through the blood of His cross.

Preached

By Christ.

Eph 2:17 And He came and preached peace to you who were afar off and to those who were near.

Through Christ.

Acts 10:36 The word which *God* sent to the children of Israel, preaching peace through Jesus Christ—He is Lord of all—

By ministers.

Is 52:7 How beautiful upon the mountains Are the feet of him who brings good news, Who proclaims peace, Who brings glad tidings of good *things,* Who proclaims salvation, Who says to Zion, "Your God reigns!"

Rom 10:15 And how shall they preach unless they are sent? As it is written: *"How beautiful are the feet of those who preach the gospel of peace, Who bring glad tidings of good things!"*

By angels.

Luke 2:14 "Glory to God in the highest, And on earth peace, goodwill toward men!"

A fruit of the Spirit.

Rom 14:17 for the kingdom of God is not eating and drinking, but righteousness and peace and joy in the Holy Spirit.

Gal 5:22 But the fruit of the Spirit is love, joy, peace, longsuffering, kindness, goodness, faithfulness,

Divine wisdom is the way of.

Prov 3:17 Her ways *are* ways of pleasantness, And all her paths *are* peace.

Accompanies

Justification.

Rom 5:1 Therefore, having been justified by faith, we have peace with God through our Lord Jesus Christ,

Faith.

Rom 15:13 Now may the God of hope fill you with all joy and peace in believing, that you may abound in hope by the power of the Holy Spirit.

Righteousness.

Is 32:17 The work of righteousness will be peace, And the effect of righteousness, quietness and assurance forever.

Acquaintance with God.

Job 22:21 "Now acquaint yourself with Him, and be at peace; Thereby good will come to you.

The love of God's law.

Ps 119:165 Great peace have those who love Your law, And nothing causes them to stumble.

Spiritual mindedness.

Rom 8:6 For to be carnally minded *is* death, but to be spiritually minded *is* life and peace.

Established by covenant.

Is 54:10 For the mountains shall depart And the hills be removed, But My kindness shall not depart from you, Nor shall My covenant of peace be removed," Says the LORD, who has mercy on you.

Ezek 34:25 "I will make a covenant of peace with them, and cause wild beasts to cease from the land; and they will dwell safely in the wilderness and sleep in the woods.

Mal 2:5 "My covenant was with him, *one* of life and peace, And I gave them to him *that he might* fear *Me;* So he feared Me And was reverent before My name.

Promised to

The Gentiles.

Zech 9:10 I will cut off the chariot from Ephraim And the horse from Jerusalem; The battle bow shall be cut off. He shall speak peace to the nations; His dominion *shall be* 'from sea to sea, And from the River to the ends of the earth.'

Believers.

Ps 72:3 The mountains will bring peace to the people, And the little hills, by righteousness.

Ps 72:7 In His days the righteous shall flourish, And abundance of peace, Until the moon is no more.

Is 26:3 You will keep *him* in perfect peace, *Whose* mind is stayed *on* You, Because he trusts in You.

Is 55:12 "For you shall go out with joy, And be led out with peace; The mountains and the hills Shall break forth into singing before you, And all the trees of the field shall clap *their* hands.

Is 66:12 For thus says the LORD: "Behold, I will extend peace to her like a river, And the glory of the Gentiles like a flowing stream. Then you shall feed; On *her* sides shall you be carried, And be dandled on *her* knees.

The meek.

Ps 37:11 But the meek shall inherit the earth, And shall delight themselves in the abundance of peace.

Returning backsliders.

Is 57:18–19 I have seen his ways, and will heal him; I will also lead him, And restore comforts to him And to his mourners. **19** "I create the fruit of the lips: Peace, peace to *him who is* far off and to *him who is* near," Says the LORD, "And I will heal him."

Believers

Should love.

Zech 8:19 "Thus says the LORD of hosts: 'The fast of the fourth *month,* The fast of the fifth, The fast of the seventh, And the fast of the tenth, Shall be joy and gladness and cheerful feasts For the house of Judah. Therefore love truth and peace.'

Have, in Christ and in God.

Is 27:5 Or let him take hold of My strength, *That* he may make peace with Me; *And* he shall make peace with Me."

John 16:33 These things I have spoken to you, that in Me you may have peace. In the world you will have tribulation; but be of good cheer, I have overcome the world."

Rom 5:1 Therefore, having been justified by faith, we have peace with God through our Lord Jesus Christ,

Enjoy blessings of.

Ps 4:8 I will both lie down in peace, and sleep; For You alone, O LORD, make me dwell in safety.

Ps 29:11 The LORD will give strength to His people; The LORD will bless His people with peace.

Ps 119:165 Great peace have those who love Your law, And nothing causes them to stumble.

Is 26:3 You will keep *him* in perfect peace, *Whose* mind *is* stayed *on* You, Because he trusts in You.

Governed by.

Phil 4:7 and the peace of God, which surpasses all understanding, will guard your hearts and minds through Christ Jesus.

Col 3:15 And let the peace of God rule in your hearts, to which also you were called in one body; and be thankful.

Die in.

Ps 37:37 Mark the blameless *man*, and observe the upright; For the future of *that* man *is* peace.

Is 57:2 He shall enter into peace; They shall rest in their beds, *Each one* walking *in* his uprightness.

Luke 2:29 "Lord, now You are letting Your servant depart in peace, According to Your word;

Wish, to each other.

Gal 6:16 And as many as walk according to this rule, peace and mercy *be* upon them, and upon the Israel of God.

Phil 1:2 Grace to you and peace from God our Father and the Lord Jesus Christ.

Col 1:2 To the saints and faithful brethren in Christ *who are* in Colosse: Grace to you and peace from God our Father and the Lord Jesus Christ.

1 Thess 1:1 Paul, Silvanus, and Timothy, To the church of the Thessalonians in God the Father and the Lord Jesus Christ: Grace to you and peace from God our Father and the Lord Jesus Christ.

Have much.

Ps 72:7 In His days the righteous shall flourish, And abundance of peace, Until the moon is no more.

Ps 119:165 Great peace have those who love Your law, And nothing causes them to stumble.

Is 54:13 All your children *shall be* taught by the LORD, And great *shall be* the peace of your children.

Jer 33:6 Behold, I will bring it health and healing; I will heal them and reveal to them the abundance of peace and truth.

Theirs is secure.

Job 34:29 When He gives quietness, who then can make trouble? And when He hides *His* face, who then can see Him, Whether *it is* against a nation or a man alone?—

Theirs passes all understanding.

Phil 4:7 and the peace of God, which surpasses all understanding, will guard your hearts and minds through Christ Jesus.

Supports them under trials.

John 14:27 Peace I leave with you, My peace I give to you; not as the world gives do I give to you. Let not your heart be troubled, neither let it be afraid.

John 16:33 These things I have spoken to you, that in Me you may have peace. In the world you will have tribulation; but be of good cheer, I have overcome the world."

The gospel is glad tidings of.

Rom 10:15 And how shall they preach unless they are sent? As it is written: *"How beautiful are the feet of those who preach the gospel of peace, Who bring glad tidings of good things!"*

The wicked

Do not know.

Luke 19:42 saying, "If you had known, even you, especially in this your day, the things *that make* for your peace! But now they are hidden from your eyes.

Rom 3:17 *And the way of peace they have not known."*

Promise, to themselves.

Deut 29:19 and so it may not happen, when he hears the words of this curse, that he blesses himself in his heart, saying, 'I shall have peace, even though I follow the dictates of my heart'—as though the drunkard could be included with the sober.

Are promised, by false teachers.

Jer 6:14 They have also healed the hurt of My people slightly, Saying, 'Peace, peace!' When *there is* no peace.

There is none for.

Is 48:22 *"There is* no peace," says the LORD, "for the wicked."

Is 57:21 *"There is* no peace," Says my God, "for the wicked."

PERDITION (DESTRUCTION).
SEE ALSO HELL
Everlasting punishment of unbelievers.

Phil 1:28 and not in any way terrified by your adversaries, which is to them a proof of perdition, but to you of salvation, and that from God.

The destiny of

Apostates.

Heb 10:39 But we are not of those who draw back to perdition, but of those who believe to the saving of the soul.

Those who desire riches.

1 Tim 6:9 But those who desire to be rich fall into temptation and a snare, and *into* many foolish and harmful lusts which drown men in destruction and perdition.

2 Pet 3:7 But the heavens and the earth *which* are now preserved by the same word, are reserved for fire until the day of judgment and perdition of ungodly men.

The Beast.

Rev 17:8 The beast that you saw was, and is not, and will ascend out of the bottomless pit and go to perdition. And those who dwell on the earth will marvel, whose names are not written in the Book of Life from the foundation of the world, when they see the beast that was, and is not, and yet is.

Rev 17:11 The beast that was, and is not, is himself also the eighth, and is of the seven, and is going to perdition.

Cf. Rev 19:20

PERFECTION (MATURITY, COMPLETION)

Is of God.

Ps 18:32 *It is* God who arms me with strength, And makes my way perfect.

Ps 138:8 The LORD will perfect *that which* concerns me; Your mercy, O LORD, *endures* forever; Do not forsake the works of Your hands.

Believers

Have in Christ.

1 Cor 2:6 However, we speak wisdom among those who are mature, yet not the wisdom of this age, nor of the rulers of this age, who are coming to nothing.

Phil 3:15 Therefore let us, as many as are mature, have this mind; and if in anything you think otherwise, God will reveal even this to you.

Col 2:10 and you are complete in Him, who is the head of all principality and power.

Commanded to aim at.

Gen 17:1 When Abram was ninety-nine years old, the LORD appeared to Abram and said to him, "I *am* Almighty God; walk before Me and be blameless.

Deut 18:13 You shall be blameless before the LORD your God.

Do not presume.

Job 9:20 Though I were righteous, my own mouth would condemn me; Though I *were* blameless, it would prove me perverse.

Phil 3:12 Not that I have already attained, or am already perfected; but I press on, that I may lay hold of that for which Christ Jesus has also laid hold of me.

Follow after.

Prov 4:18 But the path of the just *is* like the shining sun, That shines ever brighter unto the perfect day.

Phil 3:12 Not that I have already attained, or am already perfected; but I press on, that I may lay hold of that for which Christ Jesus has also laid hold of me.

Implies

Entire devotedness.

Matt 19:21 Jesus said to him, "If you want to be perfect, go, sell what you have and give to the poor, and you will have treasure in heaven; and come, follow Me."

Purity and holiness in speech.

James 3:2 For we all stumble in many things. If anyone does not stumble in word, he *is* a perfect man, able also to bridle the whole body.

Ministers appointed to lead believers to.

2 Cor 7:1 Therefore, having these promises, beloved, let us cleanse ourselves from all filthiness of the flesh and spirit, perfecting holiness in the fear of God.

2 Cor 13:11 Finally, brethren, farewell. Become complete. Be of good comfort, be of one mind, live in peace; and the God of love and peace will be with you.

Eph 4:12 for the equipping of the saints for the work of ministry, for the edifying of the body of Christ,

Col 1:28 Him we preach, warning every man and teaching every man in all wisdom, that we may present every man perfect in Christ Jesus.

Impossibility of attaining to.

2 Chr 6:36 "When they sin against You (for *there is* no one who does not sin), and You become angry with them and deliver them to the enemy, and they take them captive to a land far or near;

Ps 119:96 I have seen the consummation of all perfection, *But* Your commandment *is* exceedingly broad.

God and His Word is

The rule of.

Matt 5:48 Therefore you shall be perfect, just as your Father in heaven is perfect.

James 1:25 But he who looks into the perfect law of liberty and continues *in it*, and is not a forgetful hearer but a doer of the work, this one will be blessed in what he does.

Designed to lead us to.

2 Tim 3:16–17 All Scripture *is* given by inspiration of God, and *is* profitable for doctrine, for reproof, for correction, for instruction in righteousness, **17** that the man of God may be complete, thoroughly equipped for every good work.

Love is the bond of.

Col 3:14 But above all these things put on love, which is the bond of perfection.

Patience leads to.

James 1:4 But let patience have *its* perfect work, that you may be perfect and complete, lacking nothing.

Pray for.

Heb 13:20–21 Now may the God of peace who brought up our Lord Jesus from the dead, that great Shepherd of the sheep, through the blood of the everlasting covenant, **21** make you complete in every good work to do His will, working in you what is well pleasing in His sight, through Jesus Christ, to whom *be* glory forever and ever. Amen.

1 Pet 5:10 But may the God of all grace, who called us to His eternal glory by Christ Jesus, after you have suffered a while, perfect, establish, strengthen, and settle *you*.

The church shall attain to.

John 17:23 I in them, and You in Me; that they may be made perfect in one, and that the world may know that You have sent Me, and have loved them as You have loved Me.

Eph 4:13 till we all come to the unity of the faith and of the knowledge of the Son of God, to a perfect man, to the measure of the stature of the fullness of Christ;

Blessedness of.

Ps 37:37 Mark the blameless *man,* and observe the upright; For the future of *that* man *is* peace.

Prov 2:21 For the upright will dwell in the land, And the blameless will remain in it;

PERJURY

Described by David, against him.

Ps 27:12 Do not deliver me to the will of my adversaries; For false witnesses have risen against me, And such as breathe out violence.

Ps 35:11–21 Fierce witnesses rise up; They ask me *things* that I do not know. **12** They reward me evil for good, *To* the sorrow of my soul. **13** But as for me, when they were sick, My clothing *was* sackcloth; I humbled myself with fasting; And my prayer would return to my own heart. **14** I paced about as though *he were* my friend *or* brother; I bowed down heavily, as one who mourns *for his* mother. **15** But in my adversity they rejoiced And gathered together; Attackers gathered against me, And I did not know *it;* They tore *at me* and did not cease; **16** With ungodly mockers at feasts They gnashed at me with their teeth. **17** Lord, how long will You look on? Rescue me from their destructions, My precious *life* from the lions. **18** I will give You thanks in the great assembly; I will praise You among many people. **19** Let them not rejoice over me who are wrongfully my enemies; Nor let them wink with the eye who hate me without a cause. **20** For they do not speak peace, But they devise deceitful matters Against *the* quiet ones in the land. **21** They also opened their mouth wide against me, *And* said, "Aha, aha! Our eyes have seen *it.*"

Sin of.

Ex 20:16 "You shall not bear false witness against your neighbor.

Ex 23:1–2 "You shall not circulate a false report. Do not put your hand with the wicked to be an unrighteous witness. **2** You shall not follow a crowd to do evil; nor shall you testify in a dispute so as to turn aside after many to pervert *justice.*

Lev 19:12 And you shall not swear by My name falsely, nor shall you profane the name of your God: I *am* the LORD.

Deut 19:18–21 And the judges shall make careful inquiry, and indeed, *if* the witness *is* a false witness, who has testified falsely against his brother, **19** then you shall do to him as he thought to have done to his brother; so you shall put away the evil from among you. **20** And those who remain shall hear and fear, and hereafter they shall not again commit such evil among you. **21** Your eye shall not pity: life *shall be* for life, eye for eye, tooth for tooth, hand for hand, foot for foot.

Prov 6:19 A false witness *who* speaks lies, And one who sows discord among brethren.

Prov 12:17 He *who* speaks truth declares righteousness, But a false witness, deceit.

Prov 14:5 A faithful witness does not lie, But a false witness will utter lies.

Prov 14:25 A true witness delivers souls, But a deceitful *witness* speaks lies.

Prov 19:5 A false witness will not go unpunished, And *he who* speaks lies will not escape.

Prov 19:9 A false witness will not go unpunished, And *he who* speaks lies shall perish.

PERSECUTION

Christ submitted to patiently.

Ps 69:26 For they persecute the *ones* You have struck, And talk of the grief of those You have wounded.

Is 50:6 I gave My back to those who struck *Me,* And My cheeks to those who plucked out the beard; I did not hide My face from shame and spitting.

Is 53:7 He was oppressed and He was afflicted, Yet He opened not His mouth; He was led as a lamb to the slaughter, And as a sheep before its shearers is silent, So He opened not His mouth.

John 5:16 For this reason the Jews persecuted Jesus, and sought to kill Him, because He had done these things on the Sabbath.

Of believers

They must expect it.

Mark 10:30 who shall not receive a hundredfold now in this time—houses and brothers and sisters and mothers and children and lands, with persecutions—and in the age to come, eternal life.

Luke 21:12 But before all these things, they will lay their hands on you and persecute *you,* delivering *you* up to the synagogues and prisons. You will be brought before kings and rulers for My name's sake.

John 15:20 Remember the word that I said to you, 'A servant is not greater than his master.' If they persecuted Me, they will also persecute you. If they kept My word, they will keep yours also.

2 Tim 3:12 Yes, and all who desire to live godly in Christ Jesus will suffer persecution.

Is for God's sake.

Jer 15:15 O LORD, You know; Remember me and visit me, And take vengeance for me on my persecutors. In Your enduring patience, do not take me away. Know that for Your sake I have suffered rebuke.

Is a persecution of Christ.

Zech 2:8 For thus says the LORD of hosts: "He sent Me after glory, to the nations which plunder you; for he who touches you touches the apple of His eye.

Acts 9:4–5 Then he fell to the ground, and heard a voice saying to him, "Saul, Saul, why are you persecuting Me?" **5** And he said, "Who are You, Lord?" Then the Lord said, "I am Jesus, whom you are persecuting. It *is* hard for you to kick against the goads."

God is with them in.

Dan 3:25 "Look!" he answered, "I see four men loose, walking in the midst of the fire; and they are not hurt, and the form of the fourth is like the Son of God."

Dan 3:28 Nebuchadnezzar spoke, saying, "Blessed be the God of Shadrach, Meshach, and Abed-Nego, who sent His Angel and delivered His servants who trusted in Him, and they have frustrated the king's word, and yielded their bodies, that they should not serve nor worship any god except their own God!

Rom 8:35 Who shall separate us from the love of

Christ? *Shall* tribulation, or distress, or persecution, or famine, or nakedness, or peril, or sword?

2 Cor 1:10 who delivered us from so great a death, and does deliver us; in whom we trust that He will still deliver *us*,

2 Cor 4:9 persecuted, but not forsaken; struck down, but not destroyed—

2 Tim 3:11 persecutions, afflictions, which happened to me at Antioch, at Iconium, at Lystra—what persecutions I endured. And out of *them* all the Lord delivered me.

Sources of,

Ignorance of God and Christ.

John 16:3 And these things they will do to you because they have not known the Father nor Me.

Hated to God and Christ.

John 15:20 Remember the word that I said to you, 'A servant is not greater than his master.' If they persecuted Me, they will also persecute you. If they kept My word, they will keep yours also.

John 15:24 If I had not done among them the works which no one else did, they would have no sin; but now they have seen and also hated both Me and My Father.

Hatred to the gospel.

Matt 13:21 yet he has no root in himself, but endures only for a while. For when tribulation or persecution arises because of the word, immediately he stumbles.

Pride.

Ps 10:2 The wicked in *his* pride persecutes the poor; Let them be caught in the plots which they have devised.

Mistaken zeal.

Acts 13:50 But the Jews stirred up the devout and prominent women and the chief men of the city, raised up persecution against Paul and Barnabas, and expelled them from their region.

Acts 26:9–11 "Indeed, I myself thought I must do many things contrary to the name of Jesus of Nazareth. **10** This I also did in Jerusalem, and many of the saints I shut up in prison, having received authority from the chief priests; and when they were put to death, I cast my vote against *them*. **11** And I punished them often in every synagogue and compelled *them* to blaspheme; and being exceedingly enraged against them, I persecuted *them* even to foreign cities.

Characteristics of,

Inconsistent with spirit of the gospel.

Matt 26:52 But Jesus said to him, "Put your sword in its place, for all who take the sword will perish by the sword.

Unbelievers naturally engage in.

Gal 4:29 But, as he who was born according to the flesh then persecuted him *who was born* according to the Spirit, even so *it is* now.

Aims at gospel preachers.

Gal 5:11 And I, brethren, if I still preach circumcision, why do I still suffer persecution? Then the offense of the cross has ceased.

Sometimes causes death.

Acts 22:4 I persecuted this Way to the death, binding and delivering into prisons both men and women,

Lawful means may be used to escape.

Matt 2:13 Now when they had departed, behold, an angel of the Lord appeared to Joseph in a dream, saying, "Arise, take the young Child and His mother, flee to Egypt, and stay there until I bring you word; for Herod will seek the young Child to destroy Him."

Matt 10:23 When they persecute you in this city, flee to another. For assuredly, I say to you, you will not have gone through the cities of Israel before the Son of Man comes.

Matt 12:14–15 Then the Pharisees went out and plotted against Him, how they might destroy Him. **15** But when Jesus knew *it*, He withdrew from there. And great multitudes followed Him, and He healed them all.

Believers when suffering, should

Commit themselves to God.

1 Pet 4:19 Therefore let those who suffer according to the will of God commit their souls *to Him* in doing good, as to a faithful Creator.

Exhibit patience.

1 Cor 4:12 And we labor, working with our own hands. Being reviled, we bless; being persecuted, we endure;

Rejoice.

Matt 5:12 Rejoice and be exceedingly glad, for great *is* your reward in heaven, for so they persecuted the prophets who were before you.

1 Pet 4:13 but rejoice to the extent that you partake of Christ's sufferings, that when His glory is revealed, you may also be glad with exceeding joy.

Glorify God.

1 Pet 4:16 Yet if *anyone suffers* as a Christian, let him not be ashamed, but let him glorify God in this matter.

Pray for deliverance.

Ps 7:1 O LORD my God, in You I put my trust; Save me from all those who persecute me; And deliver me,

Ps 119:86 All Your commandments *are* faithful; They persecute me wrongfully; Help me!

Pray for those who inflict.

Matt 5:44 But I say to you, love your enemies, bless those who curse you, do good to those who hate you, and pray for those who spitefully use you and persecute you,

Return blessing for.

Rom 12:14 Bless those who persecute you; bless and do not curse.

Have courage and hope.

1 Cor 15:19 If in this life only we have hope in Christ, we are of all men the most pitiable.

1 Cor 15:32 If, in the manner of men, I have fought with beasts at Ephesus, what advantage *is it* to me? If *the* dead do not rise, *"Let us eat and drink, for tomorrow we die!"*

Heb 10:34–35 for you had compassion on me in my chains, and joyfully accepted the plundering of your goods, knowing that you have a better and an enduring possession for yourselves in heaven. **35** Therefore do not cast away your confidence, which has great reward.

Blessedness of enduring, for Christ's sake.

Matt 5:10 Blessed are those who are persecuted for righteousness' sake, For theirs is the kingdom of heaven.

Luke 6:22 Blessed are you when men hate you, And when they exclude you, And revile *you*, and cast out your name as evil, For the Son of Man's sake.

Pray for those suffering.

2 Thess 3:2 and that we may be delivered from unreasonable and wicked men; for not all have faith.

Hypocrites and the wicked

Cannot endure.

Matt 4:17 From that time Jesus began to preach and to say, "Repent, for the kingdom of heaven is at hand."

Gal 6:12 As many as desire to make a good showing in the flesh, these *would* compel you to be circumcised, only that they may not suffer persecution for the cross of Christ.

Active in.

Ps 10:2 The wicked in *his* pride persecutes the poor; Let them be caught in the plots which they have devised.

Ps 69:26 For they persecute the *ones* You have struck, And talk of the grief of those You have wounded.

Ps 143:3 For the enemy has persecuted my soul; He has crushed my life to the ground; He has made me dwell in darkness, Like those who have long been dead.

Lam 4:19 Our pursuers were swifter Than the eagles of the heavens. They pursued us on the mountains And lay in wait for us in the wilderness.

Encourage each other in.

Ps 71:11 Saying, "God has forsaken him; Pursue and take him, for *there is* none to deliver *him.*"

Rejoice in its success.

Ps 13:4 Lest my enemy say, "I have prevailed against him"; *Lest* those who trouble me rejoice when I am moved.

Rev 11:10 And those who dwell on the earth will rejoice over them, make merry, and send gifts to one another, because these two prophets tormented those who dwell on the earth.

Receive punishment for.

Ps 7:13 He also prepares for Himself instruments of death; He makes His arrows into fiery shafts.

2 Thess 1:6 since *it is* a righteous thing with God to repay with tribulation those who trouble you,

Actions illustrated.

Matt 21:33–39 "Hear another parable: There was a certain landowner who planted a vineyard and set a hedge around it, dug a winepress in it and built a tower. And he leased it to vinedressers and went into a far country. **34** Now when vintage-time drew near, he sent his servants to the vinedressers, that they might receive its fruit. **35** And the vinedressers took his servants, beat one, killed one, and stoned another. **36** Again he sent other servants, more than the first,

and they did likewise to them. **37** Then last of all he sent his son to them, saying, 'They will respect my son.' **38** But when the vinedressers saw the son, they said among themselves, 'This is the heir. Come, let us kill him and seize his inheritance.' **39** So they took him and cast *him* out of the vineyard and killed *him.*

Spirit of—exemplified by

Pharaoh, etc.

Ex 1:8–14 Now there arose a new king over Egypt, who did not know Joseph. **9** And he said to his people, "Look, the people of the children of Israel *are* more and mightier than we; **10** come, let us deal shrewdly with them, lest they multiply, and it happen, in the event of war, that they also join our enemies and fight against us, and *so* go up out of the land." **11** Therefore they set taskmasters over them to afflict them with their burdens. And they built for Pharaoh supply cities, Pithom and Raamses. **12** But the more they afflicted them, the more they multiplied and grew. And they were in dread of the children of Israel. **13** So the Egyptians made the children of Israel serve with rigor. **14** And they made their lives bitter with hard bondage—in mortar, in brick, and in all manner of service in the field. All their service in which they made them serve *was* with rigor.

Saul.

1 Sam 26:18 And he said, "Why does my lord thus pursue his servant? For what have I done, or what evil *is* in my hand?

Jezebel.

1 Kin 19:2 Then Jezebel sent a messenger to Elijah, saying, "So let the gods do *to me,* and more also, if I do not make your life as the life of one of them by tomorrow about this time."

Zedekiah, etc.

Jer 38:4–6 Therefore the princes said to the king, "Please, let this man be put to death, for thus he weakens the hands of the men of war who remain in this city, and the hands of all the people, by speaking such words to them. For this man does not seek the welfare of this people, but their harm." **5** Then Zedekiah the king said, "Look, he *is* in your hand. For the king can *do* nothing against you." **6** So they took Jeremiah and cast him into the dungeon of Malchiah the king's son, which *was* in the court of the prison, and they let Jeremiah down with ropes. And in the dungeon *there was* no water, but mire. So Jeremiah sank in the mire.

The Chaldeans. **Dan 3:8–30**

The Pharisees.

Matt 12:14 Then the Pharisees went out and plotted against Him, how they might destroy Him.

The Jews.

John 5:16 For this reason the Jews persecuted Jesus, and sought to kill Him, because He had done these things on the Sabbath.

1 Thess 2:15 who killed both the Lord Jesus and their own prophets, and have persecuted us; and they do not please God and are contrary to all men,

Herod.

Acts 12:1 Now about that time Herod the king stretched out *his* hand to harass some from the church.

The Gentiles.

Acts 14:5 And when a violent attempt was made by both the Gentiles and Jews, with their rulers, to abuse and stone them,

Paul.

Phil 3:6 concerning zeal, persecuting the church; concerning the righteousness which is in the law, blameless.

1 Tim 1:13 although I was formerly a blasphemer, a persecutor, and an insolent man; but I obtained mercy because I did *it* ignorantly in unbelief.

Suffering of—exemplified by

Micaiah.

1 Kin 22:27 and say, 'Thus says the king: "Put this *fellow* in prison, and feed him with bread of affliction and water of affliction, until I come in peace." ' "

David.

Ps 119:161 Princes persecute me without a cause, But my heart stands in awe of Your word.

Jeremiah.

Jer 32:2 For then the king of Babylon's army besieged Jerusalem, and Jeremiah the prophet was shut up in the court of the prison, which *was in* the king of Judah's house.

Daniel.

Dan 6:5–17 Then these men said, "We shall not find any charge against this Daniel unless we find *it* against him concerning the law of his God." 6 So these governors and satraps thronged before the king, and said thus to him: "King Darius, live forever! 7 All the governors of the kingdom, the administrators and satraps, the counselors and advisors, have consulted together to establish a royal statute and to make a firm decree, that whoever petitions any god or man for thirty days, except you, O king, shall be cast into the den of lions. 8 Now, O king, establish the decree and sign the writing, so that it cannot be changed, according to the law of the Medes and Persians, which does not alter." 9 Therefore King Darius signed the written decree. 10 Now when Daniel knew that the writing was signed, he went home. And in his upper room, with his windows open toward Jerusalem, he knelt down on his knees three times that day, and prayed and gave thanks before his God, as was his custom since early days. 11 Then these men assembled and found Daniel praying and making supplication before his God. 12 And they went before the king, and spoke concerning the king's decree: "Have you not signed a decree that every man who petitions any god or man within thirty days, except you, O king, shall be cast into the den of lions?" The king answered and said, "The thing *is* true, according to the law of the Medes and Persians, which does not alter." 13 So they answered and said before the king, "That Daniel, who is one of the captives from Judah, does not show due regard for you, O king, or for the decree that you have signed, but makes his petition three times a day." 14 And the king, when he heard *these* words, was greatly displeased with himself, and set *his* heart on Daniel to deliver him; and he labored till the going down of the sun to deliver him. 15 Then these men approached the king, and said to the king, "Know, O king, that *it is* the law of the

Medes and Persians that no decree or statute which the king establishes may be changed." 16 So the king gave the command, and they brought Daniel and cast *him* into the den of lions. *But* the king spoke, saying to Daniel, "Your God, whom you serve continually, He will deliver you." 17 Then a stone was brought and laid on the mouth of the den, and the king sealed it with his own signet ring and with the signets of his lords, that the purpose concerning Daniel might not be changed.

Peter, etc.

Acts 4:3 And they laid hands on them, and put *them* in custody until the next day, for it was already evening.

The apostles.

Acts 5:18 and laid their hands on the apostles and put them in the common prison.

The prophets.

Acts 7:52 Which of the prophets did your fathers not persecute? And they killed those who foretold the coming of the Just One, of whom you now have become the betrayers and murderers,

The church.

Acts 8:1 Now Saul was consenting to his death. At that time a great persecution arose against the church which was at Jerusalem; and they were all scattered throughout the regions of Judea and Samaria, except the apostles.

Paul and Barnabas.

Acts 13:50 But the Jews stirred up the devout and prominent women and the chief men of the city, raised up persecution against Paul and Barnabas, and expelled them from their region.

Paul and Silas.

Acts 16:23 And when they had laid many stripes on them, they threw *them* into prison, commanding the jailer to keep them securely.

The Jewish believers.

Heb 10:33 partly while you were made a spectacle both by reproaches and tribulations, and partly while you became companions of those who were so treated;

The believers of old.

Heb 11:36 Still others had trial of mockings and scourgings, yes, and of chains and imprisonment.

PERSEVERANCE

An evidence of salvation.

Job 17:9 Yet the righteous will hold to his way, And he who has clean hands will be stronger and stronger.

Prov 4:18 But the path of the just *is* like the shining sun, That shines ever brighter unto the perfect day.

John 8:31 Then Jesus said to those Jews who believed Him, "If you abide in My word, you are My disciples indeed.

Col 1:21–23 And you, who once were alienated and enemies in your mind by wicked works, yet now He has reconciled 22 in the body of His flesh through death, to present you holy, and blameless, and above reproach in His sight— 23 if indeed you continue in the faith, grounded and steadfast, and are not moved away from the hope of the gospel which you heard, which was preached to every creature under heaven, of which I, Paul, became a minister.

Heb 3:6 but Christ as a Son over His own house, whose house we are if we hold fast the confidence and the rejoicing of the hope firm to the end.

Heb 3:14 For we have become partakers of Christ if we hold the beginning of our confidence steadfast to the end,

To be manifested in

Seeking God.

1 Chr 16:11 Seek the LORD and His strength; Seek His face evermore!

Waiting upon God.

Hos 12:6 So you, by *the help of* your God, return; Observe mercy and justice, And wait on your God continually.

Prayer.

Rom 12:12 rejoicing in hope, patient in tribulation, continuing steadfastly in prayer;

Eph 6:18 praying always with all prayer and supplication in the Spirit, being watchful to this end with all perseverance and supplication for all the saints—

Doing good.

Rom 2:7 eternal life to those who by patient continuance in doing good seek for glory, honor, and immortality;

2 Thess 3:13 But *as for* you, brethren, do not grow weary in doing good.

Continuing in the faith.

Acts 14:22 strengthening the souls of the disciples, exhorting *them* to continue in the faith, and *saying*, "We must through many tribulations enter the kingdom of God."

Col 1:23 if indeed you continue in the faith, grounded and steadfast, and are not moved away from the hope of the gospel which you heard, which was preached to every creature under heaven, of which I, Paul, became a minister.

2 Tim 4:7 I have fought the good fight, I have finished the race, I have kept the faith.

Holding fast hope.

Heb 3:6 but Christ as a Son over His own house, whose house we are if we hold fast the confidence and the rejoicing of the hope firm to the end.

Maintained through

The power of God.

Ps 37:24 Though he fall, he shall not be utterly cast down; For the LORD upholds *him with* His hand.

Phil 1:6 being confident of this very thing, that He who has begun a good work in you will complete *it* until the day of Jesus Christ;

The power of Christ.

John 10:28 And I give them eternal life, and they shall never perish; neither shall anyone snatch them out of My hand.

The intercession of Christ.

Luke 22:31–32 And the Lord said, "Simon, Simon! Indeed, Satan has asked for you, that he may sift *you* as wheat. **32** But I have prayed for you, that your faith

should not fail; and when you have returned to *Me*, strengthen your brethren."

John 17:11 Now I am no longer in the world, but these are in the world, and I come to You. Holy Father, keep through Your name those whom You have given Me, that they may be one as We *are*.

The fear of God.

Jer 32:40 And I will make an everlasting covenant with them, that I will not turn away from doing them good; but I will put My fear in their hearts so that they will not depart from Me.

Faith.

1 Pet 1:5 who are kept by the power of God through faith for salvation ready to be revealed in the last time.

Leads to increase of knowledge.

John 8:31–32 Then Jesus said to those Jews who believed Him, "If you abide in My word, you are My disciples indeed. **32** And you shall know the truth, and the truth shall make you free."

In doing good

Leads to assurance of hope.

Heb 6:10–11 For God *is* not unjust to forget your work and labor of love which you have shown toward His name, *in that* you have ministered to the saints, and do minister. **11** And we desire that each one of you show the same diligence to the full assurance of hope until the end,

Is not in vain.

1 Cor 15:58 Therefore, my beloved brethren, be steadfast, immovable, always abounding in the work of the Lord, knowing that your labor is not in vain in the Lord.

Gal 6:9 And let us not grow weary while doing good, for in due season we shall reap if we do not lose heart.

Ministers should exhort to.

Acts 13:43 Now when the congregation had broken up, many of the Jews and devout proselytes followed Paul and Barnabas, who, speaking to them, persuaded them to continue in the grace of God.

Acts 14:22 strengthening the souls of the disciples, exhorting *them* to continue in the faith, and *saying*, "We must through many tribulations enter the kingdom of God."

Encouragement and promises to.

Matt 10:22 And you will be hated by all for My name's sake. But he who endures to the end will be saved.

Matt 24:13 But he who endures to the end shall be saved.

Heb 12:2–3 looking unto Jesus, the author and finisher of *our* faith, who for the joy that was set before Him endured the cross, despising the shame, and has sat down at the right hand of the throne of God. **3** For consider Him who endured such hostility from sinners against Himself, lest you become weary and discouraged in your souls.

Rev 2:26–28 And he who overcomes, and keeps My works until the end, to him I will give power over the nations— **27** 'He shall rule them with a rod of iron; They shall be dashed to pieces like the potter's *vessels'*— as I also have received from My Father; 28 and I will give him the morning star.

Blessedness of.

James 1:25 But he who looks into the perfect law of liberty and continues *in it,* and is not a forgetful hearer but a doer of the work, this one will be blessed in what he does.

Lack of,

Excludes from the benefits of the gospel.

Heb 6:4–6 For *it is* impossible for those who were once enlightened, and have tasted the heavenly gift, and have become partakers of the Holy Spirit, **5** and have tasted the good word of God and the powers of the age to come, **6** if they fall away, to renew them again to repentance, since they crucify again for themselves the Son of God, and put *Him* to an open shame.

Is punished.

John 15:6 If anyone does not abide in Me, he is cast out as a branch and is withered; and they gather them and throw *them* into the fire, and they are burned.

Rom 11:22 Therefore consider the goodness and severity of God: on those who fell, severity; but toward you, goodness, if you continue in *His* goodness. Otherwise you also will be cut off.

Illustrated.

Mark 4:5 Some fell on stony ground, where it did not have much earth; and immediately it sprang up because it had no depth of earth.

Mark 4:17 and they have no root in themselves, and so endure only for a time. Afterward, when tribulation or persecution arises for the word's sake, immediately they stumble.

PETER

Was Simon Bar-Jonah.

Matt 16:17 Jesus answered and said to him, "Blessed are you, Simon Bar-Jonah, for flesh and blood has not revealed *this* to you, but My Father who is in heaven.

John 21:15 So when they had eaten breakfast, Jesus said to Simon Peter, "Simon, *son* of Jonah, do you love Me more than these?" He said to Him, "Yes, Lord; You know that I love You." He said to him, "Feed My lambs."

Was fisherman with brother Andrew.

Matt 4:18 And Jesus, walking by the Sea of Galilee, saw two brothers, Simon called Peter, and Andrew his brother, casting a net into the sea; for they were fishermen.

Mark 1:16 And as He walked by the Sea of Galilee, He saw Simon and Andrew his brother casting a net into the sea; for they were fishermen.

Not highly educated.

Acts 4:13 Now when they saw the boldness of Peter and John, and perceived that they were uneducated and untrained men, they marveled. And they realized that they had been with Jesus.

Brought to Jesus.

John 1:40–42 One of the two who heard John *speak,* and followed Him, was Andrew, Simon Peter's brother. **41** He first found his own brother Simon, and said to

him, "We have found the Messiah" (which is translated, the Christ). **42** And he brought him to Jesus. Now when Jesus looked at him, He said, "You are Simon the son of Jonah. You shall be called Cephas" (which is translated, A Stone).

Called to be a disciple.

Matt 4:18–22 And Jesus, walking by the Sea of Galilee, saw two brothers, Simon called Peter, and Andrew his brother, casting a net into the sea; for they were fishermen. **19** Then He said to them, "Follow Me, and I will make you fishers of men." **20** They immediately left *their* nets and followed Him. **21** Going on from there, He saw two other brothers, James *the son* of Zebedee, and John his brother, in the boat with Zebedee their father, mending their nets. He called them, **22** and immediately they left the boat and their father, and followed Him.

Mark 1:16–18 And as He walked by the Sea of Galilee, He saw Simon and Andrew his brother casting a net into the sea; for they were fishermen. **17** Then Jesus said to them, "Follow Me, and I will make you become fishers of men." **18** They immediately left their nets and followed Him.

Walked on water.

Matt 14:28–33 And Peter answered Him and said, "Lord, if it is You, command me to come to You on the water." **29** So He said, "Come." And when Peter had come down out of the boat, he walked on the water to go to Jesus. **30** But when he saw that the wind *was* boisterous, he was afraid; and beginning to sink he cried out, saying, "Lord, save me!" **31** And immediately Jesus stretched out *His* hand and caught him, and said to him, "O you of little faith, why did you doubt?" **32** And when they got into the boat, the wind ceased. **33** Then those who were in the boat came and worshiped Him, saying, "Truly You are the Son of God."

Confessed deity of Christ.

Matt 16:13–17 When Jesus came into the region of Caesarea Philippi, He asked His disciples, saying, "Who do men say that I, the Son of Man, am?" **14** So they said, "Some *say* John the Baptist, some Elijah, and others Jeremiah or one of the prophets." **15** He said to them, "But who do you say that I am?" **16** Simon Peter answered and said, "You are the Christ, the Son of the living God." **17** Jesus answered and said to him, "Blessed are you, Simon Bar-Jonah, for flesh and blood has not revealed *this* to you, but My Father who is in heaven.

Mark 8:27–30 Now Jesus and His disciples went out to the towns of Caesarea Philippi; and on the road He asked His disciples, saying to them, "Who do men say that I am?" **28** So they answered, "John the Baptist; but some *say,* Elijah; and others, one of the prophets." **29** He said to them, "But who do you say that I am?" Peter answered and said to Him, "You are the Christ." **30** Then He strictly warned them that they should tell no one about Him.

Luke 9:18–21 And it happened, as He was alone praying, *that* His disciples joined Him, and He asked them, saying, "Who do the crowds say that I am?" **19** So they answered and said, "John the Baptist, but some *say* Elijah; and others *say* that one of the old prophets has risen again." **20** He said to them, "But who do you say that I am?" Peter answered and said, "The Christ of God." **21** And He strictly warned and commanded them to tell this to no one,

Witnessed Jesus' transfiguration.

Matt 17:1–8 Now after six days Jesus took Peter, James, and John his brother, led them up on a high mountain by themselves; **2** and He was transfigured before them. His face shone like the sun, and His clothes became as white as the light. **3** And behold, Moses and Elijah appeared to them, talking with Him. **4** Then Peter answered and said to Jesus, "Lord, it is good for us to be here; if You wish, let us make here three tabernacles: one for You, one for Moses, and one for Elijah." **5** While he was still speaking, behold, a bright cloud overshadowed them; and suddenly a voice came out of the cloud, saying, "This is My beloved Son, in whom I am well pleased. Hear Him!" **6** And when the disciples heard *it*, they fell on their faces and were greatly afraid. **7** But Jesus came and touched them and said, "Arise, and do not be afraid." **8** When they had lifted up their eyes, they saw no one but Jesus only.

2 Pet 1:17–18 For He received from God the Father honor and glory when such a voice came to Him from the Excellent Glory: "This is My beloved Son, in whom I am well pleased." **18** And we heard this voice which came from heaven when we were with Him on the holy mountain.

Cf. Mark 9:2–7; Luke 9:28–33

Did not want Jesus to wash his feet.

John 13:6–10 Then He came to Simon Peter. And *Peter* said to Him, "Lord, are You washing my feet?" **7** Jesus answered and said to him, "What I am doing you do not understand now, but you will know after this." **8** Peter said to Him, "You shall never wash my feet!" Jesus answered him, "If I do not wash you, you have no part with Me." **9** Simon Peter said to Him, "Lord, not my feet only, but also *my* hands and *my* head!" **10** Jesus said to him, "He who is bathed needs only to wash *his* feet, but is completely clean; and you are clean, but not all of you."

Denied Christ three times.

Matt 26:69–75 Now Peter sat outside in the courtyard. And a servant girl came to him, saying, "You also were with Jesus of Galilee." **70** But he denied it before *them* all, saying, "I do not know what you are saying." **71** And when he had gone out to the gateway, another *girl* saw him and said to those *who were* there, "This *fellow* also was with Jesus of Nazareth." **72** But again he denied with an oath, "I do not know the Man!" **73** And a little later those who stood by came up and said to Peter, "Surely you also are *one of* them, for your speech betrays you." **74** Then he began to curse and swear, *saying*, "I do not know the Man!" Immediately a rooster crowed. **75** And Peter remembered the word of Jesus who had said to him, "Before the rooster crows, you will deny Me three times." So he went out and wept bitterly.

Cf. Mark 14:66–72; Luke 22:55–62; John 18:15–18,25–27

Ran to Christ's tomb.

Luke 24:12 But Peter arose and ran to the tomb; and stooping down, he saw the linen cloths lying by

themselves; and he departed, marveling to himself at what had happened.

John 20:1–8 Now the first *day* of the week Mary Magdalene went to the tomb early, while it was still dark, and saw *that* the stone had been taken away from the tomb. **2** Then she ran and came to Simon Peter, and to the other disciple, whom Jesus loved, and said to them, "They have taken away the Lord out of the tomb, and we do not know where they have laid Him." **3** Peter therefore went out, and the other disciple, and were going to the tomb. **4** So they both ran together, and the other disciple outran Peter and came to the tomb first. **5** And he, stooping down and looking in, saw the linen cloths lying *there*; yet he did not go in. **6** Then Simon Peter came, following him, and went into the tomb; and he saw the linen cloths lying *there*, **7** and the handkerchief that had been around His head, not lying with the linen cloths, but folded together in a place by itself. **8** Then the other disciple, who came to the tomb first, went in also; and he saw and believed.

Called back by Christ; charged to ministry.

John 21:15–23 So when they had eaten breakfast, Jesus said to Simon Peter, "Simon, *son* of Jonah, do you love Me more than these?" He said to Him, "Yes, Lord; You know that I love You." He said to him, "Feed My lambs." **16** He said to him again a second time, "Simon, *son* of Jonah, do you love Me?" He said to Him, "Yes, Lord; You know that I love You." He said to him, "Tend My sheep." **17** He said to him the third time, "Simon, *son* of Jonah, do you love Me?" Peter was grieved because He said to him the third time, "Do you love Me?" And he said to Him, "Lord, You know all things; You know that I love You." Jesus said to him, "Feed My sheep. **18** Most assuredly, I say to you, when you were younger, you girded yourself and walked where you wished; but when you are old, you will stretch out your hands, and another will gird you and carry *you* where you do not wish." **19** This He spoke, signifying by what death he would glorify God. And when He had spoken this, He said to him, "Follow Me." **20** Then Peter, turning around, saw the disciple whom Jesus loved following, who also had leaned on His breast at the supper, and said, "Lord, who is the one who betrays You?" **21** Peter, seeing him, said to Jesus, "But Lord, what *about* this man?" **22** Jesus said to him, "If I will that he remain till I come, what *is that* to you? You follow Me." **23** Then this saying went out among the brethren that this disciple would not die. Yet Jesus did not say to him that he would not die, but, "If I will that he remain till I come, what *is that* to you?"

Led the apostles after Christ's ascension.

Acts 1:15–26 And in those days Peter stood up in the midst of the disciples (altogether the number of names was about a hundred and twenty), and said, **16** "Men *and* brethren, this Scripture had to be fulfilled, which the Holy Spirit spoke before by the mouth of David concerning Judas, who became a guide to those who arrested Jesus; **17** for he was numbered with us and obtained a part in this ministry." **18** (Now this man purchased a field with the wages of iniquity; and falling headlong, he burst open in the middle and all his entrails gushed out. **19** And it became known to all those dwelling in Jerusalem; so that field is called in their own language, Akel Dama, that is, Field of Blood.) **20** "For it is written in the Book of Psalms: *'Let his dwelling place be desolate, And let no one live in it'*; and, *'Let another take his office.'* **21** "Therefore, of these men who have accompanied us all the time that the Lord Jesus went in and out among us, **22** beginning from the baptism of John to that day when He was taken up from us, one of these must become a witness with us of His resurrection." **23** And they proposed two: Joseph called Barsabas, who was surnamed Justus, and Matthias. **24** And they prayed and said, "You, O Lord, who know the hearts of all, show which of these two You have chosen **25** to take part in this ministry and apostleship from which Judas by transgression fell, that he might go to his own place." **26** And they cast their lots, and the lot fell on Matthias. And he was numbered with the eleven apostles.

Preached on Pentecost. Acts 2:14–39
Healed lame man and others.

Acts 3:1–11 Now Peter and John went up together to the temple at the hour of prayer, the ninth *hour.* **2** And a certain man lame from his mother's womb was carried, whom they laid daily at the gate of the temple which is called Beautiful, to ask alms from those who entered the temple; **3** who, seeing Peter and John about to go into the temple, asked for alms. **4** And fixing his eyes on him, with John, Peter said, "Look at us." **5** So he gave them his attention, expecting to receive something from them. **6** Then Peter said, "Silver and gold I do not have, but what I do have I give you: In the name of Jesus Christ of Nazareth, rise up and walk." **7** And he took him by the right hand and lifted *him* up, and immediately his feet and ankle bones received strength. **8** So he, leaping up, stood and walked and entered the temple with them—walking, leaping, and praising God. **9** And all the people saw him walking and praising God. **10** Then they knew that it was he who sat begging alms at the Beautiful Gate of the temple; and they were filled with wonder and amazement at what had happened to him. **11** Now as the lame man who was healed held on to Peter and John, all the people ran together to them in the porch which is called Solomon's, greatly amazed.

Acts 5:14–16 And believers were increasingly added to the Lord, multitudes of both men and women, **15** so that they brought the sick out into the streets and laid *them* on beds and couches, that at least the shadow of Peter passing by might fall on some of them. **16** Also a multitude gathered from the surrounding cities to Jerusalem, bringing sick people and those who were tormented by unclean spirits, and they were all healed.

Arrested; preached to Jewish leaders.

Acts 4:1–12 Now as they spoke to the people, the priests, the captain of the temple, and the Sadducees came upon them, **2** being greatly disturbed that they taught the people and preached in Jesus the resurrection from the dead. **3** And they laid hands on them, and put *them* in custody until the next day, for it was already evening. **4** However, many of those who heard the word believed; and the number of the men came to be about five thousand. **5** And it came to pass, on the next day, that their rulers, elders, and scribes, **6** as well as Annas the high priest, Caiaphas, John, and Alexander, and as many as were of the family of the high priest, were gathered together at Jerusalem. **7** And when they had set them in the midst, they asked, "By what power or by what name have you done this?" **8** Then Peter, filled with the Holy Spirit, said to them, "Rulers of the people and elders of Israel: **9** If we this day are judged for a good deed *done* to a helpless man, by what means he has been made well, **10** let it be known to you all, and to all the people of Israel, that by the name of Jesus Christ of Nazareth, whom you crucified, whom God raised from the dead, by Him this man stands here before you whole. **11** This is the *'stone which was rejected by you builders, which has become the chief cornerstone.'* **12** Nor is there salvation in any other, for there is no other name under heaven given among men by which we must be saved."

Pronounced judgment on Ananias and Sapphira.

Acts 5:1–11 But a certain man named Ananias, with Sapphira his wife, sold a possession. **2** And he kept back *part* of the proceeds, his wife also being aware *of it,* and brought a certain part and laid *it* at the apostles' feet. **3** But Peter said, "Ananias, why has Satan filled your heart to lie to the Holy Spirit and keep back *part* of the price of the land for yourself? **4** While it remained, was it not your own? And after it was sold, was it not in your own control? Why have you conceived this thing in your heart? You have not lied to men but to God." **5** Then Ananias, hearing these words, fell down and breathed his last. So great fear came upon all those who heard these things. **6** And the young men arose and wrapped him up, carried *him* out, and buried *him.* **7** Now it was about three hours later when his wife came in, not knowing what had happened. **8** And Peter answered her, "Tell me whether you sold the land for so much?" She said, "Yes, for so much." **9** Then Peter said to her, "How is it that you have agreed together to test the Spirit of the Lord? Look, the feet of those who have buried your husband *are* at the door, and they will carry you out." **10** Then immediately she fell down at his feet and breathed her last. And the young men came in and found her dead, and carrying *her* out, buried *her* by her husband. **11** So great fear came upon all the church and upon all who heard these things.

Raised Dorcas from the dead.

Acts 9:36–43 At Joppa there was a certain disciple named Tabitha, which is translated Dorcas. This woman was full of good works and charitable deeds which she did. **37** But it happened in those days that she became sick and died. When they had washed her, they laid *her* in an upper room. **38** And since Lydda was near Joppa, and the disciples had heard that Peter was there, they sent two men to him, imploring *him* not to delay in coming to them. **39** Then Peter arose and went with them. When he had come, they brought *him* to the upper room. And all the widows stood by him weeping, showing the tunics and garments which Dorcas had made while she was with them. **40** But Peter put them all out, and knelt down and prayed. And turning to the body he said, "Tabitha, arise." And she opened her eyes, and when she saw Peter she sat up. **41** Then he gave her *his* hand and lifted her up; and when he had called the saints and widows, he presented her alive. **42** And it became known throughout all Joppa, and many believed on the Lord. **43** So it was that he stayed many days in Joppa with Simon, a tanner.

Eyes opened toward the Gentiles.

Acts 10:9–23 The next day, as they went on their journey and drew near the city, Peter went up on the housetop to pray, about the sixth hour. **10** Then he became very hungry and wanted to eat; but while they made ready, he fell into a trance **11** and saw heaven opened and an object like a great sheet bound at the four corners, descending to him and let down to the earth. **12** In it were all kinds of four-footed animals of the earth, wild beasts, creeping things, and birds of the air. **13** And a voice came to him, "Rise, Peter; kill and eat." **14** But Peter said, "Not so, Lord! For I have never eaten anything common or unclean." **15** And a voice *spoke* to him again the second time, "What God has cleansed you must not call common." **16** This was done three times. And the object was taken up into heaven again. **17** Now while Peter wondered within himself what this vision which he had seen meant, behold, the men who had been sent from Cornelius had made inquiry for Simon's house, and stood before the gate. **18** And they called and asked whether Simon, whose surname was Peter, was lodging there. **19** While Peter thought about the vision, the Spirit said to him, "Behold, three men are seeking you. **20** Arise therefore, go down and go with them, doubting nothing; for I have sent them." **21** Then Peter went down to the men who had been sent to him from Cornelius, and said, "Yes, I am he whom you seek. For what reason have you come?" **22** And they said, "Cornelius *the* centurion, a just man, one who fears God and has a good reputation among all the nation of the Jews, was divinely instructed by a holy angel to summon you to his house, and to hear words from you." **23** Then he invited them in and lodged *them*. On the next day Peter went away with them, and some brethren from Joppa accompanied him.

Preached to Cornelius' household.

Acts 10:34–48 Then Peter opened *his* mouth and said: "In truth I perceive that God shows no partiality. **35** But in every nation whoever fears Him and works righteousness is accepted by Him. **36** The word which *God* sent to the children of Israel, preaching peace through Jesus Christ—He is Lord of all— **37** that word you know, which was proclaimed throughout all Judea, and began from Galilee after the baptism which John preached: **38** how God anointed Jesus of Nazareth with the Holy Spirit and with power, who went about doing good and healing all who were oppressed by the devil, for God was with Him. **39** And we are witnesses of all things which He did both in the land of the Jews and in Jerusalem, whom they killed by hanging on a tree. **40** Him God raised up on the third day, and showed Him openly, **41** not to all the people, but to witnesses chosen before by God, *even* to us who ate and drank with Him after He arose from the dead. **42** And He commanded us to preach to the people, and to testify that it is He who was ordained by God *to be* Judge

of the living and the dead. **43** To Him all the prophets witness that, through His name, whoever believes in Him will receive remission of sins." **44** While Peter was still speaking these words, the Holy Spirit fell upon all those who heard the word. **45** And those of the circumcision who believed were astonished, as many as came with Peter, because the gift of the Holy Spirit had been poured out on the Gentiles also. **46** For they heard them speak with tongues and magnify God. Then Peter answered, **47** "Can anyone forbid water, that these should not be baptized who have received the Holy Spirit just as we *have?*" **48** And he commanded them to be baptized in the name of the Lord. Then they asked him to stay a few days.

Delivered from prison.

Acts 12:3–19 And because he saw that it pleased the Jews, he proceeded further to seize Peter also. Now it was *during* the Days of Unleavened Bread. **4** So when he had arrested him, he put *him* in prison, and delivered *him* to four squads of soldiers to keep him, intending to bring him before the people after Passover. **5** Peter was therefore kept in prison, but constant prayer was offered to God for him by the church. **6** And when Herod was about to bring him out, that night Peter was sleeping, bound with two chains between two soldiers; and the guards before the door were keeping the prison. **7** Now behold, an angel of the Lord stood by *him,* and a light shone in the prison; and he struck Peter on the side and raised him up, saying, "Arise quickly!" And his chains fell off *his* hands. **8** Then the angel said to him, "Gird yourself and tie on your sandals"; and so he did. And he said to him, "Put on your garment and follow me." **9** So he went out and followed him, and did not know that what was done by the angel was real, but thought he was seeing a vision. **10** When they were past the first and the second guard posts, they came to the iron gate that leads to the city, which opened to them of its own accord; and they went out and went down one street, and immediately the angel departed from him. **11** And when Peter had come to himself, he said, "Now I know for certain that the Lord has sent His angel, and has delivered me from the hand of Herod and *from* all the expectation of the Jewish people." **12** So, when he had considered *this,* he came to the house of Mary, the mother of John whose surname was Mark, where many were gathered together praying. **13** And as Peter knocked at the door of the gate, a girl named Rhoda came to answer. **14** When she recognized Peter's voice, because of *her* gladness she did not open the gate, but ran in and announced that Peter stood before the gate. **15** But they said to her, "You are beside yourself!" Yet she kept insisting that it was so. So they said, "It is his angel." **16** Now Peter continued knocking; and when they opened *the door* and saw him, they were astonished. **17** But motioning to them with his hand to keep silent, he declared to them how the Lord had brought him out of the prison. And he said, "Go, tell these things to James and to the brethren." And he departed and went to another place. **18** Then, as soon as it was day, there was no small stir among the soldiers about what had become of Peter. **19** But when Herod had searched for him and not found him, he examined the guards and commanded that *they* should be put to death. And he went down from Judea to Caesarea, and stayed *there*.

Attended Jerusalem Council.

Acts 15:7–14 And when there had been much dispute, Peter rose up and said to them: "Men and brethren, you know that a good while ago God chose among us, that by my mouth the Gentiles should hear the word of the gospel and believe. **8** So God, who knows the heart, acknowledged them by giving them the Holy Spirit, just as *He did* to us, **9** and made no distinction between us and them, purifying their hearts by faith. **10** Now therefore, why do you test God by putting a yoke on the neck of the disciples which neither our fathers nor we were able to bear? **11** But we believe that through the grace of the Lord Jesus Christ we shall be saved in the same manner as they." **12** Then all the multitude kept silent and listened to Barnabas and Paul declaring how many miracles and wonders God had worked through them among the Gentiles. **13** And after they had become silent, James answered, saying, "Men *and* brethren, listen to me: **14** Simon has declared how God at the first visited the Gentiles to take out of them a people for His name.

Interacted with Paul.

Acts 9:26–28 And when Saul had come to Jerusalem, he tried to join the disciples; but they were all afraid of him, and did not believe that he was a disciple. **27** But Barnabas took him and brought *him* to the apostles. And he declared to them how he had seen the Lord on the road, and that He had spoken to him, and how he had preached boldly at Damascus in the name of Jesus. **28** So he was with them at Jerusalem, coming in and going out.

Gal 1:17–18 nor did I go up to Jerusalem to those *who were* apostles before me; but I went to Arabia, and returned again to Damascus. **18** Then after three years I went up to Jerusalem to see Peter, and remained with him fifteen days.

Gal 2:14 But when I saw that they were not straightforward about the truth of the gospel, I said to Peter before *them* all, "If you, being a Jew, live in the manner of Gentiles and not as the Jews, why do you compel Gentiles to live as Jews?

PHARISEES, THE

A sect of the Jews.

Acts 15:5 But some of the sect of the Pharisees who believed rose up, saying, "It is necessary to circumcise them, and to command *them* to keep the law of Moses."

Acts 26:5 They knew me from the first, if they were willing to testify, that according to the strictest sect of our religion I lived a Pharisee.

By descent, especially esteemed.

Acts 23:6 But when Paul perceived that one part were Sadducees and the other Pharisees, he cried out in the council, "Men *and* brethren, I am a Pharisee, the son of a Pharisee; concerning the hope and resurrection of the dead I am being judged!"

Character of,

Zealous of the law.

Acts 15:5 But some of the sect of the Pharisees who be-

lieved rose up, saying, "It is necessary to circumcise them, and to command *them* to keep the law of Moses."

Phil 3:5 circumcised the eighth day, of the stock of Israel, *of* the tribe of Benjamin, a Hebrew of the Hebrews; concerning the law, a Pharisee;

Zealous of tradition.

Mark 7:3 For the Pharisees and all the Jews do not eat unless they wash *their* hands in a special way, holding the tradition of the elders.

Mark 7:5–8 Then the Pharisees and scribes asked Him, "Why do Your disciples not walk according to the tradition of the elders, but eat bread with unwashed hands?" **6** He answered and said to them, "Well did Isaiah prophesy of you hypocrites, as it is written: *'This people honors Me with their lips, But their heart is far from Me.* **7** *And in vain they worship Me, Teaching as doctrines the commandments of men.'* **8** For laying aside the commandment of God, you hold the tradition of men—the washing of pitchers and cups, and many other such things you do."

Gal 1:14 And I advanced in Judaism beyond many of my contemporaries in my own nation, being more exceedingly zealous for the traditions of my fathers.

Outwardly moral.

Luke 18:11 The Pharisee stood and prayed thus with himself, 'God, I thank You that I am not like other men—extortioners, unjust, adulterers, or even as this tax collector.

Phil 3:5–6 circumcised the eighth day, of the stock of Israel, *of* the tribe of Benjamin, a Hebrew of the Hebrews; concerning the law, a Pharisee; **6** concerning zeal, persecuting the church; concerning the righteousness which is in the law, blameless.

Rigid in fasting.

Luke 5:33 Then they said to Him, "Why do the disciples of John fast often and make prayers, and likewise those of the Pharisees, but Yours eat and drink?"

Luke 18:12 I fast twice a week; I give tithes of all that I possess.'

Active in proselytizing.

Matt 23:15 "Woe to you, scribes and Pharisees, hypocrites! For you travel land and sea to win one proselyte, and when he is won, you make him twice as much a son of hell as yourselves.

Self-righteous.

Luke 16:15 And He said to them, "You are those who justify yourselves before men, but God knows your hearts. For what is highly esteemed among men is an abomination in the sight of God.

Luke 18:9 Also He spoke this parable to some who trusted in themselves that they were righteous, and despised others:

Avaricious.

Matt 23:14 Woe to you, scribes and Pharisees, hypocrites! For you devour widows' houses, and for a pretense make long prayers. Therefore you will receive greater condemnation.

Luke 16:14 Now the Pharisees, who were lovers of money, also heard all these things, and they derided Him.

Ambitious of precedence.

Matt 23:6 They love the best places at feasts, the best seats in the synagogues,

Fond of public salutations and titles.

Matt 23:7–10 greetings in the marketplaces, and to be called by men, 'Rabbi, Rabbi.' 8 But you, do not be called 'Rabbi'; for One is your Teacher, the Christ, and you are all brethren. 9 Do not call anyone on earth your father; for One is your Father, He who is in heaven. 10 And do not be called teachers; for One is your Teacher, the Christ.

Particular in paying all dues.

Matt 23:23 "Woe to you, scribes and Pharisees, hypocrites! For you pay tithe of mint and anise and cummin, and have neglected the weightier *matters* of the law: justice and mercy and faith. These you ought to have done, without leaving the others undone.

Oppressive.

Matt 23:4 For they bind heavy burdens, hard to bear, and lay *them* on men's shoulders; but they *themselves* will not move them with one of their fingers.

Cruel in persecuting.

Acts 9:1–2 Then Saul, still breathing threats and murder against the disciples of the Lord, went to the high priest 2 and asked letters from him to the synagogues of Damascus, so that if he found any who were of the Way, whether men or women, he might bring them bound to Jerusalem.

Believed in the resurrection, etc.

Acts 23:8 For Sadducees say that there is no resurrection—and no angel or spirit; but the Pharisees confess both.

Made broad their phylacteries.

Matt 23:5 But all their works they do to be seen by men. They make their phylacteries broad and enlarge the borders of their garments.

Their opinions, a standard for others.

John 7:48 Have any of the rulers or the Pharisees believed in Him?

Many leading Jews were.

John 1:19 Now this is the testimony of John, when the Jews sent priests and Levites from Jerusalem to ask him, "Who are you?"

John 1:24 Now those who were sent were from the Pharisees.

John 3:1 There was a man of the Pharisees named Nicodemus, a ruler of the Jews.

Acts 5:34 Then one in the council stood up, a Pharisee named Gamaliel, a teacher of the law held in respect by all the people, and commanded them to put the apostles outside for a little while.

Acts 23:9 Then there arose a loud outcry. And the scribes of the Pharisees' party arose and protested, saying, "We find no evil in this man; but if a spirit or an angel has spoken to him, let us not fight against God."

Had disciples.

Luke 5:33 Then they said to Him, "Why do the disciples of John fast often and make prayers, and likewise those of the Pharisees, but Yours eat and drink?"

Acts 22:3 "I am indeed a Jew, born in Tarsus of Cilicia, but brought up in this city at the feet of Gamaliel, taught according to the strictness of our fathers' law, and was zealous toward God as you all are today.

Considered John's baptism.

Matt 3:7 But when he saw many of the Pharisees and Sadducees coming to his baptism, he said to them, "Brood of vipers! Who warned you to flee from the wrath to come?

Luke 7:30 But the Pharisees and lawyers rejected the will of God for themselves, not having been baptized by him.

Relationship with Christ

They often invited Him to eat with them.

Luke 7:36 Then one of the Pharisees asked Him to eat with him. And He went to the Pharisee's house, and sat down to eat.

Luke 11:37 And as He spoke, a certain Pharisee asked Him to dine with him. So He went in and sat down to eat.

They condemned Him, for associating with sinners.

Matt 9:11 And when the Pharisees saw *it*, they said to His disciples, "Why does your Teacher eat with tax collectors and sinners?"

Luke 7:39 Now when the Pharisee who had invited Him saw *this*, he spoke to himself, saying, "This Man, if He were a prophet, would know who and what manner of woman *this is* who is touching Him, for she is a sinner."

Luke 15:1–2 Then all the tax collectors and the sinners drew near to Him to hear Him. 2 And the Pharisees and scribes complained, saying, "This Man receives sinners and eats with them."

They asked Him for signs.

Matt 12:38 Then some of the scribes and Pharisees answered, saying, "Teacher, we want to see a sign from You."

Matt 16:1 Then the Pharisees and Sadducees came, and testing Him asked that He would show them a sign from heaven.

They tested Him, with questions about the law.

Matt 19:3 The Pharisees also came to Him, testing Him, and saying to Him, "Is it lawful for a man to divorce his wife for *just* any reason?"

Matt 22:15–16 Then the Pharisees went and plotted how they might entangle Him in *His* talk. 16 And they sent to Him their disciples with the Herodians, saying, "Teacher, we know that You are true, and teach the way of God in truth; nor do You care about anyone, for You do not regard the person of men.

Matt 22:35 Then one of them, a lawyer, asked Him a *question*, testing Him, and saying,

They watched Him, for evil.

Luke 6:7 So the scribes and Pharisees watched Him closely, whether He would heal on the Sabbath, that they might find an accusation against Him.

He offended them by His doctrine.

Matt 15:12 Then His disciples came and said to Him, "Do You know that the Pharisees were offended when they heard this saying?"

Matt 21:45 Now when the chief priests and Pharisees

heard His parables, they perceived that He was speaking of them.

Luke 16:14 Now the Pharisees, who were lovers of money, also heard all these things, and they derided Him.

He declared their doctrine and practice insufficient and hypocritical.

Matt 5:20 For I say to you, that unless your righteousness exceeds *the righteousness* of the scribes and Pharisees, you will by no means enter the kingdom of heaven.

Matt 16:6 Then Jesus said to them, "Take heed and beware of the leaven of the Pharisees and the Sadducees."

Matt 16:11–12 How is it you do not understand that I did not speak to you concerning bread?—*but* to beware of the leaven of the Pharisees and Sadducees." **12** Then they understood that He did not tell *them* to beware of the leaven of bread, but of the doctrine of the Pharisees and Sadducees.

Luke 12:1 In the meantime, when an innumerable multitude of people had gathered together, so that they trampled one another, He began to say to His disciples first *of all*, "Beware of the leaven of the Pharisees, which is hypocrisy.

He denounced them.

Matt 23:13–33 "But woe to you, scribes and Pharisees, hypocrites! For you shut up the kingdom of heaven against men; for you neither go in *yourselves*, nor do you allow those who are entering to go in. **14** Woe to you, scribes and Pharisees, hypocrites! For you devour widows' houses, and for a pretense make long prayers. Therefore you will receive greater condemnation. **15** "Woe to you, scribes and Pharisees, hypocrites! For you travel land and sea to win one proselyte, and when he is won, you make him twice as much a son of hell as yourselves. **16** "Woe to you, blind guides, who say, 'Whoever swears by the temple, it is nothing; but whoever swears by the gold of the temple, he is obliged *to perform it*.' **17** Fools and blind! For which is greater, the gold or the temple that sanctifies the gold? **18** And, 'Whoever swears by the altar, it is nothing; but whoever swears by the gift that is on it, he is obliged *to perform it*.' **19** Fools and blind! For which is greater, the gift or the altar that sanctifies the gift? **20** Therefore he who swears by the altar, swears by it and by all things on it. **21** He who swears by the temple, swears by it and by Him who dwells in it. **22** And he who swears by heaven, swears by the throne of God and by Him who sits on it. **23** "Woe to you, scribes and Pharisees, hypocrites! For you pay tithe of mint and anise and cummin, and have neglected the weightier *matters* of the law: justice and mercy and faith. These you ought to have done, without leaving the others undone. **24** Blind guides, who strain out a gnat and swallow a camel! **25** "Woe to you, scribes and Pharisees, hypocrites! For you cleanse the outside of the cup and dish, but inside they are full of extortion and self-indulgence. **26** Blind Pharisee, first cleanse the inside of the cup and dish, that the outside of them may be clean also. **27** "Woe to you, scribes and Pharisees, hypocrites! For you are like whitewashed tombs which indeed appear beautiful outwardly, but inside are full of dead *men's* bones and all uncleanness. **28** Even so you also outwardly appear righteous to men, but inside you are full of hypocrisy and lawlessness. **29** "Woe to you, scribes and Pharisees, hypocrites! Because you build the tombs of the prophets and adorn the monuments of the righteous, **30** and say, 'If we had lived in the days of our fathers, we would not have been partakers with them in the blood of the prophets.' **31** "Therefore you are witnesses against yourselves that you are sons of those who murdered the prophets. **32** Fill up, then, the measure of your fathers' *guilt*. **33** Serpents, brood of vipers! How can you escape the condemnation of hell?

Matt 23:39 for I say to you, you shall see Me no more till you say, '*Blessed is He who comes in the name of the* LORD!'"

Luke 11:44 Woe to you, scribes and Pharisees, hypocrites! For you are like graves which are not seen, and the men who walk over *them* are not aware *of them*."

He left Judea temporarily because of them.

John 4:1–3 Therefore, when the Lord knew that the Pharisees had heard that Jesus made and baptized more disciples than John **2** (though Jesus Himself did not baptize, but His disciples), **3** He left Judea and departed again to Galilee.

They attributed His miracles to Satan's power.

Matt 9:34 But the Pharisees said, "He casts out demons by the ruler of the demons."

Matt 12:24 Now when the Pharisees heard *it* they said, "This *fellow* does not cast out demons except by Beelzebub, the ruler of the demons."

They plotted against Him.

Matt 12:14 Then the Pharisees went out and plotted against Him, how they might destroy Him.

Matt 21:46 But when they sought to lay hands on Him, they feared the multitudes, because they took Him for a prophet.

John 7:32 The Pharisees heard the crowd murmuring these things concerning Him, and the Pharisees and the chief priests sent officers to take Him.

John 7:45 Then the officers came to the chief priests and Pharisees, who said to them, "Why have you not brought Him?"

John 11:47 Then the chief priests and the Pharisees gathered a council and said, "What shall we do? For this Man works many signs.

John 11:53 Then, from that day on, they plotted to put Him to death.

John 11:57 Now both the chief priests and the Pharisees had given a command, that if anyone knew where He was, he should report *it*, that they might seize Him.

PHILISTINES, THE

Descended from Casluhim.

Gen 10:13–14 Mizraim begot Ludim, Anamim, Lehabim, Naphtuhim, **14** Pathrusim, and Casluhim (from whom came the Philistines and Caphtorim).

Originally dwelt in the land of Caphtor.

Jer 47:4 Because of the day that comes to plunder all the Philistines, To cut off from Tyre and Sidon every helper who remains; For the LORD shall plunder the Philistines, The remnant of the country of Caphtor.

Amos 9:7 "*Are* you not like the people of Ethiopia to Me, O children of Israel?" says the LORD. "Did I not bring up Israel from the land of Egypt, The Philistines from Caphtor, And the Syrians from Kir?

Conquered the west coast of Canaan from the Avim.

Deut 2:23 And the Avim, who dwelt in villages as far as Gaza—the Caphtorim, who came from Caphtor, destroyed them and dwelt in their place.)

Called

The Caphtorim.

Deut 2:23 And the Avim, who dwelt in villages as far as Gaza—the Caphtorim, who came from Caphtor, destroyed them and dwelt in their place.)

The Cherethites.

1 Sam 30:14 We made an invasion of the southern *area* of the Cherethites, in the *territory* which *belongs* to Judah, and of the southern *area* of Caleb; and we burned Ziklag with fire."

Zeph 2:5 Woe to the inhabitants of the seacoast, The nation of the Cherethites! The word of the LORD *is* against you, O Canaan, land of the Philistines: "I will destroy you; So there shall be no inhabitant."

Country of

Called Philistia.

Ps 87:4 "I will make mention of Rahab and Babylon to those who know Me; Behold, O Philistia and Tyre, with Ethiopia: 'This *one* was born there.'"

Ps 108:9 Moab *is* My washpot; Over Edom I will cast My shoe; Over Philistia I will triumph."

Divided into five lordships.

Josh 13:3 from Sihor, which *is* east of Egypt, as far as the border of Ekron northward (*which* is counted as Canaanite); the five lords of the Philistines—the Gazites, the Ashdodites, the Ashkelonites, the Gittites, and the Ekronites; also the Avites;

Judg 3:3 *namely,* five lords of the Philistines, all the Canaanites, the Sidonians, and the Hivites who dwelt in Mount Lebanon, from Mount Baal Hermon to the entrance of Hamath.

1 Sam 6:16 So when the five lords of the Philistines had seen *it,* they returned to Ekron the same day.

Had many flourishing cities.

1 Sam 6:17 These *are* the golden tumors which the Philistines returned *as* a trespass offering to the LORD: one for Ashdod, one for Gaza, one for Ashkelon, one for Gath, one for Ekron;

Given by God to the Israelites.

Josh 13:2–3 This is the land that yet remains: all the territory of the Philistines and all *that of* the Geshurites, 3 from Sihor, which *is* east of Egypt, as far as the border of Ekron northward (*which* is counted as Canaanite); the five lords of the Philistines—the Gazites, the Ashdodites, the Ashkelonites, the Gittites, and the Ekronites; also the Avites;

Josh 15:45 Ekron, with its towns and villages;

Josh 15:47 Ashdod with its towns and villages, Gaza with its towns and villages—as far as the Brook of Egypt and the Great Sea with *its* coastline.

Governed by kings in the patriarchal age.

Gen 21:22 And it came to pass at that time that Abimelech and Phichol, the commander of his army, spoke to Abraham, saying, "God *is* with you in all that you do.

Gen 21:34 And Abraham stayed in the land of the Philistines many days.

Gen 26:8 Now it came to pass, when he had been there a long time, that Abimelech king of the Philistines looked through a window, and saw, and there was Isaac, showing endearment to Rebekah his wife.

Character of,

Proud.

Zech 9:6 "A mixed race shall settle in Ashdod, And I will cut off the pride of the Philistines.

Idolatrous.

Judg 16:23 Now the lords of the Philistines gathered together to offer a great sacrifice to Dagon their god, and to rejoice. And they said: "Our god has delivered into our hands Samson our enemy!"

1 Sam 5:2 When the Philistines took the ark of God, they brought it into the house of Dagon and set it by Dagon.

Superstitious.

Is 2:6 For You have forsaken Your people, the house of Jacob, Because they are filled with eastern ways; They *are* soothsayers like the Philistines, And they are pleased with the children of foreigners.

Warlike.

1 Sam 17:1 Now the Philistines gathered their armies together to battle, and were gathered at Sochoh, which *belongs* to Judah; they encamped between Sochoh and Azekah, in Ephes Dammim.

1 Sam 28:1 Now it happened in those days that the Philistines gathered their armies together for war, to fight with Israel. And Achish said to David, "You assuredly know that you will go out with me to battle, you and your men."

Men of great strength and stature among.

1 Sam 17:4–7 And a champion went out from the camp of the Philistines, named Goliath, from Gath, whose height *was* six cubits and a span. 5 *He had* a bronze helmet on his head, and he *was* armed with a coat of mail, and the weight of the coat *was* five thousand shekels of bronze. 6 And *he had* bronze armor on his legs and a bronze javelin between his shoulders. 7 Now the staff of his spear *was* like a weaver's beam, and his iron spearhead *weighed* six hundred shekels; and a shield-bearer went before him.

2 Sam 21:16 Then Ishbi-Benob, who *was* one of the sons of the giant, the weight of whose bronze spear *was* three hundred *shekels,* who was bearing a new *sword,* thought he could kill David.

2 Sam 21:18–20 Now it happened afterward that there was again a battle with the Philistines at Gob. Then Sibbechai the Hushathite killed Saph, who *was* one of the sons of the giant. 19 Again there was war at Gob with the Philistines, where Elhanan the son of Jaare-Oregim the Bethlehemite killed *the brother of* Goliath the Gittite, the shaft of whose spear *was* like a weaver's beam. 20 Yet again there was war at Gath, where there was a man of *great* stature, who had six fingers on each hand and six toes on each foot, twenty-four in number; and he also was born to the giant.

Some of, left to test and oppress Israel.

Judg 3:1–3 Now these *are* the nations which the LORD left, that He might test Israel by them, *that is*, all who had not known any of the wars in Canaan **2** (*this was* only so that the generations of the children of Israel might be taught to know war, at least those who had not formerly known it), **3** *namely*, five lords of the Philistines, all the Canaanites, the Sidonians, and the Hivites who dwelt in Mount Lebanon, from Mount Baal Hermon to the entrance of Hamath.

Judg 10:7–8 So the anger of the LORD was hot against Israel; and He sold them into the hands of the Philistines and into the hands of the people of Ammon. **8** From that year they harassed and oppressed the children of Israel for eighteen years—all the children of Israel who *were* on the other side of the Jordan in the land of the Amorites, in Gilead.

Judg 13:1 Again the children of Israel did evil in the sight of the LORD, and the LORD delivered them into the hand of the Philistines for forty years.

Ps 83:7 Gebal, Ammon, and Amalek; Philistia with the inhabitants of Tyre;

Is 9:11–12 Therefore the LORD shall set up The adversaries of Rezin against him, And spur his enemies on, **12** The Syrians before and the Philistines behind; And they shall devour Israel with an open mouth. For all this His anger is not turned away, But His hand *is* stretched out still.

Shamgar slew six hundred of.

Judg 3:31 After him was Shamgar the son of Anath, who killed six hundred men of the Philistines with an ox goad; and he also delivered Israel.

Samson

Promised as a deliverer from.

Judg 13:5 For behold, you shall conceive and bear a son. And no razor shall come upon his head, for the child shall be a Nazirite to God from the womb; and he shall begin to deliver Israel out of the hand of the Philistines."

Intermarried with.

Judg 14:1 Now Samson went down to Timnah, and saw a woman in Timnah of the daughters of the Philistines.

Judg 14:10 So his father went down to the woman. And Samson gave a feast there, for young men used to do so.

Killed thirty, near Askelon.

Judg 14:19 Then the Spirit of the LORD came upon him mightily, and he went down to Ashkelon and killed thirty of their men, took their apparel, and gave the changes *of clothing* to those who had explained the riddle. So his anger was aroused, and he went back up to his father's house.

Burned their vineyards, etc.

Judg 15:3–5 And Samson said to them, "This time I shall be blameless regarding the Philistines if I harm them!" **4** Then Samson went and caught three hundred foxes; and he took torches, turned *the foxes* tail to tail, and put a torch between each pair of tails. **5** When he had set the torches on fire, he let *the foxes* go into the standing grain of the Philistines, and burned up both the shocks and the standing grain, as well as the vineyards *and* olive groves.

Killed many, for burning his wife.

Judg 15:7–8 Samson said to them, "Since you would do a thing like this, I will surely take revenge on you, and after that I will cease." **8** So he attacked them hip and thigh with a great slaughter; then he went down and dwelt in the cleft of the rock of Etam.

Killed a thousand, with the jawbone of a donkey.

Judg 15:15–16 He found a fresh jawbone of a donkey, reached out his hand and took it, and killed a thousand men with it. **16** Then Samson said: "With the jawbone of a donkey, Heaps upon heaps, With the jawbone of a donkey I have slain a thousand men!"

Blinded and imprisoned by.

Judg 16:21 Then the Philistines took him and put out his eyes, and brought him down to Gaza. They bound him with bronze fetters, and he became a grinder in the prison.

Pulled down their house of Dagon at his death.

Judg 16:29–30 And Samson took hold of the two middle pillars which supported the temple, and he braced himself against them, one on his right and the other on his left. **30** Then Samson said, "Let me die with the Philistines!" And he pushed with *all his* might, and the temple fell on the lords and all the people who *were* in it. So the dead that he killed at his death were more than he had killed in his life.

Defeated Israel at Ebenezer.

1 Sam 4:1–2 And the word of Samuel came to all Israel. Now Israel went out to battle against the Philistines, and encamped beside Ebenezer; and the Philistines encamped in Aphek. **2** Then the Philistines put themselves in battle array against Israel. And when they joined battle, Israel was defeated by the Philistines, who killed about four thousand men of the army in the field.

Defeated Israel and took the ark.

1 Sam 4:3–11 And when the people had come into the camp, the elders of Israel said, "Why has the LORD defeated us today before the Philistines? Let us bring the ark of the covenant of the LORD from Shiloh to us, that when it comes among us it may save us from the hand of our enemies." **4** So the people sent to Shiloh, that they might bring from there the ark of the covenant of the LORD of hosts, who dwells *between* the cherubim. And the two sons of Eli, Hophni and Phinehas, *were* there with the ark of the covenant of God. **5** And when the ark of the covenant of the LORD came into the camp, all Israel shouted so loudly that the earth shook. **6** Now when the Philistines heard the noise of the shout, they said, "What *does* the sound of this great shout in the camp of the Hebrews *mean?*" Then they understood that the ark of the LORD had come into the camp. **7** So the Philistines were afraid, for they said, "God has come into the camp!" And they said, "Woe to us! For such a thing has never happened before. **8** Woe to us! Who will deliver us from the hand of these mighty gods? These *are* the gods who struck the Egyptians with all the plagues in the wilderness. **9** Be strong and conduct yourselves like men, you Philistines, that you do not become servants of the Hebrews, as they have been to you. Conduct yourselves like men, and fight!" 10 So the Philistines fought, and Israel was defeated, and every man fled to his tent. There was a very great slaughter, and there fell of Israel thirty thousand foot soldiers. 11 Also the ark of God was captured; and the two sons of Eli, Hophni and Phinehas, died.

Put the ark into Dagon's house.

1 Sam 5:1–4 Then the Philistines took the ark of God and brought it from Ebenezer to Ashdod. **2** When the Philistines took the ark of God, they brought it into the house of Dagon and set it by Dagon. **3** And when the people of Ashdod arose early in the morning, there was Dagon, fallen on its face to the earth before the ark of the LORD. So they took Dagon and set it in its place again. **4** And when they arose early the next morning, there was Dagon, fallen on its face to the ground before the ark of the LORD. The head of Dagon and both the palms of its hands *were* broken off on the threshold; only Dagon's torso was left of it.

Plagued for retaining the ark.

1 Sam 5:6–12 But the hand of the LORD was heavy on the people of Ashdod, and He ravaged them and struck them with tumors, *both* Ashdod and its territory. **7** And when the men of Ashdod saw how *it was*, they said, "The ark of the God of Israel must not remain with us, for His hand is harsh toward us and Dagon our god." **8** Therefore they sent and gathered to themselves all the lords of the Philistines, and said, "What shall we do with the ark of the God of Israel?" And they answered, "Let the ark of the God of Israel be carried away to Gath." So they carried the ark of the God of Israel away. **9** So it was, after they had carried it away, that the hand of the LORD was against the city with a very great destruction; and He struck the men of the city, both small and great, and tumors broke out on them. **10** Therefore they sent the ark of God to Ekron. So it was, as the ark of God came to Ekron, that the Ekronites cried out, saying, "They have brought the ark of the God of Israel to us, to kill us and our people!" **11** So they sent and gathered together all the lords of the Philistines, and said, "Send away the ark of the God of Israel, and let it go back to its own place, so that it does not kill us and our people." For there was a deadly destruction throughout all the city; the hand of God was very heavy there. **12** And the men who did not die were stricken with the tumors, and the cry of the city went up to heaven.

Sent back the ark and were healed. 1 Sam 6:1–18
Miraculously routed at Mizpah.

1 Sam 7:7–14 Now when the Philistines heard that the children of Israel had gathered together at Mizpah, the lords of the Philistines went up against Israel. And when the children of Israel heard *of it*, they were afraid of the Philistines. **8** So the children of Israel said to Samuel, "Do not cease to cry out to the LORD our God for us, that He may save us from the hand of the Philistines." **9** And Samuel took a suckling lamb and offered *it as* a whole burnt offering to the LORD. Then Samuel cried out to the LORD for Israel, and the LORD answered him. **10** Now as Samuel was offering up the burnt offering, the Philistines drew near to battle against Israel. But the LORD thundered with a loud thunder upon the Philistines that day, and so con-

fused them that they were overcome before Israel. **11** And the men of Israel went out of Mizpah and pursued the Philistines, and drove them back as far as below Beth Car. **12** Then Samuel took a stone and set *it* up between Mizpah and Shen, and called its name Ebenezer, saying, "Thus far the LORD has helped us." **13** So the Philistines were subdued, and they did not come anymore into the territory of Israel. And the hand of the LORD was against the Philistines all the days of Samuel. **14** Then the cities which the Philistines had taken from Israel were restored to Israel, from Ekron to Gath; and Israel recovered its territory from the hands of the Philistines. Also there was peace between Israel and the Amorites.

Jonathan smote a garrison of,

At Geba.

1 Sam 13:3–4 And Jonathan attacked the garrison of the Philistines that *was* in Geba, and the Philistines heard *of it*. Then Saul blew the trumpet throughout all the land, saying, "Let the Hebrews hear!" **4** Now all Israel heard it said *that* Saul had attacked a garrison of the Philistines, and *that* Israel had also become an abomination to the Philistines. And the people were called together to Saul at Gilgal.

At the passages. **1 Sam 14:1–14**

Invaded Israel with a large army.

1 Sam 13:5 Then the Philistines gathered together to fight with Israel, thirty thousand chariots and six thousand horsemen, and people as the sand which *is* on the seashore in multitude. And they came up and encamped in Michmash, to the east of Beth Aven.

1 Sam 13:17–23 Then raiders came out of the camp of the Philistines in three companies. One company turned onto the road to Ophrah, to the land of Shual, **18** another company turned to the road *to* Beth Horon, and another company turned *to* the road of the border that overlooks the Valley of Zeboim toward the wilderness. **19** Now there was no blacksmith to be found throughout all the land of Israel, for the Philistines said, "Lest the Hebrews make swords or spears." **20** But all the Israelites would go down to the Philistines to sharpen each man's plowshare, his mattock, his ax, and his sickle; **21** and the charge for a sharpening was a pim for the plowshares, the mattocks, the forks, and the axes, and to set the points of the goads. **22** So it came about, on the day of battle, that there was neither sword nor spear found in the hand of any of the people who *were* with Saul and Jonathan. But they were found with Saul and Jonathan his son. **23** And the garrison of the Philistines went out to the pass of Michmash.

Miraculously frustrated and defeated.

1 Sam 14:15–23 And there was trembling in the camp, in the field, and among all the people. The garrison and the raiders also trembled; and the earth quaked, so that it was a very great trembling. **16** Now the watchmen of Saul in Gibeah of Benjamin looked, and *there* was the multitude, melting away; and they went here and there. **17** Then Saul said to the people who *were* with him, "Now call the roll and see who has gone from us." And when they had called the roll, surprisingly, Jonathan and his armorbearer *were* not *there*. **18** And Saul said to Ahijah, "Bring the ark of God here" (for at that time the ark of God was with the children of Israel). **19** Now it happened, while Saul talked to the priest, that the noise which *was* in the camp of the Philistines continued to increase; so Saul said to the priest, "Withdraw your hand." **20** Then Saul and all the people who *were* with him assembled, and they went to the battle; and indeed every man's sword was against his neighbor, *and there was* very great confusion. **21** Moreover the Hebrews *who* were with the Philistines before that time, who went up with them into the camp *from the* surrounding *country*, they also joined the Israelites who *were* with Saul and Jonathan. **22** Likewise all the men of Israel who had hidden in the mountains of Ephraim, *when* they heard that the Philistines fled, they also followed hard after them in the battle. **23** So the LORD saved Israel that day, and the battle shifted to Beth Aven.

Saul constantly at war with.

1 Sam 14:52 Now there was fierce war with the Philistines all the days of Saul. And when Saul saw any strong man or any valiant man, he took him for himself.

Defied Israel by Goliath.

1 Sam 17:4–10 And a champion went out from the camp of the Philistines, named Goliath, from Gath, whose height *was* six cubits and a span. **5** *He had* a bronze helmet on his head, and he *was* armed with a coat of mail, and the weight of the coat *was* five thousand shekels of bronze. **6** And *he had* bronze armor on his legs and a bronze javelin between his shoulders. **7** Now the staff of his spear *was* like a weaver's beam, and his iron spearhead *weighed* six hundred shekels; and a shield-bearer went before him. **8** Then he stood and cried out to the armies of Israel, and said to them, "Why have you come out to line up for battle? *Am* I not a Philistine, and you the servants of Saul? Choose a man for yourselves, and let him come down to me. **9** If he is able to fight with me and kill me, then we will be your servants. But if I prevail against him and kill him, then you shall be our servants and serve us." **10** And the Philistine said, "I defy the armies of Israel this day; give me a man, that we may fight together."

Defeated Israel at Ephes Dammim and pursued to Ekron.

1 Sam 17:1 Now the Philistines gathered their armies together to battle, and were gathered at Sochoh, which *belongs* to Judah; they encamped between Sochoh and Azekah, in Ephes Dammim.

1 Sam 17:52 Now the men of Israel and Judah arose and shouted, and pursued the Philistines as far as the entrance of the valley and to the gates of Ekron. And the wounded of the Philistines fell along the road to Shaaraim, even as far as Gath and Ekron.

David

Killed Goliath, their champion.

1 Sam 17:40–50 Then he took his staff in his hand; and he chose for himself five smooth stones from the brook, and put them in a shepherd's bag, in a pouch which he had, and his sling was in his hand. And he drew near to the Philistine. **41** So the Philistine came, and began drawing near to David, and the man who bore the shield *went* before him. **42** And when the Philistine looked about and saw David, he disdained

him; for he was *only* a youth, ruddy and good-looking. **43** So the Philistine said to David, "*Am* I a dog, that you come to me with sticks?" And the Philistine cursed David by his gods. **44** And the Philistine said to David, "Come to me, and I will give your flesh to the birds of the air and the beasts of the field!" **45** Then David said to the Philistine, "You come to me with a sword, with a spear, and with a javelin. But I come to you in the name of the LORD of hosts, the God of the armies of Israel, whom you have defied. **46** This day the LORD will deliver you into my hand, and I will strike you and take your head from you. And this day I will give the carcasses of the camp of the Philistines to the birds of the air and the wild beasts of the earth, that all the earth may know that there is a God in Israel. **47** Then all this assembly shall know that the LORD does not save with sword and spear; for the battle *is* the LORD's, and He will give you into our hands." **48** So it was, when the Philistine arose and came and drew near to meet David, that David hurried and ran toward the army to meet the Philistine. **49** Then David put his hand in his bag and took out a stone; and he slung *it* and struck the Philistine in his forehead, so that the stone sank into his forehead, and he fell on his face to the earth. **50** So David prevailed over the Philistine with a sling and a stone, and struck the Philistine and killed him. But *there was* no sword in the hand of David.

Procured Saul's daughter for one hundred foreskins of.

1 Sam 18:25–27 Then Saul said, "Thus you shall say to David: 'The king does not desire any dowry but one hundred foreskins of the Philistines, to take vengeance on the king's enemies.' " But Saul thought to make David fall by the hand of the Philistines. **26** So when his servants told David these words, it pleased David well to become the king's son-in-law. Now the days had not expired; **27** therefore David arose and went, he and his men, and killed two hundred men of the Philistines. And David brought their foreskins, and they gave them in full count to the king, that he might become the king's son-in-law. Then Saul gave him Michal his daughter as a wife.

Often defeated them during Saul's reign.

1 Sam 19:8 And there was war again; and David went out and fought with the Philistines, and struck them with a mighty blow, and they fled from him.

1 Sam 23:1–5 Then they told David, saying, "Look, the Philistines are fighting against Keilah, and they are robbing the threshing floors." **2** Therefore David inquired of the LORD, saying, "Shall I go and attack these Philistines?" And the LORD said to David, "Go and attack the Philistines, and save Keilah." **3** But David's men said to him, "Look, we are afraid here in Judah. How much more then if we go to Keilah against the armies of the Philistines?" **4** Then David inquired of the LORD once again. And the LORD answered him and said, "Arise, go down to Keilah. For I will deliver the Philistines into your hand." **5** And David and his men went to Keilah and fought with the Philistines, struck them with a mighty blow, and took away their livestock. So David saved the inhabitants of Keilah.

Fled to them for safety.

1 Sam 27:1–7 And David said in his heart, "Now I shall perish someday by the hand of Saul. *There is* nothing better for me than that I should speedily escape to the land of the Philistines; and Saul will despair of me, to seek me anymore in any part of Israel. So I shall escape out of his hand." **2** Then David arose and went over with the six hundred men who *were* with him to Achish the son of Maoch, king of Gath. **3** So David dwelt with Achish at Gath, he and his men, each man with his household, *and* David with his two wives, Ahinoam the Jezreelitess, and Abigail the Carmelitess, Nabal's widow. **4** And it was told Saul that David had fled to Gath; so he sought him no more. **5** Then David said to Achish, "If I have now found favor in your eyes, let them give me a place in some town in the country, that I may dwell there. For why should your servant dwell in the royal city with you?" **6** So Achish gave him Ziklag that day. Therefore Ziklag has belonged to the kings of Judah to this day. **7** Now the time that David dwelt in the country of the Philistines was one full year and four months.

1 Sam 28:2 So David said to Achish, "Surely you know what your servant can do." And Achish said to David, "Therefore I will make you one of my chief guardians forever."

1 Sam 29:9 Then Achish answered and said to David, "I know that you *are* as good in my sight as an angel of God; nevertheless the princes of the Philistines have said, 'He shall not go up with us to the battle.'

Distrusted by them.

1 Sam 29:2–7 And the lords of the Philistines passed in review by hundreds and by thousands, but David and his men passed in review at the rear with Achish. **3** Then the princes of the Philistines said, "What *are* these Hebrews *doing here?*" And Achish said to the princes of the Philistines, "*Is* this not David, the servant of Saul king of Israel, who has been with me these days, or these years? And to this day I have found no fault in him since he defected *to me.*" **4** But the princes of the Philistines were angry with him; so the princes of the Philistines said to him, "Make this fellow return, that he may go back to the place which you have appointed for him, and do not let him go down with us to battle, lest in the battle he become our adversary. For with what could he reconcile himself to his master, if not with the heads of these men? **5** *Is* this not David, of whom they sang to one another in dances, saying: 'Saul has slain his thousands, And David his ten thousands'?" **6** Then Achish called David and said to him, "Surely, *as* the LORD lives, you have been upright, and your going out and your coming in with me in the army *is* good in my sight. For to this day I have not found evil in you since the day of your coming to me. Nevertheless the lords do not favor you. **7** Therefore return now, and go in peace, that you may not displease the lords of the Philistines."

Defeated them frequently during his reign.

2 Sam 5:17–23 Now when the Philistines heard that they had anointed David king over Israel, all the Philistines went up to search for David. And David heard *of it* and went down to the stronghold. **18** The Philistines also went and deployed themselves in the Valley of Rephaim. **19** So David inquired of the LORD, saying, "Shall I go up against the Philistines? Will You deliver them into my hand?" And the LORD said to David, "Go up, for I will doubtless deliver the Philistines into your hand." **20** So David went to Baal Perazim, and David defeated them there; and he said, "The LORD has broken through my enemies before me, like a breakthrough of water." Therefore he called the name of that place Baal Perazim. **21** And they left their images there, and David and his men carried them away. **22** Then the Philistines went up once again and deployed themselves in the Valley of Rephaim. **23** Therefore David inquired of the LORD, and He said, "You shall not go up; circle around behind them, and come upon them in front of the mulberry trees."

Cf. 2 Sam 8:1; 21:15–22; 23:8–12

Had a guard composed of.

2 Sam 8:18 Benaiah the son of Jehoiada *was over* both the Cherethites and the Pelethites; and David's sons were chief ministers.

Gathered all their armies to Aphek against Israel.

1 Sam 28:1 Now it happened in those days that the Philistines gathered their armies together for war, to fight with Israel. And Achish said to David, "You assuredly know that you will go out with me to battle, you and your men."

1 Sam 29:1 Then the Philistines gathered together all their armies at Aphek, and the Israelites encamped by a fountain which *is* in Jezreel.

Their city Ziklag plundered by the Amalekites.

1 Sam 30:1–2 Now it happened, when David and his men came to Ziklag, on the third day, that the Amalekites had invaded the South and Ziklag, attacked Ziklag and burned it with fire, **2** and had taken captive the women and those who *were* there, from small to great; they did not kill anyone, but carried *them* away and went their way.

1 Sam 30:16 And when he had brought him down, there they were, spread out over all the land, eating and drinking and dancing, because of all the great spoil which they had taken from the land of the Philistines and from the land of Judah.

Israel defeated by, and Saul killed.

1 Sam 31:1–10 Now the Philistines fought against Israel; and the men of Israel fled from before the Philistines, and fell slain on Mount Gilboa. **2** Then the Philistines followed hard after Saul and his sons. And the Philistines killed Jonathan, Abinadab, and Malchishua, Saul's sons. **3** The battle became fierce against Saul. The archers hit him, and he was severely wounded by the archers. **4** Then Saul said to his armorbearer, "Draw your sword, and thrust me through with it, lest these uncircumcised men come and thrust me through and abuse me." But his armorbearer would not, for he was greatly afraid. Therefore Saul took a sword and fell on it. **5** And when his armorbearer saw that Saul was dead, he also fell on his sword, and died with him. **6** So Saul, his three sons, his armorbearer, and all his men died together that same day. **7** And when the men of Israel who *were* on the other side of the valley, and *those* who *were* on the other side of the Jordan, saw that the men of Israel had fled and that Saul and his sons were dead, they forsook the cities and fled; and the Philistines came and dwelt in them. **8** So it happened the next day, when the Philistines came to strip the slain, that they found Saul and his three sons fallen on Mount Gilboa. **9** And they cut off his head and stripped off his armor, and sent *word* throughout the land of the Philistines, to proclaim *it in* the temple of their idols and among the people. **10** Then they put his armor in the temple of the Ashtoreths, and they fastened his body to the wall of Beth Shan.

Besieged in Gibbethon by Nadab.

1 Kin 15:27 Then Baasha the son of Ahijah, of the house of Issachar, conspired against him. And Baasha killed him at Gibbethon, which *belonged* to the Philistines, while Nadab and all Israel laid siege to Gibbethon.

Sent by God against Jehoram.

2 Chr 21:16–17 Moreover the LORD stirred up against Jehoram the spirit of the Philistines and the Arabians who *were* near the Ethiopians. **17** And they came up into Judah and invaded it, and carried away all the possessions that were found in the king's house, and also his sons and his wives, so that there was not a son left to him except Jehoahaz, the youngest of his sons.

Defeated by Uzziah.

2 Chr 26:6–7 Now he went out and made war against the Philistines, and broke down the wall of Gath, the wall of Jabneh, and the wall of Ashdod; and he built cities *around* Ashdod and among the Philistines. **7** God helped him against the Philistines, against the Arabians who lived in Gur Baal, and against the Meunites.

Distressed Judah under Ahaz.

2 Chr 28:18–19 The Philistines also had invaded the cities of the lowland and of the South of Judah, and had taken Beth Shemesh, Aijalon, Gederoth, Sochoh with its villages, Timnah with its villages, and Gimzo with its villages; and they dwelt there. **19** For the LORD brought Judah low because of Ahaz king of Israel, for he had encouraged moral decline in Judah and had been continually unfaithful to the LORD.

Defeated by Hezekiah.

2 Kin 18:8 He subdued the Philistines, as far as Gaza and its territory, from watchtower to fortified city.

Israel condemned for imitating.

Judg 10:6 Then the children of Israel again did evil in the sight of the LORD, and served the Baals and the Ashtoreths, the gods of Syria, the gods of Sidon, the gods of Moab, the gods of the people of Ammon, and the gods of the Philistines; and they forsook the LORD and did not serve Him.

Amos 6:2 Go over to Calneh and see; And from there go to Hamath the great; Then go down to Gath of the Philistines. *Are you* better than these kingdoms? Or is their territory greater than your territory?

Amos 9:7 "*Are* you not like the people of Ethiopia to Me, O children of Israel?" says the LORD. "Did I not bring up Israel from the land of Egypt, The Philistines from Caphtor, And the Syrians from Kir?

Prophecies respecting,

Union with Syria against Israel.

Is 9:11–12 Therefore the LORD shall set up The adversaries of Rezin against him, And spur his enemies on, **12** The Syrians before and the Philistines behind;

And they shall devour Israel with an open mouth. For all this His anger is not turned away, But His hand *is* stretched out still.

Punishment with other nations.

Jer 25:20 all the mixed multitude, all the kings of the land of Uz, all the kings of the land of the Philistines (namely, Ashkelon, Gaza, Ekron, and the remnant of Ashdod);

Dismay at ruin of Tyre.

Zech 9:3 For Tyre built herself a tower, Heaped up silver like the dust, And gold like the mire of the streets.

Zech 9:5 Ashkelon shall see *it* and fear; Gaza also shall be very sorrowful; And Ekron, for He dried up her expectation. The king shall perish from Gaza, And Ashkelon shall not be inhabited.

End of their national pride.

Zech 9:6 "A mixed race shall settle in Ashdod, And I will cut off the pride of the Philistines.

Hatred and revenge against Israel to be fully recompensed.

Ezek 25:15–17 'Thus says the Lord GOD: "Because the Philistines dealt vengefully and took vengeance with a spiteful heart, to destroy because of the old hatred," **16** therefore thus says the Lord GOD: "I will stretch out My hand against the Philistines, and I will cut off the Cherethites and destroy the remnant of the seacoast. **17** I will execute great vengeance on them with furious rebukes; and they shall know that I *am* the LORD, when I lay My vengeance upon them." ' "

Amos 1:6–8 Thus says the LORD: "For three transgressions of Gaza, and for four, I will not turn away its *punishment,* Because they took captive the whole captivity To deliver *them* up to Edom. **7** But I will send a fire upon the wall of Gaza, Which shall devour its palaces. **8** I will cut off the inhabitant from Ashdod, And the one who holds the scepter from Ashkelon; I will turn My hand against Ekron, And the remnant of the Philistines shall perish," Says the Lord GOD.

Utter destruction by Pharaoh, king of Egypt.

Jer 47:1–4 The word of the LORD that came to Jeremiah the prophet against the Philistines, before Pharaoh attacked Gaza. **2** Thus says the LORD: "Behold, waters rise out of the north, And shall be an overflowing flood; They shall overflow the land and all that is in it, The city and those who dwell within; Then the men shall cry, And all the inhabitants of the land shall wail. **3** At the noise of the stamping hooves of his strong horses, At the rushing of his chariots, *At* the rumbling of his wheels, The fathers will not look back for *their* children, Lacking courage, **4** Because of the day that comes to plunder all the Philistines, To cut off from Tyre and Sidon every helper who remains; For the LORD shall plunder the Philistines, The remnant of the country of Caphtor.

Zeph 2:5–6 Woe to the inhabitants of the seacoast, The nation of the Cherethites! The word of the LORD *is* against you, O Canaan, land of the Philistines: "I will destroy you; So there shall be no inhabitant." **6** The seacoast shall be pastures, With shelters for shepherds and folds for flocks.

Destruction and desolation of their cities.

Jer 47:5 Baldness has come upon Gaza, Ashkelon is cut off *With* the remnant of their valley. How long will you cut yourself?

Zeph 2:4 For Gaza shall be forsaken, And Ashkelon desolate; They shall drive out Ashdod at noonday, And Ekron shall be uprooted.

Their country to be a future possession to Israel.

Obad 1:19 The South shall possess the mountains of Esau, And the Lowland shall possess Philistia. They shall possess the fields of Ephraim And the fields of Samaria. Benjamin *shall possess* Gilead.

Zeph 2:7 The coast shall be for the remnant of the house of Judah; They shall feed *their* flocks there; In the houses of Ashkelon they shall lie down at evening. For the LORD their God will intervene for them, And return their captives.

To help in Israel's restoration.

Is 11:14 But they shall fly down upon the shoulder of the Philistines toward the west; Together they shall plunder the people of the East; They shall lay their hand on Edom and Moab; And the people of Ammon shall obey them.

PILLARS

The supports of a building.

Judg 16:29 And Samson took hold of the two middle pillars which supported the temple, and he braced himself against them, one on his right and the other on his left.

Used in memorials.

Gen 31:51 Then Laban said to Jacob, "Here is this heap and here is *this* pillar, which I have placed between you and me.

Made of

Marble.

Esth 1:6 *There were* white and blue linen *curtains* fastened with cords of fine linen and purple on silver rods and marble pillars; *and the* couches *were* of gold and silver on a *mosaic* pavement of alabaster, turquoise, and white and black marble.

Wood.

1 Kin 10:12 And the king made steps of the almug wood for the house of the LORD and for the king's house, also harps and stringed instruments for singers. There never again came such almug wood, nor has the like been seen to this day.

Iron.

Jer 1:18 For behold, I have made you this day A fortified city and an iron pillar, And bronze walls against the whole land— Against the kings of Judah, Against its princes, Against its priests, And against the people of the land.

Bronze.

1 Kin 7:15 And he cast two pillars of bronze, each one eighteen cubits high, and a line of twelve cubits measured the circumference of each.

Silver.

Song 3:10 He made its pillars *of* silver, Its support *of* gold, Its seat *of* purple, Its interior paved *with* love By the daughters of Jerusalem.

The veil and hangings of the tabernacle supported by.

Ex 26:32 You shall hang it upon the four pillars of acacia *wood* overlaid with gold. Their hooks *shall be* gold, upon four sockets of silver.

Ex 26:37 And you shall make for the screen five pillars of acacia *wood*, and overlay them with gold; their hooks *shall be* gold, and you shall cast five sockets of bronze for them.

Ex 36:36 He made for it four pillars of acacia *wood*, and overlaid them with gold, with their hooks of gold; and he cast four sockets of silver for them.

Ex 36:38 and its five pillars with their hooks. And he overlaid their capitals and their rings with gold, but their five sockets *were* bronze.

Two, placed in the temple porch.

1 Kin 7:15–21 And he cast two pillars of bronze, each one eighteen cubits high, and a line of twelve cubits measured the circumference of each. **16** Then he made two capitals *of* cast bronze, to set on the tops of the pillars. The height of one capital *was* five cubits, and the height of the other capital *was* five cubits. **17** *He made* a lattice network, with wreaths of chainwork, for the capitals which *were* on top of the pillars: seven chains for one capital and seven for the other capital. **18** So he made the pillars, and two rows of pomegranates above the network all around to cover the capitals that *were* on top; and thus he did for the other capital. **19** The capitals which *were* on top of the pillars in the hall *were* in the shape of lilies, four cubits. **20** The capitals on the two pillars also *had pomegranates* above, by the convex surface which *was* next to the network; and there *were* two hundred such pomegranates in rows on each of the capitals all around. **21** Then he set up the pillars by the vestibule of the temple; he set up the pillar on the right and called its name Jachin, and he set up the pillar on the left and called its name Boaz.

Of memorial

Sometimes of a single stone.

Gen 28:18 Then Jacob rose early in the morning, and took the stone that he had put at his head, set it up as a pillar, and poured oil on top of it.

Sometimes of a heap of stones.

Josh 4:8–9 And the children of Israel did so, just as Joshua commanded, and took up twelve stones from the midst of the Jordan, as the LORD had spoken to Joshua, according to the number of the tribes of the children of Israel, and carried them over with them to the place where they lodged, and laid them down there. **9** Then Joshua set up twelve stones in the midst of the Jordan, in the place where the feet of the priests who bore the ark of the covenant stood; and they are there to this day.

Josh 4:20 And those twelve stones which they took out of the Jordan, Joshua set up in Gilgal.

To witness vows.

Gen 28:18 Then Jacob rose early in the morning, and took the stone that he had put at his head, set it up as a pillar, and poured oil on top of it.

Gen 31:13 I *am* the God of Bethel, where you anointed the pillar *and* where you made a vow to Me. Now arise, get out of this land, and return to the land of your family.' "

To witness covenants.

Gen 31:52 This heap *is* a witness, and *this* pillar *is* a witness, that I will not pass beyond this heap to you, and you will not pass beyond this heap and this pillar to me, for harm.

To mark the graves of the dead.

Gen 35:20 And Jacob set a pillar on her grave, which *is* the pillar of Rachel's grave to this day.

To commemorate remarkable events.

Ex 24:4 And Moses wrote all the words of the LORD. And he rose early in the morning, and built an altar at the foot of the mountain, and twelve pillars according to the twelve tribes of Israel.

Josh 4:20 And those twelve stones which they took out of the Jordan, Joshua set up in Gilgal.

Josh 4:24 that all the peoples of the earth may know the hand of the LORD, that it *is* mighty, that you may fear the LORD your God forever."

To perpetuate names.

2 Sam 18:18 Now Absalom in his lifetime had taken and set up a pillar for himself, which *is* in the King's Valley. For he said, "I have no son to keep my name in remembrance." He called the pillar after his own name. And to this day it is called Absalom's Monument.

In honor of idols.

Lev 26:1 'You shall not make idols for yourselves; neither a carved image nor a *sacred* pillar shall you rear up for yourselves; nor shall you set up an engraved stone in your land, to bow down to it; for I *am* the LORD your God.

Deut 7:5 But thus you shall deal with them: you shall destroy their altars, and break down their *sacred* pillars, and cut down their wooden images, and burn their carved images with fire.

Often anointed.

Gen 28:18 Then Jacob rose early in the morning, and took the stone that he had put at his head, set it up as a pillar, and poured oil on top of it.

Gen 31:13 I *am* the God of Bethel, where you anointed the pillar *and* where you made a vow to Me. Now arise, get out of this land, and return to the land of your family.' "

Often had inscriptions.

Job 19:24 That they were engraved on a rock With an iron pen and lead, forever!

Represented the Lord to Israel.

Ex 13:21–22 And the LORD went before them by day in a pillar of cloud to lead the way, and by night in a pillar of fire to give them light, so as to go by day and night. **22** He did not take away the pillar of cloud by day or the pillar of fire by night *from* before the people.

Num 12:5 Then the LORD came down in the pillar of cloud and stood *in* the door of the tabernacle, and called Aaron and Miriam. And they both went forward.

Lot's wife became a pillar of salt.

Gen 19:26 But his wife looked back behind him, and she became a pillar of salt.

Illustrative of

Stability of the heavens.

Job 26:11 The pillars of heaven tremble, And are astonished at His rebuke.

Stability of the earth.

1 Sam 2:8 He raises the poor from the dust *And* lifts the beggar from the ash heap, To set *them* among princes And make them inherit the throne of glory. "For the pillars of the earth *are* the LORD's, And He has set the world upon them.

Ps 75:3 The earth and all its inhabitants are dissolved; I set up its pillars firmly. Selah

The church.

1 Tim 3:15 but if I am delayed, *I write* so that you may know how you ought to conduct yourself in the house of God, which is the church of the living God, the pillar and ground of the truth.

Stability of Christ.

Rev 10:1 I saw still another mighty angel coming down from heaven, clothed with a cloud. And a rainbow *was* on his head, his face *was* like the sun, and his feet like pillars of fire.

Ministers.

Jer 1:18 For behold, I have made you this day A fortified city and an iron pillar, And bronze walls against the whole land— Against the kings of Judah, Against its princes, Against its priests, And against the people of the land.

Gal 2:9 and when James, Cephas, and John, who seemed to be pillars, perceived the grace that had been given to me, they gave me and Barnabas the right hand of fellowship, that we *should go* to the Gentiles and they to the circumcised.

Saints who overcome in Christ.

Rev 3:12 He who overcomes, I will make him a pillar in the temple of My God, and he shall go out no more. I will write on him the name of My God and the name of the city of My God, the New Jerusalem, which comes down out of heaven from My God. And *I will write on him* My new name.

PLAGUE OR PESTILENCE

Inflicted by God.

Ezek 14:19 "Or *if* I send a pestilence into that land and pour out My fury on it in blood, and cut off from it man and beast,

Ezek 14:21 For thus says the Lord GOD: "How much more it shall be when I send My four severe judgments on Jerusalem—the sword and famine and wild beasts and pestilence—to cut off man and beast from it?

Hab 3:5 Before Him went pestilence, And fever followed at His feet.

Described as troublesome.

Ps 9:13 Have mercy on me, O LORD! Consider my trouble from those who hate me, You who lift me up from the gates of death,

Israel threatened with, as a punishment for disobedience.

Lev 26:24–25 then I also will walk contrary to you, and I will punish you yet seven times for your sins.

25 And I will bring a sword against you that will execute the vengeance of the covenant; when you are gathered together within your cities I will send pestilence among you; and you shall be delivered into the hand of the enemy.

Deut 28:21 The LORD will make the plague cling to you until He has consumed you from the land which you are going to possess.

Desolating effects of.

Ps 91:7 A thousand may fall at your side, And ten thousand at your right hand; *But* it shall not come near you.

Jer 16:6–7 Both the great and the small shall die in this land. They shall not be buried; neither shall men lament for them, cut themselves, nor make themselves bald for them. 7 Nor shall *men* break *bread* in mourning for them, to comfort them for the dead; nor shall *men* give them the cup of consolation to drink for their father or their mother.

Amos 6:9–10 Then it shall come to pass, that if ten men remain in one house, they shall die. 10 And when a relative *of the dead*, with one who will burn *the bodies*, picks up the bodies to take them out of the house, he will say to one inside the house, "*Are there* any more with you?" Then someone will say, "None." And he will say, "Hold your tongue! For we dare not mention the name of the LORD."

Equally fatal day and night.

Ps 91:5–6 You shall not be afraid of the terror by night, *Nor* of the arrow *that* flies by day, 6 *Nor* of the pestilence *that* walks in darkness, *Nor* of the destruction *that* lays waste at noonday.

Fatal to man and beast.

Ps 78:50 He made a path for His anger; He did not spare their soul from death, But gave their life over to the plague,

Jer 21:6 I will strike the inhabitants of this city, both man and beast; they shall die of a great pestilence.

Sent upon

The Egyptians.

Ex 12:29–30 And it came to pass at midnight that the LORD struck all the firstborn in the land of Egypt, from the firstborn of Pharaoh who sat on his throne to the firstborn of the captive who *was* in the dungeon, and all the firstborn of livestock. 30 So Pharaoh rose in the night, he, all his servants, and all the Egyptians; and there was a great cry in Egypt, for *there was* not a house where *there was* not one dead.

Israel for making golden calf.

Ex 32:35 So the LORD plagued the people because of what they did with the calf which Aaron made.

Israel for despising manna.

Num 11:33 But while the meat *was* still between their teeth, before it was chewed, the wrath of the LORD was aroused against the people, and the LORD struck the people with a very great plague.

Those who rebeled with Korah.

Num 16:46–50 So Moses said to Aaron, "Take a censer and put fire in it from the altar, put incense *on it*, and take it quickly to the congregation and make atonement for them; for wrath has gone out from the LORD. The plague has begun." 47 Then Aaron took *it*

as Moses commanded, and ran into the midst of the assembly; and already the plague had begun among the people. So he put in the incense and made atonement for the people. 48 And he stood between the dead and the living; so the plague was stopped. 49 Now those who died in the plague were fourteen thousand seven hundred, besides those who died in the Korah incident. 50 So Aaron returned to Moses at the door of the tabernacle of meeting, for the plague had stopped.

Israel for worshiping Baal Peor.

Num 25:18 for they harassed you with their schemes by which they seduced you in the matter of Peor and in the matter of Cozbi, the daughter of a leader of Midian, their sister, who was killed in the day of the plague because of Peor."

David's subjects for his numbering the people.

2 Sam 24:15 So the LORD sent a plague upon Israel from the morning till the appointed time. From Dan to Beersheba seventy thousand men of the people died.

Often broke out suddenly.

Ps 106:29 Thus they provoked *Him* to anger with their deeds, And the plague broke out among them.

Often followed war and famine.

Jer 27:13 Why will you die, you and your people, by the sword, by the famine, and by the pestilence, as the LORD has spoken against the nation that will not serve the king of Babylon?

Jer 28:8 The prophets who have been before me and before you of old prophesied against many countries and great kingdoms—of war and disaster and pestilence.

Jer 29:17–18 thus says the LORD of hosts: Behold, I will send on them the sword, the famine, and the pestilence, and will make them like rotten figs that cannot be eaten, they are so bad. 18 And I will pursue them with the sword, with famine, and with pestilence; and I will deliver them to trouble among all the kingdoms of the earth—to be a curse, an astonishment, a hissing, and a reproach among all the nations where I have driven them,

Egypt often afflicted with.

Jer 42:17 So shall it be with all the men who set their faces to go to Egypt to dwell there. They shall die by the sword, by famine, and by pestilence. And none of them shall remain or escape from the disaster that I will bring upon them.'

Amos 4:10 "I sent among you a plague after the manner of Egypt; Your young men I killed with a sword, Along with your captive horses; I made the stench of your camps come up into your nostrils; Yet you have not returned to Me," Says the LORD.

Especially fatal in cities.

Lev 26:25 And I will bring a sword against you that will execute the vengeance of the covenant; when you are gathered together within your cities I will send pestilence among you; and you shall be delivered into the hand of the enemy.

Jer 21:6 I will strike the inhabitants of this city, both man and beast; they shall die of a great pestilence.

Jer 21:9 He who remains in this city shall die by the sword, by famine, and by pestilence; but he who goes out and defects to the Chaldeans who besiege you, he shall live, and his life shall be as a prize to him.

Was attributed to a destroying angel.

Ex 12:23 For the LORD will pass through to strike the Egyptians; and when He sees the blood on the lintel and on the two doorposts, the LORD will pass over the door and not allow the destroyer to come into your houses to strike *you.*

2 Sam 24:16 And when the angel stretched out His hand over Jerusalem to destroy it, the LORD relented from the destruction, and said to the angel who was destroying the people, "It is enough; now restrain your hand." And the angel of the LORD was by the threshing floor of Araunah the Jebusite.

The Jews sought deliverance from, by prayer.

1 Kin 8:37–38 "When there is famine in the land, pestilence *or* blight *or* mildew, locusts *or* grasshoppers; when their enemy besieges them in the land of their cities; whatever plague or whatever sickness *there is;* **38** whatever prayer, whatever supplication is made by anyone, *or* by all Your people Israel, when each one knows the plague of his own heart, and spreads out his hands toward this temple:

2 Chr 20:9 'If disaster comes upon us—sword, judgment, pestilence, or famine—we will stand before this temple and in Your presence (for Your name *is* in this temple), and cry out to You in our affliction, and You will hear and save.'

Predicted to happen in last days.

Matt 24:7 For nation will rise against nation, and kingdom against kingdom. And there will be famines, pestilences, and earthquakes in various places.

Luke 21:11 And there will be great earthquakes in various places, and famines and pestilences; and there will be fearful sights and great signs from heaven.

Illustrative of

God's judgments upon the apostasy.

Rev 18:4 And I heard another voice from heaven saying, "Come out of her, my people, lest you share in her sins, and lest you receive of her plagues.

Rev 18:8 Therefore her plagues will come in one day—death and mourning and famine. And she will be utterly burned with fire, for strong *is* the Lord God who judges her.

The diseased state of man's heart.

1 Kin 8:38 whatever prayer, whatever supplication is made by anyone, *or* by all Your people Israel, when each one knows the plague of his own heart, and spreads out his hands toward this temple:

PLOWING

The breaking up or tilling of the earth.

Jer 4:3 For thus says the LORD to the men of Judah and Jerusalem: "Break up your fallow ground, And do not sow among thorns.

Hos 10:12 Sow for yourselves righteousness; Reap in mercy; Break up your fallow ground, For *it is* time to seek the LORD, Till He comes and rains righteousness on you.

Performed

With oxen.

Job 1:14 and a messenger came to Job and said, "The oxen were plowing and the donkeys feeding beside them,

In long and straight furrows.

Ps 129:3 The plowers plowed on my back; They made their furrows long."

Generally by foreigners and servants.

Is 61:5 Strangers shall stand and feed your flocks, And the sons of the foreigner *Shall be* your plowmen and your vinedressers.

Luke 17:7 And which of you, having a servant plowing or tending sheep, will say to him when he has come in from the field, 'Come at once and sit down to eat'?

Sometimes by the owner of the land himself.

1 Kin 19:19 So he departed from there, and found Elisha the son of Shaphat, who *was* plowing *with* twelve yoke *of oxen* before him, and he was with the twelfth. Then Elijah passed by him and threw his mantle on him.

With an ox and a donkey yoked together, forbidden to the Jews.

Deut 22:10 "You shall not plow with an ox and a donkey together.

Difficulty of, on rocky ground.

Amos 6:12 Do horses run on rocks? Does *one* plow *there* with oxen? Yet you have turned justice into gall, And the fruit of righteousness into wormwood,

Followed by harrowing and sowing.

Is 28:24–25 Does the plowman keep plowing all day to sow? Does he keep turning his soil and breaking the clods? **25** When he has leveled its surface, Does he not sow the black cummin And scatter the cummin, Plant the wheat in rows, The barley in the appointed place, And the spelt in its place?

Illustrative of

Repentance and reformation.

Jer 4:3 For thus says the LORD to the men of Judah and Jerusalem: "Break up your fallow ground, And do not sow among thorns.

Peace and prosperity.

Is 2:4 He shall judge between the nations, And rebuke many people; They shall beat their swords into plowshares, And their spears into pruning hooks; Nation shall not lift up sword against nation, Neither shall they learn war anymore.

Mic 4:3 He shall judge between many peoples, And rebuke strong nations afar off; They shall beat their swords into plowshares, And their spears into pruning hooks; Nation shall not lift up sword against nation, Neither shall they learn war anymore.

A severe course of affliction.

Hos 10:11 Ephraim *is* a trained heifer That loves to thresh *grain;* But I harnessed her fair neck, I will make Ephraim pull *a plow.* Judah shall plow; Jacob shall break his clods."

A course of sin.

Job 4:8 Even as I have seen, Those who plow iniquity And sow trouble reap the same.

Hos 10:13 You have plowed wickedness; You have reaped iniquity. You have eaten the fruit of lies, Because you trusted in your own way, In the multitude of your mighty men.

The labor of ministers.

1 Cor 9:10 Or does He say *it* altogether for our sakes? For our sakes, no doubt, *this* is written, that he who plows should plow in hope, and he who threshes in hope should be partaker of his hope.

(Attention and constancy required in) continued devotedness.

Luke 9:62 But Jesus said to him, "No one, having put his hand to the plow, and looking back, is fit for the kingdom of God."

POMEGRANATE TREE, THE

Egypt and Canaan abounded with.

Num 13:23 Then they came to the Valley of Eshcol, and there cut down a branch with one cluster of grapes; they carried it between two of them on a pole. *They* also *brought* some of the pomegranates and figs.

Num 20:5 And why have you made us come up out of Egypt, to bring us to this evil place? It *is* not a place of grain or figs or vines or pomegranates; nor *is* there any water to drink."

Deut 8:8 a land of wheat and barley, of vines and fig trees and pomegranates, a land of olive oil and honey;

The Jews

Cultivated, in orchards.

Song 4:13 Your plants *are* an orchard of pomegranates With pleasant fruits, Fragrant henna with spikenard,

Often dwelt under shade of.

1 Sam 14:2 And Saul was sitting in the outskirts of Gibeah under a pomegranate tree which *is* in Migron. The people who *were* with him *were* about six hundred men.

Drank the juice of.

Song 8:2 I would lead you *and* bring you Into the house of my mother, She *who* used to instruct me. I would cause you to drink of spiced wine, Of the juice of my pomegranate.

The blasting of, a great calamity.

Joel 1:12 The vine has dried up, And the fig tree has withered; The pomegranate tree, The palm tree also, And the apple tree— All the trees of the field are withered; Surely joy has withered away from the sons of men.

God's favor exhibited, in making fruitful.

Hag 2:19 Is the seed still in the barn? As yet the vine, the fig tree, the pomegranate, and the olive tree have not yielded *fruit. But* from this day I will bless *you.*' "

Representations of its fruit

On the high priest's robe.

Ex 39:24–26 They made on the hem of the robe pomegranates of blue, purple, and scarlet, and of fine woven *linen.* 25 And they made bells of pure gold, and put the bells between the pomegranates on the hem of the robe all around between the pomegranates: 26 a bell and a pomegranate, a bell and a pomegranate, all around the hem of the robe to minister in, as the LORD had commanded Moses.

On the pillars of the temple.

1 Kin 7:18 So he made the pillars, and two rows of pomegranates above the network all around to cover the capitals that *were* on top; and thus he did for the other capital.

POOLS AND PONDS

Made by God.

Is 35:7 The parched ground shall become a pool, And the thirsty land springs of water; In the habitation of jackals, where each lay, *There shall be* grass with reeds and rushes.

Made by man.

Eccl 2:6 I made myself water pools from which to water the growing trees of the grove.

Artificial, designed for

Supplying cities with water.

2 Kin 20:20 Now the rest of the acts of Hezekiah—all his might, and how he made a pool and a tunnel and brought water into the city—*are* they not written in the book of the chronicles of the kings of Judah?

Supplying gardens with water.

Eccl 2:6 I made myself water pools from which to water the growing trees of the grove.

Water of, brought into the city by a ditch or conduit.

2 Kin 20:20 Now the rest of the acts of Hezekiah—all his might, and how he made a pool and a tunnel and brought water into the city—*are* they not written in the book of the chronicles of the kings of Judah?

Is 22:11 You also made a reservoir between the two walls For the water of the old pool. But you did not look to its Maker, Nor did you have respect for Him who fashioned it long ago.

Filled by the rain.

Ps 84:6 *As* they pass through the Valley of Baca, They make it a spring; The rain also covers it with pools.

Scripture places mentioned

Bethesda.

John 5:2 Now there is in Jerusalem by the Sheep *Gate* a pool, which is called in Hebrew, Bethesda, having five porches.

Gibeon.

2 Sam 2:13 And Joab the son of Zeruiah, and the servants of David, went out and met them by the pool of Gibeon. So they sat down, one on one side of the pool and the other on the other side of the pool.

Hebron.

2 Sam 4:12 So David commanded his young men, and they executed them, cut off their hands and feet, and hanged *them* by the pool in Hebron. But they took the head of Ishbosheth and buried *it* in the tomb of Abner in Hebron.

Samaria.

1 Kin 22:38 Then *someone* washed the chariot at a pool in Samaria, and the dogs licked up his blood while the harlots bathed, according to the word of the LORD which He had spoken.

Siloam.

John 9:7 And He said to him, "Go, wash in the pool of

Siloam" (which is translated, Sent). So he went and washed, and came back seeing.

The upper pool.

2 Kin 18:17 Then the king of Assyria sent *the* Tartan, *the* Rabsaris, *and the* Rabshakeh from Lachish, with a great army against Jerusalem, to King Hezekiah. And they went up and came to Jerusalem. When they had come up, they went and stood by the aqueduct from the upper pool, which *was* on the highway to the Fuller's Field.

Is 7:3 Then the LORD said to Isaiah, "Go out now to meet Ahaz, you and Shear-Jashub your son, at the end of the aqueduct from the upper pool, on the highway to the Fuller's Field,

The lower pool.

Is 22:9 You also saw the damage to the city of David, That it was great; And you gathered together the waters of the lower pool.

The king's pool.

Neh 2:14 Then I went on to the Fountain Gate and to the King's Pool, but *there was* no room for the animal under me to pass.

The old pool.

Is 22:11 You also made a reservoir between the two walls For the water of the old pool. But you did not look to its Maker, Nor did you have respect for Him who fashioned it long ago.

The land of Egypt abounded in.

Ex 7:19 Then the LORD spoke to Moses, "Say to Aaron, 'Take your rod and stretch out your hand over the waters of Egypt, over their streams, over their rivers, over their ponds, and over all their pools of water, that they may become blood. And there shall be blood throughout all the land of Egypt, both in *buckets of* wood and *pitchers of* stone.' "

Illustrative of

Nineveh.

Nah 2:8 Though Nineveh of old *was* like a pool of water, Now they flee away. "Halt! Halt!" *they cry;* But no one turns back.

Spiritual renewal.

Is 35:7 The parched ground shall become a pool, And the thirsty land springs of water; In the habitation of jackals, where each lay, *There shall be* grass with reeds and rushes.

Is 41:18 I will open rivers in desolate heights, And fountains in the midst of the valleys; I will make the wilderness a pool of water, And the dry land springs of water.

(Turning cities into) great desolation.

Is 14:23 "I will also make it a possession for the porcupine, And marshes of muddy water; I will sweep it with the broom of destruction," says the LORD of hosts.

POOR, THE

Condition of, sometimes results from

Sloth.

Prov 20:13 Do not love sleep, lest you come to poverty; Open your eyes, *and* you will be satisfied with bread.

Bad company.

Prov 28:19 He who tills his land will have plenty of bread, But he who follows frivolity will have poverty enough!

Drunkenness and gluttony.

Prov 23:21 For the drunkard and the glutton will come to poverty, And drowsiness will clothe *a man* with rags.

God

Made them.

1 Sam 2:7 The LORD makes poor and makes rich; He brings low and lifts up.

Job 1:21 And he said: "Naked I came from my mother's womb, And naked shall I return there. The LORD gave, and the LORD has taken away; Blessed be the name of the LORD."

Job 34:19 Yet He is not partial to princes, Nor does He regard the rich more than the poor; For they *are* all the work of His hands.

Prov 22:2 The rich and the poor have this in common, The LORD *is* the maker of them all.

Regards them equally with the rich.

Job 34:19 Yet He is not partial to princes, Nor does He regard the rich more than the poor; For they *are* all the work of His hands.

Remembers them.

Ps 9:18 For the needy shall not always be forgotten; The expectation of the poor shall *not* perish forever.

Hears them.

Ps 69:33 For the LORD hears the poor, And does not despise His prisoners.

Is 41:17 "The poor and needy seek water, but *there is* none, Their tongues fail for thirst. I, the LORD, will hear them; I, the God of Israel, will not forsake them.

Maintains the right of.

Ps 140:12 I know that the LORD will maintain The cause of the afflicted, *And* justice for the poor.

Delivers them.

Job 36:15 He delivers the poor in their affliction, And opens their ears in oppression.

Ps 35:10 All my bones shall say, "LORD, who *is* like You, Delivering the poor from him who is too strong for him, Yes, the poor and the needy from him who plunders him?"

Protects them.

Ps 12:5 "For the oppression of the poor, for the sighing of the needy, Now I will arise," says the LORD; "I will set *him* in the safety for which he yearns."

Ps 109:31 For He shall stand at the right hand of the poor, To save *him* from those who condemn him.

Exalts them.

1 Sam 2:8 He raises the poor from the dust *And* lifts the beggar from the ash heap, To set *them* among princes And make them inherit the throne of glory. "For the pillars of the earth *are* the LORD's, And He has set the world upon them.

Ps 107:41 Yet He sets the poor on high, far from affliction, And makes *their* families like a flock.

Ps 113:7–8 He raises the poor out of the dust, And lifts the needy out of the ash heap, **8** That He may seat *him* with princes— With the princes of His people.

Is 25:4 For You have been a strength to the poor, A strength to the needy in his distress, A refuge from the storm, A shade from the heat; For the blast of the terrible ones *is* as a storm *against* the wall.

Provides for.

Ps 68:10 Your congregation dwelt in it; You, O God, provided from Your goodness for the poor.

Ps 146:7 Who executes justice for the oppressed, Who gives food to the hungry. The LORD gives freedom to the prisoners.

Despises not the prayer of.

Ps 102:17 He shall regard the prayer of the destitute, And shall not despise their prayer.

Is the refuge of.

Ps 14:6 You shame the counsel of the poor, But the LORD *is* his refuge.

Will always exist.

Deut 15:11 For the poor will never cease from the land; therefore I command you, saying, 'You shall open your hand wide to your brother, to your poor and your needy, in your land.'

Zeph 3:12 I will leave in your midst A meek and humble people, And they shall trust in the name of the LORD.

Matt 26:11 For you have the poor with you always, but Me you do not have always.

May be

Rich in faith.

James 2:5 Listen, my beloved brethren: Has God not chosen the poor of this world *to be* rich in faith and heirs of the kingdom which He promised to those who love Him?

Generous.

Mark 12:42 Then one poor widow came and threw in two mites, which make a quadrans.

2 Cor 9:12 For the administration of this service not only supplies the needs of the saints, but also is abounding through many thanksgivings to God,

Wise.

Prov 28:11 The rich man *is* wise in his own eyes, But the poor who has understanding searches him out.

Upright.

Prov 19:1 Better *is* the poor who walks in his integrity Than *one who is* perverse in his lips, and is a fool.

Christ

Lived as one of.

Matt 8:20 And Jesus said to him, "Foxes have holes and birds of the air *have* nests, but the Son of Man has nowhere to lay His head."

Preached to them.

Luke 4:18 "The Spirit of the LORD *is* upon Me, Because He has anointed Me To preach the gospel to the poor; He has sent Me to heal the brokenhearted, To proclaim liberty to the captives And recovery of sight to the blind, To set at liberty those who are oppressed;

Delivers them.

Ps 72:12 For He will deliver the needy when he cries, The poor also, and *him* who has no helper.

Offerings of, acceptable to God.

Mark 12:42–44 Then one poor widow came and threw in two mites, which make a quadrans. **43** So He called His disciples to *Himself* and said to them, "Assuredly, I say to you that this poor widow has put in more than all those who have given to the treasury; **44** for they all put in out of their abundance, but she out of her poverty put in all that she had, her whole livelihood."

2 Cor 8:2 that in a great trial of affliction the abundance of their joy and their deep poverty abounded in the riches of their liberality.

2 Cor 8:12 For if there is first a willing mind, *it is* accepted according to what one has, *and* not according to what he does not have.

Should

Rejoice in God.

Is 29:19 The humble also shall increase *their* joy in the LORD, And the poor among men shall rejoice In the Holy One of Israel.

Hope in God.

Job 5:16 So the poor have hope, And injustice shuts her mouth.

Commit themselves to God.

Ps 10:14 But You have seen, for You observe trouble and grief, To repay *it* by Your hand. The helpless commits himself to You; You are the helper of the fatherless.

When converted, rejoice in their exaltation.

James 1:9 Let the lowly brother glory in his exaltation,

Provided for under the Law.

Ex 23:11 but the seventh *year* you shall let it rest and lie fallow, that the poor of your people may eat; and what they leave, the beasts of the field may eat. In like manner you shall do with your vineyard *and* your olive grove.

Lev 19:9–10 'When you reap the harvest of your land, you shall not wholly reap the corners of your field, nor shall you gather the gleanings of your harvest. **10** And you shall not glean your vineyard, nor shall you gather *every* grape of your vineyard; you shall leave them for the poor and the stranger: I *am* the LORD your God.

Neglect toward is

Neglect of Christ.

Matt 25:42–45 for I was hungry and you gave Me no food; I was thirsty and you gave Me no drink; **43** I was a stranger and you did not take Me in, naked and you did not clothe Me, sick and in prison and you did not visit Me.' **44** "Then they also will answer Him, saying, 'Lord, when did we see You hungry or thirsty or a stranger or naked or sick or in prison, and did not minister to You?' **45** Then He will answer them, saying, 'Assuredly, I say to you, inasmuch as you did not do *it* to one of the least of these, you did not do *it* to Me.'

Inconsistent with love to God.

1 John 3:17 But whoever has this world's goods, and sees his brother in need, and shuts up his heart from him, how does the love of God abide in him?

A proof of unbelief.

James 2:15–17 If a brother or sister is naked and destitute of daily food, **16** and one of you says to them, "Depart in peace, be warmed and filled," but you do not give them the things which are needed for the body, what *does it* profit? **17** Thus also faith by itself, if it does not have works, is dead.

Commands concerning treatment of,

Do not rob.

Prov 22:22 Do not rob the poor because he *is* poor, Nor oppress the afflicted at the gate;

Do not be unjust toward.

Ex 23:6 "You shall not pervert the judgment of your poor in his dispute.

Take no usury or interest from.

Ex 22:25 "If you lend money to *any of* My people *who are* poor among you, you shall not be like a moneylender to him; you shall not charge him interest.

Lev 25:36 Take no usury or interest from him; but fear your God, that your brother may live with you.

Do not harden the heart against.

Deut 15:7 "If there is among you a poor man of your brethren, within any of the gates in your land which the LORD your God is giving you, you shall not harden your heart nor shut your hand from your poor brother,

Do not withhold generosity.

Deut 15:7 "If there is among you a poor man of your brethren, within any of the gates in your land which the LORD your God is giving you, you shall not harden your heart nor shut your hand from your poor brother,

Do not oppress.

Lev 25:39 'And if *one of* your brethren *who dwells* by you becomes poor, and sells himself to you, you shall not compel him to serve as a slave.

Lev 25:43 You shall not rule over him with rigor, but you shall fear your God.

Deut 24:14 "You shall not oppress a hired servant *who is* poor and needy, *whether* one of your brethren or one of the aliens who *is* in your land within your gates.

Zech 7:10 Do not oppress the widow or the fatherless, The alien or the poor. Let none of you plan evil in his heart Against his brother.'

Do not despise.

Prov 14:21 He who despises his neighbor sins; But he who has mercy on the poor, happy *is* he.

James 2:2–4 For if there should come into your assembly a man with gold rings, in fine apparel, and there should also come in a poor man in filthy clothes, **3** and you pay attention to the one wearing the fine clothes and say to him, "You sit here in a good place," and say to the poor man, "You stand there," or, "Sit here at my footstool," **4** have you not shown partiality among yourselves, and become judges with evil thoughts?

Relieve them.

Lev 25:35 'If one of your brethren becomes poor, and falls into poverty among you, then you shall help him, like a stranger or a sojourner, that he may live with you.

Matt 19:21 Jesus said to him, "If you want to be perfect,

go, sell what you have and give to the poor, and you will have treasure in heaven; and come, follow Me."

Defend them.

Ps 82:3–4 Defend the poor and fatherless; Do justice to the afflicted and needy. **4** Deliver the poor and needy; Free *them* from the hand of the wicked.

Do justice to them.

Ps 82:3 Defend the poor and fatherless; Do justice to the afflicted and needy.

Jer 22:3 Thus says the LORD: "Execute judgment and righteousness, and deliver the plundered out of the hand of the oppressor. Do no wrong and do no violence to the stranger, the fatherless, or the widow, nor shed innocent blood in this place.

Jer 22:16 He judged the cause of the poor and needy; Then *it was* well. *Was* not this knowing Me?" says the LORD.

Caring for,

Is characteristic of believers.

Ps 112:9 He has dispersed abroad, He has given to the poor; His righteousness endures forever; His horn will be exalted with honor.

Prov 29:7 The righteous considers the cause of the poor, *But* the wicked does not understand *such* knowledge.

2 Cor 9:9 As it is written: *"He has dispersed abroad, He has given to the poor; His righteousness endures forever."*

Is a fruit of repentance.

Luke 3:11 He answered and said to them, "He who has two tunics, let him give to him who has none; and he who has food, let him do likewise."

Should be urged.

2 Cor 8:7–8 But as you abound in everything—in faith, in speech, in knowledge, in all diligence, and in your love for us—*see* that you abound in this grace also. **8** I speak not by commandment, but I am testing the sincerity of your love by the diligence of others.

Gal 2:10 *They desired* only that we should remember the poor, the very thing which I also was eager to do.

Give to,

Not grudgingly.

Deut 15:10 You shall surely give to him, and your heart should not be grieved when you give to him, because for this thing the LORD your God will bless you in all your works and in all to which you put your hand.

2 Cor 9:7 *So let* each one *give* as he purposes in his heart, not grudgingly or of necessity; for God loves a cheerful giver.

Generously.

Deut 14:29 And the Levite, because he has no portion nor inheritance with you, and the stranger and the fatherless and the widow who *are* within your gates, may come and eat and be satisfied, that the LORD your God may bless you in all the work of your hand which you do.

Deut 15:8 but you shall open your hand wide to him and willingly lend him sufficient for his need, whatever he needs.

Deut 15:11 For the poor will never cease from the land; therefore I command you, saying, 'You shall open your hand wide to your brother, to your poor and your needy, in your land.'

Cheerfully.

2 Cor 8:12 For if there is first a willing mind, *it is* accepted according to what one has, *and* not according to what he does not have.

2 Cor 9:7 *So let* each one *give* as he purposes in his heart, not grudgingly or of necessity; for God loves a cheerful giver.

Without ostentation.

Matt 6:1 "Take heed that you do not do your charitable deeds before men, to be seen by them. Otherwise you have no reward from your Father in heaven.

Especially if they are believers.

Rom 12:13 distributing to the needs of the saints, given to hospitality.

Gal 6:10 Therefore, as we have opportunity, let us do good to all, especially to those who are of the household of faith.

Pray for.

Ps 74:19 Oh, do not deliver the life of Your turtledove to the wild beast! Do not forget the life of Your poor forever.

Ps 74:21 Oh, do not let the oppressed return ashamed! Let the poor and needy praise Your name.

They who in faith relieve,

Are happy and blessed by God.

Deut 15:10 You shall surely give to him, and your heart should not be grieved when you give to him, because for this thing the LORD your God will bless you in all your works and in all to which you put your hand.

Ps 41:1 Blessed *is* he who considers the poor; The LORD will deliver him in time of trouble.

Prov 14:21 He who despises his neighbor sins; But he who has mercy on the poor, happy *is* he.

Prov 22:9 He who has a generous eye will be blessed, For he gives of his bread to the poor.

Acts 20:35 I have shown you in every way, by laboring like this, that you must support the weak. And remember the words of the Lord Jesus, that He said, 'It is more blessed to give than to receive.' "

Heb 13:16 But do not forget to do good and to share, for with such sacrifices God is well pleased.

Have promises.

Prov 28:27 He who gives to the poor will not lack, But he who hides his eyes will have many curses.

Luke 14:13–14 But when you give a feast, invite *the* poor, *the* maimed, *the* lame, *the* blind. **14** And you will be blessed, because they cannot repay you; for you shall be repaid at the resurrection of the just."

In spirit, given the kingdom of heaven.

Matt 5:3 "Blessed *are* the poor in spirit, For theirs is the kingdom of heaven.

Luke 6:20 Then He lifted up His eyes toward His disciples, and said: "Blessed *are you* poor, For yours is the kingdom of God.

By oppressing and mocking, God is reproached.

Prov 14:31 He who oppresses the poor reproaches his Maker, But he who honors Him has mercy on the needy.

Prov 17:5 He who mocks the poor reproaches his Maker; He who is glad at calamity will not go unpunished.

The wicked

Do not care about them.

Prov 29:7 The righteous considers the cause of the poor, But the wicked does not understand *such* knowledge.

John 12:6 This he said, not that he cared for the poor, but because he was a thief, and had the money box; and he used to take what was put in it.

Oppress them.

Job 24:4–10 They push the needy off the road; All the poor of the land are forced to hide. **5** Indeed, *like* wild donkeys in the desert, They go out to their work, searching for food. The wilderness *yields* food for them *and* for *their* children. **6** They gather their fodder in the field And glean in the vineyard of the wicked. **7** They spend the night naked, without clothing, And have no covering in the cold. **8** They are wet with the showers of the mountains, And huddle around the rock for want of shelter. **9** *"Some* snatch the fatherless from the breast, And take a pledge from the poor. **10** They cause *the poor* to go naked, without clothing; And they take away the sheaves from the hungry.

Ezek 18:12 If he has oppressed the poor and needy, Robbed by violence, Not restored the pledge, Lifted his eyes to the idols, *Or* committed abomination;

Sell them.

Amos 2:6 Thus says the LORD: "For three transgressions of Israel, and for four, I will not turn away its *punishment*, Because they sell the righteous for silver, And the poor for a pair of sandals.

Crush them down.

Is 3:15 What do you mean by crushing My people And grinding the faces of the poor?" Says the Lord GOD of hosts.

Amos 4:1 Hear this word, you cows of Bashan, who *are* on the mountain of Samaria, Who oppress the poor, Who crush the needy, Who say to your husbands, "Bring *wine*, let us drink!"

Amos 5:11 Therefore, because you tread down the poor And take grain taxes from him, Though you have built houses of hewn stone, Yet you shall not dwell in them; You have planted pleasant vineyards, But you shall not drink wine from them.

Devour them.

Hab 3:14 You thrust through with his own arrows The head of his villages. They came out like a whirlwind to scatter me; Their rejoicing was like feasting on the poor in secret.

Persecute them.

Ps 10:2 The wicked in *his* pride persecutes the poor; Let them be caught in the plots which they have devised.

Defraud them.

Amos 8:5–6 Saying: "When will the New Moon be past,

That we may sell grain? And the Sabbath, That we may trade wheat? Making the ephah small and the shekel large, Falsifying the scales by deceit, **6** That we may buy the poor for silver, And the needy for a pair of sandals— Even sell the bad wheat?"

Despise the counsel of.

Ps 14:6 You shame the counsel of the poor, But the LORD *is* his refuge.

Guilt of defrauding.

James 5:4 Indeed the wages of the laborers who mowed your fields, which you kept back by fraud, cry out; and the cries of the reapers have reached the ears of the Lord of Sabaoth.

Abuses of, punished

Oppressing.

Prov 22:16 He who oppresses the poor to increase his *riches, And* he who gives to the rich, *will* surely *come* to poverty.

Ezek 22:29 The people of the land have used oppressions, committed robbery, and mistreated the poor and needy; and they wrongfully oppress the stranger.

Ezek 22:31 Therefore I have poured out My indignation on them; I have consumed them with the fire of My wrath; and I have recompensed their deeds on their own heads," says the Lord GOD.

Fleecing.

Is 3:13–15 The LORD stands up to plead, And stands to judge the people. **14** The LORD will enter into judgment With the elders of His people And His princes: "For you have eaten up the vineyard; The plunder of the poor *is* in your houses. **15** What do you mean by crushing My people And grinding the faces of the poor?" Says the Lord GOD of hosts.

Ezek 18:13 If he has exacted usury Or taken increase— Shall he then live? He shall not live! If he has done any of these abominations, He shall surely die; His blood shall be upon him.

Refusing to assist.

Job 22:7 You have not given the weary water to drink, And you have withheld bread from the hungry.

Job 22:10 Therefore snares *are* all around you, And sudden fear troubles you,

Prov 21:13 Whoever shuts his ears to the cry of the poor Will also cry himself and not be heard.

Treating with unjustice.

Job 20:19 For he has oppressed *and* forsaken the poor, He has violently seized a house which he did not build.

Job 20:29 This *is* the portion from God for a wicked man, The heritage appointed to him by God."

Job 22:6 For you have taken pledges from your brother for no reason, And stripped the naked of their clothing.

Job 22:10 Therefore snares *are* all around you, And sudden fear troubles you,

Is 10:1–3 "Woe to those who decree unrighteous decrees, Who write misfortune, *Which* they have prescribed **2** To rob the needy of justice, And to take what is right from the poor of My people, That widows may be their prey, And *that* they may rob the fa-

therless. **3** What will you do in the day of punishment, And in the desolation *which* will come from afar? To whom will you flee for help? And where will you leave your glory?

Amos 5:11–12 Therefore, because you tread down the poor And take grain taxes from him, Though you have built houses of hewn stone, Yet you shall not dwell in them; You have planted pleasant vineyards, But you shall not drink wine from them. **12** For I know your manifold transgressions And your mighty sins: Afflicting the just *and* taking bribes; Diverting the poor *from justice* at the gate.

Oppression of—illustrated.

2 Sam 12:1–6 Then the LORD sent Nathan to David. And he came to him, and said to him: "There were two men in one city, one rich and the other poor. **2** The rich *man* had exceedingly many flocks and herds. **3** But the poor *man* had nothing, except one little ewe lamb which he had bought and nourished; and it grew up together with him and with his children. It ate of his own food and drank from his own cup and lay in his bosom; and it was like a daughter to him. **4** And a traveler came to the rich man, who refused to take from his own flock and from his own herd to prepare one for the wayfaring man who had come to him; but he took the poor man's lamb and prepared it for the man who had come to him." **5** So David's anger was greatly aroused against the man, and he said to Nathan, "*As* the LORD lives, the man who has done this shall surely die! **6** And he shall restore fourfold for the lamb, because he did this thing and because he had no pity."

Care for—illustrated.

Luke 10:33–35 But a certain Samaritan, as he journeyed, came where he was. And when he saw him, he had compassion. **34** So he went to *him* and bandaged his wounds, pouring on oil and wine; and he set him on his own animal, brought him to an inn, and took care of him. **35** On the next day, when he departed, he took out two denarii, gave *them* to the innkeeper, and said to him, 'Take care of him; and whatever more you spend, when I come again, I will repay you.'

Right behavior of—exemplified by

Gideon.

Judg 6:15 So he said to Him, "O my Lord, how can I save Israel? Indeed my clan *is* the weakest in Manasseh, and I *am* the least in my father's house."

Ruth.

Ruth 2:2 So Ruth the Moabitess said to Naomi, "Please let me go to the field, and glean heads of grain after *him* in whose sight I may find favor." And she said to her, "Go, my daughter."

The widow of Zarephath.

1 Kin 17:12 So she said, "As the LORD your God lives, I do not have bread, only a handful of flour in a bin, and a little oil in a jar; and see, I *am* gathering a couple of sticks that I may go in and prepare it for myself and my son, that we may eat it, and die."

A prophet's widow.

2 Kin 4:2 So Elisha said to her, "What shall I do for you? Tell me, what do you have in the house?" And she said, "Your maidservant has nothing in the house but a jar of oil."

The believers of old.

Heb 11:37 They were stoned, they were sawn in two, were tempted, were slain with the sword. They wandered about in sheepskins and goatskins, being destitute, afflicted, tormented—

Regard for—exemplified by

Boaz.

Ruth 2:14 Now Boaz said to her at mealtime, "Come here, and eat of the bread, and dip your piece of bread in the vinegar." So she sat beside the reapers, and he passed parched *grain* to her; and she ate and was satisfied, and kept some back.

Job.

Job 29:12–16 Because I delivered the poor who cried out, The fatherless and *the one who* had no helper. **13** The blessing of a perishing *man* came upon me, And I caused the widow's heart to sing for joy. **14** I put on righteousness, and it clothed me; My justice *was* like a robe and a turban. **15** I *was* eyes to the blind, And I *was* feet to the lame. **16** I *was* a father to the poor, And I searched out the case *that* I did not know.

Nebuzaradan.

Jer 39:10 But Nebuzaradan the captain of the guard left in the land of Judah the poor people, who had nothing, and gave them vineyards and fields at the same time.

Zacchaeus.

Luke 19:8 Then Zacchaeus stood and said to the Lord, "Look, Lord, I give half of my goods to the poor; and if I have taken anything from anyone by false accusation, I restore fourfold."

Peter and John.

Acts 3:6 Then Peter said, "Silver and gold I do not have, but what I do have I give you: In the name of Jesus Christ of Nazareth, rise up and walk."

Dorcas.

Acts 9:36 At Joppa there was a certain disciple named Tabitha, which is translated Dorcas. This woman was full of good works and charitable deeds which she did.

Acts 9:39 Then Peter arose and went with them. When he had come, they brought *him* to the upper room. And all the widows stood by him weeping, showing the tunics and garments which Dorcas had made while she was with them.

Cornelius.

Acts 10:2 a devout *man* and one who feared God with all his household, who gave alms generously to the people, and prayed to God always.

The church at Antioch.

Acts 11:29–30 Then the disciples, each according to his ability, determined to send relief to the brethren dwelling in Judea. **30** This they also did, and sent it to the elders by the hands of Barnabas and Saul.

Paul.

Rom 15:25 But now I am going to Jerusalem to minister to the saints.

The churches of Macedonia and Achaia.

Rom 15:26 For it pleased those from Macedonia and Achaia to make a certain contribution for the poor among the saints who are in Jerusalem.

2 Cor 8:1–5 Moreover, brethren, we make known to you the grace of God bestowed on the churches of Macedonia: **2** that in a great trial of affliction the abundance of their joy and their deep poverty abounded in the riches of their liberality. **3** For I bear witness that according to *their* ability, yes, and beyond *their* ability, *they were* freely willing, **4** imploring us with much urgency that we would receive the gift and the fellowship of the ministering to the saints. **5** And not *only* as we had hoped, but they first gave themselves to the Lord, and *then* to us by the will of God.

POSSESSIONS

Man should honor the Lord with.

Prov 3:9–10 Honor the LORD with your possessions, And with the firstfruits of all your increase; **10** So your barns will be filled with plenty, And your vats will overflow with new wine.

Concern with material, blinds people to the gospel.

Mark 4:19 and the cares of this world, the deceitfulness of riches, and the desires for other things entering in choke the word, and it becomes unfruitful.

Jesus' command not to amass earthly.

Luke 12:33 Sell what you have and give alms; provide yourselves money bags which do not grow old, a treasure in the heavens that does not fail, where no thief approaches nor moth destroys.

Believers give up, for others when need arises.

Acts 2:44–45 Now all who believed were together, and had all things in common, **45** and sold their possessions and goods, and divided them among all, as anyone had need.

PRAISE

God

Is worthy of.

2 Sam 22:4 I will call upon the LORD, *who is worthy* to be praised; So shall I be saved from my enemies.

Is glorified by.

Ps 22:23 You who fear the LORD, praise Him! All you descendants of Jacob, glorify Him, And fear Him, all you offspring of Israel!

Ps 50:23 Whoever offers praise glorifies Me; And to him who orders *his* conduct *aright* I will show the salvation of God."

Christ

Is worthy of.

Rev 5:12 saying with a loud voice: "Worthy is the Lamb who was slain To receive power and riches and wisdom, And strength and honor and glory and blessing!"

Was offered.

John 12:13 took branches of palm trees and went out to meet Him, and cried out: "Hosanna! *'Blessed is He who comes in the name of the LORD!'* The King of Israel!"

Acceptable through Him.

Heb 13:15 Therefore by Him let us continually offer the sacrifice of praise to God, that is, the fruit of *our* lips, giving thanks to His name.

Is due to God because of

His majesty.

Ps 96:2 For the Lord is great and greatly to be praised; He is to be feared above all gods.

Ps 96:6 Honor and majesty *are* before Him; Strength and beauty *are* in His sanctuary.

Is 24:14 They shall lift up their voice, they shall sing; For the majesty of the Lord They shall cry aloud from the sea.

His glory.

Ps 138:5 Yes, they shall sing of the ways of the Lord, For great *is* the glory of the Lord.

Ezek 3:12 Then the Spirit lifted me up, and I heard behind me a great thunderous voice: "Blessed *is* the glory of the Lord from His place!"

His excellency.

Ex 15:7 And in the greatness of Your excellence You have overthrown those who rose against You; You sent forth Your wrath; It consumed them like stubble.

Ps 148:13 Let them praise the name of the Lord, For His name alone is exalted; His glory *is* above the earth and heaven.

His greatness.

1 Chr 16:25 For the Lord *is* great and greatly to be praised; He *is* also to be feared above all gods.

Ps 145:3 Great *is* the Lord, and greatly to be praised; And His greatness *is* unsearchable.

His holiness.

Ex 15:11 "Who *is* like You, O Lord, among the gods? Who *is* like You, glorious in holiness, Fearful in praises, doing wonders?

Is 6:3 And one cried to another and said: "Holy, holy, holy *is* the Lord of hosts; The whole earth *is* full of His glory!"

His wisdom.

Dan 2:20 Daniel answered and said: "Blessed be the name of God forever and ever, For wisdom and might are His.

Jude 1:25 To God our Savior, Who alone is wise, *Be* glory and majesty, Dominion and power, Both now and forever. Amen.

His power.

Ps 21:13 Be exalted, O Lord, in Your own strength! We will sing and praise Your power.

His goodness.

Ps 107:8 Oh, that *men* would give thanks to the Lord *for* His goodness, And *for* His wonderful works to the children of men!

Ps 118:1 Oh, give thanks to the Lord, for *He is* good! For His mercy *endures* forever.

Ps 136:1 Oh, give thanks to the Lord, for *He is* good! For His mercy *endures* forever.

Jer 33:11 the voice of joy and the voice of gladness, the voice of the bridegroom and the voice of the bride, the voice of those who will say: "Praise the Lord of hosts, For the Lord *is* good, For His mercy *endures* forever"— *and* of those *who will* bring the sacrifice of praise into the house of the Lord. For I will cause the captives of the land to return as at the first,' says the Lord.

His mercy.

2 Chr 20:21 And when he had consulted with the people, he appointed those who should sing to the Lord, and who should praise the beauty of holiness, as they went out before the army and were saying: "Praise the Lord, For His mercy *endures* forever."

Ps 89:1 I will sing of the mercies of the Lord forever; With my mouth will I make known Your faithfulness to all generations.

Ps 118:1–4 Oh, give thanks to the Lord, for *He is* good! For His mercy *endures* forever. **2** Let Israel now say, "His mercy *endures* forever." **3** Let the house of Aaron now say, "His mercy *endures* forever." **4** Let those who fear the Lord now say, "His mercy *endures* forever."

Cf. Ps 136:1–26

His lovingkindness and truth.

Ps 138:2 I will worship toward Your holy temple, And praise Your name For Your lovingkindness and Your truth; For You have magnified Your word above all Your name.

His faithfulness and truth.

Is 25:1 O Lord, You *are* my God. I will exalt You, I will praise Your name, For You have done wonderful *things; Your* counsels of old *are* faithfulness *and* truth.

His salvation.

Ps 18:46 The Lord lives! Blessed *be* my Rock! Let the God of my salvation be exalted.

Is 35:10 And the ransomed of the Lord shall return, And come to Zion with singing, With everlasting joy on their heads. They shall obtain joy and gladness, And sorrow and sighing shall flee away.

Is 61:10 I will greatly rejoice in the Lord, My soul shall be joyful in my God; For He has clothed me with the garments of salvation, He has covered me with the robe of righteousness, As a bridegroom decks *himself* with ornaments, And as a bride adorns *herself* with her jewels.

Luke 1:68–69 "Blessed *is* the Lord God of Israel, For He has visited and redeemed His people, **69** And has raised up a horn of salvation for us In the house of His servant David,

His wonderful works.

Ps 89:5 And the heavens will praise Your wonders, O Lord; Your faithfulness also in the assembly of the saints.

Ps 150:2 Praise Him for His mighty acts; Praise Him according to His excellent greatness!

Is 25:1 O Lord, You *are* my God. I will exalt You, I will praise Your name, For You have done wonderful *things; Your* counsels of old *are* faithfulness *and* truth.

His consolation.

Ps 42:5 Why are you cast down, O my soul? And *why* are you disquieted within me? Hope in God, for I shall yet praise Him For the help of His countenance.

Is 12:1 And in that day you will say: "O Lord, I will praise You; Though You were angry with me, Your anger is turned away, and You comfort me.

His judgment.

Ps 101:1 I will sing of mercy and justice; To You, O Lord, I will sing praises.

His counsel.

Ps 16:7 I will bless the LORD who has given me counsel; My heart also instructs me in the night seasons.

Jer 32:19 *You are* great in counsel and mighty in work, for your eyes *are* open to all the ways of the sons of men, to give everyone according to his ways and according to the fruit of his doings.

Fulfilling of his promises.

1 Kin 8:56 "Blessed *be* the LORD, who has given rest to His people Israel, according to all that He promised. There has not failed one word of all His good promise, which He promised through His servant Moses.

His pardon for sin.

Ps 103:1–3 Bless the LORD, O my soul; And all that is within me, *bless* His holy name! **2** Bless the LORD, O my soul, And forget not all His benefits: **3** Who forgives all your iniquities, Who heals all your diseases,

Hos 14:2 Take words with you, And return to the LORD. Say to Him, "Take away all iniquity; Receive *us* graciously, For we will offer the sacrifices of our lips.

His providing spiritual health.

Ps 103:3 Who forgives all your iniquities, Who heals all your diseases,

The constant preservation He provides.

Ps 71:6–8 By You I have been upheld from birth; You are He who took me out of my mother's womb. My praise *shall be* continually of You. **7** I have become as a wonder to many, But You *are* my strong refuge. **8** Let my mouth be filled *with* Your praise *And with* Your glory all the day.

His deliverance.

Ps 40:1–3 I waited patiently for the LORD; And He inclined to me, And heard my cry. **2** He also brought me up out of a horrible pit, Out of the miry clay, And set my feet upon a rock, *And* established my steps. **3** He has put a new song in my mouth— Praise to our God; Many will see *it* and fear, And will trust in the LORD.

Ps 124:6 Blessed *be* the LORD, Who has not given us *as* prey to their teeth.

His protection.

Ps 28:7 The LORD *is* my strength and my shield; My heart trusted in Him, and I am helped; Therefore my heart greatly rejoices, And with my song I will praise Him.

Ps 59:17 To You, O my Strength, I will sing praises; For God *is* my defense, My God of mercy.

His answering prayer.

Ps 28:6 Blessed *be* the LORD, Because He has heard the voice of my supplications!

Ps 118:21 I will praise You, For You have answered me, And have become my salvation.

The hope of glory.

1 Pet 1:3–4 Blessed *be* the God and Father of our Lord Jesus Christ, who according to His abundant mercy has begotten us again to a living hope through the resurrection of Jesus Christ from the dead, **4** to an inheritance incorruptible and undefiled and that does not fade away, reserved in heaven for you,

All spiritual blessings.

Ps 103:2 Bless the LORD, O my soul, And forget not all His benefits:

Eph 1:3 Blessed *be* the God and Father of our Lord Jesus Christ, who has blessed us with every spiritual blessing in the heavenly *places* in Christ,

All temporal blessings.

Ps 68:19 Blessed *be* the Lord, *Who* daily loads us *with benefits*, The God of our salvation! Selah

Ps 104:1 Bless the LORD, O my soul! O LORD my God, You are very great: You are clothed with honor and majesty,

Ps 104:14 He causes the grass to grow for the cattle, And vegetation for the service of man, That he may bring forth food from the earth,

Ps 136:25 Who gives food to all flesh, For His mercy *endures* forever.

Is obligatory upon

Angels.

Ps 103:20 Bless the LORD, you His angels, Who excel in strength, who do His word, Heeding the voice of His word.

Ps 148:2 Praise Him, all His angels; Praise Him, all His hosts!

Believers.

Ps 30:4 Sing praise to the LORD, you saints of His, And give thanks at the remembrance of His holy name.

Ps 149:5 Let the saints be joyful in glory; Let them sing aloud on their beds.

All peoples.

Ps 107:8 Oh, that *men* would give thanks to the LORD *for* His goodness, And *for* His wonderful works to the children of men!

Ps 117:1 Praise the LORD, all you Gentiles! Laud Him, all you peoples!

Ps 145:21 My mouth shall speak the praise of the LORD, And all flesh shall bless His holy name Forever and ever.

Rom 15:11 And again: *"Praise the LORD, all you Gentiles! Laud Him, all you peoples!"*

Children.

Ps 8:2 Out of the mouth of babes and nursing infants You have ordained strength, Because of Your enemies, That You may silence the enemy and the avenger.

Matt 21:16 and said to Him, "Do You hear what these are saying?" And Jesus said to them, "Yes. Have you never read, *'Out of the mouth of babes and nursing infants You have perfected praise'?"*

Those in heaven and on earth.

Ps 148:1 Praise the LORD! Praise the LORD from the heavens; Praise Him in the heights!

Ps 148:11 Kings of the earth and all peoples; Princes and all judges of the earth;

Young and old.

Ps 148:1 Praise the LORD! Praise the LORD from the heavens; Praise Him in the heights!

Ps 148:12 Both young men and maidens; Old men and children.

Small and great.

Rev 19:5 Then a voice came from the throne, saying, "Praise our God, all you His servants and those who fear Him, both small and great!"

All creation.

Ps 148:1–10 Praise the Lord! Praise the Lord from the heavens; Praise Him in the heights! **2** Praise Him, all His angels; Praise Him, all His hosts! **3** Praise Him, sun and moon; Praise Him, all you stars of light! **4** Praise Him, you heavens of heavens, And you waters above the heavens! **5** Let them praise the name of the Lord, For He commanded and they were created. **6** He also established them forever and ever; He made a decree which shall not pass away. **7** Praise the Lord from the earth, You great sea creatures and all the depths; **8** Fire and hail, snow and clouds; Stormy wind, fulfilling His word; **9** Mountains and all hills; Fruitful trees and all cedars; **10** Beasts and all cattle; Creeping things and flying fowl;

Ps 150:6 Let everything that has breath praise the Lord. Praise the Lord!

Is beautiful and pleasant.

Ps 33:1 Rejoice in the Lord, O you righteous! *For* praise from the upright is beautiful.

Ps 147:1 Praise the Lord! For *it is* good to sing praises to our God; For *it is* pleasant, *and* praise is beautiful.

Believers should offer,

To give God glory.

Is 42:12 Let them give glory to the Lord, And declare His praise in the coastlands.

Is 43:21 This people I have formed for Myself; They shall declare My praise.

Is 61:3 To console those who mourn in Zion, To give them beauty for ashes, The oil of joy for mourning, The garment of praise for the spirit of heaviness; That they may be called trees of righteousness, The planting of the Lord, that He may be glorified."

1 Pet 2:9 But you *are* a chosen generation, a royal priesthood, a holy nation, His own special people, that you may proclaim the praises of Him who called you out of darkness into His marvelous light;

During trials and affliction.

Acts 16:25 But at midnight Paul and Silas were praying and singing hymns to God, and the prisoners were listening to them.

To triumph in God.

1 Chr 16:35 And say, "Save us, O God of our salvation; Gather us together, and deliver us from the Gentiles, To give thanks to Your holy name, To triumph in Your praise."

Ps 106:47 Save us, O Lord our God, And gather us from among the Gentiles, To give thanks to Your holy name, To triumph in Your praise.

To express their joy.

James 5:13 Is anyone among you suffering? Let him pray. Is anyone cheerful? Let him sing psalms.

To invite others to.

Ps 34:3 Oh, magnify the Lord with me, And let us exalt His name together.

Ps 95:1 Oh come, let us sing to the Lord! Let us shout joyfully to the Rock of our salvation.

With prayer.

Ps 51:15 O Lord, open my lips, And my mouth shall show forth Your praise.

Ps 119:175 Let my soul live, and it shall praise You; And let Your judgments help me.

With understanding.

Ps 47:7 For God *is* the King of all the earth; Sing praises with understanding.

1 Cor 14:15 What is *the conclusion* then? I will pray with the spirit, and I will also pray with the understanding. I will sing with the spirit, and I will also sing with the understanding.

With the soul.

Ps 103:1 Bless the Lord, O my soul; And all that is within me, *bless* His holy name!

Ps 104:1 Bless the Lord, O my soul! O Lord my God, You are very great: You are clothed with honor and majesty,

Ps 104:35 May sinners be consumed from the earth, And the wicked be no more. Bless the Lord, O my soul! Praise the Lord!

With the whole heart.

Ps 9:1 I will praise *You*, O Lord, with my whole heart; I will tell of all Your marvelous works.

Ps 111:1 Praise the Lord! I will praise the Lord with *my* whole heart, In the assembly of the upright and *in* the congregation.

Ps 138:1 I will praise You with my whole heart; Before the gods I will sing praises to You.

With uprightness of heart.

Ps 119:7 I will praise You with uprightness of heart, When I learn Your righteous judgments.

With the lips.

Ps 63:3 Because Your lovingkindness *is* better than life, My lips shall praise You.

Ps 119:171 My lips shall utter praise, For You teach me Your statutes.

With the mouth.

Ps 51:15 O Lord, open my lips, And my mouth shall show forth Your praise.

Ps 63:5 My soul shall be satisfied as with marrow and fatness, And my mouth shall praise You with joyful lips.

With joy.

Ps 63:5 My soul shall be satisfied as with marrow and fatness, And my mouth shall praise You with joyful lips.

Ps 98:4 Shout joyfully to the Lord, all the earth; Break forth in song, rejoice, and sing praises.

With gladness.

2 Chr 29:30 Moreover King Hezekiah and the leaders commanded the Levites to sing praise to the Lord with the words of David and of Asaph the seer. So they sang praises with gladness, and they bowed their heads and worshiped.

Jer 33:11 the voice of joy and the voice of gladness, the voice of the bridegroom and the voice of the bride, the voice of those who will say: "Praise the Lord of hosts, For the Lord *is* good, For His mercy *endures* forever"— *and* of those *who will* bring the sacrifice of praise into the house of the LORD. For I will cause the captives of the land to return as at the first,' says the LORD.

With thankfulness.

1 Chr 16:4 And he appointed some of the Levites to minister before the ark of the LORD, to commemorate, to thank, and to praise the LORD God of Israel:

Neh 12:24 And the heads of the Levites *were* Hashabiah, Sherebiah, and Jeshua the son of Kadmiel, with their brothers across from them, to praise *and* give thanks, group alternating with group, according to the command of David the man of God.

Ps 147:7 Sing to the LORD with thanksgiving; Sing praises on the harp to our God,

Continually.

2 Chr 30:21 So the children of Israel who were present at Jerusalem kept the Feast of Unleavened Bread seven days with great gladness; and the Levites and the priests praised the LORD day by day, *singing* to the LORD, accompanied by loud instruments.

Ps 35:28 And my tongue shall speak of Your righteousness *And* of Your praise all the day long.

Ps 71:6 By You I have been upheld from birth; You are He who took me out of my mother's womb. My praise *shall be* continually of You.

Ps 71:14 But I will hope continually, And will praise You yet more and more.

Ps 104:33 I will sing to the LORD as long as I live; I will sing praise to my God while I have my being.

Ps 145:1–2 I will extol You, my God, O King; And I will bless Your name forever and ever. **2** Every day I will bless You, And I will praise Your name forever and ever.

Rev 4:8 *The* four living creatures, each having six wings, were full of eyes around and within. And they do not rest day or night, saying: "Holy, holy, holy, Lord God Almighty, Who was and is and is to come!"

Throughout the world.

Ps 113:3 From the rising of the sun to its going down The LORD's name *is* to be praised.

In psalms and hymns, etc.

Ps 105:2 Sing to Him, sing psalms to Him; Talk of all His wondrous works!

Eph 5:19 speaking to one another in psalms and hymns and spiritual songs, singing and making melody in your heart to the Lord,

Col 3:16 Let the word of Christ dwell in you richly in all wisdom, teaching and admonishing one another in psalms and hymns and spiritual songs, singing with grace in your hearts to the Lord.

Accompanied with musical instruments.

1 Chr 16:41–42 and with them Heman and Jeduthun and the rest who were chosen, who were designated by name, to give thanks to the LORD, because His mercy *endures* forever; **42** and with them Heman and Jeduthun, to sound aloud with trumpets and cymbals and the musical instruments of God. Now the sons of Jeduthun *were* gatekeepers.

Ps 150:3 Praise Him with the sound of the trumpet; Praise Him with the lute and harp!

Ps 150:5 Praise Him with loud cymbals; Praise Him with clashing cymbals!

Is a part of public worship.

Ps 9:14 That I may tell of all Your praise In the gates of the daughter of Zion. I will rejoice in Your salvation.

Ps 100:4 Enter into His gates with thanksgiving, *And* into His courts with praise. Be thankful to Him, *and* bless His name.

Ps 118:19–20 Open to me the gates of righteousness; I will go through them, *And* I will praise the LORD. **20** This is the gate of the LORD, Through which the righteous shall enter.

Heb 2:12 saying: *"I will declare Your name to My brethren; In the midst of the assembly I will sing praise to You."*

Jews offered, while standing.

1 Chr 23:30 to stand every morning to thank and praise the LORD, and likewise at evening;

Neh 9:5 And the Levites, Jeshua, Kadmiel, Bani, Hashabniah, Sherebiah, Hodijah, Shebaniah, *and* Pethahiah, said: "Stand up *and* bless the LORD your God Forever and ever! "Blessed be Your glorious name, Which is exalted above all blessing and praise!

Called the

Fruit of the lips.

Heb 13:15 Therefore by Him let us continually offer the sacrifice of praise to God, that is, the fruit of *our* lips, giving thanks to His name.

Voice of praise.

Ps 66:8 Oh, bless our God, you peoples! And make the voice of His praise to be heard,

Voice of triumph.

Ps 47:1 Oh, clap your hands, all you peoples! Shout to God with the voice of triumph!

Voice of melody.

Is 51:3 For the LORD will comfort Zion, He will comfort all her waste places; He will make her wilderness like Eden, And her desert like the garden of the LORD; Joy and gladness will be found in it, Thanksgiving and the voice of melody.

Voice of a psalm.

Ps 98:5 Sing to the LORD with the harp, With the harp and the sound of a psalm,

Garment of praise.

Is 61:3 To console those who mourn in Zion, To give them beauty for ashes, The oil of joy for mourning, The garment of praise for the spirit of heaviness; That they may be called trees of righteousness, The planting of the LORD, that He may be glorified."

Sacrifice of praise.

Heb 13:15 Therefore by Him let us continually offer the sacrifice of praise to God, that is, the fruit of *our* lips, giving thanks to His name.

Sacrifices of joy.

Ps 27:6 And now my head shall be lifted up above my enemies all around me; Therefore I will offer sacrifices of joy in His tabernacle; I will sing, yes, I will sing praises to the LORD.

Sacrifices of the lips.

Hos 14:2 Take words with you, And return to the LORD.

Say to Him, "Take away all iniquity; Receive *us* graciously, For we will offer the sacrifices of our lips.

The heavenly host engage in.

Is 6:3 And one cried to another and said: "Holy, holy, holy *is* the LORD of hosts; The whole earth *is* full of His glory!"

Luke 2:13 And suddenly there was with the angel a multitude of the heavenly host praising God and saying:

Rev 4:9–11 Whenever the living creatures give glory and honor and thanks to Him who sits on the throne, who lives forever and ever, **10** the twenty-four elders fall down before Him who sits on the throne and worship Him who lives forever and ever, and cast their crowns before the throne, saying: **11** "You are worthy, O Lord, To receive glory and honor and power; For You created all things, And by Your will they exist and were created."

Rev 5:12 saying with a loud voice: "Worthy is the Lamb who was slain To receive power and riches and wisdom, And strength and honor and glory and blessing!"

Exemplified by

Melchizedek.

Gen 14:20 And blessed be God Most High, Who has delivered your enemies into your hand." And he gave him a tithe of all.

Moses. **Ex 15:1–21**

Jethro.

Ex 18:10 And Jethro said, "Blessed *be* the LORD, who has delivered you out of the hand of the Egyptians and out of the hand of Pharaoh, *and* who has delivered the people from under the hand of the Egyptians.

The Israelites.

1 Chr 16:36 Blessed *be* the LORD God of Israel From everlasting to everlasting! And all the people said, "Amen!" and praised the LORD.

David.

1 Chr 29:10–13 Therefore David blessed the LORD before all the assembly; and David said: "Blessed are You, LORD God of Israel, our Father, forever and ever. **11** Yours, O LORD, *is* the greatness, The power and the glory, The victory and the majesty; For all *that is* in heaven and in earth *is Yours;* Yours *is* the kingdom, O LORD, And You are exalted as head over all. **12** Both riches and honor *come* from You, And You reign over all. In Your hand *is* power and might; In Your hand *it is* to make great And to give strength to all. **13** "Now therefore, our God, We thank You And praise Your glorious name.

Ps 119:164 Seven times a day I praise You, Because of Your righteous judgments.

The priests and Levites.

Ezra 3:10–11 When the builders laid the foundation of the temple of the LORD, the priests stood in their apparel with trumpets, and the Levites, the sons of Asaph, with cymbals, to praise the LORD, according to the ordinance of David king of Israel. **11** And they sang responsively, praising and giving thanks to the LORD: "For *He is* good, For His mercy *endures* forever toward Israel." Then all the people shouted with a great shout, when they praised the LORD, because the foundation of the house of the LORD was laid.

Ezra.

Neh 8:6 And Ezra blessed the LORD, the great God. Then all the people answered, "Amen, Amen!" while lifting up their hands. And they bowed their heads and worshiped the LORD with *their* faces to the ground.

Hezekiah.

Is 38:19 The living, the living man, he shall praise You, As I *do* this day; The father shall make known Your truth to the children.

Zacharias.

Luke 1:64 Immediately his mouth was opened and his tongue *loosed,* and he spoke, praising God.

The shepherds.

Luke 2:20 Then the shepherds returned, glorifying and praising God for all the things that they had heard and seen, as it was told them.

Simeon.

Luke 2:28 he took Him up in his arms and blessed God and said:

Anna.

Luke 2:38 And coming in that instant she gave thanks to the Lord, and spoke of Him to all those who looked for redemption in Jerusalem.

The multitudes.

Luke 18:43 And immediately he received his sight, and followed Him, glorifying God. And all the people, when they saw *it,* gave praise to God.

The disciples and apostles.

Luke 19:37–38 Then, as He was now drawing near the descent of the Mount of Olives, the whole multitude of the disciples began to rejoice and praise God with a loud voice for all the mighty works they had seen, **38** saying: " *'Blessed is the King who comes in the name of the LORD!'* Peace in heaven and glory in the highest!"

Luke 24:53 and were continually in the temple praising and blessing God. Amen.

The first converts.

Acts 2:47 praising God and having favor with all the people. And the Lord added to the church daily those who were being saved.

A lame man.

Acts 3:8 So he, leaping up, stood and walked and entered the temple with them—walking, leaping, and praising God.

Paul and Silas.

Acts 16:25 But at midnight Paul and Silas were praying and singing hymns to God, and the prisoners were listening to them.

PRAYER

Commanded.

Is 55:6 Seek the LORD while He may be found, Call upon Him while He is near.

Matt 7:7 "Ask, and it will be given to you; seek, and you will find; knock, and it will be opened to you.

Phil 4:6 Be anxious for nothing, but in everything by prayer and supplication, with thanksgiving, let your requests be made known to God;

To be offered

To God.

Ps 5:2 Give heed to the voice of my cry, My King and my God, For to You I will pray.

Matt 4:10 Then Jesus said to him, "Away with you, Satan! For it is written, *'You shall worship the* LORD *your God, and Him only you shall serve.'* "

To Christ.

Luke 23:42 Then he said to Jesus, "Lord, remember me when You come into Your kingdom."

Acts 7:59 And they stoned Stephen as he was calling on *God* and saying, "Lord Jesus, receive my spirit."

Through Christ.

John 14:13–14 And whatever you ask in My name, that I will do, that the Father may be glorified in the Son. 14 If you ask anything in My name, I will do *it.*

John 15:16 You did not choose Me, but I chose you and appointed you that you should go and bear fruit, and *that* your fruit should remain, that whatever you ask the Father in My name He may give you.

John 16:23–24 "And in that day you will ask Me nothing. Most assuredly, I say to you, whatever you ask the Father in My name He will give you. 24 Until now you have asked nothing in My name. Ask, and you will receive, that your joy may be full.

Eph 2:18 For through Him we both have access by one Spirit to the Father.

Heb 10:19 Therefore, brethren, having boldness to enter the Holiest by the blood of Jesus,

God hears and answers.

Ps 10:17 LORD, You have heard the desire of the humble; You will prepare their heart; You will cause Your ear to hear,

Ps 65:2 O You who hear prayer, To You all flesh will come.

Ps 99:6 Moses and Aaron were among His priests, And Samuel was among those who called upon His name; They called upon the LORD, and He answered them.

Is 58:9 Then you shall call, and the LORD will answer; You shall cry, and He will say, 'Here I *am.*' "If you take away the yoke from your midst, The pointing of the finger, and speaking wickedness,

Is described as

Bowing the knees.

Eph 3:14 For this reason I bow my knees to the Father of our Lord Jesus Christ,

Looking up.

Ps 5:3 My voice You shall hear in the morning, O LORD; In the morning I will direct *it* to You, And I will look up.

Lifting up the soul.

Ps 25:1 To You, O LORD, I lift up my soul.

Lifting up the heart.

Lam 3:41 Let us lift our hearts and hands To God in heaven.

Pouring out the heart.

Ps 62:8 Trust in Him at all times, you people; Pour out your heart before Him; God *is* a refuge for us. Selah

Pouring out the soul.

1 Sam 1:15 But Hannah answered and said, "No, my lord, I *am* a woman of sorrowful spirit. I have drunk neither wine nor intoxicating drink, but have poured out my soul before the LORD.

Calling upon the name of the Lord.

Gen 12:8 And he moved from there to the mountain east of Bethel, and he pitched his tent *with* Bethel on the west and Ai on the east; there he built an altar to the LORD and called on the name of the LORD.

Ps 80:18 Then we will not turn back from You; Revive us, and we will call upon Your name.

Ps 116:4 Then I called upon the name of the LORD: "O LORD, I implore You, deliver my soul!"

Acts 22:16 And now why are you waiting? Arise and be baptized, and wash away your sins, calling on the name of the Lord.'

Crying to God.

Ps 27:7 Hear, O LORD, *when* I cry with my voice! Have mercy also upon me, and answer me.

Ps 34:6 This poor man cried out, and the LORD heard *him,* And saved him out of all his troubles.

Drawing near to God.

Ps 73:28 But *it is* good for me to draw near to God; I have put my trust in the Lord GOD, That I may declare all Your works.

Heb 10:22 let us draw near with a true heart in full assurance of faith, having our hearts sprinkled from an evil conscience and our bodies washed with pure water.

Crying to heaven.

2 Chr 32:20 Now because of this King Hezekiah and the prophet Isaiah, the son of Amoz, prayed and cried out to heaven.

Pleading with the Lord.

Ex 32:11 Then Moses pleaded with the LORD his God, and said: "LORD, why does Your wrath burn hot against Your people whom You have brought out of the land of Egypt with great power and with a mighty hand?

Seeking God.

Job 8:5 If you would earnestly seek God And make your supplication to the Almighty,

Ps 27:8 *When You said,* "Seek My face," My heart said to You, "Your face, LORD, I will seek."

Making supplication.

Job 8:5 If you would earnestly seek God And make your supplication to the Almighty,

Jer 36:7 It may be that they will present their supplication before the LORD, and everyone will turn from his evil way. For great *is* the anger and the fury that the LORD has pronounced against this people."

Ascends to heaven.

2 Chr 30:27 Then the priests, the Levites, arose and blessed the people, and their voice was heard; and their prayer came *up* to His holy dwelling place, to heaven.

Rev 5:8 Now when He had taken the scroll, the four living creatures and the twenty-four elders fell down before the Lamb, each having a harp, and golden bowls full of incense, which are the prayers of the saints.

The Holy Spirit

Promised as a Spirit of.

Zech 12:10 "And I will pour on the house of David and on the inhabitants of Jerusalem the Spirit of grace and supplication; then they will look on Me whom they pierced. Yes, they will mourn for Him as one mourns for *his* only *son,* and grieve for Him as one grieves for a firstborn.

As the Spirit of adoption, leads to.

Rom 8:15 For you did not receive the spirit of bondage again to fear, but you received the Spirit of adoption by whom we cry out, "Abba, Father."

Gal 4:6 And because you are sons, God has sent forth the Spirit of His Son into your hearts, crying out, "Abba, Father!"

Helps our infirmities in.

Rom 8:26 Likewise the Spirit also helps in our weaknesses. For we do not know what we should pray for as we ought, but the Spirit Himself makes intercession for us with groanings which cannot be uttered.

An evidence of conversion.

Acts 9:11 So the Lord *said* to him, "Arise and go to the street called Straight, and inquire at the house of Judas for *one* called Saul of Tarsus, for behold, he is praying.

Of the righteous, avails much.

James 5:16 Confess *your* trespasses to one another, and pray for one another, that you may be healed. The effective, fervent prayer of a righteous man avails much.

Of the upright, a delight to God.

Prov 15:8 The sacrifice of the wicked *is* an abomination to the LORD, But the prayer of the upright *is* His delight.

Should be offered up

In time of affliction.

Is 26:16 LORD, in trouble they have visited You, They poured out a prayer *when* Your chastening *was* upon them.

James 5:13 Is anyone among you suffering? Let him pray. Is anyone cheerful? Let him sing psalms.

In the Holy Spirit.

Eph 6:18 praying always with all prayer and supplication in the Spirit, being watchful to this end with all perseverance and supplication for all the saints—

Jude 1:20 But you, beloved, building yourselves up on your most holy faith, praying in the Holy Spirit,

In faith.

Matt 21:22 And whatever things you ask in prayer, believing, you will receive."

Heb 10:22 let us draw near with a true heart in full assurance of faith, having our hearts sprinkled from an evil conscience and our bodies washed with pure water.

James 1:6 But let him ask in faith, with no doubting, for he who doubts is like a wave of the sea driven and tossed by the wind.

In a forgiving spirit.

Matt 6:12 And forgive us our debts, As we forgive our debtors.

With the heart.

Job 11:13 "If you would prepare your heart, And stretch out your hands toward Him;

Ps 119:58 I entreated Your favor with *my* whole heart; Be merciful to me according to Your word.

Ps 119:145 I cry out with *my* whole heart; Hear me, O LORD! I will keep Your statutes.

Jer 29:13 And you will seek Me and find *Me,* when you search for Me with all your heart.

Lam 3:41 Let us lift our hearts and hands To God in heaven.

Heb 10:22 let us draw near with a true heart in full assurance of faith, having our hearts sprinkled from an evil conscience and our bodies washed with pure water.

With the soul.

Ps 42:4 When I remember these *things,* I pour out my soul within me. For I used to go with the multitude; I went with them to the house of God, With the voice of joy and praise, With a multitude that kept a pilgrim feast.

With the spirit and understanding.

John 4:22–24 You worship what you do not know; we know what we worship, for salvation is of the Jews. **23** But the hour is coming, and now is, when the true worshipers will worship the Father in spirit and truth; for the Father is seeking such to worship Him. **24** God *is* Spirit, and those who worship Him must worship in spirit and truth."

1 Cor 14:15 What is *the conclusion* then? I will pray with the spirit, and I will also pray with the understanding. I will sing with the spirit, and I will also sing with the understanding.

With confidence in God.

Ps 56:9 When I cry out *to You,* Then my enemies will turn back; This I know, because God *is* for me.

Ps 86:7 In the day of my trouble I will call upon You, For You will answer me.

1 John 5:14 Now this is the confidence that we have in Him, that if we ask anything according to His will, He hears us.

With submission to God.

Luke 22:42 saying, "Father, if it is Your will, take this cup away from Me; nevertheless not My will, but Yours, be done."

With sincere lips.

Ps 17:1 Hear a just cause, O LORD, Attend to my cry; Give ear to my prayer *which is* not from deceitful lips.

With deliberation.

Eccl 5:2 Do not be rash with your mouth, And let not your heart utter anything hastily before God. For God *is* in heaven, and you on earth; Therefore let your words be few.

With holiness.

1 Tim 2:8 I desire therefore that the men pray everywhere, lifting up holy hands, without wrath and doubting;

With humility.

Gen 18:27 Then Abraham answered and said, "Indeed now, I who *am but* dust and ashes have taken it upon myself to speak to the Lord:

2 Chr 7:14 if My people who are called by My name will humble themselves, and pray and seek My face, and turn from their wicked ways, then I will hear from heaven, and will forgive their sin and heal their land.

2 Chr 33:12 Now when he was in affliction, he implored the LORD his God, and humbled himself greatly before the God of his fathers,

With truth.

Ps 145:18 The LORD *is* near to all who call upon Him, To all who call upon Him in truth.

John 4:24 God *is* Spirit, and those who worship Him must worship in spirit and truth."

With desire to be heard.

Neh 1:6 please let Your ear be attentive and Your eyes open, that You may hear the prayer of Your servant which I pray before You now, day and night, for the children of Israel Your servants, and confess the sins of the children of Israel which we have sinned against You. Both my father's house and I have sinned.

Ps 17:1 Hear a just cause, O LORD, Attend to my cry; Give ear to my prayer *which is* not from deceitful lips.

Ps 55:1–2 Give ear to my prayer, O God, And do not hide Yourself from my supplication. **2** Attend to me, and hear me; I am restless in my complaint, and moan noisily,

Ps 61:1 Hear my cry, O God; Attend to my prayer.

With desire to be answered.

Ps 27:7 Hear, O LORD, *when* I cry with my voice! Have mercy also upon me, and answer me.

Ps 102:2 Do not hide Your face from me in the day of my trouble; Incline Your ear to me; In the day that I call, answer me speedily.

Ps 108:6 That Your beloved may be delivered, Save *with* Your right hand, and hear me.

Ps 143:1 Hear my prayer, O LORD, Give ear to my supplications! In Your faithfulness answer me, *And* in Your righteousness.

With boldness.

Heb 4:16 Let us therefore come boldly to the throne of grace, that we may obtain mercy and find grace to help in time of need.

With earnestness.

1 Thess 3:10 night and day praying exceedingly that we may see your face and perfect what is lacking in your faith?

James 5:17 Elijah was a man with a nature like ours, and he prayed earnestly that it would not rain; and it did not rain on the land for three years and six months.

With persistence.

Gen 32:26 And He said, "Let Me go, for the day breaks." But he said, "I will not let You go unless You bless me!"

Luke 11:8–9 I say to you, though he will not rise and give to him because he is his friend, yet because of his persistence he will rise and give him as many as he needs. **9** "So I say to you, ask, and it will be given to you; seek, and you will find; knock, and it will be opened to you.

Luke 18:1–7 Then He spoke a parable to them, that men always ought to pray and not lose heart, **2** saying: "There was in a certain city a judge who did not fear God nor regard man. **3** Now there was a widow in that city; and she came to him, saying, 'Get justice for me from my adversary.' **4** And he would not for a while; but afterward he said within himself, 'Though I do not fear God nor regard man, **5** yet because this widow troubles me I will avenge her, lest by her continual coming she weary me.' " **6** Then the Lord said, "Hear what the unjust judge said. **7** And shall God not avenge His own elect who cry out day and night to Him, though He bears long with them?

Rom 12:12 rejoicing in hope, patient in tribulation, continuing steadfastly in prayer;

All the time.

1 Thess 5:17 pray without ceasing,

1 Tim 5:5 Now she who is really a widow, and left alone, trusts in God and continues in supplications and prayers night and day.

Everywhere.

1 Tim 2:8 I desire therefore that the men pray everywhere, lifting up holy hands, without wrath and doubting;

In everything.

Phil 4:6 Be anxious for nothing, but in everything by prayer and supplication, with thanksgiving, let your requests be made known to God;

For temporal blessings.

Gen 28:20 Then Jacob made a vow, saying, "If God will be with me, and keep me in this way that I am going, and give me bread to eat and clothing to put on,

Prov 30:8 Remove falsehood and lies far from me; Give me neither poverty nor riches— Feed me with the food allotted to me;

Matt 6:11 Give us this day our daily bread.

For spiritual blessings.

Matt 6:33 But seek first the kingdom of God and His righteousness, and all these things shall be added to you.

Model for.

Matt 6:9–13 In this manner, therefore, pray: Our Father in heaven, Hallowed be Your name. **10** Your kingdom come. Your will be done On earth as *it is* in heaven. **11** Give us this day our daily bread. **12** And forgive us our debts, As we forgive our debtors. **13** And do not lead us into temptation, But deliver us from the evil one. For Yours is the kingdom and the power and the glory forever. Amen.

Model to avoid.

Matt 6:5 "And when you pray, you shall not be like the

hypocrites. For they love to pray standing in the synagogues and on the corners of the streets, that they may be seen by men. Assuredly, I say to you, they have their reward.

Matt 6:7 And when you pray, do not use vain repetitions as the heathen *do*. For they think that they will be heard for their many words.

Accompanied with

Repentance.

1 Kin 8:33 "When Your people Israel are defeated before an enemy because they have sinned against You, and when they turn back to You and confess Your name, and pray and make supplication to You in this temple,

Jer 36:7 It may be that they will present their supplication before the LORD, and everyone will turn from his evil way. For great *is* the anger and the fury that the LORD has pronounced against this people."

Confession.

Neh 1:4 So it was, when I heard these words, that I sat down and wept, and mourned *for many* days; I was fasting and praying before the God of heaven.

Neh 1:7 We have acted very corruptly against You, and have not kept the commandments, the statutes, nor the ordinances which You commanded Your servant Moses.

Dan 9:4–11 And I prayed to the LORD my God, and made confession, and said, "O Lord, great and awesome God, who keeps His covenant and mercy with those who love Him, and with those who keep His commandments, **5** we have sinned and committed iniquity, we have done wickedly and rebelled, even by departing from Your precepts and Your judgments. **6** Neither have we heeded Your servants the prophets, who spoke in Your name to our kings and our princes, to our fathers and all the people of the land. **7** O Lord, righteousness *belongs* to You, but to us shame of face, as *it is* this day—to the men of Judah, to the inhabitants of Jerusalem and all Israel, those near and those far off in all the countries to which You have driven them, because of the unfaithfulness which they have committed against You. **8** "O Lord, to us *belongs* shame of face, to our kings, our princes, and our fathers, because we have sinned against You. **9** To the Lord our God *belong* mercy and forgiveness, though we have rebelled against Him. **10** We have not obeyed the voice of the LORD our God, to walk in His laws, which He set before us by His servants the prophets. **11** Yes, all Israel has transgressed Your law, and has departed so as not to obey Your voice; therefore the curse and the oath written in the Law of Moses the servant of God have been poured out on us, because we have sinned against Him.

Weeping.

Jer 31:9 They shall come with weeping, And with supplications I will lead them. I will cause them to walk by the rivers of waters, In a straight way in which they shall not stumble; For I am a Father to Israel, And Ephraim *is* My firstborn.

Hos 12:4 Yes, he struggled with the Angel and prevailed; He wept, and sought favor from Him. He found him *in* Bethel, And there He spoke to us—

Fasting.

Neh 1:4 So it was, when I heard these words, that I sat down and wept, and mourned *for many* days; I was fasting and praying before the God of heaven.

Dan 9:3 Then I set my face toward the Lord God to make request by prayer and supplications, with fasting, sackcloth, and ashes.

Acts 13:3 Then, having fasted and prayed, and laid hands on them, they sent *them* away.

Watchfulness.

Luke 21:36 Watch therefore, and pray always that you may be counted worthy to escape all these things that will come to pass, and to stand before the Son of Man."

1 Pet 4:7 But the end of all things is at hand; therefore be serious and watchful in your prayers.

Praise.

Ps 66:17 I cried to Him with my mouth, And He was extolled with my tongue.

Thanksgiving.

Phil 4:6 Be anxious for nothing, but in everything by prayer and supplication, with thanksgiving, let your requests be made known to God;

Col 4:2 Continue earnestly in prayer, being vigilant in it with thanksgiving;

Plead in the

Promises of God.

Gen 32:9–12 Then Jacob said, "O God of my father Abraham and God of my father Isaac, the LORD who said to me, 'Return to your country and to your family, and I will deal well with you': **10** I am not worthy of the least of all the mercies and of all the truth which You have shown Your servant; for I crossed over this Jordan with my staff, and now I have become two companies. **11** Deliver me, I pray, from the hand of my brother, from the hand of Esau; for I fear him, lest he come and attack me *and* the mother with the children. **12** For You said, 'I will surely treat you well, and make your descendants as the sand of the sea, which cannot be numbered for multitude.' "

Ex 32:13 Remember Abraham, Isaac, and Israel, Your servants, to whom You swore by Your own self, and said to them, 'I will multiply your descendants as the stars of heaven; and all this land that I have spoken of I give to your descendants, and they shall inherit *it* forever.' "

1 Kin 8:26 And now I pray, O God of Israel, let Your word come true, which You have spoken to Your servant David my father.

Ps 119:49 Remember the word to Your servant, Upon which You have caused me to hope.

Covenant of God.

Jer 14:21 Do not abhor *us,* for Your name's sake; Do not disgrace the throne of Your glory. Remember, do not break Your covenant with us.

Faithfulness of God.

Ps 143:1 Hear my prayer, O LORD, Give ear to my supplications! In Your faithfulness answer me, *And* in Your righteousness.

Mercy of God.

Ps 51:1 Have mercy upon me, O God, According to

Your lovingkindness; According to the multitude of Your tender mercies, Blot out my transgressions.

Dan 9:18 O my God, incline Your ear and hear; open Your eyes, and see our desolations, and the city which is called by Your name; for we do not present our supplications before You because of our righteous deeds, but because of Your great mercies.

Righteousness of God.

Dan 9:16 "O Lord, according to all Your righteousness, I pray, let Your anger and Your fury be turned away from Your city Jerusalem, Your holy mountain; because for our sins, and for the iniquities of our fathers, Jerusalem and Your people *are* a reproach to all *those* around us.

Rise early for.

Ps 5:3 My voice You shall hear in the morning, O LORD; In the morning I will direct *it* to You, And I will look up.

Ps 119:147 I rise before the dawning of the morning, And cry for help; I hope in Your word.

Seek divine teaching for.

Luke 11:1 Now it came to pass, as He was praying in a certain place, when He ceased, *that* one of His disciples said to Him, "Lord, teach us to pray, as John also taught his disciples."

Avoid hindrances in.

1 Pet 3:7 Husbands, likewise, dwell with *them* with understanding, giving honor to the wife, as to the weaker vessel, and as *being* heirs together of the grace of life, that your prayers may not be hindered.

Postures in,

Standing.

1 Kin 8:22 Then Solomon stood before the altar of the LORD in the presence of all the assembly of Israel, and spread out his hands toward heaven;

Mark 11:25 "And whenever you stand praying, if you have anything against anyone, forgive him, that your Father in heaven may also forgive you your trespasses.

Bowing down.

Ps 95:6 Oh come, let us worship and bow down; Let us kneel before the LORD our Maker.

Kneeling.

2 Chr 6:13 (for Solomon had made a bronze platform five cubits long, five cubits wide, and three cubits high, and had set it in the midst of the court; and he stood on it, knelt down on his knees before all the assembly of Israel, and spread out his hands toward heaven);

Ps 95:6 Oh come, let us worship and bow down; Let us kneel before the LORD our Maker.

Luke 22:41 And He was withdrawn from them about a stone's throw, and He knelt down and prayed,

Acts 20:36 And when he had said these things, he knelt down and prayed with them all.

Falling on the face.

Num 16:22 Then they fell on their faces, and said, "O God, the God of the spirits of all flesh, shall one man sin, and You be angry with all the congregation?"

Josh 5:14 So He said, "No, but *as* Commander of the army of the LORD I have now come." And Joshua fell on his face to the earth and worshiped, and said to Him, "What does my Lord say to His servant?"

1 Chr 21:16 Then David lifted his eyes and saw the angel of the LORD standing between earth and heaven, having in his hand a drawn sword stretched out over Jerusalem. So David and the elders, clothed in sackcloth, fell on their faces.

Matt 26:39 He went a little farther and fell on His face, and prayed, saying, "O My Father, if it is possible, let this cup pass from Me; nevertheless, not as I will, but as You *will.*"

Spreading forth the hands.

Is 1:15 When you spread out your hands, I will hide My eyes from you; Even though you make many prayers, I will not hear. Your hands are full of blood.

Lifting up the hands.

Ps 28:2 Hear the voice of my supplications When I cry to You, When I lift up my hands toward Your holy sanctuary.

Lam 2:19 "Arise, cry out in the night, At the beginning of the watches; Pour out your heart like water before the face of the Lord. Lift your hands toward Him For the life of your young children, Who faint from hunger at the head of every street."

1 Tim 2:8 I desire therefore that the men pray everywhere, lifting up holy hands, without wrath and doubting;

Incentives to,

Promises of God.

Is 65:24 "It shall come to pass That before they call, I will answer; And while they are still speaking, I will hear.

Amos 5:4 For thus says the LORD to the house of Israel: "Seek Me and live;

Zech 13:9 I will bring the *one*-third through the fire, Will refine them as silver is refined, And test them as gold is tested. They will call on My name, And I will answer them. I will say, 'This *is* My people'; And each one will say, 'The LORD *is* my God.' "

Promises of Christ.

Luke 11:9–10 "So I say to you, ask, and it will be given to you; seek, and you will find; knock, and it will be opened to you. 10 For everyone who asks receives, and he who seeks finds, and to him who knocks it will be opened.

John 14:13–14 And whatever you ask in My name, that I will do, that the Father may be glorified in the Son. 14 If you ask anything in My name, I will do *it.*

Experience of past mercies.

Ps 4:1 Hear me when I call, O God of my righteousness! You have relieved me in *my* distress; Have mercy on me, and hear my prayer.

Ps 112:2 His descendants will be mighty on earth; The generation of the upright will be blessed.

PRAYER, ANSWERS TO

God gives.

Ps 99:6 Moses and Aaron were among His priests, And Samuel was among those who called upon His name; They called upon the LORD, and He answered them.

Ps 118:5 I called on the LORD in distress; The LORD answered me *and set me* in a broad place.

Ps 138:3 In the day when I cried out, You answered me, *And* made me bold *with* strength in my soul.

Christ gives.

John 4:10 Jesus answered and said to her, "If you knew the gift of God, and who it is who says to you, 'Give Me a drink,' you would have asked Him, and He would have given you living water."

John 4:14 but whoever drinks of the water that I shall give him will never thirst. But the water that I shall give him will become in him a fountain of water springing up into everlasting life."

John 14:14 If you ask anything in My name, I will do *it*.

Christ received.

John 11:42 And I know that You always hear Me, but because of the people who are standing by I said *this*, that they may believe that You sent Me."

Heb 5:7 who, in the days of His flesh, when He had offered up prayers and supplications, with vehement cries and tears to Him who was able to save Him from death, and was heard because of His godly fear,

Granted

Through the grace of God.

Is 30:19 For the people shall dwell in Zion at Jerusalem; You shall weep no more. He will be very gracious to you at the sound of your cry; When He hears it, He will answer you.

Sometimes immediately.

Is 65:24 "It shall come to pass That before they call, I will answer; And while they are still speaking, I will hear.

Dan 9:21 yes, while I *was* speaking in prayer, the man Gabriel, whom I had seen in the vision at the beginning, being caused to fly swiftly, reached me about the time of the evening offering.

Dan 9:23 At the beginning of your supplications the command went out, and I have come to tell *you*, for you *are* greatly beloved; therefore consider the matter, and understand the vision:

Dan 10:12 Then he said to me, "Do not fear, Daniel, for from the first day that you set your heart to understand, and to humble yourself before your God, your words were heard; and I have come because of your words.

Sometimes after delay.

Luke 18:7 And shall God not avenge His own elect who cry out day and night to Him, though He bears long with them?

Sometimes differently from our desire.

2 Cor 12:8–9 Concerning this thing I pleaded with the Lord three times that it might depart from me. **9** And He said to me, "My grace is sufficient for you, for My strength is made perfect in weakness." Therefore most gladly I will rather boast in my infirmities, that the power of Christ may rest upon me.

Beyond expectation.

Jer 33:3 'Call to Me, and I will answer you, and show you great and mighty things, which you do not know.'

Eph 3:20 Now to Him who is able to do exceedingly

abundantly above all that we ask or think, according to the power that works in us,

Promised.

Ps 50:15 Call upon Me in the day of trouble; I will deliver you, and you shall glorify Me."

Ps 91:15 He shall call upon Me, and I will answer him; I *will be* with him in trouble; I will deliver him and honor him.

Is 58:9 Then you shall call, and the LORD will answer; You shall cry, and He will say, 'Here I *am*.' "If you take away the yoke from your midst, The pointing of the finger, and speaking wickedness,

Jer 29:12 Then you will call upon Me and go and pray to Me, and I will listen to you.

Matt 7:7 "Ask, and it will be given to you; seek, and you will find; knock, and it will be opened to you.

Received by those who

Seek God.

Ps 34:4 I sought the LORD, and He heard me, And delivered me from all my fears.

Seek God with all the heart.

Jer 29:12–13 Then you will call upon Me and go and pray to Me, and I will listen to you. **13** And you will seek Me and find *Me*, when you search for Me with all your heart.

Wait upon God.

Ps 40:1 I waited patiently for the LORD; And He inclined to me, And heard my cry.

Return to God.

2 Chr 7:14 if My people who are called by My name will humble themselves, and pray and seek My face, and turn from their wicked ways, then I will hear from heaven, and will forgive their sin and heal their land.

Job 22:23 If you return to the Almighty, you will be built up; You will remove iniquity far from your tents.

Job 22:27 You will make your prayer to Him, He will hear you, And you will pay your vows.

Ask in faith.

Matt 21:11 So the multitudes said, "This is Jesus, the prophet from Nazareth of Galilee."

James 5:15 And the prayer of faith will save the sick, and the Lord will raise him up. And if he has committed sins, he will be forgiven.

Ask in the name of Christ.

John 14:13 And whatever you ask in My name, that I will do, that the Father may be glorified in the Son.

Ask according to God's will.

1 John 5:14 Now this is the confidence that we have in Him, that if we ask anything according to His will, He hears us.

Call upon God in truth.

Ps 145:18 The LORD *is* near to all who call upon Him, To all who call upon Him in truth.

Fear God.

Ps 145:19 He will fulfill the desire of those who fear Him; He also will hear their cry and save them.

Set their love upon God.

Ps 91:14–15 "Because he has set his love upon Me, therefore I will deliver him; I will set him on high, because he has known My name. **15** He shall call upon Me, and I will answer him; I *will be* with him in trouble; I will deliver him and honor him.

Keep God's commandments.

1 John 3:22 And whatever we ask we receive from Him, because we keep His commandments and do those things that are pleasing in His sight.

Call upon God under oppression and affliction.

Ps 18:6 In my distress I called upon the LORD, And cried out to my God; He heard my voice from His temple, And my cry came before Him, *even* to His ears.

Ps 106:44 Nevertheless He regarded their affliction, When He heard their cry;

Is 19:20 And it will be for a sign and for a witness to the LORD of hosts in the land of Egypt; for they will cry to the LORD because of the oppressors, and He will send them a Savior and a Mighty One, and He will deliver them.

Is 30:19–20 For the people shall dwell in Zion at Jerusalem; You shall weep no more. He will be very gracious to you at the sound of your cry; When He hears it, He will answer you. **20** And *though* the Lord gives you The bread of adversity and the water of affliction, Yet your teachers will not be moved into a corner anymore, But your eyes shall see your teachers.

Abide in Christ.

John 15:7 If you abide in Me, and My words abide in you, you will ask what you desire, and it shall be done for you.

Humble themselves.

2 Chr 7:14 if My people who are called by My name will humble themselves, and pray and seek My face, and turn from their wicked ways, then I will hear from heaven, and will forgive their sin and heal their land.

Ps 9:12 When He avenges blood, He remembers them; He does not forget the cry of the humble.

Are righteous.

Ps 34:15 The eyes of the LORD *are* on the righteous, And His ears *are open* to their cry.

James 5:16 Confess *your* trespasses to one another, and pray for one another, that you may be healed. The effective, fervent prayer of a righteous man avails much.

Are poor and needy.

Is 41:17 "The poor and needy seek water, but *there is* none, Their tongues fail for thirst. I, the LORD, will hear them; *I*, the God of Israel, will not forsake them.

Believers

Are assured of.

1 John 5:15 And if we know that He hears us, whatever we ask, we know that we have the petitions that we have asked of Him.

Love and praise God for.

Ps 66:20 Blessed *be* God, Who has not turned away my prayer, Nor His mercy from me!

Ps 116:1 I love the LORD, because He has heard My voice *and* my supplications.

Ps 116:17 I will offer to You the sacrifice of thanksgiving, And will call upon the name of the LORD.

Ps 118:21 I will praise You, For You have answered me, And have become my salvation.

A motive for continued prayer.

Ps 116:2 Because He has inclined His ear to me, Therefore I will call *upon Him* as long as I live.

Denied to those who

Ask amiss.

James 4:3 You ask and do not receive, because you ask amiss, that you may spend *it* on your pleasures.

Live in sin.

Ps 66:18 If I regard iniquity in my heart, The Lord will not hear.

Is 59:2 But your iniquities have separated you from your God; And your sins have hidden *His* face from you, So that He will not hear.

John 9:31 Now we know that God does not hear sinners; but if anyone is a worshiper of God and does His will, He hears him.

Offer unworthy service to God.

Mal 1:7–9 "You offer defiled food on My altar, But say, 'In what way have we defiled You?' By saying, 'The table of the LORD is contemptible.' **8** And when you offer the blind as a sacrifice, *Is it* not evil? And when you offer the lame and sick, *Is it* not evil? Offer it then to your governor! Would he be pleased with you? Would he accept you favorably?" Says the LORD of hosts. **9** "But now entreat God's favor, That He may be gracious to us. *While* this is being *done* by your hands, Will He accept you favorably?" Says the LORD of hosts.

Forsake God.

Jer 14:10 Thus says the LORD to this people: "Thus they have loved to wander; They have not restrained their feet. Therefore the LORD does not accept them; He will remember their iniquity now, And punish their sins."

Jer 14:12 When they fast, I will not hear their cry; and when they offer burnt offering and grain offering, I will not accept them. But I will consume them by the sword, by the famine, and by the pestilence."

Reject the call of God.

Prov 1:24–25 Because I have called and you refused, I have stretched out my hand and no one regarded, **25** Because you disdained all my counsel, And would have none of my rebuke,

Prov 1:28 "Then they will call on me, but I will not answer; They will seek me diligently, but they will not find me.

Do not hear the law.

Prov 28:9 One who turns away his ear from hearing the law, Even his prayer *is* an abomination.

Zech 7:11–13 But they refused to heed, shrugged their shoulders, and stopped their ears so that they could not hear. **12** Yes, they made their hearts like flint, refusing to hear the law and the words which the LORD of hosts had sent by His Spirit through the former prophets. Thus great wrath came from the LORD of hosts. **13** Therefore it happened, *that* just as He proclaimed and they would not hear, so they called out and I would not listen," says the LORD of hosts.

Are deaf to the cry of the poor.

Prov 21:13 Whoever shuts his ears to the cry of the poor Will also cry himself and not be heard.

Shed others' blood.

Is 1:15 When you spread out your hands, I will hide My eyes from you; Even though you make many prayers, I will not hear. Your hands are full of blood.

Is 59:3 For your hands are defiled with blood, And your fingers with iniquity; Your lips have spoken lies, Your tongue has muttered perversity.

Are idolaters.

Jer 11:11–14 Therefore thus says the LORD: "Behold, I will surely bring calamity on them which they will not be able to escape; and though they cry out to Me, I will not listen to them. **12** Then the cities of Judah and the inhabitants of Jerusalem will go and cry out to the gods to whom they offer incense, but they will not save them at all in the time of their trouble. **13** For *according to* the number of your cities were your gods, O Judah; and *according to* the number of the streets of Jerusalem you have set up altars to *that* shameful thing, altars to burn incense to Baal. **14** "So do not pray for this people, or lift up a cry or prayer for them; for I will not hear *them* in the time that they cry out to Me because of their trouble.

Ezek 8:15–18 Then He said to me, "Have you seen *this*, O son of man? Turn again, you will see greater abominations than these." **16** So He brought me into the inner court of the LORD's house; and there, at the door of the temple of the LORD, between the porch and the altar, *were* about twenty-five men with their backs toward the temple of the LORD and their faces toward the east, and they were worshiping the sun toward the east. **17** And He said to me, "Have you seen *this*, O son of man? Is it a trivial thing to the house of Judah to commit the abominations which they commit here? For they have filled the land with violence; then they have returned to provoke Me to anger. Indeed they put the branch to their nose. **18** Therefore I also will act in fury. My eye will not spare nor will I have pity; and though they cry in My ears with a loud voice, I will not hear them."

Are wavering.

James 1:6–7 But let him ask in faith, with no doubting, for he who doubts is like a wave of the sea driven and tossed by the wind. **7** For let not that man suppose that he will receive anything from the Lord;

Are hypocrites.

Job 27:8–9 For what is the hope of the hypocrite, Though he may gain *much*, If God takes away his life? **9** Will God hear his cry When trouble comes upon him?

Are proud.

Job 35:12–13 There they cry out, but He does not answer, Because of the pride of evil men. **13** Surely God will not listen to empty *talk*, Nor will the Almighty regard it.

Are self-righteous.

Luke 18:11–12 The Pharisee stood and prayed thus with himself, 'God, I thank You that I am not like other men—extortioners, unjust, adulterers, or even as this tax collector. **12** I fast twice a week; I give tithes of all that I possess.'

Luke 18:14 I tell you, this man went down to his house justified *rather* than the other; for everyone who exalts himself will be humbled, and he who humbles himself will be exalted."

Are the enemies of believers.

Ps 18:40–41 You have also given me the necks of my enemies, So that I destroyed those who hated me. **41** They cried out, but *there was* none to save; *Even to* the LORD, but He did not answer them.

Mic 3:2–4 You who hate good and love evil; Who strip the skin from *My* people, And the flesh from their bones; **3** Who also eat the flesh of My people, Flay their skin from them, Break their bones, And chop *them* in pieces Like *meat* for the pot, Like flesh in the caldron." **4** Then they will cry to the LORD, But He will not hear them; He will even hide His face from them at that time, Because they have been evil in their deeds.

Exemplified in the lives of

Abraham.

Gen 17:20 And as for Ishmael, I have heard you. Behold, I have blessed him, and will make him fruitful, and will multiply him exceedingly. He shall beget twelve princes, and I will make him a great nation.

Lot.

Gen 19:19–21 Indeed now, your servant has found favor in your sight, and you have increased your mercy which you have shown me by saving my life; but I cannot escape to the mountains, lest some evil overtake me and I die. **20** See now, this city *is* near *enough* to flee to, and it *is* a little one; please let me escape there (*is* it not a little one?) and my soul shall live." **21** And he said to him, "See, I have favored you concerning this thing also, in that I will not overthrow this city for which you have spoken.

Abraham's servant.

Gen 24:15–27 And it happened, before he had finished speaking, that behold, Rebekah, who was born to Bethuel, son of Milcah, the wife of Nahor, Abraham's brother, came out with her pitcher on her shoulder. **16** Now the young woman *was* very beautiful to behold, a virgin; no man had known her. And she went down to the well, filled her pitcher, and came up. **17** And the servant ran to meet her and said, "Please let me drink a little water from your pitcher." **18** So she said, "Drink, my lord." Then she quickly let her pitcher down to her hand, and gave him a drink. **19** And when she had finished giving him a drink, she said, "I will draw *water* for your camels also, until they have finished drinking." **20** Then she quickly emptied her pitcher into the trough, ran back to the well to draw *water*, and drew for all his camels. **21** And the man, wondering at her, remained silent so as to know whether the LORD had made his journey prosperous or not. **22** So it was, when the camels had finished drinking, that the man took a golden nose ring weighing half a shekel, and two bracelets for her wrists weighing ten *shekels* of gold, **23** and said, "Whose daughter *are* you? Tell me, please, is there room *in* your father's house for us to lodge?" **24** So she said to him, "I *am* the daughter of Bethuel, Milcah's son, whom she bore to Nahor." **25** Moreover she said to him, "We have both straw and feed enough, and room to lodge." **26** Then the man bowed down his head and worshiped the LORD. **27** And he said, "Blessed *be* the LORD God of my master Abraham, who has not forsaken His mercy and His truth toward my master. As for me, being on the way, the LORD led me to the house of my master's brethren."

Jacob.

Gen 32:24–30 Then Jacob was left alone; and a Man wrestled with him until the breaking of day. **25** Now when He saw that He did not prevail against him, He touched the socket of his hip; and the socket of Jacob's hip was out of joint as He wrestled with him. **26** And He said, "Let Me go, for the day breaks." But he said, "I will not let You go unless You bless me!" **27** So He said to him, "What *is* your name?" He said, "Jacob." **28** And He said, "Your name shall no longer be called Jacob, but Israel; for you have struggled with God and with men, and have prevailed." **29** Then Jacob asked, saying, "Tell *me* Your name, I pray." And He said, "Why *is* it *that* you ask about My name?" And He blessed him there. **30** So Jacob called the name of the place Peniel: "For I have seen God face to face, and my life is preserved."

The Israelites.

Ex 2:23–24 Now it happened in the process of time that the king of Egypt died. Then the children of Israel groaned because of the bondage, and they cried out; and their cry came up to God because of the bondage. **24** So God heard their groaning, and God remembered His covenant with Abraham, with Isaac, and with Jacob.

Moses.

Ex 17:4–6 So Moses cried out to the LORD, saying, "What shall I do with this people? They are almost ready to stone me!" **5** And the LORD said to Moses, "Go on before the people, and take with you some of the elders of Israel. Also take in your hand your rod with which you struck the river, and go. **6** Behold, I will stand before you there on the rock in Horeb; and you shall strike the rock, and water will come out of it, that the people may drink." And Moses did so in the sight of the elders of Israel.

Ex 17:11–13 And so it was, when Moses held up his hand, that Israel prevailed; and when he let down his hand, Amalek prevailed. **12** But Moses' hands *became* heavy; so they took a stone and put *it* under him, and he sat on it. And Aaron and Hur supported his hands, one on one side, and the other on the other side; and his hands were steady until the going down of the sun. **13** So Joshua defeated Amalek and his people with the edge of the sword.

Ex 32:11–14 Then Moses pleaded with the LORD his God, and said: "LORD, why does Your wrath burn hot against Your people whom You have brought out of the land of Egypt with great power and with a mighty hand? **12** Why should the Egyptians speak, and say, 'He brought them out to harm them, to kill them in the mountains, and to consume them from the face of the earth'? Turn from Your fierce wrath, and relent from this harm to Your people. **13** Remember Abraham, Isaac, and Israel, Your servants, to whom You swore by Your own self, and said to them,

'I will multiply your descendants as the stars of heaven; and all this land that I have spoken of I give to your descendants, and they shall inherit *it* forever.' " **14** So the LORD relented from the harm which He said He would do to His people.

Samson.

Judg 15:18–19 Then he became very thirsty; so he cried out to the LORD and said, "You have given this great deliverance by the hand of Your servant; and now shall I die of thirst and fall into the hand of the uncircumcised?" **19** So God split the hollow place that *is* in Lehi, and water came out, and he drank; and his spirit returned, and he revived. Therefore he called its name En Hakkore, which is in Lehi to this day.

Hannah.

1 Sam 1:27 For this child I prayed, and the LORD has granted me my petition which I asked of Him.

Samuel.

1 Sam 7:9 And Samuel took a suckling lamb and offered *it as* a whole burnt offering to the LORD. Then Samuel cried out to the LORD for Israel, and the LORD answered him.

Solomon.

1 Kin 3:9 Therefore give to Your servant an understanding heart to judge Your people, that I may discern between good and evil. For who is able to judge this great people of Yours?"

1 Kin 3:12 behold, I have done according to your words; see, I have given you a wise and understanding heart, so that there has not been anyone like you before you, nor shall any like you arise after you.

A man of God.

1 Kin 13:6 Then the king answered and said to the man of God, "Please entreat the favor of the LORD your God, and pray for me, that my hand may be restored to me." So the man of God entreated the LORD, and the king's hand was restored to him, and became as before.

Elijah.

1 Kin 18:36–38 And it came to pass, at *the time of* the offering of the *evening* sacrifice, that Elijah the prophet came near and said, "LORD God of Abraham, Isaac, and Israel, let it be known this day that You *are* God in Israel and I *am* Your servant, and *that* I have done all these things at Your word. **37** Hear me, O LORD, hear me, that this people may know that You *are* the LORD God, and *that* You have turned their hearts back *to You* again." **38** Then the fire of the LORD fell and consumed the burnt sacrifice, and the wood and the stones and the dust, and it licked up the water that *was* in the trench.

James 5:17–18 Elijah was a man with a nature like ours, and he prayed earnestly that it would not rain; and it did not rain on the land for three years and six months. **18** And he prayed again, and the heaven gave rain, and the earth produced its fruit.

Elisha.

2 Kin 4:33–35 He went in therefore, shut the door behind the two of them, and prayed to the LORD. **34** And he went up and lay on the child, and put his mouth on his mouth, his eyes on his eyes, and his hands on his hands; and he stretched himself out on the child, and the flesh of the child became warm. **35** He returned and walked back and forth in the house, and again went up and stretched himself out on him; then the child sneezed seven times, and the child opened his eyes.

Jehoahaz.

2 Kin 13:4 So Jehoahaz pleaded with the LORD, and the LORD listened to him; for He saw the oppression of Israel, because the king of Syria oppressed them.

Hezekiah.

2 Kin 19:20 Then Isaiah the son of Amoz sent to Hezekiah, saying, "Thus says the LORD God of Israel: 'Because you have prayed to Me against Sennacherib king of Assyria, I have heard.'

Jabez.

1 Chr 4:10 And Jabez called on the God of Israel saying, "Oh, that You would bless me indeed, and enlarge my territory, that Your hand would be with me, and that You would keep *me* from evil, that I may not cause pain!" So God granted him what he requested.

Asa.

2 Chr 14:11–12 And Asa cried out to the LORD his God, and said, "LORD, *it is* nothing for You to help, whether with many or with those who have no power; help us, O LORD our God, for we rest on You, and in Your name we go against this multitude. O LORD, You *are* our God; do not let man prevail against You!" **12** So the LORD struck the Ethiopians before Asa and Judah, and the Ethiopians fled.

Jehoshaphat.

2 Chr 20:6–17 and said: "O LORD God of our fathers, *are* You not God in heaven, and do You *not* rule over all the kingdoms of the nations, and in Your hand *is there not* power and might, so that no one is able to withstand You? **7** *Are* You not our God, *who* drove out the inhabitants of this land before Your people Israel, and gave it to the descendants of Abraham Your friend forever? **8** And they dwell in it, and have built You a sanctuary in it for Your name, saying, **9** 'If disaster comes upon us—sword, judgment, pestilence, or famine—we will stand before this temple and in Your presence (for Your name *is* in this temple), and cry out to You in our affliction, and You will hear and save.' **10** And now, here are the people of Ammon, Moab, and Mount Seir—whom You would not let Israel invade when they came out of the land of Egypt, but they turned from them and did not destroy them— **11** here they are, rewarding us by coming to throw us out of Your possession which You have given us to inherit. **12** O our God, will You not judge them? For we have no power against this great multitude that is coming against us; nor do we know what to do, but our eyes *are* upon You." **13** Now all Judah, with their little ones, their wives, and their children, stood before the LORD. **14** Then the Spirit of the LORD came upon Jahaziel the son of Zechariah, the son of Benaiah, the son of Jeiel, the son of Mattaniah, a Levite of the sons of Asaph, in the midst of the assembly. **15** And he said, "Listen, all you of Judah and you inhabitants of Jerusalem, and you, King Jehoshaphat! Thus says the LORD to you: 'Do not be afraid nor dismayed because of this great multitude, for the battle *is* not yours, but God's. **16** Tomorrow go down against them. They will surely come up by the

Ascent of Ziz, and you will find them at the end of the brook before the Wilderness of Jeruel. **17** You will not *need* to fight in this *battle*. Position yourselves, stand still and see the salvation of the LORD, who is with you, O Judah and Jerusalem!' Do not fear or be dismayed; tomorrow go out against them, for the LORD *is* with you."

Manasseh.

2 Chr 33:13 and prayed to Him; and He received his entreaty, heard his supplication, and brought him back to Jerusalem into his kingdom. Then Manasseh knew that the LORD *was* God.

2 Chr 33:19 Also his prayer and *how God* received his entreaty, and all his sin and trespass, and the sites where he built high places and set up wooden images and carved images, before he was humbled, indeed they *are* written among the sayings of Hozai.

Ezra.

Ezra 8:21–23 Then I proclaimed a fast there at the river of Ahava, that we might humble ourselves before our God, to seek from Him the right way for us and our little ones and all our possessions. **22** For I was ashamed to request of the king an escort of soldiers and horsemen to help us against the enemy on the road, because we had spoken to the king, saying, "The hand of our God *is* upon all those for good who seek Him, but His power and His wrath *are* against all those who forsake Him." **23** So we fasted and entreated our God for this, and He answered our prayer.

Nehemiah.

Neh 4:9 Nevertheless we made our prayer to our God, and because of them we set a watch against them day and night.

Neh 4:15 And it happened, when our enemies heard that it was known to us, and *that* God had brought their plot to nothing, that all of us returned to the wall, everyone to his work.

Job.

Job 42:10 And the LORD restored Job's losses when he prayed for his friends. Indeed the LORD gave Job twice as much as he had before.

David.

Ps 18:6 In my distress I called upon the LORD, And cried out to my God; He heard my voice from His temple, And my cry came before Him, *even* to His ears.

Jeremiah.

Lam 3:55–56 I called on Your name, O LORD, From the lowest pit. **56** You have heard my voice: "Do not hide Your ear From my sighing, from my cry for help."

Daniel.

Dan 9:20–23 Now while I *was* speaking, praying, and confessing my sin and the sin of my people Israel, and presenting my supplication before the LORD my God for the holy mountain of my God, **21** yes, while I *was* speaking in prayer, the man Gabriel, whom I had seen in the vision at the beginning, being caused to fly swiftly, reached me about the time of the evening offering. **22** And he informed *me*, and talked with me, and said, "O Daniel, I have now come forth to give you skill to understand. **23** At the beginning of your supplications the command went out, and I have come to tell *you*, for you *are* greatly beloved; therefore consider the matter, and understand the vision:

Jonah.

Jon 2:2 And he said: "I cried out to the LORD because of my affliction, And He answered me. "Out of the belly of Sheol I cried, *And* You heard my voice.

Jon 2:10 So the LORD spoke to the fish, and it vomited Jonah onto dry *land.*

Zacharias.

Luke 1:13 But the angel said to him, "Do not be afraid, Zacharias, for your prayer is heard; and your wife Elizabeth will bear you a son, and you shall call his name John.

The blind man.

Luke 18:38 And he cried out, saying, "Jesus, Son of David, have mercy on me!"

Luke 18:41–43 saying, "What do you want Me to do for you?" He said, "Lord, that I may receive my sight." **42** Then Jesus said to him, "Receive your sight; your faith has made you well." **43** And immediately he received his sight, and followed Him, glorifying God. And all the people, when they saw *it,* gave praise to God.

The thief on the cross.

Luke 23:42–43 Then he said to Jesus, "Lord, remember me when You come into Your kingdom." **43** And Jesus said to him, "Assuredly, I say to you, today you will be with Me in Paradise."

The apostles.

Acts 4:29–31 Now, Lord, look on their threats, and grant to Your servants that with all boldness they may speak Your word, **30** by stretching out Your hand to heal, and that signs and wonders may be done through the name of Your holy Servant Jesus." **31** And when they had prayed, the place where they were assembled together was shaken; and they were all filled with the Holy Spirit, and they spoke the word of God with boldness.

Cornelius.

Acts 10:4 And when he observed him, he was afraid, and said, "What is it, lord?" So he said to him, "Your prayers and your alms have come up for a memorial before God.

Acts 10:31 and said, 'Cornelius, your prayer has been heard, and your alms are remembered in the sight of God.

The Christians.

Acts 12:5 Peter was therefore kept in prison, but constant prayer was offered to God for him by the church.

Acts 12:7 Now behold, an angel of the Lord stood by *him,* and a light shone in the prison; and he struck Peter on the side and raised him up, saying, "Arise quickly!" And his chains fell off *his* hands.

Paul and Silas.

Acts 16:25–26 But at midnight Paul and Silas were praying and singing hymns to God, and the prisoners were listening to them. **26** Suddenly there was a great earthquake, so that the foundations of the prison were shaken; and immediately all the doors were opened and everyone's chains were loosed.

Paul.

Acts 28:8 And it happened that the father of Publius lay sick of a fever and dysentery. Paul went in to him and prayed, and he laid his hands on him and healed him.

Lack of—illustrated by

Saul.

1 Sam 28:15 Now Samuel said to Saul, "Why have you disturbed me by bringing me up?" And Saul answered, "I am deeply distressed; for the Philistines make war against me, and God has departed from me and does not answer me anymore, neither by prophets nor by dreams. Therefore I have called you, that you may reveal to me what I should do."

Elders of Israel.

Ezek 20:3 "Son of man, speak to the elders of Israel, and say to them, 'Thus says the Lord GOD: "Have you come to inquire of Me? *As* I live," says the Lord GOD, "I will not be inquired of by you." '

Pharisees.

Matt 23:14 Woe to you, scribes and Pharisees, hypocrites! For you devour widows' houses, and for a pretense make long prayers. Therefore you will receive greater condemnation.

PRAYER, INTERCESSORY

Christ set an example of.

Luke 22:32 But I have prayed for you, that your faith should not fail; and when you have returned to *Me,* strengthen your brethren."

Luke 23:34 Then Jesus said, "Father, forgive them, for they do not know what they do." And they divided His garments and cast lots.

John 17:9–24 "I pray for them. I do not pray for the world but for those whom You have given Me, for they are Yours. **10** And all Mine are Yours, and Yours are Mine, and I am glorified in them. **11** Now I am no longer in the world, but these are in the world, and I come to You. Holy Father, keep through Your name those whom You have given Me, that they may be one as We *are.* **12** While I was with them in the world, I kept them in Your name. Those whom You gave Me I have kept; and none of them is lost except the son of perdition, that the Scripture might be fulfilled. **13** But now I come to You, and these things I speak in the world, that they may have My joy fulfilled in themselves. **14** I have given them Your word; and the world has hated them because they are not of the world, just as I am not of the world. **15** I do not pray that You should take them out of the world, but that You should keep them from the evil one. **16** They are not of the world, just as I am not of the world. **17** Sanctify them by Your truth. Your word is truth. **18** As You sent Me into the world, I also have sent them into the world. **19** And for their sakes I sanctify Myself, that they also may be sanctified by the truth. **20** "I do not pray for these alone, but also for those who will believe in Me through their word; **21** that they all may be one, as You, Father, *are* in Me, and I in You; that they also may be one in Us, that the world may believe that You sent Me. **22** And the glory which You gave Me I have given them, that they may be one just as We are one: **23** I in them, and You in Me; that they may be made perfect in one, and that the world may know that You have sent Me, and have loved them as You have loved Me. **24** "Father, I desire that they also whom You gave Me may be with Me where I am, that they may behold My glory which You have given Me; for You loved Me before the foundation of the world.

Commanded.

1 Tim 2:1 Therefore I exhort first of all that supplications, prayers, intercessions, *and* giving of thanks be made for all men,

James 5:14 Is anyone among you sick? Let him call for the elders of the church, and let them pray over him, anointing him with oil in the name of the Lord.

James 5:16 Confess *your* trespasses to one another, and pray for one another, that you may be healed. The effective, fervent prayer of a righteous man avails much.

Should be offered up for

Kings.

1 Tim 2:2 for kings and all who are in authority, that we may lead a quiet and peaceable life in all godliness and reverence.

All in authority.

1 Tim 2:2 for kings and all who are in authority, that we may lead a quiet and peaceable life in all godliness and reverence.

Ministers.

2 Cor 1:11 you also helping together in prayer for us, that thanks may be given by many persons on our behalf for the gift *granted* to us through many.

Phil 1:19 For I know that this will turn out for my deliverance through your prayer and the supply of the Spirit of Jesus Christ,

The church, by leaders.

Eph 1:16 do not cease to give thanks for you, making mention of you in my prayers:

Eph 3:14–19 For this reason I bow my knees to the Father of our Lord Jesus Christ, **15** from whom the whole family in heaven and earth is named, **16** that He would grant you, according to the riches of His glory, to be strengthened with might through His Spirit in the inner man, **17** that Christ may dwell in your hearts through faith; that you, being rooted and grounded in love, **18** may be able to comprehend with all the saints what *is* the width and length and depth and height— **19** to know the love of Christ which passes knowledge; that you may be filled with all the fullness of God.

Phil 1:4 always in every prayer of mine making request for you all with joy,

All believers.

Eph 6:18 praying always with all prayer and supplication in the Spirit, being watchful to this end with all perseverance and supplication for all the saints—

All men.

1 Tim 2:1 Therefore I exhort first of all that supplications, prayers, intercessions, *and* giving of thanks be made for all men,

Masters.

Gen 24:12–14 Then he said, "O LORD God of my master Abraham, please give me success this day, and show kindness to my master Abraham. **13** Behold, *here* I stand by the well of water, and the daughters of the men of the city are coming out to draw water. **14** Now let it be that the young woman to whom I say, 'Please let down your pitcher that I may drink,' and she says, 'Drink, and I will also give your camels a drink'—*let* her *be the one* You have appointed for Your servant Isaac. And by this I will know that You have shown kindness to my master."

Servants.

Luke 7:2–3 And a certain centurion's servant, who was dear to him, was sick and ready to die. **3** So when he heard about Jesus, he sent elders of the Jews to Him, pleading with Him to come and heal his servant.

Children.

Gen 17:18 And Abraham said to God, "Oh, that Ishmael might live before You!"

Matt 15:22 And behold, a woman of Canaan came from that region and cried out to Him, saying, "Have mercy on me, O Lord, Son of David! My daughter is severely demon-possessed."

Friends.

Job 42:8 Now therefore, take for yourselves seven bulls and seven rams, go to My servant Job, and offer up for yourselves a burnt offering; and My servant Job shall pray for you. For I will accept him, lest I deal with you *according to your* folly; because you have not spoken of Me *what is* right, as My servant Job *has.*"

Fellow countrymen.

Rom 10:1 Brethren, my heart's desire and prayer to God for Israel is that they may be saved.

The sick.

James 5:14 Is anyone among you sick? Let him call for the elders of the church, and let them pray over him, anointing him with oil in the name of the Lord.

Persecutors.

Matt 5:44 But I say to you, love your enemies, bless those who curse you, do good to those who hate you, and pray for those who spitefully use you and persecute you,

Enemies among whom we dwell.

Jer 29:7 And seek the peace of the city where I have caused you to be carried away captive, and pray to the LORD for it; for in its peace you will have peace.

Those who envy us.

Num 12:13 So Moses cried out to the LORD, saying, "Please heal her, O God, I pray!"

Those who forsake us.

2 Tim 4:16 At my first defense no one stood with me, but all forsook me. May it not be charged against them.

Those who murmur against God.

Num 11:1–2 Now *when* the people complained, it displeased the LORD; for the LORD heard *it,* and His anger was aroused. So the fire of the LORD burned among them, and consumed *some* in the outskirts of the camp. **2** Then the people cried out to Moses, and when Moses prayed to the LORD, the fire was quenched.

Num 14:13 And Moses said to the LORD: "Then the Egyptians will hear *it*, for by Your might You brought these people up from among them,

Num 14:19 Pardon the iniquity of this people, I pray, according to the greatness of Your mercy, just as You have forgiven this people, from Egypt even until now."

Encouragement to.

James 5:16 Confess *your* trespasses to one another, and pray for one another, that you may be healed. The effective, fervent prayer of a righteous man avails much.

1 John 5:16 If anyone sees his brother sinning a sin *which does* not *lead* to death, he will ask, and He will give him life for those who commit sin not *leading* to death. There is sin *leading* to death. I do not say that he should pray about that.

Beneficial to the offerer.

Job 42:10 And the LORD restored Job's losses when he prayed for his friends. Indeed the LORD gave Job twice as much as he had before.

Sin of neglecting.

1 Sam 12:23 Moreover, as for me, far be it from me that I should sin against the LORD in ceasing to pray for you; but I will teach you the good and the right way.

Believers should ask for.

1 Sam 12:19 And all the people said to Samuel, "Pray for your servants to the LORD your God, that we may not die; for we have added to all our sins the evil of asking a king for ourselves."

Heb 13:18 Pray for us; for we are confident that we have a good conscience, in all things desiring to live honorably.

Unavailing for unbelievers.

Jer 7:13–16 And now, because you have done all these works," says the LORD, "and I spoke to you, rising up early and speaking, but you did not hear, and I called you, but you did not answer, **14** therefore I will do to the house which is called by My name, in which you trust, and to this place which I gave to you and your fathers, as I have done to Shiloh. **15** And I will cast you out of My sight, as I have cast out all your brethren—the whole posterity of Ephraim. **16** "Therefore do not pray for this people, nor lift up a cry or prayer for them, nor make intercession to Me; for I will not hear you.

Jer 14:10–11 Thus says the LORD to this people: "Thus they have loved to wander; They have not restrained their feet. Therefore the LORD does not accept them; He will remember their iniquity now, And punish their sins." **11** Then the LORD said to me, "Do not pray for this people, for *their* good.

Exemplified by

Abraham.

Gen 18:23–32 And Abraham came near and said, "Would You also destroy the righteous with the wicked? **24** Suppose there were fifty righteous within the city; would You also destroy the place and not spare *it* for the fifty righteous that were in it? **25** Far be it from You to do such a thing as this, to slay the righteous with the wicked, so that the righteous should be as the wicked; far be it from You! Shall not the Judge of all the earth do right?" **26** So the LORD said, "If I find in Sodom fifty righteous within the city, then I will spare all the place for their sakes." **27** Then Abraham answered and said, "Indeed now, I who *am but* dust and ashes have taken it upon myself to speak to the Lord: **28** Suppose there were five less than the fifty righteous; would You destroy all of the city for *lack of* five?" So He said, "If I find there forty-five, I will not destroy *it*." **29** And he spoke to Him yet again and said, "Suppose there should be forty found there?" So He said, "I will not do *it* for the sake of forty." **30** Then he said, "Let not the Lord be angry, and I will speak: Suppose thirty should be found there?" So He said, "I will not do *it* if I find thirty there." **31** And he said, "Indeed now, I have taken it upon myself to speak to the Lord: Suppose twenty should be found there?" So He said, "I will not destroy *it* for the sake of twenty." **32** Then he said, "Let not the Lord be angry, and I will speak but once more: Suppose ten should be found there?" And He said, "I will not destroy *it* for the sake of ten."

Abraham's servant.

Gen 24:12–14 Then he said, "O LORD God of my master Abraham, please give me success this day, and show kindness to my master Abraham. **13** Behold, *here* I stand by the well of water, and the daughters of the men of the city are coming out to draw water. **14** Now let it be that the young woman to whom I say, 'Please let down your pitcher that I may drink,' and she says, 'Drink, and I will also give your camels a drink'—*let* her *be the one* You have appointed for Your servant Isaac. And by this I will know that You have shown kindness to my master."

Moses.

Ex 8:12 Then Moses and Aaron went out from Pharaoh. And Moses cried out to the LORD concerning the frogs which He had brought against Pharaoh.

Ex 32:11–13 Then Moses pleaded with the LORD his God, and said: "LORD, why does Your wrath burn hot against Your people whom You have brought out of the land of Egypt with great power and with a mighty hand? **12** Why should the Egyptians speak, and say, 'He brought them out to harm them, to kill them in the mountains, and to consume them from the face of the earth'? Turn from Your fierce wrath, and relent from this harm to Your people. **13** Remember Abraham, Isaac, and Israel, Your servants, to whom You swore by Your own self, and said to them, 'I will multiply your descendants as the stars of heaven; and all this land that I have spoken of I give to your descendants, and they shall inherit *it* forever.' "

Samuel.

1 Sam 7:5 And Samuel said, "Gather all Israel to Mizpah, and I will pray to the LORD for you."

Solomon.

1 Kin 8:30–36 And may You hear the supplication of Your servant and of Your people Israel, when they pray toward this place. Hear in heaven Your dwelling place; and when You hear, forgive. **31** "When anyone sins against his neighbor, and is forced to take an oath, and comes *and* takes an oath before Your altar in this temple, **32** then hear in heaven, and act, and judge Your servants, condemning the wicked, bringing his way on his head, and justifying the righteous by giving him according to his righteousness. **33** "When Your people Israel are defeated before an enemy because they have sinned against You, and when they turn back to You and confess Your name, and pray and make supplication to You in this temple, **34** then hear in heaven, and forgive the sin of Your people Israel, and bring them back to the land which You gave to their fathers. **35** "When the heavens are shut up and there is no rain because they have sinned against You, when they pray toward this place and confess Your name, and turn from their sin because You afflict them, **36** then hear in heaven, and forgive the sin of Your servants, Your people Israel, that You may teach them the good way in which they should walk; and send rain on Your land which You have given to Your people as an inheritance.

Elisha.

2 Kin 4:33 He went in therefore, shut the door behind the two of them, and prayed to the LORD.

Hezekiah.

2 Chr 30:18 For a multitude of the people, many from Ephraim, Manasseh, Issachar, and Zebulun, had not cleansed themselves, yet they ate the Passover contrary to what was written. But Hezekiah prayed for them, saying, "May the good LORD provide atonement for everyone

Isaiah.

2 Chr 32:20 Now because of this King Hezekiah and the prophet Isaiah, the son of Amoz, prayed and cried out to heaven.

Nehemiah.

Neh 1:4–11 So it was, when I heard these words, that I sat down and wept, and mourned *for many* days; I was fasting and praying before the God of heaven. **5** And I said: "I pray, LORD God of heaven, O great and awesome God, *You* who keep *Your* covenant and mercy with those who love You and observe Your commandments, **6** please let Your ear be attentive and Your eyes open, that You may hear the prayer of Your servant which I pray before You now, day and night, for the children of Israel Your servants, and confess the sins of the children of Israel which we have sinned against You. Both my father's house and I have sinned. **7** We have acted very corruptly against You, and have not kept the commandments, the statutes, nor the ordinances which You commanded Your servant Moses. **8** Remember, I pray, the word that You commanded Your servant Moses, saying, '*If* you are unfaithful, I will scatter you among the nations; **9** but *if* you return to Me, and keep My commandments and do them, though some of you were cast out to the farthest part of the heavens, *yet* I will gather them from there, and bring them to the place which I have chosen as a dwelling for My name.' **10** Now these *are* Your servants and Your people, whom You have redeemed by Your great power, and by Your strong hand. **11** O Lord, I pray, please let Your ear be attentive to the prayer of Your servant, and to the prayer of Your servants who desire to fear Your name; and let Your servant prosper this day, I

pray, and grant him mercy in the sight of this man." For I was the king's cupbearer.

David.

Ps 25:22 Redeem Israel, O God, Out of all their troubles!

Ezekiel.

Ezek 9:8 So it was, that while they were killing them, I was left *alone;* and I fell on my face and cried out, and said, "Ah, Lord GOD! Will You destroy all the remnant of Israel in pouring out Your fury on Jerusalem?"

Daniel. **Dan 9:3–19**

Stephen.

Acts 7:60 Then he knelt down and cried out with a loud voice, "Lord, do not charge them with this sin." And when he had said this, he fell asleep.

Peter and John.

Acts 8:15 who, when they had come down, prayed for them that they might receive the Holy Spirit.

The church of Jerusalem.

Acts 12:5 Peter was therefore kept in prison, but constant prayer was offered to God for him by the church.

Paul.

Col 1:9–12 For this reason we also, since the day we heard it, do not cease to pray for you, and to ask that you may be filled with the knowledge of His will in all wisdom and spiritual understanding; **10** that you may walk worthy of the Lord, fully pleasing *Him,* being fruitful in every good work and increasing in the knowledge of God; **11** strengthened with all might, according to His glorious power, for all patience and longsuffering with joy; **12** giving thanks to the Father who has qualified us to be partakers of the inheritance of the saints in the light.

2 Thess 1:11 Therefore we also pray always for you that our God would count you worthy of *this* calling, and fulfill all the good pleasure of *His* goodness and the work of faith with power,

Epaphras.

Col 4:12 Epaphras, who is *one* of you, a bondservant of Christ, greets you, always laboring fervently for you in prayers, that you may stand perfect and complete in all the will of God.

Philemon.

Philem 1:22 But, meanwhile, also prepare a guest room for me, for I trust that through your prayers I shall be granted to you.

PRAYER, PRIVATE

Christ was constant in.

Matt 14:23 And when He had sent the multitudes away, He went up on the mountain by Himself to pray. Now when evening came, He was alone there.

Matt 26:36 Then Jesus came with them to a place called Gethsemane, and said to the disciples, "Sit here while I go and pray over there."

Matt 26:39 He went a little farther and fell on His face, and prayed, saying, "O My Father, if it is possible, let this cup pass from Me; nevertheless, not as I will, but as You *will.*"

Mark 1:35 Now in the morning, having risen a long while before daylight, He went out and departed to a solitary place; and there He prayed.

Luke 9:18 And it happened, as He was alone praying, *that* His disciples joined Him, and He asked them, saying, "Who do the crowds say that I am?"

Luke 9:29 As He prayed, the appearance of His face was altered, and His robe *became* white *and* glistening.

Commanded.

Matt 6:6 But you, when you pray, go into your room, and when you have shut your door, pray to your Father who *is* in the secret *place;* and your Father who sees in secret will reward you openly.

Should be offered

At evening, morning, and noon.

Ps 55:17 Evening and morning and at noon I will pray, and cry aloud, And He shall hear my voice.

Day and night.

Ps 88:1 O LORD, God of my salvation, I have cried out day and night before You.

Without ceasing.

1 Thess 5:17 pray without ceasing,

Shall be heard.

Job 22:27 You will make your prayer to Him, He will hear you, And you will pay your vows.

Rewarded openly.

Matt 6:6 But you, when you pray, go into your room, and when you have shut your door, pray to your Father who *is* in the secret *place;* and your Father who sees in secret will reward you openly.

An evidence of conversion.

Acts 9:11 So the Lord *said* to him, "Arise and go to the street called Straight, and inquire at the house of Judas for *one* called Saul of Tarsus, for behold, he is praying.

Nothing should hinder.

Dan 6:10 Now when Daniel knew that the writing was signed, he went home. And in his upper room, with his windows open toward Jerusalem, he knelt down on his knees three times that day, and prayed and gave thanks before his God, as was his custom since early days.

Exemplified by

Lot.

Gen 19:20 See now, this city *is* near *enough* to flee to, and it *is* a little one; please let me escape there (*is* it not a little one?) and my soul shall live."

Eliezer.

Gen 24:12 Then he said, "O LORD God of my master Abraham, please give me success this day, and show kindness to my master Abraham.

Jacob.

Gen 32:9–12 Then Jacob said, "O God of my father Abraham and God of my father Isaac, the LORD who said to me, 'Return to your country and to your family, and I will deal well with you': **10** I am not worthy of the least of all the mercies and of all the truth which You have shown Your servant; for I crossed over this Jordan with my staff, and now I have become two companies. **11** Deliver me, I pray, from the hand of my brother, from the hand of Esau; for I fear him, lest he come and attack me *and* the mother with

the children. **12** For You said, 'I will surely treat you well, and make your descendants as the sand of the sea, which cannot be numbered for multitude.' "

Gideon.

Judg 6:22 Now Gideon perceived that He *was* the Angel of the LORD. So Gideon said, "Alas, O Lord GOD! For I have seen the Angel of the LORD face to face."

Judg 6:36 So Gideon said to God, "If You will save Israel by my hand as You have said—

Judg 6:39 Then Gideon said to God, "Do not be angry with me, but let me speak just once more: Let me test, I pray, just once more with the fleece; let it now be dry only on the fleece, but on all the ground let there be dew."

Hannah.

1 Sam 1:10 And she *was* in bitterness of soul, and prayed to the LORD and wept in anguish.

David.

2 Sam 7:18–29 Then King David went in and sat before the LORD; and he said: "Who *am* I, O Lord GOD? And what is my house, that You have brought me this far? **19** And yet this was a small thing in Your sight, O Lord GOD; and You have also spoken of Your servant's house for a great while to come. *Is* this the manner of man, O Lord GOD? **20** Now what more can David say to You? For You, Lord GOD, know Your servant. **21** For Your word's sake, and according to Your own heart, You have done all these great things, to make Your servant know *them.* **22** Therefore You are great, O Lord GOD. For *there is* none like You, nor *is there any* God besides You, according to all that we have heard with our ears. **23** And who *is* like Your people, like Israel, the one nation on the earth whom God went to redeem for Himself as a people, to make for Himself a name—and to do for Yourself great and awesome deeds for Your land—before Your people whom You redeemed for Yourself from Egypt, the nations, and their gods? **24** For You have made Your people Israel Your very own people forever; and You, LORD, have become their God. **25** "Now, O LORD God, the word which You have spoken concerning Your servant and concerning his house, establish *it* forever and do as You have said. **26** So let Your name be magnified forever, saying, 'The LORD of hosts *is* the God over Israel.' And let the house of Your servant David be established before You. **27** For You, O LORD of hosts, God of Israel, have revealed *this* to Your servant, saying, 'I will build you a house.' Therefore Your servant has found it in his heart to pray this prayer to You. **28** "And now, O Lord GOD, You are God, and Your words are true, and You have promised this goodness to Your servant. **29** Now therefore, let it please You to bless the house of Your servant, that it may continue before You forever; for You, O Lord GOD, have spoken *it*, and with Your blessing let the house of Your servant be blessed forever."

Hezekiah.

2 Kin 20:2 Then he turned his face toward the wall, and prayed to the LORD, saying,

Isaiah.

2 Kin 20:11 So Isaiah the prophet cried out to the LORD, and He brought the shadow ten degrees backward, by which it had gone down on the sundial of Ahaz.

Manasseh.

2 Chr 33:18–19 Now the rest of the acts of Manasseh, his prayer to his God, and the words of the seers who spoke to him in the name of the Lord God of Israel, indeed they *are written* in the book of the kings of Israel. **19** Also his prayer and *how God* received his entreaty, and all his sin and trespass, and the sites where he built high places and set up wooden images and carved images, before he was humbled, indeed they *are* written among the sayings of Hozai.

Ezra.

Ezra 9:5–6 At the evening sacrifice I arose from my fasting; and having torn my garment and my robe, I fell on my knees and spread out my hands to the Lord my God. **6** And I said: "O my God, I am too ashamed and humiliated to lift up my face to You, my God; for our iniquities have risen higher than *our* heads, and our guilt has grown up to the heavens.

Nehemiah.

Neh 2:4 Then the king said to me, "What do you request?" So I prayed to the God of heaven.

Jeremiah.

Jer 32:16–25 "Now when I had delivered the purchase deed to Baruch the son of Neriah, I prayed to the Lord, saying: **17** 'Ah, Lord God! Behold, You have made the heavens and the earth by Your great power and outstretched arm. There is nothing too hard for You. **18** *You* show lovingkindness to thousands, and repay the iniquity of the fathers into the bosom of their children after them—the Great, the Mighty God, whose name *is* the Lord of hosts. **19** *You are* great in counsel and mighty in work, for your eyes *are* open to all the ways of the sons of men, to give everyone according to his ways and according to the fruit of his doings. **20** You have set signs and wonders in the land of Egypt, to this day, and in Israel and among *other* men; and You have made Yourself a name, as it is this day. **21** You have brought Your people Israel out of the land of Egypt with signs and wonders, with a strong hand and an outstretched arm, and with great terror; **22** You have given them this land, of which You swore to their fathers to give them—"a land flowing with milk and honey." **23** And they came in and took possession of it, but they have not obeyed Your voice or walked in Your law. They have done nothing of all that You commanded them to do; therefore You have caused all this calamity to come upon them. **24** 'Look, the siege mounds! They have come to the city to take it; and the city has been given into the hand of the Chaldeans who fight against it, because of the sword and famine and pestilence. What You have spoken has happened; there You see *it!* **25** And You have said to me, O Lord God, "Buy the field for money, and take witnesses"!—yet the city has been given into the hand of the Chaldeans.' "

Daniel.

Dan 9:3 Then I set my face toward the Lord God to make request by prayer and supplications, with fasting, sackcloth, and ashes.

Dan 9:17 Now therefore, our God, hear the prayer of Your servant, and his supplications, and for the Lord's sake cause Your face to shine on Your sanctuary, which is desolate.

Jonah.

Jon 2:1 Then Jonah prayed to the Lord his God from the fish's belly.

Habakkuk.

Hab 1:2 O Lord, how long shall I cry, And You will not hear? Even cry out to You, "Violence!" And You will not save.

Anna.

Luke 2:37 and this woman *was* a widow of about eighty-four years, who did not depart from the temple, but served *God* with fastings and prayers night and day.

Paul.

Acts 9:11 So the Lord *said* to him, "Arise and go to the street called Straight, and inquire at the house of Judas for *one* called Saul of Tarsus, for behold, he is praying.

Peter.

Acts 9:40 But Peter put them all out, and knelt down and prayed. And turning to the body he said, "Tabitha, arise." And she opened her eyes, and when she saw Peter she sat up.

Acts 10:9 The next day, as they went on their journey and drew near the city, Peter went up on the housetop to pray, about the sixth hour.

Cornelius.

Acts 10:30 So Cornelius said, "Four days ago I was fasting until this hour; and at the ninth hour I prayed in my house, and behold, a man stood before me in bright clothing,

PRAYER, PUBLIC

Acceptable to God.

Is 56:7 Even them I will bring to My holy mountain, And make them joyful in My house of prayer. Their burnt offerings and their sacrifices *Will be* accepted on My altar; For My house shall be called a house of prayer for all nations."

God promises to hear.

2 Chr 7:14 if My people who are called by My name will humble themselves, and pray and seek My face, and turn from their wicked ways, then I will hear from heaven, and will forgive their sin and heal their land.

2 Chr 7:16 For now I have chosen and sanctified this house, that My name may be there forever; and My eyes and My heart will be there perpetually.

God promises to bless in.

Ex 20:24 An altar of earth you shall make for Me, and you shall sacrifice on it your burnt offerings and your peace offerings, your sheep and your oxen. In every place where I record My name I will come to you, and I will bless you.

Christ

Sanctifies by His presence.

Matt 18:20 For where two or three are gathered together in My name, I am there in the midst of them."

Attended synagogue, where public prayer took place.

Matt 12:9 Now when He had departed from there, He went into their synagogue.

Luke 4:16 So He came to Nazareth, where He had been

brought up. And as His custom was, He went into the synagogue on the Sabbath day, and stood up to read.

Promises answers to.

Matt 18:19 "Again I say to you that if two of you agree on earth concerning anything that they ask, it will be done for them by My Father in heaven.

Instituted the form of.

Luke 11:2 So He said to them, "When you pray, say: Our Father in heaven, Hallowed be Your name. Your kingdom come. Your will be done On earth as *it is* in heaven.

Should not be made in an unknown language.

1 Cor 14:14–16 For if I pray in a tongue, my spirit prays, but my understanding is unfruitful. **15** What is *the conclusion* then? I will pray with the spirit, and I will also pray with the understanding. I will sing with the spirit, and I will also sing with the understanding. **16** Otherwise, if you bless with the spirit, how will he who occupies the place of the uninformed say "Amen" at your giving of thanks, since he does not understand what you say?

Believers delight in.

Ps 42:4 When I remember these *things,* I pour out my soul within me. For I used to go with the multitude; I went with them to the house of God, With the voice of joy and praise, With a multitude that kept a pilgrim feast.

Ps 122:1 I was glad when they said to me, "Let us go into the house of the LORD."

Exhortation to.

Heb 10:25 not forsaking the assembling of ourselves together, as *is* the manner of some, but exhorting *one another,* and so much the more as you see the Day approaching.

Urge others to join in.

Ps 95:6 Oh come, let us worship and bow down; Let us kneel before the LORD our Maker.

Zech 8:21 The inhabitants of one *city* shall go to another, saying, "Let us continue to go and pray before the LORD, And seek the LORD of hosts. I myself will go also."

Exemplified by

Joshua.

Josh 7:6–9 Then Joshua tore his clothes, and fell to the earth on his face before the ark of the LORD until evening, he and the elders of Israel; and they put dust on their heads. **7** And Joshua said, "Alas, Lord GOD, why have You brought this people over the Jordan at all—to deliver us into the hand of the Amorites, to destroy us? Oh, that we had been content, and dwelt on the other side of the Jordan! **8** O Lord, what shall I say when Israel turns its back before its enemies? **9** For the Canaanites and all the inhabitants of the land will hear *it,* and surround us, and cut off our name from the earth. Then what will You do for Your great name?"

David.

1 Chr 29:10–19 Therefore David blessed the LORD before all the assembly; and David said: "Blessed are You, LORD God of Israel, our Father, forever and ever. **11** Yours, O LORD, *is* the greatness, The power and the glory, The victory and the majesty; For all *that is* in heaven and in earth *is* Yours; Yours *is* the kingdom, O LORD, And You are exalted as head over all. **12** Both riches and honor *come* from You, And You reign over all. In Your hand *is* power and might; In Your hand *it is* to make great And to give strength to all. **13** "Now therefore, our God, We thank You And praise Your glorious name. **14** But who *am* I, and who *are* my people, That we should be able to offer so willingly as this? For all things *come* from You, And of Your own we have given You. **15** For we *are* aliens and pilgrims before You, As *were* all our fathers; Our days on earth *are* as a shadow, And without hope. **16** "O LORD our God, all this abundance that we have prepared to build You a house for Your holy name is from Your hand, and *is* all Your own. **17** I know also, my God, that You test the heart and have pleasure in uprightness. As for me, in the uprightness of my heart I have willingly offered all these *things;* and now with joy I have seen Your people, who are present here to offer willingly to You. **18** O LORD God of Abraham, Isaac, and Israel, our fathers, keep this forever in the intent of the thoughts of the heart of Your people, and fix their heart toward You. **19** And give my son Solomon a loyal heart to keep Your commandments and Your testimonies and Your statutes, to do all *these things,* and to build the temple for which I have made provision."

Solomon. **2 Chr 6:1–42**

Jehoshaphat.

2 Chr 20:5–13 Then Jehoshaphat stood in the assembly of Judah and Jerusalem, in the house of the LORD, before the new court, **6** and said: "O LORD God of our fathers, *are* You not God in heaven, and do You *not* rule over all the kingdoms of the nations, and in Your hand *is there not* power and might, so that no one is able to withstand You? **7** *Are* You not our God, *who* drove out the inhabitants of this land before Your people Israel, and gave it to the descendants of Abraham Your friend forever? **8** And they dwell in it, and have built You a sanctuary in it for Your name, saying, **9** 'If disaster comes upon us—sword, judgment, pestilence, or famine—we will stand before this temple and in Your presence (for Your name *is* in this temple), and cry out to You in our affliction, and You will hear and save.' **10** And now, here are the people of Ammon, Moab, and Mount Seir—whom You would not let Israel invade when they came out of the land of Egypt, but they turned from them and did not destroy them— **11** here they are, rewarding us by coming to throw us out of Your possession which You have given us to inherit. **12** O our God, will You not judge them? For we have no power against this great multitude that is coming against us; nor do we know what to do, but our eyes *are* upon You." **13** Now all Judah, with their little ones, their wives, and their children, stood before the LORD.

Jeshua. **Neh 9:1–38**

The Jews.

Luke 1:10 And the whole multitude of the people was praying outside at the hour of incense.

The early Christians.

Acts 2:42 And they continued steadfastly in the

apostles' doctrine and fellowship, in the breaking of bread, and in prayers.

Acts 4:24 So when they heard that, they raised their voice to God with one accord and said: "Lord, You *are* God, who made heaven and earth and the sea, and all that is in them,

Acts 12:5 Peter was therefore kept in prison, but constant prayer was offered to God for him by the church.

Acts 12:12 So, when he had considered *this*, he came to the house of Mary, the mother of John whose surname was Mark, where many were gathered together praying.

Peter.

Acts 3:1 Now Peter and John went up together to the temple at the hour of prayer, the ninth *hour.*

The teachers and prophets at Antioch.

Acts 13:3 Then, having fasted and prayed, and laid hands on them, they sent *them* away.

Paul.

Acts 16:16 Now it happened, as we went to prayer, that a certain slave girl possessed with a spirit of divination met us, who brought her masters much profit by fortune-telling.

PREACHERS, PREACHING.
SEE ALSO MINISTERS

Must internalize truth before.

Ezek 3:1–3 Moreover He said to me, "Son of man, eat what you find; eat this scroll, and go, speak to the house of Israel." **2** So I opened my mouth, and He caused me to eat that scroll. **3** And He said to me, "Son of man, feed your belly, and fill your stomach with this scroll that I give you." So I ate, and it was in my mouth like honey in sweetness.

Must be sent by God.

Rom 10:15 And how shall they preach unless they are sent? As it is written: *"How beautiful are the feet of those who preach the gospel of peace, Who bring glad tidings of good things!"*

Command to.

2 Tim 4:2 Preach the word! Be ready in season *and* out of season. Convince, rebuke, exhort, with all longsuffering and teaching.

Those called as

John the Baptist.

Matt 3:1–3 In those days John the Baptist came preaching in the wilderness of Judea, **2** and saying, "Repent, for the kingdom of heaven is at hand!" **3** For this is he who was spoken of by the prophet Isaiah, saying: *"The voice of one crying in the wilderness: 'Prepare the way of the LORD; Make His paths straight.' "*

Jesus.

Matt 4:17 From that time Jesus began to preach and to say, "Repent, for the kingdom of heaven is at hand."

Eph 2:17 And He came and preached peace to you who were afar off and to those who were near.

Paul.

1 Tim 2:7 for which I was appointed a preacher and an

apostle—I am speaking the truth in Christ *and* not lying—a teacher of the Gentiles in faith and truth.

Prophets in Antioch.

Acts 13:1 Now in the church that was at Antioch there were certain prophets and teachers: Barnabas, Simeon who was called Niger, Lucius of Cyrene, Manaen who had been brought up with Herod the tetrarch, and Saul.

Goal of.

Matt 24:14 And this gospel of the kingdom will be preached in all the world as a witness to all the nations, and then the end will come.

God's Word the sole source of their.

Titus 1:3 but has in due time manifested His word through preaching, which was committed to me according to the commandment of God our Savior;

Content of their message

Repentance.

Matt 3:1–3 In those days John the Baptist came preaching in the wilderness of Judea, **2** and saying, "Repent, for the kingdom of heaven is at hand!" **3** For this is he who was spoken of by the prophet Isaiah, saying: *"The voice of one crying in the wilderness: 'Prepare the way of the LORD; Make His paths straight.' "*

Matt 4:17 From that time Jesus began to preach and to say, "Repent, for the kingdom of heaven is at hand."

Resurrection of Christ.

Acts 4:2 being greatly disturbed that they taught the people and preached in Jesus the resurrection from the dead.

The gospel of peace.

Rom 10:15 And how shall they preach unless they are sent? As it is written: *"How beautiful are the feet of those who preach the gospel of peace, Who bring glad tidings of good things!"*

Eph 2:17 And He came and preached peace to you who were afar off and to those who were near.

Should earn a living from their.

1 Cor 9:14 Even so the Lord has commanded that those who preach the gospel should live from the gospel.

Called men of God.

1 Tim 6:11 But you, O man of God, flee these things and pursue righteousness, godliness, faith, love, patience, gentleness.

2 Tim 3:17 that the man of God may be complete, thoroughly equipped for every good work.

Examples of,

Peter's sermons. **Acts 2:14–40; 3:12–26**

Paul's sermon. **Acts 13:16–41**

PRECIOUS STONES

Dug out of the earth.

Job 28:5–6 *As for* the earth, from it comes bread, But underneath it is turned up as by fire; **6** Its stones *are* the source of sapphires, And it contains gold dust.

Brought from Ophir.

1 Kin 10:11 Also, the ships of Hiram, which brought gold from Ophir, brought great *quantities* of almug wood and precious stones from Ophir.

2 Chr 9:10 Also, the servants of Hiram and the servants of Solomon, who brought gold from Ophir, brought algum wood and precious stones.

Brought from Sheba.

1 Kin 10:1–2 Now when the queen of Sheba heard of the fame of Solomon concerning the name of the LORD, she came to test him with hard questions. **2** She came to Jerusalem with a very great retinue, with camels that bore spices, very much gold, and precious stones; and when she came to Solomon, she spoke with him about all that was in her heart.

Ezek 27:22 The merchants of Sheba and Raamah *were* your merchants. They traded for your wares the choicest spices, all kinds of precious stones, and gold.

Called

Fiery stones.

Ezek 28:14 "You *were* the anointed cherub who covers; I established you; You were on the holy mountain of God; You walked back and forth in the midst of fiery stones.

Ezek 28:16 "By the abundance of your trading You became filled with violence within, And you sinned; Therefore I cast you as a profane thing Out of the mountain of God; And I destroyed you, O covering cherub, From the midst of the fiery stones.

Stones to be set.

1 Chr 29:2 Now for the house of my God I have prepared with all my might: gold for *things to be made of* gold, silver for *things of* silver, bronze for *things of* bronze, iron for *things of* iron, wood for *things of* wood, onyx stones, *stones* to be set, glistening stones of various colors, all kinds of precious stones, and marble slabs in abundance.

Jewels.

Is 61:10 I will greatly rejoice in the LORD, My soul shall be joyful in my God; For He has clothed me with the garments of salvation, He has covered me with the robe of righteousness, As a bridegroom decks *himself* with ornaments, And as a bride adorns *herself* with her jewels.

Ezek 16:12 And I put a jewel in your nose, earrings in your ears, and a beautiful crown on your head.

Precious jewels.

2 Chr 20:25 When Jehoshaphat and his people came to take away their spoil, they found among them an abundance of valuables on the dead bodies, and precious jewelry, which they stripped off for themselves, more than they could carry away; and they were three days gathering the spoil because there was so much.

Prov 20:15 There is gold and a multitude of rubies, But the lips of knowledge *are* a precious jewel.

Of great variety and colors.

1 Chr 29:2 Now for the house of my God I have prepared with all my might: gold for *things to be made of* gold, silver for *things of* silver, bronze for *things of* bronze, iron for *things of* iron, wood for *things of* wood, onyx stones, *stones* to be set, glistening stones of various colors, all kinds of precious stones, and marble slabs in abundance.

Brilliant and glistening.

1 Chr 29:2 Now for the house of my God I have pre-

pared with all my might: gold for *things to be made of* gold, silver for *things of* silver, bronze for *things of* bronze, iron for *things of* iron, wood for *things of* wood, onyx stones, *stones* to be set, glistening stones of various colors, all kinds of precious stones, and marble slabs in abundance.

Rev 21:11 having the glory of God. Her light *was* like a most precious stone, like a jasper stone, clear as crystal.

Mentioned in Scripture

Agate.

Ex 28:19 the third row, a jacinth, an agate, and an amethyst;

Amethyst.

Ex 28:19 the third row, a jacinth, an agate, and an amethyst;

Rev 21:20 the fifth sardonyx, the sixth sardius, the seventh chrysolite, the eighth beryl, the ninth topaz, the tenth chrysoprase, the eleventh jacinth, and the twelfth amethyst.

Beryl.

Ex 28:20 and the fourth row, a beryl, an onyx, and a jasper. They shall be set in gold settings.

Ezek 28:13 You were in Eden, the garden of God; Every precious stone *was* your covering: The sardius, topaz, and diamond, Beryl, onyx, and jasper, Sapphire, turquoise, and emerald with gold. The workmanship of your timbrels and pipes Was prepared for you on the day you were created.

Dan 10:6 His body *was* like beryl, his face like the appearance of lightning, his eyes like torches of fire, his arms and feet like burnished bronze in color, and the sound of his words like the voice of a multitude.

Rev 21:20 the fifth sardonyx, the sixth sardius, the seventh chrysolite, the eighth beryl, the ninth topaz, the tenth chrysoprase, the eleventh jacinth, and the twelfth amethyst.

Coral.

Job 28:18 No mention shall be made of coral or quartz, For the price of wisdom *is* above rubies.

Chalcedony.

Rev 21:19 The foundations of the wall of the city *were* adorned with all kinds of precious stones: the first foundation *was* jasper, the second sapphire, the third chalcedony, the fourth emerald,

Chrysolite and chrysoprase.

Rev 21:20 the fifth sardonyx, the sixth sardius, the seventh chrysolite, the eighth beryl, the ninth topaz, the tenth chrysoprase, the eleventh jacinth, and the twelfth amethyst.

Diamond.

Ex 28:18 the second row *shall be* a turquoise, a sapphire, and a diamond;

Jer 17:1 "The sin of Judah *is* written with a pen of iron; With the point of a diamond *it is* engraved On the tablet of their heart, And on the horns of your altars,

Ezek 28:13 You were in Eden, the garden of God; Every precious stone *was* your covering: The sardius, topaz, and diamond, Beryl, onyx, and jasper, Sapphire, turquoise, and emerald with gold. The workmanship of your timbrels and pipes Was prepared for you on the day you were created.

Emerald.

Ezek 27:16 Syria *was* your merchant because of the abundance of goods you made. They gave you for your wares emeralds, purple, embroidery, fine linen, corals, and rubies.

Ezek 28:13 You were in Eden, the garden of God; Every precious stone *was* your covering: The sardius, topaz, and diamond, Beryl, onyx, and jasper, Sapphire, turquoise, and emerald with gold. The workmanship of your timbrels and pipes Was prepared for you on the day you were created.

Rev 4:3 And He who sat there was like a jasper and a sardius stone in appearance; and *there was* a rainbow around the throne, in appearance like an emerald.

Jacinth.

Rev 21:20 the fifth sardonyx, the sixth sardius, the seventh chrysolite, the eighth beryl, the ninth topaz, the tenth chrysoprase, the eleventh jacinth, and the twelfth amethyst.

Jasper.

Ex 28:20 and the fourth row, a beryl, an onyx, and a jasper. They shall be set in gold settings.

Rev 4:3 And He who sat there was like a jasper and a sardius stone in appearance; and *there was* a rainbow around the throne, in appearance like an emerald.

Rev 21:11 having the glory of God. Her light *was* like a most precious stone, like a jasper stone, clear as crystal.

Rev 21:19 The foundations of the wall of the city *were* adorned with all kinds of precious stones: the first foundation *was* jasper, the second sapphire, the third chalcedony, the fourth emerald,

Onyx.

Ex 28:20 and the fourth row, a beryl, an onyx, and a jasper. They shall be set in gold settings.

Job 28:16 It cannot be valued in the gold of Ophir, In precious onyx or sapphire.

Ezek 28:13 You were in Eden, the garden of God; Every precious stone *was* your covering: The sardius, topaz, and diamond, Beryl, onyx, and jasper, Sapphire, turquoise, and emerald with gold. The workmanship of your timbrels and pipes Was prepared for you on the day you were created.

Pearl.

Matt 13:45–46 "Again, the kingdom of heaven is like a merchant seeking beautiful pearls, **46** who, when he had found one pearl of great price, went and sold all that he had and bought it.

Rev 21:21 The twelve gates *were* twelve pearls: each individual gate was of one pearl. And the street of the city *was* pure gold, like transparent glass.

Quartz.

Job 28:18 No mention shall be made of coral or quartz, For the price of wisdom *is* above rubies.

Ruby.

Job 28:18 No mention shall be made of coral or quartz, For the price of wisdom *is* above rubies.

Is 54:12 I will make your pinnacles of rubies, Your gates of crystal, And all your walls of precious stones.

Lam 4:7 Her Nazirites were brighter than snow And whiter than milk; They were more ruddy in body than rubies, *Like* sapphire in their appearance.

Sapphire.

Ex 24:10 and they saw the God of Israel. And *there was* under His feet as it were a paved work of sapphire stone, and it was like the very heavens in *its* clarity.

Ex 28:18 the second row *shall be* a turquoise, a sapphire, and a diamond;

Job 28:16 It cannot be valued in the gold of Ophir, In precious onyx or sapphire.

Ezek 1:26 And above the firmament over their heads *was* the likeness of a throne, in appearance like a sapphire stone; on the likeness of the throne *was* a likeness with the appearance of a man high above it.

Ezek 28:13 You were in Eden, the garden of God; Every precious stone *was* your covering: The sardius, topaz, and diamond, Beryl, onyx, and jasper, Sapphire, turquoise, and emerald with gold. The workmanship of your timbrels and pipes Was prepared for you on the day you were created.

Sardius and sardonyx.

Ex 28:17 And you shall put settings of stones in it, four rows of stones: *The first* row *shall be* a sardius, a topaz, and an emerald; *this shall be* the first row;

Ezek 28:13 You were in Eden, the garden of God; Every precious stone *was* your covering: The sardius, topaz, and diamond, Beryl, onyx, and jasper, Sapphire, turquoise, and emerald with gold. The workmanship of your timbrels and pipes Was prepared for you on the day you were created.

Rev 4:3 And He who sat there was like a jasper and a sardius stone in appearance; and *there was* a rainbow around the throne, in appearance like an emerald.

Rev 21:20 the fifth sardonyx, the sixth sardius, the seventh chrysolite, the eighth beryl, the ninth topaz, the tenth chrysoprase, the eleventh jacinth, and the twelfth amethyst.

Topaz.

Ex 28:17 And you shall put settings of stones in it, four rows of stones: *The first* row *shall be* a sardius, a topaz, and an emerald; *this shall be* the first row;

Job 28:19 The topaz of Ethiopia cannot equal it, Nor can it be valued in pure gold.

Ezek 28:13 You were in Eden, the garden of God; Every precious stone *was* your covering: The sardius, topaz, and diamond, Beryl, onyx, and jasper, Sapphire, turquoise, and emerald with gold. The workmanship of your timbrels and pipes Was prepared for you on the day you were created.

Rev 21:20 the fifth sardonyx, the sixth sardius, the seventh chrysolite, the eighth beryl, the ninth topaz, the tenth chrysoprase, the eleventh jacinth, and the twelfth amethyst.

Highly prized by the ancients.

Prov 17:8 A present *is* a precious stone in the eyes of its possessor; Wherever he turns, he prospers.

Extensive commerce in.

Ezek 27:22 The merchants of Sheba and Raamah *were* your merchants. They traded for your wares the choicest spices, all kinds of precious stones, and gold.

Rev 18:12 merchandise of gold and silver, precious stones and pearls, fine linen and purple, silk and scarlet, every kind of citron wood, every kind of object of ivory, every kind of object of most precious wood, bronze, iron, and marble;

Often given as presents.

1 Kin 10:2 She came to Jerusalem with a very great retinue, with camels that bore spices, very much gold, and precious stones; and when she came to Solomon, she spoke with him about all that was in her heart.

1 Kin 10:10 Then she gave the king one hundred and twenty talents of gold, spices in great quantity, and precious stones. There never again came such abundance of spices as the queen of Sheba gave to King Solomon.

Art of engraving and setting, known to the Jews.

Ex 28:9 "Then you shall take two onyx stones and engrave on them the names of the sons of Israel:

Ex 28:11 With the work of an engraver in stone, *like* the engravings of a signet, you shall engrave the two stones with the names of the sons of Israel. You shall set them in settings of gold.

Ex 28:20–21 and the fourth row, a beryl, an onyx, and a jasper. They shall be set in gold settings. 21 And the stones shall have the names of the sons of Israel, twelve according to their names, *like* the engravings of a signet, each one with its own name; they shall be according to the twelve tribes.

Used for

Adorning the high priest's ephod.

Ex 28:12 And you shall put the two stones on the shoulders of the ephod *as* memorial stones for the sons of Israel. So Aaron shall bear their names before the LORD on his two shoulders as a memorial.

Adorning the breastplate of judgment.

Ex 28:17–20 And you shall put settings of stones in it, four rows of stones: *The first* row *shall be* a sardius, a topaz, and an emerald; *this shall be* the first row; **18** the second row *shall be* a turquoise, a sapphire, and a diamond; **19** the third row, a jacinth, an agate, and an amethyst; **20** and the fourth row, a beryl, an onyx, and a jasper. They shall be set in gold settings.

Ex 39:10–14 And they set in it four rows of stones: a row with a sardius, a topaz, and an emerald was the first row; **11** the second row, a turquoise, a sapphire, and a diamond; **12** the third row, a jacinth, an agate, and an amethyst; **13** the fourth row, a beryl, an onyx, and a jasper. *They were* enclosed in settings of gold in their mountings. **14** *There were* twelve stones according to the names of the sons of Israel: according to their names, *engraved like* a signet, each one with its own name according to the twelve tribes.

Decorating the person.

Ezek 28:13 You were in Eden, the garden of God; Every precious stone *was* your covering: The sardius, topaz, and diamond, Beryl, onyx, and jasper, Sapphire, turquoise, and emerald with gold. The workmanship of your timbrels and pipes Was prepared for you on the day you were created.

Ornamenting royal crowns.

2 Sam 12:30 Then he took their king's crown from his head. Its weight *was* a talent of gold, with precious stones. And it was *set* on David's head. Also he brought out the spoil of the city in great abundance.

Setting in seals and rings.

Song 5:12 His eyes *are* like doves By the rivers of waters, Washed with milk, *And* fitly set.

Adorning the temple.

1 Chr 29:2 Now for the house of my God I have prepared with all my might: gold for *things to be made of* gold, silver for *things of* silver, bronze for *things of* bronze, iron for *things of* iron, wood for *things of* wood, onyx stones, *stones* to be set, glistening stones of various colors, all kinds of precious stones, and marble slabs in abundance.

1 Chr 29:8 And whoever had *precious* stones gave *them* to the treasury of the house of the LORD, into the hand of Jehiel the Gershonite.

2 Chr 3:6 And he decorated the house with precious stones for beauty, and the gold *was* gold from Parvaim.

Honoring idols.

Dan 11:38 But in their place he shall honor a god of fortresses; and a god which his fathers did not know he shall honor with gold and silver, with precious stones and pleasant things.

The treasure of kings.

2 Chr 32:27 Hezekiah had very great riches and honor. And he made himself treasuries for silver, for gold, for precious stones, for spices, for shields, and for all kinds of desirable items;

The tabernacle.

Ex 25:7 onyx stones, and stones to be set in the ephod and in the breastplate.

Illustrative of

Preciousness of Christ.

Is 28:16 Therefore thus says the Lord GOD: "Behold, I lay in Zion a stone for a foundation, A tried stone, a precious cornerstone, a sure foundation; Whoever believes will not act hastily.

1 Pet 2:6 Therefore it is also contained in the Scripture, *"Behold, I lay in Zion A chief cornerstone, elect, precious, And he who believes on Him will by no means be put to shame."*

Beauty and stability of the church.

Is 54:11–12 "O you afflicted one, Tossed with tempest, *and* not comforted, Behold, I will lay your stones with colorful gems, And lay your foundations with sapphires. **12** I will make your pinnacles of rubies, Your gates of crystal, And all your walls of precious stones.

Believers.

Mal 3:17 "They shall be Mine," says the LORD of hosts, "On the day that I make them My jewels. And I will spare them As a man spares his own son who serves him."

1 Cor 3:12 Now if anyone builds on this foundation *with* gold, silver, precious stones, wood, hay, straw,

The seductive splendor and false glory of apostasy.

Rev 17:4 The woman was arrayed in purple and scarlet, and adorned with gold and precious stones and pearls, having in her hand a golden cup full of abominations and the filthiness of her fornication.

Rev 18:16 and saying, 'Alas, alas, that great city that was clothed in fine linen, purple, and scarlet, and adorned with gold and precious stones and pearls!

Worldly glory of nations.

Ezek 28:13–16 You were in Eden, the garden of God; Every precious stone *was* your covering: The sardius, topaz, and diamond, Beryl, onyx, and jasper, Sapphire, turquoise, and emerald with gold. The workmanship of your timbrels and pipes Was prepared for you on the day you were created. **14** "You *were* the anointed cherub who covers; I established you; You were on the holy mountain of God; You walked back and forth in the midst of fiery stones. **15** You *were* perfect in your ways from the day you were created, Till iniquity was found in you. **16** "By the abundance of your trading You became filled with violence within, And you sinned; Therefore I cast you as a profane thing Out of the mountain of God; And I destroyed you, O covering cherub, From the midst of the fiery stones.

Glory and stability of heavenly Jerusalem.

Rev 21:11 having the glory of God. Her light *was* like a most precious stone, like a jasper stone, clear as crystal.

Rev 21:19 The foundations of the wall of the city *were* adorned with all kinds of precious stones: the first foundation *was* jasper, the second sapphire, the third chalcedony, the fourth emerald,

PRESENTS

Antiquity of.

Gen 32:13 So he lodged there that same night, and took what came to his hand as a present for Esau his brother:

Gen 43:15 So the men took that present and Benjamin, and they took double money in their hand, and arose and went down to Egypt; and they stood before Joseph.

Were given

To judges to secure a favorable hearing.

Prov 17:23 A wicked *man* accepts a bribe behind the back To pervert the ways of justice.

Amos 2:6 Thus says the LORD: "For three transgressions of Israel, and for four, I will not turn away its *punishment*, Because they sell the righteous for silver, And the poor for a pair of sandals.

To kings to engage their aid.

1 Kin 15:18 Then Asa took all the silver and gold *that was* left in the treasuries of the house of the LORD and the treasuries of the king's house, and delivered them into the hand of his servants. And King Asa sent them to Ben-Hadad the son of Tabrimmon, the son of Hezion, king of Syria, who dwelt in Damascus, saying,

By kings to other kings in token of submission.

1 Kin 10:25 Each man brought his present: articles of silver and gold, garments, armor, spices, horses, and mules, at a set rate year by year.

2 Chr 9:23–24 And all the kings of the earth sought the presence of Solomon to hear his wisdom, which God had put in his heart. **24** Each man brought his present: articles of silver and gold, garments, armor, spices, horses, and mules, at a set rate year by year.

Ps 72:10 The kings of Tarshish and of the isles Will bring presents; The kings of Sheba and Seba Will offer gifts.

To appease others.

Gen 32:20 and also say, 'Behold, your servant Jacob *is* behind us.' " For he said, "I will appease him with the present that goes before me, and afterward I will see his face; perhaps he will accept me."

1 Sam 25:27–28 And now this present which your maidservant has brought to my lord, let it be given to the young men who follow my lord. **28** Please forgive the trespass of your maidservant. For the LORD will certainly make for my lord an enduring house, because my lord fights the battles of the LORD, and evil is not found in you throughout your days.

1 Sam 25:35 So David received from her hand what she had brought him, and said to her, "Go up in peace to your house. See, I have heeded your voice and respected your person."

To confirm covenants.

Gen 21:28–30 And Abraham set seven ewe lambs of the flock by themselves. **29** Then Abimelech asked Abraham, "What *is the meaning of* these seven ewe lambs which you have set by themselves?" **30** And he said, "You will take *these* seven ewe lambs from my hand, that they may be my witness that I have dug this well."

To reward service.

2 Sam 18:12 But the man said to Joab, "Though I were to receive a thousand *shekels* of silver in my hand, I would not raise my hand against the king's son. For in our hearing the king commanded you and Abishai and Ittai, saying, 'Beware lest anyone *touch* the young man Absalom!'

Dan 2:6 However, if you tell the dream and its interpretation, you shall receive from me gifts, rewards, and great honor. Therefore tell me the dream and its interpretation."

Dan 2:48 Then the king promoted Daniel and gave him many great gifts; and he made him ruler over the whole province of Babylon, and chief administrator over all the wise *men* of Babylon.

To show respect.

Judg 6:18 Do not depart from here, I pray, until I come to You and bring out my offering and set *it* before You." And He said, "I will wait until you come back."

2 Kin 8:8 And the king said to Hazael, "Take a present in your hand, and go to meet the man of God, and inquire of the LORD by him, saying, 'Shall I recover from this disease?' "

In token of friendship.

Gen 33:10–11 And Jacob said, "No, please, if I have now found favor in your sight, then receive my present from my hand, inasmuch as I have seen your face as though I had seen the face of God, and you were pleased with me. **11** Please, take my blessing that is brought to you, because God has dealt graciously with me, and because I have enough." So he urged him, and he took *it.*

1 Sam 18:3–4 Then Jonathan and David made a covenant, because he loved him as his own soul. **4** And

Jonathan took off the robe that *was* on him and gave it to David, with his armor, even to his sword and his bow and his belt.

Prov 18:16 A man's gift makes room for him, And brings him before great men.

Prov 19:6 Many entreat the favor of the nobility, And every man *is* a friend to one who gives gifts.

As tribute.

Judg 3:15 But when the children of Israel cried out to the LORD, the LORD raised up a deliverer for them: Ehud the son of Gera, the Benjamite, a left-handed man. By him the children of Israel sent tribute to Eglon king of Moab.

2 Sam 8:2 Then he defeated Moab. Forcing them down to the ground, he measured them off with a line. With two lines he measured off those to be put to death, and with one full line those to be kept alive. So the Moabites became David's servants, *and* brought tribute.

2 Chr 17:5 Therefore the LORD established the kingdom in his hand; and all Judah gave presents to Jehoshaphat, and he had riches and honor in abundance.

On all occasions of public rejoicing.

Neh 8:12 And all the people went their way to eat and drink, to send portions and rejoice greatly, because they understood the words that were declared to them.

Esth 9:19 Therefore the Jews of the villages who dwelt in the unwalled towns celebrated the fourteenth day of the month of Adar *with* gladness and feasting, as a holiday, and for sending presents to one another.

At marriages.

Gen 24:53 Then the servant brought out jewelry of silver, jewelry of gold, and clothing, and gave *them* to Rebekah. He also gave precious things to her brother and to her mother.

Ps 45:12 And the daughter of Tyre *will come* with a gift; The rich among the people will seek your favor.

On recovering from sickness.

2 Kin 20:12 At that time Berodach-Baladan the son of Baladan, king of Babylon, sent letters and a present to Hezekiah, for he heard that Hezekiah had been sick.

On restoration to prosperity.

Job 42:10–11 And the LORD restored Job's losses when he prayed for his friends. Indeed the LORD gave Job twice as much as he had before. **11** Then all his brothers, all his sisters, and all those who had been his acquaintances before, came to him and ate food with him in his house; and they consoled him and comforted him for all the adversity that the LORD had brought upon him. Each one gave him a piece of silver and each a ring of gold.

On sending away friends.

Gen 45:22 He gave to all of them, to each man, changes of garments; but to Benjamin he gave three hundred *pieces* of silver and five changes of garments.

Jer 40:5 Now while Jeremiah had not yet gone back, *Nebuzaradan said,* "Go back to Gedaliah the son of Ahikam, the son of Shaphan, whom the king of Babylon has made governor over the cities of Judah, and dwell with him among the people. Or go wherever it

seems convenient for you to go." So the captain of the guard gave him rations and a gift and let him go.

Considered essential on all visits of business.

1 Sam 9:7 Then Saul said to his servant, "But look, *if* we go, what shall we bring the man? For the bread in our vessels is all gone, and *there is* no present to bring to the man of God. What do we have?"

When small or defective, refused.

Mal 1:8 And when you offer the blind as a sacrifice, *Is it* not evil? And when you offer the lame and sick, *Is it* not evil? Offer it then to your governor! Would he be pleased with you? Would he accept you favorably?" Says the LORD of hosts.

Of persons of rank, of great value and variety.

2 Kin 5:2 And the Syrians had gone out on raids, and had brought back captive a young girl from the land of Israel. She waited on Naaman's wife.

2 Chr 9:1 Now when the queen of Sheba heard of the fame of Solomon, she came to Jerusalem to test Solomon with hard questions, *having* a very great retinue, camels that bore spices, gold in abundance, and precious stones; and when she came to Solomon, she spoke with him about all that was in her heart.

Things given as,

Cattle.

Gen 32:14–15 two hundred female goats and twenty male goats, two hundred ewes and twenty rams, **15** thirty milk camels with their colts, forty cows and ten bulls, twenty female donkeys and ten foals.

Gen 32:18 then you shall say, 'They *are* your servant Jacob's. It *is* a present sent to my lord Esau; and behold, he also *is* behind us.' "

Horses and mules.

1 Kin 10:25 Each man brought his present: articles of silver and gold, garments, armor, spices, horses, and mules, at a set rate year by year.

Money.

Gen 45:22 He gave to all of them, to each man, changes of garments; but to Benjamin he gave three hundred *pieces* of silver and five changes of garments.

1 Sam 9:8 And the servant answered Saul again and said, "Look, I have here at hand one-fourth of a shekel of silver. I will give *that* to the man of God, to tell us our way."

Job 42:11 Then all his brothers, all his sisters, and all those who had been his acquaintances before, came to him and ate food with him in his house; and they consoled him and comforted him for all the adversity that the LORD had brought upon him. Each one gave him a piece of silver and each a ring of gold.

Food.

Gen 43:11 And their father Israel said to them, "If *it must be* so, then do this: Take some of the best fruits of the land in your vessels and carry down a present for the man—a little balm and a little honey, spices and myrrh, pistachio nuts and almonds.

1 Sam 25:18 Then Abigail made haste and took two hundred *loaves* of bread, two skins of wine, five sheep already dressed, five seahs of roasted *grain,* one hundred clusters of raisins, and two hundred cakes of figs, and loaded *them* on donkeys.

1 Kin 14:3 Also take with you ten loaves, *some* cakes, and a jar of honey, and go to him; he will tell you what will become of the child."

Garments.

Gen 45:22 He gave to all of them, to each man, changes of garments; but to Benjamin he gave three hundred *pieces* of silver and five changes of garments.

1 Sam 18:4 And Jonathan took off the robe that *was* on him and gave it to David, with his armor, even to his sword and his bow and his belt.

Weapons of war.

1 Sam 18:4 And Jonathan took off the robe that *was* on him and gave it to David, with his armor, even to his sword and his bow and his belt.

Ornaments.

Gen 24:22 So it was, when the camels had finished drinking, that the man took a golden nose ring weighing half a shekel, and two bracelets for her wrists weighing ten *shekels* of gold,

Gen 24:47 Then I asked her, and said, 'Whose daughter *are* you?' And she said, 'The daughter of Bethuel, Nahor's son, whom Milcah bore to him.' So I put the nose ring on her nose and the bracelets on her wrists.

Job 42:11 Then all his brothers, all his sisters, and all those who had been his acquaintances before, came to him and ate food with him in his house; and they consoled him and comforted him for all the adversity that the LORD had brought upon him. Each one gave him a piece of silver and each a ring of gold.

Gold and silver vessels.

1 Kin 10:25 Each man brought his present: articles of silver and gold, garments, armor, spices, horses, and mules, at a set rate year by year.

Precious stones.

1 Kin 10:2 She came to Jerusalem with a very great retinue, with camels that bore spices, very much gold, and precious stones; and when she came to Solomon, she spoke with him about all that was in her heart.

Servants.

Gen 20:14 Then Abimelech took sheep, oxen, and male and female servants, and gave *them* to Abraham; and he restored Sarah his wife to him.

Gen 29:24 And Laban gave his maid Zilpah to his daughter Leah *as* a maid.

Gen 29:29 And Laban gave his maid Bilhah to his daughter Rachel as a maid.

Often borne by servants.

Judg 3:18 And when he had finished presenting the tribute, he sent away the people who had carried the tribute.

Often conveyed on camels or donkeys.

1 Sam 25:18 Then Abigail made haste and took two hundred *loaves* of bread, two skins of wine, five sheep already dressed, five seahs of roasted *grain*, one hundred clusters of raisins, and two hundred cakes of figs, and loaded *them* on donkeys.

2 Kin 8:9 So Hazael went to meet him and took a present with him, of every good thing of Damascus, forty camel-loads; and he came and stood before him, and said, "Your son Ben-Hadad king of Syria

has sent me to you, saying, 'Shall I recover from this disease?' "

2 Chr 9:1 Now when the queen of Sheba heard of the fame of Solomon, she came to Jerusalem to test Solomon with hard questions, *having* a very great retinue, camels that bore spices, gold in abundance, and precious stones; and when she came to Solomon, she spoke with him about all that was in her heart.

Sometimes sent ahead of the giver.

Gen 32:21 So the present went on over before him, but he himself lodged that night in the camp.

Generally presented in person.

Gen 43:15 So the men took that present and Benjamin, and they took double money in their hand, and arose and went down to Egypt; and they stood before Joseph.

Gen 43:26 And when Joseph came home, they brought him the present which *was* in their hand into the house, and bowed down before him to the earth.

Judg 3:17 So he brought the tribute to Eglon king of Moab. (Now Eglon *was* a very fat man.)

1 Sam 25:27 And now this present which your maidservant has brought to my lord, let it be given to the young men who follow my lord.

Sometimes presented with great ceremony.

Gen 43:25 Then they made the present ready for Joseph's coming at noon, for they heard that they would eat bread there.

Judg 3:18 And when he had finished presenting the tribute, he sent away the people who had carried the tribute.

Matt 2:11 And when they had come into the house, they saw the young Child with Mary His mother, and fell down and worshiped Him. And when they had opened their treasures, they presented gifts to Him: gold, frankincense, and myrrh.

PRESUMPTION

A characteristic of the wicked.

2 Pet 2:10 and especially those who walk according to the flesh in the lust of uncleanness and despise authority. *They are* presumptuous, self-willed. They are not afraid to speak evil of dignitaries,

A characteristic of Antichrist.

2 Thess 2:4 who opposes and exalts himself above all that is called God or that is worshiped, so that he sits as God in the temple of God, showing himself that he is God.

Exhibited in

Opposing God.

Job 15:25–26 For he stretches out his hand against God, And acts defiantly against the Almighty, **26** Running stubbornly against Him With his strong, embossed shield.

Willful commission of sin.

Rom 1:32 who, knowing the righteous judgment of God, that those who practice such things are deserving of death, not only do the same but also approve of those who practice them.

Self-righteousness.

Hos 12:8 And Ephraim said, 'Surely I have become rich,

I have found wealth for myself; *In* all my labors They shall find in me no iniquity that *is* sin.'

Rev 3:17 Because you say, 'I am rich, have become wealthy, and have need of nothing'—and do not know that you are wretched, miserable, poor, blind, and naked—

Spiritual pride.

Is 65:5 Who say, 'Keep to yourself, Do not come near me, For I am holier than you!' These *are* smoke in My nostrils, A fire that burns all the day.

Luke 18:11 The Pharisee stood and prayed thus with himself, 'God, I thank You that I am not like other men—extortioners, unjust, adulterers, or even as this tax collector.

Esteeming our own ways right.

Prov 12:15 The way of a fool *is* right in his own eyes, But he who heeds counsel *is* wise.

Seeking preeminence.

Luke 14:7–11 So He told a parable to those who were invited, when He noted how they chose the best places, saying to them: 8 "When you are invited by anyone to a wedding feast, do not sit down in the best place, lest one more honorable than you be invited by him; 9 and he who invited you and him come and say to you, 'Give place to this man,' and then you begin with shame to take the lowest place. 10 But when you are invited, go and sit down in the lowest place, so that when he who invited you comes he may say to you, 'Friend, go up higher.' Then you will have glory in the presence of those who sit at the table with you. 11 For whoever exalts himself will be humbled, and he who humbles himself will be exalted."

Planning for the future.

Luke 12:18 So he said, 'I will do this: I will pull down my barns and build greater, and there I will store all my crops and my goods.

James 4:13 Come now, you who say, "Today or tomorrow we will go to such and such a city, spend a year there, buy and sell, and make a profit";

Pretending to prophesy.

Deut 18:22 when a prophet speaks in the name of the LORD, if the thing does not happen or come to pass, that *is* the thing which the LORD has not spoken; the prophet has spoken it presumptuously; you shall not be afraid of him.

Believers should avoid.

Ps 19:13 Keep back Your servant also from presumptuous *sins;* Let them not have dominion over me. Then I shall be blameless, And I shall be innocent of great transgression.

Ps 131:1 LORD, my heart is not haughty, Nor my eyes lofty. Neither do I concern myself with great matters, Nor with things too profound for me.

Punishment for.

Num 15:30 'But the person who does *anything* presumptuously, *whether he is* native-born or a stranger, that one brings reproach on the LORD, and he shall be cut off from among his people.

Rev 18:7–8 In the measure that she glorified herself and lived luxuriously, in the same measure give her torment and sorrow; for she says in her heart, 'I sit *as* queen, and am no widow, and will not see sorrow.'

8 Therefore her plagues will come in one day—death and mourning and famine. And she will be utterly burned with fire, for strong *is* the Lord God who judges her.

Illustrated by

The builders of Babel.

Gen 11:4 And they said, "Come, let us build ourselves a city, and a tower whose top *is* in the heavens; let us make a name for ourselves, lest we be scattered abroad over the face of the whole earth."

The Israelites.

Num 14:44 But they presumed to go up to the mountaintop. Nevertheless, neither the ark of the covenant of the LORD nor Moses departed from the camp.

Korah, etc.

Num 16:3 They gathered together against Moses and Aaron, and said to them, "*You take* too much upon yourselves, for all the congregation *is* holy, every one of them, and the LORD *is* among them. Why then do you exalt yourselves above the assembly of the LORD?"

Num 16:7 put fire in them and put incense in them before the LORD tomorrow, and it shall be *that* the man whom the LORD chooses *is* the holy one. *You take* too much upon yourselves, you sons of Levi!"

The men of Beth Shemesh.

1 Sam 6:19 Then He struck the men of Beth Shemesh, because they had looked into the ark of the LORD. He struck fifty thousand and seventy men of the people, and the people lamented because the LORD had struck the people with a great slaughter.

Uzzah.

2 Sam 6:6 And when they came to Nachon's threshing floor, Uzzah put out *his* hand to the ark of God and took hold of it, for the oxen stumbled.

Jeroboam.

1 Kin 13:4 So it came to pass when King Jeroboam heard the saying of the man of God, who cried out against the altar in Bethel, that he stretched out his hand from the altar, saying, "Arrest him!" Then his hand, which he stretched out toward him, withered, so that he could not pull it back to himself.

Ben-Hadad.

1 Kin 20:19 Then these young leaders of the provinces went out of the city with the army which followed them.

Uzziah.

2 Chr 26:16 But when he was strong his heart was lifted up, to *his* destruction, for he transgressed against the LORD his God by entering the temple of the LORD to burn incense on the altar of incense.

Sennacherib.

2 Chr 32:13–14 Do you not know what I and my fathers have done to all the peoples of *other* lands? Were the gods of the nations of those lands in any way able to deliver their lands out of my hand? 14 Who *was there* among all the gods of those nations that my fathers utterly destroyed that could deliver his people from my hand, that your God should be able to deliver you from my hand?

Theudas.

Acts 5:36 For some time ago Theudas rose up, claiming to be somebody. A number of men, about four hundred, joined him. He was slain, and all who obeyed him were scattered and came to nothing.

Sons of Sceva.

Acts 19:13–14 Then some of the itinerant Jewish exorcists took it upon themselves to call the name of the Lord Jesus over those who had evil spirits, saying, "We exorcise you by the Jesus whom Paul preaches." **14** Also there were seven sons of Sceva, a Jewish chief priest, who did so.

Diotrephes.

3 John 1:9 I wrote to the church, but Diotrephes, who loves to have the preeminence among them, does not receive us.

PRIDE

Is sin.

Prov 21:4 A haughty look, a proud heart, *And* the plowing of the wicked *are* sin.

Hateful to God.

Prov 6:16–17 These six *things* the LORD hates, Yes, seven *are* an abomination to Him: **17** A proud look, A lying tongue, Hands that shed innocent blood,

Prov 16:5 Everyone proud in heart *is* an abomination to the LORD; *Though they join* forces, none will go unpunished.

Hateful to Christ.

Prov 8:12–13 "I, wisdom, dwell with prudence, And find out knowledge *and* discretion. **13** The fear of the LORD *is* to hate evil; Pride and arrogance and the evil way And the perverse mouth I hate.

Often originates in

Self-righteousness.

Luke 18:11–12 The Pharisee stood and prayed thus with himself, 'God, I thank You that I am not like other men—extortioners, unjust, adulterers, or even as this tax collector. **12** I fast twice a week; I give tithes of all that I possess.'

Religious privileges.

Zeph 3:11 In that day you shall not be shamed for any of your deeds In which you transgress against Me; For then I will take away from your midst Those who rejoice in your pride, And you shall no longer be haughty In My holy mountain.

Unsanctified knowledge.

1 Cor 8:1 Now concerning things offered to idols: We know that we all have knowledge. Knowledge puffs up, but love edifies.

Inexperience.

1 Tim 3:6 not a novice, lest being puffed up with pride he fall into the *same* condemnation as the devil.

Possession of power.

Lev 26:19 I will break the pride of your power; I will make your heavens like iron and your earth like bronze.

Ezek 30:6 'Thus says the LORD: "Those who uphold Egypt shall fall, And the pride of her power shall come down. From Migdol *to* Syene Those within her shall fall by the sword," Says the Lord GOD.

Possession of wealth.

2 Kin 20:13 And Hezekiah was attentive to them, and showed them all the house of his treasures—the silver and gold, the spices and precious ointment, and all his armory—all that was found among his treasures. There was nothing in his house or in all his dominion that Hezekiah did not show them.

Forbidden.

1 Sam 2:3 "Talk no more so very proudly; Let no arrogance come from your mouth, For the LORD *is* the God of knowledge; And by Him actions are weighed.

Rom 12:3 For I say, through the grace given to me, to everyone who is among you, not to think *of himself* more highly than he ought to think, but to think soberly, as God has dealt to each one a measure of faith.

Rom 12:16 Be of the same mind toward one another. Do not set your mind on high things, but associate with the humble. Do not be wise in your own opinion.

Defiles a man.

Mark 7:20 And He said, "What comes out of a man, that defiles a man.

Mark 7:22 thefts, covetousness, wickedness, deceit, lewdness, an evil eye, blasphemy, pride, foolishness.

Hardens the mind.

Dan 5:20 But when his heart was lifted up, and his spirit was hardened in pride, he was deposed from his kingly throne, and they took his glory from him.

Believers have aversion to.

Ps 40:4 Blessed *is* that man who makes the LORD his trust, And does not respect the proud, nor such as turn aside to lies.

Ps 101:5 Whoever secretly slanders his neighbor, Him I will destroy; The one who has a haughty look and a proud heart, Him I will not endure.

Ps 131:1 LORD, my heart is not haughty, Nor my eyes lofty. Neither do I concern myself with great matters, Nor with things too profound for me.

Jer 13:17 But if you will not hear it, My soul will weep in secret for *your* pride; My eyes will weep bitterly And run down with tears, Because the LORD's flock has been taken captive.

A hindrance to knowing God.

Ps 10:4 The wicked in his proud countenance does not seek *God;* God *is* in none of his thoughts.

Prov 26:12 Do you see a man wise in his own eyes? *There is* more hope for a fool than for him.

Hos 7:10 And the pride of Israel testifies to his face, But they do not return to the LORD their God, Nor seek Him for all this.

A characteristic of

The devil.

1 Tim 3:6 not a novice, lest being puffed up with pride he fall into the *same* condemnation as the devil.

The world.

1 John 2:16 For all that *is* in the world—the lust of the flesh, the lust of the eyes, and the pride of life—is not of the Father but is of the world.

False teachers.

1 Tim 6:3–4 If anyone teaches otherwise and does not consent to wholesome words, *even* the words of our Lord Jesus Christ, and to the doctrine which accords with godliness, **4** he is proud, knowing nothing, but is obsessed with disputes and arguments over words, from which come envy, strife, reviling, evil suspicions,

The wicked.

Ps 73:6 Therefore pride serves as their necklace; Violence covers them *like* a garment.

Hab 2:4–5 "Behold the proud, His soul is not upright in him; But the just shall live by his faith. **5** "Indeed, because he transgresses by wine, *He is* a proud man, And he does not stay at home. Because he enlarges his desire as hell, And he *is* like death, and cannot be satisfied, He gathers to himself all nations And heaps up for himself all peoples.

Rom 1:30 backbiters, haters of God, violent, proud, boasters, inventors of evil things, disobedient to parents,

Comes from the heart.

Mark 7:21–23 For from within, out of the heart of men, proceed evil thoughts, adulteries, fornications, murders, **22** thefts, covetousness, wickedness, deceit, lewdness, an evil eye, blasphemy, pride, foolishness. **23** All these evil things come from within and defile a man."

Leads people to

Contempt and rejection of God's Word and ministers.

Jer 43:2 that Azariah the son of Hoshaiah, Johanan the son of Kareah, and all the proud men spoke, saying to Jeremiah, "You speak falsely! The LORD our God has not sent you to say, 'Do not go to Egypt to dwell there.'

A persecuting spirit.

Ps 10:2 The wicked in *his* pride persecutes the poor; Let them be caught in the plots which they have devised.

Wrath.

Prov 21:24 A proud *and* haughty *man*—"Scoffer" *is* his name; He acts with arrogant pride.

Contention.

Prov 13:10 By pride comes nothing but strife, But with the well-advised *is* wisdom.

Prov 28:25 He who is of a proud heart stirs up strife, But he who trusts in the LORD will be prospered.

Self-deception.

Jer 49:16 Your fierceness has deceived you, The pride of your heart, O you who dwell in the clefts of the rock, Who hold the height of the hill! Though you make your nest as high as the eagle, I will bring you down from there," says the LORD.

Obad 1:3 The pride of your heart has deceived you, *You* who dwell in the clefts of the rock, Whose habitation is high; *You* who say in your heart, 'Who will bring me down to the ground?'

Exhortation and warning against.

Is 28:1 Woe to the crown of pride, to the drunkards of Ephraim, Whose glorious beauty *is* a fading flower Which *is* at the head of the verdant valleys, To those who are overcome with wine!

Is 28:3 The crown of pride, the drunkards of Ephraim, Will be trampled underfoot;

Jer 13:15 Hear and give ear: Do not be proud, For the LORD has spoken.

Is followed by

Shame.

Prov 11:2 When pride comes, then comes shame; But with the humble *is* wisdom.

Debasement.

Prov 29:23 A man's pride will bring him low, But the humble in spirit will retain honor.

Is 28:3 The crown of pride, the drunkards of Ephraim, Will be trampled underfoot;

Destruction.

Prov 16:18 Pride *goes* before destruction, And a haughty spirit before a fall.

Prov 18:12 Before destruction the heart of a man is haughty, And before honor *is* humility.

Shall abound in the last days.

2 Tim 3:2 For men will be lovers of themselves, lovers of money, boasters, proud, blasphemers, disobedient to parents, unthankful, unholy,

They who are guilty of, shall be

Resisted.

James 4:6 But He gives more grace. Therefore He says: *"God resists the proud, But gives grace to the humble."*

Brought into contempt.

Is 23:9 The LORD of hosts has purposed it, To bring to dishonor the pride of all glory, To bring into contempt all the honorable of the earth.

Recompensed.

Ps 31:23 Oh, love the LORD, all you His saints! *For* the LORD preserves the faithful, And fully repays the proud person.

Ruined.

Jer 13:9 "Thus says the LORD: 'In this manner I will ruin the pride of Judah and the great pride of Jerusalem.

Subdued.

Ex 18:11 Now I know that the LORD *is* greater than all the gods; for in the very thing in which they behaved proudly, *He was* above them."

Is 13:11 "I will punish the world for *its* evil, And the wicked for their iniquity; I will halt the arrogance of the proud, And will lay low the haughtiness of the terrible.

Abased.

Ps 18:27 For You will save the humble people, But will bring down haughty looks.

Is 2:12 For the day of the LORD of hosts *Shall come* upon everything proud and lofty, Upon everything lifted up— And it shall be brought low—

Dan 4:37 Now I, Nebuchadnezzar, praise and extol and honor the King of heaven, all of whose works *are* truth, and His ways justice. And those who walk in pride He is able to put down.

Matt 23:12 And whoever exalts himself will be humbled, and he who humbles himself will be exalted.

Scattered.

Luke 1:51 He has shown strength with His arm; He has scattered *the* proud in the imagination of their hearts.

Punished.

Zeph 2:10–11 This they shall have for their pride, Because they have reproached and made arrogant threats Against the people of the LORD of hosts. **11** The LORD *will be* awesome to them, For He will reduce to nothing all the gods of the earth; *People* shall worship Him, Each one from his place, Indeed all the shores of the nations.

Mal 4:1 "For behold, the day is coming, Burning like an oven, And all the proud, yes, all who do wickedly will be stubble. And the day which is coming shall burn them up," Says the LORD of hosts, "That will leave them neither root nor branch.

Illustrated by

Ahithophel.

2 Sam 17:23 Now when Ahithophel saw that his advice was not followed, he saddled a donkey, and arose and went home to his house, to his city. Then he put his household in order, and hanged himself, and died; and he was buried in his father's tomb.

Hezekiah.

2 Chr 32:25 But Hezekiah did not repay according to the favor *shown* him, for his heart was lifted up; therefore wrath was looming over him and over Judah and Jerusalem.

Pharaoh.

Neh 9:10 You showed signs and wonders against Pharaoh, Against all his servants, And against all the people of his land. For You knew that they acted proudly against them. So You made a name for Yourself, as *it is* this day.

Haman.

Esth 3:5 When Haman saw that Mordecai did not bow or pay him homage, Haman was filled with wrath.

Moab.

Is 16:6 We have heard of the pride of Moab— *He is* very proud— Of his haughtiness and his pride and his wrath; *But* his lies *shall* not *be* so.

Tyre.

Is 23:9 The LORD of hosts has purposed it, To bring to dishonor the pride of all glory, To bring into contempt all the honorable of the earth.

Israel.

Is 28:1 Woe to the crown of pride, to the drunkards of Ephraim, Whose glorious beauty *is* a fading flower Which *is* at the head of the verdant valleys, To those who are overcome with wine!

Hos 5:5 The pride of Israel testifies to his face; Therefore Israel and Ephraim stumble in their iniquity; Judah also stumbles with them.

Hos 5:9 Ephraim shall be desolate in the day of rebuke; Among the tribes of Israel I make known what is sure.

Judah.

Jer 13:9 "Thus says the LORD: 'In this manner I will ruin the pride of Judah and the great pride of Jerusalem.

Babylon.

Jer 50:29 "Call together the archers against Babylon. All you who bend the bow, encamp against it all around; Let none of them escape. Repay her according to her work; According to all she has done, do to her; For she has been proud against the LORD, Against the Holy One of Israel.

Jer 50:32 The most proud shall stumble and fall, And no one will raise him up; I will kindle a fire in his cities, And it will devour all around him."

Assyria.

Ezek 31:3 Indeed Assyria *was* a cedar in Lebanon, With fine branches that shaded the forest, And of high stature; And its top was among the thick boughs.

Ezek 31:10 "Therefore thus says the Lord GOD: 'Because you have increased in height, and it set its top among the thick boughs, and its heart was lifted up in its height,

Nebuchadnezzar.

Dan 4:30 The king spoke, saying, "Is not this great Babylon, that I have built for a royal dwelling by my mighty power and for the honor of my majesty?"

Dan 5:20 But when his heart was lifted up, and his spirit was hardened in pride, he was deposed from his kingly throne, and they took his glory from him.

Belshazzar.

Dan 5:22–23 "But you his son, Belshazzar, have not humbled your heart, although you knew all this. **23** And you have lifted yourself up against the Lord of heaven. They have brought the vessels of His house before you, and you and your lords, your wives and your concubines, have drunk wine from them. And you have praised the gods of silver and gold, bronze and iron, wood and stone, which do not see or hear or know; and the God who *holds* your breath in His hand and owns all your ways, you have not glorified.

Edom.

Obad 1:3 The pride of your heart has deceived you, *You* who dwell in the clefts of the rock, Whose habitation is high; *You* who say in your heart, 'Who will bring me down to the ground?'

The scribes.

Mark 12:38–39 Then He said to them in His teaching, "Beware of the scribes, who desire to go around in long robes, *love* greetings in the marketplaces, **39** the best seats in the synagogues, and the best places at feasts,

Herod.

Acts 12:21–23 So on a set day Herod, arrayed in royal apparel, sat on his throne and gave an oration to them. **22** And the people kept shouting, "The voice of a god and not of a man!" **23** Then immediately an angel of the Lord struck him, because he did not give glory to God. And he was eaten by worms and died.

The Laodiceans.

Rev 3:17 Because you say, 'I am rich, have become wealthy, and have need of nothing'—and do not know that you are wretched, miserable, poor, blind, and naked—

PRIESTS

First persons acting as.

Gen 4:3–4 And in the process of time it came to pass that Cain brought an offering of the fruit of the ground to the LORD. 4 Abel also brought of the firstborn of his flock and of their fat. And the LORD respected Abel and his offering,

Heads of patriarchal families acted as.

Gen 8:20 Then Noah built an altar to the LORD, and took of every clean animal and of every clean bird, and offered burnt offerings on the altar.

Gen 12:8 And he moved from there to the mountain east of Bethel, and he pitched his tent *with* Bethel on the west and Ai on the east; there he built an altar to the LORD and called on the name of the LORD.

Gen 35:7 And he built an altar there and called the place El Bethel, because there God appeared to him when he fled from the face of his brother.

After the exodus, young men (firstborn) appointed to act as.

Ex 19:22 Also let the priests who come near the LORD consecrate themselves, lest the LORD break out against them."

Ex 24:5 Then he sent young men of the children of Israel, who offered burnt offerings and sacrificed peace offerings of oxen to the LORD.

The sons of Aaron appointed as, by perpetual statute.

Ex 29:9 And you shall gird them with sashes, Aaron and his sons, and put the hats on them. The priesthood shall be theirs for a perpetual statute. So you shall consecrate Aaron and his sons.

Ex 40:15 You shall anoint them, as you anointed their father, that they may minister to Me as priests; for their anointing shall surely be an everlasting priesthood throughout their generations."

Num 3:10 So you shall appoint Aaron and his sons, and they shall attend to their priesthood; but the outsider who comes near shall be put to death."

Num 16:40 *to be* a memorial to the children of Israel that no outsider, who *is* not a descendant of Aaron, should come near to offer incense before the LORD, that he might not become like Korah and his companions, just as the LORD had said to him through Moses.

Num 18:7 Therefore you and your sons with you shall attend to your priesthood for everything at the altar and behind the veil; and you shall serve. I give your priesthood *to you* as a gift for service, but the outsider who comes near shall be put to death."

Consecrated by God for the office.

Ex 28:3 So you shall speak to all *who are* gifted artisans, whom I have filled with the spirit of wisdom, that they may make Aaron's garments, to consecrate him, that he may minister to Me as priest.

Ex 29:44 So I will consecrate the tabernacle of meeting and the altar. I will also consecrate both Aaron and his sons to minister to Me as priests.

Num 3:3 These *are* the names of the sons of Aaron, the anointed priests, whom he consecrated to minister as priests.

Ceremonies at the consecration of,

Washing in water.

Ex 29:4 "And Aaron and his sons you shall bring to the door of the tabernacle of meeting, and you shall wash them with water.

Lev 8:6 Then Moses brought Aaron and his sons and washed them with water.

Clothing with the holy garments.

Ex 29:8–9 Then you shall bring his sons and put tunics on them. 9 And you shall gird them with sashes, Aaron and his sons, and put the hats on them. The priesthood shall be theirs for a perpetual statute. So you shall consecrate Aaron and his sons.

Ex 40:14 And you shall bring his sons and clothe them with tunics.

Lev 8:13 Then Moses brought Aaron's sons and put tunics on them, girded them with sashes, and put hats on them, as the LORD had commanded Moses.

Anointing with oil.

Ex 30:30 And you shall anoint Aaron and his sons, and consecrate them, that *they* may minister to Me as priests.

Ex 40:13 You shall put the holy garments on Aaron, and anoint him and consecrate him, that he may minister to Me as priest.

Offering sacrifices.

Ex 29:10–19 "You shall also have the bull brought before the tabernacle of meeting, and Aaron and his sons shall put their hands on the head of the bull. 11 Then you shall kill the bull before the LORD, *by* the door of the tabernacle of meeting. 12 You shall take *some* of the blood of the bull and put *it* on the horns of the altar with your finger, and pour all the blood beside the base of the altar. 13 And you shall take all the fat that covers the entrails, the fatty lobe *attached* to the liver, and the two kidneys and the fat that *is* on them, and burn *them* on the altar. 14 But the flesh of the bull, with its skin and its offal, you shall burn with fire outside the camp. It *is* a sin offering. 15 "You shall also take one ram, and Aaron and his sons shall put their hands on the head of the ram; 16 and you shall kill the ram, and you shall take its blood and sprinkle *it* all around on the altar. 17 Then you shall cut the ram in pieces, wash its entrails and its legs, and put *them* with its pieces and with its head. 18 And you shall burn the whole ram on the altar. It *is* a burnt offering to the LORD; it *is* a sweet aroma, an offering made by fire to the LORD. 19 "You shall also take the other ram, and Aaron and his sons shall put their hands on the head of the ram.

Cf. Lev 8:14–23

Purification by blood of a ram.

Ex 29:20–21 Then you shall kill the ram, and take some of its blood and put *it* on the tip of the right ear of Aaron and on the tip of the right ear of his sons, on the thumb of their right hand and on the big toe of their right foot, and sprinkle the blood all around on the altar. 21 And you shall take some of the blood that is on the altar, and some of the anointing oil, and sprinkle *it* on Aaron and on his garments, on his sons and on the garments of his sons with him; and he and his garments shall be hallowed, and his sons and his sons' garments with him.

Lev 8:23–24 and Moses killed *it*. Also he took *some* of its blood and put it on the tip of Aaron's right ear, on the thumb of his right hand, and on the big toe of his right foot. 24 Then he brought Aaron's sons. And Moses put *some* of the blood on the tips of their right ears, on the thumbs of their right hands, and on the big toes of their right feet. And Moses sprinkled the blood all around on the altar.

Placing in their hands the wave offering.

Ex 29:22–24 "Also you shall take the fat of the ram, the fat tail, the fat that covers the entrails, the fatty lobe *attached to* the liver, the two kidneys and the fat on them, the right thigh (for it *is* a ram of consecration), 23 one loaf of bread, one cake *made with* oil, and one wafer from the basket of the unleavened bread that *is* before the LORD; 24 and you shall put all these in the hands of Aaron and in the hands of his sons, and you shall wave them *as* a wave offering before the LORD.

Lev 8:25–27 Then he took the fat and the fat tail, all the fat that *was* on the entrails, the fatty lobe *attached to* the liver, the two kidneys and their fat, and the right thigh; 26 and from the basket of unleavened bread that was before the LORD he took one unleavened cake, a cake of bread *anointed with* oil, and one wafer, and put *them* on the fat and on the right thigh; 27 and he put all *these* in Aaron's hands and in his sons' hands, and waved them *as* a wave offering before the LORD.

Partaking of the sacrifices of consecration.

Ex 29:31–33 "And you shall take the ram of the consecration and boil its flesh in the holy place. 32 Then Aaron and his sons shall eat the flesh of the ram, and the bread that *is* in the basket, *by* the door of the tabernacle of meeting. 33 They shall eat those things with which the atonement was made, to consecrate *and* to sanctify them; but an outsider shall not eat *them,* because they *are* holy.

Lev 8:31–32 And Moses said to Aaron and his sons, "Boil the flesh *at* the door of the tabernacle of meeting, and eat it there with the bread that *is* in the basket of consecration offerings, as I commanded, saying, 'Aaron and his sons shall eat it.' 32 What remains of the flesh and of the bread you shall burn with fire.

Lasted seven days.

Ex 29:35–37 "Thus you shall do to Aaron and his sons, according to all that I have commanded you. Seven days you shall consecrate them. 36 And you shall offer a bull every day *as* a sin offering for atonement. You shall cleanse the altar when you make atonement for it, and you shall anoint it to sanctify it. 37 Seven days you shall make atonement for the altar and sanctify it. And the altar shall be most holy. Whatever touches the altar must be holy.

Lev 8:33 And you shall not go outside the door of the tabernacle of meeting *for* seven days, until the days of your consecration are ended. For seven days he shall consecrate you.

Required to remain in the tabernacle seven days after consecration.

Lev 8:33–36 And you shall not go outside the door of the tabernacle of meeting *for* seven days, until the days of your consecration are ended. For seven days he shall consecrate you. **34** As he has done this day, *so* the LORD has commanded to do, to make atonement for you. **35** Therefore you shall stay *at* the door of the tabernacle of meeting day and night for seven days, and keep the charge of the LORD, so that you may not die; for so I have been commanded." **36** So Aaron and his sons did all the things that the LORD had commanded by the hand of Moses.

No blemished or defective persons could be consecrated.

Lev 21:17–23 "Speak to Aaron, saying: 'No man of your descendants in *succeeding* generations, who has *any* defect, may approach to offer the bread of his God. **18** For any man who has a defect shall not approach: a man blind or lame, who has a marred *face* or any *limb* too long, **19** a man who has a broken foot or broken hand, **20** or is a hunchback or a dwarf, or *a man* who has a defect in his eye, or eczema or scab, or is a eunuch. **21** No man of the descendants of Aaron the priest, who has a defect, shall come near to offer the offerings made by fire to the LORD. He has a defect; he shall not come near to offer the bread of his God. **22** He may eat the bread of his God, *both* the most holy and the holy; **23** only he shall not go near the veil or approach the altar, because he has a defect, lest he profane My sanctuaries; for I the LORD sanctify them.' "

Required to prove their genealogy before they exercised the office.

Ezra 2:62 These sought their listing *among* those who were registered by genealogy, but they were not found; therefore they *were excluded* from the priesthood as defiled.

Neh 7:64 These sought their listing *among* those who were registered by genealogy, but it was not found; therefore they were excluded from the priesthood as defiled.

Garments of,

The tunic.

Ex 28:40 "For Aaron's sons you shall make tunics, and you shall make sashes for them. And you shall make hats for them, for glory and beauty.

Ex 39:27 They made tunics, artistically woven of fine linen, for Aaron and his sons,

The sash.

Ex 28:40 "For Aaron's sons you shall make tunics, and you shall make sashes for them. And you shall make hats for them, for glory and beauty.

The hat.

Ex 28:40 "For Aaron's sons you shall make tunics, and you shall make sashes for them. And you shall make hats for them, for glory and beauty.

Ex 39:28 a turban of fine linen, exquisite hats of fine linen, short trousers of fine woven linen,

The linen trousers.

Ex 28:42 And you shall make for them linen trousers to cover their nakedness; they shall reach from the waist to the thighs.

Ex 39:28 a turban of fine linen, exquisite hats of fine linen, short trousers of fine woven linen,

Worn at consecration.

Ex 29:9 And you shall gird them with sashes, Aaron and his sons, and put the hats on them. The priesthood shall be theirs for a perpetual statute. So you shall consecrate Aaron and his sons.

Ex 40:15 You shall anoint them, as you anointed their father, that they may minister to Me as priests; for their anointing shall surely be an everlasting priesthood throughout their generations."

Worn always during tabernacle service.

Ex 28:43 They shall be on Aaron and on his sons when they come into the tabernacle of meeting, or when they come near the altar to minister in the holy *place,* that they do not incur iniquity and die. *It shall be* a statute forever to him and his descendants after him.

Ex 39:41 and the garments of ministry, to minister in the holy *place:* the holy garments for Aaron the priest, and his sons' garments, to minister as priests.

Worn by the high priest on the day of atonement.

Lev 16:4 He shall put the holy linen tunic and the linen trousers on his body; he shall be girded with a linen sash, and with the linen turban he shall be attired. These *are* holy garments. Therefore he shall wash his body in water, and put them on.

Purified by sprinkling of blood.

Ex 29:21 And you shall take some of the blood that is on the altar, and some of the anointing oil, and sprinkle *it* on Aaron and on his garments, on his sons and on the garments of his sons with him; and he and his garments shall be hallowed, and his sons and his sons' garments with him.

Laid up in holy chambers.

Ezek 44:19 When they go out to the outer court, to the *outer* court to the people, they shall take off their garments in which they have ministered, leave them in the holy chambers, and put on other garments; and in their holy garments they shall not sanctify the people.

Required to wash in the bronze laver before they performed their services.

Ex 30:18–21 "You shall also make a laver of bronze, with its base also of bronze, for washing. You shall put it between the tabernacle of meeting and the altar. And you shall put water in it, **19** for Aaron and his sons shall wash their hands and their feet in water from it. **20** When they go into the tabernacle of meeting, or when they come near the altar to minister, to burn an offering made by fire to the LORD, they shall wash with water, lest they die. **21** So they shall wash their hands and their feet, lest they die. And it shall be a statute forever to them—to him and his descendants throughout their generations."

Services of,

In charge of the tabernacle.

Num 18:1 Then the LORD said to Aaron: "You and your sons and your father's house with you shall bear the iniquity *related to* the sanctuary, and you and your sons with you shall bear the iniquity *associated with* your priesthood.

Num 18:5 And you shall attend to the duties of the sanctuary and the duties of the altar, that there *may* be no more wrath on the children of Israel.

Num 18:7 Therefore you and your sons with you shall

attend to your priesthood for everything at the altar and behind the veil; and you shall serve. I give your priesthood *to you* as a gift for service, but the outsider who comes near shall be put to death."

Divided by lot.

Luke 1:9 according to the custom of the priesthood, his lot fell to burn incense when he went into the temple of the Lord.

Covering the sacred things of the sanctuary before removal.

Num 4:5–15 When the camp prepares to journey, Aaron and his sons shall come, and they shall take down the covering veil and cover the ark of the Testimony with it. **6** Then they shall put on it a covering of badger skins, and spread over *that* a cloth entirely of blue; and they shall insert its poles. **7** "On the table of showbread they shall spread a blue cloth, and put on it the dishes, the pans, the bowls, and the pitchers for pouring; and the showbread shall be on it. **8** They shall spread over them a scarlet cloth, and cover the same with a covering of badger skins; and they shall insert its poles. **9** And they shall take a blue cloth and cover the lampstand of the light, with its lamps, its wick-trimmers, its trays, and all its oil vessels, with which they service it. **10** Then they shall put it with all its utensils in a covering of badger skins, and put *it* on a carrying beam. **11** "Over the golden altar they shall spread a blue cloth, and cover it with a covering of badger skins; and they shall insert its poles. **12** Then they shall take all the utensils of service with which they minister in the sanctuary, put *them* in a blue cloth, cover them with a covering of badger skins, and put *them* on a carrying beam. **13** Also they shall take away the ashes from the altar, and spread a purple cloth over it. **14** They shall put on it all its implements with which they minister there—the firepans, the forks, the shovels, the basins, and all the utensils of the altar—and they shall spread on it a covering of badger skins, and insert its poles. **15** And when Aaron and his sons have finished covering the sanctuary and all the furnishings of the sanctuary, when the camp is set to go, then the sons of Kohath shall come to carry *them;* but they shall not touch any holy thing, lest they die. "These *are* the things in the tabernacle of meeting which the sons of Kohath are to carry.

Offering sacrifices.

2 Chr 29:34 But the priests were too few, so that they could not skin all the burnt offerings; therefore their brethren the Levites helped them until the work was ended and until the *other* priests had sanctified themselves, for the Levites were more diligent in sanctifying themselves than the priests.

2 Chr 35:11 And they slaughtered the Passover *offerings;* and the priests sprinkled *the blood* with their hands, while the Levites skinned *the animals.*

Cf. Lev 1:1—6:30

Lighting and trimming the lamps of the sanctuary.

Ex 27:20–21 "And you shall command the children of Israel that they bring you pure oil of pressed olives for the light, to cause the lamp to burn continually. **21** In the tabernacle of meeting, outside the veil which *is* before the Testimony, Aaron and his sons shall tend it from evening until morning before the

LORD. *It shall be* a statute forever to their generations on behalf of the children of Israel.

Lev 24:3–4 Outside the veil of the Testimony, in the tabernacle of meeting, Aaron shall be in charge of it from evening until morning before the LORD continually; *it shall be* a statute forever in your generations. **4** He shall be in charge of the lamps on the pure *gold* lampstand before the LORD continually.

Keeping the sacred fire always burning on the altar.

Lev 6:12–13 And the fire on the altar shall be kept burning on it; it shall not be put out. And the priest shall burn wood on it every morning, and lay the burnt offering in order on it; and he shall burn on it the fat of the peace offerings. **13** A fire shall always be burning on the altar; it shall never go out.

Burning incense.

Ex 30:7–8 Aaron shall burn on it sweet incense every morning; when he tends the lamps, he shall burn incense on it. **8** And when Aaron lights the lamps at twilight, he shall burn incense on it, a perpetual incense before the LORD throughout your generations.

Luke 1:9 according to the custom of the priesthood, his lot fell to burn incense when he went into the temple of the Lord.

Placing and removing showbread.

Lev 24:5–9 "And you shall take fine flour and bake twelve cakes with it. Two-tenths *of an ephah* shall be in each cake. **6** You shall set them in two rows, six in a row, on the pure *gold* table before the LORD. **7** And you shall put pure frankincense on *each* row, that it may be on the bread for a memorial, an offering made by fire to the LORD. **8** Every Sabbath he shall set it in order before the LORD continually, *being taken* from the children of Israel by an everlasting covenant. **9** And it shall be for Aaron and his sons, and they shall eat it in a holy place; for it *is* most holy to him from the offerings of the LORD made by fire, by a perpetual statute."

Offering firstfruits.

Lev 23:10–11 "Speak to the children of Israel, and say to them: 'When you come into the land which I give to you, and reap its harvest, then you shall bring a sheaf of the firstfruits of your harvest to the priest. **11** He shall wave the sheaf before the LORD, to be accepted on your behalf; on the day after the Sabbath the priest shall wave it.

Deut 26:3–4 And you shall go to the one who is priest in those days, and say to him, 'I declare today to the LORD your God that I have come to the country which the LORD swore to our fathers to give us.' **4** "Then the priest shall take the basket out of your hand and set it down before the altar of the LORD your God.

Blessing the people.

Num 6:23–27 "Speak to Aaron and his sons, saying, 'This is the way you shall bless the children of Israel. Say to them: **24** "The LORD bless you and keep you; **25** The LORD make His face shine upon you, And be gracious to you; **26** The LORD lift up His countenance upon you, And give you peace." ' **27** "So they shall put My name on the children of Israel, and I will bless them."

Purifying the unclean.

Lev 15:30–31 Then the priest shall offer the one *as* a sin offering and the other *as* a burnt offering, and the priest shall make atonement for her before the LORD for the discharge of her uncleanness. **31** Thus you shall separate the children of Israel from their uncleanness, lest they die in their uncleanness when they defile My tabernacle that *is* among them.

Deciding in cases of jealousy.

Num 5:14–15 if the spirit of jealousy comes upon him and he becomes jealous of his wife, who has defiled herself; or if the spirit of jealousy comes upon him and he becomes jealous of his wife, although she has not defiled herself— **15** then the man shall bring his wife to the priest. He shall bring the offering required for her, one-tenth of an ephah of barley meal; he shall pour no oil on it and put no frankincense on it, because it *is* a grain offering of jealousy, an offering for remembering, for bringing iniquity to remembrance.

Deciding in cases of leprosy. **Lev 13:2–59; 14:34–45**

Judging in cases of controversy.

Deut 17:8–13 "If a matter arises which is too hard for you to judge, between degrees of guilt for bloodshed, between one judgment or another, or between one punishment or another, matters of controversy within your gates, then you shall arise and go up to the place which the LORD your God chooses. **9** And you shall come to the priests, the Levites, and to the judge *there* in those days, and inquire *of them;* they shall pronounce upon you the sentence of judgment. **10** You shall do according to the sentence which they pronounce upon you in that place which the LORD chooses. And you shall be careful to do according to all that they order you. **11** According to the sentence of the law in which they instruct you, according to the judgment which they tell you, you shall do; you shall not turn aside *to* the right hand or *to* the left from the sentence which they pronounce upon you. **12** Now the man who acts presumptuously and will not heed the priest who stands to minister there before the LORD your God, or the judge, that man shall die. So you shall put away the evil from Israel. **13** And all the people shall hear and fear, and no longer act presumptuously.

Deut 21:5 Then the priests, the sons of Levi, shall come near, for the LORD your God has chosen them to minister to Him and to bless in the name of the LORD; by their word every controversy and every assault shall be *settled.*

Teaching the law.

Deut 33:8 And of Levi he said: "*Let* Your Thummim and Your Urim *be* with Your holy one, Whom You tested at Massah, And with whom You contended at the waters of Meribah,

Deut 33:10 They shall teach Jacob Your judgments, And Israel Your law. They shall put incense before You, And a whole burnt sacrifice on Your altar.

Mal 2:7 "For the lips of a priest should keep knowledge, And *people* should seek the law from his mouth; For he is the messenger of the LORD of hosts.

Blowing the trumpets on various occasions.

Num 10:1–10 And the LORD spoke to Moses, saying:

2 "Make two silver trumpets for yourself; you shall make them of hammered work; you shall use them for calling the congregation and for directing the movement of the camps. **3** When they blow both of them, all the congregation shall gather before you at the door of the tabernacle of meeting. **4** But if they blow *only* one, then the leaders, the heads of the divisions of Israel, shall gather to you. **5** When you sound the advance, the camps that lie on the east side shall then begin their journey. **6** When you sound the advance the second time, then the camps that lie on the south side shall begin their journey; they shall sound the call for them to begin their journeys. **7** And when the assembly is to be gathered together, you shall blow, but not sound the advance. **8** The sons of Aaron, the priests, shall blow the trumpets; and these shall be to you as an ordinance forever throughout your generations. **9** "When you go to war in your land against the enemy who oppresses you, then you shall sound an alarm with the trumpets, and you will be remembered before the LORD your God, and you will be saved from your enemies. **10** Also in the day of your gladness, in your appointed feasts, and at the beginning of your months, you shall blow the trumpets over your burnt offerings and over the sacrifices of your peace offerings; and they shall be a memorial for you before your God: I *am* the LORD your God."

Josh 6:3–4 You shall march around the city, all *you* men of war; you shall go all around the city once. This you shall do six days. **4** And seven priests shall bear seven trumpets of rams' horns before the ark. But the seventh day you shall march around the city seven times, and the priests shall blow the trumpets.

Carrying the ark.

Josh 3:6 Then Joshua spoke to the priests, saying, "Take up the ark of the covenant and cross over before the people." So they took up the ark of the covenant and went before the people.

Josh 3:17 Then the priests who bore the ark of the covenant of the LORD stood firm on dry ground in the midst of the Jordan; and all Israel crossed over on dry ground, until all the people had crossed completely over the Jordan.

Josh 6:12 And Joshua rose early in the morning, and the priests took up the ark of the LORD.

Encouraging the people when they went to war.

Deut 20:1–4 "When you go out to battle against your enemies, and see horses and chariots *and* people more numerous than you, do not be afraid of them; for the LORD your God *is* with you, who brought you up from the land of Egypt. **2** So it shall be, when you are on the verge of battle, that the priest shall approach and speak to the people. **3** And he shall say to them, 'Hear, O Israel: Today you are on the verge of battle with your enemies. Do not let your heart faint, do not be afraid, and do not tremble or be terrified because of them; **4** for the LORD your God *is* He who goes with you, to fight for you against your enemies, to save you.'

Valuing things devoted.

Lev 27:8 'But if he is too poor to pay your valuation, then he shall present himself before the priest, and the priest shall set a value for him; according to the ability of him who vowed, the priest shall value him.

Were to live by offerings of the altar, as they had no inheritance.

Deut 18:1–2 "The priests, the Levites—all the tribe of Levi—shall have no part nor inheritance with Israel; they shall eat the offerings of the LORD made by fire, and His portion. **2** Therefore they shall have no inheritance among their brethren; the LORD is their inheritance, as He said to them.

1 Cor 9:13 Do you not know that those who minister the holy things eat *of the things* of the temple, and those who serve at the altar partake of *the offerings of* the altar?

Revenues of,

Tenth of the tithes paid to the Levites.

Num 18:26 "Speak thus to the Levites, and say to them: 'When you take from the children of Israel the tithes which I have given you from them as your inheritance, then you shall offer up a heave offering of it to the LORD, a tenth of the tithe.

Num 18:28 Thus you shall also offer a heave offering to the LORD from all your tithes which you receive from the children of Israel, and you shall give the LORD's heave offering from it to Aaron the priest.

Neh 10:37–38 to bring the firstfruits of our dough, our offerings, the fruit from all kinds of trees, *the* new wine and oil, to the priests, to the storerooms of the house of our God; and to bring the tithes of our land to the Levites, for the Levites should receive the tithes in all our farming communities. **38** And the priest, the descendant of Aaron, shall be with the Levites when the Levites receive tithes; and the Levites shall bring up a tenth of the tithes to the house of our God, to the rooms of the storehouse.

Heb 7:5 And indeed those who are of the sons of Levi, who receive the priesthood, have a commandment to receive tithes from the people according to the law, that is, from their brethren, though they have come from the loins of Abraham;

Firstfruits.

Num 18:8 And the LORD spoke to Aaron: "Here, I Myself have also given you charge of My heave offerings, all the holy gifts of the children of Israel; I have given them as a portion to you and your sons, as an ordinance forever.

Num 18:12–13 "All the best of the oil, all the best of the new wine and the grain, their firstfruits which they offer to the LORD, I have given them to you. **13** Whatever first ripe fruit is in their land, which they bring to the LORD, shall be yours. Everyone who is clean in your house may eat it.

Deut 18:4 The firstfruits of your grain and your new wine and your oil, and the first of the fleece of your sheep, you shall give him.

Redemption money of the firstborn.

Num 3:48 And you shall give the money, with which the excess number of them is redeemed, to Aaron and his sons."

Num 3:51 And Moses gave their redemption money to Aaron and his sons, according to the word of the LORD, as the LORD commanded Moses.

Num 18:15–16 "Everything that first opens the womb of all flesh, which they bring to the LORD, whether man or beast, shall be yours; nevertheless the first-born of man you shall surely redeem, and the first-born of unclean animals you shall redeem. **16** And those redeemed of the devoted things you shall redeem when one month old, according to your valuation, for five shekels of silver, according to the shekel of the sanctuary, which *is* twenty gerahs.

Firstborn of animals or their substitutes.

Ex 13:12–13 that you shall set apart to the LORD all that open the womb, that is, every firstborn that comes from an animal which you have; the males *shall be* the LORD's. **13** But every firstborn of a donkey you shall redeem with a lamb; and if you will not redeem *it,* then you shall break its neck. And all the firstborn of man among your sons you shall redeem.

Num 18:17–18 But the firstborn of a cow, the firstborn of a sheep, or the firstborn of a goat you shall not redeem; they *are* holy. You shall sprinkle their blood on the altar, and burn their fat *as* an offering made by fire for a sweet aroma to the LORD. **18** And their flesh shall be yours, just as the wave breast and the right thigh are yours.

First of the wool of sheep.

Deut 18:4 The firstfruits of your grain and your new wine and your oil, and the first of the fleece of your sheep, you shall give him.

Showbread after its removal.

Lev 24:9 And it shall be for Aaron and his sons, and they shall eat it in a holy place; for it *is* most holy to him from the offerings of the LORD made by fire, by a perpetual statute."

1 Sam 21:4–6 And the priest answered David and said, "*There is* no common bread on hand; but there is holy bread, if the young men have at least kept themselves from women." **5** Then David answered the priest, and said to him, "Truly, women *have been* kept from us about three days since I came out. And the vessels of the young men are holy, and *the bread is* in effect common, even though it was consecrated in the vessel this day." **6** So the priest gave him holy *bread;* for there was no bread there but the show-bread which had been taken from before the LORD, in order to put hot bread *in its place* on the day when it was taken away.

Matt 12:4 how he entered the house of God and ate the showbread which was not lawful for him to eat, nor for those who were with him, but only for the priests?

Part of all sacrifices.

Lev 7:6–10 Every male among the priests may eat it. It shall be eaten in a holy place. It *is* most holy. **7** The trespass offering *is* like the sin offering; *there is* one law for them both: the priest who makes atonement with it shall have *it.* **8** And the priest who offers anyone's burnt offering, that priest shall have for himself the skin of the burnt offering which he has offered. **9** Also every grain offering that is baked in the oven and all that is prepared in the covered pan, or in a pan, shall be the priest's who offers it. **10** Every grain offering, *whether* mixed with oil or dry, shall belong to all the sons of Aaron, to one *as much* as the other.

Lev 7:31 And the priest shall burn the fat on the altar, but the breast shall be Aaron's and his sons'.

Lev 7:34 For the breast of the wave offering and the thigh of the heave offering I have taken from the children of Israel, from the sacrifices of their peace offerings, and I have given them to Aaron the priest and to his sons from the children of Israel by a statute forever.' "

Num 6:19–20 'And the priest shall take the boiled shoulder of the ram, one unleavened cake from the basket, and one unleavened wafer, and put *them* upon the hands of the Nazirite after he has shaved his consecrated *hair,* **20** and the priest shall wave them as a wave offering before the LORD; they *are* holy for the priest, together with the breast of the wave offering and the thigh of the heave offering. After that the Nazirite may drink wine.'

Num 18:8–11 And the LORD spoke to Aaron: "Here, I Myself have also given you charge of My heave offerings, all the holy gifts of the children of Israel; I have given them as a portion to you and your sons, as an ordinance forever. **9** This shall be yours of the most holy things *reserved* from the fire: every offering of theirs, every grain offering and every sin offering and every trespass offering which they render to Me, *shall be* most holy for you and your sons. **10** In a most holy *place* you shall eat it; every male shall eat it. It shall be holy to you. **11** "This also *is* yours: the heave offering of their gift, with all the wave offerings of the children of Israel; I have given them to you, and your sons and daughters with you, as an ordinance forever. Everyone who is clean in your house may eat it.

Deut 18:3 "And this shall be the priest's due from the people, from those who offer a sacrifice, whether *it is* bull or sheep: they shall give to the priest the shoulder, the cheeks, and the stomach.

All devoted things.

Num 18:14 "Every devoted thing in Israel shall be yours.

All restitutions when the owner could not be found.

Num 5:8 But if the man has no relative to whom restitution may be made for the wrong, the restitution for the wrong *must go* to the LORD for the priest, in addition to the ram of the atonement with which atonement is made for him.

A fixed portion of the spoil taken in war.

Num 31:29 take *it* from their half, and give *it* to Eleazar the priest as a heave offering to the LORD.

Num 31:41 So Moses gave the tribute *which was* the LORD's heave offering to Eleazar the priest, as the LORD commanded Moses.

Thirteen of the Levitical cities given to, for residence.

1 Chr 6:57–60 And to the sons of Aaron they gave *one of* the cities of refuge, Hebron; also Libnah with its common-lands, Jattir, Eshtemoa with its common-lands, **58** Hilen with its common-lands, Debir with its common-lands, **59** Ashan with its common-lands, and Beth Shemesh with its common-lands. **60** And from the tribe of Benjamin: Geba with its common-lands, Alemeth with its common-lands, and Anathoth with its common-lands. All their cities among their families *were* thirteen.

Cf. Num 35:1–8

Might purchase and hold other lands in possession.

1 Kin 2:26 And to Abiathar the priest the king said, "Go to Anathoth, to your own fields, for you *are* deserving of death; but I will not put you to death at this time, because you carried the ark of the Lord GOD before my father David, and because you were afflicted every time my father was afflicted."

Jer 32:8–9 Then Hanamel my uncle's son came to me in the court of the prison according to the word of the LORD, and said to me, 'Please buy my field that *is* in Anathoth, which *is* in the country of Benjamin; for the right of inheritance *is* yours, and the redemption *is* yours; buy *it* for yourself.' Then I knew that this was the word of the LORD. **9** So I bought the field from Hanamel, the son of my uncle who *was* in Anathoth, and weighed *out to* him the money—seventeen shekels of silver.

Special laws respecting,

Not to marry divorced or improper persons.

Lev 21:7 They shall not take a wife *who is* a harlot or a defiled woman, nor shall they take a woman divorced from her husband; for *the priest* is holy to his God.

Not to defile themselves for the dead, unless for close relatives.

Lev 21:1–6 And the LORD said to Moses, "Speak to the priests, the sons of Aaron, and say to them: 'None shall defile himself for the dead among his people, **2** except for his relatives who are nearest to him: his mother, his father, his son, his daughter, and his brother; **3** also his virgin sister who is near to him, who has had no husband, for her he may defile himself. **4** *Otherwise* he shall not defile himself, *being* a chief man among his people, to profane himself. **5** 'They shall not make any bald *place* on their heads, nor shall they shave the edges of their beards nor make any cuttings in their flesh. **6** They shall be holy to their God and not profane the name of their God, for they offer the offerings of the LORD made by fire, *and* the bread of their God; therefore they shall be holy.

Not to drink wine, etc., while attending in the tabernacle.

Lev 10:9 "Do not drink wine or intoxicating drink, you, nor your sons with you, when you go into the tabernacle of meeting, lest you die. *It shall be* a statute forever throughout your generations,

Ezek 44:21 No priest shall drink wine when he enters the inner court.

Not to defile themselves by eating what died or was torn.

Lev 22:8 Whatever dies *naturally* or is torn *by beasts* he shall not eat, to defile himself with it: I *am* the LORD.

While unclean could not perform any service.

Lev 22:1–2 Then the LORD spoke to Moses, saying, **2** "Speak to Aaron and his sons, that they separate themselves from the holy things of the children of Israel, and that they do not profane My holy name *by* what they dedicate to Me: I *am* the LORD.

Num 19:6–7 And the priest shall take cedar wood and hyssop and scarlet, and cast *them* into the midst of

the fire burning the heifer. **7** Then the priest shall wash his clothes, he shall bathe in water, and afterward he shall come into the camp; the priest shall be unclean until evening.

While unclean could not eat of the holy things.

Lev 22:3–7 Say to them: 'Whoever of all your descendants throughout your generations, who goes near the holy things which the children of Israel dedicate to the LORD, while he has uncleanness upon him, that person shall be cut off from My presence: I *am* the LORD. **4** 'Whatever man of the descendants of Aaron, who *is* a leper or has a discharge, shall not eat the holy offerings until he is clean. And whoever touches anything made unclean *by* a corpse, or a man who has had an emission of semen, **5** or whoever touches any creeping thing by which he would be made unclean, or any person by whom he would become unclean, whatever his uncleanness may be— **6** the person who has touched any such thing shall be unclean until evening, and shall not eat the holy *offerings* unless he washes his body with water. **7** And when the sun goes down he shall be clean; and afterward he may eat the holy *offerings*, because it *is* his food.

No outsider or hired servant to eat of their portion.

Lev 22:10 'No outsider shall eat the holy *offering*; one who dwells with the priest, or a hired servant, shall not eat the holy thing.

All purchased and home-born servants to eat of their portion.

Lev 22:11 But if the priest buys a person with his money, he may eat it; and one who is born in his house may eat his food.

Children of, married to strangers, not to eat of their portion.

Lev 22:12 If the priest's daughter is married to an outsider, she may not eat of the holy offerings.

Restitution to be made to, by persons ignorantly eating of their holy things.

Lev 22:14–16 'And if a man eats the holy *offering* unintentionally, then he shall restore a holy *offering* to the priest, and add one-fifth to it. **15** They shall not profane the holy *offerings* of the children of Israel, which they offer to the LORD, **16** or allow them to bear the guilt of trespass when they eat their holy *offerings*; for I the LORD sanctify them.' "

Divided by David into twenty-four divisions.

2 Chr 8:14 And, according to the order of David his father, he appointed the divisions of the priests for their service, the Levites for their duties (to praise and serve before the priests) as the duty of each day required, and the gatekeepers by their divisions at each gate; for so David the man of God had commanded.

2 Chr 35:4–5 Prepare *yourselves* according to your fathers' houses, according to your divisions, following the written instruction of David king of Israel and the written instruction of Solomon his son. **5** And stand in the holy *place* according to the divisions of the fathers' houses of your brethren the *lay* people, and *according to* the division of the father's house of the Levites.

Cf. 1 Chr 24:1–19

The four divisions which returned from Babylon subdivided into 24.

Ezra 2:36–39 The priests: the sons of Jedaiah, of the house of Jeshua, nine hundred and seventy-three; **37** the sons of Immer, one thousand and fifty-two; **38** the sons of Pashhur, one thousand two hundred and forty-seven; **39** the sons of Harim, one thousand and seventeen.

Luke 1:5 There was in the days of Herod, the king of Judea, a certain priest named Zacharias, of the division of Abijah. His wife *was* of the daughters of Aaron, and her name *was* Elizabeth.

Each division of, had its leader or chief.

1 Chr 24:6 And the scribe, Shemaiah the son of Nethanel, *one* of the Levites, wrote them down before the king, the leaders, Zadok the priest, Ahimelech the son of Abiathar, and the heads of the fathers' *houses* of the priests and Levites, one father's house taken for Eleazar and *one* for Ithamar.

1 Chr 24:31 These also cast lots just as their brothers the sons of Aaron did, in the presence of King David, Zadok, Ahimelech, and the heads of the fathers' *houses* of the priests and Levites. The chief fathers *did* just as their younger brethren.

2 Chr 36:14 Moreover all the leaders of the priests and the people transgressed more and more, *according* to all the abominations of the nations, and defiled the house of the LORD which He had consecrated in Jerusalem.

Punishment for invading the office of.

Num 18:7 Therefore you and your sons with you shall attend to your priesthood for everything at the altar and behind the veil; and you shall serve. I give your priesthood *to you* as a gift for service, but the outsider who comes near shall be put to death."

Cf. Num 16:1–35; 2 Chr 26:16–21

On special occasions persons not of Aaron's family acted as.

Judg 6:24–27 So Gideon built an altar there to the LORD, and called it The-LORD-*Is*-Peace. To this day it *is* still in Ophrah of the Abiezrites. **25** Now it came to pass the same night that the LORD said to him, "Take your father's young bull, the second bull of seven years old, and tear down the altar of Baal that your father has, and cut down the wooden image that *is* beside it; **26** and build an altar to the LORD your God on top of this rock in the proper arrangement, and take the second bull and offer a burnt sacrifice with the wood of the image which you shall cut down." **27** So Gideon took ten men from among his servants and did as the LORD had said to him. But because he feared his father's household and the men of the city too much to do *it* by day, he did *it* by night.

1 Sam 7:9 And Samuel took a suckling lamb and offered *it as* a whole burnt offering to the LORD. Then Samuel cried out to the LORD for Israel, and the LORD answered him.

1 Kin 18:33 And he put the wood in order, cut the bull in pieces, and laid *it* on the wood, and said, "Fill four waterpots with water, and pour *it* on the burnt sacrifice and on the wood."

Occasional sinfulness of,

Greediness.

1 Sam 2:13–17 And the priests' custom with the people *was that* when any man offered a sacrifice, the priest's servant would come with a three-pronged fleshhook in his hand while the meat was boiling. **14** Then he would thrust *it* into the pan, or kettle, or caldron, or pot; and the priest would take for himself all that the fleshhook brought up. So they did in Shiloh to all the Israelites who came there. **15** Also, before they burned the fat, the priest's servant would come and say to the man who sacrificed, "Give meat for roasting to the priest, for he will not take boiled meat from you, but raw." **16** And *if* the man said to him, "They should really burn the fat first; *then* you may take *as much* as your heart desires," he would then answer him, "*No,* but you must give *it* now; and if not, I will take *it* by force." **17** Therefore the sin of the young men was very great before the LORD, for men abhorred the offering of the LORD.

Drunkenness.

Is 28:7 But they also have erred through wine, And through intoxicating drink are out of the way; The priest and the prophet have erred through intoxicating drink, They are swallowed up by wine, They are out of the way through intoxicating drink; They err in vision, they stumble *in* judgment.

Profanity and immorality.

1 Sam 2:22–24 Now Eli was very old; and he heard everything his sons did to all Israel, and how they lay with the women who assembled at the door of the tabernacle of meeting. **23** So he said to them, "Why do you do such things? For I hear of your evil dealings from all the people. **24** No, my sons! For *it is* not a good report that I hear. You make the LORD's people transgress.

Injustice.

Jer 6:13 "Because from the least of them even to the greatest of them, Everyone *is* given to covetousness; And from the prophet even to the priest, Everyone deals falsely.

Corruption of the law.

Is 28:7 But they also have erred through wine, And through intoxicating drink are out of the way; The priest and the prophet have erred through intoxicating drink, They are swallowed up by wine, They are out of the way through intoxicating drink; They err in vision, they stumble *in* judgment.

Mal 2:8 But you have departed from the way; You have caused many to stumble at the law. You have corrupted the covenant of Levi," Says the LORD of hosts.

Slow to sanctify themselves for God's services.

2 Chr 29:34 But the priests were too few, so that they could not skin all the burnt offerings; therefore their brethren the Levites helped them until the work was ended and until the *other* priests had sanctified themselves, for the Levites were more diligent in sanctifying themselves than the priests.

Generally participated in punishment of the people.

Jer 14:18 If I go out to the field, Then behold, those slain with the sword! And if I enter the city, Then behold, those sick from famine! Yes, both prophet and priest go about in a land they do not know.' "

Lam 2:20 "See, O LORD, and consider! To whom have You done this? Should the women eat their offspring, The children they have cuddled? Should the priest and prophet be slain In the sanctuary of the Lord?

Appointed from every class by Jeroboam and others.

2 Kin 17:32 So they feared the LORD, and from every class they appointed for themselves priests of the high places, who sacrificed for them in the shrines of the high places.

Services of, could not remove sin.

Heb 7:11 Therefore, if perfection were through the Levitical priesthood (for under it the people received the law), what further need *was there* that another priest should rise according to the order of Melchizedek, and not be called according to the order of Aaron?

Heb 10:11 And every priest stands ministering daily and offering repeatedly the same sacrifices, which can never take away sins.

Illustrative of

Christ.

Heb 10:11–12 And every priest stands ministering daily and offering repeatedly the same sacrifices, which can never take away sins. **12** But this Man, after He had offered one sacrifice for sins forever, sat down at the right hand of God,

Believers.

Ex 19:6 And you shall be to Me a kingdom of priests and a holy nation.' These *are* the words which you shall speak to the children of Israel."

1 Pet 2:9 But you *are* a chosen generation, a royal priesthood, a holy nation, His own special people, that you may proclaim the praises of Him who called you out of darkness into His marvelous light;

PRISONS

Antiquity of.

Gen 39:20 Then Joseph's master took him and put him into the prison, a place where the king's prisoners *were* confined. And he was there in the prison.

Kinds of

State.

Gen 39:20 Then Joseph's master took him and put him into the prison, a place where the king's prisoners *were* confined. And he was there in the prison.

Jer 37:21 Then Zedekiah the king commanded that they should commit Jeremiah to the court of the prison, and that they should give him daily a piece of bread from the bakers' street, until all the bread in the city was gone. Thus Jeremiah remained in the court of the prison.

Common.

Acts 5:18 and laid their hands on the apostles and put them in the common prison.

Dungeons attached to.

Jer 38:6 So they took Jeremiah and cast him into the dungeon of Malchiah the king's son, which *was* in the court of the prison, and they let Jeremiah down

with ropes. And in the dungeon *there was* no water, but mire. So Jeremiah sank in the mire.

Zech 9:11 "As for you also, Because of the blood of your covenant, I will set your prisoners free from the waterless pit.

Had keepers.

Gen 39:21 But the LORD was with Joseph and showed him mercy, and He gave him favor in the sight of the keeper of the prison.

Used for confining

Persons accused of crimes.

Luke 23:19 who had been thrown into prison for a certain rebellion made in the city, and for murder.

Persons accused of heresy.

Acts 4:3 And they laid hands on them, and put *them* in custody until the next day, for it was already evening.

Acts 5:18 and laid their hands on the apostles and put them in the common prison.

Acts 8:3 As for Saul, he made havoc of the church, entering every house, and dragging off men and women, committing *them* to prison.

Suspected persons.

Gen 42:19 If you *are* honest *men*, let one of your brothers be confined to your prison house; but you, go and carry grain for the famine of your houses.

Condemned persons till executed.

Lev 24:12 Then they put him in custody, that the mind of the LORD might be shown to them.

Acts 12:4–5 So when he had arrested him, he put *him* in prison, and delivered *him* to four squads of soldiers to keep him, intending to bring him before the people after Passover. **5** Peter was therefore kept in prison, but constant prayer was offered to God for him by the church.

Enemies taken captive.

Judg 16:21 Then the Philistines took him and put out his eyes, and brought him down to Gaza. They bound him with bronze fetters, and he became a grinder in the prison.

2 Kin 17:4 And the king of Assyria uncovered a conspiracy by Hoshea; for he had sent messengers to So, king of Egypt, and brought no tribute to the king of Assyria, as *he had done* year by year. Therefore the king of Assyria shut him up, and bound him in prison.

Jer 52:11 He also put out the eyes of Zedekiah; and the king of Babylon bound him in bronze fetters, took him to Babylon, and put him in prison till the day of his death.

Debtors till they paid.

Matt 5:26 Assuredly, I say to you, you will by no means get out of there till you have paid the last penny.

Matt 18:30 And he would not, but went and threw him into prison till he should pay the debt.

Persons under the king's displeasure.

1 Kin 22:27 and say, 'Thus says the king: "Put this *fellow* in prison, and feed him with bread of affliction and water of affliction, until I come in peace." ' "

2 Chr 16:10 Then Asa was angry with the seer, and put

him in prison, for *he was* enraged at him because of this. And Asa oppressed *some* of the people at that time.

Mark 6:17 For Herod himself had sent and laid hold of John, and bound him in prison for the sake of Herodias, his brother Philip's wife; for he had married her.

Confinement in,

Often awarded as a punishment.

Ezra 7:26 Whoever will not observe the law of your God and the law of the king, let judgment be executed speedily on him, whether *it be* death, or banishment, or confiscation of goods, or imprisonment.

Considered a severe punishment.

Luke 22:33 But he said to Him, "Lord, I am ready to go with You, both to prison and to death."

Places used as,

Court of the king's house.

Jer 32:2 For then the king of Babylon's army besieged Jerusalem, and Jeremiah the prophet was shut up in the court of the prison, which *was in* the king of Judah's house.

House of the king's scribe.

Jer 37:15 Therefore the princes were angry with Jeremiah, and they struck him and put him in prison in the house of Jonathan the scribe. For they had made that the prison.

House of the captain of the guard.

Gen 40:3 So he put them in custody in the house of the captain of the guard, in the prison, the place where Joseph *was* confined.

Prisoner's own house.

Acts 28:16 Now when we came to Rome, the centurion delivered the prisoners to the captain of the guard; but Paul was permitted to dwell by himself with the soldier who guarded him.

Acts 28:30 Then Paul dwelt two whole years in his own rented house, and received all who came to him,

2 Tim 1:16–18 The Lord grant mercy to the household of Onesiphorus, for he often refreshed me, and was not ashamed of my chain; **17** but when he arrived in Rome, he sought me out very zealously and found *me.* **18** The Lord grant to him that he may find mercy from the Lord in that Day—and you know very well how many ways he ministered *to me* at Ephesus.

Officials had power to commit to.

1 Kin 22:27 and say, 'Thus says the king: "Put this *fellow* in prison, and feed him with bread of affliction and water of affliction, until I come in peace." ' "

Matt 5:25 Agree with your adversary quickly, while you are on the way with him, lest your adversary deliver you to the judge, the judge hand you over to the officer, and you be thrown into prison.

Persons confined in,

Said to be in custody.

Acts 4:3 And they laid hands on them, and put *them* in custody until the next day, for it was already evening.

Sometimes placed in dungeons.

Jer 37:16 When Jeremiah entered the dungeon and the cells, and Jeremiah had remained there many days,

Acts 16:24 Having received such a charge, he put them into the inner prison and fastened their feet in the stocks.

Often bound with fetters.

Gen 42:19 If you *are* honest *men,* let one of your brothers be confined to your prison house; but you, go and carry grain for the famine of your houses.

Ezek 19:9 They put him in a cage with chains, And brought him to the king of Babylon; They brought him in nets, That his voice should no longer be heard on the mountains of Israel.

Mark 6:17 For Herod himself had sent and laid hold of John, and bound him in prison for the sake of Herodias, his brother Philip's wife; for he had married her.

Sometimes chained to two soldiers.

Acts 12:6 And when Herod was about to bring him out, that night Peter was sleeping, bound with two chains between two soldiers; and the guards before the door were keeping the prison.

Sometimes fastened in stocks.

Jer 29:26 "The LORD has made you priest instead of Jehoiada the priest, so that there should be officers *in* the house of the LORD over every man *who* is demented and considers himself a prophet, that you should put him in prison and in the stocks.

Acts 16:24 Having received such a charge, he put them into the inner prison and fastened their feet in the stocks.

Sometimes did hard labor.

Judg 16:21 Then the Philistines took him and put out his eyes, and brought him down to Gaza. They bound him with bronze fetters, and he became a grinder in the prison.

Often subjected to extreme suffering.

Ps 79:11 Let the groaning of the prisoner come before You; According to the greatness of Your power Preserve those who are appointed to die;

Ps 102:20 To hear the groaning of the prisoner, To release those appointed to death,

Ps 105:18 They hurt his feet with fetters, He was laid in irons.

Fed on bread and water.

1 Kin 22:27 and say, 'Thus says the king: "Put this *fellow* in prison, and feed him with bread of affliction and water of affliction, until I come in peace." ' "

Clothed in prison dress.

2 Kin 25:29 So Jehoiachin changed from his prison garments, and he ate bread regularly before the king all the days of his life.

Sometimes allowed to be visited by their friends.

Matt 11:2 And when John had heard in prison about the works of Christ, he sent two of his disciples

Matt 25:36 I *was* naked and you clothed Me; I was sick and you visited Me; I was in prison and you came to Me.'

Acts 24:23 So he commanded the centurion to keep Paul and to let *him* have liberty, and told him not to forbid any of his friends to provide for or visit him.

Might have their condition eased by the king.

Jer 37:20–21 Therefore please hear now, O my lord the king. Please, let my petition be accepted before you, and do not make me return to the house of Jonathan the scribe, lest I die there." **21** Then Zedekiah the king commanded that they should commit Jeremiah to the court of the prison, and that they should give him daily a piece of bread from the bakers' street, until all the bread in the city was gone. Thus Jeremiah remained in the court of the prison.

Often executed in.

Gen 40:22 But he hanged the chief baker, as Joseph had interpreted to them.

Matt 14:10 So he sent and had John beheaded in prison.

Officials had power to release from.

Gen 40:21 Then he restored the chief butler to his butlership again, and he placed the cup in Pharaoh's hand.

Acts 16:35–36 And when it was day, the magistrates sent the officers, saying, "Let those men go." **36** So the keeper of the prison reported these words to Paul, saying, "The magistrates have sent to let you go. Now therefore depart, and go in peace."

Keepers of,

Strictly guarded the doors.

Acts 12:6 And when Herod was about to bring him out, that night Peter was sleeping, bound with two chains between two soldiers; and the guards before the door were keeping the prison.

Responsible for the prisoners.

Acts 16:23 And when they had laid many stripes on them, they threw *them* into prison, commanding the jailer to keep them securely.

Acts 16:27 And the keeper of the prison, awaking from sleep and seeing the prison doors open, supposing the prisoners had fled, drew his sword and was about to kill himself.

Put to death if prisoners escaped.

Acts 12:19 But when Herod had searched for him and not found him, he examined the guards and commanded that *they* should be put to death. And he went down from Judea to Caesarea, and stayed *there.*

Often used harsh measures.

Jer 37:20 Therefore please hear now, O my lord the king. Please, let my petition be accepted before you, and do not make me return to the house of Jonathan the scribe, lest I die there."

Acts 16:24 Having received such a charge, he put them into the inner prison and fastened their feet in the stocks.

Sometimes acted kindly.

Gen 39:21 But the LORD was with Joseph and showed him mercy, and He gave him favor in the sight of the keeper of the prison.

Acts 16:33–34 And he took them the same hour of the night and washed *their* stripes. And immediately he and all his family were baptized. **34** Now when he had brought them into his house, he set food before them; and he rejoiced, having believed in God with all his household.

Sometimes gave responsibility to well-conducted prisoners.

Gen 39:22–23 And the keeper of the prison committed to Joseph's hand all the prisoners who *were* in the prison; whatever they did there, it was his doing. **23** The keeper of the prison did not look into anything *that was* under Joseph's authority, because the LORD was with him; and whatever he did, the LORD made *it* prosper.

Illustrative of

Deep afflictions.

Ps 142:7 Bring my soul out of prison, That I may praise Your name; The righteous shall surround me, For You shall deal bountifully with me."

Hell.

Rev 20:7 Now when the thousand years have expired, Satan will be released from his prison

Bondage to sin and Satan.

Is 42:7 To open blind eyes, To bring out prisoners from the prison, Those who sit in darkness from the prison house.

Is 49:9 That You may say to the prisoners, 'Go forth,' To those who *are* in darkness, 'Show yourselves.' "They shall feed along the roads, And their pastures *shall be* on all desolate heights.

Is 61:1 "The Spirit of the Lord GOD *is* upon Me, Because the LORD has anointed Me To preach good tidings to the poor; He has sent Me to heal the brokenhearted, To proclaim liberty to the captives, And the opening of the prison to *those who are* bound;

PROCRASTINATION, SPIRITUAL

Condemned by Christ.

Luke 9:59–62 Then He said to another, "Follow Me." But he said, "Lord, let me first go and bury my father." **60** Jesus said to him, "Let the dead bury their own dead, but you go and preach the kingdom of God." **61** And another also said, "Lord, I will follow You, but let me first go *and* bid them farewell who are at my house." **62** But Jesus said to him, "No one, having put his hand to the plow, and looking back, is fit for the kingdom of God."

To be avoided in

Hearkening to God.

Ps 95:7–8 For He *is* our God, And we *are* the people of His pasture, And the sheep of His hand. Today, if you will hear His voice: **8** "Do not harden your hearts, as in the rebellion, As *in* the day of trial in the wilderness,

Heb 3:7–8 Therefore, as the Holy Spirit says: *"Today, if you will hear His voice, 8 Do not harden your hearts as in the rebellion, In the day of trial in the wilderness,*

Seeking God.

Ps 27:8 *When You said,* "Seek My face," My heart said to You, "Your face, LORD, I will seek."

Is 55:6 Seek the LORD while He may be found, Call upon Him while He is near.

Glorifying God.

Jer 13:16 Give glory to the LORD your God Before He causes darkness, And before your feet stumble On the dark mountains, And while you are looking for light, He turns it into the shadow of death *And* makes *it* dense darkness.

Keeping God's commandments.

Ps 119:60 I made haste, and did not delay To keep Your commandments.

Making offerings to God.

Ex 22:29 "You shall not delay *to offer* the first of your ripe produce and your juices. The firstborn of your sons you shall give to Me.

Performance of vows.

Deut 23:21 "When you make a vow to the LORD your God, you shall not delay to pay it; for the LORD your God will surely require it of you, and it would be sin to you.

Eccl 5:4 When you make a vow to God, do not delay to pay it; For *He has* no pleasure in fools. Pay what you have vowed—

Motives for avoiding

The present is the accepted time.

Eccl 12:1 Remember now your Creator in the days of your youth, Before the difficult days come, And the years draw near when you say, "I have no pleasure in them":

2 Cor 6:2 For He says: *"In an acceptable time I have heard you, And in the day of salvation I have helped you."* Behold, now *is* the accepted time; behold, now *is* the day of salvation.

The uncertainty of life.

Prov 27:1 Do not boast about tomorrow, For you do not know what a day may bring forth.

Danger of, illustrated.

Matt 5:25 Agree with your adversary quickly, while you are on the way with him, lest your adversary deliver you to the judge, the judge hand you over to the officer, and you be thrown into prison.

Luke 13:25 When once the Master of the house has risen up and shut the door, and you begin to stand outside and knock at the door, saying, 'Lord, Lord, open for us,' and He will answer and say to you, 'I do not know you, where you are from,'

Exemplified by

Lot.

Gen 19:16 And while he lingered, the men took hold of his hand, his wife's hand, and the hands of his two daughters, the LORD being merciful to him, and they brought him out and set him outside the city.

Felix.

Acts 24:25 Now as he reasoned about righteousness, self-control, and the judgment to come, Felix was afraid and answered, "Go away for now; when I have a convenient time I will call for you."

PROPERTY

Transaction for,

By Abraham.

Gen 23:3–20 Then Abraham stood up from before his dead, and spoke to the sons of Heth, saying, 4 "I *am* a foreigner and a visitor among you. Give me property for a burial place among you, that I may bury my dead out of my sight." 5 And the sons of Heth answered Abraham, saying to him, 6 "Hear us, my lord: You *are* a mighty prince among us; bury your dead in the choicest of our burial places. None of us will withhold from you his burial place, that you may bury your dead." 7 Then Abraham stood up and bowed himself to the people of the land, the sons of Heth. 8 And he spoke with them, saying, "If it is your wish that I bury my dead out of my sight, hear me, and meet with Ephron the son of Zohar for me, 9 that he may give me the cave of Machpelah which he has, which *is* at the end of his field. Let him give it to me at the full price, as property for a burial place among you." 10 Now Ephron dwelt among the sons of Heth; and Ephron the Hittite answered Abraham in the presence of the sons of Heth, all who entered at the gate of his city, saying, 11 "No, my lord, hear me: I give you the field and the cave that *is* in it; I give it to you in the presence of the sons of my people. I give it to you. Bury your dead!" 12 Then Abraham bowed himself down before the people of the land; 13 and he spoke to Ephron in the hearing of the people of the land, saying, "If you *will give it,* please hear me. I will give you money for the field; take *it* from me and I will bury my dead there." 14 And Ephron answered Abraham, saying to him, 15 "My lord, listen to me; the land *is worth* four hundred shekels of silver. What *is* that between you and me? So bury your dead." 16 And Abraham listened to Ephron; and Abraham weighed out the silver for Ephron which he had named in the hearing of the sons of Heth, four hundred shekels of silver, currency of the merchants. 17 So the field of Ephron which *was* in Machpelah, which *was* before Mamre, the field and the cave which *was* in it, and all the trees that *were* in the field, which *were* within all the surrounding borders, were deeded 18 to Abraham as a possession in the presence of the sons of Heth, before all who went in at the gate of his city. 19 And after this, Abraham buried Sarah his wife in the cave of the field of Machpelah, before Mamre (that *is,* Hebron) in the land of Canaan. 20 So the field and the cave that *is* in it were deeded to Abraham by the sons of Heth as property for a burial place.

By Jeremiah.

Jer 32:1–15 The word that came to Jeremiah from the LORD in the tenth year of Zedekiah king of Judah, which was the eighteenth year of Nebuchadnezzar. 2 For then the king of Babylon's army besieged Jerusalem, and Jeremiah the prophet was shut up in the court of the prison, which *was in* the king of Judah's house. 3 For Zedekiah king of Judah had shut him up, saying, "Why do you prophesy and say, 'Thus says the LORD: "Behold, I will give this city into the hand of the king of Babylon, and he shall take it; 4 and Zedekiah king of Judah shall not escape from the hand of the Chaldeans, but shall surely be delivered into the hand of the king of Babylon, and shall speak with him face to face, and see him eye to eye; 5 then he shall lead Zedekiah to Babylon, and there he shall be until I visit him," says the LORD; "though you fight with the Chaldeans, you shall not succeed" '?" 6 And Jeremiah said, "The word of the LORD came to me, saying, 7 'Behold, Hanamel the son of Shallum your uncle will come to you, saying, "Buy my field which is in Anathoth, for the right of redemption *is* yours to buy *it*." ' **8** Then Hanamel my uncle's son came to me in the court of the prison according to the word of the LORD, and said to me, 'Please buy my field that *is* in Anathoth, which *is* in the country of Benjamin; for the right of inheritance *is* yours, and the redemption yours; buy *it* for yourself.' Then I knew that this was the word of the LORD. **9** So I bought the field from Hanamel, the son of my uncle who *was* in Anathoth, and weighed *out to* him the money—seventeen shekels of silver. **10** And I signed the deed and sealed *it*, took witnesses, and weighed the money on the scales. **11** So I took the purchase deed, *both* that which was sealed *according* to the law and custom, and that which was open; **12** and I gave the purchase deed to Baruch the son of Neriah, son of Mahseiah, in the presence of Hanamel my uncle's *son*, and in the presence of the witnesses who signed the purchase deed, before all the Jews who sat in the court of the prison. **13** "Then I charged Baruch before them, saying, **14** 'Thus says the LORD of hosts, the God of Israel: "Take these deeds, both this purchase deed which is sealed and this deed which is open, and put them in an earthen vessel, that they may last many days." **15** For thus says the LORD of hosts, the God of Israel: "Houses and fields and vineyards shall be possessed again in this land." '

Cf. Jer 37:12

Protection of, by the law.

Ex 20:15 "You shall not steal.

Ex 20:17 "You shall not covet your neighbor's house; you shall not covet your neighbor's wife, nor his male servant, nor his female servant, nor his ox, nor his donkey, nor anything that *is* your neighbor's."

Ex 21:16 "He who kidnaps a man and sells him, or if he is found in his hand, shall surely be put to death.

Lev 19:11 'You shall not steal, nor deal falsely, nor lie to one another.

Cf. Eph 4:28; 5:3

Care of, during Year of Jubilee. Lev 25:8–34

Boundaries of, to be respected.

Deut 19:14 "You shall not remove your neighbor's landmark, which the men of old have set, in your inheritance which you will inherit in the land that the LORD your God is giving you to possess.

Prov 22:28 Do not remove the ancient landmark Which your fathers have set.

Prov 23:10 Do not remove the ancient landmark, Nor enter the fields of the fatherless;

In Israel, to be permanent.

Lev 25:10 And you shall consecrate the fiftieth year, and proclaim liberty throughout *all* the land to all its inhabitants. It shall be a Jubilee for you; and each of you shall return to his possession, and each of you shall return to his family.

Lev 25:13 'In this Year of Jubilee, each of you shall return to his possession.

Num 36:1–12 Now the chief fathers of the families of the children of Gilead the son of Machir, the son of Manasseh, of the families of the sons of Joseph, came near and spoke before Moses and before the leaders, the chief fathers of the children of Israel. **2** And they said: "The LORD commanded my lord *Moses* to give the land as an inheritance by lot to the children of Israel, and my lord was commanded by the LORD to give the inheritance of our brother Zelophehad to his daughters. **3** Now if they are married to any of the sons of the *other* tribes of the children of Israel, then their inheritance will be taken from the inheritance of our fathers, and it will be added to the inheritance of the tribe into which they marry; so it will be taken from the lot of our inheritance. **4** And when the Jubilee of the children of Israel comes, then their inheritance will be added to the inheritance of the tribe into which they marry; so their inheritance will be taken away from the inheritance of the tribe of our fathers." **5** Then Moses commanded the children of Israel according to the word of the LORD, saying: "What the tribe of the sons of Joseph speaks is right. **6** This *is* what the LORD commands concerning the daughters of Zelophehad, saying, 'Let them marry whom they think best, but they may marry only within the family of their father's tribe.' **7** So the inheritance of the children of Israel shall not change hands from tribe to tribe, for every one of the children of Israel shall keep the inheritance of the tribe of his fathers. **8** And every daughter who possesses an inheritance in any tribe of the children of Israel shall be the wife of one of the family of her father's tribe, so that the children of Israel each may possess the inheritance of his fathers. **9** Thus no inheritance shall change hands from *one* tribe to another, but every tribe of the children of Israel shall keep its own inheritance." **10** Just as the LORD commanded Moses, so did the daughters of Zelophehad; **11** for Mahlah, Tirzah, Hoglah, Milcah, and Noah, the daughters of Zelophehad, were married to the sons of their father's brothers. **12** They were married into the families of the children of Manasseh the son of Joseph, and their inheritance remained in the tribe of their father's family.

Shared by early Christians.

Acts 4:32–37 Now the multitude of those who believed were of one heart and one soul; neither did anyone say that any of the things he possessed was his own, but they had all things in common. **33** And with great power the apostles gave witness to the resurrection of the Lord Jesus. And great grace was upon them all. **34** Nor was there anyone among them who lacked; for all who were possessors of lands or houses sold them, and brought the proceeds of the things that were sold, **35** and laid *them* at the apostles' feet; and they distributed to each as anyone had need. **36** And Joses, who was also named Barnabas by the apostles (which is translated Son of Encouragement), a Levite of the country of Cyprus, **37** having land, sold *it*, and brought the money and laid *it* at the apostles' feet.

PROPHECY

Is the foretelling of future events.

Gen 49:1 And Jacob called his sons and said, "Gather together, that I may tell you what shall befall you in the last days:

Num 24:14 And now, indeed, I am going to my people. Come, I will advise you what this people will do to your people in the latter days."

God is the Author of.

Is 44:7 And who can proclaim as I do? Then let him declare it and set it in order for Me, Since I appointed the ancient people. And the things that are coming and shall come, Let them show these to them.

Is 45:21 Tell and bring forth *your case;* Yes, let them take counsel together. Who has declared this from ancient time? *Who* has told it from that time? *Have* not I, the LORD? And *there is* no other God besides Me, A just God and a Savior; *There is* none besides Me.

God gives, through Christ.

Eph 4:11 And He Himself gave some *to be* apostles, some prophets, some evangelists, and some pastors and teachers,

Rev 1:1 The Revelation of Jesus Christ, which God gave Him to show His servants—things which must shortly take place. And He sent and signified *it* by His angel to His servant John,

Rev 11:3 And I will give *power* to my two witnesses, and they will prophesy one thousand two hundred and sixty days, clothed in sackcloth."

A gift of the Holy Spirit.

1 Cor 12:10 to another the working of miracles, to another prophecy, to another discerning of spirits, to another *different* kinds of tongues, to another the interpretation of tongues.

Came not by the will of man.

2 Pet 1:21 for prophecy never came by the will of man, but holy men of God spoke *as they were* moved by the Holy Spirit.

Given from the beginning.

Luke 1:70 As He spoke by the mouth of His holy prophets, Who *have been* since the world began,

Is a sure word.

2 Pet 1:19 And so we have the prophetic word confirmed, which you do well to heed as a light that shines in a dark place, until the day dawns and the morning star rises in your hearts;

They who uttered,

Chosen and sent by God.

1 Sam 3:20 And all Israel from Dan to Beersheba knew that Samuel *had been* established as a prophet of the LORD.

2 Chr 36:15 And the LORD God of their fathers sent *warnings* to them by His messengers, rising up early and sending *them,* because He had compassion on His people and on His dwelling place.

Jer 1:5 "Before I formed you in the womb I knew you; Before you were born I sanctified you; I ordained you a prophet to the nations."

Jer 7:25 Since the day that your fathers came out of the land of Egypt until this day, I have even sent to you all My servants the prophets, daily rising up early and sending *them.*

Amos 2:11 I raised up some of your sons as prophets, And some of your young men as Nazirites. *Is it* not so, O you children of Israel?" Says the LORD.

Sent by Christ.

Matt 23:34 Therefore, indeed, I send you prophets, wise men, and scribes: *some* of them you will kill and crucify, and *some* of them you will scourge in your synagogues and persecute from city to city,

Controlled by the Holy Spirit.

Luke 1:67 Now his father Zacharias was filled with the Holy Spirit, and prophesied, saying:

Acts 1:16 "Men *and* brethren, this Scripture had to be fulfilled, which the Holy Spirit spoke before by the mouth of David concerning Judas, who became a guide to those who arrested Jesus;

Acts 11:28 Then one of them, named Agabus, stood up and showed by the Spirit that there was going to be a great famine throughout all the world, which also happened in the days of Claudius Caesar.

Acts 28:25 So when they did not agree among themselves, they departed after Paul had said one word: "The Holy Spirit spoke rightly through Isaiah the prophet to our fathers,

2 Pet 1:21 for prophecy never came by the will of man, but holy men of God spoke *as they were* moved by the Holy Spirit.

Spoke in the name of the Lord.

2 Chr 33:18 Now the rest of the acts of Manasseh, his prayer to his God, and the words of the seers who spoke to him in the name of the LORD God of Israel, indeed they *are written* in the book of the kings of Israel.

James 5:10 My brethren, take the prophets, who spoke in the name of the Lord, as an example of suffering and patience.

Spoke with authority.

1 Kin 17:1 And Elijah the Tishbite, of the inhabitants of Gilead, said to Ahab, "*As* the LORD God of Israel lives, before whom I stand, there shall not be dew nor rain these years, except at my word."

God accomplishes.

Is 44:26 Who confirms the word of His servant, And performs the counsel of His messengers; Who says to Jerusalem, 'You shall be inhabited,' To the cities of Judah, 'You shall be built,' And I will raise up her waste places;

Acts 3:18 But those things which God foretold by the mouth of all His prophets, that the Christ would suffer, He has thus fulfilled.

Christ the great subject of.

Acts 3:22–24 For Moses truly said to the fathers, '*The LORD your God will raise up for you a Prophet like me from your brethren. Him you shall hear in all things, whatever He says to you.* 23 *And it shall be that every soul who will not hear that Prophet shall be utterly destroyed from among the people.*' 24 Yes, and all the prophets, from Samuel and those who follow, as many as have spoken, have also foretold these days.

Acts 10:43 To Him all the prophets witness that, through His name, whoever believes in Him will receive remission of sins."

1 Pet 1:10–11 Of this salvation the prophets have inquired and searched carefully, who prophesied of the grace *that would come* to you, 11 searching what, or what manner of time, the Spirit of Christ who was in them was indicating when He testified beforehand the sufferings of Christ and the glories that would follow.

Fulfilled respecting Christ.

Luke 24:44 Then He said to them, "These *are* the words which I spoke to you while I was still with you, that all things must be fulfilled which were written in the Law of Moses and *the* Prophets and *the* Psalms concerning Me."

Testimony of Jesus is the spirit of.

Rev 19:10 And I fell at his feet to worship him. But he said to me, "See *that you do* not *do that!* I am your fellow servant, and of your brethren who have the testimony of Jesus. Worship God! For the testimony of Jesus is the spirit of prophecy."

Gift of, promised.

Joel 2:28 "And it shall come to pass afterward That I will pour out My Spirit on all flesh; Your sons and your daughters shall prophesy, Your old men shall dream dreams, Your young men shall see visions.

Acts 2:16–17 But this is what was spoken by the prophet Joel: **17** '*And it shall come to pass in the last days, says God, That I will pour out of My Spirit on all flesh; Your sons and your daughters shall prophesy, Your young men shall see visions, Your old men shall dream dreams.*

Is for our benefit.

1 Pet 1:12 To them it was revealed that, not to themselves, but to us they were ministering the things which now have been reported to you through those who have preached the gospel to you by the Holy Spirit sent from heaven—things which angels desire to look into.

Is a light in dark place.

2 Pet 1:19 And so we have the prophetic word confirmed, which you do well to heed as a light that shines in a dark place, until the day dawns and the morning star rises in your hearts;

Is not of private interpretation.

2 Pet 1:20 knowing this first, that no prophecy of Scripture is of any private interpretation,

Listen to.

1 Thess 5:20 Do not despise prophecies.

2 Pet 1:19 And so we have the prophetic word confirmed, which you do well to heed as a light that shines in a dark place, until the day dawns and the morning star rises in your hearts;

Receive, in faith.

2 Chr 20:20 So they rose early in the morning and went out into the Wilderness of Tekoa; and as they went out, Jehoshaphat stood and said, "Hear me, O Judah and you inhabitants of Jerusalem: Believe in the LORD your God, and you shall be established; believe His prophets, and you shall prosper."

Luke 24:25 Then He said to them, "O foolish ones, and slow of heart to believe in all that the prophets have spoken!

Blessedness of reading, hearing, and keeping.

Rev 1:3 Blessed *is* he who reads and those who hear the words of this prophecy, and keep those things which are written in it; for the time *is* near.

Rev 22:7 "Behold, I am coming quickly! Blessed *is* he who keeps the words of the prophecy of this book."

Sin of,

Pretending to the gift of.

Deut 18:20 But the prophet who presumes to speak a word in My name, which I have not commanded him to speak, or who speaks in the name of other gods, that prophet shall die.'

Jer 14:14–15 And the LORD said to me, "The prophets prophesy lies in My name. I have not sent them, commanded them, nor spoken to them; they prophesy to you a false vision, divination, a worthless thing, and the deceit of their heart. **15** Therefore thus says the LORD concerning the prophets who prophesy in My name, whom I did not send, and who say, 'Sword and famine shall not be in this land'—'By sword and famine those prophets shall be consumed!

Jer 23:13–15 "And I have seen folly in the prophets of Samaria: They prophesied by Baal And caused My people Israel to err. **14** Also I have seen a horrible thing in the prophets of Jerusalem: They commit adultery and walk in lies; They also strengthen the hands of evildoers, So that no one turns back from his wickedness. All of them are like Sodom to Me, And her inhabitants like Gomorrah. **15** "Therefore thus says the LORD of hosts concerning the prophets: 'Behold, I will feed them with wormwood, And make them drink the water of gall; For from the prophets of Jerusalem Profaneness has gone out into all the land.' "

Ezek 13:2–3 "Son of man, prophesy against the prophets of Israel who prophesy, and say to those who prophesy out of their own heart, 'Hear the word of the LORD!' " **3** Thus says the Lord GOD: "Woe to the foolish prophets, who follow their own spirit and have seen nothing!

Not giving ear to.

Neh 9:30 Yet for many years You had patience with them, And testified against them by Your Spirit in Your prophets. Yet they would not listen; Therefore You gave them into the hand of the peoples of the lands.

Adding to, or taking from.

Rev 22:18–19 For I testify to everyone who hears the words of the prophecy of this book: If anyone adds to these things, God will add to him the plagues that are written in this book; **19** and if anyone takes away from the words of the book of this prophecy, God shall take away his part from the Book of Life, from the holy city, and *from* the things which are written in this book.

Gift of, sometimes possessed by unconverted men.

Num 24:2–9 And Balaam raised his eyes, and saw Israel encamped according to their tribes; and the Spirit of God came upon him. **3** Then he took up his oracle and said: "The utterance of Balaam the son of Beor, The utterance of the man whose eyes are opened, **4** The utterance of him who hears the words of God, Who sees the vision of the Almighty, Who falls down, with eyes wide open: **5** "How lovely are your tents, O Jacob! Your dwellings, O Israel! **6** Like valleys that stretch out, Like gardens by the riverside, Like aloes planted by the LORD, Like cedars beside the waters. **7** He shall pour water from his buckets,

And his seed *shall be* in many waters. "His king shall be higher than Agag, And his kingdom shall be exalted. 8 "God brings him out of Egypt; He has strength like a wild ox; He shall consume the nations, his enemies; He shall break their bones And pierce *them* with his arrows. 9 'He bows down, he lies down as a lion; And as a lion, who shall rouse him?' "Blessed *is* he who blesses you, And cursed *is* he who curses you."

1 Sam 19:20 Then Saul sent messengers to take David. And when they saw the group of prophets prophesying, and Samuel standing *as* leader over them, the Spirit of God came upon the messengers of Saul, and they also prophesied.

1 Sam 19:23 So he went there to Naioth in Ramah. Then the Spirit of God was upon him also, and he went on and prophesied until he came to Naioth in Ramah.

Matt 7:22 Many will say to Me in that day, 'Lord, Lord, have we not prophesied in Your name, cast out demons in Your name, and done many wonders in Your name?'

John 11:49–51 And one of them, Caiaphas, being high priest that year, said to them, "You know nothing at all, **50** nor do you consider that it is expedient for us that one man should die for the people, and not that the whole nation should perish." **51** Now this he did not say on his own *authority*; but being high priest that year he prophesied that Jesus would die for the nation,

1 Cor 13:2 And though I have *the gift of* prophecy, and understand all mysteries and all knowledge, and though I have all faith, so that I could remove mountains, but have not love, I am nothing.

Validity of it is tested.

Deut 13:1–3 "If there arises among you a prophet or a dreamer of dreams, and he gives you a sign or a wonder, **2** and the sign or the wonder comes to pass, of which he spoke to you, saying, 'Let us go after other gods'—which you have not known—'and let us serve them,' **3** you shall not listen to the words of that prophet or that dreamer of dreams, for the LORD your God is testing you to know whether you love the LORD your God with all your heart and with all your soul.

Deut 18:22 when a prophet speaks in the name of the LORD, if the thing does not happen or come to pass, that *is* the thing which the LORD has not spoken; the prophet has spoken it presumptuously; you shall not be afraid of him.

PROPHETS

God spoke of old by.

Hos 12:10 I have also spoken by the prophets, And have multiplied visions; I have given symbols through the witness of the prophets."

Heb 1:1 God, who at various times and in various ways spoke in time past to the fathers by the prophets,

The messengers and servants of God.

2 Chr 36:15 And the LORD God of their fathers sent *warnings* to them by His messengers, rising up early and sending *them*, because He had compassion on His people and on His dwelling place.

Is 44:26 Who confirms the word of His servant, And

performs the counsel of His messengers; Who says to Jerusalem, 'You shall be inhabited,' To the cities of Judah, 'You shall be built,' And I will raise up her waste places;

Jer 35:15 I have also sent to you all My servants the prophets, rising up early and sending *them*, saying, 'Turn now everyone from his evil way, amend your doings, and do not go after other gods to serve them; then you will dwell in the land which I have given you and your fathers.' But you have not inclined your ear, nor obeyed Me.

The watchmen of Israel.

Ezek 3:17 "Son of man, I have made you a watchman for the house of Israel; therefore hear a word from My mouth, and give them warning from Me:

Were called

Men of God.

1 Sam 9:6 And he said to him, "Look now, *there is* in this city a man of God, and *he is* an honorable man; all that he says surely comes to pass. So let us go there; perhaps he can show us the way that we should go."

Prophets of God.

Ezra 5:2 So Zerubbabel the son of Shealtiel and Jeshua the son of Jozadak rose up and began to build the house of God which *is* in Jerusalem; and the prophets of God *were* with them, helping them.

Holy prophets.

Luke 1:70 As He spoke by the mouth of His holy prophets, Who *have been* since the world began,

Rev 18:20 "Rejoice over her, O heaven, and *you* holy apostles and prophets, for God has avenged you on her!"

Rev 22:6 Then he said to me, "These words *are* faithful and true." And the Lord God of the holy prophets sent His angel to show His servants the things which must shortly take place.

Holy men of God.

2 Kin 4:9 And she said to her husband, "Look now, I know that this *is* a holy man of God, who passes by us regularly.

2 Pet 1:21 for prophecy never came by the will of man, but holy men of God spoke *as they were* moved by the Holy Spirit.

Seers.

1 Sam 9:9 (Formerly in Israel, when a man went to inquire of God, he spoke thus: "Come, let us go to the seer"; for *he who is* now *called* a prophet was formerly called a seer.)

Women sometimes endowed as.

Joel 2:28 "And it shall come to pass afterward That I will pour out My Spirit on all flesh; Your sons and your daughters shall prophesy, Your old men shall dream dreams, Your young men shall see visions.

God communicated to them

His secret things.

Amos 3:7 Surely the Lord GOD does nothing, Unless He reveals His secret to His servants the prophets.

At various times and in different ways.

Heb 1:1 God, who at various times and in various ways spoke in time past to the fathers by the prophets,

By an audible voice.

Num 12:8 I speak with him face to face, Even plainly, and not in dark sayings; And he sees the form of the LORD. Why then were you not afraid To speak against My servant Moses?"

1 Sam 3:4–14 that the LORD called Samuel. And he answered, "Here I am!" **5** So he ran to Eli and said, "Here I am, for you called me." And he said, "I did not call; lie down again." And he went and lay down. **6** Then the LORD called yet again, "Samuel!" So Samuel arose and went to Eli, and said, "Here I am, for you called me." He answered, "I did not call, my son; lie down again." **7** (Now Samuel did not yet know the LORD, nor was the word of the LORD yet revealed to him.) **8** And the LORD called Samuel again the third time. So he arose and went to Eli, and said, "Here I am, for you did call me." Then Eli perceived that the LORD had called the boy. **9** Therefore Eli said to Samuel, "Go, lie down; and it shall be, if He calls you, that you must say, 'Speak, LORD, for Your servant hears.' " So Samuel went and lay down in his place. **10** Now the LORD came and stood and called as at other times, "Samuel! Samuel!" And Samuel answered, "Speak, for Your servant hears." **11** Then the LORD said to Samuel: "Behold, I will do something in Israel at which both ears of everyone who hears it will tingle. **12** In that day I will perform against Eli all that I have spoken concerning his house, from beginning to end. **13** For I have told him that I will judge his house forever for the iniquity which he knows, because his sons made themselves vile, and he did not restrain them. **14** And therefore I have sworn to the house of Eli that the iniquity of Eli's house shall not be atoned for by sacrifice or offering forever."

By angels.

Dan 8:15–26 Then it happened, when I, Daniel, had seen the vision and was seeking the meaning, that suddenly there stood before me one having the appearance of a man. **16** And I heard a man's voice between *the banks of* the Ulai, who called, and said, "Gabriel, make this *man* understand the vision." **17** So he came near where I stood, and when he came I was afraid and fell on my face; but he said to me, "Understand, son of man, that the vision *refers* to the time of the end." **18** Now, as he was speaking with me, I was in a deep sleep with my face to the ground; but he touched me, and stood me upright. **19** And he said, "Look, I am making known to you what shall happen in the latter time of the indignation; for at the appointed time the end *shall be.* **20** The ram which you saw, having the two horns—*they are* the kings of Media and Persia. **21** And the male goat *is* the kingdom of Greece. The large horn that *is* between its eyes *is* the first king. **22** As for the broken *horn* and the four that stood up in its place, four kingdoms shall arise out of that nation, but not with its power. **23** "And in the latter time of their kingdom, When the transgressors have reached their fullness, A king shall arise, Having fierce features, Who understands sinister schemes. **24** His power shall be mighty, but not by his own power; He shall destroy fearfully, And shall prosper and thrive; He shall destroy the mighty, and *also* the holy people. **25** "Through his cunning He shall cause deceit to prosper under his rule; And he shall exalt *himself* in his heart. He shall destroy many

in *their* prosperity. He shall even rise against the Prince of princes; But he shall be broken without *human* means. **26** "And the vision of the evenings and mornings Which was told is true; Therefore seal up the vision, For *it refers* to many days *in the future.*"

Rev 22:8–9 Now I, John, saw and heard these things. And when I heard and saw, I fell down to worship before the feet of the angel who showed me these things. **9** Then he said to me, "See *that you do* not *do that.* For I am your fellow servant, and of your brethren the prophets, and of those who keep the words of this book. Worship God."

By dreams and visions.

Num 12:6 Then He said, "Hear now My words: If there is a prophet among you, *I,* the LORD, make Myself known to him in a vision; I speak to him in a dream.

Joel 2:28 "And it shall come to pass afterward That I will pour out My Spirit on all flesh; Your sons and your daughters shall prophesy, Your old men shall dream dreams, Your young men shall see visions.

Spoke by the Holy Spirit.

Luke 1:67 Now his father Zacharias was filled with the Holy Spirit, and prophesied, saying:

2 Pet 1:21 for prophecy never came by the will of man, but holy men of God spoke *as they were* moved by the Holy Spirit.

Spoke in the name of the Lord.

2 Chr 33:18 Now the rest of the acts of Manasseh, his prayer to his God, and the words of the seers who spoke to him in the name of the LORD God of Israel, indeed they *are written* in the book of the kings of Israel.

Ezek 3:11 And go, get to the captives, to the children of your people, and speak to them and tell them, 'Thus says the Lord GOD,' whether they hear, or whether they refuse."

James 5:10 My brethren, take the prophets, who spoke in the name of the Lord, as an example of suffering and patience.

Frequently spoke in parables and riddles.

2 Sam 12:1–6 Then the LORD sent Nathan to David. And he came to him, and said to him: "There were two men in one city, one rich and the other poor. **2** The rich *man* had exceedingly many flocks and herds. **3** But the poor *man* had nothing, except one little ewe lamb which he had bought and nourished; and it grew up together with him and with his children. It ate of his own food and drank from his own cup and lay in his bosom; and it was like a daughter to him. **4** And a traveler came to the rich man, who refused to take from his own flock and from his own herd to prepare one for the wayfaring man who had come to him; but he took the poor man's lamb and prepared it for the man who had come to him." **5** So David's anger was greatly aroused against the man, and he said to Nathan, "*As* the LORD lives, the man who has done this shall surely die! **6** And he shall restore fourfold for the lamb, because he did this thing and because he had no pity."

Cf. Is 5:1–7; Ezek 17:2–10

Frequently used actions and objects as signs.

Is 20:2–4 at the same time the LORD spoke by Isaiah the

son of Amoz, saying, "Go, and remove the sackcloth from your body, and take your sandals off your feet." And he did so, walking naked and barefoot. 3 Then the LORD said, "Just as My servant Isaiah has walked naked and barefoot three years *for* a sign and a wonder against Egypt and Ethiopia, 4 so shall the king of Assyria lead away the Egyptians as prisoners and the Ethiopians as captives, young and old, naked and barefoot, with their buttocks uncovered, to the shame of Egypt.

Jer 19:1 Thus says the LORD: "Go and get a potter's earthen flask, and *take* some of the elders of the people and some of the elders of the priests.

Jer 19:10–11 "Then you shall break the flask in the sight of the men who go with you, 11 and say to them, 'Thus says the LORD of hosts: "Even so I will break this people and this city, as *one* breaks a potter's vessel, which cannot be made whole again; and they shall bury *them* in Tophet till *there is* no place to bury.

Jer 27:2–3 "Thus says the LORD to me: 'Make for yourselves bonds and yokes, and put them on your neck, 3 and send them to the king of Edom, the king of Moab, the king of the Ammonites, the king of Tyre, and the king of Sidon, by the hand of the messengers who come to Jerusalem to Zedekiah king of Judah.

Jer 43:9 "Take large stones in your hand, and hide them in the sight of the men of Judah, in the clay in the brick courtyard which *is* at the entrance to Pharaoh's house in Tahpanhes;

Jer 51:63 Now it shall be, when you have finished reading this book, *that* you shall tie a stone to it and throw it out into the Euphrates.

Cf. Ezek 4:1–13; 5:1–4; 7:23; 12:3–7; 21:6–7; 24:1–24; Hos 1:2–9

People's sin sometimes prevented God's communication to.

1 Sam 28:6 And when Saul inquired of the LORD, the LORD did not answer him, either by dreams or by Urim or by the prophets.

Lam 2:9 Her gates have sunk into the ground; He has destroyed and broken her bars. Her king and her princes *are* among the nations; The Law *is* no *more*, And her prophets find no vision from the LORD.

Ezek 7:26 Disaster will come upon disaster, And rumor will be upon rumor. Then they will seek a vision from a prophet; But the law will perish from the priest, And counsel from the elders.

Were required

To be bold and undaunted.

Ezek 2:6 "And you, son of man, do not be afraid of them nor be afraid of their words, though briers and thorns *are* with you and you dwell among scorpions; do not be afraid of their words or dismayed by their looks, though they *are* a rebellious house.

Ezek 3:8–9 Behold, I have made your face strong against their faces, and your forehead strong against their foreheads. 9 Like adamant stone, harder than flint, I have made your forehead; do not be afraid of them, nor be dismayed at their looks, though they *are* a rebellious house."

To be vigilant and faithful.

Ezek 3:17–21 "Son of man, I have made you a watch-

man for the house of Israel; therefore hear a word from My mouth, and give them warning from Me: 18 When I say to the wicked, 'You shall surely die,' and you give him no warning, nor speak to warn the wicked from his wicked way, to save his life, that same wicked *man* shall die in his iniquity; but his blood I will require at your hand. 19 Yet, if you warn the wicked, and he does not turn from his wickedness, nor from his wicked way, he shall die in his iniquity; but you have delivered your soul. 20 "Again, when a righteous *man* turns from his righteousness and commits iniquity, and I lay a stumbling block before him, he shall die; because you did not give him warning, he shall die in his sin, and his righteousness which he has done shall not be remembered; but his blood I will require at your hand. 21 Nevertheless if you warn the righteous *man* that the righteous should not sin, and he does not sin, he shall surely live because he took warning; also you will have delivered your soul."

To receive with attention all God's communications.

Ezek 3:10 Moreover He said to me: "Son of man, receive into your heart all My words that I speak to you, and hear with your ears.

To speak nothing but God's words.

Deut 18:20 But the prophet who presumes to speak a word in My name, which I have not commanded him to speak, or who speaks in the name of other gods, that prophet shall die.'

To declare everything that the Lord commanded.

Jer 26:2 "Thus says the LORD: 'Stand in the court of the LORD's house, and speak to all the cities of Judah, which come to worship *in* the LORD's house, all the words that I command you to speak to them. Do not diminish a word.

Words sometimes uttered under great bodily and mental excitement.

Jer 23:9 My heart within me is broken Because of the prophets; All my bones shake. I am like a drunken man, And like a man whom wine has overcome, Because of the LORD, And because of His holy words.

Ezek 3:14–15 So the Spirit lifted me up and took me away, and I went in bitterness, in the heat of my spirit; but the hand of the LORD was strong upon me. 15 Then I came to the captives at Tel Abib, who dwelt by the River Chebar; and I sat where they sat, and remained there astonished among them seven days.

Dan 7:28 "This *is* the end of the account. As for me, Daniel, my thoughts greatly troubled me, and my countenance changed; but I kept the matter in my heart."

Dan 10:8 Therefore I was left alone when I saw this great vision, and no strength remained in me; for my vigor was turned to frailty in me, and I retained no strength.

Hab 3:2 O LORD, I have heard Your speech *and* was afraid; O LORD, revive Your work in the midst of the years! In the midst of the years make *it* known; In wrath remember mercy.

Hab 3:16 When I heard, my body trembled; My lips quivered at *the* voice; Rottenness entered my bones; And I trembled in myself, That I might rest in the day of trouble. When he comes up to the people, He will invade them with his troops.

Sometimes spoke in verse.

Deut 32:44 So Moses came with Joshua the son of Nun and spoke all the words of this song in the hearing of the people.

Is 5:1 Now let me sing to my Well-beloved A song of my Beloved regarding His vineyard: My Well-beloved has a vineyard On a very fruitful hill.

Sometimes accompanied by music while speaking.

1 Sam 10:5 After that you shall come to the hill of God where the Philistine garrison *is.* And it will happen, when you have come there to the city, that you will meet a group of prophets coming down from the high place with a stringed instrument, a tambourine, a flute, and a harp before them; and they will be prophesying.

2 Kin 3:15 But now bring me a musician." Then it happened, when the musician played, that the hand of the LORD came upon him.

Often their words written and read.

2 Chr 21:12 And a letter came to him from Elijah the prophet, saying, Thus says the LORD God of your father David: Because you have not walked in the ways of Jehoshaphat your father, or in the ways of Asa king of Judah,

Jer 36:2 "Take a scroll of a book and write on it all the words that I have spoken to you against Israel, against Judah, and against all the nations, from the day I spoke to you, from the days of Josiah even to this day.

Luke 4:17 And He was handed the book of the prophet Isaiah. And when He had opened the book, He found the place where it was written:

Acts 13:15 And after the reading of the Law and the Prophets, the rulers of the synagogue sent to them, saying, "Men *and* brethren, if you have any word of exhortation for the people, say on."

Ordinary ones

Numerous in Israel.

1 Sam 10:5 After that you shall come to the hill of God where the Philistine garrison *is.* And it will happen, when you have come there to the city, that you will meet a group of prophets coming down from the high place with a stringed instrument, a tambourine, a flute, and a harp before them; and they will be prophesying.

1 Kin 18:4 For so it was, while Jezebel massacred the prophets of the LORD, that Obadiah had taken one hundred prophets and hidden them, fifty to a cave, and had fed them with bread and water.)

Trained up and instructed in schools.

1 Sam 19:20 Then Saul sent messengers to take David. And when they saw the group of prophets prophesying, and Samuel standing *as* leader over them, the Spirit of God came upon the messengers of Saul, and they also prophesied.

2 Kin 2:3 Now the sons of the prophets who *were* at Bethel came out to Elisha, and said to him, "Do you know that the LORD will take away your master from over you today?" And he said, "Yes, I know; keep silent!"

2 Kin 2:5 Now the sons of the prophets who *were* at Jericho came to Elisha and said to him, "Do you know

that the LORD will take away your master from over you today?" So he answered, "Yes, I know; keep silent!"

Were sacred poets of the Jews.

Ex 15:20–21 Then Miriam the prophetess, the sister of Aaron, took the timbrel in her hand; and all the women went out after her with timbrels and with dances. **21** And Miriam answered them: "Sing to the LORD, For He has triumphed gloriously! The horse and its rider He has thrown into the sea!"

1 Sam 10:5 After that you shall come to the hill of God where the Philistine garrison *is.* And it will happen, when you have come there to the city, that you will meet a group of prophets coming down from the high place with a stringed instrument, a tambourine, a flute, and a harp before them; and they will be prophesying.

1 Sam 10:10 When they came there to the hill, there was a group of prophets to meet him; then the Spirit of God came upon him, and he prophesied among them.

1 Chr 25:1 Moreover David and the captains of the army separated for the service *some* of the sons of Asaph, of Heman, and of Jeduthun, who *should* prophesy with harps, stringed instruments, and cymbals. And the number of the skilled men performing their service was:

Extraordinary ones

Specially raised up on occasions of emergency.

1 Sam 3:19–21 So Samuel grew, and the LORD was with him, and let none of his words fall to the ground. **20** And all Israel from Dan to Beersheba knew that Samuel *had been* established as a prophet of the LORD. **21** Then the LORD appeared again in Shiloh. For the LORD revealed Himself to Samuel in Shiloh by the word of the LORD.

Is 6:8–9 Also I heard the voice of the Lord, saying: "Whom shall I send, And who will go for Us?" Then I said, "Here *am* I! Send me." **9** And He said, "Go, and tell this people: 'Keep on hearing, but do not understand; Keep on seeing, but do not perceive.'

Jer 1:5 "Before I formed you in the womb I knew you; Before you were born I sanctified you; I ordained you a prophet to the nations."

Often endued with miraculous power.

Ex 4:1–4 Then Moses answered and said, "But suppose they will not believe me or listen to my voice; suppose they say, 'The LORD has not appeared to you.'" **2** So the LORD said to him, "What *is* that in your hand?" He said, "A rod." **3** And He said, "Cast it on the ground." So he cast it on the ground, and it became a serpent; and Moses fled from it. **4** Then the LORD said to Moses, "Reach out your hand and take *it* by the tail" (and he reached out his hand and caught it, and it became a rod in his hand),

1 Kin 17:23 And Elijah took the child and brought him down from the upper room into the house, and gave him to his mother. And Elijah said, "See, your son lives!"

2 Kin 5:3–8 Then she said to her mistress, "If only my master *were* with the prophet who *is* in Samaria! For he would heal him of his leprosy." **4** And *Naaman* went in and told his master, saying, "Thus and thus said the girl who *is* from the land of Israel." **5** Then the king of Syria said, "Go now, and I will send a letter to the king of Israel." So he departed and took with him ten talents of silver, six thousand *shekels* of gold, and ten changes of clothing. **6** Then he brought the letter to the king of Israel, which said, Now be advised, when this letter comes to you, that I have sent Naaman my servant to you, that you may heal him of his leprosy. **7** And it happened, when the king of Israel read the letter, that he tore his clothes and said, "*Am* I God, to kill and make alive, that this man sends a man to me to heal him of his leprosy? Therefore please consider, and see how he seeks a quarrel with me." **8** So it was, when Elisha the man of God heard that the king of Israel had torn his clothes, that he sent to the king, saying, "Why have you torn your clothes? Please let him come to me, and he shall know that there is a prophet in Israel."

Frequently were married men.

2 Kin 4:1 A certain woman of the wives of the sons of the prophets cried out to Elisha, saying, "Your servant my husband is dead, and you know that your servant feared the LORD. And the creditor is coming to take my two sons to be his slaves."

Ezek 24:18 So I spoke to the people in the morning, and at evening my wife died; and the next morning I did as I was commanded.

Sometimes wore a dress of coarse hair.

2 Kin 1:8 So they answered him, "A hairy man wearing a leather belt around his waist." And he said, "It *is* Elijah the Tishbite."

Zech 13:4 "And it shall be in that day *that* every prophet will be ashamed of his vision when he prophesies; they will not wear a robe of coarse hair to deceive.

Matt 3:4 Now John himself was clothed in camel's hair, with a leather belt around his waist; and his food was locusts and wild honey.

Rev 11:3 And I will give *power* to my two witnesses, and they will prophesy one thousand two hundred and sixty days, clothed in sackcloth."

Often led a wandering and unsettled life.

1 Kin 18:10–12 *As* the LORD your God lives, there is no nation or kingdom where my master has not sent someone to hunt for you; and when they said, '*He is* not *here*,' he took an oath from the kingdom or nation that they could not find you. **11** And now you say, 'Go, tell your master, "Elijah *is here*" '! **12** And it shall come to pass, *as soon as* I am gone from you, that the Spirit of the LORD will carry you to a place I do not know; so when I go and tell Ahab, and he cannot find you, he will kill me. But I your servant have feared the LORD from my youth.

1 Kin 19:3 And when he saw *that*, he arose and ran for his life, and went to Beersheba, which *belongs* to Judah, and left his servant there.

1 Kin 19:8 So he arose, and ate and drank; and he went in the strength of that food forty days and forty nights as far as Horeb, the mountain of God.

1 Kin 19:15 Then the LORD said to him: "Go, return on your way to the Wilderness of Damascus; and when you arrive, anoint Hazael *as* king over Syria.

2 Kin 4:10 Please, let us make a small upper room on the wall; and let us put a bed for him there, and a table and a chair and a lampstand; so it will be, whenever he comes to us, he can turn in there."

Simple in their manner of life.

Matt 3:4 Now John himself was clothed in camel's hair, with a leather belt around his waist; and his food was locusts and wild honey.

The historians for Israel.

1 Chr 29:29 Now the acts of King David, first and last, indeed they *are* written in the book of Samuel the seer, in the book of Nathan the prophet, and in the book of Gad the seer,

2 Chr 9:29 Now the rest of the acts of Solomon, first and last, *are* they not written in the book of Nathan the prophet, in the prophecy of Ahijah the Shilonite, and in the visions of Iddo the seer concerning Jeroboam the son of Nebat?

The interpreters of dreams.

Dan 1:17 As for these four young men, God gave them knowledge and skill in all literature and wisdom; and Daniel had understanding in all visions and dreams.

Were consulted in all difficulties.

1 Sam 9:6 And he said to him, "Look now, *there is* in this city a man of God, and *he is* an honorable man; all that he says surely comes to pass. So let us go there; perhaps he can show us the way that we should go."

1 Sam 28:15 Now Samuel said to Saul, "Why have you disturbed me by bringing me up?" And Saul answered, "I am deeply distressed; for the Philistines make war against me, and God has departed from me and does not answer me anymore, neither by prophets nor by dreams. Therefore I have called you, that you may reveal to me what I should do."

1 Kin 14:2–4 And Jeroboam said to his wife, "Please arise, and disguise yourself, that they may not recognize you as the wife of Jeroboam, and go to Shiloh. Indeed, Ahijah the prophet *is* there, who told me that I *would be* king over this people. **3** Also take with you ten loaves, *some* cakes, and a jar of honey, and go to him; he will tell you what will become of the child." **4** And Jeroboam's wife did so; she arose and went to Shiloh, and came to the house of Ahijah. But Ahijah could not see, for his eyes were glazed by reason of his age.

1 Kin 22:7 And Jehoshaphat said, "*Is there* not still a prophet of the LORD here, that we may inquire of Him?"

Presented with gifts by those who consulted them.

1 Sam 9:7–8 Then Saul said to his servant, "But look, *if* we go, what shall we bring the man? For the bread in our vessels is all gone, and *there is* no present to bring to the man of God. What do we have?" **8** And the servant answered Saul again and said, "Look, I have here at hand one-fourth of a shekel of silver. I will give *that* to the man of God, to tell us our way."

1 Kin 14:3 Also take with you ten loaves, *some* cakes, and a jar of honey, and go to him; he will tell you what will become of the child."

Sometimes thought it right to reject presents.

2 Kin 5:15–16 And he returned to the man of God, he and all his aides, and came and stood before him; and he said, "Indeed, now I know that *there is* no God in all the earth, except in Israel; now therefore, please take a gift from your servant." **16** But he said, "*As the* LORD *lives, before whom I stand, I will receive nothing.*" And he urged him to take *it,* but he refused.

Were sent to

Reprove the wicked and exhort to repentance.

2 Kin 17:13 Yet the LORD testified against Israel and against Judah, by all of His prophets, every seer, saying, "Turn from your evil ways, and keep My commandments *and* My statutes, according to all the law which I commanded your fathers, and which I sent to you by My servants the prophets."

2 Chr 24:19 Yet He sent prophets to them, to bring them back to the LORD; and they testified against them, but they would not listen.

Jer 25:4–5 And the LORD has sent to you all His servants the prophets, rising early and sending *them,* but you have not listened nor inclined your ear to hear. **5** They said, 'Repent now everyone of his evil way and his evil doings, and dwell in the land that the LORD has given to you and your fathers forever and ever.

Denounce the wickedness of kings.

1 Sam 15:16–19 Then Samuel said to Saul, "Be quiet! And I will tell you what the LORD said to me last night." And he said to him, "Speak on." **17** So Samuel said, "When you *were* little in your own eyes, *were* you not head of the tribes of Israel? And did not the LORD anoint you king over Israel? **18** Now the LORD sent you on a mission, and said, 'Go, and utterly destroy the sinners, the Amalekites, and fight against them until they are consumed.' **19** Why then did you not obey the voice of the LORD? Why did you swoop down on the spoil, and do evil in the sight of the LORD?"

2 Sam 12:7–12 Then Nathan said to David, "You *are* the man! Thus says the LORD God of Israel: 'I anointed you king over Israel, and I delivered you from the hand of Saul. **8** I gave you your master's house and your master's wives into your keeping, and gave you the house of Israel and Judah. And if *that had been* too little, I also would have given you much more! **9** Why have you despised the commandment of the LORD, to do evil in His sight? You have killed Uriah the Hittite with the sword; you have taken his wife *to be* your wife, and have killed him with the sword of the people of Ammon. **10** Now therefore, the sword shall never depart from your house, because you have despised Me, and have taken the wife of Uriah the Hittite to be your wife.' **11** Thus says the LORD: 'Behold, I will raise up adversity against you from your own house; and I will take your wives before your eyes and give *them* to your neighbor, and he shall lie with your wives in the sight of this sun. **12** For you did *it* secretly, but I will do this thing before all Israel, before the sun.' "

1 Kin 18:18 And he answered, "I have not troubled Israel, but you and your father's house *have,* in that you have forsaken the commandments of the LORD and have followed the Baals.

1 Kin 21:17–22 Then the word of the LORD came to Elijah the Tishbite, saying, **18** "Arise, go down to meet Ahab king of Israel, who *lives* in Samaria. There *he is,* in the vineyard of Naboth, where he has gone down to take possession of it. **19** You shall speak to him,

saying, 'Thus says the LORD: "Have you murdered and also taken possession?" ' And you shall speak to him, saying, 'Thus says the LORD: "In the place where dogs licked the blood of Naboth, dogs shall lick your blood, even yours." ' " **20** So Ahab said to Elijah, "Have you found me, O my enemy?" And he answered, "I have found *you,* because you have sold yourself to do evil in the sight of the LORD: **21** 'Behold, I will bring calamity on you. I will take away your posterity, and will cut off from Ahab every male in Israel, both bond and free. **22** I will make your house like the house of Jeroboam the son of Nebat, and like the house of Baasha the son of Ahijah, because of the provocation with which you have provoked *Me* to anger, and made Israel sin.'

Exhort to faithfulness in God's service.

2 Chr 15:1–2 Now the Spirit of God came upon Azariah the son of Oded. **2** And he went out to meet Asa, and said to him: "Hear me, Asa, and all Judah and Benjamin. The LORD *is* with you while you are with Him. If you seek Him, He will be found by you; but if you forsake Him, He will forsake you.

2 Chr 15:7 But you, be strong and do not let your hands be weak, for your work shall be rewarded!"

Predict the coming of Christ.

Luke 24:44 Then He said to them, "These *are* the words which I spoke to you while I was still with you, that all things must be fulfilled which were written in the Law of Moses and *the* Prophets and *the* Psalms concerning Me."

John 1:45 Philip found Nathanael and said to him, "We have found Him of whom Moses in the law, and also the prophets, wrote—Jesus of Nazareth, the son of Joseph."

Acts 3:24 Yes, and all the prophets, from Samuel and those who follow, as many as have spoken, have also foretold these days.

Acts 10:43 To Him all the prophets witness that, through His name, whoever believes in Him will receive remission of sins."

Predict the downfall of nations.

Is 15:1 The burden against Moab. Because in the night Ar of Moab is laid waste *And* destroyed, Because in the night Kir of Moab is laid waste *And* destroyed,

Is 17:1 The burden against Damascus. "Behold, Damascus will cease from *being* a city, And it will be a ruinous heap.

Cf. Jer 47:1—51:64

Felt deeply about some prophecies.

Is 16:9–11 Therefore I will bewail the vine of Sibmah, With the weeping of Jazer; I will drench you with my tears, O Heshbon and Elealeh; For battle cries have fallen Over your summer fruits and your harvest. **10** Gladness is taken away, And joy from the plentiful field; In the vineyards there will be no singing, Nor will there be shouting; No treaders will tread out wine in the presses; I have made their shouting cease. **11** Therefore my heart shall resound like a harp for Moab, And my inner being for Kir Heres.

Jer 9:1–7 Oh, that my head were waters, And my eyes a fountain of tears, That I might weep day and night For the slain of the daughter of my people! **2** Oh, that

I had in the wilderness A lodging place for travelers; That I might leave my people, And go from them! For they *are* all adulterers, An assembly of treacherous men. 3 "And *like* their bow they have bent their tongues *for* lies. They are not valiant for the truth on the earth. For they proceed from evil to evil, And they do not know Me," says the LORD. 4 "Everyone take heed to his neighbor, And do not trust any brother; For every brother will utterly supplant, And every neighbor will walk with slanderers. 5 Everyone will deceive his neighbor, And will not speak the truth; They have taught their tongue to speak lies; They weary themselves to commit iniquity. 6 Your dwelling place *is* in the midst of deceit; Through deceit they refuse to know Me," says the LORD. 7 Therefore thus says the LORD of hosts: "Behold, I will refine them and try them; For how shall I deal with the daughter of My people?

Words of,

Frequently proclaimed at the gate of the Lord's house.

Jer 7:2 "Stand in the gate of the LORD's house, and proclaim there this word, and say, 'Hear the word of the LORD, all *you of* Judah who enter in at these gates to worship the LORD!' "

Proclaimed in the cities and streets.

Jer 11:6 Then the LORD said to me, "Proclaim all these words in the cities of Judah and in the streets of Jerusalem, saying: 'Hear the words of this covenant and do them.

Written on tablets for the public.

Hab 2:2 Then the LORD answered me and said: "Write the vision And make *it* plain on tablets, That he may run who reads it.

Written on scrolls and read to the people.

Is 8:1 Moreover the LORD said to me, "Take a large scroll, and write on it with a man's pen concerning Maher-Shalal-Hash-Baz.

Jer 36:2 "Take a scroll of a book and write on it all the words that I have spoken to you against Israel, against Judah, and against all the nations, from the day I spoke to you, from the days of Josiah even to this day.

Were all fulfilled.

2 Kin 10:10 Know now that nothing shall fall to the earth of the word of the LORD which the LORD spoke concerning the house of Ahab; for the LORD has done what He spoke by His servant Elijah."

Is 44:26 Who confirms the word of His servant, And performs the counsel of His messengers; Who says to Jerusalem, 'You shall be inhabited,' To the cities of Judah, 'You shall be built,' And I will raise up her waste places;

Acts 3:18 But those things which God foretold by the mouth of all His prophets, that the Christ would suffer, He has thus fulfilled.

Rev 10:7 but in the days of the sounding of the seventh angel, when he is about to sound, the mystery of God would be finished, as He declared to His servants the prophets.

Assisted in national undertakings.

Ezra 5:2 So Zerubbabel the son of Shealtiel and Jeshua the son of Jozadak rose up and began to build the house of God which *is* in Jerusalem; and the prophets of God *were* with them, helping them.

Mentioned in Scripture

Enoch.

Gen 5:21–24 Enoch lived sixty-five years, and begot Methuselah. 22 After he begot Methuselah, Enoch walked with God three hundred years, and had sons and daughters. 23 So all the days of Enoch were three hundred and sixty-five years. 24 And Enoch walked with God; and he *was* not, for God took him.

Jude 1:14 Now Enoch, the seventh from Adam, prophesied about these men also, saying, "Behold, the Lord comes with ten thousands of His saints,

Noah.

Gen 9:25–27 Then he said: "Cursed *be* Canaan; A servant of servants He shall be to his brethren." 26 And he said: "Blessed *be* the LORD, The God of Shem, And may Canaan be his servant. 27 May God enlarge Japheth, And may he dwell in the tents of Shem; And may Canaan be his servant."

Abraham.

Gen 20:7 Now therefore, restore the man's wife; for he *is* a prophet, and he will pray for you and you shall live. But if you do not restore *her,* know that you shall surely die, you and all who *are* yours."

Jacob.

Gen 49:1 And Jacob called his sons and said, "Gather together, that I may tell you what shall befall you in the last days:

Aaron.

Ex 7:1 So the LORD said to Moses: "See, I have made you *as* God to Pharaoh, and Aaron your brother shall be your prophet.

Moses.

Deut 18:18 I will raise up for them a Prophet like you from among their brethren, and will put My words in His mouth, and He shall speak to them all that I command Him.

Miriam.

Ex 15:20 Then Miriam the prophetess, the sister of Aaron, took the timbrel in her hand; and all the women went out after her with timbrels and with dances.

Deborah.

Judg 4:4 Now Deborah, a prophetess, the wife of Lapidoth, was judging Israel at that time.

A prophet sent to Israel.

Judg 6:8 that the LORD sent a prophet to the children of Israel, who said to them, "Thus says the LORD God of Israel: 'I brought you up from Egypt and brought you out of the house of bondage;

A prophet sent to Eli.

1 Sam 2:27 Then a man of God came to Eli and said to him, "Thus says the LORD: 'Did I not clearly reveal Myself to the house of your father when they were in Egypt in Pharaoh's house?

Samuel.

1 Sam 3:20 And all Israel from Dan to Beersheba knew that Samuel *had been* established as a prophet of the LORD.

David.

Ps 16:8–11 I have set the LORD always before me; Because *He is* at my right hand I shall not be moved. **9** Therefore my heart is glad, and my glory rejoices; My flesh also will rest in hope. **10** For You will not leave my soul in Sheol, Nor will You allow Your Holy One to see corruption. **11** You will show me the path of life; In Your presence *is* fullness of joy; At Your right hand *are* pleasures forevermore.

Acts 2:25 For David says concerning Him: *'I foresaw the LORD always before my face, For He is at my right hand, that I may not be shaken.*

Acts 2:30 Therefore, being a prophet, and knowing that God had sworn with an oath to him that of the fruit of his body, according to the flesh, He would raise up the Christ to sit on his throne,

Nathan.

2 Sam 7:2 that the king said to Nathan the prophet, "See now, I dwell in a house of cedar, but the ark of God dwells inside tent curtains."

2 Sam 12:1 Then the LORD sent Nathan to David. And he came to him, and said to him: "There were two men in one city, one rich and the other poor.

1 Kin 1:10 But he did not invite Nathan the prophet, Benaiah, the mighty men, or Solomon his brother.

Zadok.

2 Sam 15:27 The king also said to Zadok the priest, "*Are* you *not* a seer? Return to the city in peace, and your two sons with you, Ahimaaz your son, and Jonathan the son of Abiathar.

Gad.

2 Sam 24:11 Now when David arose in the morning, the word of the LORD came to the prophet Gad, David's seer, saying,

1 Chr 29:29 Now the acts of King David, first and last, indeed they *are* written in the book of Samuel the seer, in the book of Nathan the prophet, and in the book of Gad the seer,

Ahijah.

1 Kin 11:29 Now it happened at that time, when Jeroboam went out of Jerusalem, that the prophet Ahijah the Shilonite met him on the way; and he had clothed himself with a new garment, and the two *were* alone in the field.

1 Kin 12:15 So the king did not listen to the people; for the turn *of events* was from the LORD, that He might fulfill His word, which the LORD had spoken by Ahijah the Shilonite to Jeroboam the son of Nebat.

2 Chr 9:29 Now the rest of the acts of Solomon, first and last, *are* they not written in the book of Nathan the prophet, in the prophecy of Ahijah the Shilonite, and in the visions of Iddo the seer concerning Jeroboam the son of Nebat?

A prophet of Judah.

1 Kin 13:1 And behold, a man of God went from Judah to Bethel by the word of the LORD, and Jeroboam stood by the altar to burn incense.

Iddo.

2 Chr 9:29 Now the rest of the acts of Solomon, first and last, *are* they not written in the book of Nathan the prophet, in the prophecy of Ahijah the Shilonite, and in the visions of Iddo the seer concerning Jeroboam the son of Nebat?

2 Chr 12:15 The acts of Rehoboam, first and last, *are* they not written in the book of Shemaiah the prophet, and of Iddo the seer concerning genealogies? And *there were* wars between Rehoboam and Jeroboam all their days.

Shemaiah.

1 Kin 12:22 But the word of God came to Shemaiah the man of God, saying,

2 Chr 12:7 Now when the LORD saw that they humbled themselves, the word of the LORD came to Shemaiah, saying, "They have humbled themselves; *therefore* I will not destroy them, but I will grant them some deliverance. My wrath shall not be poured out on Jerusalem by the hand of Shishak.

2 Chr 12:15 The acts of Rehoboam, first and last, *are* they not written in the book of Shemaiah the prophet, and of Iddo the seer concerning genealogies? And *there were* wars between Rehoboam and Jeroboam all their days.

Azariah the son of Oded.

2 Chr 15:2 And he went out to meet Asa, and said to him: "Hear me, Asa, and all Judah and Benjamin. The LORD *is* with you while you are with Him. If you seek Him, He will be found by you; but if you forsake Him, He will forsake you.

2 Chr 15:8 And when Asa heard these words and the prophecy of Oded the prophet, he took courage, and removed the abominable idols from all the land of Judah and Benjamin and from the cities which he had taken in the mountains of Ephraim; and he restored the altar of the LORD that *was* before the vestibule of the LORD.

Hanani.

2 Chr 16:7 And at that time Hanani the seer came to Asa king of Judah, and said to him: "Because you have relied on the king of Syria, and have not relied on the LORD your God, therefore the army of the king of Syria has escaped from your hand.

Jehu the son of Hanani.

1 Kin 16:1 Then the word of the LORD came to Jehu the son of Hanani, against Baasha, saying:

1 Kin 16:7 And also the word of the LORD came by the prophet Jehu the son of Hanani against Baasha and his house, because of all the evil that he did in the sight of the LORD in provoking Him to anger with the work of his hands, in being like the house of Jeroboam, and because he killed them.

1 Kin 16:12 Thus Zimri destroyed all the household of Baasha, according to the word of the LORD, which He spoke against Baasha by Jehu the prophet,

Elijah.

1 Kin 17:1 And Elijah the Tishbite, of the inhabitants of Gilead, said to Ahab, "*As* the LORD God of Israel lives, before whom I stand, there shall not be dew nor rain these years, except at my word."

Elisha.

1 Kin 19:16 Also you shall anoint Jehu the son of Nimshi *as* king over Israel. And Elisha the son of Shaphat of Abel Meholah you shall anoint *as* prophet in your place.

Micaiah the son of Imlah.

1 Kin 22:7–8 And Jehoshaphat said, "*Is there* not still a prophet of the LORD here, that we may inquire of Him?" **8** So the king of Israel said to Jehoshaphat, "*There is* still one man, Micaiah the son of Imlah, by whom we may inquire of the LORD; but I hate him, because he does not prophesy good concerning me, but evil." And Jehoshaphat said, "Let not the king say such things!"

Jonah.

2 Kin 14:25 He restored the territory of Israel from the entrance of Hamath to the Sea of the Arabah, according to the word of the LORD God of Israel, which He had spoken through His servant Jonah the son of Amittai, the prophet who *was* from Gath Hepher.

Jon 1:1 Now the word of the LORD came to Jonah the son of Amittai, saying,

Matt 12:39 But He answered and said to them, "An evil and adulterous generation seeks after a sign, and no sign will be given to it except the sign of the prophet Jonah.

Isaiah.

2 Kin 19:2 Then he sent Eliakim, who *was* over the household, Shebna the scribe, and the elders of the priests, covered with sackcloth, to Isaiah the prophet, the son of Amoz.

2 Chr 26:22 Now the rest of the acts of Uzziah, from first to last, the prophet Isaiah the son of Amoz wrote.

Is 1:1 The vision of Isaiah the son of Amoz, which he saw concerning Judah and Jerusalem in the days of Uzziah, Jotham, Ahaz, *and* Hezekiah, kings of Judah.

Hosea.

Hos 1:1 The word of the LORD that came to Hosea the son of Beeri, in the days of Uzziah, Jotham, Ahaz, *and* Hezekiah, kings of Judah, and in the days of Jeroboam the son of Joash, king of Israel.

Amos.

Amos 1:1 The words of Amos, who was among the sheepbreeders of Tekoa, which he saw concerning Israel in the days of Uzziah king of Judah, and in the days of Jeroboam the son of Joash, king of Israel, two years before the earthquake.

Amos 7:14–15 Then Amos answered, and said to Amaziah: "I *was* no prophet, Nor *was* I a son of a prophet, But I *was* a sheepbreeder And a tender of sycamore fruit. **15** Then the LORD took me as I followed the flock, And the LORD said to me, 'Go, prophesy to My people Israel.'

Micah.

Mic 1:1 The word of the LORD that came to Micah of Moresheth in the days of Jotham, Ahaz, *and* Hezekiah, kings of Judah, which he saw concerning Samaria and Jerusalem.

Oded.

2 Chr 28:9 But a prophet of the LORD was there, whose name *was* Oded; and he went out before the army that came to Samaria, and said to them: "Look, because the LORD God of your fathers was angry with Judah, He has delivered them into your hand; but you have killed them in a rage *that* reaches up to heaven.

Nahum.

Nah 1:1 The burden against Nineveh. The book of the vision of Nahum the Elkoshite.

Joel.

Joel 1:1 The word of the LORD that came to Joel the son of Pethuel.

Acts 2:16 But this is what was spoken by the prophet Joel:

Zephaniah.

Zeph 1:1 The word of the LORD which came to Zephaniah the son of Cushi, the son of Gedaliah, the son of Amariah, the son of Hezekiah, in the days of Josiah the son of Amon, king of Judah.

Huldah.

2 Kin 22:14 So Hilkiah the priest, Ahikam, Achbor, Shaphan, and Asaiah went to Huldah the prophetess, the wife of Shallum the son of Tikvah, the son of Harhas, keeper of the wardrobe. (She dwelt in Jerusalem in the Second Quarter.) And they spoke with her.

Jeduthun.

2 Chr 35:15 And the singers, the sons of Asaph, *were* in their places, according to the command of David, Asaph, Heman, and Jeduthun the king's seer. Also the gatekeepers were at each gate; they did not have to leave their position, because their brethren the Levites prepared portions for them.

Jeremiah.

2 Chr 36:12 He did evil in the sight of the LORD his God, *and* did not humble himself before Jeremiah the prophet, *who spoke* from the mouth of the LORD.

2 Chr 36:21 to fulfill the word of the LORD by the mouth of Jeremiah, until the land had enjoyed her Sabbaths. As long as she lay desolate she kept Sabbath, to fulfill seventy years.

Jer 1:1–2 The words of Jeremiah the son of Hilkiah, of the priests who *were* in Anathoth in the land of Benjamin, **2** to whom the word of the LORD came in the days of Josiah the son of Amon, king of Judah, in the thirteenth year of his reign.

Habakkuk.

Hab 1:1 The burden which the prophet Habakkuk saw.

Obadiah.

Obad 1:1 The vision of Obadiah. Thus says the Lord GOD concerning Edom (We have heard a report from the LORD, And a messenger has been sent among the nations, *saying,* "Arise, and let us rise up against her for battle"):

Ezekiel.

Ezek 1:3 the word of the LORD came expressly to Ezekiel the priest, the son of Buzi, in the land of the Chaldeans by the River Chebar; and the hand of the LORD was upon him there.

Daniel.

Dan 12:11 "And from the time *that* the daily *sacrifice* is taken away, and the abomination of desolation is set up, *there shall be* one thousand two hundred and ninety days.

Matt 24:15 "Therefore when you see the '*abomination of desolation,*' spoken of by Daniel the prophet, standing in the holy place" (whoever reads, let him understand),

Haggai.

Ezra 5:1 Then the prophet Haggai and Zechariah the son of Iddo, prophets, prophesied to the Jews who *were* in Judah and Jerusalem, in the name of the God of Israel, *who was* over them.

Ezra 6:14 So the elders of the Jews built, and they prospered through the prophesying of Haggai the prophet and Zechariah the son of Iddo. And they built and finished *it*, according to the commandment of the God of Israel, and according to the command of Cyrus, Darius, and Artaxerxes king of Persia.

Hag 1:1 In the second year of King Darius, in the sixth month, on the first day of the month, the word of the LORD came by Haggai the prophet to Zerubbabel the son of Shealtiel, governor of Judah, and to Joshua the son of Jehozadak, the high priest, saying,

Zechariah (son of Berechiah) son of Iddo.

Ezra 5:1 Then the prophet Haggai and Zechariah the son of Iddo, prophets, prophesied to the Jews who *were* in Judah and Jerusalem, in the name of the God of Israel, *who was* over them.

Zech 1:1 In the eighth month of the second year of Darius, the word of the LORD came to Zechariah the son of Berechiah, the son of Iddo the prophet, saying,

Malachi.

Mal 1:1 The burden of the word of the LORD to Israel by Malachi.

Zacharias the father of John.

Luke 1:67 Now his father Zacharias was filled with the Holy Spirit, and prophesied, saying:

Anna.

Luke 2:36 Now there was one, Anna, a prophetess, the daughter of Phanuel, of the tribe of Asher. She was of a great age, and had lived with a husband seven years from her virginity;

Agabus.

Acts 11:28 Then one of them, named Agabus, stood up and showed by the Spirit that there was going to be a great famine throughout all the world, which also happened in the days of Claudius Caesar.

Acts 21:10 And as we stayed many days, a certain prophet named Agabus came down from Judea.

The daughters of Philip.

Acts 21:9 Now this man had four virgin daughters who prophesied.

Paul.

1 Tim 4:1 Now the Spirit expressly says that in latter times some will depart from the faith, giving heed to deceiving spirits and doctrines of demons,

Peter.

2 Pet 2:1–2 But there were also false prophets among the people, even as there will be false teachers among you, who will secretly bring in destructive heresies, even denying the Lord who bought them, *and* bring on themselves swift destruction. **2** And many will follow their destructive ways, because of whom the way of truth will be blasphemed.

John.

Rev 1:1 The Revelation of Jesus Christ, which God gave Him to show His servants—things which must shortly take place. And He sent and signified *it* by His angel to His servant John,

One was generally attached to the king's household.

2 Sam 24:11 Now when David arose in the morning, the word of the LORD came to the prophet Gad, David's seer, saying,

2 Chr 29:25 And he stationed the Levites in the house of the LORD with cymbals, with stringed instruments, and with harps, according to the commandment of David, of Gad the king's seer, and of Nathan the prophet; for thus *was* the commandment of the LORD by his prophets.

2 Chr 35:15 And the singers, the sons of Asaph, *were* in their places, according to the command of David, Asaph, Heman, and Jeduthun the king's seer. Also the gatekeepers were at each gate; they did not have to leave their position, because their brethren the Levites prepared portions for them.

The Jews

Required to hear and believe.

Deut 18:15 "The LORD your God will raise up for you a Prophet like me from your midst, from your brethren. Him you shall hear,

2 Chr 20:20 So they rose early in the morning and went out into the Wilderness of Tekoa; and as they went out, Jehoshaphat stood and said, "Hear me, O Judah and you inhabitants of Jerusalem: Believe in the LORD your God, and you shall be established; believe His prophets, and you shall prosper."

Often tried to make them speak smooth things.

1 Kin 22:13 Then the messenger who had gone to call Micaiah spoke to him, saying, "Now listen, the words of the prophets with one accord encourage the king. Please, let your word be like the word of one of them, and speak encouragement."

Is 30:10 Who say to the seers, "Do not see," And to the prophets, "Do not prophesy to us right things; Speak to us smooth things, prophesy deceits.

Amos 2:12 "But you gave the Nazirites wine to drink, And commanded the prophets saying, 'Do not prophesy!'

Persecuted them.

2 Chr 36:16 But they mocked the messengers of God, despised His words, and scoffed at His prophets, until the wrath of the LORD arose against His people, till *there was* no remedy.

Matt 5:12 Rejoice and be exceedingly glad, for great *is* your reward in heaven, for so they persecuted the prophets who were before you.

Often imprisoned them.

1 Kin 22:27 and say, 'Thus says the king: "Put this *fellow* in prison, and feed him with bread of affliction and water of affliction, until I come in peace." ' "

Jer 32:2 For then the king of Babylon's army besieged Jerusalem, and Jeremiah the prophet was shut up in the court of the prison, which *was in* the king of Judah's house.

Jer 37:15–16 Therefore the princes were angry with Jeremiah, and they struck him and put him in prison in the house of Jonathan the scribe. For they had made that the prison. **16** When Jeremiah entered the dungeon and the cells, and Jeremiah had remained there many days,

Often put them to death.

1 Kin 18:13 Was it not reported to my lord what I did when Jezebel killed the prophets of the LORD, how I hid one hundred men of the LORD's prophets, fifty to a cave, and fed them with bread and water?

1 Kin 19:10 So he said, "I have been very zealous for the LORD God of hosts; for the children of Israel have forsaken Your covenant, torn down Your altars, and killed Your prophets with the sword. I alone am left; and they seek to take my life."

Matt 23:34–37 Therefore, indeed, I send you prophets, wise men, and scribes: *some* of them you will kill and crucify, and *some* of them you will scourge in your synagogues and persecute from city to city, **35** that on you may come all the righteous blood shed on the earth, from the blood of righteous Abel to the blood of Zechariah, son of Berechiah, whom you murdered between the temple and the altar. **36** Assuredly, I say to you, all these things will come upon this generation. **37** "O Jerusalem, Jerusalem, the one who kills the prophets and stones those who are sent to her! How often I wanted to gather your children together, as a hen gathers her chicks under *her* wings, but you were not willing!

Often left without, because of the people's sin.

1 Sam 3:1 Now the boy Samuel ministered to the LORD before Eli. And the word of the LORD was rare in those days; *there was* no widespread revelation.

Ps 74:9 We do not see our signs; *There is* no longer any prophet; Nor *is there* any among us who knows how long.

Amos 8:11–12 "Behold, the days are coming," says the Lord GOD, "That I will send a famine on the land, Not a famine of bread, Nor a thirst for water, But of hearing the words of the LORD. **12** They shall wander from sea to sea, And from north to east; They shall run to and fro, seeking the word of the LORD, But shall not find *it.*

Were mighty through faith.

Heb 11:32–40 And what more shall I say? For the time would fail me to tell of Gideon and Barak and Samson and Jephthah, also *of* David and Samuel and the prophets: **33** who through faith subdued kingdoms, worked righteousness, obtained promises, stopped the mouths of lions, **34** quenched the violence of fire, escaped the edge of the sword, out of weakness were made strong, became valiant in battle, turned to flight the armies of the aliens. **35** Women received their dead raised to life again. Others were tortured, not accepting deliverance, that they might obtain a better resurrection. **36** Still others had trial of mockings and scourgings, yes, and of chains and imprisonment. **37** They were stoned, they were sawn in two, were tempted, were slain with the sword. They wandered about in sheepskins and goatskins, being destitute, afflicted, tormented— **38** of whom the world was not worthy. They wandered in deserts and mountains, *in* dens and caves of the earth. **39** And all these, having obtained a good testimony through faith, did not receive the promise, **40** God having provided something better for us, that they should not be made perfect apart from us.

Great patience of, under suffering.

James 5:10 My brethren, take the prophets, who spoke in the name of the Lord, as an example of suffering and patience.

God avenged all injuries done to.

2 Kin 9:7 You shall strike down the house of Ahab your master, that I may avenge the blood of My servants the prophets, and the blood of all the servants of the LORD, at the hand of Jezebel.

1 Chr 16:21–22 He permitted no man to do them wrong; Yes, He rebuked kings for their sakes, **22** *Saying,* "Do not touch My anointed ones, And do My prophets no harm."

Matt 23:35–38 that on you may come all the righteous blood shed on the earth, from the blood of righteous Abel to the blood of Zechariah, son of Berechiah, whom you murdered between the temple and the altar. **36** Assuredly, I say to you, all these things will come upon this generation. **37** "O Jerusalem, Jerusalem, the one who kills the prophets and stones those who are sent to her! How often I wanted to gather your children together, as a hen gathers her chicks under *her* wings, but you were not willing! **38** See! Your house is left to you desolate;

Luke 11:50 that the blood of all the prophets which was shed from the foundation of the world may be required of this generation,

Christ exercised the office of, as predicted.

Deut 18:15 "The LORD your God will raise up for you a Prophet like me from your midst, from your brethren. Him you shall hear,

Acts 3:22 For Moses truly said to the fathers, *'The LORD your God will raise up for you a Prophet like me from your brethren. Him you shall hear in all things, whatever He says to you.*

Cf. Matt 24:1–51; 25:1–46; Mark 10:32–34

PROPHETS, FALSE

Pretended to be sent by God.

Jer 23:17–18 They continually say to those who despise Me, 'The LORD has said, "You shall have peace" '; And *to* everyone who walks according to the dictates of his own heart, they say, 'No evil shall come upon you.' " **18** For who has stood in the counsel of the LORD, And has perceived and heard His word? Who has marked His word and heard *it?*

Jer 23:31 Behold, I *am* against the prophets," says the LORD, "who use their tongues and say, 'He says.'

Not sent or commissioned by God.

Jer 14:14 And the LORD said to me, "The prophets prophesy lies in My name. I have not sent them, commanded them, nor spoken to them; they prophesy to you a false vision, divination, a worthless thing, and the deceit of their heart.

Jer 23:21 "I have not sent these prophets, yet they ran. I have not spoken to them, yet they prophesied.

Jer 29:31 Send to all those in captivity, saying, Thus says the LORD concerning Shemaiah the Nehelamite: Because Shemaiah has prophesied to you, and I have not sent him, and he has caused you to trust in a lie—

Used by God to test Israel.

Deut 13:3 you shall not listen to the words of that prophet or that dreamer of dreams, for the LORD your God is testing you to know whether you love the LORD your God with all your heart and with all your soul.

Described as

Light and treacherous.

Zeph 3:4 Her prophets are insolent, treacherous people; Her priests have polluted the sanctuary, They have done violence to the law.

Covetous.

Mic 3:11 Her heads judge for a bribe, Her priests teach for pay, And her prophets divine for money. Yet they lean on the LORD, and say, "Is not the LORD among us? No harm can come upon us."

Crafty.

Matt 7:15 "Beware of false prophets, who come to you in sheep's clothing, but inwardly they are ravenous wolves.

Drunken.

Is 28:7 But they also have erred through wine, And through intoxicating drink are out of the way; The priest and the prophet have erred through intoxicating drink, They are swallowed up by wine, They are out of the way through intoxicating drink; They err in vision, they stumble *in* judgment.

Immoral and profane.

Jer 23:11 "For both prophet and priest are profane; Yes, in My house I have found their wickedness," says the LORD.

Jer 23:14 Also I have seen a horrible thing in the prophets of Jerusalem: They commit adultery and walk in lies; They also strengthen the hands of evildoers, So that no one turns back from his wickedness. All of them are like Sodom to Me, And her inhabitants like Gomorrah.

Foxes in the desert.

Ezek 13:4 O Israel, your prophets are like foxes in the deserts.

Wind.

Jer 5:13 And the prophets become wind, For the word *is* not in them. Thus shall it be done to them."

Women sometimes acted as.

Neh 6:14 My God, remember Tobiah and Sanballat, according to these their works, and the prophetess Noadiah and the rest of the prophets who would have made me afraid.

Rev 2:20 Nevertheless I have a few things against you, because you allow that woman Jezebel, who calls herself a prophetess, to teach and seduce My servants to commit sexual immorality and eat things sacrificed to idols.

Called foolish prophets.

Ezek 13:2 "Son of man, prophesy against the prophets of Israel who prophesy, and say to those who prophesy out of their own heart, 'Hear the word of the LORD!' "

Influenced by evil spirits.

1 Kin 22:21–22 Then a spirit came forward and stood before the LORD, and said, 'I will persuade him.'

22 The LORD said to him, 'In what way?' So he said, 'I will go out and be a lying spirit in the mouth of all his prophets.' And the LORD said, 'You shall persuade *him,* and also prevail. Go out and do so.'

Prophesied

Falsely.

Jer 5:31 The prophets prophesy falsely, And the priests rule by their *own* power; And My people love to have it so. But what will you do in the end?

Lies in the name of the Lord.

Jer 14:14 And the LORD said to me, "The prophets prophesy lies in My name. I have not sent them, commanded them, nor spoken to them; they prophesy to you a false vision, divination, a worthless thing, and the deceit of their heart.

Out of their own heart.

Jer 23:16 Thus says the LORD of hosts: "Do not listen to the words of the prophets who prophesy to you. They make you worthless; They speak a vision of their own heart, Not from the mouth of the LORD.

Jer 23:26 How long will *this* be in the heart of the prophets who prophesy lies? Indeed *they are* prophets of the deceit of their own heart,

Ezek 13:2 "Son of man, prophesy against the prophets of Israel who prophesy, and say to those who prophesy out of their own heart, 'Hear the word of the LORD!' "

In the name of false gods.

Jer 2:8 The priests did not say, 'Where *is* the LORD?' And those who handle the law did not know Me; The rulers also transgressed against Me; The prophets prophesied by Baal, And walked after *things that* do not profit.

Peace, when there was no peace.

Jer 6:14 They have also healed the hurt of My people slightly, Saying, 'Peace, peace!' When *there is* no peace.

Jer 23:17 They continually say to those who despise Me, 'The LORD has said, "You shall have peace" '; And *to* everyone who walks according to the dictates of his own heart, they say, 'No evil shall come upon you.' "

Ezek 13:10 "Because, indeed, because they have seduced My people, saying, 'Peace!' when *there is* no peace—and one builds a wall, and they plaster it with untempered *mortar*—

Mic 3:5 Thus says the LORD concerning the prophets Who make my people stray; Who chant "Peace" While they chew with their teeth, But who prepare war against him Who puts nothing into their mouths:

Often practiced divination and witchcraft.

Jer 14:14 And the LORD said to me, "The prophets prophesy lies in My name. I have not sent them, commanded them, nor spoken to them; they prophesy to you a false vision, divination, a worthless thing, and the deceit of their heart.

Ezek 22:28 Her prophets plastered them with untempered *mortar,* seeing false visions, and divining lies for them, saying, 'Thus says the Lord GOD,' when the LORD had not spoken.

Acts 13:6 Now when they had gone through the island to Paphos, they found a certain sorcerer, a false prophet, a Jew whose name *was* Bar-Jesus,

Often pretended to dream.

Jer 23:28 "The prophet who has a dream, let him tell a dream; And he who has My word, let him speak My word faithfully. What *is* the chaff to the wheat?" says the LORD.

Jer 23:32 Behold, I *am* against those who prophesy false dreams," says the LORD, "and tell them, and cause My people to err by their lies and by their reckless-ness. Yet I did not send them or command them; therefore they shall not profit this people at all," says the LORD.

Often deceived by God as a judgment.

Ezek 14:9 "And if the prophet is induced to speak any-thing, I the LORD have induced that prophet, and I will stretch out My hand against him and destroy him from among My people Israel.

The Jewish people were,

Led into error by.

Jer 23:13 "And I have seen folly in the prophets of Samaria: They prophesied by Baal And caused My people Israel to err.

Mic 3:5 Thus says the LORD concerning the prophets Who make my people stray; Who chant "Peace" While they chew with their teeth, But who prepare war against him Who puts nothing into their mouths:

Involved in their own ruin by.

Is 9:15–16 The elder and honorable, he *is* the head; The prophet who teaches lies, he *is* the tail. **16** For the leaders of this people cause *them* to err, And *those who are* led by them are destroyed.

Jer 20:6 And you, Pashhur, and all who dwell in your house, shall go into captivity. You shall go to Bab-ylon, and there you shall die, and be buried there, you and all your friends, to whom you have prophe-sied lies.' "

Ezek 14:10 And they shall bear their iniquity; the pun-ishment of the prophet shall be the same as the pun-ishment of the one who inquired,

Made to forget God's name by.

Jer 23:27 who try to make My people forget My name by their dreams which everyone tells his neighbor, as their fathers forgot My name for Baal.

Deprived of God's word by.

Jer 23:30 "Therefore behold, I *am* against the prophets," says the LORD, "who steal My words every one from his neighbor.

Taught immorality and sin by.

Jer 23:14–15 Also I have seen a horrible thing in the prophets of Jerusalem: They commit adultery and walk in lies; They also strengthen the hands of evil-doers, So that no one turns back from his wicked-ness. All of them are like Sodom to Me, And her inhabitants like Gomorrah. **15** "Therefore thus says the LORD of hosts concerning the prophets: 'Behold, I will feed them with wormwood, And make them drink the water of gall; For from the prophets of Jerusalem Profaneness has gone out into all the land.' "

Oppressed and defrauded by.

Ezek 22:25 The conspiracy of her prophets in her midst is like a roaring lion tearing the prey; they have de-

voured people; they have taken treasure and precious things; they have made many widows in her midst.

Warned not to listen to.

Deut 13:3 you shall not listen to the words of that prophet or that dreamer of dreams, for the LORD your God is testing you to know whether you love the LORD your God with all your heart and with all your soul.

Jer 23:16 Thus says the LORD of hosts: "Do not listen to the words of the prophets who prophesy to you. They make you worthless; They speak a vision of their own heart, Not from the mouth of the LORD.

Jer 27:9 Therefore do not listen to your prophets, your diviners, your dreamers, your soothsayers, or your sorcerers, who speak to you, saying, "You shall not serve the king of Babylon."

Jer 27:15–16 for I have not sent them," says the LORD, "yet they prophesy a lie in My name, that I may drive you out, and that you may perish, you and the prophets who prophesy to you." **16** Also I spoke to the priests and to all this people, saying, "Thus says the LORD: 'Do not listen to the words of your proph-ets who prophesy to you, saying, "Behold, the ves-sels of the LORD's house will now shortly be brought back from Babylon"; for they prophesy a lie to you.

Encouraged and praised by.

Jer 5:31 The prophets prophesy falsely, And the priests rule by their *own* power; And My people love *to have it* so. But what will you do in the end?

Luke 6:26 Woe to you when all men speak well of you, For so did their fathers to the false prophets.

Mode of trying and detecting.

Deut 13:1–2 "If there arises among you a prophet or a dreamer of dreams, and he gives you a sign or a wonder, **2** and the sign or the wonder comes to pass, of which he spoke to you, saying, 'Let us go after other gods'—which you have not known—'and let us serve them,'

Deut 18:21–22 And if you say in your heart, 'How shall we know the word which the LORD has not spo-ken?'— **22** when a prophet speaks in the name of the LORD, if the thing does not happen or come to pass, that *is* the thing which the LORD has not spoken; the prophet has spoken it presumptuously; you shall not be afraid of him.

1 John 4:1–3 Beloved, do not believe every spirit, but test the spirits, whether they are of God; because many false prophets have gone out into the world. **2** By this you know the Spirit of God: Every spirit that confesses that Jesus Christ has come in the flesh is of God, **3** and every spirit that does not confess that Jesus Christ has come in the flesh is not of God. And this is the *spirit* of the Antichrist, which you have heard was coming, and is now already in the world.

Predicted to arise

Before destruction of Jerusalem.

Matt 24:11 Then many false prophets will rise up and deceive many.

Matt 24:24 For false christs and false prophets will rise and show great signs and wonders to deceive, if pos-sible, even the elect.

In the latter times.

2 Pet 2:1 But there were also false prophets among the people, even as there will be false teachers among you, who will secretly bring in destructive heresies, even denying the Lord who bought them, *and* bring on themselves swift destruction.

Judgments pronounced against.

Jer 8:1–2 "At that time," says the LORD, "they shall bring out the bones of the kings of Judah, and the bones of its princes, and the bones of the priests, and the bones of the prophets, and the bones of the inhabitants of Jerusalem, out of their graves. **2** They shall spread them before the sun and the moon and all the host of heaven, which they have loved and which they have served and after which they have walked, which they have sought and which they have worshiped. They shall not be gathered nor buried; they shall be like refuse on the face of the earth.

Jer 14:15 Therefore thus says the LORD concerning the prophets who prophesy in My name, whom I did not send, and who say, 'Sword and famine shall not be in this land'—'By sword and famine those prophets shall be consumed!

Jer 28:16–17 Therefore thus says the LORD: 'Behold, I will cast you from the face of the earth. This year you shall die, because you have taught rebellion against the LORD.' " **17** So Hananiah the prophet died the same year in the seventh month.

Jer 29:32 therefore thus says the LORD: Behold, I will punish Shemaiah the Nehelamite and his family: he shall not have anyone to dwell among this people, nor shall he see the good that I will do for My people, says the LORD, because he has taught rebellion against the LORD.

PROSELYTES

Described.

Esth 8:17 And in every province and city, wherever the king's command and decree came, the Jews had joy and gladness, a feast and a holiday. Then many of the people of the land became Jews, because fear of the Jews fell upon them.

Is 56:3 Do not let the son of the foreigner Who has joined himself to the LORD Speak, saying, "The LORD has utterly separated me from His people"; Nor let the eunuch say, "Here I am, a dry tree."

Required to

Give up all heathen practices.

Ezra 6:21 Then the children of Israel who had returned from the captivity ate together with all who had separated themselves from the filth of the nations of the land in order to seek the LORD God of Israel.

Give up all heathen associates.

Ruth 1:16 But Ruth said: "Entreat me not to leave you, *Or to* turn back from following after you; For wherever you go, I will go; And wherever you lodge, I will lodge; Your people *shall be* my people, And your God, my God.

Ruth 2:11 And Boaz answered and said to her, "It has been fully reported to me, all that you have done for your mother-in-law since the death of your husband, and *how* you have left your father and your mother

and the land of your birth, and have come to a people whom you did not know before.

Ps 45:10 Listen, O daughter, Consider and incline your ear; Forget your own people also, and your father's house;

Luke 14:26 "If anyone comes to Me and does not hate his father and mother, wife and children, brothers and sisters, yes, and his own life also, he cannot be My disciple.

Be circumcised.

Gen 17:13 He who is born in your house and he who is bought with your money must be circumcised, and My covenant shall be in your flesh for an everlasting covenant.

Ex 12:48 And when a stranger dwells with you *and wants* to keep the Passover to the LORD, let all his males be circumcised, and then let him come near and keep it; and he shall be as a native of the land. For no uncircumcised person shall eat it.

Enter into covenant to serve the Lord.

Deut 29:10–13 "All of you stand today before the LORD your God: your leaders and your tribes and your elders and your officers, all the men of Israel, **11** your little ones and your wives—also the stranger who *is* in your camp, from the one who cuts your wood to the one who draws your water— **12** that you may enter into covenant with the LORD your God, and into His oath, which the LORD your God makes with you today, **13** that He may establish you today as a people for Himself, and *that* He may be God to you, just as He has spoken to you, and just as He has sworn to your fathers, to Abraham, Isaac, and Jacob.

Neh 10:28–29 Now the rest of the people—the priests, the Levites, the gatekeepers, the singers, the Nethinim, and all those who had separated themselves from the peoples of the lands to the Law of God, their wives, their sons, and their daughters, everyone who had knowledge and understanding— **29** these joined with their brethren, their nobles, and entered into a curse and an oath to walk in God's Law, which was given by Moses the servant of God, and to observe and do all the commandments of the LORD our Lord, and His ordinances and His statutes:

Observe the law of Moses as Jews.

Ex 12:49 One law shall be for the native-born and for the stranger who dwells among you."

Restrictions on holding office.

Deut 23:3 "An Ammonite or Moabite shall not enter the assembly of the LORD; even to the tenth generation none of his *descendants* shall enter the assembly of the LORD forever,

Deut 23:7–8 "You shall not abhor an Edomite, for he *is* your brother. You shall not abhor an Egyptian, because you were an alien in his land. **8** The children of the third generation born to them may enter the assembly of the LORD.

Were entitled to all privileges.

Ex 12:48 And when a stranger dwells with you *and wants* to keep the Passover to the LORD, let all his males be circumcised, and then let him come near and keep it; and he shall be as a native of the land. For no uncircumcised person shall eat it.

Is 56:3–7 Do not let the son of the foreigner Who has joined himself to the LORD Speak, saying, "The LORD has utterly separated me from His people"; Nor let the eunuch say, "Here I am, a dry tree." **4** For thus says the LORD: "To the eunuchs who keep My Sabbaths, And choose what pleases Me, And hold fast My covenant, **5** Even to them I will give in My house And within My walls a place and a name Better than that of sons and daughters; I will give them an everlasting name That shall not be cut off. **6** "Also the sons of the foreigner Who join themselves to the LORD, to serve Him, And to love the name of the LORD, to be His servants— Everyone who keeps from defiling the Sabbath, And holds fast My covenant— **7** Even them I will bring to My holy mountain, And make them joyful in My house of prayer. Their burnt offerings and their sacrifices *Will be* accepted on My altar; For My house shall be called a house of prayer for all nations."

Went up to the feasts.

Acts 2:10 Phrygia and Pamphylia, Egypt and the parts of Libya adjoining Cyrene, visitors from Rome, both Jews and proselytes,

Acts 8:27 So he arose and went. And behold, a man of Ethiopia, a eunuch of great authority under Candace the queen of the Ethiopians, who had charge of all her treasury, and had come to Jerusalem to worship,

Pharisees, zealous in making.

Matt 23:15 "Woe to you, scribes and Pharisees, hypocrites! For you travel land and sea to win one proselyte, and when he is won, you make him twice as much a son of hell as yourselves.

Many embraced the gospel.

Acts 6:5 And the saying pleased the whole multitude. And they chose Stephen, a man full of faith and the Holy Spirit, and Philip, Prochorus, Nicanor, Timon, Parmenas, and Nicolas, a proselyte from Antioch,

Acts 13:43 Now when the congregation had broken up, many of the Jews and devout proselytes followed Paul and Barnabas, who, speaking to them, persuaded them to continue in the grace of God.

Later called devout Greeks.

John 12:20 Now there were certain Greeks among those who came up to worship at the feast.

Acts 17:4 And some of them were persuaded; and a great multitude of the devout Greeks, and not a few of the leading women, joined Paul and Silas.

PROSTITUTION

Used as a disguise by Tamar.

Gen 38:14–16 So she took off her widow's garments, covered *herself* with a veil and wrapped herself, and sat in an open place which *was* on the way to Timnah; for she saw that Shelah was grown, and she was not given to him as a wife. **15** When Judah saw her, he thought *was* a harlot, because she had covered her face. **16** Then he turned to her by the way, and said, "Please let me come in to you"; for he did not know that she *was* his daughter-in-law. So she said, "What will you give me, that you may come in to me?"

Forbidden in all forms.

Lev 19:29 'Do not prostitute your daughter, to cause her

to be a harlot, lest the land fall into harlotry, and the land become full of wickedness.

Deut 23:17–18 "There shall be no *ritual* harlot of the daughters of Israel, or a perverted one of the sons of Israel. **18** You shall not bring the wages of a harlot or the price of a dog to the house of the LORD your God for any vowed offering, for both of these *are* an abomination to the LORD your God.

Cf. 1 Kin 14:23–24; 2 Kin 23:7

By Eli's sons, of proper worship.

1 Sam 2:22–25 Now Eli was very old; and he heard everything his sons did to all Israel, and how they lay with the women who assembled at the door of the tabernacle of meeting. **23** So he said to them, "Why do you do such things? For I hear of your evil dealings from all the people. **24** No, my sons! For *it is* not a good report that I hear. You make the LORD's people transgress. **25** If one man sins against another, God will judge him. But if a man sins against the LORD, who will intercede for him?" Nevertheless they did not heed the voice of their father, because the LORD desired to kill them.

Israel's sins compared to.

Jer 3:6–9 The LORD said also to me in the days of Josiah the king: "Have you seen what backsliding Israel has done? She has gone up on every high mountain and under every green tree, and there played the harlot. **7** And I said, after she had done all these *things*, 'Return to Me.' But she did not return. And her treacherous sister Judah saw it. **8** Then I saw that for all the causes for which backsliding Israel had committed adultery, I had put her away and given her a certificate of divorce; yet her treacherous sister Judah did not fear, but went and played the harlot also. **9** So it came to pass, through her casual harlotry, that she defiled the land and committed adultery with stones and trees.

Ezek 16:30–42 "How degenerate is your heart!" says the Lord GOD, "seeing you do all these *things*, the deeds of a brazen harlot. **31** "You erected your shrine at the head of every road, and built your high place in every street. Yet you were not like a harlot, because you scorned payment. **32** *You are* an adulterous wife, *who* takes strangers instead of her husband. **33** Men make payment to all harlots, but you made your payments to all your lovers, and hired them to come to you from all around for your harlotry. **34** You are the opposite of *other* women in your harlotry, because no one solicited you to be a harlot. In that you gave payment but no payment was given you, therefore you are the opposite." **35** 'Now then, O harlot, hear the word of the LORD! **36** Thus says the Lord GOD: "Because your filthiness was poured out and your nakedness uncovered in your harlotry with your lovers, and with all your abominable idols, and because of the blood of your children which you gave to them, **37** surely, therefore, I will gather all your lovers with whom you took pleasure, all those you loved, *and* all those you hated; I will gather them from all around against you and will uncover your nakedness to them, that they may see all your nakedness. **38** And I will judge you as women who break wedlock or shed blood are judged; I will bring blood upon you in fury and jealousy. **39** I will also give you into their hand, and they shall throw down your shrines and break down your high places. They shall also strip you of your clothes, take your beautiful jewelry, and leave you naked and bare. **40** "They shall also bring up an assembly against you, and they shall stone you with stones and thrust you through with their swords. **41** They shall burn your houses with fire, and execute judgments on you in the sight of many women; and I will make you cease playing the harlot, and you shall no longer hire lovers. **42** So I will lay to rest My fury toward you, and My jealousy shall depart from you. I will be quiet, and be angry no more.

Ezek 20:30 Therefore say to the house of Israel, 'Thus says the Lord GOD: "Are you defiling yourselves in the manner of your fathers, and committing harlotry according to their abominations?

Hos 4:11–18 "Harlotry, wine, and new wine enslave the heart. **12** My people ask counsel from their wooden *idols*, And their staff informs them. For the spirit of harlotry has caused *them* to stray, And they have played the harlot against their God. **13** They offer sacrifices on the mountaintops, And burn incense on the hills, Under oaks, poplars, and terebinths, Because their shade *is* good. Therefore your daughters commit harlotry, And your brides commit adultery. **14** "I will not punish your daughters when they commit harlotry, Nor your brides when they commit adultery; For *the men* themselves go apart with harlots, And offer sacrifices with a ritual harlot. Therefore people *who* do not understand will be trampled. **15** "Though you, Israel, play the harlot, Let not Judah offend. Do not come up to Gilgal, Nor go up to Beth Aven, Nor swear an oath, *saying*, 'As the LORD lives'— **16** "For Israel is stubborn Like a stubborn calf; Now the LORD will let them forage Like a lamb in open country. **17** "Ephraim *is* joined to idols, Let him alone. **18** Their drink is rebellion, They commit harlotry continually. Her rulers dearly love dishonor.

Hos 5:3 I know Ephraim, And Israel is not hidden from Me; For now, O Ephraim, you commit harlotry; Israel is defiled.

Hos 6:10 I have seen a horrible thing in the house of Israel: There *is* the harlotry of Ephraim; Israel is defiled.

Hos 9:1 Do not rejoice, O Israel, with joy like *other* peoples, For you have played the harlot against your God. You have made love *for* hire on every threshing floor.

PROTECTION

Of God is

Indispensable.

Ps 127:1 Unless the LORD builds the house, They labor in vain who build it; Unless the LORD guards the city, The watchman stays awake in vain.

Timely.

Ps 46:1 God *is* our refuge and strength, A very present help in trouble.

Certain.

Deut 31:6 Be strong and of good courage, do not fear nor be afraid of them; for the LORD your God, He *is* the One who goes with you. He will not leave you nor forsake you."

Josh 1:5 No man shall *be able to* stand before you all the days of your life; as I was with Moses, *so* I will be with you. I will not leave you nor forsake you.

1 Thess 5:23–24 Now may the God of peace Himself sanctify you completely; and may your whole spirit, soul, and body be preserved blameless at the coming of our Lord Jesus Christ. **24** He who calls you *is* faithful, who also will do *it*.

2 Thess 3:3 But the Lord is faithful, who will establish you and guard *you* from the evil one.

1 Pet 1:5 who are kept by the power of God through faith for salvation ready to be revealed in the last time.

Jude 1:24 Now to Him who is able to keep you from stumbling, And to present *you* faultless Before the presence of His glory with exceeding joy,

Effectual.

John 10:28–30 And I give them eternal life, and they shall never perish; neither shall anyone snatch them out of My hand. **29** My Father, who has given *them* to Me, is greater than all; and no one is able to snatch *them* out of My Father's hand. **30** I and *My* Father are one."

2 Cor 12:9 And He said to me, "My grace is sufficient for you, for My strength is made perfect in weakness." Therefore most gladly I will rather boast in my infirmities, that the power of Christ may rest upon me.

Uninterrupted.

Ps 121:3 He will not allow your foot to be moved; He who keeps you will not slumber.

Encouraging.

Is 41:10 Fear not, for I *am* with you; Be not dismayed, for I *am* your God. I will strengthen you, Yes, I will help you, I will uphold you with My righteous right hand.'

Is 50:7 "For the Lord GOD will help Me; Therefore I will not be disgraced; Therefore I have set My face like a flint, And I know that I will not be ashamed.

Perpetual.

Ps 121:8 The LORD shall preserve your going out and your coming in From this time forth, and even forevermore.

Often afforded through weak means.

Judg 7:7 Then the LORD said to Gideon, "By the three hundred men who lapped I will save you, and deliver the Midianites into your hand. Let all the *other* people go, every man to his place."

1 Sam 17:45 Then David said to the Philistine, "You come to me with a sword, with a spear, and with a javelin. But I come to you in the name of the LORD of hosts, the God of the armies of Israel, whom you have defied.

1 Sam 17:50 So David prevailed over the Philistine with a sling and a stone, and struck the Philistine and killed him. But *there was* no sword in the hand of David.

2 Chr 14:11 And Asa cried out to the LORD his God, and said, "LORD, *it is* nothing for You to help, whether with many or with those who have no power; help us, O LORD our God, for we rest on You, and in Your name we go against this multitude. O LORD, You *are* our God; do not let man prevail against You!"

Is afforded to

Those who listen to God.

Prov 1:33 But whoever listens to me will dwell safely, And will be secure, without fear of evil."

Returning sinners.

Job 22:23 If you return to the Almighty, you will be built up; You will remove iniquity far from your tents.

Job 22:25 Yes, the Almighty will be your gold And your precious silver;

The loyal in heart.

2 Chr 16:9 For the eyes of the LORD run to and fro throughout the whole earth, to show Himself strong on behalf of *those* whose heart *is* loyal to Him. In this you have done foolishly; therefore from now on you shall have wars."

The poor.

Ps 14:6 You shame the counsel of the poor, But the LORD *is* his refuge.

Ps 72:12–14 For He will deliver the needy when he cries, The poor also, and *him* who has no helper. **13** He will spare the poor and needy, And will save the souls of the needy. **14** He will redeem their life from oppression and violence; And precious shall be their blood in His sight.

The oppressed.

Ps 9:9 The LORD also will be a refuge for the oppressed, A refuge in times of trouble.

Israel.

Ps 48:3 God *is* in her palaces; He is known as her refuge.

Zech 2:4–5 who said to him, "Run, speak to this young man, saying: 'Jerusalem shall be inhabited *as* towns without walls, because of the multitude of men and livestock in it. **5** For I,' says the LORD, 'will be a wall of fire all around her, and I will be the glory in her midst.' "

Is guaranteed to believers in

Preserving them.

Ps 145:20 The LORD preserves all who love Him, But all the wicked He will destroy.

Strengthening them.

2 Tim 4:17 But the Lord stood with me and strengthened me, so that the message might be preached fully through me, and *that* all the Gentiles might hear. Also I was delivered out of the mouth of the lion.

Upholding them.

Ps 37:17 For the arms of the wicked shall be broken, But the LORD upholds the righteous.

Ps 37:24 Though he fall, he shall not be utterly cast down; For the LORD upholds *him with* His hand.

Ps 63:8 My soul follows close behind You; Your right hand upholds me.

Guarding their feet.

1 Sam 2:9 He will guard the feet of His saints, But the wicked shall be silent in darkness. "For by strength no man shall prevail.

Prov 3:26 For the LORD will be your confidence, And will keep your foot from being caught.

Keeping them from evil.

2 Thess 3:3 But the Lord is faithful, who will establish you and guard *you* from the evil one.

Rev 3:10 Because you have kept My command to persevere, I also will keep you from the hour of trial which shall come upon the whole world, to test those who dwell on the earth.

Keeping them from falling.

Jude 1:24 Now to Him who is able to keep you from stumbling, And to present *you* faultless Before the presence of His glory with exceeding joy,

Keeping them in the way.

Ex 23:20 "Behold, I send an Angel before you to keep you in the way and to bring you into the place which I have prepared.

Providing a refuge for them.

Prov 14:26 In the fear of the LORD *there is* strong confidence, And His children will have a place of refuge.

Is 4:6 And there will be a tabernacle for shade in the daytime from the heat, for a place of refuge, and for a shelter from storm and rain.

Is 32:2 A man will be as a hiding place from the wind, And a cover from the tempest, As rivers of water in a dry place, As the shadow of a great rock in a weary land.

Defending them against their enemies.

Deut 20:1–4 "When you go out to battle against your enemies, and see horses and chariots *and* people more numerous than you, do not be afraid of them; for the LORD your God *is* with you, who brought you up from the land of Egypt. **2** So it shall be, when you are on the verge of battle, that the priest shall approach and speak to the people. **3** And he shall say to them, 'Hear, O Israel: Today you are on the verge of battle with your enemies. Do not let your heart faint, do not be afraid, and do not tremble or be terrified because of them; **4** for the LORD your God *is* He who goes with you, to fight for you against your enemies, to save you.'

Deut 33:27 The eternal God *is your* refuge, And underneath *are* the everlasting arms; He will thrust out the enemy from before you, And will say, 'Destroy!'

Is 8:10 Take counsel together, but it will come to nothing; Speak the word, but it will not stand, For God *is* with us."

Is 59:19 So shall they fear The name of the LORD from the west, And His glory from the rising of the sun; When the enemy comes in like a flood, The Spirit of the LORD will lift up a standard against him.

Times of temptation.

1 Cor 10:13 No temptation has overtaken you except such as is common to man; but God *is* faithful, who will not allow you to be tempted beyond what you are able, but with the temptation will also make the way of escape, that you may be able to bear *it*.

2 Pet 2:9 *then* the Lord knows how to deliver the godly out of temptations and to reserve the unjust under punishment for the day of judgment,

Persecution.

Luke 21:18 But not a hair of your head shall be lost.

All dangers and calamities.

Ps 57:1 Be merciful to me, O God, be merciful to me! For my soul trusts in You; And in the shadow of Your wings I will make my refuge, Until *these* calamities have passed by.

Ps 59:16 But I will sing of Your power; Yes, I will sing aloud of Your mercy in the morning; For You have been my defense And refuge in the day of my trouble.

Ps 91:3–7 Surely He shall deliver you from the snare of the fowler *And* from the perilous pestilence. **4** He shall cover you with His feathers, And under His wings you shall take refuge; His truth *shall be your* shield and buckler. **5** You shall not be afraid of the terror by night, *Nor* of the arrow *that* flies by day, **6** *Nor* of the pestilence *that* walks in darkness, *Nor* of the destruction *that* lays waste at noonday. **7** A thousand may fall at your side, And ten thousand at your right hand; *But* it shall not come near you.

All places.

Gen 28:15 Behold, I *am* with you and will keep you wherever you go, and will bring you back to this land; for I will not leave you until I have done what I have spoken to you."

2 Chr 16:9 For the eyes of the LORD run to and fro throughout the whole earth, to show Himself strong on behalf of *those* whose heart *is* loyal to Him. In this you have done foolishly; therefore from now on you shall have wars."

Sleep.

Ps 3:5 I lay down and slept; I awoke, for the LORD sustained me.

Ps 4:8 I will both lie down in peace, and sleep; For You alone, O LORD, make me dwell in safety.

Prov 3:24 When you lie down, you will not be afraid; Yes, you will lie down and your sleep will be sweet.

Death.

Ps 23:4 Yea, though I walk through the valley of the shadow of death, I will fear no evil; For You *are* with me; Your rod and Your staff, they comfort me.

Believers

Acknowledge God as their.

Ps 18:2 The LORD is my rock and my fortress and my deliverer; My God, my strength, in whom I will trust; My shield and the horn of my salvation, my stronghold.

Ps 62:2 He only *is* my rock and my salvation; *He is* my defense; I shall not be greatly moved.

Ps 89:18 For our shield *belongs* to the LORD, And our king to the Holy One of Israel.

Pray for.

Ps 17:5 Uphold my steps in Your paths, *That* my footsteps may not slip.

Ps 17:8 Keep me as the apple of Your eye; Hide me under the shadow of Your wings,

Is 51:9 Awake, awake, put on strength, O arm of the LORD! Awake as in the ancient days, In the generations of old. *Are* You not *the arm* that cut Rahab apart, *And* wounded the serpent?

Praise God for.

Ps 5:11 But let all those rejoice who put their trust in You; Let them ever shout for joy, because You defend them; Let those also who love Your name Be joyful in You.

Withdrawn from

The disobedient.

Lev 26:14–17 'But if you do not obey Me, and do not observe all these commandments, **15** and if you despise My statutes, or if your soul abhors My judgments, so that you do not perform all My commandments, *but* break My covenant, **16** I also will do this to you: I will even appoint terror over you, wasting disease and fever which shall consume the eyes and cause sorrow of heart. And you shall sow your seed in vain, for your enemies shall eat it. **17** I will set My face against you, and you shall be defeated by your enemies. Those who hate you shall reign over you, and you shall flee when no one pursues you.

The backsliding.

Josh 23:12–13 Or else, if indeed you do go back, and cling to the remnant of these nations—these that remain among you—and make marriages with them, and go in to them and they to you, **13** know for certain that the LORD your God will no longer drive out these nations from before you. But they shall be snares and traps to you, and scourges on your sides and thorns in your eyes, until you perish from this good land which the LORD your God has given you.

Judg 10:13 Yet you have forsaken Me and served other gods. Therefore I will deliver you no more.

The presumptuous.

Num 14:40–45 And they rose early in the morning and went up to the top of the mountain, saying, "Here we are, and we will go up to the place which the LORD has promised, for we have sinned!" **41** And Moses said, "Now why do you transgress the command of the LORD? For this will not succeed. **42** Do not go up, lest you be defeated by your enemies, for the LORD *is* not among you. **43** For the Amalekites and the Canaanites *are* there before you, and you shall fall by the sword; because you have turned away from the LORD, the LORD will not be with you." **44** But they presumed to go up to the mountaintop. Nevertheless, neither the ark of the covenant of the LORD nor Moses departed from the camp. **45** Then the Amalekites and the Canaanites who dwelt in that mountain came down and attacked them, and drove them back as far as Hormah.

The unbelieving.

Is 7:9 The head of Ephraim *is* Samaria, And the head of Samaria *is* Remaliah's son. If you will not believe, Surely you shall not be established." ' "

The impenitent.

Matt 23:38 See! Your house is left to you desolate;

Not to be found in

Idols.

Deut 32:37–39 He will say: 'Where *are* their gods, The rock in which they sought refuge? **38** Who ate the fat of their sacrifices, *And* drank the wine of their drink offering? Let them rise and help you, *And* be your refuge. **39** 'Now see that I, *even* I, *am* He, And *there is* no God besides Me; I kill and I make alive; I wound and I heal; Nor *is there any* who can deliver from My hand.

Is 46:7 They bear it on the shoulder, they carry it And set it in its place, and it stands; From its place it shall not move. Though *one* cries out to it, yet it cannot answer Nor save him out of his trouble.

Man.

Ps 146:3 Do not put your trust in princes, *Nor* in a son of man, in whom *there is* no help.

Is 30:7 For the Egyptians shall help in vain and to no purpose. Therefore I have called her Rahab-Hem-Shebeth.

Riches.

Prov 11:4 Riches do not profit in the day of wrath, But righteousness delivers from death.

Prov 11:28 He who trusts in his riches will fall, But the righteous will flourish like foliage.

Zeph 1:18 Neither their silver nor their gold Shall be able to deliver them In the day of the LORD's wrath; But the whole land shall be devoured By the fire of His jealousy, For He will make speedy riddance Of all those who dwell in the land.

Numbers.

Josh 11:4–8 So they went out, they and all their armies with them, *as* many people *as* the sand that *is* on the seashore in multitude, with very many horses and chariots. **5** And when all these kings had met together, they came and camped together at the waters of Merom to fight against Israel. **6** But the LORD said to Joshua, "Do not be afraid because of them, for tomorrow about this time I will deliver all of them slain before Israel. You shall hamstring their horses and burn their chariots with fire." **7** So Joshua and all the people of war with him came against them suddenly by the waters of Merom, and they attacked them. **8** And the LORD delivered them into the hand of Israel, who defeated them and chased them to Greater Sidon, to the Brook Misrephoth, and to the Valley of Mizpah eastward; they attacked them until they left none of them remaining.

Ps 33:16 No king *is* saved by the multitude of an army; A mighty man is not delivered by great strength.

Horses.

Ps 33:17 A horse *is* a vain hope for safety; Neither shall it deliver *any* by its great strength.

Prov 21:31 The horse *is* prepared for the day of battle, But deliverance *is* of the LORD.

Illustrated.

Deut 32:11 As an eagle stirs up its nest, Hovers over its young, Spreading out its wings, taking them up, Carrying them on its wings,

Ps 125:1–2 Those who trust in the LORD *Are* like Mount Zion, *Which* cannot be moved, *but* abides forever. **2** As the mountains surround Jerusalem, So the LORD surrounds His people From this time forth and forever.

Prov 18:10 The name of the LORD *is* a strong tower; The righteous run to it and are safe.

Is 25:4 For You have been a strength to the poor, A strength to the needy in his distress, A refuge from the storm, A shade from the heat; For the blast of the terrible ones *is* as a storm *against* the wall.

Is 31:5 Like birds flying about, So will the LORD of hosts defend Jerusalem. Defending, He will also deliver *it*; Passing over, He will preserve *it*."

Luke 13:34 "O Jerusalem, Jerusalem, the one who kills the prophets and stones those who are sent to her! How often I wanted to gather your children together, as a hen *gathers* her brood under *her* wings, but you were not willing!

Exemplified for

Abraham.

Gen 15:1 After these things the word of the LORD came to Abram in a vision, saying, "Do not be afraid, Abram. I *am* your shield, your exceedingly great reward."

Jacob.

Gen 48:16 The Angel who has redeemed me from all evil, Bless the lads; Let my name be named upon them, And the name of my fathers Abraham and Isaac; And let them grow into a multitude in the midst of the earth."

Joseph.

Gen 49:23–25 The archers have bitterly grieved him, Shot *at him* and hated him. **24** But his bow remained in strength, And the arms of his hands were made strong By the hands of the Mighty *God* of Jacob (From there *is* the Shepherd, the Stone of Israel), **25** By the God of your father who will help you, And by the Almighty who will bless you *With* blessings of heaven above, Blessings of the deep that lies beneath, Blessings of the breasts and of the womb.

Israel.

Josh 24:17 for the LORD our God *is* He who brought us and our fathers up out of the land of Egypt, from the house of bondage, who did those great signs in our sight, and preserved us in all the way that we went and among all the people through whom we passed.

David.

Ps 18:1–2 I will love You, O LORD, my strength. **2** The LORD is my rock and my fortress and my deliverer; My God, my strength, in whom I will trust; My shield and the horn of my salvation, my stronghold.

Daniel's friends.

Dan 3:28 Nebuchadnezzar spoke, saying, "Blessed be the God of Shadrach, Meshach, and Abed-Nego, who sent His Angel and delivered His servants who trusted in Him, and they have frustrated the king's word, and yielded their bodies, that they should not serve nor worship any god except their own God!

Daniel.

Dan 6:22 My God sent His angel and shut the lions' mouths, so that they have not hurt me, because I was found innocent before Him; and also, O king, I have done no wrong before you."

Peter.

Acts 12:4–7 So when he had arrested him, he put *him* in prison, and delivered *him* to four squads of soldiers to keep him, intending to bring him before the people after Passover. **5** Peter was therefore kept in prison, but constant prayer was offered to God for him by the church. **6** And when Herod was about to bring him out, that night Peter was sleeping, bound with two chains between two soldiers; and the guards before the door were keeping the prison. **7** Now behold, an angel of the Lord stood by *him*, and a light shone in the prison; and he struck Peter on the side and raised him up, saying, "Arise quickly!" And his chains fell off *his* hands.

Paul.

Acts 18:10 for I am with you, and no one will attack you to hurt you; for I have many people in this city."

Acts 26:17 I will deliver you from the *Jewish* people, as well as *from* the Gentiles, to whom I now send you,

PRUDENCE (UNDERSTANDING)

Exhibited in the manifestation of God's grace.

Eph 1:8 which He made to abound toward us in all wisdom and prudence,

Exemplified by Christ.

Is 52:13 Behold, My Servant shall deal prudently; He shall be exalted and extolled and be very high.

Matt 21:24–27 But Jesus answered and said to them, "I also will ask you one thing, which if you tell Me, I likewise will tell you by what authority I do these things: 25 The baptism of John—where was it from? From heaven or from men?" And they reasoned among themselves, saying, "If we say, 'From heaven,' He will say to us, 'Why then did you not believe him?' 26 But if we say, 'From men,' we fear the multitude, for all count John as a prophet." 27 So they answered Jesus and said, "We do not know." And He said to them, "Neither will I tell you by what authority I do these things.

Matt 22:15–21 Then the Pharisees went and plotted how they might entangle Him in *His* talk. 16 And they sent to Him their disciples with the Herodians, saying, "Teacher, we know that You are true, and teach the way of God in truth; nor do You care about anyone, for You do not regard the person of men. 17 Tell us, therefore, what do You think? Is it lawful to pay taxes to Caesar, or not?" 18 But Jesus perceived their wickedness, and said, "Why do you test Me, *you* hypocrites? 19 Show Me the tax money." So they brought Him a denarius. 20 And He said to them, "Whose image and inscription *is* this?" 21 They said to Him, "Caesar's." And He said to them, "Render therefore to Caesar the things that are Caesar's, and to God the things that are God's."

Intimately connected with wisdom.

Prov 8:12 "I, wisdom, dwell with prudence, And find out knowledge *and* discretion.

The wise celebrated for.

Prov 16:21 The wise in heart will be called prudent, And sweetness of the lips increases learning.

They who have,

Acquire knowledge.

Prov 14:18 The simple inherit folly, But the prudent are crowned with knowledge.

Prov 18:15 The heart of the prudent acquires knowledge, And the ear of the wise seeks knowledge.

Deal with knowledge.

Prov 13:16 Every prudent *man* acts with knowledge, But a fool lays open *his* folly.

Consider well their steps.

Prov 14:15 The simple believes every word, But the prudent considers well his steps.

Understand the ways of God.

Hos 14:9 Who *is* wise? Let him understand these things. *Who is* prudent? Let him know them. For the ways of the LORD *are* right; The righteous walk in them, But transgressors stumble in them.

Understand their own ways.

Prov 14:8 The wisdom of the prudent *is* to understand his way, But the folly of fools *is* deceit.

Not ostentatious of knowledge.

Prov 12:23 A prudent man conceals knowledge, But the heart of fools proclaims foolishness.

Foresee and avoid evil.

Prov 22:3 A prudent *man* foresees evil and hides himself, But the simple pass on and are punished.

Are preserved by it.

Prov 2:11 Discretion will preserve you; Understanding will keep you,

Suppress angry feelings.

Prov 12:16 A fool's wrath is known at once, But a prudent *man* covers shame.

Prov 19:11 The discretion of a man makes him slow to anger, And his glory *is* to overlook a transgression.

Regard correction.

Prov 15:5 A fool despises his father's instruction, But he who receives correction is prudent.

Keep silence in the evil time.

Amos 5:13 Therefore the prudent keep silent at that time, For it *is* an evil time.

Believers exercise it.

Ps 112:5 A good man deals graciously and lends; He will guide his affairs with discretion.

Matt 10:16 "Behold, I send you out as sheep in the midst of wolves. Therefore be wise as serpents and harmless as doves.

Eph 5:15 See then that you walk circumspectly, not as fools but as wise,

Col 4:5 Walk in wisdom toward those *who are* outside, redeeming the time.

Virtuous wives act with.

Prov 31:16 She considers a field and buys it; From her profits she plants a vineyard.

Prov 31:26 She opens her mouth with wisdom, And on her tongue *is* the law of kindness.

The young should cultivate.

Prov 3:21 My son, let them not depart from your eyes— Keep sound wisdom and discretion;

Of the wicked

Fails in times of perplexity.

Jer 49:7 Against Edom. Thus says the LORD of hosts: "*Is* wisdom no more in Teman? Has counsel perished from the prudent? Has their wisdom vanished?

Keeps them from the knowledge of the gospel.

Matt 11:25 At that time Jesus answered and said, "I thank You, Father, Lord of heaven and earth, that You have hidden these things from *the* wise and prudent and have revealed them to babes.

Denounced by God.

Is 5:21 Woe to *those who are* wise in their own eyes, And prudent in their own sight!

Is 29:15 Woe to those who seek deep to hide their counsel far from the LORD, And their works are in the dark; They say, "Who sees us?" and, "Who knows us?"

Defeated by God.

Is 29:14 Therefore, behold, I will again do a marvelous work Among this people, A marvelous work and a wonder; For the wisdom of their wise *men* shall perish, And the understanding of their prudent *men* shall be hidden."

1 Cor 1:19 For it is written: *"I will destroy the wisdom of the wise, And bring to nothing the understanding of the prudent."*

Necessity for—illustrated.

Matt 25:3 Those who *were* foolish took their lamps and took no oil with them,

Matt 25:9 But the wise answered, saying, '*No*, lest there should not be enough for us and you; but go rather to those who sell, and buy for yourselves.'

Luke 14:28–32 For which of you, intending to build a tower, does not sit down first and count the cost, whether he has *enough* to finish *it*— **29** lest, after he has laid the foundation, and is not able to finish, all who see *it* begin to mock him, **30** saying, 'This man began to build and was not able to finish.' **31** Or what king, going to make war against another king, does not sit down first and consider whether he is able with ten thousand to meet him who comes against him with twenty thousand? **32** Or else, while the other is still a great way off, he sends a delegation and asks conditions of peace.

Exemplified by

Jacob.

Gen 32:3–23 Then Jacob sent messengers before him to Esau his brother in the land of Seir, the country of Edom. **4** And he commanded them, saying, "Speak thus to my lord Esau, 'Thus your servant Jacob says: "I have dwelt with Laban and stayed there until now. **5** I have oxen, donkeys, flocks, and male and female servants; and I have sent to tell my lord, that I may find favor in your sight." ' " **6** Then the messengers returned to Jacob, saying, "We came to your brother Esau, and he also is coming to meet you, and four hundred men *are* with him." **7** So Jacob was greatly afraid and distressed; and he divided the people that *were* with him, and the flocks and herds and camels, into two companies. **8** And he said, "If Esau comes to the one company and attacks it, then the other company which is left will escape." **9** Then Jacob said, "O God of my father Abraham and God of my father Isaac, the LORD who said to me, 'Return to your country and to your family, and I will deal well with you': **10** I am not worthy of the least of all the mercies and of all the truth which You have shown Your servant; for I crossed over this Jordan with my staff, and now I have become two companies. **11** Deliver me, I pray, from the hand of my brother, from the hand of Esau; for I fear him, lest he come and attack me *and* the mother with the children. **12** For You said, 'I will surely treat you well, and make your descendants as the sand of the sea, which cannot be num-

bered for multitude.' " **13** So he lodged there that same night, and took what came to his hand as a present for Esau his brother: **14** two hundred female goats and twenty male goats, two hundred ewes and twenty rams, **15** thirty milk camels with their colts, forty cows and ten bulls, twenty female donkeys and ten foals. **16** Then he delivered *them* to the hand of his servants, every drove by itself, and said to his servants, "Pass over before me, and put some distance between successive droves." **17** And he commanded the first one, saying, "When Esau my brother meets you and asks you, saying, 'To whom do you belong, and where are you going? Whose *are* these in front of you?' **18** then you shall say, 'They *are* your servant Jacob's. It *is* a present sent to my lord Esau; and behold, he also *is* behind us.' " **19** So he commanded the second, the third, and all who followed the droves, saying, "In this manner you shall speak to Esau when you find him; **20** and also say, 'Behold, your servant Jacob *is* behind us.' " For he said, "I will appease him with the present that goes before me, and afterward I will see his face; perhaps he will accept me." **21** So the present went on over before him, but he himself lodged that night in the camp. **22** And he arose that night and took his two wives, his two female servants, and his eleven sons, and crossed over the ford of Jabbok. **23** He took them, sent them over the brook, and sent over what he had.

Joseph.

Gen 41:39 Then Pharaoh said to Joseph, "Inasmuch as God has shown you all this, *there is* no one as discerning and wise as you.

Jethro.

Ex 18:19–23 Listen now to my voice; I will give you counsel, and God will be with you: Stand before God for the people, so that you may bring the difficulties to God. **20** And you shall teach them the statutes and the laws, and show them the way in which they must walk and the work they must do. **21** Moreover you shall select from all the people able men, such as fear God, men of truth, hating covetousness; and place *such* over them *to be* rulers of thousands, rulers of hundreds, rulers of fifties, and rulers of tens. **22** And let them judge the people at all times. Then it will be *that* every great matter they shall bring to you, but every small matter they themselves shall judge. So it will be easier for you, for they will bear *the burden* with you. **23** If you do this thing, and God *so* commands you, then you will be able to endure, and all this people will also go to their place in peace."

Gideon.

Judg 8:1–3 Now the men of Ephraim said to him, "Why have you done this to us by not calling us when you went to fight with the Midianites?" And they reprimanded him sharply. **2** So he said to them, "What have I done now in comparison with you? *Is* not the gleaning *of the grapes* of Ephraim better than the vintage of Abiezer? **3** God has delivered into your hands the princes of Midian, Oreb and Zeeb. And what was I able to do in comparison with you?" Then their anger toward him subsided when he said that.

David.

1 Sam 16:18 Then one of the servants answered and said, "Look, I have seen a son of Jesse the Bethlehemite, *who is* skillful in playing, a mighty man of valor, a man of war, prudent in speech, and a handsome person; and the LORD *is* with him."

Abigail.

1 Sam 25:23–31 Now when Abigail saw David, she dismounted quickly from the donkey, fell on her face before David, and bowed down to the ground. **24** So she fell at his feet and said: "On me, my lord, *on* me *let* this iniquity *be!* And please let your maidservant speak in your ears, and hear the words of your maidservant. **25** Please, let not my lord regard this scoundrel Nabal. For as his name *is,* so *is* he: Nabal *is* his name, and folly *is* with him! But I, your maidservant, did not see the young men of my lord whom you sent. **26** Now therefore, my lord, *as* the LORD lives and *as* your soul lives, since the LORD has held you back from coming to bloodshed and from avenging yourself with your own hand, now then, let your enemies and those who seek harm for my lord be as Nabal. **27** And now this present which your maidservant has brought to my lord, let it be given to the young men who follow my lord. **28** Please forgive the trespass of your maidservant. For the LORD will certainly make for my lord an enduring house, because my lord fights the battles of the LORD, and evil is not found in you throughout your days. **29** Yet a man has risen to pursue you and seek your life, but the life of my lord shall be bound in the bundle of the living with the LORD your God; and the lives of your enemies He shall sling out, *as from* the pocket of a sling. **30** And it shall come to pass, when the LORD has done for my lord according to all the good that He has spoken concerning you, and has appointed you ruler over Israel, **31** that this will be no grief to you, nor offense of heart to my lord, either that you have shed blood without cause, or that my lord has avenged himself. But when the LORD has dealt well with my lord, then remember your maidservant."

Hushai.

2 Sam 15:32–34 Now it happened when David had come to the top *of the mountain,* where he worshiped God—there was Hushai the Archite coming to meet him with his robe torn and dust on his head. **33** David said to him, "If you go on with me, then you will become a burden to me. **34** But if you return to the city, and say to Absalom, 'I will be your servant, O king; *as* I *was* your father's servant previously, so I *will* now also *be* your servant,' then you may defeat the counsel of Ahithophel for me.

2 Sam 17:6–14 And when Hushai came to Absalom, Absalom spoke to him, saying, "Ahithophel has spoken in this manner. Shall we do as he says? If not, speak up." **7** So Hushai said to Absalom: "The advice that Ahithophel has given *is* not good at this time. **8** For," said Hushai, "you know your father and his men, that they *are* mighty men, and they *are* enraged in their minds, like a bear robbed of her cubs in the field; and your father *is* a man of war, and will not camp with the people. **9** Surely by now he is hidden in some pit, or in some *other* place. And it will be, when some of them are overthrown at the first, that whoever hears *it* will say, 'There is a slaughter among the people who follow Absalom.' **10** And even he *who is* valiant, whose heart *is* like the heart of

a lion, will melt completely. For all Israel knows that your father *is* a mighty man, and *those* who *are* with him *are* valiant men. **11** Therefore I advise that all Israel be fully gathered to you, from Dan to Beersheba, like the sand that *is* by the sea for multitude, and that you go to battle in person. **12** So we will come upon him in some place where he may be found, and we will fall on him as the dew falls on the ground. And of him and all the men who *are* with him there shall not be left so much as one. **13** Moreover, if he has withdrawn into a city, then all Israel shall bring ropes to that city; and we will pull it into the river, until there is not one small stone found there." **14** So Absalom and all the men of Israel said, "The advice of Hushai the Archite *is* better than the advice of Ahithophel." For the LORD had purposed to defeat the good advice of Ahithophel, to the intent that the LORD might bring disaster on Absalom.

Aged counsellors of Rehoboam.

1 Kin 12:7 And they spoke to him, saying, "If you will be a servant to these people today, and serve them, and answer them, and speak good words to them, then they will be your servants forever."

Solomon.

2 Chr 2:12 Hiram also said: Blessed *be* the LORD God of Israel, who made heaven and earth, for He has given King David a wise son, endowed with prudence and understanding, who will build a temple for the LORD and a royal house for himself!

Nehemiah.

Neh 2:12–16 Then I arose in the night, I and a few men with me; I told no one what my God had put in my heart to do at Jerusalem; nor was there any animal with me, except the one on which I rode. **13** And I went out by night through the Valley Gate to the Serpent Well and the Refuse Gate, and viewed the walls of Jerusalem which were broken down and its gates which were burned with fire. **14** Then I went on to the Fountain Gate and to the King's Pool, but *there was* no room for the animal under me to pass. **15** So I went up in the night by the valley, and viewed the wall; then I turned back and entered by the Valley Gate, and so returned. **16** And the officials did not know where I had gone or what I had done; I had not yet told the Jews, the priests, the nobles, the officials, or the others who did the work.

Neh 4:13–18 Therefore I positioned *men* behind the lower parts of the wall, at the openings; and I set the people according to their families, with their swords, their spears, and their bows. **14** And I looked, and arose and said to the nobles, to the leaders, and to the rest of the people, "Do not be afraid of them. Remember the Lord, great and awesome, and fight for your brethren, your sons, your daughters, your wives, and your houses." **15** And it happened, when our enemies heard that it was known to us, and *that* God had brought their plot to nothing, that all of us returned to the wall, everyone to his work. **16** So it was, from that time on, *that* half of my servants worked at construction, while the other half held the spears, the shields, the bows, and *wore* armor; and the leaders *were* behind all the house of Judah. **17** Those who built on the wall, and those who carried burdens, loaded themselves so that with one hand they worked at construction, and with the other held a weapon. **18** Every one of the builders had his sword girded at his side as he built. And the one who sounded the trumpet *was* beside me.

The poor wise man.

Eccl 9:15 Now there was found in it a poor wise man, and he by his wisdom delivered the city. Yet no one remembered that same poor man.

The scribe.

Mark 12:32–34 So the scribe said to Him, "Well *said*, Teacher. You have spoken the truth, for there is one God, and there is no other but He. **33** And to love Him with all the heart, with all the understanding, with all the soul, and with all the strength, and to love one's neighbor as oneself, is more than all the whole burnt offerings and sacrifices." **34** Now when Jesus saw that he answered wisely, He said to him, "You are not far from the kingdom of God." But after that no one dared question Him.

Gamaliel.

Acts 5:34–39 Then one in the council stood up, a Pharisee named Gamaliel, a teacher of the law held in respect by all the people, and commanded them to put the apostles outside for a little while. **35** And he said to them: "Men of Israel, take heed to yourselves what you intend to do regarding these men. **36** For some time ago Theudas rose up, claiming to be somebody. A number of men, about four hundred, joined him. He was slain, and all who obeyed him were scattered and came to nothing. **37** After this man, Judas of Galilee rose up in the days of the census, and drew away many people after him. He also perished, and all who obeyed him were dispersed. **38** And now I say to you, keep away from these men and let them alone; for if this plan or this work is of men, it will come to nothing; **39** but if it is of God, you cannot overthrow it—lest you even be found to fight against God."

Sergius Paulus.

Acts 13:7 who was with the proconsul, Sergius Paulus, an intelligent man. This man called for Barnabas and Saul and sought to hear the word of God.

Paul.

Acts 23:6 But when Paul perceived that one part were Sadducees and the other Pharisees, he cried out in the council, "Men *and* brethren, I am a Pharisee, the son of a Pharisee; concerning the hope and resurrection of the dead I am being judged!"

PUBLICANS. *See* TAX COLLECTORS

PUNISHMENTS

Antiquity of.

Gen 4:13–14 And Cain said to the LORD, "My punishment *is* greater than I can bear! **14** Surely You have driven me out this day from the face of the ground; I shall be hidden from Your face; I shall be a fugitive and a vagabond on the earth, and it will happen *that* anyone who finds me will kill me."

Power of inflicting, given to magistrates.

Job 31:11 For that *would be* wickedness; Yes, it *would be* iniquity *deserving of* judgment.

Acts 16:22 Then the multitude rose up together against them; and the magistrates tore off their clothes and commanded *them* to be beaten with rods.

Rom 13:4 For he is God's minister to you for good. But if you do evil, be afraid; for he does not bear the sword in vain; for he is God's minister, an avenger to *execute* wrath on him who practices evil.

Designed to be a warning to others.

Deut 13:11 So all Israel shall hear and fear, and not again do such wickedness as this among you.

Deut 17:13 And all the people shall hear and fear, and no longer act presumptuously.

Deut 19:20 And those who remain shall hear and fear, and hereafter they shall not again commit such evil among you.

Were inflicted

On the guilty.

Deut 24:16 "Fathers shall not be put to death for *their* children, nor shall children be put to death for *their* fathers; a person shall be put to death for his own sin.

Prov 17:26 Also, to punish the righteous *is* not good, Nor to strike princes for *their* uprightness.

Without pity.

Deut 19:13 Your eye shall not pity him, but you shall put away *the guilt of* innocent blood from Israel, that it may go well with you.

Deut 19:21 Your eye shall not pity: life *shall be* for life, eye for eye, tooth for tooth, hand for hand, foot for foot.

Without partiality.

Deut 13:6–8 "If your brother, the son of your mother, your son or your daughter, the wife of your bosom, or your friend who is as your own soul, secretly entices you, saying, 'Let us go and serve other gods,' which you have not known, neither you nor your fathers, **7** of the gods of the people which *are* all around you, near to you or far off from you, from *one* end of the earth to the *other* end of the earth, **8** you shall not consent to him or listen to him, nor shall your eye pity him, nor shall you spare him or conceal him;

By order of kings.

2 Sam 1:13–16 Then David said to the young man who told him, "Where *are* you from?" And he answered, "I *am* the son of an alien, an Amalekite." **14** So David said to him, "How was it you were not afraid to put forth your hand to destroy the LORD's anointed?" **15** Then David called one of the young men and said, "Go near, *and* execute him!" And he struck him so that he died. **16** So David said to him, "Your blood *is* on your own head, for your own mouth has testified against you, saying, 'I have killed the LORD's anointed.' "

Cf. 1 Kin 2:23–46

Immediately after a sentence was passed.

Deut 25:2 then it shall be, if the wicked man deserves to be beaten, that the judge will cause him to lie down and be beaten in his presence, according to his guilt, with a certain number of blows.

Josh 7:25 And Joshua said, "Why have you troubled us? The LORD will trouble you this day." So all Israel stoned him with stones; and they burned them with fire after they had stoned them with stones.

By the witnesses.

Deut 13:9 but you shall surely kill him; your hand shall be first against him to put him to death, and afterward the hand of all the people.

Deut 17:7 The hands of the witnesses shall be the first against him to put him to death, and afterward the hands of all the people. So you shall put away the evil from among you.

John 8:7 So when they continued asking Him, He raised Himself up and said to them, "He who is without sin among you, let him throw a stone at her first."

Acts 7:58–59 and they cast *him* out of the city and stoned *him*. And the witnesses laid down their clothes at the feet of a young man named Saul. **59** And they stoned Stephen as he was calling on *God* and saying, "Lord Jesus, receive my spirit."

By the people.

Num 15:35–36 Then the LORD said to Moses, "The man must surely be put to death; all the congregation shall stone him with stones outside the camp." **36** So, as the LORD commanded Moses, all the congregation brought him outside the camp and stoned him with stones, and he died.

Deut 13:9 but you shall surely kill him; your hand shall be first against him to put him to death, and afterward the hand of all the people.

By soldiers.

2 Sam 1:15 Then David called one of the young men and said, "Go near, *and* execute him!" And he struck him so that he died.

Matt 27:27–35 Then the soldiers of the governor took Jesus into the Praetorium and gathered the whole garrison around Him. **28** And they stripped Him and put a scarlet robe on Him. **29** When they had twisted a crown of thorns, they put *it* on His head, and a reed in His right hand. And they bowed the knee before Him and mocked Him, saying, "Hail, King of the Jews!" **30** Then they spat on Him, and took the reed and struck Him on the head. **31** And when they had mocked Him, they took the robe off Him, put His *own* clothes on Him, and led Him away to be crucified. **32** Now as they came out, they found a man of Cyrene, Simon by name. Him they compelled to bear His cross. **33** And when they had come to a place called Golgotha, that is to say, Place of a Skull, **34** they gave Him sour wine mingled with gall to drink. But when He had tasted *it*, He would not drink. **35** Then they crucified Him, and divided His garments, casting lots, that it might be fulfilled which was spoken by the prophet: *"They divided My garments among them, And for My clothing they cast lots."*

Sometimes deferred.

Num 15:34 They put him under guard, because it had not been explained what should be done to him.

1 Kin 2:5 "Moreover you know also what Joab the son of Zeruiah did to me, *and* what he did to the two commanders of the armies of Israel, to Abner the son of Ner and Amasa the son of Jether, whom he killed. And he shed the blood of war in peacetime, and put

the blood of war on his belt that *was* around his waist, and on his sandals that *were* on his feet.

1 Kin 2:6 Therefore do according to your wisdom, and do not let his gray hair go down to the grave in peace.

1 Kin 2:8–9 "And see, *you have* with you Shimei the son of Gera, a Benjamite from Bahurim, who cursed me with a malicious curse in the day when I went to Mahanaim. But he came down to meet me at the Jordan, and I swore to him by the LORD, saying, 'I will not put you to death with the sword.' **9** Now therefore, do not hold him guiltless, for you *are* a wise man and know what you ought to do to him; but bring his gray hair down to the grave with blood."

Secondary kinds of,

Imprisonment.

Ezra 7:26 Whoever will not observe the law of your God and the law of the king, let judgment be executed speedily on him, whether *it be* death, or banishment, or confiscation of goods, or imprisonment.

Matt 5:25 Agree with your adversary quickly, while you are on the way with him, lest your adversary deliver you to the judge, the judge hand you over to the officer, and you be thrown into prison.

Confinement in a dungeon.

Jer 38:6 So they took Jeremiah and cast him into the dungeon of Malchiah the king's son, which *was* in the court of the prison, and they let Jeremiah down with ropes. And in the dungeon *there was* no water, but mire. So Jeremiah sank in the mire.

Zech 9:11 "As for you also, Because of the blood of your covenant, I will set your prisoners free from the waterless pit.

Confinement in stocks.

Jer 20:2 Then Pashhur struck Jeremiah the prophet, and put him in the stocks that *were* in the high gate of Benjamin, which *was* by the house of the LORD.

Acts 16:24 Having received such a charge, he put them into the inner prison and fastened their feet in the stocks.

Fine, or giving of money.

Ex 21:22 "If men fight, and hurt a woman with child, so that she gives birth prematurely, yet no harm follows, he shall surely be punished accordingly as the woman's husband imposes on him; and he shall pay as the judges *determine.*

Deut 22:19 and they shall fine him one hundred *shekels* of silver and give *them* to the father of the young woman, because he has brought a bad name on a virgin of Israel. And she shall be his wife; he cannot divorce her all his days.

Restitution.

Ex 21:36 Or if it was known that the ox tended to thrust in time past, and its owner has not kept it confined, he shall surely pay ox for ox, and the dead animal shall be his own.

Ex 22:1–4 "If a man steals an ox or a sheep, and slaughters it or sells it, he shall restore five oxen for an ox and four sheep for a sheep. **2** If the thief is found breaking in, and he is struck so that he dies, *there shall be* no guilt for his bloodshed. **3** If the sun has risen on him, *there shall be* guilt for his bloodshed. He should make full restitution; if he has nothing, then he shall be sold for his theft. **4** If the theft is certainly found alive in his hand, whether it is an ox or donkey or sheep, he shall restore double.

Lev 6:4–5 then it shall be, because he has sinned and is guilty, that he shall restore what he has stolen, or the thing which he has extorted, or what was delivered to him for safekeeping, or the lost thing which he found, **5** or all that about which he has sworn falsely. He shall restore its full value, add one-fifth more to it, *and* give it to whomever it belongs, on the day of his trespass offering.

Lev 24:18 Whoever kills an animal shall make it good, animal for animal.

Retaliation or injuring according to the injury done.

Ex 21:24 eye for eye, tooth for tooth, hand for hand, foot for foot,

Deut 19:21 Your eye shall not pity: life *shall be* for life, eye for eye, tooth for tooth, hand for hand, foot for foot.

Binding with irons and fetters.

Ps 105:18 They hurt his feet with fetters, He was laid in irons.

Scourging.

Deut 25:2–3 then it shall be, if the wicked man deserves to be beaten, that the judge will cause him to lie down and be beaten in his presence, according to his guilt, with a certain number of blows. **3** Forty blows he may give him *and* no more, lest he should exceed this and beat him with many blows above these, and your brother be humiliated in your sight.

Matt 27:26 Then he released Barabbas to them; and when he had scourged Jesus, he delivered *Him* to be crucified.

Acts 22:25 And as they bound him with thongs, Paul said to the centurion who stood by, "Is it lawful for you to scourge a man who is a Roman, and uncondemned?"

2 Cor 11:24 From the Jews five times I received forty *stripes* minus one.

Selling the criminal.

Matt 18:25 But as he was not able to pay, his master commanded that he be sold, with his wife and children and all that he had, and that payment be made.

Banishment.

Ezra 7:26 Whoever will not observe the law of your God and the law of the king, let judgment be executed speedily on him, whether *it be* death, or banishment, or confiscation of goods, or imprisonment.

Rev 1:9 I, John, both your brother and companion in the tribulation and kingdom and patience of Jesus Christ, was on the island that is called Patmos for the word of God and for the testimony of Jesus Christ.

Torturing.

Matt 18:34 And his master was angry, and delivered him to the torturers until he should pay all that was due to him.

Heb 11:37 They were stoned, they were sawn in two, were tempted, were slain with the sword. They wandered about in sheepskins and goatskins, being destitute, afflicted, tormented—

Putting out the eyes.

Judg 16:21 Then the Philistines took him and put out his eyes, and brought him down to Gaza. They bound him with bronze fetters, and he became a grinder in the prison.

1 Sam 11:2 And Nahash the Ammonite answered them, "On this *condition* I will make *a covenant* with you, that I may put out all your right eyes, and bring reproach on all Israel."

Cutting off the hands and feet.

2 Sam 4:12 So David commanded his young men, and they executed them, cut off their hands and feet, and hanged *them* by the pool in Hebron. But they took the head of Ishbosheth and buried *it* in the tomb of Abner in Hebron.

Mutilating the hands and feet.

Judg 1:5–7 And they found Adoni-Bezek in Bezek, and fought against him; and they defeated the Canaanites and the Perizzites. **6** Then Adoni-Bezek fled, and they pursued him and caught him and cut off his thumbs and big toes. **7** And Adoni-Bezek said, "Seventy kings with their thumbs and big toes cut off used to gather *scraps* under my table; as I have done, so God has repaid me." Then they brought him to Jerusalem, and there he died.

Cutting off the nose and ears.

Ezek 23:25 I will set My jealousy against you, And they shall deal furiously with you; They shall remove your nose and your ears, And your remnant shall fall by the sword; They shall take your sons and your daughters, And your remnant shall be devoured by fire.

Plucking out the hair.

Neh 13:25 So I contended with them and cursed them, struck some of them and pulled out their hair, and made them swear by God, *saying,* "You shall not give your daughters as wives to their sons, nor take their daughters for your sons or yourselves.

Is 50:6 I gave My back to those who struck *Me,* And My cheeks to those who plucked out the beard; I did not hide My face from shame and spitting.

Confiscating the property.

Ezra 7:26 Whoever will not observe the law of your God and the law of the king, let judgment be executed speedily on him, whether *it be* death, or banishment, or confiscation of goods, or imprisonment.

Inflicting of capital, not permitted to the Jews by the Romans.

John 18:31 Then Pilate said to them, "You take Him and judge Him according to your law." Therefore the Jews said to him, "It is not lawful for us to put anyone to death,"

Capital kinds of,

Burning.

Gen 38:24 And it came to pass, about three months after, that Judah was told, saying, "Tamar your daughter-in-law has played the harlot; furthermore she *is* with child by harlotry." So Judah said, "Bring her out and let her be burned!"

Lev 20:14 If a man marries a woman and her mother, it *is* wickedness. They shall be burned with fire, both he and they, that there may be no wickedness among you.

Dan 3:6 and whoever does not fall down and worship shall be cast immediately into the midst of a burning fiery furnace."

Hanging.

Num 25:4 Then the LORD said to Moses, "Take all the leaders of the people and hang the offenders before the LORD, out in the sun, that the fierce anger of the LORD may turn away from Israel."

Deut 21:22–23 "If a man has committed a sin deserving of death, and he is put to death, and you hang him on a tree, **23** his body shall not remain overnight on the tree, but you shall surely bury him that day, so that you do not defile the land which the LORD your God *is* giving you *as* an inheritance; for he who is hanged *is* accursed of God.

Josh 8:29 And the king of Ai he hanged on a tree until evening. And as soon as the sun was down, Joshua commanded that they should take his corpse down from the tree, cast it at the entrance of the gate of the city, and raise over it a great heap of stones *that remains* to this day.

2 Sam 21:12 Then David went and took the bones of Saul, and the bones of Jonathan his son, from the men of Jabesh Gilead who had stolen them from the street of Beth Shan, where the Philistines had hung them up, after the Philistines had struck down Saul in Gilboa.

Esth 7:9–10 Now Harbonah, one of the eunuchs, said to the king, "Look! The gallows, fifty cubits high, which Haman made for Mordecai, who spoke good on the king's behalf, is standing at the house of Haman." Then the king said, "Hang him on it!" **10** So they hanged Haman on the gallows that he had prepared for Mordecai. Then the king's wrath subsided.

Crucifying.

Matt 20:19 and deliver Him to the Gentiles to mock and to scourge and to crucify. And the third day He will rise again."

Matt 27:35 Then they crucified Him, and divided His garments, casting lots, that it might be fulfilled which was spoken by the prophet: *"They divided My garments among them, And for My clothing they cast lots."*

Beheading.

Gen 40:19 Within three days Pharaoh will lift off your head from you and hang you on a tree; and the birds will eat your flesh from you."

Mark 6:16 But when Herod heard, he said, "This is John, whom I beheaded; he has been raised from the dead!"

Mark 6:27 Immediately the king sent an executioner and commanded his head to be brought. And he went and beheaded him in prison,

Slaying with the sword.

Acts 12:2 Then he killed James the brother of John with the sword.

Stoning.

Lev 24:14 "Take outside the camp him who has cursed; then let all who heard *him* lay their hands on his head, and let all the congregation stone him.

Deut 13:10 And you shall stone him with stones until he dies, because he sought to entice you away from

the LORD your God, who brought you out of the land of Egypt, from the house of bondage.

Acts 7:59 And they stoned Stephen as he was calling on God and saying, "Lord Jesus, receive my spirit."

Cutting in pieces.

1 Sam 15:33 But Samuel said, "As your sword has made women childless, so shall your mother be childless among women." And Samuel hacked Agag in pieces before the LORD in Gilgal.

Dan 2:5 The king answered and said to the Chaldeans, "My decision is firm: if you do not make known the dream to me, and its interpretation, you shall be cut in pieces, and your houses shall be made an ash heap.

Matt 24:51 and will cut him in two and appoint *him* his portion with the hypocrites. There shall be weeping and gnashing of teeth.

Sawing in two.

Heb 11:37 They were stoned, they were sawn in two, were tempted, were slain with the sword. They wandered about in sheepskins and goatskins, being destitute, afflicted, tormented—

Exposing to wild beasts.

Dan 6:16 So the king gave the command, and they brought Daniel and cast *him* into the den of lions. *But* the king spoke, saying to Daniel, "Your God, whom you serve continually, He will deliver you."

Dan 6:24 And the king gave the command, and they brought those men who had accused Daniel, and they cast *them* into the den of lions—them, their children, and their wives; and the lions overpowered them, and broke all their bones in pieces before they ever came to the bottom of the den.

1 Cor 15:32 If, in the manner of men, I have fought with beasts at Ephesus, what advantage *is it* to me? If *the* dead do not rise, *"Let us eat and drink, for tomorrow we die!"*

Casting headlong from a rock.

2 Chr 25:12 Also the children of Judah took captive ten thousand alive, brought them to the top of the rock, and cast them down from the top of the rock, so that they all were dashed in pieces.

Casting into the sea.

Matt 18:6 "Whoever causes one of these little ones who believe in Me to sin, it would be better for him if a millstone were hung around his neck, and he were drowned in the depth of the sea.

Strangers not exempted from.

Lev 20:2 "Again, you shall say to the children of Israel: 'Whoever of the children of Israel, or of the strangers who dwell in Israel, who gives *any* of his descendants to Molech, he shall surely be put to death. The people of the land shall stone him with stones.

Were sometimes commuted.

Ex 21:29–30 But if the ox tended to thrust with its horn in times past, and it has been made known to his owner, and he has not kept it confined, so that it has killed a man or a woman, the ox shall be stoned and its owner also shall be put to death. **30** If there is imposed on him a sum of money, then he shall pay to redeem his life, whatever is imposed on him.

For murder, not to be commuted.

Num 35:31–32 Moreover you shall take no ransom for the life of a murderer who *is* guilty of death, but he shall surely be put to death. **32** And you shall take no ransom for him who has fled to his city of refuge, that he may return to dwell in the land before the death of the priest.

PURIFICATION

Of Israel at the exodus.

Ex 14:22 So the children of Israel went into the midst of the sea on the dry *ground*, and the waters *were* a wall to them on their right hand and on their left.

1 Cor 10:2 all were baptized into Moses in the cloud and in the sea,

Of Israel before receiving the law.

Ex 19:10 Then the LORD said to Moses, "Go to the people and consecrate them today and tomorrow, and let them wash their clothes.

Of priests before consecration.

Ex 29:4 "And Aaron and his sons you shall bring to the door of the tabernacle of meeting, and you shall wash them with water.

Of Levites before consecration.

Num 8:6–7 "Take the Levites from among the children of Israel and cleanse them *ceremonially.* **7** Thus you shall do to them to cleanse them: Sprinkle water of purification on them, and let them shave all their body, and let them wash their clothes, and *so* make themselves clean.

Of high priest on Day of Atonement.

Lev 16:4 He shall put the holy linen tunic and the linen trousers on his body; he shall be girded with a linen sash, and with the linen turban he shall be attired. These *are* holy garments. Therefore he shall wash his body in water, and put them on.

Lev 16:24 And he shall wash his body with water in a holy place, put on his garments, come out and offer his burnt offering and the burnt offering of the people, and make atonement for himself and for the people.

Of things for burnt offerings.

2 Chr 4:6 He also made ten lavers, and put five on the right side and five on the left, to wash in them; such things as they offered for the burnt offering they would wash in them, but the Sea *was* for the priests to wash in.

Of individuals who were ceremonially unclean.

Lev 15:2–13 "Speak to the children of Israel, and say to them: 'When any man has a discharge from his body, his discharge *is* unclean. **3** And this shall be his uncleanness in regard to his discharge—whether his body runs with his discharge, or his body is stopped up by his discharge, it *is* his uncleanness. **4** Every bed is unclean on which he who has the discharge lies, and everything on which he sits shall be unclean. **5** And whoever touches his bed shall wash his clothes and bathe in water, and be unclean until evening. **6** He who sits on anything on which he who has the discharge sat shall wash his clothes and bathe in water, and be unclean until evening. **7** And he who touches the body of him who has the discharge shall wash his clothes and bathe in water, and be unclean until evening. **8** If he who has the discharge spits on him who is clean, then he shall wash his clothes and bathe in water, and be unclean until evening. **9** Any saddle on which he who has the discharge rides shall be unclean. **10** Whoever touches anything that was under him shall be unclean until evening. He who carries *any of* those things shall wash his clothes and bathe in water, and be unclean until evening. **11** And whomever the one who has the discharge touches, and has not rinsed his hands in water, he shall wash his clothes and bathe in water, and be unclean until evening. **12** The vessel of earth that he who has the discharge touches shall be broken, and every vessel of wood shall be rinsed in water. **13** 'And when he who has a discharge is cleansed of his discharge, then he shall count for himself seven days for his cleansing, wash his clothes, and bathe his body in running water; then he shall be clean.

Lev 17:15 "And every person who eats what died *naturally* or what was torn *by beasts, whether he is* a native of your own country or a stranger, he shall both wash his clothes and bathe in water, and be unclean until evening. Then he shall be clean.

Cf. Lev 22:4–7; Num 19:7–12,21

Of the healed leper.

Lev 14:8–9 He who is to be cleansed shall wash his clothes, shave off all his hair, and wash himself in water, that he may be clean. After that he shall come into the camp, and shall stay outside his tent seven days. **9** But on the seventh day he shall shave all the hair off his head and his beard and his eyebrows—all his hair he shall shave off. He shall wash his clothes and wash his body in water, and he shall be clean.

Of Nazirites after vow expired.

Acts 21:24 Take them and be purified with them, and pay their expenses so that they may shave *their* heads, and that all may know that those things of which they were informed concerning you are nothing, but *that* you yourself also walk orderly and keep the law.

Acts 21:26 Then Paul took the men, and the next day, having been purified with them, entered the temple to announce the expiration of the days of purification, at which time an offering should be made for each one of them.

Used by the devout before entering God's house.

Ps 26:6 I will wash my hands in innocence; So I will go about Your altar, O LORD,

Heb 10:22 let us draw near with a true heart in full assurance of faith, having our hearts sprinkled from an evil conscience and our bodies washed with pure water.

Multiplied by traditions.

Matt 15:2 "Why do Your disciples transgress the tradition of the elders? For they do not wash their hands when they eat bread."

Mark 7:3–4 For the Pharisees and all the Jews do not eat unless they wash *their* hands in a special way, holding the tradition of the elders. **4** *When they come* from the marketplace, they do not eat unless they wash. And there are many other things which they have received and hold, *like* the washing of cups, pitchers, copper vessels, and couches.

Means used for,

Water of separation.

Num 19:9 Then a man *who is* clean shall gather up the ashes of the heifer, and store *them* outside the camp in a clean place; and they shall be kept for the congregation of the children of Israel for the water of purification; it *is* for purifying from sin.

Running water.

Lev 15:13 'And when he who has a discharge is cleansed of his discharge, then he shall count for himself seven days for his cleansing, wash his clothes, and bathe his body in running water; then he shall be clean.

Water mixed with blood.

Ex 24:5–8 Then he sent young men of the children of Israel, who offered burnt offerings and sacrificed peace offerings of oxen to the LORD. **6** And Moses took half the blood and put *it* in basins, and half the blood he sprinkled on the altar. **7** Then he took the Book of the Covenant and read in the hearing of the people. And they said, "All that the LORD has said we will do, and be obedient." **8** And Moses took the blood, sprinkled *it* on the people, and said, "This is the blood of the covenant which the LORD has made with you according to all these words."

Heb 9:19 For when Moses had spoken every precept to all the people according to the law, he took the blood of calves and goats, with water, scarlet wool, and hyssop, and sprinkled both the book itself and all the people,

Was by

Sprinkling.

Num 19:13 Whoever touches the body of anyone who has died, and does not purify himself, defiles the tabernacle of the LORD. That person shall be cut off from Israel. He shall be unclean, because the water of purification was not sprinkled on him; his uncleanness *is* still on him.

Num 19:18 A clean person shall take hyssop and dip *it* in the water, sprinkle *it* on the tent, on all the vessels, on the persons who were there, or on the one who touched a bone, the slain, the dead, or a grave.

Heb 9:19 For when Moses had spoken every precept to all the people according to the law, he took the blood of calves and goats, with water, scarlet wool, and hyssop, and sprinkled both the book itself and all the people,

Washing parts of the body.

Ex 30:19 for Aaron and his sons shall wash their hands and their feet in water from it.

Washing the whole body.

Lev 8:6 Then Moses brought Aaron and his sons and washed them with water.

Lev 14:9 But on the seventh day he shall shave all the hair off his head and his beard and his eyebrows—all his hair he shall shave off. He shall wash his clothes and wash his body in water, and he shall be clean.

Of priests performed in the bronze laver.

Ex 30:18 "You shall also make a laver of bronze, with its base also of bronze, for washing. You shall put it between the tabernacle of meeting and the altar. And you shall put water in it,

2 Chr 4:6 He also made ten lavers, and put five on the right side and five on the left, to wash in them; such things as they offered for the burnt offering they would wash in them, but the Sea *was* for the priests to wash in.

Vessels in the houses of the Jews for.

John 2:6 Now there were set there six waterpots of stone, according to the manner of purification of the Jews, containing twenty or thirty gallons apiece.

Consequence of neglecting those prescribed by law.

Lev 17:16 But if he does not wash *them* or bathe his body, then he shall bear his guilt."

Num 19:13 Whoever touches the body of anyone who has died, and does not purify himself, defiles the tabernacle of the LORD. That person shall be cut off from Israel. He shall be unclean, because the water of purification was not sprinkled on him; his uncleanness *is* still on him.

Num 19:20 'But the man who is unclean and does not purify himself, that person shall be cut off from among the assembly, because he has defiled the sanctuary of the LORD. The water of purification has not been sprinkled on him; he *is* unclean.

Sanctified and purified the flesh.

Heb 9:13 For if the blood of bulls and goats and the ashes of a heifer, sprinkling the unclean, sanctifies for the purifying of the flesh,

Insufficient for spiritual purification.

Job 9:30–31 If I wash myself with snow water, And cleanse my hands with soap, **31** Yet You will plunge me into the pit, And my own clothes will abhor me.

Jer 2:22 For though you wash yourself with lye, and use much soap, *Yet* your iniquity is marked before Me," says the Lord GOD.

The Jews laid great stress on.

John 3:25 Then there arose a dispute between *some* of John's disciples and the Jews about purification.

Illustrative of

Purification by the blood of Christ.

Heb 9:9–12 It *was* symbolic for the present time in which both gifts and sacrifices are offered which cannot make him who performed the service perfect in regard to the conscience— **10** *concerned* only with foods and drinks, various washings, and fleshly ordinances imposed until the time of reformation. **11** But Christ came *as* High Priest of the good things to come, with the greater and more perfect tabernacle not made with hands, that is, not of this creation. **12** Not with the blood of goats and calves, but with His own blood He entered the Most Holy Place once for all, having obtained eternal redemption.

Regeneration.

Eph 5:26 that He might sanctify and cleanse her with the washing of water by the word,

1 John 1:7 But if we walk in the light as He is in the light, we have fellowship with one another, and the blood of Jesus Christ His Son cleanses us from all sin.

R

RAIN

Caused by condensation from the clouds.

Job 36:27–28 For He draws up drops of water, Which distill as rain from the mist, **28** Which the clouds drop down *And* pour abundantly on man.

Ps 77:17 The clouds poured out water; The skies sent out a sound; Your arrows also flashed about.

Eccl 11:3 If the clouds are full of rain, They empty *themselves* upon the earth; And if a tree falls to the south or the north, In the place where the tree falls, there it shall lie.

God

Causes it to come down.

Job 5:10 He gives rain on the earth, And sends waters on the fields.

Job 28:26 When He made a law for the rain, And a path for the thunderbolt,

Ps 147:8 Who covers the heavens with clouds, Who prepares rain for the earth, Who makes grass to grow on the mountains.

Joel 2:23 Be glad then, you children of Zion, And rejoice in the LORD your God; For He has given you the former rain faithfully, And He will cause the rain to come down for you— The former rain, And the latter rain in the first *month.*

Exhibits goodness and greatness in giving it.

Job 36:26–27 "Behold, God *is* great, and we do not know *Him;* Nor can the number of His years *be* discovered. **27** For He draws up drops of water, Which distill as rain from the mist,

Acts 14:17 Nevertheless He did not leave Himself without witness, in that He did good, gave us rain from heaven and fruitful seasons, filling our hearts with food and gladness."

Sends it upon the evil and good.

Matt 5:45 that you may be sons of your Father in heaven; for He makes His sun rise on the evil and on the good, and sends rain on the just and on the unjust.

Should be praised for it.

Ps 147:7–8 Sing to the LORD with thanksgiving; Sing praises on the harp to our God, **8** Who covers the heavens with clouds, Who prepares rain for the earth, Who makes grass to grow on the mountains.

Should be feared because of it.

Jer 5:24 They do not say in their heart, "Let us now fear the LORD our God, Who gives rain, both the former and the latter, in its season. He reserves for us the appointed weeks of the harvest."

False gods not able to give it.

Jer 14:22 Are there any among the idols of the nations that can cause rain? Or can the heavens give showers? *Are* You not He, O LORD our God? Therefore we will wait for You, Since You have made all these.

Not sent upon the earth immediately after creation.

Gen 2:5 before any plant of the field was in the earth and before any herb of the field had grown. For the LORD God had not caused it to rain on the earth, and *there was* no man to till the ground;

Rarely falls in Egypt.

Deut 11:10 For the land which you go to possess *is* not like the land of Egypt from which you have come, where you sowed your seed and watered *it* by foot, as a vegetable garden;

Zech 14:18 If the family of Egypt will not come up and enter in, they *shall have* no *rain;* they shall receive the plague with which the LORD strikes the nations who do not come up to keep the Feast of Tabernacles.

Canaan abundantly supplied with.

Deut 11:11 but the land which you cross over to possess *is* a land of hills and valleys, which drinks water from the rain of heaven,

Designed for

Refreshing the earth.

Ps 68:9 You, O God, sent a plentiful rain, Whereby You confirmed Your inheritance, When it was weary.

Ps 72:6 He shall come down like rain upon the grass before mowing, Like showers *that* water the earth.

Making the earth fruitful.

Heb 6:7 For the earth which drinks in the rain that often comes upon it, and bears herbs useful for those by whom it is cultivated, receives blessing from God;

Replenishing the springs and fountains of the earth.

Ps 104:8 They went up over the mountains; They went down into the valleys, To the place which You founded for them.

Promised in due season to the obedient.

Lev 26:4 then I will give you rain in its season, the land shall yield its produce, and the trees of the field shall yield their fruit.

Deut 11:14 then I will give *you* the rain for your land in its season, the early rain and the latter rain, that you may gather in your grain, your new wine, and your oil.

Ezek 34:26–27 I will make them and the places all around My hill a blessing; and I will cause showers to come down in their season; there shall be showers of blessing. **27** Then the trees of the field shall yield their fruit, and the earth shall yield her increase. They shall be safe in their land; and they shall know that I *am* the LORD, when I have broken the bands of their yoke and delivered them from the hand of those who enslaved them.

Frequently withheld because of sin.

Deut 11:17 lest the LORD's anger be aroused against you, and He shut up the heavens so that there be no rain, and the land yield no produce, and you perish quickly from the good land which the LORD is giving you.

Jer 3:3 Therefore the showers have been withheld, And there has been no latter rain. You have had a harlot's forehead; You refuse to be ashamed.

Jer 5:25 Your iniquities have turned these *things* away, And your sins have withheld good from you.

Amos 4:7 "I also withheld rain from you, When *there were* still three months to the harvest. I made it rain on one city, I withheld rain from another city. One part was rained upon, And where it did not rain the part withered.

The lack of,

Causes the earth to open.

Job 29:23 They waited for me *as* for the rain, And they opened their mouth wide *as* for the spring rain.

Jer 14:4 Because the ground is parched, For there was no rain in the land, The plowmen were ashamed; They covered their heads.

Dries up springs and fountains.

1 Kin 17:7 And it happened after a while that the brook dried up, because there had been no rain in the land.

Causes famine.

1 Kin 18:1–2 And it came to pass *after* many days that the word of the LORD came to Elijah, in the third year, saying, "Go, present yourself to Ahab, and I will send rain on the earth." **2** So Elijah went to present himself to Ahab; and *there was* a severe famine in Samaria.

Is removed by prayer.

1 Kin 8:35–36 "When the heavens are shut up and there is no rain because they have sinned against You, when they pray toward this place and confess Your name, and turn from their sin because You afflict them, **36** then hear in heaven, and forgive the sin of Your servants, Your people Israel, that You may teach them the good way in which they should walk; and send rain on Your land which You have given to Your people as an inheritance.

James 5:18 And he prayed again, and the heaven gave rain, and the earth produced its fruit.

Withheld for three years and six months in the days of Elijah.

1 Kin 17:1 And Elijah the Tishbite, of the inhabitants of Gilead, said to Ahab, "*As* the LORD God of Israel lives, before whom I stand, there shall not be dew nor rain these years, except at my word."

James 5:17 Elijah was a man with a nature like ours, and he prayed earnestly that it would not rain; and it did not rain on the land for three years and six months.

Divided into

Heavy.

Ezra 10:9 So all the men of Judah and Benjamin gathered at Jerusalem within three days. It *was* the ninth month, on the twentieth of the month; and all the people sat in the open square of the house of God, trembling because of *this* matter and because of heavy rain.

Plentiful.

Ps 68:9 You, O God, sent a plentiful rain, Whereby You confirmed Your inheritance, When it was weary.

Flooding.

Ezek 38:22 And I will bring him to judgment with pestilence and bloodshed; I will rain down on him, on his troops, and on the many peoples who *are* with him, flooding rain, great hailstones, fire, and brimstone.

Driving.

Prov 28:3 A poor man who oppresses the poor *Is like* a driving rain which leaves no food.

Gentle.

Job 37:6 For He says to the snow, 'Fall *on* the earth'; Likewise to the gentle rain and the heavy rain of His strength.

The former, after harvest, to prepare for planting.

Deut 11:14 then I will give *you* the rain for your land in its season, the early rain and the latter rain, that you may gather in your grain, your new wine, and your oil.

Jer 5:24 They do not say in their heart, "Let us now fear the LORD our God, Who gives rain, both the former and the latter, in its season. He reserves for us the appointed weeks of the harvest."

The latter, before harvest.

Joel 2:23 Be glad then, you children of Zion, And rejoice in the LORD your God; For He has given you the former rain faithfully, And He will cause the rain to come down for you— The former rain, And the latter rain in the first *month*.

Zech 10:1 Ask the LORD for rain In the time of the latter rain. The LORD will make flashing clouds; He will give them showers of rain, Grass in the field for everyone.

The rainbow often appears during.

Gen 9:14 It shall be, when I bring a cloud over the earth, that the rainbow shall be seen in the cloud;

Ezek 1:28 Like the appearance of a rainbow in a cloud on a rainy day, so *was* the appearance of the brightness all around it. This *was* the appearance of the likeness of the glory of the LORD. So when I saw *it*, I fell on my face, and I heard a voice of One speaking.

Often succeeded by heat and sunshine.

2 Sam 23:4 And *he shall be* like the light of the morning *when* the sun rises, A morning without clouds, *Like* the tender grass *springing* out of the earth, By clear shining after rain.'

Is 18:4 For so the LORD said to me, "I will take My rest, And I will look from My dwelling place Like clear heat in sunshine, Like a cloud of dew in the heat of harvest."

Indicated by clouds from the west.

1 Kin 18:44 Then it came to pass the seventh *time*, that he said, "There is a cloud, as small as a man's hand, rising out of the sea!" So he said, "Go up, say to Ahab, 'Prepare *your chariot*, and go down before the rain stops you.' "

Luke 12:54 Then He also said to the multitudes, "Whenever *you see* a cloud rising out of the west, immediately you say, 'A shower is coming'; and so it is.

The north wind brings forth.

Prov 25:23 The north wind brings forth rain, And a backbiting tongue an angry countenance.

Unusual in harvest time.

Prov 26:1 As snow in summer and rain in harvest, So honor is not fitting for a fool.

Storminess often accompanied.

Ps 135:7 He causes the vapors to ascend from the ends of the earth; He makes lightning for the rain; He brings the wind out of His treasuries.

Matt 7:25 and the rain descended, the floods came, and the winds blew and beat on that house; and it did not fall, for it was founded on the rock.

Matt 7:27 and the rain descended, the floods came, and the winds blew and beat on that house; and it fell. And great was its fall."

Instances of extraordinary,

Time of the Flood.

Gen 7:4 For after seven more days I will cause it to rain on the earth forty days and forty nights, and I will destroy from the face of the earth all living things that I have made."

Gen 7:12 And the rain was on the earth forty days and forty nights.

Plague of, upon Egypt.

Ex 9:18 Behold, tomorrow about this time I will cause very heavy hail to rain down, such as has not been in Egypt since its founding until now.

Ex 9:23 And Moses stretched out his rod toward heaven; and the LORD sent thunder and hail, and fire darted to the ground. And the LORD rained hail on the land of Egypt.

During wheat harvest in the days of Samuel.

1 Sam 12:17–18 *Is* today not the wheat harvest? I will call to the LORD, and He will send thunder and rain, that you may perceive and see that your wickedness *is* great, which you have done in the sight of the LORD, in asking a king for yourselves." **18** So Samuel called to the LORD, and the LORD sent thunder and rain that day; and all the people greatly feared the LORD and Samuel.

After a long drought.

1 Kin 18:45 Now it happened in the meantime that the sky became black with clouds and wind, and there was a heavy rain. So Ahab rode away and went to Jezreel.

After the captivity.

Ezra 10:9 So all the men of Judah and Benjamin gathered at Jerusalem within three days. It *was* the ninth month, on the twentieth of the month; and all the people sat in the open square of the house of God, trembling because of *this* matter and because of heavy rain.

Ezra 10:13 But *there are* many people; *it is* the season for heavy rain, and we are not able to stand outside. Nor *is this* the work of one or two days, for *there are* many of us who have transgressed in this matter.

Often impeded traveling in the east.

1 Kin 18:44 Then it came to pass the seventh *time,* that he said, "There is a cloud, as small as a man's hand, rising out of the sea!" So he said, "Go up, say to

Ahab, 'Prepare *your chariot,* and go down before the rain stops you.' "

Is 4:6 And there will be a tabernacle for shade in the daytime from the heat, for a place of refuge, and for a shelter from storm and rain.

Often destroyed houses.

Ezek 13:13–15 Therefore thus says the Lord GOD: "I will cause a stormy wind to break forth in My fury; and there shall be a flooding rain in My anger, and great hailstones in fury to consume *it.* **14** So I will break down the wall you have plastered with untempered *mortar,* and bring it down to the ground, so that its foundation will be uncovered; it will fall, and you shall be consumed in the midst of it. Then you shall know that I *am* the LORD. **15** "Thus will I accomplish My wrath on the wall and on those who have plastered it with untempered *mortar;* and I will say to you, 'The wall *is* no *more,* nor those who plastered it,

Matt 7:27 and the rain descended, the floods came, and the winds blew and beat on that house; and it fell. And great was its fall."

Illustrative of

The word of God.

Is 55:10–11 "For as the rain comes down, and the snow from heaven, And do not return there, But water the earth, And make it bring forth and bud, That it may give seed to the sower And bread to the eater, **11** So shall My word be that goes forth from My mouth; It shall not return to Me void, But it shall accomplish what I please, And it shall prosper *in the thing* for which I sent it.

The doctrine of faithful ministers.

Deut 32:2 Let my teaching drop as the rain, My speech distill as the dew, As raindrops on the tender herb, And as showers on the grass.

Christ in the communication of His graces.

Ps 72:6 He shall come down like rain upon the grass before mowing, Like showers *that* water the earth.

Hos 6:3 Let us know, Let us pursue the knowledge of the LORD. His going forth is established as the morning; He will come to us like the rain, Like the latter *and* former rain to the earth.

Spiritual blessings.

Ps 68:9 You, O God, sent a plentiful rain, Whereby You confirmed Your inheritance, When it was weary.

Ps 84:6 *As they* pass through the Valley of Baca, They make it a spring; The rain also covers it with pools.

Ezek 34:26 I will make them and the places all around My hill a blessing; and I will cause showers to come down in their season; there shall be showers of blessing.

Righteousness.

Hos 10:12 Sow for yourselves righteousness; Reap in mercy; Break up your fallow ground, For *it is* time to seek the LORD, Till He comes and rains righteousness on you.

(Destructive) God's judgments.

Job 20:23 *When* he is about to fill his stomach, *God* will cast on him the fury of His wrath, And will rain *it* on him while he is eating.

Ps 11:6 Upon the wicked He will rain coals; Fire and

brimstone and a burning wind *Shall be* the portion of their cup.

Ezek 38:22 And I will bring him to judgment with pestilence and bloodshed; I will rain down on him, on his troops, and on the many peoples who *are* with him, flooding rain, great hailstones, fire, and brimstone.

(Destructive) a poor man oppressing the poor.

Prov 28:3 A poor man who oppresses the poor *Is like* a driving rain which leaves no food.

RAPE

Of Dinah, Jacob's daughter. Gen 34:1–31

Punishment for.

Lev 19:20–22 'Whoever lies carnally with a woman who *is* betrothed to a man as a concubine, and who has not at all been redeemed nor given her freedom, for this there shall be scourging; *but* they shall not be put to death, because she was not free. **21** And he shall bring his trespass offering to the LORD, to the door of the tabernacle of meeting, a ram as a trespass offering. **22** The priest shall make atonement for him with the ram of the trespass offering before the LORD for his sin which he has committed. And the sin which he has committed shall be forgiven him.

Deut 22:23–27 "If a young woman *who is* a virgin is betrothed to a husband, and a man finds her in the city and lies with her, **24** then you shall bring them both out to the gate of that city, and you shall stone them to death with stones, the young woman because she did not cry out in the city, and the man because he humbled his neighbor's wife; so you shall put away the evil from among you. **25** "But if a man finds a betrothed young woman in the countryside, and the man forces her and lies with her, then only the man who lay with her shall die. **26** But you shall do nothing to the young woman; *there is* in the young woman no sin *deserving* of death, for just as when a man rises against his neighbor and kills him, even so *is* this matter. **27** For he found her in the countryside, *and* the betrothed young woman cried out, but *there was* no one to save her.

Cf. Matt 1:18–19

Of the Levite's concubine.

Judg 19:22–25 As they were enjoying themselves, suddenly certain men of the city, perverted men, surrounded the house *and* beat on the door. They spoke to the master of the house, the old man, saying, "Bring out the man who came to your house, that we may know him *carnally!*" **23** But the man, the master of the house, went out to them and said to them, "No, my brethren! I beg you, do not act *so* wickedly! Seeing this man has come into my house, do not commit this outrage. **24** Look, *here is* my virgin daughter and *the man's* concubine; let me bring them out now. Humble them, and do with them as you please; but to this man do not do such a vile thing!" **25** But the men would not heed him. So the man took his concubine and brought *her* out to them. And they knew her and abused her all night until morning; and when the day began to break, they let her go.

Cf. Hos 9:9; 10:9

RAPTURE OF BELIEVERS, THE

Was a mystery in the Old Testament.

1 Cor 15:51 Behold, I tell you a mystery: We shall not all sleep, but we shall all be changed—

Described as a change.

1 Cor 15:51–52 Behold, I tell you a mystery: We shall not all sleep, but we shall all be changed— **52** in a moment, in the twinkling of an eye, at the last trumpet. For the trumpet will sound, and the dead will be raised incorruptible, and we shall be changed.

Jesus' prediction of.

John 14:2–3 In My Father's house are many mansions; if *it were* not so, I would have told you. I go to prepare a place for you. **3** And if I go and prepare a place for you, I will come again and receive you to Myself; that where I am, *there* you may be also.

Paul's description of.

1 Thess 4:13–17 But I do not want you to be ignorant, brethren, concerning those who have fallen asleep, lest you sorrow as others who have no hope. **14** For if we believe that Jesus died and rose again, even so God will bring with Him those who sleep in Jesus. **15** For this we say to you by the word of the Lord, that we who are alive *and* remain until the coming of the Lord will by no means precede those who are asleep. **16** For the Lord Himself will descend from heaven with a shout, with the voice of an archangel, and with the trumpet of God. And the dead in Christ will rise first. **17** Then we who are alive *and* remain shall be caught up together with them in the clouds to meet the Lord in the air. And thus we shall always be with the Lord.

Will likely occur before the tribulation.

Rev 3:10 Because you have kept My command to persevere, I also will keep you from the hour of trial which shall come upon the whole world, to test those who dwell on the earth.

RAVEN, THE

Unclean and not to be eaten.

Lev 11:15 every raven after its kind,

Deut 14:14 every raven after its kind;

Called the raven of the valley.

Prov 30:17 The eye *that* mocks *his* father, And scorns obedience to *his* mother, The ravens of the valley will pick it out, And the young eagles will eat it.

Described as

Black.

Song 5:11 His head *is like* the finest gold; His locks *are* wavy, And black as a raven.

Solitary in disposition.

Is 34:11 But the pelican and the porcupine shall possess it, Also the owl and the raven shall dwell in it. And He shall stretch out over it The line of confusion and the stones of emptiness.

Making no provision.

Luke 12:24 Consider the ravens, for they neither sow nor reap, which have neither storehouse nor barn; and God feeds them. Of how much more value are you than the birds?

Carnivorous.

Prov 30:17 The eye *that* mocks *his* father, And scorns obedience to *his* mother, The ravens of the valley will pick it out, And the young eagles will eat it.

God provides food for.

Job 38:41 Who provides food for the raven, When its young ones cry to God, And wander about for lack of food?

Ps 147:9 He gives to the beast its food, *And* to the young ravens that cry.

Luke 12:24 Consider the ravens, for they neither sow nor reap, which have neither storehouse nor barn; and God feeds them. Of how much more value are you than the birds?

Sent by Noah from the ark.

Gen 8:7 Then he sent out a raven, which kept going to and fro until the waters had dried up from the earth.

Elijah fed by.

1 Kin 17:4–6 And it will be *that* you shall drink from the brook, and I have commanded the ravens to feed you there." **5** So he went and did according to the word of the LORD, for he went and stayed by the Brook Cherith, which flows into the Jordan. **6** The ravens brought him bread and meat in the morning, and bread and meat in the evening; and he drank from the brook.

REAPING

Is the cutting of the grain in harvest.

Job 24:6 They gather their fodder in the field And glean in the vineyard of the wicked.

Lev 23:10 "Speak to the children of Israel, and say to them: 'When you come into the land which I give to you, and reap its harvest, then you shall bring a sheaf of the firstfruits of your harvest to the priest.

The sickle used for.

Deut 16:9 "You shall count seven weeks for yourself; begin to count the seven weeks from *the time* you begin *to put* the sickle to the grain.

Mark 4:29 But when the grain ripens, immediately he puts in the sickle, because the harvest has come."

Both men and women engaged in.

Ruth 2:8–9 Then Boaz said to Ruth, "You will listen, my daughter, will you not? Do not go to glean in another field, nor go from here, but stay close by my young women. **9** *Let* your eyes *be* on the field which they reap, and go after them. Have I not commanded the young men not to touch you? And when you are thirsty, go to the vessels and drink from what the young men have drawn."

Prohibited at certain times and places

The corners of fields.

Lev 19:9 'When you reap the harvest of your land, you shall not wholly reap the corners of your field, nor shall you gather the gleanings of your harvest.

Lev 23:22 'When you reap the harvest of your land, you shall not wholly reap the corners of your field when you reap, nor shall you gather any gleaning from your harvest. You shall leave them for the poor and for the stranger: I *am* the LORD your God.' "

During the sabbatical year.

Lev 25:5 What grows of its own accord of your harvest

you shall not reap, nor gather the grapes of your untended vine, *for* it is a year of rest for the land.

During the Year of Jubilee.

Lev 25:11 That fiftieth year shall be a Jubilee to you; in it you shall neither sow nor reap what grows of its own accord, nor gather *the grapes* of your untended vine.

The fields of others.

Deut 23:25 When you come into your neighbor's standing grain, you may pluck the heads with your hand, but you shall not use a sickle on your neighbor's standing grain.

Method of, described.

Ps 129:7 With which the reaper does not fill his hand, Nor he who binds sheaves, his arms.

Is 17:5 It shall be as when the harvester gathers the grain, And reaps the heads with his arm; It shall be as he who gathers heads of grain In the Valley of Rephaim.

Grain after, was bound up into sheaves.

Gen 37:7 There we were, binding sheaves in the field. Then behold, my sheaf arose and also stood upright; and indeed your sheaves stood all around and bowed down to my sheaf."

Ps 129:7 With which the reaper does not fill his hand, Nor he who binds sheaves, his arms.

Persons engaged in,

Under the guidance of a steward.

Ruth 2:5–6 Then Boaz said to his servant who was in charge of the reapers, "Whose young woman *is* this?" **6** So the servant who was in charge of the reapers answered and said, "It *is* the young Moabite woman who came back with Naomi from the country of Moab.

Visited and fed by the master.

Ruth 2:4 Now behold, Boaz came from Bethlehem, and said to the reapers, "The LORD *be* with you!" And they answered him, "The LORD bless you!"

Ruth 2:14 Now Boaz said to her at mealtime, "Come here, and eat of the bread, and dip your piece of bread in the vinegar." So she sat beside the reapers, and he passed parched *grain* to her; and she ate and was satisfied, and kept some back.

Received wages.

John 4:36 And he who reaps receives wages, and gathers fruit for eternal life, that both he who sows and he who reaps may rejoice together.

James 5:4 Indeed the wages of the laborers who mowed your fields, which you kept back by fraud, cry out; and the cries of the reapers have reached the ears of the Lord of Sabaoth.

A time of great rejoicing.

Ps 126:5–6 Those who sow in tears Shall reap in joy. **6** He who continually goes forth weeping, Bearing seed for sowing, Shall doubtless come again with rejoicing, Bringing his sheaves *with him*.

The Jews often hindered from, because of sins.

Mic 6:15 "You shall sow, but not reap; You shall tread the olives, but not anoint yourselves with oil; And *make* sweet wine, but not drink wine.

Often unprofitable because of sin.

Jer 12:13 They have sown wheat but reaped thorns; They have put themselves to pain *but* do not profit. But be ashamed of your harvest Because of the fierce anger of the LORD."

Illustrative of

Receiving the reward of wickedness.

Job 4:8 Even as I have seen, Those who plow iniquity And sow trouble reap the same.

Prov 22:8 He who sows iniquity will reap sorrow, And the rod of his anger will fail.

Hos 8:7 "They sow the wind, And reap the whirlwind. The stalk has no bud; It shall never produce meal. If it should produce, Aliens would swallow it up.

Gal 6:8 For he who sows to his flesh will of the flesh reap corruption, but he who sows to the Spirit will of the Spirit reap everlasting life.

Receiving the reward of righteousness.

Hos 10:12 Sow for yourselves righteousness; Reap in mercy; Break up your fallow ground, For *it is* time to seek the LORD, Till He comes and rains righteousness on you.

Gal 6:8–9 For he who sows to his flesh will of the flesh reap corruption, but he who sows to the Spirit will of the Spirit reap everlasting life. **9** And let us not grow weary while doing good, for in due season we shall reap if we do not lose heart.

Ministers receiving temporal provision for spiritual labors.

1 Cor 9:11 If we have sown spiritual things for you, *is it* a great thing if we reap your material things?

Gathering in souls to God.

John 4:38 I sent you to reap that for which you have not labored; others have labored, and you have entered into their labors."

The judgments of God on the unbelieving world.

Rev 14:14–16 Then I looked, and behold, a white cloud, and on the cloud sat *One* like the Son of Man, having on His head a golden crown, and in His hand a sharp sickle. **15** And another angel came out of the temple, crying with a loud voice to Him who sat on the cloud, "Thrust in Your sickle and reap, for the time has come for You to reap, for the harvest of the earth is ripe." **16** So He who sat on the cloud thrust in His sickle on the earth, and the earth was reaped.

The final judgment.

Matt 13:30 Let both grow together until the harvest, and at the time of harvest I will say to the reapers, "First gather together the tares and bind them in bundles to burn them, but gather the wheat into my barn." ' "

Matt 13:39–43 The enemy who sowed them is the devil, the harvest is the end of the age, and the reapers are the angels. **40** Therefore as the tares are gathered and burned in the fire, so it will be at the end of this age. **41** The Son of Man will send out His angels, and they will gather out of His kingdom all things that offend, and those who practice lawlessness, **42** and will cast them into the furnace of fire. There will be wailing and gnashing of teeth. **43** Then the righteous will shine forth as the sun in the kingdom of their Father. He who has ears to hear, let him hear!

REBELLION AGAINST GOD

Forbidden.

Num 14:9 Only do not rebel against the LORD, nor fear the people of the land, for they *are* our bread; their protection has departed from them, and the LORD *is* with us. Do not fear them."

Josh 22:19 Nevertheless, if the land of your possession *is* unclean, *then* cross over to the land of the possession of the LORD, where the LORD's tabernacle stands, and take possession among us; but do not rebel against the LORD, nor rebel against us, by building yourselves an altar besides the altar of the LORD our God.

Provokes Him.

Num 16:30 But if the LORD creates a new thing, and the earth opens its mouth and swallows them up with all that belongs to them, and they go down alive into the pit, then you will understand that these men have rejected the LORD."

Neh 9:26 "Nevertheless they were disobedient And rebelled against You, Cast Your law behind their backs And killed Your prophets, who testified against them To turn them to Yourself; And they worked great provocations.

Provokes Christ.

Ex 23:20–21 "Behold, I send an Angel before you to keep you in the way and to bring you into the place which I have prepared. **21** Beware of Him and obey His voice; do not provoke Him, for He will not pardon your transgressions; for My name *is* in Him.

1 Cor 10:9 nor let us tempt Christ, as some of them also tempted, and were destroyed by serpents;

Grieves the Holy Spirit.

Is 63:10 But they rebelled and grieved His Holy Spirit; So He turned Himself against them as an enemy, *And* He fought against them.

Exhibited in

Unbelief.

Deut 9:23 Likewise, when the LORD sent you from Kadesh Barnea, saying, 'Go up and possess the land which I have given you,' then you rebelled against the commandment of the LORD your God, and you did not believe Him nor obey His voice.

Ps 106:24–25 Then they despised the pleasant land; They did not believe His word, **25** But complained in their tents, *And* did not heed the voice of the LORD.

Rejecting His government.

Josh 1:18 Whoever rebels against your command and does not heed your words, in all that you command him, shall be put to death. Only be strong and of good courage."

1 Sam 8:7 And the LORD said to Samuel, "Heed the voice of the people in all that they say to you; for they have not rejected you, but they have rejected Me, that I should not reign over them.

1 Sam 15:23 For rebellion *is as* the sin of witchcraft, And stubbornness *is as* iniquity and idolatry. Because you have rejected the word of the LORD, He also has rejected you from *being* king."

Revolting from Him.

Is 1:5 Why should you be stricken again? You will revolt more and more. The whole head is sick, And the whole heart faints.

Is 31:6 Return *to Him* against whom the children of Israel have deeply revolted.

Despising His law.

Neh 9:26 "Nevertheless they were disobedient And rebelled against You, Cast Your law behind their backs And killed Your prophets, who testified against them To turn them to Yourself; And they worked great provocations.

Despising His counsel.

Ps 107:11 Because they rebelled against the words of God, And despised the counsel of the Most High,

Distrusting His power.

Ezek 17:15 But he rebelled against him by sending his ambassadors to Egypt, that they might give him horses and many people. Will he prosper? Will he who does such *things* escape? Can he break a covenant and still be delivered?

Murmuring against Him.

Num 20:3 And the people contended with Moses and spoke, saying: "If only we had died when our brethren died before the LORD!

Num 20:10 And Moses and Aaron gathered the assembly together before the rock; and he said to them, "Hear now, you rebels! Must we bring water for you out of this rock?"

Refusing to listen to Him.

Deut 9:23 Likewise, when the LORD sent you from Kadesh Barnea, saying, 'Go up and possess the land which I have given you,' then you rebelled against the commandment of the LORD your God, and you did not believe Him nor obey His voice.

Ezek 20:8 But they rebelled against Me and would not obey Me. They did not all cast away the abominations which were before their eyes, nor did they forsake the idols of Egypt. Then I said, 'I will pour out My fury on them and fulfill My anger against them in the midst of the land of Egypt.'

Zech 7:11 But they refused to heed, shrugged their shoulders, and stopped their ears so that they could not hear.

Departing from Him.

Is 59:13 In transgressing and lying against the LORD, And departing from our God, Speaking oppression and revolt, Conceiving and uttering from the heart words of falsehood.

Dan 9:5 we have sinned and committed iniquity, we have done wickedly and rebelled, even by departing from Your precepts and Your judgments.

Departing from His instituted worship.

Ex 32:8–9 They have turned aside quickly out of the way which I commanded them. They have made themselves a molded calf, and worshiped it and sacrificed to it, and said, 'This *is* your god, O Israel, that brought you out of the land of Egypt!' " **9** And the LORD said to Moses, "I have seen this people, and indeed it *is* a stiff-necked people!

Josh 22:16–19 "Thus says the whole congregation of the LORD: 'What treachery *is* this that you have committed against the God of Israel, to turn away this day

from following the LORD, in that you have built for yourselves an altar, that you might rebel this day against the LORD? **17** *Is* the iniquity of Peor not enough for us, from which we are not cleansed till this day, although there was a plague in the congregation of the LORD, **18** but that you must turn away this day from following the LORD? And it shall be, if you rebel today against the LORD, that tomorrow He will be angry with the whole congregation of Israel. **19** Nevertheless, if the land of your possession *is* unclean, *then* cross over to the land of the possession of the LORD, where the LORD's tabernacle stands, and take possession among us; but do not rebel against the LORD, nor rebel against us, by building yourselves an altar besides the altar of the LORD our God.

Sinning against spiritual light.

Job 24:13 "There are those who rebel against the light; They do not know its ways Nor abide in its paths.

John 15:22 If I had not come and spoken to them, they would have no sin, but now they have no excuse for their sin.

Acts 13:41 *'Behold, you despisers, Marvel and perish! For I work a work in your days, A work which you will by no means believe, Though one were to declare it to you.'* "

Walking after our own thoughts.

Is 65:2 I have stretched out My hands all day long to a rebellious people, Who walk in a way *that is* not good, According to their own thoughts;

Stubbornness.

Deut 31:27 for I know your rebellion and your stiff neck. *If* today, while I am yet alive with you, you have been rebellious against the LORD, then how much more after my death?

Injustice and corruption.

Is 1:23 Your princes *are* rebellious, And companions of thieves; Everyone loves bribes, And follows after rewards. They do not defend the fatherless, Nor does the cause of the widow come before them.

Contempt of God.

Ps 107:11 Because they rebelled against the words of God, And despised the counsel of the Most High,

Man is prone to.

Deut 31:27 for I know your rebellion and your stiff neck. *If* today, while I am yet alive with you, you have been rebellious against the LORD, then how much more after my death?

Rom 7:14–18 For we know that the law is spiritual, but I am carnal, sold under sin. **15** For what I am doing, I do not understand. For what I will to do, that I do not practice; but what I hate, that I do. **16** If, then, I do what I will not to do, I agree with the law that it *is* good. **17** But now, *it is* no longer I who do it, but sin that dwells in me. **18** For I know that in me (that is, in my flesh) nothing good dwells; for to will is present with me, but *how* to perform what is good I do not find.

The heart is the seat of.

Jer 5:23 But this people has a defiant and rebellious heart; They have revolted and departed.

Matt 15:18–19 But those things which proceed out of the mouth come from the heart, and they defile a man. **19** For out of the heart proceed evil thoughts, murders, adulteries, fornications, thefts, false witness, blasphemies.

Heb 3:12 Beware, brethren, lest there be in any of you an evil heart of unbelief in departing from the living God;

Those who are guilty of,

Aggravate their sin by it.

Job 34:27 Because they turned back from Him, And would not consider any of His ways,

Practice hypocrisy to hide it.

Hos 7:14 They did not cry out to Me with their heart When they wailed upon their beds. "They assemble together for grain and new wine, They rebel against Me;

Persevere in it.

Deut 9:7 "Remember! Do not forget how you provoked the LORD your God to wrath in the wilderness. From the day that you departed from the land of Egypt until you came to this place, you have been rebellious against the LORD.

Deut 9:24 You have been rebellious against the LORD from the day that I knew you.

Increase in it, though chastised.

Is 1:5 Why should you be stricken again? You will revolt more and more. The whole head is sick, And the whole heart faints.

Warned not to exalt themselves.

Ps 66:7 He rules by His power forever; His eyes observe the nations; Do not let the rebellious exalt themselves. Selah

Denounced.

Is 30:1 "Woe to the rebellious children," says the LORD, "Who take counsel, but not of Me, And who devise plans, but not of My Spirit, That they may add sin to sin;

Have God as their enemy.

1 Sam 12:15 However, if you do not obey the voice of the LORD, but rebel against the commandment of the LORD, then the hand of the LORD will be against you, as *it was* against your fathers.

Ps 106:26–27 Therefore He raised His hand *in an oath* against them, To overthrow them in the wilderness, **27** To overthrow their descendants among the nations, And to scatter them in the lands.

Is 63:10 But they rebelled and grieved His Holy Spirit; So He turned Himself against them as an enemy, *And* He fought against them.

Impoverished for it.

Ps 68:6 God sets the solitary in families; He brings out those who are bound into prosperity; But the rebellious dwell in a dry *land.*

Brought low because of it.

Ps 107:11–12 Because they rebelled against the words of God, And despised the counsel of the Most High, **12** Therefore He brought down their heart with labor; They fell down, and *there was* none to help.

Delivered into the hands of enemies because of it.

Neh 9:26–27 "Nevertheless they were disobedient And rebelled against You, Cast Your law behind their backs And killed Your prophets, who testified against them To turn them to Yourself; And they worked great provocations. **27** Therefore You delivered them into the hand of their enemies, Who oppressed them; And in the time of their trouble, When they cried to You, You heard from heaven; And according to Your abundant mercies You gave them deliverers who saved them From the hand of their enemies.

Cast out because of it.

Ps 5:10 Pronounce them guilty, O God! Let them fall by their own counsels; Cast them out in the multitude of their transgressions, For they have rebelled against You.

Ezek 20:38 I will purge the rebels from among you, and those who transgress against Me; I will bring them out of the country where they dwell, but they shall not enter the land of Israel. Then you will know that I *am* the LORD.

Restored through Christ alone.

Ps 68:18 You have ascended on high, You have led captivity captive; You have received gifts among men, Even *from* the rebellious, That the LORD God might dwell *there.*

Heinousness of.

1 Sam 15:23 For rebellion *is as* the sin of witchcraft, And stubbornness *is as* iniquity and idolatry. Because you have rejected the word of the LORD, He also has rejected you from *being* king."

Guilt of,

Aggravated by God's fatherly care and concern.

Is 1:2 Hear, O heavens, and give ear, O earth! For the LORD has spoken: "I have nourished and brought up children, And they have rebelled against Me;

Is 65:2 I have stretched out My hands all day long to a rebellious people, Who walk in a way *that is* not good, According to their own thoughts;

To be avoided.

Josh 22:29 Far be it from us that we should rebel against the LORD, and turn from following the LORD this day, to build an altar for burnt offerings, for grain offerings, or for sacrifices, besides the altar of the LORD our God which *is* before His tabernacle."

To be confessed.

Lam 1:18 "The LORD is righteous, For I rebelled against His commandment. Hear now, all peoples, And behold my sorrow; My virgins and my young men Have gone into captivity.

Lam 1:20 "See, O LORD, that I *am* in distress; My soul is troubled; My heart is overturned within me, For I have been very rebellious. Outside the sword bereaves, At home *it is* like death.

Dan 9:5 we have sinned and committed iniquity, we have done wickedly and rebelled, even by departing from Your precepts and Your judgments.

God alone can forgive.

Neh 9:17 They refused to obey, And they were not mindful of Your wonders That You did among them. But they hardened their necks, And in their rebellion They appointed a leader To return to their bondage. But You *are* God, Ready to pardon, Gracious and merciful, Slow to anger, Abundant in kindness, And did not forsake them.

Dan 9:9 To the Lord our God *belong* mercy and forgiveness, though we have rebelled against Him.

Religious instruction designed to prevent.

Ps 78:5 For He established a testimony in Jacob, And appointed a law in Israel, Which He commanded our fathers, That they should make them known to their children;

Ps 78:8 And may not be like their fathers, A stubborn and rebellious generation, A generation *that* did not set its heart aright, And whose spirit was not faithful to God.

Promises to those who avoid.

1 Sam 12:14 If you fear the LORD and serve Him and obey His voice, and do not rebel against the commandment of the LORD, then both you and the king who reigns over you will continue following the LORD your God.

Cf. Deut 28:1–13

Forgiven upon repentance.

Neh 9:26–27 "Nevertheless they were disobedient And rebelled against You, Cast Your law behind their backs And killed Your prophets, who testified against them To turn them to Yourself; And they worked great provocations. 27 Therefore You delivered them into the hand of their enemies, Who oppressed them; And in the time of their trouble, When they cried to You, You heard from heaven; And according to Your abundant mercies You gave them deliverers who saved them From the hand of their enemies.

Ministers

Cautioned against it.

Ezek 2:8 But you, son of man, hear what I say to you. Do not be rebellious like that rebellious house; open your mouth and eat what I give you."

Often sent to people guilty of it.

Ezek 2:3–7 And He said to me: "Son of man, I am sending you to the children of Israel, to a rebellious nation that has rebelled against Me; they and their fathers have transgressed against Me to this very day. 4 For *they are* impudent and stubborn children. I am sending you to them, and you shall say to them, 'Thus says the Lord GOD.' 5 As for them, whether they hear or whether they refuse—for they *are* a rebellious house— yet they will know that a prophet has been among them. 6 "And you, son of man, do not be afraid of them nor be afraid of their words, though briers and thorns *are* with you and you dwell among scorpions; do not be afraid of their words or dismayed by their looks, though they *are* a rebellious house. 7 You shall speak My words to them, whether they hear or whether they refuse, for they *are* rebellious.

Ezek 3:4–9 Then He said to me: "Son of man, go to the house of Israel and speak with My words to them. 5 For you *are* not sent to a people of unfamiliar speech and of hard language, *but* to the house of Israel, 6 not to many people of unfamiliar speech and of hard language, whose words you cannot understand. Surely, had I sent you to them, they would have listened to you. 7 But the house of Israel will not listen to you, because they will not listen to Me; for all the house of Israel *are* impudent and hardhearted. 8 Behold, I have made your face strong against their faces, and your forehead strong against

their foreheads. 9 Like adamant stone, harder than flint, I have made your forehead; do not be afraid of them, nor be dismayed at their looks, though they *are* a rebellious house."

Mark 12:4–8 Again he sent them another servant, and at him they threw stones, wounded *him* in the head, and sent *him* away shamefully treated. 5 And again he sent another, and him they killed; and many others, beating some and killing some. 6 Therefore still having one son, his beloved, he also sent him to them last, saying, 'They will respect my son.' 7 But those vinedressers said among themselves, 'This is the heir. Come, let us kill him, and the inheritance will be ours.' 8 So they took him and killed *him* and cast *him* out of the vineyard.

Should testify against it.

Num 14:9 Only do not rebel against the LORD, nor fear the people of the land, for they *are* our bread; their protection has departed from them, and the LORD *is* with us. Do not fear them."

Is 30:8–9 Now go, write it before them on a tablet, And note it on a scroll, That it may be for time to come, Forever and ever: 9 That this *is* a rebellious people, Lying children, Children *who* will not hear the law of the LORD;

Ezek 17:12 "Say now to the rebellious house: 'Do you not know what these *things mean?*' Tell *them*, 'Indeed the king of Babylon went to Jerusalem and took its king and princes, and led them with him to Babylon.

Ezek 44:6 "Now say to the rebellious, to the house of Israel, 'Thus says the Lord GOD: "O house of Israel, let Us have no more of all your abominations.

Should remind their people of past occurrences.

Deut 9:7 "Remember! Do not forget how you provoked the LORD your God to wrath in the wilderness. From the day that you departed from the land of Egypt until you came to this place, you have been rebellious against the LORD.

Deut 31:27 for I know your rebellion and your stiff neck. *If* today, while I am yet alive with you, you have been rebellious against the LORD, then how much more after my death?

Punishment for.

1 Sam 12:15 However, if you do not obey the voice of the LORD, but rebel against the commandment of the LORD, then the hand of the LORD will be against you, as *it was* against your fathers.

Is 1:20 But if you refuse and rebel, You shall be devoured by the sword"; For the mouth of the LORD has spoken.

Jer 4:16–18 "Make mention to the nations, Yes, proclaim against Jerusalem, *That* watchers come from a far country And raise their voice against the cities of Judah. 17 Like keepers of a field they are against her all around, Because she has been rebellious against Me," says the LORD. 18 "Your ways and your doings Have procured these *things* for you. This *is* your wickedness, Because it is bitter, Because it reaches to your heart."

Ezek 20:8 But they rebelled against Me and would not obey Me. They did not all cast away the abominations which were before their eyes, nor did they forsake the idols of Egypt. Then I said, 'I will pour out

My fury on them and fulfill My anger against them in the midst of the land of Egypt.'

Ezek 20:38 I will purge the rebels from among you, and those who transgress against Me; I will bring them out of the country where they dwell, but they shall not enter the land of Israel. Then you will know that I *am* the LORD.

Cf. Lev 26:14–39

Punishment for teaching.

Jer 28:16 Therefore thus says the LORD: 'Behold, I will cast you from the face of the earth. This year you shall die, because you have taught rebellion against the LORD.' "

Ingratitude of—illustrated.

Is 1:2–3 Hear, O heavens, and give ear, O earth! For the LORD has spoken: "I have nourished and brought up children, And they have rebelled against Me; **3** The ox knows its owner And the donkey its master's crib; *But* Israel does not know, My people do not consider."

Illustrated by

Pharaoh.

Ex 5:1–2 Afterward Moses and Aaron went in and told Pharaoh, "Thus says the LORD God of Israel: 'Let My people go, that they may hold a feast to Me in the wilderness.' " **2** And Pharaoh said, "Who *is* the LORD, that I should obey His voice to let Israel go? I do not know the LORD, nor will I let Israel go."

Korah, etc.

Num 16:11 Therefore you and all your company *are* gathered together against the LORD. And what *is* Aaron that you complain against him?"

Moses and Aaron.

Num 20:12 Then the LORD spoke to Moses and Aaron, "Because you did not believe Me, to hallow Me in the eyes of the children of Israel, therefore you shall not bring this assembly into the land which I have given them."

Num 20:24 "Aaron shall be gathered to his people, for he shall not enter the land which I have given to the children of Israel, because you rebelled against My word at the water of Meribah.

The Israelites.

Deut 9:23–24 Likewise, when the LORD sent you from Kadesh Barnea, saying, 'Go up and possess the land which I have given you,' then you rebelled against the commandment of the LORD your God, and you did not believe Him nor obey His voice. **24** You have been rebellious against the LORD from the day that I knew you.

Saul.

1 Sam 15:9 But Saul and the people spared Agag and the best of the sheep, the oxen, the fatlings, the lambs, and all *that was* good, and were unwilling to utterly destroy them. But everything despised and worthless, that they utterly destroyed.

1 Sam 15:23 For rebellion *is as* the sin of witchcraft, And stubbornness *is as* iniquity and idolatry. Because you have rejected the word of the LORD, He also has rejected you from *being* king."

Jeroboam.

1 Kin 12:28–33 Therefore the king asked advice, made two calves of gold, and said to the people, "It is too much for you to go up to Jerusalem. Here are your gods, O Israel, which brought you up from the land of Egypt!" **29** And he set up one in Bethel, and the other he put in Dan. **30** Now this thing became a sin, for the people went *to worship* before the one as far as Dan. **31** He made shrines on the high places, and made priests from every class of people, who were not of the sons of Levi. **32** Jeroboam ordained a feast on the fifteenth day of the eighth month, like the feast that *was* in Judah, and offered sacrifices on the altar. So he did at Bethel, sacrificing to the calves that he had made. And at Bethel he installed the priests of the high places which he had made. **33** So he made offerings on the altar which he had made at Bethel on the fifteenth day of the eighth month, in the month which he had devised in his own heart. And he ordained a feast for the children of Israel, and offered sacrifices on the altar and burned incense.

Zedekiah.

2 Chr 36:13 And he also rebelled against King Nebuchadnezzar, who had made him swear *an oath* by God; but he stiffened his neck and hardened his heart against turning to the LORD God of Israel.

The kingdom of Israel.

Hos 7:14 They did not cry out to Me with their heart When they wailed upon their beds. "They assemble together for grain and new wine, They rebel against Me;

Hos 13:16 Samaria is held guilty, For she has rebelled against her God. They shall fall by the sword, Their infants shall be dashed in pieces, And their women with child ripped open.

REBUKE

God gives, to his own children.

2 Sam 7:14 I will be his Father, and he shall be My son. If he commits iniquity, I will chasten him with the rod of men and with the blows of the sons of men.

Job 5:17 "Behold, happy *is* the man whom God corrects; Therefore do not despise the chastening of the Almighty.

Ps 94:12 Blessed *is* the man whom You instruct, O LORD, And teach out of Your law,

Ps 119:67 Before I was afflicted I went astray, But now I keep Your word.

Ps 119:71 *It is* good for me that I have been afflicted, That I may learn Your statutes.

Ps 119:75 I know, O LORD, that Your judgments *are* right, And *that* in faithfulness You have afflicted me.

Heb 12:6–7 *For whom the LORD loves He chastens, And scourges every son whom He receives."* **7** If you endure chastening, God deals with you as with sons; for what son is there whom a father does not chasten?

God gives, to the wicked.

Ps 50:21 These *things* you have done, and I kept silent; You thought that I was altogether like you; *But* I will rebuke you, And set *them* in order before your eyes.

Is 51:20 Your sons have fainted, They lie at the head of all the streets, Like an antelope in a net; They are full of the fury of the LORD, The rebuke of your God.

Christ sent to give.

Is 2:4 He shall judge between the nations, And rebuke many people; They shall beat their swords into plowshares, And their spears into pruning hooks; Nation shall not lift up sword against nation, Neither shall they learn war anymore.

Is 11:3–4 His delight *is* in the fear of the LORD, And He shall not judge by the sight of His eyes, Nor decide by the hearing of His ears; 4 But with righteousness He shall judge the poor, And decide with equity for the meek of the earth; He shall strike the earth with the rod of His mouth, And with the breath of His lips He shall slay the wicked.

Rev 3:19 As many as I love, I rebuke and chasten. Therefore be zealous and repent.

The Holy Spirit gives.

John 16:7–8 Nevertheless I tell you the truth. It is to your advantage that I go away; for if I do not go away, the Helper will not come to you; but if I depart, I will send Him to you. 8 And when He has come, He will convict the world of sin, and of righteousness, and of judgment:

Comes because of

Impenitence.

Matt 11:20–24 Then He began to rebuke the cities in which most of His mighty works had been done, because they did not repent: 21 "Woe to you, Chorazin! Woe to you, Bethsaida! For if the mighty works which were done in you had been done in Tyre and Sidon, they would have repented long ago in sackcloth and ashes. 22 But I say to you, it will be more tolerable for Tyre and Sidon in the day of judgment than for you. 23 And you, Capernaum, who are exalted to heaven, will be brought down to Hades; for if the mighty works which were done in you had been done in Sodom, it would have remained until this day. 24 But I say to you that it shall be more tolerable for the land of Sodom in the day of judgment than for you."

Lack of spiritual understanding.

Matt 16:9 Do you not yet understand, or remember the five loaves of the five thousand and how many baskets you took up?

Matt 16:11 How is it you do not understand that I did not speak to you concerning bread?—*but* to beware of the leaven of the Pharisees and Sadducees."

Mark 7:18 So He said to them, "Are you thus without understanding also? Do you not perceive that whatever enters a man from outside cannot defile him,

Luke 24:25 Then He said to them, "O foolish ones, and slow of heart to believe in all that the prophets have spoken!

John 8:43 Why do you not understand My speech? Because you are not able to listen to My word.

John 13:7–8 Jesus answered and said to him, "What I am doing you do not understand now, but you will know after this." 8 Peter said to Him, "You shall never wash my feet!" Jesus answered him, "If I do not wash you, you have no part with Me."

Hardness of heart.

Mark 8:17 But Jesus, being aware of *it*, said to them, "Why do you reason because you have no bread? Do you not yet perceive nor understand? Is your heart still hardened?

Mark 16:14 Later He appeared to the eleven as they sat at the table; and He rebuked their unbelief and hardness of heart, because they did not believe those who had seen Him after He had risen.

Fearfulness.

Mark 4:40 But He said to them, "Why are you so fearful? How *is it* that you have no faith?"

Luke 24:37–38 But they were terrified and frightened, and supposed they had seen a spirit. 38 And He said to them, "Why are you troubled? And why do doubts arise in your hearts?

Unbelief.

Matt 17:17 Then Jesus answered and said, "O faithless and perverse generation, how long shall I be with you? How long shall I bear with you? Bring him here to Me."

Matt 17:20 So Jesus said to them, "Because of your unbelief; for assuredly, I say to you, if you have faith as a mustard seed, you will say to this mountain, 'Move from here to there,' and it will move; and nothing will be impossible for you.

Mark 16:14 Later He appeared to the eleven as they sat at the table; and He rebuked their unbelief and hardness of heart, because they did not believe those who had seen Him after He had risen.

Vain boasting.

Luke 22:34 Then He said, "I tell you, Peter, the rooster shall not crow this day before you will deny three times that you know Me."

Hypocrisy.

Matt 15:7 Hypocrites! Well did Isaiah prophesy about you, saying:

Matt 23:13 "But woe to you, scribes and Pharisees, hypocrites! For you shut up the kingdom of heaven against men; for you neither go in *yourselves,* nor do you allow those who are entering to go in.

Reviling Christ.

Luke 23:40 But the other, answering, rebuked him, saying, "Do you not even fear God, seeing you are under the same condemnation?

Unruly conduct.

1 Thess 5:14 Now we exhort you, brethren, warn those who are unruly, comfort the fainthearted, uphold the weak, be patient with all.

Oppressing our brethren.

Neh 5:7 After serious thought, I rebuked the nobles and rulers, and said to them, "Each of you is exacting usury from his brother." So I called a great assembly against them.

Sinful practices.

Matt 21:13 And He said to them, "It is written, '*My house shall be called a house of prayer,*' but you have made it a '*den of thieves.*'"

Luke 3:19 But Herod the tetrarch, being rebuked by him concerning Herodias, his brother Philip's wife, and for all the evils which Herod had done,

John 2:16 And He said to those who sold doves, "Take these things away! Do not make My Father's house a house of merchandise!"

The Scriptures are profitable for.

Ps 19:7–11 The law of the LORD *is* perfect, converting the soul; The testimony of the LORD *is* sure, making wise the simple; **8** The statutes of the LORD *are* right, rejoicing the heart; The commandment of the LORD *is* pure, enlightening the eyes; **9** The fear of the LORD *is* clean, enduring forever; The judgments of the LORD *are* true *and* righteous altogether. **10** More to be desired *are they* than gold, Yea, than much fine gold; Sweeter also than honey and the honeycomb. **11** Moreover by them Your servant is warned, *And* in keeping them *there is* great reward.

2 Tim 3:16 All Scripture *is* given by inspiration of God, and *is* profitable for doctrine, for reproof, for correction, for instruction in righteousness,

When from God,

Is for correction.

Ps 39:11 When with rebukes You correct man for iniquity, You make his beauty melt away like a moth; Surely every man *is* vapor. Selah

Is despised by the wicked.

Prov 1:30 They would have none of my counsel *And* despised my every rebuke.

Should not discourage believers.

Heb 12:5 And you have forgotten the exhortation which speaks to you as to sons: *"My son, do not despise the chastening of the LORD, Nor be discouraged when you are rebuked by Him;*

Pray that it be not be in anger.

Ps 6:1 O LORD, do not rebuke me in Your anger, Nor chasten me in Your hot displeasure.

Should be accompanied by exhortation to repentance.

1 Sam 12:20–25 Then Samuel said to the people, "Do not fear. You have done all this wickedness; yet do not turn aside from following the LORD, but serve the LORD with all your heart. **21** And do not turn aside; for *then you would go* after empty things which cannot profit or deliver, for they *are* nothing. **22** For the LORD will not forsake His people, for His great name's sake, because it has pleased the LORD to make you His people. **23** Moreover, as for me, far be it from me that I should sin against the LORD in ceasing to pray for you; but I will teach you the good and the right way. **24** Only fear the LORD, and serve Him in truth with all your heart; for consider what great things He has done for you. **25** But if you still do wickedly, you shall be swept away, both you and your king."

Declared to be

Better than secret love.

Prov 27:5 Open rebuke *is* better Than love carefully concealed.

Better than the praise of fools.

Eccl 7:5 *It is* better to hear the rebuke of the wise Than for a man to hear the song of fools.

An excellent oil.

Ps 141:5 Let the righteous strike me; *It shall be* a kindness. And let him rebuke me; *It shall be* as excellent oil; Let my head not refuse it. For still my prayer *is* against the deeds of the wicked.

More profitable to saints than stripes to a fool.

Prov 17:10 Rebuke is more effective for a wise *man* Than a hundred blows on a fool.

A proof of faithful friendship.

Prov 27:6 Faithful *are* the wounds of a friend, But the kisses of an enemy *are* deceitful.

Leads to

Prudence.

Prov 15:5 A fool despises his father's instruction, But he who receives correction is prudent.

Understanding.

Prov 15:32 He who disdains instruction despises his own soul, But he who heeds rebuke gets understanding.

Knowledge.

Prov 19:25 Strike a scoffer, and the simple will become wary; Rebuke one who has understanding, *and* he will discern knowledge.

Wisdom.

Prov 15:31 The ear that hears the rebukes of life Will abide among the wise.

Prov 29:15 The rod and rebuke give wisdom, But a child left *to* himself brings shame to his mother.

Honor.

Prov 13:18 Poverty and shame *will come* to him who disdains correction, But he who regards a rebuke will be honored.

Happiness.

Prov 6:23 For the commandment *is* a lamp, And the law a light; Reproofs of instruction *are* the way of life,

Eventually brings more respect than flattery.

Prov 28:23 He who rebukes a man will find more favor afterward Than he who flatters with the tongue.

Of those who offend, a warning to others.

Lev 19:17 'You shall not hate your brother in your heart. You shall surely rebuke your neighbor, and not bear sin because of him.

Acts 5:3–4 But Peter said, "Ananias, why has Satan filled your heart to lie to the Holy Spirit and keep back *part* of the price of the land for yourself? **4** While it remained, was it not your own? And after it was sold, was it not in your own control? Why have you conceived this thing in your heart? You have not lied to men but to God."

Acts 5:9 Then Peter said to her, "How is it that you have agreed together to test the Spirit of the Lord? Look, the feet of those who have buried your husband *are* at the door, and they will carry you out."

1 Tim 5:20 Those who are sinning rebuke in the presence of all, that the rest also may fear.

Titus 1:10 For there are many insubordinate, both idle talkers and deceivers, especially those of the circumcision,

Titus 1:13 This testimony is true. Therefore rebuke them sharply, that they may be sound in the faith,

Hypocrites not qualified to give.

Matt 7:5 Hypocrite! First remove the plank from your own eye, and then you will see clearly to remove the speck from your brother's eye.

Ministers are sent to give.

Jer 44:4 However I have sent to you all My servants the prophets, rising early and sending *them,* saying, "Oh, do not do this abominable thing that I hate!"

Ezek 3:17 "Son of man, I have made you a watchman for the house of Israel; therefore hear a word from My mouth, and give them warning from Me:

Mic 3:8 But truly I am full of power by the Spirit of the LORD, And of justice and might, To declare to Jacob his transgression And to Israel his sin.

Should be given

Openly.

1 Tim 5:20 Those who are sinning rebuke in the presence of all, that the rest also may fear.

Fearlessly.

Ezek 2:3–7 And He said to me: "Son of man, I am sending you to the children of Israel, to a rebellious nation that has rebelled against Me; they and their fathers have transgressed against Me to this very day. **4** For *they are* impudent and stubborn children. I am sending you to them, and you shall say to them, 'Thus says the Lord GOD.' **5** As for them, whether they hear or whether they refuse—for they *are* a rebellious house— yet they will know that a prophet has been among them. **6** "And you, son of man, do not be afraid of them nor be afraid of their words, though briers and thorns *are* with you and you dwell among scorpions; do not be afraid of their words or dismayed by their looks, though they *are* a rebellious house. **7** You shall speak My words to them, whether they hear or whether they refuse, for they *are* rebellious.

With all authority.

Titus 2:15 Speak these things, exhort, and rebuke with all authority. Let no one despise you.

With longsuffering, etc.

2 Tim 4:2 Preach the word! Be ready in season *and* out of season. Convince, rebuke, exhort, with all long-suffering and teaching.

Unreservedly.

Is 58:1 "Cry aloud, spare not; Lift up your voice like a trumpet; Tell My people their transgression, And the house of Jacob their sins.

Sharply, if necessary.

Titus 1:13 This testimony is true. Therefore rebuke them sharply, that they may be sound in the faith,

With Christian love.

2 Thess 3:15 Yet do not count *him* as an enemy, but admonish *him* as a brother.

Those who give, are hated by scoffers.

Prov 9:8 Do not correct a scoffer, lest he hate you; Rebuke a wise *man,* and he will love you.

Prov 15:12 A scoffer does not love one who corrects him, Nor will he go to the wise.

Hatred of,

A proof of stupidity.

Prov 12:1 Whoever loves instruction loves knowledge, But he who hates correction *is* stupid.

Leads to destruction.

Prov 15:10 Harsh discipline *is* for him who forsakes the way, *And* he who hates correction will die.

Prov 29:1 He who is often rebuked, *and* hardens *his* neck, Will suddenly be destroyed, and that without remedy.

Leads to remorse.

Prov 5:12 And say: "How I have hated instruction, And my heart despised correction!

Leads to error.

Prov 10:17 He who keeps instruction *is in* the way of life, But he who refuses correction goes astray.

Believers should

Administer.

Lev 19:17 'You shall not hate your brother in your heart. You shall surely rebuke your neighbor, and not bear sin because of him.

Eph 5:11 And have no fellowship with the unfruitful works of darkness, but rather expose *them.*

Give no occasion to receive.

Phil 2:15 that you may become blameless and harmless, children of God without fault in the midst of a crooked and perverse generation, among whom you shine as lights in the world,

Receive kindly.

Ps 141:5 Let the righteous strike me; *It shall be* a kindness. And let him rebuke me; *It shall be* as excellent oil; Let my head not refuse it. For still my prayer *is* against the deeds of the wicked.

Love those who give.

Prov 9:8 Do not correct a scoffer, lest he hate you; Rebuke a wise *man,* and he will love you.

Delight in those who give.

Prov 24:25 But those who rebuke *the wicked* will have delight, And a good blessing will come upon them.

Giving of, exemplified by

Samuel.

1 Sam 13:13 And Samuel said to Saul, "You have done foolishly. You have not kept the commandment of the LORD your God, which He commanded you. For now the LORD would have established your kingdom over Israel forever.

Nathan.

2 Sam 12:7–9 Then Nathan said to David, "You *are* the man! Thus says the LORD God of Israel: 'I anointed you king over Israel, and I delivered you from the hand of Saul. **8** I gave you your master's house and your master's wives into your keeping, and gave you the house of Israel and Judah. And if *that had been* too little, I also would have given you much more! **9** Why have you despised the commandment of the LORD, to do evil in His sight? You have killed Uriah the Hittite with the sword; you have taken his wife *to be* your wife, and have killed him with the sword of the people of Ammon.

Ahijah.

1 Kin 14:7–11 Go, tell Jeroboam, 'Thus says the LORD God of Israel: "Because I exalted you from among the people, and made you ruler over My people Israel, **8** and tore the kingdom away from the house of David, and gave it to you; and *yet* you have not been as My servant David, who kept My commandments and who followed Me with all his heart, to do only *what was* right in My eyes; **9** but you have done more evil than all who were before you, for you have gone and made for yourself other gods and molded images to provoke Me to anger, and have cast Me behind your back— 10 therefore behold! I will bring disaster on the house of Jeroboam, and will cut off from Jeroboam every male in Israel, bond and free; I will take away the remnant of the house of Jeroboam, as one takes away refuse until it is all gone. 11 The dogs shall eat whoever belongs to Jeroboam and dies in the city, and the birds of the air shall eat whoever dies in the field; for the LORD has spoken!" '

Elijah.

1 Kin 21:20 So Ahab said to Elijah, "Have you found me, O my enemy?" And he answered, "I have found *you*, because you have sold yourself to do evil in the sight of the LORD:

Elisha.

2 Kin 5:26–27 Then he said to him, "Did not my heart go *with you* when the man turned back from his chariot to meet you? *Is it* time to receive money and to receive clothing, olive groves and vineyards, sheep and oxen, male and female servants? 27 Therefore the leprosy of Naaman shall cling to you and your descendants forever." And he went out from his presence leprous, *as white* as snow.

Joab.

1 Chr 21:3 And Joab answered, "May the LORD make His people a hundred times more than they are. But, my lord the king, *are* they not all my lord's servants? Why then does my lord require this thing? Why should he be a cause of guilt in Israel?"

Shemaiah.

2 Chr 12:5 Then Shemaiah the prophet came to Rehoboam and the leaders of Judah, who were gathered together in Jerusalem because of Shishak, and said to them, "Thus says the LORD: 'You have forsaken Me, and therefore I also have left you in the hand of Shishak.' "

Hanani.

2 Chr 16:7 And at that time Hanani the seer came to Asa king of Judah, and said to him: "Because you have relied on the king of Syria, and have not relied on the LORD your God, therefore the army of the king of Syria has escaped from your hand.

Zechariah.

2 Chr 24:20 Then the Spirit of God came upon Zechariah the son of Jehoiada the priest, who stood above the people, and said to them, "Thus says God: 'Why do you transgress the commandments of the LORD, so that you cannot prosper? Because you have forsaken the LORD, He also has forsaken you.' "

Daniel.

Dan 5:22–23 "But you his son, Belshazzar, have not humbled your heart, although you knew all this. 23 And you have lifted yourself up against the Lord of heaven. They have brought the vessels of His house before you, and you and your lords, your wives and your concubines, have drunk wine from them. And you have praised the gods of silver and gold, bronze and iron, wood and stone, which do not see or hear or know; and the God who *holds* your breath in His hand and owns all your ways, you have not glorified.

John the Baptist.

Matt 3:7 But when he saw many of the Pharisees and Sadducees coming to his baptism, he said to them, "Brood of vipers! Who warned you to flee from the wrath to come?

Luke 3:19 But Herod the tetrarch, being rebuked by him concerning Herodias, his brother Philip's wife, and for all the evils which Herod had done,

Stephen.

Acts 7:51 "*You* stiff-necked and uncircumcised in heart and ears! You always resist the Holy Spirit; as your fathers *did*, so *do* you.

Peter.

Acts 8:20 But Peter said to him, "Your money perish with you, because you thought that the gift of God could be purchased with money!

Paul.

1 Cor 1:10–13 Now I plead with you, brethren, by the name of our Lord Jesus Christ, that you all speak the same thing, and *that* there be no divisions among you, but *that* you be perfectly joined together in the same mind and in the same judgment. 11 For it has been declared to me concerning you, my brethren, by those of Chloe's *household*, that there are contentions among you. 12 Now I say this, that each of you says, "I am of Paul," or "I am of Apollos," or "I am of Cephas," or "I am of Christ." 13 Is Christ divided? Was Paul crucified for you? Or were you baptized in the name of Paul?

Cf. 1 Cor 5:1–5; 6:1–8; 11:17–22; Gal 2:11

RECHABITES, THE

Descended from Hammath.

1 Chr 2:55 And the families of the scribes who dwelt at Jabez *were* the Tirathites, the Shimeathites, *and* the Suchathites. These *were* the Kenites who came from Hammath, the father of the house of Rechab.

The head of, assisted Jehu in his conspiracy against the house of Ahab.

2 Kin 10:15–17 Now when he departed from there, he met Jehonadab the son of Rechab, *coming* to meet him; and he greeted him and said to him, "Is your heart right, as my heart *is* toward your heart?" And Jehonadab answered, "It is." Jehu said, "If it is, give *me* your hand." So he gave *him* his hand, and he took him up to him into the chariot. 16 Then he said, "Come with me, and see my zeal for the LORD." So they had him ride in his chariot. 17 And when he came to Samaria, he killed all who remained to Ahab in Samaria, till he had destroyed them, according to the word of the LORD which He spoke to Elijah.

Prohibited by Jonadab from forming settlements or drinking wine.

Jer 35:6–8 But they said, "We will drink no wine, for Jonadab the son of Rechab, our father, commanded us, saying, 'You shall drink no wine, you nor your sons, forever. 7 You shall not build a house, sow seed, plant a vineyard, nor have *any of these*; but all your days you shall dwell in tents, that you may live many days in the land where you are sojourners.' 8 Thus we have obeyed the voice of Jonadab the son of Rechab, our father, in all that he charged us, to drink no wine all our days, we, our wives, our sons, or our daughters,

Obedience of, a sign to Israel.

Jer 35:12–17 Then came the word of the LORD to Jeremiah, saying, **13** "Thus says the LORD of hosts, the God of Israel: 'Go and tell the men of Judah and the inhabitants of Jerusalem, "Will you not receive instruction to obey My words?" says the LORD. **14** "The words of Jonadab the son of Rechab, which he commanded his sons, not to drink wine, are performed; for to this day they drink none, and obey their father's commandment. But although I have spoken to you, rising early and speaking, you did not obey Me. **15** I have also sent to you all My servants the prophets, rising up early and sending *them*, saying, 'Turn now everyone from his evil way, amend your doings, and do not go after other gods to serve them; then you will dwell in the land which I have given you and your fathers.' But you have not inclined your ear, nor obeyed Me. **16** Surely the sons of Jonadab the son of Rechab have performed the commandment of their father, which he commanded them, but this people has not obeyed Me." ' **17** "Therefore thus says the LORD God of hosts, the God of Israel: 'Behold, I will bring on Judah and on all the inhabitants of Jerusalem all the doom that I have pronounced against them; because I have spoken to them but they have not heard, and I have called to them but they have not answered.' "

Perpetuity of, promised.

Jer 35:18–19 And Jeremiah said to the house of the Rechabites, "Thus says the LORD of hosts, the God of Israel: 'Because you have obeyed the commandment of Jonadab your father, and kept all his precepts and done according to all that he commanded you, **19** therefore thus says the LORD of hosts, the God of Israel: "Jonadab the son of Rechab shall not lack a man to stand before Me forever." ' "

RECONCILIATION WITH GOD

Predicted.

Dan 9:24 "Seventy weeks are determined For your people and for your holy city, To finish the transgression, To make an end of sins, To make reconciliation for iniquity, To bring in everlasting righteousness, To seal up vision and prophecy, And to anoint the Most Holy.

Is 53:5 But He *was* wounded for our transgressions, *He was* bruised for our iniquities; The chastisement for our peace *was* upon Him, And by His stripes we are healed.

Proclaimed by angels at the birth of Christ.

Luke 2:14 "Glory to God in the highest, And on earth peace, goodwill toward men!"

Blotting out the legalistic requirements is necessary to.

Eph 2:14–16 For He Himself is our peace, who has made both one, and has broken down the middle wall of separation, **15** having abolished in His flesh the enmity, *that is,* the law of commandments *contained* in ordinances, so as to create in Himself one new man *from* the two, *thus* making peace, **16** and that He might reconcile them both to God in one body through the cross, thereby putting to death the enmity.

Col 2:14 having wiped out the handwriting of requirements that was against us, which was contrary to us. And He has taken it out of the way, having nailed it to the cross.

Effected for those who believe

By God in Christ.

Rom 5:11 And not only *that,* but we also rejoice in God through our Lord Jesus Christ, through whom we have now received the reconciliation.

2 Cor 5:19 that is, that God was in Christ reconciling the world to Himself, not imputing their trespasses to them, and has committed to us the word of reconciliation.

By Christ as High Priest.

Heb 2:17 Therefore, in all things He had to be made like *His* brethren, that He might be a merciful and faithful High Priest in things *pertaining* to God, to make propitiation for the sins of the people.

By the death of Christ.

Rom 5:10 For if when we were enemies we were reconciled to God through the death of His Son, much more, having been reconciled, we shall be saved by His life.

Eph 2:16 and that He might reconcile them both to God in one body through the cross, thereby putting to death the enmity.

Col 1:21–22 And you, who once were alienated and enemies in your mind by wicked works, yet now He has reconciled **22** in the body of His flesh through death, to present you holy, and blameless, and above reproach in His sight—

By the blood of Christ.

Eph 2:13 But now in Christ Jesus you who once were far off have been brought near by the blood of Christ.

Col 1:20 and by Him to reconcile all things to Himself, by Him, whether things on earth or things in heaven, having made peace through the blood of His cross.

While alienated from God.

Col 1:21 And you, who once were alienated and enemies in your mind by wicked works, yet now He has reconciled

While sinners and without spiritual strength.

Rom 5:6 For when we were still without strength, in due time Christ died for the ungodly.

Rom 5:8 But God demonstrates His own love toward us, in that while we were still sinners, Christ died for us.

Rom 5:10 For if when we were enemies we were reconciled to God through the death of His Son, much more, having been reconciled, we shall be saved by His life.

The ministry of, committed to believers.

2 Cor 5:18–20 Now all things *are* of God, who has reconciled us to Himself through Jesus Christ, and has given us the ministry of reconciliation, **19** that is, that God was in Christ reconciling the world to Himself, not imputing their trespasses to them, and has committed to us the word of reconciliation. **20** Now then, we are ambassadors for Christ, as though God were pleading through us: we implore *you* on Christ's behalf, be reconciled to God.

Effects of,

Peace with God.

Rom 5:1 Therefore, having been justified by faith, we have peace with God through our Lord Jesus Christ,

Eph 2:16–17 and that He might reconcile them both to God in one body through the cross, thereby putting to death the enmity. **17** And He came and preached peace to you who were afar off and to those who were near.

Access to God.

Rom 5:2 through whom also we have access by faith into this grace in which we stand, and rejoice in hope of the glory of God.

Eph 2:18 For through Him we both have access by one Spirit to the Father.

Union of Jews and Gentiles.

Eph 2:14 For He Himself is our peace, who has made both one, and has broken down the middle wall of separation,

Union of things in heaven and earth.

Eph 1:10 that in the dispensation of the fullness of the times He might gather together in one all things in Christ, both which are in heaven and which are on earth—in Him.

Col 1:20 and by Him to reconcile all things to Himself, by Him, whether things on earth or things in heaven, having made peace through the blood of His cross.

A pledge of final salvation.

Rom 5:10 For if when we were enemies we were reconciled to God through the death of His Son, much more, having been reconciled, we shall be saved by His life.

Necessity for—illustrated.

Matt 5:24–26 leave your gift there before the altar, and go your way. First be reconciled to your brother, and then come and offer your gift. **25** Agree with your adversary quickly, while you are on the way with him, lest your adversary deliver you to the judge, the judge hand you over to the officer, and you be thrown into prison. **26** Assuredly, I say to you, you will by no means get out of there till you have paid the last penny.

Typified.

Lev 8:15 and Moses killed *it*. Then he took the blood, and put *some* on the horns of the altar all around with his finger, and purified the altar. And he poured the blood at the base of the altar, and consecrated it, to make atonement for it.

Lev 16:20 "And when he has made an end of atoning for the Holy *Place*, the tabernacle of meeting, and the altar, he shall bring the live goat.

RED HEIFER. *SEE ALSO* CALF; OFFERING, BURNT; SACRIFICES

To be without spot or blemish.

Num 19:2 "This *is* the ordinance of the law which the LORD has commanded, saying: 'Speak to the children of Israel, that they bring you a red heifer without blemish, in which there *is* no defect *and* on which a yoke has never come.

To be given to Eleazar the second priest to offer.

Num 19:3 You shall give it to Eleazar the priest, that he may take it outside the camp, and it shall be slaughtered before him;

To be slain outside the camp.

Num 19:3 You shall give it to Eleazar the priest, that he may take it outside the camp, and it shall be slaughtered before him;

Entire body of, to be burned.

Num 19:5 Then the heifer shall be burned in his sight: its hide, its flesh, its blood, and its offal shall be burned.

Blood of, sprinkled seven times before the tabernacle.

Num 19:4 and Eleazar the priest shall take some of its blood with his finger, and sprinkle some of its blood seven times directly in front of the tabernacle of meeting.

Cedar, hyssop, burned with.

Num 19:6 And the priest shall take cedar wood and hyssop and scarlet, and cast *them* into the midst of the fire burning the heifer.

Ashes of, collected and mixed with water for purification.

Num 19:9 Then a man *who is* clean shall gather up the ashes of the heifer, and store *them* outside the camp in a clean place; and they shall be kept for the congregation of the children of Israel for the water of purification; it *is* for purifying from sin.

Cf. Num 19:11–22

Communicated uncleanness to

The priest that offered her.

Num 19:7 Then the priest shall wash his clothes, he shall bathe in water, and afterward he shall come into the camp; the priest shall be unclean until evening.

The one that burned her.

Num 19:8 And the one who burns it shall wash his clothes in water, bathe in water, and shall be unclean until evening.

The one who gathered the ashes.

Num 19:10 And the one who gathers the ashes of the heifer shall wash his clothes, and be unclean until evening. It shall be a statute forever to the children of Israel and to the stranger who dwells among them.

Could only purify the flesh.

Heb 9:13 For if the blood of bulls and goats and the ashes of a heifer, sprinkling the unclean, sanctifies for the purifying of the flesh,

A type of Christ.

Heb 9:12–14 Not with the blood of goats and calves, but with His own blood He entered the Most Holy Place once for all, having obtained eternal redemption. **13** For if the blood of bulls and goats and the ashes of a heifer, sprinkling the unclean, sanctifies for the purifying of the flesh, **14** how much more shall the blood of Christ, who through the eternal Spirit offered Himself without spot to God, cleanse your conscience from dead works to serve the living God?

REDEMPTION

Defined.

1 Cor 6:20 For you were bought at a price; therefore glorify God in your body and in your spirit, which are God's.

1 Cor 7:23 You were bought at a price; do not become slaves of men.

Is of God.

Is 43:1 But now, thus says the LORD, who created you, O Jacob, And He who formed you, O Israel: "Fear not, for I have redeemed you; I have called *you* by your name; You *are* Mine.

Is 44:21–23 "Remember these, O Jacob, And Israel, for you *are* My servant; I have formed you, you *are* My servant; O Israel, you will not be forgotten by Me! **22** I have blotted out, like a thick cloud, your transgressions, And like a cloud, your sins. Return to Me, for I have redeemed you." **23** Sing, O heavens, for the LORD has done *it!* Shout, you lower parts of the earth; Break forth into singing, you mountains, O forest, and every tree in it! For the LORD has redeemed Jacob, And glorified Himself in Israel.

Luke 1:68 "Blessed *is* the Lord God of Israel, For He has visited and redeemed His people,

Is by Christ and His blood.

Matt 20:28 just as the Son of Man did not come to be served, but to serve, and to give His life a ransom for many."

Acts 20:28 Therefore take heed to yourselves and to all the flock, among which the Holy Spirit has made you overseers, to shepherd the church of God which He purchased with His own blood.

1 Cor 1:30 But of Him you are in Christ Jesus, who became for us wisdom from God—and righteousness and sanctification and redemption—

Gal 3:13 Christ has redeemed us from the curse of the law, having become a curse for us (for it is written, "Cursed is everyone who hangs on a tree"),

Gal 4:4–5 But when the fullness of the time had come, God sent forth His Son, born of a woman, born under the law, **5** to redeem those who were under the law, that we might receive the adoption as sons.

Heb 9:12 Not with the blood of goats and calves, but with His own blood He entered the Most Holy Place once for all, having obtained eternal redemption.

1 Pet 1:19 but with the precious blood of Christ, as of a lamb without blemish and without spot.

Rev 5:9 And they sang a new song, saying: "You are worthy to take the scroll, And to open its seals; For You were slain, And have redeemed us to God by Your blood Out of every tribe and tongue and people and nation,

Is from

The bondage of the law.

Gal 4:5 to redeem those who were under the law, that we might receive the adoption as sons.

The curse of the law.

Gal 3:13 Christ has redeemed us from the curse of the law, having become a curse for us (for it is written, "Cursed is everyone who hangs on a tree"),

The power of sin.

Rom 6:18 And having been set free from sin, you became slaves of righteousness.

Rom 6:22 But now having been set free from sin, and having become slaves of God, you have your fruit to holiness, and the end, everlasting life.

The power of the grave and death.

Ps 49:15 But God will redeem my soul from the power of the grave, For He shall receive me. Selah

Hos 13:14 "I will ransom them from the power of the grave; I will redeem them from death. O Death, I will be your plagues! O Grave, I will be your destruction! Pity is hidden from My eyes."

All troubles.

Ps 25:22 Redeem Israel, O God, Out of all their troubles!

All iniquity.

Ps 130:8 And He shall redeem Israel From all his iniquities.

Titus 2:14 who gave Himself for us, that He might redeem us from every lawless deed and purify for Himself *His* own special people, zealous for good works.

All evil.

Gen 48:16 The Angel who has redeemed me from all evil, Bless the lads; Let my name be named upon them, And the name of my fathers Abraham and Isaac; And let them grow into a multitude in the midst of the earth."

The present evil age.

Gal 1:4 who gave Himself for our sins, that He might deliver us from this present evil age, according to the will of our God and Father,

Aimless conduct.

1 Pet 1:18 knowing that you were not redeemed with corruptible things, *like* silver or gold, from your aimless conduct *received* by tradition from your fathers,

Enemies.

Ps 106:10–11 He saved them from the hand of him who hated *them*, And redeemed them from the hand of the enemy. **11** The waters covered their enemies; There was not one of them left.

Jer 15:21 "I will deliver you from the hand of the wicked, And I will redeem you from the grip of the terrible."

Destruction.

Ps 103:4 Who redeems your life from destruction, Who crowns you with lovingkindness and tender mercies,

Man cannot effect.

Ps 49:7 None *of them* can by any means redeem *his* brother, Nor give to God a ransom for him—

Corruptible things cannot purchase.

1 Pet 1:18 knowing that you were not redeemed with corruptible things, *like* silver or gold, from your aimless conduct *received* by tradition from your fathers,

Procures for us

Justification.

Rom 3:24 being justified freely by His grace through the redemption that is in Christ Jesus,

Forgiveness of sin.

Eph 1:7 In Him we have redemption through His blood, the forgiveness of sins, according to the riches of His grace

Col 1:14 in whom we have redemption through His blood, the forgiveness of sins.

Adoption.

Gal 4:4–5 But when the fullness of the time had come, God sent forth His Son, born of a woman, born under the law, **5** to redeem those who were under the law, that we might receive the adoption as sons.

Purification.

Titus 2:14 who gave Himself for us, that He might redeem us from every lawless deed and purify for Himself *His* own special people, zealous for good works.

The present life, the only season for.

Job 36:18–19 Because *there is* wrath, *beware* lest He take you away with *one* blow; For a large ransom would not help you avoid *it.* **19** Will your riches, Or all the mighty forces, Keep you from distress?

Described as

Costly.

Ps 49:8 For the redemption of their souls *is* costly, And it shall cease forever—

Abundant.

Ps 130:7 O Israel, hope in the LORD; For with the LORD *there is* mercy, And with Him *is* abundant redemption.

Eternal.

Heb 9:12 Not with the blood of goats and calves, but with His own blood He entered the Most Holy Place once for all, having obtained eternal redemption.

Subjects of,

The soul.

Ps 49:8 For the redemption of their souls *is* costly, And it shall cease forever—

The body.

Rom 8:23 Not only *that,* but we also who have the firstfruits of the Spirit, even we ourselves groan within ourselves, eagerly waiting for the adoption, the redemption of our body.

The life.

Ps 103:4 Who redeems your life from destruction, Who crowns you with lovingkindness and tender mercies,

Lam 3:58 O Lord, You have pleaded the case for my soul; You have redeemed my life.

The inheritance.

Eph 1:14 who is the guarantee of our inheritance until the redemption of the purchased possession, to the praise of His glory.

Manifests the

Power of God.

Is 50:2 Why, when I came, *was there* no man? *Why,* when I called, *was there* none to answer? Is My hand shortened at all that it cannot redeem? Or have I no power to deliver? Indeed with My rebuke I dry up the sea, I make the rivers a wilderness; Their fish stink because *there is* no water, And die of thirst.

Grace of God.

Is 52:3 For thus says the LORD: "You have sold yourselves for nothing, And you shall be redeemed without money."

Love and pity of God.

Is 63:9 In all their affliction He was afflicted, And the Angel of His Presence saved them; In His love and in His pity He redeemed them; And He bore them and carried them All the days of old.

John 3:16 For God so loved the world that He gave His only begotten Son, that whoever believes in Him should not perish but have everlasting life.

Rom 6:8 Now if we died with Christ, we believe that we shall also live with Him,

1 John 4:10 In this is love, not that we loved God, but that He loved us and sent His Son *to be* the propitiation for our sins.

Those who partake of,

Include Old Testament believers.

Heb 9:15 And for this reason He is the Mediator of the new covenant, by means of death, for the redemption of the transgressions under the first covenant, that those who are called may receive the promise of the eternal inheritance.

Are the property of God.

Is 43:1 But now, thus says the LORD, who created you, O Jacob, And He who formed you, O Israel: "Fear not, for I have redeemed you; I have called *you* by your name; You *are* Mine.

1 Cor 6:20 For you were bought at a price; therefore glorify God in your body and in your spirit, which are God's.

Are firstfruits to God.

Rev 14:4 These are the ones who were not defiled with women, for they are virgins. These are the ones who follow the Lamb wherever He goes. These were redeemed from *among* men, *being* firstfruits to God and to the Lamb.

Are a special people.

2 Sam 7:23 And who *is* like Your people, like Israel, the one nation on the earth whom God went to redeem for Himself as a people, to make for Himself a name—and to do for Yourself great and awesome deeds for Your land—before Your people whom You redeemed for Yourself from Egypt, the nations, and their gods?

Titus 2:14 who gave Himself for us, that He might redeem us from every lawless deed and purify for Himself *His* own special people, zealous for good works.

1 Pet 2:9 But you *are* a chosen generation, a royal priesthood, a holy nation, His own special people, that you may proclaim the praises of Him who called you out of darkness into His marvelous light;

Have assurance.

Job 19:25 For I know *that* my Redeemer lives, And He shall stand at last on the earth;

Ps 31:5 Into Your hand I commit my spirit; You have redeemed me, O LORD God of truth.

Are sealed for the day of.

Eph 4:30 And do not grieve the Holy Spirit of God, by whom you were sealed for the day of redemption.

Are zealous for good works.

Eph 2:10 For we are His workmanship, created in Christ Jesus for good works, which God prepared beforehand that we should walk in them.

Titus 2:14 who gave Himself for us, that He might redeem us from every lawless deed and purify for Himself *His* own special people, zealous for good works.

1 Pet 2:9 But you *are* a chosen generation, a royal priesthood, a holy nation, His own special people, that you may proclaim the praises of Him who called you out of darkness into His marvelous light;

Walk safely in holiness.

Is 35:8–9 A highway shall be there, and a road, And it shall be called the Highway of Holiness. The unclean shall not pass over it, But *shall be* for others. Whoever walks the road, although a fool, Shall not go astray. 9 No lion shall be there, Nor shall *any* ravenous beast go up on it; It shall not be found there. But the redeemed shall walk *there,*

Shall return to Zion with joy.

Is 35:10 And the ransomed of the LORD shall return, And come to Zion with singing, With everlasting joy on their heads. They shall obtain joy and gladness, And sorrow and sighing shall flee away.

Alone can learn the songs of heaven.

Rev 14:3–4 They sang as it were a new song before the throne, before the four living creatures, and the elders; and no one could learn that song except the hundred *and* forty-four thousand who were redeemed from the earth. 4 These are the ones who were not defiled with women, for they are virgins. These are the ones who follow the Lamb wherever He goes. These were redeemed from *among* men, *being* firstfruits to God and to the Lamb.

Commit themselves to God.

Ps 31:5 Into Your hand I commit my spirit; You have redeemed me, O LORD God of truth.

Have a guarantee of the completion of.

2 Cor 1:22 who also has sealed us and given us the Spirit in our hearts as a guarantee.

Eph 1:14 who is the guarantee of our inheritance until the redemption of the purchased possession, to the praise of His glory.

Wait for the completion of.

Rom 8:23 Not only *that,* but we also who have the firstfruits of the Spirit, even we ourselves groan within ourselves, eagerly waiting for the adoption, the redemption of our body.

Phil 3:20–21 For our citizenship is in heaven, from which we also eagerly wait for the Savior, the Lord Jesus Christ, 21 who will transform our lowly body that it may be conformed to His glorious body, according to the working by which He is able even to subdue all things to Himself.

Titus 2:11–13 For the grace of God that brings salvation has appeared to all men, 12 teaching us that, denying ungodliness and worldly lusts, we should live soberly, righteously, and godly in the present age, 13 looking for the blessed hope and glorious appearing of our great God and Savior Jesus Christ,

Pray for the completion of.

Ps 26:11 But as for me, I will walk in my integrity; Redeem me and be merciful to me.

Ps 44:26 Arise for our help, And redeem us for Your mercies' sake.

Praise God for.

Ps 71:23 My lips shall greatly rejoice when I sing to You, And my soul, which You have redeemed.

Ps 103:4 Who redeems your life from destruction, Who crowns you with lovingkindness and tender mercies,

Is 44:22–23 I have blotted out, like a thick cloud, your transgressions, And like a cloud, your sins. Return to Me, for I have redeemed you." 23 Sing, O heavens, for the LORD has done *it!* Shout, you lower parts of the earth; Break forth into singing, you mountains, O forest, and every tree in it! For the LORD has redeemed Jacob, And glorified Himself in Israel.

Is 51:11 So the ransomed of the LORD shall return, And come to Zion with singing, With everlasting joy on their heads. They shall obtain joy and gladness; Sorrow and sighing shall flee away.

Rev 5:9 And they sang a new song, saying: "You are worthy to take the scroll, And to open its seals; For You were slain, And have redeemed us to God by Your blood Out of every tribe and tongue and people and nation,

Should glorify God for.

1 Cor 6:20 For you were bought at a price; therefore glorify God in your body and in your spirit, which are God's.

Should be without fear.

Is 43:1 But now, thus says the LORD, who created you, O Jacob, And He who formed you, O Israel: "Fear not, for I have redeemed you; I have called *you* by your name; You *are* Mine.

Typified by

Israel.

Ex 6:6 Therefore say to the children of Israel: 'I *am* the LORD; I will bring you out from under the burdens of the Egyptians, I will rescue you from their bondage, and I will redeem you with an outstretched arm and with great judgments.

Firstborn.

Ex 13:11–15 "And it shall be, when the LORD brings you into the land of the Canaanites, as He swore to you and your fathers, and gives it to you, 12 that you shall set apart to the LORD all that open the womb, that is, every firstborn that comes from an animal which you have; the males *shall be* the LORD's. 13 But every firstborn of a donkey you shall redeem with a lamb; and if you will not redeem *it,* then you shall break its neck. And all the firstborn of man among your sons you shall redeem. 14 So it shall be, when your son asks you in time to come, saying, 'What *is* this?' that you shall say to him, 'By strength of hand the LORD brought us out of Egypt, out of the house of bondage. 15 And it came to pass, when Pharaoh was stubborn about letting us go, that the LORD killed all the firstborn in the land of Egypt, both the firstborn of man and the firstborn of beast. Therefore I sacrifice to the LORD all males that open the womb, but all the firstborn of my sons I redeem.'

Num 18:15 "Everything that first opens the womb of all flesh, which they bring to the LORD, whether man or beast, shall be yours; nevertheless the firstborn of man you shall surely redeem, and the firstborn of unclean animals you shall redeem.

Atonement money.

Ex 30:12–15 "When you take the census of the children of Israel for their number, then every man shall give a ransom for himself to the LORD, when you number them, that there may be no plague among them when *you* number them. **13** This is what everyone among those who are numbered shall give: half a shekel according to the shekel of the sanctuary (a shekel *is* twenty gerahs). The half-shekel *shall be* an offering to the LORD. **14** Everyone included among those who are numbered, from twenty years old and above, shall give an offering to the LORD. **15** The rich shall not give more and the poor shall not give less than half a shekel, when *you* give an offering to the LORD, to make atonement for yourselves.

Hired servant. **Lev 25:47–54**

REGENERATION. *SEE ALSO* NEW BIRTH

Described as

Being born again.

John 3:3 Jesus answered and said to him, "Most assuredly, I say to you, unless one is born again, he cannot see the kingdom of God."

1 Pet 1:23 having been born again, not of corruptible seed but incorruptible, through the word of God which lives and abides forever,

A new creation.

2 Cor 5:17 Therefore, if anyone *is* in Christ, *he is* a new creation; old things have passed away; behold, all things have become new.

Is an active expression of God's will.

James 1:18 Of His own will He brought us forth by the word of truth, that we might be a kind of firstfruits of His creatures.

Results in

Divine cleansing from sin.

Titus 3:5 not by works of righteousness which we have done, but according to His mercy He saved us, through the washing of regeneration and renewing of the Holy Spirit,

Practical righteousness.

1 John 2:29 If you know that He is righteous, you know that everyone who practices righteousness is born of Him.

The avoidance of sin.

1 John 3:9 Whoever has been born of God does not sin, for His seed remains in him; and he cannot sin, because he has been born of God.

Overcoming the world.

1 John 5:4 For whatever is born of God overcomes the world. And this is the victory that has overcome the world—our faith.

REMARRIAGE. *SEE ALSO* DIVORCE

Not permitted, unless divorce was proper.

Matt 5:31–32 "Furthermore it has been said, 'Whoever divorces his wife, let him give her a certificate of divorce.' **32** But I say to you that whoever divorces his wife for any reason except sexual immorality causes her to commit adultery; and whoever marries a woman who is divorced commits adultery.

Matt 19:9 And I say to you, whoever divorces his wife, except for sexual immorality, and marries another, commits adultery; and whoever marries her who is divorced commits adultery."

Cf. Mark 10:10–11

Believers have certain liberty for.

1 Cor 7:15 But if the unbeliever departs, let him depart; a brother or a sister is not under bondage in such *cases*. But God has called us to peace.

Encouraged for widows.

1 Cor 7:39 A wife is bound by law as long as her husband lives; but if her husband dies, she is at liberty to be married to whom she wishes, only in the Lord.

1 Tim 5:14 Therefore I desire that *the* younger *widows* marry, bear children, manage the house, give no opportunity to the adversary to speak reproachfully.

REPENTANCE

What it is.

Is 45:22 "Look to Me, and be saved, All you ends of the earth! For I *am* God, and *there is* no other.

Acts 14:15 and saying, "Men, why are you doing these things? We also are men with the same nature as you, and preach to you that you should turn from these useless things to the living God, who made the heaven, the earth, the sea, and all things that are in them,

2 Cor 5:17 Therefore, if anyone *is* in Christ, *he is* a new creation; old things have passed away; behold, all things have become new.

Col 3:2 Set your mind on things above, not on things on the earth.

1 Thess 1:9 For they themselves declare concerning us what manner of entry we had to you, and how you turned to God from idols to serve the living and true God,

Commanded to all by God.

Ezek 18:30–32 "Therefore I will judge you, O house of Israel, every one according to his ways," says the Lord GOD. "Repent, and turn from all your transgressions, so that iniquity will not be your ruin. **31** Cast away from you all the transgressions which you have committed, and get yourselves a new heart and a new spirit. For why should you die, O house of Israel? **32** For I have no pleasure in the death of one who dies," says the Lord GOD. "Therefore turn and live!"

Acts 17:30 Truly, these times of ignorance God overlooked, but now commands all men everywhere to repent,

Commanded by Christ.

Matt 9:13 But go and learn what *this* means: 'I desire mercy and not sacrifice.' For I did not come to call the righteous, but sinners, to repentance."

Rev 2:5 Remember therefore from where you have fallen; repent and do the first works, or else I will come to you quickly and remove your lampstand from its place—unless you repent.

Rev 2:16 Repent, or else I will come to you quickly and will fight against them with the sword of My mouth.

Rev 3:3 Remember therefore how you have received and heard; hold fast and repent. Therefore if you will not watch, I will come upon you as a thief, and you will not know what hour I will come upon you.

Given by God.

Acts 11:18 When they heard these things they became silent; and they glorified God, saying, "Then God has also granted to the Gentiles repentance to life."

2 Tim 2:25 in humility correcting those who are in opposition, if God perhaps will grant them repentance, so that they may know the truth,

Christ exalted to give.

Acts 5:31 Him God has exalted to His right hand *to be* Prince and Savior, to give repentance to Israel and forgiveness of sins.

By the operation of the Holy Spirit.

Zech 12:10 "And I will pour on the house of David and on the inhabitants of Jerusalem the Spirit of grace and supplication; then they will look on Me whom they pierced. Yes, they will mourn for Him as one mourns for *his* only *son,* and grieve for Him as one grieves for a firstborn.

Called repentance to life.

Acts 11:18 When they heard these things they became silent; and they glorified God, saying, "Then God has also granted to the Gentiles repentance to life."

Called repentance to salvation.

2 Cor 7:10 For godly sorrow produces repentance *leading* to salvation, not to be regretted; but the sorrow of the world produces death.

We should be led to, by

The longsuffering of God.

Gen 6:3 And the Lord said, "My Spirit shall not strive with man forever, for he *is* indeed flesh; yet his days shall be one hundred and twenty years."

1 Pet 3:20 who formerly were disobedient, when once the Divine longsuffering waited in the days of Noah, while *the* ark was being prepared, in which a few, that is, eight souls, were saved through water.

2 Pet 3:9 The Lord is not slack concerning *His* promise, as some count slackness, but is longsuffering toward us, not willing that any should perish but that all should come to repentance.

The goodness of God.

Rom 2:4 Or do you despise the riches of His goodness, forbearance, and longsuffering, not knowing that the goodness of God leads you to repentance?

The chastisements of God.

1 Kin 8:47 *yet* when they come to themselves in the land where they were carried captive, and repent, and make supplication to You in the land of those who took them captive, saying, 'We have sinned and done wrong, we have committed wickedness';

Rev 3:19 As many as I love, I rebuke and chasten. Therefore be zealous and repent.

Godly sorrow.

2 Cor 7:10 For godly sorrow produces repentance *lead-*

ing to salvation, not to be regretted; but the sorrow of the world produces death.

Necessary to the pardon of sin.

Acts 2:38 Then Peter said to them, "Repent, and let every one of you be baptized in the name of Jesus Christ for the remission of sins; and you shall receive the gift of the Holy Spirit.

Acts 3:19 Repent therefore and be converted, that your sins may be blotted out, so that times of refreshing may come from the presence of the Lord,

Acts 8:22 Repent therefore of this your wickedness, and pray God if perhaps the thought of your heart may be forgiven you.

Conviction of sin necessary to.

1 Kin 8:38 whatever prayer, whatever supplication is made by anyone, *or* by all Your people Israel, when each one knows the plague of his own heart, and spreads out his hands toward this temple:

Prov 28:13 He who covers his sins will not prosper, But whoever confesses and forsakes *them* will have mercy.

Acts 2:37–38 Now when they heard *this,* they were cut to the heart, and said to Peter and the rest of the apostles, "Men *and* brethren, what shall we do?" **38** Then Peter said to them, "Repent, and let every one of you be baptized in the name of Jesus Christ for the remission of sins; and you shall receive the gift of the Holy Spirit.

Acts 19:18 And many who had believed came confessing and telling their deeds.

Confession and separation essential elements of.

Ezra 10:11 Now therefore, make confession to the Lord God of your fathers, and do His will; separate yourselves from the peoples of the land, and from the pagan wives."

Preached

By Christ.

Matt 4:17 From that time Jesus began to preach and to say, "Repent, for the kingdom of heaven is at hand."

Mark 1:15 and saying, "The time is fulfilled, and the kingdom of God is at hand. Repent, and believe in the gospel."

By John the Baptist.

Matt 3:2 and saying, "Repent, for the kingdom of heaven is at hand!"

Mark 1:4 John came baptizing in the wilderness and preaching a baptism of repentance for the remission of sins.

By the apostles.

Mark 6:12 So they went out and preached that *people* should repent.

Acts 20:21 testifying to Jews, and also to Greeks, repentance toward God and faith toward our Lord Jesus Christ.

In the name of Christ.

Luke 24:47 and that repentance and remission of sins should be preached in His name to all nations, beginning at Jerusalem.

Not to be regretted.

2 Cor 7:10 For godly sorrow produces repentance *lead-*

ing to salvation, not to be regretted; but the sorrow of the world produces death.

Now is the time for.

Ps 95:7–8 For He *is* our God, And we *are* the people of His pasture, And the sheep of His hand. Today, if you will hear His voice: **8** "Do not harden your hearts, as in the rebellion, As *in* the day of trial in the wilderness,

Prov 27:1 Do not boast about tomorrow, For you do not know what a day may bring forth.

Is 55:6 Seek the LORD while He may be found, Call upon Him while He is near.

2 Cor 6:2 For He says: *"In an acceptable time I have heard you, And in the day of salvation I have helped you."* Behold, now *is* the accepted time; behold, now *is* the day of salvation.

Heb 3:7–8 Therefore, as the Holy Spirit says: *"Today, if you will hear His voice,* **8** *Do not harden your hearts as in the rebellion, In the day of trial in the wilderness,*

Heb 4:7 again He designates a certain day, saying in David, *"Today,"* after such a long time, as it has been said: *"Today, if you will hear His voice, Do not harden your hearts."*

Joy in heaven over one sinner brought to.

Luke 15:7 I say to you that likewise there will be more joy in heaven over one sinner who repents than over ninety-nine just persons who need no repentance.

Luke 15:10 Likewise, I say to you, there is joy in the presence of the angels of God over one sinner who repents."

Ministers should rejoice concerning.

2 Cor 7:9 Now I rejoice, not that you were made sorry, but that your sorrow led to repentance. For you were made sorry in a godly manner, that you might suffer loss from us in nothing.

Should be evidenced by fruits.

Is 1:16–17 "Wash yourselves, make yourselves clean; Put away the evil of your doings from before My eyes. Cease to do evil, **17** Learn to do good; Seek justice, Rebuke the oppressor; Defend the fatherless, Plead for the widow.

Dan 4:27 Therefore, O king, let my advice be acceptable to you; break off your sins by *being* righteous, and your iniquities by showing mercy to *the* poor. Perhaps there may be a lengthening of your prosperity."

Matt 3:8 Therefore bear fruits worthy of repentance,

Acts 26:20 but declared first to those in Damascus and in Jerusalem, and throughout all the region of Judea, and *then* to the Gentiles, that they should repent, turn to God, and do works befitting repentance.

Should be accompanied by
Humility.

2 Chr 7:14 if My people who are called by My name will humble themselves, and pray and seek My face, and turn from their wicked ways, then I will hear from heaven, and will forgive their sin and heal their land.

James 4:9–10 Lament and mourn and weep! Let your laughter be turned to mourning and *your* joy to gloom. **10** Humble yourselves in the sight of the Lord, and He will lift you up.

Shame and confusion.

Jer 31:19 Surely, after my turning, I repented; And after I was instructed, I struck myself on the thigh; I was ashamed, yes, even humiliated, Because I bore the reproach of my youth.'

Ezek 16:61 Then you will remember your ways and be ashamed, when you receive your older and your younger sisters; for I will give them to you for daughters, but not because of My covenant with you.

Ezek 16:63 that you may remember and be ashamed, and never open your mouth anymore because of your shame, when I provide you an atonement for all you have done," says the Lord GOD.' "

Dan 9:7–8 O Lord, righteousness *belongs* to You, but to us shame of face, as *it is* this day—to the men of Judah, to the inhabitants of Jerusalem and all Israel, those near and those far off in all the countries to which You have driven them, because of the unfaithfulness which they have committed against You. **8** "O Lord, to us *belongs* shame of face, to our kings, our princes, and our fathers, because we have sinned against You.

Cf. Ezra 9:6–15

Self-abhorrence.

Job 42:6 Therefore I abhor *myself*, And repent in dust and ashes."

Confession.

Lev 26:40 *'But* if they confess their iniquity and the iniquity of their fathers, with their unfaithfulness in which they were unfaithful to Me, and that they also have walked contrary to Me,

Job 33:27 Then he looks at men and says, 'I have sinned, and perverted *what was* right, And it did not profit me.'

Faith.

Matt 21:32 For John came to you in the way of righteousness, and you did not believe him; but tax collectors and harlots believed him; and when you saw *it*, you did not afterward relent and believe him.

Mark 1:15 and saying, "The time is fulfilled, and the kingdom of God is at hand. Repent, and believe in the gospel."

Acts 20:21 testifying to Jews, and also to Greeks, repentance toward God and faith toward our Lord Jesus Christ.

Prayer.

1 Kin 8:33 "When Your people Israel are defeated before an enemy because they have sinned against You, and when they turn back to You and confess Your name, and pray and make supplication to You in this temple,

Acts 8:22 Repent therefore of this your wickedness, and pray God if perhaps the thought of your heart may be forgiven you.

Conversion.

Acts 3:19 Repent therefore and be converted, that your sins may be blotted out, so that times of refreshing may come from the presence of the Lord,

Acts 26:20 but declared first to those in Damascus and in Jerusalem, and throughout all the region of Judea, and *then* to the Gentiles, that they should repent, turn to God, and do works befitting repentance.

Turning from sin.

2 Chr 6:26 "When the heavens are shut up and there is no rain because they have sinned against You, when they pray toward this place and confess Your name, and turn from their sin because You afflict them,

Turning from idolatry.

Ezek 14:6 "Therefore say to the house of Israel, 'Thus says the Lord GOD: "Repent, turn away from your idols, and turn your faces away from all your abominations.

1 Thess 1:9 For they themselves declare concerning us what manner of entry we had to you, and how you turned to God from idols to serve the living and true God,

Greater zeal in the path of duty.

2 Cor 7:11 For observe this very thing, that you sorrowed in a godly manner: What diligence it produced in you, *what* clearing *of yourselves, what* indignation, *what* fear, *what* vehement desire, *what* zeal, *what* vindication! In all *things* you proved yourselves to be clear in this matter.

Exhortations to.

Ezek 14:6 "Therefore say to the house of Israel, 'Thus says the Lord GOD: "Repent, turn away from your idols, and turn your faces away from all your abominations.

Ezek 18:30 "Therefore I will judge you, O house of Israel, every one according to his ways," says the Lord GOD. "Repent, and turn from all your transgressions, so that iniquity will not be your ruin.

Acts 2:38 Then Peter said to them, "Repent, and let every one of you be baptized in the name of Jesus Christ for the remission of sins; and you shall receive the gift of the Holy Spirit.

Acts 3:19 Repent therefore and be converted, that your sins may be blotted out, so that times of refreshing may come from the presence of the Lord,

The wicked

Averse to.

Jer 8:6 I listened and heard, *But* they do not speak aright. No man repented of his wickedness, Saying, 'What have I done?' Everyone turned to his own course, As the horse rushes into the battle.

Matt 21:32 For John came to you in the way of righteousness, and you did not believe him; but tax collectors and harlots believed him; and when you saw it, you did not afterward relent and believe him.

Not led to, by the judgments of God.

Rev 9:20–21 But the rest of mankind, who were not killed by these plagues, did not repent of the works of their hands, that they should not worship demons, and idols of gold, silver, brass, stone, and wood, which can neither see nor hear nor walk. 21 And they did not repent of their murders or their sorceries or their sexual immorality or their thefts.

Rev 16:9 And men were scorched with great heat, and they blasphemed the name of God who has power over these plagues; and they did not repent and give Him glory.

Not led to, by miraculous intervention.

Luke 16:30–31 And he said, 'No, father Abraham; but if one goes to them from the dead, they will repent.' 31 But he said to him, 'If they do not hear Moses and the prophets, neither will they be persuaded though one rise from the dead.' "

Neglect the opportunity for.

Rev 2:21 And I gave her time to repent of her sexual immorality, and she did not repent.

Condemned for neglecting.

Matt 11:20 Then He began to rebuke the cities in which most of His mighty works had been done, because they did not repent:

Danger of neglecting.

Matt 11:20–24 Then He began to rebuke the cities in which most of His mighty works had been done, because they did not repent: 21 "Woe to you, Chorazin! Woe to you, Bethsaida! For if the mighty works which were done in you had been done in Tyre and Sidon, they would have repented long ago in sackcloth and ashes. 22 But I say to you, it will be more tolerable for Tyre and Sidon in the day of judgment than for you. 23 And you, Capernaum, who are exalted to heaven, will be brought down to Hades; for if the mighty works which were done in you had been done in Sodom, it would have remained until this day. 24 But I say to you that it shall be more tolerable for the land of Sodom in the day of judgment than for you."

Luke 13:3 I tell you, no; but unless you repent you will all likewise perish.

Luke 13:5 I tell you, no; but unless you repent you will all likewise perish."

Rom 2:5 But in accordance with your hardness and your impenitent heart you are treasuring up for yourself wrath in the day of wrath and revelation of the righteous judgment of God,

Rev 2:5 Remember therefore from where you have fallen; repent and do the first works, or else I will come to you quickly and remove your lampstand from its place—unless you repent.

Rev 2:16 Repent, or else I will come to you quickly and will fight against them with the sword of My mouth.

Rev 2:22 Indeed I will cast her into a sickbed, and those who commit adultery with her into great tribulation, unless they repent of their deeds.

Denied to apostates.

Heb 6:4–6 For *it is* impossible for those who were once enlightened, and have tasted the heavenly gift, and have become partakers of the Holy Spirit, 5 and have tasted the good word of God and the powers of the age to come, 6 if they fall away, to renew them again to repentance, since they crucify again for themselves the Son of God, and put *Him* to an open shame.

Illustrated.

Matt 21:29 He answered and said, 'I will not,' but afterward he regretted it and went.

Luke 15:18–21 I will arise and go to my father, and will say to him, "Father, I have sinned against heaven and before you, 19 and I am no longer worthy to be called your son. Make me like one of your hired servants." ' 20 "And he arose and came to his father. But when he was still a great way off, his father saw him and had compassion, and ran and fell on his neck and kissed him. **21** And the son said to him, 'Father, I have sinned against heaven and in your sight, and am no longer worthy to be called your son.'

Luke 18:13 And the tax collector, standing afar off, would not so much as raise *his* eyes to heaven, but beat his breast, saying, 'God, be merciful to me a sinner!'

Gal 1:23 But they were hearing only, "He who formerly persecuted us now preaches the faith which he once *tried to* destroy."

True—illustrated by

The Israelites.

Judg 10:15–16 And the children of Israel said to the LORD, "We have sinned! Do to us whatever seems best to You; only deliver us this day, we pray." **16** So they put away the foreign gods from among them and served the LORD. And His soul could no longer endure the misery of Israel.

David.

2 Sam 12:13 So David said to Nathan, "I have sinned against the LORD." And Nathan said to David, "The LORD also has put away your sin; you shall not die."

Manasseh.

2 Chr 33:12–13 Now when he was in affliction, he implored the LORD his God, and humbled himself greatly before the God of his fathers, **13** and prayed to Him; and He received his entreaty, heard his supplication, and brought him back to Jerusalem into his kingdom. Then Manasseh knew that the LORD *was* God.

Job.

Job 42:6 Therefore I abhor *myself,* And repent in dust and ashes."

Nineveh.

Jon 3:5–8 So the people of Nineveh believed God, proclaimed a fast, and put on sackcloth, from the greatest to the least of them. **6** Then word came to the king of Nineveh; and he arose from his throne and laid aside his robe, covered *himself* with sackcloth and sat in ashes. **7** And he caused *it* to be proclaimed and published throughout Nineveh by the decree of the king and his nobles, saying, Let neither man nor beast, herd nor flock, taste anything; do not let them eat, or drink water. **8** But let man and beast be covered with sackcloth, and cry mightily to God; yes, let every one turn from his evil way and from the violence that is in his hands.

Matt 12:41 The men of Nineveh will rise up in the judgment with this generation and condemn it, because they repented at the preaching of Jonah; and indeed a greater than Jonah *is* here.

Peter.

Matt 26:75 And Peter remembered the word of Jesus who had said to him, "Before the rooster crows, you will deny Me three times." So he went out and wept bitterly.

Zacchaeus.

Luke 19:8 Then Zacchaeus stood and said to the Lord, "Look, Lord, I give half of my goods to the poor; and if I have taken anything from anyone by false accusation, I restore fourfold."

The thief on the cross.

Luke 23:40–41 But the other, answering, rebuked him, saying, "Do you not even fear God, seeing you are under the same condemnation? **41** And we indeed justly, for we receive the due reward of our deeds; but this Man has done nothing wrong."

The Corinthians.

2 Cor 7:9–10 Now I rejoice, not that you were made sorry, but that your sorrow led to repentance. For you were made sorry in a godly manner, that you might suffer loss from us in nothing. **10** For godly sorrow produces repentance *leading* to salvation, not to be regretted; but the sorrow of the world produces death.

False—illustrated by

Saul.

1 Sam 15:24–30 Then Saul said to Samuel, "I have sinned, for I have transgressed the commandment of the LORD and your words, because I feared the people and obeyed their voice. **25** Now therefore, please pardon my sin, and return with me, that I may worship the LORD." **26** But Samuel said to Saul, "I will not return with you, for you have rejected the word of the LORD, and the LORD has rejected you from being king over Israel." **27** And as Samuel turned around to go away, *Saul* seized the edge of his robe, and it tore. **28** So Samuel said to him, "The LORD has torn the kingdom of Israel from you today, and has given it to a neighbor of yours, *who is* better than you. **29** And also the Strength of Israel will not lie nor relent. For He *is* not a man, that He should relent." **30** Then he said, "I have sinned; *yet* honor me now, please, before the elders of my people and before Israel, and return with me, that I may worship the LORD your God."

Ahab.

1 Kin 21:27–29 So it was, when Ahab heard those words, that he tore his clothes and put sackcloth on his body, and fasted and lay in sackcloth, and went about mourning. **28** And the word of the LORD came to Elijah the Tishbite, saying, **29** "See how Ahab has humbled himself before Me? Because he has humbled himself before Me, I will not bring the calamity in his days. In the days of his son I will bring the calamity on his house."

Judas.

Matt 27:3–5 Then Judas, His betrayer, seeing that He had been condemned, was remorseful and brought back the thirty pieces of silver to the chief priests and elders, **4** saying, "I have sinned by betraying innocent blood." And they said, "What *is that* to us? You see *to it!*" **5** Then he threw down the pieces of silver in the temple and departed, and went and hanged himself.

REPHAIM, THE (GIANTS)

Subdued by Chedorlaomer.

Gen 14:5 In the fourteenth year Chedorlaomer and the kings that *were* with him came and attacked the Rephaim in Ashteroth Karnaim, the Zuzim in Ham, the Emim in Shaveh Kiriathaim,

Dwelt in Canaan.

Josh 17:15 So Joshua answered them, "If you *are* a great people, *then* go up to the forest *country* and clear a place for yourself there in the land of the Perizzites and the giants, since the mountains of Ephraim are too confined for you."

Og the king of Bashan was of.

Josh 13:12 all the kingdom of Og in Bashan, who reigned in Ashtaroth and Edrei, who remained of the remnant of the giants; for Moses had defeated and cast out these.

The valley of,

A border of Judah.

Josh 15:8 And the border went up by the Valley of the Son of Hinnom to the southern slope of the Jebusite *city* (which *is* Jerusalem). The border went up to the top of the mountain that *lies* before the Valley of Hinnom westward, which *is* at the end of the Valley of Rephaim northward.

Was exceedingly fruitful.

Is 17:5 It shall be as when the harvester gathers the grain, And reaps the heads with his arm; It shall be as he who gathers heads of grain In the Valley of Rephaim.

David obtained victories over the Philistines in.

2 Sam 5:18 The Philistines also went and deployed themselves in the Valley of Rephaim.

2 Sam 5:25 And David did so, as the LORD commanded him; and he drove back the Philistines from Geba as far as Gezer.

The last of, destroyed by David and his warriors.

1 Sam 17:4 And a champion went out from the camp of the Philistines, named Goliath, from Gath, whose height *was* six cubits and a span.

1 Sam 17:49–50 Then David put his hand in his bag and took out a stone; and he slung *it* and struck the Philistine in his forehead, so that the stone sank into his forehead, and he fell on his face to the earth. **50** So David prevailed over the Philistine with a sling and a stone, and struck the Philistine and killed him. But *there was* no sword in the hand of David.

Cf. 2 Sam 21:15–22

REPTILES. *SEE ALSO* SERPENTS (SNAKES, ASPS)

Created by God.

Gen 1:24–25 Then God said, "Let the earth bring forth the living creature according to its kind: cattle and creeping thing and beast of the earth, *each* according to its kind"; and it was so. **25** And God made the beast of the earth according to its kind, cattle according to its kind, and everything that creeps on the earth according to its kind. And God saw that *it was* good.

Made for praise and glory of God.

Ps 148:10 Beasts and all cattle; Creeping things and flying fowl;

Placed under the dominion of man.

Gen 1:26 Then God said, "Let Us make man in Our image, according to Our likeness; let them have dominion over the fish of the sea, over the birds of the air, and over the cattle, over all the earth and over every creeping thing that creeps on the earth."

Unclean and not eaten.

Lev 11:31 These *are* unclean to you among all that creep.

Whoever touches them when they are dead shall be unclean until evening.

Lev 11:40–43 He who eats of its carcass shall wash his clothes and be unclean until evening. He also who carries its carcass shall wash his clothes and be unclean until evening. **41** 'And every creeping thing that creeps on the earth *shall be* an abomination. It shall not be eaten. **42** Whatever crawls on its belly, whatever goes on *all* fours, or whatever has many feet among all creeping things that creep on the earth—these you shall not eat, for they *are* an abomination. **43** You shall not make yourselves abominable with any creeping thing that creeps; nor shall you make yourselves unclean with them, lest you be defiled by them.

Acts 10:11–14 and saw heaven opened and an object like a great sheet bound at the four corners, descending to him and let down to the earth. **12** In it were all kinds of four-footed animals of the earth, wild beasts, creeping things, and birds of the air. **13** And a voice came to him, "Rise, Peter; kill and eat." **14** But Peter said, "Not so, Lord! For I have never eaten anything common or unclean."

Mentioned in Scripture

Chameleon.

Lev 11:30 the gecko, the monitor lizard, the sand reptile, the sand lizard, and the chameleon.

Cobra.

Deut 32:33 Their wine *is* the poison of serpents, And the cruel venom of cobras.

Ps 58:4 Their poison *is* like the poison of a serpent; *They are* like the deaf cobra *that* stops its ear,

Ps 91:13 You shall tread upon the lion and the cobra, The young lion and the serpent you shall trample underfoot.

Lizard.

Lev 11:29–30 'These also *shall be* unclean to you among the creeping things that creep on the earth: the mole, the mouse, and the large lizard after its kind; **30** the gecko, the monitor lizard, the sand reptile, the sand lizard, and the chameleon.

Snail.

Ps 58:8 *Let them be* like a snail which melts away as it goes, *Like* a stillborn child of a woman, that they may not see the sun.

Serpent.

Deut 8:15 who led you through that great and terrible wilderness, *in which were* fiery serpents and scorpions and thirsty land where there was no water; who brought water for you out of the flinty rock;

Job 26:13 By His Spirit He adorned the heavens; His hand pierced the fleeing serpent.

Is 30:6 The burden against the beasts of the South. Through a land of trouble and anguish, From which *came* the lioness and lion, The viper and fiery flying serpent, They will carry their riches on the backs of young donkeys, And their treasures on the humps of camels, To a people *who* shall not profit;

Matt 7:10 Or if he asks for a fish, will he give him a serpent?

Deut 32:33 Their wine *is* the poison of serpents, And the cruel venom of cobras.

Viper.

Is 59:5 They hatch vipers' eggs and weave the spider's web; He who eats of their eggs dies, And *from* that which is crushed a viper breaks out.

Acts 28:3 But when Paul had gathered a bundle of sticks and laid *them* on the fire, a viper came out because of the heat, and fastened on his hand.

Prov 23:32 At the last it bites like a serpent, And stings like a viper.

Solomon wrote a history of.

1 Kin 4:33 Also he spoke of trees, from the cedar tree of Lebanon even to the hyssop that springs out of the wall; he spoke also of animals, of birds, of creeping things, and of fish.

Worshiped by Gentiles.

Rom 1:23 and changed the glory of the incorruptible God into an image made like corruptible man—and birds and four-footed animals and creeping things.

No image or likeness of, to be made for worshiping.

Deut 4:16 lest you act corruptly and make for yourselves a carved image in the form of any figure: the likeness of male or female,

Deut 4:18 the likeness of anything that creeps on the ground or the likeness of any fish that *is* in the water beneath the earth.

Jews condemned for worshiping.

Ezek 8:10 So I went in and saw, and there—every sort of creeping thing, abominable beasts, and all the idols of the house of Israel, portrayed all around on the walls.

RESTITUTION

To the priest, for sins against property.

Lev 5:14–19 Then the LORD spoke to Moses, saying: **15** "If a person commits a trespass, and sins unintentionally in regard to the holy things of the LORD, then he shall bring to the LORD as his trespass offering a ram without blemish from the flocks, with your valuation in shekels of silver according to the shekel of the sanctuary, as a trespass offering. **16** And he shall make restitution for the harm that he has done in regard to the holy thing, and shall add one-fifth to it and give it to the priest. So the priest shall make atonement for him with the ram of the trespass offering, and it shall be forgiven him. **17** "If a person sins, and commits any of these things which are forbidden to be done by the commandments of the LORD, though he does not know *it*, yet he is guilty and shall bear his iniquity. **18** And he shall bring to the priest a ram without blemish from the flock, with your valuation, as a trespass offering. So the priest shall make atonement for him regarding his ignorance in which he erred and did not know *it*, and it shall be forgiven him. **19** It is a trespass offering; he has certainly trespassed against the LORD."

To victims.

Num 5:5–10 Then the LORD spoke to Moses, saying, **6** "Speak to the children of Israel: 'When a man or woman commits any sin that men commit in unfaithfulness against the LORD, and that person is guilty, **7** then he shall confess the sin which he has committed. He shall make restitution for his trespass in full, plus one-fifth of it, and give *it* to the one he has wronged. **8** But if the man has no relative to whom restitution may be made for the wrong, the restitution for the wrong *must go* to the LORD for the priest, in addition to the ram of the atonement with which atonement is made for him. **9** Every offering of all the holy things of the children of Israel, which they bring to the priest, shall be his. **10** And every man's holy things shall be his; whatever any man gives the priest shall be his.' "

Cf. Lev 6:1–7

For theft.

Prov 6:30–31 *People* do not despise a thief If he steals to satisfy himself when he is starving. **31** Yet *when* he is found, he must restore sevenfold; He may have to give up all the substance of his house.

Cf. Ex 22:1–15

For adultery.

Prov 6:32–35 Whoever commits adultery with a woman lacks understanding; He *who* does so destroys his own soul. **33** Wounds and dishonor he will get, And his reproach will not be wiped away. **34** For jealousy *is* a husband's fury; Therefore he will not spare in the day of vengeance. **35** He will accept no recompense, Nor will he be appeased though you give many gifts.

By Zacchaeus.

Luke 19:8 Then Zacchaeus stood and said to the Lord, "Look, Lord, I give half of my goods to the poor; and if I have taken anything from anyone by false accusation, I restore fourfold."

Offered by Paul to Philemon.

Philem 1:17–19 If then you count me as a partner, receive him as *you would* me. **18** But if he has wronged you or owes anything, put that on my account. **19** I, Paul, am writing with my own hand. I will repay—not to mention to you that you owe me even your own self besides.

RESURRECTION FROM THE DEAD, THE

A doctrine of the Old Testament.

Job 19:26 And after my skin is destroyed, this *I know,* That in my flesh I shall see God,

Ps 16:10 For You will not leave my soul in Sheol, Nor will You allow Your Holy One to see corruption.

Ps 49:15 But God will redeem my soul from the power of the grave, For He shall receive me. Selah

Is 26:19 Your dead shall live; *Together with* my dead body they shall arise. Awake and sing, you who dwell in dust; For your dew *is like* the dew of herbs, And the earth shall cast out the dead.

Dan 12:2 And many of those who sleep in the dust of the earth shall awake, Some to everlasting life, Some to shame *and* everlasting contempt.

Hos 13:14 "I will ransom them from the power of the grave; I will redeem them from death. O Death, I will be your plagues! O Grave, I will be your destruction! Pity is hidden from My eyes."

A first principle of the gospel.

1 Cor 15:13–14 But if there is no resurrection of the dead, then Christ is not risen. **14** And if Christ is not risen, then our preaching *is* empty and your faith *is* also empty.

Heb 6:1–2 Therefore, leaving the discussion of the elementary *principles* of Christ, let us go on to perfection, not laying again the foundation of repentance from dead works and of faith toward God, **2** of the doctrine of baptisms, of laying on of hands, of resurrection of the dead, and of eternal judgment.

Expected by the Jews.

John 11:24 Martha said to Him, "I know that he will rise again in the resurrection at the last day."

Heb 11:35 Women received their dead raised to life again. Others were tortured, not accepting deliverance, that they might obtain a better resurrection.

Denied by the Sadducees.

Matt 22:23 The same day the Sadducees, who say there is no resurrection, came to Him and asked Him,

Luke 20:27 Then some of the Sadducees, who deny that there is a resurrection, came to *Him* and asked Him,

Acts 23:8 For Sadducees say that there is no resurrection—and no angel or spirit; but the Pharisees confess both.

Explained away by false teachers.

2 Tim 2:18 who have strayed concerning the truth, saying that the resurrection is already past; and they overthrow the faith of some.

Called in question by some in the church.

1 Cor 15:12 Now if Christ is preached that He has been raised from the dead, how do some among you say that there is no resurrection of the dead?

Is not contrary to reason.

Mark 12:24 Jesus answered and said to them, "Are you not therefore mistaken, because you do not know the Scriptures nor the power of God?

John 12:24 Most assuredly, I say to you, unless a grain of wheat falls into the ground and dies, it remains alone; but if it dies, it produces much grain.

Acts 26:8 Why should it be thought incredible by you that God raises the dead?

Cf. 1 Cor 15:35–49

Assumed and proved by our Lord.

Matt 22:29–32 Jesus answered and said to them, "You are mistaken, not knowing the Scriptures nor the power of God. **30** For in the resurrection they neither marry nor are given in marriage, but are like angels of God in heaven. **31** But concerning the resurrection of the dead, have you not read what was spoken to you by God, saying, **32** *'I am the God of Abraham, the God of Isaac, and the God of Jacob'*? God is not the God of the dead, but of the living."

Luke 14:14 And you will be blessed, because they cannot repay you; for you shall be repaid at the resurrection of the just."

John 5:28–29 Do not marvel at this; for the hour is coming in which all who are in the graves will hear His voice **29** and come forth—those who have done good, to the resurrection of life, and those who have done evil, to the resurrection of condemnation.

Preached by the apostles.

Acts 4:2 being greatly disturbed that they taught the people and preached in Jesus the resurrection from the dead.

Acts 17:18 Then certain Epicurean and Stoic philosophers encountered him. And some said, "What does this babbler want to say?" Others said, "He seems to be a proclaimer of foreign gods," because he preached to them Jesus and the resurrection.

Acts 24:15 I have hope in God, which they themselves also accept, that there will be a resurrection of *the* dead, both of *the* just and *the* unjust.

Credibility of, shown by the resurrection of individuals.

Matt 9:25 But when the crowd was put outside, He went in and took her by the hand, and the girl arose.

Matt 27:53 and coming out of the graves after His resurrection, they went into the holy city and appeared to many.

Luke 7:14 Then He came and touched the open coffin, and those who carried *him* stood still. And He said, "Young man, I say to you, arise."

John 11:44 And he who had died came out bound hand and foot with graveclothes, and his face was wrapped with a cloth. Jesus said to them, "Loose him, and let him go."

Heb 11:35 Women received their dead raised to life again. Others were tortured, not accepting deliverance, that they might obtain a better resurrection.

Certainty of, proved by the resurrection of Christ.

1 Cor 15:12–20 Now if Christ is preached that He has been raised from the dead, how do some among you say that there is no resurrection of the dead? **13** But if there is no resurrection of the dead, then Christ is not risen. **14** And if Christ is not risen, then our preaching *is* empty and your faith *is* also empty. **15** Yes, and we are found false witnesses of God, because we have testified of God that He raised up Christ, whom He did not raise up—if in fact the dead do not rise. **16** For if *the* dead do not rise, then Christ is not risen. **17** And if Christ is not risen, your faith *is* futile; you are still in your sins! **18** Then also those who have fallen asleep in Christ have perished. **19** If in this life only we have hope in Christ, we are of all men the most pitiable. **20** But now Christ is risen from the dead, *and* has become the firstfruits of those who have fallen asleep.

Effected by the power of

God.

Matt 22:29 Jesus answered and said to them, "You are mistaken, not knowing the Scriptures nor the power of God.

Christ.

John 5:28–29 Do not marvel at this; for the hour is coming in which all who are in the graves will hear His voice **29** and come forth—those who have done good, to the resurrection of life, and those who have done evil, to the resurrection of condemnation.

John 6:39–40 This is the will of the Father who sent Me, that of all He has given Me I should lose nothing, but should raise it up at the last day. **40** And this is the will of Him who sent Me, that everyone who sees the Son and believes in Him may have everlasting life; and I will raise him up at the last day."

John 6:44 No one can come to Me unless the Father who sent Me draws him; and I will raise him up at the last day.

The Holy Spirit.

Rom 8:11 But if the Spirit of Him who raised Jesus from the dead dwells in you, He who raised Christ from the dead will also give life to your mortal bodies through His Spirit who dwells in you.

Shall be of all the dead.

John 5:28 Do not marvel at this; for the hour is coming in which all who are in the graves will hear His voice

Acts 24:15 I have hope in God, which they themselves also accept, that there will be a resurrection of *the* dead, both of *the* just and *the* unjust.

Rev 20:13 The sea gave up the dead who were in it, and Death and Hades delivered up the dead who were in them. And they were judged, each one according to his works.

Believers in, shall

Rise through Christ.

John 11:25 Jesus said to her, "I am the resurrection and the life. He who believes in Me, though he may die, he shall live.

Acts 4:2 being greatly disturbed that they taught the people and preached in Jesus the resurrection from the dead.

1 Cor 15:21–22 For since by man *came* death, by Man also *came* the resurrection of the dead. 22 For as in Adam all die, even so in Christ all shall be made alive.

Rise first.

1 Cor 15:23 But each one in his own order: Christ the firstfruits, afterward those *who are* Christ's at His coming.

1 Thess 4:16 For the Lord Himself will descend from heaven with a shout, with the voice of an archangel, and with the trumpet of God. And the dead in Christ will rise first.

Rise to eternal life.

Dan 12:2 And many of those who sleep in the dust of the earth shall awake, Some to everlasting life, Some to shame *and* everlasting contempt.

John 5:29 and come forth—those who have done good, to the resurrection of life, and those who have done evil, to the resurrection of condemnation.

Be glorified with Christ.

Col 3:4 When Christ *who is* our life appears, then you also will appear with Him in glory.

Be as the angels.

Matt 22:30 For in the resurrection they neither marry nor are given in marriage, but are like angels of God in heaven.

Have incorruptible bodies.

1 Cor 15:42 So also *is* the resurrection of the dead. *The* body is sown in corruption, it is raised in incorruption.

Have glorious bodies.

1 Cor 15:43 It is sown in dishonor, it is raised in glory. It is sown in weakness, it is raised in power.

Have powerful bodies.

1 Cor 15:43 It is sown in dishonor, it is raised in glory. It is sown in weakness, it is raised in power.

Have spiritual bodies.

1 Cor 15:44 It is sown a natural body, it is raised a spiritual body. There is a natural body, and there is a spiritual body.

Have bodies like Christ's.

Phil 3:21 who will transform our lowly body that it may be conformed to His glorious body, according to the working by which He is able even to subdue all things to Himself.

1 John 3:2 Beloved, now we are children of God; and it has not yet been revealed what we shall be, but we know that when He is revealed, we shall be like Him, for we shall see Him as He is.

Be recompensed.

Luke 14:14 And you will be blessed, because they cannot repay you; for you shall be repaid at the resurrection of the just."

Believers should look forward to.

Dan 12:13 "But you, go *your way* till the end; for you shall rest, and will arise to your inheritance at the end of the days."

Phil 3:11 if, by any means, I may attain to the resurrection from the dead.

2 Cor 5:1 For we know that if our earthly house, *this* tent, is destroyed, we have a building from God, a house not made with hands, eternal in the heavens.

Of believers, followed by change of ones still alive.

1 Cor 15:51 Behold, I tell you a mystery: We shall not all sleep, but we shall all be changed—

1 Thess 4:17 Then we who are alive *and* remain shall be caught up together with them in the clouds to meet the Lord in the air. And thus we shall always be with the Lord.

The preaching of, caused

Mocking.

Acts 17:32 And when they heard of the resurrection of the dead, some mocked, while others said, "We will hear you again on this *matter.*"

Persecution.

Acts 23:6 But when Paul perceived that one part were Sadducees and the other Pharisees, he cried out in the council, "Men *and* brethren, I am a Pharisee, the son of a Pharisee; concerning the hope and resurrection of the dead I am being judged!"

Acts 24:11–15 because you may ascertain that it is no more than twelve days since I went up to Jerusalem to worship. 12 And they neither found me in the temple disputing with anyone nor inciting the crowd, either in the synagogues or in the city. 13 Nor can they prove the things of which they now accuse me. 14 But this I confess to you, that according to the Way which they call a sect, so I worship the God of my fathers, believing all things which are written in the Law and in the Prophets. 15 I have hope in God, which they themselves also accept, that there will be a resurrection of *the* dead, both of *the* just and *the* unjust.

Blessedness of those who have part in the first.

Rev 20:6 Blessed and holy *is* he who has part in the first resurrection. Over such the second death has no power, but they shall be priests of God and of Christ, and shall reign with Him a thousand years.

Of the wicked, shall be to

Shame and everlasting contempt.

Dan 12:2 And many of those who sleep in the dust of the earth shall awake, Some to everlasting life, Some to shame *and* everlasting contempt.

Damnation.

John 5:29 and come forth—those who have done good, to the resurrection of life, and those who have done evil, to the resurrection of condemnation.

Illustrated.

John 5:25 Most assuredly, I say to you, the hour is coming, and now is, when the dead will hear the voice of the Son of God; and those who hear will live.

1 Cor 15:36–37 Foolish one, what you sow is not made alive unless it dies. **37** And what you sow, you do not sow that body that shall be, but mere grain—perhaps wheat or some other *grain.*

Cf. Ezek 37:1–10

RESURRECTION OF CHRIST. *SEE* JESUS CHRIST, RESURRECTION OF

REUBEN, THE TRIBE OF

Descended from Jacob's first son.

Gen 29:32 So Leah conceived and bore a son, and she called his name Reuben; for she said, "The LORD has surely looked on my affliction. Now therefore, my husband will love me."

Predictions respecting.

Gen 49:4 Unstable as water, you shall not excel, Because you went up to your father's bed; Then you defiled *it*— He went up to my couch.

Deut 33:6 "Let Reuben live, and not die, *Nor* let his men be few."

Persons selected from,

To number the people.

Num 1:5 "These are the names of the men who shall stand with you: from Reuben, Elizur the son of Shedeur;

To spy out the land.

Num 13:4 Now these *were* their names: from the tribe of Reuben, Shammua the son of Zaccur;

Strength of, on leaving Egypt.

Num 1:20–21 Now the children of Reuben, Israel's oldest son, their genealogies by their families, by their fathers' house, according to the number of names, every male individually, from twenty years old and above, all who *were able to* go to war: **21** those who were numbered of the tribe of Reuben *were* forty-six thousand five hundred.

Led the second division of Israel in her journeys.

Num 10:18 And the standard of the camp of Reuben set out according to their armies; over their army *was* Elizur the son of Shedeur.

Encamped with its standard south of the tabernacle.

Num 2:10 "On the south side *shall be* the standard of the forces with Reuben according to their armies, and

the leader of the children of Reuben *shall be* Elizur the son of Shedeur."

Offering of, at the dedication.

Num 7:30–35 On the fourth day Elizur the son of Shedeur, leader of the children of Reuben, *presented an offering.* **31** His offering *was* one silver platter, the weight of which *was* one hundred and thirty *shekels,* and one silver bowl of seventy shekels, according to the shekel of the sanctuary, both of them full of fine flour mixed with oil as a grain offering; **32** one gold pan of ten *shekels,* full of incense; **33** one young bull, one ram, and one male lamb in its first year, as a burnt offering; **34** one kid of the goats as a sin offering; **35** and as the sacrifice of peace offerings: two oxen, five rams, five male goats, and five male lambs in their first year. This *was* the offering of Elizur the son of Shedeur.

Families of.

Num 26:5–6 Reuben *was* the firstborn of Israel. The children of Reuben *were: of* Hanoch, the family of the Hanochites; *of* Pallu, the family of the Palluites; **6** *of* Hezron, the family of the Hezronites; *of* Carmi, the family of the Carmites.

Num 26:8–9 And the son of Pallu *was* Eliab. **9** The sons of Eliab *were* Nemuel, Dathan, and Abiram. These *are* the Dathan and Abiram, representatives of the congregation, who contended against Moses and Aaron in the company of Korah, when they contended against the LORD;

Obtained inheritance east of Jordan, on condition of helping to conquer Canaan.

Deut 3:18–20 "Then I commanded you at that time, saying: 'The LORD your God has given you this land to possess. All you men of valor shall cross over armed before your brethren, the children of Israel. **19** But your wives, your little ones, and your livestock (I know that you have much livestock) shall stay in your cities which I have given you, **20** until the LORD has given rest to your brethren as to you, and they also possess the land which the LORD your God is giving them beyond the Jordan. Then each of you may return to his possession which I have given you.'

Cf. Num 32:1–33

Bounds of its inheritance.

Deut 3:16–17 And to the Reubenites and the Gadites I gave from Gilead as far as the River Arnon, the middle of the river as *the* border, as far as the River Jabbok, the border of the people of Ammon; **17** the plain also, with the Jordan as *the* border, from Chinnereth as far as the east side of the Sea of the Arabah (the Salt Sea), below the slopes of Pisgah.

Josh 13:15–23 And Moses had given to the tribe of the children of Reuben *an inheritance* according to their families. **16** Their territory was from Aroer, which *is* on the bank of the River Arnon, and the city that *is* in the midst of the ravine, and all the plain by Medeba; **17** Heshbon and all its cities that *are* in the plain: Dibon, Bamoth Baal, Beth Baal Meon, **18** Jahaza, Kedemoth, Mephaath, **19** Kirjathaim, Sibmah, Zereth Shahar on the mountain of the valley, **20** Beth Peor, the slopes of Pisgah, and Beth Jeshimoth— **21** all the cities of the plain and all the kingdom of Sihon king of the Amorites, who reigned in Heshbon, whom

Moses had struck with the princes of Midian: Evi, Rekem, Zur, Hur, and Reba, who *were* princes of Sihon dwelling in the country. **22** The children of Israel also killed with the sword Balaam the son of Beor, the soothsayer, among those who were killed by them. **23** And the border of the children of Reuben was the bank of the Jordan. This *was* the inheritance of the children of Reuben according to their families, the cities and their villages.

Strength of, at the time of receiving its inheritance.

Num 26:7 These *are* the families of the Reubenites: those who were numbered of them were forty-three thousand seven hundred and thirty.

Cities built by.

Num 32:37–38 And the children of Reuben built Heshbon and Elealeh and Kirjathaim, **38** Nebo and Baal Meon (*their* names being changed) and Shibmah; and they gave *other* names to the cities which they built.

On Ebal, said amen to the curses.

Deut 27:13 and these shall stand on Mount Ebal to curse: Reuben, Gad, Asher, Zebulun, Dan, and Naphtali.

Dismissed by Joshua after the conquest of Canaan. Josh 22:1–9

Assisted in building the altar of witness, which offended the other tribes. Josh 22:10–29

Did not assist against Sisera.

Judg 5:15–16 And the princes of Issachar *were* with Deborah; As Issachar, so *was* Barak Sent into the valley under his command; Among the divisions of Reuben *There were* great resolves of heart. **16** Why did you sit among the sheepfolds, To hear the pipings for the flocks? The divisions of Reuben have great searchings of heart.

Some of, at David's coronation.

1 Chr 12:37–38 of the Reubenites and the Gadites and the half-tribe of Manasseh, from the other side of the Jordan, one hundred and twenty thousand armed for battle with every *kind* of weapon of war. **38** All these men of war, who could keep ranks, came to Hebron with a loyal heart, to make David king over all Israel; and all the rest of Israel *were* of one mind to make David king.

Officers appointed over, by David.

1 Chr 26:32 And his brethren *were* two thousand seven hundred able men, heads of fathers' *houses*, whom King David made officials over the Reubenites, the Gadites, and the half-tribe of Manasseh, for every matter pertaining to God and the affairs of the king.

1 Chr 27:16 Furthermore, over the tribes of Israel: the officer over the Reubenites *was* Eliezer the son of Zichri; over the Simeonites, Shephatiah the son of Maachah;

Took land of the Hagrites.

1 Chr 5:10 Now in the days of Saul they made war with the Hagrites, who fell by their hand; and they dwelt in their tents throughout the entire *area* east of Gilead.

1 Chr 5:18–22 The sons of Reuben, the Gadites, and half the tribe of Manasseh *had* forty-four thousand seven hundred and sixty valiant men, men able to bear shield and sword, to shoot with the bow, and skillful in war, who went to war. **19** They made war with the Hagrites, Jetur, Naphish, and Nodab. **20** And they were helped against them, and the Hagrites were delivered into their hand, and all who *were* with them, for they cried out to God in the battle. He heeded their prayer, because they put their trust in Him. **21** Then they took away their livestock—fifty thousand of their camels, two hundred and fifty thousand of their sheep, and two thousand of their donkeys—also one hundred thousand of their men; **22** for many fell dead, because the war *was* God's. And they dwelt in their place until the captivity.

Invaded and conquered by Hazael king of Syria.

2 Kin 10:32–33 In those days the LORD began to cut off *parts* of Israel; and Hazael conquered them in all the territory of Israel **33** from the Jordan eastward: all the land of Gilead—Gad, Reuben, and Manasseh—from Aroer, which *is* by the River Arnon, including Gilead and Bashan.

Carried away by Tiglath-Pileser.

2 Kin 15:29 In the days of Pekah king of Israel, Tiglath-Pileser king of Assyria came and took Ijon, Abel Beth Maachah, Janoah, Kedesh, Hazor, Gilead, and Galilee, all the land of Naphtali; and he carried them captive to Assyria.

1 Chr 5:6 and Beerah his son, whom Tiglath-Pileser king of Assyria carried into captivity. He *was* leader of the Reubenites.

1 Chr 5:26 So the God of Israel stirred up the spirit of Pul king of Assyria, that is, Tiglath-Pileser king of Assyria. He carried the Reubenites, the Gadites, and the half-tribe of Manasseh into captivity. He took them to Halah, Habor, Hara, and the river of Gozan to this day.

Remarkable persons of,

Dathan, Abiram, and On.

Num 16:1 Now Korah the son of Izhar, the son of Kohath, the son of Levi, with Dathan and Abiram the sons of Eliab, and On the son of Peleth, sons of Reuben, took *men;*

Num 26:9–10 The sons of Eliab *were* Nemuel, Dathan, and Abiram. These *are* the Dathan and Abiram, representatives of the congregation, who contended against Moses and Aaron in the company of Korah, when they contended against the LORD; **10** and the earth opened its mouth and swallowed them up together with Korah when that company died, when the fire devoured two hundred and fifty men; and they became a sign.

Adina, etc.

1 Chr 11:42 Adina the son of Shiza the Reubenite (a chief of the Reubenites) and thirty with him,

REVENGE

Forbidden by God.

Lev 19:18 You shall not take vengeance, nor bear any grudge against the children of your people, but you shall love your neighbor as yourself: I *am* the LORD.

Prov 24:17 Do not rejoice when your enemy falls, And do not let your heart be glad when he stumbles;

Prov 24:29 Do not say, "I will do to him just as he has done to me; I will render to the man according to his work."

Matt 5:39–41 But I tell you not to resist an evil person. But whoever slaps you on your right cheek, turn the other to him also. **40** If anyone wants to sue you and take away your tunic, let him have *your* cloak also. **41** And whoever compels you to go one mile, go with him two.

Luke 9:54–55 And when His disciples James and John saw *this*, they said, "Lord, do You want us to command fire to come down from heaven and consume them, just as Elijah did?" **55** But He turned and rebuked them, and said, "You do not know what manner of spirit you are of.

Rom 12:17 Repay no one evil for evil. Have regard for good things in the sight of all men.

Rom 12:19 Beloved, do not avenge yourselves, but *rather* give place to wrath; for it is written, *"Vengeance is Mine, I will repay,"* says the Lord.

1 Thess 5:15 See that no one renders evil for evil to anyone, but always pursue what is good both for yourselves and for all.

1 Pet 3:9 not returning evil for evil or reviling for reviling, but on the contrary blessing, knowing that you were called to this, that you may inherit a blessing.

Christ an example of forbearing.

Is 53:7 He was oppressed and He was afflicted, Yet He opened not His mouth; He was led as a lamb to the slaughter, And as a sheep before its shearers is silent, So He opened not His mouth.

1 Pet 2:23 who, when He was reviled, did not revile in return; when He suffered, He did not threaten, but committed *Himself* to Him who judges righteously;

Inconsistent with Christian spirit.

Luke 9:55 But He turned and rebuked them, and said, "You do not know what manner of spirit you are of.

Proceeds from a spiteful heart.

Ezek 25:15 'Thus says the Lord GOD: "Because the Philistines dealt vengefully and took vengeance with a spiteful heart, to destroy because of the old hatred,"

Instead of taking, we should

Trust in God.

Prov 20:22 Do not say, "I will recompense evil"; Wait for the LORD, and He will save you.

Rom 12:16 Be of the same mind toward one another. Do not set your mind on high things, but associate with the humble. Do not be wise in your own opinion.

Exhibit love.

Lev 19:18 You shall not take vengeance, nor bear any grudge against the children of your people, but you shall love your neighbor as yourself: I *am* the LORD.

Luke 6:35 But love your enemies, do good, and lend, hoping for nothing in return; and your reward will be great, and you will be sons of the Most High. For He is kind to the unthankful and evil.

Give place to wrath.

Rom 12:19 Beloved, do not avenge yourselves, but *rather* give place to wrath; for it is written, *"Vengeance is Mine, I will repay,"* says the Lord.

Exercise forbearance.

Matt 5:38–41 "You have heard that it was said, *'An eye for an eye and a tooth for a tooth.'* **39** But I tell you not to resist an evil person. But whoever slaps you on your right cheek, turn the other to him also. **40** If any-

one wants to sue you and take away your tunic, let him have *your* cloak also. **41** And whoever compels you to go one mile, go with him two.

Bless.

Rom 12:14 Bless those who persecute you; bless and do not curse.

Overcome others by kindness.

Prov 25:21–22 If your enemy is hungry, give him bread to eat; And if he is thirsty, give him water to drink; **22** For *so* you will heap coals of fire on his head, And the LORD will reward you.

Rom 12:20 Therefore *"If your enemy is hungry, feed him; If he is thirsty, give him a drink; For in so doing you will heap coals of fire on his head."*

Keep others from taking.

1 Sam 24:10 Look, this day your eyes have seen that the LORD delivered you today into my hand in the cave, and *someone* urged *me* to kill you. But *my eye* spared you, and I said, 'I will not stretch out my hand against my lord, for he *is* the LORD's anointed.'

1 Sam 26:9 But David said to Abishai, "Do not destroy him; for who can stretch out his hand against the LORD's anointed, and be guiltless?"

Cf. 1 Sam 25:24–33

The wicked are eager for.

Jer 20:10 For I heard many mocking: "Fear on every side!" "Report," *they say,* "and we will report it!" All my acquaintances watched for my stumbling, *saying,* "Perhaps he can be induced; Then we will prevail against him, And we will take our revenge on him."

Punishment for.

Ezek 25:15–17 'Thus says the Lord GOD: "Because the Philistines dealt vengefully and took vengeance with a spiteful heart, to destroy because of the old hatred," **16** therefore thus says the Lord GOD: "I will stretch out My hand against the Philistines, and I will cut off the Cherethites and destroy the remnant of the seacoast. **17** I will execute great vengeance on them with furious rebukes; and they shall know that I *am* the LORD, when I lay My vengeance upon them." ' "

Amos 1:11–12 Thus says the LORD: "For three transgressions of Edom, and for four, I will not turn away its *punishment,* Because he pursued his brother with the sword, And cast off all pity; His anger tore perpetually, And he kept his wrath forever. **12** But I will send a fire upon Teman, Which shall devour the palaces of Bozrah."

Illustrated by

Simeon and Levi.

Gen 34:25 Now it came to pass on the third day, when they were in pain, that two of the sons of Jacob, Simeon and Levi, Dinah's brothers, each took his sword and came boldly upon the city and killed all the males.

Samson.

Judg 15:7–8 Samson said to them, "Since you would do a thing like this, I will surely take revenge on you, and after that I will cease." **8** So he attacked them hip and thigh with a great slaughter; then he went down and dwelt in the cleft of the rock of Etam.

Judg 16:28–30 Then Samson called to the LORD, saying, "O Lord GOD, remember me, I pray! Strengthen me,

I pray, just this once, O God, that I may with one *blow* take vengeance on the Philistines for my two eyes!" 29 And Samson took hold of the two middle pillars which supported the temple, and he braced himself against them, one on his right and the other on his left. 30 Then Samson said, "Let me die with the Philistines!" And he pushed with *all his* might, and the temple fell on the lords and all the people who *were* in it. So the dead that he killed at his death were more than he had killed in his life.

Joab.

2 Sam 3:27 Now when Abner had returned to Hebron, Joab took him aside in the gate to speak with him privately, and there stabbed him in the stomach, so that he died for the blood of Asahel his brother.

Absalom.

2 Sam 13:23–29 And it came to pass, after two full years, that Absalom had sheepshearers in Baal Hazor, which *is* near Ephraim; so Absalom invited all the king's sons. 24 Then Absalom came to the king and said, "Kindly note, your servant has sheepshearers; please, let the king and his servants go with your servant." 25 But the king said to Absalom, "No, my son, let us not all go now, lest we be a burden to you." Then he urged him, but he would not go; and he blessed him. 26 Then Absalom said, "If not, please let my brother Amnon go with us." And the king said to him, "Why should he go with you?" 27 But Absalom urged him; so he let Amnon and all the king's sons go with him. 28 Now Absalom had commanded his servants, saying, "Watch now, when Amnon's heart is merry with wine, and when I say to you, 'Strike Amnon!' then kill him. Do not be afraid. Have I not commanded you? Be courageous and valiant." 29 So the servants of Absalom did to Amnon as Absalom had commanded. Then all the king's sons arose, and each one got on his mule and fled.

Jezebel.

1 Kin 19:2 Then Jezebel sent a messenger to Elijah, saying, "So let the gods do *to me,* and more also, if I do not make your life as the life of one of them by tomorrow about this time."

Ahab.

1 Kin 22:26 So the king of Israel said, "Take Micaiah, and return him to Amon the governor of the city and to Joash the king's son;

Haman. **Esth 3:8–15**

The Edomites.

Ezek 25:12 'Thus says the Lord GOD: "Because of what Edom did against the house of Judah by taking vengeance, and has greatly offended by avenging itself on them,"

The Philistines.

Ezek 25:15 'Thus says the Lord GOD: "Because the Philistines dealt vengefully and took vengeance with a spiteful heart, to destroy because of the old hatred,"

Herodias.

Mark 6:19–24 Therefore Herodias held it against him and wanted to kill him, but she could not; 20 for Herod feared John, knowing that he *was* a just and holy man, and he protected him. And when he heard him, he did many things, and heard him gladly.

21 Then an opportune day came when Herod on his birthday gave a feast for his nobles, the high officers, and the chief *men* of Galilee. 22 And when Herodias' daughter herself came in and danced, and pleased Herod and those who sat with him, the king said to the girl, "Ask me whatever you want, and I will give *it* to you." 23 He also swore to her, "Whatever you ask me, I will give you, up to half my kingdom." 24 So she went out and said to her mother, "What shall I ask?" And she said, "The head of John the Baptist!"

James and John.

Luke 9:54 And when His disciples James and John saw *this,* they said, "Lord, do You want us to command fire to come down from heaven and consume them, just as Elijah did?"

The chief priests.

Acts 5:33 When they heard *this,* they were furious and plotted to kill them.

The Jews.

Acts 7:54 When they heard these things they were cut to the heart, and they gnashed at him with *their* teeth.

Acts 7:59 And they stoned Stephen as he was calling on God and saying, "Lord Jesus, receive my spirit."

Acts 23:12 And when it was day, some of the Jews banded together and bound themselves under an oath, saying that they would neither eat nor drink till they had killed Paul.

REVILING AND REPROACHING

Forbidden.

1 Pet 3:9 not returning evil for evil or reviling for reviling, but on the contrary blessing, knowing that you were called to this, that you may inherit a blessing.

Of rulers, especially forbidden.

Ex 22:28 "You shall not revile God, nor curse a ruler of your people.

Acts 23:4–5 And those who stood by said, "Do you revile God's high priest?" 5 Then Paul said, "I did not know, brethren, that he was the high priest; for it is written, *'You shall not speak evil of a ruler of your people.'*"

The wicked utter, against

God.

Ps 74:22 Arise, O God, plead Your own cause; Remember how the foolish man reproaches You daily.

Ps 79:12 And return to our neighbors sevenfold into their bosom Their reproach with which they have reproached You, O Lord.

Prov 14:31 He who oppresses the poor reproaches his Maker, But he who honors Him has mercy on the needy.

Christ.

Matt 27:39 And those who passed by blasphemed Him, wagging their heads

Luke 7:34 The Son of Man has come eating and drinking, and you say, 'Look, a glutton and a winebibber, a friend of tax collectors and sinners!'

Believers.

Ps 102:8 My enemies reproach me all day long; Those who deride me swear an oath against me.

Zeph 2:8 "I have heard the reproach of Moab, And the insults of the people of Ammon, With which they have reproached My people, And made arrogant threats against their borders.

Rulers.

2 Pet 2:10–11 and especially those who walk according to the flesh in the lust of uncleanness and despise authority. *They are* presumptuous, self-willed. They are not afraid to speak evil of dignitaries, **11** whereas angels, who are greater in power and might, do not bring a reviling accusation against them before the Lord.

Jude 1:8–9 Likewise also these dreamers defile the flesh, reject authority, and speak evil of dignitaries. **9** Yet Michael the archangel, in contending with the devil, when he disputed about the body of Moses, dared not bring against him a reviling accusation, but said, "The Lord rebuke you!"

Of Christ, predicted.

Ps 69:9 Because zeal for Your house has eaten me up, And the reproaches of those who reproach You have fallen on me.

Ps 89:51 With which Your enemies have reproached, O LORD, With which they have reproached the footsteps of Your anointed.

Rom 15:3 For even Christ did not please Himself; but as it is written, *"The reproaches of those who reproached You fell on Me."*

Christ's response to.

1 Pet 2:23 who, when He was reviled, did not revile in return; when He suffered, He did not threaten, but committed *Himself* to Him who judges righteously;

Believers

Should endure.

Ps 69:7 Because for Your sake I have borne reproach; Shame has covered my face.

Luke 6:22 Blessed are you when men hate you, And when they exclude you, And revile *you,* and cast out your name as evil, For the Son of Man's sake.

1 Tim 4:10 For to this *end* we both labor and suffer reproach, because we trust in the living God, who is *the* Savior of all men, especially of those who believe.

Heb 10:33 partly while you were made a spectacle both by reproaches and tribulations, and partly while you became companions of those who were so treated;

Should expect.

Matt 10:25 It is enough for a disciple that he be like his teacher, and a servant like his master. If they have called the master of the house Beelzebub, how much more *will they call* those of his household!

Should not fear.

Is 51:7 "Listen to Me, you who know righteousness, You people in whose heart *is* My law: Do not fear the reproach of men, Nor be afraid of their insults.

Ezek 2:6 "And you, son of man, do not be afraid of them nor be afraid of their words, though briers and thorns *are* with you and you dwell among scorpions; do not be afraid of their words or dismayed by their looks, though they *are* a rebellious house.

Sometimes depressed by.

Ps 42:10–11 *As* with a breaking of my bones, My ene-

mies reproach me, While they say to me all day long, "Where *is* your God?" **11** Why are you cast down, O my soul? And why are you disquieted within me? Hope in God; For I shall yet praise Him, The help of my countenance and my God.

Ps 44:16 Because of the voice of him who reproaches and reviles, Because of the enemy and the avenger.

Ps 69:20 Reproach has broken my heart, And I am full of heaviness; I looked *for someone* to take pity, but *there was* none; And for comforters, but I found none.

May take pleasure in.

2 Cor 12:10 Therefore I take pleasure in infirmities, in reproaches, in needs, in persecutions, in distresses, for Christ's sake. For when I am weak, then I am strong.

Supported under.

2 Cor 12:10 Therefore I take pleasure in infirmities, in reproaches, in needs, in persecutions, in distresses, for Christ's sake. For when I am weak, then I am strong.

Trust in God under.

Ps 57:3 He shall send from heaven and save me; He reproaches the one who would swallow me up. Selah God shall send forth His mercy and His truth.

Ps 119:42 So shall I have an answer for him who reproaches me, For I trust in Your word.

Pray under.

2 Kin 19:4 It may be that the LORD your God will hear all the words of *the* Rabshakeh, whom his master the king of Assyria has sent to reproach the living God, and will rebuke the words which the LORD your God has heard. Therefore lift up *your* prayer for the remnant that is left.' "

2 Kin 19:16 Incline Your ear, O LORD, and hear; open Your eyes, O LORD, and see; and hear the words of Sennacherib, which he has sent to reproach the living God.

Ps 89:50 Remember, Lord, the reproach of Your servants— *How* I bear in my bosom *the reproach of* all the many peoples,

Return blessings for.

1 Cor 4:12 And we labor, working with our own hands. Being reviled, we bless; being persecuted, we endure;

1 Pet 3:9 not returning evil for evil or reviling for reviling, but on the contrary blessing, knowing that you were called to this, that you may inherit a blessing.

Benefits of enduring, for Christ's sake.

Matt 5:11 "Blessed are you when they revile and persecute you, and say all kinds of evil against you falsely for My sake.

Luke 6:22 Blessed are you when men hate you, And when they exclude you, And revile *you,* and cast out your name as evil, For the Son of Man's sake.

1 Pet 4:14 If you are reproached for the name of Christ, blessed *are you,* for the Spirit of glory and of God rests upon you. On their part He is blasphemed, but on your part He is glorified.

Practicing, excludes from heaven.

1 Cor 6:10 nor thieves, nor covetous, nor drunkards, nor revilers, nor extortioners will inherit the kingdom of God.

Punishment for.

Zeph 2:8–9
"I have heard the reproach of Moab, And the insults of the people of Ammon, With which they have reproached My people, And made arrogant threats against their borders. 9 Therefore, as I live," Says the LORD of hosts, the God of Israel, "Surely Moab shall be like Sodom, And the people of Ammon like Gomorrah— Overrun with weeds and saltpits, And a perpetual desolation. The residue of My people shall plunder them, And the remnant of My people shall possess them."

Matt 5:22
But I say to you that whoever is angry with his brother without a cause shall be in danger of the judgment. And whoever says to his brother, 'Raca!' shall be in danger of the council. But whoever says, 'You fool!' shall be in danger of hell fire.

Illustrated by

Joseph's brethren.

Gen 37:19 Then they said to one another, "Look, this dreamer is coming!

Goliath.

1 Sam 17:43 So the Philistine said to David, "*Am* I a dog, that you come to me with sticks?" And the Philistine cursed David by his gods.

Michal.

2 Sam 6:20 Then David returned to bless his household. And Michal the daughter of Saul came out to meet David, and said, "How glorious was the king of Israel today, uncovering himself today in the eyes of the maids of his servants, as one of the base fellows shamelessly uncovers himself!"

Shimei.

2 Sam 16:7–8 Also Shimei said thus when he cursed: "Come out! Come out! You bloodthirsty man, you rogue! 8 The LORD has brought upon you all the blood of the house of Saul, in whose place you have reigned; and the LORD has delivered the kingdom into the hand of Absalom your son. So now you *are caught* in your own evil, because you are a bloodthirsty man!"

Sennacherib.

Is 37:17 Incline Your ear, O LORD, and hear; open Your eyes, O LORD, and see; and hear all the words of Sennacherib, which he has sent to reproach the living God.

Is 37:23–24 "Whom have you reproached and blasphemed? Against whom have you raised *your* voice, And lifted up your eyes on high? Against the Holy One of Israel. 24 By your servants you have reproached the Lord, And said, 'By the multitude of my chariots I have come up to the height of the mountains, To the limits of Lebanon; I will cut down its tall cedars *And* its choice cypress trees; I will enter its farthest height, To its fruitful forest.

Moabites and Ammonites.

Zeph 2:8 "I have heard the reproach of Moab, And the insults of the people of Ammon, With which they have reproached My people, And made arrogant threats against their borders.

Pharisees.

Matt 12:24 Now when the Pharisees heard *it* they said, "This *fellow* does not cast out demons except by Beelzebub, the ruler of the demons."

Jews.

Matt 27:39–40 And those who passed by blasphemed Him, wagging their heads 40 and saying, "You who destroy the temple and build *it* in three days, save Yourself! If You are the Son of God, come down from the cross."

John 8:48 Then the Jews answered and said to Him, "Do we not say rightly that You are a Samaritan and have a demon?"

The criminal on the cross.

Luke 23:39 Then one of the criminals who were hanged blasphemed Him, saying, "If You are the Christ, save Yourself and us."

The Athenian philosophers.

Acts 17:18 Then certain Epicurean and Stoic philosophers encountered him. And some said, "What does this babbler want to say?" Others said, "He seems to be a proclaimer of foreign gods," because he preached to them Jesus and the resurrection.

REWARD OF BELIEVERS, THE

Is from God.

Rom 2:7 eternal life to those who by patient continuance in doing good seek for glory, honor, and immortality;

Col 3:24 knowing that from the Lord you will receive the reward of the inheritance; for you serve the Lord Christ.

Heb 11:6 But without faith *it is* impossible to please *Him*, for he who comes to God must believe that He is, and *that* He is a rewarder of those who diligently seek Him.

Is of grace, through faith alone.

Rom 4:4–5 Now to him who works, the wages are not counted as grace but as debt. 5 But to him who does not work but believes on Him who justifies the ungodly, his faith is accounted for righteousness,

Rom 4:16 Therefore *it is* of faith that *it might be* according to grace, so that the promise might be sure to all the seed, not only to those who are of the law, but also to those who are of the faith of Abraham, who is the father of us all

Rom 11:6 And if by grace, then *it is* no longer of works; otherwise grace is no longer grace. But if *it is* of works, it is no longer grace; otherwise work is no longer work.

Is of God's good pleasure.

Matt 20:14–15 Take *what is* yours and go your way. I wish to give to this last man *the same* as to you. 15 Is it not lawful for me to do what I wish with my own things? Or is your eye evil because I am good?'

Luke 12:32 "Do not fear, little flock, for it is your Father's good pleasure to give you the kingdom.

Prepared by Christ.

John 14:2 In My Father's house are many mansions; if *it were* not so, I would have told you. I go to prepare a place for you.

As servants of Christ.

Col 3:24 knowing that from the Lord you will receive the reward of the inheritance; for you serve the Lord Christ.

Based on works built on the foundation laid by Christ.

1 Cor 3:11–14 For no other foundation can anyone lay than that which is laid, which is Jesus Christ. **12** Now if anyone builds on this foundation *with* gold, silver, precious stones, wood, hay, straw, **13** each one's work will become clear; for the Day will declare it, because it will be revealed by fire; and the fire will test each one's work, of what sort it is. **14** If anyone's work which he has built on *it* endures, he will receive a reward.

Evaluation of, before judgment seat of Christ.

2 Cor 5:10 For we must all appear before the judgment seat of Christ, that each one may receive the things *done* in the body, according to what he has done, whether good or bad.

Described as

Being with Christ.

John 12:26 If anyone serves Me, let him follow Me; and where I am, there My servant will be also. If anyone serves Me, him *My* Father will honor.

John 14:3 And if I go and prepare a place for you, I will come again and receive you to Myself; that where I am, *there* you may be also.

Phil 1:23 For I am hard-pressed between the two, having a desire to depart and be with Christ, *which is* far better.

1 Thess 4:17 Then we who are alive *and* remain shall be caught up together with them in the clouds to meet the Lord in the air. And thus we shall always be with the Lord.

Beholding the face of God.

Ps 17:15 As for me, I will see Your face in righteousness; I shall be satisfied when I awake in Your likeness.

Matt 5:8 Blessed *are* the pure in heart, For they shall see God.

Rev 22:4 They shall see His face, and His name *shall be* on their foreheads.

Beholding the glory of Christ.

John 17:24 "Father, I desire that they also whom You gave Me may be with Me where I am, that they may behold My glory which You have given Me; for You loved Me before the foundation of the world.

Being glorified with Christ.

Rom 8:17–18 and if children, then heirs—heirs of God and joint heirs with Christ, if indeed we suffer with *Him*, that we may also be glorified together. **18** For I consider that the sufferings of this present time are not worthy *to be compared* with the glory which shall be revealed in us.

Phil 3:21 who will transform our lowly body that it may be conformed to His glorious body, according to the working by which He is able even to subdue all things to Himself.

Col 3:4 When Christ *who is* our life appears, then you also will appear with Him in glory.

1 John 3:2 Beloved, now we are children of God; and it has not yet been revealed what we shall be, but we know that when He is revealed, we shall be like Him, for we shall see Him as He is.

Sitting in judgment with Christ.

Dan 7:22 until the Ancient of Days came, and a judgment was made *in favor* of the saints of the Most High, and the time came for the saints to possess the kingdom.

Matt 19:28 So Jesus said to them, "Assuredly I say to you, that in the regeneration, when the Son of Man sits on the throne of His glory, you who have followed Me will also sit on twelve thrones, judging the twelve tribes of Israel.

Luke 22:30 that you may eat and drink at My table in My kingdom, and sit on thrones judging the twelve tribes of Israel."

1 Cor 6:2 Do you not know that the saints will judge the world? And if the world will be judged by you, are you unworthy to judge the smallest matters?

Reigning with Christ.

2 Tim 2:12 If we endure, We shall also reign with *Him*. If we deny *Him*, He also will deny us.

Rev 3:21 To him who overcomes I will grant to sit with Me on My throne, as I also overcame and sat down with My Father on His throne.

Rev 5:10 And have made us kings and priests to our God; And we shall reign on the earth."

Rev 20:4 And I saw thrones, and they sat on them, and judgment was committed to them. Then *I saw* the souls of those who had been beheaded for their witness to Jesus and for the word of God, who had not worshiped the beast or his image, and had not received *his* mark on their foreheads or on their hands. And they lived and reigned with Christ for a thousand years.

Rev 22:5 There shall be no night there: They need no lamp nor light of the sun, for the Lord God gives them light. And they shall reign forever and ever.

A crown of righteousness.

2 Tim 4:8 Finally, there is laid up for me the crown of righteousness, which the Lord, the righteous Judge, will give to me on that Day, and not to me only but also to all who have loved His appearing.

A crown of glory.

1 Pet 5:4 and when the Chief Shepherd appears, you will receive the crown of glory that does not fade away.

A crown of life.

James 1:12 Blessed *is* the man who endures temptation; for when he has been approved, he will receive the crown of life which the Lord has promised to those who love Him.

Rev 2:10 Do not fear any of those things which you are about to suffer. Indeed, the devil is about to throw *some* of you into prison, that you may be tested, and you will have tribulation ten days. Be faithful until death, and I will give you the crown of life.

An imperishable crown.

1 Cor 9:25 And everyone who competes *for the prize* is temperate in all things. Now they *do it* to obtain a perishable crown, but we *for* an imperishable *crown.*

Joint heirs with Christ.

Rom 8:17 and if children, then heirs—heirs of God and joint heirs with Christ, if indeed we suffer with *Him*, that we may also be glorified together.

An inheritance.

Acts 20:32 "So now, brethren, I commend you to God and to the word of His grace, which is able to build you up and give you an inheritance among all those who are sanctified.

Acts 26:18 to open their eyes, *in order* to turn *them* from darkness to light, and *from* the power of Satan to God, that they may receive forgiveness of sins and an inheritance among those who are sanctified by faith in Me.'

Col 1:12 giving thanks to the Father who has qualified us to be partakers of the inheritance of the saints in the light.

Heb 9:15 And for this reason He is the Mediator of the new covenant, by means of death, for the redemption of the transgressions under the first covenant, that those who are called may receive the promise of the eternal inheritance.

1 Pet 1:4 to an inheritance incorruptible and undefiled and that does not fade away, reserved in heaven for you,

Rev 21:7 He who overcomes shall inherit all things, and I will be his God and he shall be My son.

A kingdom.

Matt 25:34 Then the King will say to those on His right hand, 'Come, you blessed of My Father, inherit the kingdom prepared for you from the foundation of the world:

Luke 22:29 And I bestow upon you a kingdom, just as My Father bestowed *one* upon Me,

Heb 12:28 Therefore, since we are receiving a kingdom which cannot be shaken, let us have grace, by which we may serve God acceptably with reverence and godly fear.

Shining as the stars.

Dan 12:3 Those who are wise shall shine Like the brightness of the firmament, And those who turn many to righteousness Like the stars forever and ever.

Everlasting light.

Is 60:19 "The sun shall no longer be your light by day, Nor for brightness shall the moon give light to you; But the LORD will be to you an everlasting light, And your God your glory.

Eternal life.

Luke 18:30 who shall not receive many times more in this present time, and in the age to come eternal life."

John 6:40 And this is the will of Him who sent Me, that everyone who sees the Son and believes in Him may have everlasting life; and I will raise him up at the last day."

John 17:2–3 as You have given Him authority over all flesh, that He should give eternal life to as many as You have given Him. 3 And this is eternal life, that they may know You, the only true God, and Jesus Christ whom You have sent.

Rom 2:7 eternal life to those who by patient continuance in doing good seek for glory, honor, and immortality;

Rom 6:23 For the wages of sin *is* death, but the gift of God *is* eternal life in Christ Jesus our Lord.

1 John 5:11 And this is the testimony: that God has given us eternal life, and this life is in His Son.

An enduring substance.

Heb 10:34 for you had compassion on me in my chains, and joyfully accepted the plundering of your goods, knowing that you have a better and an enduring possession for yourselves in heaven.

A house eternal in the heavens.

2 Cor 5:1 For we know that if our earthly house, *this* tent, is destroyed, we have a building from God, a house not made with hands, eternal in the heavens.

A city which has foundations.

Heb 11:10 for he waited for the city which has foundations, whose builder and maker *is* God.

Entering into the joy of the Lord.

Matt 25:21 His lord said to him, 'Well *done,* good and faithful servant; you were faithful over a few things, I will make you ruler over many things. Enter into the joy of your lord.'

Heb 12:2 looking unto Jesus, the author and finisher of *our* faith, who for the joy that was set before Him endured the cross, despising the shame, and has sat down at the right hand of the throne of God.

Rest.

Heb 4:9 There remains therefore a rest for the people of God.

Rev 14:13 Then I heard a voice from heaven saying to me, "Write: 'Blessed *are* the dead who die in the Lord from now on.' " "Yes," says the Spirit, "that they may rest from their labors, and their works follow them."

Fullness of joy.

Ps 16:11 You will show me the path of life; In Your presence *is* fullness of joy; At Your right hand *are* pleasures forevermore.

The prize of the upward call.

Phil 3:14 I press toward the goal for the prize of the upward call of God in Christ Jesus.

Treasure in heaven.

Matt 19:21 Jesus said to him, "If you want to be perfect, go, sell what you have and give to the poor, and you will have treasure in heaven; and come, follow Me."

Luke 12:33 Sell what you have and give alms; provide yourselves money bags which do not grow old, a treasure in the heavens that does not fail, where no thief approaches nor moth destroys.

An eternal weight of glory.

2 Cor 4:17 For our light affliction, which is but for a moment, is working for us a far more exceeding *and* eternal weight of glory,

Is great.

Matt 5:12 Rejoice and be exceedingly glad, for great *is* your reward in heaven, for so they persecuted the prophets who were before you.

Luke 6:35 But love your enemies, do good, and lend, hoping for nothing in return; and your reward will be great, and you will be sons of the Most High. For He is kind to the unthankful and evil.

Heb 10:35 Therefore do not cast away your confidence, which has great reward.

Is full.

2 John 1:8 Look to yourselves, that we do not lose those things we worked for, but *that* we may receive a full reward.

Is sure.

Prov 11:18 The wicked *man* does deceptive work, But he who sows righteousness *will have* a sure reward.

Is satisfying.

Ps 17:15 As for me, I will see Your face in righteousness; I shall be satisfied when I awake in Your likeness.

Is inestimable.

Is 64:4 For since the beginning of the world *Men* have not heard nor perceived by the ear, Nor has the eye seen any God besides You, Who acts for the one who waits for Him.

1 Cor 2:9 But as it is written: *"Eye has not seen, nor ear heard, Nor have entered into the heart of man The things which God has prepared for those who love Him."*

Believers may feel confident of.

Ps 73:24 You will guide me with Your counsel, And afterward receive me *to* glory.

Is 25:8–9 He will swallow up death forever, And the Lord GOD will wipe away tears from all faces; The rebuke of His people He will take away from all the earth; For the LORD has spoken. **9** And it will be said in that day: "Behold, this *is* our God; We have waited for Him, and He will save us. This *is* the LORD; We have waited for Him; We will be glad and rejoice in His salvation."

2 Cor 5:1 For we know that if our earthly house, *this* tent, is destroyed, we have a building from God, a house not made with hands, eternal in the heavens.

2 Tim 4:8 Finally, there is laid up for me the crown of righteousness, which the Lord, the righteous Judge, will give to me on that Day, and not to me only but also to all who have loved His appearing.

Be careful not to lose.

2 John 1:8 Look to yourselves, that we do not lose those things we worked for, but *that* we may receive a full reward.

The prospect of, should lead to

Rejoicing.

Rom 5:2 through whom also we have access by faith into this grace in which we stand, and rejoice in hope of the glory of God.

Diligence.

2 John 1:8 Look to yourselves, that we do not lose those things we worked for, but *that* we may receive a full reward.

Pressing forward.

Phil 3:14 I press toward the goal for the prize of the upward call of God in Christ Jesus.

Enduring suffering for Christ.

2 Cor 4:16–18 Therefore we do not lose heart. Even though our outward man is perishing, yet the inward *man* is being renewed day by day. **17** For our light affliction, which is but for a moment, is working for us a far more exceeding *and* eternal weight of glory, **18** while we do not look at the things which are

seen, but at the things which are not seen. For the things which are seen *are* temporary, but the things which are not seen *are* eternal.

Heb 11:26 esteeming the reproach of Christ greater riches than the treasures in Egypt; for he looked to the reward.

Faithfulness to death.

Rev 2:10 Do not fear any of those things which you are about to suffer. Indeed, the devil is about to throw *some* of you into prison, that you may be tested, and you will have tribulation ten days. Be faithful until death, and I will give you the crown of life.

Present afflictions not to be compared with.

Rom 8:18 For I consider that the sufferings of this present time are not worthy *to be compared* with the glory which shall be revealed in us.

2 Cor 5:17 Therefore, if anyone *is* in Christ, *he is* a new creation; old things have passed away; behold, all things have become new.

Shall be given at the second coming of Christ.

Matt 16:27 For the Son of Man will come in the glory of His Father with His angels, and then He will reward each according to his works.

Rev 22:12 "And behold, I am coming quickly, and My reward *is* with Me, to give to every one according to his work.

RICHES

The true ones.

1 Cor 1:30 But of Him you are in Christ Jesus, who became for us wisdom from God—and righteousness and sanctification and redemption—

Eph 3:8 To me, who am less than the least of all the saints, this grace was given, that I should preach among the Gentiles the unsearchable riches of Christ,

Col 2:3 in whom are hidden all the treasures of wisdom and knowledge.

1 Pet 2:7 Therefore, to you who believe, *He is* precious; but to those who are disobedient, *"The stone which the builders rejected Has become the chief cornerstone,"*

God gives.

Deut 8:18 "And you shall remember the LORD your God, for *it is* He who gives you power to get wealth, that He may establish His covenant which He swore to your fathers, as *it is* this day.

1 Sam 2:7 The LORD makes poor and makes rich; He brings low and lifts up.

Prov 10:22 The blessing of the LORD makes *one* rich, And He adds no sorrow with it.

Eccl 5:19 As for every man to whom God has given riches and wealth, and given him power to eat of it, to receive his heritage and rejoice in his labor—this *is* the gift of God.

To God belongs this world's.

Hag 2:8 'The silver *is* Mine, and the gold *is* Mine,' says the LORD of hosts.

Give the worldly power.

Prov 22:7 The rich rules over the poor, And the borrower *is* servant to the lender.

Described as

Uncertain.

1 Tim 6:17 Command those who are rich in this present age not to be haughty, nor to trust in uncertain riches but in the living God, who gives us richly all things to enjoy.

Unsatisfying.

Eccl 4:8 There is one alone, without companion: He has neither son nor brother. Yet *there is* no end to all his labors, Nor is his eye satisfied with riches. *But he never asks*, "For whom do I toil and deprive myself of good?" This also *is* vanity and a grave misfortune.

Eccl 5:10 He who loves silver will not be satisfied with silver; Nor he who loves abundance, with increase. This also *is* vanity.

Perishable.

Prov 27:24 For riches *are* not forever, Nor does a crown *endure* to all generations.

Jer 48:36 Therefore My heart shall wail like flutes for Moab, And like flutes My heart shall wail For the men of Kir Heres. Therefore the riches they have acquired have perished.

James 5:2 Your riches are corrupted, and your garments are moth-eaten.

1 Pet 1:18 knowing that you were not redeemed with corruptible things, *like* silver or gold, from your aimless conduct *received* by tradition from your fathers,

Fleeting.

Prov 23:5 Will you set your eyes on that which is not? For *riches* certainly make themselves wings; They fly away like an eagle *toward* heaven.

Rev 18:16–17 and saying, 'Alas, alas, that great city that was clothed in fine linen, purple, and scarlet, and adorned with gold and precious stones and pearls! **17** For in one hour such great riches came to nothing.' Every shipmaster, all who travel by ship, sailors, and as many as trade on the sea, stood at a distance

Deceitful.

Matt 13:22 Now he who received seed among the thorns is he who hears the word, and the cares of this world and the deceitfulness of riches choke the word, and he becomes unfruitful.

Mark 4:19 and the cares of this world, the deceitfulness of riches, and the desires for other things entering in choke the word, and it becomes unfruitful.

Liable to be stolen.

Matt 6:19 "Do not lay up for yourselves treasures on earth, where moth and rust destroy and where thieves break in and steal;

Thick clay.

Hab 2:6 "Will not all these take up a proverb against him, And a taunting riddle against him, and say, 'Woe to him who increases *What is* not his—how long? And to him who loads himself with many pledges'?

Often a hindrance to the gospel.

Matt 13:22 Now he who received seed among the thorns is he who hears the word, and the cares of this world and the deceitfulness of riches choke the word, and he becomes unfruitful.

Mark 10:23–25 Then Jesus looked around and said to His disciples, "How hard it is for those who have

riches to enter the kingdom of God!" **24** And the disciples were astonished at His words. But Jesus answered again and said to them, "Children, how hard it is for those who trust in riches to enter the kingdom of God! **25** It is easier for a camel to go through the eye of a needle than for a rich man to enter the kingdom of God."

The love of, the root of all kinds of evil.

1 Tim 6:10 For the love of money is a root of all *kinds of* evil, for which some have strayed from the faith in their greediness, and pierced themselves through with many sorrows.

Often lead to

Pride.

Ezek 28:5 By your great wisdom in trade you have increased your riches, And your heart is lifted up because of your riches),"

Hos 12:8 And Ephraim said, 'Surely I have become rich, I have found wealth for myself; *In* all my labors They shall find in me no iniquity that *is* sin.'

Forgetting God.

Deut 8:13–14 and *when* your herds and your flocks multiply, and your silver and your gold are multiplied, and all that you have is multiplied; **14** when your heart is lifted up, and you forget the Lord your God who brought you out of the land of Egypt, from the house of bondage;

Rebelling against God.

Deut 32:15 "But Jeshurun grew fat and kicked; You grew fat, you grew thick, You are obese! Then he forsook God *who* made him, And scornfully esteemed the Rock of his salvation.

Neh 9:25–26 And they took strong cities and a rich land, And possessed houses full of all goods, Cisterns *already* dug, vineyards, olive groves, And fruit trees in abundance. So they ate and were filled and grew fat, And delighted themselves in Your great goodness. **26** "Nevertheless they were disobedient And rebelled against You, Cast Your law behind their backs And killed Your prophets, who testified against them To turn them to Yourself; And they worked great provocations.

Prov 30:8–9 Remove falsehood and lies far from me; Give me neither poverty nor riches— Feed me with the food allotted to me; **9** Lest I be full and deny *You*, And say, "Who *is* the Lord?" Or lest I be poor and steal, And profane the name of my God.

Rejecting Christ.

Matt 10:22 And you will be hated by all for My name's sake. But he who endures to the end will be saved.

Matt 19:22 But when the young man heard that saying, he went away sorrowful, for he had great possessions.

Self-sufficiency.

Prov 28:11 The rich man *is* wise in his own eyes, But the poor who has understanding searches him out.

Anxiety.

Eccl 5:12 The sleep of a laboring man *is* sweet, Whether he eats little or much; But the abundance of the rich will not permit him to sleep.

An overbearing spirit.

Prov 18:23 The poor *man* uses entreaties, But the rich answers roughly.

Violence.

Mic 6:12 For her rich men are full of violence, Her inhabitants have spoken lies, And their tongue is deceitful in their mouth.

Oppression.

James 2:6 But you have dishonored the poor man. Do not the rich oppress you and drag you into the courts?

Fraud.

James 5:4 Indeed the wages of the laborers who mowed your fields, which you kept back by fraud, cry out; and the cries of the reapers have reached the ears of the Lord of Sabaoth.

Sensual indulgence.

Luke 16:19 "There was a certain rich man who was clothed in purple and fine linen and fared sumptuously every day.

James 5:5 You have lived on the earth in pleasure and luxury; you have fattened your hearts as in a day of slaughter.

We should not covet.

Ps 62:10 Do not trust in oppression, Nor vainly hope in robbery; If riches increase, Do not set *your* heart *on them.*

Prov 23:4 Do not overwork to be rich; Because of your own understanding, cease!

Prov 30:8 Remove falsehood and lies far from me; Give me neither poverty nor riches— Feed me with the food allotted to me;

Luke 12:15 And He said to them, "Take heed and beware of covetousness, for one's life does not consist in the abundance of the things he possesses."

Those who covet,

Fall into temptation and hurtful lusts.

1 Tim 6:9 But those who desire to be rich fall into temptation and a snare, and *into* many foolish and harmful lusts which drown men in destruction and perdition.

Err from the faith.

1 Tim 6:10 For the love of money is a root of all *kinds of* evil, for which some have strayed from the faith in their greediness, and pierced themselves through with many sorrows.

Use unlawful means to acquire.

Prov 28:20 A faithful man will abound with blessings, But he who hastens to be rich will not go unpunished.

Bring trouble on themselves.

1 Tim 6:10 For the love of money is a root of all *kinds of* evil, for which some have strayed from the faith in their greediness, and pierced themselves through with many sorrows.

Bring trouble on their families.

Prov 15:27 He who is greedy for gain troubles his own house, But he who hates bribes will live.

Cannot secure prosperity.

James 1:11 For no sooner has the sun risen with a burning heat than it withers the grass; its flower falls, and its beautiful appearance perishes. So the rich man also will fade away in his pursuits.

Cannot redeem the soul.

Ps 49:6–9 Those who trust in their wealth And boast in the multitude of their riches, 7 None *of them* can by any means redeem *his* brother, Nor give to God a ransom for him— 8 For the redemption of their souls *is* costly, And it shall cease forever— 9 That he should continue to live eternally, *And* not see the Pit.

1 Pet 1:18 knowing that you were not redeemed with corruptible things, *like* silver or gold, from your aimless conduct *received* by tradition from your fathers,

Cannot deliver in the day of God's wrath.

Prov 11:4 Riches do not profit in the day of wrath, But righteousness delivers from death.

Zeph 1:18 Neither their silver nor their gold Shall be able to deliver them In the day of the LORD's wrath; But the whole land shall be devoured By the fire of His jealousy, For He will make speedy riddance Of all those who dwell in the land.

Rev 6:15–17 And the kings of the earth, the great men, the rich men, the commanders, the mighty men, every slave and every free man, hid themselves in the caves and in the rocks of the mountains, 16 and said to the mountains and rocks, "Fall on us and hide us from the face of Him who sits on the throne and from the wrath of the Lamb! 17 For the great day of His wrath has come, and who is able to stand?"

Those who possess, should

Ascribe them to God.

1 Chr 29:12 Both riches and honor *come* from You, And You reign over all. In Your hand *is* power and might; In Your hand *it is* to make great And to give strength to all.

Not trust in them.

Job 31:24 "If I have made gold my hope, Or said to fine gold, '*You are* my confidence';

1 Tim 6:17 Command those who are rich in this present age not to be haughty, nor to trust in uncertain riches but in the living God, who gives us richly all things to enjoy.

Not boast of obtaining them.

Deut 8:17 then you say in your heart, 'My power and the might of my hand have gained me this wealth.'

Jer 9:23 Thus says the LORD: "Let not the wise *man* glory in his wisdom, Let not the mighty *man* glory in his might, Nor let the rich *man* glory in his riches;

Not hoard them.

Matt 6:19 "Do not lay up for yourselves treasures on earth, where moth and rust destroy and where thieves break in and steal;

Devote them to God's service.

1 Chr 29:3 Moreover, because I have set my affection on the house of my God, I have given to the house of my God, over and above all that I have prepared for the holy house, my own special treasure of gold and silver:

Mark 12:42–44 Then one poor widow came and threw in two mites, which make a quadrans. 43 So He called His disciples to *Himself* and said to them, "Assuredly, I say to you that this poor widow has put in more than all those who have given to the treasury; 44 for they all put in out of their abundance, but she out of her poverty put in all that she had, her whole livelihood."

Give of them to the poor.

Matt 19:21 Jesus said to him, "If you want to be perfect, go, sell what you have and give to the poor, and you will have treasure in heaven; and come, follow Me."

1 John 3:17 But whoever has this world's goods, and sees his brother in need, and shuts up his heart from him, how does the love of God abide in him?

Use them in promoting the salvation of others.

Luke 16:9 "And I say to you, make friends for yourselves by unrighteous mammon, that when you fail, they may receive you into an everlasting home.

Be generous in all things.

1 Chr 29:14 But who *am* I, and who *are* my people, That we should be able to offer so willingly as this? For all things *come* from You, And of Your own we have given You.

1 Tim 6:18 *Let them* do good, that they be rich in good works, ready to give, willing to share,

Not be haughty.

1 Tim 6:17 Command those who are rich in this present age not to be haughty, nor to trust in uncertain riches but in the living God, who gives us richly all things to enjoy.

When converted, rejoice in being humbled.

James 1:9–10 Let the lowly brother glory in his exaltation, 10 but the rich in his humiliation, because as a flower of the field he will pass away.

Heavenly treasures superior to.

Matt 6:19–20 "Do not lay up for yourselves treasures on earth, where moth and rust destroy and where thieves break in and steal; 20 but lay up for yourselves treasures in heaven, where neither moth nor rust destroys and where thieves do not break in and steal.

Of the wicked, stored up for the righteous.

Prov 13:22 A good *man* leaves an inheritance to his children's children, But the wealth of the sinner is stored up for the righteous.

The wicked

Often increase in.

Ps 73:12 Behold, these *are* the ungodly, Who are always at ease; They increase *in* riches.

Often spend their day in.

Job 21:13 They spend their days in wealth, And in a moment go down to the grave.

Swallow them down.

Job 20:15 He swallows down riches And vomits them up again; God casts them out of his belly.

Trust in the abundance of.

Ps 52:7 "Here is the man *who* did not make God his strength, But trusted in the abundance of his riches, *And* strengthened himself in his wickedness."

Prov 11:28 He who trusts in his riches will fall, But the righteous will flourish like foliage.

Heap them up.

Job 27:16 Though he heaps up silver like dust, And piles up clothing like clay—

Ps 39:6 Surely every man walks about like a shadow; Surely they busy themselves in vain; He heaps up *riches,* And does not know who will gather them.

Eccl 2:26 For *God* gives wisdom and knowledge and joy to a man who *is* good in His sight; but to the sinner He gives the work of gathering and collecting, that he may give to *him who is* good before God. This also *is* vanity and grasping for the wind.

Keep, to their hurt.

Eccl 5:13 There is a severe evil *which* I have seen under the sun: Riches kept for their owner to his hurt.

Boast about their.

Ps 49:6 Those who trust in their wealth And boast in the multitude of their riches,

Ps 52:7 "Here is the man *who* did not make God his strength, But trusted in the abundance of his riches, *And* strengthened himself in his wickedness."

Do not profit by.

Prov 11:4 Riches do not profit in the day of wrath, But righteousness delivers from death.

Prov 13:7 There is one who makes himself rich, yet *has* nothing; *And* one who makes himself poor, yet *has* great riches.

Eccl 5:11 When goods increase, They increase who eat them; So what profit have the owners Except to see *them* with their eyes?

Have trouble with.

Prov 15:6 *In* the house of the righteous *there is* much treasure, But in the revenue of the wicked is trouble.

1 Tim 6:9–10 But those who desire to be rich fall into temptation and a snare, and *into* many foolish and harmful lusts which drown men in destruction and perdition. 10 For the love of money is a root of all *kinds of* evil, for which some have strayed from the faith in their greediness, and pierced themselves through with many sorrows.

Must leave them to others.

Ps 49:10 For he sees wise men die; Likewise the fool and the senseless person perish, And leave their wealth to others.

Vanity of heaping up.

Ps 39:6 Surely every man walks about like a shadow; Surely they busy themselves in vain; He heaps up *riches,* And does not know who will gather them.

Eccl 5:10–11 He who loves silver will not be satisfied with silver; Nor he who loves abundance, with increase. This also *is* vanity. 11 When goods increase, They increase who eat them; So what profit have the owners Except to see *them* with their eyes?

Guilt of trusting in.

Job 31:24–25 "If I have made gold my hope, Or said to fine gold, *'You are* my confidence'; 25 If I have rejoiced because my wealth *was* great, And because my hand had gained much;

Ezek 28:4–5 With your wisdom and your understanding You have gained riches for yourself, And gathered gold and silver into your treasuries; 5 By your great wisdom in trade you have increased your riches, And your heart is lifted up because of your riches),"

Ezek 28:8 They shall throw you down into the Pit, And

you shall die the death of the slain In the midst of the seas.

Denunciations against those who

Gain them dishonestly.

Prov 13:11 Wealth *gained by* dishonesty will be diminished, But he who gathers by labor will increase.

Prov 21:6 Getting treasures by a lying tongue *Is* the fleeting fantasy of those who seek death.

Jer 17:11 "*As* a partridge that broods but does not hatch, *So is* he who gets riches, but not by right; It will leave him in the midst of his days, And at his end he will be a fool."

Increase, by oppression.

Prov 22:16 He who oppresses the poor to increase his *riches, And* he who gives to the rich, *will* surely *come* to poverty.

Hab 2:6–8 "Will not all these take up a proverb against him, And a taunting riddle against him, and say, 'Woe to him who increases *What* is not his—how long? And to him who loads himself with many pledges'? 7 Will not your creditors rise up suddenly? Will they not awaken who oppress you? And you will become their booty. 8 Because you have plundered many nations, All the remnant of the people shall plunder you, Because of men's blood And the violence of the land *and* the city, And of all who dwell in it.

Mic 2:2–3 They covet fields and take *them* by violence, Also houses, and seize *them*. So they oppress a man and his house, A man and his inheritance. 3 Therefore thus says the LORD: "Behold, against this family I am devising disaster, From which you cannot remove your necks; Nor shall you walk haughtily, For this *is* an evil time.

Hoard up riches.

Eccl 5:13–14 There is a severe evil *which* I have seen under the sun: Riches kept for their owner to his hurt. 14 But those riches perish through misfortune; When he begets a son, *there is* nothing in his hand.

James 5:3 Your gold and silver are corroded, and their corrosion will be a witness against you and will eat your flesh like fire. You have heaped up treasure in the last days.

Trust in.

Prov 11:28 He who trusts in his riches will fall, But the righteous will flourish like foliage.

Luke 6:24 "But woe to you who are rich, For you have received your consolation.

Abuse.

James 5:1 Come now, *you* rich, weep and howl for your miseries that are coming upon *you!*

James 5:5 You have lived on the earth in pleasure and luxury; you have fattened your hearts as in a day of slaughter.

Spend, upon their appetite.

Job 20:15–17 He swallows down riches And vomits them up again; God casts them out of his belly. 16 He will suck the poison of cobras; The viper's tongue will slay him. 17 He will not see the streams, The rivers flowing with honey and cream.

Folly and danger of trusting in—illustrated.

Luke 12:16–21 Then He spoke a parable to them, say-ing: "The ground of a certain rich man yielded plentifully. 17 And he thought within himself, saying, 'What shall I do, since I have no room to store my crops?' 18 So he said, 'I will do this: I will pull down my barns and build greater, and there I will store all my crops and my goods. 19 And I will say to my soul, "Soul, you have many goods laid up for many years; take your ease; eat, drink, *and* be merry." ' 20 But God said to him, 'Fool! This night your soul will be required of you; then whose will those things be which you have provided?' 21 "So *is* he who lays up treasure for himself, and is not rich toward God."

Danger of misusing—illustrated.

Luke 16:19–25 "There was a certain rich man who was clothed in purple and fine linen and fared sumptuously every day. 20 But there was a certain beggar named Lazarus, full of sores, who was laid at his gate, 21 desiring to be fed with the crumbs which fell from the rich man's table. Moreover the dogs came and licked his sores. 22 So it was that the beggar died, and was carried by the angels to Abraham's bosom. The rich man also died and was buried. 23 And being in torments in Hades, he lifted up his eyes and saw Abraham afar off, and Lazarus in his bosom. 24 "Then he cried and said, 'Father Abraham, have mercy on me, and send Lazarus that he may dip the tip of his finger in water and cool my tongue; for I am tormented in this flame.' 25 But Abraham said, 'Son, remember that in your lifetime you received your good things, and likewise Lazarus evil things; but now he is comforted and you are tormented.

Examples of believers possessing,

Abram.

Gen 13:2 Abram *was* very rich in livestock, in silver, and in gold.

Lot.

Gen 13:5–6 Lot also, who went with Abram, had flocks and herds and tents. 6 Now the land was not able to support them, that they might dwell together, for their possessions were so great that they could not dwell together.

Isaac.

Gen 26:13–14 The man began to prosper, and continued prospering until he became very prosperous; 14 for he had possessions of flocks and possessions of herds and a great number of servants. So the Philistines envied him.

Jacob.

Gen 32:5 I have oxen, donkeys, flocks, and male and female servants; and I have sent to tell my lord, that I may find favor in your sight." ' "

Gen 32:10 I am not worthy of the least of all the mercies and of all the truth which You have shown Your servant; for I crossed over this Jordan with my staff, and now I have become two companies.

Joseph.

Gen 45:8 So now *it was* not you *who* sent me here, but God; and He has made me a father to Pharaoh, and lord of all his house, and a ruler throughout all the land of Egypt.

Gen 45:13 So you shall tell my father of all my glory in

Egypt, and of all that you have seen; and you shall hurry and bring my father down here."

Boaz.

Ruth 2:1 There was a relative of Naomi's husband, a man of great wealth, of the family of Elimelech. His name *was* Boaz.

Barzillai.

2 Sam 19:32 Now Barzillai was a very aged man, eighty years old. And he had provided the king with supplies while he stayed at Mahanaim, for he *was* a very rich man.

The Shunammite.

2 Kin 4:8 Now it happened one day that Elisha went to Shunem, where there *was* a notable woman, and she persuaded him to eat some food. So it was, as often as he passed by, he would turn in there to eat some food.

David.

1 Chr 29:28 So he died in a good old age, full of days and riches and honor; and Solomon his son reigned in his place.

Jehoshaphat.

2 Chr 17:5 Therefore the LORD established the kingdom in his hand; and all Judah gave presents to Jehoshaphat, and he had riches and honor in abundance.

Hezekiah.

2 Chr 32:27–29 Hezekiah had very great riches and honor. And he made himself treasuries for silver, for gold, for precious stones, for spices, for shields, and for all kinds of desirable items; **28** storehouses for the harvest of grain, wine, and oil; and stalls for all kinds of livestock, and folds for flocks. **29** Moreover he provided cities for himself, and possessions of flocks and herds in abundance; for God had given him very much property.

Job.

Job 1:3 Also, his possessions were seven thousand sheep, three thousand camels, five hundred yoke of oxen, five hundred female donkeys, and a very large household, so that this man was the greatest of all the people of the East.

Joseph of Arimathea.

Matt 27:57 Now when evening had come, there came a rich man from Arimathea, named Joseph, who himself had also become a disciple of Jesus.

Zacchaeus.

Luke 19:2 Now behold, *there was* a man named Zacchaeus who was a chief tax collector, and he was rich.

Dorcas.

Acts 9:36 At Joppa there was a certain disciple named Tabitha, which is translated Dorcas. This woman was full of good works and charitable deeds which she did.

Examples of those truly rich.

Matt 5:8 Blessed *are* the pure in heart, For they shall see God.

Matt 8:10 When Jesus heard *it*, He marveled, and said to those who followed, "Assuredly, I say to you, I have not found such great faith, not even in Israel!

Matt 13:45–46 "Again, the kingdom of heaven is like a merchant seeking beautiful pearls, **46** who, when he

had found one pearl of great price, went and sold all that he had and bought it.

Luke 10:42 But one thing is needed, and Mary has chosen that good part, which will not be taken away from her."

John 1:45 Philip found Nathanael and said to him, "We have found Him of whom Moses in the law, and also the prophets, wrote—Jesus of Nazareth, the son of Joseph."

Phil 3:8 Yet indeed I also count all things loss for the excellence of the knowledge of Christ Jesus my Lord, for whom I have suffered the loss of all things, and count them as rubbish, that I may gain Christ

James 2:5 Listen, my beloved brethren: Has God not chosen the poor of this world *to be* rich in faith and heirs of the kingdom which He promised to those who love Him?

1 Pet 2:7 Therefore, to you who believe, *He is* precious; but to those who are disobedient, *"The stone which the builders rejected Has become the chief cornerstone,"*

Rev 3:18 I counsel you to buy from Me gold refined in the fire, that you may be rich; and white garments, that you may be clothed, *that* the shame of your nakedness may not be revealed; and anoint your eyes with eye salve, that you may see.

Examples of unbelievers possessing,

Laban.

Gen 30:30 For what you had before I *came was* little, and it has increased to a great amount; the LORD has blessed you since my coming. And now, when shall I also provide for my own house?"

Esau.

Gen 36:7 For their possessions were too great for them to dwell together, and the land where they were strangers could not support them because of their livestock.

Nabal.

1 Sam 25:2 Now *there was* a man in Maon whose business *was* in Carmel, and the man *was* very rich. He had three thousand sheep and a thousand goats. And he was shearing his sheep in Carmel.

Haman.

Esth 5:11 Then Haman told them of his great riches, the multitude of his children, everything in which the king had promoted him, and how he had advanced him above the officials and servants of the king.

The Ammonites.

Jer 49:4 Why do you boast in the valleys, Your flowing valley, O backsliding daughter? Who trusted in her treasures, *saying,* 'Who will come against me?'

The people of Tyre.

Ezek 28:5 By your great wisdom in trade you have increased your riches, And your heart is lifted up because of your riches),"

A young man.

Matt 19:22 But when the young man heard that saying, he went away sorrowful, for he had great possessions.

RIDICULING AND MOCKING

The sufferings of Christ by, predicted.

Ps 22:6–8 But I *am* a worm, and no man; A reproach of men, and despised by the people. **7** All those who see Me ridicule Me; They shoot out the lip, they shake the head, *saying,* **8** "He trusted in the LORD, let Him rescue Him; Let Him deliver Him, since He delights in Him!"

Is 53:3 He is despised and rejected by men, A Man of sorrows and acquainted with grief. And we hid, as it were, *our* faces from Him; He was despised, and we did not esteem Him.

Luke 18:32 For He will be delivered to the Gentiles and will be mocked and insulted and spit upon.

Christ endured.

Matt 9:24 He said to them, "Make room, for the girl is not dead, but sleeping." And they ridiculed Him.

Matt 27:29 When they had twisted a crown of thorns, they put *it* on His head, and a reed in His right hand. And they bowed the knee before Him and mocked Him, saying, "Hail, King of the Jews!"

Believers endure, because of

Being children of God.

Gen 21:9 And Sarah saw the son of Hagar the Egyptian, whom she had borne to Abraham, scoffing.

Gal 4:29 But, as he who was born according to the flesh then persecuted him *who was born* according to the Spirit, even so *it is* now.

Their uprightness.

Job 12:4 "I am one mocked by his friends, Who called on God, and He answered him, The just and blameless *who is* ridiculed.

Their faith.

Heb 11:36 Still others had trial of mockings and scourgings, yes, and of chains and imprisonment.

Their faithfulness in declaring the word of God.

Jer 20:7–8 O LORD, You induced me, and I was persuaded; You are stronger than I, and have prevailed. I am in derision daily; Everyone mocks me. **8** For when I spoke, I cried out; I shouted, "Violence and plunder!" Because the word of the LORD was made to me A reproach and a derision daily.

Their zeal for God's work.

Neh 2:19 But when Sanballat the Horonite, Tobiah the Ammonite official, and Geshem the Arab heard *of it,* they laughed at us and despised us, and said, "What *is* this thing that you are doing? Will you rebel against the king?"

The wicked engage in, against

The second coming of Christ.

2 Pet 3:3–4 knowing this first: that scoffers will come in the last days, walking according to their own lusts, **4** and saying, "Where is the promise of His coming? For since the fathers fell asleep, all things continue as *they were* from the beginning of creation."

The gifts of the Spirit.

Acts 2:13 Others mocking said, "They are full of new wine."

God's threatening.

Is 5:19 That say, "Let Him make speed *and* hasten His

work, That we may see *it;* And let the counsel of the Holy One of Israel draw near and come, That we may know *it.*"

Jer 17:15 Indeed they say to me, "Where *is* the word of the LORD? Let it come now!"

God's ministers.

2 Chr 36:16 But they mocked the messengers of God, despised His words, and scoffed at His prophets, until the wrath of the LORD arose against His people, till *there was* no remedy.

God's ordinances.

Lam 1:7 In the days of her affliction and roaming, Jerusalem remembers all her pleasant things That she had in the days of old. When her people fell into the hand of the enemy, With no one to help her, The adversaries saw her *And* mocked at her downfall.

Believers.

Ps 123:4 Our soul is exceedingly filled With the scorn of those who are at ease, With the contempt of the proud.

Lam 3:14 I have become the ridicule of all my people— Their taunting song all the day.

Lam 3:63 Look at their sitting down and their rising up; I *am* their taunting song.

The resurrection of the dead.

Acts 17:32 And when they heard of the resurrection of the dead, some mocked, while others said, "We will hear you again on this *matter.*"

All solemn admonitions.

2 Chr 30:6–10 Then the runners went throughout all Israel and Judah with the letters from the king and his leaders, and spoke according to the command of the king: "Children of Israel, return to the LORD God of Abraham, Isaac, and Israel; then He will return to the remnant of you who have escaped from the hand of the kings of Assyria. **7** And do not be like your fathers and your brethren, who trespassed against the LORD God of their fathers, so that He gave them up to desolation, as you see. **8** Now do not be stiff-necked, as your fathers *were, but* yield yourselves to the LORD; and enter His sanctuary, which He has sanctified forever, and serve the LORD your God, that the fierceness of His wrath may turn away from you. **9** For if you return to the LORD, your brethren and your children *will be treated* with compassion by those who lead them captive, so that they may come back to this land; for the LORD your God *is* gracious and merciful, and will not turn *His* face from you if you return to Him." **10** So the runners passed from city to city through the country of Ephraim and Manasseh, as far as Zebulun; but they laughed at them and mocked them.

Idolaters addicted to.

Is 57:3–6 "But come here, You sons of the sorceress, You offspring of the adulterer and the harlot! **4** Whom do you ridicule? Against whom do you make a wide mouth *And* stick out the tongue? *Are* you not children of transgression, Offspring of falsehood, **5** Inflaming yourselves with gods under every green tree, Slaying the children in the valleys, Under the clefts of the rocks? **6** Among the smooth *stones* of the stream *Is* your portion; They, they, *are* your lot! Even to them you have poured a drink offering, You have offered a grain offering. Should I receive comfort in these?

Drunkards addicted to.

Ps 69:12 Those who sit in the gate speak against me, And I *am* the song of the drunkards.

Hos 7:5 In the day of our king Princes have made *him* sick, inflamed with wine; He stretched out his hand with scoffers.

Those who are addicted to,

Delight in it.

Prov 1:22 "How long, you simple ones, will you love simplicity? For scorners delight in their scorning, And fools hate knowledge.

Are contentious.

Prov 22:10 Cast out the scoffer, and contention will leave; Yes, strife and reproach will cease.

Are scorned by God.

Prov 3:34 Surely He scorns the scornful, But gives grace to the humble.

Are hated by men.

Prov 24:9 The devising of foolishness *is* sin, And the scoffer *is* an abomination to men.

Are avoided by believers.

Ps 1:1 Blessed *is* the man Who walks not in the counsel of the ungodly, Nor stands in the path of sinners, Nor sits in the seat of the scornful;

Jer 15:17 I did not sit in the assembly of the mockers, Nor did I rejoice; I sat alone because of Your hand, For You have filled me with indignation.

Walk after their own lusts.

2 Pet 3:3 knowing this first: that scoffers will come in the last days, walking according to their own lusts,

Are proud and haughty.

Prov 21:24 A proud *and* haughty *man*—"Scoffer" *is* his name; He acts with arrogant pride.

Do not listen to rebuke.

Prov 13:1 A wise son *heeds* his father's instruction, But a scoffer does not listen to rebuke.

Do not love those who correct.

Prov 9:8 Do not correct a scoffer, lest he hate you; Rebuke a wise *man,* and he will love you.

Prov 15:12 A scoffer does not love one who corrects him, Nor will he go to the wise.

Will not go to the wise.

Prov 15:12 A scoffer does not love one who corrects him, Nor will he go to the wise.

Bring others into danger.

Prov 29:8 Scoffers set a city aflame, But wise *men* turn away wrath.

Shall themselves endure it.

Ezek 23:32 "Thus says the Lord GOD: 'You shall drink of your sister's cup, The deep and wide one; You shall be laughed to scorn And held in derision; It contains much.

Characteristic of the last days.

2 Pet 3:3 knowing this first: that scoffers will come in the last days, walking according to their own lusts,

Jude 1:18 how they told you that there would be mock-ers in the last time who would walk according to their own ungodly lusts.

Woe pronounced against.

Is 5:18–19 Woe to those who draw iniquity with cords of vanity, And sin as if with a cart rope; **19** That say, "Let Him make speed *and* hasten His work, That we may see *it;* And let the counsel of the Holy One of Is-rael draw near and come, That we may know *it.*"

Punishment for.

2 Chr 36:17 Therefore He brought against them the king of the Chaldeans, who killed their young men with the sword in the house of their sanctuary, and had no compassion on young man or virgin, on the aged or the weak; He gave *them* all into his hand.

Prov 19:29 Judgments are prepared for scoffers, And beatings for the backs of fools.

Is 29:20 For the terrible one is brought to nothing, The scornful one is consumed, And all who watch for in-iquity are cut off—

Lam 3:64–66 Repay them, O LORD, According to the work of their hands. **65** Give them a veiled heart; Your curse *be* upon them! **66** In Your anger, Pursue and destroy them From under the heavens of the LORD.

Illustrated by

Ishmael.

Gen 21:9 And Sarah saw the son of Hagar the Egyptian, whom she had borne to Abraham, scoffing.

The children at Bethel.

2 Kin 2:23 Then he went up from there to Bethel; and as he was going up the road, some youths came from the city and mocked him, and said to him, "Go up, you baldhead! Go up, you baldhead!"

Ephraim and Manasseh.

2 Chr 30:10 So the runners passed from city to city through the country of Ephraim and Manasseh, as far as Zebulun; but they laughed at them and mocked them.

The chiefs of Judah.

2 Chr 36:16 But they mocked the messengers of God, despised His words, and scoffed at His prophets, until the wrath of the LORD arose against His people, till *there was* no remedy.

Sanballat.

Neh 4:1 But it so happened, when Sanballat heard that we were rebuilding the wall, that he was furious and very indignant, and mocked the Jews.

The enemies of Job.

Job 30:1 "But now they mock at me, *men* younger than I, Whose fathers I disdained to put with the dogs of my flock.

Job 30:9 "And now I am their taunting song; Yes, I am their byword.

The enemies of David.

Ps 35:15–16 But in my adversity they rejoiced And gath-ered together; Attackers gathered against me, And I did not know *it;* They tore *at me* and did not cease; **16** With ungodly mockers at feasts They gnashed at me with their teeth.

The rulers of Israel.

Is 28:14 Therefore hear the word of the L<small>ORD</small>, you scornful men, Who rule this people who *are* in Jerusalem,

The Ammonites.

Ezek 25:3 Say to the Ammonites, 'Hear the word of the Lord G<small>OD</small>! Thus says the Lord G<small>OD</small>: "Because you said, 'Aha!' against My sanctuary when it was profaned, and against the land of Israel when it was desolate, and against the house of Judah when they went into captivity,

The people of Tyre.

Ezek 26:2 "Son of man, because Tyre has said against Jerusalem, 'Aha! She is broken who *was* the gateway of the peoples; now she is turned over to me; I shall be filled; she is laid waste.'

The heathen.

Ezek 36:2–3 Thus says the Lord G<small>OD</small>: "Because the enemy has said of you, 'Aha! The ancient heights have become our possession,' " ' **3** therefore prophesy, and say, 'Thus says the Lord G<small>OD</small>: "Because they made *you* desolate and swallowed you up on every side, so that you became the possession of the rest of the nations, and you are taken up by the lips of talkers and slandered by the people"—

The soldiers who punished Christ.

Matt 27:28–30 And they stripped Him and put a scarlet robe on Him. **29** When they had twisted a crown of thorns, they put *it* on His head, and a reed in His right hand. And they bowed the knee before Him and mocked Him, saying, "Hail, King of the Jews!" **30** Then they spat on Him, and took the reed and struck Him on the head.

Luke 23:36 The soldiers also mocked Him, coming and offering Him sour wine,

The chief priests.

Matt 27:41 Likewise the chief priests also, mocking with the scribes and elders, said,

The Pharisees.

Luke 16:14 Now the Pharisees, who were lovers of money, also heard all these things, and they derided Him.

The men who held Jesus.

Luke 22:63–64 Now the men who held Jesus mocked Him and beat Him. **64** And having blindfolded Him, they struck Him on the face and asked Him, saying, "Prophesy! Who is the one who struck You?"

Herod.

Luke 23:11 Then Herod, with his men of war, treated Him with contempt and mocked *Him,* arrayed Him in a gorgeous robe, and sent Him back to Pilate.

The people and rulers at the crucifixion.

Luke 23:35 And the people stood looking on. But even the rulers with them sneered, saying, "He saved others; let Him save Himself if He is the Christ, the chosen of God."

Some of the Pentecost multitude.

Acts 2:13 Others mocking said, "They are full of new wine."

The Athenians listening to Paul.

Acts 17:32 And when they heard of the resurrection of the dead, some mocked, while others said, "We will hear you again on this *matter.*"

RIGHTEOUSNESS

Is obedience to God's law.

Deut 6:25 Then it will be righteousness for us, if we are careful to observe all these commandments before the L<small>ORD</small> our God, as He has commanded us.'

Ps 1:2 But his delight *is* in the law of the L<small>ORD</small>, And in His law he meditates day and night.

Rom 10:5 For Moses writes about the righteousness which is of the law, *"The man who does those things shall live by them."*

Luke 1:6 And they were both righteous before God, walking in all the commandments and ordinances of the Lord blameless.

God loves.

Ps 11:7 For the L<small>ORD</small> *is* righteous, He loves righteousness; His countenance beholds the upright.

God looks for.

Is 5:7 For the vineyard of the L<small>ORD</small> of hosts *is* the house of Israel, And the men of Judah are His pleasant plant. He looked for justice, but behold, oppression; For righteousness, but behold, a cry *for help.*

Exhortation to seek.

Matt 6:33 But seek first the kingdom of God and His righteousness, and all these things shall be added to you.

Christ

Called "The Sun of."

Mal 4:2 But to you who fear My name The Sun of Righteousness shall arise With healing in His wings; And you shall go out And grow fat like stall-fed calves.

Loves.

Ps 45:7 You love righteousness and hate wickedness; Therefore God, Your God, has anointed You With the oil of gladness more than Your companions.

Heb 1:9 *You have loved righteousness and hated lawlessness; Therefore God, Your God, has anointed You With the oil of gladness more than Your companions."*

Was girded with.

Is 11:5 Righteousness shall be the belt of His loins, And faithfulness the belt of His waist.

Put on, as a breastplate.

Is 59:17 For He put on righteousness as a breastplate, And a helmet of salvation on His head; He put on the garments of vengeance for clothing, And was clad with zeal as a cloak.

Was sustained by.

Is 59:16 He saw that *there was* no man, And wondered that *there was* no intercessor; Therefore His own arm brought salvation for Him; And His own righteousness, it sustained Him.

Preached.

Ps 40:9 I have proclaimed the good news of righteousness In the great assembly; Indeed, I do not restrain my lips, O L<small>ORD</small>, You Yourself know.

Fulfilled all.

Matt 3:15 But Jesus answered and said to him, "Permit

it *to be so* now, for thus it is fitting for us to fulfill all righteousness." Then he allowed Him.

Became.

1 Cor 1:30 But of Him you are in Christ Jesus, who became for us wisdom from God—and righteousness and sanctification and redemption—

Is the end of the law for.

Rom 10:4 For Christ *is* the end of the law for righteousness to everyone who believes.

Has brought in everlasting.

Dan 9:24 "Seventy weeks are determined For your people and for your holy city, To finish the transgression, To make an end of sins, To make reconciliation for iniquity, To bring in everlasting righteousness, To seal up vision and prophecy, And to anoint the Most Holy.

Shall judge with.

Ps 72:2 He will judge Your people with righteousness, And Your poor with justice.

Is 11:4 But with righteousness He shall judge the poor, And decide with equity for the meek of the earth; He shall strike the earth with the rod of His mouth, And with the breath of His lips He shall slay the wicked.

Acts 17:31 because He has appointed a day on which He will judge the world in righteousness by the Man whom He has ordained. He has given assurance of this to all by raising Him from the dead."

Rev 19:11 Now I saw heaven opened, and behold, a white horse. And He who sat on him *was* called Faithful and True, and in righteousness He judges and makes war.

Shall reign in.

Ps 45:6 Your throne, O God, *is* forever and ever; A scepter of righteousness *is* the scepter of Your kingdom.

Is 32:1 Behold, a king will reign in righteousness, And princes will rule with justice.

Heb 1:8 But to the Son *He says:* "Your throne, O God, *is* forever and ever; A scepter of righteousness is the scepter of Your kingdom.

Shall execute.

Ps 99:4 The King's strength also loves justice; You have established equity; You have executed justice and righteousness in Jacob.

Jer 23:6 In His days Judah will be saved, And Israel will dwell safely; Now this *is* His name by which He will be called: THE LORD OUR RIGHTEOUSNESS.

None, by nature, have.

Job 15:14 "What *is* man, that he could be pure? And *he who is* born of a woman, that he could be righteous?

Ps 14:3 They have all turned aside, They have together become corrupt; *There is* none who does good, No, not one.

Rom 3:10 As it is written: *"There is none righteous, no, not one;*

Cannot come by the law.

Gal 2:21 I do not set aside the grace of God; for if righteousness *comes* through the law, then Christ died in vain."

Gal 3:21 *Is* the law then against the promises of God? Certainly not! For if there had been a law given

which could have given life, truly righteousness would have been by the law.

No salvation by works of.

Rom 3:20 Therefore by the deeds of the law no flesh will be justified in His sight, for by the law *is* the knowledge of sin.

Rom 9:31–32 but Israel, pursuing the law of righteousness, has not attained to the law of righteousness. **32** Why? Because *they did* not *seek it* by faith, but as it were, by the works of the law. For they stumbled at that stumbling stone.

Gal 2:16 knowing that a man is not justified by the works of the law but by faith in Jesus Christ, even we have believed in Christ Jesus, that we might be justified by faith in Christ and not by the works of the law; for by the works of the law no flesh shall be justified.

Eph 2:8–9 For by grace you have been saved through faith, and that not of yourselves; *it is* the gift of God, **9** not of works, lest anyone should boast.

2 Tim 1:9 who has saved us and called *us* with a holy calling, not according to our works, but according to His own purpose and grace which was given to us in Christ Jesus before time began,

Titus 3:5 not by works of righteousness which we have done, but according to His mercy He saved us, through the washing of regeneration and renewing of the Holy Spirit,

Unregenerate man seeks justification by works of.

Luke 18:9 Also He spoke this parable to some who trusted in themselves that they were righteous, and despised others:

Rom 10:3 For they being ignorant of God's righteousness, and seeking to establish their own righteousness, have not submitted to the righteousness of God.

The blessing of God is not to be attributed to our works of.

Deut 9:5 *It is* not because of your righteousness or the uprightness of your heart *that* you go in to possess their land, but because of the wickedness of these nations *that* the LORD your God drives them out from before you, and that He may fulfill the word which the LORD swore to your fathers, to Abraham, Isaac, and Jacob.

Believers

Have, in Christ.

Is 45:24 He shall say, 'Surely in the LORD I have righteousness and strength. To Him *men* shall come, And all shall be ashamed Who are incensed against Him.

Is 54:17 No weapon formed against you shall prosper, And every tongue *which* rises against you in judgment You shall condemn. This *is* the heritage of the servants of the LORD, And their righteousness *is* from Me," Says the LORD.

2 Cor 5:21 For He made Him who knew no sin *to be* sin for us, that we might become the righteousness of God in Him.

Have, imputed.

Rom 4:11 And he received the sign of circumcision, a seal of the righteousness of the faith which *he had while still* uncircumcised, that he might be the father of all those who believe, though they are uncircumcised, that righteousness might be imputed to them also,

Rom 4:22 And therefore *"it was accounted to him for righteousness."*

Are covered with the robe of.

Is 61:10 I will greatly rejoice in the LORD, My soul shall be joyful in my God; For He has clothed me with the garments of salvation, He has covered me with the robe of righteousness, As a bridegroom decks *himself* with ornaments, And as a bride adorns *herself* with her jewels.

Receive, from God.

Ps 24:5 He shall receive blessing from the LORD, And righteousness from the God of his salvation.

Are renewed in.

Eph 4:24 and that you put on the new man which was created according to God, in true righteousness and holiness.

Are led in the paths of.

Ps 23:3 He restores my soul; He leads me in the paths of righteousness For His name's sake.

Are servants of.

Rom 6:16 Do you not know that to whom you present yourselves slaves to obey, you are that one's slaves whom you obey, whether of sin *leading* to death, or of obedience *leading* to righteousness?

Rom 6:18 And having been set free from sin, you became slaves of righteousness.

Characterized by.

Gen 18:25 Far be it from You to do such a thing as this, to slay the righteous with the wicked, so that the righteous should be as the wicked; far be it from You! Shall not the Judge of all the earth do right?"

Ps 1:5–6 Therefore the ungodly shall not stand in the judgment, Nor sinners in the congregation of the righteous. 6 For the LORD knows the way of the righteous, But the way of the ungodly shall perish.

Know.

Is 51:7 "Listen to Me, you who know righteousness, You people in whose heart *is* My law: Do not fear the reproach of men, Nor be afraid of their insults.

Do.

1 John 2:29 If you know that He is righteous, you know that everyone who practices righteousness is born of Him.

1 John 3:7 Little children, let no one deceive you. He who practices righteousness is righteous, just as He is righteous.

Work, by faith.

Heb 11:33 who through faith subdued kingdoms, worked righteousness, obtained promises, stopped the mouths of lions,

Follow after.

Is 51:1 "Listen to Me, you who follow after righteousness, You who seek the LORD: Look to the rock *from which* you were hewn, And to the hole of the pit *from which* you were dug.

Put on.

Job 29:14 I put on righteousness, and it clothed me; My justice *was* like a robe and a turban.

Desire.

Ps 51:10 Create in me a clean heart, O God, And renew a steadfast spirit within me.

Matt 5:6 Blessed *are* those who hunger and thirst for righteousness, For they shall be filled.

Gal 5:5 For we through the Spirit eagerly wait for the hope of righteousness by faith.

Walk before God in.

1 Kin 3:6 And Solomon said: "You have shown great mercy to Your servant David my father, because he walked before You in truth, in righteousness, and in uprightness of heart with You; You have continued this great kindness for him, and You have given him a son to sit on his throne, as *it is* this day.

Offer the sacrifice of.

Ps 4:5 Offer the sacrifices of righteousness, And put your trust in the LORD.

Ps 51:19 Then You shall be pleased with the sacrifices of righteousness, With burnt offering and whole burnt offering; Then they shall offer bulls on Your altar.

Put no trust in their own.

Is 64:6 But we are all like an unclean *thing*, And all our righteousnesses *are* like filthy rags; We all fade as a leaf, And our iniquities, like the wind, Have taken us away.

Phil 3:6–8 concerning zeal, persecuting the church; concerning the righteousness which is in the law, blameless. 7 But what things were gain to me, these I have counted loss for Christ. 8 Yet indeed I also count all things loss for the excellence of the knowledge of Christ Jesus my Lord, for whom I have suffered the loss of all things, and count them as rubbish, that I may gain Christ

Should live in.

Zeph 2:3 Seek the LORD, all you meek of the earth, Who have upheld His justice. Seek righteousness, seek humility. It may be that you will be hidden In the day of the LORD's anger.

Luke 1:75 In holiness and righteousness before Him all the days of our life.

Titus 2:12 teaching us that, denying ungodliness and worldly lusts, we should live soberly, righteously, and godly in the present age,

1 Pet 2:24 who Himself bore our sins in His own body on the tree, that we, having died to sins, might live for righteousness—by whose stripes you were healed.

Should yield their members to.

Rom 6:13 And do not present your members *as* instruments of unrighteousness to sin, but present yourselves to God as being alive from the dead, and your members *as* instruments of righteousness to God.

Rom 6:19 I speak in human *terms* because of the weakness of your flesh. For just as you presented your members *as* slaves of uncleanness, and of lawlessness *leading* to *more* lawlessness, so now present your members *as* slaves *of* righteousness for holiness.

Should have on the breastplate of.

Eph 6:14 Stand therefore, having girded your waist with truth, having put on the breastplate of righteousness,

Shall receive a crown of.

2 Tim 4:8 Finally, there is laid up for me the crown of righteousness, which the Lord, the righteous Judge, will give to me on that Day, and not to me only but also to all who have loved His appearing.

Shall see God's face in.

Ps 17:15 As for me, I will see Your face in righteousness; I shall be satisfied when I awake in Your likeness.

Of believers endures forever.

Ps 112:3 Wealth and riches *will be* in his house, And his righteousness endures forever.

Ps 112:9 He has dispersed abroad, He has given to the poor; His righteousness endures forever; His horn will be exalted with honor.

2 Cor 9:9 As it is written: *"He has dispersed abroad, He has given to the poor; His righteousness endures forever."*

An evidence of the new birth.

1 John 2:29 If you know that He is righteous, you know that everyone who practices righteousness is born of Him.

The kingdom of God is.

Rom 14:17 for the kingdom of God is not eating and drinking, but righteousness and peace and joy in the Holy Spirit.

The fruit of the Spirit is in all.

Eph 5:9 (for the fruit of the Spirit *is* in all goodness, righteousness, and truth),

The Scriptures instruct in.

2 Tim 3:16 All Scripture *is* given by inspiration of God, and *is* profitable for doctrine, for reproof, for correction, for instruction in righteousness,

Judgments designed to lead to.

Is 26:9 With my soul I have desired You in the night, Yes, by my spirit within me I will seek You early; For when Your judgments *are* in the earth, The inhabitants of the world will learn righteousness.

Chastisements yield the fruit of.

Heb 12:11 Now no chastening seems to be joyful for the present, but painful; nevertheless, afterward it yields the peaceable fruit of righteousness to those who have been trained by it.

Has no fellowship with unrighteousness.

2 Cor 6:14 Do not be unequally yoked together with unbelievers. For what fellowship has righteousness with lawlessness? And what communion has light with darkness?

Ministers should

Be preachers of.

2 Pet 2:5 and did not spare the ancient world, but saved Noah, *one of* eight *people,* a preacher of righteousness, bringing in the flood on the world of the ungodly;

Reason about.

Acts 24:25 Now as he reasoned about righteousness, self-control, and the judgment to come, Felix was afraid and answered, "Go away for now; when I have a convenient time I will call for you."

Follow after.

1 Tim 6:11 But you, O man of God, flee these things and pursue righteousness, godliness, faith, love, patience, gentleness.

2 Tim 2:22 Flee also youthful lusts; but pursue righteousness, faith, love, peace with those who call on the Lord out of a pure heart.

Be clothed with.

Ps 132:9 Let Your priests be clothed with righteousness, And let Your saints shout for joy.

Be armed with.

2 Cor 6:7 by the word of truth, by the power of God, by the armor of righteousness on the right hand and on the left,

Pray for the fruit of, in their people.

2 Cor 9:10 Now may He who supplies seed to the sower, and bread for food, supply and multiply the seed you have *sown* and increase the fruits of your righteousness,

Phil 1:11 being filled with the fruits of righteousness which *are* by Jesus Christ, to the glory and praise of God.

Protects and directs believers.

Prov 11:5 The righteousness of the blameless will direct his way aright, But the wicked will fall by his own wickedness.

Prov 13:6 Righteousness guards *him whose* way is blameless, But wickedness overthrows the sinner.

Judgment should be executed in.

Lev 19:15 'You shall do no injustice in judgment. You shall not be partial to the poor, nor honor the person of the mighty. In righteousness you shall judge your neighbor.

Those who walk in and follow,

Are righteous.

1 John 3:7 Little children, let no one deceive you. He who practices righteousness is righteous, just as He is righteous.

Are the excellent of the earth.

Ps 16:3 As for the saints who *are* on the earth, "They are the excellent ones, in whom is all my delight."

Prov 12:26 The righteous should choose his friends carefully, For the way of the wicked leads them astray.

Are loved by God.

Ps 5:12 For You, O LORD, will bless the righteous; With favor You will surround him as *with* a shield.

Ps 146:8 The LORD opens *the eyes of* the blind; The LORD raises those who are bowed down; The LORD loves the righteous.

Prov 15:9 The way of the wicked *is* an abomination to the LORD, But He loves him who follows righteousness.

Acts 10:35 But in every nation whoever fears Him and works righteousness is accepted by Him.

Are objects of God's watchful care.

Job 36:7 He does not withdraw His eyes from the righteous; But *they are* on the throne with kings, For He has seated them forever, And they are exalted.

Ps 34:15 The eyes of the LORD *are* on the righteous, And His ears *are* open to their cry.

Prov 10:3 The LORD will not allow the righteous soul to famish, But He casts away the desire of the wicked.

1 Pet 3:12 *For the eyes of the LORD are on the righteous, And His ears are open to their prayers; But the face of the LORD is against those who do evil."*

Are tried by God.

Ps 11:5 The LORD tests the righteous, But the wicked and the one who loves violence His soul hates.

Are exalted by God.

Job 36:7 He does not withdraw His eyes from the righteous; But *they are* on the throne with kings, For He has seated them forever, And they are exalted.

Dwell in security.

Is 33:15–16 He who walks righteously and speaks uprightly, He who despises the gain of oppressions, Who gestures with his hands, refusing bribes, Who stops his ears from hearing of bloodshed, And shuts his eyes from seeing evil: **16** He will dwell on high; His place of defense *will be* the fortress of rocks; Bread will be given him, His water *will be* sure.

Are bold as a lion.

Prov 28:1 The wicked flee when no one pursues, But the righteous are bold as a lion.

Are delivered out of all troubles.

Ps 34:19 Many *are* the afflictions of the righteous, But the LORD delivers him out of them all.

Prov 11:8 The righteous is delivered from trouble, And it comes to the wicked instead.

Are never forsaken by God.

Ps 37:25 I have been young, and *now* am old; Yet I have not seen the righteous forsaken, Nor his descendants begging bread.

Are abundantly provided for.

Ps 112:3 Wealth and riches *will be* in his house, And his righteousness endures forever.

Prov 13:25 The righteous eats to the satisfying of his soul, But the stomach of the wicked shall be in want.

Prov 15:6 *In* the house of the righteous *there is* much treasure, But in the revenue of the wicked is trouble.

Matt 6:25–33 "Therefore I say to you, do not worry about your life, what you will eat or what you will drink; nor about your body, what you will put on. Is not life more than food and the body more than clothing? **26** Look at the birds of the air, for they neither sow nor reap nor gather into barns; yet your heavenly Father feeds them. Are you not of more value than they? **27** Which of you by worrying can add one cubit to his stature? **28** "So why do you worry about clothing? Consider the lilies of the field, how they grow: they neither toil nor spin; **29** and yet I say to you that even Solomon in all his glory was not arrayed like one of these. **30** Now if God so clothes the grass of the field, which today is, and tomorrow is thrown into the oven, *will He* not much more *clothe* you, O you of little faith? **31** "Therefore do not worry, saying, 'What shall we eat?' or 'What shall we drink?' or 'What shall we wear?' **32** For after all these things the Gentiles seek. For your heavenly Father knows that you need all these things. **33** But seek first the kingdom of God and His righteousness, and all these things shall be added to you.

Think and desire good.

Prov 11:23 The desire of the righteous *is* only good, But the expectation of the wicked *is* wrath.

Prov 12:5 The thoughts of the righteous *are* right, But the counsels of the wicked *are* deceitful.

Know the secret of the Lord.

Ps 25:14 The secret of the LORD *is* with those who fear Him, And He will show them His covenant.

Prov 3:32 For the perverse *person is* an abomination to the LORD, But His secret counsel *is* with the upright.

Have their prayers heard.

Ps 34:17 *The* righteous cry out, and the LORD hears, And delivers them out of all their troubles.

Prov 15:29 The LORD *is* far from the wicked, But He hears the prayer of the righteous.

Luke 18:7 And shall God not avenge His own elect who cry out day and night to Him, though He bears long with them?

James 5:16 Confess *your* trespasses to one another, and pray for one another, that you may be healed. The effective, fervent prayer of a righteous man avails much.

1 Pet 3:12 *For the eyes of the LORD are on the righteous, And His ears are open to their prayers; But the face of the LORD is against those who do evil."*

Have their desires granted.

Prov 10:24 The fear of the wicked will come upon him, And the desire of the righteous will be granted.

Find it with life and honor.

Prov 21:21 He who follows righteousness and mercy Finds life, righteousness and honor.

Shall hold to their way.

Job 17:9 Yet the righteous will hold to his way, And he who has clean hands will be stronger and stronger.

Shall never be moved.

Ps 15:2 He who walks uprightly, And works righteousness, And speaks the truth in his heart;

Ps 15:5 He *who* does not put out his money at usury, Nor does he take a bribe against the innocent. He who does these *things* shall never be moved.

Ps 55:22 Cast your burden on the LORD, And He shall sustain you; He shall never permit the righteous to be moved.

Prov 10:30 The righteous will never be removed, But the wicked will not inhabit the earth.

Prov 12:3 A man is not established by wickedness, But the root of the righteous cannot be moved.

Shall be remembered.

Ps 112:6 Surely he will never be shaken; The righteous will be in everlasting remembrance.

Shall flourish as a branch.

Prov 11:28 He who trusts in his riches will fall, But the righteous will flourish like foliage.

Shall be glad in the Lord.

Ps 64:10 The righteous shall be glad in the LORD, and trust in Him. And all the upright in heart shall glory.

Brings its own reward.

Prov 11:18 The wicked *man* does deceptive work, But he who sows righteousness *will have* a sure reward.

Is 3:10 "Say to the righteous that *it shall be* well *with them*, For they shall eat the fruit of their doings.

Leads to life.

Prov 11:19 As righteousness *leads* to life, So he who pursues evil *pursues it* to his own death.

Prov 12:28 In the way of righteousness *is* life, And in *its* pathway *there is* no death.

The work of, shall be peace, etc.

Is 32:17 The work of righteousness will be peace, And the effect of righteousness, quietness and assurance forever.

Is a crown of glory to the aged.

Prov 16:31 The silver-haired head *is* a crown of glory, *If* it is found in the way of righteousness.

The wicked

Are far from.

Ps 119:150 They draw near who follow after wickedness; They are far from Your law.

Is 46:12 "Listen to Me, you stubborn-hearted, Who *are* far from righteousness:

Rom 6:20 For when you were slaves of sin, you were free in regard to righteousness.

Are enemies of.

Acts 13:10 and said, "O full of all deceit and all fraud, *you* son of the devil, *you* enemy of all righteousness, will you not cease perverting the straight ways of the Lord?

Set aside.

Ps 36:3 The words of his mouth *are* wickedness and deceit; He has ceased to be wise *and* to do good.

Amos 5:7 You who turn justice to wormwood, And lay righteousness to rest in the earth!"

Do not practice.

Rom 2:8 but to those who are self-seeking and do not obey the truth, but obey unrighteousness—indignation and wrath,

Rom 9:30 What shall we say then? That Gentiles, who did not pursue righteousness, have attained to righteousness, even the righteousness of faith;

2 Thess 2:12 that they all may be condemned who did not believe the truth but had pleasure in unrighteousness.

1 John 3:10 In this the children of God and the children of the devil are manifest: Whoever does not practice righteousness is not of God, nor *is* he who does not love his brother.

Love lying rather than.

Ps 52:3 You love evil more than good, Lying rather than speaking righteousness. Selah

Mention God, but not it.

Is 48:1 "Hear this, O house of Jacob, Who are called by the name of Israel, And have come forth from the wellsprings of Judah; Who swear by the name of the LORD, And make mention of the God of Israel, *But* not in truth or in righteousness;

Do not take opportunities to learn it.

Ps 106:43 Many times He delivered them; But they rebelled in their counsel, And were brought low for their iniquity.

Is 26:10 Let grace be shown to the wicked, *Yet* he will not learn righteousness; In the land of uprightness he will deal unjustly, And will not behold the majesty of the LORD.

Hate those who follow.

Ps 31:18 Let the lying lips be put to silence, Which speak insolent things proudly and contemptuously against the righteous.

Ps 34:21 Evil shall slay the wicked, And those who hate the righteous shall be condemned.

Ps 37:32 The wicked watches the righteous, And seeks to slay him.

Matt 23:35 that on you may come all the righteous blood shed on the earth, from the blood of righteous Abel to the blood of Zechariah, son of Berechiah, whom you murdered between the temple and the altar.

Matt 27:39–44 And those who passed by blasphemed Him, wagging their heads **40** and saying, "You who destroy the temple and build *it* in three days, save Yourself! If You are the Son of God, come down from the cross." **41** Likewise the chief priests also, mocking with the scribes and elders, said, **42** "He saved others; Himself He cannot save. If He is the King of Israel, let Him now come down from the cross, and we will believe Him. **43** He trusted in God; let Him deliver Him now if He will have Him; for He said, 'I am the Son of God.' " **44** Even the robbers who were crucified with Him reviled Him with the same thing.

1 John 3:12 not as Cain *who* was of the wicked one and murdered his brother. And why did he murder him? Because his works were evil and his brother's righteous.

Should awaken to.

Dan 4:27 Therefore, O king, let my advice be acceptable to you; break off your sins by *being* righteous, and your iniquities by showing mercy to *the* poor. Perhaps there may be a lengthening of your prosperity.

Hos 10:12 Sow for yourselves righteousness; Reap in mercy; Break up your fallow ground, For *it is* time to seek the LORD, Till He comes and rains righteousness on you.

1 Cor 15:34 Awake to righteousness, and do not sin; for some do not have the knowledge of God. I speak *this* to your shame.

Vainly wish to die as those who follow.

Num 23:10 "Who can count the dust of Jacob, Or number one-fourth of Israel? Let me die the death of the righteous, And let my end be like his!"

The throne of kings established by.

Prov 16:12 *It is* an abomination for kings to commit wickedness, For a throne is established by righteousness.

Prov 25:5 Take away the wicked from before the king, And his throne will be established in righteousness.

Nations exalted by.

Prov 14:34 Righteousness exalts a nation, But sin *is* a reproach to *any* people.

Blessedness of,

By having it imputed, without works.

Rom 4:6 just as David also describes the blessedness of

the man to whom God imputes righteousness apart from works:

By doing.

Ps 106:3 Blessed *are* those who keep justice, *And* he who does righteousness at all times!

By hungering and thirsting after.

Matt 5:6 Blessed *are* those who hunger and thirst for righteousness, For they shall be filled.

By suffering for.

1 Pet 3:14 But even if you should suffer for righteousness' sake, *you are* blessed. *"And do not be afraid of their threats, nor be troubled."*

By being persecuted for.

Matt 5:10 Blessed are those who are persecuted for righteousness' sake, For theirs is the kingdom of heaven.

By turning others to.

Dan 12:3 Those who are wise shall shine Like the brightness of the firmament, And those who turn many to righteousness Like the stars forever and ever.

Promised to believers.

Is 32:16 Then justice will dwell in the wilderness, And righteousness remain in the fruitful field.

Is 45:8 "Rain down, you heavens, from above, And let the skies pour down righteousness; Let the earth open, let them bring forth salvation, And let righteousness spring up together. I, the LORD, have created it.

Is 60:21 Also your people *shall* all *be* righteous; They shall inherit the land forever, The branch of My planting, The work of My hands, That I may be glorified.

Is 61:3 To console those who mourn in Zion, To give them beauty for ashes, The oil of joy for mourning, The garment of praise for the spirit of heaviness; That they may be called trees of righteousness, The planting of the LORD, that He may be glorified."

Is 61:11 For as the earth brings forth its bud, As the garden causes the things that are sown in it to spring forth, So the Lord GOD will cause righteousness and praise to spring forth before all the nations.

Is 62:1 For Zion's sake I will not hold My peace, And for Jerusalem's sake I will not rest, Until her righteousness goes forth as brightness, And her salvation as a lamp *that* burns.

Exemplified by

Jacob.

Gen 30:33 So my righteousness will answer for me in time to come, when the subject of my wages comes before you: every one that *is* not speckled and spotted among the goats, and brown among the lambs, will be considered stolen, if *it is* with me."

David.

2 Sam 22:21 "The LORD rewarded me according to my righteousness; According to the cleanness of my hands He has recompensed me.

Zacharias.

Luke 1:6 And they were both righteous before God, walking in all the commandments and ordinances of the Lord blameless.

Abel.

Heb 11:4 By faith Abel offered to God a more excellent sacrifice than Cain, through which he obtained witness that he was righteous, God testifying of his gifts; and through it he being dead still speaks.

Lot.

2 Pet 2:8 (for that righteous man, dwelling among them, tormented *his* righteous soul from day to day by seeing and hearing *their* lawless deeds)—

RIGHTEOUSNESS, IMPUTED

Predicted.

Is 56:1 Thus says the LORD: "Keep justice, and do righteousness, For My salvation *is* about to come, And My righteousness to be revealed.

Ezek 16:14 Your fame went out among the nations because of your beauty, for it *was* perfect through My splendor which I had bestowed on you," says the Lord GOD.

Revealed in the gospel.

Rom 1:17 For in it the righteousness of God is revealed from faith to faith; as it is written, *"The just shall live by faith."*

Is of the Lord.

Is 54:17 No weapon formed against you shall prosper, And every tongue *which* rises against you in judgment You shall condemn. This *is* the heritage of the servants of the LORD, And their righteousness *is* from Me," Says the LORD.

Described as

The righteousness of faith.

Rom 4:13 For the promise that he would be the heir of the world *was* not to Abraham or to his seed through the law, but through the righteousness of faith.

Rom 9:30 What shall we say then? That Gentiles, who did not pursue righteousness, have attained to righteousness, even the righteousness of faith;

Rom 10:6 But the righteousness of faith speaks in this way, *"Do not say in your heart, 'Who will ascend into heaven?'"* (that is, to bring Christ down *from above*)

The righteousness of God, apart from the law.

Rom 3:21 But now the righteousness of God apart from the law is revealed, being witnessed by the Law and the Prophets,

The righteousness of God by faith in Christ.

Rom 3:22 even the righteousness of God, through faith in Jesus Christ, to all and on all who believe. For there is no difference;

Christ being made righteousness for us.

1 Cor 1:30 But of Him you are in Christ Jesus, who became for us wisdom from God—and righteousness and sanctification and redemption—

Our being made the righteousness of God, in Christ.

2 Cor 5:21 For He made Him who knew no sin *to be* sin for us, that we might become the righteousness of God in Him.

Christ being the end of the law for righteousness.

Rom 10:4 For Christ *is* the end of the law for righteousness to everyone who believes.

Christ being "The Lord our righteousness."

Jer 23:6 In His days Judah will be saved, And Israel will dwell safely; Now this is His name by which He will be called: THE LORD OUR RIGHTEOUSNESS.

Christ bringing in an everlasting righteousness.

Dan 9:24 "Seventy weeks are determined For your people and for your holy city, To finish the transgression, To make an end of sins, To make reconciliation for iniquity, To bring in everlasting righteousness, To seal up vision and prophecy, And to anoint the Most Holy.

Is a free gift.

Rom 5:17 For if by the one man's offense death reigned through the one, much more those who receive abundance of grace and of the gift of righteousness will reign in life through the One, Jesus Christ.)

God's, never to be abolished.

Is 5:16 But the LORD of hosts shall be exalted in judgment, And God who is holy shall be hallowed in righteousness.

The promises made through.

Rom 4:13 For the promise that he would be the heir of the world was not to Abraham or to his seed through the law, but through the righteousness of faith.

Believers

Receive, on believing.

Rom 4:5 But to him who does not work but believes on Him who justifies the ungodly, his faith is accounted for righteousness,

Rom 4:11 And he received the sign of circumcision, a seal of the righteousness of the faith which he had while still uncircumcised, that he might be the father of all those who believe, though they are uncircumcised, that righteousness might be imputed to them also,

Rom 4:24 but also for us. It shall be imputed to us who believe in Him who raised up Jesus our Lord from the dead,

Clothed with the robe of righteousness.

Is 61:10 I will greatly rejoice in the LORD, My soul shall be joyful in my God; For He has clothed me with the garments of salvation, He has covered me with the robe of righteousness, As a bridegroom decks himself with ornaments, And as a bride adorns herself with her jewels.

Exalted in righteousness.

Ps 89:16 In Your name they rejoice all day long, And in Your righteousness they are exalted.

Desire to be found in.

Phil 3:9 and be found in Him, not having my own righteousness, which is from the law, but that which is through faith in Christ, the righteousness which is from God by faith;

Glory in having.

Is 45:24–25 He shall say, 'Surely in the LORD I have righteousness and strength. To Him men shall come, And all shall be ashamed Who are incensed against Him. 25 In the LORD all the descendants of Israel Shall be justified, and shall glory.' "

The Gentiles attained to.

Rom 9:30 What shall we say then? That Gentiles, who did not pursue righteousness, have attained to righteousness, even the righteousness of faith;

Blessedness of those who have.

Rom 4:6 just as David also describes the blessedness of the man to whom God imputes righteousness apart from works:

The Jews

Ignorant of.

Rom 10:3 For they being ignorant of God's righteousness, and seeking to establish their own righteousness, have not submitted to the righteousness of God.

Stumble at the concept of.

Rom 9:32 Why? Because they did not seek it by faith, but as it were, by the works of the law. For they stumbled at that stumbling stone.

Do not submit to.

Rom 10:3 For they being ignorant of God's righteousness, and seeking to establish their own righteousness, have not submitted to the righteousness of God.

Exemplified by

Abraham.

Rom 4:9 Does this blessedness then come upon the circumcised only, or upon the uncircumcised also? For we say that faith was accounted to Abraham for righteousness.

Rom 4:22 And therefore "it was accounted to him for righteousness."

Gal 3:6 just as Abraham "believed God, and it was accounted to him for righteousness."

Paul.

Phil 3:7–9 But what things were gain to me, these I have counted loss for Christ. 8 Yet indeed I also count all things loss for the excellence of the knowledge of Christ Jesus my Lord, for whom I have suffered the loss of all things, and count them as rubbish, that I may gain Christ 9 and be found in Him, not having my own righteousness, which is from the law, but that which is through faith in Christ, the righteousness which is from God by faith;

RINGS OR BRACELETS

Antiquity of.

Gen 24:22 So it was, when the camels had finished drinking, that the man took a golden nose ring weighing half a shekel, and two bracelets for her wrists weighing ten shekels of gold,

Gen 38:18 Then he said, "What pledge shall I give you?" So she said, "Your signet and cord, and your staff that is in your hand." Then he gave them to her, and went in to her, and she conceived by him.

Made of gold and set with precious stones.

Num 31:50–51 Therefore we have brought an offering for the LORD, what every man found of ornaments of gold: armlets and bracelets and signet rings and earrings and necklaces, to make atonement for ourselves before the LORD." 51 So Moses and Eleazar the priest received the gold from them, all the fashioned ornaments.

Were worn

On the hands.

Gen 41:42 Then Pharaoh took his signet ring off his hand and put it on Joseph's hand; and he clothed him in garments of fine linen and put a gold chain around his neck.

On the arms.

2 Sam 1:10 So I stood over him and killed him, because I was sure that he could not live after he had fallen. And I took the crown that *was* on his head and the bracelet that *was* on his arm, and have brought them here to my lord."

In the ears.

Job 42:11 Then all his brothers, all his sisters, and all those who had been his acquaintances before, came to him and ate food with him in his house; and they consoled him and comforted him for all the adversity that the LORD had brought upon him. Each one gave him a piece of silver and each a ring of gold.

Hos 2:13 I will punish her For the days of the Baals to which she burned incense. She decked herself with her earrings and jewelry, And went after her lovers; But Me she forgot," says the LORD.

Ezek 16:12 And I put a jewel in your nose, earrings in your ears, and a beautiful crown on your head.

In the nose.

Is 3:21 and the rings; The nose jewels,

Rich men distinguished by.

James 2:2 For if there should come into your assembly a man with gold rings, in fine apparel, and there should also come in a poor man in filthy clothes,

Women of high rank adorned with.

Is 3:16 Moreover the LORD says: "Because the daughters of Zion are haughty, And walk with outstretched necks And wanton eyes, Walking and mincing *as* they go, Making a jingling with their feet,

Is 3:21 and the rings; The nose jewels,

Of kings

Used for sealing decrees.

Esth 3:12 Then the king's scribes were called on the thirteenth day of the first month, and *a decree* was written according to all that Haman commanded—to the king's satraps, to the governors who *were* over each province, to the officials of all people, to every province according to its script, and to every people in their language. In the name of King Ahasuerus it was written, and sealed with the king's signet ring.

Esth 8:8 You yourselves write *a decree* concerning the Jews, as you please, in the king's name, and seal *it* with the king's signet ring; for whatever is written in the king's name and sealed with the king's signet ring no one can revoke."

Esth 8:10 And he wrote in the name of King Ahasuerus, sealed *it* with the king's signet ring, and sent letters by couriers on horseback, riding on royal horses bred from swift steeds.

Honored favorite people with them.

Gen 41:42 Then Pharaoh took his signet ring off his hand and put it on Joseph's hand; and he clothed him in garments of fine linen and put a gold chain around his neck.

Esth 3:10 So the king took his signet ring from his hand and gave it to Haman, the son of Hammedatha the Agagite, the enemy of the Jews.

Esth 8:2 So the king took off his signet ring, which he had taken from Haman, and gave it to Mordecai; and Esther appointed Mordecai over the house of Haman.

Numbers of, taken from Midianites.

Num 31:50 Therefore we have brought an offering for the LORD, what every man found of ornaments of gold: armlets and bracelets and signet rings and earrings and necklaces, to make atonement for ourselves before the LORD."

Illustrative of favor.

Luke 15:22 "But the father said to his servants, 'Bring out the best robe and put *it* on him, and put a ring on his hand and sandals on *his* feet.

RIVERS

Source of.

Job 28:10 He cuts out channels in the rocks, And his eye sees every precious thing.

Ps 104:8 They went up over the mountains; They went down into the valleys, To the place which You founded for them.

Ps 104:10 He sends the springs into the valleys; They flow among the hills.

Enclosed within banks.

Dan 12:5 Then I, Daniel, looked; and there stood two others, one on this riverbank and the other on that riverbank.

Flow through valleys.

Ps 104:8 They went up over the mountains; They went down into the valleys, To the place which You founded for them.

Ps 104:10 He sends the springs into the valleys; They flow among the hills.

Some were

Great and mighty.

Gen 15:18 On the same day the LORD made a covenant with Abram, saying: "To your descendants I have given this land, from the river of Egypt to the great river, the River Euphrates—

Ps 74:15 You broke open the fountain and the flood; You dried up mighty rivers.

Deep.

Ezek 47:5 Again he measured one thousand, *and it was* a river that I could not cross; for the water was too deep, water in which one must swim, a river that could not be crossed.

Zech 10:11 He shall pass through the sea with affliction, And strike the waves of the sea: All the depths of the River shall dry up. Then the pride of Assyria shall be brought down, And the scepter of Egypt shall depart.

Broad.

Is 33:21 But there the majestic LORD *will be* for us A place of broad rivers *and* streams, In which no galley with oars will sail, Nor majestic ships pass by

Rapid.

Judg 5:21 The torrent of Kishon swept them away, That ancient torrent, the torrent of Kishon. O my soul, march on in strength!

Parted into many streams.

Gen 2:10 Now a river went out of Eden to water the garden, and from there it parted and became four riverheads.

Is 11:15 The LORD will utterly destroy the tongue of the

Sea of Egypt; With His mighty wind He will shake His fist over the River, And strike it in the seven streams, And make *men* cross over dry-shod.

Run into the sea.

Eccl 1:7 All the rivers run into the sea, Yet the sea *is* not full; To the place from which the rivers come, There they return again.

Ezek 47:8 Then he said to me: "This water flows toward the eastern region, goes down into the valley, and enters the sea. *When it* reaches the sea, *its* waters are healed.

God's power over, unlimited.

Is 50:2 Why, when I came, *was there* no man? *Why,* when I called, *was there* none to answer? Is My hand shortened at all that it cannot redeem? Or have I no power to deliver? Indeed with My rebuke I dry up the sea, I make the rivers a wilderness; Their fish stink because *there is* no water, And die of thirst.

Nah 1:4 He rebukes the sea and makes it dry, And dries up all the rivers. Bashan and Carmel wither, And the flower of Lebanon wilts.

Useful for

Supplying drink to the people.

Jer 2:18 And now why take the road to Egypt, To drink the waters of Sihor? Or why take the road to Assyria, To drink the waters of the River?

Commerce.

Is 23:3 And on great waters the grain of Shihor, The harvest of the River, *is* her revenue; And she is a marketplace for the nations.

Promoting vegetation.

Gen 2:10 Now a river went out of Eden to water the garden, and from there it parted and became four riverheads.

Bathing.

Ex 2:5 Then the daughter of Pharaoh came down to bathe at the river. And her maidens walked along the riverside; and when she saw the ark among the reeds, she sent her maid to get it.

Baptism often performed in.

Matt 3:6 and were baptized by him in the Jordan, confessing their sins.

Of Canaan, abounded with fish.

Lev 11:9–10 'These you may eat of all that *are* in the water: whatever in the water has fins and scales, whether in the seas or in the rivers—that you may eat. **10** But all in the seas or in the rivers that do not have fins and scales, all that move in the water or any living thing which *is* in the water, they *are* an abomination to you.

Banks of,

Covered with reeds.

Ex 2:3 But when she could no longer hide him, she took an ark of bulrushes for him, daubed it with asphalt and pitch, put the child in it, and laid *it* in the reeds by the river's bank.

Ex 2:5 Then the daughter of Pharaoh came down to bathe at the river. And her maidens walked along the riverside; and when she saw the ark among the reeds, she sent her maid to get it.

Planted with trees.

Ezek 47:7 When I returned, there, along the bank of the river, *were* very many trees on one side and the other.

Frequented by doves.

Song 5:12 His eyes *are* like doves By the rivers of waters, Washed with milk, *And* fitly set.

Frequented by wild beasts.

Jer 49:19 "Behold, he shall come up like a lion from the floodplain of the Jordan Against the dwelling place of the strong; But I will suddenly make him run away from her. And who *is* a chosen *man that* I may appoint over her? For who *is* like Me? Who will arraign Me? And who *is* that shepherd Who will withstand Me?"

Places of common resort.

Ps 137:1 By the rivers of Babylon, There we sat down, yea, we wept When we remembered Zion.

Frequently overflowed.

Josh 3:15 and as those who bore the ark came to the Jordan, and the feet of the priests who bore the ark dipped in the edge of the water (for the Jordan overflows all its banks during the whole time of harvest),

1 Chr 12:15 These *are* the ones who crossed the Jordan in the first month, when it had overflowed all its banks; and they put to flight all *those* in the valleys, to the east and to the west.

Especially fruitful.

Ps 1:3 He shall be like a tree Planted by the rivers of water, That brings forth its fruit in its season, Whose leaf also shall not wither; And whatever he does shall prosper.

Is 32:20 Blessed *are* you who sow beside all waters, Who send out freely the feet of the ox and the donkey.

Gardens often made beside.

Num 24:6 Like valleys that stretch out, Like gardens by the riverside, Like aloes planted by the LORD, Like cedars beside the waters.

Cities often built beside.

Ps 46:4 *There is* a river whose streams shall make glad the city of God, The holy *place* of the tabernacle of the Most High.

Ps 137:1 By the rivers of Babylon, There we sat down, yea, we wept When we remembered Zion.

Often the boundaries of kingdoms.

Josh 22:25 For the LORD has made the Jordan a border between you and us, *you* children of Reuben and children of Gad. You have no part in the LORD." So your descendants would make our descendants cease fearing the LORD.'

1 Kin 4:24 For he had dominion over all *the region* on this side of the River from Tiphsah even to Gaza, namely over all the kings on this side of the River; and he had peace on every side all around him.

Ones mentioned in Scripture,

Of Eden.

Gen 2:10 Now a river went out of Eden to water the garden, and from there it parted and became four riverheads.

Of Jotbathah.

Deut 10:7 From there they journeyed to Gudgodah, and from Gudgodah to Jotbathah, a land of rivers of water.

Of Ethiopia.

Is 18:1 Woe to the land shadowed with buzzing wings, Which *is* beyond the rivers of Ethiopia,

Of Babylon.

Ps 137:1 By the rivers of Babylon, There we sat down, yea, we wept When we remembered Zion.

Of Egypt.

Gen 15:18 On the same day the LORD made a covenant with Abram, saying: "To your descendants I have given this land, from the river of Egypt to the great river, the River Euphrates—

Of Damascus.

2 Kin 5:12 *Are* not the Abanah and the Pharpar, the rivers of Damascus, better than all the waters of Israel? Could I not wash in them and be clean?" So he turned and went away in a rage.

Of Ahava.

Ezra 8:15 Now I gathered them by the river that flows to Ahava, and we camped there three days. And I looked among the people and the priests, and found none of the sons of Levi there.

Of Judah.

Joel 3:18 And it will come to pass in that day *That* the mountains shall drip with new wine, The hills shall flow with milk, And all the brooks of Judah shall be flooded with water; A fountain shall flow from the house of the LORD And water the Valley of Acacias.

Of Philippi.

Acts 16:13 And on the Sabbath day we went out of the city to the riverside, where prayer was customarily made; and we sat down and spoke to the women who met *there.*

Abanah.

2 Kin 5:12 *Are* not the Abanah and the Pharpar, the rivers of Damascus, better than all the waters of Israel? Could I not wash in them and be clean?" So he turned and went away in a rage.

Arnon.

Deut 2:36 From Aroer, which *is* on the bank of the River Arnon, and *from* the city that *is* in the ravine, as far as Gilead, there was not one city too strong for us; the LORD our God delivered all to us.

Josh 12:1 These *are* the kings of the land whom the children of Israel defeated, and whose land they possessed on the other side of the Jordan toward the rising of the sun, from the River Arnon to Mount Hermon, and all the eastern Jordan plain:

Chebar.

Ezek 1:1 Now it came to pass in the thirtieth year, in the fourth *month,* on the fifth *day* of the month, as I *was* among the captives by the River Chebar, *that* the heavens were opened and I saw visions of God.

Ezek 1:3 the word of the LORD came expressly to Ezekiel the priest, the son of Buzi, in the land of the Chaldeans by the River Chebar; and the hand of the LORD was upon him there.

Ezek 10:15 And the cherubim were lifted up. This *was* the living creature I saw by the River Chebar.

Ezek 10:20 This *is* the living creature I saw under the God of Israel by the River Chebar, and I knew they *were* cherubim.

Euphrates.

Gen 2:14 The name of the third river *is* Hiddekel; it *is* the one which goes toward the east of Assyria. The fourth river *is* the Euphrates.

Gihon.

Gen 2:13 The name of the second river *is* Gihon; it *is* the one which goes around the whole land of Cush.

Gozan.

2 Kin 17:6 In the ninth year of Hoshea, the king of Assyria took Samaria and carried Israel away to Assyria, and placed them in Halah and by the Habor, the River of Gozan, and in the cities of the Medes.

1 Chr 5:26 So the God of Israel stirred up the spirit of Pul king of Assyria, that is, Tiglath-Pileser king of Assyria. He carried the Reubenites, the Gadites, and the half-tribe of Manasseh into captivity. He took them to Halah, Habor, Hara, and the river of Gozan to this day.

Hiddekel.

Gen 2:14 The name of the third river *is* Hiddekel; it *is* the one which goes toward the east of Assyria. The fourth river *is* the Euphrates.

Jabbok.

Deut 2:37 Only you did not go near the land of the people of Ammon—anywhere along the River Jabbok, or to the cities of the mountains, or wherever the LORD our God had forbidden us.

Josh 12:2 *One king was* Sihon king of the Amorites, who dwelt in Heshbon *and* ruled half of Gilead, from Aroer, which is on the bank of the River Arnon, from the middle of that river, even as far as the River Jabbok, *which is* the border of the Ammonites,

Jordan.

Josh 3:8 You shall command the priests who bear the ark of the covenant, saying, 'When you have come to the edge of the water of the Jordan, you shall stand in the Jordan.' "

2 Kin 5:10 And Elisha sent a messenger to him, saying, "Go and wash in the Jordan seven times, and your flesh shall be restored to you, and *you shall* be clean."

Kanah.

Josh 16:8 The border went out from Tappuah westward to the Brook Kanah, and it ended at the sea. This *was* the inheritance of the tribe of the children of Ephraim according to their families.

Kishon.

Judg 5:21 The torrent of Kishon swept them away, That ancient torrent, the torrent of Kishon. O my soul, march on in strength!

Pharpar.

2 Kin 5:12 *Are* not the Abanah and the Pharpar, the rivers of Damascus, better than all the waters of Israel? Could I not wash in them and be clean?" So he turned and went away in a rage.

Pishon.

Gen 2:11 The name of the first *is* Pishon; it *is* the one which skirts the whole land of Havilah, where *there is* gold.

Ulai.

Dan 8:16 And I heard a man's voice between *the banks*

of the Ulai, who called, and said, "Gabriel, make this *man* understand the vision."

Fordable in certain places.

Gen 32:22 And he arose that night and took his two wives, his two female servants, and his eleven sons, and crossed over the ford of Jabbok.

Josh 2:7 Then the men pursued them by the road to the Jordan, to the fords. And as soon as those who pursued them had gone out, they shut the gate.

Is 16:2 For it shall be as a wandering bird thrown out of the nest; *So* shall be the daughters of Moab at the fords of the Arnon.

Illustrative of

Christ's abundant grace.

Is 32:2 A man will be as a hiding place from the wind, And a cover from the tempest, As rivers of water in a dry place, As the shadow of a great rock in a weary land.

John 1:16 And of His fullness we have all received, and grace for grace.

The gifts and graces of the Holy Spirit.

Ps 46:4 *There is* a river whose streams shall make glad the city of God, The holy *place* of the tabernacle of the Most High.

Is 41:18 I will open rivers in desolate heights, And fountains in the midst of the valleys; I will make the wilderness a pool of water, And the dry land springs of water.

Is 43:19–20 Behold, I will do a new thing, Now it shall spring forth; Shall you not know it? I will even make a road in the wilderness *And* rivers in the desert. **20** The beast of the field will honor Me, The jackals and the ostriches, Because I give waters in the wilderness *And* rivers in the desert, To give drink to My people, My chosen.

John 7:38–39 He who believes in Me, as the Scripture has said, out of his heart will flow rivers of living water." **39** But this He spoke concerning the Spirit, whom those believing in Him would receive; for the Holy Spirit was not yet *given*, because Jesus was not yet glorified.

Heavy afflictions.

Ps 69:2 I sink in deep mire, Where *there is* no standing; I have come into deep waters, Where the floods overflow me.

Is 43:2 When you pass through the waters, I *will be* with you; And through the rivers, they shall not overflow you. When you walk through the fire, you shall not be burned, Nor shall the flame scorch you.

Abundance.

Job 20:17 He will not see the streams, The rivers flowing with honey and cream.

Job 29:6 When my steps were bathed with cream, And the rock poured out rivers of oil for me!

People fleeing from judgments.

Is 23:10 Overflow through your land like the River, O daughter of Tarshish; *There is* no more strength.

(Steady course of) peace of believers.

Is 66:12 For thus says the LORD: "Behold, I will extend peace to her like a river, And the glory of the Gentiles

like a flowing stream. Then you shall feed; On *her* sides shall you be carried, And be dandled on *her* knees.

(Fruitfulness of trees planted by) the permanent prosperity of believers.

Ps 1:3 He shall be like a tree Planted by the rivers of water, That brings forth its fruit in its season, Whose leaf also shall not wither; And whatever he does shall prosper.

Jer 17:8 For he shall be like a tree planted by the waters, Which spreads out its roots by the river, And will not fear when heat comes; But its leaf will be green, And will not be anxious in the year of drought, Nor will cease from yielding fruit.

(Drying up of) God's judgments.

Jer 51:36 Therefore thus says the LORD: "Behold, I will plead your case and take vengeance for you. I will dry up her sea and make her springs dry.

Nah 1:4 He rebukes the sea and makes it dry, And dries up all the rivers. Bashan and Carmel wither, And the flower of Lebanon wilts.

Zech 10:11 He shall pass through the sea with affliction, And strike the waves of the sea: All the depths of the River shall dry up. Then the pride of Assyria shall be brought down, And the scepter of Egypt shall depart.

Cf. Is 19:1–8

(Overflowing of) God's judgments.

Is 8:7–8 Now therefore, behold, the Lord brings up over them The waters of the River, strong and mighty— The king of Assyria and all his glory; He will go up over all his channels And go over all his banks. **8** He will pass through Judah, He will overflow and pass over, He will reach up to the neck; And the stretching out of his wings Will fill the breadth of Your land, O Immanuel.

Is 28:2 Behold, the Lord has a mighty and strong one, Like a tempest of hail and a destroying storm, Like a flood of mighty waters overflowing, Who will bring *them* down to the earth with *His* hand.

Is 28:18 Your covenant with death will be annulled, And your agreement with Sheol will not stand; When the overflowing scourge passes through, Then you will be trampled down by it.

Jer 47:2 Thus says the LORD: "Behold, waters rise out of the north, And shall be an overflowing flood; They shall overflow the land and all that is in it, The city and those who dwell within; Then the men shall cry, And all the inhabitants of the land shall wail.

ROCKS

Described as

Flinty.

Deut 8:15 who led you through that great and terrible wilderness, *in which were* fiery serpents and scorpions and thirsty land where there was no water; who brought water for you out of the flinty rock;

Deut 32:13 "He made him ride in the heights of the earth, That he might eat the produce of the fields; He made him draw honey from the rock, And oil from the flinty rock;

Hard.

Jer 5:3 O LORD, *are* not Your eyes on the truth? You have stricken them, But they have not grieved; You have consumed them, But they have refused to receive correction. They have made their faces harder than rock; They have refused to return.

Durable.

Job 19:24 That they were engraved on a rock With an iron pen and lead, forever!

Barren.

Ezek 26:4 And they shall destroy the walls of Tyre and break down her towers; I will also scrape her dust from her, and make her like the top of a rock.

Ezek 26:14 I will make you like the top of a rock; you shall be *a place for* spreading nets, and you shall never be rebuilt, for I the LORD have spoken,' says the Lord GOD.

Amos 6:12 Do horses run on rocks? Does *one* plow *there* with oxen? Yet you have turned justice into gall, And the fruit of righteousness into wormwood,

Luke 8:6 Some fell on rock; and as soon as it sprang up, it withered away because it lacked moisture.

Often sharp-pointed and craggy.

1 Sam 14:4 Between the passes, by which Jonathan sought to go over to the Philistines' garrison, *there was* a sharp rock on one side and a sharp rock on the other side. And the name of one *was* Bozez, and the name of the other Seneh.

Often had clefts.

Ex 33:22 So it shall be, while My glory passes by, that I will put you in the cleft of the rock, and will cover you with My hand while I pass by.

Were a defense to a country.

Is 33:16 He will dwell on high; His place of defense *will be* the fortress of rocks; Bread will be given him, His water *will be* sure.

Dreaded by sailors.

Acts 27:20 Now when neither sun nor stars appeared for many days, and no small tempest beat on *us*, all hope that we would be saved was finally given up.

Inhabited by

Wild goats.

Job 39:1 "Do you know the time when the wild mountain goats bear young? *Or* can you mark when the deer gives birth?

Badgers.

Ps 104:18 The high hills *are* for the wild goats; The cliffs are a refuge for the rock badgers.

Prov 30:26 The rock badgers are a feeble folk, Yet they make their homes in the crags;

Doves.

Song 2:14 "O my dove, in the clefts of the rock, In the secret *places* of the cliff, Let me see your face, Let me hear your voice; For your voice *is* sweet, And your face *is* lovely."

Jer 48:28 You who dwell in Moab, Leave the cities and dwell in the rock, And be like the dove *which* makes her nest In the sides of the cave's mouth.

Eagles.

Job 39:28 On the rock it dwells and resides, On the crag of the rock and the stronghold.

Jer 49:16 Your fierceness has deceived you, The pride of your heart, O you who dwell in the clefts of the rock,

Who hold the height of the hill! Though you make your nest as high as the eagle, I will bring you down from there," says the LORD.

The olive tree flourished among.

Deut 32:13 "He made him ride in the heights of the earth, That he might eat the produce of the fields; He made him draw honey from the rock, And oil from the flinty rock;

Job 29:6 When my steps were bathed with cream, And the rock poured out rivers of oil for me!

Bees often made their honey among.

Deut 32:13 "He made him ride in the heights of the earth, That he might eat the produce of the fields; He made him draw honey from the rock, And oil from the flinty rock;

Ps 81:16 He would have fed them also with the finest of wheat; And with honey from the rock I would have satisfied you."

Used as

Altars.

Judg 6:20–21 The Angel of God said to him, "Take the meat and the unleavened bread and lay *them* on this rock, and pour out the broth." And he did so. **21** Then the Angel of the LORD put out the end of the staff that *was* in His hand, and touched the meat and the unleavened bread; and fire rose out of the rock and consumed the meat and the unleavened bread. And the Angel of the LORD departed out of his sight.

Judg 6:26 and build an altar to the LORD your God on top of this rock in the proper arrangement, and take the second bull and offer a burnt sacrifice with the wood of the image which you shall cut down."

Judg 13:19 So Manoah took the young goat with the grain offering, and offered it upon the rock to the LORD. And He did a wondrous thing while Manoah and his wife looked on—

Places for idolatrous worship.

Is 57:5 Inflaming yourselves with gods under every green tree, Slaying the children in the valleys, Under the clefts of the rocks?

Places of observation.

Ex 33:21 And the LORD said, "Here is a place by Me, and you shall stand on the rock.

Num 23:9 For from the top of the rocks I see him, And from the hills I behold him; There! A people dwelling alone, Not reckoning itself among the nations.

Places of safety.

1 Sam 13:6 When the men of Israel saw that they were in danger (for the people were distressed), then the people hid in caves, in thickets, in rocks, in holes, and in pits.

Is 2:19 They shall go into the holes of the rocks, And into the caves of the earth, From the terror of the LORD And the glory of His majesty, When He arises to shake the earth mightily.

Jer 16:16 "Behold, I will send for many fishermen," says the LORD, "and they shall fish them; and afterward I will send for many hunters, and they shall hunt them from every mountain and every hill, and out of the holes of the rocks.

Rev 6:15 And the kings of the earth, the great men, the

rich men, the commanders, the mighty men, every slave and every free man, hid themselves in the caves and in the rocks of the mountains,

Places of shelter for the poor.

Job 24:8 They are wet with the showers of the mountains, And huddle around the rock for want of shelter.

Job 30:3 *They are* gaunt from want and famine, Fleeing late to the wilderness, desolate and waste,

Job 30:6 *They had* to live in the clefts of the valleys, *In* caves of the earth and the rocks.

Houses often built on.

Matt 7:24–25 "Therefore whoever hears these sayings of Mine, and does them, I will liken him to a wise man who built his house on the rock: **25** and the rain descended, the floods came, and the winds blew and beat on that house; and it did not fall, for it was founded on the rock.

Tombs often hewn out of.

Is 22:16 'What have you here, and whom have you here, That you have hewn a sepulcher here, *As* he who hews himself a sepulcher on high, Who carves a tomb for himself in a rock?

Matt 27:60 and laid it in his new tomb which he had hewn out of the rock; and he rolled a large stone against the door of the tomb, and departed.

Important events often engraved on.

Job 19:24 That they were engraved on a rock With an iron pen and lead, forever!

Ones mentioned in Scripture

Adullam.

1 Chr 11:15 Now three of the thirty chief men went down to the rock to David, into the cave of Adullam; and the army of the Philistines encamped in the Valley of Rephaim.

Bozez.

1 Sam 14:4 Between the passes, by which Jonathan sought to go over to the Philistines' garrison, *there was* a sharp rock on one side and a sharp rock on the other side. And the name of one *was* Bozez, and the name of the other Seneh.

En Gedi.

1 Sam 24:1–2 Now it happened, when Saul had returned from following the Philistines, that it was told him, saying, "Take note! David *is* in the Wilderness of En Gedi." **2** Then Saul took three thousand chosen men from all Israel, and went to seek David and his men on the Rocks of the Wild Goats.

Etam.

Judg 15:8 So he attacked them hip and thigh with a great slaughter; then he went down and dwelt in the cleft of the rock of Etam.

Horeb in Rephidim.

Ex 17:1–6 Then all the congregation of the children of Israel set out on their journey from the Wilderness of Sin, according to the commandment of the LORD, and camped in Rephidim; but *there was* no water for the people to drink. **2** Therefore the people contended with Moses, and said, "Give us water, that we may drink." So Moses said to them, "Why do you contend with me? Why do you tempt the LORD?" **3** And the people thirsted there for water, and the people com-

plained against Moses, and said, "Why *is* it you have brought us up out of Egypt, to kill us and our children and our livestock with thirst?" **4** So Moses cried out to the LORD, saying, "What shall I do with this people? They are almost ready to stone me!" **5** And the LORD said to Moses, "Go on before the people, and take with you some of the elders of Israel. Also take in your hand your rod with which you struck the river, and go. **6** Behold, I will stand before you there on the rock in Horeb; and you shall strike the rock, and water will come out of it, that the people may drink." And Moses did so in the sight of the elders of Israel.

Meribah in Kadesh. **Num 20:1–11**

Oreb.

Judg 7:25 And they captured two princes of the Midianites, Oreb and Zeeb. They killed Oreb at the rock of Oreb, and Zeeb they killed at the winepress of Zeeb. They pursued Midian and brought the heads of Oreb and Zeeb to Gideon on the other side of the Jordan.

Is 10:26 And the LORD of hosts will stir up a scourge for him like the slaughter of Midian at the rock of Oreb; *as* His rod was on the sea, so will He lift it up in the manner of Egypt.

Rimmon.

Judg 20:45 Then they turned and fled toward the wilderness to the rock of Rimmon; and they cut down five thousand of them on the highways. Then they pursued them relentlessly up to Gidom, and killed two thousand of them.

Seneh.

1 Sam 14:4 Between the passes, by which Jonathan sought to go over to the Philistines' garrison, *there was* a sharp rock on one side and a sharp rock on the other side. And the name of one *was* Bozez, and the name of the other Seneh.

Rock of Escape in the Wilderness of Maon.

1 Sam 23:25 When Saul and his men went to seek *him*, they told David. Therefore he went down to the rock, and stayed in the Wilderness of Maon. And when Saul heard *that*, he pursued David in the Wilderness of Maon.

1 Sam 23:28 Therefore Saul returned from pursuing David, and went against the Philistines; so they called that place the Rock of Escape.

Sela in the Valley of Salt.

2 Kin 14:7 He killed ten thousand Edomites in the Valley of Salt, and took Sela by war, and called its name Joktheel to this day.

2 Chr 25:11–12 Then Amaziah strengthened himself, and leading his people, he went to the Valley of Salt and killed ten thousand of the people of Seir. **12** Also the children of Judah took captive ten thousand alive, brought them to the top of the rock, and cast them down from the top of the rock, so that they all were dashed in pieces.

Man's industry in cutting through.

Job 28:9–10 He puts his hand on the flint; He overturns the mountains at the roots. **10** He cuts out channels in the rocks, And his eye sees every precious thing.

Hammers used for breaking.

Jer 23:29 "Is not My word like a fire?" says the LORD, "And like a hammer *that* breaks the rock in pieces?

Casting down from, a punishment.

2 Chr 25:12 Also the children of Judah took captive ten thousand alive, brought them to the top of the rock, and cast them down from the top of the rock, so that they all were dashed in pieces.

Miracles connected with,

Water brought from.

Ex 17:6 Behold, I will stand before you there on the rock in Horeb; and you shall strike the rock, and water will come out of it, that the people may drink." And Moses did so in the sight of the elders of Israel.

Num 20:11 Then Moses lifted his hand and struck the rock twice with his rod; and water came out abundantly, and the congregation and their animals drank.

Fire ascended out of.

Judg 6:21 Then the Angel of the LORD put out the end of the staff that *was* in His hand, and touched the meat and the unleavened bread; and fire rose out of the rock and consumed the meat and the unleavened bread. And the Angel of the LORD departed out of his sight.

Broken in pieces by the wind.

1 Kin 19:11 Then He said, "Go out, and stand on the mountain before the LORD." And behold, the LORD passed by, and a great and strong wind tore into the mountains and broke the rocks in pieces before the LORD, *but* the LORD *was* not in the wind; and after the wind an earthquake, *but* the LORD *was* not in the earthquake;

Split at the death of Christ.

Matt 27:51 Then, behold, the veil of the temple was torn in two from top to bottom; and the earth quaked, and the rocks were split,

God's power exhibited in removing.

Job 14:18 "But *as* a mountain falls *and* crumbles away, And *as* a rock is moved from its place;

Nah 1:6 Who can stand before His indignation? And who can endure the fierceness of His anger? His fury is poured out like fire, And the rocks are thrown down by Him.

Illustrative of

God as creator of His people.

Deut 32:18 Of the Rock *who* begot you, you are unmindful, And have forgotten the God who fathered you.

God as the strength of His people.

Ps 18:1–2 I will love You, O LORD, my strength. **2** The LORD is my rock and my fortress and my deliverer; My God, my strength, in whom I will trust; My shield and the horn of my salvation, my stronghold.

Ps 62:7 In God *is* my salvation and my glory; The rock of my strength, *And* my refuge, *is* in God.

Is 17:10 Because you have forgotten the God of your salvation, And have not been mindful of the Rock of your stronghold, Therefore you will plant pleasant plants And set out foreign seedlings;

God as defense of His people.

Ps 31:2–3 Bow down Your ear to me, Deliver me speedily; Be my rock of refuge, A fortress of defense to save me. **3** For You *are* my rock and my fortress; Therefore, for Your name's sake, Lead me and guide me.

God as refuge of His people.

Ps 94:22 But the LORD has been my defense, And my God the rock of my refuge.

God as salvation of His people.

Deut 32:15 "But Jeshurun grew fat and kicked; You grew fat, you grew thick, You are obese! Then he forsook God *who* made him, And scornfully esteemed the Rock of his salvation.

Ps 89:26 He shall cry to Me, 'You *are* my Father, My God, and the rock of my salvation.'

Ps 95:1 Oh come, let us sing to the LORD! Let us shout joyfully to the Rock of our salvation.

Christ as refuge of His people.

Is 32:2 A man will be as a hiding place from the wind, And a cover from the tempest, As rivers of water in a dry place, As the shadow of a great rock in a weary land.

Christ as foundation of His church.

Matt 16:18 And I also say to you that you are Peter, and on this rock I will build My church, and the gates of Hades shall not prevail against it.

1 Pet 2:6 Therefore it is also contained in the Scripture, *"Behold, I lay in Zion A chief cornerstone, elect, precious, And he who believes on Him will by no means be put to shame."*

Christ as source of spiritual gifts.

1 Cor 10:4 and all drank the same spiritual drink. For they drank of that spiritual Rock that followed them, and that Rock was Christ.

Christ as a stumbling stone to the wicked.

Is 8:14 He will be as a sanctuary, But a stone of stumbling and a rock of offense To both the houses of Israel, As a trap and a snare to the inhabitants of Jerusalem.

Rom 9:33 As it is written: *"Behold, I lay in Zion a stumbling stone and rock of offense, And whoever believes on Him will not be put to shame."*

1 Pet 2:8 and *"A stone of stumbling And a rock of offense."* They stumble, being disobedient to the word, to which they also were appointed.

A place of safety.

Ps 27:5 For in the time of trouble He shall hide me in His pavilion; In the secret place of His tabernacle He shall hide me; He shall set me high upon a rock.

Ps 40:2 He also brought me up out of a horrible pit, Out of the miry clay, And set my feet upon a rock, *And* established my steps.

Whatever we trust in.

Deut 32:31 For their rock *is* not like our Rock, Even our enemies themselves *being* judges.

Deut 32:37 He will say: 'Where *are* their gods, The rock in which they sought refuge?

The ancestor of a nation.

Is 51:1 "Listen to Me, you who follow after righteousness, You who seek the LORD: Look to the rock *from which* you were hewn, And to the hole of the pit *from which* you were dug.

ROMAN EMPIRE, THE

Called the world.

Luke 2:1 And it came to pass in those days *that* a decree went out from Caesar Augustus that all the world should be registered.

Represented by

Legs of iron in Nebuchadnezzar's vision.

Dan 2:33 its legs of iron, its feet partly of iron and partly of clay.

Dan 2:40 And the fourth kingdom shall be as strong as iron, inasmuch as iron breaks in pieces and shatters everything; and like iron that crushes, *that kingdom* will break in pieces and crush all the others.

Terrible beast in Daniel's vision.

Dan 7:7 "After this I saw in the night visions, and behold, a fourth beast, dreadful and terrible, exceedingly strong. It had huge iron teeth; it was devouring, breaking in pieces, and trampling the residue with its feet. It *was* different from all the beasts that *were* before it, and it had ten horns.

Dan 7:19 "Then I wished to know the truth about the fourth beast, which was different from all the others, exceedingly dreadful, *with* its teeth of iron and its nails of bronze, *which* devoured, broke in pieces, and trampled the residue with its feet;

Rome the capital of.

Acts 18:2 And he found a certain Jew named Aquila, born in Pontus, who had recently come from Italy with his wife Priscilla (because Claudius had commanded all the Jews to depart from Rome); and he came to them.

Acts 19:21 When these things were accomplished, Paul purposed in the Spirit, when he had passed through Macedonia and Achaia, to go to Jerusalem, saying, "After I have been there, I must also see Rome."

Judea a province of, under a procurator or governor.

Luke 3:2 while Annas and Caiaphas were high priests, the word of God came to John the son of Zacharias in the wilderness.

Acts 23:34 And when the governor had read *it*, he asked what province he was from. And when he understood that *he was* from Cilicia,

Acts 23:26 Claudius Lysias, To the most excellent governor Felix: Greetings.

Acts 25:1 Now when Festus had come to the province, after three days he went up from Caesarea to Jerusalem.

Allusions to military affairs of,

Strict obedience to superiors.

Matt 8:8–9 The centurion answered and said, "Lord, I am not worthy that You should come under my roof. But only speak a word, and my servant will be healed. 9 For I also am a man under authority, having soldiers under me. And I say to this *one*, 'Go,' and he goes; and to another, 'Come,' and he comes; and to my servant, 'Do this,' and he does *it*."

Use of the panoply or defensive armor.

Rom 13:12 The night is far spent, the day is at hand. Therefore let us cast off the works of darkness, and let us put on the armor of light.

2 Cor 6:7 by the word of truth, by the power of God, by the armor of righteousness on the right hand and on the left,

Eph 6:11–17 Put on the whole armor of God, that you may be able to stand against the wiles of the devil. 12 For we do not wrestle against flesh and blood, but against principalities, against powers, against the rulers of the darkness of this age, against spiritual *hosts* of wickedness in the heavenly *places*. 13 Therefore take up the whole armor of God, that you may be able to withstand in the evil day, and having done all, to stand. 14 Stand therefore, having girded your waist with truth, having put on the breastplate of righteousness, 15 and having shod your feet with the preparation of the gospel of peace; 16 above all, taking the shield of faith with which you will be able to quench all the fiery darts of the wicked one. 17 And take the helmet of salvation, and the sword of the Spirit, which is the word of God;

The soldier's harsh life.

2 Tim 2:3–4 You therefore must endure hardship as a good soldier of Jesus Christ. 4 No one engaged in warfare entangles himself with the affairs of *this* life, that he may please him who enlisted him as a soldier.

The soldier's special comrade who shared his toils and dangers.

Phil 2:25 Yet I considered it necessary to send to you Epaphroditus, my brother, fellow worker, and fellow soldier, but your messenger and the one who ministered to my need;

Danger of sentinels' sleeping.

Matt 28:13–14 saying, "Tell them, 'His disciples came at night and stole Him *away* while we slept.' 14 And if this comes to the governor's ears, we will appease him and make you secure."

Removing from the muster roll names of soldiers guilty of crimes.

Rev 3:5 He who overcomes shall be clothed in white garments, and I will not blot out his name from the Book of Life; but I will confess his name before My Father and before His angels.

Crowning of soldiers who distinguished themselves.

2 Tim 4:7–8 I have fought the good fight, I have finished the race, I have kept the faith. 8 Finally, there is laid up for me the crown of righteousness, which the Lord, the righteous Judge, will give to me on that Day, and not to me only but also to all who have loved His appearing.

Triumphs of victorious generals.

2 Cor 2:14–16 Now thanks *be* to God who always leads us in triumph in Christ, and through us diffuses the fragrance of His knowledge in every place. 15 For we are to God the fragrance of Christ among those who are being saved and among those who are perishing. 16 To the one *we are* the aroma of death *leading* to death, and to the other the aroma of life *leading* to life. And who *is* sufficient for these things?

Col 2:15 Having disarmed principalities and powers, He made a public spectacle of them, triumphing over them in it.

Different military officers.

Acts 21:31 Now as they were seeking to kill him, news came to the commander of the garrison that all Jerusalem was in an uproar.

Acts 23:23–24 And he called for two centurions, saying,

"Prepare two hundred soldiers, seventy horsemen, and two hundred spearmen to go to Caesarea at the third hour of the night; 24 and provide mounts to set Paul on, and bring *him* safely to Felix the governor."

Italian and Augustan regiments.

Acts 10:1 There was a certain man in Caesarea called Cornelius, a centurion of what was called the Italian Regiment,

Acts 27:1 And when it was decided that we should sail to Italy, they delivered Paul and some other prisoners to *one* named Julius, a centurion of the Augustan Regiment.

Allusions to judicial affairs of,

Person accused, examined by scourging.

Acts 22:24 the commander ordered him to be brought into the barracks, and said that he should be examined under scourging, so that he might know why they shouted so against him.

Acts 22:29 Then immediately those who were about to examine him withdrew from him; and the commander was also afraid after he found out that he was a Roman, and because he had bound him.

Criminals delivered over to the soldiers for execution.

Matt 27:26–27 Then he released Barabbas to them; and when he had scourged Jesus, he delivered *Him* to be crucified. 27 Then the soldiers of the governor took Jesus into the Praetorium and gathered the whole garrison around Him.

Accusation in writing placed over the head of those executed.

John 19:19 Now Pilate wrote a title and put *it* on the cross. And the writing was: JESUS OF NAZARETH, THE KING OF THE JEWS.

Garments of those executed given to the soldiers.

Matt 27:35 Then they crucified Him, and divided His garments, casting lots, that it might be fulfilled which was spoken by the prophet: *"They divided My garments among them, And for My clothing they cast lots."*

John 19:23 Then the soldiers, when they had crucified Jesus, took His garments and made four parts, to each soldier a part, and also the tunic. Now the tunic was without seam, woven from the top in one piece.

Prisoners chained to soldiers for safety.

Acts 21:33 Then the commander came near and took him, and commanded *him* to be bound with two chains; and he asked who he was and what he had done.

Acts 12:6 And when Herod was about to bring him out, that night Peter was sleeping, bound with two chains between two soldiers; and the guards before the door were keeping the prison.

2 Tim 1:16 The Lord grant mercy to the household of Onesiphorus, for he often refreshed me, and was not ashamed of my chain;

Acts 28:16 Now when we came to Rome, the centurion delivered the prisoners to the captain of the guard; but Paul was permitted to dwell by himself with the soldier who guarded him.

Accusers and accused confronted together.

Acts 23:35 he said, "I will hear you when your accusers

also have come." And he commanded him to be kept in Herod's Praetorium.

Acts 25:16–19 To them I answered, 'It is not the custom of the Romans to deliver any man to destruction before the accused meets the accusers face to face, and has opportunity to answer for himself concerning the charge against him.' 17 Therefore when they had come together, without any delay, the next day I sat on the judgment seat and commanded the man to be brought in. 18 When the accusers stood up, they brought no accusation against him of such things as I supposed, 19 but had some questions against him about their own religion and about a certain Jesus, who had died, whom Paul affirmed to be alive.

Accused person protected from popular violence.

Acts 23:20 And he said, "The Jews have agreed to ask that you bring Paul down to the council tomorrow, as though they were going to inquire more fully about him.

Acts 23:24–27 and provide mounts to set Paul on, and bring *him* safely to Felix the governor." 25 He wrote a letter in the following manner: 26 Claudius Lysias, To the most excellent governor Felix: Greetings. 27 This man was seized by the Jews and was about to be killed by them. Coming with the troops I rescued him, having learned that he was a Roman.

Power of life and death vested in its authorities.

John 18:31 Then Pilate said to them, "You take Him and judge Him according to your law." Therefore the Jews said to him, "It is not lawful for us to put anyone to death,"

John 18:39–40 "But you have a custom that I should release someone to you at the Passover. Do you therefore want me to release to you the King of the Jews?" 40 Then they all cried again, saying, "Not this Man, but Barabbas!" Now Barabbas was a robber.

John 19:10 Then Pilate said to Him, "Are You not speaking to me? Do You not know that I have power to crucify You, and power to release You?"

All appeals made to the emperor.

Acts 25:11–12 For if I am an offender, or have committed anything deserving of death, I do not object to dying; but if there is nothing in these things of which these men accuse me, no one can deliver me to them. I appeal to Caesar." 12 Then Festus, when he had conferred with the council, answered, "You have appealed to Caesar? To Caesar you shall go!"

Those who appealed to Caesar, to be brought before him.

Acts 26:32 Then Agrippa said to Festus, "This man might have been set free if he had not appealed to Caesar."

Allusions to citizenship of,

Obtained by purchase.

Acts 22:28 The commander answered, "With a large sum I obtained this citizenship." And Paul said, "But I was born *a citizen*."

Obtained by birth.

Acts 22:28 The commander answered, "With a large sum I obtained this citizenship." And Paul said, "But I was born *a citizen*."

Brought exemption from scourging.

Acts 16:37–38 But Paul said to them, "They have beaten us openly, uncondemned Romans, *and* have thrown *us* into prison. And now do they put us out secretly? No indeed! Let them come themselves and get us out." **38** And the officers told these words to the magistrates, and they were afraid when they heard that they were Romans.

Acts 22:25 And as they bound him with thongs, Paul said to the centurion who stood by, "Is it lawful for you to scourge a man who is a Roman, and uncondemned?"

Allusions to Greek games adapted by

Gladiatorial fights.

1 Cor 4:9 For I think that God has displayed us, the apostles, last, as men condemned to death; for we have been made a spectacle to the world, both to angels and to men.

1 Cor 15:32 If, in the manner of men, I have fought with beasts at Ephesus, what advantage *is it* to me? If *the* dead do not rise, *"Let us eat and drink, for tomorrow we die!"*

Foot races.

1 Cor 9:24 Do you not know that those who run in a race all run, but one receives the prize? Run in such a way that you may obtain *it*.

Phil 2:16 holding fast the word of life, so that I may rejoice in the day of Christ that I have not run in vain or labored in vain.

Phil 3:11–14 if, by any means, I may attain to the resurrection from the dead. **12** Not that I have already attained, or am already perfected; but I press on, that I may lay hold of that for which Christ Jesus has also laid hold of me. **13** Brethren, I do not count myself to have apprehended; but one thing I *do*, forgetting those things which are behind and reaching forward to those things which are ahead, **14** I press toward the goal for the prize of the upward call of God in Christ Jesus.

Heb 12:1–2 Therefore we also, since we are surrounded by so great a cloud of witnesses, let us lay aside every weight, and the sin which so easily ensnares *us*, and let us run with endurance the race that is set before us, **2** looking unto Jesus, the author and finisher of *our* faith, who for the joy that was set before Him endured the cross, despising the shame, and has sat down at the right hand of the throne of God.

Wrestling.

Eph 6:12 For we do not wrestle against flesh and blood, but against principalities, against powers, against the rulers of the darkness of this age, against spiritual *hosts* of wickedness in the heavenly *places*.

Training of combatants.

1 Cor 9:25 And everyone who competes *for the prize* is temperate in all things. Now they *do it* to obtain a perishable crown, but we *for* an imperishable *crown*.

1 Cor 9:27 But I discipline my body and bring *it* into subjection, lest, when I have preached to others, I myself should become disqualified.

Crowning of conquerors.

1 Cor 9:25 And everyone who competes *for the prize* is temperate in all things. Now they *do it* to obtain a perishable crown, but we *for* an imperishable *crown*.

Phil 3:14 I press toward the goal for the prize of the upward call of God in Christ Jesus.

2 Tim 4:8 Finally, there is laid up for me the crown of righteousness, which the Lord, the righteous Judge, will give to me on that Day, and not to me only but also to all who have loved His appearing.

Competing according to rules.

2 Tim 2:5 And also if anyone competes in athletics, he is not crowned unless he competes according to the rules.

Emperors of, mentioned

Tiberius.

Luke 3:1 Now in the fifteenth year of the reign of Tiberius Caesar, Pontius Pilate being governor of Judea, Herod being tetrarch of Galilee, his brother Philip tetrarch of Iturea and the region of Trachonitis, and Lysanias tetrarch of Abilene,

Augustus.

Luke 2:1 And it came to pass in those days *that* a decree went out from Caesar Augustus that all the world should be registered.

Claudius.

Acts 11:28 Then one of them, named Agabus, stood up and showed by the Spirit that there was going to be a great famine throughout all the world, which also happened in the days of Claudius Caesar.

Nero (as Caesar).

Acts 25:10 So Paul said, "I stand at Caesar's judgment seat, where I ought to be judged. To the Jews I have done no wrong, as you very well know.

Phil 4:22 All the saints greet you, but especially those who are of Caesar's household.

Predictions respecting,

Its universal dominion.

Dan 7:23 "Thus he said: 'The fourth beast shall be A fourth kingdom on earth, Which shall be different from all *other* kingdoms, And shall devour the whole earth, Trample it and break it in pieces.

Its division into ten parts.

Dan 2:41–43 Whereas you saw the feet and toes, partly of potter's clay and partly of iron, the kingdom shall be divided; yet the strength of the iron shall be in it, just as you saw the iron mixed with ceramic clay. **42** And *as* the toes of the feet *were* partly of iron and partly of clay, *so* the kingdom shall be partly strong and partly fragile. **43** As you saw iron mixed with ceramic clay, they will mingle with the seed of men; but they will not adhere to one another, just as iron does not mix with clay.

Dan 7:20 and the ten horns that *were* on its head, and the other *horn* which came up, before which three fell, namely, that horn which had eyes and a mouth which spoke pompous words, whose appearance *was* greater than his fellows.

Dan 7:24 The ten horns *are* ten kings *Who* shall arise from this kingdom. And another shall rise after them; He shall be different from the first *ones*, And shall subdue three kings.

SABBATH, THE

Instituted by God.

Gen 2:3 Then God blessed the seventh day and sanctified it, because in it He rested from all His work which God had created and made.

Grounds of its institution.

Gen 2:2–3 And on the seventh day God ended His work which He had done, and He rested on the seventh day from all His work which He had done. 3 Then God blessed the seventh day and sanctified it, because in it He rested from all His work which God had created and made.

Ex 20:11 For *in* six days the LORD made the heavens and the earth, the sea, and all that *is* in them, and rested the seventh day. Therefore the LORD blessed the Sabbath day and hallowed it.

The seventh day observed as.

Ex 20:9–11 Six days you shall labor and do all your work, **10** but the seventh day *is* the Sabbath of the LORD your God. *In it* you shall do no work: you, nor your son, nor your daughter, nor your male servant, nor your female servant, nor your cattle, nor your stranger who *is* within your gates. **11** For *in* six days the LORD made the heavens and the earth, the sea, and all that *is* in them, and rested the seventh day. Therefore the LORD blessed the Sabbath day and hallowed it.

Made for man.

Mark 2:27 And He said to them, "The Sabbath was made for man, and not man for the Sabbath.

God

Blessed.

Gen 2:3 Then God blessed the seventh day and sanctified it, because in it He rested from all His work which God had created and made.

Ex 20:11 For *in* six days the LORD made the heavens and the earth, the sea, and all that *is* in them, and rested the seventh day. Therefore the LORD blessed the Sabbath day and hallowed it.

Sanctified.

Gen 2:3 Then God blessed the seventh day and sanctified it, because in it He rested from all His work which God had created and made.

Ex 31:15 Work shall be done for six days, but the seventh *is* the Sabbath of rest, holy to the LORD. Whoever does *any* work on the Sabbath day, he shall surely be put to death.

Hallowed.

Ex 20:11 For *in* six days the LORD made the heavens and the earth, the sea, and all that *is* in them, and rested the seventh day. Therefore the LORD blessed the Sabbath day and hallowed it.

Commanded its observance.

Ex 20:8 "Remember the Sabbath day, to keep it holy.

Lev 19:3 'Every one of you shall revere his mother and his father, and keep My Sabbaths: I *am* the LORD your God.

Lev 19:30 'You shall keep My Sabbaths and reverence My sanctuary: I *am* the LORD.

Observance of, remembers His goodness.

Deut 5:15 And remember that you were a slave in the land of Egypt, and the LORD your God brought you out from there by a mighty hand and by an outstretched arm; therefore the LORD your God commanded you to keep the Sabbath day.

Shows favor in appointing.

Ex 23:12 Six days you shall do your work, and on the seventh day you shall rest, that your ox and your donkey may rest, and the son of your female servant and the stranger may be refreshed.

Neh 9:14 You made known to them Your holy Sabbath, And commanded them precepts, statutes and laws, By the hand of Moses Your servant.

A sign of the covenant.

Ex 31:13 "Speak also to the children of Israel, saying: 'Surely My Sabbaths you shall keep, for it *is* a sign between Me and you throughout your generations, that *you* may know that I *am* the LORD who sanctifies you.

Ex 31:17 It *is* a sign between Me and the children of Israel forever; for *in* six days the LORD made the heavens and the earth, and on the seventh day He rested and was refreshed.' "

A type of the heavenly rest.

Heb 4:4 For He has spoken in a certain place of the seventh *day* in this way: "*And God rested on the seventh day from all His works*";

Heb 4:9 There remains therefore a rest for the people of God.

Christ

Is Lord of.

Mark 2:28 Therefore the Son of Man is also Lord of the Sabbath."

Was accustomed to observe.

Luke 4:16 So He came to Nazareth, where He had been brought up. And as His custom was, He went into the synagogue on the Sabbath day, and stood up to read.

Taught on.

Luke 4:31 Then He went down to Capernaum, a city of Galilee, and was teaching them on the Sabbaths.

Luke 6:6 Now it happened on another Sabbath, also, that He entered the synagogue and taught. And a man was there whose right hand was withered.

Healed on.

Matt 12:6–14 Yet I say to you that in this place there is *One* greater than the temple. **7** But if you had known what *this* means, *'I desire mercy and not sacrifice,'* you would not have condemned the guiltless. **8** For the Son of Man is Lord even of the Sabbath." **9** Now when He had departed from there, He went into their synagogue. **10** And behold, there was a man who had a withered hand. And they asked Him, saying, "Is it lawful to heal on the Sabbath?"—that they might accuse Him. **11** Then He said to them, "What man is there among you who has one sheep, and if it falls into a pit on the Sabbath, will not lay hold of it and lift *it* out? **12** Of how much more value then is a man than a sheep? Therefore it is lawful to do good on the Sabbath." **13** Then He said to the man, "Stretch out your hand." And he stretched *it* out, and it was restored as whole as the other. **14** Then the Pharisees went out and plotted against Him, how they might destroy Him.

Cf. Mark 3:1–6; Luke 6:5–11; 14:1–5

Servants and cattle should be allowed to rest on.

Ex 20:10 but the seventh day *is* the Sabbath of the LORD your God. *In it* you shall do no work: you, nor your son, nor your daughter, nor your male servant, nor your female servant, nor your cattle, nor your stranger who *is* within your gates.

Deut 5:14 but the seventh day *is* the Sabbath of the LORD your God. *In it* you shall do no work: you, nor your son, nor your daughter, nor your male servant, nor your female servant, nor your ox, nor your donkey, nor any of your cattle, nor your stranger who *is* within your gates, that your male servant and your female servant may rest as well as you.

No manner of work to be done on.

Ex 20:10 but the seventh day *is* the Sabbath of the LORD your God. *In it* you shall do no work: you, nor your son, nor your daughter, nor your male servant, nor your female servant, nor your cattle, nor your stranger who *is* within your gates.

Lev 23:3 'Six days shall work be done, but the seventh day *is* a Sabbath of solemn rest, a holy convocation. You shall do no work *on it; it is* the Sabbath of the LORD in all your dwellings.

No purchases to be made on.

Neh 10:31 *if* the peoples of the land brought wares or any grain to sell on the Sabbath day, we would not buy it from them on the Sabbath, or on a holy day; and we would forego the seventh year's *produce* and the exacting of every debt.

Neh 13:15–17 In those days I saw *people* in Judah treading wine presses on the Sabbath, and bringing in sheaves, and loading donkeys with wine, grapes, figs, and all *kinds of* burdens, which they brought into Jerusalem on the Sabbath day. And I warned *them* about the day on which they were selling provisions. **16** Men of Tyre dwelt there also, who brought in fish and all kinds of goods, and sold *them* on the Sabbath to the children of Judah, and in Jerusalem. **17** Then I contended with the nobles of Judah, and said to

them, "What evil thing *is* this that you do, by which you profane the Sabbath day?

No burdens to be carried on.

Neh 13:19 So it was, at the gates of Jerusalem, as it began to be dark before the Sabbath, that I commanded the gates to be shut, and charged that they must not be opened till after the Sabbath. Then I posted *some* of my servants at the gates, *so that* no burdens would be brought in on the Sabbath day.

Jer 17:21 Thus says the LORD: "Take heed to yourselves, and bear no burden on the Sabbath day, nor bring *it* in by the gates of Jerusalem;

Divine worship to be celebrated on.

Ezek 46:3 Likewise the people of the land shall worship at the entrance to this gateway before the LORD on the Sabbaths and the New Moons.

Acts 16:13 And on the Sabbath day we went out of the city to the riverside, where prayer was customarily made; and we sat down and spoke to the women who met *there.*

The Scriptures to be read on.

Acts 13:27 For those who dwell in Jerusalem, and their rulers, because they did not know Him, nor even the voices of the Prophets which are read every Sabbath, have fulfilled *them* in condemning *Him.*

Acts 15:21 For Moses has had throughout many generations those who preach him in every city, being read in the synagogues every Sabbath."

The Word of God to be preached on.

Acts 13:14–15 But when they departed from Perga, they came to Antioch in Pisidia, and went into the synagogue on the Sabbath day and sat down. **15** And after the reading of the Law and the Prophets, the rulers of the synagogue sent to them, saying, "Men *and* brethren, if you have any word of exhortation for the people, say on."

Acts 13:44 On the next Sabbath almost the whole city came together to hear the word of God.

Acts 17:2 Then Paul, as his custom was, went in to them, and for three Sabbaths reasoned with them from the Scriptures,

Acts 18:4 And he reasoned in the synagogue every Sabbath, and persuaded both Jews and Greeks.

Works connected with religious service lawful on.

Num 28:9 'And on the Sabbath day two lambs in their first year, without blemish, and two-tenths *of an ephah* of fine flour as a grain offering, mixed with oil, with its drink offering—

Matt 12:5 Or have you not read in the law that on the Sabbath the priests in the temple profane the Sabbath, and are blameless?

John 7:23 If a man receives circumcision on the Sabbath, so that the law of Moses should not be broken, are you angry with Me because I made a man completely well on the Sabbath?

Works of mercy lawful on.

Matt 12:12 Of how much more value then is a man than a sheep? Therefore it is lawful to do good on the Sabbath."

Luke 13:16 So ought not this woman, being a daughter of Abraham, whom Satan has bound—think of it—

for eighteen years, be loosed from this bond on the Sabbath?"

John 9:14 Now it was a Sabbath when Jesus made the clay and opened his eyes.

Necessary wants may be supplied on.

Matt 12:1 At that time Jesus went through the grainfields on the Sabbath. And His disciples were hungry, and began to pluck heads of grain and to eat.

Luke 13:15 The Lord then answered him and said, "Hypocrite! Does not each one of you on the Sabbath loose his ox or donkey from the stall, and lead *it* away to water it?

Luke 14:1 Now it happened, as He went into the house of one of the rulers of the Pharisees to eat bread on the Sabbath, that they watched Him closely.

Called

The Sabbath of the Lord.

Ex 20:10 but the seventh day *is* the Sabbath of the LORD your God. *In it* you shall do no work: you, nor your son, nor your daughter, nor your male servant, nor your female servant, nor your cattle, nor your stranger who *is* within your gates.

Lev 23:3 'Six days shall work be done, but the seventh day *is* a Sabbath of solemn rest, a holy convocation. You shall do no work *on it*; it *is* the Sabbath of the LORD in all your dwellings.

Deut 5:14 but the seventh day *is* the Sabbath of the LORD your God. *In it* you shall do no work: you, nor your son, nor your daughter, nor your male servant, nor your female servant, nor your ox, nor your donkey, nor any of your cattle, nor your stranger who *is* within your gates, that your male servant and your female servant may rest as well as you.

The Sabbath of rest.

Ex 31:15 Work shall be done for six days, but the seventh *is* the Sabbath of rest, holy to the LORD. Whoever does *any* work on the Sabbath day, he shall surely be put to death.

A holy Sabbath to the Lord.

Ex 16:23 Then he said to them, "This *is what* the LORD has said: 'Tomorrow *is* a Sabbath rest, a holy Sabbath to the LORD. Bake what you will bake *today,* and boil what you will boil; and lay up for yourselves all that remains, to be kept until morning.' "

God's holy day.

Is 58:13 "If you turn away your foot from the Sabbath, *From* doing your pleasure on My holy day, And call the Sabbath a delight, The holy *day* of the LORD honorable, And shall honor Him, not doing your own ways, Nor finding your own pleasure, Nor speaking *your own* words,

The Lord's Day.

Rev 1:10 I was in the Spirit on the Lord's Day, and I heard behind me a loud voice, as of a trumpet,

Old Testament saints were to

Observe.

Neh 13:22 And I commanded the Levites that they should cleanse themselves, and that they should go and guard the gates, to sanctify the Sabbath day. Remember me, O my God, *concerning* this also, and spare me according to the greatness of Your mercy!

Is 58:13 "If you turn away your foot from the Sabbath, *From* doing your pleasure on My holy day, And call the Sabbath a delight, The holy *day* of the LORD honorable, And shall honor Him, not doing your own ways, Nor finding your own pleasure, Nor speaking *your own* words,

Rejoice in.

Ps 118:24 This *is* the day the LORD has made; We will rejoice and be glad in it.

Is 58:13 "If you turn away your foot from the Sabbath, *From* doing your pleasure on My holy day, And call the Sabbath a delight, The holy *day* of the LORD honorable, And shall honor Him, not doing your own ways, Nor finding your own pleasure, Nor speaking *your own* words,

Testify against those who desecrated.

Neh 13:15 In those days I saw *people* in Judah treading wine presses on the Sabbath, and bringing in sheaves, and loading donkeys with wine, grapes, figs, and all *kinds of* burdens, which they brought into Jerusalem on the Sabbath day. And I warned *them* about the day on which they were selling provisions.

Neh 13:20–21 Now the merchants and sellers of all kinds of wares lodged outside Jerusalem once or twice. **21** Then I warned them, and said to them, "Why do you spend the night around the wall? If you do *so* again, I will lay hands on you!" From that time on they came no *more* on the Sabbath.

Observance of, to be perpetual.

Ex 31:16–17 Therefore the children of Israel shall keep the Sabbath, to observe the Sabbath throughout their generations *as* a perpetual covenant. **17** It *is* a sign between Me and the children of Israel forever; for *in* six days the LORD made the heavens and the earth, and on the seventh day He rested and was refreshed.' "

Matt 5:17–18 "Do not think that I came to destroy the Law or the Prophets. I did not come to destroy but to fulfill. **18** For assuredly, I say to you, till heaven and earth pass away, one jot or one tittle will by no means pass from the law till all is fulfilled.

Blessedness of honoring.

Is 56:2 Blessed *is* the man *who* does this, And the son of man *who* lays hold on it; Who keeps from defiling the Sabbath, And keeps his hand from doing any evil."

Is 56:6 "Also the sons of the foreigner Who join themselves to the LORD, to serve Him, and to love the name of the LORD, to be His servants— Everyone who keeps from defiling the Sabbath, And holds fast My covenant—

Is 58:13–14 "If you turn away your foot from the Sabbath, *From* doing your pleasure on My holy day, And call the Sabbath a delight, The holy *day* of the LORD honorable, And shall honor Him, not doing your own ways, Nor finding your own pleasure, Nor speaking *your own* words, **14** Then you shall delight yourself in the LORD; And I will cause you to ride on the high hills of the earth, And feed you with the heritage of Jacob your father. The mouth of the LORD has spoken."

Denunciations against those who profane.

Neh 13:18 Did not your fathers do thus, and did not our God bring all this disaster on us and on this city? Yet you bring added wrath on Israel by profaning the Sabbath."

Jer 17:27 "But if you will not heed Me to hallow the Sabbath day, such as not carrying a burden when entering the gates of Jerusalem on the Sabbath day, then I will kindle a fire in its gates, and it shall devour the palaces of Jerusalem, and it shall not be quenched." ' "

Punishment of those who profane.

Ex 31:14–15 You shall keep the Sabbath, therefore, for *it is* holy to you. Everyone who profanes it shall surely be put to death; for whoever does *any* work on it, that person shall be cut off from among his people. **15** Work shall be done for six days, but the seventh *is* the Sabbath of rest, holy to the LORD. Whoever does *any* work on the Sabbath day, he shall surely be put to death.

Num 15:32–36 Now while the children of Israel were in the wilderness, they found a man gathering sticks on the Sabbath day. **33** And those who found him gathering sticks brought him to Moses and Aaron, and to all the congregation. **34** They put him under guard, because it had not been explained what should be done to him. **35** Then the LORD said to Moses, "The man must surely be put to death; all the congregation shall stone him with stones outside the camp." **36** So, as the LORD commanded Moses, all the congregation brought him outside the camp and stoned him with stones, and he died.

The wicked

Defile.

Is 56:2 Blessed *is* the man *who* does this, And the son of man *who* lays hold on it; Who keeps from defiling the Sabbath, And keeps his hand from doing any evil.

Ezek 20:13 Yet the house of Israel rebelled against Me in the wilderness; they did not walk in My statutes; they despised My judgments, 'which, *if* a man does, he shall live by them'; and they greatly defiled My Sabbaths. Then I said I would pour out My fury on them in the wilderness, to consume them.

Profane.

Neh 13:17 Then I contended with the nobles of Judah, and said to them, "What evil thing *is* this that you do, by which you profane the Sabbath day?

Ezek 22:8 You have despised My holy things and profaned My Sabbaths.

Ezek 20:16 because they despised My judgments and did not walk in My statutes, but profaned My Sabbaths; for their heart went after their idols.

Wearied by.

Amos 8:5 Saying: "When will the New Moon be past, That we may sell grain? And the Sabbath, That we may trade wheat? Making the ephah small and the shekel large, Falsifying the scales by deceit,

Hide their eyes from.

Ezek 22:26 Her priests have violated My law and profaned My holy things; they have not distinguished between the holy and unholy, nor have they made known *the difference* between the unclean and the clean; and they have hidden their eyes from My Sabbaths, so that I am profaned among them.

Do their own pleasure on.

Is 58:13 "If you turn away your foot from the Sabbath, *From* doing your pleasure on My holy day, And call the Sabbath a delight, The holy *day* of the LORD honorable, And shall honor Him, not doing your own ways, Nor finding your own pleasure, Nor speaking *your own* words,

Do work and business on.

Neh 10:31 *if* the peoples of the land brought wares or any grain to sell on the Sabbath day, we would not buy it from them on the Sabbath, or on a holy day; and we would forego the seventh year's *produce* and the exacting of every debt.

Neh 13:15–16 In those days I saw *people* in Judah treading wine presses on the Sabbath, and bringing in sheaves, and loading donkeys with wine, grapes, figs, and all *kinds of* burdens, which they brought into Jerusalem on the Sabbath day. And I warned *them* about the day on which they were selling provisions. **16** Men of Tyre dwelt there also, who brought in fish and all kinds of goods, and sold *them* on the Sabbath to the children of Judah, and in Jerusalem.

Sometimes pretend zeal for.

Luke 13:14 But the ruler of the synagogue answered with indignation, because Jesus had healed on the Sabbath; and he said to the crowd, "There are six days on which men ought to work; therefore come and be healed on them, and not on the Sabbath day."

John 9:16 Therefore some of the Pharisees said, "This Man is not from God, because He does not keep the Sabbath." Others said, "How can a man who is a sinner do such signs?" And there was a division among them.

May be judicially deprived of.

Lam 2:6 He has done violence to His tabernacle, *As if it were* a garden; He has destroyed His place of assembly; The LORD has caused The appointed feasts and Sabbaths to be forgotten in Zion. In His burning indignation He has spurned the king and the priest.

Hos 2:11 I will also cause all her mirth to cease, Her feast days, Her New Moons, Her Sabbaths— All her appointed feasts.

Honoring of—exemplified by

Moses.

Num 15:32–34 Now while the children of Israel were in the wilderness, they found a man gathering sticks on the Sabbath day. **33** And those who found him gathering sticks brought him to Moses and Aaron, and to all the congregation. **34** They put him under guard, because it had not been explained what should be done to him.

Nehemiah.

Neh 13:15 In those days I saw *people* in Judah treading wine presses on the Sabbath, and bringing in sheaves, and loading donkeys with wine, grapes, figs, and all *kinds of* burdens, which they brought into Jerusalem on the Sabbath day. And I warned *them* about the day on which they were selling provisions.

Neh 13:21 Then I warned them, and said to them, "Why do you spend the night around the wall? If you do *so* again, I will lay hands on you!" From that time on they came no *more* on the Sabbath.

The women.

Luke 23:56 Then they returned and prepared spices and fragrant oils. And they rested on the Sabbath according to the commandment.

Paul.

Acts 13:14 But when they departed from Perga, they came to Antioch in Pisidia, and went into the synagogue on the Sabbath day and sat down.

The disciples.

Acts 16:13 And on the Sabbath day we went out of the city to the riverside, where prayer was customarily made; and we sat down and spoke to the women who met *there.*

John.

Rev 1:10 I was in the Spirit on the Lord's Day, and I heard behind me a loud voice, as of a trumpet,

Dishonoring of—illustrated by

The gatherers of manna.

Ex 16:27 Now it happened *that some* of the people went out on the seventh day to gather, but they found none.

The gatherers of sticks.

Num 15:32 Now while the children of Israel were in the wilderness, they found a man gathering sticks on the Sabbath day.

The men of Tyre.

Neh 13:16 Men of Tyre dwelt there also, who brought in fish and all kinds of goods, and sold *them* on the Sabbath to the children of Judah, and in Jerusalem.

The inhabitants of Jerusalem.

Jer 17:21–23 Thus says the LORD: "Take heed to yourselves, and bear no burden on the Sabbath day, nor bring *it* in by the gates of Jerusalem; **22** nor carry a burden out of your houses on the Sabbath day, nor do any work, but hallow the Sabbath day, as I commanded your fathers. **23** But they did not obey nor incline their ear, but made their neck stiff, that they might not hear nor receive instruction.

SABBATICAL YEAR, THE

A sabbath for the land.

Lev 25:2 "Speak to the children of Israel, and say to them: 'When you come into the land which I give you, then the land shall keep a sabbath to the LORD.

Kept every seventh year.

Ex 23:11 but the seventh *year* you shall let it rest and lie fallow, that the poor of your people may eat; and what they leave, the beasts of the field may eat. In like manner you shall do with your vineyard *and* your olive grove.

Lev 25:4 but in the seventh year there shall be a sabbath of solemn rest for the land, a sabbath to the LORD. You shall neither sow your field nor prune your vineyard.

Surplus of sixth year to provide for.

Lev 25:20–22 'And if you say, "What shall we eat in the seventh year, since we shall not sow nor gather in our produce?" **21** Then I will command My blessing on you in the sixth year, and it will bring forth produce enough for three years. **22** And you shall sow in the eighth year, and eat old produce until the ninth year; until its produce comes in, you shall eat *of* the old *harvest.*

Enactments respecting,

Cessation of all field labor.

Lev 25:4–5 but in the seventh year there shall be a sabbath of solemn rest for the land, a sabbath to the LORD. You shall neither sow your field nor prune your vineyard. **5** What grows of its own accord of your harvest you shall not reap, nor gather the grapes of your untended vine, *for* it is a year of rest for the land.

The fruits of the earth to be common property.

Ex 23:11 but the seventh *year* you shall let it rest and lie fallow, that the poor of your people may eat; and what they leave, the beasts of the field may eat. In like manner you shall do with your vineyard *and* your olive grove.

Lev 25:6–7 And the sabbath *produce* of the land shall be food for you: for you, your male and female servants, your hired man, and the stranger who dwells with you, **7** for your livestock and the beasts that *are* in your land—all its produce shall be for food.

Remission of debts.

Deut 15:1–3 "At the end of *every* seven years you shall grant a release *of debts.* **2** And this *is* the form of the release: Every creditor who has lent *anything* to his neighbor shall release *it*; he shall not require *it* of his neighbor or his brother, because it is called the LORD's release. **3** Of a foreigner you may require *it*; but you shall give up your claim to what is owed by your brother,

Neh 10:31 *if* the peoples of the land brought wares or any grain to sell on the Sabbath day, we would not buy it from them on the Sabbath, or on a holy day; and we would forego the seventh year's *produce* and the exacting of every debt.

Release of all Hebrew servants.

Ex 21:2 If you buy a Hebrew servant, he shall serve six years; and in the seventh he shall go out free and pay nothing.

Deut 15:12 "If your brother, a Hebrew man, or a Hebrew woman, is sold to you and serves you six years, then in the seventh year you shall let him go free from you.

Public reading of the law at the Feast of Tabernacles.

Deut 31:10–13 And Moses commanded them, saying: "At the end of *every* seven years, at the appointed time in the year of release, at the Feast of Tabernacles, **11** when all Israel comes to appear before the LORD your God in the place which He chooses, you shall read this law before all Israel in their hearing. **12** Gather the people together, men and women and little ones, and the stranger who *is* within your gates, that they may hear and that they may learn to fear the LORD your God and carefully observe all the words of this law, **13** and *that* their children, who have not known it, may hear and learn to fear the LORD your God as long as you live in the land which you cross the Jordan to possess."

No release to strangers during.

Deut 15:3 Of a foreigner you may require *it*; but you shall give up your claim to what is owed by your brother,

Release during, not to hinder the exercise of benevolence.

Deut 15:9–11 Beware lest there be a wicked thought in your heart, saying, 'The seventh year, the year of release, is at hand,' and your eye be evil against your poor brother and you give him nothing, and he cry out to the LORD against you, and it become sin among you. **10** You shall surely give to him, and your heart should not be grieved when you give to him, because for this thing the LORD your God will bless you in all your works and in all to which you put your hand. **11** For the poor will never cease from the land; therefore I command you, saying, 'You shall open your hand wide to your brother, to your poor and your needy, in your land.'

Jews warned about neglecting.

Lev 26:34–35 Then the land shall enjoy its sabbaths as long as it lies desolate and you *are* in your enemies' land; then the land shall rest and enjoy its sabbaths. **35** As long as *it* lies desolate it shall rest— for the time it did not rest on your sabbaths when you dwelt in it.

Lev 26:43 The land also shall be left empty by them, and will enjoy its sabbaths while it lies desolate without them; they will accept their guilt, because they despised My judgments and because their soul abhorred My statutes.

Cf. Jer 34:13–18

The seventy years of captivity a punishment for neglecting.

2 Chr 36:20–21 And those who escaped from the sword he carried away to Babylon, where they became servants to him and his sons until the rule of the kingdom of Persia, **21** to fulfill the word of the LORD by the mouth of Jeremiah, until the land had enjoyed her Sabbaths. As long as she lay desolate she kept Sabbath, to fulfill seventy years.

Restored after the captivity.

Neh 10:31 *if* the peoples of the land brought wares or any grain to sell on the Sabbath day, we would not buy it from them on the Sabbath, or on a holy day; and we would forego the seventh year's *produce* and the exacting of every debt.

SACKCLOTH

Made of coarse hair.

Matt 3:4 Now John himself was clothed in camel's hair, with a leather belt around his waist; and his food was locusts and wild honey.

Zech 13:4 "And it shall be in that day *that* every prophet will be ashamed of his vision when he prophesies; they will not wear a robe of coarse hair to deceive.

Rev 6:12 I looked when He opened the sixth seal, and behold, there was a great earthquake; and the sun became black as sackcloth of hair, and the moon became like blood.

Of a black color.

Rev 6:12 I looked when He opened the sixth seal, and behold, there was a great earthquake; and the sun became black as sackcloth of hair, and the moon became like blood.

Was worn

By God's prophets.

2 Kin 1:8 So they answered him, "A hairy man wearing a leather belt around his waist." And he said, "It *is* Elijah the Tishbite."

Is 20:2 at the same time the LORD spoke by Isaiah the son of Amoz, saying, "Go, and remove the sackcloth from your body, and take your sandals off your feet." And he did so, walking naked and barefoot.

Matt 3:4 Now John himself was clothed in camel's hair, with a leather belt around his waist; and his food was locusts and wild honey.

Rev 11:3 And I will give *power* to my two witnesses, and they will prophesy one thousand two hundred and sixty days, clothed in sackcloth."

By persons in affliction.

2 Sam 21:10 Now Rizpah the daughter of Aiah took sackcloth and spread it for herself on the rock, from the beginning of harvest until the late rains poured on them from heaven. And she did not allow the birds of the air to rest on them by day nor the beasts of the field by night.

1 Kin 21:27 So it was, when Ahab heard those words, that he tore his clothes and put sackcloth on his body, and fasted and lay in sackcloth, and went about mourning.

Neh 9:1 Now on the twenty-fourth day of this month the children of Israel were assembled with fasting, in sackcloth, and with dust on their heads.

Ps 69:11 I also made sackcloth my garment; I became a byword to them.

Joel 1:13 Gird yourselves and lament, you priests; Wail, you who minister before the altar; Come, lie all night in sackcloth, You who minister to my God; For the grain offering and the drink offering Are withheld from the house of your God.

Jon 3:5 So the people of Nineveh believed God, proclaimed a fast, and put on sackcloth, from the greatest to the least of them.

Around the waist.

Gen 37:34 Then Jacob tore his clothes, put sackcloth on his waist, and mourned for his son many days.

1 Kin 20:31 Then his servants said to him, "Look now, we have heard that the kings of the house of Israel *are* merciful kings. Please, let us put sackcloth around our waists and ropes around our heads, and go out to the king of Israel; perhaps he will spare your life."

Frequently next to the skin in deep afflictions.

1 Kin 21:27 So it was, when Ahab heard those words, that he tore his clothes and put sackcloth on his body, and fasted and lay in sackcloth, and went about mourning.

2 Kin 6:30 Now it happened, when the king heard the words of the woman, that he tore his clothes; and as he passed by on the wall, the people looked, and there underneath *he had* sackcloth on his body.

Job 16:15 "I have sewn sackcloth over my skin, And laid my head in the dust.

Often over the whole person.

2 Kin 19:1–2 And so it was, when King Hezekiah heard *it*, that he tore his clothes, covered himself with sackcloth, and went into the house of the LORD. **2** Then he sent Eliakim, who *was* over the household, Shebna the scribe, and the elders of the priests, covered with sackcloth, to Isaiah the prophet, the son of Amoz.

With ashes on the head.

Esth 4:1 When Mordecai learned all that had happened, he tore his clothes and put on sackcloth and ashes, and went out into the midst of the city. He cried out with a loud and bitter cry.

Along with ropes around the head.

1 Kin 20:31 Then his servants said to him, "Look now, we have heard that the kings of the house of Israel *are* merciful kings. Please, let us put sackcloth around our waists and ropes around our heads, and go out to the king of Israel; perhaps he will spare your life."

In the streets.

Is 15:3 In their streets they will clothe themselves with sackcloth; On the tops of their houses And in their streets Everyone will wail, weeping bitterly.

At funerals.

2 Sam 3:31 Then David said to Joab and to all the people who were with him, "Tear your clothes, gird yourselves with sackcloth, and mourn for Abner." And King David followed the coffin.

No one clothed in, allowed into the palaces of kings.

Esth 4:2 He went as far as the front of the king's gate, for no one *might* enter the king's gate clothed with sackcloth.

Illustrative of

(Girding with) heavy afflictions.

Is 3:24 And so it shall be: Instead of a sweet smell there will be a stench; Instead of a sash, a rope; Instead of well-set hair, baldness; Instead of a rich robe, a girding of sackcloth; And branding instead of beauty.

Is 22:12 And in that day the Lord GOD of hosts Called for weeping and for mourning, For baldness and for girding with sackcloth.

Is 32:11 Tremble, you *women* who are at ease; Be troubled, you complacent ones; Strip yourselves, make yourselves bare, And gird *sackcloth* on *your* waists.

(Clothing the heavens with) severe judgments.

Is 50:3 I clothe the heavens with blackness, And I make sackcloth their covering."

(Sun becoming as) severe judgments.

Rev 6:12 I looked when He opened the sixth seal, and behold, there was a great earthquake; and the sun became black as sackcloth of hair, and the moon became like blood.

(Putting off) joy and gladness.

Ps 30:11 You have turned for me my mourning into dancing; You have put off my sackcloth and clothed me with gladness,

SACRIFICES.
SEE ALSO CALF, LAMB, PRIESTS
Divine institution of.

Gen 1:29 And God said, "See, I have given you every herb *that* yields seed which *is* on the face of all the earth, and every tree whose fruit yields seed; to you it shall be for food.

Gen 3:21 Also for Adam and his wife the LORD God made tunics of skin, and clothed them.

Gen 4:4–5 Abel also brought of the firstborn of his flock and of their fat. And the LORD respected Abel and his offering, **5** but He did not respect Cain and his offering. And Cain was very angry, and his countenance fell.

Gen 9:3 Every moving thing that lives shall be food for you. I have given you all things, even as the green herbs.

Heb 11:4 By faith Abel offered to God a more excellent sacrifice than Cain, through which he obtained witness that he was righteous, God testifying of his gifts; and through it he being dead still speaks.

To be offered to God alone as supreme.

Ex 22:20 "He who sacrifices to *any* god, except to the LORD only, he shall be utterly destroyed.

Judg 13:16 And the Angel of the LORD said to Manoah, "Though you detain Me, I will not eat your food. But if you offer a burnt offering, you must offer it to the LORD." (For Manoah did not know He *was* the Angel of the LORD.)

2 Kin 5:17 So Naaman said, "Then, if not, please let your servant be given two mule-loads of earth; for your servant will no longer offer either burnt offering or sacrifice to other gods, but to the LORD.

2 Kin 17:36 but the LORD, who brought you up from the land of Egypt with great power and an outstretched arm, Him you shall fear, Him you shall worship, and to Him you shall offer sacrifice.

Jon 1:16 Then the men feared the LORD exceedingly, and offered a sacrifice to the LORD and took vows.

Consisted of

Clean animals or bloody sacrifices.

Gen 8:20 Then Noah built an altar to the LORD, and took of every clean animal and of every clean bird, and offered burnt offerings on the altar.

The fruits of the earth or sacrifices without blood.

Gen 4:4 Abel also brought of the firstborn of his flock and of their fat. And the LORD respected Abel and his offering,

Lev 2:1 'When anyone offers a grain offering to the LORD, his offering shall be *of* fine flour. And he shall pour oil on it, and put frankincense on it.

Always offered upon altars.

Ex 20:24 An altar of earth you shall make for Me, and you shall sacrifice on it your burnt offerings and your peace offerings, your sheep and your oxen. In every place where I record My name I will come to you, and I will bless you.

The offering of, an acknowledgment of sin.

Heb 10:3 But in those *sacrifices there is* a reminder of sins every year.

Were offered

From the earliest age.

Gen 4:3–4 And in the process of time it came to pass that Cain brought an offering of the fruit of the ground to the LORD. **4** Abel also brought of the first-born of his flock and of their fat. And the LORD respected Abel and his offering,

By the patriarchs.

Gen 22:2 Then He said, "Take now your son, your only *son* Isaac, whom you love, and go to the land of Moriah, and offer him there as a burnt offering on one of the mountains of which I shall tell you."

Gen 22:13 Then Abraham lifted his eyes and looked, and there behind *him was* a ram caught in a thicket by its horns. So Abraham went and took the ram, and offered it up for a burnt offering instead of his son.

Gen 31:54 Then Jacob offered a sacrifice on the mountain, and called his brethren to eat bread. And they ate bread and stayed all night on the mountain.

Gen 46:1 So Israel took his journey with all that he had, and came to Beersheba, and offered sacrifices to the God of his father Isaac.

Job 1:5 So it was, when the days of feasting had run their course, that Job would send and sanctify them, and he would rise early in the morning and offer burnt offerings *according to* the number of them all. For Job said, "It may be that my sons have sinned and cursed God in their hearts." Thus Job did regularly.

After the departure of Israel from Egypt.

Ex 5:3 So they said, "The God of the Hebrews has met with us. Please, let us go three days' journey into the desert and sacrifice to the LORD our God, lest He fall upon us with pestilence or with the sword."

Ex 5:17 But he said, "You *are* idle! Idle! Therefore you say, 'Let us go *and* sacrifice to the LORD.'

Ex 18:12 Then Jethro, Moses' father-in-law, took a burnt offering and *other* sacrifices *to offer* to God. And Aaron came with all the elders of Israel to eat bread with Moses' father-in-law before God.

Ex 24:5 Then he sent young men of the children of Israel, who offered burnt offerings and sacrificed peace offerings of oxen to the LORD.

Under the Mosaic age.

Heb 10:1–3 For the law, having a shadow of the good things to come, *and* not the very image of the things, can never with these same sacrifices, which they offer continually year by year, make those who approach perfect. **2** For then would they not have ceased to be offered? For the worshipers, once purified, would have had no more consciousness of sins. **3** But in those *sacrifices there is* a reminder of sins every year.

Cf. Lev 1:1–7:38

Daily.

Ex 29:38–39 "Now this *is* what you shall offer on the altar: two lambs of the first year, day by day continually. **39** One lamb you shall offer in the morning, and the other lamb you shall offer at twilight.

Num 28:3–4 "And you shall say to them, 'This *is* the offering made by fire which you shall offer to the LORD: two male lambs in their first year without blemish,

day by day, as a regular burnt offering. **4** The one lamb you shall offer in the morning, the other lamb you shall offer in the evening,

Weekly.

Num 28:9–10 'And on the Sabbath day two lambs in their first year, without blemish, and two-tenths *of an ephah* of fine flour as a grain offering, mixed with oil, with its drink offering— **10** *this is* the burnt offering for every Sabbath, besides the regular burnt offering with its drink offering.

Monthly.

Num 28:11 'At the beginnings of your months you shall present a burnt offering to the LORD: two young bulls, one ram, and seven lambs in their first year, without blemish;

Yearly.

Lev 16:3 "Thus Aaron shall come into the Holy *Place:* with *the blood of* a young bull as a sin offering, and *of* a ram as a burnt offering.

1 Sam 1:3 This man went up from his city yearly to worship and sacrifice to the LORD of hosts in Shiloh. Also the two sons of Eli, Hophni and Phinehas, the priests of the LORD, *were* there.

1 Sam 1:21 Now the man Elkanah and all his house went up to offer to the LORD the yearly sacrifice and his vow.

1 Sam 20:6 If your father misses me at all, then say, 'David earnestly asked *permission* of me that he might run over to Bethlehem, his city, for *there is* a yearly sacrifice there for all the family.'

At all the feasts.

Num 10:10 Also in the day of your gladness, in your appointed feasts, and at the beginning of your months, you shall blow the trumpets over your burnt offerings and over the sacrifices of your peace offerings; and they shall be a memorial for you before your God: I *am* the LORD your God."

For the whole nation.

1 Chr 29:21 And they made sacrifices to the LORD and offered burnt offerings to the LORD on the next day: a thousand bulls, a thousand rams, a thousand lambs, with their drink offerings, and sacrifices in abundance for all Israel.

Cf. Lev 16:15–30

For individuals.

Lev 1:2 "Speak to the children of Israel, and say to them: 'When any one of you brings an offering to the LORD, you shall bring your offering of the livestock— of the herd and of the flock.

Lev 17:8 "Also you shall say to them: 'Whatever man of the house of Israel, or of the strangers who dwell among you, who offers a burnt offering or sacrifice,

In faith of a coming Savior.

Heb 11:4 By faith Abel offered to God a more excellent sacrifice than Cain, through which he obtained witness that he was righteous, God testifying of his gifts; and through it he being dead still speaks.

Heb 11:17 By faith Abraham, when he was tested, offered up Isaac, and he who had received the promises offered up his only begotten *son,*

Heb 11:28 By faith he kept the Passover and the sprinkling of blood, lest he who destroyed the firstborn should touch them.

Required to be perfect and without blemish.

Lev 22:19 *you shall offer* of your own free will a male without blemish from the cattle, from the sheep, or from the goats.

Deut 15:21 But if there is a defect in it, *if it is* lame or blind *or has* any serious defect, you shall not sacrifice it to the LORD your God.

Deut 17:1 "You shall not sacrifice to the LORD your God a bull or sheep which has any blemish *or* defect, for that *is* an abomination to the LORD your God.

Mal 1:8 And when you offer the blind as a sacrifice, *Is it* not evil? And when you offer the lame and sick, *Is it* not evil? Offer it then to your governor! Would he be pleased with you? Would he accept you favorably?" Says the LORD of hosts.

Mal 1:14 "But cursed *be* the deceiver Who has in his flock a male, And takes a vow, But sacrifices to the Lord what is blemished— For I *am* a great King," Says the LORD of hosts, "And My name *is to be* feared among the nations.

Generally the best of their kind.

Gen 4:4 Abel also brought of the firstborn of his flock and of their fat. And the LORD respected Abel and his offering,

1 Sam 15:22 So Samuel said: "Has the LORD *as great* delight in burnt offerings and sacrifices, As in obeying the voice of the LORD? Behold, to obey is better than sacrifice, *And* to heed than the fat of rams.

Ps 66:15 I will offer You burnt sacrifices of fat animals, With the sweet aroma of rams; I will offer bulls with goats. Selah

Is 1:11 "To what purpose *is* the multitude of your sacrifices to Me?" Says the LORD. "I have had enough of burnt offerings of rams And the fat of fed cattle. I do not delight in the blood of bulls, Or of lambs or goats.

Different kinds of,

Burnt offering wholly consumed by fire.

1 Kin 18:38 Then the fire of the LORD fell and consumed the burnt sacrifice, and the wood and the stones and the dust, and it licked up the water that *was* in the trench.

Cf. Lev 1:1–17

Sin offering for sins of ignorance. **Lev 4:1–35**

Trespass offering for intentional sins.

Lev 6:1–7 And the LORD spoke to Moses, saying: 2 "If a person sins and commits a trespass against the LORD by lying to his neighbor about what was delivered to him for safekeeping, or about a pledge, or about a robbery, or if he has extorted from his neighbor, 3 or if he has found what was lost and lies concerning it, and swears falsely—in any one of these things that a man may do in which he sins: 4 then it shall be, because he has sinned and is guilty, that he shall restore what he has stolen, or the thing which he has extorted, or what was delivered to him for safekeeping, or the lost thing which he found, 5 or all that about which he has sworn falsely. He shall restore its full value, add one-fifth more to it, *and* give it to whomever it belongs, on the day of his trespass offering. 6 And he shall bring his trespass offering to

the LORD, a ram without blemish from the flock, with your valuation, as a trespass offering, to the priest. 7 So the priest shall make atonement for him before the LORD, and he shall be forgiven for any one of these things that he may have done in which he trespasses."

Cf. Lev 7:1–7

Peace offering. **Lev 3:1–17**

To be brought to the place appointed by God.

Deut 12:6 There you shall take your burnt offerings, your sacrifices, your tithes, the heave offerings of your hand, your vowed offerings, your freewill offerings, and the firstborn of your herds and flocks.

2 Chr 7:12 Then the LORD appeared to Solomon by night, and said to him: "I have heard your prayer, and have chosen this place for Myself as a house of sacrifice.

Were bound to the horns of the altar.

Ps 118:27 God *is* the LORD, And He has given us light; Bind the sacrifice with cords to the horns of the altar.

Were seasoned with salt.

Lev 2:13 And every offering of your grain offering you shall season with salt; you shall not allow the salt of the covenant of your God to be lacking from your grain offering. With all your offerings you shall offer salt.

Mark 9:49 "For everyone will be seasoned with fire, and every sacrifice will be seasoned with salt.

Sometimes consumed by fire from heaven.

Lev 9:24 and fire came out from before the LORD and consumed the burnt offering and the fat on the altar. When all the people saw *it*, they shouted and fell on their faces.

1 Kin 18:38 Then the fire of the LORD fell and consumed the burnt sacrifice, and the wood and the stones and the dust, and it licked up the water that *was* in the trench.

2 Chr 7:1 When Solomon had finished praying, fire came down from heaven and consumed the burnt offering and the sacrifices; and the glory of the LORD filled the temple.

When bloody, accompanied with grain and drink offering.

Num 15:3–12 and you make an offering by fire to the LORD, a burnt offering or a sacrifice, to fulfill a vow or as a freewill offering or in your appointed feasts, to make a sweet aroma to the LORD, from the herd or the flock, 4 then he who presents his offering to the LORD shall bring a grain offering of one-tenth *of an ephah* of fine flour mixed with one-fourth of a hin of oil; 5 and one-fourth of a hin of wine as a drink offering you shall prepare with the burnt offering or the sacrifice, for each lamb. 6 Or for a ram you shall prepare as a grain offering two-tenths *of an ephah* of fine flour mixed with one-third of a hin of oil; 7 and as a drink offering you shall offer one-third of a hin of wine as a sweet aroma to the LORD. 8 And when you prepare a young bull as a burnt offering, or as a sacrifice to fulfill a vow, or as a peace offering to the LORD, 9 then shall be offered with the young bull a grain offering of three-tenths *of an ephah* of fine flour mixed with half a hin of oil; 10 and you shall bring as the drink offering half a hin of wine as an offering made by fire, a sweet aroma to the LORD. **11** Thus it shall be done for each young bull, for each ram, or for each lamb or young goat. **12** According to the number that you prepare, so you shall do with everyone according to their number.

No leaven offered with, except for peace offering.

Ex 23:18 "You shall not offer the blood of My sacrifice with leavened bread; nor shall the fat of My sacrifice remain until morning.

Lev 7:13 Besides the cakes, *as* his offering he shall offer leavened bread with the sacrifice of thanksgiving of his peace offering.

Fat of, not to remain until morning.

Ex 23:8 And you shall take no bribe, for a bribe blinds the discerning and perverts the words of the righteous.

The priests

Appointed to offer.

1 Sam 2:28 Did I not choose him out of all the tribes of Israel *to be* My priest, to offer upon My altar, to burn incense, and to wear an ephod before Me? And did I not give to the house of your father all the offerings of the children of Israel made by fire?

Ezek 44:11 Yet they shall be ministers in My sanctuary, *as* gatekeepers of the house and ministers of the house; they shall slay the burnt offering and the sacrifice for the people, and they shall stand before them to minister to them.

Ezek 44:15 "But the priests, the Levites, the sons of Zadok, who kept charge of My sanctuary when the children of Israel went astray from Me, they shall come near Me to minister to Me; and they shall stand before Me to offer to Me the fat and the blood," says the Lord GOD.

Heb 5:1 For every high priest taken from among men is appointed for men in things *pertaining* to God, that he may offer both gifts and sacrifices for sins.

Heb 8:3 For every high priest is appointed to offer both gifts and sacrifices. Therefore *it is* necessary that this One also have something to offer.

Had a portion of, and lived by.

Ex 29:27–28 And from the ram of the consecration you shall consecrate the breast of the wave offering which is waved, and the thigh of the heave offering which is raised, of *that* which *is* for Aaron and of *that* which is for his sons. **28** It shall be from the children of Israel *for* Aaron and his sons by a statute forever. For it is a heave offering; it shall be a heave offering from the children of Israel from the sacrifices of their peace offerings, *that is*, their heave offering to the LORD.

Deut 18:3 "And this shall be the priest's due from the people, from those who offer a sacrifice, whether *it is* bull or sheep: they shall give to the priest the shoulder, the cheeks, and the stomach.

Josh 13:14 Only to the tribe of Levi he had given no inheritance; the sacrifices of the LORD God of Israel made by fire *are* their inheritance, as He said to them.

1 Cor 9:13 Do you not know that those who minister the holy things eat *of the things* of the temple, and those who serve at the altar partake of *the offerings of the* altar?

Were typical of Christ's sacrifice.

1 Cor 5:7 Therefore purge out the old leaven, that you may be a new lump, since you truly are unleavened. For indeed Christ, our Passover, was sacrificed for us.

Eph 5:2 And walk in love, as Christ also has loved us and given Himself for us, an offering and a sacrifice to God for a sweet-smelling aroma.

Heb 10:1 For the law, having a shadow of the good things to come, *and* not the very image of the things, can never with these same sacrifices, which they offer continually year by year, make those who approach perfect.

Heb 10:11–12 And every priest stands ministering daily and offering repeatedly the same sacrifices, which can never take away sins. **12** But this Man, after He had offered one sacrifice for sins forever, sat down at the right hand of God,

Were accepted when offered in sincerity and faith.

Gen 4:4 Abel also brought of the firstborn of his flock and of their fat. And the LORD respected Abel and his offering,

Gen 8:21 And the LORD smelled a soothing aroma. Then the LORD said in His heart, "I will never again curse the ground for man's sake, although the imagination of man's heart *is* evil from his youth; nor will I again destroy every living thing as I have done.

Heb 11:4 By faith Abel offered to God a more excellent sacrifice than Cain, through which he obtained witness that he was righteous, God testifying of his gifts; and through it he being dead still speaks.

Of the wicked, were not accepted.

Is 1:11 "To what purpose *is* the multitude of your sacrifices to Me?" Says the LORD. "I have had enough of burnt offerings of rams And the fat of fed cattle. I do not delight in the blood of bulls, Or of lambs or goats.

Is 66:3 "He who kills a bull *is as if* he slays a man; He who sacrifices a lamb, *as if* he breaks a dog's neck; He who offers a grain offering, *as if he offers* swine's blood; He who burns incense, *as if* he blesses an idol. Just as they have chosen their own ways, And their soul delights in their abominations,

Imparted a legal purification.

Heb 9:13 For if the blood of bulls and goats and the ashes of a heifer, sprinkling the unclean, sanctifies for the purifying of the flesh,

Heb 9:22 And according to the law almost all things are purified with blood, and without shedding of blood there is no remission.

Could not take away sin.

Ps 40:6 Sacrifice and offering You did not desire; My ears You have opened. Burnt offering and sin offering You did not require.

Heb 9:9 It *was* symbolic for the present time in which both gifts and sacrifices are offered which cannot make him who performed the service perfect in regard to the conscience—

Cf. Heb 10:1–11

Without obedience, worthless.

1 Sam 15:22 So Samuel said: "Has the LORD *as great* delight in burnt offerings and sacrifices, As in obeying the voice of the LORD? Behold, to obey is better than sacrifice, *And* to heed than the fat of rams.

Prov 21:3 To do righteousness and justice *Is* more acceptable to the LORD than sacrifice.

Mark 12:33 And to love Him with all the heart, with all the understanding, with all the soul, and with all the strength, and to love one's neighbor as oneself, is more than all the whole burnt offerings and sacrifices."

The covenants of God confirmed by.

Gen 15:9–17 So He said to him, "Bring Me a three-year-old heifer, a three-year-old female goat, a three-year-old ram, a turtledove, and a young pigeon." **10** Then he brought all these to Him and cut them in two, down the middle, and placed each piece opposite the other; but he did not cut the birds in two. **11** And when the vultures came down on the carcasses, Abram drove them away. **12** Now when the sun was going down, a deep sleep fell upon Abram; and behold, horror *and* great darkness fell upon him. **13** Then He said to Abram: "Know certainly that your descendants will be strangers in a land *that is* not theirs, and will serve them, and they will afflict them four hundred years. **14** And also the nation whom they serve I will judge; afterward they shall come out with great possessions. **15** Now as for you, you shall go to your fathers in peace; you shall be buried at a good old age. **16** But in the fourth generation they shall return here, for the iniquity of the Amorites *is* not yet complete." **17** And it came to pass, when the sun went down and it was dark, that behold, there appeared a smoking oven and a burning torch that passed between those pieces.

Ex 24:5–8 Then he sent young men of the children of Israel, who offered burnt offerings and sacrificed peace offerings of oxen to the LORD. **6** And Moses took half the blood and put *it* in basins, and half the blood he sprinkled on the altar. **7** Then he took the Book of the Covenant and read in the hearing of the people. And they said, "All that the LORD has said we will do, and be obedient." **8** And Moses took the blood, sprinkled *it* on the people, and said, "This is the blood of the covenant which the LORD has made with you according to all these words."

Ps 50:5 "Gather My saints together to Me, Those who have made a covenant with Me by sacrifice."

Heb 9:19–20 For when Moses had spoken every precept to all the people according to the law, he took the blood of calves and goats, with water, scarlet wool, and hyssop, and sprinkled both the book itself and all the people, **20** saying, *"This is the blood of the covenant which God has commanded you."*

The Jews

Condemned for not treating, with respect.

1 Sam 2:29 Why do you kick at My sacrifice and My offering which I have commanded *in My* dwelling place, and honor your sons more than Me, to make yourselves fat with the best of all the offerings of Israel My people?'

Mal 1:12 "But you profane it, In that you say, 'The table of the LORD is defiled; And its fruit, its food, *is* contemptible.'

Condemned for bringing defective and blemished.

Mal 1:13–14 You also say, 'Oh, what a weariness!' And you sneer at it," Says the LORD of hosts. "And you bring the stolen, the lame, and the sick; Thus you bring an offering! Should I accept this from your hand?" Says the LORD. **14** "But cursed *be* the deceiver Who has in his flock a male, And takes a vow, But sacrifices to the Lord what is blemished— For I *am* a great King," Says the LORD of hosts, "And My name *is to be* feared among the nations.

Condemned for not offering.

Is 43:23–24 You have not brought Me the sheep for your burnt offerings, Nor have you honored Me with your sacrifices. I have not caused you to serve with grain offerings, Nor wearied you with incense. **24** You have bought Me no sweet cane with money, Nor have you satisfied Me with the fat of your sacrifices; But you have burdened Me with your sins, You have wearied Me with your iniquities.

Unaccepted in, because of sin.

Is 1:11 "To what purpose *is* the multitude of your sacrifices to Me?" Says the LORD. "I have had enough of burnt offerings of rams And the fat of fed cattle. I do not delight in the blood of bulls, Or of lambs or goats.

Is 1:15 When you spread out your hands, I will hide My eyes from you; Even though you make many prayers, I will not hear. Your hands are full of blood.

Is 66:3 "He who kills a bull *is as if* he slays a man; He who sacrifices a lamb, *as if* he breaks a dog's neck; He who offers a grain offering, *as if he offers* swine's blood; He who burns incense, *as if* he blesses an idol. Just as they have chosen their own ways, And their soul delights in their abominations,

Hos 8:13 *For* the sacrifices of My offerings they sacrifice flesh and eat *it, But* the LORD does not accept them. Now He will remember their iniquity and punish their sins. They shall return to Egypt.

Condemned for offering, to idols.

2 Chr 34:25 because they have forsaken Me and burned incense to other gods, that they might provoke Me to anger with all the works of their hands. Therefore My wrath will be poured out on this place, and not be quenched.' " '

Is 65:3 A people who provoke Me to anger continually to My face; Who sacrifice in gardens, And burn incense on altars of brick;

Is 65:7 Your iniquities and the iniquities of your fathers together," Says the LORD, "Who have burned incense on the mountains And blasphemed Me on the hills; Therefore I will measure their former work into their bosom."

Ezek 20:28 When I brought them into the land *concerning* which I had raised My hand in an oath to give them, and they saw all the high hills and all the thick trees, there they offered their sacrifices and provoked Me with their offerings. There they also sent up their sweet aroma and poured out their drink offerings.

Ezek 20:31 For when you offer your gifts and make your sons pass through the fire, you defile yourselves with all your idols, even to this day. So shall I be inquired of by you, O house of Israel? *As* I live," says the Lord GOD, "I will not be inquired of by you.

Offered to false gods, are offered to devils.

Lev 17:7 They shall no more offer their sacrifices to demons, after whom they have played the harlot. This shall be a statute forever for them throughout their generations." '

Deut 32:17 They sacrificed to demons, not to God, *To gods* they did not know, To new *gods,* new arrivals That your fathers did not fear.

Ps 106:37 They even sacrificed their sons And their daughters to demons,

1 Cor 10:20 Rather, that the things which the Gentiles sacrifice they sacrifice to demons and not to God, and I do not want you to have fellowship with demons.

On great occasions, very numerous.

2 Chr 5:6 Also King Solomon, and all the congregation of Israel who were assembled with him before the ark, were sacrificing sheep and oxen that could not be counted or numbered for multitude.

2 Chr 7:5 King Solomon offered a sacrifice of twenty-two thousand bulls and one hundred and twenty thousand sheep. So the king and all the people dedicated the house of God.

For public use often provided by the state.

2 Chr 31:3 The king also *appointed* a portion of his possessions for the burnt offerings: for the morning and evening burnt offerings, the burnt offerings for the Sabbaths and the New Moons and the set feasts, as *it is* written in the Law of the LORD.

Illustrative of

Prayer.

Ps 141:2 Let my prayer be set before You *as* incense, The lifting up of my hands *as* the evening sacrifice.

Thanksgiving.

Ps 27:6 And now my head shall be lifted up above my enemies all around me; Therefore I will offer sacrifices of joy in His tabernacle; I will sing, yes, I will sing praises to the LORD.

Ps 107:22 Let them sacrifice the sacrifices of thanksgiving, And declare His works with rejoicing.

Ps 116:17 I will offer to You the sacrifice of thanksgiving, And will call upon the name of the LORD.

Heb 13:15 Therefore by Him let us continually offer the sacrifice of praise to God, that is, the fruit of *our* lips, giving thanks to His name.

Devotedness.

Rom 12:1 I beseech you therefore, brethren, by the mercies of God, that you present your bodies a living sacrifice, holy, acceptable to God, *which is* your reasonable service.

Phil 2:17 Yes, and if I am being poured out *as a drink offering* on the sacrifice and service of your faith, I am glad and rejoice with you all.

Benevolence.

Phil 4:18 Indeed I have all and abound. I am full, having received from Epaphroditus the things *sent* from you, a sweet-smelling aroma, an acceptable sacrifice, well pleasing to God.

Heb 13:16 But do not forget to do good and to share, for with such sacrifices God is well pleased.

Righteousness.

Ps 4:5 Offer the sacrifices of righteousness, And put your trust in the LORD.

Ps 51:19 Then You shall be pleased with the sacrifices of righteousness, With burnt offering and whole burnt offering; Then they shall offer bulls on Your altar.

A broken spirit.

Ps 51:17 The sacrifices of God *are* a broken spirit, A broken and a contrite heart— These, O God, You will not despise.

Martyrdom.

Phil 2:7 but made Himself of no reputation, taking the form of a bondservant, *and* coming in the likeness of men.

2 Tim 4:6 For I am already being poured out as a drink offering, and the time of my departure is at hand.

SACRIFICE, THE DAILY

Ordained at Mount Sinai.

Num 28:6 *It is* a regular burnt offering which was ordained at Mount Sinai for a sweet aroma, an offering made by fire to the LORD.

A lamb as a burnt offering morning and evening.

Ex 29:38–39 "Now this *is* what you shall offer on the altar: two lambs of the first year, day by day continually. 39 One lamb you shall offer in the morning, and the other lamb you shall offer at twilight.

Num 28:3–4 "And you shall say to them, 'This *is* the offering made by fire which you shall offer to the LORD: two male lambs in their first year without blemish, day by day, as a regular burnt offering. 4 The one lamb you shall offer in the morning, the other lamb you shall offer in the evening,

Doubled on the Sabbath.

Num 28:9–10 'And on the Sabbath day two lambs in their first year, without blemish, and two-tenths *of an ephah* of fine flour as a grain offering, mixed with oil, with its drink offering— 10 *this is* the burnt offering for every Sabbath, besides the regular burnt offering with its drink offering.

Required to be

With a grain and drink offering.

Ex 29:40–41 With the one lamb shall be one-tenth *of an ephah* of flour mixed with one-fourth of a hin of pressed oil, and one-fourth of a hin of wine *as* a drink offering. 41 And the other lamb you shall offer at twilight; and you shall offer with it the grain offering and the drink offering, as in the morning, for a sweet aroma, an offering made by fire to the LORD.

Num 28:5–8 and one-tenth of an ephah of fine flour as a grain offering mixed with one-fourth of a hin of pressed oil. 6 *It is* a regular burnt offering which was ordained at Mount Sinai for a sweet aroma, an offering made by fire to the LORD. 7 And its drink offering *shall be* one-fourth of a hin for each lamb; in a holy *place* you shall pour out the drink to the LORD as an offering. 8 The other lamb you shall offer in the evening; as the morning grain offering and its drink offering, you shall offer *it* as an offering made by fire, a sweet aroma to the LORD.

Slowly and entirely consumed.

Lev 6:9–12 "Command Aaron and his sons, saying, 'This *is* the law of the burnt offering: The burnt offering *shall be* on the hearth upon the altar all night until morning, and the fire of the altar shall be kept burning on it. **10** And the priest shall put on his linen garment, and his linen trousers he shall put on his body, and take up the ashes of the burnt offering which the fire has consumed on the altar, and he shall put them beside the altar. **11** Then he shall take off his garments, put on other garments, and carry the ashes outside the camp to a clean place. **12** And the fire on the altar shall be kept burning on it; it shall not be put out. And the priest shall burn wood on it every morning, and lay the burnt offering in order on it; and he shall burn on it the fat of the peace offerings.

Perpetually observed.

Ex 29:42 *This shall be* a continual burnt offering throughout your generations *at* the door of the tabernacle of meeting before the Lord, where I will meet you to speak with you.

Num 28:6 *It is* a regular burnt offering which was ordained at Mount Sinai for a sweet aroma, an offering made by fire to the Lord.

Distinctively acceptable.

Num 28:8 The other lamb you shall offer in the evening; as the morning grain offering and its drink offering, you shall offer *it* as an offering made by fire, a sweet aroma to the Lord.

Ps 141:2 Let my prayer be set before You *as* incense, The lifting up of my hands *as* the evening sacrifice.

Secured God's presence and favor.

Ex 29:43–44 And there I will meet with the children of Israel, and *the tabernacle* shall be sanctified by My glory. **44** So I will consecrate the tabernacle of meeting and the altar. I will also consecrate both Aaron and his sons to minister to Me as priests.

Times of offering, were devoted to prayer.

Ezra 9:5 At the evening sacrifice I arose from my fasting; and having torn my garment and my robe, I fell on my knees and spread out my hands to the Lord my God.

Dan 9:20–21 Now while I *was* speaking, praying, and confessing my sin and the sin of my people Israel, and presenting my supplication before the Lord my God for the holy mountain of my God, **21** yes, while I *was* speaking in prayer, the man Gabriel, whom I had seen in the vision at the beginning, being caused to fly swiftly, reached me about the time of the evening offering.

Acts 3:1 Now Peter and John went up together to the temple at the hour of prayer, the ninth *hour.*

Restored after the captivity.

Ezra 3:3 Though fear *had come* upon them because of the people of those countries, they set the altar on its bases; and they offered burnt offerings on it to the Lord, *both* the morning and evening burnt offerings.

The abolition of, foretold.

Dan 9:26–27 "And after the sixty-two weeks Messiah shall be cut off, but not for Himself; And the people of the prince who is to come Shall destroy the city and the sanctuary. The end of it *shall be* with a flood, And till the end of the war desolations are determined. **27** Then he shall confirm a covenant with many for one week; But in the middle of the week He shall bring an end to sacrifice and offering. And on the wing of abominations shall be one who makes desolate, Even until the consummation, which is determined, Is poured out on the desolate."

Dan 11:31 And forces shall be mustered by him, and they shall defile the sanctuary fortress; then they shall take away the daily *sacrifices,* and place *there* the abomination of desolation.

Illustrative of

Christ.

John 1:29 The next day John saw Jesus coming toward him, and said, "Behold! The Lamb of God who takes away the sin of the world!

John 1:36 And looking at Jesus as He walked, he said, "Behold the Lamb of God!"

1 Pet 1:19 but with the precious blood of Christ, as of a lamb without blemish and without spot.

Acceptable prayer.

Ps 141:2 Let my prayer be set before You *as* incense, The lifting up of my hands *as* the evening sacrifice.

Sadducees, The

A sect of the Jews.

Acts 5:17 Then the high priest rose up, and all those who *were* with him (which is the sect of the Sadducees), and they were filled with indignation,

Denied the resurrection and a future state.

Matt 22:23 The same day the Sadducees, who say there is no resurrection, came to Him and asked Him,

Luke 20:27 Then some of the Sadducees, who deny that there is a resurrection, came to *Him* and asked Him,

The resurrection a cause of dispute between them and the Pharisees.

Acts 23:6–9 But when Paul perceived that one part were Sadducees and the other Pharisees, he cried out in the council, "Men *and* brethren, I am a Pharisee, the son of a Pharisee; concerning the hope and resurrection of the dead I am being judged!" **7** And when he had said this, a dissension arose between the Pharisees and the Sadducees; and the assembly was divided. **8** For Sadducees say that there is no resurrection—and no angel or spirit; but the Pharisees confess both. **9** Then there arose a loud outcry. And the scribes of the Pharisees' party arose and protested, saying, "We find no evil in this man; but if a spirit or an angel has spoken to him, let us not fight against God."

Were refused baptism by John.

Matt 3:7 But when he saw many of the Pharisees and Sadducees coming to his baptism, he said to them, "Brood of vipers! Who warned you to flee from the wrath to come?

Christ

Was tested by them.

Matt 16:1 Then the Pharisees and Sadducees came, and testing Him asked that He would show them a sign from heaven.

Cautioned His disciples against their principles.

Matt 16:6 Then Jesus said to them, "Take heed and beware of the leaven of the Pharisees and the Sadducees."

Matt 16:11–12 How is it you do not understand that I did not speak to you concerning bread?—*but* to beware of the leaven of the Pharisees and Sadducees." **12** Then they understood that He did not tell *them* to beware of the leaven of bread, but of the doctrine of the Pharisees and Sadducees.

Defended the resurrection to them.

Matt 22:24–32 saying: "Teacher, Moses said that if a man dies, having no children, his brother shall marry his wife and raise up offspring for his brother. **25** Now there were with us seven brothers. The first died after he had married, and having no offspring, left his wife to his brother. **26** Likewise the second also, and the third, even to the seventh. **27** Last of all the woman died also. **28** Therefore, in the resurrection, whose wife of the seven will she be? For they all had her." **29** Jesus answered and said to them, "You are mistaken, not knowing the Scriptures nor the power of God. **30** For in the resurrection they neither marry nor are given in marriage, but are like angels of God in heaven. **31** But concerning the resurrection of the dead, have you not read what was spoken to you by God, saying, **32** *'I am the God of Abraham, the God of Isaac, and the God of Jacob'*? God is not the God of the dead, but of the living."

Cf. Mark 12:19–27

Silenced them.

Matt 22:34 But when the Pharisees heard that He had silenced the Sadducees, they gathered together.

Persecuted the Christians.

Acts 4:1 Now as they spoke to the people, the priests, the captain of the temple, and the Sadducees came upon them,

Acts 5:17–18 Then the high priest rose up, and all those who *were* with him (which is the sect of the Sadducees), and they were filled with indignation, **18** and laid their hands on the apostles and put them in the common prison.

Acts 5:40 And they agreed with him, and when they had called for the apostles and beaten *them*, they commanded that they should not speak in the name of Jesus, and let them go.

SALT

Characterized as good and useful.

Mark 9:50 Salt *is* good, but if the salt loses its flavor, how will you season it? Have salt in yourselves, and have peace with one another."

Used for

Seasoning food.

Job 6:6 Can flavorless food be eaten without salt? Or is there *any* taste in the white of an egg?

Seasoning sacrifices.

Lev 2:13 And every offering of your grain offering you shall season with salt; you shall not allow the salt of the covenant of your God to be lacking from your grain offering. With all your offerings you shall offer salt.

Ezra 6:9 And whatever they need—young bulls, rams, and lambs for the burnt offerings of the God of heaven, wheat, salt, wine, and oil, according to the request of the priests who *are* in Jerusalem—let it be given them day by day without fail,

Ezek 43:24 When you offer them before the LORD, the priests shall throw salt on them, and they will offer them up *as* a burnt offering to the LORD.

Ratifying covenants.

Num 18:19 "All the heave offerings of the holy things, which the children of Israel offer to the LORD, I have given to you and your sons and daughters with you as an ordinance forever; it *is* a covenant of salt forever before the LORD with you and your descendants with you."

2 Chr 13:5 Should you not know that the LORD God of Israel gave the dominion over Israel to David forever, to him and his sons, by a covenant of salt?

Strengthening newborn infants.

Ezek 16:4 *As for* your nativity, on the day you were born your navel cord was not cut, nor were you washed in water to cleanse *you;* you were not rubbed with salt nor wrapped in swaddling cloths.

Lost its flavor when exposed to the air.

Matt 5:13 "You are the salt of the earth; but if the salt loses its flavor, how shall it be seasoned? It is then good for nothing but to be thrown out and trampled underfoot by men.

Mark 9:50 Salt *is* good, but if the salt loses its flavor, how will you season it? Have salt in yourselves, and have peace with one another."

Often found

In pits.

Zeph 2:9 Therefore, as I live," Says the LORD of hosts, the God of Israel, "Surely Moab shall be like Sodom, And the people of Ammon like Gomorrah— Overrun with weeds and saltpits, And a perpetual desolation. The residue of My people shall plunder them, And the remnant of My people shall possess them."

In springs.

James 3:12 Can a fig tree, my brethren, bear olives, or a grapevine bear figs? Thus no spring yields both salt water and fresh.

Near the Dead (Salt) Sea.

Num 34:12 the border shall go down along the Jordan, and it shall end at the Salt Sea. This shall be your land with its surrounding boundaries.' "

Deut 3:17 the plain also, with the Jordan as *the* border, from Chinnereth as far as the east side of the Sea of the Arabah (the Salt Sea), below the slopes of Pisgah.

Places where it abounded barren and unfruitful.

Jer 17:6 For he shall be like a shrub in the desert, And shall not see when good comes, But shall inhabit the parched places in the wilderness, *In* a salt land *which is* not inhabited.

Ezek 47:11 But its swamps and marshes will not be healed; they will be given over to salt.

The valley of, celebrated for victories.

2 Sam 8:13 And David made *himself* a name when he returned from killing eighteen thousand Syrians in the Valley of Salt.

2 Kin 14:7 He killed ten thousand Edomites in the Valley of Salt, and took Sela by war, and called its name Joktheel to this day.

1 Chr 18:12 Moreover Abishai the son of Zeruiah killed eighteen thousand Edomites in the Valley of Salt.

Ps 60:title To the Chief Musician. Set to "Lily of the Testimony." A Michtam of David. For teaching. When he fought against Mesopotamia and Syria of Zobah, and Joab returned and killed twelve thousand Edomites in the Valley of Salt.

Miracles connected with,

Lot's wife turned into a pillar of.

Gen 19:26 But his wife looked back behind him, and she became a pillar of salt.

Elisha healed the bad water with.

2 Kin 2:20–21 And he said, Bring me a new cruse, and put salt therein. And they brought *it* to him. **21** Then he went out to the source of the water, and cast in the salt there, and said, "Thus says the LORD: 'I have healed this water; from it there shall be no more death or barrenness.' "

Places sown with, to denote perpetual desolation.

Judg 9:45 So Abimelech fought against the city all that day; he took the city and killed the people who *were* in it; and he demolished the city and sowed it with salt.

Liberally afforded to the Jews after the captivity.

Ezra 6:9 And whatever they need—young bulls, rams, and lambs for the burnt offerings of the God of heaven, wheat, salt, wine, and oil, according to the request of the priests who *are* in Jerusalem—let it be given them day by day without fail,

Ezra 7:22 up to one hundred talents of silver, one hundred kors of wheat, one hundred baths of wine, one hundred baths of oil, and salt without prescribed limit.

Illustrative of

Believers.

Matt 5:13 "You are the salt of the earth; but if the salt loses its flavor, how shall it be seasoned? It is then good for nothing but to be thrown out and trampled underfoot by men.

Grace in the heart.

Mark 9:50 Salt *is* good, but if the salt loses its flavor, how will you season it? Have salt in yourselves, and have peace with one another."

Wisdom in speech.

Col 4:6 *Let* your speech always *be* with grace, seasoned with salt, that you may know how you ought to answer each one.

(Without flavor) false professors.

Matt 5:13 "You are the salt of the earth; but if the salt loses its flavor, how shall it be seasoned? It is then good for nothing but to be thrown out and trampled underfoot by men.

Mark 9:50 Salt *is* good, but if the salt loses its flavor, how will you season it? Have salt in yourselves, and have peace with one another."

(Pits of) desolation.

Zeph 2:9 Therefore, as I live," Says the LORD of hosts, the God of Israel, "Surely Moab shall be like Sodom, And the people of Ammon like Gomorrah— Overrun with weeds and saltpits, And a perpetual desolation. The residue of My people shall plunder them, And the remnant of My people shall possess them."

(Seasoned with fire) preparation of the wicked for destruction.

Mark 9:49 "For everyone will be seasoned with fire, and every sacrifice will be seasoned with salt.

SALUTATIONS

Antiquity of.

Gen 18:2 So he lifted his eyes and looked, and behold, three men were standing by him; and when he saw *them,* he ran from the tent door to meet them, and bowed himself to the ground,

Gen 19:1 Now the two angels came to Sodom in the evening, and Lot was sitting in the gate of Sodom. When Lot saw *them,* he rose to meet them, and he bowed himself with his face toward the ground.

Were given

By brethren to each other.

1 Sam 17:22 And David left his supplies in the hand of the supply keeper, ran to the army, and came and greeted his brothers.

By inferiors to their superiors.

Gen 47:7 Then Joseph brought in his father Jacob and set him before Pharaoh; and Jacob blessed Pharaoh.

By superiors to inferiors.

1 Sam 30:21 Now David came to the two hundred men who had been so weary that they could not follow David, whom they also had made to stay at the Brook Besor. So they went out to meet David and to meet the people who *were* with him. And when David came near the people, he greeted them.

By all passers-by.

1 Sam 10:3–4 Then you shall go on forward from there and come to the terebinth tree of Tabor. There three men going up to God at Bethel will meet you, one carrying three young goats, another carrying three loaves of bread, and another carrying a skin of wine. **4** And they will greet you and give you two *loaves* of bread, which you shall receive from their hands.

Ps 129:8 Neither let those who pass by them say, "The blessing of the LORD *be* upon you; We bless you in the name of the LORD!"

On entering a house.

Judg 18:15 So they turned aside there, and came to the house of the young Levite man—to the house of Micah—and greeted him.

Matt 10:12 And when you go into a household, greet it.

Luke 1:40–41 and entered the house of Zacharias and greeted Elizabeth. **41** And it happened, when Elizabeth heard the greeting of Mary, that the babe leaped in her womb; and Elizabeth was filled with the Holy Spirit.

Luke 1:44 For indeed, as soon as the voice of your greeting sounded in my ears, the babe leaped in my womb for joy.

Often sent through messengers.

1 Sam 25:5 David sent ten young men; and David said

to the young men, "Go up to Carmel, go to Nabal, and greet him in my name.

1 Sam 25:14 Now one of the young men told Abigail, Nabal's wife, saying, "Look, David sent messengers from the wilderness to greet our master; and he reviled them.

2 Sam 8:10 then Toi sent Joram his son to King David, to greet him and bless him, because he had fought against Hadadezer and defeated him (for Hadadezer had been at war with Toi); and *Joram* brought with him articles of silver, articles of gold, and articles of bronze.

Often sent by letter.

Rom 16:21–23 Timothy, my fellow worker, and Lucius, Jason, and Sosipater, my countrymen, greet you. **22** I, Tertius, who wrote *this* epistle, greet you in the Lord. **23** Gaius, my host and *the host* of the whole church, greets you. Erastus, the treasurer of the city, greets you, and Quartus, a brother.

1 Cor 16:21 The salutation with my own hand—Paul's.

Col 4:18 This salutation by my own hand—Paul. Remember my chains. Grace *be* with you. Amen.

2 Thess 3:17 The salutation of Paul with my own hand, which is a sign in every epistle; so I write.

Denied to persons of bad character.

2 John 1:10 If anyone comes to you and does not bring this doctrine, do not receive him into your house nor greet him;

Persons in haste excused from giving or receiving.

2 Kin 4:29 Then he said to Gehazi, "Get yourself ready, and take my staff in your hand, and be on your way. If you meet anyone, do not greet him; and if anyone greets you, do not answer him; but lay my staff on the face of the child."

Luke 10:24 for I tell you that many prophets and kings have desired to see what you see, and have not seen *it*, and to hear what you hear, and have not heard *it*."

Expressions used as,

Peace be with you.

Judg 19:20 And the old man said, "Peace *be* with you! However, *let* all your needs *be* my responsibility; only do not spend the night in the open square."

Peace to you, peace to your house, and peace to all that you have.

1 Sam 25:6 And thus you shall say to him who lives in prosperity: 'Peace *be* to you, peace to your house, and peace to all that you have!

Peace to this house.

Luke 10:5 But whatever house you enter, first say, 'Peace to this house.'

The Lord be with you.

Ruth 2:4 Now behold, Boaz came from Bethlehem, and said to the reapers, "The LORD *be* with you!" And they answered him, "The LORD bless you!"

The Lord bless you.

Ruth 2:4 Now behold, Boaz came from Bethlehem, and said to the reapers, "The LORD *be* with you!" And they answered him, "The LORD bless you!"

The blessing of the Lord be upon you.

Ps 129:8 Neither let those who pass by them say, "The blessing of the LORD *be* upon you; We bless you in the name of the LORD!"

Blessed are you of the Lord.

1 Sam 15:13 Then Samuel went to Saul, and Saul said to him, "Blessed *are* you of the LORD! I have performed the commandment of the LORD."

God be gracious to you.

Gen 43:29 Then he lifted his eyes and saw his brother Benjamin, his mother's son, and said, "*Is* this your younger brother of whom you spoke to me?" And he said, "God be gracious to you, my son."

Are you in health?

2 Sam 20:9 Then Joab said to Amasa, "*Are* you in health, my brother?" And Joab took Amasa by the beard with his right hand to kiss him.

Greetings.

Matt 26:49 Immediately he went up to Jesus and said, "Greetings, Rabbi!" and kissed Him.

Rejoice.

Matt 28:9 And as they went to tell His disciples, behold, Jesus met them, saying, "Rejoice!" So they came and held Him by the feet and worshiped Him.

Luke 1:28 And having come in, the angel said to her, "Rejoice, highly favored *one*, the Lord *is* with you; blessed *are* you among women!"

Often dishonest.

2 Sam 20:9 Then Joab said to Amasa, "*Are* you in health, my brother?" And Joab took Amasa by the beard with his right hand to kiss him.

Matt 26:49 Immediately he went up to Jesus and said, "Greetings, Rabbi!" and kissed Him.

Given to Christ in derision.

Matt 15:18 But those things which proceed out of the mouth come from the heart, and they defile a man.

Matt 27:29 When they had twisted a crown of thorns, they put *it* on His head, and a reed in His right hand. And they bowed the knee before Him and mocked Him, saying, "Hail, King of the Jews!"

Often accompanied by

Falling on the neck and kissing.

Gen 33:4 But Esau ran to meet him, and embraced him, and fell on his neck and kissed him, and they wept.

Gen 45:14–15 Then he fell on his brother Benjamin's neck and wept, and Benjamin wept on his neck. **15** Moreover he kissed all his brothers and wept over them, and after that his brothers talked with him.

Luke 15:20 "And he arose and came to his father. But when he was still a great way off, his father saw him and had compassion, and ran and fell on his neck and kissed him.

Laying hold of the beard with the right hand.

2 Sam 20:9 Then Joab said to Amasa, "*Are* you in health, my brother?" And Joab took Amasa by the beard with his right hand to kiss him.

Bowing frequently to the ground.

Gen 33:3 Then he crossed over before them and bowed himself to the ground seven times, until he came near to his brother.

Embracing and kissing the feet.

Matt 28:9 And as they went to tell His disciples, behold, Jesus met them, saying, "Rejoice!" So they came and held Him by the feet and worshiped Him.

Luke 7:38 and stood at His feet behind *Him* weeping; and she began to wash His feet with her tears, and wiped *them* with the hair of her head; and she kissed His feet and anointed *them* with the fragrant oil.

Luke 7:45 You gave Me no kiss, but this woman has not ceased to kiss My feet since the time I came in.

Touching the hem of the garment.

Matt 14:36 and begged Him that they might only touch the hem of His garment. And as many as touched *it* were made perfectly well.

Falling prostrate on the ground.

Esth 8:3 Now Esther spoke again to the king, fell down at his feet, and implored him with tears to counteract the evil of Haman the Agagite, and the scheme which he had devised against the Jews.

Matt 2:11 And when they had come into the house, they saw the young Child with Mary His mother, and fell down and worshiped Him. And when they had opened their treasures, they presented gifts to Him: gold, frankincense, and myrrh.

Luke 8:41 And behold, there came a man named Jairus, and he was a ruler of the synagogue. And he fell down at Jesus' feet and begged Him to come to his house,

Licking the dust.

Ps 72:9 Those who dwell in the wilderness will bow before Him, And His enemies will lick the dust.

Is 49:23 Kings shall be your foster fathers, And their queens your nursing mothers; They shall bow down to you with *their* faces to the earth, And lick up the dust of your feet. Then you will know that I *am* the LORD, For they shall not be ashamed who wait for Me."

The Jews condemned for giving, only to their countrymen.

Matt 5:47 And if you greet your brethren only, what do you do more *than others?* Do not even the tax collectors do so?

The Pharisees condemned for seeking, in public.

Matt 23:7 greetings in the marketplaces, and to be called by men, 'Rabbi, Rabbi.'

Mark 12:38 Then He said to them in His teaching, "Beware of the scribes, who desire to go around in long robes, *love* greetings in the marketplaces,

SALVATION

Is of God.

Ps 3:8 Salvation *belongs* to the LORD. Your blessing *is* upon Your people. Selah

Ps 37:39 But the salvation of the righteous *is* from the LORD; *He is* their strength in the time of trouble.

Jer 3:23 Truly, in vain *is salvation hoped for* from the hills, *And from* the multitude of mountains; Truly, in the LORD our God *Is* the salvation of Israel.

1 Thess 5:9 For God did not appoint us to wrath, but to obtain salvation through our Lord Jesus Christ,

1 Tim 2:4 who desires all men to be saved and to come to the knowledge of the truth.

2 Tim 1:9 who has saved us and called *us* with a holy calling, not according to our works, but according to His own purpose and grace which was given to us in Christ Jesus before time began,

Is by Christ.

Is 45:21–22 Tell and bring forth *your case;* Yes, let them take counsel together. Who has declared this from ancient time? *Who* has told it from that time? *Have* not I, the LORD? And *there is* no other God besides Me, A just God and a Savior; *There is* none besides Me. 22 "Look to Me, and be saved, All you ends of the earth! For I *am* God, and *there is* no other.

Is 59:16 He saw that *there was* no man, And wondered that *there was* no intercessor; Therefore His own arm brought salvation for Him; And His own righteousness, it sustained Him.

Is 63:9 In all their affliction He was afflicted, And the Angel of His Presence saved them; In His love and in His pity He redeemed them; And He bore them and carried them All the days of old.

Acts 4:12 Nor is there salvation in any other, for there is no other name under heaven given among men by which we must be saved."

Eph 5:23 For the husband is head of the wife, as also Christ is head of the church; and He is the Savior of the body.

Is through faith in Christ.

Mark 16:16 He who believes and is baptized will be saved; but he who does not believe will be condemned.

Acts 16:31 So they said, "Believe on the Lord Jesus Christ, and you will be saved, you and your household."

Rom 10:9 that if you confess with your mouth the Lord Jesus and believe in your heart that God has raised Him from the dead, you will be saved.

Eph 2:8 For by grace you have been saved through faith, and that not of yourselves; *it is* the gift of God,

1 Pet 1:5 who are kept by the power of God through faith for salvation ready to be revealed in the last time.

Confession of Christ necessary to.

Rom 10:10 For with the heart one believes unto righteousness, and with the mouth confession is made unto salvation.

Announced after the Fall.

Gen 3:15 And I will put enmity Between you and the woman, And between your seed and her Seed; He shall bruise your head, And you shall bruise His heel."

Of Israel, predicted.

Is 35:4 Say to those *who are* fearful-hearted, "Be strong, do not fear! Behold, your God will come *with* vengeance, *With* the recompense of God; He will come and save you."

Is 45:17 *But* Israel shall be saved by the LORD With an everlasting salvation; You shall not be ashamed or disgraced Forever and ever.

Zech 9:16 The LORD their God will save them in that

day, As the flock of His people. For they *shall be like* the jewels of a crown, Lifted like a banner over His land—

Rom 11:26 And so all Israel will be saved, as it is written: *"The Deliverer will come out of Zion, And He will turn away ungodliness from Jacob;*

Of the Gentiles, predicted.

Is 45:22 "Look to Me, and be saved, All you ends of the earth! For I *am* God, and *there is* no other.

Is 49:6 Indeed He says, 'It is too small a thing that You should be My Servant To raise up the tribes of Jacob, And to restore the preserved ones of Israel; I will also give You as a light to the Gentiles, That You should be My salvation to the ends of the earth.' "

Is 52:10 The LORD has made bare His holy arm In the eyes of all the nations; And all the ends of the earth shall see The salvation of our God.

Revealed in the gospel.

Rom 1:16 For I am not ashamed of the gospel of Christ, for it is the power of God to salvation for everyone who believes, for the Jew first and also for the Greek.

1 Cor 1:18 For the message of the cross is foolishness to those who are perishing, but to us who are being saved it is the power of God.

Eph 1:13 In Him you also *trusted,* after you heard the word of truth, the gospel of your salvation; in whom also, having believed, you were sealed with the Holy Spirit of promise,

2 Tim 1:10 but has now been revealed by the appearing of our Savior Jesus Christ, *who* has abolished death and brought life and immortality to light through the gospel,

Came to the Gentiles through the fall of the Jews.

Rom 11:11 I say then, have they stumbled that they should fall? Certainly not! But through their fall, to provoke them to jealousy, salvation *has come* to the Gentiles.

Christ

The captain of.

Heb 2:10 For it was fitting for Him, for whom *are* all things and by whom *are* all things, in bringing many sons to glory, to make the captain of their salvation perfect through sufferings.

The author of.

Heb 5:9 And having been perfected, He became the author of eternal salvation to all who obey Him,

Appointed for.

Is 49:6 Indeed He says, 'It is too small a thing that You should be My Servant To raise up the tribes of Jacob, And to restore the preserved ones of Israel; I will also give You as a light to the Gentiles, That You should be My salvation to the ends of the earth.' "

Raised up for.

Luke 1:69 And has raised up a horn of salvation for us In the house of His servant David,

Has.

Zech 9:9 "Rejoice greatly, O daughter of Zion! Shout, O daughter of Jerusalem! Behold, your King is coming to you; He *is* just and having salvation, Lowly and riding on a donkey, A colt, the foal of a donkey.

Brings, with Him.

Is 62:11 Indeed the LORD has proclaimed To the end of the world: "Say to the daughter of Zion, 'Surely your salvation is coming; Behold, His reward *is* with Him, And His work before Him.' "

Luke 19:9 And Jesus said to him, "Today salvation has come to this house, because he also is a son of Abraham;

Came and died to effect.

Is 63:1 Who *is* this who comes from Edom, With dyed garments from Bozrah, This *One who is* glorious in His apparel, Traveling in the greatness of His strength?— "I who speak in righteousness, mighty to save."

Matt 18:11 For the Son of Man has come to save that which was lost.

John 3:14–15 And as Moses lifted up the serpent in the wilderness, even so must the Son of Man be lifted up, **15** that whoever believes in Him should not perish but have eternal life.

Gal 1:4 who gave Himself for our sins, that He might deliver us from this present evil age, according to the will of our God and Father,

1 Tim 1:15 This *is* a faithful saying and worthy of all acceptance, that Christ Jesus came into the world to save sinners, of whom I am chief.

Heb 7:25 Therefore He is also able to save to the uttermost those who come to God through Him, since He always lives to make intercession for them.

Exalted to give.

Acts 5:31 Him God has exalted to His right hand *to be* Prince and Savior, to give repentance to Israel and forgiveness of sins.

Described as

Not by works.

Rom 11:6 And if by grace, then *it is* no longer of works; otherwise grace is no longer grace. But if *it is* of works, it is no longer grace; otherwise work is no longer work.

Eph 2:9 not of works, lest anyone should boast.

2 Tim 1:9 who has saved us and called *us* with a holy calling, not according to our works, but according to His own purpose and grace which was given to us in Christ Jesus before time began,

Titus 3:5 not by works of righteousness which we have done, but according to His mercy He saved us, through the washing of regeneration and renewing of the Holy Spirit,

Of grace.

Eph 2:5 even when we were dead in trespasses, made us alive together with Christ (by grace you have been saved),

Eph 2:8 For by grace you have been saved through faith, and that not of yourselves; *it is* the gift of God,

2 Tim 1:9 who has saved us and called *us* with a holy calling, not according to our works, but according to His own purpose and grace which was given to us in Christ Jesus before time began,

Titus 2:11 For the grace of God that brings salvation has appeared to all men,

Of love.

Rom 5:8 But God demonstrates His own love toward us, in that while we were still sinners, Christ died for us.

1 John 4:9–10 In this the love of God was manifested toward us, that God has sent His only begotten Son into the world, that we might live through Him. **10** In this is love, not that we loved God, but that He loved us and sent His Son *to be* the propitiation for our sins.

Of mercy.

Ps 6:4 Return, O Lord, deliver me! Oh, save me for Your mercies' sake!

Titus 3:5 not by works of righteousness which we have done, but according to His mercy He saved us, through the washing of regeneration and renewing of the Holy Spirit,

Of the longsuffering of God.

2 Pet 3:15 and consider *that* the longsuffering of our Lord *is* salvation—as also our beloved brother Paul, according to the wisdom given to him, has written to you,

Great.

Heb 2:3 how shall we escape if we neglect so great a salvation, which at the first began to be spoken by the Lord, and was confirmed to us by those who heard *Him,*

Glorious.

2 Tim 2:10 Therefore I endure all things for the sake of the elect, that they also may obtain the salvation which is in Christ Jesus with eternal glory.

Common among believers.

Jude 1:3 Beloved, while I was very diligent to write to you concerning our common salvation, I found it necessary to write to you exhorting you to contend earnestly for the faith which was once for all delivered to the saints.

From generation to generation.

Is 51:8 For the moth will eat them up like a garment, And the worm will eat them like wool; But My righteousness will be forever, And My salvation from generation to generation."

To the uttermost.

Heb 7:25 Therefore He is also able to save to the uttermost those who come to God through Him, since He always lives to make intercession for them.

Eternal.

Is 45:17 *But* Israel shall be saved by the Lord With an everlasting salvation; You shall not be ashamed or disgraced Forever and ever.

Is 51:6 Lift up your eyes to the heavens, And look on the earth beneath. For the heavens will vanish away like smoke, The earth will grow old like a garment, And those who dwell in it will die in like manner; But My salvation will be forever, And My righteousness will not be abolished.

Heb 5:9 And having been perfected, He became the author of eternal salvation to all who obey Him,

Reconciliation to God, a pledge of.

Rom 5:10 For if when we were enemies we were reconciled to God through the death of His Son, much more, having been reconciled, we shall be saved by His life.

Is deliverance from

Sin.

Matt 1:21 And she will bring forth a Son, and you shall call His name Jesus, for He will save His people from their sins."

1 John 3:5 And you know that He was manifested to take away our sins, and in Him there is no sin.

Uncleanness.

Ezek 36:29 I will deliver you from all your uncleannesses. I will call for the grain and multiply it, and bring no famine upon you.

The devil.

Col 2:15 Having disarmed principalities and powers, He made a public spectacle of them, triumphing over them in it.

Heb 2:14–15 Inasmuch then as the children have partaken of flesh and blood, He Himself likewise shared in the same, that through death He might destroy him who had the power of death, that is, the devil, **15** and release those who through fear of death were all their lifetime subject to bondage.

Wrath.

Rom 5:9 Much more then, having now been justified by His blood, we shall be saved from wrath through Him.

1 Thess 1:10 and to wait for His Son from heaven, whom He raised from the dead, *even* Jesus who delivers us from the wrath to come.

This present evil age.

Gal 1:4 who gave Himself for our sins, that He might deliver us from this present evil age, according to the will of our God and Father,

Enemies.

Luke 1:71 That we should be saved from our enemies And from the hand of all who hate us,

Luke 1:74 To grant us that we, Being delivered from the hand of our enemies, Might serve Him without fear,

Eternal death.

John 3:16–17 For God so loved the world that He gave His only begotten Son, that whoever believes in Him should not perish but have everlasting life. **17** For God did not send His Son into the world to condemn the world, but that the world through Him might be saved.

Regeneration necessary to.

John 3:3 Jesus answered and said to him, "Most assuredly, I say to you, unless one is born again, he cannot see the kingdom of God."

Final perseverance necessary to.

Matt 10:22 And you will be hated by all for My name's sake. But he who endures to the end will be saved.

Searched into and exhibited by the prophets.

1 Pet 1:10 Of this salvation the prophets have inquired and searched carefully, who prophesied of the grace *that would come* to you,

The Scriptures are able to lead one to.

1 Cor 1:21 For since, in the wisdom of God, the world through wisdom did not know God, it pleased God through the foolishness of the message preached to save those who believe.

2 Tim 3:15 and that from childhood you have known the Holy Scriptures, which are able to make you wise for salvation through faith which is in Christ Jesus.

James 1:21 Therefore lay aside all filthiness and overflow of wickedness, and receive with meekness the implanted word, which is able to save your souls.

Now is the day of.

Is 49:8 Thus says the LORD: "In an acceptable time I have heard You, And in the day of salvation I have helped You; I will preserve You and give You As a covenant to the people, To restore the earth, To cause them to inherit the desolate heritages;

2 Cor 6:2 For He says: *"In an acceptable time I have heard you, And in the day of salvation I have helped you."* Behold, now *is* the accepted time; behold, now *is* the day of salvation.

From sin, to be worked out with fear and trembling.

Phil 2:12 Therefore, my beloved, as you have always obeyed, not as in my presence only, but now much more in my absence, work out your own salvation with fear and trembling;

Believers

Appointed to obtain.

1 Thess 5:9 For God did not appoint us to wrath, but to obtain salvation through our Lord Jesus Christ,

2 Thess 2:13 But we are bound to give thanks to God always for you, brethren beloved by the Lord, because God from the beginning chose you for salvation through sanctification by the Spirit and belief in the truth,

2 Tim 1:9 who has saved us and called *us* with a holy calling, not according to our works, but according to His own purpose and grace which was given to us in Christ Jesus before time began,

Are heirs of.

Heb 1:14 Are they not all ministering spirits sent forth to minister for those who will inherit salvation?

Have, through grace.

Acts 15:11 But we believe that through the grace of the Lord Jesus Christ we shall be saved in the same manner as they."

Have a token of, in their patient suffering for Christ.

Phil 1:28–29 and not in any way terrified by your adversaries, which is to them a proof of perdition, but to you of salvation, and that from God. 29 For to you it has been granted on behalf of Christ, not only to believe in Him, but also to suffer for His sake,

Kept by the power of God to.

1 Pet 1:5 who are kept by the power of God through faith for salvation ready to be revealed in the last time.

Beautified with.

Ps 149:4 For the LORD takes pleasure in His people; He will beautify the humble with salvation.

Clothed with.

Is 61:10 I will greatly rejoice in the LORD, My soul shall be joyful in my God; For He has clothed me with the garments of salvation, He has covered me with the robe of righteousness, As a bridegroom decks *himself*

with ornaments, And as a bride adorns *herself* with her jewels.

Satisfied by.

Luke 2:30 For my eyes have seen Your salvation

Love.

Ps 40:16 Let all those who seek You rejoice and be glad in You; Let such as love Your salvation say continually, "The LORD be magnified!"

Hope for.

Lam 3:26 *It is* good that *one* should hope and wait quietly For the salvation of the LORD.

Rom 8:24 For we were saved in this hope, but hope that is seen is not hope; for why does one still hope for what he sees?

Wait for.

Gen 49:18 I have waited for your salvation, O LORD!

Ps 119:81 My soul faints for Your salvation, But I hope in Your word.

Ps 119:123 My eyes fail *from seeking* Your salvation And Your righteous word.

Ps 119:174 I long for Your salvation, O LORD, And Your law *is* my delight.

Lam 3:26 *It is* good that *one* should hope and wait quietly For the salvation of the LORD.

Daily approach nearer to.

Rom 13:11 And *do* this, knowing the time, that now *it is* high time to awake out of sleep; for now our salvation *is* nearer than when we *first* believed.

Receive, as the end of their faith.

1 Pet 1:9 receiving the end of your faith—the salvation of *your* souls.

Welcome the news of.

Is 52:7 How beautiful upon the mountains Are the feet of him who brings good news, Who proclaims peace, Who brings glad tidings of good *things*, Who proclaims salvation, Who says to Zion, "Your God reigns!"

Rom 10:15 And how shall they preach unless they are sent? As it is written: *"How beautiful are the feet of those who preach the gospel of peace, Who bring glad tidings of good things!"*

Pray to be visited with.

Ps 85:7 Show us Your mercy, LORD, And grant us Your salvation.

Ps 106:4 Remember me, O LORD, with the favor *You have toward* Your people. Oh, visit me with Your salvation,

Ps 119:41 Let Your mercies come also to me, O LORD— Your salvation according to Your word.

Pray for the assurance of.

Ps 35:3 Also draw out the spear, And stop those who pursue me. Say to my soul, "I *am* your salvation."

Pray for a joyful sense of.

Ps 51:12 Restore to me the joy of Your salvation, And uphold me *by Your* generous Spirit.

Evidence, by works.

Heb 6:9–10 But, beloved, we are confident of better things concerning you, yes, things that accompany salvation, though we speak in this manner. 10 For God *is* not unjust to forget your work and labor of love which you have shown toward His name, *in that* you have ministered to the saints, and do minister.

Ascribe, to God.

Ps 25:5 Lead me in Your truth and teach me, For You *are* the God of my salvation; On You I wait all the day.

Is 12:2 Behold, God *is* my salvation, I will trust and not be afraid; 'For YAH, the LORD, *is* my strength and song; He also has become my salvation.' "

Praise God for.

1 Chr 16:23 Sing to the LORD, all the earth; Proclaim the good news of His salvation from day to day.

Ps 96:2 Sing to the LORD, bless His name; Proclaim the good news of His salvation from day to day.

Ps 116:12 What shall I render to the LORD For all His benefits toward me?

Rejoice and glory in.

Ps 9:14 That I may tell of all Your praise In the gates of the daughter of Zion. I will rejoice in Your salvation.

Ps 21:1 The king shall have joy in Your strength, O LORD; And in Your salvation how greatly shall he rejoice!

Is 25:9 And it will be said in that day: "Behold, this *is* our God; We have waited for Him, and He will save us. This *is* the LORD; We have waited for Him; We will be glad and rejoice in His salvation."

1 Cor 1:31 that, as it is written, *"He who glories, let him glory in the LORD."*

Gal 6:14 But God forbid that I should boast except in the cross of our Lord Jesus Christ, by whom the world has been crucified to me, and I to the world.

Declare.

Ps 40:10 I have not hidden Your righteousness within my heart; I have declared Your faithfulness and Your salvation; I have not concealed Your lovingkindness and Your truth From the great assembly.

Ps 71:15 My mouth shall tell of Your righteousness *And* Your salvation all the day, For I do not know *their* limits.

Godly sorrow works repentance to.

2 Cor 7:10 For godly sorrow produces repentance *leading* to salvation, not to be regretted; but the sorrow of the world produces death.

All the earth shall see.

Is 52:10 The LORD has made bare His holy arm In the eyes of all the nations; And all the ends of the earth shall see The salvation of our God.

Luke 3:6 *And all flesh shall see the salvation of God.' "*

Ministers

Give the knowledge of.

Luke 1:77 To give knowledge of salvation to His people By the remission of their sins,

Show the way of.

Acts 16:17 This girl followed Paul and us, and cried out, saying, "These men are the servants of the Most High God, who proclaim to us the way of salvation."

Should exhort to.

Ezek 3:18–19 When I say to the wicked, 'You shall surely die,' and you give him no warning, nor speak to warn the wicked from his wicked way, to save his life, that same wicked *man* shall die in his iniquity;

but his blood I will require at your hand. **19** Yet, if you warn the wicked, and he does not turn from his wickedness, nor from his wicked way, he shall die in his iniquity; but you have delivered your soul.

Acts 2:40 And with many other words he testified and exhorted them, saying, "Be saved from this perverse generation."

Should labor to lead others to.

Rom 11:14 if by any means I may provoke to jealousy *those who are* my flesh and save some of them.

Should be clothed in.

2 Chr 6:41 "Now therefore, Arise, O LORD God, to Your resting place, You and the ark of Your strength. Let Your priests, O LORD God, be clothed with salvation, And let Your saints rejoice in goodness.

Ps 132:16 I will also clothe her priests with salvation, And her saints shall shout aloud for joy.

Should use self-denial to lead others to.

1 Cor 9:22 to the weak I became as weak, that I might win the weak. I have become all things to all *men,* that I might by all means save some.

Should endure suffering that the elect may obtain.

2 Tim 2:10 Therefore I endure all things for the sake of the elect, that they also may obtain the salvation which is in Christ Jesus with eternal glory.

Are a fragrance of Christ to God, in those who obtain.

2 Cor 2:15 For we are to God the fragrance of Christ among those who are being saved and among those who are perishing.

The heavenly host ascribe, to God.

Rev 7:10 and crying out with a loud voice, saying, "Salvation *belongs* to our God who sits on the throne, and to the Lamb!"

Rev 19:1 After these things I heard a loud voice of a great multitude in heaven, saying, "Alleluia! Salvation and glory and honor and power *belong* to the Lord our God!

Sought in vain from

Idols.

Is 45:20 "Assemble yourselves and come; Draw near together, You *who have* escaped from the nations. They have no knowledge, Who carry the wood of their carved image, And pray to a god *that* cannot save.

Jer 2:28 But where *are* your gods that you have made for yourselves? Let them arise, If they can save you in the time of your trouble; For *according to* the number of your cities Are your gods, O Judah.

Earthly power.

Jer 3:23 Truly, in vain *is salvation hoped for* from the hills, *And from* the multitude of mountains; Truly, in the LORD our God *Is* the salvation of Israel.

No escape for those who neglect.

Heb 2:3 how shall we escape if we neglect so great a salvation, which at the first began to be spoken by the Lord, and was confirmed to us by those who heard Him,

Is far off from the wicked.

Ps 119:155 Salvation *is* far from the wicked, For they do not seek Your statutes.

Is 59:11 We all growl like bears, And moan sadly like

doves; We look for justice, but *there is* none; For salvation, *but* it is far from us.

Illustrated by

A rock.

Deut 32:15 "But Jeshurun grew fat and kicked; You grew fat, you grew thick, You are obese! Then he forsook God *who* made him, And scornfully esteemed the Rock of his salvation.

2 Sam 22:47 "The LORD lives! Blessed *be* my Rock! Let God be exalted, The Rock of my salvation!

Ps 95:1 Oh come, let us sing to the LORD! Let us shout joyfully to the Rock of our salvation.

A horn.

Ps 18:2 The LORD is my rock and my fortress and my deliverer; My God, my strength, in whom I will trust; My shield and the horn of my salvation, my stronghold.

Luke 1:69 And has raised up a horn of salvation for us In the house of His servant David,

A tower.

2 Sam 22:51 "*He is* the tower of salvation to His king, And shows mercy to His anointed, To David and his descendants forevermore."

A helmet.

Is 59:17 For He put on righteousness as a breastplate, And a helmet of salvation on His head; He put on the garments of vengeance for clothing, And was clad with zeal as a cloak.

Eph 6:17 And take the helmet of salvation, and the sword of the Spirit, which is the word of God;

A shield.

2 Sam 22:36 "You have also given me the shield of Your salvation; Your gentleness has made me great.

A lamp.

Is 62:1 For Zion's sake I will not hold My peace, And for Jerusalem's sake I will not rest, Until her righteousness goes forth as brightness, And her salvation as a lamp *that* burns.

A cup.

Ps 116:13 I will take up the cup of salvation, And call upon the name of the LORD.

Clothing.

2 Chr 6:41 "Now therefore, Arise, O LORD God, to Your resting place, You and the ark of Your strength. Let Your priests, O LORD God, be clothed with salvation, And let Your saints rejoice in goodness.

Ps 132:16 I will also clothe her priests with salvation, And her saints shall shout aloud for joy.

Ps 149:4 For the LORD takes pleasure in His people; He will beautify the humble with salvation.

Is 61:10 I will greatly rejoice in the LORD, My soul shall be joyful in my God; For He has clothed me with the garments of salvation, He has covered me with the robe of righteousness, As a bridegroom decks *himself* with ornaments, And as a bride adorns *herself* with her jewels.

Wells.

Is 12:3 Therefore with joy you will draw water From the wells of salvation.

Walls and bulwarks.

Is 26:1 In that day this song will be sung in the land of Judah: "We have a strong city; *God* will appoint salvation *for* walls and bulwarks.

Is 60:18 Violence shall no longer be heard in your land, Neither wasting nor destruction within your borders; But you shall call your walls Salvation, And your gates Praise.

Chariots.

Hab 3:8 O LORD, were *You* displeased with the rivers, *Was* Your anger against the rivers, *Was* Your wrath against the sea, That You rode on Your horses, Your chariots of salvation?

A victory.

1 Cor 15:57 But thanks *be* to God, who gives us the victory through our Lord Jesus Christ.

Typified.

Num 21:4–9 Then they journeyed from Mount Hor by the Way of the Red Sea, to go around the land of Edom; and the soul of the people became very discouraged on the way. **5** And the people spoke against God and against Moses: "Why have you brought us up out of Egypt to die in the wilderness? For *there is* no food and no water, and our soul loathes this worthless bread." **6** So the LORD sent fiery serpents among the people, and they bit the people; and many of the people of Israel died. **7** Therefore the people came to Moses, and said, "We have sinned, for we have spoken against the LORD and against you; pray to the LORD that He take away the serpents from us." So Moses prayed for the people. **8** Then the LORD said to Moses, "Make a fiery *serpent*, and set it on a pole; and it shall be that everyone who is bitten, when he looks at it, shall live." **9** So Moses made a bronze serpent, and put it on a pole; and so it was, if a serpent had bitten anyone, when he looked at the bronze serpent, he lived.

John 3:14–15 And as Moses lifted up the serpent in the wilderness, even so must the Son of Man be lifted up, **15** that whoever believes in Him should not perish but have eternal life.

SAMARIA (OLD TESTAMENT)

The territory of Ephraim and Manasseh.

Josh 17:17–18 And Joshua spoke to the house of Joseph—to Ephraim and Manasseh—saying, "You *are* a great people and have great power; you shall not have *only* one lot, **18** but the mountain country shall be yours. Although it *is* wooded, you shall cut it down, and its farthest extent shall be yours; for you shall drive out the Canaanites, though they have iron chariots *and* are strong."

Is 28:1 Woe to the crown of pride, to the drunkards of Ephraim, Whose glorious beauty *is* a fading flower Which *is* at the head of the verdant valleys, To those who are overcome with wine!

The whole kingdom of Israel sometimes called.

Ezek 16:46 "Your elder sister *is* Samaria, who dwells with her daughters to the north of you; and your younger sister, who dwells to the south of you, *is* Sodom and her daughters.

Ezek 16:51 "Samaria did not commit half of your sins;

but you have multiplied your abominations more than they, and have justified your sisters by all the abominations which you have done.

Hos 8:5–6 Your calf is rejected, O Samaria! My anger is aroused against them— How long until they attain to innocence? 6 For from Israel *is* even this: A workman made it, and it *is* not God; But the calf of Samaria shall be broken to pieces.

Had many cities.

1 Kin 13:32 For the saying which he cried out by the word of the Lord against the altar in Bethel, and against all the shrines on the high places which *are* in the cities of Samaria, will surely come to pass."

City of Samaria the capital of,

Built by Omri and named after Shemer.

1 Kin 16:23–24 In the thirty-first year of Asa king of Judah, Omri became king over Israel, *and reigned* twelve years. Six years he reigned in Tirzah. 24 And he bought the hill of Samaria from Shemer for two talents of silver; then he built on the hill, and called the name of the city which he built, Samaria, after the name of Shemer, owner of the hill.

Called the mountain of Samaria.

Amos 4:1 Hear this word, you cows of Bashan, who *are* on the mountain of Samaria, Who oppress the poor, Who crush the needy, Who say to your husbands, "Bring *wine*, let us drink!"

Amos 6:1 Woe to you *who are* at ease in Zion, And trust in Mount Samaria, Notable persons in the chief nation, To whom the house of Israel comes!

Called the head of Ephraim.

Is 7:9 The head of Ephraim *is* Samaria, And the head of Samaria *is* Remaliah's son. If you will not believe, Surely you shall not be established." ' "

Kings of Israel sometimes took their titles from.

1 Kin 21:1 And it came to pass after these things *that* Naboth the Jezreelite had a vineyard which *was* in Jezreel, next to the palace of Ahab king of Samaria.

2 Kin 1:3 But the angel of the Lord said to Elijah the Tishbite, "Arise, go up to meet the messengers of the king of Samaria, and say to them, 'Is it because *there is* no God in Israel *that* you are going to inquire of Baal-Zebub, the god of Ekron?'

The residence of the kings of Israel.

1 Kin 16:29 In the thirty-eighth year of Asa king of Judah, Ahab the son of Omri became king over Israel; and Ahab the son of Omri reigned over Israel in Samaria twenty-two years.

2 Kin 1:2 Now Ahaziah fell through the lattice of his upper room in Samaria, and was injured; so he sent messengers and said to them, "Go, inquire of Baal-Zebub, the god of Ekron, whether I shall recover from this injury."

2 Kin 3:1 Now Jehoram the son of Ahab became king over Israel at Samaria in the eighteenth year of Jehoshaphat king of Judah, and reigned twelve years.

2 Kin 3:6 So King Jehoram went out of Samaria at that time and mustered all Israel.

The burial place of the kings of Israel.

1 Kin 16:28 So Omri rested with his fathers and was

buried in Samaria. Then Ahab his son reigned in his place.

1 Kin 22:37 So the king died, and was brought to Samaria. And they buried the king in Samaria.

2 Kin 13:13 So Joash rested with his fathers. Then Jeroboam sat on his throne. And Joash was buried in Samaria with the kings of Israel.

Was well fortified.

2 Kin 10:2 Now as soon as this letter comes to you, since your master's sons *are* with you, and you have chariots and horses, a fortified city also, and weapons,

The pool of Samaria near to.

1 Kin 22:38 Then *someone* washed the chariot at a pool in Samaria, and the dogs licked up his blood while the harlots bathed, according to the word of the Lord which He had spoken.

The prophet Elisha dwelt in.

2 Kin 2:25 Then he went from there to Mount Carmel, and from there he returned to Samaria.

2 Kin 5:3 Then she said to her mistress, "If only my master *were* with the prophet who *is* in Samaria! For he would heal him of his leprosy."

Besieged by Ben-Hadad. **1 Kin 20:1–12**

Deliverance of, predicted.

1 Kin 20:13–14 Suddenly a prophet approached Ahab king of Israel, saying, "Thus says the Lord: 'Have you seen all this great multitude? Behold, I will deliver it into your hand today, and you shall know that I *am* the Lord.' " 14 So Ahab said, "By whom?" And he said, "Thus says the Lord: 'By the young leaders of the provinces.' " Then he said, "Who will set the battle in order?" And he answered, "You."

Deliverance of, effected.

1 Kin 20:15–21 Then he mustered the young leaders of the provinces, and there were two hundred and thirty-two; and after them he mustered all the people, all the children of Israel—seven thousand. 16 So they went out at noon. Meanwhile Ben-Hadad and the thirty-two kings helping him were getting drunk at the command post. 17 The young leaders of the provinces went out first. And Ben-Hadad sent out *a patrol*, and they told him, saying, "Men are coming out of Samaria!" 18 So he said, "If they have come out for peace, take them alive; and if they have come out for war, take them alive." 19 Then these young leaders of the provinces went out of the city with the army which followed them. 20 And each one killed his man; so the Syrians fled, and Israel pursued them; and Ben-Hadad the king of Syria escaped on a horse with the cavalry. 21 Then the king of Israel went out and attacked the horses and chariots, and killed the Syrians with a great slaughter.

Besieged again by Ben-Hadad.

2 Kin 6:24 And it happened after this that Ben-Hadad king of Syria gathered all his army, and went up and besieged Samaria.

Suffered severely from famine.

2 Kin 6:25–29 And there was a great famine in Samaria; and indeed they besieged it until a donkey's head was *sold* for eighty *shekels* of silver, and one-fourth of a kab of dove droppings for five *shekels* of silver.

26 Then, as the king of Israel was passing by on the wall, a woman cried out to him, saying, "Help, my lord, O king!" 27 And he said, "If the LORD does not help you, where can I find help for you? From the threshing floor or from the winepress?" 28 Then the king said to her, "What is troubling you?" And she answered, "This woman said to me, 'Give your son, that we may eat him today, and we will eat my son tomorrow.' 29 So we boiled my son, and ate him. And I said to her on the next day, 'Give your son, that we may eat him'; but she has hidden her son."

Elisha predicted return of city's trade.

2 Kin 7:1–2 Then Elisha said, "Hear the word of the LORD. Thus says the LORD: 'Tomorrow about this time a seah of fine flour *shall be sold* for a shekel, and two seahs of barley for a shekel, at the gate of Samaria.' " 2 So an officer on whose hand the king leaned answered the man of God and said, "Look, *if* the LORD would make windows in heaven, could this thing be?" And he said, "In fact, you shall see *it* with your eyes, but you shall not eat of it."

Delivered by miraculous means.

2 Kin 7:6–7 For the LORD had caused the army of the Syrians to hear the noise of chariots and the noise of horses—the noise of a great army; so they said to one another, "Look, the king of Israel has hired against us the kings of the Hittites and the kings of the Egyptians to attack us!" 7 Therefore they arose and fled at twilight, and left the camp intact—their tents, their horses, and their donkeys—and they fled for their lives.

Remarkable prosperity in, as foretold by Elisha.

2 Kin 7:16–20 Then the people went out and plundered the tents of the Syrians. So a seah of fine flour was *sold* for a shekel, and two seahs of barley for a shekel, according to the word of the LORD. 17 Now the king had appointed the officer on whose hand he leaned to have charge of the gate. But the people trampled him in the gate, and he died, just as the man of God had said, who spoke when the king came down to him. 18 So it happened just as the man of God had spoken to the king, saying, "Two seahs of barley for a shekel, and a seah of fine flour for a shekel, shall be *sold* tomorrow about this time in the gate of Samaria." 19 Then that officer had answered the man of God, and said, "Now look, *if* the LORD would make windows in heaven, could such a thing be?" And he had said, "In fact, you shall see *it* with your eyes, but you shall not eat of it." 20 And so it happened to him, for the people trampled him in the gate, and he died.

Besieged and taken by Shalmaneser.

2 Kin 17:5–6 Now the king of Assyria went throughout all the land, and went up to Samaria and besieged it for three years. 6 In the ninth year of Hoshea, the king of Assyria took Samaria and carried Israel away to Assyria, and placed them in Halah and by the Habor, the River of Gozan, and in the cities of the Medes.

2 Kin 18:9–10 Now it came to pass in the fourth year of King Hezekiah, which *was* the seventh year of Hoshea the son of Elah, king of Israel, *that* Shalmaneser king of Assyria came up against Samaria and besieged it. 10 And at the end of three years they took it. In the sixth year of Hezekiah, that *is*, the ninth year of Hoshea king of Israel, Samaria was taken.

A mountainous country.

Jer 31:5 You shall yet plant vines on the mountains of Samaria; The planters shall plant and eat *them* as ordinary food.

Amos 3:9 "Proclaim in the palaces at Ashdod, And in the palaces in the land of Egypt, and say: 'Assemble on the mountains of Samaria; See great tumults in her midst, And the oppressed within her.

People of, characterized as

Proud and arrogant.

Is 9:9 All the people will know— Ephraim and the inhabitant of Samaria— Who say in pride and arrogance of heart:

Corrupt and wicked.

Ezek 16:46–47 "Your elder sister *is* Samaria, who dwells with her daughters to the north of you; and your younger sister, who dwells to the south of you, *is* Sodom and her daughters. 47 You did not walk in their ways nor act according to their abominations; but, as *if that were* too little, you became more corrupt than they in all your ways.

Hos 7:1 "When I would have healed Israel, Then the iniquity of Ephraim was uncovered, And the wickedness of Samaria. For they have committed fraud; A thief comes in; A band of robbers takes spoil outside.

Amos 3:9–10 "Proclaim in the palaces at Ashdod, And in the palaces in the land of Egypt, and say: 'Assemble on the mountains of Samaria; See great tumults in her midst, And the oppressed within her. 10 For they do not know to do right,' Says the LORD, 'Who store up violence and robbery in their palaces.' "

Idolatrous.

Ezek 23:5 "Oholah played the harlot even though she was Mine; And she lusted for her lovers, the neighboring Assyrians,

Amos 8:14 Those who swear by the sin of Samaria, Who say, 'As your god lives, O Dan!' And, 'As the way of Beersheba lives!' They shall fall and never rise again."

Mic 1:7 All her carved images shall be beaten to pieces, And all her pay as a harlot shall be burned with the fire; All her idols I will lay desolate, For she gathered *it* from the pay of a harlot, And they shall return to the pay of a harlot."

Predictions respecting its destruction.

Is 8:4 for before the child shall have knowledge to cry 'My father' and 'My mother,' the riches of Damascus and the spoil of Samaria will be taken away before the king of Assyria."

Is 9:11–12 Therefore the LORD shall set up The adversaries of Rezin against him, And spur his enemies on, 12 The Syrians before and the Philistines behind; And they shall devour Israel with an open mouth. For all this His anger is not turned away, But His hand *is* stretched out still.

Hos 13:16 Samaria is held guilty, For she has rebelled against her God. They shall fall by the sword, Their infants shall be dashed in pieces, And their women with child ripped open.

Amos 3:11–12 Therefore thus says the Lord GOD: "An adversary *shall be* all around the land; He shall sap your strength from you, And your palaces shall be plundered." **12** Thus says the Lord: "As a shepherd takes from the mouth of a lion Two legs or a piece of an ear, So shall the children of Israel be taken out Who dwell in Samaria— In the corner of a bed and on the edge of a couch!

Mic 1:6 "Therefore I will make Samaria a heap of ruins in the field, Places for planting a vineyard; I will pour down her stones into the valley, And I will uncover her foundations.

Inhabitants of, carried captive to Assyria.

2 Kin 17:6 In the ninth year of Hoshea, the king of Assyria took Samaria and carried Israel away to Assyria, and placed them in Halah and by the Habor, the River of Gozan, and in the cities of the Medes.

2 Kin 17:23 until the Lord removed Israel out of His sight, as He had said by all His servants the prophets. So Israel was carried away from their own land to Assyria, *as it is* to this day.

2 Kin 18:11 Then the king of Assyria carried Israel away captive to Assyria, and put them in Halah and by the Habor, the River of Gozan, and in the cities of the Medes,

Repopulated from Assyria.

2 Kin 17:24–25 Then the king of Assyria brought *people* from Babylon, Cuthah, Ava, Hamath, and from Sepharvaim, and placed *them* in the cities of Samaria instead of the children of Israel; and they took possession of Samaria and dwelt in its cities. **25** And it was so, at the beginning of their dwelling there, *that* they did not fear the Lord; therefore the Lord sent lions among them, which killed *some* of them.

Samaria (New Testament)
Situated between Judea and Galilee.

Luke 17:11 Now it happened as He went to Jerusalem that He passed through the midst of Samaria and Galilee.

John 4:3–4 He left Judea and departed again to Galilee. **4** But He needed to go through Samaria.

Had many cities.

Matt 10:5 These twelve Jesus sent out and commanded them, saying: "Do not go into the way of the Gentiles, and do not enter a city of the Samaritans.

Luke 9:52 and sent messengers before His face. And as they went, they entered a village of the Samaritans, to prepare for Him.

Cities of, mentioned in Scripture
Samaria.

Acts 8:5 Then Philip went down to the city of Samaria and preached Christ to them.

Sychar.

John 4:5 So He came to a city of Samaria which is called Sychar, near the plot of ground that Jacob gave to his son Joseph.

Antipatris.

Acts 23:31 Then the soldiers, as they were commanded, took Paul and brought *him* by night to Antipatris.

Christ preached in.

John 4:39–42 And many of the Samaritans of that city believed in Him because of the word of the woman who testified, "He told me all that I *ever* did." **40** So

when the Samaritans had come to Him, they urged Him to stay with them; and He stayed there two days. **41** And many more believed because of His own word. **42** Then they said to the woman, "Now we believe, not because of what you said, for we ourselves have heard *Him* and we know that this is indeed the Christ, the Savior of the world."

Christ at first forbade His disciples to visit.

Matt 10:5 These twelve Jesus sent out and commanded them, saying: "Do not go into the way of the Gentiles, and do not enter a city of the Samaritans.

Christ, after His resurrection, commanded the gospel to be preached in.

Acts 1:8 But you shall receive power when the Holy Spirit has come upon you; and you shall be witnesses to Me in Jerusalem, and in all Judea and Samaria, and to the end of the earth."

Inhabitants of,
Their true descent.

2 Kin 17:24 Then the king of Assyria brought *people* from Babylon, Cuthah, Ava, Hamath, and from Sepharvaim, and placed *them* in the cities of Samaria instead of the children of Israel; and they took possession of Samaria and dwelt in its cities.

Ezra 4:9–10 From Rehum the commander, Shimshai the scribe, and the rest of their companions—*representatives* of the Dinaites, the Apharsathchites, the Tarpelites, the people of Persia and Erech and Babylon and Shushan, the Dehavites, the Elamites, **10** and the rest of the nations whom the great and noble Osnapper took captive and settled in the cities of Samaria and the remainder beyond the River—and so forth.

Boasted descent from Jacob.

John 4:12 Are You greater than our father Jacob, who gave us the well, and drank from it himself, as well as his sons and his livestock?"

Professed to worship God.

Ezra 4:2 they came to Zerubbabel and the heads of the fathers' *houses*, and said to them, "Let us build with you, for we seek your God as you *do*; and we have sacrificed to Him since the days of Esarhaddon king of Assyria, who brought us here."

Their religion mixed with idolatry.

2 Kin 17:41 So these nations feared the Lord, yet served their carved images; also their children and their children's children have continued doing as their fathers did, even to this day.

John 4:22 You worship what you do not know; we know what we worship, for salvation is of the Jews.

Worshiped on Mount Gerizim.

John 4:20 Our fathers worshiped on this mountain, and you *Jews* say that in Jerusalem is the place where one ought to worship."

Expected the Messiah.

John 4:25 The woman said to Him, "I know that Messiah is coming" (who is called Christ). "When He comes, He will tell us all things."

John 4:29 "Come, see a Man who told me all things that I ever did. Could this be the Christ?"

Were superstitious.

Acts 8:9–11 But there was a certain man called Simon,

who previously practiced sorcery in the city and astonished the people of Samaria, claiming that he was someone great, **10** to whom they all gave heed, from the least to the greatest, saying, "This man is the great power of God." **11** And they heeded him because he had astonished them with his sorceries for a long time.

More humane and grateful than the Jews.

Luke 10:33–36 But a certain Samaritan, as he journeyed, came where he was. And when he saw him, he had compassion. **34** So he went to *him* and bandaged his wounds, pouring on oil and wine; and he set him on his own animal, brought him to an inn, and took care of him. **35** On the next day, when he departed, he took out two denarii, gave *them* to the innkeeper, and said to him, 'Take care of him; and whatever more you spend, when I come again, I will repay you.' **36** So which of these three do you think was neighbor to him who fell among the thieves?"

Luke 17:16–18 and fell down on *his* face at His feet, giving Him thanks. And he was a Samaritan. **17** So Jesus answered and said, "Were there not ten cleansed? But where *are* the nine? **18** Were there not any found who returned to give glory to God except this foreigner?"

Abhorred by the Jews.

John 8:48 Then the Jews answered and said to Him, "Do we not say rightly that You are a Samaritan and have a demon?"

Had no dealings with the Jews.

Luke 9:52–53 and sent messengers before His face. And as they went, they entered a village of the Samaritans, to prepare for Him. **53** But they did not receive Him, because His face was *set* for the journey to Jerusalem.

John 4:9 Then the woman of Samaria said to Him, "How is it that You, being a Jew, ask a drink from me, a Samaritan woman?" For Jews have no dealings with Samaritans.

Ready to hear and embrace the gospel.

John 4:39–42 And many of the Samaritans of that city believed in Him because of the word of the woman who testified, "He told me all that I *ever* did." **40** So when the Samaritans had come to Him, they urged Him to stay with them; and He stayed there two days. **41** And many more believed because of His own word. **42** Then they said to the woman, "Now we believe, not because of what you said, for we ourselves have heard *Him* and we know that this is indeed the Christ, the Savior of the world."

Acts 8:6–8 And the multitudes with one accord heeded the things spoken by Philip, hearing and seeing the miracles which he did. **7** For unclean spirits, crying with a loud voice, came out of many who were possessed; and many who were paralyzed and lame were healed. **8** And there was great joy in that city.

The persecuted Christians fled to.

Acts 8:1 Now Saul was consenting to his death. At that time a great persecution arose against the church which was at Jerusalem; and they were all scattered throughout the regions of Judea and Samaria, except the apostles.

The gospel first preached in, by Philip.

Acts 8:5 Then Philip went down to the city of Samaria and preached Christ to them.

Many Christian churches in.

Acts 9:31 Then the churches throughout all Judea, Galilee, and Samaria had peace and were edified. And walking in the fear of the Lord and in the comfort of the Holy Spirit, they were multiplied.

SAMUEL

Birth and consecration of. 1 Sam 1:19–28

God's word first came to him. 1 Sam 3:2–18

Recognized as prophet and leader for Israel.

1 Sam 3:19–21 So Samuel grew, and the LORD was with him and let none of his words fall to the ground. **20** And all Israel from Dan to Beersheba knew that Samuel *had been* established as a prophet of the LORD. **21** Then the LORD appeared again in Shiloh. For the LORD revealed Himself to Samuel in Shiloh by the word of the LORD.

Became circuit judge.

1 Sam 7:15–17 And Samuel judged Israel all the days of his life. **16** He went from year to year on a circuit to Bethel, Gilgal, and Mizpah, and judged Israel in all those places. **17** But he always returned to Ramah, for his home *was* there. There he judged Israel, and there he built an altar to the LORD.

Called Israel to repentance.

1 Sam 7:3–6 Then Samuel spoke to all the house of Israel, saying, "If you return to the LORD with all your hearts, *then* put away the foreign gods and the Ashtoreths from among you, and prepare your hearts for the LORD, and serve Him only; and He will deliver you from the hand of the Philistines." **4** So the children of Israel put away the Baals and the Ashtoreths, and served the LORD only. **5** And Samuel said, "Gather all Israel to Mizpah, and I will pray to the LORD for you." **6** So they gathered together at Mizpah, drew water, and poured *it* out before the LORD. And they fasted that day, and said there, "We have sinned against the LORD." And Samuel judged the children of Israel at Mizpah.

Warned Israel about dangers of having a king.
1 Sam 8:10–18

Used by God to choose Saul as king.

1 Sam 10:1 Then Samuel took a flask of oil and poured *it* on his head, and kissed him and said: "*Is it* not because the LORD has anointed you commander over His inheritance?

Cf. 1 Sam 9:15–27

Told Saul he must forfeit royal office.
1 Sam 15:10–31

Death of.

1 Sam 25:1 Then Samuel died; and the Israelites gathered together and lamented for him, and buried him at his home in Ramah. And David arose and went down to the Wilderness of Paran.

Called up from the grave; warned Saul.

1 Sam 28:11–19 Then the woman said, "Whom shall I bring up for you?" And he said, "Bring up Samuel for me." **12** When the woman saw Samuel, she cried out with a loud voice. And the woman spoke to Saul, saying, "Why have you deceived me? For you *are* Saul!" **13** And the king said to her, "Do not be afraid. What did you see?" And the woman said to Saul, "I saw a spirit ascending out of the earth." **14** So he said to her, "What *is* his form?" And she said, "An old man is coming up, and he *is* covered with a mantle." And Saul perceived that it *was* Samuel, and he stooped with *his* face to the ground and bowed down. **15** Now Samuel said to Saul, "Why have you disturbed me by bringing me up?" And Saul answered, "I am deeply distressed; for the Philistines make war against me, and God has departed from me and does not answer me anymore, neither by prophets nor by dreams. Therefore I have called you, that you may reveal to me what I should do." **16** Then Samuel said: "So why do you ask me, seeing the LORD has departed from you and has become your enemy? **17** And the LORD has done for Himself as He spoke by me. For the LORD has torn the kingdom out of your hand and given it to your neighbor, David. **18** Because you did not obey the voice of the LORD nor execute His fierce wrath upon Amalek, therefore the LORD has done this thing to you this day. **19** Moreover the LORD will also deliver Israel with you into the hand of the Philistines. And tomorrow you and your sons *will be* with me. The LORD will also deliver the army of Israel into the hand of the Philistines."

SANCTIFICATION

Is separation to the service of God.

Ps 4:3 But know that the LORD has set apart for Himself him who is godly; The LORD will hear when I call to Him.

2 Cor 6:17 Therefore *"Come out from among them And be separate, says the Lord. Do not touch what is unclean, And I will receive you."*

Effected by

God.

Ezek 37:28 The nations also will know that I, the LORD, sanctify Israel, when My sanctuary is in their midst forevermore." ' "

1 Thess 5:23 Now may the God of peace Himself sanctify you completely; and may your whole spirit, soul, and body be preserved blameless at the coming of our Lord Jesus Christ.

Jude 1:1 Jude, a bondservant of Jesus Christ, and brother of James, To those who are called, sanctified by God the Father, and preserved in Jesus Christ:

Christ.

Heb 2:11 For both He who sanctifies and those who are being sanctified *are* all of one, for which reason He is not ashamed to call them brethren,

Heb 13:12 Therefore Jesus also, that He might sanctify the people with His own blood, suffered outside the gate.

The Holy Spirit.

Rom 15:16 that I might be a minister of Jesus Christ to the Gentiles, ministering the gospel of God, that the offering of the Gentiles might be acceptable, sanctified by the Holy Spirit.

1 Cor 6:11 And such were some of you. But you were

washed, but you were sanctified, but you were justified in the name of the Lord Jesus and by the Spirit of our God.

2 Thess 2:13 But we are bound to give thanks to God always for you, brethren beloved by the Lord, because God from the beginning chose you for salvation through sanctification by the Spirit and belief in the truth,

1 Pet 1:2 elect according to the foreknowledge of God the Father, in sanctification of the Spirit, for obedience and sprinkling of the blood of Jesus Christ: Grace to you and peace be multiplied.

In Christ.

1 Cor 1:2 To the church of God which is at Corinth, to those who are sanctified in Christ Jesus, called *to be* saints, with all who in every place call on the name of Jesus Christ our Lord, both theirs and ours:

1 Cor 1:30 But of Him you are in Christ Jesus, who became for us wisdom from God—and righteousness and sanctification and redemption—

Through the atonement of Christ.

Heb 10:10 By that will we have been sanctified through the offering of the body of Jesus Christ once *for all.*

Heb 13:12 Therefore Jesus also, that He might sanctify the people with His own blood, suffered outside the gate.

Through the Word of God.

John 17:17 Sanctify them by Your truth. Your word is truth.

John 17:19 And for their sakes I sanctify Myself, that they also may be sanctified by the truth.

Eph 5:26 that He might sanctify and cleanse her with the washing of water by the word,

All believers are growing in.

Acts 20:32 "So now, brethren, I commend you to God and to the word of His grace, which is able to build you up and give you an inheritance among all those who are sanctified.

Acts 26:18 to open their eyes, *in order* to turn *them* from darkness to light, and *from* the power of Satan to God, that they may receive forgiveness of sins and an inheritance among those who are sanctified by faith in Me.'

1 Cor 6:11 And such were some of you. But you were washed, but you were sanctified, but you were justified in the name of the Lord Jesus and by the Spirit of our God.

The church made glorious by.

Eph 5:26–27 that He might sanctify and cleanse her with the washing of water by the word, **27** that He might present her to Himself a glorious church, not having spot or wrinkle or any such thing, but that she should be holy and without blemish.

Described.

Rom 13:14 But put on the Lord Jesus Christ, and make no provision for the flesh, to *fulfill its* lusts.

Purpose of.

Eph 5:1 Therefore be imitators of God as dear children.

Process of, working out salvation.

Phil 2:12 Therefore, my beloved, as you have always

obeyed, not as in my presence only, but now much more in my absence, work out your own salvation with fear and trembling;

Should lead to

Mortification of sin.

1 Thess 4:3–4 For this is the will of God, your sanctification: that you should abstain from sexual immorality; **4** that each of you should know how to possess his own vessel in sanctification and honor,

Fruitful living.

Rom 6:22 But now having been set free from sin, and having become slaves of God, you have your fruit to holiness, and the end, everlasting life.

Eph 5:7–9 Therefore do not be partakers with them. **8** For you were once darkness, but now *you are* light in the Lord. Walk as children of light **9** (for the fruit of the Spirit *is* in all goodness, righteousness, and truth),

Believers fitted for the service of God by.

2 Tim 2:21 Therefore if anyone cleanses himself from the latter, he will be a vessel for honor, sanctified and useful for the Master, prepared for every good work.

Ministers

Set apart to God's service by.

Jer 1:5 "Before I formed you in the womb I knew you; Before you were born I sanctified you; I ordained you a prophet to the nations."

Should pray that their people enjoy complete.

1 Thess 5:23 Now may the God of peace Himself sanctify you completely; and may your whole spirit, soul, and body be preserved blameless at the coming of our Lord Jesus Christ.

Should exhort their people to walk in.

1 Thess 4:1 Finally then, brethren, we urge and exhort in the Lord Jesus that you should abound more and more, just as you received from us how you ought to walk and to please God;

1 Thess 4:3 For this is the will of God, your sanctification: that you should abstain from sexual immorality;

None can inherit the kingdom of God without.

1 Cor 6:9–11 Do you not know that the unrighteous will not inherit the kingdom of God? Do not be deceived. Neither fornicators, nor idolaters, nor adulterers, nor homosexuals, nor sodomites, **10** nor thieves, nor covetous, nor drunkards, nor revilers, nor extortioners will inherit the kingdom of God. **11** And such were some of you. But you were washed, but you were sanctified, but you were justified in the name of the Lord Jesus and by the Spirit of our God.

Typified.

Gen 2:3 Then God blessed the seventh day and sanctified it, because in it He rested from all His work which God had created and made.

Ex 13:2 "Consecrate to Me all the firstborn, whatever opens the womb among the children of Israel, *both of* man and beast; it is Mine."

Ex 19:14 So Moses went down from the mountain to the people and sanctified the people, and they washed their clothes.

Ex 40:9–15 "And you shall take the anointing oil, and anoint the tabernacle and all that *is* in it; and you shall hallow it and all its utensils, and it shall be holy. **10** You shall anoint the altar of the burnt offering and all its utensils, and consecrate the altar. The altar shall be most holy. **11** And you shall anoint the laver and its base, and consecrate it. **12** "Then you shall bring Aaron and his sons to the door of the tabernacle of meeting and wash them with water. **13** You shall put the holy garments on Aaron, and anoint him and consecrate him, that he may minister to Me as priest. **14** And you shall bring his sons and clothe them with tunics. **15** You shall anoint them, as you anointed their father, that they may minister to Me as priests; for their anointing shall surely be an everlasting priesthood throughout their generations."

Lev 27:14–16 'And when a man dedicates his house *to be* holy to the LORD, then the priest shall set a value for it, whether it is good or bad; as the priest values it, so it shall stand. **15** If he who dedicated it *wants to* redeem his house, then he must add one-fifth of the money of your valuation to it, and it shall be his. **16** 'If a man dedicates to the LORD *part* of a field of his possession, then your valuation shall be according to the seed for it. A homer of barley seed *shall be valued* at fifty shekels of silver.

SANHEDRIN

Probably derived from the seventy elders appointed by Moses.

Ex 24:9 Then Moses went up, also Aaron, Nadab, and Abihu, and seventy of the elders of Israel,

Num 11:16–17 So the LORD said to Moses: "Gather to Me seventy men of the elders of Israel, whom you know to be the elders of the people and officers over them; bring them to the tabernacle of meeting, that they may stand there with you. **17** Then I will come down and talk with you there. I will take of the Spirit that *is* upon you and will put *the same* upon them; and they shall bear the burden of the people with you, that you may not bear *it* yourself alone.

Cf. Num 11:24–30

Mentioned in the New Testament.

Luke 22:66 As soon as it was day, the elders of the people, both chief priests and scribes, came together and led Him into their council, saying,

John 11:47 Then the chief priests and the Pharisees gathered a council and said, "What shall we do? For this Man works many signs.

Acts 5:27 And when they had brought them, they set *them* before the council. And the high priest asked them,

Consisted of chief priest, etc.

Matt 26:57 And those who had laid hold of Jesus led *Him* away to Caiaphas the high priest, where the scribes and the elders were assembled.

Matt 26:59 Now the chief priests, the elders, and all the council sought false testimony against Jesus to put Him to death,

Presided over by high priest.

Matt 26:62–66 And the high priest arose and said to Him, "Do You answer nothing? What *is it* these men testify against You?" **63** But Jesus kept silent. And the high priest answered and said to Him, "I put You under oath by the living God: Tell us if You are the Christ, the Son of God!" **64** Jesus said to him, "*It is as you said.* Nevertheless, I say to you, hereafter you will see the Son of Man sitting at the right hand of the Power, and coming on the clouds of heaven." **65** Then the high priest tore his clothes, saying, "He has spoken blasphemy! What further need do we have of witnesses? Look, now you have heard His blasphemy! **66** What do you think?" They answered and said, "He is deserving of death."

Sat in high priest's palace.

Matt 26:57–58 And those who had laid hold of Jesus led *Him* away to Caiaphas the high priest, where the scribes and the elders were assembled. **58** But Peter followed Him at a distance to the high priest's courtyard. And he went in and sat with the servants to see the end.

SAUL (OLD TESTAMENT)

Son of Kish.

1 Sam 9:1–2 There was a man of Benjamin whose name *was* Kish the son of Abiel, the son of Zeror, the son of Bechorath, the son of Aphiah, a Benjamite, a mighty man of power. **2** And he had a choice and handsome son whose name *was* Saul. *There was* not a more handsome person than he among the children of Israel. From his shoulders upward *he was* taller than any of the people.

First met Samuel. 1 Sam 9:15–27

Anointed as king. 1 Sam 10:1–16

His family and early exploits named.

1 Sam 14:47–52 So Saul established his sovereignty over Israel, and fought against all his enemies on every side, against Moab, against the people of Ammon, against Edom, against the kings of Zobah, and against the Philistines. Wherever he turned, he harassed *them.* **48** And he gathered an army and attacked the Amalekites, and delivered Israel from the hands of those who plundered them. **49** The sons of Saul were Jonathan, Jishui, and Malchishua. And the names of his two daughters *were these:* the name of the firstborn Merab, and the name of the younger Michal. **50** The name of Saul's wife *was* Ahinoam the daughter of Ahimaaz. And the name of the commander of his army *was* Abner the son of Ner, Saul's uncle. **51** Kish *was* the father of Saul, and Ner the father of Abner *was* the son of Abiel. **52** Now there was fierce war with the Philistines all the days of Saul. And when Saul saw any strong man or any valiant man, he took him for himself.

Incomplete obedience and loss of the kingdom.
1 Sam 15:1–31

Resented David.

1 Sam 18:6–13 Now it had happened as they were coming *home,* when David was returning from the slaughter of the Philistine, that the women had come out of all the cities of Israel, singing and dancing, to meet King Saul, with tambourines, with joy, and with musical instruments. **7** So the women sang as they danced, and said: "Saul has slain his thousands, And David his ten thousands." **8** Then Saul was very angry, and the saying displeased him; and he said, "They have ascribed to David ten thousands, and to

me they have ascribed *only* thousands. Now *what* more can he have but the kingdom?" **9** So Saul eyed David from that day forward. **10** And it happened on the next day that the distressing spirit from God came upon Saul, and he prophesied inside the house. So David played *music* with his hand, as at other times; but *there was* a spear in Saul's hand. **11** And Saul cast the spear, for he said, "I will pin David to the wall!" But David escaped his presence twice. **12** Now Saul was afraid of David, because the LORD was with him, but had departed from Saul. **13** Therefore Saul removed him from his presence, and made him his captain over a thousand; and he went out and came in before the people.

Sought to kill David. 1 Sam 19:1–24

Chased David. 1 Sam 23:13–29; 1 Sam 24:1–2

Spared from death. 1 Sam 24:8–15; 1 Sam 26:6–12

God departed from him.

1 Sam 28:3–6 Now Samuel had died, and all Israel had lamented for him and buried him in Ramah, in his own city. And Saul had put the mediums and the spiritists out of the land. **4** Then the Philistines gathered together, and came and encamped at Shunem. So Saul gathered all Israel together, and they encamped at Gilboa. **5** When Saul saw the army of the Philistines, he was afraid, and his heart trembled greatly. **6** And when Saul inquired of the LORD, the LORD did not answer him, either by dreams or by Urim or by the prophets.

Visited a medium at En Dor. 1 Sam 28:7–25

Death of. 1 Sam 31:1–13; 1 Chr 10:1–14

SCAPEGOAT, THE

Part of the sin offering on the day of atonement.

Lev 16:5 And he shall take from the congregation of the children of Israel two kids of the goats as a sin offering, and one ram as a burnt offering.

Lev 16:7 He shall take the two goats and present them before the LORD *at* the door of the tabernacle of meeting.

Chosen by lot.

Lev 16:8 Then Aaron shall cast lots for the two goats: one lot for the LORD and the other lot for the scapegoat.

The high priest transferred the sins of Israel to.

Lev 16:21 Aaron shall lay both his hands on the head of the live goat, confess over it all the iniquities of the children of Israel, and all their transgressions, concerning all their sins, putting them on the head of the goat, and shall send *it* away into the wilderness by the hand of a suitable man.

Sent into the wilderness by the hands of a suitable man.

Lev 16:21–22 Aaron shall lay both his hands on the head of the live goat, confess over it all the iniquities of the children of Israel, and all their transgressions, concerning all their sins, putting them on the head of the goat, and shall send *it* away into the wilderness by the hand of a suitable man. **22** The goat shall bear on itself all their iniquities to an uninhabited land; and he shall release the goat in the wilderness.

Communicated uncleanness to

The high priest.

Lev 16:24 And he shall wash his body with water in a holy place, put on his garments, come out and offer his burnt offering and the burnt offering of the people, and make atonement for himself and for the people.

The man who lead him away.

Lev 16:26 And he who released the goat as the scapegoat shall wash his clothes and bathe his body in water, and afterward he may come into the camp.

Typical of Christ.

Is 53:6 All we like sheep have gone astray; We have turned, every one, to his own way; And the LORD has laid on Him the iniquity of us all.

Is 53:11–12 He shall see the labor of His soul, *and* be satisfied. By His knowledge My righteous Servant shall justify many, For He shall bear their iniquities. **12** Therefore I will divide Him a portion with the great, And He shall divide the spoil with the strong, Because He poured out His soul unto death, And He was numbered with the transgressors, And He bore the sin of many, And made intercession for the transgressors.

SCIENCES (ALLUDED TO)

Architecture.

Deut 8:12 lest—*when* you have eaten and are full, and have built beautiful houses and dwell *in them;*

1 Chr 29:19 And give my son Solomon a loyal heart to keep Your commandments and Your testimonies and Your statutes, to do all *these things,* and to build the temple for which I have made provision."

Mathematics.

Gen 15:5 Then He brought him outside and said, "Look now toward heaven, and count the stars if you are able to number them." And He said to him, "So shall your descendants be."

Lev 26:8 Five of you shall chase a hundred, and a hundred of you shall put ten thousand to flight; your enemies shall fall by the sword before you.

Job 29:18 "Then I said, 'I shall die in my nest, And multiply *my* days as the sand.

Astronomy.

Job 38:31–32 "Can you bind the cluster of the Pleiades, Or loose the belt of Orion? **32** Can you bring out Mazzaroth in its season? Or can you guide the Great Bear with its cubs?

Is 13:10 For the stars of heaven and their constellations Will not give their light; The sun will be darkened in its going forth, And the moon will not cause its light to shine.

Astrology.

Is 47:13 You are wearied in the multitude of your counsels; Let now the astrologers, the stargazers, *And* the monthly prognosticators Stand up and save you From what shall come upon you.

Botany.

1 Kin 4:33 Also he spoke of trees, from the cedar tree of Lebanon even to the hyssop that springs out of the wall; he spoke also of animals, of birds, of creeping things, and of fish.

Geography. Gen 10:1–30; Is 11:11

History and chronology.

1 Kin 22:39 Now the rest of the acts of Ahab, and all that he did, the ivory house which he built and all the cities that he built, *are* they not written in the book of the chronicles of the kings of Israel?

2 Kin 1:18 Now the rest of the acts of Ahaziah which he did, *are* they not written in the book of the chronicles of the kings of Israel?

1 Chr 9:1 So all Israel was recorded by genealogies, and indeed, they *were* inscribed in the book of the kings of Israel. But Judah was carried away captive to Babylon because of their unfaithfulness.

1 Chr 29:29 Now the acts of King David, first and last, indeed they *are* written in the book of Samuel the seer, in the book of Nathan the prophet, and in the book of Gad the seer,

Mechanics.

Gen 6:14–16 Make yourself an ark of gopherwood; make rooms in the ark, and cover it inside and outside with pitch. **15** And this is how you shall make it: The length of the ark *shall be* three hundred cubits, its width fifty cubits, and its height thirty cubits. **16** You shall make a window for the ark, and you shall finish it to a cubit from above; and set the door of the ark in its side. You shall make it *with* lower, second, and third *decks.*

Gen 11:4 And they said, "Come, let us build ourselves a city, and a tower whose top *is* in the heavens; let us make a name for ourselves, lest we be scattered abroad over the face of the whole earth."

Ex 14:6–7 So he made ready his chariot and took his people with him. **7** Also, he took six hundred choice chariots, and all the chariots of Egypt with captains over every one of them.

Medicine.

Jer 8:22 *Is there* no balm in Gilead, *Is there* no physician there? Why then is there no recovery For the health of the daughter of my people?

Mark 5:26 and had suffered many things from many physicians. She had spent all that she had and was no better, but rather grew worse.

Music.

1 Chr 16:4–7 And he appointed some of the Levites to minister before the ark of the LORD, to commemorate, to thank, and to praise the LORD God of Israel: **5** Asaph the chief, and next to him Zechariah, *then* Jeiel, Shemiramoth, Jehiel, Mattithiah, Eliab, Benaiah, and Obed-Edom: Jeiel with stringed instruments and harps, but Asaph made music with cymbals; **6** Benaiah and Jahaziel the priests regularly *blew* the trumpets before the ark of the covenant of God. **7** On that day David first delivered *this psalm* into the hand of Asaph and his brethren, to thank the LORD:

1 Chr 25:6 All these *were* under the direction of their father for the music *in* the house of the LORD, with cymbals, stringed instruments, and harps, for the service of the house of God. Asaph, Jeduthun, and Heman *were* under the authority of the king.

Navigation.

1 Kin 9:27 Then Hiram sent his servants with the fleet,

seamen who knew the sea, to work with the servants of Solomon.

Ps 107:23 Those who go down to the sea in ships, Who do business on great waters,

Surveying.

Neh 2:12–16 Then I arose in the night, I and a few men with me; I told no one what my God had put in my heart to do at Jerusalem; nor was there any animal with me, except the one on which I rode. **13** And I went out by night through the Valley Gate to the Serpent Well and the Refuse Gate, and viewed the walls of Jerusalem which were broken down and its gates which were burned with fire. **14** Then I went on to the Fountain Gate and to the King's Pool, but *there was* no room for the animal under me to pass. **15** So I went up in the night by the valley, and viewed the wall; then I turned back and entered by the Valley Gate, and so returned. **16** And the officials did not know where I had gone or what I had done; I had not yet told the Jews, the priests, the nobles, the officials, or the others who did the work.

Ezek 40:5–6 Now there was a wall all around the outside of the temple. In the man's hand was a measuring rod six cubits *long, each being a* cubit and a handbreadth; and he measured the width of the wall structure, one rod; and the height, one rod. **6** Then he went to the gateway which faced east; and he went up its stairs and measured the threshold of the gateway, *which was* one rod wide, and the other threshold *was* one rod wide.

Zech 2:2 So I said, "Where are you going?" And he said to me, "To measure Jerusalem, to see what *is* its width and what *is* its length."

Cf. Josh 18:4–9

Zoology.

1 Kin 4:33 Also he spoke of trees, from the cedar tree of Lebanon even to the hyssop that springs out of the wall; he spoke also of animals, of birds, of creeping things, and of fish.

SCORPION, THE

Sting of, sharp and caused torment.

Rev 9:5 And they were not given *authority* to kill them, but to torment them *for* five months. Their torment *was* like the torment of a scorpion when it strikes a man.

Rev 9:10 They had tails like scorpions, and there were stings in their tails. Their power *was* to hurt men five months.

Abounded in the great desert.

Deut 8:15 who led you through that great and terrible wilderness, *in which were* fiery serpents and scorpions and thirsty land where there was no water; who brought water for you out of the flinty rock;

Unfit for food.

Luke 11:12 Or if he asks for an egg, will he offer him a scorpion?

Illustrative of

Wicked men.

Ezek 2:6 "And you, son of man, do not be afraid of them nor be afraid of their words, though briers and thorns *are* with you and you dwell among scorpions;

do not be afraid of their words or dismayed by their looks, though they *are* a rebellious house.

Ministers of Antichrist.

Rev 9:3 Then out of the smoke locusts came upon the earth. And to them was given power, as the scorpions of the earth have power.

Rev 9:5 And they were not given *authority* to kill them, but to torment them *for* five months. Their torment *was* like the torment of a scorpion when it strikes a man.

Rev 9:10 They had tails like scorpions, and there were stings in their tails. Their power *was* to hurt men five months.

Christ gave His disciples power over.

Luke 10:19 Behold, I give you the authority to trample on serpents and scorpions, and over all the power of the enemy, and nothing shall by any means hurt you.

SCRIBES, THE

Antiquity of.

2 Sam 8:17 Zadok the son of Ahitub and Ahimelech the son of Abiathar *were* the priests; Seraiah *was* the scribe;

Wore inkhorns at their sides.

Ezek 9:2–3 And suddenly six men came from the direction of the upper gate, which faces north, each with his battle-ax in his hand. One man among them *was* clothed with linen and had a writer's inkhorn at his side. They went in and stood beside the bronze altar. **3** Now the glory of the God of Israel had gone up from the cherub, where it had been, to the threshold of the temple. And He called to the man clothed with linen, who *had* the writer's inkhorn at his side;

Families celebrated for furnishing,

Kenites.

1 Chr 2:55 And the families of the scribes who dwelt at Jabez *were* the Tirathites, the Shimeathites, *and* the Suchathites. These *were* the Kenites who came from Hammath, the father of the house of Rechab.

Levi.

1 Chr 24:6 And the scribe, Shemaiah the son of Nethanel, *one of* the Levites, wrote them down before the king, the leaders, Zadok the priest, Ahimelech the son of Abiathar, and the heads of the fathers' *houses* of the priests and Levites, one father's house taken for Eleazar and *one* for Ithamar.

2 Chr 34:13 *were* over the burden bearers and *were* overseers of all who did work in any kind of service. And *some* of the Levites *were* scribes, officers, and gatekeepers.

Generally men of great wisdom.

1 Chr 27:32 Also Jehonathan, David's uncle, *was* a counselor, a wise man, and a scribe; and Jehiel the son of Hachmoni *was* with the king's sons.

Often learned in the law.

Ezra 7:6 this Ezra came up from Babylon; and he *was* a skilled scribe in the Law of Moses, which the LORD God of Israel had given. The king granted him all his request, according to the hand of the LORD his God upon him.

Were ready writers.

Ps 45:1 My heart is overflowing with a good theme; I recite my composition concerning the King; My tongue *is* the pen of a ready writer.

Acted as

Secretaries to kings.

2 Sam 8:17 Zadok the son of Ahitub and Ahimelech the son of Abiathar *were* the priests; Seraiah *was* the scribe;

2 Sam 20:25 Sheva *was* scribe; Zadok and Abiathar *were* the priests;

2 Kin 12:10 So it was, whenever they saw that *there was* much money in the chest, that the king's scribe and the high priest came up and put it in bags, and counted the money that was found in the house of the LORD.

Esth 3:12 Then the king's scribes were called on the thirteenth day of the first month, and *a decree* was written according to all that Haman commanded—to the king's satraps, to the governors who *were* over each province, to the officials of all people, to every province according to its script, and to every people in their language. In the name of King Ahasuerus it was written, and sealed with the king's signet ring.

Secretaries to prophets.

Jer 36:5 And Jeremiah commanded Baruch, saying, "I *am* confined, I cannot go into the house of the LORD.

Jer 36:26 And the king commanded Jerahmeel the king's son, Seraiah the son of Azriel, and Shelemiah the son of Abdeel, to seize Baruch the scribe and Jeremiah the prophet, but the LORD hid them.

Notaries in courts of justice.

Jer 32:11–12 So I took the purchase deed, *both* that which was sealed *according* to the law and custom, and that which was open; **12** and I gave the purchase deed to Baruch the son of Neriah, son of Mahseiah, in the presence of Hanamel my uncle's *son,* and in the presence of the witnesses who signed the purchase deed, before all the Jews who sat in the court of the prison.

Religious teachers.

Neh 8:2–6 So Ezra the priest brought the Law before the assembly of men and women and all who *could* hear with understanding on the first day of the seventh month. **3** Then he read from it in the open square that *was* in front of the Water Gate from morning until midday, before the men and women and those who could understand; and the ears of all the people *were* attentive to the Book of the Law. **4** So Ezra the scribe stood on a platform of wood which they had made for the purpose; and beside him, at his right hand, stood Mattithiah, Shema, Anaiah, Urijah, Hilkiah, and Maaseiah; and at his left hand Pedaiah, Mishael, Malchijah, Hashum, Hashbadana, Zechariah, *and* Meshullam. **5** And Ezra opened the book in the sight of all the people, for he was *standing* above all the people; and when he opened it, all the people stood up. **6** And Ezra blessed the LORD, the great God. Then all the people answered, "Amen, Amen!" while lifting up their hands. And they bowed their heads and worshiped the LORD with *their* faces to the ground.

Writers of public documents.

1 Chr 24:6 And the scribe, Shemaiah the son of Nethanel, *one of* the Levites, wrote them down before the king, the leaders, Zadok the priest, Ahimelech the son of Abiathar, and the heads of the fathers' *houses* of the priests and Levites, one father's house taken for Eleazar and *one* for Ithamar.

Keepers of the muster-rolls of the host.

2 Kin 25:19 He also took out of the city an officer who had charge of the men of war, five men of the king's close associates who were found in the city, the chief recruiting officer of the army, who mustered the people of the land, and sixty men of the people of the land *who were* found in the city.

2 Chr 26:11 Moreover Uzziah had an army of fighting men who went out to war by companies, according to the number on their roll as prepared by Jeiel the scribe and Maaseiah the officer, under the hand of Hananiah, *one* of the king's captains.

Jer 52:25 He also took out of the city an officer who had charge of the men of war, seven men of the king's close associates who were found in the city, the principal scribe of the army who mustered the people of the land, and sixty men of the people of the land who were found in the midst of the city.

In the New Testament,

Were doctors of the law.

Mark 12:28 Then one of the scribes came, and having heard them reasoning together, perceiving that He had answered them well, asked Him, "Which is the first commandment of all?"

Matt 22:35 Then one of them, a lawyer, asked *Him a question,* testing Him, and saying,

Wore long robes and loved preeminence.

Mark 12:38–39 Then He said to them in His teaching, "Beware of the scribes, who desire to go around in long robes, *love* greetings in the marketplaces, **39** the best seats in the synagogues, and the best places at feasts,

Sat in Moses' seat.

Matt 23:2 saying: "The scribes and the Pharisees sit in Moses' seat.

Were frequently Pharisees.

Acts 23:9 Then there arose a loud outcry. And the scribes of the Pharisees' party arose and protested, saying, "We find no evil in this man; but if a spirit or an angel has spoken to him, let us not fight against God."

Esteemed wise and learned.

1 Cor 1:20 Where *is* the wise? Where *is* the scribe? Where *is* the disputer of this age? Has not God made foolish the wisdom of this world?

Regarded as interpreters of Scripture.

Matt 2:4 And when he had gathered all the chief priests and scribes of the people together, he inquired of them where the Christ was to be born.

Matt 17:10 And His disciples asked Him, saying, "Why then do the scribes say that Elijah must come first?"

Mark 12:35 Then Jesus answered and said, while He taught in the temple, "How *is it* that the scribes say that the Christ is the Son of David?

Their manner of teaching contrasted with that of Christ.

Matt 7:29 for He taught them as one having authority, and not as the scribes.

Mark 1:22 And they were astonished at His teaching, for He taught them as one having authority, and not as the scribes.

Condemned by Christ for hypocrisy.

Matt 23:15 "Woe to you, scribes and Pharisees, hypocrites! For you travel land and sea to win one proselyte, and when he is won, you make him twice as much a son of hell as yourselves.

Often offended at our Lord's conduct and teaching.

Matt 21:15 But when the chief priests and scribes saw the wonderful things that He did, and the children crying out in the temple and saying, "Hosanna to the Son of David!" they were indignant

Mark 2:6–7 And some of the scribes were sitting there and reasoning in their hearts, 7 "Why does this *Man* speak blasphemies like this? Who can forgive sins but God alone?"

Mark 2:16 And when the scribes and Pharisees saw Him eating with the tax collectors and sinners, they said to His disciples, "How *is it* that He eats and drinks with tax collectors and sinners?"

Mark 3:22 And the scribes who came down from Jerusalem said, "He has Beelzebub," and, "By the ruler of the demons He casts out demons."

Tested our Lord.

John 8:3 Then the scribes and Pharisees brought to Him a woman caught in adultery. And when they had set her in the midst,

Active in procuring our Lord's death.

Matt 26:3 Then the chief priests, the scribes, and the elders of the people assembled at the palace of the high priest, who was called Caiaphas,

Luke 23:10 And the chief priests and scribes stood and vehemently accused Him.

Persecuted the Christians.

Acts 4:5 And it came to pass, on the next day, that their rulers, elders, and scribes,

Acts 6:12 And they stirred up the people, the elders, and the scribes; and they came upon *him,* seized him, and brought *him* to the council.

Acts 18:21 but took leave of them, saying, "I must by all means keep this coming feast in Jerusalem; but I will return again to you, God willing." And he sailed from Ephesus.

Illustrative of well-instructed ministers of the gospel.

Matt 13:52 Then He said to them, "Therefore every scribe instructed concerning the kingdom of heaven is like a householder who brings out of his treasure *things* new and old."

SCRIPTURES, THE

Given by inspiration of God.

Acts 1:16 "Men *and* brethren, this Scripture had to be fulfilled, which the Holy Spirit spoke before by the mouth of David concerning Judas, who became a guide to those who arrested Jesus;

2 Tim 3:16 All Scripture *is* given by inspiration of God, and *is* profitable for doctrine, for reproof, for correction, for instruction in righteousness,

Heb 3:7 Therefore, as the Holy Spirit says: *"Today, if you will hear His voice,*

2 Pet 1:21 for prophecy never came by the will of man, but holy men of God spoke *as they were* moved by the Holy Spirit.

Christ sanctioned, by appealing to them.

Matt 4:4 But He answered and said, "It is written, *'Man shall not live by bread alone, but by every word that proceeds from the mouth of God.'"*

Mark 12:10 Have you not even read this Scripture: *'The stone which the builders rejected Has become the chief cornerstone.*

Luke 24:27 And beginning at Moses and all the Prophets, He expounded to them in all the Scriptures the things concerning Himself.

John 7:42 Has not the Scripture said that the Christ comes from the seed of David and from the town of Bethlehem, where David was?"

Names for,

Word.

James 1:21–23 Therefore lay aside all filthiness and overflow of wickedness, and receive with meekness the implanted word, which is able to save your souls. **22** But be doers of the word, and not hearers only, deceiving yourselves. **23** For if anyone is a hearer of the word and not a doer, he is like a man observing his natural face in a mirror;

1 Pet 2:2 as newborn babes, desire the pure milk of the word, that you may grow thereby,

Word of God.

Luke 11:28 But He said, "More than that, blessed *are* those who hear the word of God and keep it!"

Heb 4:12 For the word of God *is* living and powerful, and sharper than any two-edged sword, piercing even to the division of soul and spirit, and of joints and marrow, and is a discerner of the thoughts and intents of the heart.

Word of Christ.

Col 3:16 Let the word of Christ dwell in you richly in all wisdom, teaching and admonishing one another in psalms and hymns and spiritual songs, singing with grace in your hearts to the Lord.

Word of truth.

James 1:18 Of His own will He brought us forth by the word of truth, that we might be a kind of firstfruits of His creatures.

Holy Scriptures.

Rom 1:2 which He promised before through His prophets in the Holy Scriptures,

2 Tim 3:15 and that from childhood you have known the Holy Scriptures, which are able to make you wise for salvation through faith which is in Christ Jesus.

Scripture of truth.

Dan 10:21 But I will tell you what is noted in the Scripture of Truth. (No one upholds me against these, except Michael your prince.

Book.

Ps 40:7 Then I said, "Behold, I come; In the scroll of the book *it is* written of me.

Rev 22:19 and if anyone takes away from the words of the book of this prophecy, God shall take away his part from the Book of Life, from the holy city, and *from* the things which are written in this book.

Book of the Lord.

Is 34:16 "Search from the book of the LORD, and read: Not one of these shall fail; Not one shall lack her mate. For My mouth has commanded it, and His Spirit has gathered them.

Book of the Law.

Neh 8:3 Then he read from it in the open square that *was* in front of the Water Gate from morning until midday, before the men and women and those who could understand; and the ears of all the people *were* attentive to the Book of the Law.

Gal 3:10 For as many as are of the works of the law are under the curse; for it is written, *"Cursed is everyone who does not continue in all things which are written in the book of the law, to do them."*

Law of the Lord.

Ps 1:2 But his delight *is* in the law of the LORD, And in His law he meditates day and night.

Is 30:9 That this *is* a rebellious people, Lying children, Children *who* will not hear the law of the LORD;

Sword of the Spirit.

Eph 6:17 And take the helmet of salvation, and the sword of the Spirit, which is the word of God;

Oracles of God.

Rom 3:2 Much in every way! Chiefly because to them were committed the oracles of God.

1 Pet 4:11 If anyone speaks, *let him speak* as the oracles of God. If anyone ministers, *let him do it* as with the ability which God supplies, that in all things God may be glorified through Jesus Christ, to whom belong the glory and the dominion forever and ever. Amen.

Contain the promises of the gospel.

Rom 1:2 which He promised before through His prophets in the Holy Scriptures,

Reveal the laws, statutes, and judgments of God.

Ex 24:3–4 So Moses came and told the people all the words of the LORD and all the judgments. And all the people answered with one voice and said, "All the words which the LORD has said we will do." 4 And Moses wrote all the words of the LORD. And he rose early in the morning, and built an altar at the foot of the mountain, and twelve pillars according to the twelve tribes of Israel.

Deut 4:5 "Surely I have taught you statutes and judgments, just as the LORD my God commanded me, that you should act according *to them* in the land which you go to possess.

Deut 4:14 And the LORD commanded me at that time to teach you statutes and judgments, that you might observe them in the land which you cross over to possess.

Record divine prophecies.

2 Pet 1:19–21 And so we have the prophetic word con-

firmed, which you do well to heed as a light that shines in a dark place, until the day dawns and the morning star rises in your hearts; 20 knowing this first, that no prophecy of Scripture is of any private interpretation, 21 for prophecy never came by the will of man, but holy men of God spoke *as they were* moved by the Holy Spirit.

Testify of Christ.

John 5:39 You search the Scriptures, for in them you think you have eternal life; and these are they which testify of Me.

Acts 10:43 To Him all the prophets witness that, through His name, whoever believes in Him will receive remission of sins."

Acts 18:28 for he vigorously refuted the Jews publicly, showing from the Scriptures that Jesus is the Christ.

1 Cor 15:3 For I delivered to you first of all that which I also received: that Christ died for our sins according to the Scriptures,

Are full and sufficient.

Luke 16:29 Abraham said to him, 'They have Moses and the prophets; let them hear them.'

Luke 16:31 But he said to him, 'If they do not hear Moses and the prophets, neither will they be persuaded though one rise from the dead.' "

Are an unerring guide.

Prov 6:23 For the commandment *is* a lamp, And the law a light; Reproofs of instruction *are* the way of life,

2 Pet 1:19 And so we have the prophetic word confirmed, which you do well to heed as a light that shines in a dark place, until the day dawns and the morning star rises in your hearts;

Instruct about salvation.

2 Tim 3:15 and that from childhood you have known the Holy Scriptures, which are able to make you wise for salvation through faith which is in Christ Jesus.

Are profitable both for doctrine and practice.

2 Tim 3:16–17 All Scripture *is* given by inspiration of God, and *is* profitable for doctrine, for reproof, for correction, for instruction in righteousness, 17 that the man of God may be complete, thoroughly equipped for every good work.

Described as

Pure.

Ps 12:6 The words of the LORD *are* pure words, *Like* silver tried in a furnace of earth, Purified seven times.

Ps 119:140 Your word *is* very pure; Therefore Your servant loves it.

Prov 30:5 Every word of God *is* pure; He *is* a shield to those who put their trust in Him.

True.

Ps 119:160 The entirety of Your word *is* truth, And every one of Your righteous judgments *endures* forever.

John 17:17 Sanctify them by Your truth. Your word is truth.

Perfect.

Ps 19:7 The law of the LORD *is* perfect, converting the soul; The testimony of the Lord *is* sure, making wise the simple;

Precious.

Ps 19:10 More to be desired *are they* than gold, Yea, than much fine gold; Sweeter also than honey and the honeycomb.

Living and powerful.

Heb 4:12 For the word of God *is* living and powerful, and sharper than any two-edged sword, piercing even to the division of soul and spirit, and of joints and marrow, and is a discerner of the thoughts and intents of the heart.

Written for our instruction.

Rom 15:4 For whatever things were written before were written for our learning, that we through the patience and comfort of the Scriptures might have hope.

Intended for the use of all men.

Rom 16:26 but now made manifest, and by the prophetic Scriptures made known to all nations, according to the commandment of the everlasting God, for obedience to the faith—

Nothing to be taken from, or added to.

Deut 4:2 You shall not add to the word which I command you, nor take from it, that you may keep the commandments of the Lord your God which I command you.

Deut 12:32 "Whatever I command you, be careful to observe it; you shall not add to it nor take away from it.

One portion of, to be compared with another.

1 Cor 2:13 These things we also speak, not in words which man's wisdom teaches but which the Holy Spirit teaches, comparing spiritual things with spiritual.

Designed for

Regenerating.

James 1:18 Of His own will He brought us forth by the word of truth, that we might be a kind of firstfruits of His creatures.

1 Pet 1:23 having been born again, not of corruptible seed but incorruptible, through the word of God which lives and abides forever,

Giving life.

Ps 119:50 This *is* my comfort in my affliction, For Your word has given me life.

Ps 119:93 I will never forget Your precepts, For by them You have given me life.

Illuminating.

Ps 119:130 The entrance of Your words gives light; It gives understanding to the simple.

Converting the soul.

Ps 19:7 The law of the Lord *is* perfect, converting the soul; The testimony of the Lord *is* sure, making wise the simple;

Making wise the simple.

Ps 19:7 The law of the Lord *is* perfect, converting the soul; The testimony of the Lord *is* sure, making wise the simple;

Sanctifying.

John 17:17 Sanctify them by Your truth. Your word is truth.

Eph 5:26 that He might sanctify and cleanse her with the washing of water by the word,

Producing faith.

John 20:31 but these are written that you may believe that Jesus is the Christ, the Son of God, and that believing you may have life in His name.

Producing hope.

Ps 119:49 Remember the word to Your servant, Upon which You have caused me to hope.

Rom 15:4 For whatever things were written before were written for our learning, that we through the patience and comfort of the Scriptures might have hope.

Producing obedience.

Deut 17:19–20 And it shall be with him, and he shall read it all the days of his life, that he may learn to fear the Lord his God and be careful to observe all the words of this law and these statutes, **20** that his heart may not be lifted above his brethren, that he may not turn aside from the commandment *to* the right hand or *to* the left, and that he may prolong *his* days in his kingdom, he and his children in the midst of Israel.

Cleansing the heart and life.

Ps 119:9 How can a young man cleanse his way? By taking heed according to Your word.

John 15:3 You are already clean because of the word which I have spoken to you.

Eph 5:26 that He might sanctify and cleanse her with the washing of water by the word,

Keeping from destructive paths.

Ps 17:4 Concerning the works of men, By the word of Your lips, I have kept away from the paths of the destroyer.

Supporting life.

Deut 8:3 So He humbled you, allowed you to hunger, and fed you with manna which you did not know nor did your fathers know, that He might make you know that man shall not live by bread alone; but man lives by every *word* that proceeds from the mouth of the Lord.

Matt 4:4 But He answered and said, "It is written, 'Man shall not live by bread alone, but by every word that proceeds from the mouth of God.' "

Promoting growth in grace.

1 Pet 2:2 as newborn babes, desire the pure milk of the word, that you may grow thereby,

Building up in the faith.

Acts 20:32 "So now, brethren, I commend you to God and to the word of His grace, which is able to build you up and give you an inheritance among all those who are sanctified.

Admonishing.

Ps 19:11 Moreover by them Your servant is warned, *And* in keeping them *there is* great reward.

1 Cor 10:11 Now all these things happened to them as examples, and they were written for our admonition, upon whom the ends of the ages have come.

Comforting.

Ps 119:82 My eyes fail *from searching* Your word, Saying, "When will You comfort me?"

Rom 15:4 For whatever things were written before were written for our learning, that we through the patience and comfort of the Scriptures might have hope.

Rejoicing the heart.

Ps 19:8 The statutes of the LORD *are* right, rejoicing the heart; The commandment of the LORD *is* pure, enlightening the eyes;

Ps 119:111 Your testimonies I have taken as a heritage forever, For they *are* the rejoicing of my heart.

Work effectually in them that believe.

1 Thess 2:13 For this reason we also thank God without ceasing, because when you received the word of God which you heard from us, you welcomed *it* not *as* the word of men, but as it is in truth, the word of God, which also effectively works in you who believe.

The letter of, without the Spirit, killeth.

John 6:63 It is the Spirit who gives life; the flesh profits nothing. The words that I speak to you are spirit, and *they* are life.

2 Cor 3:6 who also made us sufficient as ministers of the new covenant, not of the letter but of the Spirit; for the letter kills, but the Spirit gives life.

Ignorance of, a source of error.

Matt 22:29 Jesus answered and said to them, "You are mistaken, not knowing the Scriptures nor the power of God.

Acts 13:27 For those who dwell in Jerusalem, and their rulers, because they did not know Him, nor even the voices of the Prophets which are read every Sabbath, have fulfilled *them* in condemning *Him.*

Christ enables us to understand.

Luke 24:45 And He opened their understanding, that they might comprehend the Scriptures.

The Holy Spirit enables us to understand.

John 16:13 However, when He, the Spirit of truth, has come, He will guide you into all truth; for He will not speak on His own *authority*, but whatever He hears He will speak; and He will tell you things to come.

1 Cor 2:10–14 But God has revealed *them* to us through His Spirit. For the Spirit searches all things, yes, the deep things of God. **11** For what man knows the things of a man except the spirit of the man which is in him? Even so no one knows the things of God except the Spirit of God. **12** Now we have received, not the spirit of the world, but the Spirit who is from God, that we might know the things that have been freely given to us by God. **13** These things we also speak, not in words which man's wisdom teaches but which the Holy Spirit teaches, comparing spiritual things with spiritual. **14** But the natural man does not receive the things of the Spirit of God, for they are foolishness to him; nor can he know *them*, because they are spiritually discerned.

No prophecy of, is of any private interpretation.

2 Pet 1:20 knowing this first, that no prophecy of Scripture is of any private interpretation,

Everything should be tried by.

Is 8:20 To the law and to the testimony! If they do not speak according to this word, *it is* because *there is* no light in them.

Acts 17:11 These were more fair-minded than those in Thessalonica, in that they received the word with all readiness, and searched the Scriptures daily *to find out* whether these things were so.

Should be

The standard of teaching.

1 Pet 4:11 If anyone speaks, *let him speak* as the oracles of God. If anyone ministers, *let him do it* as with the ability which God supplies, that in all things God may be glorified through Jesus Christ, to whom belong the glory and the dominion forever and ever. Amen.

Believed.

John 2:22 Therefore, when He had risen from the dead, His disciples remembered that He had said this to them; and they believed the Scripture and the word which Jesus had said.

Appealed to.

1 Cor 1:31 that, as it is written, *"He who glories, let him glory in the LORD."*

1 Pet 1:16 because it is written, *"Be holy, for I am holy."*

Read.

Deut 17:19 And it shall be with him, and he shall read it all the days of his life, that he may learn to fear the LORD his God and be careful to observe all the words of this law and these statutes,

Is 34:16 "Search from the book of the LORD, and read: Not one of these shall fail; Not one shall lack her mate. For My mouth has commanded it, and His Spirit has gathered them.

Read publicly to all.

Deut 31:11–13 when all Israel comes to appear before the LORD your God in the place which He chooses, you shall read this law before all Israel in their hearing. **12** Gather the people together, men and women and little ones, and the stranger who *is* within your gates, that they may hear and that they may learn to fear the LORD your God and carefully observe all the words of this law, **13** and *that* their children, who have not known it, may hear and learn to fear the LORD your God as long as you live in the land which you cross the Jordan to possess."

Neh 8:3 Then he read from it in the open square that *was* in front of the Water Gate from morning until midday, before the men and women and those who could understand; and the ears of all the people *were* attentive to the Book of the Law.

Jer 36:6 You go, therefore, and read from the scroll which you have written at my instruction, the words of the LORD, in the hearing of the people in the LORD's house on the day of fasting. And you shall also read them in the hearing of all Judah who come from their cities.

Acts 13:15 And after the reading of the Law and the

Prophets, the rulers of the synagogue sent to them, saying, "Men *and* brethren, if you have any word of exhortation for the people, say on."

Known.

2 Tim 3:15 and that from childhood you have known the Holy Scriptures, which are able to make you wise for salvation through faith which is in Christ Jesus.

Received, not as the word of men, but as the Word of God.

1 Thess 2:13 For this reason we also thank God without ceasing, because when you received the word of God which you heard from us, you welcomed *it* not *as* the word of men, but as it is in truth, the word of God, which also effectively works in you who believe.

Received with meekness.

James 1:21 Therefore lay aside all filthiness and overflow of wickedness, and receive with meekness the implanted word, which is able to save your souls.

Searched.

John 5:39 You search the Scriptures, for in them you think you have eternal life; and these are they which testify of Me.

John 7:52 They answered and said to him, "Are you also from Galilee? Search and look, for no prophet has arisen out of Galilee."

Acts 17:11 These were more fair-minded than those in Thessalonica, in that they received the word with all readiness, and searched the Scriptures daily *to find out* whether these things were so.

Laid up in the heart.

Deut 6:6 "And these words which I command you today shall be in your heart.

Deut 11:18 "Therefore you shall lay up these words of mine in your heart and in your soul, and bind them as a sign on your hand, and they shall be as frontlets between your eyes.

Taught to children.

Deut 6:7 You shall teach them diligently to your children, and shall talk of them when you sit in your house, when you walk by the way, when you lie down, and when you rise up.

Deut 11:19 You shall teach them to your children, speaking of them when you sit in your house, when you walk by the way, when you lie down, and when you rise up.

2 Tim 3:15 and that from childhood you have known the Holy Scriptures, which are able to make you wise for salvation through faith which is in Christ Jesus.

Taught to all.

2 Chr 17:7–9 Also in the third year of his reign he sent his leaders, Ben-Hail, Obadiah, Zechariah, Nethanel, and Michaiah, to teach in the cities of Judah. 8 And with them *he sent* Levites: Shemaiah, Nethaniah, Zebadiah, Asahel, Shemiramoth, Jehonathan, Adonijah, Tobijah, and Tobadonijah—the Levites; and with them Elishama and Jehoram, the priests. 9 So they taught in Judah, and *had* the Book of the Law of the LORD with them; they went throughout all the cities of Judah and taught the people.

Neh 8:7–8 Also Jeshua, Bani, Sherebiah, Jamin, Akkub, Shabbethai, Hodijah, Maaseiah, Kelita, Azariah, Jozabad, Hanan, Pelaiah, and the Levites, helped the people to understand the Law; and the people *stood* in their place. 8 So they read distinctly from the book, in the Law of God; and they gave the sense, and helped *them* to understand the reading.

Talked of continually.

Deut 6:7 You shall teach them diligently to your children, and shall talk of them when you sit in your house, when you walk by the way, when you lie down, and when you rise up.

Not handled deceitfully.

2 Cor 4:2 But we have renounced the hidden things of shame, not walking in craftiness nor handling the word of God deceitfully, but by manifestation of the truth commending ourselves to every man's conscience in the sight of God.

Not only heard, but obeyed.

Matt 7:24 "Therefore whoever hears these sayings of Mine, and does them, I will liken him to a wise man who built his house on the rock:

Luke 11:28 But He said, "More than that, blessed *are* those who hear the word of God and keep it!"

James 1:22 But be doers of the word, and not hearers only, deceiving yourselves.

Used to answer spiritual enemies.

Matt 4:4 But He answered and said, "It is written, 'Man shall not live by bread alone, but by every word that proceeds from the mouth of God.'"

Matt 4:7 Jesus said to him, "It is written again, 'You shall not tempt the LORD your God.'"

Matt 4:10 Then Jesus said to him, "Away with you, Satan! For it is written, 'You shall worship the LORD your God, and Him only you shall serve.'"

Eph 6:11 Put on the whole armor of God, that you may be able to stand against the wiles of the devil.

Eph 6:17 And take the helmet of salvation, and the sword of the Spirit, which is the word of God;

All should desire to hear.

Neh 8:1 Now all the people gathered together as one man in the open square that *was* in front of the Water Gate; and they told Ezra the scribe to bring the Book of the Law of Moses, which the LORD had commanded Israel.

Advantage of possessing.

Rom 3:2 Much in every way! Chiefly because to them were committed the oracles of God.

Believers

Love exceedingly.

Ps 119:97 Oh, how I love Your law! It *is* my meditation all the day.

Ps 119:113 I hate the double-minded, But I love Your law.

Ps 119:159 Consider how I love Your precepts; Revive me, O LORD, according to Your lovingkindness.

Ps 119:167 My soul keeps Your testimonies, And I love them exceedingly.

Delight in.

Ps 1:2 But his delight *is* in the law of the LORD, And in His law he meditates day and night.

Regard, as sweet.

Ps 119:103 How sweet are Your words to my taste, *Sweeter* than honey to my mouth!

Esteem, above all things.

Job 23:12 I have not departed from the commandment of His lips; I have treasured the words of His mouth More than my necessary *food.*

Long after.

Ps 119:82 My eyes fail *from searching* Your word, Saying, "When will You comfort me?"

Stand in awe of.

Ps 119:161 Princes persecute me without a cause, But my heart stands in awe of Your word.

Is 66:2 For all those *things* My hand has made, And all those *things* exist," Says the LORD. "But on this *one* will I look: On *him who is* poor and of a contrite spirit, And who trembles at My word.

Keep, in remembrance.

Ps 119:16 I will delight myself in Your statutes; I will not forget Your word.

Grieve when men disobey.

Ps 119:158 I see the treacherous, and am disgusted, Because they do not keep Your word.

Hide, in their hearts.

Ps 119:11 Your word I have hidden in my heart, That I might not sin against You.

Hope in.

Ps 119:74 Those who fear You will be glad when they see me, Because I have hoped in Your word.

Ps 119:81 My soul faints for Your salvation, But I hope in Your word.

Ps 119:147 I rise before the dawning of the morning, And cry for help; I hope in Your word.

Meditate in.

Ps 1:2 But his delight *is* in the law of the LORD, And in His law he meditates day and night.

Ps 119:99 I have more understanding than all my teachers, For Your testimonies *are* my meditation.

Ps 119:148 My eyes are awake through the *night* watches, That I may meditate on Your word.

Rejoice in.

Ps 119:162 I rejoice at Your word As one who finds great treasure.

Jer 15:16 Your words were found, and I ate them, And Your word was to me the joy and rejoicing of my heart; For I am called by Your name, O LORD God of hosts.

Trust in.

Ps 119:42 So shall I have an answer for him who reproaches me, For I trust in Your word.

Obey.

Ps 119:67 Before I was afflicted I went astray, But now I keep Your word.

Luke 8:21 But He answered and said to them, "My mother and My brothers are these who hear the word of God and do it."

John 17:6 "I have manifested Your name to the men whom You have given Me out of the world. They were Yours, You gave them to Me, and they have kept Your word.

Speak of.

Ps 119:172 My tongue shall speak of Your word, For all Your commandments *are* righteousness.

Esteem, as a light.

Ps 119:105 Your word *is* a lamp to my feet And a light to my path.

Pray to be taught.

Ps 119:12–13 Blessed *are* You, O LORD! Teach me Your statutes. **13** With my lips I have declared All the judgments of Your mouth.

Ps 119:33 Teach me, O LORD, the way of Your statutes, And I shall keep it *to* the end.

Ps 119:66 Teach me good judgment and knowledge, For I believe Your commandments.

Pray to be conformed to.

Ps 119:133 Direct my steps by Your word, And let no iniquity have dominion over me.

Plead the promises of, in prayer.

Ps 119:25 My soul clings to the dust; Revive me according to Your word.

Ps 119:28 My soul melts from heaviness; Strengthen me according to Your word.

Ps 119:41 Let Your mercies come also to me, O LORD— Your salvation according to Your word.

Ps 119:76 Let, I pray, Your merciful kindness be for my comfort, According to Your word to Your servant.

Ps 119:169 Let my cry come before You, O LORD; Give me understanding according to Your word.

Those who search, are truly noble.

Acts 17:11 These were more fair-minded than those in Thessalonica, in that they received the word with all readiness, and searched the Scriptures daily *to find out* whether these things were so.

Blessedness of hearing and obeying.

Luke 11:28 But He said, "More than that, blessed *are* those who hear the word of God and keep it!"

James 1:25 But he who looks into the perfect law of liberty and continues *in it*, and is not a forgetful hearer but a doer of the work, this one will be blessed in what he does.

Let them dwell richly in you.

Col 3:16 Let the word of Christ dwell in you richly in all wisdom, teaching and admonishing one another in psalms and hymns and spiritual songs, singing with grace in your hearts to the Lord.

The wicked

Corrupt.

2 Cor 2:17 For we are not, as so many, peddling the word of God; but as of sincerity, but as from God, we speak in the sight of God in Christ.

Make, of none effect through their traditions.

Mark 7:9–13 He said to them, "*All too* well you reject the commandment of God, that you may keep your tradition. **10** For Moses said, *'Honor your father and your mother'*; and, *'He who curses father or mother, let him be put to death.'* **11** But you say, 'If a man says to his father or mother, "Whatever profit you might have received from me *is* Corban"—' (that is, a gift *to God*), **12** then you no longer let him do anything for his father or his mother, **13** making the word of God of no effect through your tradition which you have handed down. And many such things you do."

Reject.

Jer 8:9 The wise men are ashamed, They are dismayed and taken. Behold, they have rejected the word of the LORD; So what wisdom do they have?

Stumble at.

1 Pet 2:8 and *"A stone of stumbling And a rock of offense."* They stumble, being disobedient to the word, to which they also were appointed.

Do not obey.

Ps 119:158 I see the treacherous, and am disgusted, Because they do not keep Your word.

Frequently twist, to their own destruction.

2 Pet 3:16 as also in all his epistles, speaking in them of these things, in which are some things hard to understand, which untaught and unstable *people* twist to their own destruction, as *they do* also the rest of the Scriptures.

Consequences for those who tamper with or destroy.

Jer 36:29–31 And you shall say to Jehoiakim king of Judah, 'Thus says the LORD: "You have burned this scroll, saying, 'Why have you written in it that the king of Babylon will certainly come and destroy this land, and cause man and beast to cease from here?' " **30** Therefore thus says the LORD concerning Jehoiakim king of Judah: "He shall have no one to sit on the throne of David, and his dead body shall be cast out to the heat of the day and the frost of the night. **31** I will punish him, his family, and his servants for their iniquity; and I will bring on them, on the inhabitants of Jerusalem, and on the men of Judah all the doom that I have pronounced against them; but they did not heed." ' "

Rev 22:18–19 For I testify to everyone who hears the words of the prophecy of this book: If anyone adds to these things, God will add to him the plagues that are written in this book; **19** and if anyone takes away from the words of the book of this prophecy, God shall take away his part from the Book of Life, from the holy city, and *from* the things which are written in this book.

SEA, THE

The gathering together of the waters originally called.

Gen 1:10 And God called the dry *land* Earth, and the gathering together of the waters He called Seas. And God saw that *it was* good.

Great rivers often called.

Is 11:15 The LORD will utterly destroy the tongue of the Sea of Egypt; With His mighty wind He will shake His fist over the River, And strike it in the seven streams, And make *men* cross over dryshod.

Jer 51:36 Therefore thus says the LORD: "Behold, I will plead your case and take vengeance for you. I will dry up her sea and make her springs dry.

Lakes often called.

Deut 3:17 the plain also, with the Jordan as *the* border, from Chinnereth as far as the east side of the Sea of the Arabah (the Salt Sea), below the slopes of Pisgah.

Matt 8:24 And suddenly a great tempest arose on the sea, so that the boat was covered with the waves. But He was asleep.

Matt 8:27 So the men marveled, saying, "Who can this be, that even the winds and the sea obey Him?"

Matt 8:32 And He said to them, "Go." So when they had come out, they went into the herd of swine. And suddenly the whole herd of swine ran violently down the steep place into the sea, and perished in the water.

God

Created.

Ex 20:11 For *in* six days the LORD made the heavens and the earth, the sea, and all that *is* in them, and rested the seventh day. Therefore the LORD blessed the Sabbath day and hallowed it.

Ps 95:5 The sea *is* His, for He made it; And His hands formed the dry *land*.

Acts 14:15 and saying, "Men, why are you doing these things? We also are men with the same nature as you, and preach to you that you should turn from these useless things to the living God, who made the heaven, the earth, the sea, and all things that are in them,

Made the animals of.

Gen 1:20–22 Then God said, "Let the waters abound with an abundance of living creatures, and let birds fly above the earth across the face of the firmament of the heavens." **21** So God created great sea creatures and every living thing that moves, with which the waters abounded, according to their kind, and every winged bird according to its kind. And God saw that *it was* good. **22** And God blessed them, saying, "Be fruitful and multiply, and fill the waters in the seas, and let birds multiply on the earth."

Founded the earth upon.

Ps 24:2 For He has founded it upon the seas, And established it upon the waters.

Set bounds to, by a perpetual decree.

Job 26:10 He drew a circular horizon on the face of the waters, At the boundary of light and darkness.

Job 38:8 "Or *who* shut in the sea with doors, When it burst forth *and* issued from the womb;

Job 38:10–11 When I fixed My limit for it, And set bars and doors; **11** When I said, 'This far you may come, but no farther, And here your proud waves must stop!'

Prov 8:27 When He prepared the heavens, I *was* there, When He drew a circle on the face of the deep,

Prov 8:29 When He assigned to the sea its limit, So that the waters would not transgress His command, When He marked out the foundations of the earth,

Measures the waters of.

Is 40:12 Who has measured the waters in the hollow of His hand, Measured heaven with a span And calculated the dust of the earth in a measure? Weighed the mountains in scales And the hills in a balance?

Does what He pleases in.

Ps 135:6 Whatever the LORD pleases He does, In heaven and in earth, In the seas and in all deep places.

Dries up, by His rebuke.

Is 50:2 Why, when I came, *was there* no man? *Why,* when I called, *was there* none to answer? Is My hand shortened at all that it cannot redeem? Or have I no power to deliver? Indeed with My rebuke I dry up the sea, I make the rivers a wilderness; Their fish stink because *there is* no water, And die of thirst.

Nah 1:4 He rebukes the sea and makes it dry, And dries up all the rivers. Bashan and Carmel wither, And the flower of Lebanon wilts.

Shakes, by His word.

Hag 2:6 "For thus says the LORD of hosts: 'Once more (it *is* a little while) I will shake heaven and earth, the sea and dry land;

Stills, by His power.

Ps 65:7 You who still the noise of the seas, The noise of their waves, And the tumult of the peoples.

Ps 89:9 You rule the raging of the sea; When its waves rise, You still them.

Ps 107:29 He calms the storm, So that its waves are still.

Of immense extent.

Job 11:9 Their measure *is* longer than the earth And broader than the sea.

Ps 104:25 This great and wide sea, In which *are* innumerable teeming things, Living things both small and great.

Of great depth.

Ps 68:22 The Lord said, "I will bring back from Bashan, I will bring *them* back from the depths of the sea,

Rivers supplied by exhalations from.

Eccl 1:7 All the rivers run into the sea, Yet the sea *is* not full; To the place from which the rivers come, There they return again.

Replenished by rivers.

Eccl 1:7 All the rivers run into the sea, Yet the sea *is* not full; To the place from which the rivers come, There they return again.

Ezek 47:8 Then he said to me: "This water flows toward the eastern region, goes down into the valley, and enters the sea. *When it* reaches the sea, *its* waters are healed.

Names for,

The deep.

Job 41:31 He makes the deep boil like a pot; He makes the sea like a pot of ointment.

Ps 107:24 They see the works of the LORD, And His wonders in the deep.

2 Cor 11:25 Three times I was beaten with rods; once I was stoned; three times I was shipwrecked; a night and a day I have been in the deep;

Great waters.

Ps 77:19 Your way *was* in the sea, Your path in the great waters, And Your footsteps were not known.

Great and wide sea.

Ps 104:25 This great and wide sea, In which *are* innu-

merable teeming things, Living things both small and great.

The clouds the garment of.

Job 38:9 When I made the clouds its garment, And thick darkness its swaddling band;

Darkness the swaddling band of.

Job 38:9 When I made the clouds its garment, And thick darkness its swaddling band;

Sand the barrier of.

Jer 5:22 Do you not fear Me?' says the LORD. 'Will you not tremble at My presence, Who have placed the sand as the bound of the sea, By a perpetual decree, that it cannot pass beyond it? And though its waves toss to and fro, Yet they cannot prevail; Though they roar, yet they cannot pass over it.

Inhabited by innumerable creatures.

Ps 104:25–26 This great and wide sea, In which *are* innumerable teeming things, Living things both small and great. **26** There the ships sail about; *There is* that Leviathan Which You have made to play there.

The wonders of God seen in.

Ps 107:24 They see the works of the LORD, And His wonders in the deep.

Made to glorify God.

Ps 69:34 Let heaven and earth praise Him, The seas and everything that moves in them.

Ps 148:7 Praise the LORD from the earth, You great sea creatures and all the depths;

Mentioned in Scripture

The Adriatic or Sea of Adria.

Acts 27:27 Now when the fourteenth night had come, as we were driven up and down in the Adriatic *Sea,* about midnight the sailors sensed that they were drawing near some land.

Mediterranean or Great Sea.

Num 34:6 'As for the western border, you shall have the Great Sea for a border; this shall be your western border.

Deut 11:24 Every place on which the sole of your foot treads shall be yours: from the wilderness and Lebanon, from the river, the River Euphrates, even to the Western Sea, shall be your territory.

Deut 34:2 all Naphtali and the land of Ephraim and Manasseh, all the land of Judah as far as the Western Sea,

Zech 14:8 And in that day it shall be *That* living waters shall flow from Jerusalem, Half of them toward the eastern sea And half of them toward the western sea; In both summer and winter it shall occur.

Red Sea.

Ex 10:19 And the LORD turned a very strong west wind, which took the locusts away and blew them into the Red Sea. There remained not one locust in all the territory of Egypt.

Ex 13:18 So God led the people around *by* way of the wilderness of the Red Sea. And the children of Israel went up in orderly ranks out of the land of Egypt.

Ex 23:31 And I will set your bounds from the Red Sea to the sea, Philistia, and from the desert to the River. For

I will deliver the inhabitants of the land into your hand, and you shall drive them out before you.

Sea of Joppa or Sea of the Philistines.

Ex 23:31 And I will set your bounds from the Red Sea to the sea, Philistia, and from the desert to the River. For I will deliver the inhabitants of the land into your hand, and you shall drive them out before you.

Ezra 3:7 They also gave money to the masons and the carpenters, and food, drink, and oil to the people of Sidon and Tyre to bring cedar logs from Lebanon to the sea, to Joppa, according to the permission which they had from Cyrus king of Persia.

Salt or Dead Sea.

Gen 14:3 All these joined together in the Valley of Siddim (that is, the Salt Sea).

Num 34:12 the border shall go down along the Jordan, and it shall end at the Salt Sea. This shall be your land with its surrounding boundaries.' "

Sea of Galilee.

Matt 4:18 And Jesus, walking by the Sea of Galilee, saw two brothers, Simon called Peter, and Andrew his brother, casting a net into the sea; for they were fishermen.

Matt 8:32 And He said to them, "Go." So when they had come out, they went into the herd of swine. And suddenly the whole herd of swine ran violently down the steep place into the sea, and perished in the water.

John 6:1 After these things Jesus went over the Sea of Galilee, which is *the Sea* of Tiberias.

Sea of Jazer.

Jer 48:32 O vine of Sibmah! I will weep for you with the weeping of Jazer. Your plants have gone over the sea, They reach to the sea of Jazer. The plunderer has fallen on your summer fruit and your vintage.

Raised by the wind.

Ps 107:25–26 For He commands and raises the stormy wind, Which lifts up the waves of the sea. **26** They mount up to the heavens, They go down again to the depths; Their soul melts because of trouble.

Jon 1:4 But the LORD sent out a great wind on the sea, and there was a mighty tempest on the sea, so that the ship was about to be broken up.

Caused to foam by Leviathan.

Job 41:31–32 He makes the deep boil like a pot; He makes the sea like a pot of ointment. **32** He leaves a shining wake behind him; *One* would think the deep had white hair.

The waves of,

Raised upon high.

Ps 93:3 The floods have lifted up, O LORD, The floods have lifted up their voice; The floods lift up their waves.

Ps 107:25 For He commands and raises the stormy wind, Which lifts up the waves of the sea.

Tossed to and fro.

Jer 5:22 Do you not fear Me?' says the LORD. 'Will you not tremble at My presence, Who have placed the sand as the bound of the sea, By a perpetual decree, that it cannot pass beyond it? And though its waves toss to and fro, Yet they cannot prevail; Though they roar, yet they cannot pass over it.

Multitudinous.

Jer 51:42 The sea has come up over Babylon; She is covered with the multitude of its waves.

Mighty.

Ps 93:4 The LORD on high *is* mightier Than the noise of many waters, *Than* the mighty waves of the sea.

Acts 27:41 But striking a place where two seas met, they ran the ship aground; and the prow stuck fast and remained immovable, but the stern was being broken up by the violence of the waves.

Tumultuous.

Luke 21:25 "And there will be signs in the sun, in the moon, and in the stars; and on the earth distress of nations, with perplexity, the sea and the waves roaring;

Jude 1:13 raging waves of the sea, foaming up their own shame; wandering stars for whom is reserved the blackness of darkness forever.

The shore of, covered with sand.

Gen 22:17 blessing I will bless you, and multiplying I will multiply your descendants as the stars of the heaven and as the sand which *is* on the seashore; and your descendants shall possess the gate of their enemies.

1 Kin 4:29 And God gave Solomon wisdom and exceedingly great understanding, and largeness of heart like the sand on the seashore.

Job 6:3 For then it would be heavier than the sand of the sea— Therefore my words have been rash.

Ps 78:27 He also rained meat on them like the dust, Feathered fowl like the sand of the seas;

Numerous islands in.

Ezek 26:18 Now the coastlands tremble on the day of your fall; Yes, the coastlands by the sea are troubled at your departure." '

Passed over in ships.

Ps 104:26 There the ships sail about; *There is* that Leviathan Which You have made to play there.

Ps 107:23 Those who go down to the sea in ships, Who do business on great waters,

Sailing on, dangerous.

Acts 27:9 Now when much time had been spent, and sailing was now dangerous because the Fast was already over, Paul advised them,

Acts 27:20 Now when neither sun nor stars appeared for many days, and no small tempest beat on *us,* all hope that we would be saved was finally given up.

2 Cor 11:26 *in* journeys often, *in* perils of waters, *in* perils of robbers, *in* perils of *my own* countrymen, *in* perils of the Gentiles, *in* perils in the city, *in* perils in the wilderness, *in* perils in the sea, *in* perils among false brethren;

Commercial nations

Often built cities on the borders of.

Gen 49:13 "Zebulun shall dwell by the haven of the sea; He *shall become* a haven for ships, And his border shall adjoin Sidon.

Ezek 27:3 and say to Tyre, 'You who are situated at the entrance of the sea, merchant of the peoples on many coastlands, thus says the Lord GOD: "O Tyre, you have said, 'I *am* perfect in beauty.'

Nah 3:8 Are you better than No Amon *That was* situated by the River, That had the waters around her, Whose rampart *was* the sea, Whose wall *was* the sea?

Derived great wealth from.

Deut 33:19 They shall call the peoples *to* the mountain; There they shall offer sacrifices of righteousness; For they shall partake *of* the abundance of the seas And *of* treasures hidden in the sand."

Shall give up its dead at the last day.

Rev 20:13 The sea gave up the dead who were in it, and Death and Hades delivered up the dead who were in them. And they were judged, each one according to his works.

The renewed earth shall be without.

Rev 21:1 Now I saw a new heaven and a new earth, for the first heaven and the first earth had passed away. Also there was no more sea.

Illustrative of

Heavy afflictions.

Is 43:2 When you pass through the waters, I *will be* with you; And through the rivers, they shall not overflow you. When you walk through the fire, you shall not be burned, Nor shall the flame scorch you.

Lam 2:13 How shall I console you? To what shall I liken you, O daughter of Jerusalem? What shall I compare with you, that I may comfort you, O virgin daughter of Zion? For your ruin *is* spread wide as the sea; Who can heal you?

(Troubled) the wicked.

Is 57:20 But the wicked *are* like the troubled sea, When it cannot rest, Whose waters cast up mire and dirt.

(Roaring) hostile armies.

Is 5:30 In that day they will roar against them Like the roaring of the sea. And if *one* looks to the land, Behold, darkness *and* sorrow; And the light is darkened by the clouds.

Jer 6:23 They will lay hold on bow and spear; They *are* cruel and have no mercy; Their voice roars like the sea; And they ride on horses, As men of war set in array against you, O daughter of Zion."

(Waves of) righteousness.

Is 48:18 Oh, that you had heeded My commandments! Then your peace would have been like a river, And your righteousness like the waves of the sea.

(Waves of) devastating armies.

Ezek 26:3–4 "Therefore thus says the Lord GOD: 'Behold, I *am* against you, O Tyre, and will cause many nations to come up against you, as the sea causes its waves to come up. 4 And they shall destroy the walls of Tyre and break down her towers; I will also scrape her dust from her, and make her like the top of a rock.

(Waves of) the unsteady.

James 1:6 But let him ask in faith, with no doubting, for he who doubts is like a wave of the sea driven and tossed by the wind.

(Covered with waters) the diffusion of spiritual knowledge over the earth in the last days.

Is 11:9 They shall not hurt nor destroy in all My holy

mountain, For the earth shall be full of the knowledge of the LORD As the waters cover the sea.

Hab 2:14 For the earth will be filled With the knowledge of the glory of the LORD, As the waters cover the sea.

(Smooth as glass) the peace of heaven.

Rev 4:6 Before the throne *there was* a sea of glass, like crystal. And in the midst of the throne, and around the throne, *were* four living creatures full of eyes in front and in back.

Rev 15:2 And I saw *something* like a sea of glass mingled with fire, and those who have the victory over the beast, over his image and over his mark *and* over the number of his name, standing on the sea of glass, having harps of God.

SEALS (OFFICIAL)

Called signets.

Gen 38:18 Then he said, "What pledge shall I give you?" So she said, "Your signet and cord, and your staff that *is* in your hand." Then he gave *them* to her, and went in to her, and she conceived by him.

Gen 38:25 When she *was* brought out, she sent to her father-in-law, saying, "By the man to whom these belong, I *am* with child." And she said, "Please determine whose these *are*—the signet and cord, and staff."

Precious stones set in gold used as.

Ex 28:11 With the work of an engraver in stone, *like* the engravings of a signet, you shall engrave the two stones with the names of the sons of Israel. You shall set them in settings of gold.

Inscriptions upon, alluded to.

2 Tim 2:19 Nevertheless the solid foundation of God stands, having this seal: "The Lord knows those who are His," and, "Let everyone who names the name of Christ depart from iniquity."

Generally worn as rings or bracelets.

Jer 22:24 "*As* I live," says the LORD, "though Coniah the son of Jehoiakim, king of Judah, were the signet on My right hand, yet I would pluck you off;

Impressions of,

Frequently taken in clay.

Job 38:14 It takes on form like clay *under* a seal, And stands out like a garment.

Used for security.

Dan 6:17 Then a stone was brought and laid on the mouth of the den, and the king sealed it with his own signet ring and with the signets of his lords, that the purpose concerning Daniel might not be changed.

Matt 27:66 So they went and made the tomb secure, sealing the stone and setting the guard.

Attached to all royal decrees.

1 Kin 21:8 And she wrote letters in Ahab's name, sealed *them* with his seal, and sent the letters to the elders and the nobles who *were* dwelling in the city with Naboth.

Esth 3:12 Then the king's scribes were called on the thirteenth day of the first month, and a decree was written according to all that Haman commanded—to the king's satraps, to the governors who *were* over each province, to the officials of all people, to every province according to its script, and to every people in their language. In the name of King Ahasuerus it was written, and sealed with the king's signet ring.

Esth 8:8 You yourselves write *a decree* concerning the Jews, as you please, in the king's name, and seal *it* with the king's signet ring; for whatever is written in the king's name and sealed with the king's signet ring no one can revoke."

Attached to covenants.

Neh 9:38 "And because of all this, We make a sure *covenant* and write *it;* Our leaders, our Levites, *and* our priests seal *it.*"

Neh 10:1 Now those who placed *their* seal on *the document were:* Nehemiah the governor, the son of Hacaliah, and Zedekiah,

Attached to lease and transfers of property.

Jer 32:9–12 So I bought the field from Hanamel, the son of my uncle who *was* in Anathoth, and weighed *out to* him the money—seventeen shekels of silver. **10** And I signed the deed and sealed *it,* took witnesses, and weighed the money on the scales. **11** So I took the purchase deed, *both* that which was sealed *according* to the law and custom, and that which was open; **12** and I gave the purchase deed to Baruch the son of Neriah, son of Mahseiah, in the presence of Hanamel my uncle's *son,* and in the presence of the witnesses who signed the purchase deed, before all the Jews who sat in the court of the prison.

Jer 32:44 Men will buy fields for money, sign deeds and seal *them,* and take witnesses, in the land of Benjamin, in the places around Jerusalem, in the cities of Judah, in the cities of the mountains, in the cities of the lowland, and in the cities of the South; for I will cause their captives to return,' says the LORD."

Set upon treasures.

Deut 32:34 *'Is* this not laid up in store with Me, Sealed up among My treasures?

Attached to the victims approved for sacrifice, alluded to.

John 6:27 Do not labor for the food which perishes, but for the food which endures to everlasting life, which the Son of Man will give you, because God the Father has set His seal on Him."

Were given by kings as a badge of authority.

Gen 41:41–42 And Pharaoh said to Joseph, "See, I have set you over all the land of Egypt." **42** Then Pharaoh took his signet ring off his hand and put it on Joseph's hand; and he clothed him in garments of fine linen and put a gold chain around his neck.

Illustrative of

Circumcision.

Rom 4:11 And he received the sign of circumcision, a seal of the righteousness of the faith which *he had while still* uncircumcised, that he might be the father of all those who believe, though they are uncircumcised, that righteousness might be imputed to them also,

Converts.

1 Cor 9:2 If I am not an apostle to others, yet doubtless I am to you. For you are the seal of my apostleship in the Lord.

What is dear or valued.

Song 8:6 Set me as a seal upon your heart, As a seal upon your arm; For love *is as* strong as death, Jealousy *as* cruel as the grave; Its flames *are* flames of fire, A most vehement flame.

Jer 22:24 *"As* I live," says the LORD, "though Coniah the son of Jehoiakim, king of Judah, were the signet on My right hand, yet I would pluck you off;

Hag 2:23 'In that day,' says the LORD of hosts, 'I will take you, Zerubbabel My servant, the son of Shealtiel,' says the LORD, 'and will make you like a signet *ring;* for I have chosen you,' says the LORD of hosts."

Secrecy.

Dan 12:4 "But you, Daniel, shut up the words, and seal the book until the time of the end; many shall run to and fro, and knowledge shall increase."

Rev 5:1 And I saw in the right *hand* of Him who sat on the throne a scroll written inside and on the back, sealed with seven seals.

Rev 10:4 Now when the seven thunders uttered their voices, I was about to write; but I heard a voice from heaven saying to me, "Seal up the things which the seven thunders uttered, and do not write them."

Security.

Song 4:12 A garden enclosed *Is* my sister, *my* spouse, A spring shut up, A fountain sealed.

2 Tim 2:19 Nevertheless the solid foundation of God stands, having this seal: "The Lord knows those who are His," and, "Let everyone who names the name of Christ depart from iniquity."

Rev 7:2–8 Then I saw another angel ascending from the east, having the seal of the living God. And he cried with a loud voice to the four angels to whom it was granted to harm the earth and the sea, **3** saying, "Do not harm the earth, the sea, or the trees till we have sealed the servants of our God on their foreheads." **4** And I heard the number of those who were sealed. One hundred *and* forty-four thousand of all the tribes of the children of Israel *were* sealed: **5** of the tribe of Judah twelve thousand *were* sealed; of the tribe of Reuben twelve thousand *were* sealed; of the tribe of Gad twelve thousand *were* sealed; **6** of the tribe of Asher twelve thousand *were* sealed; of the tribe of Naphtali twelve thousand *were* sealed; of the tribe of Manasseh twelve thousand *were* sealed; **7** of the tribe of Simeon twelve thousand *were* sealed; of the tribe of Levi twelve thousand *were* sealed; of the tribe of Issachar twelve thousand *were* sealed; **8** of the tribe of Zebulun twelve thousand *were* sealed; of the tribe of Joseph twelve thousand *were* sealed; of the tribe of Benjamin twelve thousand *were* sealed.

Rev 20:3 and he cast him into the bottomless pit, and shut him up, and set a seal on him, so that he should deceive the nations no more till the thousand years were finished. But after these things he must be released for a little while.

Full approval.

John 3:33 He who has received His testimony has certified that God is true.

Act as restraints.

Job 9:7 He commands the sun, and it does not rise; He seals off the stars;

Job 37:7 He seals the hand of every man, That all men may know His work.

Rev 20:3 and he cast him into the bottomless pit, and shut him up, and set a seal on him, so that he should deceive the nations no more till the thousand years were finished. But after these things he must be released for a little while.

SECOND COMING OF CHRIST.
SEE JESUS CHRIST, SECOND COMING OF

SECURITY, ETERNAL.
SEE ALSO ASSURANCE

Described.

Ps 97:10 You who love the LORD, hate evil! He preserves the souls of His saints; He delivers them out of the hand of the wicked.

Depends on Christ.

John 10:28–29 And I give them eternal life, and they shall never perish; neither shall anyone snatch them out of My hand. **29** My Father, who has given *them* to Me, is greater than all; and no one is able to snatch *them* out of My Father's hand.

Paul's explanation of.

Rom 8:31–39 What then shall we say to these things? If God *is* for us, who *can be* against us? **32** He who did not spare His own Son, but delivered Him up for us all, how shall He not with Him also freely give us all things? **33** Who shall bring a charge against God's elect? *It is* God who justifies. **34** Who *is* he who condemns? *It is* Christ who died, and furthermore is also risen, who is even at the right hand of God, who also makes intercession for us. **35** Who shall separate us from the love of Christ? *Shall* tribulation, or distress, or persecution, or famine, or nakedness, or peril, or sword? **36** As it is written: *"For Your sake we are killed all day long; We are accounted as sheep for the slaughter."* **37** Yet in all these things we are more than conquerors through Him who loved us. **38** For I am persuaded that neither death nor life, nor angels nor principalities nor powers, nor things present nor things to come, **39** nor height nor depth, nor any other created thing, shall be able to separate us from the love of God which is in Christ Jesus our Lord.

Is guaranteed by the Holy Spirit.

Eph 1:13–14 In Him you also *trusted*, after you heard the word of truth, the gospel of your salvation; in whom also, having believed, you were sealed with the Holy Spirit of promise, **14** who is the guarantee of our inheritance until the redemption of the purchased possession, to the praise of His glory.

SEED

Every herb, tree, and grass yields its own.

Gen 1:11–12 Then God said, "Let the earth bring forth grass, the herb *that* yields seed, *and* the fruit tree *that* yields fruit according to its kind, whose seed *is* in itself, on the earth"; and it was so. **12** And the earth brought forth grass, the herb *that* yields seed according to its kind, and the tree *that* yields fruit, whose seed *is* in itself according to its kind. And God saw that *it was* good.

Gen 1:29 And God said, "See, I have given you every herb *that* yields seed which *is* on the face of all the earth, and every tree whose fruit yields seed; to you it shall be for food.

Each kind of, has its own body.

1 Cor 15:38 But God gives it a body as He pleases, and to each seed its own body.

Sowing of,

Time for, called seedtime.

Gen 8:22 "While the earth remains, Seedtime and harvest, Cold and heat, Winter and summer, And day and night Shall not cease."

Necessary to its productiveness.

John 12:24 Most assuredly, I say to you, unless a grain of wheat falls into the ground and dies, it remains alone; but if it dies, it produces much grain.

1 Cor 15:36 Foolish one, what you sow is not made alive unless it dies.

Required constant diligence.

Eccl 11:4 He who observes the wind will not sow, And he who regards the clouds will not reap.

Eccl 11:6 In the morning sow your seed, And in the evening do not withhold your hand; For you do not know which will prosper, Either this or that, Or whether both alike *will be* good.

Often attended with great waste.

Matt 13:4–5 And as he sowed, some *seed* fell by the wayside; and the birds came and devoured them. **5** Some fell on stony places, where they did not have much earth; and they immediately sprang up because they had no depth of earth.

Matt 13:7 And some fell among thorns, and the thorns sprang up and choked them.

Often attended with danger.

Ps 126:5–6 Those who sow in tears Shall reap in joy. **6** He who continually goes forth weeping, Bearing seed for sowing, Shall doubtless come again with rejoicing, Bringing his sheaves *with him.*

Yearly return of seedtime, secured by covenant.

Gen 8:21–22 And the LORD smelled a soothing aroma. Then the LORD said in His heart, "I will never again curse the ground for man's sake, although the imagination of man's heart *is* evil from his youth; nor will I again destroy every living thing as I have done. **22** "While the earth remains, Seedtime and harvest, Cold and heat, Winter and summer, And day and night Shall not cease."

The ground carefully plowed and prepared for.

Is 28:24–25 Does the plowman keep plowing all day to sow? Does he keep turning his soil and breaking the clods? **25** When he has leveled its surface, Does he not sow the black cummin And scatter the cummin, Plant the wheat in rows, The barley in the appointed place, And the spelt in its place?

Often sown beside rivers.

Eccl 11:1 Cast your bread upon the waters, For you will find it after many days.

Is 32:20 Blessed *are* you who sow beside all waters, Who send out freely the feet of the ox and the donkey.

Often trodden into the ground, by the feet of livestock.

Is 32:20 Blessed *are* you who sow beside all waters, Who send out freely the feet of the ox and the donkey.

Required to be watered by the rain.

Is 55:10 "For as the rain comes down, and the snow from heaven, And do not return there, But water the earth, And make it bring forth and bud, That it may give seed to the sower And bread to the eater,

In Egypt required to be artificially watered.

Deut 11:10 For the land which you go to possess *is* not like the land of Egypt from which you have come, where you sowed your seed and watered *it* by foot, as a vegetable garden;

Yielded an abundant increase in Canaan.

Gen 26:12 Then Isaac sowed in that land, and reaped in the same year a hundredfold; and the LORD blessed him.

Mosaic laws respecting,

Different kinds of, not to be sown in the same field.

Lev 19:19 'You shall keep My statutes. You shall not let your livestock breed with another kind. You shall not sow your field with mixed seed. Nor shall a garment of mixed linen and wool come upon you.

Deut 22:9 "You shall not sow your vineyard with different kinds of seed, lest the yield of the seed which you have sown and the fruit of your vineyard be defiled.

If dry, exempted from uncleanness though touched by an unclean thing.

Lev 11:37 And if a part of *any such* carcass falls on any planting seed which is to be sown, it *remains* clean.

If wet, rendered unclean by contact with an unclean thing.

Lev 11:38 But if water is put on the seed, and if *a part* of *any such* carcass falls on it, it *becomes* unclean to you.

The tithe of, to be given to God.

Lev 27:30 And all the tithe of the land, *whether* of the seed of the land *or* of the fruit of the tree, *is* the LORD's. It *is* holy to the LORD.

Not to be sown during the sabbatical year.

Lev 25:4 but in the seventh year there shall be a sabbath of solemn rest for the land, a sabbath to the LORD. You shall neither sow your field nor prune your vineyard.

Lev 25:20 'And if you say, "What shall we eat in the seventh year, since we shall not sow nor gather in our produce?"

Not to be sown in Year of Jubilee.

Lev 25:11 That fiftieth year shall be a Jubilee to you; in it you shall neither sow nor reap what grows of its own accord, nor gather *the grapes* of your untended vine.

Difference between, and the plant which grows from it, noticed.

1 Cor 15:37–38 And what you sow, you do not sow that body that shall be, but mere grain—perhaps wheat or some other *grain.* **38** But God gives it a body as He pleases, and to each seed its own body.

The Jews punished by

Its rotting in the ground.

Joel 1:17 The seed shrivels under the clods, Storehouses are in shambles; Barns are broken down, For the grain has withered.

Mal 2:3 "Behold, I will rebuke your descendants And spread refuse on your faces, The refuse of your solemn feasts; And *one* will take you away with it.

Its yielding a small increase.

Is 5:10 For ten acres of vineyard shall yield one bath, And a homer of seed shall yield one ephah."

Hag 1:6 "You have sown much, and bring in little; You eat, but do not have enough; You drink, but you are not filled with drink; You clothe yourselves, but no one is warm; And he who earns wages, Earns wages *to put* into a bag with holes."

Its increase being consumed by locusts.

Deut 28:38 "You shall carry much seed out to the field but gather little in, for the locust shall consume it.

Joel 1:4 What the chewing locust left, the swarming locust has eaten; What the swarming locust left, the crawling locust has eaten; And what the crawling locust left, the consuming locust has eaten.

Its increase being consumed by enemies.

Lev 26:16 I also will do this to you: I will even appoint terror over you, wasting disease and fever which shall consume the eyes and cause sorrow of heart. And you shall sow your seed in vain, for your enemies shall eat it.

Deut 28:33 A nation whom you have not known shall eat the fruit of your land and the produce of your labor, and you shall be only oppressed and crushed continually.

Deut 28:51 And they shall eat the increase of your livestock and the produce of your land, until you are destroyed; they shall not leave you grain or new wine or oil, *or* the increase of your cattle or the offspring of your flocks, until they have destroyed you.

Its being choked by thorns.

Jer 12:13 They have sown wheat but reaped thorns; They have put themselves to pain *but* do not profit. But be ashamed of your harvest Because of the fierce anger of the LORD."

Illustrative of

The Word of God.

Luke 8:11 "Now the parable is this: The seed is the word of God.

1 Pet 1:23 having been born again, not of corruptible seed but incorruptible, through the word of God which lives and abides forever,

Spiritual life.

1 John 3:9 Whoever has been born of God does not sin, for His seed remains in him; and he cannot sin, because he has been born of God.

Sowing, illustrative of

Preaching the gospel.

Matt 13:3 Then He spoke many things to them in parables, saying: "Behold, a sower went out to sow.

Matt 13:32 which indeed is the least of all the seeds; but when it is grown it is greater than the herbs and becomes a tree, so that the birds of the air come and nest in its branches."

1 Cor 9:11 If we have sown spiritual things for you, *is it* a great thing if we reap your material things?

Scattering or dispersing a people.

Zech 10:9 "I will sow them among the peoples, And they shall remember Me in far countries; They shall live, together with their children, And they shall return.

Christian generosity.

Eccl 11:6 In the morning sow your seed, And in the evening do not withhold your hand; For you do not know which will prosper, Either this or that, Or whether both alike *will be* good.

2 Cor 9:6 But this *I say:* He who sows sparingly will also reap sparingly, and he who sows bountifully will also reap bountifully.

Men's works producing a corresponding fruit.

Job 4:8 Even as I have seen, Those who plow iniquity And sow trouble reap the same.

Hos 10:12 Sow for yourselves righteousness; Reap in mercy; Break up your fallow ground, For *it is* time to seek the LORD, Till He comes and rains righteousness on you.

Gal 6:7–8 Do not be deceived, God is not mocked; for whatever a man sows, that he will also reap. **8** For he who sows to his flesh will of the flesh reap corruption, but he who sows to the Spirit will of the Spirit reap everlasting life.

The death of Christ and its effects.

John 12:24 Most assuredly, I say to you, unless a grain of wheat falls into the ground and dies, it remains alone; but if it dies, it produces much grain.

The burial of the body.

1 Cor 15:36–38 Foolish one, what you sow is not made alive unless it dies. **37** And what you sow, you do not sow that body that shall be, but mere grain—perhaps wheat or some other *grain*. **38** But God gives it a body as He pleases, and to each seed its own body.

SEEKING GOD

Commanded.

Is 55:6 Seek the LORD while He may be found, Call upon Him while He is near.

Matt 7:7 "Ask, and it will be given to you; seek, and you will find; knock, and it will be opened to you.

Includes seeking

His name.

Ps 83:16 Fill their faces with shame, That they may seek Your name, O LORD.

His Word.

Is 34:16 "Search from the book of the LORD, and read: Not one of these shall fail; Not one shall lack her mate. For My mouth has commanded it, and His Spirit has gathered them.

His face.

Ps 27:8 *When You said,* "Seek My face," My heart said to You, "Your face, LORD, I will seek."

Ps 105:4 Seek the LORD and His strength; Seek His face evermore!

His strength.

1 Chr 16:11 Seek the LORD and His strength; Seek His face evermore!

Ps 105:4 Seek the LORD and His strength; Seek His face evermore!

His commandments.

1 Chr 28:8 Now therefore, in the sight of all Israel, the assembly of the LORD, and in the hearing of our God, be careful to seek out all the commandments of the LORD your God, that you may possess this good land, and leave *it* as an inheritance for your children after you forever.

Mal 2:7 "For the lips of a priest should keep knowledge, And *people* should seek the law from his mouth; For he is the messenger of the LORD of hosts.

His precepts.

Ps 119:45 And I will walk at liberty, For I seek Your precepts.

Ps 119:94 I *am* Yours, save me; For I have sought Your precepts.

His kingdom.

Matt 6:33 But seek first the kingdom of God and His righteousness, and all these things shall be added to you.

Luke 12:31 But seek the kingdom of God, and all these things shall be added to you.

His righteousness.

Matt 6:33 But seek first the kingdom of God and His righteousness, and all these things shall be added to you.

Christ.

Mal 3:1 "Behold, I send My messenger, And he will prepare the way before Me. And the Lord, whom you seek, Will suddenly come to His temple, Even the Messenger of the covenant, In whom you delight. Behold, He is coming," Says the LORD of hosts.

Luke 2:15–16 So it was, when the angels had gone away from them into heaven, that the shepherds said to one another, "Let us now go to Bethlehem and see this thing that has come to pass, which the Lord has made known to us." **16** And they came with haste and found Mary and Joseph, and the Babe lying in a manger.

Honor that comes from Him.

John 5:44 How can you believe, who receive honor from one another, and do not seek the honor that *comes* from the only God?

Justification by Christ.

Gal 2:16–17 knowing that a man is not justified by the works of the law but by faith in Jesus Christ, even we have believed in Christ Jesus, that we might be justified by faith in Christ and not by the works of the law; for by the works of the law no flesh shall be justified. **17** "But if, while we seek to be justified by Christ, we ourselves also are found sinners, *is* Christ therefore a minister of sin? Certainly not!

The city He has prepared.

Heb 11:10 for he waited for the city which has foundations, whose builder and maker *is* God.

Heb 11:16 But now they desire a better, that is, a heavenly *country*. Therefore God is not ashamed to be called their God, for He has prepared a city for them.

Heb 13:14 For here we have no continuing city, but we seek the one to come.

By prayer.

Job 8:5 If you would earnestly seek God And make your supplication to the Almighty,

Dan 9:3 Then I set my face toward the Lord God to make request by prayer and supplications, with fasting, sackcloth, and ashes.

In His house.

Deut 12:5 "But you shall seek the place where the LORD your God chooses, out of all your tribes, to put His name for His dwelling place; and there you shall go.

Ps 27:4 One *thing* I have desired of the LORD, That will I seek: That I may dwell in the house of the LORD All the days of my life, To behold the beauty of the LORD, And to inquire in His temple.

Should be

Immediate.

Hos 10:12 Sow for yourselves righteousness; Reap in mercy; Break up your fallow ground, For *it is* time to seek the LORD, Till He comes and rains righteousness on you.

Evermore.

Ps 105:4 Seek the LORD and His strength; Seek His face evermore!

While He may be found.

Is 55:6 Seek the LORD while He may be found, Call upon Him while He is near.

With diligence.

Heb 11:6 But without faith *it is* impossible to please Him, for he who comes to God must believe that He is, and *that* He is a rewarder of those who diligently seek Him.

With the heart.

Deut 4:29 But from there you will seek the LORD your God, and you will find *Him* if you seek Him with all your heart and with all your soul.

1 Chr 22:19 Now set your heart and your soul to seek the LORD your God. Therefore arise and build the sanctuary of the LORD God, to bring the ark of the covenant of the LORD and the holy articles of God into the house that is to be built for the name of the LORD."

In the day of trouble.

Ps 77:2 In the day of my trouble I sought the Lord; My hand was stretched out in the night without ceasing; My soul refused to be comforted.

Ensures

His being found.

Deut 4:29 But from there you will seek the LORD your God, and you will find *Him* if you seek Him with all your heart and with all your soul.

1 Chr 28:9 "As for you, my son Solomon, know the God of your father, and serve Him with a loyal heart and with a willing mind; for the LORD searches all hearts and understands all the intent of the thoughts. If you seek Him, He will be found by you; but if you forsake Him, He will cast you off forever.

Prov 8:17 I love those who love me, And those who seek me diligently will find me.

Jer 29:13 And you will seek Me and find *Me,* when you search for Me with all your heart.

His favor.

Lam 3:25 The LORD *is* good to those who wait for Him, To the soul *who* seeks Him.

His protection.

Ezra 8:22 For I was ashamed to request of the king an escort of soldiers and horsemen to help us against the enemy on the road, because we had spoken to the king, saying, "The hand of our God *is* upon all those for good who seek Him, but His power and His wrath *are* against all those who forsake Him."

His not forsaking us.

Ps 9:10 And those who know Your name will put their trust in You; For You, LORD, have not forsaken those who seek You.

Life.

Ps 69:32 The humble shall see *this and* be glad; And you who seek God, your hearts shall live.

Amos 5:4 For thus says the LORD to the house of Israel: "Seek Me and live;

Amos 5:6 Seek the LORD and live, Lest He break out like fire *in* the house of Joseph, And devour *it,* With no one to quench *it* in Bethel—

Prosperity.

Job 8:5–6 If you would earnestly seek God And make your supplication to the Almighty, **6** If you *were* pure and upright, Surely now He would awake for you, And prosper your rightful dwelling place.

Ps 34:10 The young lions lack and suffer hunger; But those who seek the LORD shall not lack any good *thing.*

Being heard of Him.

Ps 34:4 I sought the LORD, and He heard me, And delivered me from all my fears.

Understanding all things.

Prov 28:5 Evil men do not understand justice, But those who seek the LORD understand all.

Gifts of righteousness.

Hos 10:12 Sow for yourselves righteousness; Reap in mercy; Break up your fallow ground, For *it is* time to seek the LORD, Till He comes and rains righteousness on you.

Imperative on all.

Is 8:19 And when they say to you, "Seek those who are mediums and wizards, who whisper and mutter," should not a people seek their God? *Should they seek* the dead on behalf of the living?

Afflictions designed to lead to.

Ps 78:33–34 Therefore their days He consumed in futility, And their years in fear. **34** When He slew them, then they sought Him; And they returned and sought earnestly for God.

Hos 5:15 I will return again to My place Till they acknowledge their offense. Then they will seek My face; In their affliction they will earnestly seek Me."

None, by nature, are found to be engaged in.

Ps 14:2 The LORD looks down from heaven upon the children of men, To see if there are any who understand, who seek God.

Rom 3:11 *There is none who understands; There is none who seeks after God.*

Luke 12:23 *Life is more than food, and the body is more than clothing.*

Luke 12:30 *For all these things the nations of the world seek after, and your Father knows that you need these things.*

Believers

Especially exhorted to.

Zeph 2:3 Seek the LORD, all you meek of the earth, Who have upheld His justice. Seek righteousness, seek humility. It may be that you will be hidden In the day of the LORD's anger.

Desirous of.

Job 5:8 "But as for me, I would seek God, And to God I would commit my cause—

Purpose to, in their hearts.

2 Chr 11:16 And after *the Levites left*, those from all the tribes of Israel, such as set their heart to seek the LORD God of Israel, came to Jerusalem to sacrifice to the LORD God of their fathers.

2 Chr 30:19 *who* prepares his heart to seek God, the LORD God of his fathers, though *he is* not *cleansed* according to the purification of the sanctuary."

Ps 27:8 When You said, "Seek My face," My heart said to You, "Your face, LORD, I will seek."

Engage in, with the whole heart.

2 Chr 15:12 Then they entered into a covenant to seek the LORD God of their fathers with all their heart and with all their soul;

Ps 119:10 With my whole heart I have sought You; Oh, let me not wander from Your commandments!

Early in.

Ps 63:1 O God, You *are* my God; Early will I seek You; My soul thirsts for You; My flesh longs for You In a dry and thirsty land Where there is no water.

Is 26:9 With my soul I have desired You in the night, Yes, by my spirit within me I will seek You early; For when Your judgments *are* in the earth, The inhabitants of the world will learn righteousness.

Earnest in.

Job 8:5 If you would earnestly seek God And make your supplication to the Almighty,

Characterized by.

Ps 24:6 This *is* Jacob, the generation of those who seek Him, Who seek Your face. Selah

Is never in vain.

Is 45:19 I have not spoken in secret, In a dark place of the earth; I did not say to the seed of Jacob, 'Seek Me in vain'; I, the LORD, speak righteousness, I declare things that are right.

Blessedness of.

Ps 119:2 Blessed *are* those who keep His testimonies, Who seek Him with the whole heart!

Leads to joy.

Ps 70:4 Let all those who seek You rejoice and be glad in You; And let those who love Your salvation say continually, "Let God be magnified!"

Ps 105:3 Glory in His holy name; Let the hearts of those rejoice who seek the LORD!

Ends in praise.

Ps 22:26 The poor shall eat and be satisfied; Those who seek Him will praise the LORD. Let your heart live forever!

Promise connected with.

Ps 69:32 The humble shall see *this and* be glad; And you who seek God, your hearts shall live.

Shall be rewarded.

Heb 11:6 But without faith *it is* impossible to please *Him*, for he who comes to God must believe that He is, and *that* He is a rewarder of those who diligently seek Him.

The wicked

Are gone out of the way of.

Ps 14:2-3 The LORD looks down from heaven upon the children of men, To see if there are any who understand, who seek God. 3 They have all turned aside, They have together become corrupt; *There is* none who does good, No, not one.

Rom 3:11-12 *There is none who understands; There is none who seeks after God. 12 They have all turned aside; They have together become unprofitable; There is none who does good, no, not one."*

Prepare not their hearts for.

2 Chr 12:14 And he did evil, because he did not prepare his heart to seek the LORD.

Refuse, through pride.

Ps 10:4 The wicked in his proud countenance does not seek *God*; God *is* in none of his thoughts.

Not led to, by affliction.

Is 9:13 For the people do not turn to Him who strikes them, Nor do they seek the LORD of hosts.

Sometimes pretend to.

Ezra 4:2 they came to Zerubbabel and the heads of the fathers' *houses*, and said to them, "Let us build with you, for we seek your God as you *do;* and we have sacrificed to Him since the days of Esarhaddon king of Assyria, who brought us here."

Is 58:2 Yet they seek Me daily, And delight to know My ways, As a nation that did righteousness, And did not forsake the ordinance of their God. They ask of Me the ordinances of justice; They take delight in approaching God.

Are rejected, when too late in.

Prov 1:28 "Then they will call on me, but I will not answer; They will seek me diligently, but they will not find me.

Those who neglect, denounced and punished.

Is 31:1 Woe to those who go down to Egypt for help, *And* rely on horses, Who trust in chariots because *they are* many, And in horsemen because they are very strong, But who do not look to the Holy One of Israel, Nor seek the LORD!

Zeph 1:4-6 "I will stretch out My hand against Judah, And against all the inhabitants of Jerusalem. I will cut off every trace of Baal from this place, The names of the idolatrous priests with the *pagan* priests— 5 Those who worship the host of heaven on the housetops; Those who worship and swear *oaths* by the LORD, But who *also* swear by Milcom; 6 Those who have turned back from *following* the LORD, And have not sought the LORD, nor inquired of Him."

Exemplified by

Asa.

2 Chr 14:7 Therefore he said to Judah, "Let us build these cities and make walls around *them*, and towers, gates, and bars, *while* the land *is* yet before us, because we have sought the LORD our God; we have sought *Him*, and He has given us rest on every side." So they built and prospered.

Jehoshaphat.

2 Chr 17:3–4 Now the LORD was with Jehoshaphat, because he walked in the former ways of his father David; he did not seek the Baals, **4** but sought the God of his father, and walked in His commandments and not according to the acts of Israel.

Uzziah.

2 Chr 26:5 He sought God in the days of Zechariah, who had understanding in the visions of God; and as long as he sought the LORD, God made him prosper.

Hezekiah.

2 Chr 31:21 And in every work that he began in the service of the house of God, in the law and in the commandment, to seek his God, he did *it* with all his heart. So he prospered.

Josiah.

2 Chr 34:3 For in the eighth year of his reign, while he was still young, he began to seek the God of his father David; and in the twelfth year he began to purge Judah and Jerusalem of the high places, the wooden images, the carved images, and the molded images.

Ezra.

Ezra 7:10 For Ezra had prepared his heart to seek the Law of the LORD, and to do *it*, and to teach statutes and ordinances in Israel.

David.

Ps 34:4 I sought the LORD, and He heard me, And delivered me from all my fears.

Daniel.

Dan 9:3–4 Then I set my face toward the Lord God to make request by prayer and supplications, with fasting, sackcloth, and ashes. **4** And I prayed to the LORD my God, and made confession, and said, "O Lord, great and awesome God, who keeps His covenant and mercy with those who love Him, and with those who keep His commandments,

SELF-CONTROL

Is crucial to victory.

1 Cor 9:25 And everyone who competes *for the prize* is temperate in all things. Now they *do it* to obtain a perishable crown, but we *for* an imperishable *crown.*

Is a fruit of the Spirit.

Gal 5:23 gentleness, self-control. Against such there is no law.

Refers to sober-mindedness.

1 Pet 1:13 Therefore gird up the loins of your mind, be sober, and rest *your* hope fully upon the grace that is to be brought to you at the revelation of Jesus Christ;

A virtue believers add to their faith.

2 Pet 1:6 to knowledge self-control, to self-control perseverance, to perseverance godliness,

SELF-DELUSION

A characteristic of the wicked.

Ps 49:18 Though while he lives he blesses himself (For *men* will praise you when you do well for yourself),

Prosperity frequently leads to.

Ps 30:6 Now in my prosperity I said, "I shall never be moved."

Hos 12:8 And Ephraim said, 'Surely I have become rich, I have found wealth for myself; *In* all my labors They shall find in me no iniquity that *is* sin.'

Luke 12:17–19 And he thought within himself, saying, 'What shall I do, since I have no room to store my crops?' **18** So he said, 'I will do this: I will pull down my barns and build greater, and there I will store all my crops and my goods. **19** And I will say to my soul, "Soul, you have many goods laid up for many years; take your ease; eat, drink, *and* be merry."'

Obstinate sinners often given up to.

Ps 81:11–12 "But My people would not heed My voice, And Israel would *have* none of Me. **12** So I gave them over to their own stubborn heart, To walk in their own counsels.

Hos 4:17 "Ephraim *is* joined to idols, Let him alone.

2 Thess 2:10–11 and with all unrighteous deception among those who perish, because they did not receive the love of the truth, that they might be saved. **11** And for this reason God will send them strong delusion, that they should believe the lie,

Exhibited in thinking that

Our own ways are right.

Prov 14:12 There is a way *that seems* right to a man, But its end *is* the way of death.

We should adhere to established wicked practices.

Jer 44:17 But we will certainly do whatever has gone out of our own mouth, to burn incense to the queen of heaven and pour out drink offerings to her, as we have done, we and our fathers, our kings and our princes, in the cities of Judah and in the streets of Jerusalem. For *then* we had plenty of food, were well-off, and saw no trouble.

We are pure.

Prov 30:12 *There is* a generation *that is* pure in its own eyes, *Yet* is not washed from its filthiness.

We are better than others.

Luke 18:11 The Pharisee stood and prayed thus with himself, 'God, I thank You that I am not like other men—extortioners, unjust, adulterers, or even as this tax collector.

We are rich in spiritual things.

Rev 3:17 Because you say, 'I am rich, have become wealthy, and have need of nothing'—and do not know that you are wretched, miserable, poor, blind, and naked—

We may have peace while in sin.

Deut 29:19 and so it may not happen, when he hears the words of this curse, that he blesses himself in his heart, saying, 'I shall have peace, even though I follow the dictates of my heart'—as though the drunkard could be included with the sober.

We are above adversity.

Ps 10:6 He has said in his heart, "I shall not be moved; I shall never be in adversity."

Gifts entitle us to heaven.

Matt 7:21–22 "Not everyone who says to Me, 'Lord, Lord,' shall enter the kingdom of heaven, but he who does the will of My Father in heaven. **22** Many will say to Me in that day, 'Lord, Lord, have we not prophesied in Your name, cast out demons in Your name, and done many wonders in Your name?'

Privileges entitle us to heaven.

Matt 3:9 and do not think to say to yourselves, 'We have Abraham as *our* father.' For I say to you that God is able to raise up children to Abraham from these stones.

Luke 13:25–26 When once the Master of the house has risen up and shut the door, and you begin to stand outside and knock at the door, saying, 'Lord, Lord, open for us,' and He will answer and say to you, 'I do not know you, where you are from,' **26** then you will begin to say, 'We ate and drank in Your presence, and You taught in our streets.'

God will not punish our sins.

Ps 10:11 He has said in his heart, "God has forgotten; He hides His face; He will never see."

Jer 5:12 They have lied about the LORD, And said, "*It is* not He. Neither will evil come upon us, Nor shall we see sword or famine.

Christ shall not come to judge.

2 Pet 3:4 and saying, "Where is the promise of His coming? For since the fathers fell asleep, all things continue as *they were* from the beginning of creation."

Our lives shall be prolonged.

Is 56:12 "Come," *one says*, "I will bring wine, And we will fill ourselves with intoxicating drink; Tomorrow will be as today, *And* much more abundant."

Luke 12:19 And I will say to my soul, "Soul, you have many goods laid up for many years; take your ease; eat, drink, *and* be merry." '

James 4:13 Come now, you who say, "Today or tomorrow we will go to such and such a city, spend a year there, buy and sell, and make a profit";

Frequently preserved in, to the last.

Matt 7:22 Many will say to Me in that day, 'Lord, Lord, have we not prophesied in Your name, cast out demons in Your name, and done many wonders in Your name?'

Matt 25:11–12 "Afterward the other virgins came also, saying, 'Lord, Lord, open to us!' **12** But he answered and said, 'Assuredly, I say to you, I do not know you.'

Luke 13:24–25 "Strive to enter through the narrow gate, for many, I say to you, will seek to enter and will not be able. **25** When once the Master of the house has risen up and shut the door, and you begin to stand outside and knock at the door, saying, 'Lord, Lord, open for us,' and He will answer and say to you, 'I do not know you, where you are from,'

Fatal consequences of.

Matt 7:23 And then I will declare to them, 'I never knew you; depart from Me, you who practice lawlessness!'

Matt 24:48–51 But if that evil servant says in his heart, 'My master is delaying his coming,' **49** and begins to beat *his* fellow servants, and to eat and drink with the drunkards, **50** the master of that servant will come on a day when he is not looking for *him* and at an hour that he is not aware of, **51** and will cut him in two and appoint *him* his portion with the hypocrites. There shall be weeping and gnashing of teeth.

Luke 12:20 But God said to him, 'Fool! This night your soul will be required of you; then whose will those things be which you have provided?'

1 Thess 5:3 For when they say, "Peace and safety!" then sudden destruction comes upon them, as labor pains upon a pregnant woman. And they shall not escape.

Illustrated by

Ahab.

1 Kin 20:27 And the children of Israel were mustered and given provisions, and they went against them. Now the children of Israel encamped before them like two little flocks of goats, while the Syrians filled the countryside.

1 Kin 20:34 So *Ben-Hadad* said to him, "The cities which my father took from your father I will restore; and you may set up marketplaces for yourself in Damascus, as my father did in Samaria." Then *Ahab said*, "I will send you away with this treaty." So he made a treaty with him and sent him away.

The Israelites.

Hos 12:8 And Ephraim said, 'Surely I have become rich, I have found wealth for myself; *In* all my labors They shall find in me no iniquity that *is* sin.'

The Jews.

John 8:33 They answered Him, "We are Abraham's descendants, and have never been in bondage to anyone. How *can* You say, 'You will be made free'?"

John 8:41 You do the deeds of your father." Then they said to Him, "We were not born of fornication; we have one Father—God."

The church of Laodicea.

Rev 3:17 Because you say, 'I am rich, have become wealthy, and have need of nothing'—and do not know that you are wretched, miserable, poor, blind, and naked—

Babylon.

Is 47:7–11 And you said, 'I shall be a lady forever,' *So* that you did not take these *things* to heart, Nor remember the latter end of them. **8** "Therefore hear this now, *you who are* given to pleasures, Who dwell securely, Who say in your heart, 'I *am*, and *there is* no one else besides me; I shall not sit *as* a widow, Nor shall I know the loss of children'; **9** But these two *things* shall come to you In a moment, in one day: The loss of children, and widowhood. They shall come upon you in their fullness Because of the multitude of your sorceries, For the great abundance of your enchantments. **10** "For you have trusted in your wickedness; You have said, 'No one sees me'; Your wisdom and your knowledge have warped you; And you have said in your heart, 'I *am*, and *there is* no one else besides me.' **11** Therefore evil shall come upon you; You shall not know from where it arises. And trouble shall fall upon you; You will not be able to put it off. And desolation shall come upon you suddenly, *Which* you shall not know.

SELF-DENIAL. *SEE ALSO* HUMILITY
Christ exemplified.

Matt 4:8–10 Again, the devil took Him up on an exceedingly high mountain, and showed Him all the kingdoms of the world and their glory. **9** And he said to Him, "All these things I will give You if You will fall down and worship me." **10** Then Jesus said to him, "Away with you, Satan! For it is written, *'You shall worship the* LORD *your God, and Him only you shall serve.'"*

Matt 8:20 And Jesus said to him, "Foxes have holes and birds of the air *have* nests, but the Son of Man has nowhere to lay *His* head."

John 6:38 For I have come down from heaven, not to do My own will, but the will of Him who sent Me.

Rom 15:3 For even Christ did not please Himself; but as it is written, *"The reproaches of those who reproached You fell on Me."*

Phil 2:6–8 who, being in the form of God, did not consider it robbery to be equal with God, **7** but made Himself of no reputation, taking the form of a bondservant, *and* coming in the likeness of men. **8** And being found in appearance as a man, He humbled Himself and became obedient to *the point of* death, even the death of the cross.

Necessary
In following Christ.

Matt 10:37–38 He who loves father or mother more than Me is not worthy of Me. And he who loves son or daughter more than Me is not worthy of Me. **38** And he who does not take his cross and follow after Me is not worthy of Me.

Luke 9:23–24 Then He said to *them* all, "If anyone desires to come after Me, let him deny himself, and take up his cross daily, and follow Me. **24** For whoever desires to save his life will lose it, but whoever loses his life for My sake will save it.

Luke 14:27–33 And whoever does not bear his cross and come after Me cannot be My disciple. **28** For which of you, intending to build a tower, does not sit down first and count the cost, whether he has *enough* to finish *it*— **29** lest, after he has laid the foundation, and is not able to finish, all who see *it* begin to mock him, **30** saying, 'This man began to build and was not able to finish.' **31** Or what king, going to make war against another king, does not sit down first and consider whether he is able with ten thousand to meet him who comes against him with twenty thousand? **32** Or else, while the other is still a great way off, he sends a delegation and asks conditions of peace. **33** So likewise, whoever of you does not forsake all that he has cannot be My disciple.

In the warfare of saints.

2 Tim 2:4 No one engaged in warfare entangles himself with the affairs of *this* life, that he may please him who enlisted him as a soldier.

To the triumph of saints.

1 Cor 9:25–27 And everyone who competes *for the prize* is temperate in all things. Now they *do it* to obtain a perishable crown, but we *for* an imperishable *crown.* **26** Therefore I run thus: not with uncertainty. Thus I fight: not as *one who* beats the air. **27** But I discipline my body and bring *it* into subjection, lest, when I have preached to others, I myself should become disqualified.

Ministers especially called to exercise.

2 Cor 6:4–5 But in all *things* we commend ourselves as ministers of God: in much patience, in tribulations, in needs, in distresses, **5** in stripes, in imprisonments, in tumults, in labors, in sleeplessness, in fastings;

Should be exercised in
Denying ungodliness and worldly lusts.

Rom 6:12 Therefore do not let sin reign in your mortal body, that you should obey it in its lusts.

Titus 2:12 teaching us that, denying ungodliness and worldly lusts, we should live soberly, righteously, and godly in the present age,

Controlling the appetite.

Prov 23:2 And put a knife to your throat If you *are* a man given to appetite.

Abstaining from fleshly lusts.

1 Pet 2:11 Beloved, I beg *you* as sojourners and pilgrims, abstain from fleshly lusts which war against the soul,

No longer living to lusts of men.

1 Pet 4:2 that he no longer should live the rest of *his* time in the flesh for the lusts of men, but for the will of God.

Mortifying sinful lusts.

Mark 9:43 If your hand causes you to sin, cut it off. It is better for you to enter into life maimed, rather than having two hands, to go to hell, into the fire that shall never be quenched—

Col 3:5 Therefore put to death your members which are on the earth: fornication, uncleanness, passion, evil desire, and covetousness, which is idolatry.

Mortifying deeds of the body.

Rom 8:13 For if you live according to the flesh you will die; but if by the Spirit you put to death the deeds of the body, you will live.

Not pleasing ourselves.

Rom 15:1–3 We then who are strong ought to bear with the scruples of the weak, and not to please ourselves. **2** Let each of us please *his* neighbor for *his* good, leading to edification. **3** For even Christ did not please Himself; but as it is written, *"The reproaches of those who reproached You fell on Me."*

Not seeking out own profit.

1 Cor 10:24 Let no one seek his own, but each one the other's *well-being.*

1 Cor 10:33 just as I also please all *men* in all *things,* not seeking my own profit, but the *profit* of many, that they may be saved.

1 Cor 13:5 does not behave rudely, does not seek its own, is not provoked, thinks no evil;

Phil 2:4 Let each of you look out not only for his own interests, but also for the interests of others.

Preferring the profit of others.

Rom 14:20–21 Do not destroy the work of God for the sake of food. All things indeed *are* pure, but *it is* evil for the man who eats with offense. **21** *It is* good neither to eat meat nor drink wine nor *do anything* by which your brother stumbles or is offended or is made weak.

1 Cor 10:24 Let no one seek his own, but each one the other's *well-being.*

1 Cor 10:33 just as I also please all *men* in all *things*, not seeking my own profit, but the *profit* of many, that they may be saved.

Assisting others.

Luke 3:11 He answered and said to them, "He who has two tunics, let him give to him who has none; and he who has food, let him do likewise."

Even lawful things.

1 Cor 10:23 All things are lawful for me, but not all things are helpful; all things are lawful for me, but not all things edify.

Forsaking all.

Luke 14:33 So likewise, whoever of you does not forsake all that he has cannot be My disciple.

Taking up the cross and following Christ.

Matt 10:38 And he who does not take his cross and follow after Me is not worthy of Me.

Matt 16:24 Then Jesus said to His disciples, "If anyone desires to come after Me, let him deny himself, and take up his cross, and follow Me.

Crucifying the flesh.

Gal 5:24 And those *who are* Christ's have crucified the flesh with its passions and desires.

Being crucified with Christ.

Rom 6:6 knowing this, that our old man was crucified with *Him*, that the body of sin might be done away with, that we should no longer be slaves of sin.

Being crucified to the world.

Gal 6:14 But God forbid that I should boast except in the cross of our Lord Jesus Christ, by whom the world has been crucified to me, and I to the world.

Putting off the old man which is corrupt.

Eph 4:22 that you put off, concerning your former conduct, the old man which grows corrupt according to the deceitful lusts,

Col 3:9 Do not lie to one another, since you have put off the old man with his deeds,

Preferring Christ to all earthly relations.

Matt 8:21–22 Then another of His disciples said to Him, "Lord, let me first go and bury my father." **22** But Jesus said to him, "Follow Me, and let the dead bury their own dead."

Luke 14:26 "If anyone comes to Me and does not hate his father and mother, wife and children, brothers and sisters, yes, and his own life also, he cannot be My disciple.

True of strangers and pilgrims.

Heb 11:13–15 These all died in faith, not having received the promises, but having seen them afar off were assured of them, embraced *them* and confessed that they were strangers and pilgrims on the earth.

14 For those who say such things declare plainly that they seek a homeland. **15** And truly if they had called to mind that *country* from which they had come out, they would have had opportunity to return.

1 Pet 2:11 Beloved, I beg *you* as sojourners and pilgrims, abstain from fleshly lusts which war against the soul,

Danger of neglecting.

Matt 16:25–26 For whoever desires to save his life will lose it, but whoever loses his life for My sake will find it. **26** For what profit is it to a man if he gains the whole world, and loses his own soul? Or what will a man give in exchange for his soul?

1 Cor 9:27 But I discipline my body and bring *it* into subjection, lest, when I have preached to others, I myself should become disqualified.

Reward of.

Matt 19:28–29 So Jesus said to them, "Assuredly I say to you, that in the regeneration, when the Son of Man sits on the throne of His glory, you who have followed Me will also sit on twelve thrones, judging the twelve tribes of Israel. **29** And everyone who has left houses or brothers or sisters or father or mother or wife or children or lands, for My name's sake, shall receive a hundredfold, and inherit eternal life.

Rom 8:13 For if you live according to the flesh you will die; but if by the Spirit you put to death the deeds of the body, you will live.

Happy result of.

2 Pet 1:4 by which have been given to us exceedingly great and precious promises, that through these you may be partakers of the divine nature, having escaped the corruption *that is* in the world through lust.

Exemplified by

Abraham.

Gen 13:9 *Is* not the whole land before you? Please separate from me. If *you take* the left, then I will go to the right; or, if *you go* to the right, then I will go to the left."

Heb 11:8–9 By faith Abraham obeyed when he was called to go out to the place which he would receive as an inheritance. And he went out, not knowing where he was going. **9** By faith he dwelt in the land of promise as *in* a foreign country, dwelling in tents with Isaac and Jacob, the heirs with him of the same promise;

The widow of Zarephath.

1 Kin 17:12–15 So she said, "As the Lord your God lives, I do not have bread, only a handful of flour in a bin, and a little oil in a jar; and see, I *am* gathering a couple of sticks that I may go in and prepare it for myself and my son, that we may eat it, and die." **13** And Elijah said to her, "Do not fear; go *and* do as you have said, but make me a small cake from it first, and bring *it* to me; and afterward make *some* for yourself and your son. **14** For thus says the Lord God of Israel: 'The bin of flour shall not be used up, nor shall the jar of oil run dry, until the day the Lord sends rain on the earth.' " **15** So she went away and did according to the word of Elijah; and she and he and her household ate for *many* days.

Esther.

Esth 4:16 "Go, gather all the Jews who are present in Shushan, and fast for me; neither eat nor drink for three days, night or day. My maids and I will fast likewise. And so I will go to the king, which *is* against the law; and if I perish, I perish!"

The Rechabites.

Jer 35:6–7 But they said, "We will drink no wine, for Jonadab the son of Rechab, our father, commanded us, saying, 'You shall drink no wine, you nor your sons, forever. **7** You shall not build a house, sow seed, plant a vineyard, nor have *any of these;* but all your days you shall dwell in tents, that you may live many days in the land where you are sojourners.'

Daniel.

Dan 1:8–16 But Daniel purposed in his heart that he would not defile himself with the portion of the king's delicacies, nor with the wine which he drank; therefore he requested of the chief of the eunuchs that he might not defile himself. **9** Now God had brought Daniel into the favor and goodwill of the chief of the eunuchs. **10** And the chief of the eunuchs said to Daniel, "I fear my lord the king, who has appointed your food and drink. For why should he see your faces looking worse than the young men who *are* your age? Then you would endanger my head before the king." **11** So Daniel said to the steward whom the chief of the eunuchs had set over Daniel, Hananiah, Mishael, and Azariah, **12** "Please test your servants for ten days, and let them give us vegetables to eat and water to drink. **13** Then let our appearance be examined before you, and the appearance of the young men who eat the portion of the king's delicacies; and as you see fit, *so* deal with your servants." **14** So he consented with them in this matter, and tested them ten days. **15** And at the end of ten days their features appeared better and fatter in flesh than all the young men who ate the portion of the king's delicacies. **16** Thus the steward took away their portion of delicacies and the wine that they were to drink, and gave them vegetables.

The apostles.

Matt 19:27 Then Peter answered and said to Him, "See, we have left all and followed You. Therefore what shall we have?"

Simon, Andrew, James, and John.

Mark 1:16–20 And as He walked by the Sea of Galilee, He saw Simon and Andrew his brother casting a net into the sea; for they were fishermen. **17** Then Jesus said to them, "Follow Me, and I will make you become fishers of men." **18** They immediately left their nets and followed Him. **19** When He had gone a little farther from there, He saw James the *son* of Zebedee, and John his brother, who also *were* in the boat mending their nets. **20** And immediately He called them, and they left their father Zebedee in the boat with the hired servants, and went after Him.

A poor widow.

Luke 21:4 for all these out of their abundance have put in offerings for God, but she out of her poverty put in all the livelihood that she had."

The early Christians.

Acts 2:45 and sold their possessions and goods, and divided them among all, as anyone had need.

Acts 4:34 Nor was there anyone among them who lacked; for all who were possessors of lands or houses sold them, and brought the proceeds of the things that were sold,

Barnabas.

Acts 4:36–37 And Joses, who was also named Barnabas by the apostles (which is translated Son of Encouragement), a Levite of the country of Cyprus, **37** having land, sold *it,* and brought the money and laid *it* at the apostles' feet.

Paul.

Acts 20:24 But none of these things move me; nor do I count my life dear to myself, so that I may finish my race with joy, and the ministry which I received from the Lord Jesus, to testify to the gospel of the grace of God.

1 Cor 9:19 For though I am free from all *men,* I have made myself a servant to all, that I might win the more;

1 Cor 9:27 But I discipline my body and bring *it* into subjection, lest, when I have preached to others, I myself should become disqualified.

Moses.

Heb 11:24–25 By faith Moses, when he became of age, refused to be called the son of Pharaoh's daughter, **25** choosing rather to suffer affliction with the people of God than to enjoy the passing pleasures of sin,

SELF-EXAMINATION

Enjoined.

2 Cor 13:5 Examine yourselves *as to* whether you are in the faith. Test yourselves. Do you not know yourselves, that Jesus Christ is in you?—unless indeed you are disqualified.

Necessary before the Lord's Table.

1 Cor 11:28 But let a man examine himself, and so let him eat of the bread and drink of the cup.

A difficult process.

Jer 17:9 "The heart *is* deceitful above all *things,* And desperately wicked; Who can know it?

Believers should be engaged in

With holy awe.

Ps 4:4 Be angry, and do not sin. Meditate within your heart on your bed, and be still. Selah

With diligent search.

Ps 77:6 I call to remembrance my song in the night; I meditate within my heart, And my spirit makes diligent search.

Lam 3:40 Let us search out and examine our ways, And turn back to the LORD;

With prayer for divine searching.

Ps 26:2 Examine me, O LORD, and prove me; Try my mind and my heart.

Ps 139:23–24 Search me, O God, and know my heart; Try me, and know my anxieties; **24** And see if *there is any* wicked way in me, And lead me in the way everlasting.

With the purpose of repentance.

Ps 119:59 I thought about my ways, And turned my feet to Your testimonies.

Lam 3:40 Let us search out and examine our ways, And turn back to the LORD;

Advantages of.

1 Cor 11:31 For if we would judge ourselves, we would not be judged.

Gal 6:4 But let each one examine his own work, and then he will have rejoicing in himself alone, and not in another.

1 John 3:20–22 For if our heart condemns us, God is greater than our heart, and knows all things. **21** Beloved, if our heart does not condemn us, we have confidence toward God. **22** And whatever we ask we receive from Him, because we keep His commandments and do those things that are pleasing in His sight.

SELFISHNESS

Contrary to the law of God.

Lev 19:18 You shall not take vengeance, nor bear any grudge against the children of your people, but you shall love your neighbor as yourself: I *am* the LORD.

Matt 22:39 And *the* second *is* like it: *'You shall love your neighbor as yourself.'*

James 2:8 If you really fulfill *the* royal law according to the Scripture, *"You shall love your neighbor as yourself,"* you do well;

Christ's example opposes it.

John 4:34 Jesus said to them, "My food is to do the will of Him who sent Me, and to finish His work.

Rom 15:3 For even Christ did not please Himself; but as it is written, *"The reproaches of those who reproached You fell on Me."*

2 Cor 8:9 For you know the grace of our Lord Jesus Christ, that though He was rich, yet for your sakes He became poor, that you through His poverty might become rich.

God hates.

Mal 1:10 "Who *is there* even among you who would shut the doors, So that you would not kindle fire *on* My altar in vain? I have no pleasure in you," Says the LORD of hosts, "Nor will I accept an offering from your hands.

Exhibited in

Being lovers of ourselves.

2 Tim 3:2 For men will be lovers of themselves, lovers of money, boasters, proud, blasphemers, disobedient to parents, unthankful, unholy,

Pleasing ourselves.

Rom 15:1 We then who are strong ought to bear with the scruples of the weak, and not to please ourselves.

Seeking our own.

1 Cor 10:33 just as I also please all *men* in all *things*, not seeking my own profit, but the *profit* of many, that they may be saved.

Phil 2:21 For all seek their own, not the things which are of Christ Jesus.

Seeking after gain.

Is 56:11 Yes, *they are* greedy dogs *Which* never have enough. And they *are* shepherds Who cannot understand; They all look to their own way, Every one for his own gain, From his *own* territory.

Seeking undue preeminence.

Matt 20:21 And He said to her, "What do you wish?" She said to Him, "Grant that these two sons of mine may sit, one on Your right hand and the other on the left, in Your kingdom."

Living to ourselves.

2 Cor 5:15 and He died for all, that those who live should live no longer for themselves, but for Him who died for them and rose again.

Neglect of the poor.

1 John 3:17 But whoever has this world's goods, and sees his brother in need, and shuts up his heart from him, how does the love of God abide in him?

Serving God for reward.

Mal 1:10 "Who *is there* even among you who would shut the doors, So that you would not kindle fire *on* My altar in vain? I have no pleasure in you," Says the LORD of hosts, "Nor will I accept an offering from your hands.

Performing duty for reward.

Mic 3:11 Her heads judge for a bribe, Her priests teach for pay, And her prophets divine for money. Yet they lean on the LORD, and say, "Is not the LORD among us? No harm can come upon us."

Inconsistent with Christian love and fellowship.

Rom 12:4–5 For as we have many members in one body, but all the members do not have the same function, **5** so we, *being* many, are one body in Christ, and individually members of one another.

1 Cor 10:24 Let no one seek his own, but each one the other's *well-being.*

1 Cor 13:5 does not behave rudely, does not seek its own, is not provoked, thinks no evil;

Phil 2:4 Let each of you look out not only for his own interests, but also for the interests of others.

Cf. 1 Cor 12:12–27

The love of Christ should constrain us to avoid.

2 Cor 5:14–15 For the love of Christ compels us, because we judge thus: that if One died for all, then all died; **15** and He died for all, that those who live should live no longer for themselves, but for Him who died for them and rose again.

Ministers should be devoid of.

1 Cor 9:19–23 For though I am free from all *men*, I have made myself a servant to all, that I might win the more; **20** and to the Jews I became as a Jew, that I might win Jews; to those *who are* under the law, as under the law, that I might win those *who are* under the law; **21** to those *who are* without law, as without law (not being without law toward God, but under law toward Christ), that I might win those *who are* without law; **22** to the weak I became as weak, that I might win the weak. I have become all things to all *men*, that I might by all means save some. **23** Now this I do for the gospel's sake, that I may be partaker of it with *you*.

1 Cor 10:33 just as I also please all *men* in all *things*, not seeking my own profit, but the *profit* of many, that they may be saved.

All people naturally prone to.

Eph 2:3 among whom also we all once conducted ourselves in the lusts of our flesh, fulfilling the desires of the flesh and of the mind, and were by nature children of wrath, just as the others.

Phil 2:21 For all seek their own, not the things which are of Christ Jesus.

Believers sometimes falsely accused of.

Job 1:9–11 So Satan answered the LORD and said, "Does Job fear God for nothing? 10 Have You not made a hedge around him, around his household, and around all that he has on every side? You have blessed the work of his hands, and his possessions have increased in the land. 11 But now, stretch out Your hand and touch all that he has, and he will surely curse You to Your face!"

Characteristic of the last days.

2 Tim 3:1–2 But know this, that in the last days perilous times will come: 2 For men will be lovers of themselves, lovers of money, boasters, proud, blasphemers, disobedient to parents, unthankful, unholy,

Illustrated by

Cain.

Gen 4:9 Then the LORD said to Cain, "Where *is* Abel your brother?" He said, "I do not know. *Am* I my brother's keeper?"

Nabal.

1 Sam 25:3 The name of the man *was* Nabal, and the name of his wife Abigail. And *she was* a woman of good understanding and beautiful appearance; but the man *was* harsh and evil in *his* doings. He *was of the house of* Caleb.

1 Sam 25:11 Shall I then take my bread and my water and my meat that I have killed for my shearers, and give *it* to men when I do not know where they *are* from?"

Haman.

Esth 6:6 So Haman came in, and the king asked him, "What shall be done for the man whom the king delights to honor?" Now Haman thought in his heart, "Whom would the king delight to honor more than me?"

Priests.

Is 56:11 Yes, *they are* greedy dogs *Which* never have enough. And they *are* shepherds Who cannot understand; They all look to their own way, Every one for his own gain, From his *own* territory.

The Jews.

Zech 7:6 When you eat and when you drink, do you not eat and drink *for yourselves*?

James and John.

Mark 10:37 They said to Him, "Grant us that we may sit, one on Your right hand and the other on Your left, in Your glory."

The multitude.

John 6:26 Jesus answered them and said, "Most assuredly, I say to you, you seek Me, not because you saw the signs, but because you ate of the loaves and were filled.

SELF-RIGHTEOUSNESS

Man is prone to.

Prov 20:6 Most men will proclaim each his own goodness, But who can find a faithful man?

Prov 30:12 *There is* a generation *that is* pure in its own eyes, *Yet* is not washed from its filthiness.

Is hateful to God.

Luke 16:15 And He said to them, "You are those who justify yourselves before men, but God knows your hearts. For what is highly esteemed among men is an abomination in the sight of God.

Is useless because it is

But external.

Matt 23:25–28 "Woe to you, scribes and Pharisees, hypocrites! For you cleanse the outside of the cup and dish, but inside they are full of extortion and self-indulgence. 26 Blind Pharisee, first cleanse the inside of the cup and dish, that the outside of them may be clean also. 27 "Woe to you, scribes and Pharisees, hypocrites! For you are like whitewashed tombs which indeed appear beautiful outwardly, but inside are full of dead *men's* bones and all uncleanness. 28 Even so you also outwardly appear righteous to men, but inside you are full of hypocrisy and lawlessness.

Luke 11:39–44 Then the Lord said to him, "Now you Pharisees make the outside of the cup and dish clean, but your inward part is full of greed and wickedness. 40 Foolish ones! Did not He who made the outside make the inside also? 41 But rather give alms of such things as you have; then indeed all things are clean to you. 42 "But woe to you Pharisees! For you tithe mint and rue and all manner of herbs, and pass by justice and the love of God. These you ought to have done, without leaving the others undone. 43 Woe to you Pharisees! For you love the best seats in the synagogues and greetings in the marketplaces. 44 Woe to you, scribes and Pharisees, hypocrites! For you are like graves which are not seen, and the men who walk over *them* are not aware *of them*."

But partial.

Matt 23:25 "Woe to you, scribes and Pharisees, hypocrites! For you cleanse the outside of the cup and dish, but inside they are full of extortion and self-indulgence.

Luke 11:44 Woe to you, scribes and Pharisees, hypocrites! For you are like graves which are not seen, and the men who walk over *them* are not aware *of them*."

No better than filthy rags.

Is 64:6 But we are all like an unclean *thing*, And all our righteousnesses *are* like filthy rags; We all fade as a leaf, And our iniquities, like the wind, Have taken us away.

Ineffectual for salvation.

Job 9:30–31 If I wash myself with snow water, And cleanse my hands with soap, 31 Yet You will plunge me into the pit, And my own clothes will abhor me.

Matt 5:20 For I say to you, that unless your righteousness exceeds *the righteousness* of the scribes and Pharisees, you will by no means enter the kingdom of heaven.

Rom 3:20 Therefore by the deeds of the law no flesh will be justified in His sight, for by the law *is* the knowledge of sin.

Unprofitable.

Is 57:12 I will declare your righteousness And your works, For they will not profit you.

Is boastful.

Matt 23:30 and say, 'If we had lived in the days of our fathers, we would not have been partakers with them in the blood of the prophets.'

Those who are given to,

Audaciously approach God.

Luke 18:11 The Pharisee stood and prayed thus with himself, 'God, I thank You that I am not like other men—extortioners, unjust, adulterers, or even as this tax collector.

Seek to justify themselves.

Luke 10:29 But he, wanting to justify himself, said to Jesus, "And who is my neighbor?"

Seek to justify themselves before men.

Luke 16:15 And He said to them, "You are those who justify yourselves before men, but God knows your hearts. For what is highly esteemed among men is an abomination in the sight of God.

Reject the righteousness of God.

Rom 10:3 For they being ignorant of God's righteousness, and seeking to establish their own righteousness, have not submitted to the righteousness of God.

Condemn others.

Matt 9:11–13 And when the Pharisees saw *it*, they said to His disciples, "Why does your Teacher eat with tax collectors and sinners?" **12** When Jesus heard *that*, He said to them, "Those who are well have no need of a physician, but those who are sick. **13** But go and learn what *this* means: '*I desire mercy and not sacrifice.*' For I did not come to call the righteous, but sinners, to repentance."

Luke 7:39 Now when the Pharisee who had invited Him saw *this*, he spoke to himself, saying, "This Man, if He were a prophet, would know who and what manner of woman *this is* who is touching Him, for she is a sinner."

Consider their own way right.

Prov 21:2 Every way of a man *is* right in his own eyes, But the LORD weighs the hearts.

Despise others.

Is 65:5 Who say, 'Keep to yourself, Do not come near me, For I am holier than you!' These *are* smoke in My nostrils, A fire that burns all the day.

Luke 18:9 Also He spoke this parable to some who trusted in themselves that they were righteous, and despised others:

Proclaim their own goodness.

Prov 20:6 Most men will proclaim each his own goodness, But who can find a faithful man?

Are pure in their own eyes.

Prov 30:12 *There is* a generation *that is* pure in its own eyes, Yet is not washed from its filthiness.

Are abominable before God.

Is 65:5 Who say, 'Keep to yourself, Do not come near me, For I am holier than you!' These *are* smoke in My nostrils, A fire that burns all the day.

Folly of.

Job 9:20 Though I were righteous, my own mouth would condemn me; Though I *were* blameless, it would prove me perverse.

Believers renounce.

Phil 3:7–10 But what things were gain to me, these I have counted loss for Christ. **8** Yet indeed I also count all things loss for the excellence of the knowledge of Christ Jesus my Lord, for whom I have suffered the loss of all things, and count them as rubbish, that I may gain Christ **9** and be found in Him, not having my own righteousness, which *is* from the law, but that which *is* through faith in Christ, the righteousness which is from God by faith; **10** that I may know Him and the power of His resurrection, and the fellowship of His sufferings, being conformed to His death,

Those who judge it in others, condemn themselves.

Rom 2:1 Therefore you are inexcusable, O man, whoever you are who judge, for in whatever you judge another you condemn yourself; for you who judge practice the same things.

Reveals misunderstanding of God's law.

1 Tim 1:9 knowing this: that the law is not made for a righteous person, but for *the* lawless and insubordinate, for *the* ungodly and for sinners, for *the* unholy and profane, for murderers of fathers and murderers of mothers, for manslayers,

Warnings against.

Deut 9:4 "Do not think in your heart, after the LORD your God has cast them out before you, saying, 'Because of my righteousness the LORD has brought me in to possess this land'; but *it is* because of the wickedness of these nations *that* the LORD is driving them out from before you.

Eccl 7:16 Do not be overly righteous, Nor be overly wise: Why should you destroy yourself?

Matt 23:27–28 "Woe to you, scribes and Pharisees, hypocrites! For you are like whitewashed tombs which indeed appear beautiful outwardly, but inside are full of dead *men's* bones and all uncleanness. **28** Even so you also outwardly appear righteous to men, but inside you are full of hypocrisy and lawlessness.

Illustrated.

Luke 18:10–12 "Two men went up to the temple to pray, one a Pharisee and the other a tax collector. **11** The Pharisee stood and prayed thus with himself, 'God, I thank You that I am not like other men—extortioners, unjust, adulterers, or even as this tax collector. **12** I fast twice a week; I give tithes of all that I possess.'

Examples of,

Saul.

1 Sam 15:13 Then Samuel went to Saul, and Saul said to him, "Blessed *are* you of the LORD! I have performed the commandment of the LORD."

A young man.

Matt 19:20 The young man said to Him, "All these things I have kept from my youth. What do I still lack?"

A lawyer.

Luke 10:25 And behold, a certain lawyer stood up and tested Him, saying, "Teacher, what shall I do to inherit eternal life?"

Luke 10:29 But he, wanting to justify himself, said to Jesus, "And who is my neighbor?"

The Pharisees.

Luke 11:39 Then the Lord said to him, "Now you Pharisees make the outside of the cup and dish clean, but your inward part is full of greed and wickedness.

John 8:33 They answered Him, "We are Abraham's descendants, and have never been in bondage to anyone. How *can* You say, 'You will be made free'?"

John 9:28 Then they reviled him and said, "You are His disciple, but we are Moses' disciples.

Israel.

Rom 10:3 For they being ignorant of God's righteousness, and seeking to establish their own righteousness, have not submitted to the righteousness of God.

The church of Laodicea.

Rev 3:17 Because you say, 'I am rich, have become wealthy, and have need of nothing'—and do not know that you are wretched, miserable, poor, blind, and naked—

Self-Will and Stubbornness

Forbidden.

2 Chr 30:8 Now do not be stiff-necked, as your fathers *were, but* yield yourselves to the Lord; and enter His sanctuary, which He has sanctified forever, and serve the Lord your God, that the fierceness of His wrath may turn away from you.

Ps 75:5 Do not lift up your horn on high; Do *not* speak with a stiff neck.' "

Ps 95:8 "Do not harden your hearts, as in the rebellion, As *in* the day of trial in the wilderness,

Sources of

Unbelief.

2 Kin 17:14 Nevertheless they would not hear, but stiffened their necks, like the necks of their fathers, who did not believe in the Lord their God.

Pride.

Neh 9:16 "But they and our fathers acted proudly, Hardened their necks, And did not heed Your commandments,

Neh 9:29 And testified against them, That You might bring them back to Your law. Yet they acted proudly, And did not heed Your commandments, But sinned against Your judgments, 'Which if a man does, he shall live by them.' And they shrugged their shoulders, Stiffened their necks, And would not hear.

An evil heart.

Jer 7:24 Yet they did not obey or incline their ear, but followed the counsels *and* the dictates of their evil hearts, and went backward and not forward.

God knows about.

Is 48:4 Because I knew that you *were* obstinate, And your neck *was* an iron sinew, And your brow bronze,

Exhibited in

Refusing to hearken to God.

Prov 1:24 Because I have called and you refused, I have stretched out my hand and no one regarded,

Refusing to hearken to the messengers of God.

1 Sam 8:19 Nevertheless the people refused to obey the voice of Samuel; and they said, "No, but we will have a king over us,

Jer 44:16 "*As for* the word that you have spoken to us in the name of the Lord, we will not listen to you!

Zech 7:11 But they refused to heed, shrugged their shoulders, and stopped their ears so that they could not hear.

Refusing to walk in the ways of God.

Neh 9:17 They refused to obey, And they were not mindful of Your wonders That You did among them. But they hardened their necks, And in their rebellion They appointed a leader To return to their bondage. But You *are* God, Ready to pardon, Gracious and merciful, Slow to anger, Abundant in kindness, And did not forsake them.

Ps 78:10 They did not keep the covenant of God; They refused to walk in His law,

Is 42:24 Who gave Jacob for plunder, and Israel to the robbers? Was it not the Lord, He against whom we have sinned? For they would not walk in His ways, Nor were they obedient to His law.

Jer 6:16 Thus says the Lord: "Stand in the ways and see, And ask for the old paths, where the good way *is*, And walk in it; Then you will find rest for your souls. But they said, 'We will not walk *in it.*'

Refusing to hearken to parents.

Deut 21:18–19 "If a man has a stubborn and rebellious son who will not obey the voice of his father or the voice of his mother, and *who*, when they have chastened him, will not heed them, **19** then his father and his mother shall take hold of him and bring him out to the elders of his city, to the gate of his city.

Refusing to receive correction.

Deut 21:18 "If a man has a stubborn and rebellious son who will not obey the voice of his father or the voice of his mother, and *who*, when they have chastened him, will not heed them,

Jer 5:3 O Lord, *are* not Your eyes on the truth? You have stricken them, But they have not grieved; You have consumed them, But they have refused to receive correction. They have made their faces harder than rock; They have refused to return.

Jer 7:28 "So you shall say to them, 'This *is* a nation that does not obey the voice of the Lord their God nor receive correction. Truth has perished and has been cut off from their mouth.

Rebelling against God.

Deut 31:27 for I know your rebellion and your stiff neck. *If* today, while I am yet alive with you, you have been rebellious against the Lord, then how much more after my death?

Ps 78:8 And may not be like their fathers, A stubborn

and rebellious generation, A generation *that* did not set its heart aright, And whose spirit was not faithful to God.

Resisting the Holy Spirit.

Acts 7:51 "*You* stiff-necked and uncircumcised in heart and ears! You always resist the Holy Spirit; as your fathers *did*, so *do* you.

Walking in the counsels of an evil heart.

Jer 7:24 Yet they did not obey or incline their ear, but followed the counsels *and* the dictates of their evil hearts, and went backward and not forward.

Jer 23:17 They continually say to those who despise Me, 'The LORD has said, "You shall have peace" '; And *to* everyone who walks according to the dictates of his own heart, they say, 'No evil shall come upon you.' "

Hardening the neck.

Neh 9:16 "But they and our fathers acted proudly, Hardened their necks, And did not heed Your commandments.

Hardening the heart.

2 Chr 36:13 And he also rebelled against King Nebuchadnezzar, who had made him swear *an oath* by God; but he stiffened his neck and hardened his heart against turning to the LORD God of Israel.

Going backward and not forward.

Jer 7:24 Yet they did not obey or incline their ear, but followed the counsels *and* the dictates of their evil hearts, and went backward and not forward.

Heinousness of.

1 Sam 15:23 For rebellion *is as* the sin of witchcraft, And stubbornness *is as* iniquity and idolatry. Because you have rejected the word of the LORD, He also has rejected you from *being* king."

Ministers should

Be without.

Titus 1:7 For a bishop must be blameless, as a steward of God, not self-willed, not quick-tempered, not given to wine, not violent, not greedy for money,

Warn their people against.

Heb 3:7–12 Therefore, as the Holy Spirit says: *"Today, if you will hear His voice,* **8** *Do not harden your hearts as in the rebellion, In the day of trial in the wilderness,* **9** *Where your fathers tested Me, tried Me, And saw My works forty years.* **10** *Therefore I was angry with that generation, And said, 'They always go astray in their heart, And they have not known My ways.'* **11** *So I swore in My wrath, 'They shall not enter My rest.'* " **12** Beware, brethren, lest there be in any of you an evil heart of unbelief in departing from the living God;

Pray that their people may be forgiven for.

Ex 34:9 Then he said, "If now I have found grace in Your sight, O Lord, let my Lord, I pray, go among us, even though we *are* a stiff-necked people; and pardon our iniquity and our sin, and take us as Your inheritance."

Deut 9:27 Remember Your servants, Abraham, Isaac, and Jacob; do not look on the stubbornness of this people, or on their wickedness or their sin,

Characteristic of the wicked.

Prov 7:11 She *was* loud and rebellious, Her feet would not stay at home.

2 Pet 2:10 and especially those who walk according to the flesh in the lust of uncleanness and despise authority. *They are* presumptuous, self-willed. They are not afraid to speak evil of dignitaries,

The wicked do not cease from.

Judg 2:19 And it came to pass, when the judge was dead, that they reverted and behaved more corruptly than their fathers, by following other gods, to serve them and bow down to them. They did not cease from their own doings nor from their stubborn way.

Punishment for.

Deut 21:21 Then all the men of his city shall stone him to death with stones; so you shall put away the evil from among you, and all Israel shall hear and fear.

Prov 29:1 He who is often rebuked, *and* hardens *his* neck, Will suddenly be destroyed, and that without remedy.

Illustrated.

Ps 32:9 Do not be like the horse *or* like the mule, *Which* have no understanding, Which must be harnessed with bit and bridle, Else they will not come near you.

Jer 31:18 "I have surely heard Ephraim bemoaning himself: 'You have chastised me, and I was chastised, Like an untrained bull; Restore me, and I will return, For You *are* the LORD my God.

Examples of,

Simeon and Levi.

Gen 49:6 Let not my soul enter their council; Let not my honor be united to their assembly; For in their anger they slew a man, And in their self-will they hamstrung an ox.

The Israelites.

Ex 32:9 And the LORD said to Moses, "I have seen this people, and indeed it *is* a stiff-necked people!

Deut 9:6 Therefore understand that the LORD your God is not giving you this good land to possess because of your righteousness, for you *are* a stiff-necked people.

Deut 9:13 "Furthermore the LORD spoke to me, saying, 'I have seen this people, and indeed they are a stiff-necked people.

Saul.

1 Sam 15:19–23 Why then did you not obey the voice of the LORD? Why did you swoop down on the spoil, and do evil in the sight of the LORD?" **20** And Saul said to Samuel, "But I have obeyed the voice of the LORD, and gone on the mission on which the LORD sent me, and brought back Agag king of Amalek; I have utterly destroyed the Amalekites. **21** But the people took of the plunder, sheep and oxen, the best of the things which should have been utterly destroyed, to sacrifice to the LORD your God in Gilgal." **22** So Samuel said: "Has the LORD *as great* delight in burnt offerings and sacrifices, As in obeying the voice of the LORD? Behold, to obey is better than sacrifice, *And* to heed than the fat of rams. **23** For rebellion *is as* the sin of witchcraft, And stubbornness *is as* iniquity and idolatry. Because you have rejected the word of the LORD, He also has rejected you from *being* king."

David.

2 Sam 24:4 Nevertheless the king's word prevailed against Joab and against the captains of the army. Therefore Joab and the captains of the army went out from the presence of the king to count the people of Israel.

Josiah.

2 Chr 35:22 Nevertheless Josiah would not turn his face from him, but disguised himself so that he might fight with him, and did not heed the words of Necho from the mouth of God. So he came to fight in the Valley of Megiddo.

Zedekiah.

2 Chr 36:13 And he also rebelled against King Nebuchadnezzar, who had made him swear *an oath* by God; but he stiffened his neck and hardened his heart against turning to the LORD God of Israel.

SERPENTS (SNAKES, ASPS).
SEE ALSO REPTILES

Created by God.

Job 26:13 By His Spirit He adorned the heavens; His hand pierced the fleeing serpent.

Characterized as cunning.

Gen 3:1 Now the serpent was more cunning than any beast of the field which the LORD God had made. And he said to the woman, "Has God indeed said, 'You shall not eat of every tree of the garden'?"

Matt 10:16 "Behold, I send you out as sheep in the midst of wolves. Therefore be wise as serpents and harmless as doves.

Called fleeing.

Job 26:13 By His Spirit He adorned the heavens; His hand pierced the fleeing serpent.

Is 27:1 In that day the LORD with His severe sword, great and strong, Will punish Leviathan the fleeing serpent, Leviathan that twisted serpent; And He will slay the reptile that *is* in the sea.

Unclean and unfit for food.

Matt 7:10 Or if he asks for a fish, will he give him a serpent?

Places of habitation

Hedges.

Eccl 10:8 He who digs a pit will fall into it, And whoever breaks through a wall will be bitten by a serpent.

Holes in walls.

Amos 5:19 It *will be* as though a man fled from a lion, And a bear met him! Or *as though* he went into the house, Leaned his hand on the wall, And a serpent bit him!

Deserts.

Deut 8:15 who led you through that great and terrible wilderness, *in which were* fiery serpents and scorpions and thirsty land where there was no water; who brought water for you out of the flinty rock;

Produced from eggs.

Is 59:5 They hatch vipers' eggs and weave the spider's web; He who eats of their eggs dies, And *from* that which is crushed a viper breaks out.

Cursed above all creatures.

Gen 3:14 So the LORD God said to the serpent: "Because you have done this, You *are* cursed more than all cattle, And more than every beast of the field; On your belly you shall go, And you shall eat dust All the days of your life.

Doomed to eat their food mingled with dust.

Gen 3:14 So the LORD God said to the serpent: "Because you have done this, You *are* cursed more than all cattle, And more than every beast of the field; On your belly you shall go, And you shall eat dust All the days of your life.

Is 65:25 The wolf and the lamb shall feed together, The lion shall eat straw like the ox, And dust *shall be* the serpent's food. They shall not hurt nor destroy in all My holy mountain," Says the LORD.

Mic 7:17 They shall lick the dust like a serpent; They shall crawl from their holes like snakes of the earth. They shall be afraid of the LORD our God, And shall fear because of You.

Many kinds are poisonous.

Deut 32:24 *They shall be* wasted with hunger, Devoured by pestilence and bitter destruction; I will also send against them the teeth of beasts, With the poison of serpents of the dust.

Ps 58:4 Their poison *is* like the poison of a serpent; *They are* like the deaf cobra *that* stops its ear,

All kinds of, can be tamed.

James 3:7 For every kind of beast and bird, of reptile and creature of the sea, is tamed and has been tamed by mankind.

Were often charmed.

Eccl 10:11 A serpent may bite when *it is* not charmed; The babbler is no different.

Dangerous to travelers.

Gen 49:17 Dan shall be a serpent by the way, A viper by the path, That bites the horse's heels So that its rider shall fall backward.

Man's aversion and hatred to.

Gen 3:15 And I will put enmity Between you and the woman, And between your seed and her Seed; He shall bruise your head, And you shall bruise His heel."

Often sent as a punishment.

Num 21:6 So the LORD sent fiery serpents among the people, and they bit the people; and many of the people of Israel died.

Deut 32:24 *They shall be* wasted with hunger, Devoured by pestilence and bitter destruction; I will also send against them the teeth of beasts, With the poison of serpents of the dust.

1 Cor 10:9 nor let us tempt Christ, as some of them also tempted, and were destroyed by serpents;

Miracles connected with

Moses' rod turned into.

Ex 4:3 And He said, "Cast it on the ground." So he cast it on the ground, and it became a serpent; and Moses fled from it.

Ex 7:9 "When Pharaoh speaks to you, saying, 'Show a miracle for yourselves,' then you shall say to Aaron, 'Take your rod and cast *it* before Pharaoh, *and* let it become a serpent.' "

Ex 7:15 Go to Pharaoh in the morning, when he goes out to the water, and you shall stand by the river's bank to meet him; and the rod which was turned to a serpent you shall take in your hand.

Bronze one on a pole.

Num 21:8–9 Then the LORD said to Moses, "Make a fiery *serpent,* and set it on a pole; and it shall be that everyone who is bitten, when he looks at it, shall live." **9** So Moses made a bronze serpent, and put it on a pole; and so it was, if a serpent had bitten anyone, when he looked at the bronze serpent, he lived.

John 3:14–15 And as Moses lifted up the serpent in the wilderness, even so must the Son of Man be lifted up, **15** that whoever believes in Him should not perish but have eternal life.

Power over, given to the disciples.

Mark 16:18 they will take up serpents; and if they drink anything deadly, it will by no means hurt them; they will lay hands on the sick, and they will recover."

Luke 10:19 Behold, I give you the authority to trample on serpents and scorpions, and over all the power of the enemy, and nothing shall by any means hurt you.

Illustrative of

The devil.

Gen 3:1 Now the serpent was more cunning than any beast of the field which the LORD God had made. And he said to the woman, "Has God indeed said, 'You shall not eat of every tree of the garden'?"

2 Cor 11:3 But I fear, lest somehow, as the serpent deceived Eve by his craftiness, so your minds may be corrupted from the simplicity that is in Christ.

Rev 12:9 So the great dragon was cast out, that serpent of old, called the Devil and Satan, who deceives the whole world; he was cast to the earth, and his angels were cast out with him.

Rev 20:2 He laid hold of the dragon, that serpent of old, who is *the* Devil and Satan, and bound him for a thousand years;

Hypocrites.

Matt 23:33 Serpents, brood of vipers! How can you escape the condemnation of hell?

The tribe of Dan.

Gen 49:17 Dan shall be a serpent by the way, A viper by the path, That bites the horse's heels So that its rider shall fall backward.

Enemies who harass and destroy.

Is 14:29 "Do not rejoice, all you of Philistia, Because the rod that struck you is broken; For out of the serpent's roots will come forth a viper, And its offspring *will be* a fiery flying serpent.

Jer 8:17 "For behold, I will send serpents among you, Vipers which cannot be charmed, And they shall bite you," says the LORD.

(Sharp tongue of) malice of the wicked.

Ps 140:3 They sharpen their tongues like a serpent; The poison of asps *is* under their lips. Selah

(Poisonous bite of) baneful effects of wine.

Prov 23:21 For the drunkard and the glutton will come to poverty, And drowsiness will clothe *a man* with rags.

Prov 23:32 At the last it bites like a serpent, And stings like a viper.

SERVANTS

Early mention of.

Gen 9:25–26 Then he said: "Cursed *be* Canaan; A servant of servants He shall be to his brethren." **26** And he said: "Blessed *be* the LORD, The God of Shem, And may Canaan be his servant.

Categories of,

Male.

Gen 24:34 So he said, "I *am* Abraham's servant.

Gen 32:5 I have oxen, donkeys, flocks, and male and female servants; and I have sent to tell my lord, that I may find favor in your sight." ' "

Female.

Gen 16:6 So Abram said to Sarai, "Indeed your maid *is* in your hand; do to her as you please." And when Sarai dealt harshly with her, she fled from her presence.

Gen 32:5 I have oxen, donkeys, flocks, and male and female servants; and I have sent to tell my lord, that I may find favor in your sight." ' "

Slaves.

Gen 43:18 Now the men were afraid because they were brought into Joseph's house; and they said, "*It is* because of the money, which was returned in our sacks the first time, that we are brought in, so that he may make a case against us and seize us, to take us as slaves with our donkeys."

Lev 25:46 And you may take them as an inheritance for your children after you, to inherit *them as* a possession; they shall be your permanent slaves. But regarding your brethren, the children of Israel, you shall not rule over one another with rigor.

Hired.

Mark 1:20 And immediately He called them, and they left their father Zebedee in the boat with the hired servants, and went after Him.

Luke 15:17 "But when he came to himself, he said, 'How many of my father's hired servants have bread enough and to spare, and I perish with hunger!

Are persons devoted to the service of another.

Ps 119:49 Remember the word to Your servant, Upon which You have caused me to hope.

Is 56:6 "Also the sons of the foreigner Who join themselves to the LORD, to serve Him, And to love the name of the LORD, to be His servants— Everyone who keeps from defiling the Sabbath, And holds fast My covenant—

Are the subjects of a prince or king.

Ex 9:20 He who feared the word of the LORD among the servants of Pharaoh made his servants and his livestock flee to the houses.

Ex 11:8 And all these your servants shall come down to me and bow down to me, saying, 'Get out, and all

the people who follow you!' After that I will go out."
Then he went out from Pharaoh in great anger.

Are persons of low condition.

Eccl 10:7 I have seen servants on horses, While princes
walk on the ground like servants.

Are persons devoted to God.

Ps 119:49 Remember the word to Your servant, Upon
which You have caused me to hope.

Is 56:6 "Also the sons of the foreigner Who join themselves to the LORD, to serve Him, And to love the
name of the LORD, to be His servants— Everyone
who keeps from defiling the Sabbath, And holds fast
My covenant—

Rom 1:1 Paul, a bondservant of Jesus Christ, called *to be*
an apostle, separated to the gospel of God

The term often used to express humility.

Gen 18:3 and said, "My Lord, if I have now found favor
in Your sight, do not pass on by Your servant.

Gen 33:5 And he lifted his eyes and saw the women
and children, and said, "Who *are* these with you?" So
he said, "The children whom God has graciously
given your servant."

1 Sam 20:7 If he says thus: '*It is* well,' your servant will
be safe. But if he is very angry, be sure that evil is determined by him.

1 Kin 20:32 So they wore sackcloth around their waists
and *put* ropes around their heads, and came to the
king of Israel and said, "Your servant Ben-Hadad
says, 'Please let me live.' " And he said, "Is he still
alive? He *is* my brother."

Hired,

Called hirelings.

John 10:12–13 But a hireling, *he who is* not the shepherd,
one who does not own the sheep, sees the wolf coming and leaves the sheep and flees; and the wolf
catches the sheep and scatters them. **13** The hireling
flees because he is a hireling and does not care about
the sheep.

Engaged by the year.

Lev 25:53 He shall be with him as a yearly hired servant, and he shall not rule with rigor over him in
your sight.

Is 16:14 But now the LORD has spoken, saying, "Within
three years, as the years of a hired man, the glory of
Moab will be despised with all that great multitude,
and the remnant *will be* very small *and* feeble."

Engaged by the day.

Job 7:1 "*Is there* not a time of hard service for man on
earth? *Are not* his days also like the days of a hired
man?

Matt 20:2 Now when he had agreed with the laborers
for a denarius a day, he sent them into his vineyard.

Not to be oppressed.

Deut 24:14 "You shall not oppress a hired servant *who
is* poor and needy, *whether* one of your brethren or
one of the aliens who *is* in your land within your
gates.

*To be paid without delay at the expiration of their
service.*

Lev 19:13 'You shall not cheat your neighbor, nor rob

him. The wages of him who is hired shall not remain
with you all night until morning.

Deut 24:15 Each day you shall give *him* his wages, and
not let the sun go down on it, for he *is* poor and has
set his heart on it; lest he cry out against you to the
LORD, and it be sin to you.

To be esteemed worthy of their wages.

Luke 10:7 And remain in the same house, eating and
drinking such things as they give, for the laborer is
worthy of his wages. Do not go from house to house.

*To partake of the produce of the land in the sabbatical
year.*

Lev 25:6 And the sabbath *produce* of the land shall be
food for you: for you, your male and female servants,
your hired man, and the stranger who dwells with
you,

*If foreigners, not allowed to partake of the Passover
or holy things.*

Ex 12:45 A sojourner and a hired servant shall not eat it.

Lev 22:10 'No outsider shall eat the holy *offering;* one
who dwells with the priest, or a hired servant, shall
not eat the holy thing.

Anxiety of, for the end of their daily toil, alluded to.

Job 7:2 Like a servant who earnestly desires the shade,
And like a hired man who eagerly looks for his
wages,

Hebrew slaves serving their brethren to be treated as.

Lev 25:39–40 'And if *one of* your brethren *who dwells* by
you becomes poor, and sells himself to you, you shall
not compel him to serve as a slave. **40** As a hired servant *and* a sojourner he shall be with you, *and* shall
serve you until the Year of Jubilee.

Hebrew slaves serving strangers to be treated as.

Lev 25:47 'Now if a sojourner or stranger close to you
becomes rich, and *one of* your brethren *who dwells* by
him becomes poor, and sells himself to the stranger
or sojourner close to you, or to a member of the
stranger's family,

Lev 25:53 He shall be with him as a yearly hired servant, and he shall not rule with rigor over him in
your sight.

*Often stood in the marketplace waiting for employ-
ment.*

Matt 20:1–3 "For the kingdom of heaven is like a
landowner who went out early in the morning to
hire laborers for his vineyard. **2** Now when he had
agreed with the laborers for a denarius a day, he sent
them into his vineyard. **3** And he went out about the
third hour and saw others standing idle in the marketplace,

Often well fed.

Luke 15:17 "But when he came to himself, he said,
'How many of my father's hired servants have bread
enough and to spare, and I perish with hunger!

Often oppressed and their wages kept back.

Mal 3:5 And I will come near you for judgment; I will
be a swift witness Against sorcerers, Against adulterers, Against perjurers, Against those who exploit
wage earners and widows and orphans, And against
those who turn away an alien— Because they do not
fear Me," Says the LORD of hosts.

James 5:4 Indeed the wages of the laborers who mowed your fields, which you kept back by fraud, cry out; and the cries of the reapers have reached the ears of the Lord of Sabaoth.

Slaves or servants,

Joseph's brothers willing to be.

Gen 43:18 Now the men were afraid because they were brought into Joseph's house; and they said, "*It is* because of the money, which was returned in our sacks the first time, that we are brought in, so that he may make a case against us and seize us, to take us as slaves with our donkeys."

Gen 44:9 With whomever of your servants it is found, let him die, and we also will be my lord's slaves."

Some served from birth.

Gen 14:14 Now when Abram heard that his brother was taken captive, he armed his three hundred and eighteen trained *servants* who were born in his own house, and went in pursuit as far as Dan.

Ps 116:16 O LORD, truly I *am* Your servant; I *am* Your servant, the son of Your maidservant; You have loosed my bonds.

Jer 2:14 "*Is* Israel a servant? *Is* he a homeborn *slave?* Why is he plundered?

Some purchased.

Gen 17:27 and all the men of his house, born in the house or bought with money from a foreigner, were circumcised with him.

Gen 37:36 Now the Midianites had sold him in Egypt to Potiphar, an officer of Pharaoh *and* captain of the guard.

Captives taken in war often kept as.

Deut 20:14 But the women, the little ones, the livestock, and all that is in the city, all its spoil, you shall plunder for yourself; and you shall eat the enemies' plunder which the LORD your God gives you.

2 Kin 5:2 And the Syrians had gone out on raids, and had brought back captive a young girl from the land of Israel. She waited on Naaman's wife.

Strangers dwelling in Israel might be purchased as.

Lev 25:45 Moreover you may buy the children of the strangers who dwell among you, and their families who are with you, which they beget in your land; and they shall become your property.

Foreigners might be purchased as.

Lev 25:44 And as for your male and female slaves whom you may have—from the nations that are around you, from them you may buy male and female slaves.

Persons unable to pay their debts liable to be sold as.

2 Kin 4:1 A certain woman of the wives of the sons of the prophets cried out to Elisha, saying, "Your servant my husband is dead, and you know that your servant feared the LORD. And the creditor is coming to take my two sons to be his slaves."

Neh 5:4–5 There were also those who said, "We have borrowed money for the king's tax *on* our lands and vineyards. **5** Yet now our flesh *is* as the flesh of our brethren, our children as their children; and indeed we are forcing our sons and our daughters to be slaves, and *some* of our daughters have been brought

into slavery. *It is* not in our power *to redeem them*, for other men have our lands and vineyards."

Matt 18:25 But as he was not able to pay, his master commanded that he be sold, with his wife and children and all that he had, and that payment be made.

Thieves unable to make restitution were sold as.

Ex 22:3 If the sun has risen on him, *there shall be* guilt for his bloodshed. He should make full restitution; if he has nothing, then he shall be sold for his theft.

Slaves more valuable than hired servants.

Deut 15:18 It shall not seem hard to you when you send him away free from you; for he has been worth a double hired servant in serving you six years. Then the LORD your God will bless you in all that you do.

When Israelites, not to be treated harshly.

Lev 25:39–40 'And if *one of* your brethren *who dwells* by you becomes poor, and sells himself to you, you shall not compel him to serve as a slave. **40** As a hired servant *and* a sojourner he shall be with you, *and* shall serve you until the Year of Jubilee.

Lev 25:46 And you may take them as an inheritance for your children after you, to inherit *them as* a possession; they shall be your permanent slaves. But regarding your brethren, the children of Israel, you shall not rule over one another with rigor.

When Israelites, to have their liberty after six years of service.

Ex 21:2 If you buy a Hebrew servant, he shall serve six years; and in the seventh he shall go out free and pay nothing.

Deut 15:12 "If your brother, a Hebrew man, or a Hebrew woman, is sold to you and serves you six years, then in the seventh year you shall let him go free from you.

Israelites sold as, refusing their liberty, to have their ears bored to the door.

Ex 21:5–6 But if the servant plainly says, 'I love my master, my wife, and my children; I will not go out free,' **6** then his master shall bring him to the judges. He shall also bring him to the door, or to the doorpost, and his master shall pierce his ear with an awl; and he shall serve him forever.

Deut 15:16–17 And if it happens that he says to you, 'I will not go away from you,' because he loves you and your house, since he prospers with you, **17** then you shall take an awl and thrust *it* through his ear to the door, and he shall be your servant forever. Also to your female servant you shall do likewise.

Israelites sold to strangers as, might be redeemed by their nearest of kin.

Lev 25:47–55 'Now if a sojourner or stranger close to you becomes rich, and *one of* your brethren *who dwells* by him becomes poor, and sells himself to the stranger *or* sojourner close to you, or to a member of the stranger's family, **48** after he is sold he may be redeemed again. One of his brothers may redeem him; **49** or his uncle or his uncle's son may redeem him; or *anyone* who is near of kin to him in his family may redeem him; or if he is able he may redeem himself. **50** Thus he shall reckon with him who bought him: The price of his release shall be according to the number of years, from the year that he was sold to him until the Year of Jubilee; *it shall be* according to the time of a hired servant for him. **51** If *there are* still many years *remaining,* according to them he shall repay the price of his redemption from the money with which he was bought. **52** And if there remain but a few years until the Year of Jubilee, then he shall reckon with him, *and* according to his years he shall repay him the price of his redemption. **53** He shall be with him as a yearly hired servant, and he shall not rule with rigor over him in your sight. **54** And if he is not redeemed in these *years,* then he shall be released in the Year of Jubilee—he and his children with him. **55** For the children of Israel *are* servants to Me; they *are* My servants whom I brought out of the land of Egypt: I *am* the L ORD your God.

All Israelites sold as, to be free at the Jubilee.

Lev 25:10 And you shall consecrate the fiftieth year, and proclaim liberty throughout *all* the land to all its inhabitants. It shall be a Jubilee for you; and each of you shall return to his possession, and each of you shall return to his family.

Lev 25:40–41 As a hired servant *and* a sojourner he shall be with you, *and* shall serve you until the Year of Jubilee. **41** And *then* he shall depart from you—he and his children with him—and shall return to his own family. He shall return to the possession of his fathers.

Lev 25:54 And if he is not redeemed in these *years,* then he shall be released in the Year of Jubilee—he and his children with him.

Could not, when set free, demand wives or children procured during servitude.

Ex 21:3–4 If he comes in by himself, he shall go out by himself; if he *comes in* married, then his wife shall go out with him. **4** If his master has given him a wife, and she has borne him sons or daughters, the wife and her children shall be her master's, and he shall go out by himself.

To be furnished generously, when their servitude expired.

Deut 15:13–14 And when you send him away free from you, you shall not let him go away empty-handed; **14** you shall supply him liberally from your flock, from your threshing floor, and from your winepress. *From what* the L ORD has blessed you with, you shall give to him.

When foreigners, to be circumcised.

Gen 17:13 He who is born in your house and he who is bought with your money must be circumcised, and My covenant shall be in your flesh for an everlasting covenant.

Gen 17:27 and all the men of his house, born in the house or bought with money from a foreigner, were circumcised with him.

Ex 12:44 But every man's servant who is bought for money, when you have circumcised him, then he may eat it.

To be allowed to rest on the Sabbath.

Ex 20:10 but the seventh day *is* the Sabbath of the L ORD your God. *In it* you shall do no work: you, nor your son, nor your daughter, nor your male servant, nor your female servant, nor your cattle, nor your stranger who *is* within your gates.

To participate in all national rejoicings.

Deut 12:18 But you must eat them before the L ORD your God in the place which the L ORD your God chooses, you and your son and your daughter, your male servant and your female servant, and the Levite who *is* within your gates; and you shall rejoice before the L ORD your God in all to which you put your hands.

Deut 16:11 You shall rejoice before the L ORD your God, you and your son and your daughter, your male servant and your female servant, the Levite who *is* within your gates, the stranger and the fatherless and the widow who *are* among you, at the place where the L ORD your God chooses to make His name abide.

Deut 16:14 And you shall rejoice in your feast, you and your son and your daughter, your male servant and your female servant and the Levite, the stranger and the fatherless and the widow, who *are* within your gates.

Persons of distinction had many.

Gen 14:14 Now when Abram heard that his brother was taken captive, he armed his three hundred and eighteen trained *servants* who were born in his own house, and went in pursuit as far as Dan.

Eccl 2:7 I acquired male and female servants, and had servants born in my house. Yes, I had greater possessions of herds and flocks than all who were in Jerusalem before me.

Engaged in the most menial offices.

1 Sam 25:41 Then she arose, bowed her face to the earth, and said, "Here is your maidservant, a servant to wash the feet of the servants of my lord."

John 13:4–5 rose from supper and laid aside His garments, took a towel and girded Himself. **5** After that, He poured water into a basin and began to wash the disciples' feet, and to wipe *them* with the towel with which He was girded.

Maimed or injured by masters, to have their freedom.

Ex 21:26–27 "If a man strikes the eye of his male or female servant, and destroys it, he shall let him go free for the sake of his eye. **27** And if he knocks out the tooth of his male or female servant, he shall let him go free for the sake of his tooth.

Masters to be recompensed for injury done to.

Ex 21:32 If the ox gores a male or female servant, he shall give to their master thirty shekels of silver, and the ox shall be stoned.

Laws respecting the killing of.

Ex 21:20–21 "And if a man beats his male or female servant with a rod, so that he dies under his hand, he shall surely be punished. **21** Notwithstanding, if he remains alive a day or two, he shall not be punished; for he *is* his property.

Of others, not to be coveted or enticed away.

Ex 20:17 "You shall not covet your neighbor's house; you shall not covet your neighbor's wife, nor his male servant, nor his female servant, nor his ox, nor his donkey, nor anything that *is* your neighbor's."

Deut 5:21 'You shall not covet your neighbor's wife; and you shall not desire your neighbor's house, his field, his male servant, his female servant, his ox, his donkey, or anything that *is* your neighbor's.'

Seeking protection, not to be delivered up to masters.

Deut 23:15 "You shall not give back to his master the slave who has escaped from his master to you.

Custom of branding, alluded to.

Gal 6:17 From now on let no one trouble me, for I bear in my body the marks of the Lord Jesus.

Sometimes rose to higher position.

Eccl 10:7 I have seen servants on horses, While princes walk on the ground like servants.

Sometimes intermarried with their master's family.

1 Chr 2:34–35 Now Sheshan had no sons, only daughters. And Sheshan had an Egyptian servant whose name *was* Jarha. **35** Sheshan gave his daughter to Jarha his servant as wife, and she bore him Attai.

Laws respecting marriage with female.

Ex 21:7–11 "And if a man sells his daughter to be a female slave, she shall not go out as the male slaves do. **8** If she does not please her master, who has betrothed her to himself, then he shall let her be redeemed. He shall have no right to sell her to a foreign people, since he has dealt deceitfully with her. **9** And if he has betrothed her to his son, he shall deal with her according to the custom of daughters. **10** If he takes another *wife*, he shall not diminish her food, her clothing, and her marriage rights. **11** And if he does not do these three for her, then she shall go out free, without *paying* money.

Seizing and stealing of men for, condemned and punished by the law.

Ex 21:16 "He who kidnaps a man and sells him, or if he is found in his hand, shall surely be put to death.

Deut 24:7 "If a man is found kidnapping any of his brethren of the children of Israel, and mistreats him or sells him, then that kidnapper shall die; and you shall put away the evil from among you.

1 Tim 1:10 for fornicators, for sodomites, for kidnappers, for liars, for perjurers, and if there is any other thing that is contrary to sound doctrine,

Laws respecting, often violated. **Jer 34:8–16**

Bond, illustrative of

Christ.

Ps 40:6 Sacrifice and offering You did not desire; My ears You have opened. Burnt offering and sin offering You did not require.

Phil 2:7–8 but made Himself of no reputation, taking the form of a bondservant, *and* coming in the likeness of men. **8** And being found in appearance as a man, He humbled Himself and became obedient to *the point of* death, even the death of the cross.

Heb 10:5 Therefore, when He came into the world, He said: *"Sacrifice and offering You did not desire, But a body You have prepared for Me.*

Believers.

1 Cor 6:20 For you were bought at a price; therefore glorify God in your body and in your spirit, which are God's.

1 Cor 7:23 You were bought at a price; do not become slaves of men.

The wicked.

Rom 6:16 Do you not know that to whom you present

yourselves slaves to obey, you are that one's slaves whom you obey, whether of sin *leading* to death, or of obedience *leading* to righteousness?

Rom 6:19 I speak in human *terms* because of the weakness of your flesh. For just as you presented your members *as* slaves of uncleanness, and of lawlessness *leading* to *more* lawlessness, so now present your members *as* slaves *of* righteousness for holiness.

2 Pet 2:19 While they promise them liberty, they themselves are slaves of corruption; for by whom a person is overcome, by him also he is brought into bondage.

Christ condescended to the office of.

Matt 20:28 just as the Son of Man did not come to be served, but to serve, and to give His life a ransom for many."

Luke 22:27 For who *is* greater, he who sits at the table, or he who serves? *Is* it not he who sits at the table? Yet I am among you as the One who serves.

John 13:5 After that, He poured water into a basin and began to wash the disciples' feet, and to wipe *them* with the towel with which He was girded.

Phil 2:7 but made Himself of no reputation, taking the form of a bondservant, *and* coming in the likeness of men.

Are inferior to their masters.

Luke 22:27 For who *is* greater, he who sits at the table, or he who serves? *Is* it not he who sits at the table? Yet I am among you as the One who serves.

Should follow Christ's example.

1 Pet 2:21 For to this you were called, because Christ also suffered for us, leaving us an example, that you should follow His steps:

Duties of, to masters

To pray for them.

Gen 24:12 Then he said, "O LORD God of my master Abraham, please give me success this day, and show kindness to my master Abraham.

To honor them.

Mal 1:6 "A son honors *his* father, And a servant *his* master. If then I am the Father, Where *is* My honor? And if I *am* a Master, Where *is* My reverence? Says the LORD of hosts To you priests who despise My name. Yet you say, 'In what way have we despised Your name?'

1 Tim 6:1 Let as many bondservants as are under the yoke count their own masters worthy of all honor, so that the name of God and *His* doctrine may not be blasphemed.

To revere them the more when they are believers.

1 Tim 6:2 And those who have believing masters, let them not despise *them* because they are brethren, but rather serve *them* because those who are benefited are believers and beloved. Teach and exhort these things.

To submit to and obey them.

Eph 6:5 Bondservants, be obedient to those who are your masters according to the flesh, with fear and trembling, in sincerity of heart, as to Christ;

Titus 2:9 *Exhort* bondservants to be obedient to their own masters, to be well pleasing in all *things,* not answering back,

1 Pet 2:18 Servants, *be* submissive to *your* masters with all fear, not only to the good and gentle, but also to the harsh.

To attend to their call.

Ps 123:2 Behold, as the eyes of servants *look* to the hand of their masters, As the eyes of a maid to the hand of her mistress, So our eyes *look* to the LORD our God, Until He has mercy on us.

To sympathize with them.

2 Sam 12:18 Then on the seventh day it came to pass that the child died. And the servants of David were afraid to tell him that the child was dead. For they said, "Indeed, while the child was alive, we spoke to him, and he would not heed our voice. How can we tell him that the child is dead? He may do some harm!"

To prefer their business to their own food.

Gen 24:33 *Food* was set before him to eat, but he said, "I will not eat until I have told about my errand." And he said, "Speak on."

To bless God for mercies shown to them.

Gen 24:27 And he said, "Blessed *be* the LORD God of my master Abraham, who has not forsaken His mercy and His truth toward my master. As for me, being on the way, the LORD led me to the house of my master's brethren."

Gen 24:48 And I bowed my head and worshiped the LORD, and blessed the LORD God of my master Abraham, who had led me in the way of truth to take the daughter of my master's brother for his son.

To be faithful to them.

Luke 16:10–12 He who *is* faithful in *what is* least is faithful also in much; and he who is unjust in *what is* least is unjust also in much. **11** Therefore if you have not been faithful in the unrighteous mammon, who will commit to your trust the true *riches?* **12** And if you have not been faithful in what is another man's, who will give you what is your own?

1 Cor 4:2 Moreover it is required in stewards that one be found faithful.

Titus 2:10 not pilfering, but showing all good fidelity, that they may adorn the doctrine of God our Savior in all things.

To be profitable to them.

Luke 19:15–16 "And so it was that when he returned, having received the kingdom, he then commanded these servants, to whom he had given the money, to be called to him, that he might know how much every man had gained by trading. **16** Then came the first, saying, 'Master, your mina has earned ten minas.'

Luke 19:18 And the second came, saying, 'Master, your mina has earned five minas.'

Philem 1:11 who once was unprofitable to you, but now is profitable to you and to me.

To be anxious for their welfare.

1 Sam 25:14–17 Now one of the young men told Abigail, Nabal's wife, saying, "Look, David sent messengers from the wilderness to greet our master; and he reviled them. **15** But the men *were* very good to us, and we were not hurt, nor did we miss anything as long as we accompanied them, when we were in the fields. **16** They were a wall to us both by night and day, all the time we were with them keeping the sheep. **17** Now therefore, know and consider what you will do, for harm is determined against our master and against all his household. For he *is such* a scoundrel that *one* cannot speak to him."

2 Kin 5:2–3 And the Syrians had gone out on raids, and had brought back captive a young girl from the land of Israel. She waited on Naaman's wife. **3** Then she said to her mistress, "If only my master *were* with the prophet who *is* in Samaria! For he would heal him of his leprosy."

To be earnest in transacting their business.

Gen 24:54–56 And he and the men who *were* with him ate and drank and stayed all night. Then they arose in the morning, and he said, "Send me away to my master." **55** But her brother and her mother said, "Let the young woman stay with us *a few* days, at least ten; after that she may go." **56** And he said to them, "Do not hinder me, since the LORD has prospered my way; send me away so that I may go to my master."

To be prudent in the management of their affairs.
Gen 24:34–49

To be industrious in laboring for them.

Neh 4:16 So it was, from that time on, *that* half of my servants worked at construction, while the other half held the spears, the shields, the bows, and *wore* armor; and the leaders *were* behind all the house of Judah.

Neh 4:23 So neither I, my brethren, my servants, nor the men of the guard who followed me took off our clothes, *except* that everyone took them off for washing.

To be kind and attentive to their guests.

Gen 43:23–24 But he said, "Peace *be* with you, do not be afraid. Your God and the God of your father has given you treasure in your sacks; I had your money." Then he brought Simeon out to them. **24** So the man brought the men into Joseph's house and gave *them* water, and they washed their feet; and he gave their donkeys feed.

To be submissive even to the harsh.

Gen 16:6 So Abram said to Sarai, "Indeed your maid *is* in your hand; do to her as you please." And when Sarai dealt harshly with her, she fled from her presence.

Gen 16:9 The Angel of the LORD said to her, "Return to your mistress, and submit yourself under her hand."

1 Pet 2:18 Servants, *be* submissive to *your* masters with all fear, not only to the good and gentle, but also to the harsh.

Not to answer them rudely.

Titus 2:9 *Exhort* bondservants to be obedient to their own masters, to be well pleasing in all *things*, not answering back,

Not to serve them with eyeservice, as men-pleasers.

Eph 6:6 not with eyeservice, as men-pleasers, but as bondservants of Christ, doing the will of God from the heart,

Col 3:22 Bondservants, obey in all things your masters according to the flesh, not with eyeservice, as men-pleasers, but in sincerity of heart, fearing God.

Not to defraud them.

Titus 2:10 not pilfering, but showing all good fidelity, that they may adorn the doctrine of God our Savior in all things.

Should be content in their situation.

1 Cor 7:20–21 Let each one remain in the same calling in which he was called. **21** Were you called *while* a slave? Do not be concerned about it; but if you can be made free, rather use *it.*

Should be compassionate to their fellow servants.

Matt 18:33 Should you not also have had compassion on your fellow servant, just as I had pity on you?'

Should serve

With conscience toward God.

1 Pet 2:19 For this *is* commendable, if because of conscience toward God one endures grief, suffering wrongfully.

In the fear of God.

Eph 6:5 Bondservants, be obedient to those who are your masters according to the flesh, with fear and trembling, in sincerity of heart, as to Christ;

Col 3:22 Bondservants, obey in all things your masters according to the flesh, not with eyeservice, as men-pleasers, but in sincerity of heart, fearing God.

As the servants of Christ.

Eph 6:5–6 Bondservants, be obedient to those who are your masters according to the flesh, with fear and trembling, in sincerity of heart, as to Christ; **6** not with eyeservice, as men-pleasers, but as bondservants of Christ, doing the will of God from the heart,

Heartily, as to the Lord, and not to men.

Eph 6:7 with goodwill doing service, as to the Lord, and not to men,

Col 3:23 And whatever you do, do it heartily, as to the Lord and not to men,

As doing the will of God from the heart.

Eph 6:6 not with eyeservice, as men-pleasers, but as bondservants of Christ, doing the will of God from the heart,

In singleness of heart.

Eph 6:5 Bondservants, be obedient to those who are your masters according to the flesh, with fear and trembling, in sincerity of heart, as to Christ;

Col 3:22 Bondservants, obey in all things your masters according to the flesh, not with eyeservice, as men-pleasers, but in sincerity of heart, fearing God.

When patient under injury, are commendable before God.

1 Pet 2:19–20 For this *is* commendable, if because of conscience toward God one endures grief, suffering wrongfully. **20** For what credit *is it* if, when you are beaten for your faults, you take it patiently? But when you do good and suffer, if you take it patiently, this *is* commendable before God.

When good,

Are the servants of Christ.

Col 3:24 knowing that from the Lord you will receive the reward of the inheritance; for you serve the Lord Christ.

Are brethren beloved in the Lord.

Philem 1:16 no longer as a slave but more than a slave—a beloved brother, especially to me but how much more to you, both in the flesh and in the Lord.

Are the Lord's freedmen.

1 Cor 7:22 For he who is called in the Lord *while* a slave is the Lord's freedman. Likewise he who is called *while* free is Christ's slave.

Are partakers of gospel privileges.

1 Cor 12:13 For by one Spirit we were all baptized into one body—whether Jews or Greeks, whether slaves or free—and have all been made to drink into one Spirit.

Gal 3:28 There is neither Jew nor Greek, there is neither slave nor free, there is neither male nor female; for you are all one in Christ Jesus.

Eph 6:8 knowing that whatever good anyone does, he will receive the same from the Lord, whether *he is* a slave or free.

Col 3:11 where there is neither Greek nor Jew, circumcised nor uncircumcised, barbarian, Scythian, slave *nor* free, but Christ *is* all and in all.

Deserve the confidence of their masters.

Gen 24:2 So Abraham said to the oldest servant of his house, who ruled over all that he had, "Please, put your hand under my thigh,

Gen 24:4 but you shall go to my country and to my family, and take a wife for my son Isaac."

Gen 24:10 Then the servant took ten of his master's camels and departed, for all his master's goods *were in* his hand. And he arose and went to Mesopotamia, to the city of Nahor.

Gen 39:4 So Joseph found favor in his sight, and served him. Then he made him overseer of his house, and all *that* he had he put under his authority.

Often exalted.

Gen 41:40 You shall be over my house, and all my people shall be ruled according to your word; only in regard to the throne will I be greater than you."

Prov 17:2 A wise servant will rule over a son who causes shame, And will share an inheritance among the brothers.

Often advanced by their master.

Gen 39:4–5 So Joseph found favor in his sight, and served him. Then he made him overseer of his house, and all *that* he had he put under his authority. **5** So it was, from the time *that* he had made him overseer of his house and all that he had, that the LORD blessed the Egyptian's house for Joseph's sake; and the blessing of the LORD was on all that he had in the house and in the field.

To be honored.

Gen 24:31 And he said, "Come in, O blessed of the LORD! Why do you stand outside? For I have prepared the house, and a place for the camels."

Prov 27:18 Whoever keeps the fig tree will eat its fruit; So he who waits on his master will be honored.

Bring God's blessing upon their masters.

Gen 30:27 And Laban said to him, "Please *stay*, if I have found favor in your eyes, *for* I have learned by experience that the LORD has blessed me for your sake."

Gen 30:30 For what you had before I *came was* little, and it has increased to a great amount; the LORD has blessed you since my coming. And now, when shall I also provide for my own house?"

Gen 39:3 And his master saw that the LORD *was* with him and that the LORD made all he did to prosper in his hand.

Adorn the doctrine of God their Savior in all things.

Titus 2:10 not pilfering, but showing all good fidelity, that they may adorn the doctrine of God our Savior in all things.

Have God with them.

Gen 24:7 The LORD God of heaven, who took me from my father's house and from the land of my family, and who spoke to me and swore to me, saying, 'To your descendants I give this land,' He will send His angel before you, and you shall take a wife for my son from there.

Gen 24:27 And he said, "Blessed *be* the LORD God of my master Abraham, who has not forsaken His mercy and His truth toward my master. As for me, being on the way, the LORD led me to the house of my master's brethren."

Gen 31:7 Yet your father has deceived me and changed my wages ten times, but God did not allow him to hurt me.

Gen 31:42 Unless the God of my father, the God of Abraham and the Fear of Isaac, had been with me, surely now you would have sent me away empty-handed. God has seen my affliction and the labor of my hands, and rebuked *you* last night."

Gen 39:3 And his master saw that the LORD *was* with him and that the LORD made all he did to prosper in his hand.

Gen 39:21 But the LORD was with Joseph and showed him mercy, and He gave him favor in the sight of the keeper of the prison.

Acts 7:9–10 "And the patriarchs, becoming envious, sold Joseph into Egypt. But God was with him **10** and delivered him out of all his troubles, and gave him favor and wisdom in the presence of Pharaoh, king of Egypt; and he made him governor over Egypt and all his house.

Are blessed by God.

Matt 24:46 Blessed *is* that servant whom his master, when he comes, will find so doing.

Are mourned over after death.

Gen 35:8 Now Deborah, Rebekah's nurse, died, and she was buried below Bethel under the terebinth tree. So the name of it was called Allon Bachuth.

Shall be rewarded.

Eph 6:8 knowing that whatever good anyone does, he will receive the same from the Lord, whether *he is* a slave or free.

Col 3:24 knowing that from the Lord you will receive the reward of the inheritance; for you serve the Lord Christ.

Master's property increased by faithful ones.

Gen 30:29–30 So *Jacob* said to him, "You know how I have served you and how your livestock has been with me. **30** For what you had before I *came was* little,

and it has increased to a great amount; the LORD has blessed you since my coming. And now, when shall I also provide for my own house?"

Characteristics of unbelieving ones,

Concerned with appearances.

Eph 6:6 not with eyeservice, as men-pleasers, but as bondservants of Christ, doing the will of God from the heart,

Col 3:22 Bondservants, obey in all things your masters according to the flesh, not with eyeservice, as men-pleasers, but in sincerity of heart, fearing God.

Deceit.

2 Sam 19:26 And he answered, "My lord, O king, my servant deceived me. For your servant said, 'I will saddle a donkey for myself, that I may ride on it and go to the king,' because your servant *is* lame.

Ps 101:6–7 My eyes *shall be* on the faithful of the land, That they may dwell with me; He who walks in a perfect way, He shall serve me. **7** He who works deceit shall not dwell within my house; He who tells lies shall not continue in my presence.

Quarrelsomeness.

Gen 26:20 But the herdsmen of Gerar quarreled with Isaac's herdsmen, saying, "The water *is* ours." So he called the name of the well Esek, because they quarreled with him.

Covetousness.

2 Kin 5:20 But Gehazi, the servant of Elisha the man of God, said, "Look, my master has spared Naaman this Syrian, while not receiving from his hands what he brought; but *as* the LORD lives, I will run after him and take something from him."

Lying.

2 Kin 5:22 And he said, "All *is* well. My master has sent me, saying, 'Indeed, just now two young men of the sons of the prophets have come to me from the mountains of Ephraim. Please give them a talent of silver and two changes of garments.' "

2 Kin 5:24 When he came to the citadel, he took *them* from their hand, and stored *them* away in the house; then he let the men go, and they departed.

Stealing.

Titus 2:10 not pilfering, but showing all good fidelity, that they may adorn the doctrine of God our Savior in all things.

Violence and greed.

Matt 24:49 and begins to beat *his* fellow servants, and to eat and drink with the drunkards,

Unmerciful to their fellows.

Matt 18:30 And he would not, but went and threw him into prison till he should pay the debt.

Will not submit to correction.

Prov 29:19 A servant will not be corrected by mere words; For though he understands, he will not respond.

Do not rule graciously.

Prov 30:21–22 For three *things* the earth is perturbed, Yes, for four it cannot bear up: **22** For a servant when he reigns, A fool when he is filled with food,

Is 3:5 The people will be oppressed, Every one by another and every one by his neighbor; The child will be insolent toward the elder, And the base toward the honorable."

Shall be punished.

Matt 24:50 the master of that servant will come on a day when he is not looking for *him* and at an hour that he is not aware of,

Examples of good ones,

Eliezer. Gen 24:1–67

Deborah.

Gen 24:59 So they sent away Rebekah their sister and her nurse, and Abraham's servant and his men.

Gen 35:8 Now Deborah, Rebekah's nurse, died, and she was buried below Bethel under the terebinth tree. So the name of it was called Allon Bachuth.

Jacob.

Gen 31:36–40 Then Jacob was angry and rebuked Laban, and Jacob answered and said to Laban: "What *is* my trespass? What *is* my sin, that you have so hotly pursued me? **37** Although you have searched all my things, what part of your household things have you found? Set *it* here before my brethren and your brethren, that they may judge between us both! **38** These twenty years I *have been* with you; your ewes and your female goats have not miscarried their young, and I have not eaten the rams of your flock. **39** That which was torn *by beasts* I did not bring to you; I bore the loss of it. You required it from my hand, *whether* stolen by day or stolen by night. **40** *There* I was! In the day the drought consumed me, and the frost by night, and my sleep departed from my eyes.

Joseph.

Gen 39:3 And his master saw that the LORD *was* with him and that the LORD made all he did to prosper in his hand.

Acts 7:10 and delivered him out of all his troubles, and gave him favor and wisdom in the presence of Pharaoh, king of Egypt; and he made him governor over Egypt and all his house.

The servants of Boaz.

Ruth 2:4 Now behold, Boaz came from Bethlehem, and said to the reapers, "The LORD *be* with you!" And they answered him, "The LORD bless you!"

Jonathan's armorbearer.

1 Sam 14:6–7 Then Jonathan said to the young man who bore his armor, "Come, let us go over to the garrison of these uncircumcised; it may be that the LORD will work for us. For nothing restrains the LORD from saving by many or by few." **7** So his armorbearer said to him, "Do all that is in your heart. Go then; here I am with you, according to your heart."

David's servants.

2 Sam 12:18 Then on the seventh day it came to pass that the child died. And the servants of David were afraid to tell him that the child was dead. For they said, "Indeed, while the child was alive, we spoke to him, and he would not heed our voice. How can we tell him that the child is dead? He may do some harm!"

A captive young girl.

2 Kin 5:2–4 And the Syrians had gone out on raids, and had brought back captive a young girl from the land of Israel. She waited on Naaman's wife. **3** Then she said to her mistress, "If only my master *were* with the prophet who *is* in Samaria! For he would heal him of his leprosy." **4** And *Naaman* went in and told his master, saying, "Thus and thus said the girl who *is* from the land of Israel."

The servants of Naaman.

2 Kin 5:13 And his servants came near and spoke to him, and said, "My father, *if* the prophet had told you *to do* something great, would you not have done *it?* How much more then, when he says to you, 'Wash, and be clean'?"

The servants of a centurion.

Matt 8:9 For I also am a man under authority, having soldiers under me. And I say to this *one,* 'Go,' and he goes; and to another, 'Come,' and he comes; and to my servant, 'Do this,' and he does *it.*"

The servants of Cornelius.

Acts 10:7 And when the angel who spoke to him had departed, Cornelius called two of his household servants and a devout soldier from among those who waited on him continually.

Onesimus after his conversion.

Philem 1:11 who once was unprofitable to you, but now is profitable to you and to me.

Examples of bad ones,

The servants of Abraham and Lot.

Gen 13:7 And there was strife between the herdsmen of Abram's livestock and the herdsmen of Lot's livestock. The Canaanites and the Perizzites then dwelt in the land.

The servants of Abimelech.

Gen 21:25 Then Abraham rebuked Abimelech because of a well of water which Abimelech's servants had seized.

Absalom's servants.

2 Sam 13:28–29 Now Absalom had commanded his servants, saying, "Watch now, when Amnon's heart is merry with wine, and when I say to you, 'Strike Amnon!' then kill him. Do not be afraid. Have I not commanded you? Be courageous and valiant." **29** So the servants of Absalom did to Amnon as Absalom had commanded. Then all the king's sons arose, and each one got on his mule and fled.

2 Sam 14:30 So he said to his servants, "See, Joab's field is near mine, and he has barley there; go and set it on fire." And Absalom's servants set the field on fire.

Ziba.

2 Sam 16:1–4 When David was a little past the top *of the mountain,* there was Ziba the servant of Mephibosheth, who met him with a couple of saddled donkeys, and on them two hundred *loaves* of bread, one hundred clusters of raisins, one hundred summer fruits, and a skin of wine. **2** And the king said to Ziba, "What do you mean to do with these?" So Ziba said, "The donkeys *are* for the king's household to ride on, the bread and summer fruit for the young men to eat, and the wine for those who are faint in the wilderness to drink." **3** Then the king said, "And where *is* your master's son?" And Ziba said to the king, "Indeed he is staying in Jerusalem, for he said,

'Today the house of Israel will restore the kingdom of my father to me.' " **4** So the king said to Ziba, "Here, all that *belongs* to Mephibosheth *is* yours." And Ziba said, "I humbly bow before you, *that* I may find favor in your sight, my lord, O king!"

The servants of Shimei.

1 Kin 2:39 Now it happened at the end of three years, that two slaves of Shimei ran away to Achish the son of Maachah, king of Gath. And they told Shimei, saying, "Look, your slaves *are* in Gath!"

Jeroboam.

1 Kin 11:26 Then Solomon's servant, Jeroboam the son of Nebat, an Ephraimite from Zereda, whose mother's name *was* Zeruah, a widow, also rebelled against the king.

Zimri.

1 Kin 16:9 Now his servant Zimri, commander of half *his* chariots, conspired against him as he was in Tirzah drinking himself drunk in the house of Arza, steward of *his* house in Tirzah.

Gehazi.

2 Kin 5:20 But Gehazi, the servant of Elisha the man of God, said, "Look, my master has spared Naaman this Syrian, while not receiving from his hands what he brought; but *as* the LORD lives, I will run after him and take something from him."

The servants of Amon.

2 Kin 21:23 Then the servants of Amon conspired against him, and killed the king in his own house.

Job's servants.

Job 19:16 I call my servant, but he gives no answer; I beg him with my mouth.

The servants of the high priest.

Mark 14:65 Then some began to spit on Him, and to blindfold Him, and to beat Him, and to say to Him, "Prophesy!" And the officers struck Him with the palms of their hands.

Onesimus before his conversion.

Philem 1:11 who once was unprofitable to you, but now is profitable to you and to me.

SEX

For believers, must be enjoyed in proper context.

1 Cor 6:12–20 All things are lawful for me, but all things are not helpful. All things are lawful for me, but I will not be brought under the power of any. **13** Foods for the stomach and the stomach for foods, but God will destroy both it and them. Now the body *is* not for sexual immorality but for the Lord, and the Lord for the body. **14** And God both raised up the Lord and will also raise us up by His power. **15** Do you not know that your bodies are members of Christ? Shall I then take the members of Christ and make *them* members of a harlot? Certainly not! **16** Or do you not know that he who is joined to a harlot is one body *with her*? For *"the two,"* He says, *"shall become one flesh."* **17** But he who is joined to the Lord is one spirit *with Him.* **18** Flee sexual immorality. Every sin that a man does is outside the body, but he who commits sexual immorality sins against his own body. **19** Or do you not know that your body is the temple of the Holy Spirit *who is* in you, whom you have from God,

and you are not your own? **20** For you were bought at a price; therefore glorify God in your body and in your spirit, which are God's.

1 Thess 4:1–8 Finally then, brethren, we urge and exhort in the Lord Jesus that you should abound more and more, just as you received from us how you ought to walk and to please God; **2** for you know what commandments we gave you through the Lord Jesus. **3** For this is the will of God, your sanctification: that you should abstain from sexual immorality; **4** that each of you should know how to possess his own vessel in sanctification and honor, **5** not in passion of lust, like the Gentiles who do not know God; **6** that no one should take advantage of and defraud his brother in this matter, because the Lord *is* the avenger of all such, as we also forewarned you and testified. **7** For God did not call us to uncleanness, but in holiness. **8** Therefore he who rejects *this* does not reject man, but God, who has also given us His Holy Spirit.

Marriage provides proper channel for.

1 Cor 7:1–8 Now concerning the things of which you wrote to me: *It is* good for a man not to touch a woman. **2** Nevertheless, because of sexual immorality, let each man have his own wife, and let each woman have her own husband. **3** Let the husband render to his wife the affection due her, and likewise also the wife to her husband. **4** The wife does not have authority over her own body, but the husband *does.* And likewise the husband does not have authority over his own body, but the wife *does.* **5** Do not deprive one another except with consent for a time, that you may give yourselves to fasting and prayer; and come together again so that Satan does not tempt you because of your lack of self-control. **6** But I say this as a concession, not as a commandment. **7** For I wish that all men were even as I myself. But each one has his own gift from God, one in this manner and another in that. **8** But I say to the unmarried and to the widows: It is good for them if they remain even as I am;

SEXUAL IMMORALITY (FORNICATION)

Desire for, comes from within man.

Mark 7:21 For from within, out of the heart of men, proceed evil thoughts, adulteries, fornications, murders,

Is a work of the flesh.

Gal 5:19 Now the works of the flesh are evident, which are: adultery, fornication, uncleanness, lewdness,

God did not design the body for.

1 Cor 6:13 Foods for the stomach and the stomach for foods, but God will destroy both it and them. Now the body *is* not for sexual immorality but for the Lord, and the Lord for the body.

1 Cor 6:18 Flee sexual immorality. Every sin that a man does is outside the body, but he who commits sexual immorality sins against his own body.

Believers are to flee.

1 Cor 6:18 Flee sexual immorality. Every sin that a man does is outside the body, but he who commits sexual immorality sins against his own body.

Inherent danger for single people.

1 Cor 7:2 Nevertheless, because of sexual immorality,

let each man have his own wife, and let each woman have her own husband.

Gentiles were instructed to abstain from, associated with idol worship.

Acts 15:20 but that we write to them to abstain from things polluted by idols, *from* sexual immorality, *from* things strangled, and *from* blood.

Reason for divorce.

Matt 5:32 But I say to you that whoever divorces his wife for any reason except sexual immorality causes her to commit adultery; and whoever marries a woman who is divorced commits adultery.

Matt 19:9 And I say to you, whoever divorces his wife, except for sexual immorality, and marries another, commits adultery; and whoever marries her who is divorced commits adultery."

Occurred in the Corinthian church.

1 Cor 5:1 It is actually reported *that there is* sexual immorality among you, and such sexual immorality as is not even named among the Gentiles—that a man has his father's wife!

Other terms for,

Lewdness and lust.

Rom 13:13 Let us walk properly, as in the day, not in revelry and drunkenness, not in lewdness and lust, not in strife and envy.

Jude 1:4 For certain men have crept in unnoticed, who long ago were marked out for this condemnation, ungodly men, who turn the grace of our God into lewdness and deny the only Lord God and our Lord Jesus Christ.

Fornication.

1 Cor 6:9 Do you not know that the unrighteous will not inherit the kingdom of God? Do not be deceived. Neither fornicators, nor idolaters, nor adulterers, nor homosexuals, nor sodomites,

Eph 5:5 For this you know, that no fornicator, unclean person, nor covetous man, who is an idolater, has any inheritance in the kingdom of Christ and God.

Col 3:5 Therefore put to death your members which are on the earth: fornication, uncleanness, passion, evil desire, and covetousness, which is idolatry.

Illustrated by

Esau.

Heb 12:16 lest there *be* any fornicator or profane person like Esau, who for one morsel of food sold his birthright.

David.

2 Sam 11:1–4 It happened in the spring of the year, at the time when kings go out *to battle,* that David sent Joab and his servants with him, and all Israel; and they destroyed the people of Ammon and besieged Rabbah. But David remained at Jerusalem. 2 Then it happened one evening that David arose from his bed and walked on the roof of the king's house. And from the roof he saw a woman bathing, and the woman *was* very beautiful to behold. 3 So David sent and inquired about the woman. And *someone* said, "*Is* this not Bathsheba, the daughter of Eliam, the wife of Uriah the Hittite?" 4 Then David sent messengers, and took her; and she came to him, and he

lay with her, for she was cleansed from her impurity; and she returned to her house.

The harlot.

Prov 2:16–19 To deliver you from the immoral woman, From the seductress *who* flatters with her words, 17 Who forsakes the companion of her youth, And forgets the covenant of her God. 18 For her house leads down to death, And her paths to the dead; 19 None who go to her return, Nor do they regain the paths of life—

Cf. Prov 7:6–23; 23:27–28

Sodom and Gomorrah.

Jude 1:7 as Sodom and Gomorrah, and the cities around them in a similar manner to these, having given themselves over to sexual immorality and gone after strange flesh, are set forth as an example, suffering the vengeance of eternal fire.

SHEEP

Clean animals, may be eaten.

Deut 14:4 These *are* the animals which you may eat: the ox, the sheep, the goat,

Described as

Innocent.

2 Sam 24:17 Then David spoke to the LORD when he saw the angel who was striking the people, and said, "Surely I have sinned, and I have done wickedly; but these sheep, what have they done? Let Your hand, I pray, be against me and against my father's house."

Knowing their shepherds.

John 10:4–5 And when he brings out his own sheep, he goes before them; and the sheep follow him, for they know his voice. 5 Yet they will by no means follow a stranger, but will flee from him, for they do not know the voice of strangers."

Agile.

Ps 114:4 The mountains skipped like rams, The little hills like lambs.

Ps 114:6 O mountains, *that* you skipped like rams? O little hills, like lambs?

Being covered with fleece.

Job 31:20 If his heart has not blessed me, And *if he was not* warmed with the fleece of my sheep;

Remarkably prolific.

Ps 107:41 Yet He sets the poor on high, far from affliction, And makes *their* families like a flock.

Ps 144:13 *That* our barns *may be* full, Supplying all kinds of produce; *That* our sheep may bring forth thousands And ten thousands in our fields;

Song 4:2 Your teeth *are* like a flock of shorn *sheep* Which have come up from the washing, Every one of which bears twins, And none is barren among them.

Ezek 36:37 'Thus says the Lord GOD: "I will also let the house of Israel inquire of Me to do this for them: I will increase their men like a flock.

Bleating of, alluded to.

Judg 5:16 Why did you sit among the sheepfolds, To hear the pipings for the flocks? The divisions of Reuben have great searchings of heart.

1 Sam 15:14 But Samuel said, "What then *is* this bleating of the sheep in my ears, and the lowing of the oxen which I hear?"

Under man's care from the earliest age.

Gen 4:4 Abel also brought of the firstborn of his flock and of their fat. And the LORD respected Abel and his offering,

Constituted a great part of patriarchal wealth.

Gen 13:5 Lot also, who went with Abram, had flocks and herds and tents.

Gen 24:25 Moreover she said to him, "We have both straw and feed enough, and room to lodge."

Gen 26:14 for he had possessions of flocks and possessions of herds and a great number of servants. So the Philistines envied him.

Males of, called rams.

1 Sam 15:22 So Samuel said: "Has the LORD *as great* delight in burnt offerings and sacrifices, As in obeying the voice of the LORD? Behold, to obey is better than sacrifice, *And* to heed than the fat of rams.

Jer 51:40 "I will bring them down Like lambs to the slaughter, Like rams with male goats.

Females of, called ewes.

Gen 31:38 These twenty years I *have been* with you; your ewes and your female goats have not miscarried their young, and I have not eaten the rams of your flock.

Ps 78:71 From following the ewes that had young He brought him, To shepherd Jacob His people, And Israel His inheritance.

Young of, called lambs.

Ex 12:3 Speak to all the congregation of Israel, saying: 'On the tenth of this month every man shall take for himself a lamb, according to the house of *his* father, a lamb for a household.

Is 11:6 "The wolf also shall dwell with the lamb, The leopard shall lie down with the young goat, The calf and the young lion and the fatling together; And a little child shall lead them.

Places celebrated for,

Kedar.

Ezek 27:21 Arabia and all the princes of Kedar *were* your regular merchants. They traded with you in lambs, rams, and goats.

Bashan.

Deut 32:14 Curds from the cattle, and milk of the flock, With fat of lambs; And rams of the breed of Bashan, and goats, With the choicest wheat; And you drank wine, the blood of the grapes.

Nebaioth.

Is 60:7 All the flocks of Kedar shall be gathered together to you, The rams of Nebaioth shall minister to you; They shall ascend with acceptance on My altar, And I will glorify the house of My glory.

Flesh of, extensively used as food.

1 Sam 25:18 Then Abigail made haste and took two hundred *loaves* of bread, two skins of wine, five sheep already dressed, five seahs of roasted *grain,* one hundred clusters of raisins, and two hundred cakes of figs, and loaded *them* on donkeys.

1 Kin 1:19 He has sacrificed oxen and fattened cattle and sheep in abundance, and has invited all the sons of the king, Abiathar the priest, and Joab the commander of the army; but Solomon your servant he has not invited.

1 Kin 4:23 ten fatted oxen, twenty oxen from the pastures, and one hundred sheep, besides deer, gazelles, roebucks, and fatted fowl.

Neh 5:18 Now *that* which was prepared daily *was* one ox *and* six choice sheep. Also fowl were prepared for me, and once every ten days an abundance of all kinds of wine. Yet in spite of this I did not demand the governor's provisions, because the bondage was heavy on this people.

Is 22:13 But instead, joy and gladness, Slaying oxen and killing sheep, Eating meat and drinking wine: "Let us eat and drink, for tomorrow we die!"

Milk of, used as food.

Deut 32:14 Curds from the cattle, and milk of the flock, With fat of lambs; And rams of the breed of Bashan, and goats, With the choicest wheat; And you drank wine, the blood of the grapes.

Is 7:21–22 It shall be in that day *That* a man will keep alive a young cow and two sheep; **22** So it shall be, from the abundance of milk they give, That he will eat curds; For curds and honey everyone will eat who is left in the land.

1 Cor 9:7 Who ever goes to war at his own expense? Who plants a vineyard and does not eat of its fruit? Or who tends a flock and does not drink of the milk of the flock?

Skins of, worn as clothing by the poor.

Heb 11:37 They were stoned, they were sawn in two, were tempted, were slain with the sword. They wandered about in sheepskins and goatskins, being destitute, afflicted, tormented—

Skins of, made into a covering for the tabernacle.

Ex 25:5 ram skins dyed red, badger skins, and acacia wood;

Ex 36:19 Then he made a covering for the tent of ram skins dyed red, and a covering of badger skins above *that.*

Ex 39:34 the covering of ram skins dyed red, the covering of badger skins, and the veil of the covering;

Wool of, made into clothing.

Job 31:20 If his heart has not blessed me, And *if* he was *not* warmed with the fleece of my sheep;

Prov 31:13 She seeks wool and flax, And willingly works with her hands.

Ezek 34:3 You eat the fat and clothe yourselves with the wool; you slaughter the fatlings, *but* you do not feed the flock.

Offered in sacrifice from the earliest age.

Gen 4:4 Abel also brought of the firstborn of his flock and of their fat. And the LORD respected Abel and his offering,

Gen 8:20 Then Noah built an altar to the LORD, and took of every clean animal and of every clean bird, and offered burnt offerings on the altar.

Gen 15:9–10 So He said to him, "Bring Me a three-year-old heifer, a three-year-old female goat, a three-year-old ram, a turtledove, and a young pigeon." **10** Then he brought all these to Him and cut them in two, down the middle, and placed each piece opposite the other; but he did not cut the birds in two.

Offered in sacrifice under the law.

Ex 20:24 An altar of earth you shall make for Me, and you shall sacrifice on it your burnt offerings and your peace offerings, your sheep and your oxen. In every place where I record My name I will come to you, and I will bless you.

Lev 1:10 'If his offering *is* of the flocks—of the sheep or of the goats—as a burnt sacrifice, he shall bring a male without blemish.

1 Kin 8:5 Also King Solomon, and all the congregation of Israel who were assembled with him, *were* with him before the ark, sacrificing sheep and oxen that could not be counted or numbered for multitude.

1 Kin 8:63 And Solomon offered a sacrifice of peace offerings, which he offered to the LORD, twenty-two thousand bulls and one hundred and twenty thousand sheep. So the king and all the children of Israel dedicated the house of the LORD.

Flocks of,

Attended by members of the family.

Gen 29:9 Now while he was still speaking with them, Rachel came with her father's sheep, for she was a shepherdess.

Ex 2:16 Now the priest of Midian had seven daughters. And they came and drew water, and they filled the troughs to water their father's flock.

1 Sam 16:11 And Samuel said to Jesse, "Are all the young men here?" Then he said, "There remains yet the youngest, and there he is, keeping the sheep." And Samuel said to Jesse, "Send and bring him. For we will not sit down till he comes here."

Attended by servants.

1 Sam 17:20 So David rose early in the morning, left the sheep with a keeper, and took *the things* and went as Jesse had commanded him. And he came to the camp as the army was going out to the fight and shouting for the battle.

Is 61:5 Strangers shall stand and feed your flocks, And the sons of the foreigner *Shall be* your plowmen and your vinedressers.

Guarded by dogs.

Job 30:1 "But now they mock at me, *men* younger than I, Whose fathers I disdained to put with the dogs of my flock.

Kept in folds.

1 Sam 24:3 So he came to the sheepfolds by the road, where there *was* a cave; and Saul went in to attend to his needs. (David and his men were staying in the recesses of the cave.)

2 Sam 7:8 Now therefore, thus shall you say to My servant David, 'Thus says the LORD of hosts: "I took you from the sheepfold, from following the sheep, to be ruler over My people, over Israel.

John 10:1 "Most assuredly, I say to you, he who does not enter the sheepfold by the door, but climbs up some other way, the same is a thief and a robber.

Conducted to the richest pastures.

Ps 23:2 He makes me to lie down in green pastures; He leads me beside the still waters.

Fed on the mountains.

Ex 3:1 Now Moses was tending the flock of Jethro his father-in-law, the priest of Midian. And he led the flock to the back of the desert, and came to Horeb, the mountain of God.

Ezek 34:6 My sheep wandered through all the mountains, and on every high hill; yes, My flock was scattered over the whole face of the earth, and no one was seeking or searching *for them.*"

Ezek 34:13 And I will bring them out from the peoples and gather them from the countries, and will bring them to their own land; I will feed them on the mountains of Israel, in the valleys and in all the inhabited places of the country.

Fed in the valleys.

Is 65:10 Sharon shall be a fold of flocks, And the Valley of Achor a place for herds to lie down, For My people who have sought Me.

Frequently covered the pastures.

Ps 65:13 The pastures are clothed with flocks; The valleys also are covered with grain; They shout for joy, they also sing.

Watered every day.

Gen 29:8–10 But they said, "We cannot until all the flocks are gathered together, and they have rolled the stone from the well's mouth; then we water the sheep." **9** Now while he was still speaking with them, Rachel came with her father's sheep, for she was a shepherdess. **10** And it came to pass, when Jacob saw Rachel the daughter of Laban his mother's brother, and the sheep of Laban his mother's brother, that Jacob went near and rolled the stone from the well's mouth, and watered the flock of Laban his mother's brother.

Ex 2:16–17 Now the priest of Midian had seven daughters. And they came and drew water, and they filled the troughs to water their father's flock. **17** Then the shepherds came and drove them away; but Moses stood up and helped them, and watered their flock.

Made to rest at noon.

Ps 23:2 He makes me to lie down in green pastures; He leads me beside the still waters.

Song 1:7 Tell me, O you whom I love, Where you feed *your flock,* Where you make *it* rest at noon. For why should I be as one who veils herself By the flocks of your companions?

Followed the shepherd.

John 10:4 And when he brings out his own sheep, he goes before them; and the sheep follow him, for they know his voice.

John 10:27 My sheep hear My voice, and I know them, and they follow Me.

Fled from strangers.

John 10:5 Yet they will by no means follow a stranger, but will flee from him, for they do not know the voice of strangers."

Washed and shorn every year.

Song 4:2 Your teeth *are* like a flock of shorn *sheep* Which have come up from the washing, Every one of which bears twins, And none *is* barren among them.

Firstborn of,

Not to be shorn.

Deut 15:19 "All the firstborn males that come from your herd and your flock you shall sanctify to the LORD your God; you shall do no work with the firstborn of your herd, nor shear the firstborn of your flock.

Not to be redeemed.

Num 18:17 But the firstborn of a cow, the firstborn of a sheep, or the firstborn of a goat you shall not redeem; they *are* holy. You shall sprinkle their blood on the altar, and burn their fat *as* an offering made by fire for a sweet aroma to the LORD.

Could not be dedicated as a freewill offering.

Lev 27:26 'But the firstborn of the animals, which should be the LORD's firstborn, no man shall dedicate; whether *it is* an ox or sheep, it *is* the LORD's.

Tithe of, given to the Levites.

2 Chr 31:4–6 Moreover he commanded the people who dwelt in Jerusalem to contribute support for the priests and the Levites, that they might devote themselves to the Law of the LORD. **5** As soon as the commandment was circulated, the children of Israel brought in abundance the firstfruits of grain and wine, oil and honey, and of all the produce of the field; and they brought in abundantly the tithe of everything. **6** And the children of Israel and Judah, who dwelt in the cities of Judah, brought the tithe of oxen and sheep; also the tithe of holy things which were consecrated to the LORD their God they laid in heaps.

First wool of, given to the priests.

Deut 18:4 The firstfruits of your grain and your new wine and your oil, and the first of the fleece of your sheep, you shall give him.

Shearing of, a time of rejoicing.

1 Sam 25:2 Now *there was* a man in Maon whose business *was* in Carmel, and the man *was* very rich. He had three thousand sheep and a thousand goats. And he was shearing his sheep in Carmel.

1 Sam 25:11 Shall I then take my bread and my water and my meat that I have killed for my shearers, and give *it* to men when I do not know where they *are* from?"

1 Sam 25:36 Now Abigail went to Nabal, and there he was, holding a feast in his house, like the feast of a king. And Nabal's heart *was* merry within him, for he *was* very drunk; therefore she told him nothing, little or much, until morning light.

2 Sam 13:23 And it came to pass, after two full years, that Absalom had sheepshearers in Baal Hazor, which *is* near Ephraim; so Absalom invited all the king's sons.

Were frequently

Given as presents.

2 Sam 17:29 honey and curds, sheep and cheese of the herd, for David and the people who *were* with him to eat. For they said, "The people are hungry and weary and thirsty in the wilderness."

1 Chr 12:40 Moreover those who were near to them,

from as far away as Issachar and Zebulun and Naphtali, were bringing food on donkeys and camels, on mules and oxen—provisions of flour and cakes of figs and cakes of raisins, wine and oil and oxen and sheep abundantly, for *there was* joy in Israel.

Given as tribute.

2 Kin 3:4 Now Mesha king of Moab was a sheep-breeder, and he regularly paid the king of Israel one hundred thousand lambs and the wool of one hundred thousand rams.

2 Chr 17:11 Also *some* of the Philistines brought Jehoshaphat presents and silver as tribute; and the Arabians brought him flocks, seven thousand seven hundred rams and seven thousand seven hundred male goats.

Destroyed by wild beasts.

Jer 50:17 "Israel *is* like scattered sheep; The lions have driven *him* away. First the king of Assyria devoured him; Now at last this Nebuchadnezzar king of Babylon has broken his bones."

Mic 5:8 And the remnant of Jacob Shall be among the Gentiles, In the midst of many peoples, Like a lion among the beasts of the forest, Like a young lion among flocks of sheep, Who, if he passes through, Both treads down and tears in pieces, And none can deliver.

John 10:12 But a hireling, *he who is* not the shepherd, one who does not own the sheep, sees the wolf coming and leaves the sheep and flees; and the wolf catches the sheep and scatters them.

Taken in great numbers in war.

Judg 6:4 Then they would encamp against them and destroy the produce of the earth as far as Gaza, and leave no sustenance for Israel, neither sheep nor ox nor donkey.

1 Sam 14:32 And the people rushed on the spoil, and took sheep, oxen, and calves, and slaughtered *them* on the ground; and the people ate *them* with the blood.

1 Chr 5:21 Then they took away their livestock—fifty thousand of their camels, two hundred and fifty thousand of their sheep, and two thousand of their donkeys—also one hundred thousand of their men;

2 Chr 14:15 They also attacked the livestock enclosures, and carried off sheep and camels in abundance, and returned to Jerusalem.

Cut off by disease.

Ex 9:3 behold, the hand of the LORD will be on your cattle in the field, on the horses, on the donkeys, on the camels, on the oxen, and on the sheep—a very severe pestilence.

False prophets assume the simple appearance of.

Matt 7:15 "Beware of false prophets, who come to you in sheep's clothing, but inwardly they are ravenous wolves.

Illustrative of

The people of God.

Ps 74:1 O God, why have You cast *us* off forever? *Why* does Your anger smoke against the sheep of Your pasture?

Ps 78:52 But He made His own people go forth like sheep, And guided them in the wilderness like a flock;

Ps 79:13 So we, Your people and sheep of Your pasture, Will give You thanks forever; We will show forth Your praise to all generations.

John 21:16–17 He said to him again a second time, "Simon, *son* of Jonah, do you love Me?" He said to Him, "Yes, Lord; You know that I love You." He said to him, "Tend My sheep." **17** He said to him the third time, "Simon, *son* of Jonah, do you love Me?" Peter was grieved because He said to him the third time, "Do you love Me?" And he said to Him, "Lord, You know all things; You know that I love You." Jesus said to him, "Feed My sheep.

Heb 13:20 Now may the God of peace who brought up our Lord Jesus from the dead, that great Shepherd of the sheep, through the blood of the everlasting covenant,

1 Pet 5:2 Shepherd the flock of God which is among you, serving as overseers, not by compulsion but willingly, not for dishonest gain but eagerly;

Cf. John 10:7–26

Those under God's judgment.

Ps 44:1 We have heard with our ears, O God, Our fathers have told us, The deeds You did in their days, In days of old:

(In patience and simplicity) Christ's patience.

Is 53:7 He was oppressed and He was afflicted, Yet He opened not His mouth; He was led as a lamb to the slaughter, And as a sheep before its shearers is silent, So He opened not His mouth.

(In proneness to wander) those who are apart from God.

Ps 119:176 I have gone astray like a lost sheep; Seek Your servant, For I do not forget Your commandments.

Is 53:6 All we like sheep have gone astray; We have turned, every one, to his own way; And the LORD has laid on Him the iniquity of us all.

Ezek 34:16 "I will seek what was lost and bring back what was driven away, bind up the broken and strengthen what was sick; but I will destroy the fat and the strong, and feed them in judgment."

(Lost) the unregenerate.

Matt 10:6 But go rather to the lost sheep of the house of Israel.

(When found) restored sinners.

Luke 15:5 And when he has found *it,* he lays *it* on his shoulders, rejoicing.

Luke 15:7 I say to you that likewise there will be more joy in heaven over one sinner who repents than over ninety-nine just persons who need no repentance.

(Separation from the goats) the separation of believers from the wicked.

Matt 25:32–33 All the nations will be gathered before Him, and He will separate them one from another, as a shepherd divides *his* sheep from the goats. **33** And He will set the sheep on His right hand, but the goats on the left.

SHEKINAH (PRESENCE OF GOD).
SEE ALSO GOD, GLORY OF

Adam and Eve hid themselves from.

Gen 3:8 And they heard the sound of the LORD God walking in the garden in the cool of the day, and Adam and his wife hid themselves from the presence of the LORD God among the trees of the garden.

Was God's glory cloud.

Ex 24:16–17 Now the glory of the LORD rested on Mount Sinai, and the cloud covered it six days. And on the seventh day He called to Moses out of the midst of the cloud. **17** The sight of the glory of the LORD *was* like a consuming fire on the top of the mountain in the eyes of the children of Israel.

Ex 34:5–8 Now the LORD descended in the cloud and stood with him there, and proclaimed the name of the LORD. **6** And the LORD passed before him and proclaimed, "The LORD, the LORD God, merciful and gracious, longsuffering, and abounding in goodness and truth, **7** keeping mercy for thousands, forgiving iniquity and transgression and sin, by no means clearing *the guilty,* visiting the iniquity of the fathers upon the children and the children's children to the third and the fourth generation." **8** So Moses made haste and bowed his head toward the earth, and worshiped.

Filled the tabernacle.

Ex 40:34–35 Then the cloud covered the tabernacle of meeting, and the glory of the LORD filled the tabernacle. **35** And Moses was not able to enter the tabernacle of meeting, because the cloud rested above it, and the glory of the LORD filled the tabernacle.

Determined when Israel would journey.

Ex 40:36–38 Whenever the cloud was taken up from above the tabernacle, the children of Israel would go onward in all their journeys. **37** But if the cloud was not taken up, then they did not journey till the day that it was taken up. **38** For the cloud of the LORD *was* above the tabernacle by day, and fire was over it by night, in the sight of all the house of Israel, throughout all their journeys.

Filled the temple.

1 Kin 8:10 And it came to pass, when the priests came out of the holy *place,* that the cloud filled the house of the LORD,

Was the physical manifestation of God's presence.

Hab 3:3–4 God came from Teman, The Holy One from Mount Paran. Selah His glory covered the heavens, And the earth was full of His praise. **4** *His* brightness was like the light; He had rays *flashing* from His hand, And there His power *was* hidden.

Appeared at Christ's transfiguration.

Mark 9:7 And a cloud came and overshadowed them; and a voice came out of the cloud, saying, "This is My beloved Son. Hear Him!"

Will be completely visible when Christ returns.

Rev 1:7 Behold, He is coming with clouds, and every eye will see Him, even they who pierced Him. And all the tribes of the earth will mourn because of Him. Even so, Amen.

SHEPHERDS

Early mention of.

Gen 4:2 Then she bore again, this time his brother Abel. Now Abel was a keeper of sheep, but Cain was a tiller of the ground.

Usually carried a scrip or bag.

1 Sam 17:40 Then he took his staff in his hand; and he chose for himself five smooth stones from the brook, and put them in a shepherd's bag, in a pouch which he had, and his sling was in his hand. And he drew near to the Philistine.

Carried a staff or rod.

Lev 27:32 And concerning the tithe of the herd or the flock, of whatever passes under the rod, the tenth one shall be holy to the LORD.

Ps 23:4 Yea, though I walk through the valley of the shadow of death, I will fear no evil; For You *are* with me; Your rod and Your staff, they comfort me.

Dwelt in tents while tending their flocks.

Song 1:8 If you do not know, O fairest among women, Follow in the footsteps of the flock, And feed your little goats Beside the shepherds' tents.

Is 38:12 My life span is gone, Taken from me like a shepherd's tent; I have cut off my life like a weaver. He cuts me off from the loom; From day until night You make an end of me.

Members of the family, both male and female, acted as.

Gen 29:6 So he said to them, "Is he well?" And they said, *"He is* well. And look, his daughter Rachel is coming with the sheep."

1 Sam 16:11 And Samuel said to Jesse, "Are all the young men here?" Then he said, "There remains yet the youngest, and there he is, keeping the sheep." And Samuel said to Jesse, "Send and bring him. For we will not sit down till he comes here."

1 Sam 17:15 But David occasionally went and returned from Saul to feed his father's sheep at Bethlehem.

Had hired keepers under them.

1 Sam 17:20 So David rose early in the morning, left the sheep with a keeper, and took *the things* and went as Jesse had commanded him. And he came to the camp as the army was going out to the fight and shouting for the battle.

The unfaithfulness of hireling, alluded to.

John 10:12 But a hireling, *he who is* not the shepherd, one who does not own the sheep, sees the wolf coming and leaves the sheep and flees; and the wolf catches the sheep and scatters them.

Care of the sheep by, exhibited in

Knowing them.

John 10:14 I am the good shepherd; and I know My *sheep,* and am known by My own.

Going before and leading them.

Ps 77:20 You led Your people like a flock By the hand of Moses and Aaron.

Ps 78:52 But He made His own people go forth like sheep, And guided them in the wilderness like a flock;

Ps 80:1 Give ear, O Shepherd of Israel, You who lead Jo-

seph like a flock; You who dwell *between* the cherubim, shine forth!

Seeking out good pasture for them.

1 Chr 4:39–41 So they went to the entrance of Gedor, as far as the east side of the valley, to seek pasture for their flocks. **40** And they found rich, good pasture, and the land *was* broad, quiet, and peaceful; for some Hamites formerly lived there. **41** These recorded by name came in the days of Hezekiah king of Judah; and they attacked their tents and the Meunites who were found there, and utterly destroyed them, as it is to this day. So they dwelt in their place, because *there was* pasture for their flocks there.

Ps 23:2 He makes me to lie down in green pastures; He leads me beside the still waters.

Numbering them when they return from pasture.

Jer 33:13 In the cities of the mountains, in the cities of the lowland, in the cities of the South, in the land of Benjamin, in the places around Jerusalem, and in the cities of Judah, the flocks shall again pass under the hands of him who counts *them,*' says the LORD.

Watching over them by night.

Luke 2:8 Now there were in the same country shepherds living out in the fields, keeping watch over their flock by night.

Tenderness to the ewes and lambs.

Gen 33:13–14 But Jacob said to him, "My lord knows that the children *are* weak, and the flocks and herds which are nursing *are* with me. And if the men should drive them hard one day, all the flock will die. **14** Please let my lord go on ahead before his servant. I will lead on slowly at a pace which the livestock that go before me, and the children, are able to endure, until I come to my lord in Seir."

Ps 78:71 From following the ewes that had young He brought him, To shepherd Jacob His people, And Israel His inheritance.

Defending them when attacked by wild beasts.

1 Sam 17:34–36 But David said to Saul, "Your servant used to keep his father's sheep, and when a lion or a bear came and took a lamb out of the flock, **35** I went out after it and struck it, and delivered *the lamb* from its mouth; and when it arose against me, I caught *it* by its beard, and struck and killed it. **36** Your servant has killed both lion and bear; and this uncircumcised Philistine will be like one of them, seeing he has defied the armies of the living God."

Amos 3:12 Thus says the LORD: "As a shepherd takes from the mouth of a lion Two legs or a piece of an ear, So shall the children of Israel be taken out Who dwell in Samaria— In the corner of a bed and on the edge of a couch!

Searching them out when lost and straying.

Ezek 34:12 As a shepherd seeks out his flock on the day he is among his scattered sheep, so will I seek out My sheep and deliver them from all the places where they were scattered on a cloudy and dark day.

Luke 15:4–5 "What man of you, having a hundred sheep, if he loses one of them, does not leave the ninety-nine in the wilderness, and go after the one which is lost until he finds it? **5** And when he has found *it,* he lays *it* on his shoulders, rejoicing.

Attending them when sick.

Ezek 34:16 "I will seek what was lost and bring back what was driven away, bind up the broken and strengthen what was sick; but I will destroy the fat and the strong, and feed them in judgment."

An abomination to the Egyptians.

Gen 46:34 that you shall say, 'Your servants' occupation has been with livestock from our youth even till now, both we *and* also our fathers,' that you may dwell in the land of Goshen; for every shepherd *is* an abomination to the Egyptians."

Illustrative of

God as leader of Israel.

Ps 77:20 You led Your people like a flock By the hand of Moses and Aaron.

Ps 80:1 Give ear, O Shepherd of Israel, You who lead Joseph like a flock; You who dwell *between* the cherubim, shine forth!

Christ as the good shepherd.

Ezek 34:23 I will establish one shepherd over them, and he shall feed them—My servant David. He shall feed them and be their shepherd.

Zech 13:7 "Awake, O sword, against My Shepherd, Against the Man who is My Companion," Says the LORD of hosts. "Strike the Shepherd, And the sheep will be scattered; Then I will turn My hand against the little ones.

John 10:14 I am the good shepherd; and I know My *sheep,* and am known by My own.

Heb 13:20 Now may the God of peace who brought up our Lord Jesus from the dead, that great Shepherd of the sheep, through the blood of the everlasting covenant,

Kings as the leaders of the people.

Is 44:28 Who says of Cyrus, '*He is* My shepherd, And he shall perform all My pleasure, Saying to Jerusalem, "You shall be built," And to the temple, "Your foundation shall be laid." '

Jer 6:3 The shepherds with their flocks shall come to her. They shall pitch *their* tents against her all around. Each one shall pasture in his own place."

Jer 49:19 "Behold, he shall come up like a lion from the floodplain of the Jordan Against the dwelling place of the strong; But I will suddenly make him run away from her. And who *is* a chosen *man that* I may appoint over her? For who *is* like Me? Who will arraign Me? And who *is* that shepherd Who will withstand Me?"

Ministers of the gospel.

Jer 23:4 I will set up shepherds over them who will feed them; and they shall fear no more, nor be dismayed, nor shall they be lacking," says the LORD.

(Searching out straying sheep) Christ seeking the lost.

Ezek 34:12 As a shepherd seeks out his flock on the day he is among his scattered sheep, so will I seek out My sheep and deliver them from all the places where they were scattered on a cloudy and dark day.

Luke 15:2–7 And the Pharisees and scribes complained, saying, "This Man receives sinners and eats with them." 3 So He spoke this parable to them, saying:

4 "What man of you, having a hundred sheep, if he loses one of them, does not leave the ninety-nine in the wilderness, and go after the one which is lost until he finds it? 5 And when he has found *it,* he lays *it* on his shoulders, rejoicing. 6 And when he comes home, he calls together *his* friends and neighbors, saying to them, 'Rejoice with me, for I have found my sheep which was lost!' 7 I say to you that likewise there will be more joy in heaven over one sinner who repents than over ninety-nine just persons who need no repentance.

(Their care and tenderness) tenderness of Christ.

Is 40:11 He will feed His flock like a shepherd; He will gather the lambs with His arm, And carry *them* in His bosom, *And* gently lead those who are with young.

Ezek 34:13–16 And I will bring them out from the peoples and gather them from the countries, and will bring them to their own land; I will feed them on the mountains of Israel, in the valleys and in all the inhabited places of the country. 14 I will feed them in good pasture, and their fold shall be on the high mountains of Israel. There they shall lie down in a good fold and feed in rich pasture on the mountains of Israel. 15 I will feed My flock, and I will make them lie down," says the Lord GOD. 16 "I will seek what was lost and bring back what was driven away, bind up the broken and strengthen what was sick; but I will destroy the fat and the strong, and feed them in judgment."

(Ignorant and foolish) bad ministers.

Is 56:11 Yes, *they are* greedy dogs *Which* never have enough. And they *are* shepherds Who cannot understand; They all look to their own way, Every one for his own gain, From his *own* territory.

Jer 50:6 "My people have been lost sheep. Their shepherds have led them astray; They have turned them away *on* the mountains. They have gone from mountain to hill; They have forgotten their resting place.

Ezek 34:2 "Son of man, prophesy against the shepherds of Israel, prophesy and say to them, 'Thus says the Lord GOD to the shepherds: "Woe to the shepherds of Israel who feed themselves! Should not the shepherds feed the flocks?

Ezek 34:10 Thus says the Lord GOD: "Behold, I *am* against the shepherds, and I will require My flock at their hand; I will cause them to cease feeding the sheep, and the shepherds shall feed themselves no more; for I will deliver My flock from their mouths, that they may no longer be food for them."

Zech 11:7–8 So I fed the flock for slaughter, in particular the poor of the flock. I took for myself two staffs: the one I called Beauty, and the other I called Bonds; and I fed the flock. 8 I dismissed the three shepherds in one month. My soul loathed them, and their soul also abhorred me.

Zech 11:15–17 And the LORD said to me, "Next, take for yourself the implements of a foolish shepherd. 16 For indeed I will raise up a shepherd in the land *who* will not care for those who are cut off, nor seek the young, nor heal those that are broken, nor feed those that still stand. But he will eat the flesh of the fat and tear their hooves in pieces. 17 "Woe to the worthless shepherd, Who leaves the flock! A sword *shall be* against his arm And against his right eye; His arm shall completely wither, And his right eye shall be totally blinded."

SHOWBREAD

Twelve cakes of fine flour.

Lev 24:5 "And you shall take fine flour and bake twelve cakes with it. Two-tenths *of an ephah* shall be in each cake.

Called hallowed bread.

1 Sam 21:4 And the priest answered David and said, "*There is* no common bread on hand; but there is holy bread, if the young men have at least kept themselves from women."

Materials for, provided by the people.

Lev 24:8 Every Sabbath he shall set it in order before the LORD continually, *being taken* from the children of Israel by an everlasting covenant.

Neh 10:32–33 Also we made ordinances for ourselves, to exact from ourselves yearly one-third of a shekel for the service of the house of our God: **33** for the showbread, for the regular grain offering, for the regular burnt offering of the Sabbaths, the New Moons, and the set feasts; for the holy things, for the sin offerings to make atonement for Israel, and all the work of the house of our God.

Prepared by Levites.

1 Chr 9:32 And some of their brethren of the sons of the Kohathites *were* in charge of preparing the showbread for every Sabbath.

1 Chr 23:29 both with the showbread and the fine flour for the grain offering, with the unleavened cakes and *what is baked in* the pan, with what is mixed and with all kinds of measures and sizes;

Placed in two rows on the table before the Lord.

Ex 25:30 And you shall set the showbread on the table before Me always.

Ex 40:23 and he set the bread in order upon it before the LORD, as the LORD had commanded Moses.

Lev 24:6 You shall set them in two rows, six in a row, on the pure *gold* table before the LORD.

Table of,

Dimensions.

Ex 25:23 "You shall also make a table of acacia wood; two cubits *shall be* its length, a cubit its width, and a cubit and a half its height.

Covered with gold.

Ex 25:24 And you shall overlay it with pure gold, and make a molding of gold all around.

Had an ornamental border.

Ex 25:25 You shall make for it a frame of a handbreadth all around, and you shall make a gold molding for the frame all around.

Had poles of acacia wood covered with gold.

Ex 25:28 And you shall make the poles of acacia wood, and overlay them with gold, that the table may be carried with them.

Had rings of gold in the corners for the poles.

Ex 25:26–27 And you shall make for it four rings of gold, and put the rings on the four corners that *are* at its four legs. **27** The rings shall be close to the frame, as holders for the poles to bear the table.

Had dishes, spoons, covers, and bowls of gold.

Ex 25:29 You shall make its dishes, its pans, its pitchers, and its bowls for pouring. You shall make them of pure gold.

Placed in the north side of the tabernacle.

Ex 40:22 He put the table in the tabernacle of meeting, on the north side of the tabernacle, outside the veil;

Heb 9:2 For a tabernacle was prepared: the first *part*, in which *was* the lampstand, the table, and the showbread, which is called the sanctuary;

Directions for removing.

Num 4:7 "On the table of showbread they shall spread a blue cloth, and put on it the dishes, the pans, the bowls, and the pitchers for pouring; and the showbread shall be on it.

Pure frankincense placed on.

Lev 24:7 And you shall put pure frankincense on *each* row, that it may be on the bread for a memorial, an offering made by fire to the LORD.

Was changed every Sabbath day.

Lev 24:8 Every Sabbath he shall set it in order before the LORD continually, *being taken* from the children of Israel by an everlasting covenant.

After removal from the table, given to the priests.

Lev 24:9 And it shall be for Aaron and his sons, and they shall eat it in a holy place; for it *is* most holy to him from the offerings of the LORD made by fire, by a perpetual statute."

Not lawful for any but the priests to eat, except in extreme cases.

1 Sam 21:4–6 And the priest answered David and said, "*There is* no common bread on hand; but there is holy bread, if the young men have at least kept themselves from women." **5** Then David answered the priest, and said to him, "Truly, women *have been* kept from us about three days since I came out. And the vessels of the young men are holy, and *the bread is* in effect common, even though it was consecrated in the vessel this day." **6** So the priest gave him holy bread; for there was no bread there but the showbread which had been taken from before the LORD, in order to put hot bread *in its place* on the day when it was taken away.

Matt 12:4 how he entered the house of God and ate the showbread which was not lawful for him to eat, nor for those who were with him, but only for the priests?

Illustrative of

Christ as the bread of life.

John 6:48 I am the bread of life.

The church.

1 Cor 5:7 Therefore purge out the old leaven, that you may be a new lump, since you truly are unleavened. For indeed Christ, our Passover, was sacrificed for us.

1 Cor 10:17 For we, *though* many, are one bread *and* one body; for we all partake of that one bread.

SHIELDS

A part of defensive armor.

Ps 115:9 O Israel, trust in the LORD; He *is* their help and their shield.

Ps 140:7 O GOD the Lord, the strength of my salvation, You have covered my head in the day of battle.

Frequently made of, or covered with

Gold.

2 Sam 8:7 And David took the shields of gold that had belonged to the servants of Hadadezer, and brought them to Jerusalem.

1 Kin 10:17 He also *made* three hundred shields *of* hammered gold; three minas of gold went into each shield. The king put them in the House of the Forest of Lebanon.

Bronze.

1 Kin 14:27 Then King Rehoboam made bronze shields in their place, and committed *them* to the hands of the captains of the guard, who guarded the doorway of the king's house.

Said to belong to God.

Ps 47:9 The princes of the people have gathered together, The people of the God of Abraham. For the shields of the earth *belong* to God; He is greatly exalted.

Kinds of,

Defensive tool in war.

1 Chr 5:18 The sons of Reuben, the Gadites, and half the tribe of Manasseh *had* forty-four thousand seven hundred and sixty valiant men, men able to bear shield and sword, to shoot with the bow, and skillful in war, who went to war.

2 Chr 9:15–16 And King Solomon made two hundred large shields of hammered gold; six hundred *shekels* of hammered gold went into each shield. **16** *He* also *made* three hundred shields of hammered gold; three hundred *shekels* of gold went into each shield. The king put them in the House of the Forest of Lebanon.

Ezek 26:8 He will slay with the sword your daughter *villages* in the fields; he will heap up a siege mound against you, build a wall against you, and raise a defense against you.

Often borne by an shield-bearer.

1 Sam 17:7 Now the staff of his spear *was* like a weaver's beam, and his iron spearhead *weighed* six hundred shekels; and a shield-bearer went before him.

Before war, were

Gathered together.

Jer 51:11 Make the arrows bright! Gather the shields! The LORD has raised up the spirit of the kings of the Medes. For His plan *is* against Babylon to destroy it, Because it *is* the vengeance of the LORD, The vengeance for His temple.

Uncovered.

Is 22:6 Elam bore the quiver With chariots of men *and* horsemen, And Kir uncovered the shield.

Prepared.

Jer 46:3 "Order the buckler and shield, And draw near to battle!

Anointed.

2 Sam 1:21 "O mountains of Gilboa, *Let there be* no dew nor rain upon you, Nor fields of offerings. For the shield of the mighty is cast away there! The shield of Saul, not anointed with oil.

Is 21:5 Prepare the table, Set a watchman in the tower, Eat and drink. Arise, you princes, Anoint the shield!

Often made red.

Nah 2:3 The shields of his mighty men *are* made red, The valiant men *are* in scarlet. The chariots *come* with flaming torches In the day of his preparation, And the spears are brandished.

Provided by the kings of Israel in great abundance.

2 Chr 11:12 Also in every city *he put* shields and spears, and made them very strong, having Judah and Benjamin on his side.

2 Chr 26:14 Then Uzziah prepared for them, for the entire army, shields, spears, helmets, body armor, bows, and slings *to cast* stones.

2 Chr 32:5 And he strengthened himself, built up all the wall that was broken, raised *it* up to the towers, and *built* another wall outside; also he repaired the Millo *in* the City of David, and made weapons and shields in abundance.

A disgrace to lose, or throw away.

2 Sam 1:21 "O mountains of Gilboa, *Let there be* no dew nor rain upon you, Nor fields of offerings. For the shield of the mighty is cast away there! The shield of Saul, not anointed with oil.

Of the defeated, often burned.

Ezek 39:9 "Then those who dwell in the cities of Israel will go out and set on fire and burn the weapons, both the shields and bucklers, the bows and arrows, the javelins and spears; and they will make fires with them for seven years.

In times of peace were hung up in towers or armories.

Song 4:4 Your neck *is* like the tower of David, Built for an armory, On which hang a thousand bucklers, All shields of mighty men.

Ezek 27:10 "Those from Persia, Lydia, and Libya Were in your army as men of war; They hung shield and helmet in you; They gave splendor to you.

Were scarce in Israel in the days of Deborah and Barak.

Judg 5:8 They chose new gods; Then *there was* war in the gates; Not a shield or spear was seen among forty thousand in Israel.

Many of the Israelites used, with expertness.

1 Chr 12:8 *Some* Gadites joined David at the stronghold in the wilderness, mighty men of valor, men trained for battle, who could handle shield and spear, whose faces *were like* the faces of lions, and *were* as swift as gazelles on the mountains:

1 Chr 12:24 of the sons of Judah bearing shield and spear, six thousand eight hundred armed for war;

1 Chr 12:34 of Naphtali one thousand captains, and with them thirty-seven thousand with shield and spear;

2 Chr 14:8 And Asa had an army of three hundred thousand from Judah who carried shields and spears, and from Benjamin two hundred and eighty thousand men who carried shields and drew bows; all these *were* mighty men of valor.

2 Chr 25:5 Moreover Amaziah gathered Judah together and set over them captains of thousands and captains of hundreds, according to *their* fathers' houses, throughout all Judah and Benjamin; and he numbered them from twenty years old and above, and found them to be three hundred thousand choice men, *able* to go to war, who could handle spear and shield.

Illustrative of
Protection of God.

Gen 15:1 After these things the word of the LORD came to Abram in a vision, saying, "Do not be afraid, Abram. I *am* your shield, your exceedingly great reward."

Ps 33:20 Our soul waits for the LORD; He *is* our help and our shield.

Favor of God.

Ps 5:12 For You, O LORD, will bless the righteous; With favor You will surround him as *with* a shield.

Truth of God.

Ps 91:4 He shall cover you with His feathers, And under His wings you shall take refuge; His truth *shall be your* shield and buckler.

Salvation of God.

2 Sam 22:36 "You have also given me the shield of Your salvation; Your gentleness has made me great.

Ps 18:35 You have also given me the shield of Your salvation; Your right hand has held me up, Your gentleness has made me great.

Faith.

Eph 6:16 above all, taking the shield of faith with which you will be able to quench all the fiery darts of the wicked one.

SHIPS

Noah's ark was prototype.

Gen 6:14–16 Make yourself an ark of gopherwood; make rooms in the ark, and cover it inside and outside with pitch. **15** And this is how you shall make it: The length of the ark *shall be* three hundred cubits, its width fifty cubits, and its height thirty cubits. **16** You shall make a window for the ark, and you shall finish it to a cubit from above; and set the door of the ark in its side. You shall make it *with* lower, second, and third *decks*.

Gen 7:17–18 Now the flood was on the earth forty days. The waters increased and lifted up the ark, and it rose high above the earth. **18** The waters prevailed and greatly increased on the earth, and the ark moved about on the surface of the waters.

Antiquity of, among the Jews.

Gen 49:13 "Zebulun shall dwell by the haven of the sea; He *shall become* a haven for ships, And his border shall adjoin Sidon.

Judg 5:17 Gilead stayed beyond the Jordan, And why did Dan remain on ships? Asher continued at the seashore, And stayed by his inlets.

Described as
Majestic.

Is 33:21 But there the majestic LORD *will be* for us A place of broad rivers *and* streams, In which no galley with oars will sail, Nor majestic ships pass by

Large.

James 3:4 Look also at ships: although they are so large and are driven by fierce winds, they are turned by a very small rudder wherever the pilot desires.

Strong.

Is 23:14 Wail, you ships of Tarshish! For your strength is laid waste.

Swift.

Job 9:26 They pass by like swift ships, Like an eagle swooping on its prey.

Solomon built a fleet of.

1 Kin 9:26 King Solomon also built a fleet of ships at Ezion Geber, which *is* near Elath on the shore of the Red Sea, in the land of Edom.

Mentioned in Scripture,
Of Cyprus.

Num 24:24 But ships *shall come* from the coasts of Cyprus, And they shall afflict Asshur and afflict Eber, And so shall *Amalek*, until he perishes."

Dan 11:30 For ships from Cyprus shall come against him; therefore he shall be grieved, and return in rage against the holy covenant, and do *damage*. "So he shall return and show regard for those who forsake the holy covenant.

Of Tarshish.

Is 23:1 The burden against Tyre. Wail, you ships of Tarshish! For it is laid waste, So that there is no house, no harbor; From the land of Cyprus it is revealed to them.

Is 60:9 Surely the coastlands shall wait for Me; And the ships of Tarshish *will come* first, To bring your sons from afar, Their silver and their gold with them, To the name of the LORD your God, And to the Holy One of Israel, Because He has glorified you.

Of Adramyttium.

Acts 27:2 So, entering a ship of Adramyttium, we put to sea, meaning to sail along the coasts of Asia. Aristarchus, a Macedonian of Thessalonica, was with us.

Of Alexandria.

Acts 27:6 There the centurion found an Alexandrian ship sailing to Italy, and he put us on board.

Of Chaldea.

Is 43:14 Thus says the LORD, your Redeemer, The Holy One of Israel: "For your sake I will send to Babylon, And bring them all down as fugitives— The Chaldeans, who rejoice in their ships.

Of Tyre.

2 Chr 8:18 And Hiram sent him ships by the hand of his servants, and servants who knew the sea. They went with the servants of Solomon to Ophir, and acquired four hundred and fifty talents of gold from there, and brought it to King Solomon.

Generally made of the fir tree.

Ezek 27:5 They made all *your* planks of fir trees from

Senir; They took a cedar from Lebanon to make you a mast.

Sometimes made of reed.

Is 18:2 Which sends ambassadors by sea, Even in vessels of reed on the waters, *saying,* "Go, swift messengers, to a nation tall and smooth *of skin,* To a people terrible from their beginning onward, A nation powerful and treading down, Whose land the rivers divide."

The seams of, were caulked.

Ezek 27:9 Elders of Gebal and its wise men Were in you to caulk your seams; All the ships of the sea And their oarsmen were in you To market your merchandise.

Ezek 27:27 "Your riches, wares, and merchandise, Your mariners and pilots, Your caulkers and merchandisers, All your men of war who *are* in you, And the entire company which *is* in your midst, Will fall into the midst of the seas on the day of your ruin.

Parts of, mentioned

The prow and stern.

Acts 27:29–30 Then, fearing lest we should run aground on the rocks, they dropped four anchors from the stern, and prayed for day to come. **30** And as the sailors were seeking to escape from the ship, when they had let down the skiff into the sea, under pretense of putting out anchors from the prow,

Acts 27:41 But striking a place where two seas met, they ran the ship aground; and the prow stuck fast and remained immovable, but the stern was being broken up by the violence of the waves.

The hold or between the sides.

Jon 1:5 Then the mariners were afraid; and every man cried out to his god, and threw the cargo that *was* in the ship into the sea, to lighten the load. But Jonah had gone down into the lowest parts of the ship, had lain down, and was fast asleep.

The mast.

Is 33:23 Your tackle is loosed, They could not strengthen their mast, They could not spread the sail. Then the prey of great plunder is divided; The lame take the prey.

Ezek 27:5 They made all *your* planks of fir trees from Senir; They took a cedar from Lebanon to make you a mast.

The sails.

Is 33:23 Your tackle is loosed, They could not strengthen their mast, They could not spread the sail. Then the prey of great plunder is divided; The lame take the prey.

Ezek 27:7 Fine embroidered linen from Egypt was what you spread for your sail; Blue and purple from the coasts of Elishah was what covered you.

The tackle.

Is 33:23 Your tackle is loosed, They could not strengthen their mast, They could not spread the sail. Then the prey of great plunder is divided; The lame take the prey.

Acts 27:19 On the third *day* we threw the ship's tackle overboard with our own hands.

The rudder or helm.

James 3:4 Look also at ships: although they are so large and are driven by fierce winds, they are turned by a very small rudder wherever the pilot desires.

The rudder ropes.

Acts 27:40 And they let go the anchors and left *them* in the sea, meanwhile loosing the rudder ropes; and they hoisted the mainsail to the wind and made for shore.

The anchors.

Acts 27:29 Then, fearing lest we should run aground on the rocks, they dropped four anchors from the stern, and prayed for day to come.

Acts 27:40 And they let go the anchors and left *them* in the sea, meanwhile loosing the rudder ropes; and they hoisted the mainsail to the wind and made for shore.

The skiffs.

Acts 27:30 And as the sailors were seeking to escape from the ship, when they had let down the skiff into the sea, under pretense of putting out anchors from the prow,

Acts 27:32 Then the soldiers cut away the ropes of the skiff and let it fall off.

The oars.

Is 33:21 But there the majestic LORD *will be* for us A place of broad rivers *and* streams, In which no galley with oars will sail, Nor majestic ships pass by

Ezek 27:6 *Of* oaks from Bashan they made your oars; The company of Ashurites have inlaid your planks *With* ivory from the coasts of Cyprus.

Often the property of individuals.

Acts 27:11 Nevertheless the centurion was more persuaded by the helmsman and the owner of the ship than by the things spoken by Paul.

Commanded by a master.

Jon 1:6 So the captain came to him, and said to him, "What do you mean, sleeper? Arise, call on your God; perhaps your God will consider us, so that we may not perish."

Acts 27:11 Nevertheless the centurion was more persuaded by the helmsman and the owner of the ship than by the things spoken by Paul.

Guided in their course by pilots.

Ezek 27:8 "Inhabitants of Sidon and Arvad were your oarsmen; Your wise men, O Tyre, were in you; They became your pilots.

Ezek 27:27–29 "Your riches, wares, and merchandise, Your mariners and pilots, Your caulkers and merchandisers, All your men of war who *are* in you, And the entire company which *is* in you, Will fall into the midst of the seas on the day of your ruin. **28** The common-land will shake at the sound of the cry of your pilots. **29** "All who handle the oar, The mariners, All the pilots of the sea Will come down from their ships *and* stand on the shore.

Governed and directed by the helm.

James 3:4 Look also at ships: although they are so large and are driven by fierce winds, they are turned by a very small rudder wherever the pilot desires.

Course of frequently directed by the heavenly bodies.

Acts 27:20 Now when neither sun nor stars appeared

for many days, and no small tempest beat on *us*, all hope that we would be saved was finally given up.

Worked by mariners or sailors.

Ezek 27:9 Elders of Gebal and its wise men Were in you to caulk your seams; All the ships of the sea And their oarsmen were in you To market your merchandise.

Ezek 27:27 "Your riches, wares, and merchandise, Your mariners and pilots, Your caulkers and merchandisers, All your men of war who *are* in you, And the entire company which *is* in your midst, Will fall into the midst of the seas on the day of your ruin.

Jon 1:5 Then the mariners were afraid; and every man cried out to his god, and threw the cargo that *was* in the ship into the sea, to lighten the load. But Jonah had gone down into the lowest parts of the ship, had lain down, and was fast asleep.

Acts 27:30 And as the sailors were seeking to escape from the ship, when they had let down the skiff into the sea, under pretense of putting out anchors from the prow,

Propelled by wind and sails.

Acts 27:2–7 So, entering a ship of Adramyttium, we put to sea, meaning to sail along the coasts of Asia. Aristarchus, a Macedonian of Thessalonica, was with us. 3 And the next *day* we landed at Sidon. And Julius treated Paul kindly and gave *him* liberty to go to his friends and receive care. 4 When we had put to sea from there, we sailed under *the shelter of* Cyprus, because the winds were contrary. 5 And when we had sailed over the sea which is off Cilicia and Pamphylia, we came to Myra, *a city* of Lycia. 6 There the centurion found an Alexandrian ship sailing to Italy, and he put us on board. 7 When we had sailed slowly many days, and arrived with difficulty off Cnidus, the wind not permitting us to proceed, we sailed under *the shelter of* Crete off Salmone.

Often propelled by oars.

Jon 1:13 Nevertheless the men rowed hard to return to land, but they could not, for the sea continued to grow more tempestuous against them.

John 6:19 So when they had rowed about three or four miles, they saw Jesus walking on the sea and drawing near the boat; and they were afraid.

Navigated

Rivers.

Is 33:21 But there the majestic LORD *will be* for us A place of broad rivers *and* streams, In which no galley with oars will sail, Nor majestic ships pass by

Lakes.

Luke 5:1–2 So it was, as the multitude pressed about Him to hear the word of God, that He stood by the Lake of Gennesaret, 2 and saw two boats standing by the lake; but the fishermen had gone from them and were washing *their* nets.

The ocean.

Ps 104:26 There the ships sail about; *There is* that Leviathan Which You have made to play there.

Ps 107:23 Those who go down to the sea in ships, Who do business on great waters,

Soundings usually taken for, in dangerous places.

Acts 27:28 And they took soundings and found *it* to be twenty fathoms; and when they had gone a little farther, they took soundings again and found *it* to be fifteen fathoms.

Usually distinguished by signs or figure heads.

Acts 28:11 After three months we sailed in an Alexandrian ship whose figurehead was the Twin Brothers, which had wintered at the island.

Course of, through the midst of the sea, wonderful.

Prov 30:18–19 There are three *things which* are too wonderful for me, Yes, four *which* I do not understand: 19 The way of an eagle in the air, The way of a serpent on a rock, The way of a ship in the midst of the sea, And the way of a man with a virgin.

Employed in

Trading.

1 Kin 22:48 Jehoshaphat made merchant ships to go to Ophir for gold; but they never sailed, for the ships were wrecked at Ezion Geber.

2 Chr 8:18 And Hiram sent him ships by the hand of his servants, and servants who knew the sea. They went with the servants of Solomon to Ophir, and acquired four hundred and fifty talents of gold from there, and brought it to King Solomon.

2 Chr 9:21 For the king's ships went to Tarshish with the servants of Hiram. Once every three years the merchant ships came, bringing gold, silver, ivory, apes, and monkeys.

Fishing.

Matt 4:21 Going on from there, He saw two other brothers, James *the son* of Zebedee, and John his brother, in the boat with Zebedee their father, mending their nets. He called them,

Luke 5:4–9 When He had stopped speaking, He said to Simon, "Launch out into the deep and let down your nets for a catch." 5 But Simon answered and said to Him, "Master, we have toiled all night and caught nothing; nevertheless at Your word I will let down the net." 6 And when they had done this, they caught a great number of fish, and their net was breaking. 7 So they signaled to *their* partners in the other boat to come and help them. And they came and filled both the boats, so that they began to sink. 8 When Simon Peter saw *it*, he fell down at Jesus' knees, saying, "Depart from me, for I am a sinful man, O Lord!" 9 For he and all who were with him were astonished at the catch of fish which they had taken;

John 21:3–8 Simon Peter said to them, "I am going fishing." They said to him, "We are going with you also." They went out and immediately got into the boat, and that night they caught nothing. 4 But when the morning had now come, Jesus stood on the shore; yet the disciples did not know that it was Jesus. 5 Then Jesus said to them, "Children, have you any food?" They answered Him, "No." 6 And He said to them, "Cast the net on the right side of the boat, and you will find *some*." So they cast, and now they were not able to draw it in because of the multitude of fish. 7 Therefore that disciple whom Jesus loved said to Peter, "It is the Lord!" Now when Simon Peter heard that it was the Lord, he put on *his* outer garment (for he had removed it), and plunged into the sea. 8 But the other disciples came in the little boat (for they were not far from land, but about two hundred cubits), dragging the net with fish.

War.

Num 24:24 But ships *shall come* from the coasts of Cyprus, And they shall afflict Asshur and afflict Eber, And so shall *Amalek*, until he perishes."

Dan 11:30 For ships from Cyprus shall come against him; therefore he shall be grieved, and return in rage against the holy covenant, and do *damage*. "So he shall return and show regard for those who forsake the holy covenant.

Dan 11:40 "At the time of the end the king of the South shall attack him; and the king of the North shall come against him like a whirlwind, with chariots, horsemen, and with many ships; and he shall enter the countries, overwhelm *them*, and pass through.

Carrying passengers.

Jon 1:3 But Jonah arose to flee to Tarshish from the presence of the LORD. He went down to Joppa, and found a ship going to Tarshish; so he paid the fare, and went down into it, to go with them to Tarshish from the presence of the LORD.

Acts 27:2 So, entering a ship of Adramyttium, we put to sea, meaning to sail along the coasts of Asia. Aristarchus, a Macedonian of Thessalonica, was with us.

Acts 27:6 There the centurion found an Alexandrian ship sailing to Italy, and he put us on board.

Acts 28:11 After three months we sailed in an Alexandrian ship whose figurehead was the Twin Brothers, which had wintered at the island.

Endangered by

Storms.

Jon 1:4 But the LORD sent out a great wind on the sea, and there was a mighty tempest on the sea, so that the ship was about to be broken up.

Mark 4:37–38 And a great windstorm arose, and the waves beat into the boat, so that it was already filling. 38 But He was in the stern, asleep on a pillow. And they awoke Him and said to Him, "Teacher, do You not care that we are perishing?"

Quicksands.

Acts 27:17 When they had taken it on board, they used cables to undergird the ship; and fearing lest they should run aground on the Syrtis *Sands*, they struck sail and so were driven.

Rocks.

Acts 27:29 Then, fearing lest we should run aground on the rocks, they dropped four anchors from the stern, and prayed for day to come.

When damaged were sometimes undergirded with cables.

Acts 27:17 When they had taken it on board, they used cables to undergird the ship; and fearing lest they should run aground on the Syrtis *Sands*, they struck sail and so were driven.

Were often wrecked.

1 Kin 22:48 Jehoshaphat made merchant ships to go to Ophir for gold; but they never sailed, for the ships were wrecked at Ezion Geber.

Ps 48:7 *As when* You break the ships of Tarshish With an east wind.

Acts 27:41–44 But striking a place where two seas met, they ran the ship aground; and the prow stuck fast and remained immovable, but the stern was being broken up by the violence of the waves. 42 And the soldiers' plan was to kill the prisoners, lest any of them should swim away and escape. 43 But the centurion, wanting to save Paul, kept them from *their* purpose, and commanded that those who could swim should jump *overboard* first and get to land, 44 and the rest, some on boards and some on *parts* of the ship. And so it was that they all escaped safely to land.

2 Cor 11:25 Three times I was beaten with rods; once I was stoned; three times I was shipwrecked; a night and a day I have been in the deep;

Illustrative of

Industrious women.

Prov 31:14 She is like the merchant ships, She brings her food from afar.

(Wrecked) departure from the faith.

1 Tim 1:19 having faith and a good conscience, which some having rejected, concerning the faith have suffered shipwreck,

SHOES

Early use of.

Gen 14:23 that I *will take* nothing, from a thread to a sandal strap, and that I will not take anything that *is* yours, lest you should say, 'I have made Abram rich'—

Called sandals.

Mark 6:9 but to wear sandals, and not to put on two tunics.

Acts 12:8 Then the angel said to him, "Gird yourself and tie on your sandals"; and so he did. And he said to him, "Put on your garment and follow me."

Soles of, sometimes plated with bronze or iron.

Deut 33:25 Your sandals *shall be* iron and bronze; As your days, *so shall* your strength *be*.

Bound round the feet with straps or ties.

John 1:27 It is He who, coming after me, is preferred before me, whose sandal strap I am not worthy to loose."

Acts 12:8 Then the angel said to him, "Gird yourself and tie on your sandals"; and so he did. And he said to him, "Put on your garment and follow me."

Of ladies of distinction,

Often made of badgers' skins.

Ezek 16:10 I clothed you in embroidered cloth and gave you sandals of badger skin; I clothed you with fine linen and covered you with silk.

Often highly ornamental.

Song 7:1 How beautiful are your feet in sandals, O prince's daughter! The curves of your thighs *are* like jewels, The work of the hands of a skillful workman.

Probably often adorned with tinkling ornaments.

Is 3:18 In that day the Lord will take away the finery: The jingling anklets, the scarves, and the crescents;

Loosing of for another, a degrading office.

John 1:27 It is He who, coming after me, is preferred before me, whose sandal strap I am not worthy to loose."

Bearing for another, a degrading office; performed only by slaves.

Matt 3:11 I indeed baptize you with water unto repentance, but He who is coming after me is mightier than I, whose sandals I am not worthy to carry. He will baptize you with the Holy Spirit and fire.

The Jews

Put on, before beginning a journey.

Ex 12:11 And thus you shall eat it: *with* a belt on your waist, your sandals on your feet, and your staff in your hand. So you shall eat it in haste. It *is* the LORD's Passover.

Never wore, in mourning.

2 Sam 15:30 So David went up by the Ascent of the *Mount of* Olives, and wept as he went up; and he had his head covered and went barefoot. And all the people who *were* with him covered their heads and went up, weeping as they went up.

Is 20:2–3 at the same time the LORD spoke by Isaiah the son of Amoz, saying, "Go, and remove the sackcloth from your body, and take your sandals off your feet." And he did so, walking naked and barefoot. **3** Then the LORD said, "Just as My servant Isaiah has walked naked and barefoot three years *for* a sign and a wonder against Egypt and Ethiopia,

Ezek 24:17 Sigh in silence, make no mourning for the dead; bind your turban on your head, and put your sandals on your feet; do not cover *your* lips, and do not eat man's bread *of sorrow*."

Ezek 24:23 Your turbans shall be on your heads and your sandals on your feet; you shall neither mourn nor weep, but you shall pine away in your iniquities and mourn with one another.

Put off, when they entered sacred places.

Ex 3:5 Then He said, "Do not draw near this place. Take your sandals off your feet, for the place where you stand *is* holy ground."

Josh 5:15 Then the Commander of the LORD's army said to Joshua, "Take your sandal off your foot, for the place where you stand *is* holy." And Joshua did so.

Wore out by a long journey.

Josh 9:5 old and patched sandals on their feet, and old garments on themselves; and all the bread of their provision was dry *and* moldy.

Josh 9:13 And these wineskins which we filled *were* new, and see, they are torn; and these our garments and our sandals have become old because of the very long journey."

Of Israel preserved for forty years, while journeying in the wilderness.

Deut 29:5 And I have led you forty years in the wilderness. Your clothes have not worn out on you, and your sandals have not worn out on your feet.

Often given as bribes.

Amos 2:6 Thus says the LORD: "For three transgressions of Israel, and for four, I will not turn away its *punishment*, Because they sell the righteous for silver, And the poor for a pair of sandals.

Amos 8:6 That we may buy the poor for silver, And the needy for a pair of sandals— Even sell the bad wheat?"

Customs connected with,

A man who refused to marry a deceased brother's wife disgraced by pulling off his shoes.

Deut 25:9–10 then his brother's wife shall come to him in the presence of the elders, remove his sandal from his foot, spit in his face, and answer and say, 'So shall it be done to the man who will not build up his brother's house.' **10** And his name shall be called in Israel, 'The house of him who had his sandal removed.'

The right of redemption resigned by a man's giving one of his shoes to the next of kin.

Ruth 4:7–8 Now this *was the custom* in former times in Israel concerning redeeming and exchanging, to confirm anything: one man took off his sandal and gave *it* to the other, and this *was* a confirmation in Israel. **8** Therefore the close relative said to Boaz, "Buy *it* for yourself." So he took off his sandal.

The apostles prohibited from taking more than ones they had on.

Matt 10:10 nor bag for *your* journey, nor two tunics, nor sandals, nor staffs; for a worker is worthy of his food.

Mark 6:9 but to wear sandals, and not to put on two tunics.

Luke 10:4 Carry neither money bag, knapsack, nor sandals; and greet no one along the road.

Illustrative of

The preparation of the gospel.

Eph 6:15 and having shod your feet with the preparation of the gospel of peace;

The beauty conferred on believers.

Song 7:1 How beautiful are your feet in sandals, O prince's daughter! The curves of your thighs *are* like jewels, The work of the hands of a skillful workman.

Luke 15:22 "But the father said to his servants, 'Bring out the best robe and put *it* on him, and put a ring on his hand and sandals on his feet.

(Having blood on) being engaged in war and slaughter.

1 Kin 2:5 "Moreover you know also what Joab the son of Zeruiah did to me, *and* what he did to the two commanders of the armies of Israel, to Abner the son of Ner and Amasa the son of Jether, whom he killed. And he shed the blood of war in peacetime, and put the blood of war on his belt that *was* around his waist, and on his sandals that *were* on his feet.

(Taken off) an ignominious and servile condition.

Is 47:2 Take the millstones and grind meal. Remove your veil, Take off the skirt, Uncover the thigh, Pass through the rivers.

Jer 2:25 Withhold your foot from being unshod, and your throat from thirst. But you said, 'There is no hope. No! For I have loved aliens, and after them I will go.'

(Thrown over a place) subjection.

Ps 60:8 Moab *is* My washpot; Over Edom I will cast My shoe; Philistia, shout in triumph because of Me."

Ps 108:9 Moab *is* My washpot; Over Edom I will cast My shoe; Over Philistia I will triumph."

SICKNESS

Sent by God.

Deut 28:59–61 then the LORD will bring upon you and your descendants extraordinary plagues—great and prolonged plagues—and serious and prolonged sicknesses. **60** Moreover He will bring back on you all the diseases of Egypt, of which you were afraid, and they shall cling to you. **61** Also every sickness and every plague, which *is* not written in this Book of the Law, will the LORD bring upon you until you are destroyed.

Deut 32:39 'Now see that I, *even* I, *am* He, And *there is* no God besides Me; I kill and I make alive; I wound and I heal; Nor *is there any* who can deliver from My hand.

2 Sam 12:15 Then Nathan departed to his house. And the LORD struck the child that Uriah's wife bore to David, and it became ill.

Acts 12:23 Then immediately an angel of the Lord struck him, because he did not give glory to God. And he was eaten by worms and died.

The devil sometimes permitted to inflict.

Job 2:6–7 And the LORD said to Satan, "Behold, he *is* in your hand, but spare his life." **7** So Satan went out from the presence of the LORD, and struck Job with painful boils from the sole of his foot to the crown of his head.

Luke 9:39 And behold, a spirit seizes him, and he suddenly cries out; it convulses him so that he foams *at the mouth;* and it departs from him with great difficulty, bruising him.

Luke 13:16 So ought not this woman, being a daughter of Abraham, whom Satan has bound—think of it—for eighteen years, be loosed from this bond on the Sabbath?"

Often brought on by intemperance.

Hos 7:5 In the day of our king Princes have made *him* sick, inflamed with wine; He stretched out his hand with scoffers.

Sometimes sent as a punishment of sin.

Lev 26:14–16 'But if you do not obey Me, and do not observe all these commandments, **15** and if you despise My statutes, or if your soul abhors My judgments, so that you do not perform all My commandments, *but* break My covenant, **16** I also will do this to you: I will even appoint terror over you, wasting disease and fever which shall consume the eyes and cause sorrow of heart. And you shall sow your seed in vain, for your enemies shall eat it.

2 Chr 21:12–15 And a letter came to him from Elijah the prophet, saying, Thus says the LORD God of your father David: Because you have not walked in the ways of Jehoshaphat your father, or in the ways of Asa king of Judah, **13** but have walked in the way of

the kings of Israel, and have made Judah and the inhabitants of Jerusalem to play the harlot like the harlotry of the house of Ahab, and also have killed your brothers, those of your father's household, *who were* better than yourself, **14** behold, the LORD will strike your people with a serious affliction—your children, your wives, and all your possessions; **15** and you *will become* very sick with a disease of your intestines, until your intestines come out by reason of the sickness, day by day.

1 Cor 11:30 For this reason many *are* weak and sick among you, and many sleep.

One of God's four harsh judgments on a guilty land.

Ezek 14:19–21 "Or *if* I send a pestilence into that land and pour out My fury on it in blood, and cut off from it man and beast, **20** even *though* Noah, Daniel, and Job *were* in it, *as* I live," says the Lord GOD, "they would deliver neither son nor daughter; they would deliver *only* themselves by their righteousness." **21** For thus says the Lord GOD: "How much more it shall be when I send My four severe judgments on Jerusalem—the sword and famine and wild beasts and pestilence—to cut off man and beast from it?

God

Promises to heal.

Ex 23:25 "So you shall serve the LORD your God, and He will bless your bread and your water. And I will take sickness away from the midst of you.

2 Kin 20:5 "Return and tell Hezekiah the leader of My people, 'Thus says the LORD, the God of David your father: "I have heard your prayer, I have seen your tears; surely I will heal you. On the third day you shall go up to the house of the LORD.

Heals.

Deut 32:39 'Now see that I, *even* I, *am* He, And *there is* no God besides Me; I kill and I make alive; I wound and I heal; Nor *is there any* who can deliver from My hand.

Ps 103:3 Who forgives all your iniquities, Who heals all your diseases,

Is 38:5 "Go and tell Hezekiah, 'Thus says the LORD, the God of David your father: "I have heard your prayer, I have seen your tears; surely I will add to your days fifteen years.

Is 38:9 This is the writing of Hezekiah king of Judah, when he had been sick and had recovered from his sickness:

Exhibits His mercy in healing.

Phil 2:27 For indeed he was sick almost unto death; but God had mercy on him, and not only on him but on me also, lest I should have sorrow upon sorrow.

Exhibits His power in healing.

Luke 5:17 Now it happened on a certain day, as He was teaching, that there were Pharisees and teachers of the law sitting by, who had come out of every town of Galilee, Judea, and Jerusalem. And the power of the Lord was *present* to heal them.

Exhibits His love in healing.

Is 38:17 Indeed *it was* for *my own* peace *That* I had great bitterness; But You have lovingly *delivered* my soul from the pit of corruption, For You have cast all my sins behind Your back.

Often manifests saving grace to sinners during.

Job 33:19–24 "Man is also chastened with pain on his bed, And with strong *pain* in many of his bones, **20** So that his life abhors bread, And his soul succulent food. **21** His flesh wastes away from sight, And his bones stick out *which once* were not seen. **22** Yes, his soul draws near the Pit, And his life to the executioners. **23** "If there is a messenger for him, A mediator, one among a thousand, To show man His uprightness, **24** Then He is gracious to him, and says, 'Deliver him from going down to the Pit; I have found a ransom';

Ps 107:17–21 Fools, because of their transgression, And because of their iniquities, were afflicted. **18** Their soul abhorred all manner of food, And they drew near to the gates of death. **19** Then they cried out to the LORD in their trouble, *And* He saved them out of their distresses. **20** He sent His word and healed them, And delivered *them* from their destructions. **21** Oh, that *men* would give thanks to the LORD *for* His goodness, And *for* His wonderful works to the children of men!

Permits believers to be tried by.

Job 2:5–6 But stretch out Your hand now, and touch his bone and his flesh, and he will surely curse You to Your face!" **6** And the LORD said to Satan, "Behold, he *is* in your hand, but spare his life."

Strengthens believers in.

Ps 41:3 The LORD will strengthen him on his bed of illness; You will sustain him on his sickbed.

Comforts believers in.

Ps 41:3 The LORD will strengthen him on his bed of illness; You will sustain him on his sickbed.

Hears the prayers of those in.

Ps 30:2 O LORD my God, I cried out to You, And You healed me.

Ps 107:18–20 Their soul abhorred all manner of food, And they drew near to the gates of death. **19** Then they cried out to the LORD in their trouble, *And* He saved them out of their distresses. **20** He sent His word and healed them, And delivered *them* from their destructions.

Preserves believers in time of.

Ps 91:3–7 Surely He shall deliver you from the snare of the fowler *And* from the perilous pestilence. **4** He shall cover you with His feathers, And under His wings you shall take refuge; His truth *shall be your* shield and buckler. **5** You shall not be afraid of the terror by night, *Nor* of the arrow *that* flies by day, **6** *Nor* of the pestilence *that* walks in darkness, *Nor* of the destruction *that* lays waste at noonday. **7** A thousand may fall at your side, And ten thousand at your right hand; *But* it shall not come near you.

Abandons the wicked to.

Jer 34:17 "Therefore thus says the LORD: 'You have not obeyed Me in proclaiming liberty, every one to his brother and every one to his neighbor. Behold, I proclaim liberty to you,' says the LORD—'to the sword, to pestilence, and to famine! And I will deliver you to trouble among all the kingdoms of the earth.

Persecutes the wicked by.

Jer 29:18 And I will pursue them with the sword, with famine, and with pestilence; and I will deliver them to trouble among all the kingdoms of the earth—to be a curse, an astonishment, a hissing, and a reproach among all the nations where I have driven them,

Healing of, lawful on the Sabbath.

Luke 13:14–16 But the ruler of the synagogue answered with indignation, because Jesus had healed on the Sabbath; and he said to the crowd, "There are six days on which men ought to work; therefore come and be healed on them, and not on the Sabbath day." **15** The Lord then answered him and said, "Hypocrite! Does not each one of you on the Sabbath loose his ox or donkey from the stall, and lead *it* away to water it? **16** So ought not this woman, being a daughter of Abraham, whom Satan has bound—think of it—for eighteen years, be loosed from this bond on the Sabbath?"

Christ compassionate toward those in.

Is 53:4 Surely He has borne our griefs And carried our sorrows; Yet we esteemed Him stricken, Smitten by God, and afflicted.

Matt 8:16–17 When evening had come, they brought to Him many who were demon-possessed. And He cast out the spirits with a word, and healed all who were sick, **17** that it might be fulfilled which was spoken by Isaiah the prophet, saying: *"He Himself took our infirmities And bore our sicknesses."*

Christ healed, by

Being present.

Matt 4:23 And Jesus went about all Galilee, teaching in their synagogues, preaching the gospel of the kingdom, and healing all kinds of sickness and all kinds of disease among the people.

Mark 1:31 So He came and took her by the hand and lifted her up, and immediately the fever left her. And she served them.

Not being present.

Matt 8:13 Then Jesus said to the centurion, "Go your way; and as you have believed, *so* let it be done for you." And his servant was healed that same hour.

Laying on hands.

Mark 6:5 Now He could do no mighty work there, except that He laid His hands on a few sick people and healed *them.*

Luke 13:13 And He laid *His* hands on her, and immediately she was made straight, and glorified God.

A touch.

Matt 8:3 Then Jesus put out *His* hand and touched him, saying, "I am willing; be cleansed." Immediately his leprosy was cleansed.

Someone's touching His garment.

Matt 14:35–36 And when the men of that place recognized Him, they sent out into all that surrounding region, brought to Him all who were sick, **36** and begged Him that they might only touch the hem of His garment. And as many as touched *it* were made perfectly well.

Mark 5:27–34 When she heard about Jesus, she came

behind *Him* in the crowd and touched His garment. **28** For she said, "If only I may touch His clothes, I shall be made well." **29** Immediately the fountain of her blood was dried up, and she felt in *her* body that she was healed of the affliction. **30** And Jesus, immediately knowing in Himself that power had gone out of Him, turned around in the crowd and said, "Who touched My clothes?" **31** But His disciples said to Him, "You see the multitude thronging You, and You say, 'Who touched Me?'" **32** And He looked around to see her who had done this thing. **33** But the woman, fearing and trembling, knowing what had happened to her, came and fell down before Him and told Him the whole truth. **34** And He said to her, "Daughter, your faith has made you well. Go in peace, and be healed of your affliction."

A word.

Matt 8:8 The centurion answered and said, "Lord, I am not worthy that You should come under my roof. But only speak a word, and my servant will be healed.

Matt 8:13 Then Jesus said to the centurion, "Go your way; and as you have believed, *so* let it be done for you." And his servant was healed that same hour.

Faith required in those healed of, by Christ.

Matt 9:28–29 And when He had come into the house, the blind men came to Him. And Jesus said to them, "Do you believe that I am able to do this?" They said to Him, "Yes, Lord." **29** Then He touched their eyes, saying, "According to your faith let it be to you."

Mark 5:34 And He said to her, "Daughter, your faith has made you well. Go in peace, and be healed of your affliction."

Mark 10:52 Then Jesus said to him, "Go your way; your faith has made you well." And immediately he received his sight and followed Jesus on the road.

Often incurable by human means.

Deut 28:27 The LORD will strike you with the boils of Egypt, with tumors, with the scab, and with the itch, from which you cannot be healed.

2 Chr 21:18 After all this the LORD struck him in his intestines with an incurable disease.

The apostles were endued with power to heal.

Matt 10:1 And when He had called His twelve disciples to *Him*, He gave them power *over* unclean spirits, to cast them out, and to heal all kinds of sickness and all kinds of disease.

Mark 16:18 they will take up serpents; and if they drink anything deadly, it will by no means hurt them; they will lay hands on the sick, and they will recover."

Mark 16:20 And they went out and preached everywhere, the Lord working with *them* and confirming the word through the accompanying signs. Amen.

The power of healing, a miraculous gift of the early church.

1 Cor 12:9 to another faith by the same Spirit, to another gifts of healings by the same Spirit,

1 Cor 12:30 Do all have gifts of healings? Do all speak with tongues? Do all interpret?

Believers

Acknowledge that it comes from God.

Ps 31:1–8 In You, O LORD, I put my trust; Let me never

be ashamed; Deliver me in Your righteousness. **2** Bow down Your ear to me, Deliver me speedily; Be my rock of refuge, A fortress of defense to save me. **3** For You *are* my rock and my fortress; Therefore, for Your name's sake, Lead me and guide me. **4** Pull me out of the net which they have secretly laid for me, For You *are* my strength. **5** Into Your hand I commit my spirit; You have redeemed me, O LORD God of truth. **6** I have hated those who regard useless idols; But I trust in the LORD. **7** I will be glad and rejoice in Your mercy, For You have considered my trouble; You have known my soul in adversities, **8** And have not shut me up into the hand of the enemy; You have set my feet in a wide place.

Is 38:12 My life span is gone, Taken from me like a shepherd's tent; I have cut off my life like a weaver. He cuts me off from the loom; From day until night You make an end of me.

Is 38:15 "What shall I say? He has both spoken to me, And He Himself has done *it*. I shall walk carefully all my years In the bitterness of my soul.

Are resigned under.

Job 2:10 But he said to her, "You speak as one of the foolish women speaks. Shall we indeed accept good from God, and shall we not accept adversity?" In all this Job did not sin with his lips.

Mourn under, with prayer.

Is 38:14 Like a crane *or* a swallow, so I chattered; I mourned like a dove; My eyes fail *from looking* upward. O LORD, I am oppressed; Undertake for me!

Pray for recovery from.

Is 38:2–3 Then Hezekiah turned his face toward the wall, and prayed to the LORD, **3** and said, "Remember now, O LORD, I pray, how I have walked before You in truth and with a loyal heart, and have done *what is* good in Your sight." And Hezekiah wept bitterly.

Ascribe recovery from, to God.

Ps 103:1–3 Bless the LORD, O my soul; And all that is within me, *bless* His holy name! **2** Bless the LORD, O my soul, And forget not all His benefits: **3** Who forgives all your iniquities, Who heals all your diseases,

Is 38:19–20 The living, the living man, he shall praise You, As I *do* this day; The father shall make known Your truth to the children. **20** "The LORD *was ready* to save me; Therefore we will sing my songs with stringed instruments All the days of our life, in the house of the LORD."

Luke 17:15 And one of them, when he saw that he was healed, returned, and with a loud voice glorified God,

Acts 3:8 So he, leaping up, stood and walked and entered the temple with them—walking, leaping, and praising God.

Feel for others in.

Ps 35:13 But as for me, when they were sick, My clothing *was* sackcloth; I humbled myself with fasting; And my prayer would return to my own heart.

Visit those in.

Matt 25:36 I *was* naked and you clothed Me; I was sick and you visited Me; I was in prison and you came to Me.'

Pray for those afflicted with.

Acts 28:8 And it happened that the father of Publius lay sick of a fever and dysentery. Paul went in to him and prayed, and he laid his hands on him and healed him.

James 5:14–15 Is anyone among you sick? Let him call for the elders of the church, and let them pray over him, anointing him with oil in the name of the Lord. **15** And the prayer of faith will save the sick, and the Lord will raise him up. And if he has committed sins, he will be forgiven.

Visiting those in, an evidence of belonging to Christ.

Matt 25:34 Then the King will say to those on His right hand, 'Come, you blessed of My Father, inherit the kingdom prepared for you from the foundation of the world:

Matt 25:36 I *was* naked and you clothed Me; I was sick and you visited Me; I was in prison and you came to Me.'

Matt 25:40 And the King will answer and say to them, 'Assuredly, I say to you, inasmuch as you did *it* to one of the least of these My brethren, you did *it* to Me.'

God's aid should be sought in.

2 Chr 16:12 And in the thirty-ninth year of his reign, Asa became diseased in his feet, and his malady was severe; yet in his disease he did not seek the LORD, but the physicians.

The wicked

Have much sorrow with.

Eccl 5:17 All his days he also eats in darkness, And *he has* much sorrow and sickness and anger.

Forsake those in.

1 Sam 30:13 Then David said to him, "To whom do you *belong*, and where *are* you from?" And he said, "I *am* a young man from Egypt, servant of an Amalekite; and my master left me behind, because three days ago I fell sick.

Do not visit those in.

Matt 25:43 I was a stranger and you did not take Me in, naked and you did not clothe Me, sick and in prison and you did not visit Me.'

Matt 25:45 Then He will answer them, saying, 'Assuredly, I say to you, inasmuch as you did not do *it* to one of the least of these, you did not do *it* to Me.'

Illustrative of sin.

Lev 13:45–46 "Now the leper on whom the sore *is*, his clothes shall be torn and his head bare; and he shall cover his mustache, and cry, 'Unclean! Unclean!' **46** He shall be unclean. All the days he has the sore he shall be unclean. He *is* unclean, and he shall dwell alone; his dwelling *shall be* outside the camp.

Is 1:5 Why should you be stricken again? You will revolt more and more. The whole head is sick, And the whole heart faints.

Jer 8:22 *Is there* no balm in Gilead, *Is there* no physician there? Why then is there no recovery For the health of the daughter of my people?

Matt 9:12 When Jesus heard *that*, He said to them,

"Those who are well have no need of a physician, but those who are sick.

SIDONIANS, THE

Descended from Sidon, son of Canaan.

Gen 10:15 Canaan begot Sidon his firstborn, and Heth;

1 Chr 1:13 Canaan begot Sidon, his firstborn, and Heth;

Formerly a part of the Phoenician nation.

Matt 15:21–22 Then Jesus went out from there and departed to the region of Tyre and Sidon. **22** And behold, a woman of Canaan came from that region and cried out to Him, saying, "Have mercy on me, O Lord, Son of David! My daughter is severely demon-possessed."

Mark 7:24 From there He arose and went to the region of Tyre and Sidon. And He entered a house and wanted no one to know *it*, but He could not be hidden.

Mark 7:26 The woman was a Greek, a Syro-Phoenician by birth, and she kept asking Him to cast the demon out of her daughter.

Dwelt on the seacoast.

Luke 6:17 And He came down with them and stood on a level place with a crowd of His disciples and a great multitude of people from all Judea and Jerusalem, and from the seacoast of Tyre and Sidon, who came to hear Him and be healed of their diseases,

Acts 27:3 And the next *day* we landed at Sidon. And Julius treated Paul kindly and gave *him* liberty to go to his friends and receive care.

Cities of, mentioned

Sidon.

Josh 11:8 And the LORD delivered them into the hand of Israel, who defeated them and chased them to Greater Sidon, to the Brook Misrephoth, and to the Valley of Mizpah eastward; they attacked them until they left none of them remaining.

Josh 19:28 including Ebron, Rehob, Hammon, and Kanah, as far as Greater Sidon.

Zarephath.

1 Kin 17:9 "Arise, go to Zarephath, which *belongs* to Sidon, and dwell there. See, I have commanded a widow there to provide for you."

Luke 4:26 but to none of them was Elijah sent except to Zarephath, *in the region* of Sidon, to a woman *who was* a widow.

Governed by kings.

Jer 25:22 all the kings of Tyre, all the kings of Sidon, and the kings of the coastlands which *are* across the sea;

Jer 27:3 and send them to the king of Edom, the king of Moab, the king of the Ammonites, the king of Tyre, and the king of Sidon, by the hand of the messengers who come to Jerusalem to Zedekiah king of Judah.

Character of,

Quiet and secure.

Judg 18:7 So the five men departed and went to Laish. They saw the people who *were* there, how they dwelt safely, in the manner of the Sidonians, quiet and secure. *There were* no rulers in the land who might put *them* to shame for anything. They *were* far from the Sidonians, and they had no ties with anyone.

Idolatrous.

1 Kin 11:5 For Solomon went after Ashtoreth the goddess of the Sidonians, and after Milcom the abomination of the Ammonites.

Superstitious.

Jer 27:3 and send them to the king of Edom, the king of Moab, the king of the Ammonites, the king of Tyre, and the king of Sidon, by the hand of the messengers who come to Jerusalem to Zedekiah king of Judah.

Jer 27:9 Therefore do not listen to your prophets, your diviners, your dreamers, your soothsayers, or your sorcerers, who speak to you, saying, "You shall not serve the king of Babylon."

Wicked and impenitent.

Matt 11:21–22 "Woe to you, Chorazin! Woe to you, Bethsaida! For if the mighty works which were done in you had been done in Tyre and Sidon, they would have repented long ago in sackcloth and ashes. 22 But I say to you, it will be more tolerable for Tyre and Sidon in the day of judgment than for you.

Engaged in extensive commerce.

Is 23:2 Be still, you inhabitants of the coastland, You merchants of Sidon, Whom those who cross the sea have filled.

Were skillful sailors.

Ezek 27:8 "Inhabitants of Sidon and Arvad were your oarsmen; Your wise men, O Tyre, were in you; They became your pilots.

Supplied the Jews with timber.

1 Chr 22:4 and cedar trees in abundance; for the Sidonians and those from Tyre brought much cedar wood to David.

Ezra 3:7 They also gave money to the masons and the carpenters, and food, drink, and oil to the people of Sidon and Tyre to bring cedar logs from Lebanon to the sea, to Joppa, according to the permission which they had from Cyrus king of Persia.

Were supplied from Judea with provisions.

Ezek 27:17 Judah and the land of Israel *were* your traders. They traded for your merchandise wheat of Minnith, millet, honey, oil, and balm.

Acts 12:20 Now Herod had been very angry with the people of Tyre and Sidon; but they came to him with one accord, and having made Blastus the king's personal aide their friend, they asked for peace, because their country was supplied with food by the king's *country.*

Territory of,

Bordered on the land of Canaan.

Gen 10:19 And the border of the Canaanites was from Sidon as you go toward Gerar, as far as Gaza; then as you go toward Sodom, Gomorrah, Admah, and Zeboiim, as far as Lasha.

Given by God to Israel.

Gen 49:13 "Zebulun shall dwell by the haven of the sea; He *shall become* a haven for ships, And his border shall adjoin Sidon.

Josh 13:6 all the inhabitants of the mountains from Lebanon as far as the Brook Misrephoth, *and* all the Sidonians—them I will drive out from before the children of Israel; only divide it by lot to Israel as an inheritance, as I have commanded you.

Allotted to the tribe of Asher.

Josh 19:24 The fifth lot came out for the tribe of the children of Asher according to their families.

Josh 19:28 including Ebron, Rehob, Hammon, and Kanah, as far as Greater Sidon.

Visited by our Lord.

Matt 15:21 Then Jesus went out from there and departed to the region of Tyre and Sidon.

Israel unable to expel.

Judg 1:31 Nor did Asher drive out the inhabitants of Acco or the inhabitants of Sidon, or of Ahlab, Achzib, Helbah, Aphik, or Rehob.

Judg 3:3 *namely,* five lords of the Philistines, all the Canaanites, the Sidonians, and the Hivites who dwelt in Mount Lebanon, from Mount Baal Hermon to the entrance of Hamath.

Hostile and oppressive to God's people.

Judg 10:12 Also the Sidonians and Amalekites and Maonites oppressed you; and you cried out to Me, and I delivered you from their hand.

Ezek 28:22 and say, 'Thus says the Lord GOD: "Behold, I *am* against you, O Sidon; I will be glorified in your midst; And they shall know that I *am* the LORD, When I execute judgments in her and am hallowed in her.

Ezek 28:24 "And there shall no longer be a pricking brier or a painful thorn for the house of Israel from among all *who are* around them, who despise them. Then they shall know that I *am* the Lord GOD."

Joel 3:5–6 Because you have taken My silver and My gold, And have carried into your temples My prized possessions. 6 Also the people of Judah and the people of Jerusalem You have sold to the Greeks, That you may remove them far from their borders.

Solomon intermarried with.

1 Kin 11:1 But King Solomon loved many foreign women, as well as the daughter of Pharaoh: women of the Moabites, Ammonites, Edomites, Sidonians, *and* Hittites—

Ahab intermarried with.

1 Kin 16:31 And it came to pass, as though it had been a trivial thing for him to walk in the sins of Jeroboam the son of Nebat, that he took as wife Jezebel the daughter of Ethbaal, king of the Sidonians; and he went and served Baal and worshiped him.

Israel followed the idolatry of.

Judg 10:6 Then the children of Israel again did evil in the sight of the LORD, and served the Baals and the Ashtoreths, the gods of Syria, the gods of Sidon, the gods of Moab, the gods of the people of Ammon, and the gods of the Philistines; and they forsook the LORD and did not serve Him.

1 Kin 11:33 because they have forsaken Me, and worshiped Ashtoreth the goddess of the Sidonians, Chemosh the god of the Moabites, and Milcom the god of the people of Ammon, and have not walked in My ways to do *what is* right in My eyes and *keep* My statutes and My judgments, as *did* his father David.

Predictions respecting,

Territory of, to be given to Nebuchadnezzar, king of Babylon.

Jer 27:3 and send them to the king of Edom, the king of Moab, the king of the Ammonites, the king of Tyre, and the king of Sidon, by the hand of the messengers who come to Jerusalem to Zedekiah king of Judah.

Jer 27:6 And now I have given all these lands into the hand of Nebuchadnezzar the king of Babylon, My servant; and the beasts of the field I have also given him to serve him.

Partaking with the other nations of God's judgments.

Jer 25:22–28 all the kings of Tyre, all the kings of Sidon, and the kings of the coastlands which *are* across the sea; **23** Dedan, Tema, Buz, and all *who are* in the farthest corners; **24** all the kings of Arabia and all the kings of the mixed multitude who dwell in the desert; **25** all the kings of Zimri, all the kings of Elam, and all the kings of the Medes; **26** all the kings of the north, far and near, one with another; and all the kingdoms of the world which *are* on the face of the earth. Also the king of Sheshach shall drink after them. **27** "Therefore you shall say to them, 'Thus says the LORD of hosts, the God of Israel: "Drink, be drunk, and vomit! Fall and rise no more, because of the sword which I will send among you." ' **28** And it shall be, if they refuse to take the cup from your hand to drink, then you shall say to them, 'Thus says the LORD of hosts: "You shall certainly drink!

Ezek 32:20 "They shall fall in the midst of *those* slain by the sword; She is delivered to the sword, Drawing her and all her multitudes.

All their helpers to be cut off.

Jer 47:4 Because of the day that comes to plunder all the Philistines, To cut off from Tyre and Sidon every helper who remains; For the LORD shall plunder the Philistines, The remnant of the country of Caphtor.

That God should be glorified in the judgments upon them.

Ezek 28:21–23 "Son of man, set your face toward Sidon, and prophesy against her, **22** and say, 'Thus says the Lord GOD: "Behold, I *am* against you, O Sidon; I will be glorified in your midst; And they shall know that I *am* the LORD, When I execute judgments in her and am hallowed in her. **23** For I will send pestilence upon her, And blood in her streets; The wounded shall be judged in her midst By the sword against her on every side; Then they shall know that I *am* the LORD.

Their spoiling and oppression of the Jews to be fully recompensed.

Joel 3:4 "Indeed, what have you to do with Me, O Tyre and Sidon, and all the coasts of Philistia? Will you retaliate against Me? But if you retaliate against Me, Swiftly and speedily I will return your retaliation upon your own head;

Joel 3:8 I will sell your sons and your daughters Into the hand of the people of Judah, And they will sell them to the Sabeans, To a people far off; For the LORD has spoken."

Many of, attended Christ's ministry.

Mark 3:8 and Jerusalem and Idumea and beyond the Jordan; and those from Tyre and Sidon, a great multitude, when they heard how many things He was doing, came to Him.

Having revolted from Herod, were obliged to propitiate him.

Acts 12:20 Now Herod had been very angry with the people of Tyre and Sidon; but they came to him with one accord, and having made Blastus the king's personal aide their friend, they asked for peace, because their country was supplied with food by the king's *country.*

SIEGES

Fenced cities subjected to.

2 Kin 18:13 And in the fourteenth year of King Hezekiah, Sennacherib king of Assyria came up against all the fortified cities of Judah and took them.

Threatened as a punishment.

Deut 28:52 "They shall besiege you at all your gates until your high and fortified walls, in which you trust, come down throughout all your land; and they shall besiege you at all your gates throughout all your land which the LORD your God has given you.

Described as

Encamping against.

2 Sam 12:28 Now therefore, gather the rest of the people together and encamp against the city and take it, lest I take the city and it be called after my name."

2 Kin 25:1 Now it came to pass in the ninth year of his reign, in the tenth month, on the tenth *day* of the month, *that* Nebuchadnezzar king of Babylon and all his army came against Jerusalem and encamped against it; and they built a siege wall against it all around.

2 Chr 32:1 After these deeds of faithfulness, Sennacherib king of Assyria came and entered Judah; he encamped against the fortified cities, thinking to win them over to himself.

Surrounding with armies.

2 Kin 6:14 Therefore he sent horses and chariots and a great army there, and they came by night and surrounded the city.

Jer 51:2 And I will send winnowers to Babylon, Who shall winnow her and empty her land. For in the day of doom They shall be against her all around.

Luke 21:20 "But when you see Jerusalem surrounded by armies, then know that its desolation is near.

Setting in array against.

Jer 50:9 For behold, I will raise and cause to come up against Babylon An assembly of great nations from the north country, And they shall array themselves against her; From there she shall be captured. Their arrows *shall be* like *those* of an expert warrior; None shall return in vain.

Often lasted for a long time.

2 Kin 17:5 Now the king of Assyria went throughout all the land, and went up to Samaria and besieged it for three years.

Great noise and tumult of, alluded to.

Joel 2:5 With a noise like chariots Over mountaintops they leap, Like the noise of a flaming fire that devours the stubble, Like a strong people set in battle array.

Those engaged in,

Built camps and mounds.

Ezek 4:2 Lay siege against it, build a siege wall against it, and heap up a mound against it; set camps against it also, and place battering rams against it all around.

Ezek 26:8 He will slay with the sword your daughter *villages* in the fields; he will heap up a siege mound against you, build a wall against you, and raise a defense against you.

Built an embankment around the city.

Luke 19:43 For days will come upon you when your enemies will build an embankment around you, surround you and close you in on every side,

Faced the city on every side.

Ezek 23:24 And they shall come against you With chariots, wagons, and war-horses, With a horde of people. They shall array against you Buckler, shield, and helmet all around. 'I will delegate judgment to them, And they shall judge you according to their judgments.

Cut off all supplies.

2 Kin 19:24 I have dug and drunk strange water, And with the soles of my feet I have dried up All the brooks of defense."

Frequently laid ambushes.

Judg 9:34 So Abimelech and all the people who *were* with him rose by night, and lay in wait against Shechem in four companies.

Called upon the city to surrender.

1 Kin 20:2–3 Then he sent messengers into the city to Ahab king of Israel, and said to him, "Thus says Ben-Hadad: 3 'Your silver and your gold *are* mine; your loveliest wives and children are mine.' "

2 Kin 18:18 And when they had called to the king, Eliakim the son of Hilkiah, who *was* over the household, Shebna the scribe, and Joah the son of Asaph, the recorder, came out to them.

2 Kin 18:20 You speak of *having* plans and power for war; but *they are* mere words. And in whom do you trust, that you rebel against me?

Employed battering rams against the walls.

Ezek 4:2 Lay siege against it, build a siege wall against it, and heap up a mound against it; set camps against it also, and place battering rams against it all around.

Ezek 26:9 He will direct his battering rams against your walls, and with his axes he will break down your towers.

Shot arrows and other missiles into the city.

2 Kin 19:32 "Therefore thus says the LORD concerning the king of Assyria: 'He shall not come into this city, Nor shoot an arrow there, Nor come before it with shield, Nor build a siege mound against it.

Often suffered much during.

Ezek 29:18 "Son of man, Nebuchadnezzar king of Babylon caused his army to labor strenuously against Tyre; every head *was* made bald, and every shoulder rubbed raw; yet neither he nor his army received wages from Tyre, for the labor which they expended on it.

The Jews forbidden to cut down fruit trees for the purpose of.

Deut 20:19–20 "When you besiege a city for a long time, while making war against it to take it, you shall not destroy its trees by wielding an ax against them; if you can eat of them, do not cut them down to use in the siege, for the tree of the field *is* man's *food.* 20 Only the trees which you know *are* not trees for food you may destroy and cut down, to build siegeworks against the city that makes war with you, until it is subdued.

Extreme difficulty of taking cities by, alluded to.

Prov 18:19 A brother offended *is harder to win* than a strong city, And contentions *are* like the bars of a castle.

Cities subjected to,

Were repaired and newly fortified beforehand.

2 Chr 32:5 And he strengthened himself, built up all the wall that was broken, raised *it* up to the towers, and *built* another wall outside; also he repaired the Millo in the City of David, and made weapons and shields in abundance.

Is 22:9–10 You also saw the damage to the city of David, That it was great; And you gathered together the waters of the lower pool. 10 You numbered the houses of Jerusalem, And the houses you broke down To fortify the wall.

Nah 3:14 Draw your water for the siege! Fortify your strongholds! Go into the clay and tread the mortar! Make strong the brick kiln!

Were supplied with water beforehand.

Nah 3:14 Draw your water for the siege! Fortify your strongholds! Go into the clay and tread the mortar! Make strong the brick kiln!

The inhabitants, cut off outside water beforehand.

2 Chr 32:3–4 he consulted with his leaders and commanders to stop the water from the springs which *were* outside the city; and they helped him. 4 Thus many people gathered together who stopped all the springs and the brook that ran through the land, saying, "Why should the kings of Assyria come and find much water?"

Were securely shut up.

Josh 6:1 Now Jericho was securely shut up because of the children of Israel; none went out, and none came in.

Walls of, defended by the inhabitants.

2 Sam 11:20–21 if it happens that the king's wrath rises, and he says to you: 'Why did you approach so near to the city when you fought? Did you not know that they would shoot from the wall? 21 Who struck Abimelech the son of Jerubbesheth? Was it not a woman who cast a piece of a millstone on him from the wall, so that he died in Thebez? Why did you go near the wall?'—then you shall say, 'Your servant Uriah the Hittite is dead also.' "

2 Kin 18:26 Then Eliakim the son of Hilkiah, Shebna, and Joah said to *the* Rabshakeh, "Please speak to your servants in Aramaic, for we understand *it;* and do not speak to us in Hebrew in the hearing of the people who *are* on the wall."

2 Chr 32:18 Then they called out with a loud voice in

Hebrew to the people of Jerusalem who *were* on the wall, to frighten them and trouble them, that they might take the city.

Sometimes used ambushes.

Jer 51:12 Set up the standard on the walls of Babylon; Make the guard strong, Set up the watchmen, Prepare the ambushes. For the LORD has both devised and done What He spoke against the inhabitants of Babylon.

Often suffered from famine.

2 Kin 6:26–29 Then, as the king of Israel was passing by on the wall, a woman cried out to him, saying, "Help, my lord, O king!" **27** And he said, "If the LORD does not help you, where can I find help for you? From the threshing floor or from the winepress?" **28** Then the king said to her, "What is troubling you?" And she answered, "This woman said to me, 'Give your son, that we may eat him today, and we will eat my son tomorrow.' **29** So we boiled my son, and ate him. And I said to her on the next day, 'Give your son, that we may eat him'; but she has hidden her son."

2 Kin 25:3 By the ninth *day* of the *fourth* month the famine had become so severe in the city that there was no food for the people of the land.

Ezek 6:12 He who is far off shall die by the pestilence, he who is near shall fall by the sword, and he who remains and is besieged shall die by the famine. Thus will I spend My fury upon them.

Often suffered from pestilence.

Jer 21:6 I will strike the inhabitants of this city, both man and beast; they shall die of a great pestilence.

Jer 32:24 'Look, the siege mounds! They have come to the city to take it; and the city has been given into the hand of the Chaldeans who fight against it, because of the sword and famine and pestilence. What You have spoken has happened; there You see *it*!

Often demanded terms of peace.

1 Sam 11:1–3 Then Nahash the Ammonite came up and encamped against Jabesh Gilead; and all the men of Jabesh said to Nahash, "Make a covenant with us, and we will serve you." **2** And Nahash the Ammonite answered them, "On this *condition* I will make *a covenant* with you, that I may put out all your right eyes, and bring reproach on all Israel." **3** Then the elders of Jabesh said to him, "Hold off for seven days, that we may send messengers to all the territory of Israel. And then, if *there is* no one to save us, we will come out to you."

Frequently taken by ambush.

Judg 9:43–44 So he took his people, divided them into three companies, and lay in wait in the field. And he looked, and there were the people, coming out of the city; and he rose against them and attacked them. **44** Then Abimelech and the company that *was* with him rushed forward and stood at the entrance of the gate of the city; and the *other* two companies rushed upon all who *were* in the fields and killed them.

Frequently taken by assault.

Josh 10:35 They took it on that day and struck it with the edge of the sword; all the people who *were* in it

he utterly destroyed that day, according to all that he had done to Lachish.

2 Sam 12:29 So David gathered all the people together and went to Rabbah, fought against it, and took it.

Frequently helped by allies.

1 Sam 11:11 So it was, on the next day, that Saul put the people in three companies; and they came into the midst of the camp in the morning watch, and killed Ammonites until the heat of the day. And it happened that those who survived were scattered, so that no two of them were left together.

1 Sam 23:5 And David and his men went to Keilah and fought with the Philistines, struck them with a mighty blow, and took away their livestock. So David saved the inhabitants of Keilah.

Inhabitants of, exhorted to be courageous.

2 Chr 32:6–8 Then he set military captains over the people, gathered them together to him in the open square of the city gate, and gave them encouragement, saying, **7** "Be strong and courageous; do not be afraid nor dismayed before the king of Assyria, nor before all the multitude that *is* with him; for *there are* more with us than with him. **8** With him *is* an arm of flesh; but with us *is* the LORD our God, to help us and to fight our battles." And the people were strengthened by the words of Hezekiah king of Judah.

Cities taken by,

Given up to pillage.

Jer 50:26–27 Come against her from the farthest border; Open her storehouses; Cast her up as heaps of ruins, And destroy her utterly; Let nothing of her be left. **27** Slay all her bulls, Let them go down to the slaughter. Woe to them! For their day has come, the time of their punishment.

Inhabitants of, often put to the sword.

Josh 10:28 On that day Joshua took Makkedah, and struck it and its king with the edge of the sword. He utterly destroyed them—all the people who *were* in it. He let none remain. He also did to the king of Makkedah as he had done to the king of Jericho.

Josh 10:30 And the LORD also delivered it and its king into the hand of Israel; he struck it and all the people who *were* in it with the edge of the sword. He let none remain in it, but did to its king as he had done to the king of Jericho.

Josh 10:32 And the LORD delivered Lachish into the hand of Israel, who took it on the second day, and struck it and all the people who *were* in it with the edge of the sword, according to all that he had done to Libnah.

Josh 10:35 They took it on that day and struck it with the edge of the sword; all the people who *were* in it he utterly destroyed that day, according to all that he had done to Lachish.

Jer 50:30 Therefore her young men shall fall in the streets, And all her men of war shall be cut off in that day," says the LORD.

Frequently broken down.

Judg 9:45 So Abimelech fought against the city all that day; he took the city and killed the people who *were* in it; and he demolished the city and sowed it with salt.

Frequently destroyed by fire.

Josh 8:19 So *those in* ambush arose quickly out of their place; they ran as soon as he had stretched out his hand, and they entered the city and took it, and hurried to set the city on fire.

Sometimes sown with salt.

Judg 9:45 So Abimelech fought against the city all that day; he took the city and killed the people who *were* in it; and he demolished the city and sowed it with salt.

Sometimes named after the captor.

2 Sam 12:28 Now therefore, gather the rest of the people together and encamp against the city and take it, lest I take the city and it be called after my name."

Mentioned in Scripture

Jericho. **Josh 6:2–20**

Ai.

Josh 7:2–4 Now Joshua sent men from Jericho to Ai, which *is* beside Beth Aven, on the east side of Bethel, and spoke to them, saying, "Go up and spy out the country." So the men went up and spied out Ai. 3 And they returned to Joshua and said to him, "Do not let all the people go up, but let about two or three thousand men go up and attack Ai. Do not weary all the people there, for *the people of Ai are* few." 4 So about three thousand men went up there from the people, but they fled before the men of Ai.

Cf. **Josh 8:1–19**

Makkedah.

Josh 10:28 On that day Joshua took Makkedah, and struck it and its king with the edge of the sword. He utterly destroyed them—all the people who *were* in it. He let none remain. He also did to the king of Makkedah as he had done to the king of Jericho.

Libnah.

Josh 10:29–30 Then Joshua passed from Makkedah, and all Israel with him, to Libnah; and they fought against Libnah. 30 And the LORD also delivered it and its king into the hand of Israel; he struck it and all the people who *were* in it with the edge of the sword. He let none remain in it, but did to its king as he had done to the king of Jericho.

Lachish.

Josh 10:31–32 Then Joshua passed from Libnah, and all Israel with him, to Lachish; and they encamped against it and fought against it. 32 And the LORD delivered Lachish into the hand of Israel, who took it on the second day, and struck it and all the people who *were* in it with the edge of the sword, according to all that he had done to Libnah.

Eglon.

Josh 10:34–35 From Lachish Joshua passed to Eglon, and all Israel with him; and they encamped against it and fought against it. 35 They took it on that day and struck it with the edge of the sword; all the people who *were* in it he utterly destroyed that day, according to all that he had done to Lachish.

Hebron.

Josh 10:36–37 So Joshua went up from Eglon, and all Israel with him, to Hebron; and they fought against it. 37 And they took it and struck it with the edge of the

sword—its king, all its cities, and all the people who *were* in it; he left none remaining, according to all that he had done to Eglon, but utterly destroyed it and all the people who *were* in it.

Debir.

Josh 10:38–39 Then Joshua returned, and all Israel with him, to Debir; and they fought against it. 39 And he took it and its king and all its cities; they struck them with the edge of the sword and utterly destroyed all the people who *were* in it. He left none remaining; as he had done to Hebron, so he did to Debir and its king, as he had done also to Libnah and its king.

Shechem.

Judg 9:34 So Abimelech and all the people who *were* with him rose by night, and lay in wait against Shechem in four companies.

Judg 9:45 So Abimelech fought against the city all that day; he took the city and killed the people who *were* in it; and he demolished the city and sowed it with salt.

Thebez.

Judg 9:50 Then Abimelech went to Thebez, and he encamped against Thebez and took it.

Jabesh Gilead.

1 Sam 11:1 Then Nahash the Ammonite came up and encamped against Jabesh Gilead; and all the men of Jabesh said to Nahash, "Make a covenant with us, and we will serve you."

Keilah.

1 Sam 23:1 Then they told David, saying, "Look, the Philistines are fighting against Keilah, and they are robbing the threshing floors."

Ziklag.

1 Sam 30:1–2 Now it happened, when David and his men came to Ziklag, on the third day, that the Amalekites had invaded the South and Ziklag, attacked Ziklag and burned it with fire, 2 and had taken captive the women and those who *were* there, from small to great; they did not kill anyone, but carried *them* away and went their way.

Rabbah.

2 Sam 11:1 It happened in the spring of the year, at the time when kings go out *to battle,* that David sent Joab and his servants with him, and all Israel; and they destroyed the people of Ammon and besieged Rabbah. But David remained at Jerusalem.

2 Sam 12:26–29 Now Joab fought against Rabbah of the people of Ammon, and took the royal city. 27 And Joab sent messengers to David, and said, "I have fought against Rabbah, and I have taken the city's water *supply.* 28 Now therefore, gather the rest of the people together and encamp against the city and take it, lest I take the city and it be called after my name." 29 So David gathered all the people together and went to Rabbah, fought against it, and took it.

Gibbethon.

1 Kin 16:15 In the twenty-seventh year of Asa king of Judah, Zimri had reigned in Tirzah seven days. And the people *were* encamped against Gibbethon, which *belonged* to the Philistines.

Tirzah.

1 Kin 16:17 Then Omri and all Israel with him went up from Gibbethon, and they besieged Tirzah.

Samaria.

1 Kin 20:1 Now Ben-Hadad the king of Syria gathered all his forces together; thirty-two kings *were* with him, with horses and chariots. And he went up and besieged Samaria, and made war against it.

2 Kin 6:24 And it happened after this that Ben-Hadad king of Syria gathered all his army, and went up and besieged Samaria.

2 Kin 17:5 Now the king of Assyria went throughout all the land, and went up to Samaria and besieged it for three years.

Ramoth Gilead.

1 Kin 22:4 So he said to Jehoshaphat, "Will you go with me to fight at Ramoth Gilead?" Jehoshaphat said to the king of Israel, "I *am* as you *are*, my people as your people, my horses as your horses."

1 Kin 22:29 So the king of Israel and Jehoshaphat the king of Judah went up to Ramoth Gilead.

Cities of Israel in Galilee.

2 Kin 15:29 In the days of Pekah king of Israel, Tiglath-Pileser king of Assyria came and took Ijon, Abel Beth Maachah, Janoah, Kedesh, Hazor, Gilead, and Galilee, all the land of Naphtali; and he carried them captive to Assyria.

Cities of Judah.

2 Kin 18:13 And in the fourteenth year of King Hezekiah, Sennacherib king of Assyria came up against all the fortified cities of Judah and took them.

Jerusalem.

2 Kin 24:10–11 At that time the servants of Nebuchadnezzar king of Babylon came up against Jerusalem, and the city was besieged. **11** And Nebuchadnezzar king of Babylon came against the city, as his servants were besieging it.

2 Kin 25:1–2 Now it came to pass in the ninth year of his reign, in the tenth month, on the tenth *day* of the month, *that* Nebuchadnezzar king of Babylon and all his army came against Jerusalem and encamped against it; and they built a siege wall against it all around. **2** So the city was besieged until the eleventh year of King Zedekiah.

Illustrative of

The omnipresence of God.

Ps 139:5 You have hedged me behind and before, And laid Your hand upon me.

The judgments of God.

Mic 5:1 Now gather yourself in troops, O daughter of troops; He has laid siege against us; They will strike the judge of Israel with a rod on the cheek.

Zion in her affliction.

Is 1:8 So the daughter of Zion is left as a booth in a vineyard, As a hut in a garden of cucumbers, As a besieged city.

SIGNS AND WONDERS

Given by prophets.

Deut 13:2 and the sign or the wonder comes to pass, of which he spoke to you, saying, 'Let us go after other gods'—which you have not known—'and let us serve them,'

Performed by false prophets.

Matt 7:22 Many will say to Me in that day, 'Lord, Lord, have we not prophesied in Your name, cast out demons in Your name, and done many wonders in Your name?'

Mark 13:22 For false christs and false prophets will rise and show signs and wonders to deceive, if possible, even the elect.

Promised to apostolic community by Christ.

Mark 16:17–18 And these signs will follow those who believe: In My name they will cast out demons; they will speak with new tongues; **18** they will take up serpents; and if they drink anything deadly, it will by no means hurt them; they will lay hands on the sick, and they will recover."

A manifestation of Christ's glory.

John 2:11 This beginning of signs Jesus did in Cana of Galilee, and manifested His glory; and His disciples believed in Him.

The need to see, displays one's unbelief.

John 4:48 Then Jesus said to him, "Unless you *people* see signs and wonders, you will by no means believe."

Of Jesus

Provoked curiosity among the people.

John 6:2 Then a great multitude followed Him, because they saw His signs which He performed on those who were diseased.

Validated Him as the Messiah.

Acts 2:22 "Men of Israel, hear these words: Jesus of Nazareth, a Man attested by God to you by miracles, wonders, and signs which God did through Him in your midst, as you yourselves also know—

Heb 2:4 God also bearing witness both with signs and wonders, with various miracles, and gifts of the Holy Spirit, according to His own will?

By the apostles, to authenticate them as messengers of God.

Acts 2:18–19 And on My menservants and on My maidservants I will pour out My Spirit in those days; And they shall prophesy. **19** I will show wonders in heaven above And signs in the earth beneath: Blood and fire and vapor of smoke.

2 Cor 12:12 Truly the signs of an apostle were accomplished among you with all perseverance, in signs and wonders and mighty deeds.

Heb 2:4 God also bearing witness both with signs and wonders, with various miracles, and gifts of the Holy Spirit, according to His own will?

Jews requested, but still didn't believe in Christ.

Matt 12:38–44 Then some of the scribes and Pharisees answered, saying, "Teacher, we want to see a sign from You." **39** But He answered and said to them, "An evil and adulterous generation seeks after a sign, and no sign will be given to it except the sign of the prophet Jonah. **40** For as Jonah was three days and three nights in the belly of the great fish, so will the Son of Man be three days and three nights in the heart of the earth. **41** The men of Nineveh will rise up in the judgment with this generation and condemn it, because they repented at the preaching of Jonah; and indeed a greater than Jonah *is* here. **42** The queen of the South will rise up in the judgment with this generation and condemn it, for she came from the ends of the earth to hear the wisdom of Solomon; and indeed a greater than Solomon *is* here. **43** "When an unclean spirit goes out of a man, he goes through dry places, seeking rest, and finds none. **44** Then he says, 'I will return to my house from which I came.' And when he comes, he finds *it* empty, swept, and put in order.

1 Cor 1:22 For Jews request a sign, and Greeks seek after wisdom;

SILVER

Veins of, found in the earth.

Job 28:1 "Surely there is a mine for silver, And a place *where* gold is refined.

Generally found in an impure state.

Prov 25:4 Take away the dross from silver, And it will go to the silversmith *for* jewelry.

Comparative value of.

Is 60:17 "Instead of bronze I will bring gold, Instead of iron I will bring silver, Instead of wood, bronze, And instead of stones, iron. I will also make your officers peace, And your magistrates righteousness.

Described as

White and shining.

Ps 68:13–14 Though you lie down among the sheepfolds, *You will be* like the wings of a dove covered with silver, And her feathers with yellow gold." **14** When the Almighty scattered kings in it, It was *white* as snow in Zalmon.

Capable of being melted.

Ezek 22:20 *As men* gather silver, bronze, iron, lead, and tin into the midst of a furnace, to blow fire on it, to melt *it;* so I will gather *you* in My anger and in My fury, and I will leave *you there* and melt you.

Ezek 22:22 As silver is melted in the midst of a furnace, so shall you be melted in its midst; then you shall know that I, the LORD, have poured out My fury on you.' "

Malleable.

Jer 10:9 Silver is beaten into plates; It is brought from Tarshish, And gold from Uphaz, The work of the craftsman And of the hands of the metalsmith; Blue and purple *are* their clothing; They *are* all the work of skillful *men.*

Purified by fire.

Prov 17:3 The refining pot *is* for silver and the furnace for gold, But the LORD tests the hearts.

Zech 13:9 I will bring the *one*-third through the fire, Will refine them as silver is refined, And test them as gold is tested. They will call on My name, And I will answer them. I will say, 'This *is* My people'; And each one will say, 'The LORD *is* my God.' "

Purified, called

Refined silver.

1 Chr 29:4 three thousand talents of gold, of the gold of Ophir, and seven thousand talents of refined silver, to overlay the walls of the houses;

Choice silver.

Prov 8:19 My fruit *is* better than gold, yes, than fine gold, And my revenue than choice silver.

Tarshish carried on extensive commerce in.

Jer 10:9 Silver is beaten into plates; It is brought from Tarshish, And gold from Uphaz, The work of the craftsman And of the hands of the metalsmith; Blue and purple *are* their clothing; They *are* all the work of skillful *men.*

Ezek 27:12 "Tarshish *was* your merchant because of your many luxury goods. They gave you silver, iron, tin, and lead for your goods.

The patriarchs rich in.

Gen 13:2 Abram *was* very rich in livestock, in silver, and in gold.

Gen 24:35 The LORD has blessed my master greatly, and he has become great; and He has given him flocks and herds, silver and gold, male and female servants, and camels and donkeys.

Used as money from the earliest times.

Gen 23:15–16 "My lord, listen to me; the land *is worth* four hundred shekels of silver. What *is* that between you and me? So bury your dead." **16** And Abraham listened to Ephron; and Abraham weighed out the silver for Ephron which he had named in the hearing of the sons of Heth, four hundred shekels of silver, currency of the merchants.

Gen 37:28 Then Midianite traders passed by; so *the brothers* pulled Joseph up and lifted him out of the pit, and sold him to the Ishmaelites for twenty *shekels* of silver. And they took Joseph to Egypt.

1 Kin 16:24 And he bought the hill of Samaria from Shemer for two talents of silver; then he built on the hill, and called the name of the city which he built, Samaria, after the name of Shemer, owner of the hill.

Very abundant in the reign of Solomon.

1 Kin 10:21–22 All King Solomon's drinking vessels *were* gold, and all the vessels of the House of the Forest of Lebanon *were* pure gold. Not *one was* silver, for this was accounted as nothing in the days of Solomon. **22** For the king had merchant ships at sea with the fleet of Hiram. Once every three years the merchant ships came bringing gold, silver, ivory, apes, and monkeys.

1 Kin 10:27 The king made silver *as common* in Jerusalem as stones, and he made cedar trees as abundant as the sycamores which *are* in the lowland.

2 Chr 9:20–21 All King Solomon's drinking vessels *were* gold, and all the vessels of the House of the Forest of Lebanon *were* pure gold. Not *one was* silver, for this was accounted as nothing in the days of Solomon. **21** For the king's ships went to Tarshish with the servants of Hiram. Once every three years the merchant ships came, bringing gold, silver, ivory, apes, and monkeys.

2 Chr 9:27 The king made silver *as common* in Jerusalem as stones, and he made cedar trees as abundant as the sycamores which *are* in the lowland.

The working in, a trade.

Acts 19:24 For a certain man named Demetrius, a silversmith, who made silver shrines of Diana, brought no small profit to the craftsmen.

Made into

Cups.

Gen 44:2 Also put my cup, the silver cup, in the mouth of the sack of the youngest, and his grain money." So he did according to the word that Joseph had spoken.

Dishes.

Num 7:13 His offering *was* one silver platter, the weight of which *was* one hundred and thirty *shekels*, and one silver bowl of seventy shekels, according to the shekel of the sanctuary, both of them full of fine flour mixed with oil as a grain offering;

Num 7:84–85 This *was* the dedication *offering* for the altar from the leaders of Israel, when it was anointed: twelve silver platters, twelve silver bowls, and twelve gold pans. 85 Each silver platter *weighed* one hundred and thirty *shekels* and each bowl seventy *shekels*. All the silver of the vessels *weighed* two thousand four hundred *shekels*, according to the shekel of the sanctuary.

Bowls.

Num 7:13 His offering *was* one silver platter, the weight of which *was* one hundred and thirty *shekels*, and one silver bowl of seventy shekels, according to the shekel of the sanctuary, both of them full of fine flour mixed with oil as a grain offering;

Num 7:84 This *was* the dedication *offering* for the altar from the leaders of Israel, when it was anointed: twelve silver platters, twelve silver bowls, and twelve gold pans.

Thin plates.

Jer 10:9 Silver is beaten into plates; It is brought from Tarshish, And gold from Uphaz, The work of the craftsman And of the hands of the metalsmith; Blue and purple *are* their clothing; They *are* all the work of skillful *men*.

Chains.

Is 40:19 The workman molds an image, The goldsmith overspreads it with gold, And the silversmith casts silver chains.

Wires (alluded to).

Eccl 12:6 *Remember your Creator* before the silver cord is loosed, Or the golden bowl is broken, Or the pitcher shattered at the fountain, Or the wheel broken at the well.

Sockets for the boards of the tabernacle.

Ex 26:19 You shall make forty sockets of silver under the twenty boards: two sockets under each of the boards for its two tenons.

Ex 26:25 So there shall be eight boards with their sockets of silver—sixteen sockets—two sockets under each of the boards.

Ex 26:32 You shall hang it upon the four pillars of acacia *wood* overlaid with gold. Their hooks *shall be* gold, upon four sockets of silver.

Ex 36:24 Forty sockets of silver he made to go under the twenty boards: two sockets under each of the boards for its two tenons.

Ex 36:26 and their forty sockets of silver: two sockets under each of the boards.

Ex 36:30 So there were eight boards and their sockets—

sixteen sockets of silver—two sockets under each of the boards.

Ex 36:36 He made for it four pillars of acacia *wood*, and overlaid them with gold, with their hooks of gold; and he cast four sockets of silver for them.

Ornaments and hooks for the pillars of the tabernacle.

Ex 27:17 All the pillars around the court shall have bands of silver; their hooks *shall be* of silver and their sockets of bronze.

Ex 38:19 And *there were* four pillars *with* their four sockets of bronze; their hooks *were* silver, and the overlay of their capitals and their bands *was* silver.

Lampstands.

1 Chr 28:15 the weight for the lampstands of gold, and their lamps of gold, by weight for each lampstand and its lamps; for the lampstands of silver by weight, for the lampstand and its lamps, according to the use of each lampstand.

Tables.

1 Chr 28:16 And by weight *he gave* gold for the tables of the showbread, for each table, and silver for the tables of silver;

Beds or couches.

Esth 1:6 *There were* white and blue linen *curtains* fastened with cords of fine linen and purple on silver rods and marble pillars; *and the* couches *were* of gold and silver on a *mosaic* pavement of alabaster, turquoise, and white and black marble.

Articles.

2 Sam 8:10 then Toi sent Joram his son to King David, to greet him and bless him, because he had fought against Hadadezer and defeated him (for Hadadezer had been at war with Toi); and *Joram* brought with him articles of silver, articles of gold, and articles of bronze.

Ezra 6:5 Also let the gold and silver articles of the house of God, which Nebuchadnezzar took from the temple which *is* in Jerusalem and brought to Babylon, be restored and taken back to the temple which *is* in Jerusalem, *each* to its place; and deposit *them* in the house of God"—

Idols.

Ps 115:4 Their idols *are* silver and gold, The work of men's hands.

Is 2:20 In that day a man will cast away his idols of silver And his idols of gold, Which they made, *each* for himself to worship, To the moles and bats,

Is 30:22 You will also defile the covering of your images of silver, And the ornament of your molded images of gold. You will throw them away as an unclean thing; You will say to them, "Get away!"

Ornaments for the person.

Ex 3:22 But every woman shall ask of her neighbor, namely, of her who dwells near her house, articles of silver, articles of gold, and clothing; and you shall put *them* on your sons and on your daughters. So you shall plunder the Egyptians."

Given by the Israelites for making the tabernacle.

Ex 25:3 And this *is* the offering which you shall take from them: gold, silver, and bronze;

Ex 35:24 Everyone who offered an offering of silver or bronze brought the Lord's offering. And everyone with whom was found acacia wood for any work of the service, brought *it*.

Given by David and his subjects for making the temple.

1 Chr 28:14 *He* gave gold by weight for *things* of gold, for all articles used in every kind of service; also *silver* for all articles of silver by weight, for all articles used in every kind of service;

1 Chr 29:2 Now for the house of my God I have prepared with all my might: gold for *things to be made of* gold, silver for *things of* silver, bronze for *things of* bronze, iron for *things of* iron, wood for *things of* wood, onyx stones, *stones* to be set, glistening stones of various colors, all kinds of precious stones, and marble slabs in abundance.

1 Chr 29:6–9 Then the leaders of the fathers' *houses*, leaders of the tribes of Israel, the captains of thousands and of hundreds, with the officers over the king's work, offered willingly. **7** They gave for the work of the house of God five thousand talents and ten thousand darics of gold, ten thousand talents of silver, eighteen thousand talents of bronze, and one hundred thousand talents of iron. **8** And whoever had *precious* stones gave *them* to the treasury of the house of the Lord, into the hand of Jehiel the Gershonite. **9** Then the people rejoiced, for they had offered willingly, because with a loyal heart they had offered willingly to the Lord; and King David also rejoiced greatly.

Taken in war consecrated to God.

Josh 6:19 But all the silver and gold, and vessels of bronze and iron, *are* consecrated to the Lord; they shall come into the treasury of the Lord."

2 Sam 8:11 King David also dedicated these to the Lord, along with the silver and gold that he had dedicated from all the nations which he had subdued—

1 Kin 15:15 He also brought into the house of the Lord the things which his father had dedicated, and the things which he himself had dedicated: silver and gold and utensils.

Taken in war purified by fire.

Num 31:22–23 "Only the gold, the silver, the bronze, the iron, the tin, and the lead, **23** everything that can endure fire, you shall put through the fire, and it shall be clean; and it shall be purified with the water of purification. But all that cannot endure fire you shall put through water.

Often given as presents.

1 Kin 10:25 Each man brought his present: articles of silver and gold, garments, armor, spices, horses, and mules, at a set rate year by year.

2 Kin 5:5 Then the king of Syria said, "Go now, and I will send a letter to the king of Israel." So he departed and took with him ten talents of silver, six thousand *shekels* of gold, and ten changes of clothing.

2 Kin 5:23 So Naaman said, "Please, take two talents." And he urged him, and bound two talents of silver in two bags, with two changes of garments, and handed *them* to two of his servants; and they carried *them* on ahead of him.

Tribute often paid in.

2 Chr 17:11 Also *some* of the Philistines brought Jehoshaphat presents and silver as tribute; and the Arabians brought him flocks, seven thousand seven hundred rams and seven thousand seven hundred male goats.

Neh 5:15 But the former governors who *were* before me laid burdens on the people, and took from them bread and wine, besides forty shekels of silver. Yes, even their servants bore rule over the people, but I did not do so, because of the fear of God.

Illustrative of

The words of the Lord.

Ps 12:6 The words of the Lord *are* pure words, *Like* silver tried in a furnace of earth, Purified seven times.

The tongue of the righteous.

Prov 10:20 The tongue of the righteous *is* choice silver; The heart of the wicked *is worth* little.

Good rulers.

Is 1:22–23 Your silver has become dross, Your wine mixed with water. **23** Your princes *are* rebellious, And companions of thieves; Everyone loves bribes, And follows after rewards. They do not defend the fatherless, Nor does the cause of the widow come before them.

The Medo-Persian kingdom.

Dan 2:32 This image's head *was* of fine gold, its chest and arms of silver, its belly and thighs of bronze,

Dan 2:39 But after you shall arise another kingdom inferior to yours; then another, a third kingdom of bronze, which shall rule over all the earth.

Believers purified by affliction.

Ps 66:10 For You, O God, have tested us; You have refined us as silver is refined.

Zech 13:9 I will bring the *one*-third through the fire, Will refine them as silver is refined, And test them as gold is tested. They will call on My name, And I will answer them. I will say, 'This *is* My people'; And each one will say, 'The Lord *is* my God.' "

(Search for her) diligence required for attaining knowledge.

Prov 2:4 If you seek her as silver, And search for her as *for* hidden treasures;

(Rejected, dross of) the wicked.

Is 1:22 Your silver has become dross, Your wine mixed with water.

Jer 6:30 *People* will call them rejected silver, Because the Lord has rejected them."

Ezek 22:18 "Son of man, the house of Israel has become dross to Me; they *are* all bronze, tin, iron, and lead, in the midst of a furnace; they have become dross from silver.

Wisdom to be esteemed more than.

Job 28:15 It cannot be purchased for gold, Nor can silver be weighed *for* its price.

Prov 3:14 For her proceeds *are* better than the profits of silver, And her gain than fine gold.

Prov 8:10 Receive my instruction, and not silver, And knowledge rather than choice gold;

Prov 8:19 My fruit *is* better than gold, yes, than fine gold, And my revenue than choice silver.

Prov 16:16 How much better to get wisdom than gold! And to get understanding is to be chosen rather than silver.

SIMEON, THE TRIBE OF

Descended from Jacob's second son by Leah.

Gen 29:33 Then she conceived again and bore a son, and said, "Because the LORD has heard that I *am* unloved, He has therefore given me this *son* also." And she called his name Simeon.

Predictions respecting.

Gen 49:5–7 "Simeon and Levi *are* brothers; Instruments of cruelty *are in* their dwelling place. **6** Let not my soul enter their council; Let not my honor be united to their assembly; For in their anger they slew a man, And in their self-will they hamstrung an ox. **7** Cursed *be* their anger, for *it is* fierce; And their wrath, for it is cruel! I will divide them in Jacob And scatter them in Israel.

Persons selected from,

To number the people.

Num 1:6 from Simeon, Shelumiel the son of Zurishaddai;

To spy out the land.

Num 13:5 from the tribe of Simeon, Shaphat the son of Hori;

To divide the land.

Num 34:20 from the tribe of the children of Simeon, Shemuel the son of Ammihud;

Formed part of the second division of Israel in her journeys.

Num 10:18–19 And the standard of the camp of Reuben set out according to their armies; over their army *was* Elizur the son of Shedeur. **19** Over the army of the tribe of the children of Simeon *was* Shelumiel the son of Zurishaddai.

Encamped under the standard of Reuben south of the tabernacle.

Num 2:12 "Those who camp next to him *shall be* the tribe of Simeon, and the leader of the children of Simeon *shall be* Shelumiel the son of Zurishaddai."

Strength of, on leaving Egypt.

Num 1:22–23 From the children of Simeon, their genealogies by their families, by their fathers' house, of those who were numbered, according to the number of names, every male individually, from twenty years old and above, all who *were able to* go to war: **23** those who were numbered of the tribe of Simeon *were* fifty-nine thousand three hundred.

Num 2:13 And his army was numbered at fifty-nine thousand three hundred.

Offering of, at the dedication.

Num 7:36–41 On the fifth day Shelumiel the son of Zurishaddai, leader of the children of Simeon, *presented an offering*. **37** His offering *was* one silver platter, the weight of which *was* one hundred and thirty *shekels*, and one silver bowl of seventy shekels, according to the shekel of the sanctuary, both of them full of fine flour mixed with oil as a grain offering; **38** one gold pan of ten *shekels*, full of incense; **39** one young bull, one ram, and one male lamb in its first year, as a burnt offering; **40** one kid of the goats as a sin offering; **41** and as the sacrifice of peace offerings: two oxen, five rams, five male goats, and five male lambs in their first year. This *was* the offering of Shelumiel the son of Zurishaddai.

Families of.

Num 26:12–13 The sons of Simeon according to their families *were: of* Nemuel, the family of the Nemuelites; *of* Jamin, the family of the Jaminites; *of* Jachin, the family of the Jachinites; **13** *of* Zerah, the family of the Zarhites; *of* Shaul, the family of the Shaulites.

Strength of, on entering Canaan.

Num 26:14 These *are* the families of the Simeonites: twenty-two thousand two hundred.

Plagued for following the idolatry of Midian, which accounts for tribe's decrease.

Num 25:9 And those who died in the plague were twenty-four thousand.

Num 25:14 Now the name of the Israelite who was killed, who was killed with the Midianite woman, *was* Zimri the son of Salu, a leader of a father's house among the Simeonites.

Num 26:14 These *are* the families of the Simeonites: twenty-two thousand two hundred.

Num 1:23 those who were numbered of the tribe of Simeon *were* fifty-nine thousand three hundred.

On Mount Gerizim, said amen to the blessings.

Deut 27:12 "These shall stand on Mount Gerizim to bless the people, when you have crossed over the Jordan: Simeon, Levi, Judah, Issachar, Joseph, and Benjamin;

Inheritance of, within Judah.

Josh 19:1–8 The second lot came out for Simeon, for the tribe of the children of Simeon according to their families. And their inheritance was within the inheritance of the children of Judah. **2** They had in their inheritance Beersheba (Sheba), Moladah, **3** Hazar Shual, Balah, Ezem, **4** Eltolad, Bethul, Hormah, **5** Ziklag, Beth Marcaboth, Hazar Susah, **6** Beth Lebaoth, and Sharuhen: thirteen cities and their villages; **7** Ain, Rimmon, Ether, and Ashan: four cities and their villages; **8** and all the villages that *were* all around these cities as far as Baalath Beer, Ramah of the South. This *was* the inheritance of the tribe of the children of Simeon according to their families.

Bounds of her inheritance with cities and villages.

Josh 19:2–8 They had in their inheritance Beersheba (Sheba), Moladah, **3** Hazar Shual, Balah, Ezem, **4** Eltolad, Bethul, Hormah, **5** Ziklag, Beth Marcaboth, Hazar Susah, **6** Beth Lebaoth, and Sharuhen: thirteen cities and their villages; **7** Ain, Rimmon, Ether, and Ashan: four cities and their villages; **8** and all the villages that *were* all around these cities as far as Baalath Beer, Ramah of the South. This *was* the inheritance of the tribe of the children of Simeon according to their families.

1 Chr 4:28–33 They dwelt at Beersheba, Moladah, Hazar Shual, **29** Bilhah, Ezem, Tolad, **30** Bethuel, Hormah, Ziklag, **31** Beth Marcaboth, Hazar Susim, Beth Biri, and at Shaaraim. These *were* their cities until the reign of David. **32** And their villages *were* Etam, Ain, Rimmon, Tochen, and Ashan—five cities as far as Baal. These *were* their dwelling places, and they maintained their genealogy:

United with Judah in expelling the Canaanites from tribe's inheritance.

Judg 1:3 So Judah said to Simeon his brother, "Come up with me to my allotted territory, that we may fight against the Canaanites; and I will likewise go with you to your allotted territory." And Simeon went with him.

Judg 1:17 And Judah went with his brother Simeon, and they attacked the Canaanites who inhabited Zephath, and utterly destroyed it. So the name of the city was called Hormah.

Many of, at the coronation of David.

1 Chr 12:25 of the sons of Simeon, mighty men of valor fit for war, seven thousand one hundred;

Officer appointed over, by David.

1 Chr 27:16 Furthermore, over the tribes of Israel: the officer over the Reubenites *was* Eliezer the son of Zichri; over the Simeonites, Shephatiah the son of Maachah;

Part of, united with Judah under Asa.

2 Chr 15:9 Then he gathered all Judah and Benjamin, and those who dwelt with them from Ephraim, Manasseh, and Simeon, for they came over to him in great numbers from Israel when they saw that the LORD his God was with him.

Josiah purged her land of idols.

2 Chr 34:6 And *so he did* in the cities of Manasseh, Ephraim, and Simeon, as far as Naphtali and all around, with axes.

Part of, destroyed the remnant of the Amalekites, and dwelt in their land.

1 Chr 4:39–43 So they went to the entrance of Gedor, as far as the east side of the valley, to seek pasture for their flocks. **40** And they found rich, good pasture, and the land *was* broad, quiet, and peaceful; for some Hamites formerly lived there. **41** These recorded by name came in the days of Hezekiah king of Judah; and they attacked their tents and the Meunites who were found there, and utterly destroyed them, as it is to this day. So they dwelt in their place, because *there was* pasture for their flocks there. **42** Now *some* of them, five hundred men of the sons of Simeon, went to Mount Seir, having as their captains Pelatiah, Neariah, Rephaiah, and Uzziel, the sons of Ishi. **43** And they defeated the rest of the Amalekites who had escaped. They have dwelt there to this day.

SIMPLICITY

Is opposed to fleshly wisdom.

2 Cor 1:12 For our boasting is this: the testimony of our conscience that we conducted ourselves in the world in simplicity and godly sincerity, not with fleshly wisdom but by the grace of God, and more abundantly toward you.

Necessity for.

Matt 18:2–3 Then Jesus called a little child to Him, set him in the midst of them, **3** and said, "Assuredly, I say to you, unless you are converted and become as little children, you will by no means enter the kingdom of heaven.

Should be exhibited

In preaching the gospel.

1 Thess 2:3–7 For our exhortation *did* not *come* from error or uncleanness, nor *was it* in deceit. **4** But as we have been approved by God to be entrusted with the gospel, even so we speak, not as pleasing men, but God who tests our hearts. **5** For neither at any time did we use flattering words, as you know, nor a cloak for covetousness—God *is* witness. **6** Nor did we seek glory from men, either from you or from others, when we might have made demands as apostles of Christ. **7** But we were gentle among you, just as a nursing *mother* cherishes her own children.

In acts of benevolence.

Rom 12:8 he who exhorts, in exhortation; he who gives, with liberality; he who leads, with diligence; he who shows mercy, with cheerfulness.

In all our conduct.

2 Cor 1:12 For our boasting is this: the testimony of our conscience that we conducted ourselves in the world in simplicity and godly sincerity, not with fleshly wisdom but by the grace of God, and more abundantly toward you.

Concerning our own wisdom.

1 Cor 3:18 Let no one deceive himself. If anyone among you seems to be wise in this age, let him become a fool that he may become wise.

Concerning evil.

Rom 16:19 For your obedience has become known to all. Therefore I am glad on your behalf; but I want you to be wise in what is good, and simple concerning evil.

Concerning malice.

1 Cor 14:20 Brethren, do not be children in understanding; however, in malice be babes, but in understanding be mature.

Exhortation to.

Rom 16:19 For your obedience has become known to all. Therefore I am glad on your behalf; but I want you to be wise in what is good, and simple concerning evil.

1 Pet 2:2 as newborn babes, desire the pure milk of the word, that you may grow thereby,

Those who have the grace of,

Are made wise by God.

Matt 11:25 At that time Jesus answered and said, "I thank You, Father, Lord of heaven and earth, that You have hidden these things from *the* wise and prudent and have revealed them to babes.

Are made wise by the Word of God.

Ps 19:7 The law of the LORD *is* perfect, converting the soul; The testimony of the LORD *is* sure, making wise the simple;

Ps 119:130 The entrance of Your words gives light; It gives understanding to the simple.

Are preserved by God.

Ps 116:6 The LORD preserves the simple; I was brought low, and He saved me.

Made circumspect by instruction.

Prov 1:4 To give prudence to the simple, To the young man knowledge and discretion—

Profit by the correction of others.

Prov 19:25 Strike a scoffer, and the simple will become wary; Rebuke one who has understanding, *and* he will discern knowledge.

Prov 21:11 When the scoffer is punished, the simple is made wise; But when the wise is instructed, he receives knowledge.

Beware of being corrupted from that, which is in Christ.

2 Cor 11:3 But I fear, lest somehow, as the serpent deceived Eve by his craftiness, so your minds may be corrupted from the simplicity that is in Christ.

Illustrated.

Matt 6:22 "The lamp of the body is the eye. If therefore your eye is good, your whole body will be full of light.

Exemplified by

David.

Ps 131:1–2 LORD, my heart is not haughty, Nor my eyes lofty. Neither do I concern myself with great matters, Nor with things too profound for me. **2** Surely I have calmed and quieted my soul, Like a weaned child with his mother; Like a weaned child *is* my soul within me.

Jeremiah.

Jer 1:6 Then said I: "Ah, Lord GOD! Behold, I cannot speak, for I *am* a youth."

The early Christians.

Acts 2:46 So continuing daily with one accord in the temple, and breaking bread from house to house, they ate their food with gladness and simplicity of heart,

Acts 4:32 Now the multitude of those who believed were of one heart and one soul; neither did anyone say that any of the things he possessed was his own, but they had all things in common.

Paul.

2 Cor 1:12 For our boasting is this: the testimony of our conscience that we conducted ourselves in the world in simplicity and godly sincerity, not with fleshly wisdom but by the grace of God, and more abundantly toward you.

SIN

Is the transgression of the law.

1 John 3:4 Whoever commits sin also commits lawlessness, and sin is lawlessness.

Is of the devil.

John 8:44 You are of *your* father the devil, and the desires of your father you want to do. He was a murderer from the beginning, and does not stand in the truth, because there is no truth in him. When he speaks a lie, he speaks from his own *resources,* for he is a liar and the father of it.

1 John 3:8 He who sins is of the devil, for the devil has sinned from the beginning. For this purpose the Son of God was manifested, that He might destroy the works of the devil.

All unrighteousness is.

1 John 5:17 All unrighteousness is sin, and there is sin not *leading* to death.

Is the omission of what we know to be good.

James 4:17 Therefore, to him who knows to do good and does not do *it,* to him it is sin.

Whatever is not of faith is.

Rom 14:23 But he who doubts is condemned if he eats, because *he does* not *eat* from faith; for whatever *is* not from faith is sin.

The thought of foolishness is.

Prov 24:9 The devising of foolishness *is* sin, And the scoffer *is* an abomination to men.

All the imaginations of the unrenewed heart are.

Gen 6:5 Then the LORD saw that the wickedness of man *was* great in the earth, and *that* every intent of the thoughts of his heart *was* only evil continually.

Gen 8:21 And the LORD smelled a soothing aroma. Then the LORD said in His heart, "I will never again curse the ground for man's sake, although the imagination of man's heart *is* evil from his youth; nor will I again destroy every living thing as I have done.

Described as

Coming from the heart.

Matt 15:19 For out of the heart proceed evil thoughts, murders, adulteries, fornications, thefts, false witness, blasphemies.

The fruit of lust.

James 1:15 Then, when desire has conceived, it gives birth to sin; and sin, when it is full-grown, brings forth death.

The sting of death.

1 Cor 15:56 The sting of death *is* sin, and the strength of sin *is* the law.

Rebellion against God.

Deut 9:7 "Remember! Do not forget how you provoked the LORD your God to wrath in the wilderness. From the day that you departed from the land of Egypt until you came to this place, you have been rebellious against the LORD.

Josh 1:18 Whoever rebels against your command and does not heed your words, in all that you command him, shall be put to death. Only be strong and of good courage."

Works of darkness.

Eph 5:11 And have no fellowship with the unfruitful works of darkness, but rather expose *them.*

Dead works.

Heb 6:1 Therefore, leaving the discussion of the elementary *principles* of Christ, let us go on to perfection, not laying again the foundation of repentance from dead works and of faith toward God,

Heb 9:14 how much more shall the blood of Christ, who through the eternal Spirit offered Himself without spot to God, cleanse your conscience from dead works to serve the living God?

An abomination to God.

Prov 15:9 The way of the wicked *is* an abomination to the LORD, But He loves him who follows righteousness.

Jer 44:4 However I have sent to you all My servants the prophets, rising early and sending *them*, saying, "Oh, do not do this abominable thing that I hate!"

Jer 44:11 "Therefore thus says the Lord of hosts, the God of Israel: 'Behold, I will set My face against you for catastrophe and for cutting off all Judah.

Reproaching the Lord.

Num 15:30 'But the person who does *anything* presumptuously, *whether he is* native-born or a stranger, that one brings reproach on the Lord, and he shall be cut off from among his people.

Ps 74:18 Remember this, *that* the enemy has reproached, O Lord, And *that* a foolish people has blasphemed Your name.

Defiling.

Prov 30:12 *There is* a generation *that is* pure in its own eyes, *Yet* is not washed from its filthiness.

Is 59:3 For your hands are defiled with blood, And your fingers with iniquity; Your lips have spoken lies, Your tongue has muttered perversity.

Deceitful.

Heb 3:13 but exhort one another daily, while it is called "Today," lest any of you be hardened through the deceitfulness of sin.

A reproach.

Prov 14:34 Righteousness exalts a nation, But sin *is* a reproach to *any* people.

Often very great.

Ex 32:20 Then he took the calf which they had made, burned *it* in the fire, and ground *it* to powder; and he scattered *it* on the water and made the children of Israel drink *it*.

1 Sam 2:17 Therefore the sin of the young men was very great before the Lord, for men abhorred the offering of the Lord.

Often mighty.

Amos 5:12 For I know your manifold transgressions And your mighty sins: Afflicting the just *and* taking bribes; Diverting the poor *from justice* at the gate.

Often manifold.

Amos 5:12 For I know your manifold transgressions And your mighty sins: Afflicting the just *and* taking bribes; Diverting the poor *from justice* at the gate.

Often presumptuous.

Ps 19:13 Keep back Your servant also from presumptuous *sins*; Let them not have dominion over me. Then I shall be blameless, And I shall be innocent of great transgression.

Sometimes open and manifest.

1 Tim 5:24 Some men's sins are clearly evident, preceding *them* to judgment, but those of some *men* follow later.

Sometimes secret.

Ps 90:8 You have set our iniquities before You, Our secret *sins* in the light of Your countenance.

1 Tim 5:24 Some men's sins are clearly evident, preceding *them* to judgment, but those of some *men* follow later.

Besetting.

Heb 12:1 Therefore we also, since we are surrounded by so great a cloud of witnesses, let us lay aside every weight, and the sin which so easily ensnares *us*, and let us run with endurance the race that is set before us,

Like scarlet and crimson.

Is 1:18 "Come now, and let us reason together," Says the Lord, "Though your sins are like scarlet, They shall be as white as snow; Though they are red like crimson, They shall be as wool.

Reaching to heaven.

Rev 18:5 For her sins have reached to heaven, and God has remembered her iniquities.

Entered into the world by Adam.

Gen 3:6–7 So when the woman saw that the tree *was* good for food, that it *was* pleasant to the eyes, and a tree desirable to make *one* wise, she took of its fruit and ate. She also gave to her husband with her, and he ate. 7 Then the eyes of both of them were opened, and they knew that they *were* naked; and they sewed fig leaves together and made themselves coverings.

Rom 5:12 Therefore, just as through one man sin entered the world, and death through sin, and thus death spread to all men, because all sinned—

All men are conceived and born in.

Gen 5:3 And Adam lived one hundred and thirty years, and begot *a son* in his own likeness, after his image, and named him Seth.

Job 15:14 "What *is* man, that he could be pure? And *he who is* born of a woman, that he could be righteous?

Job 25:4 How then can man be righteous before God? Or how can he be pure *who is* born of a woman?

Ps 51:5 Behold, I was brought forth in iniquity, And in sin my mother conceived me.

Scripture concludes all under.

Gal 3:22 But the Scripture has confined all under sin, that the promise by faith in Jesus Christ might be given to those who believe.

No man is without.

1 Kin 8:46 "When they sin against You (for *there is* no one who does not sin), and You become angry with them and deliver them to the enemy, and they take them captive to the land of the enemy, far or near;

Eccl 7:20 For *there is* not a just man on earth who does good And does not sin.

Christ alone is without.

2 Cor 5:21 For He made Him who knew no sin *to be* sin for us, that we might become the righteousness of God in Him.

Heb 4:15 For we do not have a High Priest who cannot sympathize with our weaknesses, but was in all *points* tempted as *we are, yet* without sin.

Heb 7:26 For such a High Priest was fitting for us, *who is* holy, harmless, undefiled, separate from sinners, and has become higher than the heavens;

1 John 3:5 And you know that He was manifested to take away our sins, and in Him there is no sin.

God

Abominates.

Deut 25:16 For all who do such things, all who behave

unrighteously, *are* an abomination to the LORD your God.

Prov 6:16–19 These six *things* the LORD hates, Yes, seven *are* an abomination to Him: **17** A proud look, A lying tongue, Hands that shed innocent blood, **18** A heart that devises wicked plans, Feet that are swift in running to evil, **19** A false witness *who* speaks lies, And one who sows discord among brethren.

Marks.

Job 10:14 If I sin, then You mark me, And will not acquit me of my iniquity.

Remembers.

Rev 18:5 For her sins have reached to heaven, and God has remembered her iniquities.

Is provoked to jealousy by.

1 Kin 14:22 Now Judah did evil in the sight of the LORD, and they provoked Him to jealousy with their sins which they committed, more than all that their fathers had done.

Is provoked to anger by.

1 Kin 16:2 "Inasmuch as I lifted you out of the dust and made you ruler over My people Israel, and you have walked in the way of Jeroboam, and have made My people Israel sin, to provoke Me to anger with their sins,

Alone can forgive.

Ex 34:7 keeping mercy for thousands, forgiving iniquity and transgression and sin, by no means clearing *the guilty,* visiting the iniquity of the fathers upon the children and the children's children to the third and the fourth generation."

Dan 9:9 To the Lord our God *belong* mercy and forgiveness, though we have rebelled against Him.

Mic 7:18 Who *is* a God like You, Pardoning iniquity And passing over the transgression of the remnant of His heritage? He does not retain His anger forever, Because He delights *in* mercy.

Mark 2:7 "Why does this *Man* speak blasphemies like this? Who can forgive sins but God alone?"

Recompenses those who live in.

Jer 16:18 And first I will repay double for their iniquity and their sin, because they have defiled My land; they have filled My inheritance with the carcasses of their detestable and abominable idols."

Rev 18:6 Render to her just as she rendered to you, and repay her double according to her works; in the cup which she has mixed, mix double for her.

Punishes.

Is 13:11 "I will punish the world for *its* evil, And the wicked for their iniquity; I will halt the arrogance of the proud, And will lay low the haughtiness of the terrible.

Amos 3:2 "You only have I known of all the families of the earth; Therefore I will punish you for all your iniquities."

The law

Is transgressed by every act of.

James 2:10–11 For whoever shall keep the whole law, and yet stumble in one *point,* he is guilty of all. **11** For He who said, *"Do not commit adultery,"* also said, *"Do not murder."* Now if you do not commit adul-

tery, but you do murder, you have become a transgressor of the law.

1 John 3:4 Whoever commits sin also commits lawlessness, and sin is lawlessness.

Gives knowledge of.

Rom 3:20 Therefore by the deeds of the law no flesh will be justified in His sight, for by the law *is* the knowledge of sin.

Rom 7:7 What shall we say then? *Is* the law sin? Certainly not! On the contrary, I would not have known sin except through the law. For I would not have known covetousness unless the law had said, *"You shall not covet."*

Shows exceeding sinfulness of.

Rom 7:13 Has then what is good become death to me? Certainly not! But sin, that it might appear sin, was producing death in me through what is good, so that sin through the commandment might become exceedingly sinful.

Made to restrain.

1 Tim 1:9–10 knowing this: that the law is not made for a righteous person, but for *the* lawless and insubordinate, for *the* ungodly and for sinners, for *the* unholy and profane, for murderers of fathers and murderers of mothers, for manslayers, **10** for fornicators, for sodomites, for kidnappers, for liars, for perjurers, and if there is any other thing that is contrary to sound doctrine,

Arouses tendency toward.

Rom 7:5 For when we were in the flesh, the sinful passions which were aroused by the law were at work in our members to bear fruit to death.

Rom 7:8 But sin, taking opportunity by the commandment, produced in me all *manner of evil* desire. For apart from the law sin *was* dead.

Rom 7:11 For sin, taking occasion by the commandment, deceived me, and by it killed *me.*

Is the strength of.

1 Cor 15:56 The sting of death *is* sin, and the strength of sin *is* the law.

Curses those guilty of.

Gal 3:10 For as many as are of the works of the law are under the curse; for it is written, *"Cursed is everyone who does not continue in all things which are written in the book of the law, to do them."*

No man can cleanse himself from.

Job 9:30–31 If I wash myself with snow water, And cleanse my hands with soap, **31** Yet You will plunge me into the pit, And my own clothes will abhor me.

Prov 20:9 Who can say, "I have made my heart clean, I am pure from my sin"?

Jer 2:22 For though you wash yourself with lye, and use much soap, *Yet* your iniquity is marked before Me," says the Lord GOD.

No man can atone for.

Mic 6:7 Will the LORD be pleased with thousands of rams, Ten thousand rivers of oil? Shall I give my firstborn *for* my transgression, The fruit of my body *for* the sin of my soul?

God has opened a fountain for cleansing from.

Zech 13:1 "In that day a fountain shall be opened for the house of David and for the inhabitants of Jerusalem, for sin and for uncleanness.

Christ was manifested to take away.

John 1:29 The next day John saw Jesus coming toward him, and said, "Behold! The Lamb of God who takes away the sin of the world!

1 John 3:5 And you know that He was manifested to take away our sins, and in Him there is no sin.

Christ's blood redeems and cleanses from.

Eph 1:7 In Him we have redemption through His blood, the forgiveness of sins, according to the riches of His grace

1 John 1:7 But if we walk in the light as He is in the light, we have fellowship with one another, and the blood of Jesus Christ His Son cleanses us from all sin.

Believers

Made free from.

Rom 6:18 And having been set free from sin, you became slaves of righteousness.

Dead to.

Rom 6:2 Certainly not! How shall we who died to sin live any longer in it?

Rom 6:11 Likewise you also, reckon yourselves to be dead indeed to sin, but alive to God in Christ Jesus our Lord.

1 Pet 2:24 who Himself bore our sins in His own body on the tree, that we, having died to sins, might live for righteousness—by whose stripes you were healed.

Profess to have ceased from.

1 Pet 4:1 Therefore, since Christ suffered for us in the flesh, arm yourselves also with the same mind, for he who has suffered in the flesh has ceased from sin,

Cannot live in.

1 John 3:9 Whoever has been born of God does not sin, for His seed remains in him; and he cannot sin, because he has been born of God.

1 John 5:18 We know that whoever is born of God does not sin; but he who has been born of God keeps himself, and the wicked one does not touch him.

Resolve against.

Job 34:32 Teach me *what* I do not see; If I have done iniquity, I will do no more'?

Ashamed of having committed.

Rom 6:21 What fruit did you have then in the things of which you are now ashamed? For the end of those things *is* death.

Abhor themselves because of.

Job 42:6 Therefore I abhor *myself*, And repent in dust and ashes."

Ezek 20:43 And there you shall remember your ways and all your doings with which you were defiled; and you shall loathe yourselves in your own sight because of all the evils that you have committed.

Have yet the remains of, in them.

Rom 7:17 But now, *it is* no longer I who do it, but sin that dwells in me.

Rom 7:23 But I see another law in my members, warring against the law of my mind, and bringing me into captivity to the law of sin which is in my members.

Gal 5:17 For the flesh lusts against the Spirit, and the Spirit against the flesh; and these are contrary to one another, so that you do not do the things that you wish.

The fear of God restrains.

Ex 20:20 And Moses said to the people, "Do not fear; for God has come to test you, and that His fear may be before you, so that you may not sin."

Ps 4:4 Be angry, and do not sin. Meditate within your heart on your bed, and be still. Selah

Prov 16:6 In mercy and truth Atonement is provided for iniquity; And by the fear of the LORD *one* departs from evil.

The Word of God keeps people from.

Ps 17:4 Concerning the works of men, By the word of Your lips, I have kept away from the paths of the destroyer.

Ps 119:11 Your word I have hidden in my heart, That I might not sin against You.

The Holy Spirit convinces of.

John 16:8–9 And when He has come, He will convict the world of sin, and of righteousness, and of judgment: **9** of sin, because they do not believe in Me;

If we say that we have no, we make God a liar.

1 John 1:10 If we say that we have not sinned, we make Him a liar, and His word is not in us.

Shame belongs to those guilty of.

Dan 9:7–8 O Lord, righteousness *belongs* to You, but to us shame of face, as *it is* this day—to the men of Judah, to the inhabitants of Jerusalem and all Israel, those near and those far off in all the countries to which You have driven them, because of the unfaithfulness which they have committed against You. **8** "O Lord, to us *belongs* shame of face, to our kings, our princes, and our fathers, because we have sinned against You.

Should be

Confessed.

Job 33:27 Then he looks at men and says, 'I have sinned, and perverted *what was* right, And it did not profit me.'

Prov 28:13 He who covers his sins will not prosper, But whoever confesses and forsakes *them* will have mercy.

Mourned over.

Ps 38:18 For I will declare my iniquity; I will be in anguish over my sin.

Jer 3:21 A voice was heard on the desolate heights, Weeping *and* supplications of the children of Israel. For they have perverted their way; They have forgotten the LORD their God.

Hated.

Ps 97:10 You who love the LORD, hate evil! He preserves the souls of His saints; He delivers them out of the hand of the wicked.

Prov 8:13 The fear of the LORD *is* to hate evil; Pride and arrogance and the evil way And the perverse mouth I hate.

Amos 5:15 Hate evil, love good; Establish justice in the gate. It may be that the LORD God of hosts Will be gracious to the remnant of Joseph.

Rom 12:9 *Let* love *be* without hypocrisy. Abhor what is evil. Cling to what is good.

Put away.

Job 11:14 If iniquity *were* in your hand, *and you* put it far away, And would not let wickedness dwell in your tents;

Departed from.

Ps 34:14 Depart from evil and do good; Seek peace and pursue it.

2 Tim 2:19 Nevertheless the solid foundation of God stands, having this seal: "The Lord knows those who are His," and, "Let everyone who names the name of Christ depart from iniquity."

Avoided even in appearance.

1 Thess 5:22 Abstain from every form of evil.

Guarded against.

Ps 4:4 Be angry, and do not sin. Meditate within your heart on your bed, and be still. Selah

Ps 39:1 I said, "I will guard my ways, Lest I sin with my tongue; I will restrain my mouth with a muzzle, While the wicked are before me."

Striven against.

Heb 12:4 You have not yet resisted to bloodshed, striving against sin.

Put to death.

Rom 6:6 knowing this, that our old man was crucified with *Him,* that the body of sin might be done away with, that we should no longer be slaves of sin.

Rom 8:13 For if you live according to the flesh you will die; but if by the Spirit you put to death the deeds of the body, you will live.

Col 3:5 Therefore put to death your members which are on the earth: fornication, uncleanness, passion, evil desire, and covetousness, which is idolatry.

Especially strive against besetting.

Heb 12:1 Therefore we also, since we are surrounded by so great a cloud of witnesses, let us lay aside every weight, and the sin which so easily ensnares *us,* and let us run with endurance the race that is set before us,

Aggravated by neglecting advantages.

Luke 12:47 And that servant who knew his master's will, and did not prepare *himself* or do according to his will, shall be beaten with many *stripes.*

John 15:22 If I had not come and spoken to them, they would have no sin, but now they have no excuse for their sin.

Guilt concerning.

Job 31:33 If I have covered my transgressions as Adam, By hiding my iniquity in my bosom,

Prov 28:13 He who covers his sins will not prosper, But whoever confesses and forsakes *them* will have mercy.

We should pray to God

To search for, in our hearts.

Ps 139:23–24 Search me, O God, and know my heart; Try me, and know my anxieties; 24 And see if *there is any* wicked way in me, And lead me in the way everlasting.

To make us know our.

Job 13:23 How many *are* my iniquities and sins? Make me know my transgression and my sin.

To forgive our.

Ex 34:9 Then he said, "If now I have found grace in Your sight, O Lord, let my Lord, I pray, go among us, even though we *are* a stiff-necked people; and pardon our iniquity and our sin, and take us as Your inheritance."

Luke 11:4 And forgive us our sins, For we also forgive everyone who is indebted to us. And do not lead us into temptation, But deliver us from the evil one."

To keep us from.

Ps 19:13 Keep back Your servant also from presumptuous *sins;* Let them not have dominion over me. Then I shall be blameless, And I shall be innocent of great transgression.

To deliver us from.

Matt 6:13 And do not lead us into temptation, But deliver us from the evil one. For Yours is the kingdom and the power and the glory forever. Amen.

To cleanse us from.

Ps 51:2 Wash me thoroughly from my iniquity, And cleanse me from my sin.

Prayer hindered by.

Ps 66:18 If I regard iniquity in my heart, The Lord will not hear.

Is 59:2 But your iniquities have separated you from your God; And your sins have hidden *His* face from you, So that He will not hear.

Blessings withheld on account of.

Jer 5:25 Your iniquities have turned these *things* away, And your sins have withheld good from you.

The wicked

Are servants to.

John 8:34 Jesus answered them, "Most assuredly, I say to you, whoever commits sin is a slave of sin.

Rom 6:16 Do you not know that to whom you present yourselves slaves to obey, you are that one's slaves whom you obey, whether of sin *leading* to death, or of obedience *leading* to righteousness?

Are dead in.

Eph 2:1 And you He made alive, who were dead in trespasses and sins,

Are guilty of, in everything they do.

Prov 21:4 A haughty look, a proud heart, *And* the plowing of the wicked *are* sin.

Ezek 21:24 "Therefore thus says the Lord GOD: 'Because you have made your iniquity to be remembered, in that your transgressions are uncovered, so that in all your doings your sins appear—because you have come to remembrance, you shall be taken in hand.

Plead necessity for.

1 Sam 13:11–12 And Samuel said, "What have you

done?" Saul said, "When I saw that the people were scattered from me, and *that* you did not come within the days appointed, and *that* the Philistines gathered together at Michmash, **12** then I said, 'The Philistines will now come down on me at Gilgal, and I have not made supplication to the LORD.' Therefore I felt compelled, and offered a burnt offering."

Excuse.

Gen 3:12–13 Then the man said, "The woman whom You gave *to be* with me, she gave me of the tree, and I ate." **13** And the LORD God said to the woman, "What *is* this you have done?" The woman said, "The serpent deceived me, and I ate."

1 Sam 15:13–15 Then Samuel went to Saul, and Saul said to him, "Blessed *are* you of the LORD! I have performed the commandment of the LORD." **14** But Samuel said, "What then *is* this bleating of the sheep in my ears, and the lowing of the oxen which I hear?" **15** And Saul said, "They have brought them from the Amalekites; for the people spared the best of the sheep and the oxen, to sacrifice to the LORD your God; and the rest we have utterly destroyed."

Encourage themselves in.

Ps 64:5 They encourage themselves *in* an evil matter; They talk of laying snares secretly; They say, "Who will see them?"

Defy God in committing.

Is 5:18–19 Woe to those who draw iniquity with cords of vanity, And sin as if with a cart rope; **19** That say, "Let Him make speed *and* hasten His work, That we may see *it;* And let the counsel of the Holy One of Israel draw near and come, That we may know *it."*

Boast of.

Is 3:9 The look on their countenance witnesses against them, And they declare their sin as Sodom; They do not hide *it.* Woe to their soul! For they have brought evil upon themselves.

Mock.

Prov 14:9 Fools mock at sin, But among the upright *there is* favor.

Expect impunity in.

Ps 10:11 He has said in his heart, "God has forgotten; He hides His face; He will never see."

Ps 50:21 These *things* you have done, and I kept silent; You thought that I was altogether like you; *But* I will rebuke you, And set *them* in order before your eyes.

Ps 94:7 Yet they say, "The LORD does not see, Nor does the God of Jacob understand."

Cannot cease from.

2 Pet 2:14 having eyes full of adultery and that cannot cease from sin, enticing unstable souls. *They have* a heart trained in covetous practices, *and are* accursed children.

Commit more and more.

Ps 78:17 But they sinned even more against Him By rebelling against the Most High in the wilderness.

Is 30:1 "Woe to the rebellious children," says the LORD, "Who take counsel, but not of Me, And who devise plans, but not of My Spirit, That they may add sin to sin;

Are encouraged in, by prosperity.

Job 21:7–15 Why do the wicked live *and* become old, Yes, become mighty in power? **8** Their descendants are established with them in their sight, And their offspring before their eyes. **9** Their houses *are* safe from fear, Neither *is* the rod of God upon them. **10** Their bull breeds without failure; Their cow calves without miscarriage. **11** They send forth their little ones like a flock, And their children dance. **12** They sing to the tambourine and harp, And rejoice to the sound of the flute. **13** They spend their days in wealth, And in a moment go down to the grave. **14** Yet they say to God, 'Depart from us, For we do not desire the knowledge of Your ways. **15** Who *is* the Almighty, that we should serve Him? And what profit do we have if we pray to Him?'

Prov 10:16 The labor of the righteous *leads* to life, The wages of the wicked to sin.

Are led by despair to continue in.

Jer 2:25 Withhold your foot from being unshod, and your throat from thirst. But you said, 'There is no hope. No! For I have loved aliens, and after them I will go.'

Jer 18:12 And they said, "That is hopeless! So we will walk according to our own plans, and we will every one obey the dictates of his evil heart."

Try to conceal, from God.

Gen 3:8 And they heard the sound of the LORD God walking in the garden in the cool of the day, and Adam and his wife hid themselves from the presence of the LORD God among the trees of the garden.

Gen 3:10 So he said, "I heard Your voice in the garden, and I was afraid because I was naked; and I hid myself."

Job 31:33 If I have covered my transgressions as Adam, By hiding my iniquity in my bosom,

Throw the blame of, on God.

Gen 3:12 Then the man said, "The woman whom You gave *to be* with me, she gave me of the tree, and I ate."

Jer 7:10 and *then* come and stand before Me in this house which is called by My name, and say, 'We are delivered to do all these abominations'?

Throw the blame of, on others.

Gen 3:12–13 Then the man said, "The woman whom You gave *to be* with me, she gave me of the tree, and I ate." **13** And the LORD God said to the woman, "What *is* this you have done?" The woman said, "The serpent deceived me, and I ate."

Ex 32:22–24 So Aaron said, "Do not let the anger of my lord become hot. You know the people, that they *are set* on evil. **23** For they said to me, 'Make us gods that shall go before us; *as for* this Moses, the man who brought us out of the land of Egypt, we do not know what has become of him.' **24** And I said to them, 'Whoever has any gold, let them break *it* off.' So they gave *it* to me, and I cast it into the fire, and this calf came out."

Tempt others to.

Gen 3:6 So when the woman saw that the tree *was* good for food, that it *was* pleasant to the eyes, and a tree desirable to make *one* wise, she took of its fruit and ate. She also gave to her husband with her, and he ate.

1 Kin 16:2 "Inasmuch as I lifted you out of the dust and made you ruler over My people Israel, and you have walked in the way of Jeroboam, and have made My people Israel sin, to provoke Me to anger with their sins,

1 Kin 21:25 But there was no one like Ahab who sold himself to do wickedness in the sight of the LORD, because Jezebel his wife stirred him up.

Prov 1:10–14 My son, if sinners entice you, Do not consent. **11** If they say, "Come with us, Let us lie in wait to *shed* blood; Let us lurk secretly for the innocent without cause; **12** Let us swallow them alive like Sheol, And whole, like those who go down to the Pit; **13** We shall find all *kinds* of precious possessions, We shall fill our houses with spoil; **14** Cast in your lot among us, Let us all have one purse"—

Delight in those who commit.

Ps 10:3 For the wicked boasts of his heart's desire; He blesses the greedy *and* renounces the LORD.

Hos 7:3 They make a king glad with their wickedness, And princes with their lies.

Rom 1:32 who, knowing the righteous judgment of God, that those who practice such things are deserving of death, not only do the same but also approve of those who practice them.

Shall bear the shame of.

Ezek 16:52 You who judged your sisters, bear your own shame also, because the sins which you committed were more abominable than theirs; they are more righteous than you. Yes, be disgraced also, and bear your own shame, because you justified your sisters.

Shall find out the wicked.

Num 32:23 But if you do not do so, then take note, you have sinned against the LORD; and be sure your sin will find you out.

Ministers should warn the wicked to forsake.

Ezek 33:9 Nevertheless if you warn the wicked to turn from his way, and he does not turn from his way, he shall die in his iniquity; but you have delivered your soul.

Dan 4:27 Therefore, O king, let my advice be acceptable to you; break off your sins by *being* righteous, and your iniquities by showing mercy to *the* poor. Perhaps there may be a lengthening of your prosperity."

Leads to

Shame.

Rom 6:21 What fruit did you have then in the things of which you are now ashamed? For the end of those things *is* death.

Disquiet.

Ps 38:3 *There is* no soundness in my flesh Because of Your anger, Nor *any* health in my bones Because of my sin.

Disease.

Job 20:11 His bones are full of his youthful vigor, But it will lie down with him in the dust.

The ground was cursed on account of.

Gen 3:17–18 Then to Adam He said, "Because you have heeded the voice of your wife, and have eaten from

the tree of which I commanded you, saying, 'You shall not eat of it': "Cursed *is* the ground for your sake; In toil you shall eat *of* it All the days of your life. **18** Both thorns and thistles it shall bring forth for you, And you shall eat the herb of the field.

Toil and sorrow originated in.

Gen 3:16–17 To the woman He said: "I will greatly multiply your sorrow and your conception; In pain you shall bring forth children; Your desire *shall be* for your husband, And he shall rule over you." **17** Then to Adam He said, "Because you have heeded the voice of your wife, and have eaten from the tree of which I commanded you, saying, 'You shall not eat of it': "Cursed *is* the ground for your sake; In toil you shall eat *of* it All the days of your life.

Gen 3:19 In the sweat of your face you shall eat bread Till you return to the ground, For out of it you were taken; For dust you *are*, And to dust you shall return."

Job 14:1 "Man *who is* born of woman Is of few days and full of trouble.

Excludes from heaven.

1 Cor 6:9–10 Do you not know that the unrighteous will not inherit the kingdom of God? Do not be deceived. Neither fornicators, nor idolaters, nor adulterers, nor homosexuals, nor sodomites, **10** nor thieves, nor covetous, nor drunkards, nor revilers, nor extortioners will inherit the kingdom of God.

Gal 5:19–21 Now the works of the flesh are evident, which are: adultery, fornication, uncleanness, lewdness, **20** idolatry, sorcery, hatred, contentions, jealousies, outbursts of wrath, selfish ambitions, dissensions, heresies, **21** envy, murders, drunkenness, revelries, and the like; of which I tell you beforehand, just as I also told *you* in time past, that those who practice such things will not inherit the kingdom of God.

Eph 5:5 For this you know, that no fornicator, unclean person, nor covetous man, who is an idolater, has any inheritance in the kingdom of Christ and God.

Rev 21:27 But there shall by no means enter it anything that defiles, or causes an abomination or a lie, but only those who are written in the Lamb's Book of Life.

When finished brings forth death.

James 1:15 Then, when desire has conceived, it gives birth to sin; and sin, when it is full-grown, brings forth death.

Death is

The wages of.

Rom 6:23 For the wages of sin *is* death, but the gift of God *is* eternal life in Christ Jesus our Lord.

The punishment of.

Gen 2:17 but of the tree of the knowledge of good and evil you shall not eat, for in the day that you eat of it you shall surely die."

Ezek 18:4 "Behold, all souls are Mine; The soul of the father As well as the soul of the son is Mine; The soul who sins shall die.

SINCERITY

Christ was an example of.

1 Pet 2:22 *"Who committed no sin, Nor was deceit found in His mouth";*

Ministers should be examples of.

Titus 2:7 in all things showing yourself *to be* a pattern of good works; in doctrine *showing* integrity, reverence, incorruptibility,

Opposed to fleshly wisdom.

2 Cor 1:12 For our boasting is this: the testimony of our conscience that we conducted ourselves in the world in simplicity and godly sincerity, not with fleshly wisdom but by the grace of God, and more abundantly toward you.

Should characterize

Our love to God.

2 Cor 8:8 I speak not by commandment, but I am testing the sincerity of your love by the diligence of others.

2 Cor 8:24 Therefore show to them, and before the churches the proof of your love and of our boasting on your behalf.

Our love to Christ.

Eph 6:24 Grace *be* with all those who love our Lord Jesus Christ in sincerity. Amen.

Our service to God.

Josh 24:14 "Now therefore, fear the LORD, serve Him in sincerity and in truth, and put away the gods which your fathers served on the other side of the River and in Egypt. Serve the LORD!

John 4:23–24 But the hour is coming, and now is, when the true worshipers will worship the Father in spirit and truth; for the Father is seeking such to worship Him. 24 God *is* Spirit, and those who worship Him must worship in spirit and truth."

Our faith.

1 Tim 1:5 Now the purpose of the commandment is love from a pure heart, *from* a good conscience, and *from* sincere faith,

Our love to one another.

Rom 12:9 *Let* love *be* without hypocrisy. Abhor what is evil. Cling to what is good.

1 Pet 1:22 Since you have purified your souls in obeying the truth through the Spirit in sincere love of the brethren, love one another fervently with a pure heart,

1 John 3:18 My little children, let us not love in word or in tongue, but in deed and in truth.

Our whole conduct.

2 Cor 1:12 For our boasting is this: the testimony of our conscience that we conducted ourselves in the world in simplicity and godly sincerity, not with fleshly wisdom but by the grace of God, and more abundantly toward you.

The preaching of the gospel.

2 Cor 2:17 For we are not, as so many, peddling the word of God; but as of sincerity, but as from God, we speak in the sight of God in Christ.

1 Thess 2:3–5 For our exhortation *did* not *come* from error or uncleanness, nor *was it* in deceit. 4 But as we have been approved by God to be entrusted with the gospel, even so we speak, not as pleasing men, but God who tests our hearts. 5 For neither at any time did we use flattering words, as you know, nor a cloak for covetousness—God *is* witness.

A characteristic of the doctrines of the gospel.

1 Pet 2:2 as newborn babes, desire the pure milk of the word, that you may grow thereby,

The gospel sometimes preached without.

Phil 1:16 The former preach Christ from selfish ambition, not sincerely, supposing to add affliction to my chains;

The wicked devoid of.

Ps 5:9 For *there is* no faithfulness in their mouth; Their inward part *is* destruction; Their throat *is* an open tomb; They flatter with their tongue.

Ps 55:21 *The words* of his mouth were smoother than butter, But war *was* in his heart; His words were softer than oil, Yet they *were* drawn swords.

Exhortations to.

Ps 34:13 Keep your tongue from evil, And your lips from speaking deceit.

1 Cor 5:8 Therefore let us keep the feast, not with old leaven, nor with the leaven of malice and wickedness, but with the unleavened *bread* of sincerity and truth.

1 Pet 2:1 Therefore, laying aside all malice, all deceit, hypocrisy, envy, and all evil speaking,

Pray for, on behalf of others.

Phil 1:10 that you may approve the things that are excellent, that you may be sincere and without offense till the day of Christ,

Blessedness of.

Ps 32:2 Blessed *is* the man to whom the LORD does not impute iniquity, And in whose spirit *there is* no deceit.

Exemplified by

The men of Zebulun.

1 Chr 12:33 of Zebulun there were fifty thousand who went out to battle, expert in war with all weapons of war, stouthearted men who could keep ranks;

Hezekiah.

Is 38:3 and said, "Remember now, O LORD, I pray, how I have walked before You in truth and with a loyal heart, and have done *what is* good in Your sight." And Hezekiah wept bitterly.

Nathanael.

John 1:47 Jesus saw Nathanael coming toward Him, and said of him, "Behold, an Israelite indeed, in whom is no deceit!"

Paul.

2 Cor 1:12 For our boasting is this: the testimony of our conscience that we conducted ourselves in the world in simplicity and godly sincerity, not with fleshly wisdom but by the grace of God, and more abundantly toward you.

Timothy.

2 Tim 1:5 when I call to remembrance the genuine faith that is in you, which dwelt first in your grandmother Lois and your mother Eunice, and I am persuaded is in you also.

Lois and Eunice.

2 Tim 1:5 when I call to remembrance the genuine faith that is in you, which dwelt first in your grandmother Lois and your mother Eunice, and I am persuaded is in you also.

The Redeemed.

Rev 14:5 And in their mouth was found no deceit, for they are without fault before the throne of God.

SINS, THE FORGIVENESS OF

Blessedness of those who receive.

Ps 32:1–2 Blessed *is he whose* transgression *is* forgiven, *Whose* sin *is* covered. **2** Blessed *is* the man to whom the LORD does not impute iniquity, And in whose spirit *there is* no deceit.

Causes reverence for God.

Ps 130:3–4 If You, LORD, should mark iniquities, O Lord, who could stand? **4** But *there is* forgiveness with You, That You may be feared.

Available to those who confess their sin.

Ps 32:5 I acknowledged my sin to You, And my iniquity I have not hidden. I said, "I will confess my transgressions to the LORD," And You forgave the iniquity of my sin. Selah

1 John 1:9 If we confess our sins, He is faithful and just to forgive us *our* sins and to cleanse us from all unrighteousness.

The result of repentance.

Is 1:18–19 "Come now, and let us reason together," Says the LORD, "Though your sins are like scarlet, They shall be as white as snow; Though they are red like crimson, They shall be as wool. **19** If you are willing and obedient, You shall eat the good of the land;

Available to those God redeems through the work of Christ.

Is 43:25 "I, *even* I, *am* He who blots out your transgressions for My own sake; And I will not remember your sins.

Is 44:22 I have blotted out, like a thick cloud, your transgressions, And like a cloud, your sins. Return to Me, for I have redeemed you."

The readiness of.

Ps 86:5 For You, Lord, *are* good, and ready to forgive, And abundant in mercy to all those who call upon You.

God removes sin as far as the east is from the west.

Ps 103:12 As far as the east is from the west, *So* far has He removed our transgressions from us.

People should pray for.

Matt 6:12 And forgive us our debts, As we forgive our debtors.

Christ shed His blood for.

Matt 26:28 For this is My blood of the new covenant, which is shed for many for the remission of sins.

Gives knowledge of salvation.

Luke 1:77 To give knowledge of salvation to His people By the remission of their sins,

Compared to wiping ink from a document.

Acts 3:19 Repent therefore and be converted, that your sins may be blotted out, so that times of refreshing may come from the presence of the Lord,

Col 2:13–14 And you, being dead in your trespasses and the uncircumcision of your flesh, He has made alive together with Him, having forgiven you all trespasses, **14** having wiped out the handwriting of requirements that was against us, which was contrary to us. And He has taken it out of the way, having nailed it to the cross.

Is the result of salvation.

Acts 26:18 to open their eyes, *in order* to turn *them* from darkness to light, and *from* the power of Satan to God, that they may receive forgiveness of sins and an inheritance among those who are sanctified by faith in Me.'

Eph 1:7 In Him we have redemption through His blood, the forgiveness of sins, according to the riches of His grace

Col 1:14 in whom we have redemption through His blood, the forgiveness of sins.

Col 2:13 And you, being dead in your trespasses and the uncircumcision of your flesh, He has made alive together with Him, having forgiven you all trespasses,

Believers should grant to others.

Eph 4:32 And be kind to one another, tenderhearted, forgiving one another, even as God in Christ forgave you.

SINS, NATIONAL

Pervade all ranks.

Is 1:5 Why should you be stricken again? You will revolt more and more. The whole head is sick, And the whole heart faints.

Jer 5:1–5 "Run to and fro through the streets of Jerusalem; See now and know; And seek in her open places If you can find a man, If there is *anyone* who executes judgment, Who seeks the truth, And I will pardon her. **2** Though they say, '*As* the LORD lives,' Surely they swear falsely." **3** O LORD, *are* not Your eyes on the truth? You have stricken them, But they have not grieved; You have consumed them, But they have refused to receive correction. They have made their faces harder than rock; They have refused to return. **4** Therefore I said, "Surely these *are* poor. They are foolish; For they do not know the way of the LORD, The judgment of their God. **5** I will go to the great men and speak to them, For they have known the way of the LORD, The judgment of their God." But these have altogether broken the yoke *And* burst the bonds.

Jer 6:13 "Because from the least of them even to the greatest of them, Everyone *is* given to covetousness; And from the prophet even to the priest, Everyone deals falsely.

Often caused and encouraged by rulers.

1 Kin 14:16 And He will give Israel up because of the sins of Jeroboam, who sinned and who made Israel sin."

2 Chr 21:11–13 Moreover he made high places in the mountains of Judah, and caused the inhabitants of Jerusalem to commit harlotry, and led Judah astray.

12 And a letter came to him from Elijah the prophet, saying, Thus says the LORD God of your father David: Because you have not walked in the ways of Jehoshaphat your father, or in the ways of Asa king of Judah, **13** but have walked in the way of the kings of Israel, and have made Judah and the inhabitants of Jerusalem to play the harlot like the harlotry of the house of Ahab, and also have killed your brothers, those of your father's household, *who were* better than yourself,

Prov 29:12 If a ruler pays attention to lies, All his servants *become* wicked.

Cf. 1 Kin 12:26–33

Often caused by prosperity.

Deut 32:15 "But Jeshurun grew fat and kicked; You grew fat, you grew thick, You are obese! Then he forsook God *who* made him, And scornfully esteemed the Rock of his salvation.

Neh 9:28 "But after they had rest, They again did evil before You. Therefore You left them in the hand of their enemies, So that they had dominion over them; Yet when they returned and cried out to You, You heard from heaven; And many times You delivered them according to Your mercies,

Jer 48:11 "Moab has been at ease from his youth; He has settled on his dregs, And has not been emptied from vessel to vessel, Nor has he gone into captivity. Therefore his taste remained in him, And his scent has not changed.

Ezek 16:49 Look, this was the iniquity of your sister Sodom: She and her daughter had pride, fullness of food, and abundance of idleness; neither did she strengthen the hand of the poor and needy.

Ezek 28:5 By your great wisdom in trade you have increased your riches, And your heart is lifted up because of your riches),"

Defile

The land.

Lev 18:25 For the land is defiled; therefore I visit the punishment of its iniquity upon it, and the land vomits out its inhabitants.

Num 35:33–34 So you shall not pollute the land where you *are;* for blood defiles the land, and no atonement can be made for the land, for the blood that is shed on it, except by the blood of him who shed it. **34** Therefore do not defile the land which you inhabit, in the midst of which I dwell; for I the LORD dwell among the children of Israel.' "

Ps 106:38 And shed innocent blood, The blood of their sons and daughters, Whom they sacrificed to the idols of Canaan; And the land was polluted with blood.

Is 24:5 The earth is also defiled under its inhabitants, Because they have transgressed the laws, Changed the ordinance, Broken the everlasting covenant.

Mic 2:10 "Arise and depart, For this *is* not *your* rest; Because it is defiled, it shall destroy, Yes, with utter destruction.

The people.

Lev 18:24 'Do not defile yourselves with any of these things; for by all these the nations are defiled, which I am casting out before you.

Ezek 14:11 that the house of Israel may no longer stray from Me, nor be profaned anymore with all their transgressions, but that they may be My people and I may be their God," says the Lord GOD.' "

National worship.

Is 1:10–15 Hear the word of the LORD, You rulers of Sodom; Give ear to the law of our God, You people of Gomorrah: **11** "To what purpose *is* the multitude of your sacrifices to Me?" Says the LORD. "I have had enough of burnt offerings of rams And the fat of fed cattle. I do not delight in the blood of bulls, Or of lambs or goats. **12** "When you come to appear before Me, Who has required this from your hand, To trample My courts? **13** Bring no more futile sacrifices; Incense is an abomination to Me. The New Moons, the Sabbaths, and the calling of assemblies— I cannot endure iniquity and the sacred meeting. **14** Your New Moons and your appointed feasts My soul hates; They are a trouble to Me, I am weary of bearing *them.* **15** When you spread out your hands, I will hide My eyes from you; Even though you make many prayers, I will not hear. Your hands are full of blood.

Amos 5:21–22 "I hate, I despise your feast days, And I do not savor your sacred assemblies. **22** Though you offer Me burnt offerings and your grain offerings, I will not accept *them,* Nor will I regard your fattened peace offerings.

Hag 2:14 Then Haggai answered and said, " 'So is this people, and so is this nation before Me,' says the LORD, 'and so is every work of their hands; and what they offer there is unclean.

Aggravated by privileges.

Is 5:4–7 What more could have been done to My vineyard That I have not done in it? Why then, when I expected *it* to bring forth *good* grapes, Did it bring forth wild grapes? **5** And now, please let Me tell you what I will do to My vineyard: I will take away its hedge, and it shall be burned; *And* break down its wall, and it shall be trampled down. **6** I will lay it waste; It shall not be pruned or dug, But there shall come up briers and thorns. I will also command the clouds That they rain no rain on it." **7** For the vineyard of the LORD of hosts *is* the house of Israel, And the men of Judah are His pleasant plant. He looked for justice, but behold, oppression; For righteousness, but behold, a cry *for help.*

Ezek 20:11–13 And I gave them My statutes and showed them My judgments, 'which, *if* a man does, he shall live by them.' **12** Moreover I also gave them My Sabbaths, to be a sign between them and Me, that they might know that I *am* the LORD who sanctifies them. **13** Yet the house of Israel rebelled against Me in the wilderness; they did not walk in My statutes; they despised My judgments, 'which, *if* a man does, he shall live by them'; and they greatly defiled My Sabbaths. Then I said I would pour out My fury on them in the wilderness, to consume them.

Amos 2:4 Thus says the LORD: "For three transgressions of Judah, and for four, I will not turn away its *punishment,* Because they have despised the law of the LORD, And have not kept His commandments. Their lies lead them astray, *Lies* which their fathers followed.

Amos 3:1–2 Hear this word that the LORD has spoken against you, O children of Israel, against the whole family which I brought up from the land of Egypt, saying: **2** "You only have I known of all the families of the earth; Therefore I will punish you for all your iniquities."

Matt 11:21–24 "Woe to you, Chorazin! Woe to you, Bethsaida! For if the mighty works which were done in you had been done in Tyre and Sidon, they would have repented long ago in sackcloth and ashes. **22** But I say to you, it will be more tolerable for Tyre and Sidon in the day of judgment than for you. **23** And you, Capernaum, who are exalted to heaven, will be brought down to Hades; for if the mighty works which were done in you had been done in Sodom, it would have remained until this day. **24** But I say to you that it shall be more tolerable for the land of Sodom in the day of judgment than for you."

Lead the heathen to blaspheme.

Ezek 36:20 When they came to the nations, wherever they went, they profaned My holy name—when they said of them, 'These *are* the people of the LORD, *and* yet they have gone out of His land.'

Ezek 36:23 And I will sanctify My great name, which has been profaned among the nations, which you have profaned in their midst; and the nations shall know that I *am* the LORD," says the Lord GOD, "when I am hallowed in you before their eyes.

Rom 2:24 For *"the name of God is blasphemed among the Gentiles because of you,"* as it is written.

Are a reproach to a people.

Prov 14:34 Righteousness exalts a nation, But sin *is* a reproach to *any* people.

Should be

Repented of.

Jer 18:8 if that nation against whom I have spoken turns from its evil, I will relent of the disaster that I thought to bring upon it.

Jon 3:5 So the people of Nineveh believed God, proclaimed a fast, and put on sackcloth, from the greatest to the least of them.

Mourned over.

Joel 2:12 "Now, therefore," says the LORD, "Turn to Me with all your heart, With fasting, with weeping, and with mourning."

Confessed.

Lev 26:40 '*But* if they confess their iniquity and the iniquity of their fathers, with their unfaithfulness in which they were unfaithful to Me, and that they also have walked contrary to Me,

Deut 30:2 and you return to the LORD your God and obey His voice, according to all that I command you today, you and your children, with all your heart and with all your soul,

Judg 10:10 And the children of Israel cried out to the LORD, saying, "We have sinned against You, because we have both forsaken our God and served the Baals!"

1 Kin 8:47–48 *yet* when they come to themselves in the land where they were carried captive, and repent, and make supplication to You in the land of those who took them captive, saying, 'We have sinned and done wrong, we have committed wickedness'; **48** and *when* they return to You with all their heart and with all their soul in the land of their enemies who led them away captive, and pray to You toward their land which You gave to their fathers, the city which You have chosen and the temple which I have built for Your name:

Turned from.

Is 1:16 "Wash yourselves, make yourselves clean; Put away the evil of your doings from before My eyes. Cease to do evil,

Hos 14:1–2 O Israel, return to the LORD your God, For you have stumbled because of your iniquity; **2** Take words with you, and return to the LORD. Say to Him, "Take away all iniquity; Receive *us* graciously, For we will offer the sacrifices of our lips.

Jon 3:10 Then God saw their works, that they turned from their evil way; and God relented from the disaster that He had said He would bring upon them, and He did not do it.

Believers especially mourn over.

Ps 119:136 Rivers of water run down from my eyes, Because *men* do not keep Your law.

Ezek 9:4 and the LORD said to him, "Go through the midst of the city, through the midst of Jerusalem, and put a mark on the foreheads of the men who sigh and cry over all the abominations that are done within it."

Ministers should

Mourn over.

Ezra 10:6 Then Ezra rose up from before the house of God, and went into the chamber of Jehohanan the son of Eliashib; and *when* he came there, he ate no bread and drank no water, for he mourned because of the guilt of those from the captivity.

Jer 13:17 But if you will not hear it, My soul will weep in secret for *your* pride; My eyes will weep bitterly And run down with tears, Because the LORD's flock has been taken captive.

Ezek 6:11 'Thus says the Lord GOD: "Pound your fists and stamp your feet, and say, 'Alas, for all the evil abominations of the house of Israel! For they shall fall by the sword, by famine, and by pestilence.

Joel 2:17 Let the priests, who minister to the LORD, Weep between the porch and the altar; Let them say, "Spare Your people, O LORD, And do not give Your heritage to reproach, That the nations should rule over them. Why should they say among the peoples, 'Where *is* their God?' "

Testify against.

Is 30:8–9 Now go, write it before them on a tablet, And note it on a scroll, That it may be for time to come, Forever and ever: **9** That this *is* a rebellious people, Lying children, Children *who* will not hear the law of the LORD;

Is 58:1 "Cry aloud, spare not; Lift up your voice like a trumpet; Tell My people their transgression, And the house of Jacob their sins.

Ezek 2:3–5 And He said to me: "Son of man, I am sending you to the children of Israel, to a rebellious nation that has rebelled against Me; they and their fathers have transgressed against Me to this very day. **4** For *they are* impudent and stubborn children. I am sending you to them, and you shall say to them, 'Thus says the Lord GOD.' 5 As for them, whether they hear or whether they refuse—for they *are* a rebellious house—yet they will know that a prophet has been among them.

Ezek 22:2 "Now, son of man, will you judge, will you judge the bloody city? Yes, show her all her abominations!

Jon 1:2 "Arise, go to Nineveh, that great city, and cry out against it; for their wickedness has come up before Me."

Try to turn the people from.

Jer 23:22 But if they had stood in My counsel, And had caused My people to hear My words, Then they would have turned them from their evil way And from the evil of their doings.

Pray for forgiveness of.

Ex 32:31–32 Then Moses returned to the LORD and said, "Oh, these people have committed a great sin, and have made for themselves a god of gold! 32 Yet now, if You will forgive their sin—but if not, I pray, blot me out of Your book which You have written."

Joel 2:17 Let the priests, who minister to the LORD, Weep between the porch and the altar; Let them say, "Spare Your people, O LORD, And do not give Your heritage to reproach, That the nations should rule over them. Why should they say among the peoples, 'Where *is* their God?' "

National prayer rejected because of.

Is 1:15 When you spread out your hands, I will hide My eyes from you; Even though you make many prayers, I will not hear. Your hands are full of blood.

Is 59:2 But your iniquities have separated you from your God; And your sins have hidden *His* face from you, So that He will not hear.

National worship rejected on account of.

Is 1:10–14 Hear the word of the LORD, You rulers of Sodom; Give ear to the law of our God, You people of Gomorrah: 11 "To what purpose *is* the multitude of your sacrifices to Me?" Says the LORD. "I have had enough of burnt offerings of rams And the fat of fed cattle. I do not delight in the blood of bulls, Or of lambs or goats. 12 "When you come to appear before Me, Who has required this from your hand, To trample My courts? 13 Bring no more futile sacrifices; Incense is an abomination to Me. The New Moons, the Sabbaths, and the calling of assemblies— I cannot endure iniquity and the sacred meeting. 14 Your New Moons and your appointed feasts My soul hates; They are a trouble to Me, I am weary of bearing *them*.

Jer 6:19–20 Hear, O earth! Behold, I will certainly bring calamity on this people— The fruit of their thoughts, Because they have not heeded My words Nor My law, but rejected it. 20 For what purpose to Me Comes frankincense from Sheba, And sweet cane from a far country? Your burnt offerings *are* not acceptable, Nor your sacrifices sweet to Me."

Jer 7:9–14 Will you steal, murder, commit adultery, swear falsely, burn incense to Baal, and walk after other gods whom you do not know, 10 and *then* come and stand before Me in this house which is called by My name, and say, 'We are delivered to do all these abominations'? 11 Has this house, which is called by My name, become a den of thieves in your eyes? Behold, I, even I, have seen *it*," says the LORD. 12 "But go now to My place which *was* in Shiloh, where I set My name at the first, and see what I did to it because of the wickedness of My people Israel. 13 And now, because you have done all these works," says the LORD, "and I spoke to you, rising up early and speaking, but you did not hear, and I called you, but you did not answer, 14 therefore I will do to the house which is called by My name, in which you trust, and to this place which I gave to you and your fathers, as I have done to Shiloh.

Cause the withdrawal of privileges.

Lam 2:9 Her gates have sunk into the ground; He has destroyed and broken her bars. Her king and her princes *are* among the nations; The Law *is* no *more*, And her prophets find no vision from the LORD.

Amos 8:11 "Behold, the days are coming," says the Lord GOD, "That I will send a famine on the land, Not a famine of bread, Nor a thirst for water, But of hearing the words of the LORD.

Matt 23:37–39 "O Jerusalem, Jerusalem, the one who kills the prophets and stones those who are sent to her! How often I wanted to gather your children together, as a hen gathers her chicks under *her* wings, but you were not willing! 38 See! Your house is left to you desolate; 39 for I say to you, you shall see Me no more till you say, '*Blessed is He who comes in the name of the LORD!*' "

Bring down national judgments.

Matt 23:35–36 that on you may come all the righteous blood shed on the earth, from the blood of righteous Abel to the blood of Zechariah, son of Berechiah, whom you murdered between the temple and the altar. 36 Assuredly, I say to you, all these things will come upon this generation.

Matt 27:25 And all the people answered and said, "His blood *be* on us and on our children."

Denunciations against.

Is 1:24 Therefore the Lord says, The LORD of hosts, the Mighty One of Israel, "Ah, I will rid Myself of My adversaries, And take vengeance on My enemies.

Is 30:1 "Woe to the rebellious children," says the LORD, "Who take counsel, but not of Me, And who devise plans, but not of My Spirit, That they may add sin to sin;

Jer 5:9 Shall I not punish *them* for these *things?*" says the LORD. "And shall I not avenge Myself on such a nation as this?

Jer 6:27–30 "I have set you *as* an assayer *and* a fortress among My people, That you may know and test their way. 28 They *are* all stubborn rebels, walking as slanderers. *They are* bronze and iron, They *are* all corrupters; 29 The bellows blow fiercely, The lead is consumed by the fire; The smelter refines in vain, For the wicked are not drawn off. 30 *People* will call them rejected silver, Because the LORD has rejected them."

Punishment for.

Is 3:8 For Jerusalem stumbled, And Judah is fallen, Because their tongue and their doings *Are* against the LORD, To provoke the eyes of His glory.

Jer 12:17 But if they do not obey, I will utterly pluck up and destroy that nation," says the LORD.

Jer 25:12 'Then it will come to pass, when seventy years are completed, *that* I will punish the king of Babylon and that nation, the land of the Chaldeans, for their iniquity,' says the LORD; 'and I will make it a perpetual desolation.

Ezek 28:7–10 Behold, therefore, I will bring strangers against you, The most terrible of the nations; And they shall draw their swords against the beauty of your wisdom, And defile your splendor. **8** They shall throw you down into the Pit, And you shall die the death of the slain In the midst of the seas. **9** "Will you still say before him who slays you, 'I *am* a god'? But you *shall be* a man, and not a god, In the hand of him who slays you. **10** You shall die the death of the uncircumcised By the hand of aliens; For I have spoken," says the Lord GOD.' "

Punishment for, averted on repentance.

Judg 10:15–16 And the children of Israel said to the LORD, "We have sinned! Do to us whatever seems best to You; only deliver us this day, we pray." **16** So they put away the foreign gods from among them and served the LORD. And His soul could no longer endure the misery of Israel.

2 Chr 12:6–7 So the leaders of Israel and the king humbled themselves; and they said, "The LORD *is* righteous." **7** Now when the LORD saw that they humbled themselves, the word of the LORD came to Shemaiah, saying, "They have humbled themselves; *therefore* I will not destroy them, but I will grant them some deliverance. My wrath shall not be poured out on Jerusalem by the hand of Shishak.

Ps 106:43–46 Many times He delivered them; But they rebelled in their counsel, And were brought low for their iniquity. **44** Nevertheless He regarded their affliction, When He heard their cry; **45** And for their sake He remembered His covenant, And relented according to the multitude of His mercies. **46** He also made them to be pitied By all those who carried them away captive.

Jon 3:10 Then God saw their works, that they turned from their evil way; and God relented from the disaster that He had said He would bring upon them, and He did not do it.

Illustrated by

Sodom and Gomorrah.

Gen 18:20 And the LORD said, "Because the outcry against Sodom and Gomorrah is great, and because their sin is very grave,

2 Pet 2:6 and turning the cities of Sodom and Gomorrah into ashes, condemned *them* to destruction, making *them* an example to those who afterward would live ungodly;

The children of Israel.

Ex 16:8 Also Moses said, "*This shall be seen* when the LORD gives you meat to eat in the evening, and in the morning bread to the full; for the LORD hears your complaints which you make against Him. And what *are* we? Your complaints *are* not against us but against the LORD."

Ex 32:31 Then Moses returned to the LORD and said,

"Oh, these people have committed a great sin, and have made for themselves a god of gold!

The nations of Canaan.

Deut 9:4 "Do not think in your heart, after the LORD your God has cast them out before you, saying, 'Because of my righteousness the LORD has brought me in to possess this land'; but *it is* because of the wickedness of these nations *that* the LORD is driving them out from before you.

The kingdom of Israel.

2 Kin 17:8–12 and had walked in the statutes of the nations whom the LORD had cast out from before the children of Israel, and of the kings of Israel, which they had made. **9** Also the children of Israel secretly did against the LORD their God things that *were* not right, and they built for themselves high places in all their cities, from watchtower to fortified city. **10** They set up for themselves *sacred* pillars and wooden images on every high hill and under every green tree. **11** There they burned incense on all the high places, like the nations whom the LORD had carried away before them; and they did wicked things to provoke the LORD to anger, **12** for they served idols, of which the LORD had said to them, "You shall not do this thing."

Hos 4:1–2 Hear the word of the LORD, You children of Israel, For the LORD *brings* a charge against the inhabitants of the land: "There is no truth or mercy Or knowledge of God in the land. **2** *By* swearing and lying, Killing and stealing and committing adultery, They break all restraint, With bloodshed upon bloodshed.

The kingdom of Judah.

2 Kin 17:19 Also Judah did not keep the commandments of the LORD their God, but walked in the statutes of Israel which they made.

Is 1:2–7 Hear, O heavens, and give ear, O earth! For the LORD has spoken: "I have nourished and brought up children, And they have rebelled against Me; **3** The ox knows its owner And the donkey its master's crib; *But* Israel does not know, My people do not consider." **4** Alas, sinful nation, A people laden with iniquity, A brood of evildoers, Children who are corrupters! They have forsaken the LORD, They have provoked to anger The Holy One of Israel, They have turned away backward. **5** Why should you be stricken again? You will revolt more and more. The whole head is sick, And the whole heart faints. **6** From the sole of the foot even to the head, *There is* no soundness in it, *But* wounds and bruises and putrefying sores; They have not been closed or bound up, Or soothed with ointment. **7** Your country *is* desolate, Your cities *are* burned with fire; Strangers devour your land in your presence; And *it is* desolate, as overthrown by strangers.

Moab.

Jer 48:29–30 "We have heard the pride of Moab (He *is* exceedingly proud), Of his loftiness and arrogance and pride, And of the haughtiness of his heart." **30** "I know his wrath," says the LORD, "But *it is* not right; His lies have made nothing right.

Babylon.

Jer 51:6 Flee from the midst of Babylon, And every one save his life! Do not be cut off in her iniquity, For this *is* the time of the LORD's vengeance; He shall recompense her.

Jer 51:13 O you who dwell by many waters, Abundant in treasures, Your end has come, The measure of your covetousness.

Jer 51:52 "Therefore behold, the days are coming," says the LORD, "That I will bring judgment on her carved images, And throughout all her land the wounded shall groan.

Tyre.

Ezek 28:2 "Son of man, say to the prince of Tyre, 'Thus says the Lord GOD: "Because your heart *is* lifted up, And you say, 'I *am* a god, I sit *in* the seat of gods, In the midst of the seas,' Yet you *are* a man, and not a god, Though you set your heart as the heart of a god

Nineveh.

Nah 3:1 Woe to the bloody city! It *is* all full of lies *and* robbery. *Its* victim never departs.

SLANDER

An abomination to God.

Prov 6:16 These six *things* the LORD hates, Yes, seven *are* an abomination to Him:

Prov 6:19 A false witness *who* speaks lies, And one who sows discord among brethren.

Forbidden.

Ex 23:1 "You shall not circulate a false report. Do not put your hand with the wicked to be an unrighteous witness.

Eph 4:31 Let all bitterness, wrath, anger, clamor, and evil speaking be put away from you, with all malice.

James 4:11 Do not speak evil of one another, brethren. He who speaks evil of a brother and judges his brother, speaks evil of the law and judges the law. But if you judge the law, you are not a doer of the law but a judge.

Includes

Whispering.

Rom 1:29 being filled with all unrighteousness, sexual immorality, wickedness, covetousness, maliciousness; full of envy, murder, strife, deceit, evil-mindedness; *they are* whisperers,

2 Cor 12:20 For I fear lest, when I come, I shall not find you such as I wish, and *that* I shall be found by you such as you do not wish; lest *there be* contentions, jealousies, outbursts of wrath, selfish ambitions, backbitings, whisperings, conceits, tumults;

Backbiting.

Rom 1:30 backbiters, haters of God, violent, proud, boasters, inventors of evil things, disobedient to parents,

2 Cor 12:20 For I fear lest, when I come, I shall not find you such as I wish, and *that* I shall be found by you such as you do not wish; lest *there be* contentions, jealousies, outbursts of wrath, selfish ambitions, backbitings, whisperings, conceits, tumults;

Evil surmising.

1 Tim 6:4 he is proud, knowing nothing, but is obsessed with disputes and arguments over words, from which come envy, strife, reviling, evil suspicions,

Talebearing.

Lev 19:16 You shall not go about *as* a talebearer among your people; nor shall you take a stand against the life of your neighbor: I *am* the LORD.

Babbling.

Eccl 10:11 A serpent may bite when *it is* not charmed; The babbler is no different.

Tattling.

1 Tim 5:13 And besides they learn *to be* idle, wandering about from house to house, and not only idle but also gossips and busybodies, saying things which they ought not.

Evil speaking.

Ps 41:5 My enemies speak evil of me: "When will he die, and his name perish?"

Ps 109:20 *Let* this *be* the LORD's reward to my accusers, And to those who speak evil against my person.

Defaming.

Jer 20:10 For I heard many mocking: "Fear on every side!" "Report," *they say*, "and we will report it!" All my acquaintances watched for my stumbling, *saying*, "Perhaps he can be induced; Then we will prevail against him, And we will take our revenge on him."

1 Cor 4:13 being defamed, we entreat. We have been made as the filth of the world, the offscouring of all things until now.

Bearing false witness.

Ex 20:16 "You shall not bear false witness against your neighbor.

Deut 5:20 'You shall not bear false witness against your neighbor.

Luke 3:14 Likewise the soldiers asked him, saying, "And what shall we do?" So he said to them, "Do not intimidate anyone or accuse falsely, and be content with your wages."

Judging uncharitably.

James 4:11–12 Do not speak evil of one another, brethren. He who speaks evil of a brother and judges his brother, speaks evil of the law and judges the law. But if you judge the law, you are not a doer of the law but a judge. **12** There is one Lawgiver, who is able to save and to destroy. Who are you to judge another?

Circulating false reports.

Ex 23:1 "You shall not circulate a false report. Do not put your hand with the wicked to be an unrighteous witness.

Repeating matters.

Prov 17:9 He who covers a transgression seeks love, But he who repeats a matter separates friends.

Is a deceitful work.

Ps 52:2 Your tongue devises destruction, Like a sharp razor, working deceitfully.

Comes from the evil heart.

Matt 15:19 For out of the heart proceed evil thoughts, murders, adulteries, fornications, thefts, false witness, blasphemies.

Luke 6:45 A good man out of the good treasure of his heart brings forth good; and an evil man out of the evil treasure of his heart brings forth evil. For out of the abundance of the heart his mouth speaks.

Often arises from hatred.

Ps 41:7 All who hate me whisper together against me; Against me they devise my hurt.

Ps 109:3 They have also surrounded me with words of hatred, And fought against me without a cause.

Idleness leads to.

1 Tim 5:13 And besides they learn *to be* idle, wandering about from house to house, and not only idle but also gossips and busybodies, saying things which they ought not.

The wicked addicted to.

Ps 50:20 You sit *and* speak against your brother; You slander your own mother's son.

Ps 52:4 You love all devouring words, *You* deceitful tongue.

Prov 11:9 The hypocrite with *his* mouth destroys his neighbor, But through knowledge the righteous will be delivered.

Jer 6:28 They *are* all stubborn rebels, walking as slanderers. *They are* bronze and iron, They *are* all corrupters;

Jer 9:4 "Everyone take heed to his neighbor, And do not trust any brother; For every brother will utterly supplant, And every neighbor will walk with slanderers.

A characteristic of the devil.

Rev 12:10 Then I heard a loud voice saying in heaven, "Now salvation, and strength, and the kingdom of our God, and the power of His Christ have come, for the accuser of our brethren, who accused them before our God day and night, has been cast down.

Those who indulge in, are fools.

Prov 10:18 Whoever hides hatred *has* lying lips, And whoever spreads slander *is* a fool.

Those who indulge in, not to be trusted.

Jer 9:4 "Everyone take heed to his neighbor, And do not trust any brother; For every brother will utterly supplant, And every neighbor will walk with slanderers.

Women warned against.

Titus 2:3 the older women likewise, that they be reverent in behavior, not slanderers, not given to much wine, teachers of good things—

Minister's wives should avoid.

1 Tim 3:11 Likewise, *their* wives *must be* reverent, not slanderers, temperate, faithful in all things.

Those exposed to,

Christ.

Ps 35:11 Fierce witnesses rise up; They ask me *things* that I do not know.

Matt 26:60 but found none. Even though many false witnesses came forward, they found none. But at last two false witnesses came forward

Authorities.

2 Pet 2:10 and especially those who walk according to the flesh in the lust of uncleanness and despise authority. *They are* presumptuous, self-willed. They are not afraid to speak evil of dignitaries,

Jude 1:8 Likewise also these dreamers defile the flesh, reject authority, and speak evil of dignitaries.

Ministers.

Rom 3:8 And *why* not say, "Let us do evil that good may come"?—as we are slanderously reported and as some affirm that we say. Their condemnation is just.

2 Cor 6:8 by honor and dishonor, by evil report and good report; as deceivers, and *yet* true;

Close relatives.

Ps 50:20 You sit *and* speak against your brother; You slander your own mother's son.

Believers.

Ps 38:12 Those also who seek my life lay snares *for me;* Those who seek my hurt speak of destruction, And plan deception all the day long.

Ps 109:2 For the mouth of the wicked and the mouth of the deceitful Have opened against me; They have spoken against me with a lying tongue.

1 Pet 4:4 In regard to these, they think it strange that you do not run with *them* in the same flood of dissipation, speaking evil of *you.*

Believers

Should keep their tongue from.

Ps 34:13 Keep your tongue from evil, And your lips from speaking deceit.

1 Pet 3:10 For *"He who would love life And see good days, Let him refrain his tongue from evil, And his lips from speaking deceit.*

Should lay aside.

Eph 4:31 Let all bitterness, wrath, anger, clamor, and evil speaking be put away from you, with all malice.

1 Pet 2:1 Therefore, laying aside all malice, all deceit, hypocrisy, envy, and all evil speaking,

Should be warned against.

Titus 3:1–2 Remind them to be subject to rulers and authorities, to obey, to be ready for every good work, **2** to speak evil of no one, to be peaceable, gentle, showing all humility to all men.

Should give no occasion for.

1 Pet 2:12 having your conduct honorable among the Gentiles, that when they speak against you as evildoers, they may, by *your* good works which they observe, glorify God in the day of visitation.

1 Pet 3:16 having a good conscience, that when they defame you as evildoers, those who revile your good conduct in Christ may be ashamed.

Should return good for.

1 Cor 4:13 being defamed, we entreat. We have been made as the filth of the world, the offscouring of all things until now.

Blessed in enduring.

Matt 5:11 "Blessed are you when they revile and persecute you, and say all kinds of evil against you falsely for My sake.

Characterized as avoiding.

Ps 15:1 LORD, who may abide in Your tabernacle? Who may dwell in Your holy hill?

Ps 15:3 He *who* does not backbite with his tongue, Nor does evil to his neighbor, Nor does he take up a reproach against his friend;

Should not be listened to.

1 Sam 24:9 And David said to Saul: "Why do you listen to the words of men who say, 'Indeed David seeks your harm'?

Deserves frowning disapproval.

Prov 25:23 The north wind brings forth rain, And a backbiting tongue an angry countenance.

Effects of,

Separates friends.

Prov 16:28 A perverse man sows strife, And a whisperer separates the best of friends.

Prov 17:9 He who covers a transgression seeks love, But he who repeats a matter separates friends.

Produces wounds.

Prov 18:8 The words of a talebearer *are* like tasty trifles, And they go down into the inmost body.

Prov 26:22 The words of a talebearer *are* like tasty trifles, And they go down into the inmost body.

Creates strife.

Prov 26:20 Where *there is* no wood, the fire goes out; And where *there is* no talebearer, strife ceases.

Sows discord among brethren.

Prov 6:19 A false witness *who* speaks lies, And one who sows discord among brethren.

Can lead to murder.

Ps 31:13 For I hear the slander of many; Fear *is* on every side; While they take counsel together against me, They scheme to take away my life.

Ezek 22:9 In you are men who slander to cause bloodshed; in you are those who eat on the mountains; in your midst they commit lewdness.

The tongue of, is a scourge.

Job 5:21 You shall be hidden from the scourge of the tongue, And you shall not be afraid of destruction when it comes.

Is venomous.

Ps 140:3 They sharpen their tongues like a serpent; The poison of asps *is* under their lips. Selah

Eccl 10:11 A serpent may bite when *it is* not charmed; The babbler is no different.

Is destructive.

Prov 11:9 The hypocrite with *his* mouth destroys his neighbor, But through knowledge the righteous will be delivered.

End of, is mischievous madness.

Eccl 10:13 The words of his mouth begin with foolishness, And the end of his talk *is* raving madness.

Men shall give account for.

Matt 12:36 But I say to you that for every idle word men may speak, they will give account of it in the day of judgment.

James 1:26 If anyone among you thinks he is religious, and does not bridle his tongue but deceives his own heart, this one's religion *is* useless.

Punishment for.

Deut 19:16–21 If a false witness rises against any man to testify against him of wrongdoing, **17** then both men in the controversy shall stand before the LORD, before the priests and the judges who serve in those days.

18 And the judges shall make careful inquiry, and indeed, *if* the witness *is* a false witness, who has testified falsely against his brother, **19** then you shall do to him as he thought to have done to his brother; so you shall put away the evil from among you. **20** And those who remain shall hear and fear, and hereafter they shall not again commit such evil among you. **21** Your eye shall not pity: life *shall be* for life, eye for eye, tooth for tooth, hand for hand, foot for foot.

Ps 101:5 Whoever secretly slanders his neighbor, Him I will destroy; The one who has a haughty look and a proud heart, Him I will not endure.

Illustrated.

Prov 12:18 There is one who speaks like the piercings of a sword, But the tongue of the wise *promotes* health.

Prov 25:18 A man who bears false witness against his neighbor *Is like* a club, a sword, and a sharp arrow.

Examples of,

Laban's sons.

Gen 31:1 Now *Jacob* heard the words of Laban's sons, saying, "Jacob has taken away all that was our father's, and from what was our father's he has acquired all this wealth."

Doeg.

1 Sam 22:9–11 Then answered Doeg the Edomite, who was set over the servants of Saul, and said, "I saw the son of Jesse going to Nob, to Ahimelech the son of Ahitub. **10** And he inquired of the LORD for him, gave him provisions, and gave him the sword of Goliath the Philistine." **11** So the king sent to call Ahimelech the priest, the son of Ahitub, and all his father's house, the priests who *were* in Nob. And they all came to the king.

The princes of Ammon.

2 Sam 10:3 And the princes of the people of Ammon said to Hanun their lord, "Do you think that David really honors your father because he has sent comforters to you? Has David not *rather* sent his servants to you to search the city, to spy it out, and to overthrow it?"

Ziba.

2 Sam 16:3 Then the king said, "And where *is* your master's son?" And Ziba said to the king, "Indeed he is staying in Jerusalem, for he said, 'Today the house of Israel will restore the kingdom of my father to me.' "

The witnesses against Naboth.

1 Kin 21:13 And two men, scoundrels, came in and sat before him; and the scoundrels witnessed against him, against Naboth, in the presence of the people, saying, "Naboth has blasphemed God and the king!" Then they took him outside the city and stoned him with stones, so that he died.

The enemies of the Jews. **Ezra 4:7–16**

Geshem.

Neh 6:6 In it *was* written: It is reported among the nations, and Geshem says, *that* you and the Jews plan to rebel; therefore, according to these rumors, you are rebuilding the wall, that you may be their king.

Haman.

Esth 3:8 Then Haman said to King Ahasuerus, "There is

a certain people scattered and dispersed among the people in all the provinces of your kingdom; their laws *are* different from all *other* people's, and they do not keep the king's laws. Therefore it *is* not fitting for the king to let them remain.

David's enemies.

Ps 31:13 For I hear the slander of many; Fear *is* on every side; While they take counsel together against me, They scheme to take away my life.

Jeremiah's enemies.

Jer 38:4 Therefore the princes said to the king, "Please, let this man be put to death, for thus he weakens the hands of the men of war who remain in this city, and the hands of all the people, by speaking such words to them. For this man does not seek the welfare of this people, but their harm."

The Jews.

Matt 11:18–19 For John came neither eating nor drinking, and they say, 'He has a demon.' **19** The Son of Man came eating and drinking, and they say, 'Look, a glutton and a winebibber, a friend of tax collectors and sinners!' But wisdom is justified by her children."

The witnesses against Christ.

Matt 26:59–61 Now the chief priests, the elders, and all the council sought false testimony against Jesus to put Him to death, **60** but found none. Even though many false witnesses came forward, they found none. But at last two false witnesses came forward **61** and said, "This *fellow* said, 'I am able to destroy the temple of God and to build it in three days.' "

The priests.

Mark 15:3 And the chief priests accused Him of many things, but He answered nothing.

The enemies of Stephen.

Acts 6:11 Then they secretly induced men to say, "We have heard him speak blasphemous words against Moses and God."

The enemies of Paul.

Acts 17:7 Jason has harbored them, and these are all acting contrary to the decrees of Caesar, saying there is another king—Jesus."

Tertullus.

Acts 24:2 And when he was called upon, Tertullus began his accusation, saying: "Seeing that through you we enjoy great peace, and prosperity is being brought to this nation by your foresight,

Acts 24:5 For we have found this man a plague, a creator of dissension among all the Jews throughout the world, and a ringleader of the sect of the Nazarenes.

SLAVERY

Joseph sold into.

Gen 37:25–28 And they sat down to eat a meal. Then they lifted their eyes and looked, and there was a company of Ishmaelites, coming from Gilead with their camels, bearing spices, balm, and myrrh, on their way to carry *them* down to Egypt. **26** So Judah said to his brothers, "What profit *is there* if we kill our brother and conceal his blood? **27** Come and let us sell him to the Ishmaelites, and let not our hand be

upon him, for he *is* our brother *and* our flesh." And his brothers listened. **28** Then Midianite traders passed by; so *the brothers* pulled Joseph up and lifted him out of the pit, and sold him to the Ishmaelites for twenty *shekels* of silver. And they took Joseph to Egypt.

Israel's, in Egypt, described. Ex 1:8–22

Principles for dealing with, under the law. Lev 25:39–55

Jeremiah's prophecy of, for Jews. Jer 2:14–25

To sin.

John 8:31–36 Then Jesus said to those Jews who believed Him, "If you abide in My word, you are My disciples indeed. **32** And you shall know the truth, and the truth shall make you free." **33** They answered Him, "We are Abraham's descendants, and have never been in bondage to anyone. How *can* You say, 'You will be made free'?" **34** Jesus answered them, "Most assuredly, I say to you, whoever commits sin is a slave of sin. **35** And a slave does not abide in the house forever, *but* a son abides forever. **36** Therefore if the Son makes you free, you shall be free indeed.

Rom 6:17–18 But God be thanked that *though* you were slaves of sin, yet you obeyed from the heart that form of doctrine to which you were delivered. **18** And having been set free from sin, you became slaves of righteousness.

Cf. 1 John 3:4,8–9

Was not to hinder serving Christ.

1 Cor 7:20–24 Let each one remain in the same calling in which he was called. **21** Were you called *while* a slave? Do not be concerned about it; but if you can be made free, rather use *it*. **22** For he who is called in the Lord *while* a slave is the Lord's freedman. Likewise he who is called *while* free is Christ's slave. **23** You were bought at a price; do not become slaves of men. **24** Brethren, let each one remain with God in that *state* in which he was called.

Believers freed from (spiritual).

Gal 3:13 Christ has redeemed us from the curse of the law, having become a curse for us (for it is written, *"Cursed is everyone who hangs on a tree"*),

Gal 4:5 to redeem those who were under the law, that we might receive the adoption as sons.

Titus 2:14 who gave Himself for us, that He might redeem us from every lawless deed and purify for Himself *His* own special people, zealous for good works.

1 Pet 1:18–19 knowing that you were not redeemed with corruptible things, *like* silver or gold, from your aimless conduct *received* by tradition from your fathers, **19** but with the precious blood of Christ, as of a lamb without blemish and without spot.

Cf. Rom 3:24; 1 Cor 1:30; Eph 1:7; Col 1:14; Heb 9:12

Was not to be practiced abusively.

Ex 21:16 "He who kidnaps a man and sells him, or if he is found in his hand, shall surely be put to death.

Ex 21:26–27 "If a man strikes the eye of his male or female servant, and destroys it, he shall let him go free for the sake of his eye. **27** And if he knocks out the tooth of his male or female servant, he shall let him go free for the sake of his tooth.

Lev 25:10 And you shall consecrate the fiftieth year, and proclaim liberty throughout *all* the land to all its inhabitants. It shall be a Jubilee for you; and each of you shall return to his possession, and each of you shall return to his family.

Deut 23:15–16 "You shall not give back to his master the slave who has escaped from his master to you. **16** He may dwell with you in your midst, in the place which he chooses within one of your gates, where it seems best to him; you shall not oppress him.

SOBRIETY

Commanded.

1 Pet 1:13 Therefore gird up the loins of your mind, be sober, and rest *your* hope fully upon the grace that is to be brought to you at the revelation of Jesus Christ;

1 Pet 5:8 Be sober, be vigilant; because your adversary the devil walks about like a roaring lion, seeking whom he may devour.

The gospel designed to teach.

Titus 2:11–12 For the grace of God that brings salvation has appeared to all men, **12** teaching us that, denying ungodliness and worldly lusts, we should live soberly, righteously, and godly in the present age,

Should be practiced with

Watchfulness.

1 Thess 5:6 Therefore let us not sleep, as others *do*, but let us watch and be sober.

Prayer.

1 Pet 4:7 But the end of all things is at hand; therefore be serious and watchful in your prayers.

Required in

Ministers.

1 Tim 3:2–3 A bishop then must be blameless, the husband of one wife, temperate, sober-minded, of good behavior, hospitable, able to teach; **3** not given to wine, not violent, not greedy for money, but gentle, not quarrelsome, not covetous;

Titus 1:8 but hospitable, a lover of what is good, sober-minded, just, holy, self-controlled,

Wives of ministers.

1 Tim 3:11 Likewise, *their* wives *must be* reverent, not slanderers, temperate, faithful in all things.

Aged men.

Titus 2:2 that the older men be sober, reverent, temperate, sound in faith, in love, in patience;

Young men.

Titus 2:6 Likewise, exhort the young men to be sober-minded,

Young women.

Titus 2:4 that they admonish the young women to love their husbands, to love their children,

All believers.

1 Thess 5:6 Therefore let us not sleep, as others *do*, but let us watch and be sober.

1 Thess 5:8 But let us who are of the day be sober, putting on the breastplate of faith and love, and *as* a helmet the hope of salvation.

Women should exhibit, in dress.

1 Tim 2:9 in like manner also, that the women adorn themselves in modest apparel, with propriety and moderation, not with braided hair or gold or pearls or costly clothing,

We should estimate our character and talents with.

Rom 12:3 For I say, through the grace given to me, to everyone who is among you, not to think *of himself* more highly than he ought to think, but to think soberly, as God has dealt to each one a measure of faith.

Motives to.

1 Pet 4:7 But the end of all things is at hand; therefore be serious and watchful in your prayers.

1 Pet 5:8 Be sober, be vigilant; because your adversary the devil walks about like a roaring lion, seeking whom he may devour.

SOLOMON

Son of David, by Bathsheba.

2 Sam 12:24 Then David comforted Bathsheba his wife, and went in to her and lay with her. So she bore a son, and he called his name Solomon. Now the LORD loved him,

Anointed king. 1 Kin 1:28–48; 1 Chr 29:21–25

Received final instruction from father David.

1 Kin 2:1–10 Now the days of David drew near that he should die, and he charged Solomon his son, saying: **2** "I go the way of all the earth; be strong, therefore, and prove yourself a man. **3** And keep the charge of the LORD your God: to walk in His ways, to keep His statutes, His commandments, His judgments, and His testimonies, as it is written in the Law of Moses, that you may prosper in all that you do and wherever you turn; **4** that the LORD may fulfill His word which He spoke concerning me, saying, 'If your sons take heed to their way, to walk before Me in truth with all their heart and with all their soul,' He said, 'you shall not lack a man on the throne of Israel.' **5** "Moreover you know also what Joab the son of Zeruiah did to me, *and* what he did to the two commanders of the armies of Israel, to Abner the son of Ner and Amasa the son of Jether, whom he killed. And he shed the blood of war in peacetime, and put the blood of war on his belt that *was* around his waist, and on his sandals that *were* on his feet. **6** Therefore do according to your wisdom, and do not let his gray hair go down to the grave in peace. **7** "But show kindness to the sons of Barzillai the Gileadite, and let them be among those who eat at your table, for so they came to me when I fled from Absalom your brother. **8** "And see, *you have* with you Shimei the son of Gera, a Benjamite from Bahurim, who cursed me with a malicious curse in the day when I went to Mahanaim. But he came down to meet me at the Jordan, and I swore to him by the LORD, saying, 'I will not put you to death with the sword.' **9** Now therefore, do not hold him guiltless, for you *are* a wise man and know what you ought to do to him; but bring his gray hair down to the grave with blood." **10** So David rested with his fathers, and was buried in the City of David.

Cf. 1 Chr 22:6–19

Prayed for wisdom. 1 Kin 3:4–15; 2 Chr 1:7–13
Enjoyed prosperity and fame.

1 Kin 4:20–34 Judah and Israel *were* as numerous as the sand by the sea in multitude, eating and drinking and rejoicing. **21** So Solomon reigned over all kingdoms from the River *to* the land of the Philistines, as far as the border of Egypt. *They* brought tribute and served Solomon all the days of his life. **22** Now Solomon's provision for one day was thirty kors of fine flour, sixty kors of meal, **23** ten fatted oxen, twenty oxen from the pastures, and one hundred sheep, besides deer, gazelles, roebucks, and fatted fowl. **24** For he had dominion over all *the region* on this side of the River from Tiphsah even to Gaza, namely over all the kings on this side of the River; and he had peace on every side all around him. **25** And Judah and Israel dwelt safely, each man under his vine and his fig tree, from Dan as far as Beersheba, all the days of Solomon. **26** Solomon had forty thousand stalls of horses for his chariots, and twelve thousand horsemen. **27** And these governors, each man in his month, provided food for King Solomon and for all who came to King Solomon's table. There was no lack in their supply. **28** They also brought barley and straw to the proper place, for the horses and steeds, each man according to his charge. **29** And God gave Solomon wisdom and exceedingly great understanding, and largeness of heart like the sand on the seashore. **30** Thus Solomon's wisdom excelled the wisdom of all the men of the East and all the wisdom of Egypt. **31** For he was wiser than all men—than Ethan the Ezrahite, and Heman, Chalcol, and Darda, the sons of Mahol; and his fame was in all the surrounding nations. **32** He spoke three thousand proverbs, and his songs were one thousand and five. **33** Also he spoke of trees, from the cedar tree of Lebanon even to the hyssop that springs out of the wall; he spoke also of animals, of birds, of creeping things, and of fish. **34** And men of all nations, from all the kings of the earth who had heard of his wisdom, came to hear the wisdom of Solomon.

Dedicated the temple. 1 Kin 8:22–66; 2 Chr 6:12—7:10
God appeared to him a second time.

1 Kin 9:1–9 And it came to pass, when Solomon had finished building the house of the LORD and the king's house, and all Solomon's desire which he wanted to do, **2** that the LORD appeared to Solomon the second time, as He had appeared to him at Gibeon. **3** And the LORD said to him: "I have heard your prayer and your supplication that you have made before Me; I have consecrated this house which you have built to put My name there forever, and My eyes and My heart will be there perpetually. **4** Now if you walk before Me as your father David walked, in integrity of heart and in uprightness, to do according to all that I have commanded you, *and* if you keep My statutes and My judgments, **5** then I will establish the throne of your kingdom over Israel forever, as I promised David your father, saying, 'You shall not fail to have a man on the throne of Israel.' **6** *But* if you or your sons at all turn from following Me, and do not keep My commandments *and* My statutes which I have set before you, but go and serve other gods and worship them, **7** then I will cut off Israel from the land which I have given them; and this house which I have con-

secrated for My name I will cast out of My sight. Israel will be a proverb and a byword among all peoples. **8** And *as for* this house, *which* is exalted, everyone who passes by it will be astonished and will hiss, and say, 'Why has the LORD done thus to this land and to this house?' **9** Then they will answer, 'Because they forsook the LORD their God, who brought their fathers out of the land of Egypt, and have embraced other gods, and worshiped them and served them; therefore the LORD has brought all this calamity on them.' "

Cf. 2 Chr 7:11–22

Visited by queen of Sheba. 1 Kin 10:1–13; 2 Chr 9:1–12

Fell away from God's standards.

1 Kin 11:1–13 But King Solomon loved many foreign women, as well as the daughter of Pharaoh: women of the Moabites, Ammonites, Edomites, Sidonians, *and* Hittites— **2** from the nations of whom the LORD had said to the children of Israel, "You shall not intermarry with them, nor they with you. Surely they will turn away your hearts after their gods." Solomon clung to these in love. **3** And he had seven hundred wives, princesses, and three hundred concubines; and his wives turned away his heart. **4** For it was so, when Solomon was old, that his wives turned his heart after other gods; and his heart was not loyal to the LORD his God, as *was* the heart of his father David. **5** For Solomon went after Ashtoreth the goddess of the Sidonians, and after Milcom the abomination of the Ammonites. **6** Solomon did evil in the sight of the LORD, and did not fully follow the LORD, as *did* his father David. **7** Then Solomon built a high place for Chemosh the abomination of Moab, on the hill that *is* east of Jerusalem, and for Molech the abomination of the people of Ammon. **8** And he did likewise for all his foreign wives, who burned incense and sacrificed to their gods. **9** So the LORD became angry with Solomon, because his heart had turned from the LORD God of Israel, who had appeared to him twice, **10** and had commanded him concerning this thing, that he should not go after other gods; but he did not keep what the LORD had commanded. **11** Therefore the LORD said to Solomon, "Because you have done this, and have not kept My covenant and My statutes, which I have commanded you, I will surely tear the kingdom away from you and give it to your servant. **12** Nevertheless I will not do it in your days, for the sake of your father David; I will tear it out of the hand of your son. **13** However I will not tear away the whole kingdom; I will give one tribe to your son for the sake of my servant David, and for the sake of Jerusalem which I have chosen."

Jeroboam rebelled against him. 1 Kin 11:26–40

2 Chr 13:6 Yet Jeroboam the son of Nebat, the servant of Solomon the son of David, rose up and rebelled against his lord.

Death of.

1 Kin 11:41–43 Now the rest of the acts of Solomon, all that he did, and his wisdom, *are* they not written in the book of the acts of Solomon? **42** And the period that Solomon reigned in Jerusalem over all Israel *was* forty years. **43** Then Solomon rested with his fathers, and was buried in the City of David his father. And Rehoboam his son reigned in his place.

Cf. 2 Chr 9:29–31

SOUL

Wisdom gives life to.

Prov 3:22 So they will be life to your soul And grace to your neck.

Destiny of one's, dependent on response to Christ.

Mark 8:34–38 When He had called the people to *Himself*, with His disciples also, He said to them, "Whoever desires to come after Me, let him deny himself, and take up his cross, and follow Me. **35** For whoever desires to save his life will lose it, but whoever loses his life for My sake and the gospel's will save it. **36** For what will it profit a man if he gains the whole world, and loses his own soul? **37** Or what will a man give in exchange for his soul? **38** For whoever is ashamed of Me and My words in this adulterous and sinful generation, of him the Son of Man also will be ashamed when He comes in the glory of His Father with the holy angels."

Described as the heart.

2 Cor 4:6 For it is the God who commanded light to shine out of darkness, who has shone in our hearts to *give* the light of the knowledge of the glory of God in the face of Jesus Christ.

Used interchangeably with spirit.

1 Thess 5:23 Now may the God of peace Himself sanctify you completely; and may your whole spirit, soul, and body be preserved blameless at the coming of our Lord Jesus Christ.

Heb 4:12 For the word of God *is* living and powerful, and sharper than any two-edged sword, piercing even to the division of soul and spirit, and of joints and marrow, and is a discerner of the thoughts and intents of the heart.

SOVEREIGN PLAN OF GOD, THE

Can't be thwarted.

Job 42:2 "I know that You can do everything, And that no purpose *of Yours* can be withheld from You.

Over the affairs of men.

Gen 50:20 But as for you, you meant evil against me; *but* God meant it for good, in order to bring it about as *it is* this day, to save many people alive.

Eccl 2:24 Nothing *is* better for a man *than* that he should eat and drink, and *that* his soul should enjoy good in his labor. This also, I saw, was from the hand of God.

Human responsibility is subject to.

Prov 16:1 The preparations of the heart *belong* to man, But the answer of the tongue *is* from the LORD.

Over creation.

Matt 10:29–30 Are not two sparrows sold for a copper coin? And not one of them falls to the ground apart from your Father's will. **30** But the very hairs of your head are all numbered.

Security of salvation depends on.

John 6:37 All that the Father gives Me will come to Me, and the one who comes to Me I will by no means cast out.

Every event in life is orchestrated by.

Rom 8:28 And we know that all things work together for good to those who love God, to those who are the called according to *His* purpose.

Salvation of elect is a result of.

Acts 13:48 Now when the Gentiles heard this, they were glad and glorified the word of the Lord. And as many as had been appointed to eternal life believed.

Rom 9:11 (for *the children* not yet being born, nor having done any good or evil, that the purpose of God according to election might stand, not of works but of Him who calls),

Eph 1:11 In Him also we have obtained an inheritance, being predestined according to the purpose of Him who works all things according to the counsel of His will,

SPEAR, THE

An offensive weapon.

2 Sam 23:8 These *are* the names of the mighty men whom David had: Josheb-Basshebeth the Tachmonite, chief among the captains. He was called Adino the Eznite, because he had killed eight hundred men at one time.

2 Sam 23:18 Now Abishai the brother of Joab, the son of Zeruiah, was chief of *another* three. He lifted his spear against three hundred *men*, killed *them*, and won a name among *these* three.

First mention of, in Scripture.

Josh 8:18 Then the LORD said to Joshua, "Stretch out the spear that *is* in your hand toward Ai, for I will give it into your hand." And Joshua stretched out the spear that *was* in his hand toward the city.

Parts of, mentioned

The staff of wood.

1 Sam 17:7 Now the staff of his spear *was* like a weaver's beam, and his iron spearhead *weighed* six hundred shekels; and a shield-bearer went before him.

The head of iron or bronze.

1 Sam 17:7 Now the staff of his spear *was* like a weaver's beam, and his iron spearhead *weighed* six hundred shekels; and a shield-bearer went before him.

2 Sam 21:16 Then Ishbi-Benob, who *was* one of the sons of the giant, the weight of whose bronze spear *was* three hundred *shekels*, who was bearing a new *sword*, thought he could kill David.

Probably pointed at both ends.

2 Sam 2:23 However, he refused to turn aside. Therefore Abner struck him in the stomach with the blunt end of the spear, so that the spear came out of his back; and he fell down there and died on the spot. So it was *that* as many as came to the place where Asahel fell down and died, stood still.

Called glittering.

Job 39:23 The quiver rattles against him, The glittering spear and javelin.

Hab 3:11 The sun and moon stood still in their habitation; At the light of Your arrows they went, At the shining of Your glittering spear.

Different kinds of,

Lances.

Jer 50:42 They shall hold the bow and the lance; They *are* cruel and shall not show mercy. Their voice shall roar like the sea; They shall ride on horses, Set in array, like a man for the battle, Against you, O daughter of Babylon.

Javelins.

Num 25:7 Now when Phinehas the son of Eleazar, the son of Aaron the priest, saw *it,* he rose from among the congregation and took a javelin in his hand;

1 Sam 18:10 And it happened on the next day that the distressing spirit from God came upon Saul, and he prophesied inside the house. So David played *music* with his hand, as at other times; but *there was* a spear in Saul's hand.

Darts.

2 Sam 18:14 Then Joab said, "I cannot linger with you." And he took three spears in his hand and thrust them through Absalom's heart, while he was *still* alive in the midst of the terebinth tree.

Job 41:26 *Though* the sword reaches him, it cannot avail; Nor does spear, dart, or javelin.

Job 41:29 Darts are regarded as straw; He laughs at the threat of javelins.

Those who used, called spearmen.

Acts 23:23 And he called for two centurions, saying, "Prepare two hundred soldiers, seventy horsemen, and two hundred spearmen to go to Caesarea at the third hour of the night;

Frequently used by horse soldiers.

Nah 3:3 Horsemen charge with bright sword and glittering spear. *There is* a multitude of slain, A great number of bodies, Countless corpses— They stumble over the corpses—

Prepared before war.

Jer 46:4 Harness the horses, And mount up, you horsemen! Stand forth with *your* helmets, Polish the spears, Put on the armor!

Pruning hooks made into, before war.

Joel 3:10 Beat your plowshares into swords And your pruning hooks into spears; Let the weak say, 'I *am* strong.' "

Made into pruning hooks in peace.

Is 2:4 He shall judge between the nations, And rebuke many people; They shall beat their swords into plowshares, And their spears into pruning hooks; Nation shall not lift up sword against nation, Neither shall they learn war anymore.

Mic 4:3 He shall judge between many peoples, And rebuke strong nations afar off; They shall beat their swords into plowshares, And their spears into pruning hooks; Nation shall not lift up sword against nation, Neither shall they learn war anymore.

The Israelites

Were acquainted with the making of.

1 Sam 13:19 Now there was no blacksmith to be found

throughout all the land of Israel, for the Philistines said, "Lest the Hebrews make swords or spears."

Frequently used.

Neh 4:13 Therefore I positioned *men* behind the lower parts of the wall, at the openings; and I set the people according to their families, with their swords, their spears, and their bows.

Neh 4:16 So it was, from that time on, *that* half of my servants worked at construction, while the other half held the spears, the shields, the bows, and *wore* armor; and the leaders *were* behind all the house of Judah.

Had none, in the times of Deborah and Saul.

Judg 5:8 They chose new gods; Then *there was* war in the gates; Not a shield or spear was seen among forty thousand in Israel.

1 Sam 13:22 So it came about, on the day of battle, that there was neither sword nor spear found in the hand of any of the people who *were* with Saul and Jonathan. But they were found with Saul and Jonathan his son.

Spears provided by their kings in great abundance.

2 Chr 11:12 Also in every city *he put* shields and spears, and made them very strong, having Judah and Benjamin on his side.

2 Chr 32:5 And he strengthened himself, built up all the wall that was broken, raised *it* up to the towers, and *built* another wall outside; also he repaired the Millo *in* the City of David, and made weapons and shields in abundance.

Frequently thrown from the hand.

1 Sam 18:11 And Saul cast the spear, for he said, "I will pin David to the wall!" But David escaped his presence twice.

1 Sam 19:10 Then Saul sought to pin David to the wall with the spear, but he slipped away from Saul's presence; and he drove the spear into the wall. So David fled and escaped that night.

Often retained in the hand of the person using.

Num 25:7 Now when Phinehas the son of Eleazar, the son of Aaron the priest, saw *it,* he rose from among the congregation and took a javelin in his hand;

2 Sam 2:23 However, he refused to turn aside. Therefore Abner struck him in the stomach with the blunt end of the spear, so that the spear came out of his back; and he fell down there and died on the spot. So it was *that* as many as came to the place where Asahel fell down and died, stood still.

Stuck in the ground beside the head during sleep.

1 Sam 26:7–11 So David and Abishai came to the people by night; and there Saul lay sleeping within the camp, with his spear stuck in the ground by his head. And Abner and the people lay all around him. **8** Then Abishai said to David, "God has delivered your enemy into your hand this day. Now therefore, please, let me strike him at once with the spear, right to the earth; and I will not *have to strike* him a second time!" **9** But David said to Abishai, "Do not destroy him; for who can stretch out his hand against the LORD's anointed, and be guiltless?" **10** David said furthermore, "*As* the LORD lives, the LORD shall strike him, or his day shall come to die, or he shall go out to battle and perish. **11** The LORD forbid that I should stretch out my hand against the LORD's anointed. But please, take now the spear and the jug of water that *are* by his head, and let us go."

Illustrative of the bitterness of the wicked.

Ps 57:4 My soul *is* among lions; I lie *among* the sons of men Who are set on fire, Whose teeth *are* spears and arrows, And their tongue a sharp sword.

SPEECH. *SEE ALSO* TONGUE(S)

Too much, risks sin.

Prov 10:19 In the multitude of words sin is not lacking, But he who restrains his lips *is* wise.

Discernment in, characteristic of the wise.

Prov 16:21 The wise in heart will be called prudent, And sweetness of the lips increases learning.

Of the wise, brings a blessing.

Prov 18:4 The words of a man's mouth *are* deep waters; The wellspring of wisdom *is* a flowing brook.

Everyone must give an account for their.

Matt 12:36 But I say to you that for every idle word men may speak, they will give account of it in the day of judgment.

Should edify others.

Eph 4:29 Let no corrupt word proceed out of your mouth, but what is good for necessary edification, that it may impart grace to the hearers.

Should act as a purifying influence.

Col 4:6 *Let* your speech always *be* with grace, seasoned with salt, that you may know how you ought to answer each one.

Reveals the purity of one's heart.

James 1:26 If anyone among you thinks he is religious, and does not bridle his tongue but deceives his own heart, this one's religion *is* useless.

The spiritually mature can control their.

James 3:2 For we all stumble in many things. If anyone does not stumble in word, he *is* a perfect man, able also to bridle the whole body.

SPIRITUAL GIFTS

Foretold as miraculous.

Is 35:4–6 Say to those *who are* fearful-hearted, "Be strong, do not fear! Behold, your God will come *with* vengeance, *With* the recompense of God; He will come and save you." **5** Then the eyes of the blind shall be opened, And the ears of the deaf shall be unstopped. **6** Then the lame shall leap like a deer, And the tongue of the dumb sing. For waters shall burst forth in the wilderness, And streams in the desert.

Joel 2:28–29 "And it shall come to pass afterward That I will pour out My Spirit on all flesh; Your sons and your daughters shall prophesy, Your old men shall dream dreams, Your young men shall see visions. **29** And also on *My* menservants and on *My* maidservants I will pour out My Spirit in those days

Different kinds of, enumerated.

1 Cor 12:4–6 There are diversities of gifts, but the same Spirit. **5** There are differences of ministries, but the same Lord. **6** And there are diversities of activities, but it is the same God who works all in all.

1 Cor 12:8–10 for to one is given the word of wisdom through the Spirit, to another the word of knowledge through the same Spirit, **9** to another faith by the same Spirit, to another gifts of healings by the same Spirit, **10** to another the working of miracles, to another prophecy, to another discerning of spirits, to another *different* kinds of tongues, to another the interpretation of tongues.

1 Cor 12:28 And God has appointed these in the church: first apostles, second prophets, third teachers, after that miracles, then gifts of healings, helps, administrations, varieties of tongues.

1 Cor 14:1 Pursue love, and desire spiritual *gifts,* but especially that you may prophesy.

Christ was endued with.

Matt 12:28 But if I cast out demons by the Spirit of God, surely the kingdom of God has come upon you.

Poured out on the day of Pentecost.

Acts 2:1–4 When the Day of Pentecost had fully come, they were all with one accord in one place. **2** And suddenly there came a sound from heaven, as of a rushing mighty wind, and it filled the whole house where they were sitting. **3** Then there appeared to them divided tongues, as of fire, and *one* sat upon each of them. **4** And they were all filled with the Holy Spirit and began to speak with other tongues, as the Spirit gave them utterance.

Conferred on the preaching of the gospel.

Acts 10:44–46 While Peter was still speaking these words, the Holy Spirit fell upon all those who heard the word. **45** And those of the circumcision who believed were astonished, as many as came with Peter, because the gift of the Holy Spirit had been poured out on the Gentiles also. **46** For they heard them speak with tongues and magnify God. Then Peter answered,

Given by the laying on of the apostles' hands.

Acts 8:17–18 Then they laid hands on them, and they received the Holy Spirit. **18** And when Simon saw that through the laying on of the apostles' hands the Holy Spirit was given, he offered them money,

Acts 19:6 And when Paul had laid hands on them, the Holy Spirit came upon them, and they spoke with tongues and prophesied.

For the edification of the church.

1 Cor 12:7 But the manifestation of the Spirit is given to each one for the profit *of all:*

1 Cor 14:12–13 Even so you, since you are zealous for spiritual *gifts, let it be* for the edification of the church *that* you seek to excel. **13** Therefore let him who speaks in a tongue pray that he may interpret.

Dispensed according to His sovereign will.

1 Cor 12:11 But one and the same Spirit works all these things, distributing to each one individually as He wills.

Were to be sought after.

1 Cor 12:31 But earnestly desire the best gifts. And yet I show you a more excellent way.

1 Cor 14:1 Pursue love, and desire spiritual *gifts,* but especially that you may prophesy.

Temporary nature of.

1 Cor 13:8 Love never fails. But whether *there are* prophecies, they will fail; whether *there are* tongues, they will cease; whether *there is* knowledge, it will vanish away.

Were not to be

Neglected.

1 Tim 4:14 Do not neglect the gift that is in you, which was given to you by prophecy with the laying on of the hands of the eldership.

2 Tim 1:6 Therefore I remind you to stir up the gift of God which is in you through the laying on of my hands.

Despised.

1 Thess 5:20 Do not despise prophecies.

Purchased.

Acts 8:20 But Peter said to him, "Your money perish with you, because you thought that the gift of God could be purchased with money!

Might seem to be present without saving grace.

Matt 7:22–23 Many will say to Me in that day, 'Lord, Lord, have we not prophesied in Your name, cast out demons in Your name, and done many wonders in Your name?' 23 And then I will declare to them, 'I never knew you; depart from Me, you who practice lawlessness!'

1 Cor 13:1–2 Though I speak with the tongues of men and of angels, but have not love, I have become sounding brass or a clanging cymbal. 2 And though I have *the gift of* prophecy, and understand all mysteries and all knowledge, and though I have all faith, so that I could remove mountains, but have not love, I am nothing.

Counterfeited by Antichrist.

Matt 24:24 For false christs and false prophets will rise and show great signs and wonders to deceive, if possible, even the elect.

2 Thess 2:9 The coming of the *lawless one* is according to the working of Satan, with all power, signs, and lying wonders,

Rev 13:13–14 He performs great signs, so that he even makes fire come down from heaven on the earth in the sight of men. 14 And he deceives those who dwell on the earth by those signs which he was granted to do in the sight of the beast, telling those who dwell on the earth to make an image to the beast who was wounded by the sword and lived.

STARS, THE

Infinite in number.

Gen 15:5 Then He brought him outside and said, "Look now toward heaven, and count the stars if you are able to number them." And He said to him, "So shall your descendants be."

Jer 33:22 As the host of heaven cannot be numbered, nor the sand of the sea measured, so will I multiply the descendants of David My servant and the Levites who minister to Me.' "

God

Created.

Gen 1:16–17 Then God made two great lights: the greater light to rule the day, and the lesser light to rule the night. *He made* the stars also. 17 God set them in the firmament of the heavens to give light on the earth,

Ps 8:3 When I consider Your heavens, the work of Your fingers, The moon and the stars, which You have ordained,

Ps 148:5 Let them praise the name of the LORD, For He commanded and they were created.

Appointed them to give light by night.

Gen 1:14 Then God said, "Let there be lights in the firmament of the heavens to divide the day from the night; and let them be for signs and seasons, and for days and years;

Gen 1:16 Then God made two great lights: the greater light to rule the day, and the lesser light to rule the night. *He made* the stars also.

Ps 136:9 The moon and stars to rule by night, For His mercy *endures* forever.

Jer 31:35 Thus says the LORD, Who gives the sun for a light by day, The ordinances of the moon and the stars for a light by night, Who disturbs the sea, And its waves roar (The LORD of hosts *is* His name):

Gave them numbers and names.

Ps 147:4 He counts the number of the stars; He calls them all by name.

Established, forever.

Ps 148:3 Praise Him, sun and moon; Praise Him, all you stars of light!

Ps 148:6 He also established them forever and ever; He made a decree which shall not pass away.

Jer 31:36 "If those ordinances depart From before Me, says the LORD, *Then* the seed of Israel shall also cease From being a nation before Me forever."

Sometimes obscures them.

Job 9:7 He commands the sun, and it does not rise; He seals off the stars;

They exhibit the greatness of His power.

Ps 8:3 When I consider Your heavens, the work of Your fingers, The moon and the stars, which You have ordained,

Is 40:26 Lift up your eyes on high, And see who has created these *things,* Who brings out their host by number; He calls them all by name, By the greatness of His might And the strength of *His* power; Not one is missing.

They are made to praise Him.

Ps 148:3 Praise Him, sun and moon; Praise Him, all you stars of light!

They are impure compared to Him.

Job 25:5 If even the moon does not shine, And the stars are not pure in His sight,

Revolve in fixed orbits.

Judg 5:20 They fought from the heavens; The stars from their courses fought against Sisera.

Shine in the firmament of heaven.

Dan 12:3 Those who are wise shall shine Like the

brightness of the firmament, And those who turn many to righteousness Like the stars forever and ever.

Are of different magnitudes.

1 Cor 15:41 *There is* one glory of the sun, another glory of the moon, and another glory of the stars; for *one* star differs from *another* star in glory.

Appear after sunset.

Neh 4:21 So we labored in the work, and half of *the men* held the spears from daybreak until the stars appeared.

Job 3:9 May the stars of its morning be dark; May it look for light, but *have* none, And not see the dawning of the day;

Called

The host of heaven.

Deut 17:3 who has gone and served other gods and worshiped them, either the sun or moon or any of the host of heaven, which I have not commanded,

Jer 33:22 As the host of heaven cannot be numbered, nor the sand of the sea measured, so will I multiply the descendants of David My servant and the Levites who minister to Me.' "

Stars of light.

Ps 148:3 Praise Him, sun and moon; Praise Him, all you stars of light!

Stars of heaven.

Is 13:10 For the stars of heaven and their constellations Will not give their light; The sun will be darkened in its going forth, And the moon will not cause its light to shine.

When grouped together, called constellations.

2 Kin 23:5 Then he removed the idolatrous priests whom the kings of Judah had ordained to burn incense on the high places in the cities of Judah and in the places all around Jerusalem, and those who burned incense to Baal, to the sun, to the moon, to the constellations, and to all the host of heaven.

Is 13:10 For the stars of heaven and their constellations Will not give their light; The sun will be darkened in its going forth, And the moon will not cause its light to shine.

Ones mentioned in Scripture

Morning star.

Rev 2:28 and I will give him the morning star.

The Bear (Arcturus).

Job 9:9 He made the Bear, Orion, and the Pleiades, And the chambers of the south;

Job 38:32 Can you bring out Mazzaroth in its season? Or can you guide the Great Bear with its cubs?

Pleiades.

Job 9:9 He made the Bear, Orion, and the Pleiades, And the chambers of the south;

Job 38:31 "Can you bind the cluster of the Pleiades, Or loose the belt of Orion?

Amos 5:8 He made the Pleiades and Orion; He turns the shadow of death into morning And makes the day dark as night; He calls for the waters of the sea And pours them out on the face of the earth; The LORD *is* His name.

Orion.

Job 9:9 He made the Bear, Orion, and the Pleiades, And the chambers of the south;

Job 38:31 "Can you bind the cluster of the Pleiades, Or loose the belt of Orion?

Amos 5:8 He made the Pleiades and Orion; He turns the shadow of death into morning And makes the day dark as night; He calls for the waters of the sea And pours them out on the face of the earth; The LORD *is* His name.

Mazzaroth.

Job 38:32 Can you bring out Mazzaroth in its season? Or can you guide the Great Bear with its cubs?

One of extraordinary brightness appeared at Christ's birth.

Matt 2:2 saying, "Where is He who has been born King of the Jews? For we have seen His star in the East and have come to worship Him."

Matt 2:9 When they heard the king, they departed; and behold, the star which they had seen in the East went before them, till it came and stood over where the young Child was.

Idolaters worshiped.

Jer 8:2 They shall spread them before the sun and the moon and all the host of heaven, which they have loved and which they have served and after which they have walked, which they have sought and which they have worshiped. They shall not be gathered nor buried; they shall be like refuse on the face of the earth.

Jer 19:13 And the houses of Jerusalem and the houses of the kings of Judah shall be defiled like the place of Tophet, because of all the houses on whose roofs they have burned incense to all the host of heaven, and poured out drink offerings to other gods." ' "

Amos 5:26 You also carried Sikkuth your king And Chiun, your idols, The star of your gods, Which you made for yourselves.

Acts 7:43 *You also took up the tabernacle of Moloch, And the star of your god Remphan, Images which you made to worship; And I will carry you away beyond Babylon.'*

The Israelites forbidden to worship.

Deut 4:19 And *take heed,* lest you lift your eyes to heaven, and *when* you see the sun, the moon, and the stars, all the host of heaven, you feel driven to worship them and serve them, which the LORD your God has given to all the peoples under the whole heaven as a heritage.

Deut 17:2–4 "If there is found among you, within any of your gates which the LORD your God gives you, a man or a woman who has been wicked in the sight of the LORD your God, in transgressing His covenant, 3 who has gone and served other gods and worshiped them, either the sun or moon or any of the host of heaven, which I have not commanded, 4 and it is told you, and you hear *of it,* then you shall inquire diligently. And if *it is* indeed true *and* certain that such an abomination has been committed in Israel,

Punishment for worshiping.

Deut 17:5–7 then you shall bring out to your gates that

man or woman who has committed that wicked thing, and shall stone to death that man or woman with stones. **6** Whoever is deserving of death shall be put to death on the testimony of two or three witnesses; he shall not be put to death on the testimony of one witness. **7** The hands of the witnesses shall be the first against him to put him to death, and afterward the hands of all the people. So you shall put away the evil from among you.

Astrology and stargazing practiced by the Babylonians.

Is 47:13 You are wearied in the multitude of your counsels; Let now the astrologers, the stargazers, *And* the monthly prognosticators Stand up and save you From what shall come upon you.

Use of, in navigation, alluded to.

Acts 27:20 Now when neither sun nor stars appeared for many days, and no small tempest beat on *us,* all hope that we would be saved was finally given up.

Illustrative of

Christ.

Num 24:17 "I see Him, but not now; I behold Him, but not near; A Star shall come out of Jacob; A Scepter shall rise out of Israel, And batter the brow of Moab, And destroy all the sons of tumult.

Rev 22:16 "I, Jesus, have sent My angel to testify to you these things in the churches. I am the Root and the Offspring of David, the Bright and Morning Star."

Angels.

Job 38:7 When the morning stars sang together, And all the sons of God shouted for joy?

Ministers.

Rev 1:16 He had in His right hand seven stars, out of His mouth went a sharp two-edged sword, and His countenance *was* like the sun shining in its strength.

Rev 1:20 The mystery of the seven stars which you saw in My right hand, and the seven golden lampstands: The seven stars are the angels of the seven churches, and the seven lampstands which you saw are the seven churches.

Rev 2:1 "To the angel of the church of Ephesus write, 'These things says He who holds the seven stars in His right hand, who walks in the midst of the seven golden lampstands:

Princes and subordinate governors.

Dan 8:10 And it grew up to the host of heaven; and it cast down *some* of the host and *some* of the stars to the ground, and trampled them.

Rev 8:12 Then the fourth angel sounded: And a third of the sun was struck, a third of the moon, and a third of the stars, so that a third of them were darkened. A third of the day did not shine, and likewise the night.

(Morning star) glory to be given to faithful believers.

Rev 2:28 and I will give him the morning star.

(Shining of) the reward of faithful ministers.

Dan 12:3 Those who are wise shall shine Like the brightness of the firmament, And those who turn many to righteousness Like the stars forever and ever.

(Withdrawing their light) severe judgments.

Is 13:10 For the stars of heaven and their constellations Will not give their light; The sun will be darkened in its going forth, And the moon will not cause its light to shine.

Ezek 32:7 When *I* put out your light, I will cover the heavens, and make its stars dark; I will cover the sun with a cloud, And the moon shall not give her light.

Joel 2:10 The earth quakes before them, The heavens tremble; The sun and moon grow dark, And the stars diminish their brightness.

Joel 3:15 The sun and moon will grow dark, And the stars will diminish their brightness.

(Setting the nest among) pride and carnal security.

Obad 1:4 Though you ascend *as* high as the eagle, And though you set your nest among the stars, From there I will bring you down," says the LORD.

(Wandering) false teachers.

Jude 1:13 raging waves of the sea, foaming up their own shame; wandering stars for whom is reserved the blackness of darkness forever.

STEADFASTNESS

Exhibited by God.

Num 23:19 "God *is* not a man, that He should lie, Nor a son of man, that He should repent. Has He said, and will He not do? Or has He spoken, and will He not make it good?

Dan 6:26 I make a decree that in every dominion of my kingdom *men must* tremble and fear before the God of Daniel. For He *is* the living God, And steadfast forever; His kingdom *is the one* which shall not be destroyed, And His dominion *shall endure* to the end.

James 1:17 Every good gift and every perfect gift is from above, and comes down from the Father of lights, with whom there is no variation or shadow of turning.

Commanded.

Phil 4:1 Therefore, my beloved and longed-for brethren, my joy and crown, so stand fast in the Lord, beloved.

2 Thess 2:15 Therefore, brethren, stand fast and hold the traditions which you were taught, whether by word or our epistle.

James 1:6–8 But let him ask in faith, with no doubting, for he who doubts is like a wave of the sea driven and tossed by the wind. **7** For let not that man suppose that he will receive anything from the Lord; **8** *he is* a double-minded man, unstable in all his ways.

Godliness necessary for.

Job 11:13–15 "If you would prepare your heart, And stretch out your hands toward Him; **14** If iniquity *were* in your hand, *and you* put it far away, And would not let wickedness dwell in your tents; **15** Then surely you could lift up your face without spot; Yes, you could be steadfast, and not fear;

Secured by

The power of God.

Ps 55:22 Cast your burden on the LORD, And He shall sustain you; He shall never permit the righteous to be moved.

Ps 62:2 He only *is* my rock and my salvation; *He is* my defense; I shall not be greatly moved.

1 Pet 1:5 who are kept by the power of God through faith for salvation ready to be revealed in the last time.

Jude 1:24 Now to Him who is able to keep you from stumbling, And to present *you* faultless Before the presence of His glory with exceeding joy,

The presence of God.

Ps 16:8 I have set the LORD always before me; Because *He is* at my right hand I shall not be moved.

Trust in God.

Ps 26:1 Vindicate me, O LORD, For I have walked in my integrity. I have also trusted in the LORD; I shall not slip.

The intercession of Christ.

Luke 22:31–32 And the Lord said, "Simon, Simon! Indeed, Satan has asked for you, that he may sift *you* as wheat. 32 But I have prayed for you, that your faith should not fail; and when you have returned to *Me*, strengthen your brethren."

Should be manifested in

Cleaving to God.

Deut 10:20 You shall fear the LORD your God; you shall serve Him, and to Him you shall hold fast, and take oaths in His name.

Acts 11:23 When he came and had seen the grace of God, he was glad, and encouraged them all that with purpose of heart they should continue with the Lord.

The work of the Lord.

1 Cor 15:58 Therefore, my beloved brethren, be steadfast, immovable, always abounding in the work of the Lord, knowing that your labor is not in vain in the Lord.

Continuing in the apostles' doctrine.

Acts 2:42 And they continued steadfastly in the apostles' doctrine and fellowship, in the breaking of bread, and in prayers.

Holding fast our confession.

Heb 4:14 Seeing then that we have a great High Priest who has passed through the heavens, Jesus the Son of God, let us hold fast *our* confession.

Heb 10:23 Let us hold fast the confession of *our* hope without wavering, for He who promised *is* faithful.

Holding fast the confidence and rejoicing of the hope.

Heb 3:6 but Christ as a Son over His own house, whose house we are if we hold fast the confidence and the rejoicing of the hope firm to the end.

Heb 3:14 For we have become partakers of Christ if we hold the beginning of our confidence steadfast to the end,

Keeping the faith.

1 Cor 16:13 Watch, stand fast in the faith, be brave, be strong.

Col 2:5 For though I am absent in the flesh, yet I am with you in spirit, rejoicing to see your *good* order and the steadfastness of your faith in Christ.

1 Pet 5:9 Resist him, steadfast in the faith, knowing that the same sufferings are experienced by your brotherhood in the world.

Holding fast what is good.

1 Thess 5:21 Test all things; hold fast what is good.

Maintaining Christian liberty.

Gal 5:1 Stand fast therefore in the liberty by which Christ has made us free, and do not be entangled again with a yoke of bondage.

Striving for the faith of the gospel.

Phil 1:27 Only let your conduct be worthy of the gospel of Christ, so that whether I come and see you or am absent, I may hear of your affairs, that you stand fast in one spirit, with one mind striving together for the faith of the gospel,

Jude 1:3 Beloved, while I was very diligent to write to you concerning our common salvation, I found it necessary to write to you exhorting you to contend earnestly for the faith which was once for all delivered to the saints.

In affliction.

Ps 44:17–19 All this has come upon us; But we have not forgotten You, Nor have we dealt falsely with Your covenant. 18 Our heart has not turned back, Nor have our steps departed from Your way; 19 But You have severely broken us in the place of jackals, And covered us with the shadow of death.

Rom 8:35–37 Who shall separate us from the love of Christ? *Shall* tribulation, or distress, or persecution, or famine, or nakedness, or peril, or sword? 36 As it is written: *"For Your sake we are killed all day long; We are accounted as sheep for the slaughter."* 37 Yet in all these things we are more than conquerors through Him who loved us.

1 Thess 3:3 that no one should be shaken by these afflictions; for you yourselves know that we are appointed to this.

Believers

Pray for.

Ps 17:5 Uphold my steps in Your paths, *That* my footsteps may not slip.

Praise God for.

Ps 116:8 For You have delivered my soul from death, My eyes from tears, *And* my feet from falling.

A characteristic of.

Job 17:9 Yet the righteous will hold to his way, And he who has clean hands will be stronger and stronger.

John 8:31 Then Jesus said to those Jews who believed Him, "If you abide in My word, you are My disciples indeed.

Ministers

Exhorted to.

2 Tim 1:13–14 Hold fast the pattern of sound words which you have heard from me, in faith and love which are in Christ Jesus. 14 That good thing which was committed to you, keep by the Holy Spirit who dwells in us.

Titus 1:9 holding fast the faithful word as he has been taught, that he may be able, by sound doctrine, both to exhort and convict those who contradict.

Should exhort others to.

Acts 13:43 Now when the congregation had broken up, many of the Jews and devout proselytes followed

Paul and Barnabas, who, speaking to them, persuaded them to continue in the grace of God.

Acts 14:22 strengthening the souls of the disciples, exhorting *them* to continue in the faith, and *saying,* "We must through many tribulations enter the kingdom of God."

Should pray for, in their people.

1 Thess 3:13 so that He may establish your hearts blameless in holiness before our God and Father at the coming of our Lord Jesus Christ with all His saints.

2 Thess 2:17 comfort your hearts and establish you in every good word and work.

Encouraged by, in their people.

1 Thess 3:8 For now we live, if you stand fast in the Lord.

Rejoice to see, in their people.

Col 2:5 For though I am absent in the flesh, yet I am with you in spirit, rejoicing to see your *good* order and the steadfastness of your faith in Christ.

The wicked devoid of.

Ps 78:8 And may not be like their fathers, A stubborn and rebellious generation, A generation *that* did not set its heart aright, And whose spirit was not faithful to God.

Ps 78:37 For their heart was not steadfast with Him, Nor were they faithful in His covenant.

Principle of—illustrated.

Matt 7:24–25 "Therefore whoever hears these sayings of Mine, and does them, I will liken him to a wise man who built his house on the rock: **25** and the rain descended, the floods came, and the winds blew and beat on that house; and it did not fall, for it was founded on the rock.

John 15:4 Abide in Me, and I in you. As the branch cannot bear fruit of itself, unless it abides in the vine, neither can you, unless you abide in Me.

Col 2:7 rooted and built up in Him and established in the faith, as you have been taught, abounding in it with thanksgiving.

Lack of—illustrated.

Luke 8:6 Some fell on rock; and as soon as it sprang up, it withered away because it lacked moisture.

Luke 8:13 But the ones on the rock *are those* who, when they hear, receive the word with joy; and these have no root, who believe for a while and in time of temptation fall away.

John 15:6 If anyone does not abide in Me, he is cast out as a branch and is withered; and they gather them and throw *them* into the fire, and they are burned.

2 Pet 2:17 These are wells without water, clouds carried by a tempest, for whom is reserved the blackness of darkness forever.

Jude 1:12 These are spots in your love feasts, while they feast with you without fear, serving *only* themselves. *They are* clouds without water, carried about by the winds; late autumn trees without fruit, twice dead, pulled up by the roots;

Exemplified by

Caleb.

Num 14:24 But My servant Caleb, because he has a dif-

ferent spirit in him and has followed Me fully, I will bring into the land where he went, and his descendants shall inherit it.

Joshua.

Josh 24:15 And if it seems evil to you to serve the LORD, choose for yourselves this day whom you will serve, whether the gods which your fathers served that *were* on the other side of the River, or the gods of the Amorites, in whose land you dwell. But as for me and my house, we will serve the LORD."

Josiah.

2 Kin 22:2 And he did *what was* right in the sight of the LORD, and walked in all the ways of his father David; he did not turn aside to the right hand or to the left.

Job.

Job 2:3 Then the LORD said to Satan, "Have you considered My servant Job, that *there is* none like him on the earth, a blameless and upright man, one who fears God and shuns evil? And still he holds fast to his integrity, although you incited Me against him, to destroy him without cause."

David.

Ps 18:21–22 For I have kept the ways of the LORD, And have not wickedly departed from my God. **22** For all His judgments *were* before me, And I did not put away His statutes from me.

Shadrach.

Dan 3:18 But if not, let it be known to you, O king, that we do not serve your gods, nor will we worship the gold image which you have set up."

Daniel.

Dan 6:10 Now when Daniel knew that the writing was signed, he went home. And in his upper room, with his windows open toward Jerusalem, he knelt down on his knees three times that day, and prayed and gave thanks before his God, as was his custom since early days.

The early Christians.

Acts 2:42 And they continued steadfastly in the apostles' doctrine and fellowship, in the breaking of bread, and in prayers.

The Corinthians.

1 Cor 15:1 Moreover, brethren, I declare to you the gospel which I preached to you, which also you received and in which you stand,

The Colossians.

Col 2:5 For though I am absent in the flesh, yet I am with you in spirit, rejoicing to see your *good* order and the steadfastness of your faith in Christ.

Those who overcame Satan.

Rev 12:11 And they overcame him by the blood of the Lamb and by the word of their testimony, and they did not love their lives to the death.

STEWARD

Paul was one, of the mysteries of God.

1 Cor 4:1 Let a man so consider us, as servants of Christ and stewards of the mysteries of God.

Col 1:25 of which I became a minister according to the stewardship from God which was given to me for you, to fulfill the word of God,

Must be faithful.

1 Cor 4:2 Moreover it is required in stewards that one be found faithful.

Elders serve God as.

Titus 1:7 For a bishop must be blameless, as a steward of God, not self-willed, not quick-tempered, not given to wine, not violent, not greedy for money,

Believers serve God as, in handling His gifts.

1 Pet 4:10 As each one has received a gift, minister it to one another, as good stewards of the manifold grace of God.

STRANGERS AND PILGRIMS

Described.

John 17:16 They are not of the world, just as I am not of the world.

Believers are called to be.

Gen 12:1 Now the LORD had said to Abram: "Get out of your country, From your family And from your father's house, To a land that I will show you.

Ps 39:12 "Hear my prayer, O LORD, And give ear to my cry; Do not be silent at my tears; For I *am* a stranger with You, A sojourner, as all my fathers *were.*

Luke 14:26–27 "If anyone comes to Me and does not hate his father and mother, wife and children, brothers and sisters, yes, and his own life also, he cannot be My disciple. **27** And whoever does not bear his cross and come after Me cannot be My disciple.

Luke 14:33 So likewise, whoever of you does not forsake all that he has cannot be My disciple.

Acts 7:3 and said to him, *'Get out of your country and from your relatives, and come to a land that I will show you.'*

1 Pet 1:1 Peter, an apostle of Jesus Christ, To the pilgrims of the Dispersion in Pontus, Galatia, Cappadocia, Asia, and Bithynia,

Saints confess themselves.

1 Chr 29:15 For we *are* aliens and pilgrims before You, As *were* all our fathers; Our days on earth *are* as a shadow, And without hope.

Ps 39:12 "Hear my prayer, O LORD, And give ear to my cry; Do not be silent at my tears; For I *am* a stranger with You, A sojourner, as all my fathers *were.*

Ps 119:19 I *am* a stranger in the earth; Do not hide Your commandments from me.

Heb 11:13 These all died in faith, not having received the promises, but having seen them afar off were assured of them, embraced *them* and confessed that they were strangers and pilgrims on the earth.

As saints they

Have the example of Christ.

Luke 9:58 And Jesus said to him, "Foxes have holes and birds of the air *have* nests, but the Son of Man has nowhere to lay *His* head."

Are strengthened by God.

Deut 33:25 Your sandals *shall be* iron and bronze; As your days, *so shall* your strength *be.*

Ps 84:6–7 *As they* pass through the Valley of Baca, They make it a spring; The rain also covers it with pools.

7 They go from strength to strength; *Each one* appears before God in Zion.

Are actuated by faith.

Heb 11:9 By faith he dwelt in the land of promise as *in* a foreign country, dwelling in tents with Isaac and Jacob, the heirs with him of the same promise;

Have their faces toward Zion.

Jer 50:5 They shall ask the way to Zion, With their faces toward it, *saying,* 'Come and let us join ourselves to the LORD *In* a perpetual covenant *That* will not be forgotten.'

Keep the promises in view.

Heb 11:13 These all died in faith, not having received the promises, but having seen them afar off were assured of them, embraced *them* and confessed that they were strangers and pilgrims on the earth.

Forsake all for Christ.

Matt 19:27 Then Peter answered and said to Him, "See, we have left all and followed You. Therefore what shall we have?"

Look for a heavenly country.

Heb 11:16 But now they desire a better, that is, a heavenly *country.* Therefore God is not ashamed to be called their God, for He has prepared a city for them.

Look for a heavenly city.

Heb 11:10 for he waited for the city which has foundations, whose builder and maker *is* God.

Pass their sojourning in fear.

1 Pet 1:17 And if you call on the Father, who without partiality judges according to each one's work, conduct yourselves throughout the time of your stay *here* in fear;

Rejoice in the statutes of God.

Ps 119:54 Your statutes have been my songs In the house of my pilgrimage.

Pray for direction.

Ps 43:3 Oh, send out Your light and Your truth! Let them lead me; Let them bring me to Your holy hill And to Your tabernacle.

Jer 50:5 They shall ask the way to Zion, With their faces toward it, *saying,* 'Come and let us join ourselves to the LORD *In* a perpetual covenant *That* will not be forgotten.'

Have a heavenly citizenship.

Phil 3:20 For our citizenship is in heaven, from which we also eagerly wait for the Savior, the Lord Jesus Christ,

Hate worldly fellowship.

Ps 120:5–6 Woe is me, that I dwell in Meshech, *That* I dwell among the tents of Kedar! **6** My soul has dwelt too long With one who hates peace.

Are not mindful of this world.

Heb 11:15 And truly if they had called to mind that *country* from which they had come out, they would have had opportunity to return.

Are not at home in this world.

Heb 11:9 By faith he dwelt in the land of promise as *in* a foreign country, dwelling in tents with Isaac and Jacob, the heirs with him of the same promise;

Shine as lights in the world.

Phil 2:15 that you may become blameless and harmless, children of God without fault in the midst of a crooked and perverse generation, among whom you shine as lights in the world,

Invite others to go with them.

Num 10:29 Now Moses said to Hobab the son of Reuel the Midianite, Moses' father-in-law, "We are setting out for the place of which the LORD said, 'I will give it to you.' Come with us, and we will treat you well; for the LORD has promised good things to Israel."

Are exposed to persecution.

Ps 120:5–7 Woe is me, that I dwell in Meshech, *That I* dwell among the tents of Kedar! **6** My soul has dwelt too long With one who hates peace. **7** I *am for* peace; But when I speak, they *are* for war.

John 17:14 I have given them Your word; and the world has hated them because they are not of the world, just as I am not of the world.

Should abstain from fleshly lusts.

1 Pet 2:11 Beloved, I beg *you* as sojourners and pilgrims, abstain from fleshly lusts which war against the soul,

Should have their treasure in heaven.

Matt 6:19 "Do not lay up for yourselves treasures on earth, where moth and rust destroy and where thieves break in and steal;

Luke 12:33 Sell what you have and give alms; provide yourselves money bags which do not grow old, a treasure in the heavens that does not fail, where no thief approaches nor moth destroys.

Col 3:1–2 If then you were raised with Christ, seek those things which are above, where Christ is, sitting at the right hand of God. **2** Set your mind on things above, not on things on the earth.

Should not be over anxious about worldly things.

Matt 6:25 "Therefore I say to you, do not worry about your life, what you will eat or what you will drink; nor about your body, what you will put on. Is not life more than food and the body more than clothing?

Long for their pilgrimage to end.

Ps 55:6 So I said, "Oh, that I had wings like a dove! I would fly away and be at rest.

2 Cor 5:1–8 For we know that if our earthly house, *this* tent, is destroyed, we have a building from God, a house not made with hands, eternal in the heavens. **2** For in this we groan, earnestly desiring to be clothed with our habitation which is from heaven, **3** if indeed, having been clothed, we shall not be found naked. **4** For we who are in *this* tent groan, being burdened, not because we want to be unclothed, but further clothed, that mortality may be swallowed up by life. **5** Now He who has prepared us for this very thing *is* God, who also has given us the Spirit as a guarantee. **6** So *we are* always confident, knowing that while we are at home in the body we are absent from the Lord. **7** For we walk by faith, not by sight. **8** We are confident, yes, well pleased rather to be absent from the body and to be present with the Lord.

Die in faith.

Heb 11:13 These all died in faith, not having received the promises, but having seen them afar off were as-

sured of them, embraced *them* and confessed that they were strangers and pilgrims on the earth.

The world is not worthy of.

Heb 11:38 of whom the world was not worthy. They wandered in deserts and mountains, *in* dens and caves of the earth.

God is not ashamed to be called their God.

Heb 11:16 But now they desire a better, that is, a heavenly *country.* Therefore God is not ashamed to be called their God, for He has prepared a city for them.

Typified by

Israel.

Ex 6:4 I have also established My covenant with them, to give them the land of Canaan, the land of their pilgrimage, in which they were strangers.

Ex 12:11 And thus you shall eat it: *with* a belt on your waist, your sandals on your feet, and your staff in your hand. So you shall eat it in haste. It *is* the LORD's Passover.

Exemplified

Abraham.

Gen 23:4 "I *am* a foreigner and a visitor among you. Give me property for a burial place among you, that I may bury my dead out of my sight."

Acts 7:4–5 Then he came out of the land of the Chaldeans and dwelt in Haran. And from there, when his father was dead, He moved him to this land in which you now dwell. **5** And *God* gave him no inheritance in it, not even *enough* to set his foot on. But even when *Abraham* had no child, He promised to give it to him for a possession, and to his descendants after him.

Jacob.

Gen 47:9 And Jacob said to Pharaoh, "The days of the years of my pilgrimage *are* one hundred and thirty years; few and evil have been the days of the years of my life, and they have not attained to the days of the years of the life of my fathers in the days of their pilgrimage."

The saints of old.

1 Chr 29:15 For we *are* aliens and pilgrims before You, As *were* all our fathers; Our days on earth *are* as a shadow, And without hope.

Heb 11:13 These all died in faith, not having received the promises, but having seen them afar off were assured of them, embraced *them* and confessed that they were strangers and pilgrims on the earth.

Heb 11:38 of whom the world was not worthy. They wandered in deserts and mountains, *in* dens and caves of the earth.

David.

Ps 39:12 "Hear my prayer, O LORD, And give ear to my cry; Do not be silent at my tears; For I *am* a stranger with You, A sojourner, as all my fathers *were.*

The apostles.

Matt 19:27 Then Peter answered and said to Him, "See, we have left all and followed You. Therefore what shall we have?"

STRANGERS IN ISRAEL

All foreigners sojourning in Israel were counted as.

Ex 12:49 One law shall be for the native-born and for the stranger who dwells among you."

Under the care and protection of God.

Deut 10:18 He administers justice for the fatherless and the widow, and loves the stranger, giving him food and clothing.

Ps 146:9 The LORD watches over the strangers; He relieves the fatherless and widow; But the way of the wicked He turns upside down.

Very numerous in Solomon's reign.

2 Chr 2:17 Then Solomon numbered all the aliens who *were* in the land of Israel, after the census in which David his father had numbered them; and there were found to be one hundred and fifty-three thousand six hundred.

Chiefly consisted of

The remnant of the mixed multitude that came out of Egypt.

Ex 12:38 A mixed multitude went up with them also, and flocks and herds—a great deal of livestock.

The remnant of the nations of the land.

1 Kin 9:20 All the people *who were* left of the Amorites, Hittites, Perizzites, Hivites, and Jebusites, who *were* not of the children of Israel—

2 Chr 8:7 All the people *who were* left of the Hittites, Amorites, Perizzites, Hivites, and Jebusites, who *were* not of Israel—

Captives taken in war.

Deut 21:10 "When you go out to war against your enemies, and the LORD your God delivers them into your hand, and you take them captive,

Foreign servants.

Lev 25:44–45 And as for your male and female slaves whom you may have—from the nations that are around you, from them you may buy male and female slaves. **45** Moreover you may buy the children of the strangers who dwell among you, and their families who are with you, which they beget in your land; and they shall become your property.

Persons who sought employment among the Jews.

1 Kin 7:13 Now King Solomon sent and brought Huram from Tyre.

1 Kin 9:27 Then Hiram sent his servants with the fleet, seamen who knew the sea, to work with the servants of Solomon.

Persons who came into Israel for the sake of religious privileges.

1 Kin 8:41 "Moreover, concerning a foreigner, who *is* not of Your people Israel, but has come from a far country for Your name's sake

Laws respecting

Not to practice idolatrous rites.

Lev 20:2 "Again, you shall say to the children of Israel: 'Whoever of the children of Israel, or of the strangers who dwell in Israel, who gives *any* of his descendants to Molech, he shall surely be put to death. The people of the land shall stone him with stones.

Not to blaspheme God.

Lev 24:16 And whoever blasphemes the name of the LORD shall surely be put to death. All the congregation shall certainly stone him, the stranger as well as him who is born in the land. When he blasphemes the name *of the LORD,* he shall be put to death.

Not to eat blood.

Lev 17:10–12 'And whatever man of the house of Israel, or of the strangers who dwell among you, who eats any blood, I will set My face against that person who eats blood, and will cut him off from among his people. **11** For the life of the flesh *is* in the blood, and I have given it to you upon the altar to make atonement for your souls; for it *is* the blood *that* makes atonement for the soul.' **12** Therefore I said to the children of Israel, 'No one among you shall eat blood, nor shall any stranger who dwells among you eat blood.'

Not to eat the Passover while uncircumcised.

Ex 12:43–44 And the LORD said to Moses and Aaron, "This *is* the ordinance of the Passover: No foreigner shall eat it. **44** But every man's servant who is bought for money, when you have circumcised him, then he may eat it.

Not to work on the Sabbath.

Ex 20:10 but the seventh day *is* the Sabbath of the LORD your God. *In it* you shall do no work: you, nor your son, nor your daughter, nor your male servant, nor your female servant, nor your cattle, nor your stranger who *is* within your gates.

Ex 23:12 Six days you shall do your work, and on the seventh day you shall rest, that your ox and your donkey may rest, and the son of your female servant and the stranger may be refreshed.

Deut 5:14 but the seventh day *is* the Sabbath of the LORD your God. *In it* you shall do no work: you, nor your son, nor your daughter, nor your male servant, nor your female servant, nor your ox, nor your donkey, nor any of your cattle, nor your stranger who *is* within your gates, that your male servant and your female servant may rest as well as you.

Not to be mistreated or oppressed.

Ex 22:21 "You shall neither mistreat a stranger nor oppress him, for you were strangers in the land of Egypt.

Ex 23:9 "Also you shall not oppress a stranger, for you know the heart of a stranger, because you were strangers in the land of Egypt.

Lev 19:33 'And if a stranger dwells with you in your land, you shall not mistreat him.

Not to be chosen as kings in Israel.

Deut 17:15 you shall surely set a king over you whom the LORD your God chooses; *one* from among your brethren you shall set as king over you; you may not set a foreigner over you, who *is* not your brother.

To be loved.

Lev 19:34 The stranger who dwells among you shall be to you as one born among you, and you shall love him as yourself; for you were strangers in the land of Egypt: I *am* the LORD your God.

Deut 10:19 Therefore love the stranger, for you were strangers in the land of Egypt.

To be relieved in distress.

Lev 25:35 'If one of your brethren becomes poor, and falls into poverty among you, then you shall help him, like a stranger or a sojourner, that he may live with you.

Subject to the civil law.

Lev 24:22 You shall have the same law for the stranger and for one from your own country; for I *am* the LORD your God.' "

To have justice done to them in all disputes.

Deut 1:16 "Then I commanded your judges at that time, saying, 'Hear *the cases* between your brethren, and judge righteously between a man and his brother or the stranger who is with him.

Deut 24:17 "You shall not pervert justice due the stranger or the fatherless, nor take a widow's garment as a pledge.

To enjoy the benefit of the cities of refuge.

Num 35:15 These six cities shall be for refuge for the children of Israel, for the stranger, and for the sojourner among them, that anyone who kills a person accidentally may flee there.

To have the gleaning of the harvest.

Lev 19:10 And you shall not glean your vineyard, nor shall you gather *every* grape of your vineyard; you shall leave them for the poor and the stranger: I *am* the LORD your God.

Lev 23:22 'When you reap the harvest of your land, you shall not wholly reap the corners of your field when you reap, nor shall you gather any gleaning from your harvest. You shall leave them for the poor and for the stranger: I *am* the LORD your God.' "

Deut 24:19–22 "When you reap your harvest in your field, and forget a sheaf in the field, you shall not go back to get it; it shall be for the stranger, the fatherless, and the widow, that the LORD your God may bless you in all the work of your hands. **20** When you beat your olive trees, you shall not go over the boughs again; it shall be for the stranger, the fatherless, and the widow. **21** When you gather the grapes of your vineyard, you shall not glean *it* afterward; it shall be for the stranger, the fatherless, and the widow. **22** And you shall remember that you were a slave in the land of Egypt; therefore I command you to do this thing.

To participate in the rejoicings of the people.

Deut 14:29 And the Levite, because he has no portion nor inheritance with you, and the stranger and the fatherless and the widow who *are* within your gates, may come and eat and be satisfied, that the LORD your God may bless you in all the work of your hand which you do.

Deut 16:11 You shall rejoice before the LORD your God, you and your son and your daughter, your male servant and your female servant, the Levite who *is* within your gates, the stranger and the fatherless and the widow who *are* among you, at the place where the LORD your God chooses to make His name abide.

Deut 16:14 And you shall rejoice in your feast, you and your son and your daughter, your male servant and your female servant and the Levite, the stranger

and the fatherless and the widow, who *are* within your gates.

Deut 26:11 So you shall rejoice in every good *thing* which the LORD your God has given to you and your house, you and the Levite and the stranger who *is* among you.

To have the law read to them.

Deut 31:12 Gather the people together, men and women and little ones, and the stranger who *is* within your gates, that they may hear and that they may learn to fear the LORD your God and carefully observe all the words of this law,

Josh 8:32–35 And there, in the presence of the children of Israel, he wrote on the stones a copy of the law of Moses, which he had written. **33** Then all Israel, with their elders and officers and judges, stood on either side of the ark before the priests, the Levites, who bore the ark of the covenant of the LORD, the stranger as well as he who was born among them. Half of them *were* in front of Mount Gerizim and half of them in front of Mount Ebal, as Moses the servant of the LORD had commanded before, that they should bless the people of Israel. **34** And afterward he read all the words of the law, the blessings and the cursings, according to all that is written in the Book of the Law. **35** There was not a word of all that Moses had commanded which Joshua did not read before all the assembly of Israel, with the women, the little ones, and the strangers who were living among them.

The Jews might purchase and have them as slaves.

Lev 25:44–45 And as for your male and female slaves whom you may have—from the nations that are around you, from them you may buy male and female slaves. **45** Moreover you may buy the children of the strangers who dwell among you, and their families who are with you, which they beget in your land; and they shall become your property.

The Jews might charge interest to.

Deut 23:20 To a foreigner you may charge interest, but to your brother you shall not charge interest, that the LORD your God may bless you in all to which you set your hand in the land which you are entering to possess.

Might purchase Hebrew servants subject to release.

Lev 25:47–48 'Now if a sojourner or stranger close to you becomes rich, and *one of* your brethren *who dwells* by him becomes poor, and sells himself to the stranger *or* sojourner close to you, or to a member of the stranger's family, **48** after he is sold he may be redeemed again. One of his brothers may redeem him;

Might offer their burnt offerings on the altar of God.

Lev 17:8 "Also you shall say to them: 'Whatever man of the house of Israel, or of the strangers who dwell among you, who offers a burnt offering or sacrifice,

Lev 22:18 "Speak to Aaron and his sons, and to all the children of Israel, and say to them: 'Whatever man of the house of Israel, or of the strangers in Israel, who offers his sacrifice for any of his vows or for any of his freewill offerings, which they offer to the LORD as a burnt offering—

Num 15:14 And if a stranger dwells with you, or whoever *is* among you throughout your generations, and would present an offering made by fire, a sweet aroma to the LORD, just as you do, so shall he do.

Allowed to eat what died of itself.

Deut 14:21 "You shall not eat anything that dies *of itself;* you may give it to the alien who *is* within your gates, that he may eat it, or you may sell it to a foreigner; for you *are* a holy people to the LORD your God. "You shall not boil a young goat in its mother's milk.

Motives urged on the Jews for being kind to.

Ex 22:21 "You shall neither mistreat a stranger nor oppress him, for you were strangers in the land of Egypt.

Ex 23:9 "Also you shall not oppress a stranger, for you know the heart of a stranger, because you were strangers in the land of Egypt.

Admitted to worship in the outer court of the temple.

1 Kin 8:41–43 "Moreover, concerning a foreigner, who *is* not of Your people Israel, but has come from a far country for Your name's sake **42** (for they will hear of Your great name and Your strong hand and Your outstretched arm), when he comes and prays toward this temple, **43** hear in heaven Your dwelling place, and do according to all for which the foreigner calls to You, that all peoples of the earth may know Your name and fear You, as *do* Your people Israel, and that they may know that this temple which I have built is called by Your name.

Eph 2:14 For He Himself is our peace, who has made both one, and has broken down the middle wall of separation,

Rev 11:2 But leave out the court which is outside the temple, and do not measure it, for it has been given to the Gentiles. And they will tread the holy city underfoot *for* forty-two months.

Were frequently employed in public works.

1 Chr 22:2 So David commanded to gather the aliens who *were* in the land of Israel; and he appointed masons to cut hewn stones to build the house of God.

2 Chr 2:18 And he made seventy thousand of them bearers of burdens, eighty thousand stonecutters in the mountain, and three thousand six hundred overseers to make the people work.

The Jews condemned for oppressing.

Ps 94:6 They slay the widow and the stranger, And murder the fatherless.

Ezek 22:7 In you they have made light of father and mother; in your midst they have oppressed the stranger; in you they have mistreated the fatherless and the widow.

Ezek 22:29 The people of the land have used oppressions, committed robbery, and mistreated the poor and needy; and they wrongfully oppress the stranger.

STRIFE

Christ, an example of avoiding.

Is 42:2 He will not cry out, nor raise *His voice,* Nor cause His voice to be heard in the street.

Matt 12:15–19 But when Jesus knew *it,* He withdrew from there. And great multitudes followed Him, and

He healed them all. **16** Yet He warned them not to make Him known, **17** that it might be fulfilled which was spoken by Isaiah the prophet, saying: **18** *"Behold! My Servant whom I have chosen, My Beloved in whom My soul is well pleased! I will put My Spirit upon Him, And He will declare justice to the Gentiles.* **19** *He will not quarrel nor cry out, Nor will anyone hear His voice in the streets.*

Luke 9:52–56 and sent messengers before His face. And as they went, they entered a village of the Samaritans, to prepare for Him. **53** But they did not receive Him, because His face was *set* for the journey to Jerusalem. **54** And when His disciples James and John saw *this,* they said, "Lord, do You want us to command fire to come down from heaven and consume them, just as Elijah did?" **55** But He turned and rebuked them, and said, "You do not know what manner of spirit you are of. **56** For the Son of Man did not come to destroy men's lives but to save *them."* And they went to another village.

1 Pet 2:23 who, when He was reviled, did not revile in return; when He suffered, He did not threaten, but committed *Himself* to Him who judges righteously;

Forbidden.

Prov 3:30 Do not strive with a man without cause, If he has done you no harm.

Prov 25:8 Do not go hastily to court; For what will you do in the end, When your neighbor has put you to shame?

A work of the flesh.

1 Cor 3:3 for you are still carnal. For where *there are* envy, strife, and divisions among you, are you not carnal and behaving like *mere* men?

Gal 5:20 idolatry, sorcery, hatred, contentions, jealousies, outbursts of wrath, selfish ambitions, dissensions, heresies,

Existed in the church.

1 Cor 1:11 For it has been declared to me concerning you, my brethren, by those of Chloe's *household,* that there are contentions among you.

Caused by

Hatred.

Prov 10:12 Hatred stirs up strife, But love covers all sins.

Pride.

Prov 13:10 By pride comes nothing but strife, But with the well-advised *is* wisdom.

Prov 28:25 He who is of a proud heart stirs up strife, But he who trusts in the LORD will be prospered.

Wrath.

Prov 15:18 A wrathful man stirs up strife, But *he who is* slow to anger allays contention.

Prov 30:33 For *as* the churning of milk produces butter, And wringing the nose produces blood, So the forcing of wrath produces strife.

Contrariness.

Prov 16:28 A perverse man sows strife, And a whisperer separates the best of friends.

A contentious disposition.

Prov 26:21 *As* charcoal *is* to burning coals, and wood to fire, So *is* a contentious man to kindle strife.

Talebearing.

Prov 26:20 Where *there is* no wood, the fire goes out; And where *there is* no talebearer, strife ceases.

Drunkenness.

Prov 23:29–30 Who has woe? Who has sorrow? Who has contentions? Who has complaints? Who has wounds without cause? Who has redness of eyes? **30** Those who linger long at the wine, Those who go in search of mixed wine.

Lusts.

James 4:1 Where do wars and fights *come* from among you? Do *they* not *come* from your *desires for* pleasure that war in your members?

Obscure questions.

1 Tim 6:4 he is proud, knowing nothing, but is obsessed with disputes and arguments over words, from which come envy, strife, reviling, evil suspicions,

2 Tim 2:23 But avoid foolish and ignorant disputes, knowing that they generate strife.

Scoffing.

Prov 22:10 Cast out the scoffer, and contention will leave; Yes, strife and reproach will cease.

Difficulty of stopping, a reason for avoiding it.

Prov 17:14 The beginning of strife *is like* releasing water; Therefore stop contention before a quarrel starts.

Shameful in believers.

2 Cor 12:20 For I fear lest, when I come, I shall not find you such as I wish, and *that* I shall be found by you such as you do not wish; lest *there be* contentions, jealousies, outbursts of wrath, selfish ambitions, backbitings, whisperings, conceits, tumults;

James 3:14 But if you have bitter envy and self-seeking in your hearts, do not boast and lie against the truth.

Believers should

Avoid it altogether.

Gen 13:8 So Abram said to Lot, "Please let there be no strife between you and me, and between my herdsmen and your herdsmen; for we *are* brethren.

Eph 4:3 endeavoring to keep the unity of the Spirit in the bond of peace.

Avoid questions that lead to.

2 Tim 2:14 Remind *them* of these things, charging *them* before the Lord not to strive about words to no profit, to the ruin of the hearers.

Not walk in.

Rom 13:13 Let us walk properly, as in the day, not in revelry and drunkenness, not in lewdness and lust, not in strife and envy.

Not act from.

Phil 2:3 *Let* nothing *be done* through selfish ambition or conceit, but in lowliness of mind let each esteem others better than himself.

Do all things without.

Phil 2:14 Do all things without complaining and disputing,

Submit to wrong rather than engage in.

Prov 20:22 Do not say, "I will recompense evil"; Wait for the LORD, and He will save you.

Matt 5:39–40 But I tell you not to resist an evil person. But whoever slaps you on your right cheek, turn the other to him also. **40** If anyone wants to sue you and take away your tunic, let him have *your* cloak also.

1 Cor 6:7 Now therefore, it is already an utter failure for you that you go to law against one another. Why do you not rather accept wrong? Why do you not rather *let yourselves* be cheated?

Seek God's protection from.

2 Sam 22:44 "You have also delivered me from the strivings of my people; You have kept me as the head of the nations. A people I have not known shall serve me.

Ps 18:43 You have delivered me from the strivings of the people; You have made me the head of the nations; A people I have not known shall serve me.

Ps 31:20 You shall hide them in the secret place of Your presence From the plots of man; You shall keep them secretly in a pavilion From the strife of tongues.

Praise God for protection from.

Ps 35:1 Plead *my cause,* O LORD, with those who strive with me; Fight against those who fight against me.

Jer 18:19 Give heed to me, O LORD, And listen to the voice of those who contend with me!

Ministers should

Avoid altogether.

1 Tim 3:3 not given to wine, not violent, not greedy for money, but gentle, not quarrelsome, not covetous;

2 Tim 2:24 And a servant of the Lord must not quarrel but be gentle to all, able to teach, patient,

Avoid questions that lead to.

2 Tim 2:23 But avoid foolish and ignorant disputes, knowing that they generate strife.

Titus 3:9 But avoid foolish disputes, genealogies, contentions, and strivings about the law; for they are unprofitable and useless.

Not preach from position of.

Phil 1:15–16 Some indeed preach Christ even from envy and strife, and some also from goodwill: **16** The former preach Christ from selfish ambition, not sincerely, supposing to add affliction to my chains;

Warn against.

1 Cor 1:10 Now I plead with you, brethren, by the name of our Lord Jesus Christ, that you all speak the same thing, and *that* there be no divisions among you, but *that* you be perfectly joined together in the same mind and in the same judgment.

2 Tim 2:14 Remind *them* of these things, charging *them* before the Lord not to strive about words to no profit, to the ruin of the hearers.

Admonish against.

1 Cor 1:11–12 For it has been declared to me concerning you, my brethren, by those of Chloe's *household,* that there are contentions among you. **12** Now I say this, that each of you says, "I am of Paul," or "I am of Apollos," or "I am of Cephas," or "I am of Christ."

1 Cor 3:3 for you are still carnal. For where *there are* envy, strife, and divisions among you, are you not carnal and behaving like *mere* men?

1 Cor 11:17–18 Now in giving these instructions I do not praise *you,* since you come together not for the better but for the worse. **18** For first of all, when you come together as a church, I hear that there are divisions among you, and in part I believe it.

Appeased by slowness to anger.

Prov 15:18 A wrathful man stirs up strife, But *he who is* slow to anger allays contention.

It is honorable to cease from.

Prov 20:3 *It is* honorable for a man to stop striving, Since any fool can start a quarrel.

Hypocrites make religion a pretense for.

Is 58:4 Indeed you fast for strife and debate, And to strike with the fist of wickedness. You will not fast as *you do* this day, To make your voice heard on high.

Fools engage in.

Prov 18:6 A fool's lips enter into contention, And his mouth calls for blows.

Evidences a love of transgression.

Prov 17:19 He who loves transgression loves strife, And he who exalts his gate seeks destruction.

Leads to

Blasphemy.

Lev 24:10–11 Now the son of an Israelite woman, whose father *was* an Egyptian, went out among the children of Israel; and this Israelite *woman's* son and a man of Israel fought each other in the camp. **11** And the Israelite woman's son blasphemed the name *of the* L ORD and cursed; and so they brought him to Moses. (His mother's name *was* Shelomith the daughter of Dibri, of the tribe of Dan.)

Injustice.

Hab 1:3–4 Why do You show me iniquity, And cause *me* to see trouble? For plundering and violence *are* before me; There is strife, and contention arises. **4** Therefore the law is powerless, And justice never goes forth. For the wicked surround the righteous; Therefore perverse judgment proceeds.

Confusion and every evil work.

James 3:16 For where envy and self-seeking *exist,* confusion and every evil thing *are* there.

Violence.

Ex 21:18 "If men contend with each other, and one strikes the other with a stone or with *his* fist, and he does not die but is confined to *his* bed,

Ex 21:22 "If men fight, and hurt a woman with child, so that she gives birth prematurely, yet no harm follows, he shall surely be punished accordingly as the woman's husband imposes on him; and he shall pay as the judges *determine.*

Mutual destruction.

Gal 5:15 But if you bite and devour one another, beware lest you be consumed by one another!

Temporal blessing embittered by.

Prov 17:1 Better *is* a dry morsel with quietness, Than a house full of feasting *with* strife.

Excludes from heaven.

Gal 5:20–21 idolatry, sorcery, hatred, contentions, jealousies, outbursts of wrath, selfish ambitions, dissensions, heresies, **21** envy, murders, drunkenness, revelries, and the like; of which I tell you beforehand, just as I also told *you* in time past, that those who

practice such things will not inherit the kingdom of God.

Promoters of, should be expelled.

Prov 22:10 Cast out the scoffer, and contention will leave; Yes, strife and reproach will cease.

Punishment for.

Ps 55:9 Destroy, O Lord, *and* divide their tongues, For I have seen violence and strife in the city.

Strength and violence of—illustrated.

Prov 17:14 The beginning of strife *is like* releasing water; Therefore stop contention before a quarrel starts.

Prov 18:19 A brother offended *is harder to win* than a strong city, And contentions *are* like the bars of a castle.

Danger of joining in—illustrated.

Prov 26:17 He who passes by *and* meddles in a quarrel not his own *Is like* one who takes a dog by the ears.

Examples of,

The herdsmen of Abram and of Lot.

Gen 13:7 And there was strife between the herdsmen of Abram's livestock and the herdsmen of Lot's livestock. The Canaanites and the Perizzites then dwelt in the land.

The herdsmen of Gerar and of Isaac.

Gen 26:20 But the herdsmen of Gerar quarreled with Isaac's herdsmen, saying, "The water *is* ours." So he called the name of the well Esek, because they quarreled with him.

Laban and Jacob.

Gen 31:36 Then Jacob was angry and rebuked Laban, and Jacob answered and said to Laban: "What *is* my trespass? What *is* my sin, that you have so hotly pursued me?

Two Hebrews.

Ex 2:13 And when he went out the second day, behold, two Hebrew men were fighting, and he said to the one who did the wrong, "Why are you striking your companion?"

The Israelites.

Deut 1:12 How can I alone bear your problems and your burdens and your complaints?

Judah and Israel.

2 Sam 19:41–43 Just then all the men of Israel came to the king, and said to the king, "Why have our brethren, the men of Judah, stolen you away and brought the king, his household, and all David's men with him across the Jordan?" **42** So all the men of Judah answered the men of Israel, "Because the king *is* a close relative of ours. Why then are you angry over this matter? Have we ever eaten at the king's *expense?* Or has he given us any gift?" **43** And the men of Israel answered the men of Judah, and said, "We have ten shares in the king; therefore we also have more *right* to David than you. Why then do you despise us—were we not the first to advise bringing back our king?" Yet the words of the men of Judah were fiercer than the words of the men of Israel.

The disciples.

Luke 22:24 Now there was also a dispute among them, as to which of them should be considered the greatest.

Judaizing teachers.

Acts 15:2 Therefore, when Paul and Barnabas had no small dissension and dispute with them, they determined that Paul and Barnabas and certain others of them should go up to Jerusalem, to the apostles and elders, about this question.

Paul and Barnabas.

Acts 15:39 Then the contention became so sharp that they parted from one another. And so Barnabas took Mark and sailed to Cyprus;

Pharisees and Sadducees.

Acts 23:7 And when he had said this, a dissension arose between the Pharisees and the Sadducees; and the assembly was divided.

The Corinthians.

1 Cor 1:11 For it has been declared to me concerning you, my brethren, by those of Chloe's *household*, that there are contentions among you.

1 Cor 6:6 But brother goes to law against brother, and that before unbelievers!

SUBMISSION TO GOD

Christ set an example of.

Matt 26:39–44 He went a little farther and fell on His face, and prayed, saying, "O My Father, if it is possible, let this cup pass from Me; nevertheless, not as I will, but as You *will*." **40** Then He came to the disciples and found them sleeping, and said to Peter, "What! Could you not watch with Me one hour? **41** Watch and pray, lest you enter into temptation. The spirit indeed *is* willing, but the flesh *is* weak." **42** Again, a second time, He went away and prayed, saying, "O My Father, if this cup cannot pass away from Me unless I drink it, Your will be done." **43** And He came and found them asleep again, for their eyes were heavy. **44** So He left them, went away again, and prayed the third time, saying the same words.

John 12:27 "Now My soul is troubled, and what shall I say? 'Father, save Me from this hour'? But for this purpose I came to this hour.

John 18:11 So Jesus said to Peter, "Put your sword into the sheath. Shall I not drink the cup which My Father has given Me?"

Commanded.

Ps 37:7 Rest in the LORD, and wait patiently for Him; Do not fret because of him who prospers in his way, Because of the man who brings wicked schemes to pass.

Ps 46:10 Be still, and know that I *am* God; I will be exalted among the nations, I will be exalted in the earth!

Should be exhibited in

Obedience to the will of God.

2 Sam 15:26 But if He says thus: 'I have no delight in you,' here I am, let Him do to me as seems good to Him."

Matt 6:10 Your kingdom come. Your will be done On earth as *it is* in heaven.

Recognition of the sovereignty of God in His purposes.

Ps 32:5 I acknowledged my sin to You, And my iniquity I have not hidden. I said, "I will confess my transgressions to the LORD," And You forgave the iniquity of my sin. Selah

Ps 32:11 Be glad in the LORD and rejoice, you righteous; And shout for joy, all *you* upright in heart!

Rom 9:20–21 But indeed, O man, who are you to reply against God? Will the thing formed say to him who formed *it*, "Why have you made me like this?" **21** Does not the potter have power over the clay, from the same lump to make one vessel for honor and another for dishonor?

The prospect of death.

Acts 21:13 Then Paul answered, "What do you mean by weeping and breaking my heart? For I am ready not only to be bound, but also to die at Jerusalem for the name of the Lord Jesus."

2 Cor 4:16–18 Therefore we do not lose heart. Even though our outward man is perishing, yet the inward *man* is being renewed day by day. **17** For our light affliction, which is but for a moment, is working for us a far more exceeding *and* eternal weight of glory, **18** while we do not look at the things which are seen, but at the things which are not seen. For the things which are seen *are* temporary, but the things which are not seen *are* eternal.

2 Cor 5:1 For we know that if our earthly house, *this* tent, is destroyed, we have a building from God, a house not made with hands, eternal in the heavens.

Loss of goods.

Job 1:15–16 when the Sabeans raided *them* and took them away—indeed they have killed the servants with the edge of the sword; and I alone have escaped to tell you!" **16** While he *was* still speaking, another also came and said, "The fire of God fell from heaven and burned up the sheep and the servants, and consumed them; and I alone have escaped to tell you!"

Job 1:20–21 Then Job arose, tore his robe, and shaved his head; and he fell to the ground and worshiped. **21** And he said: "Naked I came from my mother's womb, And naked shall I return there. The LORD gave, and the LORD has taken away; Blessed be the name of the LORD."

Loss of children.

Job 1:18–21 While he *was* still speaking, another also came and said, "Your sons and daughters *were* eating and drinking wine in their oldest brother's house, **19** and suddenly a great wind came from across the wilderness and struck the four corners of the house, and it fell on the young people, and they are dead; and I alone have escaped to tell you!" **20** Then Job arose, tore his robe, and shaved his head; and he fell to the ground and worshiped. **21** And he said: "Naked I came from my mother's womb, And naked shall I return there. The LORD gave, and the LORD has taken away; Blessed be the name of the LORD."

Chastisements.

Heb 12:9 Furthermore, we have had human fathers who corrected *us*, and we paid *them* respect. Shall we not much more readily be in subjection to the Father of spirits and live?

Bodily suffering.

Job 2:8–10 And he took for himself a potsherd with which to scrape himself while he sat in the midst of the ashes. **9** Then his wife said to him, "Do you still hold fast to your integrity? Curse God and die!" **10** But he said to her, "You speak as one of the foolish women speaks. Shall we indeed accept good from God, and shall we not accept adversity?" In all this Job did not sin with his lips.

The wicked are devoid of.

Prov 19:3 The foolishness of a man twists his way, And his heart frets against the LORD.

Exhortation to.

Ps 37:1–11 Do not fret because of evildoers, Nor be envious of the workers of iniquity. **2** For they shall soon be cut down like the grass, And wither as the green herb. **3** Trust in the LORD, and do good; Dwell in the land, and feed on His faithfulness. **4** Delight yourself also in the LORD, And He shall give you the desires of your heart. **5** Commit your way to the LORD, Trust also in Him, And He shall bring *it* to pass. **6** He shall bring forth your righteousness as the light, And your justice as the noonday. **7** Rest in the LORD, and wait patiently for Him; Do not fret because of him who prospers in his way, Because of the man who brings wicked schemes to pass. **8** Cease from anger, and forsake wrath; Do not fret—*it* only *causes* harm. **9** For evildoers shall be cut off; But those who wait on the LORD, They shall inherit the earth. **10** For yet a little while and the wicked *shall be* no *more;* Indeed, you will look carefully for his place, But it *shall be* no *more.* **11** But the meek shall inherit the earth, And shall delight themselves in the abundance of peace.

Motives to,

God's greatness.

Ps 46:10 Be still, and know that I *am* God; I will be exalted among the nations, I will be exalted in the earth!

God's love.

Heb 12:6 *For whom the LORD loves He chastens, And scourges every son whom He receives."*

God's justice.

Neh 9:33 However You *are* just in all that has befallen us; For You have dealt faithfully, But we have done wickedly.

God's wisdom.

Rom 11:32–33 For God has committed them all to disobedience, that He might have mercy on all. **33** Oh, the depth of the riches both of the wisdom and knowledge of God! How unsearchable *are* His judgments and His ways past finding out!

God's faithfulness.

1 Pet 4:19 Therefore let those who suffer according to the will of God commit their souls *to Him* in doing good, as to a faithful Creator.

Our own sinfulness.

Lam 3:38–39 *Is it* not from the mouth of the Most High That woe and well-being proceed? **39** Why should a living man complain, A man for the punishment of his sins?

Mic 7:9 I will bear the indignation of the LORD, Because I have sinned against Him, Until He pleads my case And executes justice for me. He will bring me forth to the light; I will see His righteousness.

Exemplified by

Jacob.

Gen 43:14 And may God Almighty give you mercy before the man, that he may release your other brother and Benjamin. If I am bereaved, I am bereaved!"

Aaron.

Lev 10:3 And Moses said to Aaron, "This is what the LORD spoke, saying: 'By those who come near Me I must be regarded as holy; And before all the people I must be glorified.' " So Aaron held his peace.

The Israelites.

Judg 10:15 And the children of Israel said to the LORD, "We have sinned! Do to us whatever seems best to You; only deliver us this day, we pray."

Eli.

1 Sam 3:18 Then Samuel told him everything, and hid nothing from him. And he said, "It *is* the LORD. Let Him do what seems good to Him."

David.

2 Sam 12:23 But now he is dead; why should I fast? Can I bring him back again? I shall go to him, but he shall not return to me."

Hezekiah.

2 Kin 20:19 So Hezekiah said to Isaiah, "The word of the LORD which you have spoken *is* good!" For he said, "Will there not be peace and truth at least in my days?"

Job.

Job 2:10 But he said to her, "You speak as one of the foolish women speaks. Shall we indeed accept good from God, and shall we not accept adversity?" In all this Job did not sin with his lips.

Stephen.

Acts 7:59 And they stoned Stephen as he was calling on *God* and saying, "Lord Jesus, receive my spirit."

Paul.

Acts 21:13 Then Paul answered, "What do you mean by weeping and breaking my heart? For I am ready not only to be bound, but also to die at Jerusalem for the name of the Lord Jesus."

The disciples.

Acts 21:14 So when he would not be persuaded, we ceased, saying, "The will of the Lord be done."

Peter.

2 Pet 1:14 knowing that shortly I *must* put off my tent, just as our Lord Jesus Christ showed me.

SUBSTITUTIONARY DEATH OF CHRIST

As a ransom for believers.

Matt 20:28 just as the Son of Man did not come to be served, but to serve, and to give His life a ransom for many."

Mark 10:45 For even the Son of Man did not come to be served, but to serve, and to give His life a ransom for many."

1 Tim 2:6 who gave Himself a ransom for all, to be testified in due time,

Expression of the truth of.

2 Cor 5:14 For the love of Christ compels us, because we judge thus: that if One died for all, then all died;

Manifested in His bearing the punishment believers deserved.

1 Pet 2:24 who Himself bore our sins in His own body on the tree, that we, having died to sins, might live for righteousness—by whose stripes you were healed.

1 Pet 3:18 For Christ also suffered once for sins, the just for the unjust, that He might bring us to God, being put to death in the flesh but made alive by the Spirit,

SUFFERING

And believers,

Reasons for.

John 9:1–3 Now as *Jesus* passed by, He saw a man who was blind from birth. **2** And His disciples asked Him, saying, "Rabbi, who sinned, this man or his parents, that he was born blind?" **3** Jesus answered, "Neither this man nor his parents sinned, but that the works of God should be revealed in him.

1 Cor 11:30 For this reason many *are* weak and sick among you, and many sleep.

2 Cor 1:3–7 Blessed *be* the God and Father of our Lord Jesus Christ, the Father of mercies and God of all comfort, **4** who comforts us in all our tribulation, that we may be able to comfort those who are in any trouble, with the comfort with which we ourselves are comforted by God. **5** For as the sufferings of Christ abound in us, so our consolation also abounds through Christ. **6** Now if we are afflicted, *it is* for your consolation and salvation, which is effective for enduring the same sufferings which we also suffer. Or if we are comforted, *it is* for your consolation and salvation. **7** And our hope for you *is* steadfast, because we know that as you are partakers of the sufferings, so also *you will partake* of the consolation.

2 Cor 12:7–10 And lest I should be exalted above measure by the abundance of the revelations, a thorn in the flesh was given to me, a messenger of Satan to buffet me, lest I be exalted above measure. **8** Concerning this thing I pleaded with the Lord three times that it might depart from me. **9** And He said to me, "My grace is sufficient for you, for My strength is made perfect in weakness." Therefore most gladly I will rather boast in my infirmities, that the power of Christ may rest upon me. **10** Therefore I take pleasure in infirmities, in reproaches, in needs, in persecutions, in distresses, for Christ's sake. For when I am weak, then I am strong.

Heb 12:5–12 And you have forgotten the exhortation which speaks to you as to sons: *"My son, do not despise the chastening of the LORD, Nor be discouraged when you are rebuked by Him;* **6** *For whom the LORD loves He chastens, And scourges every son whom He receives."* **7** If you endure chastening, God deals with you as with sons; for what son is there whom a father does not chasten? **8** But if you are without chastening, of which all have become partakers, then you are illegitimate and not sons. **9** Furthermore, we

have had human fathers who corrected *us,* and we paid *them* respect. Shall we not much more readily be in subjection to the Father of spirits and live? **10** For they indeed for a few days chastened *us* as seemed *best* to them, but He for *our* profit, that *we* may be partakers of His holiness. **11** Now no chastening seems to be joyful for the present, but painful; nevertheless, afterward it yields the peaceable fruit of righteousness to those who have been trained by it. **12** Therefore strengthen the hands which hang down, and the feeble knees,

James 5:15 And the prayer of faith will save the sick, and the Lord will raise him up. And if he has committed sins, he will be forgiven.

1 Pet 5:10 But may the God of all grace, who called us to His eternal glory by Christ Jesus, after you have suffered a while, perfect, establish, strengthen, and settle *you.*

As part of God's plan.

Ex 4:11 So the LORD said to him, "Who has made man's mouth? Or who makes the mute, the deaf, the seeing, or the blind? *Have* not I, the LORD?

Num 12:10–12 And when the cloud departed from above the tabernacle, suddenly Miriam *became* leprous, as *white as* snow. Then Aaron turned toward Miriam, and there she was, a leper. **11** So Aaron said to Moses, "Oh, my lord! Please do not lay *this* sin on us, in which we have done foolishly and in which we have sinned. **12** Please do not let her be as one dead, whose flesh is half consumed when he comes out of his mother's womb!"

Deut 8:15–16 who led you through that great and terrible wilderness, *in which were* fiery serpents and scorpions and thirsty land where there was no water; who brought water for you out of the flinty rock; **16** who fed you in the wilderness with manna, which your fathers did not know, that He might humble you and that He might test you, to do you good in the end—

Rom 8:28 And we know that all things work together for good to those who love God, to those who are the called according to *His* purpose.

1 Pet 4:19 Therefore let those who suffer according to the will of God commit their souls *to Him* in doing good, as to a faithful Creator.

Cf. Gen 50:19–20

Outweighed by future glory and rewards.

Rom 8:17–18 and if children, then heirs—heirs of God and joint heirs with Christ, if indeed we suffer with *Him,* that we may also be glorified together. **18** For I consider that the sufferings of this present time are not worthy *to be compared* with the glory which shall be revealed in us.

1 Pet 1:6–7 In this you greatly rejoice, though now for a little while, if need be, you have been grieved by various trials, **7** that the genuineness of your faith, *being* much more precious than gold that perishes, though it is tested by fire, may be found to praise, honor, and glory at the revelation of Jesus Christ,

1 Pet 4:13 but rejoice to the extent that you partake of Christ's sufferings, that when His glory is revealed, you may also be glad with exceeding joy.

Should be expected.

Matt 5:10–12 Blessed are those who are persecuted for righteousness' sake, For theirs is the kingdom of heaven. **11** "Blessed are you when they revile and persecute you, and say all kinds of evil against you falsely for My sake. **12** Rejoice and be exceedingly glad, for great *is* your reward in heaven, for so they persecuted the prophets who were before you.

John 15:18–21 "If the world hates you, you know that it hated Me before *it hated* you. **19** If you were of the world, the world would love its own. Yet because you are not of the world, but I chose you out of the world, therefore the world hates you. **20** Remember the word that I said to you, 'A servant is not greater than his master.' If they persecuted Me, they will also persecute you. If they kept My word, they will keep yours also. **21** But all these things they will do to you for My name's sake, because they do not know Him who sent Me.

Acts 5:41 So they departed from the presence of the council, rejoicing that they were counted worthy to suffer shame for His name.

Acts 14:22 strengthening the souls of the disciples, exhorting *them* to continue in the faith, and *saying*, "We must through many tribulations enter the kingdom of God."

Phil 1:29–30 For to you it has been granted on behalf of Christ, not only to believe in Him, but also to suffer for His sake, **30** having the same conflict which you saw in me and now hear *is* in me.

2 Tim 3:12 Yes, and all who desire to live godly in Christ Jesus will suffer persecution.

1 Pet 2:20–21 For what credit *is it* if, when you are beaten for your faults, you take it patiently? But when you do good and suffer, if you take it patiently, this *is* commendable before God. **21** For to this you were called, because Christ also suffered for us, leaving us an example, that you should follow His steps:

Cf. Matt 10:38–39; 16:24–25; Mark 8:34–35; Luke 9:23–24; 14:27; 17:33; John 12:25; Phil 3:10; Col 1:24

Patience in, evidence of spiritual maturity.

2 Thess 1:4–6 so that we ourselves boast of you among the churches of God for your patience and faith in all your persecutions and tribulations that you endure, **5** *which is* manifest evidence of the righteous judgment of God, that you may be counted worthy of the kingdom of God, for which you also suffer; **6** since *it is* a righteous thing with God to repay with tribulation those who trouble you,

James 1:2–4 My brethren, count it all joy when you fall into various trials, **3** knowing that the testing of your faith produces patience. **4** But let patience have *its* perfect work, that you may be perfect and complete, lacking nothing.

James 5:11 Indeed we count them blessed who endure. You have heard of the perseverance of Job and seen the end *intended by* the Lord—that the Lord is very compassionate and merciful.

1 Pet 2:20–25 For what credit *is it* if, when you are beaten for your faults, you take it patiently? But when you do good and suffer, if you take it patiently, this *is* commendable before God. **21** For to this you were called, because Christ also suffered for us, leaving us

an example, that you should follow His steps: **22** *"Who committed no sin, Nor was deceit found in His mouth"*; **23** who, when He was reviled, did not revile in return; when He suffered, He did not threaten, but committed *Himself* to Him who judges righteously; **24** who Himself bore our sins in His own body on the tree, that we, having died to sins, might live for righteousness—by whose stripes you were healed. **25** For you were like sheep going astray, but have now returned to the Shepherd and Overseer of your souls.

1 Pet 5:10 But may the God of all grace, who called us to His eternal glory by Christ Jesus, after you have suffered a while, perfect, establish, strengthen, and settle *you*.

Cf. Heb 6:9–12,18–20; Rev 13:10

We should remember that of others.

Heb 13:3 Remember the prisoners as if chained with them—those who are mistreated—since you yourselves are in the body also.

James 1:27 Pure and undefiled religion before God and the Father is this: to visit orphans and widows in their trouble, *and* to keep oneself unspotted from the world.

Cf. Matt 25:33–45; James 2:14–17

Remedy for.

Ps 27:13–14 *I would have lost heart,* unless I had believed That I would see the goodness of the Lᴏʀᴅ In the land of the living. **14** Wait on the Lᴏʀᴅ; Be of good courage, And He shall strengthen your heart; Wait, I say, on the Lᴏʀᴅ!

Ps 55:22 Cast your burden on the Lᴏʀᴅ, And He shall sustain you; He shall never permit the righteous to be moved.

Jon 2:7 "When my soul fainted within me, I remembered the Lᴏʀᴅ; And my prayer went *up* to You, Into Your holy temple.

Phil 4:6 Be anxious for nothing, but in everything by prayer and supplication, with thanksgiving, let your requests be made known to God;

James 5:13 Is anyone among you suffering? Let him pray. Is anyone cheerful? Let him sing psalms.

1 Pet 5:7 casting all your care upon Him, for He cares for you.

Sometimes must be endured for doing right.

1 Pet 3:13–17 And who *is* he who will harm you if you become followers of what is good? **14** But even if you should suffer for righteousness' sake, *you are* blessed. *"And do not be afraid of their threats, nor be troubled."* **15** But sanctify the Lord God in your hearts, and always *be* ready to *give* a defense to everyone who asks you a reason for the hope that is in you, with meekness and fear; **16** having a good conscience, that when they defame you as evildoers, those who revile your good conduct in Christ may be ashamed. **17** For *it is* better, if it is the will of God, to suffer for doing good than for doing evil.

1 Pet 4:12–16 Beloved, do not think it strange concerning the fiery trial which is to try you, as though some strange thing happened to you; **13** but rejoice to the extent that you partake of Christ's sufferings, that when His glory is revealed, you may also be glad with exceeding joy. **14** If you are reproached for the name of Christ, blessed *are you,* for the Spirit of glory and of God rests upon you. On their part He is blasphemed, but on your part He is glorified. **15** But let none of you suffer as a murderer, a thief, an evildoer, or as a busybody in other people's matters. **16** Yet if *anyone suffers* as a Christian, let him not be ashamed, but let him glorify God in this matter.

Exemplified by,

Job.

Job 1:13–22 Now there was a day when his sons and daughters *were* eating and drinking wine in their oldest brother's house; **14** and a messenger came to Job and said, "The oxen were plowing and the donkeys feeding beside them, **15** when the Sabeans raided *them* and took them away—indeed they have killed the servants with the edge of the sword; and I alone have escaped to tell you!" **16** While he *was* still speaking, another also came and said, "The fire of God fell from heaven and burned up the sheep and the servants, and consumed them; and I alone have escaped to tell you!" **17** While he *was* still speaking, another also came and said, "The Chaldeans formed three bands, raided the camels and took them away, yes, and killed the servants with the edge of the sword; and I alone have escaped to tell you!" **18** While he *was* still speaking, another also came and said, "Your sons and daughters *were* eating and drinking wine in their oldest brother's house, **19** and suddenly a great wind came from across the wilderness and struck the four corners of the house, and it fell on the young people, and they are dead; and I alone have escaped to tell you!" **20** Then Job arose, tore his robe, and shaved his head; and he fell to the ground and worshiped. **21** And he said: "Naked I came from my mother's womb, And naked shall I return there. The Lord gave, and the Lord has taken away; Blessed be the name of the Lord." **22** In all this Job did not sin nor charge God with wrong.

Job 2:1–9 Again there was a day when the sons of God came to present themselves before the Lord, and Satan came also among them to present himself before the Lord. **2** And the Lord said to Satan, "From where do you come?" Satan answered the Lord and said, "From going to and fro on the earth, and from walking back and forth on it." **3** Then the Lord said to Satan, "Have you considered My servant Job, that *there is* none like him on the earth, a blameless and upright man, one who fears God and shuns evil? And still he holds fast to his integrity, although you incited Me against him, to destroy him without cause." **4** So Satan answered the Lord and said, "Skin for skin! Yes, all that a man has he will give for his life. **5** But stretch out Your hand now, and touch his bone and his flesh, and he will surely curse You to Your face!" **6** And the Lord said to Satan, "Behold, he *is* in your hand, but spare his life." **7** So Satan went out from the presence of the Lord, and struck Job with painful boils from the sole of his foot to the crown of his head. **8** And he took for himself a potsherd with which to scrape himself while he sat in the midst of the ashes. **9** Then his wife said to him, "Do you still hold fast to your integrity? Curse God and die!"

Job 2:13 So they sat down with him on the ground seven days and seven nights, and no one spoke a word to him, for they saw that *his* grief was very great.

Job 3:24 For my sighing comes before I eat, And my groanings pour out like water.

Job 7:5 My flesh is caked with worms and dust, My skin is cracked and breaks out afresh.

Job 7:14 Then You scare me with dreams And terrify me with visions,

Job 13:28 "*Man* decays like a rotten thing, Like a garment that is moth-eaten.

Job 16:8 You have shriveled me up, And it is a witness *against me;* My leanness rises up against me *And* bears witness to my face.

Job 19:17 My breath is offensive to my wife, And I am repulsive to the children of my own body.

Job 30:17 My bones are pierced in me at night, And my gnawing pains take no rest.

Job 30:30 My skin grows black and falls from me; My bones burn with fever.

Job 33:21 His flesh wastes away from sight, And his bones stick out *which once* were not seen.

Jeremiah.

Jer 11:18–19 Now the Lord gave me knowledge *of it,* and I know *it;* for You showed me their doings. **19** But I *was* like a docile lamb brought to the slaughter; and I did not know that they had devised schemes against me, *saying,* "Let us destroy the tree with its fruit, and let us cut him off from the land of the living, that his name may be remembered no more."

Cf. Jer 20:1–18

Paul.

2 Cor 4:8–12 *We are* hard-pressed on every side, yet not crushed; *we are* perplexed, but not in despair; **9** persecuted, but not forsaken; struck down, but not destroyed— **10** always carrying about in the body the dying of the Lord Jesus, that the life of Jesus also may be manifested in our body. **11** For we who live are always delivered to death for Jesus' sake, that the life of Jesus also may be manifested in our mortal flesh. **12** So then death is working in us, but life in you.

2 Cor 6:4–10 But in all *things* we commend ourselves as ministers of God: in much patience, in tribulations, in needs, in distresses, **5** in stripes, in imprisonments, in tumults, in labors, in sleeplessness, in fastings; **6** by purity, by knowledge, by longsuffering, by kindness, by the Holy Spirit, by sincere love, **7** by the word of truth, by the power of God, by the armor of righteousness on the right hand and on the left, **8** by honor and dishonor, by evil report and good report; as deceivers, and *yet* true; **9** as unknown, and *yet* well known; as dying, and behold we live; as chastened, and *yet* not killed; **10** as sorrowful, yet always rejoicing; as poor, yet making many rich; as having nothing, and *yet* possessing all things.

2 Cor 11:22–33 Are they Hebrews? So *am* I. Are they Israelites? So *am* I. Are they the seed of Abraham? So *am* I. **23** Are they ministers of Christ?—I speak as a fool—I *am* more: in labors more abundant, in stripes above measure, in prisons more frequently, in deaths often. **24** From the Jews five times I received forty *stripes* minus one. **25** Three times I was beaten with rods; once I was stoned; three times I was shipwrecked; a night and a day I have been in the deep; **26** *in* journeys often, *in* perils of waters, *in* perils of robbers, *in* perils of *my own* countrymen, *in* perils of the Gentiles, *in* perils in the city, *in* perils in the wilderness, *in* perils in the sea, *in* perils among false brethren; **27** in weariness and toil, in sleeplessness often, in hunger and thirst, in fastings often, in cold and nakedness— **28** besides the other things, what comes upon me daily: my deep concern for all the churches. **29** Who is weak, and I am not weak? Who is made to stumble, and I do not burn *with indignation?* **30** If I must boast, I will boast in the things which concern my infirmity. **31** The God and Father of our Lord Jesus Christ, who is blessed forever, knows that I am not lying. **32** In Damascus the governor, under Aretas the king, was guarding the city of the Damascenes with a garrison, desiring to arrest me; **33** but I was let down in a basket through a window in the wall, and escaped from his hands.

SUICIDE

By Saul and his armorbearer.

1 Sam 31:4–6 Then Saul said to his armorbearer, "Draw your sword, and thrust me through with it, lest these uncircumcised men come and thrust me through and abuse me." But his armorbearer would not, for he was greatly afraid. Therefore Saul took a sword and fell on it. **5** And when his armorbearer saw that Saul was dead, he also fell on his sword, and died with him. **6** So Saul, his three sons, his armorbearer, and all his men died together that same day.

Of Ahithophel.

2 Sam 17:23 Now when Ahithophel saw that his advice was not followed, he saddled a donkey, and arose and went home to his house, to his city. Then he put his household in order, and hanged himself, and died; and he was buried in his father's tomb.

Of Judas Iscariot.

Matt 27:3–10 Then Judas, His betrayer, seeing that He had been condemned, was remorseful and brought back the thirty pieces of silver to the chief priests and elders, **4** saying, "I have sinned by betraying innocent blood." And they said, "What *is that* to us? You see *to it!*" **5** Then he threw down the pieces of silver in the temple and departed, and went and hanged himself. **6** But the chief priests took the silver pieces and said, "It is not lawful to put them into the treasury, because they are the price of blood." **7** And they consulted together and bought with them the potter's field, to bury strangers in. **8** Therefore that field has been called the Field of Blood to this day. **9** Then was fulfilled what was spoken by Jeremiah the prophet, saying, *"And they took the thirty pieces of silver, the value of Him who was priced,* whom they of the children of Israel priced, **10** *and gave them for the potter's field, as the* LORD *directed me."*

Acts 1:18–19 (Now this man purchased a field with the wages of iniquity; and falling headlong, he burst open in the middle and all his entrails gushed out. **19** And it became known to all those dwelling in Jerusalem; so that field is called in their own language, Akel Dama, that is, Field of Blood.)

Jews' opposition to.

John 8:22 So the Jews said, "Will He kill Himself, because He says, 'Where I go you cannot come'?"

In the last days, unbelievers will seek it unsuccessfully.

Rev 9:6 In those days men will seek death and will not find it; they will desire to die, and death will flee from them.

SUMMER

Made by God.

Ps 74:17 You have set all the borders of the earth; You have made summer and winter.

Yearly return of, secured by covenant.

Gen 8:22 "While the earth remains, Seedtime and harvest, Cold and heat, Winter and summer, And day and night Shall not cease."

Characterized by

Excessive heat.

Jer 17:8 For he shall be like a tree planted by the waters, Which spreads out its roots by the river, And will not fear when heat comes; But its leaf will be green, And will not be anxious in the year of drought, Nor will cease from yielding fruit.

Excessive drought.

Ps 32:4 For day and night Your hand was heavy upon me; My vitality was turned into the drought of summer. Selah

Approach of, indicated by new leaves on trees.

Matt 24:32 "Now learn this parable from the fig tree: When its branch has already become tender and puts forth leaves, you know that summer *is* near.

Many kinds of fruit were ripe and used during.

2 Sam 16:1 When David was a little past the top *of the mountain,* there was Ziba the servant of Mephibosheth, who met him with a couple of saddled donkeys, and on them two hundred *loaves* of bread, one hundred clusters of raisins, one hundred summer fruits, and a skin of wine.

Jer 40:10 As for me, I will indeed dwell at Mizpah and serve the Chaldeans who come to us. But you, gather wine and summer fruit and oil, put *them* in your vessels, and dwell in your cities that you have taken."

Jer 48:32 O vine of Sibmah! I will weep for you with the weeping of Jazer. Your plants have gone over the sea, They reach to the sea of Jazer. The plunderer has fallen on your summer fruit and your vintage.

The ancients had houses or apartments suited to.

Judg 3:20 So Ehud came to him (now he was sitting upstairs in his cool private chamber). Then Ehud said, "I have a message from God for you." So he arose from *his* seat.

Judg 3:24 When he had gone out, *Eglon's* servants came to look, and to *their* surprise, the doors of the upper room were locked. So they said, "He is probably attending to his needs in the cool chamber."

Amos 3:15 I will destroy the winter house along with the summer house; The houses of ivory shall perish, And the great houses shall have an end," Says the LORD.

The ant provided her winter food during.

Prov 6:8 Provides her supplies in the summer, *And* gathers her food in the harvest.

Prov 30:25 The ants *are* a people not strong, Yet they prepare their food in the summer;

The wise are diligent during.

Prov 10:5 He who gathers in summer *is* a wise son; He who sleeps in harvest *is* a son who causes shame.

Illustrative of seasons of grace.

Jer 8:20 "The harvest is past, The summer is ended, And we are not saved!"

SUN, THE

Called the greater light.

Gen 1:16 Then God made two great lights: the greater light to rule the day, and the lesser light to rule the night. *He made* the stars also.

God

Created.

Gen 1:14 Then God said, "Let there be lights in the firmament of the heavens to divide the day from the night; and let them be for signs and seasons, and for days and years;

Gen 1:16 Then God made two great lights: the greater light to rule the day, and the lesser light to rule the night. *He made* the stars also.

Ps 74:16 The day *is* Yours, the night also *is* Yours; You have prepared the light and the sun.

Placed it in the firmament.

Gen 1:17 God set them in the firmament of the heavens to give light on the earth,

Appointed it to rule the day.

Gen 1:16 Then God made two great lights: the greater light to rule the day, and the lesser light to rule the night. *He made* the stars also.

Ps 136:8 The sun to rule by day, For His mercy *endures* forever;

Jer 31:35 Thus says the LORD, Who gives the sun for a light by day, The ordinances of the moon and the stars for a light by night, Who disturbs the sea, And its waves roar (The LORD of hosts *is* His name):

Appointed it to divide seasons.

Gen 1:14 Then God said, "Let there be lights in the firmament of the heavens to divide the day from the night; and let them be for signs and seasons, and for days and years;

Exercises sovereign power over.

Job 9:7 He commands the sun, and it does not rise; He seals off the stars;

Causes, to rise both on evil and good.

Matt 5:45 that you may be sons of your Father in heaven; for He makes His sun rise on the evil and on the good, and sends rain on the just and on the unjust.

Causes, to know its time of setting.

Ps 104:19 He appointed the moon for seasons; The sun knows its going down.

Made to praise and glorify God.

Ps 148:3 Praise Him, sun and moon; Praise Him, all you stars of light!

The power and brilliancy of its rising alluded to.

Judg 5:31 "Thus let all Your enemies perish, O LORD! But *let* those who love Him *be* like the sun When it comes out in full strength." So the land had rest for forty years.

2 Sam 23:4 And *he shall be* like the light of the morning *when* the sun rises, A morning without clouds, *Like* the tender grass *springing* out of the earth, By clear shining after rain.'

Clearness of its light alluded to.

Song 6:10 Who is she who looks forth as the morning, Fair as the moon, Clear as the sun, Awesome as *an army* with banners?

Compared to a bridegroom coming forth from his chamber.

Ps 19:5 Which *is* like a bridegroom coming out of his chamber, *And* rejoices like a strong man to run its race.

Compared to a strong man rejoicing to run a race.

Ps 19:5 Which *is* like a bridegroom coming out of his chamber, *And* rejoices like a strong man to run its race.

Diffuses light and heat to all the earth.

Ps 19:6 Its rising *is* from one end of heaven, And its circuit to the other end; And there is nothing hidden from its heat.

The rays of,

Pleasant to man.

Job 30:28 I go about mourning, but not in the sun; I stand up in the assembly *and* cry out for help.

Eccl 11:7 Truly the light is sweet, And *it is* pleasant for the eyes to behold the sun;

Produce and ripen fruits.

Deut 33:14 With the precious fruits of the sun, With the precious produce of the months,

Soften and melt some substances.

Ex 16:21 So they gathered it every morning, every man according to his need. And when the sun became hot, it melted.

Wither and burn up the herbs of the field.

Mark 4:6 But when the sun was up it was scorched, and because it had no root it withered away.

James 1:11 For no sooner has the sun risen with a burning heat than it withers the grass; its flower falls, and its beautiful appearance perishes. So the rich man also will fade away in his pursuits.

Change the color of the skin.

Song 1:6 Do not look upon me, because I *am* dark, Because the sun has tanned me. My mother's sons were angry with me; They made me the keeper of the vineyards, *But* my own vineyard I have not kept.

Frequently destructive to human life.

Ps 121:6 The sun shall not strike you by day, Nor the moon by night.

Is 49:10 They shall neither hunger nor thirst, Neither heat nor sun shall strike them; For He who has mercy on them will lead them, Even by the springs of water He will guide them.

Indicates the the time of day.

2 Kin 20:9 Then Isaiah said, "This is the sign to you from the LORD, that the LORD will do the thing which He has spoken: *shall* the shadow go forward ten degrees or go backward ten degrees?"

The Jews

Commenced their day with the rising of.

Gen 19:23–24 The sun had risen upon the earth when Lot entered Zoar. **24** Then the LORD rained brimstone and fire on Sodom and Gomorrah, from the LORD out of the heavens.

Gen 19:27–28 And Abraham went early in the morning to the place where he had stood before the LORD. **28** Then he looked toward Sodom and Gomorrah, and toward all the land of the plain; and he saw, and behold, the smoke of the land which went up like the smoke of a furnace.

Judg 9:33 And it shall be, as soon as the sun is up in the morning, *that* you shall rise early and rush upon the city; and *when* he and the people who are with him come out against you, you may then do to them as you find opportunity."

Commenced their evening with the setting of.

Gen 28:11 So he came to a certain place and stayed there all night, because the sun had set. And he took one of the stones of that place and put it at his head, and he lay down in that place to sleep.

Deut 24:13 You shall in any case return the pledge to him again when the sun goes down, that he may sleep in his own garment and bless you; and it shall be righteousness to you before the LORD your God.

Mark 1:32 At evening, when the sun had set, they brought to Him all who were sick and those who were demon-possessed.

Defined the east by rising of.

Num 21:11 And they journeyed from Oboth and camped at Ije Abarim, in the wilderness which *is* east of Moab, toward the sunrise.

Deut 4:41 Then Moses set apart three cities on this side of the Jordan, toward the rising of the sun,

Deut 4:47 And they took possession of his land and the land of Og king of Bashan, two kings of the Amorites, who *were* on this side of the Jordan, toward the rising of the sun,

Josh 12:1 These *are* the kings of the land whom the children of Israel defeated, and whose land they possessed on the other side of the Jordan toward the rising of the sun, from the River Arnon to Mount Hermon, and all the eastern Jordan plain:

Defined the west by setting of.

Josh 1:4 From the wilderness and this Lebanon as far as the great river, the River Euphrates, all the land of the Hittites, and to the Great Sea toward the going down of the sun, shall be your territory.

Defined the whole earth by its movements.

Ps 50:1 The Mighty One, God the LORD, Has spoken and called the earth From the rising of the sun to its going down.

Ps 113:3 From the rising of the sun to its going down The LORD's name *is* to be praised.

Is 45:6 That they may know from the rising of the sun

to its setting That *there is* none besides Me. I *am* the LORD, and *there is* no other;

Forbidden to worship.

Deut 4:19 And *take heed*, lest you lift your eyes to heaven, and *when* you see the sun, the moon, and the stars, all the host of heaven, you feel driven to worship them and serve them, which the LORD your God has given to all the peoples under the whole heaven as a heritage.

Deut 17:3 who has gone and served other gods and worshiped them, either the sun or moon or any of the host of heaven, which I have not commanded,

Made images of.

2 Chr 14:5 He also removed the high places and the incense altars from all the cities of Judah, and the kingdom was quiet under him.

2 Chr 34:4 They broke down the altars of the Baals in his presence, and the incense altars which *were* above them he cut down; and the wooden images, the carved images, and the molded images he broke in pieces, and made dust of them and scattered *it* on the graves of those who had sacrificed to them.

Consecrated chariots and horses, as symbols of.

2 Kin 23:11 Then he removed the horses that the kings of Judah had dedicated to the sun, at the entrance to the house of the LORD, by the chamber of Nathan-Melech, the officer who *was* in the court; and he burned the chariots of the sun with fire.

Sometimes worshiped.

2 Kin 23:5 Then he removed the idolatrous priests whom the kings of Judah had ordained to burn incense on the high places in the cities of Judah and in the places all around Jerusalem, and those who burned incense to Baal, to the sun, to the moon, to the constellations, and to all the host of heaven.

Jer 8:2 They shall spread them before the sun and the moon and all the host of heaven, which they have loved and which they have served and after which they have walked, which they have sought and which they have worshiped. They shall not be gathered nor buried; they shall be like refuse on the face of the earth.

Worshipers of, turned their faces toward the east.

Ezek 8:16 So He brought me into the inner court of the LORD's house; and there, at the door of the temple of the LORD, between the porch and the altar, *were* about twenty-five men with their backs toward the temple of the LORD and their faces toward the east, and they were worshiping the sun toward the east.

Miracles connected with,

Stood still for a whole day in the Valley of Aijalon.

Josh 10:12–13 Then Joshua spoke to the LORD in the day when the LORD delivered up the Amorites before the children of Israel, and he said in the sight of Israel: "Sun, stand still over Gibeon; And Moon, in the Valley of Aijalon." **13** So the sun stood still, And the moon stopped, Till the people had revenge Upon their enemies. *Is* this not written in the Book of Jasher? So the sun stood still in the midst of heaven, and did not hasten to go *down* for about a whole day.

Shadow put back on the dial.

2 Kin 20:11 So Isaiah the prophet cried out to the LORD, and He brought the shadow ten degrees backward, by which it had gone down on the sundial of Ahaz.

Darkened at the crucifixion.

Luke 23:44–45 Now it was about the sixth hour, and there was darkness over all the earth until the ninth hour. **45** Then the sun was darkened, and the veil of the temple was torn in two.

Illustrative of

God's favor.

Ps 84:11 For the LORD God *is* a sun and shield; The LORD will give grace and glory; No good *thing* will He withhold From those who walk uprightly.

Christ's coming.

Mal 4:2 But to you who fear My name The Sun of Righteousness shall arise With healing in His wings; And you shall go out And grow fat like stall-fed calves.

The glory of Christ.

Matt 17:2 and He was transfigured before them. His face shone like the sun, and His clothes became as white as the light.

Rev 1:16 He had in His right hand seven stars, out of His mouth went a sharp two-edged sword, and His countenance *was* like the sun shining in its strength.

Rev 10:1 I saw still another mighty angel coming down from heaven, clothed with a cloud. And a rainbow *was* on his head, his face *was* like the sun, and his feet like pillars of fire.

Supreme rulers.

Gen 37:9 Then he dreamed still another dream and told it to his brothers, and said, "Look, I have dreamed another dream. And this time, the sun, the moon, and the eleven stars bowed down to me."

Is 13:10 For the stars of heaven and their constellations Will not give their light; The sun will be darkened in its going forth, And the moon will not cause its light to shine.

(Its brightness) the future glory of believers.

Dan 12:3 Those who are wise shall shine Like the brightness of the firmament, And those who turn many to righteousness Like the stars forever and ever.

Matt 13:43 Then the righteous will shine forth as the sun in the kingdom of their Father. He who has ears to hear, let him hear!

(Its power) the triumph of believers.

Judg 5:31 "Thus let all Your enemies perish, O LORD! But *let* those who love Him *be* like the sun When it comes out in full strength." So the land had rest for forty years.

(Darkened) severe calamities.

Ezek 32:7 When *I* put out your light, I will cover the heavens, and make its stars dark; I will cover the sun with a cloud, And the moon shall not give her light.

Joel 2:10 The earth quakes before them, The heavens tremble; The sun and moon grow dark, And the stars diminish their brightness.

Joel 2:31 The sun shall be turned into darkness, And the moon into blood, Before the coming of the great and awesome day of the LORD.

Matt 24:29 "Immediately after the tribulation of those days the sun will be darkened, and the moon will not give its light; the stars will fall from heaven, and the powers of the heavens will be shaken.

Rev 9:2 And he opened the bottomless pit, and smoke arose out of the pit like the smoke of a great furnace. So the sun and the air were darkened because of the smoke of the pit.

(Going down at noon) premature destruction.

Jer 15:9 "She languishes who has borne seven; She has breathed her last; Her sun has gone down While *it was* yet day; She has been ashamed and confounded. And the remnant of them I will deliver to the sword Before their enemies," says the LORD.

Amos 8:9 "And it shall come to pass in that day," says the Lord GOD, "That I will make the sun go down at noon, And I will darken the earth in broad daylight;

(No more going down) perpetual blessedness.

Is 60:20 Your sun shall no longer go down, Nor shall your moon withdraw itself; For the LORD will be your everlasting light, And the days of your mourning shall be ended.

(Before or in sight of) public ignominy.

2 Sam 12:11–12 Thus says the LORD: 'Behold, I will raise up adversity against you from your own house; and I will take your wives before your eyes and give *them* to your neighbor, and he shall lie with your wives in the sight of this sun. **12** For you did *it* secretly, but I will do this thing before all Israel, before the sun.' "

Jer 8:2 They shall spread them before the sun and the moon and all the host of heaven, which they have loved and which they have served and after which they have walked, which they have sought and which they have worshiped. They shall not be gathered nor buried; they shall be like refuse on the face of the earth.

SWEARING FALSELY

Forbidden.

Lev 19:12 And you shall not swear by My name falsely, nor shall you profane the name of your God: I *am* the LORD.

Num 30:2 If a man makes a vow to the LORD, or swears an oath to bind himself by some agreement, he shall not break his word; he shall do according to all that proceeds out of his mouth.

Matt 5:33 "Again you have heard that it was said to those of old, 'You shall not swear falsely, but shall perform your oaths to the Lord.'

Hateful to God.

Zech 8:17 Let none of you think evil in your heart against your neighbor; And do not love a false oath. For all these *are things* that I hate,' Says the LORD."

We should not love.

Zech 8:17 Let none of you think evil in your heart against your neighbor; And do not love a false oath. For all these *are things* that I hate,' Says the LORD."

Fraud often leads to.

Lev 6:2–3 "If a person sins and commits a trespass

against the LORD by lying to his neighbor about what was delivered to him for safekeeping, or about a pledge, or about a robbery, or if he has extorted from his neighbor, **3** or if he has found what was lost and lies concerning it, and swears falsely—in any one of these things that a man may do in which he sins:

Believers abstain from, and are blessed.

Josh 9:20 This we will do to them: We will let them live, lest wrath be upon us because of the oath which we swore to them."

Ps 15:4 In whose eyes a vile person is despised, But he honors those who fear the LORD; He *who* swears to his own hurt and does not change;

Ps 24:4–5 He who has clean hands and a pure heart, Who has not lifted up his soul to an idol, Nor sworn deceitfully. **5** He shall receive blessing from the LORD, And righteousness from the God of his salvation.

The wicked

Are addicted to the practice of.

Jer 5:2 Though they say, '*As* the LORD lives,' Surely they swear falsely."

Hos 10:4 They have spoken words, Swearing falsely in making a covenant. Thus judgment springs up like hemlock in the furrows of the field.

Plead excuses for.

Jer 7:9–10 Will you steal, murder, commit adultery, swear falsely, burn incense to Baal, and walk after other gods whom you do not know, **10** and *then* come and stand before Me in this house which is called by My name, and say, 'We are delivered to do all these abominations'?

Shall be judged on account of.

Mal 3:5 And I will come near you for judgment; I will be a swift witness Against sorcerers, Against adulterers, Against perjurers, Against those who exploit wage earners and widows and orphans, And against those who turn away an alien— Because they do not fear Me," Says the LORD of hosts.

Shall be cut off for.

Zech 5:3 Then he said to me, "This *is* the curse that goes out over the face of the whole earth: 'Every thief shall be expelled,' according *to* this side of *the scroll;* and, 'Every perjurer shall be expelled,' according *to* that side of it."

Shall have a curse upon their houses for.

Zech 5:4 "I will send out *the curse,*" says the LORD of hosts; "It shall enter the house of the thief And the house of the one who swears falsely by My name. It shall remain in the midst of his house And consume it, with its timber and stones."

False witnesses guilty of.

Deut 19:16 If a false witness rises against any man to testify against him of wrongdoing,

Deut 19:18 And the judges shall make careful inquiry, and indeed, *if* the witness *is* a false witness, who has testified falsely against his brother,

Illustrated by

Saul.

1 Sam 19:6 So Saul heeded the voice of Jonathan, and Saul swore, "*As* the LORD lives, he shall not be killed."

1 Sam 19:10 Then Saul sought to pin David to the wall with the spear, but he slipped away from Saul's presence; and he drove the spear into the wall. So David fled and escaped that night.

Shimei.

1 Kin 2:41–43 And Solomon was told that Shimei had gone from Jerusalem to Gath and had come back. **42** Then the king sent and called for Shimei, and said to him, "Did I not make you swear by the LORD, and warn you, saying, 'Know for certain that on the day you go out and travel anywhere, you shall surely die'? And you said to me, 'The word I have heard *is* good.' **43** Why then have you not kept the oath of the LORD and the commandment that I gave you?"

The Jews.

Ezek 16:59 For thus says the Lord GOD: "I will deal with you as you have done, who despised the oath by breaking the covenant.

Zedekiah.

Ezek 17:13–19 And he took the king's offspring, made a covenant with him, and put him under oath. He also took away the mighty of the land, **14** that the kingdom might be brought low and not lift itself up, *but* that by keeping his covenant it might stand. **15** But he rebelled against him by sending his ambassadors to Egypt, that they might give him horses and many people. Will he prosper? Will he who does such *things* escape? Can he break a covenant and still be delivered? **16** '*As* I live,' says the Lord GOD, 'surely in the place *where* the king *dwells* who made him king, whose oath he despised and whose covenant he broke—with him in the midst of Babylon he shall die. **17** Nor will Pharaoh with *his* mighty army and great company do anything in the war, when they heap up a siege mound and build a wall to cut off many persons. **18** Since he despised the oath by breaking the covenant, and in fact gave his hand and still did all these *things,* he shall not escape.' " **19** Therefore thus says the Lord GOD: "*As* I live, surely My oath which he despised, and My covenant which he broke, I will recompense on his own head.

Peter.

Matt 26:72 But again he denied with an oath, "I do not know the Man!"

Matt 26:74 Then he began to curse and swear, *saying,* "I do not know the Man!" Immediately a rooster crowed.

SWEARING, PROFANE

Of all kinds is forbidden.

Ex 20:7 "You shall not take the name of the LORD your God in vain, for the LORD will not hold *him* guiltless who takes His name in vain.

Matt 5:34–36 But I say to you, do not swear at all: neither by heaven, for it is God's throne; **35** nor by the earth, for it is His footstool; nor by Jerusalem, for it is the city of the great King. **36** Nor shall you swear by your head, because you cannot make one hair white or black.

Matt 23:21–22 He who swears by the temple, swears by it and by Him who dwells in it. **22** And he who swears by heaven, swears by the throne of God and by Him who sits on it.

James 5:12 But above all, my brethren, do not swear, either by heaven or by earth or with any other oath. But let your "Yes" be "Yes," and *your* "No," "No," lest you fall into judgment.

The wicked

Are addicted to.

Ps 10:7 His mouth is full of cursing and deceit and oppression; Under his tongue *is* trouble and iniquity.

Rom 3:14 *"Whose mouth is full of cursing and bitterness."*

Love.

Ps 109:17 As he loved cursing, so let it come to him; As he did not delight in blessing, so let it be far from him.

Clothe themselves with.

Ps 109:18 As he clothed himself with cursing as with his garment, So let it enter his body like water, And like oil into his bones.

Guilt of.

Ex 20:7 "You shall not take the name of the LORD your God in vain, for the LORD will not hold *him* guiltless who takes His name in vain.

Deut 5:11 'You shall not take the name of the LORD your God in vain, for the LORD will not hold *him* guiltless who takes His name in vain.

Woe pronounced against.

Matt 23:16 "Woe to you, blind guides, who say, 'Whoever swears by the temple, it is nothing; but whoever swears by the gold of the temple, he is obliged *to perform it.*'

Nations visited for.

Jer 23:10 For the land is full of adulterers; For because of a curse the land mourns. The pleasant places of the wilderness are dried up. Their course of life is evil, And their might *is* not right.

Hos 4:1–3 Hear the word of the LORD, You children of Israel, For the LORD *brings* a charge against the inhabitants of the land: "There is no truth or mercy Or knowledge of God in the land. **2** *By* swearing and lying, Killing and stealing and committing adultery, They break all restraint, With bloodshed upon bloodshed. **3** Therefore the land will mourn; And everyone who dwells there will waste away With the beasts of the field And the birds of the air; Even the fish of the sea will be taken away.

Punishment for.

Lev 24:16 And whoever blasphemes the name of the LORD shall surely be put to death. All the congregation shall certainly stone him, the stranger as well as him who is born in the land. When he blasphemes the name *of the LORD*, he shall be put to death.

Lev 24:23 Then Moses spoke to the children of Israel; and they took outside the camp him who had cursed, and stoned him with stones. So the children of Israel did as the LORD commanded Moses.

Ps 59:12 *For* the sin of their mouth *and* the words of their lips, Let them even be taken in their pride, And for the cursing and lying *which* they speak.

Ps 109:17–18 As he loved cursing, so let it come to him; As he did not delight in blessing, so let it be far from him. **18** As he clothed himself with cursing as with

his garment, So let it enter his body like water, And like oil into his bones.

Illustrated by

The son of an Israelite woman.

Lev 24:11 And the Israelite woman's son blasphemed the name *of the* LORD and cursed; and so they brought him to Moses. (His mother's name *was* Shelomith the daughter of Dibri, of the tribe of Dan.)

Gehazi.

2 Kin 5:20 But Gehazi, the servant of Elisha the man of God, said, "Look, my master has spared Naaman this Syrian, while not receiving from his hands what he brought; but *as* the LORD lives, I will run after him and take something from him."

Peter.

Matt 26:74 Then he began to curse and swear, *saying,* "I do not know the Man!" Immediately a rooster crowed.

SWINE

When wild, inhabited the woods.

Ps 80:13 The boar out of the woods uproots it, And the wild beast of the field devours it.

Unclean and not to be eaten.

Lev 11:7–8 and the swine, though it divides the hoof, having cloven hooves, yet does not chew the cud, *is* unclean to you. **8** Their flesh you shall not eat, and their carcasses you shall not touch. They *are* unclean to you.

Described as

Fierce and ungrateful.

Matt 7:6 "Do not give what is holy to the dogs; nor cast your pearls before swine, lest they trample them under their feet, and turn and tear you in pieces.

Filthy in their habits.

2 Pet 2:22 But it has happened to them according to the true proverb: *"A dog returns to his own vomit,"* and, "a sow, having washed, to her wallowing in the mire."

Destructive to agriculture.

Ps 80:13 The boar out of the woods uproots it, And the wild beast of the field devours it.

Eating pods.

Luke 15:16 And he would gladly have filled his stomach with the pods that the swine ate, and no one gave him *anything.*

Sacrificing of, an abomination.

Is 66:3 "He who kills a bull *is as if* he slays a man; He who sacrifices a lamb, *as if* he breaks a dog's neck; He who offers a grain offering, *as if he offers* swine's blood; He who burns incense, *as if* he blesses an idol. Just as they have chosen their own ways, And their soul delights in their abominations,

Kept in large herds.

Matt 8:30 Now a good way off from them there was a herd of many swine feeding.

Tending of, considered degradation to a Jew (implied).

Luke 15:15 Then he went and joined himself to a citizen of that country, and he sent him into his fields to feed swine.

Those of the Gergesenes demonized.

Matt 8:31–32 So the demons begged Him, saying, "If You cast us out, permit us to go away into the herd of swine." **32** And He said to them, "Go." So when they had come out, they went into the herd of swine. And suddenly the whole herd of swine ran violently down the steep place into the sea, and perished in the water.

Mark 5:11 Now a large herd of swine was feeding there near the mountains.

Mark 5:14 So those who fed the swine fled, and they told *it* in the city and in the country. And they went out to see what it was that had happened.

The ungodly Jews condemned for eating.

Is 65:4 Who sit among the graves, And spend the night in the tombs; Who eat swine's flesh, And the broth of abominable things is *in* their vessels;

Is 66:17 "Those who sanctify themselves and purify themselves, *To go* to the gardens After an *idol* in the midst, Eating swine's flesh and the abomination and the mouse, Shall be consumed together," says the LORD.

Illustrative of

The wicked.

Matt 7:6 "Do not give what is holy to the dogs; nor cast your pearls before swine, lest they trample them under their feet, and turn and tear you in pieces.

Hypocrites.

2 Pet 2:22 But it has happened to them according to the true proverb: *"A dog returns to his own vomit,"* and, "a sow, having washed, to her wallowing in the mire."

SWORD, THE

Probable origin.

Gen 3:24 So He drove out the man; and He placed cherubim at the east of the garden of Eden, and a flaming sword which turned every way, to guard the way to the tree of life.

Was pointed.

Ezek 21:15 I have set the point of the sword against all their gates, That the heart may melt and many may stumble. Ah! *It is* made bright; *It is* grasped for slaughter:

Frequently had two edges.

Ps 149:6 *Let* the high praises of God *be* in their mouth, And a two-edged sword in their hand,

Described as

Sharp.

Ps 57:4 My soul *is* among lions; I lie *among* the sons of men Who are set on fire, Whose teeth *are* spears and arrows, And their tongue a sharp sword.

Bright.

Nah 3:3 Horsemen charge with bright sword and glittering spear. *There is* a multitude of slain, A great number of bodies, Countless corpses— They stumble over the corpses—

Glittering.

Deut 32:41 If I whet My glittering sword, And My hand

takes hold on judgment, I will render vengeance to My enemies, And repay those who hate Me.

Job 20:25 It is drawn, and comes out of the body; Yes, the glittering *point comes* out of his gall. Terrors *come* upon him;

Oppressive.

Jer 46:16 He made many fall; Yes, one fell upon another. And they said, 'Arise! Let us go back to our own people And to the land of our nativity From the oppressing sword.'

Hurtful.

Ps 144:10 *The One* who gives salvation to kings, Who delivers David His servant From the deadly sword.

Carried in a sheath or scabbard.

1 Chr 21:27 So the LORD commanded the angel, and he returned his sword to its sheath.

Jer 47:6 "O you sword of the LORD, How long until you are quiet? Put yourself up into your scabbard, Rest and be still!

Ezek 21:3–5 and say to the land of Israel, 'Thus says the LORD: "Behold, I *am* against you, and I will draw My sword out of its sheath and cut off both righteous and wicked from you. **4** Because I will cut off both righteous and wicked from you, therefore My sword shall go out of its sheath against all flesh from south *to* north, **5** that all flesh may know that I, the LORD, have drawn My sword out of its sheath; it shall not return anymore." '

Suspended from the belt or side.

1 Sam 17:39 David fastened his sword to his armor and tried to walk, for he had not tested *them*. And David said to Saul, "I cannot walk with these, for I have not tested *them*." So David took them off.

2 Sam 20:8 When they *were* at the large stone which *is* in Gibeon, Amasa came before them. Now Joab was dressed in battle armor; on it was a belt *with* a sword fastened in its sheath at his hips; and as he was going forward, it fell out.

Neh 4:18 Every one of the builders had his sword girded at his side as he built. And the one who sounded the trumpet *was* beside me.

Ps 45:3 Gird Your sword upon *Your* thigh, O Mighty One, With Your glory and Your majesty.

Was used

By the patriarchs.

Gen 34:25 Now it came to pass on the third day, when they were in pain, that two of the sons of Jacob, Simeon and Levi, Dinah's brothers, each took his sword and came boldly upon the city and killed all the males.

Gen 48:22 Moreover I have given to you one portion above your brothers, which I took from the hand of the Amorite with my sword and my bow."

By the Jews.

Judg 20:2 And the leaders of all the people, all the tribes of Israel, presented themselves in the assembly of the people of God, four hundred thousand foot soldiers who drew the sword.

2 Sam 24:9 Then Joab gave the sum of the number of the people to the king. And there were in Israel eight hundred thousand valiant men who drew the sword, and the men of Judah were five hundred thousand men.

By heathen nations.

Judg 7:22 When the three hundred blew the trumpets, the LORD set every man's sword against his companion throughout the whole camp; and the army fled to Beth Acacia, toward Zererah, as far as the border of Abel Meholah, by Tabbath.

1 Sam 15:33 But Samuel said, "As your sword has made women childless, so shall your mother be childless among women." And Samuel hacked Agag in pieces before the LORD in Gilgal.

For self-defense.

Luke 22:36 Then He said to them, "But now, he who has a money bag, let him take *it,* and likewise a knapsack; and he who has no sword, let him sell his garment and buy one.

For destruction of enemies.

Num 21:24 Then Israel defeated him with the edge of the sword, and took possession of his land from the Arnon to the Jabbok, as far as the people of Ammon; for the border of the people of Ammon *was* fortified.

Josh 6:21 And they utterly destroyed all that *was* in the city, both man and woman, young and old, ox and sheep and donkey, with the edge of the sword.

For punishing criminals.

1 Sam 15:33 But Samuel said, "As your sword has made women childless, so shall your mother be childless among women." And Samuel hacked Agag in pieces before the LORD in Gilgal.

Acts 12:2 Then he killed James the brother of John with the sword.

Sometimes for self-destruction.

1 Sam 31:4–5 Then Saul said to his armorbearer, "Draw your sword, and thrust me through with it, lest these uncircumcised men come and thrust me through and abuse me." But his armorbearer would not, for he was greatly afraid. Therefore Saul took a sword and fell on it. **5** And when his armorbearer saw that Saul was dead, he also fell on his sword, and died with him.

Acts 16:27 And the keeper of the prison, awaking from sleep and seeing the prison doors open, supposing the prisoners had fled, drew his sword and was about to kill himself.

Hebrews early acquainted with making of.

1 Sam 13:19 Now there was no blacksmith to be found throughout all the land of Israel, for the Philistines said, "Lest the Hebrews make swords or spears."

In time of war, plowshares made into.

Joel 3:10 Beat your plowshares into swords And your pruning hooks into spears; Let the weak say, 'I *am* strong.' "

In time of peace, made into plowshares.

Is 2:4 He shall judge between the nations, And rebuke many people; They shall beat their swords into plowshares, And their spears into pruning hooks; Nation shall not lift up sword against nation, Neither shall they learn war anymore.

Mic 4:3 He shall judge between many peoples, And rebuke strong nations afar off; They shall beat their swords into plowshares, And their spears into pruning hooks; Nation shall not lift up sword against nation, Neither shall they learn war anymore.

Sharpened and furbished before going to war.

Ps 7:12 If he does not turn back, He will sharpen His sword; He bends His bow and makes it ready.

Ezek 21:9 "Son of man, prophesy and say, 'Thus says the LORD!' Say: 'A sword, a sword is sharpened And also polished!

Was brandished over the head.

Ezek 32:10 Yes, I will make many peoples astonished at you, and their kings shall be horribly afraid of you when I brandish My sword before them; and they shall tremble *every* moment, every man for his own life, in the day of your fall.'

Was thrust through enemies.

Ezek 16:40 "They shall also bring up an assembly against you, and they shall stone you with stones and thrust you through with their swords.

Often threatened or sent as a punishment.

Lev 26:25 And I will bring a sword against you that will execute the vengeance of the covenant; when you are gathered together within your cities I will send pestilence among you; and you shall be delivered into the hand of the enemy.

Lev 26:33 I will scatter you among the nations and draw out a sword after you; your land shall be desolate and your cities waste.

Deut 32:25 The sword shall destroy outside; *There shall be* terror within For the young man and virgin, The nursing child with the man of gray hairs.

Ezra 9:7 Since the days of our fathers to this day we *have been* very guilty, and for our iniquities we, our kings, *and* our priests have been delivered into the hand of the kings of the lands, to the sword, to captivity, to plunder, and to humiliation, as *it is* this day.

Ps 78:62 He also gave His people over to the sword, And was furious with His inheritance.

Was one of God's four severe judgments.

Ezek 14:21 For thus says the Lord GOD: "How much more it shall be when I send My four severe judgments on Jerusalem—the sword and famine and wild beasts and pestilence—to cut off man and beast from it?

Those slain by, communicated ceremonial uncleanness.

Num 19:16 Whoever in the open field touches one who is slain by a sword or who has died, or a bone of a man, or a grave, shall be unclean seven days.

Illustrative of

The Word of God.

Eph 6:17 And take the helmet of salvation, and the sword of the Spirit, which is the word of God;

Heb 4:12 For the word of God *is* living and powerful, and sharper than any two-edged sword, piercing even to the division of soul and spirit, and of joints and marrow, and is a discerner of the thoughts and intents of the heart.

The word of Christ.

Is 49:2 And He has made My mouth like a sharp sword; In the shadow of His hand He has hidden Me, And made Me a polished shaft; In His quiver He has hidden Me."

Rev 1:16 He had in His right hand seven stars, out of His mouth went a sharp two-edged sword, and His countenance *was* like the sun shining in its strength.

The justice of God.

Deut 32:41 If I whet My glittering sword, And My hand takes hold on judgment, I will render vengeance to My enemies, And repay those who hate Me.

Zech 13:7 "Awake, O sword, against My Shepherd, Against the Man who is My Companion," Says the LORD of hosts. "Strike the Shepherd, And the sheep will be scattered; Then I will turn My hand against the little ones.

The protection of God.

Deut 33:29 Happy *are* you, O Israel! Who *is* like you, a people saved by the LORD, The shield of your help And the sword of your majesty! Your enemies shall submit to you, And you shall tread down their high places."

War and contention.

Matt 10:34 "Do not think that I came to bring peace on earth. I did not come to bring peace but a sword.

Severe and heavy calamities.

Ezek 5:2 You shall burn with fire one-third in the midst of the city, when the days of the siege are finished; then you shall take one-third and strike around *it* with the sword, and one-third you shall scatter in the wind: I will draw out a sword after them.

Ezek 5:17 So I will send against you famine and wild beasts, and they will bereave you. Pestilence and blood shall pass through you, and I will bring the sword against you. I, the LORD, have spoken.' "

Ezek 14:17 "Or if I bring a sword on that land, and say, 'Sword, go through the land,' and I cut off man and beast from it,

Ezek 21:9 "Son of man, prophesy and say, 'Thus says the LORD!' Say: 'A sword, a sword is sharpened And also polished!

Deep mental affliction.

Luke 2:35 (yes, a sword will pierce through your own soul also), that the thoughts of many hearts may be revealed."

The wicked.

Ps 17:13 Arise, O LORD, Confront him, cast him down; Deliver my life from the wicked with Your sword,

The tongue of the wicked.

Ps 57:4 My soul *is* among lions; I lie *among* the sons of men Who are set on fire, Whose teeth *are* spears and arrows, And their tongue a sharp sword.

Ps 64:3 Who sharpen their tongue like a sword, And bend *their bows to shoot* their arrows—bitter words,

Prov 12:18 There is one who speaks like the piercings of a sword, But the tongue of the wise *promotes* health.

Persecuting spirit of the wicked.

Ps 37:14 The wicked have drawn the sword And have bent their bow, To cast down the poor and needy, To slay those who are of upright conduct.

The end of the wicked.

Prov 5:4 But in the end she is bitter as wormwood, Sharp as a two-edged sword.

False witnesses.

Prov 25:18 A man who bears false witness against his neighbor *Is like* a club, a sword, and a sharp arrow.

Judicial authority.

Rom 13:4 For he is God's minister to you for good. But if you do evil, be afraid; for he does not bear the sword in vain; for he is God's minister, an avenger to *execute* wrath on him who practices evil.

(Drawing of) war and destruction.

Lev 26:33 I will scatter you among the nations and draw out a sword after you; your land shall be desolate and your cities waste.

Ezek 21:3–5 and say to the land of Israel, 'Thus says the LORD: "Behold, I *am* against you, and I will draw My sword out of its sheath and cut off both righteous and wicked from you. **4** Because I will cut off both righteous and wicked from you, therefore My sword shall go out of its sheath against all flesh from south *to* north, **5** that all flesh may know that I, the LORD, have drawn My sword out of its sheath; it shall not return anymore." '

(Putting, into its scabbard) peace and friendship.

Jer 47:6 "O you sword of the LORD, How long until you are quiet? Put yourself up into your scabbard, Rest and be still!

(Living by) fighting.

Gen 27:40 By your sword you shall live, And you shall serve your brother; And it shall come to pass, when you become restless, That you shall break his yoke from your neck."

(Not departing from one's house) perpetual calamity.

2 Sam 12:10 Now therefore, the sword shall never depart from your house, because you have despised Me, and have taken the wife of Uriah the Hittite to be your wife.'

SYNAGOGUES

Places in which the Jews assembled for worship.

Acts 13:5 And when they arrived in Salamis, they preached the word of God in the synagogues of the Jews. They also had John as *their* assistant.

Acts 13:14 But when they departed from Perga, they came to Antioch in Pisidia, and went into the synagogue on the Sabbath day and sat down.

Early notice of their existence.

Ps 74:8 They said in their hearts, "Let us destroy them altogether." They have burned up all the meeting places of God in the land.

Probably originated in the schools of the prophets.

1 Sam 19:18–24 So David fled and escaped, and went to Samuel at Ramah, and told him all that Saul had done to him. And he and Samuel went and stayed in Naioth. **19** Now it was told Saul, saying, "Take note, David *is* at Naioth in Ramah!" **20** Then Saul sent messengers to take David. And when they saw the group of prophets prophesying, and Samuel standing *as* leader over them, the Spirit of God came upon the messengers of Saul, and they also prophesied. **21** And when Saul was told, he sent other messengers, and they prophesied likewise. Then Saul sent messengers again the third time, and they prophesied also. **22** Then he also went to Ramah, and came to the great well that *is* at Sechu. So he asked, and said, "Where *are* Samuel and David?" And *someone* said, "Indeed *they are* at Naioth in Ramah." **23** So he went there to Naioth in Ramah. Then the Spirit of God was upon him also, and he went on and prophesied until he came to Naioth in Ramah. **24** And he also stripped off his clothes and prophesied before Samuel in like manner, and lay down naked all that day and all that night. Therefore they say, "*Is* Saul also among the prophets?"

2 Kin 4:23 So he said, "Why are you going to him today? *It is* neither the New Moon nor the Sabbath." And she said, "*It is* well."

Revival of, after the captivity.

Neh 8:1–8 Now all the people gathered together as one man in the open square that *was* in front of the Water Gate; and they told Ezra the scribe to bring the Book of the Law of Moses, which the LORD had commanded Israel. **2** So Ezra the priest brought the Law before the assembly of men and women and all who *could* hear with understanding on the first day of the seventh month. **3** Then he read from it in the open square that *was* in front of the Water Gate from morning until midday, before the men and women and those who could understand; and the ears of all the people *were attentive* to the Book of the Law. **4** So Ezra the scribe stood on a platform of wood which they had made for the purpose; and beside him, at his right hand, stood Mattithiah, Shema, Anaiah, Urijah, Hilkiah, and Maaseiah; and at his left hand Pedaiah, Mishael, Malchijah, Hashum, Hashbadana, Zechariah, *and* Meshullam. **5** And Ezra opened the book in the sight of all the people, for he was *standing* above all the people; and when he opened it, all the people stood up. **6** And Ezra blessed the LORD, the great God. Then all the people answered, "Amen, Amen!" while lifting up their hands. And they bowed their heads and worshiped the LORD with *their* faces to the ground. **7** Also Jeshua, Bani, Sherebiah, Jamin, Akkub, Shabbethai, Hodijah, Maaseiah, Kelita, Azariah, Jozabad, Hanan, Pelaiah, and the Levites, helped the people to understand the Law; and the people *stood* in their place. **8** So they read distinctly from the book, in the Law of God; and they gave the sense, and helped *them* to understand the reading.

Service of, consisted of
Prayer.
Matt 6:5 "And when you pray, you shall not be like the hypocrites. For they love to pray standing in the synagogues and on the corners of the streets, that they may be seen by men. Assuredly, I say to you, they have their reward.

Reading the Word of God.
Neh 8:18 Also day by day, from the first day until the last day, he read from the Book of the Law of God. And they kept the feast seven days; and on the eighth day *there was* a sacred assembly, according to the *prescribed* manner.

Neh 9:3 And they stood up in their place and read from

the Book of the Law of the LORD their God *for one-*fourth of the day; and *for another* fourth they confessed and worshiped the LORD their God.

Neh 13:1 On that day they read from the Book of Moses in the hearing of the people, and in it was found written that no Ammonite or Moabite should ever come into the assembly of God,

Acts 15:21 For Moses has had throughout many generations those who preach him in every city, being read in the synagogues every Sabbath."

Expounding the Word of God.
Neh 8:8 So they read distinctly from the book, in the Law of God; and they gave the sense, and helped *them* to understand the reading.

Luke 4:21 And He began to say to them, "Today this Scripture is fulfilled in your hearing."

Praise and thanksgiving.
Neh 9:5 And the Levites, Jeshua, Kadmiel, Bani, Hashabniah, Sherebiah, Hodijah, Shebaniah, *and* Pethahiah, said: "Stand up *and* bless the LORD your God Forever and ever! "Blessed be Your glorious name, Which is exalted above all blessing and praise!

Service in, on the Sabbath day.
Luke 4:16 So He came to Nazareth, where He had been brought up. And as His custom was, He went into the synagogue on the Sabbath day, and stood up to read.

Acts 13:14 But when they departed from Perga, they came to Antioch in Pisidia, and went into the synagogue on the Sabbath day and sat down.

Governed by
A president or chief ruler.
Acts 18:8 Then Crispus, the ruler of the synagogue, believed on the Lord with all his household. And many of the Corinthians, hearing, believed and were baptized.

Acts 18:17 Then all the Greeks took Sosthenes, the ruler of the synagogue, and beat *him* before the judgment seat. But Gallio took no notice of these things.

Ordinary rulers.
Mark 5:22 And behold, one of the rulers of the synagogue came, Jairus by name. And when he saw Him, he fell at His feet

Acts 13:15 And after the reading of the Law and the Prophets, the rulers of the synagogue sent to them, saying, "Men *and* brethren, if you have any word of exhortation for the people, say on."

Provided with a minister, who had charge of the sacred books.
Luke 4:17 And He was handed the book of the prophet Isaiah. And when He had opened the book, He found the place where it was written:

Luke 4:20 Then He closed the book, and gave *it* back to the attendant and sat down. And the eyes of all who were in the synagogue were fixed on Him.

Seating
For the congregation.
Acts 13:14 But when they departed from Perga, they came to Antioch in Pisidia, and went into the synagogue on the Sabbath day and sat down.

Best, reserved for the elders.

Matt 23:6 They love the best places at feasts, the best seats in the synagogues,

Daily Scripture portion sometimes read by one of the congregation.

Luke 4:16 So He came to Nazareth, where He had been brought up. And as His custom was, He went into the synagogue on the Sabbath day, and stood up to read.

Strangers were invited to address the congregation.

Acts 13:15 And after the reading of the Law and the Prophets, the rulers of the synagogue sent to them, saying, "Men *and* brethren, if you have any word of exhortation for the people, say on."

Christ often

Attended.

Luke 4:16 So He came to Nazareth, where He had been brought up. And as His custom was, He went into the synagogue on the Sabbath day, and stood up to read.

Preached and taught in.

Matt 4:23 And Jesus went about all Galilee, teaching in their synagogues, preaching the gospel of the kingdom, and healing all kinds of sickness and all kinds of disease among the people.

Mark 1:39 And He was preaching in their synagogues throughout all Galilee, and casting out demons.

Luke 13:10 Now He was teaching in one of the synagogues on the Sabbath.

Performed miracles in.

Matt 12:9–10 Now when He had departed from there, He went into their synagogue. **10** And behold, there was a man who had a withered hand. And they asked Him, saying, "Is it lawful to heal on the Sabbath?"—that they might accuse Him.

Mark 1:23 Now there was a man in their synagogue with an unclean spirit. And he cried out,

Luke 13:11 And behold, there was a woman who had a spirit of infirmity eighteen years, and was bent over and could in no way raise *herself* up.

The apostles frequently taught and preached in.

Acts 9:20 Immediately he preached the Christ in the synagogues, that He is the Son of God.

Acts 13:5 And when they arrived in Salamis, they preached the word of God in the synagogues of the Jews. They also had John as *their* assistant.

Acts 17:1 Now when they had passed through Amphipolis and Apollonia, they came to Thessalonica, where there was a synagogue of the Jews.

Acts 17:17 Therefore he reasoned in the synagogue with the Jews and with the *Gentile* worshipers, and in the marketplace daily with those who happened to be there.

Often used as courts of justice.

Acts 9:2 and asked letters from him to the synagogues of Damascus, so that if he found any who were of the Way, whether men or women, he might bring them bound to Jerusalem.

James 2:2 For if there should come into your assembly a man with gold rings, in fine apparel, and there should also come in a poor man in filthy clothes,

Offenders were often

Given up to, for trial.

Luke 12:11 "Now when they bring you to the synagogues and magistrates and authorities, do not worry about how or what you should answer, or what you should say.

Luke 21:12 But before all these things, they will lay their hands on you and persecute *you*, delivering *you* up to the synagogues and prisons. You will be brought before kings and rulers for My name's sake.

Punished in.

Matt 10:17 But beware of men, for they will deliver you up to councils and scourge you in their synagogues.

Matt 23:34 Therefore, indeed, I send you prophets, wise men, and scribes: *some* of them you will kill and crucify, and *some* of them you will scourge in your synagogues and persecute from city to city,

Acts 22:19 So I said, 'Lord, they know that in every synagogue I imprisoned and beat those who believe on You.

Expelled from.

John 9:22 His parents said these *things* because they feared the Jews, for the Jews had agreed already that if anyone confessed *that* He *was* Christ, he would be put out of the synagogue.

John 9:34 They answered and said to him, "You were completely born in sins, and are you teaching us?" And they cast him out.

John 12:42 Nevertheless even among the rulers many believed in Him, but because of the Pharisees they did not confess *Him*, lest they should be put out of the synagogue;

John 16:2 They will put you out of the synagogues; yes, the time is coming that whoever kills you will think that he offers God service.

The building of, considered a good work.

Luke 7:5 "for he loves our nation, and has built us a synagogue."

Sometimes several, in the same city.

Acts 6:9 Then there arose some from what is called the Synagogue of the Freedmen (Cyrenians, Alexandrians, and those from Cilicia and Asia), disputing with Stephen.

Acts 9:2 and asked letters from him to the synagogues of Damascus, so that if he found any who were of the Way, whether men or women, he might bring them bound to Jerusalem.

Each sect had its own.

Acts 6:9 Then there arose some from what is called the Synagogue of the Freedmen (Cyrenians, Alexandrians, and those from Cilicia and Asia), disputing with Stephen.

SYRIA

Originally included Mesopotamia.

Gen 25:20 Isaac was forty years old when he took Rebekah as wife, the daughter of Bethuel the Syrian of Padan Aram, the sister of Laban the Syrian.

Gen 28:5 So Isaac sent Jacob away, and he went to

Padan Aram, to Laban the son of Bethuel the Syrian, the brother of Rebekah, the mother of Jacob and Esau.

Deut 26:5 And you shall answer and say before the LORD your God: 'My father *was* a Syrian, about to perish, and he went down to Egypt and dwelt there, few in number; and there he became a nation, great, mighty, and populous.

Acts 7:2 And he said, "Brethren and fathers, listen: The God of glory appeared to our father Abraham when he was in Mesopotamia, before he dwelt in Haran,

The country around Damascus, the capital.

2 Sam 8:6 Then David put garrisons in Syria of Damascus; and the Syrians became David's servants, *and* brought tribute. So the LORD preserved David wherever he went.

Is 7:8 For the head of Syria *is* Damascus, And the head of Damascus *is* Rezin. Within sixty-five years Ephraim will be broken, *So that it will* not *be* a people.

Abanah and Pharpar are rivers of.

2 Kin 5:12 *Are* not the Abanah and the Pharpar, the rivers of Damascus, better than all the waters of Israel? Could I not wash in them and be clean?" So he turned and went away in a rage.

Governed by kings.

1 Kin 22:31 Now the king of Syria had commanded the thirty-two captains of his chariots, saying, "Fight with no one small or great, but only with the king of Israel."

2 Kin 5:1 Now Naaman, commander of the army of the king of Syria, was a great and honorable man in the eyes of his master, because by him the LORD had given victory to Syria. He was also a mighty man of valor, *but* a leper.

Inhabitants of,

Called Syrians (of Damascus).

2 Sam 8:5 When the Syrians of Damascus came to help Hadadezer king of Zobah, David killed twenty-two thousand of the Syrians.

2 Sam 10:11 Then he said, "If the Syrians are too strong for me, then you shall help me; but if the people of Ammon are too strong for you, then I will come and help you.

2 Kin 5:20 But Gehazi, the servant of Elisha the man of God, said, "Look, my master has spared Naaman this Syrian, while not receiving from his hands what he brought; but *as* the LORD lives, I will run after him and take something from him."

An idolatrous people.

Judg 10:6 Then the children of Israel again did evil in the sight of the LORD, and served the Baals and the Ashtoreths, the gods of Syria, the gods of Sidon, the gods of Moab, the gods of the people of Ammon, and the gods of the Philistines; and they forsook the LORD and did not serve Him.

2 Kin 5:18 Yet in this thing may the LORD pardon your servant: when my master goes into the temple of Rimmon to worship there, and he leans on my hand, and I bow down in the temple of Rimmon—when I bow down in the temple of Rimmon, may the LORD please pardon your servant in this thing."

A warlike people.

1 Kin 20:23 Then the servants of the king of Syria said to him, "Their gods *are* gods of the hills. Therefore they were stronger than we; but if we fight against them in the plain, surely we will be stronger than they.

1 Kin 20:25 and you shall muster an army like the army that you have lost, horse for horse and chariot for chariot. Then we will fight against them in the plain; surely we will be stronger than they." And he listened to their voice and did so.

A commercial people.

Ezek 27:18 Damascus *was* your merchant because of the abundance of goods you made, because of your many luxury items, with the wine of Helbon and with white wool.

Spoke the Aramaic language.

2 Kin 18:26 Then Eliakim the son of Hilkiah, Shebna, and Joah said to *the* Rabshakeh, "Please speak to your servants in Aramaic, for we understand *it;* and do not speak to us in Hebrew in the hearing of the people who *are* on the wall."

Ezra 4:7 In the days of Artaxerxes also, Bishlam, Mithredath, Tabel, and the rest of their companions wrote to Artaxerxes king of Persia; and the letter *was* written in Aramaic script, and translated into the Aramaic language.

Dan 2:4 Then the Chaldeans spoke to the king in Aramaic, "O king, live forever! Tell your servants the dream, and we will give the interpretation."

Israel followed the idolatry of.

Judg 10:6 Then the children of Israel again did evil in the sight of the LORD, and served the Baals and the Ashtoreths, the gods of Syria, the gods of Sidon, the gods of Moab, the gods of the people of Ammon, and the gods of the Philistines; and they forsook the LORD and did not serve Him.

David

Destroyed the army of, which assisted Hadadezer.

2 Sam 8:5 When the Syrians of Damascus came to help Hadadezer king of Zobah, David killed twenty-two thousand of the Syrians.

Garrisoned there and received tribute.

2 Sam 8:6 Then David put garrisons in Syria of Damascus; and the Syrians became David's servants, *and* brought tribute. So the LORD preserved David wherever he went.

Dedicated the spoils of.

2 Sam 8:11–12 King David also dedicated these to the LORD, along with the silver and gold that he had dedicated from all the nations which he had subdued— **12** from Syria, from Moab, from the people of Ammon, from the Philistines, from Amalek, and from the spoil of Hadadezer the son of Rehob, king of Zobah.

Obtained renown by his victory over.

2 Sam 8:13 And David made *himself* a name when he returned from killing eighteen thousand Syrians in the Valley of Salt.

Sent Joab against the armies of, hired by the Ammonites. **2 Sam 10:6–14**

Destroyed a second army of.

2 Sam 10:15–19 When the Syrians saw that they had been defeated by Israel, they gathered together. **16** Then Hadadezer sent and brought out the Syrians who *were* beyond the River, and they came to Helam. And Shobach the commander of Hadadezer's army *went* before them. **17** When it was told David, he gathered all Israel, crossed over the Jordan, and came to Helam. And the Syrians set themselves in battle array against David and fought with him. **18** Then the Syrians fled before Israel; and David killed seven hundred charioteers and forty thousand horsemen of the Syrians, and struck Shobach the commander of their army, who died there. **19** And when all the kings *who were* servants to Hadadezer saw that they were defeated by Israel, they made peace with Israel and served them. So the Syrians were afraid to help the people of Ammon anymore.

Asa sought aid of, against Israel.

1 Kin 15:18–20 Then Asa took all the silver and gold *that was* left in the treasuries of the house of the LORD and the treasuries of the king's house, and delivered them into the hand of his servants. And King Asa sent them to Ben-Hadad the son of Tabrimmon, the son of Hezion, king of Syria, who dwelt in Damascus, saying, **19** "*Let there be* a treaty between you and me, as there was between my father and your father. See, I have sent you a present of silver and gold. Come and break your treaty with Baasha king of Israel, so that he will withdraw from me." **20** So Ben-Hadad heeded King Asa, and sent the captains of his armies against the cities of Israel. He attacked Ijon, Dan, Abel Beth Maachah, and all Chinneroth, with all the land of Naphtali.

Elijah anointed Hazael king over, by divine direction.

1 Kin 19:15 Then the LORD said to him: "Go, return on your way to the Wilderness of Damascus; and when you arrive, anoint Hazael *as* king over Syria.

Ben-Hadad king of, besieged Samaria.
1 Kin 20:1–12

The Israelites

Under Ahab, encouraged and assisted by God, overcame.

1 Kin 20:13–20 Suddenly a prophet approached Ahab king of Israel, saying, "Thus says the LORD: 'Have you seen all this great multitude? Behold, I will deliver it into your hand today, and you shall know that I *am* the LORD.' " **14** So Ahab said, "By whom?" And he said, "Thus says the LORD: 'By the young leaders of the provinces.' " Then he said, "Who will set the battle in order?" And he answered, "You." **15** Then he mustered the young leaders of the provinces, and there were two hundred and thirty-two; and after them he mustered all the people, all the children of Israel—seven thousand. **16** So they went out at noon. Meanwhile Ben-Hadad and the thirty-two kings helping him were getting drunk at the command post. **17** The young leaders of the provinces went out first. And Ben-Hadad sent out *a patrol*, and they told him, saying, "Men are coming out of Samaria!" **18** So he said, "If they have come out for peace, take them alive; and if they have come out for war, take them alive." **19** Then these young leaders of the provinces went out of the city with the army which followed them. **20** And each one killed his man; so the Syrians fled, and Israel pursued them; and Ben-Hadad the king of Syria escaped on a horse with the cavalry.

Forewarned of invasion by, at the return of the year.

1 Kin 20:22–25 And the prophet came to the king of Israel and said to him, "Go, strengthen yourself; take note, and see what you should do, for in the spring of the year the king of Syria will come up against you." **23** Then the servants of the king of Syria said to him, "Their gods *are* gods of the hills. Therefore they were stronger than we; but if we fight against them in the plain, surely we will be stronger than they." **24** So do this thing: Dismiss the kings, each from his position, and put captains in their places; **25** and you shall muster an army like the army that you have lost, horse for horse and chariot for chariot. Then we will fight against them in the plain; surely we will be stronger than they." And he listened to their voice and did so.

Syrians greatly outnumbered them.

1 Kin 20:26–27 So it was, in the spring of the year, that Ben-Hadad mustered the Syrians and went up to Aphek to fight against Israel. **27** And the children of Israel were mustered and given provisions, and they went against them. Now the children of Israel encamped before them like two little flocks of goats, while the Syrians filled the countryside.

Encouraged and assisted by God, overcame the Syrians a second time.

1 Kin 20:28–30 Then a man of God came and spoke to the king of Israel, and said, "Thus says the LORD: 'Because the Syrians have said, "The LORD *is* God of the hills, but He *is* not God of the valleys," therefore I will deliver all this great multitude into your hand, and you shall know that I *am* the LORD.' " **29** And they encamped opposite each other for seven days. So it was that on the seventh day the battle was joined; and the children of Israel killed one hundred thousand foot soldiers *of* the Syrians in one day. **30** But the rest fled to Aphek, into the city; then a wall fell on twenty-seven thousand of the men *who were* left. And Ben-Hadad fled and went into the city, into an inner chamber.

Craftily drawn into a league with. **1 Kin 20:31–43**

At peace with, for three years.

1 Kin 22:1 Now three years passed without war between Syria and Israel.

Under Ahab, sought to recover Ramoth Gilead from.
1 Kin 22:3–29

Defeated by, and Ahab slain.

1 Kin 22:30–36 And the king of Israel said to Jehoshaphat, "I will disguise myself and go into battle; but you put on your robes." So the king of Israel disguised himself and went into battle. **31** Now the king of Syria had commanded the thirty-two captains of his chariots, saying, "Fight with no one small or great, but only with the king of Israel." **32** So it was, when the captains of the chariots saw Jehoshaphat, that they said, "Surely it *is* the king of Israel!" Therefore they turned aside to fight against him, and Jehoshaphat cried out. **33** And it happened, when the captains of the chariots saw that it *was* not the king of Israel, that they turned back from pursuing him. **34** Now a *certain* man drew a bow at random, and struck the king of Israel between the joints of his armor. So he said to the driver of his chariot, "Turn around and take me out of the battle, for I am wounded." **35** The battle increased that day; and the king was propped up in his chariot, facing the Syrians, and died at evening. The blood ran out from the wound onto the floor of the chariot. **36** Then, as the sun was going down, a shout went throughout the army, saying, "Every man to his city, and every man to his own country!"

Harassed by frequent incursions of.

2 Kin 5:2 And the Syrians had gone out on raids, and had brought back captive a young girl from the land of Israel. She waited on Naaman's wife.

2 Kin 6:23 Then he prepared a great feast for them; and after they ate and drank, he sent them away and they went to their master. So the bands of Syrian *raiders* came no more into the land of Israel.

Heard the secrets of, from Elisha.

2 Kin 6:8–12 Now the king of Syria was making war against Israel; and he consulted with his servants, saying, "My camp *will be* in such and such a place." **9** And the man of God sent to the king of Israel, saying, "Beware that you do not pass this place, for the Syrians are coming down there." **10** Then the king of Israel sent *someone* to the place of which the man of God had told him. Thus he warned him, and he was watchful there, not just once or twice. **11** Therefore the heart of the king of Syria was greatly troubled by this thing; and he called his servants and said to them, "Will you not show me which of us *is* for the king of Israel?" **12** And one of his servants said, "None, my lord, O king; but Elisha, the prophet who *is* in Israel, tells the king of Israel the words that you speak in your bedroom."

God smote with blindness those sent against Elisha by the king of.

2 Kin 6:14 Therefore he sent horses and chariots and a great army there, and they came by night and surrounded the city.

2 Kin 6:18–20 So when *the Syrians* came down to him, Elisha prayed to the LORD, and said, "Strike this people, I pray, with blindness." And He struck them with blindness according to the word of Elisha. **19** Now Elisha said to them, "This *is* not the way, nor *is* this the city. Follow me, and I will bring you to the man whom you seek." But he led them to Samaria. **20** So it was, when they had come to Samaria, that Elisha said, "LORD, open the eyes of these *men*, that they may see." And the LORD opened their eyes, and they saw; and there *they were*, inside Samaria!

Besieged Samaria again.

2 Kin 6:24–29 And it happened after this that Ben-Hadad king of Syria gathered all his army, and went up and besieged Samaria. **25** And there was a great famine in Samaria; and indeed they besieged it until a donkey's head was *sold* for eighty *shekels* of silver, and one-fourth of a kab of dove droppings for five *shekels* of silver. **26** Then, as the king of Israel was passing by on the wall, a woman cried out to him, saying, "Help, my lord, O king!" **27** And he said, "If

the LORD does not help you, where can I find help for you? From the threshing floor or from the winepress?" **28** Then the king said to her, "What is troubling you?" And she answered, "This woman said to me, 'Give your son, that we may eat him today, and we will eat my son tomorrow.' **29** So we boiled my son, and ate him. And I said to her on the next day, 'Give your son, that we may eat him'; but she has hidden her son."

Army of, miraculously routed.

2 Kin 7:5–6 And they rose at twilight to go to the camp of the Syrians; and when they had come to the outskirts of the Syrian camp, to their surprise no one *was* there. **6** For the LORD had caused the army of the Syrians to hear the noise of chariots and the noise of horses—the noise of a great army; so they said to one another, "Look, the king of Israel has hired against us the kings of the Hittites and the kings of the Egyptians to attack us!"

Death of the king of, and the cruelty of his successor foretold by Elisha.

2 Kin 8:7 Then Elisha went to Damascus, and Ben-Hadad king of Syria was sick; and it was told him, saying, "The man of God has come here."

2 Kin 8:15 But it happened on the next day that he took a thick cloth and dipped *it* in water, and spread *it* over his face so that he died; and Hazael reigned in his place.

Joram king of Israel, in seeking to recover Ramoth Gilead from, severely wounded.

2 Kin 8:28–29 Now he went with Joram the son of Ahab to war against Hazael king of Syria at Ramoth Gilead; and the Syrians wounded Joram. **29** Then King Joram went back to Jezreel to recover from the wounds which the Syrians had inflicted on him at Ramah, when he fought against Hazael king of Syria. And Ahaziah the son of Jehoram, king of Judah, went down to see Joram the son of Ahab in Jezreel, because he was sick.

2 Kin 9:15 But King Joram had returned to Jezreel to recover from the wounds which the Syrians had inflicted on him when he fought with Hazael king of Syria.) And Jehu said, "If you are so minded, let no one leave *or* escape from the city to go and tell *it* in Jezreel."

Israel delivered into the hands of, for the sins of Jehoahaz.

2 Kin 13:3 Then the anger of the LORD was aroused against Israel, and He delivered them into the hand of Hazael king of Syria, and into the hand of Ben-Hadad the son of Hazael, all *their* days.

2 Kin 13:7 For He left of the army of Jehoahaz only fifty horsemen, ten chariots, and ten thousand foot soldiers; for the king of Syria had destroyed them and made them like the dust at threshing.

2 Kin 13:22 And Hazael king of Syria oppressed Israel all the days of Jehoahaz.

A deliverer raised up for Israel against.

2 Kin 13:5 Then the LORD gave Israel a deliverer, so that they escaped from under the hand of the Syrians; and the children of Israel dwelt in their tents as before.

2 Kin 13:23–25 But the LORD was gracious to them, had compassion on them, and regarded them, because of His covenant with Abraham, Isaac, and Jacob, and would not yet destroy them or cast them from His presence. 24 Now Hazael king of Syria died. Then Ben-Hadad his son reigned in his place. 25 And Jehoash the son of Jehoahaz recaptured from the hand of Ben-Hadad, the son of Hazael, the cities which he had taken out of the hand of Jehoahaz his father by war. Three times Joash defeated him and recaptured the cities of Israel.

Elisha predicted to Joash his three victories over.

2 Kin 13:14–19 Elisha had become sick with the illness of which he would die. Then Joash the king of Israel came down to him, and wept over his face, and said, "O my father, my father, the chariots of Israel and their horsemen!" 15 And Elisha said to him, "Take a bow and some arrows." So he took himself a bow and some arrows. 16 Then he said to the king of Israel, "Put your hand on the bow." So he put his hand *on it*, and Elisha put his hands on the king's hands. 17 And he said, "Open the east window"; and he opened *it*. Then Elisha said, "Shoot"; and he shot. And he said, "The arrow of the LORD's deliverance and the arrow of deliverance from Syria; for you must strike the Syrians at Aphek till you have destroyed *them*." 18 Then he said, "Take the arrows"; so he took *them*. And he said to the king of Israel, "Strike the ground"; so he struck three times, and stopped. 19 And the man of God was angry with him, and said, "You should have struck five or six times; then you would have struck Syria till you had destroyed *it!* But now you will strike Syria *only* three times."

Joined with Israel against Ahaz and besieged Jerusalem.

2 Kin 16:5 Then Rezin king of Syria and Pekah the son of Remaliah, king of Israel, came up to Jerusalem to *make* war; and they besieged Ahaz but could not overcome *him.*

Is 7:12 But Ahaz said, "I will not ask, nor will I test the LORD!"

Retook Elath and drove out the Jews.

2 Kin 16:6 At that time Rezin king of Syria captured Elath for Syria, and drove the men of Judah from Elath. Then the Edomites went to Elath, and dwell there to this day.

Subdued, and its inhabitants taken captive by Assyria.

2 Kin 16:9 So the king of Assyria heeded him; for the king of Assyria went up against Damascus and took it, carried *its people* captive to Kir, and killed Rezin.

Prophecies respecting,

Destruction of Rezin, king of.

Is 7:8 For the head of Syria *is* Damascus, And the head of Damascus *is* Rezin. Within sixty-five years Ephraim will be broken, *So that it will* not *be* a people.

Is 7:16 For before the Child shall know to refuse the evil and choose the good, the land that you dread will be forsaken by both her kings.

It would cease to be a kingdom.

Is 17:1–3 The burden against Damascus. "Behold, Damascus will cease from *being* a city, And it will be a ruinous heap. 2 The cities of Aroer *are* forsaken; They will be for flocks Which lie down, and no one will make *them* afraid. 3 The fortress also will cease from Ephraim, The kingdom from Damascus, And the remnant of Syria; They will be as the glory of the children of Israel," Says the LORD of hosts.

Terror and dismay in, prompted by foreign invasion.

Jer 49:23–24 Against Damascus. "Hamath and Arpad are shamed, For they have heard bad news. They are fainthearted; *There is* trouble on the sea; It cannot be quiet. 24 Damascus has grown feeble; She turns to flee, And fear has seized *her.* Anguish and sorrows have taken her like a woman in labor.

Destruction of its inhabitants.

Jer 49:26 Therefore her young men shall fall in her streets, And all the men of war shall be cut off in that day," says the LORD of hosts.

Plundering and burning of Damascus.

Is 8:4 for before the child shall have knowledge to cry 'My father' and 'My mother,' the riches of Damascus and the spoil of Samaria will be taken away before the king of Assyria."

Jer 49:27 "I will kindle a fire in the wall of Damascus, And it shall consume the palaces of Ben-Hadad."

Amos 1:4 But I will send a fire into the house of Hazael, Which shall devour the palaces of Ben-Hadad.

Its calamities, the punishments of its sins.

Amos 1:3 Thus says the LORD: "For three transgressions of Damascus, and for four, I will not turn away its *punishment,* Because they have threshed Gilead with implements of iron.

Its inhabitants to be captives.

Amos 1:3 Thus says the LORD: "For three transgressions of Damascus, and for four, I will not turn away its *punishment,* Because they have threshed Gilead with implements of iron.

Its history in connection with the Macedonian Empire. **Dan 11:6–45**

Subdued and governed by the Romans.

Luke 2:2 This census first took place while Quirinius was governing Syria.

Gospel preached and many churches founded in.

Acts 15:23 They wrote this *letter* by them: The apostles, the elders, and the brethren, To the brethren who are of the Gentiles in Antioch, Syria, and Cilicia: Greetings.

Acts 15:41 And he went through Syria and Cilicia, strengthening the churches.

TABERNACLE, THE

Moses was commanded to construct after a divine pattern.

Ex 25:9 According to all that I show you, *that is,* the pattern of the tabernacle and the pattern of all its furnishings, just so you shall make *it.*

Ex 26:30 And you shall raise up the tabernacle according to its pattern which you were shown on the mountain.

Heb 8:5 who serve the copy and shadow of the heavenly things, as Moses was divinely instructed when he was about to make the tabernacle. For He said, *"See that you make all things according to the pattern shown you on the mountain."*

Made of the freewill offerings of the people.

Ex 25:1–8 Then the LORD spoke to Moses, saying: **2** "Speak to the children of Israel, that they bring Me an offering. From everyone who gives it willingly with his heart you shall take My offering. **3** And this *is* the offering which you shall take from them: gold, silver, and bronze; **4** blue, purple, and scarlet *thread,* fine linen, and goats' *hair;* **5** ram skins dyed red, badger skins, and acacia wood; **6** oil for the light, and spices for the anointing oil and for the sweet incense; **7** onyx stones, and stones to be set in the ephod and in the breastplate. **8** And let them make Me a sanctuary, that I may dwell among them.

Ex 35:4–5 And Moses spoke to all the congregation of the children of Israel, saying, "This *is* the thing which the LORD commanded, saying: **5** 'Take from among you an offering to the LORD. Whoever *is* of a willing heart, let him bring it as an offering to the LORD: gold, silver, and bronze;

Ex 35:21–29 Then everyone came whose heart was stirred, and everyone whose spirit was willing, *and* they brought the LORD's offering for the work of the tabernacle of meeting, for all its service, and for the holy garments. **22** They came, both men and women, as many as had a willing heart, *and* brought earrings and nose rings, rings and necklaces, all jewelry of gold, that is, every man who *made* an offering of gold to the LORD. **23** And every man, with whom was found blue, purple, and scarlet *thread,* fine linen, goats' *hair,* red skins of rams, and badger skins, brought *them.* **24** Everyone who offered an offering of silver or bronze brought the LORD's offering. And everyone with whom was found acacia wood for any work of the service, brought *it.* **25** All the women *who were* gifted artisans spun yarn with their hands, and brought what they had spun, of blue, purple, *and* scarlet, and fine linen. **26** And all the women whose hearts stirred with wisdom spun yarn of goats' *hair.* **27** The rulers brought onyx stones, and the stones to

be set in the ephod and in the breastplate, **28** and spices and oil for the light, for the anointing oil, and for the sweet incense. **29** The children of Israel brought a freewill offering to the LORD, all the men and women whose hearts were willing to bring *material* for all kinds of work which the LORD, by the hand of Moses, had commanded to be done.

Divine wisdom given to Bezalel to make.

Ex 31:2–7 "See, I have called by name Bezalel the son of Uri, the son of Hur, of the tribe of Judah. **3** And I have filled him with the Spirit of God, in wisdom, in understanding, in knowledge, and in all *manner of* workmanship, **4** to design artistic works, to work in gold, in silver, in bronze, **5** in cutting jewels for setting, in carving wood, and to work in all *manner of* workmanship. **6** "And I, indeed I, have appointed with him Aholiab the son of Ahisamach, of the tribe of Dan; and I have put wisdom in the hearts of all the gifted artisans, that they may make all that I have commanded you: **7** the tabernacle of meeting, the ark of the Testimony and the mercy seat that *is* on it, and all the furniture of the tabernacle—

Ex 35:30–35 And Moses said to the children of Israel, "See, the LORD has called by name Bezalel the son of Uri, the son of Hur, of the tribe of Judah; **31** and He has filled him with the Spirit of God, in wisdom and understanding, in knowledge and all manner of workmanship, **32** to design artistic works, to work in gold and silver and bronze, **33** in cutting jewels for setting, in carving wood, and to work in all manner of artistic workmanship. **34** "And He has put in his heart the ability to teach, *in* him and Aholiab the son of Ahisamach, of the tribe of Dan. **35** He has filled them with skill to do all manner of work of the engraver and the designer and the tapestry maker, in blue, purple, and scarlet *thread,* and fine linen, and of the weaver—those who do every work and those who design artistic works.

Ex 36:1 "And Bezalel and Aholiab, and every gifted artisan in whom the LORD has put wisdom and understanding, to know how to do all manner of work for the service of the sanctuary, shall do according to all that the LORD has commanded."

Names for,

Tabernacle of the Lord.

Josh 22:19 Nevertheless, if the land of your possession *is* unclean, *then* cross over to the land of the possession of the LORD, where the LORD's tabernacle stands, and take possession among us; but do not rebel against the LORD, nor rebel against us, by building yourselves an altar besides the altar of the LORD our God.

1 Sam 1:9 So Hannah arose after they had finished eating and drinking in Shiloh. Now Eli the priest was sitting on the seat by the doorpost of the tabernacle of the LORD.

1 Sam 3:3 and before the lamp of God went out in the tabernacle of the LORD where the ark of God *was*, and while Samuel was lying down,

1 Kin 2:28 Then news came to Joab, for Joab had defected to Adonijah, though he had not defected to Absalom. So Joab fled to the tabernacle of the LORD, and took hold of the horns of the altar.

1 Chr 16:39 and Zadok the priest and his brethren the priests, before the tabernacle of the LORD at the high place that *was* at Gibeon,

Tabernacle of Testimony or witness.

Ex 38:21 This is the inventory of the tabernacle, the tabernacle of the Testimony, which was counted according to the commandment of Moses, for the service of the Levites, by the hand of Ithamar, son of Aaron the priest.

Num 1:50 but you shall appoint the Levites over the tabernacle of the Testimony, over all its furnishings, and over all things that belong to it; they shall carry the tabernacle and all its furnishings; they shall attend to it and camp around the tabernacle.

Num 17:7–8 And Moses placed the rods before the LORD in the tabernacle of witness. 8 Now it came to pass on the next day that Moses went into the tabernacle of witness, and behold, the rod of Aaron, of the house of Levi, had sprouted and put forth buds, had produced blossoms and yielded ripe almonds.

2 Chr 24:6 So the king called Jehoiada the chief *priest*, and said to him, "Why have you not required the Levites to bring in from Judah and from Jerusalem the collection, *according to the commandment* of Moses the servant of the LORD and of the assembly of Israel, for the tabernacle of witness?"

Acts 7:44 "Our fathers had the tabernacle of witness in the wilderness, as He appointed, instructing Moses to make it according to the pattern that he had seen,

Tabernacle of meeting.

Ex 27:21 In the tabernacle of meeting, outside the veil which *is* before the Testimony, Aaron and his sons shall tend it from evening until morning before the LORD. *It shall be* a statute forever to their generations on behalf of the children of Israel.

Ex 33:7 Moses took his tent and pitched it outside the camp, far from the camp, and called it the tabernacle of meeting. And it came to pass *that* everyone who sought the LORD went out to the tabernacle of meeting which *was* outside the camp.

Ex 40:26 He put the gold altar in the tabernacle of meeting in front of the veil;

Tabernacle of Shiloh.

Ps 78:60 So that He forsook the tabernacle of Shiloh, The tent He had placed among men,

House of the Lord.

Josh 6:24 But they burned the city and all that *was* in it with fire. Only the silver and gold, and the vessels of bronze and iron, they put into the treasury of the house of the LORD.

1 Sam 1:7 So it was, year by year, when she went up to the house of the LORD, that she provoked her; therefore she wept and did not eat.

1 Sam 1:24 Now when she had weaned him, she took him up with her, with three bulls, one ephah of flour, and a skin of wine, and brought him to the house of the LORD in Shiloh. And the child *was* young.

Was a moveable tent suited to the unsettled condition of Israel.

2 Sam 7:6–7 For I have not dwelt in a house since the time that I brought the children of Israel up from Egypt, even to this day, but have moved about in a tent and in a tabernacle. 7 Wherever I have moved about with all the children of Israel, have I ever spoken a word to anyone from the tribes of Israel, whom I commanded to shepherd My people Israel, saying, 'Why have you not built Me a house of cedar?' " '

Designed for manifestation of God's presence and for His worship.

Ex 25:8 And let them make Me a sanctuary, that I may dwell among them.

Ex 29:42–43 *This shall be* a continual burnt offering throughout your generations *at* the door of the tabernacle of meeting before the LORD, where I will meet you to speak with you. 43 And there I will meet with the children of Israel, and *the tabernacle* shall be sanctified by My glory.

The boards of

Supported by bars of acacia wood resting in rings of gold.

Ex 26:26–29 "And you shall make bars of acacia wood: five for the boards on one side of the tabernacle, 27 five bars for the boards on the other side of the tabernacle, and five bars for the boards of the side of the tabernacle, for the far side westward. 28 The middle bar shall pass through the midst of the boards from end to end. 29 You shall overlay the boards with gold, make their rings of gold *as* holders for the bars, and overlay the bars with gold.

Ex 36:31–33 And he made bars of acacia wood: five for the boards on one side of the tabernacle, 32 five bars for the boards on the other side of the tabernacle, and five bars for the boards of the tabernacle on the far side westward. 33 And he made the middle bar to pass through the boards from one end to the other.

With the bars, covered with gold.

Ex 26:26–29 "And you shall make bars of acacia wood: five for the boards on one side of the tabernacle, 27 five bars for the boards on the other side of the tabernacle, and five bars for the boards of the side of the tabernacle, for the far side westward. 28 The middle bar shall pass through the midst of the boards from end to end. 29 You shall overlay the boards with gold, make their rings of gold *as* holders for the bars, and overlay the bars with gold.

Ex 36:34 He overlaid the boards with gold, made their rings of gold *to be* holders for the bars, and overlaid the bars with gold.

The door of, a screen suspended from five pillars of acacia wood.

Ex 26:36–37 "You shall make a screen for the door of the tabernacle, *woven of* blue, purple, and scarlet *thread*, and fine woven linen, made by a weaver. 37 And you shall make for the screen five pillars of acacia *wood*, and overlay them with gold; their hooks *shall be* gold, and you shall cast five sockets of bronze for them.

Ex 36:37–38 He also made a screen for the tabernacle door, of blue, purple, and scarlet *thread*, and fine woven linen, made by a weaver, 38 and its five pillars with their hooks. And he overlaid their capitals and their rings with gold, but their five sockets *were* bronze.

Coverings of,

The first or inner, ten curtains of linen joined with loops and golden clasps.

Ex 26:1–6 "Moreover you shall make the tabernacle *with* ten curtains *of* fine woven linen and blue, purple, and scarlet *thread*; with artistic designs of cherubim you shall weave them. 2 The length of each curtain *shall be* twenty-eight cubits, and the width of each curtain four cubits. And every one of the curtains shall have the same measurements. 3 Five curtains shall be coupled to one another, and *the other* five curtains *shall be* coupled to one another. 4 And you shall make loops of blue *yarn* on the edge of the curtain on the selvedge of *one* set, and likewise you shall do on the outer edge of *the other* curtain of the second set. 5 Fifty loops you shall make in the one curtain, and fifty loops you shall make on the edge of the curtain that *is* on the end of the second set, that the loops may be clasped to one another. 6 And you shall make fifty clasps of gold, and couple the curtains together with the clasps, so that it may be one tabernacle.

Ex 36:8–13 Then all the gifted artisans among them who worked on the tabernacle made ten curtains woven of fine linen, and of blue, purple, and scarlet thread; *with* artistic designs of cherubim they made them. 9 The length of each curtain *was* twenty-eight cubits, and the width of each curtain four cubits; the curtains *were* all the same size. 10 And he coupled five curtains to one another, and *the other* five curtains he coupled to one another. 11 He made loops of blue *yarn* on the edge of the curtain on the selvedge of one set; likewise he did on the outer edge of *the other* curtain of the second set. 12 Fifty loops he made on one curtain, and fifty loops he made on the edge of the curtain on the end of the second set; the loops held one *curtain* to another. 13 And he made fifty clasps of gold, and coupled the curtains to one another with the clasps, that it might be one tabernacle.

The second, eleven curtains of goats' hair.

Ex 26:7–13 "You shall also make curtains of goats' *hair*, to be a tent over the tabernacle. You shall make eleven curtains. 8 The length of each curtain *shall be* thirty cubits, and the width of each curtain four cubits; and the eleven curtains shall all have the same measurements. 9 And you shall couple five curtains by themselves and six curtains by themselves, and you shall double over the sixth curtain at the forefront of the tent. 10 You shall make fifty loops on the edge of the curtain that is outermost in *one* set, and fifty loops on the edge of the curtain of the second set. 11 And you shall make fifty bronze clasps, put the clasps into the loops, and couple the tent together, that it may be one. 12 The remnant that remains of the curtains of the tent, the half curtain that remains, shall hang over the back of the tabernacle. 13 And a cubit on one side and a cubit on the other side, of what remains of the length of the curtains of the tent, shall hang over the sides of the tabernacle, on this side and on that side, to cover it.

Ex 36:14–18 He made curtains of goats' *hair* for the tent over the tabernacle; he made eleven curtains. 15 The length of each curtain *was* thirty cubits, and the width of each curtain four cubits; the eleven curtains *were* the same size. 16 He coupled five curtains by themselves and six curtains by themselves. 17 And he made fifty loops on the edge of the curtain that is outermost in one set, and fifty loops he made on the edge of the curtain of the second set. 18 He also made fifty bronze clasps to couple the tent together, that it might be one.

The third, rams' skins dyed red.

Ex 26:14 "You shall also make a covering of ram skins dyed red for the tent, and a covering of badger skins above that.

Ex 36:19 Then he made a covering for the tent of ram skins dyed red, and a covering of badger skins above *that.*

The fourth or outward, badgers' skins.

Ex 26:14 "You shall also make a covering of ram skins dyed red for the tent, and a covering of badger skins above that.

Ex 36:19 Then he made a covering for the tent of ram skins dyed red, and a covering of badger skins above *that.*

Divided by a veil, suspended from four pillars of acacia.

Ex 26:31–33 "You shall make a veil woven of blue, purple, and scarlet *thread*, and fine woven linen. It shall be woven with an artistic design of cherubim. 32 You shall hang it upon the four pillars of acacia *wood* overlaid with gold. Their hooks *shall be* gold, upon four sockets of silver. 33 And you shall hang the veil from the clasps. Then you shall bring the ark of the Testimony in there, behind the veil. The veil shall be a divider for you between the holy *place* and the Most Holy.

Ex 36:35–36 And he made a veil of blue, purple, and scarlet *thread*, and fine woven linen; it was worked *with* an artistic design of cherubim. 36 He made for it four pillars of acacia *wood*, and overlaid them with gold, with their hooks of gold; and he cast four sockets of silver for them.

Ex 40:21 And he brought the ark into the tabernacle, hung up the veil of the covering, and partitioned off the ark of the Testimony, as the LORD had commanded Moses.

Divided into

The holy place.

Ex 26:33 And you shall hang the veil from the clasps. Then you shall bring the ark of the Testimony in there, behind the veil. The veil shall be a divider for you between the holy *place* and the Most Holy.

Heb 9:2–6 For a tabernacle was prepared: the first *part*, in which *was* the lampstand, the table, and the showbread, which is called the sanctuary; 3 and behind the second veil, the part of the tabernacle which is called the Holiest of All, 4 which had the golden censer and the ark of the covenant overlaid on all sides with gold, in which *were* the golden pot that had the manna, Aaron's rod that budded, and the tablets of the covenant; 5 and above it were the cherubim of glory overshadowing the mercy seat. Of these things we cannot now speak in detail. **6** Now when these things had been thus prepared, the priests always went into the first part of the tabernacle, performing *the services.*

The Most Holy Place.

Ex 26:34 You shall put the mercy seat upon the ark of the Testimony in the Most Holy.

Heb 9:3 and behind the second veil, the part of the tabernacle which is called the Holiest of All,

Heb 9:7 But into the second part the high priest *went* alone once a year, not without blood, which he offered for himself and *for* the people's sins *committed* in ignorance;

Had a court all around.

Ex 40:8 You shall set up the court all around, and hang up the screen at the court gate.

Table of showbread, golden lampstand, and altar of incense were in the holy place.

Ex 26:35 You shall set the table outside the veil, and the lampstand across from the table on the side of the tabernacle toward the south; and you shall put the table on the north side.

Ex 40:22 He put the table in the tabernacle of meeting, on the north side of the tabernacle, outside the veil;

Ex 40:24 He put the lampstand in the tabernacle of meeting, across from the table, on the south side of the tabernacle;

Ex 40:26 He put the gold altar in the tabernacle of meeting in front of the veil;

Heb 9:2 For a tabernacle was prepared: the first *part,* in which *was* the lampstand, the table, and the showbread, which is called the sanctuary;

Ark and mercy seat in the Most Holy Place.

Ex 26:33–34 And you shall hang the veil from the clasps. Then you shall bring the ark of the Testimony in there, behind the veil. The veil shall be a divider for you between the holy *place* and the Most Holy. **34** You shall put the mercy seat upon the ark of the Testimony in the Most Holy.

Ex 40:20–21 He took the Testimony and put *it* into the ark, inserted the poles through the rings of the ark, and put the mercy seat on top of the ark. **21** And he brought the ark into the tabernacle, hung up the veil of the covering, and partitioned off the ark of the Testimony, as the LORD had commanded Moses.

Heb 9:4 which had the golden censer and the ark of the covenant overlaid on all sides with gold, in which *were* the golden pot that had the manna, Aaron's rod that budded, and the tablets of the covenant;

Court of,

One hundred cubits long and fifty cubits wide.

Ex 27:18 The length of the court *shall be* one hundred cubits, the width fifty throughout, and the height five cubits, *made of* fine woven linen, and its sockets of bronze.

Surrounded by linen hangings suspended from pillars in bronze sockets.

Ex 27:9–15 "You shall also make the court of the tabernacle. For the south side *there shall be* hangings for the court *made of* fine woven linen, one hundred cubits long for one side. **10** And its twenty pillars and

their twenty sockets *shall be* bronze. The hooks of the pillars and their bands *shall be* silver. **11** Likewise along the length of the north side *there shall be* hangings one hundred *cubits* long, with its twenty pillars and their twenty sockets of bronze, and the hooks of the pillars and their bands of silver. **12** "And along the width of the court on the west side *shall be* hangings of fifty cubits, with their ten pillars and their ten sockets. **13** The width of the court on the east side *shall be* fifty cubits. **14** The hangings on *one* side *of the gate shall be* fifteen cubits, *with* their three pillars and their three sockets. **15** And on the other side *shall be* hangings of fifteen *cubits,* *with* their three pillars and their three sockets.

Ex 38:9–16 Then he made the court on the south side; the hangings of the court *were of* fine woven linen, one hundred cubits long. **10** There *were* twenty pillars for them, with twenty bronze sockets. The hooks of the pillars and their bands *were* silver. **11** On the north side *the hangings were* one hundred cubits *long,* with twenty pillars and their twenty bronze sockets. The hooks of the pillars and their bands *were* silver. **12** And on the west side *there were* hangings of fifty cubits, with ten pillars and their ten sockets. The hooks of the pillars and their bands *were* silver. **13** For the east side *the hangings were* fifty cubits. **14** The hangings of one side *of the gate were* fifteen cubits *long,* *with* their three pillars and their three sockets, **15** and the same for the other side of the court gate; on this side and that *were* hangings of fifteen cubits, *with* their three pillars and their three sockets. **16** All the hangings of the court all around *were of* fine woven linen.

The gate of, a screen of linen suspended from four pillars.

Ex 27:16 "For the gate of the court *there shall be* a screen twenty cubits long, *woven of* blue, purple, and scarlet *thread,* and fine woven linen, made by a weaver. It *shall have* four pillars and four sockets.

Ex 38:18 The screen for the gate of the court *was* woven of blue, purple, and scarlet *thread,* and of fine woven linen. The length *was* twenty cubits, and the height along its width *was* five cubits, corresponding to the hangings of the court.

Contained the bronze altar and bronze laver.

Ex 40:29–30 And he put the altar of burnt offering *before* the door of the tabernacle of the tent of meeting, and offered upon it the burnt offering and the grain offering, as the LORD had commanded Moses. **30** He set the laver between the tabernacle of meeting and the altar, and put water there for washing;

All the pillars of, overlaid with silver, etc.

Ex 27:17 All the pillars around the court shall have bands of silver; their hooks *shall be* of silver and their sockets of bronze.

Ex 38:17 The sockets for the pillars *were* bronze, the hooks of the pillars and their bands *were* silver, and the overlay of their capitals *was* silver; and all the pillars of the court had bands of silver.

All the utensils of, made of bronze.

Ex 27:19 All the utensils of the tabernacle for all its service, all its pegs, and all the pegs of the court, *shall be* of bronze.

Was set up

Initially on the first day of the second year after the exodus.

Ex 40:2 "On the first day of the first month you shall set up the tabernacle of the tent of meeting.

Ex 40:17 And it came to pass in the first month of the second year, on the first *day* of the month, *that* the tabernacle was raised up.

By Moses at Mount Sinai.

Ex 40:18–19 So Moses raised up the tabernacle, fastened its sockets, set up its boards, put in its bars, and raised up its pillars. 19 And he spread out the tent over the tabernacle and put the covering of the tent on top of it, as the LORD had commanded Moses.

Num 10:11–12 Now it came to pass on the twentieth *day* of the second month, in the second year, that the cloud was taken up from above the tabernacle of the Testimony. 12 And the children of Israel set out from the Wilderness of Sinai on their journeys; then the cloud settled down in the Wilderness of Paran.

At Gilgal.

Josh 5:10–11 Now the children of Israel camped in Gilgal, and kept the Passover on the fourteenth day of the month at twilight on the plains of Jericho. 11 And they ate of the produce of the land on the day after the Passover, unleavened bread and parched grain, on the very same day.

In Shiloh.

Josh 18:1 Now the whole congregation of the children of Israel assembled together at Shiloh, and set up the tabernacle of meeting there. And the land was subdued before them.

Josh 19:51 These *were* the inheritances which Eleazar the priest, Joshua the son of Nun, and the heads of the fathers of the tribes of the children of Israel divided as an inheritance by lot in Shiloh before the LORD, at the door of the tabernacle of meeting. So they made an end of dividing the country.

In Nob.

1 Sam 21:1–6 Now David came to Nob, to Ahimelech the priest. And Ahimelech was afraid when he met David, and said to him, "Why *are* you alone, and no one is with you?" 2 So David said to Ahimelech the priest, "The king has ordered me on some business, and said to me, 'Do not let anyone know anything about the business on which I send you, or what I have commanded you.' And I have directed *my* young men to such and such a place. 3 Now therefore, what have you on hand? Give *me* five *loaves of* bread in my hand, or whatever can be found." 4 And the priest answered David and said, "*There is* no common bread on hand; but there is holy bread, if the young men have at least kept themselves from women." 5 Then David answered the priest, and said to him, "Truly, women *have been* kept from us about three days since I came out. And the vessels of the young men are holy, and *the bread is* in effect common, even though it was consecrated in the vessel this day." 6 So the priest gave him holy *bread;* for there was no bread there but the showbread which had been taken from before the LORD, in order to put hot bread *in its place* on the day when it was taken away.

Finally at Gibeon.

1 Chr 16:39 and Zadok the priest and his brethren the priests, before the tabernacle of the LORD at the high place that *was* at Gibeon,

1 Chr 21:29 For the tabernacle of the LORD and the altar of the burnt offering, which Moses had made in the wilderness, *were* at that time at the high place in Gibeon.

Anointed and consecrated with oil.

Ex 40:9 "And you shall take the anointing oil, and anoint the tabernacle and all that *is* in it; and you shall hallow it and all its utensils, and it shall be holy.

Lev 8:10 Also Moses took the anointing oil, and anointed the tabernacle and all that *was* in it, and consecrated them.

Num 7:1 Now it came to pass, when Moses had finished setting up the tabernacle, that he anointed it and consecrated it and all its furnishings, and the altar and all its utensils; so he anointed them and consecrated them.

Sprinkled and purified with blood.

Heb 9:21 Then likewise he sprinkled with blood both the tabernacle and all the vessels of the ministry.

Sanctified by the glory of the Lord.

Ex 29:43 And there I will meet with the children of Israel, and *the tabernacle* shall be sanctified by My glory.

Ex 40:34 Then the cloud covered the tabernacle of meeting, and the glory of the LORD filled the tabernacle.

Num 9:15 Now on the day that the tabernacle was raised up, the cloud covered the tabernacle, the tent of the Testimony; from evening until morning it was above the tabernacle like the appearance of fire.

The Lord appeared in, over the mercy seat.

Ex 25:22 And there I will meet with you, and I will speak with you from above the mercy seat, from between the two cherubim which *are* on the ark of the Testimony, about everything which I will give you in commandment to the children of Israel.

Lev 16:2 and the LORD said to Moses: "Tell Aaron your brother not to come at *just* any time into the Holy *Place* inside the veil, before the mercy seat which *is* on the ark, lest he die; for I will appear in the cloud above the mercy seat.

Num 7:89 Now when Moses went into the tabernacle of meeting to speak with Him, he heard the voice of One speaking to him from above the mercy seat that *was* on the ark of the Testimony, from between the two cherubim; thus He spoke to him.

In the wilderness, the cloud of glory rested on.

Ex 40:36–38 Whenever the cloud was taken up from above the tabernacle, the children of Israel would go onward in all their journeys. 37 But if the cloud was not taken up, then they did not journey till the day that it was taken up. 38 For the cloud of the LORD *was* above the tabernacle by day, and fire was over it by night, in the sight of all the house of Israel, throughout all their journeys.

Num 9:15–16 Now on the day that the tabernacle was raised up, the cloud covered the tabernacle, the tent of the Testimony; from evening until morning it was above the tabernacle like the appearance of fire. 16 So it was always: the cloud covered it *by day*, and the appearance of fire by night.

The priests

Alone could enter.

Num 18:3 They shall attend to your needs and all the needs of the tabernacle; but they shall not come near the articles of the sanctuary and the altar, lest they die—they and you also.

Num 18:5 And you shall attend to the duties of the sanctuary and the duties of the altar, that there *may* be no more wrath on the children of Israel.

Performed all services in.

Num 3:10 So you shall appoint Aaron and his sons, and they shall attend to their priesthood; but the outsider who comes near shall be put to death."

Num 18:1–2 Then the LORD said to Aaron: "You and your sons and your father's house with you shall bear the iniquity *related to* the sanctuary, and you and your sons with you shall bear the iniquity *associated with* your priesthood. 2 Also bring with you your brethren of the tribe of Levi, the tribe of your father, that they may be joined with you and serve you while you and your sons *are* with you before the tabernacle of witness.

Heb 9:6 Now when these things had been thus prepared, the priests always went into the first part of the tabernacle, performing *the services.*

Were the ministers of.

Heb 8:2 a Minister of the sanctuary and of the true tabernacle which the Lord erected, and not man.

The Levites

Appointed over, and had charge of.

Num 1:50 but you shall appoint the Levites over the tabernacle of the Testimony, over all its furnishings, and over all things that belong to it; they shall carry the tabernacle and all its furnishings; they shall attend to it and camp around the tabernacle.

Num 8:24 "This *is* what *pertains* to the Levites: From twenty-five years old and above one may enter to perform service in the work of the tabernacle of meeting;

Num 18:2–4 Also bring with you your brethren of the tribe of Levi, the tribe of your father, that they may be joined with you and serve you while you and your sons *are* with you before the tabernacle of witness. 3 They shall attend to your needs and all the needs of the tabernacle; but they shall not come near the articles of the sanctuary and the altar, lest they die—they and you also. 4 They shall be joined with you and attend to the needs of the tabernacle of meeting, for all the work of the tabernacle; but an outsider shall not come near you.

Did the inferior service of.

Num 3:6–8 "Bring the tribe of Levi near, and present them before Aaron the priest, that they may serve him. 7 And they shall attend to his needs and the needs of the whole congregation before the tabernacle of meeting, to do the work of the tabernacle. 8 Also they shall attend to all the furnishings of the tabernacle of meeting, and to the needs of the children of Israel, to do the work of the tabernacle.

Took it down and put it up.

Num 1:51 And when the tabernacle is to go forward, the Levites shall take it down; and when the tabernacle is to be set up, the Levites shall set it up. The outsider who comes near shall be put to death.

Carried.

Num 4:15 And when Aaron and his sons have finished covering the sanctuary and all the furnishings of the sanctuary, when the camp is set to go, then the sons of Kohath shall come to carry *them;* but they shall not touch any holy thing, lest they die. "These *are* the things in the tabernacle of meeting which the sons of Kohath are to carry.

Num 4:25 They shall carry the curtains of the tabernacle and the tabernacle of meeting *with* its covering, the covering of badger skins that *is* on it, the screen for the door of the tabernacle of meeting,

Num 4:31 And this *is* what they must carry as all their service for the tabernacle of meeting: the boards of the tabernacle, its bars, its pillars, its sockets,

Pitched their tents around.

Num 1:53 but the Levites shall camp around the tabernacle of the Testimony, that there may be no wrath on the congregation of the children of Israel; and the Levites shall keep charge of the tabernacle of the Testimony."

Num 3:23 The families of the Gershonites were to camp behind the tabernacle westward.

Num 3:29 The families of the children of Kohath were to camp on the south side of the tabernacle.

Num 3:35 The leader of the fathers' house of the families of Merari *was* Zuriel the son of Abihail. These *were* to camp on the north side of the tabernacle.

Freewill offerings made at the first rearing of.

Num 7:1–9 Now it came to pass, when Moses had finished setting up the tabernacle, that he anointed it and consecrated it and all its furnishings, and the altar and all its utensils; so he anointed them and consecrated them. 2 Then the leaders of Israel, the heads of their fathers' houses, who *were* the leaders of the tribes and over those who were numbered, made an offering. 3 And they brought their offering before the LORD, six covered carts and twelve oxen, a cart for *every* two of the leaders, and for each one an ox; and they presented them before the tabernacle. 4 Then the LORD spoke to Moses, saying, 5 "Accept *these* from them, that they may be used in doing the work of the tabernacle of meeting; and you shall give them to the Levites, *to* every man according to his service." 6 So Moses took the carts and the oxen, and gave them to the Levites. 7 Two carts and four oxen he gave to the sons of Gershon, according to their service; 8 and four carts and eight oxen he gave to the sons of Merari, according to their service, under the authority of Ithamar the son of Aaron the priest. 9 But to the sons of Kohath he gave none, because theirs *was* the service of the holy things, *which* they carried on their shoulders.

Free-will offerings made at the dedication of the altar of. Num 7:10-87

All offerings to be made at.

Lev 17:4 and does not bring it to the door of the tabernacle of meeting to offer an offering to the LORD before the tabernacle of the LORD, the guilt of bloodshed shall be imputed to that man. He has shed blood; and that man shall be cut off from among his people,

Deut 12:5–6 "But you shall seek the place where the LORD your God chooses, out of all your tribes, to put His name for His dwelling place; and there you shall go. **6** There you shall take your burnt offerings, your sacrifices, your tithes, the heave offerings of your hand, your vowed offerings, your freewill offerings, and the firstborn of your herds and flocks.

Deut 12:11 then there will be the place where the LORD your God chooses to make His name abide. There you shall bring all that I command you: your burnt offerings, your sacrifices, your tithes, the heave offerings of your hand, and all your choice offerings which you vow to the LORD.

Deut 12:13–14 Take heed to yourself that you do not offer your burnt offerings in every place that you see; **14** but in the place which the LORD chooses, in one of your tribes, there you shall offer your burnt offerings, and there you shall do all that I command you.

Punishment for defiling.

Lev 15:31 'Thus you shall separate the children of Israel from their uncleanness, lest they die in their uncleanness when they defile My tabernacle that *is* among them.

Num 19:13 Whoever touches the body of anyone who has died, and does not purify himself, defiles the tabernacle of the LORD. That person shall be cut off from Israel. He shall be unclean, because the water of purification was not sprinkled on him; his uncleanness *is* still on him.

A permanent house substituted for, when the kingdom was established.

2 Sam 7:5–13 "Go and tell My servant David, 'Thus says the LORD: "Would you build a house for Me to dwell in? **6** For I have not dwelt in a house since the time that I brought the children of Israel up from Egypt, even to this day, but have moved about in a tent and in a tabernacle. **7** Wherever I have moved about with all the children of Israel, have I ever spoken a word to anyone from the tribes of Israel, whom I commanded to shepherd My people Israel, saying, 'Why have you not built Me a house of cedar?' " " ' **8** Now therefore, thus shall you say to My servant David, 'Thus says the LORD of hosts: "I took you from the sheepfold, from following the sheep, to be ruler over My people, over Israel. **9** And I have been with you wherever you have gone, and have cut off all your enemies from before you, and have made you a great name, like the name of the great men who *are* on the earth. **10** Moreover I will appoint a place for My people Israel, and will plant them, that they may dwell in a place of their own and move no more; nor shall the sons of wickedness oppress them anymore, as previously, **11** since the time that I commanded judges *to be* over My people Israel, and have caused you to rest from all your enemies. Also the LORD tells you that He will make you a house. **12** "When your days are fulfilled and you rest with your fathers, I will set up your seed after you, who will come from your body, and I will establish his kingdom. **13** He shall build a house for My name, and I will establish the throne of his kingdom forever.

Illustrative of

Christ.

Is 4:6 And there will be a tabernacle for shade in the daytime from the heat, for a place of refuge, and for a shelter from storm and rain.

John 1:14 And the Word became flesh and dwelt among us, and we beheld His glory, the glory as of the only begotten of the Father, full of grace and truth.

Heb 9:8–9 the Holy Spirit indicating this, that the way into the Holiest of All was not yet made manifest while the first tabernacle was still standing. **9** It *was* symbolic for the present time in which both gifts and sacrifices are offered which cannot make him who performed the service perfect in regard to the conscience—

Heb 9:11 But Christ came *as* High Priest of the good things to come, with the greater and more perfect tabernacle not made with hands, that is, not of this creation.

The people of God.

Ps 15:1 LORD, who may abide in Your tabernacle? Who may dwell in Your holy hill?

Is 16:5 In mercy the throne will be established; And One will sit on it in truth, in the tabernacle of David, Judging and seeking justice and hastening righteousness."

Is 54:2 "Enlarge the place of your tent, And let them stretch out the curtains of your dwellings; Do not spare; Lengthen your cords, And strengthen your stakes.

Heb 8:2 a Minister of the sanctuary and of the true tabernacle which the Lord erected, and not man.

Rev 21:2–3 Then I, John, saw the holy city, New Jerusalem, coming down out of heaven from God, prepared as a bride adorned for her husband. **3** And I heard a loud voice from heaven saying, "Behold, the tabernacle of God *is* with men, and He will dwell with them, and they shall be His people. God Himself will be with them *and be* their God.

The human body.

2 Cor 5:1 For we know that if our earthly house, *this* tent, is destroyed, we have a building from God, a house not made with hands, eternal in the heavens.

2 Pet 1:13 Yes, I think it is right, as long as I am in this tent, to stir you up by reminding *you,*

(The Most Holy Place) heaven.

Heb 6:19–20 This *hope* we have as an anchor of the soul, both sure and steadfast, and which enters the Presence *behind* the veil, **20** where the forerunner has entered for us, *even* Jesus, having become High Priest forever according to the order of Melchizedek.

Heb 9:12 Not with the blood of goats and calves, but with His own blood He entered the Most Holy Place once for all, having obtained eternal redemption.

Heb 9:24 For Christ has not entered the holy places made with hands, *which are* copies of the true, but into heaven itself, now to appear in the presence of God for us;

Heb 10:19 Therefore, brethren, having boldness to enter the Holiest by the blood of Jesus,

(The veil) Christ's body.

Heb 10:20 by a new and living way which He consecrated for us, through the veil, that is, His flesh,

(The veil) the shadows of the Mosaic age.

Heb 9:8 the Holy Spirit indicating this, that the way into the Holiest of All was not yet made manifest while the first tabernacle was still standing.

Heb 9:10 *concerned* only with foods and drinks, various washings, and fleshly ordinances imposed until the time of reformation.

Rom 16:25–26 Now to Him who is able to establish you according to my gospel and the preaching of Jesus Christ, according to the revelation of the mystery kept secret since the world began **26** but now made manifest, and by the prophetic Scriptures made known to all nations, according to the commandment of the everlasting God, for obedience to the faith—

Rev 11:19 Then the temple of God was opened in heaven, and the ark of His covenant was seen in His temple. And there were lightnings, noises, thunderings, an earthquake, and great hail.

TAX COLLECTORS

Prone to extortion.

Luke 3:13 And he said to them, "Collect no more than what is appointed for you."

Luke 19:8 Then Zacchaeus stood and said to the Lord, "Look, Lord, I give half of my goods to the poor; and if I have taken anything from anyone by false accusation, I restore fourfold."

Chiefs of, were very rich.

Luke 19:2 Now behold, *there was* a man named Zacchaeus who was a chief tax collector, and he was rich.

The Jews

Despised them.

Luke 18:11 The Pharisee stood and prayed thus with himself, 'God, I thank You that I am not like other men—extortioners, unjust, adulterers, or even as this tax collector.

Classed them with the most infamous characters.

Matt 11:19 The Son of Man came eating and drinking, and they say, 'Look, a glutton and a winebibber, a friend of tax collectors and sinners!' But wisdom is justified by her children."

Matt 21:32 For John came to you in the way of righteousness, and you did not believe him; but tax collectors and harlots believed him; and when you saw *it*, you did not afterward relent and believe him.

Despised our Lord for associating with them.

Matt 9:11 And when the Pharisees saw *it*, they said to His disciples, "Why does your Teacher eat with tax collectors and sinners?"

Matt 11:19 The Son of Man came eating and drinking, and they say, 'Look, a glutton and a winebibber, a friend of tax collectors and sinners!' But wisdom is justified by her children."

Kind and hospitable to their friends.

Matt 5:46–47 For if you love those who love you, what reward have you? Do not even the tax collectors do the same? **47** And if you greet your brethren only, what do you do more *than others?* Do not even the tax collectors do so?

Luke 5:29 Then Levi gave Him a great feast in his own house. And there were a great number of tax collectors and others who sat down with them.

Luke 19:6 So he made haste and came down, and received Him joyfully.

Many of them

Believed the preaching of John.

Matt 21:32 For John came to you in the way of righteousness, and you did not believe him; but tax collectors and harlots believed him; and when you saw *it*, you did not afterward relent and believe him.

Received John's baptism.

Luke 3:12 Then tax collectors also came to be baptized, and said to him, "Teacher, what shall we do?"

Luke 7:29 And when all the people heard *Him*, even the tax collectors justified God, having been baptized with the baptism of John.

Attended the preaching of Christ.

Mark 2:15 Now it happened, as He was dining in *Levi's* house, that many tax collectors and sinners also sat together with Jesus and His disciples; for there were many, and they followed Him.

Luke 15:1 Then all the tax collectors and the sinners drew near to Him to hear Him.

Embraced the gospel.

Matt 21:31 Which of the two did the will of *his* father?" They said to Him, "The first." Jesus said to them, "Assuredly, I say to you that tax collectors and harlots enter the kingdom of God before you.

Matthew the apostle was a.

Matt 10:3 Philip and Bartholomew; Thomas and Matthew the tax collector; James the *son* of Alphaeus, and Lebbaeus, whose surname was Thaddaeus;

Luke 5:27 After these things He went out and saw a tax collector named Levi, sitting at the tax office. And He said to him, "Follow Me."

TAXES

Must not be excessive.

1 Kin 12:3–7 that they sent and called him. Then Jeroboam and the whole assembly of Israel came and spoke to Rehoboam, saying, **4** "Your father made our yoke heavy; now therefore, lighten the burdensome service of your father, and his heavy yoke which he put on us, and we will serve you." **5** So he said to them, "Depart *for* three days, then come back to me." And the people departed. **6** Then King Rehoboam consulted the elders who stood before his father Solomon while he still lived, and he said, "How do you advise *me* to answer these people?" **7** And they spoke to him, saying, "If you will be a servant to these people today, and serve them, and answer them, and speak good words to them, then they will be your servants forever."

Must be paid.

Matt 22:15–21 Then the Pharisees went and plotted how they might entangle Him in *His* talk. **16** And they sent to Him their disciples with the Herodians, saying, "Teacher, we know that You are true, and teach the way of God in truth; nor do You care about anyone, for You do not regard the person of men. **17** Tell us, therefore, what do You think? Is it lawful to pay taxes to Caesar, or not?" **18** But Jesus perceived their wickedness, and said, "Why do you test Me, *you* hypocrites? **19** Show Me the tax money." So they brought Him a denarius. **20** And He said to them, "Whose image and inscription *is* this?" **21** They said to Him, "Caesar's." And He said to them, "Render therefore to Caesar the things that are Caesar's, and to God the things that are God's."

Mark 12:13–17 Then they sent to Him some of the Pharisees and the Herodians, to catch Him in *His* words. **14** When they had come, they said to Him, "Teacher, we know that You are true, and care about no one; for You do not regard the person of men, but teach the way of God in truth. Is it lawful to pay taxes to Caesar, or not? **15** Shall we pay, or shall we not pay?" But He, knowing their hypocrisy, said to them, "Why do you test Me? Bring Me a denarius that I may see *it*." **16** So they brought *it*. And He said to them, "Whose image and inscription *is* this?" They said to Him, "Caesar's." **17** And Jesus answered and said to them, "Render to Caesar the things that are Caesar's, and to God the things that are God's." And they marveled at Him.

Luke 20:20–26 So they watched *Him*, and sent spies who pretended to be righteous, that they might seize on His words, in order to deliver Him to the power and the authority of the governor. **21** Then they asked Him, saying, "Teacher, we know that You say and teach rightly, and You do not show personal favoritism, but teach the way of God in truth: **22** Is it lawful for us to pay taxes to Caesar or not?" **23** But He perceived their craftiness, and said to them, "Why do you test Me? **24** Show Me a denarius. Whose image and inscription does it have?" They answered and said, "Caesar's." **25** And He said to them, "Render therefore to Caesar the things that are Caesar's, and to God the things that are God's." **26** But they could not catch Him in His words in the presence of the people. And they marveled at His answer and kept silent.

Rom 13:6–7 For because of this you also pay taxes, for they are God's ministers attending continually to this very thing. **7** Render therefore to all their due: taxes to whom taxes *are due,* customs to whom customs, fear to whom fear, honor to whom honor.

Cf. 1 Pet 2:13–17

Jesus falsely accused of not paying.

Luke 23:2 And they began to accuse Him, saying, "We found this *fellow* perverting the nation, and forbidding to pay taxes to Caesar, saying that He Himself is Christ, a King."

Cf. Matt 17:24–27

TEMPLE, THE FIRST (SOLOMON'S)

Began on Mount Moriah, on the threshing floor of Ornan.

1 Chr 21:28–30 At that time, when David saw that the LORD had answered him on the threshing floor of Ornan the Jebusite, he sacrificed there. **29** For the tabernacle of the LORD and the altar of the burnt offering, which Moses had made in the wilderness, *were* at that time at the high place in Gibeon. **30** But David could not go before it to inquire of God, for he was afraid of the sword of the angel of the LORD.

1 Chr 22:2 So David commanded to gather the aliens who *were* in the land of Israel; and he appointed masons to cut hewn stones to build the house of God.

2 Chr 3:1 Now Solomon began to build the house of the LORD at Jerusalem on Mount Moriah, where *the* LORD had appeared to his father David, at the place that David had prepared on the threshing floor of Ornan the Jebusite.

David

Anxious to build.

2 Sam 7:2 that the king said to Nathan the prophet, "See now, I dwell in a house of cedar, but the ark of God dwells inside tent curtains."

1 Chr 22:7 And David said to Solomon: "My son, as for me, it was in my mind to build a house to the name of the LORD my God;

1 Chr 29:3 Moreover, because I have set my affection on the house of my God, I have given to the house of my God, over and above all that I have prepared for the holy house, my own special treasure of gold and silver:

Ps 132:2–5 How he swore to the LORD, *And* vowed to the Mighty One of Jacob: **3** "Surely I will not go into the chamber of my house, Or go up to the comfort of my bed; **4** I will not give sleep to my eyes Or slumber to my eyelids, **5** Until I find a place for the LORD, A dwelling place for the Mighty One of Jacob."

Being a man of war, not permitted to build.

2 Sam 7:5–9 "Go and tell My servant David, 'Thus says the LORD: "Would you build a house for Me to dwell in? **6** For I have not dwelt in a house since the time that I brought the children of Israel up from Egypt, even to this day, but have moved about in a tent and in a tabernacle. **7** Wherever I have moved about with all the children of Israel, have I ever spoken a word to anyone from the tribes of Israel, whom I commanded to shepherd My people Israel, saying, 'Why have you not built Me a house of cedar?' " ' **8** Now therefore, thus shall you say to My servant David, 'Thus says the LORD of hosts: "I took you from the sheepfold, from following the sheep, to be ruler over My people, over Israel. **9** And I have been with you wherever you have gone, and have cut off all your enemies from before you, and have made you a great name, like the name of the great men who *are* on the earth.

1 Kin 5:3 You know how my father David could not build a house for the name of the LORD his God because of the wars which were fought against him on every side, until the LORD put *his foes* under the soles of his feet.

1 Chr 22:8 but the word of the LORD came to me, saying, 'You have shed much blood and have made great wars; you shall not build a house for My name, because you have shed much blood on the earth in My sight.

Told by the prophet that Solomon should build.

2 Sam 7:12–13 "When your days are fulfilled and you rest with your fathers, I will set up your seed after you, who will come from your body, and I will establish his kingdom. **13** He shall build a house for My name, and I will establish the throne of his kingdom forever.

1 Chr 17:12 He shall build Me a house, and I will establish his throne forever.

Made preparations for building.

1 Chr 22:2–5 So David commanded to gather the aliens who *were* in the land of Israel; and he appointed masons to cut hewn stones to build the house of God. **3** And David prepared iron in abundance for the nails of the doors of the gates and for the joints, and bronze in abundance beyond measure, **4** and cedar trees in abundance; for the Sidonians and those from Tyre brought much cedar wood to David. **5** Now David said, "Solomon my son *is* young and inexperienced, and the house to be built for the LORD *must be* exceedingly magnificent, famous and glorious throughout all countries. I will now make preparation for it." So David made abundant preparations before his death.

1 Chr 22:14–16 Indeed I have taken much trouble to prepare for the house of the LORD one hundred thousand talents of gold and one million talents of silver, and bronze and iron beyond measure, for it is so abundant. I have prepared timber and stone also, and you may add to them. **15** Moreover *there are* workmen with you in abundance: woodsmen and stonecutters, and all types of skillful men for every kind of work. **16** Of gold and silver and bronze and iron *there is* no limit. Arise and begin working, and the LORD be with you."

1 Chr 29:2–5 Now for the house of my God I have prepared with all my might: gold for *things to be made of* gold, silver for *things of* silver, bronze for *things of* bronze, iron for *things of* iron, wood for *things of* wood, onyx stones, *stones* to be set, glistening stones of various colors, all kinds of precious stones, and marble slabs in abundance. **3** Moreover, because I have set my affection on the house of my God, I have given to the house of my God, over and above all that I have prepared for the holy house, my own special treasure of gold and silver: **4** three thousand talents of gold, of the gold of Ophir, and seven thousand talents of refined silver, to overlay the walls of the houses; **5** the gold for *things of* gold and the silver for *things of* silver, and for all kinds of work *to be done* by the hands of craftsmen. Who *then* is willing to consecrate himself this day to the LORD?"

Charged Solomon to build.

1 Chr 22:6–7 Then he called for his son Solomon, and charged him to build a house for the LORD God of Israel. **7** And David said to Solomon: "My son, as for me, it was in my mind to build a house to the name of the LORD my God;

1 Chr 22:11 Now, my son, may the LORD be with you; and may you prosper, and build the house of the LORD your God, as He has said to you.

Prayed that Solomon might have wisdom to build.

1 Chr 29:19 And give my son Solomon a loyal heart to keep Your commandments and Your testimonies and Your statutes, to do all *these things,* and to build the temple for which I have made provision."

Charged his princes to assist in building.

1 Chr 22:17–19 David also commanded all the leaders of Israel to help Solomon his son, *saying,* **18** "Is not the LORD your God with you? And has He *not* given you rest on every side? For He has given the inhabitants of the land into my hand, and the land is subdued before the LORD and before His people. **19** Now set your heart and your soul to seek the LORD your God. Therefore arise and build the sanctuary of the LORD God, to bring the ark of the covenant of the LORD and the holy articles of God into the house that is to be built for the name of the LORD."

Collected freewill offerings of the people for the building.

1 Chr 29:6–9 Then the leaders of the fathers' *houses,* leaders of the tribes of Israel, the captains of thousands and of hundreds, with the officers over the king's work, offered willingly. **7** They gave for the work of the house of God five thousand talents and ten thousand darics of gold, ten thousand talents of silver, eighteen thousand talents of bronze, and one hundred thousand talents of iron. **8** And whoever had *precious* stones gave *them* to the treasury of the house of the LORD, into the hand of Jehiel the Gershonite. **9** Then the people rejoiced, for they had offered willingly, because with a loyal heart they had offered willingly to the LORD; and King David also rejoiced greatly.

Solomon

Determined to build.

2 Chr 2:1 Then Solomon determined to build a temple for the name of the LORD, and a royal house for himself.

Specially instructed for.

2 Chr 3:3 This is the foundation which Solomon laid for building the house of God: The length *was* sixty cubits (by cubits according to the former measure) and the width twenty cubits.

Employed all the aliens in preparing for.

2 Chr 2:2 Solomon selected seventy thousand men to bear burdens, eighty thousand to quarry *stone* in the mountains, and three thousand six hundred to oversee them.

2 Chr 2:17–18 Then Solomon numbered all the aliens who *were* in the land of Israel, after the census in which David his father had numbered them; and there were found to be one hundred and fifty-three thousand six hundred. **18** And he made seventy thousand of them bearers of burdens, eighty thousand stonecutters in the mountain, and three thousand six hundred overseers to make the people work.

Cf. 1 Kin 5:15

Applied to Hiram for a skillful workman to superintend, etc. the building of.

2 Chr 2:7 Therefore send me at once a man skillful to work in gold and silver, in bronze and iron, in purple and crimson and blue, who has skill to engrave with the skillful men who are with me in Judah and Jerusalem, whom David my father provided.

2 Chr 2:13–14 And now I have sent a skillful man, endowed with understanding, Huram my master *craftsman* **14** (the son of a woman of the daughters of Dan, and his father was a man of Tyre), skilled to work in gold and silver, bronze and iron, stone and wood, purple and blue, fine linen and crimson, and to make any engraving and to accomplish any plan which may be given to him, with your skillful men and with the skillful men of my lord David your father.

Employed thirty thousand Israelites in the work.

1 Kin 5:13–14 Then King Solomon raised up a labor force out of all Israel; and the labor force was thirty thousand men. **14** And he sent them to Lebanon, ten thousand a month in shifts: they were one month in Lebanon *and* two months at home; Adoniram *was* in charge of the labor force.

Contracted with Hiram for wood, stone, and labor.

1 Kin 5:6–12 Now therefore, command that they cut down cedars for me from Lebanon; and my servants will be with your servants, and I will pay you wages for your servants according to whatever you say. For you know *there is* none among us who has skill to cut timber like the Sidonians. **7** So it was, when Hiram heard the words of Solomon, that he rejoiced greatly and said, Blessed *be* the LORD this day, for He has given David a wise son over this great people! **8** Then Hiram sent to Solomon, saying: I have considered *the message* which you sent me, *and* I will do all you desire concerning the cedar and cypress logs. **9** My servants shall bring *them* down from Lebanon to the sea; I will float them in rafts by sea to the place you indicate to me, and will have them broken apart there; then you can take *them* away. And you shall fulfill my desire by giving food for my household. **10** Then Hiram gave Solomon cedar and cypress logs *according to* all his desire. **11** And Solomon gave Hiram twenty thousand kors of wheat *as* food for his household, and twenty kors of pressed oil. Thus Solomon gave to Hiram year by year. **12** So the LORD gave Solomon wisdom, as He had promised him; and there was peace between Hiram and Solomon, and the two of them made a treaty together.

2 Chr 2:8–10 Also send me cedar and cypress and algum logs from Lebanon, for I know that your servants have skill to cut timber in Lebanon; and indeed my servants *will be* with your servants, **9** to prepare timber for me in abundance, for the temple which I am about to build *shall be* great and wonderful. **10** And indeed I will give to your servants, the woodsmen who cut timber, twenty thousand kors of ground wheat, twenty thousand kors of barley, twenty thousand baths of wine, and twenty thousand baths of oil.

Commenced second day of second month of fourth year of his reign.

1 Kin 6:1 And it came to pass in the four hundred and eightieth year after the children of Israel had come out of the land of Egypt, in the fourth year of Solomon's reign over Israel, in the month of Ziv, which *is* the second month, that he began to build the house of the LORD.

1 Kin 6:37 In the fourth year the foundation of the house of the LORD was laid, in the month of Ziv.

2 Chr 3:2 And he began to build on the second *day* of the second month in the fourth year of his reign.

Did not disturb temple worship.

1 Kin 6:7 And the temple, when it was being built, was built with stone finished at the quarry, so that no hammer or chisel *or* any iron tool was heard in the temple while it was being built.

Divided into

The sanctuary or larger room.

2 Chr 3:5 The larger room he paneled with cypress

which he overlaid with fine gold, and he carved palm trees and chainwork on it.

The inner sanctuary or Most Holy Place.

1 Kin 6:19 And he prepared the inner sanctuary inside the temple, to set the ark of the covenant of the LORD there.

The vestibule.

2 Chr 3:4 And the vestibule that *was* in front *of the sanctuary* was twenty cubits long across the width of the house, and the height *was* one hundred and twenty. He overlaid the inside with pure gold.

Three stories of chambers on the right side connect with the interior.

1 Kin 6:5–6 Against the wall of the temple he built chambers all around, *against* the walls of the temple, all around the sanctuary and the inner sanctuary. Thus he made side chambers all around it. **6** The lowest chamber *was* five cubits wide, the middle *was* six cubits wide, and the third *was* seven cubits wide; for he made narrow ledges around the outside of the temple, so that *the support beams* would not be fastened into the walls of the temple.

1 Kin 6:8 The doorway for the middle story *was* on the right side of the temple. They went up by stairs to the middle *story*, and from the middle to the third.

1 Kin 6:10 And he built side chambers against the entire temple, each five cubits high; they were attached to the temple with cedar beams.

Surrounded with spacious courts.

1 Kin 6:36 And he built the inner court with three rows of hewn stone and a row of cedar beams.

2 Chr 4:9 Furthermore he made the court of the priests, and the great court and doors for the court; and he overlaid these doors with bronze.

Was sixty cubits longs, twenty wide, and thirty high.

1 Kin 6:2 Now the house which King Solomon built for the LORD, its length *was* sixty cubits, its width twenty, and its height thirty cubits.

2 Chr 3:3 This is the foundation which Solomon laid for building the house of God: The length *was* sixty cubits (by cubits according to the former measure) and the width twenty cubits.

Was lighted by narrow windows.

1 Kin 6:4 And he made for the house windows with beveled frames.

Was roofed with cedar.

1 Kin 6:9 So he built the temple and finished it, and he paneled the temple with beams and boards of cedar.

The house or nave in front of the sanctuary

Was forty cubits long.

1 Kin 6:17 And in front of it the temple sanctuary was forty cubits *long*.

Had folding doors of cypress wood carved and golden.

1 Kin 6:34–35 And the two doors *were* of cypress wood; two panels *comprised* one folding door, and two panels *comprised* the other folding door. **35** Then he carved cherubim, palm trees, and open flowers *on them*, and overlaid *them* with gold applied evenly on the carved work.

Had door posts of olive wood carved and gilded.

1 Kin 6:33 So for the door of the sanctuary he also made doorposts *of* olive wood, one-fourth *of the wall.*

2 Chr 3:7 He also overlaid the house—the beams and doorposts, its walls and doors—with gold; and he carved cherubim on the walls.

The inner sanctuary or Most Holy Place

Was twenty cubits for each dimension.

1 Kin 6:16 Then he built the twenty-cubit room at the rear of the temple, from floor to ceiling, with cedar boards; he built *it* inside as the inner sanctuary, as the Most Holy *Place.*

1 Kin 6:20 The inner sanctuary *was* twenty cubits long, twenty cubits wide, and twenty cubits high. He overlaid it with pure gold, and overlaid the altar of cedar.

Two cherubims of gilded olive wood made within.

1 Kin 6:23–28 Inside the inner sanctuary he made two cherubim *of* olive wood, *each* ten cubits high. **24** One wing of the cherub *was* five cubits, and the other wing of the cherub five cubits: ten cubits from the tip of one wing to the tip of the other. **25** And the other cherub *was* ten cubits; both cherubim *were* of the same size and shape. **26** The height of one cherub *was* ten cubits, and so *was* the other cherub. **27** Then he set the cherubim inside the inner room; and they stretched out the wings of the cherubim so that the wing of the one touched *one* wall, and the wing of the other cherub touched the other wall. And their wings touched each other in the middle of the room. **28** Also he overlaid the cherubim with gold.

2 Chr 3:11–13 The wings of the cherubim *were* twenty cubits in *overall* length: one wing *of the one cherub was* five cubits, touching the wall of the room, and the other wing *was* five cubits, touching the wing of the other cherub; **12** *one* wing of the other cherub *was* five cubits, touching the wall of the room, and the other wing *also was* five cubits, touching the wing of the other cherub. **13** The wings of these cherubim spanned twenty cubits overall. They stood on their feet, and they faced inward.

A partition of chains of gold between it and nave.

1 Kin 6:21 So Solomon overlaid the inside of the temple with pure gold. He stretched gold chains across the front of the inner sanctuary, and overlaid it with gold.

The doors and the posts of, of olive wood carved and gilded.

1 Kin 6:31–32 For the entrance of the inner sanctuary he made doors *of* olive wood; the lintel *and* doorposts *were* one-fifth *of the wall.* **32** The two doors *were of* olive wood; and he carved on them figures of cherubim, palm trees, and open flowers, and overlaid *them* with gold; and he spread gold on the cherubim and on the palm trees.

Separated from the nave by a veil.

2 Chr 3:14 And he made the veil of blue, purple, crimson, and fine linen, and wove cherubim into it.

The floor and walls of, covered with cedar and cypress wood.

1 Kin 6:15 And he built the inside walls of the temple with cedar boards; from the floor of the temple to the ceiling he paneled the inside with wood; and he covered the floor of the temple with planks of cypress.

Cedar of, carved with flowers, etc.

1 Kin 6:18 The inside of the temple was cedar, carved with ornamental buds and open flowers. All *was* cedar; there was no stone *to be* seen.

Paneled with cypress wood and gilded.

2 Chr 3:5 The larger room he paneled with cypress which he overlaid with fine gold, and he carved palm trees and chainwork on it.

The whole inside and outside covered with gold.

1 Kin 6:21–22 So Solomon overlaid the inside of the temple with pure gold. He stretched gold chains across the front of the inner sanctuary, and overlaid it with gold. **22** The whole temple he overlaid with gold, until he had finished all the temple; also he overlaid with gold the entire altar that *was* by the inner sanctuary.

2 Chr 3:7 He also overlaid the house—the beams and doorposts, its walls and doors—with gold; and he carved cherubim on the walls.

Decorated with precious stones.

2 Chr 3:6 And he decorated the house with precious stones for beauty, and the gold *was* gold from Parvaim.

The vestibule of

Twenty cubits long and ten wide.

1 Kin 6:3 The vestibule in front of the sanctuary of the house *was* twenty cubits long across the width of the house, *and* the width of *the vestibule extended* ten cubits from the front of the house.

One hundred and twenty cubits high.

2 Chr 3:4 And the vestibule that *was* in front *of the sanctuary* was twenty cubits long across the width of the house, and the height *was* one hundred and twenty. He overlaid the inside with pure gold.

Pillars of, with their capitals described.

1 Kin 7:15–22 And he cast two pillars of bronze, each one eighteen cubits high, and a line of twelve cubits measured the circumference of each. **16** Then he made two capitals *of* cast bronze, to set on the tops of the pillars. The height of one capital *was* five cubits, and the height of the other capital *was* five cubits. **17** *He made* a lattice network, with wreaths of chainwork, for the capitals which *were* on top of the pillars: seven chains for one capital and seven for the other capital. **18** So he made the pillars, and two rows of pomegranates above the network all around to cover the capitals that *were* on top; and thus he did for the other capital. **19** The capitals which *were* on top of the pillars in the hall *were* in the shape of lilies, four cubits. **20** The capitals on the two pillars also *had* pomegranates above, by the convex surface which *was* next to the network; and there *were* two hundred such pomegranates in rows on each of the capitals all around. **21** Then he set up the pillars by the vestibule of the temple; he set up the pillar on the right and called its name Jachin, and he set up the pillar on the left and called its name Boaz. **22** The tops of the pillars were in the shape of lilies. So the work of the pillars was finished.

2 Chr 3:15–17 Also he made in front of the temple two pillars thirty-five cubits high, and the capital that *was* on the top of each of *them* was five cubits. **16** He made wreaths of chainwork, as in the inner sanctuary, and put *them* on top of the pillars; and he made one hundred pomegranates, and put *them* on the wreaths of chainwork. **17** Then he set up the pillars before the temple, one on the right hand and the other on the left; he called the name of the one on the right hand Jachin, and the name of the one on the left Boaz.

Its magnificence.

2 Chr 2:5 And the temple which I build *will be* great, for our God is greater than all gods.

2 Chr 2:9 to prepare timber for me in abundance, for the temple which I am about to build *shall be* great and wonderful.

Was seven years in building.

1 Kin 6:38 And in the eleventh year, in the month of Bul, which is the eighth month, the house was finished in all its details and according to all its plans. So he was seven years in building it.

Was finished in the eighth month of the eleventh year of Solomon.

1 Kin 6:38 And in the eleventh year, in the month of Bul, which is the eighth month, the house was finished in all its details and according to all its plans. So he was seven years in building it.

Was called

The house of the Lord.

2 Chr 23:5 one-third *shall be* at the king's house; and one-third at the Gate of the Foundation. All the people *shall be* in the courts of the house of the Lord.

2 Chr 23:12 Now when Athaliah heard the noise of the people running and praising the king, she came to the people *in* the temple of the Lord.

The mountain of the Lord's house.

Is 2:2 Now it shall come to pass in the latter days *That* the mountain of the Lord's house Shall be established on the top of the mountains, And shall be exalted above the hills; And all nations shall flow to it.

House of the God of Jacob.

Is 2:3 Many people shall come and say, "Come, and let us go up to the mountain of the Lord, To the house of the God of Jacob; He will teach us His ways, And we shall walk in His paths." For out of Zion shall go forth the law, And the word of the Lord from Jerusalem.

Zion.

Ps 84:1–7 How lovely *is* Your tabernacle, O Lord of hosts! **2** My soul longs, yes, even faints For the courts of the Lord; My heart and my flesh cry out for the living God. **3** Even the sparrow has found a home, And the swallow a nest for herself, Where she may lay her young— *Even* Your altars, O Lord of hosts, My King and my God. **4** Blessed *are* those who dwell in Your house; They will still be praising You. Selah **5** Blessed *is* the man whose strength *is* in You, Whose heart *is* set on pilgrimage. **6** *As they* pass through the Valley of Baca, They make it a spring; The rain also covers it with pools. **7** They go from strength to strength; *Each one* appears before God in Zion.

Mount Zion.

Ps 74:2 Remember Your congregation, *which* You have purchased of old, The tribe of Your inheritance, *which* You have redeemed— This Mount Zion where You have dwelt.

Appointed as a house of sacrifice.

2 Chr 7:12 Then the Lord appeared to Solomon by night, and said to him: "I have heard your prayer, and have chosen this place for Myself as a house of sacrifice.

Appointed as a house of prayer.

Is 56:7 Even them I will bring to My holy mountain, And make them joyful in My house of prayer. Their burnt offerings and their sacrifices *Will be* accepted on My altar; For My house shall be called a house of prayer for all nations."

Matt 21:13 And He said to them, "It is written, *'My house shall be called a house of prayer,'* but you have made it a *'den of thieves.'*"

God promised to dwell in.

1 Kin 6:12–13 "*Concerning* this temple which you are building, if you walk in My statutes, execute My judgments, keep all My commandments, and walk in them, then I will perform My word with you, which I spoke to your father David. **13** And I will dwell among the children of Israel, and will not forsake My people Israel."

All dedicated things placed in.

2 Chr 5:1 So all the work that Solomon had done for the house of the Lord was finished; and Solomon brought in the things which his father David had dedicated: the silver and the gold and all the furnishings. And he put *them* in the treasuries of the house of God.

The ark of God brought into with great solemnity.

1 Kin 8:1–9 Now Solomon assembled the elders of Israel and all the heads of the tribes, the chief fathers of the children of Israel, to King Solomon in Jerusalem, that they might bring up the ark of the covenant of the Lord from the City of David, which *is* Zion. **2** Therefore all the men of Israel assembled with King Solomon at the feast in the month of Ethanim, which *is* the seventh month. **3** So all the elders of Israel came, and the priests took up the ark. **4** Then they brought up the ark of the Lord, the tabernacle of meeting, and all the holy furnishings that *were* in the tabernacle. The priests and the Levites brought them up. **5** Also King Solomon, and all the congregation of Israel who were assembled with him, *were* with him before the ark, sacrificing sheep and oxen that could not be counted or numbered for multitude. **6** Then the priests brought in the ark of the covenant of the Lord to its place, into the inner sanctuary of the temple, to the Most Holy *Place,* under the wings of the cherubim. **7** For the cherubim spread *their* two wings over the place of the ark, and the cherubim overshadowed the ark and its poles. **8** The poles extended so that the ends of the poles could be seen from the holy *place,* in front of the inner sanctuary; but they could not be seen from outside. And they are there to this day. **9** Nothing *was* in the ark except the two tablets of stone which Moses put there at Horeb, when the Lord made *a covenant* with the children of Israel, when they came out of the land of Egypt.

Cf. 2 Chr 5:2–10

Filled with the cloud of glory.

1 Kin 8:10–11 And it came to pass, when the priests came out of the holy *place,* that the cloud filled the house of the LORD, **11** so that the priests could not continue ministering because of the cloud; for the glory of the LORD filled the house of the LORD.

2 Chr 5:13 indeed it came to pass, when the trumpeters and singers *were* as one, to make one sound to be heard in praising and thanking the LORD, and when they lifted up their voice with the trumpets and cymbals and instruments of music, and praised the LORD, *saying:* "For He is good, For His mercy *endures* forever," that the house, the house of the LORD, was filled with a cloud,

2 Chr 7:2 And the priests could not enter the house of the LORD, because the glory of the LORD had filled the LORD's house.

Solemnly dedicated to God by Solomon.
1 Kin 8:12-66; 2 Chr 6:1-42

Sacred fire sent down from heaven at its dedication.

2 Chr 7:3 When all the children of Israel saw how the fire came down, and the glory of the LORD on the temple, they bowed their faces to the ground on the pavement, and worshiped and praised the LORD, *saying:* "For *He is* good, For His mercy *endures* forever."

God not restricted to.

Acts 7:47-48 But Solomon built Him a house. **48** "However, the Most High does not dwell in temples made with hands, as the prophet says:

Complete destruction of, predicted.

Jer 26:18 "Micah of Moresheth prophesied in the days of Hezekiah king of Judah, and spoke to all the people of Judah, saying, 'Thus says the LORD of hosts: "Zion shall be plowed *like* a field, Jerusalem shall become heaps of ruins, And the mountain of the temple Like the bare hills of the forest." '

Mic 3:12 Therefore because of you Zion shall be plowed *like* a field, Jerusalem shall become heaps of ruins, And the mountain of the temple Like the bare hills of the forest.

Historical references to,

Pillaged by Shishak king of Egypt.

1 Kin 14:25-26 It happened in the fifth year of King Rehoboam *that* Shishak king of Egypt came up against Jerusalem. **26** And he took away the treasures of the house of the LORD and the treasures of the king's house; he took away everything. He also took away all the gold shields which Solomon had made.

2 Chr 12:9 So Shishak king of Egypt came up against Jerusalem, and took away the treasures of the house of the LORD and the treasures of the king's house; he took everything. He also carried away the gold shields which Solomon had made.

Repaired by Jehoash at the institution of Jehoiada.
2 Kin 12:4-14; 2 Chr 24:4-13

Treasures of given by Jehoash to appease the Syrians.

2 Kin 12:17-18 Hazael king of Syria went up and fought against Gath, and took it; then Hazael set his face to go up to Jerusalem. **18** And Jehoash king of Judah took all the sacred things that his fathers, Jehoshaphat and Jehoram and Ahaziah, kings of Judah, had dedicated, and his own sacred things, and all the gold found in the treasuries of the house of the

LORD and in the king's house, and sent *them* to Hazael king of Syria. Then he went away from Jerusalem.

Defiled and its treasures given by Ahaz to the king of Assyria.

2 Kin 16:14 He also brought the bronze altar which *was* before the LORD, from the front of the temple—from between the *new* altar and the house of the LORD—and put it on the north side of the *new* altar.

2 Kin 16:18 Also he removed the Sabbath pavilion which they had built in the temple, and he removed the king's outer entrance from the house of the LORD, on account of the king of Assyria.

2 Chr 28:20-21 Also Tiglath-Pileser king of Assyria came to him and distressed him, and did not assist him. **21** For Ahaz took part *of the treasures* from the house of the LORD, from the house of the king, and from the leaders, and he gave *it* to the king of Assyria; but he did not help him.

Purified and divine worship restored under Hezekiah.
2 Chr 29:3-35

Its treasures given by Hezekiah to the Assyrians to procure a treaty.

2 Kin 18:13-16 And in the fourteenth year of King Hezekiah, Sennacherib king of Assyria came up against all the fortified cities of Judah and took them. **14** Then Hezekiah king of Judah sent to the king of Assyria at Lachish, saying, "I have done wrong; turn away from me; whatever you impose on me I will pay." And the king of Assyria assessed Hezekiah king of Judah three hundred talents of silver and thirty talents of gold. **15** So Hezekiah gave *him* all the silver that was found in the house of the LORD and in the treasuries of the king's house. **16** At that time Hezekiah stripped *the gold from* the doors of the temple of the LORD, and *from* the pillars which Hezekiah king of Judah had overlaid, and gave it to the king of Assyria.

Polluted by the idolatrous worship of Manasseh.

2 Kin 21:4-7 He also built altars in the house of the LORD, of which the LORD had said, "In Jerusalem I will put My name." **5** And he built altars for all the host of heaven in the two courts of the house of the LORD. **6** Also he made his son pass through the fire, practiced soothsaying, used witchcraft, and consulted spiritists and mediums. He did much evil in the sight of the LORD, to provoke *Him* to anger. **7** He even set a carved image of Asherah that he had made, in the house of which the LORD had said to David and to Solomon his son, "In this house and in Jerusalem, which I have chosen out of all the tribes of Israel, I will put My name forever;

2 Chr 33:4-5 He also built altars in the house of the LORD, of which the LORD had said, "In Jerusalem shall My name be forever." **5** And he built altars for all the host of heaven in the two courts of the house of the LORD.

2 Chr 33:7 He even set a carved image, the idol which he had made, in the house of God, of which God had said to David and to Solomon his son, "In this house and in Jerusalem, which I have chosen out of all the tribes of Israel, I will put My name forever;

Repaired by Josiah.

2 Kin 22:3-7 Now it came to pass, in the eighteenth year of King Josiah, *that* the king sent Shaphan the scribe, the son of Azaliah, the son of Meshullam, to the house of the Lord, saying: **4** "Go up to Hilkiah the high priest, that he may count the money which has been brought into the house of the Lord, which the doorkeepers have gathered from the people. **5** And let them deliver it into the hand of those doing the work, who are the overseers in the house of the Lord; let them give it to those who *are* in the house of the Lord doing the work, to repair the damages of the house— **6** to carpenters and builders and masons—and to buy timber and hewn stone to repair the house. **7** However there need be no accounting made with them of the money delivered into their hand, because they deal faithfully."

Cf. 2 Chr 34:8–13

Purified by Josiah.

2 Kin 23:4–7 And the king commanded Hilkiah the high priest, the priests of the second order, and the doorkeepers, to bring out of the temple of the Lord all the articles that were made for Baal, for Asherah, and for all the host of heaven; and he burned them outside Jerusalem in the fields of Kidron, and carried their ashes to Bethel. **5** Then he removed the idolatrous priests whom the kings of Judah had ordained to burn incense on the high places in the cities of Judah and in the places all around Jerusalem, and those who burned incense to Baal, to the sun, to the moon, to the constellations, and to all the host of heaven. **6** And he brought out the wooden image from the house of the Lord, to the Brook Kidron outside Jerusalem, burned it at the Brook Kidron and ground *it* to ashes, and threw its ashes on the graves of the common people. **7** Then he tore down the *ritual* booths of the perverted persons that *were* in the house of the Lord, where the women wove hangings for the wooden image.

2 Kin 23:11–12 Then he removed the horses that the kings of Judah had dedicated to the sun, at the entrance to the house of the Lord, by the chamber of Nathan-Melech, the officer who *was* in the court; and he burned the chariots of the sun with fire. **12** The altars that *were* on the roof, the upper chamber of Ahaz, which the kings of Judah had made, and the altars which Manasseh had made in the two courts of the house of the Lord, the king broke down and pulverized there, and threw their dust into the Brook Kidron.

Pillaged and burned by the Babylonians.

2 Kin 25:9 He burned the house of the Lord and the king's house; all the houses of Jerusalem, that is, all the houses of the great, he burned with fire.

2 Kin 25:13–17 The bronze pillars that *were* in the house of the Lord, and the carts and the bronze Sea that *were* in the house of the Lord, the Chaldeans broke in pieces, and carried their bronze to Babylon. **14** They also took away the pots, the shovels, the trimmers, the spoons, and all the bronze utensils with which the priests ministered. **15** The firepans and the basins, the things of solid gold and solid silver, the captain of the guard took away. **16** The two pillars, one Sea, and the carts, which Solomon had made for the house of the Lord, the bronze of all these articles was beyond measure. **17** The height of one pillar *was*

eighteen cubits, and the capital on it *was* of bronze. The height of the capital was three cubits, and the network and pomegranates all around the capital were all of bronze. The second pillar was the same, with a network.

2 Chr 36:18–19 And all the articles from the house of God, great and small, the treasures of the house of the Lord, and the treasures of the king and of his leaders, all *these* he took to Babylon. **19** Then they burned the house of God, broke down the wall of Jerusalem, burned all its palaces with fire, and destroyed all its precious possessions.

Illustrative of

Christ.

John 2:19 Jesus answered and said to them, "Destroy this temple, and in three days I will raise it up."

John 2:21 But He was speaking of the temple of His body.

The universal church.

1 Cor 3:16 Do you not know that you are the temple of God and *that* the Spirit of God dwells in you?

2 Cor 6:16 And what agreement has the temple of God with idols? For you are the temple of the living God. As God has said: *"I will dwell in them And walk among them. I will be their God, And they shall be My people."*

Eph 2:20–22 having been built on the foundation of the apostles and prophets, Jesus Christ Himself being the chief corner*stone*, **21** in whom the whole building, being fitted together, grows into a holy temple in the Lord, **22** in whom you also are being built together for a dwelling place of God in the Spirit.

The bodies of believers.

1 Cor 6:19 Or do you not know that your body is the temple of the Holy Spirit *who is* in you, whom you have from God, and you are not your own?

TEMPLE, THE SECOND
Built on the site of the first temple.

Ezra 6:2–12 And at Achmetha, in the palace that *is* in the province of Media, a scroll was found, and in it a record *was* written thus: **3** In the first year of King Cyrus, King Cyrus issued a decree *concerning* the house of God at Jerusalem: "Let the house be rebuilt, the place where they offered sacrifices; and let the foundations of it be firmly laid, its height sixty cubits *and* its width sixty cubits, **4** *with* three rows of heavy stones and one row of new timber. Let the expenses be paid from the king's treasury. **5** Also let the gold and silver articles of the house of God, which Nebuchadnezzar took from the temple which *is* in Jerusalem and brought to Babylon, be restored and taken back to the temple which *is* in Jerusalem, *each* to its place; and deposit *them* in the house of God"— **6** Now *therefore*, Tattenai, governor of *the region* beyond the River, and Shethar-Boznai, and your companions the Persians who *are* beyond the River, keep yourselves far from there. **7** Let the work of this house of God alone; let the governor of the Jews and the elders of the Jews build this house of God on its site. **8** Moreover I issue a decree *as to* what you shall do for the elders of these Jews, for the building of this house of God: Let the cost be paid at the king's expense from taxes *on the region* beyond the River; this is to be given immediately to these men, so that they are not hindered. **9** And whatever they need—young bulls, rams, and lambs for the burnt offerings of the God of heaven, wheat, salt, wine, and oil, according to the request of the priests who *are* in Jerusalem—let it be given them day by day without fail, **10** that they may offer sacrifices of sweet aroma to the God of heaven, and pray for the life of the king and his sons. **11** Also I issue a decree that whoever alters this edict, let a timber be pulled from his house and erected, and let him be hanged on it; and let his house be made a refuse heap because of this. **12** And may the God who causes His name to dwell there destroy any king or people who put their hand to alter it, or to destroy this house of God which is in Jerusalem. I Darius issue a decree; let it be done diligently.

Cyrus

His decree for building, predicted.

Is 44:28 Who says of Cyrus, '*He is* My shepherd, And he shall perform all My pleasure, Saying to Jerusalem, "You shall be built," And to the temple, "Your foundation shall be laid." '

Gave a decree for building, in the first year of his reign.

Ezra 1:1–2 Now in the first year of Cyrus king of Persia, that the word of the LORD by the mouth of Jeremiah might be fulfilled, the LORD stirred up the spirit of Cyrus king of Persia, so that he made a proclamation throughout all his kingdom, and also *put it* in writing, saying, **2** Thus says Cyrus king of Persia: All the kingdoms of the earth the LORD God of heaven has given me. And He has commanded me to build Him a house at Jerusalem which *is* in Judah.

Ezra 6:3 In the first year of King Cyrus, King Cyrus issued a decree *concerning* the house of God at Jerusalem: "Let the house be rebuilt, the place where they offered sacrifices; and let the foundations of it be firmly laid, its height sixty cubits *and* its width sixty cubits,

Gave permission to the Jews to go to Jerusalem to build.

Ezra 1:3 Who *is* among you of all His people? May his God be with him, and let him go up to Jerusalem which *is* in Judah, and build the house of the LORD God of Israel (He *is* God), which *is* in Jerusalem.

Furnished means for building.

Ezra 6:4 *with* three rows of heavy stones and one row of new timber. Let the expenses be paid from the king's treasury.

Ordered those who remained in Babylon to contribute to the building of.

Ezra 1:4 And whoever is left in any place where he dwells, let the men of his place help him with silver and gold, with goods and livestock, besides the freewill offerings for the house of God which *is* in Jerusalem.

Gave the articles of the first temple for.

Ezra 1:7–11 King Cyrus also brought out the articles of the house of the LORD, which Nebuchadnezzar had taken from Jerusalem and put in the temple of his gods; **8** and Cyrus king of Persia brought them out by the hand of Mithredath the treasurer, and count-

ed them out to Sheshbazzar the prince of Judah. **9** This *is* the number of them: thirty gold platters, one thousand silver platters, twenty-nine knives, **10** thirty gold basins, four hundred and ten silver basins of a similar *kind, and* one thousand other articles. **11** All the articles of gold and silver *were* five thousand four hundred. All *these* Sheshbazzar took with the captives who were brought from Babylon to Jerusalem.

Ezra 6:5 Also let the gold and silver articles of the house of God, which Nebuchadnezzar took from the temple which *is* in Jerusalem and brought to Babylon, be restored and taken back to the temple which *is* in Jerusalem, *each* to its place; and deposit *them* in the house of God"—

Divine worship commenced before the foundation was laid.

Ezra 3:1–6 And when the seventh month had come, and the children of Israel *were* in the cities, the people gathered together as one man to Jerusalem. **2** Then Jeshua the son of Jozadak and his brethren the priests, and Zerubbabel the son of Shealtiel and his brethren, arose and built the altar of the God of Israel, to offer burnt offerings on it, as *it is* written in the Law of Moses the man of God. **3** Though fear *had come* upon them because of the people of those countries, they set the altar on its bases; and they offered burnt offerings on it to the LORD, *both* the morning and evening burnt offerings. **4** They also kept the Feast of Tabernacles, as *it is* written, and *offered* the daily burnt offerings in the number required by ordinance for each day. **5** Afterwards *they offered* the regular burnt offering, and *those* for New Moons and for all the appointed feasts of the LORD that were consecrated, and *those* of everyone who willingly offered a freewill offering to the LORD. **6** From the first day of the seventh month they began to offer burnt offerings to the LORD, although the foundation of the temple of the LORD had not been laid.

Materials for building, procured from Tyre and Sidon.

Ezra 3:7 They also gave money to the masons and the carpenters, and food, drink, and oil to the people of Sidon and Tyre to bring cedar logs from Lebanon to the sea, to Joppa, according to the permission which they had from Cyrus king of Persia.

Foundation of, laid the second month of second year after the captivity.

Ezra 3:8 Now in the second month of the second year of their coming to the house of God at Jerusalem, Zerubbabel the son of Shealtiel, Jeshua the son of Jozadak, and the rest of their brethren the priests and the Levites, and all those who had come out of the captivity to Jerusalem, began *work* and appointed the Levites from twenty years old and above to oversee the work of the house of the LORD.

Solemnities connected with laying the foundation of.

Ezra 3:9–11 Then Jeshua *with* his sons and brothers, Kadmiel *with* his sons, and the sons of Judah, arose as one to oversee those working on the house of God: the sons of Henadad *with* their sons and their brethren the Levites. **10** When the builders laid the foundation of the temple of the LORD, the priests stood in their apparel with trumpets, and the Levites, the sons of Asaph, with cymbals, to praise the LORD, according to the ordinance of David king of Israel. **11** And they sang responsively, praising and giving thanks to the LORD: "For *He is* good, For His mercy *endures* forever toward Israel." Then all the people shouted with a great shout, when they praised the LORD, because the foundation of the house of the LORD was laid.

Its dimensions.

Ezra 6:3–4 In the first year of King Cyrus, King Cyrus issued a decree *concerning* the house of God at Jerusalem: "Let the house be rebuilt, the place where they offered sacrifices; and let the foundations of it be firmly laid, its height sixty cubits *and* its width sixty cubits, **4** *with* three rows of heavy stones and one row of new timber. Let the expenses be paid from the king's treasury.

Grief of those who had seen the first temple.

Ezra 3:12 But many of the priests and Levites and heads of the fathers' *houses,* old men who had seen the first temple, wept with a loud voice when the foundation of this temple was laid before their eyes. Yet many shouted aloud for joy,

Hag 2:3 'Who is left among you who saw this temple in its former glory? And how do you see it now? In comparison with it, *is this* not in your eyes as nothing?

Joy of those who had not seen the first temple.

Ezra 3:13 so that the people could not discern the noise of the shout of joy from the noise of the weeping of the people, for the people shouted with a loud shout, and the sound was heard afar off.

The Samaritans

Proposed to assist in building.

Ezra 4:1–2 Now when the adversaries of Judah and Benjamin heard that the descendants of the captivity were building the temple of the LORD God of Israel, **2** they came to Zerubbabel and the heads of the fathers' *houses,* and said to them, "Let us build with you, for we seek your God as you *do;* and we have sacrificed to Him since the days of Esarhaddon king of Assyria, who brought us here."

Their help refused by the Jews.

Ezra 4:3 But Zerubbabel and Jeshua and the rest of the heads of the fathers' *houses* of Israel said to them, "You may do nothing with us to build a house for our God; but we alone will build to the LORD God of Israel, as King Cyrus the king of Persia has commanded us."

Attempted to frustrate the Jews in building.

Ezra 4:4–5 Then the people of the land tried to discourage the people of Judah. They troubled them in building, **5** and hired counselors against them to frustrate their purpose all the days of Cyrus king of Persia, even until the reign of Darius king of Persia.

Wrote to Artaxerxes Smerdis to interrupt the building.
Ezra 4:6–16

Procured its interruption for fifteen years.

Ezra 4:24 Thus the work of the house of God which *is* at Jerusalem ceased, and it was discontinued until the second year of the reign of Darius king of Persia.

The Jews reproved and punished for not persevering in building.

Hag 1:1–6 In the second year of King Darius, in the sixth month, on the first day of the month, the word of the LORD came by Haggai the prophet to Zerubbabel the son of Shealtiel, governor of Judah, and to Joshua the son of Jehozadak, the high priest, saying, **2** "Thus speaks the LORD of hosts, saying: 'This people says, "The time has not come, the time that the LORD's house should be built." ' " **3** Then the word of the LORD came by Haggai the prophet, saying, **4** *Is it* time for you yourselves to dwell in your paneled houses, and this temple *to lie* in ruins?" **5** Now therefore, thus says the LORD of hosts: "Consider your ways! **6** "You have sown much, and bring in little; You eat, but do not have enough; You drink, but you are not filled with drink; You clothe yourselves, but no one is warm; And he who earns wages, Earns wages *to put* into a bag with holes."

Hag 1:9–11 "*You* looked for much, but indeed *it came to* little; and when you brought it home, I blew it away. Why?" says the LORD of hosts. "Because of My house that *is in* ruins, while every one of you runs to his own house. **10** Therefore the heavens above you withhold the dew, and the earth withholds its fruit. **11** For I called for a drought on the land and the mountains, on the grain and the new wine and the oil, on whatever the ground brings forth, on men and livestock, and on all the labor of *your* hands."

Hag 2:15 'And now, carefully consider from this day forward: from before stone was laid upon stone in the temple of the LORD—

Hag 2:17 I struck you with blight and mildew and hail in all the labors of your hands; yet you did not *turn* to Me,' says the LORD.

Zech 8:10 For before these days *There were* no wages for man nor any hire for beast; *There was* no peace from the enemy for whoever went out or came in; For I set all men, everyone, against his neighbor.

The Jews encouraged to proceed in building.

Hag 1:8 Go up to the mountains and bring wood and build the temple, that I may take pleasure in it and be glorified," says the LORD.

Hag 2:19 Is the seed still in the barn? As yet the vine, the fig tree, the pomegranate, and the olive tree have not yielded *fruit. But* from this day I will bless *you.*' "

Zech 8:9 "Thus says the LORD of hosts: 'Let your hands be strong, You who have been hearing in these days These words by the mouth of the prophets, Who *spoke* in the day the foundation was laid For the house of the LORD of hosts, That the temple might be built.

Resumed by Zerubbabel and Jeshua.

Ezra 5:2 So Zerubbabel the son of Shealtiel and Jeshua the son of Jozadak rose up and began to build the house of God which *is* in Jerusalem; and the prophets of God *were* with them, helping them.

Its completion by Zerubbabel foretold, to encourage the Jews.

Zech 4:4–10 So I answered and spoke to the angel who talked with me, saying, "What *are* these, my lord?" **5** Then the angel who talked with me answered and said to me, "Do you not know what these are?" And

I said, "No, my lord." **6** So he answered and said to me: "This *is* the word of the LORD to Zerubbabel: 'Not by might nor by power, but by My Spirit,' Says the LORD of hosts. **7** 'Who *are* you, O great mountain? Before Zerubbabel *you shall become* a plain! And he shall bring forth the capstone With shouts of "Grace, grace to it!" ' " **8** Moreover the word of the LORD came to me, saying: **9** "The hands of Zerubbabel Have laid the foundation of this temple; His hands shall also finish *it*. Then you will know That the LORD of hosts has sent Me to you. **10** For who has despised the day of small things? For these seven rejoice to see The plumb line in the hand of Zerubbabel. They are the eyes of the LORD, Which scan to and fro throughout the whole earth."

Future glory of, predicted.

Hag 2:7–9 and I will shake all nations, and they shall come to the Desire of All Nations, and I will fill this temple with glory,' says the LORD of hosts. **8** 'The silver *is* Mine, and the gold *is* Mine,' says the LORD of hosts. **9** 'The glory of this latter temple shall be greater than the former,' says the LORD of hosts. 'And in this place I will give peace,' says the LORD of hosts."

Tattenai the governor asks about Darius's sanction for it. Ezra 5:3–17

The decree of Cyrus found and confirmed by Darius.

Ezra 6:1–2 Then King Darius issued a decree, and a search was made in the archives, where the treasures were stored in Babylon. **2** And at Achmetha, in the palace that *is* in the province of Media, a scroll was found, and in it a record *was* written thus:

Ezra 6:6–12 Now *therefore*, Tattenai, governor of *the region* beyond the River, and Shethar-Boznai, and your companions the Persians who *are* beyond the River, keep yourselves far from there. **7** Let the work of this house of God alone; let the governor of the Jews and the elders of the Jews build this house of God on its site. **8** Moreover I issue a decree *as to* what you shall do for the elders of these Jews, for the building of this house of God: Let the cost be paid at the king's expense from taxes *on the region* beyond the River; this is to be given immediately to these men, so that they are not hindered. **9** And whatever they need—young bulls, rams, and lambs for the burnt offerings of the God of heaven, wheat, salt, wine, and oil, according to the request of the priests who *are* in Jerusalem—let it be given them day by day without fail, **10** that they may offer sacrifices of sweet aroma to the God of heaven, and pray for the life of the king and his sons. **11** Also I issue a decree that whoever alters this edict, let a timber be pulled from his house and erected, and let him be hanged on it; and let his house be made a refuse heap because of this. **12** And may the God who causes His name to dwell there destroy any king or people who put their hand to alter it, or to destroy this house of God which is in Jerusalem. I Darius issue a decree; let it be done diligently.

Finished the third day of the twelfth month in the sixth year of Darius.

Ezra 6:15 Now the temple was finished on the third day of the month of Adar, which was in the sixth year of the reign of King Darius.

Dedication of, celebrated with joy and thankfulness.

Ezra 6:16–18 Then the children of Israel, the priests and the Levites and the rest of the descendants of the captivity, celebrated the dedication of this house of God with joy. **17** And they offered sacrifices at the dedication of this house of God, one hundred bulls, two hundred rams, four hundred lambs, and as a sin offering for all Israel twelve male goats, according to the number of the tribes of Israel. **18** They assigned the priests to their divisions and the Levites to their divisions, over the service of God in Jerusalem, as it is written in the Book of Moses.

Repaired and beautified by Herod.

John 2:20 Then the Jews said, "It has taken forty-six years to build this temple, and will You raise it up in three days?"

The magnificence of its building and ornaments.

Mark 13:1 Then as He went out of the temple, one of His disciples said to Him, "Teacher, see what manner of stones and what buildings *are here!*"

Luke 21:5 Then, as some spoke of the temple, how it was adorned with beautiful stones and donations, He said,

John 2:20 Then the Jews said, "It has taken forty-six years to build this temple, and will You raise it up in three days?"

Beautiful gate of, mentioned.

Acts 3:2 And a certain man lame from his mother's womb was carried, whom they laid daily at the gate of the temple which is called Beautiful, to ask alms from those who entered the temple;

Solomon's porch connected with.

John 10:23 And Jesus walked in the temple, in Solomon's porch.

Acts 3:11 Now as the lame man who was healed held on to Peter and John, all the people ran together to them in the porch which is called Solomon's, greatly amazed.

Christ

To appear in.

Hag 2:7 and I will shake all nations, and they shall come to the Desire of All Nations, and I will fill this temple with glory,' says the LORD of hosts.

Mal 3:1 "Behold, I send My messenger, And he will prepare the way before Me. And the Lord, whom you seek, Will suddenly come to His temple, Even the Messenger of the covenant, In whom you delight. Behold, He is coming," Says the LORD of hosts.

Presented in.

Luke 2:22 Now when the days of her purification according to the law of Moses were completed, they brought Him to Jerusalem to present *Him* to the Lord

Luke 2:27 So he came by the Spirit into the temple. And when the parents brought in the Child Jesus, to do for Him according to the custom of the law,

Miraculously transported to a pinnacle of.

Matt 4:5 Then the devil took Him up into the holy city, set Him on the pinnacle of the temple,

Luke 4:9 Then he brought Him to Jerusalem, set Him on the pinnacle of the temple, and said to Him, "If You are the Son of God, throw Yourself down from here.

Frequently taught in.

Mark 14:49 I was daily with you in the temple teaching, and you did not seize Me. But the Scriptures must be fulfilled."

Purified, at the commencement of his ministry.

John 2:15–17 When He had made a whip of cords, He drove them all out of the temple, with the sheep and the oxen, and poured out the changers' money and overturned the tables. **16** And He said to those who sold doves, "Take these things away! Do not make My Father's house a house of merchandise!" **17** Then His disciples remembered that it was written, *"Zeal for Your house has eaten Me up."*

Purified, at the close of his ministry.

Matt 21:12–13 Then Jesus went into the temple of God and drove out all those who bought and sold in the temple, and overturned the tables of the money changers and the seats of those who sold doves. **13** And He said to them, "It is written, *'My house shall be called a house of prayer,'* but you have made it a *'den of thieves.'*"

Predicted its destruction.

Matt 24:2 And Jesus said to them, "Do you not see all these things? Assuredly, I say to you, not *one* stone shall be left here upon another, that shall not be thrown down."

Mark 13:2 And Jesus answered and said to him, "Do you see these great buildings? Not *one* stone shall be left upon another, that shall not be thrown down."

Luke 21:6 "These things which you see—the days will come in which not *one* stone shall be left upon another that shall not be thrown down."

The veil of, torn at His death.

Matt 27:51 Then, behold, the veil of the temple was torn in two from top to bottom; and the earth quaked, and the rocks were split,

Separation between the outer or Gentile court and that of the Jews alluded to.

Eph 2:13–14 But now in Christ Jesus you who once were far off have been brought near by the blood of Christ. **14** For He Himself is our peace, who has made both one, and has broken down the middle wall of separation,

No Gentile allowed to enter the inner courts of.

Acts 21:27–30 Now when the seven days were almost ended, the Jews from Asia, seeing him in the temple, stirred up the whole crowd and laid hands on him, **28** crying out, "Men of Israel, help! This is the man who teaches all *men* everywhere against the people, the law, and this place; and furthermore he also brought Greeks into the temple and has defiled this holy place." **29** (For they had previously seen Trophimus the Ephesian with him in the city, whom they supposed that Paul had brought into the temple.) **30** And all the city was disturbed; and the people ran together, seized Paul, and dragged him out of the temple; and immediately the doors were shut.

The Jews

Prayed outside of, while the priest offered incense within.

Luke 1:10 And the whole multitude of the people was praying outside at the hour of incense.

Luke 18:10 "Two men went up to the temple to pray, one a Pharisee and the other a tax collector.

Considered it blasphemy to speak against.

Matt 26:61 and said, "This *fellow* said, 'I am able to destroy the temple of God and to build it in three days.'"

Acts 6:13 They also set up false witnesses who said, "This man does not cease to speak blasphemous words against this holy place and the law;

Acts 21:28 crying out, "Men of Israel, help! This is the man who teaches all *men* everywhere against the people, the law, and this place; and furthermore he also brought Greeks into the temple and has defiled this holy place."

Desecrated by selling animals within.

John 2:14 And He found in the temple those who sold oxen and sheep and doves, and the money changers doing business.

Desecration of, foretold.

Dan 9:27 Then he shall confirm a covenant with many for one week; But in the middle of the week He shall bring an end to sacrifice and offering. And on the wing of abominations shall be one who makes desolate, Even until the consummation, which is determined, Is poured out on the desolate."

Dan 11:31 And forces shall be mustered by him, and they shall defile the sanctuary fortress; then they shall take away the daily *sacrifices*, and place *there* the abomination of desolation.

Desecrated by the Romans.

Dan 9:27 Then he shall confirm a covenant with many for one week; But in the middle of the week He shall bring an end to sacrifice and offering. And on the wing of abominations shall be one who makes desolate, Even until the consummation, which is determined, Is poured out on the desolate."

Matt 24:15 "Therefore when you see the *'abomination of desolation,'* spoken of by Daniel the prophet, standing in the holy place" (whoever reads, let him understand),

TEMPTATION

Does not come from God.

James 1:13 Let no one say when he is tempted, "I am tempted by God"; for God cannot be tempted by evil, nor does He Himself tempt anyone.

Comes from

Lusts.

James 1:14 But each one is tempted when he is drawn away by his own desires and enticed.

Covetousness.

Prov 28:20 A faithful man will abound with blessings, But he who hastens to be rich will not go unpunished.

1 Tim 6:9–10 But those who desire to be rich fall into temptation and a snare, and *into* many foolish and harmful lusts which drown men in destruction and perdition. **10** For the love of money is a root of all *kinds of* evil, for which some have strayed from the faith in their greediness, and pierced themselves through with many sorrows.

The devil is the author of.

1 Chr 21:1 Now Satan stood up against Israel, and moved David to number Israel.

Matt 4:1 Then Jesus was led up by the Spirit into the wilderness to be tempted by the devil.

John 13:2 And supper being ended, the devil having already put it into the heart of Judas Iscariot, Simon's *son*, to betray Him,

1 Thess 3:5 For this reason, when I could no longer endure it, I sent to know your faith, lest by some means the tempter had tempted you, and our labor might be in vain.

Evil associates, the instruments of.

Prov 1:10 My son, if sinners entice you, Do not consent.

Prov 7:6 For at the window of my house I looked through my lattice,

Prov 16:29 A violent man entices his neighbor, And leads him in a way *that is* not good.

Often arises through

Poverty.

Prov 30:9 Lest I be full and deny *You*, And say, "Who *is* the LORD?" Or lest I be poor and steal, And profane the name of my God.

Matt 4:2–3 And when He had fasted forty days and forty nights, afterward He was hungry. **3** Now when the tempter came to Him, he said, "If You are the Son of God, command that these stones become bread."

Prosperity.

Prov 30:9 Lest I be full and deny *You*, And say, "Who *is* the LORD?" Or lest I be poor and steal, And profane the name of my God.

Matt 4:8 Again, the devil took Him up on an exceedingly high mountain, and showed Him all the kingdoms of the world and their glory.

Worldly glory.

Num 22:17 for I will certainly honor you greatly, and I will do whatever you say to me. Therefore please come, curse this people for me.' "

Dan 4:30 The king spoke, saying, "Is not this great Babylon, that I have built for a royal dwelling by my mighty power and for the honor of my majesty?"

Dan 5:2 While he tasted the wine, Belshazzar gave the command to bring the gold and silver vessels which his father Nebuchadnezzar had taken from the temple which *had been* in Jerusalem, that the king and his lords, his wives, and his concubines might drink from them.

Matt 4:8 Again, the devil took Him up on an exceedingly high mountain, and showed Him all the kingdoms of the world and their glory.

Objectives of

To distrust God's providence.

Matt 4:3 Now when the tempter came to Him, he said, "If You are the Son of God, command that these stones become bread."

Presumption.

Matt 4:6 and said to Him, "If You are the Son of God, throw Yourself down. For it is written: *'He shall give His angels charge over you,'* and, *'In their hands they shall bear you up, Lest you dash your foot against a stone.'* "

Worshiping Satan.

Matt 4:9 And he said to Him, "All these things I will give You if You will fall down and worship me."

Often strengthened by the perversion of God's Word.

Matt 4:6 and said to Him, "If You are the Son of God, throw Yourself down. For it is written: *'He shall give His angels charge over you,'* and, *'In their hands they shall bear you up, Lest you dash your foot against a stone.'* "

Permitted as a trial of

Faith.

James 1:2–3 My brethren, count it all joy when you fall into various trials, **3** knowing that the testing of your faith produces patience.

1 Pet 1:7 that the genuineness of your faith, *being* much more precious than gold that perishes, though it is tested by fire, may be found to praise, honor, and glory at the revelation of Jesus Christ,

Dedication.

Job 1:9–12 So Satan answered the LORD and said, "Does Job fear God for nothing? **10** Have You not made a hedge around him, around his household, and around all that he has on every side? You have blessed the work of his hands, and his possessions have increased in the land. **11** But now, stretch out Your hand and touch all that he has, and he will surely curse You to Your face!" **12** And the LORD said to Satan, "Behold, all that he has *is* in your power; only do not lay a hand on his *person*." So Satan went out from the presence of the LORD.

Always conformable to human nature.

1 Cor 10:13 No temptation has overtaken you except such as is common to man; but God *is* faithful, who will not allow you to be tempted beyond what you are able, but with the temptation will also make the way of escape, that you may be able to bear *it*.

Often ends in sin and death.

1 Tim 6:9 But those who desire to be rich fall into temptation and a snare, and *into* many foolish and harmful lusts which drown men in destruction and perdition.

James 1:15 Then, when desire has conceived, it gives birth to sin; and sin, when it is full-grown, brings forth death.

Christ

Endured, from the devil.

Mark 1:13 And He was there in the wilderness forty days, tempted by Satan, and was with the wild beasts; and the angels ministered to Him.

Endured, from the wicked.

Matt 16:1 Then the Pharisees and Sadducees came, and testing Him asked that He would show them a sign from heaven.

Matt 22:18 But Jesus perceived their wickedness, and said, "Why do you test Me, *you* hypocrites?

Luke 10:25 And behold, a certain lawyer stood up and tested Him, saying, "Teacher, what shall I do to inherit eternal life?"

Resisted it by the Word of God.

Matt 4:4 But He answered and said, "It is written, *'Man shall not live by bread alone, but by every word that proceeds from the mouth of God.'*"

Matt 4:7 Jesus said to him, "It is written again, *'You shall not tempt the LORD your God.'*"

Matt 4:10 Then Jesus said to him, "Away with you, Satan! For it is written, *'You shall worship the LORD your God, and Him only you shall serve.'*"

Overcame it.

Matt 4:11 Then the devil left Him, and behold, angels came and ministered to Him.

Sympathizes with those under.

Heb 4:15 For we do not have a High Priest who cannot sympathize with our weaknesses, but was in all *points* tempted as *we are, yet* without sin.

Is able to help those under.

Heb 2:18 For in that He Himself has suffered, being tempted, He is able to aid those who are tempted.

Intercedes for His people under.

Luke 22:31–32 And the Lord said, "Simon, Simon! Indeed, Satan has asked for you, that he may sift *you* as wheat. **32** But I have prayed for you, that your faith should not fail; and when you have returned to *Me,* strengthen your brethren."

John 17:15 I do not pray that You should take them out of the world, but that You should keep them from the evil one.

Will not be greater than believers can endure.

1 Cor 10:13 No temptation has overtaken you except such as is common to man; but God *is* faithful, who will not allow you to be tempted beyond what you are able, but with the temptation will also make the way of escape, that you may be able to bear *it.*

God delivers believers from.

2 Pet 2:9 *then* the Lord knows how to deliver the godly out of temptations and to reserve the unjust under punishment for the day of judgment,

Believers

May be in heaviness through.

1 Pet 1:6 In this you greatly rejoice, though now for a little while, if need be, you have been grieved by various trials,

Should resist, in faith.

Eph 6:16 above all, taking the shield of faith with which you will be able to quench all the fiery darts of the wicked one.

1 Pet 5:9 Resist him, steadfast in the faith, knowing that the same sufferings are experienced by your brotherhood in the world.

Should watch against.

Matt 26:41 Watch and pray, lest you enter into temptation. The spirit indeed *is* willing, but the flesh *is* weak."

1 Pet 5:8 Be sober, be vigilant; because your adversary the devil walks about like a roaring lion, seeking whom he may devour.

Should pray to be kept from.

Matt 6:13 And do not lead us into temptation, But deliver us from the evil one. For Yours is the kingdom and the power and the glory forever. Amen.

Matt 26:41 Watch and pray, lest you enter into temptation. The spirit indeed *is* willing, but the flesh *is* weak."

Should not cause for others.

Rom 14:13 Therefore let us not judge one another anymore, but rather resolve this, not to put a stumbling block or a cause to fall in *our* brother's way.

Should restore those overcome by.

Gal 6:1 Brethren, if a man is overtaken in any trespass, you who *are* spiritual restore such a one in a spirit of gentleness, considering yourself lest you also be tempted.

Should avoid.

Prov 4:14–15 Do not enter the path of the wicked, And do not walk in the way of evil. **15** Avoid it, do not travel on it; Turn away from it and pass on.

The devil will renew.

Luke 4:13 Now when the devil had ended every temptation, he departed from Him until an opportune time.

Weakness of the flesh makes it stronger.

Matt 26:41 Watch and pray, lest you enter into temptation. The spirit indeed *is* willing, but the flesh *is* weak."

Nominal Christians fall away in time of.

Luke 8:13 But the ones on the rock *are those* who, when they hear, receive the word with joy; and these have no root, who believe for a while and in time of temptation fall away.

Blessedness of those who meet and overcome.

James 1:2–4 My brethren, count it all joy when you fall into various trials, **3** knowing that the testing of your faith produces patience. **4** But let patience have *its* perfect work, that you may be perfect and complete, lacking nothing.

James 1:12 Blessed *is* the man who endures temptation; for when he has been approved, he will receive the crown of life which the Lord has promised to those who love Him.

Those who encountered,

Eve.

Gen 3:1 Now the serpent was more cunning than any beast of the field which the LORD God had made. And he said to the woman, "Has God indeed said, 'You shall not eat of every tree of the garden'?"

Gen 3:4–5 Then the serpent said to the woman, "You will not surely die. **5** For God knows that in the day you eat of it your eyes will be opened, and you will be like God, knowing good and evil."

Joseph.

Gen 39:7 And it came to pass after these things that his master's wife cast longing eyes on Joseph, and she said, "Lie with me."

Balaam.

Num 22:17 for I will certainly honor you greatly, and I will do whatever you say to me. Therefore please come, curse this people for me.'"

Achan.

Josh 7:21 When I saw among the spoils a beautiful Babylonian garment, two hundred shekels of silver, and a wedge of gold weighing fifty shekels, I coveted them and took them. And there they are, hidden in the earth in the midst of my tent, with the silver under it."

David.

2 Sam 11:2 Then it happened one evening that David arose from his bed and walked on the roof of the king's house. And from the roof he saw a woman bathing, and the woman *was* very beautiful to behold.

Jeroboam.

1 Kin 15:30 because of the sins of Jeroboam, which he had sinned and by which he had made Israel sin, because of his provocation with which he had provoked the LORD God of Israel to anger.

Peter.

Mark 14:67–71 And when she saw Peter warming himself, she looked at him and said, "You also were with Jesus of Nazareth." **68** But he denied it, saying, "I neither know nor understand what you are saying." And he went out on the porch, and a rooster crowed. **69** And the servant girl saw him again, and began to say to those who stood by, "This is one of them." **70** But he denied it again. And a little later those who stood by said to Peter again, "Surely you are *one* of them; for you are a Galilean, and your speech shows *it.*" **71** Then he began to curse and swear, "I do not know this Man of whom you speak!"

Paul.

2 Cor 12:7 And lest I should be exalted above measure by the abundance of the revelations, a thorn in the flesh was given to me, a messenger of Satan to buffet me, lest I be exalted above measure.

Gal 4:14 And my trial which was in my flesh you did not despise or reject, but you received me as an angel of God, *even* as Christ Jesus.

TEN COMMANDMENTS, THE

Spoken by God.

Ex 20:1 And God spoke all these words, saying:

Deut 5:4 The LORD talked with you face to face on the mountain from the midst of the fire.

Deut 5:22 "These words the LORD spoke to all your assembly, in the mountain from the midst of the fire, the cloud, and the thick darkness, with a loud voice; and He added no more. And He wrote them on two tablets of stone and gave them to me.

Written by God.

Ex 32:16 Now the tablets *were* the work of God, and the writing *was* the writing of God engraved on the tablets.

Ex 34:1 And the LORD said to Moses, "Cut two tablets of stone like the first *ones,* and I will write on *these* tablets the words that were on the first tablets which you broke.

Ex 34:28 So he was there with the LORD forty days and forty nights; he neither ate bread nor drank water. And He wrote on the tablets the words of the covenant, the Ten Commandments.

Deut 4:13 So He declared to you His covenant which He commanded you to perform, the Ten Commandments; and He wrote them on two tablets of stone.

Deut 10:4 And He wrote on the tablets according to the first writing, the Ten Commandments, which the LORD had spoken to you in the mountain from the midst of the fire in the day of the assembly; and the LORD gave them to me.

Enumerated.

Ex 20:3–17 "You shall have no other gods before Me. **4** "You shall not make for yourself a carved image—any likeness *of anything* that *is* in heaven above, or that *is* in the earth beneath, or that *is* in the water under the earth; **5** you shall not bow down to them nor serve them. For I, the LORD your God, *am* a jealous God, visiting the iniquity of the fathers upon the children to the third and fourth *generations* of those who hate Me, **6** but showing mercy to thousands, to those who love Me and keep My commandments. **7** "You shall not take the name of the LORD your God in vain, for the LORD will not hold *him* guiltless who takes His name in vain. **8** "Remember the Sabbath day, to keep it holy. **9** Six days you shall labor and do all your work, **10** but the seventh day *is* the Sabbath of the LORD your God. *In it* you shall do no work: you, nor your son, nor your daughter, nor your male servant, nor your female servant, nor your cattle, nor your stranger who *is* within your gates. **11** For *in* six days the LORD made the heavens and the earth, the sea, and all that *is* in them, and rested the seventh day. Therefore the LORD blessed the Sabbath day and hallowed it. **12** "Honor your father and your mother, that your days may be long upon the land which the LORD your God is giving you. **13** "You shall not murder. **14** "You shall not commit adultery. **15** "You shall not steal. **16** "You shall not bear false witness against your neighbor. **17** "You shall not covet your neighbor's house; you shall not covet your neighbor's wife, nor his male servant, nor his female servant, nor his ox, nor his donkey, nor anything that *is* your neighbor's."

Summarized by Christ.

Matt 22:35–40 Then one of them, a lawyer, asked *Him a question,* testing Him, and saying, **36** "Teacher, which *is* the great commandment in the law?" **37** Jesus said to him, " *'You shall love the LORD your God with all your heart, with all your soul, and with all your mind.'* **38** This is *the* first and great commandment. **39** And *the* second *is* like it: *'You shall love your neighbor as yourself.'* **40** On these two commandments hang all the Law and the Prophets."

Law of, is spiritual. See "Law of God."

Matt 5:28 But I say to you that whoever looks at a woman to lust for her has already committed adultery with her in his heart.

Rom 7:14 For we know that the law is spiritual, but I am carnal, sold under sin.

TENTS

Origin and antiquity of.

Gen 4:20 And Adah bore Jabal. He was the father of those who dwell in tents and have livestock.

Num 24:5 "How lovely are your tents, O Jacob! Your dwellings, O Israel!

Job 12:6 The tents of robbers prosper, And those who provoke God are secure— In what God provides by His hand.

Heb 11:9 By faith he dwelt in the land of promise as *in* a foreign country, dwelling in tents with Isaac and Jacob, the heirs with him of the same promise;

Were spread out.

Is 40:22 *It is* He who sits above the circle of the earth, And its inhabitants *are* like grasshoppers, Who stretches out the heavens like a curtain, And spreads them out like a tent to dwell in.

Is 54:2 "Enlarge the place of your tent, And let them stretch out the curtains of your dwellings; Do not spare; Lengthen your cords, And strengthen your stakes.

Fastened by cords to stakes or pegs.

Judg 4:21 Then Jael, Heber's wife, took a tent peg and took a hammer in her hand, and went softly to him and drove the peg into his temple, and it went down into the ground; for he was fast asleep and weary. So he died.

Is 54:2 "Enlarge the place of your tent, And let them stretch out the curtains of your dwellings; Do not spare; Lengthen your cords, And strengthen your stakes.

Jer 10:20 My tent is plundered, And all my cords are broken; My children have gone from me, And they *are* no more. *There is* no one to pitch my tent anymore, Or set up my curtains.

Were used by

The patriarchs.

Gen 13:5 Lot also, who went with Abram, had flocks and herds and tents.

Gen 25:27 So the boys grew. And Esau was a skillful hunter, a man of the field; but Jacob was a mild man, dwelling in tents.

Heb 11:9 By faith he dwelt in the land of promise as *in* a foreign country, dwelling in tents with Isaac and Jacob, the heirs with him of the same promise;

Israel in the desert.

Ex 33:8 So it was, whenever Moses went out to the tabernacle, *that* all the people rose, and each man stood *at* his tent door and watched Moses until he had gone into the tabernacle.

Num 24:2 And Balaam raised his eyes, and saw Israel encamped according to their tribes; and the Spirit of God came upon him.

The people of Israel in all their wars.

1 Sam 4:3 And when the people had come into the camp, the elders of Israel said, "Why has the Lord defeated us today before the Philistines? Let us bring the ark of the covenant of the Lord from Shiloh to us, that when it comes among us it may save us from the hand of our enemies."

1 Sam 4:10 So the Philistines fought, and Israel was defeated, and every man fled to his tent. There was a very great slaughter, and there fell of Israel thirty thousand foot soldiers.

1 Sam 29:1 Then the Philistines gathered together all their armies at Aphek, and the Israelites encamped by a fountain which *is* in Jezreel.

1 Kin 16:16 Now the people *who were* encamped heard it said, "Zimri has conspired and also has killed the king." So all Israel made Omri, the commander of the army, king over Israel that day in the camp.

The Rechabites.

Jer 35:7 You shall not build a house, sow seed, plant a vineyard, nor have *any of these*; but all your days you shall dwell in tents, that you may live many days in the land where you are sojourners.'

Jer 35:10 But we have dwelt in tents, and have obeyed and done according to all that Jonadab our father commanded us.

The Arabs.

Is 13:20 It will never be inhabited, Nor will it be settled from generation to generation; Nor will the Arabian pitch tents there, Nor will the shepherds make their sheepfolds there.

Shepherds while tending their flocks.

Song 1:8 If you do not know, O fairest among women, Follow in the footsteps of the flock, And feed your little goats Beside the shepherds' tents.

Is 38:12 My life span is gone, Taken from me like a shepherd's tent; I have cut off my life like a weaver. He cuts me off from the loom; From day until night You make an end of me.

All Middle Eastern nations.

Judg 6:5 For they would come up with their livestock and their tents, coming in as numerous as locusts; both they and their camels were without number; and they would enter the land to destroy it.

1 Sam 17:4 And a champion went out from the camp of the Philistines, named Goliath, from Gath, whose height *was* six cubits and a span.

2 Kin 7:7 Therefore they arose and fled at twilight, and left the camp intact—their tents, their horses, and their donkeys—and they fled for their lives.

1 Chr 5:10 Now in the days of Saul they made war with the Hagrites, who fell by their hand; and they dwelt in their tents throughout the entire *area* east of Gilead.

Separate, for women of the family.

Gen 24:67 Then Isaac brought her into his mother Sarah's tent; and he took Rebekah and she became his wife, and he loved her. So Isaac was comforted after his mother's *death*.

Separate, for the servants.

Gen 31:33 And Laban went into Jacob's tent, into Leah's tent, and into the two maids' tents, but he did not find *them*. Then he went out of Leah's tent and entered Rachel's tent.

Were pitched

With order and regularity.

Num 1:52 The children of Israel shall pitch their tents, everyone by his own camp, everyone by his own standard, according to their armies;

In the neighborhood of wells, etc.

Gen 13:10 And Lot lifted his eyes and saw all the plain of Jordan, that it *was* well watered everywhere (before the Lord destroyed Sodom and Gomorrah) like the garden of the LORD, like the land of Egypt as you go toward Zoar.

Gen 13:12 Abram dwelt in the land of Canaan, and Lot dwelt in the cities of the plain and pitched *his* tent even as far as Sodom.

Gen 26:17–18 Then Isaac departed from there and pitched his tent in the Valley of Gerar, and dwelt there. **18** And Isaac dug again the wells of water which they had dug in the days of Abraham his father, for the Philistines had stopped them up after the death of Abraham. He called them by the names which his father had called them.

1 Sam 29:1 Then the Philistines gathered together all their armies at Aphek, and the Israelites encamped by a fountain which *is* in Jezreel.

Under trees.

Gen 18:1 Then the LORD appeared to him by the terebinth trees of Mamre, as he was sitting in the tent door in the heat of the day.

Gen 18:4 Please let a little water be brought, and wash your feet, and rest yourselves under the tree.

Judg 4:5 And she would sit under the palm tree of Deborah between Ramah and Bethel in the mountains of Ephraim. And the children of Israel came up to her for judgment.

On the tops of houses.

2 Sam 16:22 So they pitched a tent for Absalom on the top of the house, and Absalom went in to his father's concubines in the sight of all Israel.

Sending persons to seek a convenient place for, alluded to.

Deut 1:33 who went in the way before you to search out a place for you to pitch your tents, to show you the way you should go, in the fire by night and in the cloud by day.

Ease and rapidity of their removal, alluded to.

Is 38:12 My life span is gone, Taken from me like a shepherd's tent; I have cut off my life like a weaver. He cuts me off from the loom; From day until night You make an end of me.

Of the Jews, contrasted with those of the Gentiles.

Num 24:5 "How lovely are your tents, O Jacob! Your dwellings, O Israel!

Song 1:5 I *am* dark, but lovely, O daughters of Jerusalem, Like the tents of Kedar, Like the curtains of Solomon.

Custom of sitting and standing at the door of.

Gen 18:1 Then the LORD appeared to him by the terebinth trees of Mamre, as he was sitting in the tent door in the heat of the day.

Judg 4:20 And he said to her, "Stand at the door of the tent, and if any man comes and inquires of you, and says, 'Is there any man here?' you shall say, 'No.' "

Illustrative of

(Spread out) the heavens.

Is 40:22 *It is* He who sits above the circle of the earth, And its inhabitants *are* like grasshoppers, Who stretches out the heavens like a curtain, And spreads them out like a tent to dwell in.

(Enlarging of) the extension of God's people.

Is 54:2 "Enlarge the place of your tent, And let them stretch out the curtains of your dwellings; Do not spare; Lengthen your cords, And strengthen your stakes.

THANKSGIVING

Christ set an example of.

Matt 11:25 At that time Jesus answered and said, "I thank You, Father, Lord of heaven and earth, that You have hidden these things from *the* wise and prudent and have revealed them to babes.

Matt 26:27 Then He took the cup, and gave thanks, and gave *it* to them, saying, "Drink from it, all of you.

John 6:11 And Jesus took the loaves, and when He had given thanks He distributed *them* to the disciples, and the disciples to those sitting down; and likewise of the fish, as much as they wanted.

John 11:41 Then they took away the stone *from the place* where the dead man was lying. And Jesus lifted up *His* eyes and said, "Father, I thank You that You have heard Me.

The heavenly host engaged in.

Rev 4:9 Whenever the living creatures give glory and honor and thanks to Him who sits on the throne, who lives forever and ever,

Rev 7:11–12 All the angels stood around the throne and the elders and the four living creatures, and fell on their faces before the throne and worshiped God, **12** saying: "Amen! Blessing and glory and wisdom, Thanksgiving and honor and power and might, *Be* to our God forever and ever. Amen."

Rev 11:16–17 And the twenty-four elders who sat before God on their thrones fell on their faces and worshiped God, **17** saying: "We give You thanks, O Lord God Almighty, The One who is and who was and who is to come, Because You have taken Your great power and reigned.

Commanded.

Ps 50:14 Offer to God thanksgiving, And pay your vows to the Most High.

Phil 4:6 Be anxious for nothing, but in everything by prayer and supplication, with thanksgiving, let your requests be made known to God;

Should be offered

To God.

Ps 50:14 Offer to God thanksgiving, And pay your vows to the Most High.

Ps 92:1 *It is* good to give thanks to the LORD, And to sing praises to Your name, O Most High;

To Christ.

1 Tim 1:12 And I thank Christ Jesus our Lord who has enabled me, because He counted me faithful, putting *me* into the ministry,

Through Christ.

Rom 1:8 First, I thank my God through Jesus Christ for you all, that your faith is spoken of throughout the whole world.

Col 3:17 And *whatever* you do in word or deed, *do* all in the name of the Lord Jesus, giving thanks to God the Father through Him.

Heb 13:15 Therefore by Him let us continually offer the sacrifice of praise to God, that is, the fruit of *our* lips, giving thanks to His name.

In the name of Christ.

Eph 5:20 giving thanks always for all things to God the Father in the name of our Lord Jesus Christ,

On behalf of ministers.

2 Cor 1:11 you also helping together in prayer for us, that thanks may be given by many persons on our behalf for the gift *granted* to us through many.

In private worship.

Dan 6:10 Now when Daniel knew that the writing was signed, he went home. And in his upper room, with his windows open toward Jerusalem, he knelt down on his knees three times that day, and prayed and gave thanks before his God, as was his custom since early days.

In public worship.

Ps 35:18 I will give You thanks in the great assembly; I will praise You among many people.

In and for everything.

2 Cor 9:11 while *you are* enriched in everything for all liberality, which causes thanksgiving through us to God.

Eph 5:20 giving thanks always for all things to God the Father in the name of our Lord Jesus Christ,

1 Thess 5:18 in everything give thanks; for this is the will of God in Christ Jesus for you.

Upon the completion of great undertakings.

Neh 12:31 So I brought the leaders of Judah up on the wall, and appointed two large thanksgiving choirs. *One* went to the right hand on the wall toward the Refuse Gate.

Neh 12:40 So the two thanksgiving choirs stood in the house of God, likewise I and the half of the rulers with me;

Before taking food.

John 6:11 And Jesus took the loaves, and when He had given thanks He distributed *them* to the disciples, and the disciples to those sitting down; and likewise of the fish, as much as they wanted.

Acts 27:35 And when he had said these things, he took bread and gave thanks to God in the presence of them all; and when he had broken *it* he began to eat.

Always.

Eph 1:16 do not cease to give thanks for you, making mention of you in my prayers:

Eph 5:20 giving thanks always for all things to God the Father in the name of our Lord Jesus Christ,

1 Thess 1:2 We give thanks to God always for you all, making mention of you in our prayers,

At the remembrance of God's holiness.

Ps 30:4 Sing praise to the LORD, you saints of His, And give thanks at the remembrance of His holy name.

Ps 97:12 Rejoice in the LORD, you righteous, And give thanks at the remembrance of His holy name.

For the goodness and mercy of God.

Ps 106:1 Praise the LORD! Oh, give thanks to the LORD, for *He is* good! For His mercy *endures* forever.

Ps 107:1 Oh, give thanks to the LORD, for *He is* good! For His mercy *endures* forever.

Ps 136:1–3 Oh, give thanks to the LORD, for *He is* good! For His mercy *endures* forever. **2** Oh, give thanks to the God of gods! For His mercy *endures* forever. **3** Oh, give thanks to the Lord of lords! For His mercy *endures* forever:

For the gift of Christ.

2 Cor 9:15 Thanks *be* to God for His indescribable gift!

For Christ's power and reign.

Rev 11:17 saying: "We give You thanks, O Lord God Almighty, The One who is and who was and who is to come, Because You have taken Your great power and reigned.

For the working of God's Word in others.

1 Thess 2:13 For this reason we also thank God without ceasing, because when you received the word of God which you heard from us, you welcomed *it* not *as* the word of men, but as it is in truth, the word of God, which also effectively works in you who believe.

For deliverance through Christ from indwelling sin.

Rom 7:23–25 But I see another law in my members, warring against the law of my mind, and bringing me into captivity to the law of sin which is in my members. **24** O wretched man that I am! Who will deliver me from this body of death? **25** I thank God— through Jesus Christ our Lord! So then, with the mind I myself serve the law of God, but with the flesh the law of sin.

For victory over death and the grave.

1 Cor 15:57 But thanks *be* to God, who gives us the victory through our Lord Jesus Christ.

For wisdom and might.

Dan 2:23 "I thank You and praise You, O God of my fathers; You have given me wisdom and might, And have now made known to me what we asked of You, For You have made known to us the king's demand."

For the triumph of the gospel.

2 Cor 2:14 Now thanks *be* to God who always leads us in triumph in Christ, and through us diffuses the fragrance of His knowledge in every place.

For the conversion of others.

Rom 6:17 But God be thanked that *though* you were slaves of sin, yet you obeyed from the heart that form of doctrine to which you were delivered.

For faith exhibited by others.

Rom 1:8 First, I thank my God through Jesus Christ for you all, that your faith is spoken of throughout the whole world.

2 Thess 1:3 We are bound to thank God always for you, brethren, as it is fitting, because your faith grows exceedingly, and the love of every one of you all abounds toward each other,

For love exhibited by others.

2 Thess 1:3 We are bound to thank God always for you, brethren, as it is fitting, because your faith grows exceedingly, and the love of every one of you all abounds toward each other,

For the grace bestowed on others.

1 Cor 1:4 I thank my God always concerning you for the grace of God which was given to you by Christ Jesus,

Phil 1:3–5 I thank my God upon every remembrance of you, **4** always in every prayer of mine making request for you all with joy, **5** for your fellowship in the gospel from the first day until now,

Col 1:3–6 We give thanks to the God and Father of our Lord Jesus Christ, praying always for you, **4** since we heard of your faith in Christ Jesus and of your love for all the saints; **5** because of the hope which is laid up for you in heaven, of which you heard before in the word of the truth of the gospel, **6** which has come to you, as *it has* also in all the world, and is bringing forth fruit, as *it is* also among you since the day you heard and knew the grace of God in truth;

For the zeal exhibited by others.

2 Cor 8:16 But thanks *be* to God who puts the same earnest care for you into the heart of Titus.

For the nearness of God's presence.

Ps 75:1 We give thanks to You, O God, we give thanks! For Your wondrous works declare *that* Your name is near.

For appointment to the ministry.

1 Tim 1:12 And I thank Christ Jesus our Lord who has enabled me, because He counted me faithful, putting *me* into the ministry,

For willingness to offer our property for God's service.

1 Chr 29:6–14 Then the leaders of the fathers' *houses*, leaders of the tribes of Israel, the captains of thousands and of hundreds, with the officers over the king's work, offered willingly. **7** They gave for the work of the house of God five thousand talents and ten thousand darics of gold, ten thousand talents of silver, eighteen thousand talents of bronze, and one hundred thousand talents of iron. **8** And whoever had *precious* stones gave *them* to the treasury of the house of the LORD, into the hand of Jehiel the Gershonite. **9** Then the people rejoiced, for they had offered willingly, because with a loyal heart they had offered willingly to the LORD; and King David also rejoiced greatly. **10** Therefore David blessed the LORD before all the assembly; and David said: "Blessed are You, LORD God of Israel, our Father, forever and ever. **11** Yours, O LORD, *is* the greatness, The power and the glory, The victory and the majesty; For all *that is* in heaven and in earth *is* Yours; Yours *is* the kingdom, O LORD, And You are exalted as head over all. **12** Both riches and honor *come* from You, And You reign over all. In Your hand *is* power and might; In Your hand *it is* to make great And to give strength to all. **13** "Now therefore, our God, We thank You And praise Your glorious name. **14** But who *am* I, and who *are* my people, That we should be able to offer so willingly as this? For all things *come* from You, And of Your own we have given You.

For the supply of our bodily wants.

Rom 14:6–7 He who observes the day, observes *it* to the Lord; and he who does not observe the day, to the Lord he does not observe *it*. He who eats, eats to the Lord, for he gives God thanks; and he who does not eat, to the Lord he does not eat, and gives God

thanks. **7** For none of us lives to himself, and no one dies to himself.

1 Tim 4:3–4 forbidding to marry, *and commanding* to abstain from foods which God created to be received with thanksgiving by those who believe and know the truth. **4** For every creature of God *is* good, and nothing is to be refused if it is received with thanksgiving;

For all men.

1 Tim 2:1 Therefore I exhort first of all that supplications, prayers, intercessions, *and* giving of thanks be made for all men,

With intercession for others.

1 Tim 2:1 Therefore I exhort first of all that supplications, prayers, intercessions, *and* giving of thanks be made for all men,

2 Tim 1:3 I thank God, whom I serve with a pure conscience, as *my* forefathers *did*, as without ceasing I remember you in my prayers night and day,

Philem 1:4 I thank my God, making mention of you always in my prayers,

With any prayer.

Neh 11:17 Mattaniah the son of Micha, the son of Zabdi, the son of Asaph, the leader *who* began the thanksgiving with prayer; Bakbukiah, the second among his brethren; and Abda the son of Shammua, the son of Galal, the son of Jeduthun.

Phil 4:6 Be anxious for nothing, but in everything by prayer and supplication, with thanksgiving, let your requests be made known to God;

Col 4:2 Continue earnestly in prayer, being vigilant in it with thanksgiving;

With praise.

Ps 92:1 *It is* good to give thanks to the LORD, And to sing praises to Your name, O Most High;

Heb 13:15 Therefore by Him let us continually offer the sacrifice of praise to God, that is, the fruit of *our* lips, giving thanks to His name.

Expressed in psalms.

1 Chr 16:7 On that day David first delivered *this psalm* into the hand of Asaph and his brethren, to thank the LORD:

Ministers appointed to offer, in public.

1 Chr 16:4 And he appointed some of the Levites to minister before the ark of the LORD, to commemorate, to thank, and to praise the LORD God of Israel:

1 Chr 16:7 On that day David first delivered *this psalm* into the hand of Asaph and his brethren, to thank the LORD:

1 Chr 23:30 to stand every morning to thank and praise the LORD, and likewise at evening;

2 Chr 31:2 And Hezekiah appointed the divisions of the priests and the Levites according to their divisions, each man according to his service, the priests and Levites for burnt offerings and peace offerings, to serve, to give thanks, and to praise in the gates of the camp of the LORD.

Believers

Exhorted to.

Ps 105:1 Oh, give thanks to the LORD! Call upon His name; Make known His deeds among the peoples!

Col 3:15 And let the peace of God rule in your hearts, to which also you were called in one body; and be thankful.

Resolved to offer.

Ps 18:49 Therefore I will give thanks to You, O Lord, among the Gentiles, And sing praises to Your name.

Ps 30:12 To the end that *my* glory may sing praise to You and not be silent. O Lord my God, I will give thanks to You forever.

Habitually offer.

Dan 6:10 Now when Daniel knew that the writing was signed, he went home. And in his upper room, with his windows open toward Jerusalem, he knelt down on his knees three times that day, and prayed and gave thanks before his God, as was his custom since early days.

Offer sacrifices of.

Ps 116:17 I will offer to You the sacrifice of thanksgiving, And will call upon the name of the Lord.

Abound in the faith with.

Col 2:7 rooted and built up in Him and established in the faith, as you have been taught, abounding in it with thanksgiving.

Magnify God by.

Ps 69:30 I will praise the name of God with a song, And will magnify Him with thanksgiving.

Come before God with.

Ps 95:2 Let us come before His presence with thanksgiving; Let us shout joyfully to Him with psalms.

Should enter God's gate with.

Ps 100:4 Enter into His gates with thanksgiving, *And* into His courts with praise. Be thankful to Him, *and* bless His name.

Of hypocrites, full of boasting.

Luke 18:11 The Pharisee stood and prayed thus with himself, 'God, I thank You that I am not like other men—extortioners, unjust, adulterers, or even as this tax collector.

The wicked averse to.

Rom 1:21 because, although they knew God, they did not glorify *Him* as God, nor were thankful, but became futile in their thoughts, and their foolish hearts were darkened.

Exemplified by

David.

1 Chr 29:12 Both riches and honor *come* from You, And You reign over all. In Your hand *is* power and might; In Your hand it *is* to make great And to give strength to all.

The Levites.

2 Chr 5:12–13 and the Levites *who were* the singers, all those of Asaph and Heman and Jeduthun, with their sons and their brethren, stood at the east end of the altar, clothed in white linen, having cymbals, stringed instruments and harps, and with them one hundred and twenty priests sounding with trumpets— **13** indeed it came to pass, when the trumpeters and singers *were* as one, to make one sound to be heard in praising and thanking the Lord, and when they lifted up their voice with the trumpets

and cymbals and instruments of music, and praised the Lord, *saying:* "For He is good, For His mercy endures forever," that the house, the house of the Lord, was filled with a cloud,

Daniel.

Dan 2:23 "I thank You and praise You, O God of my fathers; You have given me wisdom and might, And have now made known to me what we asked of You, For You have made known to us the king's demand."

Jonah.

Jon 2:9 But I will sacrifice to You With the voice of thanksgiving; I will pay what I have vowed. Salvation *is* of the Lord."

Simeon.

Luke 2:28 he took Him up in his arms and blessed God and said:

Anna.

Luke 2:38 And coming in that instant she gave thanks to the Lord, and spoke of Him to all those who looked for redemption in Jerusalem.

Paul.

Acts 28:15 And from there, when the brethren heard about us, they came to meet us as far as Appii Forum and Three Inns. When Paul saw them, he thanked God and took courage.

THEFT

Is an abomination.

Jer 7:9–10 Will you steal, murder, commit adultery, swear falsely, burn incense to Baal, and walk after other gods whom you do not know, **10** and *then* come and stand before Me in this house which is called by My name, and say, 'We are delivered to do all these abominations'?

Forbidden.

Ex 20:15 "You shall not steal.

Mark 10:19 You know the commandments: *'Do not commit adultery,' 'Do not murder,' 'Do not steal,' 'Do not bear false witness,' 'Do not defraud,' 'Honor your father and your mother.'"*

Rom 13:9 For the commandments, *"You shall not commit adultery," "You shall not murder," "You shall not steal," "You shall not bear false witness," "You shall not covet,"* and if *there is* any other commandment, are *all* summed up in this saying, namely, *"You shall love your neighbor as yourself."*

From the poor, especially forbidden.

Is 10:2 To rob the needy of justice, And to take what is right from the poor of My people, That widows may be their prey, And *that* they may rob the fatherless.

Includes fraud in general.

Lev 19:13 'You shall not cheat your neighbor, nor rob *him*. The wages of him who is hired shall not remain with you all night until morning.

Includes fraud concerning wages.

Lev 19:13 'You shall not cheat your neighbor, nor rob *him*. The wages of him who is hired shall not remain with you all night until morning.

Mal 3:5 And I will come near you for judgment; I will be a swift witness Against sorcerers, Against adulterers, Against perjurers, Against those who exploit wage earners and widows and orphans, And against those who turn away an alien— Because they do not fear Me," Says the LORD of hosts.

James 5:4 Indeed the wages of the laborers who mowed your fields, which you kept back by fraud, cry out; and the cries of the reapers have reached the ears of the Lord of Sabaoth.

Proceeds from the heart.

Matt 15:19 For out of the heart proceed evil thoughts, murders, adulteries, fornications, thefts, false witness, blasphemies.

Defiles a man.

Matt 15:20 These are *the things* which defile a man, but to eat with unwashed hands does not defile a man."

The wicked

Are addicted to.

Ps 119:61 The cords of the wicked have bound me, *But* I have not forgotten Your law.

Store up the fruits of.

Amos 3:10 For they do not know to do right,' Says the LORD, 'Who store up violence and robbery in their palaces.' "

Lie in wait to commit.

Hos 6:9 As bands of robbers lie in wait for a man, *So* the company of priests murder on the way to Shechem; Surely they commit lewdness.

Commit, under shelter of the night.

Job 24:14 The murderer rises with the light; He kills the poor and needy; And in the night he is like a thief.

Obad 1:5 "If thieves had come to you, If robbers by night— Oh, how you will be cut off!— Would they not have stolen till they had enough? If grape-gatherers had come to you, Would they not have left *some* gleanings?

Join those who commit.

Ps 50:18 When you saw a thief, you consented with him, And have been a partaker with adulterers.

Associate with those who commit.

Is 1:23 Your princes *are* rebellious, And companions of thieves; Everyone loves bribes, And follows after rewards. They do not defend the fatherless, Nor does the cause of the widow come before them.

May, for a season, prosper in.

Job 12:6 The tents of robbers prosper, And those who provoke God are secure— In what God provides by His hand.

Plead excuses for.

Jer 7:9–10 Will you steal, murder, commit adultery, swear falsely, burn incense to Baal, and walk after other gods whom you do not know, **10** and *then* come and stand before Me in this house which is called by My name, and say, 'We are delivered to do all these abominations'?

Do not repent of.

Rev 9:21 And they did not repent of their murders or their sorceries or their sexual immorality or their thefts.

Destroy themselves by.

Prov 21:7 The violence of the wicked will destroy them, Because they refuse to do justice.

Connected with murder.

Jer 7:9 Will you steal, murder, commit adultery, swear falsely, burn incense to Baal, and walk after other gods whom you do not know,

Hos 4:2 *By* swearing and lying, Killing and stealing and committing adultery, They break all restraint, With bloodshed upon bloodshed.

Shame follows the detection of.

Jer 2:26 "As the thief is ashamed when he is found out, So is the house of Israel ashamed; They and their kings and their princes, and their priests and their prophets,

Brings a curse on those who commit it.

Hos 4:2–3 *By* swearing and lying, Killing and stealing and committing adultery, They break all restraint, With bloodshed upon bloodshed. **3** Therefore the land will mourn; And everyone who dwells there will waste away With the beasts of the field And the birds of the air; Even the fish of the sea will be taken away.

Zech 5:3–4 Then he said to me, "This *is* the curse that goes out over the face of the whole earth: 'Every thief shall be expelled,' according *to* this side of *the scroll;* and, 'Every perjurer shall be expelled,' according *to* that side of it." **4** "I will send out *the curse,*" says the LORD of hosts; "It shall enter the house of the thief And the house of the one who swears falsely by My name. It shall remain in the midst of his house And consume it, with its timber and stones."

Mal 3:5 And I will come near you for judgment; I will be a swift witness Against sorcerers, Against adulterers, Against perjurers, Against those who exploit wage earners and widows and orphans, And against those who turn away an alien— Because they do not fear Me," Says the LORD of hosts.

Brings the wrath of God upon those who commit it.

Ezek 22:29 The people of the land have used oppressions, committed robbery, and mistreated the poor and needy; and they wrongfully oppress the stranger.

Ezek 22:31 Therefore I have poured out My indignation on them; I have consumed them with the fire of My wrath; and I have recompensed their deeds on their own heads," says the Lord GOD.

Excludes from heaven.

1 Cor 6:10 nor thieves, nor covetous, nor drunkards, nor revilers, nor extortioners will inherit the kingdom of God.

Those who connive at,

Hate their own souls.

Prov 29:24 Whoever is a partner with a thief hates his own life; He swears to tell the truth, but reveals nothing.

Shall be reproved of God.

Ps 50:18 When you saw a thief, you consented with him, And have been a partaker with adulterers.

Ps 50:21 These *things* you have done, and I kept silent; You thought that I was altogether like you; *But* I will rebuke you, And set *them* in order before your eyes.

Mosaic law respecting.

Ex 22:1–8 "If a man steals an ox or a sheep, and slaughters it or sells it, he shall restore five oxen for an ox and four sheep for a sheep. **2** If the thief is found breaking in, and he is struck so that he dies, *there shall be* no guilt for his bloodshed. **3** If the sun has risen on him, *there shall be* guilt for his bloodshed. He should make full restitution; if he has nothing, then he shall be sold for his theft. **4** If the theft is certainly found alive in his hand, whether it is an ox or donkey or sheep, he shall restore double. **5** "If a man causes a field or vineyard to be grazed, and lets loose his animal, and it feeds in another man's field, he shall make restitution from the best of his own field and the best of his own vineyard. **6** "If fire breaks out and catches in thorns, so that stacked grain, standing grain, or the field is consumed, he who kindled the fire shall surely make restitution. **7** "If a man delivers to his neighbor money or articles to keep, and it is stolen out of the man's house, if the thief is found, he shall pay double. **8** If the thief is not found, then the master of the house shall be brought to the judges *to see* whether he has put his hand into his neighbor's goods.

Believers warned against.

Eph 4:28 Let him who stole steal no longer, but rather let him labor, working with *his* hands what is good, that he may have something to give him who has need.

1 Pet 4:15 But let none of you suffer as a murderer, a thief, an evildoer, or as a busybody in other people's matters.

All earthly treasure exposed to.

Matt 6:19 "Do not lay up for yourselves treasures on earth, where moth and rust destroy and where thieves break in and steal;

Heavenly treasure secure from.

Matt 6:20 but lay up for yourselves treasures in heaven, where neither moth nor rust destroys and where thieves do not break in and steal.

Luke 12:33 Sell what you have and give alms; provide yourselves money bags which do not grow old, a treasure in the heavens that does not fail, where no thief approaches nor moth destroys.

Woe pronounced against.

Is 10:2 To rob the needy of justice, And to take what is right from the poor of My people, That widows may be their prey, And *that* they may rob the fatherless.

Nah 3:1 Woe to the bloody city! It *is* all full of lies *and* robbery. *Its* victim never departs.

Illustrates the guilt of false teachers.

Jer 23:30 "Therefore behold, I *am* against the prophets," says the LORD, "who steal My words every one from his neighbor.

John 10:1 "Most assuredly, I say to you, he who does not enter the sheepfold by the door, but climbs up some other way, the same is a thief and a robber.

John 10:8 All who *ever* came before Me are thieves and robbers, but the sheep did not hear them.

John 10:10 The thief does not come except to steal, and to kill, and to destroy. I have come that they may have life, and that they may have *it* more abundantly.

Those who committed,

Rachel.

Gen 31:19 Now Laban had gone to shear his sheep, and Rachel had stolen the household idols that were her father's.

Achan.

Josh 7:21 When I saw among the spoils a beautiful Babylonian garment, two hundred shekels of silver, and a wedge of gold weighing fifty shekels, I coveted them and took them. And there they are, hidden in the earth in the midst of my tent, with the silver under it."

The Shechemites.

Judg 9:25 And the men of Shechem set men in ambush against him on the tops of the mountains, and they robbed all who passed by them along that way; and it was told Abimelech.

Micah.

Judg 17:2 And he said to his mother, "The eleven hundred *shekels* of silver that were taken from you, and on which you put a curse, even saying it in my ears— here *is* the silver with me; I took it." And his mother said, "*May you be* blessed by the LORD, my son!"

THEOCRACY, ISRAEL AS A

Lasted from the deliverance out of Egypt until the appointment of kings.

Ex 19:4–6 'You have seen what I did to the Egyptians, and *how* I bore you on eagles' wings and brought you to Myself. **5** Now therefore, if you will indeed obey My voice and keep My covenant, then you shall be a special treasure to Me above all people; for all the earth *is* Mine. **6** And you shall be to Me a kingdom of priests and a holy nation.' These *are* the words which you shall speak to the children of Israel."

1 Sam 8:7 And the LORD said to Samuel, "Heed the voice of the people in all that they say to you; for they have not rejected you, but they have rejected Me, that I should not reign over them.

Was established on

The right of redemption.

Ex 6:6–7 Therefore say to the children of Israel: 'I *am* the LORD; I will bring you out from under the burdens of the Egyptians, I will rescue you from their bondage, and I will redeem you with an outstretched arm and with great judgments. **7** I will take you as My people, and I will be your God. Then you shall know that I *am* the LORD your God who brings you out from under the burdens of the Egyptians.

2 Sam 7:23 And who *is* like Your people, like Israel, the one nation on the earth whom God went to redeem for Himself as a people, to make for Himself a name—and to do for Yourself great and awesome deeds for Your land—before Your people whom You redeemed for Yourself from Egypt, the nations, and their gods?

Is 43:3 For I *am* the LORD your God, The Holy One of Israel, your Savior; I gave Egypt for your ransom, Ethiopia and Seba in your place.

The right of covenant.

Deut 26:17–19 Today you have proclaimed the LORD to be your God, and that you will walk in His ways and keep His statutes, His commandments, and His judgments, and that you will obey His voice. **18** Also today the LORD has proclaimed you to be His special people, just as He promised you, that *you* should keep all His commandments, **19** and that He will set you high above all nations which He has made, in praise, in name, and in honor, and that you may be a holy people to the LORD your God, just as He has spoken."

Consisted in God's

Promulgating laws. Ex 20:1-23:33

Directing the movements of the nation.

Ex 40:36-37 Whenever the cloud was taken up from above the tabernacle, the children of Israel would go onward in all their journeys. **37** But if the cloud was not taken up, then they did not journey till the day that it was taken up.

Num 9:17-23 Whenever the cloud was taken up from above the tabernacle, after that the children of Israel would journey; and in the place where the cloud settled, there the children of Israel would pitch their tents. **18** At the command of the LORD the children of Israel would journey, and at the command of the LORD they would camp; as long as the cloud stayed above the tabernacle they remained encamped. **19** Even when the cloud continued long, many days above the tabernacle, the children of Israel kept the charge of the LORD and did not journey. **20** So it was, when the cloud was above the tabernacle a few days: according to the command of the LORD they would remain encamped, and according to the command of the LORD they would journey. **21** So it was, when the cloud remained only from evening until morning: when the cloud was taken up in the morning, then they would journey; whether by day or by night, whenever the cloud was taken up, they would journey. **22** *Whether it was* two days, a month, or a year that the cloud remained above the tabernacle, the children of Israel would remain encamped and not journey; but when it was taken up, they would journey. **23** At the command of the LORD they remained encamped, and at the command of the LORD they journeyed; they kept the charge of the LORD, at the command of the LORD by the hand of Moses.

Proclaiming war.

Ex 17:14-16 Then the LORD said to Moses, "Write this *for* a memorial in the book and recount *it* in the hearing of Joshua, that I will utterly blot out the remembrance of Amalek from under heaven." **15** And Moses built an altar and called its name, The-LORD-Is-My-Banner; **16** for he said, "Because the LORD has sworn: the LORD *will have* war with Amalek from generation to generation."

Num 31:1-2 And the LORD spoke to Moses, saying: **2** "Take vengeance on the Midianites for the children of Israel. Afterward you shall be gathered to your people."

Josh 6:2-3 And the LORD said to Joshua: "See! I have given Jericho into your hand, its king, *and* the mighty men of valor. **3** You shall march around the city, all *you* men of war; you shall go all around the city once. This you shall do six days.

Josh 8:1 Now the LORD said to Joshua: "Do not be afraid, nor be dismayed; take all the people of war with you, and arise, go up to Ai. See, I have given into your hand the king of Ai, his people, his city, and his land.

Appointing civil officers.

Ex 3:10 Come now, therefore, and I will send you to Pharaoh that you may bring My people, the children of Israel, out of Egypt."

Num 27:18 And the LORD said to Moses: "Take Joshua the son of Nun with you, a man in whom *is* the Spirit, and lay your hand on him;

Num 27:20 And you shall give *some* of your authority to him, that all the congregation of the children of Israel may be obedient.

Appointing ecclesiastical officers.

Ex 28:1 "Now take Aaron your brother, and his sons with him, from among the children of Israel, that he may minister to Me as priest, Aaron *and* Aaron's sons: Nadab, Abihu, Eleazar, and Ithamar.

Ex 40:12-15 "Then you shall bring Aaron and his sons to the door of the tabernacle of meeting and wash them with water. **13** You shall put the holy garments on Aaron, and anoint him and consecrate him, that he may minister to Me as priest. **14** And you shall bring his sons and clothe them with tunics. **15** You shall anoint them, as you anointed their father, that they may minister to Me as priests; for their anointing shall surely be an everlasting priesthood throughout their generations."

Being the supreme judge.

Num 9:8-11 And Moses said to them, "Stand still, that I may hear what the LORD will command concerning you." **9** Then the LORD spoke to Moses, saying, **10** "Speak to the children of Israel, saying: 'If anyone of you or your posterity is unclean because of a corpse, or *is* far away on a journey, he may still keep the LORD's Passover. **11** On the fourteenth day of the second month, at twilight, they may keep it. They shall eat it with unleavened bread and bitter herbs.

Num 15:34-35 They put him under guard, because it had not been explained what should be done to him. **35** Then the LORD said to Moses, "The man must surely be put to death; all the congregation shall stone him with stones outside the camp."

Num 27:5-11 So Moses brought their case before the LORD. **6** And the LORD spoke to Moses, saying: **7** "The daughters of Zelophehad speak *what is* right; you shall surely give them a possession of inheritance among their father's brothers, and cause the inheritance of their father to pass to them. **8** And you shall speak to the children of Israel, saying: 'If a man dies and has no son, then you shall cause his inheritance to pass to his daughter. **9** If he has no daughter, then you shall give his inheritance to his brothers. **10** If he has no brothers, then you shall give his inheritance to his father's brothers. **11** And if his father has no brothers, then you shall give his inheritance to the relative closest to him in his family, and he shall possess it.' " And it shall be to the children of Israel a statute of judgment, just as the LORD commanded Moses.

Exercising mercy.

Num 14:20 Then the LORD said: "I have pardoned, according to your word;

Deut 9:18-20 And I fell down before the LORD, as at the first, forty days and forty nights; I neither ate bread nor drank water, because of all your sin which you committed in doing wickedly in the sight of the LORD, to provoke Him to anger. **19** For I was afraid of the anger and hot displeasure with which the LORD was angry with you, to destroy you. But the LORD listened to me at that time also. **20** And the LORD was very angry with Aaron *and* would have destroyed him; so I prayed for Aaron also at the same time.

Distributing the conquered lands.

Josh 13:1–7 Now Joshua was old, advanced in years. And the LORD said to him: "You are old, advanced in years, and there remains very much land yet to be possessed. **2** This is the land that yet remains: all the territory of the Philistines and all *that of* the Geshurites, **3** from Sihor, which *is* east of Egypt, as far as the border of Ekron northward (*which* is counted as Canaanite); the five lords of the Philistines—the Gazites, the Ashdodites, the Ashkelonites, the Gittites, and the Ekronites; also the Avites; **4** from the south, all the land of the Canaanites, and Mearah that belongs to the Sidonians as far as Aphek, to the border of the Amorites; **5** the land of the Gebalites, and all Lebanon, toward the sunrise, from Baal Gad below Mount Hermon as far as the entrance to Hamath; **6** all the inhabitants of the mountains from Lebanon as far as the Brook Misrephoth, *and* all the Sidonians—them I will drive out from before the children of Israel; only divide it by lot to Israel as an inheritance, as I have commanded you. **7** Now therefore, divide this land as an inheritance to the nine tribes and half the tribe of Manasseh."

Exacting tribute.

Lev 27:30 And all the tithe of the land, *whether* of the seed of the land *or* of the fruit of the tree, *is* the LORD's. It *is* holy to the LORD.

Deut 16:16 "Three times a year all your males shall appear before the LORD your God in the place which He chooses: at the Feast of Unleavened Bread, at the Feast of Weeks, and at the Feast of Tabernacles; and they shall not appear before the LORD empty-handed.

Deut 26:1–4 "And it shall be, when you come into the land which the LORD your God is giving you *as* an inheritance, and you possess it and dwell in it, **2** that you shall take some of the first of all the produce of the ground, which you shall bring from your land that the LORD your God is giving you, and put *it* in a basket and go to the place where the LORD your God chooses to make His name abide. **3** And you shall go to the one who is priest in those days, and say to him, 'I declare today to the LORD your God that I have come to the country which the LORD swore to our fathers to give us.' **4** "Then the priest shall take the basket out of your hand and set it down before the altar of the LORD your God.

Cf. Ex 35:4–29

Residing in and appearing over the tabernacle.

Ex 25:8 And let them make Me a sanctuary, that I may dwell among them.

Lev 26:11–12 I will set My tabernacle among you, and My soul shall not abhor you. **12** I will walk among you and be your God, and you shall be My people.

Num 9:15–16 Now on the day that the tabernacle was raised up, the cloud covered the tabernacle, the tent of the Testimony; from evening until morning it was above the tabernacle like the appearance of fire. **16** So it was always: the cloud covered it *by day*, and the appearance of fire by night.

Guilt of Israel in rejecting.

1 Sam 8:6–9 But the thing displeased Samuel when they said, "Give us a king to judge us." So Samuel prayed to the LORD. **7** And the LORD said to Samuel, "Heed the voice of the people in all that they say to you; for they have not rejected you, but they have rejected Me, that I should not reign over them. **8** According to all the works which they have done since the day that I brought them up out of Egypt, even to this day—with which they have forsaken Me and served other gods—so they are doing to you also. **9** Now therefore, heed their voice. However, you shall solemnly forewarn them, and show them the behavior of the king who will reign over them."

THRESHING

The removing or separating of wheat or grain from the straw.

1 Chr 21:20 Now Ornan turned and saw the angel; and his four sons *who were* with him hid themselves, but Ornan continued threshing wheat.

Was performed

By a rod or stick.

Is 28:27 For the black cummin is not threshed with a threshing sledge, Nor is a cartwheel rolled over the cummin; But the black cummin is beaten out with a stick, And the cummin with a rod.

By cartwheels.

Is 28:27–28 For the black cummin is not threshed with a threshing sledge, Nor is a cartwheel rolled over the cummin; But the black cummin is beaten out with a stick, And the cummin with a rod. **28** Bread *flour* must be ground; Therefore he does not thresh it forever, Break *it with* his cartwheel, Or crush it *with* his horsemen.

By implements with sharp teeth.

Is 41:15 "Behold, I will make you into a new threshing sledge with sharp teeth; You shall thresh the mountains and beat *them* small, And make the hills like chaff.

Amos 1:3 Thus says the LORD: "For three transgressions of Damascus, and for four, I will not turn away its *punishment*, Because they have threshed Gilead with implements of iron.

By the feet of horses and oxen.

2 Sam 24:22 Now Araunah said to David, "Let my lord the king take and offer up whatever *seems* good to him. Look, *here are* oxen for burnt sacrifice, and threshing implements and the yokes of the oxen for wood.

Is 28:28 Bread *flour* must be ground; Therefore he does not thresh it forever, Break *it with* his cartwheel, Or crush it *with* his horsemen.

Hos 10:11 Ephraim *is* a trained heifer That loves to thresh *grain*; But I harnessed her fair neck, I will make Ephraim pull *a plow*. Judah shall plow; Jacob shall break his clods."

Cattle employed in, not to be muzzled.

Deut 25:4 "You shall not muzzle an ox while it treads out *the grain*.

1 Cor 9:9 For it is written in the law of Moses, "You

shall not muzzle an ox while it treads out the grain." Is it oxen God is concerned about?

1 Tim 5:18 For the Scripture says, *"You shall not muzzle an ox while it treads out the grain,"* and, "The laborer *is* worthy of his wages."

Continued until the vintage in years of abundance.

Lev 26:5 Your threshing shall last till the time of vintage, and the vintage shall last till the time of sowing; you shall eat your bread to the full, and dwell in your land safely.

The place for,

Called the threshing floor.

Num 18:27 And your heave offering shall be reckoned to you as though *it were* the grain of the threshing floor and as the fullness of the winepress.

Judg 6:37 look, I shall put a fleece of wool on the threshing floor; if there is dew on the fleece only, and *it is* dry on all the ground, then I shall know that You will save Israel by my hand, as You have said."

2 Sam 24:18 And Gad came that day to David and said to him, "Go up, erect an altar to the LORD on the threshing floor of Araunah the Jebusite."

2 Kin 6:27 And he said, "If the LORD does not help you, where can I find help for you? From the threshing floor or from the winepress?"

Is 21:10 Oh, my threshing and the grain of my floor! That which I have heard from the LORD of hosts, The God of Israel, I have declared to you.

Hos 9:1 Do not rejoice, O Israel, with joy like *other* peoples, For you have played the harlot against your God. You have made love *for* hire on every threshing floor.

Was large and roomy (implied).

Gen 50:10 Then they came to the threshing floor of Atad, which *is* beyond the Jordan, and they mourned there with a great and very solemn lamentation. He observed seven days of mourning for his father.

Generally on high ground.

1 Chr 21:18 Therefore, the angel of the LORD commanded Gad to say to David that David should go and erect an altar to the LORD on the threshing floor of Ornan the Jebusite.

2 Chr 3:1 Now Solomon began to build the house of the LORD at Jerusalem on Mount Moriah, where *the LORD* had appeared to his father David, at the place that David had prepared on the threshing floor of Ornan the Jebusite.

Sometimes beside the winepress for concealment.

Judg 6:11 Now the Angel of the LORD came and sat under the terebinth tree which *was* in Ophrah, which *belonged* to Joash the Abiezrite, while his son Gideon threshed wheat in the winepress, in order to hide *it* from the Midianites.

Used for winnowing the grain.

Ruth 3:2 Now Boaz, whose young women you were with, *is he* not our relative? In fact, he is winnowing barley tonight at the threshing floor.

Often robbed.

1 Sam 23:1 Then they told David, saying, "Look, the Philistines are fighting against Keilah, and they are robbing the threshing floors."

The Jews slept there, during the time of.

Ruth 3:7 And after Boaz had eaten and drunk, and his heart was cheerful, he went to lie down at the end of the heap of grain; and she came softly, uncovered his feet, and lay down.

Fullness of, promised as a blessing.

Joel 2:24 The threshing floors shall be full of wheat, And the vats shall overflow with new wine and oil.

Scarcity in, a punishment.

Hos 9:2 The threshing floor and the winepress Shall not feed them, And the new wine shall fail in her.

Followed by winnowing with a shovel or fan.

Is 30:24 Likewise the oxen and the young donkeys that work the ground Will eat cured fodder, Which has been winnowed with the shovel and fan.

Is 41:16 You shall winnow them, the wind shall carry them away, And the whirlwind shall scatter them; You shall rejoice in the LORD, *And* glory in the Holy One of Israel.

Matt 3:12 His winnowing fan *is* in His hand, and He will thoroughly clean out His threshing floor, and gather His wheat into the barn; but He will burn up the chaff with unquenchable fire."

Illustrative of

The judgments of God.

Is 21:10 Oh, my threshing and the grain of my floor! That which I have heard from the LORD of hosts, The God of Israel, I have declared to you.

Jer 51:33 For thus says the LORD of hosts, the God of Israel: "The daughter of Babylon *is* like a threshing floor *When it is* time to thresh her; Yet a little while And the time of her harvest will come."

Hab 3:12 You marched through the land in indignation; You trampled the nations in anger.

The labors of ministers.

1 Cor 9:9–10 For it is written in the law of Moses, *"You shall not muzzle an ox while it treads out the grain."* Is it oxen God is concerned about? **10** Or does He say *it* altogether for our sakes? For our sakes, no doubt, *this* is written, that he who plows should plow in hope, and he who threshes in hope should be partaker of his hope.

Israel in her conquests.

Is 41:15–16 "Behold, I will make you into a new threshing sledge with sharp teeth; You shall thresh the mountains and beat *them* small, And make the hills like chaff. **16** You shall winnow them, the wind shall carry them away, And the whirlwind shall scatter them; You shall rejoice in the LORD, *And* glory in the Holy One of Israel.

Mic 4:13 "Arise and thresh, O daughter of Zion; For I will make your horn iron, And I will make your hooves bronze; You shall beat in pieces many peoples; I will consecrate their gain to the LORD, And their substance to the Lord of the whole earth."

(Gathering the sheaves for) preparing the enemies of God's people for judgments.

Mic 4:12 But they do not know the thoughts of the LORD, Nor do they understand His counsel; For He will gather them like sheaves to the threshing floor.

(Dust made by) complete destruction.

2 Kin 13:7 For He left of the army of Jehoahaz only fifty horsemen, ten chariots, and ten thousand foot soldiers; for the king of Syria had destroyed them and made them like the dust at threshing.

Is 41:15 "Behold, I will make you into a new threshing sledge with sharp teeth; You shall thresh the mountains and beat *them* small, And make the hills like chaff.

(An implement for, with teeth) Israel overcoming opposition.

Is 41:15 "Behold, I will make you into a new threshing sledge with sharp teeth; You shall thresh the mountains and beat *them* small, And make the hills like chaff.

TIME

The duration of the world.

Job 22:16 Who were cut down before their time, Whose foundations were swept away by a flood?

Rev 10:6 and swore by Him who lives forever and ever, who created heaven and the things that are in it, the earth and the things that are in it, and the sea and the things that are in it, that there should be delay no longer,

The measure of the continuance of anything.

Judg 18:31 So they set up for themselves Micah's carved image which he made, all the time that the house of God was in Shiloh.

An appointed season.

Neh 2:6 Then the king said to me (the queen also sitting beside him), "How long will your journey be? And when will you return?" So it pleased the king to send me; and I set him a time.

Eccl 3:1 To everything *there is* a season, A time for every purpose under heaven:

Eccl 3:17 I said in my heart, "God shall judge the righteous and the wicked, For *there is* a time there for every purpose and for every work."

Ways of measuring,

Years.

Gen 15:13 Then He said to Abram: "Know certainly that your descendants will be strangers in a land *that is* not theirs, and will serve them, and they will afflict them four hundred years.

2 Sam 21:1 Now there was a famine in the days of David for three years, year after year; and David inquired of the LORD. And the LORD answered, "*It is* because of Saul and *his* bloodthirsty house, because he killed the Gibeonites."

Dan 9:2 in the first year of his reign I, Daniel, understood by the books the number of the years *specified* by the word of the LORD through Jeremiah the prophet, that He would accomplish seventy years in the desolations of Jerusalem.

Months.

Num 10:10 Also in the day of your gladness, in your appointed feasts, and at the beginning of your months, you shall blow the trumpets over your burnt offerings and over the sacrifices of your peace offerings;

and they shall be a memorial for you before your God: I *am* the LORD your God."

1 Chr 27:1 And the children of Israel, according to their number, the heads of fathers' *houses*, the captains of thousands and hundreds and their officers, served the king in every matter of the *military* divisions. *These divisions* came in and went out month by month throughout all the months of the year, each division *having* twenty-four thousand.

Job 3:6 *As for* that night, may darkness seize it; May it not rejoice among the days of the year, May it not come into the number of the months.

Weeks.

Dan 10:2 In those days I, Daniel, was mourning three full weeks.

Luke 18:12 I fast twice a week; I give tithes of all that I possess.'

Days.

Gen 8:3 And the waters receded continually from the earth. At the end of the hundred and fifty days the waters decreased.

Job 1:4 And his sons would go and feast *in their* houses, each on his *appointed* day, and would send and invite their three sisters to eat and drink with them.

Luke 11:3 Give us day by day our daily bread.

Hours, after the captivity.

Dan 5:5 In the same hour the fingers of a man's hand appeared and wrote opposite the lampstand on the plaster of the wall of the king's palace; and the king saw the part of the hand that wrote.

John 11:9 Jesus answered, "Are there not twelve hours in the day? If anyone walks in the day, he does not stumble, because he sees the light of this world.

Moments of.

Ex 33:5 For the LORD had said to Moses, "Say to the children of Israel, 'You *are* a stiff-necked people. I could come up into your midst in one moment and consume you. Now therefore, take off your ornaments, that I may know what to do to you.' "

Luke 4:5 Then the devil, taking Him up on a high mountain, showed Him all the kingdoms of the world in a moment of time.

1 Cor 15:52 in a moment, in the twinkling of an eye, at the last trumpet. For the trumpet will sound, and the dead will be raised incorruptible, and we shall be changed.

The heavenly bodies, appointed as a means for computing.

Gen 1:14 Then God said, "Let there be lights in the firmament of the heavens to divide the day from the night; and let them be for signs and seasons, and for days and years;

The sundial invented for determining.

2 Kin 20:9–11 Then Isaiah said, "This is the sign to you from the LORD, that the LORD will do the thing which He has spoken: *shall* the shadow go forward ten degrees or go backward ten degrees?" **10** And Hezekiah answered, "It is an easy thing for the shadow to go down ten degrees; no, but let the shadow go backward ten degrees." **11** So Isaiah the prophet cried out to the LORD, and He brought the shadow ten degrees backward, by which it had gone down on the sundial of Ahaz.

Eras from which, computed

Nativity of the patriarchs during the patriarchal age.

Gen 7:11 In the six hundredth year of Noah's life, in the second month, the seventeenth day of the month, on that day all the fountains of the great deep were broken up, and the windows of heaven were opened.

Gen 8:13 And it came to pass in the six hundred and first year, in the first *month,* the first *day* of the month, that the waters were dried up from the earth; and Noah removed the covering of the ark and looked, and indeed the surface of the ground was dry.

Gen 17:1 When Abram was ninety-nine years old, the LORD appeared to Abram and said to him, "I *am* Almighty God; walk before Me and be blameless.

The exodus from Egypt.

Ex 19:1 In the third month after the children of Israel had gone out of the land of Egypt, on the same day, they came *to* the Wilderness of Sinai.

Ex 40:17 And it came to pass in the first month of the second year, on the first *day* of the month, *that* the tabernacle was raised up.

Num 9:1 Now the LORD spoke to Moses in the Wilderness of Sinai, in the first month of the second year after they had come out of the land of Egypt, saying:

Num 33:38 Then Aaron the priest went up to Mount Hor at the command of the LORD, and died there in the fortieth year after the children of Israel had come out of the land of Egypt, on the first *day* of the fifth month.

1 Kin 6:1 And it came to pass in the four hundred and eightieth year after the children of Israel had come out of the land of Egypt, in the fourth year of Solomon's reign over Israel, in the month of Ziv, which *is* the second month, that he began to build the house of the LORD.

The Jubilee.

Lev 25:15 According to the number of years after the Jubilee you shall buy from your neighbor, and according to the number of years of crops he shall sell to you.

Accession of kings.

1 Kin 15:1 In the eighteenth year of King Jeroboam the son of Nebat, Abijam became king over Judah.

Is 36:1 Now it came to pass in the fourteenth year of King Hezekiah *that* Sennacherib king of Assyria came up against all the fortified cities of Judah and took them.

Jer 1:2 to whom the word of the LORD came in the days of Josiah the son of Amon, king of Judah, in the thirteenth year of his reign.

Luke 3:1 Now in the fifteenth year of the reign of Tiberius Caesar, Pontius Pilate being governor of Judea, Herod being tetrarch of Galilee, his brother Philip tetrarch of Iturea and the region of Trachonitis, and Lysanias tetrarch of Abilene,

Building of the temple.

1 Kin 9:10 Now it happened at the end of twenty years, when Solomon had built the two houses, the house of the LORD and the king's house

2 Chr 8:1 It came to pass at the end of twenty years,

when Solomon had built the house of the LORD and his own house,

The captivity.

Ezek 1:1 Now it came to pass in the thirtieth year, in the fourth *month,* on the fifth *day* of the month, as I *was* among the captives by the River Chebar, *that* the heavens were opened and I saw visions of God.

Ezek 33:21 And it came to pass in the twelfth year of our captivity, in the tenth *month,* on the fifth *day* of the month, *that* one who had escaped from Jerusalem came to me and said, "The city has been captured!"

Ezek 40:1 In the twenty-fifth year of our captivity, at the beginning of the year, on the tenth *day* of the month, in the fourteenth year after the city was captured, on the very same day the hand of the LORD was upon me; and He took me there.

In prophetic language, means a prophetic year, or 360 natural days.

Dan 12:7 Then I heard the man clothed in linen, who *was* above the waters of the river, when he held up his right hand and his left hand to heaven, and swore by Him who lives forever, that *it shall be* for a time, times, and half *a time;* and when the power of the holy people has been completely shattered, all these *things* shall be finished.

Rev 12:14 But the woman was given two wings of a great eagle, that she might fly into the wilderness to her place, where she is nourished for a time and times and half a time, from the presence of the serpent.

Shortness of man's portion of.

Ps 89:47 Remember how short my time is; For what futility have You created all the children of men?

Should be redeemed.

Eph 5:16 redeeming the time, because the days are evil.

Col 4:5 Walk in wisdom toward those *who are* outside, redeeming the time.

Should be spent in fear of God.

1 Pet 1:17 And if you call on the Father, who without partiality judges according to each one's work, conduct yourselves throughout the time of your stay *here* in fear;

Particular periods of, mentioned

The ancient time.

Is 45:21 Tell and bring forth *your case;* Yes, let them take counsel together. Who has declared this from ancient time? *Who* has told it from that time? *Have* not I, the LORD? And *there is* no other God besides Me, A just God and a Savior; *There is* none besides Me.

The accepted time.

Is 49:8 Thus says the LORD: "In an acceptable time I have heard You, And in the day of salvation I have helped You; I will preserve You and give You As a covenant to the people, To restore the earth, To cause them to inherit the desolate heritages;

2 Cor 6:2 For He says: *"In an acceptable time I have heard you, And in the day of salvation I have helped you."* Behold, now *is* the accepted time; behold, now *is* the day of salvation.

The time of punishment.

Jer 46:21 Also her mercenaries are in her midst like fat bulls, For they also are turned back, They have fled away together. They did not stand, For the day of their calamity had come upon them, The time of their punishment.

Jer 50:27 Slay all her bulls, Let them go down to the slaughter. Woe to them! For their day has come, the time of their punishment.

The time of refreshing.

Acts 3:19 Repent therefore and be converted, that your sins may be blotted out, so that times of refreshing may come from the presence of the Lord,

The time of restoration of all things.

Acts 3:21 whom heaven must receive until the times of restoration of all things, which God has spoken by the mouth of all His holy prophets since the world began.

The time of reformation.

Heb 9:10 *concerned* only with foods and drinks, various washings, and fleshly ordinances imposed until the time of reformation.

The time of healing.

Jer 14:19 Have You utterly rejected Judah? Has Your soul loathed Zion? Why have You stricken us so that *there is* no healing for us? We looked for peace, but *there was* no good; And for the time of healing, and there was trouble.

The time of need.

Heb 4:16 Let us therefore come boldly to the throne of grace, that we may obtain mercy and find grace to help in time of need.

The time of temptation.

Luke 8:13 But the ones on the rock *are those* who, when they hear, receive the word with joy; and these have no root, who believe for a while and in time of temptation fall away.

The evil time.

Ps 37:19 They shall not be ashamed in the evil time, And in the days of famine they shall be satisfied.

Eccl 9:12 For man also does not know his time: Like fish taken in a cruel net, Like birds caught in a snare, So the sons of men *are* snared in an evil time, When it falls suddenly upon them.

The time of trouble.

Ps 27:5 For in the time of trouble He shall hide me in His pavilion; In the secret place of His tabernacle He shall hide me; He shall set me high upon a rock.

Jer 14:8 O the Hope of Israel, his Savior in time of trouble, Why should You be like a stranger in the land, And like a traveler *who* turns aside to tarry for a night?

All events of, preappointed by God.

Acts 17:26 And He has made from one blood every nation of men to dwell on all the face of the earth, and has determined their preappointed times and the boundaries of their dwellings,

All God's purposes accomplish at fullness of.

Mark 1:15 and saying, "The time is fulfilled, and the kingdom of God is at hand. Repent, and believe in the gospel."

Gal 4:4 But when the fullness of the time had come, God sent forth His Son, born of a woman, born under the law,

TIMOTHY

Had mixed parentage.

Acts 16:1 Then he came to Derbe and Lystra. And behold, a certain disciple was there, named Timothy, *the* son of a certain Jewish woman who believed, but his father *was* Greek.

Acts 16:3 Paul wanted to have him go on with him. And he took *him* and circumcised him because of the Jews who were in that region, for they all knew that his father was Greek.

Became a believer as a child.

2 Tim 1:5 when I call to remembrance the genuine faith that is in you, which dwelt first in your grandmother Lois and your mother Eunice, and I am persuaded is in you also.

2 Tim 3:15 and that from childhood you have known the Holy Scriptures, which are able to make you wise for salvation through faith which is in Christ Jesus.

Joined Paul's ministry.

Acts 16:1–3 Then he came to Derbe and Lystra. And behold, a certain disciple was there, named Timothy, *the* son of a certain Jewish woman who believed, but his father *was* Greek. **2** He was well spoken of by the brethren who were at Lystra and Iconium. **3** Paul wanted to have him go on with him. And he took *him* and circumcised him because of the Jews who were in that region, for they all knew that his father was Greek.

Set apart for ministry.

1 Tim 4:14 Do not neglect the gift that is in you, which was given to you by prophecy with the laying on of the hands of the eldership.

Rejoined Paul at Corinth.

Acts 18:1–5 After these things Paul departed from Athens and went to Corinth. **2** And he found a certain Jew named Aquila, born in Pontus, who had recently come from Italy with his wife Priscilla (because Claudius had commanded all the Jews to depart from Rome); and he came to them. **3** So, because he was of the same trade, he stayed with them and worked; for by occupation they were tentmakers. **4** And he reasoned in the synagogue every Sabbath, and persuaded both Jews and Greeks. **5** When Silas and Timothy had come from Macedonia, Paul was compelled by the Spirit, and testified to the Jews *that* Jesus *is* the Christ.

Went with Paul to Jerusalem.

Acts 20:1–5 After the uproar had ceased, Paul called the disciples to *himself*, embraced *them*, and departed to go to Macedonia. **2** Now when he had gone over that region and encouraged them with many words, he came to Greece **3** and stayed three months. And when the Jews plotted against him as he was about to sail to Syria, he decided to return through Macedonia. **4** And Sopater of Berea accompanied him to Asia—also Aristarchus and Secundus of the Thessalonians, and Gaius of Derbe, and Timothy, and Tychicus and Trophimus of Asia. **5** These men, going ahead, waited for us at Troas.

Sent to Thessalonica.

1 Thess 3:1–2 Therefore, when we could no longer endure it, we thought it good to be left in Athens alone,

2 and sent Timothy, our brother and minister of God, and our fellow laborer in the gospel of Christ, to establish you and encourage you concerning your faith,

1 Thess 3:6 But now that Timothy has come to us from you, and brought us good news of your faith and love, and that you always have good remembrance of us, greatly desiring to see us, as we also *to see* you—

With Paul in Rome.

Phil 1:1 Paul and Timothy, bondservants of Jesus Christ, To all the saints in Christ Jesus who are in Philippi, with the bishops and deacons:

Phil 2:19 But I trust in the Lord Jesus to send Timothy to you shortly, that I also may be encouraged when I know your state.

Phil 2:23 Therefore I hope to send him at once, as soon as I see how it goes with me.

Instructed and exhorted by Paul.

1 Tim 4:12–16 Let no one despise your youth, but be an example to the believers in word, in conduct, in love, in spirit, in faith, in purity. 13 Till I come, give attention to reading, to exhortation, to doctrine. 14 Do not neglect the gift that is in you, which was given to you by prophecy with the laying on of the hands of the eldership. 15 Meditate on these things; give yourself entirely to them, that your progress may be evident to all. 16 Take heed to yourself and to the doctrine. Continue in them, for in doing this you will save both yourself and those who hear you.

1 Tim 6:20–21 O Timothy! Guard what was committed to your trust, avoiding the profane *and* idle babblings and contradictions of what is falsely called knowledge— 21 by professing it some have strayed concerning the faith. Grace *be* with you. Amen.

2 Tim 1:6–9 Therefore I remind you to stir up the gift of God which is in you through the laying on of my hands. 7 For God has not given us a spirit of fear, but of power and of love and of a sound mind. 8 Therefore do not be ashamed of the testimony of our Lord, nor of me His prisoner, but share with me in the sufferings for the gospel according to the power of God, 9 who has saved us and called *us* with a holy calling, not according to our works, but according to His own purpose and grace which was given to us in Christ Jesus before time began,

TITHE

The tenth of anything.

1 Sam 8:15 He will take a tenth of your grain and your vintage, and give it to his officers and servants.

1 Sam 8:17 He will take a tenth of your sheep. And you will be his servants.

Antiquity of the custom of giving one to God's ministers.

Gen 14:20 And blessed be God Most High, Who has delivered your enemies into your hand." And he gave him a tithe of all.

Heb 7:6 but he whose genealogy is not derived from them received tithes from Abraham and blessed him who had the promises.

Considered a just return to God for his blessings.

Gen 28:22 And this stone which I have set as a pillar shall be God's house, and of all that You give me I will surely give a tenth to You."

Under the law belonged to God.

Lev 27:30 And all the tithe of the land, *whether* of the seed of the land *or* of the fruit of the tree, *is* the LORD's. It *is* holy to the LORD.

Various forms of,

All the produce of the land.

Lev 27:30 And all the tithe of the land, *whether* of the seed of the land *or* of the fruit of the tree, *is* the LORD's. It *is* holy to the LORD.

All cattle.

Lev 27:32 And concerning the tithe of the herd or the flock, of whatever passes under the rod, the tenth one shall be holy to the LORD.

Holy things dedicated.

2 Chr 31:6 And the children of Israel and Judah, who dwelt in the cities of Judah, brought the tithe of oxen and sheep; also the tithe of holy things which were consecrated to the LORD their God they laid in heaps.

Given by God to the Levites for their services.

Num 18:21 "Behold, I have given the children of Levi all the tithes in Israel as an inheritance in return for the work which they perform, the work of the tabernacle of meeting.

Num 18:24 For the tithes of the children of Israel, which they offer up *as* a heave offering to the LORD, I have given to the Levites as an inheritance; therefore I have said to them, 'Among the children of Israel they shall have no inheritance.' "

Neh 10:37 to bring the firstfruits of our dough, our offerings, the fruit from all kinds of trees, *the* new wine and oil, to the priests, to the storerooms of the house of our God; and to bring the tithes of our land to the Levites, for the Levites should receive the tithes in all our farming communities.

The tenth of, offered by the Levites as a heave offering to God.

Num 18:26–27 "Speak thus to the Levites, and say to them: 'When you take from the children of Israel the tithes which I have given you from them as your inheritance, then you shall offer up a heave offering of it to the LORD, a tenth of the tithe. 27 And your heave offering shall be reckoned to you as though *it were* the grain of the threshing floor and as the fullness of the winepress.

The tenth of, given by the Levites to the priests as their portion.

Num 18:26 "Speak thus to the Levites, and say to them: 'When you take from the children of Israel the tithes which I have given you from them as your inheritance, then you shall offer up a heave offering of it to the LORD, a tenth of the tithe.

Num 18:28 Thus you shall also offer a heave offering to the LORD from all your tithes which you receive from the children of Israel, and you shall give the LORD's heave offering from it to Aaron the priest.

Neh 10:38 And the priest, the descendant of Aaron, shall be with the Levites when the Levites receive tithes; and the Levites shall bring up a tenth of the tithes to the house of our God, to the rooms of the storehouse.

Reasonableness of appointing, for the Levites.

Num 18:20 Then the LORD said to Aaron: "You shall have no inheritance in their land, nor shall you have any portion among them; I *am* your portion and your inheritance among the children of Israel.

Num 18:23–24 But the Levites shall perform the work of the tabernacle of meeting, and they shall bear their iniquity; *it shall be* a statute forever, throughout your generations, that among the children of Israel they shall have no inheritance. **24** For the tithes of the children of Israel, which they offer up *as* a heave offering to the LORD, I have given to the Levites as an inheritance; therefore I have said to them, 'Among the children of Israel they shall have no inheritance.' "

Josh 13:33 But to the tribe of Levi Moses had given no inheritance; the LORD God of Israel *was* their inheritance, as He had said to them.

When redeemed, a fifth part of the value to be added.

Lev 27:31 If a man wants at all to redeem *any* of his tithes, he shall add one-fifth to it.

Punishment for changing.

Lev 27:33 He shall not inquire whether it is good or bad, nor shall he exchange it; and if he exchanges it at all, then both it and the one exchanged for it shall be holy; it shall not be redeemed.' "

The Jews slow in giving.

Neh 13:10 I also realized that the portions for the Levites had not been given *them;* for each of the Levites and the singers who did the work had gone back to his field.

The Jews reproved for withholding.

Mal 3:8 "Will a man rob God? Yet you have robbed Me! But you say, 'In what way have we robbed You?' In tithes and offerings.

The pious rulers of Israel caused the payment of.

2 Chr 31:5 As soon as the commandment was circulated, the children of Israel brought in abundance the firstfruits of grain and wine, oil and honey, and of all the produce of the field; and they brought in abundantly the tithe of everything.

Neh 13:11–12 So I contended with the rulers, and said, "Why is the house of God forsaken?" And I gathered them together and set them in their place. **12** Then all Judah brought the tithe of the grain and the new wine and the oil to the storehouse.

Treasurers appointed over, for distributing.

2 Chr 31:12 Then they faithfully brought in the offerings, the tithes, and the dedicated things; Cononiah the Levite had charge of them, and Shimei his brother *was* the next.

Neh 13:13 And I appointed as treasurers over the storehouse Shelemiah the priest and Zadok the scribe, and of the Levites, Pedaiah; and next to them *was* Hanan the son of Zaccur, the son of Mattaniah; for they were considered faithful, and their task *was* to distribute to their brethren.

The Pharisees scrupulous in paying.

Luke 11:42 "But woe to you Pharisees! For you tithe mint and rue and all manner of herbs, and pass by justice and the love of God. These you ought to have done, without leaving the others undone.

Luke 18:12 I fast twice a week; I give tithes of all that I possess.'

A second,

Its value yearly brought to the tabernacle and a portion eaten before the Lord.

Deut 12:6–7 There you shall take your burnt offerings, your sacrifices, your tithes, the heave offerings of your hand, your vowed offerings, your freewill offerings, and the firstborn of your herds and flocks. **7** And there you shall eat before the LORD your God, and you shall rejoice in all to which you have put your hand, you and your households, in which the LORD your God has blessed you.

Deut 12:17–19 You may not eat within your gates the tithe of your grain or your new wine or your oil, of the firstborn of your herd or your flock, of any of your offerings which you vow, of your freewill offerings, or of the heave offering of your hand. **18** But you must eat them before the LORD your God in the place which the LORD your God chooses, you and your son and your daughter, your male servant and your female servant, and the Levite who *is* within your gates; and you shall rejoice before the LORD your God in all to which you put your hands. **19** Take heed to yourself that you do not forsake the Levite as long as you live in your land.

Deut 14:22–27 "You shall truly tithe all the increase of your grain that the field produces year by year. **23** And you shall eat before the LORD your God, in the place where He chooses to make His name abide, the tithe of your grain and your new wine and your oil, of the firstborn of your herds and your flocks, that you may learn to fear the LORD your God always. **24** But if the journey is too long for you, so that you are not able to carry *the tithe, or* if the place where the LORD your God chooses to put His name is too far from you, when the LORD your God has blessed you, **25** then you shall exchange *it* for money, take the money in your hand, and go to the place which the LORD your God chooses. **26** And you shall spend that money for whatever your heart desires: for oxen or sheep, for wine or similar drink, for whatever your heart desires; you shall eat there before the LORD your God, and you shall rejoice, you and your household. **27** You shall not forsake the Levite who *is* within your gates, for he has no part nor inheritance with you.

To be consumed at home every third year to promote hospitality and charity.

Deut 14:28–29 "At the end of *every* third year you shall bring out the tithe of your produce of that year and store *it* up within your gates. **29** And the Levite, because he has no portion nor inheritance with you, and the stranger and the fatherless and the widow who *are* within your gates, may come and eat and be satisfied, that the LORD your God may bless you in all the work of your hand which you do.

Deut 26:12–15 "When you have finished laying aside all the tithe of your increase in the third year—the year of tithing—and have given *it* to the Levite, the stranger, the fatherless, and the widow, so that they may eat within your gates and be filled, **13** then you shall say before the LORD your God: 'I have removed the holy *tithe* from *my* house, and also have given them to the Levite, the stranger, the fatherless, and the widow, according to all Your commandments which You have commanded me; I have not transgressed Your commandments, nor have I forgotten *them*. **14** I have not eaten any of it when in mourning, nor have I removed *any* of it for an unclean *use*, nor given *any* of it for the dead. I have obeyed the voice of the LORD my God, and have done according to all that You have commanded me. **15** Look down from Your holy habitation, from heaven, and bless Your people Israel and the land which You have given us, just as You swore to our fathers, "a land flowing with milk and honey." '

TONGUE(S). *SEE ALSO* SPEECH

Sinfulness of the.

Ps 5:9 For *there is* no faithfulness in their mouth; Their inward part *is* destruction; Their throat *is* an open tomb; They flatter with their tongue.

Ps 34:13 Keep your tongue from evil, And your lips from speaking deceit.

Ps 39:1 I said, "I will guard my ways, Lest I sin with my tongue; I will restrain my mouth with a muzzle, While the wicked are before me."

Ps 52:4 You love all devouring words, *You* deceitful tongue.

Ps 109:2 For the mouth of the wicked and the mouth of the deceitful Have opened against me; They have spoken against me with a lying tongue.

Ps 120:2–3 Deliver my soul, O LORD, from lying lips *And* from a deceitful tongue. **3** What shall be given to you, Or what shall be done to you, You false tongue?

Prov 6:12 A worthless person, a wicked man, Walks with a perverse mouth;

Prov 6:17 A proud look, A lying tongue, Hands that shed innocent blood,

Prov 10:6 Blessings *are* on the head of the righteous, But violence covers the mouth of the wicked.

Prov 10:8 The wise in heart will receive commands, But a prating fool will fall.

Prov 10:13–14 Wisdom is found on the lips of him who has understanding, But a rod *is* for the back of him who is devoid of understanding. **14** Wise *people* store up knowledge, But the mouth of the foolish *is* near destruction.

Prov 10:18–19 Whoever hides hatred *has* lying lips, And whoever spreads slander *is* a fool. **19** In the multitude of words sin is not lacking, But he who restrains his lips *is* wise.

Prov 10:31–32 The mouth of the righteous brings forth wisdom, But the perverse tongue will be cut out. **32** The lips of the righteous know what is acceptable, But the mouth of the wicked *what is* perverse.

Prov 12:23 A prudent man conceals knowledge, But the heart of fools proclaims foolishness.

Prov 13:3 He who guards his mouth preserves his life, *But* he who opens wide his lips shall have destruction.

Prov 15:1–2 A soft answer turns away wrath, But a harsh word stirs up anger. **2** The tongue of the wise uses knowledge rightly, But the mouth of fools pours forth foolishness.

Prov 15:23 A man has joy by the answer of his mouth, And a word *spoken* in due season, how good *it is!*

Prov 15:26 The thoughts of the wicked *are* an abomination to the LORD, But *the words* of the pure *are* pleasant.

Prov 15:28 The heart of the righteous studies how to answer, But the mouth of the wicked pours forth evil.

Prov 15:31–33 The ear that hears the rebukes of life Will abide among the wise. **32** He who disdains instruction despises his own soul, But he who heeds rebuke gets understanding. **33** The fear of the LORD *is* the instruction of wisdom, And before honor *is* humility.

Prov 17:20 He who has a deceitful heart finds no good, And he who has a perverse tongue falls into evil.

Prov 17:28 Even a fool is counted wise when he holds his peace; *When* he shuts his lips, *he is considered* perceptive.

Prov 18:2 A fool has no delight in understanding, But in expressing his own heart.

Prov 18:6–8 A fool's lips enter into contention, And his mouth calls for blows. **7** A fool's mouth *is* his destruction, And his lips *are* the snare of his soul. **8** The words of a talebearer *are* like tasty trifles, And they go down into the inmost body.

Prov 26:28 A lying tongue hates *those who are* crushed by it, And a flattering mouth works ruin.

Prov 28:23 He who rebukes a man will find more favor afterward Than he who flatters with the tongue.

Is 59:3 For your hands are defiled with blood, And your fingers with iniquity; Your lips have spoken lies, Your tongue has muttered perversity.

James 1:26 If anyone among you thinks he is religious, and does not bridle his tongue but deceives his own heart, this one's religion *is* useless.

James 3:1–12 My brethren, let not many of you become teachers, knowing that we shall receive a stricter judgment. **2** For we all stumble in many things. If anyone does not stumble in word, he *is* a perfect man, able also to bridle the whole body. **3** Indeed, we put bits in horses' mouths that they may obey us, and we turn their whole body. **4** Look also at ships: although they are so large and are driven by fierce winds, they are turned by a very small rudder wherever the pilot desires. **5** Even so the tongue is a little member and boasts great things. See how great a forest a little fire kindles! **6** And the tongue *is* a fire, a world of iniquity. The tongue is so set among our members that it defiles the whole body, and sets on fire the course of nature; and it is set on fire by hell. **7** For every kind of beast and bird, of reptile and creature of the sea, is tamed and has been tamed by mankind. **8** But no man can tame the tongue. *It is* an unruly evil, full of deadly poison. **9** With it we bless our God and Father, and with it we curse men, who have been made in the similitude of God. **10** Out of the same mouth proceed blessing and cursing. My brethren, these things ought not to be so. **11** Does a spring send forth fresh *water* and bitter from the same opening? **12** Can a fig tree, my brethren, bear olives, or a grapevine bear figs? Thus no spring yields both salt water and fresh.

Cf. Ps 39:1; Matt 12:36; Rom 3:9–18

Related to the heart.

Prov 10:20 The tongue of the righteous *is* choice silver; The heart of the wicked *is worth* little.

Matt 12:35 A good man out of the good treasure of his heart brings forth good things, and an evil man out of the evil treasure brings forth evil things.

Matt 15:18–19 But those things which proceed out of the mouth come from the heart, and they defile a man. **19** For out of the heart proceed evil thoughts, murders, adulteries, fornications, thefts, false witness, blasphemies.

Luke 6:45 A good man out of the good treasure of his heart brings forth good; and an evil man out of the evil treasure of his heart brings forth evil. For out of the abundance of the heart his mouth speaks.

Cf. Prov 18:21

Gift of, as language.

Acts 2:4–12 And they were all filled with the Holy Spirit and began to speak with other tongues, as the Spirit gave them utterance. **5** And there were dwelling in Jerusalem Jews, devout men, from every nation under heaven. **6** And when this sound occurred, the multitude came together, and were confused, because everyone heard them speak in his own language. **7** Then they were all amazed and marveled, saying to one another, "Look, are not all these who speak Galileans? **8** And how *is it that* we hear, each in our own language in which we were born? **9** Parthians and Medes and Elamites, those dwelling in Mesopotamia, Judea and Cappadocia, Pontus and Asia, **10** Phrygia and Pamphylia, Egypt and the parts of Libya adjoining Cyrene, visitors from Rome, both Jews and proselytes, **11** Cretans and Arabs—we hear them speaking in our own tongues the wonderful works of God." **12** So they were all amazed and perplexed, saying to one another, "Whatever could this mean?"

1 Cor 12:10 to another the working of miracles, to another prophecy, to another discerning of spirits, to another *different* kinds of tongues, to another the interpretation of tongues.

Cf. 1 Cor 13:8; 14:2–39

TOWERS

Origin and antiquity of.

Gen 11:4 And they said, "Come, let us build ourselves a city, and a tower whose top *is* in the heavens; let us make a name for ourselves, lest we be scattered abroad over the face of the whole earth."

Were built

In cities.

Judg 9:51 But there was a strong tower in the city, and all the men and women—all the people of the city—fled there and shut themselves in; then they went up to the top of the tower.

On the walls of cities.

2 Chr 14:7 Therefore he said to Judah, "Let us build these cities and make walls around *them*, and towers, gates, and bars, *while* the land *is* yet before us, because we have sought the LORD our God; we have sought *Him*, and He has given us rest on every side." So they built and prospered.

2 Chr 26:9 And Uzziah built towers in Jerusalem at the Corner Gate, at the Valley Gate, and at the corner buttress of the wall; then he fortified them.

In the forests.

2 Chr 27:4 Moreover he built cities in the mountains of Judah, and in the forests he built fortresses and towers.

In the deserts.

2 Chr 26:10 Also he built towers in the desert. He dug many wells, for he had much livestock, both in the lowlands and in the plains; *he also had* farmers and vinedressers in the mountains and in Carmel, for he loved the soil.

In vineyards.

Is 5:2 He dug it up and cleared out its stones, And planted it with the choicest vine. He built a tower in its midst, And also made a winepress in it; So He expected *it* to bring forth *good* grapes, But it brought forth wild grapes.

Matt 21:33 "Hear another parable: There was a certain landowner who planted a vineyard and set a hedge around it, dug a winepress in it and built a tower. And he leased it to vinedressers and went into a far country.

Frequently very high.

Is 2:15 Upon every high tower, And upon every fortified wall;

Frequently strong and well fortified.

Judg 9:51 But there was a strong tower in the city, and all the men and women—all the people of the city—fled there and shut themselves in; then they went up to the top of the tower.

2 Chr 26:9 And Uzziah built towers in Jerusalem at the Corner Gate, at the Valley Gate, and at the corner buttress of the wall; then he fortified them.

Were used as armories.

Song 4:4 Your neck *is* like the tower of David, Built for an armory, On which hang a thousand bucklers, All shields of mighty men.

Were used as citadels in time of war.

Judg 9:51 But there was a strong tower in the city, and all the men and women—all the people of the city—fled there and shut themselves in; then they went up to the top of the tower.

Ezek 27:11 Men of Arvad with your army *were* on your walls *all* around, And the men of Gammad were in your towers; They hung their shields on your walls *all* around; They made your beauty perfect.

Watchmen posted on, in times of danger.

2 Kin 9:17 Now a watchman stood on the tower in Jezreel, and he saw the company of Jehu as he came, and said, "I see a company of men." And Joram said, "Get a horseman and send him to meet them, and let him say, '*Is it* peace?' "

Hab 2:1 I will stand my watch And set myself on the rampart, And watch to see what He will say to me, And what I will answer when I am corrected.

Names of,

Babel.

Gen 11:9 Therefore its name is called Babel, because there the LORD confused the language of all the earth;

and from there the LORD scattered them abroad over the face of all the earth.

Eder.

Gen 35:21 Then Israel journeyed and pitched his tent beyond the tower of Eder.

Penuel.

Judg 8:17 Then he tore down the tower of Penuel and killed the men of the city.

Shechem.

Judg 9:46 Now when all the men of the tower of Shechem had heard *that,* they entered the stronghold of the temple of the god Berith.

Thebez.

Judg 9:50–51 Then Abimelech went to Thebez, and he encamped against Thebez and took it. **51** But there was a strong tower in the city, and all the men and women—all the people of the city—fled there and shut themselves in; then they went up to the top of the tower.

David.

Song 4:4 Your neck *is* like the tower of David, Built for an armory, On which hang a thousand bucklers, All shields of mighty men.

Lebanon.

Song 7:4 Your neck *is* like an ivory tower, Your eyes *like* the pools in Heshbon By the gate of Bath Rabbim. Your nose *is* like the tower of Lebanon Which looks toward Damascus.

Of the Ovens.

Neh 3:11 Malchijah the son of Harim and Hashub the son of Pahath-Moab repaired another section, as well as the Tower of the Ovens.

Of the Hundred.

Neh 12:39 and above the Gate of Ephraim, above the Old Gate, above the Fish Gate, the Tower of Hananel, the Tower of the Hundred, as far as the Sheep Gate; and they stopped by the Gate of the Prison.

Jezreel.

2 Kin 9:17 Now a watchman stood on the tower in Jezreel, and he saw the company of Jehu as he came, and said, "I see a company of men." And Joram said, "Get a horseman and send him to meet them, and let him say, '*Is it* peace?' "

Hananel.

Jer 31:38 "Behold, the days are coming, says the LORD, that the city shall be built for the LORD from the Tower of Hananel to the Corner Gate.

Zech 14:10 All the land shall be turned into a plain from Geba to Rimmon south of Jerusalem. *Jerusalem* shall be raised up and inhabited in her place from Benjamin's Gate to the place of the First Gate and the Corner Gate, and *from* the Tower of Hananel to the king's winepresses.

Syene.

Ezek 29:10 Indeed, therefore, I *am* against you and against your rivers, and I will make the land of Egypt utterly waste and desolate, from Migdol *to* Syene, as far as the border of Ethiopia.

Ezek 30:6 'Thus says the LORD: "Those who uphold Egypt shall fall, And the pride of her power shall come down. From Migdol *to* Syene Those within her shall fall by the sword," Says the Lord GOD.

Siloam.

Luke 13:4 Or those eighteen on whom the tower in Siloam fell and killed them, do you think that they were worse sinners than all *other* men who dwelt in Jerusalem?

Of Jerusalem, remarkable for number, strength, and beauty.

Ps 48:12 Walk about Zion, And go all around her. Count her towers;

Frequently broken down in war.

Judg 8:17 Then he tore down the tower of Penuel and killed the men of the city.

Judg 9:49 So each of the people likewise cut down his own bough and followed Abimelech, put *them* against the stronghold, and set the stronghold on fire above them, so that all the people of the tower of Shechem died, about a thousand men and women.

Ezek 26:4 And they shall destroy the walls of Tyre and break down her towers; I will also scrape her dust from her, and make her like the top of a rock.

Frequently left desolate.

Is 32:14 Because the palaces will be forsaken, The bustling city will be deserted. The forts and towers will become lairs forever, A joy of wild donkeys, a pasture of flocks—

Zeph 3:6 "I have cut off nations, Their fortresses are devastated; I have made their streets desolate, With none passing by. Their cities are destroyed; *There is* no one, no inhabitant.

Illustrative of

God as the protector of His people.

2 Sam 22:3 The God of my strength, in whom I will trust; My shield and the horn of my salvation, My stronghold and my refuge; My Savior, You save me from violence.

2 Sam 22:51 "*He is* the tower of salvation to His king, And shows mercy to His anointed, To David and his descendants forevermore."

Ps 18:2 The LORD is my rock and my fortress and my deliverer; My God, my strength, in whom I will trust; My shield and the horn of my salvation, my stronghold.

Ps 61:3 For You have been a shelter for me, A strong tower from the enemy.

The name of the Lord.

Prov 18:10 The name of the LORD *is* a strong tower; The righteous run to it and are safe.

Ministers.

Jer 6:27 "I have set you *as* an assayer *and* a fortress among My people, That you may know and test their way.

Mount Zion.

Mic 4:8 And you, O tower of the flock, The stronghold of the daughter of Zion, To you shall it come, Even the former dominion shall come, The kingdom of the daughter of Jerusalem."

The proud and haughty.

Is 2:15 Upon every high tower, And upon every fortified wall;

Is 30:25 There will be on every high mountain And on every high hill Rivers *and* streams of waters, In the day of the great slaughter, When the towers fall.

TRAVELERS

General references to.

Judg 19:17 And when he raised his eyes, he saw the traveler in the open square of the city; and the old man said, "Where are you going, and where do you come from?"

Is 35:8 A highway shall be there, and a road, And it shall be called the Highway of Holiness. The unclean shall not pass over it, But it *shall be* for others. Whoever walks the road, although a fool, Shall not go astray.

Preparations made by, alluded to.

Ezek 12:3–4 "Therefore, son of man, prepare your belongings for captivity, and go into captivity by day in their sight. You shall go from your place into captivity to another place in their sight. It may be that they will consider, though they *are* a rebellious house. 4 By day you shall bring out your belongings in their sight, as though going into captivity; and at evening you shall go in their sight, like those who go into captivity.

Often collected together and formed caravans.

Gen 37:25 And they sat down to eat a meal. Then they lifted their eyes and looked, and there was a company of Ishmaelites, coming from Gilead with their camels, bearing spices, balm, and myrrh, on their way to carry *them* down to Egypt.

Is 21:13 The burden against Arabia. In the forest in Arabia you will lodge, O you traveling companies of Dedanites.

Luke 2:44 but supposing Him to have been in the company, they went a day's journey, and sought Him among *their* relatives and acquaintants.

Often hired persons as guides.

Num 10:31–32 So *Moses* said, "Please do not leave, inasmuch as you know how we are to camp in the wilderness, and you can be our eyes. 32 And it shall be, if you go with us—indeed it shall be—that whatever good the LORD will do to us, the same we will do to you."

Job 29:15 I *was* eyes to the blind, And I *was* feet to the lame.

Friends of,

Often supplied them with provision.

Gen 21:14 So Abraham rose early in the morning, and took bread and a skin of water; and putting *it* on her shoulder, he gave *it* and the boy to Hagar, and sent her away. Then she departed and wandered in the Wilderness of Beersheba.

Gen 44:1 And he commanded the steward of his house, saying, "Fill the men's sacks with food, as much as they can carry, and put each man's money in the mouth of his sack.

Jer 40:5 Now while Jeremiah had not yet gone back, *Nebuzaradan said,* "Go back to Gedaliah the son of Ahikam, the son of Shaphan, whom the king of Babylon has made governor over the cities of Judah, and

dwell with him among the people. Or go wherever it seems convenient for you to go." So the captain of the guard gave him rations and a gift and let him go.

Sometimes accompanied them a short way.

2 Sam 19:31 And Barzillai the Gileadite came down from Rogelim and went across the Jordan with the king, to escort him across the Jordan.

Acts 20:38 sorrowing most of all for the words which he spoke, that they would see his face no more. And they accompanied him to the ship.

Acts 21:5 When we had come to the end of those days, we departed and went on our way; and they all accompanied us, with wives and children, till *we were* out of the city. And we knelt down on the shore and prayed.

Frequently commended them to protection of God.

Gen 43:13–14 Take your brother also, and arise, go back to the man. **14** And may God Almighty give you mercy before the man, that he may release your other brother and Benjamin. If I am bereaved, I am bereaved!"

Acts 21:5 When we had come to the end of those days, we departed and went on our way; and they all accompanied us, with wives and children, till *we were* out of the city. And we knelt down on the shore and prayed.

Frequently took leave of them with sorrow.

Acts 20:37 Then they all wept freely, and fell on Paul's neck and kissed him,

Acts 21:6 When we had taken our leave of one another, we boarded the ship, and they returned home.

Often sent them away with music.

Gen 31:27 Why did you flee away secretly, and steal away from me, and not tell me; for I might have sent you away with joy and songs, with timbrel and harp?

Generally commenced their journey early in the morning.

Judg 19:5 Then it came to pass on the fourth day that they arose early in the morning, and he stood to depart; but the young woman's father said to his son-in-law, "Refresh your heart with a morsel of bread, and afterward go your way."

Generally rested at noon.

Gen 18:1–3 Then the LORD appeared to him by the terebinth trees of Mamre, as he was sitting in the tent door in the heat of the day. 2 So he lifted his eyes and looked, and behold, three men were standing by him; and when he saw *them,* he ran from the tent door to meet them, and bowed himself to the ground, 3 and said, "My Lord, if I have now found favor in Your sight, do not pass on by Your servant.

John 4:6 Now Jacob's well was there. Jesus therefore, being wearied from *His* journey, sat thus by the well. It was about the sixth hour.

Halted at evening.

Gen 24:11 And he made his camels kneel down outside the city by a well of water at evening time, the time when women go out to draw *water.*

Generally halted at wells or streams.

Gen 24:11 And he made his camels kneel down outside the city by a well of water at evening time, the time when women go out to draw *water.*

Gen 32:21 So the present went on over before him, but he himself lodged that night in the camp.

Gen 32:23 He took them, sent them over the brook, and sent over what he had.

Ex 15:27 Then they came to Elim, where there *were* twelve wells of water and seventy palm trees; so they camped there by the waters.

1 Sam 30:21 Now David came to the two hundred men who had been so weary that they could not follow David, whom they also had made to stay at the Brook Besor. So they went out to meet David and to meet the people who *were* with him. And when David came near the people, he greeted them.

John 4:6 Now Jacob's well was there. Jesus therefore, being wearied from *His* journey, sat thus by the well. It was about the sixth hour.

Carried with them

Provisions for the way.

Josh 9:11–12 Therefore our elders and all the inhabitants of our country spoke to us, saying, 'Take provisions with you for the journey, and go to meet them, and say to them, "We *are* your servants; now therefore, make a covenant with us." ' **12** This bread of ours we took hot *for* our provision from our houses on the day we departed to come to you. But now look, it is dry and moldy.

Judg 19:19 although we have both straw and fodder for our donkeys, and bread and wine for myself, for your female servant, and for the young man *who is* with your servant; *there is* no lack of anything."

Feed for their beasts of burden.

Gen 42:27 But as one *of them* opened his sack to give his donkey feed at the encampment, he saw his money; and there it was, in the mouth of his sack.

Judg 19:19 although we have both straw and fodder for our donkeys, and bread and wine for myself, for your female servant, and for the young man *who is* with your servant; *there is* no lack of anything."

Skins filled with water, wine, etc.

Gen 21:14–15 So Abraham rose early in the morning, and took bread and a skin of water; and putting *it* on her shoulder, he gave *it* and the boy to Hagar, and sent her away. Then she departed and wandered in the Wilderness of Beersheba. **15** And the water in the skin was used up, and she placed the boy under one of the shrubs.

Josh 9:13 And these wineskins which we filled *were* new, and see, they are torn; and these our garments and our sandals have become old because of the very long journey."

Presents for those who entertained them.

Gen 43:15 So the men took that present and Benjamin, and they took double money in their hand, and arose and went down to Egypt; and they stood before Joseph.

1 Kin 10:2 She came to Jerusalem with a very great retinue, with camels that bore spices, very much gold, and precious stones; and when she came to Solomon, she spoke with him about all that was in her heart.

2 Kin 5:5 Then the king of Syria said, "Go now, and I will send a letter to the king of Israel." So he departed and took with him ten talents of silver, six thousand *shekels* of gold, and ten changes of clothing.

Matt 2:11 And when they had come into the house, they saw the young Child with Mary His mother, and fell down and worshiped Him. And when they had opened their treasures, they presented gifts to Him: gold, frankincense, and myrrh.

Often traveled on foot.

Gen 28:10 Now Jacob went out from Beersheba and went toward Haran.

Gen 32:10 I am not worthy of the least of all the mercies and of all the truth which You have shown Your servant; for I crossed over this Jordan with my staff, and now I have become two companies.

Ex 12:37 Then the children of Israel journeyed from Rameses to Succoth, about six hundred thousand men on foot, besides children.

Acts 20:13 Then we went ahead to the ship and sailed to Assos, there intending to take Paul on board; for so he had given orders, intending himself to go on foot.

On foot, how attired.

Ex 12:11 And thus you shall eat it: *with* a belt on your waist, your sandals on your feet, and your staff in your hand. So you shall eat it in haste. It *is* the LORD's Passover.

After a long journey, described.

Josh 9:4–5 they worked craftily, and went and pretended to be ambassadors. And they took old sacks on their donkeys, old wineskins torn and mended, **5** old and patched sandals on their feet, and old garments on themselves; and all the bread of their provision was dry *and* moldy.

Josh 9:13 And these wineskins which we filled *were* new, and see, they are torn; and these our garments and our sandals have become old because of the very long journey."

Of distinction

Rode on donkeys, camels, etc.

Gen 22:3 So Abraham rose early in the morning and saddled his donkey, and took two of his young men with him, and Isaac his son; and he split the wood for the burnt offering, and arose and went to the place of which God had told him.

Gen 24:64 Then Rebekah lifted her eyes, and when she saw Isaac she dismounted from her camel;

Num 22:21 So Balaam rose in the morning, saddled his donkey, and went with the princes of Moab.

Rode in chariots.

2 Kin 5:9 Then Naaman went with his horses and chariot, and he stood at the door of Elisha's house.

Acts 8:27–28 So he arose and went. And behold, a man of Ethiopia, a eunuch of great authority under Candace the queen of the Ethiopians, who had charge of all her treasury, and had come to Jerusalem to worship, **28** was returning. And sitting in his chariot, he was reading Isaiah the prophet.

Generally attended by running footmen.

1 Sam 25:27 And now this present which your maidservant has brought to my lord, let it be given to the young men who follow my lord.

1 Kin 18:46 Then the hand of the Lord came upon Elijah; and he girded up his loins and ran ahead of Ahab to the entrance of Jezreel.

2 Kin 4:24 Then she saddled a donkey, and said to her servant, "Drive, and go forward; do not slacken the pace for me unless I tell you."

Eccl 10:7 I have seen servants on horses, While princes walk on the ground like servants.

Often preceded by heralds, etc., to have the roads prepared.

Is 40:3–4 The voice of one crying in the wilderness: "Prepare the way of the Lord; Make straight in the desert A highway for our God. 4 Every valley shall be exalted And every mountain and hill brought low; The crooked places shall be made straight And the rough places smooth;

Mark 1:2–3 As it is written in the Prophets: *"Behold, I send My messenger before Your face, Who will prepare Your way before You."* 3 *"The voice of one crying in the wilderness: 'Prepare the way of the Lord; Make His paths straight.' "*

Generally performed their journey with a large retinue.

1 Kin 10:2 She came to Jerusalem with a very great retinue, with camels that bore spices, very much gold, and precious stones; and when she came to Solomon, she spoke with him about all that was in her heart.

2 Kin 5:5 Then the king of Syria said, "Go now, and I will send a letter to the king of Israel." So he departed and took with him ten talents of silver, six thousand *shekels* of gold, and ten changes of clothing.

2 Kin 5:9 Then Naaman went with his horses and chariot, and he stood at the door of Elisha's house.

Frequently demanded provisions by the way.

Judg 8:5 Then he said to the men of Succoth, "Please give loaves of bread to the people who follow me, for they are exhausted, and I am pursuing Zebah and Zalmunna, kings of Midian."

Judg 8:8 Then he went up from there to Penuel and spoke to them in the same way. And the men of Penuel answered him as the men of Succoth had answered.

1 Sam 25:4–13 When David heard in the wilderness that Nabal was shearing his sheep, 5 David sent ten young men; and David said to the young men, "Go up to Carmel, go to Nabal, and greet him in my name. 6 And thus you shall say to him who lives *in prosperity*: 'Peace *be* to you, peace to your house, and peace to all that you have! 7 Now I have heard that you have shearers. Your shepherds were with us, and we did not hurt them, nor was there anything missing from them all the while they were in Carmel. 8 Ask your young men, and they will tell you. Therefore let *my* young men find favor in your eyes, for we come on a feast day. Please give whatever comes to your hand to your servants and to your son David.' " 9 So when David's young men came, they spoke to Nabal according to all these words in the name of David, and waited. 10 Then Nabal answered David's servants, and said, "Who *is* David, and who *is* the son of Jesse? There are many servants nowadays who break away each one from his master. 11 Shall I then take my bread and my water and my meat that

I have killed for my shearers, and give *it* to men when I do not know where they *are* from?" 12 So David's young men turned on their heels and went back; and they came and told him all these words. 13 Then David said to his men, "Every man gird on his sword." So every man girded on his sword, and David also girded on his sword. And about four hundred men went with David, and two hundred stayed with the supplies.

Before setting out gave employment, etc. to their servants.

Matt 25:14 "For *the kingdom of heaven is* like a man traveling to a far country, *who* called his own servants and delivered his goods to them.

Generally treated with great hospitality.

Gen 18:2–8 So he lifted his eyes and looked, and behold, three men were standing by him; and when he saw *them*, he ran from the tent door to meet them, and bowed himself to the ground, 3 and said, "My Lord, if I have now found favor in Your sight, do not pass on by Your servant. 4 Please let a little water be brought, and wash your feet, and rest yourselves under the tree. 5 And I will bring a morsel of bread, that you may refresh your hearts. After that you may pass by, inasmuch as you have come to your servant." They said, "Do as you have said." 6 So Abraham hurried into the tent to Sarah and said, "Quickly, make ready three measures of fine meal; knead *it* and make cakes." 7 And Abraham ran to the herd, took a tender and good calf, gave *it* to a young man, and he hastened to prepare it. 8 So he took butter and milk and the calf which he had prepared, and set *it* before them; and he stood by them under the tree as they ate.

Gen 19:2 And he said, "Here now, my lords, please turn in to your servant's house and spend the night, and wash your feet; then you may rise early and go on your way." And they said, "No, but we will spend the night in the open square."

Gen 24:18–19 So she said, "Drink, my lord." Then she quickly let her pitcher down to her hand, and gave him a drink. 19 And when she had finished giving him a drink, she said, "I will draw *water* for your camels also, until they have finished drinking."

Gen 24:24 So she said to him, "I *am* the daughter of Bethuel, Milcah's son, whom she bore to Nahor."

Gen 24:32–33 Then the man came to the house. And he unloaded the camels, and provided straw and feed for the camels, and water to wash his feet and the feet of the men who *were* with him. 33 *Food* was set before him to eat, but he said, "I will not eat until I have told about my errand." And he said, "Speak on."

Ex 2:20 So he said to his daughters, "And where *is* he? Why *is* it *that* you have left the man? Call him, that he may eat bread."

Judg 19:20–21 And the old man said, "Peace *be* with you! However, *let* all your needs *be* my responsibility; only do not spend the night in the open square." 21 So he brought him into his house, and gave fodder to the donkeys. And they washed their feet, and ate and drank.

Job 31:32 (*But* no sojourner had to lodge in the street, *For* I have opened my doors to the traveler);

Heb 13:2 Do not forget to entertain strangers, for by so *doing* some have unwittingly entertained angels.

Places to stay over.

Gen 42:27 But as one *of them* opened his sack to give his donkey feed at the encampment, he saw his money; and there it was, in the mouth of his sack.

Ex 4:24 And it came to pass on the way, at the encampment, that the LORD met him and sought to kill him.

Luke 2:7 And she brought forth her firstborn Son, and wrapped Him in swaddling cloths, and laid Him in a manger, because there was no room for them in the inn.

Luke 10:34 So he went to *him* and bandaged his wounds, pouring on oil and wine; and he set him on his own animal, brought him to an inn, and took care of him.

Were frequently asked destination, identity.

Judg 19:17 And when he raised his eyes, he saw the traveler in the open square of the city; and the old man said, "Where are you going, and where do you come from?"

Protected by those who entertained them.

Gen 19:6–8 So Lot went out to them through the doorway, shut the door behind him, **7** and said, "Please, my brethren, do not do so wickedly! **8** See now, I have two daughters who have not known a man; please, let me bring them out to you, and you may do to them as you wish; only do nothing to these men, since this is the reason they have come under the shadow of my roof."

Judg 19:23 But the man, the master of the house, went out to them and said to them, "No, my brethren! I beg you, do not act *so* wickedly! Seeing this man has come into my house, do not commit this outrage.

For security, sometimes left the highways.

Judg 5:6 "In the days of Shamgar, son of Anath, In the days of Jael, The highways were deserted, And the travelers walked along the byways.

On errands requiring dispatch

Went with great speed.

Esth 8:10 And he wrote in the name of King Ahasuerus, sealed *it* with the king's signet ring, and sent letters by couriers on horseback, riding on royal horses bred from swift steeds.

Job 9:25 "Now my days are swifter than a runner; They flee away, they see no good.

Greeted no one by the way.

2 Kin 4:29 Then he said to Gehazi, "Get yourself ready, and take my staff in your hand, and be on your way. If you meet anyone, do not greet him; and if anyone greets you, do not answer him; but lay my staff on the face of the child."

Luke 10:4 Carry neither money bag, knapsack, nor sandals; and greet no one along the road.

Journeys of, measured in days.

Gen 31:23 Then he took his brethren with him and pursued him for seven days' journey, and he overtook him in the mountains of Gilead.

Deut 1:2 *It is* eleven days' *journey* from Horeb by way of Mount Seir to Kadesh Barnea.

2 Kin 3:9 So the king of Israel went with the king of Judah and the king of Edom, and they marched on that roundabout route seven days; and there was no water for the army, nor for the animals that followed them.

The Jews prohibited from taking long journeys on the Sabbath.

Ex 20:10 but the seventh day *is* the Sabbath of the LORD your God. *In it* you shall do no work: you, nor your son, nor your daughter, nor your male servant, nor your female servant, nor your cattle, nor your stranger who *is* within your gates.

Acts 1:12 Then they returned to Jerusalem from the mount called Olivet, which is near Jerusalem, a Sabbath day's journey.

Ceasing of, threatened as a calamity.

Is 33:8 The highways lie waste, The traveling man ceases. He has broken the covenant, He has despised the cities, He regards no man.

TREES

Originally created by God.

Gen 1:11–12 Then God said, "Let the earth bring forth grass, the herb *that* yields seed, *and* the fruit tree *that* yields fruit according to its kind, whose seed *is* in itself, on the earth"; and it was so. **12** And the earth brought forth grass, the herb *that* yields seed according to its kind, and the tree *that* yields fruit, whose seed *is* in itself according to its kind. And God saw that *it was* good.

Gen 2:9 And out of the ground the LORD God made every tree grow that is pleasant to the sight and good for food. The tree of life *was* also in the midst of the garden, and the tree of the knowledge of good and evil.

Made for the glory of God.

Ps 148:9 Mountains and all hills; Fruitful trees and all cedars;

Different kinds, mentioned

Of the wood.

Song 2:3 Like an apple tree among the trees of the woods, So *is* my beloved among the sons. I sat down in his shade with great delight, And his fruit *was* sweet to my taste.

Of the forest.

Is 10:19 Then the rest of the trees of his forest Will be so few in number That a child may write them.

Bearing fruit.

Neh 9:25 And they took strong cities and a rich land, And possessed houses full of all goods, Cisterns already dug, vineyards, olive groves, And fruit trees in abundance. So they ate and were filled and grew fat, And delighted themselves in Your great goodness.

Eccl 2:5 I made myself gardens and orchards, and I planted all *kinds* of fruit trees in them.

Ezek 47:12 Along the bank of the river, on this side and that, will grow all *kinds of* trees used for food; their leaves will not wither, and their fruit will not fail. They will bear fruit every month, because their water flows from the sanctuary. Their fruit will be for food, and their leaves for medicine."

Evergreen.

Ps 37:35 I have seen the wicked in great power, And spreading himself like a native green tree.

Jer 17:2 While their children remember Their altars and their wooden images By the green trees on the high hills.

Deciduous or those that shed leaves.

Is 6:13 But yet a tenth *will be* in it, And will return and be for consuming, As a terebinth tree or as an oak, Whose stump *remains* when it is cut down. So the holy seed *shall be* its stump."

Of various sizes.

Ezek 17:24 And all the trees of the field shall know that I, the LORD, have brought down the high tree and exalted the low tree, dried up the green tree and made the dry tree flourish; I, the LORD, have spoken and have done *it.*"

Given as food to the animal creation.

Gen 1:29–30 And God said, "See, I have given you every herb *that* yields seed which *is* on the face of all the earth, and every tree whose fruit yields seed; to you it shall be for food. **30** Also, to every beast of the earth, to every bird of the air, and to everything that creeps on the earth, in which *there is* life, *I have given* every green herb for food"; and it was so.

Deut 20:19 "When you besiege a city for a long time, while making war against it to take it, you shall not destroy its trees by wielding an ax against them; if you can eat of them, do not cut them down to use in the siege, for the tree of the field *is* man's *food.*

Designed to beautify the earth.

Gen 2:9 And out of the ground the LORD God made every tree grow that is pleasant to the sight and good for food. The tree of life *was* also in the midst of the garden, and the tree of the knowledge of good and evil.

Parts of, mentioned

The roots.

Jer 17:8 For he shall be like a tree planted by the waters, Which spreads out its roots by the river, And will not fear when heat comes; But its leaf will be green, And will not be anxious in the year of drought, Nor will cease from yielding fruit.

The stem or trunk.

Is 11:1 There shall come forth a Rod from the stem of Jesse, And a Branch shall grow out of his roots.

Is 44:19 And no one considers in his heart, Nor *is there* knowledge nor understanding to say, "I have burned half of it in the fire, Yes, I have also baked bread on its coals; I have roasted meat and eaten *it*; And shall I make the rest of it an abomination? Shall I fall down before a block of wood?"

The branches.

Lev 23:40 And you shall take for yourselves on the first day the fruit of beautiful trees, branches of palm trees, the boughs of leafy trees, and willows of the brook; and you shall rejoice before the LORD your God for seven days.

Dan 4:14 He cried aloud and said thus: 'Chop down the

tree and cut off its branches, Strip off its leaves and scatter its fruit. Let the beasts get out from under it, And the birds from its branches.

The tender shoots.

Luke 21:29–30 Then He spoke to them a parable: "Look at the fig tree, and all the trees. **30** When they are already budding, you see and know for yourselves that summer is now near.

The leaves.

Dan 4:12 Its leaves *were* lovely, Its fruit abundant, And in it *was* food for all. The beasts of the field found shade under it, The birds of the heavens dwelt in its branches, And all flesh was fed from it.

Matt 21:19 And seeing a fig tree by the road, He came to it and found nothing on it but leaves, and said to it, "Let no fruit grow on you ever again." Immediately the fig tree withered away.

The fruit or seeds.

Lev 27:30 And all the tithe of the land, *whether* of the seed of the land *or* of the fruit of the tree, *is* the LORD's. It *is* holy to the LORD.

Ezek 36:30 And I will multiply the fruit of your trees and the increase of your fields, so that you need never again bear the reproach of famine among the nations.

Each kind has its own seed.

Gen 1:11–12 Then God said, "Let the earth bring forth grass, the herb *that* yields seed, *and* the fruit tree *that* yields fruit according to its kind, whose seed *is* in itself, on the earth"; and it was so. **12** And the earth brought forth grass, the herb *that* yields seed according to its kind, and the tree *that* yields fruit, whose seed *is* in itself according to its kind. And God saw that *it was* good.

Often propagated by birds who carry the seeds.

Ezek 17:3 and say, 'Thus says the Lord GOD: "A great eagle with large wings and long pinions, Full of feathers of various colors, Came to Lebanon And took from the cedar the highest branch.

Ezek 17:5 Then he took some of the seed of the land And planted it in a fertile field; He placed *it* by abundant waters *And* set it like a willow tree.

Planted by man.

Lev 19:23 'When you come into the land, and have planted all kinds of trees for food, then you shall count their fruit as uncircumcised. Three years it shall be as uncircumcised to you. *It* shall not be eaten.

Each kind of, known by its fruit.

Matt 12:33 "Either make the tree good and its fruit good, or else make the tree bad and its fruit bad; for a tree is known by *its* fruit.

Nourished

By the earth.

Gen 1:12 And the earth brought forth grass, the herb *that* yields seed according to its kind, and the tree *that* yields fruit, whose seed *is* in itself according to its kind. And God saw that *it was* good.

Gen 2:9 And out of the ground the LORD God made every tree grow that is pleasant to the sight and good for food. The tree of life *was* also in the midst of the garden, and the tree of the knowledge of good and evil.

By the rain from heaven.

Is 44:14 He cuts down cedars for himself, And takes the cypress and the oak; He secures *it* for himself among the trees of the forest. He plants a pine, and the rain nourishes *it.*

Through their own sap.

Ps 104:16 The trees of the LORD are full *of sap,* The cedars of Lebanon which He planted,

Especially flourished beside the rivers and streams of water.

Ezek 47:12 Along the bank of the river, on this side and that, will grow all *kinds of* trees used for food; their leaves will not wither, and their fruit will not fail. They will bear fruit every month, because their water flows from the sanctuary. Their fruit will be for food, and their leaves for medicine."

When cut down, often sprouted from their roots again.

Job 14:7 "For there is hope for a tree, If it is cut down, that it will sprout again, And that its tender shoots will not cease.

Were sold with the land on which they grew.

Gen 23:17 So the field of Ephron which *was* in Machpelah, which *was* before Mamre, the field and the cave which *was* in it, and all the trees that *were* in the field, which *were* within all the surrounding borders, were deeded

Sometimes suffered from

Locusts.

Ex 10:5 And they shall cover the face of the earth, so that no one will be able to see the earth; and they shall eat the residue of what is left, which remains to you from the hail, and they shall eat every tree which grows up for you out of the field.

Ex 10:15 For they covered the face of the whole earth, so that the land was darkened; and they ate every herb of the land and all the fruit of the trees which the hail had left. So there remained nothing green on the trees or on the plants of the field throughout all the land of Egypt.

Deut 28:42 Locusts shall consume all your trees and the produce of your land.

Hail and frost.

Ex 9:25 And the hail struck throughout the whole land of Egypt, all that *was* in the field, both man and beast; and the hail struck every herb of the field and broke every tree of the field.

Ps 78:47 He destroyed their vines with hail, And their sycamore trees with frost.

Fire.

Joel 1:19 O LORD, to You I cry out; For fire has devoured the open pastures, And a flame has burned all the trees of the field.

Desolating armies.

2 Kin 19:23 By your messengers you have reproached the Lord, And said: "By the multitude of my chariots I have come up to the height of the mountains, To the limits of Lebanon; I will cut down its tall cedars *And*

its choice cypress trees; I will enter the extremity of its borders, *To* its fruitful forest.

Is 10:34 He will cut down the thickets of the forest with iron, And Lebanon will fall by the Mighty One.

Provided shade.

Gen 18:4 Please let a little water be brought, and wash your feet, and rest yourselves under the tree.

Job 40:21 He lies under the lotus trees, In a covert of reeds and marsh.

Were cut down

With axes.

Deut 19:5 as when *a man* goes to the woods with his neighbor to cut timber, and his hand swings a stroke with the ax to cut down the tree, and the head slips from the handle and strikes his neighbor so that he dies—he shall flee to one of these cities and live;

Ps 74:5 They seem like men who lift up Axes among the thick trees.

Matt 3:10 And even now the ax is laid to the root of the trees. Therefore every tree which does not bear good fruit is cut down and thrown into the fire.

For building.

2 Kin 6:2 Please, let us go to the Jordan, and let every man take a beam from there, and let us make there a place where we may dwell." So he answered, "Go."

2 Chr 2:8 Also send me cedar and cypress and algum logs from Lebanon, for I know that your servants have skill to cut timber in Lebanon; and indeed my servants *will be* with your servants,

2 Chr 2:10 And indeed I will give to your servants, the woodsmen who cut timber, twenty thousand kors of ground wheat, twenty thousand kors of barley, twenty thousand baths of wine, and twenty thousand baths of oil.

By besieging armies to build forts.

Deut 20:20 Only the trees which you know *are* not trees for food you may destroy and cut down, to build siegeworks against the city that makes war with you, until it is subdued.

Jer 6:6 For thus has the LORD of hosts said: "Cut down trees, And build a mound against Jerusalem. This *is* the city to be punished. She *is* full of oppression in her midst.

For making idols.

Is 40:20 Whoever *is* too impoverished for *such* a contribution Chooses a tree *that* will not rot; He seeks for himself a skillful workman To prepare a carved image *that* will not totter.

Is 44:14 He cuts down cedars for himself, And takes the cypress and the oak; He secures *it* for himself among the trees of the forest. He plants a pine, and the rain nourishes *it.*

Is 44:17 And the rest of it he makes into a god, His carved image. He falls down before it and worships *it,* Prays to it and says, "Deliver me, for you *are* my god!"

For fuel.

Is 44:14–16 He cuts down cedars for himself, And takes the cypress and the oak; He secures *it* for himself among the trees of the forest. He plants a pine, and the rain nourishes *it.* **15** Then it shall be for a man to burn, For he will take some of it and warm himself; Yes, he kindles *it* and bakes bread; Indeed he makes a god and worships *it;* He makes it a carved image, and falls down to it. **16** He burns half of it in the fire; With this half he eats meat; He roasts a roast, and is satisfied. He even warms *himself* and says, "Ah! I am warm, I have seen the fire."

Matt 3:10 And even now the ax is laid to the root of the trees. Therefore every tree which does not bear good fruit is cut down and thrown into the fire.

God increases and multiplies the fruit of, for His people.

Lev 26:4 then I will give you rain in its season, the land shall yield its produce, and the trees of the field shall yield their fruit.

Ezek 34:27 Then the trees of the field shall yield their fruit, and the earth shall yield her increase. They shall be safe in their land; and they shall know that I *am* the LORD, when I have broken the bands of their yoke and delivered them from the hand of those who enslaved them.

Joel 2:22 Do not be afraid, you beasts of the field; For the open pastures are springing up, And the tree bears its fruit; The fig tree and the vine yield their strength.

God often renders, barren as a punishment.

Lev 26:20 And your strength shall be spent in vain; for your land shall not yield its produce, nor shall the trees of the land yield their fruit.

Early custom of planting, in consecrated grounds.

Gen 21:33 Then *Abraham* planted a tamarisk tree in Beersheba, and there called on the name of the LORD, the Everlasting God.

The Jews

Were prohibited from planting in consecrated places.

Deut 16:21 "You shall not plant for yourself any tree, as a wooden image, near the altar which you build for yourself to the LORD your God.

Were prohibited from cutting down fruit bearing, for sieges.

Deut 20:19 "When you besiege a city for a long time, while making war against it to take it, you shall not destroy its trees by wielding an ax against them; if you can eat of them, do not cut them down to use in the siege, for the tree of the field *is* man's *food.*

Often pitched their tents under.

Gen 18:1 Then the LORD appeared to him by the terebinth trees of Mamre, as he was sitting in the tent door in the heat of the day.

Gen 18:4 Please let a little water be brought, and wash your feet, and rest yourselves under the tree.

Judg 4:5 And she would sit under the palm tree of Deborah between Ramah and Bethel in the mountains of Ephraim. And the children of Israel came up to her for judgment.

1 Sam 22:6 When Saul heard that David and the men who *were* with him had been discovered—now Saul was staying in Gibeah under a tamarisk tree in Ramah, with his spear in his hand, and all his servants standing about him—

Often were buried under.

Gen 35:8 Now Deborah, Rebekah's nurse, died, and she was buried below Bethel under the terebinth tree. So the name of it was called Allon Bachuth.

1 Sam 31:13 Then they took their bones and buried *them* under the tamarisk tree at Jabesh, and fasted seven days.

Often executed criminals on.

Gen 40:19 Within three days Pharaoh will lift off your head from you and hang you on a tree; and the birds will eat your flesh from you."

Deut 21:22–23 "If a man has committed a sin deserving of death, and he is put to death, and you hang him on a tree, **23** his body shall not remain overnight on the tree, but you shall surely bury him that day, so that you do not defile the land which the LORD your God is giving you *as* an inheritance; for he who is hanged *is* accursed of God.

Josh 10:26 And afterward Joshua struck them and killed them, and hanged them on five trees; and they were hanging on the trees until evening.

Gal 3:13 Christ has redeemed us from the curse of the law, having become a curse for us (for it is written, *"Cursed is everyone who hangs on a tree"*),

Considered those on which criminals were executed abominable.

Is 14:19 But you are cast out of your grave Like an abominable branch, *Like* the garment of those who are slain, Thrust through with a sword, Who go down to the stones of the pit, Like a corpse trodden underfoot.

Mentioned in Scripture

Acacia.

Ex 36:20 For the tabernacle he made boards of acacia wood, standing upright.

Is 41:19 I will plant in the wilderness the cedar and the acacia tree, The myrtle and the oil tree; I will set in the desert the cypress tree *and* the pine And the box tree together,

Almond.

Gen 43:11 And their father Israel said to them, "If *it must be* so, then do this: Take some of the best fruits of the land in your vessels and carry down a present for the man—a little balm and a little honey, spices and myrrh, pistachio nuts and almonds.

Eccl 12:5 Also they are afraid of height, And of terrors in the way; When the almond tree blossoms, The grasshopper is a burden, And desire fails. For man goes to his eternal home, And the mourners go about the streets.

Jer 1:11 Moreover the word of the LORD came to me, saying, "Jeremiah, what do you see?" And I said, "I see a branch of an almond tree."

Almug.

1 Kin 10:11–12 Also, the ships of Hiram, which brought gold from Ophir, brought great *quantities* of almug wood and precious stones from Ophir. **12** And the king made steps of the almug wood for the house of the LORD and for the king's house, also harps and stringed instruments for singers. There never again came such almug wood, nor has the like been seen to this day.

2 Chr 9:10–11 Also, the servants of Hiram and the servants of Solomon, who brought gold from Ophir, brought algum wood and precious stones. **11** And the king made walkways *of* the algum wood for the house of the LORD and for the king's house, also harps and stringed instruments for singers; and there were none such *as these* seen before in the land of Judah.

Aloes.

Num 24:6 Like valleys that stretch out, Like gardens by the riverside, Like aloes planted by the LORD, Like cedars beside the waters.

Apple.

Song 2:3 Like an apple tree among the trees of the woods, So *is* my beloved among the sons. I sat down in his shade with great delight, And his fruit *was* sweet to my taste.

Song 8:5 Who *is* this coming up from the wilderness, Leaning upon her beloved? I awakened you under the apple tree. There your mother brought you forth; There she *who* bore you brought *you* forth.

Joel 1:12 The vine has dried up, And the fig tree has withered; The pomegranate tree, The palm tree also, And the apple tree— All the trees of the field are withered; Surely joy has withered away from the sons of men.

Box.

Is 41:19 I will plant in the wilderness the cedar and the acacia tree, The myrtle and the oil tree; I will set in the desert the cypress tree *and* the pine And the box tree together,

Broom.

1 Kin 19:4–5 But he himself went a day's journey into the wilderness, and came and sat down under a broom tree. And he prayed that he might die, and said, "It is enough! Now, LORD, take my life, for I *am* no better than my fathers!" **5** Then as he lay and slept under a broom tree, suddenly an angel touched him, and said to him, "Arise *and* eat."

Cedar.

1 Kin 5:10 Then Hiram gave Solomon cedar and cypress logs *according to* all his desire.

1 Kin 10:27 The king made silver *as common* in Jerusalem as stones, and he made cedar trees as abundant as the sycamores which *are* in the lowland.

Chestnut.

Ezek 31:8 The cedars in the garden of God could not hide it; The fir trees were not like its boughs, And the chestnut trees were not like its branches; No tree in the garden of God was like it in beauty.

Cypress.

Is 44:14 He cuts down cedars for himself, And takes the cypress and the oak; He secures *it* for himself among the trees of the forest. He plants a pine, and the rain nourishes *it*.

Fig.

Deut 8:8 a land of wheat and barley, of vines and fig trees and pomegranates, a land of olive oil and honey;

Fir.

2 Kin 19:23 By your messengers you have reproached

the Lord, And said: "By the multitude of my chariots I have come up to the height of the mountains, To the limits of Lebanon; I will cut down its tall cedars *And* its choice cypress trees; I will enter the extremity of its borders, *To* its fruitful forest.

Ps 104:17 Where the birds make their nests; The stork has her home in the fir trees.

Green.

Ps 37:35 I have seen the wicked in great power, And spreading himself like a native green tree.

Mulberry.

2 Sam 5:23–24 Therefore David inquired of the LORD, and He said, "You shall not go up; circle around behind them, and come upon them in front of the mulberry trees. **24** And it shall be, when you hear the sound of marching in the tops of the mulberry trees, then you shall advance quickly. For then the LORD will go out before you to strike the camp of the Philistines."

Myrtle.

Is 41:19 I will plant in the wilderness the cedar and the acacia tree, The myrtle and the oil tree; I will set in the desert the cypress tree *and* the pine And the box tree together,

Is 55:13 Instead of the thorn shall come up the cypress tree, And instead of the brier shall come up the myrtle tree; And it shall be to the LORD for a name, For an everlasting sign *that* shall not be cut off."

Zech 1:8 I saw by night, and behold, a man riding on a red horse, and it stood among the myrtle trees in the hollow; and behind him *were* horses: red, sorrel, and white.

Mustard.

Matt 13:31–32 Another parable He put forth to them, saying: "The kingdom of heaven is like a mustard seed, which a man took and sowed in his field, **32** which indeed is the least of all the seeds; but when it is grown it is greater than the herbs and becomes a tree, so that the birds of the air come and nest in its branches."

Oil.

Is 41:19 I will plant in the wilderness the cedar and the acacia tree, The myrtle and the oil tree; I will set in the desert the cypress tree *and* the pine And the box tree together,

Olive.

Deut 6:11 houses full of all good things, which you did not fill, hewn-out wells which you did not dig, vineyards and olive trees which you did not plant— when you have eaten and are full—

Palm.

Ex 15:27 Then they came to Elim, where there *were* twelve wells of water and seventy palm trees; so they camped there by the waters.

Pine.

Is 41:19 I will plant in the wilderness the cedar and the acacia tree, The myrtle and the oil tree; I will set in the desert the cypress tree *and* the pine And the box tree together,

Is 44:14 He cuts down cedars for himself, And takes the cypress and the oak; He secures *it* for himself among the trees of the forest. He plants a pine, and the rain nourishes *it*.

Pomegranate.

Deut 8:8 a land of wheat and barley, of vines and fig trees and pomegranates, a land of olive oil and honey;

Joel 1:12 The vine has dried up, And the fig tree has withered; The pomegranate tree, The palm tree also, And the apple tree— All the trees of the field are withered; Surely joy has withered away from the sons of men.

Sycamore.

1 Kin 10:27 The king made silver *as common* in Jerusalem as stones, and he made cedar trees as abundant as the sycamores which *are* in the lowland.

Ps 78:47 He destroyed their vines with hail, And their sycamore trees with frost.

Amos 7:14 Then Amos answered, and said to Amaziah: "I *was* no prophet, Nor *was* I a son of a prophet, But I *was* a sheepbreeder And a tender of sycamore fruit.

Luke 19:4 So he ran ahead and climbed up into a sycamore tree to see Him, for He was going to pass that *way.*

Terebinth.

Is 1:30 For you shall be as a terebinth whose leaf fades, And as a garden that has no water.

Is 6:13 But yet a tenth *will be* in it, And will return and be for consuming, As a terebinth tree or as an oak, Whose stump *remains* when it is cut down. So the holy seed *shall be* its stump."

Willow.

Is 44:4 They will spring up among the grass Like willows by the watercourses.'

Ezek 17:5 Then he took some of the seed of the land And planted it in a fertile field; He placed *it* by abundant waters *And* set it like a willow tree.

Solomon wrote the history of.

1 Kin 4:33 Also he spoke of trees, from the cedar tree of Lebanon even to the hyssop that springs out of the wall; he spoke also of animals, of birds, of creeping things, and of fish.

Illustrative of

Christ.

Rom 11:24 For if you were cut out of the olive tree which is wild by nature, and were grafted contrary to nature into a cultivated olive tree, how much more will these, who *are* natural *branches*, be grafted into their own olive tree?

Rev 2:7 "He who has an ear, let him hear what the Spirit says to the churches. To him who overcomes I will give to eat from the tree of life, which is in the midst of the Paradise of God." '

Rev 22:2 In the middle of its street, and on either side of the river, *was* the tree of life, which bore twelve fruits, each *tree* yielding its fruit every month. The leaves of the tree *were* for the healing of the nations.

Rev 22:14 Blessed *are* those who do His commandments, that they may have the right to the tree of life, and may enter through the gates into the city.

Wisdom.

Prov 3:18 She *is* a tree of life to those who take hold of her, And happy *are all* who retain her.

Kings, etc.

Is 10:34 He will cut down the thickets of the forest with iron, And Lebanon will fall by the Mighty One.

Ezek 17:24 And all the trees of the field shall know that I, the Lord, have brought down the high tree and exalted the low tree, dried up the green tree and made the dry tree flourish; I, the Lord, have spoken and have done *it.*"

Ezek 31:7–10 'Thus it was beautiful in greatness and in the length of its branches, Because its roots reached to abundant waters. **8** The cedars in the garden of God could not hide it; The fir trees were not like its boughs, And the chestnut trees were not like its branches; No tree in the garden of God was like it in beauty. **9** I made it beautiful with a multitude of branches, So that all the trees of Eden envied it, That *were* in the garden of God.' **10** "Therefore thus says the Lord God: 'Because you have increased in height, and it set its top among the thick boughs, and its heart was lifted up in its height,

Dan 4:10–14 These *were* the visions of my head *while* on my bed: I was looking, and behold, A tree in the midst of the earth, And its height was great. **11** The tree grew and became strong; Its height reached to the heavens, And it could be seen to the ends of all the earth. **12** Its leaves *were* lovely, Its fruit abundant, And in it *was* food for all. The beasts of the field found shade under it, The birds of the heavens dwelt in its branches, And all flesh was fed from it. **13** "I saw in the visions of my head *while* on my bed, and there was a watcher, a holy one, coming down from heaven. **14** He cried aloud and said thus: 'Chop down the tree and cut off its branches, Strip off its leaves and scatter its fruit. Let the beasts get out from under it, And the birds from its branches.

The life and conversation of the righteous.

Prov 11:30 The fruit of the righteous *is a* tree of life, And he who wins souls *is* wise.

Prov 15:4 A wholesome tongue *is* a tree of life, But perverseness in it breaks the spirit.

(Green) the innocence of Christ.

Luke 23:31 For if they do these things in the green wood, what will be done in the dry?"

(Good and fruitful) believers and their works.

Num 24:6 Like valleys that stretch out, Like gardens by the riverside, Like aloes planted by the Lord, Like cedars beside the waters.

Ps 1:1–3 Blessed *is* the man Who walks not in the counsel of the ungodly, Nor stands in the path of sinners, Nor sits in the seat of the scornful; **2** But his delight *is* in the law of the Lord, And in His law he meditates day and night. **3** He shall be like a tree Planted by the rivers of water, That brings forth its fruit in its season, Whose leaf also shall not wither; And whatever he does shall prosper.

Is 61:3 To console those who mourn in Zion, To give them beauty for ashes, The oil of joy for mourning, The garment of praise for the spirit of heaviness;

That they may be called trees of righteousness, The planting of the LORD, that He may be glorified."

Jer 17:8 For he shall be like a tree planted by the waters, Which spreads out its roots by the river, And will not fear when heat comes; But its leaf will be green, And will not be anxious in the year of drought, Nor will cease from yielding fruit.

Matt 7:17–18 Even so, every good tree bears good fruit, but a bad tree bears bad fruit. **18** A good tree cannot bear bad fruit, nor *can* a bad tree bear good fruit.

(Duration of) continued prosperity of believers.

Is 65:22 They shall not build and another inhabit; They shall not plant and another eat; For as the days of a tree, *so shall be* the days of My people, And My elect shall long enjoy the work of their hands.

(Casting their leaves yet retaining their substance) the elect remnant in Israel.

Is 6:13 But yet a tenth *will be* in it, And will return and be for consuming, As a terebinth tree or as an oak, Whose stump *remains* when it is cut down. So the holy seed *shall be* its stump."

(Barren) the wicked.

Hos 9:16 Ephraim is stricken, Their root is dried up; They shall bear no fruit. Yes, were they to bear children, I would kill the darlings of their womb."

(Shaking of the leaves off) the terror of the wicked.

Is 7:2 And it was told to the house of David, saying, "Syria's forces are deployed in Ephraim." So his heart and the heart of his people were moved as the trees of the woods are moved with the wind.

(Producing evil fruit) the wicked.

Matt 7:17–19 Even so, every good tree bears good fruit, but a bad tree bears bad fruit. **18** A good tree cannot bear bad fruit, nor *can* a bad tree bear good fruit. **19** Every tree that does not bear good fruit is cut down and thrown into the fire.

(Dry) useless persons.

Is 56:3 Do not let the son of the foreigner Who has joined himself to the LORD Speak, saying, "The LORD has utterly separated me from His people"; Nor let the eunuch say, "Here I am, a dry tree."

(Dry) the wicked ripe for judgment.

Luke 23:31 For if they do these things in the green wood, what will be done in the dry?"

TRIALS, TRIBULATIONS

God allows.

Luke 22:31 And the Lord said, "Simon, Simon! Indeed, Satan has asked for you, that he may sift *you* as wheat.

Produces perseverance.

Rom 5:3 And not only *that*, but we also glory in tribulations, knowing that tribulation produces perseverance;

God comforts believers during.

2 Cor 1:4 who comforts us in all our tribulation, that we may be able to comfort those who are in any trouble, with the comfort with which we ourselves are comforted by God.

Believers should expect to suffer.

1 Thess 3:4 For, in fact, we told you before when we were with you that we would suffer tribulation, just as it happened, and you know.

Evidence of God's love for believers.

Heb 12:5–6 And you have forgotten the exhortation which speaks to you as to sons: *"My son, do not despise the chastening of the LORD, Nor be discouraged when you are rebuked by Him; 6 For whom the LORD loves He chastens, And scourges every son whom He receives."*

Believers are to face them with joy.

James 1:2 My brethren, count it all joy when you fall into various trials,

God uses them to prove and strengthen one's faith.

James 1:3–12 knowing that the testing of your faith produces patience. **4** But let patience have *its* perfect work, that you may be perfect and complete, lacking nothing. **5** If any of you lacks wisdom, let him ask of God, who gives to all liberally and without reproach, and it will be given to him. **6** But let him ask in faith, with no doubting, for he who doubts is like a wave of the sea driven and tossed by the wind. **7** For let not that man suppose that he will receive anything from the Lord; **8** *he is* a double-minded man, unstable in all his ways. **9** Let the lowly brother glory in his exaltation, **10** but the rich in his humiliation, because as a flower of the field he will pass away. **11** For no sooner has the sun risen with a burning heat than it withers the grass; its flower falls, and its beautiful appearance perishes. So the rich man also will fade away in his pursuits. **12** Blessed *is* the man who endures temptation; for when he has been approved, he will receive the crown of life which the Lord has promised to those who love Him.

1 Pet 1:6–7 In this you greatly rejoice, though now for a little while, if need be, you have been grieved by various trials, **7** that the genuineness of your faith, *being* much more precious than gold that perishes, though it is tested by fire, may be found to praise, honor, and glory at the revelation of Jesus Christ,

TRIBUTE

Sometimes exacted by kings from their own subjects.

1 Sam 8:10–17 So Samuel told all the words of the LORD to the people who asked him for a king. **11** And he said, "This will be the behavior of the king who will reign over you: He will take your sons and appoint *them* for his own chariots and *to be* his horsemen, and *some* will run before his chariots. **12** He will appoint captains over his thousands and captains over his fifties, *will set some* to plow his ground and reap his harvest, and *some* to make his weapons of war and equipment for his chariots. **13** He will take your daughters *to be* perfumers, cooks, and bakers. **14** And he will take the best of your fields, your vineyards, and your olive groves, and give *them* to his servants. **15** He will take a tenth of your grain and your vintage, and give it to his officers and servants. **16** And he will take your male servants, your female servants, your finest young men, and your donkeys, and put *them* to his work. **17** He will take a tenth of your sheep. And you will be his servants.

Exacted from all conquered nations.

Josh 16:10 And they did not drive out the Canaanites who dwelt in Gezer; but the Canaanites dwell among the Ephraimites to this day and have become forced laborers.

Judg 1:30 Nor did Zebulun drive out the inhabitants of Kitron or the inhabitants of Nahalol; so the Canaanites dwelt among them, and were put under tribute.

Judg 1:33 Nor did Naphtali drive out the inhabitants of Beth Shemesh or the inhabitants of Beth Anath; but they dwelt among the Canaanites, the inhabitants of the land. Nevertheless the inhabitants of Beth Shemesh and Beth Anath were put under tribute to them.

Judg 1:35 and the Amorites were determined to dwell in Mount Heres, in Aijalon, and in Shaalbim; yet when the strength of the house of Joseph became greater, they were put under tribute.

2 Kin 23:33 Now Pharaoh Necho put him in prison at Riblah in the land of Hamath, that he might not reign in Jerusalem; and he imposed on the land a tribute of one hundred talents of silver and a talent of gold.

2 Kin 23:35 So Jehoiakim gave the silver and gold to Pharaoh; but he taxed the land to give money according to the command of Pharaoh; he exacted the silver and gold from the people of the land, from every one according to his assessment, to give *it* to Pharaoh Necho.

Often exacted in

Labor.

1 Kin 5:13–14 Then King Solomon raised up a labor force out of all Israel; and the labor force was thirty thousand men. **14** And he sent them to Lebanon, ten thousand a month in shifts: they were one month in Lebanon *and* two months at home; Adoniram *was* in charge of the labor force.

1 Kin 9:15 And this *is* the reason for the labor force which King Solomon raised: to build the house of the LORD, his own house, the Millo, the wall of Jerusalem, Hazor, Megiddo, and Gezer.

1 Kin 9:21 that is, their descendants who were left in the land after them, whom the children of Israel had not been able to destroy completely—from these Solomon raised forced labor, as it is to this day.

Produce of land, etc.

1 Sam 8:15 He will take a tenth of your grain and your vintage, and give it to his officers and servants.

1 Kin 4:7 And Solomon had twelve governors over all Israel, who provided food for the king and his household; each one made provision for one month of the year.

Gold and silver.

2 Kin 23:33 Now Pharaoh Necho put him in prison at Riblah in the land of Hamath, that he might not reign in Jerusalem; and he imposed on the land a tribute of one hundred talents of silver and a talent of gold.

2 Kin 23:35 So Jehoiakim gave the silver and gold to Pharaoh; but he taxed the land to give money according to the command of Pharaoh; he exacted the silver and gold from the people of the land, from

every one according to his assessment, to give *it* to Pharaoh Necho.

The Jews required to pay half a shekel to God as.

Ex 30:12–16 "When you take the census of the children of Israel for their number, then every man shall give a ransom for himself to the LORD, when you number them, that there may be no plague among them when *you* number them. **13** This is what everyone among those who are numbered shall give: half a shekel according to the shekel of the sanctuary (a shekel *is* twenty gerahs). The half-shekel *shall be* an offering to the LORD. **14** Everyone included among those who are numbered, from twenty years old and above, shall give an offering to the LORD. **15** The rich shall not give more and the poor shall not give less than half a shekel, when *you* give an offering to the LORD, to make atonement for yourselves. **16** And you shall take the atonement money of the children of Israel, and shall appoint it for the service of the tabernacle of meeting, that it may be a memorial for the children of Israel before the LORD, to make atonement for yourselves."

Christ, to avoid offense, wrought a miracle to pay for Himself and Peter.

Matt 17:24–27 When they had come to Capernaum, those who received the *temple* tax came to Peter and said, "Does your Teacher not pay the *temple* tax?" **25** He said, "Yes." And when he had come into the house, Jesus anticipated him, saying, "What do you think, Simon? From whom do the kings of the earth take customs or taxes, from their sons or from strangers?" **26** Peter said to Him, "From strangers." Jesus said to him, "Then the sons are free. **27** Nevertheless, lest we offend them, go to the sea, cast in a hook, and take the fish that comes up first. And when you have opened its mouth, you will find a piece of money; take that and give it to them for Me and you."

Kings of Israel

Forbidden to levy unnecessary or oppressive.

Deut 17:17 Neither shall he multiply wives for himself, lest his heart turn away; nor shall he greatly multiply silver and gold for himself.

Set officers over.

2 Sam 20:24 Adoram *was* in charge of revenue; Jehoshaphat the son of Ahilud *was* recorder;

1 Kin 4:6–7 Ahishar, over the household; and Adoniram the son of Abda, over the labor force. **7** And Solomon had twelve governors over all Israel, who provided food for the king and his household; each one made provision for one month of the year.

Often oppressed the people with.

1 Kin 12:4 "Your father made our yoke heavy; now therefore, lighten the burdensome service of your father, and his heavy yoke which he put on us, and we will serve you."

1 Kin 12:11 And now, whereas my father put a heavy yoke on you, I will add to your yoke; my father chastised you with whips, but I will chastise you with scourges!' "

When oppressive, sometimes led to rebellion.

1 Kin 12:14–20 and he spoke to them according to the advice of the young men, saying, "My father made your yoke heavy, but I will add to your yoke; my father chastised you with whips, but I will chastise you with scourges!" **15** So the king did not listen to the people; for the turn *of events* was from the LORD, that He might fulfill His word, which the LORD had spoken by Ahijah the Shilonite to Jeroboam the son of Nebat. **16** Now when all Israel saw that the king did not listen to them, the people answered the king, saying: "What share have we in David? *We have* no inheritance in the son of Jesse. To your tents, O Israel! Now, see to your own house, O David!" So Israel departed to their tents. **17** But Rehoboam reigned over the children of Israel who dwelt in the cities of Judah. **18** Then King Rehoboam sent Adoram, who *was* in charge of the revenue; but all Israel stoned him with stones, and he died. Therefore King Rehoboam mounted his chariot in haste to flee to Jerusalem. **19** So Israel has been in rebellion against the house of David to this day. **20** Now it came to pass when all Israel heard that Jeroboam had come back, they sent for him and called him to the congregation, and made him king over all Israel. There was none who followed the house of David, but the tribe of Judah only.

Priests and Levites exempted from.

Ezra 7:24 Also we inform you that it shall not be lawful to impose tax, tribute, or custom *on* any of the priests, Levites, singers, gatekeepers, Nethinim, or servants of this house of God.

Roman,

Decree of Augustus for.

Luke 2:1 And it came to pass in those days *that* a decree went out from Caesar Augustus that all the world should be registered.

First levied in Judea when Quirinius was governor.

Luke 2:2 This census first took place while Quirinius was governing Syria.

Persons registered for, in the native place of their tribe and family.

Luke 2:3–5 So all went to be registered, everyone to his own city. **4** Joseph also went up from Galilee, out of the city of Nazareth, into Judea, to the city of David, which is called Bethlehem, because he was of the house and lineage of David, **5** to be registered with Mary, his betrothed wife, who was with child.

Collected by the Publicans.

Luke 3:12–13 Then tax collectors also came to be baptized, and said to him, "Teacher, what shall we do?" **13** And he said to them, "Collect no more than what is appointed for you."

Luke 5:27 After these things He went out and saw a tax collector named Levi, sitting at the tax office. And He said to him, "Follow Me."

Was paid in Roman coin.

Matt 22:19–20 Show Me the tax money." So they brought Him a denarius. **20** And He said to them, "Whose image and inscription *is* this?"

Was resisted by the Galileans under Judas of Galilee.

Luke 13:1 There were present at that season some who told Him about the Galileans whose blood Pilate had mingled with their sacrifices.

Acts 5:37 After this man, Judas of Galilee rose up in the

days of the census, and drew away many people after him. He also perished, and all who obeyed him were dispersed.

Christ showed to the Pharisees and Herodians the propriety of paying.

Matt 22:15–22 Then the Pharisees went and plotted how they might entangle Him in *His* talk. **16** And they sent to Him their disciples with the Herodians, saying, "Teacher, we know that You are true, and teach the way of God in truth; nor do You care about anyone, for You do not regard the person of men. **17** Tell us, therefore, what do You think? Is it lawful to pay taxes to Caesar, or not?" **18** But Jesus perceived their wickedness, and said, "Why do you test Me, *you* hypocrites? **19** Show Me the tax money." So they brought Him a denarius. **20** And He said to them, "Whose image and inscription *is* this?" **21** They said to Him, "Caesar's." And He said to them, "Render therefore to Caesar the things that are Caesar's, and to God the things that are God's." **22** When they had heard *these words*, they marveled, and left Him and went their way.

Mark 12:13–17 Then they sent to Him some of the Pharisees and the Herodians, to catch Him in *His* words. **14** When they had come, they said to Him, "Teacher, we know that You are true, and care about no one; for You do not regard the person of men, but teach the way of God in truth. Is it lawful to pay taxes to Caesar, or not? **15** Shall we pay, or shall we not pay?" But He, knowing their hypocrisy, said to them, "Why do you test Me? Bring Me a denarius that I may see *it*." **16** So they brought *it*. And He said to them, "Whose image and inscription *is* this?" They said to Him, "Caesar's." **17** And Jesus answered and said to them, "Render to Caesar the things that are Caesar's, and to God the things that are God's." And they marveled at Him.

Our Lord falsely accused of forbidding to pay.

Rom 13:6–7 For because of this you also pay taxes, for they are God's ministers attending continually to this very thing. **7** Render therefore to all their due: taxes to whom taxes *are due*, customs to whom customs, fear to whom fear, honor to whom honor.

All believers exhorted to pay.

Rom 13:6–7 For because of this you also pay taxes, for they are God's ministers attending continually to this very thing. **7** Render therefore to all their due: taxes to whom taxes *are due*, customs to whom customs, fear to whom fear, honor to whom honor.

TRINITY, THE

Doctrine of, proved from Scripture.

Is 11:2 The Spirit of the LORD shall rest upon Him, The Spirit of wisdom and understanding, The Spirit of counsel and might, The Spirit of knowledge and of the fear of the LORD.

Is 61:1 "The Spirit of the Lord GOD *is* upon Me, Because the LORD has anointed Me To preach good tidings to the poor; He has sent Me to heal the brokenhearted, To proclaim liberty to the captives, And the opening of the prison to *those who are* bound;

Matt 3:16–17 When He had been baptized, Jesus came up immediately from the water; and behold, the heavens were opened to Him, and He saw the Spirit of God descending like a dove and alighting upon Him. **17** And suddenly a voice *came* from heaven, saying, "This is My beloved Son, in whom I am well pleased."

Matt 28:19 Go therefore and make disciples of all the nations, baptizing them in the name of the Father and of the Son and of the Holy Spirit,

Luke 3:22 And the Holy Spirit descended in bodily form like a dove upon Him, and a voice came from heaven which said, "You are My beloved Son; in You I am well pleased."

Rom 8:9 But you are not in the flesh but in the Spirit, if indeed the Spirit of God dwells in you. Now if anyone does not have the Spirit of Christ, he is not His.

1 Cor 12:3–6 Therefore I make known to you that no one speaking by the Spirit of God calls Jesus accursed, and no one can say that Jesus is Lord except by the Holy Spirit. **4** There are diversities of gifts, but the same Spirit. **5** There are differences of ministries, but the same Lord. **6** And there are diversities of activities, but it is the same God who works all in all.

2 Cor 1:21–22 Now He who establishes us with you in Christ and has anointed us *is* God, **22** who also has sealed us and given us the Spirit in our hearts as a guarantee.

2 Cor 13:14 The grace of the Lord Jesus Christ, and the love of God, and the communion of the Holy Spirit *be* with you all. Amen.

Eph 4:4–6 *There is* one body and one Spirit, just as you were called in one hope of your calling; **5** one Lord, one faith, one baptism; **6** one God and Father of all, who *is* above all, and through all, and in you all.

1 Pet 1:2 elect according to the foreknowledge of God the Father, in sanctification of the Spirit, for obedience and sprinkling of the blood of Jesus Christ: Grace to you and peace be multiplied.

Jude 1:20–21 But you, beloved, building yourselves up on your most holy faith, praying in the Holy Spirit, **21** keep yourselves in the love of God, looking for the mercy of our Lord Jesus Christ unto eternal life.

Rev 1:4–5 John, to the seven churches which are in Asia: Grace to you and peace from Him who is and who was and who is to come, and from the seven Spirits who are before His throne, **5** and from Jesus Christ, the faithful witness, the firstborn from the dead, and the ruler over the kings of the earth. To Him who loved us and washed us from our sins in His own blood,

Divine titles applied to the three persons in.

Ex 20:2 "I *am* the Lord your God, who brought you out of the land of Egypt, out of the house of bondage.

John 20:28 And Thomas answered and said to Him, "My Lord and my God!"

Acts 5:3–4 But Peter said, "Ananias, why has Satan filled your heart to lie to the Holy Spirit and keep back *part* of the price of the land for yourself? **4** While it remained, was it not your own? And after it was sold, was it not in your own control? Why have you conceived this thing in your heart? You have not lied to men but to God."

Each person in, described as

Eternal.

Rom 16:26 but now made manifest, and by the prophetic Scriptures made known to all nations, according to the commandment of the everlasting God, for obedience to the faith—

Heb 9:14 how much more shall the blood of Christ, who through the eternal Spirit offered Himself without spot to God, cleanse your conscience from dead works to serve the living God?

Rev 22:13 I am the Alpha and the Omega, *the* Beginning and *the* End, the First and the Last."

Holy.

Acts 3:14 But you denied the Holy One and the Just, and asked for a murderer to be granted to you,

1 John 2:20 But you have an anointing from the Holy One, and you know all things.

Rev 4:8 *The* four living creatures, each having six wings, were full of eyes around and within. And they do not rest day or night, saying: "Holy, holy, holy, Lord God Almighty, Who was and is and is to come!"

Rev 15:4 Who shall not fear You, O Lord, and glorify Your name? For *You* alone *are* holy. For all nations shall come and worship before You, For Your judgments have been manifested."

True.

John 7:28 Then Jesus cried out, as He taught in the temple, saying, "You both know Me, and you know where I am from; and I have not come of Myself, but He who sent Me is true, whom you do not know.

Rev 3:7 "And to the angel of the church in Philadelphia write, 'These things says He who is holy, He who is true, *"He who has the key of David, He who opens and no one shuts, and shuts and no one opens"*:

Omnipresent.

Ps 139:7 Where can I go from Your Spirit? Or where can I flee from Your presence?

Jer 23:24 Can anyone hide himself in secret places, So I shall not see him?" says the Lord; "Do I not fill heaven and earth?" says the Lord.

Eph 1:23 which is His body, the fullness of Him who fills all in all.

Omnipotent.

Gen 17:1 When Abram was ninety-nine years old, the Lord appeared to Abram and said to him, "I *am* Almighty God; walk before Me and be blameless.

Jer 32:17 'Ah, Lord God! Behold, You have made the heavens and the earth by Your great power and outstretched arm. There is nothing too hard for You.

Luke 1:35 And the angel answered and said to her, "*The* Holy Spirit will come upon you, and the power of the Highest will overshadow you; therefore, also, that Holy One who is to be born will be called the Son of God.

Rom 15:19 in mighty signs and wonders, by the power of the Spirit of God, so that from Jerusalem and round about to Illyricum I have fully preached the gospel of Christ.

Heb 1:3 who being the brightness of *His* glory and the express image of His person, and upholding all things by the word of His power, when He had by

Himself purged our sins, sat down at the right hand of the Majesty on high,

Rev 1:8 "I am the Alpha and the Omega, *the* Beginning and *the* End," says the Lord, "who is and who was and who is to come, the Almighty."

Omniscient.

John 21:17 He said to him the third time, "Simon, *son of* Jonah, do you love Me?" Peter was grieved because He said to him the third time, "Do you love Me?" And he said to Him, "Lord, You know all things; You know that I love You." Jesus said to him, "Feed My sheep.

Acts 15:18 "Known to God from eternity are all His works.

1 Cor 2:10–11 But God has revealed *them* to us through His Spirit. For the Spirit searches all things, yes, the deep things of God. **11** For what man knows the things of a man except the spirit of the man which is in him? Even so no one knows the things of God except the Spirit of God.

Creator.

Gen 1:1 In the beginning God created the heavens and the earth.

Job 26:13 By His Spirit He adorned the heavens; His hand pierced the fleeing serpent.

Job 33:4 The Spirit of God has made me, And the breath of the Almighty gives me life.

Ps 148:5 Let them praise the name of the LORD, For He commanded and they were created.

John 1:3 All things were made through Him, and without Him nothing was made that was made.

Col 1:16 For by Him all things were created that are in heaven and that are on earth, visible and invisible, whether thrones or dominions or principalities or powers. All things were created through Him and for Him.

Sanctifier.

Heb 2:11 For both He who sanctifies and those who are being sanctified *are* all of one, for which reason He is not ashamed to call them brethren,

1 Pet 1:2 elect according to the foreknowledge of God the Father, in sanctification of the Spirit, for obedience and sprinkling of the blood of Jesus Christ: Grace to you and peace be multiplied.

Jude 1:1 Jude, a bondservant of Jesus Christ, and brother of James, To those who are called, sanctified by God the Father, and preserved in Jesus Christ:

Author of all spiritual operations.

1 Cor 12:11 But one and the same Spirit works all these things, distributing to each one individually as He wills.

Col 1:29 To this *end* I also labor, striving according to His working which works in me mightily.

Heb 13:21 make you complete in every good work to do His will, working in you what is well pleasing in His sight, through Jesus Christ, to whom *be* glory forever and ever. Amen.

Source of eternal life.

John 10:28 And I give them eternal life, and they shall never perish; neither shall anyone snatch them out of My hand.

Rom 6:23 For the wages of sin *is* death, but the gift of God *is* eternal life in Christ Jesus our Lord.

Gal 6:8 For he who sows to his flesh will of the flesh reap corruption, but he who sows to the Spirit will of the Spirit reap everlasting life.

Teacher.

Is 48:17 Thus says the LORD, your Redeemer, The Holy One of Israel: "I *am* the LORD your God, Who teaches you to profit, Who leads you by the way you should go.

Is 54:13 All your children *shall be* taught by the LORD, And great *shall be* the peace of your children.

Luke 21:15 for I will give you a mouth and wisdom which all your adversaries will not be able to contradict or resist.

John 14:26 But the Helper, the Holy Spirit, whom the Father will send in My name, He will teach you all things, and bring to your remembrance all things that I said to you.

Gal 1:12 For I neither received it from man, nor was I taught *it*, but *it came* through the revelation of Jesus Christ.

1 John 2:20 But you have an anointing from the Holy One, and you know all things.

Raising Christ from the dead.

John 2:19 Jesus answered and said to them, "Destroy this temple, and in three days I will raise it up."

1 Cor 6:14 And God both raised up the Lord and will also raise us up by His power.

1 Pet 3:18 For Christ also suffered once for sins, the just for the unjust, that He might bring us to God, being put to death in the flesh but made alive by the Spirit,

Inspiring the prophets, etc.

Mark 13:11 But when they arrest *you* and deliver you up, do not worry beforehand, or premeditate what you will speak. But whatever is given you in that hour, speak that; for it is not you who speak, but the Holy Spirit.

2 Cor 13:3 since you seek a proof of Christ speaking in me, who is not weak toward you, but mighty in you.

Heb 1:1 God, who at various times and in various ways spoke in time past to the fathers by the prophets,

Supplying ministers to the church.

Jer 3:15 And I will give you shepherds according to My heart, who will feed you with knowledge and understanding.

Jer 26:5 to heed the words of My servants the prophets whom I sent to you, both rising up early and sending *them* (but you have not heeded),

Matt 10:5 These twelve Jesus sent out and commanded them, saying: "Do not go into the way of the Gentiles, and do not enter a city of the Samaritans.

Acts 13:2 As they ministered to the Lord and fasted, the Holy Spirit said, "Now separate to Me Barnabas and Saul for the work to which I have called them."

Acts 20:28 Therefore take heed to yourselves and to all the flock, among which the Holy Spirit has made you overseers, to shepherd the church of God which He purchased with His own blood.

Eph 4:11 And He Himself gave some *to be* apostles,

some prophets, some evangelists, and some pastors and teachers,

Salvation is work of.

2 Thess 2:13–14 But we are bound to give thanks to God always for you, brethren beloved by the Lord, because God from the beginning chose you for salvation through sanctification by the Spirit and belief in the truth, **14** to which He called you by our gospel, for the obtaining of the glory of our Lord Jesus Christ.

Titus 3:4–6 But when the kindness and the love of God our Savior toward man appeared, **5** not by works of righteousness which we have done, but according to His mercy He saved us, through the washing of regeneration and renewing of the Holy Spirit, **6** whom He poured out on us abundantly through Jesus Christ our Savior,

1 Pet 1:2 elect according to the foreknowledge of God the Father, in sanctification of the Spirit, for obedience and sprinkling of the blood of Jesus Christ: Grace to you and peace be multiplied.

Baptism administered in name of.

Matt 28:19 Go therefore and make disciples of all the nations, baptizing them in the name of the Father and of the Son and of the Holy Spirit,

Benediction given in name of.

2 Cor 13:14 The grace of the Lord Jesus Christ, and the love of God, and the communion of the Holy Spirit *be* with you all. Amen.

TRUMPET, THE

An instrument of music.

1 Chr 13:8 Then David and all Israel played *music* before God with all *their* might, with singing, on harps, on stringed instruments, on tambourines, on cymbals, and with trumpets.

Made of

Rams' horns.

Josh 6:4 And seven priests shall bear seven trumpets of rams' horns before the ark. But the seventh day you shall march around the city seven times, and the priests shall blow the trumpets.

Silver.

Num 10:2 "Make two silver trumpets for yourself; you shall make them of hammered work; you shall use them for calling the congregation and for directing the movement of the camps.

Required to give an intelligible and understood sound.

1 Cor 14:8 For if the trumpet makes an uncertain sound, who will prepare for battle?

Used for

Regulating the journeys of the children of Israel.

Num 10:2 "Make two silver trumpets for yourself; you shall make them of hammered work; you shall use them for calling the congregation and for directing the movement of the camps.

Num 10:5–6 When you sound the advance, the camps that lie on the east side shall then begin their journey. **6** When you sound the advance the second time, then the camps that lie on the south side shall begin

their journey; they shall sound the call for them to begin their journeys.

Calling assemblies.

Num 10:2–3 "Make two silver trumpets for yourself; you shall make them of hammered work; you shall use them for calling the congregation and for directing the movement of the camps. **3** When they blow both of them, all the congregation shall gather before you at the door of the tabernacle of meeting.

Num 10:7 And when the assembly is to be gathered together, you shall blow, but not sound the advance.

Blowing over the sacrifices on the feast day.

Num 10:10 Also in the day of your gladness, in your appointed feasts, and at the beginning of your months, you shall blow the trumpets over your burnt offerings and over the sacrifices of your peace offerings; and they shall be a memorial for you before your God: I *am* the LORD your God."

Ps 81:3 Blow the trumpet at the time of the New Moon, At the full moon, on our solemn feast day.

Blowing at all religious processions and ceremonies.

1 Chr 13:8 Then David and all Israel played *music* before God with all *their* might, with singing, on harps, on stringed instruments, on tambourines, on cymbals, and with trumpets.

1 Chr 15:24 Shebaniah, Joshaphat, Nethanel, Amasai, Zechariah, Benaiah, and Eliezer, the priests, were to blow the trumpets before the ark of God; and Obed-Edom and Jehiah, doorkeepers for the ark.

1 Chr 15:28 Thus all Israel brought up the ark of the covenant of the LORD with shouting and with the sound of the horn, with trumpets and with cymbals, making music with stringed instruments and harps.

2 Chr 5:13 indeed it came to pass, when the trumpeters and singers *were* as one, to make one sound to be heard in praising and thanking the LORD, and when they lifted up their voice with the trumpets and cymbals and instruments of music, and praised the LORD, *saying:* "For He is good, For His mercy *endures* forever," that the house, the house of the LORD, was filled with a cloud,

2 Chr 15:14 Then they took an oath before the LORD with a loud voice, with shouting and trumpets and rams' horns.

Assembling the people to war.

Judg 3:27 And it happened, when he arrived, that he blew the trumpet in the mountains of Ephraim, and the children of Israel went down with him from the mountains; and he led them.

Sounding for a memorial when the people went into battle.

Num 10:9 "When you go to war in your land against the enemy who oppresses you, then you shall sound an alarm with the trumpets, and you will be remembered before the LORD your God, and you will be saved from your enemies.

Num 31:6–7 Then Moses sent them to the war, one thousand from *each* tribe; he sent them to the war with Phinehas the son of Eleazar the priest, with the holy articles and the signal trumpets in his hand. **7** And they warred against the Midianites, just as the

LORD commanded Moses, and they killed all the males.

Proclaiming kings.

2 Kin 9:13 Then each man hastened to take his garment and put *it* under him on the top of the steps; and they blew trumpets, saying, "Jehu is king!"

2 Kin 11:14 When she looked, there was the king standing by a pillar according to custom; and the leaders and the trumpeters were by the king. All the people of the land were rejoicing and blowing trumpets. So Athaliah tore her clothes and cried out, "Treason! Treason!"

Giving alarm in cases of danger.

Ezek 33:2–6 "Son of man, speak to the children of your people, and say to them: 'When I bring the sword upon a land, and the people of the land take a man from their territory and make him their watchman, **3** when he sees the sword coming upon the land, if he blows the trumpet and warns the people, **4** then whoever hears the sound of the trumpet and does not take warning, if the sword comes and takes him away, his blood shall be on his *own* head. **5** He heard the sound of the trumpet, but did not take warning; his blood shall be upon himself. But he who takes warning will save his life. **6** But if the watchman sees the sword coming and does not blow the trumpet, and the people are not warned, and the sword comes and takes *any* person from among them, he is taken away in his iniquity; but his blood I will require at the watchman's hand.'

Moses commanded to make two, for the tabernacle.

Num 10:2 "Make two silver trumpets for yourself; you shall make them of hammered work; you shall use them for calling the congregation and for directing the movement of the camps.

Solomon made a great many, for the service of the temple.

2 Chr 5:12 and the Levites *who were* the singers, all those of Asaph and Heman and Jeduthun, with their sons and their brethren, stood at the east end of the altar, clothed in white linen, having cymbals, stringed instruments and harps, and with them one hundred and twenty priests sounding with trumpets—

The priests to blow the sacred.

Num 10:8 The sons of Aaron, the priests, shall blow the trumpets; and these shall be to you as an ordinance forever throughout your generations.

2 Chr 5:12 and the Levites *who were* the singers, all those of Asaph and Heman and Jeduthun, with their sons and their brethren, stood at the east end of the altar, clothed in white linen, having cymbals, stringed instruments and harps, and with them one hundred and twenty priests sounding with trumpets—

2 Chr 7:6 And the priests attended to their services; the Levites also with instruments of the music of the LORD, which King David had made to praise the LORD, saying, "For His mercy *endures* forever," whenever David offered praise by their ministry. The priests sounded trumpets opposite them, while all Israel stood.

The feast of trumpets celebrated by blowing of.

Lev 23:24 "Speak to the children of Israel, saying: 'In the seventh month, on the first *day* of the month, you shall have a sabbath-*rest,* a memorial of blowing of trumpets, a holy convocation.

Num 29:1 'And in the seventh month, on the first *day* of the month, you shall have a holy convocation. You shall do no customary work. For you it is a day of blowing the trumpets.

The Jubilee introduced by blowing of.

Lev 25:9 Then you shall cause the trumpet of the Jubilee to sound on the tenth *day* of the seventh month; on the Day of Atonement you shall make the trumpet to sound throughout all your land.

Miracles connected with,

Falling of the walls of Jericho.

Josh 6:20 So the people shouted when *the priests* blew the trumpets. And it happened when the people heard the sound of the trumpet, and the people shouted with a great shout, that the wall fell down flat. Then the people went up into the city, every man straight before him, and they took the city.

Heard at Mount Sinai at giving of the law.

Ex 19:16 Then it came to pass on the third day, in the morning, that there were thunderings and lightnings, and a thick cloud on the mountain; and the sound of the trumpet was very loud, so that all the people who *were* in the camp trembled.

Ex 20:18 Now all the people witnessed the thunderings, the lightning flashes, the sound of the trumpet, and the mountain smoking; and when the people saw *it,* they trembled and stood afar off.

Confusion produced in the camp of the Midianites by sound of.

Judg 7:16 Then he divided the three hundred men *into* three companies, and he put a trumpet into every man's hand, with empty pitchers, and torches inside the pitchers.

Judg 7:22 When the three hundred blew the trumpets, the LORD set every man's sword against his companion throughout the whole camp; and the army fled to Beth Acacia, toward Zererah, as far as the border of Abel Meholah, by Tabbath.

The war horse acquainted with the sound of.

Job 39:24–25 He devours the distance with fierceness and rage; Nor does he come to a halt because the trumpet *has* sounded. **25** At *the blast of* the trumpet he says, 'Aha!' He smells the battle from afar, The thunder of captains and shouting.

Sounding of, illustrative of

God's power to raise the dead.

1 Cor 15:52 in a moment, in the twinkling of an eye, at the last trumpet. For the trumpet will sound, and the dead will be raised incorruptible, and we shall be changed.

1 Thess 4:16 For the Lord Himself will descend from heaven with a shout, with the voice of an archangel, and with the trumpet of God. And the dead in Christ will rise first.

The proclamation of the gospel.

Ps 89:15 Blessed *are* the people who know the joyful

sound! They walk, O LORD, in the light of Your countenance.

The bold and faithful preaching of ministers.

Is 58:1 "Cry aloud, spare not; Lift up your voice like a trumpet; Tell My people their transgression, And the house of Jacob their sins.

Hos 8:1 "*Set* the trumpet to your mouth! *He shall come* like an eagle against the house of the LORD, Because they have transgressed My covenant And rebelled against My law.

Joel 2:1 Blow the trumpet in Zion, And sound an alarm in My holy mountain! Let all the inhabitants of the land tremble; For the day of the LORD is coming, For it is at hand:

Judgments in the last days.

Rev 8:2 And I saw the seven angels who stand before God, and to them were given seven trumpets.

Rev 8:13 And I looked, and I heard an angel flying through the midst of heaven, saying with a loud voice, "Woe, woe, woe to the inhabitants of the earth, because of the remaining blasts of the trumpet of the three angels who are about to sound!"

TRUST

God is the true object of.

Ps 65:5 *By* awesome deeds in righteousness You will answer us, O God of our salvation, *You who are* the confidence of all the ends of the earth, And of the far-off seas;

The fear of God leads to.

Prov 14:26 In the fear of the LORD *there is* strong confidence, And His children will have a place of refuge.

Encouragements to,

The everlasting strength of God.

Is 26:4 Trust in the LORD forever, For in YAH, the LORD, *is* everlasting strength.

The goodness of God.

Nah 1:7 The LORD *is* good, A stronghold in the day of trouble; And He knows those who trust in Him.

The lovingkindness of God.

Ps 36:7 How precious *is* Your lovingkindness, O God! Therefore the children of men put their trust under the shadow of Your wings.

The rich bounty of God.

1 Tim 6:17 Command those who are rich in this present age not to be haughty, nor to trust in uncertain riches but in the living God, who gives us richly all things to enjoy.

The care of God for us.

1 Pet 5:7 casting all your care upon Him, for He cares for you.

Previous deliverances.

Ps 9:10 And those who know Your name will put their trust in You; For You, LORD, have not forsaken those who seek You.

2 Cor 1:10 who delivered us from so great a death, and does deliver us; in whom we trust that He will still deliver *us,*

Should be with the whole heart.

Prov 3:5 Trust in the LORD with all your heart, And lean not on your own understanding;

Should be from youth up.

Ps 71:5 For You are my hope, O Lord GOD; *You are* my trust from my youth.

Of believers is

Not in the flesh.

Phil 3:3–4 For we are the circumcision, who worship God in the Spirit, rejoice in Christ Jesus, and have no confidence in the flesh, **4** though I also might have confidence in the flesh. If anyone else thinks he may have confidence in the flesh, I more so:

Not in themselves.

2 Cor 1:9 Yes, we had the sentence of death in ourselves, that we should not trust in ourselves but in God who raises the dead,

Not in carnal weapons.

1 Sam 17:38–39 So Saul clothed David with his armor, and he put a bronze helmet on his head; he also clothed him with a coat of mail. **39** David fastened his sword to his armor and tried to walk, for he had not tested *them.* And David said to Saul, "I cannot walk with these, for I have not tested *them.*" So David took them off.

1 Sam 17:45 Then David said to the Philistine, "You come to me with a sword, with a spear, and with a javelin. But I come to you in the name of the LORD of hosts, the God of the armies of Israel, whom you have defied.

Ps 44:6 For I will not trust in my bow, Nor shall my sword save me.

2 Cor 10:4 For the weapons of our warfare *are* not carnal but mighty in God for pulling down strongholds,

In God.

Ps 11:1 In the LORD I put my trust; How can you say to my soul, "Flee *as* a bird to your mountain"?

Ps 31:14 But as for me, I trust in You, O LORD; I say, "You *are* my God."

2 Cor 1:9 Yes, we had the sentence of death in ourselves, that we should not trust in ourselves but in God who raises the dead,

In the Word of God.

Ps 119:42 So shall I have an answer for him who reproaches me, For I trust in Your word.

In the mercy of God.

Ps 13:5 But I have trusted in Your mercy; My heart shall rejoice in Your salvation.

Ps 52:8 But I *am* like a green olive tree in the house of God; I trust in the mercy of God forever and ever.

In Christ.

Eph 3:12 in whom we have boldness and access with confidence through faith in Him.

Through Christ.

2 Cor 3:4 And we have such trust through Christ toward God.

Grounded in God's covenant.

2 Sam 23:5 "Although my house *is* not so with God, Yet He has made with me an everlasting covenant, Ordered in all *things* and secure. For *this is* all my salvation and all *my* desire; Will He not make *it* increase?

Strong in the prospect of death.

Ps 23:4 Yea, though I walk through the valley of the shadow of death, I will fear no evil; For You *are* with me; Your rod and Your staff, they comfort me.

Fixed.

2 Sam 22:3 The God of my strength, in whom I will trust; My shield and the horn of my salvation, My stronghold and my refuge; My Savior, You save me from violence.

Job 13:15 Though He slay me, yet will I trust Him. Even so, I will defend my own ways before Him.

Ps 112:7 He will not be afraid of evil tidings; His heart is steadfast, trusting in the LORD.

Despised by the wicked.

Is 36:4 Then *the* Rabshakeh said to them, "Say now to Hezekiah, 'Thus says the great king, the king of Assyria: "What confidence is this in which you trust?

Is 36:7 "But if you say to me, 'We trust in the LORD our God,' *is it* not He whose high places and whose altars Hezekiah has taken away, and said to Judah and Jerusalem, 'You shall worship before this altar'?" '

Forever.

Ps 52:8 But I *am* like a green olive tree in the house of God; I trust in the mercy of God forever and ever.

Ps 62:8 Trust in Him at all times, you people; Pour out your heart before Him; God *is* a refuge for us. Selah

Is 26:4 Trust in the LORD forever, For in YAH, the LORD, *is* everlasting strength.

Believers plead for, in prayer.

Ps 25:20 Keep my soul, and deliver me; Let me not be ashamed, for I put my trust in You.

Ps 31:1 In You, O LORD, I put my trust; Let me never be ashamed; Deliver me in Your righteousness.

Ps 141:8 But my eyes *are* upon You, O GOD the Lord; In You I take refuge; Do not leave my soul destitute.

The Lord knows those who have.

Nah 1:7 The LORD *is* good, A stronghold in the day of trouble; And He knows those who trust in Him.

Exhortations to.

Ps 4:5 Offer the sacrifices of righteousness, And put your trust in the LORD.

Ps 115:9–11 O Israel, trust in the LORD; He *is* their help and their shield. **10** O house of Aaron, trust in the LORD; He *is* their help and their shield. **11** You who fear the LORD, trust in the LORD; He *is* their help and their shield.

Leads to

Being encompassed with mercy.

Ps 32:10 Many sorrows *shall be* to the wicked; But he who trusts in the LORD, mercy shall surround him.

Enjoyment of perfect peace.

Is 26:3 You will keep *him* in perfect peace, *Whose* mind is stayed *on You,* Because he trusts in You.

Enjoyment of all temporal and spiritual blessings.

Is 57:13 When you cry out, Let your collection *of idols* deliver you. But the wind will carry them all away, A breath will take *them.* But he who puts his trust in Me

shall possess the land, And shall inherit My holy mountain."

Enjoyment of happiness.

Prov 16:20 He who heeds the word wisely will find good, And whoever trusts in the LORD, happy *is* he.

Rejoicing in God.

Ps 5:11 But let all those rejoice who put their trust in You; Let them ever shout for joy, because You defend them; Let those also who love Your name Be joyful in You.

Ps 33:21 For our heart shall rejoice in Him, Because we have trusted in His holy name.

Fulfillment of all holy desires.

Ps 37:5 Commit your way to the LORD, Trust also in Him, And He shall bring *it* to pass.

Deliverance from enemies.

Ps 37:40 And the LORD shall help them and deliver them; He shall deliver them from the wicked, And save them, Because they trust in Him.

Safety in times of danger.

Prov 29:25 The fear of man brings a snare, But whoever trusts in the LORD shall be safe.

Stability.

Ps 125:1 Those who trust in the LORD *Are* like Mount Zion, *Which* cannot be moved, *but* abides forever.

Prosperity.

Prov 28:25 He who is of a proud heart stirs up strife, But he who trusts in the LORD will be prospered.

Keeps from

Fear.

Ps 56:11 In God I have put my trust; I will not be afraid. What can man do to me?

Is 12:2 Behold, God *is* my salvation, I will trust and not be afraid; 'For YAH, the LORD, *is* my strength and song; He also has become my salvation.' "

Heb 13:6 So we may boldly say: *"The LORD is my helper; I will not fear. What can man do to me?"*

Slipping.

Ps 26:1 Vindicate me, O LORD, For I have walked in my integrity. I have also trusted in the LORD; I shall not slip.

Condemnation.

Ps 34:22 The LORD redeems the soul of His servants, And none of those who trust in Him shall be condemned.

To be accompanied by doing good.

Ps 37:3 Trust in the LORD, and do good; Dwell in the land, and feed on His faithfulness.

Blessedness of placing, in God.

Ps 2:12 Kiss the Son, lest He be angry, And you perish *in* the way, When His wrath is kindled but a little. Blessed *are* all those who put their trust in Him.

Ps 34:8 Oh, taste and see that the LORD *is* good; Blessed *is* the man *who* trusts in Him!

Ps 40:4 Blessed *is* that man who makes the LORD his trust, And does not respect the proud, nor such as turn aside to lies.

Jer 17:7 "Blessed *is* the man who trusts in the LORD, And whose hope is the LORD.

Of the wicked,

Is not in God.

Ps 78:22 Because they did not believe in God, And did not trust in His salvation.

Zeph 3:2 She has not obeyed *His* voice, She has not received correction; She has not trusted in the LORD, She has not drawn near to her God.

Is in idols.

Is 42:17 They shall be turned back, They shall be greatly ashamed, Who trust in carved images, Who say to the molded images, 'You *are* our gods.'

Hab 2:18 "What profit is the image, that its maker should carve it, The molded image, a teacher of lies, That the maker of its mold should trust in it, To make mute idols?

Is in man.

Judg 9:26 Now Gaal the son of Ebed came with his brothers and went over to Shechem; and the men of Shechem put their confidence in him.

Ps 118:8–9 *It is* better to trust in the LORD Than to put confidence in man. **9** *It is* better to trust in the LORD Than to put confidence in princes.

Is in their own heart.

Prov 28:26 He who trusts in his own heart is a fool, But whoever walks wisely will be delivered.

Is in their own righteousness.

Luke 18:9 Also He spoke this parable to some who trusted in themselves that they were righteous, and despised others:

Luke 18:12 I fast twice a week; I give tithes of all that I possess.'

Is in futile things.

Job 15:31 Let him not trust in futile *things,* deceiving himself, For futility will be his reward.

Is 59:4 No one calls for justice, Nor does *any* plead for truth. They trust in empty words and speak lies; They conceive evil and bring forth iniquity.

Is in falsehood.

Is 28:15 Because you have said, "We have made a covenant with death, And with Sheol we are in agreement. When the overflowing scourge passes through, It will not come to us, For we have made lies our refuge, And under falsehood we have hidden ourselves."

Jer 13:25 This is your lot, The portion of your measures from Me," says the LORD, "Because you have forgotten Me And trusted in falsehood.

Is in earthly alliances.

Is 30:2 Who walk to go down to Egypt, And have not asked My advice, To strengthen themselves in the strength of Pharaoh, And to trust in the shadow of Egypt!

Ezek 17:15 But he rebelled against him by sending his ambassadors to Egypt, that they might give him horses and many people. Will he prosper? Will he who does such *things* escape? Can he break a covenant and still be delivered?

Is in wealth.

Ps 49:6 Those who trust in their wealth And boast in the multitude of their riches,

Ps 52:7 "Here is the man *who* did not make God his strength, But trusted in the abundance of his riches, And strengthened himself in his wickedness."

Prov 11:28 He who trusts in his riches will fall, But the righteous will flourish like foliage.

Jer 48:7 For because you have trusted in your works and your treasures, You also shall be taken. And Chemosh shall go forth into captivity, His priests and his princes together.

Mark 10:24 And the disciples were astonished at His words. But Jesus answered again and said to them, "Children, how hard it is for those who trust in riches to enter the kingdom of God!

Is vain and delusive.

Is 30:7 For the Egyptians shall help in vain and to no purpose. Therefore I have called her Rahab-Hem-Shebeth.

Jer 2:37 Indeed you will go forth from him With your hands on your head; For the LORD has rejected your trusted allies, And you will not prosper by them.

Shall make them ashamed.

Is 20:5 Then they shall be afraid and ashamed of Ethiopia their expectation and Egypt their glory.

Is 30:3 Therefore the strength of Pharaoh Shall be your shame, And trust in the shadow of Egypt Shall be *your* humiliation.

Is 30:5 They were all ashamed of a people *who* could not benefit them, Or be help or benefit, But a shame and also a reproach."

Jer 48:13 Moab shall be ashamed of Chemosh, As the house of Israel was ashamed of Bethel, their confidence.

Shall be destroyed.

Job 18:14 He is uprooted from the shelter of his tent, And they parade him before the king of terrors.

Is 28:18 Your covenant with death will be annulled, And your agreement with Sheol will not stand; When the overflowing scourge passes through, Then you will be trampled down by it.

Woe and curse of false.

Is 30:1–2 "Woe to the rebellious children," says the LORD, "Who take counsel, but not of Me, And who devise plans, but not of My Spirit, That they may add sin to sin; **2** Who walk to go down to Egypt, And have not asked My advice, To strengthen themselves in the strength of Pharaoh, And to trust in the shadow of Egypt!

Is 31:1–3 Woe to those who go down to Egypt for help, *And* rely on horses, Who trust in chariots because *they are* many, And in horsemen because they are very strong, But who do not look to the Holy One of Israel, Nor seek the LORD! **2** Yet He also *is* wise and will bring disaster, And will not call back His words, But will arise against the house of evildoers, And against the help of those who work iniquity. **3** Now the Egyptians *are* men, and not God; And their horses are flesh, and not spirit. When the LORD stretches out His hand, Both he who helps will fall, And he who is helped will fall down; They all will perish together.

Jer 17:5 Thus says the LORD: "Cursed *is* the man who

trusts in man And makes flesh his strength, Whose heart departs from the LORD.

Of believers—described.

Ps 91:12 In *their* hands they shall bear you up, Lest you dash your foot against a stone.

Prov 18:10 The name of the LORD *is* a strong tower; The righteous run to it and are safe.

Of the wicked—described.

2 Kin 18:21 Now look! You are trusting in the staff of this broken reed, Egypt, on which if a man leans, it will go into his hand and pierce it. So *is* Pharaoh king of Egypt to all who trust in him.

Job 8:14 Whose confidence shall be cut off, And whose trust *is* a spider's web.

Of believers—exemplified by

David.

1 Sam 17:45 Then David said to the Philistine, "You come to me with a sword, with a spear, and with a javelin. But I come to you in the name of the LORD of hosts, the God of the armies of Israel, whom you have defied.

1 Sam 30:6 Now David was greatly distressed, for the people spoke of stoning him, because the soul of all the people was grieved, every man for his sons and his daughters. But David strengthened himself in the LORD his God.

Hezekiah.

2 Kin 18:5 He trusted in the LORD God of Israel, so that after him was none like him among all the kings of Judah, nor who were before him.

Jehoshaphat.

2 Chr 20:12 O our God, will You not judge them? For we have no power against this great multitude that is coming against us; nor do we know what to do, but our eyes *are* upon You.

Shadrach, Meshach, and Abed-Nego.

Dan 3:28 Nebuchadnezzar spoke, saying, "Blessed be the God of Shadrach, Meshach, and Abed-Nego, who sent His Angel and delivered His servants who trusted in Him, and they have frustrated the king's word, and yielded their bodies, that they should not serve nor worship any god except their own God!

Paul.

2 Tim 1:12 For this reason I also suffer these things; nevertheless I am not ashamed, for I know whom I have believed and am persuaded that He is able to keep what I have committed to Him until that Day.

Of the wicked—illustrated by

Goliath.

1 Sam 17:43–45 So the Philistine said to David, "*Am* I a dog, that you come to me with sticks?" And the Philistine cursed David by his gods. 44 And the Philistine said to David, "Come to me, and I will give your flesh to the birds of the air and the beasts of the field!" **45** Then David said to the Philistine, "You come to me with a sword, with a spear, and with a javelin. But I come to you in the name of the LORD of hosts, the God of the armies of Israel, whom you have defied.

Ben-Hadad.

1 Kin 20:10 Then Ben-Hadad sent to him and said, "The

gods do so to me, and more also, if enough dust is left of Samaria for a handful for each of the people who follow me."

Sennacherib.

2 Chr 32:8 With him *is* an arm of flesh; but with us *is* the LORD our God, to help us and to fight our battles." And the people were strengthened by the words of Hezekiah king of Judah.

The Israelites.

Is 31:1 Woe to those who go down to Egypt for help, *And* rely on horses, Who trust in chariots because *they are* many, And in horsemen because they are very strong, But who do not look to the Holy One of Israel, Nor seek the LORD!

TRUTH

God is a God of.

Deut 32:4 *He is* the Rock, His work *is* perfect; For all His ways *are* justice, A God of truth and without injustice; Righteous and upright *is* He.

Ps 31:15 My times *are* in Your hand; Deliver me from the hand of my enemies, And from those who persecute me.

Christ is.

John 1:14 And the Word became flesh and dwelt among us, and we beheld His glory, the glory as of the only begotten of the Father, full of grace and truth.

John 7:18 He who speaks from himself seeks his own glory; but He who seeks the glory of the One who sent Him is true, and no unrighteousness is in Him.

John 14:6 Jesus said to him, "I am the way, the truth, and the life. No one comes to the Father except through Me.

Christ spoke.

John 8:45 But because I tell the truth, you do not believe Me.

The Holy Spirit is the Spirit of.

John 14:17 the Spirit of truth, whom the world cannot receive, because it neither sees Him nor knows Him; but you know Him, for He dwells with you and will be in you.

The Holy Spirit guides into all.

John 16:13 However, when He, the Spirit of truth, has come, He will guide you into all truth; for He will not speak on His own *authority,* but whatever He hears He will speak; and He will tell you things to come.

The Word of God is.

Dan 10:21 But I will tell you what is noted in the Scripture of Truth. (No one upholds me against these, except Michael your prince.

John 17:17 Sanctify them by Your truth. Your word is truth.

God regards, with favor.

Jer 5:3 O LORD, *are* not Your eyes on the truth? You have stricken them, But they have not grieved; You have consumed them, But they have refused to receive correction. They have made their faces harder than rock; They have refused to return.

The judgments of God are according to.

Ps 96:13 For He is coming, for He is coming to judge the earth. He shall judge the world with righteousness, And the peoples with His truth.

Rom 2:2 But we know that the judgment of God is according to truth against those who practice such things.

Believers should

Worship God in.

Ps 145:18 The LORD *is* near to all who call upon Him, To all who call upon Him in truth.

John 4:24 God *is* Spirit, and those who worship Him must worship in spirit and truth."

Serve God in.

Josh 24:14 "Now therefore, fear the LORD, serve Him in sincerity and in truth, and put away the gods which your fathers served on the other side of the River and in Egypt. Serve the LORD!

1 Sam 12:24 Only fear the LORD, and serve Him in truth with all your heart; for consider what great things He has done for you.

Walk before God in.

1 Kin 2:4 that the LORD may fulfill His word which He spoke concerning me, saying, 'If your sons take heed to their way, to walk before Me in truth with all their heart and with all their soul,' He said, 'you shall not lack a man on the throne of Israel.'

2 Kin 20:3 "Remember now, O LORD, I pray, how I have walked before You in truth and with a loyal heart, and have done *what was* good in Your sight." And Hezekiah wept bitterly.

Keep religious feasts with.

1 Cor 5:8 Therefore let us keep the feast, not with old leaven, nor with the leaven of malice and wickedness, but with the unleavened *bread* of sincerity and truth.

Esteem, as priceless.

Prov 23:23 Buy the truth, and do not sell *it, Also* wisdom and instruction and understanding.

Rejoice in.

1 Cor 13:6 does not rejoice in iniquity, but rejoices in the truth;

Speak, to one another.

Zech 8:16 These *are* the things you shall do: Speak each man the truth to his neighbor; Give judgment in your gates for truth, justice, and peace;

Eph 4:25 Therefore, putting away lying, *"Let each one of you speak truth with his neighbor,"* for we are members of one another.

Meditate upon.

Phil 4:8 Finally, brethren, whatever things are true, whatever things *are* noble, whatever things *are* just, whatever things *are* pure, whatever things *are* lovely, whatever things *are* of good report, if *there is* any virtue and if *there is* anything praiseworthy—meditate on these things.

Write, upon the tablets of the heart.

Prov 3:3 Let not mercy and truth forsake you; Bind them around your neck, Write them on the tablet of your heart,

God desires in the heart.

Ps 51:6 Behold, You desire truth in the inward parts,

And in the hidden *part* You will make me to know wisdom.

The fruit of the Spirit is in.

Eph 5:9 (for the fruit of the Spirit *is* in all goodness, righteousness, and truth),

Ministers should

Speak.

2 Cor 12:6 For though I might desire to boast, I will not be a fool; for I will speak the truth. But I refrain, lest anyone should think of me above what he sees me *to be* or hears from me.

Gal 4:16 Have I therefore become your enemy because I tell you the truth?

Teach in.

1 Tim 2:7 for which I was appointed a preacher and an apostle—I am speaking the truth in Christ *and* not lying—a teacher of the Gentiles in faith and truth.

Approve themselves by.

2 Cor 4:2 But we have renounced the hidden things of shame, not walking in craftiness nor handling the word of God deceitfully, but by manifestation of the truth commending ourselves to every man's conscience in the sight of God.

2 Cor 6:7–8 by the word of truth, by the power of God, by the armor of righteousness on the right hand and on the left, **8** by honor and dishonor, by evil report and good report; as deceivers, and *yet* true;

2 Cor 7:14 For if in anything I have boasted to him about you, I am not ashamed. But as we spoke all things to you in truth, even so our boasting to Titus was found true.

Magistrates should be men of.

Ex 18:21 Moreover you shall select from all the people able men, such as fear God, men of truth, hating covetousness; and place *such* over them *to be* rulers of thousands, rulers of hundreds, rulers of fifties, and rulers of tens.

Kings are preserved by.

Prov 20:28 Mercy and truth preserve the king, And by lovingkindness he upholds his throne.

Those who speak,

Show forth righteousness.

Prov 12:17 He *who* speaks truth declares righteousness, But a false witness, deceit.

Shall be established.

Prov 12:19 The truthful lip shall be established forever, But a lying tongue *is* but for a moment.

Are the delight of God.

Prov 12:22 Lying lips *are* an abomination to the LORD, But those who deal truthfully *are* His delight.

The wicked

Do not speak or practice.

Is 59:14–15 Justice is turned back, And righteousness stands afar off; For truth is fallen in the street, And equity cannot enter. **15** So truth fails, And he *who* departs from evil makes himself a prey. Then the LORD saw *it,* and it displeased Him That *there was* no justice.

Jer 9:5 Everyone will deceive his neighbor, And will not speak the truth; They have taught their tongue to speak lies; They weary themselves to commit iniquity.

Hos 4:1 Hear the word of the LORD, You children of Israel, For the LORD *brings* a charge against the inhabitants of the land: "There is no truth or mercy Or knowledge of God in the land.

Do not plead for.

Is 59:4 No one calls for justice, Nor does *any* plead for truth. They trust in empty words and speak lies; They conceive evil and bring forth iniquity.

Are not valiant for.

Jer 9:3 "And *like* their bow they have bent their tongues *for* lies. They are not valiant for the truth on the earth. For they proceed from evil to evil, And they do not know Me," says the LORD.

Punished for lack of.

Jer 9:5 Everyone will deceive his neighbor, And will not speak the truth; They have taught their tongue to speak lies; They weary themselves to commit iniquity.

Jer 9:9 Shall I not punish them for these *things?*" says the LORD. "Shall I not avenge Myself on such a nation as this?"

Hos 4:1 Hear the word of the LORD, You children of Israel, For the LORD *brings* a charge against the inhabitants of the land: "There is no truth or mercy Or knowledge of God in the land.

Came by Jesus Christ (gospel).

John 1:17 For the law was given through Moses, *but* grace and truth came through Jesus Christ.

John 18:37 Pilate therefore said to Him, "Are You a king then?" Jesus answered, "You say *rightly* that I am a king. For this cause I was born, and for this cause I have come into the world, that I should bear witness to the truth. Everyone who is of the truth hears My voice."

Rom 9:1 I tell the truth in Christ, I am not lying, my conscience also bearing me witness in the Holy Spirit,

1 Tim 2:7 for which I was appointed a preacher and an apostle—I am speaking the truth in Christ *and* not lying—a teacher of the Gentiles in faith and truth.

John bears witness to.

John 5:33 You have sent to John, and he has borne witness to the truth.

Is according to godliness.

Titus 1:1 Paul, a bondservant of God and an apostle of Jesus Christ, according to the faith of God's elect and the acknowledgment of the truth which accords with godliness,

Is sanctifying.

John 17:17 Sanctify them by Your truth. Your word is truth.

John 17:19 And for their sakes I sanctify Myself, that they also may be sanctified by the truth.

Is purifying.

1 Pet 1:22 Since you have purified your souls in obeying the truth through the Spirit in sincere love of the brethren, love one another fervently with a pure heart,

Is part of Christian armor.

Eph 6:14 Stand therefore, having girded your waist with truth, having put on the breastplate of righteousness,

Is available to believers.

Jer 33:6 Behold, I will bring it health and healing; I will heal them and reveal to them the abundance of peace and truth.

2 John 1:2 because of the truth which abides in us and will be with us forever:

Should be acknowledged and believed.

2 Thess 2:12–13 that they all may be condemned who did not believe the truth but had pleasure in unrighteousness. **13** But we are bound to give thanks to God always for you, brethren beloved by the Lord, because God from the beginning chose you for salvation through sanctification by the Spirit and belief in the truth,

1 Tim 4:3 forbidding to marry, *and commanding* to abstain from foods which God created to be received with thanksgiving by those who believe and know the truth.

2 Tim 2:25 in humility correcting those who are in opposition, if God perhaps will grant them repentance, so that they may know the truth,

Should be loved and obeyed.

Rom 2:8 but to those who are self-seeking and do not obey the truth, but obey unrighteousness—indignation and wrath,

Gal 3:1 O foolish Galatians! Who has bewitched you that you should not obey the truth, before whose eyes Jesus Christ was clearly portrayed among you as crucified?

2 Thess 2:10 and with all unrighteous deception among those who perish, because they did not receive the love of the truth, that they might be saved.

Should be manifested.

2 Cor 4:2 But we have renounced the hidden things of shame, not walking in craftiness nor handling the word of God deceitfully, but by manifestation of the truth commending ourselves to every man's conscience in the sight of God.

Should be rightly divided.

2 Tim 2:15 Be diligent to present yourself approved to God, a worker who does not need to be ashamed, rightly dividing the word of truth.

The wicked opposed to.

1 Tim 6:5 useless wranglings of men of corrupt minds and destitute of the truth, who suppose that godliness is a *means of* gain. From such withdraw yourself.

2 Tim 3:8 Now as Jannes and Jambres resisted Moses, so do these also resist the truth: men of corrupt minds, disapproved concerning the faith;

2 Tim 4:4 and they will turn *their* ears away from the truth, and be turned aside to fables.

The church is the pillar and ground of.

1 Tim 3:15 but if I am delayed, *I write* so that you may know how you ought to conduct yourself in the house of God, which is the church of the living God, the pillar and ground of the truth.

The devil is devoid of.

John 8:44 You are of *your* father the devil, and the desires of your father you want to do. He was a murderer from the beginning, and does not stand in the truth, because there is no truth in him. When he speaks a lie, he speaks from his own *resources*, for he is a liar and the father of it.

TYRE

Antiquity of.

Josh 19:29 And the border turned to Ramah and to the fortified city of Tyre; then the border turned to Hosah, and ended at the sea by the region of Achzib.

Is 23:7 *Is* this your joyous *city*, Whose antiquity *is* from ancient days, Whose feet carried her far off to dwell?

Other names for,

The daughter of Sidon.

Is 23:12 And He said, "You will rejoice no more, O you oppressed virgin daughter of Sidon. Arise, cross over to Cyprus; There also you will have no rest."

The daughter of Tarshish.

Is 23:10 Overflow through your land like the River, O daughter of Tarshish; *There is* no more strength.

The joyous city.

Is 23:7 *Is* this your joyous *city*, Whose antiquity *is* from ancient days, Whose feet carried her far off to dwell?

The crowning city.

Is 23:8 Who has taken this counsel against Tyre, the crowning *city*, Whose merchants *are* princes, Whose traders *are* the honorable of the earth?

The renowned city.

Ezek 26:17 And they will take up a lamentation for you, and say to you: "How you have perished, O one inhabited by seafaring men, O renowned city, Who was strong at sea, She and her inhabitants, Who caused their terror *to be* on all her inhabitants!

Insular position of.

Ezek 26:17 And they will take up a lamentation for you, and say to you: "How you have perished, O one inhabited by seafaring men, O renowned city, Who was strong at sea, She and her inhabitants, Who caused their terror *to be* on all her inhabitants!

Ezek 27:4 Your borders *are* in the midst of the seas. Your builders have perfected your beauty.

Ezek 27:25 "The ships of Tarshish were carriers of your merchandise. You were filled and very glorious in the midst of the seas.

Strongly fortified.

Josh 19:29 And the border turned to Ramah and to the fortified city of Tyre; then the border turned to Hosah, and ended at the sea by the region of Achzib.

2 Sam 24:7 and they came to the stronghold of Tyre and to all the cities of the Hivites and the Canaanites. Then they went out to South Judah *as far as* Beersheba.

Ezek 26:17 And they will take up a lamentation for you, and say to you: "How you have perished, O one inhabited by seafaring men, O renowned city, Who was strong at sea, She and her inhabitants, Who caused their terror *to be* on all her inhabitants!

Zech 9:3 For Tyre built herself a tower, Heaped up silver like the dust, And gold like the mire of the streets.

Governed by kings.

1 Kin 5:1 Now Hiram king of Tyre sent his servants to Solomon, because he heard that they had anointed him king in place of his father, for Hiram had always loved David.

Jer 25:22 all the kings of Tyre, all the kings of Sidon, and the kings of the coastlands which *are* across the sea;

Celebrated for

Its beauty.

Ezek 27:3–4 and say to Tyre, 'You who are situated at the entrance of the sea, merchant of the peoples on many coastlands, thus says the Lord GOD: "O Tyre, you have said, 'I *am* perfect in beauty.' **4** Your borders *are* in the midst of the seas. Your builders have perfected your beauty.

Its commerce.

Is 23:2–3 Be still, you inhabitants of the coastland, You merchants of Sidon, Whom those who cross the sea have filled. **3** And on great waters the grain of Shihor, The harvest of the River, *is* her revenue; And she is a marketplace for the nations.

Ezek 27:3 and say to Tyre, 'You who are situated at the entrance of the sea, merchant of the peoples on many coastlands, thus says the Lord GOD: "O Tyre, you have said, 'I *am* perfect in beauty.'

Cf. Ezek 27:12–25

Its wealth.

Ezek 27:33 'When your wares went out by sea, You satisfied many people; You enriched the kings of the earth With your many luxury goods and your merchandise.

Ezek 28:4–5 With your wisdom and your understanding You have gained riches for yourself, And gathered gold and silver into your treasuries; **5** By your great wisdom in trade you have increased your riches, And your heart is lifted up because of your riches),"

Zech 9:3 For Tyre built herself a tower, Heaped up silver like the dust, And gold like the mire of the streets.

Strength and beauty of its ships.

Ezek 27:5–7 They made all *your* planks of fir trees from Senir; They took a cedar from Lebanon to make you a mast. **6** *Of* oaks from Bashan they made your oars; The company of Ashurites have inlaid your planks *With* ivory from the coasts of Cyprus. **7** Fine embroidered linen from Egypt was what you spread for your sail; Blue and purple from the coasts of Elishah was what covered you.

Soldiers of, supplied by Persia, etc.

Ezek 27:10–11 "Those from Persia, Lydia, and Libya Were in your army as men of war; They hung shield and helmet in you; They gave splendor to you. **11** Men of Arvad with your army *were* on your walls *all* around, And the men of Gammad were in your towers; They hung their shields on your walls *all* around; They made your beauty perfect.

Inhabitants of,

Seafaring men.

Ezek 26:17 And they will take up a lamentation for you, and say to you: "How you have perished, O one inhabited by seafaring men, O renowned city, Who was strong at sea, And her inhabitants, Who caused their terror *to be* on all her inhabitants!

Merchants and traders.

Is 23:8 Who has taken this counsel against Tyre, the crowning *city*, Whose merchants *are* princes, Whose traders *are* the honorable of the earth?

Proud and haughty.

Is 23:9 The Lord of hosts has purposed it, To bring to dishonor the pride of all glory, To bring into contempt all the honorable of the earth.

Ezek 28:2 "Son of man, say to the prince of Tyre, 'Thus says the Lord God: "Because your heart *is* lifted up, And you say, 'I *am* a god, I sit *in* the seat of gods, In the midst of the seas,' Yet you *are* a man, and not a god, Though you set your heart as the heart of a god

Ezek 28:17 "Your heart was lifted up because of your beauty; You corrupted your wisdom for the sake of your splendor; I cast you to the ground, I laid you before kings, That they might gaze at you.

Self-conceited.

Ezek 28:3–5 (Behold, you *are* wiser than Daniel! There is no secret that can be hidden from you! **4** With your wisdom and your understanding You have gained riches for yourself, And gathered gold and silver into your treasuries; **5** By your great wisdom in trade you have increased your riches, And your heart is lifted up because of your riches),"

Superstitious.

Jer 27:2–3 "Thus says the Lord to me: 'Make for yourselves bonds and yokes, and put them on your neck, **3** and send them to the king of Edom, the king of Moab, the king of the Ammonites, the king of Tyre, and the king of Sidon, by the hand of the messengers who come to Jerusalem to Zedekiah king of Judah.

Jer 27:9 Therefore do not listen to your prophets, your diviners, your dreamers, your soothsayers, or your sorcerers, who speak to you, saying, "You shall not serve the king of Babylon."

Wicked.

Ezek 28:18 "You defiled your sanctuaries By the multitude of your iniquities, By the iniquity of your trading; Therefore I brought fire from your midst; It devoured you, And I turned you to ashes upon the earth In the sight of all who saw you.

Often confederated against the Jews.

Ps 83:7 Gebal, Ammon, and Amalek; Philistia with the inhabitants of Tyre;

Ezek 26:2 "Son of man, because Tyre has said against Jerusalem, 'Aha! She is broken who *was* the gateway of the peoples; now she is turned over to me; I shall be filled; she is laid waste.'

Amos 1:9 Thus says the Lord: "For three transgressions of Tyre, and for four, I will not turn away its *punishment*, Because they delivered up the whole captivity to Edom, And did not remember the covenant of brotherhood.

David and Solomon formed alliances with.

1 Kin 5:1 Now Hiram king of Tyre sent his servants to Solomon, because he heard that they had anointed him king in place of his father, for Hiram had always loved David.

2 Chr 2:3 Then Solomon sent to Hiram king of Tyre, saying: As you have dealt with David my father, and sent him cedars to build himself a house to dwell in, *so deal with me.*

Supplied

Seamen for Solomon's navy.

1 Kin 9:27 Then Hiram sent his servants with the fleet, seamen who knew the sea, to work with the servants of Solomon.

2 Chr 8:18 And Hiram sent him ships by the hand of his servants, and servants who knew the sea. They went with the servants of Solomon to Ophir, and acquired four hundred and fifty talents of gold from there, and brought it to King Solomon.

Master craftsmen.

2 Chr 2:7 Therefore send me at once a man skillful to work in gold and silver, in bronze and iron, in purple and crimson and blue, who has skill to engrave with the skillful men who are with me in Judah and Jerusalem, whom David my father provided.

2 Chr 2:13 And now I have sent a skillful man, endowed with understanding, Huram my master *craftsman*

Timber for building the temple.

1 Kin 5:6 Now therefore, command that they cut down cedars for me from Lebanon; and my servants will be with your servants, and I will pay you wages for your servants according to whatever you say. For you know *there is* none among us who has skill to cut timber like the Sidonians.

1 Kin 5:9 My servants shall bring *them* down from Lebanon to the sea; I will float them in rafts by sea to the place you indicate to me, and will have them broken apart there; then you can take *them* away. And you shall fulfill my desire by giving food for my household.

2 Chr 2:8–9 Also send me cedar and cypress and algum logs from Lebanon, for I know that your servants have skill to cut timber in Lebanon; and indeed my servants *will be* with your servants, **9** to prepare timber for me in abundance, for the temple which I am about to build *shall be* great and wonderful.

2 Chr 2:16 And we will cut wood from Lebanon, as much as you need; we will bring it to you in rafts by sea to Joppa, and you will carry it up to Jerusalem.

Timber for rebuilding the temple and city.

Ezra 3:7 They also gave money to the masons and the carpenters, and food, drink, and oil to the people of Sidon and Tyre to bring cedar logs from Lebanon to the sea, to Joppa, according to the permission which they had from Cyrus king of Persia.

The Jews condemned for purchasing from the people of, on the Sabbath.

Neh 13:16 Men of Tyre dwelt there also, who brought in fish and all kinds of goods, and sold *them* on the Sabbath to the children of Judah, and in Jerusalem.

Christ

Alluded to city's depravity.

Matt 11:21–22 "Woe to you, Chorazin! Woe to you, Bethsaida! For if the mighty works which were done in you had been done in Tyre and Sidon, they would have repented long ago in sackcloth and ashes. **22** But I say to you, it will be more tolerable for Tyre and Sidon in the day of judgment than for you.

Visited the coasts of.

Matt 15:21 Then Jesus went out from there and departed to the region of Tyre and Sidon.

Mark 7:24 From there He arose and went to the region of Tyre and Sidon. And He entered a house and wanted no one to know *it*, but He could not be hidden.

Was followed by many from.

Mark 3:8 and Jerusalem and Idumea and beyond the Jordan; and those from Tyre and Sidon, a great multitude, when they heard how many things He was doing, came to Him.

Luke 6:17 And He came down with them and stood on a level place with a crowd of His disciples and a great multitude of people from all Judea and Jerusalem, and from the seacoast of Tyre and Sidon, who came to hear Him and be healed of their diseases,

Paul found disciples at.

Acts 21:3–4 When we had sighted Cyprus, we passed it on the left, sailed to Syria, and landed at Tyre; for there the ship was to unload her cargo. **4** And finding disciples, we stayed there seven days. They told Paul through the Spirit not to go up to Jerusalem.

Depended for provision upon Galilee.

Acts 12:20 Now Herod had been very angry with the people of Tyre and Sidon; but they came to him with one accord, and having made Blastus the king's personal aide their friend, they asked for peace, because their country was supplied with food by the king's *country*.

Appeased the anger of Herod.

Acts 12:20 Now Herod had been very angry with the people of Tyre and Sidon; but they came to him with one accord, and having made Blastus the king's personal aide their friend, they asked for peace, because their country was supplied with food by the king's *country*.

Prophecies respecting,

Envy against the Jews a cause of its destruction.

Ezek 26:2 "Son of man, because Tyre has said against Jerusalem, 'Aha! She is broken who *was* the gateway of the peoples; now she is turned over to me; I shall be filled; she is laid waste.'

Pride a cause of its destruction.

Ezek 28:2–6 "Son of man, say to the prince of Tyre, 'Thus says the Lord GOD: "Because your heart *is* lifted up, And you say, 'I *am* a god, I sit *in* the seat of gods, In the midst of the seas,' Yet you *are* a man, and not a god, Though you set your heart as the heart of a god **3** (Behold, you *are* wiser than Daniel! There is no secret that can be hidden from you! **4** With your wisdom and your understanding You have gained riches for yourself, And gathered gold and silver into your treasuries; **5** By your great wisdom in trade you

have increased your riches, And your heart is lifted up because of your riches)," **6** 'Therefore thus says the Lord GOD: "Because you have set your heart as the heart of a god,

To be destroyed by the king of Babylon.

Is 23:13–14 Behold, the land of the Chaldeans, This people *which* was not; Assyria founded it for wild beasts of the desert. They set up its towers, They raised up its palaces, *And* brought it to ruin. **14** Wail, you ships of Tarshish! For your strength is laid waste.

Jer 27:3 and send them to the king of Edom, the king of Moab, the king of the Ammonites, the king of Tyre, and the king of Sidon, by the hand of the messengers who come to Jerusalem to Zedekiah king of Judah.

Jer 27:6 And now I have given all these lands into the hand of Nebuchadnezzar the king of Babylon, My servant; and the beasts of the field I have also given him to serve him.

Ezek 26:7–13 "For thus says the Lord GOD: 'Behold, I will bring against Tyre from the north Nebuchadnezzar king of Babylon, king of kings, with horses, with chariots, and with horsemen, and an army with many people. **8** He will slay with the sword your daughter *villages* in the fields; he will heap up a siege mound against you, build a wall against you, and raise a defense against you. **9** He will direct his battering rams against your walls, and with his axes he will break down your towers. **10** Because of the abundance of his horses, their dust will cover you; your walls will shake at the noise of the horsemen, the wagons, and the chariots, when he enters your gates, as men enter a city that has been breached. **11** With the hooves of his horses he will trample all your streets; he will slay your people by the sword, and your strong pillars will fall to the ground. **12** They will plunder your riches and pillage your merchandise; they will break down your walls and destroy your pleasant houses; they will lay your stones, your timber, and your soil in the midst of the water. **13** I will put an end to the sound of your songs, and the sound of your harps shall be heard no more.

Inhabitants of, would emigrate to other countries.

Is 23:12 And He said, "You will rejoice no more, O you oppressed virgin daughter of Sidon. Arise, cross over to Cyprus; There also you will have no rest."

To be scraped as the top of a rock, and to be a place for the spreading nets.

Ezek 26:3–5 "Therefore thus says the Lord GOD: 'Behold, I *am* against you, O Tyre, and will cause many nations to come up against you, as the sea causes its waves to come up. **4** And they shall destroy the walls of Tyre and break down her towers; I will also scrape her dust from her, and make her like the top of a rock. **5** It shall be *a place for* spreading nets in the midst of the sea, for I have spoken,' says the Lord GOD; 'it shall become plunder for the nations.

Ezek 26:14 I will make you like the top of a rock; you shall be *a place for* spreading nets, and you shall never be rebuilt, for I the LORD have spoken,' says the Lord GOD.

The king of Babylon rewarded for his service against.

Ezek 29:18–20 "Son of man, Nebuchadnezzar king of

Babylon caused his army to labor strenuously against Tyre; every head *was* made bald, and every shoulder rubbed raw; yet neither he nor his army received wages from Tyre, for the labor which they expended on it. **19** Therefore thus says the Lord GOD: 'Surely I will give the land of Egypt to Nebuchadnezzar king of Babylon; he shall take away her wealth, carry off her spoil, and remove her pillage; and that will be the wages for his army. **20** I have given him the land of Egypt *for* his labor, because they worked for Me,' says the Lord GOD.

To lie in waste and be forgotten for seventy years.

Is 23:15 Now it shall come to pass in that day that Tyre will be forgotten seventy years, according to the days of one king. At the end of seventy years it will happen to Tyre as *in* the song of the harlot:

Its restoration to commercial greatness after seventy years.

Is 23:16–17 "Take a harp, go about the city, You forgotten harlot; Make sweet melody, sing many songs, That you may be remembered." **17** And it shall be, at the end of seventy years, that the LORD will deal with Tyre. She will return to her hire, and commit fornication with all the kingdoms of the world on the face of the earth.

Its second destruction by the Macedonians.

Ezek 27:32 In their wailing for you They will take up a lamentation, And lament for you: 'What *city is* like Tyre, Destroyed in the midst of the sea?

Ezek 28:7–8 Behold, therefore, I will bring strangers against you, The most terrible of the nations; And they shall draw their swords against the beauty of your wisdom, And defile your splendor. **8** They shall throw you down into the Pit, And you shall die the death of the slain In the midst of the seas.

Ezek 28:18 "You defiled your sanctuaries By the multitude of your iniquities, By the iniquity of your trading; Therefore I brought fire from your midst; It devoured you, And I turned you to ashes upon the earth In the sight of all who saw you.

Zech 9:2–4 Also *against* Hamath, *which* borders on it, And *against* Tyre and Sidon, though they are very wise. **3** For Tyre built herself a tower, Heaped up silver like the dust, And gold like the mire of the streets. **4** Behold, the LORD will cast her out; He will destroy her power in the sea, And she will be devoured by fire.

The ruins of the first city employed in destroying the second city.

Ezek 26:12 They will plunder your riches and pillage your merchandise; they will break down your walls and destroy your pleasant houses; they will lay your stones, your timber, and your soil in the midst of the water.

Never to recover its greatness.

Ezek 26:21 I will make you a terror, and you *shall be* no *more;* though you are sought for, you will never be found again,' says the Lord GOD."

Its inhabitants sold as slaves, as a recompence for their selling the Jews.

Joel 3:4–8 "Indeed, what have you to do with Me, O Tyre and Sidon, and all the coasts of Philistia? Will you retaliate against Me? But if you retaliate against Me, Swiftly and speedily I will return your retaliation upon your own head; **5** Because you have taken My silver and My gold, And have carried into your temples My prized possessions. **6** Also the people of Judah and the people of Jerusalem You have sold to the Greeks, That you may remove them far from their borders. **7** "Behold, I will raise them Out of the place to which you have sold them, And will return your retaliation upon your own head. **8** I will sell your sons and your daughters Into the hand of the people of Judah, And they will sell them to the Sabeans, To a people far off; For the LORD has spoken."

All nations terrified at its destruction.

Ezek 26:15–18 "Thus says the Lord GOD to Tyre: 'Will the coastlands not shake at the sound of your fall, when the wounded cry, when slaughter is made in the midst of you? **16** Then all the princes of the sea will come down from their thrones, lay aside their robes, and take off their embroidered garments; they will clothe themselves with trembling; they will sit on the ground, tremble *every* moment, and be astonished at you. **17** And they will take up a lamentation for you, and say to you: "How you have perished, O one inhabited by seafaring men, O renowned city, Who was strong at sea, She and her inhabitants, Who caused their terror *to be* on all her inhabitants! **18** Now the coastlands tremble on the day of your fall; Yes, the coastlands by the sea are troubled at your departure." '

Ezek 27:29–36 "All who handle the oar, The mariners, All the pilots of the sea Will come down from their ships *and* stand on the shore. **30** They will make their voice heard because of you; They will cry bitterly and cast dust on their heads; They will roll about in ashes; **31** They will shave themselves completely bald because of you, Gird themselves with sackcloth, And weep for you With bitterness of heart *and* bitter wailing. **32** In their wailing for you They will take up a lamentation, And lament for you: 'What *city is* like Tyre, Destroyed in the midst of the sea? **33** 'When your wares went out by sea, You satisfied many people; You enriched the kings of the earth With your many luxury goods and your merchandise. **34** But you are broken by the seas in the depths of the waters; Your merchandise and the entire company will fall in your midst. **35** All the inhabitants of the isles will be astonished at you; Their kings will be greatly afraid, And *their* countenance will be troubled. **36** The merchants among the peoples will hiss at you; You will become a horror, and *be* no more forever.' " ' "

Zech 9:5 Ashkelon shall see *it* and fear; Gaza also shall be very sorrowful; And Ekron, for He dried up her expectation. The king shall perish from Gaza, And Ashkelon shall not be inhabited.

Would participate in the blessings of the gospel.

Ps 45:12 And the daughter of Tyre *will come* with a gift; The rich among the people will seek your favor.

Is 23:18 Her gain and her pay will be set apart for the LORD; it will not be treasured nor laid up, for her gain will be for those who dwell before the LORD, to eat sufficiently, and for fine clothing.

UNBELIEF

Is defined as sin.

John 16:9 of sin, because they do not believe in Me;

Defilement inseparable from.

Titus 1:15 To the pure all things are pure, but to those who are defiled and unbelieving nothing is pure; but even their mind and conscience are defiled.

All, by nature, committed to.

Rom 11:32 For God has committed them all to disobedience, that He might have mercy on all.

Proceeds from

An evil heart.

Heb 3:12 Beware, brethren, lest there be in any of you an evil heart of unbelief in departing from the living God;

Slowness of heart.

Luke 24:25 Then He said to them, "O foolish ones, and slow of heart to believe in all that the prophets have spoken!

Hardness of heart.

Mark 16:14 Later He appeared to the eleven as they sat at the table; and He rebuked their unbelief and hardness of heart, because they did not believe those who had seen Him after He had risen.

Acts 19:9 But when some were hardened and did not believe, but spoke evil of the Way before the multitude, he departed from them and withdrew the disciples, reasoning daily in the school of Tyrannus.

Not listening to the truth.

John 8:45–46 But because I tell the truth, you do not believe Me. **46** Which of you convicts Me of sin? And if I tell the truth, why do you not believe Me?

Judicial blindness.

John 12:39–40 Therefore they could not believe, because Isaiah said again: **40** *"He has blinded their eyes and hardened their hearts, Lest they should see with their eyes, Lest they should understand with their hearts and turn, So that I should heal them."*

Not being Christ's sheep.

John 10:26 But you do not believe, because you are not of My sheep, as I said to you.

The devil blinding the mind.

2 Cor 4:4 whose minds the god of this age has blinded, who do not believe, lest the light of the gospel of the glory of Christ, who is the image of God, should shine on them.

The devil stealing the word out of the heart.

Luke 8:12 Those by the wayside are the ones who hear; then the devil comes and takes away the word out of their hearts, lest they should believe and be saved.

Seeking honor from men.

John 5:44 How can you believe, who receive honor from one another, and do not seek the honor that *comes* from the only God?

Makes God a liar.

1 John 5:10 He who believes in the Son of God has the witness in himself; he who does not believe God has made Him a liar, because he has not believed the testimony that God has given of His Son.

Exhibited in

Rejecting Christ.

John 16:9 of sin, because they do not believe in Me;

Rejecting the word of God.

Ps 106:24 Then they despised the pleasant land; They did not believe His word,

Rejecting the gospel.

Is 53:1 Who has believed our report? And to whom has the arm of the LORD been revealed?

John 12:38 that the word of Isaiah the prophet might be fulfilled, which he spoke: *"Lord, who has believed our report? And to whom has the arm of the LORD been revealed?"*

Rejecting evidence of miracles.

John 12:37 But although He had done so many signs before them, they did not believe in Him,

Departing from God.

Heb 3:12 Beware, brethren, lest there be in any of you an evil heart of unbelief in departing from the living God;

Questioning the power of God.

2 Kin 7:2 So an officer on whose hand the king leaned answered the man of God and said, "Look, *if* the LORD would make windows in heaven, could this thing be?" And he said, "In fact, you shall see *it* with your eyes, but you shall not eat of it."

Ps 78:19–20 Yes, they spoke against God: They said, "Can God prepare a table in the wilderness? **20** Behold, He struck the rock, So that the waters gushed out, And the streams overflowed. Can He give bread also? Can He provide meat for His people? "

Not believing the works of God.

Ps 78:32 In spite of this they still sinned, And did not believe in His wondrous works.

Wavering at the promise of God.

Rom 4:20 He did not waver at the promise of God through unbelief, but was strengthened in faith, giving glory to God,

Rebuked by Christ.

Matt 17:17 Then Jesus answered and said, "O faithless and perverse generation, how long shall I be with you? How long shall I bear with you? Bring him here to Me."

John 20:27 Then He said to Thomas, "Reach your finger here, and look at My hands; and reach your hand *here,* and put *it* into My side. Do not be unbelieving, but believing."

Was an impediment to the performance of miracles.

Matt 17:20 So Jesus said to them, "Because of your unbelief; for assuredly, I say to you, if you have faith as a mustard seed, you will say to this mountain, 'Move from here to there,' and it will move; and nothing will be impossible for you.

Mark 6:5 Now He could do no mighty work there, except that He laid His hands on a few sick people and healed *them.*

Miracles designed to convince those in.

John 10:37–38 If I do not do the works of My Father, do not believe Me; **38** but if I do, though you do not believe Me, believe the works, that you may know and believe that the Father *is* in Me, and I in Him."

1 Cor 14:22 Therefore tongues are for a sign, not to those who believe but to unbelievers; but prophesying is not for unbelievers but for those who believe.

The Jews rejected because of.

Rom 11:20 Well *said.* Because of unbelief they were broken off, and you stand by faith. Do not be haughty, but fear.

Believers should have no fellowship with those in.

2 Cor 6:14 Do not be unequally yoked together with unbelievers. For what fellowship has righteousness with lawlessness? And what communion has light with darkness?

Those who are guilty of,

Do not have the word of God in them.

John 5:38 But you do not have His word abiding in you, because whom He sent, Him you do not believe.

Cannot please God.

Heb 11:6 But without faith *it is* impossible to please *Him,* for he who comes to God must believe that He is, and *that* He is a rewarder of those who diligently seek Him.

Malign the gospel.

Acts 19:9 But when some were hardened and did not believe, but spoke evil of the Way before the multitude, he departed from them and withdrew the disciples, reasoning daily in the school of Tyrannus.

Persecute the ministers of God.

Rom 15:31 that I may be delivered from those in Judea who do not believe, and that my service for Jerusalem may be acceptable to the saints,

Excite others against believers.

Acts 14:2 But the unbelieving Jews stirred up the Gentiles and poisoned their minds against the brethren.

Persevere in it.

John 12:37 But although He had done so many signs before them, they did not believe in Him,

Stiffen their necks.

2 Kin 17:14 Nevertheless they would not hear, but stiffened their necks, like the necks of their fathers, who did not believe in the LORD their God.

Are condemned already.

John 3:18 "He who believes in Him is not condemned; but he who does not believe is condemned already, because he has not believed in the name of the only begotten Son of God.

Have the wrath of God abiding upon them.

John 3:36 He who believes in the Son has everlasting life; and he who does not believe the Son shall not see life, but the wrath of God abides on him."

Shall not be established.

Is 7:9 The head of Ephraim *is* Samaria, And the head of Samaria *is* Remaliah's son. If you will not believe, Surely you shall not be established." ' "

Shall die in their sins.

John 8:24 Therefore I said to you that you will die in your sins; for if you do not believe that I am *He,* you will die in your sins."

Shall not enter rest.

Heb 3:19 So we see that they could not enter in because of unbelief.

Heb 4:11 Let us therefore be diligent to enter that rest, lest anyone fall according to the same example of disobedience.

Shall be condemned.

Mark 16:16 He who believes and is baptized will be saved; but he who does not believe will be condemned.

2 Thess 2:12 that they all may be condemned who did not believe the truth but had pleasure in unrighteousness.

Shall be destroyed.

Jude 1:5 But I want to remind you, though you once knew this, that the Lord, having saved the people out of the land of Egypt, afterward destroyed those who did not believe.

Shall be cast into the lake of fire.

Rev 21:8 But the cowardly, unbelieving, abominable, murderers, sexually immoral, sorcerers, idolaters, and all liars shall have their part in the lake which burns with fire and brimstone, which is the second death."

Warnings against.

Heb 3:12 Beware, brethren, lest there be in any of you an evil heart of unbelief in departing from the living God;

Heb 4:11 Let us therefore be diligent to enter that rest, lest anyone fall according to the same example of disobedience.

Prayer for help against.

Mark 9:24 Immediately the father of the child cried out and said with tears, "Lord, I believe; help my unbelief!"

The portion of, awarded to all unfaithful servants.

Luke 12:46 the master of that servant will come on a day when he is not looking for *him,* and at an hour when he is not aware, and will cut him in two and appoint *him* his portion with the unbelievers.

Examples of,

Eve.

Gen 3:4–6 Then the serpent said to the woman, "You will not surely die. **5** For God knows that in the day you eat of it your eyes will be opened, and you will be like God, knowing good and evil." **6** So when the woman saw that the tree *was* good for food, that it *was* pleasant to the eyes, and a tree desirable to make *one* wise, she took of its fruit and ate. She also gave to her husband with her, and he ate.

Moses and Aaron.

Num 20:12 Then the LORD spoke to Moses and Aaron, "Because you did not believe Me, to hallow Me in the eyes of the children of Israel, therefore you shall not bring this assembly into the land which I have given them."

The Israelites.

Deut 9:23 Likewise, when the LORD sent you from Kadesh Barnea, saying, 'Go up and possess the land which I have given you,' then you rebelled against the commandment of the LORD your God, and you did not believe Him nor obey His voice.

Naaman.

2 Kin 5:12 *Are* not the Abanah and the Pharpar, the rivers of Damascus, better than all the waters of Israel? Could I not wash in them and be clean?" So he turned and went away in a rage.

A Samaritan officer.

2 Kin 7:2 So an officer on whose hand the king leaned answered the man of God and said, "Look, *if* the LORD would make windows in heaven, could this thing be?" And he said, "In fact, you shall see *it* with your eyes, but you shall not eat of it."

The disciples.

Matt 17:17 Then Jesus answered and said, "O faithless and perverse generation, how long shall I be with you? How long shall I bear with you? Bring him here to Me."

Luke 24:11 And their words seemed to them like idle tales, and they did not believe them.

Luke 24:25 Then He said to them, "O foolish ones, and slow of heart to believe in all that the prophets have spoken!

Zacharias.

Luke 1:20 But behold, you will be mute and not able to speak until the day these things take place, because you did not believe my words which will be fulfilled in their own time."

The chief priests.

Luke 22:67 "If You are the Christ, tell us." But He said to them, "If I tell you, you will by no means believe.

The Jews.

John 5:38 But you do not have His word abiding in you, because whom He sent, Him you do not believe.

The brothers of Christ.

John 7:5 For even His brothers did not believe in Him.

Thomas.

John 20:25 The other disciples therefore said to him, "We have seen the Lord." So he said to them, "Unless I see in His hands the print of the nails, and put my finger into the print of the nails, and put my hand into His side, I will not believe."

The Jews of Iconium.

Acts 14:2 But the unbelieving Jews stirred up the Gentiles and poisoned their minds against the brethren.

The Thessalonian Jews.

Acts 17:5 But the Jews who were not persuaded, becoming envious, took some of the evil men from the marketplace, and gathering a mob, set all the city in an uproar and attacked the house of Jason, and sought to bring them out to the people.

The Ephesians.

Acts 19:9 But when some were hardened and did not believe, but spoke evil of the Way before the multitude, he departed from them and withdrew the disciples, reasoning daily in the school of Tyrannus.

Saul.

1 Tim 1:13 although I was formerly a blasphemer, a persecutor, and an insolent man; but I obtained mercy because I did *it* ignorantly in unbelief.

The people of Jericho.

Heb 11:31 By faith the harlot Rahab did not perish with those who did not believe, when she had received the spies with peace.

UNBELIEVING NATIONS

Are without God and Christ.

Eph 2:12 that at that time you were without Christ, being aliens from the commonwealth of Israel and strangers from the covenants of promise, having no hope and without God in the world.

Described as

Ignorant.

1 Cor 1:21 For since, in the wisdom of God, the world through wisdom did not know God, it pleased God through the foolishness of the message preached to save those who believe.

Eph 4:18 having their understanding darkened, being alienated from the life of God, because of the ignorance that is in them, because of the blindness of their heart;

Idolatrous.

Ps 135:15 The idols of the nations *are* silver and gold, The work of men's hands.

Rom 1:23 and changed the glory of the incorruptible God into an image made like corruptible man—and birds and four-footed animals and creeping things.

Rom 1:25 who exchanged the truth of God for the lie, and worshiped and served the creature rather than the Creator, who is blessed forever. Amen.

Worshipers of demons.

1 Cor 10:20 Rather, that the things which the Gentiles sacrifice they sacrifice to demons and not to God, and I do not want you to have fellowship with demons.

Cruel.

Ps 74:20 Have respect to the covenant; For the dark places of the earth are full of the haunts of cruelty.

Filthy.

Ezra 6:21 Then the children of Israel who had returned from the captivity ate together with all who had separated themselves from the filth of the nations of the land in order to seek the LORD God of Israel.

Eph 4:19 who, being past feeling, have given themselves over to lewdness, to work all uncleanness with greediness.

Eph 5:12 For it is shameful even to speak of those things which are done by them in secret.

Persecuting.

Ps 2:1–2 Why do the nations rage, And the people plot a vain thing? **2** The kings of the earth set themselves, And the rulers take counsel together, Against the LORD and against His Anointed, *saying,*

2 Cor 11:26 *in* journeys often, *in* perils of waters, *in* perils of robbers, *in* perils of *my own* countrymen, *in* perils of the Gentiles, *in* perils in the city, *in* perils in the wilderness, *in* perils in the sea, *in* perils among false brethren;

Scoffing at believers.

Ps 79:10 Why should the nations say, "Where *is* their God?" Let there be known among the nations in our sight The avenging of the blood of Your servants *which has been* shed.

Strangers to the covenant of promise.

Eph 2:12 that at that time you were without Christ, being aliens from the commonwealth of Israel and strangers from the covenants of promise, having no hope and without God in the world.

Having no hope.

Eph 2:12 that at that time you were without Christ, being aliens from the commonwealth of Israel and strangers from the covenants of promise, having no hope and without God in the world.

Selling slaves.

Lev 25:44 And as for your male and female slaves whom you may have—from the nations that are around you, from them you may buy male and female slaves.

Aware of certain truths

Evidence of the power of God.

Acts 17:27 so that they should seek the Lord, in the hope that they might grope for Him and find Him, though He is not far from each one of us;

Rom 1:19–20 because what may be known of God is manifest in them, for God has shown *it* to them. **20** For since the creation of the world His invisible *attributes* are clearly seen, being understood by the things that are made, *even* His eternal power and Godhead, so that they are without excuse,

Evidence of the goodness of God.

Acts 14:17 Nevertheless He did not leave Himself without witness, in that He did good, gave us rain from heaven and fruitful seasons, filling our hearts with food and gladness."

The testimony of conscience.

Rom 2:14–15 for when Gentiles, who do not have the law, by nature do the things in the law, these, although not having the law, are a law to themselves, **15** who show the work of the law written in their hearts, their conscience also bearing witness, and between themselves *their* thoughts accusing or else excusing *them*)

Evil of imitating.

2 Kin 16:3 But he walked in the way of the kings of Israel; indeed he made his son pass through the fire, according to the abominations of the nations whom the LORD had cast out from before the children of Israel.

Ps 106:35 But they mingled with the Gentiles And learned their works;

Jer 10:2 Thus says the LORD: "Do not learn the way of the Gentiles; Do not be dismayed at the signs of heaven, For the Gentiles are dismayed at them.

Ezek 11:12 And you shall know that I *am* the LORD; for you have not walked in My statutes nor executed My judgments, but have done according to the customs of the Gentiles which *are* all around you." ' "

Matt 6:7 And when you pray, do not use vain repetitions as the heathen *do.* For they think that they will be heard for their many words.

Employed to chastise God's people.

Lev 26:33 I will scatter you among the nations and draw out a sword after you; your land shall be desolate and your cities waste.

Jer 49:14 I have heard a message from the LORD, And an ambassador has been sent to the nations: "Gather together, come against her, And rise up to battle!

Lam 1:3 Judah has gone into captivity, Under affliction and hard servitude; She dwells among the nations, She finds no rest; All her persecutors overtake her in dire straits.

Ezek 7:24 Therefore I will bring the worst of the Gentiles, And they will possess their houses; I will cause the pomp of the strong to cease, And their holy places shall be defiled.

Ezek 25:7 indeed, therefore, I will stretch out My hand against you, and give you as plunder to the nations; I will cut you off from the peoples, and I will cause you to perish from the countries; I will destroy you, and you shall know that I *am* the LORD."

Dan 4:27 Therefore, O king, let my advice be acceptable to you; break off your sins by *being* righteous, and your iniquities by showing mercy to *the* poor. Perhaps there may be a lengthening of your prosperity."

Hab 1:5–9 "Look among the nations and watch—Be utterly astounded! For *I will* work a work in your days *Which* you would not believe, though it were told *you.* **6** For indeed I am raising up the Chaldeans, A bitter and hasty nation Which marches through the breadth of the earth, To possess dwelling places *that are* not theirs. **7** They are terrible and dreadful; Their judgment and their dignity proceed from themselves. **8** Their horses also are swifter than leopards, And more fierce than evening wolves. Their chargers charge ahead; Their cavalry comes from afar; They fly as the eagle *that* hastens to eat. **9** "They all come for violence; Their faces are set *like* the east wind. They gather captives like sand.

Israel shall be avenged of.

Ps 149:7 To execute vengeance on the nations, And punishments on the peoples;

Jer 10:25 Pour out Your fury on the Gentiles, who do not know You, And on the families who do not call on Your name; For they have eaten up Jacob, Devoured him and consumed him, And made his dwelling place desolate.

Obad 1:15 "For the day of the LORD upon all the nations *is* near; As you have done, it shall be done to you; Your reprisal shall return upon your own head.

God

Rules over.

2 Chr 20:6 and said: "O LORD God of our fathers, *are* You not God in heaven, and do You *not* rule over all the kingdoms of the nations, and in Your hand *is there not* power and might, so that no one is able to withstand You?

Ps 47:8 God reigns over the nations; God sits on His holy throne.

Brings to nothing the counsels of.

Ps 33:10 The LORD brings the counsel of the nations to nothing; He makes the plans of the peoples of no effect.

Will be exalted among.

Ps 46:10 Be still, and know that I *am* God; I will be exalted among the nations, I will be exalted in the earth!

Ps 102:15 So the nations shall fear the name of the LORD, And all the kings of the earth Your glory.

Punishes.

Ps 44:2 You drove out the nations with Your hand, But them You planted; You afflicted the peoples, and cast them out.

Joel 3:11–13 Assemble and come, all you nations, And gather together all around. Cause Your mighty ones to go down there, O LORD. **12** "Let the nations be wakened, and come up to the Valley of Jehoshaphat; For there I will sit to judge all the surrounding nations. **13** Put in the sickle, for the harvest is ripe. Come, go down; For the winepress is full, The vats overflow— For their wickedness *is* great."

Mic 5:15 And I will execute vengeance in anger and fury On the nations that have not heard."

Hab 3:12 You marched through the land in indignation; You trampled the nations in anger.

Zech 14:18 If the family of Egypt will not come up and enter in, they *shall have* no *rain;* they shall receive the plague with which the LORD strikes the nations who do not come up to keep the Feast of Tabernacles.

Will finally judge.

Rom 2:12–16 For as many as have sinned without law will also perish without law, and as many as have sinned in the law will be judged by the law **13** (for not the hearers of the law *are* just in the sight of God, but the doers of the law will be justified; **14** for when Gentiles, who do not have the law, by nature do the things in the law, these, although not having the law,

are a law to themselves, **15** who show the work of the law written in their hearts, their conscience also bearing witness, and between themselves *their* thoughts accusing or else excusing *them*) **16** in the day when God will judge the secrets of men by Jesus Christ, according to my gospel.

Given to Christ.

Ps 2:8 Ask of Me, and I will give *You* The nations *for* Your inheritance, And the ends of the earth *for* Your possession.

Dan 7:14 Then to Him was given dominion and glory and a kingdom, That all peoples, nations, and languages should serve Him. His dominion *is* an everlasting dominion, Which shall not pass away, And His kingdom *the one* Which shall not be destroyed.

Salvation of, foretold.

Gen 12:3 I will bless those who bless you, And I will curse him who curses you; And in you all the families of the earth shall be blessed."

Is 2:2–4 Now it shall come to pass in the latter days *That* the mountain of the LORD's house Shall be established on the top of the mountains, And shall be exalted above the hills; And all nations shall flow to it. **3** Many people shall come and say, "Come, and let us go up to the mountain of the LORD, To the house of the God of Jacob; He will teach us His ways, And we shall walk in His paths." For out of Zion shall go forth the law, And the word of the LORD from Jerusalem. **4** He shall judge between the nations, And rebuke many people; They shall beat their swords into plowshares, And their spears into pruning hooks; Nation shall not lift up sword against nation, Neither shall they learn war anymore.

Is 52:10 The LORD has made bare His holy arm In the eyes of all the nations; And all the ends of the earth shall see The salvation of our God.

Is 60:1–8 Arise, shine; For your light has come! And the glory of the LORD is risen upon you. **2** For behold, the darkness shall cover the earth, And deep darkness the people; But the LORD will arise over you, And His glory will be seen upon you. **3** The Gentiles shall come to your light, And kings to the brightness of your rising. **4** "Lift up your eyes all around, and see: They all gather together, they come to you; Your sons shall come from afar, And your daughters shall be nursed at *your* side. **5** Then you shall see and become radiant, And your heart shall swell with joy; Because the abundance of the sea shall be turned to you, The wealth of the Gentiles shall come to you. **6** The multitude of camels shall cover your *land,* The dromedaries of Midian and Ephah; All those from Sheba shall come; They shall bring gold and incense, And they shall proclaim the praises of the LORD. **7** All the flocks of Kedar shall be gathered together to you, The rams of Nebaioth shall minister to you; They shall ascend with acceptance on My altar, And I will glorify the house of My glory. **8** "Who *are* these *who* fly like a cloud, And like doves to their roosts?

Acts 28:28 "Therefore let it be known to you that the salvation of God has been sent to the Gentiles, and they will hear it!"

Rom 15:9–12 and that the Gentiles might glorify God for *His* mercy, as it is written: *"For this reason I will confess to You among the Gentiles, And sing to*

Your name." **10** And again he says: *"Rejoice, O Gentiles, with His people!"* **11** And again: *"Praise the* LORD, *all you Gentiles! Laud Him, all you peoples!"* **12** And again, Isaiah says: *"There shall be a root of Jesse; And He who shall rise to reign over the Gentiles, In Him the Gentiles shall hope."*

Gal 3:8 And the Scripture, foreseeing that God would justify the Gentiles by faith, preached the gospel to Abraham beforehand, *saying, "In you all the nations shall be blessed."*

The gospel to be preached to.

1 Chr 16:24 Declare His glory among the nations, His wonders among all peoples.

Ps 96:3 Declare His glory among the nations, His wonders among all peoples.

Matt 24:14 And this gospel of the kingdom will be preached in all the world as a witness to all the nations, and then the end will come.

Matt 28:19 Go therefore and make disciples of all the nations, baptizing them in the name of the Father and of the Son and of the Holy Spirit,

Rom 10:14 How then shall they call on Him in whom they have not believed? And how shall they believe in Him of whom they have not heard? And how shall they hear without a preacher?

Rom 16:26 but now made manifest, and by the prophetic Scriptures made known to all nations, according to the commandment of the everlasting God, for obedience to the faith—

Gal 1:16 to reveal His Son in me, that I might preach Him among the Gentiles, I did not immediately confer with flesh and blood,

The gospel received by.

Acts 11:1 Now the apostles and brethren who were in Judea heard that the Gentiles had also received the word of God.

Acts 13:48 Now when the Gentiles heard this, they were glad and glorified the word of the Lord. And as many as had been appointed to eternal life believed.

Acts 15:3 So, being sent on their way by the church, they passed through Phoenicia and Samaria, describing the conversion of the Gentiles; and they caused great joy to all the brethren.

Acts 15:23 They wrote this *letter* by them: The apostles, the elders, and the brethren, To the brethren who are of the Gentiles in Antioch, Syria, and Cilicia: Greetings.

Baptism to be administered to.

Matt 28:19 Go therefore and make disciples of all the nations, baptizing them in the name of the Father and of the Son and of the Holy Spirit,

The Holy Spirit poured out upon.

Acts 10:44–45 While Peter was still speaking these words, the Holy Spirit fell upon all those who heard the word. **45** And those of the circumcision who believed were astonished, as many as came with Peter, because the gift of the Holy Spirit had been poured out on the Gentiles also.

Acts 15:8 So God, who knows the heart, acknowledged them by giving them the Holy Spirit, just as *He did* to us,

Believers should

Praise God for success of the gospel among.

Ps 98:1–3 Oh, sing to the LORD a new song! For He has done marvelous things; His right hand and His holy arm have gained Him the victory. **2** The LORD has made known His salvation; His righteousness He has revealed in the sight of the nations. **3** He has remembered His mercy and His faithfulness to the house of Israel; All the ends of the earth have seen the salvation of our God.

Acts 11:18 When they heard these things they became silent; and they glorified God, saying, "Then God has also granted to the Gentiles repentance to life."

Pray for.

Ps 67:2–5 That Your way may be known on earth, Your salvation among all nations. **3** Let the peoples praise You, O God; Let all the peoples praise You. **4** Oh, let the nations be glad and sing for joy! For You shall judge the people righteously, And govern the nations on earth. Selah **5** Let the peoples praise You, O God; Let all the peoples praise You.

Aid missions to.

2 Cor 11:9 And when I was present with you, and in need, I was a burden to no one, for what I lacked the brethren who came from Macedonia supplied. And in everything I kept myself from being burdensome to you, and so I will keep *myself.*

3 John 1:6–7 who have borne witness of your love before the church. *If* you send them forward on their journey in a manner worthy of God, you will do well, **7** because they went forth for His name's sake, taking nothing from the Gentiles.

Conversion of, acceptable to God.

Acts 10:35 But in every nation whoever fears Him and works righteousness is accepted by Him.

Rom 15:16 that I might be a minister of Jesus Christ to the Gentiles, ministering the gospel of God, that the offering of the Gentiles might be acceptable, sanctified by the Holy Spirit.

UPRIGHTNESS

God is perfect in.

Is 26:7 The way of the just *is* uprightness; O Most Upright, You weigh the path of the just.

God has pleasure in.

1 Chr 29:17 I know also, my God, that You test the heart and have pleasure in uprightness. As for me, in the uprightness of my heart I have willingly offered all these *things;* and now with joy I have seen Your people, who are present here to offer willingly to You.

Man has deviated from.

Eccl 7:29 Truly, this only I have found: That God made man upright, But they have sought out many schemes."

Should be in

Heart.

2 Chr 29:34 But the priests were too few, so that they could not skin all the burnt offerings; therefore their brethren the Levites helped them until the work was ended and until the *other* priests had sanctified themselves, for the Levites were more diligent in sanctifying themselves than the priests.

Ps 125:4 Do good, O Lord, to *those who are* good, And to *those who are* upright in their hearts.

Speech.

Is 33:15 He who walks righteously and speaks uprightly, He who despises the gain of oppressions, Who gestures with his hands, refusing bribes, Who stops his ears from hearing of bloodshed, And shuts his eyes from seeing evil:

Walk.

Prov 14:2 He who walks in his uprightness fears the Lord, But *he who is* perverse in his ways despises Him.

Judging.

Ps 58:1 Do you indeed speak righteousness, you silent ones? Do you judge uprightly, you sons of men?

Ps 75:2 "When I choose the proper time, I will judge uprightly.

Ruling.

Ps 78:72 So he shepherded them according to the integrity of his heart, And guided them by the skillfulness of his hands.

Being kept from presumptuous sins is necessary to.

Ps 19:13 Keep back Your servant also from presumptuous *sins;* Let them not have dominion over me. Then I shall be blameless, And I shall be innocent of great transgression.

Those who walk in,

Fear God.

Prov 14:2 He who walks in his uprightness fears the Lord, But *he who is* perverse in his ways despises Him.

Favored by God.

Ps 11:7 For the Lord *is* righteous, He loves righteousness; His countenance beholds the upright.

Delighted in by God.

Prov 11:20 Those who are of a perverse heart *are* an abomination to the Lord, But *the* blameless in their ways *are* His delight.

Prov 15:8 The sacrifice of the wicked *is* an abomination to the Lord, But the prayer of the upright *is* His delight.

Prospered by God.

Job 8:6 If you *were* pure and upright, Surely now He would awake for you, And prosper your rightful dwelling place.

Prov 14:11 The house of the wicked will be overthrown, But the tent of the upright will flourish.

Defended by God.

Prov 2:7 He stores up sound wisdom for the upright; *He is* a shield to those who walk uprightly;

Recompensed by God.

Ps 18:23–24 I was also blameless before Him, And I kept myself from my iniquity. **24** Therefore the Lord has recompensed me according to my righteousness, According to the cleanness of my hands in His sight.

Find strength in God's way.

Prov 10:29 The way of the Lord *is* strength for the up-

right, But destruction *will come* to the workers of iniquity.

Obtain good from God's work.

Mic 2:7 You who are named the house of Jacob: "Is the Spirit of the Lord restricted? *Are* these His doings? Do not My words do good To him who walks uprightly?

Obtain light in darkness.

Ps 112:4 Unto the upright there arises light in the darkness; *He is* gracious, and full of compassion, and righteous.

Guided by integrity.

Prov 11:3 The integrity of the upright will guide them, But the perversity of the unfaithful will destroy them.

Direct their way.

Prov 21:29 A wicked man hardens his face, But *as for* the upright, he establishes his way.

Kept by righteousness.

Prov 13:6 Righteousness guards *him whose* way is blameless, But wickedness overthrows the sinner.

Scorned by the wicked.

Job 12:4 "I am one mocked by his friends, Who called on God, and He answered him, The just and blameless *who is* ridiculed.

Hated by the wicked.

Prov 29:10 The bloodthirsty hate the blameless, But the upright seek his well-being.

Amos 5:10 They hate the one who rebukes in the gate, And they abhor the one who speaks uprightly.

Persecuted by the wicked.

Ps 37:14 The wicked have drawn the sword And have bent their bow, To cast down the poor and needy, To slay those who are of upright conduct.

Praise from them is beautiful.

Ps 33:1 Rejoice in the Lord, O you righteous! *For* praise from the upright is beautiful.

A blessing to others.

Prov 11:11 By the blessing of the upright the city is exalted, But it is overthrown by the mouth of the wicked.

The truly wise walk in.

Prov 15:21 Folly *is* joy to *him who is* destitute of discernment, But a man of understanding walks uprightly.

The way of, is to depart from evil.

Prov 16:17 The highway of the upright *is* to depart from evil; He who keeps his way preserves his soul.

Those who walk in, shall

Possess good things.

Prov 28:10 Whoever causes the upright to go astray in an evil way, He himself will fall into his own pit; But the blameless will inherit good.

Have nothing good withheld.

Ps 84:11 For the Lord God *is* a sun and shield; The Lord will give grace and glory; No good *thing* will He withhold From those who walk uprightly.

Dwell in the land.

Prov 2:21 For the upright will dwell in the land, And the blameless will remain in it;

Dwell on high and be provided for.

Is 33:16 He will dwell on high; His place of defense *will be* the fortress of rocks; Bread will be given him, His water *will be* sure.

Dwell with God.

Ps 15:2 He who walks uprightly, And works righteousness, And speaks the truth in his heart;

Ps 140:13 Surely the righteous shall give thanks to Your name; The upright shall dwell in Your presence.

Be blessed.

Ps 112:2 His descendants will be mighty on earth; The generation of the upright will be blessed.

Be delivered by righteousness.

Prov 11:6 The righteousness of the upright will deliver them, But the unfaithful will be caught by *their* lust.

Be delivered by their wisdom.

Prov 12:6 The words of the wicked *are,* "Lie in wait for blood," But the mouth of the upright will deliver them.

Be saved.

Prov 28:18 Whoever walks blamelessly will be saved, But *he who is* perverse *in his* ways will suddenly fall.

Enter into peace.

Ps 37:37 Mark the blameless *man,* and observe the upright; For the future of *that* man *is* peace.

Is 57:2 He shall enter into peace; They shall rest in their beds, *Each one* walking *in* his uprightness.

Have dominion over the wicked.

Ps 49:14 Like sheep they are laid in the grave; Death shall feed on them; The upright shall have dominion over them in the morning; And their beauty shall be consumed in the grave, far from their dwelling.

Have inheritance forever.

Ps 37:18 The LORD knows the days of the upright, And their inheritance shall be forever.

A characteristic of believers.

Ps 111:1 Praise the LORD! I will praise the LORD with *my* whole heart, In the assembly of the upright and *in* the congregation.

Is 26:7 The way of the just *is* uprightness; O Most Upright, You weigh the path of the just.

The wicked

Do not have in their hearts.

Hab 2:4 "Behold the proud, His soul is not upright in him; But the just shall live by his faith.

Leave the path of.

Prov 2:13 From those who leave the paths of uprightness To walk in the ways of darkness;

Do not act with.

Mic 7:2 The faithful *man* has perished from the earth, And *there is* no one upright among men. They all lie in wait for blood; Every man hunts his brother with a net.

Mic 7:4 The best of them *is* like a brier; The most upright *is sharper* than a thorn hedge; The day of your watchman and your punishment comes; Now shall be their perplexity.

Pray for those who walk in.

Ps 125:4 Do good, O LORD, to *those who are* good, And to *those who are* upright in their hearts.

Reprove those who deviate from.

Gal 2:14 But when I saw that they were not straightforward about the truth of the gospel, I said to Peter before *them* all, "If you, being a Jew, live in the manner of Gentiles and not as the Jews, why do you compel Gentiles to live as Jews?

URIM AND THUMMIM

Placed in the breastplate of the high priest.

Ex 28:30 And you shall put in the breastplate of judgment the Urim and the Thummim, and they shall be over Aaron's heart when he goes in before the LORD. So Aaron shall bear the judgment of the children of Israel over his heart before the LORD continually.

Lev 8:8 Then he put the breastplate on him, and he put the Urim and the Thummim in the breastplate.

God to be consulted by.

Num 27:21 He shall stand before Eleazar the priest, who shall inquire before the LORD for him by the judgment of the Urim. At his word they shall go out, and at his word they shall come in, he and all the children of Israel with him—all the congregation."

Instances of consulting God by.

Judg 1:1 Now after the death of Joshua it came to pass that the children of Israel asked the LORD, saying, "Who shall be first to go up for us against the Canaanites to fight against them?"

Judg 20:18 Then the children of Israel arose and went up to the house of God to inquire of God. They said, "Which of us shall go up first to battle against the children of Benjamin?" The LORD said, "Judah first!"

Judg 20:28 and Phinehas the son of Eleazar, the son of Aaron, stood before it in those days), saying, "Shall I yet again go out to battle against the children of my brother Benjamin, or shall I cease?" And the LORD said, "Go up, for tomorrow I will deliver them into your hand."

1 Sam 23:9–11 When David knew that Saul plotted evil against him, he said to Abiathar the priest, "Bring the ephod here." 10 Then David said, "O LORD God of Israel, Your servant has certainly heard that Saul seeks to come to Keilah to destroy the city for my sake. 11 Will the men of Keilah deliver me into his hand? Will Saul come down, as Your servant has heard? O LORD God of Israel, I pray, tell Your servant." And the LORD said, "He will come down."

1 Sam 30:7–8 Then David said to Abiathar the priest, Ahimelech's son, "Please bring the ephod here to me." And Abiathar brought the ephod to David. 8 So David inquired of the LORD, saying, "Shall I pursue this troop? Shall I overtake them?" And He answered him, "Pursue, for you shall surely overtake *them* and without fail recover *all.*"

Sometimes no answer by, in consequence of the sin of those consulting.

1 Sam 28:6 And when Saul inquired of the LORD, the LORD did not answer him, either by dreams or by Urim or by the prophets.

Were not in the second temple.

Ezra 2:63 And the governor said to them that they should not eat of the most holy things till a priest could consult with the Urim and Thummim.

Neh 7:65 And the governor said to them that they should not eat of the most holy things till a priest could consult with the Urim and Thummim.

Illustrative of the light and perfection of Christ, the true high priest.

Deut 33:8 And of Levi he said: *"Let* Your Thummim and Your Urim *be* with Your holy one, Whom You tested at Massah, And with whom You contended at the waters of Meribah,

John 1:4 In Him was life, and the life was the light of men.

John 1:9 That was the true Light which gives light to every man coming into the world.

John 1:17 For the law was given through Moses, *but* grace and truth came through Jesus Christ.

Col 2:3 in whom are hidden all the treasures of wisdom and knowledge.

V

VALLEYS
Tracts of land between mountains.
1 Sam 17:3 The Philistines stood on a mountain on one side, and Israel stood on a mountain on the other side, with a valley between them.

Called
Lowlands.

Deut 1:7 Turn and take your journey, and go to the mountains of the Amorites, to all the neighboring *places* in the plain, in the mountains and in the lowland, in the South and on the seacoast, to the land of the Canaanites and to Lebanon, as far as the great river, the River Euphrates.

Josh 10:40 So Joshua conquered all the land: the mountain country and the South and the lowland and the wilderness slopes, and all their kings; he left none remaining, but utterly destroyed all that breathed, as the LORD God of Israel had commanded.

Verdant valleys, when fruitful.

Is 28:1 Woe to the crown of pride, to the drunkards of Ephraim, Whose glorious beauty *is* a fading flower Which *is* at the head of the verdant valleys, To those who are overcome with wine!

Is 28:4 And the glorious beauty is a fading flower Which *is* at the head of the verdant valley, Like the first fruit before the summer, Which an observer sees; He eats it up while it is still in his hand.

Watered by mountain streams.
Deut 21:4 The elders of that city shall bring the heifer down to a valley with flowing water, which is neither plowed nor sown, and they shall break the heifer's neck there in the valley.

Ps 104:8 They went up over the mountains; They went down into the valleys, To the place which You founded for them.

Ps 104:10 He sends the springs into the valleys; They flow among the hills.

Canaan abounded in.
Deut 11:11 but the land which you cross over to possess *is* a land of hills and valleys, which drinks water from the rain of heaven,

Abounded with
Fountains and springs.

Deut 8:7 For the LORD your God is bringing you into a good land, a land of brooks of water, of fountains and springs, that flow out of valleys and hills;

Is 41:18 I will open rivers in desolate heights, And fountains in the midst of the valleys; I will make the wilderness a pool of water, And the dry land springs of water.

Rocks and caves.

Job 30:6 *They had* to live in the clefts of the valleys, *In* caves of the earth and the rocks.

Is 57:5 Inflaming yourselves with gods under every green tree, Slaying the children in the valleys, Under the clefts of the rocks?

Trees.

1 Kin 10:27 The king made silver *as common* in Jerusalem as stones, and he made cedar trees as abundant as the sycamores which *are* in the lowland.

Flowers.

Song 2:1 I *am* the rose of Sharon, *And* the lily of the valleys.

Ravens.

Prov 30:17 The eye *that* mocks *his* father, And scorns obedience to *his* mother, The ravens of the valley will pick it out, And the young eagles will eat it.

Doves.

Ezek 7:16 'Those who survive will escape and be on the mountains Like doves of the valleys, All of them mourning, Each for his iniquity.

Of Israel, well tilled and fruitful.
1 Sam 6:13 Now *the people of* Beth Shemesh *were* reaping their wheat harvest in the valley; and they lifted their eyes and saw the ark, and rejoiced to see *it.*

Ps 65:13 The pastures are clothed with flocks; The valleys also are covered with grain; They shout for joy, they also sing.

Often the scenes of idolatrous rites.
Is 57:5 Inflaming yourselves with gods under every green tree, Slaying the children in the valleys, Under the clefts of the rocks?

The heathen supposed that certain deities presided over.
1 Kin 20:23 Then the servants of the king of Syria said to him, "Their gods *are* gods of the hills. Therefore they were stronger than we; but if we fight against them in the plain, surely we will be stronger than they.

1 Kin 20:28 Then a man of God came and spoke to the king of Israel, and said, "Thus says the LORD: 'Because the Syrians have said, "The LORD *is* God of the hills, but He *is* not God of the valleys," therefore I will deliver all this great multitude into your hand, and you shall know that I *am* the LORD.' "

The Canaanites held possession of, against Judah.
Judg 1:19 So the LORD was with Judah. And they drove out the mountaineers, but they could not drive out the inhabitants of the lowland, because they had chariots of iron.

Often the scenes of great battles.

Judg 5:15 And the princes of Issachar *were* with Deborah; As Issachar, so *was* Barak Sent into the valley under his command; Among the divisions of Reuben *There were* great resolves of heart.

Judg 7:8 So the people took provisions and their trumpets in their hands. And he sent away all *the rest of* Israel, every man to his tent, and retained those three hundred men. Now the camp of Midian was below him in the valley.

Judg 7:22 When the three hundred blew the trumpets, the LORD set every man's sword against his companion throughout the whole camp; and the army fled to Beth Acacia, toward Zererah, as far as the border of Abel Meholah, by Tabbath.

1 Sam 17:19 Now Saul and they and all the men of Israel *were* in the Valley of Elah, fighting with the Philistines.

Those mentioned in Scripture,

Acacias.

Joel 3:18 And it will come to pass in that day *That* the mountains shall drip with new wine, The hills shall flow with milk, And all the brooks of Judah shall be flooded with water; A fountain shall flow from the house of the LORD And water the Valley of Acacias.

Achor.

Josh 7:24 Then Joshua, and all Israel with him, took Achan the son of Zerah, the silver, the garment, the wedge of gold, his sons, his daughters, his oxen, his donkeys, his sheep, his tent, and all that he had, and they brought them to the Valley of Achor.

Is 65:10 Sharon shall be a fold of flocks, And the Valley of Achor a place for herds to lie down, For My people who have sought Me.

Hos 2:15 I will give her her vineyards from there, And the Valley of Achor as a door of hope; She shall sing there, As in the days of her youth, As in the day when she came up from the land of Egypt.

Aijalon.

Josh 10:12 Then Joshua spoke to the LORD in the day when the LORD delivered up the Amorites before the children of Israel, and he said in the sight of Israel: "Sun, stand still over Gibeon; And Moon, in the Valley of Aijalon."

Baca.

Ps 84:6 *As they* pass through the Valley of Baca, They make it a spring; The rain also covers it with pools.

Berachah.

2 Chr 20:26 And on the fourth day they assembled in the Valley of Berachah, for there they blessed the LORD; therefore the name of that place was called The Valley of Berachah until this day.

Bochim.

Judg 2:5 Then they called the name of that place Bochim; and they sacrificed there to the LORD.

Elah.

1 Sam 17:2 And Saul and the men of Israel were gathered together, and they encamped in the Valley of Elah, and drew up in battle array against the Philistines.

1 Sam 17:19 Now Saul and they and all the men of Israel *were* in the Valley of Elah, fighting with the Philistines.

1 Sam 21:9 So the priest said, "The sword of Goliath the Philistine, whom you killed in the Valley of Elah, there it is, wrapped in a cloth behind the ephod. If you will take that, take *it*. For *there is* no other except that one here." And David said, "*There is* none like it; give it to me."

Eshcol.

Num 32:9 For when they went up to the Valley of Eshcol and saw the land, they discouraged the heart of the children of Israel, so that they did not go into the land which the LORD had given them.

Deut 1:24 And they departed and went up into the mountains, and came to the Valley of Eshcol, and spied it out.

Gad.

2 Sam 24:5 And they crossed over the Jordan and camped in Aroer, on the right side of the town which *is* in the midst of the ravine of Gad, and toward Jazer.

Gerar.

Gen 26:17 Then Isaac departed from there and pitched his tent in the Valley of Gerar, and dwelt there.

Gibeon.

Is 28:21 For the LORD will rise up as *at* Mount Perazim, He will be angry as in the Valley of Gibeon—That He may do His work, His awesome work, And bring to pass His act, His unusual act.

Hamon Gog.

Ezek 39:11 "It will come to pass in that day *that* I will give Gog a burial place there in Israel, the valley of those who pass by east of the sea; and it will obstruct travelers, because there they will bury Gog and all his multitude. Therefore they will call *it* the Valley of Hamon Gog.

Hebron.

Gen 37:14 Then he said to him, "Please go and see if it is well with your brothers and well with the flocks, and bring back word to me." So he sent him out of the Valley of Hebron, and he went to Shechem.

Hinnom.

Josh 18:16 Then the border came down to the end of the mountain that *lies* before the Valley of the Son of Hinnom, which *is* in the Valley of the Rephaim on the north, descended to the Valley of Hinnom, to the side of the Jebusite *city* on the south, and descended to En Rogel.

2 Kin 23:10 And he defiled Topheth, which *is* in the Valley of the Son of Hinnom, that no man might make his son or his daughter pass through the fire to Molech.

2 Chr 28:3 He burned incense in the Valley of the Son of Hinnom, and burned his children in the fire, according to the abominations of the nations whom the LORD had cast out before the children of Israel.

Jer 7:32 "Therefore behold, the days are coming," says the LORD, "when it will no more be called Tophet, or the Valley of the Son of Hinnom, but the Valley of Slaughter; for they will bury in Tophet until there is no room.

Jehoshaphat or decision.

Joel 3:2 I will also gather all nations, And bring them down to the Valley of Jehoshaphat; And I will enter into judgment with them there On account of My people, My heritage Israel, Whom they have also scattered among the nations; They have also divided up My land.

Joel 3:14 Multitudes, multitudes in the valley of decision! For the day of the LORD *is* near in the valley of decision.

Jericho.

Deut 34:3 the South, and the plain of the Valley of Jericho, the city of palm trees, as far as Zoar.

Jezreel.

Hos 1:5 It shall come to pass in that day That I will break the bow of Israel in the Valley of Jezreel."

Jiphthah El.

Josh 19:14 Then the border went around it on the north side of Hannathon, and it ended in the Valley of Jiphthah El.

Josh 19:27 It turned toward the sunrise to Beth Dagon; and it reached to Zebulun and to the Valley of Jiphthah El, then northward beyond Beth Emek and Neiel, bypassing Cabul *which was* on the left,

Lebanon.

Josh 11:17 from Mount Halak and the ascent to Seir, even as far as Baal Gad in the Valley of Lebanon below Mount Hermon. He captured all their kings, and struck them down and killed them.

Megiddo.

2 Chr 35:22 Nevertheless Josiah would not turn his face from him, but disguised himself so that he might fight with him, and did not heed the words of Necho from the mouth of God. So he came to fight in the Valley of Megiddo.

Zech 12:11 In that day there shall be a great mourning in Jerusalem, like the mourning at Hadad Rimmon in the plain of Megiddo.

Moab where Moses was buried.

Deut 34:6 And He buried him in a valley in the land of Moab, opposite Beth Peor; but no one knows his grave to this day.

Rephaim.

Josh 15:8 And the border went up by the Valley of the Son of Hinnom to the southern slope of the Jebusite *city* (which *is* Jerusalem). The border went up to the top of the mountain that *lies* before the Valley of Hinnom westward, which *is* at the end of the Valley of Rephaim northward.

Josh 18:16 Then the border came down to the end of the mountain that *lies* before the Valley of the Son of Hinnom, which *is* in the Valley of the Rephaim on the north, descended to the Valley of Hinnom, to the side of the Jebusite *city* on the south, and descended to En Rogel.

2 Sam 5:18 The Philistines also went and deployed themselves in the Valley of Rephaim.

Is 17:5 It shall be as when the harvester gathers the grain, And reaps the heads with his arm; It shall be as he who gathers heads of grain In the Valley of Rephaim.

Salt.

2 Sam 8:13 And David made *himself* a name when he returned from killing eighteen thousand Syrians in the Valley of Salt.

2 Kin 14:7 He killed ten thousand Edomites in the Valley of Salt, and took Sela by war, and called its name Joktheel to this day.

Shaveh or King's Valley.

Gen 14:17 And the king of Sodom went out to meet him at the Valley of Shaveh (that *is,* the King's Valley), after his return from the defeat of Chedorlaomer and the kings who *were* with him.

2 Sam 18:18 Now Absalom in his lifetime had taken and set up a pillar for himself, which *is* in the King's Valley. For he said, "I have no son to keep my name in remembrance." He called the pillar after his own name. And to this day it is called Absalom's Monument.

Siddim.

Gen 14:3 All these joined together in the Valley of Siddim (that is, the Salt Sea).

Gen 14:8 And the king of Sodom, the king of Gomorrah, the king of Admah, the king of Zeboiim, and the king of Bela (that *is,* Zoar) went out and joined together in battle in the Valley of Siddim

Sorek.

Judg 16:4 Afterward it happened that he loved a woman in the Valley of Sorek, whose name *was* Delilah.

Succoth.

Ps 60:6 God has spoken in His holiness: "I will rejoice; I will divide Shechem And measure out the Valley of Succoth.

Zeboim.

1 Sam 13:18 another company turned to the road *to* Beth Horon, and another company turned *to* the road of the border that overlooks the Valley of Zeboim toward the wilderness.

Zephathah.

2 Chr 14:10 So Asa went out against him, and they set the troops in battle array in the Valley of Zephathah at Mareshah.

Zered.

Num 21:12 From there they moved and camped in the Valley of Zered.

To be filled with hostile chariots, threatened as a punishment.

Is 22:7 It shall come to pass *that* your choicest valleys Shall be full of chariots, And the horsemen shall set themselves in array at the gate.

Miracles connected with,

The moon made to stand still over Aijalon.

Josh 10:12 Then Joshua spoke to the LORD in the day when the LORD delivered up the Amorites before the children of Israel, and he said in the sight of Israel: "Sun, stand still over Gibeon; And Moon, in the Valley of Aijalon."

Ditches in, filled with water.

2 Kin 3:16–17 And he said, "Thus says the LORD: 'Make this valley full of ditches.' **17** For thus says the LORD:

'You shall not see wind, nor shall you see rain; yet that valley shall be filled with water, so that you, your cattle, and your animals may drink.'

Water in, made to appear to the Moabites like blood.

2 Kin 3:22–23 Then they rose up early in the morning, and the sun was shining on the water; and the Moabites saw the water on the other side *as* red as blood. 23 And they said, "This is blood; the kings have surely struck swords and have killed one another; now therefore, Moab, to the spoil!"

Illustrative of

(Fruitful and well watered) the tents of Israel.

Num 24:6 Like valleys that stretch out, Like gardens by the riverside, Like aloes planted by the LORD, Like cedars beside the waters.

Affliction and death.

Ps 23:4 Yea, though I walk through the valley of the shadow of death, I will fear no evil; For You *are* with me; Your rod and Your staff, they comfort me.

(Filling up of) removing all obstructions to the gospel.

Is 40:4 Every valley shall be exalted And every mountain and hill brought low; The crooked places shall be made straight And the rough places smooth;

Luke 3:5 *Every valley shall be filled And every mountain and hill brought low; The crooked places shall be made straight And the rough ways smooth;*

VANITY (FUTILITY OF LIFE)

Everyone has experienced.

Ps 39:5 Indeed, You have made my days *as* handbreadths, And my age *is* as nothing before You; Certainly every man at his best state *is* but vapor. Selah

Ps 39:11 When with rebukes You correct man for iniquity, You make his beauty melt away like a moth; Surely every man *is* vapor. Selah

Ps 62:9 Surely men of low degree *are* a vapor, Men of high degree *are* a lie; If they are weighed on the scales, They *are* altogether *lighter* than vapor.

Ps 94:11 The LORD knows the thoughts of man, That they *are* futile.

Rom 8:20 For the creation was subjected to futility, not willingly, but because of Him who subjected *it* in hope;

The days of man witness.

Ps 39:11 When with rebukes You correct man for iniquity, You make his beauty melt away like a moth; Surely every man *is* vapor. Selah

Eccl 6:12 For who knows what *is* good for man in life, all the days of his vain life which he passes like a shadow? Who can tell a man what will happen after him under the sun?

Eccl 11:10 Therefore remove sorrow from your heart, And put away evil from your flesh, For childhood and youth *are* vanity.

Worldly truth attests to.

Ps 39:6 Surely every man walks about like a shadow; Surely they busy themselves in vain; He heaps up *riches,* And does not know who will gather them.

Ps 127:2 *It is* vain for you to rise up early, To sit up late, To eat the bread of sorrows; *For* so He gives His beloved sleep.

Eccl 1:2 "Vanity of vanities," says the Preacher; "Vanity of vanities, all *is* vanity."

Eccl 2:1 I said in my heart, "Come now, I will test you with mirth; therefore enjoy pleasure"; but surely, this also *was* vanity.

Eccl 2:15 So I said in my heart, "As it happens to the fool, It also happens to me, And why was I then more wise?" Then I said in my heart, "This also *is* vanity."

Eccl 2:21 For there is a man whose labor *is* with wisdom, knowledge, and skill; yet he must leave his heritage to a man who has not labored for it. This also *is* vanity and a great evil.

Eccl 4:4 Again, I saw that for all toil and every skillful work a man is envied by his neighbor. This also *is* vanity and grasping for the wind.

Lam 4:17 Still our eyes failed us, *Watching* vainly for our help; In our watching we watched For a nation *that* could not save *us.*

1 Cor 3:20 and again, *"The LORD knows the thoughts of the wise, that they are futile."*

Cf. Eccl 2:3–11

Concern for wealth is reflection of.

Eccl 2:26 For *God* gives wisdom and knowledge and joy to a man who *is* good in His sight; but to the sinner He gives the work of gathering and collecting, that he may give to *him who is* good before God. This also *is* vanity and grasping for the wind.

Eccl 4:8 There is one alone, without companion: He has neither son nor brother. Yet *there is* no end to all his labors, Nor is his eye satisfied with riches. *But he never asks,* "For whom do I toil and deprive myself of good?" This also *is* vanity and a grave misfortune.

Eccl 5:10 He who loves silver will not be satisfied with silver; Nor he who loves abundance, with increase. This also *is* vanity.

Eccl 6:2 A man to whom God has given riches and wealth and honor, so that he lacks nothing for himself of all he desires; yet God does not give him power to eat of it, but a foreigner consumes it. This *is* vanity, and it *is* an evil affliction.

Foolish questions, etc. represent.

1 Tim 1:6–7 from which some, having strayed, have turned aside to idle talk, 7 desiring to be teachers of the law, understanding neither what they say nor the things which they affirm.

1 Tim 6:20 O Timothy! Guard what was committed to your trust, avoiding the profane *and* idle babblings and contradictions of what is falsely called knowledge—

2 Tim 2:14 Remind *them* of these things, charging *them* before the Lord not to strive about words to no profit, to the ruin of the hearers.

2 Tim 2:16 But shun profane *and* idle babblings, for they will increase to more ungodliness.

Titus 3:9 But avoid foolish disputes, genealogies, contentions, and strivings about the law; for they are unprofitable and useless.

Actions of unbelievers prove it.

2 Kin 17:15 And they rejected His statutes and His covenant that He had made with their fathers, and His testimonies which He had testified against them;

they followed idols, became idolaters, and *went* after the nations who *were* all around them, *concerning* whom the LORD had charged them that they should not do like them.

Job 11:11–12 For He knows deceitful men; He sees wickedness also. Will He not then consider *it?* **12** For an empty-headed man will be wise, When a wild donkey's colt is born a man.

Job 15:31 Let him not trust in futile *things,* deceiving himself, For futility will be his reward.

Job 21:15 Who *is* the Almighty, that we should serve Him? And what profit do we have if we pray to Him?'

Ps 2:1 Why do the nations rage, And the people plot a vain thing?

Ps 4:2 How long, O you sons of men, *Will you turn* my glory to shame? *How long* will you love worthlessness *And* seek falsehood? Selah

Ps 10:7 His mouth is full of cursing and deceit and oppression; Under his tongue *is* trouble and iniquity.

Ps 12:2 They speak idly everyone with his neighbor; *With* flattering lips *and* a double heart they speak.

Ps 31:6 I have hated those who regard useless idols; But I trust in the LORD.

Ps 36:4 He devises wickedness on his bed; He sets himself in a way *that is* not good; He does not abhor evil.

Ps 39:6 Surely every man walks about like a shadow; Surely they busy themselves in vain; He heaps up *riches,* And does not know who will gather them.

Ps 41:6 And if he comes to see *me,* he speaks lies; His heart gathers iniquity to itself; *When* he goes out, he tells *it.*

Ps 78:33 Therefore their days He consumed in futility, And their years in fear.

Prov 12:11 He who tills his land will be satisfied with bread, But he who follows frivolity *is* devoid of understanding.

Prov 22:8 He who sows iniquity will reap sorrow, And the rod of his anger will fail.

Prov 28:19 He who tills his land will have plenty of bread, But he who follows frivolity will have poverty enough!

Is 44:9–10 Those who make an image, all of them *are* useless, And their precious things shall not profit; They *are* their own witnesses; They neither see nor know, that they may be ashamed. **10** Who would form a god or mold an image *That* profits him nothing?

Is 57:13 When you cry out, Let your collection *of idols* deliver you. But the wind will carry them all away, A breath will take *them.* But he who puts his trust in Me shall possess the land, And shall inherit My holy mountain."

Jer 2:5 Thus says the LORD: "What injustice have your fathers found in Me, That they have gone far from Me, Have followed idols, And have become idolaters?

Jer 7:8 "Behold, you trust in lying words that cannot profit.

Jer 10:8 But they are altogether dull-hearted and foolish; A wooden idol *is* a worthless doctrine.

Jer 12:13 They have sown wheat but reaped thorns;

They have put themselves to pain *but* do not profit. But be ashamed of your harvest Because of the fierce anger of the LORD."

Jer 16:19 O LORD, my strength and my fortress, My refuge in the day of affliction, The Gentiles shall come to You From the ends of the earth and say, "Surely our fathers have inherited lies, Worthlessness and unprofitable *things.*"

Jer 18:15 "Because My people have forgotten Me, They have burned incense to worthless idols. And they have caused themselves to stumble in their ways, *From* the ancient paths, To walk in pathways and not on a highway,

Jer 23:32 Behold, I *am* against those who prophesy false dreams," says the LORD, "and tell them, and cause My people to err by their lies and by their recklessness. Yet I did not send them or command them; therefore they shall not profit this people at all," says the LORD.

Mal 3:14 You have said, 'It is useless to serve God; What profit *is it* that we have kept His ordinance, And that we have walked as mourners Before the LORD of hosts?

Matt 6:7 And when you pray, do not use vain repetitions as the heathen *do.* For they think that they will be heard for their many words.

Acts 4:25 who by the mouth of Your servant David have said: *'Why did the nations rage, And the people plot vain things?*

Rom 1:21 because, although they knew God, they did not glorify *Him* as God, nor were thankful, but became futile in their thoughts, and their foolish hearts were darkened.

1 Cor 13:3 And though I bestow all my goods to feed *the poor,* and though I give my body to be burned, but have not love, it profits me nothing.

Eph 4:17 This I say, therefore, and testify in the Lord, that you should no longer walk as the rest of the Gentiles walk, in the futility of their mind,

1 Tim 4:8 For bodily exercise profits a little, but godliness is profitable for all things, having promise of the life that now is and of that which is to come.

Heb 13:9 Do not be carried about with various and strange doctrines. For *it is* good that the heart be established by grace, not with foods which have not profited those who have been occupied with them.

James 1:26 If anyone among you thinks he is religious, and does not bridle his tongue but deceives his own heart, this one's religion *is* useless.

James 2:14 What *does it* profit, my brethren, if someone says he has faith but does not have works? Can faith save him?

2 Pet 2:18 For when they speak great swelling *words* of emptiness, they allure through the lusts of the flesh, through lewdness, the ones who have actually escaped from those who live in error.

Believers

Hate the thoughts of.

Ps 119:113 I hate the double-minded, But I love Your law.

Pray to be kept from.

Ps 119:37 Turn away my eyes from looking at worthless things, *And* revive me in Your way.

Prov 30:8 Remove falsehood and lies far from me; Give me neither poverty nor riches— Feed me with the food allotted to me;

Avoid.

Ps 24:4 He who has clean hands and a pure heart, Who has not lifted up his soul to an idol, Nor sworn deceitfully.

Avoid those given to.

Ps 26:4 I have not sat with idolatrous mortals, Nor will I go in with hypocrites.

VEIL

A covering for the head usually worn by women.

Gen 38:14 So she took off her widow's garments, covered *herself* with a veil and wrapped herself, and sat in an open place which *was* on the way to Timnah; for she saw that Shelah was grown, and she was not given to him as a wife.

Reasons for wearing,

As a token of modesty.

Gen 24:65 for she had said to the servant, "Who *is* this man walking in the field to meet us?" The servant said, "It *is* my master." So she took a veil and covered herself.

As a token of subjection.

1 Cor 11:3 But I want you to know that the head of every man is Christ, the head of woman *is* man, and the head of Christ *is* God.

1 Cor 11:6–7 For if a woman is not covered, let her also be shorn. But if it is shameful for a woman to be shorn or shaved, let her be covered. 7 For a man indeed ought not to cover *his* head, since he is the image and glory of God; but woman is the glory of man.

1 Cor 11:10 For this reason the woman ought to have *a symbol of* authority on *her* head, because of the angels.

For concealment.

Gen 38:14 So she took off her widow's garments, covered *herself* with a veil and wrapped herself, and sat in an open place which *was* on the way to Timnah; for she saw that Shelah was grown, and she was not given to him as a wife.

The removing of, considered rude and insolent.

Song 5:7 The watchmen who went about the city found me. They struck me, they wounded me; The keepers of the walls Took my veil away from me.

Removing of, threatened as a punishment to ungodly women.

Is 3:18–19 In that day the Lord will take away the finery: The jingling anklets, the scarves, and the crescents; 19 The pendants, the bracelets, and the veils;

One concealed glory of Moses' face.

Ex 34:33 And when Moses had finished speaking with them, he put a veil on his face.

2 Cor 3:13 unlike Moses, *who* put a veil over his face so that the children of Israel could not look steadily at the end of what was passing away.

Illustrative of

The spiritual blindness of the Gentile nations.

Is 25:7 And He will destroy on this mountain The surface of the covering cast over all people, And the veil that is spread over all nations.

The spiritual blindness of the Jewish nation.

2 Cor 3:14–16 But their minds were blinded. For until this day the same veil remains unlifted in the reading of the Old Testament, because the *veil* is taken away in Christ. 15 But even to this day, when Moses is read, a veil lies on their heart. 16 Nevertheless when one turns to the Lord, the veil is taken away.

VEIL, THE SACRED

In the tabernacle

Moses commanded to have linen woven for use in.

Ex 26:31 "You shall make a veil woven of blue, purple, and scarlet *thread,* and fine woven linen. It shall be woven with an artistic design of cherubim.

Ex 36:35 And he made a veil of blue, purple, and scarlet *thread*, and fine woven linen; it was worked *with* an artistic design of cherubim.

Suspended from four pillars of acacia wood overlaid with gold.

Ex 26:32 You shall hang it upon the four pillars of acacia *wood* overlaid with gold. Their hooks *shall be* gold, upon four sockets of silver.

Hung between the holy and Most Holy Place.

Ex 26:33 And you shall hang the veil from the clasps. Then you shall bring the ark of the Testimony in there, behind the veil. The veil shall be a divider for you between the holy *place* and the Most Holy.

Heb 9:3 and behind the second veil, the part of the tabernacle which is called the Holiest of All,

Designed to conceal the ark, mercy seat, and the symbol of the divine presence.

Ex 40:3 You shall put in it the ark of the Testimony, and partition off the ark with the veil.

The high priest

Alone allowed to go inside the.

Heb 9:6–7 Now when these things had been thus prepared, the priests always went into the first part of the tabernacle, performing *the services.* 7 But into the second part the high priest *went* alone once a year, not without blood, which he offered for himself and *for* the people's sins *committed* in ignorance;

Allowed to go inside the veil but once a year.

Lev 16:2 and the LORD said to Moses: "Tell Aaron your brother not to come at *just* any time into the Holy Place inside the veil, before the mercy seat which *is* on the ark, lest he die; for I will appear in the cloud above the mercy seat.

Heb 9:7 But into the second part the high priest *went* alone once a year, not without blood, which he offered for himself and *for* the people's sins *committed* in ignorance;

Could not go inside the veil without blood.

Lev 16:3 "Thus Aaron shall come into the Holy *Place:* with *the blood of* a young bull as a sin offering, and *of* a ram as a burnt offering.

Heb 9:7 But into the second part the high priest *went* alone once a year, not without blood, which he offered for himself and *for* the people's sins *committed* in ignorance;

Made by Solomon for the temple.

2 Chr 3:14 And he made the veil of blue, purple, crimson, and fine linen, and wove cherubim into it.

Was torn at the death of our Lord.

Matt 27:51 Then, behold, the veil of the temple was torn in two from top to bottom; and the earth quaked, and the rocks were split,

Mark 15:38 Then the veil of the temple was torn in two from top to bottom.

Luke 23:45 Then the sun was darkened, and the veil of the temple was torn in two.

Illustrative of

The obscurity of the Mosaic age.

Heb 9:8 the Holy Spirit indicating this, that the way into the Holiest of All was not yet made manifest while the first tabernacle was still standing.

The flesh of Christ, which concealed His divinity.

Is 53:2 For He shall grow up before Him as a tender plant, And as a root out of dry ground. He has no form or comeliness; And when we see Him, *There is* no beauty that we should desire Him.

Heb 10:20 by a new and living way which He consecrated for us, through the veil, that is, His flesh,

(Tearing of) the death of Christ, which opened heaven to believers.

Heb 9:24 For Christ has not entered the holy places made with hands, *which are* copies of the true, but into heaven itself, now to appear in the presence of God for us;

Heb 10:19–20 Therefore, brethren, having boldness to enter the Holiest by the blood of Jesus, **20** by a new and living way which He consecrated for us, through the veil, that is, His flesh,

VENGEANCE

Is God's prerogative.

Deut 32:35 Vengeance is Mine, and recompense; Their foot shall slip in *due* time; For the day of their calamity *is* at hand, And the things to come hasten upon them.'

Is just retribution for trespasses against God's law.

Ps 94:1–2 O LORD God, to whom vengeance belongs— O God, to whom vengeance belongs, shine forth! **2** Rise up, O Judge of the earth; Render punishment to the proud.

Believers are to refrain from taking their own.

Rom 12:19 Beloved, do not avenge yourselves, but *rather* give place to wrath; for it is written, "Vengeance is Mine, I will repay," says the Lord.

Paul left it to God.

2 Tim 4:14 Alexander the coppersmith did me much harm. May the Lord repay him according to his works.

VINE, THE

Often found wild.

2 Kin 4:39 So one went out into the field to gather herbs, and found a wild vine, and gathered from it a lapful of wild gourds, and came and sliced *them* into the pot of stew, though they did not know *what they were.*

Hos 9:10 "I found Israel Like grapes in the wilderness; I saw your fathers As the firstfruits on the fig tree in its first season. *But* they went to Baal Peor, And separated themselves *to that* shame; They became an abomination like the thing they loved.

Cultivated

In vineyards from the time of Noah.

Gen 9:20 And Noah began *to be* a farmer, and he planted a vineyard.

On the sides of hills.

Jer 31:5 You shall yet plant vines on the mountains of Samaria; The planters shall plant and eat *them* as ordinary food.

In the valleys.

Song 6:11 I went down to the garden of nuts To see the verdure of the valley, To see whether the vine had budded *And* the pomegranates had bloomed.

By the walls of houses.

Ps 128:3 Your wife *shall be* like a fruitful vine In the very heart of your house, Your children like olive plants All around your table.

Required to be dressed and pruned to increase its fruitfulness.

Lev 25:3 Six years you shall sow your field, and six years you shall prune your vineyard, and gather its fruit;

2 Chr 26:10 Also he built towers in the desert. He dug many wells, for he had much livestock, both in the lowlands and in the plains; *he also had* farmers and vinedressers in the mountains and in Carmel, for he loved the soil.

Is 18:5 For before the harvest, when the bud is perfect And the sour grape is ripening in the flower, He will both cut off the sprigs with pruning hooks And take away *and* cut down the branches.

Canaan abounded in.

Deut 6:11 houses full of all good things, which you did not fill, hewn-out wells which you did not dig, vineyards and olive trees which you did not plant— when you have eaten and are full—

Deut 8:8 a land of wheat and barley, of vines and fig trees and pomegranates, a land of olive oil and honey;

Places celebrated for,

Eshcol.

Num 13:23–24 Then they came to the Valley of Eshcol, and there cut down a branch with one cluster of grapes; they carried it between two of them on a pole. *They* also *brought* some of the pomegranates and figs. **24** The place was called the Valley of Eshcol, because of the cluster which the men of Israel cut down there.

Sibmah.

Is 16:8–9 For the fields of Heshbon languish, *And* the vine of Sibmah; The lords of the nations have broken down its choice plants, Which have reached to Jazer And wandered through the wilderness. Her branches are stretched out, They are gone over the sea. **9** Therefore I will bewail the vine of Sibmah,

With the weeping of Jazer; I will drench you with my tears, O Heshbon and Elealeh; For battle cries have fallen Over your summer fruits and your harvest.

Lebanon.

Hos 14:7 Those who dwell under his shadow shall return; They shall be revived *like* grain, And grow like a vine. Their scent *shall be* like the wine of Lebanon.

Egypt.

Ps 78:47 He destroyed their vines with hail, And their sycamore trees with frost.

Ps 80:8 You have brought a vine out of Egypt; You have cast out the nations, and planted it.

The low and spreading vine particularly esteemed.

Ezek 17:6 And it grew and became a spreading vine of low stature; Its branches turned toward him, But its roots were under it. So it became a vine, Brought forth branches, And put forth shoots.

Of Sodom and Gomorrah bad and unfit for use.

Deut 32:32 For their vine *is* of the vine of Sodom And of the fields of Gomorrah; Their grapes *are* grapes of gall, Their clusters *are* bitter.

Often degenerated.

Is 5:2 He dug it up and cleared out its stones, And planted it with the choicest vine. He built a tower in its midst, And also made a winepress in it; So He expected *it* to bring forth *good* grapes, But it brought forth wild grapes.

Jer 2:21 Yet I had planted you a noble vine, a seed of highest quality. How then have you turned before Me Into the degenerate plant of an alien vine?

Frequently injured by hail and frost.

Ps 78:47 He destroyed their vines with hail, And their sycamore trees with frost.

Ps 105:32–33 He gave them hail for rain, *And* flaming fire in their land. **33** He struck their vines also, and their fig trees, And splintered the trees of their territory.

Foxes destructive to.

Song 2:15 Catch us the foxes, The little foxes that spoil the vines, For our vines *have* tender grapes.

The wild boar destructive to.

Ps 80:13 The boar out of the woods uproots it, And the wild beast of the field devours it.

The fruit of,

Called grapes.

Gen 40:10 and in the vine *were* three branches; it *was* as though it budded, its blossoms shot forth, and its clusters brought forth ripe grapes.

Very sour when unripe.

Jer 31:30 But every one shall die for his own iniquity; every man who eats the sour grapes, his teeth shall be set on edge.

Eaten fresh from the branches.

Deut 23:24 "When you come into your neighbor's vineyard, you may eat your fill of grapes at your pleasure, but you shall not put *any* in your container.

Eaten dried (raisins).

1 Sam 25:18 Then Abigail made haste and took two hundred *loaves* of bread, two skins of wine, five

sheep already dressed, five seahs of roasted *grain,* one hundred clusters of raisins, and two hundred cakes of figs, and loaded *them* on donkeys.

1 Sam 30:12 And they gave him a piece of a cake of figs and two clusters of raisins. So when he had eaten, his strength came back to him; for he had eaten no bread nor drunk water for three days and three nights.

Sold in the markets.

Neh 13:15 In those days I saw *people* in Judah treading wine presses on the Sabbath, and bringing in sheaves, and loading donkeys with wine, grapes, figs, and all *kinds of* burdens, which they brought into Jerusalem on the Sabbath day. And I warned *them* about the day on which they were selling provisions.

Made into wine.

Deut 32:14 Curds from the cattle, and milk of the flock, With fat of lambs; And rams of the breed of Bashan, and goats, With the choicest wheat; And you drank wine, the blood of the grapes.

Matt 26:29 But I say to you, I will not drink of this fruit of the vine from now on until that day when I drink it new with you in My Father's kingdom."

The wood of, fit only for burning.

Ezek 15:2–5 "Son of man, how is the wood of the vine *better* than any other wood, the vine branch which is among the trees of the forest? **3** Is wood taken from it to make any object? Or can *men* make a peg from it to hang any vessel on? **4** Instead, it is thrown into the fire for fuel; the fire devours both ends of it, and its middle is burned. Is it useful for *any* work? **5** Indeed, when it was whole, no object could be made from it. How much less will it be useful for *any* work when the fire has devoured it, and it is burned?

Garments sometimes washed in juice of fruit.

Gen 49:11 Binding his donkey to the vine, And his donkey's colt to the choice vine, He washed his garments in wine, And his clothes in the blood of grapes.

Probably produced two crops of fruit in the year.

Num 13:20 whether the land *is* rich or poor; and whether there are forests there or not. Be of good courage. And bring some of the fruit of the land." Now the time *was* the season of the first ripe grapes.

Perfumed the air with the fragrance of its flowers.

Song 2:13 The fig tree puts forth her green figs, And the vines *with* the tender grapes Give a good smell. Rise up, my love, my fair one, And come away!

Hos 14:7 Those who dwell under his shadow shall return; They shall be revived *like* grain, And grow like a vine. Their scent *shall be* like the wine of Lebanon.

God made, fruitful for His people when obedient.

Joel 2:22 Do not be afraid, you beasts of the field; For the open pastures are springing up, And the tree bears its fruit; The fig tree and the vine yield their strength.

Zech 8:12 'For the seed *shall be* prosperous, The vine shall give its fruit, The ground shall give her increase, And the heavens shall give their dew— I will cause the remnant of this people To possess all these.

Frequently made unfruitful as a punishment.

Jer 8:13 "I will surely consume them," says the LORD. "No grapes *shall be* on the vine, Nor figs on the fig tree, And the leaf shall fade; And *the things* I have given them shall pass away from them." ' "

Hos 2:12 "And I will destroy her vines and her fig trees, Of which she has said, 'These *are* my wages that my lovers have given me.' So I will make them a forest, And the beasts of the field shall eat them.

Joel 1:7 He has laid waste My vine, And ruined My fig tree; He has stripped it bare and thrown *it* away; Its branches are made white.

Joel 1:12 The vine has dried up, And the fig tree has withered; The pomegranate tree, The palm tree also, And the apple tree— All the trees of the field are withered; Surely joy has withered away from the sons of men.

Hag 2:19 Is the seed still in the barn? As yet the vine, the fig tree, the pomegranate, and the olive tree have not yielded *fruit. But* from this day I will bless *you*.' "

Sometimes lost its fruit prematurely.

Job 15:33 He will shake off his unripe grape like a vine, And cast off his blossom like an olive tree.

Mal 3:11 "And I will rebuke the devourer for your sakes, So that he will not destroy the fruit of your ground, Nor shall the vine fail to bear fruit for you in the field," Says the LORD of hosts;

Nazirites prohibited eating any part of.

Num 6:3–4 he shall separate himself from wine and *similar* drink; he shall drink neither vinegar made from wine nor vinegar made from *similar* drink; neither shall he drink any grape juice, nor eat fresh grapes or raisins. 4 All the days of his separation he shall eat nothing that is produced by the grapevine, from seed to skin.

Illustrative of

Christ.

John 15:1–2 "I am the true vine, and My Father is the vinedresser. 2 Every branch in Me that does not bear fruit He takes away; and every *branch* that bears fruit He prunes, that it may bear more fruit.

Israel.

Ps 80:8 You have brought a vine out of Egypt; You have cast out the nations, and planted it.

Is 5:2 He dug it up and cleared out its stones, And planted it with the choicest vine. He built a tower in its midst, And also made a winepress in it; So He expected *it* to bring forth *good* grapes, But it brought forth wild grapes.

Is 5:7 For the vineyard of the LORD of hosts *is* the house of Israel, And the men of Judah are His pleasant plant. He looked for justice, but behold, oppression; For righteousness, but behold, a cry *for help.*

(Its fruitful branches) believers.

John 15:5 "I am the vine, you *are* the branches. He who abides in Me, and I in him, bears much fruit; for without Me you can do nothing.

(Unfruitful branches) merely professing Christians.

John 15:2 Every branch in Me that does not bear fruit He takes away; and every *branch* that bears fruit He prunes, that it may bear more fruit.

John 15:6 If anyone does not abide in Me, he is cast out as a branch and is withered; and they gather them and throw *them* into the fire, and they are burned.

(Its quick growth) the growth of believers in grace.

Hos 14:7 Those who dwell under his shadow shall return; They shall be revived *like* grain, And grow like a vine. Their scent *shall be* like the wine of Lebanon.

(Pruning of) God's purifying His people by afflictions.

John 15:2 Every branch in Me that does not bear fruit He takes away; and every *branch* that bears fruit He prunes, that it may bear more fruit.

(Worthlessness of its wood) the unprofitableness of the wicked.

Ezek 15:6–7 "Therefore thus says the Lord GOD: 'Like the wood of the vine among the trees of the forest, which I have given to the fire for fuel, so I will give up the inhabitants of Jerusalem; 7 and I will set My face against them. They will go out from *one* fire, but *another* fire shall devour them. Then you shall know that I *am* the LORD, when I set My face against them.

(Unfruitful) the wicked.

Hos 10:1 Israel empties *his* vine; He brings forth fruit for himself. According to the multitude of his fruit He has increased the altars; According to the bounty of his land They have embellished *his* sacred pillars.

(Sitting under one's own) peace and prosperity.

1 Kin 4:25 And Judah and Israel dwelt safely, each man under his vine and his fig tree, from Dan as far as Beersheba, all the days of Solomon.

Mic 4:4 But everyone shall sit under his vine and under his fig tree, And no one shall make *them* afraid; For the mouth of the LORD of hosts has spoken.

Zech 3:10 In that day,' says the LORD of hosts, 'Everyone will invite his neighbor Under his vine and under his fig tree.' "

Proverbial allusion to fathers eating the unripe fruit of.

Jer 31:29–30 In those days they shall say no more: 'The fathers have eaten sour grapes, And the children's teeth are set on edge.' 30 But every one shall die for his own iniquity; every man who eats the sour grapes, his teeth shall be set on edge.

Ezek 18:2 "What do you mean when you use this proverb concerning the land of Israel, saying: 'The fathers have eaten sour grapes, And the children's teeth are set on edge'?

VINEYARDS

Origin and antiquity of.

Gen 9:20 And Noah began *to be* a farmer, and he planted a vineyard.

The design of planting.

Ps 107:37 And sow fields and plant vineyards, That they may yield a fruitful harvest.

1 Cor 9:7 Who ever goes to war at his own expense? Who plants a vineyard and does not eat of its fruit? Or who tends a flock and does not drink of the milk of the flock?

Frequently walled or fenced with hedges.

Num 22:24 Then the Angel of the LORD stood in a narrow path between the vineyards, *with* a wall on this side and a wall on that side.

Prov 24:31 And there it was, all overgrown with thorns; Its surface was covered with nettles; Its stone wall was broken down.

Is 5:2 He dug it up and cleared out its stones, And planted it with the choicest vine. He built a tower in its midst, And also made a winepress in it; So He expected *it* to bring forth *good* grapes, But it brought forth wild grapes.

Is 5:5 And now, please let Me tell you what I will do to My vineyard: I will take away its hedge, and it shall be burned; *And* break down its wall, and it shall be trampled down.

Cottages built in, for the keepers.

Is 1:8 So the daughter of Zion is left as a booth in a vineyard, As a hut in a garden of cucumbers, As a besieged city.

Provided with the apparatus for making wine.

Is 5:2 He dug it up and cleared out its stones, And planted it with the choicest vine. He built a tower in its midst, And also made a winepress in it; So He expected *it* to bring forth *good* grapes, But it brought forth wild grapes.

Matt 21:33 "Hear another parable: There was a certain landowner who planted a vineyard and set a hedge around it, dug a winepress in it and built a tower. And he leased it to vinedressers and went into a far country.

Laws respecting,

Not to be planted with different kinds of seed.

Deut 22:9 "You shall not sow your vineyard with different kinds of seed, lest the yield of the seed which you have sown and the fruit of your vineyard be defiled.

Not to be cultivated in the sabbatical year.

Ex 23:11 but the seventh *year* you shall let it rest and lie fallow, that the poor of your people may eat; and what they leave, the beasts of the field may eat. In like manner you shall do with your vineyard *and* your olive grove.

Lev 25:4 but in the seventh year there shall be a sabbath of solemn rest for the land, a sabbath to the LORD. You shall neither sow your field nor prune your vineyard.

The spontaneous fruit of, not to be gathered during the sabbatical year.

Lev 25:5 What grows of its own accord of your harvest you shall not reap, nor gather the grapes of your untended vine, *for* it is a year of rest for the land.

Lev 25:11 That fiftieth year shall be a Jubilee to you; in it you shall neither sow nor reap what grows of its own accord, nor gather *the grapes* of your untended vine.

Compensation in kind to be made for injury done to.

Ex 22:5 "If a man causes a field or vineyard to be grazed, and lets loose his animal, and it feeds in another man's field, he shall make restitution from the best of his own field and the best of his own vineyard.

Strangers entering, allowed to eat fruit of, but not to take any away.

Deut 23:24 "When you come into your neighbor's vineyard, you may eat your fill of grapes at your pleasure, but you shall not put *any* in your container.

The gleaning of, to be left for the poor.

Lev 19:10 And you shall not glean your vineyard, nor shall you gather *every* grape of your vineyard; you shall leave them for the poor and the stranger: I *am* the LORD your God.

Deut 24:21 When you gather the grapes of your vineyard, you shall not glean *it* afterward; it shall be for the stranger, the fatherless, and the widow.

The fruit of new, not to be eaten for three years.

Lev 19:23 'When you come into the land, and have planted all kinds of trees for food, then you shall count their fruit as uncircumcised. Three years it shall be as uncircumcised to you. *It* shall not be eaten.

The fruit of new, to be holy to the Lord in the fourth year.

Lev 19:24 But in the fourth year all its fruit shall be holy, a praise to the LORD.

The fruit of new, to be eaten by the owners from the fifth year.

Lev 19:25 And in the fifth year you may eat its fruit, that it may yield to you its increase: I *am* the LORD your God.

Planters of, not liable to military service till they had eaten of the fruit.

Deut 20:6 Also what man *is there* who has planted a vineyard and has not eaten of it? Let him go and return to his house, lest he die in the battle and another man eat of it.

Frequently let out to vinedressers or keepers.

Song 8:11 Solomon had a vineyard at Baal Hamon; He leased the vineyard to keepers; Everyone was to bring for its fruit A thousand silver coins.

Matt 21:33 "Hear another parable: There was a certain landowner who planted a vineyard and set a hedge around it, dug a winepress in it and built a tower. And he leased it to vinedressers and went into a far country.

Rent of, frequently paid by part of the fruit.

Matt 21:34 Now when vintage-time drew near, he sent his servants to the vinedressers, that they might receive its fruit.

Were often mortgaged.

Neh 5:3–4 There were also *some* who said, "We have mortgaged our lands and vineyards and houses, that we might buy grain because of the famine." 4 There were also those who said, "We have borrowed money for the king's tax *on* our lands and vineyards.

Estimated rent of.

Song 8:11 Solomon had a vineyard at Baal Hamon; He leased the vineyard to keepers; Everyone was to bring for its fruit A thousand silver coins.

Is 7:23 It shall happen in that day, *That* wherever there could be a thousand vines *Worth* a thousand *shekels* of silver, It will be for briers and thorns.

Estimated profit arising from, to the cultivators.

Song 8:12 My own vineyard *is* before me. You, O Solomon, *may have* a thousand, And those who tend its fruit two hundred.

Matt 20:1–2 "For the kingdom of heaven is like a landowner who went out early in the morning to hire laborers for his vineyard. **2** Now when he had agreed with the laborers for a denarius a day, he sent them into his vineyard.

The poor engaged in the cultivation of.

2 Kin 25:12 But the captain of the guard left *some* of the poor of the land as vinedressers and farmers.

Is 61:5 Strangers shall stand and feed your flocks, And the sons of the foreigner *Shall be* your plowmen and your vinedressers.

Sometimes involved in family disputes.

Song 1:6 Do not look upon me, because I *am* dark, Because the sun has tanned me. My mother's sons were angry with me; They made me the keeper of the vineyards, *But* my own vineyard I have not kept.

Matt 21:28–30 "But what do you think? A man had two sons, and he came to the first and said, 'Son, go, work today in my vineyard.' **29** He answered and said, 'I will not,' but afterward he regretted it and went. **30** Then he came to the second and said likewise. And he answered and said, 'I *go*, sir,' but he did not go.

Of the kings of Israel, superintended by officers of state.

1 Chr 27:27 And Shimei the Ramathite *was* over the vineyards, and Zabdi the Shiphmite was over the produce of the vineyards for the supply of wine.

The vintage or ingathering of,

Was a time of great rejoicing.

Is 16:10 Gladness is taken away, And joy from the plentiful field; In the vineyards there will be no singing, Nor will there be shouting; No treaders will tread out wine in the presses; I have made their shouting cease.

Sometimes continued to the time of sowing seed.

Lev 26:5 Your threshing shall last till the time of vintage, and the vintage shall last till the time of sowing; you shall eat your bread to the full, and dwell in your land safely.

Failure in, brought great grief.

Is 16:9–10 Therefore I will bewail the vine of Sibmah, With the weeping of Jazer; I will drench you with my tears, O Heshbon and Elealeh; For battle cries have fallen Over your summer fruits and your harvest. **10** Gladness is taken away, And joy from the plentiful field; In the vineyards there will be no singing, Nor will there be shouting; No treaders will tread out wine in the presses; I have made their shouting cease.

Of red grapes, particularly esteemed.

Is 27:2 In that day sing to her, "A vineyard of red wine!

The produce of, was frequently destroyed by enemies.

Jer 48:32 O vine of Sibmah! I will weep for you with the weeping of Jazer. Your plants have gone over the sea, They reach to the sea of Jazer. The plunderer has fallen on your summer fruit and your vintage.

The whole produce of, often destroyed by blight and insects.

Deut 28:39 You shall plant vineyards and tend *them*, but you shall neither drink *of* the wine nor gather the *grapes;* for the worms shall eat them.

Amos 4:9 "I blasted you with blight and mildew. When your gardens increased, Your vineyards, Your fig trees, And your olive trees, The locust devoured *them;* Yet you have not returned to Me," Says the Lord.

In unfavorable seasons, produced little wine.

Is 5:10 For ten acres of vineyard shall yield one bath, And a homer of seed shall yield one ephah."

Hag 1:9 "*You* looked for much, but indeed *it came to* little; and when you brought it home, I blew it away. Why?" says the Lord of hosts. "Because of My house that *is in* ruins, while every one of you runs to his own house.

Hag 1:11 For I called for a drought on the land and the mountains, on the grain and the new wine and the oil, on whatever the ground brings forth, on men and livestock, and on all the labor of *your* hands."

The wicked judicially deprived of the enjoyment of.

Amos 5:11 Therefore, because you tread down the poor And take grain taxes from him, Though you have built houses of hewn stone, Yet you shall not dwell in them; You have planted pleasant vineyards, But you shall not drink wine from them.

Zeph 1:13 Therefore their goods shall become booty, And their houses a desolation; They shall build houses, but not inhabit *them;* They shall plant vineyards, but not drink their wine."

The Rechabites forbidden to plant.

Jer 35:7–9 You shall not build a house, sow seed, plant a vineyard, nor have *any of these;* but all your days you shall dwell in tents, that you may live many days in the land where you are sojourners.' **8** Thus we have obeyed the voice of Jonadab the son of Rechab, our father, in all that he charged us, to drink no wine all our days, we, our wives, our sons, or our daughters, **9** nor to build ourselves houses to dwell in; nor do we have vineyard, field, or seed.

Of the lazy man, care of neglected.

Prov 24:30–31 I went by the field of the lazy *man*, And by the vineyard of the man devoid of understanding; **31** And there it was, all overgrown with thorns; Its surface was covered with nettles; Its stone wall was broken down.

Illustrative of

The nation Israel.

Is 5:7 For the vineyard of the Lord of hosts *is* the house of Israel, And the men of Judah are His pleasant plant. He looked for justice, but behold, oppression; For righteousness, but behold, a cry *for help.*

Is 27:2 In that day sing to her, "A vineyard of red wine!

Jer 12:10 "Many rulers have destroyed My vineyard, They have trodden My portion underfoot; They have made My pleasant portion a desolate wilderness.

Matt 21:33 "Hear another parable: There was a certain landowner who planted a vineyard and set a hedge around it, dug a winepress in it and built a tower. And he leased it to vinedressers and went into a far country.

(Failure of) severe calamities.

Is 32:10 In a year and *some* days You will be troubled, you complacent women; For the vintage will fail, The gathering will not come.

(Gleaning grapes of) the elect.

Is 24:13 When it shall be thus in the midst of the land among the people, *It shall be* like the shaking of an olive tree, Like the gleaning of grapes when the vintage is done.

VISIONS

God often made known His will by.

Ps 89:19 Then You spoke in a vision to Your holy one, And said: "I have given help to *one who is* mighty; I have exalted one chosen from the people.

God especially made Himself known to prophets by.

Num 12:6 Then He said, "Hear now My words: If there is a prophet among you, *I*, the LORD, make Myself known to him in a vision; I speak to him in a dream.

Often accompanied by

A representative of the divine person and glory.

Is 6:1 In the year that King Uzziah died, I saw the Lord sitting on a throne, high and lifted up, and the train of His *robe* filled the temple.

An audible voice from heaven.

Gen 15:1 After these things the word of the LORD came to Abram in a vision, saying, "Do not be afraid, Abram. I *am* your shield, your exceedingly great reward."

1 Sam 3:4–5 that the LORD called Samuel. And he answered, "Here I am!" **5** So he ran to Eli and said, "Here I am, for you called me." And he said, "I did not call; lie down again." And he went and lay down.

An appearance of angels.

Luke 1:11 Then an angel of the Lord appeared to him, standing on the right side of the altar of incense.

Luke 1:22 But when he came out, he could not speak to them; and they perceived that he had seen a vision in the temple, for he beckoned to them and remained speechless.

Luke 24:23 When they did not find His body, they came saying that they had also seen a vision of angels who said He was alive.

Acts 10:3 About the ninth hour of the day he saw clearly in a vision an angel of God coming in and saying to him, "Cornelius!"

An appearance of human beings.

Acts 9:12 And in a vision he has seen a man named Ananias coming in and putting *his* hand on him, so that he might receive his sight."

Acts 16:9 And a vision appeared to Paul in the night. A man of Macedonia stood and pleaded with him, saying, "Come over to Macedonia and help us."

Frequently difficult and perplexing to those who received them.

Dan 7:15 "I, Daniel, was grieved in my spirit within *my* body, and the visions of my head troubled me.

Dan 8:15 Then it happened, when I, Daniel, had seen the vision and was seeking the meaning, that suddenly there stood before me one having the appearance of a man.

Acts 10:17 Now while Peter wondered within himself what this vision which he had seen meant, behold, the men who had been sent from Cornelius had made inquiry for Simon's house, and stood before the gate.

Often communicated

In the night.

Gen 46:2 Then God spoke to Israel in the visions of the night, and said, "Jacob, Jacob!" And he said, "Here I am."

Dan 2:19 Then the secret was revealed to Daniel in a night vision. So Daniel blessed the God of heaven.

In a trance.

Num 24:16 The utterance of him who hears the words of God, And has the knowledge of the Most High, *Who* sees the vision of the Almighty, *Who* falls down, with eyes wide open:

Acts 11:5 "I was in the city of Joppa praying; and in a trance I saw a vision, an object descending like a great sheet, let down from heaven by four corners; and it came to me.

Often recorded for the benefit of the people.

Hab 2:2 Then the LORD answered me and said: "Write the vision And make *it* plain on tablets, That he may run who reads it.

Often multiplied for the benefit of the people.

Hos 12:10 I have also spoken by the prophets, And have multiplied visions; I have given symbols through the witness of the prophets."

Given in Scripture to

Abram.

Gen 15:1 After these things the word of the LORD came to Abram in a vision, saying, "Do not be afraid, Abram. I *am* your shield, your exceedingly great reward."

Jacob.

Gen 46:2 Then God spoke to Israel in the visions of the night, and said, "Jacob, Jacob!" And he said, "Here I am."

Moses.

Ex 3:2–3 And the Angel of the LORD appeared to him in a flame of fire from the midst of a bush. So he looked, and behold, the bush was burning with fire, but the bush *was* not consumed. **3** Then Moses said, "I will now turn aside and see this great sight, why the bush does not burn."

Acts 7:30–32 "And when forty years had passed, an Angel of the Lord appeared to him in a flame of fire in a bush, in the wilderness of Mount Sinai. **31** When Moses saw *it*, he marveled at the sight; and as he drew near to observe, the voice of the Lord came to him, **32** saying, 'I am the God of your fathers—the

God of Abraham, the God of Isaac, and the God of Jacob.' And Moses trembled and dared not look.

Samuel.

1 Sam 3:2–15 And it came to pass at that time, while Eli *was* lying down in his place, and when his eyes had begun to grow so dim that he could not see, **3** and before the lamp of God went out in the tabernacle of the LORD where the ark of God *was,* and while Samuel was lying down, **4** that the LORD called Samuel. And he answered, "Here I am!" **5** So he ran to Eli and said, "Here I am, for you called me." And he said, "I did not call; lie down again." And he went and lay down. **6** Then the LORD called yet again, "Samuel!" So Samuel arose and went to Eli, and said, "Here I am, for you called me." He answered, "I did not call, my son; lie down again." **7** (Now Samuel did not yet know the LORD, nor was the word of the LORD yet revealed to him.) **8** And the LORD called Samuel again the third time. So he arose and went to Eli, and said, "Here I am, for you did call me." Then Eli perceived that the LORD had called the boy. **9** Therefore Eli said to Samuel, "Go, lie down; and it shall be, if He calls you, that you must say, 'Speak, LORD, for Your servant hears.' " So Samuel went and lay down in his place. **10** Now the LORD came and stood and called as at other times, "Samuel! Samuel!" And Samuel answered, "Speak, for Your servant hears." **11** Then the LORD said to Samuel: "Behold, I will do something in Israel at which both ears of everyone who hears it will tingle. **12** In that day I will perform against Eli all that I have spoken concerning his house, from beginning to end. **13** For I have told him that I will judge his house forever for the iniquity which he knows, because his sons made themselves vile, and he did not restrain them. **14** And therefore I have sworn to the house of Eli that the iniquity of Eli's house shall not be atoned for by sacrifice or offering forever." **15** So Samuel lay down until morning, and opened the doors of the house of the LORD. And Samuel was afraid to tell Eli the vision.

Nathan.

2 Sam 7:4 But it happened that night that the word of the LORD came to Nathan, saying,

2 Sam 7:17 According to all these words and according to all this vision, so Nathan spoke to David.

Eliphaz.

Job 4:13–16 In disquieting thoughts from the visions of the night, When deep sleep falls on men, **14** Fear came upon me, and trembling, Which made all my bones shake. **15** Then a spirit passed before my face; The hair on my body stood up. **16** It stood still, But I could not discern its appearance. A form *was* before my eyes; *There was* silence; Then I heard a voice *saying:*

Isaiah.

Is 6:1–8 In the year that King Uzziah died, I saw the Lord sitting on a throne, high and lifted up, and the train of His *robe* filled the temple. **2** Above it stood seraphim; each one had six wings: with two he covered his face, with two he covered his feet, and with two he flew. **3** And one cried to another and said: "Holy, holy, holy *is* the LORD of hosts; The whole earth *is* full of His glory!" **4** And the posts of the door were shaken by the voice of him who cried out, and

the house was filled with smoke. **5** So I said: "Woe *is* me, for I am undone! Because I *am* a man of unclean lips, And I dwell in the midst of a people of unclean lips; For my eyes have seen the King, The LORD of hosts." **6** Then one of the seraphim flew to me, having in his hand a live coal *which* he had taken with the tongs from the altar. **7** And he touched my mouth *with it,* and said: "Behold, this has touched your lips; Your iniquity is taken away, And your sin purged." **8** Also I heard the voice of the Lord, saying: "Whom shall I send, And who will go for Us?" Then I said, "Here *am* I! Send me."

Ezekiel.

Ezek 1:4–14 Then I looked, and behold, a whirlwind was coming out of the north, a great cloud with raging fire engulfing itself; and brightness *was* all around it and radiating out of its midst like the color of amber, out of the midst of the fire. **5** Also from within it *came* the likeness of four living creatures. And this *was* their appearance: they had the likeness of a man. **6** Each one had four faces, and each one had four wings. **7** Their legs *were* straight, and the soles of their feet *were* like the soles of calves' feet. They sparkled like the color of burnished bronze. **8** The hands of a man *were* under their wings on their four sides; and each of the four had faces and wings. **9** Their wings touched one another. *The creatures* did not turn when they went, but each one went straight forward. **10** As for the likeness of their faces, *each* had the face of a man; each of the four had the face of a lion on the right side, each of the four had the face of an ox on the left side, and each of the four had the face of an eagle. **11** Thus *were* their faces. Their wings stretched upward; two *wings* of each one touched one another, and two covered their bodies. **12** And each one went straight forward; they went wherever the spirit wanted to go, and they did not turn when they went. **13** As for the likeness of the living creatures, their appearance *was* like burning coals of fire, like the appearance of torches going back and forth among the living creatures. The fire was bright, and out of the fire went lightning. **14** And the living creatures ran back and forth, in appearance like a flash of lightning.

Ezek 8:2–14 Then I looked, and there was a likeness, like the appearance of fire—from the appearance of His waist and downward, fire; and from His waist and upward, like the appearance of brightness, like the color of amber. **3** He stretched out the form of a hand, and took me by a lock of my hair; and the Spirit lifted me up between earth and heaven, and brought me in visions of God to Jerusalem, to the door of the north gate of the inner *court,* where the seat of the image of jealousy *was,* which provokes to jealousy. **4** And behold, the glory of the God of Israel *was* there, like the vision that I saw in the plain. **5** Then He said to me, "Son of man, lift your eyes now toward the north." So I lifted my eyes toward the north, and there, north of the altar gate, was this image of jealousy in the entrance. **6** Furthermore He said to me, "Son of man, do you see what they are doing, the great abominations that the house of Israel commits here, to make Me go far away from My sanctuary? Now turn again, you will see greater abominations." **7** So He brought me to the door of the court; and when I looked, there was a hole in the wall. **8** Then He said to me, "Son of man, dig into the wall"; and when I dug into the wall, there was a door. **9** And He said to me, "Go in, and see the wicked abominations which they are doing there." **10** So I went in and saw, and there—every sort of creeping thing, abominable beasts, and all the idols of the house of Israel, portrayed all around on the walls. **11** And there stood before them seventy men of the elders of the house of Israel, and in their midst stood Jaazaniah the son of Shaphan. Each man had a censer in his hand, and a thick cloud of incense went up. **12** Then He said to me, "Son of man, have you seen what the elders of the house of Israel do in the dark, every man in the room of his idols? For they say, 'The LORD does not see us, the LORD has forsaken the land.' " **13** And He said to me, "Turn again, *and* you will see greater abominations that they are doing." **14** So He brought me to the door of the north gate of the LORD's house; and to my dismay, women were sitting there weeping for Tammuz.

Ezek 11:24–25 Then the Spirit took me up and brought me in a vision by the Spirit of God into Chaldea, to those in captivity. And the vision that I had seen went up from me. **25** So I spoke to those in captivity of all the things the LORD had shown me.

Ezek 37:1–10 The hand of the LORD came upon me and brought me out in the Spirit of the LORD, and set me down in the midst of the valley; and it *was* full of bones. **2** Then He caused me to pass by them all around, and behold, *there were* very many in the open valley; and indeed *they were* very dry. **3** And He said to me, "Son of man, can these bones live?" So I answered, "O Lord GOD, You know." **4** Again He said to me, "Prophesy to these bones, and say to them, 'O dry bones, hear the word of the LORD! **5** Thus says the Lord GOD to these bones: "Surely I will cause breath to enter into you, and you shall live. **6** I will put sinews on you and bring flesh upon you, cover you with skin and put breath in you; and you shall live. Then you shall know that I *am* the LORD." ' " **7** So I prophesied as I was commanded; and as I prophesied, there was a noise, and suddenly a rattling; and the bones came together, bone to bone. **8** Indeed, as I looked, the sinews and the flesh came upon them, and the skin covered them over; but *there was* no breath in them. **9** Also He said to me, "Prophesy to the breath, prophesy, son of man, and say to the breath, 'Thus says the Lord GOD: "Come from the four winds, O breath, and breathe on these slain, that they may live." ' " **10** So I prophesied as He commanded me, and breath came into them, and they lived, and stood upon their feet, an exceedingly great army.

Cf. Ezek 10; 40—48

Nebuchadnezzar.

Dan 2:28 But there is a God in heaven who reveals secrets, and He has made known to King Nebuchadnezzar what will be in the latter days. Your dream, and the visions of your head upon your bed, were these:

Dan 4:5 I saw a dream which made me afraid, and the thoughts on my bed and the visions of my head troubled me.

Daniel.

Dan 2:19 Then the secret was revealed to Daniel in a night vision. So Daniel blessed the God of heaven.

Cf. Dan 7—8,10

Amos.

Amos 7:1–9 Thus the Lord GOD showed me: Behold, He formed locust swarms at the beginning of the late crop; indeed *it was* the late crop after the king's mowings. **2** And so it was, when they had finished eating the grass of the land, that I said: "O Lord GOD, forgive, I pray! Oh, that Jacob may stand, For he *is* small!" **3** *So* the LORD relented concerning this. "It shall not be," said the LORD. **4** Thus the Lord GOD showed me: Behold, the Lord GOD called for conflict by fire, and it consumed the great deep and devoured the territory. **5** Then I said: "O Lord GOD, cease, I pray! Oh, that Jacob may stand, For he *is* small!" **6** *So* the LORD relented concerning this. "This also shall not be," said the Lord GOD. **7** Thus He showed me: Behold, the Lord stood on a wall *made* with a plumb line, with a plumb line in His hand. **8** And the LORD said to me, "Amos, what do you see?" And I said, "A plumb line." Then the Lord said: "Behold, I am setting a plumb line In the midst of My people Israel; I will not pass by them anymore. **9** The high places of Isaac shall be desolate, And the sanctuaries of Israel shall be laid waste. I will rise with the sword against the house of Jeroboam."

Amos 8:1–6 Thus the Lord GOD showed me: Behold, a basket of summer fruit. **2** And He said, "Amos, what do you see?" So I said, "A basket of summer fruit." Then the LORD said to me: "The end has come upon My people Israel; I will not pass by them anymore. **3** And the songs of the temple Shall be wailing in that day," Says the Lord GOD— "Many dead bodies everywhere, They shall be thrown out in silence." **4** Hear this, you who swallow up the needy, And make the poor of the land fail, **5** Saying: "When will the New Moon be past, That we may sell grain? And the Sabbath, That we may trade wheat? Making the ephah small and the shekel large, Falsifying the scales by deceit, **6** That we may buy the poor for silver, And the needy for a pair of sandals— Even sell the bad wheat?"

Amos 9:1 I saw the Lord standing by the altar, and He said: "Strike the doorposts, that the thresholds may shake, And break them on the heads of them all. I will slay the last of them with the sword. He who flees from them shall not get away, And he who escapes from them shall not be delivered.

Zechariah.

Zech 1:8 I saw by night, and behold, a man riding on a red horse, and it stood among the myrtle trees in the hollow; and behind him *were* horses: red, sorrel, and white.

Zech 3:1 Then he showed me Joshua the high priest standing before the Angel of the LORD, and Satan standing at his right hand to oppose him.

Zech 4:2 And he said to me, "What do you see?" So I said, "I am looking, and there *is* a lampstand of solid gold with a bowl on top of it, and on the *stand* seven lamps with seven pipes to the seven lamps.

Zech 5:2 And he said to me, "What do you see?" So I

answered, "I see a flying scroll. Its length *is* twenty cubits and its width ten cubits."

Zech 6:1 Then I turned and raised my eyes and looked, and behold, four chariots *were* coming from between two mountains, and the mountains *were* mountains of bronze.

Paul.

Acts 9:3 As he journeyed he came near Damascus, and suddenly a light shone around him from heaven.

Acts 9:6 So he, trembling and astonished, said, "Lord, what do You want me to do?" Then the Lord *said* to him, "Arise and go into the city, and you will be told what you must do."

Acts 16:9 And a vision appeared to Paul in the night. A man of Macedonia stood and pleaded with him, saying, "Come over to Macedonia and help us."

Acts 18:9 Now the Lord spoke to Paul in the night by a vision, "Do not be afraid, but speak, and do not keep silent;

Acts 22:18 and saw Him saying to me, 'Make haste and get out of Jerusalem quickly, for they will not receive your testimony concerning Me.'

Acts 27:23 For there stood by me this night an angel of the God to whom I belong and whom I serve,

2 Cor 12:1–4 It is doubtless not profitable for me to boast. I will come to visions and revelations of the Lord: **2** I know a man in Christ who fourteen years ago—whether in the body I do not know, or whether out of the body I do not know, God knows—such a one was caught up to the third heaven. **3** And I know such a man—whether in the body or out of the body I do not know, God knows— **4** how he was caught up into Paradise and heard inexpressible words, which it is not lawful for a man to utter.

Ananias.

Acts 9:10–11 Now there was a certain disciple at Damascus named Ananias; and to him the Lord said in a vision, "Ananias." And he said, "Here I am, Lord." **11** So the Lord *said* to him, "Arise and go to the street called Straight, and inquire at the house of Judas for *one* called Saul of Tarsus, for behold, he is praying."

Cornelius.

Acts 10:3 About the ninth hour of the day he saw clearly in a vision an angel of God coming in and saying to him, "Cornelius!"

Peter.

Acts 10:9–17 The next day, as they went on their journey and drew near the city, Peter went up on the housetop to pray, about the sixth hour. **10** Then he became very hungry and wanted to eat; but while they made ready, he fell into a trance **11** and saw heaven opened and an object like a great sheet bound at the four corners, descending to him and let down to the earth. **12** In it were all kinds of four-footed animals of the earth, wild beasts, creeping things, and birds of the air. **13** And a voice came to him, "Rise, Peter; kill and eat." **14** But Peter said, "Not so, Lord! For I have never eaten anything common or unclean." **15** And a voice *spoke* to him again the second time, "What God has cleansed you must not call common." **16** This was done three times. And the object was taken up into heaven again. **17** Now while Peter wondered

within himself what this vision which he had seen meant, behold, the men who had been sent from Cornelius had made inquiry for Simon's house, and stood before the gate.

John.

Rev 1:12 Then I turned to see the voice that spoke with me. And having turned I saw seven golden lampstands,

Cf. Rev 4—22

Sometimes withheld for a long season.

1 Sam 3:1 Now the boy Samuel ministered to the Lᴏʀᴅ before Eli. And the word of the Lᴏʀᴅ was rare in those days; *there was* no widespread revelation.

The withholding of, a great calamity.

Prov 29:18 Where *there is* no revelation, the people cast off restraint; But happy *is* he who keeps the law.

Lam 2:9 Her gates have sunk into the ground; He has destroyed and broken her bars. Her king and her princes *are* among the nations; The Law *is* no *more,* And her prophets find no vision from the Lᴏʀᴅ.

False prophets pretended to have seen.

Jer 14:14 And the Lᴏʀᴅ said to me, "The prophets prophesy lies in My name. I have not sent them, commanded them, nor spoken to them; they prophesy to you a false vision, divination, a worthless thing, and the deceit of their heart.

Jer 23:16 Thus says the Lᴏʀᴅ of hosts: "Do not listen to the words of the prophets who prophesy to you. They make you worthless; They speak a vision of their own heart, Not from the mouth of the Lᴏʀᴅ.

The prophets of God skilled in interpreting.

2 Chr 26:5 He sought God in the days of Zechariah, who had understanding in the visions of God; and as long as he sought the Lᴏʀᴅ, God made him prosper.

Dan 1:17 As for these four young men, God gave them knowledge and skill in all literature and wisdom; and Daniel had understanding in all visions and dreams.

Vows

Solemn promises made to God.

Ps 76:11 Make vows to the Lᴏʀᴅ your God, and pay *them;* Let all who are around Him bring presents to Him who ought to be feared.

Were made in reference to

Devoting the person to God.

Num 6:2 "Speak to the children of Israel, and say to them: 'When either a man or woman consecrates an offering to take the vow of a Nazirite, to separate himself to the Lᴏʀᴅ,

Dedicating children to God.

1 Sam 1:11 Then she made a vow and said, "O Lᴏʀᴅ of hosts, if You will indeed look on the affliction of Your maidservant and remember me, and not forget Your maidservant, but will give Your maidservant a male child, then I will give him to the Lᴏʀᴅ all the days of his life, and no razor shall come upon his head."

Devoting property to God.

Gen 28:22 And this stone which I have set as a pillar shall be God's house, and of all that You give me I will surely give a tenth to You."

Offering sacrifices.

Lev 7:16 But if the sacrifice of his offering *is* a vow or a voluntary offering, it shall be eaten the same day that he offers his sacrifice; but on the next day the remainder of it also may be eaten;

Lev 22:18 "Speak to Aaron and his sons, and to all the children of Israel, and say to them: 'Whatever man of the house of Israel, or of the strangers in Israel, who offers his sacrifice for any of his vows or for any of his freewill offerings, which they offer to the LORD as a burnt offering—

Lev 22:22 Those *that are* blind or broken or maimed, or have an ulcer or eczema or scabs, you shall not offer to the LORD, nor make an offering by fire of them on the altar to the LORD.

Num 15:3 and you make an offering by fire to the LORD, a burnt offering or a sacrifice, to fulfill a vow or as a freewill offering or in your appointed feasts, to make a sweet aroma to the LORD, from the herd or the flock,

Afflicting the soul.

Num 30:13 Every vow and every binding oath to afflict her soul, her husband may confirm it, or her husband may make it void.

To be voluntary.

Deut 23:21–22 "When you make a vow to the LORD your God, you shall not delay to pay it; for the LORD your God will surely require it of you, and it would be sin to you. 22 But if you abstain from vowing, it shall not be sin to you.

To be performed faithfully.

Num 30:2 If a man makes a vow to the LORD, or swears an oath to bind himself by some agreement, he shall not break his word; he shall do according to all that proceeds out of his mouth.

To be performed without delay.

Deut 23:21 "When you make a vow to the LORD your God, you shall not delay to pay it; for the LORD your God will surely require it of you, and it would be sin to you.

Deut 23:23 That which has gone from your lips you shall keep and perform, for you voluntarily vowed to the LORD your God what you have promised with your mouth.

Danger of inconsiderately making.

Prov 20:25 *It is* a snare for a man to devote rashly *something as* holy, And afterward to reconsider *his* vows.

Of children, void without the consent of parents.

Num 30:3–5 "Or if a woman makes a vow to the LORD, and binds *herself* by some agreement while in her father's house in her youth, 4 and her father hears her vow and the agreement by which she has bound herself, and her father holds his peace, then all her vows shall stand, and every agreement with which she has bound herself shall stand. 5 But if her father overrules her on the day that he hears, then none of her vows nor her agreements by which she has bound herself shall stand; and the LORD will release her, because her father overruled her.

Of married women, void without consent of husbands.

Num 30:6–8 "If indeed she takes a husband, while bound by her vows or by a rash utterance from her lips by which she bound herself, 7 and her husband hears *it*, and makes no response to her on the day that he hears, then her vows shall stand, and her agreements by which she bound herself shall stand. 8 But if her husband overrules her on the day that he hears *it*, he shall make void her vow which she took and what she uttered with her lips, by which she bound herself, and the LORD will release her.

Num 30:10–13 "If she vowed in her husband's house, or bound herself by an agreement with an oath, 11 and her husband heard *it*, and made no response to her *and* did not overrule her, then all her vows shall stand, and every agreement by which she bound herself shall stand. 12 But if her husband truly made them void on the day he heard *them*, then whatever proceeded from her lips concerning her vows or concerning the agreement binding her, it shall not stand; her husband has made them void, and the LORD will release her. 13 Every vow and every binding oath to afflict her soul, her husband may confirm it, or her husband may make it void.

Of widows and women divorced from their husbands, binding.

Num 30:9 "Also any vow of a widow or a divorced woman, by which she has bound herself, shall stand against her.

Of wives, could be objected to only at the time of making.

Num 30:14–15 Now if her husband makes no response whatever to her from day to day, then he confirms all her vows or all the agreements that bind her; he confirms them, because he made no response to her on the day that he heard *them*. 15 But if he does make them void after he has heard *them*, then he shall bear her guilt."

Might be redeemed by paying a suitable compensation.

Lev 27:1–8 Now the LORD spoke to Moses, saying, 2 "Speak to the children of Israel, and say to them: 'When a man consecrates by a vow certain persons to the LORD, according to your valuation, 3 if your valuation is of a male from twenty years old up to sixty years old, then your valuation shall be fifty shekels of silver, according to the shekel of the sanctuary. 4 If it *is* a female, then your valuation shall be thirty shekels; 5 and if from five years old up to twenty years old, then your valuation for a male shall be twenty shekels, and for a female ten shekels; 6 and if from a month old up to five years old, then your valuation for a male shall be five shekels of silver, and for a female your valuation shall be three shekels of silver; 7 and if from sixty years old and above, if it *is* a male, then your valuation shall be fifteen shekels, and for a female ten shekels. 8 'But if he is too poor to pay your valuation, then he shall present himself before the priest, and the priest shall set a value for him; according to the ability of him who vowed, the priest shall value him.

Cf. Lev 27:11–23

Clean beasts the subjects of, not to be redeemed.

Lev 27:9–10 'If *it is* an animal that men may bring as an offering to the LORD, all that *anyone* gives to the LORD shall be holy. 10 He shall not substitute it or exchange it, good for bad or bad for good; and if he at all exchanges animal for animal, then both it and the one exchanged for it shall be holy.

Those recorded in Scripture, of

Jacob.

Gen 28:20–22 Then Jacob made a vow, saying, "If God will be with me, and keep me in this way that I am going, and give me bread to eat and clothing to put on, **21** so that I come back to my father's house in peace, then the LORD shall be my God. **22** And this stone which I have set as a pillar shall be God's house, and of all that You give me I will surely give a tenth to You."

Gen 31:13 I *am* the God of Bethel, where you anointed the pillar *and* where you made a vow to Me. Now arise, get out of this land, and return to the land of your family.' "

The Israelites.

Num 21:2 So Israel made a vow to the LORD, and said, "If You will indeed deliver this people into my hand, then I will utterly destroy their cities."

Jephthah.

Judg 11:30–31 And Jephthah made a vow to the LORD, and said, "If You will indeed deliver the people of Ammon into my hands, **31** then it will be that whatever comes out of the doors of my house to meet me, when I return in peace from the people of Ammon, shall surely be the LORD's, and I will offer it up as a burnt offering."

Hannah.

1 Sam 1:11 Then she made a vow and said, "O LORD of hosts, if You will indeed look on the affliction of Your maidservant and remember me, and not forget Your maidservant, but will give Your maidservant a male child, then I will give him to the LORD all the days of his life, and no razor shall come upon his head."

Elkanah.

1 Sam 1:3–4 This man went up from his city yearly to worship and sacrifice to the LORD of hosts in Shiloh. Also the two sons of Eli, Hophni and Phinehas, the priests of the LORD, *were* there. **4** And whenever the time came for Elkanah to make an offering, he would give portions to Peninnah his wife and to all her sons and daughters.

David.

Ps 132:2–5 How he swore to the LORD, *And* vowed to the Mighty One of Jacob: **3** "Surely I will not go into the chamber of my house, Or go up to the comfort of my bed; **4** I will not give sleep to my eyes *Or* slumber to my eyelids, **5** Until I find a place for the LORD, A dwelling place for the Mighty One of Jacob."

The sailors who cast out Jonah.

Jon 1:16 Then the men feared the LORD exceedingly, and offered a sacrifice to the LORD and took vows.

Jonah.

Jon 2:9 But I will sacrifice to You With the voice of thanksgiving; I will pay what I have vowed. Salvation *is* of the LORD."

Lemuel's mother.

Prov 31:1–2 The words of King Lemuel, the utterance which his mother taught him: **2** What, my son? And what, son of my womb? And what, son of my vows?

Paul.

Acts 18:18 So Paul still remained a good while. Then he took leave of the brethren and sailed for Syria, and Priscilla and Aquila *were* with him. He had *his* hair cut off at Cenchrea, for he had taken a vow.

Certain Jews with Paul.

Acts 21:23–24 Therefore do what we tell you: We have four men who have taken a vow. **24** Take them and be purified with them, and pay their expenses so that they may shave *their* heads, and that all may know that those things of which they were informed concerning you are nothing, but *that* you yourself also walk orderly and keep the law.

Acts 21:26 Then Paul took the men, and the next day, having been purified with them, entered the temple to announce the expiration of the days of purification, at which time an offering should be made for each one of them.

All things dedicated by, to be brought to the tabernacle.

Deut 12:6 There you shall take your burnt offerings, your sacrifices, your tithes, the heave offerings of your hand, your vowed offerings, your freewill offerings, and the firstborn of your herds and flocks.

Deut 12:11 then there will be the place where the LORD your God chooses to make His name abide. There you shall bring all that I command you: your burnt offerings, your sacrifices, your tithes, the heave offerings of your hand, and all your choice offerings which you vow to the LORD.

Deut 12:17–18 You may not eat within your gates the tithe of your grain or your new wine or your oil, of the firstborn of your herd or your flock, of any of your offerings which you vow, of your freewill offerings, or of the heave offering of your hand. **18** But you must eat them before the LORD your God in the place which the LORD your God chooses, you and your son and your daughter, your male servant and your female servant, and the Levite who *is* within your gates; and you shall rejoice before the LORD your God in all to which you put your hands.

Deut 12:26 Only the holy things which you have, and your vowed offerings, you shall take and go to the place which the LORD chooses.

Of things corrupt or blemished, an insult to God.

Lev 22:23 Either a bull or a lamb that has any limb too long or too short you may offer *as* a freewill offering, but for a vow it shall not be accepted.

Mal 1:14 "But cursed *be* the deceiver Who has in his flock a male, And takes a vow, But sacrifices to the Lord what is blemished— For I *am* a great King," Says the LORD of hosts, "And My name *is to be* feared among the nations.

The hire of a harlot or price of a dog could not be the subject of.

Deut 23:18 You shall not bring the wages of a harlot or the price of a dog to the house of the LORD your God for any vowed offering, for both of these *are* an abomination to the LORD your God.

WAGES

Were paid one day at a time.

Lev 19:13 'You shall not cheat your neighbor, nor rob *him*. The wages of him who is hired shall not remain with you all night until morning.

Deut 24:14–15 "You shall not oppress a hired servant *who is* poor and needy, *whether* one of your brethren or one of the aliens who *is* in your land within your gates. 15 Each day you shall give *him* his wages, and not let the sun go down on it, for he *is* poor and has set his heart on it; lest he cry out against you to the LORD, and it be sin to you.

Matt 20:1–2 "For the kingdom of heaven is like a landowner who went out early in the morning to hire laborers for his vineyard. 2 Now when he had agreed with the laborers for a denarius a day, he sent them into his vineyard.

As the result of sin.

Rom 6:23 For the wages of sin *is* death, but the gift of God *is* eternal life in Christ Jesus our Lord.

Cf. Acts 1:18; 2 Pet 2:13,15

Must not be withheld.

James 5:4 Indeed the wages of the laborers who mowed your fields, which you kept back by fraud, cry out; and the cries of the reapers have reached the ears of the Lord of Sabaoth.

Ministers must receive appropriate level of.

1 Cor 9:3–14 My defense to those who examine me is this: 4 Do we have no right to eat and drink? 5 Do we have no right to take along a believing wife, as *do* also the other apostles, the brothers of the Lord, and Cephas? 6 Or *is* it only Barnabas and I *who* have no right to refrain from working? 7 Who ever goes to war at his own expense? Who plants a vineyard and does not eat of its fruit? Or who tends a flock and does not drink of the milk of the flock? 8 Do I say these things as a *mere* man? Or does not the law say the same also? 9 For it is written in the law of Moses, *"You shall not muzzle an ox while it treads out the grain."* Is it oxen God is concerned about? 10 Or does He say *it* altogether for our sakes? For our sakes, no doubt, *this* is written, that he who plows should plow in hope, and he who threshes in hope should be partaker of his hope. 11 If we have sown spiritual things for you, *is it* a great thing if we reap your material things? 12 If others are partakers of *this* right over you, *are* we not even more? Nevertheless we have not used this right, but endure all things lest we hinder the gospel of Christ. 13 Do you not know that those who minister the holy things eat *of the things* of the temple, and those who serve at the altar partake of *the offerings of* the altar? 14 Even so the Lord has commanded that those who preach the gospel should live from the gospel.

1 Tim 5:17–18 Let the elders who rule well be counted worthy of double honor, especially those who labor in the word and doctrine. 18 For the Scripture says, *"You shall not muzzle an ox while it treads out the grain,"* and, "The laborer *is* worthy of his wages."

Cf. Gal 6:6; 2 Tim 2:6

WAITING ON GOD

As the God of providence.

Jer 14:22 Are there any among the idols of the nations that can cause rain? Or can the heavens give showers? *Are* You not He, O LORD our God? Therefore we will wait for You, Since You have made all these.

As the God of salvation.

Ps 25:5 Lead me in Your truth and teach me, For You *are* the God of my salvation; On You I wait all the day.

As the giver of all temporal blessings.

Ps 104:27–28 These all wait for You, That You may give *them* their food in due season. 28 *What* You give them they gather in; You open Your hand, they are filled with good.

Ps 145:15–16 The eyes of all look expectantly to You, And You give them their food in due season. 16 You open Your hand And satisfy the desire of every living thing.

The objects of

Mercy.

Ps 123:2 Behold, as the eyes of servants *look* to the hand of their masters, As the eyes of a maid to the hand of her mistress, So our eyes *look* to the LORD our God, Until He has mercy on us.

Pardon.

Ps 39:7–8 "And now, Lord, what do I wait for? My hope *is* in You. 8 Deliver me from all my transgressions; Do not make me the reproach of the foolish.

The Consolation of Israel.

Luke 2:25 And behold, there was a man in Jerusalem whose name was Simeon, and this man was just and devout, waiting for the Consolation of Israel, and the Holy Spirit was upon him.

Salvation.

Gen 49:18 I have waited for your salvation, O LORD!

Ps 62:1–2 Truly my soul silently *waits* for God; From Him *comes* my salvation. 2 He only *is* my rock and my salvation; *He is* my defense; I shall not be greatly moved.

Guidance and teaching.

Ps 25:5 Lead me in Your truth and teach me, For You *are* the God of my salvation; On You I wait all the day.

Protection.

Ps 33:20 Our soul waits for the LORD; He *is* our help and our shield.

Ps 59:9–10 I will wait for You, O You his Strength; For God *is* my defense. **10** My God of mercy shall come to meet me; God shall let me see *my desire* on my enemies.

The fulfillment of His word.

Hab 2:3 For the vision *is* yet for an appointed time; But at the end it will speak, and it will not lie. Though it tarries, wait for it; Because it will surely come, It will not tarry.

The fulfillment of His promises.

Acts 1:4 And being assembled together with *them,* He commanded them not to depart from Jerusalem, but to wait for the Promise of the Father, "which," *He said,* "you have heard from Me;

Hope of righteousness by faith.

Gal 5:5 For we through the Spirit eagerly wait for the hope of righteousness by faith.

Coming of Christ.

1 Cor 1:7 so that you come short in no gift, eagerly waiting for the revelation of our Lord Jesus Christ,

1 Thess 1:10 and to wait for His Son from heaven, whom He raised from the dead, *even* Jesus who delivers us from the wrath to come.

Is good.

Ps 52:9 I will praise You forever, Because You have done *it;* And in the presence of Your saints I will wait on Your name, for *it is* good.

Exhortations and encouragements to.

Ps 27:14 Wait on the LORD; Be of good courage, And He shall strengthen your heart; Wait, I say, on the LORD!

Ps 37:7 Rest in the LORD, and wait patiently for Him; Do not fret because of him who prospers in his way, Because of the man who brings wicked schemes to pass.

Hos 12:6 So you, by *the help of* your God, return; Observe mercy and justice, And wait on your God continually.

Zeph 3:8 "Therefore wait for Me," says the LORD, "Until the day I rise up for plunder; My determination *is* to gather the nations To My assembly of kingdoms, To pour on them My indignation, All My fierce anger; All the earth shall be devoured With the fire of My jealousy.

Should be

With the soul.

Ps 62:1 Truly my soul silently *waits* for God; From Him *comes* my salvation.

Ps 62:5 My soul, wait silently for God alone, For my expectation *is* from Him.

With earnest desire.

Ps 130:6 My soul *waits* for the Lord More than those who watch for the morning— *Yes, more than* those who watch for the morning.

With patience.

Ps 37:7 Rest in the LORD, and wait patiently for Him; Do not fret because of him who prospers in his way, Because of the man who brings wicked schemes to pass.

Ps 40:1 I waited patiently for the LORD; And He inclined to me, And heard my cry.

With resignation.

Lam 3:26 *It is* good that *one* should hope and wait quietly For the salvation of the LORD.

With hope in His word.

Ps 130:5 I wait for the LORD, my soul waits, And in His word I do hope.

With full confidence.

Mic 7:7 Therefore I will look to the LORD; I will wait for the God of my salvation; My God will hear me.

Continually.

Hos 12:6 So you, by *the help of* your God, return; Observe mercy and justice, And wait on your God continually.

All the day.

Ps 25:5 Lead me in Your truth and teach me, For You *are* the God of my salvation; On You I wait all the day.

Especially in adversity.

Ps 59:1–9 Deliver me from my enemies, O my God; Defend me from those who rise up against me. **2** Deliver me from the workers of iniquity, And save me from bloodthirsty men. **3** For look, they lie in wait for my life; The mighty gather against me, Not *for* my transgression nor *for* my sin, O LORD. **4** They run and prepare themselves through no fault *of mine.* Awake to help me, and behold! **5** You therefore, O LORD God of hosts, the God of Israel, Awake to punish all the nations; Do not be merciful to any wicked transgressors. Selah **6** At evening they return, They growl like a dog, And go all around the city. **7** Indeed, they belch with their mouth; Swords *are* in their lips; For *they say,* "Who hears?" **8** But You, O LORD, shall laugh at them; You shall have all the nations in derision. **9** I will wait for You, O You his Strength; For God *is* my defense.

Is 8:17 And I will wait on the LORD, Who hides His face from the house of Jacob; And I will hope in Him.

In the way of His judgments.

Is 26:8 Yes, in the way of Your judgments, O LORD, we have waited for You; The desire of *our* soul *is* for Your name And for the remembrance of You.

Believers

Resolve to.

Ps 52:9 I will praise You forever, Because You have done *it;* And in the presence of Your saints I will wait on Your name, for *it is* good.

Ps 59:9 I will wait for You, O You his Strength; For God *is* my defense.

Have expectation from.

Ps 62:5 My soul, wait silently for God alone, For my expectation *is* from Him.

Plead for, in prayer.

Ps 25:21 Let integrity and uprightness preserve me, For I wait for You.

Is 33:2 O Lord, be gracious to us; We have waited for You. Be their arm every morning, Our salvation also in the time of trouble.

The patience of, often tried in.

Ps 69:3 I am weary with my crying; My throat is dry; My eyes fail while I wait for my God.

Those who engage in,

Are heard.

Ps 40:1 I waited patiently for the Lord; And He inclined to me, And heard my cry.

Are blessed.

Is 30:18 Therefore the Lord will wait, that He may be gracious to you; And therefore He will be exalted, that He may have mercy on you. For the Lord *is* a God of justice; Blessed *are* all those who wait for Him.

Dan 12:12 Blessed *is* he who waits, and comes to the one thousand three hundred and thirty-five days.

Experience His goodness.

Lam 3:25 The Lord *is* good to those who wait for Him, To the soul *who* seeks Him.

Shall not be ashamed.

Ps 25:3 Indeed, let no one who waits on You be ashamed; Let those be ashamed who deal treacherously without cause.

Is 49:23 Kings shall be your foster fathers, And their queens your nursing mothers; They shall bow down to you with *their* faces to the earth, And lick up the dust of your feet. Then you will know that I *am* the Lord, For they shall not be ashamed who wait for Me."

Shall renew their strength.

Is 40:31 But those who wait on the Lord Shall renew *their* strength; They shall mount up with wings like eagles, They shall run and not be weary, They shall walk and not faint.

Shall inherit the earth.

Ps 37:9 For evildoers shall be cut off; But those who wait on the Lord, They shall inherit the earth.

Shall be saved.

Prov 20:22 Do not say, "I will recompense evil"; Wait for the Lord, and He will save you.

Is 25:9 And it will be said in that day: "Behold, this *is* our God; We have waited for Him, and He will save us. This *is* the Lord; We have waited for Him; We will be glad and rejoice in His salvation."

Shall receive the glorious things prepared by God for them.

Is 64:4 For since the beginning of the world Men have not heard nor perceived by the ear, Nor has the eye seen any God besides You, Who acts for the one who waits for Him.

Predicted of the Gentiles.

Is 42:4 He will not fail nor be discouraged, Till He has established justice in the earth; And the coastlands shall wait for His law."

Is 60:9 Surely the coastlands shall wait for Me; And the ships of Tarshish *will come* first, To bring your sons from afar, Their silver and their gold with them, To the name of the Lord your God, And to the Holy One of Israel, Because He has glorified you.

Illustrated.

Ps 123:2 Behold, as the eyes of servants *look* to the hand of their masters, As the eyes of a maid to the hand of her mistress, So our eyes *look* to the Lord our God, Until He has mercy on us.

Luke 12:36 and you yourselves be like men who wait for their master, when he will return from the wedding, that when he comes and knocks they may open to him immediately.

James 5:7 Therefore be patient, brethren, until the coming of the Lord. See *how* the farmer waits for the precious fruit of the earth, waiting patiently for it until it receives the early and latter rain.

Exemplified by

Jacob.

Gen 49:18 I have waited for your salvation, O Lord!

Hannah.

1 Sam 1:2 And he had two wives: the name of one *was* Hannah, and the name of the other Peninnah. Peninnah had children, but Hannah had no children.

David.

Ps 39:7 "And now, Lord, what do I wait for? My hope *is* in You.

Isaiah.

Is 8:17 And I will wait on the Lord, Who hides His face from the house of Jacob; And I will hope in Him.

Micah.

Mic 7:7 Therefore I will look to the Lord; I will wait for the God of my salvation; My God will hear me.

Joseph of Arimathea.

Mark 15:43 Joseph of Arimathea, a prominent council member, who was himself waiting for the kingdom of God, coming and taking courage, went in to Pilate and asked for the body of Jesus.

WALK, THE CHRISTIAN

Means to live according to God's will.

Deut 10:12–13 "And now, Israel, what does the Lord your God require of you, but to fear the Lord your God, to walk in all His ways and to love Him, to serve the Lord your God with all your heart and with all your soul, 13 *and* to keep the commandments of the Lord and His statutes which I command you today for your good?

In the law of God.

Ps 119:1 Blessed *are* the undefiled in the way, Who walk in the law of the Lord!

Not in the way of the wicked.

Prov 1:15 My son, do not walk in the way with them, Keep your foot from their path;

God requires a humble.

Mic 6:8 He has shown you, O man, what *is* good; And what does the Lord require of you But to do justly, To love mercy, And to walk humbly with your God?

According to the Spirit.

Rom 8:4 that the righteous requirement of the law might be fulfilled in us who do not walk according to the flesh but according to the Spirit.

Gal 5:16 I say then: Walk in the Spirit, and you shall not fulfill the lust of the flesh.

Should be proper.

Rom 13:13 Let us walk properly, as in the day, not in revelry and drunkenness, not in lewdness and lust, not in strife and envy.

Should be worthy.

Eph 4:1 I, therefore, the prisoner of the Lord, beseech you to walk worthy of the calling with which you were called,

Col 1:10 that you may walk worthy of the Lord, fully pleasing *Him*, being fruitful in every good work and increasing in the knowledge of God;

Not as unbelievers.

Eph 4:17 This I say, therefore, and testify in the Lord, that you should no longer walk as the rest of the Gentiles walk, in the futility of their mind,

Should be progressing spiritually.

Phil 3:16 Nevertheless, to *the degree* that we have already attained, let us walk by the same rule, let us be of the same mind.

Should be in the light of truth and holiness.

1 John 1:7 But if we walk in the light as He is in the light, we have fellowship with one another, and the blood of Jesus Christ His Son cleanses us from all sin.

WALLS

Designed for separation.

Ezek 43:8 When they set their threshold by My threshold, and their doorpost by My doorpost, with a wall between them and Me, they defiled My holy name by the abominations which they committed; therefore I have consumed them in My anger.

Eph 2:14 For He Himself is our peace, who has made both one, and has broken down the middle wall of separation,

Designed for defense.

1 Sam 25:16 They were a wall to us both by night and day, all the time we were with them keeping the sheep.

Mentioned in Scripture

Of cities.

Num 13:28 Nevertheless the people who dwell in the land *are* strong; the cities *are* fortified *and* very large; moreover we saw the descendants of Anak there.

Of temples.

1 Chr 29:4 three thousand talents of gold, of the gold of Ophir, and seven thousand talents of refined silver, to overlay the walls of the houses;

Is 56:5 Even to them I will give in My house And within My walls a place and a name Better than that of sons and daughters; I will give them an everlasting name That shall not be cut off.

Of houses.

1 Sam 18:11 And Saul cast the spear, for he said, "I will pin David to the wall!" But David escaped his presence twice.

Of vineyards.

Num 22:24 Then the Angel of the Lord stood in a narrow path between the vineyards, *with* a wall on this side and a wall on that side.

Prov 24:31 And there it was, all overgrown with thorns; Its surface was covered with nettles; Its stone wall was broken down.

Frequently made of stone and wood together.

Ezra 5:8 Let it be known to the king that we went into the province of Judea, to the temple of the great God, which is being built with heavy stones, and timber is being laid in the walls; and this work goes on diligently and prospers in their hands.

Hab 2:11 For the stone will cry out from the wall, And the beam from the timbers will answer it.

Often strengthened with plates of iron or bronze.

Jer 15:20 And I will make you to this people a fortified bronze wall; And they will fight against you, But they shall not prevail against you; For I *am* with you to save you And deliver you," says the Lord.

Ezek 4:3 Moreover take for yourself an iron plate, and set it *as* an iron wall between you and the city. Set your face against it, and it shall be besieged, and you shall lay siege against it. This *will be* a sign to the house of Israel.

Of cities

Often very high.

Deut 1:28 Where can we go up? Our brethren have discouraged our hearts, saying, "The people *are* greater and taller than we; the cities *are* great and fortified up to heaven; moreover we have seen the sons of the Anakim there." '

Deut 3:5 All these cities *were* fortified with high walls, gates, and bars, besides a great many rural towns.

Strongly fortified.

Is 2:15 Upon every high tower, And upon every fortified wall;

Is 25:12 The fortress of the high fort of your walls He will bring down, lay low, *And* bring to the ground, down to the dust.

Had towers built on them.

2 Chr 26:9 And Uzziah built towers in Jerusalem at the Corner Gate, at the Valley Gate, and at the corner buttress of the wall; then he fortified them.

2 Chr 32:5 And he strengthened himself, built up all the wall that was broken, raised *it* up to the towers, and *built* another wall outside; also he repaired the Millo *in* the City of David, and made weapons and shields in abundance.

Ps 48:12 Walk about Zion, And go all around her. Count her towers;

Houses often built on.

Josh 2:15 Then she let them down by a rope through the window, for her house *was* on the city wall; she dwelt on the wall.

Were broad and places of public resort.

2 Kin 6:26 Then, as the king of Israel was passing by on the wall, a woman cried out to him, saying, "Help, my lord, O king!"

2 Kin 6:30 Now it happened, when the king heard the words of the woman, that he tore his clothes; and as he passed by on the wall, the people looked, and there underneath *he had* sackcloth on his body.

Ps 55:10 Day and night they go around it on its walls; Iniquity and trouble *are* also in the midst of it.

Were strongly manned in war.

2 Kin 18:26 Then Eliakim the son of Hilkiah, Shebna, and Joah said to *the* Rabshakeh, "Please speak to your servants in Aramaic, for we understand *it*; and do not speak to us in Hebrew in the hearing of the people who *are* on the wall."

Kept by watchmen night and day.

Song 5:7 The watchmen who went about the city found me. They struck me, they wounded me; The keepers of the walls Took my veil away from me.

Is 62:6 I have set watchmen on your walls, O Jerusalem; They shall never hold their peace day or night. You who make mention of the LORD, do not keep silent,

Houses sometimes broken down to repair and fortify.

Is 22:10 You numbered the houses of Jerusalem, And the houses you broke down To fortify the wall.

Danger of approaching too near to, in time of war.

2 Sam 11:20–21 if it happens that the king's wrath rises, and he says to you: 'Why did you approach so near to the city when you fought? Did you not know that they would shoot from the wall? **21** Who struck Abimelech the son of Jerubbesheth? Was it not a woman who cast a piece of a millstone on him from the wall, so that he died in Thebez? Why did you go near the wall?'—then you shall say, 'Your servant Uriah the Hittite is dead also.' "

Were battered by besieging armies.

2 Sam 20:15 Then they came and besieged him in Abel of Beth Maachah; and they cast up a siege mound against the city, and it stood by the rampart. And all the people who *were* with Joab battered the wall to throw it down.

Ezek 4:2–3 Lay siege against it, build a siege wall against it, and heap up a mound against it; set camps against it also, and place battering rams against it all around. **3** Moreover take for yourself an iron plate, and set it *as* an iron wall between you and the city. Set your face against it, and it shall be besieged, and you shall lay siege against it. This *will be* a sign to the house of Israel.

Adroitness of soldiers in scaling alluded to.

Joel 2:7–9 They run like mighty men, They climb the wall like men of war; Every one marches in formation, And they do not break ranks. **8** They do not push one another; Every one marches in his own column. Though they lunge between the weapons, They are not cut down. **9** They run to and fro in the city, They run on the wall; They climb into the houses, They enter at the windows like a thief.

Sometimes burned.

Jer 49:27 "I will kindle a fire in the wall of Damascus, And it shall consume the palaces of Ben-Hadad."

Amos 1:7 But I will send a fire upon the wall of Gaza, Which shall devour its palaces.

Of Jerusalem, sometimes laid in ruins.

2 Chr 25:23 Then Joash the king of Israel captured Amaziah king of Judah, the son of Joash, the son of Je-

hoahaz, at Beth Shemesh; and he brought him to Jerusalem, and broke down the wall of Jerusalem from the Gate of Ephraim to the Corner Gate—four hundred cubits.

2 Chr 36:19 Then they burned the house of God, broke down the wall of Jerusalem, burned all its palaces with fire, and destroyed all its precious possessions.

Jer 50:15 Shout against her all around; She has given her hand, Her foundations have fallen, Her walls are thrown down; For it *is* the vengeance of the LORD. Take vengeance on her. As she has done, so do to her.

Destruction of, a punishment and cause of grief.

Deut 28:52 "They shall besiege you at all your gates until your high and fortified walls, in which you trust, come down throughout all your land; and they shall besiege you at all your gates throughout all your land which the LORD your God has given you.

Neh 1:3 And they said to me, "The survivors who are left from the captivity in the province *are* there in great distress and reproach. The wall of Jerusalem *is* also broken down, and its gates *are* burned with fire."

Neh 2:12–17 Then I arose in the night, I and a few men with me; I told no one what my God had put in my heart to do at Jerusalem; nor was there any animal with me, except the one on which I rode. **13** And I went out by night through the Valley Gate to the Serpent Well and the Refuse Gate, and viewed the walls of Jerusalem which were broken down and its gates which were burned with fire. **14** Then I went on to the Fountain Gate and to the King's Pool, but *there was* no room for the animal under me to pass. **15** So I went up in the night by the valley, and viewed the wall; then I turned back and entered by the Valley Gate, and so returned. **16** And the officials did not know where I had gone or what I had done; I had not yet told the Jews, the priests, the nobles, the officials, or the others who did the work. **17** Then I said to them, "You see the distress that we *are* in, how Jerusalem *lies* waste, and its gates are burned with fire. Come and let us build the wall of Jerusalem, that we may no longer be a reproach."

The falling of, sometimes caused great destruction.

1 Kin 20:30 But the rest fled to Aphek, into the city; then a wall fell on twenty-seven thousand of the men *who were* left. And Ben-Hadad fled and went into the city, into an inner chamber.

The bodies of enemies sometimes fastened on, as a disgrace.

1 Sam 31:10 Then they put his armor in the temple of the Ashtoreths, and they fastened his body to the wall of Beth Shan.

Custom of dedicating.

Neh 12:27 Now at the dedication of the wall of Jerusalem they sought out the Levites in all their places, to bring them to Jerusalem to celebrate the dedication with gladness, both with thanksgivings and singing, *with* cymbals and stringed instruments and harps.

Idolatrous rites performed on.

2 Kin 3:27 Then he took his eldest son who would have reigned in his place, and offered him *as* a burnt offering upon the wall; and there was great indignation against Israel. So they departed from him and returned to *their own* land.

Instances of persons let down from.

Josh 2:15 Then she let them down by a rope through the window, for her house *was* on the city wall; she dwelt on the wall.

Acts 9:24–25 But their plot became known to Saul. And they watched the gates day and night, to kill him. **25** Then the disciples took him by night and let *him* down through the wall in a large basket.

2 Cor 11:33 but I was let down in a basket through a window in the wall, and escaped from his hands.

Small towns and villages were not surrounded by.

Lev 25:31 However the houses of villages which have no wall around them shall be counted as the fields of the country. They may be redeemed, and they shall be released in the Jubilee.

Deut 3:5 All these cities *were* fortified with high walls, gates, and bars, besides a great many rural towns.

Of houses

Usually plastered.

Ezek 13:10 "Because, indeed, because they have seduced My people, saying, 'Peace!' when *there is* no peace—and one builds a wall, and they plaster it with untempered *mortar*—

Dan 5:5 In the same hour the fingers of a man's hand appeared and wrote opposite the lampstand on the plaster of the wall of the king's palace; and the king saw the part of the hand that wrote.

Had nails or pegs fastened into them when built.

Eccl 12:11 The words of the wise are like goads, and the words of scholars are like well-driven nails, given by one Shepherd.

Is 22:23 I will fasten him *as* a peg in a secure place, And he will become a glorious throne to his father's house.

Liable to leprosy.

Lev 14:37 And he shall examine the plague; and indeed *if* the plague *is* on the walls of the house with ingrained streaks, greenish or reddish, which appear to be deep in the wall,

Sometimes occupied by serpents.

Amos 5:19 It *will be* as though a man fled from a lion, And a bear met him! Or *as though* he went into the house, Leaned his hand on the wall, And a serpent bit him!

Could be easily dug through.

Ezek 8:7–8 So He brought me to the door of the court; and when I looked, there was a hole in the wall. **8** Then He said to me, "Son of man, dig into the wall"; and when I dug into the wall, there was a door.

Ezek 12:5 Dig through the wall in their sight, and carry your belongings out through it.

The seat next, was the place of distinction.

1 Sam 20:25 Now the king sat on his seat, as at other times, on a seat by the wall. And Jonathan arose, and Abner sat by Saul's side, but David's place was empty.

Hyssop frequently grew on.

1 Kin 4:33 Also he spoke of trees, from the cedar tree of Lebanon even to the hyssop that springs out of the wall; he spoke also of animals, of birds, of creeping things, and of fish.

Miracles connected with,

Falling of the walls of Jericho.

Josh 6:20 So the people shouted when *the priests* blew the trumpets. And it happened when the people heard the sound of the trumpet, and the people shouted with a great shout, that the wall fell down flat. Then the people went up into the city, every man straight before him, and they took the city.

Handwriting on the wall of Belshazzar's palace.

Dan 5:5 In the same hour the fingers of a man's hand appeared and wrote opposite the lampstand on the plaster of the wall of the king's palace; and the king saw the part of the hand that wrote.

Dan 5:25–28 "And this is the inscription that was written: MENE, MENE, TEKEL, UPHARSIN. **26** This *is* the interpretation of *each* word. MENE: God has numbered your kingdom, and finished it; **27** TEKEL: You have been weighed in the balances, and found wanting; **28** PERES: Your kingdom has been divided, and given to the Medes and Persians."

Illustrative of

Salvation.

Is 26:1 In that day this song will be sung in the land of Judah: "We have a strong city; *God* will appoint salvation *for* walls and bulwarks.

Is 60:18 Violence shall no longer be heard in your land, Neither wasting nor destruction within your borders; But you shall call your walls Salvation, And your gates Praise.

The protection of God.

Zech 2:5 For I,' says the LORD, 'will be a wall of fire all around her, and I will be the glory in her midst.' "

Those who afford protection.

1 Sam 25:16 They were a wall to us both by night and day, all the time we were with them keeping the sheep.

Is 2:15 Upon every high tower, And upon every fortified wall;

Ordinances as a protection to God's people.

Is 5:5 And now, please let Me tell you what I will do to My vineyard: I will take away its hedge, and it shall be burned; *And* break down its wall, and it shall be trampled down.

The wealth of the rich in his own esteem.

Prov 18:11 The rich man's wealth *is* his strong city, And like a high wall in his own esteem.

(Bronze) prophets in their testimony against the wicked.

Jer 15:20 And I will make you to this people a fortified bronze wall; And they will fight against you, But they shall not prevail against you; For I *am* with you to save you And deliver you," says the LORD.

(Leaning or tottering) the wicked under judgments.

Ps 62:3 How long will you attack a man? You shall be

slain, all of you, Like a leaning wall and a tottering fence.

Is 30:13 Therefore this iniquity shall be to you Like a breach ready to fall, A bulge in a high wall, Whose breaking comes suddenly, in an instant.

Separation of Jews and Gentiles.

Eph 2:14 For He Himself is our peace, who has made both one, and has broken down the middle wall of separation,

(Plastered with untempered mortar) the teaching of false prophets.

Ezek 13:10–15 "Because, indeed, because they have seduced My people, saying, 'Peace!' when *there is* no peace—and one builds a wall, and they plaster it with untempered *mortar*— **11** say to those who plaster *it* with untempered *mortar*, that it will fall. There will be flooding rain, and you, O great hailstones, shall fall; and a stormy wind shall tear *it* down. **12** Surely, when the wall has fallen, will it not be said to you, 'Where *is* the mortar with which you plastered *it?'* " **13** Therefore thus says the Lord GOD: "I will cause a stormy wind to break forth in My fury; and there shall be a flooding rain in My anger, and great hailstones in fury to consume *it.* **14** So I will break down the wall you have plastered with untempered *mortar,* and bring it down to the ground, so that its foundation will be uncovered; it will fall, and you shall be consumed in the midst of it. Then you shall know that I *am* the LORD. **15** "Thus will I accomplish My wrath on the wall and on those who have plastered it with untempered *mortar;* and I will say to you, 'The wall *is* no *more,* nor those who plastered it,

(Whitewashed) hypocrites.

Acts 23:3 Then Paul said to him, "God will strike you, *you* whitewashed wall! For you sit to judge me according to the law, and do you command me to be struck contrary to the law?"

WAR

Antiquity of.

Gen 14:2 *that* they made war with Bera king of Sodom, Birsha king of Gomorrah, Shinab king of Admah, Shemeber king of Zeboiim, and the king of Bela (that is, Zoar).

Originates in man-centered desires.

James 4:1 Where do wars and fights *come* from among you? Do *they* not *come* from your *desires for* pleasure that war in your members?

A time for.

Eccl 3:8 A time to love, And a time to hate; A time of war, And a time of peace.

God

Frequently ordered.

Ex 17:16 for he said, "Because the LORD has sworn: the LORD *will have* war with Amalek from generation to generation."

Num 31:1–2 And the LORD spoke to Moses, saying: **2** "Take vengeance on the Midianites for the children of Israel. Afterward you shall be gathered to your people."

Deut 7:1–2 "When the LORD your God brings you into the land which you go to possess, and has cast out many nations before you, the Hittites and the Girgashites and the Amorites and the Canaanites and the Perizzites and the Hivites and the Jebusites, seven nations greater and mightier than you, **2** and when the LORD your God delivers them over to you, you shall conquer them *and* utterly destroy them. You shall make no covenant with them nor show mercy to them.

1 Sam 15:1–3 Samuel also said to Saul, "The LORD sent me to anoint you king over His people, over Israel. Now therefore, heed the voice of the words of the LORD. **2** Thus says the LORD of hosts: 'I will punish Amalek *for* what he did to Israel, how he ambushed him on the way when he came up from Egypt. **3** Now go and attack Amalek, and utterly destroy all that they have, and do not spare them. But kill both man and woman, infant and nursing child, ox and sheep, camel and donkey.' "

Taught His people the art of.

2 Sam 22:35 He teaches my hands to make war, So that my arms can bend a bow of bronze.

Strengthens His people for.

Lev 26:7–8 You will chase your enemies, and they shall fall by the sword before you. **8** Five of you shall chase a hundred, and a hundred of you shall put ten thousand to flight; your enemies shall fall by the sword before you.

Gives the victory in.

Num 21:3 And the LORD listened to the voice of Israel and delivered up the Canaanites, and they utterly destroyed them and their cities. So the name of that place was called Hormah.

Deut 2:33 And the LORD our God delivered him over to us; so we defeated him, his sons, and all his people.

Deut 3:3 "So the LORD our God also delivered into our hands Og king of Bashan, with all his people, and we attacked him until he had no survivors remaining.

2 Sam 23:10 He arose and attacked the Philistines until his hand was weary, and his hand stuck to the sword. The LORD brought about a great victory that day; and the people returned after him only to plunder.

Prov 21:31 The horse *is* prepared for the day of battle, But deliverance *is* of the LORD.

Causes to cease.

Ps 46:9 He makes wars cease to the end of the earth; He breaks the bow and cuts the spear in two; He burns the chariot in the fire.

Scatters those who delight in.

Ps 68:30 Rebuke the beasts of the reeds, The herd of bulls with the calves of the peoples, *Till everyone* submits himself with pieces of silver. Scatter the peoples *who* delight in war.

Large armies frequently engaged in.

2 Chr 13:3 Abijah set the battle in order with an army of valiant warriors, four hundred thousand choice men. Jeroboam also drew up in battle formation against him with eight hundred thousand choice men, mighty men of valor.

2 Chr 14:9 Then Zerah the Ethiopian came out against them with an army of a million men and three hundred chariots, and he came to Mareshah.

Weapons were used in.

Josh 1:14 Your wives, your little ones, and your livestock shall remain in the land which Moses gave you on this side of the Jordan. But you shall pass before your brethren armed, all your mighty men of valor, and help them,

Judg 18:11 And six hundred men of the family of the Danites went from there, from Zorah and Eshtaol, armed with weapons of war.

Preceded by

Consultation.

Prov 24:6 For by wise counsel you will wage your own war, And in a multitude of counselors *there is* safety.

Luke 14:31 Or what king, going to make war against another king, does not sit down first and consider whether he is able with ten thousand to meet him who comes against him with twenty thousand?

Great preparation.

Joel 3:9 Proclaim this among the nations: "Prepare for war! Wake up the mighty men, Let all the men of war draw near, Let them come up.

Rumors.

Jer 4:19 O my soul, my soul! I am pained in my very heart! My heart makes a noise in me; I cannot hold my peace, Because you have heard, O my soul, The sound of the trumpet, The alarm of war.

Matt 24:6 And you will hear of wars and rumors of wars. See that you are not troubled; for all *these things* must come to pass, but the end is not yet.

Frequently lengthy.

2 Sam 3:1 Now there was a long war between the house of Saul and the house of David. But David grew stronger and stronger, and the house of Saul grew weaker and weaker.

Frequently harsh and bloody.

1 Sam 14:22 Likewise all the men of Israel who had hidden in the mountains of Ephraim, *when* they heard that the Philistines fled, they also followed hard after them in the battle.

1 Chr 5:22 for many fell dead, because the war *was* God's. And they dwelt in their place until the captivity.

2 Chr 14:13 And Asa and the people who *were* with him pursued them to Gerar. So the Ethiopians were overthrown, and they could not recover, for they were broken before the LORD and His army. And they carried away very much spoil.

2 Chr 28:6 For Pekah the son of Remaliah killed one hundred and twenty thousand in Judah in one day, all valiant men, because they had forsaken the LORD God of their fathers.

Often attended by

Famine.

Is 51:19 These two *things* have come to you; Who will be sorry for you?— Desolation and destruction, famine and sword— By whom will I comfort you?

Jer 14:15 Therefore thus says the LORD concerning the prophets who prophesy in My name, whom I did not send, and who say, 'Sword and famine shall not be in this land'—'By sword and famine those prophets shall be consumed!

Lam 5:10 Our skin is hot as an oven, Because of the fever of famine.

Pestilence.

Jer 27:13 Why will you die, you and your people, by the sword, by the famine, and by the pestilence, as the LORD has spoken against the nation that will not serve the king of Babylon?

Jer 28:8 The prophets who have been before me and before you of old prophesied against many countries and great kingdoms—of war and disaster and pestilence.

Cruelty.

Jer 18:21 Therefore deliver up their children to the famine, And pour out their *blood* By the force of the sword; Let their wives *become* widows And bereaved of their children. Let their men be put to death, Their young men *be* slain By the sword in battle.

Lam 5:11–14 They ravished the women in Zion, The maidens in the cities of Judah. **12** Princes were hung up by their hands, And elders were not respected. **13** Young men ground at the millstones; Boys staggered under *loads of* wood. **14** The elders have ceased *gathering at* the gate, And the young men from their music.

Devastation.

Is 1:7 Your country *is* desolate, Your cities *are* burned with fire; Strangers devour your land in your presence; And *it is* desolate, as overthrown by strangers.

Records often kept of.

Num 21:14 Therefore it is said in the Book of the Wars of the LORD: "Waheb in Suphah, The brooks of the Arnon,

Often sent as a punishment for sin.

Judg 5:8 They chose new gods; Then *there was* war in the gates; Not a shield or spear was seen among forty thousand in Israel.

The Jews

Were experts in.

1 Chr 12:33 of Zebulun there were fifty thousand who went out to battle, expert in war with all weapons of war, stouthearted men who could keep ranks;

1 Chr 12:35–36 of the Danites who could keep battle formation, twenty-eight thousand six hundred; **36** of Asher, those who could go out to war, able to keep battle formation, forty thousand;

Song 3:8 They all hold swords, *Being* expert in war. Every man *has* his sword on his thigh Because of fear in the night.

Frequently engaged in.

1 Kin 14:30 And there was war between Rehoboam and Jeroboam all *their* days.

1 Kin 15:7 Now the rest of the acts of Abijam, and all that he did, *are* they not written in the book of the chronicles of the kings of Judah? And there was war between Abijam and Jeroboam.

1 Kin 15:16 Now there was war between Asa and Baasha king of Israel all their days.

Cf. Josh 6–11

Illustrative of

Our contest with death.

Eccl 8:8 No one has power over the spirit to retain the spirit, And no one has power in the day of death. *There is* no release from that war, And wickedness will not deliver those who are given to it.

The contest of believers with the enemies of their salvation.

Rom 7:23 But I see another law in my members, warring against the law of my mind, and bringing me into captivity to the law of sin which is in my members.

2 Cor 10:3 For though we walk in the flesh, we do not war according to the flesh.

Eph 6:12 For we do not wrestle against flesh and blood, but against principalities, against powers, against the rulers of the darkness of this age, against spiritual *hosts* of wickedness in the heavenly *places.*

1 Tim 1:18 This charge I commit to you, son Timothy, according to the prophecies previously made concerning you, that by them you may wage the good warfare,

The contest between Antichrist and the church.

Rev 11:7 When they finish their testimony, the beast that ascends out of the bottomless pit will make war against them, overcome them, and kill them.

Rev 13:4 So they worshiped the dragon who gave authority to the beast; and they worshiped the beast, saying, "Who *is* like the beast? Who is able to make war with him?"

Rev 13:7 It was granted to him to make war with the saints and to overcome them. And authority was given him over every tribe, tongue, and nation.

The malignity of the wicked.

Ps 55:21 *The words* of his mouth were smoother than butter, But war *was* in his heart; His words were softer than oil, Yet they *were* drawn swords.

WAR, WEAPONS OF

Made of iron or bronze.

1 Sam 17:5–6 *He had* a bronze helmet on his head, and he *was* armed with a coat of mail, and the weight of the coat *was* five thousand shekels of bronze. **6** And *he had* bronze armor on his legs and a bronze javelin between his shoulders.

Job 20:24 He will flee from the iron weapon; A bronze bow will pierce him through.

Offensive,

Sword.

Judg 20:15 And from their cities at that time the children of Benjamin numbered twenty-six thousand men who drew the sword, besides the inhabitants of Gibeah, who numbered seven hundred select men.

Ezek 32:27 They do not lie with the mighty *Who are* fallen of the uncircumcised, Who have gone down to hell with their weapons of war; They have laid their swords under their heads, But their iniquities will be on their bones, Because of the terror of the mighty in the land of the living.

Two-edged sword.

Ps 149:6 *Let* the high praises of God *be* in their mouth, And a two-edged sword in their hand,

Prov 5:4 But in the end she is bitter as wormwood, Sharp as a two-edged sword.

Dagger.

Judg 3:16 Now Ehud made himself a dagger (it was double-edged and a cubit in length) and fastened it under his clothes on his right thigh.

Judg 3:21–22 Then Ehud reached with his left hand, took the dagger from his right thigh, and thrust it into his belly. **22** Even the hilt went in after the blade, and the fat closed over the blade, for he did not draw the dagger out of his belly; and his entrails came out.

Spear or lance.

1 Sam 18:10–11 And it happened on the next day that the distressing spirit from God came upon Saul, and he prophesied inside the house. So David played *music* with his hand, as at other times; but *there was* a spear in Saul's hand. **11** And Saul cast the spear, for he said, "I will pin David to the wall!" But David escaped his presence twice.

1 Sam 26:7 So David and Abishai came to the people by night; and there Saul lay sleeping within the camp, with his spear stuck in the ground by his head. And Abner and the people lay all around him.

2 Sam 18:14 Then Joab said, "I cannot linger with you." And he took three spears in his hand and thrust them through Absalom's heart, while he was *still* alive in the midst of the terebinth tree.

Jer 50:42 They shall hold the bow and the lance; They *are* cruel and shall not show mercy. Their voice shall roar like the sea; They shall ride on horses, Set in array, like a man for the battle, Against you, O daughter of Babylon.

Battle-ax.

Jer 51:20 "You *are* My battle-ax *and* weapons of war: For with you I will break the nation in pieces; With you I will destroy kingdoms;

Ezek 26:9 He will direct his battering rams against your walls, and with his axes he will break down your towers.

Bow and arrows.

Gen 48:22 Moreover I have given to you one portion above your brothers, which I took from the hand of the Amorite with my sword and my bow."

1 Kin 22:34 Now a *certain* man drew a bow at random, and struck the king of Israel between the joints of his armor. So he said to the driver of his chariot, "Turn around and take me out of the battle, for I am wounded."

Sling.

1 Sam 17:50 So David prevailed over the Philistine with a sling and a stone, and struck the Philistine and killed him. But *there was* no sword in the hand of David.

2 Kin 3:25 Then they destroyed the cities, and each man threw a stone on every good piece of land and filled it; and they stopped up all the springs of water and cut down all the good trees. But they left the stones of Kir Haraseth *intact*. However the slingers surrounded and attacked it.

Club.

Matt 26:47 And while He was still speaking, behold, Judas, one of the twelve, with a great multitude with swords and clubs, came from the chief priests and elders of the people.

Called weapons of war.

2 Sam 1:27 "How the mighty have fallen, And the weapons of war perished!"

1 Chr 12:33 of Zebulun there were fifty thousand who went out to battle, expert in war with all weapons of war, stouthearted men who could keep ranks;

1 Chr 12:37 of the Reubenites and the Gadites and the half-tribe of Manasseh, from the other side of the Jordan, one hundred and twenty thousand armed for battle with every *kind* of weapon of war.

Called instruments of death.

Ps 7:13 He also prepares for Himself instruments of death; He makes His arrows into fiery shafts.

Defensive,

Helmet.

1 Sam 17:5 *He had* a bronze helmet on his head, and he *was* armed with a coat of mail, and the weight of the coat *was* five thousand shekels of bronze.

1 Sam 17:38 So Saul clothed David with his armor, and he put a bronze helmet on his head; he also clothed him with a coat of mail.

2 Chr 26:14 Then Uzziah prepared for them, for the entire army, shields, spears, helmets, body armor, bows, and slings *to cast* stones.

Coat of mail, breastplate.

Ex 28:32 There shall be an opening for his head in the middle of it; it shall have a woven binding all around its opening, like the opening in a coat of mail, so that it does not tear.

1 Sam 17:5 *He had* a bronze helmet on his head, and he *was* armed with a coat of mail, and the weight of the coat *was* five thousand shekels of bronze.

1 Sam 17:38 So Saul clothed David with his armor, and he put a bronze helmet on his head; he also clothed him with a coat of mail.

Jer 46:4 Harness the horses, And mount up, you horsemen! Stand forth with *your* helmets, Polish the spears, Put on the armor!

Rev 9:9 And they had breastplates like breastplates of iron, and the sound of their wings *was* like the sound of chariots with many horses running into battle.

Belt.

1 Sam 18:4 And Jonathan took off the robe that *was* on him and gave it to David, with his armor, even to his sword and his bow and his belt.

2 Sam 18:11 So Joab said to the man who told him, "You just saw *him!* And why did you not strike him there to the ground? I would have given you ten *shekels* of silver and a belt."

Shield.

1 Kin 10:16–17 And King Solomon made two hundred large shields *of* hammered gold; six hundred *shekels* of gold went into each shield. **17** He also *made* three

hundred shields *of* hammered gold; three minas of gold went into each shield. The king put them in the House of the Forest of Lebanon.

1 Kin 14:26–27 And he took away the treasures of the house of the LORD and the treasures of the king's house; he took away everything. He also took away all the gold shields which Solomon had made. **27** Then King Rehoboam made bronze shields in their place, and committed *them* to the hands of the captains of the guard, who guarded the doorway of the king's house.

1 Chr 5:18 The sons of Reuben, the Gadites, and half the tribe of Manasseh *had* forty-four thousand seven hundred and sixty valiant men, men able to bear shield and sword, to shoot with the bow, and skillful in war, who went to war.

Called armor.

1 Sam 17:6 And *he had* bronze armor on his legs and a bronze javelin between his shoulders.

Luke 11:22 But when a stronger than he comes upon him and overcomes him, he takes from him all his armor in which he trusted, and divides his spoils.

For sieges,

Battering rams.

2 Sam 20:15 Then they came and besieged him in Abel of Beth Maachah; and they cast up a siege mound against the city, and it stood by the rampart. And all the people who *were* with Joab battered the wall to throw it down.

Ezek 4:2 Lay siege against it, build a siege wall against it, and heap up a mound against it; set camps against it also, and place battering rams against it all around.

Devices for casting stones, etc.

2 Chr 26:15 And he made devices in Jerusalem, invented by skillful men, to be on the towers and the corners, to shoot arrows and large stones. So his fame spread far and wide, for he was marvelously helped till he became strong.

Not worn in ordinary times.

1 Sam 21:8 And David said to Ahimelech, "Is there not here on hand a spear or a sword? For I have brought neither my sword nor my weapons with me, because the king's business required haste."

Put on at the first alarm.

Is 8:9 "Be shattered, O you peoples, and be broken in pieces! Give ear, all you from far countries. Gird yourselves, but be broken in pieces; Gird yourselves, but be broken in pieces.

Jer 46:3–4 "Order the buckler and shield, And draw near to battle! **4** Harness the horses, And mount up, you horsemen! Stand forth with *your* helmets, Polish the spears, Put on the armor!

Armories built for.

2 Kin 20:13 And Hezekiah was attentive to them, and showed them all the house of his treasures—the silver and gold, the spices and precious ointment, and all his armory—all that was found among his treasures. There was nothing in his house or in all his dominion that Hezekiah did not show them.

Song 4:4 Your neck *is* like the tower of David, Built for an armory, On which hang a thousand bucklers, All shields of mighty men.

Great stores of, prepared.

2 Chr 32:5 And he strengthened himself, built up all the wall that was broken, raised *it* up to the towers, and *built* another wall outside; also he repaired the Millo *in* the City of David, and made weapons and shields in abundance.

Were provided from the public arsenals.

2 Chr 11:12 Also in every city *he put* shields and spears, and made them very strong, having Judah and Benjamin on his side.

2 Chr 26:14 Then Uzziah prepared for them, for the entire army, shields, spears, helmets, body armor, bows, and slings *to cast* stones.

Often given as presents.

1 Kin 10:25 Each man brought his present: articles of silver and gold, garments, armor, spices, horses, and mules, at a set rate year by year.

Before using

Tried and proved.

1 Sam 17:39 David fastened his sword to his armor and tried to walk, for he had not tested *them*. And David said to Saul, "I cannot walk with these, for I have not tested *them*." So David took them off.

Polished.

Jer 46:4 Harness the horses, And mount up, you horsemen! Stand forth with *your* helmets, Polish the spears, Put on the armor!

Ezek 21:9–11 "Son of man, prophesy and say, 'Thus says the LORD!' Say: 'A sword, a sword is sharpened And also polished! **10** Sharpened to make a dreadful slaughter, Polished to flash like lightning! Should we then make mirth? It despises the scepter of My son, *As it does* all wood. **11** And He has given it to be polished, That it may be handled; This sword is sharpened, and it is polished To be given into the hand of the slayer.'

Ezek 21:28 "And you, son of man, prophesy and say, 'Thus says the Lord GOD concerning the Ammonites and concerning their reproach,' and say: 'A sword, a sword *is* drawn, Polished for slaughter, For consuming, for flashing—

Anointed.

Is 21:5 Prepare the table, Set a watchman in the tower, Eat and drink. Arise, you princes, Anoint the shield!

Part of, borne by armorbearers.

Judg 9:54 Then he called quickly to the young man, his armorbearer, and said to him, "Draw your sword and kill me, lest men say of me, 'A woman killed him.' " So his young man thrust him through, and he died.

1 Sam 14:1 Now it happened one day that Jonathan the son of Saul said to the young man who bore his armor, "Come, let us go over to the Philistines' garrison that *is* on the other side." But he did not tell his father.

1 Sam 16:21 So David came to Saul and stood before him. And he loved him greatly, and he became his armorbearer.

Hung on the walls of cities.

Ezek 27:10–11 "Those from Persia, Lydia, and Libya Were in your army as men of war; They hung shield and helmet in you; They gave splendor to you. **11** Men of Arvad with your army *were* on your walls *all* around, And the men of Gammad were in your towers; They hung their shields on your walls *all* around; They made your beauty perfect.

Of the vanquished,

Taken off them.

2 Sam 2:21 And Abner said to him, "Turn aside to your right hand or to your left, and lay hold on one of the young men and take his armor for yourself." But Asahel would not turn aside from following him.

Luke 11:22 But when a stronger than he comes upon him and overcomes him, he takes from him all his armor in which he trusted, and divides his spoils.

Sometimes kept as trophies.

1 Sam 17:54 And David took the head of the Philistine and brought it to Jerusalem, but he put his armor in his tent.

Sometimes burned.

Ezek 39:9–10 "Then those who dwell in the cities of Israel will go out and set on fire and burn the weapons, both the shields and bucklers, the bows and arrows, the javelins and spears; and they will make fires with them for seven years. **10** They will not take wood from the field nor cut down *any* from the forests, because they will make fires with the weapons; and they will plunder those who plundered them, and pillage those who pillaged them," says the Lord GOD.

Of conquered nations taken away to prevent rebellion.

Judg 5:8 They chose new gods; Then *there was* war in the gates; Not a shield or spear was seen among forty thousand in Israel.

1 Sam 13:19–22 Now there was no blacksmith to be found throughout all the land of Israel, for the Philistines said, "Lest the Hebrews make swords or spears." **20** But all the Israelites would go down to the Philistines to sharpen each man's plowshare, his mattock, his ax, and his sickle; **21** and the charge for a sharpening was a pim for the plowshares, the mattocks, the forks, and the axes, and to set the points of the goads. **22** So it came about, on the day of battle, that there was neither sword nor spear found in the hand of any of the people who *were* with Saul and Jonathan. But they were found with Saul and Jonathan his son.

Inferior to wisdom.

Eccl 9:18 Wisdom *is* better than weapons of war; But one sinner destroys much good."

Illustrative of

Spiritual armor.

Rom 13:12 The night is far spent, the day is at hand. Therefore let us cast off the works of darkness, and let us put on the armor of light.

2 Cor 6:7 by the word of truth, by the power of God, by the armor of righteousness on the right hand and on the left,

Eph 6:11–14 Put on the whole armor of God, that you

may be able to stand against the wiles of the devil. **12** For we do not wrestle against flesh and blood, but against principalities, against powers, against the rulers of the darkness of this age, against spiritual *hosts* of wickedness in the heavenly *places*. **13** Therefore take up the whole armor of God, that you may be able to withstand in the evil day, and having done all, to stand. **14** Stand therefore, having girded your waist with truth, having put on the breastplate of righteousness,

1 Thess 5:8 But let us who are of the day be sober, putting on the breastplate of faith and love, and *as* a helmet the hope of salvation.

Spiritual weapons.

2 Cor 10:4 For the weapons of our warfare *are* not carnal but mighty in God for pulling down strongholds,

Eph 6:17 And take the helmet of salvation, and the sword of the Spirit, which is the word of God;

Judgments of God.

Is 13:5 They come from a far country, From the end of heaven— The LORD and His weapons of indignation, To destroy the whole land.

Jer 50:25 The LORD has opened His armory, And has brought out the weapons of His indignation; For this *is* the work of the Lord GOD of hosts In the land of the Chaldeans.

WATCHFULNESS

Christ an example of.

Matt 26:38 Then He said to them, "My soul is exceedingly sorrowful, even to death. Stay here and watch with Me."

Matt 26:40 Then He came to the disciples and found them sleeping, and said to Peter, "What! Could you not watch with Me one hour?

Luke 6:12 Now it came to pass in those days that He went out to the mountain to pray, and continued all night in prayer to God.

Commanded.

Mark 13:37 And what I say to you, I say to all: Watch!"

1 Thess 5:6 Therefore let us not sleep, as others *do,* but let us watch and be sober.

1 Pet 4:7 But the end of all things is at hand; therefore be serious and watchful in your prayers.

Rev 3:2 Be watchful, and strengthen the things which remain, that are ready to die, for I have not found your works perfect before God.

God especially requires, in ministers.

Ezek 3:17 "Son of man, I have made you a watchman for the house of Israel; therefore hear a word from My mouth, and give them warning from Me:

Is 62:6 I have set watchmen on your walls, O Jerusalem; They shall never hold their peace day or night. You who make mention of the LORD, do not keep silent,

Mark 13:34 *It is* like a man going to a far country, who left his house and gave authority to his servants, and to each his work, and commanded the doorkeeper to watch.

Acts 20:31 Therefore watch, and remember that for three years I did not cease to warn everyone night and day with tears.

2 Tim 4:5 But you be watchful in all things, endure afflictions, do the work of an evangelist, fulfill your ministry.

Faithful ministers exercise.

Heb 13:17 Obey those who rule over you, and be submissive, for they watch out for your souls, as those who must give account. Let them do so with joy and not with grief, for that would be unprofitable for you.

Faithful servants marked by.

Matt 24:45–46 "Who then is a faithful and wise servant, whom his master made ruler over his household, to give them food in due season? **46** Blessed *is* that servant whom his master, when he comes, will find so doing.

Luke 12:41–44 Then Peter said to Him, "Lord, do You speak this parable *only* to us, or to all *people?*" **42** And the Lord said, "Who then is that faithful and wise steward, whom *his* master will make ruler over his household, to give *them their* portion of food in due season? **43** Blessed *is* that servant whom his master will find so doing when he comes. **44** Truly, I say to you that he will make him ruler over all that he has.

Should be

With prayer.

Ps 141:3 Set a guard, O LORD, over my mouth; Keep watch over the door of my lips.

Luke 21:36 Watch therefore, and pray always that you may be counted worthy to escape all these things that will come to pass, and to stand before the Son of Man."

Eph 6:18 praying always with all prayer and supplication in the Spirit, being watchful to this end with all perseverance and supplication for all the saints—

With thanksgiving.

Col 4:2 Continue earnestly in prayer, being vigilant in it with thanksgiving;

With steadfastness in the faith.

1 Cor 16:13 Watch, stand fast in the faith, be brave, be strong.

With heedfulness.

Mark 13:33 Take heed, watch and pray; for you do not know when the time is.

With sobriety.

1 Thess 5:6 Therefore let us not sleep, as others *do,* but let us watch and be sober.

1 Pet 4:7 But the end of all things is at hand; therefore be serious and watchful in your prayers.

Daily.

Prov 8:34 Blessed is the man who listens to me, Watching daily at my gates, Waiting at the posts of my doors.

In all things.

2 Tim 4:5 But you be watchful in all things, endure afflictions, do the work of an evangelist, fulfill your ministry.

Motives to,

Receiving guidance from God.

Hab 2:1 I will stand my watch And set myself on the rampart, And watch to see what He will say to me,

And what I will answer when I am corrected.

Uncertain time of Christ's return.

Matt 24:42 Watch therefore, for you do not know what hour your Lord is coming.

Matt 25:13 "Watch therefore, for you know neither the day nor the hour in which the Son of Man is coming.

Mark 13:35–36 Watch therefore, for you do not know when the master of the house is coming—in the evening, at midnight, at the crowing of the rooster, or in the morning— **36** lest, coming suddenly, he find you sleeping.

Incessant assaults of the devil.

1 Pet 5:8 Be sober, be vigilant; because your adversary the devil walks about like a roaring lion, seeking whom he may devour.

Liability to temptation.

Matt 26:41 Watch and pray, lest you enter into temptation. The spirit indeed *is* willing, but the flesh *is* weak."

Blessedness of.

Luke 12:37 Blessed *are* those servants whom the master, when he comes, will find watching. Assuredly, I say to you that he will gird himself and have them sit down *to eat,* and will come and serve them.

Rev 16:15 "Behold, I am coming as a thief. Blessed *is* he who watches, and keeps his garments, lest he walk naked and they see his shame."

Unfaithful ministers devoid of.

Is 56:10 His watchmen *are* blind, They are all ignorant; They *are* all dumb dogs, They cannot bark; Sleeping, lying down, loving to slumber.

The wicked averse to.

1 Thess 5:7 For those who sleep, sleep at night, and those who get drunk are drunk at night.

Danger of neglecting.

Matt 24:48–51 But if that evil servant says in his heart, 'My master is delaying his coming,' **49** and begins to beat *his* fellow servants, and to eat and drink with the drunkards, **50** the master of that servant will come on a day when he is not looking for *him* and at an hour that he is not aware of, **51** and will cut him in two and appoint *him* his portion with the hypocrites. There shall be weeping and gnashing of teeth.

Matt 25:5 But while the bridegroom was delayed, they all slumbered and slept.

Matt 25:8 And the foolish said to the wise, 'Give us *some* of your oil, for our lamps are going out.'

Matt 25:12 But he answered and said, 'Assuredly, I say to you, I do not know you.'

Rev 3:3 Remember therefore how you have received and heard; hold fast and repent. Therefore if you will not watch, I will come upon you as a thief, and you will not know what hour I will come upon you.

Illustrated.

Luke 12:35–36 "Let your waist be girded and *your* lamps burning; **36** and you yourselves be like men who wait for their master, when he will return from the wedding, that when he comes and knocks they may open to him immediately.

Exemplified by

David.

Ps 102:7 I lie awake, And am like a sparrow alone on the housetop.

Anna.

Luke 2:37 and this woman *was* a widow of about eighty-four years, who did not depart from the temple, but served *God* with fastings and prayers night and day.

Paul.

2 Cor 11:27 in weariness and toil, in sleeplessness often, in hunger and thirst, in fastings often, in cold and nakedness—

WATCHMEN

Soldiers generally acted as.

Matt 27:65–66 Pilate said to them, "You have a guard; go your way, make *it* as secure as you know how." **66** So they went and made the tomb secure, sealing the stone and setting the guard.

Citizens sometimes acted as.

Neh 7:3 And I said to them, "Do not let the gates of Jerusalem be opened until the sun is hot; and while they stand *guard,* let them shut and bar the doors; and appoint guards from among the inhabitants of Jerusalem, one at his watch station and another in front of his own house."

Were stationed

On towers.

2 Kin 9:17 Now a watchman stood on the tower in Jezreel, and he saw the company of Jehu as he came, and said, "I see a company of men." And Joram said, "Get a horseman and send him to meet them, and let him say, 'Is *it* peace?' "

Is 21:5 Prepare the table, Set a watchman in the tower, Eat and drink. Arise, you princes, Anoint the shield!

On the walls of cities.

Is 62:6 I have set watchmen on your walls, O Jerusalem; They shall never hold their peace day or night. You who make mention of the LORD, do not keep silent,

In the streets of cities.

Ps 127:1 Unless the LORD builds the house, They labor in vain who build it; Unless the LORD guards the city, The watchman stays awake in vain.

Around the temple in Jerusalem on special occasions.

2 Kin 11:6 one-third *shall be* at the gate of Sur, and one-third at the gate behind the escorts. You shall keep the watch of the house, lest it be broken down.

Paraded the streets at night to preserve order.

Song 3:3 The watchmen who go about the city found me; *I said,* "Have you seen the one I love?"

Song 5:7 The watchmen who went about the city found me. They struck me, they wounded me; The keepers of the walls Took my veil away from me.

In time of danger,

Increase in number.

Jer 51:12 Set up the standard on the walls of Babylon; Make the guard strong, Set up the watchmen, Prepare the ambushes. For the LORD has both devised and done What He spoke against the inhabitants of Babylon.

Were vigilant day and night.

Neh 4:9 Nevertheless we made our prayer to our God, and because of them we set a watch against them day and night.

Is 21:8 Then he cried, "A lion, my Lord! I stand continually on the watchtower in the daytime; I have sat at my post every night.

Reported the approach of all strangers.

2 Sam 18:24–27 Now David was sitting between the two gates. And the watchman went up to the roof over the gate, to the wall, lifted his eyes and looked, and there was a man, running alone. **25** Then the watchman cried out and told the king. And the king said, "If he *is* alone, *there is* news in his mouth." And he came rapidly and drew near. **26** Then the watchman saw *another* man running, and the watchman called to the gatekeeper and said, "There is *another* man, running alone!" And the king said, "He also brings news." **27** So the watchman said, "I think the running of the first is like the running of Ahimaaz the son of Zadok." And the king said, "He *is* a good man, and comes with good news."

2 Kin 9:18–20 So the horseman went to meet him, and said, "Thus says the king: '*Is it* peace?'" And Jehu said, "What have you to do with peace? Turn around and follow me." So the watchman reported, saying, "The messenger went to them, but is not coming back." **19** Then he sent out a second horseman who came to them, and said, "Thus says the king: '*Is it* peace?'" And Jehu answered, "What have you to do with peace? Turn around and follow me." **20** So the watchman reported, saying, "He went up to them and is not coming back; and the driving *is* like the driving of Jehu the son of Nimshi, for he drives furiously!"

Is 21:6–7 For thus has the Lord said to me: "Go, set a watchman, Let him declare what he sees." **7** And he saw a chariot *with* a pair of horsemen, A chariot of donkeys, *and* a chariot of camels, And he listened earnestly with great care.

Is 21:9 And look, here comes a chariot of men *with* a pair of horsemen!" Then he answered and said, "Babylon is fallen, is fallen! And all the carved images of her gods He has broken to the ground."

Sounded an alarm at the approach of enemies.

Ezek 33:2–3 "Son of man, speak to the children of your people, and say to them: 'When I bring the sword upon a land, and the people of the land take a man from their territory and make him their watchman, **3** when he sees the sword coming upon the land, if he blows the trumpet and warns the people,

Vigilance of, vain without God's protection.

Ps 127:1 Unless the LORD builds the house, They labor in vain who build it; Unless the LORD guards the city, The watchman stays awake in vain.

Were relieved by turns.

Neh 7:3 And I said to them, "Do not let the gates of Jerusalem be opened until the sun is hot; and while they stand *guard*, let them shut and bar the doors; and appoint guards from among the inhabitants of Jerusalem, one at his watch station and another in front of his own house."

Danger of sleeping at their posts, referred to.

Matt 28:13–14 saying, "Tell them, 'His disciples came at night and stole Him *away* while we slept.' **14** And if this comes to the governor's ears, we will appease him and make you secure."

Neglecting to give warning, punished with death.

Ezek 33:6 But if the watchman sees the sword coming and does not blow the trumpet, and the people are not warned, and the sword comes and takes *any* person from among them, he is taken away in his iniquity; but his blood I will require at the watchman's hand.'

Often interrogated by travelers.

Is 21:11 The burden against Dumah. He calls to me out of Seir, "Watchman, what of the night? Watchman, what of the night?"

Illustrative of

Ministers.

Is 52:8 Your watchmen shall lift up their voices, With *their* voices they shall sing together; For they shall see eye to eye When the LORD brings back Zion.

Is 62:6 I have set watchmen on your walls, O Jerusalem; They shall never hold their peace day or night. You who make mention of the LORD, do not keep silent,

Ezek 3:17 "Son of man, I have made you a watchman for the house of Israel; therefore hear a word from My mouth, and give them warning from Me:

Heb 13:17 Obey those who rule over you, and be submissive, for they watch out for your souls, as those who must give account. Let them do so with joy and not with grief, for that would be unprofitable for you.

(Blind) careless ministers.

Is 56:10 His watchmen *are* blind, They are all ignorant; They *are* all dumb dogs, They cannot bark; Sleeping, lying down, loving to slumber.

(Looking for the morning) eager waiting for God.

Ps 130:5–6 I wait for the LORD, my soul waits, And in His word I do hope. **6** My soul *waits* for the Lord More than those who watch for the morning— *Yes, more than* those who watch for the morning.

WATER

One of the elements of the world.

Gen 1:2 The earth was without form, and void; and darkness *was* on the face of the deep. And the Spirit of God was hovering over the face of the waters.

God's original work with,

Created the firmament to divide.

Gen 1:6–7 Then God said, "Let there be a firmament in the midst of the waters, and let it divide the waters from the waters." **7** Thus God made the firmament, and divided the waters which *were* under the firmament from the waters which *were* above the firmament; and it was so.

Collected it into one place.

Gen 1:9 Then God said, "Let the waters under the heavens be gathered together into one place, and let the dry *land* appear"; and it was so.

Created birds and fishes, etc. from.

Gen 1:20–21 Then God said, "Let the waters abound with an abundance of living creatures, and let birds fly above the earth across the face of the firmament of the heavens." **21** So God created great sea creatures and every living thing that moves, with which the waters abounded, according to their kind, and every winged bird according to its kind. And God saw that *it was* good.

Necessary to vegetation.

Gen 2:5–6 before any plant of the field was in the earth and before any herb of the field had grown. For the LORD God had not caused it to rain on the earth, and *there was* no man to till the ground; **6** but a mist went up from the earth and watered the whole face of the ground.

Job 14:9 Yet at the scent of water it will bud And bring forth branches like a plant.

Is 1:30 For you shall be as a terebinth whose leaf fades, And as a garden that has no water.

Some plants particularly require.

Job 8:11 "Can the papyrus grow up without a marsh? Can the reeds flourish without water?

Necessary to the comfort and happiness of man.

Is 41:17 "The poor and needy seek water, but *there is* none, Their tongues fail for thirst. I, the LORD, will hear them; *I*, the God of Israel, will not forsake them.

Zech 9:11 "As for you also, Because of the blood of your covenant, I will set your prisoners free from the waterless pit.

Collected in

Springs.

Josh 15:19 She answered, "Give me a blessing; since you have given me land in the South, give me also springs of water." So he gave her the upper springs and the lower springs.

1 Kin 18:5 And Ahab had said to Obadiah, "Go into the land to all the springs of water and to all the brooks; perhaps we may find grass to keep the horses and mules alive, so that we will not have to kill any livestock."

2 Chr 32:3 he consulted with his leaders and commanders to stop the water from the springs which *were* outside the city; and they helped him.

Pools.

1 Kin 22:38 Then *someone* washed the chariot at a pool in Samaria, and the dogs licked up his blood while the harlots bathed, according to the word of the LORD which He had spoken.

Neh 2:14 Then I went on to the Fountain Gate and to the King's Pool, but *there was* no room for the animal under me to pass.

Ponds.

Ex 7:19 Then the LORD spoke to Moses, "Say to Aaron, 'Take your rod and stretch out your hand over the waters of Egypt, over their streams, over their rivers, over their ponds, and over all their pools of water, that they may become blood. And there shall

be blood throughout all the land of Egypt, both in *buckets of* wood and *pitchers of* stone.' "

Is 19:10 And its foundations will be broken. All who make wages *will be* troubled of soul.

Wells.

Gen 21:19 Then God opened her eyes, and she saw a well of water. And she went and filled the skin with water, and gave the lad a drink.

Fountains.

1 Sam 29:1 Then the Philistines gathered together all their armies at Aphek, and the Israelites encamped by a fountain which is in Jezreel.

Brooks.

2 Sam 17:20 And when Absalom's servants came to the woman at the house, they said, "Where *are* Ahimaaz and Jonathan?" So the woman said to them, "They have gone over the water brook." And when they had searched and could not find *them*, they returned to Jerusalem.

1 Kin 18:5 And Ahab had said to Obadiah, "Go into the land to all the springs of water and to all the brooks; perhaps we may find grass to keep the horses and mules alive, so that we will not have to kill any livestock."

Streams.

Ps 78:16 He also brought streams out of the rock, And caused waters to run down like rivers.

Is 35:6 Then the lame shall leap like a deer, And the tongue of the dumb sing. For waters shall burst forth in the wilderness, And streams in the desert.

Rivers.

Is 8:7 Now therefore, behold, the Lord brings up over them The waters of the River, strong and mighty— The king of Assyria and all his glory; He will go up over all his channels And go over all his banks.

Jer 2:18 And now why take the road to Egypt, To drink the waters of Sihor? Or why take the road to Assyria, To drink the waters of the River?

The sea.

Gen 1:9–10 Then God said, "Let the waters under the heavens be gathered together into one place, and let the dry *land* appear"; and it was so. **10** And God called the dry *land* Earth, and the gathering together of the waters He called Seas. And God saw that *it was* good.

Is 11:9 They shall not hurt nor destroy in all My holy mountain, For the earth shall be full of the knowledge of the LORD As the waters cover the sea.

The clouds.

Gen 1:7 Thus God made the firmament, and divided the waters which *were* under the firmament from the waters which *were* above the firmament; and it was so.

Job 26:8–9 He binds up the water in His thick clouds, Yet the clouds are not broken under it. **9** He covers the face of *His* throne, *And* spreads His cloud over it.

Returns to its source.

Eccl 1:7 All the rivers run into the sea, Yet the sea *is* not full; To the place from which the rivers come, There they return again.

Ps 104:8 They went up over the mountains; They went down into the valleys, To the place which You founded for them.

Drops from the clouds in rain.

Deut 11:11 but the land which you cross over to possess *is* a land of hills and valleys, which drinks water from the rain of heaven,

2 Sam 21:10 Now Rizpah the daughter of Aiah took sackcloth and spread it for herself on the rock, from the beginning of harvest until the late rains poured on them from heaven. And she did not allow the birds of the air to rest on them by day nor the beasts of the field by night.

Described as

Fluid.

Ps 78:16 He also brought streams out of the rock, And caused waters to run down like rivers.

Prov 30:4 Who has ascended into heaven, or descended? Who has gathered the wind in His fists? Who has bound the waters in a garment? Who has established all the ends of the earth? What *is* His name, and what *is* His Son's name, If you know?

Unstable.

Gen 49:4 Unstable as water, you shall not excel, Because you went up to your father's bed; Then you defiled it— He went up to my couch.

Penetrating.

Ps 109:18 As he clothed himself with cursing as with his garment, So let it enter his body like water, And like oil into his bones.

Reflecting images.

Prov 27:19 As in water face *reflects* face, So a man's heart *reveals* the man.

Wearing the hardest substances.

Job 14:19 *As* water wears away stones, *And as* torrents wash away the soil of the earth; So You destroy the hope of man.

Cleansing.

Ezek 36:25 Then I will sprinkle clean water on you, and you shall be clean; I will cleanse you from all your filthiness and from all your idols.

Eph 5:26 that He might sanctify and cleanse her with the washing of water by the word,

Refreshing.

Job 22:7 You have not given the weary water to drink, And you have withheld bread from the hungry.

Prov 25:25 *As* cold water to a weary soul, So *is* good news from a far country.

Congealed by cold.

Job 38:29 From whose womb comes the ice? And the frost of heaven, who gives it birth?

Ps 147:16–17 He gives snow like wool; He scatters the frost like ashes; 17 He casts out His hail like morsels; Who can stand before His cold?

Was used by Jews

As their principal beverage.

Gen 24:43 behold, I stand by the well of water; and it shall come to pass that when the virgin comes out to draw *water*, and I say to her, "Please give me a little water from your pitcher to drink,"

1 Kin 13:19 So he went back with him, and ate bread in his house, and drank water.

1 Kin 13:22 but you came back, ate bread, and drank

water in the place of which *the* LORD said to you, "Eat no bread and drink no water," your corpse shall not come to the tomb of your fathers.' "

1 Kin 18:4 For so it was, while Jezebel massacred the prophets of the LORD, that Obadiah had taken one hundred prophets and hidden them, fifty to a cave, and had fed them with bread and water.)

Hos 2:5 For their mother has played the harlot; She who conceived them has behaved shamefully. For she said, 'I will go after my lovers, Who give *me* my bread and my water, My wool and my linen, My oil and my drink.'

For culinary purposes.

Ex 12:9 Do not eat it raw, nor boiled at all with water, but roasted in fire—its head with its legs and its entrails.

For washing the person.

Gen 18:4 Please let a little water be brought, and wash your feet, and rest yourselves under the tree.

Gen 24:32 Then the man came to the house. And he unloaded the camels, and provided straw and feed for the camels, and water to wash his feet and the feet of the men who *were* with him.

For legal purification.

Ex 29:4 "And Aaron and his sons you shall bring to the door of the tabernacle of meeting, and you shall wash them with water.

Heb 9:10 *concerned* only with foods and drinks, various washings, and fleshly ordinances imposed until the time of reformation.

Heb 9:19 For when Moses had spoken every precept to all the people according to the law, he took the blood of calves and goats, with water, scarlet wool, and hyssop, and sprinkled both the book itself and all the people,

Kept for purification in large pots.

John 2:6 Now there were set there six waterpots of stone, according to the manner of purification of the Jews, containing twenty or thirty gallons apiece.

Carried in vessels.

Gen 21:14 So Abraham rose early in the morning, and took bread and a skin of water; and putting *it* on her shoulder, he gave *it* and the boy to Hagar, and sent her away. Then she departed and wandered in the Wilderness of Beersheba.

1 Sam 26:11 The LORD forbid that I should stretch out my hand against the LORD's anointed. But please, take now the spear and the jug of water that *are* by his head, and let us go."

Mark 14:13 And He sent out two of His disciples and said to them, "Go into the city, and a man will meet you carrying a pitcher of water; follow him.

Artificial mode of conveying, into large cities.

2 Kin 20:20 Now the rest of the acts of Hezekiah—all his might, and how he made a pool and a tunnel and brought water into the city—*are* they not written in the book of the chronicles of the kings of Judah?

Frequently bitter and unfit for use.

Ex 15:23 Now when they came to Marah, they could not drink the waters of Marah, for they *were* bitter. Therefore the name of it was called Marah.

2 Kin 2:19 Then the men of the city said to Elisha, "Please notice, the situation of this city *is* pleasant, as my lord sees; but the water *is* bad, and the ground barren."

The lack of, considered a great calamity.

Ex 17:1–3 Then all the congregation of the children of Israel set out on their journey from the Wilderness of Sin, according to the commandment of the LORD, and camped in Rephidim; but *there was* no water for the people to drink. **2** Therefore the people contended with Moses, and said, "Give us water, that we may drink." So Moses said to them, "Why do you contend with me? Why do you tempt the LORD?" **3** And the people thirsted there for water, and the people complained against Moses, and said, "Why *is* it you have brought us up out of Egypt, to kill us and our children and our livestock with thirst?"

Num 20:2 Now there was no water for the congregation; so they gathered together against Moses and Aaron.

2 Kin 3:9–10 So the king of Israel went with the king of Judah and the king of Edom, and they marched on that roundabout route seven days; and there was no water for the army, nor for the animals that followed them. **10** And the king of Israel said, "Alas! For the LORD has called these three kings together to deliver them into the hand of Moab."

Is 3:1 For behold, the Lord, the LORD of hosts, Takes away from Jerusalem and from Judah The stock and the store, The whole supply of bread and the whole supply of water;

In times of scarcity, sold at an enormous price.

Lam 5:4 We pay for the water we drink, And our wood comes at a price.

Miracles connected with,

Turned into blood.

Ex 7:17 Thus says the LORD: "By this you shall know that I *am* the LORD. Behold, I will strike the waters which *are* in the river with the rod that *is* in my hand, and they shall be turned to blood.

Ex 7:20 And Moses and Aaron did so, just as the LORD commanded. So he lifted up the rod and struck the waters that *were* in the river, in the sight of Pharaoh and in the sight of his servants. And all the waters that *were* in the river were turned to blood.

Turned into wine.

John 2:7–9 Jesus said to them, "Fill the waterpots with water." And they filled them up to the brim. **8** And He said to them, "Draw *some* out now, and take *it* to the master of the feast." And they took *it*. **9** When the master of the feast had tasted the water that was made wine, and did not know where it came from (but the servants who had drawn the water knew), the master of the feast called the bridegroom.

Brought from the rock.

Ex 17:6 Behold, I will stand before you there on the rock in Horeb; and you shall strike the rock, and water will come out of it, that the people may drink." And Moses did so in the sight of the elders of Israel.

Num 20:11 Then Moses lifted his hand and struck the rock twice with his rod; and water came out abundantly, and the congregation and their animals drank.

Brought from the hollow place in Lehi.

Judg 15:19 So God split the hollow place that *is* in Lehi, and water came out, and he drank; and his spirit returned, and he revived. Therefore he called its name En Hakkore, which is in Lehi to this day.

Consumed by fire from heaven.

1 Kin 18:38 Then the fire of the LORD fell and consumed the burnt sacrifice, and the wood and the stones and the dust, and it licked up the water that *was* in the trench.

Divided and made to stand as a wall or heap.

Ex 14:21–22 Then Moses stretched out his hand over the sea; and the LORD caused the sea to go *back* by a strong east wind all that night, and made the sea into dry *land*, and the waters were divided. **22** So the children of Israel went into the midst of the sea on the dry *ground*, and the waters *were* a wall to them on their right hand and on their left.

Josh 3:16 that the waters which came down from upstream stood *still*, *and* rose in a heap very far away at Adam, the city that *is* beside Zaretan. So the waters that went down into the Sea of the Arabah, the Salt Sea, failed, *and* were cut off; and the people crossed over opposite Jericho.

Valley filled with.

2 Kin 3:17–22 For thus says the LORD: 'You shall not see wind, nor shall you see rain; yet that valley shall be filled with water, so that you, your cattle, and your animals may drink.' **18** And this is a simple matter in the sight of the LORD; He will also deliver the Moabites into your hand. **19** Also you shall attack every fortified city and every choice city, and shall cut down every good tree, and stop up every spring of water, and ruin every good piece of land with stones." **20** Now it happened in the morning, when the grain offering was offered, that suddenly water came by way of Edom, and the land was filled with water. **21** And when all the Moabites heard that the kings had come up to fight against them, all who were able to bear arms and older were gathered; and they stood at the border. **22** Then they rose up early in the morning, and the sun was shining on the water; and the Moabites saw the water on the other side *as* red as blood.

Iron made to float in.

2 Kin 6:5–6 But as one was cutting down a tree, the iron *ax head* fell into the water; and he cried out and said, "Alas, master! For it was borrowed." **6** So the man of God said, "Where did it fall?" And he showed him the place. So he cut off a stick, and threw *it* in there; and he made the iron float.

Christ and Peter walking on.

Matt 14:26–29 And when the disciples saw Him walking on the sea, they were troubled, saying, "It is a ghost!" And they cried out for fear. **27** But immediately Jesus spoke to them, saying, "Be of good cheer! It is I; do not be afraid." **28** And Peter answered Him and said, "Lord, if it is You, command me to come to You on the water." **29** So He said, "Come." And when Peter had come down out of the boat, he walked on the water to go to Jesus.

Healing powers communicated to.

2 Kin 5:14 So he went down and dipped seven times in the Jordan, according to the saying of the man of God; and his flesh was restored like the flesh of a little child, and he was clean.

John 5:4 For an angel went down at a certain time into the pool and stirred up the water; then whoever stepped in first, after the stirring of the water, was made well of whatever disease he had.

John 9:7 And He said to him, "Go, wash in the pool of Siloam" (which is translated, Sent). So he went and washed, and came back seeing.

The world and its inhabitants once destroyed by.

Gen 7:20–23 The waters prevailed fifteen cubits upward, and the mountains were covered. **21** And all flesh died that moved on the earth: birds and cattle and beasts and every creeping thing that creeps on the earth, and every man. **22** All in whose nostrils *was* the breath of the spirit of life, all that *was* on the dry *land,* died. **23** So He destroyed all living things which were on the face of the ground: both man and cattle, creeping thing and bird of the air. They were destroyed from the earth. Only Noah and those who *were* with him in the ark remained *alive.*

2 Pet 3:6 by which the world *that* then existed perished, being flooded with water.

The world not to be again destroyed by.

Gen 9:8–15 Then God spoke to Noah and to his sons with him, saying: **9** "And as for Me, behold, I establish My covenant with you and with your descendants after you, **10** and with every living creature that *is* with you: the birds, the cattle, and every beast of the earth with you, of all that go out of the ark, every beast of the earth. **11** Thus I establish My covenant with you: Never again shall all flesh be cut off by the waters of the flood; never again shall there be a flood to destroy the earth." **12** And God said: "This *is* the sign of the covenant which I make between Me and you, and every living creature that *is* with you, for perpetual generations: **13** I set My rainbow in the cloud, and it shall be for the sign of the covenant between Me and the earth. **14** It shall be, when I bring a cloud over the earth, that the rainbow shall be seen in the cloud; **15** and I will remember My covenant which *is* between Me and you and every living creature of all flesh; the waters shall never again become a flood to destroy all flesh.

2 Pet 3:7 But the heavens and the earth *which* are now preserved by the same word, are reserved for fire until the day of judgment and perdition of ungodly men.

Illustrative of

The support of God.

Is 8:6 "Inasmuch as these people refused The waters of Shiloah that flow softly, And rejoice in Rezin and in Remaliah's son;

The gifts and graces of the Holy Spirit.

Is 41:17–18 "The poor and needy seek water, but *there is* none, Their tongues fail for thirst. I, the Lᴏʀᴅ, will hear them; *I,* the God of Israel, will not forsake them.

18 I will open rivers in desolate heights, And fountains in the midst of the valleys; I will make the wilderness a pool of water, And the dry land springs of water.

Is 44:3 For I will pour water on him who is thirsty, And floods on the dry ground; I will pour My Spirit on your descendants, And My blessing on your offspring;

Ezek 36:25 Then I will sprinkle clean water on you, and you shall be clean; I will cleanse you from all your filthiness and from all your idols.

John 7:38–39 He who believes in Me, as the Scripture has said, out of his heart will flow rivers of living water." **39** But this He spoke concerning the Spirit, whom those believing in Him would receive; for the Holy Spirit was not yet *given,* because Jesus was not yet glorified.

Persecutors.

Ps 124:4–5 Then the waters would have overwhelmed us, The stream would have gone over our soul; **5** Then the swollen waters Would have gone over our soul."

Persecutions.

Ps 88:17 They came around me all day long like water; They engulfed me altogether.

Hostile armies.

Is 8:7 Now therefore, behold, the Lord brings up over them The waters of the River, strong and mighty— The king of Assyria and all his glory; He will go up over all his channels And go over all his banks.

Is 17:13 The nations will rush like the rushing of many waters; But *God* will rebuke them and they will flee far away, And be chased like the chaff of the mountains before the wind, Like a rolling thing before the whirlwind.

Severe affliction.

Ps 66:12 You have caused men to ride over our heads; We went through fire and through water; But You brought us out to rich *fulfillment.*

Ps 69:1 Save me, O God! For the waters have come up to *my* neck.

Is 30:20 And *though* the Lord gives you The bread of adversity and the water of affliction, Yet your teachers will not be moved into a corner anymore, But your eyes shall see your teachers.

Is 43:2 When you pass through the waters, I *will be* with you; And through the rivers, they shall not overflow you. When you walk through the fire, you shall not be burned, Nor shall the flame scorch you.

(Still) the ordinances of the gospel.

Ps 23:2 He makes me to lie down in green pastures; He leads me beside the still waters.

(Deep) counsel in the heart.

Prov 20:5 Counsel in the heart of man *is* like deep water, But a man of understanding will draw it out.

(Deep) the words of wisdom.

Prov 18:4 The words of a man's mouth *are* deep waters; The wellspring of wisdom *is* a flowing brook.

(Poured out) the wrath of God.

Hos 5:10 "The princes of Judah are like those who remove a landmark; I will pour out my wrath on them like water.

(Poured out) faintness by terror.

Ps 22:14 I am poured out like water, And all My bones are out of joint; My heart is like wax; It has melted within Me.

(Pouring out of buckets) a numerous progeny.

Num 24:7 He shall pour water from his buckets, And his seed *shall be* in many waters. "His king shall be higher than Agag, And his kingdom shall be exalted.

(Spilled on the ground) death.

2 Sam 14:14 For we will surely die and *become* like water spilled on the ground, which cannot be gathered up again. Yet God does not take away a life; but He devises means, so that His banished ones are not expelled from Him.

(Its instability) a wavering disposition.

Gen 49:4 Unstable as water, you shall not excel, Because you went up to your father's bed; Then you defiled *it*— He went up to my couch.

(Its weakness) faintness and cowardice.

Josh 7:5 And the men of Ai struck down about thirty-six men, for they chased them *from* before the gate as far as Shebarim, and struck them down on the descent; therefore the hearts of the people melted and became like water.

Ezek 7:17 Every hand will be feeble, And every knee will be *as* weak *as* water.

(Difficulty of stopping) strife and contention.

Prov 17:14 The beginning of strife *is like* releasing water; Therefore stop contention before a quarrel starts.

(Rapidly flowing away) the career of the wicked.

Job 24:18 "They *should be* swift on the face of the waters, Their portion *should be* cursed in the earth, *So that* no one *would* turn into the way of their vineyards.

Ps 58:7 Let them flow away as waters *which* run continually; *When* he bends *his bow,* Let his arrows be as if cut in pieces.

(Many) different nations and people.

Jer 51:13 O you who dwell by many waters, Abundant in treasures, Your end has come, The measure of your covetousness.

Rev 17:1 Then one of the seven angels who had the seven bowls came and talked with me, saying to me, "Come, I will show you the judgment of the great harlot who sits on many waters,

Rev 17:15 Then he said to me, "The waters which you saw, where the harlot sits, are peoples, multitudes, nations, and tongues.

(Many) a variety of afflictions.

2 Sam 22:17 "He sent from above, He took me, He drew me out of many waters.

(Sound of many) the word of Christ.

Rev 1:15 His feet *were* like fine brass, as if refined in a furnace, and His voice as the sound of many waters;

(Covering the sea) the general diffusion of the knowledge of God.

Is 11:9 They shall not hurt nor destroy in all My holy mountain, For the earth shall be full of the knowledge of the LORD As the waters cover the sea.

Hab 2:14 For the earth will be filled With the knowledge of the glory of the LORD, As the waters cover the sea.

WEAKNESS

Of man demonstrates the power of God.

1 Cor 2:3–5 I was with you in weakness, in fear, and in much trembling. **4** And my speech and my preaching *were* not with persuasive words of human wisdom, but in demonstration of the Spirit and of power, **5** that your faith should not be in the wisdom of men but in the power of God.

Strength of God made perfect in.

2 Cor 12:9 And He said to me, "My grace is sufficient for you, for My strength is made perfect in weakness." Therefore most gladly I will rather boast in my infirmities, that the power of Christ may rest upon me.

Men made strong in.

Heb 11:34 quenched the violence of fire, escaped the edge of the sword, out of weakness were made strong, became valiant in battle, turned to flight the armies of the aliens.

WEEKS

A period of time consisting of seven days.

Lev 23:15–16 'And you shall count for yourselves from the day after the Sabbath, from the day that you brought the sheaf of the wave offering: seven Sabbaths shall be completed. **16** Count fifty days to the day after the seventh Sabbath; then you shall offer a new grain offering to the LORD.

Luke 18:12 I fast twice a week; I give tithes of all that I possess.'

A span of seven years sometimes so called.

Gen 29:27–28 Fulfill her week, and we will give you this one also for the service which you will serve with me still another seven years." **28** Then Jacob did so and fulfilled her week. So he gave him his daughter Rachel as wife also.

Dan 9:24–25 "Seventy weeks are determined For your people and for your holy city, To finish the transgression, To make an end of sins, To make reconciliation for iniquity, To bring in everlasting righteousness, To seal up vision and prophecy, And to anoint the Most Holy. **25** "Know therefore and understand, *That* from the going forth of the command To restore and build Jerusalem Until Messiah the Prince, *There shall be* seven weeks and sixty-two weeks; The street shall be built again, and the wall, Even in troublesome times.

Dan 9:27 Then he shall confirm a covenant with many for one week; But in the middle of the week He shall bring an end to sacrifice and offering. And on the wing of abominations shall be one who makes desolate, Even until the consummation, which is determined, Is poured out on the desolate."

Origin of computing time by.

Gen 2:2 And on the seventh day God ended His work which He had done, and He rested on the seventh day from all His work which He had done.

The Feast of Pentecost called the Feast of Weeks.

Ex 34:22 "And you shall observe the Feast of Weeks, of the firstfruits of wheat harvest, and the Feast of Ingathering at the year's end.

Acts 2:1 When the Day of Pentecost had fully come, they were all with one accord in one place.

WEEP, WEEPING

Believers are to, with others.

Rom 12:15 Rejoice with those who rejoice, and weep with those who weep.

Is the result of sorrow over sin.

James 4:8–9 Draw near to God and He will draw near to you. Cleanse *your* hands, *you* sinners; and purify *your* hearts, *you* double-minded. **9** Lament and mourn and weep! Let your laughter be turned to mourning and *your* joy to gloom.

Demonstrated by

Joseph.

Gen 43:30 Now his heart yearned for his brother; so Joseph made haste and sought *somewhere* to weep. And he went into *his* chamber and wept there.

David and his men.

2 Sam 1:11–12 Therefore David took hold of his own clothes and tore them, and *so did* all the men who *were* with him. **12** And they mourned and wept and fasted until evening for Saul and for Jonathan his son, for the people of the LORD and for the house of Israel, because they had fallen by the sword.

Jesus.

Matt 9:36 But when He saw the multitudes, He was moved with compassion for them, because they were weary and scattered, like sheep having no shepherd.

Luke 19:41–42 Now as He drew near, He saw the city and wept over it, **42** saying, "If you had known, even you, especially in this your day, the things *that make* for your peace! But now they are hidden from your eyes.

John 11:35 Jesus wept.

A prostitute.

Luke 7:37–38 And behold, a woman in the city who was a sinner, when she knew that *Jesus* sat at the table in the Pharisee's house, brought an alabaster flask of fragrant oil, **38** and stood at His feet behind *Him* weeping; and she began to wash His feet with her tears, and wiped *them* with the hair of her head; and she kissed His feet and anointed *them* with the fragrant oil.

Paul.

Acts 20:19 serving the Lord with all humility, with many tears and trials which happened to me by the plotting of the Jews;

Acts 20:31 Therefore watch, and remember that for three years I did not cease to warn everyone night and day with tears.

Phil 3:18 For many walk, of whom I have told you often, and now tell you even weeping, *that they are* the enemies of the cross of Christ:

The Ephesian elders.

Acts 20:37–38 Then they all wept freely, and fell on Paul's neck and kissed him, **38** sorrowing most of all for the words which he spoke, that they would see his face no more. And they accompanied him to the ship.

WEIGHTS

Generally regulated by the standard shekel of the sanctuary.

Ex 30:24 five hundred *shekels* of cassia, according to the shekel of the sanctuary, and a hin of olive oil.

Sometimes regulated by the king's standard.

2 Sam 14:26 And when he cut the hair of his head—at the end of every year he cut *it* because it was heavy on him—when he cut it, he weighed the hair of his head at two hundred shekels according to the king's standard.

Were frequently used in scales or balances.

Job 31:6 Let me be weighed on honest scales, That God may know my integrity.

Is 40:12 Who has measured the waters in the hollow of His hand, Measured heaven with a span And calculated the dust of the earth in a measure? Weighed the mountains in scales And the hills in a balance?

Units of, mentioned in Scripture

Gerah.

Ex 30:13 This is what everyone among those who are numbered shall give: half a shekel according to the shekel of the sanctuary (a shekel *is* twenty gerahs). The half-shekel *shall be* an offering to the LORD.

Ezek 45:12 The shekel *shall be* twenty gerahs; twenty shekels, twenty-five shekels, *and* fifteen shekels shall be your mina.

Half a shekel.

Gen 24:22 So it was, when the camels had finished drinking, that the man took a golden nose ring weighing half a shekel, and two bracelets for her wrists weighing ten *shekels* of gold,

Shekel.

Ex 30:13 This is what everyone among those who are numbered shall give: half a shekel according to the shekel of the sanctuary (a shekel *is* twenty gerahs). The half-shekel *shall be* an offering to the LORD.

Ezek 45:12 The shekel *shall be* twenty gerahs; twenty shekels, twenty-five shekels, *and* fifteen shekels shall be your mina.

Drachma.

Neh 7:70–72 And some of the heads of the fathers' houses gave to the work. The governor gave to the treasury one thousand gold drachmas, fifty basins, and five hundred and thirty priestly garments. **71** Some of the heads of the fathers' *houses* gave to the treasury of the work twenty thousand gold drachmas, and two thousand two hundred silver minas. **72** And that which the rest of the people gave *was* twenty thousand gold drachmas, two thousand silver minas, and sixty-seven priestly garments.

Mina.

Neh 7:71 Some of the heads of the fathers' *houses* gave to the treasury of the work twenty thousand gold drachmas, and two thousand two hundred silver minas.

Ezek 45:12 The shekel *shall be* twenty gerahs; twenty

shekels, twenty-five shekels, *and* fifteen shekels shall be your mina.

Talent.

2 Sam 12:30 Then he took their king's crown from his head. Its weight *was* a talent of gold, with precious stones. And it was *set* on David's head. Also he brought out the spoil of the city in great abundance.

Rev 16:21 And great hail from heaven fell upon men, *each hailstone* about the weight of a talent. Men blasphemed God because of the plague of the hail, since that plague was exceedingly great.

Value of money estimated according to.

Gen 23:16 And Abraham listened to Ephron; and Abraham weighed out the silver for Ephron which he had named in the hearing of the sons of Heth, four hundred shekels of silver, currency of the merchants.

Gen 43:21 but it happened, when we came to the encampment, that we opened our sacks, and there, *each* man's money *was* in the mouth of his sack, our money in full weight; so we have brought it back in our hand.

Jer 32:9 So I bought the field from Hanamel, the son of my uncle who *was* in Anathoth, and weighed *out* to him the money—seventeen shekels of silver.

All metals were given by.

Ex 37:24 Of a talent of pure gold he made it, with all its utensils.

1 Chr 28:14 *He gave* gold by weight for *things* of gold, for all articles used in every kind of service; also *silver* for all articles of silver by weight, for all articles used in every kind of service;

Provisions were sold by, in times of scarcity.

Lev 26:26 When I have cut off your supply of bread, ten women shall bake your bread in one oven, and they shall bring back your bread by weight, and you shall eat and not be satisfied.

Ezek 4:10 And your food which you eat *shall be* by weight, twenty shekels a day; from time to time you shall eat it.

Ezek 4:16 Moreover He said to me, "Son of man, surely I will cut off the supply of bread in Jerusalem; they shall eat bread by weight and with anxiety, and shall drink water by measure and with dread,

The Jews

Forbidden to have various.

Deut 25:13–14 "You shall not have in your bag differing weights, a heavy and a light. **14** You shall not have in your house differing measures, a large and a small.

Forbidden to have unjust.

Lev 19:35–36 'You shall do no injustice in judgment, in measurement of length, weight, or volume. **36** You shall have honest scales, honest weights, an honest ephah, and an honest hin: I *am* the LORD your God, who brought you out of the land of Egypt.

Frequently used unjustly.

Mic 6:11 Shall I count pure *those* with the wicked scales, And with the bag of deceitful weights?

Illustrative of

Sins.

Heb 12:1 Therefore we also, since we are surrounded by

so great a cloud of witnesses, let us lay aside every weight, and the sin which so easily ensnares *us*, and let us run with endurance the race that is set before us,

The restraints put on the elements.

Job 28:25 To establish a weight for the wind, And apportion the waters by measure.

(Heavy) the exceeding glory reserved for saints.

2 Cor 4:17 For our light affliction, which is but for a moment, is working for us a far more exceeding *and* eternal weight of glory,

WELLS

First mention of.

Gen 16:14 Therefore the well was called Beer Lahai Roi; observe, *it is* between Kadesh and Bered.

Frequently made

Near encampments.

Gen 21:30 And he said, "You will take *these* seven ewe lambs from my hand, that they may be my witness that I have dug this well."

Gen 26:18 And Isaac dug again the wells of water which they had dug in the days of Abraham his father, for the Philistines had stopped them up after the death of Abraham. He called them by the names which his father had called them.

Outside cities.

Gen 24:11 And he made his camels kneel down outside the city by a well of water at evening time, the time when women go out to draw *water*.

John 4:6–8 Now Jacob's well was there. Jesus therefore, being wearied from *His* journey, sat thus by the well. It was about the sixth hour. **7** A woman of Samaria came to draw water. Jesus said to her, "Give Me a drink." **8** For His disciples had gone away into the city to buy food.

In the courts of houses.

2 Sam 17:18 Nevertheless a lad saw them, and told Absalom. But both of them went away quickly and came to a man's house in Bahurim, who had a well in his court; and they went down into it.

In the desert.

2 Chr 26:10 Also he built towers in the desert. He dug many wells, for he had much livestock, both in the lowlands and in the plains; *he also had* farmers and vinedressers in the mountains and in Carmel, for he loved the soil.

Supplied by springs.

Prov 16:22 Understanding *is* a wellspring of life to him who has it. But the correction of fools *is* folly.

Supplied by the rain.

Ps 84:6 *As they* pass through the Valley of Baca, They make it a spring; The rain also covers it with pools.

Surrounded by trees.

Gen 49:22 "Joseph *is* a fruitful bough, A fruitful bough by a well; His branches run over the wall.

Ex 15:27 Then they came to Elim, where there *were* twelve wells of water and seventy palm trees; so they camped there by the waters.

Names often given to.

Gen 16:14 Therefore the well was called Beer Lahai Roi; observe, *it is* between Kadesh and Bered.

Gen 21:30–31 And he said, "You will take *these* seven ewe lambs from my hand, that they may be my witness that I have dug this well." **31** Therefore he called that place Beersheba, because the two of them swore an oath there.

Canaan abounded with.

Deut 6:11 houses full of all good things, which you did not fill, hewn-out wells which you did not dig, vineyards and olive trees which you did not plant—when you have eaten and are full—

Many supplied from Lebanon.

Song 4:15 A fountain of gardens, A well of living waters, And streams from Lebanon.

Ones mentioned in Scripture

Beer Lahai Roi.

Gen 16:14 Therefore the well was called Beer Lahai Roi; observe, *it is* between Kadesh and Bered.

Bethlehem.

2 Sam 23:15 And David said with longing, "Oh, that someone would give me a drink of the water from the well of Bethlehem, which *is* by the gate!"

1 Chr 11:17–18 And David said with longing, "Oh, that someone would give me a drink of water from the well of Bethlehem, which is by the gate!" **18** So the three broke through the camp of the Philistines, drew water from the well of Bethlehem that *was* by the gate, and took *it* and brought *it* to David. Nevertheless David would not drink it, but poured it out to the LORD.

Beer (east of Jordan).

Num 21:16–18 From there *they went* to Beer, which *is* the well where the LORD said to Moses, "Gather the people together, and I will give them water." **17** Then Israel sang this song: "Spring up, O well! All of you sing to it— **18** The well the leaders sank, Dug by the nation's nobles, By the lawgiver, with their staves." And from the wilderness *they went* to Mattanah,

Beersheba.

Gen 21:30–31 And he said, "You will take *these* seven ewe lambs from my hand, that they may be my witness that I have dug this well." **31** Therefore he called that place Beersheba, because the two of them swore an oath there.

Elim.

Ex 15:27 Then they came to Elim, where there *were* twelve wells of water and seventy palm trees; so they camped there by the waters.

Esek.

Gen 26:20 But the herdsmen of Gerar quarreled with Isaac's herdsmen, saying, "The water *is* ours." So he called the name of the well Esek, because they quarreled with him.

Hagar.

Gen 21:19 Then God opened her eyes, and she saw a well of water. And she went and filled the skin with water, and gave the lad a drink.

Haran.

Gen 29:3–4 Now all the flocks would be gathered there; and they would roll the stone from the well's mouth, water the sheep, and put the stone back in its place on the well's mouth. **4** And Jacob said to them, "My brethren, where *are* you from?" And they said, "We *are* from Haran."

Jacob.

John 4:6 Now Jacob's well was there. Jesus therefore, being wearied from *His* journey, sat thus by the well. It was about the sixth hour.

Rehoboth.

Gen 26:22 And he moved from there and dug another well, and they did not quarrel over it. So he called its name Rehoboth, because he said, "For now the LORD has made room for us, and we shall be fruitful in the land."

Sitnah.

Gen 26:21 Then they dug another well, and they quarreled over that *one* also. So he called its name Sitnah.

Often deep and difficult to draw from.

John 4:11 The woman said to Him, "Sir, You have nothing to draw with, and the well is deep. Where then do You get that living water?

Often covered to prevent their being filled with sand.

Gen 29:2–3 And he looked, and saw a well in the field; and behold, there *were* three flocks of sheep lying by it; for out of that well they watered the flocks. A large stone *was* on the well's mouth. **3** Now all the flocks would be gathered there; and they would roll the stone from the well's mouth, water the sheep, and put the stone back in its place on the well's mouth.

Had troughs placed near for watering livestock.

Gen 24:19–20 And when she had finished giving him a drink, she said, "I will draw *water* for your camels also, until they have finished drinking." **20** Then she quickly emptied her pitcher into the trough, ran back to the well to draw *water*, and drew for all his camels.

Ex 2:16 Now the priest of Midian had seven daughters. And they came and drew water, and they filled the troughs to water their father's flock.

Frequented by

Women who came to draw water.

Gen 24:13–14 Behold, *here* I stand by the well of water, and the daughters of the men of the city are coming out to draw water. **14** Now let it be that the young woman to whom I say, 'Please let down your pitcher that I may drink,' and she says, 'Drink, and I will also give your camels a drink'—*let* her *be the one* You have appointed for Your servant Isaac. And by this I will know that You have shown kindness to my master."

John 4:7 A woman of Samaria came to draw water. Jesus said to her, "Give Me a drink."

Travelers.

Gen 24:11 And he made his camels kneel down outside the city by a well of water at evening time, the time when women go out to draw *water*.

Gen 24:13 Behold, *here* I stand by the well of water, and the daughters of the men of the city are coming out to draw water.

Gen 24:42 "And this day I came to the well and said, 'O LORD God of my master Abraham, if You will now prosper the way in which I go,

John 4:6 Now Jacob's well was there. Jesus therefore, being wearied from *His* journey, sat thus by the well. It was about the sixth hour.

Strangers not to draw from, without permission.

Num 20:17 Please let us pass through your country. We will not pass through fields or vineyards, nor will we drink water from wells; we will go along the King's Highway; we will not turn aside to the right hand or to the left until we have passed through your territory.' "

Water of, frequently sold.

Num 20:19 So the children of Israel said to him, "We will go by the Highway, and if I or my livestock drink any of your water, then I will pay for it; let me only pass through on foot, nothing *more*."

Were a frequent cause of strife.

Gen 21:25 Then Abraham rebuked Abimelech because of a well of water which Abimelech's servants had seized.

Gen 26:21–22 Then they dug another well, and they quarreled over that *one* also. So he called its name Sitnah. **22** And he moved from there and dug another well, and they did not quarrel over it. So he called its name Rehoboth, because he said, "For now the LORD has made room for us, and we shall be fruitful in the land."

Ex 2:16–17 Now the priest of Midian had seven daughters. And they came and drew water, and they filled the troughs to water their father's flock. **17** Then the shepherds came and drove them away; but Moses stood up and helped them, and watered their flock.

Were often stopped up by enemies.

Gen 26:15 Now the Philistines had stopped up all the wells which his father's servants had dug in the days of Abraham his father, and they had filled them with earth.

Gen 26:18 And Isaac dug again the wells of water which they had dug in the days of Abraham his father, for the Philistines had stopped them up after the death of Abraham. He called them by the names which his father had called them.

2 Kin 3:19 Also you shall attack every fortified city and every choice city, and shall cut down every good tree, and stop up every spring of water, and ruin every good piece of land with stones."

2 Kin 3:25 Then they destroyed the cities, and each man threw a stone on every good piece of land and filled it; and they stopped up all the springs of water and cut down all the good trees. But they left the stones of Kir Haraseth *intact*. However the slingers surrounded and attacked it.

Often afforded no water.

Jer 14:3 Their nobles have sent their lads for water; They went to the cisterns *and* found no water. They returned with their vessels empty; They were ashamed and confounded And covered their heads.

Zech 9:11 "As for you also, Because of the blood of your covenant, I will set your prisoners free from the waterless pit.

Illustrative of

Salvation.

Is 12:3 Therefore with joy you will draw water From the wells of salvation.

The Holy Spirit in believers.

John 4:14 but whoever drinks of the water that I shall give him will never thirst. But the water that I shall give him will become in him a fountain of water springing up into everlasting life."

John 7:37–38 On the last day, that great *day* of the feast, Jesus stood and cried out, saying, "If anyone thirsts, let him come to Me and drink. **38** He who believes in Me, as the Scripture has said, out of his heart will flow rivers of living water."

The mouth of the righteous.

Prov 10:11 The mouth of the righteous *is* a well of life, But violence covers the mouth of the wicked.

Wisdom and understanding in man.

Prov 16:22 Understanding *is* a wellspring of life to him who has it. But the correction of fools *is* folly.

Prov 18:4 The words of a man's mouth *are* deep waters; The wellspring of wisdom *is* a flowing brook.

(A fruitful bough by) Joseph's numerous posterity.

Gen 49:22 "Joseph *is* a fruitful bough, A fruitful bough by a well; His branches run over the wall.

(Drinking from one's own) enjoyment of marital happiness.

Prov 5:15 Drink water from your own cistern, And running water from your own well.

(Without water) hypocrites.

2 Pet 2:17 These are wells without water, clouds carried by a tempest, for whom is reserved the blackness of darkness forever.

WHIRLWIND, THE

Generally came from the south.

Job 37:9 From the chamber *of the south* comes the whirlwind, And cold from the scattering winds *of the north*.

Is 21:1 The burden against the Wilderness of the Sea. As whirlwinds in the South pass through, *So* it comes from the desert, from a terrible land.

Zech 9:14 Then the LORD will be seen over them, And His arrow will go forth like lightning. The Lord GOD will blow the trumpet, And go with whirlwinds from the south.

Sometimes came from the north.

Ezek 1:4 Then I looked, and behold, a whirlwind was coming out of the north, a great cloud with raging fire engulfing itself; and brightness *was* all around it and radiating out of its midst like the color of amber, out of the midst of the fire.

Called the whirlwind of God.

Jer 23:19 Behold, a whirlwind of the LORD has gone forth in fury— A violent whirlwind! It will fall violently on the head of the wicked.

Jer 30:23 Behold, the whirlwind of the LORD Goes forth with fury, A continuing whirlwind; It will fall violently on the head of the wicked.

Arose up from the earth.

Jer 25:32 Thus says the LORD of hosts: "Behold, disaster shall go forth From nation to nation, And a great whirlwind shall be raised up From the farthest parts of the earth.

Miracles connected with,

Elijah taken to heaven in.

2 Kin 2:1 And it came to pass, when the LORD was about to take up Elijah into heaven by a whirlwind, that Elijah went with Elisha from Gilgal.

2 Kin 2:11 Then it happened, as they continued on and talked, that suddenly a chariot of fire *appeared* with horses of fire, and separated the two of them; and Elijah went up by a whirlwind into heaven.

God spoke to Job from.

Job 38:1 Then the LORD answered Job out of the whirlwind, and said:

Cf. Job 40:6

Frequently continued for a long time.

Jer 30:23 Behold, the whirlwind of the LORD Goes forth with fury, A continuing whirlwind; It will fall violently on the head of the wicked.

Destructive nature of.

Prov 1:27 When your terror comes like a storm, And your destruction comes like a whirlwind, When distress and anguish come upon you.

Illustrative of the

Speed with which God executes His purposes.

Nah 1:3 The LORD *is* slow to anger and great in power, And will not at all acquit *the wicked.* The LORD has His way In the whirlwind and in the storm, And the clouds *are* the dust of His feet.

Velocity of Christ's second coming.

Is 66:15 For behold, the LORD will come with fire And with His chariots, like a whirlwind, To render His anger with fury, And His rebuke with flames of fire.

Velocity of the chariots in hostile armies.

Is 5:28 Whose arrows *are* sharp, And all their bows bent; Their horses' hooves will seem like flint, And their wheels like a whirlwind.

Jer 4:13 "Behold, he shall come up like clouds, And his chariots like a whirlwind. His horses are swifter than eagles. Woe to us, for we are plundered!"

Fury of God's judgments.

Jer 25:32 Thus says the LORD of hosts: "Behold, disaster shall go forth From nation to nation, And a great whirlwind shall be raised up From the farthest parts of the earth.

Jer 30:23 Behold, the whirlwind of the LORD Goes forth with fury, A continuing whirlwind; It will fall violently on the head of the wicked.

Sudden destruction of the wicked.

Ps 58:9 Before your pots can feel *the burning* thorns, He shall take them away as with a whirlwind, As in His living and burning wrath.

Prov 1:27 When your terror comes like a storm, And your destruction comes like a whirlwind, When distress and anguish come upon you.

Is 17:13 The nations will rush like the rushing of many waters; But *God* will rebuke them and they will flee far away, And be chased like the chaff of the mountains before the wind, Like a rolling thing before the whirlwind.

Is 40:24 Scarcely shall they be planted, Scarcely shall they be sown, Scarcely shall their stock take root in the earth, When He will also blow on them, And they will wither, And the whirlwind will take them away like stubble.

Is 41:16 You shall winnow them, the wind shall carry them away, And the whirlwind shall scatter them; You shall rejoice in the LORD, *And* glory in the Holy One of Israel.

Jer 30:23 Behold, the whirlwind of the LORD Goes forth with fury, A continuing whirlwind; It will fall violently on the head of the wicked.

Unavoidable fruit of a life of sin and vanity.

Hos 8:7 "They sow the wind, And reap the whirlwind. The stalk has no bud; It shall never produce meal. If it should produce, Aliens would swallow it up.

WICKED, AFFLICTIONS OF THE

God is glorified in.

Ex 14:4 Then I will harden Pharaoh's heart, so that he will pursue them; and I will gain honor over Pharaoh and over all his army, that the Egyptians may know that I *am* the LORD." And they did so.

Ezek 38:22–23 And I will bring him to judgment with pestilence and bloodshed; I will rain down on him, on his troops, and on the many peoples who *are* with him, flooding rain, great hailstones, fire, and brimstone. **23** Thus I will magnify Myself and sanctify Myself, and I will be known in the eyes of many nations. Then they shall know that I *am* the LORD." '

God holds in derision.

Ps 37:13 The Lord laughs at him, For He sees that his day is coming.

Prov 1:26–27 I also will laugh at your calamity; I will mock when your terror comes, **27** When your terror comes like a storm, And your destruction comes like a whirlwind, When distress and anguish come upon you.

Are multiplied.

Deut 31:17 Then My anger shall be aroused against them in that day, and I will forsake them, and I will hide My face from them, and they shall be devoured. And many evils and troubles shall befall them, so that they will say in that day, 'Have not these evils come upon us because our God *is* not among us?'

Job 20:12–18 "Though evil is sweet in his mouth, *And* he hides it under his tongue, **13** *Though* he spares it and does not forsake it, But still keeps it in his mouth, **14** *Yet* his food in his stomach turns sour; It becomes cobra venom within him. **15** He swallows down riches And vomits them up again; God casts them out of his belly. **16** He will suck the poison of cobras; The viper's tongue will slay him. **17** He will not see the streams, The rivers flowing with honey and cream. **18** He will restore that for which he labored, And will not swallow *it* down; From the proceeds of business He will get no enjoyment.

Ps 32:10 Many sorrows *shall be* to the wicked; But he who trusts in the LORD, mercy shall surround him.

Are continual.

Job 15:20 The wicked man writhes with pain all *his* days, And the number of years is hidden from the oppressor.

Eccl 2:23 For all his days *are* sorrowful, and his work burdensome; even in the night his heart takes no rest. This also is vanity.

Are often sudden.

Prov 6:15 Therefore his calamity shall come suddenly; Suddenly he shall be broken without remedy.

Is 30:13 Therefore this iniquity shall be to you Like a breach ready to fall, A bulge in a high wall, Whose breaking comes suddenly, in an instant.

Rev 18:10 standing at a distance for fear of her torment, saying, 'Alas, alas, that great city Babylon, that mighty city! For in one hour your judgment has come.'

Are often judicially sent.

Job 21:17 "How often is the lamp of the wicked put out? *How often* does their destruction come upon them, The sorrows *God* distributes in His anger?

Ps 107:17 Fools, because of their transgression, And because of their iniquities, were afflicted.

Jer 30:15 Why do you cry about your affliction? Your sorrow *is* incurable. Because of the multitude of your iniquities, *Because* your sins have increased, I have done these things to you.

Are for examples to others.

Ps 64:7–9 But God shall shoot at them *with* an arrow; Suddenly they shall be wounded. 8 So He will make them stumble over their own tongue; All who see them shall flee away. 9 All men shall fear, And shall declare the work of God; For they shall wisely consider His doing.

Zeph 3:6–7 "I have cut off nations, Their fortresses are devastated; I have made their streets desolate, With none passing by. Their cities are destroyed; *There is* no one, no inhabitant. 7 I said, 'Surely you will fear Me, You will receive instruction'— So that her dwelling would not be cut off, *Despite* everything for which I punished her. But they rose early and corrupted all their deeds.

1 Cor 10:5–11 But with most of them God was not well pleased, for *their bodies* were scattered in the wilderness. 6 Now these things became our examples, to the intent that we should not lust after evil things as they also lusted. 7 And do not become idolaters as *were* some of them. As it is written, *"The people sat down to eat and drink, and rose up to play."* 8 Nor let us commit sexual immorality, as some of them did, and in one day twenty-three thousand fell; 9 nor let us tempt Christ, as some of them also tempted, and were destroyed by serpents; 10 nor complain, as some of them also complained, and were destroyed by the destroyer. 11 Now all these things happened to them as examples, and they were written for our admonition, upon whom the ends of the ages have come.

2 Pet 2:6 and turning the cities of Sodom and Gomorrah into ashes, condemned *them* to destruction, making *them* an example to those who afterward would live ungodly;

Are ineffectual of themselves, for conversion.

Ex 9:30 But as for you and your servants, I know that you will not yet fear the LORD God."

Is 9:13 For the people do not turn to Him who strikes them, Nor do they seek the LORD of hosts.

Jer 2:30 "In vain I have chastened your children; They received no correction. Your sword has devoured your prophets Like a destroying lion.

Hag 2:17 I struck you with blight and mildew and hail in all the labors of your hands; yet you did not *turn* to Me,' says the LORD.

Their persecution of believers, a cause of.

Deut 30:7 "Also the LORD your God will put all these curses on your enemies and on those who hate you, who persecuted you.

Ps 55:19 God will hear, and afflict them, Even He who abides from of old. Selah Because they do not change, Therefore they do not fear God.

Zech 2:9 For surely I will shake My hand against them, and they shall become spoil for their servants. Then you will know that the LORD of hosts has sent Me.

2 Thess 1:6 since *it is* a righteous thing with God to repay with tribulation those who trouble you,

Impenitence is a cause of.

Prov 1:30–31 They would have none of my counsel *And* despised my every rebuke. 31 Therefore they shall eat the fruit of their own way, And be filled to the full with their own fancies.

Ezek 24:13 In your filthiness *is* lewdness. Because I have cleansed you, and you were not cleansed, You will not be cleansed of your filthiness anymore, Till I have caused My fury to rest upon you.

Amos 4:6–12 "Also I gave you cleanness of teeth in all your cities. And lack of bread in all your places; Yet you have not returned to Me," Says the LORD. 7 "I also withheld rain from you, When *there were* still three months to the harvest. I made it rain on one city, I withheld rain from another city. One part was rained upon, And where it did not rain the part withered. 8 So two *or* three cities wandered to another city to drink water, But they were not satisfied; Yet you have not returned to Me," Says the LORD. 9 "I blasted you with blight and mildew. When your gardens increased, Your vineyards, Your fig trees, And your olive trees, The locust devoured *them;* Yet you have not returned to Me," Says the LORD. 10 "I sent among you a plague after the manner of Egypt; Your young men I killed with a sword, Along with your captive horses; I made the stench of your camps come up into your nostrils; Yet you have not returned to Me," Says the LORD. 11 "I overthrew *some* of you, As God overthrew Sodom and Gomorrah, And you were like a firebrand plucked from the burning; Yet you have not returned to Me," Says the LORD. 12 "Therefore thus will I do to you, O Israel; Because I will do this to you, Prepare to meet your God, O Israel!"

Zech 7:11–12 But they refused to heed, shrugged their shoulders, and stopped their ears so that they could not hear. 12 Yes, they made their hearts like flint, refusing to hear the law and the words which the LORD of hosts had sent by His Spirit through the former prophets. Thus great wrath came from the LORD of hosts.

Rev 2:21–22 And I gave her time to repent of her sexual immorality, and she did not repent. **22** Indeed I will cast her into a sickbed, and those who commit adultery with her into great tribulation, unless they repent of their deeds.

Sometimes humble them.

1 Kin 21:27 So it was, when Ahab heard those words, that he tore his clothes and put sackcloth on his body, and fasted and lay in sackcloth, and went about mourning.

Frequently harden.

Neh 9:28–29 "But after they had rest, They again did evil before You. Therefore You left them in the hand of their enemies, So that they had dominion over them; Yet when they returned and cried out to You, You heard from heaven; And many times You delivered them according to Your mercies, **29** And testified against them, That You might bring them back to Your law. Yet they acted proudly, And did not heed Your commandments, But sinned against Your judgments, 'Which if a man does, he shall live by them.' And they shrugged their shoulders, Stiffened their necks, And would not hear.

Jer 5:3 O LORD, *are* not Your eyes on the truth? You have stricken them, But they have not grieved; You have consumed them, But they have refused to receive correction. They have made their faces harder than rock; They have refused to return.

Produce slavish fear.

Job 15:24 Trouble and anguish make him afraid; They overpower him, like a king ready for battle.

Ps 73:19 Oh, how they are *brought* to desolation, as in a moment! They are utterly consumed with terrors.

Jer 49:3 "Wail, O Heshbon, for Ai is plundered! Cry, you daughters of Rabbah, Gird yourselves with sackcloth! Lament and run to and fro by the walls; For Milcom shall go into captivity With his priests and his princes together.

Jer 49:5 Behold, I will bring fear upon you," Says the Lord GOD of hosts, "From all those who are around you; You shall be driven out, everyone headlong, And no one will gather those who wander off.

Saints should not be alarmed at.

Prov 3:25–26 Do not be afraid of sudden terror, Nor of trouble from the wicked when it comes; **26** For the LORD will be your confidence, And will keep your foot from being caught.

Exemplified by

Pharaoh and the Egyptians.

Ex 9:14–15 for at this time I will send all My plagues to your very heart, and on your servants and on your people, that you may know that *there is* none like Me in all the earth. **15** Now if I had stretched out My hand and struck you and your people with pestilence, then you would have been cut off from the earth.

Ex 14:24–25 Now it came to pass, in the morning watch, that the LORD looked down upon the army of the Egyptians through the pillar of fire and cloud, and He troubled the army of the Egyptians. **25** And He

took off their chariot wheels, so that they drove them with difficulty; and the Egyptians said, "Let us flee from the face of Israel, for the LORD fights for them against the Egyptians."

Ahaziah.

2 Kin 1:1–4 Moab rebelled against Israel after the death of Ahab. **2** Now Ahaziah fell through the lattice of his upper room in Samaria, and was injured; so he sent messengers and said to them, "Go, inquire of Baal-Zebub, the god of Ekron, whether I shall recover from this injury." **3** But the angel of the LORD said to Elijah the Tishbite, "Arise, go up to meet the messengers of the king of Samaria, and say to them, '*Is it* because *there is* no God in Israel *that* you are going to inquire of Baal-Zebub, the god of Ekron?' **4** Now therefore, thus says the LORD: 'You shall not come down from the bed to which you have gone up, but you shall surely die.' " So Elijah departed.

Gehazi.

2 Kin 5:27 Therefore the leprosy of Naaman shall cling to you and your descendants forever." And he went out from his presence leprous, *as white* as snow.

Jehoram. **2 Chr 21:12–19**

Uzziah.

2 Chr 26:19–21 Then Uzziah became furious; and he *had* a censer in his hand to burn incense. And while he was angry with the priests, leprosy broke out on his forehead, before the priests in the house of the LORD, beside the incense altar. **20** And Azariah the chief priest and all the priests looked at him, and there, on his forehead, he *was* leprous; so they thrust him out of that place. Indeed he also hurried to get out, because the LORD had struck him. **21** King Uzziah was a leper until the day of his death. He dwelt in an isolated house, because he was a leper; for he was cut off from the house of the LORD. Then Jotham his son *was* over the king's house, judging the people of the land.

Ahaz, etc.

2 Chr 28:5–8 Therefore the LORD his God delivered him into the hand of the king of Syria. They defeated him, and carried away a great multitude of them as captives, and brought *them* to Damascus. Then he was also delivered into the hand of the king of Israel, who defeated him with a great slaughter. **6** For Pekah the son of Remaliah killed one hundred and twenty thousand in Judah in one day, all valiant men, because they had forsaken the LORD God of their fathers. **7** Zichri, a mighty man of Ephraim, killed Maaseiah the king's son, Azrikam the officer over the house, and Elkanah *who was* second to the king. **8** And the children of Israel carried away captive of their brethren two hundred thousand women, sons, and daughters; and they also took away much spoil from them, and brought the spoil to Samaria.

2 Chr 28:22 Now in the time of his distress King Ahaz became increasingly unfaithful to the LORD. This *is that* King Ahaz.

WICKED, CHARACTER OF THE

Abominable.

Rev 21:8 But the cowardly, unbelieving, abominable, murderers, sexually immoral, sorcerers, idolaters, and all liars shall have their part in the lake which burns with fire and brimstone, which is the second death."

Alienated from God.

Eph 4:18 having their understanding darkened, being alienated from the life of God, because of the ignorance that is in them, because of the blindness of their heart;

Col 1:21 And you, who once were alienated and enemies in your mind by wicked works, yet now He has reconciled

Blasphemous.

Luke 22:65 And many other things they blasphemously spoke against Him.

Rev 16:9 And men were scorched with great heat, and they blasphemed the name of God who has power over these plagues; and they did not repent and give Him glory.

Blinded.

2 Cor 4:4 whose minds the god of this age has blinded, who do not believe, lest the light of the gospel of the glory of Christ, who is the image of God, should shine on them.

Eph 4:18 having their understanding darkened, being alienated from the life of God, because of the ignorance that is in them, because of the blindness of their heart;

Boastful.

Ps 5:5 The boastful shall not stand in Your sight; You hate all workers of iniquity.

Ps 10:3 For the wicked boasts of his heart's desire; He blesses the greedy *and* renounces the LORD.

Ps 49:6 Those who trust in their wealth And boast in the multitude of their riches,

Conspiring against God's people.

Neh 4:8 and all of them conspired together to come *and* attack Jerusalem and create confusion.

Neh 6:2 that Sanballat and Geshem sent to me, saying, "Come, let us meet together among the villages in the plain of Ono." But they thought to do me harm.

Ps 38:12 Those also who seek my life lay snares *for me;* Those who seek my hurt speak of destruction, And plan deception all the day long.

Covetous.

Mic 2:2 They covet fields and take *them* by violence, Also houses, and seize *them.* So they oppress a man and his house, A man and his inheritance.

Rom 1:29 being filled with all unrighteousness, sexual immorality, wickedness, covetousness, maliciousness; full of envy, murder, strife, deceit, evil-mindedness; *they are* whisperers,

Deceitful.

Ps 5:6 You shall destroy those who speak falsehood; The LORD abhors the bloodthirsty and deceitful man.

Rom 3:13 *"Their throat is an open tomb; With their tongues they have practiced deceit"; "The poison of asps is under their lips";*

Delighting in the iniquity of others.

Prov 2:14 Who rejoice in doing evil, *And* delight in the perversity of the wicked;

Rom 1:32 who, knowing the righteous judgment of God, that those who practice such things are deserving of death, not only do the same but also approve of those who practice them.

Despising the works of the faithful.

Neh 2:19 But when Sanballat the Horonite, Tobiah the Ammonite official, and Geshem the Arab heard *of it,* they laughed at us and despised us, and said, "What *is* this thing that you are doing? Will you rebel against the king?"

Neh 4:2 And he spoke before his brethren and the army of Samaria, and said, "What are these feeble Jews doing? Will they fortify themselves? Will they offer sacrifices? Will they complete it in a day? Will they revive the stones from the heaps of rubbish—*stones* that are burned?"

2 Tim 3:3–4 unloving, unforgiving, slanderers, without self-control, brutal, despisers of good, **4** traitors, headstrong, haughty, lovers of pleasure rather than lovers of God,

Destructive.

Is 59:7 Their feet run to evil, And they make haste to shed innocent blood; Their thoughts *are* thoughts of iniquity; Wasting and destruction *are* in their paths.

Disobedient.

Neh 9:26 "Nevertheless they were disobedient And rebelled against You, Cast Your law behind their backs And killed Your prophets, who testified against them To turn them to Yourself; And they worked great provocations.

Titus 3:3 For we ourselves were also once foolish, disobedient, deceived, serving various lusts and pleasures, living in malice and envy, hateful and hating one another.

1 Pet 2:7 Therefore, to you who believe, *He is* precious; but to those who are disobedient, *"The stone which the builders rejected Has become the chief cornerstone,"*

Enticing to evil.

Prov 1:10–14 My son, if sinners entice you, Do not consent. **11** If they say, "Come with us, Let us lie in wait to *shed* blood; Let us lurk secretly for the innocent without cause; **12** Let us swallow them alive like Sheol, And whole, like those who go down to the Pit; **13** We shall find all *kinds* of precious possessions, We shall fill our houses with spoil; **14** Cast in your lot among us, Let us all have one purse"—

2 Tim 3:6 For of this sort are those who creep into households and make captives of gullible women loaded down with sins, led away by various lusts,

Envious.

Neh 2:10 When Sanballat the Horonite and Tobiah the Ammonite official heard *of it,* they were deeply disturbed that a man had come to seek the well-being of the children of Israel.

Titus 3:3 For we ourselves were also once foolish, disobedient, deceived, serving various lusts and pleasures, living in malice and envy, hateful and hating one another.

Fearful.

Prov 28:1 The wicked flee when no one pursues, But the righteous are bold as a lion.

Rev 21:8 But the cowardly, unbelieving, abominable, murderers, sexually immoral, sorcerers, idolaters, and all liars shall have their part in the lake which burns with fire and brimstone, which is the second death."

Fierce.

Prov 16:29 A violent man entices his neighbor, And leads him in a way *that is* not good.

2 Tim 3:3 unloving, unforgiving, slanderers, without self-control, brutal, despisers of good,

Foolish.

Deut 32:6 Do you thus deal with the LORD, O foolish and unwise people? *Is* He not your Father, *who* bought you? Has He not made you and established you?

Forgetting God.

Job 8:13 So *are* the paths of all who forget God; And the hope of the hypocrite shall perish,

Fraudulent.

Ps 37:21 The wicked borrows and does not repay, But the righteous shows mercy and gives.

Mic 6:11 Shall I count pure *those* with the wicked scales, And with the bag of deceitful weights?

Glorying in their shame.

Phil 3:19 whose end *is* destruction, whose god *is their* belly, and *whose* glory *is* in their shame—who set their mind on earthly things.

Hard-hearted.

Ezek 3:7 But the house of Israel will not listen to you, because they will not listen to Me; for all the house of Israel *are* impudent and hard-hearted.

Hating the light.

Job 24:13 "There are those who rebel against the light; They do not know its ways Nor abide in its paths.

John 3:20 For everyone practicing evil hates the light and does not come to the light, lest his deeds should be exposed.

Headstrong and haughty.

2 Tim 3:4 traitors, headstrong, haughty, lovers of pleasure rather than lovers of God,

Hostile to God.

Rom 8:7 Because the carnal mind *is* enmity against God; for it is not subject to the law of God, nor indeed can be.

Col 1:21 And you, who once were alienated and enemies in your mind by wicked works, yet now He has reconciled

Hypocritical.

Is 29:13 Therefore the Lord said: "Inasmuch as these people draw near with their mouths And honor Me with their lips, But have removed their hearts far from Me, And their fear toward Me is taught by the commandment of men,

2 Tim 3:5 having a form of godliness but denying its power. And from such people turn away!

Ignorant of God.

Hos 4:1 Hear the word of the LORD, You children of Israel, For the LORD *brings* a charge against the inhabitants of the land: "There is no truth or mercy Or knowledge of God in the land.

2 Thess 1:8 in flaming fire taking vengeance on those who do not know God, and on those who do not obey the gospel of our Lord Jesus Christ.

Impudent.

Ezek 2:4 For *they are* impudent and stubborn children. I am sending you to them, and you shall say to them, 'Thus says the Lord GOD.'

Infidel.

Ps 10:4 The wicked in his proud countenance does not seek *God*; God *is* in none of his thoughts.

Ps 14:1 The fool has said in his heart, "*There is* no God." They are corrupt, They have done abominable works, There is none who does good.

Loathsome.

Prov 13:5 A righteous *man* hates lying, But a wicked *man* is loathsome and comes to shame.

Lovers of pleasure more than of God.

2 Tim 3:4 traitors, headstrong, haughty, lovers of pleasure rather than lovers of God,

Lying.

Ps 58:3 The wicked are estranged from the womb; They go astray as soon as they are born, speaking lies.

Ps 62:4 They only consult to cast *him* down from his high position; They delight in lies; They bless with their mouth, But they curse inwardly. Selah

Is 59:4 No one calls for justice, Nor does *any* plead for truth. They trust in empty words and speak lies; They conceive evil and bring forth iniquity.

Mischievous.

Prov 24:8 He who plots to do evil Will be called a schemer.

Mic 7:3 That they may successfully do evil with both hands— The prince asks *for gifts,* The judge *seeks* a bribe, And the great *man* utters his evil desire; So they scheme together.

Murderous.

Ps 10:8 He sits in the lurking places of the villages; In the secret places he murders the innocent; His eyes are secretly fixed on the helpless.

Ps 94:6 They slay the widow and the stranger, And murder the fatherless.

Rom 1:29 being filled with all unrighteousness, sexual immorality, wickedness, covetousness, maliciousness; full of envy, murder, strife, deceit, evil-mindedness; *they are* whisperers,

Prayerless.

Job 21:15 Who *is* the Almighty, that we should serve Him? And what profit do we have if we pray to Him?'

Ps 53:4 Have the workers of iniquity no knowledge, Who eat up my people *as* they eat bread, And do not call upon God?

Persecuting.

Ps 69:26 For they persecute the *ones* You have struck, And talk of the grief of those You have wounded.

Ps 109:16 Because he did not remember to show mercy, But persecuted the poor and needy man, That he might even slay the broken in heart.

Perverse.

Deut 32:5 "They have corrupted themselves; *They are*

not His children, Because of their blemish: A perverse and crooked generation.

Prov 21:8 The way of a guilty man *is* perverse; But *as for* the pure, his work *is* right.

Is 57:17 For the iniquity of his covetousness I was angry and struck him; I hid and was angry, And he went on backsliding in the way of his heart.

Acts 2:40 And with many other words he testified and exhorted them, saying, "Be saved from this perverse generation."

Proud.

Ps 59:12 *For* the sin of their mouth *and* the words of their lips, Let them even be taken in their pride, And for the cursing and lying *which* they speak.

Obad 1:3 The pride of your heart has deceived you, *You* who dwell in the clefts of the rock, Whose habitation is high; *You* who say in your heart, 'Who will bring me down to the ground?'

2 Tim 3:2 For men will be lovers of themselves, lovers of money, boasters, proud, blasphemers, disobedient to parents, unthankful, unholy,

Rejoicing in the affliction of saints.

Ps 35:15 But in my adversity they rejoiced And gathered together; Attackers gathered against me, And I did not know *it;* They tore *at me* and did not cease;

Reprobate.

2 Cor 13:5 Examine yourselves *as to* whether you are in the faith. Test yourselves. Do you not know yourselves, that Jesus Christ is in you?—unless indeed you are disqualified.

2 Tim 3:8 Now as Jannes and Jambres resisted Moses, so do these also resist the truth: men of corrupt minds, disapproved concerning the faith;

Titus 1:16 They profess to know God, but in works they deny Him, being abominable, disobedient, and disqualified for every good work.

Selfish.

2 Tim 3:2 For men will be lovers of themselves, lovers of money, boasters, proud, blasphemers, disobedient to parents, unthankful, unholy,

Sensual.

Phil 3:19 whose end *is* destruction, whose god *is their* belly, and *whose* glory *is* in their shame—who set their mind on earthly things.

Jude 1:19 These are sensual persons, who cause divisions, not having the Spirit.

Sold under sin.

1 Kin 21:20 So Ahab said to Elijah, "Have you found me, O my enemy?" And he answered, "I have found *you,* because you have sold yourself to do evil in the sight of the LORD:

2 Kin 17:17 And they caused their sons and daughters to pass through the fire, practiced witchcraft and soothsaying, and sold themselves to do evil in the sight of the LORD, to provoke Him to anger.

Stiff-necked.

Ex 33:5 For the LORD had said to Moses, "Say to the children of Israel, 'You *are* a stiff-necked people. I could come up into your midst in one moment and consume you. Now therefore, take off your ornaments, that I may know what to do to you.' "

Acts 7:51 "You stiff-necked and uncircumcised in heart and ears! You always resist the Holy Spirit; as your fathers *did,* so *do* you.

Uncircumcised in heart.

Jer 9:26 Egypt, Judah, Edom, the people of Ammon, Moab, and all *who are* in the farthest corners, who dwell in the wilderness. For all *these* nations *are* uncircumcised, and all the house of Israel *are* uncircumcised in the heart."

Acts 7:51 "You stiff-necked and uncircumcised in heart and ears! You always resist the Holy Spirit; as your fathers *did,* so *do* you.

Unjust.

Prov 11:7 When a wicked man dies, *his* expectation will perish, And the hope of the unjust perishes.

Is 26:10 Let grace be shown to the wicked, *Yet* he will not learn righteousness; In the land of uprightness he will deal unjustly, And will not behold the majesty of the LORD.

Unmerciful.

Rom 1:31 undiscerning, untrustworthy, unloving, unforgiving, unmerciful;

Ungodly.

Prov 16:27 An ungodly man digs up evil, And *it is* on his lips like a burning fire.

Unholy.

2 Tim 3:2 For men will be lovers of themselves, lovers of money, boasters, proud, blasphemers, disobedient to parents, unthankful, unholy,

Unprofitable.

Matt 25:30 And cast the unprofitable servant into the outer darkness. There will be weeping and gnashing of teeth.'

Rom 3:12 *They have all turned aside; They have together become unprofitable; There is none who does good, no, not one."*

Unruly.

Titus 1:10 For there are many insubordinate, both idle talkers and deceivers, especially those of the circumcision,

Unthankful.

Luke 6:35 But love your enemies, do good, and lend, hoping for nothing in return; and your reward will be great, and you will be sons of the Most High. For He is kind to the unthankful and evil.

2 Tim 3:2 For men will be lovers of themselves, lovers of money, boasters, proud, blasphemers, disobedient to parents, unthankful, unholy,

Unwise.

Deut 32:6 Do you thus deal with the LORD, O foolish and unwise people? *Is* He not your Father, *who* bought you? Has He not made you and established you?

Without self-control.

2 Tim 3:3 unloving, unforgiving, slanderers, without self-control, brutal, despisers of good,

WICKED, THE (COMPARED WITH)
Abominable branches.

Is 14:19 But you are cast out of your grave Like an

abominable branch, *Like* the garment of those who are slain, Thrust through with a sword, Who go down to the stones of the pit, Like a corpse trodden underfoot.

Ashes under the feet.

Mal 4:3 You shall trample the wicked, For they shall be ashes under the soles of your feet On the day that I do *this,*" Says the LORD of hosts.

Bad figs.

Jer 24:8 'And as the bad figs which cannot be eaten, they are so bad'—surely thus says the LORD—'so will I give up Zedekiah the king of Judah, his princes, the residue of Jerusalem who remain in this land, and those who dwell in the land of Egypt.

Bad fish.

Matt 13:48 which, when it was full, they drew to shore; and they sat down and gathered the good into vessels, but threw the bad away.

Bad trees.

Luke 6:43 "For a good tree does not bear bad fruit, nor does a bad tree bear good fruit.

Beasts.

Ps 49:12 Nevertheless man, *though* in honor, does not remain; He is like the beasts *that* perish.

2 Pet 2:12 But these, like natural brute beasts made to be caught and destroyed, speak evil of the things they do not understand, and will utterly perish in their own corruption,

Blind.

Zeph 1:17 "I will bring distress upon men, And they shall walk like blind men, Because they have sinned against the LORD; Their blood shall be poured out like dust, And their flesh like refuse."

Matt 15:14 Let them alone. They are blind leaders of the blind. And if the blind leads the blind, both will fall into a ditch."

Bronze, iron, etc.

Jer 6:28 They *are* all stubborn rebels, walking as slanderers. *They are* bronze and iron, They *are* all corrupters;

Ezek 22:18 "Son of man, the house of Israel has become dross to Me; they *are* all bronze, tin, iron, and lead, in the midst of a furnace; they have become dross from silver.

Briers and thorns.

Is 55:13 Instead of the thorn shall come up the cypress tree, And instead of the brier shall come up the myrtle tree; And it shall be to the LORD for a name, For an everlasting sign *that* shall not be cut off."

Ezek 2:6 "And you, son of man, do not be afraid of them nor be afraid of their words, though briers and thorns *are* with you and you dwell among scorpions; do not be afraid of their words or dismayed by their looks, though they *are* a rebellious house.

Bulls of Bashan.

Ps 22:12 Many bulls have surrounded Me; Strong *bulls* of Bashan have encircled Me.

Chaff.

Job 21:18 They are like straw before the wind, And like chaff that a storm carries away.

Ps 1:4 The ungodly *are* not so, But *are* like the chaff which the wind drives away.

Matt 3:12 His winnowing fan *is* in His hand, and He will thoroughly clean out His threshing floor, and gather His wheat into the barn; but He will burn up the chaff with unquenchable fire."

Clouds without water.

Jude 1:12 These are spots in your love feasts, while they feast with you without fear, serving *only* themselves. *They are* clouds without water, carried about by the winds; late autumn trees without fruit, twice dead, pulled up by the roots;

Corpses trodden underfoot.

Is 14:19 But you are cast out of your grave Like an abominable branch, *Like* the garment of those who are slain, Thrust through with a sword, Who go down to the stones of the pit, Like a corpse trodden underfoot.

Deaf cobras.

Ps 58:4 Their poison *is* like the poison of a serpent; *They are* like the deaf cobra *that* stops its ear,

Dogs.

Prov 26:11 As a dog returns to his own vomit, *So* a fool repeats his folly.

Matt 7:6 "Do not give what is holy to the dogs; nor cast your pearls before swine, lest they trample them under their feet, and turn and tear you in pieces.

2 Pet 2:22 But it has happened to them according to the true proverb: *"A dog returns to his own vomit,"* and, "a sow, having washed, to her wallowing in the mire."

Dross.

Ps 119:119 You put away all the wicked of the earth *like* dross; Therefore I love Your testimonies.

Ezek 22:18–19 "Son of man, the house of Israel has become dross to Me; they *are* all bronze, tin, iron, and lead, in the midst of a furnace; they have become dross from silver. 19 Therefore thus says the Lord GOD: 'Because you have all become dross, therefore behold, I will gather you into the midst of Jerusalem.

Early dew that passes away.

Hos 13:3 Therefore they shall be like the morning cloud And like the early dew that passes away, Like chaff blown off from a threshing floor And like smoke from a chimney.

Earthenware covered with dross.

Prov 26:23 Fervent lips with a wicked heart *Are like* earthenware covered with silver dross.

Fading leaves.

Is 1:30 For you shall be as a terebinth whose leaf fades, And as a garden that has no water.

Fiery oven.

Ps 21:9 You shall make them as a fiery oven in the time of Your anger; The LORD shall swallow them up in His wrath, And the fire shall devour them.

Hos 7:4 "They *are* all adulterers. Like an oven heated by a baker— He ceases stirring *the fire* after kneading the dough, Until it is leavened.

Fire of thorns.

Ps 118:12 They surrounded me like bees; They were

quenched like a fire of thorns; For in the name of the LORD I will destroy them.

Fools building upon sand.

Matt 7:26 "But everyone who hears these sayings of Mine, and does not do them, will be like a foolish man who built his house on the sand:

Fuel of fire.

Is 9:19 Through the wrath of the LORD of hosts The land is burned up, And the people shall be as fuel for the fire; No man shall spare his brother.

Garden without water.

Is 1:30 For you shall be as a terebinth whose leaf fades, And as a garden that has no water.

Goats.

Matt 25:32 All the nations will be gathered before Him, and He will separate them one from another, as a shepherd divides *his* sheep from the goats.

Grain blighted.

2 Kin 19:26 Therefore their inhabitants had little power; They were dismayed and confounded; They were *as* the grass of the field And the green herb, *As* the grass on the housetops And *grain* blighted before it is grown.

Grass.

Ps 37:2 For they shall soon be cut down like the grass, And wither as the green herb.

Ps 92:7 When the wicked spring up like grass, And when all the workers of iniquity flourish, *It is* that they may be destroyed forever.

Grass on the housetop.

2 Kin 19:26 Therefore their inhabitants had little power; They were dismayed and confounded; They were *as* the grass of the field And the green herb, *As* the grass on the housetops And *grain* blighted before it is grown.

Green trees.

Ps 37:35 I have seen the wicked in great power, And spreading himself like a native green tree.

Green herbs.

Ps 37:2 For they shall soon be cut down like the grass, And wither as the green herb.

Horses rushing into the battle.

Jer 8:6 I listened and heard, *But* they do not speak aright. No man repented of his wickedness, Saying, 'What have I done?' Everyone turned to his own course, As the horse rushes into the battle.

Idols.

Ps 115:8 Those who make them are like them; *So is* everyone who trusts in them.

Lions eager for prey.

Ps 17:12 As a lion is eager to tear his prey, And like a young lion lurking in secret places.

Melting wax.

Ps 68:2 As smoke is driven away, So drive *them* away; As wax melts before the fire, *So* let the wicked perish at the presence of God.

Morning clouds.

Hos 13:3 Therefore they shall be like the morning cloud And like the early dew that passes away, Like chaff blown off from a threshing floor And like smoke from a chimney.

Moth-eaten garments.

Is 50:9 Surely the Lord GOD will help Me; Who *is* he *who* will condemn Me? Indeed they will all grow old like a garment; The moth will eat them up.

Is 51:8 For the moth will eat them up like a garment, And the worm will eat them like wool; But My righteousness will be forever, And My salvation from generation to generation."

Passing whirlwinds.

Prov 10:25 When the whirlwind passes by, the wicked *is* no *more*, But the righteous *has* an everlasting foundation.

Raging waves of the sea.

Jude 1:13 raging waves of the sea, foaming up their own shame; wandering stars for whom is reserved the blackness of darkness forever.

Rejected silver.

Jer 6:30 *People* will call them rejected silver, Because the LORD has rejected them."

Scorpions.

Ezek 2:6 "And you, son of man, do not be afraid of them nor be afraid of their words, though briers and thorns *are* with you and you dwell among scorpions; do not be afraid of their words or dismayed by their looks, though they *are* a rebellious house.

Serpents.

Ps 58:4 Their poison *is* like the poison of a serpent; *They are* like the deaf cobra *that* stops its ear,

Matt 23:33 Serpents, brood of vipers! How can you escape the condemnation of hell?

Shrub in the desert.

Jer 17:6 For he shall be like a shrub in the desert, And shall not see when good comes, But shall inhabit the parched places in the wilderness, *In* a salt land *which is* not inhabited.

Smoke.

Hos 13:3 Therefore they shall be like the morning cloud And like the early dew that passes away, Like chaff blown off from a threshing floor And like smoke from a chimney.

Stony ground.

Matt 13:5 Some fell on stony places, where they did not have much earth; and they immediately sprang up because they had no depth of earth.

Stubble.

Mal 4:1 "For behold, the day is coming, Burning like an oven, And all the proud, yes, all who do wickedly will be stubble. And the day which is coming shall burn them up," Says the LORD of hosts, "That will leave them neither root nor branch.

Swine.

Matt 7:6 "Do not give what is holy to the dogs; nor cast your pearls before swine, lest they trample them under their feet, and turn and tear you in pieces.

2 Pet 2:22 But it has happened to them according to the true proverb: *"A dog returns to his own vomit,"* and, "a sow, having washed, to her wallowing in the mire."

Tares.

Matt 13:38 The field is the world, the good seeds are the sons of the kingdom, but the tares are the sons of the wicked *one*.

Troubled sea.

Is 57:20 But the wicked *are* like the troubled sea, When it cannot rest, Whose waters cast up mire and dirt.

Visions of the night.

Job 20:8 He will fly away like a dream, and not be found; Yes, he will be chased away like a vision of the night.

Wandering stars.

Jude 1:13 raging waves of the sea, foaming up their own shame; wandering stars for whom is reserved the blackness of darkness forever.

Wayward children.

Matt 11:16 "But to what shall I liken this generation? It is like children sitting in the marketplaces and calling to their companions,

Wells without water.

2 Pet 2:17 These are wells without water, clouds carried by a tempest, for whom is reserved the blackness of darkness forever.

Whirling dust.

Ps 83:13 O my God, make them like the whirling dust, Like the chaff before the wind!

Whitewashed tombs.

Matt 23:27 "Woe to you, scribes and Pharisees, hypocrites! For you are like whitewashed tombs which indeed appear beautiful outwardly, but inside are full of dead *men's* bones and all uncleanness.

Wild donkey's colt.

Job 11:12 For an empty-headed man will be wise, When a wild donkey's colt is born a man.

WICKED, DEATH OF THE

Is in their sins.

Ezek 3:19 Yet, if you warn the wicked, and he does not turn from his wickedness, nor from his wicked way, he shall die in his iniquity; but you have delivered your soul.

John 8:21 Then Jesus said to them again, "I am going away, and you will seek Me, and will die in your sin. Where I go you cannot come."

Is without hope.

Prov 11:7 When a wicked man dies, *his* expectation will perish, And the hope of the unjust perishes.

Sometimes without fear.

2 Chr 36:11–13 Zedekiah *was* twenty-one years old when he became king, and he reigned eleven years in Jerusalem. **12** He did evil in the sight of the LORD his God, *and* did not humble himself before Jeremiah the prophet, *who spoke* from the mouth of the LORD. **13** And he also rebelled against King Nebuchadnezzar, who had made him swear *an oath* by God; but he stiffened his neck and hardened his heart against turning to the LORD God of Israel.

Jer 34:5 You shall die in peace; as in the ceremonies of your fathers, the former kings who were before you, so they shall burn incense for you and lament for

you, *saying*, "Alas, lord!" For I have pronounced the word, says the LORD.' "

Frequently sudden and unexpected.

Job 21:13 They spend their days in wealth, And in a moment go down to the grave.

Job 21:23 One dies in his full strength, Being wholly at ease and secure;

Job 27:21 The east wind carries him away, and he is gone; It sweeps him out of his place.

Prov 29:1 He who is often rebuked, *and* hardens *his* neck, Will suddenly be destroyed, and that without remedy.

Frequently marked by terror.

Job 18:11–15 Terrors frighten him on every side, And drive him to his feet. **12** His strength is starved, And destruction *is* ready at his side. **13** It devours patches of his skin; The firstborn of death devours his limbs. **14** He is uprooted from the shelter of his tent, And they parade him before the king of terrors. **15** They dwell in his tent *who are* none of his; Brimstone is scattered on his dwelling.

Job 27:19–21 The rich man will lie down, But not be gathered *up;* He opens his eyes, And he *is* no more. **20** Terrors overtake him like a flood; A tempest steals him away in the night. **21** The east wind carries him away, and he is gone; It sweeps him out of his place.

Ps 73:19 Oh, how they are *brought* to desolation, as in a moment! They are utterly consumed with terrors.

Punishment follows.

Is 14:9 "Hell from beneath is excited about you, To meet *you* at your coming; It stirs up the dead for you, All the chief ones of the earth; It has raised up from their thrones All the kings of the nations.

Acts 1:25 to take part in this ministry and apostleship from which Judas by transgression fell, that he might go to his own place."

The remembrance of them perishes.

Job 18:17 The memory of him perishes from the earth, And he has no name among the renowned.

Ps 34:16 The face of the LORD *is* against those who do evil, To cut off the remembrance of them from the earth.

Prov 10:7 The memory of the righteous *is* blessed, But the name of the wicked will rot.

God has no pleasure in.

Ezek 18:23 Do I have any pleasure at all that the wicked should die?" says the Lord GOD, "*and* not that he should turn from his ways and live?

Ezek 18:32 For I have no pleasure in the death of one who dies," says the Lord GOD. "Therefore turn and live!"

Like the death of beasts.

Ps 49:14 Like sheep they are laid in the grave; Death shall feed on them; The upright shall have dominion over them in the morning; And their beauty shall be consumed in the grave, far from their dwelling.

Illustrated.

Luke 12:20 But God said to him, 'Fool! This night your soul will be required of you; then whose will those things be which you have provided?'

Luke 16:22–23 So it was that the beggar died, and was carried by the angels to Abraham's bosom. The rich man also died and was buried. **23** And being in torments in Hades, he lifted up his eyes and saw Abraham afar off, and Lazarus in his bosom.

Examples of,

Korah, etc.

Num 16:32 and the earth opened its mouth and swallowed them up, with their households and all the men with Korah, with all *their* goods.

Absalom.

2 Sam 18:9–10 Then Absalom met the servants of David. Absalom rode on a mule. The mule went under the thick boughs of a great terebinth tree, and his head caught in the terebinth; so he was left hanging between heaven and earth. And the mule which *was* under him went on. **10** Now a certain man saw *it* and told Joab, and said, "I just saw Absalom hanging in a terebinth tree!"

Ahab.

1 Kin 22:34 Now a *certain* man drew a bow at random, and struck the king of Israel between the joints of his armor. So he said to the driver of his chariot, "Turn around and take me out of the battle, for I am wounded."

Jezebel.

2 Kin 9:33 Then he said, "Throw her down." So they threw her down, and *some* of her blood spattered on the wall and on the horses; and he trampled her underfoot.

Athaliah.

2 Chr 23:15 So they seized her; and she went by way of the entrance of the Horse Gate *into* the king's house, and they killed her there.

Haman.

Esth 7:10 So they hanged Haman on the gallows that he had prepared for Mordecai. Then the king's wrath subsided.

Belshazzar.

Dan 5:30 That very night Belshazzar, king of the Chaldeans, was slain.

Judas Iscariot.

Matt 27:5 Then he threw down the pieces of silver in the temple and departed, and went and hanged himself.

Acts 1:18 (Now this man purchased a field with the wages of iniquity; and falling headlong, he burst open in the middle and all his entrails gushed out.

Ananias and Sapphira.

Acts 5:5 Then Ananias, hearing these words, fell down and breathed his last. So great fear came upon all those who heard these things.

Acts 5:9–10 Then Peter said to her, "How is it that you have agreed together to test the Spirit of the Lord? Look, the feet of those who have buried your husband *are* at the door, and they will carry you out." **10** Then immediately she fell down at his feet and breathed her last. And the young men came in and found her dead, and carrying *her* out, buried *her* by her husband.

Herod.

Acts 12:23 Then immediately an angel of the Lord struck him, because he did not give glory to God. And he was eaten by worms and died.

WICKED, HAPPINESS OF THE

Is limited to this life.

Ps 17:14 With Your hand from men, O LORD, From men of the world *who have* their portion in *this* life, And whose belly You fill with Your hidden treasure. They are satisfied with children, And leave the rest of their *possession* for their babes.

Luke 16:25 But Abraham said, 'Son, remember that in your lifetime you received your good things, and likewise Lazarus evil things; but now he is comforted and you are tormented.

Is short.

Job 20:5 That the triumphing of the wicked is short, And the joy of the hypocrite is *but* for a moment?

Is uncertain.

Luke 12:20 But God said to him, 'Fool! This night your soul will be required of you; then whose will those things be which you have provided?'

James 4:13–14 Come now, you who say, "Today or tomorrow we will go to such and such a city, spend a year there, buy and sell, and make a profit"; **14** whereas you do not know what *will happen* tomorrow. For what *is* your life? It is even a vapor that appears for a little time and then vanishes away.

Is vanity.

Eccl 2:1 I said in my heart, "Come now, I will test you with mirth; therefore enjoy pleasure"; but surely, this also *was* vanity.

Eccl 7:6 For like the crackling of thorns under a pot, So *is* the laughter of the fool. This also is vanity.

Is derived from

Their power.

Job 21:7 Why do the wicked live *and* become old, Yes, become mighty in power?

Ps 37:35 I have seen the wicked in great power, And spreading himself like a native green tree.

Their worldly prosperity.

Job 21:13 They spend their days in wealth, And in a moment go down to the grave.

Ps 17:14 With Your hand from men, O LORD, From men of the world *who have* their portion in *this* life, And whose belly You fill with Your hidden treasure. They are satisfied with children, And leave the rest of their *possession* for their babes.

Ps 52:7 "Here is the man *who* did not make God his strength, But trusted in the abundance of his riches, *And* strengthened himself in his wickedness."

Ps 73:3–4 For I *was* envious of the boastful, When I saw the prosperity of the wicked. **4** For *there are* no pangs in their death, But their strength *is* firm.

Ps 73:7 Their eyes bulge with abundance; They have more than heart could wish.

Popular applause.

Acts 12:22 And the people kept shouting, "The voice of a god and not of a man!"

Gluttony.

Is 22:13 But instead, joy and gladness, Slaying oxen and killing sheep, Eating meat and drinking wine: "Let us eat and drink, for tomorrow we die!"

Hab 1:16 Therefore they sacrifice to their net, And burn incense to their dragnet; Because by them their share *is* sumptuous And their food plentiful.

Drunkenness.

Is 5:11 Woe to those who rise early in the morning, *That* they may follow intoxicating drink; Who continue until night, *till* wine inflames them!

Is 56:12 "Come," *one says,* "I will bring wine, And we will fill ourselves with intoxicating drink; Tomorrow will be as today, *And* much more abundant."

Frivolous pleasure.

Job 21:12 They sing to the tambourine and harp, And rejoice to the sound of the flute.

Is 5:12 The harp and the strings, The tambourine and flute, And wine are in their feasts; But they do not regard the work of the LORD, Nor consider the operation of His hands.

Successful oppression of others.

Hab 1:15 They take up all of them with a hook, They catch them in their net, And gather them in their dragnet. Therefore they rejoice and are glad.

James 5:6 You have condemned, you have murdered the just; he does not resist you.

Marred by jealousy.

Esth 5:13 Yet all this avails me nothing, so long as I see Mordecai the Jew sitting at the king's gate."

Often interrupted by judgments.

Num 11:33 But while the meat *was* still between their teeth, before it was chewed, the wrath of the LORD was aroused against the people, and the LORD struck the people with a very great plague.

Job 15:21 Dreadful sounds *are* in his ears; In prosperity the destroyer comes upon him.

Ps 73:18–20 Surely You set them in slippery places; You cast them down to destruction. **19** Oh, how they are *brought* to desolation, as in a moment! They are utterly consumed with terrors. **20** As a dream when *one* awakes, *So,* Lord, when You awake, You shall despise their image.

Jer 25:10–11 Moreover I will take from them the voice of mirth and the voice of gladness, the voice of the bridegroom and the voice of the bride, the sound of the millstones and the light of the lamp. **11** And this whole land shall be a desolation *and* an astonishment, and these nations shall serve the king of Babylon seventy years.

Leads to sorrow.

Prov 14:13 Even in laughter the heart may sorrow, And the end of mirth *may be* grief.

Leads to recklessness.

Is 22:13 But instead, joy and gladness, Slaying oxen and killing sheep, Eating meat and drinking wine: "Let us eat and drink, for tomorrow we die!"

Sometimes a stumbling block to believers.

Ps 73:3 For I *was* envious of the boastful, When I saw the prosperity of the wicked.

Ps 73:16 When I thought *how* to understand this, It *was* too painful for me—

Jer 12:1 Righteous *are* You, O LORD, when I plead with You; Yet let me talk with You about *Your* judgments. Why does the way of the wicked prosper? *Why* are those happy who deal so treacherously?

Hab 1:13 *You are* of purer eyes than to behold evil, And cannot look on wickedness. Why do You look on those who deal treacherously, *And* hold Your tongue when the wicked devours A *person* more righteous than he?

Believers

Often permitted to see the end of.

Ps 73:17–20 Until I went into the sanctuary of God; *Then* I understood their end. **18** Surely You set them in slippery places; You cast them down to destruction. **19** Oh, how they are *brought* to desolation, as in a moment! They are utterly consumed with terrors. **20** As a dream when *one* awakes, *So,* Lord, when You awake, You shall despise their image.

Should not envy.

Ps 37:1 Do not fret because of evildoers, Nor be envious of the workers of iniquity.

Illustrated.

Ps 37:35–36 I have seen the wicked in great power, And spreading himself like a native green tree. **36** Yet he passed away, and behold, he *was* no *more;* Indeed I sought him, but he could not be found.

Luke 12:16–20 Then He spoke a parable to them, saying: "The ground of a certain rich man yielded plentifully. **17** And he thought within himself, saying, 'What shall I do, since I have no room to store my crops?' **18** So he said, 'I will do this: I will pull down my barns and build greater, and there I will store all my crops and my goods. **19** And I will say to my soul, "Soul, you have many goods laid up for many years; take your ease; eat, drink, *and* be merry." ' **20** But God said to him, 'Fool! This night your soul will be required of you; then whose will those things be which you have provided?'

Luke 16:19–25 "There was a certain rich man who was clothed in purple and fine linen and fared sumptuously every day. **20** But there was a certain beggar named Lazarus, full of sores, who was laid at his gate, **21** desiring to be fed with the crumbs which fell from the rich man's table. Moreover the dogs came and licked his sores. **22** So it was that the beggar died, and was carried by the angels to Abraham's bosom. The rich man also died and was buried. **23** And being in torments in Hades, he lifted up his eyes and saw Abraham afar off, and Lazarus in his bosom. **24** "Then he cried and said, 'Father Abraham, have mercy on me, and send Lazarus that he may dip the tip of his finger in water and cool my tongue; for I am tormented in this flame.' **25** But Abraham said, 'Son, remember that in your lifetime you received your good things, and likewise Lazarus evil things; but now he is comforted and you are tormented.

Examples of,

Unbelievers in Israel.

Num 11:33 But while the meat *was* still between their teeth, before it was chewed, the wrath of the LORD was aroused against the people, and the LORD struck the people with a very great plague.

Haman.

Esth 5:9–11 So Haman went out that day joyful and with a glad heart; but when Haman saw Mordecai in the king's gate, and that he did not stand or tremble before him, he was filled with indignation against Mordecai. **10** Nevertheless Haman restrained himself and went home, and he sent and called for his friends and his wife Zeresh. **11** Then Haman told them of his great riches, the multitude of his children, everything in which the king had promoted him, and how he had advanced him above the officials and servants of the king.

Belshazzar.

Dan 5:1 Belshazzar the king made a great feast for a thousand of his lords, and drank wine in the presence of the thousand.

Herod.

Acts 12:21–23 So on a set day Herod, arrayed in royal apparel, sat on his throne and gave an oration to them. **22** And the people kept shouting, "The voice of a god and not of a man!" **23** Then immediately an angel of the Lord struck him, because he did not give glory to God. And he was eaten by worms and died.

WICKED, PUNISHMENT OF THE

Is from God.

Lev 26:18 'And after all this, if you do not obey Me, then I will punish you seven times more for your sins.

Is 13:11 "I will punish the world for *its* evil, And the wicked for their iniquity; I will halt the arrogance of the proud, And will lay low the haughtiness of the terrible.

2 Thess 1:6 since *it is* a righteous thing with God to repay with tribulation those who trouble you,

Because of their

Sin and iniquity.

Jer 36:31 I will punish him, his family, and his servants for their iniquity; and I will bring on them, on the inhabitants of Jerusalem, and on the men of Judah all the doom that I have pronounced against them; but they did not heed." ' "

Lam 3:39 Why should a living man complain, A man for the punishment of his sins?

Ezek 3:17–18 "Son of man, I have made you a watchman for the house of Israel; therefore hear a word from My mouth, and give them warning from Me: **18** When I say to the wicked, 'You shall surely die,' and you give him no warning, nor speak to warn the wicked from his wicked way, to save his life, that same wicked *man* shall die in his iniquity; but his blood I will require at your hand.

Ezek 18:4 "Behold, all souls are Mine; The soul of the father As well as the soul of the son is Mine; The soul who sins shall die.

Ezek 18:13 If he has exacted usury Or taken increase— Shall he then live? He shall not live! If he has done any of these abominations, He shall surely die; His blood shall be upon him.

Ezek 18:20 The soul who sins shall die. The son shall not bear the guilt of the father, nor the father bear the guilt of the son. The righteousness of the righteous

shall be upon himself, and the wickedness of the wicked shall be upon himself.

Amos 3:2 "You only have I known of all the families of the earth; Therefore I will punish you for all your iniquities."

Idolatry.

Lev 26:30 I will destroy your high places, cut down your incense altars, and cast your carcasses on the lifeless forms of your idols; and My soul shall abhor you.

Is 10:10–11 As my hand has found the kingdoms of the idols, Whose carved images excelled those of Jerusalem and Samaria, **11** As I have done to Samaria and her idols, Shall I not do also to Jerusalem and her idols?' "

Rejection of the law of God.

1 Sam 15:23 For rebellion *is as* the sin of witchcraft, And stubbornness *is as* iniquity and idolatry. Because you have rejected the word of the LORD, He also has rejected you from *being* king."

Hos 4:6–9 My people are destroyed for lack of knowledge. Because you have rejected knowledge, I also will reject you from being priest for Me; Because you have forgotten the law of your God, I also will forget your children. **7** "The more they increased, The more they sinned against Me; I will change their glory into shame. **8** They eat up the sin of My people; They set their heart on their iniquity. **9** And it shall be: like people, like priest. So I will punish them for their ways, And reward them for their deeds.

Disobedience of God.

Neh 9:26–27 "Nevertheless they were disobedient And rebelled against You, Cast Your law behind their backs And killed Your prophets, who testified against them To turn them to Yourself; And they worked great provocations. **27** Therefore You delivered them into the hand of their enemies, Who oppressed them; And in the time of their trouble, When they cried to You, You heard from heaven; And according to Your abundant mercies You gave them deliverers who saved them From the hand of their enemies.

Eph 5:6 Let no one deceive you with empty words, for because of these things the wrath of God comes upon the sons of disobedience.

2 Thess 1:8 in flaming fire taking vengeance on those who do not know God, and on those who do not obey the gospel of our Lord Jesus Christ.

Evil ways and doings.

Jer 21:14 But I will punish you according to the fruit of your doings," says the LORD; "I will kindle a fire in its forest, And it shall devour all things around it." ' "

Hos 4:9 And it shall be: like people, like priest. So I will punish them for their ways, And reward them for their deeds.

Hos 12:2 "The LORD also *brings* a charge against Judah, And will punish Jacob according to his ways; According to his deeds He will recompense him.

Pride.

Is 10:12 Therefore it shall come to pass, when the Lord has performed all His work on Mount Zion and on Jerusalem, *that He will say,* "I will punish the fruit of the arrogant heart of the king of Assyria, and the glory of his haughty looks."

Is 24:21 It shall come to pass in that day *That* the LORD will punish on high the host of exalted ones, And on the earth the kings of the earth.

Luke 14:11 For whoever exalts himself will be humbled, and he who humbles himself will be exalted."

Unbelief.

Mark 16:16 He who believes and is baptized will be saved; but he who does not believe will be condemned.

Rom 11:20 Well *said.* Because of unbelief they were broken off, and you stand by faith. Do not be haughty, but fear.

Heb 3:18–19 And to whom did He swear that they would not enter His rest, but to those who did not obey? **19** So we see that they could not enter in because of unbelief.

Heb 4:2 For indeed the gospel was preached to us as well as to them; but the word which they heard did not profit them, not being mixed with faith in those who heard *it.*

Covetousness.

Is 57:17 For the iniquity of his covetousness I was angry and struck him; I hid and was angry, And he went on backsliding in the way of his heart.

Jer 51:13 O you who dwell by many waters, Abundant in treasures, Your end has come, The measure of your covetousness.

Oppression.

Is 49:26 I will feed those who oppress you with their own flesh, And they shall be drunk with their own blood as with sweet wine. All flesh shall know That I, the LORD, *am* your Savior, And your Redeemer, the Mighty One of Jacob."

Jer 30:16 Therefore all those who devour you shall be devoured; And all your adversaries, every one of them, shall go into captivity; Those who plunder you shall become plunder, And all who prey upon you I will make a prey.

Jer 30:20 Their children also shall be as before, And their congregation shall be established before Me; And I will punish all who oppress them.

Persecuting.

Jer 11:21–22 "Therefore thus says the LORD concerning the men of Anathoth who seek your life, saying, 'Do not prophesy in the name of the LORD, lest you die by our hand'— **22** therefore thus says the LORD of hosts: 'Behold, I will punish them. The young men shall die by the sword, their sons and their daughters shall die by famine;

Matt 23:34–36 Therefore, indeed, I send you prophets, wise men, and scribes: *some* of them you will kill and crucify, and *some* of them you will scourge in your synagogues and persecute from city to city, **35** that on you may come all the righteous blood shed on the earth, from the blood of righteous Abel to the blood of Zechariah, son of Berechiah, whom you murdered between the temple and the altar. **36** Assuredly, I say to you, all these things will come upon this generation.

Is the fruit of their sin.

Job 4:8 Even as I have seen, Those who plow iniquity And sow trouble reap the same.

Prov 22:8 He who sows iniquity will reap sorrow, And the rod of his anger will fail.

Rom 6:21 What fruit did you have then in the things of which you are now ashamed? For the end of those things *is* death.

Gal 6:8 For he who sows to his flesh will of the flesh reap corruption, but he who sows to the Spirit will of the Spirit reap everlasting life.

Is the reward of their sin.

Ps 91:8 Only with your eyes shall you look, And see the reward of the wicked.

Is 3:11 Woe to the wicked! *It shall be* ill *with him,* For the reward of his hands shall be given him.

Jer 16:18 And first I will repay double for their iniquity and their sin, because they have defiled My land; they have filled My inheritance with the carcasses of their detestable and abominable idols."

Rom 6:23 For the wages of sin *is* death, but the gift of God *is* eternal life in Christ Jesus our Lord.

Heb 2:2 For if the word spoken through angels proved steadfast, and every transgression and disobedience received a just reward,

Often brought about by their evil designs.

Esth 7:10 So they hanged Haman on the gallows that he had prepared for Mordecai. Then the king's wrath subsided.

Ps 37:15 Their sword shall enter their own heart, And their bows shall be broken.

Ps 57:6 They have prepared a net for my steps; My soul is bowed down; They have dug a pit before me; Into the midst of it they *themselves* have fallen. Selah

Often begins on earth.

Prov 11:31 If the righteous will be recompensed on the earth, How much more the ungodly and the sinner.

In this life by

Sickness.

Lev 26:16 I also will do this to you: I will even appoint terror over you, wasting disease and fever which shall consume the eyes and cause sorrow of heart. And you shall sow your seed in vain, for your enemies shall eat it.

Ps 78:50 He made a path for His anger; He did not spare their soul from death, But gave their life over to the plague,

Famine.

Lev 26:19–20 I will break the pride of your power; I will make your heavens like iron and your earth like bronze. **20** And your strength shall be spent in vain; for your land shall not yield its produce, nor shall the trees of the land yield their fruit.

Lev 26:26 When I have cut off your supply of bread, ten women shall bake your bread in one oven, and they shall bring back your bread by weight, and you shall eat and not be satisfied.

Lev 26:29 You shall eat the flesh of your sons, and you shall eat the flesh of your daughters.

Ps 107:34 A fruitful land into barrenness, For the wickedness of those who dwell in it.

Wild beasts.

Lev 26:22 I will also send wild beasts among you, which shall rob you of your children, destroy your livestock, and make you few in number; and your highways shall be desolate.

War.

Lev 26:25 And I will bring a sword against you that will execute the vengeance of the covenant; when you are gathered together within your cities I will send pestilence among you; and you shall be delivered into the hand of the enemy.

Lev 26:32–33 I will bring the land to desolation, and your enemies who dwell in it shall be astonished at it. **33** I will scatter you among the nations and draw out a sword after you; your land shall be desolate and your cities waste.

Jer 6:4 "Prepare war against her; Arise, and let us go up at noon. Woe to us, for the day goes away, For the shadows of the evening are lengthening.

Deliverance to enemies.

Neh 9:27 Therefore You delivered them into the hand of their enemies, Who oppressed them; And in the time of their trouble, When they cried to You, You heard from heaven; And according to Your abundant mercies You gave them deliverers who saved them From the hand of their enemies.

Fear.

Lev 26:36–37 'And as for those of you who are left, I will send faintness into their hearts in the lands of their enemies; the sound of a shaken leaf shall cause them to flee; they shall flee as though fleeing from a sword, and they shall fall when no one pursues. **37** They shall stumble over one another, as it were before a sword, when no one pursues; and you shall have no *power* to stand before your enemies.

Job 18:11 Terrors frighten him on every side, And drive him to his feet.

Receiving debased mind.

Rom 1:28 And even as they did not like to retain God in *their* knowledge, God gave them over to a debased mind, to do those things which are not fitting;

Being put in slippery places. **Ps 73:3–19**

Trouble and distress.

Is 8:22 Then they will look to the earth, and see trouble and darkness, gloom of anguish; and *they will be* driven into darkness.

Zeph 1:15 That day *is* a day of wrath, A day of trouble and distress, A day of devastation and desolation, A day of darkness and gloominess, A day of clouds and thick darkness,

Being cut off.

Ps 94:23 He has brought on them their own iniquity, And shall cut them off in their own wickedness; The LORD our God shall cut them off.

Pride being brought low.

Is 13:11 "I will punish the world for *its* evil, And the wicked for their iniquity; I will halt the arrogance of the proud, And will lay low the haughtiness of the terrible.

Future described as

Being awarded by Christ.

Matt 16:27 For the Son of Man will come in the glory of His Father with His angels, and then He will reward each according to his works.

Matt 25:31 "When the Son of Man comes in His glory, and all the holy angels with Him, then He will sit on the throne of His glory.

Hell.

Ps 9:17 The wicked shall be turned into hell, *And* all the nations that forget God.

Matt 5:29 If your right eye causes you to sin, pluck it out and cast *it* from you; for it is more profitable for you that one of your members perish, than for your whole body to be cast into hell.

Luke 12:5 But I will show you whom you should fear: Fear Him who, after He has killed, has power to cast into hell; yes, I say to you, fear Him!

Luke 16:23 And being in torments in Hades, he lifted up his eyes and saw Abraham afar off, and Lazarus in his bosom.

Darkness.

Matt 8:12 But the sons of the kingdom will be cast out into outer darkness. There will be weeping and gnashing of teeth."

2 Pet 2:17 These are wells without water, clouds carried by a tempest, for whom is reserved the blackness of darkness forever.

Resurrection of condemnation, shame, and contempt.

Dan 12:2 And many of those who sleep in the dust of the earth shall awake, Some to everlasting life, Some to shame *and* everlasting contempt.

John 5:29 and come forth—those who have done good, to the resurrection of life, and those who have done evil, to the resurrection of condemnation.

Everlasting destruction.

Ps 52:5 God shall likewise destroy you forever; He shall take you away, and pluck you out of *your* dwelling place, And uproot you from the land of the living. Selah

Ps 92:7 When the wicked spring up like grass, And when all the workers of iniquity flourish, *It is* that they may be destroyed forever.

2 Thess 1:9 These shall be punished with everlasting destruction from the presence of the Lord and from the glory of His power,

Everlasting fire.

Matt 25:41 "Then He will also say to those on the left hand, 'Depart from Me, you cursed, into the everlasting fire prepared for the devil and his angels:

Jude 1:7 as Sodom and Gomorrah, and the cities around them in a similar manner to these, having given themselves over to sexual immorality and gone after strange flesh, are set forth as an example, suffering the vengeance of eternal fire.

Second death.

Rev 2:11 "He who has an ear, let him hear what the Spirit says to the churches. He who overcomes shall not be hurt by the second death." '

Rev 21:8 But the cowardly, unbelieving, abominable,

murderers, sexually immoral, sorcerers, idolaters, and all liars shall have their part in the lake which burns with fire and brimstone, which is the second death."

Condemnation of hell.

Matt 23:33 Serpents, brood of vipers! How can you escape the condemnation of hell?

Eternal condemnation.

Mark 3:29 but he who blasphemes against the Holy Spirit never has forgiveness, but is subject to eternal condemnation"—

Blackness of darkness.

2 Pet 2:17 These are wells without water, clouds carried by a tempest, for whom is reserved the blackness of darkness forever.

Jude 1:13 raging waves of the sea, foaming up their own shame; wandering stars for whom is reserved the blackness of darkness forever.

Everlasting burnings.

Is 33:14 The sinners in Zion are afraid; Fearfulness has seized the hypocrites: "Who among us shall dwell with the devouring fire? Who among us shall dwell with everlasting burnings?"

The wrath of God.

John 3:36 He who believes in the Son has everlasting life; and he who does not believe the Son shall not see life, but the wrath of God abides on him."

Wine of the wrath of God.

Rev 14:10 he himself shall also drink of the wine of the wrath of God, which is poured out full strength into the cup of His indignation. He shall be tormented with fire and brimstone in the presence of the holy angels and in the presence of the Lamb.

Torment with fire.

Rev 14:10 he himself shall also drink of the wine of the wrath of God, which is poured out full strength into the cup of His indignation. He shall be tormented with fire and brimstone in the presence of the holy angels and in the presence of the Lamb.

Torment forever and ever.

Rev 14:11 And the smoke of their torment ascends forever and ever; and they have no rest day or night, who worship the beast and his image, and whoever receives the mark of his name."

Often sudden and unexpected.

Ps 35:8 Let destruction come upon him unexpectedly, And let his net that he has hidden catch himself; Into that very destruction let him fall.

Ps 64:7 But God shall shoot at them *with* an arrow; Suddenly they shall be wounded.

Prov 29:1 He who is often rebuked, *and* hardens *his* neck, Will suddenly be destroyed, and that without remedy.

Luke 12:20 But God said to him, 'Fool! This night your soul will be required of you; then whose will those things be which you have provided?'

1 Thess 5:3 For when they say, "Peace and safety!" then sudden destruction comes upon them, as labor pains upon a pregnant woman. And they shall not escape.

Shall be

According to their deeds.

Matt 16:27 For the Son of Man will come in the glory of His Father with His angels, and then He will reward each according to his works.

Rom 2:6 who *"will render to each one according to his deeds":*

Rom 2:9 tribulation and anguish, on every soul of man who does evil, of the Jew first and also of the Greek;

2 Cor 5:10 For we must all appear before the judgment seat of Christ, that each one may receive the things *done* in the body, according to what he has done, whether good or bad.

According to the knowledge possessed by them.

Luke 12:47–48 And that servant who knew his master's will, and did not prepare *himself* or do according to his will, shall be beaten with many *stripes.* **48** But he who did not know, yet committed things deserving of stripes, shall be beaten with few. For everyone to whom much is given, from him much will be required; and to whom much has been committed, of him they will ask the more.

Increased by neglect of privileges.

Matt 11:21–24 "Woe to you, Chorazin! Woe to you, Bethsaida! For if the mighty works which were done in you had been done in Tyre and Sidon, they would have repented long ago in sackcloth and ashes. **22** But I say to you, it will be more tolerable for Tyre and Sidon in the day of judgment than for you. **23** And you, Capernaum, who are exalted to heaven, will be brought down to Hades; for if the mighty works which were done in you had been done in Sodom, it would have remained until this day. **24** But I say to you that it shall be more tolerable for the land of Sodom in the day of judgment than for you."

Luke 10:13–15 "Woe to you, Chorazin! Woe to you, Bethsaida! For if the mighty works which were done in you had been done in Tyre and Sidon, they would have repented long ago, sitting in sackcloth and ashes. **14** But it will be more tolerable for Tyre and Sidon at the judgment than for you. **15** And you, Capernaum, who are exalted to heaven, will be brought down to Hades.

Relentless.

Luke 16:23–26 And being in torments in Hades, he lifted up his eyes and saw Abraham afar off, and Lazarus in his bosom. **24** "Then he cried and said, 'Father Abraham, have mercy on me, and send Lazarus that he may dip the tip of his finger in water and cool my tongue; for I am tormented in this flame.' **25** But Abraham said, 'Son, remember that in your lifetime you received your good things, and likewise Lazarus evil things; but now he is comforted and you are tormented. **26** And besides all this, between us and you there is a great gulf fixed, so that those who want to pass from here to you cannot, nor can those from there pass to us.'

Accompanied by remorse.

Is 66:24 "And they shall go forth and look Upon the corpses of the men Who have transgressed against Me. For their worm does not die, And their fire is not quenched. They shall be an abhorrence to all flesh."

Mark 9:44 where *'Their worm does not die And the fire is not quenched.'*

No combination avails against.

Prov 11:21 *Though they join* forces, the wicked will not go unpunished; But the posterity of the righteous will be delivered.

Deferred, emboldens them in sin.

Eccl 8:11 Because the sentence against an evil work is not executed speedily, therefore the heart of the sons of men is fully set in them to do evil.

Should be a warning to others.

Num 26:10 and the earth opened its mouth and swallowed them up together with Korah when that company died, when the fire devoured two hundred and fifty men; and they became a sign.

1 Cor 10:6–11 Now these things became our examples, to the intent that we should not lust after evil things as they also lusted. **7** And do not become idolaters as *were* some of them. As it is written, *"The people sat down to eat and drink, and rose up to play."* **8** Nor let us commit sexual immorality, as some of them did, and in one day twenty-three thousand fell; **9** nor let us tempt Christ, as some of them also tempted, and were destroyed by serpents; **10** nor complain, as some of them also complained, and were destroyed by the destroyer. **11** Now all these things happened to them as examples, and they were written for our admonition, upon whom the ends of the ages have come.

Jude 1:7 as Sodom and Gomorrah, and the cities around them in a similar manner to these, having given themselves over to sexual immorality and gone after strange flesh, are set forth as an example, suffering the vengeance of eternal fire.

Consummated at the day of judgment.

Matt 25:31 "When the Son of Man comes in His glory, and all the holy angels with Him, then He will sit on the throne of His glory.

Matt 25:46 And these will go away into everlasting punishment, but the righteous into eternal life."

Rom 2:5 But in accordance with your hardness and your impenitent heart you are treasuring up for yourself wrath in the day of wrath and revelation of the righteous judgment of God,

Rom 2:16 in the day when God will judge the secrets of men by Jesus Christ, according to my gospel.

2 Pet 2:9 *then* the Lord knows how to deliver the godly out of temptations and to reserve the unjust under punishment for the day of judgment,

WICKED, TITLES AND NAMES OF THE

Accursed children.

2 Pet 2:14 having eyes full of adultery and that cannot cease from sin, enticing unstable souls. *They have* a heart trained in covetous practices, *and are* accursed children.

Adversaries of the Lord.

1 Sam 2:10 The adversaries of the LORD shall be broken in pieces; From heaven He will thunder against them. The LORD will judge the ends of the earth. "He will give strength to His king, And exalt the horn of His anointed."

Brood of evildoers.

Is 1:4 Alas, sinful nation, A people laden with iniquity, A brood of evildoers, Children who are corrupters! They have forsaken The LORD, They have provoked to anger The Holy One of Israel, They have turned away backward.

Is 14:20 You will not be joined with them in burial, Because you have destroyed your land *And* slain your people. The brood of evildoers shall never be named.

Brood of vipers.

Matt 3:7 But when he saw many of the Pharisees and Sadducees coming to his baptism, he said to them, "Brood of vipers! Who warned you to flee from the wrath to come?

Matt 12:34 Brood of vipers! How can you, being evil, speak good things? For out of the abundance of the heart the mouth speaks.

Children of the devil.

Acts 13:10 and said, "O full of all deceit and all fraud, *you* son of the devil, *you* enemy of all righteousness, will you not cease perverting the straight ways of the Lord?

1 John 3:10 In this the children of God and the children of the devil are manifest: Whoever does not practice righteousness is not of God, nor *is* he who does not love his brother.

Children of vile men.

Job 30:8 *They were* sons of fools, Yes, sons of vile men; They were scourged from the land.

Children of foreigners.

Is 2:6 For You have forsaken Your people, the house of Jacob, Because they are filled with eastern ways; They *are* soothsayers like the Philistines, And they are pleased with the children of foreigners.

Children of transgression.

Is 57:4 Whom do you ridicule? Against whom do you make a wide mouth *And* stick out the tongue? *Are* you not children of transgression, Offspring of falsehood,

Children in whom is no faith.

Deut 32:20 And He said: 'I will hide My face from them, I will see what their end *will be,* For they *are* a perverse generation, Children in whom *is* no faith.

Children of the flesh.

Rom 9:8 That is, those who *are* the children of the flesh, these *are* not the children of God; but the children of the promise are counted as the seed.

Children of iniquity.

Hos 10:9 "O Israel, you have sinned from the days of Gibeah; There they stood. The battle in Gibeah against the children of iniquity Did not overtake them.

Children who will not hear the law of the Lord.

Is 30:9 That this *is* a rebellious people, Lying children, Children *who* will not hear the law of the LORD;

Children of pride.

Job 41:34 He beholds every high *thing;* He *is* king over all the children of pride."

Children of wrath.

Eph 2:3 among whom also we all once conducted ourselves in the lusts of our flesh, fulfilling the desires of the flesh and of the mind, and were by nature children of wrath, just as the others.

Children that are corrupters.

Is 1:4 Alas, sinful nation, A people laden with iniquity, A brood of evildoers, Children who are corrupters! They have forsaken the LORD, They have provoked to anger The Holy One of Israel, They have turned away backward.

Corrupt men.

Deut 13:13 'Corrupt men have gone out from among you and enticed the inhabitants of their city, saying, "Let us go and serve other gods" '—which you have not known—

Corrupt scoundrels.

1 Sam 2:12 Now the sons of Eli *were* corrupt; they did not know the LORD.

1 Kin 21:10 and seat two men, scoundrels, before him to bear witness against him, saying, You have blasphemed God and the king. *Then* take him out, and stone him, that he may die.

Descendants of the wicked.

Ps 37:28 For the LORD loves justice, And does not forsake His saints; They are preserved forever, But the descendants of the wicked shall be cut off.

Disqualified.

2 Cor 13:5–7 Examine yourselves *as to* whether you are in the faith. Test yourselves. Do you not know yourselves, that Jesus Christ is in you?—unless indeed you are disqualified. **6** But I trust that you will know that we are not disqualified. **7** Now I pray to God that you do no evil, not that we should appear approved, but that you should do what is honorable, though we may seem disqualified.

Enemies of God.

Ps 37:20 But the wicked shall perish; And the enemies of the LORD, Like the splendor of the meadows, shall vanish. Into smoke they shall vanish away.

James 4:4 Adulterers and adulteresses! Do you not know that friendship with the world is enmity with God? Whoever therefore wants to be a friend of the world makes himself an enemy of God.

Enemies of the cross of Christ.

Phil 3:18 For many walk, of whom I have told you often, and now tell you even weeping, *that they are* the enemies of the cross of Christ:

Enemies of all righteousness.

Acts 13:10 and said, "O full of all deceit and all fraud, *you* son of the devil, *you* enemy of all righteousness, will you not cease perverting the straight ways of the Lord?

Evildoers.

Ps 37:1 Do not fret because of evildoers, Nor be envious of the workers of iniquity.

Ps 101:8 Early I will destroy all the wicked of the land, That I may cut off all the evildoers from the city of the LORD.

Prov 17:4 An evildoer gives heed to false lips; A liar listens eagerly to a spiteful tongue.

1 Pet 2:14 or to governors, as to those who are sent by him for the punishment of evildoers and *for the* praise of those who do good.

Evil men.

Prov 4:14 Do not enter the path of the wicked, And do not walk in the way of evil.

2 Tim 3:13 But evil men and impostors will grow worse and worse, deceiving and being deceived.

Evil generation.

Deut 1:35 'Surely not one of these men of this evil generation shall see that good land of which I swore to give to your fathers,

Evil and adulterous generation.

Matt 12:39 But He answered and said to them, "An evil and adulterous generation seeks after a sign, and no sign will be given to it except the sign of the prophet Jonah.

Fools.

Prov 1:7 The fear of the LORD *is* the beginning of knowledge, *But* fools despise wisdom and instruction.

Rom 1:22 Professing to be wise, they became fools,

Foreigners.

Ps 144:7 Stretch out Your hand from above; Rescue me and deliver me out of great waters, From the hand of foreigners,

Haters of God.

Ps 81:15 The haters of the LORD would pretend submission to Him, But their fate would endure forever.

Rom 1:30 backbiters, haters of God, violent, proud, boasters, inventors of evil things, disobedient to parents,

Impudent and stubborn children.

Ezek 2:4 For *they are* impudent and stubborn children. I am sending you to them, and you shall say to them, 'Thus says the Lord GOD.'

Inventors of evil things.

Rom 1:30 backbiters, haters of God, violent, proud, boasters, inventors of evil things, disobedient to parents,

Lying children.

Is 30:9 That this *is* a rebellious people, Lying children, Children *who* will not hear the law of the LORD;

Men of the world.

Ps 17:14 With Your hand from men, O LORD, From men of the world *who have* their portion in *this* life, And whose belly You fill with Your hidden treasure. They are satisfied with children, And leave the rest of their *possession* for their babes.

Offspring of falsehood.

Is 57:4 Whom do you ridicule? Against whom do you make a wide mouth *And* stick out the tongue? *Are* you not children of transgression, Offspring of falsehood,

People loaded with iniquity.

Is 1:4 Alas, sinful nation, A people laden with iniquity, A brood of evildoers, Children who are corrupters! They have forsaken the LORD, They have provoked to anger The Holy One of Israel, They have turned away backward.

Perverse generation.

Deut 32:20 And He said: 'I will hide My face from them, I will see what their end *will be*, For they *are* a perverse generation, Children in whom *is* no faith.

Acts 2:40 And with many other words he testified and exhorted them, saying, "Be saved from this perverse generation."

Perverse and crooked (faithless) generation.

Deut 32:5 "They have corrupted themselves; *They are* not His children, Because of their blemish: A perverse and crooked generation.

Matt 17:17 Then Jesus answered and said, "O faithless and perverse generation, how long shall I be with you? How long shall I bear with you? Bring him here to Me."

Phil 2:15 that you may become blameless and harmless, children of God without fault in the midst of a crooked and perverse generation, among whom you shine as lights in the world,

Rebellious children.

Is 30:1 "Woe to the rebellious children," says the LORD, "Who take counsel, but not of Me, And who devise plans, but not of My Spirit, That they may add sin to sin;

Rebellious people.

Is 30:9 That this *is* a rebellious people, Lying children, Children *who* will not hear the law of the LORD;

Is 65:2 I have stretched out My hands all day long to a rebellious people, Who walk in a way *that is* not good, According to their own thoughts;

Rebellious house.

Ezek 2:5 As for them, whether they hear or whether they refuse—for they *are* a rebellious house—yet they will know that a prophet has been among them.

Ezek 2:8 But you, son of man, hear what I say to you. Do not be rebellious like that rebellious house; open your mouth and eat what I give you."

Ezek 12:2 "Son of man, you dwell in the midst of a rebellious house, which has eyes to see but does not see, and ears to hear but does not hear; for they *are* a rebellious house.

Scornful.

Ps 1:1 Blessed *is* the man Who walks not in the counsel of the ungodly, Nor stands in the path of sinners, Nor sits in the seat of the scornful;

Serpents.

Matt 23:33 Serpents, brood of vipers! How can you escape the condemnation of hell?

Silly children.

Jer 4:22 "For My people *are* foolish, They have not known Me. They *are* silly children, And they have no understanding. They *are* wise to do evil, But to do good they have no knowledge."

Sinners.

Ps 26:9 Do not gather my soul with sinners, Nor my life with bloodthirsty men,

Prov 1:10 My son, if sinners entice you, Do not consent.

Slaves of corruption.

2 Pet 2:19 While they promise them liberty, they themselves are slaves of corruption; for by whom a person is overcome, by him also he is brought into bondage.

Slaves of sin.

John 8:34 Jesus answered them, "Most assuredly, I say to you, whoever commits sin is a slave of sin.

Rom 6:20 For when you were slaves of sin, you were free in regard to righteousness.

Sons of the wicked one.

Matt 13:38 The field is the world, the good seeds are the sons of the kingdom, but the tares are the sons of the wicked *one*.

Sons of hell.

Matt 23:15 "Woe to you, scribes and Pharisees, hypocrites! For you travel land and sea to win one proselyte, and when he is won, you make him twice as much a son of hell as yourselves.

Sons of fools.

Job 30:8 *They were* sons of fools, Yes, sons of vile men; They were scourged from the land.

Sons of disobedience.

Eph 2:2 in which you once walked according to the course of this world, according to the prince of the power of the air, the spirit who now works in the sons of disobedience,

Col 3:6 Because of these things the wrath of God is coming upon the sons of disobedience,

Sons of this world.

Luke 16:8 So the master commended the unjust steward because he had dealt shrewdly. For the sons of this world are more shrewd in their generation than the sons of light.

Sons of wickedness.

2 Sam 7:10 Moreover I will appoint a place for My people Israel, and will plant them, that they may dwell in a place of their own and move no more; nor shall the sons of wickedness oppress them anymore, as previously,

Stubborn and rebellious generation.

Ps 78:8 And may not be like their fathers, A stubborn and rebellious generation, A generation *that* did not set its heart aright, And whose spirit was not faithful to God.

Stubborn rebels.

Jer 6:28 They *are* all stubborn rebels, walking as slanderers. *They are* bronze and iron, They *are* all corrupters;

Transgressors.

Ps 37:38 But the transgressors shall be destroyed together; The future of the wicked shall be cut off.

Ps 51:13 *Then* I will teach transgressors Your ways, And sinners shall be converted to You.

Ungodly.

Ps 1:1 Blessed *is* the man Who walks not in the counsel of the ungodly, Nor stands in the path of sinners, Nor sits in the seat of the scornful;

Ungodly men.

Jude 1:4 For certain men have crept in unnoticed, who long ago were marked out for this condemnation, ungodly men, who turn the grace of our God into lewdness and deny the only Lord God and our Lord Jesus Christ.

Unprofitable servants.

Matt 25:30 And cast the unprofitable servant into the outer darkness. There will be weeping and gnashing of teeth.'

Vessels of wrath.

Rom 9:22 *What* if God, wanting to show *His* wrath and to make His power known, endured with much longsuffering the vessels of wrath prepared for destruction,

Wicked of the earth.

Ps 75:8 For in the hand of the LORD *there is* a cup, And the wine is red; It is fully mixed, and He pours it out; Surely its dregs shall all the wicked of the earth Drain *and* drink down.

Wicked transgressors.

Ps 59:5 You therefore, O LORD God of hosts, the God of Israel, Awake to punish all the nations; Do not be merciful to any wicked transgressors. Selah

Wicked and lazy servants.

Matt 25:26 "But his lord answered and said to him, 'You wicked and lazy servant, you knew that I reap where I have not sown, and gather where I have not scattered seed.

Wicked and adulterous generation.

Matt 12:45 Then he goes and takes with him seven other spirits more wicked than himself, and they enter and dwell there; and the last *state* of that man is worse than the first. So shall it also be with this wicked generation."

Matt 16:4 A wicked and adulterous generation seeks after a sign, and no sign shall be given to it except the sign of the prophet Jonah." And He left them and departed.

Wicked women.

Jer 2:33 "Why do you beautify your way to seek love? Therefore you have also taught The wicked women your ways.

Workers of iniquity.

Ps 28:3 Do not take me away with the wicked And with the workers of iniquity, Who speak peace to their neighbors, But evil *is* in their hearts.

Ps 36:12 There the workers of iniquity have fallen; They have been cast down and are not able to rise.

Worthless rogues.

2 Chr 13:7 Then worthless rogues gathered to him, and strengthened themselves against Rehoboam the son of Solomon, when Rehoboam was young and inexperienced and could not withstand them.

WIDOWS

Character of true.

Luke 2:37 and this woman *was* a widow of about eighty-four years, who did not depart from the temple, but served *God* with fastings and prayers night and day.

1 Tim 5:5 Now she who is really a widow, and left alone, trusts in God and continues in supplications and prayers night and day.

1 Tim 5:10 well reported for good works: if she has brought up children, if she has lodged strangers, if she has washed the saints' feet, if she has relieved the afflicted, if she has diligently followed every good work.

God

Surely hears the cry of.

Ex 22:23 If you afflict them in any way, *and* they cry at all to Me, I will surely hear their cry;

Judges for.

Deut 10:18 He administers justice for the fatherless and the widow, and loves the stranger, giving him food and clothing.

Ps 68:5 A father of the fatherless, a defender of widows, Is God in His holy habitation.

Relieves.

Ps 146:9 The LORD watches over the strangers; He relieves the fatherless and widow; But the way of the wicked He turns upside down.

Establishes the border of.

Prov 15:25 The LORD will destroy the house of the proud, But He will establish the boundary of the widow.

Will witness against oppressors of.

Mal 3:5 And I will come near you for judgment; I will be a swift witness Against sorcerers, Against adulterers, Against perjurers, Against those who exploit wage earners and widows and orphans, And against those who turn away an alien— Because they do not fear Me," Says the LORD of hosts.

Exhorted to trust in God.

Jer 49:11 Leave your fatherless children, I will preserve *them* alive; And let your widows trust in Me."

Should not be

Afflicted.

Ex 22:22 "You shall not afflict any widow or fatherless child.

Oppressed.

Jer 7:6 *if* you do not oppress the stranger, the fatherless, and the widow, and do not shed innocent blood in this place, or walk after other gods to your hurt,

Zech 7:10 Do not oppress the widow or the fatherless, The alien or the poor. Let none of you plan evil in his heart Against his brother.'

Treated with violence.

Jer 22:3 Thus says the LORD: "Execute judgment and righteousness, and deliver the plundered out of the hand of the oppressor. Do no wrong and do no violence to the stranger, the fatherless, or the widow, nor shed innocent blood in this place.

Deprived of garment in pledge.

Deut 24:17 "You shall not pervert justice due the stranger or the fatherless, nor take a widow's garment as a pledge.

Should be

Pleaded for.

Is 1:17 Learn to do good; Seek justice, Rebuke the oppressor; Defend the fatherless, Plead for the widow.

Honored, if widows indeed.

1 Tim 5:3 Honor widows who are really widows.

Relieved by their friends and family.

1 Tim 5:4 But if any widow has children or grand-children, let them first learn to show piety at home and to repay their parents; for this is good and acceptable before God.

1 Tim 5:16 If any believing man or woman has widows, let them relieve them, and do not let the church be burdened, that it may relieve those who are really widows.

Relieved by the church.

Acts 6:1 Now in those days, when *the number of* the disciples was multiplying, there arose a complaint against the Hebrews by the Hellenists, because their widows were neglected in the daily distribution.

1 Tim 5:9 Do not let a widow under sixty years old be taken into the number, *and not unless* she has been the wife of one man,

Visited in affliction.

James 1:27 Pure and undefiled religion before God and the Father is this: to visit orphans and widows in their trouble, *and* to keep oneself unspotted from the world.

Allowed to share in our blessings.

Deut 14:29 And the Levite, because he has no portion nor inheritance with you, and the stranger and the fatherless and the widow who *are* within your gates, may come and eat and be satisfied, that the Lord your God may bless you in all the work of your hand which you do.

Deut 16:11 You shall rejoice before the Lord your God, you and your son and your daughter, your male servant and your female servant, the Levite who *is* within your gates, the stranger and the fatherless and the widow who *are* among you, at the place where the Lord your God chooses to make His name abide.

Deut 16:14 And you shall rejoice in your feast, you and your son and your daughter, your male servant and your female servant and the Levite, the stranger and the fatherless and the widow, who *are* within your gates.

Deut 24:19–21 "When you reap your harvest in your field, and forget a sheaf in the field, you shall not go back to get it; it shall be for the stranger, the fatherless, and the widow, that the Lord your God may bless you in all the work of your hands. **20** When you beat your olive trees, you shall not go over the boughs again; it shall be for the stranger, the fatherless, and the widow. **21** When you gather the grapes of your vineyard, you shall not glean *it* afterward; it shall be for the stranger, the fatherless, and the widow.

Though poor, may be generous.

Mark 12:42–43 Then one poor widow came and threw in two mites, which make a quadrans. **43** So He called His disciples to *Himself* and said to them, "Assuredly, I say to you that this poor widow has put in more than all those who have given to the treasury;

When young, exposed to many temptations.

1 Tim 5:11–14 But refuse *the* younger widows; for when they have begun to grow wanton against Christ, they desire to marry, **12** having condemnation because they have cast off their first faith. **13** And besides they learn *to be* idle, wandering about from house to house, and not only idle but also gossips and busybodies, saying things which they ought not. **14** Therefore I desire that *the* younger *widows* marry, bear children, manage the house, give no opportunity to the adversary to speak reproachfully.

Believers' relationship to,

Sympathize with them.

Acts 9:39 Then Peter arose and went with them. When he had come, they brought *him* to the upper room. And all the widows stood by him weeping, showing the tunics and garments which Dorcas had made while she was with them.

Give joy to them.

Job 29:13 The blessing of a perishing *man* came upon me, And I caused the widow's heart to sing for joy.

Do not disappoint them.

Job 31:16 "If I have kept the poor from *their* desire, Or caused the eyes of the widow to fail,

The wicked's relationship to,

Do no good to them.

Job 24:21 For he preys on the barren *who* do not bear, And does no good for the widow.

Send them away empty.

Job 22:9 You have sent widows away empty, And the strength of the fatherless was crushed.

Take pledges from.

Job 24:3 They drive away the donkey of the fatherless; They take the widow's ox as a pledge.

Reject the cause of.

Is 1:23 Your princes *are* rebellious, And companions of thieves; Everyone loves bribes, And follows after rewards. They do not defend the fatherless, Nor does the cause of the widow come before them.

Mistreat them.

Ezek 22:7 In you they have made light of father and mother; in your midst they have oppressed the stranger; in you they have mistreated the fatherless and the widow.

Make a prey of.

Is 10:2 To rob the needy of justice, And to take what is right from the poor of My people, That widows may be their prey, And *that* they may rob the fatherless.

Matt 23:14 Woe to you, scribes and Pharisees, hypocrites! For you devour widows' houses, and for a pretense make long prayers. Therefore you will receive greater condemnation.

Slay them.

Ps 94:6 They slay the widow and the stranger, And murder the fatherless.

Curse for perverting judgment of.

Deut 27:19 'Cursed *is* the one who perverts the justice due the stranger, the fatherless, and widow.' "And all the people shall say, 'Amen!'

Woe to those who oppress.

Is 10:1–2 "Woe to those who decree unrighteous decrees, Who write misfortune, *Which* they have prescribed **2** To rob the needy of justice, And to take what is right from the poor of My people, That widows may be their prey, And *that* they may rob the fatherless.

Blessings on those who relieve.

Deut 14:29 And the Levite, because he has no portion nor inheritance with you, and the stranger and the fatherless and the widow who *are* within your gates, may come and eat and be satisfied, that the LORD your God may bless you in all the work of your hand which you do.

A type of Zion in affliction.

Lam 5:3 We have become orphans and waifs, Our mothers *are* like widows.

Were released from all obligation to former husbands.

Rom 7:3 So then if, while *her* husband lives, she marries another man, she will be called an adulteress; but if her husband dies, she is free from that law, so that she is no adulteress, though she has married another man.

Were clothed in mourning after the decease of husbands.

Gen 38:14 So she took off her widow's garments, covered *herself* with a veil and wrapped herself, and sat in an open place which *was* on the way to Timnah; for she saw that Shelah was grown, and she was not given to him as a wife.

Gen 38:19 So she arose and went away, and laid aside her veil and put on the garments of her widowhood.

2 Sam 14:2 And Joab sent to Tekoa and brought from there a wise woman, and said to her, "Please pretend to be a mourner, and put on mourning apparel; do not anoint yourself with oil, but act like a woman who has been mourning a long time for the dead.

2 Sam 14:5 Then the king said to her, "What troubles you?" And she answered, "Indeed I *am* a widow, my husband is dead.

Reproach connected with.

Is 54:4 "Do not fear, for you will not be ashamed; Neither be disgraced, for you will not be put to shame; For you will forget the shame of your youth, And will not remember the reproach of your widowhood anymore.

Increase of, threatened as a punishment.

Ex 22:24 and My wrath will become hot, and I will kill you with the sword; your wives shall be widows, and your children fatherless.

Jer 15:8 Their widows will be increased to Me more than the sand of the seas; I will bring against them, Against the mother of the young men, A plunderer at noonday; I will cause anguish and terror to fall on them suddenly.

Jer 18:21 Therefore deliver up their children to the famine, And pour out their *blood* By the force of the sword; Let their wives *become* widows And bereaved of their children. Let their men be put to death, Their young men *be* slain By the sword in battle.

Laws respecting,

Not to be oppressed.

Ex 22:22 "You shall not afflict any widow or fatherless child.

Deut 27:19 'Cursed *is* the one who perverts the justice due the stranger, the fatherless, and widow.' "And all the people shall say, 'Amen!'

Garment of, not to be taken in pledge by creditors.

Deut 24:17 "You shall not pervert justice due the stranger or the fatherless, nor take a widow's garment as a pledge.

Bound to perform their vows.

Num 30:9 "Also any vow of a widow or a divorced woman, by which she has bound herself, shall stand against her.

Not to intermarry with priests.

Lev 21:14 A widow or a divorced woman or a defiled woman *or* a harlot—these he shall not marry; but he shall take a virgin of his own people as wife.

To be allowed to glean in fields and vineyards.

Deut 24:19 "When you reap your harvest in your field, and forget a sheaf in the field, you shall not go back to get it; it shall be for the stranger, the fatherless, and the widow, that the LORD your God may bless you in all the work of your hands.

To have a share of the triennial tithe.

Deut 14:28–29 "At the end of *every* third year you shall bring out the tithe of your produce of that year and store *it* up within your gates. **29** And the Levite, because he has no portion nor inheritance with you, and the stranger and the fatherless and the widow who *are* within your gates, may come and eat and be satisfied, that the LORD your God may bless you in all the work of your hand which you do.

Deut 26:12–13 "When you have finished laying aside all the tithe of your increase in the third year—the year of tithing—and have given *it* to the Levite, the stranger, the fatherless, and the widow, so that they may eat within your gates and be filled, **13** then you shall say before the LORD your God: 'I have removed the holy *tithe* from *my* house, and also have given them to the Levite, the stranger, the fatherless, and the widow, according to all Your commandments which You have commanded me; I have not transgressed Your commandments, nor have I forgotten *them.*

To share in public rejoicings.

Deut 16:11 You shall rejoice before the LORD your God, you and your son and your daughter, your male servant and your female servant, the Levite who *is* within your gates, the stranger and the fatherless and the widow who *are* among you, at the place where the LORD your God chooses to make His name abide.

Deut 16:14 And you shall rejoice in your feast, you and your son and your daughter, your male servant and your female servant and the Levite, the stranger and the fatherless and the widow, who *are* within your gates.

When daughters of priests and childless, to partake of the holy things.

Lev 22:13 But if the priest's daughter is a widow or divorced, and has no child, and has returned to her father's house as in her youth, she may eat her father's food; but no outsider shall eat it.

When left childless, to be married by their husband's nearest male relative.

Deut 25:5–6 "If brothers dwell together, and one of them dies and has no son, the widow of the dead man shall not be *married* to a stranger outside *the family;* her husband's brother shall go in to her, take her as his wife, and perform the duty of a husband's brother to her. 6 And it shall be *that* the firstborn son which she bears will succeed to the name of his dead brother, that his name may not be blotted out of Israel.

Ruth 3:10–13 Then he said, "Blessed *are* you of the LORD, my daughter! For you have shown more kindness at the end than at the beginning, in that you did not go after young men, whether poor or rich. 11 And now, my daughter, do not fear. I will do for you all that you request, for all the people of my town know that you *are* a virtuous woman. 12 Now it is true that I *am* a close relative; however, there is a relative closer than I. 13 Stay this night, and in the morning it shall be *that* if he will perform the duty of a close relative for you—good; let him do it. But if he does not want to perform the duty for you, then I will perform the duty for you, *as* the LORD lives! Lie down until morning."

Ruth 4:4–5 And I thought to inform you, saying, 'Buy *it* back in the presence of the inhabitants and the elders of my people. If you will redeem *it,* redeem *it;* but if you will not redeem *it, then* tell me, that I may know; for *there is* no one but you to redeem *it,* and I *am* next after you.' " And he said, "I will redeem *it.*" 5 Then Boaz said, "On the day you buy the field from the hand of Naomi, you must also buy *it* from Ruth the Moabitess, the wife of the dead, to perpetuate the name of the dead through his inheritance."

Matt 22:24–26 saying: "Teacher, Moses said that if a man dies, having no children, his brother shall marry his wife and raise up offspring for his brother. 25 Now there were with us seven brothers. The first died after he had married, and having no offspring, left his wife to his brother. 26 Likewise the second also, and the third, even to the seventh.

Allowed to marry again.

Rom 7:3 So then if, while *her* husband lives, she marries another man, she will be called an adulteress; but if her husband dies, she is free from that law, so that she is no adulteress, though she has married another man.

Intermarrying with certain kings was considered treason.

1 Kin 2:21–24 So she said, "Let Abishag the Shunammite be given to Adonijah your brother as wife." 22 And King Solomon answered and said to his mother, "Now why do you ask Abishag the Shunammite for Adonijah? Ask for him the kingdom also—for he *is* my older brother—for him, and for Abiathar the priest, and for Joab the son of Zeruiah." 23 Then King Solomon swore by the LORD, saying, "May God do so to me, and more also, if Adonijah has not spoken this word against his own life! 24 Now therefore, *as* the LORD lives, who has confirmed me and set me

on the throne of David my father, and who has established a house for me, as He promised, Adonijah shall be put to death today!"

Lack of mourning by, considered a great calamity.

Job 27:15 Those who survive him shall be buried in death, And their widows shall not weep,

Ps 78:64 Their priests fell by the sword, And their widows made no lamentation.

Were under the special protection of God.

Deut 10:18 He administers justice for the fatherless and the widow, and loves the stranger, giving him food and clothing.

Ps 68:5 A father of the fatherless, a defender of widows, *Is* God in His holy habitation.

Were frequently oppressed and persecuted.

Job 24:3 They drive away the donkey of the fatherless; They take the widow's ox as a pledge.

Ezek 22:7 In you they have made light of father and mother; in your midst they have oppressed the stranger; in you they have mistreated the fatherless and the widow.

Often devoted themselves entirely to God's service.

Luke 2:37 and this woman *was* a widow of about eighty-four years, who did not depart from the temple, but served *God* with fastings and prayers night and day.

1 Tim 5:10 well reported for good works: if she has brought up children, if she has lodged strangers, if she has washed the saints' feet, if she has relieved the afflicted, if she has diligently followed every good work.

Instances of great generosity in.

1 Kin 17:9–15 "Arise, go to Zarephath, which *belongs* to Sidon, and dwell there. See, I have commanded a widow there to provide for you." 10 So he arose and went to Zarephath. And when he came to the gate of the city, indeed a widow *was* there gathering sticks. And he called to her and said, "Please bring me a little water in a cup, that I may drink." 11 And as she was going to get *it,* he called to her and said, "Please bring me a morsel of bread in your hand." 12 So she said, "As the LORD your God lives, I do not have bread, only a handful of flour in a bin, and a little oil in a jar; and see, I *am* gathering a couple of sticks that I may go in and prepare it for myself and my son, that we may eat it, and die." 13 And Elijah said to her, "Do not fear; go *and* do as you have said, but make me a small cake from it first, and bring *it* to me; and afterward make *some* for yourself and your son. 14 For thus says the LORD God of Israel: 'The bin of flour shall not be used up, nor shall the jar of oil run dry, until the day the LORD sends rain on the earth.' " 15 So she went away and did according to the word of Elijah; and she and he and her household ate for *many* days.

Mark 12:42–43 Then one poor widow came and threw in two mites, which make a quadrans. 43 So He called His disciples to *Himself* and said to them, "Assuredly, I say to you that this poor widow has put in more than all those who have given to the treasury;

Illustrative of

A desolate condition.

Is 47:8–9 "Therefore hear this now, *you who are* given to pleasures, Who dwell securely, Who say in your heart, 'I *am,* and *there is* no one else besides me; I shall not sit *as* a widow, Nor shall I know the loss of children'; **9** But these two *things* shall come to you In a moment, in one day: The loss of children, and widowhood. They shall come upon you in their fullness Because of the multitude of your sorceries, For the great abundance of your enchantments.

Zion in captivity.

Lam 1:1 How lonely sits the city *That was* full of people! *How* like a widow is she, Who *was* great among the nations! The princess among the provinces Has become a slave!

WILD OX

Had two horns.

Deut 33:17 His glory *is like* a firstborn bull, And his horns *like* the horns of the wild ox; Together with them He shall push the peoples To the ends of the earth; They *are* the ten thousands of Ephraim, And they *are* the thousands of Manasseh."

Described as

Intractable in disposition.

Job 39:9–10 "Will the wild ox be willing to serve you? Will he bed by your manger? **10** Can you bind the wild ox in the furrow with ropes? Or will he plow the valleys behind you?

Job 39:12 Will you trust him to bring home your grain, And gather it to your threshing floor?

Of great strength.

Job 39:11 Will you trust him because his strength *is* great? Or will you leave your labor to him?

The young of, remarkable for agility.

Ps 29:6 He makes them also skip like a calf, Lebanon and Sirion like a young wild ox.

Illustrative of

God as strength of psalmist.

Ps 92:10 But my horn You have exalted like a wild ox; I have been anointed with fresh oil.

God as the strength of Israel.

Num 23:22 God brings them out of Egypt; He has strength like a wild ox.

Num 24:8 "God brings him out of Egypt; He has strength like a wild ox; He shall consume the nations, his enemies; He shall break their bones And pierce *them* with his arrows.

The wicked.

Is 34:7 The wild oxen shall come down with them, And the young bulls with the mighty bulls; Their land shall be soaked with blood, And their dust saturated with fatness."

(Horns of) the strength of the descendants of Joseph.

Deut 33:17 His glory *is like* a firstborn bull, And his horns *like* the horns of the wild ox; Together with them He shall push the peoples To the ends of the earth; They *are* the ten thousands of Ephraim, And they *are* the thousands of Manasseh."

(Horns of) the strength of powerful enemies.

Ps 22:21 Save Me from the lion's mouth And from the horns of the wild oxen! You have answered Me.

(The position of its horns) the exaltation of believers.

Ps 92:10 But my horn You have exalted like a wild ox; I have been anointed with fresh oil.

WIND, THE

Variable nature of.

Eccl 1:6 The wind goes toward the south, And turns around to the north; The wind whirls about continually, And comes again on its circuit.

God

Created.

Amos 4:13 For behold, He who forms mountains, And creates the wind, Who declares to man what his thought *is,* And makes the morning darkness, Who treads the high places of the earth— The LORD God of hosts *is* His name.

Restrains.

Job 28:25 To establish a weight for the wind, And apportion the waters by measure.

Ps 107:29 He calms the storm, So that its waves are still.

Brings it forth out of His treasuries.

Ps 135:7 He causes the vapors to ascend from the ends of the earth; He makes lightning for the rain; He brings the wind out of His treasuries.

Jer 10:13 When He utters His voice, *There is* a multitude of waters in the heavens: "And He causes the vapors to ascend from the ends of the earth. He makes lightning for the rain, He brings the wind out of His treasuries."

Raises.

Ps 107:25 For He commands and raises the stormy wind, Which lifts up the waves of the sea.

Jon 4:8 And it happened, when the sun arose, that God prepared a vehement east wind; and the sun beat on Jonah's head, so that he grew faint. Then he wished death for himself, and said, "*It is* better for me to die than to live."

Changes.

Ps 78:26 He caused an east wind to blow in the heavens; And by His power He brought in the south wind.

Calms.

Matt 8:26 But He said to them, "Why are you fearful, O you of little faith?" Then He arose and rebuked the winds and the sea, and there was a great calm.

Matt 14:32 And when they got into the boat, the wind ceased.

Gathers it in His hand.

Prov 30:4 Who has ascended into heaven, or descended? Who has gathered the wind in His fists? Who has bound the waters in a garment? Who has established all the ends of the earth? What *is* His name, and what *is* His Son's name, If you know?

Accomplishes God's purposes.

Ps 148:8 Fire and hail, snow and clouds; Stormy wind, fulfilling His word;

Theory of, above man's comprehension.

John 3:8 The wind blows where it wishes, and you hear the sound of it, but cannot tell where it comes from and where it goes. So is everyone who is born of the Spirit."

Names of, mentioned in Scripture

North.

Prov 25:23 The north wind brings forth rain, And a backbiting tongue an angry countenance.

Song 4:16 Awake, O north *wind,* And come, O south! Blow upon my garden, *That* its spices may flow out. Let my beloved come to his garden And eat its pleasant fruits.

South.

Job 37:17 Why *are* your garments hot, When He quiets the earth by the south *wind?*

Luke 12:55 And when you see the south wind blow, you say, 'There will be hot weather'; and there is.

East.

Job 27:21 The east wind carries him away, and he is gone; It sweeps him out of his place.

Ezek 17:10 Behold, *it is* planted, Will it thrive? Will it not utterly wither when the east wind touches it? It will wither in the garden terrace where it grew." ' "

Hos 13:15 Though he is fruitful among *his* brethren, An east wind shall come; The wind of the LORD shall come up from the wilderness. Then his spring shall become dry, And his fountain shall be dried up. He shall plunder the treasury of every desirable prize.

West.

Ex 10:19 And the LORD turned a very strong west wind, which took the locusts away and blew them into the Red Sea. There remained not one locust in all the territory of Egypt.

Euroclydon.

Acts 27:14 But not long after, a tempestuous head wind arose, called Euroclydon.

Dry wind.

Jer 4:11 At that time it will be said To this people and to Jerusalem, "A dry wind of the desolate heights *blows* in the wilderness Toward the daughter of My people— Not to fan or to cleanse—

Whirlwind. See Whirlwind, The.

Drying nature of.

Gen 8:1 Then God remembered Noah, and every living thing, and all the animals that *were* with him in the ark. And God made a wind to pass over the earth, and the waters subsided.

Ex 14:21 Then Moses stretched out his hand over the sea; and the LORD caused the sea to go *back* by a strong east wind all that night, and made the sea into dry *land,* and the waters were divided.

Is 11:15 The LORD will utterly destroy the tongue of the Sea of Egypt; With His mighty wind He will shake His fist over the River, And strike it in the seven streams, And make *men* cross over dryshod.

Purifying nature of.

Job 37:21 Even now *men* cannot look at the light *when it is* bright in the skies, When the wind has passed and cleared them.

Jer 4:11 At that time it will be said To this people and to Jerusalem, "A dry wind of the desolate heights *blows* in the wilderness Toward the daughter of My people— Not to fan or to cleanse—

When violent, called

Tempest.

Job 9:17 For He crushes me with a tempest, And multiplies my wounds without cause.

Job 27:20 Terrors overtake him like a flood; A tempest steals him away in the night.

Jon 1:4 But the LORD sent out a great wind on the sea, and there was a mighty tempest on the sea, so that the ship was about to be broken up.

Storm.

Job 21:18 They are like straw before the wind, And like chaff that a storm carries away.

Ps 83:15 So pursue them with Your tempest, And frighten them with Your storm.

Stormy wind.

Ps 148:8 Fire and hail, snow and clouds; Stormy wind, fulfilling His word;

Ezek 13:11 say to those who plaster *it* with untempered *mortar,* that it will fall. There will be flooding rain, and you, O great hailstones, shall fall; and a stormy wind shall tear *it* down.

Ezek 13:13 Therefore thus says the Lord GOD: "I will cause a stormy wind to break forth in My fury; and there shall be a flooding rain in My anger, and great hailstones in fury to consume *it.*

Windy storm.

Ps 55:8 I would hasten my escape From the windy storm *and* tempest."

Great and strong wind.

1 Kin 19:11 Then He said, "Go out, and stand on the mountain before the LORD." And behold, the LORD passed by, and a great and strong wind tore into the mountains and broke the rocks in pieces before the LORD, *but* the LORD *was* not in the wind; and after the wind an earthquake, *but* the LORD *was* not in the earthquake;

Mighty wind.

Acts 2:2 And suddenly there came a sound from heaven, as of a rushing mighty wind, and it filled the whole house where they were sitting.

Rev 6:13 And the stars of heaven fell to the earth, as a fig tree drops its late figs when it is shaken by a mighty wind.

Fierce wind.

James 3:4 Look also at ships: although they are so large and are driven by fierce winds, they are turned by a very small rudder wherever the pilot desires.

Rough wind.

Is 27:8 In measure, by sending it away, You contended with it. He removes *it* by His rough wind In the day of the east wind.

Frequently brings rain.

1 Kin 18:44–45 Then it came to pass the seventh *time,* that he said, "There is a cloud, as small as a man's hand, rising out of the sea!" So he said, "Go up, say to Ahab, 'Prepare *your chariot,* and go down before the rain stops you.' " **45** Now it happened in the meantime that the sky became black with clouds and wind, and there was a heavy rain. So Ahab rode away and went to Jezreel.

2 Kin 3:17 For thus says the LORD: 'You shall not see wind, nor shall you see rain; yet that valley shall be filled with water, so that you, your cattle, and your animals may drink.'

Prov 25:23 The north wind brings forth rain, And a backbiting tongue an angry countenance.

Often blighting.

Ps 103:16 For the wind passes over it, and it is gone, And its place remembers it no more.

Is 40:7 The grass withers, the flower fades, Because the breath of the LORD blows upon it; Surely the people *are* grass.

Movement of the trees by it, noticed.

Is 7:2 And it was told to the house of David, saying, "Syria's forces are deployed in Ephraim." So his heart and the heart of his people were moved as the trees of the woods are moved with the wind.

Matt 11:7 As they departed, Jesus began to say to the multitudes concerning John: "What did you go out into the wilderness to see? A reed shaken by the wind?

Rev 6:13 And the stars of heaven fell to the earth, as a fig tree drops its late figs when it is shaken by a mighty wind.

Tempestuousness of,

Raises the sea in waves.

Ps 107:25 For He commands and raises the stormy wind, Which lifts up the waves of the sea.

John 6:18 Then the sea arose because a great wind was blowing.

Drives about the largest ships.

Matt 14:24 But the boat was now in the middle of the sea, tossed by the waves, for the wind was contrary.

Acts 27:18 And because we were exceedingly tempest-tossed, the next *day* they lightened the ship.

James 3:4 Look also at ships: although they are so large and are driven by fierce winds, they are turned by a very small rudder wherever the pilot desires.

Destroys houses.

Job 1:19 and suddenly a great wind came from across the wilderness and struck the four corners of the house, and it fell on the young people, and they are dead; and I alone have escaped to tell you!"

Matt 7:27 and the rain descended, the floods came, and the winds blew and beat on that house; and it fell. And great was its fall."

Miracles connected with,

Locusts brought by.

Ex 10:13 So Moses stretched out his rod over the land of Egypt, and the LORD brought an east wind on the land all that day and all *that* night. When it was morning, the east wind brought the locusts.

Locusts removed by.

Ex 10:19 And the LORD turned a very strong west wind, which took the locusts away and blew them into the

Red Sea. There remained not one locust in all the territory of Egypt.

Red sea divided by.

Ex 14:21 Then Moses stretched out his hand over the sea; and the LORD caused the sea to go *back* by a strong east wind all that night, and made the sea into dry *land*, and the waters were divided.

Quails brought by.

Num 11:31 Now a wind went out from the LORD, and it brought quail from the sea and left *them* fluttering near the camp, about a day's journey on this side and about a day's journey on the other side, all around the camp, and about two cubits above the surface of the ground.

Rocks and mountains torn by.

1 Kin 19:11 Then He said, "Go out, and stand on the mountain before the LORD." And behold, the LORD passed by, and a great and strong wind tore into the mountains and broke the rocks in pieces before the LORD, *but* the LORD *was* not in the wind; and after the wind an earthquake, *but* the LORD *was* not in the earthquake;

Sent because of Jonah.

Jon 1:4 But the LORD sent out a great wind on the sea, and there was a mighty tempest on the sea, so that the ship was about to be broken up.

Calmed by casting out Jonah.

Jon 1:15 So they picked up Jonah and threw him into the sea, and the sea ceased from its raging.

Calmed by Christ.

Matt 8:26 But He said to them, "Why are you fearful, O you of little faith?" Then He arose and rebuked the winds and the sea, and there was a great calm.

Matt 14:32 And when they got into the boat, the wind ceased.

Illustrative of

The operations of the Holy Spirit.

Ezek 37:9 Also He said to me, "Prophesy to the breath, prophesy, son of man, and say to the breath, 'Thus says the Lord GOD: "Come from the four winds, O breath, and breathe on these slain, that they may live." ' "

John 3:8 The wind blows where it wishes, and you hear the sound of it, but cannot tell where it comes from and where it goes. So is everyone who is born of the Spirit."

Acts 2:2 And suddenly there came a sound from heaven, as of a rushing mighty wind, and it filled the whole house where they were sitting.

The life of man.

Job 7:7 Oh, remember that my life *is* a breath! My eye will never again see good.

The speeches of the desperate.

Job 6:26 Do you intend to rebuke *my* words, And the speeches of a desperate one, *which are* as wind?

Terrors that pursue the soul.

Job 30:15 Terrors are turned upon me; They pursue my honor as the wind, And my prosperity has passed like a cloud.

Molded images.

Is 41:29 Indeed they *are* all worthless; Their works *are* nothing; Their molded images *are* wind and confusion.

Iniquity that leads to destruction.

Is 64:6 But we are all like an unclean *thing,* And all our righteousnesses *are* like filthy rags; We all fade as a leaf, And our iniquities, like the wind, Have taken us away.

False doctrines.

Eph 4:14 that we should no longer be children, tossed to and fro and carried about with every wind of doctrine, by the trickery of men, in the cunning craftiness of deceitful plotting,

(Chaff or stubble before) the wicked.

Job 21:18 They are like straw before the wind, And like chaff that a storm carries away.

Ps 1:4 The ungodly *are* not so, But *are* like the chaff which the wind drives away.

(Without rain) one who boasts of a false gift.

Prov 25:14 Whoever falsely boasts of giving *Is like* clouds and wind without rain.

(When destructive) the judgments of God.

Is 27:8 In measure, by sending it away, You contended with it. He removes *it* by His rough wind In the day of the east wind.

Is 29:6 You will be punished by the LORD of hosts With thunder and earthquake and great noise, *With* storm and tempest And the flame of devouring fire.

Is 41:16 You shall winnow them, the wind shall carry them away, And the whirlwind shall scatter them; You shall rejoice in the LORD, *And* glory in the Holy One of Israel.

(Sowing) a course of sin.

Hos 8:7 "They sow the wind, And reap the whirlwind. The stalk has no bud; It shall never produce meal. If it should produce, Aliens would swallow it up.

(Feeding upon) vain hopes.

Hos 12:1 "Ephraim feeds on the wind, And pursues the east wind; He daily increases lies and desolation. Also they make a covenant with the Assyrians, And oil is carried to Egypt.

(Bringing forth) disappointed expectations.

Is 26:18 We have been with child, we have been in pain; We have, as it were, brought forth wind; We have not accomplished any deliverance in the earth, Nor have the inhabitants of the world fallen.

WINE

First mention of.

Gen 9:20–21 And Noah began *to be* a farmer, and he planted a vineyard. **21** Then he drank of the wine and was drunk, and became uncovered in his tent.

Was made of

The juice of the grape.

Gen 49:11 Binding his donkey to the vine, And his donkey's colt to the choice vine, He washed his garments in wine, And his clothes in the blood of grapes.

The juice of the pomegranate.

Song 8:2 I would lead you *and* bring you Into the house of my mother, She *who* used to instruct me. I would cause you to drink of spiced wine, Of the juice of my pomegranate.

Method of producing fruit, first alluded to.

Gen 40:11 Then Pharaoh's cup *was* in my hand; and I took the grapes and pressed them into Pharaoh's cup, and placed the cup in Pharaoh's hand."

Generally made by treading the grapes in a press.

Neh 13:15 In those days I saw *people* in Judah treading wine presses on the Sabbath, and bringing in sheaves, and loading donkeys with wine, grapes, figs, and all *kinds of* burdens, which they brought into Jerusalem on the Sabbath day. And I warned *them* about the day on which they were selling provisions.

Is 63:2–3 Why *is* Your apparel red, And Your garments like one who treads in the winepress? **3** "I have trodden the winepress alone, And from the peoples no one *was* with Me. For I have trodden them in My anger, And trampled them in My fury; Their blood is sprinkled upon My garments, And I have stained all My robes.

Refining of, alluded to.

Is 25:6 And in this mountain The LORD of hosts will make for all people A feast of choice pieces, A feast of wines on the lees, Of fat things full of marrow, Of well-refined wines on the lees.

Improved by age.

Luke 5:39 And no one, having drunk old *wine,* immediately desires new; for he says, 'The old is better.' "

Places celebrated for,

Canaan in general.

Deut 33:28 Then Israel shall dwell in safety, The fountain of Jacob alone, In a land of grain and new wine; His heavens shall also drop dew.

Possessions of Judah.

Gen 49:8 "Judah, you *are he* whom your brothers shall praise; Your hand *shall be* on the neck of your enemies; Your father's children shall bow down before you.

Gen 49:11–12 Binding his donkey to the vine, And his donkey's colt to the choice vine, He washed his garments in wine, And his clothes in the blood of grapes. **12** His eyes *are* darker than wine, And his teeth whiter than milk.

Lebanon.

Hos 14:7 Those who dwell under his shadow shall return; They shall be revived *like* grain, And grow like a vine. Their scent *shall be* like the wine of Lebanon.

Helbon.

Ezek 27:18 Damascus *was* your merchant because of the abundance of goods you made, because of your many luxury items, with the wine of Helbon and with white wool.

Assyria.

2 Kin 18:32 until I come and take you away to a land like your own land, a land of grain and new wine, a land of bread and vineyards, a land of olive groves and honey, that you may live and not die. But do not listen to Hezekiah, lest he persuade you, saying, "The LORD will deliver us."

Is 36:17 until I come and take you away to a land like your own land, a land of grain and new wine, a land of bread and vineyards.

Moab.

Is 16:8–10 For the fields of Heshbon languish, *And* the vine of Sibmah; The lords of the nations have broken down its choice plants, Which have reached to Jazer And wandered through the wilderness. Her branches are stretched out, They are gone over the sea. **9** Therefore I will bewail the vine of Sibmah, With the weeping of Jazer; I will drench you with my tears, O Heshbon and Elealeh; For battle cries have fallen Over your summer fruits and your harvest. **10** Gladness is taken away, And joy from the plentiful field; In the vineyards there will be no singing, Nor will there be shouting; No treaders will tread out wine in the presses; I have made their shouting cease.

Jer 48:32–33 O vine of Sibmah! I will weep for you with the weeping of Jazer. Your plants have gone over the sea, They reach to the sea of Jazer. The plunderer has fallen on your summer fruit and your vintage. **33** Joy and gladness are taken From the plentiful field And from the land of Moab; I have caused wine to fail from the winepresses; No one will tread with joyous shouting— Not joyous shouting!

Many kinds of.

Neh 5:18 Now *that* which was prepared daily *was* one ox *and* six choice sheep. Also fowl were prepared for me, and once every ten days an abundance of all kinds of wine. Yet in spite of this I did not demand the governor's provisions, because the bondage was heavy on this people.

Sweet, esteemed for flavor and strength.

Is 49:26 I will feed those who oppress you with their own flesh, And they shall be drunk with their own blood as with sweet wine. All flesh shall know That I, the LORD, *am* your Savior, And your Redeemer, the Mighty One of Jacob."

Amos 9:13 "Behold, the days are coming," says the LORD, "When the plowman shall overtake the reaper, And the treader of grapes him who sows seed; The mountains shall drip with sweet wine, And all the hills shall flow *with it.*

Mic 6:15 "You shall sow, but not reap; You shall tread the olives, but not anoint yourselves with oil; And *make* sweet wine, but not drink wine.

Red, most esteemed.

Prov 23:31 Do not look on the wine when it is red, When it sparkles in the cup, *When* it swirls around smoothly;

Is 27:2 In that day sing to her, "A vineyard of red wine!

Often spiced to increase its strength, etc.

Prov 9:2 She has slaughtered her meat, She has mixed her wine, She has also furnished her table.

Prov 9:5 "Come, eat of my bread And drink of the wine I have mixed.

Prov 23:30 Those who linger long at the wine, Those who go in search of mixed wine.

Song 8:2 I would lead you *and* bring you Into the house of my mother, She *who* used to instruct me. I would

cause you to drink of spiced wine, Of the juice of my pomegranate.

Uses of,

As a beverage, from the earliest times.

Gen 9:21 Then he drank of the wine and was drunk, and became uncovered in his tent.

Gen 27:25 He said, "Bring *it* near to me, and I will eat of my son's game, so that my soul may bless you." So he brought *it* near to him, and he ate; and he brought him wine, and he drank.

At all feasts and entertainments.

Esth 1:7 And they served drinks in golden vessels, each vessel being different from the other, with royal wine in abundance, according to the generosity of the king.

Esth 5:6 At the banquet of wine the king said to Esther, "What *is* your petition? It shall be granted you. What *is* your request, up to half the kingdom? It shall be done!"

Is 5:12 The harp and the strings, The tambourine and flute, And wine are in their feasts; But they do not regard the work of the LORD, Nor consider the operation of His hands.

Dan 5:1–4 Belshazzar the king made a great feast for a thousand of his lords, and drank wine in the presence of the thousand. **2** While he tasted the wine, Belshazzar gave the command to bring the gold and silver vessels which his father Nebuchadnezzar had taken from the temple which *had been* in Jerusalem, that the king and his lords, his wives, and his concubines might drink from them. **3** Then they brought the gold vessels that had been taken from the temple of the house of God which *had been* in Jerusalem; and the king and his lords, his wives, and his concubines drank from them. **4** They drank wine, and praised the gods of gold and silver, bronze and iron, wood and stone.

John 2:3 And when they ran out of wine, the mother of Jesus said to Him, "They have no wine."

For drink offerings in the worship of God.

Ex 29:40 With the one lamb shall be one-tenth *of an ephah* of flour mixed with one-fourth of a hin of pressed oil, and one-fourth of a hin of wine *as* a drink offering.

Num 15:4–10 then he who presents his offering to the LORD shall bring a grain offering of one-tenth *of an ephah* of fine flour mixed with one-fourth of a hin of oil; **5** and one-fourth of a hin of wine as a drink offering you shall prepare with the burnt offering or the sacrifice, for each lamb. **6** Or for a ram you shall prepare as a grain offering two-tenths *of an ephah* of fine flour mixed with one-third of a hin of oil; **7** and as a drink offering you shall offer one-third of a hin of wine as a sweet aroma to the LORD. **8** And when you prepare a young bull as a burnt offering, or as a sacrifice to fulfill a vow, or as a peace offering to the LORD, **9** then shall be offered with the young bull a grain offering of three-tenths *of an ephah* of fine flour mixed with half a hin of oil; **10** and you shall bring as the drink offering half a hin of wine as an offering made by fire, a sweet aroma to the LORD.

For drink offerings in idolatrous worship.

Deut 32:37–38 He will say: 'Where *are* their gods, The rock in which they sought refuge? **38** Who ate the fat of their sacrifices, *And* drank the wine of their drink offering? Let them rise and help you, *And* be your refuge.

As a medicine.

Luke 10:34 So he went to *him* and bandaged his wounds, pouring on oil and wine; and he set him on his own animal, brought him to an inn, and took care of him.

1 Tim 5:23 No longer drink only water, but use a little wine for your stomach's sake and your frequent infirmities.

Firstfruits of, to be offered to God.

Deut 18:4 The firstfruits of your grain and your new wine and your oil, and the first of the fleece of your sheep, you shall give him.

2 Chr 31:5 As soon as the commandment was circulated, the children of Israel brought in abundance the firstfruits of grain and wine, oil and honey, and of all the produce of the field; and they brought in abundantly the tithe of everything.

With grain and oil, denoted all temporal blessings.

Gen 27:28 Therefore may God give you Of the dew of heaven, Of the fatness of the earth, And plenty of grain and wine.

Gen 27:37 Then Isaac answered and said to Esau, "Indeed I have made him your master, and all his brethren I have given to him as servants; with grain and wine I have sustained him. What shall I do now for you, my son?"

Ps 4:7 You have put gladness in my heart, More than in the season that their grain and wine increased.

Hos 2:8 For she did not know That I gave her grain, new wine, and oil, And multiplied her silver and gold— *Which* they prepared for Baal.

Joel 2:19 The LORD will answer and say to His people, "Behold, I will send you grain and new wine and oil, And you will be satisfied by them; I will no longer make you a reproach among the nations.

Given in abundance to the Jews when obedient.

Hos 2:22 The earth shall answer With grain, With new wine, And with oil; They shall answer Jezreel.

Joel 2:19 The LORD will answer and say to His people, "Behold, I will send you grain and new wine and oil, And you will be satisfied by them; I will no longer make you a reproach among the nations.

Joel 2:24 The threshing floors shall be full of wheat, And the vats shall overflow with new wine and oil.

Zech 9:17 For how great is its goodness And how great its beauty! Grain shall make the young men thrive, And new wine the young women.

The Jews frequently deprived of, as a punishment.

Is 24:7 The new wine fails, the vine languishes, All the merry-hearted sigh.

Is 24:11 *There is* a cry for wine in the streets, All joy is darkened, The mirth of the land is gone.

Hos 2:9 "Therefore I will return and take away My grain in its time And My new wine in its season, And will take back My wool and My linen, *Given* to cover her nakedness.

Joel 1:10 The field is wasted, The land mourns; For the grain is ruined, The new wine is dried up, The oil fails.

Hag 1:11 For I called for a drought on the land and the mountains, on the grain and the new wine and the oil, on whatever the ground brings forth, on men and livestock, and on all the labor of *your* hands."

Hag 2:16 since those *days*, when *one* came to a heap of twenty ephahs, there were *but* ten; when *one* came to the wine vat to draw out fifty baths from the press, there were *but* twenty.

The Jews frequently drank, to excess.

Is 5:11 Woe to those who rise early in the morning, *That* they may follow intoxicating drink; Who continue until night, *till* wine inflames them!

Joel 3:3 They have cast lots for My people, Have given a boy *as payment* for a harlot, And sold a girl for wine, that they may drink.

Amos 6:6 Who drink wine from bowls, And anoint yourselves with the best ointments, But are not grieved for the affliction of Joseph.

In times of scarcity, was mixed with water.

Is 1:22 Your silver has become dross, Your wine mixed with water.

Sometimes mixed with milk as a beverage.

Song 5:1 I have come to my garden, my sister, *my* spouse; I have gathered my myrrh with my spice; I have eaten my honeycomb with my honey; I have drunk my wine with my milk. Eat, O friends! Drink, yes, drink deeply, O beloved ones!

Characterized as

Cheering God and man.

Judg 9:13 But the vine said to them, 'Should I cease my new wine, Which cheers *both* God and men, And go to sway over trees?'

Zech 9:17 For how great is its goodness And how great its beauty! Grain shall make the young men thrive, And new wine the young women.

Gladdening the heart.

Ps 104:15 And wine *that* makes glad the heart of man, Oil to make *his* face shine, And bread *which* strengthens man's heart.

Strengthening.

2 Sam 16:2 And the king said to Ziba, "What do you mean to do with these?" So Ziba said, "The donkeys *are* for the king's household to ride on, the bread and summer fruit for the young men to eat, and the wine for those who are faint in the wilderness to drink."

Making happy.

Esth 1:10 On the seventh day, when the heart of the king was merry with wine, he commanded Mehuman, Biztha, Harbona, Bigtha, Abagtha, Zethar, and Carcas, seven eunuchs who served in the presence of King Ahasuerus,

Eccl 10:19 A feast is made for laughter, And wine makes merry; But money answers everything.

Custom of presenting to travelers.

Gen 14:18 Then Melchizedek king of Salem brought out bread and wine; he *was* the priest of God Most High.

1 Sam 25:18 Then Abigail made haste and took two hundred *loaves* of bread, two skins of wine, five sheep already dressed, five seahs of roasted *grain*, one hundred clusters of raisins, and two hundred cakes of figs, and loaded *them* on donkeys.

Custom of giving, mixed with drugs, to persons in pain or suffering.

Prov 31:6 Give strong drink to him who is perishing, And wine to those who are bitter of heart.

Mark 15:23 Then they gave Him wine mingled with myrrh to drink, but He did not take *it*.

Forbidden to the priests while engaged in the tabernacle.

Lev 10:9 "Do not drink wine or intoxicating drink, you, nor your sons with you, when you go into the tabernacle of meeting, lest you die. *It shall be* a statute forever throughout your generations,

Forbidden to Nazirites during their separation.

Num 6:3 he shall separate himself from wine and *similar* drink; he shall drink neither vinegar made from wine nor vinegar made from *similar* drink; neither shall he drink any grape juice, nor eat fresh grapes or raisins.

The Rechabites never drank.

Jer 35:5–6 Then I set before the sons of the house of the Rechabites bowls full of wine, and cups; and I said to them, "Drink wine." **6** But they said, "We will drink no wine, for Jonadab the son of Rechab, our father, commanded us, saying, 'You shall drink no wine, you nor your sons, forever.

In excess

Forbidden.

Eph 5:18 And do not be drunk with wine, in which is dissipation; but be filled with the Spirit,

Generates anger.

Prov 20:1 Wine *is* a mocker, Strong drink *is* a brawler, And whoever is led astray by it is not wise.

Impairs the health.

1 Sam 25:37 So it was, in the morning, when the wine had gone from Nabal, and his wife had told him these things, that his heart died within him, and he became *like* a stone.

Hos 4:11 "Harlotry, wine, and new wine enslave the heart.

Impairs the judgment and memory.

Prov 31:4–5 *It is* not for kings, O Lemuel, *It is* not for kings to drink wine, Nor for princes intoxicating drink; **5** Lest they drink and forget the law, And pervert the justice of all the afflicted.

Is 28:7 But they also have erred through wine, And through intoxicating drink are out of the way; The priest and the prophet have erred through intoxicating drink, They are swallowed up by wine, They are out of the way through intoxicating drink; They err in vision, they stumble *in* judgment.

Inflames the passions.

Is 5:11 Woe to those who rise early in the morning, *That*

they may follow intoxicating drink; Who continue until night, *till* wine inflames them!

Leads to sorrow and contention.

Prov 23:29–30 Who has woe? Who has sorrow? Who has contentions? Who has complaints? Who has wounds without cause? Who has redness of eyes? **30** Those who linger long at the wine, Those who go in search of mixed wine.

Leads to remorse.

Prov 23:31–32 Do not look on the wine when it is red, When it sparkles in the cup, *When* it swirls around smoothly; **32** At the last it bites like a serpent, And stings like a viper.

An article of extensive commerce.

Ezek 27:18 Damascus *was* your merchant because of the abundance of goods you made, because of your many luxury items, with the wine of Helbon and with white wool.

Was stored in cellars.

1 Chr 27:27 And Shimei the Ramathite *was* over the vineyards, and Zabdi the Shiphmite was over the produce of the vineyards for the supply of wine.

Was kept in skins.

1 Sam 25:18 Then Abigail made haste and took two hundred *loaves* of bread, two skins of wine, five sheep already dressed, five seahs of roasted *grain*, one hundred clusters of raisins, and two hundred cakes of figs, and loaded *them* on donkeys.

Hab 2:15 "Woe to him who gives drink to his neighbor, Pressing *him to* your bottle, Even to make *him* drunk, That you may look on his nakedness!

Consequence of putting (when new), into old skins.

Mark 2:22 And no one puts new wine into old wineskins; or else the new wine bursts the wineskins, the wine is spilled, and the wineskins are ruined. But new wine must be put into new wineskins."

Water miraculously turned into.

John 2:9 When the master of the feast had tasted the water that was made wine, and did not know where it came from (but the servants who had drawn the water knew), the master of the feast called the bridegroom.

Illustrative of

The blood of Christ.

Matt 26:27–29 Then He took the cup, and gave thanks, and gave *it* to them, saying, "Drink from it, all of you. **28** For this is My blood of the new covenant, which is shed for many for the remission of sins. **29** But I say to you, I will not drink of this fruit of the vine from now on until that day when I drink it new with you in My Father's kingdom."

The blessing of the gospel.

Is 25:6 And in this mountain The LORD of hosts will make for all people A feast of choice pieces, A feast of wines on the lees, Of fat things full of marrow, Of well-refined wines on the lees.

Is 55:1 "Ho! Everyone who thirsts, Come to the waters; And you who have no money, Come, buy and eat. Yes, come, buy wine and milk Without money and without price.

The wrath and judgments of God.

Ps 60:3 You have shown Your people hard things; You have made us drink the wine of confusion.

Ps 75:8 For in the hand of the LORD *there is* a cup, And the wine is red; It is fully mixed, and He pours it out; Surely its dregs shall all the wicked of the earth Drain *and* drink down.

Jer 13:12–14 "Therefore you shall speak to them this word: 'Thus says the LORD God of Israel: "Every bottle shall be filled with wine." ' " "And they will say to you, 'Do we not certainly know that every bottle will be filled with wine?' **13** "Then you shall say to them, 'Thus says the LORD: "Behold, I will fill all the inhabitants of this land—even the kings who sit on David's throne, the priests, the prophets, and all the inhabitants of Jerusalem—with drunkenness! **14** And I will dash them one against another, even the fathers and the sons together," says the LORD. "I will not pity nor spare nor have mercy, but will destroy them." ' "

Jer 25:15–18 For thus says the LORD God of Israel to me: "Take this wine cup of fury from My hand, and cause all the nations, to whom I send you, to drink it. **16** And they will drink and stagger and go mad because of the sword that I will send among them." **17** Then I took the cup from the LORD's hand, and made all the nations drink, to whom the LORD had sent me: **18** Jerusalem and the cities of Judah, its kings and its princes, to make them a desolation, an astonishment, a hissing, and a curse, as *it is* this day;

The abominations of the last days.

Rev 17:2 with whom the kings of the earth committed fornication, and the inhabitants of the earth were made drunk with the wine of her fornication."

Rev 18:3 For all the nations have drunk of the wine of the wrath of her fornication, the kings of the earth have committed fornication with her, and the merchants of the earth have become rich through the abundance of her luxury."

Violence and destruction.

Prov 4:17 For they eat the bread of wickedness, And drink the wine of violence.

WINTER

God makes.

Ps 74:17 You have set all the borders of the earth; You have made summer and winter.

Yearly return of, promised.

Gen 8:22 "While the earth remains, Seedtime and harvest, Cold and heat, Winter and summer, And day and night Shall not cease."

Coldness and inclemency of, noticed.

Prov 20:4 The lazy *man* will not plow because of winter; He will beg during harvest and *have* nothing.

John 10:22 Now it was the Feast of Dedication in Jerusalem, and it was winter.

Unsuited for

Traveling.

Matt 24:20 And pray that your flight may not be in winter or on the Sabbath.

2 Tim 4:21 Do your utmost to come before winter. Eu-

bulus greets you, as well as Pudens, Linus, Claudia, and all the brethren.

Navigation.

Acts 27:9 Now when much time had been spent, and sailing was now dangerous because the Fast was already over, Paul advised them,

Ships were laid up in port during.

Acts 27:12 And because the harbor was not suitable to winter in, the majority advised to set sail from there also, if by any means they could reach Phoenix, a harbor of Crete opening toward the southwest and northwest, *and* winter *there.*

Acts 28:11 After three months we sailed in an Alexandrian ship whose figurehead was the Twin Brothers, which had wintered at the island.

The Jews frequently had special houses for.

Jer 36:22 Now the king was sitting in the winter house in the ninth month, with *a fire* burning on the hearth before him.

Amos 3:15 I will destroy the winter house along with the summer house; The houses of ivory shall perish, And the great houses shall have an end," Says the LORD.

Illustrative of seasons of spiritual adversity.

Song 2:11 For lo, the winter is past, The rain is over *and* gone.

WISDOM

The fear of the Lord is.

Job 28:28 And to man He said, 'Behold, the fear of the Lord, that *is* wisdom, And to depart from evil *is* understanding.' "

Prov 15:33 The fear of the LORD *is* the instruction of wisdom, And before honor *is* humility.

Described.

Prov 1:2–6 To know wisdom and instruction, To perceive the words of understanding, **3** To receive the instruction of wisdom, Justice, judgment, and equity; **4** To give prudence to the simple, To the young man knowledge and discretion— **5** A wise *man* will hear and increase learning, And a man of understanding will attain wise counsel, **6** To understand a proverb and an enigma, The words of the wise and their riddles.

Unbelievers despise.

Prov 1:7 The fear of the LORD *is* the beginning of knowledge, *But* fools despise wisdom and instruction.

Evaluating one's use of time is.

Ps 90:12 So teach *us* to number our days, That we may gain a heart of wisdom.

Solomon sought.

1 Kin 3:9 Therefore give to Your servant an understanding heart to judge Your people, that I may discern between good and evil. For who is able to judge this great people of Yours?"

Paul's prayer for believers to have spiritual.

Eph 1:17–18 that the God of our Lord Jesus Christ, the Father of glory, may give to you the spirit of wisdom and revelation in the knowledge of Him, **18** the eyes of your understanding being enlightened; that you may know what is the hope of His calling, what are the riches of the glory of His inheritance in the saints,

Believers should ask God for.

James 1:5 If any of you lacks wisdom, let him ask of God, who gives to all liberally and without reproach, and it will be given to him.

Demonstrated by good conduct and works.

James 3:13 Who *is* wise and understanding among you? Let him show by good conduct *that* his works *are done* in the meekness of wisdom.

Qualities of godly.

James 3:17 But the wisdom that is from above is first pure, then peaceable, gentle, willing to yield, full of mercy and good fruits, without partiality and without hypocrisy.

WIVES

Not to be selected from among the ungodly.

Gen 24:3 and I will make you swear by the LORD, the God of heaven and the God of the earth, that you will not take a wife for my son from the daughters of the Canaanites, among whom I dwell;

Gen 26:34–35 When Esau was forty years old, he took as wives Judith the daughter of Beeri the Hittite, and Basemath the daughter of Elon the Hittite. 35 And they were a grief of mind to Isaac and Rebekah.

Gen 28:1 Then Isaac called Jacob and blessed him, and charged him, and said to him: "You shall not take a wife from the daughters of Canaan.

Union of husbands and, established by God.

Gen 2:24 Therefore a man shall leave his father and mother and be joined to his wife, and they shall become one flesh.

Excellent ones are crowns of their husbands.

Prov 12:4 An excellent wife *is* the crown of her husband, But she who causes shame *is* like rottenness in his bones.

Duties to husbands

To love them.

Titus 2:4 that they admonish the young women to love their husbands, to love their children,

To reverence them.

Eph 5:33 Nevertheless let each one of you in particular so love his own wife as himself, and let the wife *see* that she respects *her* husband.

To be faithful to them.

1 Cor 7:3–5 Let the husband render to his wife the affection due her, and likewise also the wife to her husband. 4 The wife does not have authority over her own body, but the husband *does.* And likewise the husband does not have authority over his own body, but the wife *does.* 5 Do not deprive one another except with consent for a time, that you may give yourselves to fasting and prayer; and come together again so that Satan does not tempt you because of your lack of self-control.

1 Cor 7:10 Now to the married I command, *yet* not I but the Lord: A wife is not to depart from *her* husband.

To be submissive to them.

Gen 3:16 To the woman He said: "I will greatly multiply your sorrow and your conception; In pain you shall bring forth children; Your desire *shall be* for your husband, And he shall rule over you."

Eph 5:22 Wives, submit to your own husbands, as to the Lord.

Eph 5:24 Therefore, just as the church is subject to Christ, so *let* the wives *be* to their own husbands in everything.

1 Pet 3:1 Wives, likewise, *be* submissive to your own husbands, that even if some do not obey the word, they, without a word, may be won by the conduct of their wives,

To obey them.

1 Cor 14:34 Let your women keep silent in the churches, for they are not permitted to speak; but *they are* to be submissive, as the law also says.

Titus 2:5 to be discreet, chaste, homemakers, good, obedient to their own husbands, that the word of God may not be blasphemed.

To remain with them for life.

Rom 7:2–3 For the woman who has a husband is bound by the law to *her* husband as long as he lives. But if the husband dies, she is released from the law of *her* husband. 3 So then if, while *her* husband lives, she marries another man, she will be called an adulteress; but if her husband dies, she is free from that law, so that she is no adulteress, though she has married another man.

Should be adorned

Not with adornment.

1 Tim 2:9 in like manner also, that the women adorn themselves in modest apparel, with propriety and moderation, not with braided hair or gold or pearls or costly clothing,

1 Pet 3:3 Do not let your adornment be *merely* outward—arranging the hair, wearing gold, or putting on *fine* apparel—

With modesty and sobriety.

1 Tim 2:9 in like manner also, that the women adorn themselves in modest apparel, with propriety and moderation, not with braided hair or gold or pearls or costly clothing,

With a gentle and quiet spirit.

1 Pet 3:4–5 rather *let it be* the hidden person of the heart, with the incorruptible *beauty* of a gentle and quiet spirit, which is very precious in the sight of God. 5 For in this manner, in former times, the holy women who trusted in God also adorned themselves, being submissive to their own husbands,

With good works.

1 Tim 2:10 but, which is proper for women professing godliness, with good works.

1 Tim 5:10 well reported for good works: if she has brought up children, if she has lodged strangers, if she has washed the saints' feet, if she has relieved the afflicted, if she has diligently followed every good work.

Good ones

Are from the Lord.

Prov 19:14 Houses and riches *are* an inheritance from fathers, But a prudent wife *is* from the LORD.

Indicate the favor of God.

Prov 18:22 He who finds a wife finds a good *thing*, And obtains favor from the LORD.

Are a blessing to husbands.

Prov 12:4 An excellent wife *is* the crown of her husband, But she who causes shame *is* like rottenness in his bones.

Prov 31:10 Who can find a virtuous wife? For her worth *is* far above rubies.

Prov 31:12 She does him good and not evil All the days of her life.

Bring honor on husbands.

Prov 31:23 Her husband is known in the gates, When he sits among the elders of the land.

Secure confidence of husbands.

Prov 31:11 The heart of her husband safely trusts her; So he will have no lack of gain.

Are praised by husbands.

Prov 31:28 Her children rise up and call her blessed; Her husband *also*, and he praises her:

Are diligent and prudent.

Prov 31:13–27 She seeks wool and flax, And willingly works with her hands. **14** She is like the merchant ships, She brings her food from afar. **15** She also rises while it is yet night, And provides food for her household, And a portion for her maidservants. **16** She considers a field and buys it; From her profits she plants a vineyard. **17** She girds herself with strength, And strengthens her arms. **18** She perceives that her merchandise *is* good, And her lamp does not go out by night. **19** She stretches out her hands to the distaff, And her hand holds the spindle. **20** She extends her hand to the poor, Yes, she reaches out her hands to the needy. **21** She is not afraid of snow for her household, For all her household *is* clothed with scarlet. **22** She makes tapestry for herself; Her clothing *is* fine linen and purple. **23** Her husband is known in the gates, When he sits among the elders of the land. **24** She makes linen garments and sells *them*, And supplies sashes for the merchants. **25** Strength and honor *are* her clothing; She shall rejoice in time to come. **26** She opens her mouth with wisdom, And on her tongue *is* the law of kindness. **27** She watches over the ways of her household, And does not eat the bread of idleness.

Are benevolent to the poor.

Prov 31:20 She extends her hand to the poor, Yes, she reaches out her hands to the needy.

Duty of, to unbelieving husbands.

1 Cor 7:13–14 And a woman who has a husband who does not believe, if he is willing to live with her, let her not divorce him. **14** For the unbelieving husband is sanctified by the wife, and the unbelieving wife is sanctified by the husband; otherwise your children would be unclean, but now they are holy.

1 Cor 7:16 For how do you know, O wife, whether you will save *your* husband? Or how do you know, O husband, whether you will save *your* wife?

1 Pet 3:1–2 Wives, likewise, *be* submissive to your own husbands, that even if some do not obey the word, they, without a word, may be won by the conduct of their wives, **2** when they observe your chaste conduct *accompanied* by fear.

Should be silent in the churches.

1 Cor 14:34 Let your women keep silent in the churches, for they are not permitted to speak; but *they are* to be submissive, as the law also says.

Should seek religious instruction from their husbands.

1 Cor 14:35 And if they want to learn something, let them ask their own husbands at home; for it is shameful for women to speak in church.

Of ministers, should be exemplary.

1 Tim 3:11 Likewise, *their* wives *must be* reverent, not slanderers, temperate, faithful in all things.

Good—examples of,

The wife of Manoah.

Judg 13:10 Then the woman ran in haste and told her husband, and said to him, "Look, the Man who came to me the *other* day has just now appeared to me!"

Orpah and Ruth.

Ruth 1:4 Now they took wives of the women of Moab: the name of the one *was* Orpah, and the name of the other Ruth. And they dwelt there about ten years.

Ruth 1:8 And Naomi said to her two daughters-in-law, "Go, return each to her mother's house. The LORD deal kindly with you, as you have dealt with the dead and with me.

Abigail.

1 Sam 25:3 The name of the man *was* Nabal, and the name of his wife Abigail. And *she was* a woman of good understanding and beautiful appearance; but the man *was* harsh and evil in *his* doings. He *was of the house of* Caleb.

Esther.

Esth 2:15–17 Now when the turn came for Esther the daughter of Abihail the uncle of Mordecai, who had taken her as his daughter, to go in to the king, she requested nothing but what Hegai the king's eunuch, the custodian of the women, advised. And Esther obtained favor in the sight of all who saw her. **16** So Esther was taken to King Ahasuerus, into his royal palace, in the tenth month, which *is* the month of Tebeth, in the seventh year of his reign. **17** The king loved Esther more than all the *other* women, and she obtained grace and favor in his sight more than all the virgins; so he set the royal crown upon her head and made her queen instead of Vashti.

Elizabeth.

Luke 1:6 And they were both righteous before God, walking in all the commandments and ordinances of the Lord blameless.

Priscilla.

Acts 18:2 And he found a certain Jew named Aquila, born in Pontus, who had recently come from Italy with his wife Priscilla (because Claudius had commanded all the Jews to depart from Rome); and he came to them.

Acts 18:26 So he began to speak boldly in the synagogue. When Aquila and Priscilla heard him, they took him aside and explained to him the way of God more accurately.

Sarah.

1 Pet 3:6 as Sarah obeyed Abraham, calling him lord, whose daughters you are if you do good and are not afraid with any terror.

Bad—examples of,

Samson's wife.

Judg 14:15–17 But it came to pass on the seventh day that they said to Samson's wife, "Entice your husband, that he may explain the riddle to us, or else we will burn you and your father's house with fire. Have you invited us in order to take what is ours? *Is that* not *so?*" **16** Then Samson's wife wept on him, and said, "You only hate me! You do not love me! You have posed a riddle to the sons of my people, but you have not explained *it* to me." And he said to her, "Look, I have not explained *it* to my father or my mother; so should I explain *it* to you?" **17** Now she had wept on him the seven days while their feast lasted. And it happened on the seventh day that he told her, because she pressed him so much. Then she explained the riddle to the sons of her people.

Michal.

2 Sam 6:16 Now as the ark of the LORD came into the City of David, Michal, Saul's daughter, looked through a window and saw King David leaping and whirling before the LORD; and she despised him in her heart.

Jezebel.

1 Kin 21:25 But there was no one like Ahab who sold himself to do wickedness in the sight of the LORD, because Jezebel his wife stirred him up.

Zeresh.

Esth 5:14 Then his wife Zeresh and all his friends said to him, "Let a gallows be made, fifty cubits high, and in the morning suggest to the king that Mordecai be hanged on it; then go merrily with the king to the banquet." And the thing pleased Haman; so he had the gallows made.

Job's wife.

Job 2:9 Then his wife said to him, "Do you still hold fast to your integrity? Curse God and die!"

Herodias.

Mark 6:17 For Herod himself had sent and laid hold of John, and bound him in prison for the sake of Herodias, his brother Philip's wife; for he had married her.

Sapphira.

Acts 5:1–2 But a certain man named Ananias, with Sapphira his wife, sold a possession. **2** And he kept back *part* of the proceeds, his wife also being aware *of it,* and brought a certain part and laid *it* at the apostles' feet.

WOLF, THE

Ravenous nature of.

Gen 49:27 "Benjamin is a ravenous wolf; In the morning he shall devour the prey, And at night he shall divide the spoil."

Fierce destroyers, particularly in the evening.

Jer 5:6 Therefore a lion from the forest shall slay them, A wolf of the deserts shall destroy them; A leopard will watch over their cities. Everyone who goes out from there shall be torn in pieces, Because their transgressions are many; Their backslidings have increased.

Hab 1:8 Their horses also are swifter than leopards, And more fierce than evening wolves. Their chargers charge ahead; Their cavalry comes from afar; They fly as the eagle *that* hastens to eat.

Destructive to flocks of sheep.

John 10:12 But a hireling, *he who is* not the shepherd, one who does not own the sheep, sees the wolf coming and leaves the sheep and flees; and the wolf catches the sheep and scatters them.

Illustrative of

The wicked.

Matt 10:16 "Behold, I send you out as sheep in the midst of wolves. Therefore be wise as serpents and harmless as doves.

Luke 10:3 Go your way; behold, I send you out as lambs among wolves.

Wicked rulers.

Ezek 22:27 Her princes in her midst *are* like wolves tearing the prey, to shed blood, to destroy people, and to get dishonest gain.

Zeph 3:3 Her princes in her midst *are* roaring lions; Her judges *are* evening wolves That leave not a bone till morning.

False prophets.

Matt 7:15 "Beware of false prophets, who come to you in sheep's clothing, but inwardly they are ravenous wolves.

Acts 20:29 For I know this, that after my departure savage wolves will come in among you, not sparing the flock.

The devil.

John 10:12 But a hireling, *he who is* not the shepherd, one who does not own the sheep, sees the wolf coming and leaves the sheep and flees; and the wolf catches the sheep and scatters them.

The tribe of Benjamin.

Gen 49:27 "Benjamin is a ravenous wolf; In the morning he shall devour the prey, And at night he shall divide the spoil."

Fierce enemies.

Jer 5:6 Therefore a lion from the forest shall slay them, A wolf of the deserts shall destroy them; A leopard will watch over their cities. Everyone who goes out from there shall be torn in pieces, Because their transgressions are many; Their backslidings have increased.

Hab 1:8 Their horses also are swifter than leopards, And more fierce than evening wolves. Their chargers charge ahead; Their cavalry comes from afar; They fly as the eagle *that* hastens to eat.

(Taming of) the change effected by conversion.

Is 11:6 "The wolf also shall dwell with the lamb, The leopard shall lie down with the young goat, The calf and the young lion and the fatling together; And a little child shall lead them.

Is 65:25 The wolf and the lamb shall feed together, The lion shall eat straw like the ox, And dust *shall be* the serpent's food. They shall not hurt nor destroy in all My holy mountain," Says the LORD.

WOMAN. *SEE ALSO* WIVES

Origin and source of the name.

Gen 2:23 And Adam said: "This *is* now bone of my bones And flesh of my flesh; She shall be called Woman, Because she was taken out of Man."

Originally made

By God in His own image.

Gen 1:27 So God created man in His *own* image; in the image of God He created him; male and female He created them.

From one of Adam's ribs.

Gen 2:21–22 And the LORD God caused a deep sleep to fall on Adam, and he slept; and He took one of his ribs, and closed up the flesh in its place. **22** Then the rib which the LORD God had taken from man He made into a woman, and He brought her to the man.

For man.

1 Cor 11:9 Nor was man created for the woman, but woman for the man.

To be a helper for man.

Gen 2:18 And the LORD God said, "*It is* not good that man should be alone; I will make him a helper comparable to him."

Gen 2:20 So Adam gave names to all cattle, to the birds of the air, and to every beast of the field. But for Adam there was not found a helper comparable to him.

Subordinate to man.

1 Cor 11:3 But I want you to know that the head of every man is Christ, the head of woman *is* man, and the head of Christ *is* God.

To be the glory of man.

1 Cor 11:7 For a man indeed ought not to cover *his* head, since he is the image and glory of God; but woman is the glory of man.

Deceived by Satan.

Gen 3:1–6 Now the serpent was more cunning than any beast of the field which the LORD God had made. And he said to the woman, "Has God indeed said, 'You shall not eat of every tree of the garden'?" **2** And the woman said to the serpent, "We may eat the fruit of the trees of the garden; **3** but of the fruit of the tree which *is* in the midst of the garden, God has said, 'You shall not eat it, nor shall you touch it, lest you die.' " **4** Then the serpent said to the woman, "You will not surely die. **5** For God knows that in the day you eat of it your eyes will be opened, and you will be like God, knowing good and evil." **6** So when the woman saw that the tree *was* good for food, that it *was* pleasant to the eyes, and a tree desirable to make *one* wise, she took of its fruit and ate. She also gave to her husband with her, and he ate.

2 Cor 11:3 But I fear, lest somehow, as the serpent deceived Eve by his craftiness, so your minds may be corrupted from the simplicity that is in Christ.

1 Tim 2:14 And Adam was not deceived, but the woman being deceived, fell into transgression.

Led man to disobey God.

Gen 3:6 So when the woman saw that the tree *was* good for food, that it *was* pleasant to the eyes, and a tree desirable to make *one* wise, she took of its fruit and ate. She also gave to her husband with her, and he ate.

Gen 3:11–12 And He said, "Who told you that you *were* naked? Have you eaten from the tree of which I commanded you that you should not eat?" **12** Then the man said, "The woman whom You gave *to be* with me, she gave me of the tree, and I ate."

Curse pronounced on.

Gen 3:16 To the woman He said: "I will greatly multiply your sorrow and your conception; In pain you shall bring forth children; Your desire *shall be* for your husband, And he shall rule over you."

Salvation promised through the seed of.

Gen 3:15 And I will put enmity Between you and the woman, And between your seed and her Seed; He shall bruise your head, And you shall bruise His heel."

Is 7:14 Therefore the Lord Himself will give you a sign: Behold, the virgin shall conceive and bear a Son, and shall call His name Immanuel.

Safety in childbirth promised to the faithful and holy.

1 Tim 2:15 Nevertheless she will be saved in childbearing if they continue in faith, love, and holiness, with self-control.

Characterized as

Weaker than man.

1 Pet 3:7 Husbands, likewise, dwell with *them* with understanding, giving honor to the wife, as to the weaker vessel, and as *being* heirs together of the grace of life, that your prayers may not be hindered.

Timid.

Is 19:16 In that day Egypt will be like women, and will be afraid and fear because of the waving of the hand of the LORD of hosts, which He waves over it.

Jer 50:37 A sword *is* against their horses, Against their chariots, And against all the mixed peoples who *are* in her midst; And they will become like women. A sword *is* against her treasures, and they will be robbed.

Jer 51:30 The mighty men of Babylon have ceased fighting, They have remained in their strongholds; Their might has failed, They became *like* women; They have burned her dwelling places, The bars of her *gate* are broken.

Nah 3:13 Surely, your people in your midst *are* women! The gates of your land are wide open for your enemies; Fire shall devour the bars of your *gates*.

Loving and affectionate.

2 Sam 1:26 I am distressed for you, my brother Jonathan; You have been very pleasant to me; Your love to me was wonderful, Surpassing the love of women.

Tender and constant to her children.

Is 49:15 "Can a woman forget her nursing child, And not have compassion on the son of her womb? Surely they may forget, Yet I will not forget you.

Lam 4:10 The hands of the compassionate women Have

cooked their own children; They became food for them In the destruction of the daughter of my people.

To wear her hair long as a covering.

1 Cor 11:15 But if a woman has long hair, it is a glory to her; for *her* hair is given to her for a covering.

Virtuous, held in high estimation.

Ruth 3:11 And now, my daughter, do not fear. I will do for you all that you request, for all the people of my town know that you *are* a virtuous woman.

Prov 31:10 Who can find a virtuous wife? For her worth *is* far above rubies.

Prov 31:30 Charm *is* deceitful and beauty *is* passing, But a woman *who* fears the LORD, she shall be praised.

Could be

Fond of self-indulgence.

Is 32:9–11 Rise up, you women who are at ease, Hear my voice; You complacent daughters, Give ear to my speech. **10** In a year and *some* days You will be troubled, you complacent women; For the vintage will fail, The gathering will not come. **11** Tremble, you *women* who are at ease; Be troubled, you complacent ones; Strip yourselves, make yourselves bare, And gird *sackcloth* on *your* waists.

Subtle and deceitful.

Prov 7:10 And there a woman met him, *With* the attire of a harlot, and a crafty heart.

Eccl 7:26 And I find more bitter than death The woman whose heart *is* snares and nets, Whose hands *are* fetters. He who pleases God shall escape from her, But the sinner shall be trapped by her.

Gullible and easily led into error.

2 Tim 3:6 For of this sort are those who creep into households and make captives of gullible women loaded down with sins, led away by various lusts,

Zealous in promoting superstition and idolatry.

Jer 7:18 The children gather wood, the fathers kindle the fire, and the women knead dough, to make cakes for the queen of heaven; and *they* pour out drink offerings to other gods, that they may provoke Me to anger.

Ezek 13:17 "Likewise, son of man, set your face against the daughters of your people, who prophesy out of their own heart; prophesy against them,

Ezek 13:23 Therefore you shall no longer envision futility nor practice divination; for I will deliver My people out of your hand, and you shall know that I *am* the LORD." ' "

Active in instigating to sin.

Num 31:15–16 And Moses said to them: "Have you kept all the women alive? **16** Look, these *women* caused the children of Israel, through the counsel of Balaam, to trespass against the LORD in the incident of Peor, and there was a plague among the congregation of the LORD.

1 Kin 21:25 But there was no one like Ahab who sold himself to do wickedness in the sight of the LORD, because Jezebel his wife stirred him up.

Neh 13:26 Did not Solomon king of Israel sin by these things? Yet among many nations there was no king like him, who was beloved of his God; and God

made him king over all Israel. Nevertheless pagan women caused even him to sin.

Generally wore a veil in the presence of men.

Gen 24:65 for she had said to the servant, "Who *is* this man walking in the field to meet us?" The servant said, "It *is* my master." So she took a veil and covered herself.

Generally lived in a separate apartment or tent.

Gen 18:9 Then they said to him, "Where *is* Sarah your wife?" So he said, "Here, in the tent."

Gen 24:67 Then Isaac brought her into his mother Sarah's tent; and he took Rebekah and she became his wife, and he loved her. So Isaac was comforted after his mother's *death.*

Esth 2:9 Now the young woman pleased him, and she obtained his favor; so he readily gave beauty preparations to her, besides her allowance. Then seven choice maidservants were provided for her from the king's palace, and he moved her and her maidservants to the best *place* in the house of the women.

Esth 2:11 And every day Mordecai paced in front of the court of the women's quarters, to learn of Esther's welfare and what was happening to her.

Of distinction

Fair and graceful.

Gen 12:11 And it came to pass, when he was close to entering Egypt, that he said to Sarai his wife, "Indeed I know that you *are* a woman of beautiful countenance.

Gen 24:16 Now the young woman *was* very beautiful to behold, a virgin; no man had known her. And she went down to the well, filled her pitcher, and came up.

Song 1:8 If you do not know, O fairest among women, Follow in the footsteps of the flock, And feed your little goats Beside the shepherds' tents.

Amos 8:13 "In that day the fair virgins And strong young men Shall faint from thirst.

Haughty.

Is 3:16 Moreover the LORD says: "Because the daughters of Zion are haughty, And walk with outstretched necks And wanton eyes, Walking and mincing *as* they go, Making a jingling with their feet,

Fond of dress and finery.

Is 3:17–23 Therefore the Lord will strike with a scab The crown of the head of the daughters of Zion, And the LORD will uncover their secret parts." **18** In that day the Lord will take away the finery: The jingling anklets, the scarves, and the crescents; **19** The pendants, the bracelets, and the veils; **20** The headdresses, the leg ornaments, and the headbands; The perfume boxes, the charms, **21** and the rings; The nose jewels, **22** the festal apparel, and the mantles; The outer garments, the purses, **23** and the mirrors; The fine linen, the turbans, and the robes.

Wore their hair plaited and adorned with gold and pearls.

Is 3:24 And so it shall be: Instead of a sweet smell there will be a stench; Instead of a sash, a rope; Instead of well-set hair, baldness; Instead of a rich robe, a girding of sackcloth; And branding instead of beauty.

1 Tim 2:9 in like manner also, that the women adorn themselves in modest apparel, with propriety and moderation, not with braided hair or gold or pearls or costly clothing,

Of the poorer classes, tanned from exposure to the sun.

Song 1:5–6 I *am* dark, but lovely, O daughters of Jerusalem, Like the tents of Kedar, Like the curtains of Solomon. **6** Do not look upon me, because I *am* dark, Because the sun has tanned me. My mother's sons were angry with me; They made me the keeper of the vineyards, *But* my own vineyard I have not kept.

Young,

Called maiden or girl.

Ex 2:8 And Pharaoh's daughter said to her, "Go." So the maiden went and called the child's mother.

Luke 8:51–52 When He came into the house, He permitted no one to go in except Peter, James, and John, and the father and mother of the girl. **52** Now all wept and mourned for her; but He said, "Do not weep; she is not dead, but sleeping."

Called virgins.

Gen 24:16 Now the young woman *was* very beautiful to behold, a virgin; no man had known her. And she went down to the well, filled her pitcher, and came up.

Lam 1:4 The roads to Zion mourn Because no one comes to the set feasts. All her gates are desolate; Her priests sigh, Her virgins are afflicted, And she *is* in bitterness.

Were happy and rejoicing.

Judg 11:34 When Jephthah came to his house at Mizpah, there was his daughter, coming out to meet him with timbrels and dancing; and she *was his* only child. Besides her he had neither son nor daughter.

Judg 21:21 and watch; and just when the daughters of Shiloh come out to perform their dances, then come out from the vineyards, and every man catch a wife for himself from the daughters of Shiloh; then go to the land of Benjamin.

Jer 31:13 "Then shall the virgin rejoice in the dance, And the young men and the old, together; For I will turn their mourning to joy, Will comfort them, And make them rejoice rather than sorrow.

Zech 9:17 For how great is its goodness And how great its beauty! Grain shall make the young men thrive, And new wine the young women.

Were fond of ornaments.

Jer 2:32 Can a virgin forget her ornaments, *Or* a bride her attire? Yet My people have forgotten Me days without number.

Required to learn from and imitate their elders.

Titus 2:4 that they admonish the young women to love their husbands, to love their children,

Inherited parents' property when there was no male heir.

Num 27:8 And you shall speak to the children of Israel, saying: 'If a man dies and has no son, then you shall cause his inheritance to pass to his daughter.

Could not marry without consent of parents.

Gen 24:3–4 and I will make you swear by the LORD, the God of heaven and the God of the earth, that you will not take a wife for my son from the daughters of the Canaanites, among whom I dwell; **4** but you shall go to my country and to my family, and take a wife for my son Isaac."

Gen 34:6 Then Hamor the father of Shechem went out to Jacob to speak with him.

Ex 22:17 If her father utterly refuses to give her to him, he shall pay money according to the bride-price of virgins.

Considered it a calamity to remain unmarried.

Judg 11:37 Then she said to her father, "Let this thing be done for me: let me alone for two months, that I may go and wander on the mountains and bewail my virginity, my friends and I."

Ps 78:63 The fire consumed their young men, And their maidens were not given in marriage.

Is 4:1 And in that day seven women shall take hold of one man, saying, "We will eat our own food and wear our own apparel; Only let us be called by your name, To take away our reproach."

Sometimes taken captive.

Lam 1:18 "The LORD is righteous, For I rebelled against His commandment. Hear now, all peoples, And behold my sorrow; My virgins and my young men Have gone into captivity.

Ezek 30:17–18 The young men of Aven and Pi Beseth shall fall by the sword, And these *cities* shall go into captivity. **18** At Tehaphnehes the day shall also be darkened, When I break the yokes of Egypt there. And her arrogant strength shall cease in her; As for her, a cloud shall cover her, And her daughters shall go into captivity.

Punishment for seducing, when betrothed.

Deut 22:23–27 "If a young woman *who is* a virgin is betrothed to a husband, and a man finds her in the city and lies with her, **24** then you shall bring them both out to the gate of that city, and you shall stone them to death with stones, the young woman because she did not cry out in the city, and the man because he humbled his neighbor's wife; so you shall put away the evil from among you. **25** "But if a man finds a betrothed young woman in the countryside, and the man forces her and lies with her, then only the man who lay with her shall die. **26** But you shall do nothing to the young woman; *there is* in the young woman no sin *deserving* of death, for just as when a man rises against his neighbor and kills him, even so *is* this matter. **27** For he found her in the countryside, *and* the betrothed young woman cried out, but *there was* no one to save her.

Punishment for seducing, when not betrothed.

Ex 22:16–17 "If a man entices a virgin who is not betrothed, and lies with her, he shall surely pay the bride-price for her *to be* his wife. **17** If her father utterly refuses to give her to him, he shall pay money according to the bride-price of virgins.

Deut 22:28–29 "If a man finds a young woman *who is* a virgin, who is not betrothed, and he seizes her and lies with her, and they are found out, **29** then the man who lay with her shall give to the young woman's father fifty *shekels* of silver, and she shall be his wife because he has humbled her; he shall not be permitted to divorce her all his days.

Often treated with great cruelty in war.

Deut 32:25 The sword shall destroy outside; *There shall be* terror within For the young man and virgin, The nursing child with the man of gray hairs.

Lam 2:21 "Young and old lie On the ground in the streets; My virgins and my young men Have fallen by the sword; You have slain *them* in the day of Your anger, You have slaughtered *and* not pitied.

Lam 5:11 They ravished the women in Zion, The maidens in the cities of Judah.

Of distinction, dressed in robes of various colors.

2 Sam 13:18 Now she had on a robe of many colors, for the king's virgin daughters wore such apparel. And his servant put her out and bolted the door behind her.

Ps 45:14 She shall be brought to the King in robes of many colors; The virgins, her companions who follow her, shall be brought to You.

Were required to hear and obey the law.

Josh 8:35 There was not a word of all that Moses had commanded which Joshua did not read before all the assembly of Israel, with the women, the little ones, and the strangers who were living among them.

Had a court of the tabernacle assigned to them.

Ex 38:8 He made the laver of bronze and its base of bronze, from the bronze mirrors of the serving women who assembled at the door of the tabernacle of meeting.

1 Sam 2:22 Now Eli was very old; and he heard everything his sons did to all Israel, and how they lay with the women who assembled at the door of the tabernacle of meeting.

Allowed to join in the temple music from the time of David.

1 Chr 25:5–6 All these *were* the sons of Heman the king's seer in the words of God, to exalt his horn. For God gave Heman fourteen sons and three daughters. **6** All these *were* under the direction of their father for the music *in* the house of the LORD, with cymbals, stringed instruments, and harps, for the service of the house of God. Asaph, Jeduthun, and Heman *were* under the authority of the king.

Ezra 2:65 besides their male and female servants, of whom *there were* seven thousand three hundred and thirty-seven; and they had two hundred men and women singers.

Neh 7:67 besides their male and female servants, of whom *there were* seven thousand three hundred and thirty-seven; and they had two hundred and forty-five men and women singers.

Forms of employment,

Household work.

Gen 18:6 So Abraham hurried into the tent to Sarah and said, "Quickly, make ready three measures of fine meal; knead *it* and make cakes."

Prov 31:15 She also rises while it is yet night, And pro-

vides food for her household, And a portion for her maidservants.

Agriculture.

Ruth 2:8 Then Boaz said to Ruth, "You will listen, my daughter, will you not? Do not go to glean in another field, nor go from here, but stay close by my young women.

Song 1:6 Do not look upon me, because I *am* dark, Because the sun has tanned me. My mother's sons were angry with me; They made me the keeper of the vineyards, *But* my own vineyard I have not kept.

Tending sheep.

Gen 29:9 Now while he was still speaking with them, Rachel came with her father's sheep, for she was a shepherdess.

Ex 2:16 Now the priest of Midian had seven daughters. And they came and drew water, and they filled the troughs to water their father's flock.

Drawing and carrying water.

Gen 24:11 And he made his camels kneel down outside the city by a well of water at evening time, the time when women go out to draw *water.*

Gen 24:13 Behold, *here* I stand by the well of water, and the daughters of the men of the city are coming out to draw water.

Gen 24:15–16 And it happened, before he had finished speaking, that behold, Rebekah, who was born to Bethuel, son of Milcah, the wife of Nahor, Abraham's brother, came out with her pitcher on her shoulder. **16** Now the young woman *was* very beautiful to behold, a virgin; no man had known her. And she went down to the well, filled her pitcher, and came up.

1 Sam 9:11 As they went up the hill to the city, they met some young women going out to draw water, and said to them, "Is the seer here?"

John 4:7 A woman of Samaria came to draw water. Jesus said to her, "Give Me a drink."

Grinding grain.

Matt 24:41 Two *women will be* grinding at the mill: one will be taken and the other left.

Luke 17:35 Two *women* will be grinding together: the one will be taken and the other left.

Spinning.

Prov 31:13–14 She seeks wool and flax, And willingly works with her hands. **14** She is like the merchant ships, She brings her food from afar.

Embroidery.

Prov 31:22 She makes tapestry for herself; Her clothing *is* fine linen and purple.

Celebrating the victories of the nation.

Ex 15:20–21 Then Miriam the prophetess, the sister of Aaron, took the timbrel in her hand; and all the women went out after her with timbrels and with dances. **21** And Miriam answered them: "Sing to the LORD, For He has triumphed gloriously! The horse and its rider He has thrown into the sea!"

Judg 11:34 When Jephthah came to his house at Mizpah, there was his daughter, coming out to meet him with timbrels and dancing; and she *was his* only child. Besides her he had neither son nor daughter.

1 Sam 18:6–7 Now it had happened as they were coming *home*, when David was returning from the slaughter of the Philistine, that the women had come out of all the cities of Israel, singing and dancing, to meet King Saul, with tambourines, with joy, and with musical instruments. **7** So the women sang as they danced, and said: "Saul has slain his thousands, And David his ten thousands."

Attending funerals as mourners.

Jer 9:17 Thus says the LORD of hosts: "Consider and call for the mourning women, That they may come; And send for skillful wailing women, That they may come.

Jer 9:20 Yet hear the word of the LORD, O women, And let your ear receive the word of His mouth; Teach your daughters wailing, And everyone her neighbor a lamentation.

Vows of, when married, not binding upon the husband.

Num 30:6–8 "If indeed she takes a husband, while bound by her vows or by a rash utterance from her lips by which she bound herself, **7** and her husband hears *it*, and makes no response to her on the day that he hears, then her vows shall stand, and her agreements by which she bound herself shall stand. **8** But if her husband overrules her on the day that he hears *it*, he shall make void her vow which she took and what she uttered with her lips, by which she bound herself, and the LORD will release her.

Unfaithfulness of, when married, discovered by the waters of jealousy. Num 5:14–28

Punishment for injuring, when with child.

Ex 21:22–25 "If men fight, and hurt a woman with child, so that she gives birth prematurely, yet no harm follows, he shall surely be punished accordingly as the woman's husband imposes on him; and he shall pay as the judges *determine*. **23** But if *any* harm follows, then you shall give life for life, **24** eye for eye, tooth for tooth, hand for hand, foot for foot, **25** burn for burn, wound for wound, stripe for stripe.

To be governed by, Jews considered a calamity.

Is 3:12 *As for* My people, children *are* their oppressors, And women rule over them. O My people! Those who lead you cause *you* to err, And destroy the way of your paths."

To be slain by, considered a great disgrace.

Judg 9:54 Then he called quickly to the young man, his armorbearer, and said to him, "Draw your sword and kill me, lest men say of me, 'A woman killed him.' " So his young man thrust him through, and he died.

Considered a valuable captive in war.

Deut 20:14 But the women, the little ones, the livestock, and all that is in the city, all its spoil, you shall plunder for yourself; and you shall eat the enemies' plunder which the LORD your God gives you.

1 Sam 30:2 and had taken captive the women and those who *were* there, from small to great; they did not kill anyone, but carried *them* away and went their way.

Often wounded or killed in war.

2 Kin 8:12 And Hazael said, "Why is my lord weeping?" He answered, "Because I know the evil that you will do to the children of Israel: Their strong-

holds you will set on fire, and their young men you will kill with the sword; and you will dash their children, and rip open their women with child."

Lam 5:11 They ravished the women in Zion, The maidens in the cities of Judah.

Ezek 9:6 Utterly slay old *and* young men, maidens and little children and women; but do not come near anyone on whom *is* the mark; and begin at My sanctuary." So they began with the elders who *were* before the temple.

Hos 13:16 Samaria is held guilty, For she has rebelled against her God. They shall fall by the sword, Their infants shall be dashed in pieces, And their women with child ripped open.

Illustrative of

(Gloriously arrayed) the people of God.

Ps 45:13 The royal daughter *is* all glorious within *the* palace; Her clothing *is* woven with gold.

Gal 4:26 but the Jerusalem above is free, which is the mother of us all.

Rev 12:1 Now a great sign appeared in heaven: a woman clothed with the sun, with the moon under her feet, and on her head a garland of twelve stars.

(Delicate) backsliding Israel.

Jer 6:2 I have likened the daughter of Zion To a lovely and delicate woman.

(Chaste and holy) believers.

Song 1:3 Because of the fragrance of your good ointments, Your name *is* ointment poured forth; Therefore the virgins love you.

2 Cor 11:2 For I am jealous for you with godly jealousy. For I have betrothed you to one husband, that I may present *you as* a chaste virgin to Christ.

Rev 14:4 These are the ones who were not defiled with women, for they are virgins. These are the ones who follow the Lamb wherever He goes. These were redeemed from *among* men, *being* firstfruits to God and to the Lamb.

(Lewd) religious apostasy.

Rev 17:4 The woman was arrayed in purple and scarlet, and adorned with gold and precious stones and pearls, having in her hand a golden cup full of abominations and the filthiness of her fornication.

Rev 17:18 And the woman whom you saw is that great city which reigns over the kings of the earth."

(Wise) those who know Christ.

Matt 25:1–2 "Then the kingdom of heaven shall be likened to ten virgins who took their lamps and went out to meet the bridegroom. **2** Now five of them were wise, and five *were* foolish.

Matt 25:4 but the wise took oil in their vessels with their lamps.

(Foolish) merely professing Christians.

Matt 25:1–3 "Then the kingdom of heaven shall be likened to ten virgins who took their lamps and went out to meet the bridegroom. **2** Now five of them were wise, and five *were* foolish. **3** Those who *were* foolish took their lamps and took no oil with them,

(At ease and careless) a state of carnal security.

Is 32:9 Rise up, you women who are at ease, Hear my

voice; You complacent daughters, Give ear to my speech.

Is 32:11 Tremble, you *women* who are at ease; Be troubled, you complacent ones; Strip yourselves, make yourselves bare, And gird *sackcloth* on *your* waists.

(Forsaken) Israel in her captivity.

Is 54:6 For the LORD has called you Like a woman forsaken and grieved in spirit, Like a youthful wife when you were refused," Says your God.

WORK

Instituted by God before the Fall.

Gen 2:15 Then the LORD God took the man and put him in the garden of Eden to tend and keep it.

Attitude of believers in their.

Col 3:22–23 Bondservants, obey in all things your masters according to the flesh, not with eyeservice, as men-pleasers, but in sincerity of heart, fearing God. **23** And whatever you do, do it heartily, as to the Lord and not to men,

Commitment to, a testimony to unbelievers.

1 Thess 4:11 that you also aspire to lead a quiet life, to mind your own business, and to work with your own hands, as we commanded you,

Paul's instructions concerning those who would not.

2 Thess 3:10–12 For even when we were with you, we commanded you this: If anyone will not work, neither shall he eat. **11** For we hear that there are some who walk among you in a disorderly manner, not working at all, but are busybodies. **12** Now those who are such we command and exhort through our Lord Jesus Christ that they work in quietness and eat their own bread.

WORKS. *SEE* SALVATION, NOT BY WORKS.

WORSHIP

Of God

Defined.

John 4:20–24 Our fathers worshiped on this mountain, and you *Jews* say that in Jerusalem is the place where one ought to worship." **21** Jesus said to her, "Woman, believe Me, the hour is coming when you will neither on this mountain, nor in Jerusalem, worship the Father. **22** You worship what you do not know; we know what we worship, for salvation is of the Jews. **23** But the hour is coming, and now is, when the true worshipers will worship the Father in spirit and truth; for the Father is seeking such to worship Him. **24** God *is* Spirit, and those who worship Him must worship in spirit and truth."

Corrupted.

2 Kin 21:3 For he rebuilt the high places which Hezekiah his father had destroyed; he raised up altars for Baal, and made a wooden image, as Ahab king of Israel had done; and he worshiped all the host of heaven and served them.

2 Kin 21:21 So he walked in all the ways that his father had walked; and he served the idols that his father had served, and worshiped them.

Rom 1:25 who exchanged the truth of God for the lie, and worshiped and served the creature rather than the Creator, who is blessed forever. Amen.

Elijah's object lesson in. **1 Kin 18:21–39**

Of Christ by

Angels.

Heb 1:6 But when He again brings the firstborn into the world, He says: *"Let all the angels of God worship Him."*

Wise men.

Matt 2:1–2 Now after Jesus was born in Bethlehem of Judea in the days of Herod the king, behold, wise men from the East came to Jerusalem, **2** saying, "Where is He who has been born King of the Jews? For we have seen His star in the East and have come to worship Him."

Matt 2:11 And when they had come into the house, they saw the young Child with Mary His mother, and fell down and worshiped Him. And when they had opened their treasures, they presented gifts to Him: gold, frankincense, and myrrh.

The man born blind.

John 9:30–38 The man answered and said to them, "Why, this is a marvelous thing, that you do not know where He is from; yet He has opened my eyes! **31** Now we know that God does not hear sinners; but if anyone is a worshiper of God and does His will, He hears him. **32** Since the world began it has been unheard of that anyone opened the eyes of one who was born blind. **33** If this Man were not from God, He could do nothing." **34** They answered and said to him, "You were completely born in sins, and are you teaching us?" And they cast him out. **35** Jesus heard that they had cast him out; and when He had found him, He said to him, "Do you believe in the Son of God?" **36** He answered and said, "Who is He, Lord, that I may believe in Him?" **37** And Jesus said to him, "You have both seen Him and it is He who is talking with you." **38** Then he said, "Lord, I believe!" And he worshiped Him.

The disciples.

Matt 28:16–17 Then the eleven disciples went away into Galilee, to the mountain which Jesus had appointed for them. **17** When they saw Him, they worshiped Him; but some doubted.

The heavenly choir.

Rev 4:10–11 the twenty-four elders fall down before Him who sits on the throne and worship Him who lives forever and ever, and cast their crowns before the throne, saying: **11** "You are worthy, O Lord, To receive glory and honor and power; For You created all things, And by Your will they exist and were created."

YEAR OF JUBILEE, THE

Occurred every fiftieth year.

Lev 25:8 'And you shall count seven sabbaths of years for yourself, seven times seven years; and the time of the seven sabbaths of years shall be to you forty-nine years.

Lev 25:10 And you shall consecrate the fiftieth year, and proclaim liberty throughout *all* the land to all its inhabitants. It shall be a Jubilee for you; and each of you shall return to his possession, and each of you shall return to his family.

Began on the Day of Atonement.

Lev 25:9 Then you shall cause the trumpet of the Jubilee to sound on the tenth *day* of the seventh month; on the Day of Atonement you shall make the trumpet to sound throughout all your land.

Other names for,

Year of liberty.

Ezek 46:17 But if he gives a gift of some of his inheritance to one of his servants, it shall be his until the year of liberty, after which it shall return to the prince. But his inheritance shall belong to his sons; it shall become theirs.

Year of the redeemed.

Is 63:4 For the day of vengeance *is* in My heart, And the year of My redeemed has come.

Acceptable year.

Is 61:2 To proclaim the acceptable year of the LORD, And the day of vengeance of our God; To comfort all who mourn,

Was especially holy.

Lev 25:12 For it *is* the Jubilee; it shall be holy to you; you shall eat its produce from the field.

Proclaimed by trumpets.

Lev 25:9 Then you shall cause the trumpet of the Jubilee to sound on the tenth *day* of the seventh month; on the Day of Atonement you shall make the trumpet to sound throughout all your land.

Ps 89:15 Blessed *are* the people who know the joyful sound! They walk, O LORD, in the light of Your countenance.

Enactments respecting,

Cessation of all field labor.

Lev 25:11 That fiftieth year shall be a Jubilee to you; in it you shall neither sow nor reap what grows of its own accord, nor gather *the grapes* of your untended vine.

The fruits of the earth to be common property.

Lev 25:12 For it *is* the Jubilee; it shall be holy to you; you shall eat its produce from the field.

Redemption of sold property.

Lev 25:23–27 'The land shall not be sold permanently, for the land *is* Mine; for you *are* strangers and sojourners with Me. 24 And in all the land of your possession you shall grant redemption of the land. 25 'If one of your brethren becomes poor, and has sold *some* of his possession, and if his redeeming relative comes to redeem it, then he may redeem what his brother sold. 26 Or if the man has no one to redeem it, but he himself becomes able to redeem it, 27 then let him count the years since its sale, and restore the remainder to the man to whom he sold it, that he may return to his possession.

Restoration of all inheritances.

Lev 25:10 And you shall consecrate the fiftieth year, and proclaim liberty throughout *all* the land to all its inhabitants. It shall be a Jubilee for you; and each of you shall return to his possession, and each of you shall return to his family.

Lev 25:13 'In this Year of Jubilee, each of you shall return to his possession.

Lev 25:28 But if he is not able to have *it* restored to himself, then what was sold shall remain in the hand of him who bought it until the Year of Jubilee; and in the Jubilee it shall be released, and he shall return to his possession.

Lev 27:24 In the Year of Jubilee the field shall return to him from whom it was bought, to the one who *owned* the land as a possession.

Release of Hebrew servants.

Lev 25:40–41 As a hired servant *and* a sojourner he shall be with you, *and* shall serve you until the Year of Jubilee. 41 And *then* he shall depart from you—he and his children with him—and shall return to his own family. He shall return to the possession of his fathers.

Lev 25:54 And if he is not redeemed in these *years,* then he shall be released in the Year of Jubilee—he and his children with him.

Houses in walled cities not redeemed within a year, exempted from the benefit of.

Lev 25:30 But if it is not redeemed within the space of a full year, then the house in the walled city shall belong permanently to him who bought it, throughout his generations. It shall not be released in the Jubilee.

Sale of property calculated from.

Lev 25:15–16 According to the number of years after the Jubilee you shall buy from your neighbor, and according to the number of years of crops he shall sell to you. 16 According to the multitude of years you shall increase its price, and according to the fewer number of years you shall diminish its price; for he sells to you *according* to the number *of the years* of the crops.

Value of devoted property calculated from.

Lev 27:14–23 'And when a man dedicates his house *to be* holy to the LORD, then the priest shall set a value for it, whether it is good or bad; as the priest values it, so it shall stand. **15** If he who dedicated it *wants to* redeem his house, then he must add one-fifth of the money of your valuation to it, and it shall be his. **16** 'If a man dedicates to the LORD *part* of a field of his possession, then your valuation shall be according to the seed for it. A homer of barley seed *shall be valued* at fifty shekels of silver. **17** If he dedicates his field from the Year of Jubilee, according to your valuation it shall stand. **18** But if he dedicates his field after the Jubilee, then the priest shall reckon to him the money due according to the years that remain till the Year of Jubilee, and it shall be deducted from your valuation. **19** And if he who dedicates the field ever wishes to redeem it, then he must add one-fifth of the money of your valuation to it, and it shall belong to him. **20** But if he does not want to redeem the field, or if he has sold the field to another man, it shall not be redeemed anymore; **21** but the field, when it is released in the Jubilee, shall be holy to the LORD, as a devoted field; it shall be the possession of the priest. **22** 'And if a man dedicates to the LORD a field which he has bought, which is not the field of his possession, **23** then the priest shall reckon to him the worth of your valuation, up to the Year of Jubilee, and he shall give your valuation on that day *as* a holy *offering* to the LORD.

Illustrative of the gospel.

Is 61:1–2 "The Spirit of the Lord GOD *is* upon Me, Because the LORD has anointed Me To preach good tidings to the poor; He has sent Me to heal the brokenhearted, To proclaim liberty to the captives, And the opening of the prison to *those who are* bound; **2** To proclaim the acceptable year of the LORD, And the day of vengeance of our God; To comfort all who mourn,

Luke 4:18–19 *"The Spirit of the LORD is upon Me, Because He has anointed Me To preach the gospel to the poor; He has sent Me to heal the brokenhearted, To proclaim liberty to the captives And recovery of sight to the blind, To set at liberty those who are oppressed;* **19** *To proclaim the acceptable year of the LORD."*

YEARS

The sun and moon appointed to mark out.

Gen 1:14 Then God said, "Let there be lights in the firmament of the heavens to divide the day from the night; and let them be for signs and seasons, and for days and years;

Early computation of time by.

Gen 5:3 And Adam lived one hundred and thirty years, and begot *a son* in his own likeness, after his image, and named him Seth.

Divided into

Seasons.

Gen 8:22 "While the earth remains, Seedtime and har-

vest, Cold and heat, Winter and summer, And day and night Shall not cease."

Months.

Gen 7:11 In the six hundredth year of Noah's life, in the second month, the seventeenth day of the month, on that day all the fountains of the great deep were broken up, and the windows of heaven were opened.

1 Chr 27:1 And the children of Israel, according to their number, the heads of fathers' *houses,* the captains of thousands and hundreds and their officers, served the king in every matter of the *military* divisions. *These divisions* came in and went out month by month throughout all the months of the year, each division *having* twenty-four thousand.

Weeks.

Luke 18:12 I fast twice a week; I give tithes of all that I possess.'

Days.

Esth 9:27 the Jews established and imposed it upon themselves and their descendants and all who would join them, that without fail they should celebrate these two days every year, according to the written *instructions* and according to the *prescribed* time,

References to, during the patriarchal age.

Gen 7:11 In the six hundredth year of Noah's life, in the second month, the seventeenth day of the month, on that day all the fountains of the great deep were broken up, and the windows of heaven were opened.

Gen 7:24 And the waters prevailed on the earth one hundred and fifty days.

Gen 8:13 And it came to pass in the six hundred and first year, in the first *month,* the first *day* of the month, that the waters were dried up from the earth; and Noah removed the covering of the ark and looked, and indeed the surface of the ground was dry.

Gen 8:3 And the waters receded continually from the earth. At the end of the hundred and fifty days the waters decreased.

Beginning of, changed after the exodus.

Ex 12:2 "This month *shall be* your beginning of months; it *shall be* the first month of the year to you.

Remarkable ones

Sabbatical.

Lev 25:4 but in the seventh year there shall be a sabbath of solemn rest for the land, a sabbath to the LORD. You shall neither sow your field nor prune your vineyard.

Jubilee.

Lev 25:11 That fiftieth year shall be a Jubilee to you; in it you shall neither sow nor reap what grows of its own accord, nor gather *the grapes* of your untended vine.

In prophetic computation, days and weeks reckoned as.

Dan 9:27 Then he shall confirm a covenant with many for one week; But in the middle of the week He shall bring an end to sacrifice and offering. And on the wing of abominations shall be one who makes desolate, Even until the consummation, which is determined, Is poured out on the desolate."

Dan 12:11–12 "And from the time *that* the daily *sacrifice* is taken away, and the abomination of desolation is set up, *there shall be* one thousand two hundred and ninety days. **12** Blessed *is* he who waits, and comes to the one thousand three hundred and thirty-five days.

Illustrative of

(Became of age) manhood.

Heb 11:24 By faith Moses, when he became of age, refused to be called the son of Pharaoh's daughter,

(Well advanced in) old age.

Luke 1:7 But they had no child, because Elizabeth was barren, and they were both well advanced in years.

(Being full of) old age.

Gen 25:8 Then Abraham breathed his last and died in a good old age, an old man and full *of years,* and was gathered to his people.

(Acceptable) the time of the gospel.

Is 61:2 To proclaim the acceptable year of the LORD, And the day of vengeance of our God; To comfort all who mourn,

Luke 4:19 *To proclaim the acceptable year of the LORD."*

(Of the right hand of the Most High) prosperity.

Ps 77:10 And I said, "This *is* my anguish; *But I will remember* the years of the right hand of the Most High."

(Of the redeemed) redemption by Christ.

Is 63:4 For the day of vengeance *is* in My heart, And the year of My redeemed has come.

(Of punishment) severe judgments.

Jer 11:23 and there shall be no remnant of them, for I will bring catastrophe on the men of Anathoth, *even* the year of their punishment.' "

Jer 23:12 "Therefore their way shall be to them Like slippery *ways;* In the darkness they shall be driven on And fall in them; For I will bring disaster on them, The year of their punishment," says the LORD.

(Of recompences) judgments.

Is 34:8 For *it is* the day of the LORD's vengeance, The year of recompense for the cause of Zion.

YOUTH

Eagle as symbol for.

Ps 103:5 Who satisfies your mouth with good *things,* So *that* your youth is renewed like the eagle's.

Is 40:29–31 He gives power to the weak, And to *those who have* no might He increases strength. **30** Even the youths shall faint and be weary, And the young men shall utterly fall, **31** But those who wait on the LORD Shall renew *their* strength; They shall mount up with wings like eagles, They shall run and not be weary, They shall walk and not faint.

Of Jesus, briefly described.

Luke 2:41–52 His parents went to Jerusalem every year at the Feast of the Passover. **42** And when He was twelve years old, they went up to Jerusalem according to the custom of the feast. **43** When they had finished the days, as they returned, the Boy Jesus lingered behind in Jerusalem. And Joseph and His mother did not know *it;* **44** but supposing Him to have been in the company, they went a day's journey, and sought Him among *their* relatives and acquaintances. **45** So when they did not find Him, they returned to Jerusalem, seeking Him. **46** Now so it was *that* after three days they found Him in the temple, sitting in the midst of the teachers, both listening to them and asking them questions. **47** And all who heard Him were astonished at His understanding and answers. **48** So when they saw Him, they were amazed; and His mother said to Him, "Son, why have You done this to us? Look, Your father and I have sought You anxiously." **49** And He said to them, "Why did you seek Me? Did you not know that I must be about My Father's business?" **50** But they did not understand the statement which He spoke to them. **51** Then He went down with them and came to Nazareth, and was subject to them, but His mother kept all these things in her heart. **52** And Jesus increased in wisdom and stature, and in favor with God and men.

Need not hinder one's ministry.

1 Tim 4:12 Let no one despise your youth, but be an example to the believers in word, in conduct, in love, in spirit, in faith, in purity.

Z

ZEAL

Christ an example of.

Ps 69:9 Because zeal for Your house has eaten me up, And the reproaches of those who reproach You have fallen on me.

John 2:17 Then His disciples remembered that it was written, *"Zeal for Your house has eaten Me up."*

Godly sorrow leads to.

2 Cor 7:10–11 For godly sorrow produces repentance *leading* to salvation, not to be regretted; but the sorrow of the world produces death. 11 For observe this very thing, that you sorrowed in a godly manner: What diligence it produced in you, *what* clearing *of yourselves, what* indignation, *what* fear, *what* vehement desire, *what* zeal, *what* vindication! In all *things* you proved yourselves to be clear in this matter.

Of believers is ardent.

Ps 119:139 My zeal has consumed me, Because my enemies have forgotten Your words.

Provokes others to do good.

2 Cor 9:2 for I know your willingness, about which I boast of you to the Macedonians, that Achaia was ready a year ago; and your zeal has stirred up the majority.

Should be exhibited

In spirit.

Rom 12:11 not lagging in diligence, fervent in spirit, serving the Lord;

In well-doing.

Gal 4:18 But it is good to be zealous in a good thing always, and not only when I am present with you.

Titus 2:14 who gave Himself for us, that He might redeem us from every lawless deed and purify for Himself *His* own special people, zealous for good works.

In desiring the salvation of others.

Acts 26:29 And Paul said, "I would to God that not only you, but also all who hear me today, might become both almost and altogether such as I am, except for these chains."

Rom 10:1 Brethren, my heart's desire and prayer to God for Israel is that they may be saved.

In contending for the faith.

Jude 1:3 Beloved, while I was very diligent to write to you concerning our common salvation, I found it necessary to write to you exhorting you to contend earnestly for the faith which was once for all delivered to the saints.

In missionary labors.

Rom 15:19 in mighty signs and wonders, by the power of the Spirit of God, so that from Jerusalem and round about to Illyricum I have fully preached the gospel of Christ.

Rom 15:23 But now no longer having a place in these parts, and having a great desire these many years to come to you,

For the glory of God.

Num 25:11 "Phinehas the son of Eleazar, the son of Aaron the priest, has turned back My wrath from the children of Israel, because he was zealous with My zeal among them, so that I did not consume the children of Israel in My zeal.

Num 25:13 and it shall be to him and his descendants after him a covenant of an everlasting priesthood, because he was zealous for his God, and made atonement for the children of Israel.' "

For the welfare of other believers.

Col 4:13 For I bear him witness that he has a great zeal for you, and those who are in Laodicea, and those in Hierapolis.

Against idolatry. **2 Kin 23:4–14**

Sometimes wrongly directed.

2 Sam 21:2 So the king called the Gibeonites and spoke to them. Now the Gibeonites *were* not of the children of Israel, but of the remnant of the Amorites; the children of Israel had sworn protection to them, but Saul had sought to kill them in his zeal for the children of Israel and Judah.

Acts 22:3–4 "I am indeed a Jew, born in Tarsus of Cilicia, but brought up in this city at the feet of Gamaliel, taught according to the strictness of our fathers' law, and was zealous toward God as you all are today. 4 I persecuted this Way to the death, binding and delivering into prisons both men and women,

Phil 3:6 concerning zeal, persecuting the church; concerning the righteousness which is in the law, blameless.

Sometimes not according to knowledge.

Acts 21:20 And when they heard *it*, they glorified the Lord. And they said to him, "You see, brother, how many myriads of Jews there are who have believed, and they are all zealous for the law;

Rom 10:2 For I bear them witness that they have a zeal for God, but not according to knowledge.

Gal 1:14 And I advanced in Judaism beyond many of my contemporaries in my own nation, being more exceedingly zealous for the traditions of my fathers.

Ungodly men sometimes pretend.

2 Kin 10:16 Then he said, "Come with me, and see my zeal for the LORD." So they had him ride in his chariot.

Matt 23:15 "Woe to you, scribes and Pharisees, hypocrites! For you travel land and sea to win one proselyte, and when he is won, you make him twice as much a son of hell as yourselves.

Exhortation to.

Rom 12:11 not lagging in diligence, fervent in spirit, serving the Lord;

Rev 3:19 As many as I love, I rebuke and chasten. Therefore be zealous and repent.

Holy—exemplified by

Phinehas.

Num 25:11 "Phinehas the son of Eleazar, the son of Aaron the priest, has turned back My wrath from the children of Israel, because he was zealous with My zeal among them, so that I did not consume the children of Israel in My zeal.

Num 25:13 and it shall be to him and his descendants after him a covenant of an everlasting priesthood, because he was zealous for his God, and made atonement for the children of Israel.' "

Josiah.

2 Kin 23:19–25 Now Josiah also took away all the shrines of the high places that *were* in the cities of Samaria, which the kings of Israel had made to provoke the LORD to anger; and he did to them according to all the deeds he had done in Bethel. **20** He executed all the priests of the high places who *were* there, on the altars, and burned men's bones on them; and he returned to Jerusalem. **21** Then the king commanded all the people, saying, "Keep the Passover to the LORD your God, as *it is* written in this Book of the Covenant." **22** Such a Passover surely had never been held since the days of the judges who judged Israel, nor in all the days of the kings of Israel and the kings of Judah. **23** But in the eighteenth year of King Josiah this Passover was held before the LORD in Jerusalem. **24** Moreover Josiah put away those who consulted mediums and spiritists, the household gods and idols, all the abominations that were seen in the land of Judah and in Jerusalem, that he might perform the words of the law which were written in the book that Hilkiah the priest found in the house of the LORD. **25** Now before him there was no king like him, who turned to the LORD with all his heart, with all his soul, and with all his might, according to all the Law of Moses; nor after him did *any* arise like him.

Apollos.

Acts 18:25 This man had been instructed in the way of the Lord; and being fervent in spirit, he spoke and taught accurately the things of the Lord, though he knew only the baptism of John.

Corinthians.

1 Cor 14:12 Even so you, since you are zealous for spiritual *gifts, let it be* for the edification of the church *that* you seek to excel.

Epaphras.

Col 4:12–13 Epaphras, who is *one* of you, a bondservant of Christ, greets you, always laboring fervently for you in prayers, that you may stand perfect and complete in all the will of God. **13** For I bear him witness

that he has a great zeal for you, and those who are in Laodicea, and those in Hierapolis.

ZEBULUN, THE TRIBE OF

Descended from Jacob's tenth son.

Gen 30:19–20 Then Leah conceived again and bore Jacob a sixth son. **20** And Leah said, "God has endowed me *with* a good endowment; now my husband will dwell with me, because I have borne him six sons." So she called his name Zebulun.

Predictions respecting.

Gen 49:13 "Zebulun shall dwell by the haven of the sea; He *shall become* a haven for ships, And his border shall adjoin Sidon.

Deut 33:18–19 And of Zebulun he said: "Rejoice, Zebulun, in your going out, And Issachar in your tents! **19** They shall call the peoples *to* the mountain; There they shall offer sacrifices of righteousness; For they shall partake *of* the abundance of the seas And *of* treasures hidden in the sand."

Persons selected from,

To number the people.

Num 1:9 from Zebulun, Eliab the son of Helon;

To spy out the land.

Num 13:10 from the tribe of Zebulun, Gaddiel the son of Sodi;

To divide the land.

Num 34:25 a leader from the tribe of the children of Zebulun, Elizaphan the son of Parnach;

Strength of, on leaving Egypt.

Num 1:30–31 From the children of Zebulun, their genealogies by their families, by their fathers' house, according to the number of names, from twenty years old and above, all who *were able to* go to war: **31** those who were numbered of the tribe of Zebulun *were* fifty-seven thousand four hundred.

Formed the rear of the first division of the army of Israel in its journeys.

Num 10:14 The standard of the camp of the children of Judah set out first according to their armies; over their army was Nahshon the son of Amminadab.

Num 10:16 And over the army of the tribe of the children of Zebulun *was* Eliab the son of Helon.

Encamped under the standard of Judah, east of the tabernacle.

Num 2:3 On the east side, toward the rising of the sun, those of the standard of the forces with Judah shall camp according to their armies; and Nahshon the son of Amminadab *shall be* the leader of the children of Judah."

Num 2:7 "Then *comes* the tribe of Zebulun, and Eliab the son of Helon *shall be* the leader of the children of Zebulun."

Offering of, at the dedication.

Num 7:24–29 On the third day Eliab the son of Helon, leader of the children of Zebulun, *presented an offering.* **25** His offering *was* one silver platter, the weight of which *was* one hundred and thirty *shekels,* and one silver bowl of seventy shekels, according to the shekel of the sanctuary, both of them full of fine flour mixed with oil as a grain offering; **26** one gold pan of ten *shekels*, full of incense; **27** one young bull, one ram, and one male lamb in its first year, as a burnt offering; **28** one kid of the goats as a sin offering; **29** and for the sacrifice of peace offerings: two oxen, five rams, five male goats, and five male lambs in their first year. This *was* the offering of Eliab the son of Helon.

Families of.

Num 26:26–27 The sons of Zebulun according to their families *were*: of Sered, the family of the Sardites; of Elon, the family of the Elonites; of Jahleel, the family of the Jahleelites. **27** These *are* the families of the Zebulunites according to those who were numbered of them: sixty thousand five hundred.

Strength of, on entering Canaan.

Num 26:27 These *are* the families of the Zebulunites according to those who were numbered of them: sixty thousand five hundred.

On Ebal, said amen to the curses.

Deut 27:13 and these shall stand on Mount Ebal to curse: Reuben, Gad, Asher, Zebulun, Dan, and Naphtali.

A naval and commercial people.

Gen 49:13 "Zebulun shall dwell by the haven of the sea; He *shall become* a haven for ships, And his border shall adjoin Sidon.

Bounds of their inheritance.

Josh 19:10–16 The third lot came out for the children of Zebulun according to their families, and the border of their inheritance was as far as Sarid. **11** Their border went toward the west and to Maralah, went to Dabbasheth, and extended along the brook that is east of Jokneam. **12** Then from Sarid it went eastward toward the sunrise along the border of Chisloth Tabor, and went out toward Daberath, bypassing Japhia. **13** And from there it passed along on the east of Gath Hepher, toward Eth Kazin, and extended to Rimmon, which borders on Neah. **14** Then the border went around it on the north side of Hannathon, and it ended in the Valley of Jiphthah El. **15** Included were Kattath, Nahallal, Shimron, Idalah, and Bethlehem: twelve cities with their villages. **16** This *was* the inheritance of the children of Zebulun according to their families, these cities with their villages.

Unable to drive out the Canaanites from their cities, but made them tributary.

Judg 1:30 Nor did Zebulun drive out the inhabitants of Kitron or the inhabitants of Nahalol; so the Canaanites dwelt among them, and were put under tribute.

Praised for assisting Deborah and Barak in opposing Sisera.

Judg 4:10 And Barak called Zebulun and Naphtali to Kedesh; he went up with ten thousand men under his command, and Deborah went up with him.

Judg 5:14 From Ephraim *were* those whose roots were in Amalek. After you, Benjamin, with your peoples, From Machir rulers came down, And from Zebulun those who bear the recruiter's staff.

Judg 5:18 Zebulun *is* a people *who* jeopardized their lives to the point of death, Naphtali also, on the heights of the battlefield.

Aided Gideon against the army of the Midianites.

Judg 6:35 And he sent messengers throughout all Manasseh, who also gathered behind him. He also sent messengers to Asher, Zebulun, and Naphtali; and they came up to meet them.

Furnished a judge to Israel.

Judg 12:11–12 After him, Elon the Zebulunite judged Israel. He judged Israel ten years. **12** And Elon the Zebulunite died and was buried at Aijalon in the country of Zebulun.

Some of, at David's coronation.

1 Chr 12:33 of Zebulun there were fifty thousand who went out to battle, expert in war with all weapons of war, stouthearted men who could keep ranks;

Officer appointed over by David.

1 Chr 27:19 *over* Zebulun, Ishmaiah the son of Obadiah; *over* Naphtali, Jerimoth the son of Azriel;

Only some of them, assisted in Hezekiah's reformation.

2 Chr 30:10–11 So the runners passed from city to city through the country of Ephraim and Manasseh, as far as Zebulun; but they laughed at them and mocked them. **11** Nevertheless some from Asher, Manasseh, and Zebulun humbled themselves and came to Jerusalem.

2 Chr 30:18 For a multitude of the people, many from Ephraim, Manasseh, Issachar, and Zebulun, had not cleansed themselves, yet they ate the Passover contrary to what was written. But Hezekiah prayed for them, saying, "May the good LORD provide atonement for everyone

Land of, blessed with the presence and instruction of Christ.

Is 9:1 Nevertheless the gloom *will* not *be* upon her who *is* distressed, As when at first He lightly esteemed The land of Zebulun and the land of Naphtali, And afterward more heavily oppressed *her*, By the way of the sea, beyond the Jordan, In Galilee of the Gentiles.

Matt 4:13–15 And leaving Nazareth, He came and dwelt in Capernaum, which is by the sea, in the regions of Zebulun and Naphtali, **14** that it might be fulfilled which was spoken by Isaiah the prophet, saying: **15** *"The land of Zebulun and the land of Naphtali, By the way of the sea, beyond the Jordan, Galilee of the Gentiles:*